THE CONCISE OXFORD DICTIONARY

# The Concise Oxford Dictionary

TENTH EDITION, REVISED

*Edited by*

Judy Pearsall

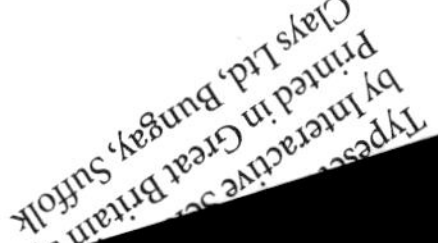

OXFORD
UNIVERSITY PRESS

Great Clarendon Street, Oxford OX2 6DP

Oxford University Press is a department of the University of Oxford.
It furthers the University's objective of excellence in research, scholarship, and education by publishing worldwide in

Oxford New York

Athens Auckland Bangkok Bogotá Buenos Aires
Cape Town Chennai Dar es Salaam Delhi Florence Hong Kong Istanbul
Karachi Kolkata Kuala Lumpur Madrid Melbourne Mexico City Mumbai
Nairobi Paris São Paulo Shanghai Singapore Taipei Tokyo Toronto Warsaw

with associated companies in Berlin Ibadan



Published in the United States by Oxford University Press Inc., New York



First edition 1911
New edition (revised) 1929
Third edition (with Addenda) 1934
Fourth edition 1951
Fifth edition 1964
Sixth edition 1976
Seventh edition 1982
Eighth edition 1990
Ninth edition 1995
Tenth edition 1999
Tenth (revised) edition 2001



British Library Cataloguing in Publication Data
Data available

Library of Congress Cataloging in Publication Data
The concise Oxford dictionary.—10th ed./edited by Judy Pearsall.
p. cm. Rev. ed. of: The concise Oxford dictionary of current English. 9th ed. 1995
1. English language—20th century–Dictionaries. 2. English language—New words—Dictionaries. I. Pearsall, Judy. II. Concise Oxford dictionary of current English.
PE1628.C68 1999 423—dc21 99-20834

ISBN 0-19-860438-6
ISBN 0-19-860436-X (thumb index)
ISBN 0-19-860470-X (dictionary with CD-ROM)

10 9 8 7 6 5 4 3 2 1

...set in Arial, Nimrod, and Minion
...Sciences Ltd, Gloucester
...by

# *Contents*

# *Editorial team*

***Editor***
Judy Pearsall

***Chief Science Editor***
Bill Trumble

***Associate Editors***
Catherine Soanes
Angus Stevenson

***Senior Editors***
Julia Elliott
Sara Hawker

***Senior Assistant Editor***
Catherine Bailey

***Administrative Co-ordinator***
Sarah O'Connor

***Editorial Assistants and Keyboarders***
Jonathan Blaney

Kirsten Hayman
Lisa Johnston
Muriel Ranivoalison
Susan Wilkin

# *Preface to the Tenth Edition*

The tenth edition of the *Concise Oxford Dictionary* is a very important one. This is the first edition of the dictionary which has been able to draw on the research and analysis of the language reflected in the ground-breaking *New Oxford Dictionary of English*. As with the very first edition of the *Concise Oxford Dictionary*, published in 1911, which made use of the 'materials' and 'methods' by which the editors of the *Oxford English Dictionary* had 'revolutionized lexicography', so the tenth edition makes use of the innovative principles and methodology devised for the *New Oxford Dictionary of English*.

The new *Concise Oxford Dictionary* takes to heart the new approaches to presentation and understanding of meaning which form such an integral part of the *New Oxford Dictionary of English*, modifying them to the needs of a smaller one-volume dictionary and at the same time preserving the unique traditions of the *Concise*. Each entry is built around the core sense or senses of the word in current English, as based on rigorous analysis of large amounts of real, modern evidence available in computerized form. Subsenses are shown in their relation to the core senses by the use of a special 'arrow' design feature (➤). Definitions are sharp and crisp, and the new open layout makes finding individual senses, sections, and entries easier than ever before. In all respects the new *Concise Oxford Dictionary* benefits from the extensive research carried out for the *New Oxford Dictionary of English*, producing the most accurate, up to date, and objective description of the language.

The dictionary definitions retain the hallmark of conciseness, although this is balanced by an emphasis on clarity and accessibility, using ordinary modern English to explain technical and complex terms, with no abbreviations. The tenth edition adopts much of the innovatory style from the *New Oxford Dictionary of English* in presentation of technical vocabulary, with, for example, genus information for plants and animals being placed in a separate and easily recognizable format.

The tenth edition of the *Concise Oxford Dictionary* is firmly based on the evidence, which informs everything we are able to say about the language and the words within it, whether it is in giving information about spelling, in ensuring accurate and precise definitions, or in establishing currency or level of formality. The editors have made use of huge amounts of corpus material and other computerized evidence, including the 100-million word British National Corpus, and the citation database of the Oxford World Reading Programme, currently standing at around 48 million words and growing at a rate of around 5 million words per year.

Special attention has been given to enhancing the overall vocabulary coverage of the dictionary, so that the number of words entered as headwords has been increased without increasing the overall size. This has been done by looking closely at what is likely to be most useful to users. Entries for very common words such as 'be' or 'go' have been included in brief form, typically occupying around half the space allocated to them in previous editions. In addition, some compounds which are easily analysable into their component parts, such as 'beach ball' or 'hen house', have been omitted. This combination of condensing some entries and choosing to omit others allows the inclusion of many more words and meanings in current use which are less familiar, especially those belonging to specialist and scientific fields. The result is the inclusion of all those words, phrases, and meanings that form the central vocabulary of English in the modern world.

The richness and variety of the English language is of interest not only to lexicographers but also to many other native speakers of English. In the tenth edition specially created 'word-formation' panels have been included to illustrate the many ways in which new (and old) words are formed from other linguistic elements. Word-formation elements such as '-phobia', '-saurus', and '-graphy' are given expanded treatment, highlighting and explaining the formation of words as diverse as 'hagiography', 'anatomy', 'apatosaurus', and 'Europhobia'.

The editors are grateful to many people for their help in the preparation of this dictionary. Those not forming part of the editorial team who deserve mention include: Frank Abate and Elizabeth Jewell for various comments and suggestions, especially on North American English, and Tony Deverson, Bruce Moore, and Penny Silva, for their additional contributions on (respectively) New Zealand, Australian, and South African English. In addition, we are indebted to Michael Proffitt and the continuing work of the New Words team of the *Oxford English Dictionary*, for their help in identifying and drafting new words as they come into the language.

## PREFACE TO THE REVISED EDITION

This revised edition contains many extra entries for words which have entered the language since the Tenth Edition was published in 1999, together with a section of appendices. Besides useful tables of factual information, the appendix includes a glossary of abbreviations used in electronic text messaging (SMS), a list of short or unusual words for word games, and a Guide to Good English.

# Introduction

The *Concise Oxford Dictionary* is designed to be as straightforward and self-explanatory as possible and the use of special dictionary symbols and conventions has been kept to a minimum. Those that are used are explained below. In addition, the following notes are designed to enable the reader to understand more fully the principles involved in and the thinking behind the making of this dictionary.

## ENTRY STRUCTURE: CORE SENSE AND SUBSENSES

Within each part of speech the first definition given is the core sense. This represents the typical, central, or 'core' meaning of the word in modern standard English. The core meaning is not necessarily the oldest meaning, nor is it always the most frequent meaning, because figurative and extended senses are sometimes the most frequent. It is the meaning accepted by native speakers as the one which is most established as literal and central.

Each word has at least one core sense, which acts as a gateway to other, related subsenses. The relationship between core sense and subsense is indicated in the dictionary entry by the placing of the subsenses immediately after the core sense, introduced by a solid arrow symbol. Many entries have more than one core sense. Each new core sense is introduced by a bold sense number, and each may have its own subsense or subsenses relating to it.

**capital**[1] ● n. **1** the most important city or town of a country or region, usually its seat of government and administrative centre. ➤ a place particularly associated with a specified activity: *the fashion capital of the world.* **2** wealth owned by a person or organization or invested, lent, or borrowed. ➤ the excess of a company's assets over its liabilities. **3** a capital letter. ● adj. **1** (of an offence or charge) liable to the death penalty. **2** (of a letter of the alphabet) large in size and of the form used to begin sentences and names. **3** informal, dated excellent.
– PHRASES **make capital out of** use to one's own advantage. **with a capital ——** used for emphasis: *she was ugly with a capital U.*
– DERIVATIVES **capitally** adv.
– ORIGIN ME (as adj. in the sense 'relating to the head or top'): via OFr. from L. *capitalis*, from *caput* 'head'.

**cap** ● n. **1** a soft, flat hat without a brim and usually with a peak. ➤ a soft, close-fitting head covering worn for a particular purpose: *a shower cap.* ➤ an academic mortar board. **2** a protective lid or cover for a bottle, pen, etc. ➤ Dentistry an artificial protective covering for a tooth. **3** an upper limit imposed on spending or borrowing. **4** chiefly Brit. a cap awarded to members of a sports team, especially a national team. **5** (also **Dutch cap**) Brit. informal a contraceptive diaphragm. **6** the broad upper part of the fruiting body of a mushroom or toadstool. **7** short for PERCUSSION CAP. ● v. (**capped**, **capping**) **1** put or form a lid or cover on. ➤ put a cap on (a tooth). **2** provide a fitting climax or conclusion to. ➤ follow or reply to (a story or remark) with a still better one. **3** place a limit on (prices, expenditure, etc.). **4** (**be capped**) chiefly Brit. be chosen as a member of a sports team, especially a national one. **5** Scottish & NZ confer a university degree on.
– PHRASES **cap in hand** humbly asking for a favour. **set one's cap at** (or US **for**) dated (of a woman) try to attract (a particular man) as a suitor. **to cap it all** as the final unfortunate incident in a long series.
– DERIVATIVES **capful** n. (pl. **-fuls**). **capper** n.
– ORIGIN OE *cæppe* 'hood', from late L. *cappa*, perh. from L. *caput* 'head'.

The organization of core senses and subsenses is designed to show direct, logical relationships between the uses of a word. The aim is to help the user, not only to navigate the entries more easily and to find the relevant sense more readily, but also to build up an understanding in general of the way in which different meanings of a word relate to each other.

## LABELS

Unless otherwise stated, the words and senses recorded in this dictionary are all part of standard English. Some words, however, are appropriate only to certain situations or are found only in certain contexts, and where this is the case a label (or combination of labels) is used.

### Register labels

Register labels refer to the particular level of use in the language—indicating whether a term is formal or informal, historical or archaic, and so on:

**formal:** normally used only in writing, in contexts such as official documents.

**informal:** normally used only in spoken contexts or informal written contexts.

**dated:** no longer used by the majority of English speakers, but still encountered, especially among the older generation.

**archaic:** old-fashioned language, not in ordinary use today, though sometimes used to give a deliberately old-fashioned effect and also encountered in the literature of the past.

**historical:** still used today, but only in reference to some practice or artefact that is no longer part of the modern world, e.g. **banneret** or **umbo**.

**poetic/literary:** found only or mainly in poetry, or in literature written in a consciously 'literary' style.

**technical:** normally used only in technical and specialist language, though not necessarily restricted to any specific subject field.

**rare:** not in normal use.

**humorous:** used with the intention of sounding funny or playful.

**euphemistic:** used in place of a more direct or vulgar term.

**dialect:** not used in the standard language, but still widely used in certain local regions of the English-speaking world.

**offensive:** likely to cause offence, especially racial offence, whether the speaker intends it or not.

**derogatory:** intended to convey a low opinion or cause personal offence.

**vulgar slang:** very informal language, especially that relating to sexual activity or other bodily functions, which is widely regarded as taboo and may cause offence.

### Geographical labels

The main regional standards for the language of English are British, US and Canadian, Australian and New Zealand, South African, Indian, and West Indian. The vast majority of words and senses listed in the dictionary are common to all the major regional standard varieties of English, but where important local differences exist these are recorded.

The geographical label 'Brit.' implies that the use is found typically in standard British English but is not found in standard American English, though it may be found in other varieties such as Australian or South African English. The label 'US', on the other hand, implies that the use is typically US and is not standard in British English, though it may be found elsewhere.

## Subject labels

Subject labels are used to indicate that a word or sense is associated with a particular subject field or specialist activity, such as Medicine, Aeronautics, or Baseball.

## GRAMMAR

The dictionary is based on a rigorous analysis of the grammar and syntactical structures of the language. This information is used to structure and organize the dictionary entry but, for the most part, it remains implicit in the text itself. Grammar is made explicit where it causes difficulty or is the source of controversy, or is likely to be of particular interest to the user.

1. Strong or obligatory syntactical patterns are presented directly, in bold text preceding the definition, e.g.

> **close** ... **3** ... (**close in**) (of days) get successively shorter with the approach of the winter solstice.
>
> **sound** ... **3** (**sound off**) express one's opinions loudly or forcefully.
>
> **bristle** ... **3** (**bristle with**) be covered with or abundant in.

Where the structure is a verb structure including a direct object, this is also indicated in bold text (notice that the direct object is included unbracketed in the definition text in these cases):

> **cash** ... **2** (**cash something in**) convert an insurance policy, savings account, etc. into money.
>
> **pad** ... **3** (**pad something out**) lengthen a speech or piece of writing with unnecessary material.
>
> **egg** ... (**egg someone on**) urge or encourage someone to do something foolish or risky.

A similar presentation is used to show an obligatory plural form:

> **work** ... **5** (**works**) ... a place where industrial or manufacturing processes are carried out.

2. Where a verbal noun ending in *-ing* or a verbal adjective ending in *-ed* or *-ing* is an important or the most important component of the verb use, this is indicated:

> **accommodate** ... **2** ... [as adj. **accommodating**] fitting in helpfully with another's wishes or demands.
>
> **abash** ... [usu. as adj. **abashed**] cause to feel embarrassed, disconcerted, or ashamed.

3. A small number of other explicit grammar labels are used:

[**treated as sing. or pl.**]: used to indicate nouns which may be used with either a singular or a plural verb without any change in meaning, normally collective nouns, e.g.

> **staff** **n. 1** [treated as sing. or pl.] the employees of a particular organization.

[**treated as sing.**]: used to indicate nouns which have a plural form but are normally used with a singular verb (many of which are words ending in *-ics* which relate to sports or subjects of study), e.g.

> **genetics** **pl. n. 1** [treated as sing.] the study of heredity and the variation of inherited characteristics.

**acrobatics** **pl. n.** [usu. treated as sing.] spectacular gymnastic feats.

**mumps** **pl. n.** [treated as sing.] a viral disease mainly affecting children, causing swelling of the parotid salivary glands of the face.

[**as modifier**]: used to indicate noun senses in which the noun is normally placed in front of another noun in order to modify its meaning, e.g.

**scattergun** ... [as modifier] covering a broad range in a random and unsystematic way: *the scattergun approach*.

**bayonet** ... **2** [as modifier] denoting a type of fitting for a light bulb or other appliance which is pushed into a socket and then twisted into place.

[**postpos.**]: used to indicate an adjective which is used postpositively, i.e. which comes immediately after the noun which it modifies (often an adjective which has been adopted from a language where postpositive use is standard), e.g.

**par excellence** ... [postpos.] better or more than all others of the same kind: *Nash is the Regency architect par excellence.*

**elect** ... **2** [postpos.] elected to a position but not yet in office: *the President Elect.*

[**with neg.**]: used to indicate words and senses which are typically used in negative constructions, e.g.

**clever** ... **2** [with neg.] Brit. informal healthy; well: *I didn't feel too clever.*

**fathom** ... **1** [usu. with neg.] understand (something) after much thought.

## SPELLING AND INFLECTION

The *Concise Oxford Dictionary* gives advice and information on spelling, in particular for those cases which are irregular or which otherwise cause difficulty for native speakers. The main categories are summarized below.

### Variant spellings

The main form of each word given is the standard British spelling or form. Standard variants, e.g. standard US spellings, are indicated at the top of the entry and cross-referred if the alphabetical position is more than four entries distant from the main entry.

**anaemia** (US **anemia**)
**anemia** US spelling of **ANAEMIA**.

**abulia** (also **aboulia**)
**aboulia** variant spelling of **ABULIA**.

Other variants, such as archaic, old-fashioned, or informal spellings, are cross-referred to the main entry, but are not themselves listed at the parent entry.

**Esquimau** archaic spelling of **ESKIMO**.

## Hyphenation

Although standard spelling in English is fixed, the use of hyphenation is not. In standard English a few general rules are followed, and these are outlined below.

**Noun compounds**: there are no hard-and-fast rules to determine the use of one-word, two-word, or hyphenated forms (except when used to show grammatical function: see below): whether, for example, to write **airstream**, **air-stream**, or **air stream**. All three forms are found in use in standard texts. However, the evidence of modern English indicates a tendency towards avoiding hyphenation in general, showing a preference for **airstream** rather than **air-stream** and for **air raid** rather than **air-raid**. There is an additional tendency for the form to be one word in US English and two words in British English, e.g. **air fare** tends to be the more common form in British English, while **airfare** tends to be more common in US English.

To save space and avoid confusion, only one of the three possible forms—the standard British one—is entered in the dictionary. This does not, however, imply that other forms are incorrect or not used.

**Grammatical function**: hyphens are also used to serve certain grammatical functions. When a noun compound made up of two separate words (e.g. **credit card**) is placed before another noun and used to modify it, the general rule is that the noun compound becomes hyphenated, e.g. *I used my credit card* but *credit-card debt*. This sort of regular alternation will be seen in example sentences but is not otherwise explicitly mentioned in the dictionary entries.

A similar alternation is found in compound adjectives such as **well known**. When used predicatively, i.e. after the verb, such adjectives are generally unhyphenated, but when used attributively, i.e. before the noun, they are generally hyphenated: *he is not well known* but *a well-known painter*.

A general rule governing verb compounds means that, where a noun compound is two words (e.g. **beta test**), any verb derived from it is normally hyphenated (**to beta-test**). This alternation is shown explicitly in the dictionary text for relevant entries.

## Inflection

English has comparatively few inflections compared to other European languages, and those that exist are remarkably regular. An *-s* is added to most nouns to make a plural; *-ed* is added to most verbs to make a past tense or past participle, and *-ing* is added to make a present participle.

Where difficulties arise, for example, because the inflection is not regular, or because the spelling change even in a regular inflection is not straightforward, full guidance is given. The main areas outlined are covered below.

**Verbs:** the following forms are regarded as regular and are therefore not shown in the dictionary:

- third person singular present forms adding *-s* to the stem (or *-es* to stems ending in *-s*, *-x*, *-z*, *-sh*, or soft *-ch*), e.g. **find** → **finds** or **change** → **changes**.
- past tenses and past participles dropping a final silent e and adding *-ed* to the stem, e.g. **change** → **changed** or **dance** → **danced**.
- present participles dropping a final silent *e* and adding *-ing* to the stem, e.g. **change** → **changing** or **dance** → **dancing**.

Other forms are given in the dictionary, notably for:

- verbs which inflect by doubling a consonant, e.g. **bat** → **batted, batting**
- verbs ending in *-y* which inflect by changing *-y* to *-i*, e.g. **try** → **tries, tried**
- verbs in which past tense and past participle do not follow the regular *-ed* pattern, e.g. **feel** → past and past part. **felt; awake** → past **awoke;** past part. **awoken**
- present participles which add *-ing* but retain a final *e* (in order to make clear that the pronunciation of *g* remains soft), e.g. **singe** → **singeing**

**Nouns:** plurals formed by adding *-s* (or *-es* when they end in *-s*, *-x*, *-z*, *-sh*, or soft *-ch*) are regarded as regular and are not shown.

Other plural forms are given in the dictionary, notably for:

- nouns ending in *-i* or *-o*, e.g. **agouti** → **agoutis, albino** → **albinos**
- nouns ending in *-a*, *-um*, or *-us* which are or appear to be Latinate forms, e.g. **areola** → **areolae, spectrum** → **spectra, alveolus** → **alveoli**
- nouns ending in *-y*, e.g. **fly** → **flies**
- nouns with more than one plural form, e.g. **storey** → **storeys** or **stories**
- nouns with plurals showing a change in the stem, e.g. **foot** → **feet**
- nouns with plurals unchanged from the singular form, e.g. **sheep** → **sheep**

**Adjectives:** the following forms for comparative and superlative are regarded as regular and are not shown in the dictionary:

- words of one syllable adding *-er* and *-est*, e.g. **great** → **greater, greatest**
- words of one syllable ending in silent *e*, which drop the *-e* and add *-er* and *-est*, e.g. **brave** → **braver, bravest**
- words which form the comparative and superlative by adding 'more' and 'most'

Other forms are given in the dictionary, notably for:

- adjectives which form the comparative and superlative by doubling a final consonant, e.g. **hot** → **hotter, hottest**
- two-syllable adjectives which form the comparative and superlative with *-er* and *-est* (typically adjectives ending in *-y* and their negative forms), e.g. **happy** → **happier, happiest; unhappy** → **unhappier, unhappiest**

## PRONUNCIATIONS

Pronunciations are not given for ordinary, everyday words such as **bake**, **baby**, **beach**, **bewilder**, **boastful**, or **budget**, since it is assumed that native speakers of English do not, as a rule, have problems with the pronunciation of such words.

In the *Concise Oxford Dictionary*, the principle followed is that pronunciations are given only where they are likely to cause problems for the native speaker of English, in particular for foreign words, scientific and other technical terms, rare words, words with unusual stress patterns, and words in which the standard pronunciation is disputed. For example, full pronunciations are given for the following words: **baba ganoush**, **baccalaureate**, **beatific**, **bijouterie**, **bucolic**, and **buddleia**.

The International Phonetic Alphabet (IPA) is used in representing the standard accent of English as spoken in the south of England (sometimes called Received Pronunciation or RP). It is recognized that, although the English of southern England is the pronunciation given, many variations are heard in standard speech in other parts of the English-speaking world.

The symbols used for English words, with their values, are given below.

## Consonants

The following have their usual English values: *b, d, f, h, k, l, m, n, p, r, s, t, v, w,* and *z* .

Other symbols are used as follows:

| | | | | | | | |
|---|---|---|---|---|---|---|---|
| g | **g**et | x | lo**ch** | ð | **th**is | j | **y**es |
| tʃ | **ch**ip | ŋ | ri**ng** | ʃ | **sh**e | | |
| dʒ | **j**ar | θ | **th**in | ʒ | deci**s**ion | | |

## Vowels

| SHORT VOWELS | | LONG VOWELS (ː indicates length) | | DIPHTHONGS | | TRIPHTHONGS | |
|---|---|---|---|---|---|---|---|
| a | c**a**t | ɑː | **ar**m | ʌɪ | m**y** | ʌɪə | f**ire** |
| ɛ | b**e**d | ɛː | h**air** | aʊ | h**ow** | aʊə | s**our** |
| ə | **a**go | əː | h**er** | eɪ | d**ay** | | |
| ɪ | s**i**t | iː | s**ee** | əʊ | n**o** | | |
| i | cos**y** | ɔː | s**aw** | ɪə | n**ear** | | |
| ɒ | h**o**t | uː | t**oo** | ɔɪ | b**oy** | | |
| ʌ | r**u**n | | | ʊə | p**oor** | | |
| ʊ | p**u**t | | | | | | |

(ə) before /l/, /m/, or /n/ indicates that the syllable may be realized with a syllabic **l**, **m**, or **n**, rather than with a vowel and a consonant, e.g. /ˈbʌt(ə)n/ rather than /ˈbʌtən/.

(r) indicates an **r** that is sometimes sounded when a vowel follows, as in dra**w**er, cha-ch**a**ing.

## Foreign pronunciations

Foreign words and phrases, whether naturalized or not, are always given an anglicized pronunciation. The anglicized pronunciation represents the normal pronunciation used by native speakers of standard English when using the word in an English context. A foreign pronunciation is also given for words taken from other languages (principally French, Dutch, German, Italian, Russian, and Spanish) where this is appreciably different from the anglicized form and where the other language is familiar to a reasonable number of English speakers.

Foreign-language transcriptions are based on current national standards. Regional variations have not been given, except in the case of Spanish transcriptions, where both Castilian and American Spanish variants are given. Transcriptions are broad, and many symbols, identical to those used for transcribing English, have similar values to those of RP. In a few cases, where there is no English equivalent to a foreign sound, a symbol has been added to the inventory. The additional symbols used to represent foreign pronunciations are given below.

## Consonants

| | | |
|---|---|---|
| ç | | gemütli**ch** |
| ɲ | | Monsei**gn**eur |
| β | | boli**v**ar |
| ɣ | | al**g**uacil |
| ʀ | French 'r' | aube**r**ge |

## Vowels

| SHORT VOWELS | LONG VOWELS (ː indicates length) | NASALIZED VOWELS (~ indicates nasality) | DIPHTHONGS |
|---|---|---|---|
| ɐ Abitu**r** | aː Autob**ah**n | ã p**in**cette | aɪ Gl**ei**chschaltung |
| | | ɒ̃ cord**on** bleu | |
| e abb**é** | eː W**eh**rmacht | ɑ̃ ch**an**son | |
| | | ɛ̃ coup de m**ain** | |
| o cabild**o** | oː verb**o**ten | œ̃ vingt-et-**un** | |
| ɔ durchk**o**mponiert | | ɔ̃ arr**on**dissement | |
| œ douc**eu**r | | | |
| ø vi**eux** **jeu** | øː Gasth**ö**fe | | |
| u c**u**randero | | | |
| y cr**u** | yː gem**ü**tlich | | |
| ʲ Dái**l** | | | |
| ʾ **h**auteur | | | |

# Guide to the use of the dictionary

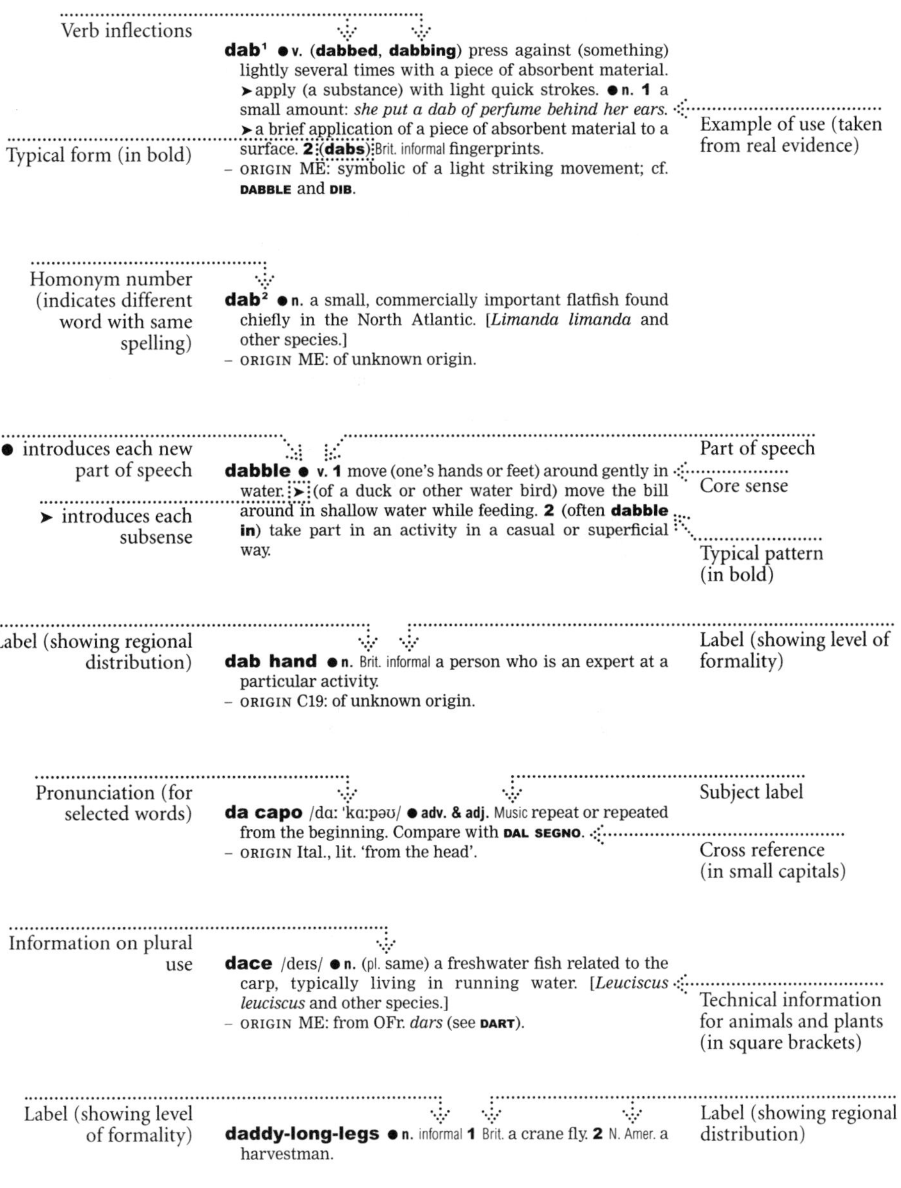

Variant pronunciations

Cross-reference entry (cross reference in small capitals)

**daikon** /ˈdʌɪk(ə)n, -kɒn/ ● **n.** another term for MOOLI.
– ORIGIN Japanese, from *dai* 'large' + *kon* 'root'.

Variant spelling

**daimyo** /ˈdʌɪmɪəʊ, ˈdʌɪmjəʊ/ (also **daimio**) ● **n.** (pl. **-os**) (in feudal Japan) one of the great lords who were vassals of the shogun.
– ORIGIN Japanese, from *dai* 'great' + *myō* 'name'.

Plural form

**daisy** ● **n.** (pl. **-ies**) a small grassland plant with composite flowers having a yellow disc and white rays. [*Bellis perennis.*] ➤ used in names of other plants of the same family, e.g. **Michaelmas daisy**.

Phrases and idioms

– PHRASES **pushing up (the) daisies** informal dead and buried.
– ORIGIN OE *dæges ēage* 'day's eye' (because the flower opens in the morning and closes at night).

Word origin

**damp** ● **adj.** slightly wet. ● **n. 1** moisture in the air, on a surface, or in a solid, typically with detrimental or unpleasant effects. ➤ (**damps**) archaic damp air or atmosphere. **2** archaic a check or discouragement. ● **v. 1** make damp. **2** control or restrain (a feeling or a situation). **3** make (a fire) burn less strongly by reducing its air supply. **4** reduce or stop the vibration of (the strings of a musical instrument). ➤ Physics progressively reduce the amplitude of (an oscillation or vibration).

Label (showing currency)

Subject label

– DERIVATIVES **dampish** adj. **damply** adv. **dampness** n.
– ORIGIN ME (in the sense 'noxious inhalation'): of W. Gmc origin.

Derivatives (in alphabetical order)

Grammatical information (in square brackets)

**darts** ● **pl. n.** [usu. treated as sing.] an indoor game in which darts are thrown at a dartboard to score points.

# Abbreviations used in the dictionary

Abbreviations in general use, such as 'etc.', 'i.e.', and 'p.m.', are listed and explained as entries in the dictionary itself.

| | |
|---|---|
| abbrev. | abbreviation |
| Aborig. | Aboriginal |
| adj. | adjective |
| adv. | adverb |
| Afr. | African |
| Afrik. | Afrikaans |
| alt. | alteration, altered |
| Amer. | American |
| appar. | apparently |
| Arab. | Arabic |
| assoc. | associated, association |
| aux. | auxiliary |
| b. | born |
| back-form. | back-formation |
| C (as in C18, C19, etc.) | century |
| Canad. | Canadian |
| cent. | century |
| cf. | compare with |
| Chin. | Chinese |
| colloq. | colloquial |
| comb. form | combining form |
| compar. | comparative |
| conj. | conjunction |
| contr. | contraction |
| corresp. | corresponding |
| Dan. | Danish |
| det. | determiner |
| dial. | dialect |
| dimin. | diminutive |
| Du. | Dutch |
| E. | East |
| eccles. | ecclesiastical |
| Engl. | English |
| exclam. | exclamation |
| fem. | feminine |
| Fr. | French |
| freq. | frequently |
| Ger. | German |
| Gk | Greek |
| Gmc | Germanic |
| Heb. | Hebrew |
| imper. | imperative |
| Ind. | Indian |
| Indo-Eur. | Indo-European |
| infin. | infinitive |
| interrog. | interrogative |
| Ir. | Irish |
| Ital. | Italian |
| L. | Latin |
| lang. | language |
| langs | languages |
| Latin Amer. Sp. | Latin American Spanish |
| lit. | literally |
| masc. | masculine |
| MDu. | Middle Dutch |
| ME | Middle English |
| med. | medieval |
| Mex. Sp. | Mexican Spanish |
| Mid. High Ger. | Middle High German |
| Mid. Low Ger. | Middle Low German |
| mod. | modern |
| n. | noun |
| N. | North |
| naut. | nautical |
| neg. | negative |
| neut. | neuter |
| north. Engl. | northern English |
| Norw. | Norwegian |
| obs. | obsolete |
| OE | Old English |
| OFr. | Old French |
| ON | Old Norse |
| ONorth. Fr. | Old Northern French |
| orig. | originally |
| part. | participle |
| perh. | perhaps |
| Pers. | Persian |
| phr. | phrase |
| phrs | phrases |
| pl. | plural |
| pop. | popular |
| Port. | Portuguese |

| | | | |
|---|---|---|---|
| possess. | possessive | Scand. | Scandinavian |
| postpos. | postpositive | sing. | singular |
| predet. | predeterminer | sl. | slang |
| prep. | preposition | Sp. | Spanish |
| pres. | present | Swed. | Swedish |
| prob. | probably | symb. | symbol |
| pron. | pronoun | Turk. | Turkish |
| pronunc. | pronunciation | ult. | ultimately |
| ref. | reference | usu. | usually |
| rel. | related | v. | verb |
| Russ. | Russian | var. | variant |
| S. | South | vars | variants |
| Sc. | Scottish | W. | West |

## Note on trademarks and proprietary status

This dictionary includes some words which have, or are asserted to have, proprietary status as trademarks or otherwise. Their inclusion does not imply that they have acquired for legal purposes a non-proprietary or general significance, nor any other judgement concerning their legal status. In cases where the editorial staff have some evidence that a word has proprietary status this is indicated in the entry for that word by the label trademark, but no judgement concerning the legal status of such words is made or implied thereby.

# A a

**A**[1] (also **a**) ● n. (pl. **As** or **A's**) **1** the first letter of the alphabet. **2** denoting the first, best, or most important in a set. **3** Music the sixth note of the diatonic scale of C major, having a standard frequency of 440 Hz. **4** the human blood type (in the ABO system) containing the A antigen and lacking the B.
– PHRASES **from A to B** from one's starting point to one's destination. **from A to Z** over the entire range.

**A**[2] ● **abbrev. 1** (in card games) ace. **2** (in showing goals or points conceded) against. **3** ampere(s). **4** (**Å**) ångstrom(s). **5** answer. **6** (in names of sports clubs) Athletic. **7** Austria (international vehicle registration).

**a**[1] (**an** before a vowel sound) ● **det. 1** used when mentioning someone or something for the first time; the indefinite article. ➤one single: *a hundred.* ➤used when mentioning someone one does not know. ➤someone like (the name specified). **2** per: *typing 60 words a minute.*
– ORIGIN ME: weak form of OE *ān* 'one'.

**a**[2] ● **abbrev. 1** (in travel timetables) arrives. **2** atto- ($10^{-18}$). **3** Brit. (with reference to sporting fixtures) away. **4** (used before a date) before. [from L. *ante.*] ● **symb.** (***a***) Physics acceleration.

**a-**[1] (often **an-** before a vowel) ● **prefix** not; without: *atheistic.*
– ORIGIN from Gk.

**a-**[2] ● **prefix 1** to; towards: *aside.* **2** in the process of: *a-hunting.* ➤in a specified state: *aflutter.*
– ORIGIN OE, unstressed form of **ON**.

**a-**[3] ● **prefix** variant spelling of **AD-** before *sc, sp,* and *st* (as in *ascend, aspire* and *astringent*).

**a-**[4] ● **prefix 1** of: *anew.* **2** utterly: *abash.*
– ORIGIN unstressed form of **OF** (sense 1); Anglo-Norman Fr. *a-*, from L. *ex* (sense 2).

**-a**[1] ● **suffix** forming: **1** ancient or Latinized modern names of animals and plants: *primula.* **2** names of oxides: *baryta.* **3** geographical names: *Africa.* **4** ancient or Latinized modern feminine forenames: *Lydia.* **5** nouns from Italian, Portuguese, and Spanish: *stanza.*
– ORIGIN representing a Gk, L., or Romance fem. sing.

**-a**[2] ● **suffix** forming plural nouns: **1** from Greek or Latin neuter plurals corresponding to a singular in *-um* or *-on* (such as *addenda, phenomena*). **2** in names (often from modern Latin) of zoological groups: *Insectivora.*

**-a**[3] ● **suffix** informal **1** of: *coupla.* **2** have: *mighta.* **3** to: *oughta.*

**@** ● **symb.** 'at', used: **1** to indicate cost or rate per unit: *30 items @ £29.99 each.* **2** in Internet addresses between the user's name and the domain name: *jsmith@oup.co.uk.*

**A1** ● **adj.** informal excellent.

**A3** ● **n.** a standard European size of paper, 420 × 297 mm.

**A4** ● **n.** a standard European size of paper, 297 × 210 mm.

**A5** ● **n.** a standard European size of paper, 210 × 148 mm.

**AA** ● **abbrev. 1** Alcoholics Anonymous. **2** anti-aircraft. **3** Automobile Association.

**aa** /ˈɑːɑː/ ● **n.** Geology basaltic lava forming very rough, jagged masses with a light frothy texture. Often contrasted with **PAHOEHOE**.
– ORIGIN C19: from Hawaiian *'a-'a.*

**AAA** ● **abbrev. 1** Amateur Athletic Association. **2** American (or Australian) Automobile Association.

**AAAS** ● **abbrev.** American Association for the Advancement of Science.

**AAM** ● **abbrev.** air-to-air missile.

**A & E** ● **abbrev.** accident and emergency.

**A & M** ● **abbrev.** Hymns Ancient and Modern.

**A & R** ● **abbrev.** artist(s) and repertoire (or recording), the department of a record company responsible for selecting new artists.

**aardvark** /ˈɑːdvɑːk/ ● **n.** a badger-sized African burrowing mammal, with long ears, a tubular snout, and a long extensible tongue, feeding on ants and termites. [*Orycteropus afer.*]
– ORIGIN C18: S. Afr. Du., from *aarde* 'earth' + *vark* 'pig'.

**aardwolf** /ˈɑːdwʊlf/ ● **n.** (pl. **aardwolves**) a black-striped African mammal of the hyena family, feeding mainly on termites. [*Proteles cristatus.*]
– ORIGIN C19: S. Afr. Du., from *aarde* 'earth' + *wolf* 'wolf'.

**aargh** /ɑː/ ● **exclam.** an expression of anguish, horror, rage, or other strong emotion.

**Aaron's beard** /ˈɛːrən/ ● **n.** a name given to the rose of Sharon and other plants.
– ORIGIN C19: alluding to the long beard of *Aaron* in the Bible, because of the hairy stamens or long runners of such plants.

**Aaron's rod** ● **n.** the great mullein.
– ORIGIN C18: alluding to *Aaron* in the Bible, whose staff was said to have flowered (Num. 17:8).

**AARP** ● **abbrev.** American Association of Retired Persons.

**A'asia** ● **abbrev.** Australasia.

**AAU** ● **abbrev.** Amateur Athletic Union.

**AAUP** ● **abbrev.** American Association of University Professors.

**AB**[1] ● **n.** the human blood type (in the ABO system) containing both the A and B antigens.

**AB**[2] ● **abbrev. 1** able seaman. **2** Alberta (in official postal use). **3** US Bachelor of Arts. [from L. *Artium Baccalaureus.*]

**Ab**[1] (also **Av**) ● **n.** (in the Jewish calendar) the eleventh month of the civil and fifth of the religious year, usually coinciding with parts of July and August.
– ORIGIN from Heb. *'āḇ.*

**Ab**[2] ● **abbrev.** Biology antibody.

**ab** ● **n.** informal an abdominal muscle.

**ab-** (also **abs-**) ● **prefix** away; from: *abdicate.*
– ORIGIN from L.

**ABA** ● **abbrev. 1** Amateur Boxing Association. **2** American Bar Association. **3** American Booksellers' Association.

**abaca** /ˈabəkə/ ● **n.** a large herbaceous Asian plant of the banana family, yielding Manila hemp. [*Musa textilis.*]
– ORIGIN C18: via Sp. from Tagalog *abaká.*

**aback** ● **adv. 1** archaic towards or situated to the rear. **2** Sailing with the sail pressed back against the mast by a headwind.
– PHRASES **take someone aback** shock or surprise someone.

**abacus** /ˈabəkəs/ ● **n.** (pl. **abacuses**) **1** a frame with rows of wires or grooves along which beads are slid, used for calculating. **2** Architecture the flat slab on top of a capital, supporting the architrave.
– ORIGIN ME: from L., from Gk *abax, abak-* 'slab, drawing board', of Semitic origin.

**abaft** /əˈbɑːft/ ● **adv. & prep.** Nautical in or behind the stern of a ship.
– ORIGIN ME: from **A-**[2] + archaic *baft* 'in the rear'.

**abalone** /ˌabəˈləʊni/ ● **n.** an edible mollusc of warm seas, with a shallow ear-shaped shell lined with mother-of-pearl. [Genus *Haliotis.*]
– ORIGIN C19: from Amer. Sp. *abulones*, pl. of *abulón*, from

*aulón*, the name in an Amer. Ind. lang. for Monterey Bay, California.

**abandon** ● v. **1** give up (an action or practice) completely. **2** desert or leave permanently. **3** (**abandon oneself to**) indulge in (a desire or impulse) without restraint. ➤ [as adj. **abandoned**] unrestrained; uninhibited: *a wild, abandoned dance.* ● n. lack of inhibition or restraint.
– PHRASES **abandon ship** leave a ship because it is sinking.
– DERIVATIVES **abandonment** n.
– ORIGIN ME: from OFr. *abandoner*, from *a-* (from L. *ad* 'to, at') + *bandon* 'control' (rel. to **BAN**[1]).

**abase** /ə'beɪs/ ● v. belittle or degrade.
– DERIVATIVES **abasement** n.
– ORIGIN ME: from OFr. *abaissier*, from *a-* (from L. *ad* 'to, at') + *baissier* 'to lower'.

**abash** ● v. [usu. as adj. **abashed**] cause to feel embarrassed, disconcerted, or ashamed.
– DERIVATIVES **abashment** n.
– ORIGIN ME: from Anglo-Norman Fr. *abaiss-*; cf. OFr. *esbaiss-*, *esbair*, from *es-* 'utterly' + *bair* 'astound'.

**abate** /ə'beɪt/ ● v. **1** (of something bad) become less intense or widespread. **2** Law reduce or remove (a nuisance).
– DERIVATIVES **abatement** n.
– ORIGIN ME: from OFr. *abatre* 'to fell', based on L. *battere*, *battuere* 'to beat'.

**abatis** /'abətɪs/ (also **abattis**) ● n. (pl. same, **abatises**, or **abattises**) historical a defence made of felled trees placed together with the boughs pointing outwards.
– ORIGIN C18: from Fr., lit. 'felled (trees)', from OFr. *abatre* 'to fell'.

**abattoir** /'abətwɑː/ ● n. a slaughterhouse.
– ORIGIN C19: from Fr., from *abattre* 'to fell'.

**abaxial** /ab'aksɪəl/ ● adj. Botany facing away from the stem (in particular denoting the lower surface of a leaf). The opposite of **ADAXIAL**.

**abaya** /ə'beɪjə/ ● n. a full-length, sleeveless outer garment worn by Arabs.
– ORIGIN C19: from Arab. *'abāya*.

**Abba** /'abə/ ● n. **1** (in the New Testament) God as father. **2** (in the Syrian Orthodox and Coptic Churches) a title given to bishops and patriarchs.
– ORIGIN via Gk from Aramaic *'abbā* 'father'.

**abbacy** /'abəsi/ ● n. (pl. **-ies**) the office of an abbot or abbess.
– ORIGIN ME: from eccles. L. *abbacia*, from *abbas*, *abbat-* (see **ABBOT**).

**Abbasid** /ə'basɪd, 'abəsɪd/ ● n. a member of a dynasty of caliphs who ruled in Baghdad 750–1258.
– ORIGIN named after Muhammad's uncle *Abbas*, founder of the dynasty.

**abbatial** /ə'beɪʃ(ə)l/ ● adj. of or relating to an abbey, abbot, or abbess.
– ORIGIN C17: from med. L. *abbatialis*, from *abbas*, *abbat-* (see **ABBOT**).

**abbé** /'abeɪ, French abe/ ● n. (in France) an abbot or other cleric.
– ORIGIN C16: Fr., from eccles. L. *abbas*, *abbat-* (see **ABBOT**).

**abbess** /'abɛs/ ● n. a woman who is the head of an abbey of nuns.
– ORIGIN ME: from OFr. *abbesse* 'female abbot'.

**abbey** ● n. (pl. **-eys**) an establishment occupied by a community of monks or nuns.
– ORIGIN ME: from OFr. *abbeie*, from med. L. *abbatia* 'abbacy', from *abbas*, *abbat-* (see **ABBOT**).

**abbot** ● n. a man who is the head of an abbey of monks.
– DERIVATIVES **abbotship** n.
– ORIGIN OE *abbod*, from eccles. L. *abbas*, *abbat-*, from Gk *abbas* 'father', from Aramaic *'abbā* (see **ABBA**).

**abbreviate** /ə'briːvɪeɪt/ ● v. shorten (a word, phrase, or text).
– DERIVATIVES **abbreviation** n.
– ORIGIN ME: from late L. *abbreviat-*, *abbreviare* 'shorten', from L. *brevis* 'short'.

**ABC**[1] ● n. **1** the alphabet. **2** an alphabetical guide. ➤ the rudiments of a subject.

**ABC**[2] ● abbrev. **1** American Broadcasting Company. **2** Australian Broadcasting Corporation.

**abdabs** (also **habdabs**) ● pl. n. Brit. informal (often in phr. **the screaming abdabs**) nervous anxiety or irritation.
– ORIGIN 1940s: of unknown origin.

**abdicate** /'abdɪkeɪt/ ● v. **1** (of a monarch) renounce the throne. **2** fail to fulfil or undertake (a duty).
– DERIVATIVES **abdication** n. **abdicator** n.
– ORIGIN C16: from L. *abdicat-*, *abdicare* 'renounce', from *ab-* 'away, from' + *dicare* 'declare'.

**abdomen** /'abdəmən, ab'dəʊmən/ ● n. the part of the body containing the digestive and reproductive organs; the belly. ➤ Zoology the hinder part of the body of an arthropod.
– DERIVATIVES **abdominal** /ab'dɒmɪn(ə)l/ adj. **abdominally** adv.
– ORIGIN C16: from L.

**abducens nerves** /ab'djuːs(ə)nz/ ● pl. n. Anatomy the pair of cranial nerves supplying the muscles concerned with lateral movement of the eyes.
– ORIGIN C19: *abducens* (mod. L., 'leading away'), from L. *abducere* (see **ABDUCT**).

**abduct** ● v. **1** take (someone) away illegally by force or deception. **2** Physiology (of a muscle) move (a limb or part) away from the midline of the body or from another part. The opposite of **ADDUCT**[1].
– DERIVATIVES **abductee** n. **abduction** n. **abductor** n.
– ORIGIN C17: from L. *abduct-*, *abducere* 'lead away'.

**abeam** ● adv. on a line at right angles to a ship's or an aircraft's length. ➤ (**abeam of**) opposite the middle of (a ship or aircraft).
– ORIGIN C19: from **A-**[2] + **BEAM**.

**abed** ● adv. archaic in bed.

**abelia** /ə'biːlɪə/ ● n. an East Asian shrub of the honeysuckle family. [Genus *Abelia*.]
– ORIGIN mod. L.; named after the Engl. botanist Clarke *Abel* (1780–1826).

**abelian** /ə'biːlɪən/ ● adj. Mathematics (of a group) having members related by a commutative operation (i.e. $a*b = b*a$).
– ORIGIN C19: from the name of the Norw. mathematician Niels Henrik *Abel* + **-IAN**.

**Abenaki** /ˌabə'naki/ ● n. & adj. variant spelling of **ABNAKI**.

**Aberdeen Angus** ● n. a breed of hornless black beef cattle originating in Scotland.

**Aberdonian** /ˌabə'dəʊnɪən/ ● adj. of or relating to Aberdeen. ● n. a native or citizen of Aberdeen.
– ORIGIN C17: from med. L. *Aberdonia*.

**aberrant** /ə'bɛr(ə)nt/ ● adj. departing from an accepted standard. ➤ chiefly Biology diverging from the normal type.
– DERIVATIVES **aberrance** n. **aberrancy** n. **aberrantly** adv.

**aberration** /ˌabə'reɪʃ(ə)n/ ● n. an unwelcome or unacceptable deviation from what is normal. ➤ Biology a characteristic that deviates from the normal type. ➤ Optics the failure of rays to converge at one focus because of a defect in a lens or mirror. ➤ Astronomy the apparent displacement of a celestial object from its true position, caused by the relative motion of the observer and the object.
– DERIVATIVES **aberrational** adj.
– ORIGIN C16: from L. *aberratio(n-)*, from *aberrare* 'to stray'.

**abet** /ə'bɛt/ ● v. (**abetted**, **abetting**) (usu. in phr. **aid and abet**) encourage or assist (someone) to do something wrong, in particular to commit a crime.
– DERIVATIVES **abetment** n. **abetter** (also **abettor**) n.
– ORIGIN ME: from OFr. *abeter*, from *a-* (from L. *ad* 'to, at') + *beter* 'hound, urge on'.

**abeyance** /ə'beɪəns/ ● n. a state of temporary disuse or suspension. ➤ Law the position of being without an owner or claimant.
– DERIVATIVES **abeyant** adj.
– ORIGIN C16: from OFr. *abeance* 'aspiration to a title', from *abeer* 'aspire after', from *a-* 'towards' + *beer* 'to gape'.

**ABH** ● abbrev. actual bodily harm.

**abhor** /əb'hɔː/ ● v. (**abhorred**, **abhorring**) detest; hate.

– DERIVATIVES **abhorrer** n.
– ORIGIN ME: from L. *abhorrere*, from *ab-* 'away from' + *horrere* 'to shudder'.

**abhorrent** ● **adj.** inspiring disgust and loathing.
– DERIVATIVES **abhorrence** n.

**abide** ● **v. 1** (**abide by**) accept or act in accordance with (a rule or decision). **2** (**can/could not abide**) informal be unable to tolerate. **3** [often as adj. **abiding**] (of a feeling or memory) endure. **4** archaic live; dwell.
– DERIVATIVES **abidance** n. (archaic). **abidingly** adv.
– ORIGIN OE *ābīdan* 'wait', from *ā-* 'onwards' + *bīdan* (see **BIDE**).

**ability** ● **n.** (pl. **-ies**) **1** the capacity to do something. **2** skill or talent.
– ORIGIN ME: from OFr. *ablete*, from L. *habilitas*, from *habilis* 'able'.

**-ability** ● **suffix** forming nouns of quality corresponding to adjectives ending in *-able* (such as *suitability* corresponding to *suitable*).
– ORIGIN from Fr. *-abilité* or L. *-abilitas*.

**ab initio** /ˌab ɪˈnɪʃɪəʊ/ ● **adv. & adj.** from the beginning.
– ORIGIN from L.

**abiogenesis** /ˌeɪbʌɪə(ʊ)ˈdʒɛnɪsɪs/ ● **n.** technical term for **SPONTANEOUS GENERATION**.
– DERIVATIVES **abiogenic** adj.
– ORIGIN C19: from **A-**[1] + Gk *bios* 'life' + **GENESIS**.

**abiotic** /ˌeɪbʌɪˈɒtɪk/ ● **adj.** not involving or derived from living organisms.

**Abitur** /ˌabɪˈtʊə, German ˌabiˈtuːɐ/ ● **n.** (in Germany) a set of examinations taken in the final year of secondary school.
– ORIGIN from Ger., abbrev. of *Abiturientenexamen* 'leavers' examination'.

**abject** /ˈabdʒɛkt/ ● **adj. 1** extremely unpleasant and degrading: *living in abject poverty.* **2** completely without pride or dignity: *an abject apology.*
– DERIVATIVES **abjection** n. **abjectly** adv. **abjectness** n.
– ORIGIN ME (in the sense 'rejected'): from L. *abjectus*, *abicere* 'reject', from *ab-* 'away' + *jacere* 'to throw'.

**abjure** /əbˈdʒʊə/ ● **v.** formal solemnly renounce (a belief or claim).
– PHRASES **abjure the realm** historical swear an oath to leave a country forever.
– DERIVATIVES **abjuration** n.
– ORIGIN ME: from L. *abjurare*, from *ab-* 'away' + *jurare* 'swear'.

**Abkhaz** /abˈkɑːz/ ● **n.** (pl. same) **1** a member of a people living mainly in the autonomous territory of Abkhazia in NW Georgia. **2** the North Caucasian language of this people.
– DERIVATIVES **Abkhazian** adj. & n.

**ablation** /əˈbleɪʃ(ə)n/ ● **n. 1** the loss of solid material (especially ice) by melting or evaporation. ➤ the erosion of rock by wind action. **2** the surgical removal of body tissue.
– DERIVATIVES **ablate** v.
– ORIGIN ME: from late L. *ablatio(n-)*, from L. *ablat-*, *auferre* 'take away'.

**ablative** /ˈablətɪv/ ● **adj. 1** Grammar denoting a case indicating an agent, instrument, or source, expressed by 'by', 'with', or 'from' in English. **2** involving ablation. ● **n.** Grammar a word in the ablative case.
– ORIGIN ME: from OFr. *ablative* (fem. of *ablatif*), L. *ablativus*, from *ablat-*, *auferre* (see **ABLATION**).

**ablative absolute** ● **n.** a construction in Latin which consists of a noun and participle or adjective in the ablative case and which functions as a sentence adverb, for example *mirabile dictu* 'wonderful to relate'.

**ablaut** /ˈablaʊt/ ● **n.** alternation in the vowels of related word forms, especially in Germanic strong verbs (e.g. in *sing*, *sang*, *sung*).
– ORIGIN C19: from Ger., from *ab* 'off' + *Laut* 'sound'.

**ablaze** ● **adj.** burning fiercely.

**able** ● **adj.** (**-er**, **-est**) **1** having the power, skill, or means to do something. **2** having considerable proficiency or intelligence.
– DERIVATIVES **ably** adv.
– ORIGIN ME: from OFr. *hable*, from L. *habilis* 'handy', from *habere* 'to hold'.

**-able** ● **suffix** forming adjectives meaning: **1** able to be: *calculable.* **2** subject to; relevant to: *taxable.* **3** having the quality to: *suitable.*
– DERIVATIVES **-ably** suffix forming corresponding adverbs.
– ORIGIN from Fr. *-able* or L. *-abilis*.

**able-bodied** ● **adj.** not physically unfit or disabled.

**able seaman** ● **n.** a rank of sailor in the Royal Navy above ordinary seaman and below leading seaman.

**abloom** ● **adj.** in bloom.

**ablution** /əˈbluːʃ(ə)n/ ● **n. 1** formal or humorous an act of washing. ➤ a ceremonial act of washing parts of the body or sacred containers. **2** (**ablutions**) Brit. (in army slang) a room with washing places and toilets.
– DERIVATIVES **ablutionary** adj.
– ORIGIN ME: from L. *ablutio(n-)*, from *abluere*, from *ab-* 'away' + *luere* 'wash'.

**ABM** ● **abbrev.** anti-ballistic-missile.

**Abnaki** /abˈnaki/ (also **Abenaki** /abəˈnaki/) ● **n.** (pl. same or **Abnakis**) a member of an American Indian people of Maine and southern Quebec.
– ORIGIN from Fr. *Abénaqui*, from Montagnais *ouabanăkionek* 'people of the eastern land'.

**abnegate** /ˈabnɪgeɪt/ ● **v.** formal renounce or reject (something desired or valuable).
– DERIVATIVES **abnegation** n. **abnegator** n.
– ORIGIN C17 (earlier (ME) as *abnegation*): from L. *abnegat-*, *abnegare* 'renounce', from *ab-* 'away, off' + *negare* 'deny'.

**Abney level** ● **n.** Surveying a kind of clinometer consisting of a sighting tube, spirit level, and graduated scale.
– ORIGIN C19: named after the Engl. scientist Sir William *Abney*.

**abnormal** ● **adj.** deviating from what is normal.
– DERIVATIVES **abnormality** n. **abnormally** adv.
– ORIGIN C19: alt. of C16 *anormal*, from Fr., var. of *anomal*, via L. from Gk *anōmalos* (see **ANOMALY**).

**Abo** /ˈabəʊ/ ● **n.** (pl. **Abos**) Austral. informal, offensive an Aboriginal.

**aboard** ● **adv. & prep. 1** on or into (a ship, train, or other vehicle). **2** Baseball on base.
– ORIGIN ME: from **A-**[2] + **BOARD**, reinforced by OFr. *à bord*.

**abode**[1] ● **n.** formal or poetic/literary a house or home. ➤ residence: *their right of abode in Britain.*
– ORIGIN ME: verbal noun from **ABIDE**.

**abode**[2] ● **v.** archaic past of **ABIDE**.

**abolish** ● **v.** formally put an end to (a practice or institution).
– DERIVATIVES **abolishable** adj. **abolisher** n. **abolishment** n. **abolition** n.
– ORIGIN ME: from OFr. *aboliss-*, lengthened stem of *abolir*, from L. *abolere* 'destroy'.

**abolitionist** ● **n.** a person who favours the abolition of something, especially capital punishment or (formerly) slavery.
– DERIVATIVES **abolitionism** n.

**abomasum** /ˌabəʊˈmeɪsəm/ ● **n.** (pl. **abomasa** /-sə/) Zoology the fourth stomach of a ruminant, which receives food from the omasum and passes it to the small intestine.
– ORIGIN C17: mod. L., from *ab-* 'away, from' + *omasum* (see **OMASUM**).

**A-bomb** ● **n.** short for **ATOM BOMB**.

**abominable** ● **adj.** causing moral revulsion. ➤ informal terrible.
– DERIVATIVES **abominably** adv.
– ORIGIN ME: via OFr. from L. *abominabilis*, from *abominari* 'deprecate', from *ab-* 'away, from' + *omen*, *omin-* 'omen'.

**Abominable Snowman** ● **n.** (pl. **-men**) another term for **YETI**.

**abominate** /əˈbɒmɪneɪt/ ● **v.** formal detest.
– DERIVATIVES **abominator** n.

**abomination** ● **n.** a cause of disgust or hatred. ➤ a feeling of hatred.

**aboral** /abˈɔːr(ə)l/ ● **adj.** Zoology furthest from or leading

away from the mouth.
– DERIVATIVES **aborally** adv.

**aboriginal** ● adj. inhabiting or existing in a land from the earliest times or from before the arrival of colonists; indigenous. ➤ (**Aboriginal**) of or relating to the Australian Aboriginals or their languages. ● n. **1** an aboriginal inhabitant. ➤ (**Aboriginal**) a person belonging to one of the indigenous peoples of Australia. **2** (**Aboriginal**) any of the Australian Aboriginal languages.
– ORIGIN C17: from L. *aborigines* (see **ABORIGINE**) + **-AL**.

**aborigine** /abə'rɪdʒɪni:/ ● n. an aboriginal person, animal, or plant. ➤ (**Aborigine**) an Australian aboriginal.
– ORIGIN C19: back-form. from C16 *aborigines* 'original inhabitants', from L. *ab origine* 'from the beginning'.

**aborning** /ə'bɔ:nɪŋ/ ● adv. chiefly N. Amer. while being born or produced.
– ORIGIN 1930s: from *a-* 'in the process of' + US dial. *born* 'to be born'.

**abort** ● v. **1** carry out or undergo the abortion of (a fetus). **2** Biology (of an embryonic organ or organism) remain undeveloped; fail to mature. **3** bring to a premature end because of a problem or fault. ● n. informal or technical an act of aborting a flight or other enterprise.
– ORIGIN C16: from L. *aboriri* 'miscarry', from *ab-* 'away, from' + *oriri* 'be born'.

**abortifacient** /ə,bɔ:tɪ'feɪʃ(ə)nt/ Medicine ● adj. (of a drug) causing abortion. ● n. an abortifacient drug.

**abortion** ● n. **1** the deliberate termination of a human pregnancy. ➤ the natural expulsion of a fetus from the womb before it is able to survive independently. **2** Biology the arrest of the development of an organ, especially a seed or fruit. **3** informal, derogatory something imperfectly planned or made.
– DERIVATIVES **abortionist** n. (chiefly derogatory).

**abortive** ● adj. **1** failing to produce the intended result. **2** Biology, dated (of an organ or organism) rudimentary; arrested in development. **3** Medicine (of a virus infection) failing to produce symptoms.
– DERIVATIVES **abortively** adv.

**abortus fever** /ə'bɔ:təs/ ● n. Medicine the commonest form of undulant fever in humans, caused by the brucellosis bacterium.
– ORIGIN 1920s: from L. *abortus* 'miscarriage'.

**ABO system** ● n. a system of four basic types (A, AB, B, and O) into which human blood may be classified, based on the presence or absence of inherited antigens.

**aboulia** ● n. variant spelling of **ABULIA**.

**abound** ● v. exist in large numbers or amounts. ➤ (**abound in/with**) have in large numbers or amounts.
– ORIGIN ME: from OFr. *abunder*, from L. *abundare* 'overflow', from *ab-* 'from' + *undare* 'surge'.

**about** ● prep. & adv. **1** [as prep.] on the subject of; concerning. **2** used to indicate movement within a particular area or location in a particular place. **3** [as adv.] approximately.
– PHRASES **be about to** be on the point of. **know what one is about** informal be sensible and self-possessed.
– ORIGIN OE *onbūtan*, from *on* 'in, on' + *būtan* 'outside of' (see **BUT**[2]).

**about-face** ● n. chiefly N. Amer. another term for **ABOUT-TURN**.

**about-turn** ● n. Brit. **1** Military a turn made so as to face the opposite direction. **2** informal a complete change of opinion or policy.

**above** ● prep. & adv. **1** at a higher level than. **2** in preference to. **3** [as adv.] (in printed text) mentioned earlier.
– PHRASES **above all** (**else**) more so than anything else. **above board** legitimate and honest. **above oneself** conceited. **not be above** be capable of stooping to (an unworthy act).
– ORIGIN OE *abufan*, from *a-* 'on' + *bufan* (from *bi* 'by' + *ufan* 'above').

**ab ovo** /ab 'əʊvəʊ/ ● adv. from the very beginning.
– ORIGIN L., lit. 'from the egg'.

**Abp** ● abbrev. Archbishop.

**abracadabra** ● exclam. a word said by conjurors when performing a magic trick.
– ORIGIN C17: from L., from a Gk base.

**abrade** /ə'breɪd/ ● v. scrape or wear away by friction or erosion.
– DERIVATIVES **abrader** n.
– ORIGIN C17: from L. *abradere*, from *ab-* 'away, from' + *radere* 'to scrape'.

**abrasion** /ə'breɪʒ(ə)n/ ● n. the action or process of abrading or being abraded.

**abrasive** /ə'breɪsɪv/ ● adj. **1** (of a substance) capable of polishing or cleaning a hard surface by rubbing or grinding. **2** harsh or rough in manner. ● n. a substance used for abrading.
– DERIVATIVES **abrasively** adv. **abrasiveness** n.
– ORIGIN C19: from L. *abras-*, *abradere* (see **ABRADE**) + **-IVE**.

**abreaction** ● n. Psychoanalysis the expression and consequent release of a previously repressed emotion, achieved through hypnosis or suggestion.
– DERIVATIVES **abreact** v. **abreactive** adj.

**abreast** ● adv. **1** side by side and facing the same way. **2** alongside. **3** (**abreast of**) up to date with.

**abridge** ● v. **1** shorten (a text or film) without losing the sense. **2** Law curtail (a right or privilege).
– DERIVATIVES **abridgeable** adj. **abridgement** (also **abridgment**) n. **abridger** n.
– ORIGIN ME: from OFr. *abregier*, from late L. *abbreviare* (see **ABBREVIATE**).

**abroad** ● adv. **1** in or to a foreign country or countries. **2** in different directions; over a wide area. ➤ (of a feeling or rumour) widely current. **3** archaic out of doors. ● n. foreign countries collectively.
– ORIGIN ME: from **A-**[2] + **BROAD**.

**abrogate** /'abrəgeɪt/ ● v. formal repeal or do away with (a law or agreement).
– DERIVATIVES **abrogation** n. **abrogator** n.
– ORIGIN C16: from L. *abrogat-*, *abrogare* 'repeal', from *ab-* 'away, from' + *rogare* 'propose a law'.

**abrupt** ● adj. **1** sudden and unexpected. **2** brief to the point of rudeness; curt. **3** steep.
– DERIVATIVES **abruptly** adv. **abruptness** n.
– ORIGIN C16: from L. *abruptus* 'broken off, steep', from *abrumpere*, from *ab-* 'away, from' + *rumpere* 'break'.

**abruption** ● n. technical the sudden breaking away of a portion from a mass. ➤ Medicine premature separation of the placenta from the wall of the womb during pregnancy.

**ABS** ● abbrev. **1** acrylonitrile-butadiene-styrene, a hard composite plastic. **2** anti-lock braking system.

**abs-** ● prefix variant spelling of **AB-** before *c*, *q*, and *t* (as in *abscond*, *abstain*).

**abscess** ● n. a swollen area within body tissue, containing an accumulation of pus.
– DERIVATIVES **abscessed** adj.
– ORIGIN C16: from L. *abscessus*, from *abscedere*, from *ab-* 'away from' + *cedere* 'go'.

**abscisic acid** /ab'sɪsɪk/ ● n. Biochemistry a plant hormone which promotes leaf detachment, induces seed and bud dormancy, and inhibits germination.
– ORIGIN 1960s: from **ABSCISSION**.

**abscissa** /ab'sɪsə/ ● n. (pl. **abscissae** /-si:/ or **abscissas**) Mathematics the distance from a point on a graph to the vertical or *y*-axis; the *x*-coordinate. Compare with **ORDINATE**.
– ORIGIN C17: from mod. L. *abscissa* (*linea*) 'cut-off (line)', fem. past part. of *abscindere* (see **ABSCISSION**).

**abscission** /əb'sɪʃ(ə)n/ ● n. Botany the process by which parts of a plant break off naturally, e.g. dead leaves.
– DERIVATIVES **abscise** /əb'sʌɪz/ v.
– ORIGIN C17: from L. *abscissio(n-)*, from *abscindere*, from *ab-* 'off' + *scindere* 'to cut'.

**abscond** /əb'skɒnd, ab-/ ● v. **1** leave hurriedly and secretly to escape from custody or avoid arrest. **2** (of bees) entirely abandon a hive.
– DERIVATIVES **absconder** n.
– ORIGIN C16: from L. *abscondere* 'hide', from *ab-* 'away, from' + *condere* 'stow'.

**abseil** /'abseɪl, -zʌɪl/ ● v. descend a near-vertical surface using a rope coiled round the body and fixed at a higher point.
– DERIVATIVES **abseiler** n. **abseiling** n.

– ORIGIN 1930s: from Ger. *abseilen*, from *ab* 'down' + *Seil* 'rope'.

**absence** • n. **1** the state of being away from a place or person. **2** (**absence of**) the non-existence or lack of.

**absent** • adj. /ˈabs(ə)nt/ **1** not present. **2** showing a lack of attention. • v. /abˈsɛnt/ (**absent oneself**) stay or go away. • prep. /ˈabs(ə)nt/ N. Amer. without.
– DERIVATIVES **absently** adv.
– ORIGIN ME: via OFr. from L. *absens, absent-*, pres. part. of *abesse*, from *ab-* 'from, away' + *esse* 'to be'.

**absentee** • n. a person who is absent.

**absenteeism** • n. the practice of regularly staying away from work or school without good reason.

**absent-minded** • adj. forgetful.
– DERIVATIVES **absent-mindedly** adv. **absent-mindedness** n.

**absinth** /ˈabsɪnθ/ • n. **1** the shrub wormwood. **2** (usu. **absinthe**) a green aniseed-flavoured liqueur formerly made with wormwood.
– ORIGIN ME: from Fr. *absinthe*, via L. from Gk *apsinthion* 'wormwood'.

**absit omen** /ˌabsɪt ˈəʊmən/ • exclam. used to express the hope that what is threatened may not become fact.
– ORIGIN L., lit. 'may this (evil) omen be absent'.

**absolute** /ˈabsəluːt/ • adj. **1** not qualified or diminished in any way; total. ➤not subject to any limitation of power: *an absolute ruler.* **2** not relative or comparative. **3** Grammar (of a construction) syntactically independent of the rest of the sentence, as in *dinner being over, we left the table.* ➤(of a transitive verb) used without an expressed object (e.g. *guns kill*). ➤(of an adjective) used without an expressed noun (e.g. *the brave*). **4** Law (of a decree) final. See also **DECREE ABSOLUTE**. • n. Philosophy a value or principle regarded as universally valid or able to be viewed without relation to other things.
– DERIVATIVES **absoluteness** n.
– ORIGIN ME: from L. *absolutus* 'freed, unrestricted', from *absolvere* (see **ABSOLVE**).

**absolute advantage** • n. Economics the ability of one individual or group to carry out an economic activity more efficiently than another individual or group.

**absolute alcohol** • n. ethanol containing less than one per cent of water by weight.

**absolutely** • adv. **1** with no qualification, restriction, or limitation. **2** used for emphasis or to express agreement. **3** not viewed in relation to other things or factors. **4** Grammar (of a verb) without a stated object.

**absolute magnitude** • n. Astronomy the magnitude (brightness) of a celestial object as it would be seen at a standard distance of 10 parsecs.

**absolute majority** • n. a majority over all rivals combined; more than half.

**absolute music** • n. instrumental music not intended to represent or illustrate anything. Compare with **PROGRAMME MUSIC**.

**absolute pitch** • n. Music **1** perfect pitch. **2** pitch according to a fixed standard defined by the frequency of the sound vibration.

**absolute temperature** • n. a temperature measured from absolute zero in kelvins.

**absolute title** • n. Law the guarantee of title to the ownership of a property or lease.

**absolute value** • n. **1** Mathematics the magnitude of a real number without regard to its sign. **2** technical the actual magnitude of a numerical value or measurement, irrespective of its relation to other values.

**absolute zero** • n. the lowest temperature theoretically possible (zero kelvins, −273.15°C), at which the motion of particles which constitutes heat is minimal.

**absolution** • n. formal release from guilt, obligation, or punishment. ➤ecclesiastical declaration of forgiveness of sins.
– ORIGIN ME: via OFr. from L. *absolutio(n-)*, from *absolvere* (see **ABSOLVE**).

**absolutism** • n. belief in absolute principles in politics, philosophy, or theology.
– DERIVATIVES **absolutist** n. & adj.

**absolutize** (also **-ise**) • v. chiefly Philosophy & Theology make or treat as absolute.
– DERIVATIVES **absolutization** n.

**absolve** /əbˈzɒlv/ • v. declare free from guilt or responsibility. ➤give absolution for (a sin).
– ORIGIN ME: from L. *absolvere* 'set free, acquit', from *ab-* 'from' + *solvere* 'loosen'.

**absorb** /əbˈzɔːb, -ˈsɔːb/ • v. **1** soak up (liquid or another substance). **2** take in (information). **3** assimilate (a less powerful entity). **4** use up (time or resources). **5** reduce the effect or intensity of (sound or an impact). **6** [usu. as adj. **absorbed** or **absorbing**] engross the attention of.
– DERIVATIVES **absorbability** n. **absorbable** adj. **absorbedly** adv. **absorber** n. **absorbingly** adv.
– ORIGIN ME: from L. *absorbere*, from *ab-* 'from' + *sorbere* 'suck in'.

**absorbance** • n. Physics a measure of the capacity of a substance to absorb light of a specified wavelength.

**absorbent** • adj. able to soak up liquid easily. • n. an absorbent substance or item.
– DERIVATIVES **absorbency** n.

**absorptiometer** /əbˌzɔːpʃɪˈɒmɪtə, -ˌsɔːp-/ • n. Physics an instrument for measuring the absorption of light or other radiation.
– DERIVATIVES **absorptiometric** adj. **absorptiometry** n.

**absorption** /əbˈzɔːpʃ(ə)n, -ˈsɔːp-/ • n. the process of absorbing or the action of being absorbed.
– DERIVATIVES **absorptive** adj.

**absorption costing** • n. a method of calculating the cost of a product or enterprise by taking into account overheads as well as direct costs.

**absquatulate** /əbˈskwɒtjʊleɪt/ • v. humorous, chiefly N. Amer. leave abruptly.
– DERIVATIVES **absquatulation** n.
– ORIGIN C19: blend of **ABSCOND**, *squattle* 'depart', and **PERAMBULATE**.

**abstain** • v. **1** restrain oneself from doing something. **2** formally decline to vote.
– DERIVATIVES **abstainer** n.
– ORIGIN ME: from OFr. *abstenir*, from L. *abstinere*, from *ab-* 'from' + *tenere* 'hold'.

**abstemious** /əbˈstiːmɪəs/ • adj. not self-indulgent, especially as regards eating and drinking.
– DERIVATIVES **abstemiously** adv. **abstemiousness** n.
– ORIGIN C17: from L. *abstemius* (from *ab-* 'from' + a word rel. to *temetum* 'alcoholic liquor') + **-ous**.

**abstention** /əbˈstɛnʃ(ə)n/ • n. **1** an instance of abstaining from a vote. **2** abstinence.
– DERIVATIVES **abstentionism** n.
– ORIGIN C16: from late L. *abstentio(n-)*, from *abstinere* (see **ABSTAIN**).

**abstinence** /ˈabstɪnəns/ • n. the fact or practice of abstaining, especially from drinking alcohol.
– DERIVATIVES **abstinent** adj. **abstinently** adv.
– ORIGIN ME: from OFr., from L. *abstinentia*, from *abstinere* (see **ABSTAIN**).

**abstract** • adj. /ˈabstrakt/ **1** theoretical rather than physical or concrete. **2** relating to or denoting art that does not attempt to represent external, recognizable reality. • v. /əbˈstrakt/ **1** consider theoretically or separately from something else. **2** extract or remove. ➤(**abstract oneself**) withdraw. **3** [as adj. **abstracted**] not concentrating. **4** make a written summary of. • n. /ˈabstrakt/ **1** a summary of a book or article. **2** an abstract work of art.
– DERIVATIVES **abstractedly** adv. **abstractly** adv. **abstractor** n.
– ORIGIN ME: from L. *abstract-, abstrahere*, from *ab-* 'from' + *trahere* 'draw off'.

**abstract expressionism** • n. a development of abstract art which aimed at subjective emotional expression with particular emphasis on spontaneous creativity (e.g. action painting).
– DERIVATIVES **abstract expressionist** n. & adj.

**abstraction** • n. **1** the quality or process of dealing with ideas rather than events. ➤something which exists only as an idea. **2** a state of preoccupation. **3** abstract qualities in art. **4** the process of abstracting something.

**abstractionism** • n. **1** the principles and practice of

abstract art. **2** the presentation of ideas in abstract terms.
– DERIVATIVES **abstractionist** n. & adj.

**abstract of title** • n. Law a summary of the title deeds and documents relating to the ownership of a piece of land.

**abstruse** /əb'stru:s/ • adj. difficult to understand.
– DERIVATIVES **abstrusely** adv. **abstruseness** n.
– ORIGIN C16: from L. *abstrus-*, *abstrudere* 'conceal', from *ab-* 'from' + *trudere* 'to push'.

**absurd** • adj. wildly unreasonable, illogical, or inappropriate.
– DERIVATIVES **absurdity** n. **absurdly** adv.
– ORIGIN C16: from L. *absurdus* 'out of tune', hence 'irrational'; rel. to *surdus* 'deaf, dull'.

**absurdism** • n. the belief that human beings exist in a purposeless, chaotic universe.
– DERIVATIVES **absurdist** adj. & n.

**ABTA** • abbrev. Association of British Travel Agents.

**abulia** /ə'bu:lɪə/ (also **aboulia**) • n. Psychiatry an absence of will power or an inability to act decisively.
– DERIVATIVES **abulic** adj.
– ORIGIN C19: coined from **A-**[1] + Gk *boulē* 'the will'.

**Abuna** /ə'bu:nə/ • n. a title given to the Patriarch of the Ethiopian Orthodox Church.
– ORIGIN Amharic, from Arab. *'abūnā* 'our father'.

**abundance** /ə'bʌnd(ə)ns/ • n. **1** a very large quantity of something. ➤plentifulness; prosperity. **2** the amount of something present in a particular area or sample. **3** (in solo whist) a bid by which a player undertakes to make nine or more tricks.
– ORIGIN ME: from L. *abundantia*, from *abundant-*, *abundare* (see **ABOUND**).

**abundant** • adj. plentiful. ➤(**abundant in**) having plenty of.
– DERIVATIVES **abundantly** adv.

**abura** /ə'bjʊ:rə/ • n. a West African tree which yields soft pale wood, and leaves that are used in herbal medicine. [*Mitragyna stipulosa*.]
– ORIGIN C20: from Yoruba.

**abuse** • v. /ə'bju:z/ **1** use to bad effect or for a bad purpose. **2** treat with cruelty or violence. ➤assault sexually. **3** address in an insulting and offensive way. • n. /ə'bju:s/ **1** the improper use of something. **2** cruel and violent treatment. ➤sexual assault. **3** insulting and offensive language.
– DERIVATIVES **abuser** n.
– ORIGIN ME: via OFr. from L. *abus-*, *abuti* 'misuse', from *ab-* 'away' + *uti* 'to use'.

**abusive** • adj. **1** extremely offensive and insulting. **2** characterized by illegality or physical abuse.
– DERIVATIVES **abusively** adv. **abusiveness** n.

**abut** /ə'bʌt/ • v. (**abutted**, **abutting**) **1** (of land or a building) be next to or have a common boundary with. **2** touch or lean on.
– ORIGIN ME: from Anglo-Latin *abuttare*, from *a-* 'to' + OFr. *but* 'end'; sense 2 is from OFr. *abouter*, from *a-* + *bouter* (see **BUTT**[1]).

**abutilon** /ə'bju:tɪlɒn/ • n. a herbaceous plant or shrub of warm climates, with showy yellow, red, or mauve flowers. [Genus *Abutilon*.]
– ORIGIN mod. L., from Arab. *ūbūṭīlūn* 'Indian mallow'.

**abutment** • n. **1** a structure supporting the lateral pressure of an arch or span. **2** a point at which something abuts something else.

**abutter** • n. chiefly US the owner of an adjoining property.

**abuzz** • adj. filled with a continuous humming sound.

**ABV** • abbrev. alcohol by volume.

**abysm** /ə'bɪz(ə)m/ • n. poetic/literary an abyss.
– ORIGIN ME: from OFr. *abisme*, med. L. *abysmus*, alt. of late L. *abyssus* 'bottomless pit'.

**abysmal** • adj. **1** informal extremely bad. **2** poetic/literary very deep.
– DERIVATIVES **abysmally** adv.

**abyss** /ə'bɪs/ • n. a very deep chasm. ➤(**the abyss**) a catastrophic situation seen as likely to occur.
– ORIGIN ME: via late L. from Gk *abussos* 'bottomless', from *a-* 'without' + *bussos* 'depth'.

**abyssal** • adj. **1** relating to or denoting the depths of the ocean. **2** Geology plutonic.

**Abyssinian** • adj. historical of or relating to Abyssinia (the former name of Ethiopia). • n. **1** historical a native of Abyssinia. **2** a cat of a breed having long ears and short brown hair flecked with grey.

**AC** • abbrev. **1** (**ac.**) N. Amer. acre. **2** (also **ac**) air conditioning. **3** Aircraftman. **4** (also **ac**) alternating current. **5** appellation contrôlée. **6** athletic club. **7** before Christ. [from L. *ante Christum*.] **8** Companion of the Order of Australia.

**Ac** • symb. the chemical element actinium.

**a/c** • abbrev. **1** account. **2** (also **A/C**) air conditioning.

**ac-** • prefix variant spelling of **AD-** assimilated before *c*, *k*, and *q* (as in *accept*, *acquit*, and *acquiesce*).

**-ac** • suffix forming adjectives which are often also (or only) used as nouns, such as *maniac*. Compare with **-ACAL**.
– ORIGIN via L. *-acus* or Fr. *-aque* from Gk *-akos*.

**acacia** /ə'keɪʃə, -sɪə/ • n. a tree or shrub of warm climates which has yellow or white flowers and is typically thorny. [Genus *Acacia*: numerous species.]
– ORIGIN ME: via L. from Gk *akakia*.

**academe** /'akədi:m/ • n. (often in phr. **the groves of academe**) academia.
– ORIGIN C16: from L. *academia* (see **ACADEMY**).

**academia** /ˌakə'di:mɪə/ • n. the academic environment or community.
– ORIGIN 1950s: from L. (see **ACADEMY**).

**academic** • adj. **1** of or relating to education and scholarship. ➤scholarly rather than technical or practical. **2** (of an art form) conventional in an idealized or excessively formal way. **3** not of practical relevance. • n. a teacher or scholar in an institute of higher education.
– DERIVATIVES **academically** adv.
– ORIGIN C16: from Fr. *académique* or med. L. *academicus*, from *academia* (see **ACADEMY**).

**academical** • adj. of or relating to a college or university. • n. (**academicals**) Brit. dated formal university attire.

**academician** /əˌkadə'mɪʃ(ə)n/ • n. **1** a member of an academy. **2** N. Amer. an academic.

**academicism** /ˌakə'dɛmɪsɪz(ə)m/ (also **academism**) • n. adherence to formal or conventional rules and traditions in art or literature.

**academy** • n. (pl. **-ies**) **1** a place of study or training in a special field. ➤[chiefly in names] US & Scottish a secondary school. **2** a society or institution of distinguished scholars, artists, or scientists.
– ORIGIN ME: from Fr. *académie* or L. *academia*, from Gk *akadēmeia*, from *Akadēmos*, the hero after whom the garden where Plato taught was named.

**Academy award** • n. an award given by the Academy of Motion Picture Arts and Sciences for achievement in the film industry; an Oscar.

**Acadian** chiefly historical • adj. of or relating to the former French colony of Acadia (now Nova Scotia) in Canada. • n. a native or inhabitant of Acadia, or a descendant of the Acadians.

**acajou** /'akəʒu:/ • n. another term for **CASHEW**.
– ORIGIN C16: from Fr., via Port. from Tupi *acajú*.

**-acal** • suffix forming adjectives such as *maniacal*, often making a distinction from nouns ending in *-ac* (as in *maniacal* compared with *maniac*).

**acalculia** /ˌeɪkal'kju:lɪə/ • n. Medicine loss of the ability to perform simple calculations, as a result of brain injury or disease.
– ORIGIN C20: from **A-**[1] + L. *calculare* 'calculate' + **-IA**[1].

**acanthamoeba** /əˌkanθə'mi:bə/ • n. (pl. **acanthamoebae** /-'mi:bi:/) an amoeba of a genus which includes a number that can cause opportunistic infections in humans. [Genus *Acanthamoeba*.]

**acantho-** /ə'kanθəʊ/ (also **acanth-** before a vowel) • comb. form having thorn-like characteristics.
– ORIGIN from Gk *akantha* 'thorn'.

**acanthus** /ə'kanθəs/ • n. **1** a herbaceous plant or shrub

with bold flower spikes and spiny decorative leaves, found in warm regions of the Old World. [Genus *Acanthus*: many species.] **2** Architecture a representation of an acanthus leaf, used especially as a decoration for Corinthian column capitals.
– ORIGIN via L. from Gk *akanthos*, from *akantha* 'thorn', from *akē* 'sharp point'.

**a cappella** /ˌa kəˈpɛlə, ˌɑː/ ● **adj. & adv.** (of music) sung without instrumental accompaniment.
– ORIGIN Ital., lit. 'in chapel style'.

**acara** /əˈkɑːrə/ ● **n.** a small cichlid fish of Central and South America with long dorsal and anal fins. [Genera *Aequidens* and *Cichlisoma*.]
– ORIGIN from Port. *acará*, from Tupi.

**Acari** /əˈkɑːri/ ● **pl. n.** Zoology a large order of small arachnids which comprises the mites and ticks.
– DERIVATIVES **acarid** /ˈakərɪd/ n. & adj. **acarine** /ˈakərʌɪn/ n. & adj.
– ORIGIN mod. L., from *acarus*, from Gk *akari* 'mite, tick'.

**acaricide** /ˈakərɪsʌɪd/ ● **n.** a substance poisonous to mites or ticks.
– ORIGIN C19: from Gk *akari* 'mite, tick' + **-CIDE**.

**acaroid** /ˈakərɔɪd/ (also **accaroid**) ● **n.** a resin obtained in Australia from some kinds of grass tree, used in making varnish.
– ORIGIN C19: of unknown origin.

**acarology** /ˌakəˈrɒlədʒi/ ● **n.** the study of mites and ticks.
– DERIVATIVES **acarologist** n.
– ORIGIN C20: from Gk *akari* 'mite, tick' + **-LOGY**.

**ACAS** /ˈeɪkas/ ● **abbrev.** Advisory, Conciliation, and Arbitration Service.

**acausal** ● **adj.** not governed or operating by the laws of cause and effect.

**accede** /əkˈsiːd/ ● **v.** (usu. **accede to**) formal **1** assent or agree to. **2** assume (an office or position).
– ORIGIN ME: from L. *accedere*, from *ad-* 'to' + *cedere* 'give way, yield'.

**accelerando** /əkˌsɛləˈrandəʊ, əˌtʃɛl-/ ● **adv. & adj.** Music with a gradual increase of speed.
– ORIGIN from Ital.

**accelerant** ● **n.** a substance used to aid the spread of fire. ● **adj.** technical accelerating or causing acceleration.

**accelerate** /əkˈsɛləreɪt/ ● **v.** begin to move more quickly. ➤ increase in rate, amount, or extent. ➤ Physics undergo a change in velocity.
– DERIVATIVES **acceleration** n. **accelerative** adj.
– ORIGIN C16 (earlier (C15) as *acceleration*): from L. *accelerat-*, *accelerare* 'hasten', from *ad-* 'towards' + *celer* 'swift'.

**accelerator** ● **n. 1** a foot pedal which controls the speed of a vehicle's engine. **2** Physics an apparatus for accelerating charged particles to high velocities. **3** a substance that speeds up a chemical process.

**accelerometer** /əkˌsɛləˈrɒmɪtə/ ● **n.** an instrument for measuring acceleration.

**accent** ● **n.** /ˈaks(ə)nt, -sɛnt/ **1** a particular way of pronouncing a language, associated with a country, area, or social class. **2** an emphasis given to a syllable, word, or note in speech or music. **3** a special or particular emphasis. **4** a mark on a letter or word indicating pitch, stress, or the quality of a vowel. ● **v.** /akˈsɛnt/ **1** [as adj. **accented**] spoken with a particular accent. **2** stress (a word, syllable, or note). **3** emphasize.
– DERIVATIVES **accentual** adj.
– ORIGIN ME: from L. *accentus* 'tone, signal, or intensity', translating Gk *prosōidia* 'song, intonation'.

**accentor** /əkˈsɛntə/ ● **n.** a small brown and grey songbird of a family including the dunnock. [Family Prunellidae, genus *Prunella*.]
– ORIGIN C19: from late L., from *ad-* 'to' + *cantor* 'singer'.

**accentuate** /əkˈsɛntʃʊeɪt, -tjʊ-/ ● **v.** make more noticeable or prominent.
– DERIVATIVES **accentuation** n.
– ORIGIN C18 (earlier (C15) as *accentuation*): from med. L. *accentuat-*, *accentuare*, from L. *accentus* (see **ACCENT**).

**accept** ● **v. 1** consent to receive (something offered). **2** regard favourably or with approval. **3** believe to be valid or correct. **4** take on (a responsibility or liability). ➤ tolerate or submit to.
– DERIVATIVES **acceptance** n. **acceptant** adj. (rare). **acceptor** (also **-er**) n.
– ORIGIN ME: from L. *acceptare*, from *accipere*, from *ad-* 'to' + *capere* 'take'.

**acceptable** ● **adj. 1** able to be accepted. **2** adequate.
– DERIVATIVES **acceptability** n. **acceptableness** n. **acceptably** adv.

**acceptation** /ˌaksɛpˈteɪʃ(ə)n/ ● **n.** the accepted meaning of a word or phrase.

**access** ● **n. 1** the means or opportunity to approach or enter a place. ➤ the right or opportunity to use something or see someone. **2** retrieval of information stored in a computer's memory. **3** an attack or outburst of an emotion: *an access of rage*. ● **v. 1** gain access to; make accessible. ➤ Computing obtain, examine, or retrieve (data). **2** approach or enter (a place).
– ORIGIN ME: from L. *accessus*, from *accedere* (see **ACCEDE**).

**accessary** ● **n. & adj.** variant spelling of **ACCESSORY**.

**accessible** ● **adj. 1** able to be accessed. **2** friendly and easy to talk to; approachable. **3** easily understood or appreciated.
– DERIVATIVES **accessibility** n. **accessibly** adv.

**accession** ● **n. 1** the attainment of a position of rank. **2** the formal acceptance of a treaty or joining of an association. **3** a new item added to a collection of books or artefacts. ● **v.** record the addition of (a new item) to a library or museum.

**accessorize** (also **-ise**) ● **v.** provide (a garment) with a fashion accessory.

**accessory** (also **accessary**) ● **n.** (pl. **-ies**) **1** a thing which can be added to something else in order to make it more useful, versatile, or attractive. ➤ a small article carried or worn to complement a garment. **2** Law a person who assists the perpetrator of a crime without taking part in it. ● **adj.** chiefly technical subsidiary or supplementary.
– DERIVATIVES **accessorial** adj. (chiefly Law).
– ORIGIN ME: from med. L. *accessorius* 'additional thing', from L. *access-*, *accedere* (see **ACCEDE**).

**accessory nerves** ● **pl. n.** Anatomy a pair of cranial nerves supplying certain muscles in the neck and shoulder.

**acciaccatura** /əˌtʃakəˈtjʊərə/ ● **n.** (pl. **acciaccaturas** or **acciaccature**) Music a grace note performed as quickly as possible before an essential note of a melody.
– ORIGIN Ital., from *acciaccare* 'to crush'.

**accidence** /ˈaksɪd(ə)ns/ ● **n.** dated the part of grammar concerned with the inflections of words.
– ORIGIN C16: from late L. *accidentia*, from L. *accidere* (see **ACCIDENT**).

**accident** ● **n. 1** an unfortunate incident that happens unexpectedly and unintentionally. **2** something that happens by chance or without apparent cause. ➤ chance. **3** Philosophy a property of a thing which is not essential to its nature.
– ORIGIN ME (in the sense 'an event'): via OFr. from L. *accident-*, *accidere*, from *ad-* 'towards, to' + *cadere* 'to fall'.

**accidental** ● **adj. 1** happening by accident. **2** incidental. **3** Philosophy relating to or denoting properties not essential to a thing's nature. ● **n. 1** Music a sign indicating a momentary departure from the key signature by raising or lowering a note. **2** Ornithology another term for **VAGRANT**.
– DERIVATIVES **accidentally** adv.

**accidie** /ˈaksɪdi/ ● **n.** spiritual or mental sloth.
– ORIGIN ME: via OFr. from med. L. *accidia*, alt. of **ACEDIA**.

**accipiter** /akˈsɪpɪtə/ ● **n.** Ornithology a hawk of a group distinguished by short, broad wings, such as the goshawk. [*Accipiter* and other genera.]
– DERIVATIVES **accipitrine** adj.
– ORIGIN from L., 'hawk, bird of prey'.

**acclaim** ● **v.** praise enthusiastically and publicly. ● **n.** enthusiastic public praise.
– DERIVATIVES **acclamation** n.
– ORIGIN C17: from L. *acclamare*, from *ad-* 'to' + *clamare* 'to

shout'.

**acclimate** /ˈaklɪmeɪt, əˈklʌɪmət/ ● **v.** chiefly N. Amer. acclimatize.
– DERIVATIVES **acclimation** n.
– ORIGIN C18: from Fr. *acclimater*, from *a-* (from L. *ad* 'to, at') + *climat* 'climate'.

**acclimatize** (also **-ise**) ● **v. 1** become accustomed to a new climate or new conditions. **2** Biology respond to changes in environmental factors. **3** Botany & Horticulture harden off (a plant).
– DERIVATIVES **acclimatization** n.
– ORIGIN C19: from Fr. *acclimater* 'acclimatize' + **-IZE**.

**acclivity** /əˈklɪvɪti/ ● **n.** (pl. **-ies**) an upward slope.
– DERIVATIVES **acclivitous** adj.
– ORIGIN C17: from L. *acclivitas*, from *acclivis*, from *ad-* 'towards' + *clivus* 'a slope'.

**accolade** /ˈakəleɪd, ˌakəˈleɪd/ ● **n. 1** something granted as a special honour or in recognition of merit. **2** a ceremonial touch on a person's shoulders with a sword at the bestowing of a knighthood.
– ORIGIN C17: from Fr., from Provençal *acolada*, lit. 'embrace around the neck (when bestowing knighthood)', from L. *ad-* 'at, to' + *collum* 'neck'.

**accommodate** ● **v. 1** provide lodging or sufficient space for. **2** fit in with the wishes or needs of. ➤ [as adj. **accommodating**] fitting in helpfully with another's wishes or demands.
– DERIVATIVES **accommodatingly** n. **accommodative** adj.
– ORIGIN C16: from L. *accommodat-*, *accommodare* 'make fitting', from *ad-* 'to' + *commodus* 'fitting'.

**accommodation** ● **n. 1** a room, building, or space in which someone may live or stay. ➤ (**accommodations**) chiefly N. Amer. lodgings. **2** a settlement or compromise. **3** adjustment to or reconciliation of changing circumstances. **4** the automatic adjustment of the focus of the eye by the lens.
– ORIGIN C17: from L. *accommodatio(n-)*, from *accommodare* (see **ACCOMMODATE**).

**accommodation address** ● **n.** Brit. an address for correspondence used by a person unable or unwilling to give a permanent address.

**accommodationist** ● **n.** US a person who seeks compromise.

**accommodation ladder** ● **n.** a ladder up the side of a ship allowing access from a small boat or a quayside.

**accompaniment** ● **n. 1** a musical part which supports or partners an instrument, voice, or group. **2** something that supplements or complements something else.
– ORIGIN C18: from Fr. *accompagnement*, from *accompagner* 'accompany'.

**accompanist** ● **n.** a person who provides a musical accompaniment.

**accompany** ● **v.** (**-ies**, **-ied**) **1** go somewhere with. **2** be present or occur at the same time as. ➤ provide something as a complement to. **3** play a musical accompaniment for.
– ORIGIN ME: from OFr. *accompagner*, from *a-* (from L. *ad* 'to, at') + *compagne*, from OFr. *compaignon* 'companion'.

**accomplice** /əˈkʌmplɪs, əˈkɒm-/ ● **n.** a person who helps another commit a crime.
– ORIGIN C16: alt. of ME *complice* 'an associate', via OFr. from late L. *complex*, *complic-* 'allied'.

**accomplish** ● **v.** achieve or complete successfully.
– ORIGIN ME: from OFr. *acompliss-*, *acomplir*, based on L. *ad-* 'to' + *complere* 'to complete'.

**accomplished** ● **adj.** highly trained or skilled.

**accomplishment** ● **n. 1** something that has been achieved successfully. **2** an activity that one can do well.

**accord** ● **v. 1** give or grant someone (power or recognition). **2** (**accord with**) be harmonious or consistent with. ● **n. 1** an official agreement or treaty. **2** agreement or harmony.
– PHRASES **of one's own accord** voluntarily or without outside intervention. **with one accord** in a united way.
– ORIGIN OE, from OFr. *acorder* 'reconcile', from L. *ad-* 'to' + *cor*, *cord-* 'heart'; influenced by **CONCORD**.

**accordance** ● **n.** (in phr. **in accordance with**) in a manner conforming with.

**accordant** ● **adj.** archaic agreeing or compatible.

**according** ● **adv. 1** (**according to**) as stated by or in. ➤ in a manner corresponding or in proportion to. **2** (**according as**) depending on whether.

**accordingly** ● **adv. 1** appropriately. **2** consequently.

**accordion** /əˈkɔːdɪən/ ● **n.** a musical instrument played by stretching and squeezing with the hands to work a bellows that blows air over reeds, the melody and chords being sounded by buttons or keys.
– DERIVATIVES **accordionist** n.
– ORIGIN C19: from Ger. *Akkordion*, from Ital. *accordare* 'to tune'.

**accost** ● **v.** approach and address boldly or aggressively.
– ORIGIN C16 (orig. in the sense 'lie or go alongside'): from Fr. *accoster*, from Ital. *accostare*, from L. *ad-* 'to' + *costa* 'rib, side'.

**accouchement** /əˈkuːʃmɒ̃/ ● **n.** archaic the action of giving birth.
– ORIGIN C18: Fr., from *accoucher* 'act as midwife', from *a-* (from L. *ad* 'to, at') + *coucher* (see **COUCH**[1]).

**accoucheur** /ˌakuːˈʃəː/ ● **n.** a male midwife.
– ORIGIN C18: Fr., from *accoucher* (see **ACCOUCHEMENT**).

**account** ● **n. 1** a description of an event or experience. **2** a record of financial expenditure and receipts. ➤ chiefly Brit. a bill taking the form of such a record. **3** a service through a bank or similar organization by which funds are held on behalf of a client or goods or services are supplied on credit. **4** a facility allowing access to a computer or computational facility. **5** importance: *money was of no account to her.* ● **v. 1** consider or regard in a specified way. **2** (**account for**) supply or make up (a specified amount). **3** (**account for**) give a satisfactory record or explanation of. **4** (**account for**) succeed in killing or defeating.
– PHRASES **call** (or **bring**) **to account** require (someone) to explain a mistake or poor performance. **money of account** denominations of money used in reckoning but not current as coins. **on someone's account** for a specified person's benefit. **on account of** because of. **on no account** under no circumstances. **on one's own account** with one's own money or assets. **take account of** consider along with other factors before reaching a decision. **turn to (good) account** turn to one's advantage.
– ORIGIN ME (in the sense 'counting', 'to count'): from OFr. *acont* (n.), *aconter* (v.), based on *conter* 'to count'.

**accountable** ● **adj. 1** required or expected to justify actions or decisions. **2** explicable; understandable.
– DERIVATIVES **accountability** n. **accountably** adv.

**accountancy** ● **n.** the profession or duties of an accountant.

**accountant** ● **n.** a person who keeps or inspects financial accounts.
– ORIGIN ME: from legal Fr., pres. part. of OFr. *aconter* (see **ACCOUNT**).

**accounting** ● **n.** the action of keeping financial accounts.

**accoutre** /əˈkuːtə/ (US **accouter**) ● **v.** (**accoutred**, **accoutring**; US **accoutered**, **accoutering**) (usu. **be accoutred**) clothe or equip, especially in something noticeable or impressive.
– ORIGIN C16: from Fr. *accoutrer*, from OFr. *acoustrer*, from *a-* (from L. *ad* 'to, at') + *cousture* 'sewing'.

**accoutrement** /əˈkuːtəm(ə)nt, -trə-/ (US **accouterment**) ● **n. 1** an additional item of dress or equipment. **2** (**accoutrements**) a soldier's outfit other than weapons and garments.

**accra** /ˈakrə, əˈkrɑː/ (also **akara**) ● **n.** (in West Africa and the Caribbean) a fritter made using black-eyed peas.
– ORIGIN from Yoruba *àkàrà* 'bean cake'.

**accredit** ● **v.** (**accredited**, **accrediting**) **1** give credit to (someone) for something. ➤ (**accredit something to**) attribute something to. **2** [often as adj. **accredited**] give official authorization or sanction to. **3** send (a diplomat or journalist) to a particular place or post.
– DERIVATIVES **accreditation** n.

– ORIGIN C17: from Fr. *accréditer*, from *a-* (from L. *ad* 'to, at') + *crédit* 'credit'.

**accrete** /əˈkriːt/ • **v.** grow or form by accumulation or coalescence.
– DERIVATIVES **accretion** n. **accretionary** adj. **accretive** adj.
– ORIGIN C18: from L. *accret-*, *accrescere* 'grow', from *ad-* 'to' + *crescere* 'grow'.

**accrue** /əˈkruː/ • **v.** (**accrues, accrued, accruing**) **1** (of a benefit or sum of money) be received in regular or increasing amounts. **2** make provision for (a charge) at the end of a financial period.
– DERIVATIVES **accrual** n.
– ORIGIN ME: from OFr. *acreue*, past part. of *acreistre* 'increase', from L. *accrescere* (see **ACCRETE**).

**acculturate** /əˈkʌltʃəreɪt/ • **v.** assimilate or cause to assimilate a different culture.
– DERIVATIVES **acculturation** n. **acculturative** adj.

**accumulate** /əˈkjuːmjʊleɪt/ • **v.** gather together a number or quantity of. ➤build up.
– DERIVATIVES **accumulation** n. **accumulative** adj.
– ORIGIN C15: from L. *accumulat-*, *accumulare* 'heap up', from *ad-* 'to' + *cumulus* 'a heap'.

**accumulator** • **n. 1** a person or thing that accumulates. **2** Brit. a large rechargeable electric cell. **3** Brit. a bet placed on a series of events, the winnings and stake from each being placed on the next.

**accurate** /ˈakjʊrət/ • **adj. 1** correct in all details. **2** capable of or successful in reaching the intended target.
– DERIVATIVES **accuracy** n. **accurately** adv.
– ORIGIN C16: from L. *accurat-*, *accurare* 'do with care', from *ad-* 'towards' + *cura* 'care'.

**accursed** /əˈkəːsɪd, əˈkəːst/ • **adj. 1** poetic/literary under a curse. **2** informal detestable.
– ORIGIN ME: past part. of obs. *accurse*, from *a-* (expressing intensity) + **CURSE**.

**accusal** • **n.** another term for **ACCUSATION**.

**accusation** • **n.** a charge or claim that someone has done something illegal or wrong.

**accusative** /əˈkjuːzətɪv/ Grammar • **adj.** denoting a case which expresses the object of an action or the goal of motion. • **n.** a word in the accusative case.
– ORIGIN ME: from L. (*casus*) *accusativus*, translating Gk (*ptōsis*) *aitiatikē* '(the case) showing cause'.

**accusatorial** /əˌkjuːzəˈtɔːrɪəl/ • **adj.** Law involving accusation by a prosecutor and a verdict reached by an impartial judge or jury. Compare with **ADVERSARIAL, INQUISITORIAL**.

**accuse** • **v.** charge with an offence or crime. ➤(**accuse someone of**) claim that someone has done something wrong.
– DERIVATIVES **accusatory** adj. **accuser** n. **accusing** adj. **accusingly** adv.
– ORIGIN ME: from OFr. *acuser*, from L. *accusare* 'call to account', from *ad-* 'towards' + *causa* 'reason, motive, lawsuit'.

**accustom** • **v. 1** make used to. ➤(**be accustomed to**) be used to. **2** [as adj. **accustomed**] customary.
– ORIGIN ME: from OFr. *acostumer*, from *a-* (from L. *ad* 'to, at') + *costume* 'custom'.

**AC/DC** • **adj. 1** alternating current/direct current. **2** informal bisexual.

**ace** • **n. 1** a playing card with a single spot on it, the highest card in its suit in most games. **2** informal a person who excels at a particular activity. **3** Tennis a service that an opponent is unable to return. **4** Golf a hole in one. • **adj.** informal very good. • **v.** informal **1** (in tennis) serve an ace against. **2** Golf score an ace on. **3** N. Amer. get an A or its equivalent in (a test or exam).
– PHRASES **ace up one's sleeve** (or N. Amer. **in the hole**) a plan or piece of information kept secret until required. **hold all the aces** have all the advantages. **within an ace of** very close to.
– ORIGIN ME (denoting the 'one' on dice): via OFr. from L. *as* 'unity, a unit'.

**-acea** • **suffix** Zoology forming the names of zoological groups: *Crustacea*. Compare with **-ACEAN**.
– ORIGIN from L., 'of the nature of', neut. pl. adj. ending.

**-aceae** • **suffix** Botany forming the names of families of plants: *Liliaceae*.
– ORIGIN from L., 'of the nature of', fem. pl. adj. ending.

**-acean** • **suffix** Zoology forming the singular of group names ending in *-acea* (such as *crustacean* from *Crustacea*).
– ORIGIN from L. *-aceus* 'of the nature of' + **-AN**.

**acedia** /əˈsiːdɪə/ • **n.** another term for **ACCIDIE**.
– ORIGIN C17: via late L. from Gk *akēdia* 'listlessness'.

**acellular** • **adj.** Biology not divided into or containing cells. ➤consisting of one cell only.

**acentric** • **adj. 1** without a centre; not centralized. **2** Genetics (of a chromosome) having no centromere.

**-aceous** • **suffix 1** Botany forming adjectives from family names: *ericaceous*. **2** chiefly Biology & Geology forming adjectives describing similarity: *olivaceous*.
– ORIGIN from L. *-aceus* 'of the nature of' + **-OUS**.

**acephalous** /eɪˈsɛf(ə)ləs, -ˈkɛf-/ • **adj. 1** without a head. **2** Prosody lacking syllables in the first foot.
– ORIGIN C18: via med. L. from Gk *akephalos* 'headless' + **-OUS**.

**acer** /ˈeɪsə/ • **n.** a maple or related tree, with five-lobed leaves. [Genus *Acer*.]
– ORIGIN from L., 'maple'.

**acerb** /əˈsəːb/ • **adj.** chiefly US another term for **ACERBIC**.

**acerbic** • **adj. 1** sharp and forthright. **2** archaic or technical tasting sour or bitter.
– DERIVATIVES **acerbically** adv. **acerbity** n.
– ORIGIN C19: from L. *acerbus* 'sour-tasting' + **-IC**.

**acesulfame** /ˌasɪˈsʌlfeɪm/ • **n.** a sulphur-containing compound used as a low-calorie artificial sweetener.
– ORIGIN 1980s: of unknown origin.

**acet-** • **comb. form** see **ACETO-**.

**acetabulum** /ˌasɪˈtabjʊləm/ • **n.** (pl. **acetabula** /-lə/) **1** Anatomy the socket of the hip bone, into which the head of the femur fits. **2** Zoology a sucker or other cup-shaped structure.
– ORIGIN ME (denoting a vinegar cup): from L., from *acetum* 'vinegar' + *-abulum*, denoting a container.

**acetal** /ˈasɪtal/ • **n.** Chemistry an organic compound formed by the condensation of two alcohol molecules with an aldehyde molecule.
– ORIGIN C19: from **ACETIC ACID** + *al* from **ALCOHOL**.

**acetaldehyde** /ˌasɪtˈaldɪhʌɪd/ • **n.** Chemistry a colourless volatile liquid aldehyde obtained by oxidizing ethanol.

**acetamide** /əˈsiːtəmʌɪd, əˈsɛt-/ • **n.** Chemistry a crystalline solid with a characteristic musty odour, the amide of acetic acid.

**acetaminophen** /əˌsiːtəˈmɪnəfɛn, əˌsɛtə-, ˌasɪtə-/ • **n.** North American term for **PARACETAMOL**.
– ORIGIN 1960s: from para-*acetylaminophen*ol.

**acetanilide** /ˌasɪˈtanɪlʌɪd/ • **n.** Chemistry a crystalline solid prepared by acetylation of aniline, used in dye manufacture.

**acetate** /ˈasɪteɪt/ • **n. 1** Chemistry a salt or ester of acetic acid: *lead acetate*. **2** textile fibre or plastic made of cellulose acetate. ➤a transparency made of cellulose acetate film. ➤a direct-cut recording disc coated with cellulose acetate.

**acetic acid** /əˈsiːtɪk, əˈsɛt-/ • **n.** Chemistry the acid that gives vinegar its characteristic taste. [$CH_3COOH$.]
– ORIGIN C18: *acetic* from Fr. *acétique*, from L. *acetum* 'vinegar'.

**aceto-** (also **acet-** before a vowel) • **comb. form** Chemistry representing **ACETIC ACID** or **ACETYL**.

**acetobacter** /əˌsiːtə(ʊ)ˈbaktə, ˌasɪtəʊ-/ • **n.** bacteria that oxidize organic compounds to acetic acid, as in vinegar formation. [Genus *Acetobacter*.]
– ORIGIN mod. L., from **ACETO-** + **BACTERIUM**.

**acetogenic** /əˌsiːtə(ʊ)ˈdʒɛnɪk, ˌasɪtəʊ-/ • **adj.** (of bacteria) forming acetic acid or acetates as a product of metabolism.

**acetonaemia** /ˌasɪtə(ʊ)ˈniːmɪə/ • **n.** another term for **KETOSIS**.

**acetone** /ˈasɪtəʊn/ • **n.** Chemistry a colourless volatile liquid ketone used as a solvent and synthetic reagent.
– ORIGIN C19: from **ACETIC ACID** + **-ONE**.

**acetonitrile** /əˌsiːtə(ʊ)ˈnʌɪtrʌɪl, ˌasɪtəʊ-/ ● **n.** Chemistry a toxic odoriferous liquid, used as a solvent in high-performance liquid chromatography.

**acetous** /əˈsiːtəs/ ● **adj.** producing or resembling vinegar.
– ORIGIN ME: from late L. *acetosus* 'sour', from L. *acetum* 'vinegar'.

**acetyl** /ˈasɪtʌɪl, -tɪl/ ● **n.** [as modifier] Chemistry of or denoting the acyl radical $-C(O)CH_3$, derived from acetic acid.

**acetylate** /əˈsɛtɪleɪt/ ● **v.** Chemistry introduce an acetyl group into (a molecule).
– DERIVATIVES **acetylation** n.

**acetylcholine** /ˌasɪtʌɪlˈkəʊliːn, -tɪl-/ ● **n.** Biochemistry a compound occurring in the nervous system, in which it functions as a neurotransmitter.

**acetylcholinesterase** /ˌasɪtʌɪlˌkəʊlɪnˈɛstəreɪz, -tɪl-/ ● **n.** Biochemistry an enzyme that breaks down acetylcholine, stopping excitation of a nerve after transmission of an impulse.

**acetylene** /əˈsɛtɪliːn/ ● **n.** Chemistry a hydrocarbon gas which burns with a bright flame, used in welding and formerly in lighting. [$C_2H_2$.]
– ORIGIN C19: from **ACETIC ACID** + **-YL** + **-ENE**.

**acetylide** /əˈsɛtɪlʌɪd/ ● **n.** Chemistry a salt-like compound formed from acetylene and a metal, typically unstable or explosive: *silver acetylide.*

**acetylsalicylic acid** /ˌasɪtʌɪlˌsalɪˈsɪlɪk, -tɪl-/ ● **n.** systematic chemical name for **ASPIRIN**.

**Achaean** ● **n.** an inhabitant of Achaea in ancient Greece. ➤ poetic/literary a Greek. ● **adj.** of or relating to Achaea or the Achaeans.

**Achaemenid** /əˈkiːmənɪd/ (also **Achaemenian** /ˌakɪˈmiːnɪən/) ● **n.** a member of the dynasty ruling in Persia from Cyrus I to Darius III (553–330 BC).
– ORIGIN named after *Achaemenes*, the reputed ancestor of the dynasty.

**achalasia** /ˌakəˈleɪzɪə/ ● **n.** Medicine a condition in which the muscles of the lower part of the oesophagus fail to relax, preventing food from passing into the stomach.
– ORIGIN C20: from **A-**[1] + Gk *khalasis* 'loosening' + **-IA**[1].

**acharnement** /əˈʃɑːnmɒ̃/ ● **n.** archaic bloodthirsty fury or ferocity.
– ORIGIN Fr., from *acharner* 'give animals a taste of flesh', ult. from L. *caro, carn-* 'flesh'.

**ache** ● **n.** a continuous or prolonged dull pain. ● **v. 1** suffer from an ache. **2** yearn.
– DERIVATIVES **aching** adj. **achingly** adv.
– ORIGIN OE *æce* (n.), *acan* (v.); the mod. spelling is due to a mistaken assumption that the word is derived from Gk *akhos* 'pain'.

**achene** /əˈkiːn/ ● **n.** Botany a small, dry one-seeded fruit that does not open to release the seed.
– ORIGIN C19: from mod. L. *achaenium*, from *a-* 'not' + Gk *khainein* 'to gape'.

**Acheulian** /əˈʃuːlɪən/ (also **Acheulean**) ● **adj.** Archaeology relating to or denoting the main Lower Palaeolithic culture in Europe (preceding the Mousterian), dated to about 1,500,000–150,000 years ago.
– ORIGIN from *St-Acheul* near Amiens in northern France, where objects from this culture were found.

**achieve** ● **v.** bring about or accomplish by effort, skill, or courage.
– DERIVATIVES **achievable** adj. **achiever** n.
– ORIGIN ME: from OFr. *achever* 'come or bring to a head', from *a chief* 'to a head'.

**achievement** ● **n. 1** a thing that is achieved. **2** the process or fact of achieving. **3** Heraldry a representation of a coat of arms with all the adjuncts to which a bearer of arms is entitled.

**achillea** /ˌakɪˈliːə, əˈkɪlɪə/ ● **n.** yarrow or a related plant, with white or yellow flowers and fern-like leaves. [Genus *Achillea*.]
– ORIGIN via L. from Gk *Akhilleios*, denoting a plant supposed to have been used medicinally by Achilles.

**Achilles heel** ● **n.** a weakness or vulnerable point.
– ORIGIN C19: alluding to the mythological Gk hero *Achilles*, whose mother plunged him into the River Styx when he was a baby, thus making his body invulnerable except for the heel by which she held him.

**Achilles tendon** ● **n.** the tendon connecting calf muscles to the heel.

**achimenes** /əˈkɪmənɪːz/ ● **n.** (pl. same) a Central American plant with tubular or trumpet-shaped flowers. [Genus *Achimenes*.]
– ORIGIN mod. L., either from Gk *akhaimenis* (denoting the plant euphorbia) or from *a-* 'not' + *kheimanein* 'expose to the cold'.

**Achinese** /ˈatʃɪniːz/ ● **n.** (pl. same) **1** a member of a people living in northern Sumatra. **2** the Indonesian language of this people. ● **adj.** of or relating to this people or their language.
– ORIGIN from *Acheh, Atjeh*, a territory in northern Sumatra + *-n-* + **-ESE**.

**achiote** /ˌatʃɪˈɒti/ ● **n.** North American term for **ANNATTO**.
– ORIGIN C17: from Sp., from Nahuatl *achiotl*.

**achiral** /eɪˈkʌɪr(ə)l/ ● **adj.** Chemistry (of a molecule) able to be superimposed on its mirror image; not chiral.

**achkan** /ˈatʃk(ə)n/ ● **n.** a knee-length coat buttoned in front, worn by men from the Indian subcontinent.
– ORIGIN from Hindi *ackan*.

**achlorhydria** /ˌeɪklɔːˈhʌɪdrɪə, ˌaklɔː-/ ● **n.** Medicine absence of hydrochloric acid in the gastric secretions.

**Acholi** /əˈtʃəʊli/ ● **n.** (pl. same) **1** a member of a farming and pastoral people of northern Uganda and southern Sudan. **2** the Nilotic language of this people.
– ORIGIN the name in Acholi.

**achondrite** /əˈkɒndrʌɪt/ ● **n.** a stony meteorite containing no small mineral granules (chondrules).

**achondroplasia** /əˌkɒndrə(ʊ)ˈpleɪzɪə, eɪ-/ ● **n.** Medicine a hereditary condition in which the growth of long bones is retarded, resulting in short limbs.
– DERIVATIVES **achondroplasic** adj. **achondroplastic** adj.
– ORIGIN C19: from **A-**[1] + Gk *khondros* 'cartilage' + *plasis* 'moulding' + **-IA**[1].

**achromat** /ˈakrə(ʊ)mat/ ● **n.** an achromatic lens.

**achromatic** /ˌakrə(ʊ)ˈmatɪk/ ● **adj. 1** relating to or denoting lenses that transmit light without separating it into constituent colours. **2** without colour.
– DERIVATIVES **achromaticity** n. **achromatism** n.
– ORIGIN C18: via Fr. from Gk *a-* 'without' + *khrōmatikos* (from *khrōma* 'colour').

**achy** ● **adj.** (**-ier, -est**) suffering from an ache or aches.

**acicular** /əˈsɪkjʊlə/ ● **adj.** technical needle-shaped.
– ORIGIN C18: from late L. *acicula* 'small needle' + **-AR**[1].

**acid** ● **n. 1** a substance (typically, a corrosive or sour-tasting liquid) with particular chemical properties including turning litmus red, neutralizing alkalis, and dissolving some metals. ➤ Chemistry any molecule able to donate a proton or accept electrons in reactions. **2** informal the drug LSD. ● **adj. 1** containing or having the properties of an acid; having a pH of less than 7. ➤ Geology & Metallurgy rich in silica. **2** sharp-tasting or sour. **3** (of remarks) bitter or cutting.
– DERIVATIVES **acidic** adj. **acidification** n. **acidify** v. **acidity** n. **acidly** adv. **acidy** adj.
– ORIGIN C17: from L. *acidus*, from *acere* 'be sour'.

**acid drop** ● **n.** Brit. a boiled sweet with a sharp taste.

**acid house** ● **n.** a kind of synthesized dance music with a fast repetitive beat, associated with the taking of drugs.

**acidimetry** /ˌasɪˈdɪmɪtri/ ● **n.** measurement of the strengths of acids.

**acid jazz** ● **n.** a kind of dance music incorporating elements of jazz, funk, soul, and hip hop.

**acidophilic** /ˌasɪdə(ʊ)ˈfɪlɪk, əˌsɪd-/ ● **adj.** Biology **1** relating to or denoting cells readily stained with acid dyes. **2** growing best in acidic conditions.

**acidophilus** /ˌasɪˈdɒfɪləs/ ● **n.** a bacterium used to make yogurt. [*Lactobacillus acidophilus*.]
– ORIGIN 1920s: mod. L., lit. 'acid-loving'.

**acidosis** /ˌasɪˈdəʊsɪs/ ● **n.** Medicine an excessively acid condition of the body fluids or tissues.
– DERIVATIVES **acidotic** adj.

**acid rain** ● **n.** rainfall made acidic by atmospheric sulphur and nitrogen oxides from the industrial burning of fossil fuels.

**acid rock** ● **n.** a style of rock music popular in the late 1960s, associated with hallucinogenic drugs.

**acid salt** ● **n.** Chemistry a salt formed by incomplete replacement of the hydrogen of an acid, e.g. potassium hydrogen sulphate ($KHSO_4$).

**acid test** ● **n.** a conclusive test of success or value.
– ORIGIN figuratively, from the original use denoting a test for gold using nitric acid.

**acidulate** /əˈsɪdjʊleɪt/ ● **v.** make slightly acidic.
– DERIVATIVES **acidulated** adj. **acidulation** n.
– ORIGIN C18: from L. *acidulus* (from *acidus* 'sour') + **-ATE**[3].

**acidulous** /əˈsɪdjʊləs/ ● **adj.** sharp-tasting; sour.

**acinus** /ˈasɪnəs/ ● **n.** (pl. **acini** /-nʌɪ/) Anatomy **1** a small sac-like cavity in a gland, surrounded by secretory cells. **2** a region of the lung supplied with air from one of the terminal bronchioles.
– ORIGIN C18: L., lit. 'a kernel'.

**-acious** ● **suffix** (forming adjectives) inclined to; having as a capacity: *capacious*.
– ORIGIN from L. *-ax*, *-ac-* + **-OUS**.

**-acity** ● **suffix** forming nouns of quality or state corresponding to adjectives ending in *-acious* (such as *audacity* corresponding to *audacious*).
– ORIGIN from Fr. *-acité* or L. *-acitas*.

**ack-ack** ● **n.** Military, informal anti-aircraft gunfire or guns.
– ORIGIN signallers' name for the letters *AA*; *ack* for *A* was replaced in military use by *able* in 1942.

**ackee** /ˈaki/ (also **akee**) ● **n. 1** a tropical West African tree which is cultivated for its fruit. [*Blighia sapida*.] **2** the fruit of this tree, which is poisonous until fully ripe.
– ORIGIN C18: from Kru *ākee*.

**ack emma** ● **adv.** Brit. dated informal term for **A.M.**
– ORIGIN First World War: signallers' name for these letters.

**ackers** /ˈakəz/ ● **pl. n.** Brit. informal money.
– ORIGIN 1930s (orig. used by Brit. troops in Egypt as a name for the piastre): prob. alt. of Arab. *fakka* 'small change, coins'.

**acknowledge** ● **v. 1** accept or admit the existence or truth of. **2** confirm receipt of or gratitude for. **3** greet with words or gestures.
– DERIVATIVES **acknowledgeable** adj.
– ORIGIN C15: from the obs. ME verb *knowledge*, influenced by obs. *acknow* 'acknowledge, confess'.

**acknowledgement** (also **acknowledgment**) ● **n. 1** the action or fact of acknowledging. **2** (**acknowledgements**) a statement printed at the beginning of a book expressing the author's gratitude to others.

**ACL** ● **abbrev.** anterior cruciate ligament.

**aclinic line** /əˈklɪnɪk/ ● **n.** another term for **MAGNETIC EQUATOR**.
– ORIGIN C19: *aclinic* from Gk *aklinēs*, from *a-* 'not' + *klinein* 'to bend'.

**ACLU** ● **abbrev.** American Civil Liberties Union.

**acme** /ˈakmi/ ● **n.** the highest point of achievement or excellence.
– ORIGIN C16: from Gk *akmē* 'highest point'.

**Acmeist** /ˈakmiːɪst/ ● **adj.** denoting an early 20th-century movement in Russian poetry which favoured formal technique and clarity of exposition. ● **n.** a member of this movement.
– DERIVATIVES **Acmeism** n.

**acne** ● **n.** a skin condition marked by numerous red pimples resulting from inflamed sebaceous glands.
– DERIVATIVES **acned** adj.
– ORIGIN C19: via mod. L. from Gk *aknas*, a misreading of *akmas*, accusative pl. of *akmē* 'highest point, peak, or facial eruption'; cf. **ACME**.

**acne rosacea** ● **n.** see **ROSACEA**.

**Acol** /ˈakɒl/ ● **n.** Bridge a commonly used British system of bidding designed to enable partners with weaker hands to find suitable contracts.
– ORIGIN 1930s: from *Acol* Road in Hampstead, London, where the system was devised.

**acolyte** /ˈakəlʌɪt/ ● **n. 1** an assistant or follower. **2** a person assisting a priest in a religious service.
– ORIGIN ME: from OFr. *acolyt* or eccles. L. *acolytus*, from Gk *akolouthos* 'follower'.

**aconite** /ˈakənʌɪt/ ● **n. 1** a poisonous plant bearing spikes of hooded pink or purple flowers. [Genus *Aconitum*: many species, including monkshood.] **2** (also **winter aconite**) a small plant bearing yellow flowers in early spring. [*Eranthis hyemalis*.]
– ORIGIN C16: via Fr. and L. from Gk *akoniton*.

**acorn** ● **n.** the fruit of the oak, a smooth oval nut in a cup-like base.
– ORIGIN OE *æcern*, of Gmc origin; rel. to **ACRE**, later assoc. with **OAK** and **CORN**[1].

**acorn barnacle** ● **n.** a stalkless barnacle which attaches itself in large numbers to rocks, ships, and marine animals. [Genus *Balanus*.]

**acorn squash** ● **n.** a winter squash of a variety with ridged dark green to orange rind and yellow flesh.

**acorn worm** ● **n.** a burrowing worm-like marine animal with a proboscis, a collar, and a long trunk with gill slits. [Class Enteropneusta.]

**acouchi** /əˈkuːtʃi/ ● **n.** (pl. **acouchis**) a large forest rodent resembling an agouti, found in the Amazon basin. [Genus *Myoprocta*: two species.]
– ORIGIN C18: from Fr., from Tupi.

**acoustic** /əˈkuːstɪk/ ● **adj. 1** relating to sound or hearing. ➤(of building materials) used for soundproofing or modifying sound. ➤(of a device or system) utilizing sound energy. ➤(of an explosive mine) set off by sound waves. **2** (of popular music or musical instruments) not having electrical amplification. ● **n. 1** the properties of a room or building that determine how sound is transmitted in it. **2** (**acoustics**) [treated as sing.] the branch of physics concerned with the properties of sound.
– DERIVATIVES **acoustical** adj. **acoustically** adv. **acoustician** n.
– ORIGIN C17: from Gk *akoustikos*, from *akouein* 'hear'.

**acoustic coupler** ● **n.** Electronics a modem which converts digital signals into audible signals and vice versa so that they can be transmitted and received over telephone lines.

**acoustic impedance** ● **n.** Physics the ratio of the pressure over an imaginary surface in a sound wave to the rate of particle flow across the surface.

**acoustic shock** ● **n.** damaged hearing suffered by the user of an earphone as a result of sudden excessive noise in the device.

**acquaint** ● **v. 1** (**acquaint someone with**) make someone aware of or familiar with. **2** (**be acquainted with**) know personally. ➤(**be acquainted**) (of two or more people) know each other personally.
– ORIGIN ME: from OFr. *acointier* 'make known', from late L. *accognitare*, from L. *accognoscere*, from *ad-* 'to' + *cognoscere* 'come to know'.

**acquaintance** ● **n. 1** the fact or state of being acquainted. **2** a person one knows slightly.
– DERIVATIVES **acquaintanceship** n.

**acquiesce** /ˌakwɪˈɛs/ ● **v.** accept or consent to something without protest.
– DERIVATIVES **acquiescence** n. **acquiescent** adj.
– ORIGIN C17: from L. *acquiescere*, from *ad-* 'to, at' + *quiescere* 'to rest'.

**acquire** ● **v.** come to possess. ➤learn or develop (a skill, quality, etc.).
– PHRASES **acquired taste** a thing that one learns to like over time.
– DERIVATIVES **acquirable** adj. **acquiree** n. (Finance). **acquirement** n. **acquirer** n.
– ORIGIN ME *acquere*, from OFr. *aquerre*, based on L. *acquirere* 'get in addition', from *ad-* 'to' + *quaerere* 'seek'.

**acquired character** (also **acquired characteristic**) ● **n.** Biology a change in an organ or tissue due to use, disuse, or environmental effects, and not inherited.

**acquired immune deficiency syndrome** ● **n.** see **AIDS**.

**acquisition** /ˌakwɪˈzɪʃ(ə)n/ ● **n. 1** a recently acquired asset or object. **2** the act of acquiring.

**acquisition accounting** ● **n.** a procedure in accounting in which the value of the assets of a company is changed from book to fair market level after a takeover.

**acquisitive** ● **adj.** excessively interested in acquiring money or material things.
– DERIVATIVES **acquisitively** adv. **acquisitiveness** n.
– ORIGIN C19: from Fr. *acquisitif, -ive*, from late L. *acquisitivus*, from L. *acquisit-*, *acquirere* (see **ACQUIRE**).

**acquit** ● **v.** (**acquitted**, **acquitting**) **1** formally declare not guilty of a criminal charge. **2** (**acquit oneself**) conduct oneself or perform in a specified way. ➤(**acquit oneself of**) archaic discharge (a duty or responsibility).
– DERIVATIVES **acquittal** n.
– ORIGIN ME: from OFr. *acquiter*, from med. L. *acquitare* 'pay a debt', from *ad-* 'to' + *quitare* 'set free'.

**acquittance** ● **n.** Law, dated a written receipt attesting the settlement of a fine or debt.

**acrasia** ● **n.** variant spelling of **AKRASIA**.

**acre** /ˈeɪkə/ ● **n.** a unit of land area equal to 4,840 square yards (0.405 hectare).
– DERIVATIVES **acreage** n. **-acred** adj.
– ORIGIN OE *æcer* (denoting the amount of land a yoke of oxen could plough in a day), of Gmc origin.

**acre-foot** ● **n.** (pl. **acre-feet**) a unit of volume equal to the volume of a sheet of water one acre (0.405 hectare) in area and one foot (30.48 cm) in depth; 43,560 cubic feet (1233.5 cubic metres).

**acrid** /ˈakrɪd/ ● **adj.** unpleasantly bitter or pungent.
– DERIVATIVES **acridity** n. **acridly** adv.
– ORIGIN C18: formed irregularly from L. *acer, acri-* 'sharp, pungent' + **-ID**[1]; prob. influenced by *acid*.

**acridine** /ˈakrɪdiːn/ ● **n.** Chemistry a colourless solid compound obtained from coal tar, used in the manufacture of dyes and drugs.

**acriflavine** /ˌakrɪˈfleɪvɪn, -iːn/ ● **n.** a bright orange-red dye derived from acridine, used as an antiseptic.
– ORIGIN C20: from **ACRIDINE** + L. *flavus* 'yellow' + **-INE**[4].

**acrimony** /ˈakrɪməni/ ● **n.** bitterness or ill feeling.
– DERIVATIVES **acrimonious** adj. **acrimoniously** adv.
– ORIGIN C16 (in the sense 'bitter taste or smell'): from Fr. *acrimonie* or L. *acrimonia*, from *acer, acri-* 'pungent, acrid'.

**acrobat** ● **n.** an entertainer who performs acrobatics.
– DERIVATIVES **acrobatic** adj. **acrobatically** adv.
– ORIGIN C19: from Fr. *acrobate*, from Gk *akrobatēs*, from *akrobatos* 'walking on tiptoe', from *akron* 'tip' + *bainein* 'to walk'.

**acrobatics** ● **pl. n.** [usu. treated as sing.] spectacular gymnastic feats.

**acrocyanosis** /ˌakrə(ʊ)sʌɪəˈnəʊsɪs/ ● **n.** Medicine bluish or purple colouring of the hands and feet caused by slow circulation.
– ORIGIN C19: from Gk *akron* 'tip' + **CYANOSIS**.

**acrolect** /ˈakrə(ʊ)lɛkt/ ● **n.** Linguistics the most prestigious dialect or variety of a language. Contrasted with **BASILECT**.
– DERIVATIVES **acrolectal** adj.
– ORIGIN 1960s: from Gk *akron* 'summit' + *-lect* as in *dialect*.

**acromegaly** /ˌakrə(ʊ)ˈmɛgəli/ ● **n.** Medicine abnormal growth of the hands, feet, and face, caused by overproduction of growth hormone by the pituitary gland.
– DERIVATIVES **acromegalic** /-mɪˈgalɪk/ adj.
– ORIGIN C19: coined in Fr. from Gk *akron* 'tip, extremity' + *megas, megal-* 'great'.

**acronym** /ˈakrənɪm/ ● **n.** a word formed from the initial letters of other words (e.g. *laser, Aids*).
– ORIGIN 1940s: from Gk *akron* 'end, tip' + *onoma* 'name'.

**acropetal** /əˈkrɒpɪt(ə)l/ ● **adj.** Botany relating to or denoting growth upwards from the base or point of attachment. Often contrasted with **BASIPETAL**.
– DERIVATIVES **acropetally** adv.
– ORIGIN C19: from Gk *akron* 'tip' + L. *petere* 'seek' + **-AL**.

**acrophobia** /ˌakrəˈfəʊbɪə/ ● **n.** extreme or irrational fear of heights.
– DERIVATIVES **acrophobic** adj.
– ORIGIN C19: from Gk *akron* 'summit' + **-PHOBIA**.

**acropolis** /əˈkrɒpəlɪs/ ● **n.** a citadel or fortified part of an ancient Greek city, built on high ground.
– ORIGIN Gk, from *akron* 'summit' + *polis* 'city'.

**across** ● **prep. & adv.** from one side to the other of (something). ➤expressing movement over a place or region. ➤on or towards the other side of.
– PHRASES **across the board** applying to all.
– ORIGIN ME (as adv. meaning 'in the form of a cross'): from OFr. *a croix, en croix* 'in or on a cross'.

**acrostic** /əˈkrɒstɪk/ ● **n.** a poem or puzzle in which certain letters in each line form a word or words.
– ORIGIN C16: from Fr. *acrostiche*, from Gk *akrostikhis*, from *akron* 'end' + *stikhos* 'row, line of verse'.

**acrylamide** /əˈkrɪləmʌɪd/ ● **n.** Chemistry a colourless crystalline solid which readily forms water-soluble polymers.
– ORIGIN C19: from **ACRYLIC** + **AMIDE**.

**acrylic** ● **adj.** denoting a synthetic resin or textile fibre made from polymers of acrylic acid or acrylates.
– ORIGIN C19: from the liquid aldehyde *acrolein* (from L. *acer, acri-* 'pungent' + *ol(eum)* 'oil' + **-IN**[1]) + **-YL** + **-IC**.

**acrylic acid** ● **n.** Chemistry a pungent liquid organic acid which can be polymerized to make synthetic resins.
– DERIVATIVES **acrylate** n.

**acrylonitrile** /ˌakrɪlə(ʊ)ˈnʌɪtrʌɪl/ ● **n.** Chemistry a pungent, toxic liquid used in making artificial fibres and other polymers.

**ACT** ● **abbrev. 1** advance corporation tax. **2** Australian Capital Territory.

**act** ● **v. 1** take action; do something. ➤(**act up**) informal behave badly. **2** (**act for/on behalf of**) represent on a contractual or legal basis. ➤[as adj. **acting**] temporarily doing the duties of another. **3** take effect or have a particular effect. **4** perform a fictional role in a play or film. ➤behave so as to appear to be: *I acted dumb.* ➤(**act something out**) perform a narrative as if it were a play. ● **n. 1** a thing done. **2** a simulation or pretence. ➤a particular type of behaviour or routine: *he did his Sir Galahad act.* **3** Law a written ordinance of Parliament, Congress, etc. **4** dated a record of the decisions or proceedings of a committee or an academic body. **5** a main division of a play, ballet, or opera. **6** a set performance.
– PHRASES **act of God** an instance of uncontrollable natural forces in operation. **act of grace** a privilege or concession that cannot be claimed as a right. **get** (or **be**) **in on the act** informal become (or be) involved in a particular activity, in order to gain an advantage.
– DERIVATIVES **actability** n. **actable** adj. **acting** n.
– ORIGIN ME: from L. *actus* 'event, thing done', from *act-*, *agere* 'do, act', reinforced by Fr. *acte*.

**actant** /ˈaktənt/ ● **n. 1** Grammar a noun or noun phrase involved in the action expressed by a verb. **2** (in literary theory) a person, creature, or object playing an active role in a narrative.

**ACTH** ● **abbrev.** Biochemistry adrenocorticotrophic hormone.

**actin** /ˈaktɪn/ ● **n.** Biochemistry a protein which forms (together with myosin) the contractile filaments of muscle cells.
– ORIGIN 1940: from Gk *aktis, aktin-* 'ray' + **-IN**[1].

**acting pilot officer** ● **n.** a rank in the RAF above warrant officer and below pilot officer.

**actinian** /akˈtɪnɪən/ ● **n.** Zoology a sea anemone.
– ORIGIN C18: from the mod. L. genus name *Actinia* (from Gk *aktis, aktin-* 'ray') + **-AN**.

**actinic** /akˈtɪnɪk/ ● **adj.** technical (of light or lighting) able to cause photochemical reactions, as in photography, through having a significant short-wavelength or ultraviolet component.
– DERIVATIVES **actinism** n.
– ORIGIN C19: from Gk *aktis, aktin-* 'ray' + **-IC**.

**actinide** /ˈaktɪnʌɪd/ ● **n.** Chemistry any of the series of fifteen radioactive metallic elements from actinium (atomic number 89) to lawrencium (atomic number 103) in the periodic table.
– ORIGIN 1940s: from **ACTINIUM** + **-IDE**, on the pattern of *lanthanide*.

**actinium** /akˈtɪnɪəm/ ● **n.** the chemical element of atomic number 89, a rare radioactive metallic element of

the actinide series that occurs as an impurity in uranium ores. (Symbol: **Ac**)
– ORIGIN C20: from Gk *aktis, aktin-* 'ray' + **-IUM**.

**actinolite** /ak'tɪnəlʌɪt/ ● n. a green mineral of the amphibole group containing calcium, magnesium, and iron and occurring chiefly in metamorphic rocks and as a form of asbestos.
– ORIGIN C18: from Gk *aktis, aktin-* 'ray' + *lithos* 'stone' (because of the ray-like crystals).

**actinometer** /ˌaktɪ'nɒmɪtə/ ● n. Physics an instrument for measuring the intensity of radiation.
– ORIGIN C19: from Gk *aktis, aktin-* 'ray' + **-METER**.

**actinomorphic** /ˌaktɪnə(ʊ)'mɔːfɪk/ ● adj. Biology characterized by radial symmetry, such as a starfish. Compare with **ZYGOMORPHIC**.
– DERIVATIVES **actinomorphy** n.
– ORIGIN C19: from Gk *aktis, aktin-* 'ray' + *morphē* 'form' + **-IC**.

**actinomycete** /ˌaktɪnə(ʊ)'mʌɪsiːt/ ● n. a filamentous bacterium of an order (Actinomycetales) including the streptomycetes.
– ORIGIN 1920s: mod. L. *actinomycetes*, from Gk *aktis, aktin-* 'ray' + *mukētes*, pl. of *mukēs* 'fungus'.

**action** ● n. **1** the process of doing something to achieve an aim. **2** a thing done. **3** the effect or influence of something such as a chemical. **4** a legal process; a lawsuit. **5** armed conflict. **6** the way in which something works or moves. ● v. take action on.
– PHRASES **in action** engaged in an activity; in operation. **out of action** not working.
– ORIGIN ME: via OFr. from L. *actio(n-)*, from *agere* 'do, act'.

**actionable** ● adj. Law giving sufficient reason to take legal action.

**actioner** ● n. informal a film predominantly consisting of exciting action and adventure.

**action painting** ● n. a technique and style of painting in which paint is thrown or poured on to the canvas.

**action potential** ● n. Physiology the change in electrical potential associated with the passage of an impulse along the membrane of a muscle cell or nerve cell.

**action replay** ● n. Brit. a playback of part of a television broadcast, especially one in slow motion.

**action stations** ● pl. n. chiefly Brit. the positions taken up by military personnel in preparation for action.

**activate** ● v. make active or operative. ➤convert (a substance, molecule, etc.) into a reactive form.
– DERIVATIVES **activation** n. **activator** n.

**activated carbon** (also **activated charcoal**) ● n. charcoal that has been heated or otherwise treated to increase its adsorptive power.

**activated sludge** ● n. aerated sewage containing aerobic micro-organisms which help to break it down.

**active** ● adj. **1** moving or tending to move about vigorously or frequently. ➤(of a person's mind or imagination) alert and lively. **2** participating in a particular sphere or activity. **3** working. **4** (of an electric circuit) capable of modifying its state or characteristics automatically in response to input or feedback. **5** (of a volcano) erupting or having erupted in the historical times. **6** (of a disease) not in remission or latent. **7** having a chemical or biological effect on something. **8** Grammar denoting a voice of verbs in which the subject is typically the person or thing performing the action and which can take a direct object (e.g. *she loved him* as opposed to *he was loved*). The opposite of **PASSIVE**. ● n. Grammar an active form of a verb.
– DERIVATIVES **actively** adv.
– ORIGIN ME: from L. *activus*, from *act-*, *agere* 'act, do'.

**active immunity** ● n. Physiology immunity which results from the production of antibodies by the immune system.

**active layer** ● n. Geography the seasonally thawed surface layer above permafrost.

**active list** ● n. a list of the officers in an armed service who are liable to be called on for duty.

**active matrix** ● n. Electronics a display system in which each pixel is individually controlled.

**active service** ● n. direct participation in military operations as a member of the armed forces.

**active site** ● n. Biochemistry a region on an enzyme that binds to a protein or other substance during a reaction.

**active transport** ● n. Biology the movement of ions or molecules across a cell membrane into a region of higher concentration, assisted by enzymes and requiring energy.

**activism** ● n. the use of vigorous campaigning to bring about political or social change.
– DERIVATIVES **activist** n. & adj.

**activity** ● n. (pl. **-ies**) **1** a condition in which things are happening or being done. ➤busy or vigorous action or movement. **2** an action taken in pursuit of an objective. ➤a recreational pursuit. **3** the degree to which something displays its characteristic property or behaviour.

**act of contrition** ● n. (in the Roman Catholic Church) a penitential prayer.

**actomyosin** /ˌaktə(ʊ)'mʌɪəsɪn/ ● n. Biochemistry a complex of actin and myosin of which the contractile protein filaments of muscle tissue are composed.

**actor** ● n. **1** a person whose profession is acting. **2** a participant in an action or process.

**actress** ● n. a female actor.
– DERIVATIVES **actressy** adj.

**actual** /'aktʃʊəl, -tjʊəl/ ● adj. **1** existing in fact. **2** current.
– DERIVATIVES **actuality** n. **actualization** (also **-isation**) n. **actualize** (also **-ise**) v.
– ORIGIN ME: from OFr. *actuel* 'active, practical', from late L. *actualis*, from *actus* (see **ACT**).

**actual bodily harm** ● n. Law minor injury inflicted on a person by the deliberate action of another, considered less serious than grievous bodily harm.

**actually** ● adv. **1** as the truth or facts of a situation. **2** as a matter of fact; even.

**actuary** /'aktʃʊəri, -tjʊ-/ ● n. (pl. **-ies**) a person who compiles and analyses statistics in order to calculate insurance risks and premiums.
– DERIVATIVES **actuarial** adj. **actuarially** (also **actuarily**) adv.
– ORIGIN C16: from L. *actuarius* 'bookkeeper', from *actus* (see **ACT**).

**actuate** /'aktʃʊeɪt, -tjʊ-/ ● v. **1** cause to operate. **2** motivate to act in a particular way.
– DERIVATIVES **actuation** n. **actuator** n.
– ORIGIN C16: from med. L. *actuat-*, *actuare*, from L. *actus* (see **ACT**).

**actus reus** /ˌaktəs 'reɪəs/ ● n. Law action or conduct which is a constituent element of a crime, as opposed to the mental state of the accused. Compare with **MENS REA**.
– ORIGIN L., lit. 'guilty act'.

**acuity** /ə'kjuːɪti/ ● n. sharpness or keenness of thought, vision, or hearing.
– ORIGIN ME: from OFr. *acuite* or med. L. *acuitas*, from L. *acuere* (see **ACUTE**).

**aculeate** /ə'kjuːlɪət/ ● adj. **1** Entomology denoting hymenopterous insects with stings, e.g. bees and wasps. **2** Botany sharply pointed; prickly.
– ORIGIN C17: from L. *aculeatus*, from *aculeus* 'a sting', dimin. of *acus* 'needle'.

**acumen** /'akjʊmən, ə'kjuːmən/ ● n. the ability to make good judgements and take quick decisions.
– ORIGIN C16: from L., 'sharpness, point', from *acuere* (see **ACUTE**).

**acuminate** /ə'kjuːmɪnət/ ● adj. Biology (of a plant or animal structure) tapering to a point.
– ORIGIN C16: from late L. *acuminat-*, *acuminare*, from *acuere* (see **ACUTE**).

**acupressure** /'akjʊˌprɛʃə/ ● n. a system of complementary medicine in which manual pressure is applied to the body at specific points along supposed lines of energy.
– ORIGIN 1950s: blend of **ACUPUNCTURE** and **PRESSURE**.

**acupuncture** /'akjʊˌpʌŋ(k)tʃə/ ● n. a system of complementary medicine in which fine needles are inserted in

the skin at specific points along supposed lines of energy.
– DERIVATIVES **acupuncturist** n.
– ORIGIN C17: from L. *acu* 'with a needle' + PUNCTURE.

**acushla** /əˈkʊʃlə/ ● n. Irish dated an affectionate form of address.
– ORIGIN C19: from Ir. *a chuisle* (*moi chroi*) 'O pulse (of my heart)!'

**acutance** /əˈkjuːt(ə)ns/ ● n. the sharpness of a photographic or printed image.

**acute** ● adj. **1** critical; serious. ➤(of an illness) coming sharply to a crisis; severe. Often contrasted with CHRONIC. **2** perceptive; shrewd. ➤(of a physical sense or faculty) highly developed. **3** (of an angle) less than 90°. **4** (of a sound) high; shrill. ● n. short for ACUTE ACCENT.
– DERIVATIVES **acutely** adv. **acuteness** n.
– ORIGIN ME: from L. *acut-*, *acuere* 'sharpen', from *acus* 'needle'.

**acute abdomen** ● n. Medicine a condition of severe abdominal pain caused by acute disease of or injury to the internal organs.

**acute accent** ● n. a mark (´) placed over certain letters in some languages to indicate a feature such as altered sound quality (e.g. in *fiancée*).

**acute rheumatism** ● n. rheumatic fever.

**ACW** ● abbrev. aircraftwoman.

**-acy** ● suffix forming nouns of state or quality: *celibacy.*
– ORIGIN var. of -CY, from L. *-atia* (med. L. *-acia*), or from Gk *-ateia*.

**acyclic** /eɪˈsʌɪklɪk, -ˈsɪk-/ ● adj. **1** not displaying or forming part of a cycle. ➤(of a woman) not having a menstrual cycle. **2** Chemistry (of a compound or molecule) containing no rings of atoms.

**acyclovir** /eɪˈsʌɪklə(ʊ),vɪə/ ● n. Medicine an antiviral drug used chiefly in the treatment of herpes and Aids.
– ORIGIN 1970s: from *acycl(ic)* + *vir(al DNA)*.

**acyl** /ˈeɪsʌɪl, ˈasɪl/ ● n. [as modifier] Chemistry of or denoting a radical of general formula –C(O)R, where R is an alkyl group, derived from a carboxylic acid.
– ORIGIN C19: coined in Ger., from L. *acidus* (see ACID) + -YL.

**acylate** /ˈeɪsʌɪleɪt, ˈasɪl-/ ● v. Chemistry introduce an acyl group into (a molecule or compound).
– DERIVATIVES **acylation** n.

**AD** ● abbrev. Anno Domini (placed after a date, indicating that it comes the specified number of years after the traditional date of Christ's birth).
– ORIGIN L. 'in the year of the Lord'.

**A/D** ● abbrev. Electronics analogue to digital.

**ad** ● n. informal **1** an advertisement. **2** Tennis advantage.

**ad-** (also **a-** before *sc, sp, st*; **ac-** before *c, k, q*; **af-** before *f*; **ag-** before *g*; **al-** before *l*; **an-** before *n*; **ap-** before *p*; **ar-** before *r*; **as-** before *s*; **at-** before *t*) ● prefix **1** denoting motion or direction to: *advance.* **2** denoting reduction or change into: *adulterate.* **3** denoting addition or increase: *adjunct.*
– ORIGIN from L. *ad* 'to'.

**-ad**[1] /ad, əd/ ● suffix forming nouns: **1** in collective numerals: *myriad.* **2** in names of females in classical mythology: *dryad.* **3** in names of poems and similar compositions: *Iliad.* **4** forming names of members of some taxonomic groupings: *bromeliad.*
– ORIGIN from the Gk ending *-as, -ad-*.

**-ad**[2] /əd/ ● suffix forming nouns such as *ballad, salad.* Compare with -ADE[2].
– ORIGIN from Fr. *-ade*.

**Ada** /ˈeɪdə/ ● n. a high-level computer programming language used chiefly in real-time computerized control systems, e.g. for aircraft navigation.
– ORIGIN 1980s: named after the C19 Engl. mathematician *Ada* Lovelace.

**adage** /ˈadɪdʒ/ ● n. a proverb or short statement expressing a general truth.
– ORIGIN C16: from Fr., from L. *adagium* 'saying', based on an early form of *aio* 'I say'.

**adagio** /əˈdɑː(d)ʒɪəʊ/ Music ● adv. & adj. in slow time. ● n. (pl. **-os**) an adagio passage.
– ORIGIN Ital., from *ad agio* 'at ease'.

**adamant** ● adj. refusing to be persuaded or to change one's mind. ● n. archaic a legendary rock or mineral associated at times with both diamond and lodestones.
– DERIVATIVES **adamance** n. **adamancy** n. **adamantly** adv.
– ORIGIN OE (as n.), from OFr. *adamaunt-*, via L. from Gk *adamas, adamant-*, 'untameable, invincible' (later used to denote the hardest metal or stone, hence diamond), from *a-* 'not' + *daman* 'to tame'.

**adamantine** /,adəˈmantʌɪn/ ● adj. poetic/literary unbreakable.

**Adam's ale** ● n. dated, humorous water.

**Adam's apple** ● n. a projection at the front of the neck formed by the thyroid cartilage of the larynx, often prominent in men.
– ORIGIN C18: so named from the notion that a piece of the forbidden fruit became lodged in Adam's throat.

**Adam's needle** ● n. another term for YUCCA.

**adapt** ● v. **1** make suitable for a new use or purpose. **2** become adjusted to new conditions.
– DERIVATIVES **adaptability** n. **adaptable** adj. **adaptably** adv. **adaptive** adj.
– ORIGIN ME: from Fr. *adapter*, from L. *adaptare*, from *ad-* 'to' + *aptare* (from *aptus* 'fit').

**adaptation** ● n. **1** the action or process of adapting or being adapted. **2** a film or play adapted from a written work. **3** Biology a change or the process of change by which an organism or species becomes better suited to its environment.

**adaptationism** ● n. Biology the axiom or assumption that each feature of an organism is the result of evolutionary adaptation for a particular function.
– DERIVATIVES **adaptationist** n. & adj.

**adaption** ● n. another term for ADAPTATION.

**adaptive radiation** ● n. Biology the diversification of a group of organisms into forms filling different ecological niches.

**adaptogen** /əˈdaptədʒ(ə)n/ ● n. (in herbal medicine) a natural substance considered to help the body adapt to stress.
– DERIVATIVES **adaptogenic** adj.

**adaptor** (also **adapter**) ● n. **1** a device for connecting pieces of equipment. ➤Brit. a device for connecting more than one plug at a time or plugs of a non-standard type to an electrical socket. **2** a person who adapts a text for filming, broadcasting, or the stage.

**Adar** /əˈdɑː/ ● n. (in the Jewish calendar) the sixth month of the civil and twelfth of the religious year, usually coinciding with parts of February and March.
– ORIGIN from Heb. *ʼăḏār.*

**ADAS** /ˈeɪdas/ ● abbrev. Agricultural Development and Advisory Service.

**adaxial** /adˈaksɪəl/ ● adj. Botany facing toward the stem (in particular denoting the upper surface of a leaf). The opposite of ABAXIAL.

**ADC** ● abbrev. **1** aide-de-camp. **2** analogue to digital converter.

**add** ● v. **1** join to or put with something else. ➤(**add up**) increase in amount, number, or degree. **2** put together (two or more numbers or amounts) to calculate their total value. ➤(**add up to**) amount to. **3** (**add up**) informal make sense. **4** say as a further remark.
– ORIGIN ME: from L. *addit-*, *addere*, from *ad-* 'to' + the base of *dare* 'put'.

**addax** /ˈadaks/ ● n. a large antelope with a mainly greyish and white coat, native to the deserts of North Africa. [*Addax nasomaculatus.*]
– ORIGIN C17: from L., from an Afr. word recorded by Pliny.

**addendum** /əˈdɛndəm/ ● n. (pl. **addenda** /-də/) **1** an extra item added at the end of a book or text. **2** Engineering the radial distance from the pitch circle of a cogwheel or wormwheel to the crests of the teeth or ridges. Compare with DEDENDUM.
– ORIGIN C17: L., 'that which is to be added', gerundive of *addere* (see ADD).

**adder**[1] • **n.** a small venomous snake which has a dark zigzag pattern on its back and bears live young. [*Vipera berus.*] ➤ used in names of similar or related snakes, e.g. **death adder, puff adder.**
– ORIGIN OE *nædre* 'serpent, adder', of Gmc origin; the initial *n* was lost in ME by wrong division of *a naddre.*

**adder**[2] • **n.** Electronics a unit which adds together two input variables.

**adder's tongue** (also US **adder tongue**) • **n. 1** a fern with a single pointed oval frond and an unbranched spore-bearing stem. [Genus *Ophioglossum.*] **2** North American term for **DOG'S-TOOTH VIOLET.**

**addict** • **n.** a person who is addicted to something.
– ORIGIN C20: from the obs. verb *addict*, which was a back-form. from **ADDICTED.**

**addicted** • **adj. 1** physically dependent on a particular substance. **2** devoted to a particular interest or activity.
– ORIGIN C16: from the obs. adj. *addict* 'bound or devoted', from L. *addict-*, *addicere* 'assign', from *ad-* 'to' + *dicere* 'say'.

**addiction** • **n.** the fact or condition of being addicted.

**addictive** • **adj.** causing or likely to cause addiction.

**Addisonian anaemia** • **n.** another term for **PERNICIOUS ANAEMIA.**

**Addison's disease** • **n.** a disease characterized by progressive anaemia and bronze discoloration of the skin, caused by inadequate secretion of hormones by the adrenal cortex.
– DERIVATIVES **Addisonian** adj.
– ORIGIN C19: named after the Engl. physician Thomas *Addison.*

**addition** • **n. 1** the action or process of adding. ➤ a person or thing added. **2** the process of adding numbers or amounts. ➤ Mathematics the process of combining matrices, vectors, or other quantities under specific rules to obtain their sum or resultant.
– DERIVATIVES **additional** adj. **additionally** adv.

**additional member system** • **n.** a type of proportional representation in which each elector votes separately for a party and for a representative.

**addition reaction** • **n.** Chemistry a reaction in which one molecule combines with another to form a larger molecule with no other products.

**additive** • **n.** a substance added to improve or preserve something. • **adj. 1** characterized by, relating to, or produced by addition. **2** technical of or relating to the reproduction of colours by the superimposition of primary colours.

**addle** • **v.** [often as adj. **addled**] **1** confuse. **2** (of an egg) become rotten, producing no chick. • **adj. 1** unsound; muddled: *the film is addle-brained.* **2** archaic (of an egg) rotten.
– ORIGIN ME: from OE *adela* 'liquid filth', of Gmc origin.

**addorsed** /əˈdɔːst/ • **adj.** chiefly Heraldry back to back.
– ORIGIN C16: from L. *ad* 'to' + *dorsum* 'back' + **-ED**[2].

**address** • **n. 1** the particulars of the place where someone lives or an organization is situated. **2** Computing a binary number identifying a location in a data storage system or computer memory. **3** a formal speech. ➤ archaic a person's manner of speaking. ➤ (**addresses**) archaic courteous or amorous approaches. **4** dated skill, dexterity, or readiness. • **v. 1** write someone's name and address on (an envelope or parcel). **2** speak formally to. ➤ (**address something to**) direct one's remarks to. **3** think about and begin to deal with. **4** Golf prepare to hit (the ball).
– DERIVATIVES **addressee** n. **addresser** n.
– ORIGIN ME (as v. in the senses 'set upright' and 'guide, direct'): from OFr., based on L. *ad-* 'towards' + *directus* (see **DIRECT**).

**addressable** • **adj.** Computing relating to or denoting a memory unit in which all locations can be separately accessed by a particular program.

**adduce** /əˈdjuːs/ • **v.** cite as evidence.
– DERIVATIVES **adducible** adj.
– ORIGIN ME: from L. *adducere*, from *ad-* 'towards' + *ducere* 'to lead'.

**adduct**[1] /əˈdʌkt/ • **v.** (of a muscle) move (a limb or other part) towards the midline of the body or towards another part. The opposite of **ABDUCT.**
– DERIVATIVES **adduction** n. **adductor** n.
– ORIGIN C19: back-form. from ME *adduction*, from late L. *adductio(n-)* 'bringing forward', from *adducere* (see **ADDUCE**).

**adduct**[2] /ˈadʌkt/ • **n.** Chemistry the product of an addition reaction between two compounds.
– ORIGIN 1940s: from Ger. *Addukt* (blend of *Addition* and *Produkt*).

**-ade**[1] • **suffix** forming nouns: **1** denoting an action that is completed: *blockade.* **2** denoting the body concerned in an action or process: *brigade.* **3** denoting the product or result of an action or process: *arcade.*
– ORIGIN from Fr., via Port., Provençal, and Sp. *-ada* or via Ital. *-ata*, from L. *-atus* (past participial suffix of verbs ending in *-are*).

**-ade**[2] • **suffix** forming nouns such as *decade.*
– ORIGIN var. of **-AD**[1], from Fr. *-ade*, from Gk *-as, -ad-.*

**-ade**[3] • **suffix** forming nouns: **1** equivalent in sense to nouns ending in **-ADE**[1]: *brocade.* **2** denoting a person: *renegade.*
– ORIGIN from Sp. or Port. *-ado*, masc. form of *-ada* (see **-ADE**[1]).

**adenine** /ˈadɪniːn/ • **n.** Biochemistry a compound which is one of the four constituent bases of nucleic acids.
– ORIGIN C19: from Gk *adēn* 'gland' + **-INE**[4].

**adeno-** • **comb. form** relating to a gland or glands: *adenocarcinoma.*
– ORIGIN from Gk *adēn* 'gland'.

**adenocarcinoma** /ˌadɪnəʊˌkɑːsɪˈnəʊmə/ • **n.** (pl. **adenocarcinomas** or **adenocarcinomata** /-mətə/) Medicine a malignant tumour formed from glandular structures in epithelial tissue.

**adenoids** /ˈadɪnɔɪdz/ • **pl. n.** a mass of enlarged lymphatic tissue between the back of the nose and the throat.
– DERIVATIVES **adenoidal** adj.
– ORIGIN C19: *adenoid* from Gk *adēn* 'gland' + **-OID.**

**adenoma** /ˌadɪˈnəʊmə/ • **n.** (pl. **adenomas** or **adenomata** /-mətə/) Medicine a benign tumour formed from glandular structures in epithelial tissue.
– ORIGIN C19: mod. L., from Gk *adēn* 'gland'.

**adenosine** /əˈdɛnə(ʊ)siːn/ • **n.** Biochemistry a nucleoside consisting of adenine combined with ribose.

**adenosine monophosphate** • **n.** another term for **ADENYLIC ACID.**

**adenosine triphosphate** • **n.** Biochemistry a compound which by its breakdown in the body (to **adenosine diphosphate**) provides energy for physiological processes such as muscular contraction.

**adenovirus** /ˈadɪnəʊˌvʌɪrəs/ • **n.** Medicine any of a group of DNA viruses first discovered in adenoid tissue, most of which cause respiratory diseases.

**adenylate cyclase** /əˌdɛnɪleɪt ˈsʌɪkleɪz, ˈsɪk-/ • **n.** Biochemistry an enzyme that catalyses the formation of cyclic adenylic acid from adenosine triphosphate.

**adenylic acid** /ˌadɪˈnɪlɪk/ • **n.** Biochemistry a compound consisting of adenosine bonded to a single phosphate group, present in most DNA and RNA.
– DERIVATIVES **adenylate** n.

**adept** • **adj.** /ˈadɛpt, əˈdɛpt/ very skilled or proficient. • **n.** /ˈadɛpt/ a person who is adept at something.
– DERIVATIVES **adeptly** adv. **adeptness** n.
– ORIGIN C17: from L. *adept-*, *adipisci* 'obtain, attain'.

**adequate** • **adj.** satisfactory or acceptable.
– DERIVATIVES **adequacy** n. **adequately** adv.
– ORIGIN C17: from L. *adaequat-*, *adaequare* 'make equal to', from *ad-* 'to' + *aequus* 'equal'.

**à deux** /ɑː ˈdəː, French a dø/ • **adv.** for or involving two people.
– ORIGIN from Fr.

**ADF** • **abbrev.** automatic direction-finder.

**ad fin.** /ad ˈfɪn/ • **adv.** at or near the end of a piece of writing.
– ORIGIN from L. *ad finem* 'at the end'.

**ADH** • **abbrev.** Biochemistry antidiuretic hormone.

**ADHD** • **abbrev.** attention deficit hyperactivity disorder.

**adhere** /ədˈhɪə/ • **v.** (**adhere to**) **1** stick fast to. **2** believe in and follow the practices of. **3** represent truthfully and

in detail.
– DERIVATIVES **adherence** n. **adherent** n.
– ORIGIN C15: from L. *adhaerere*, from *ad-* 'to' + *haerere* 'to stick'.

**adhesion** /əd'hiːʒ(ə)n/ ● n. the action or process of adhering. ➤ Physics the sticking together of particles of different substances. ➤ Medicine an abnormal union of surfaces due to inflammation or injury.

**adhesive** /əd'hiːsɪv, -zɪv/ ● adj. causing adherence; sticky. ● n. an adhesive substance.
– DERIVATIVES **adhesively** adv. **adhesiveness** n.

**adhibit** /əd'hɪbɪt/ ● v. (**adhibited**, **adhibiting**) formal apply or affix to something else.
– DERIVATIVES **adhibition** n.
– ORIGIN C16: from L. *adhibit-*, *adhibere* 'bring in', from *ad-* 'to' + *habere* 'hold, have'.

**ad hoc** /ad 'hɒk/ ● adj. & adv. formed, arranged, or done for a particular purpose only.
– ORIGIN L., lit. 'to this'.

**adhocracy** /ad'hɒkrəsi/ ● n. the replacement of a rigid bureaucracy with flexible and informal forms of organization.

**ad hominem** /ad 'hɒmɪnɛm/ ● adv. & adj. **1** associated with a particular person. **2** (of an argument) personal rather than objective.
– ORIGIN L., lit. 'to the person'.

**adiabatic** /ˌeɪdʌɪə'batɪk, ˌadɪə-/ ● adj. Physics **1** relating to or denoting a process or condition in which heat does not enter or leave the system concerned. **2** impassable to heat.
– DERIVATIVES **adiabatically** adv.
– ORIGIN C19: from Gk *adiabatos* 'impassable', from *a-* 'not' + *dia* 'through' + *batos* 'passable'.

**adieu** /ə'djuː/ ● exclam. chiefly poetic/literary goodbye.
– ORIGIN ME: from OFr., from *a* 'to' + *Dieu* 'God'.

**ad infinitum** /ˌad ɪnfɪ'nʌɪtəm/ ● adv. endlessly; forever.
– ORIGIN L., lit. 'to infinity'.

**ad interim** /ad 'ɪntərɪm/ ● adv. for the meantime.
– ORIGIN L., from *ad* 'to' and *interim* 'meanwhile', used as a noun.

**adios** /ˌadɪ'ɒs, Spanish a'ðjos/ ● exclam. Spanish term for GOODBYE.
– ORIGIN Sp. *adiós*, from *a* 'to' + *Dios* 'God'.

**adipic acid** /ə'dɪpɪk/ ● n. Chemistry a crystalline fatty acid obtained from natural fats, used in making nylon.
– DERIVATIVES **adipate** n.
– ORIGIN C19: from L. *adeps*, *adip-* 'fat' + -IC.

**adipocere** /ˌadɪpə(ʊ)'sɪə/ ● n. a greyish waxy substance formed by the decomposition of soft tissue in dead bodies subjected to moisture.
– ORIGIN C19: from Fr. *adipocire*, from L. *adeps*, *adip-* 'fat' + Fr. *cire* 'wax'.

**adipocyte** /'adɪpə(ʊ)sʌɪt/ ● n. Biology a cell specialized for the storage of fat, found in connective tissue.
– ORIGIN 1930s: from ADIPOSE + -CYTE.

**adipose** /'adɪpəʊs, -z/ ● adj. technical denoting body tissue used for the storage of fat.
– DERIVATIVES **adiposity** n.
– ORIGIN C18: from mod. L. *adiposus*, from *adeps*, *adip-* 'fat'.

**adipose fin** ● n. Zoology a small, rayless, fleshy dorsal fin present in certain fishes, notably in the salmon family.

**adit** /'adɪt/ ● n. an access or drainage passage leading horizontally into a mine.
– ORIGIN C17: from L. *aditus* 'approach, entrance'.

**Adivasi** /ˌɑːdɪ'vɑːsi/ ● n. (pl. same or **Adivasis**) a member of an aboriginal tribal people of India.
– ORIGIN from mod. Sanskrit *ādivāsī*, from *ādi* 'the beginning' + *vāsin* 'inhabitant'.

**Adj.** ● abbrev. adjutant.

**adjacent** /ə'dʒeɪs(ə)nt/ ● adj. **1** next to or adjoining something else. **2** Geometry (of a pair of angles) formed on the same side of a straight line when intersected by another line.
– DERIVATIVES **adjacency** n.
– ORIGIN ME: from L. *adjacent-*, *adjacere* 'lie near to', from *ad-* 'to' + *jacere* 'lie down'.

**adjective** ● n. Grammar a word naming an attribute of a noun, such as *sweet*, *red*, or *technical*.
– DERIVATIVES **adjectival** adj. **adjectivally** adv.
– ORIGIN ME: from OFr. *adjectif*, *-ive*, from L. *adject-*, *adicere*, 'add'.

**adjigo** /'adʒɪgəʊ/ (also **adjiko** /'adʒɪkəʊ/) ● n. a yam with edible tubers, native to SW Australian coastal areas. [*Dioscorea hastifolia*.]
– ORIGIN C19: prob. from Nhanta (an Aborig. lang.) *ajuga* 'vegetable food'.

**adjoin** ● v. [often as adj. **adjoining**] be next to and joined with.
– ORIGIN ME: from OFr. *ajoindre*, from L. *adjungere*, from *ad-* 'to' + *jungere* 'to join'.

**adjoint** ● adj. Mathematics related to a given function, matrix, or quantity by a particular process of transposition.
– ORIGIN C19: from Fr., lit. 'joined to', from *adjoindre* (see ADJOIN).

**adjourn** /ə'dʒəːn/ ● v. **1** break off (a meeting) with the intention of resuming it later. **2** postpone (a resolution or sentence).
– DERIVATIVES **adjournment** n.
– ORIGIN ME (in the sense 'summon someone to appear on a particular day'): from OFr. *ajorner*, from the phr. *a jorn (nome)* 'to an (appointed) day'.

**Adjt** ● abbrev. adjutant.

**adjudge** ● v. **1** consider or declare to be true or the case. **2** (in legal use) award (compensation). **3** (in legal use) condemn to pay a penalty.
– DERIVATIVES **adjudgement** (also **adjudgment**) n.
– ORIGIN ME: from OFr. *ajuger*, from L. *adjudicare*, from *ad-* 'to' + *judicare*, from *judex*, *judic-* 'a judge'.

**adjudicate** /ə'dʒuːdɪkeɪt/ ● v. make a formal judgement on a disputed matter. ➤ act as a judge in a competition.
– DERIVATIVES **adjudication** n. **adjudicative** adj. **adjudicator** n.
– ORIGIN C18: from L. *adjudicat-*, *adjudicare* (see ADJUDGE).

**adjunct** /'adʒʌŋ(k)t/ ● n. **1** an additional and supplementary part. **2** an assistant. **3** Grammar a word or phrase in a sentence other than the verb or predicate. ● adj. connected or added in an auxiliary way.
– DERIVATIVES **adjunctive** adj.
– ORIGIN C16: from L. *adjunct-*, *adjungere* (see ADJOIN).

**adjunction** ● n. **1** Mathematics the joining of two sets to form a larger set. **2** Logic the asserting in a single formula of two previously asserted formulae.

**adjure** /ə'dʒʊə/ ● v. formal solemnly urge to do something.
– DERIVATIVES **adjuration** n. **adjuratory** /-rət(ə)ri/ adj.
– ORIGIN ME: from L. *adjurare*, from *ad-* 'to' + *jurare* 'swear'.

**adjust** ● v. **1** alter slightly in order to achieve a correct or desired result. ➤ adapt or become used to a new situation. **2** assess (loss or damages) when settling an insurance claim.
– DERIVATIVES **adjustability** n. **adjustable** adj. **adjuster** n. **adjustment** n.
– ORIGIN C17: from obs. Fr. *adjuster*, from OFr. *ajoster* 'to approximate', based on L. *ad-* 'to' + *juxta* 'near'.

**adjutant** /'adʒʊt(ə)nt/ ● n. **1** a military officer acting as an administrative assistant to a senior officer. **2** a large black-and-white stork with a massive bill and a bare head and neck, found in India and SE Asia. [Genus *Leptoptilos*: two species.]
– DERIVATIVES **adjutancy** n.
– ORIGIN C17: from L. *adjutant-*, *adjutare*, frequentative of *adjuvare* (see ADJUVANT).

**adjutant general** ● n. (pl. **adjutants general**) (in the British army) a high-ranking administrative officer. ➤ (in the US army) the chief administrative officer.

**adjuvant** /'adʒʊv(ə)nt/ Medicine ● adj. (of therapy) applied after initial treatment for cancer to suppress secondary tumour formation. ● n. a substance which enhances the body's immune response to an antigen.
– ORIGIN C16: from L. *adjuvant-*, *adjuvare*, from *ad-* 'towards' + *juvare* to 'help'.

**ad-lib** ● v. (**ad-libbed**, **ad-libbing**) speak or perform in public without preparing in advance. ● adv. & adj.

**1** spoken without advance preparation. **2** Music with free rhythm and expression. **3** as much and as often as desired. ● **n.** an ad-lib remark or speech.
– ORIGIN C19: abbrev. of **AD LIBITUM**.

**ad libitum** /ad ˈlɪbɪtəm/ ● **adv. & adj.** more formal term for **AD-LIB**.
– ORIGIN L., lit. 'according to pleasure'.

**ad litem** /ad ˈlʌɪtɛm/ ● **adj.** Law acting in a lawsuit on behalf of a child or an adult who cannot represent themself.
– ORIGIN L., lit. 'for the lawsuit'.

**Adm.** ● **abbrev.** Admiral.

**adman** ● **n.** (pl. **-men**) informal a person who works in advertising.

**admass** ● **n.** dated, chiefly Brit. the section of the community regarded as readily influenced by advertising and the mass media.

**admeasure** ● **v.** archaic apportion.
– DERIVATIVES **admeasurement** n.
– ORIGIN C16: from OFr. *amesurer*, from med. L. *admensurare*, based on L. *metiri* 'to measure'.

**admin** ● **n.** informal, chiefly Brit. administration.

**administer** ● **v. 1** attend to the organization or implementation of. **2** dispense (a drug or remedy). ➤deal out (punishment). **3** (of a priest) perform the rites of (a sacrament). **4** archaic or Law direct the taking of (an oath).
– DERIVATIVES **administrable** adj.
– ORIGIN ME: via OFr. from L. *administrare*, from *ad-* 'to' + *ministrare* 'wait upon'.

**administrate** ● **v.** administer; carry out administration.
– DERIVATIVES **administrative** adj. **administratively** adv. **administrator** n.

**administration** ● **n. 1** the organization and running of a business or system. **2** the government in power. ➤chiefly N. Amer. the term of office of a political leader or government. ➤(in the US) a government agency. **3** Law the management and disposal of the property of a deceased person or debtor, or of an insolvent company, by a legally appointed administrator. **4** the action of administering.

**administratrix** /ədˌmɪnɪˈstreɪtrɪks/ ● **n.** (pl. **administratrixes**, **administratrices** /-trɪsiːz/) Law a female administrator of an estate.

**admirable** ● **adj.** deserving respect and approval.
– DERIVATIVES **admirably** adv.

**admiral** ● **n.** the most senior commander of a fleet or navy. ➤(**Admiral**) a naval officer of the second most senior rank, above vice admiral and below Admiral of the Fleet or Fleet Admiral.
– DERIVATIVES **admiralship** n.
– ORIGIN ME: from OFr. *amiral*, *admirail*, via med. L. from Arab. *'amīr* 'commander'.

**Admiral of the Fleet** ● **n.** the highest rank of admiral in the Royal Navy.

**Admiralty** ● **n.** (pl. **-ies**) **1** (in the UK) the government department that formerly administered the Royal Navy, now used only in titles. **2** (**admiralty**) Law the jurisdiction of courts of law over cases concerning ships or the sea.

**admire** ● **v.** regard with respect or warm approval. ➤look at with pleasure.
– DERIVATIVES **admiration** n. **admirer** n. **admiring** adj. **admiringly** adv.
– ORIGIN C16 (earlier (ME) as *admiration*): from L. *admirari*, from *ad-* 'at' + *mirari* 'wonder'.

**admissible** ● **adj. 1** acceptable or valid. **2** having the right to be admitted to a place.
– DERIVATIVES **admissibility** n.

**admission** ● **n. 1** a confession. **2** the process or fact of being admitted to a place.

**admit** ● **v.** (**admitted**, **admitting**) **1** confess to be true or to be the case. ➤confess to or acknowledge (a crime, fault, or failure). **2** allow to enter. ➤receive into a hospital for treatment. **3** accept as valid. **4** (**admit of**) allow the possibility of.
– DERIVATIVES **admitted** adj. **admittedly** adv.
– ORIGIN ME: from L. *admittere*, from *ad-* 'to' + *mittere* 'send'.

**admittance** ● **n. 1** the process or fact of entering or being allowed to enter. **2** Physics a measure of electrical conduction, numerically equal to the reciprocal of the impedance.

**admix** ● **v.** chiefly technical mix with something else.
– DERIVATIVES **admixture** n.

**admonish** ● **v.** reprimand firmly. ➤earnestly urge or warn.
– DERIVATIVES **admonishment** n. **admonition** n. **admonitor** n. **admonitory** adj.
– ORIGIN ME *amonest* 'urge, exhort', from OFr. *amonester*, based on L. *admonere* 'urge by warning'.

**ADN** ● **abbrev.** Yemen (international vehicle registration).
– ORIGIN from *Aden*, the name of a port in Yemen which was capital of the former South Yemen.

**adnate** /ˈadneɪt/ ● **adj.** Botany joined by having grown together.
– ORIGIN C17: from L. *adnatus*, var. of *agnatus* (see **AGNATE**), by assoc. with **AD-**.

**ad nauseam** /ad ˈnɔːzɪam, -sɪam/ ● **adv.** to a tiresomely excessive degree.
– ORIGIN L., lit. 'to sickness'.

**adnexa** /adˈnɛksə/ ● **pl. n.** Anatomy the parts adjoining an organ.
– DERIVATIVES **adnexal** adj.
– ORIGIN C19: L., neut. pl. of *adnexus* 'joined', from *adnectere* 'fasten to'.

**ado** ● **n.** trouble; fuss.
– ORIGIN ME (orig. in the sense 'action, business'): from northern ME *at do* 'to do', from ON *at* (used to mark an infin.) and **DO**[1].

**-ado** /ˈeɪdəʊ, ˈɑː-/ ● **suffix** forming nouns such as *bravado*, *desperado*. Compare with **-ADE**[3].
– ORIGIN from Sp. and Port. *-ado*, based on L. *-atus*.

**adobe** /əˈdəʊbi, əˈdəʊb/ ● **n.** a kind of clay used to make sun-dried bricks.
– ORIGIN C18: from Sp., from *adobar* 'to plaster', from Arab. *aṭ-ṭūb*, from *al* 'the' + *ṭūb* 'bricks'.

**adolescent** ● **adj.** in the process of developing from a child into an adult. ● **n.** an adolescent boy or girl.
– DERIVATIVES **adolescence** n.
– ORIGIN ME: via Fr. from L. *adolescent-*, *adolescere*, from *ad-* 'to' + *alescere* 'grow, grow up'.

**Adonai** /ˌadɒˈnʌɪ, -ˈneɪʌɪ/ ● **n.** a Hebrew name for God.
– ORIGIN from Heb. *'ăḏōnāy*; see also **JEHOVAH**.

**Adonis** /əˈdəʊnɪs/ ● **n.** an extremely handsome young man.
– ORIGIN from the name of a beautiful youth in Gk mythology.

**Adonis blue** ● **n.** a small butterfly, the male of which has vivid sky-blue wings. [*Lysandra bellargus*.]

**adopt** ● **v. 1** legally take (another's child) and bring it up as one's own. **2** choose to take up or follow (an option or course of action). **3** Brit. choose as a candidate for office. ➤formally approve or accept. **4** Brit. (of a local authority) accept responsibility for the maintenance of (a road). **5** assume (an attitude or position).
– DERIVATIVES **adoptable** adj. **adoptee** n. **adopter** n. **adoption** n.
– ORIGIN C15 (earlier (ME) as *adoption*): via Fr. from L. *adoptare*, from *ad-* 'to' + *optare* 'choose'.

**adoptive** ● **adj. 1** (of a child or parent) in that relationship by adoption. **2** denoting a place chosen as one's permanent place of residence.
– DERIVATIVES **adoptively** adv.

**adorable** ● **adj.** inspiring great affection.
– DERIVATIVES **adorability** n. **adorableness** n. **adorably** adv.

**adoral** /adˈɔːr(ə)l/ ● **adj.** Zoology relating to or denoting the side or end where the mouth is situated.
– DERIVATIVES **adorally** adv.
– ORIGIN C19: from **AD-** + **ORAL**.

**adore** ● **v. 1** love and respect deeply. **2** worship or venerate (a deity).
– DERIVATIVES **adoration** n. **adorer** n. **adoring** adj. **adoringly** adv.
– ORIGIN ME: via OFr. from L. *adorare* 'to worship', from *ad-* 'to' + *orare* 'speak, pray'.

**adorn** ● **v.** decorate.
– DERIVATIVES **adorner** n. **adornment** n.
– ORIGIN ME: via OFr. from L. *adornare*, from *ad-* 'to' + *ornare* 'deck, add lustre'.

**ADP** ● **abbrev.** **1** Biochemistry adenosine diphosphate. **2** automatic data processing.

**ad personam** /ˌad pəːˈsəʊnam/ ● **adv.** formal on an individual basis.
– ORIGIN L., lit. 'to the person'.

**adpressed** ● **adj.** Botany lying closely against an adjacent part or the ground.

**ADR** ● **abbrev.** alternative dispute resolution.

**ad rem** /ad ˈrɛm/ ● **adv. & adj.** formal to the point.
– ORIGIN C16: L., lit. 'to the matter'.

**adrenal** /əˈdriːn(ə)l/ ● **adj.** relating to or denoting a pair of ductless glands situated above the kidneys which secrete adrenalin, noradrenaline, and corticosteroid hormones. ● **n.** an adrenal gland.

**adrenalin** /əˈdrɛn(ə)lɪn/ (also **adrenaline**) ● **n.** a hormone secreted by the adrenal glands that increases rates of blood circulation, breathing, and carbohydrate metabolism.
– ORIGIN C20: from **ADRENAL** + **-IN**[1].

**adrenalized** (also **-ised**) ● **adj.** excited, tense, or highly charged.

**adrenergic** /ˌadrɪˈnəːdʒɪk/ ● **adj.** Physiology relating to or denoting nerve cells in which adrenalin, noradrenaline, or a similar substance acts as a neurotransmitter.
– ORIGIN 1930s: from **ADRENALIN** + Gk *ergon* 'work' + **-IC**.

**adrenocorticotrophic hormone** /əˌdriːnə(ʊ)ˌkɔːtɪkə(ʊ)ˈtrəʊfɪk, -ˈtrɒfɪk/ (also **adrenocorticotropic hormone** /-ˈtrəʊpɪk, -ˈtrɒpɪk/) ● **n.** a hormone stimulating the adrenal cortex, secreted by the pituitary gland.

**adret** /ˈadreɪ/ ● **n.** Geography a mountain slope which faces the sun. Compare with **UBAC**.
– ORIGIN from Fr., from dial. vars of *à* 'to' and *droit* 'straight'.

**Adriatic** /ˌeɪdrɪˈatɪk/ ● **adj.** of or relating to the region comprising the Adriatic Sea and its coasts and islands. ● **n.** (**the Adriatic**) this region.

**adrift** ● **adj. & adv. 1** (of a boat) drifting without control. **2** Brit. informal no longer fixed in position.

**adroit** /əˈdrɔɪt/ ● **adj.** skilful.
– DERIVATIVES **adroitly** adv. **adroitness** n.
– ORIGIN C17: from Fr., from *à droit* 'according to right'.

**adscititious** /ˌadsɪˈtɪʃəs/ ● **adj.** rare additional.
– ORIGIN C17: from L. *adscit-*, *adsciscere* 'admit, adopt', + **-ITIOUS**[2], on the pattern of *adventitious*.

**ADSL** ● **abbrev.** asymmetric digital subscriber line, a technology for transmitting digital information over standard telephone lines, using most of the bandwidth to transmit information to the user and only a small part to receive it from them.

**adsorb** /ədˈzɔːb, -ˈsɔːb/ ● **v.** (of a solid) hold (molecules of a gas, liquid, or solute) as a thin film on surfaces outside or within the material.
– DERIVATIVES **adsorbable** adj. **adsorbate** n. **adsorption** n. **adsorptive** adj.
– ORIGIN C19: blend of **AD-** (expressing adherence) + **ABSORB**.

**adsorbent** ● **n.** a substance which adsorbs another. ● **adj.** able to adsorb substances.

**adstratum** /ˈadstrɑːtəm, adˈstrɑːtəm/ ● **n.** (pl. **adstrata**) Linguistics a language or group of elements within it responsible for changes in a neighbouring language.
– DERIVATIVES **adstrate** adj.
– ORIGIN 1930s: mod. L., from L. *ad* 'to' + *stratum* 'something laid down'.

**ADT** ● **abbrev.** Atlantic Daylight Time.

**aduki** /əˈduːki/ ● **n.** variant of **ADZUKI**.

**adulation** /adjʊˈleɪʃ(ə)n/ ● **n.** excessive admiration.
– DERIVATIVES **adulate** v. **adulator** n. **adulatory** adj.
– ORIGIN ME: from L. *adulatio(n)-*, from *adulat-*, *adulari* 'fawn on'.

**adult** /ˈadʌlt, əˈdʌlt/ ● **n.** a person who is fully grown and developed. ➤ Law a person who has reached the age of majority. ● **adj.** fully grown and developed. ➤ of, for, or characteristic of adults.
– DERIVATIVES **adulthood** n. **adultly** adv.
– ORIGIN C16: from L. *adult-*, *adolescere* (see **ADOLESCENT**).

**adulterate** ● **v.** /əˈdʌltəreɪt/ render poorer in quality by adding another substance. ● **adj.** /əˈdʌlt(ə)rət/ archaic not pure or genuine.
– DERIVATIVES **adulterant** n. **adulteration** n. **adulterator** n.
– ORIGIN C16 (as adj.): from L. *adulterat-*, *adulterare* 'corrupt'.

**adulterer** ● **n.** (fem. **adulteress**) a person who has committed adultery.
– ORIGIN C16: from obs. *adulter* 'commit adultery', from L. *adulterare* 'debauch, corrupt'.

**adulterine** /əˈdʌlt(ə)rʌɪn/ ● **adj. 1** (of a child) born as the result of an adulterous relationship. **2** archaic illegal, unlicensed, or counterfeit.

**adultery** ● **n.** voluntary sexual intercourse between a married person and a person who is not their spouse.
– DERIVATIVES **adulterous** adj. **adulterously** adv.
– ORIGIN C15: from obs. *adulter*, from L. *adulter* 'adulterer'.

**adultescent** /adʌlˈtɛs(ə)nt/ ● **n.** informal a middle-aged person whose clothes, interests, and activities are typically associated with youth culture.
– ORIGIN 1990s: blend of **ADULT** and **ADOLESCENT**.

**adumbrate** /ˈadʌmbreɪt/ ● **v.** formal **1** give a faint or general idea of. ➤ foreshadow. **2** overshadow.
– DERIVATIVES **adumbration** n. **adumbrative** adj.
– ORIGIN C16: from L. *adumbrat-*, *adumbrare*, from *ad-* 'to' (as an intensifier) + *umbrare* 'cast a shadow'.

**adust** /əˈdʌst/ ● **adj.** archaic **1** burnt. **2** gloomy.
– ORIGIN ME: from Fr. *aduste* or L. *adustus* 'burnt', from *adurere* 'to burn'.

**ad valorem** /ˌad vəˈlɔːrɛm/ ● **adv. & adj.** (of the levying of taxes or duties) in proportion to the value of the goods or transaction concerned.
– ORIGIN L., 'according to the value'.

**advance** ● **v. 1** move forwards. ➤ cause to occur at an earlier date than planned. **2** make or cause to make progress. **3** put forward (a theory or suggestion). **4** hand over (payment) to (someone) as a loan or before it is due. ● **n. 1** a forward movement. **2** a development or improvement. **3** an amount of money advanced. **4** an approach made with the aim of initiating a sexual or amorous relationship. ● **adj.** done, sent, or supplied beforehand.
– PHRASES **in advance** ahead in time.
– DERIVATIVES **advancer** n.
– ORIGIN ME: from OFr. *avance* (n.), *avancer* (v.), from late L. *abante* 'in front', from *ab* 'from' + *ante* 'before'.

**advanced** ● **adj. 1** far on in progress or life. **2** complex; not elementary. **3** very modern.

**advanced gas-cooled reactor** ● **n.** a nuclear reactor in which the coolant is carbon dioxide, with uranium oxide fuel clad in steel and using graphite as a moderator.

**advanced level** ● **n.** (in the UK except Scotland) the higher of the two main levels of the GCE examination.

**advanced subsidiary level** ● **n.** (in the UK except Scotland) a GCE examination at a level between GCSE and advanced level.

**advance guard** ● **n.** a body of soldiers preceding and making preparations for the main body of an army.

**advancement** ● **n. 1** the process of promoting a cause or plan. **2** the promotion of a person in rank or status. **3** a development or improvement.

**advantage** ● **n. 1** a condition or circumstance that puts one in a favourable position. ➤ benefit; profit. **2** Tennis a score marking a point interim between deuce and winning the game. ● **v.** be of benefit to. ➤ [as adj. **advantaged**] prosperous.
– PHRASES **take advantage of 1** make unfair use of for one's own benefit. **2** dated seduce. **3** make good use of the opportunities offered by. **to advantage** in a way which displays or uses the best aspects.
– DERIVATIVES **advantageous** /adv(ə)nˈteɪdʒəs/ adj. **advantageously** adv.

– ORIGIN ME: from OFr. *avantage*, from *avant* 'in front', from late L. *abante* (see **ADVANCE**).

**advection** /əd'vɛkʃ(ə)n/ • **n.** the transfer of heat or matter by the flow of a fluid, especially horizontally in the atmosphere or the sea.
– DERIVATIVES **advect** v. **advective** adj.
– ORIGIN C20: from L. *advectio(n-)*, from *advehere* 'bring', from *ad-* 'to' + *vehere* 'carry'.

**advent** /'adv(ə)nt, -vɛnt/ • **n. 1** the arrival of a notable person or thing. **2** (**Advent**) Christian Theology the coming or second coming of Christ. ➤the first season of the Church year, leading up to Christmas and including the four preceding Sundays.
– ORIGIN OE, from L. *adventus* 'arrival', from *advenire*, from *ad-* 'to' + *venire* 'come'.

**Advent calendar** • **n.** a calendar containing small numbered flaps, one of which is opened on each day of Advent to reveal a picture appropriate to the season.

**Adventist** • **n.** a member of a Christian sect emphasizing belief in the imminent second coming of Christ.
– DERIVATIVES **Adventism** n.

**adventitia** /,advɛn'tɪʃə/ • **n.** the outermost layer of the wall of a blood vessel.
– DERIVATIVES **adventitial** adj.
– ORIGIN C19: shortening of mod. L. *tunica adventitia* 'additional sheath'.

**adventitious** /,adv(ə)n'tɪʃəs/ • **adj. 1** happening according to chance. **2** coming from outside; not native. **3** Biology formed accidentally or in an unusual position. **4** Botany (of a root) growing directly from the stem or other upper part of a plant.
– DERIVATIVES **adventitiously** adv.
– ORIGIN C17: from L. *adventicius* 'coming to us from abroad' + **-ous** (see also **-ITIOUS**[2]).

**Advent Sunday** • **n.** the first Sunday in Advent.

**adventure** • **n. 1** an unusual, exciting, and daring experience. ➤excitement arising from this. **2** archaic a commercial speculation. • **v.** dated engage in an adventure.
– DERIVATIVES **adventurer** n. **adventuresome** adj. **adventuress** n.
– ORIGIN ME: from OFr. *aventure* (n.), *aventurer* (v.), based on L. *adventurus* 'about to happen', from *advenire* 'arrive'.

**adventure playground** • **n.** Brit. a playground containing structures encouraging physically challenging play.

**adventurism** • **n.** willingness to take risks in business or politics.
– DERIVATIVES **adventurist** n. & adj.

**adventurous** • **adj.** open to or involving new or daring methods or experiences.
– DERIVATIVES **adventurously** adv. **adventurousness** n.

**adverb** • **n.** Grammar a word or phrase that modifies the meaning of an adjective, verb, or other adverb, or of a sentence (e.g *gently, very, fortunately*).
– ORIGIN ME: from L. *adverbium*, from *ad-* 'to' (expressing addition) + *verbum* 'word, verb'.

**adverbial** Grammar • **n.** a word or phrase functioning as a major clause constituent and typically expressing place (*in the garden*), time (*in May*), or manner (*in a strange way*). • **adj.** relating to or functioning as an adverb or adverbial.
– DERIVATIVES **adverbially** adv.

**adversarial** /,advə'sɛːrɪəl/ • **adj. 1** involving or characterized by conflict or opposition. **2** Law (of a legal procedure) in which the parties in a dispute have the responsibility for finding and presenting evidence. Compare with **ACCUSATORIAL**, **INQUISITORIAL**.
– DERIVATIVES **adversarially** adv.

**adversary** /'advəs(ə)ri/ • **n.** (pl. **-ies**) an opponent. • **adj.** /'advəs(ə)ri, ad'vəːsəri/ another term for **ADVERSARIAL**.
– ORIGIN ME: from OFr. *adversarie*, from L. *adversarius* 'opposed, opponent', from *adversus* (see **ADVERSE**).

**adversative** /əd'vəːsətɪv/ • **adj.** Grammar (of a word or phrase) expressing opposition or antithesis.

**adverse** /'advəːs/ • **adj.** harmful; unfavourable.
– DERIVATIVES **adversely** adv.
– ORIGIN ME: from OFr. *advers*, from L. *adversus* 'against, opposite', from *advertere*, from *ad-* 'to' + *vertere* 'to turn'.

**USAGE** adverse

A common error is to use **adverse** instead of **averse**, as in *I am not adverse to helping out*, rather than the correct form *I am not averse to helping out*. Around 15 per cent of citations in the British National Corpus show this incorrect use of **adverse**.

**adversity** • **n.** (pl. **-ies**) difficulty; misfortune.

**advert**[1] /'advəːt/ • **n.** Brit. informal an advertisement.

**advert**[2] /əd'vəːt/ • **v.** (**advert to**) formal refer to.
– ORIGIN ME: from OFr. *avertire*, from L. *advertere* (see **ADVERSE**).

**advertise** • **v. 1** promote or publicize. **2** archaic notify.
– DERIVATIVES **advertiser** n. **advertising** n.
– ORIGIN ME: from OFr. *advertiss-*, lengthened stem of *advertir*, from L. *advertere* (see **ADVERT**[2]).

**advertisement** • **n. 1** a notice or display advertising something. **2** archaic a notice to readers in a book.

**advertorial** /,advəː'tɔːrɪəl/ • **n.** an advertisement in the style of an editorial or objective journalistic article.

**advice** • **n. 1** guidance or recommendations offered with regard to future action. **2** a formal notice of a sale, delivery, or other transaction. **3** (**advices**) archaic news.
– ORIGIN ME: from OFr. *avis*, based on L. *ad* 'to' + *visum*, past part. of *videre* 'to see'.

**advisable** • **adj.** to be recommended; sensible.
– DERIVATIVES **advisability** n. **advisably** adv.

**advise** • **v. 1** recommend (a course of action). ➤offer advice to. **2** inform about a fact or situation.
– DERIVATIVES **adviser** (also **advisor**) n.
– ORIGIN ME: from OFr. *aviser*, based on L. *ad-* 'to' + *visere*, frequentative of *videre* 'to see'.

**advised** • **adj.** prudent. ➤considered.
– DERIVATIVES **advisedly** adv.

**advisement** • **n.** archaic or N. Amer. careful consideration. ➤advice or counsel.
– PHRASES **take something under advisement** N. Amer. reserve judgement while considering something.

**advisory** • **adj.** having the power to make recommendations but not to enforce them. ➤recommended. • **n.** (pl. **-ies**) N. Amer. an official announcement or warning.

**advocaat** /'advəkɑː/ • **n.** a liqueur made with eggs, sugar, and brandy.
– ORIGIN 1930s: from Du., lit. 'advocate' (being orig. considered a lawyer's drink).

**advocate** • **n.** /'advəkət/ **1** a person who publicly supports or recommends a particular cause or policy. **2** a person who pleads a case on someone else's behalf. ➤Scottish term for **BARRISTER**. • **v.** /'advəkeɪt/ publicly recommend or support.
– DERIVATIVES **advocacy** n. **advocateship** n. **advocation** n.
– ORIGIN ME: from OFr. *avocat*, from L. *advocat-*, *advocare* 'call (to one's aid)', from *ad-* 'to' + *vocare* 'to call'.

**advocate-depute** • **n.** (in Scotland) any of a number of officers who assist the Lord Advocate in prosecutions.

**advocate-general** • **n.** (pl. **advocates-general**) any of a number of officers assisting the judges in the European Court of Justice.

**advowson** /əd'vaʊz(ə)n/ • **n.** Brit. (in ecclesiastical law) the right to recommend a member of the Anglican clergy for a vacant benefice, or to make such an appointment.
– ORIGIN ME: from OFr. *avoeson*, from L. *advocatio(n-)*, from *advocare* (see **ADVOCATE**).

**advt** • **abbrev.** advertisement.

**Adyghe** /'adɪgeɪ, ,ɑːdɪ'geɪ/ (also **Adygei**) • **n.** (pl. same) **1** a member of a mainly Sunni Muslim people of the NW Caucasus, especially Adygea. **2** the North Caucasian language of this people.

**adytum** /'adɪtəm/ • **n.** (pl. **adyta** /-tə/) the innermost sanctuary of an ancient Greek temple.
– ORIGIN L., from Gk *aduton*, neut. sing. of *adutos* 'impenetrable'.

**adze** /adz/ (US **adz**) • **n.** a tool similar to an axe, with an arched blade at right angles to the handle.
– ORIGIN OE *adesa*, of unknown origin.

## Word *Formation*

**-aemia** (also **-haemia**) 'blood', from Greek *haima* 'blood'

Most **-aemia** words relate to the presence or absence of a particular substance in the blood.

➤ Some **-aemia** words in current use (full entries and definitions to be found in this dictionary):

| | | |
|---|---|---|
| anaemia | deficiency of red blood cells or haemoglobin | Gk *an* 'without' |
| hyperaemia | excess of blood | Gk *huper* 'over' |
| hyperglycaemia | excess glucose in the blood | Gk *huper* 'over' + *glukus* 'sweet' |
| hyperlipaemia | excess fat in the blood | Gk *huper* 'over' + *lipos* 'fat' |
| hypocalcaemia | deficiency of calcium in the blood | Gk *hupo* 'under' |
| hypoglycaemia | deficiency of glucose in the blood | Gk *hupo* 'under' + *glukus* 'sweet' |
| hypovolaemia | a decrease in the volume of circulating blood | Gk *hupo* 'under' + VOLUME |
| ischaemia | inadequate blood supply | Gk *iskhein* 'keep back' |
| leukaemia | malignant disease involving overproduction of white blood cells | Gk *leukos* 'white' |
| lipaemia | excess emulsified fat in the blood | Gk *lipos* 'fat' |
| septicaemia | blood poisoning | Gk *sēpein* 'make rotten' |

The US standard spelling is usually **-emia**, hence ***anemia***, ***leukemia***, and ***septicemia***.

The prefixes **haemo-** and **haemato-** are also based on Greek *haima* 'blood', giving rise to such words as ***haemoglobin***, ***haemophiliac***, and ***haemorrhoid***.

**adzuki** /əd'zuːki/ (also **aduki**) ● **n.** (pl. **adzukis**) **1** a small, round dark-red edible bean. **2** the bushy Asian plant which produces this bean. [*Vigna angularis*.]
– ORIGIN C18: from Japanese *azuki*.

**AE** ● **abbrev.** auto-exposure.

**Æ** (also **æ**) ● **n.** a letter used in Old English to represent a vowel intermediate between a and e (see ASH[2]).

**-ae** /iː, ʌɪ/ ● **suffix** forming plural nouns: **1** used in names of animal and plant families and other groups: *Felidae*. **2** used instead of *-as* in the plural of many non-naturalized nouns ending in *-a* derived from Latin or Greek: *larvae*.
– ORIGIN L. pl. suffix, or representing the Gk pl. ending *-ai*.

**AEA** ● **abbrev.** Atomic Energy Authority.

**AEC** ● **abbrev.** historical Atomic Energy Commission.

**aedile** /'iːdʌɪl/ ● **n.** (in ancient Rome) either of two (later four) magistrates responsible for public buildings and other matters.
– DERIVATIVES **aedileship** n.
– ORIGIN C16: from L. *aedilis* 'concerned with buildings', from *aedes* 'building'.

**AEEU** ● **abbrev.** Amalgamated Engineering and Electrical Union.

**Aegean** /iː'dʒiːən, ɪ-/ ● **adj.** relating to or denoting the region comprising the Aegean Sea and its coasts and islands. ● **n.** (**the Aegean**) this region.

**aegis** /'iːdʒɪs/ ● **n.** **1** the protection, backing, or support of someone. **2** (in classical art and mythology) an attribute of certain gods represented as a goatskin shield.
– ORIGIN C17: via L. from Gk *aigis* 'shield of Zeus'.

**aegrotat** /ʌɪ'grə(ʊ)tat, 'iː-, iː'grə(ʊ)-/ ● **n.** Brit. a certificate stating that a student is too ill to take an exam.
– ORIGIN C18: L., lit. 'he is sick'.

**-aemia** (also **-haemia**, US **-emia** or **-hemia**) ● **comb. form** in nouns denoting that a substance is present in the blood: *septicaemia*. See word-formation panel.
– ORIGIN mod. L., from Gk *-aimia*, from *haima* 'blood'.

**aeolian** /iː'əʊlɪən/ (US **eolian**) ● **adj.** chiefly Geology relating to or arising from the action of the wind.
– ORIGIN C17: from *Aeolus*, the name of the god of the winds in Gk mythology, + -IAN.

**aeolian harp** ● **n.** a stringed instrument that produces musical sounds when a current of air passes through it.

**Aeolian mode** /iː'əʊlɪən/ ● **n.** Music the mode represented by the natural diatonic scale A–A (containing a minor 3rd, 6th, and 7th).
– ORIGIN C18: from L. *Aeolius*, 'from *Aeolis*' (an ancient coastal district of Asia Minor) + -AN.

**aeon** /'iːən/ ● **n.** (US or technical also **eon**) **1** an indefinite and very long period. **2** Astronomy & Geology a period of a thousand million years. **3** Geology a major division of geological time, subdivided into eras. **4** Philosophy (in Neoplatonism, Platonism, and Gnosticism) a power existing outside time, deriving from the supreme deity.
– ORIGIN C17: via eccles. L. from Gk *aiōn* 'age'.

**aepyornis** /ˌiːpɪ'ɔːnɪs/ ● **n.** an extinct giant flightless bird, found in Madagascar. [Genus *Aepyornis*.]
– ORIGIN C19: mod. L., from Gk *aipus* 'high' + *ornis* 'bird'.

**aerate** /'ɛːreɪt/ ● **v.** introduce air into.
– DERIVATIVES **aeration** n. **aerator** n.
– ORIGIN C18: from L. *aer* 'air' + -ATE[3], influenced by Fr. *aérer*.

**aerated** ● **adj.** **1** (of a liquid) made effervescent by being charged with carbon dioxide or some other gas. **2** Brit. informal agitated, angry, or over-excited.

**aerenchyma** /ɛː'rɛŋkɪmə/ ● **n.** Botany a soft plant tissue containing air spaces, found especially in many aquatic plants.
– DERIVATIVES **aerenchymatous** adj.
– ORIGIN C19: from Gk *aēr* 'air' + *enkhuma* 'infusion'.

**aerial** /'ɛːrɪəl/ ● **n.** **1** a structure that transmits or receives radio or television signals. **2** (**aerials**) a type of freestyle skiing in which the skier jumps from a ramp and carries out manoeuvres in the air. ● **adj.** **1** existing or taking place in the air or atmosphere. ➤ (of a bird) spending much of its time in flight. **2** involving the use of aircraft. **3** (of a part of a plant) growing above ground.
– DERIVATIVES **aeriality** n. **aerially** adv.
– ORIGIN C16: via L. *aerius* from Gk *aerios* (from *aēr* 'air') + -AL.

**aerialist** ● **n.** a person who performs acrobatics high above the ground on a tightrope or trapezes.

**aerie** ● **n.** US spelling of EYRIE.

**aero-** /'ɛːrəʊ/ ● **comb. form** **1** of or relating to air: *aerobic*. **2** of or relating to aircraft: *aerodrome*.
– ORIGIN from Gk *aēr* 'air'.

**aerobatics** ● **pl. n.** [treated as sing. or pl.] feats of flying performed for an audience on the ground.
– DERIVATIVES **aerobatic** adj.
– ORIGIN First World War: from AERO- + a shortened form of ACROBATICS.

**aerobe** /'ɛːrəʊb/ ● **n.** Biology an aerobic micro-organism.

– ORIGIN C19: coined in Fr. from Gk *aēr* + *bios* 'life'.

**aerobic** /ɛːˈrəʊbɪk/ ● **adj. 1** denoting physical exercise intended to improve the efficiency of the cardiovascular system in absorbing and transporting oxygen. **2** Biology relating to, involving, or requiring free oxygen.
– DERIVATIVES **aerobically** adv.
– ORIGIN C19: from **AERO-** + Gk *bios* 'life' + **-IC**.

**aerobics** ● **pl. n.** [treated as sing. or pl.] aerobic exercises.

**aerobiology** ● **n.** the study of the aerial transport of micro-organisms, spores, seeds, etc.

**aerobraking** ● **n.** the process of slowing down a spacecraft by flying through a planet's atmosphere to produce aerodynamic drag.

**aerodrome** ● **n.** Brit. a small airport or airfield.

**aerodynamic** ● **adj. 1** of or relating to aerodynamics. **2** having a shape which reduces the drag from air moving past.
– DERIVATIVES **aerodynamically** adv.

**aerodynamics** ● **pl. n. 1** [treated as sing.] the branch of science concerned with the properties of moving air and the interaction between the air and solid bodies moving through it. **2** [treated as pl.] aerodynamic properties.
– DERIVATIVES **aerodynamicist** n.

**aeroelasticity** ● **n.** the branch of science concerned with the interaction between aerodynamic forces and non-rigid structures.
– DERIVATIVES **aeroelastic** adj.

**aerofoil** ● **n.** Brit. a structure with curved surfaces designed to give the most favourable ratio of lift to drag in flight.

**aerogel** ● **n.** a solid material of extremely low density, produced by removing the liquid component from a conventional gel.

**aerogramme** (US **aerogram**) ● **n.** another term for **AIR LETTER**.

**aerolite** ● **n.** a meteorite made of rock.

**aerology** ● **n.** dated the study of the atmosphere.
– DERIVATIVES **aerological** adj.

**aeromagnetic** ● **adj.** relating to or denoting the measurement of the earth's magnetic field using airborne instruments.

**aeromedical** ● **adj.** of or relating to the use of aircraft for medical purposes.

**aeronaut** ● **n.** dated a traveller in a hot-air balloon, airship, or other flying craft.
– ORIGIN C18: from Fr. *aéronaute*, from Gk *aēr* 'air' + *nautēs* 'sailor'.

**aeronautics** ● **pl. n.** [usu. treated as sing.] the study or practice of travel through the air.
– DERIVATIVES **aeronautic** adj. **aeronautical** adj.
– ORIGIN C19: from mod. L. *aeronautica* 'matters relating to aeronautics', from Gk (see **AERONAUT**).

**aeronomy** /ɛːˈrɒnəmi/ ● **n.** the branch of science concerned with the properties of the upper atmosphere.

**aerophagy** /ɛːˈrɒfədʒi/ ● **n.** Medicine the swallowing of air.

**aerophone** ● **n.** Music, technical a wind instrument.

**aeroplane** ● **n.** chiefly Brit. a powered flying vehicle with fixed wings and a weight greater than that of the air it displaces.
– ORIGIN C19: from Fr. *aéroplane*, from *aéro-* 'air' + Gk *-planos* 'wandering'.

**aeroshell** ● **n.** a casing which protects a spacecraft during re-entry.

**aerosol** ● **n. 1** a substance enclosed under pressure and released as a fine spray by means of a propellant gas. **2** Chemistry a colloidal suspension of particles dispersed in air or gas.
– DERIVATIVES **aerosolize** (also **-ise**) v.
– ORIGIN 1920s: from **AERO-** + **SOL**².

**aerospace** ● **n.** the branch of technology and industry concerned with aviation and space flight.

**aerostat** /ˈɛːrəstat/ ● **n.** an airship or hot-air balloon.
– ORIGIN C18: from Fr. *aérostat*, from Gk *aēr* 'air' + *statos* 'standing'.

**Aesculapian** /ˌiːskjʊˈleɪpɪən/ ● **adj.** of or relating to medicine or physicians.
– ORIGIN C16: from L. *Aesculapius*, the name of the Roman god of medicine, + **-IAN**.

**aesthete** /ˈiːsθiːt, ˈɛs-/ (US also **esthete**) ● **n.** a person who is appreciative of or sensitive to art and beauty.
– ORIGIN C19: from Gk *aisthētēs* 'a person who perceives', or from **AESTHETIC**.

**aesthetic** /iːsˈθɛtɪk, ɛs-/ (US also **esthetic**) ● **adj.** concerned with beauty or the appreciation of beauty. ➤of pleasing appearance. ➤(**Aesthetic**) relating to or denoting a literary and artistic movement in England during the 1880s, devoted to 'art for art's sake' and rejecting the notion that art should have a social or moral purpose. ● **n.** a set of principles underlying the work of a particular artist or artistic movement.
– DERIVATIVES **aesthetically** adv. **aestheticism** n. **aestheticize** (also **-ise**) v.
– ORIGIN C18: from Gk *aisthētikos*, from *aisthēta* 'perceptible things', from *aisthesthai* 'perceive'.

**aesthetician** (US also **esthetician**) ● **n. 1** a person who is knowledgeable about aesthetics. **2** N. Amer. a beautician.

**aesthetics** (US also **esthetics**) ● **pl. n.** [usu. treated as sing.] a set of principles concerned with the nature and appreciation of beauty, especially in art. ➤the branch of philosophy which deals with questions of beauty and artistic taste.

**aestival** /ˈiːstɪv(ə)l, iːˈstʌɪv(ə)l, ˈɛst-, ɛˈstʌɪv(ə)l/ (US also **estival**) ● **adj.** technical belonging to or appearing in summer.
– ORIGIN ME: from L. *aestivalis*, from *aestivus*, from *aestus* 'heat'.

**aestivation** /ˌiːstɪˈveɪʃ(ə)n, ˌɛst-/ (US **estivation**) ● **n. 1** Zoology prolonged torpor or dormancy of an insect, fish, or amphibian during a hot or dry period. **2** Botany the arrangement of petals and sepals in a flower bud before it opens. Compare with **VERNATION**.
– DERIVATIVES **aestivate** v.
– ORIGIN C17: from L. *aestivat-*, *aestivare* 'spend the summer', from *aestus* 'heat' + **-ATION**.

**aet.** (also **aetat.**) ● **abbrev.** aetatis.

**a.e.t.** ● **abbrev.** after extra time (in a soccer match).

**aetatis** /ʌɪˈtɑːtɪs, iː-/ ● **adj.** of or at the age of.
– ORIGIN from L.

**aether** ● **n.** variant spelling of **ETHER** (in senses 3 and 4).

**aetiology** /ˌiːtɪˈɒlədʒi/ (US **etiology**) ● **n. 1** Medicine the cause, set of causes, or manner of causation of a disease or condition. **2** the investigation or attribution of cause or a reason.
– DERIVATIVES **aetiologic** adj. **aetiological** adj. **aetiologically** adv.
– ORIGIN C16: via med. L. from Gk *aitiologia*, from *aitia* 'a cause' + *-logia* (see **-LOGY**).

**AF** ● **abbrev. 1** audio frequency. **2** autofocus.

**af-** ● **prefix** variant spelling of **AD-** assimilated before *f* (as in *affiliate*, *affirm*).

**Afar** /ˈɑːfɑː/ ● **n.** (pl. same or **Afars**) **1** a member of a people living in Djibouti and NE Ethiopia. **2** the Cushitic language of this people.
– ORIGIN from Afar *qafar*.

**afar** ● **adv.** chiefly poetic/literary at or to a distance.
– ORIGIN ME *of feor* 'from far'.

**AFC** ● **abbrev. 1** Air Force Cross. **2** Association Football Club. **3** automatic frequency control.

**afeared** ● **adj.** archaic or dialect afraid.
– ORIGIN OE, from *āfǣran* 'frighten'.

**affable** ● **adj.** good-natured and sociable.
– DERIVATIVES **affability** n. **affably** adv.
– ORIGIN ME: via OFr. from L. *affabilis*, from *affari*, from *ad-* 'to' + *fari* 'speak'.

**affair** ● **n. 1** an event or sequence of events of a specified kind or that has previously been referred to. **2** a matter that is a particular person's concern or responsibility. ➤(**affairs**) matters of public interest and importance. ➤(**affairs**) business and financial dealings. **3** a love affair.
– ORIGIN ME: from OFr. *afaire*, from *à faire* 'to do'; cf. **ADO**.

**affaire** /a'fɛː, French afɛʀ/ (also **affaire de** or **du cœur** /də 'kəː, djuː, French də, dy kœʀ/) ● **n.** a love affair.
– ORIGIN C19: Fr., lit. 'affair (of the heart)'.

**affairé** /a'fɛːreɪ, French afeʀe/ ● **adj.** busy; involved.
– ORIGIN Fr., from *affaire*, from *à* 'to' + *faire* 'do'.

**affect**[1] /ə'fɛkt/ ● **v.** have an effect on; make a difference to. ➤ touch the feelings of.
– DERIVATIVES **affecting** adj. **affectingly** adv.
– ORIGIN ME (in the sense 'attack as a disease'): from Fr. *affecter* or L. *affect-*, *afficere* (see **AFFECT**[2]).

**USAGE** affect

Affect and **effect** are commonly confused. **Affect** is primarily a verb meaning 'make a difference to'. **Effect** is used both as a noun and a verb, meaning 'a result' or 'bring about (a result)'.

**affect**[2] /ə'fɛkt/ ● **v.** pretend to have or feel. ➤ use, wear, or assume pretentiously or so as to impress.
– ORIGIN ME (in the sense 'like, love'): from Fr. *affecter* or L. *affectare* 'aim at', frequentative of *afficere* 'affect, influence'.

**affect**[3] /'afɛkt/ ● **n.** Psychology emotion or desire as influencing behaviour.
– DERIVATIVES **affectless** adj. **affectlessness** n.
– ORIGIN C19: from Ger. *Affekt* from L. *affectus* 'disposition', from *afficere* (see **AFFECT**[2]).

**affectation** ● **n.** behaviour, speech, or writing that is artificial and designed to impress. ➤ a studied display of feeling.
– ORIGIN C16: from L. *affectatio(n-)*, from *affectare* (see **AFFECT**[2]).

**affected** ● **adj. 1** artificial, pretentious, and designed to impress. **2** archaic disposed or inclined in a specified way.
– DERIVATIVES **affectedly** adv. **affectedness** n.

**affection** ● **n. 1** a feeling of fondness or liking. **2** archaic the action or process of affecting or being affected. ➤ a disease. ➤ a mental state; an emotion.
– DERIVATIVES **affectional** adj.
– ORIGIN ME: via OFr. from L. *affectio(n-)*, from *afficere* (see **AFFECT**[2]).

**affectionate** ● **adj.** readily showing affection.
– DERIVATIVES **affectionately** adv.

**affective** ● **adj.** chiefly Psychology relating to moods, feelings, and attitudes.
– DERIVATIVES **affectively** adv. **affectivity** n.
– ORIGIN ME: via Fr. from late L. *affectivus*, from *afficere* (see **AFFECT**[2]).

**affenpinscher** /'afən,pɪnʃə/ ● **n.** a dog of a small breed resembling the griffon.
– ORIGIN C20: from Ger., from *Affe* 'monkey' + *Pinscher* 'terrier'.

**afferent** /'af(ə)r(ə)nt/ Physiology ● **adj.** relating to or denoting the conduction of nerve impulses or blood inwards or towards something. The opposite of **EFFERENT**. ● **n.** an afferent nerve fibre or vessel.
– ORIGIN C19: from L. *afferent-*, *afferre* 'bring towards'.

**affiance** /ə'fʌɪəns/ ● **v.** (**be affianced**) poetic/literary be engaged to marry.
– ORIGIN C15: from OFr. *afiancer*, from *afier* 'promise, entrust', from med. L. *affidare* 'declare on oath'.

**affiant** /ə'fʌɪənt/ ● **n.** US Law a person who makes an affidavit.
– ORIGIN C19: from Fr., pres. part. of *afier*, from med. L. *affidare* (see **AFFIANCE**).

**affidavit** /,afɪ'deɪvɪt/ ● **n.** Law a written statement confirmed by oath or affirmation, for use as evidence in court.
– ORIGIN C16: from med. L., lit. 'he has stated on oath', from *affidare*.

**affiliate** ● **v.** /ə'fɪlɪeɪt/ (usu. **be affiliated to/with**) officially attach or connect to an organization. ➤ (of an organization) admit as a member. ● **n.** /ə'fɪlɪət/ an affiliated person or organization.
– DERIVATIVES **affiliation** n. **affiliative** adj.
– ORIGIN C18: from med. L. *affiliat-*, *affiliare* 'adopt as a son'.

**affiliation order** ● **n.** UK Law, historical an order that the man judged to be the father of an illegitimate child must help to support it.

**affinal** /ə'fʌɪn(ə)l/ ● **adj.** Anthropology concerning or having a family relationship by marriage.
– ORIGIN C19: from L. *affinis* (see **AFFINITY**) + **-AL**.

**affine** /ə'fʌɪn/ ● **adj.** Mathematics allowing for or preserving parallel relationships. ● **n.** Anthropology a relative by marriage.
– ORIGIN C16 (as n.): from OFr. *afin* or L. *affinis* (see **AFFINITY**).

**affined** ● **adj.** archaic related or connected.
– ORIGIN C16: from L. *affinis* (see **AFFINITY**) + **-ED**[1].

**affinity** ● **n.** (pl. **-ies**) **1** a spontaneous or natural liking or sympathy. ➤ a close relationship based on a common origin or structure. ➤ relationship by marriage. **2** chiefly Biochemistry the degree to which a substance tends to combine with another.
– ORIGIN ME: via OFr. from L. *affinitas*, from *affinis* 'related' (lit. 'bordering on').

**affinity card** ● **n.** a cheque card or credit card for which the bank donates a portion of the money spent using the card to a specific charity.

**affirm** ● **v.** state emphatically or publicly. ➤ Law ratify (a judgement or agreement). ➤ Law make a formal declaration rather than taking an oath.
– DERIVATIVES **affirmation** n. **affirmatory** adj. **affirmer** n.
– ORIGIN ME (in the sense 'make firm'): via OFr. from L. *affirmare*, from *ad-* 'to' + *firmus* 'strong'.

**affirmative** ● **adj. 1** agreeing with or consenting to a statement or request. ➤ Grammar & Logic stating that a fact is so. Contrasted with **NEGATIVE** and **INTERROGATIVE**. **2** relating to or denoting proposed legislation which must receive an affirmative parliamentary vote before it can come into force. ● **n.** an affirmative statement or word. ➤ Logic a statement asserting that something is true of the subject of a proposition. ● **exclam.** chiefly N. Amer. yes.
– PHRASES **in the affirmative** so as to accept or agree to a statement or request.
– DERIVATIVES **affirmatively** adv.
– ORIGIN ME (in the sense 'assertive, positive'): via OFr. from late L. *affirmativus*, from *affirmare* (see **AFFIRM**).

**affirmative action** ● **n.** chiefly N. Amer. action favouring those who tend to suffer from discrimination.

**affix** ● **v.** /ə'fɪks/ attach or fasten to something else. ● **n.** /'afɪks/ Grammar an addition to the base form or stem of a word in order to modify its meaning or create a new word.
– DERIVATIVES **affixation** n.
– ORIGIN ME: from OFr. *affixer* or med. L. *affixare*, frequentative of L. *affigere*, from *ad-* 'to' + *figere* 'to fix'.

**afflatus** /ə'fleɪtəs/ ● **n.** formal a divine creative impulse or inspiration.
– ORIGIN C17: from L., from *afflare*, from *ad-* 'to' + *flare* 'to blow'.

**afflict** ● **v.** cause pain or suffering to.
– DERIVATIVES **affliction** n. **afflictive** adj. (archaic).
– ORIGIN ME: from L. *afflictare* 'knock about, harass', or *afflict-*, *affligere* 'knock down, weaken'.

**affluent** ● **adj. 1** wealthy. **2** archaic (of water) flowing freely or copiously. ● **n.** archaic a tributary stream.
– DERIVATIVES **affluence** n. **affluently** adv.
– ORIGIN ME: via OFr. from L. *affluent-*, *affluere* 'flow towards, flow freely'.

**afflux** /'aflʌks/ ● **n.** archaic a flow of water or air.
– ORIGIN C17: from med. L. *affluxus*, from *affluere* (see **AFFLUENT**).

**afford** ● **v. 1** (**can/could afford**) have sufficient money, time, or means for. ➤ be able to do something without risk of adverse consequences. **2** provide (an opportunity or facility).
– DERIVATIVES **affordability** n. **affordable** adj.
– ORIGIN OE *geforthian* 'promote, perform', later 'manage to do', from *ge-* (prefix implying completeness) + *forthian* 'to further', from **FORTH**.

**afforest** /ə'fɒrɪst/ ● **v. 1** convert (land) into forest for commercial exploitation. **2** Brit. historical bring (woodland) under the jurisdiction of forest law for the purpose of hunting.
– DERIVATIVES **afforestation** n.

**affranchise** • **v.** archaic release from servitude.
– ORIGIN C15: from OFr. *afranchiss-*, lengthened stem of *afranchir*, from *a-* (from L. *ad* 'to, at') + *franc* 'free'.

**affray** • **n.** Law, dated a breach of the peace by fighting in a public place.
– ORIGIN ME: from Anglo-Norman Fr. *afrayer* 'disturb, startle', based on an element of Gmc origin rel. to OE *frithu* 'peace, safety'.

**affricate** /ˈafrɪkət/ • **n.** Phonetics a phoneme which combines a plosive with an immediately following fricative or spirant sharing the same place of articulation, e.g. *ch* as in *chair* and *j* as in *jar*.
– ORIGIN C19: from L. *affricat-*, *affricare*, from *ad-* 'to' + *fricare* 'to rub'.

**affright** archaic • **v.** frighten. • **n.** fright.

**affront** • **n.** an action or remark that causes outrage or offence. • **v.** offend the modesty or values of.
– ORIGIN ME: from OFr. *afronter* 'to slap in the face, insult', based on L. *ad frontem* 'to the face'.

**affronté** /əˈfrʌnti/ (also **affronty**) • **adj.** [often postpos.] Heraldry (especially of an animal's head) facing the observer.
– ORIGIN C16: Fr., past part. of *affronter* 'to face'.

**Afghan** /ˈafgan/ • **n.** **1** a native or national of Afghanistan, or a person of Afghan descent. **2** another term for **PASHTO**. **3** (**afghan**) a knitted or crocheted blanket or shawl. • **adj.** of or relating to Afghanistan or the Pashto language.
– ORIGIN from Pashto *afghānī*.

**Afghan coat** • **n.** Brit. a kind of sheepskin coat with the skin outside, typically having a shaggy border.

**Afghan hound** • **n.** a tall hunting dog of a breed with long silky hair.

**afghani** /afˈgɑːni/ • **n.** (pl. **afghanis**) the basic monetary unit of Afghanistan, equal to 100 puls.
– ORIGIN from Pashto *afghānī*.

**aficionado** /əˌfɪsjəˈnɑːdəʊ, -ˌfɪʃjə-/ • **n.** (pl. **-os**) a person who is very knowledgeable and enthusiastic about an activity or subject.
– ORIGIN C19 (denoting a devotee of bullfighting): from Sp., 'amateur', past part. of *aficioner* 'become fond of' used as a noun, based on L. *affectio(n-)* (see **AFFECTION**).

**afield** • **adv.** **1** to or at a distance. **2** in the field (in reference to hunting).

**afire** • **adv. & adj.** chiefly poetic/literary on fire.

**AFL** • **abbrev.** Australian Football League.

**aflame** • **adv. & adj.** in flames.

**aflatoxin** /ˌafləˈtɒksɪn/ • **n.** Chemistry a toxic compound produced by certain moulds found in food, which can cause liver damage and cancer.
– ORIGIN 1960s: from elements of the mod. L. taxonomic name of a mould (*Aspergillus flavus*) + **TOXIN**.

**AFL-CIO** • **abbrev.** American Federation of Labor and Congress of Industrial Organizations.

**afloat** • **adj. & adv.** **1** floating in water. ➤on board a ship or boat. **2** out of debt or difficulty.

**AFM** • **abbrev.** Air Force Medal.

**afoot** • **adv. & adj.** **1** in preparation or progress. **2** chiefly N. Amer. on foot.

**afore** • **prep.** archaic or dialect before.

**afore-** • **prefix** before; previously: *aforementioned*.

**aforementioned** • **adj.** denoting a person or thing previously mentioned.

**a fortiori** /ˌeɪ fɔːtɪˈɔːrʌɪ, ˌɑː, -riː/ • **adv. & adj.** with a yet stronger reason than a conclusion previously accepted.
– ORIGIN C17: L., from *a fortiori argumento* 'from stronger argument'.

**afoul** • **adv.** N. Amer. into conflict or difficulty with.

**afraid** • **adj.** (often **afraid of/to do**) fearful or anxious. ➤(**afraid for**) anxious about the well-being of.
– PHRASES **I'm afraid** expressing polite apology or regret.
– ORIGIN ME: past part. of the obs. verb *affray*, from Anglo-Norman Fr. *afrayer* (see **AFFRAY**).

**A-frame** • **n.** a timber frame shaped like a capital letter A. ➤N. Amer. a house built around such a frame.

**afreet** /ˈafriːt/ (also **afrit**) • **n.** (in Arabian and Muslim mythology) a powerful jinn or demon.
– ORIGIN C18: from Arab. *ʻifrīt*.

**afresh** • **adv.** in a new or different way.

**African** • **n.** a person from Africa, especially a black person. ➤a person of black African descent. • **adj.** of or relating to Africa or people of African descent.

**Africana** /ˌafrɪˈkɑːnə/ • **pl. n.** things connected with Africa.

**African American** chiefly US • **n.** an American of African origin. • **adj.** of or relating to African Americans.

**Africander** /ˌafrɪˈkandə/ • **n.** variant spelling of **AFRIKANDER**.

**Africanism** • **n.** **1** a feature of language or culture regarded as characteristically African. **2** the belief that black Africans and their culture should predominate in Africa.
– DERIVATIVES **Africanist** n. & adj.

**Africanize** (also **-ise**) • **v.** **1** make African in character. ➤(in Africa) restructure (an organization) by replacing white employees with black Africans. **2** [usu. as adj. **Africanized**] hybridize (honeybees of European stock) with bees of African stock, producing an aggressive strain.
– DERIVATIVES **Africanization** n.

**African violet** • **n.** a small East African plant with heart-shaped velvety leaves and violet, pink, or white flowers. [Genus *Saintpaulia*: several species.]

**Afrikaans** /ˌafrɪˈkɑːns/ • **n.** a language of southern Africa derived from Dutch, an official language of South Africa. • **adj.** of or relating to the Afrikaner people or their language.
– ORIGIN the name in Afrik., from Du., lit. 'African'.

**Afrikander** /ˌafrɪˈkɑːndə/ (also **Africander**) • **n.** an animal of a South African breed of sheep or longhorn cattle.
– ORIGIN C19 (an early form of **AFRIKANER**): via Afrik. from S. Afr. Du.

**Afrikaner** /ˌafrɪˈkɑːnə/ • **n.** **1** an Afrikaans-speaking white person in South Africa, especially one of Dutch or Huguenot descent. **2** S. African a gladiolus or related plant.
– DERIVATIVES **Afrikanerdom** n.
– ORIGIN Afrik., from S. Afr. Du. *Africander*, from Du. *Afrikaan* 'an African' + the personal suffix *-der*.

**afrit** • **n.** variant spelling of **AFREET**.

**Afro** • **n.** a hairstyle consisting of a mass of very tight curls all round the head, like the natural hair of some black people.

**Afro-** • **comb. form** African; African and ...: *Afro-Asiatic*. ➤relating to Africa: *Afrocentric*.

**Afro-American** • **adj. & n.** chiefly N. Amer. another term for **AFRICAN AMERICAN**.

**Afro-Asiatic** • **adj.** relating to or denoting a family of languages spoken in the Middle East and North Africa.

**Afro-Caribbean** • **n.** a person of African descent living in or coming from the Caribbean. • **adj.** of or relating to Afro-Caribbeans.

**Afrocentric** • **adj.** regarding African or black culture as pre-eminent.
– DERIVATIVES **Afrocentrism** n. **Afrocentrist** n.

**afrormosia** /ˌafrɔːˈməʊzɪə/ • **n.** **1** the wood of a tropical tree, resembling teak and used for furniture. **2** the tree that yields this wood, occurring mainly in West Africa. [Genus *Pericopsis* (formerly *Afrormosia*).]
– ORIGIN 1920s: mod. L., from **AFRO-** + the related genus name *Ormosia*, from Gk *hormos* 'necklace' (because necklaces were strung with the seeds).

**aft** /ɑːft/ • **adv. & adj.** at, near, or towards the stern of a ship or tail of an aircraft.
– ORIGIN C17: prob. from obs. *baft* (see **ABAFT**), influenced by Low Ger. and Du. *achter* 'abaft, after'.

**after** • **prep.** **1** in the time following (an event or another period of time). ➤N. Amer. past (used in specifying a time). **2** behind. ➤in the direction of someone who is moving away. **3** in pursuit or quest of. **4** next to and following in order or importance. **5** in allusion or reference to: *he was named after his grandfather*. ➤in the style or following the example of. • **conj. & adv.** in the time following (an event). • **adj.** **1** archaic later. **2** nearer the stern of a ship.
– PHRASES **after all** in spite of any indications or expectations to the contrary. **after hours** after normal working

or opening hours. **after you** a polite formula offering precedence. **be after doing something** Irish be on the point of doing something or have just done it.
– ORIGIN OE *æfter*, of Gmc origin.

**afterbirth** • n. the placenta and fetal membranes discharged from the womb after a birth.

**afterburner** • n. an auxiliary burner in which extra fuel is burned in the exhaust of a jet engine to increase thrust.

**aftercare** • n. **1** care of a person after a stay in hospital or on release from prison. **2** support or advice offered to a customer following a purchase.

**afterdamp** • n. choking gas left after an explosion of firedamp in a mine.

**afterdeck** • n. an open deck toward the stern of a ship.

**after-effect** • n. an effect that follows after the primary action of something.

**afterglow** • n. **1** light remaining in the sky after the sun has set. **2** good feelings remaining after a pleasurable experience.

**after-image** • n. an impression of a vivid image retained by the eye after the stimulus has ceased.

**afterlife** • n. **1** (in some religions) life after death. **2** later life.

**aftermarket** • n. **1** chiefly N. Amer. the market for spare parts and accessories for motor vehicles. **2** Stock Exchange the market for shares and bonds after their original issue.

**aftermath** • n. **1** the consequences of an unpleasant or disastrous event. **2** Farming new grass growing after mowing or harvest.
– ORIGIN C15: from AFTER + dial. *math* 'mowing', of Gmc origin.

**aftermost** • adj. nearest the stern of a ship or tail of an aircraft.

**afternoon** • n. the time from noon or lunchtime to evening. • adv. (**afternoons**) informal in the afternoon; every afternoon.

**afterpains** • pl. n. pains after childbirth caused by contraction of the womb.

**afters** • pl. n. Brit. informal the dessert course of a meal.

**aftershave** • n. an astringent scented lotion for applying to the skin after shaving.

**aftershock** • n. a smaller earthquake following the main shock of a large earthquake.

**aftersun** • adj. denoting a product applied to the skin after exposure to the sun.

**aftertaste** • n. a strong or unpleasant taste lingering in the mouth after eating or drinking.

**afterthought** • n. something thought of or added later.

**aftertouch** • n. a facility on an electronic music keyboard by which an effect is produced by depressing a key after striking it.

**afterwards** (US also **afterward** /-wəd/) • adv. at a later or future time.
– ORIGIN OE *æftewearde*, from *æftan* 'aft' + -WARDS, influenced by AFTER.

**afterword** • n. a concluding section in a book, typically by a person other than the author.

**afterworld** • n. a world entered after death.

**AG** • abbrev. **1** Adjutant General. **2** Attorney General.

**Ag**[1] • symb. the chemical element silver.
– ORIGIN from L. *argentum*.

**Ag**[2] • abbrev. Biochemistry antigen.

**ag-** • prefix variant spelling of AD- assimilated before *g* (as in *aggravate, aggression*).

**Aga** /'ɑːgə/ • n. Brit. trademark a type of heavy heat-retaining cooking stove or range intended for continuous heating.
– ORIGIN 1930s: from the original maker's name (*Svenskaa*) *A*(*ktiebolaget*) *Ga*(*sackumulator*) 'Swedish Gas Accumulator Company'.

**aga** /'ɑːgə/ • n. (in Muslim countries, especially under the Ottoman Empire) a military commander or official.
– ORIGIN C16: from Turk. *ağa* 'master, lord', from Mongolian *aqa*.

**again** /ə'gɛn, ə'geɪn/ • adv. **1** once more. **2** returning to a previous position or condition. **3** in addition to what has already been mentioned. ➤ on the other hand.
– PHRASES **again and again** repeatedly.
– ORIGIN OE *ongēan, ongægn*, of Gmc origin.

**against** /ə'gɛnst, ə'geɪnst/ • prep. **1** in opposition to. ➤ to the disadvantage of. ➤ in resistance to. **2** in anticipation of and preparation for (a difficulty). ➤ (in betting) in anticipation of the failure of: *the odds were 5–1 against England.* **3** in relation to (money owed, due, or lent) so as to reduce, cancel, or secure it. **4** in or into contact with. **5** in contrast to.
– PHRASES **have something against** dislike or bear a grudge against.
– ORIGIN ME: from AGAIN + *-s* (adverbial genitive) + *-t*, prob. by assoc. with superlatives (as in *amongst*).

**Aga Khan** /ˌɑːgə 'kɑːn/ • n. the title of the spiritual leader of the Nizari sect of Ismaili Muslims.

**agal** /a'gɑːl/ • n. a headband worn by Bedouin Arab men to keep the keffiyeh in place.
– ORIGIN C19: representing a Bedouin pronunc. of Arab. '*ikāl* 'bond, hobble'.

**agama** /ə'gɑːmə/ • n. a lizard of a large group with long tails and large heads. [Genus *Agama*, family Agamidae.]
– DERIVATIVES **agamid** n.
– ORIGIN C18: perh. from Carib.

**agamic** /ə'gamɪk/ • adj. Biology asexual; reproducing asexually.
– ORIGIN C19: from Gk *agamos* 'unmarried' + -IC.

**agammaglobulinaemia** /eɪˌgaməˌglɒbjʊlɪ'niːmɪə/ (also **agammaglobulinemia**) • n. Medicine lack of gamma globulin in the blood plasma, causing immune deficiency.

**agamospermy** /'agəmə(ʊ)ˌspəːmi/ • n. Botany asexual reproduction in which seeds are produced from unfertilized ovules.
– DERIVATIVES **agamospermous** adj.
– ORIGIN 1930s: from Gk *agamos* 'unmarried' + *sperma* 'seed'.

**agapanthus** /ˌagə'panθəs/ • n. a South African plant of the lily family, with funnel-shaped bluish flowers which grow in rounded clusters. [Genus *Agapanthus*.]
– ORIGIN mod. L., from Gk *agapē* 'love' + *anthos* 'flower'.

**agape**[1] /ə'geɪp/ • adj. (of a person's mouth) wide open.

**agape**[2] /'agəpi, -peɪ/ • n. **1** Christian Theology Christian love as distinct from erotic love or simple affection. **2** a communal meal in token of Christian fellowship.
– ORIGIN C17: from Gk *agapē* 'brotherly love'.

**agar** /'eɪgɑː/ (also **agar-agar** /eɪgɑːr'eɪgɑː/) • n. a gelatinous substance obtained from various kinds of red seaweed and used in biological culture media and as a thickener in foods.
– ORIGIN C19: from Malay.

**agaric** /'ag(ə)rɪk, ə'gɑːrɪk/ • n. a fungus of an order (Agaricales) including all those with a cap with gills on the underside, e.g. mushrooms.
– ORIGIN ME: from L. *agaricum*, from Gk *agarikon* 'tree fungus'.

**agarose** /'agərəʊz, -s/ • n. Biochemistry a polysaccharide which is the main constituent of agar.

**agate** /'agət/ • n. an ornamental stone consisting of a hard variety of chalcedony, typically banded in appearance.
– ORIGIN C15: from Fr., via L. from Gk *akhatēs*.

**agave** /ə'geɪvi/ • n. a succulent plant with rosettes of narrow spiny leaves and tall flower spikes, native to the southern US and tropical America. [Genus *Agave*: numerous species.]
– ORIGIN L., from Gk *Agauē*, the name of one of the daughters of Cadmus in Gk mythology.

**AGC** • abbrev. Electronics automatic gain control.

**age** • n. **1** the length of time that a person or thing has existed. ➤ a particular stage in someone's life. ➤ old age. **2** a distinct period of history. ➤ a division of geological time that is a subdivision of an epoch. ➤ archaic a lifetime taken as a measure of time. ➤ (**ages/an age**) informal a very long time. • v. (**ageing** or **aging**) grow or cause to appear old or older. ➤ (with reference to an alcoholic drink, cheese, etc.) mature.

– PHRASES **act** (or **be**) **one's age** behave in a manner appropriate to someone of one's age. **come of age** reach adult status (in UK law at 18). **of an age 1** old enough to be able or expected to do something. **2** (of two or more people or things) of a similar age.
– DERIVATIVES **ageing** n. & adj.
– ORIGIN ME: from OFr., based on L. *aetas, aetat-*, from *aevum* 'age, era'.

**-age** ● **suffix** forming nouns: **1** denoting an action or its result: *leverage*. ➤a function; a sphere of action: *homage*. ➤a state or condition: *bondage*. **2** denoting an aggregate or number of: *mileage*. ➤a set of group of: *baggage*. ➤fees payable for: *postage*. **3** denoting a place: *vicarage*.
– ORIGIN from OFr., based on L. *-aticum*, neut. form of the adjectival ending *-aticus*.

**aged** ● **adj. 1** /eɪdʒd/ of a specified age: *he died aged 60*. ➤(of a horse or farm animal) over a certain defined age of maturity, typically 6 to 12 years for horses, 3 or 4 years for cattle. **2** /'eɪdʒɪd/ old. **3** /eɪdʒd/ having been subjected to ageing.

**age group** ● **n.** a number of people or things classed together as being of similar age.

**age hardening** ● **n.** spontaneous hardening of a metal which occurs if it is quenched and then stored at ambient temperature or treated with mild heat.
– DERIVATIVES **age-hardened** adj.

**ageism** (also **agism**) ● **n.** prejudice or discrimination on the grounds of age.
– DERIVATIVES **ageist** adj. & n.

**ageless** ● **adj.** not ageing or appearing to age.
– DERIVATIVES **agelessness** n.

**agency** ● **n. 1** a business or organization providing a particular service. ➤a government office or department providing a specific service for a state. **2** action or intervention so as to produce a particular result. ➤a thing or person that acts to produce a particular result.
– ORIGIN C17: from med. L. *agentia*, from *agent-* (see **AGENT**).

**agenda** /ə'dʒɛndə/ ● **n.** a list of items to be discussed at a meeting. ➤a list of matters to be addressed.
– ORIGIN C17: from L., neut. pl. of *agendum*, gerundive of *agere* 'do'.

**agent** ● **n. 1** a person that provides a particular service, typically one organizing transactions between two other parties. ➤a person who manages financial or contractual matters for an actor, performer, or writer. **2** a person who works in secret to obtain information for a government. **3** a person or thing that takes an active role or produces a specified effect. ➤Grammar the doer of an action. **4** Computing an independently operating Internet program, typically one set up to locate information on a specified subject and deliver it on a regular basis.
– DERIVATIVES **agentive** adj. (Grammar).
– ORIGIN ME: from L. *agent-, agere* 'to do'.

**agent general** ● **n.** (pl. **agents general**) the representative of an Australian state or Canadian province in a major foreign city.

**agent noun** ● **n.** a noun denoting a person or thing that performs the action of a verb, usually ending in *-er* or *-or*, e.g. *worker, accelerator*.

**Agent Orange** ● **n.** a defoliant chemical used by the US in the Vietnam War.

**agent provocateur** /ˌaʒɒ̃ prəˌvɒkə'təː, French aʒɑ̃ pʀɔvɔkatøʀ/ ● **n.** (pl. **agents provocateurs** pronunc. same) a person employed to induce suspected offenders to commit criminal acts and thus be convicted.
– ORIGIN C19: Fr., lit. 'provocative agent'.

**age of consent** ● **n.** the age at which a person's consent to sexual intercourse is valid in law.

**age of discretion** ● **n.** the age at which someone is considered able to take responsibility for their actions or affairs.

**age of reason** ● **n. 1** the Enlightenment. **2** (especially in the Roman Catholic Church) the age at which a child is held capable of discerning right from wrong.

**age-old** ● **adj.** having existed for a very long time.

**agglomerate** ● **v.** /ə'glɒməreɪt/ collect or form into a mass or group. ● **n.** /ə'glɒmərət/ **1** a mass or collection of things. **2** Geology a volcanic rock consisting of large fragments bonded together. ● **adj.** /ə'glɒmərət/ collected or formed into a mass.
– DERIVATIVES **agglomeration** n. **agglomerative** adj.
– ORIGIN C17: from L. *agglomerat-, agglomerare* 'add to', from *ad-* 'to' + *glomerare* (from *glomus* 'ball').

**agglutinate** /ə'gluːtɪneɪt/ ● **v. 1** firmly stick or be stuck together to form a mass. **2** Linguistics (of a language) combine (word elements) to express compound ideas.
– DERIVATIVES **agglutination** n. **agglutinative** adj. (Linguistics).
– ORIGIN C16: from L. *agglutinat-, agglutinare* 'cause to adhere'.

**agglutinin** /ə'gluːtɪnɪn/ ● **n.** Biology an antibody, lectin, or other substance that causes agglutination.

**aggradation** /ˌagrə'deɪʃ(ə)n/ ● **n.** Geology the deposition of material by a river, stream, or current.
– ORIGIN C19: from **AG-** + *(de)gradation*.

**aggrandize** /ə'grandʌɪz/ (also **-ise**) ● **v.** increase the power, status, or wealth of. ➤artificially enhance the reputation of.
– DERIVATIVES **aggrandizement** n. **aggrandizer** n.
– ORIGIN C17: from Fr. *agrandiss-, agrandir*, prob. from Ital. *aggrandire*, from L. *grandis* 'large'.

**aggravate** ● **v. 1** make worse. **2** informal annoy.
– DERIVATIVES **aggravating** adj. **aggravatingly** adv. **aggravation** n.
– ORIGIN C16: from L. *aggravat-, aggravare* 'make heavy'.

**USAGE** aggravate

Aggravate in the sense 'annoy' is in widespread use in modern English and dates back to the 17th century, but the use is still regarded as incorrect by some traditionalists.

**aggravated** ● **adj.** Law (of an offence) made more serious by attendant circumstances. ➤(of a penalty) made more severe in recognition of the seriousness of an offence.

**aggregate** ● **n.** /'agrɪgət/ **1** a whole formed by combining several disparate elements. **2** the total score of a player or team in a fixture comprising more than one game or round. **3** a material or structure formed from a loosely compacted mass of fragments or particles. ➤pieces of broken or crushed stone or gravel used to make concrete. ● **adj.** /'agrɪgət/ **1** formed or calculated by the combination of many separate units or items. **2** Botany (of a group of species) comprising several very similar species formerly regarded as a single species. **3** Economics denoting the total supply or demand for goods and services in an economy at a particular time. ● **v.** /'agrɪgeɪt/ combine into a whole.
– DERIVATIVES **aggregation** n. **aggregative** /'agrɪgətɪv/ adj.
– ORIGIN ME: from L. *aggregat-, aggregare* 'herd together', from *ad-* 'towards' + *grex, greg-* 'a flock'.

**aggregate fruit** ● **n.** Botany a fruit formed from several carpels derived from the same flower, e.g. a raspberry.

**aggression** ● **n.** hostile or violent behaviour or attitudes. ➤the action of attacking without provocation, especially in beginning a war.
– DERIVATIVES **aggressor** n.
– ORIGIN C17: from L. *aggressio(n-)*, from *aggredi* 'to attack', from *ad-* 'towards' + *gradi* 'proceed, walk'.

**aggressive** ● **adj.** characterized by or resulting from aggression. ➤unduly forceful.
– DERIVATIVES **aggressively** adv. **aggressiveness** n.

**aggrieved** ● **adj.** resentful because of unfair treatment.
– DERIVATIVES **aggrievedly** adv.
– ORIGIN ME (in the sense 'distressed'): past part. of *aggrieve*, from OFr. *agrever* 'make heavier', based on L. *aggravare* (see **AGGRAVATE**).

**aggro** ● **n.** Brit. informal **1** aggressive behaviour. **2** difficulties.
– ORIGIN 1960s: abbrev. of *aggravation* (see **AGGRAVATE**), or of **AGGRESSION**.

**aghast** /ə'gɑːst/ ● **adj.** filled with horror or shock.
– ORIGIN ME: past part. of the obs. verb *agast, gast* 'frighten', from OE *gǣsten*.

**agile** ● **adj.** able to move quickly and easily.
– DERIVATIVES **agilely** adv. **agility** n.

– ORIGIN ME: via Fr. from L. *agilis*, from *agere* 'do'.

**agile gibbon** ● **n.** a gibbon of SE Asia with colour varying from light buff to black. [*Hylobates agilis*.]

**agin** /ə'gɪn/ ● **prep.** dialect form of AGAINST.
– ORIGIN C19: var. of the obs. prep. *again*, with the same meaning.

**aging** ● **adj. & n.** variant spelling of *ageing* (see AGE).

**agism** ● **n.** variant spelling of AGEISM.

**agist** /ə'dʒɪst/ ● **v.** take in and feed (livestock) for payment.
– DERIVATIVES **agister** n. **agistment** n.
– ORIGIN ME: from OFr. *agister*, from *a-* + *gister*, from *giste* 'lodging'.

**agitate** ● **v. 1** [often as adj. **agitated**] make troubled or nervous. **2** campaign to arouse public concern about an issue. **3** stir or disturb (a liquid) briskly.
– DERIVATIVES **agitatedly** adv. **agitation** n. **agitator** n.
– ORIGIN ME (in the sense 'drive away'): from L. *agitat-*, *agitare* 'agitate, drive', frequentative of *agere* 'do, drive'.

**agitato** /ˌadʒɪ'tɑːtəʊ/ ● **adv. & adj.** Music agitated in manner.
– ORIGIN Ital., lit. 'agitated'.

**agitprop** /'adʒɪtprɒp, 'ag-/ ● **n.** political propaganda, especially in art or literature.
– ORIGIN 1930s: Russ., blend of *agitatsiya* 'agitation' and *propaganda* 'propaganda'.

**aglet** /'aglət/ ● **n.** a metal or plastic tube fixed tightly round each end of a shoelace.
– ORIGIN ME: from Fr. *aiguillette* 'small needle', dimin. of *aiguille* (see AIGUILLE).

**agley** /ə'gleɪ, ə'gliː/ ● **adv.** Scottish askew; awry.
– ORIGIN C18: from A-[2] + Scots *gley* 'squint'.

**aglow** ● **adj.** glowing.

**AGM** ● **abbrev.** annual general meeting.

**agma** /'agmə/ ● **n.** the speech sound of 'ng' as in *thing*, a velar nasal consonant. ➤the symbol /ŋ/, used to represent this sound in the International Phonetic Alphabet.
– ORIGIN 1950s: from late Gk, from Gk, lit. 'fragment'.

**agnate** /'agneɪt/ chiefly Law ● **n.** a person descended from the same male ancestor as another, especially through the male line. ● **adj.** descended in this way. Compare with COGNATE (in sense 2). ➤of the same clan or nation.
– DERIVATIVES **agnatic** /-'natɪk/ adj. **agnation** n.
– ORIGIN C15: from L. *agnatus*, from *ad-* 'to' + *gnatus*, *natus* 'born'.

**Agnatha** /ag'neɪθə/ ● **pl. n.** Zoology a group of primitive jawless vertebrates which includes the lampreys, hagfishes, and many fossil fishlike forms.
– DERIVATIVES **agnathan** n. & adj.
– ORIGIN from mod. L. *Agnatha*, from A-[1] + Gk *gnathos* 'jaw'.

**agnolotti** /ˌanjə'lɒti/ ● **pl. n.** small filled pasta squares.
– ORIGIN from Ital.

**agnosia** /əg'nəʊsɪə/ ● **n.** Medicine inability to interpret sensations and hence to recognize things, typically as a result of brain damage.
– ORIGIN C20: coined in Ger. from Gk *agnōsia* 'ignorance'.

**agnostic** /ag'nɒstɪk/ ● **n.** a person who believes that nothing is known or can be known of the existence or nature of God. ● **adj.** of or relating to agnostics or agnosticism.
– DERIVATIVES **agnosticism** n.
– ORIGIN C19: from A-[1] + GNOSTIC.

**Agnus Dei** /ˌagnʊs 'deɪiː, ˌanjʊs, 'diːʌɪ/ ● **n. 1** a figure of a lamb bearing a cross or flag, as an emblem of Christ. **2** Christian Church an invocation beginning with the words 'Lamb of God' forming a set part of the Mass.
– ORIGIN ME: from L., lit. 'Lamb of God'.

**ago** ● **adv.** before the present (used with a measurement of time).
– ORIGIN ME *ago*, *agone*, past part. of the obs. verb *ago* 'pass', used to express passage of time.

**agog** ● **adj.** very eager to hear or see something.
– ORIGIN C16: from OFr. *en gogues*, from *en* 'in' + the pl. of *gogue* 'fun'.

**agogic** /ə'gɒdʒɪk/ Music ● **adj.** relating to or denoting accentuation within musical phrases by slight lengthening of notes. ● **n.** (**agogics**) [usu. treated as sing.] the use of agogic accents.
– ORIGIN C19: from Ger. *agogisch*, from Gk *agōgos* 'leading', from *agein* 'to lead', + -IC.

**agogo** /ə'gəʊgəʊ/ ● **n.** (pl. **-os**) a small bell made of two joined metal cones, used as a percussion instrument in African and Latin music.
– ORIGIN from Yoruba.

**a gogo** /ə 'gəʊgəʊ/ ● **adj.** [postpos.] informal in abundance.
– ORIGIN 1960s: from Fr. *à gogo*, from OFr. *gogue* 'fun'.

**agonic line** /ə'gɒnɪk/ ● **n.** an imaginary line round the earth passing through both the north pole and the north magnetic pole, at any point on which a compass needle points to true north.
– ORIGIN C19: from Gk *agōnios*, *agōnos* (from *a-* 'without' + *gonia* 'angle') + -IC.

**agonist** /'agənɪst/ ● **n. 1** Biochemistry a substance which initiates a physiological response when combined with a receptor. **2** Anatomy a muscle whose contraction moves a part of the body directly. **3** a protagonist.
– DERIVATIVES **agonism** n.
– ORIGIN C20: from Gk *agōnistēs* 'contestant', from *agōn* 'contest'; cf. ANTAGONIST.

**agonistic** ● **adj. 1** polemical; combative. ➤Zoology (of animal behaviour) associated with conflict. **2** Biochemistry of, relating to, or acting as an agonist.
– DERIVATIVES **agonistically** adv.
– ORIGIN C17: via late L. from Gk *agōnistikos*, from *agōnistēs* 'contestant', from *agōn* 'contest'.

**agonize** (also **-ise**) ● **v. 1** undergo great mental anguish through worrying over something. **2** [usu. as adj. **agonizing**] cause agony to.
– DERIVATIVES **agonizingly** adv.
– ORIGIN C16: from Fr. *agoniser* or late L. *agonizare*, from Gk *agōnizesthai* 'contend', from *agōn* 'contest'.

**agony** ● **n.** (pl. **-ies**) extreme suffering.
– ORIGIN ME: via OFr. and late L. from Gk *agōnia*, from *agōn* 'contest'.

**agony aunt** (or **agony uncle**) ● **n.** Brit. informal a person who answers letters in an agony column.

**agony column** ● **n.** Brit. informal a column in a newspaper or magazine offering advice on readers' personal problems.

**agora**[1] /'agɒrə/ ● **n.** (pl. **agorae** /-riː/ or **agoras**) (in ancient Greece) a public open space used for assemblies and markets.
– ORIGIN from Gk.

**agora**[2] /ˌagə'rɑː/ ● **n.** (pl. **agorot** or **agoroth** /ˌagə'rəʊt, -rəʊθ/) a monetary unit of Israel, equal to one hundredth of a shekel.
– ORIGIN from Heb. *'ăgōrāh* 'small coin'.

**agoraphobia** /ˌag(ə)rə'fəʊbɪə/ ● **n.** extreme or irrational fear of open or public places.
– DERIVATIVES **agoraphobe** n. **agoraphobic** adj. & n.
– ORIGIN C19: from Gk *agora* (see AGORA[1]) + -PHOBIA.

**agouti** /ə'guːti/ ● **n.** (pl. same or **agoutis**) **1** a large long-legged burrowing rodent related to the guinea pig, native to Central and South America. [Genera *Agouti* and *Dasyprocta*: several species.] **2** fur in which each hair has alternate dark and light bands, producing a grizzled appearance. **3** a mouse having fur of this type.
– ORIGIN C16: via Fr. or from Sp. *aguti*, from Tupi *akuti*.

**AGR** ● **abbrev.** advanced gas-cooled (nuclear) reactor.

**agrammatism** /ə'gramətɪz(ə)m/ ● **n.** Medicine a tendency to form sentences without the correct inflectional structure, as a result of brain damage.

**agranulocytosis** /əˌgranjʊlə(ʊ)sʌɪ'təʊsɪs/ ● **n.** Medicine a deficiency of granulocytes in the blood, causing increased vulnerability to infection.

**agraphia** /ə'grafɪə, eɪ-/ ● **n.** Medicine inability to write, as a language disorder resulting from brain damage.
– ORIGIN C19: from A-[1] + Gk *-graphia* 'writing'.

**agrarian** /ə'grɛːrɪən/ ● **adj.** of or relating to cultivated land or agriculture. ➤relating to landed property. ● **n.** a

person who advocates a redistribution of landed property.
– ORIGIN C17: from L. *agrarius*, from *ager*, *agr-* 'field'.

**agree** ● v. (**agrees**, **agreed**, **agreeing**) **1** have the same opinion about something. ➤(**be agreed**) (of two or more parties) be in agreement. **2** (**agree to/to do something**) consent to do something. ➤chiefly Brit. reach agreement about. **3** (**agree with**) be consistent with. ➤[usu. with neg.] be good for. ➤Grammar have the same number, gender, case, or person as.
– ORIGIN ME: from OFr. *agreer*, based on L. *ad-* 'to' + *gratus* 'pleasing'.

**agreeable** ● adj. **1** pleasant. **2** willing to agree to something. ➤acceptable.
– DERIVATIVES **agreeableness** n. **agreeably** adv.

**agreement** ● n. **1** accordance in opinion or feeling. ➤consistency. ➤Grammar the condition of agreeing with another word. **2** a negotiated and typically legally binding arrangement.

**agribusiness** ● n. **1** agriculture conducted on strictly commercial principles. **2** the group of industries concerned with agricultural produce and services.
– DERIVATIVES **agribusinessman** n. (pl. **-men**).

**agriculture** ● n. the science or practice of farming, including the rearing of crops and animals.
– DERIVATIVES **agricultural** adj. **agriculturalist** n. **agriculturally** adv. **agriculturist** n.
– ORIGIN ME: from L. *agricultura*, from *ager*, *agr-* 'field' + *cultura* 'growing, cultivation'.

**agrimony** /'agrɪməni/ ● n. (pl. **-ies**) a plant of the rose family with slender flower spikes of yellow flowers. [Genus *Agrimonia*.]
– ORIGIN ME: via OFr. from L. *agrimonia*, alt. of *argemonia*, from Gk *argemōnē* 'poppy'.

**agrion** /'agrɪɒn/ ● n. a large damselfly that has a body with a metallic sheen. [Genus *Agrion*: numerous species.]
– ORIGIN Gk, neut. of *agrios* 'wild'.

**agriscience** ● n. the application of science to agriculture.
– DERIVATIVES **agriscientist** n.

**agro-** /'agrəʊ/ ● comb. form agricultural: *agro-industry*. ➤agriculture and ...: *agroforestry*.
– ORIGIN from Gk *agros* 'field'.

**agrobiology** ● n. the branch of biology concerned with soil science and plant nutrition and its application to crop production.
– DERIVATIVES **agrobiological** adj. **agrobiologist** n.

**agrochemical** ● n. a chemical used in agriculture.

**agroforestry** ● n. agriculture incorporating the cultivation of trees.

**agro-industry** ● n. industry connected with agriculture. ➤agriculture developed along industrial lines.
– DERIVATIVES **agro-industrial** adj.

**agronomy** /ə'grɒnəmi/ ● n. the science of soil management and crop production.
– DERIVATIVES **agronomic** adj. **agronomical** adj. **agronomically** adv. **agronomist** n.
– ORIGIN C19: from Fr. *agronomie*, from *agronome* 'agriculturist', from Gk *agros* 'field' + *-nomos* 'arranging' (from *nemoein* 'arrange').

**agrostology** /ˌagrə'stɒlədʒi/ ● n. the branch of botany concerned with grasses.
– ORIGIN C19: from Gk *agrōstis* (denoting a kind of grass) + **-LOGY**.

**aground** ● adj. & adv. (with reference to a ship) on or on to the bottom in shallow water.

**aguardiente** /əˌgwɑːdɪ'ɛnteɪ, Spanish aɣwar'ðjente/ ● n. (in Spanish-speaking countries) a distilled liquor resembling brandy.
– ORIGIN from Sp., from *agua* 'water' + *ardiente* 'fiery'.

**ague** /'eɪgjuː/ ● n. archaic malaria or some other illness involving fever and shivering. ➤a fever or shivering fit.
– DERIVATIVES **agued** adj. **aguish** adj.
– ORIGIN ME: via OFr. from med. L. *acuta* (*febris*) 'acute (fever)'.

**AH** ● abbrev. in the year of the Hegira (used in the Muslim calendar for reckoning years).
– ORIGIN from L. *anno Hegirae*.

**ah** (also **aah**) ● exclam. expressing surprise, sympathy, realization, etc.

**AHA** ● abbrev. alpha-hydroxy acid.

**aha** ● exclam. expressing triumph or surprise.

**ahead** ● adv. further forward in space or time. ➤in advance. ➤in the lead.
– PHRASES **ahead of 1** before: *we have a long drive ahead of us*. **2** in advance of.

**ahem** ● exclam. used to attract attention or express disapproval or embarrassment.

**ahimsa** /ə'hɪmsɑː/ ● n. (in the Hindu, Buddhist, and Jainist tradition) respect for all living things and avoidance of violence towards others.
– ORIGIN Sanskrit, from *a* 'non-, without' + *hiṃsā* 'violence'.

**ahistorical** ● adj. lacking historical perspective or context.

**-aholic** (also **-oholic**) ● suffix denoting a person addicted to something: *shopaholic*.
– ORIGIN on the pattern of (*alc*)*oholic*.

**ahoy** ● exclam. Nautical a call to attract attention.

**AI** ● abbrev. **1** Amnesty International. **2** artificial insemination. **3** artificial intelligence.

**ai** /'ɑːi/ ● n. (pl. **ais**) the three-toed sloth.
– ORIGIN C17: from Tupi, imitative of its cry.

**AID** ● abbrev. artificial insemination by donor.

**aid** ● n. **1** help or support. **2** material help given to a country in need. **3** historical a grant of subsidy or tax to a king. ● v. help.
– PHRASES **in aid of** chiefly Brit. in support of. **what's (all) this in aid of?** Brit. informal what is the purpose of this?
– ORIGIN ME: from OFr. *aide* (n.), *aidier* (v.), based on L. *adjuvare*, from *ad-* 'towards' + *juvare* 'to help'.

**aida** /'eɪdə/ ● n. a material consisting of a mesh of small holes, used in cross-stitch embroidery.

**aid climbing** ● n. rock climbing using objects such as pegs placed in the rock. Compare with **FREE CLIMBING**.
– DERIVATIVES **aid climb** n. & v.

**aide** /eɪd/ ● n. an assistant to a political leader. ➤short for **AIDE-DE-CAMP**.

**aide-de-camp** /ˌeɪddə'kɒ̃/ ● n. (pl. **aides-de-camp** pronunc. same) a military officer acting as a confidential assistant to a senior officer.
– ORIGIN C17: from Fr., 'camp adjutant'.

**aide-memoire** /ˌeɪd mɛm'wɑː, French ɛd mɛmwaʀ/ ● n. (pl. **aides-memoires** or **aides-memoire** pronunc. same) **1** a book or note used to aid the memory. **2** a diplomatic memorandum.
– ORIGIN C19: from Fr. *aide-mémoire*, from *aider* 'to help' and *mémoire* 'memory'.

**Aids** (also **AIDS**) ● n. a disease, caused by a virus transmitted in body fluids, in which there is a severe loss of cellular immunity leaving the sufferer susceptible to infection and malignancy.
– ORIGIN 1980s: acronym from *acquired immune deficiency syndrome*.

**Aids-related complex** ● n. the symptoms of a person who is affected with the Aids virus but does not necessarily develop the disease.

**aigrette** /'eɪgrɛt, eɪ'grɛt/ ● n. a headdress consisting of a white egret's feather or other decoration such as a spray of gems.
– ORIGIN C18: from Fr., 'egret'.

**aiguille** /'eɪgwiːl/ ● n. a sharp pinnacle of rock in a mountain range.
– ORIGIN C18: from Fr., lit. 'needle'.

**aiguillette** /ˌeɪgwɪ'lɛt/ ● n. an ornament on some military and naval uniforms, consisting of braided loops ending in tagged points hanging from the shoulder.
– ORIGIN C16: from Fr., lit. 'small needle'.

**AIH** ● abbrev. artificial insemination by husband.

**aikido** /ʌɪ'kiːdəʊ/ ● n. a Japanese form of self-defence and martial art that uses locks, holds, throws, and the opponent's own movements.
– ORIGIN 1950s: from Japanese *aikidō*, lit. 'way of adapting the spirit', from *ai* 'together, unify' + *ki* 'spirit' + *dō*

'way'.

**ail** ● v. archaic trouble or afflict in mind or body.
– ORIGIN OE *eglian, eglan*, from *egle* 'troublesome', of Gmc origin.

**ailanthus** /eɪ'lanθəs/ ● n. a tall large-leaved deciduous tree native to Asia and Australasia, especially the tree of heaven. [Genus *Ailanthus*: several species.]
– ORIGIN mod. L., from Fr. *ailante*, from Amboinese *ailanto*, lit. 'tree of heaven' (the ending is influenced by names ending with *-anthus*, from Gk *anthos* 'flower').

**aileron** /'eɪlərɒn/ ● n. a hinged surface in the trailing edge of an aircraft's wing, used to control the roll of the aircraft about its longitudinal axis.
– ORIGIN C20: from Fr., lit. 'small wing'.

**ailing** ● adj. in poor health.

**ailment** ● n. a minor illness.

**ailurophobia** /ˌʌɪljʊrə'fəʊbɪə/ ● n. extreme or irrational fear of cats.
– DERIVATIVES **ailurophobe** n.
– ORIGIN C20: from Gk *ailuros* 'cat' + **-PHOBIA**.

**AIM** ● abbrev. Alternative Investment Market.

**aim** ● v. **1** point (a weapon or camera) at a target. ➤direct at someone or something. **2** try to achieve something. ● n. **1** a purpose or intention. **2** the aiming of a weapon or missile.
– PHRASES **take aim** point a weapon or camera at a target.
– DERIVATIVES **aimless** adj. **aimlessly** adv. **aimlessness** n.
– ORIGIN ME: from OFr. *amer*, var. of *esmer*, from L. *aestimare* 'assess, estimate'.

**ain't** ● contr. informal **1** am not; are not; is not. **2** has not; have not.

**USAGE ain't**

In modern English the use of **ain't** is non-standard, despite being widespread in many dialects and in informal speech.

**Ainu** /'eɪnuː/ ● n. (pl. same or **Ainus**) **1** a member of an aboriginal people of northern Japan. **2** the language of this people, perhaps related to Altaic.
– ORIGIN the name in Ainu, lit. 'man, person'.

**aïoli** /ʌɪ'əʊli/ (also **aioli**) ● n. mayonnaise seasoned with garlic.
– ORIGIN Fr., from Provençal *ai* 'garlic' + *oli* 'oil'.

**air** ● n. **1** the invisible gaseous substance surrounding the earth, a mixture mainly of oxygen and nitrogen. **2** the open space above the surface of the earth. ➤[as modifier] indicating the use of aircraft. ➤the earth's atmosphere as a medium for transmitting radio waves. **3** one of the four elements in ancient and medieval philosophy and in astrology. **4** a breeze or light wind. **5** (**air of**) an impression given. ➤(**airs**) an annoyingly affected and condescending manner. **6** Music a tune or short melodious composition. ● v. **1** express (an opinion or grievance) publicly. ➤broadcast (a programme) on radio or television. **2** expose (a room) to the open air. ➤Brit. put (washed laundry) in the open air or a warm place to remove dampness.
– PHRASES **airs and graces** an affectation of superiority. **in the air** noticeable all around. **on** (or **off**) **the air** being (or not being) broadcast on radio or television. **take the air** go out of doors. **up in the air** unresolved. **walk** (or **tread**) **on air** feel elated.
– DERIVATIVES **airing** n. **airless** adj. **airlessness** n.
– ORIGIN ME: from OFr. *air*, from L. *aer*, from Gk *aēr*; sense 5 prob. from OFr. *aire* 'site, disposition'; sense 6 from Ital. *aria*.

**air bag** ● n. a safety device that inflates rapidly on impact to protect the occupants of a vehicle in a collision.

**air ball** ● n. Basketball a shot which misses the basket and backboard entirely.

**airbase** ● n. a base for military aircraft.

**air bearing** ● n. a bearing in which moving surfaces are kept apart by a layer of air provided by jets.

**air bed** ● n. Brit. an inflatable mattress.

**air bladder** ● n. an air-filled bladder or sac found in certain animals and plants.

**airboat** ● n. a shallow-draught boat powered by an aircraft engine, for use in swamps.

**airborne** ● adj. **1** transported by air. **2** (of an aircraft) flying.

**air brake** ● n. **1** a brake worked by air pressure. **2** a movable flap or other device on an aircraft to reduce its speed.

**airbrick** ● n. Brit. a brick perforated with small holes for ventilation.

**air bridge** ● n. Brit. a portable bridge or walkway put against an aircraft door.

**airbrush** ● n. an artist's device for spraying paint by means of compressed air. ● v. paint with an airbrush. ➤alter or conceal (a photograph) using an airbrush.

**airburst** ● n. an explosion in the air, especially of a nuclear bomb.

**air chief marshal** ● n. a high rank of RAF officer, above air marshal and below Marshal of the RAF.

**air commodore** ● n. a rank of RAF officer, above group captain and below air vice-marshal.

**air conditioning** ● n. a system for controlling the humidity, ventilation, and temperature in a building or vehicle.
– DERIVATIVES **air-conditioned** adj. **air conditioner** n.

**air corridor** ● n. a route over a foreign country to which aircraft are restricted.

**air cover** ● n. protection by aircraft for land-based or naval operations in war situations.

**aircraft** ● n. (pl. same) an aeroplane, helicopter, or other machine capable of flight.

**aircraft carrier** ● n. a large warship equipped to serve as a base for aircraft.

**aircraftman** (or **aircraftwoman**) ● n. (pl. **-men** or **-women**) the lowest RAF rank, below leading aircraftman (or leading aircraftwoman).

**aircrew** ● n. (pl. **aircrews**) [treated as sing. or pl.] the crew manning an aircraft. ➤(pl. same) a member of such a crew.

**air cushion** ● n. **1** an inflatable cushion. **2** the layer of air supporting a hovercraft or similar vehicle.

**airdrop** ● n. an act of dropping supplies, troops, or equipment by parachute. ● v. (**-dropped**, **-dropping**) drop by parachute.

**air-dry** ● v. make or become dry through contact with air.

**Airedale** /'ɛːdeɪl/ ● n. a large terrier of a rough-coated black-and-tan breed.
– ORIGIN C19: from *Airedale*, a district in Yorkshire.

**airer** ● n. Brit. a frame or stand for airing or drying laundry.

**airfield** ● n. an area of land set aside for the take-off, landing, and maintenance of aircraft.

**air filter** ● n. a device for filtering particles from the air passing into an internal-combustion engine.

**airflow** ● n. the flow of air encountered by a moving aircraft or vehicle.

**airfoil** ● n. North American term for **AEROFOIL**.

**air force** ● n. a branch of the armed forces concerned with fighting or defence in the air.

**airframe** ● n. the body of an aircraft as distinct from its engine.

**airfreight** ● n. the carriage of goods by aircraft. ➤goods carried by aircraft. ● v. carry or send by aircraft.

**air-freshener** ● n. a scented substance or device for masking unpleasant odours in a room.

**airglow** ● n. a glow in the night sky caused by radiation from the upper atmosphere.

**air guitar** ● n. informal the actions of a person playing an imaginary guitar.

**air gun** ● n. **1** a gun which uses compressed air to fire pellets. **2** a tool using very hot air to strip paint.

**airhead**[1] ● n. Military a base close to the area of active operations where supplies and troops can be received and evacuated by air.
– ORIGIN Second World War: on the pattern of *bridgehead*.

**airhead**[2] ● **n.** informal a stupid person.
**air hostess** ● **n.** Brit. a stewardess in a passenger aircraft.
**air-kiss** ● **v.** purse the lips as if kissing, without making contact. ● **n.** (**air kiss**) a kiss of this kind.
**air layering** ● **n.** Horticulture layering of a plant in which the branch is potted or wrapped in a moist growing medium to promote root growth.
**air letter** ● **n.** a sheet of light paper folded and sealed to form a letter for sending by airmail.
**airlift** ● **n.** an act of transporting supplies by aircraft, typically in an emergency. ● **v.** transport in this way.
**airline** ● **n. 1** an organization providing a regular passenger air service. **2** (usu. **air line**) a pipe supplying air.
**airliner** ● **n.** a large passenger aircraft.
**airlock** ● **n. 1** a stoppage of the flow in a pump or pipe, caused by an air bubble. **2** a compartment with controlled pressure and parallel sets of doors, to permit movement between areas at different pressures.
**airmail** ● **n.** a system of transporting mail overseas by air. ● **v.** send by airmail.
**airman** (or **airwoman**) ● **n.** (pl. **-men** or **-women**) a pilot or member of the crew of an aircraft in an air force. ➤ a member of the RAF below commissioned rank. ➤ a member of the US air force of the lowest rank, below staff sergeant. ➤ a member of the US navy whose general duties are concerned with aircraft.
– DERIVATIVES **airmanship** n.
**air marshal** ● **n.** a high rank of RAF officer, above air vice-marshal and below air chief marshal.
**air mass** ● **n.** Meteorology a body of air with horizontally uniform levels of temperature, humidity, and pressure.
**air mattress** ● **n.** North American term for **AIR BED**.
**air mile** ● **n. 1** a nautical mile used as a measure of distance flown by aircraft. **2** (**Air Miles**) trademark points (equivalent to miles of free air travel) accumulated by buyers of airline tickets and other products.
**airmiss** ● **n.** Brit. an instance of two or more aircraft in flight on different routes being less than a prescribed safe distance apart.
**airmobile** /ɛːˈməʊbʌɪl/ ● **adj.** (of troops) moved about by air.
**air officer** ● **n.** any rank of RAF officer above that of group captain.
**air pistol** (or **air rifle**) ● **n.** a gun which uses compressed air to fire pellets.
**airplane** ● **n.** North American term for **AEROPLANE**.
**air plant** ● **n.** an epiphytic tropical American plant with long narrow leaves that absorb water and nutrients from the atmosphere. [Genus *Tillandsia*: several species.]
**airplay** ● **n.** broadcasting time devoted to a particular record, performer, or musical genre.
**air pocket** ● **n. 1** a cavity containing air. **2** a region of low pressure causing an aircraft to lose height suddenly.
**airport** ● **n.** a complex for civil aircraft comprising runways, hangars, and passenger facilities.
**air pump** ● **n.** a device for pumping air into or out of an enclosed space.
**air quality** ● **n.** the degree to which the ambient air is pollution-free.
**air raid** ● **n.** an attack in which bombs are dropped from aircraft on to a ground target.
**air sac** ● **n.** an alveolus. ➤ an extension of a bird's lung cavity into a bone or other part of the body.
**airscrew** ● **n.** Brit. an aircraft propeller.
**air-sea rescue** ● **n.** a rescue from the sea using aircraft.
**airship** ● **n.** a power-driven aircraft kept buoyant by a body of gas (usually helium) which is lighter than air.
**air shot** ● **n.** informal a missed attempt to hit or kick a ball.
**airsick** ● **adj.** affected with nausea due to air travel.
– DERIVATIVES **airsickness** n.
**airside** ● **n.** the area beyond passport and customs control in an airport terminal.
**airspace** ● **n.** the part of the air above and subject to the jurisdiction of a particular country.
**airspeed** ● **n.** the speed of an aircraft relative to the air through which it is moving.
**airstream** ● **n.** a current of air.
**airstrip** ● **n.** a strip of ground for the take-off and landing of aircraft.
**airtight** ● **adj.** not allowing air to escape or pass through.
**airtime** ● **n.** time during which a broadcast is being transmitted.
**air-to-air** ● **adj.** directed or operating from one aircraft to another in flight.
**air-to-ground** ● **adj.** directed or operating from an aircraft in flight to the land surface.
**air-to-surface** ● **adj.** directed or operating from an aircraft in flight to the surface of the sea.
**air traffic control** ● **n.** the ground-based personnel and equipment concerned with controlling and monitoring air traffic within a particular area.
– DERIVATIVES **air traffic controller** n.
**air vice-marshal** ● **n.** a high rank of RAF officer, above air commodore and below air marshal.
**airwaves** ● **pl. n.** the radio frequencies used for broadcasting.
**airway** ● **n. 1** the passage by which air reaches the lungs. ➤ a tube for supplying air to the lungs in an emergency. **2** a recognized route followed by aircraft.
**airworthy** ● **adj.** (of an aircraft) safe to fly.
– DERIVATIVES **airworthiness** n.
**airy** ● **adj.** (**-ier**, **-iest**) **1** spacious and well ventilated. **2** light as air; delicate. **3** casual; dismissive.
– DERIVATIVES **airily** adv. **airiness** n.
**airy-fairy** ● **adj.** informal, chiefly Brit. foolishly idealistic and vague.
**aisle** /ʌɪl/ ● **n. 1** a passage between rows of seats, pews, or supermarket shelves. **2** Architecture a lateral division of a church parallel to, and divided by pillars from, a nave, choir, or transept.
– PHRASES **lead someone up the aisle** get married to someone.
– DERIVATIVES **aisled** adj.
– ORIGIN ME *ele*, *ile*, from OFr. *ele*, from L. *ala* 'wing'.
**ait** /eɪt/ (also **eyot**) ● **n.** [in place names] Brit. a small island in a river.
– ORIGIN OE *iggath*, *īgeth*, based on *īeg* 'island' + a dimin. suffix.
**aitch** ● **n.** the letter H.
– PHRASES **drop one's aitches** fail to pronounce the letter *h* at the beginning of words.
– ORIGIN C16: from OFr. *ache*.
**aitchbone** ● **n.** the buttock or rump bone of cattle. ➤ a cut of beef lying over this.
– ORIGIN C15, from dial. *nache* 'rump', from OFr., based on L. *natis* 'buttock(s)', + **BONE**; the initial *n* was lost by wrong division of *a nache bone*.
**ajar** ● **adv. & adj.** (of a door or window) slightly open.
– ORIGIN C17: from **A-**[2] + obs. *char* (OE *cerr*) 'a turn'.
**ajuga** /əˈdʒuːgə/ ● **n.** a plant of a genus that includes bugle. [Genus *Ajuga*.]
– ORIGIN mod. L., from med. L.
**AK** ● **abbrev.** Alaska (in official postal use).
**aka** ● **abbrev.** also known as.
**Akali** /əˈkɑːli/ ● **n.** (pl. **Akalis**) a member of a militant Sikh political group.
– ORIGIN from Punjabi *akālī*, lit. 'follower of the Immortal One'.
**Akan** /ˈɑːk(ə)n/ ● **n.** (pl. same) **1** a member of a people inhabiting southern Ghana and adjacent parts of Ivory Coast. **2** the language of this people, belonging to the Kwa group.
– ORIGIN the name in Akan.
**akara** /əˈkarə/ ● **n.** variant spelling of **ACCRA**.
**akasha** /ɑːˈkɑːʃə/ ● **n.** (chiefly in Hinduism) a supposed all-pervading field in the ether in which a record of past events is imprinted.
– DERIVATIVES **akashic** adj.

– ORIGIN from Sanskrit *ākāśa*.

**akebia** /əˈkiːbɪə/ ● **n.** an East Asian climbing shrub with purplish flowers and deeply divided leaves. [Genus *Akebia*.]
– ORIGIN C19: mod. L., from Japanese *akebi*.

**akee** ● **n.** variant spelling of **ACKEE**.

**Akela** /ɑːˈkeɪlə/ ● **n.** informal the adult leader of a group of Cub Scouts.
– ORIGIN 1920s: from the name of the leader of a wolf pack in Kipling's *Jungle Books*.

**akimbo** /əˈkɪmbəʊ/ ● **adv.** with hands on the hips and elbows turned outwards.
– ORIGIN ME *in kenebowe*: prob. from ON.

**akin** ● **adj. 1** of similar character. **2** related by blood.
– ORIGIN C16: contracted form of *of kin*.

**akinesia** /ˌeɪkɪˈniːsɪə, a-/ ● **n.** Medicine loss or impairment of the power of voluntary movement.
– DERIVATIVES **akinetic** adj.
– ORIGIN C19: from Gk *akinēsia* 'quiescence'.

**Akita** /əˈkiːtə/ ● **n.** a spitz (dog) of a Japanese breed.
– ORIGIN C20: from *Akita*, the name of a district in northern Japan.

**Akkadian** /əˈkeɪdɪən, -ˈkad-/ ● **n. 1** an inhabitant of Akkad in ancient Babylonia. **2** the extinct Semitic language of Akkad. ● **adj.** of or relating to Akkad, its people, or their language.

**akrasia** /əˈkreɪzɪə, əˈkrasɪə/ (also **acrasia**) ● **n.** chiefly Philosophy weakness of will, leading to someone acting against their better judgement.
– DERIVATIVES **akratic** adj.
– ORIGIN C19: from Gk, from *a-* 'without' + *kratos* 'power, strength'.

**akvavit** /ˈakvəvɪt/ ● **n.** variant spelling of **AQUAVIT**.

**AL** ● **abbrev. 1** Alabama (in official postal use). **2** American League (in baseball).

**Al** ● **symb.** the chemical element aluminium.

**al-** ● **prefix** variant spelling of **AD-** assimilated before *-l* (as in *alleviate*).

**-al** ● **suffix 1** (forming adjectives from Latin, Greek, or English words) relating to; of the kind of: *tidal*. **2** forming nouns chiefly denoting verbal action: *arrival*.
– ORIGIN sense 1 from Fr. *-el* or L. *-alis*; sense 2 from Fr. *-aille* or from L. *-alis* functioning as a noun ending.

**Ala.** ● **abbrev.** Alabama.

**à la** /ɑː lɑː, a la/ ● **prep.** cooked or prepared in a specified style or manner: *fish cooked à la meunière*.
– ORIGIN Fr., from **À LA MODE**.

**Alabaman** ● **n.** a native or inhabitant of the US state of Alabama. ● **adj.** of or relating to Alabama.

**alabaster** /ˈaləbɑːstə, -bastə, ˌaləˈbɑːstə, -ˈbastə/ ● **n. 1** a translucent form of gypsum, typically white, often carved into ornaments. **2** [as modifier] poetic/literary smooth and white.
– ORIGIN ME: via OFr. from L. *alabaster, alabastrum*, from Gk *alabastos, alabastros*.

**à la carte** /ɑː lɑː ˈkɑːt, a la, French a la kaʀt/ ● **adj.** (of a menu) listing food that can be ordered as separate items, rather than part of a set meal. ● **adv.** as à la carte items from a menu.
– ORIGIN C19: Fr., lit. 'according to the (menu) card'.

**alack** (also **alack-a-day**) ● **exclam.** archaic an expression of regret or dismay.
– ORIGIN ME: prob. from **AH** + **LACK**.

**alacrity** /əˈlakrɪti/ ● **n.** brisk and cheerful readiness.
– ORIGIN ME: from L. *alacritas*, from *alacer* 'brisk'.

**Aladdin's cave** ● **n.** a place filled with a great number of interesting or precious items.
– ORIGIN from *Aladdin* in the *Arabian Nights' Entertainments*.

**Aladdin's lamp** ● **n.** a talisman enabling its holder to gratify any wish.

**alameda** /ˌaləˈmeɪdə/ ● **n.** (in Spanish-speaking countries) a tree-lined public promenade.
– ORIGIN C18: from Sp.

**à la mode** /ɑː lɑː ˈməʊd, a la/ ● **adv. & adj. 1** up to date. **2** (of beef) braised in wine with vegetables. **3** N. Amer. served with ice cream.
– ORIGIN C16: Fr., lit. 'in the fashion'.

**alanine** /ˈaləniːn/ ● **n.** Biochemistry an amino acid which is a constituent of most proteins.
– ORIGIN C19: from Ger. as *Alanin*, from **ALDEHYDE** + *-an* + **-INE**[4].

**alannah** /əˈlanə/ ● **n.** Irish my child.
– ORIGIN C19: from Ir. *a leanbh* 'O child'.

**alap** /ɑːˈlɑːp/ ● **n.** (in Indian music) the improvised section of a raga, forming a prologue to the formal expression.
– ORIGIN from Hindi *alāp*.

**Alar** /ˈeɪlɑː/ ● **n.** trademark a growth retardant sprayed on fruit and vegetables to enhance the quality of the crop.
– ORIGIN 1960s: of unknown origin.

**alar** /ˈeɪlə/ ● **adj. 1** chiefly Zoology of or relating to a wing or wings. ➤ Anatomy wing-like or wing-shaped. **2** Botany axillary.
– ORIGIN C19: from L. *alaris*, from *ala* 'wing'.

**alarm** ● **n. 1** anxious or frightened awareness of danger. ➤ a warning of danger. **2** a warning sound or device. ● **v. 1** frighten or disturb. **2** (**be alarmed**) be fitted or protected with an alarm.
– DERIVATIVES **alarming** adj. **alarmingly** adv.
– ORIGIN ME (as exclam. meaning 'to arms!'): from OFr. *alarme*, from Ital. *allarme*, from *all' arme!*

**alarm clock** ● **n.** a clock with a device that can be made to sound at the time set in advance.

**alarmist** ● **n.** a person who exaggerates a danger, so causing needless alarm. ● **adj.** creating needless alarm.
– DERIVATIVES **alarmism** n.

**alarum** /əˈlɑːrəm/ ● **n.** archaic term for **ALARM**.
– PHRASES **alarums and excursions** humorous confused activity and uproar.

**Alas.** ● **abbrev.** Alaska.

**alas** ● **exclam.** poetic/literary or humorous an expression of grief, pity, or concern.
– ORIGIN ME: from OFr. *a las, a lasse*, from *a* 'ah' + *las(se)* (from L. *lassus* 'weary').

**Alaskan** ● **n.** a native or inhabitant of the US state of Alaska. ● **adj.** of or relating to Alaska.

**alate** /ˈeɪleɪt/ ● **adj.** Botany & Entomology (chiefly of insects or seeds) having wings or wing-like appendages.
– ORIGIN C17: from L. *alatus*, from *ala* 'wing'.

**alb** /alb/ ● **n.** a white vestment reaching to the feet, worn by clergy and servers in some Christian Churches.
– ORIGIN OE *albe*, from eccles. L. *tunica* (or *vestis*) *alba* 'white garment'.

**alba** /ˈalbə/ ● **n.** a shrub rose of a variety with grey-green leaves and pinkish-white, sweet-scented flowers.
– ORIGIN C19: from L. *alba*, fem. of *albus* 'white', from the name *rosa alba*, an old white garden rose.

**albacore** /ˈalbəkɔː/ ● **n.** a tuna of warm seas which travels in large schools and is an important food fish. [*Thunnus alalunga*.]
– ORIGIN C16: from Port. *albacora*, from Arab. *al-bakūra*, perh. from *al* 'the' + *bakūr* 'premature, precocious'.

**Albanian** ● **n. 1** a native or national of Albania, or a person of Albanian descent. **2** the Indo-European language of Albania. ● **adj.** of or relating to Albania or its language.

**albatross** /ˈalbətrɒs/ ● **n.** (pl. **albatrosses**) **1** a very large seabird with long narrow wings, found chiefly in the southern oceans. [Genera *Diomedea* and *Phoebetria*.] **2** a burden or encumbrance (in allusion to Coleridge's *The Rime of the Ancient Mariner*). **3** Golf a double eagle.
– ORIGIN C17: alt. (influenced by L. *albus* 'white') of C16 *alcatras*, applied to various seabirds, from Sp. and Port. *alcatraz*, from Arab. *al-ġaṭṭās* 'the diver'.

**albedo** /alˈbiːdəʊ/ ● **n.** (pl. **-os**) chiefly Astronomy the proportion of the incident light or radiation that is reflected by a surface.
– ORIGIN C19: eccles. L., 'whiteness', from L. *albus* 'white'.

**albeit** /ɔːlˈbiːɪt/ ● **conj.** though.
– ORIGIN ME: from the phr. *all be it* 'although it be (that)'.

**albert** (also **albert chain**) ● **n.** Brit. a watch chain with a bar at one end for attaching to a buttonhole.
– ORIGIN C19: named after Prince *Albert* (1819–61), consort

of Queen Victoria.

**albescent** /al'bɛs(ə)nt/ ● **adj.** poetic/literary growing or shading into white.
– ORIGIN C18: from L. *albescent-*, *albescere* 'become white'.

**Albigenses** /ˌalbɪ'gɛnsiːz, -'dʒɛn-/ ● **pl. n.** the members of a heretic sect in southern France in the 12th–13th centuries, believing in a form of Manichaean dualism.
– DERIVATIVES **Albigensian** adj.
– ORIGIN from med. L., from *Albiga*, the L. name of *Albi* in southern France.

**albino** /al'biːnəʊ/ ● **n.** (pl. **-os**) a person or animal having a congenital absence of pigment in the skin and hair (which are white) and the eyes (which are usually pink).
– DERIVATIVES **albinism** /'albɪnɪz(ə)m/ n.
– ORIGIN C18: from Port. and Sp., from *albo* (from L. *albus* 'white') + *-ino* (see **-INE**[1]).

**Albion** /'albɪən/ ● **n.** poetic/literary Britain or England.
– ORIGIN OE, from L., prob. of Celtic origin and rel. to L. *albus* 'white' (in allusion to the white cliffs of Dover).

**albite** /'albʌɪt/ ● **n.** a sodium-rich, typically white mineral of the feldspar group.
– ORIGIN C19: from L. *albus* 'white' + **-ITE**[1].

**albizzia** /al'bɪzɪə/ ● **n.** a leguminous tree or shrub of warm climates, with feathery leaves and plume-like flowers. [Genus *Albizia*.]
– ORIGIN mod. L., named after the Ital. nobleman Filippo delgi *Albizzi*.

**album** ● **n.** **1** a blank book for the insertion of photographs, stamps, or pictures. **2** a collection of recordings issued as a single item.
– ORIGIN C17: from L., neut. of *albus* 'white' used as noun meaning 'a blank tablet'.

**albumen** /'albjʊmɪn/ ● **n.** egg white, or the protein contained in it.
– ORIGIN C16: from L., from *albus* 'white'.

**albumin** /'albjʊmɪn/ ● **n.** Biochemistry a water-soluble form of protein, coagulable by heat, found especially in blood serum and egg white.
– DERIVATIVES **albuminous** /al'bjuːmɪnəs/ adj.
– ORIGIN C19: from Fr. *albumine*, based on L. *albumen*, *albumin-* (see **ALBUMEN**).

**albuminuria** /ˌalbjʊmɪ'njʊərɪə/ ● **n.** Medicine the presence of albumin in the urine, typically as a symptom of kidney disease.

**alcahest** ● **n.** variant spelling of **ALKAHEST**.

**alcaic** /al'keɪɪk/ Prosody ● **adj.** written in or denoting a verse metre occurring in four-line stanzas. ● **n.** (**alcaics**) verse written in such a metre.
– ORIGIN C17: via late L. from Gk *alkaikos*, from *Alkaios* Alcaeus (*c.*620–*c.*580 BC), Gk lyric poet.

**alcalde** /al'kaldeɪ/ ● **n.** a magistrate or mayor in a Spanish, Portuguese, or Latin American town.
– ORIGIN C16: Sp., from Arab. *al-ḳāḍī* (see **CADI**).

**alcazar** /ˌalkə'zɑː/ ● **n.** a Spanish palace or fortress of Moorish origin.
– ORIGIN C17: from Sp. *alcázar*, from Arab. *al-ḳaṣr* 'the castle'.

**alchemilla** /ˌalkə'mɪlə/ ● **n.** lady's mantle or a related plant. [Genus *Alchemilla*.]
– ORIGIN mod. L., from a med. L. dimin. of *alchimia* 'alchemy', from the belief that dew from the leaves of the plant could turn base metals into gold.

**alchemy** /'alkɪmi/ ● **n.** **1** the medieval forerunner of chemistry, concerned particularly with attempts to convert base metals into gold or to find a universal elixir. **2** a process by which paradoxical results are achieved or incompatible elements combined.
– DERIVATIVES **alchemic** /al'kɛmɪk/ adj. **alchemical** adj. **alchemist** n. **alchemize** (also **-ise**) v.
– ORIGIN ME: via OFr. and med. L. from Arab. *alkīmiyā'*, from *al* 'the' + *kīmiyā'* (from Gk *khēmia*, *khēmeia* 'art of transmuting metals').

**alcheringa** /ˌaltʃə'rɪŋgə/ ● **n.** (in the mythology of some Australian Aboriginals) the 'golden age' when the first ancestors were created.
– ORIGIN C19: from Aranda *aljerre-nge* 'in the dreamtime'.

**alcid** /'alsɪd/ ● **n.** Ornithology a bird of the auk family (Alcidae).
– ORIGIN C19: from mod. L. *Alcidae*, from the genus name *Alca*, from ON *álka* 'razorbill'; cf. **AUK**.

**alcohol** ● **n.** **1** a colourless volatile flammable liquid which is the intoxicating constituent of wine, beer, spirits, etc. Also called **ETHANOL**, **ETHYL ALCOHOL**. [$C_2H_5OH$.] **2** drink containing this. **3** Chemistry any organic compound containing a hydroxyl group –OH: *propyl alcohol*.
– ORIGIN C16 (in the sense 'a fine powder, especially kohl, produced by sublimation'): Fr., or from med. L., from Arab. *al-kuḥl* 'the kohl'.

**alcoholic** ● **adj.** containing, relating to, or caused by the consumption of alcohol. ● **n.** a person suffering from alcoholism.

**alcoholism** ● **n.** addiction to alcoholic liquor.

**alcoholometer** /ˌalkəhɒ'lɒmɪtə/ ● **n.** an instrument for measuring the concentration of alcohol in a liquid.
– DERIVATIVES **alcoholometry** n.

**alcopop** ● **n.** Brit. informal a ready-mixed soft drink containing alcohol.

**alcove** ● **n.** a recess, typically in the wall of a room.
– ORIGIN C16: from Fr. *alcôve*, from Sp. *alcoba*, from Arab. *al-ḳubba* 'the vault'.

**aldehyde** /'aldɪhʌɪd/ ● **n.** Chemistry an organic compound containing the group –CHO, formed by the oxidation of alcohols.
– DERIVATIVES **aldehydic** /ˌaldɪ'hɪdɪk/ adj.
– ORIGIN C19: shortened from L. *alcohol dehydrogenatum* 'alcohol deprived of hydrogen'.

**al dente** /al 'dɛnteɪ, -ti/ ● **adj. & adv.** (of food) cooked so as to be still firm when bitten.
– ORIGIN Ital., lit. 'to the tooth'.

**alder** /'ɔːldə/ ● **n.** a catkin-bearing tree of the birch family with toothed leaves, found especially on damp ground and riverbanks. [*Alnus glutinosa* and other species.]
– ORIGIN OE *alor*, *aler*, of Gmc origin.

**alder buckthorn** ● **n.** a deciduous shrub which bears glossy leaves and black berries. [*Frangula alnus*.]

**alderfly** ● **n.** (pl. **-flies**) a brownish neuropterous insect that lives near water and has predatory aquatic larvae. [*Sialis* and other genera.]

**alderman** ● **n.** (pl. **-men**) **1** chiefly historical a co-opted member of an English county or borough council, next in status to the Mayor. **2** (or **alderwoman**) (pl. **-women**) N. Amer. & Austral. an elected member of a city council.
– DERIVATIVES **aldermanic** adj. **aldermanship** n.
– ORIGIN OE *aldormann* (in the sense 'a man of high rank'), from *aldor*, *ealdor* 'chief, patriarch' (from *ald* 'old') + **MAN**.

**aldicarb** /'aldɪkɑːb/ ● **n.** a systemic agricultural pesticide used particularly against some mites, insects, and nematode worms.
– ORIGIN 1970s: blend of **ALDEHYDE** + *carbamide* (from **CARBO-** + **AMIDE**).

**Aldis lamp** /'ɔːldɪs/ ● **n.** trademark a hand-held lamp for signalling in Morse code.
– ORIGIN First World War: named after the Brit. inventor Arthur C. W. *Aldis*.

**aldol** /'aldɒl/ ● **n.** Chemistry a viscous compound with alcohol and aldehyde groups, obtained when acetaldehyde dimerizes.
– ORIGIN C19: from *al(dehyde)* + **-OL**.

**aldosterone** /al'dɒstərəʊn/ ● **n.** Biochemistry a corticosteroid hormone which stimulates absorption of sodium by the kidneys and so regulates water and salt balance.
– ORIGIN 1950s: blend of **ALDEHYDE** and **STEROID**, + **-ONE**.

**aldosteronism** /ˌaldə(ʊ)'stɛrənɪz(ə)m/ ● **n.** Medicine a condition in which there is excessive secretion of aldosterone, disturbing the salt balance of the blood and leading to high blood pressure.

**aldrin** /'ɔːldrɪn/ ● **n.** a compound of the chlorinated hydrocarbon type, formerly used as an insecticide.
– ORIGIN 1940s: from the name of the Ger. chemist Kurt *Alder* + **-IN**[1].

**ale** ● **n.** chiefly Brit. beer other than lager, stout, or porter. ➤ N. Amer. beer brewed by top fermentation.
– ORIGIN OE *alu*, *ealu*, of Gmc origin.

**aleatory** /'eɪlɪət(ə)ri, 'al-/ (also **aleatoric**) ● **adj.** **1** depending on the throw of a die or on chance. **2** relating to or denoting music or other forms of art involving elements of random choice during their composition or performance.
– ORIGIN C17: from L. *aleatorius*, from *aleator* 'dice player', from *alea* 'die'.

**alec** /'alɪk/ (also **aleck**) ● **n.** Austral. informal a stupid person.
– ORIGIN C20: shortening of **SMART ALEC**.

**alecost** /'eɪlkɒst/ ● **n.** another term for **COSTMARY**.
– ORIGIN C16: from **ALE** + obs. *cost* **COSTMARY**.

**alee** /ə'li:/ ● **adj. & adv.** Nautical on the leeward side of a ship. ➤(of the helm) moved round to leeward.

**alehouse** ● **n.** dated an inn or public house.

**alembic** /ə'lɛmbɪk/ ● **n.** an apparatus formerly used for distilling, consisting of a gourd-shaped container and a cap with a long beak for conveying the products to a receiver.
– ORIGIN ME: via OFr. from med. L. *alembicus*, from Arab. *al-'anbīḳ*, from *al-* 'the' + *'anbīḳ* 'still' (from Gk *ambix*, *ambik-* 'cup').

**aleph** /'ɑ:lɛf/ ● **n.** the first letter of the Hebrew alphabet.
– ORIGIN ME: from Heb. *'ālep*, lit. 'ox' (the character in Phoenician and ancient Heb. possibly being derived from a hieroglyph of an ox's head).

**Aleppo gall** ● **n.** a hard nut-like gall, a source of gallic acid and tannin, that forms on the valonia oak (formerly known as the Aleppo oak).

**alerce** /ə'lə:si/ ● **n.** a cypress tree, found especially in southern Spain and north Africa, which is the source of gum sandarac. [*Tetraclinis articulata* and other species.]
– ORIGIN C19: from Sp., 'larch'.

**alert** ● **adj.** quick to notice and respond to potential danger or problems. ➤intellectually active. ● **n.** **1** (often in phr. **on the alert**) the state of being alert. **2** a warning of danger. **3** a reminder or prompt. ● **v.** warn of a danger or problem.
– DERIVATIVES **alertly** adv. **alertness** n.
– ORIGIN C16 (orig. in military use): from Fr. *alerte*, from Ital. *all' erta* 'to the watchtower'.

**-ales** /'eɪli:z/ ● **suffix** Botany forming the names of orders of plants: *Rosales*.
– ORIGIN from the pl. of the L. adjectival suffix *-alis*.

**alethic** /ə'li:θɪk/ ● **adj.** Philosophy denoting modalities of truth, such as necessity, contingency, or impossibility.
– ORIGIN 1950s: from Gk *alētheia* 'truth' + **-IC**.

**aleurone** /ə'ljʊərəʊn/ ● **n.** Botany protein stored as granules in the cells of plant seeds.
– ORIGIN C19: from Gk *aleuron* 'flour'.

**Aleut** /ə'lju:t, 'alɪu:t/ ● **n.** **1** a member of a people chiefly inhabiting the Aleutian Islands and parts of western Alaska. **2** the language of this people, related to Eskimo.
– ORIGIN of unknown origin.

**A level** ● **n.** Brit. short for **ADVANCED LEVEL**.

**alevin** /'aləvɪn/ ● **n.** a newly spawned salmon or trout still carrying the yolk.
– ORIGIN C19: from Fr., based on L. *allevare* 'raise up'.

**alewife** ● **n.** (pl. **alewives**) a NW Atlantic fish of the herring family, swimming up rivers to spawn. [*Alosa pseudoharengus*.]
– ORIGIN C17: perh. from earlier *alewife* 'woman who keeps an ale house', with ref. to the fish's large belly.

**alexanders** ● **pl. n.** [treated as sing.] a plant of the parsley family with yellowish flowers, formerly used in salads. [*Smyrnium olusatrum*.]
– ORIGIN OE *alexandre*, from med. L. *alexandrum*.

**Alexander technique** ● **n.** a system designed to promote well-being by retraining one's awareness and habits of posture to ensure minimum effort and strain.
– ORIGIN 1930s: named after the Australian-born actor and elocutionist Frederick Matthias *Alexander*.

**Alexandrian** ● **adj.** of or relating to Alexandria in Egypt. ➤belonging to or characteristic of the schools of literature and philosophy of ancient Alexandria, especially in being allusive or imitative.

**alexandrine** /,alɪg'zɑ:ndrɪn, -ʌɪn/ Prosody ● **adj.** (of a line of verse) having six iambic feet. ● **n.** an alexandrine line.
– ORIGIN C16: from Fr. *alexandrin*, from *Alexandre* referring to Alexander the Great, the subject of an OFr. poem in this metre.

**alexandrite** /,alɪg'zɑ:ndrʌɪt/ ● **n.** a gem variety of chrysoberyl which appears green in daylight and red in artificial light.
– ORIGIN C19: from the name of Tsar *Alexander* II of Russia + **-ITE**[1].

**alexia** /ə'lɛksɪə, eɪ-/ ● **n.** Medicine inability to recognize or read written words or letters, typically as a result of brain damage. Compare with **DYSLEXIA**.
– ORIGIN C19: from **A-**[1] + Gk *lexis* 'speech', from *legein* 'speak', which was confused with L. *legere* 'read'.

**Alf** ● **n.** Austral. informal an uneducated and unthinkingly conservative Australian man.
– ORIGIN 1960s: abbrev. of *Alfred*.

**alfalfa** /al'falfə/ ● **n.** a leguminous plant with clover-like leaves and bluish flowers, native to SW Asia and grown for fodder. [*Medicago sativa*.]
– ORIGIN C19: from Sp., from Arab. *al-faṣfaṣa*, a green fodder.

**alfisol** /'alfɪsɒl/ ● **n.** Soil Science a leached basic or slightly acid soil with a clay-enriched B horizon.
– ORIGIN 1960s: from the arbitrary element *Alfi-* + **-SOL**.

**Alfredo** /al'freɪdəʊ/ ● **n.** a sauce for pasta incorporating butter, cream, garlic, and Parmesan cheese.
– ORIGIN named after the Ital. chef and restaurateur *Alfredo* di Lelio.

**alfresco** /al'frɛskəʊ/ ● **adv. & adj.** in the open air.
– ORIGIN C18: from Ital. *al fresco* 'in the fresh (air)'.

**Alfvén wave** ● **n.** Physics a transverse magnetohydrodynamic wave travelling in the direction of the magnetic field in a magnetized plasma.
– ORIGIN 1950s: named after the Swed. physicist Hannes *Alfvén*.

**alga** /'algə/ ● **n.** (pl. **algae** /'aldʒi:, 'algi:/) any of a large group of simple, non-flowering plants containing chlorophyll but lacking true stems, roots, leaves, and vascular tissue, e.g. the seaweeds and many single-celled forms.
– DERIVATIVES **algal** adj.
– ORIGIN C16: from L., 'seaweed'.

**algebra** /'aldʒɪbrə/ ● **n.** the part of mathematics in which letters and other general symbols are used to represent numbers and quantities in formulae and equations. ➤a system of this based on given axioms.
– DERIVATIVES **algebraic** /aldʒɪ'breɪɪk/ adj. **algebraical** adj. **algebraically** adv. **algebraist** n.
– ORIGIN ME: from Ital., Sp., and med. L., from Arab. *al-jabr* 'the reunion of broken parts', from *jabara* 'reunite, restore'.

**Algerian** /al'dʒɪərɪən/ ● **n.** a native or inhabitant of Algeria. ● **adj.** of or relating to Algeria.

**-algia** ● **comb. form** denoting pain in a specified part of the body: *neuralgia*. See word-formation panel.
– DERIVATIVES **-algic** comb. form in corresponding adjectives.
– ORIGIN from Gk *algos* 'pain'.

**algicide** /'aldʒɪsʌɪd, 'algɪ-/ ● **n.** a substance which is poisonous to algae.

**alginic acid** /al'dʒɪnɪk/ ● **n.** Chemistry an insoluble gelatinous carbohydrate found in many brown seaweeds, chiefly as salts which are used as thickening agents.
– DERIVATIVES **alginate** n.
– ORIGIN C19: *alginic* from **ALGA** + **-IN**[1] + **-IC**.

**Algol** /'algɒl/ ● **n.** an early, high-level computer programming language which was devised to carry out scientific calculations.
– ORIGIN 1950s: from *algo(rithmic)* + the initial letter of **LANGUAGE**.

**algolagnia** /,algə(ʊ)'lagnɪə/ ● **n.** Psychiatry sadomasochism.
– ORIGIN C20: from Ger. *Algolagnie*, from Gk *algos* 'pain' + *lagneia* 'lust'.

**algology** /əl'gɒlədʒi/ ● **n.** the study of algae.
– DERIVATIVES **algological** adj. **algologist** n.

**Algonquian** /al'gɒŋkwɪən, -kɪ-/ (also **Algonkian** /-kɪən/)

## Word *Formation*

**-algia** 'pain', from Greek *algos* 'pain'

➤ **-algia** words in current use (full entries and definitions to be found in this dictionary):

| | | |
|---|---|---|
| arthralgia | pain in a joint | Gk *arthron* 'joint' |
| causalgia | severe pain in a limb | Gk *kausos* 'heat, fever' |
| myalgia | pain in a muscle | Gk *mus* 'muscle' |
| neuralgia | pain along a nerve | Gk *neuron* 'nerve' |
| otalgia | earache | Gk *ous, ōt-* 'ear' |

The word ***nostalgia***, with its current sense 'sentimental longing or affection for the past', originally (18th century) meant 'homesickness', formed on the Greek element *nostos* 'return home'.

➤ Some other words based on Greek *algos* 'pain':

| | | |
|---|---|---|
| algolagnia | technical term in psychiatry for sadomasochism | Gk *algos* + *lagneia* 'lust' |
| analgesia, analgesic | relief of pain using drugs; relieving pain | Gk *an-* 'not' + *algein* 'feel pain' |
| hyperalgesia | heightened sensitivity to pain | Gk *huperalgein* 'be in great pain' |

● **n.** **1** a large family of North American Indian languages, including Cree, Blackfoot, and Cheyenne. **2** a speaker of any of these languages. ● **adj.** relating to or denoting this family of languages or its speakers.

**Algonquin** /al'gɒŋkwɪn/ (also **Algonkin**) ● **n.** **1** a member of an American Indian people living in Canada along the Ottawa River and its tributaries and westward to the north of Lake Superior. **2** the Algonquian language of this people. ● **adj.** of or relating to this people or their language.
– ORIGIN C17 Fr., contr. of obs. *Algoumequin*, from a Micmac word meaning 'at the place of spearing fish and eels'.

**algorithm** /'algərɪð(ə)m/ ● **n.** a process or set of rules to be followed in calculations or other problem-solving operations, especially by a computer.
– DERIVATIVES **algorithmic** adj. **algorithmically** adv.
– ORIGIN C17 (denoting the Arabic or decimal notation of numbers): var. of ME *algorism*, via OFr. from med. L. *algorismus*, Arab. *al-Ḵwārizmī* 'the man of Ḵwārizm', the cognomen of a C9 mathematician.

**alguacil** /ˌalgwa'θiːl, Spanish ˌalɣwa'θil, -'sil/ ● **n.** (pl. **alguaciles** /ˌalgwa'θiːlɪz, Spanish ˌalɣwa'θiles, -'siles/) each of a pair of mounted officials at a bullfight.
– ORIGIN Sp., from Arab. *al-wazīr* 'the helper, aide, or vizier'.

**alhaji** /al'hadʒi/ ● **n.** (pl. **alhajis**) (fem. **alhaja**) (in West Africa) a Muslim who has been to Mecca as a pilgrim.
– ORIGIN Hausa, from Pers. and Turk., from *al* 'the' + *hājī* 'pilgrim'.

**alias** /'eɪlɪəs/ ● **adv.** also known as. ● **n.** **1** a false or assumed identity. **2** Computing an alternative name or label that refers to a file, command, or address, and can be used to locate or access it. **3** Physics & Telecommunications each of a set of signal frequencies which, when sampled at a given uniform rate, would give the same set of sampled values and thus be indistinguishable. ● **v.** Physics & Telecommunications misidentify (a signal frequency), introducing distortion or error.
– DERIVATIVES **aliasing** n.
– ORIGIN ME: from L., 'at another time, otherwise'.

**alibi** /'alɪbʌɪ/ ● **n.** (pl. **alibis**) a claim or piece of evidence that one was elsewhere when an alleged act took place. ➤ informal an excuse. ● **v.** (**alibis**, **alibied**, **alibiing**) informal provide an alibi for.
– ORIGIN C17: from L., 'elsewhere'.

**Alice band** ● **n.** a flexible band worn to hold back the hair.
– ORIGIN from the name of the heroine of *Alice's Adventures in Wonderland* by Lewis Carroll.

**alicyclic** /ˌalɪ'sʌɪklɪk, -'sɪk-/ ● **adj.** Chemistry relating to or denoting organic compounds which combine cyclic structure with aliphatic properties (e.g. cyclohexane).

**alidade** /'alɪdeɪd/ ● **n.** a sighting device or pointer for determining directions or measuring angles, used in surveying.
– ORIGIN ME: via Fr. and Sp. from Arab. *al-'iḍāda* 'the revolving radius'.

**alien** ● **adj.** **1** belonging to a foreign country. **2** unfamiliar and distasteful. **3** (of a plant or animal species) introduced from another country and later naturalized. **4** relating to or denoting beings from other worlds. ● **n.** **1** a foreigner, especially one who is not a naturalized citizen of the country where they are living. **2** an alien plant or animal species. **3** a being from another world.
– DERIVATIVES **alienage** n. **alienness** n.
– ORIGIN ME: via OFr. from L. *alienus* 'belonging to another', from *alius* 'other'.

**alienable** ● **adj.** Law able to be transferred to new ownership.
– DERIVATIVES **alienability** n.

**alienate** ● **v.** **1** cause to feel isolated. ➤ lose or destroy the support or sympathy of. **2** Law transfer ownership of (property rights) to another.
– PHRASES **alienate someone's affections** US Law induce someone to transfer their affection from a person with legal rights or claims on them.
– DERIVATIVES **alienator** n.
– ORIGIN C16: from L. *alienat-*, *alienare* 'estrange', from *alienus* (see **ALIEN**).

**alienation** ● **n.** **1** the state or experience of being alienated. ➤ Psychiatry a state of depersonalization or loss of identity in which the self seems unreal. **2** Theatre an effect, sought by some dramatists, whereby the audience remains objective and does not identify with the actors. **3** Law the transfer of the ownership of property rights.

**alienist** ● **n.** former term for **PSYCHIATRIST**. ➤ chiefly US a psychiatrist who assesses the competence of a defendant in a law court.
– ORIGIN C19: from Fr. *aliéniste*, based on L. *alienus* (see **ALIEN**).

**aliform** /'eɪlɪfɔːm/ ● **adj.** wing-shaped.
– ORIGIN C18: from mod. L. *aliformis*, from L. *ala* 'wing' + *-formis* (see **-FORM**).

**alight**[1] ● **v.** **1** formal, chiefly Brit. descend from public transport. **2** (**alight on**) chance to notice.
– ORIGIN OE *ālīhtan*, from *ā-* (as an intensifier) + *līhtan* 'descend' (see **LIGHT**[3]).

**alight**[2] ● **adv. & adj.** **1** on fire. **2** shining brightly.
– ORIGIN ME: prob. from the phr. *on a light* (= lighted) *fire*.

**align** ● **v.** **1** place or arrange in a straight line or into correct relative positions. **2** (**align oneself with**) ally oneself to. ➤ come together in alliance.
– DERIVATIVES **alignment** n.
– ORIGIN C17: from Fr. *aligner*, from *à ligne* 'into line'.

**alike** ● **adj.** similar. ● **adv.** in a similar way.
– ORIGIN OE *gelīc*, of Gmc origin; reinforced in ME by ON

*álíkr* (adj.) and *álíka* (adv.).

**aliment** /ˈalɪm(ə)nt/ ● **n.** **1** archaic food; nourishment. **2** Scots Law maintenance; alimony.
– ORIGIN C15: from L. *alimentum*, from *alere* 'nourish'.

**alimentary** ● **adj.** of or providing nourishment or sustenance.

**alimentary canal** ● **n.** the whole passage along which food passes through the body from mouth to anus during digestion.

**alimentation** ● **n.** formal the provision of nourishment or other necessities of life.

**alimony** /ˈalɪməni/ ● **n.** chiefly N. Amer. maintenance for a spouse after separation or divorce.
– ORIGIN C17 (in the sense 'nourishment, means of subsistence'): from L. *alimonia* 'nutriment', from *alere* 'nourish'.

**A-line** ● **adj.** (of a garment) slightly flared from a narrow waist or shoulders.

**aliphatic** /ˌalɪˈfatɪk/ ● **adj.** Chemistry relating to or denoting organic compounds in which carbon atoms form open chains (as in the alkanes), not aromatic rings.
– ORIGIN C19: from Gk *aleiphar, aleiphat-* 'fat' + **-IC**.

**aliquot** /ˈalɪkwɒt/ ● **n.** **1** a portion of a larger whole, especially a sample taken for chemical analysis or other treatment. **2** (also **aliquot part** or **portion**) Mathematics a quantity which can be divided into another an integral number of times. ● **v.** divide (a whole) into aliquots; take aliquots from (a whole).
– ORIGIN C16: from Fr. *aliquote*, from L. *aliquot* 'some, so many', from *alius* 'one of two' + *quot* 'how many'.

**alisphenoid** /ˌalɪˈsfiːnɔɪd/ ● **n.** Anatomy a wing-like cartilaginous bone within the skull, forming part of the socket of the eye.
– ORIGIN C19: from L. *ala* 'wing' + **SPHENOID**.

**aliterate** /eɪˈlɪt(ə)rət/ ● **adj.** unwilling to read, although able to do so. ● **n.** an aliterate person.
– DERIVATIVES **aliteracy** n.

**alive** ● **adj.** **1** living, not dead. ➤ continuing in existence or use. **2** alert and active. ➤ having interest and meaning. ➤ (**alive to**) aware of and interested in. **3** (**alive with**) swarming or teeming with.
– PHRASES **alive and kicking** informal prevalent and very active. **alive and well** still existing or active.
– DERIVATIVES **aliveness** n.
– ORIGIN OE *on līfe*, lit. 'in life'.

**aliyah** /ˈalɪjə/ ● **n.** (pl. **aliyoth** /ˈalɪjəʊt/) Judaism **1** immigration to Israel. **2** the honour of being called upon to read from the Torah.
– ORIGIN from Heb. *'ălīyyāh* 'ascent'.

**alizarin** /əˈlɪz(ə)rɪn/ ● **n.** Chemistry a red pigment present in madder root, used in making dyes.
– ORIGIN C19: from Fr. *alizarine*, from *alizari* 'madder', from Arab. *al-'iṣāra* 'pressed juice'.

**alkahest** /ˈalkəhɛst/ (also **alcahest**) ● **n.** historical the hypothetical universal solvent sought by alchemists.
– ORIGIN C17: sham Arab., prob. invented by the C16 Swiss physician Paracelsus.

**alkali** /ˈalkəlʌɪ/ ● **n.** (pl. **alkalis** or US also **alkalies**) a compound, e.g. lime or caustic soda, with particular chemical properties including turning litmus blue and neutralizing or effervescing with acids.
– DERIVATIVES **alkalization** (also **-isation**) n. **alkalize** (also **-ise**) v.
– ORIGIN ME (denoting a saline substance derived from the ashes of plants): from med. L., from Arab. *al-ḳalī*, from *ḳalā* 'fry, roast'.

**alkalic** /alˈkalɪk/ ● **adj.** Geology (of a rock or mineral) richer in sodium and/or potassium than is usual for its type.

**alkali feldspar** ● **n.** Geology any of the group of feldspars rich in sodium and/or potassium.

**alkali metal** ● **n.** Chemistry any of the reactive metals lithium, sodium, potassium, rubidium, caesium, and francium, occupying Group IA (1) of the periodic table and forming strongly alkaline hydroxides.

**alkaline** ● **adj.** containing an alkali or having the properties of an alkali; having a pH greater than 7.
– DERIVATIVES **alkalinity** n.

**alkaline earth** ● **n.** Chemistry any of the reactive metals beryllium, magnesium, calcium, strontium, barium, and radium, occupying Group IIA (2) of the periodic table and forming basic oxides and hydroxides.

**alkaloid** /ˈalkəlɔɪd/ ● **n.** Chemistry any of a class of nitrogenous organic compounds of plant origin which have pronounced physiological actions on humans.

**alkalosis** /ˌalkəˈləʊsɪs/ ● **n.** Medicine an excessively alkaline condition of the body fluids or tissues, which may cause weakness or cramp.

**alkane** /ˈalkeɪn/ ● **n.** Chemistry any of the series of saturated hydrocarbons including methane, ethane, propane, and higher members.
– ORIGIN C19: from **ALKYL** + **-ANE**[2].

**alkanet** /ˈalkənɛt/ ● **n.** a plant of the borage family with a hairy stem and blue flowers. [*Pentaglottis sempervirens* and other species.]
– ORIGIN ME: from colloq. Arab. *al-ḥannat* (Arab. *al-ḥinnā'*) 'the henna shrub'.

**alkene** /ˈalkiːn/ ● **n.** Chemistry any of the series of unsaturated hydrocarbons containing a double bond, including ethylene and propene.
– ORIGIN C19: from **ALKYL** + **-ENE**.

**alkyd** /ˈalkɪd/ ● **n.** Chemistry any of a group of synthetic polyester resins.
– ORIGIN 1920s: blend of **ALKYL** and **ACID**.

**alkyl** /ˈalkʌɪl, -kɪl/ ● **n.** [as modifier] Chemistry of or denoting a hydrocarbon radical derived from an alkane by removal of a hydrogen atom.
– ORIGIN C19: Ger., from *Alkohol* 'alcohol' + **-YL**.

**alkylate** /ˈalkɪleɪt/ ● **v.** Chemistry introduce an alkyl group into (a molecule).
– DERIVATIVES **alkylation** n.

**alkyne** /ˈalkʌɪn/ ● **n.** Chemistry any of the series of unsaturated hydrocarbons containing a triple bond, including acetylene.
– ORIGIN C20: from **ALKYL** + **-YNE**.

**all** ● **predet., det., & pron.** the whole quantity or extent of. ➤ [det.] any whatever. ➤ [det.] the greatest possible. ➤ [pron.] everything. ● **adv.** **1** completely. **2** (in games) used after a number to indicate an equal score.
– PHRASES **all along** from the beginning. **all and sundry** everyone. **all but 1** very nearly. **2** all except. **all for** informal strongly in favour of. **all in** informal exhausted. **all in all** on the whole. **all of** often ironic as much as. **all one to** making no difference to. **all out** using all one's strength or resources. **all over 1** informal everywhere. **2** informal typical of the person mentioned: *that's our management all over!* **all over the place** (or N. Amer. also **map**, Brit. also **shop**) informal **1** everywhere. **2** in a state of disorder. **all round 1** in all respects. **2** for or by each person. **all there** [with neg.] informal in full possession of one's mental faculties: *he's not quite all there.* **all together** all in one place or in a group. **all told** in total. **all very well** informal used to express criticism or scepticism. **all the way** informal without limit or reservation. **at all** [with neg. or in questions] in any way; to any extent. **for all** —— in spite of ——. **in all** in total. **on all fours** on hands and knees. **one's all** one's whole strength or resources.
– ORIGIN OE *all, eall*, of Gmc origin.

**alla breve** /ˌalə ˈbreɪvi, ˈbrɛveɪ/ ● **n.** Music a time signature indicating 2 or 4 minim beats in a bar.
– ORIGIN Ital., lit. 'according to the breve'.

**alla cappella** /kəˈpɛlə/ ● **adj. & adv.** another term for **A CAPPELLA**.

**Allah** /ˈalə, əlˈlɑː/ ● **n.** the name of God among Muslims (and Arab Christians).
– ORIGIN from Arab. *'all'h*, contr. of *al-'il'h* 'the god'.

**allamanda** /ˌaləˈmandə/ ● **n.** a tropical shrub or climber with showy flowers, typically of yellow or purple. [*Allamanda cathartica* and other species.]
– ORIGIN mod. L., named after the Swiss naturalist Jean-Nicholas-Sébastien *Allamand*.

**all-American** ● **adj.** US denoting a sports player honoured as one of the best amateur competitors in the US.

**allanite** /ˈalənʌɪt/ ● **n.** a brownish-black mineral of the epidote group, consisting of a silicate of rare-earth metals, aluminium, and iron.

– ORIGIN C19: named after the Sc. mineralogist Thomas *Allan* + **-ITE**[1].

**allantoin** /əˈlantəʊɪn/ ● **n.** Biochemistry a crystalline compound formed in the nitrogen metabolism of many mammals.
– ORIGIN C19: from **ALLANTOIS** (because it was discovered in the allantoic fluid of cows) + **-IN**[1].

**allantois** /əˈlantəʊɪs/ ● **n.** (pl. **allantoides** /-ɪdiːz/) the fetal membrane lying below the chorion in many vertebrates, formed as an outgrowth of the embryo's gut.
– DERIVATIVES **allantoic** adj. **allantoid** adj.
– ORIGIN C17: mod. L., based on Gk *allantoeidēs* 'sausage-shaped'.

**allargando** /ˌalɑːˈgandəʊ/ ● **adv. & adj.** Music getting slower and broader.
– ORIGIN Ital., lit. 'broadening'.

**all-around** ● **adj.** US term for **ALL-ROUND**.

**allay** /əˈleɪ/ ● **v.** diminish or end (fear or concern). ➤ alleviate (pain or hunger).
– ORIGIN OE *ālecgan* 'lay down or aside', of Gmc origin.

**all-clear** ● **n.** a signal that danger or difficulty is over.

**allée** /ˈaleɪ/ ● **n.** an alley in a formal garden or park, bordered by trees or bushes.
– ORIGIN C18: from Fr.

**allege** /əˈlɛdʒ/ ● **v.** claim that someone has done something wrong, typically without proof.
– DERIVATIVES **allegation** n. **alleged** adj. **allegedly** adv.
– ORIGIN ME (in the sense 'declare on oath'): from OFr. *esligier*, based on L. *lis, lit-* 'lawsuit'; confused in sense with L. *allegare* 'allege'.

**allegiance** ● **n.** loyalty or commitment of a subordinate to a superior or of an individual to a group or cause.
– ORIGIN ME: from Anglo-Norman Fr., var. of OFr. *ligeance*, from *lige, liege* (see **LIEGE**), perh. by assoc. with Anglo-Latin *alligantia* 'alliance'.

**allegorical** ● **adj.** constituting or containing allegory.
– DERIVATIVES **allegoric** adj. **allegorically** adv.

**allegory** ● **n.** (pl. **-ies**) a story, poem, or picture which can be interpreted to reveal a hidden meaning.
– DERIVATIVES **allegorist** n. **allegorization** (also **-isation**) n. **allegorize** (also **-ise**) v.
– ORIGIN ME: from OFr. *allegorie*, via L. from Gk *allēgoria*, from *allos* 'other' + *-agoria* 'speaking'.

**allegretto** /ˌalɪˈgrɛtəʊ/ ● **adv. & adj.** Music at a fairly brisk speed.
– ORIGIN Ital., dimin. of **ALLEGRO**.

**allegro** /əˈlɛgrəʊ, -ˈleɪg-/ Music ● **adv. & adj.** at a brisk speed. ● **n.** (pl. **-os**) an allegro movement, passage, or composition.
– ORIGIN Ital., lit. 'lively'.

**allele** /ˈaliːl/ ● **n.** Genetics one of two or more alternative forms of a gene that arise by mutation and are found at the same place on a chromosome.
– DERIVATIVES **allelic** adj.
– ORIGIN 1930s: from Ger. *Allel*, abbrev. of **ALLELOMORPH**.

**allelochemical** /əˌliːləʊˈkɛmɪk(ə)l/ ● **n.** Biology a chemical produced by a living organism which exerts a detrimental physiological effect on another species.
– ORIGIN 1970s: from Gk *allēl-* 'one another' + **CHEMICAL**.

**allelomorph** /əˈliːləʊmɔːf/ ● **n.** another term for **ALLELE**.
– DERIVATIVES **allelomorphic** adj.
– ORIGIN C20: from Gk *allēl-* 'one another' + *morphē* 'form'.

**allelopathy** /ˌaliːˈlɒpəθi/ ● **n.** Ecology the inhibition of the growth of a plant by the action of substances released by another plant.
– DERIVATIVES **allelopathic** /əˌliːlə(ʊ)ˈpaθɪk/ adj.
– ORIGIN 1950s: from Gk *allēl-* 'one another' + **-PATHY**.

**alleluia** /ˌalɪˈluːjə/ ● **exclam. & n.** variant spelling of **HALLELUJAH**.

**allemande** /ˈalmɑːnd/ ● **n. 1** a German court dance popular in the 16th century. **2** a figure in country dancing in which adjacent dancers make a turn.
– ORIGIN C17: from Fr., 'German (dance)'.

**Allen key** ● **n.** trademark a spanner designed to fit into and turn an Allen screw.

**Allen screw** ● **n.** trademark a screw with a hexagonal socket in the head.
– ORIGIN 1930s: from the name of the *Allen* Manufacturing Company, Connecticut.

**allergen** /ˈalədʒ(ə)n/ ● **n.** a substance that causes an allergic reaction.
– DERIVATIVES **allergenic** adj. **allergenicity** n.

**allergic** /əˈləːdʒɪk/ ● **adj.** of, caused by, or relating to an allergy. ➤ having an allergy: *allergic to bee stings.*

**allergy** /ˈalədʒi/ ● **n.** (pl. **-ies**) a damaging immune response by the body to a substance to which it has become hypersensitive.
– DERIVATIVES **allergist** n.
– ORIGIN C20: from Ger. *Allergie*, from Gk *allos* 'other', on the pattern of *Energie* 'energy'.

**alleviate** /əˈliːvɪeɪt/ ● **v.** make (pain or difficulty) less severe.
– DERIVATIVES **alleviation** n. **alleviative** adj. **alleviator** n.
– ORIGIN ME: from late L. *alleviat-, alleviare* 'lighten', from L. *allevare*, from *ad-* 'to' + *levare* 'raise', influenced by *levis* 'light'.

**alley**[1] ● **n.** (pl. **-eys**) **1** a narrow passageway between or behind buildings. ➤ a path in a park or garden. **2** a long, narrow area in which skittles and bowling are played. **3** N. Amer. Tennis either of the two side strips between the service court and the sidelines. ➤ Baseball the area between the outfielders in left-centre or right-centrefield.
– ORIGIN ME: from OFr. *alee* 'walking or passage', from *aler* 'go', from L. *ambulare* 'to walk'.

**alley**[2] ● **n.** (pl. **-eys**) variant spelling of **ALLY**[2].

**alley cat** ● **n.** a stray urban cat.

**alley-oop** ● **exclam.** used to encourage or draw attention to the performance of an acrobatic feat. ● **n.** (also **alley-oop pass**) Basketball a high pass caught by a leaping teammate who tries to dunk the ball before landing.
– ORIGIN C20: perh. from Fr. *allez!* 'go on!' + a supposedly Fr. pronunc. of **UP**.

**alleyway** ● **n.** another term for **ALLEY**[1] (in sense 1).

**All Fools' Day** ● **n.** another term for **APRIL FOOL'S DAY**.

**All Hallows** ● **n.** another term for **ALL SAINTS' DAY**.

**alliaceous** /ˌalɪˈeɪʃəs/ ● **adj.** Botany relating to or denoting plants of a group that comprises the onions and other alliums.
– ORIGIN C18: from L. *allium* 'garlic' + **-ACEOUS**.

**alliance** ● **n. 1** a union or association formed for mutual benefit. ➤ a relationship based on an affinity. ➤ the state of being joined or associated. **2** Ecology a group of closely related plant associations.
– ORIGIN ME: from OFr. *aliance*, from *alier* (see **ALLY**[1]).

**allicin** /ˈalɪsɪn/ ● **n.** Chemistry a pungent oily liquid with antibacterial properties, present in garlic.
– ORIGIN 1940s: from L. *allium* 'garlic' + **-IN**[1].

**allied** /ˈalʌɪd, əˈlʌɪd/ ● **adj. 1** joined by or relating to an alliance. ➤ (usu. **Allied**) of or relating to Britain and its allies in the First and Second World Wars and after. **2** (**allied to/with**) in combination or working together with. ➤ connected or related.

**alligator** ● **n. 1** a large semiaquatic reptile similar to a crocodile but with a broader and shorter head, native to the Americas and China. [Genus *Alligator*: two species.] **2** the skin of the alligator.
– ORIGIN C16: from Sp. *el lagarto* 'the lizard'.

**alligator clip** ● **n.** chiefly N. Amer. another term for **CROCODILE CLIP**.

**alligator fish** ● **n.** a small, slender bottom-dwelling fish of the NW Atlantic, with an armour of bony plates and two curved spines on the snout. [*Aspidophoroides monopterygius.*]

**alligator lizard** ● **n.** a heavily built slow-moving lizard native to North America and Mexico. [Genus *Gerrhonotus*: several species.]

**alligator pear** ● **n.** North American term for **AVOCADO**.

**alligator snapper** ● **n.** a large snapping turtle occurring in fresh water around the Gulf of Mexico. [*Macroclemys temminckii.*]

**all-in** ● **adj.** Brit. (especially of a price) inclusive of everything.

**all-in-one** ● **adj.** combining two or more items or functions in a single unit.

**all-in wrestling** ● **n.** chiefly Brit. wrestling with few or no restrictions.

**allis shad** /ˈalɪs/ ● **n.** a shad (fish) with a deep blue back and silvery sides. [*Alosa alosa*.]
– ORIGIN C16: *allis* from OFr. *alose*, from late L. *alausa*.

**alliteration** ● **n.** the occurrence of the same letter or sound at the beginning of adjacent or closely connected words.
– DERIVATIVES **alliterate** v. **alliterative** adj. **alliteratively** adv.
– ORIGIN C17: from med. L. *alliteratio(n-)*, from L. *ad-* (expressing addition) + *littera* 'letter'.

**allium** /ˈalɪəm/ ● **n.** (pl. **alliums**) a bulbous plant of a genus that includes the onion and its relatives (e.g. garlic and chives). [Genus *Allium*.]
– ORIGIN L., 'garlic'.

**all-nighter** ● **n.** informal an event or task that continues throughout the night.

**allo-** /ˈaləʊ/ ● **comb. form** other; different: *allopatric*.
– ORIGIN from Gk *allos* 'other'.

**allocate** ● **v.** assign or distribute (resources or duties) to.
– DERIVATIVES **allocable** adj. **allocation** n. **allocative** adj. **allocator** n.
– ORIGIN C17 (earlier (ME) as *allocation*): from med. L. *allocat-*, *allocare* 'allot'.

**allochthonous** /əˈlɒkθənəs/ ● **adj.** Geology denoting a deposit or formation that originated at a distance from its present position. Often contrasted with **AUTOCHTHONOUS**.
– ORIGIN C20: from **ALLO-** + Gk *khthōn* 'earth' + **-OUS**.

**allocution** /ˌaləˈkjuːʃ(ə)n/ ● **n.** a formal speech giving advice or a warning.
– ORIGIN C17: from L. *allocutio(n-)*, from *alloqui* 'speak to'.

**allod** /ˈalɒd/ (also **allodium** /əˈləʊdɪəm/) ● **n.** historical an estate held in absolute ownership, without acknowledgement to a superior.
– DERIVATIVES **allodial** adj.
– ORIGIN C17 (as *allodium*): from med. L. *al(l)odium*, from a Gmc cognate of **ALL** + *ōd* 'estate'.

**allogamy** /əˈlɒgəmi/ ● **n.** Botany the fertilization of a flower by pollen from another flower, especially one on a different plant. Compare with **AUTOGAMY**.
– DERIVATIVES **allogamous** adj.
– ORIGIN C19: from **ALLO-** + Gk *gamos* 'marriage'.

**allogeneic** /ˌalə(ʊ)dʒɪˈniːɪk, -dʒɪˈneɪɪk/ ● **adj.** Physiology relating to or denoting tissues which are genetically dissimilar and hence immunologically incompatible, although from individuals of the same species.
– ORIGIN 1960s: from **ALLO-** + Gk *genea* 'race, stock' + **-IC**.

**allogenic** /ˌaləˈdʒɛnɪk/ ● **adj. 1** Geology (of a mineral or sediment) transported to its present position from elsewhere. Often contrasted with **AUTHIGENIC**. **2** Ecology (of a successional change) caused by non-living factors in the environment.

**allograft** /ˈaləgrɑːft/ ● **n.** a tissue graft from a donor of the same species as the recipient but not genetically identical.

**allograph** /ˈaləgrɑːf/ ● **n. 1** Linguistics each of two or more alternative forms of a letter of an alphabet or other unit of a writing system. **2** Phonetics each of two or more letters or letter combinations representing a single phoneme in different words (e.g. the (f) of 'fake' and the (ph) of 'phase').
– ORIGIN 1950s: from **ALLO-** + **GRAPHEME**.

**allometry** /əˈlɒmɪtri/ ● **n.** Biology the growth of body parts at different rates, resulting in a change of proportions.
– DERIVATIVES **allometric** adj.

**allomorph** /ˈaləmɔːf/ ● **n.** Linguistics any of two or more representations of a morpheme, such as the plural endings /s/ (as in *bats*) and /z/ (as in *bugs*).
– DERIVATIVES **allomorphic** adj.
– ORIGIN 1940s: from **ALLO-** + **MORPHEME**.

**allopathy** /əˈlɒpəθi/ ● **n.** the treatment of disease by conventional means, i.e. with drugs having effects opposite to the symptoms. Often contrasted with **HOMEOPATHY**.
– DERIVATIVES **allopath** n. **allopathic** adj. **allopathist** n.

**allopatric** /ˌaləˈpatrɪk/ ● **adj.** Biology (of animal or plant species or populations) occurring in separate non-overlapping geographical areas. Compare with **SYMPATRIC**.
– DERIVATIVES **allopatry** n.
– ORIGIN 1940s: from **ALLO-** + Gk *patra* 'fatherland' + **-IC**.

**allophone** /ˈaləfəʊn/ ● **n.** Phonetics any of the various phonetic realizations of a phoneme in a language, which do not contribute to distinctions of meaning.
– DERIVATIVES **allophonic** adj.
– ORIGIN 1930s: from **ALLO-** + **PHONEME**.

**allopurinol** /ˌalə(ʊ)ˈpjʊərɪnɒl/ ● **n.** Medicine a synthetic drug which inhibits uric acid formation in the body and is used to treat gout and related conditions.

**All Ordinaries index** ● **n.** (on the Australian stock exchanges) an index based on the weighted average of selected ordinary share prices.

**allosaurus** /ˌaləˈsɔːrəs/ ● **n.** a large bipedal carnivorous dinosaur of the late Jurassic period.
– ORIGIN mod. L., from Gk *allos* 'other' + *sauros* 'lizard'.

**allosteric** /ˌaləˈstɛrɪk, -ˈstɪərɪk/ ● **adj.** Biochemistry relating to or denoting the alteration of the activity of an enzyme by means of a conformational change induced by a different molecule.
– DERIVATIVES **allosterically** adv.

**allot** ● **v.** (**allotted**, **allotting**) apportion or assign (something) to someone.
– DERIVATIVES **allottee** n.
– ORIGIN C15: from OFr. *aloter*, from *a-* (from L. *ad* 'to') + *loter* 'divide into lots'.

**allotment** ● **n. 1** Brit. a plot of land rented by an individual from a local authority, for growing vegetables or flowers. **2** the action of allotting. ➤ an amount of something allotted.

**allotrope** /ˈalətrəʊp/ ● **n.** Chemistry each of two or more different physical forms in which an element can exist (e.g. graphite, charcoal, and diamond as forms of carbon).
– DERIVATIVES **allotropic** adj. **allotropy** /əˈlɒtrəpi/n.
– ORIGIN C19: from Gk *allotropos* 'of another form', from *allo-* 'other' + *tropos* 'manner'.

**allow** ● **v. 1** admit as legal or acceptable. ➤ permit to do something. **2** (often **allow for**) take into consideration when making plans or calculations. ➤ provide or set aside for a particular purpose. **3** admit the truth of.
– DERIVATIVES **allowable** adj. **allowably** adv.
– ORIGIN ME: from OFr. *alouer*, from L. *allaudare* 'to praise', reinforced by med. L. *allocare* (see **ALLOCATE**).

**allowance** ● **n.** the amount of something allowed. ➤ a sum of money paid regularly to a person, typically to meet specified expenses. ➤ an amount of money that can be earned or received free of tax. ➤ Horse Racing a deduction in the weight that a horse is required to carry in a race. ● **v.** archaic give (someone) a sum of money regularly as an allowance.
– PHRASES **make allowance(s) for 1** take into consideration. **2** treat leniently on account of mitigating circumstances.

**allowedly** ● **adv.** as is generally admitted to be true.

**alloxan** /əˈlɒks(ə)n/ ● **n.** Chemistry an acidic compound obtained by the oxidation of uric acid.
– ORIGIN C19: from *all(antoin)* + *ox(alic)* + **-AN**.

**alloy** ● **n.** /ˈalɔɪ/ a metal made by combining two or more metallic elements, especially to give greater strength or resistance to corrosion. ➤ an inferior metal mixed with a precious one. ● **v.** /əˈlɔɪ/ **1** mix (metals) to make an alloy. **2** spoil by adding something inferior.
– ORIGIN C16: from OFr. *aloi* (n.) and Fr. *aloyer* (v.), both from OFr. *aloier*, *aleier* 'combine', from L. *alligare* 'bind'.

**all-points bulletin** ● **n.** (in the US) a radio message sent to every officer in a police force giving details of a suspected criminal or stolen vehicle.

**all right** ● **adj.** satisfactory; acceptable. ➤ permissible. ● **adv.** fairly well. ● **exclam.** expressing or asking for agreement or acceptance.

**all-round** ● **adj.** chiefly Brit. having a great many abilities or uses. ➤ in many or all respects.

**all-rounder** ● **n.** Brit. a person competent in a range of skills, especially a cricketer who can both bat and bowl well.

**All Saints' Day** ● **n.** a Christian festival in honour of all the saints, held (in the Western Church) on 1 November.

**all-seater** ● **adj.** Brit. (of a sports stadium) having a seat for every spectator and no standing places.

**allseed** ● **n.** a small plant with white flowers, producing a large number of seeds. [*Radiola linoides.*]

**All Souls' Day** ● **n.** a Catholic festival with prayers for the souls of the dead in purgatory, held on 2 November.

**allspice** ● **n.** **1** the dried aromatic fruit of a Caribbean tree, used as a culinary spice. **2** a tree of the myrtle family from which this spice is obtained. [*Pimenta dioica.*] **3** an aromatic North American tree or shrub. [Genus *Calycanthus.*]

**all-terrain vehicle** ● **n.** a small open motor vehicle fitted with large tyres, designed for use on rough ground.

**all-ticket** ● **adj.** denoting or relating to a sports match for which tickets must be bought in advance.

**all-time** ● **adj.** hitherto unsurpassed: *the all-time record.*

**allude** ● **v.** (**allude to**) hint at. ➤ mention in passing.
– ORIGIN C15: from L. *allus-*, *alludere*, from *ad-* 'towards' + *ludere* 'to play'.

**all-up weight** ● **n.** chiefly Brit. the total weight of an aircraft, with passengers, cargo, and fuel.

**allure** ● **n.** powerful attraction or fascination. ● **v.** [often as adj. **alluring**] powerfully attract.
– DERIVATIVES **allurement** n. **alluringly** adv.
– ORIGIN ME: from OFr. *aleurier* 'attract', from *a-* (from L. *ad* 'to') + *luere* 'a lure' (orig. a falconry term).

**allusion** ● **n.** the practice or device of making indirect or implicit references. ➤ a reference of this type.
– DERIVATIVES **allusive** adj. **allusively** adv. **allusiveness** n.

**alluvion** /əˈl(j)uːvɪən/ ● **n.** Law the formation of new land by deposition of sediment by the sea or a river. Compare with **AVULSION**.
– ORIGIN C16: from Fr., from L. *alluvio(n-)*, from *ad-* 'towards' + *luere* 'to wash'.

**alluvium** /əˈl(j)uːvɪəm/ ● **n.** a deposit of clay, silt, and sand left by flowing flood water in a river valley or delta, typically producing fertile soil.
– DERIVATIVES **alluvial** adj.
– ORIGIN C17: L., neut. of *alluvius* 'washed against', from *ad-* 'towards' + *luere* 'to wash'.

**all-wheel drive** ● **n.** North American term for **FOUR-WHEEL DRIVE**.

**ally**[1] /ˈalʌɪ/ ● **n.** (pl. **-ies**) a person or organization that cooperates with another. ➤ a state formally cooperating with another for a military or other purpose. ➤ (**the Allies**) the countries that fought with Britain in the First and Second World Wars. ● **v.** /also əˈlʌɪ/ (**-ies**, **-ied**) (**ally something to/with**) combine a resource or commodity with (another) for mutual benefit. ➤ (**ally oneself with**) side with.
– ORIGIN ME: from OFr. *alier*, from L. *alligare* 'bind together'; cf. **ALLOY**.

**ally**[2] /ˈali/ (also **alley**) ● **n.** (pl. **-ies**) a toy marble.
– ORIGIN C18: perh. a dimin. of **ALABASTER**, choice marbles being made orig. of alabaster or marble rather than terracotta.

**-ally** ● **suffix** forming adverbs from adjectives ending in *-al* (such as *radically* from *radical*).

**allyl** /ˈalʌɪl, -lɪl/ ● **n.** [as modifier] Chemistry of or denoting the unsaturated hydrocarbon radical $-C_3H_5$.
– DERIVATIVES **allylic** adj.
– ORIGIN C19: from L. *allium* 'garlic' (because identified in compounds from alliums) + **-YL**.

**Almagest** /ˈalmədʒɛst/ ● **n.** (**the Almagest**) an Arabic version of Ptolemy's astronomical treatise.
– ORIGIN ME: from OFr. *almageste*, based on Arab., from *al* 'the' + Gk *megistē* 'greatest (composition)'.

**alma mater** /ˌalmə ˈmɑːtə, ˈmeɪt-/ ● **n.** the school, college, or university that one once attended.
– ORIGIN C17 (in the general sense 'a source of nourishment'): L., lit. 'bounteous mother'.

**almanac** /ˈɔːlmənak, ˈɒl-/ (also **almanack**) ● **n.** an annual calendar containing important dates and statistical information such as astronomical data. ➤ an annual handbook containing information of general or specialist interest.
– ORIGIN ME: via med. L. from Gk *almenikhiaka*, of unknown origin.

**almandine** /ˈalməndiːn, -dʌɪn/ ● **n.** a kind of garnet with a violet tint.
– ORIGIN ME: from obs. Fr., alt. of *alabandine*, from med. L. *alabandina (gemma)*, 'jewel from *Alabanda*', an ancient city in Asia Minor where these stones were cut.

**almighty** ● **adj.** **1** omnipotent. **2** informal enormous. ● **n.** (**the Almighty**) a name or title for God.

**Almohad** /ˈalməhad/ (also **Almohade** /-heɪd/) ● **n.** (pl. **Almohads**) a member of a Berber Muslim movement and dynasty that conquered the Almoravid empire in the 12th century.
– ORIGIN Sp., ult. from Arab. *al-muwaḥḥidun* 'those who affirm the unity of God'.

**almond** ● **n.** **1** the oval edible nut-like kernel of the almond tree, growing in a woody shell. **2** the tree that produces this, related to the peach and plum. [*Prunus dulcis.*]
– ORIGIN ME: from OFr. *alemande*, from med. L. *amandula*, from Gk *amugdalē*.

**almond eyes** ● **pl. n.** eyes that are narrow and oval with pointed ends.

**almond oil** ● **n.** oil obtained from bitter almonds, used in cosmetic and medicinal preparations and as a flavouring.

**almond paste** ● **n.** marzipan.

**almoner** /ˈɑːmənə, ˈalm-/ ● **n.** historical an official distributor of alms.
– DERIVATIVES **almonry** n.
– ORIGIN ME: from OFr. *aumonier*, based on med. L. *eleemosynarius*, from *eleemosyna* (see **ALMS**).

**Almoravid** /alˈmɔːrəvɪd/ (also **Almoravide** /-vʌɪd/) ● **n.** (pl. **Almoravids**) a member of a federation of Muslim Berber peoples that established an empire in Morocco, Algeria, and Spain in the 11th century.
– ORIGIN Sp., from Arab. *al-murābit*, lit. 'one who is bound'.

**almost** ● **adv.** very nearly.
– ORIGIN OE *æl mǣst* 'for the most part' (see **ALL**, **MOST**).

**alms** /ɑːmz/ ● **pl. n.** (in historical contexts) charitable donations of money or food to the poor.
– ORIGIN OE *ælmysse*, *ælmesse*, from Christian L. *eleemosyna*, from Gk *eleēmosunē* 'compassion', from *eleēmōn* 'compassionate', from *eleos* 'mercy'.

**almshouse** ● **n.** a house founded by charity, offering accommodation for the poor.

**almucantar** /ˌalməˈkantə/ ● **n.** Astronomy **1** a circle on the celestial sphere parallel to the horizon. **2** a telescope mounted on a float resting on mercury, used to determine stellar altitude and azimuth.
– ORIGIN ME: from med. L. *almucantarath* or obs. Fr. *almucantara*, from Arab. *almuḳanṭarāt* 'lines of celestial latitude', based on *al* 'the' + *ḳanṭara* 'arch'.

**aloe** /ˈaləʊ/ ● **n.** **1** a succulent tropical plant with a rosette of thick tapering leaves and bell-shaped or tubular flowers on long stems. [Genus *Aloe.*] ➤ (**aloes** or **bitter aloes**) a strong laxative obtained from the bitter juice of various kinds of aloe. ➤ (also **American aloe**) another term for **CENTURY PLANT**. **2** (also **aloes wood**) the fragrant heartwood of a tropical Asian tree. ➤ the resin obtained from this wood, used in perfume, incense, and medicine.
– ORIGIN OE *alewe*, *alwe*, via L. from Gk *aloē*; reinforced in late ME by OFr. *aloes* 'aloe', hence freq. used in the pl.

**aloe vera** /ˈvɪərə/ ● **n.** **1** a gelatinous substance obtained from a kind of aloe, used in cosmetics as an emollient. **2** the plant that yields this substance, grown chiefly in the Caribbean and the southern US. [*Aloe vera.*]
– ORIGIN C20: mod. L., lit. 'true aloe', prob. in contrast to

the Amer. agave, which closely resembles aloe vera.

**aloft** • **adj. & adv.** up in or into the air. ➤up the mast or into the rigging of a ship.
– ORIGIN ME: from ON *á lopt, á lopti*, from *á* 'in, on, to' + *lopt* 'air'.

**alogical** • **adj.** opposed to or lacking in logic.

**aloha** /ə'ləʊhə/ • **exclam. & n.** a Hawaiian word used when greeting or parting.
– ORIGIN C19: from Maori *aroha* 'love, affection, pity'.

**aloha shirt** • **n.** a loose, brightly patterned Hawaiian shirt.

**alone** • **adj. & adv. 1** on one's own; by oneself. ➤isolated and lonely. **2** only; exclusively.
– PHRASES **go it alone** informal act without assistance. **leave** (or **let**) **alone 1** abandon or desert. **2** stop interfering with.
– DERIVATIVES **aloneness** n.
– ORIGIN ME: from ALL + ONE.

**along** • **prep. & adv. 1** moving in a constant direction on (a more or less horizontal surface). **2** extending in a more or less horizontal line on. **3** in or into company with others.
– PHRASES **along about** N. Amer. informal or dialect approximately. **along of** archaic or dialect **1** on account of. **2** with. **along with** in company with or at the same time as. **be** (or **come**) **along** arrive.
– ORIGIN OE *andlang*, of W. Gmc origin; rel. to LONG[1].

**alongshore** • **adv.** along or by the shore.

**alongside** • **prep.** (N. Amer. also **alongside of**) close to the side of; next to. ➤at the same time as or in coexistence with.

**aloo** /'ɑːluː, 'aluː/ • **n.** Indian potato.
– ORIGIN from Hindi, Urdu, and Sanskrit *ālū*.

**aloof** • **adj.** cool and distant.
– DERIVATIVES **aloofly** adv. **aloofness** n.
– ORIGIN C16: from A-[2] + LUFF, orig. in naut. use meaning 'away and to windward!', i.e. with the ship's head kept close to the wind away from a lee shore or other hazard.

**alopecia** /ˌalə'piːʃə/ • **n.** Medicine the absence of hair from areas of the body where it normally grows.
– ORIGIN ME: via L. from Gk *alōpekia*, lit. 'fox mange', from *alōpēx* 'fox'.

**aloud** • **adv.** audibly. ➤archaic loudly.

**alow** /ə'ləʊ/ • **adv.** archaic or dialect below; downwards.

**ALP** • **abbrev.** Australian Labor Party.

**alp** • **n.** a high mountain. ➤(**the Alps**) the high range of mountains in Switzerland and adjoining countries. ➤(in Switzerland) an area of green pasture on a mountainside.
– ORIGIN ME (orig. pl.): via Fr. from L. *Alpes*, from Gk *Alpeis*.

**alpaca** /al'pakə/ • **n.** (pl. same or **alpacas**) a long-haired domesticated South American mammal related to the llama. [*Lama pacos*.] ➤the wool of the alpaca, or fabric made from it.
– ORIGIN C18: from Sp., from Aymara *allpaca*.

**alpargata** /ˌalpɑː'gɑːtə/ • **n.** an espadrille.
– ORIGIN C19: from Sp.

**alpenglow** /'alpəngləʊ/ • **n.** the rosy light of the setting or rising sun seen on high mountains.
– ORIGIN C19: a partial translation of Ger. *Alpenglühen*, lit. 'Alp glow'.

**alpenhorn** /'alpənhɔːn/ (also **alphorn**) • **n.** a very long valveless wooden wind instrument played like a horn and used for signalling in the Alps.
– ORIGIN C19: from Ger., lit. 'Alp horn'.

**alpenstock** /'alpənstɒk/ • **n.** a long iron-tipped stick used by hillwalkers.
– ORIGIN C19: from Ger., lit. 'Alp stick'.

**alpha** /'alfə/ • **n. 1** the first letter of the Greek alphabet (Α, α), transliterated as 'a'. ➤[as modifier] denoting the first of a series of items or categories. ➤Brit. a first-class mark given for a piece of work. **2** a code word representing the letter A, used in radio communication.
– PHRASES **alpha and omega** the beginning and the end (used by Christians as a title for Jesus).
– ORIGIN via L. from Gk.

**alphabet** • **n.** a set of letters or symbols in a fixed order used to represent the basic set of speech sounds of a language.
– DERIVATIVES **alphabetization** (also **-isation**) n. **alphabetize** (also **-ise**) v.
– ORIGIN C16: from late L. *alphabetum*, from Gk *alpha, bēta*, the first two letters of the Gk alphabet.

**alphabetical** • **adj.** of or relating to an alphabet. ➤in the order of the letters of the alphabet.
– DERIVATIVES **alphabetic** adj. **alphabetically** adv.

**alphabet soup** • **n.** informal a confusing or confused mixture of things.
– ORIGIN C20: alluding to a kind of clear soup containing pasta in the shapes of letters.

**alpha blocker** • **n.** Medicine any of a class of drugs which prevent the stimulation of the adrenergic receptors responsible for increased blood pressure.

**alphafetoprotein** /ˌalfəˌfiːtəʊ'prəʊtiːn/ • **n.** Medicine a protein produced by a fetus which is present in amniotic fluid and the bloodstream of the mother, levels of which can be measured to detect certain congenital defects such as spina bifida.

**alpha-hydroxy acid** • **n.** Chemistry an organic acid containing a hydroxyl group adjacent to the carboxylic acid group, especially any of a group used in skincare preparations for their exfoliating properties.

**alphanumeric** • **adj.** consisting of or using both letters and numerals. • **n.** a character that is either a letter or a number.
– DERIVATIVES **alphanumerical** adj.

**alpha particle** • **n.** Physics a helium nucleus, especially as emitted by some radioactive substances.

**alpha radiation** • **n.** ionizing radiation consisting of alpha particles, emitted by some substances undergoing radioactive decay.

**alpha rhythm** • **n.** Physiology the normal electrical activity of the brain when conscious and relaxed, consisting of oscillations (**alpha waves**) with a frequency of 8 to 13 hertz.

**alpha test** • **n.** a trial of machinery or software carried out before a product is made available for beta-testing. • **v.** (**alpha-test**) subject to an alpha test.

**alphorn** /'alphɔːn/ • **n.** another term for ALPENHORN.

**alpine** • **adj. 1** of or relating to high mountains. ➤(in the names of plants and animals) growing or found on high mountains. ➤(**Alpine**) of or relating to the Alps. **2** (also **Alpine**) relating to or denoting skiing downhill. • **n. 1** an alpine plant. **2** a North American butterfly which has brownish-black wings with orange-red markings. [Genus *Erebia*.]

**alpinist** • **n.** a climber of high mountains, especially in the Alps.

**alprazolam** /al'preɪzə(ʊ)lam/ • **n.** Medicine a drug of the benzodiazepine group, used in the treatment of anxiety.
– ORIGIN 1970s: from *al-* of unknown origin + *p(henyl)* + *(t)r(i)azol(e)* + *(-azep)am*.

**already** • **adv. 1** before the time in question. ➤as surprisingly soon or early as this. **2** N. Amer. informal an expression of impatience: *enough already with these crazy kids!*
– ORIGIN ME: from ALL + READY; sense 2 is influenced by Yiddish use.

**alright** • **adj., adv., & exclam.** variant spelling of ALL RIGHT.

**USAGE alright**

The spelling **alright** (rather than **all right**) is still considered by many to be unacceptable in formal writing, even though other single-word forms such as **altogether** have long been accepted.

**Alsatian** • **n. 1** Brit. a German shepherd dog. **2** a native or inhabitant of Alsace. • **adj.** of or relating to Alsace.

**alsike** /'alsɪk/ • **n.** a tall clover which is widely grown for fodder. [*Trifolium hybridum*.]
– ORIGIN C19: named after *Alsike* in Sweden.

**also** • **adv.** in addition.

– ORIGIN OE *alswā* 'quite so, in that manner, similarly' (see **ALL, SO**[1]).

**also-ran** ● n. a loser in a race or contest.

**alstroemeria** /ˌalstrəˈmɪərɪə/ ● n. a South American plant widely cultivated for its showy lily-like flowers. [Genus *Alstroemeria*.]
– ORIGIN C18: mod. L., named after the Swed. naturalist Klas von *Alstroemer*.

**Alta** ● abbrev. Alberta.

**Altaic** /alˈteɪɪk/ ● adj. **1** of or relating to the Altai Mountains in central Asia. **2** relating to or denoting a phylum of languages which includes Turkic, Mongolian, Tungusic, and Manchu. ● n. the Altaic phylum of languages.

**altar** /ˈɔːltə, ˈɒl-/ ● n. the table in a Christian church at which the bread and wine are consecrated in communion services. ➤a table or flat-topped block used as the focus for a religious ritual.
– PHRASES **lead to the altar** marry (a woman).
– ORIGIN OE *altar, alter*, based on late L. *altar, altarium*, from L. *altus* 'high'.

**altar boy** ● n. a boy who acts as a priest's assistant during a service.

**altarpiece** ● n. a painting or other work of art designed to be set above and behind an altar.

**altazimuth** /alˈtazɪməθ/ ● n. **1** Astronomy a telescope mounting that moves in azimuth (about a vertical axis) and in altitude (about a horizontal axis). Compare with **EQUATORIAL MOUNT**. **2** a surveying instrument for measuring vertical and horizontal angles.
– ORIGIN C19: blend of **ALTITUDE** and **AZIMUTH**.

**alter** /ˈɔːltə, ˈɒl-/ ● v. change in character, appearance, direction, etc. ➤N. Amer. & Austral. castrate or spay (a domestic animal).
– DERIVATIVES **alterable** adj. **alteration** n.
– ORIGIN ME: from OFr. *alterer*, from late L. *alterare*, from L. *alter* 'other'.

**altercation** ● n. a noisy argument or disagreement.
– DERIVATIVES **altercate** v. (archaic).
– ORIGIN ME: from L. *altercatio(n-)*, from *altercari* 'to wrangle'.

**alter ego** /ˌaltər ˈɛgəʊ, ˌɒlt-, ˈiːg-/ ● n. **1** a person's secondary or alternative personality. **2** a close friend who is very like oneself.
– ORIGIN C16: L., 'other self'.

**alterity** /alˈtɛrɪti, ɒl-/ ● n. formal the state of being other or different.
– ORIGIN C17: from late L. *alteritas*, from *alter* 'other'.

**alternant** /ɔːlˈtəːnənt, ɒl-/ ● n. a variant of a word or other linguistic unit. ● adj. alternating.

**alternate** ● v. /ˈɔːltəneɪt, ˈɒl-/ occur or do in turn repeatedly. ➤(of a thing) change repeatedly between two contrasting conditions. ● adj. /ɔːlˈtəːnət, ɒl-/ **1** every other. ➤(of two things) each following and succeeded by the other in a regular pattern. ➤Botany (of leaves or shoots) placed alternately on the two sides of the stem. **2** chiefly N. Amer. another term for **ALTERNATIVE**. ● n. /ɔːlˈtəːnət, ɒl-/ N. Amer. a deputy or substitute.
– DERIVATIVES **alternately** adv. **alternation** n.
– ORIGIN C16 (earlier (ME) as *alternation*): from L. *alternat-*, *alternare* 'do by turns', from *alternus* 'every other', from *alter* 'other'.

**USAGE** alternate

The use of **alternate** to mean **alternative** is common in North American English, though still regarded as incorrect by many in Britain.

**alternate angles** ● pl. n. Mathematics two equal angles formed when a line crosses two parallel lines, lying on opposite sides of the transversal line and on opposite relative sides of the other lines.

**alternating current** (abbrev.: **AC**) ● n. an electric current that reverses its direction many times a second at regular intervals. Compare with **DIRECT CURRENT**.

**alternation of generations** ● n. Biology a pattern of reproduction shown by some lower plants and invertebrates, involving a regular alternation between sexual and asexual forms (as in ferns) or dioecious and parthenogenetic forms (as in some jellyfishes).

**alternative** ● adj. **1** (of one or more things) available as another possibility. ➤(of two things) mutually exclusive. **2** of or relating to activities that depart from or challenge traditional norms. ● n. one of two or more available possibilities.
– DERIVATIVES **alternatively** adv.
– ORIGIN C16: from Fr. *alternatif, -ive* or med. L. *alternativus*, from L. *alternare* (see **ALTERNATE**).

**alternative dispute resolution** ● n. chiefly N. Amer. the use of methods such as mediation to resolve a dispute without resort to litigation.

**alternative energy** ● n. energy fuelled in ways that do not use up the earth's natural resources or otherwise harm the environment, especially by avoiding the use of fossil fuels or nuclear power.

**alternative fuel** ● n. a fuel other than petrol or diesel for powering motor vehicles, such as natural gas or electricity.

**alternative medicine** ● n. medical therapy regarded as unorthodox by the medical profession, e.g. herbalism and naturopathy. See also **COMPLEMENTARY MEDICINE**.

**alternator** ● n. a dynamo that generates an alternating current.

**althorn** /ˈalthɔːn/ ● n. a musical instrument of the saxhorn family, especially the alto or tenor saxhorn in E flat.
– ORIGIN C19: from Ger., from *alt* 'high' (from L. *altus*) + *Horn* 'horn'.

**although** ● conj. **1** in spite of the fact that. **2** but.

**altimeter** /ˈaltɪmiːtə/ ● n. an instrument for determining altitude attained, especially a barometric or radar device fitted in an aircraft.
– ORIGIN C20: from L. *altus* 'high' + **-METER**.

**altimetry** /alˈtɪmɪtri/ ● n. the measurement of height or altitude.
– DERIVATIVES **altimetric** adj. **altimetrically** adv.
– ORIGIN ME: from med. L. *altimetria*.

**altiplano** /ˌaltɪˈplɑːnəʊ/ ● n. (pl. **-os**) the high tableland of central South America.
– ORIGIN C20: from Sp.

**altissimo** /alˈtɪsɪməʊ/ ● adj. Music very high in pitch.
– ORIGIN Ital., superlative of *alto* 'high'.

**altitude** ● n. the height of an object or point in relation to sea level or ground level. ➤Astronomy the apparent height of a celestial object above the horizon, measured in angular distance. ➤Geometry the length of the perpendicular line from a vertex to the opposite side of a figure.
– DERIVATIVES **altitudinal** adj.
– ORIGIN ME: from L. *altitudo*, from *altus* 'high'.

**altitude sickness** ● n. illness caused by ascent to high altitude, characterized chiefly by hyperventilation, nausea, and exhaustion resulting from shortage of oxygen.

**Alt key** ● n. Computing a key on a keyboard which, when pressed simultaneously with another key, gives the latter an alternative function.

**alto** /ˈaltəʊ/ ● n. (pl. **-os**) **1** (especially in church music) the highest adult male singing voice. ➤the lowest female singing voice; contralto. **2** [as modifier] denoting the member of a family of instruments pitched second or third highest.
– ORIGIN C16: from Ital. *alto (canto)* 'high (song)'.

**alto clef** ● n. Music a clef placing middle C on the middle line of the stave, used chiefly for viola music.

**altocumulus** ● n. (pl. **-cumuli**) cloud forming a layer of rounded masses with a level base, occurring at medium altitude (typically 2 to 7 km, 6,500 to 23,000 ft).
– ORIGIN C19: from mod. L. *alto-* (from L. *altus* 'high') + **CUMULUS**.

**altogether** ● adv. completely. ➤in total. ➤on the whole.
– PHRASES **in the altogether** informal naked.

**alto-relievo** /ˌaltəʊrɪˈliːvəʊ/ (also **alto-rilievo** /-rɪˈljeɪvəʊ/) ● n. (pl. **-os**) Art high relief.
– ORIGIN C17: from Ital. *alto-rilievo*.

**altostratus** ● n. cloud forming a continuous uniform layer which resembles stratus but occurs at medium altitude (typically 2 to 7 km, 6,500 to 23,000 ft).

– ORIGIN C19: from mod. L. *alto-* (from L. *altus* 'high') + **STRATUS**.

**altricial** /al'trɪʃ(ə)l/ ● **adj.** Zoology relating to or denoting a bird or other animal whose young are hatched or born in an undeveloped state and require care and feeding by the parents. Often contrasted with **PRECOCIAL**.
– ORIGIN C19: from L. *altrix, altric-*, fem. of *altor* 'nourisher', from *alere* 'nourish'.

**altruism** /'altruɪz(ə)m/ ● **n.** selfless concern for the well-being of others. ➤ Zoology behaviour of an animal that benefits another at its own expense.
– DERIVATIVES **altruist** n. **altruistic** adj. **altruistically** adv.
– ORIGIN C19: from Fr. *altruisme*, from Ital. *altrui* 'somebody else', from L. *alteri huic* 'to this other'.

**ALU** ● **abbrev.** Computing arithmetic logic unit.

**aludel** /'aljʊdɛl/ ● **n.** a pear-shaped ceramic or glass pot, open at both ends to enable a series to be fitted one above another, formerly used in chemical processes.
– ORIGIN ME: from OFr. *alutel*, via Sp. from Arab. *al-'uṯāl* 'the sublimation vessel'.

**alula** /'aljʊlə/ ● **n.** (pl. **alulae** /'aljʊliː/) technical term for **BASTARD WING**.
– ORIGIN C18: mod. L., lit. 'small wing', dimin. of *ala*.

**alum** /'aləm/ ● **n.** Chemistry **1** (also **potash alum**) a colourless astringent compound which is a hydrated double sulphate of aluminium and potassium, used in solution in dyeing and tanning. **2** any of a series of analogous compounds of other metals.
– ORIGIN ME: via OFr. from L. *alumen, alumin-*, rel. to *aluta* 'tawed leather'.

**alumina** /ə'luːmɪnə/ ● **n.** aluminium oxide, a white solid that is a major constituent of many clays and is found crystallized as corundum and sapphire. [$Al_2O_3$.]
– ORIGIN C18: from L. *alumen* (see **ALUM**), on the pattern of words such as *magnesia*.

**aluminium** /al(j)ʊ'mɪnɪəm/ (US **aluminum**) ● **n.** a strong, light, corrosion-resistant silvery-grey metal, the chemical element of atomic number 13. (Symbol: **Al**)
– DERIVATIVES **aluminize** /ə'l(j)uːmɪnʌɪz/ (also **-ise**) v. **aluminous** adj.
– ORIGIN C19: from **ALUMINA** + **-IUM**.

**aluminium bronze** ● **n.** an alloy of copper and aluminium.

**aluminosilicate** /əˌluːmɪnə(ʊ)'sɪlɪkeɪt/ ● **n.** Chemistry a silicate in which aluminium replaces some of the silicon, especially as a constituent of minerals such as feldspar.

**aluminum** /ə'luːmɪnəm/ ● **n.** US spelling of **ALUMINIUM**.

**alumnus** /ə'lʌmnəs/ ● **n.** (fem. **alumna**; pl. **alumni** /-ni/ or fem. **alumnae** /-niː/) a former pupil or student of a particular school, college, or university.
– ORIGIN C17: from L., 'nursling, pupil', from *alere* 'nourish'.

**alum root** ● **n.** chiefly N. Amer. another term for **HEUCHERA**.

**alveolar** /al'vɪələ, ˌalvɪ'əʊlə/ ● **adj. 1** Anatomy of or relating to an alveolus. **2** Phonetics (of a consonant) pronounced with the tip of the tongue on or near the bony ridge containing the alveoli of the upper teeth (e.g. *n, s, d, t*). ● **n.** Phonetics an alveolar consonant.

**alveolitis** /ˌalvɪə(ʊ)'lʌɪtɪs/ ● **n.** Medicine inflammation of the air sacs of the lungs.

**alveolus** /al'vɪələs, ˌalvɪ'əʊləs/ ● **n.** (pl. **alveoli** /-lʌɪ, -liː/) Anatomy **1** any of the many tiny air sacs of the lungs which allow for rapid gaseous exchange. **2** the bony socket for the root of a tooth. **3** an acinus in a gland.
– DERIVATIVES **alveolate** /al'vɪələt/ adj.
– ORIGIN C17: from L., 'small cavity', dimin. of *alveus*.

**alway** ● **adv.** archaic form of **ALWAYS**.

**always** ● **adv. 1** on all occasions. ➤ throughout a long period of the past. ➤ forever. ➤ repeatedly. **2** failing all else.
– ORIGIN ME: genitive case of *all way*.

**alyssum** /'alɪs(ə)m, ə'lɪs(ə)m/ ● **n.** (pl. **alyssums**) a herbaceous plant which typically bears small white or yellow flowers. [Genera *Alyssum* and *Lobularia*: many species.]
– ORIGIN C16: mod. L., from L. *alysson*, from Gk *alusson*, from *a-* 'without' + *lussa* 'rabies' (referring to early herbalist use).

**Alzheimer's disease** /'altshʌɪməz/ ● **n.** a form of progressive mental deterioration due to generalized degeneration of the brain, occurring in middle or old age.
– ORIGIN C20: named after the Ger. neurologist Alois *Alzheimer*.

**AM** ● **abbrev. 1** amplitude modulation. **2** US Master of Arts. [L. *artium magister*.] **3** Member of the Order of Australia.

**Am** ● **symb.** the chemical element americium.

**am** first person singular present of **BE**.

**a.m.** ● **abbrev.** before noon.
– ORIGIN from L. *ante meridiem*.

**amacrine cell** /'aməkrʌɪn, -krɪn/ ● **n.** Anatomy a small nerve cell within the retina which has dendrites but no axon.
– ORIGIN C20: from **A-**[1] + Gk *makros* 'large' + *is, in-* 'sinew or strip'.

**amadavat** /'amədəvat/ ● **n.** variant spelling of **AVADAVAT**.

**amadou** /'amədu:/ ● **n.** a spongy substance made from dried fungi, formerly used as an absorbent in medicine and as tinder.
– ORIGIN C18: from Fr., from L. *amator* 'lover' (because it easily ignites).

**amah** /'ɑːmə/ ● **n.** a nursemaid or maid in the Far East or India.
– ORIGIN from Port. *ama* 'nurse'.

**amalgam** /ə'malgəm/ ● **n. 1** a mixture or blend. **2** Chemistry an alloy of mercury with another metal, especially one used for dental fillings.
– ORIGIN C15: from Fr. *amalgame* or med. L. *amalgama*, from Gk *malagma* 'an emollient'.

**amalgamate** /ə'malgəmeɪt/ ● **v. 1** combine or unite to form one organization or structure. **2** Chemistry alloy (a metal) with mercury.
– DERIVATIVES **amalgamation** n.
– ORIGIN C17: from med. L. *amalgamat-, amalgamare* 'form into a soft mass', from *amalgama* (see **AMALGAM**).

**amanuensis** /əˌmanjʊ'ɛnsɪs/ ● **n.** (pl. **amanuenses** /-siːz/) a literary assistant, in particular one who takes dictation.
– ORIGIN C17: L., from *(servus) a manu* '(slave) at hand(writing), secretary' + *-ensis* 'belonging to'.

**amaranth** /'amərænθ/ ● **n.** a plant of a chiefly tropical family (Amaranthaceae) that includes love-lies-bleeding.
– DERIVATIVES **amaranthine** /ˌamə'ranθʌɪn/ adj.
– ORIGIN C16: from Fr. *amarante* or mod. L. *amaranthus*, alt. (on the pattern of plant names ending in *-anthus*) of L. *amarantus*, from Gk *amarantos* 'not fading'.

**amaretti** /ˌamə'rɛti/ ● **pl. n.** Italian almond-flavoured biscuits.
– ORIGIN Ital., based on *amaro* 'bitter'; cf. **AMARETTO**.

**amaretto** /ˌamə'rɛtəʊ/ ● **n.** a brown almond-flavoured liqueur produced in Italy.
– ORIGIN Ital., dimin. of *amaro* 'bitter' (with ref. to bitter almonds).

**amaryllis** /ˌamə'rɪlɪs/ ● **n.** a bulbous plant with showy trumpet-shaped flowers and strap-shaped leaves. [*Amaryllis belladonna* (S. Africa) or genus *Hippeastrum* (S. America).]
– ORIGIN mod. L., from L. *Amaryllis* (from Gk *Amarullis*), a name for a country girl in pastoral poetry.

**amass** ● **v.** accumulate over time. ➤ archaic (of people) gather together.
– DERIVATIVES **amasser** n.
– ORIGIN C15: from Fr. *amasser* or med. L. *amassare*, based on L. *massa* (see **MASS**).

**amateur** /'amətə, -tʃə, -tjʊə, ˌamə'təː/ ● **n.** a person who engages in a pursuit, especially a sport, on an unpaid basis. ➤ a person considered inept at a particular activity. ● **adj.** non-professional. ➤ inept.
– DERIVATIVES **amateurism** n.
– ORIGIN C18: from Fr., from Ital. *amatore*, from L. *amator* 'lover', from *amare* 'to love'.

**amateurish** ● **adj.** inept.
– DERIVATIVES **amateurishly** adv. **amateurishness** n.

**amatol** /'amətɒl/ ● **n.** a high explosive consisting of a mixture of TNT and ammonium nitrate.

– ORIGIN C20: formed irregularly from *am(monium)* + *tol(uene)*.

**amatory** /ˈamət(ə)ri/ • **adj.** relating to or induced by sexual love or desire.

– ORIGIN C16: from L. *amatorius*, from *amator* (see **AMATEUR**).

**amaurosis** /ˌamɔːˈrəʊsɪs/ • **n.** Medicine partial or total blindness without visible change in the eye, typically due to disease of the optic nerve, spinal cord, or brain.

– DERIVATIVES **amaurotic** adj.

– ORIGIN C17: from Gk *amaurōsis*, from *amauroun* 'darken', from *amauros* 'dim'.

**amaze** • **v.** surprise greatly.

– DERIVATIVES **amazement** n. **amazing** adj. **amazingly** n. **amazingness** n.

– ORIGIN OE *āmasian*, of unknown origin.

**Amazon** /ˈaməz(ə)n/ • **n. 1** a member of a legendary race of female warriors believed by the ancient Greeks to exist in Scythia or elsewhere. ➤ a very tall, strong woman. **2** (**amazon**) a green parrot with a broad rounded tail, found in Central and South America. [Genus *Amazona*.]

– ORIGIN ME: via L. from Gk *Amazōn*, explained by the Greeks as 'breastless' (as if from *a-* 'without' + *mazos* 'breast'), referring to the fable that the Amazons cut off the right breast so as to draw a bow more easily, but prob. a folk etymology of an unknown foreign word.

**amazon ant** • **n.** a small reddish ant which captures the pupae of other ant colonies to raise as slaves. [Genus *Polyergus*.]

**Amazonian** /aməˈzəʊnɪən/ • **adj. 1** of or relating to the River Amazon. **2** (of a woman) very tall and strong.

**ambassador** • **n.** a diplomat sent by a state as its permanent representative in a foreign country. ➤ a representative or promoter of a specified activity.

– DERIVATIVES **ambassadorial** adj. **ambassadorship** n. **ambassadress** n.

– ORIGIN ME: from Fr. *ambassadeur*, from Ital. *ambasciator*, based on L. *ambactus* 'servant'.

**ambassador-at-large** • **n.** N. Amer. an ambassador with special duties not appointed to a particular country.

**ambatch** /ˈambatʃ/ • **n.** a tropical African tree with light spongy wood that is used chiefly for rafts and floats. [*Aeschynomene elaphroxylon*.]

– ORIGIN C19: of Ethiopic origin.

**amber** • **n. 1** hard translucent fossilized resin originating from extinct coniferous trees, typically yellowish in colour and used in jewellery. **2** a honey-yellow colour. ➤ a yellow light used as a cautionary signal between green for 'go' and red for 'stop'.

– ORIGIN ME: from OFr. *ambre*, from Arab. *ʿanbar* 'ambergris', later 'amber'.

**ambergris** /ˈambəgrɪs, -iːs/ • **n.** a wax-like secretion of the intestines of the sperm whale, found floating in tropical seas and used in perfume manufacture.

– ORIGIN ME: from OFr. *ambre gris* 'grey amber', as distinct from *amber jaune* 'yellow amber' (the resin).

**amberjack** • **n.** a large game fish with a yellowish tail, found in inshore tropical and subtropical waters of the Atlantic and South Pacific. [Genus *Seriola*: several species.]

**ambidextrous** /ˌambɪˈdɛkstrəs/ • **adj.** able to use the right and left hands equally well.

– DERIVATIVES **ambidexterity** n. **ambidextrously** adv. **ambidextrousness** n.

– ORIGIN C17: from late L. *ambidexter* (from L. *ambi-* 'on both sides' + *dexter* 'right-handed') + **-OUS**.

**ambience** /ˈambɪəns/ (also **ambiance**) • **n. 1** the character and atmosphere of a place. **2** quality or character given to a sound recording by the space in which the sound occurs.

**ambient** /ˈambɪənt/ • **adj. 1** of or relating to the immediate environs of something. **2** denoting a style of instrumental music with electronic textures and no persistent beat, used to create atmosphere.

– ORIGIN C16: from Fr. *ambiant* or L. *ambient-*, *ambire* 'go round'.

**ambiguous** /amˈbɪgjʊəs/ • **adj.** (of language) having more than one meaning. ➤ unclear because not distinguishing between alternatives.

– DERIVATIVES **ambiguity** /ambɪˈgjuːɪti/ n. **ambiguously** adv. **ambiguousness** n.

– ORIGIN C16: from L. *ambiguus* 'doubtful' (from *ambigere* 'waver, go around', from *ambi-* 'both ways' + *agere* 'to drive') + **-OUS**.

**ambisexual** /ˌambɪˈsɛksjʊəl, -ʃʊəl/ • **adj.** bisexual; androgynous.

– DERIVATIVES **ambisexually** adv.

– ORIGIN 1930s: from L. *ambi-* 'on both sides' + **SEXUAL**.

**ambisonic** • **adj.** denoting or relating to a high-fidelity audio system that reproduces the directional and acoustic properties of recorded sound using two or more channels. • **n.** (**ambisonics**) [treated as sing.] ambisonic reproduction or systems.

– ORIGIN 1970s: from L. *ambi-* 'on both sides' + **SONIC**.

**ambit** /ˈambɪt/ • **n.** the scope, extent, or bounds of something.

– ORIGIN ME (in the sense 'precincts, environs'): from L. *ambitus* 'circuit', from *ambire* 'go round'.

**ambition** • **n.** a strong desire to do or achieve something. ➤ desire for success, wealth, or fame.

– ORIGIN ME: via OFr. from L. *ambitio(n-)*, from *ambire* 'go around (canvassing for votes)'.

**ambitious** • **adj.** having or showing ambition. ➤ (of a plan or piece of work) intended to satisfy high aspirations and therefore difficult to achieve.

– DERIVATIVES **ambitiously** adv. **ambitiousness** n.

**ambivalent** /amˈbɪv(ə)l(ə)nt/ • **adj.** having mixed feelings or contradictory ideas about something or someone.

– DERIVATIVES **ambivalence** n. **ambivalently** adv.

– ORIGIN C20: from *ambivalence* (from Ger. *Ambivalenz*), on the pattern of *equivalent*.

**ambivert** /ˈambɪvəːt/ • **n.** Psychology a person who has a balance of extrovert and introvert features in their personality.

– DERIVATIVES **ambiversion** n.

– ORIGIN 1920s: from L. *ambi-* 'on both sides', on the pattern of *extrovert* and *introvert*.

**amble** • **v.** walk or move at a leisurely pace. • **n.** a leisurely walk.

– DERIVATIVES **ambler** n.

– ORIGIN ME: from OFr. *ambler*, from L. *ambulare* 'to walk'.

**amblyopia** /ˌamblɪˈəʊpɪə/ • **n.** Medicine impaired or dim vision without obvious defect or change in the eye.

– DERIVATIVES **amblyopic** adj.

– ORIGIN C18: from Gk *ambluōpia* 'dim-sightedness', from *ambluōpos* (adj.), from *amblus* 'dull' + *ōps*, *ōp-* 'eye'.

**ambo** /ˈambəʊ/ • **n.** (pl. **ambos** or **ambones** /-ˈbəʊniːz/) (in an early Christian church) an oblong pulpit with steps at each end.

– ORIGIN C17: via med. L. from Gk *ambōn* 'rim' (in med. Gk 'pulpit').

**amboyna** /amˈbɔɪnə/ • **n.** the decorative wood of a fast-growing SE Asian tree (*Pterocarpus indicus*), used for cabinetmaking.

– ORIGIN C19: named after *Amboina* Island in Indonesia.

**ambrosia** • **n. 1** Greek & Roman Mythology the food of the gods. ➤ something very pleasing to taste or smell. **2** a fungal product used as food by ambrosia beetles or their larvae. ➤ another term for **BEE BREAD**.

– DERIVATIVES **ambrosial** adj.

– ORIGIN C16: via L. from Gk, 'elixir of life', from *ambrotos* 'immortal'.

**ambrosia beetle** • **n.** a small dark wood-boring beetle which feeds on ambrosia produced by a fungus in the wood. [*Xyleborus* and other genera.]

**ambry** /ˈambri/ • **n.** variant spelling of **AUMBRY**.

**ambulacrum** /ˌambjʊˈleɪkrəm, -ˈlakrəm/ • **n.** (pl. **ambulacra** /-ˈleɪkrə, -ˈlakrə/) Zoology (in an echinoderm) each of the radially arranged bands through which the double rows of tube feet protrude.

– DERIVATIVES **ambulacral** adj.

– ORIGIN C19: L., 'avenue', from *ambulare* 'to walk'.

**ambulance** • **n.** a vehicle equipped for taking sick or

injured people to and from hospital. • **v.** convey in an ambulance.
– ORIGIN C19: Fr., from *hôpital ambulant* 'mobile field hospital', from L. *ambulant-* (see **AMBULANT**).

**ambulance-chaser** • **n.** derogatory, chiefly N. Amer. a lawyer who specializes in bringing cases seeking damages for personal injury.

**ambulant** /ˈambjʊl(ə)nt/ • **adj.** Medicine able to walk about; not confined to bed.
– ORIGIN C17: from L. *ambulant-*, *ambulare* 'walk'.

**ambulate** /ˈambjʊleɪt/ • **v.** formal or technical walk; move about.
– DERIVATIVES **ambulation** n.
– ORIGIN C17: from L. *ambulat-*, *ambulare* 'walk'.

**ambulatory** /ˈambjʊlət(ə)ri/ • **adj. 1** relating to walking or able to walk. **2** movable; mobile. • **n.** (pl. **-ies**) an aisle or cloister in a church or monastery.

**ambuscade** /ˌambəˈskeɪd/ • **n.** an ambush. • **v.** archaic lie in wait; ambush.
– ORIGIN C16: from Fr. *embuscade*, based on a late L. word meaning 'to place in a wood'; rel. to **BUSH**[1].

**ambush** • **n.** a surprise attack by people lying in wait in a concealed position. • **v.** attack in such a way.
– ORIGIN ME: from OFr. *embusche* (n.), *embuschier* (v.), based on a late L. word meaning 'to place in a wood'; rel. to **BUSH**[1].

**ameba** • **n.** (pl. **amebae** or **amebas**) US spelling of **AMOEBA**.

**amebiasis** • **n.** US spelling of **AMOEBIASIS**.

**amelanchier** /ˌaməˈlaŋkɪə/ • **n.** a shrub of a genus that includes juneberry and snowy mespilus, typically bearing white flowers. [Genus *Amelanchier.*]
– ORIGIN from Fr. dial. *amelancier* 'medlar'.

**ameliorate** /əˈmiːlɪəreɪt/ • **v.** make better; reduce the undesirable effect of.
– DERIVATIVES **amelioration** n. **ameliorative** adj. **ameliorator** n.
– ORIGIN C18: alt. of **MELIORATE**, influenced by Fr. *améliorer*, from *meilleur* 'better'.

**amen** /ɑːˈmɛn, eɪ-/ • **exclam.** said at the end of a prayer or hymn, meaning 'so be it'.
– ORIGIN OE, from eccles. L., from Gk *amēn*, from Heb. *'āmēn* 'truth, certainty'.

**amenable** /əˈmiːnəb(ə)l/ • **adj.** responsive to suggestion. ➤(**amenable to**) capable of being acted on.
– DERIVATIVES **amenability** n. **amenably** adv.
– ORIGIN C16 (in the sense 'liable to answer to a law or tribunal'): from OFr. *amener* 'bring to' from *a-* 'to' + *mener* 'bring' (from L. *minari* 'threaten').

**amend** • **v. 1** make minor improvements to (a document, proposal, etc.). **2** archaic put right.
– DERIVATIVES **amendable** adj. **amender** n.
– ORIGIN ME: from OFr. *amender*, based on L. *emendare* (see **EMEND**).

**amende honorable** /əˌmɒ̃d ɒnɔːˈrɑːbl(ə), French amɑ̃d ɔnɔʀabl/ • **n.** (pl. **amendes honorables** pronunc. same) poetic/literary a public apology or reparation.
– ORIGIN Fr., lit. 'honourable reparation'.

**amendment** • **n. 1** a minor improvement. ➤the action of amending something. **2** (**Amendment**) an article added to the US Constitution.

**amends** • **pl. n.** (in phr. **make amends**) compensate or make up for a wrongdoing.
– PHRASES **offer of amends** Law an offer to publish a correction and an apology for an act of libel.
– ORIGIN ME: from OFr. *amendes* 'penalties, fine', pl. of *amende* 'reparation', from *amender* (see **AMEND**).

**amenity** /əˈmiːnɪti, -ˈmɛn-/ • **n.** (pl. **-ies**) a useful or desirable feature of a place. ➤the pleasantness or attractiveness of a place.
– ORIGIN ME: from OFr. *amenite* or L. *amoenitas*, from *amoenus* 'pleasant'.

**amenity bed** • **n.** Brit. a hospital bed in a private room available for a payment to a patient receiving National Health treatment.

**amenorrhoea** /əˌmɛnəˈriːə/ (US **amenorrhea**) • **n.** an abnormal absence of menstruation.

**ament** /ˈeɪmɛnt, əˈmɛnt/ • **n.** Botany a catkin.
– ORIGIN C18: from L. *amentum* 'thong'.

**amentia** /eɪˈmɛnʃə, ə-/ • **n.** Medicine, dated severe congenital mental handicap.
– ORIGIN ME: from L., lit. 'madness', from *amens*, *ament-* 'mad', from *a-* 'without' + *mens* 'the mind'.

**Amerasian** /ˌaməˈreɪʃ(ə)n, -ʒ(ə)n/ • **adj.** having one American and one Asian parent. • **n.** an Amerasian person.

**amercement** /əˈməːsmənt/ • **n.** English Law, historical a fine.
– DERIVATIVES **amerce** v.
– ORIGIN ME: from Anglo-Norman Fr. *amerciment*, based on *estre amercie* 'be at the mercy of another', from *a merci* 'at (the) mercy'.

**American** • **adj.** relating to or characteristic of the United States. ➤relating to the continents of America. • **n.** a native or citizen of the United States. ➤a native or inhabitant of any of the countries of North, South, or Central America.
– PHRASES **the American dream** the ideal by which equality of opportunity is available to any American, allowing the highest aspirations and goals to be achieved.
– DERIVATIVES **Americanization** (also **-isation**) n. **Americanize** (also **-ise**) v. **Americanness** n.

**Americana** /əˌmɛrɪˈkɑːnə/ • **pl. n.** things associated with the United States.

**American aloe** • **n.** another term for **CENTURY PLANT**.

**American football** • **n.** a kind of football played with an oval ball by teams of eleven players, on a field marked out as a gridiron.

**American Indian** • **n.** a member of any of the groups of indigenous peoples of North, Central, and South America, especially those of North America.

**USAGE American Indian**

The term **American Indian** has been steadily replaced in the US by the term **Native American**, especially in official contexts; **American Indian** is still widespread in general use even in the US, however, and is not normally regarded as offensive by American Indians themselves.

**Americanism** • **n. 1** a word or phrase peculiar to or originating in the United States. **2** the qualities typical of America and Americans.

**American organ** • **n.** a type of reed organ resembling the harmonium but in which air is sucked (not blown) through reeds.

**American plan** • **n.** North American term for **FULL BOARD**.

**americium** /ˌaməˈrɪsjəm/ • **n.** the chemical element of atomic number 95, an artificially made radioactive metal of the actinide series. (Symbol: **Am**)
– ORIGIN 1940s: from *America* (where it was first made) + **-IUM**.

**Amerindian** /ˌaməˈrɪndɪən/ (also **Amerind** /ˈamərɪnd/) • **n.** another term for **AMERICAN INDIAN**, used chiefly in anthropological and linguistic contexts.

**amethyst** /ˈaməθɪst/ • **n.** a precious stone consisting of a violet or purple variety of quartz.
– DERIVATIVES **amethystine** /-ˈθɪstiːn/ adj.
– ORIGIN ME: via OFr. from L. *amethystus*, from Gk *amethustos* 'not drunken' (because the stone was believed to prevent intoxication).

**amethyst deceiver** • **n.** an edible woodland mushroom with a lilac cap and stem. [*Laccaria amethystea.*]

**Amex** • **abbrev. 1** trademark American Express. **2** American Stock Exchange.

**Amhara** /amˈhɑːrə/ • **n.** (pl. same or **Amharas**) a member of a Semitic people of central Ethiopia.
– ORIGIN from *Amhara*, the name of a region of central Ethiopia.

**Amharic** /amˈharɪk/ • **n.** the official language of Ethiopia, a Semitic language descended from Ge'ez.

**amiable** • **adj.** friendly and pleasant in manner.
– DERIVATIVES **amiability** n. **amiableness** n. **amiably** adv.
– ORIGIN ME (in the senses 'kind' and 'lovely, lovable'): via

OFr. from late L. *amicabilis* (see **AMICABLE**).

**amianthus** /ˌamɪˈanθəs/ ● **n.** a variety of asbestos with fine silky fibres which can be woven.
– ORIGIN C17: from L. *amiantus*, from Gk *amiantos* 'not defiled'.

**amicable** /ˈamɪkəb(ə)l/ ● **adj.** characterized by friendliness and absence of discord.
– DERIVATIVES **amicability** n. **amicableness** n. **amicably** adv.
– ORIGIN ME (in the sense 'pleasant'): from late L. *amicabilis*, from L. *amicus* 'friend'.

**amicable numbers** ● **pl. n.** Mathematics a pair of numbers each of which is the sum of the factors of the other (e.g. 220 and 284).

**amice**[1] /ˈamɪs/ ● **n.** a white linen cloth worn on the neck and shoulders, under the alb, by a priest celebrating the Eucharist.
– ORIGIN ME: from med. L. *amicia, amisia*.

**amice**[2] /ˈamɪs/ ● **n.** a cap, hood, or cape worn by members of certain religious orders.
– ORIGIN ME: from OFr. *aumusse*, from med. L. *almucia*.

**amicus** /əˈmʌɪkəs/ (in full **amicus curiae** /ˈkjʊərɪiː/) ● **n.** (pl. **amici** /-siː/) an impartial adviser to a court of law in a particular case.
– ORIGIN C17: mod. L., lit. 'friend (of the court)'.

**amid** ● **prep.** surrounded by; in the middle of.

**Amidah** /əˈmiːdə/ ● **n.** Judaism a prayer consisting of a varying number of blessings recited while the worshippers stand.
– ORIGIN C19: Heb., lit. 'standing'.

**amide** /ˈeɪmʌɪd, ˈamʌɪd/ ● **n.** Chemistry **1** an organic compound containing the group $-C(O)NH_2$. **2** a salt-like compound containing the anion $NH_2^-$.
– ORIGIN C19: from **AMMONIA** + **-IDE**.

**amidships** (US also **amidship**) ● **adv. & adj.** in the middle of a ship, either longitudinally or laterally.
– ORIGIN C17: from **A-**[2] + **MIDSHIP**, influenced by **AMID**.

**amidst** ● **prep.** poetic/literary variant of **AMID**.

**amigo** /əˈmiːgəʊ/ ● **n.** (pl. **-os**) informal, chiefly N. Amer. (especially in Spanish-speaking areas) a friend.
– ORIGIN C19: from Sp.

**amine** /ˈeɪmiːn/ ● **n.** Chemistry an organic compound derived from ammonia by replacement of one or more hydrogen atoms by organic radicals.
– ORIGIN C19: from **AMMONIA** + **-INE**[4].

**amino acid** ● **n.** Biochemistry any of a class of about twenty simple organic compounds which form the basic constituents of proteins and contain both a carboxyl ($-COOH$) and an amino ($-NH_2$) group.

**amino group** /əˈmiːnəʊ, əˈmʌɪnəʊ/ ● **n.** Chemistry the group $-NH_2$, present in amino acids, amides, and many amines.

**amir** /əˈmiːə/ ● **n.** variant spelling of **EMIR**.
– ORIGIN C16: from Pers. and Urdu, from Arab. *'amīr* 'commander'; cf. **EMIR**.

**Amish** /ˈamɪʃ, ˈɑː-, ˈeɪ-/ ● **pl. n.** (**the Amish**) a strict US Mennonite sect living mainly in Pennsylvania and Ohio. ● **adj.** of or relating to this sect.
– ORIGIN C19: appar. from Ger. *amisch*, from the name of the Swiss preacher Jakob *Amman*.

**amiss** ● **adj.** not quite right; inappropriate. ● **adv.** wrongly or inappropriately.
– PHRASES **take something amiss** be offended through misinterpreting something said. **not go** (or **come**) **amiss** be welcome and useful.
– ORIGIN ME: prob. from ON *á mis* 'so as to miss', from *á* 'on' + *mis* (rel. to **MISS**[1]).

**amitotic** /ˌeɪmʌɪˈtɒtɪk, ˌamʌɪ-/ ● **adj.** Biology relating to or denoting the division of a cell nucleus without mitosis.
– DERIVATIVES **amitosis** n. **amitotically** adv.

**amitriptyline** /ˌamɪˈtrɪptɪliːn/ ● **n.** Medicine a mild tranquillizer of the tricyclic antidepressant group.
– ORIGIN 1960s: from *ami(ne)* + **TRI-** + *(he)ptyl* + **-INE**[4].

**amity** /ˈamɪti/ ● **n.** friendly relations.
– ORIGIN ME: from OFr. *amitie*, based on L. *amicus* 'friend'.

**ammeter** /ˈamɪtə/ ● **n.** an instrument for measuring electric current in amperes.

**ammo** /ˈaməʊ/ ● **n.** informal ammunition.

**ammonia** /əˈməʊnɪə/ ● **n.** a colourless, intensely pungent gas which dissolves in water to give a strongly alkaline solution. [$NH_3$.] ➤a solution of this, used as a cleaning fluid.
– DERIVATIVES **ammoniacal** adj.
– ORIGIN C18: mod. L., from *sal ammoniacus* (see **SAL AMMONIAC**).

**ammoniated** ● **adj.** combined or treated with ammonia.

**ammonite** /ˈamənʌɪt/ ● **n.** Palaeontology an extinct marine cephalopod mollusc with a flat-coiled spiral shell, found as fossils chiefly in Jurassic and Cretaceous deposits.
– DERIVATIVES **ammonoid** n.
– ORIGIN C18: from mod. L. *ammonites*, from med. L. *cornu Ammonis* 'horn of Ammon', from the fossil's resemblance to the ram's horn assoc. with the god Jupiter Ammon.

**ammonium** /əˈməʊnɪəm/ ● **n.** [as modifier] Chemistry of or denoting the cation $NH_4^+$, present in solutions of ammonia and in salts derived from ammonia.

**ammunition** ● **n.** a supply or quantity of bullets and shells.
– ORIGIN C16: from obs. Fr. *amunition*, alt. (by wrong division) of *la munition* (see **MUNITION**).

**amnesia** /amˈniːzɪə/ ● **n.** a partial or total loss of memory.
– DERIVATIVES **amnesiac** n. & adj. **amnesic** adj. & n.
– ORIGIN C18: from Gk *amnēsia* 'forgetfulness'.

**amnesty** ● **n.** (pl. **-ies**) an official pardon for people convicted of political offences. ➤an undertaking by the authorities to take no action against specified offences during a fixed period. ● **v.** (**-ies**, **-ied**) grant an amnesty to.
– ORIGIN C16: via L. from Gk *amnēstia* 'forgetfulness'.

**amniocentesis** /ˌamnɪəʊsɛnˈtiːsɪs/ ● **n.** (pl. **amniocenteses** /-siːz/) a process in which amniotic fluid is sampled using a hollow needle inserted into the uterus, to screen for abnormalities in the developing fetus.
– ORIGIN 1950s: from **AMNION** + Gk *kentēsis* 'pricking'.

**amnion** /ˈamnɪən/ ● **n.** (pl. **amnions** or **amnia**) the innermost membrane that encloses the embryo of a mammal, bird, or reptile.
– DERIVATIVES **amniotic** adj.
– ORIGIN C17: from Gk, 'caul', dimin. of *amnos* 'lamb'.

**amniote** /ˈamnɪəʊt/ ● **n.** Zoology an animal whose embryo develops in an amnion and chorion and has an allantois, i.e. a mammal, bird, or reptile.
– ORIGIN C19: from mod. L. *Amniota*, back-form. from *amniotic* (see **AMNION**).

**amniotic fluid** ● **n.** the fluid surrounding a fetus within the amnion.

**amoeba** /əˈmiːbə/ (US also **ameba**) ● **n.** (pl. **amoebas** or **amoebae** /-biː/) a single-celled animal which catches food and moves about by extending finger-like projections of protoplasm. [Phylum Rhizopoda.]
– DERIVATIVES **amoebic** adj. **amoeboid** adj.
– ORIGIN C19: mod. L., from Gk *amoibē* 'change, alternation'.

**amoebiasis** /ˌamiːˈbʌɪəsɪs/ (US also **amebiasis**) ● **n.** Medicine infection with amoebas, especially as causing dysentery.

**amok** /əˈmɒk/ (also **amuck**) ● **adv.** (in phr. **run amok**) behave uncontrollably and disruptively.
– ORIGIN C17: via Port. *amouco*, from Malay *amok* 'rushing in a frenzy'.

**among** (chiefly Brit. also **amongst**) ● **prep. 1** situated more or less centrally in relation to (several others). **2** being a member or members of (a larger set). **3** occurring in or practised by (some members of a community). **4** indicating a division, choice, or differentiation involving three or more participants.
– ORIGIN OE *ongemang* (from *on* 'in' + *gemang* 'assemblage, mingling').

**amontillado** /əˌmɒntɪˈlɑːdəʊ, -ˈljɑː-/ ● **n.** (pl. **-os**) a medium dry sherry.
– ORIGIN Sp., from *Montilla*, a town in southern Spain.

**amoral** /eɪˈmɒr(ə)l/ ● **adj.** lacking a moral sense; unconcerned whether something is right or wrong.
– DERIVATIVES **amoralism** n. **amoralist** n. **amorality** n.

**amoretto** /ˌaməˈrɛtəʊ/ ● **n.** (pl. **amoretti** /-ti/) a representation of Cupid in a work of art.
– ORIGIN Ital., dimin. of *amore* 'love', from L. *amor.*

**amorist** /ˈamərɪst/ ● **n.** a person who is in love or who writes about love.
– ORIGIN C16: from L. *amor* or Fr. *amour* 'love' + **-IST**.

**Amorite** /ˈamərʌɪt/ ● **n.** a member of an ancient people living in Mesopotamia, Palestine, and Syria in the 3rd millennium BC.
– ORIGIN from Heb. *'ĕmōrī* + **-ITE**[1].

**amoroso**[1] /ˌaməˈrəʊzəʊ, -səʊ/ ● **adv. & adj.** Music in a loving or tender manner.
– ORIGIN Ital., from med. L. *amorosus* (see **AMOROUS**).

**amoroso**[2] /ˌaməˈrəʊzəʊ, -səʊ/ ● **n.** a dark, sweet sherry.
– ORIGIN from Sp., lit. 'amorous', from med. L. *amorosus* (see **AMOROUS**).

**amorous** ● **adj.** showing or feeling sexual desire.
– DERIVATIVES **amorously** adv. **amorousness** n.
– ORIGIN ME: via OFr. from med. L. *amorosus*, from L. *amor* 'love'.

**amorphous** /əˈmɔːfəs/ ● **adj. 1** without a clearly defined shape or form. **2** Mineralogy & Chemistry not crystalline, or not apparently crystalline.
– DERIVATIVES **amorphously** adv. **amorphousness** n.
– ORIGIN C18: from mod. L. *amorphus*, from Gk *amorphos* 'shapeless' (from *a-* 'without' + *morphē* 'form') + **-OUS**.

**amortize** /əˈmɔːtʌɪz/ (also **-ise**) ● **v. 1** gradually write off the initial cost of (an asset) over a period. ➤reduce or cancel (a debt) by money regularly put aside. **2** historical transfer (land) to a corporation in mortmain.
– DERIVATIVES **amortization** n.
– ORIGIN ME: from OFr. *amortiss-*, *amortir*, based on L. *ad* 'to, at' + *mors, mort-* 'death'.

**amosite** /ˈeɪməsʌɪt/ ● **n.** an iron-rich amphibole asbestos.
– ORIGIN C20: from the initial letters of *A*sbestos *M*ines *o*f *S*outh *A*frica.

**amount** ● **n.** the total of something in number, size, value, or extent. ➤a quantity: *a small amount of water.* ● **v.** (**amount to**) **1** come to be (a total) when added together. **2** be the equivalent of.
– PHRASES **any amount of** a great deal or number of.
– ORIGIN ME: from OFr. *amunter*, from *amont* 'upward', lit. 'uphill', from L. *ad montem*.

**amour** /əˈmʊə/ ● **n.** a love affair or lover, especially a secret one.
– ORIGIN ME: via OFr. from L. *amor* 'love'.

**amour fou** /əˌmʊə ˈfuː, French amuʀ fu/ ● **n.** uncontrollable or obsessive passion.
– ORIGIN 1970s: Fr., 'insane love'.

**amour propre** /aˌmʊə ˈprɒpr(ə), French amuʀ pʀɔpʀ/ ● **n.** self-respect.
– ORIGIN from Fr.

**amoxycillin** /əˌmɒksɪˈsɪlɪn/ (also **amoxicillin**) ● **n.** Medicine a semi-synthetic penicillin closely related to ampicillin and with similar properties.
– ORIGIN 1970s: from ***am(ino-)*** + **OXY-**[2] + **(PENI)CILLIN**.

**AMP** ● **abbrev.** Biochemistry adenosine monophosphate.

**amp**[1] ● **n.** short for **AMPERE**.

**amp**[2] ● **n.** informal short for **AMPLIFIER**.

**Ampakine** /ˈampəkʌɪn/ ● **n.** (trademark in the US) any of a class of synthetic compounds which facilitate transmission of nerve impulses in the brain and appear to improve memory and learning capacity.
– ORIGIN from *AMPA* (an acronym denoting certain receptors in the brain) + Gk *kinein* 'to move'.

**ampelopsis** /ˌampɪˈlɒpsɪs/ ● **n.** (pl. same) a bushy climbing plant of the vine family. [Genus *Ampelopsis*: two species.]
– ORIGIN mod. L., from Gk *ampelos* 'vine' + *opsis* 'appearance'.

**amperage** /ˈamp(ə)rɪdʒ/ ● **n.** the strength of an electric current in amperes.

**ampere** /ˈampɛː/ (abbrev.: **A**) ● **n.** the SI base unit of electric current, equal to a flow of one coulomb per second.
– ORIGIN C19: after the Fr. physicist André-Marie *Ampère*.

**ampersand** /ˈampəsand/ ● **n.** the sign & (standing for *and*, as in *Smith & Co.*, or the Latin *et*, as in *&c.*).
– ORIGIN C19: alt. of *and per se and* '& by itself is *and*', chanted as an aid to learning the sign.

**amphetamine** /amˈfɛtəmiːn, -ɪn/ ● **n.** a synthetic mood-altering drug, used illegally as a stimulant.
– ORIGIN 1930s: abbrev. of its chemical name, *a(lpha)-m(ethyl) phe(ne)t(hyl)amine*.

**amphi-** /ˈamfi/ ● **comb. form 1** both: *amphibian.* ➤of both kinds: *amphipod.* ➤on both sides: *amphiprostyle.* **2** around: *amphitheatre.*
– ORIGIN from Gk.

**amphibian** ● **n. 1** Zoology a cold-blooded vertebrate animal of a class (Amphibia) that comprises the frogs, toads, newts, salamanders, and caecilians, distinguished by an aquatic gill-breathing larval stage followed by a terrestrial lung-breathing adult stage. **2** a seaplane, tank, or other vehicle that can operate on land and on water.
– ORIGIN C17 (in the sense 'of double or doubtful nature'): from mod. L. *amphibium* 'an amphibian', from Gk *amphibion* (noun use of *amphibios* 'living both in water and on land', from *amphi* 'both' + *bios* 'life').

**amphibious** /amˈfɪbɪəs/ ● **adj. 1** living in or suited for both land and water. **2** (of a military operation) involving forces landed from the sea.
– DERIVATIVES **amphibiously** adv.

**amphibole** /ˈamfɪbəʊl/ ● **n.** any of a class of rock-forming silicate or aluminosilicate minerals typically occurring as fibrous or columnar crystals.
– ORIGIN C19: from Fr., from L. *amphibolus* 'ambiguous' (because of the varied structure of the minerals).

**amphibolite** /amˈfɪbəlʌɪt/ ● **n.** Geology a granular metamorphic rock consisting mainly of hornblende and plagioclase.

**amphibology** /ˌamfɪˈbɒlədʒi/ ● **n.** (pl. **-ies**) a phrase or sentence that is grammatically ambiguous.
– ORIGIN ME: from OFr. *amphibologie*, from late L. *amphibologia*, from L. *amphibolia*, from Gk *amphibolos* 'ambiguous'.

**amphibrach** /ˈamfɪbrak/ ● **n.** Prosody a metrical foot consisting of a stressed syllable between two unstressed syllables or (in Greek and Latin) a long syllable between two short syllables.
– ORIGIN C16: via L. from Gk *amphibrakhus* 'short at both ends'.

**amphimixis** /ˌamfɪˈmɪksɪs/ ● **n.** Botany sexual reproduction involving the fusion of two different gametes to form a zygote. Often contrasted with **APOMIXIS**.
– DERIVATIVES **amphimictic** adj.
– ORIGIN C19: from **AMPHI-** + Gk *mixis* 'mingling'.

**amphioxus** /ˌamfɪˈɒksəs/ ● **n.** a small lancelet (fish), caught for food in Asia. [Genus *Branchiostoma*.]
– ORIGIN C19: mod. L., from **AMPHI-** + Gk *oxus* 'sharp'.

**amphipathic** /ˌamfɪˈpaθɪk/ ● **adj.** Biochemistry (of a molecule, especially a protein) having both hydrophilic and hydrophobic parts.
– ORIGIN 1930s: from **AMPHI-** + Gk *pathikos* (from *pathos* 'experience').

**amphiphilic** /ˌamfɪˈfɪlɪk/ ● **adj.** Biochemistry another term for **AMPHIPATHIC**.

**Amphipoda** /ˌamfɪˈpəʊdə/ ● **pl. n.** Zoology an order of chiefly marine crustaceans with a laterally compressed body and a large number of leg-like appendages.
– DERIVATIVES **amphipod** /ˈamfɪpɒd/ n.
– ORIGIN mod. L., from **AMPHI-** 'of both kinds' (because some legs are specialized for swimming and some for feeding) + Gk *pous, pod-* 'foot'.

**amphiprostyle** /amˈfɪprəstʌɪl/ ● **adj.** (of a classical building) having a portico at each end but not at the sides.
– ORIGIN C18: via L. from Gk *amphiprostulos*, from *amphi-* 'both, on both sides'+ *prostulos* (see **PROSTYLE**).

**amphisbaena** /ˌamfɪsˈbiːnə/ ● **n.** a mythical serpent with a head at each end.
– ORIGIN ME: via L. from Gk *amphisbaina*, from *amphis* 'both ways' + *bainein* 'go'.

**Amphisbaenia** /ˌamfɪsˈbiːnɪə/ • **pl. n.** Zoology a suborder of reptiles which comprises the worm lizards.
– DERIVATIVES **amphisbaenian** n. & adj.
– ORIGIN mod. L., from Gk *amphisbaina* (see **AMPHISBAENA**).

**amphitheatre** (US **amphitheater**) • **n.** a round building consisting of tiers of seats surrounding a central space for dramatic or sporting events. ➤ a semicircular seating gallery in a theatre.
– ORIGIN ME: via L. from Gk *amphitheatron*, from *amphi* 'on both sides' + *theatron* (see **THEATRE**).

**amphiuma** /ˌamfɪˈjuːmə/ • **n.** a fully aquatic eel-like amphibian of the south-eastern US. [Genus *Amphiuma*.]
– ORIGIN mod. L., prob. from **AMPHI-** + Gk *pneuma* 'breath'.

**amphora** /ˈamf(ə)rə/ • **n.** (pl. **amphorae** /-riː/ or **amphoras**) a tall ancient Greek or Roman jar or jug with two handles and a narrow neck.
– ORIGIN L., from Gk *amphoreus*, from **AMPHI-** + *phoreus* 'bearer' from *pherein* 'to bear'.

**amphoteric** /ˌamfəˈtɛrɪk/ • **adj.** Chemistry able to react both as a base and as an acid.
– ORIGIN C19: from Gk *amphoteros*, comp. of *amphō* 'both', + **-IC**.

**ampicillin** /ˌampɪˈsɪlɪn/ • **n.** Medicine a semi-synthetic form of penicillin used chiefly to treat respiratory and urinary infections.
– ORIGIN 1960s: blend of *amino* (see **AMINO GROUP**) and a contr. of **PENICILLIN**.

**ample** • **adj.** (**-er**, **-est**) enough or more than enough; plentiful. ➤ large and accommodating.
– DERIVATIVES **ampleness** n. **amply** adv.
– ORIGIN ME: via Fr. from L. *amplus* 'large, abundant'.

**amplexus** /amˈplɛksəs/ • **n.** Zoology the mating position of frogs and toads, in which the male clasps the female about the back.
– ORIGIN 1930s: from L., 'an embrace'.

**amplifier** • **n. 1** an electronic device for increasing the amplitude of electrical signals, used chiefly in sound reproduction. **2** a device of this kind combined with a loudspeaker, used to amplify electric guitars and other musical instruments.

**amplify** • **v.** (**-ies**, **-ied**) **1** increase the volume of (sound), especially using an amplifier. ➤ increase the amplitude of (an electrical signal or other oscillation). **2** add detail to (a story or statement). **3** Genetics make multiple copies of (a gene or DNA sequence).
– DERIVATIVES **amplification** n.
– ORIGIN ME: from OFr. *amplifier*, from L. *amplificare*, from *amplus* 'large, abundant'.

**amplitude** • **n. 1** Physics the maximum extent or magnitude of a vibration or other oscillating phenomenon, measured from the equilibrium position or average value. **2** breadth, range, or magnitude. **3** Astronomy the angular distance of a celestial object from the true east or west point of the horizon at rising or setting.
– ORIGIN C16: from L. *amplitudo*, from *amplus* 'large, abundant'.

**amplitude modulation** • **n.** the modulation of a wave by varying its amplitude, used especially as a means of broadcasting an audio signal by combining it with a radio carrier wave.

**ampoule** /ˈampuːl/ (US also **ampul** or **ampule** /ˈampjuːl/) • **n.** Medicine a small sealed glass capsule containing a measured quantity of liquid ready for injecting.
– ORIGIN C20: from Fr., from L. *ampulla* (see **AMPULLA**).

**ampulla** /amˈpʊlə/ • **n.** (pl. **ampullae** /-liː/) **1** a roughly spherical ancient Roman flask with two handles. ➤ a flask for holding consecrated oil. **2** Anatomy & Zoology a cavity or enclosure shaped like a Roman ampulla.
– ORIGIN ME: from L., dimin. of *ampora*, var. of *amphora* (see **AMPHORA**).

**amputate** /ˈampjʊteɪt/ • **v.** cut off (a limb) by surgical operation.
– DERIVATIVES **amputation** n. **amputator** n.
– ORIGIN C16: from L. *amputat-*, *amputare* 'lop off'.

**amputee** • **n.** a person who has had a limb amputated.

**AMRAAM** • **abbrev.** advanced medium range air-to-air missile.

**amrit** /ˈʌmrɪt/ (also **amrita** /ˈʌmriːta/) • **n.** a syrup considered divine by Sikhs and taken by them at baptism and in religious observances.
– ORIGIN from Sanskrit *amṛta* 'immortal'.

**AMT** • **abbrev.** US alternative minimum tax.

**amtrac** /ˈamtrak/ (also **amtrak**) • **n.** US an amphibious tracked vehicle used for landing assault troops on a shore.

**amu** • **abbrev.** atomic mass unit.

**amuck** /əˈmʌk/ • **adv.** variant spelling of **AMOK**.

**amulet** /ˈamjʊlɪt/ • **n.** an ornament or small piece of jewellery thought to give protection against evil or danger.
– ORIGIN C16: from L. *amuletum*, of unknown origin.

**amuse** • **v. 1** cause to laugh or smile. **2** entertain.
– DERIVATIVES **amused** adj. **amusedly** adv. **amusing** adj. **amusingly** adv.
– ORIGIN C15 (in the sense 'delude, deceive'): from OFr. *amuser* 'entertain, deceive', from *a-* (expressing causal effect) + *muser* 'stare stupidly'.

**amuse-gueule** /əˌmjuːzˈɡəːl, French amyzgœl/ • **n.** (pl. **amuse-gueules** or same) a small savoury item of food served as an appetizer.
– ORIGIN Fr., lit. 'amuse mouth'.

**amusement** • **n. 1** the state or experience of finding something funny. **2** the provision or enjoyment of entertainment. ➤ Brit. a game machine or other mechanical device for providing entertainment.

**amusement arcade** • **n.** Brit. an indoor area containing coin-operated game machines.

**amusement park** • **n.** a large outdoor area with fairground rides and other entertainments.

**amygdala** /əˈmɪɡdələ/ • **n.** (pl. **amygdalae** /əˈmɪɡdəliː/) Anatomy a roughly almond-shaped mass of grey matter deep inside each hemisphere of the brain, associated with the sense of smell.
– DERIVATIVES **amygdaloid** adj.
– ORIGIN ME: via L. from Gk *amugdalē* 'almond'.

**amygdale** /əˈmɪɡdeɪl/ • **n.** Geology a vesicle in an igneous rock, containing secondary minerals.
– DERIVATIVES **amygdaloidal** adj.
– ORIGIN C19: from Fr., from L. *amygdala* (see **AMYGDALA**).

**amygdalin** /əˈmɪɡd(ə)lɪn/ • **n.** Chemistry a bitter crystalline organic compound found in almonds and the stones of peaches, apricots, and other fruit.
– ORIGIN C19: from L. *amygdala* 'almond' + **-IN**[1].

**amyl** /ˈeɪmʌɪl, ˈamɪl/ • **n. 1** [as modifier] Chemistry of or denoting the straight-chain pentyl radical $-C_5H_{11}$. **2** informal short for **AMYL NITRITE**.
– ORIGIN C19: from L. *amylum* 'starch' + **-YL**.

**amylase** /ˈamɪleɪz/ • **n.** Biochemistry an enzyme, found chiefly in saliva and pancreatic fluid, that converts starch and glycogen into simple sugars.

**amyl nitrate** • **n.** Chemistry a colourless synthetic liquid used as an additive in diesel fuel to improve its ignition properties.

**amyl nitrite** • **n.** Chemistry a yellowish volatile synthetic liquid used medicinally as a vasodilator and sometimes inhaled for its stimulatory effects.

**amyloid** /ˈamɪlɔɪd/ • **n.** Medicine a starch-like protein which is deposited in the liver, kidneys, spleen, or other tissues in certain diseases.
– DERIVATIVES **amyloidosis** n.

**amylopectin** /ˌamɪləʊˈpɛktɪn/ • **n.** Biochemistry the non-crystallizable form of starch, consisting of branched polysaccharide chains.

**amylose** /ˈamɪləʊs/ • **n.** Biochemistry the crystallizable form of starch, consisting of long unbranched polysaccharide chains.

**amyotrophic lateral sclerosis** • **n.** a form of motor neuron disease.

**amyotrophy** /ˌamɪˈɒtrəfi/ • **n.** Medicine atrophy of muscular tissue.
– DERIVATIVES **amyotrophic** adj.
– ORIGIN C19: from **A-**[1] + Gk *mus*, *muo-* 'muscle' + Gk *trophē* 'nourishment'.

**Amytal** /ˈamɪt(ə)l/ ● **n.** trademark a barbiturate drug used as a sedative and a hypnotic.

**an** ● **det.** the form of the indefinite article (see **A**[1]) used before words beginning with a vowel sound.

**an-**[1] ● **prefix** variant spelling of **A-**[1] before a vowel (as in *anaemia*).

**an-**[2] ● **prefix** variant spelling of **AD-** assimilated before *n* (as in *annihilate, annotate*).

**an-**[3] ● **prefix** variant spelling of **ANA-** shortened before a vowel (as in *aneurysm*).

**-an** ● **suffix** **1** forming adjectives and nouns, especially from: ➤names of places: *Cuban.* ➤names of systems: *Anglican.* ➤names of zoological classes or orders: *crustacean.* ➤names of founders: *Lutheran.* **2** /an/ Chemistry forming names of organic compounds, chiefly polysaccharides: *dextran.*
– ORIGIN from L. *-anus, -ana, -anum.*

**ana-** (usu. **an-** before a vowel) ● **prefix** **1** up: *anabatic.* **2** back: *anamnesis.* **3** again: *anabiosis.*
– ORIGIN from Gk *ana* 'up'.

**-ana** ● **suffix** (forming plural nouns) denoting things associated with a person, place, or field of interest: *Victoriana.*
– ORIGIN from L., neut. pl. of *-anus*, adj. ending.

**Anabaptism** /ˌanəˈbaptɪz(ə)m/ ● **n.** the doctrine that baptism should only be administered to believing adults, held by a Protestant sect of the 16th century.
– DERIVATIVES **Anabaptist** n. & adj.
– ORIGIN C16: via eccles. L. from Gk *anabaptismos*, from *ana-* 'over again' + *baptismos* 'baptism'.

**anabatic** /ˌanəˈbatɪk/ ● **adj.** Meteorology (of a wind) caused by local upward motion of warm air.
– ORIGIN C20: from Gk *anabatikos*, from *anabatēs* 'a person who ascends'.

**anabiosis** /ˌanəbʌɪˈəʊsɪs/ ● **n.** Zoology a temporary state of suspended animation or greatly reduced metabolism.
– DERIVATIVES **anabiotic** /-ˈɒtɪk/ adj.
– ORIGIN C19: from Gk *anabiōsis*, from *anabioein* 'return to life'.

**anabolic steroid** ● **n.** any of a class of synthetic steroid hormones which are used medicinally to promote the growth of muscle and (illegally) to enhance performance in athletics and other sports.

**anabolism** /əˈnabəlɪz(ə)m/ ● **n.** Biochemistry the synthesis of complex molecules in living organisms from simpler ones together with the storage of energy.
– DERIVATIVES **anabolic** adj.
– ORIGIN C19: from Gk *anabolē* 'ascent', from *ana-* 'up' + *ballein* 'to throw'.

**anachronism** /əˈnakrəˌnɪz(ə)m/ ● **n.** **1** a thing appropriate to a period other than that in which it exists. **2** the attribution of something to a period to which it does not belong.
– DERIVATIVES **anachronic** /ˌanəˈkrɒnɪk/ adj. **anachronistic** adj. **anachronistically** adv.
– ORIGIN C17: from Gk *anakhronismos*, from *ana-* 'backwards' + *khronos* 'time'.

**anaclitic** /ˌanəˈklɪtɪk/ ● **adj.** Psychoanalysis relating to or characterized by a strong emotional dependence on another or others.
– ORIGIN 1920s: from Gk *anaklitos* 'for reclining'.

**anacoluthon** /ˌanəkəˈluːθɒn, -θ(ə)n/ ● **n.** (pl. **anacolutha** /-θə/) a construction in which the expected grammatical sequence is absent, for example *while in the garden, the door banged shut.*
– DERIVATIVES **anacoluthic** adj.
– ORIGIN C18: via late L. from Gk *anakolouthon*, from *an-* 'not' + *akolouthos* 'following'.

**anaconda** /ˌanəˈkɒndə/ ● **n.** a very large semiaquatic snake of the boa family, native to tropical South America. [*Eunectes murinus* and other species.]
– ORIGIN C18: alt. of L. *anacandaia* 'python', from Sinhalese *henakan̆dayā.*

**anacrusis** /ˌanəˈkruːsɪs/ ● **n.** (pl. **anacruses** /-siːz/) Prosody one or more unstressed syllables at the beginning of a verse.
– ORIGIN C19: mod. L., from Gk *anakrousis* 'prelude', from *ana-* 'up' + *krousis* 'striking'.

**anadromous** /əˈnadrəməs/ ● **adj.** Zoology (of a fish) migrating up rivers from the sea to spawn. The opposite of **CATADROMOUS.**
– ORIGIN C18: from Gk *anadromos* (from *ana-* 'up' + *dromos* 'running') + **-OUS.**

**anaemia** /əˈniːmɪə/ (US **anemia**) ● **n.** a condition in which there is a deficiency of red cells or haemoglobin in the blood, resulting in pallor and weariness.
– DERIVATIVES **anaemic** adj.
– ORIGIN C19: via mod. L. from Gk *anaimia*, from *an-* 'without' + *haima* 'blood'.

**anaerobe** /ˈanərəʊb, əˈnɛːrəʊb/ ● **n.** Biology an anaerobic micro-organism.

**anaerobic** ● **adj.** Biology relating to, involving, or requiring the absence of free oxygen.
– DERIVATIVES **anaerobically** adv.

**anaesthesia** /ˌanɪsˈθiːzɪə/ (US **anesthesia**) ● **n.** insensitivity to pain, especially as artificially induced by the administration of gases or drugs before a surgical operation.
– DERIVATIVES **anaesthesiologist** n. **anaesthesiology** n.
– ORIGIN C18: mod. L., from Gk *anaisthēsia*, from *an-* 'without' + *aisthēsis* 'sensation'.

**anaesthetic** /ˌanɪsˈθɛtɪk/ (US **anesthetic**) ● **n.** **1** a substance that induces insensitivity to pain. **2** (**anaesthetics**) [treated as sing.] the study or practice of anaesthesia. ● **adj.** inducing or relating to anaesthesia.

**anaesthetist** /əˈniːsθətɪst/ (US **anesthetist**) ● **n.** a medical specialist who administers anaesthetics.
– DERIVATIVES **anaesthetization** (also **-isation**) n. **anaesthetize** (also **-ise**) v.

**anagen** /ˈanədʒ(ə)n/ ● **n.** Physiology the growing phase of a hair follicle.
– ORIGIN 1920s: from **ANA-** + **-GEN.**

**anagenesis** /ˌanəˈdʒɛnɪsɪs/ ● **n.** Biology species formation without branching of the evolutionary line of descent.
– DERIVATIVES **anagenetic** adj.

**anaglyph** /ˈanəglɪf/ ● **n.** **1** a stereoscopic photograph having two images superimposed and printed in different colours, producing a stereo effect when viewed with appropriate filters over each eye. **2** an object, such as a cameo, embossed or carved in low relief.
– DERIVATIVES **anaglyphic** adj.
– ORIGIN C16: from Gk *anagluphē*, from *ana-* 'up' + *gluphein* 'carve'.

**anagram** /ˈanəgram/ ● **n.** a word, phrase, or name formed by rearranging the letters of another, such as *spar*, formed from *rasp.* ● **v.** (**anagrammed, anagramming**) make an anagram of.
– DERIVATIVES **anagrammatic** adj. **anagrammatical** adj. **anagrammatization** (also **-isation**) n. **anagrammatize** (also **-ise**) v.
– ORIGIN C16: from Fr. *anagramme* or mod. L. *anagramma*, from Gk *ana-* 'back, anew' + *gramma* 'letter'.

**anal** /ˈeɪn(ə)l/ ● **adj.** **1** of, relating to, or situated near the anus. **2** Psychoanalysis denoting a stage of infantile psychosexual development in which defecation is the major source of sensuous pleasure. ➤anal-retentive.
– DERIVATIVES **anally** adv.

**analects** /ˈanəlɛkts/ (also **analecta** /ˌanəˈlɛktə/) ● **pl. n.** a collection of short literary or philosophical extracts.
– ORIGIN ME: via L. from Gk *analekta* 'things gathered up', from *ana-* 'up' + *legein* 'gather'.

**analeptic** /ˌanəˈlɛptɪk/ Medicine ● **adj.** restorative, especially through stimulating the central nervous system. ● **n.** an analeptic drug.
– ORIGIN C16: via late L. from Gk *analēptikos.*

**anal fin** ● **n.** Zoology an unpaired fin located on the underside of a fish posterior to the anus.

**analgesia** /ˌan(ə)lˈdʒiːzɪə/ ● **n.** Medicine relief of pain through administration of drugs or other methods.
– ORIGIN C18: from Gk *analgēsia* 'painlessness', from *an-* 'not' + *algein* 'feel pain'.

**analgesic** /ˌan(ə)lˈdʒiːzɪk, -sɪk/ Medicine ● **adj.** acting to relieve pain. ● **n.** an analgesic drug.

**analogize** /əˈnalədʒʌɪz/ (also **-ise**) ● **v.** compare by analogy.

**analogous** /əˈnaləɡəs/ ● **adj. 1** comparable in certain respects. **2** Biology performing a similar function but having a different evolutionary origin, such as the wings of insects and birds. Often contrasted with **HOMOLOGOUS**.
– DERIVATIVES **analogously** adv.
– ORIGIN C17: via L. from Gk *analogos* 'proportionate' + **-OUS**.

**analogue** /ˈanəlɒɡ/ (US also **analog**) ● **n.** a person or thing seen as analogous to another. ● **adj.** (also **analog**) relating to or using information represented by a continuously variable physical quantity (such as spatial position, voltage, etc.) rather than digitally.
– ORIGIN C19: from Fr., from Gk *analogon*, neut. of *analogos* 'proportionate'.

**analogy** /əˈnalədʒi/ ● **n.** (pl. **-ies**) a comparison between one thing and another made for the purpose of explanation or clarification. ➤ the process of making such a comparison. ➤ a thing regarded as analogous to another; an analogue.
– DERIVATIVES **analogical** adj. **analogically** adv.
– ORIGIN ME: from Fr. *analogie*, L. *analogia* 'proportion', from Gk, from *analogos* 'proportionate'.

**analphabetic** ● **adj. 1** representing sounds by composite signs rather than by single letters or symbols. **2** completely illiterate.

**anal-retentive** ● **adj.** Psychoanalysis excessively orderly and fussy (supposedly owing to conflict over toilet-training in infancy).
– DERIVATIVES **anal retention** n. **anal retentiveness** n.

**anal-sadistic** ● **adj.** Psychoanalysis displaying abnormal aggressive and destructive tendencies supposedly caused by anal fixation.
– DERIVATIVES **anal-sadism** n.

**analysand** /əˈnalɪsand/ ● **n.** a person undergoing psychoanalysis.

**analyse** (US **analyze**) ● **v. 1** examine methodically and in detail the constitution or structure of. ➤ identify and measure the chemical constituents of. **2** psychoanalyse.
– DERIVATIVES **analysable** adj. **analyser** n.
– ORIGIN C16: influenced by Fr. *analyser*, from med. L. *analysis* (see **ANALYSIS**).

**analysis** /əˈnalɪsɪs/ ● **n.** (pl. **analyses** /-siːz/) **1** a detailed examination of the elements or structure of something. **2** the process of separating something into its constituent elements. Often contrasted with **SYNTHESIS**. ➤ the process of analysing the chemical constituents of a substance. **3** short for **PSYCHOANALYSIS**. **4** Mathematics the part of mathematics concerned with the theory of functions and the use of limits, continuity, and the operations of calculus.
– ORIGIN C16: via med. L. from Gk *analusis*, from *analuein* 'unloose'.

**analyst** ● **n. 1** a person who conducts analysis. **2** a psychoanalyst.

**analytic** ● **adj. 1** another term for **ANALYTICAL**. **2** Logic true by virtue of the meaning of the words or concepts used to express it, so that its denial would be a self-contradiction. Compare with **SYNTHETIC**. **3** Linguistics (of a language) tending to use word order to express grammatical structure. Contrasted with **SYNTHETIC**.
– ORIGIN C17: via L. from Gk *analutikos*, from *analuein* 'unloose'.

**analytical** ● **adj.** relating to or using analysis or logical reasoning.
– DERIVATIVES **analytically** adv.

**analytical geometry** ● **n.** geometry using coordinates.

**analytical philosophy** ● **n.** a method of approaching philosophical problems through analysis of the terms in which they are expressed.

**analytical psychology** ● **n.** the psychoanalytical system of psychology developed and practised by the Swiss psychologist Carl Jung (1875–1961).

**analyze** ● **v.** US spelling of **ANALYSE**.

**anamnesis** /ˌanəmˈniːsɪs/ ● **n.** (pl. **anamneses** /-siːz/) **1** recollection, especially of a supposed previous existence. **2** Christian Church the part of the Eucharist in which the Passion, Resurrection, and Ascension of Christ are recalled.
– ORIGIN C16: from Gk *anamnēsis*.

**anamnestic** /ˌanəmˈnɛstɪk/ ● **adj.** Medicine denoting an enhanced reaction of the body's immune system to an antigen related to one previously encountered.

**anamorphosis** /ˌanəˈmɔːfəsɪs/ ● **n.** a distorted image which appears normal when viewed from a particular point or with a suitable mirror or lens. ➤ the process by which such images are produced.
– DERIVATIVES **anamorphic** adj.
– ORIGIN C18: from Gk *anamorphōsis* 'transformation'.

**ananda** /ɑːˈnʌndə/ ● **n.** (in Hinduism, Buddhism, and Jainism) extreme happiness, as one of the highest states of being.
– ORIGIN from Sanskrit *ānanda*.

**Anangu** /ˈɑːnɑːŋuː/ ● **n.** (pl. same) Austral. an Aboriginal, especially one from central Australia.
– ORIGIN from an Aborig. word meaning 'person'.

**anapaest** /ˈanəpiːst, -pɛst/ (US **anapest**) ● **n.** Prosody a metrical foot consisting of two short or unstressed syllables followed by one long or stressed syllable.
– DERIVATIVES **anapaestic** /-ˈpiːstɪk, -ˈpɛstɪk/ adj.
– ORIGIN C16: via L. from Gk *anapaistos* 'reversed', from *ana-* 'back' + *paiein* 'strike' (because it is the reverse of a dactyl).

**anaphase** /ˈanəfeɪz/ ● **n.** Genetics the third stage of cell division, between metaphase and telophase, during which the chromosomes move away from one another to opposite poles of the spindle.

**anaphora** /əˈnaf(ə)rə/ ● **n. 1** Grammar the use of a word referring back to a word used earlier in a text or conversation, to avoid repetition, for example the pronouns *he, she, it*, and *they* and the verb *do* in *I like it and so do they.* Compare with **CATAPHORA**. **2** Rhetoric the repetition of a word or phrase at the beginning of successive clauses. **3** Christian Church the part of the Eucharist which contains the consecration, anamnesis, and communion.
– DERIVATIVES **anaphoric** /ˌanəˈfɒrɪk/ adj. **anaphorically** adv.
– ORIGIN C16: via L. from Gk, 'repetition', from *ana-* 'back' + *pherein* 'to bear'.

**anaphrodisiac** /əˌnafrəˈdɪzɪak/ Medicine ● **adj.** tending to reduce sexual desire. ● **n.** an anaphrodisiac drug.

**anaphylaxis** /ˌanəfɪˈlaksɪs/ ● **n.** Medicine an extreme allergic reaction to an antigen to which the body has become hypersensitive following an earlier exposure.
– DERIVATIVES **anaphylactic** adj.
– ORIGIN C20: mod. L., from Gk *ana-* 'again' + *phulaxis* 'guarding'.

**anaptyxis** /ˌanəpˈtɪksɪs/ ● **n.** Phonetics the insertion of a vowel between two consonants to aid pronunciation, as in *he went thataway.*
– DERIVATIVES **anaptyctic** adj.
– ORIGIN C19: mod. L., from Gk *anaptuxis* 'unfolding'.

**anarch** /ˈanɑːk/ poetic/literary ● **n.** an anarchist. ● **adj.** anarchic.
– ORIGIN C17: from Gk *anarkhos* (see **ANARCHY**).

**anarchic** ● **adj.** with no controlling rules or principles to give order.
– DERIVATIVES **anarchical** adj. **anarchically** adv.

**anarchism** ● **n.** belief in the abolition of all government and the organization of society on a voluntary, cooperative basis.
– DERIVATIVES **anarchist** n. & adj. **anarchistic** adj.
– ORIGIN C17: from Gk *anarkhos* (see **ANARCHY**) + **-ISM**; later influenced by Fr. *anarchisme*.

**anarchy** ● **n. 1** a state of disorder due to lack of government or control. **2** a society or political system founded on the principles of anarchism.
– ORIGIN C16: via med. L. from Gk *anarkhia*, from *anarkhos*, from *an-* 'without' + *arkhos* 'chief, ruler'.

**Anasazi** /ˌanəˈsɑːzi/ ● **n.** (pl. same or **Anasazis**) a member of an ancient American Indian people of the southwestern US.
– ORIGIN from Navajo, 'ancient one' or 'enemy ancestor'.

**anastigmat** /əˈnastɪɡmat/ ● **n.** an anastigmatic lens system.

**anastigmatic** /ˌanəstɪɡˈmatɪk/ ● **adj.** (of a lens system) constructed so that the astigmatism of each element is cancelled out.

**anastomose** /ə'nastəməʊz/ ● **v.** chiefly Medicine link or be linked by anastomosis.

**anastomosis** /əˌnastə'məʊsɪs/ ● **n.** (pl. **anastomoses** /-siːz/) technical a cross-connection between adjacent channels, tubes, fibres, or other parts of a network. ➤ Medicine a connection made surgically between adjacent blood vessels, parts of the intestine, or other channels of the body.
– DERIVATIVES **anastomotic** adj. & n.
– ORIGIN C16: mod. L., from Gk *anastomōsis*, from *anastomoun* 'provide with a mouth'.

**anastrophe** /ə'nastrəfi/ ● **n.** Rhetoric the inversion of the usual order of words or clauses.
– ORIGIN C16: from Gk *anastrophē* 'turning back'.

**anathema** /ə'naθəmə/ ● **n.** **1** something that one vehemently dislikes: *racism was anathema to her.* **2** a formal curse of the Church, excommunicating a person or denouncing a doctrine.
– ORIGIN C16: from eccles. L., from Gk *anathema* 'thing dedicated', (later) 'thing devoted to evil', from *anatithenai* 'to set up'.

**anathematize** /ə'naθəmətʌɪz/ (also **-ise**) ● **v.** curse; condemn.

**Anatolian** ● **n.** **1** a native or inhabitant of Anatolia in western Asia Minor. **2** an extinct group of ancient languages constituting a branch of the Indo-European language family. ● **adj.** of or relating to Anatolia.

**anatomize** (also **-ise**) ● **v.** **1** dissect (a body). **2** examine and analyse in detail.
– ORIGIN ME: from med. L. *anatomizare*, from *anatomia* (see **ANATOMY**).

**anatomy** ● **n.** (pl. **-ies**) **1** the branch of biology and medicine concerned with bodily structure, especially as revealed by dissection. ➤ the bodily structure of a person, animal, or plant. **2** a detailed examination: *the anatomy of change.* ➤ a complex structure.
– DERIVATIVES **anatomical** adj. **anatomically** adv. **anatomist** n.
– ORIGIN ME: from OFr. *anatomie* or late L. *anatomia*, from Gk, from *ana-* 'up' + *tomia* 'cutting'.

**anatto** ● **n.** variant spelling of **ANNATTO**.

**ANC** ● **abbrev.** African National Congress.

**-ance** ● **suffix** forming nouns: **1** denoting a quality or state: *perseverance.* **2** denoting an action: *utterance.*
– ORIGIN from Fr. *-ance*, from L. *-antia*, *-entia* (from pres. participial stems *-ant-*, *-ent-*).

**ancestor** ● **n.** a person, typically one more remote than a grandparent, from whom one is descended. ➤ something from which a later species or version has evolved.
– DERIVATIVES **ancestral** adj. **ancestrally** adv. **ancestress** n.
– ORIGIN ME: from OFr. *ancestre*, from L. *antecessor*, from *antecedere*, from *ante* 'before' + *cedere* 'go'.

**ancestry** ● **n.** (pl. **-ies**) a person's ancestors or ethnic descent.

**ancho** /'antʃəʊ/ ● **n.** a large aromatic variety of chilli, used in Mexican dishes.
– ORIGIN from Mex. Sp. (*chile*) *ancho*, 'wide (chilli)'.

**anchor** ● **n.** **1** a heavy object used to moor a ship to the sea bottom, typically having a metal shank with a pair of curved, barbed flukes. ➤ (**anchors**) Brit. informal the brakes of a car. **2** an anchorman or anchorwoman. ● **v.** **1** moor with an anchor. ➤ secure firmly in position. **2** present and coordinate (a television or radio programme).
– PHRASES **at anchor** moored with an anchor.
– ORIGIN OE *ancor*, *ancra*, via L. from Gk *ankura*; reinforced in ME by OFr. *ancre*.

**anchorage** ● **n.** **1** an area suitable for a ship to anchor at. ➤ the action or state of anchoring or being anchored. **2** historical an anchorite's dwelling place.

**anchor escapement** ● **n.** a form of escapement in clocks and watches in which the teeth of the crown- or balance-wheel act on the pallets by recoil.

**anchorite** /'aŋkərʌɪt/ ● **n.** historical a religious recluse.
– DERIVATIVES **anchoress** n. **anchoritic** adj.
– ORIGIN ME: from med. L. *anchorita*, from eccles. Gk *anakhōrētēs*, from *anakhōrein* 'retire'.

**anchorman** (or **anchorwoman**) ● **n.** (pl. **-men** or **-women**) **1** a person who presents and coordinates a live television or radio programme involving other contributors. **2** the member of a relay team who runs the last leg.

**anchoveta** /ˌantʃə(ʊ)'vɛtə/ ● **n.** an anchovy found off the Pacific coasts of South America. [*Engraulis ringens.*]
– ORIGIN 1940s: from Sp., dimin. of *anchova* (see **ANCHOVY**).

**anchovy** /'antʃəvi, an'tʃəʊvi/ ● **n.** (pl. **-ies**) a small shoaling fish of the herring family, an important food fish with a strong flavour. [Genus *Engraulis*: several species.]
– ORIGIN C16: from Sp. and Port. *anchova*.

**anchusa** /əŋ'kjuːzə, an'tʃuːzə/ ● **n.** a plant of the borage family with bright, typically blue, flowers. [Genus *Anchusa.*]
– ORIGIN via L. from Gk *ankhousa*.

**ancien régime** /ˌɒsiã reɪ'ʒiːm, French ɑ̃sjɛ̃ ʀeʒim/ ● **n.** (pl. **anciens régimes** pronunc. same) a political or social system that has been displaced by a more modern one. ➤ (**the Ancien Régime**) the political and social system in France before the Revolution of 1789.
– ORIGIN Fr., lit. 'old rule'.

**ancient**[1] ● **adj.** belonging to or originating in the very distant past. ➤ chiefly humorous very old. ● **n.** **1** archaic or humorous an old man. **2** (**the ancients**) the people of ancient times, especially the classical Greeks and Romans.
– PHRASES **the Ancient of Days** a biblical title for God.
– DERIVATIVES **anciently** adv. **ancientness** n.
– ORIGIN ME: from OFr. *ancien*, based on L. *ante* 'before'.

**ancient**[2] ● **n.** archaic a standard, flag, or ensign.
– ORIGIN C16: alt. of **ENSIGN** by assoc. with *ancien*, an early form of **ANCIENT**[1].

**ancient demesne** ● **n.** land recorded in Domesday Book as belonging to the Crown.

**ancient lights** ● **pl. n.** [treated as sing.] English Law the right of access to light of a property, established by custom and used to prevent the construction of buildings which would obstruct such access.

**ancient monument** ● **n.** Brit. an old building or site that is preserved by an official agency.

**ancillary** /an'sɪləri/ ● **adj.** providing support to the primary activities of an organization. ➤ additional; subsidiary. ● **n.** (pl. **-ies**) an ancillary person or thing.
– ORIGIN C17: from L. *ancillaris*, from *ancilla* 'maidservant'.

**ancon** /'aŋkɒn, -k(ə)n/ ● **n.** (pl. **ancones** /aŋ'kəʊniːz/) Architecture **1** a console, typically consisting of two volutes, that supports or appears to support a cornice. **2** each of a pair of projections on either side of a block of stone or other material, used for lifting it.
– ORIGIN C18: via L. from Gk *ankōn* 'bend, elbow'.

**Ancona** /ən'kəʊnə/ ● **n.** a chicken of a breed with black-and-white mottled plumage.
– ORIGIN C19: from the name of the port of *Ancona* in Italy.

**-ancy** ● **suffix** (forming nouns) denoting a quality or state: *expectancy.*
– ORIGIN from L. *-antia* (see also **-ENCY**).

**ancylostomiasis** /ˌaŋkɪlə(ʊ)stə(ʊ)'mʌɪəsɪs, ˌansɪ-/ (also **ankylostomiasis**) ● **n.** Medicine hookworm infection of the small intestine, often leading to anaemia.
– ORIGIN C19: from mod. L. *Ancylostoma* a genus of hookworms + **-IASIS**.

**AND** ● **abbrev.** Andorra (international vehicle registration).

**and** ● **conj.** **1** used to connect words of the same part of speech, clauses, or sentences. ➤ connecting two identical comparatives, to emphasize a progressive change. ➤ connecting two identical words, implying great duration or great extent. **2** used to connect two numbers to indicate that they are being added together. ➤ archaic connecting two numbers, implying succession. **3** used to introduce an additional comment or interjection. **4** informal used after some verbs and before another verb to indicate intention, instead of 'to'. ● **n.** (**AND**) **1** a logical operation which gives the value one if and only if all the operands

are one, and otherwise gives a value of zero. **2** [as modifier] Electronics denoting a gate circuit which produces an output only when signals are received simultaneously through all input connections.
– ORIGIN OE *and*, *ond*, of Gmc origin.

**-and** ● **suffix** (forming nouns) denoting a person or thing to be treated in a specified way: *analysand*.
– ORIGIN from L. gerundive ending *-andus*.

**Andalusian** /ˌandəˈluːzɪən, -sɪən/ ● **n. 1** a native or inhabitant of Andalusia in southern Spain. **2** the dialect of Spanish spoken in Andalusia. ● **adj.** relating to Andalusia.

**andalusite** /ˌandəˈluːsʌɪt/ ● **n.** a grey, green, brown, or pink aluminosilicate mineral occurring as elongated rhombic prisms.

**andante** /anˈdanteɪ/ Music ● **adv. & adj.** in a moderately slow tempo. ● **n.** an andante passage.
– ORIGIN Ital., lit. 'going', pres. part. of *andare*.

**andantino** /ˌandanˈtiːnəʊ/ ● **adv. & adj.** Music lighter than andante, and usually quicker.
– ORIGIN Ital., dimin. of **ANDANTE**.

**Andean** /anˈdiːən, ˈandɪən/ ● **adj.** of or relating to the Andes. ● **n.** a native or inhabitant of the Andes.

**Anderson shelter** ● **n.** an air-raid shelter of a type built in the UK during the Second World War.
– ORIGIN 1930s: named after Sir John *Anderson*, Home Secretary 1939–40.

**andesite** /ˈandɪzʌɪt, -sʌɪt/ ● **n.** Geology a dark, fine-grained volcanic rock.
– DERIVATIVES **andesitic** adj.
– ORIGIN C19: named after the *Andes* mountains.

**andiron** /ˈandʌɪən/ ● **n.** a metal support, typically one of a pair, for wood burning in a fireplace.
– ORIGIN ME: from OFr. *andier*.

**Andorran** /anˈdɔːrən/ ● **n.** a native or inhabitant of the small autonomous principality of Andorra in the southern Pyrenees. ● **adj.** of or relating to Andorra.

**andouille** /ɒ̃ˈduːj/ ● **n.** (in France) a pork sausage made from chitterlings. ➤(in Cajun cooking) a spicy smoked-pork sausage.
– ORIGIN from Fr.

**andradite** /ˈandrədʌɪt/ ● **n.** a mineral of the garnet group, containing calcium and iron and occurring as yellow, green, brown, or black crystals.
– ORIGIN C19: named after the Brazilian geologist J. B. de *Andrada* e Silva.

**andro-** ● **comb. form** of men; male: *androcentric*.
– ORIGIN from Gk *anēr*, *andr-* 'man'.

**androcentric** /ˌandrə(ʊ)ˈsɛntrɪk/ ● **adj.** focused or centred on men.

**androcracy** /anˈdrɒkrəsi/ ● **n.** (pl. **-ies**) a social system ruled or dominated by men.
– DERIVATIVES **androcratic** adj.

**androecium** /anˈdriːsɪəm/ ● **n.** (pl. **androecia** /-sɪə/) Botany the stamens of a flower collectively.
– ORIGIN C19: mod. L., from **ANDRO-** + *oikion* 'house'.

**androgen** /ˈandrədʒ(ə)n/ ● **n.** Biochemistry a male sex hormone, such as testosterone.
– DERIVATIVES **androgenic** adj.
– ORIGIN 1930s: from Gk *anēr*, *andr-* 'man' + **-GEN**.

**androgenize** /anˈdrɒdʒənʌɪz/ (also **-ise**) ● **v.** treat with or expose to male sex hormones.
– DERIVATIVES **androgenization** n.

**androgyne** /ˈandrədʒʌɪn/ ● **n.** an androgynous individual. ➤a hermaphrodite.

**androgynous** /anˈdrɒdʒɪnəs/ ● **adj.** partly male and partly female in appearance; of indeterminate sex. ➤hermaphrodite.
– DERIVATIVES **androgyny** n.
– ORIGIN C17 (earlier (C16) as *androgyne*): via L. *androgynus* from Gk *androgunos* (from *anēr*, *andr-* 'man' + *gunē* 'woman') + **-OUS**.

**android** /ˈandrɔɪd/ ● **n.** (in science fiction) a robot with a human appearance.

**andromeda** /anˈdrɒmɪdə/ ● **n.** another term for **BOG ROSEMARY**.
– ORIGIN mod. L (genus name), named after the princess *Andromeda* in Gk mythology.

**andropause** ● **n.** the occurrence in some older men of a collection of symptoms such as fatigue and loss of libido, attributed to lower testosterone levels.
– ORIGIN 1990s: from **ANDRO-**, on the pattern of **MENOPAUSE**.

**androstenedione** /ˌandrɒstiːnˈdaɪəʊn/ ● **n.** Biochemistry a compound from which testosterone and certain oestrogens are produced in humans.
– ORIGIN 1930s: from **ANDROSTERONE** + **-ENE** + **DI-**[1] + **-ONE**.

**androsterone** /ˌandrə(ʊ)ˈstɪərəʊn, anˈdrɒstərəʊn/ ● **n.** Biochemistry a relatively inactive male sex hormone produced by metabolism of testosterone.

**-androus** ● **comb. form** Botany having male organs or stamens of a specified number: *polyandrous*.
– ORIGIN from mod. L. *-andrus* from Gk *-andros* 'male' + **-OUS**.

**-ane**[1] ● **suffix** variant spelling of **-AN**, often with a distinction of sense (such as *humane* compared with *human*).

**-ane**[2] ● **suffix** Chemistry forming names of saturated hydrocarbons: *propane*.

**anecdotage** /ˈanɪkdəʊtɪdʒ/ ● **n. 1** anecdotes collectively. **2** humorous old age in someone who is garrulous.

**anecdote** /ˈanɪkdəʊt/ ● **n.** a short entertaining story about a real incident or person. ➤an account regarded as unreliable or as being hearsay.
– DERIVATIVES **anecdotal** adj. **anecdotalist** n. **anecdotally** adv.
– ORIGIN C17: from Fr., or via mod. L. from Gk *anekdota* 'things unpublished'.

**anechoic** /ˌanɪˈkəʊɪk/ ● **adj.** technical free from echo; tending to absorb or deaden sound.

**anele** /əˈniːl/ ● **v.** archaic anoint, especially as part of the Christian rite of extreme unction.
– ORIGIN ME: from *an-* 'on' + archaic *elien* 'to oil'.

**anemia** ● **n.** US spelling of **ANAEMIA**.

**anemic** ● **adj.** US spelling of ***anaemic*** (see **ANAEMIA**).

**anemograph** /əˈnɛməgrɑːf/ ● **n.** an anemometer which records the speed, duration, and sometimes also the direction of the wind.

**anemometer** /ˌanɪˈmɒmɪtə/ ● **n.** an instrument for measuring the speed of the wind or other flowing gas.
– DERIVATIVES **anemometric** adj. **anemometry** n.
– ORIGIN C18: from Gk *anemos* 'wind' + **-METER**.

**anemone** /əˈnɛməni/ ● **n. 1** a plant of the buttercup family, which typically has brightly coloured flowers and deeply divided leaves. [Genus *Anemone*: numerous species.] **2** short for **SEA ANEMONE**.
– ORIGIN C16: from L., said to be from Gk *anemōnē* 'wind-flower', appar. because the flowers open only when the wind blows.

**anemone fish** ● **n.** another term for **CLOWNFISH**.

**anemophilous** /ˌanɪˈmɒfɪləs/ ● **adj.** Botany pollinated by the wind.
– DERIVATIVES **anemophily** n.
– ORIGIN C19: from Gk *anemos* 'wind' + *-philous* (see **-PHILIA**).

**anencephalic** /ˌanɛnsɪˈfalɪk, -kɛˈfalɪk/ ● **adj.** Medicine having part or all of the cerebral hemispheres and the rear of the skull congenitally absent.
– DERIVATIVES **anencephaly** n.
– ORIGIN C19: from Gk *anenkephalos* 'without brain' + **-IC**.

**anent** /əˈnɛnt/ ● **prep.** archaic or Scottish concerning; about.
– ORIGIN OE *on efen* 'in line with, in company with'.

**-aneous** ● **suffix** forming adjectives from Latin words: *spontaneous*.
– ORIGIN from the L. suffix *-aneus* + **-OUS**.

**anergia** /aˈnəːdʒɪə/ ● **n.** Psychiatry abnormal lack of energy.
– ORIGIN C19: mod. L., from Gk *an-* 'without' + *ergon* 'work'.

**anergy** /ˈanədʒi/ ● **n.** Medicine absence of the normal immune response to a particular antigen or allergen.
– ORIGIN C20: from Ger. *Anergie*, from Gk *an-* 'not', on the pattern of *Allergie* 'allergy'.

**aneroid** /ˈanərɔɪd/ ● **adj.** relating to or denoting a barometer that measures air pressure by the action of the

air in deforming the elastic lid of an evacuated box.
– ORIGIN C19: coined in Fr. from Gk *a-* 'without' + *nēros* 'water'.

**anesthesia** etc. ● n. US spelling of **ANAESTHESIA** etc.

**aneurysm** /ˈanjʊrɪz(ə)m/ (also **aneurism**) ● n. Medicine an excessive localized swelling of the wall of an artery.
– DERIVATIVES **aneurysmal** adj.
– ORIGIN ME: from Gk *aneurusma* 'dilatation'.

**anew** ● adv. chiefly poetic/literary in a new or different way. ➤ once more; again.

**anfractuous** /ənˈfraktjʊəs/ ● adj. sinuous or circuitous.
– DERIVATIVES **anfractuosity** n.
– ORIGIN C16: from late L. *anfractuosus*.

**angel** ● n. **1** a spiritual being believed to act as an attendant or messenger of God, conventionally represented as being of human form with wings. **2** a person of great beauty, kindness, or virtue. **3** informal (especially in the theatre) a financial backer. **4** (**angels**) aviation slang used with a numeral to indicate an aircraft's altitude in thousands of feet: *we rendezvous at angels nine.* **5** a former English coin bearing the figure of the archangel Michael killing a dragon. **6** informal an unexplained radar signal.
– PHRASES **on the side of the angels** on the side of what is right.
– ORIGIN OE *engel*, ult. via eccles. L. from Gk *angelos* 'messenger'.

**angel cake** (N. Amer. also **angel food cake**) ● n. a very light, pale sponge cake typically baked in a ring shape and covered with soft icing.

**angel dust** ● n. informal **1** the hallucinogenic drug phencyclidine hydrochloride. **2** another term for **CLENBUTEROL**.

**Angeleno** /ˌandʒəˈliːnəʊ/ (also **Los Angeleno**, **Angelino**) ● n. (pl. **-os**) a native or inhabitant of Los Angeles.
– ORIGIN C19: from Amer. Sp.

**angelfish** ● n. (pl. same or **-fishes**) a fish with a deep, laterally compressed body and large dorsal and anal fins, often vividly coloured or patterned. [*Pterophyllum scalare* (Amazon basin) and other species.]

**angel hair** ● n. a type of pasta consisting of very fine long strands.

**angelic** ● adj. **1** of or relating to angels. **2** exceptionally beautiful, innocent, or kind.
– DERIVATIVES **angelical** adj. **angelically** adv.

**angelica** /anˈdʒɛlɪkə/ ● n. a tall aromatic plant of the parsley family, the candied stalks of which are used in confectionery and cake decoration. [Genus *Angelica*: many species.]
– ORIGIN C16: from med. L. (*herba*) *angelica* 'angelic (herb)', so named because it was believed to be efficacious against poisoning and disease.

**angelica tree** ● n. a tree of the ginseng family, with large leaves and black berries. [Genus *Aralia*: several species.]

**Angelino** ● n. variant spelling of **ANGELENO**.

**Angelman's syndrome** ● n. a rare congenital disorder characterized by mental retardation and a tendency to jerky movement.
– ORIGIN 1970s: named after the Brit. doctor Harold *Angelman*.

**angelology** ● n. theological doctrine concerning angels.

**angel shark** ● n. a large, active bottom-dwelling cartilaginous fish with broad wing-like pectoral fins. [*Squatina squatina* and other species.]

**angels on horseback** ● pl. n. Brit. an appetizer consisting of oysters individually wrapped in bacon and served on toast.

**angel's trumpet** ● n. a South American shrub or small tree with large pendulous trumpet-shaped flowers. [Genus *Brugmansia*.]

**angelus** /ˈandʒ(ə)ləs/ ● n. a Roman Catholic devotion commemorating the Incarnation of Jesus and including the Hail Mary. ➤ a ringing of bells announcing this.
– ORIGIN C17: from the L. phr. *Angelus domini* 'the angel of the Lord', the opening words of the devotion.

**angel wings** ● pl. n. [treated as sing.] a large white edible piddock (mollusc) found in the Caribbean and on the east coast of North America. [*Barnea costata*.]

**anger** ● n. a strong feeling of annoyance, displeasure, or hostility. ● v. provoke anger in.
– ORIGIN ME: from ON *angr* 'grief', *angra* 'vex'.

**Angevin** /ˈandʒəvɪn/ ● n. **1** a native, inhabitant, or ruler of Anjou in western France. **2** any of the Plantagenet kings of England, especially those who were also counts of Anjou (Henry II, Richard I, and John).
– ORIGIN from Fr., meaning 'of Angers' (the former capital of Anjou).

**angina** /anˈdʒʌɪnə/ ● n. Medicine **1** (also **angina pectoris** /ˈpɛkt(ə)rɪs/) a condition marked by severe pain in the chest, arising from an inadequate blood supply to the heart. **2** used in names of disorders involving pain in the throat: *Ludwig's angina*.
– ORIGIN C16: from L., 'quinsy', from Gk *ankhonē* 'strangling'; *pectoris* means 'of the chest'.

**angio-** ● comb. form **1** relating to blood vessels: *angiography*. **2** relating to seed vessels: *angiosperm*.
– ORIGIN from Gk *angeion* 'vessel'.

**angiogenesis** ● n. Physiology the development of new blood vessels.

**angiogram** /ˈandʒɪə(ʊ)gram/ ● n. an X-ray photograph of blood or lymph vessels, made by angiography.

**angiography** /ˌandʒɪˈɒgrəfi/ ● n. radiography of blood or lymph vessels, carried out after introduction of a radiopaque substance.
– DERIVATIVES **angiographic** adj. **angiographically** adv.

**angioma** /ˌandʒɪˈəʊmə/ ● n. (pl. **angiomas** or **angiomata** /-mətə/) Medicine an abnormal growth produced by the dilatation or new formation of blood vessels.

**angioneurotic** ● adj. Medicine (of oedema) marked by swelling and itching of areas of skin.

**angioplasty** /ˈandʒɪə(ʊ)ˌplasti/ ● n. (pl. **-ies**) Medicine surgical repair or unblocking of a blood vessel, especially a coronary artery.

**angiosperm** ● n. Botany a plant of a large group (subdivision Angiospermae) that comprises those that have flowers and produce seeds enclosed within a carpel, including herbaceous plants, shrubs, grasses, and most trees. Compare with **GYMNOSPERM**.
– DERIVATIVES **angiospermous** /-ˈspəːməs/ adj.

**angiotensin** /ˌandʒɪə(ʊ)ˈtɛnsɪn/ ● n. Biochemistry a protein whose presence in the blood promotes aldosterone secretion and tends to lead to hypertension.

**Angle** ● n. a member of an ancient Germanic people that founded English kingdoms in Mercia, Northumbria, and East Anglia.
– ORIGIN from L. *Anglus* 'inhabitant of *Angul*' (in northern Germany); rel. to **ANGLE**[2], **ENGLISH**.

**angle**[1] ● n. **1** the space (usually measured in degrees) between two intersecting lines or surfaces at or close to the point where they meet. ➤ a corner, especially an external projection or internal recess. ➤ a measure of the inclination of one line or surface with respect to another. **2** a position from which something is viewed or along which it travels or acts. ➤ a particular way of approaching an issue or problem. **3** Astrology each of the four cardinal points of a chart. **4** angle iron or a similar constructional material. ● v. **1** direct, move, or incline at an angle. **2** present (information) to reflect a particular view or have a particular focus.
– DERIVATIVES **angled** adj.
– ORIGIN ME: from OFr., from L. *angulus* 'corner'.

**angle**[2] ● v. **1** [often as noun **angling**] fish with a rod and line. **2** seek something desired by indirectly prompting someone to offer it: *she was angling for sympathy.* ● n. archaic a fish hook.
– DERIVATIVES **angler** n.
– ORIGIN OE *angul* (n.).

**angle bead** ● n. a strip of metal or wood fixed to an external corner before it is plastered to reinforce it.

**angle bracket** ● n. **1** either of a pair of marks in the form < >, used to enclose words or figures so as to separate them from their context. **2** another term for **BRACKET**

(in sense 3).

**angle grinder** ● **n.** a device with a rotating abrasive disc, used to grind, polish, or cut metal and other materials.

**angle iron** ● **n.** a constructional material consisting of pieces of iron or steel with an L-shaped cross section, able to be bolted together.

**angle of attack** ● **n.** Aeronautics the angle between the line of the chord of an aerofoil and the relative airflow.

**angle of incidence** ● **n.** Physics the angle which an incident line or ray makes with a perpendicular to the surface at the point of incidence.

**angle of reflection** ● **n.** Physics the angle made by a reflected ray with a perpendicular to the reflecting surface.

**angle of refraction** ● **n.** Physics the angle made by a refracted ray with a perpendicular to the refracting surface.

**angle of repose** ● **n.** the steepest angle at which a sloping surface formed of loose material is stable.

**anglerfish** ● **n.** (pl. same or **-fishes**) a marine fish that lures prey within reach of its mouth with a fleshy lobe on a filament arising from its snout. [*Lophius piscatorius* and many other species.]

**angle shades** ● **pl. n.** [treated as sing.] a moth with wings patterned in muted green, red, and pink. [*Phlogophora meticulosa*.]

**angle wings** ● **pl. n.** [treated as sing.] a North American butterfly that is related to and resembles the comma. [Genus *Polygonia*: several species.]

**Anglian** /ˈaŋglɪən/ ● **adj.** of or relating to the ancient Angles.

**Anglican** ● **adj.** relating to or denoting the Church of England or any Church in communion with it. ● **n.** a member of any of these Churches.
– DERIVATIVES **Anglicanism** n.
– ORIGIN C17: from med. L. *Anglicanus*, from L. *Anglus* 'Angle'.

**Anglican chant** ● **n.** a method of singing unmetrical psalms and canticles to short harmonized melodies, the first note being extended to accommodate as many syllables as necessary.

**Anglican communion** ● **n.** the group of Christian Churches derived from or related to the Church of England.

**anglice** /ˈaŋglɪsi/ ● **adv.** formal in English.
– ORIGIN from med. L., from L. *Anglus* 'Angle'.

**Anglicism** ● **n. 1** a word or phrase that is peculiar to British English. **2** the quality of being typically English or of favouring English things.

**anglicize** (also **-ise**) ● **v.** [often as adj. **anglicized**] make English in form or character.
– DERIVATIVES **anglicization** n.

**Anglo** ● **n.** (pl. **Anglos**) **1** a white English-speaking person, especially one of British or (US) non-Hispanic origin. **2** Brit. informal a person selected for a Scottish, Irish, or Welsh national sports team who plays for an English club.

**Anglo-** ● **comb. form** English: *anglophone*. ➤of English origin: *Anglo-Saxon*. ➤English and ...: *Anglo-Latin*. ➤British and ...: *Anglo-Indian*.
– ORIGIN mod. L., from L. *Anglus* 'English'.

**Anglo-Catholicism** ● **n.** a tradition within the Anglican Church which is close to Catholicism in its doctrine and worship and is broadly identified with High Church Anglicanism.
– DERIVATIVES **Anglo-Catholic** adj. & n.

**Anglo-Celt** ● **n.** a person of British or Irish descent.
– DERIVATIVES **Anglo-Celtic** adj.

**Anglocentric** ● **adj.** centred on or considered in terms of England or Britain.

**Anglo-Indian** ● **adj.** relating to or involving both Britain and India. ➤of mixed British and Indian parentage. ➤chiefly historical of British descent or birth but having lived long in India. ● **n.** an Anglo-Indian person.

**Anglo-Irish** ● **adj.** of or relating to both Britain and Ireland (or specifically the Republic of Ireland). ➤of English descent but born or resident in Ireland. ➤of mixed English and Irish parentage.

**Anglo-Latin** ● **n.** Latin as used in medieval England.

**Anglomania** ● **n.** excessive admiration of English customs.
– DERIVATIVES **Anglomaniac** n.

**Anglo-Norman French** ● **n.** the variety of Norman French used in England after the Norman Conquest.

**Anglo-Nubian** ● **n.** a goat of a breed with a short glossy coat and lop ears, kept for its rich milk.

**Anglophile** ● **n.** a person who is fond of or greatly admires England or Britain.
– DERIVATIVES **Anglophilia** n.

**Anglophobe** ● **n.** a person who hates or fears England or Britain.
– DERIVATIVES **Anglophobia** n.

**anglophone** ● **adj.** English-speaking. ● **n.** an English-speaking person.

**Anglo-Saxon** ● **n. 1** a Germanic inhabitant of England between the 5th century and the Norman Conquest. ➤a person of English descent. ➤chiefly N. Amer. any white, English-speaking person. **2** the Old English language. ➤informal plain English, in particular vulgar slang.

**Angolan** /aŋˈgəʊlən/ ● **n.** a native or inhabitant of Angola, a country in SW Africa. ● **adj.** of or relating to Angola.

**angora** /aŋˈgɔːrə/ ● **n. 1** a cat, goat, or rabbit of a long-haired breed. **2** a fabric made from the hair of the angora goat or rabbit.
– ORIGIN C19: from *Angora* (now Ankara) in Turkey.

**angora wool** ● **n.** a mixture of sheep's wool and angora rabbit hair.

**angostura** /ˌaŋgəˈstjʊərə/ ● **n. 1** an aromatic bitter bark from South America, used as a flavouring. **2** (also **Angostura bitters** trademark) a kind of tonic.
– ORIGIN C18: from *Angostura* (now Ciudad Bolívar) in Venezuela.

**angry** ● **adj.** (**-ier, -iest**) **1** feeling or showing anger. **2** (of a wound or sore) red and inflamed.
– DERIVATIVES **angrily** adv.

**angst** /aŋst/ ● **n.** a profound feeling of generalized anxiety or dread.
– DERIVATIVES **angsty** adj.
– ORIGIN 1920s: from Ger., 'fear'.

**angstrom** /ˈaŋstrəm/ (also **ångström** /ˈɒŋstrəːm/) (abbrev.: **Å**) ● **n.** Physics a unit of length equal to one hundred-millionth of a centimetre, $10^{-10}$ metre.
– ORIGIN C19: named after the Swed. physicist A. J. *Ångström*.

**Anguillan** /aŋˈgwɪlən/ ● **n.** a native or inhabitant of Anguilla, an island in the Leeward Islands. ● **adj.** of or relating to Anguilla.

**anguilliform** /aŋˈgwɪlɪfɔːm/ ● **adj.** Zoology relating to or denoting eels or related fish.
– ORIGIN C17: from L. *anguilla* 'eel' + **-IFORM**.

**anguish** ● **n.** severe mental or physical pain or suffering.
– ORIGIN ME: via OFr. from L. *angustia* 'tightness', (pl.) 'straits, distress', from *angustus* 'narrow'.

**anguished** ● **adj.** experiencing or expressing anguish.
– ORIGIN C17: past part. of rare v. *anguish*, from OFr. *anguissier*, from eccles. L. *angustiare*, from L. *angustia* (see **ANGUISH**).

**angular** /ˈaŋgjʊlə/ ● **adj.** having angles or sharp corners. ➤(of a person) lean and having a prominent bone structure. ➤placed or directed at an angle. ➤Physics measured with reference to angles, especially those associated with rotation: *angular momentum*.
– DERIVATIVES **angularity** n. **angularly** adv.
– ORIGIN ME: from L. *angularis*, from *angulus* (see **ANGLE[1]**).

**angulate** /ˈaŋgjʊleɪt/ ● **v.** technical hold or bend (a part of the body) so as to form an angle or angles. ➤Skiing incline (the upper body) sideways and outwards during a turn.
– DERIVATIVES **angulation** n.
– ORIGIN C15: from L. *angulat-*, *angulare*, from *angulus* 'angle'.

**Angus** /ˈaŋgəs/ ● **n.** short for **ABERDEEN ANGUS**.

**angwantibo** /əŋˈgwɒntɪbəʊ/ ● **n.** (pl. **-os**) a small rare nocturnal primate of west central Africa, related to the potto. [*Arctocebus calabarensis*.]
– ORIGIN C19: from Efik.

**anharmonic** ● **adj.** Physics relating to or denoting motion that is not simple harmonic.
– DERIVATIVES **anharmonicity** n.

**anhedonia** /ˌanhɪˈdəʊnɪə/ ● **n.** Psychiatry inability to feel pleasure in normally pleasurable activities.
– DERIVATIVES **anhedonic** adj.
– ORIGIN C19: from Fr. *anhédonie*, from Gk *an-* 'without' + *hēdonē* 'pleasure'.

**anhedral** /anˈhiːdr(ə)l, -ˈhɛd-/ ● **adj.** chiefly Geology (of a crystal) having no plane faces. ● **n.** Aeronautics downward inclination of an aircraft's wing.
– ORIGIN C19: from **AN-**[1] + *-hedral* (see **-HEDRON**).

**anhinga** /anˈhɪŋgə/ ● **n.** chiefly N. Amer. another term for **DARTER** (in sense 1).
– ORIGIN C18: from Port., from Tupi *áyinga*.

**anhydride** /anˈhʌɪdrʌɪd/ ● **n.** Chemistry a compound obtained by removing the elements of water from a particular acid: *acetic anhydride*.
– ORIGIN C19: from Gk *anudros* (see **ANHYDROUS**) + **-IDE**.

**anhydrite** /anˈhʌɪdrʌɪt/ ● **n.** a white mineral consisting of anhydrous calcium sulphate.
– ORIGIN C19: from Gk *anudros* (see **ANHYDROUS**) + **-ITE**[1].

**anhydrous** /anˈhʌɪdrəs/ ● **adj.** Chemistry containing no water.
– ORIGIN C19: from Gk *anudros* (from *an-* 'without' + *hudōr* 'water') + **-OUS**.

**ani** /ˈɑːni/ ● **n.** (pl. **anis**) a glossy black long-tailed bird of the cuckoo family found in Central and South America. [Genus *Crotophaga*: three species.]
– ORIGIN C19: from Sp. *ani*, Port. *anum*, from Tupi *anū*.

**aniline** /ˈanɪliːn, -lɪn/ ● **n.** Chemistry a colourless oily liquid present in coal tar, used in the manufacture of dyes, drugs, and plastics.
– ORIGIN C19: from *anil* 'indigo' (from which it was orig. obtained), via Fr. and Port. from Arab. *an-nīl*.

**anilingus** /ˌeɪnɪˈlɪŋgəs/ ● **n.** sexual stimulation of the anus by the tongue or mouth.
– ORIGIN 1960s: on the pattern of *cunnilingus*.

**anima** /ˈanɪmə/ ● **n.** Psychoanalysis **1** (in Jungian psychology) the feminine part of a man's personality. Compare with **ANIMUS**. **2** the part of the psyche which is directed inwards, in touch with the subconscious. Compare with **PERSONA**.
– ORIGIN 1920s: from L., 'mind, soul'.

**animadvert** /ˌanɪmədˈvəːt/ ● **v.** (**animadvert on/upon/against**) formal criticize or censure.
– DERIVATIVES **animadversion** n.
– ORIGIN ME (in the sense 'pay attention to'): from L. *animadvertere*, from *animus* 'mind' + *advertere* 'to turn'.

**animal** ● **n. 1** a living organism which is typically distinguished from a plant by feeding on organic matter, having specialized sense organs and nervous system, and being able to move about and to respond rapidly to stimuli. ➤a mammal, as opposed to a bird, reptile, fish, or insect. **2** a very cruel, violent, or uncivilized person. **3** [as modifier] of the flesh rather than the spirit or intellect: *animal lust*. **4** a particular type of person or thing: *a political animal*. ● **adj.** Biology denoting the pole or extremity of an embryo containing the more active cytoplasm. The opposite of **VEGETAL**.
– DERIVATIVES **animalization** (also **-isation**) n. **animalize** (also **-ise**) v.
– ORIGIN ME: from L. *animal*, based on *animalis* 'having breath' from *anima* 'breath'.

**animalcule** /ˌanɪˈmalkjuːl/ ● **n.** archaic a microscopic animal.
– DERIVATIVES **animalcular** adj.

**animalism** ● **n. 1** behaviour characteristic of animals; animality. **2** religious worship of or concerning animals.
– DERIVATIVES **animalistic** adj.

**animalist** ● **n.** an animal liberationist.

**animality** ● **n.** behaviour or nature characteristic of animals, especially in being physical and instinctive.

**animal liberation** ● **n.** the freeing of animals from exploitation and cruel treatment by humans.
– DERIVATIVES **animal liberationist** n.

**animal magnetism** ● **n. 1** a quality of powerful sexual attractiveness. **2** historical a supposed emanation to which the action of mesmerism was ascribed.

**animal spirits** ● **pl. n.** natural exuberance.

**animate** ● **v.** /ˈanɪmeɪt/ **1** bring to life or activity. **2** give (a film or character) the appearance of movement using animation techniques. ● **adj.** /ˈanɪmət/ alive; having life.
– DERIVATIVES **animator** n.
– ORIGIN ME: from L. *animat-*, *animare*, from *anima* 'life, soul'.

**animated** ● **adj. 1** lively. **2** (of a film) made using animation techniques.
– DERIVATIVES **animatedly** adv.

**animated stick** ● **n.** a stick insect of eastern Australia, sometimes reaching 25 cm in length. [*Acrophylla titan*.]

**animateur** /ˌanɪməˈtəː/ ● **n.** a person who promotes or encourages something, especially artistic projects.
– ORIGIN 1950s: Fr., from med. L. *animator*.

**animation** ● **n. 1** the state of being full of life or vigour. ➤chiefly archaic the state of being alive. **2** the technique of filming successive drawings, or positions of models, to create a film giving an illusion of movement. ➤(also **computer animation**) the manipulation of electronic images by means of a computer to create moving images.

**animato** /ˌanɪˈmɑːtəʊ/ ● **adv. & adj.** Music in an animated manner.
– ORIGIN from Ital.

**animatronics** /ˌanɪməˈtrɒnɪks/ ● **pl. n.** [treated as sing.] the technique of making and operating lifelike robots, especially for use in films.
– DERIVATIVES **animatronic** adj.

**anime** /ˈanɪmeɪ, ˈanɪmə/ ● **n.** Japanese film and television animation, typically having a science fiction theme.
– ORIGIN 1980s: Japanese.

**animism** /ˈanɪmɪz(ə)m/ ● **n. 1** the attribution of a living soul to plants, inanimate objects, and natural phenomena. **2** belief in a supernatural power that organizes and animates the material universe.
– DERIVATIVES **animist** n. **animistic** adj.
– ORIGIN C19: from L. *anima* 'life, soul' + **-ISM**.

**animosity** /ˌanɪˈmɒsɪti/ ● **n.** (pl. **-ies**) strong hostility.
– ORIGIN ME (in the sense 'spirit, courage'): from OFr. *animosite* or late L. *animositas*, from *animosus* 'spirited', from L. *animus* 'spirit, mind'.

**animus** /ˈanɪməs/ ● **n. 1** hostility or ill feeling. **2** motivation to do something. **3** Psychoanalysis (in Jungian psychology) the masculine part of a woman's personality. Compare with **ANIMA**.
– ORIGIN C19: from L., 'spirit, mind'.

**anion** /ˈanʌɪən/ ● **n.** Chemistry a negatively charged ion. The opposite of **CATION**.
– DERIVATIVES **anionic** adj.
– ORIGIN C19: from **ANODE** or **ANA-**, + **ION**.

**anise** /ˈanɪs/ ● **n. 1** a Mediterranean plant of the parsley family, cultivated for its aromatic seeds (aniseed). [*Pimpinella anisum*.] **2** used in names of Asian or American trees or shrubs bearing fruit with an aniseed-like odour, e.g. **star anise**. [Genus *Illicium*.]
– ORIGIN ME: via OFr. from L. *anisum*, from Gk *anison* 'anise, dill'.

**anise cap** ● **n.** a pale greenish mushroom which has a funnel-shaped cap and smells strongly of aniseed. [*Clitocybe odora*.]

**aniseed** ● **n.** the seed of the anise, used as a flavouring and in herbal medicine.

**anisette** /ˌanɪˈzɛt/ ● **n.** a liqueur flavoured with aniseed.
– ORIGIN C19: from Fr., dimin. of *anis* 'anise'.

**anisogamy** /ˌanʌɪˈsɒgəmi/ ● **n.** Biology sexual reproduction by the fusion of dissimilar gametes. Compare with **ISOGAMY**.
– DERIVATIVES **anisogamous** adj.
– ORIGIN C19: from Gk *anisos* 'unequal' + *gamos* 'mar-

riage'.

**Anisoptera** /ˌanʌɪˈzɒptərə/ ● **pl. n.** Entomology a suborder of insects which comprises the dragonflies.
– DERIVATIVES **anisopteran** n. & adj.
– ORIGIN mod. L., from Gk *anisos* 'unequal' + *pteron* 'wing'.

**anisotropic** /ˌanʌɪsə(ʊ)ˈtrɒpɪk/ ● **adj.** Physics having a different magnitude or properties when measured in different directions.
– DERIVATIVES **anisotropically** adv. **anisotropy** /-ˈsɒtrəpi/ n.
– ORIGIN C19: from Gk *anisos* 'unequal' + *tropos* 'turn' + **-IC**.

**ankh** /aŋk/ ● **n.** an object or design resembling a cross with a loop instead of the top arm, used in ancient Egypt as a symbol of life.
– ORIGIN C19: from Egyptian, lit. 'life, soul'.

**ankle** ● **n.** the joint connecting the foot with the leg. ➤the narrow part of the leg between this and the calf. ● **v.** informal, chiefly US walk. ➤leave.
– DERIVATIVES **ankled** adj.
– ORIGIN OE *ancleow*, of Gmc origin.

**ankle-biter** ● **n.** humorous, chiefly N. Amer. & Austral./NZ a child.

**ankle bone** ● **n.** the talus.

**anklet** ● **n. 1** an ornament worn round an ankle. **2** chiefly N. Amer. a sock that reaches just above the ankle.

**ankylosaur** /ˈaŋkɪləsɔː/ ● **n.** a heavily built quadrupedal herbivorous dinosaur of the Cretaceous period, armoured with bony plates.
– ORIGIN C20: from mod. L. *Ankylosaurus*, from Gk *ankulos* (see **ANKYLOSIS**) + *sauros* 'lizard'.

**ankylose** /ˈaŋkɪləʊz/ ● **v.** (**be/become ankylosed**) Medicine (of bones or a joint) be or become stiffened or united by ankylosis.
– ORIGIN C18: back-form. from **ANKYLOSIS**.

**ankylosing spondylitis** ● **n.** Medicine a form of spinal arthritis, chiefly affecting young males, that eventually causes ankylosis of vertebral and sacro-iliac joints.

**ankylosis** /ˌaŋkɪˈləʊsɪs/ ● **n.** Medicine abnormal stiffening and immobility of a joint due to fusion of the bones.
– DERIVATIVES **ankylotic** adj.
– ORIGIN C18: from Gk *ankulōsis*, from *ankuloun* 'to crook', from *ankulos* 'crooked'.

**ankylostomiasis** /ˌaŋkɪlə(ʊ)stə(ʊ)ˈmʌɪəsɪs/ ● **n.** variant spelling of **ANCYLOSTOMIASIS**.

**anlage** /ˈanlɑːɡə/ ● **n.** (pl. **anlagen** /-ɡ(ə)n/) Biology the rudimentary basis of a particular organ or other part, especially in an embryo.
– ORIGIN C19: from Ger., 'foundation, basis'.

**anna** /ˈanə/ ● **n.** a former monetary unit of India and Pakistan, equal to one sixteenth of a rupee.
– ORIGIN from Hindi *ānā*.

**annal** /ˈan(ə)l/ ● **n.** a record of the events of one year. ➤a record of one item in a chronicle.
– DERIVATIVES **annalist** n. **annalistic** adj. **annalistically** adv.
– ORIGIN C17: back-form. from **ANNALS**.

**annals** ● **pl. n.** a record of events year by year. ➤historical records.
– ORIGIN C16: from L. *annales* (*libri*) 'yearly (books)', from *annus* 'year'.

**annates** /ˈaneɪts/ ● **pl. n.** chiefly historical a year's revenue of a Roman Catholic see or benefice, paid to the Pope by a bishop or other cleric newly appointed to the see or benefice.
– ORIGIN C16: from Fr., from med. L. *annata* 'year's proceeds', from *annus* 'year'.

**annatto** /əˈnatəʊ/ (also **anatto**) ● **n.** (pl. **-os**) **1** an orange-red dye obtained from the seed coat of a tropical fruit, used for colouring foods. **2** the tropical American tree from which this fruit is obtained. [*Bixa orellana*.]
– ORIGIN C17: from Carib.

**anneal** /əˈniːl/ ● **v. 1** heat (metal or glass) and allow it to cool slowly, in order to remove internal stresses and make it less brittle. **2** Biochemistry recombine (DNA) in the double-stranded form.
– DERIVATIVES **annealer** n.
– ORIGIN OE *onǣlan* 'set on fire', from *on* + *ǣlan* 'burn, bake' from *āl* 'fire, burning'.

**Annelida** /əˈnɛlɪdə/ ● **pl. n.** Zoology a large phylum that comprises the segmented worms, which include earthworms, lugworms, ragworms, and leeches.
– DERIVATIVES **annelid** /ˈan(ə)lɪd/ n. & adj. **annelidan** n. & adj.
– ORIGIN mod. L., from Fr. (*animaux*) *annelés* 'ringed (animals)', from OFr. *anel* 'a ring', from L. *anellus*, dimin. of *anulus* 'a ring'.

**annex** ● **v.** /əˈnɛks/ add as an extra or subordinate part. ➤add (territory) to one's own territory by appropriation. ● **n.** /ˈanɛks/ (chiefly Brit. also **annexe**) (pl. **annexes**) **1** a building joined to or associated with a main building. **2** an addition to a document.
– DERIVATIVES **annexation** n. **annexationist** n. & adj.
– ORIGIN ME: from OFr. *annexer*, from L. *annectere* 'connect'.

**annihilate** /əˈnʌɪɪleɪt/ ● **v. 1** destroy utterly. ➤informal defeat utterly. **2** Physics convert (matter) into radiant energy, especially by collision of a particle with an antiparticle.
– DERIVATIVES **annihilation** n. **annihilator** n.
– ORIGIN ME: from late L. *annihilat-*, *annihilare* 'reduce to nothing'.

**anniversary** ● **n.** (pl. **-ies**) the date on which an event took place in a previous year or in the past.
– ORIGIN ME: from L. *anniversarius* 'returning yearly', from *annus* 'year' + *versus* 'turning'.

**Anno Domini** /ˌanəʊ ˈdɒmɪnʌɪ/ ● **adv.** full form of **AD**.
– ORIGIN L., 'in the year of the Lord'.

**annotate** /ˈanəteɪt/ ● **v.** add notes to (a text or diagram) giving explanation or comment.
– DERIVATIVES **annotatable** adj. **annotation** n. **annotative** adj. **annotator** n.
– ORIGIN C16 (earlier (ME) as *annotation*): from L. *annotat-*, *annotare* 'mark'.

**announce** ● **v.** make a formal public declaration about a fact, occurrence, or intention. ➤make known the arrival of (a guest) at a formal social occasion.
– DERIVATIVES **announcement** n. **announcer** n.
– ORIGIN C15: from Fr. *annoncer*, from L. *annuntiare*, from *ad-* 'to' + *nuntiare* 'declare, announce'.

**annoy** ● **v. 1** make a little angry. **2** archaic harm or attack repeatedly.
– DERIVATIVES **annoyance** n. **annoyer** n. **annoying** adj. **annoyingly** adv.
– ORIGIN ME: from OFr. *anoier* (v.), *anoi* (n.), based on L. *in odio* in the phr. *mihi in odio est* 'it is hateful to me'.

**annual** ● **adj. 1** occurring once every year. **2** calculated over or covering a year. **3** (of a plant) living only for a year or less, perpetuating itself by seed. Compare with **BIENNIAL**, **PERENNIAL**. ● **n. 1** a book or magazine of a series published once a year. **2** an annual plant.
– DERIVATIVES **annually** adv.
– ORIGIN ME: from OFr. *annuel*, from late L. *annualis*, based on L. *annus* 'year'.

**annual general meeting** ● **n.** Brit. a yearly meeting of the members or shareholders of an organization.

**annualized** ● **adj.** (of a rate of return or inflation) recalculated as an annual rate.

**annuitant** /əˈnjuːɪt(ə)nt/ ● **n.** formal a person who receives an annuity.

**annuity** ● **n.** (pl. **-ies**) a fixed sum of money paid to someone each year, typically for the rest of their life. ➤a form of insurance or investment entitling the investor to a series of annual sums.
– ORIGIN ME: from Fr. *annuité*, from med. L. *annuitas*, from L. *annuus* 'yearly', from *annus* 'year'.

**annul** /əˈnʌl/ ● **v.** (**annulled**, **annulling**) declare (a law or contract, especially that of marriage) invalid.
– DERIVATIVES **annulment** n.
– ORIGIN ME: from OFr. *anuller*, from late L. *annullare*, from *ad-* 'to' + *nullum* 'nothing'.

**annular** /ˈanjʊlə/ ● **adj.** technical ring-shaped.
– DERIVATIVES **annularly** adv.
– ORIGIN C16: from Fr. *annulaire* or L. *annularis*, from *anulus* (see **ANNULUS**).

**annular eclipse** ● **n.** an eclipse of the sun in which the edge of the sun remains visible as a bright ring around the moon.

**annulate** /ˈanjʊlət/ ● **adj.** chiefly Zoology marked with or formed of rings.
– DERIVATIVES **annulated** adj. **annulation** n.
– ORIGIN C19: from L. *annulatus*, from *anulus* (see **ANNULUS**).

**annulet** /ˈanjʊlɪt/ ● **n. 1** Architecture a small band encircling a column. **2** Heraldry a charge in the form of a small ring.
– ORIGIN ME: from OFr. *anelet*, from L. *anulus* (see **ANNULUS**) + **-ET**[1].

**annulus** /ˈanjʊləs/ ● **n.** (pl. **annuli** /-lʌɪ, -liː/) technical a ring-shaped object, structure, or region.
– ORIGIN C16: from L. *anulus, annulus*.

**annunciate** /əˈnʌnsɪeɪt/ ● **v.** chiefly archaic announce.
– ORIGIN ME: from med. L. *annunciat-*, var. of L. *annuntiat-*, *annuntiare* 'announce'.

**annunciation** ● **n. 1** (**the Annunciation**) the announcement of the Incarnation by the angel Gabriel to Mary (Luke 1:26–38). ➤a Church festival commemorating this, held on 25 March (Lady Day). **2** formal or archaic the announcement of something.

**annunciator** ● **n.** a device such as a bell or light that indicates which of several electric circuits has been activated.

**annus horribilis** /ˌanəs hɒˈriːbɪlɪs/ ● **n.** a year of disaster or misfortune.
– ORIGIN mod. L., suggested by **ANNUS MIRABILIS**.

**annus mirabilis** /mɪˈrɑːbɪlɪs/ ● **n.** a remarkable or auspicious year.
– ORIGIN mod. L., 'wonderful year'.

**anoa** /əˈnəʊə/ ● **n.** (pl. same or **anoas**) a small deer-like water buffalo, native to Sulawesi. [Genus *Bubalus*: two species.]
– ORIGIN C19: a local word.

**anode** /ˈanəʊd/ ● **n.** a positively charged electrode. The opposite of **CATHODE**.
– DERIVATIVES **anodal** adj. **anodic** adj.
– ORIGIN C19: from Gk *anodos* 'way up'.

**anodize** /ˈanədʌɪz/ (also **-ise**) ● **v.** [usu. as adj. **anodized**] coat (a metal, especially aluminium) with a protective oxide layer by an electrolytic process in which the metal forms the anode.
– DERIVATIVES **anodizer** n.

**anodyne** /ˈanədʌɪn/ ● **adj.** unlikely to cause offence or disagreement but somewhat dull. ● **n.** a painkilling drug or medicine.
– ORIGIN C16: via L. from Gk *anōdunos* 'painless'.

**anogenital** /ˌeɪnəʊˈdʒɛnɪt(ə)l/ ● **adj.** Medicine & Anatomy of or relating to the anus and genitals.

**anoint** ● **v.** smear or rub with oil, especially as part of a religious ceremony. ➤ceremonially confer office on (a priest or monarch) by anointing. ➤[often as adj. **anointed**] nominate as successor: *his officially anointed heir.*
– PHRASES **Anointing of the Sick** (in the Roman Catholic Church) the sacramental anointing of the ill or infirm with blessed oil; unction.
– DERIVATIVES **anointer** n.
– ORIGIN ME: from OFr. *enoint*, *enoindre*, from L. *inungere*, from *in-* 'upon' + *ungere* 'anoint, smear with oil'.

**anole** /əˈnəʊli/ ● **n.** a small arboreal American lizard with a throat fan, often brightly coloured. [Genus *Anolis*.]
– ORIGIN C18: from Carib.

**anomalistic month** ● **n.** Astronomy a month measured between successive perigees of the moon (approximately 27½ days).

**anomalistic year** ● **n.** Astronomy a year measured between successive perihelia of the earth (approximately 365¼ days).

**anomaly** /əˈnɒm(ə)li/ ● **n.** (pl. **-ies**) **1** something that deviates from what is standard, normal, or expected. **2** Astronomy the angular distance of a planet or satellite from its last perihelion or perigee.
– DERIVATIVES **anomalous** n. **anomalously** adv. **anomalousness** n.
– ORIGIN C16: via L. from Gk *anōmalia*, from *anōmalos* (from *an-* + *homalos* 'even') + **-Y**[3].

**anomia** /əˈnəʊmɪə/ ● **n.** Medicine a form of aphasia in which the patient is unable to recall the names of everyday objects.
– DERIVATIVES **anomic** adj.
– ORIGIN C20: from **A-**[1] + L. *nomen* 'name' + **-IA**[1].

**anomie** /ˈanəmi/ (also **anomy**) ● **n.** lack of the usual social or ethical standards.
– DERIVATIVES **anomic** /əˈnɒmɪk/ adj.
– ORIGIN 1930s: from Fr., from Gk *anomia*, from *anomos* 'lawless'.

**anon** ● **adv.** archaic or informal soon; shortly.
– ORIGIN OE *on ān, on āne* 'in or into (one state or course)'.

**anon.** ● **abbrev.** anonymous.

**anonym** ● **n. 1** an anonymous person or publication. **2** a pseudonym.
– ORIGIN C19: from Fr. *anonyme*, from Gk *anōnumos* (see **ANONYMOUS**).

**anonymize** (also **-ise**) ● **v.** Medicine remove identifying particulars from (test results) for statistical or other purposes.

**anonymous** ● **adj. 1** not identified by name; of unknown identity. **2** having no individual or unusual features.
– DERIVATIVES **anonymity** /anəˈnɪmɪti/ n. **anonymously** adv.
– ORIGIN C16: via late L. from Gk *anōnumos* 'nameless' (from *an-* 'without' + *onoma* 'name') + **-OUS**.

**anopheles** /əˈnɒfɪliːz/ ● **n.** a mosquito of a genus which includes the species that transmits the malarial parasite to humans.
– DERIVATIVES **anopheline** /əˈnɒfɪlʌɪn, -liːn/ adj. & n.
– ORIGIN C19: mod. L. genus name, from Gk *anōphelēs* 'unprofitable, useless'.

**Anoplura** /ˌanə(ʊ)ˈplʊərə/ ● **pl. n.** Entomology an order of insects that comprises the sucking lice.
– DERIVATIVES **anopluran** n. & adj.
– ORIGIN mod. L., from *anoplos* 'unarmed' + *oura* 'tail'.

**anorak** ● **n. 1** a waterproof jacket, usually with a hood. **2** Brit. informal a socially inept person with unfashionable and largely solitary interests.
– ORIGIN 1920s: from Greenland Eskimo *anoraq*.

**anorectal** /ˌeɪnəʊˈrɛkt(ə)l/ ● **adj.** Medicine & Anatomy of or relating to the anus and rectum.

**anorexia** /ˌanəˈrɛksɪə/ ● **n.** lack of appetite for food, in particular (also **anorexia nervosa**) an emotional disorder characterized by an obsessive desire to lose weight by refusing to eat.
– ORIGIN C16: via late L. from Gk, from *an-* 'without' + *orexis* 'appetite'.

**anorexic** (also **anorectic**) ● **adj.** relating to or suffering from anorexia. ● **n. 1** a person suffering from anorexia. **2** (**anorectic**) a medicine which produces a loss of appetite.

**anorgasmia** /ˌanɔːˈgazmɪə/ ● **n.** Medicine persistent inability to achieve orgasm despite responding to sexual stimulation.
– DERIVATIVES **anorgasmic** adj.

**anorthite** /əˈnɔːθʌɪt/ ● **n.** a calcium-rich mineral of the feldspar group, typically white.
– ORIGIN C19: from **AN-**[1] + Gk *orthos* 'straight' + **-ITE**[1].

**anorthosite** /əˈnɔːθəsʌɪt/ ● **n.** Geology a granular igneous rock composed largely of labradorite or another plagioclase.
– ORIGIN C19: from Fr. *anorthose* 'plagioclase' + **-ITE**[1].

**anosmia** /aˈnɒzmɪə/ ● **n.** Medicine the loss of the sense of smell, caused by head injury, infection, or blockage of the nose.
– DERIVATIVES **anosmic** adj.
– ORIGIN C19: from **AN-**[2] + Gk *osmē* 'smell'.

**another** ● **det. & pron. 1** one more; a further. **2** used to refer to a different person or thing from one already referred to.
– PHRASES **another place** Brit. the other House of Parliament (used in the Commons to refer to the Lords, and vice versa).
– ORIGIN ME: orig. *an other*.

**anothery** (also **anotherie**) ● **n.** Austral. informal another one.

**ANOVA** /aˈnəʊvə/ ● **n.** analysis of variance, a statistical

method in which the variation in a set of observations is divided into distinct components.
– ORIGIN 1960s: acronym.

**anovulant** /a'nɒvjʊl(ə)nt/ ● **adj.** Medicine denoting a drug or other agent that prevents ovulation.

**anovulatory** /ˌanɒvjʊ'leɪt(ə)ri/ ● **adj.** Medicine (of a menstrual cycle) in which ovulation does not occur.

**anoxia** /a'nɒksɪə/ ● **n.** chiefly Medicine an absence or deficiency of oxygen in a tissue, medium, etc.
– DERIVATIVES **anoxic** adj.

**ANS** ● **abbrev.** autonomic nervous system.

**Anschluss** /'anʃlʊs/ ● **n.** the annexation of Austria by Germany in 1938.
– ORIGIN Ger., from *anschliessen* 'to join'.

**anserine** /'ansərʌɪn/ ● **adj.** of or like a goose.
– ORIGIN C19: from L. *anserinus*, from *anser* 'goose'.

**ANSI** ● **abbrev.** American National Standards Institute.

**answer** ● **n.** **1** something said, written, or done as a reaction to a question, statement, or situation. **2** the solution to a problem or dilemma. ● **v.** **1** respond with an answer. ➤(**answer back**) respond impudently. ➤(**answer to**) be responsible or report to. ➤(**answer to the name of**) be called. **2** defend oneself against (a charge or accusation). ➤(**answer for**) be responsible or to blame for. **3** be suitable for fulfilling (a need); satisfy.
– PHRASES **have** (or **know**) **all the answers** informal be very confident in one's knowledge. **in answer to** as a response to or as a result of.
– ORIGIN OE *andswaru* (n.), *andswarian* (v.), of Gmc origin; from a base shared by **SWEAR**.

**answerable** ● **adj.** **1** (**answerable to/for**) responsible to or for. **2** (of a question) able to be answered.

**answering machine** ● **n.** a device which supplies a recorded answer to a telephone call and can record a message from the caller.

**answering service** ● **n.** a business that receives and answers telephone calls for its clients.

**answerphone** ● **n.** Brit. a telephone answering machine.

**ant** ● **n.** a small insect, usually wingless and with a sting, living in a complex social colony with one or more breeding queens. [Family Formicidae.]
– PHRASES **have ants in one's pants** informal be fidgety.
– ORIGIN OE *ǣmete*, of W. Gmc origin: cf. **EMMET**.

**ant-** ● **prefix** variant spelling of **ANTI-** shortened before a vowel or *h* (as in *Antarctic*).

**-ant** ● **suffix** **1** (forming adjectives) denoting attribution of an action or state: *arrogant*. **2** (forming nouns) denoting an agent: *deodorant*.
– ORIGIN from Fr. or L. pres. participial verb stems (see also **-ENT**).

**antacid** /an'tasɪd/ ● **adj.** preventing or correcting acidity in the stomach. ● **n.** an antacid medicine.

**antagonism** /an'tag(ə)nɪz(ə)m/ ● **n.** active hostility or opposition.

**antagonist** ● **n.** **1** a person who actively opposes or is hostile. **2** Biochemistry a substance which interferes with the physiological action of another. **3** Anatomy a muscle whose action counteracts that of another muscle.
– DERIVATIVES **antagonistic** adj. **antagonistically** adv.
– ORIGIN C16: from Fr. *antagoniste* or late L. *antagonista*, from Gk *antagōnistēs*, from *antagōnizesthai* (see **ANTAGONIZE**); cf. **AGONIST**.

**antagonize** (also **-ise**) ● **v.** **1** cause to become hostile. **2** Biochemistry act as an antagonist of.
– ORIGIN C18 (in the sense 'struggle against'): from Gk *antagōnizesthai*, from *ant-* 'against' + *agōnizesthai* 'struggle'.

**Antarctic** ● **adj.** of or relating to the south polar region or Antarctica.
– ORIGIN ME: from OFr. *antartique* or L. *antarcticus*, from Gk *antarktikos* 'opposite to the north', from *ant-* 'against' + *arktikos* (see **ARCTIC**).

**antbear** ● **n.** another term for **AARDVARK**.

**antbird** ● **n.** a long-legged, short-tailed insectivorous bird found mainly in the tropical forests of South America. [Family Formicariidae: many species.]

**ante** /'anti/ ● **n.** a stake put up by a player in poker or brag before receiving cards. ● **v.** (**antes**, **anted**, **anteing**) (**ante up**) put up (an amount) as an ante in poker or brag. ➤N. Amer. informal pay an amount of money in advance.
– PHRASES **up** (or **raise**) **the ante** increase what is at stake or under discussion.
– ORIGIN C19: from L., lit. 'before'.

**ante-** /'anti/ ● **prefix** before; preceding: *antecedent*.
– ORIGIN from L. *ante* 'before'.

**anteater** ● **n.** a mammal that feeds on ants and termites, with a long snout and sticky tongue. [Many species, chiefly in family Myrmecophagidae (Central and S. America).]

**antebellum** /ˌantɪ'bɛləm/ ● **adj.** occurring or existing before a particular war, especially the US Civil War.
– ORIGIN C19: from L., from *ante* 'before' and *bellum* 'war'.

**antecedent** /ˌantɪ'siːd(ə)nt/ ● **n.** **1** a thing that existed before or logically precedes another. **2** (**antecedents**) a person's ancestors and social background. **3** Grammar an earlier word, phrase, or clause to which a following pronoun refers back. **4** Logic the statement contained in the 'if' clause of a conditional proposition. ● **adj.** preceding in time or order.
– DERIVATIVES **antecedence** n. **antecedently** adv.
– ORIGIN ME: from OFr. or from L. *antecedent-*, *antecedere*, from *ante* 'before' + *cedere* 'go'.

**antechamber** ● **n.** a small room leading to a main one.
– ORIGIN C17: from Fr. *antichambre*, from Ital. *anticamera*, from *anti-* 'preceding' + *camera* (see **CHAMBER**).

**antechapel** ● **n.** a distinct part of a college chapel between the entrance and the nave or choir.

**antechinus** /ˌantɪ'kʌɪnəs/ ● **n.** a shrew-like marsupial mouse found in Australia, New Guinea, and Tasmania. [Genus *Antechinus*.]
– ORIGIN mod. L., from Gk *anti-* 'simulating' + *ekhinos* 'hedgehog' (from its bristly fur).

**antedate** ● **v.** come before in date. ➤indicate that (a document or event) should be assigned to an earlier date.

**antediluvian** /ˌantɪdɪ'luːvɪən/ ● **adj.** **1** of or belonging to the time before the biblical Flood. **2** chiefly humorous ridiculously old-fashioned.
– ORIGIN C17: from **ANTE-** + L. *diluvium* 'deluge' + **-AN**.

**antelope** ● **n.** (pl. same or **antelopes**) a swift-running deer-like ruminant animal with upward-pointing horns, of a group including the gazelles, impala, gnu, and eland.
– ORIGIN ME (orig. the name of a fierce mythical creature): via OFr. and med. L. from late Gk *antholops*, of unknown origin and meaning.

**ante-mortem** ● **adj.** & **adv.** before death.
– ORIGIN from L.

**antenatal** ● **adj.** before birth; during or relating to pregnancy. ● **n.** informal a medical examination during pregnancy.
– DERIVATIVES **antenatally** adv.

**antenna** ● **n.** (pl. **antennae** /-niː/) **1** Zoology a long, thin sensory appendage found in pairs on the heads of insects and some other arthropods. **2** (pl. also **antennas**) chiefly N. Amer. or technical an aerial.
– DERIVATIVES **antennal** adj. **antennary** adj.
– ORIGIN C17: from L., alt. of *antemna* 'yard' (of a ship), used in pl. to translate Gk *keraioi* 'horns (of insects)'.

**antennule** /an'tɛnjuːl/ ● **n.** Zoology a small antenna, especially either of the first pair of antennae in a crustacean.

**antenuptial** ● **adj.** chiefly Brit. another term for **PRENUPTIAL**.
– ORIGIN C19: from late L. *antenuptialis* (see **ANTE-**, **NUPTIAL**).

**antepartum** /antɪ'pɑːtəm/ ● **adj.** Medicine occurring not long before childbirth.
– ORIGIN C19: from L., 'before birth'.

**antepenultimate** ● **adj.** last but two in a series.

**ante-post** ● **adj.** Brit. (of a bet on a horse race) placed before the runners are known, on a horse thought likely to be entered.

**anterior** • **adj.** **1** chiefly Anatomy & Biology nearer the front, especially in the front of the body or nearer to the head. The opposite of **POSTERIOR**. ➤ Botany situated further away from the main stem. **2** (**anterior to**) formal prior to. **3** Phonetics pronounced with an obstruction located in front of the palato-alveolar region of the mouth, e.g. *b, p, d, t*.
– DERIVATIVES **anteriority** n. **anteriorly** adv.
– ORIGIN C16: from Fr. *antérieur* or L. *anterior*, compar. of *ante* 'before'.

**antero-** /'antərəʊ/ • **comb. form** chiefly Anatomy representing **ANTERIOR**: *anteroposterior*.

**anterograde** • **adj.** directed forwards in time.
– ORIGIN C19: from **ANTERIOR**, on the pattern of *retrograde*.

**anterolateral** • **adj.** chiefly Anatomy both anterior and lateral.

**ante-room** • **n.** an antechamber, especially one serving as a waiting room. ➤ a large room in an officers' mess adjacent to the dining room.

**anteroposterior** • **adj.** chiefly Anatomy relating to or directed towards both front and back.

**anteverted** /'antɪvəːtɪd/ • **adj.** Anatomy & Medicine (of an organ of the body, especially the womb) inclined forward.
– ORIGIN C19: from L. *antevertere*, from *ante* 'before' + *vertere* 'to turn' + **-ED²**.

**ant heap** • **n.** another term for **ANTHILL**.

**anthelion** /ant'hiːlɪən, an'θiːl-/ • **n.** (pl. **anthelia** /-lɪə/) a luminous halo round a shadow projected by the sun on to a cloud or fog bank. ➤ a parhelion seen opposite the sun in the sky.
– ORIGIN C17: from Gk *anthēlios* 'opposite to the sun'.

**anthelmintic** /ˌanθ(ə)l'mɪntɪk/ • **adj.** Medicine denoting a preparation used to destroy parasitic worms.
– ORIGIN C17: from *anth-* (var. of *anti* 'against') + Gk *helmins, helminth-* 'worm' + **-IC**.

**anthem** • **n.** **1** a rousing or uplifting song identified with a particular group or cause. ➤ (also **national anthem**) a solemn patriotic song adopted as an expression of national identity. **2** a musical setting of a religious text to be sung by a choir during a church service.
– DERIVATIVES **anthemic** adj.
– ORIGIN OE *antefn, antifne*, from late L. *antiphona* (see **ANTIPHON**).

**anthemion** /an'θiːmɪən/ • **n.** (pl. **anthemia** /-mɪə/) an ornamental design of alternating motifs resembling clusters of narrow leaves or honeysuckle petals.
– ORIGIN C19: from Gk, lit. 'flower'.

**anther** • **n.** Botany the part of a stamen that contains the pollen.
– ORIGIN C18: from Fr. *anthère* or mod. L. *anthera*, from Gk *anthēra* 'flowery'.

**antheridium** /ˌanθə'rɪdɪəm/ • **n.** (pl. **antheridia** /-dɪə/) Botany the male sex organ of algae, mosses, ferns, fungi, and other non-flowering plants.
– DERIVATIVES **antheridial** adj.
– ORIGIN C19: mod. L., from *anthera* (see **ANTHER**) + *-idium* (from the Gk dimin. suffix *-idion*).

**antherozoid** /ˌanθ(ə)rə(ʊ)'zəʊɪd/ • **n.** Botany another term for **SPERMATOZOID**.

**anthesis** /an'θiːsɪs/ • **n.** Botany the flowering period of a plant, from the opening of the flower bud.
– ORIGIN C19: from Gk *anthēsis* 'flowering'.

**anthill** • **n.** a nest in the form of a mound built by ants or termites.

**antho-** /'anθəʊ/ • **comb. form** of or relating to flowers: *anthophilous*.
– ORIGIN from Gk *anthos* 'flower'.

**anthocyanin** /ˌanθə(ʊ)'sʌɪənɪn/ • **n.** Chemistry a blue, violet, or red flavonoid pigment found in plants.
– ORIGIN C19: from Ger. *Anthocyan*, from Gk *anthos* 'flower' + *kuanos* 'blue' + **-IN¹**.

**anthology** • **n.** (pl. **-ies**) a collection of poems or other pieces of writing or music.
– DERIVATIVES **anthologist** n. **anthologize** (also **-ise**) v.
– ORIGIN C17: via Fr. or med. L. from Gk *anthologia*, from *anthos* 'flower' (i.e. 'flowers' of verse) + *-logia* 'collection'.

**anthophilous** /an'θɒfɪləs/ • **adj.** Zoology (of insects or other animals) frequenting flowers.

**Anthozoa** /ˌanθə'zəʊə/ • **pl. n.** Zoology a large class of marine coelenterates that includes the sea anemones and corals.
– DERIVATIVES **anthozoan** n. & adj.
– ORIGIN mod. L., from Gk *anthos* 'flower' + *zōia* 'animals'.

**anthracene** /'anθrəsiːn/ • **n.** Chemistry a crystalline aromatic hydrocarbon obtained by the distillation of crude oils. [$C_{14}H_{10}$.]
– ORIGIN C19: from Gk *anthrax, anthrak-* 'coal' + **-ENE**.

**anthracite** /'anθrəsʌɪt/ • **n.** coal of a hard variety that contains relatively pure carbon and burns with little flame and smoke.
– DERIVATIVES **anthracitic** adj.
– ORIGIN C16 (denoting a gem resembling coal): from Gk *anthrakitēs*, from *anthrax, anthrak-* 'coal'.

**anthracnose** /an'θraknəʊs/ • **n.** a mainly fungal disease of plants, causing dark lesions.
– ORIGIN C19: coined in Fr. from Gk *anthrax, anthrak-* 'coal' + *nosos* 'disease'.

**anthranilic acid** /ˌanθrə'nɪlɪk/ • **n.** Chemistry a colourless or yellow crystalline compound obtained by hydrolysis of indigo.
– DERIVATIVES **anthranilate** n.
– ORIGIN C19: *anthranilic* from Gk *anthrax* 'coal' + *anil* (see **ANILINE**) + **-IC**.

**anthraquinone** /ˌanθrə'kwɪnəʊn/ • **n.** Chemistry a yellow crystalline compound made by oxidizing anthracene, the basis of many dyes.

**anthrax** /'anθraks/ • **n.** a serious bacterial disease of sheep and cattle, typically affecting the skin and lungs and able to be transmitted to humans.
– ORIGIN ME, 'carbuncle': from L., from Gk *anthrax, anthrak-* 'coal, carbuncle'.

**anthropic principle** /an'θrɒpɪk/ • **n.** the cosmological principle that theories of the universe are constrained by the necessity to allow human existence.
– ORIGIN 1970s: *anthropic* from Gk *anthrōpikos*, from *anthrōpos* 'human being'.

**anthropo-** /'anθrəpəʊ/ • **comb. form** human; relating to human beings: *anthropology*.
– ORIGIN from Gk *anthrōpos* 'human being'.

**anthropocentric** • **adj.** regarding humankind as the most important element of existence.
– DERIVATIVES **anthropocentrically** adv. **anthropocentrism** n.

**anthropogenic** /ˌanθrəpə(ʊ)'dʒɛnɪk/ • **adj.** (chiefly of pollution) originating in human activity.
– DERIVATIVES **anthropogenically** adv.

**anthropoid** • **adj.** **1** resembling a human being in form. **2** Zoology relating to the group of higher primates including monkeys, apes, and humans. ➤ (of an ape) belonging to the family of great apes. • **n.** Zoology a higher primate, especially an ape or apeman.
– ORIGIN C19: from Gk *anthrōpoeidēs*, from *anthrōpos* 'human being' + **-OID**.

**anthropology** /ˌanθrə'pɒlədʒi/ • **n.** the study of humankind, including the comparative study of societies and cultures and the science of human zoology and evolution.
– DERIVATIVES **anthropological** adj. **anthropologist** n.

**anthropometry** /ˌanθrə'pɒmɪtri/ (also **anthropometrics**) • **n.** the scientific study of the measurements and proportions of the human body.
– DERIVATIVES **anthropometric** adj.

**anthropomorphic** /anθrəpə'mɔːfɪk/ • **adj.** relating to or characterized by anthropomorphism. ➤ having human characteristics.
– DERIVATIVES **anthropomorphically** adv.

**anthropomorphism** /ˌanθrəpə'mɔːfɪz(ə)m/ • **n.** the attribution of human characteristics or behaviour to a god, animal, or object.
– DERIVATIVES **anthropomorphize** (also **-ise**) v.

**anthropomorphous** • **adj.** human in form or nature.

– ORIGIN C18: from Gk *anthrōpomorphos* (from *anthrōpos* 'human being' + *morphē* 'form') + **-ous**.

**anthropopathy** /ˌanθrəˈpɒpəθi/ ● **n.** the attribution of human emotions to a god.
– ORIGIN C17: from **ANTHROPO-** + **-PATHY**.

**anthropophagi** /ˌanθrəˈpɒfəgʌɪ/ ● **pl. n.** (in legends or fables) cannibals.
– ORIGIN C16: from L., from Gk *anthrōpophagos* 'man-eating'.

**anthropophagy** /ˌanθrəˈpɒfədʒi/ ● **n.** cannibalism.
– DERIVATIVES **anthropophagous** /-gəs/ adj.
– ORIGIN C17: from Gk *anthrōpophagia*, from *anthrōpophagos* (see **ANTHROPOPHAGI**).

**anthroposophy** /ˌanθrəˈpɒsəfi/ ● **n.** a system established by the Austrian philosopher Rudolf Steiner that seeks to optimize physical and mental health and well-being.
– DERIVATIVES **anthroposophical** adj.
– ORIGIN C20: from **ANTHROPO-** + Gk *sophia* 'wisdom'.

**anthurium** /anˈθ(j)ʊərɪəm/ ● **n.** (pl. **anthuriums**) a tropical American plant grown for its ornamental foliage or brightly coloured flowering spathes. [Genus *Anthurium*.]
– ORIGIN mod. L., from Gk *anthos* 'flower' + *oura* 'tail'.

**anti** ● **prep.** opposed to; against. ● **n.** (pl. **antis**) informal an opponent of something.

**anti-** (also **ant-**) ● **prefix 1** opposed to; against: *anti-aircraft*. ➤preventing or relieving: *antibacterial*. ➤the opposite of: *anticlimax*. ➤acting as a rival: *antipope*. **2** Physics the antiparticle of a specified particle.
– ORIGIN from Gk *anti* 'against'.

**anti-aircraft** ● **adj.** (of a gun or missile) used to attack enemy aircraft.

**antibacterial** ● **adj.** active against bacteria.

**antibiosis** /ˌantɪbʌɪˈəʊsɪs/ ● **n.** Biology an antagonistic association between two organisms (especially micro-organisms), in which one is adversely affected. Compare with **SYMBIOSIS**.
– ORIGIN C19: from **ANTI-** + **SYMBIOSIS**.

**antibiotic** ● **n.** a medicine that inhibits the growth of or destroys micro-organisms.
– ORIGIN C19: from **ANTI-** + Gk *biōtikos* 'fit for life' (from *bios* 'life').

**antibody** ● **n.** (pl. **-ies**) a blood protein produced by the body in response to and counteracting an antigen.

**antic** ● **adj.** archaic grotesque or bizarre.
– ORIGIN C16: from Ital. *antico* 'antique', also 'grotesque'.

**anticholinergic** /ˌantɪˌkəʊlɪˈnəːdʒɪk/ Medicine ● **adj.** inhibiting the action of the neurotransmitter acetylcholine. ● **n.** an anticholinergic drug.

**Antichrist** ● **n.** **(the Antichrist)** a postulated opponent of Christ expected by the early Church to appear before the end of the world.

**anticipate** ● **v. 1** be aware of (a future event) and take action. ➤regard as probable. ➤look forward to. **2** act or happen before.
– DERIVATIVES **anticipation** n. **anticipative** adj. **anticipator** n. **anticipatory** adj.
– ORIGIN C16 (earlier (ME) as *anticipation*): from L. *anticipat-*, *anticipare*, from *ante-* 'before' + *capere* 'take'.

**anticlerical** ● **adj.** chiefly historical opposed to the power or influence of the clergy.
– DERIVATIVES **anticlericalism** n.

**anticlimax** ● **n.** a disappointing end to an exciting series of events.
– DERIVATIVES **anticlimactic** adj. **anticlimactically** adv.

**anticline** /ˈantɪklʌɪn/ ● **n.** Geology a ridge or fold of stratified rock in which the strata slope downwards from the crest. Compare with **SYNCLINE**.
– DERIVATIVES **anticlinal** adj.
– ORIGIN C19: from **ANTI-** + Gk *klinein* 'lean', on the pattern of *incline*.

**anticlockwise** ● **adv. & adj.** Brit. in the opposite direction to the way in which the hands of a clock move round.

**anticoagulant** ● **adj.** having the effect of retarding the coagulation of the blood. ● **n.** an anticoagulant substance.

**anticodon** /ˌantɪˈkəʊdɒn/ ● **n.** Biochemistry a sequence of three nucleotides forming a unit of genetic code in a transfer RNA molecule, corresponding to a complementary codon in messenger RNA.

**anticonvulsant** ● **adj.** preventing or reducing the severity of epileptic fits or other convulsions. ● **n.** an anticonvulsant drug.

**antics** ● **pl. n.** foolish, outrageous, or amusing behaviour.
– ORIGIN C16: from **ANTIC**.

**anticyclone** ● **n.** a weather system with high barometric pressure at its centre, around which air slowly circulates (typically associated with calm, fine weather).
– DERIVATIVES **anticyclonic** adj.

**antidepressant** ● **adj.** used to alleviate depression. ● **n.** an antidepressant drug.

**antidiarrhoeal** ● **adj.** used to alleviate diarrhoea.

**antidiuretic hormone** ● **n.** another term for **VASOPRESSIN**.

**antidote** ● **n. 1** a medicine taken to counteract a particular poison. **2** something that counteracts an unpleasant feeling or situation: *laughter is a good antidote to stress.*
– DERIVATIVES **antidotal** adj.
– ORIGIN ME: via L., from Gk *antidoton*, from *anti-* 'against' + *didonai* 'give'.

**antidromic** /ˌantɪˈdrəʊmɪk/ ● **adj.** Physiology (of an impulse) travelling in the opposite direction to that normal in a nerve fibre. The opposite of **ORTHODROMIC**.
– ORIGIN C20: from **ANTI-** + Gk *dromos* 'running' + **-IC**.

**anti-emetic** ● **adj.** preventing vomiting. ● **n.** an anti-emetic drug.

**antifeedant** ● **n.** a naturally occurring substance in certain plants which adversely affects animals which eat them.

**antiferromagnetic** ● **adj.** Physics denoting or exhibiting a weak form of magnetism in which there is an antiparallel alignment of adjacent electron spins in a crystal lattice.

**antifouling** ● **n.** a substance applied to a boat's hull to prevent fouling.

**antifreeze** ● **n.** a liquid added to water to lower the freezing point, especially in the radiator of a motor vehicle.

**anti-g** ● **adj.** short for **ANTIGRAVITY**.

**antigen** ● **n.** a substance which the body recognizes as alien and which induces an immune response. Compare with **ANTIBODY**.
– DERIVATIVES **antigenic** adj.
– ORIGIN C20: via Ger. from Fr. *antigène* (see **ANTI-**, **-GEN**).

**antigenic determinant** ● **n.** Biochemistry another term for **EPITOPE**.

**antigorite** /anˈtɪgərʌɪt/ ● **n.** a mineral of the serpentine group, occurring typically as thin green plates.
– ORIGIN from *Antigorio*, a valley in Piedmont, Italy, + **-ITE**[1].

**antigravity** ● **n.** Physics a hypothetical force opposing gravity. ● **adj.** designed to counteract the effects of high acceleration.

**Antiguan** /anˈtiːgwən/ ● **n.** a native or inhabitant of Antigua, or the country of Antigua and Barbuda, in the West Indies. ● **adj.** of or relating to Antigua or Antigua and Barbuda.

**anti-hero** (or **anti-heroine**) ● **n.** a central character in a story, film, or drama who lacks conventional heroic attributes.

**antihistamine** ● **n.** a drug or other compound that inhibits the physiological effects of histamine, used especially in the treatment of allergies.

**anti-infective** ● **adj.** used to prevent infection. ● **n.** an anti-infective drug.

**anti-inflammatory** ● **adj.** (of a drug) used to reduce inflammation. ● **n.** (pl. **-ies**) an anti-inflammatory drug.

**anti-knock** ● **n.** a substance added to petrol to inhibit pre-ignition.

**anti-lock** ● **adj.** (of brakes) designed so as to prevent the wheels locking and the vehicle skidding if applied suddenly.

**antilogarithm** • **n.** the number of which a given number is the logarithm.

**antilogy** /an'tɪlədʒi/ • **n.** (pl. **-ies**) archaic a contradiction in terms or ideas.
– ORIGIN C17: from Fr. *antilogie*, from Gk *antilogia*, from *anti-* 'against' + *-logia* (see **-LOGY**).

**antimacassar** /ˌantɪmə'kasə/ • **n.** a piece of cloth put over the back of an upholstered chair to protect it from grease and dirt.
– ORIGIN C19: from **ANTI-** + **MACASSAR**.

**antimatter** • **n.** Physics matter consisting of elementary particles which are the antiparticles of those making up normal matter.

**antimetabolite** • **n.** Physiology a substance that interferes with the normal metabolic processes within cells.

**antimony** /'antɪməni/ • **n.** the chemical element of atomic number 51, a brittle silvery-white semimetal. (Symbol: **Sb**)
– DERIVATIVES **antimonial** adj. **antimonic** adj. **antimonious** adj.
– ORIGIN ME (denoting the ore stibnite): from med. L. *antimonium*, of unknown origin.

**antinode** • **n.** Physics the position of maximum displacement in a standing wave system.

**antinomian** /antɪ'nəʊmɪən/ • **adj.** holding or relating to the view that Christians are released by grace from the obligation of observing the moral law. • **n.** a person holding such a view.
– DERIVATIVES **antinomianism** n.
– ORIGIN C17: from med. L. *Antinomi*, a C16 Ger. sect, from Gk *anti-* 'against' + *nomos* 'law'.

**antinomy** /an'tɪnəmi/ • **n.** (pl. **-ies**) a paradox.
– ORIGIN C16: from L. *antinomia*, from Gk, from *anti* 'against' + *nomos* 'law'.

**antioxidant** • **n.** a substance that prevents or inhibits oxidation.

**antiparallel** • **adj.** Physics parallel but moving or oriented in opposite directions.

**antiparticle** • **n.** Physics a subatomic particle with the same mass as a given particle but opposite electric or magnetic properties (e.g. a positron in relation to an electron).

**antipasto** /ˌantɪ'pastəʊ/ • **n.** (pl. **antipasti** /-ti/) (in Italian cookery) an hors d'oeuvre.
– ORIGIN Ital., from *anti-* 'before' + *pasto* (from L. *pastus* 'food').

**antipathy** /an'tɪpəθi/ • **n.** (pl. **-ies**) a deep-seated feeling of aversion.
– DERIVATIVES **antipathetic** adj.
– ORIGIN C16: from Fr. *antipathie*, or via L. from Gk *antipatheia*, from *antipathēs* 'opposed in feeling'.

**anti-personnel** • **adj.** (of weapons) designed to kill or injure people rather than to damage buildings or equipment.

**antiperspirant** • **n.** a substance applied to prevent or reduce perspiration.

**antiphon** /'antɪf(ə)n/ • **n.** a short sentence sung or recited before or after a psalm or canticle. ➤a musical setting of an antiphon.
– ORIGIN ME: via eccles. L. from Gk *antiphōna* 'harmonies', neut. pl. of *antiphōnos* 'responsive', from *anti* 'in return' + *phōnē* 'sound'.

**antiphonal** • **adj.** (of church music) sung, recited, or played alternately by two groups. • **n.** another term for **ANTIPHONARY**.
– DERIVATIVES **antiphonally** adv.

**antiphonary** /an'tɪf(ə)nəri/ • **n.** (pl. **-ies**) a book of plainsong for the Divine Office.

**antiphony** • **n.** antiphonal singing, playing, or chanting.

**Antipodes** /an'tɪpədiːz/ • **pl. n. 1** (**the Antipodes**) Australia and New Zealand (used by inhabitants of the northern hemisphere). **2** (**antipodes** or **antipode**) the direct opposite of something.
– DERIVATIVES **antipodal** adj. **Antipodean** adj. & n.
– ORIGIN ME: via Fr. or late L. from Gk *antipodes* 'having the feet opposite', from *anti* 'against, opposite' + *pous, pod-* 'foot'.

**antipope** • **n.** a person established as pope in opposition to one held by others to be canonically chosen.
– ORIGIN ME *antipape*, via Fr. from med. L. *antipapa* (on the pattern of *Antichrist*).

**antiproton** • **n.** Physics the negatively charged antiparticle of a proton.

**antipruritic** /ˌantɪprʊ'rɪtɪk/ • **adj.** used to relieve itching. • **n.** an antipruritic drug.
– ORIGIN C19: from **ANTI-** + *pruritic* (see **PRURITUS**).

**antipsychotic** • **adj.** used to treat psychotic disorders. • **n.** an antipsychotic drug.

**antipyretic** • **adj.** used to prevent or reduce fever. • **n.** an antipyretic drug.

**antiquarian** /ˌantɪ'kwɛːrɪən/ • **adj.** relating to or studying antiques, rare books, or antiquities. • **n.** (also **antiquary**) a person who studies or collects antiques or antiquities.
– DERIVATIVES **antiquarianism** n.
– ORIGIN C17: from L. *antiquarius*, from *antiquus* (see **ANTIQUE**).

**antiquark** • **n.** Physics the antiparticle of a quark.

**antiquated** • **adj.** old-fashioned or outdated.
– ORIGIN C16: from eccles. L. *antiquare* 'make old', from *antiquus* (see **ANTIQUE**).

**antique** • **n.** a decorative object or piece of furniture that is valuable because of its age. • **adj. 1** valuable because of its age. **2** belonging to the distant past. ➤old-fashioned or outdated. • **v.** (**antiques, antiqued, antiquing**) cause to resemble an antique by artificial means.
– ORIGIN C15: from L. *antiquus, anticus* 'former, ancient', from *ante* 'before'.

**antiquity** • **n.** (pl. **-ies**) **1** the distant past, especially the classical and other civilizations before the Middle Ages. **2** (usu. **antiquities**) an object or building from the distant past. **3** great age.
– ORIGIN ME: from OFr. *antiquite*, from L. *antiquitas*, from *antiquus* (see **ANTIQUE**).

**anti-roll bar** • **n.** a rubber-mounted bar fitted in the suspension of a vehicle to increase its stability, especially when cornering.

**antirrhinum** /ˌantɪ'rʌɪnəm/ • **n.** (pl. **antirrhinums**) a plant of a genus that includes the snapdragon. [Genus *Antirrhinum*.]
– ORIGIN from L., from Gk *antirrhinon*, from *anti-* 'counterfeiting' + *rhis, rhin-* 'nose', from the resemblance of the flower to an animal's snout.

**antiscorbutic** Medicine • **adj.** preventing or curing scurvy. • **n.** an antiscorbutic food or drug.

**anti-self** • **n.** an adopted persona that is the opposite of one's conscious normal self. • **adj.** Physiology (of antibodies) directed against the body's own tissues.

**anti-Semitism** • **n.** hostility to or prejudice against Jews.
– DERIVATIVES **anti-Semite** n. **anti-Semitic** adj.

**antisense** • **adj.** Genetics relating to or denoting a sequence of nucleotides in DNA or RNA complementary to (and hence capable of binding to) a coding (or sense) sequence.

**antisepsis** • **n.** the practice of using antiseptics to eliminate the micro-organisms that cause disease. Compare with **ASEPSIS**.

**antiseptic** • **adj. 1** relating to or denoting substances that prevent the growth of disease-causing micro-organisms. **2** so clean or pure as to be bland or characterless. • **n.** an antiseptic compound or preparation.
– DERIVATIVES **antiseptically** adv.

**antiserum** • **n.** (pl. **antisera**) a blood serum containing antibodies against specific antigens, injected to treat or protect against specific diseases.

**antisocial** • **adj. 1** contrary to the customs of society and causing annoyance to others. ➤Psychiatry sociopathic. **2** not sociable.
– DERIVATIVES **antisocially** adv.

**antispasmodic** • **adj.** used to relieve spasm of involuntary muscle. ● **n.** an antispasmodic drug.

**anti-static** ● **adj.** preventing the build-up of static electricity or reducing its effects.

**antistrophe** /an'tɪstrəfi/ ● **n.** the second section of an ancient Greek choral ode or of one division of it. Compare with **STROPHE**.
– ORIGIN C16: via late L. from Gk *antistrophē*, from *antistrephein* 'turn against'.

**antisymmetric** ● **adj.** Mathematics & Physics unaltered in magnitude but changed in sign by an arithmetical or symmetry operation.

**antithesis** /an'tɪθəsɪs/ ● **n.** (pl. **antitheses** /-siːz/) **1** a person or thing that is the direct opposite of another. ➤ a contrast or opposition between two things. **2** a rhetorical or literary device in which an opposition or contrast of ideas is expressed. **3** (in Hegelian philosophy) the negation of the thesis as the second stage in the process of dialectical reasoning. Compare with **SYNTHESIS**.
– ORIGIN ME: from late L., from Gk *antitithenai* 'set against'.

**antithetical** /ˌantɪ'θɛtɪk(ə)l/ ● **adj.** **1** mutually incompatible. **2** relating to or using the rhetorical device of antithesis.
– DERIVATIVES **antithetic** adj. **antithetically** adv.
– ORIGIN C16: from Gk *antithetikos*, from *antithetos* 'placed in opposition'.

**antitoxin** ● **n.** Physiology an antibody that counteracts a toxin.
– DERIVATIVES **antitoxic** adj.

**antitrade winds** ● **pl. n.** steady winds that blow in the opposite direction to and overlie the trade winds.

**antitrust** ● **adj.** chiefly US (of legislation) preventing or controlling monopolies.

**antitype** ● **n.** a person or thing that represents the opposite of another.
– DERIVATIVES **antitypical** adj.
– ORIGIN C17: from late L. *antitypus*, from Gk *antitupos*, from *anti* 'against, opposite' + *tupos* 'type, a stamp'.

**antivenin** /ˌantɪ'vɛnɪn/ ● **n.** an antiserum containing antibodies against specific poisons, especially those in the venom of snakes.
– DERIVATIVES **antivenom** n.
– ORIGIN C19: from **ANTI-** + *ven(om)* + **IN**[1].

**antiviral** ● **adj.** Medicine (of a drug or treatment) effective against viruses.

**antivirus** ● **adj.** Computing (of software) designed to detect and destroy computer viruses.

**antivivisection** ● **adj.** opposed to the use of live animals for scientific research.
– DERIVATIVES **antivivisectionism** n. **antivivisectionist** n. & adj.

**antler** ● **n.** a branched horn on the head of an adult deer. ➤ one of the branches on an antler.
– DERIVATIVES **antlered** adj.
– ORIGIN ME: from Anglo-Norman Fr., var. of OFr. *antoillier*, of unknown origin.

**ant lion** ● **n.** an insect that resembles a dragonfly, with predatory larvae that construct conical pits into which insects fall. [Family Myrmeleontidae.]

**antonomasia** /ˌantənə'meɪzɪə, anˌtɒnə-/ ● **n.** Linguistics the substitution of an epithet or title for a proper name. ➤ the use of a proper name to express a general idea (e.g. *a Scrooge* for a miser).
– ORIGIN C16: via L. from Gk, from *antonomazein* 'name instead'.

**antonym** /'antənɪm/ ● **n.** a word opposite in meaning to another.
– DERIVATIVES **antonymous** adj.
– ORIGIN C19: from Fr. *antonyme*, from *ant-* (from Gk *anti-* 'against') + Gk *onoma* 'a name'.

**antrectomy** /an'trɛktəmi/ ● **n.** surgical removal of the antrum of the stomach.

**antrum** /'antrəm/ ● **n.** (pl. **antra** /-trə/) Anatomy **1** a natural chamber or cavity in a bone. **2** the pyloric end of the stomach.
– DERIVATIVES **antral** adj.
– ORIGIN C19: from L., from Gk *antron* 'cave'.

**antsy** /'antsi/ ● **adj.** (**-ier**, **-iest**) N. Amer. informal agitated, impatient, or restless.
– ORIGIN C19: prob. from the phr. *have ants in one's pants* (see **ANT**).

**Anura** /ə'njʊərə/ ● **pl. n.** Zoology an order of tailless amphibians that comprises the frogs and toads.
– DERIVATIVES **anuran** n. & adj.
– ORIGIN mod. L., from **AN-**[1] + Gk *oura* 'tail'.

**anuria** /ə'njʊərɪə/ ● **n.** Medicine failure of the kidneys to produce urine.
– DERIVATIVES **anuric** adj.

**anus** /'eɪnəs/ ● **n.** the opening at the end of the alimentary canal through which solid waste matter leaves the body.
– ORIGIN ME: from L., orig. 'a ring'.

**anvil** ● **n.** **1** a heavy iron block on which metal can be hammered and shaped. **2** the horizontally extended upper part of a cumulonimbus cloud. **3** Anatomy another term for **INCUS**.
– ORIGIN OE *anfilte*, from the Gmc base of **ON** + a verbal stem meaning 'beat'.

**anxiety** ● **n.** (pl. **-ies**) a feeling of being anxious. ➤ Psychiatry a nervous disorder marked by excessive uneasiness.
– ORIGIN C16: from Fr. *anxiété* or L. *anxietas*, from *anxius* (see **ANXIOUS**).

**anxiolytic** /ˌaŋzɪə'lɪtɪk/ Medicine ● **adj.** used to reduce anxiety. ● **n.** an anxiolytic drug.

**anxious** ● **adj.** **1** experiencing worry or unease. **2** very eager and concerned to do something.
– DERIVATIVES **anxiously** adv. **anxiousness** n.
– ORIGIN C17: from L. *anxius* (from *angere* 'to choke') + **-OUS**.

**any** ● **det. & pron.** **1** used to refer to one or some of a thing or number of things, no matter how much or how many. **2** whichever of a specified class might be chosen. ● **adv.** at all; in some degree (used for emphasis).
– PHRASES **any more** (also chiefly N. Amer. **anymore**) to any further extent; any longer. **any time** (also **anytime**) at whatever time. **any time** (or **day** or **minute**) **now** informal very soon. **be not having any** (**of it**) informal be unwilling to cooperate.
– ORIGIN OE *ǣnig* (see **ONE**, **-Y**[1]), of Gmc origin.

**anybody** ● **pron.** anyone.

**anyhow** ● **adv.** **1** another term for **ANYWAY**. **2** in a careless or haphazard way.

**anymore** ● **adv.** chiefly N. Amer. variant of ***any more*** (see **ANY**).

**anyone** ● **pron.** any person or people.

**anyplace** ● **adv.** N. Amer. informal term for **ANYWHERE**.

**any road** ● **adv.** chiefly N. English informal term for **ANYWAY**.

**anything** ● **pron.** used to refer to a thing, no matter what.
– PHRASES **anything but** not at all (used for emphasis). **anything like** —— [with neg.] at all like a specified thing (used for emphasis). (**as**) —— **as anything** informal extremely ——.

**anytime** ● **adv.** chiefly N. Amer. variant of ***any time*** (see **ANY**).

**anyway** ● **adv.** **1** used to confirm or support a point. **2** used in conversations to change the subject or to resume after interruption. **3** used to indicate that something happened or will happen in spite of something else.

**anyways** ● **adv.** N. Amer. informal or dialect form of **ANYWAY**.

**anywhere** ● **adv.** in or to any place. ● **pron.** any place.

**anywheres** ● **adv. & pron.** chiefly N. Amer. informal or dialect form of **ANYWHERE**.

**anywise** ● **adv.** archaic in any manner or way.

**Anzac** ● **n.** a soldier in the Australian and New Zealand Army Corps (1914–18). ➤ informal a person from Australia or New Zealand.

**AOB** ● **abbrev.** Brit. (at the end of an agenda for a meeting) any other business.

**AOC** ● **abbrev.** appellation d'origine contrôlée (see **APPELLATION CONTRÔLÉE**).

**ao dai** /'aʊ ˌdʌɪ/ ● **n.** (pl. **ao dais**) a Vietnamese woman's traditional long-sleeved tunic with ankle-length panels at front and back, worn over trousers.

– ORIGIN 1960s: Vietnamese.

**A-OK** (also **A-okay**) ● **adj. & adv.** N. Amer. informal in a good order or manner; all right.
– ORIGIN 1960s (orig. an astronauts' term): from *a*ll systems *OK*.

**AOR** ● **n.** a style of popular music in which a hard rock background is combined with more melodic elements.
– ORIGIN 1970s (orig. US): from *album-oriented rock* or *adult-oriented rock*.

**aorist** /ˈeɪərɪst, ˈɛːr-/ Grammar ● **adj.** relating to or denoting a past tense of a verb (especially in Greek) which does not contain any reference to duration or completion of the action. ● **n.** a word in the aorist tense.
– DERIVATIVES **aoristic** adj.
– ORIGIN C16: from Gk *aoristos* 'indefinite'.

**aorta** /eɪˈɔːtə/ ● **n.** the main artery of the body, supplying oxygenated blood from the heart to the circulatory system.
– DERIVATIVES **aortic** adj.
– ORIGIN C16: from Gk *aortē*, from *aeirein* 'raise'.

**aoudad** /ˈɑːʊdad/ ● **n.** another term for **BARBARY SHEEP**.
– ORIGIN C19: from Fr., from Berber *udād*.

**à outrance** /ɑː ˈuːtrɒ̃s, French a utrɑ̃s/ ● **adv.** poetic/literary to the death or the very end.
– ORIGIN Fr., lit. 'to the utmost'.

**AP** ● **abbrev.** Associated Press.

**ap-**[1] ● **prefix** variant spelling of **AD-** assimilated before *p* (as in *apposite*, *apprehend*).

**ap-**[2] ● **prefix** variant spelling of **APO-** shortened before a vowel or *h* (as in *aphelion*).

**apace** ● **adv.** poetic/literary swiftly; quickly.
– ORIGIN ME: from OFr. *a pas* 'at (a considerable) pace'.

**Apache** /əˈpatʃi/ ● **n.** (pl. same or **Apaches**) **1** a member of an American Indian people living chiefly in New Mexico and Arizona. **2** any of the Athabaskan languages of this people.
– ORIGIN from Mex. Sp., prob. from Zuñi *Apachu*, lit. 'enemy'.

**apanage** ● **n.** variant spelling of **APPANAGE**.

**apart** ● **adv.** **1** separated by a specified distance. ➤ no longer living together or close emotionally. **2** to or on one side. **3** into pieces.
– PHRASES **apart from 1** except for. **2** as well as.
– DERIVATIVES **apartness** n.
– ORIGIN ME: from OFr., from L. *a parte* 'at the side'.

**apartheid** /əˈpɑːtheɪt, əˈpɑːtʌɪd/ ● **n.** the system of segregation or discrimination on grounds of race in force in South Africa 1948–91.
– ORIGIN 1940s: from Afrik., lit. 'separateness', from Du. *apart* 'separate' + *-heid* (equivalent of **-HOOD**).

**aparthotel** (also **apartotel**) ● **n.** a type of hotel providing self-catering apartments as well as ordinary hotel facilities.

**apartment** ● **n.** **1** chiefly N. Amer. a suite of rooms forming one residence; a flat. ➤ a block of apartments. **2** (**apartments**) a private suite of rooms in a very large house.
– ORIGIN C17: from Fr. *appartement*, from Ital. *appartamento*, from *appartare* 'to separate'.

**apathetic** ● **adj.** not interested or enthusiastic.
– DERIVATIVES **apathetically** adv.

**apathy** /ˈapəθi/ ● **n.** lack of interest or enthusiasm.
– ORIGIN C17: from Fr. *apathie*, via L. from Gk *apatheia*, from *apathēs* 'without feeling'.

**apatite** /ˈapətʌɪt/ ● **n.** a pale green to purple mineral consisting chiefly of calcium phosphate.
– ORIGIN C19: from Gk *apatē* 'deceit' (from the mineral's diverse forms and colours).

**apatosaurus** /əˌpatəˈsɔːrəs/ ● **n.** a huge herbivorous dinosaur of the late Jurassic period, with a long neck and tail.
– ORIGIN mod. L., from Gk *apatē* 'deceit' (because of a deceptive similarity between some of its bones and those of other dinosaurs) + *sauros* 'lizard'.

**APB** ● **abbrev.** US all-points bulletin.

**APC** ● **abbrev.** armoured personnel carrier.

**ape** ● **n.** **1** a large tailless primate of a group including the gorilla, chimpanzees, orang-utan, and gibbons. [Families Pongidae and Hylobatidae.] **2** informal an unintelligent or clumsy person. **3** archaic an inferior imitator. ● **v.** imitate, especially in an absurd or unthinking way.
– PHRASES **go ape** (or N. Amer. vulgar slang **apeshit**) informal go wild.
– ORIGIN OE *apa*, of Gmc origin.

**APEC** ● **abbrev.** Asia Pacific Economic Cooperation.

**apeman** ● **n.** (pl. **-men**) an extinct ape-like primate believed to be related to present-day humans.

**aperçu** /ˌapɛːˈsjuː/ ● **n.** (pl. **aperçus**) a comment which makes an illuminating or entertaining point.
– ORIGIN C19: from Fr., past part. of *apercevoir* 'perceive'.

**aperient** /əˈpɪərɪənt/ Medicine ● **adj.** used to relieve constipation. ● **n.** an aperient drug.
– ORIGIN C17: from L. *aperient-*, *aperire* 'to open'.

**aperiodic** ● **adj.** chiefly Physics **1** not periodic; irregular. **2** damped to prevent oscillation or vibration.
– DERIVATIVES **aperiodicity** n.

**aperitif** /əˈpɛrɪtiːf, əˌpɛrɪˈtiːf/ ● **n.** an alcoholic drink taken before a meal to stimulate the appetite.
– ORIGIN C19: from Fr. *apéritif*, from med. L. *aperitivus*, based on L. *aperire* 'to open'.

**aperture** /ˈapətʃə, -tj(ʊ)ə/ ● **n.** chiefly technical an opening, hole, or gap. ➤ the variable opening by which light enters a camera.
– ORIGIN ME: from L. *apertura*, from *apert-*, *aperire* 'to open'.

**apery** /ˈeɪpəri/ ● **n.** archaic absurd or unthinking mimicry.

**apetalous** /eɪˈpɛt(ə)ləs, ə-/ ● **adj.** Botany having no petals.
– ORIGIN C18: from mod. L. *apetalus*, from Gk *apetalos* 'leafless' + **-OUS**.

**APEX** ● **abbrev.** Association of Professional, Executive, Clerical, and Computer Staff.

**Apex** /ˈeɪpɛks/ ● **n.** a system of reduced fares for scheduled airline flights and railway journeys which must be booked and paid for in advance.
– ORIGIN 1970s: from *A*dvance *P*urchase *Ex*cursion.

**apex** /ˈeɪpɛks/ ● **n.** (pl. **apexes** or **apices** /ˈeɪpɪsiːz/) **1** the top or highest part of something, especially one forming a point. ➤ Botany the growing point of a shoot. **2** the highest level of a hierarchy. ● **v.** reach a high point or climax.
– ORIGIN C17: from L., 'peak, tip'.

**Apgar score** /ˈapgə/ ● **n.** Medicine a number expressing the physical condition of a newborn infant (a score of ten representing the best possible condition).
– ORIGIN 1960s: named after the Amer. anaesthesiologist Virginia *Apgar*.

**aphasia** /əˈfeɪzɪə/ ● **n.** Medicine inability to understand or produce speech as a result of brain damage.
– DERIVATIVES **aphasic** adj. & n.
– ORIGIN C19: from Gk, from *aphatos* 'speechless'.

**aphelion** /apˈhiːlɪən/ ● **n.** (pl. **aphelia** /-lɪə/) Astronomy the point in a body's orbit at which it is furthest from the sun. The opposite of **PERIHELION**.
– ORIGIN C17: alt. of mod. L. *aphelium*, from Gk *aph' hēlion* 'from the sun'.

**apheresis** /əˈfɪərɪsɪs/ ● **n.** **1** Linguistics omission of the initial sound of a word, as when *he is* is pronounced *he's*. **2** Medicine a technique by which a particular substance or component is removed from the blood.
– ORIGIN C16: via late L. from Gk *aphairesis*, from *aphairein* 'take away'.

**aphesis** /ˈafɪsɪs/ ● **n.** Linguistics the gradual loss of an unstressed vowel at the beginning of a word (e.g. of *e* from *esquire* to form *squire*).
– DERIVATIVES **aphetic** /əˈfɛtɪk/ adj. **aphetically** adv.
– ORIGIN C19: from Gk, lit. 'letting go', from *apo* 'from' + *hienai* 'let go, send'.

**aphicide** /ˈeɪfɪsʌɪd/ ● **n.** an insecticide used against aphids.

**aphid** /ˈeɪfɪd/ ● **n.** a small bug which feeds by sucking sap from plants, especially a blackfly or greenfly. [*Aphis* and other genera: many species.]
– ORIGIN C19: back-form. from *aphides*, pl. of **APHIS**.

**aphis** /ˈeɪfɪs/ ● **n.** (pl. **aphides** /-diːz/) another term for

**APHID.**
– ORIGIN C18: mod. L., from Gk, perh. a misreading of *koris* 'bug' (interpreting the characters κορ 'kor' as αφ 'aph').

**aphonia** /eɪ'fəʊnɪə, ə-/ (also **aphony** /'af(ə)ni/) ● **n.** Medicine inability to speak through disease of or damage to the larynx or mouth.
– ORIGIN C17: mod. L., from Gk *aphōnia*, from *aphōnos* 'voiceless'.

**aphorism** /'afərɪz(ə)m/ ● **n.** a pithy observation which contains a general truth.
– DERIVATIVES **aphorist** n. **aphoristic** adj. **aphoristically** adv. **aphorize** (also **-ise**) v.
– ORIGIN C16: from Fr. *aphorisme* or late L. *aphorismus*, from Gk *aphorismos* 'definition'.

**aphrodisiac** /ˌafrə'dɪzɪak/ ● **n.** a food, drink, or drug that stimulates sexual desire.
– ORIGIN C18: from Gk *aphrodisiakos*, from *aphrodisios*, from *Aphroditē* 'Aphrodite', the goddess of love.

**aphtha** /'afθə/ ● **n.** (pl. **aphthae** /'afθiː/) Medicine a small ulcer occurring in groups in the mouth or on the tongue.
– DERIVATIVES **aphthous** adj.
– ORIGIN C17: via L. from Gk, rel. to *haptein* 'set on fire'.

**API** ● **abbrev.** Computing application programming interface.

**apian** /'eɪpɪən/ ● **adj.** of or relating to bees.
– ORIGIN C19: from L. *apianus*, from *apis* 'bee'.

**apiary** /'eɪpɪəri/ ● **n.** (pl. **-ies**) a place where bees are kept.
– DERIVATIVES **apiarian** adj. **apiarist** n.
– ORIGIN C17: from L. *apiarium*, from *apis* 'bee'.

**apical** /'eɪpɪk(ə)l, 'ap-/ ● **adj. 1** technical relating to or denoting an apex. **2** Phonetics (of a consonant) formed with the tip of the tongue at or near the front teeth or the alveolar ridge, for example *th* or trilled *r*.
– ORIGIN C19: from L. *apex*, *apic-* (see **APEX**) + **-AL**.

**apices** plural form of **APEX**.

**apiculture** /'eɪpɪˌkʌltʃə/ ● **n.** technical term for **BEE-KEEPING**.
– DERIVATIVES **apicultural** adj. **apiculturist** n.
– ORIGIN C19: from L. *apis* 'bee' + **CULTURE**.

**apiece** ● **adv.** to, for, or by each one.

**apish** /'eɪpɪʃ/ ● **adj.** resembling or likened to an ape. ➤foolish or silly.
– DERIVATIVES **apishly** adv. **apishness** n.

**aplanat** /'aplənat/ ● **n.** Physics a reflecting or refracting surface which is free from spherical aberration.
– DERIVATIVES **aplanatic** adj.
– ORIGIN C19: coined in Ger. from Gk *aplanētos*, from *a-* 'not' + *planan* 'wander'.

**aplasia** /ə'pleɪzɪə/ ● **n.** Medicine the failure of an organ or tissue to develop or to function normally.
– DERIVATIVES **aplastic** adj.
– ORIGIN C19: from **A-**[1] + Gk *plasis* 'formation'.

**aplastic anaemia** ● **n.** Medicine deficiency of all types of blood cell caused by failure of bone marrow development.

**aplenty** ● **adj.** [postpos.] in abundance: *he has work aplenty.*

**aplomb** /ə'plɒm/ ● **n.** self-confidence or assurance.
– ORIGIN C18 (in the sense 'perpendicularity, steadiness'): from Fr., from *à plomb* 'according to a plummet'.

**apnoea** /ap'niːə/ (US **apnea**) ● **n.** Medicine temporary cessation of breathing, especially during sleep.
– ORIGIN C18: mod. L., from Gk *apnoia*, from *apnous* 'breathless'.

**apo-** /'apəʊ/ ● **prefix 1** away from or separate: *apocrine.* **2** Astronomy denoting the furthest point in the orbit of a body in relation to the primary: *apolune.* Compare with **PERI-**.
– ORIGIN from Gk *apo* 'from, away, quite, un-'.

**Apoc.** ● **abbrev. 1** Apocalypse. **2** Apocrypha.

**apocalypse** /ə'pɒkəlɪps/ ● **n. 1** an event involving destruction or damage on a catastrophic scale. **2** (**the Apocalypse**) the complete final destruction of the world, as described in the biblical book of Revelation. ➤(especially in the Vulgate Bible) the book of Revelation.
– ORIGIN OE, via OFr. and eccles. L. from Gk *apokalupsis*, from *apokaluptein* 'uncover, reveal'.

**apocalyptic** ● **adj. 1** momentous or catastrophic. **2** of or resembling the biblical Apocalypse.
– DERIVATIVES **apocalyptically** adv.

**apocarpous** /ˌapə'kɑːpəs/ ● **adj.** Botany having distinct carpels that are not joined together.
– ORIGIN C19: from **APO-** + Gk *karpos* 'fruit' + **-OUS**.

**apochromat** /'apəkrəmat/ ● **n.** Physics a lens or lens system that reduces spherical and chromatic aberration.
– DERIVATIVES **apochromatic** adj.

**apocope** /ə'pɒkəpi/ ● **n.** Linguistics omission of the final sound of a word, as when *cup of tea* is pronounced as *cuppa tea.*
– ORIGIN C16: from late L., from Gk *apokoptein* 'cut off'.

**Apocr.** ● **abbrev.** Apocrypha.

**apocrine** /'apəkrʌɪn, -krɪn/ ● **adj.** Physiology relating to or denoting glands which release some cytoplasm in their secretions, especially sweat glands in the armpits and pubic regions.
– ORIGIN C20: from **APO-** + Gk *krinein* 'to separate'.

**Apocrypha** /ə'pɒkrɪfə/ ● **pl. n.** [treated as sing. or pl.] **1** (**the Apocrypha**) biblical or related writings appended to the Old Testament in the Septuagint and Vulgate versions, not forming part of the accepted canon of Scripture. **2** (**apocrypha**) writings or reports not considered genuine.
– ORIGIN ME: from eccles. L. *apocrypha* (*scripta*) 'hidden (writings)', from Gk *apokruphos*, from *apokruptein* 'hide away'.

**apocryphal** ● **adj. 1** (of a report) of doubtful authenticity, although widely circulated as being true. **2** of or belonging to the Apocrypha.

**apodictic** /ˌapə'dɪktɪk/ (also **apodeictic** /-'dʌɪktɪk/) ● **adj.** formal clearly established or beyond dispute.
– ORIGIN C17: via L. from Gk *apodeiktikos*, from *apodeiknunai* 'show off, demonstrate'.

**apodosis** /ə'pɒdəsɪs/ ● **n.** (pl. **apodoses** /-siːz/) Grammar the main clause of a conditional sentence (e.g. *I would agree* in *if you asked me I would agree*). Contrasted with **PROTASIS**.
– ORIGIN C17: via late L. from Gk, from *apodidonai* 'give back'.

**apodous** /'apədəs/ ● **adj.** Zoology without feet or having only rudimentary feet.
– ORIGIN C19: from Gk *apous*, *apod-* 'footless' + **-OUS**.

**apogee** /'apədʒiː/ ● **n. 1** Astronomy the point in the orbit of the moon or a satellite at which it is furthest from the earth. The opposite of **PERIGEE**. **2** the culmination or climax of something.
– ORIGIN C16: from Fr. *apogée* or mod. L. *apogaeum*, from Gk *apogaion* (*diastēma*), '(distance) away from earth'.

**apolar** ● **adj.** chiefly Biochemistry having no electrical polarity.

**apolitical** ● **adj.** not interested or involved in politics.

**apollo** ● **n.** (pl. **-os**) a large creamy-white butterfly with black and red spots, found chiefly in the mountains of Europe. [*Parnassius apollo.*]
– ORIGIN C19: from *Apollo*, the Gk god of the sun.

**Apollonian** /ˌapə'ləʊnɪən/ ● **adj. 1** Greek Mythology of or relating to the god Apollo. **2** of or relating to the rational, ordered, and self-disciplined aspects of human nature. Compare with **DIONYSIAC**.

**apologetic** ● **adj. 1** expressing an apology. **2** constituting a formal justification of a theory or doctrine.
– DERIVATIVES **apologetically** adv.

**apologetics** ● **pl. n.** [treated as sing. or pl.] reasoned arguments in justification of a theory or doctrine.

**apologia** /ˌapə'ləʊdʒɪə/ ● **n.** a formal written defence of one's opinions or conduct.
– ORIGIN C18: from L. (see **APOLOGY**).

**apologist** ● **n.** a person who offers an argument in defence of something controversial.

**apologize** (also **-ise**) ● **v.** express regret for something that one has done wrong.

**apologue** /'apəlɒg/ ● **n.** a moral fable, especially one with animals as characters.

– ORIGIN C16: from Fr., via L. from Gk *apologos* 'story'.

**apology** ● n. (pl. **-ies**) **1** a regretful acknowledgement of an offence or failure. ➤(**apologies**) a formal expression of regret at being unable to attend a meeting or social function. **2** (**an apology for**) a very poor example of. **3** a justification or defence.
– ORIGIN C16: from Fr. *apologie*, or via late L. from Gk *apologia* 'a speech in one's own defence', from *apo* 'away'+ *-logia* (see **-LOGY**).

**apolune** /ˈapə(ʊ)luːn/ ● n. the point at which a spacecraft in lunar orbit is furthest from the moon. The opposite of **PERILUNE**.
– ORIGIN 1960s: from **APO-** + L. *luna* 'moon', on the pattern of *apogee*.

**apomict** /ˈapəmɪkt/ ● n. Botany a plant which reproduces by apomixis.

**apomixis** /ˌapəˈmɪksɪs/ ● n. Botany asexual reproduction in plants, in particular agamospermy. Often contrasted with **AMPHIMIXIS**.
– DERIVATIVES **apomictic** adj.
– ORIGIN C20: from **APO-** + Gk *mixis* 'mingling'.

**apomorphine** /ˌapəˈmɔːfiːn/ ● n. Medicine a compound derived from morphine, used as an emetic and in the treatment of Parkinsonism.

**aponeurosis** /ˌapənjʊˈrəʊsɪs/ ● n. (pl. **aponeuroses** /-siːz/) Anatomy a sheet of fibrous tissue which takes the place of a tendon in sheet-like muscles having a wide area of attachment.
– DERIVATIVES **aponeurotic** adj.
– ORIGIN C17: mod. L., from Gk *aponeurōsis*, from *apo* 'off, away' + *neuron* 'sinew' + **-OSIS**.

**apophatic** /ˌapəˈfatɪk/ ● adj. Theology (of knowledge of God) obtained through negation. The opposite of **CATAPHATIC**.
– ORIGIN C19: from Gk *apophatikos* 'negative', from *apophasis* 'denial'.

**apophthegm** /ˈapəθɛm/ (US **apothegm**) ● n. a concise saying or maxim.
– DERIVATIVES **apophthegmatic** /-θɛgˈmatɪk/ adj.
– ORIGIN C16: from Fr. *apophthegme* or mod. L. *apothegma*, from Gk, from *apophthengesthai* 'speak out'.

**apophyllite** /əˈpɒfɪlʌɪt/ ● n. a white mineral consisting of a hydrated silicate and fluoride of calcium and potassium.
– ORIGIN C19: from **APO-** + Gk *phullon* 'leaf' + **-ITE**[1].

**apophysis** /əˈpɒfɪsɪs/ ● n. (pl. **apophyses**) chiefly Zoology & Anatomy a natural protuberance or swelling, especially one on a bone for the attachment of muscles.
– DERIVATIVES **apophyseal** adj.
– ORIGIN C16: mod. L., from Gk *apophusis* 'offshoot'.

**apoplectic** /ˌapəˈplɛktɪk/ ● adj. **1** informal overcome with anger. **2** dated relating to or denoting apoplexy (stroke).
– DERIVATIVES **apoplectically** adv.

**apoplexy** /ˈapəplɛksi/ ● n. (pl. **-ies**) **1** dated unconsciousness or incapacity resulting from a cerebral haemorrhage or stroke. **2** informal inability to act or speak caused by extreme anger.
– ORIGIN ME: from OFr. *apoplexie*, from late L. *apoplexia*, from Gk *apoplēxia*, from *apoplēssein* 'disable by a stroke'.

**apoprotein** /ˌapəˈprəʊtiːn/ ● n. Biochemistry a protein which together with a prosthetic group forms a particular biochemical molecule such as a hormone or enzyme.

**apoptosis** /ˌapə(p)ˈtəʊsɪs/ ● n. Physiology the death of cells which occurs as a normal part of an organism's development.
– DERIVATIVES **apoptotic** /-ˈtɒtɪk/ adj.
– ORIGIN 1970s: from Gk *apoptōsis* 'falling off'.

**aporia** /əˈpɔːrɪə, əˈpɒrɪə/ ● n. **1** an irresolvable internal contradiction or logical disjunction in a text, argument, or theory. **2** Rhetoric the expression of doubt.
– ORIGIN C16: via late L. from Gk, from *aporos* 'impassable'.

**aposematic** /ˌapə(ʊ)sɪˈmatɪk/ ● adj. Zoology denoting coloration or markings serving to warn or repel predators.
– DERIVATIVES **aposematism** n.
– ORIGIN C19: from **APO-** + Gk *sēma* 'sign' + **-ATIC**.

**aposiopesis** /ˌapə(ʊ)ˌsʌɪəˈpiːsɪs/ ● n. (pl. **aposiopeses** /-siːz/) Rhetoric the device of suddenly breaking off in speech.
– DERIVATIVES **aposiopetic** adj.
– ORIGIN C16: via L. from Gk *aposiōpēsis*, from *aposiōpan* 'be silent'.

**apostasy** /əˈpɒstəsi/ ● n. the abandonment or renunciation of a belief or principle.
– ORIGIN ME: from eccles. L. *apostasia*, from late Gk alt. of Gk *apostasis* 'defection'.

**apostate** /ˈapəsteɪt/ ● n. a person who renounces a belief or principle. ● adj. abandoning a belief or principle.
– DERIVATIVES **apostatical** adj.
– ORIGIN ME: from eccles. L. *apostata*, from Gk *apostatēs* 'apostate, runaway slave'.

**apostatize** /əˈpɒstətʌɪz/ (also **-ise**) ● v. renounce a belief or principle.

**a posteriori** /eɪ, ɑː, pɒˌstɛrɪˈɔːrʌɪ, pɒˌstɪə-/ ● adj. & adv. **1** (with reference to reasoning or knowledge) proceeding from observations or experiences to the deduction of probable causes. **2** as an afterthought or with hindsight.
– ORIGIN C17: L., 'from what comes after'.

**apostle** ● n. **1** (**Apostle**) each of the twelve chief disciples of Jesus Christ. ➤an important early Christian teacher or missionary. **2** a vigorous and pioneering supporter of an idea or cause.
– DERIVATIVES **apostleship** n.
– ORIGIN OE *apostol*, via eccles. L. from Gk *apostolos* 'messenger', from *apostellein* 'send forth'.

**apostlebird** ● n. a gregarious Australian bird with grey, brown, and black plumage. [*Struthidea cinerea*.]
– ORIGIN C20: named from the supposed habit of these birds of going about in flocks of twelve.

**Apostle spoon** ● n. a teaspoon with the figure of an Apostle or saint on the handle.

**apostolate** /əˈpɒstəleɪt/ ● n. **1** the position or authority of an apostle. ➤a group of apostles. **2** evangelistic activity or works.

**apostolic** /ˌapəˈstɒlɪk/ ● adj. **1** of or relating to the Apostles. **2** of or relating to the Pope, especially when he is regarded as the successor to St Peter.

**Apostolic Fathers** ● pl. n. the Christian leaders immediately succeeding the Apostles.

**apostolic succession** ● n. the uninterrupted transmission of spiritual authority from the Apostles through successive popes and bishops, taught by the Roman Catholic Church but denied by most Protestants.

**apostrophe**[1] /əˈpɒstrəfi/ ● n. a punctuation mark (') used to indicate either possession (e.g. *Harry's book*) or the omission of letters or numbers (e.g. *can't*; *1 Jan. '99*).
– ORIGIN C16: via late L., from Gk *apostrophos*, from *apostrephein* 'turn away'.

**apostrophe**[2] /əˈpɒstrəfi/ ● n. Rhetoric an exclamatory passage in a speech or poem addressed to a person or personified thing.
– ORIGIN C16: via L. from Gk *apostrophē* 'turning away', from *apostrephein* 'turn away'.

**apostrophize** /əˈpɒstrəfʌɪz/ (also **-ise**) ● v. **1** Rhetoric address with an exclamatory passage. **2** punctuate with an apostrophe.

**apothecaries' measure** (also **apothecaries' weight**) ● n. historical a system of units formerly used in pharmacy for liquid volume (or weight), based on the fluid ounce and the ounce troy.

**apothecary** /əˈpɒθɪk(ə)ri/ ● n. (pl. **-ies**) archaic a person who prepared and sold medicines.
– ORIGIN ME: via OFr. from late L. *apothecarius*, from L. *apotheca*, from Gk *apothēkē* 'storehouse'.

**apothegm** ● n. US spelling of **APOPHTHEGM**.

**apothem** /ˈapəθɛm/ ● n. Geometry a line from the centre of a regular polygon at right angles to any of its sides.
– ORIGIN C19: from Gk *apotithenai* 'put aside, deposit'.

**apotheosis** /əˌpɒθɪˈəʊsɪs/ ● n. (pl. **apotheoses** /-siːz/) **1** the highest point in the development of something. **2** elevation to divine status.
– DERIVATIVES **apotheosize** (also **-ise**) v.
– ORIGIN C16: via eccles. L. from Gk *apotheōsis*, from *apotheoun* 'make a god of', from *apo-* 'from' + *theos*

'god'.

**apotropaic** /ˌapətrəˈpeɪɪk/ • **adj.** supposedly having the power to avert evil or bad luck.
– DERIVATIVES **apotropaically** adv.
– ORIGIN C19: from Gk *apotropaios*, from *apotrepein* 'turn away or from' + **-IC**.

**app.** • **abbrev. 1** appendix (in a book). **2** Computing application.

**appal** (US **appall**) • **v.** (**appalled**, **appalling**) **1** greatly dismay or horrify. **2** [as adj. **appalling**] informal very bad or displeasing.
– DERIVATIVES **appallingly** adv.
– ORIGIN ME: from OFr. *apalir* 'grow pale'.

**Appaloosa** /ˌapəˈluːsə/ • **n.** a horse of a North American breed having dark spots on a light background.
– ORIGIN 1920s: from *Opelousas* in Louisiana, or *Palouse*, a river in Idaho.

**appanage** /ˈap(ə)nɪdʒ/ (also **apanage**) • **n. 1** historical a provision made for the maintenance of the younger children of kings and princes. **2** archaic a benefit or right.
– ORIGIN C17: from Fr., based on med. L. *appanare* 'provide with the means of subsistence', from *ad-* 'to' + *panis* 'bread'.

**apparat** /ˌapəˈrɑːt/ • **n.** chiefly historical the administrative system of a communist party.
– ORIGIN Russ., from Ger., lit. 'apparatus'.

**apparatchik** /ˌapəˈratʃɪk/ • **n.** (pl. **apparatchiks** or **apparatchiki** /-kiː/) **1** chiefly historical a member of a communist party apparat. **2** derogatory or humorous an official in a large political organization.
– ORIGIN 1940s: from Russ., from *apparat* (see **APPARAT**).

**apparatus** /ˌapəˈreɪtəs/ • **n.** (pl. **apparatuses**) **1** the equipment needed for a particular activity or purpose. **2** a complex structure within an organization: *the apparatus of government.* **3** (also **critical apparatus**, **apparatus criticus**) a collection of notes accompanying a printed text.
– ORIGIN C17: from L., from *apparat-*, *apparare* 'make ready for'.

**apparel** /əˈparəl/ • **n.** formal clothing. ➤ (**apparels**) embroidered ornamentation on ecclesiastical vestments. • **v.** (**apparelled**, **apparelling**; US **appareled**, **appareling**) archaic clothe.
– ORIGIN ME (as v. meaning 'make ready or fit', as n. meaning 'furnishings, equipment'): from OFr. *apareillier*, based on L. *ad-* 'to' (expressing change) + *par* 'equal'.

**apparent** • **adj. 1** readily perceived or understood; obvious. **2** seeming real or true.
– DERIVATIVES **apparently** adv.
– ORIGIN ME: from OFr. *aparant*, from L. *apparent-*, *apparere* (see **APPEAR**).

**apparent horizon** • **n.** see **HORIZON** (sense 1).

**apparent magnitude** • **n.** Astronomy the magnitude of a celestial object as it is measured from the earth.

**apparent time** • **n.** time as indicated by the actual position of the sun. Compare with **MEAN SOLAR TIME**.

**apparent wind** • **n.** the wind as it is experienced on board a moving sailing vessel.

**apparition** • **n.** a remarkable thing making a sudden appearance. ➤ a ghost.
– DERIVATIVES **apparitional** adj.
– ORIGIN ME (in the sense 'the action of appearing'): from L. *apparitio(n-)*, from *apparere* (see **APPEAR**).

**appeal** • **v. 1** make a serious or heartfelt request. ➤ Cricket (of the bowler or fielders) call on the umpire to declare a batsman out. **2** Law apply to a higher court for a reversal of the decision of a lower court. **3** (usu. **appeal to**) be attractive or interesting. • **n. 1** an act of appealing. **2** Law an application to a higher court for a decision to be reversed. **3** the quality of being attractive or interesting.
– DERIVATIVES **appealable** adj. **appealer** n. **appealing** adj. **appealingly** adv.
– ORIGIN ME (in legal contexts): from OFr. *apel* (n.), *apeler* (v.), from L. *appellare* 'to address'.

**appear** • **v. 1** come into sight. ➤ come into existence or use. ➤ be published. ➤ informal arrive. **2** present oneself publicly or formally, especially on stage or as the accused or counsel in a law court. **3** seem; give a specified impression.
– ORIGIN ME: from OFr. *apareir*, from L. *apparere*, from *ad-* 'towards' + *parere* 'come into view'.

**appearance** • **n. 1** the way that someone or something appears. ➤ an impression given: *she read it with every appearance of interest.* **2** an act of performing in a public event. **3** an act of arriving or becoming visible.
– PHRASES **keep up appearances** maintain an impression of wealth or well-being. **make** (or **put in**) **an appearance** attend an event briefly. **to** (or **by**) **all appearances** as far as can be seen.

**appease** • **v.** placate (someone) by acceding to their demands.
– DERIVATIVES **appeasement** n. **appeaser** n.
– ORIGIN ME: from OFr. *apaisier*, from *a-* (from L. *ad* 'to, at') + *pais* 'peace'.

**appellant** /əˈpɛl(ə)nt/ • **n.** Law a person who appeals against a court ruling.
– ORIGIN ME: from Fr. *apelant*, lit. 'appealing', from *apeler* (see **APPEAL**).

**appellate** /əˈpɛlət/ • **adj.** Law (of a court) dealing with appeals.
– ORIGIN ME (in the sense 'appealed against, accused'): from L. *appellat-*, *appellare* (see **APPEAL**).

**appellation** /ˌapəˈleɪʃ(ə)n/ • **n.** formal a name or title.
– ORIGIN ME: via OFr. from L. *appellatio(n-)*, from *appellare* (see **APPEAL**).

**appellation contrôlée** /apəˌlasjɒ̃ kənˈtrɒleɪ, French apɛlasjɔ̃ kɔ̃tʀole/ (also **appellation d'origine** /ˌdɒrɪˈʒiːn, French dɔʀiʒin/ **contrôlée**) • **n.** a guarantee of the description of a French wine, in conformity with statutory regulations as to its origin.
– ORIGIN Fr., lit. 'controlled appellation'.

**appellative** /əˈpɛlətɪv/ • **adj.** formal relating to or denoting the giving of a name. • **n.** Grammar a common noun used as a vocative.
– ORIGIN ME: from late L. *appellativus*, from L. *appellat-*, *appellare* (see **APPEAL**).

**appellee** /ˌapəˈliː, ˌapɛˈliː/ • **n.** Law, chiefly US the defendant in a case taken to a higher court.
– ORIGIN C16: from Fr. *appelé*, past part. of *appeler*, from L. *appellare* (see **APPEAL**).

**append** • **v.** add to the end of a document or piece of writing.
– ORIGIN ME: from L. *appendere* 'hang on'.

**appendage** • **n. 1** a thing attached to something larger or more important. **2** Biology a projecting part of an organism, with a distinct appearance or function.

**appendant** formal or archaic • **adj.** attached. • **n.** a subordinate person or thing.

**appendectomy** /ˌap(ə)nˈdɛktəmi/ (Brit. also **appendicectomy** /əˌpɛndɪˈsɛktəmi/) • **n.** (pl. **-ies**) a surgical operation to remove the appendix.

**appendicitis** • **n.** inflammation of the appendix.

**appendicular** /ˌap(ə)nˈdɪkjʊlə/ • **adj.** technical relating to or denoting an appendage or appendages.

**appendix** • **n.** (pl. **appendices** or **appendixes**) **1** (also **vermiform appendix**) Anatomy a tube-shaped sac attached to the lower end of the large intestine. **2** a section of subsidiary matter at the end of a book.
– ORIGIN C16 (in sense 2): from L., from *appendere* (see **APPEND**).

**apperception** • **n.** Psychology assimilation into the mind of a new concept.
– DERIVATIVES **apperceptive** adj.
– ORIGIN C18: from Fr. *aperception* or mod. L. *aperceptio(n-)*, from L. *ad-* 'to' + *percipere* 'perceive'.

**appertain** /ˌapəˈteɪn/ • **v. 1** (**appertain to**) relate to. **2** be appropriate.
– ORIGIN ME: from OFr. *apertenir*, from late L. *appertinere*, from *ad-* 'to' + L. *pertinere* 'to pertain'.

**appestat** /ˈapɪstat/ • **n.** Physiology the region of the hypothalamus believed to control appetite.
– ORIGIN 1950s: from **APPETITE**, prob. on the pattern of *thermostat*.

**appetency** /ˈapɪt(ə)nsi/ • **n.** (pl. **-ies**) archaic a longing or desire.
– ORIGIN C17: from L. *appetentia*, from *appetere* (see **APPE-**

**TITE**).

**appetite** • n. a natural desire to satisfy a bodily need, especially for food.
– DERIVATIVES **appetitive** adj.
– ORIGIN ME: from OFr. *apetit* (mod. *appétit*), from L. *appetitus* 'desire for', from *appetere* 'seek after'.

**appetizer** (also **-iser**) • n. a small dish of food or a drink taken before a meal to stimulate the appetite.

**appetizing** (also **-ising**) • adj. stimulating the appetite.
– DERIVATIVES **appetizingly** adv.
– ORIGIN C17: from Fr. *appétissant*, irregular formation from *appétit* (see **APPETITE**).

**applaud** • v. show approval by clapping. ➤praise or approve of.
– ORIGIN C15: from L. *applaudere*, from *ad-* 'to' + *plaudere* 'to clap', reinforced by Fr. *applaudir*.

**applause** • n. approval expressed by clapping.
– ORIGIN ME: from med. L. *applausus*, from *applaudere* (see **APPLAUD**).

**apple** • n. **1** the rounded fruit of a tree of the rose family, with green or red skin and crisp flesh. **2** the tree bearing such fruit. [Genus *Malus*: numerous cultivated forms.] **3** used in names of similar unrelated fruits, e.g. **custard apple**.
– PHRASES **the apple of one's eye** a person of whom one is extremely fond and proud. [orig. denoting the pupil of the eye, extended as a symbol of something cherished.] **apples and pears** Brit. rhyming slang stairs. **a rotten** (or **bad**) **apple** informal a corrupt person in a group, likely to have a detrimental influence on the others. **upset the apple cart** spoil a plan.
– DERIVATIVES **appley** adj.
– ORIGIN OE *æppel*, of Gmc origin.

**apple butter** • n. N. Amer. a paste of spiced stewed apple.

**apple-cheeked** • adj. having round rosy cheeks.

**applejack** • n. N. Amer. a spirit distilled from cider.

**apple-pie bed** • n. a bed which, as a practical joke, has been made with a sheet folded so that the legs cannot be stretched out.

**apple-pie order** • n. perfect order.

**applesauce** • n. **1** (**apple sauce**) a purée of stewed apples, typically served with pork or as a dessert. **2** N. Amer. informal nonsense.

**applet** /'aplɪt/ • n. Computing a small application running within a larger program.

**appliance** • n. **1** a device designed to perform a specific task. **2** a fire engine. **3** Brit. the action of applying something.
– DERIVATIVES **applianced** adj.

**applicable** • adj. relevant; appropriate.
– DERIVATIVES **applicability** n. **applicably** adv.
– ORIGIN C16 (in the sense 'compliant'): from OFr., or from med. L. *applicabilis*, from *applicare* (see **APPLY**).

**applicant** • n. a person who applies for something.

**application** • n. **1** a formal request to an authority. **2** the action of putting something into operation. ➤practical use or relevance. **3** the action of applying something to a surface. **4** sustained effort. **5** Computing a program or piece of software designed to fulfil a particular purpose.
– DERIVATIVES **applicational** adj.

**application programming interface** • n. Computing a system of tools and resources in an operating system, enabling creation of software applications.

**applicative** /'aplɪkeɪtɪv, -kətɪv/ • adj. (of a subject) applied.

**applicator** • n. a device for inserting something or applying a substance to a surface.

**applied** • adj. (of a subject) practical rather than theoretical. Compare with **PURE**.

**appliqué** /ə'pliːkeɪ/ • n. ornamental needlework in which pieces of fabric are attached to a fabric ground. • v. (**appliqués**, **appliquéd**, **appliquéing**) decorate with appliqué.
– ORIGIN C18: from Fr., past part. of *appliquer* 'apply', from L. *applicare* (see **APPLY**).

**apply** • v. (**-ies**, **-ied**) **1** make a formal request. ➤put oneself forward as a candidate for a job. **2** bring into operation or use. ➤be relevant. **3** put (a substance) on a surface. **4** (**apply oneself**) work hard.
– DERIVATIVES **applier** n.
– ORIGIN ME: from OFr. *aplier*, from L. *applicat-*, *applicare* 'fold, fasten to'.

**appoggiatura** /əˌpɒdʒə'tjʊərə/ • n. (pl. **appoggiaturas** or **appoggiature**) Music a grace note which delays the next note of the melody, taking half or more of its written time value.
– ORIGIN Ital., from *appoggiare* 'lean upon, rest'.

**appoint** • v. **1** assign a job or role to. **2** determine or decide on (a time or place). ➤archaic decree. **3** Law determine the disposal of (property) under powers granted by the owner.
– DERIVATIVES **appointee** n. **appointer** n.
– ORIGIN ME: from OFr. *apointer*, from *a point* 'to a point'.

**appointed** • adj. **1** (of a time or place) designated. **2** equipped or furnished in a specified way.

**appointive** • adj. N. Amer. (of a job) relating to or filled by appointment rather than election.

**appointment** • n. **1** an arrangement to meet at a particular time and place. **2** a job or position. ➤the action or process of appointing someone. **3** (**appointments**) furniture or fittings.
– PHRASES **by appointment** (**to the Queen**) selling goods or services to the Queen.

**apport** /ə'pɔːt/ • n. an object produced supposedly by occult means at a seance.
– ORIGIN C19: from Fr. *apport* 'something brought', from *apporter* 'bring to'.

**apportion** • v. share out; assign.
– DERIVATIVES **apportionable** adj.
– ORIGIN C16: from OFr. *apportionner* or med. L. *apportionare*, from *ad-* 'to' + *portionare* 'divide into portions'.

**apportionment** • n. the action or result of apportioning. ➤the determination of the proportional number of members each US state sends to the House of Representatives.

**appose** /ə'pəʊz/ • v. technical place next to.
– ORIGIN C16: from L. *apponere*, on the pattern of words such as *compose*, *expose*.

**apposite** /'apəzɪt/ • adj. (especially of language) very appropriate; apt.
– DERIVATIVES **appositely** adv. **appositeness** n.
– ORIGIN C16: from L. *apposit-*, *apponere* 'apply'.

**apposition** • n. **1** chiefly technical the positioning of things next to each other. **2** Grammar a relationship between two or more words in which the units are grammatically parallel and have the same referent (e.g. *my friend Sue*).
– DERIVATIVES **appositional** adj. & n. **appositive** adj. & n.
– ORIGIN ME: from late L. *appositio(n-)*, from *apponere* (see **APPOSITE**).

**appraisal** • n. an assessment of someone or something, especially the performance of an employee.

**appraise** • v. assess the value, quality, or performance of. ➤(of an official valuer) set a price on.
– DERIVATIVES **appraisable** adj. **appraisee** n. **appraisement** n. **appraiser** n. **appraising** adj. **appraisingly** adv. **appraisive** adj.
– ORIGIN ME: alt. of **APPRIZE**, by assoc. with **PRAISE**.

**USAGE** appraise

**Appraise** is frequently confused with **apprise**. **Appraise** means 'assess', while **apprise** means 'inform' and is often used in the structure **apprise someone of something**.

**appreciable** • adj. large or important enough to be noticed.
– DERIVATIVES **appreciably** adv.

**appreciate** /ə'priːʃɪeɪt, -sɪ-/ • v. **1** recognize the value or significance of. ➤be grateful for. **2** rise in value or price.
– DERIVATIVES **appreciator** n. **appreciatory** /-ʃ(ɪ)ət(ə)ri/ adj.
– ORIGIN C16: from late L. *appretiat-*, *appretiare* 'set at a price, appraise', from *ad-* 'to' + *pretium* 'price'.

**appreciation** • n. **1** recognition of the value or significance of something. ➤gratitude. **2** a written assessment of an artist or work, especially a favourable one. **3** increase in monetary value.

**appreciative** ● **adj.** feeling or showing gratitude or pleasure.
– DERIVATIVES **appreciatively** adv. **appreciativeness** n.

**apprehend** ● **v. 1** intercept (someone) in the course of harmful or illicit action. ➤seize or arrest (someone). **2** understand; perceive. **3** archaic anticipate with uneasiness or fear.
– ORIGIN ME: from Fr. *appréhender* or L. *apprehendere*, from *ad-* 'towards' + *prehendere* 'lay hold of'.

**apprehensible** ● **adj.** archaic or poetic/literary capable of being understood or perceived.

**apprehension** ● **n. 1** anxious or fearful anticipation. **2** understanding. **3** the action of arresting someone.

**apprehensive** ● **adj. 1** anticipating with anxiety or fear. **2** archaic or poetic/literary of or relating to perception or understanding.
– DERIVATIVES **apprehensively** adv. **apprehensiveness** n.
– ORIGIN ME: from Fr. *appréhensif* or med. L. *apprehensivus*, from L. *apprehendere* (see APPREHEND).

**apprentice** ● **n.** a person learning a trade from a skilled employer. ● **v.** employ as an apprentice.
– DERIVATIVES **apprenticeship** n.
– ORIGIN ME: from OFr. *aprentis*, from *apprendre* 'learn', from L. *apprehendere* (see APPREHEND).

**appress** /ə'prɛs/ ● **v.** technical [usu. as adj. **appressed**] press (something) close to something else.
– ORIGIN C17: from L. *appress-*, *apprimere* 'press close'.

**apprise** /ə'prʌɪz/ ● **v.** (usu. **apprise someone of**) inform; tell.
– ORIGIN C17: from Fr. *appris*, *apprise*, past part. of *apprendre* 'learn, teach', from L. *apprehendere* (see APPREHEND).

**USAGE** apprise
On the confusion of **apprise** with **appraise**, see APPRAISE.

**apprize** /ə'prʌɪz/ (also **-ise**) ● **v.** archaic put a price on.
– ORIGIN ME: from OFr. *aprisier*, from *a-* (from L. *ad* 'to, at') + *prisier* 'to price, prize', from *pris* (see PRICE).

**approach** ● **v. 1** come near or nearer to in distance, time, or standard. ➤archaic bring nearer. **2** make an initial proposal to or request of. **3** start to deal with in a certain way. ● **n. 1** a way of dealing with something. **2** an initial proposal or request. **3** the action of approaching. ➤a way leading to a place: *the northern approaches to London.*
– ORIGIN ME: from OFr. *aprochier*, *aprocher*, from eccles. L. *appropiare* 'draw near'.

**approachable** ● **adj. 1** friendly and easy to talk to. **2** able to be reached from a particular direction or by a particular means.
– DERIVATIVES **approachability** n.

**approach shot** ● **n.** Golf a stroke which sends the ball from the fairway on to or nearer the green.

**approbation** ● **n.** approval; praise.
– DERIVATIVES **approbate** v. (US rare). **approbative** adj. **approbatory** adj.
– ORIGIN ME: via OFr. from L. *approbatio(n-)*, from *approbare* 'approve', from *ad-* 'to' + *probare* 'try, test'.

**appropriate** ● **adj.** /ə'prəʊprɪət/ **1** suitable; proper. **2** archaic assigned to a particular person. ● **v.** /ə'prəʊprɪeɪt/ **1** take for one's own use without permission. **2** devote (money) to a special purpose.
– DERIVATIVES **appropriately** adv. **appropriateness** n. **appropriation** n. **appropriator** n.
– ORIGIN ME: from late L. *appropriat-*, *appropriare* 'make one's own', from *ad-* 'to' + *proprius* 'own, proper'.

**approval** ● **n.** the action of approving of something. ➤a favourable opinion.
– PHRASES **on approval** (of goods) able to be returned if unsatisfactory. **seal** (or **stamp**) **of approval** an official indication that something is approved of.

**approve** ● **v. 1** officially accept as satisfactory. ➤(often **approve of**) believe that someone or something is good or acceptable. **2** archaic prove.
– DERIVATIVES **approving** adj. **approvingly** adv.
– ORIGIN ME: from OFr. *aprover*, from L. *approbare* (see APPROBATION).

**approved school** ● **n.** Brit. historical a residential institution for young offenders.

**approx.** ● **abbrev.** approximate(ly).

**approximate** ● **adj.** /ə'prɒksɪmət/ fairly accurate but not totally precise. ● **v.** /ə'prɒksɪmeɪt/ come close in quality or quantity. ➤estimate fairly accurately.
– DERIVATIVES **approximately** adv. **approximation** n. **approximative** adj.
– ORIGIN ME: from late L. *approximat-*, *approximare*, from *ad-* 'to' + *proximus* 'very near'.

**appurtenance** /ə'pəːt(ɪ)nəns/ ● **n.** an accessory associated with a particular activity.
– ORIGIN ME: from OFr. *apertenance*, based on late L. *appertinere* (see APPERTAIN).

**appurtenant** ● **adj.** formal belonging.
– ORIGIN ME: from OFr. *apartenant* 'appertaining', from *apartenir* (see APPERTAIN).

**APR** ● **abbrev.** annual(ized) percentage rate.

**Apr.** ● **abbrev.** April.

**apraxia** /ə'praksɪə/ ● **n.** Medicine inability to perform particular activities as a result of brain damage.
– DERIVATIVES **apraxic** adj.
– ORIGIN C19: from Ger. *Apraxie*, from Gk *apraxia* 'inaction'.

**après-ski** ● **n.** social activities following a day's skiing.
– ORIGIN 1950s: from Fr., lit. 'after skiing'.

**apricot** /'eɪprɪkɒt, 'aprɪ-/ ● **n. 1** an orange-yellow soft fruit, resembling a small peach. **2** the tree bearing this fruit. [*Prunus armeniaca*.] **3** an orange-yellow colour.
– ORIGIN C16: from Port. *albricoque* or Sp. *albaricoque*, from Sp. Arab. *al* 'the' + *barḳūḳ*, via late Gk from L. *praecoquum*, var. of *praecox* 'early-ripe'.

**April** ● **n.** the fourth month of the year.
– ORIGIN OE, from L. *Aprilis*.

**April Fool** ● **n.** a victim of a hoax on April Fool's Day. ➤a trick played on April Fool's Day.

**April Fool's Day** ● **n.** 1 April, traditionally an occasion for playing tricks.

**a priori** /ˌeɪ prʌɪ'ɔːrʌɪ, ˌɑː prɪ'ɔːri/ ● **adj. & adv.** based on theoretical deduction rather than empirical observation.
– DERIVATIVES **apriorism** /eɪ'prʌɪərɪz(ə)m/ n.
– ORIGIN C16: L., 'from what is before'.

**apron** ● **n. 1** a protective garment covering the front of one's clothes and tied at the back. **2** a small area adjacent to another larger area or structure. ➤an area on an airfield used for manoeuvring or parking aircraft. ➤(also **apron stage**) a strip of stage projecting in front of the curtain. **3** an endless conveyor made of overlapping plates.
– PHRASES **tied to someone's apron strings** under someone's influence and control to an excessive extent.
– DERIVATIVES **aproned** adj.
– ORIGIN ME *naperon*, from OFr., dimin. of *nape*, *nappe* 'tablecloth', from L. *mappa* 'napkin'; the *n* was lost by wrong division of *a napron*.

**apropos** /ˌaprə'pəʊ, 'aprəpəʊ/ ● **prep.** with reference to.
– PHRASES **apropos of nothing** having no relevance to any previous discussion or situation.
– ORIGIN C17: from Fr. *à propos* '(with regard) to (this) purpose'.

**apse** /aps/ ● **n. 1** a large semicircular or polygonal recess with a domed roof, typically at a church's eastern end. **2** another term for APSIS.
– DERIVATIVES **apsidal** /'apsɪd(ə)l/ adj.
– ORIGIN C19: from L. *apsis* (see APSIS).

**apsis** /'apsɪs/ ● **n.** (pl. **apsides** /-diːz/) Astronomy either of the two points in a body's orbit that are nearest to or furthest from the larger body round which it moves.
– DERIVATIVES **apsidal** adj.
– ORIGIN C17: via L. from Gk *apsis*, *hapsis* 'arch, vault'.

**apt** ● **adj. 1** appropriate; suitable. **2** (**apt to do something**) having a specified tendency. **3** quick to learn.
– DERIVATIVES **aptly** adv. **aptness** n.
– ORIGIN ME: from L. *aptus* 'fitted', from *apere* 'fasten'.

**apterous** /ˈapt(ə)rəs/ ● **adj.** Entomology (of an insect) having no wings.
– ORIGIN C18: from Gk *apteros* (from *a-* 'without' + *pteron* 'wing') + **-OUS**.

**Apterygota** /apˈtɛrɪˌɡəʊtə/ ● **pl. n.** Entomology a group of primitive wingless insects including the bristletails and springtails.
– DERIVATIVES **apterygote** n.
– ORIGIN mod. L. *Apterygota*, from Gk *a-* 'not' + *pterugōtos* 'winged'.

**aptitude** ● **n.** a natural ability or propensity.
– ORIGIN ME: via OFr. from late L. *aptitudo*, from L. *aptus* (see **APT**).

**APU** ● **abbrev.** auxiliary power unit.

**aqua** /ˈakwə/ ● **n.** the colour aquamarine.

**aqua-** /ˈakwə/ ● **comb. form** relating to water: *aquaculture.*
– ORIGIN from L. *aqua* 'water'.

**aqua aura** ● **n.** quartz or another mineral covered with a thin film of gold, having a blue iridescent colour.
– ORIGIN from L. *aqua* 'water' + *aura*, representing L. *aurum* 'gold'.

**aquaculture** ● **n.** the rearing or cultivation of aquatic animals or plants.

**aqua fortis** /ˈfɔːtɪs/ ● **n.** archaic term for **NITRIC ACID**.
– ORIGIN C15: from L., lit. 'strong water'.

**aqualung** ● **n.** a portable breathing apparatus for divers, which feeds compressed air from cylinders on the diver's back through a mask or mouthpiece.

**aquamanile** /ˌakwəməˈnʌɪli, -ˈniːli/ ● **n.** a medieval water container in the form of a mammal or bird.
– ORIGIN C19: from late L., from L. *aquaemanalis*, lit. 'ewer of water'.

**aquamarine** ● **n.** **1** a light bluish-green variety of beryl. **2** a light bluish-green colour.
– ORIGIN C18: from L. *aqua marina* 'seawater'.

**aquanaut** ● **n.** a diver.
– ORIGIN C19: from L. *aqua* 'water' + Gk *nautēs* 'sailor'.

**aquaplane** ● **n.** a board for riding on water, pulled by a speedboat. ● **v.** **1** ride on an aquaplane. **2** (of a vehicle) slide uncontrollably on a wet surface.

**aqua regia** /ˈriːdʒə/ ● **n.** Chemistry a highly corrosive mixture of concentrated nitric and hydrochloric acids.
– ORIGIN C17: L., lit. 'royal water'.

**aquarelle** /ˌakwəˈrɛl/ ● **n.** the technique of painting with thin, transparent watercolours.
– ORIGIN C19: from Fr., from Ital. *acquarella* 'watercolour'.

**aquarist** /ˈakwərɪst/ ● **n.** a person who keeps an aquarium.

**aquarium** ● **n.** (pl. **aquaria** /-rɪə/ or **aquariums**) a transparent tank of water in which live fish and other water creatures and plants are kept.
– ORIGIN C19: from L., neut. of *aquarius* 'of water', on the pattern of *vivarium*.

**Aquarius** /əˈkwɛːrɪəs/ ● **n.** **1** Astronomy a large constellation (the Water Carrier or Water Bearer), said to represent a man pouring water from a jar. **2** Astrology the eleventh sign of the zodiac, which the sun enters about 21 January.
– PHRASES **Age of Aquarius** an astrological age which is about to begin, marked by the precession of the vernal equinox into Aquarius, believed to herald worldwide peace and harmony.
– DERIVATIVES **Aquarian** n. & adj.
– ORIGIN L. *aquarius* 'of water'.

**aquarobics** /ˌakwəˈrəʊbɪks/ ● **pl. n.** [treated as sing. or pl.] aerobic exercises performed in water.

**aquatic** /əˈkwatɪk, -ˈkwɒt-/ ● **adj.** of or relating to water. ➤ living in or near water. ● **n.** an aquatic plant or animal.
– ORIGIN C15 (in the sense 'watery, rainy'): from OFr. *aquatique* or L. *aquaticus*, from *aqua* 'water'.

**aquatint** ● **n.** a print resembling a watercolour, made using a copper plate etched with nitric acid.
– ORIGIN C18: from Fr. *aquatinte*, from Ital. *acqua tinta* 'coloured water'.

**aquavit** /ˌakwəˈviːt/ (also **akvavit**) ● **n.** an alcoholic spirit made from potatoes.
– ORIGIN C19: from Norw., Swed., and Dan. *akvavit*, lit. 'water of life'.

**aqua vitae** /ˈvʌɪtiː, ˈviːtʌɪ/ ● **n.** strong alcoholic spirit, especially brandy.
– ORIGIN ME: from L., lit. 'water of life'.

**aqueduct** /ˈakwɪdʌkt/ ● **n.** **1** an artificial channel for conveying water, especially a bridge or viaduct carrying a waterway. **2** Anatomy a small duct containing fluid in the body.
– ORIGIN C16: from obs. Fr., from L. *aquae ductus* 'conduit', from *aqua* 'water' + *ducere* 'to lead'.

**aqueous** /ˈeɪkwɪəs/ ● **adj.** of, resembling, or containing water.
– ORIGIN C17: from med. L. *aqueus*, from L. *aqua* 'water'.

**aqueous humour** ● **n.** the clear fluid in the eyeball in front of the lens.

**aquifer** /ˈakwɪfə/ ● **n.** a body of permeable rock able to hold or transmit water.
– ORIGIN C20: from L. *aqui-* (from *aqua* 'water') + *-fer* 'bearing'.

**aquilegia** /ˌakwɪˈliːdʒə/ ● **n.** a plant bearing showy flowers with backward-pointing spurs. [Genus *Aquilegia*.]
– ORIGIN from med. L., prob. from L. *aquilegus* 'water-collecting'.

**aquiline** /ˈakwɪlʌɪn/ ● **adj.** **1** like an eagle. **2** (of a nose) curved like an eagle's beak.
– ORIGIN C17: from L. *aquilinus*, from *aquila* 'eagle'.

**AR** ● **abbrev.** **1** US Arkansas (in official postal use). **2** Autonomous Republic.

**Ar** ● **symb.** the chemical element argon.

**ar-** ● **prefix** variant spelling of **AD-** assimilated before *r* (as in *arrive*).

**-ar**[1] ● **suffix** **1** (forming adjectives) of the kind specified: *molecular.* **2** forming nouns such as *scholar.* Compare with **-ER**[5].
– ORIGIN from OFr. *-aire, -ier*, or from L. *-aris*.

**-ar**[2] ● **suffix** forming nouns such as *pillar.*
– ORIGIN via OFr. from L. *-are* (neut. of *-aris*).

**-ar**[3] ● **suffix** forming nouns such as *bursar.*
– ORIGIN from OFr. *-aire, -ier*, or from L. *-arius, -arium*.

**-ar**[4] ● **suffix** alteration of **-ER**[1], **-OR**[1] (as in *liar*).

**ARA** ● **abbrev.** Associate of the Royal Academy.

**Arab** /ˈarəb, ˈeɪrab/ ● **n.** **1** a member of a Semitic people inhabiting much of the Middle East and North Africa. **2** a horse of a breed originating in Arabia.
– DERIVATIVES **Arabization** (also **-isation**) n. **Arabize** (also **-ise**) v.
– ORIGIN via L. and Gk from Arab. *'arab.*

**arabesque** /ˌarəˈbɛsk/ ● **n.** **1** Ballet a posture in which one leg is extended horizontally backwards, the torso extended forwards, and the arms outstretched. **2** an ornamental design consisting of intertwined flowing lines. ➤ Music a passage with a highly ornamented melody.
– ORIGIN C17: from Fr., from Ital. *arabesco* 'in the Arabic style', from *arabo* 'Arab'.

**Arabian** ● **n.** **1** historical a native or inhabitant of Arabia. **2** an Arab horse. ● **adj.** of or relating to Arabia or its people.

**Arabic** ● **n.** the Semitic language of the Arabs, spoken in many dialects in much of North Africa and the Middle East and written from right to left in a cursive script also used for other languages such as Persian, Urdu, and Malay. ● **adj.** of or relating to the Arabs or Arabic.

**arabica** /əˈrabɪkə/ ● **n.** coffee beans from a widely grown coffee plant native to the Old World tropics (*Coffea arabica*).
– ORIGIN 1920s: from L., fem. of *arabicus* 'Arabic'.

**Arabic numeral** ● **n.** any of the numerals 0, 1, 2, 3, 4, 5, 6, 7, 8, and 9.

**arabinose** /ˈarəbɪnəʊz, -s/ ● **n.** Chemistry a sugar which is a constituent of many plant gums.
– ORIGIN C19: from **ARABICA** + **-IN**[1] + **-OSE**[2].

**arabis** /ˈarəbɪs/ ● **n.** a herbaceous plant bearing white or pink flowers. [Genus *Arabis*.]
– ORIGIN via med. L. from Gk, fem. of *Araps, Arab-* (see

**ARAB**).

**Arabism** ● **n. 1** Arab culture or identity. **2** an Arabic word or phrase.
– DERIVATIVES **Arabist** n. & adj.

**arable** ● **adj.** (of land) suitable for growing crops. ➤(of crops) able to be grown on such land. ● **n.** arable land or crops.
– ORIGIN ME: from OFr., or from L. *arabilis*, from *arare* 'to plough'.

**aracari** /ˌarəˈsɑːri, ˌarəˈkɑːri/ ● **n.** (pl. **aracaris**) a small colourful toucan with a serrated bill. [Genus *Pteroglossus*: several species.]
– ORIGIN C19: via Port. from Tupi *arasaʼri*.

**arachidonic acid** /əˌrakɪˈdɒnɪk/ ● **n.** Biochemistry a fatty acid present in animal fats which is an essential constituent of the human diet.
– ORIGIN C20: from mod. L *arachis, arachid* 'peanut', from Gk *arak(h)os, -kis* + **-ONE** + **-IC**.

**Arachnida** /əˈraknɪdə/ ● **pl. n.** Zoology a class of arthropods including spiders, scorpions, mites, and ticks.
– DERIVATIVES **arachnid** n. & adj.
– ORIGIN mod. L., from Gk *arakhnē* 'spider'.

**arachnoid** /əˈraknɔɪd/ ● **adj.** like a spider or arachnid. ● **n.** (also **arachnoid membrane**) Anatomy the fine middle membrane of the three surrounding the brain and spinal cord, situated between the dura mater and the pia mater.
– ORIGIN C18: from mod. L. *arachnoides*, from Gk *arakhnoeidēs* 'like a cobweb', from *arakhnē* 'spider'.

**arachnophobia** /əˌraknəˈfəʊbɪə/ ● **n.** extreme or irrational fear of spiders.
– DERIVATIVES **arachnophobe** n. **arachnophobic** adj.
– ORIGIN 1920s: mod. L., from Gk *arakhnē* 'spider' + **-PHOBIA**.

**aragonite** /ˈarəg(ə)nʌɪt/ ● **n.** a mineral consisting of calcium carbonate, occurring as colourless prisms in deposits from hot springs.
– ORIGIN C19: from the region of *Aragon* in Spain + **-ITE**[1].

**arak** /əˈrak/ ● **n.** variant spelling of **ARRACK**.

**aralia** /əˈreɪlɪə/ ● **n.** a tree or shrub of a diverse group cultivated for their foliage, profuse tiny flowers, or herbal properties. [Genus *Aralia*.]
– ORIGIN mod. L., of unknown origin.

**Aramaean** /ˌarəˈmiːən/ (also **Aramean**) ● **n.** a member of a people inhabiting ancient Aram (modern Syria) and Mesopotamia in the 11th–8th centuries BC. ● **adj.** of or relating to Aram or the Aramaeans.

**Aramaic** /ˌarəˈmeɪɪk/ ● **n.** a branch of the Semitic family of languages, used as a lingua franca in the Near East from the 6th century BC and still spoken in some communities. ● **adj.** of or relating to this language.
– ORIGIN C19: from Gk *Aramaios* 'of Aram' (the biblical name of Syria) + **-IC**.

**arame** /ˈarəmi/ ● **n.** an edible Pacific seaweed used in Japanese cookery. [*Ecklonia bicyclis*.]
– ORIGIN from Japanese.

**Aran** /ˈar(ə)n/ ● **adj.** denoting a type of knitwear with patterns of cable stitch and large diamond designs, traditionally associated with the Aran Islands off the west coast of Ireland.

**Aranda** /əˈrʌntə, aˈruːndə/ (also **Arunta** or **Arrernte**) ● **n.** (pl. same or **Arandas**) **1** a member of an Aboriginal people of central Australia. **2** the language of this people.
– ORIGIN the name in Aranda.

**araneid** /əˈreɪnɪɪd/ ● **n.** Zoology an invertebrate of the order (Araneae) that comprises the spiders.
– ORIGIN C19: from mod. L. *Araneida* (former order name), from *aranea* 'spider'.

**Arapaho** /əˈrapəhəʊ/ ● **n.** (pl. same or **-os**) **1** a member of a North American Indian people living on the Great Plains. **2** the Algonquian language of this people.
– ORIGIN from Crow *alappahó*, lit. 'many tattoo marks'.

**arapaima** /ˌarəˈpʌɪmə/ ● **n.** a very large edible freshwater fish native to tropical South America. [*Arapaima gigas*.]
– ORIGIN C19: from Tupi.

**arational** ● **adj.** unconcerned with or outside rationality.

**Araucanian** /ˌarɔːˈkeɪnɪən/ ● **n. 1** a member of a group of American Indian peoples of Chile and parts of Argentina. **2** the language of these peoples. ● **adj.** relating to or denoting these peoples or their language.
– ORIGIN from Sp. *Araucania*, a region in Chile.

**araucaria** /ˌarɔːˈkɛːrɪə/ ● **n.** an evergreen conifer with stiff sharp leaves, e.g. the monkey puzzle. [Genus *Araucaria*.]
– ORIGIN mod. L., from Sp. *Arauco*, a province of Araucania, Chile.

**Arawak** /ˈarəwak/ ● **n.** (pl. same or **Arawaks**) **1** a member of a group of native peoples of the Greater Antilles and northern and western South America. **2** any of the languages of these peoples.
– DERIVATIVES **Arawakan** adj. & n.
– ORIGIN from Carib *aruac*.

**arbalest** /ˈɑːbəlɛst/ (also **arblast**) ● **n.** historical a crossbow with a mechanism for drawing back and releasing the string.
– ORIGIN OE *arblast*, from OFr. *arbaleste*, from late L. *arcubalista*, from L. *arcus* 'bow' + *ballista* (see **BALLISTA**).

**arbiter** /ˈɑːbɪtə/ ● **n. 1** a person who settles a dispute. **2** a person who has influence over something: *an arbiter of taste.*
– ORIGIN ME: from L., 'judge, supreme ruler'.

**arbitrage** /ˈɑːbɪtrɪdʒ, ˌɑːbɪˈtrɑːʒ/ ● **n.** Economics the simultaneous buying and selling of assets in different markets or in derivative forms, taking advantage of the differing prices.
– DERIVATIVES **arbitrageur** n.
– ORIGIN ME, from Fr., from *arbitrer* 'give judgement'.

**arbitral** /ˈɑːbɪtr(ə)l/ ● **adj.** of, relating to, or resulting from the use of an arbitrator.

**arbitrament** /ɑːˈbɪtrəm(ə)nt/ ● **n.** the settling of a dispute by an arbitrator.

**arbitrary** /ˈɑːbɪt(rə)ri/ ● **adj. 1** based on random choice or personal whim. **2** (of power or a ruling body) autocratic. **3** Mathematics (of a constant or other quantity) of unspecified value.
– DERIVATIVES **arbitrarily** adv. **arbitrariness** n.
– ORIGIN ME: from L. *arbitrarius*, from *arbiter* 'judge, supreme ruler'.

**arbitration** ● **n.** the use of an arbitrator to settle a dispute.
– DERIVATIVES **arbitrate** v.
– ORIGIN ME: from L. *arbitratio(n-)*, from *arbitrat-*, *arbitrari*, from *arbiter* 'judge, supreme ruler'.

**arbitrator** ● **n.** an independent person or body officially appointed to settle a dispute.

**arblast** /ˈɑːblɑːst/ ● **n.** variant spelling of **ARBALEST**.

**arbor**[1] /ˈɑːbə/ ● **n.** an axle on which something revolves. ➤a device holding a tool in a lathe.
– ORIGIN C17: from Fr. *arbre* 'tree, axis', influenced by L. *arbor* 'tree'.

**arbor**[2] ● **n.** US spelling of **ARBOUR**.

**arboreal** /ɑːˈbɔːrɪəl/ ● **adj.** of, relating to, or living in trees.
– DERIVATIVES **arboreality** n.
– ORIGIN C17: from L. *arboreus*, from *arbor* 'tree', + **-AL**.

**arborescent** /ˌɑːbəˈrɛs(ə)nt/ ● **adj.** Botany tree-like.
– DERIVATIVES **arborescence** n.
– ORIGIN C17: from L. *arborescent-*, *arborescere* 'grow into a tree', from *arbor* 'tree'.

**arboretum** /ˌɑːbəˈriːtəm/ ● **n.** (pl. **arboretums** or **arboreta** /-tə/) a botanical garden devoted to trees.
– ORIGIN C19: from L., 'a place with trees', from *arbor* 'tree'.

**arboriculture** /ˈɑːb(ə)rɪˌkʌltʃə, ɑːˈbɔː-/ ● **n.** the cultivation of trees and shrubs.
– DERIVATIVES **arboricultural** adj. **arboriculturist** n.

**Arborio** /ɑːˈbɔːrɪəʊ/ ● **n.** a variety of round-grained Italian rice used in making risotto.
– ORIGIN named after *Arborio* in northern Italy.

**arborization** /ˌɑːb(ə)rʌɪˈzeɪʃ(ə)n/ (also **-isation**) ● **n.** Anatomy a fine branching structure at the end of a nerve fibre.

**arbor vitae** /ˌɑːbə ˈvʌɪtiː, ˈviːtʌɪ/ ● **n.** another term for **THUJA**.
– ORIGIN C16: from L., lit. 'tree of life', prob. with ref. to its medicinal use.

**arbour** /ˈɑːbə/ (US **arbor**) ● **n.** a garden alcove with the sides and roof formed by trees or climbing plants.
– DERIVATIVES **arboured** adj.
– ORIGIN ME: from OFr. *erbier*, from *erbe* 'grass, herb', from L. *herba*; influenced by L. *arbor* 'tree'.

**arbovirus** /ˈɑːbə(ʊ)ˌvʌɪrəs/ ● **n.** Medicine any of a group of viruses (e.g. that causing yellow fever) transmitted by mosquitoes, ticks, or other arthropods.
– ORIGIN 1950s: from *ar(thropod)-bo(rne)* + **VIRUS**.

**arbutus** /ɑːˈbjuːtəs, ˈɑːbjʊtəs/ ● **n.** an evergreen tree or shrub of a genus that includes the strawberry tree. [Genus *Arbutus*.]
– ORIGIN from L.

**ARC** ● **abbrev.** Medicine Aids-related complex.

**arc** /ɑːk/ ● **n. 1** a curve forming part of the circumference of a circle or other figure. ➤ a curving trajectory. ➤ [as modifier] Mathematics indicating the inverse of a trigonometrical function: *arc cosine*. **2** a luminous electrical discharge between two points. ● **v.** (**arced** /ɑːkt/, **arcing** /ˈɑːkɪŋ/) **1** move with a curving trajectory. **2** [as noun **arcing**] the forming of an electric arc.
– ORIGIN ME: via OFr. from L. *arcus* 'bow, curve'.

**arcade** ● **n. 1** a covered passage with arches along one or both sides. ➤ chiefly Brit. a covered walk with shops along one or both sides. ➤ Architecture a series of arches supporting a wall. **2** short for **AMUSEMENT ARCADE**.
– DERIVATIVES **arcaded** adj. **arcading** n.
– ORIGIN C17: from Fr., from Provençal *arcada* or Ital. *arcata*, based on L. *arcus* 'bow'.

**Arcadian** ● **n. 1** a native of Arcadia, a mountainous region of southern Greece. **2** poetic/literary an idealized country dweller. ● **adj.** of or relating to Arcadia, especially as regarded as an ideal rustic paradise.

**Arcady** /ˈɑːkədi/ ● **n.** poetic/literary an ideal rustic paradise.
– ORIGIN C16: from Gk *Arkadia* 'Arcadia', a region of Greece.

**arcana** /ɑːˈkeɪnə/ ● **pl. n.** [treated as sing. or pl.] (sing. **arcanum**) **1** secrets; mysteries. **2** either of the two groups of cards in a tarot pack: the twenty-two trumps (the **major arcana**) and the fifty-six suit cards (the **minor arcana**).
– ORIGIN C16: from L., neut. pl. of *arcanus* (see **ARCANE**).

**arcane** /ɑːˈkeɪn/ ● **adj.** understood by few; mysterious.
– DERIVATIVES **arcanely** adv.
– ORIGIN C16: from L. *arcanus*, from *arcere* 'to shut up', from *arca* 'chest'.

**arch**[1] ● **n. 1** a curved symmetrical structure spanning an opening and supporting the weight of a bridge, roof, or wall. ➤ an arch-shaped curve. **2** the inner side of the foot. ● **v.** form or cause to form an arch.
– DERIVATIVES **arched** adj.
– ORIGIN ME: from OFr. *arche*, based on L. *arcus* 'bow'.

**arch**[2] ● **adj.** self-consciously playful or teasing.
– DERIVATIVES **archly** adv. **archness** n.
– ORIGIN C17: from **ARCH-**, by assoc. with the sense 'rogue' in combinations such as *arch-scoundrel*.

**arch-** ● **comb. form** chief; principal: *archbishop*. ➤ pre-eminent of its kind: *arch-enemy*.
– ORIGIN via L. from Gk *arkhi-*, from *arkhos* 'chief'.

**-arch** /ɑːk/ ● **comb. form** (forming nouns) denoting a ruler or leader: *monarch*.
– ORIGIN Gk *arkhos* 'ruling', from *arkhein* 'to rule'.

**archaea** /ɑːˈkiːə/ ● **pl. n.** Biology micro-organisms which are similar to bacteria in size and simplicity of structure but constitute an ancient group intermediate between the bacteria and eukaryotes.
– DERIVATIVES **archaean** adj. & n.
– ORIGIN mod. L., from Gk *arkhaios* 'primitive'.

**Archaean** /ɑːˈkiːən/ (US **Archean**) ● **adj.** Geology relating to or denoting the earlier part of the Precambrian aeon (before about 2,500 million years ago), in which there was no life on the earth.
– ORIGIN C19: from Gk *arkhaios* 'ancient' + **-AN**.

**archaebacteria** /ˌɑːkɪbakˈtɪərɪə/ ● **pl. n.** (sing. **archaebacterium**) another term for **ARCHAEA**.
– DERIVATIVES **archaebacterial** adj.

**archaeo-** /ˈɑːkɪəʊ/ ● **comb. form** relating to archaeology or prehistoric times: *archaeoastronomy*.
– ORIGIN from Gk *arkhaios* 'ancient'.

**archaeoastronomy** ● **n.** the investigation of the astronomical knowledge of prehistoric cultures.

**archaeology** (US also **archeology**) ● **n.** the study of human history and prehistory through the excavation of sites and the analysis of physical remains.
– DERIVATIVES **archaeologic** adj. **archaeological** adj. **archaeologically** adv. **archaeologist** n. **archaeologize** (also **-ise**) v.

**archaeomagnetism** ● **n.** magnetism possessed by components of clay and rocks which have in the past been heated, especially as studied in a method of geological or archaeological dating.
– DERIVATIVES **archaeomagnetic** adj.

**archaeometry** /ˌɑːkɪˈɒmətri/ ● **n.** the application of scientific techniques to the dating of archaeological remains.
– DERIVATIVES **archaeometric** adj.

**archaeopteryx** /ˌɑːkɪˈɒptərɪks/ ● **n.** the oldest known fossil bird, of the late Jurassic period, which had feathers and wings like a bird, but teeth and a bony tail like a dinosaur.
– ORIGIN from **ARCHAEO-** + Gk *pterux* 'wing'.

**archaic** /ɑːˈkeɪɪk/ ● **adj.** very old or old-fashioned. ➤ (of language) used to give an old-fashioned flavour. ➤ belonging to an early period of art or culture.
– DERIVATIVES **archaically** adv.
– ORIGIN C19: from Fr. *archaïque*, from Gk *arkhaikos*, from *arkhaios* (see **ARCHAISM**).

**archaism** /ˈɑːkeɪɪz(ə)m/ ● **n.** a thing that is archaic, especially a word or style of art. ➤ the use of archaic features in language or art.
– DERIVATIVES **archaistic** adj.
– ORIGIN C17: from mod. L. *archaismus*, from Gk *arkhaismos*, based on *arkhaios* 'ancient'.

**archaize** (also **-ise**) ● **v.** consciously imitate an archaic word or style of art.

**archangel** /ˈɑːkeɪndʒ(ə)l, ɑːkˈeɪn-/ ● **n. 1** an angel of high rank. **2** (also **yellow archangel**) a yellow-flowered deadnettle found in woodland. [*Lamiastrum galeobdolon*.]
– DERIVATIVES **archangelic** adj.

**archbishop** ● **n.** the chief bishop responsible for a large district.

**archbishopric** ● **n.** the office or district of an archbishop.

**archdeacon** ● **n.** a senior Christian cleric to whom a bishop delegates certain responsibilities.

**archdeaconry** ● **n.** (pl. **-ies**) the office or district of an archdeacon.

**archdiocese** ● **n.** the district for which an archbishop is responsible.
– DERIVATIVES **archdiocesan** adj.

**archduchess** ● **n.** historical **1** the wife or widow of an archduke. **2** a daughter of the Emperor of Austria.

**archduke** ● **n.** a chief duke, in particular (historical) the son of the Emperor of Austria.
– DERIVATIVES **archducal** adj. **archduchy** n.

**Archean** ● **adj.** US spelling of **ARCHAEAN**.

**archegonium** /ˌɑːkɪˈgəʊnɪəm/ ● **n.** (pl. **archegonia** /-ɪə/) Botany the female sex organ in mosses, liverworts, ferns, and most conifers.
– ORIGIN C19: mod. L., from Gk *arkhegonos*, from *arkhe-* 'chief' + *gonos* 'race'.

**arch-enemy** ● **n.** a chief enemy.

**archeology** ● **n.** US spelling of **ARCHAEOLOGY**.

**archer** ● **n.** a person who shoots with a bow and arrows.
– ORIGIN ME: from OFr. *archier*, based on L. *arcus* 'bow'.

**archerfish** ● **n.** (pl. same or **-fishes**) a freshwater fish, native to Asia, Australia, and the Philippines, that knocks insect prey off vegetation by shooting water from its mouth. [Genus *Toxotes*: several species.]

**archery** ● **n.** shooting with a bow and arrows.

## Word *Formation*

**-archy** 'rule or government', from Greek *arkhein* 'to rule'

➤ Some of the most common **-archy** words:

| | | |
|---|---|---|
| anarchy | a state of disorder | Gk *an-* 'without' |
| hierarchy | a system ranked according to status | Gk *hieros* 'sacred' (because it was originally used to denote the system of orders of angels and other heavenly beings) |
| matriarchy | a social organization in which the mother is head of the family | L. *mater, matr-* 'mother' |
| monarchy | government by a king or queen | Gk *monos* 'alone' |
| oligarchy | a small group of people holding power | Gk *oligoi* 'few' |
| patriarchy | a social organization in which the father is head of the family | Gk *patria* 'family' |
| squirearchy | landowners as the dominant class | based on SQUIRE + HIERARCHY |

A number of **-archy** words have equivalents ending in **-arch** (forming nouns, i.e. 'a ruler'), for example ***monarch***, ***matriarch***, and ***patriarch***. In modern English, the elements **-arch** and **-archy** are no longer productive, i.e. they are no longer used to form new words.

**archetype** /'ɑːkɪtʌɪp/ ● **n.** **1** a very typical example. **2** an original model. **3** Psychoanalysis (in Jungian theory) a primitive mental image inherited from the earliest human ancestors and supposed to be present in the collective unconscious. **4** a recurrent motif in literature or art.
– DERIVATIVES **archetypal** adj. **archetypally** adv. **archetypical** adj.
– ORIGIN C16: via L. from Gk *arkhetupon* 'something moulded first as a model', from *arkhe-* 'primitive' + *tupos* 'a model'.

**archidiaconal** /ˌɑːkɪdʌɪ'ak(ə)n(ə)l/ ● **adj.** of or relating to an archdeacon.

**archiepiscopal** /ˌɑːkɪɪ'pɪskəp(ə)l/ ● **adj.** of or relating to an archbishop.
– DERIVATIVES **archiepiscopacy** n. (pl. **-ies**) **archiepiscopate** n.

**archil** /'ɑːtʃɪl/ ● **n.** archaic spelling of ORCHIL.

**archimandrite** /ˌɑːkɪ'mandrʌɪt/ ● **n.** the superior of a large monastery or group of monasteries in the Orthodox Church. ➤ an honorary title given to a monastic priest.
– ORIGIN C17: via eccles. L., from eccles. Gk *arkhimandritēs*, from *arkhi-* 'chief' + *mandra* 'monastery'.

**Archimedean** /ˌɑːkɪ'miːdɪən/ ● **adj.** of or relating to the Greek mathematician Archimedes (*c.*287–212 BC).

**Archimedean screw** ● **n.** a device invented by Archimedes for raising water by means of a helix rotating within a tube.

**Archimedes' principle** /ˌɑːkɪ'miːdiːz/ ● **n.** Physics a law stating that a body immersed in a fluid is subject to an upward force equal in magnitude to the weight of fluid it displaces.

**archipelago** /ˌɑːkɪ'pɛləgəʊ/ ● **n.** (pl. **-os** or **-oes**) an extensive group of islands.
– ORIGIN C16: from Ital. *arcipelago*, from Gk *arkhi-* 'chief' + *pelagos* 'sea' (orig. a name for the Aegean Sea, notable for its large number of islands).

**architect** ● **n.** **1** a person who designs buildings and supervises their construction. **2** a person responsible for the invention or realization of something. ● **v.** Computing design and make (a program or system).
– ORIGIN C16: from Fr. *architecte*, from Ital. *architetto*, via L. from Gk *arkhitektōn* 'chief builder'.

**architectonic** /ˌɑːkɪtɛk'tɒnɪk/ ● **adj.** **1** of or relating to architecture or architects. **2** having a clearly defined and artistically pleasing structure. ● **n.** (**architectonics**) [treated as sing.] **1** the scientific study of architecture. **2** musical, literary, or artistic structure.
– DERIVATIVES **architectonically** adv.
– ORIGIN C17: via L. from Gk *arkhitektonikos*, from *arkhitektōn* (see ARCHITECT).

**architecture** ● **n.** **1** the art or practice of designing and constructing buildings. ➤ the style in which a building is designed and constructed. **2** the complex structure of something. ➤ the conceptual structure and logical organization of a computer or computer-based system.
– DERIVATIVES **architectural** adj. **architecturally** adv.

**architrave** /'ɑːkɪtreɪv/ ● **n.** **1** (in classical architecture) a main beam resting across the tops of columns. **2** the frame around a doorway or window. ➤ a moulding round the exterior of an arch.
– ORIGIN C16: from Fr., from Ital., from *archi-* 'chief' + *-trave* from L. *trabs, trab-* 'a beam'.

**archive** /'ɑːkʌɪv/ ● **n.** a collection of historical documents or records. ● **v.** place in an archive. ➤ Computing transfer (data) to a less frequently used storage medium, e.g. magnetic tape.
– DERIVATIVES **archival** adj.
– ORIGIN C17: from Fr. *archives* (pl.), from L. *archiva, archia*, from Gk *arkheia* 'public records'.

**archivist** /'ɑːkɪvɪst/ ● **n.** a person who maintains and is in charge of archives.

**archivolt** /'ɑːkɪvəʊlt/ ● **n.** a band of mouldings round the lower curve of an arch. ➤ the lower curve itself.
– ORIGIN C17: from Fr. *archivolte* or Ital. *archivolto*, based on L. *arcus* 'bow, arch' + *volvere* 'to roll'.

**archlute** ● **n.** a bass lute with an extended neck which supports unstopped bass strings.

**archon** /'ɑːkən/ ● **n.** each of the nine chief magistrates in ancient Athens.
– DERIVATIVES **archonship** n.
– ORIGIN C16: from Gk *arkhōn* 'ruler'.

**archosaur** /'ɑːkəsɔː/ ● **n.** Zoology & Palaeontology a reptile of a large group that includes the crocodilians together with the extinct dinosaurs and pterosaurs.
– ORIGIN 1930s: from mod. L. *Archosauria*, from Gk *arkhos* 'chief' or *arkhōn* 'ruler' + -SAUR.

**archway** ● **n.** a curved structure forming a passage or entrance.

**-archy** /'ɑːrki/ ● **comb. form** (forming nouns) denoting a type of rule or government, corresponding to nouns ending in *-arch*: *monarchy.* See word-formation panel.

**arc lamp** (also **arc light**) ● **n.** a light source using an electric arc.

**arco** /'ɑːkəʊ/ ● **adv. & adj.** Music played on a violin or other stringed instrument using the bow.

**arcology** /ɑː'kɒlədʒi/ ● **n.** (pl. **-ies**) an ideal city contained within a massive vertical structure, allowing maximum conservation of its environment.
– ORIGIN 1969: blend of ARCHITECTURE and ECOLOGY.

**arcos** ● **abbrev.** the inverse of a cosine.

**arcsin** ● **abbrev.** the inverse of a sine.

**arctan** ● **abbrev.** the inverse of a tangent.

**Arctic** • **adj.** **1** of or relating to the regions around the North Pole. ➤ living or growing in such regions. **2** (**arctic**) informal (of weather) very cold. • **n.** **1** (**the Arctic**) the regions around the North Pole. **2** N. Amer. a thick waterproof overshoe. **3** (**arctic**) a drab-coloured hairy butterfly of the arctic and subarctic regions of the New World. [Genus *Oenis*.]
– ORIGIN ME: via OFr. from L. *arcticus*, *articus*, based on Gk *arktos* 'bear, Ursa Major, pole star'.

**Arctogaean** /ˌɑːktəˈdʒiːən/ (US **Arctogean**) • **adj.** Zoology relating to or denoting the zoogeographical area Arctogaea, comprising the Palaearctic, Nearctic, Ethiopian, and Oriental regions.
– ORIGIN from mod. L. *Arctogaea*, from Gk *arktos* 'northern' + *gaia* 'earth'.

**arcuate** /ˈɑːkjʊət/ • **adj.** technical curved.
– ORIGIN ME: from L. *arcuat-*, *arcuare* 'to curve'.

**arcus senilis** /ˌɑːkəs sɪˈnʌɪlɪs/ • **n.** Medicine a narrow opaque band encircling the cornea, common in old age.
– ORIGIN L., lit. 'senile bow'.

**arc welding** • **n.** welding using the heat generated by an electric arc.

**-ard** • **suffix** **1** forming nouns such as *bollard*. **2** forming nouns having a depreciatory sense: *drunkard*.
– ORIGIN from OFr., from Ger. *-hard* 'hard, hardy'.

**ardent** /ˈɑːd(ə)nt/ • **adj.** **1** very enthusiastic or passionate. **2** archaic or poetic/literary burning; glowing.
– DERIVATIVES **ardency** n. **ardently** adv.
– ORIGIN ME: from OFr. *ardant* from L. *ardent-*, *ardens*, from *ardere* 'to burn'.

**ardour** /ˈɑːdə/ (US **ardor**) • **n.** great enthusiasm or passion.
– ORIGIN ME: via OFr. from L. *ardor*, from *ardere* 'to burn'.

**arduous** /ˈɑːdjʊəs/ • **adj.** difficult and tiring.
– DERIVATIVES **arduously** adv. **arduousness** n.
– ORIGIN C16: from L. *arduus* 'steep, difficult' + **-OUS**.

**are**[1] second person singular present and first, second, third person plural present of **BE**.

**are**[2] /ɑː/ • **n.** historical a metric unit of measurement, equal to 100 square metres. Compare with **HECTARE**.
– ORIGIN C18: from Fr., from L. *area* (see **AREA**).

**area** • **n.** **1** a region of an expanse or surface. ➤ a space allocated for a specific use. **2** a subject or range of activity. **3** the extent or measurement of a surface. **4** a sunken enclosure giving access to a basement.
– DERIVATIVES **areal** adj.
– ORIGIN C16: from L., lit. 'vacant piece of level ground'.

**area code** • **n.** another term for **DIALLING CODE**.

**areaway** • **n.** N. Amer. **1** a sunken enclosure giving access to a basement. **2** a passageway between buildings.

**areca palm** /ˈarɪkə, əˈriːkə/ • **n.** a tropical Asian palm yielding astringent nuts which are chewed with betel leaves. [Genus *Areca*.]
– ORIGIN via Port. from Malayalam *āḍekka*.

**areg** plural form of **ERG**[2].

**arena** • **n.** **1** a level area surrounded by seating, in which public events and entertainments are held. **2** a sphere of activity.
– ORIGIN C17: from L. *harena*, *arena* 'sand, sand-strewn place of combat'.

**arenaceous** /ˌarɪˈneɪʃəs/ • **adj.** Geology consisting of sand or sand-like particles. ➤ Biology living or growing in sand.
– ORIGIN C17: from L. *arenaceus*, from *arena* 'sand'.

**arenavirus** /əˈriːnəˌvʌɪrəs/ • **n.** Medicine any of a group of RNA viruses (e.g. that causing Lassa fever) appearing to contain sand-like granules.
– ORIGIN 1970s: from L. *arenosus* 'sandy' + **VIRUS**.

**aren't** • **contr.** **1** are not. **2** am not (only used in questions).

**areola** /əˈriːələ/ • **n.** (pl. **areolae** /-liː/) **1** Anatomy a small circular area, in particular the pigmented skin surrounding a nipple. ➤ Medicine a reddened patch around a spot or papule. **2** Biology any of the small spaces between lines or cracks on a leaf or an insect's wing.
– DERIVATIVES **areolar** adj. **areolate** adj.
– ORIGIN C17 (in the sense 'small space or interstice'): from L., lit. 'small open space', dimin. of *area* (see **AREA**).

**areole** /ˈɛːrɪəʊl/ • **n.** Biology an areola, especially a small area bearing spines or hairs on a cactus.
– ORIGIN C19: from Fr. *aréole*, from L. (see **AREOLA**).

**areology** /ɛːrɪˈɒlədʒi/ • **n.** the study of the planet Mars.
– DERIVATIVES **areological** adj. **areologist** n. & adj.
– ORIGIN from *Ares* Gk god of war (equivalent to the Roman God Mars) + **-OLOGY**.

**arête** /əˈrɛt, əˈreɪt/ • **n.** a sharp mountain ridge.
– ORIGIN C19: from Fr., from L. *arista* 'ear of corn, spine'.

**argali** /ˈɑːg(ə)li/ • **n.** (pl. same) a large Asian mountain sheep with massive horns. [*Ovis ammon*.]
– ORIGIN C18: from Mongolian.

**Argand diagram** /ˈɑːgənd/ • **n.** Mathematics a graph on which complex numbers can be represented, the horizontal coordinate representing the real part of the number and the vertical coordinate the imaginary part.
– ORIGIN C20: named after the Fr. mathematician J. R. *Argand*.

**Argand lamp** • **n.** historical an oil or gas lamp with a cylindrical burner allowing air to pass to both inner and outer surfaces of the flame.
– ORIGIN C18: named after the Fr. physicist Aimé *Argand*.

**argent** /ˈɑːdʒ(ə)nt/ • **adj.** & **n.** poetic/literary & Heraldry silver.
– ORIGIN ME (denoting silver coins): via OFr. from L. *argentum* 'silver'.

**argentiferous** /ˌɑːdʒ(ə)nˈtɪf(ə)rəs/ • **adj.** (of rocks or minerals) containing silver.
– ORIGIN C18: from L. *argentum* 'silver' + **-FEROUS**.

**Argentine** • **n.** & **adj.** another term for **ARGENTINIAN**.

**argentine** /ˈɑːdʒ(ə)ntʌɪn/ • **adj.** archaic of or resembling silver. • **n.** a small marine fish with a silvery sheen. [*Argentina silus* and other species.]
– ORIGIN ME: from OFr. *argentin*, *argentine*, from *argent* 'silver', from L. *argentum*.

**Argentine ant** • **n.** a predatory ant native to South America and introduced elsewhere. [*Iridomyrmex humilis*.]

**Argentinian** /ˌɑːdʒənˈtɪnɪən/ • **n.** a native or national of Argentina, or a person of Argentinian descent. • **adj.** of or relating to Argentina.

**argillaceous** /ˌɑːdʒɪˈleɪʃəs/ • **adj.** Geology (of rocks or sediment) consisting of or containing clay.
– ORIGIN C17: from L. *argillaceus* (from *argilla* 'clay') + **-OUS**.

**argillite** /ˈɑːdʒɪlʌɪt/ • **n.** Geology a sedimentary rock formed from consolidated clay.
– ORIGIN C18: from L. *argilla* 'clay' + **-ITE**[1].

**arginine** /ˈɑːdʒɪniːn/ • **n.** Biochemistry a basic amino acid which is an essential nutrient in the diet of vertebrates.
– ORIGIN C19: from Ger. *Arginin*, perh. from Gk *arginoeis* 'bright-shining, white'.

**Argive** /ˈɑːgʌɪv, -dʒʌɪv/ • **adj.** of or relating to the ancient city of Argos in Greece. ➤ (especially in Homer) Greek. • **n.** a citizen of Argos. ➤ (especially in Homer) a Greek person.

**argle-bargle** • **n.** **1** copious but meaningless talk. **2** another term for **ARGY-BARGY**.
– ORIGIN C19: reduplication of dial. *argle*, alt. of **ARGUE**.

**argol** /ˈɑːg(ə)l/ • **n.** tartar obtained from wine fermentation.
– ORIGIN ME: from Anglo-Norman Fr. *argoile*, of unknown origin.

**argon** /ˈɑːgɒn/ • **n.** the chemical element of atomic number 18, an inert gaseous element of the noble gas group. (Symbol: **Ar**)
– ORIGIN C19: from Gk, neut. of *argos* 'idle', from *a-* 'without' + *ergon* 'work'.

**argonaut** /ˈɑːg(ə)nɔːt/ • **n.** Zoology another term for **PAPER NAUTILUS**.
– ORIGIN from L. *argonauta* from Gk *argonautēs* 'sailor in the ship *Argo*' (the ship in which Jason and his companions went in search of the Golden Fleece).

**argosy** /ˈɑːgəsi/ • **n.** (pl. **-ies**) poetic/literary a large merchant ship, originally one from Ragusa (now Dubrovnik) or Venice.

– ORIGIN C16: appar. from Ital. *Ragusea* (*nave*) '(vessel) of *Ragusa*'.

**argot** /ˈɑːɡəʊ/ ● **n.** the jargon or slang of a particular group.
– ORIGIN C19 (orig. denoting criminals' jargon): from Fr.

**arguable** ● **adj.** able to be argued or asserted. ➤ open to disagreement.
– DERIVATIVES **arguably** adv.

**argue** ● **v.** (**argues**, **argued**, **arguing**) **1** exchange diverging or opposite views heatedly. **2** give reasons or cite evidence in support of something.
– PHRASES **argue the toss** informal, chiefly Brit. dispute a decision already made.
– DERIVATIVES **arguer** n.
– ORIGIN ME: from OFr. *arguer*, from L. *argutari* 'prattle', frequentative of *arguere* 'make clear, prove, accuse'.

**argufy** /ˈɑːɡjʊfʌɪ/ ● **v.** (**-ies**, **-ied**) humorous or dialect argue about something trivial.
– ORIGIN C17: fanciful formation from **ARGUE**; cf. *speechify*.

**argument** ● **n. 1** a heated exchange of diverging or opposite views. **2** a set of reasons given in support of something. **3** Mathematics & Logic an independent variable associated with a function or proposition and determining its value, e.g. $x$ in $y = F(x)$. **4** Linguistics any of the noun phrases in a clause that are related directly to the verb. **5** archaic a summary of the subject matter of a book.
– PHRASES **argument from design** Christian Theology the argument that God's existence is demonstrable from the evidence of design in the universe.
– ORIGIN ME: via OFr. from L. *argumentum*, from *arguere* 'make clear, prove, accuse'.

**argumentation** ● **n.** the action of reasoning systematically in support of something.

**argumentative** ● **adj. 1** given to arguing. **2** using or characterized by systematic reasoning.
– DERIVATIVES **argumentatively** adv. **argumentativeness** n.

**argus** /ˈɑːɡəs/ ● **n. 1** a large long-tailed Asian pheasant with eye-like markings on its wings. [*Argusianus argus*.] **2** a small brown or bluish butterfly with eye-like markings. [*Aricia* and other genera.]
– ORIGIN ME: from L., from Gk *Argos*, the name of a mythical watchman with a hundred eyes.

**argute** /ɑːˈɡjuːt/ ● **adj.** rare shrewd.
– ORIGIN C16: from L. *argutus* 'made clear, proved, accused', from *arguere*.

**argy-bargy** /ˌɑːdʒɪˈbɑːdʒi, ˌɑːɡɪˈbɑːɡi/ ● **n.** (pl. **-ies**) informal, chiefly Brit. noisy quarrelling.
– ORIGIN C19: rhyming jingle based on **ARGUE**.

**argyle** /ɑːˈɡʌɪl/ ● **n.** a pattern on knitted garments composed of coloured diamonds on a plain background.
– ORIGIN 1940s: from the *Argyll* branch of the Sc. Campbell clan, on whose tartan the pattern is based.

**arhat** /ˈɑːhat/ ● **n.** (in Buddhism and Jainism) a saint of one of the highest ranks.
– ORIGIN from Sanskrit, lit. 'meritorious'.

**arhythmic** ● **adj.** variant spelling of **ARRHYTHMIC**.

**aria** /ˈɑːrɪə/ ● **n.** Music a long accompanied song for a solo voice in an opera or oratorio.
– ORIGIN C18: from Ital., from L. *aer* 'air'.

**Arian** /ˈɛːrɪən/ ● **n. 1** an adherent of Arianism. **2** (also **Arien**) a person born under the sign of Aries. ● **adj. 1** of or concerning Arianism. **2** (also **Arien**) of or relating to a person born under the sign of Aries.

**-arian** ● **suffix** (forming adjectives and corresponding nouns) having a concern or belief in a specified thing: *vegetarian*.
– ORIGIN from the L. suffix *-arius*.

**Arianism** ● **n.** Christian Theology the main heresy denying the divinity of Christ, originating with the Alexandrian priest Arius (*c*.250–*c*.336).

**arid** /ˈarɪd/ ● **adj. 1** (of land or a climate) very dry; having little or no rain. **2** uninteresting: *arid verse*.
– DERIVATIVES **aridity** n. **aridly** adv. **aridness** n.
– ORIGIN C17: from Fr. *aride* or L. *aridus*, from *arere* 'be dry or parched'.

**aridisol** /əˈrɪdɪsɒl/ ● **n.** Soil Science a saline or alkaline soil with very little organic matter, characteristic of arid regions.

**Arien** ● **n. & adj.** variant spelling of **ARIAN** (in sense 2).

**Aries** /ˈɛːriːz/ ● **n. 1** Astronomy a small constellation (the Ram), said to represent the ram whose Golden Fleece was sought by Jason and the Argonauts. **2** Astrology the first sign of the zodiac, which the sun enters about 20 March.
– PHRASES **First Point of Aries** Astronomy the point on the celestial sphere (formerly in Aries but now in Pisces owing to precession) where the path of the sun crosses the celestial equator at the vernal equinox.
– ORIGIN from L.

**aright** ● **adv.** dialect correctly; properly.
– ORIGIN OE *on riht*, *ariht* (see **A-**[2] + **RIGHT**).

**aril** /ˈarɪl/ ● **n.** Botany an extra seed covering, typically coloured and hairy or fleshy.
– DERIVATIVES **arillate** adj.
– ORIGIN C18: from mod. L. *arillus*, of unknown origin.

**arioso** /ˌarɪˈəʊzəʊ, -səʊ/ Music ● **n.** (especially in opera and oratorio) a style of vocal performance less formal than an aria. ● **adj. & adv.** in such a style or manner.
– ORIGIN Ital., from **ARIA**.

**-arious** ● **suffix** forming adjectives such as *gregarious*.
– ORIGIN from the L. suffix *-arius* + **-OUS**.

**arise** ● **v.** (past **arose**; past part. **arisen**) **1** originate or become apparent. ➤ (**arise from/out of**) occur as a result of. **2** formal or poetic/literary get or stand up.
– ORIGIN OE *ārīsan*, from *ā-* 'away' (as an intensifier) + **RISE**.

**arisings** ● **pl. n.** materials forming the secondary or waste products of industrial operations.

**aristocracy** ● **n.** (pl. **-ies**) [treated as sing. or pl.] the highest class in some societies, comprising people of noble birth with hereditary titles. ➤ a form of government in which power is held by the nobility.
– ORIGIN C15: from OFr. *aristocratie*, from Gk *aristokratia*, from *aristos* 'best' + *-kratia* 'power'.

**aristocrat** /ˈarɪstəkrat, əˈrɪst-/ ● **n.** a member of the aristocracy.
– DERIVATIVES **aristocratic** adj. **aristocratically** adv.

**Aristotelian** /ˌarɪstəˈtiːlɪən/ ● **adj.** of or relating to the Greek philosopher Aristotle (384–322 BC) or his theories. ● **n.** a student or follower of Aristotle or his philosophy.

**Aristotelian logic** ● **n.** the traditional system of logic expounded by Aristotle and developed in the Middle Ages.

**Aristotle's lantern** /ˈarɪstɒt(ə)lz/ ● **n.** Zoology a conical structure of calcareous plates and muscles supporting the teeth of a sea urchin.

**Arita** /əˈriːtə/ ● **n.** a type of Japanese porcelain characterized by asymmetric decoration.
– ORIGIN C19: named after *Arita*, the town in Japan where it is made.

**arithmetic** ● **n.** /əˈrɪθmətɪk/ the branch of mathematics concerned with the properties and manipulation of numbers. ➤ the use of numbers in counting and calculation. ● **adj.** /ˌarɪθˈmɛtɪk/ of or relating to arithmetic.
– DERIVATIVES **arithmetical** adj. **arithmetically** adv. **arithmetician** n.
– ORIGIN ME: from OFr. *arismetique*, based on L. *arithmetica*, from Gk *arithmētikē* (*tekhnē*) '(art) of counting', from *arithmos* 'number'.

**arithmetic mean** ● **n.** see **MEAN**[3] (sense 1).

**arithmetic progression** (also **arithmetic series**) ● **n.** a sequence of numbers in which each differs from the preceding one by a constant quantity (e.g. 1, 2, 3, 4, etc.; 9, 7, 5, 3, etc.).

**arithmetize** /əˈrɪθmətʌɪz/ (also **-ise**) ● **v.** express arithmetically.

**-arium** /ˈɛːrɪəm/ ● **suffix** forming nouns usually denoting a place: *planetarium*. See word-formation panel.
– ORIGIN from L., neut. of *-arius*, adjectival ending.

**Ariz.** ● **abbrev.** Arizona.

**Arizonan** ● **n.** a native or inhabitant of the US state of Arizona. ● **adj.** of or relating to Arizona.

**Ark.** ● **abbrev.** Arkansas.

## Word *Formation*

### -arium 'a place'

The form **-arium** derives from an adjectival ending in Latin.

➤ Some **-arium** words in current use:

| | | |
|---|---|---|
| aquarium | a tank for aquatic fauna and flora | L. *aqua* 'water' |
| columbarium | a repository with niches for storing funeral urns | L. *columba* 'dove' (with allusion to the niches in a dovecote) |
| dolphinarium | an aquarium for dolphins | based on DOLPHIN |
| herbarium | a collection of dried plants | L. *herba* 'grass, green crop' |
| insectarium | a container for the study of insects | based on INSECT |
| leprosarium | a leper hospital | Gk *lepros* 'scaly' |
| oceanarium | a large seawater aquarium | based on OCEAN |
| planetarium | a domed building used to project images of the sky showing the stars and planets | based on PLANET |
| rosarium | a rose garden | based on ROSE |
| sacrarium | the sanctuary of a church; a shrine | L. *sacer, sacr-* 'holy' |
| solarium | a room with sunbeds or sunlamps | L. *sol* 'sun' |
| termitarium | a termite colony | based on TERMITE |
| terrarium | a glass case for keeping small land animals, esp. frogs, snakes, etc. | L. *terra* 'earth' |
| vivarium | an enclosure for keeping animals under observation | L. *vivus* 'living' |

➤ The term is specifically used to designate rooms of varying temperatures forming part of an ancient Roman bathhouse:

| | | |
|---|---|---|
| caldarium | the hot room | L. *calidus* 'hot' |
| frigidarium | the cold room | L. *frigere* 'be cold' |
| tepidarium | the warm room | L. *tepere* 'be warm' |

Some words ending in **-arium** in this dictionary, such as the chemical elements ***barium*** and ***samarium***, are etymologically unrelated.

**ark** ● **n. 1** (in the Bible) the ship built by Noah to save his family and two of every kind of animal from the Flood. **2** short for **ARK OF THE COVENANT**. ➤(also **Holy Ark**) a chest or cupboard housing the Torah scrolls in a synagogue.
– PHRASES **out of the ark** informal very old or old-fashioned.
– ORIGIN OE *ærc*, from L. *arca* 'chest'.

**Arkansan** /ɑːˈkanz(ə)n/ ● **n.** a native or inhabitant of the US state of Arkansas. ● **adj.** of or relating to Arkansas.

**Ark of the Covenant** (also **Ark of the Testimony**) ● **n.** the wooden chest which contained the tablets of the laws of the ancient Israelites.

**arkose** /ˈɑːkəʊs, -z/ ● **n.** Geology a coarse-grained sandstone which is at least 25 per cent feldspar.
– DERIVATIVES **arkosic** adj.
– ORIGIN C19: from Fr., prob. from Gk *arkhaios* 'ancient'.

**ark shell** ● **n.** a small bivalve mollusc which attaches itself to rocks with byssus threads. [*Arca* and other genera.]

**arm**[1] ● **n. 1** each of the two upper limbs of the human body from the shoulder to the hand. ➤a limb of an octopus, starfish, or other animal. **2** a side part of a chair supporting a sitter's arm. **3** a narrow strip of water or land projecting from a larger body. **4** a branch or division of an organization. ➤one of the types of troops of which an army is composed. **5** Mathematics each of the lines enclosing an angle.
– PHRASES **arm in arm** with arms linked. **cost an arm and a leg** informal be extremely expensive. **would give one's right arm for** informal wish for desperately. **in arms** (of a baby) too young to walk. **keep at arm's length** avoid intimacy or close contact with. **the long** (or **strong**) **arm of the law** the far-reaching power of the law. **put the arm on** N. Amer. informal attempt to coerce (someone) to do something. **with open arms** with great affection or enthusiasm.
– DERIVATIVES **armful** n. (pl. **-fuls**). **armless** adj.
– ORIGIN OE *arm, earm*, of Gmc origin.

**arm**[2] ● **v. 1** supply with weapons. ➤provide with essential equipment for a task or situation. **2** activate the fuse of (a bomb) so that it is ready to explode.
– ORIGIN ME: from OFr. *armer*, from L. *armare*, from *arma* 'armour, arms'.

**armada** /ɑːˈmɑːdə/ ● **n.** a fleet of warships.
– ORIGIN C16: from Sp., from L. *armata*, fem. past part. of *armare* 'to arm'.

**armadillo** /ˌɑːməˈdɪləʊ/ ● **n.** (pl. **-os**) a nocturnal insectivorous mammal native to Central and South America, with large claws and a body covered in bony plates. [Family Dasypodidae: numerous species.]
– ORIGIN C16: from Sp. *armado* 'armed man', from L. *armat-, armare* 'to arm'.

**Armageddon** /ˌɑːməˈɡɛd(ə)n/ ● **n. 1** (in the New Testament) the last battle between good and evil before the Day of Judgement. **2** a catastrophic conflict.
– ORIGIN Gk, from Heb. *har měgiddōn* 'hill of Megiddo' (Rev. 16:16).

**Armagnac** /ˈɑːmənjak/ ● **n.** a type of brandy made in Aquitaine in SW France.
– ORIGIN from the former name of a district in Aquitaine.

**armament** /ˈɑːməm(ə)nt/ ● **n. 1** (also **armaments**) military weapons and equipment. **2** the process of equipping military forces for war.
– ORIGIN C17: from L. *armamentum*, from *armare* (see **ARM**[2]).

**armamentarium** /ˌɑːməmɛnˈtɛːrɪəm/ ● **n.** (pl. **armamentaria** /-rɪə/) **1** the medicines, equipment, and techniques available to a medical practitioner. **2** a collection of resources available for a purpose.
– ORIGIN C19: from L., 'arsenal, armoury'.

**armature** /ˈɑːmətʃə, -tj(ʊ)ə/ ● **n. 1** the rotating coil or coils of a dynamo or electric motor. ➤any moving part of an electrical machine in which a voltage is induced by a

magnetic field. ➤a piece of iron acting as a keeper for a magnet. **2** a framework on which a clay sculpture is moulded. **3** Biology the protective covering of an animal or plant. **4** archaic armour.
– ORIGIN ME: from Fr., from L. *armatura* 'armour', from *armare* (see **ARM**[2]).

**armband** ● **n. 1** a band worn around the upper arm to hold up a shirtsleeve or as a form of identification. **2** an inflatable plastic band worn around the upper arm as a swimming aid.

**armchair** ● **n. 1** a large, comfortable chair with side supports for the sitter's arms. **2** [as modifier] lacking direct experience of or involvement in a particular subject or activity: *an armchair traveller.*

**Armco** /'ɑːmkəʊ/ ● **n.** trademark a very pure soft iron used for roadside crash barriers.
– ORIGIN C20: acronym from *American Rolling Mill Company.*

**armed** ● **adj. 1** equipped with or involving a firearm or firearms. **2** Heraldry having claws or a beak of a specified tincture.

**armed forces** (also **armed services**) ● **pl. n.** a country's army, navy, and air force.

**Armenian** /ɑː'miːnɪən/ ● **n. 1** a native of Armenia or a person of Armenian descent. **2** the Indo-European language of Armenia. ● **adj.** of or relating to Armenia, its language, or its Church.

**Armenian Church** (also **Armenian Apostolic Orthodox Church**) ● **n.** an independent Christian Church in Armenia, influenced by Roman, Byzantine, and Syrian traditions.

**armhole** ● **n.** an opening in a garment through which the wearer puts an arm.

**armiger** /'ɑːmɪdʒə/ ● **n.** a person entitled to heraldic arms.
– DERIVATIVES **armigerous** adj.
– ORIGIN C16: L., lit. 'bearing arms'.

**armillaria** /ˌɑːmɪ'lɛːrɪə/ ● **n.** a fungus found chiefly in woodland, having mycelia that can grow for a considerable distance. [Genus *Armillaria.*]
– ORIGIN mod. L.: from L. *armilla* 'bracelet' (because of the bracelet-like frill on the fruiting bodies).

**armillary sphere** ● **n.** a revolving model of the celestial sphere constructed from metal rings representing the equator, the tropics, etc.
– ORIGIN C17: from mod. L. *armillaris* 'relating to an *armilla*', a similar astronomical instrument used by ancient astronomers, from L. *armilla* 'bracelet'.

**Arminian** /ɑː'mɪnɪən/ ● **adj.** of or relating to the doctrines of Jacobus Arminius (1560–1609), a Dutch Protestant theologian who rejected the Calvinist doctrine of predestination. ● **n.** an adherent of these doctrines.
– DERIVATIVES **Arminianism** n.

**armistice** /'ɑːmɪstɪs/ ● **n.** a truce.
– ORIGIN C18: from Fr., or from mod. L. *armistitium*, from *arma* (see **ARM**[2]) + *-stitium* 'stoppage'.

**Armistice Day** ● **n.** the anniversary of the armistice of 11 November 1918, now replaced by Remembrance Sunday in the UK.

**armlet** ● **n.** a bracelet worn round the upper arm.

**armlock** ● **n.** a method of restraining someone by holding their arm tightly behind their back.

**armoire** /ɑː'mwɑː/ ● **n.** a cupboard or wardrobe.
– ORIGIN C16: from Fr., from OFr. *armarie* (see **AUMBRY**).

**armor** ● **n.** US spelling of **ARMOUR**.

**armorer** ● **n.** US spelling of **ARMOURER**.

**Armorican** /ɑː'mɒrɪk(ə)n/ ● **adj. 1** of or relating to Armorica, an ancient region of France. **2** Geology another term for **HERCYNIAN**.

**armory**[1] /'ɑːməri/ ● **n.** heraldry.
– DERIVATIVES **armorial** adj.
– ORIGIN ME: from OFr. *armoierie* (see **ARMOURY**).

**armory**[2] ● **n.** US spelling of **ARMOURY**.

**armour** (US **armor**) ● **n. 1** the metal coverings formerly worn by soldiers to protect the body in battle. **2** (also **armour plate**) the tough metal layer covering a military vehicle or ship. ➤military vehicles collectively. **3** the protective layer or shell of some animals and plants.
– DERIVATIVES **armoured** adj. **armour-plated** adj.
– ORIGIN ME: from OFr. *armure*, from L. *armatura*, from *armare* (see **ARM**[2]).

**armourer** (US **armorer**) ● **n. 1** a maker or supplier of weapons or armour. **2** an official in charge of the arms of a warship or regiment.

**armoury** (US **armory**) ● **n.** (pl. **-ies**) **1** a store or supply of arms. ➤US a place where arms are manufactured. **2** an array of resources available for a particular purpose. **3** N. Amer. a place where militia units drill and train.
– ORIGIN ME (in the sense 'armour'): from OFr. *armoirie*, *armoierie*, from *armoier* 'to blazon', from *arme* (see **ARMS**).

**armpit** ● **n. 1** a hollow under the arm at the shoulder. **2** informal, chiefly N. Amer. an extremely unpleasant place.
– PHRASES **up to one's armpits** deeply involved in something unpleasant.

**armrest** ● **n.** an arm of a chair.

**arms** ● **pl. n. 1** weapons; armaments. **2** distinctive emblems originally borne on shields in battle and now forming heraldic insignia.
– PHRASES **a call to arms** a call to make ready for fighting. **in arms** prepared to fight. **under arms** equipped and ready for war or battle. **up in arms** (**about** or **over**) protesting vigorously (about).
– ORIGIN ME: from OFr. *armes*, from L. *arma*.

**arms control** ● **n.** international disarmament or arms limitation, especially by mutual consent.

**arms race** ● **n.** a competition between nations for superiority in the development and accumulation of weapons.

**arm-twisting** ● **n.** informal persuasion by the use of physical force or moral pressure.

**arm-wrestling** ● **n.** a contest in which two people sit opposite each other with one elbow resting on a table and try to force each other's arm down on to the table.
– DERIVATIVES **arm-wrestle** v.

**army** ● **n.** (pl. **-ies**) [treated as sing. or pl.] **1** an organized military force equipped for fighting on land. **2** a large number of similar people or things.
– ORIGIN ME: from OFr. *armee*, from *armata*, fem. past part. of L. *armare* 'to arm'.

**army ant** ● **n.** a blind nomadic tropical ant that forages in large columns, preying on insects. [Subfamily Dorylinae: many species.]

**Army List** ● **n.** (in the UK) an official list of commissioned officers.

**army worm** ● **n. 1** the caterpillars of some moths, which feed on crops and move en masse when the food is exhausted. **2** the small maggots of certain gnats, which move in large numbers within secreted slime.

**arnica** /'ɑːnɪkə/ ● **n. 1** a plant of the daisy family which bears yellow, daisy-like flowers. [Genus *Arnica*: many species.] **2** a preparation of this plant used medicinally for the treatment of bruises.
– ORIGIN C18: mod. L., of unknown origin.

**aroid** /'ɛːrɔɪd/ ● **n.** Botany a plant of the arum family (Araceae).

**aroma** ● **n.** a pleasant and distinctive smell.
– ORIGIN ME: via L. from Gk *arōma* 'spice'.

**aromatherapy** ● **n.** the use of aromatic plant extracts and essential oils for therapeutic purposes.
– DERIVATIVES **aromatherapeutic** adj. **aromatherapist** n.

**aromatic** ● **adj. 1** having an aroma. **2** Chemistry (of an organic compound) containing a planar unsaturated ring of atoms which is stabilized by an interaction of the bonds forming the ring. ● **n.** an aromatic plant, substance, or compound.
– DERIVATIVES **aromatically** adv. **aromaticity** n. (Chemistry).

**aromatize** (also **-ise**) ● **v. 1** Chemistry convert (a compound) into an aromatic structure. **2** cause to have an aroma.
– DERIVATIVES **aromatization** n.

**arose** past of **ARISE**.

**around** ● **adv. 1** located or situated on every side. **2** so as

to face in the opposite direction. **3** in or to many places throughout a locality. **4** here and there. **5** available or present. **6** approximately. ● **prep. 1** on every side of. **2** in or to many places throughout (a locality). **3** so as to encircle or embrace. ➤following an approximately circular route.
– ORIGIN ME: from **A-²** + **ROUND**.

**arouse** ● **v. 1** evoke (a feeling or response). ➤provoke to anger or strong emotions. ➤excite sexually. **2** awaken from sleep.
– DERIVATIVES **arousable** adj. **arousal** n.
– ORIGIN C16: from **ROUSE**, on the pattern of the pair of *rise, arise*.

**ARP** ● **abbrev.** Brit. historical air-raid precautions.

**arpeggiate** /ɑː'pɛdʒɪeɪt/ ● **v.** Music play (a chord) as a series of ascending or descending notes.
– DERIVATIVES **arpeggiation** n. **arpeggiator** n.

**arpeggio** /ɑː'pɛdʒɪəʊ/ ● **n.** (pl. **-os**) Music the notes of a chord played in rapid succession.
– ORIGIN Ital., from *arpeggiare* 'play the harp', from *arpa* 'harp'.

**arpeggione** /ɑːˌpɛdʒɪ'əʊneɪ, -ni/ ● **n.** an early 19th-century stringed instrument resembling a guitar and having six strings and frets, but played with a bow like a cello.
– ORIGIN C19: from Ger., from **ARPEGGIO**.

**arquebus** /'ɑːkwɪbəs/ ● **n.** variant spelling of **HARQUEBUS**.

**arr.** ● **abbrev. 1** (of a piece of music) arranged by. **2** (in a transport timetable) arrives.

**arrack** /'arək, ə'rak/ (also **arak**) ● **n.** an alcoholic spirit made from the sap of the coco palm or from rice.
– ORIGIN C17: from Arab. *'arak* 'sweat', from the phr. *'arak al-tamr*, denoting an alcoholic spirit made from dates.

**arraign** /ə'reɪn/ ● **v.** call before a court to answer a criminal charge.
– DERIVATIVES **arraignment** n.
– ORIGIN ME: from OFr. *araisnier*, based on L. *ad-* 'to' + *ratio(n-)* 'reason, account'.

**arrange** ● **v. 1** put in a neat, attractive, or required order. **2** organize or plan. ➤reach agreement about an action or event in advance: *they arranged to meet at eleven o'clock*. **3** Music adapt (a composition) for performance with instruments or voices other than those originally specified. **4** archaic settle (a dispute or claim).
– DERIVATIVES **arrangeable** adj. **arranger** n.
– ORIGIN ME: from OFr. *arangier*, from *a-* (from L. *ad* 'to, at') + *rangier* (see **RANGE**).

**arrangement** ● **n. 1** the action, process, or result of arranging. **2** a plan for a future event. **3** Music an arranged composition. **4** archaic a settlement of a dispute or claim.

**arrant** /'ar(ə)nt/ ● **adj.** utter; complete: *what arrant nonsense!*
– DERIVATIVES **arrantly** adv.
– ORIGIN ME: var. of **ERRANT**, orig. in phrs such as *arrant thief* ('outlawed, roving thief').

**arras** /'arəs/ ● **n.** a tapestry wall hanging.
– ORIGIN ME: named after the Fr. town of *Arras*.

**array** /ə'reɪ/ ● **n. 1** an impressive display or range of a particular thing. **2** an ordered arrangement of troops. **3** Mathematics an arrangement of quantities or symbols in rows and columns; a matrix. **4** Computing an ordered set of related elements. **5** Law a list of jurors impanelled. **6** poetic/literary elaborate or beautiful clothing. ● **v. 1** display or arrange in a neat or impressive way. **2** (**be arrayed in**) be elaborately clothed in. **3** Law impanel (a jury).
– ORIGIN ME: from OFr. *arei* (n.), *areer* (v.), based on L. *ad-* 'towards' + a Gmc base meaning 'prepare'.

**arrears** ● **pl. n.** payments or debts that are outstanding and due.
– PHRASES **in arrears** (also chiefly Law **in arrear**) **1** behind with paying money that is owed. ➤(of wages or rent) paid at the end of each period of work or occupation. **2** (of a competitor in a race) falling behind others.
– DERIVATIVES **arrearage** n.
– ORIGIN ME: from *arrear* (adv.) 'behind, overdue', from OFr. *arere*, from med. L. *adretro*, from *ad-* 'towards' + *retro* 'backwards'.

**Arrernte** /ə'rʌntə, a'ruːndə/ ● **n.** variant form of **ARANDA**.

**arrest** ● **v. 1** seize (someone) by legal authority and take them into custody. ➤seize and detain (a ship) by legal authority. **2** stop or check (progress or a process). **3** [usu. as adj. **arresting**] attract the attention of. ● **n. 1** the action of arresting. **2** a sudden cessation of motion.
– PHRASES **arrest of judgement** Law the suspension of proceedings in a criminal trial between the verdict and the sentence on the grounds of a material irregularity in the course of the trial.
– DERIVATIVES **arrestee** n. (chiefly N. Amer.). **arrestingly** adv.
– ORIGIN ME: from OFr. *arester*, based on L. *ad-* 'at, to' + *restare* 'remain, stop'.

**arrestable offence** ● **n.** Law an offence for which the offender may be arrested without a warrant; a felony.

**arrester** (also **arrestor**) ● **n.** a device which prevents or stops. ➤a device on an aircraft carrier that slows down aircraft after landing by means of a hook and cable.

**arrestment** ● **n.** Scots Law an attachment of property for the satisfaction of a debt.

**Arretine** /'arətʌɪn/ ● **adj.** denoting Samian ware made at Arretium (modern Arezzo) in Italy.

**arrhythmia** /ə'rɪðmɪə/ ● **n.** Medicine a condition in which the heart beats with an irregular or abnormal rhythm.
– ORIGIN C19: from Gk *arruthmia* 'lack of rhythm', from *a-* 'without' + *rhuthmos* (see **RHYTHM**).

**arrhythmic** (also **arhythmic**) ● **adj.** not rhythmic. ➤Medicine relating to or suffering from cardiac arrhythmia.
– DERIVATIVES **arrhythmical** adj. **arrhythmically** adv.

**arrière-pensée** /ˌarɪɛː 'pɒ̃seɪ, French arjɛʀ pɑ̃se/ ● **n.** a concealed thought or intention.
– ORIGIN Fr., lit. 'behind thought'.

**arris** /'arɪs/ ● **n.** Architecture a sharp edge formed by the meeting of two flat or curved surfaces.
– ORIGIN C17: alt. of early mod. Fr. *areste* 'sharp ridge', earlier form of **ARÊTE**.

**arris rail** ● **n.** a fence rail with a triangular cross section.

**arrive** ● **v. 1** reach a destination. **2** be brought or delivered. **3** (of a particular moment) come about. **4** (**arrive at**) reach (a conclusion or decision). **5** informal become successful and well known.
– DERIVATIVES **arrival** n.
– ORIGIN ME (in the sense 'reach the shore after a voyage'): from OFr. *ariver*, based on L. *ad-* 'to' + *ripa* 'shore'.

**arriviste** /ˌariː'viːst/ ● **n.** a person bent on improving their social or financial status; a parvenu.
– DERIVATIVES **arrivisme** /ˌariː'viːzm(ə)/ n.
– ORIGIN C20: from Fr., from *arriver* (see **ARRIVE**).

**arrogant** ● **adj.** having an exaggerated sense of one's own importance or abilities.
– DERIVATIVES **arrogance** n. **arrogantly** adv.
– ORIGIN ME: via OFr. from L. *arrogare* (see **ARROGATE**).

**arrogate** /'arəgeɪt/ ● **v.** take or claim for oneself without justification.
– DERIVATIVES **arrogation** n.
– ORIGIN C16: from L. *arrogat-*, *arrogare* 'claim for oneself', from *ad-* 'to' + *rogare* 'ask'.

**arrondissement** /a'rɒndiːsmɑ̃, ˌarɒn'diːsmɑ̃, French arɔ̃dismɑ̃/ ● **n.** (in France) a subdivision of a local government department. ➤an administrative district of Paris.
– ORIGIN Fr., from *arrondir* 'make round'.

**arrow** ● **n.** a stick with a sharp pointed head, designed to be shot from a bow. ➤a symbol resembling this, used to show direction or position. ● **v.** move swiftly and directly.
– DERIVATIVES **arrowed** adj. **arrowy** adj.
– ORIGIN OE *arewe*, *arwe*, from ON.

**arrowgrass** ● **n.** a grass-like marsh plant with a slender spike of tiny flowers. [Genus *Triglochin*.]

**arrowhead** ● **n. 1** Geometry a quadrilateral in which one internal angle is more than 180°. **2** a water plant with arrow-shaped leaves above the water surface. [Genus *Sagittaria*: several species.]

**arrowroot** ● **n. 1** a fine-grained starch used in cookery

and medicine. **2** the herbaceous Caribbean plant from which this starch is prepared. [*Maranta arundinacea*.]
– ORIGIN C17: alt. of Arawak *aru-aru* (lit. 'meal of meals') by assoc. with **ARROW** and **ROOT**[1], the plant's tubers being used to absorb poison from arrow wounds.

**arrow worm** • n. a slender transparent worm-like marine animal with spines on the head for grasping prey, common in plankton. [Phylum Chaetognatha: many species.]

**arroyo** /əˈrɔɪəʊ/ • n. (pl. **-os**) US a dry, steep-sided gully cut by a river or stream.
– ORIGIN C19: from Sp.

**arse** Brit. vulgar slang • n. a person's buttocks or anus. • v. **1** (**arse about/around**) behave in a stupid way. **2** (**can't/couldn't be arsed**) not be bothered to do something.
– ORIGIN OE *ærs*, of Gmc origin.

**arsehole** • n. Brit. vulgar slang a person's anus.

**arsenal** • n. a store of weapons and ammunition. ➤a military establishment where weapons and ammunition are made and stored.
– ORIGIN C16 (in the sense 'a dockyard'): from Fr., or from obs. Ital. *arzanale*, based on Arab. *dār-aṣ-ṣināʻa*, from *dār* 'house' + *al-* '(of) the' + *sināʻa* 'art, industry'.

**arsenic** /ˈɑːs(ə)nɪk/ • n. the chemical element of atomic number 33, a brittle steel-grey semimetal with many highly poisonous compounds. (Symbol: **As**)
– DERIVATIVES **arsenical** adj. **arsenide** n.
– ORIGIN ME (in sense 'orpiment'): via OFr. from L. *arsenicum*, from Gk *arsenikon*, from Arab. *al-zarnīḵ*.

**arsenic acid** /ɑːˈsenɪk/ • n. Chemistry a weakly acidic crystalline solid with oxidizing properties. [$H_3AsO_4$.]
– DERIVATIVES **arsenate** n.

**arsenopyrite** /ˌɑːs(ə)nəʊˈpʌɪrʌɪt/ • n. a silvery-grey mineral consisting of an arsenide and sulphide of iron and cobalt.

**arsine** /ˈɑːsiːn/ • n. Chemistry a poisonous gas made by the reaction of some arsenic compounds with acids. [$AsH_3$.]
– ORIGIN C19: from **ARSENIC**, on the pattern of *amine*.

**arsis** /ˈɑːsɪs/ • n. (pl. **arses** /-siːz/) Prosody a stressed syllable or part of a metrical foot in Greek or Latin verse. Often contrasted with **THESIS**.
– ORIGIN ME: via late L. from Gk, lit. 'lifting', from *airein* 'raise'.

**arson** • n. the criminal act of deliberately setting fire to property.
– DERIVATIVES **arsonist** n.
– ORIGIN C17: an Anglo-Norman Fr. legal term, from med. L. *arsio(n-)*, from L. *ardere* 'to burn'.

**arsphenamine** /ɑːsˈfɛnəmiːn, -ɪn/ • n. Medicine a synthetic organic arsenic compound formerly used to treat syphilis.

**art**[1] • n. **1** the expression or application of creative skill and imagination, especially through a visual medium such as painting or sculpture. ➤works produced in this way. **2** (**the arts**) the various branches of creative activity, such as painting, music, literature, and dance. **3** (**arts**) subjects of study primarily concerned with human culture (as contrasted with scientific or technical subjects). **4** a skill at doing a specified thing.
– ORIGIN ME: via OFr. from L. *ars*, *art-*.

**art**[2] archaic or dialect second person singular present of **BE**.

**art.** • abbrev. article.

**art deco** /ˈdɛkəʊ/ • n. a style of decorative art characterized by precise and boldly delineated geometric shapes.
– ORIGIN 1960s: shortened from Fr. *art décoratif* 'decorative art', from the 1925 *Exposition des Arts décoratifs* in Paris.

**artefact** /ˈɑːtɪfakt/ (US **artifact**) • n. **1** an object made by a human being. **2** something observed in a scientific investigation that is not naturally present but occurs as a result of the investigative procedure.
– DERIVATIVES **artefactual** adj.
– ORIGIN C19: from L. *arte* 'by or using art' + *factum* 'something made'.

**artel** /ɑːˈtɛl/ • n. (pl. **artels**, **arteli**) (in pre-revolutionary Russia) a cooperative association of craftsmen living and working together.
– ORIGIN from Russ. *artel'*.

**artemisia** /ˌɑːtɪˈmɪzɪə/ • n. an aromatic or bitter-tasting plant of a genus that includes wormwood, some species of which are used in herbal medicine. [Genus *Artemisia*.]
– ORIGIN ME: via L. from Gk, 'wormwood', named after the Gk goddess Artemis.

**artemisinin** /ˌɑːtɪˈmiːsɪnɪn/ • n. a terpene-based antimalarial substance obtained from an artemisia and used in Chinese medicine.

**arterialized** (also **-ised**) • adj. Physiology (of blood) converted from venous to arterial by oxygenation.
– DERIVATIVES **arterialization** n.

**arterio-** • comb. form of or relating to the arteries: *arteriosclerosis*.

**arteriography** /ɑːˌtɪərɪˈɒgrəfi/ • n. Medicine radiography of an artery, carried out after injection of a radiopaque substance.

**arteriole** /ɑːˈtɪərɪəʊl/ • n. Anatomy a small branch of an artery leading into capillaries.
– DERIVATIVES **arteriolar** adj.
– ORIGIN C19: from Fr. *artériole*, dimin. of *artère* (see **ARTERY**).

**arteriosclerosis** /ɑːˌtɪərɪəʊsklɪəˈrəʊsɪs, -skləˈ-/ • n. Medicine thickening and hardening of the walls of the arteries.
– DERIVATIVES **arteriosclerotic** adj.

**arteriovenous** /ɑːˌtɪərɪəʊˈviːnəs/ • adj. Anatomy of, relating to, or affecting an artery and a vein.

**artery** • n. (pl. **-ies**) **1** any of the muscular-walled tubes forming part of the circulation system by which blood is conveyed from the heart to all parts of the body. **2** an important route in a traffic or transport system.
– DERIVATIVES **arterial** adj. **arteritis** n.
– ORIGIN ME: from L. *arteria*, from Gk *artēria*, prob. from *airein* 'raise'.

**artesian** /ɑːˈtiːzɪən, -ʒ(ə)n/ • adj. relating to or denoting a well that is bored perpendicularly into water-bearing strata lying at an angle, so that water is supplied by natural pressure.
– ORIGIN C19: from Fr. *artésien*, 'from *Artois*', a region in France.

**Artex** /ˈɑːtɛks/ • n. trademark a kind of plaster applied to walls and ceilings to give a textured finish.
– ORIGIN 1950s: blend of **ART**[1] and **TEXTURE**.

**art form** • n. a conventionally established form of artistic composition, such as the novel.

**artful** • adj. cunningly clever or skilful.
– DERIVATIVES **artfully** adv. **artfulness** n.

**art history** • n. the academic study of the history and development of the visual arts.
– DERIVATIVES **art historian** n. **art historical** adj.

**art house** • n. a cinema which shows artistic or experimental films.

**arthralgia** /ɑːˈθraldʒə/ • n. Medicine pain in a joint.
– ORIGIN C19: from Gk *arthron* 'joint' + **-ALGIA**.

**arthritis** /ɑːˈθrʌɪtɪs/ • n. a disease causing painful inflammation and stiffness of the joints.
– DERIVATIVES **arthritic** adj. & n.
– ORIGIN C16: via L. from Gk, from *arthron* 'joint'.

**arthro-** • comb. form of a joint; relating to joints: *arthroscope*.
– ORIGIN from Gk *arthron* 'joint'.

**arthrodesis** /ɑːˈθrɒdɪsɪs/ • n. surgical immobilization of a joint by fusion of the bones.
– ORIGIN C20: from **ARTHRO-** + Gk *desis* 'binding together'.

**Arthropoda** /ˌɑːθrəˈpəʊdə/ • pl. n. Zoology a large phylum of invertebrate animals having a segmented body, external skeleton, and jointed limbs, including insects, spiders, and crustaceans.
– DERIVATIVES **arthropod** /ˈɑːθrəpɒd/ n.
– ORIGIN mod. L., from Gk *arthron* 'joint' + *pous*, *pod-* 'foot'.

**arthroscope** /ˈɑːθrəskəʊp/ • n. Medicine an instrument for inspecting or operating on the interior of a joint.
– DERIVATIVES **arthroscopic** adj. **arthroscopy** n.

**Arthurian** /ɑːˈθjʊərɪən/ ● **adj.** of or relating to the reign of the legendary King Arthur of Britain.

**artichoke** /ˈɑːtɪtʃəʊk/ ● **n.** **1** a plant with large, thistle-like flower heads. [*Cynara scolymus*.] **2** (also **globe artichoke**) the unopened flower head of this plant, of which the heart and the fleshy bases of the bracts are edible. **3** see **JERUSALEM ARTICHOKE**.
– ORIGIN C16: from northern Ital. *articiocco*, from Sp. *alcarchofa*, from Arab. *al-ḵaršūfa*.

**article** ● **n.** **1** a particular object. **2** a piece of writing included with others in a newspaper or magazine. **3** a separate clause or paragraph of a legal document. **4** (**articles**) a period of training with a firm as a solicitor, architect, surveyor, or accountant. ➤the terms on which crew members take service on a ship. **5** Grammar the definite or indefinite article. ● **v.** bind by articles in order to become qualified.
– PHRASES **an article of faith** a firmly held belief.
– ORIGIN ME: from OFr., from L. *articulus* 'small connecting part', dimin. of *artus* 'joint'.

**articled clerk** ● **n.** Brit. a trainee solicitor.

**articular** /ɑːˈtɪkjʊlə/ ● **adj.** Anatomy of or relating to a joint.
– ORIGIN ME: from L. *articularis*, from *articulus* (see **ARTICLE**).

**articulate** ● **adj.** /ɑːˈtɪkjʊlət/ **1** fluent and clear in speech. **2** technical having joints or jointed segments. ➤Zoology denoting a brachiopod which has projections and sockets that form a hinge joining the two halves of the shell. ● **v.** /ɑːˈtɪkjʊleɪt/ **1** pronounce (words) distinctly. ➤clearly express (an idea or feeling). **2** form a joint. ➤(**be articulated**) be connected by joints.
– DERIVATIVES **articulable** adj. **articulacy** n. **articulated** adj. **articulately** adv. **articulateness** n. **articulatory** n.
– ORIGIN C16: from L. *articulat-*, *articulare* 'divide into joints, utter distinctly', from *articulus* (see **ARTICLE**).

**articulation** ● **n.** **1** the action of articulating. ➤Music clarity in the production of successive notes. ➤Phonetics the formation of a speech sound by constriction of the air flow in the vocal organs. **2** the state of being jointed. ➤a specified joint.

**articulator** ● **n.** any of the vocal organs above the larynx, including the tongue, lips, teeth, and hard palate.

**artifact** ● **n.** US spelling of **ARTEFACT**.

**artifice** /ˈɑːtɪfɪs/ ● **n.** clever devices or expedients, especially to trick or deceive others.
– ORIGIN ME (in the sense 'workmanship'): from OFr., from L. *artificium*, based on *ars* 'art' + *facere* 'make'.

**artificer** /ɑːˈtɪfɪsə/ ● **n.** a skilled mechanic in the armed forces.

**artificial** ● **adj.** **1** made as a copy of something natural. **2** contrived or affected. **3** Bridge (of a bid) conventional as opposed to natural.
– DERIVATIVES **artificiality** n. **artificially** adv.
– ORIGIN ME: from OFr. *artificiel* or L. *artificialis*, from *artificium* (see **ARTIFICE**).

**artificial horizon** ● **n.** a gyroscopic instrument or a fluid surface providing the pilot of an aircraft with a horizontal reference plane for navigational measurement when the natural horizon is obscured.

**artificial insemination** ● **n.** the veterinary or medical procedure of injecting semen into the vagina or uterus.

**artificial intelligence** ● **n.** the performance by computer systems of tasks normally requiring human intelligence, such as visual perception or decision-making.

**artificial respiration** ● **n.** the restoration or maintenance of someone's breathing by manual, mechanical, or mouth-to-mouth methods.

**artillery** /ɑːˈtɪləri/ ● **n.** (pl. **-ies**) large-calibre guns used in warfare on land. ➤a branch of the armed forces trained to use artillery.
– DERIVATIVES **artillerist** n.
– ORIGIN ME: from OFr. *artillerie*, from *artiller*, alt. of *atillier* 'equip, arm', prob. a var. of *atirier*, from *a-* + *tire* 'rank, order'.

**Artiodactyla** /ˌɑːtɪə(ʊ)ˈdaktɪlə/ ● **pl. n.** Zoology an order of mammals that comprises the ruminants, camels, pigs, and hippopotamuses (the even-toed ungulates).
– DERIVATIVES **artiodactyl** n. & adj.
– ORIGIN mod. L., from Gk *artios* 'even' + *daktulos* 'finger, toe'.

**artisan** /ˌɑːtɪˈzan, ˈɑːtɪzan/ ● **n.** a skilled worker who makes things by hand.
– DERIVATIVES **artisanal** adj.
– ORIGIN C16: from Fr., from Ital. *artigiano*, based on L. *artire* 'instruct in the arts'.

**artist** ● **n.** **1** a person who paints or draws as a profession or hobby. ➤a person who practises or performs any of the creative arts. **2** informal a habitual practitioner of a specified activity: *a con artist.*
– DERIVATIVES **artistic** adj. **artistically** adv. **artistry** n.
– ORIGIN C16: from Fr. *artiste*, from Ital. *artista*, from *arte* 'art', from L. *ars, art-*.

**artiste** /ɑːˈtiːst/ ● **n.** a professional entertainer, especially a singer or dancer.
– ORIGIN C19: from Fr. (see **ARTIST**).

**artless** ● **adj.** **1** without guile or pretension. **2** clumsy.
– DERIVATIVES **artlessly** adv.

**art nouveau** /ˌɑː(t) nuːˈvəʊ/ ● **n.** a style of decorative art and architecture characterized by intricate linear designs and flowing curves.
– ORIGIN C20: from Fr., lit. 'new art'.

**arts and crafts** ● **pl. n.** decorative design and handicraft.

**artwork** ● **n.** illustrations or other non-textual material prepared for inclusion in a publication.

**arty** (chiefly N. Amer. also **artsy**) ● **adj.** (**-ier**, **-iest**) informal artistic or interested in the arts, especially in a pretentious or affected way.
– DERIVATIVES **artiness** n.

**arty-farty** (also **artsy-fartsy**) ● **adj.** informal pretentiously or affectedly artistic.

**arugula** /əˈruːgjʊlə/ ● **n.** N. Amer. the salad vegetable rocket.
– ORIGIN 1970s: from Ital. dial. *arucula*, *aruca*, from Ital. *rucola*, dimin. of *ruca* **ROCKET**[2].

**arum** /ˈɛːrəm/ ● **n.** a plant of a large family with typically arrow-shaped leaves and a broad leafy spathe enclosing a club-shaped spadix. [*Arum maculatum* (**wild arum**, cuckoo pint) and other species, family Araceae.]
– ORIGIN ME: from L., from Gk *aron*.

**arum lily** ● **n.** chiefly Brit. a tall lily-like African plant which bears a large showy spathe. [Genus *Zantedeschia*.]

**Arunta** /əˈrʌntə, aˈruːndə/ ● **n.** variant spelling of **ARANDA**.

**arvo** /ˈɑːvəʊ/ ● **n.** (pl. **-os**) Austral./NZ informal afternoon.

**-ary**[1] ● **suffix** **1** forming adjectives such as *budgetary.* **2** forming nouns such as *dictionary.*
– ORIGIN from Fr. *-aire* or L. *-arius* 'connected with'.

**-ary**[2] ● **suffix** forming adjectives such as *capillary.*
– ORIGIN from Fr. *-aire* or L. *-aris* 'relating to'.

**Aryan** /ˈɛːrɪən/ ● **n.** **1** a member of a people speaking an Indo-European language who invaded northern India in the 2nd millennium BC. **2** the language of this people. **3** (in Nazi ideology) a person of Caucasian race not of Jewish descent. ● **adj.** relating to or denoting the Aryan people or their language.
– ORIGIN from Sanskrit *ārya* 'noble' + **-AN**.

**aryl** /ˈarʌɪl, -rɪl/ ● **n.** [as modifier] Chemistry of or denoting a radical derived from an aromatic hydrocarbon by removal of a hydrogen atom.
– ORIGIN C20: from **AROMATIC** + **-YL**.

**arytenoid** /ˌarɪˈtiːnɔɪd/ ● **adj.** Anatomy relating to or denoting cartilage at the back of the larynx used in the production of different kinds of voice quality.
– ORIGIN C18: from mod. L. *arytaenoides*, from Gk *arutainoeidēs*, from *arutaina* 'funnel'.

**AS** ● **abbrev.** Anglo-Saxon.

**As** ● **symb.** the chemical element arsenic.

**as**[1] /az, əz/ ● **adv.** used in comparisons to refer to the extent or degree of something. ➤used to emphasize an amount. ● **conj.** **1** used to indicate simultaneous occurrence. **2** used to indicate by comparison the way that something happens. **3** because. **4** even though. ● **prep.** **1** used to refer to the function or character of someone or

something. **2** during the time of being.
– PHRASES **as for** (or **to**) with regard to. **as from** (or **of**) chiefly Brit. from a particular time or date. **as if** (or **though**) as would be the case if. **as (it) is** in the existing circumstances. **as yet** until now or that time.
– ORIGIN ME: reduced form of OE *alswā* 'similarly' (see **ALSO**).

**as²** /as/ ● **n.** an ancient Roman copper coin.
– ORIGIN L., 'a unit'.

**as-** ● **prefix** variant spelling of **AD-** assimilated before *s* (as in *assemble*).

**ASA** ● **abbrev. 1** Advertising Standards Authority. **2** Amateur Swimming Association. **3** American Standards Association.

**asafoetida** /ˌasəˈfiːtɪdə, -ˈfɛt-/ (US **asafetida**) ● **n. 1** a fetid resinous gum obtained from the roots of a herbaceous plant, used in herbal medicine and Indian cooking. **2** a plant of the parsley family, from which this gum is obtained. [*Ferula assa-foetida*.]
– ORIGIN ME: from med. L., from *asa* (from Pers. *azā* 'mastic') + *foetida* (see **FETID**).

**asana** /ˈɑːsənə/ ● **n.** a posture adopted in hatha yoga.
– ORIGIN from Sanskrit *āsana*.

**asap** ● **abbrev.** as soon as possible.

**ASB** ● **abbrev.** Alternative Service Book.

**asbestos** /azˈbɛstɒs, as-, -təs/ ● **n.** a highly heat-resistant fibrous silicate mineral able to be woven into fabrics, used in brake linings and in fire-resistant and insulating materials.
– ORIGIN C17, via L. from Gk *asbestos* 'unquenchable'.

**asbestosis** /ˌazbɛˈstəʊsɪs, ˌas-/ ● **n.** a lung disease resulting from the inhalation of asbestos particles, marked by severe fibrosis and a high risk of cancer of the pleura.

**ascarid** /ˈaskərɪd/ (also **ascaris** /-rɪs/) ● **n.** Zoology a member of a family of parasitic nematode worms (Ascaridae) that live in the intestines of vertebrates.
– ORIGIN C17: from mod. L. *Ascaridae*, from Gk *askarides*, pl. of *askaris* 'intestinal worm'.

**ascend** ● **v. 1** go up; climb or rise. **2** rise in status. **3** (of a voice or sound) rise in pitch.
– PHRASES **ascend the throne** become king or queen.
– ORIGIN ME: from L. *ascendere*, from *ad-* 'to' + *scandere* 'to climb'.

**ascendant** (also **ascendent**) ● **adj. 1** holding a position of increasing status or influence. **2** Astrology (of a planet, zodiacal degree, or sign) on or close to the intersection of the ecliptic with the eastern horizon. ● **n.** Astrology the ascendant point.
– PHRASES **in the ascendant** rising in power or influence.
– DERIVATIVES **ascendancy** n.

**ascender** ● **n. 1** a person or thing that ascends. **2** a lower-case letter (or part of it) that extends above the level of the top of an *x* (such as *b* and *f*). **3** Climbing a device which can be clipped to a rope to act as a foothold or handhold.

**ascension** ● **n. 1** the action of ascending in status. **2** (**Ascension**) the ascent of Christ into heaven on the fortieth day after the Resurrection.
– DERIVATIVES **ascensional** adj.
– ORIGIN ME: via OFr. from L. *ascensio(n-)*, from *ascendere* (see **ASCEND**).

**Ascension Day** ● **n.** the Thursday forty days after Easter, on which Christ's Ascension is celebrated in the Christian Church.

**Ascensiontide** ● **n.** the period of ten days from Ascension Day to Whitsun Eve.

**ascent** ● **n.** an instance of ascending. ➤ a climb to the summit of a mountain. ➤ an upward slope.
– ORIGIN C16: from **ASCEND**, on the pattern of the pair of *descend, descent*.

**ascertain** /ˌasəˈteɪn/ ● **v.** find out for certain.
– DERIVATIVES **ascertainable** adj. **ascertainment** n.
– ORIGIN ME: from OFr. *acertener*, based on L. *certus* 'settled, sure'.

**ascesis** /əˈsiːsɪs/ ● **n.** the practice of severe self-discipline.
– ORIGIN C19: from Gk *askēsis* 'training'.

**ascetic** /əˈsɛtɪk/ ● **adj.** characterized by the practice of severe self-discipline. ● **n.** an ascetic person.
– DERIVATIVES **ascetically** adv. **asceticism** n.
– ORIGIN C17: from med. L. *asceticus* or Gk *askētikos*, from *askētēs* 'monk', from *askein* 'to exercise'.

**aschelminth** /ˈaʃhɛlmɪnθ, ˈask-/ ● **n.** (pl. **aschelminths** or **aschelminthes**) Zoology a typically worm-like invertebrate of a large group that lack a well-developed coelom and blood vessels and include the nematodes, rotifers, and water bears.
– ORIGIN from mod. L. *Aschelminthes* (former phylum name), from Gk *askos* 'sac' + *helminth* 'worm' (from the former belief that animals of this group had a fluid-filled internal sac).

**asci** plural form of **ASCUS**.

**ascidian** /əˈsɪdɪən/ ● **n.** Zoology a sea squirt.
– ORIGIN C19: from mod. L. pl. *Ascidia* (genus name), from Gk *askidion*, dimin. of *askos* 'wineskin'.

**ASCII** /ˈaski/ ● **abbrev.** Computing American Standard Code for Information Interchange.

**ascites** /əˈsʌɪtiːz/ ● **n.** Medicine the accumulation of fluid in the peritoneal cavity, causing abdominal swelling.
– DERIVATIVES **ascitic** adj.
– ORIGIN ME: via late L. from Gk *askitēs*, from *askos* 'wineskin'.

**ascomycete** /ˌaskəˈmʌɪsiːt/ ● **n.** (pl. **ascomycetes** /-ˈmʌɪsiːts, -mʌɪˈsiːtiːz/) Botany a fungus of a large group whose spores develop within asci and which includes most moulds, mildews, and yeasts, the fungal component of most lichens, and the morels and truffles.
– ORIGIN C19: from mod. L. *Ascomycetes* (former class name), from Gk *askos* 'sac' + *mukētes* 'fungi'.

**ascorbic acid** /əˈskɔːbɪk/ ● **n.** vitamin C, a compound found in citrus fruits and green vegetables which is essential in maintaining healthy connective tissue and of which a deficiency causes scurvy.
– DERIVATIVES **ascorbate** n.
– ORIGIN 1930s: from **A-¹** + med. L. *scorbutus* 'scurvy' + **-IC**.

**ascribe** ● **v.** (**ascribe something to**) attribute something to (a particular cause, person or period). ➤ regard a quality as belonging to.
– DERIVATIVES **ascribable** adj. **ascription** n.
– ORIGIN ME: from L. *ascribere*, from *ad-* 'to' + *scribere* 'write'.

**ascus** /ˈaskəs/ ● **n.** (pl. **asci** /ˈaskʌɪ, -iː/) Botany a sac in which the spores of ascomycete fungi develop.
– ORIGIN C19: mod. L., from Gk *askos* 'bag'.

**asdic** /ˈazdɪk/ ● **n.** chiefly Brit. a form of sonar developed in the Second World War to detect enemy submarines.
– ORIGIN acronym from *Allied Submarine Detection Investigation Committee.*

**-ase** ● **suffix** Biochemistry forming names of enzymes: *amylase.*
– ORIGIN from *(diast)ase.*

**ASEAN** /ˈasɪən/ ● **abbrev.** Association of South-East Asian Nations.

**aseismic** /eɪˈsʌɪzmɪk/ ● **adj.** Geology not characterized by earthquake activity.

**asepsis** /eɪˈsɛpsɪs/ ● **n.** the absence or exclusion of bacteria, viruses, and other micro-organisms. Compare with **ANTISEPSIS**.
– DERIVATIVES **aseptic** adj.

**asexual** ● **adj. 1** Biology without sex or sexual organs. ➤ (of reproduction) not involving the fusion of gametes. **2** without sexual feelings or associations.
– DERIVATIVES **asexuality** n. **asexually** adv.

**ASH** ● **abbrev.** Action on Smoking and Health.

**ash¹** ● **n. 1** the powdery residue left after the burning of a substance. ➤ (**ashes**) the remains of a human body after cremation or burning. ➤ (in chemical analysis) the mineral component of an organic substance (indicated by the residue left after burning). **2** (**the Ashes**) a notional cricket trophy awarded for a test match series between England and Australia. [from a mock obituary notice referring to the symbolical remains of English cricket.] ● **v. 1** (in chemical analysis) burn to ash. **2** cover or sprinkle with ash.

– PHRASES **ashes in one's mouth** something that is bitterly disappointing or worthless. **rise from the ashes** be renewed after destruction.
– DERIVATIVES **ashy** adj.
– ORIGIN OE *æsce, aexe*, of Gmc origin.

**ash²** • n. **1** a tree with compound leaves, winged fruits, and hard pale wood. [Genus *Fraxinus*: many species.] ➤ used in names of other trees, e.g. **mountain ash**. **2** an Old English runic letter, ᚫ. ➤ the symbol æ or Æ, used in the Roman alphabet in place of the runic letter and as a phonetic symbol. See also **Æ**.
– ORIGIN OE *æsc*, of Gmc origin.

**ashamed** • adj. feeling embarrassed or guilty.
– DERIVATIVES **ashamedly** adv.
– ORIGIN OE *āscamod*, past part. of *āscamian* 'feel shame', from *ā-* (as an intensifier) + **SHAME**.

**Ashanti** /əˈʃanti/ (also **Asante**) • n. (pl. same) **1** a member of a people of south central Ghana. **2** the dialect of Akan spoken by the Ashanti.
– ORIGIN the name in Akan.

**ash blonde** (also **ash blond**) • adj. denoting hair that is a very pale blonde colour.

**ashcan** • n. US a dustbin.

**ashen¹** • adj. **1** (of a person's face) very pale with shock, fear, or illness. **2** poetic/literary ash-coloured.

**ashen²** • adj. archaic or poetic/literary made of wood from the ash tree.

**ashet** /ˈaʃɪt/ • n. Scottish & N. English a large plate or dish.
– ORIGIN C16: from Fr. *assiette*.

**Ashkenazi** /ˌaʃkəˈnɑːzi/ • n. (pl. **Ashkenazim** /-zɪm/) a Jew of central or eastern European descent. Compare with **SEPHARDI**.
– DERIVATIVES **Ashkenazic** adj.
– ORIGIN from mod. Heb., from *Ashkenaz*, grandson of Japheth, one of the sons of Noah (Gen. 10:3).

**ash key** • n. Brit. the winged fruit of an ash tree, growing in clusters resembling keys.

**ashlar** /ˈaʃlə/ • n. masonry made of large square-cut stones, generally used as a facing material.
– ORIGIN ME: from OFr. *aisselier* from L. *axilla*, dimin. of *axis* 'plank'.

**ashlaring** • n. **1** ashlar masonry. **2** upright boarding fixed from the joists to the rafters of an attic to cut off the acute angle between the roof and the floor.

**ashore** • adv. to or on the shore or land from the direction of the sea. ➤ on land as opposed to at sea.

**ashplant** • n. a sapling from an ash tree used as a walking stick or whip.

**ashram** /ˈaʃrəm/ • n. a place of religious retreat or community life in or modelled on those in India.
– ORIGIN from Sanskrit *āśrama* 'hermitage'.

**ashrama** /ˈaʃrəmə/ • n. Hinduism any of the four stages of an ideal life, ascending from the status of pupil to the total renunciation of the world.
– ORIGIN from Sanskrit *āśrama*.

**ashtray** • n. a small receptacle for tobacco ash and cigarette ends.

**Ash Wednesday** • n. the first day of Lent in the Western Christian Church, marked by services of penitence.
– ORIGIN from the custom of marking the foreheads of penitents with ashes on that day.

**ASI** • abbrev. airspeed indicator.

**Asian** /ˈeɪʃ(ə)n, -ʒ(ə)n/ • n. a native of Asia or a person of Asian descent. • adj. relating to Asia or its people.

**USAGE** Asian

In Britain **Asian** is used to refer to people who come from (or whose parents came from) the Indian subcontinent, while in North America it is used to refer to people from the Far East.

**Asian American** • n. an American who is of Asian (chiefly Far Eastern) descent. • adj. of or relating to Asian Americans.

**Asiatic** /ˌeɪʃɪˈatɪk, ˌeɪzɪ-/ • adj. relating to or deriving from Asia.

**ASIC** • abbrev. Electronics application specific integrated circuit.

**A-side** • n. the side of a pop single regarded as the main one.

**aside** • adv. **1** to one side; out of the way. **2** in reserve or out of consideration. • n. **1** an actor's remark that is heard by the audience but is supposed not to be heard by the other characters. **2** an incidental remark.
– PHRASES **aside from** apart from. **set something aside** **1** remove land from agricultural production for fallow or other use. **2** annul a legal decision or process.
– ORIGIN ME (orig. *on side*): see **A²**, **SIDE**.

**asinine** /ˈasɪnʌɪn/ • adj. extremely stupid or foolish.
– DERIVATIVES **asininity** n.
– ORIGIN C15: from L. *asininus*, from *asinus* 'ass'.

**-asis** (often **-iasis**) • suffix forming the names of diseases: *psoriasis*.
– ORIGIN via L. from Gk.

**ask** • v. **1** say something in order to obtain an answer or some information. ➤ (**ask after** or Scottish **for**) enquire about the well-being of. **2** request to do or give something. ➤ request permission. ➤ (**ask for**) request to speak to. ➤ request (a specified amount) as a price for selling something. **3** expect or demand (something) of someone. **4** invite to a social occasion. ➤ (**ask someone out**) invite someone out on a date. • n. chiefly N. Amer. the asking price of a financial security.
– PHRASES **a big ask** Austral./NZ informal a difficult demand to fulfil. **for the asking** for little or no effort or cost. **I ask you!** informal an exclamation of shock or disapproval.
– DERIVATIVES **asker** n.
– ORIGIN OE *āscian, āhsian, ācxian*, of W. Gmc origin.

**askance** /əˈskans, əˈskɑːns/ (also **askant** /-ˈskant, -ˈskɑːnt/) • adv. with a look of suspicion or disapproval.
– ORIGIN C15: of unknown origin.

**askari** /əˈskɑːri/ • n. (pl. same or **askaris**) (in East Africa) a soldier or police officer.
– ORIGIN C19: from Arab. *ʿaskarī* 'soldier'.

**askew** /əˈskjuː/ • adv. & adj. not in a straight or level position.
– ORIGIN C16: from **A-²** + **SKEW**.

**asking price** • n. the price at which something is offered for sale.

**ASL** • abbrev. American Sign Language.

**aslant** • adv. at a slant. • prep. across at a slant.

**asleep** • adj. & adv. **1** in or into a state of sleep. ➤ not attentive or alert. **2** (of a limb) numb.

**ASLEF** /ˈazlɛf/ • abbrev. Associated Society of Locomotive Engineers and Firemen.

**AS level** • n. (in the UK except Scotland) an examination or a pass at advanced subsidiary level.

**aslope** • adj. & adv. poetic/literary in a sloping position.
– ORIGIN ME: origin uncertain; this form appears earlier than **SLOPE**.

**ASM** • abbrev. **1** air-to-surface missile. **2** assistant stage manager.

**asocial** • adj. avoiding or inconsiderate of others.

**ASP** • abbrev. application service provider, a company providing Internet access to software applications that would otherwise have to be installed on individual computers.

**asp** /asp/ • n. **1** (also **asp viper**) a small viper with an upturned snout. [*Vipera aspis*.] **2** the Egyptian cobra. [*Naja haje*.] **3** a large predatory freshwater fish of the carp family. [*Aspius aspius*.]
– ORIGIN ME: from L. *aspis*, from Gk.

**asparagine** /əˈsparədʒiːn/ • n. Biochemistry a hydrophilic amino acid which is a constituent of most proteins.
– ORIGIN C19: from **ASPARAGUS** (which contains it) + **-INE⁴**.

**asparagus** /əˈsparəgəs/ • n. **1** the tender young shoots of a plant, eaten as a vegetable. **2** the tall plant with feathery foliage from which these shoots are obtained. [*Asparagus officinalis*.]
– ORIGIN C16: via L. from Gk *asparagos*.

**asparagus fern** • n. a decorative plant with feathery foliage, related to the edible asparagus. [Genus *Asparagus*: several species.]

**aspartame** /əˈspɑːteɪm/ • n. an artificial sweetener derived from aspartic acid and phenylalanine.

**aspartic acid** /ə'spɑːtɪk/ ● **n.** Biochemistry an acidic amino acid present in many proteins and in sugar cane, important in the metabolism of nitrogen in animals and also acting as a neurotransmitter.
– DERIVATIVES **aspartate** n.
– ORIGIN C19: *aspartic* from Fr. *aspartique*, L. *asparagus* (see **ASPARAGUS**).

**aspect** ● **n. 1** a particular part or feature. ➤ a particular appearance or quality. **2** the positioning of a building in a particular direction. ➤ the side of a building facing a particular direction. **3** Astrology any of a number of particular angular relationships between one celestial body or point on the ecliptic and another. **4** Grammar a category or form of a verb which expresses a feature of the action related to time, such as completion or duration. ● **v.** Astrology (of a planet) form an aspect with (another celestial body).
– DERIVATIVES **aspectual** adj.
– ORIGIN ME: from L. *aspectus*, from *aspicere* 'look at'.

**aspect ratio** ● **n. 1** the ratio of the width to the height of an image on a television screen. **2** Aeronautics the ratio of the span to the mean chord of an aerofoil.

**aspen** ● **n.** a poplar tree with small rounded long-stalked leaves noted for trembling in the breeze. [*Populus tremula* (Europe), *P. tremuloides* (N. America), and other species.]
– ORIGIN ME: from dial. *asp* + **-EN**², forming an adjective later used as a noun.

**Asperger's syndrome** /'aspəːdʒəz/ ● **n.** Psychiatry a mild autistic disorder characterized by awkwardness in social interaction, pedantry in speech, and preoccupation with very narrow interests.
– ORIGIN C20 named after the Austrian psychiatrist Hans *Asperger*.

**asperges** /ə'spəːdʒiːz/ ● **n.** Christian Church the rite of sprinkling holy water at the beginning of the Mass. ➤ another term for **ASPERGILLUM**.
– ORIGIN C16: the first word of the Latin text of Psalms 50(51):9 (lit. 'thou shalt purge'), recited during the sprinkling of the holy water.

**aspergillosis** /ˌaspədʒɪ'ləʊsɪs/ ● **n.** Medicine a condition in which certain fungi infect the lungs or other tissues, especially through inhalation of spores from mouldy hay.
– ORIGIN C19: from mod. L. *Aspergillus* (genus name of the fungi), from **ASPERGILLUM**, + **-OSIS**.

**aspergillum** /ˌaspə'dʒɪləm/ ● **n.** (pl. **aspergilla** or **aspergillums**) an implement for sprinkling holy water.
– ORIGIN C17: from L.

**asperity** /ə'spɛrɪti/ ● **n.** (pl. **-ies**) **1** harshness of tone or manner. ➤ (**asperities**) harsh qualities or conditions. **2** a rough edge on a surface.
– ORIGIN ME: from OFr. *asperite*, or L. *asperitas*, from *asper* 'rough'.

**asperse** /ə'spəːs/ ● **v.** rare cast aspersions on.

**aspersion** /ə'spəːʃ(ə)n/ ● **n.** an attack on someone's character or reputation.
– ORIGIN ME (denoting the sprinkling of water at baptism): from L. *aspersio(n-)*, from *aspergere* 'sprinkle'.

**asphalt** /'asfalt, -əlt/ ● **n.** a dark bituminous pitch occurring naturally or derived from crude oil, used in surfacing roads or as waterproofing in building. ● **v.** surface with asphalt.
– DERIVATIVES **asphaltic** adj.
– ORIGIN ME: from Fr. *asphalte*, based on late L. *asphalton*, *asphaltum*, from Gk *asphalton*.

**aspherical** ● **adj.** not spherical.
– DERIVATIVES **aspheric** adj.

**asphodel** /'asfədɛl/ ● **n. 1** a plant of the lily family with long, slender leaves and flowers borne on a spike. [*Asphodelus* and other genera.] **2** poetic/literary an everlasting flower said to grow in the Elysian fields.
– ORIGIN ME: via L. from Gk *asphodelos*; cf. **DAFFODIL**.

**asphyxia** /əs'fɪksɪə/ ● **n.** a condition arising when the body is deprived of oxygen, causing unconsciousness or death.
– DERIVATIVES **asphyxial** adj. **asphyxiant** adj. & n.
– ORIGIN C18 (in the sense 'stopping of the pulse'): mod. L., from Gk *asphuxia*, from *a-* 'without' + *sphuxis* 'pulse'.

**asphyxiate** ● **v.** kill or be killed by asphyxia.
– DERIVATIVES **asphyxiation** n. **asphyxiator** n.

**aspic** ● **n.** a clear savoury jelly made with meat stock.
– ORIGIN C18: from Fr., lit. 'asp', from the colours of the jelly as compared with those of the snake.

**aspidistra** /ˌaspɪ'dɪstrə/ ● **n.** a bulbous plant of the lily family with broad tapering leaves, native to East Asia. [Genus *Aspidistra*.]
– ORIGIN C19: mod. L., from Gk *aspis*, *aspid-* 'shield' (because of the shape of the stigma).

**aspirant** /ə'spʌɪər(ə)nt, 'asp(ɪ)r-/ ● **adj.** aspiring towards a particular achievement or status. ● **n.** a person who has such aspirations.

**aspirate** ● **v.** /'aspəreɪt/ **1** Phonetics pronounce (a sound) with an exhalation of breath. ➤ pronounce the sound of *h* at the beginning of a word. **2** chiefly Medicine draw (fluid) by suction from a bodily vessel or cavity. **3** inhale. **4** [as adj. **aspirated**] (of an internal-combustion engine) provided with air. ● **n.** /'asp(ə)rət/ **1** Phonetics an aspirated consonant. ➤ a sound of *h*. **2** Medicine matter that has been drawn from the body by aspiration. ● **adj.** /'asp(ə)rət/ Phonetics aspirated.
– ORIGIN C16: from L. *aspiratus* 'breathed', from *aspirare* (see **ASPIRE**).

**aspiration** ● **n. 1** a hope or ambition. **2** the action of aspirating.
– DERIVATIVES **aspirational** adj.

**aspirator** ● **n.** Medicine an instrument or apparatus for aspirating fluid from a vessel or cavity.

**aspire** ● **v.** (usu. **aspire to/to do something**) **1** direct one's hopes or ambitions towards achieving something. **2** poetic/literary rise high; tower.
– ORIGIN ME: from Fr. *aspirer* or L. *aspirant-*, *aspirare*, from *ad-* 'to' + *spirare* 'breathe'.

**aspirin** ● **n.** (pl. same or **aspirins**) a synthetic compound (acetylsalicylic acid) used to relieve pain and reduce fever and inflammation.
– ORIGIN C19: from Ger., from *acetylierte Spirsäure* 'acetylated salicylic acid'.

**asquint** ● **adv. & adj.** with a glance to one side or from the corner of the eyes.
– ORIGIN ME: perh. from **A-**² + a Low Ger. or Du. word rel. to mod. Du. *schuinte* 'slant'.

**ass**¹ /as/ ● **n. 1** an animal of the horse family which is smaller than a horse and has longer ears and a braying call. [*Equus africanus* (Africa) and *E. hemionus* (Asia).] ➤ (in general use) a donkey. **2** informal a foolish or stupid person.
– ORIGIN OE *assa*, from a Celtic word rel. to Welsh *asyn*, Breton *azen*, based on L. *asinus*.

**ass**² /ɑːs, as/ ● **n.** N. Amer. vulgar slang a person's buttocks or anus.
– ORIGIN var. of **ARSE**.

**assagai** ● **n. & v.** variant spelling of **ASSEGAI**.

**assai** /a'sʌɪ/ ● **adv.** [usu. postpos.] Music very: *allegro assai*.
– ORIGIN Ital., 'very much'.

**assail** /ə'seɪl/ ● **v. 1** make a concerted or violent attack on. **2** (of an unpleasant feeling) come upon (someone) strongly.
– DERIVATIVES **assailable** adj.
– ORIGIN ME: from OFr. *asaill-*, stressed stem of *asalir*, from med. L. *assalire*, from L. *assilire*, from *ad-* 'to' + *salire* 'to leap'.

**assailant** ● **n.** a person who physically attacks another.

**Assamese** /ˌasə'miːz/ ● **n.** (pl. same) **1** a native or inhabitant of Assam. **2** the official language of Assam, an Indic language related to Bengali. ● **adj.** of or relating to Assam, its people, or their language.

**assart** /ə'sɑːt/ Brit. historical ● **n.** a piece of land converted from forest to arable use. ● **v.** convert to arable use.
– ORIGIN ME: from OFr. *essarter*, from med. L. *ex(s)artare*, based on *ex* 'out' + *sar(r)ire* 'to weed'.

**assassin** /ə'sasɪn/ ● **n. 1** a person who assassinates. **2** (**Assassin**) a member of the fanatical Nizari branch of Ismaili Muslims dominant at the time of the Crusades.
– ORIGIN C16: from Fr., or from med. L. *assassinus*, from Arab. *ḥašīšī* 'hashish-eater', with ref. to the Assassins'

reputed use of hashish before murder missions.

**assassinate** • **v.** murder (a political or religious leader).
– DERIVATIVES **assassination** n.

**assassin bug** • **n.** a long-legged predatory or bloodsucking bug occurring chiefly in the tropics, some kinds of which can transmit diseases to humans. [Family Reduviidae: numerous species.]

**assault** • **n.** **1** a violent attack. ➤Law an act that threatens physical harm to a person, whether or not actual harm is done. **2** a concerted attempt to do something demanding. • **v.** make an assault on.
– DERIVATIVES **assaulter** n. **assaultive** adj.
– ORIGIN ME: from OFr. *asaut* (n.), *assauter* (v.), based on L. *ad-* 'to' + *saltare*, from *salire* 'to leap'.

**assault and battery** • **n.** Law the action of threatening a person together with making physical contact with them.

**assault course** • **n.** Brit. a course providing a series of physical challenges, used for training soldiers.

**assay** /ə'seɪ, 'aseɪ/ • **n.** **1** the testing of a metal or ore to determine its ingredients and quality. **2** a procedure for measuring the biochemical or immunological activity of a sample. • **v.** **1** carry out an assay on. **2** archaic attempt.
– DERIVATIVES **assayer** n.
– ORIGIN ME: from OFr. *assai* (n.), *assaier* (v.), var. of *essai* 'trial', *essayer* (see **ESSAY**).

**assay office** • **n.** **1** an establishment for the assaying of ores and metals. **2** Brit. an institution authorized to award hallmarks to articles made from precious metals.

**assegai** /'asəɡʌɪ/ (also **assagai**) • **n.** (pl. **assegais**) **1** a slender iron-tipped hardwood spear used chiefly by southern African peoples. **2** (also **assegai wood**) a South African tree of the dogwood family, yielding a hard wood. [*Curtisia dentata*.]
– ORIGIN C17: from obs. Fr. *azagaie* or Port. *azagaia*, from Arab. *az-zaġāyah*, from *az*, *al* 'the' + Berber *zaġāyah* 'spear'.

**assemblage** • **n.** a collection or gathering. ➤a machine or object made of pieces fitted together. ➤a work of art made by grouping together found or unrelated objects.

**assemble** • **v.** **1** come or bring together. **2** fit together the component parts of. **3** Computing translate (a program) from a symbolic language into machine code.
– ORIGIN ME: from OFr. *asembler*, based on L. *ad-* 'to' + *simul* 'together'.

**assemblé** /ˌasɒ̃'bleɪ/ • **n.** (pl. pronounced same) Ballet a leap in which the feet are brought together before landing.
– ORIGIN Fr., past part. of *assembler* 'assemble, put together'.

**assembler** • **n.** **1** a person who assembles component parts. **2** Computing a program for converting instructions written in symbolic code into machine code. ➤another term for **ASSEMBLY LANGUAGE**.

**assembly** • **n.** (pl. **-ies**) **1** a group of people gathered together. ➤a group having legislative or decision-making powers. ➤a regular gathering of teachers and pupils in a school. **2** the action of assembling component parts. ➤a unit consisting of assembled components. **3** Computing the conversion of instructions in symbolic code to machine code by an assembler.

**assembly language** • **n.** Computing the symbolic code converted by an assembler.

**assembly line** • **n.** a series of workers and machines in a factory by which a succession of identical items is progressively assembled.

**assembly rooms** • **pl. n.** chiefly Brit. a public room or hall in which meetings or social functions are held.

**assent** /ə'sɛnt/ • **n.** the expression of approval or agreement. • **v.** (usu. **assent to**) express assent.
– ORIGIN ME: from OFr. *as(s)enter* (v.), *as(s)ente* (n.), based on L. *assentire*, from *ad-* 'towards' + *sentire* 'feel, think'.

**assenter** (also **assentor**) • **n.** **1** a person who assents. **2** (usu. **assentor**) Brit. any of the people, other than the proposer and seconder, who are required to sign the nomination papers for a candidate in parliamentary or local government elections.

**assert** • **v.** **1** state a fact or belief confidently and forcefully. **2** cause others to recognize (one's authority or a right) by confident and forceful behaviour. ➤(**assert oneself**) behave or speak confidently and forcefully.
– DERIVATIVES **asserter** (also **-or**) n. **assertion** n.
– ORIGIN C17 (earlier (ME) as *assertion*): from L. *asserere* 'claim, affirm', from *ad-* 'to' + *serere* 'to join'.

**assertive** • **adj.** having or showing a confident and forceful personality.
– DERIVATIVES **assertively** adv. **assertiveness** n.

**asses** plural form of **AS**[2], **ASS**[1], **ASS**[2].

**asses' bridge** • **n.** English term for **PONS ASINORUM**.

**assess** • **v.** evaluate or estimate the nature, value, or quality of. ➤set the value of a tax, fine, etc., for (a person or property) at a specified level.
– DERIVATIVES **assessable** adj. **assessment** n.
– ORIGIN ME: from OFr. *assesser*, based on L. *assidere* 'sit by' (in med. L. 'levy tax'), from *ad-* 'to, at' + *sedere* 'sit'.

**assessor** • **n.** **1** a person who assesses. **2** a specialist who is called upon for advice by a judge or committee of inquiry.

**asset** • **n.** **1** a useful or valuable thing or person. **2** (**assets**) property owned by a person or company, regarded as having value and being available to meet debts, commitments, or legacies.
– ORIGIN C16 (in the pl. in the sense 'sufficient estate to allow discharge of a will'): from Anglo-Norman Fr., from OFr. *asez* 'enough', based on L. *ad* 'to' + *satis* 'enough'.

**asset-backed** • **adj.** denoting securities having as collateral the return on a series of mortgages, credit agreements, or other forms of lending.

**asset-stripping** • **n.** the practice of taking over a company in financial difficulties and selling each of its assets at a profit.
– DERIVATIVES **asset-stripper** n.

**asseveration** /əˌsɛvə'reɪʃ(ə)n/ • **n.** a solemn or emphatic declaration or statement.
– DERIVATIVES **asseverate** v.
– ORIGIN C16: from L. *asseveratio(n-)*, from *asseverare*, from *ad-* 'to' + *severus* 'serious'.

**asshole** • **n.** vulgar slang US spelling of **ARSEHOLE**.

**assibilate** /ə'sɪbɪleɪt/ • **v.** Phonetics pronounce (a sound) as a sibilant or affricate ending in a sibilant (e.g. sound *t* as *ts*).
– DERIVATIVES **assibilation** n.
– ORIGIN C19: from L. *assibilat-*, *assibilare*, from *ad-* 'to' + *sibilare* 'to hiss'.

**assiduity** /ˌasɪ'djuːɪti/ • **n.** (pl. **-ies**) constant or close attention to what one is doing. ➤(**assiduities**) archaic or poetic/literary constant attentions to someone.
– ORIGIN ME: from L. *assiduitas*, from *assiduus* (see **ASSIDUOUS**).

**assiduous** /ə'sɪdjʊəs/ • **adj.** showing great care and perseverance.
– DERIVATIVES **assiduously** adv. **assiduousness** n.
– ORIGIN C16: from L. *assiduus*, from *assidere* (see **ASSESS**), + **-OUS**.

**assign** • **v.** **1** allocate (a task or duty) to someone. ➤appoint to a particular task. **2** designate or set aside for a specific purpose. ➤attribute (something) to a group or person. **3** transfer (legal rights or liabilities). • **n.** Law another term for **ASSIGNEE**.
– DERIVATIVES **assignable** adj. **assigner** n. **assignor** n.
– ORIGIN ME: from OFr. *asigner*, *assiner*, from L. *assignare*, from *ad-* 'to' + *signare* 'to sign'.

**assignation** • **n.** **1** a secret arrangement to meet. **2** the action of assigning.

**assignee** • **n.** chiefly Law **1** a person to whom a right or liability is legally transferred. **2** a person appointed to act for another.

**assignment** • **n.** **1** a task or duty assigned as part of a job or course of study. **2** the action of assigning or fact of being assigned. **3** an act of assigning a right or liability. ➤a document effecting such a transfer.

**assimilate** • **v.** **1** take in and fully understand (information or ideas). ➤(of a society or culture) absorb and integrate (people, ideas, or culture). **2** absorb and digest (food or nutrients). **3** regard as similar. **4** Phonetics make (a

sound) more like another in the same or next word.
– DERIVATIVES **assimilable** adj. **assimilation** n. **assimilative** adj. **assimilator** n. **assimilatory** adj.
– ORIGIN ME: from L. *assimilat-*, *assimilare* 'absorb, incorporate', from *ad-* 'to' + *similis* 'like'.

**assimilationist** ● n. a person who advocates or participates in racial or cultural integration.

**assist** ● v. help by doing a share of work or by providing money or information. ● n. chiefly N. Amer. **1** an act of helping, especially by providing money. **2** (chiefly in ice hockey, basketball, or baseball) an act of touching the ball in a play in which a teammate scores or an opposing batter is put out.
– DERIVATIVES **assister** n.
– ORIGIN ME: from OFr. *assister*, from L. *assistere* 'take one's stand by'.

**assistance** ● n. the provision of money, resources, or information to help someone. ➤ the action of helping.

**assistant** ● n. **1** a person who ranks below a senior person. **2** a person who helps in particular work.

**assistant professor** ● n. N. Amer. an academic ranking immediately below an associate professor.

**assisted area** ● n. (in the UK) a region receiving government grants or loans for industrial development.

**assisted place** ● n. (in the UK) a place in an independent school for a pupil whose fees are wholly or partially subsidized by the state.

**assize** /ə'sʌɪz/ ● n. historical a court which sat at intervals in each county of England and Wales to administer the civil and criminal law.
– ORIGIN ME: from OFr. *assise*, fem. past part. of *asseeir* 'sit, settle, assess', from L. *assidere* (see **ASSESS**).

**Assoc.** ● abbrev. Association.

**associate** ● v. /ə'səʊʃɪeɪt, -sɪeɪt/ **1** make a conceptual connection between. **2** (usu. **associate with**) meet or have dealings with. ➤ (**associate oneself with**) allow oneself to be connected with or seen to be supportive of. ➤ (**be associated with**) be involved with. ● n. /ə'səʊʃɪət, -sɪət/ **1** a partner or companion in business or at work. **2** a person with limited or subordinate membership of an organization. **3** chiefly Psychology a concept connected with another. ● adj. /ə'səʊʃɪət, -sɪət/ **1** connected with an organization or business. **2** having shared function or membership but with a lesser status.
– DERIVATIVES **associability** n. **associable** adj. **associateship** n. **associator** n.
– ORIGIN ME: from L. *associat-*, *associare* 'join', from *ad-* 'to' + *socius* 'sharing, allied'.

**associate professor** ● n. N. Amer. an academic ranking immediately below full professor.

**association** ● n. **1** a group of people organized for a joint purpose. **2** a connection or cooperative link between people or organizations. ➤ Chemistry a weak interaction between molecules, such as hydrogen bonding. **3** a conceptual connection. **4** Ecology a stable plant community including a characteristic group of dominant plant species.
– DERIVATIVES **associational** adj.

**Association Football** ● n. more formal term for **SOCCER**.

**associationism** ● n. a theory in philosophy or psychology which regards the simple association of ideas or sensations as the primary basis of meaning, thought, or learning.
– DERIVATIVES **associationist** n. & adj.

**associative** ● adj. **1** of or involving association. **2** Mathematics involving the condition that a group of quantities connected by operators gives the same result in whichever order the operations are performed, as long as the order of the quantities remains the same, e.g. $(a \times b) \times c = a \times (b \times c)$.

**assonance** /'as(ə)nəns/ ● n. the resemblance of sound between syllables in nearby words arising from the rhyming of stressed vowels (e.g. *sonnet, porridge*), and also from the use of identical consonants with different vowels (e.g. *killed, cold, culled*).
– DERIVATIVES **assonant** adj. **assonate** /-neɪt/ v.
– ORIGIN C18: from Fr., from L. *assonare* 'respond to'.

**assort** ● v. **1** Genetics (of genes or characteristics) become distributed among cells or progeny. **2** archaic classify.
– ORIGIN C15: from OFr. *assorter*, from *a-* + *sorte* 'sort, kind'.

**assortative** ● adj. denoting or involving the preferential mating of animals or marriage between people with similar characteristics.

**assorted** ● adj. of various sorts put together.

**assortment** ● n. a miscellaneous collection.

**ASSR** ● abbrev. historical Autonomous Soviet Socialist Republic.

**Asst** ● abbrev. Assistant.

**assuage** /ə'sweɪdʒ/ ● v. **1** make (an unpleasant feeling) less intense. **2** satisfy (an appetite or desire).
– DERIVATIVES **assuagement** n.
– ORIGIN ME: from OFr. *assouagier*, based on L. *ad-* 'to' + *suavis* 'sweet'.

**assume** ● v. **1** accept as true without proof. **2** take (responsibility or control). **3** begin to have (a specified quality, appearance, or extent). ➤ adopt falsely.
– DERIVATIVES **assumable** adj. **assumed** adj. **assumedly** adv.
– ORIGIN ME: from L. *assumere*, from *ad-* 'towards' + *sumere* 'take'.

**assuming** ● conj. based on the assumption. ● adj. archaic arrogant or presumptuous.

**assumption** ● n. **1** a thing that is assumed as true. **2** the action of assuming responsibility or control. **3** (**Assumption**) the reception of the Virgin Mary bodily into heaven, according to Roman Catholic doctrine. ➤ the feast in honour of this, celebrated on 15 August. **4** archaic arrogance or presumption.

**assumptive** ● adj. **1** rare of the nature of an assumption. **2** archaic arrogant or presumptuous.

**assurance** ● n. **1** a positive declaration intended to give confidence. **2** confidence in one's own abilities. ➤ certainty. **3** chiefly Brit. life insurance (with reference to policies under whose terms a payment is guaranteed).

**assure** ● v. **1** tell someone something positively in order to dispel potential doubts. **2** make (something) certain to happen. **3** chiefly Brit. cover by assurance. ➤ secure the future payment of (an amount) with insurance.
– DERIVATIVES **assurer** n.
– ORIGIN ME: from OFr. *assurer*, based on L. *ad-* 'to' + *securus* (see **SECURE**).

**assured** ● adj. **1** confident. **2** protected against discontinuance or change.
– DERIVATIVES **assuredly** adv.

**Assyrian** ● n. **1** an inhabitant of ancient Assyria. **2** the Akkadian language of ancient Assyria. **3** a dialect of Aramaic still spoken in parts of Syria and northern Iraq. ● adj. **1** of or relating to ancient Assyria or its language. **2** relating to or denoting modern Assyrian or its speakers.

**Assyriology** /əˌsɪrɪ'ɒlədʒɪ/ ● n. the study of the language, history, and antiquities of ancient Assyria.
– DERIVATIVES **Assyriological** adj. **Assyriologist** n.

**AST** ● abbrev. Atlantic Standard Time.

**astable** /ə'steɪb(ə)l, eɪ-/ ● adj. chiefly Electronics of or relating to a system or electric circuit which oscillates spontaneously between unstable states.

**astatic** /ə'statɪk/ ● adj. Physics (of a system or instrument) consisting of or employing a combination of magnets suspended in a uniform magnetic field on a single wire or thread in such a way that no torque is present.
– ORIGIN C19: from Gk *astatos* 'unstable' + **-IC**.

**astatine** /'astətiːn/ ● n. the chemical element of atomic number 85, a very unstable radioactive member of the halogen group. (Symbol: **At**)
– ORIGIN 1940s: from Gk *astatos* 'unstable' + **-INE**[4].

**aster** /'astə/ ● n. a plant of a large genus that includes the Michaelmas daisy, with characteristic purple or pink rayed flowers. [Genus *Aster*: numerous species.]
– ORIGIN C17: via L. from Gk *astēr* 'star'.

**-aster** ● suffix forming nouns: **1** denoting poor quality: *poetaster*. **2** Botany denoting incomplete resemblance: *oleaster*.

– ORIGIN from L.

**asterisk** ● **n.** a symbol (*) used in text as a pointer to an annotation or footnote. ● **v.** mark with an asterisk.
– ORIGIN ME: via late L. from Gk *asteriskos* 'small star', dimin. of *astēr.*

**asterism** /ˈastərɪz(ə)m/ ● **n. 1** Astronomy a prominent pattern or group of stars that is smaller than a constellation. **2** a group of three asterisks (⁂) drawing attention to following text.
– ORIGIN C16: from Gk *asterismos*, from *astēr* 'star'.

**astern** ● **adv.** behind or towards the rear of a ship or aircraft. ➤(of a ship's engine) backwards.

**asteroid** /ˈastərɔɪd/ ● **n. 1** a small rocky body orbiting the sun. **2** Zoology an echinoderm of a class (Asteroidea) comprising the starfishes.
– DERIVATIVES **asteroidal** adj.
– ORIGIN C19: from Gk *asteroeidēs* 'starlike', from *astēr* 'star'.

**asthenia** /əsˈθiːnɪə/ ● **n.** Medicine abnormal physical weakness or lack of energy.
– DERIVATIVES **asthenic** adj.
– ORIGIN C18: mod. L., from Gk *astheneia*, from *asthenēs* 'weak'.

**asthenosphere** /əsˈθɛnəsfɪə/ ● **n.** Geology the upper layer of the earth's mantle, below the lithosphere, in which there is relatively low resistance to plastic flow and convection is thought to occur.
– DERIVATIVES **asthenospheric** adj.
– ORIGIN C20: from Gk *asthenēs* 'weak' + **SPHERE**.

**asthma** /ˈasmə/ ● **n.** a respiratory condition marked by attacks of spasm in the bronchi of the lungs, causing difficulty in breathing and usually associated with allergic reaction.
– DERIVATIVES **asthmatic** adj. & n. **asthmatically** adv.
– ORIGIN ME: from med. L. *asma*, from Gk *asthma*, from *azein* 'breathe hard'.

**astigmatism** /əˈstɪgmətɪz(ə)m/ ● **n.** a deviation in the spherical curvature of the eye or a lens, resulting in distorted images.
– DERIVATIVES **astigmatic** /astɪgˈmatɪk/ adj.
– ORIGIN C19: from **A-**[1] + Gk *stigma* 'point' + **-ISM**.

**astilbe** /əˈstɪlbi/ ● **n.** a plant of the saxifrage family, with plumes of tiny white, pink, or red flowers. [Genus *Astilbe.*]
– ORIGIN mod. L., from Gk *a-* 'not' + *stilbē*, fem. of *stilbos* 'glittering'.

**astir** ● **adj. 1** in a state of excited movement. **2** awake and out of bed.

**astonish** ● **v.** surprise or impress greatly.
– DERIVATIVES **astonishing** adj. **astonishingly** adv. **astonishment** n.
– ORIGIN C16: from obs. *astone* 'stun, stupefy', from OFr. *estoner*, based on L. *ex-* 'out' + *tonare* 'to thunder'.

**astound** ● **v.** shock or greatly surprise.
– DERIVATIVES **astounding** adj. **astoundingly** adv.
– ORIGIN ME: from *astoned*, past part. of obs. *astone* (see **ASTONISH**).

**astragal** /ˈastrəg(ə)l/ ● **n. 1** Architecture a convex moulding or wooden strip, of semi-circular section. **2** a bar separating panes of glass in cabinetmaking.
– ORIGIN C17: from **ASTRAGALUS**, partly via Fr. *astragale.*

**astragalus** /əˈstrag(ə)ləs/ ● **n.** (pl. **astragali** /-lʌɪ/) **1** chiefly Zoology another term for **TALUS**[1]. **2** a plant of a genus that includes milk vetch. [Genus *Astragalus.*]
– ORIGIN C16: via L. from Gk *astragalos* 'ankle bone, moulding', also the name of a plant.

**astrakhan** /ˌastrəˈkan/ ● **n.** the dark curly fleece of young karakul lambs from central Asia.
– ORIGIN C18: named after the city of *Astrakhan* in Russia.

**astral** /ˈastr(ə)l/ ● **adj. 1** of, relating to, or resembling the stars. **2** of or relating to a supposed non-physical realm of existence to which various psychic and paranormal phenomena are ascribed, and in which the physical human body is said to have a counterpart.
– ORIGIN C17: from late L. *astralis*, from *astrum* 'star'.

**astrantia** /əˈstrantɪə/ ● **n.** a plant of the parsley family with small compact starlike heads of tiny flowers surrounded by prominent bracts. [Genus *Astrantia*: several species.]
– ORIGIN mod. L., perh. from Gk *astēr* 'star'.

**astray** ● **adv.** away from the correct path or direction.
– PHRASES **go astray** become lost or mislaid.
– ORIGIN ME: from an Anglo-Norman Fr. var. of OFr. *estraie*, past part. of *estraier*, based on L. *extra* 'out of bounds' + *vagari* 'wander'.

**astride** ● **prep. & adv.** with a leg on each side of. ➤[adv.] (of a person's legs) apart.

**astringent** /əˈstrɪn(d)ʒ(ə)nt/ ● **adj. 1** causing the contraction of skin cells and other body tissues. **2** sharp or severe in manner or style. ➤(of taste or smell) sharp or bitter. ● **n.** an astringent lotion applied to the skin for cosmetic purposes or to reduce bleeding from minor abrasions.
– DERIVATIVES **astringency** n. **astringently** adv.
– ORIGIN C16: from Fr., from L. *astringent-*, *astringere* 'pull tight'.

**astro-** /ˈastrəʊ/ ● **comb. form** relating to the stars or celestial objects: *astrodome.* ➤relating to outer space: *astrochemistry.*
– ORIGIN from Gk *astron* 'star'.

**astro-archaeology** ● **n.** another term for **ARCHAEOASTRONOMY**.

**astrochemistry** ● **n.** the study of molecules and ions occurring in stars and interstellar space.
– DERIVATIVES **astrochemical** adj. **astrochemist** n.

**astrocyte** /ˈastrə(ʊ)sʌɪt/ ● **n.** Anatomy a star-shaped glial cell of the central nervous system.
– DERIVATIVES **astrocytic** adj.

**astrodome** ● **n. 1** chiefly US an enclosed stadium with a domed roof. **2** a domed window in an aircraft for astronomical observations.

**astroid** /ˈastrɔɪd/ ● **n.** Mathematics a hypocycloid with four cusps (like a square with concave sides).

**astrolabe** /ˈastrəleɪb/ ● **n.** an instrument formerly used in making astronomical measurements and in navigation for calculating latitude, consisting of a disc with the edge marked in degrees and a pivoted pointer.
– ORIGIN ME: from OFr. *astrelabe*, from med. L. *astrolabium*, from Gk *astrolabon*, neut. of *astrolabos* 'star-taking'.

**astrology** ● **n.** the study of the movements and relative positions of celestial bodies interpreted as having an influence on human affairs and the natural world.
– DERIVATIVES **astrologer** n. **astrological** adj. **astrologically** adv. **astrologist** n.

**astrometry** ● **n.** the measurement of the positions, motions, and magnitudes of stars.
– DERIVATIVES **astrometric** adj.

**astronaut** ● **n.** a person trained to travel in a spacecraft.
– DERIVATIVES **astronautical** adj.
– ORIGIN 1920s: from **ASTRO-**, on the pattern of *aeronaut* and *aquanaut.*

**astronautics** ● **pl. n.** [treated as sing.] the science and technology of space travel and exploration.

**astronomical** ● **adj. 1** of or relating to astronomy. **2** informal (of an amount) extremely large.
– DERIVATIVES **astronomic** adj. **astronomically** adv.

**astronomical unit** ● **n.** Astronomy a unit of measurement equal to 149.6 million kilometres, the mean distance from the centre of the earth to the centre of the sun.

**astronomical year** ● **n.** another term for **SOLAR YEAR**.

**astronomy** ● **n.** the branch of science which deals with celestial objects, space, and the physical universe as a whole.
– DERIVATIVES **astronomer** n.

**astrophysics** ● **pl. n.** [treated as sing.] the branch of astronomy concerned with the physical nature of stars and other celestial bodies, and the application of the laws and theories of physics to the interpretation of astronomical observations.
– DERIVATIVES **astrophysical** adj. **astrophysicist** n.

**AstroTurf** ● **n.** trademark an artificial grass surface, used

for sports fields.
– ORIGIN 1960s: from sense 1 of **ASTRODOME** + **TURF**.

**astute** ● **adj.** having an ability to assess situations or people accurately.
– DERIVATIVES **astutely** adv. **astuteness** n.
– ORIGIN C17: obs. Fr. *astut* or L. *astutus*, from *astus* 'craft'.

**astylar** /ə'stʌɪlə/ ● **adj.** Architecture (of a classical building) lacking columns or pilasters.
– ORIGIN C19: from **A-**[1] + Gk *stulos* 'column' + **-AR**[1].

**asunder** ● **adv.** archaic or poetic/literary apart.
– ORIGIN OE *on sundran* 'in or into a separate place'.

**asura** /'ʌsʊrə/ ● **n.** (in Vedic religion) a member of a class of divine beings which in Indian mythology tend to be evil and in Zoroastrianism are benevolent. Compare with **DEVA**.
– ORIGIN Skr., prob. from *ásu* 'breath, life'.

**ASV** ● **abbrev.** American Standard Version (of the Bible).

**asylum** ● **n. 1** the protection granted by a state to someone who has left their native country as a political refugee. ➤shelter or protection from danger. **2** dated an institution for the care of the mentally ill.
– ORIGIN ME: via L. from Gk *asulon* 'refuge', from *asulos* 'inviolable', from *a-* 'without' + *sulon* 'right of seizure'.

**asymmetric bars** ● **pl. n.** a pair of bars of different heights used in women's gymnastics.

**asymmetry** /ə'sɪmɪtri, eɪ-/ ● **n.** (pl. **-ies**) lack of symmetry.
– DERIVATIVES **asymmetric** adj. **asymmetrical** adj. **asymmetrically** adv.

**asymptomatic** ● **adj.** Medicine producing or showing no symptoms.

**asymptote** /'asɪm(p)təʊt/ ● **n.** a straight line that continually approaches a given curve but does not meet it at any finite distance.
– DERIVATIVES **asymptotic** /ˌasɪm(p)'tɒtɪk/ adj. **asymptotically** adv.
– ORIGIN C17: from mod. L. *asymptota* (*linea*) '(line) not meeting', from Gk *asumptōtos* 'not falling together'.

**asynchronous** ● **adj. 1** not existing or occurring at the same time. **2** Computing & Telecommunications making use of pulses to control the timing of operations that are sent when the previous operation is completed, rather than at regular intervals. **3** (of a machine or motor) not working in time with the alternations of current. **4** Astronomy (of a satellite) revolving round the parent planet at a different rate from that at which the planet rotates.
– DERIVATIVES **asynchronously** adv.

**asyndeton** /ə'sɪndɪt(ə)n/ ● **n.** (pl. **asyndeta** /-tə/) the omission or absence of a conjunction between parts of a sentence, as in *I came, I saw, I conquered*.
– DERIVATIVES **asyndetic** /asɪn'dɛtɪk/ adj.
– ORIGIN C16: mod. L., from Gk *asundeton*, neut. of *asundetos* 'unconnected'.

**At** ● **symb.** the chemical element astatine.

**at**[1] ● **prep. 1** expressing location or arrival in a particular place or position. **2** expressing the time when an event takes place. **3** expressing attendance of an educational institution or a workplace. **4** denoting a particular point or segment on a scale. ➤referring to someone's age. **5** expressing a particular state or condition. ➤expressing a relationship between an individual and a skill. **6** expressing the object or target of a look, shot, action, or plan. ➤expressing an incomplete or attempted action. **7** expressing the means by which something is done.
– PHRASES **at that** in addition; furthermore. **where it's at** informal the focus of fashion or style.
– ORIGIN OE *æt*, of Gmc origin.

**at**[2] /ɑːt, at/ ● **n.** a monetary unit of Laos, equal to one hundredth of a kip.
– ORIGIN from Thai.

**at-** ● **prefix** variant spelling of **AD-** assimilated before *t* (as in *attend*).

**ataman** /'atəman/ ● **n.** (pl. **atamans**) a Cossack leader.
– ORIGIN C19: from Russ.

**ataraxy** /'atəraksi/ (also **ataraxia** /ˌatə'raksɪə/) ● **n.** a state of serene calmness.
– DERIVATIVES **ataractic** adj. **ataraxic** adj.
– ORIGIN C17: from Fr. *ataraxie*, from Gk *ataraxia* 'impassiveness', from *a-* 'not' + *tarassein* 'disturb'.

**atavistic** /ˌatə'vɪstɪk/ ● **adj.** relating to or characterized by reversion to something ancient or ancestral.
– DERIVATIVES **atavism** n. **atavistically** adv.
– ORIGIN C19: based on L. *atavus* 'forefather' + the adjectival suffix *-istic*.

**ataxia** /ə'taksɪə/ (also **ataxy** /-si/) ● **n.** Medicine the loss of full control of bodily movements.
– DERIVATIVES **ataxic** adj.
– ORIGIN C19: mod. L., from Gk, from *a-* 'without' + *taxis* 'order'.

**ATB** ● **abbrev.** all-terrain bike.

**ATC** ● **abbrev. 1** air traffic control or controller. **2** Air Training Corps.

**ATE** ● **abbrev.** automated test equipment.

**ate** past of **EAT**.

**-ate**[1] ● **suffix** forming nouns: **1** denoting status or office: *doctorate*. ➤denoting a state or function: *mandate*. **2** denoting a group: *electorate*. **3** Chemistry denoting a salt or ester, especially of an acid with a corresponding name ending in *-ic*: *chlorate*. **4** denoting a product of a chemical process: *condensate*.
– ORIGIN from OFr. *-at* or L. *-atus*, *-ata*, *-atum*.

**-ate**[2] ● **suffix 1** forming adjectives and nouns such as *associate*. **2** forming adjectives from Latin: *caudate*.
– ORIGIN from L. *-atus*, *-ata*, *-atum*.

**-ate**[3] ● **suffix** forming verbs such as *fascinate*.
– ORIGIN from **-ATE**[2]; orig. on the basis of past participial adjectives ending in *-atus*, later extended to Latin verbs ending in *-are* and French verbs ending in *-er*.

**atelectasis** /ˌatɪ'lɛktəsɪs/ ● **n.** Medicine partial collapse or incomplete inflation of the lung.
– ORIGIN C19: from Gk *atelēs* 'imperfect' + *ektasis* 'extension'.

**atelier** /ə'tɛlɪeɪ/ ● **n.** a workshop or studio.
– ORIGIN C17: from Fr., from OFr. *astelle* 'splinter of wood'.

**a tempo** /ɑː 'tɛmpəʊ/ ● **adv. & adj.** Music in the previous tempo.
– ORIGIN Ital., lit. 'in time'.

**ATF** ● **abbrev.** (in the US) (Federal Bureau of) Alcohol, Tobacco, and Firearms.

**Athabaskan** /ˌaθə'bask(ə)n/ (also **Athapaskan**) ● **n. 1** a family of North American Indian languages, including Navajo and Apache. **2** a speaker of any of these languages. ● **adj.** of or relating to these languages.
– ORIGIN from *Athabasca*, the name of a lake in western Canada + **-AN**.

**athanor** /'aθənɔː/ ● **n.** historical a type of furnace used by alchemists.
– ORIGIN C15: from Arab. *at-tannūr*, from *al-* 'the' + *tannūr* 'baker's oven'.

**Atharva Veda** /əˌtɑːvə 'veɪdə, 'viːdə/ ● **n.** a collection of hymns and ritual utterances added at a later stage to the existing Veda material.
– ORIGIN from Sanskrit *Atharvan* (the name of Brahma's eldest son, said to be the author of the collection) + **VEDA**.

**atheism** /'eɪθɪɪz(ə)m/ ● **n.** the theory or belief that God does not exist.
– DERIVATIVES **atheist** n. **atheistic** adj. **atheistical** adj.
– ORIGIN C16: from Fr. *athéisme*, from Gk *atheos*, from *a-* 'without' + *theos* 'god'.

**atheling** /'aθ(ə)lɪŋ/ ● **n.** a prince or lord in Anglo-Saxon England.
– ORIGIN OE *ætheling*, of W. Gmc origin, from a base meaning 'race, family'.

**athematic** /ˌaθɪ'matɪk, ˌeɪ-/ ● **adj. 1** Music (of a composition) not thematic. **2** Grammar (of a verb form) having a suffix attached to the stem without a connecting (thematic) vowel.

**Athenaeum** /ˌaθɪ'niːəm/ (US also **Atheneum**) ● **n.** used in the names of libraries or institutions for literary or scientific study.
– ORIGIN C18: via L. from Gk *Athēnaion*, denoting the temple of the goddess Athene.

**Athenian** ● **n.** a native or inhabitant of Athens. ● **adj.** of or relating to Athens.

**atherogenic** /ˌaθərə(ʊ)ˈdʒɛnɪk/ • **adj.** Physiology tending to promote the formation of fatty plaques in the arteries.
– DERIVATIVES **atherogenesis** n.
– ORIGIN 1950s: from **ATHEROMA** + **-GENIC**.

**atheroma** /ˌaθəˈrəʊmə/ • **n.** Medicine degeneration of the walls of the arteries, leading to restriction of the circulation and a risk of thrombosis.
– DERIVATIVES **atheromatous** adj.
– ORIGIN C16: via L. from Gk *athērōma*, from *athērē* 'groats'.

**atherosclerosis** /ˌaθərəʊsklɪəˈrəʊsɪs, -sklə-/ • **n.** Medicine a disease of the arteries characterized by the deposition of plaques of fatty material on their inner walls.
– DERIVATIVES **atherosclerotic** adj.
– ORIGIN C20: from Gk *athērē* 'groats' + *sklērōsis* (see **SCLEROSIS**).

**athetosis** /ˌaθɪˈtəʊsɪs/ • **n.** Medicine a condition in which abnormal muscle contraction causes involuntary writhing movements.
– DERIVATIVES **athetoid** adj. **athetotic** adj.
– ORIGIN C19: from Gk *athetos* 'without position' + **-OSIS**.

**athlete** • **n.** a person who is proficient in sports, especially one who competes in track and field events.
– DERIVATIVES **athletic** adj. **athletically** adv. **athleticism** n.
– ORIGIN ME: from L. *athleta*, from Gk *athlētēs*, from *athlein* 'compete for a prize', from *athlon* 'prize'.

**athlete's foot** • **n.** a form of ringworm infection affecting mainly the skin between the toes.

**athletics** • **pl. n.** [usu. treated as sing.] **1** chiefly Brit. the sport of competing in track and field events. **2** N. Amer. physical sports and games of any kind.

**at-home** • **n.** a social gathering in a person's home.

**athwart** /əˈθwɔːt/ • **prep. 1** from side to side of; across. **2** counter to. • **adv. 1** across from side to side; transversely. **2** so as to be perverse or contradictory.
– ORIGIN ME: from **A-**[2] + **THWART**.

**-atic** • **suffix** forming adjectives and nouns: *aquatic*.
– ORIGIN from Fr. *-atique* or L. *-aticus*, sometimes based on Gk *-atikos*.

**-ation** • **suffix** (forming nouns) denoting an action or its result: *exploration*.
– ORIGIN from Fr. *-ation* or L. *-ation-*.

**-ative** • **suffix** (forming adjectives) denoting a characteristic or propensity: *pejorative*.
– ORIGIN from Fr. *-atif, -ative* or L. *-ativus* (from past part. stems ending in *-at*).

**Atlantean** • **adj.** of or relating to the legendary island of Atlantis.

**atlantes** plural form of **ATLAS** (sense 3).

**Atlantic** • **adj. 1** of or adjoining the Atlantic Ocean. **2** Geology relating to or denoting the third climatic stage of the postglacial period in northern Europe (about 7,500 to 5,000 years ago), with a moist oceanic climate.
– ORIGIN ME: via L. from Gk *Atlantikos*, from *Atlas, Atlant-* (see **ATLAS**). The term orig. referred to Mount Atlas in Libya.

**Atlanticism** /atˈlantɪˌsɪz(ə)m/ • **n.** belief in a close relationship between western Europe and the US, or particularly in Nato.
– DERIVATIVES **Atlanticist** n. & adj.

**atlas** • **n. 1** a book of maps or charts. **2** Anatomy the topmost vertebra of the backbone, articulating with the occipital bone of the skull. **3** (pl. **atlantes** /atˈlantiːz/) Architecture a stone carving of a male figure, used as a column to support the entablature of a Greek or Greek-style building.
– ORIGIN C16: via L. from Gk *Atlas*, the Gk god who held up the pillars of the universe, whose picture appeared at the front of early atlases.

**atlas moth** • **n.** a very large boldly marked tropical silk moth. [*Attacus atlas*.]

**ATM** • **abbrev. 1** Telecommunications asynchronous transfer mode. **2** automated teller machine.

**atman** /ˈɑːtmən/ • **n.** Hinduism the spiritual life principle of the universe, especially when regarded as immanent in the real self of the individual. ➤a person's soul.
– ORIGIN from Sanskrit *ātman*, lit. 'essence'.

**atmosphere** • **n. 1** the envelope of gases surrounding the earth or another planet. ➤the air in a particular place. **2** a pervading tone or mood. ➤a pleasurable and interesting or exciting mood. **3** Physics a unit of pressure equal to mean atmospheric pressure at sea level, 101,325 pascals (roughly 14.7 pounds per square inch).
– DERIVATIVES **atmospheric** adj. **atmospherical** adj. (archaic). **atmospherically** adv.
– ORIGIN C17: from mod. L. *atmosphaera*, from Gk *atmos* 'vapour' + *sphaira* 'globe'.

**atmospherics** • **pl. n.** electrical disturbances in the atmosphere, especially as they interfere with telecommunications.

**ATOL** /ˈatɒl/ • **abbrev.** (in the UK) Air Travel Organizer's Licence.

**atoll** /ˈatɒl, əˈtɒl/ • **n.** a ring-shaped reef or chain of islands formed of coral.
– ORIGIN C17: from Maldivian *atoḷu*.

**atom** • **n. 1** the smallest particle of a chemical element, consisting of a positively charged nucleus (containing protons and typically also neutrons) surrounded by negatively charged electrons. **2** [usu. with neg.] an extremely small amount.
– ORIGIN C15: from OFr. *atome*, via L. from Gk *atomos* 'indivisible', based on *a-* 'not' + *temnein* 'to cut'.

**atom bomb** (also **atomic bomb**) • **n.** a bomb which derives its destructive power from the rapid release of energy by fission of heavy atomic nuclei.

**atomic** • **adj. 1** of or relating to an atom or atoms. **2** of or forming a single irreducible unit or component in a larger system. **3** relating to or denoting nuclear energy.
– DERIVATIVES **atomically** adv.

**atomic clock** • **n.** an extremely accurate type of clock which is regulated by the vibrations of an atomic or molecular system such as caesium or ammonia.

**atomicity** • **n. 1** Chemistry the number of atoms in the molecule of an element. **2** the state or fact of being composed of atoms.

**atomic mass** • **n.** the mass of an atom of a chemical element expressed in atomic mass units.

**atomic mass unit** • **n.** a unit of mass used to express atomic and molecular weights, equal to one twelfth of the mass of an atom of carbon-12.

**atomic number** • **n.** Chemistry the number of protons in the nucleus of an atom, which is characteristic of a chemical element and determines its place in the periodic table.

**atomic theory** • **n.** the theory that all matter is made up of tiny indivisible particles (atoms).

**atomic volume** • **n.** Chemistry the volume occupied by one gram-atom of an element under standard conditions.

**atomic weight** • **n.** Chemistry another term for **RELATIVE ATOMIC MASS**.

**atomism** • **n.** chiefly Philosophy a theoretical approach that regards something as interpretable through analysis into distinct, separable, and independent elementary components. The opposite of **HOLISM**.
– DERIVATIVES **atomist** n. **atomistic** adj.

**atomize** (also **-ise**) • **v. 1** convert (a substance) into very fine particles or droplets. **2** fragment.
– DERIVATIVES **atomization** n. **atomizer** n.

**atomy** /ˈatəmi/ • **n.** (pl. **-ies**) archaic a skeleton or emaciated body.
– ORIGIN C16: from **ANATOMY**, taken as *an atomy*.

**atonal** /eɪˈtəʊn(ə)l, ə-/ • **adj.** Music not written in any key or mode.
– DERIVATIVES **atonalism** n. **atonalist** n. **atonality** n.

**atone** • **v.** (**atone for**) make amends or reparation for.
– ORIGIN ME: from *at one* in early use; later by back-form. from **ATONEMENT**.

**atonement** • **n. 1** reparation for a wrong or injury. **2** (**the Atonement**) Christian Theology the reconciliation of God and mankind through the death of Jesus Christ.
– ORIGIN C16: from *at one* + **-MENT**.

**atonic** /əˈtɒnɪk/ • **adj. 1** Linguistics (of a syllable) without

accent or stress. **2** Physiology lacking muscular tone.
– DERIVATIVES **atony** /ˈatəni/ n.

**atop** poetic/literary ● **prep.** on the top of. ● **adv.** on the top.

**atopic** /eɪˈtɒpɪk/ ● **adj.** denoting a form of allergy in which a hypersensitivity reaction such as eczema or asthma may occur in a part of the body not in contact with the allergen.
– DERIVATIVES **atopy** /ˈatəpi/ n.
– ORIGIN C20: from Gk *atopia* 'unusualness'.

**-ator** ● **suffix** forming agent nouns such as *agitator*.
– ORIGIN from L., or sometimes representing Fr. *-ateur*.

**-atory** ● **suffix** (forming adjectives) relating to or involving an action: *explanatory*.
– ORIGIN from L. *-atorius*.

**ATP** ● **abbrev.** **1** Biochemistry adenosine triphosphate. **2** Brit. automatic train protection.

**atrabilious** /ˌatrəˈbɪlɪəs/ ● **adj.** poetic/literary melancholy or ill-tempered.
– DERIVATIVES **atrabiliousness** n.
– ORIGIN C17: from L. *atra bilis* 'black bile', translation of Gk *melankholia* 'melancholy', + **-IOUS**.

**atraumatic** ● **adj.** (of a medical or surgical procedure) causing minimal tissue injury.

**atrazine** /ˈatrəziːn/ ● **n.** a synthetic compound derived from triazine, used as an agricultural herbicide.
– ORIGIN 1960s: blend of *amino* and **TRIAZINE**.

**atresia** /əˈtriːʃə, -zɪə/ ● **n.** **1** Medicine absence or abnormal narrowing of an opening or passage in the body. **2** Physiology the degeneration of those Graafian follicles which do not ovulate during the menstrual cycle.
– ORIGIN C19: from **A-**[1] + Gk *trēsis* 'perforation' + **-IA**[1].

**atrioventricular** /ˌeɪtrɪə(ʊ)vɛnˈtrɪkjʊlə/ ● **adj.** Anatomy & Physiology of or relating to the atrial and ventricular chambers of the heart.

**atrium** /ˈeɪtrɪəm/ ● **n.** (pl. **atria** /ˈeɪtrɪə/ or **atriums**) **1** Architecture an open-roofed central court in an ancient Roman house. ➤a central hall or court in a modern building, typically rising through several stories and having a glazed roof. **2** Anatomy each of the two upper cavities of the heart from which blood is passed to the ventricles.
– DERIVATIVES **atrial** adj.
– ORIGIN C16: from L.

**atrocious** ● **adj.** **1** horrifyingly wicked. **2** informal extremely bad or unpleasant.
– DERIVATIVES **atrociously** adv. **atrociousness** n.
– ORIGIN C17: from L. *atrox, atroc-* 'cruel' + **-IOUS**.

**atrocity** ● **n.** (pl. **-ies**) an extremely wicked or cruel act.
– ORIGIN C16: from Fr. *atrocité* or L. *atrocitas*, from *atrox, atroc-* 'cruel'.

**atrophy** /ˈatrəfi/ ● **v.** (**-ies**, **-ied**) **1** (of body tissue or an organ) waste away, especially as a result of the degeneration of cells, or become vestigial during evolution. **2** gradually decline in effectiveness or vigour. ● **n.** (pl. **-ies**) the condition or process of atrophying.
– DERIVATIVES **atrophic** /əˈtrɒfɪk/ adj.
– ORIGIN C16: from Fr. *atrophier* (v.), *atrophie* (n.), from late L. *atrophia*, from Gk, 'lack of food'.

**atropine** /ˈatrəpiːn, -ɪn/ ● **n.** Chemistry a poisonous compound found in deadly nightshade, used in medicine as a muscle relaxant.
– ORIGIN C19: mod. L. *Atropa belladonna* 'deadly nightshade', from *Atropos* 'inflexible', the name of one of the Fates + **-INE**[4].

**at sign** ● **n.** the symbol @.

**attaboy** ● **exclam.** an informal expression of encouragement or admiration.
– ORIGIN C20: prob. representing a casual pronunc. of *that's the boy*.

**attach** ● **v.** **1** fasten; join. ➤include (a condition) as part of an agreement. ➤assign or attribute. **2** [as adj. **attached**] full of affection or fondness. **3** appoint for special or temporary duties. **4** Law, archaic seize (a person or property) by legal authority.
– DERIVATIVES **attachable** adj.
– ORIGIN ME: from OFr. *atachier* 'fasten, fix'.

**attaché** /əˈtaʃeɪ/ ● **n.** a person on the staff of an ambassador, having a specialized area of responsibility.
– ORIGIN C19: from Fr., lit. 'attached', past part. of *attacher*.

**attaché case** ● **n.** a small, flat briefcase for carrying documents.

**attachment** ● **n.** **1** an extra part or extension attached to perform a function. ➤a computer file appended to an email. **2** affection or fondness. ➤an affectionate relationship. **3** the action of attaching. **4** Brit. temporary secondment to an organization.
– PHRASES **attachment of earnings** English Law payment of debts by direct deduction from the debtor's earnings, under a court order.

**attack** ● **v.** **1** take aggressive action against. ➤(of a disease, chemical, etc.) act harmfully on. **2** criticize or oppose fiercely and publicly. **3** begin to deal with (a problem or task) in a determined way. **4** (in sport) make a forceful attempt to score goals or points. ● **n.** **1** an instance of attacking. ➤destructive action by a disease or chemical. **2** a sudden short bout of an illness or disorder. **3** the players in a team whose role is to attack.
– DERIVATIVES **attacker** n.
– ORIGIN C17: from Fr. *attaque* (n.), *attaquer* (v.), from Ital. *attacco* 'an attack', *attaccare* 'join battle'.

**attain** ● **v.** **1** succeed in accomplishing. **2** reach (a specified age, size, or amount).
– DERIVATIVES **attainability** n. **attainable** adj. **attainableness** n. **attainment** n.
– ORIGIN ME: from OFr. *ateindre*, from L. *attingere*, from *ad-* 'at, to' + *tangere* 'to touch'.

**attainder** /əˈteɪndə/ ● **n.** historical the forfeiture of land and civil rights suffered as a consequence of a sentence of death for treason or felony.
– PHRASES **act** (or **bill**) **of attainder** an item of legislation inflicting attainder without judicial process.
– ORIGIN ME: from Anglo-Norman Fr., var. of OFr. *ateindre* in the sense 'convict, bring to justice' (see **ATTAIN**).

**attaint** ● **v.** **1** historical subject to attainder. **2** archaic (of a disease) affect or infect.
– ORIGIN ME (in the sense 'touch, attain'): from obs. *attaint* (adj.), from OFr. *ataint, ateint*, past part. of *ateindre* (see **ATTAIN**).

**Attalid** /ˈatəlɪd/ ● **n.** a member of a Hellenistic dynasty named after Attalus I (reigned 241–197 BC), which flourished in the 3rd and 2nd centuries BC.

**attar** /ˈatə/ (also **otto**) ● **n.** a fragrant essential oil, typically made from rose petals.
– ORIGIN C17: via Pers. from Arab. *'iṭr* 'perfume, essence'.

**attempt** ● **v.** make an effort to achieve or complete. ➤try to climb to the top of (a mountain). ● **n.** an act of attempting. ➤a bid to kill someone.
– DERIVATIVES **attemptable** adj.
– ORIGIN ME: from OFr. *attempter*, from L. *attemptare*, from *ad-* 'to' + *temptare* 'to tempt'.

**attend** ● **v.** **1** be present at. ➤go regularly to (a school, church, or clinic). **2** (**attend to**) deal with. ➤pay attention to. **3** (usu. **be attended**) occur at the same time as or as a result of. **4** escort and wait on (a member of royalty or other important person).
– DERIVATIVES **attendee** n. **attender** n.
– ORIGIN ME: from OFr. *atendre*, from L. *attendere*, from *ad-* 'to' + *tendere* 'stretch'.

**attendance** ● **n.** **1** the action or state of attending. **2** the number of people present at a particular occasion.

**attendant** ● **n.** **1** a person employed to provide a service to the public. ➤an assistant to an important person. **2** a person who attends a particular occasion. ● **adj.** occurring at the same time or as a result of.

**attention** ● **n.** **1** the mental faculty of considering or taking notice. ➤notice taken. **2** special care or consideration. ➤(**attentions**) a person's behaviour to another as an indication of affection or sexual interest. **3** Military a position assumed by a soldier, standing very straight with the feet together and the arms straight down the sides of the body.
– DERIVATIVES **attentional** adj.
– ORIGIN ME: from L. *attentio(n-)*, from *attendere* (see **ATTEND**).

**attention deficit disorder** • n. any of a range of behavioural disorders occurring primarily in children, including such symptoms as poor concentration, hyperactivity, and learning difficulties.

**attentive** • adj. **1** paying close attention. **2** assiduously attending to the comfort or wishes of others.
– DERIVATIVES **attentively** adv. **attentiveness** n.
– ORIGIN ME: from OFr. *attentif*, *-ive*, from *atendre* (see ATTEND).

**attenuate** • v. /əˈtɛnjʊeɪt/ **1** reduce the strength, effect, or value of. **2** make thin or thinner.
– DERIVATIVES **attenuation** n.
– ORIGIN C16: from L. *attenuat-*, *attenuare* 'make slender'.

**attenuator** • n. a device which reduces the strength of a radio or audio signal.

**attest** /əˈtɛst/ • v. **1** provide or serve as clear evidence of. **2** declare that something exists or is the case.
– DERIVATIVES **attestable** adj. **attestation** n. **attestor** n.
– ORIGIN C16: from Fr. *attester*, from L. *attestari*, from *ad-* 'to' + *testari* 'to witness'.

**Attic** /ˈatɪk/ • adj. of or relating to Attica in Eastern Greece, or ancient Athens, or the dialect of Greek spoken there. • n. the Attic dialect spoken in ancient Athens.
– ORIGIN C16: via L. from Gk *Attikos*.

**attic** • n. a space or room inside or partly inside the roof of a building.
– ORIGIN C17 (as an architectural term designating a small order (column and entablature) above a taller one): from Fr. *attique*, from L. *Atticus*.

**Atticism** /ˈatɪsɪz(ə)m/ • n. a word or form characteristic of Attic Greek, regarded as having particular literary elegance.

**attire** • n. clothes, especially fine or formal ones. • v. (**be attired**) be dressed in clothes of a specified kind.
– ORIGIN ME: from OFr. *atirier*, *atirer* 'equip', from *a tire* 'in order'.

**attitude** • n. **1** a settled way of thinking or feeling. ➤ a position of the body indicating a particular mental state. **2** informal, chiefly N. Amer. truculent behaviour. ➤ self-confident behaviour: *she snapped her fingers with attitude*. **3** the orientation of an aircraft or spacecraft.
– DERIVATIVES **attitudinal** adj.
– ORIGIN C17: from Fr., from Ital. *attitudine* 'fitness, posture'.

**attitudinize** /ˌatɪˈtjuːdɪnʌɪz/ (also **-ise**) • v. adopt or express a particular attitude or attitudes, typically just for effect.
– DERIVATIVES **attitudinizer** n.

**atto-** /ˈatəʊ/ • comb. form denoting a factor of $10^{-18}$: *attowatt*.
– ORIGIN from Dan. or Norw. *atten* 'eighteen'.

**attorn** /əˈtəːn/ • v. Law formally make or acknowledge a transfer.
– ORIGIN ME (in the senses 'turn, change'): from OFr. *atorner* (see ATTORNEY).

**attorney** /əˈtəːni/ • n. (pl. **-eys**) a person, typically a lawyer, appointed to act for another in legal matters. ➤ chiefly US a qualified lawyer.
– DERIVATIVES **attorneyship** n.
– ORIGIN ME: from OFr. *atorne*, past part. of *atorner* 'assign', from *a* 'towards' + *torner* 'turn'.

**Attorney-General** • n. (pl. **Attorneys General**) the principal legal officer who represents the Crown or a state in legal proceedings and gives legal advice to the government.

**attract** • v. **1** draw or bring in by offering something of interest or advantage. **2** evoke (a specified reaction). ➤ (often **be attracted to**) cause to have a liking for or interest in. **3** exert a pull on.
– DERIVATIVES **attractable** adj. **attractor** n.
– ORIGIN ME: from L. *attract-*, *attrahere* 'draw near'.

**attractant** • n. a substance which attracts. • adj. tending to attract.

**attraction** • n. **1** the action or power of attracting. ➤ a quality or feature that attracts. ➤ a building or place which draws visitors. **2** Physics a force under the influence of which objects tend to move towards each other.

**attractive** • adj. **1** pleasing or appealing to the senses. ➤ having qualities or features which arouse interest. **2** of or relating to attraction between physical objects.
– DERIVATIVES **attractively** adv. **attractiveness** n.

**attribute** • v. /əˈtrɪbjuːt/ (**attribute something to**) regard something as belonging to or being caused by. • n. /ˈatrɪbjuːt/ **1** a quality or feature regarded as characteristic or inherent. **2** a material object recognized as representative of a person, status, or office.
– DERIVATIVES **attributable** /əˈtrɪbjʊtəb(ə)l/ adj. **attribution** n.
– ORIGIN C15: the noun from OFr. *attribut*; the verb from L. *attribut-* 'allotted': both from *attribuere*, from *ad-* 'to' + *tribuere* 'assign'.

**attributive** /əˈtrɪbjʊtɪv/ • adj. Grammar (of an adjective or other modifier) preceding the word that it modifies and expressing an attribute, as *old* in *the old dog*. Contrasted with PREDICATIVE.
– DERIVATIVES **attributively** adv.

**attrit** /əˈtrɪt/ • v. (**attritted**, **attritting**) US informal wear down (an opponent) by sustained action.
– ORIGIN 1950s: back-form. from ATTRITION.

**attrition** /əˈtrɪʃ(ə)n/ • n. **1** the action or process of gradually wearing down through sustained attack or pressure. **2** wearing away by friction. **3** (in scholastic theology) sorrow for sin falling short of contrition.
– DERIVATIVES **attritional** adj.
– ORIGIN ME: from late L. *attritio(n-)*, from *atterere* 'to rub'.

**attune** • v. adjust or accustom to a particular situation.
– ORIGIN C16: from AT- + TUNE.

**Atty** • abbrev. Attorney.

**ATV** • abbrev. all-terrain vehicle.

**atypical** • adj. not typical.
– DERIVATIVES **atypically** adv.

**AU** • abbrev. **1** ångström unit(s). **2** (also **a.u.**) astronomical unit(s).

**Au** • symb. the chemical element gold.
– ORIGIN from L. *aurum*.

**aubade** /əʊˈbɑːd/ • n. a poem or piece of music appropriate to the dawn.
– ORIGIN C17: from Fr., from Sp. *albada*, from *alba* 'dawn'.

**auberge** /əʊˈbɛːʒ, French obɛʀʒ/ • n. an inn in French-speaking countries.
– ORIGIN Fr., from Provençal *alberga* 'lodging'.

**aubergine** /ˈəʊbəʒiːn/ • n. chiefly Brit. **1** the purple egg-shaped fruit of a tropical plant, eaten as a vegetable. **2** the plant of the nightshade family which bears this fruit. [*Solanum melongena*.]
– ORIGIN C18: from Fr., from Catalan *alberginia*, from Arab. *al-bāḏinjān*.

**aubretia** /ɔːˈbriːʃə/ (also **aubrietia**) • n. a dwarf evergreen trailing plant with dense masses of foliage and purple, pink, or white flowers. [*Aubrieta deltoidea*.]
– ORIGIN C19: mod. L., named after the Fr. botanist Claude *Aubriet*.

**auburn** /ˈɔːbən, ˈɔːbəːn/ • n. a reddish-brown colour.
– ORIGIN ME: from OFr. *auborne*, from L. *alburnus* 'whitish', from *albus* 'white' (the word became assoc. with *brown* because in the 16th and 17th cents. it was often written *abrune* or *abroun*).

**AUC** • abbrev. used to indicate a date reckoned from 753 BC, the year of the foundation of Rome.
– ORIGIN from L. *ab urbe condita* 'from the foundation of the city'.

**au courant** /ˌəʊ kʊˈrɒ̃/ • adj. up to date and well informed.
– ORIGIN C18: from Fr., lit. 'in the (regular) course'.

**auction** /ˈɔːkʃ(ə)n/ • n. **1** a public sale in which goods or property are sold to the highest bidder. **2** Bridge the part of the game in which players bid to decide the contract in which the hand shall be played. • v. sell or offer for sale at an auction.
– ORIGIN C16: from L. *auctio(n-)* 'increase, auction'.

**auction bridge** • n. an obsolete form of the card game bridge, in which all tricks won counted towards the game whether bid or not.

**auctioneer** • n. a person who conducts auctions by ac-

cepting bids and declaring goods sold.
– DERIVATIVES **auctioneering** n.

**audacious** /ɔːˈdeɪʃəs/ ● adj. **1** recklessly daring. **2** impudent.
– DERIVATIVES **audaciously** adv. **audaciousness** n. **audacity** n.
– ORIGIN C16: from L. *audax, audac-* 'bold' + **-IOUS**.

**audial** /ˈɔːdɪəl/ ● adj. relating to or perceived through the sense of hearing.
– ORIGIN C20: formed irregularly from L. *audire* 'hear', on the pattern of *visual*.

**audible** ● adj. able to be heard. ● n. American Football a change of playing tactics called by the quarterback at the line of scrimmage.
– DERIVATIVES **audibility** n. **audibly** adv.
– ORIGIN C15: from late L. *audibilis*, from *audire* 'hear'.

**audience** ● n. **1** the assembled spectators or listeners at an event. **2** the readership of a book, magazine, or newspaper. **3** a formal interview with a person in authority.
– ORIGIN ME: from OFr., from L. *audientia*, from *audire* 'hear'.

**audio-** ● comb. form relating to hearing or sound, especially when recorded, transmitted, or reproduced: *audiovisual*.
– ORIGIN from L. *audire* 'hear'.

**audiobook** ● n. an audio cassette recording of a reading of a book.

**audio frequency** ● n. a frequency of oscillation capable of being perceived by the human ear, generally between 20 and 20,000 Hz.

**audiogram** ● n. a graphic record produced by audiometry.

**audiology** /ˌɔːdɪˈɒlədʒi/ ● n. the branch of science and medicine concerned with the sense of hearing.
– DERIVATIVES **audiological** adj. **audiologist** n.

**audiometry** /ˌɔːdɪˈɒmɪtri/ ● n. measurement of the range and sensitivity of a person's sense of hearing.
– DERIVATIVES **audiometer** n. **audiometric** adj.

**audiophile** ● n. a hi-fi enthusiast.

**audio tape** ● n. magnetic tape on which sound can be recorded. ● v. (**audiotape**) record (sound) on tape.

**audio typist** ● n. a typist who transcribes from recorded dictation.

**audio-visual** ● adj. using both sight and sound, typically in the form of slides or video and speech or music.

**audit** ● n. an official inspection of an organization's accounts, typically by an independent body. ● v. (**audited, auditing**) **1** conduct an audit of. **2** N. Amer. attend (a class) informally, without working for credit.
– ORIGIN ME: from L. *auditus* 'hearing', from *audire* 'hear', in med. L. *auditus (compoti)* 'audit (of an account)', an audit orig. being presented orally.

**audition** /ɔːˈdɪʃ(ə)n/ ● n. **1** an interview for a musician, actor, etc., consisting of a practical demonstration of the candidate's suitability and skill. **2** archaic the power of hearing. ● v. assess or be assessed by an audition.
– ORIGIN C16: from L. *auditio(n-)*, from *audire* 'hear'.

**auditor** ● n. **1** a person who conducts an audit. **2** a listener. **3** N. Amer. a person who attends a class informally without working for credit.
– DERIVATIVES **auditorial** adj.

**auditorium** ● n. (pl. **auditoriums** or **auditoria**) **1** the part of a theatre or hall in which the audience sits. **2** chiefly N. Amer. a large hall used for public gatherings.
– ORIGIN C17: from L., neut. of *auditorius* (see **AUDITORY**).

**auditory** ● adj. of or relating to the sense of hearing.
– ORIGIN C16: from L. *auditorius*, from *audire* 'hear'.

**au fait** /əʊ ˈfeɪ, French o fɛ(t)/ ● adj. (**au fait with**) having a good or detailed knowledge of.
– ORIGIN C18: from Fr., lit. 'to the point'.

**au fond** /əʊ ˈfɒ̃, French o fɔ̃/ ● adv. in essence.
– ORIGIN from Fr.

**Aug.** ● abbrev. August.

**auger** /ˈɔːɡə/ ● n. a tool resembling a large corkscrew, for boring holes.
– ORIGIN OE *nafogār*, from *nafu* (see **NAVE**[2]) + *gār* 'piercer'; the *n* was lost by wrong division of *a nauger*.

**Auger effect** /ˈəʊʒeɪ/ ● n. Physics an effect whereby an atom which has been ionized by removal of an electron from an inner shell loses energy by emitting an electron from an outer shell.
– ORIGIN 1930s: named after the Fr. physicist Pierre V. *Auger*.

**auger shell** ● n. a marine mollusc with a slender tapering spiral shell, often brightly coloured. [*Terebra* and other genera.]

**aught**[1] /ɔːt/ (also **ought**) ● pron. archaic anything at all.
– ORIGIN OE *āwiht* (see **AYE**[2], **WIGHT**).

**aught**[2] ● n. variant spelling of **OUGHT**[2].

**augite** /ˈɔːdʒʌɪt/ ● n. a dark green or black aluminosilicate mineral found in many igneous rocks.
– ORIGIN C19: from L. *augites*, denoting a precious stone, from Gk *augitēs*, from *augē* 'lustre'.

**augment** /ɔːɡˈmɛnt/ ● v. **1** make greater by addition; increase. **2** [as adj. **augmented**] Music denoting an interval which is one semitone greater than the corresponding major or perfect interval.
– DERIVATIVES **augmenter** n.
– ORIGIN ME: from OFr. *augmenter* (v.), *augment* (n.), or late L. *augmentare*, from L. *augere* 'to increase'.

**augmentation** ● n. the action or process of augmenting. ➤ Music the lengthening of the time values of notes in a melodic part.

**augmentative** ● adj. Linguistics (of an affix or derived word) reinforcing the idea of the original word, especially by meaning 'a large one of its kind'.

**au gratin** /əʊ ˈɡratã, French o ɡʀatɛ̃/ ● adj. [postpos.] sprinkled with breadcrumbs or grated cheese and browned.
– ORIGIN Fr., lit. 'by grating', from *gratter* 'to grate'.

**augur** /ˈɔːɡə/ ● v. portend (a specified outcome): *the end of the cold war seemed to augur well*. ● n. (in ancient Rome) a religious official who interpreted natural signs so as to determine divine approval or disapproval of a proposed action.
– DERIVATIVES **augural** /ˈɔːɡjʊr(ə)l/ adj. (archaic).
– ORIGIN ME: from L., 'diviner'.

**augury** /ˈɔːɡjʊri/ ● n. (pl. **-ies**) **1** an omen. **2** the interpretation of omens.

**August** ● n. the eighth month of the year.
– ORIGIN OE, from L. *augustus* 'consecrated, venerable'; named after *Augustus* Caesar, the first Roman emperor.

**august** /ɔːˈɡʌst/ ● adj. inspiring respect and admiration.
– DERIVATIVES **augustly** adv. **augustness** n.
– ORIGIN C17: from Fr. *auguste* or L. *augustus* 'consecrated, venerable'.

**Augustan** /ɔːˈɡʌst(ə)n/ ● adj. **1** connected with or occurring during the reign of the Roman emperor Augustus, especially as a notable period of Latin literature. **2** relating to or denoting a refined and classical style of 17th- and 18th-century English literature. ● n. a writer of the Augustan age.

**Augustine** /ɔːˈɡʌstɪn/ ● n. an Augustinian friar.

**Augustinian** /ˌɔːɡəˈstɪnɪən/ ● adj. of or relating to St Augustine (354-430) or his doctrines. ➤ relating to or denoting a religious order observing a rule derived from St Augustine's writings. ● n. a member of an Augustinian order. ➤ an adherent of the doctrines of St Augustine.

**auk** /ɔːk/ ● n. a short-winged diving seabird of a family including the guillemot and puffin, typically black and white. [Family Alcidae.]
– ORIGIN C17: from ON *álka* 'razorbill'.

**auld** /ɔːld, ɑːld/ ● adj. Scottish form of **OLD**.
– PHRASES **auld lang syne** times long past.
– ORIGIN OE *ald*, Anglian form of **OLD**.

**aumbry** /ˈɔːmbri/ (also **ambry**) ● n. (pl. **-ies**) a small recess or cupboard in the wall of a church.
– ORIGIN ME: from OFr. *armarie*, from L. *armarium* 'closet', from *arma* 'utensils'.

**au naturel** /ˌəʊ natjʊˈrɛl, French o natyʀɛl/ ● adj. & adv. in the most simple or natural way.
– ORIGIN from Fr.

**aunt** ● n. **1** the sister of one's father or mother or the wife of one's uncle. **2** informal an unrelated adult female friend of a child.

– ORIGIN ME: from OFr. *ante*, from L. *amita*.

**auntie** (also **aunty**) ● n. (pl. **-ies**) informal **1** aunt. **2** (**Auntie**) Brit. the BBC.

**Aunt Sally** ● n. (pl. **-ies**) **1** a game played in parts of Britain in which players throw sticks or balls at a wooden dummy (formerly a figure of a woman). **2** a person or thing set up as an easy target for criticism.

**au pair** /əʊ 'pɛː/ ● n. a young foreign person, typically a woman, who helps with housework and childcare in exchange for board and lodging.
– ORIGIN C19: from Fr., lit. 'on equal terms'.

**aura** /'ɔːrə/ ● n. (pl. **aurae** /-riː/ or **auras**) **1** the distinctive atmosphere or quality that seems to be generated by someone or something. **2** (in spiritualism and some forms of alternative medicine) a supposed emanation surrounding the body of a living creature. **3** Medicine a warning sensation experienced before an attack of epilepsy or migraine.
– ORIGIN ME, lit. 'a gentle breeze': via L. from Gk, 'breeze, breath'.

**aural** /'ɔːr(ə)l/ ● adj. of or relating to the ear or the sense of hearing.
– DERIVATIVES **aurally** adv.
– ORIGIN C19: from L. *auris* 'ear' + **-AL**.

**aurar** plural form of **EYRIR**.

**aureate** /'ɔːrɪət/ ● adj. made of or having the colour of gold.
– ORIGIN ME: from late L. *aureatus*, from L. *aureus* 'golden', from *aurum* 'gold'.

**aureole** /'ɔːrɪəʊl/ (also **aureola** /ɔː'rɪələ/) ● n. **1** (in paintings) a radiant circle surrounding a person's head or body as a way of representing holiness. **2** a corona around the sun or moon. **3** Geology the zone of metamorphosed rock surrounding an igneous intrusion.
– ORIGIN ME: from OFr. *aureole*, from L. *aureola* (*corona*) 'golden (crown)', fem. of *aureolus* (dimin. of *aureus*, from *aurum* 'gold').

**aureus** /'ɔːrɪəs/ ● n. (pl. **aurei**) an ancient Roman coin worth 25 silver denarii.
– ORIGIN L., noun use of *aureus* 'golden', from *aurum* 'gold'.

**au revoir** /ˌəʊ rə'vwɑː, French o ʀəvwaʀ/ ● exclam. goodbye.
– ORIGIN C17: from Fr., lit. 'to the seeing again'.

**auric**[1] /'ɔːrɪk/ ● adj. of or relating to an aura.

**auric**[2] /'ɔːrɪk/ ● adj. Chemistry of gold with a valency of three; of gold(III).
– ORIGIN C19: from L. *aurum* 'gold' + **-IC**.

**auricle** /'ɔːrɪk(ə)l/ ● n. Anatomy & Zoology **1** the external part or pinna of the ear. **2** an atrium of the heart.
– DERIVATIVES **auriculate** adj.
– ORIGIN ME: from L. *auricula*, dimin. of *auris* 'ear'.

**auricula** /ɔː'rɪkjʊlə/ ● n. an Alpine primula with leaves said to resemble bears' ears. [*Primula auricula*.]
– ORIGIN C17: from L., dimin. of *auris* 'ear'.

**auricular** /ɔː'rɪkjʊlə/ ● adj. **1** of or relating to the ear or hearing. **2** of, relating to, or shaped like an auricle.
– ORIGIN ME: from late L. *auricularis*, from *auricula*, dimin. of *auris* 'ear'.

**auriferous** /ɔː'rɪf(ə)rəs/ ● adj. (of rocks or minerals) containing gold.
– ORIGIN C17: from L. *aurifer* 'gold-bearing' + **-OUS**.

**Aurignacian** /ˌɔːrɪ'njeɪʃ(ə)n, ˌɔːrɪg'neɪ-/ ● adj. Archaeology relating to or denoting the early stages of the Upper Palaeolithic culture in Europe and the Near East, dated to about 34,000–29,000 years ago.
– ORIGIN C20: from Fr. *Aurignacien*, from *Aurignac* in SW France, where objects from this culture were found.

**aurochs** /'ɔːrɒks, 'aʊ-/ ● n. (pl. same) a large extinct wild ox that was the ancestor of domestic cattle. [*Bos primigenius*.]
– ORIGIN C18: from Ger., var. of *Auerochs*, from Old High Ger. *ūrohso*, from *ūr* + *ohso* 'ox'.

**aurora** /ɔː'rɔːrə/ ● n. (pl. **auroras** or **aurorae** /-riː/) **1** the northern lights (**aurora borealis**) or southern lights (**aurora australis**), a natural phenomenon characterized by the appearance of streamers of coloured light in the sky near the earth's magnetic poles and caused by the interaction of charged particles from the sun with atoms in the upper atmosphere. **2** poetic/literary the dawn.
– DERIVATIVES **auroral** adj.
– ORIGIN ME: from L., 'dawn, goddess of the dawn'.

**AUS** ● abbrev. Australia (international vehicle registration).

**auscultation** /ˌɔːsk(ə)l'teɪʃ(ə)n/ ● n. the action of listening to sounds from the heart, lungs, or other organs with a stethoscope.
– DERIVATIVES **auscultate** v. **auscultatory** /ɔː'skʌltət(ə)ri/ adj.
– ORIGIN C17: from L. *auscultatio(n-)*, from *auscultare* 'listen to'.

**Auslese** /'aʊsleɪzə/ ● n. a white wine of German origin or style made from selected bunches of grapes picked later than the general harvest.
– ORIGIN from Ger., from *aus* 'out' + *Lese* 'picking'.

**auspice** /'ɔːspɪs/ ● n. archaic an omen.
– PHRASES **under the auspices of** with the support or protection of.
– ORIGIN C16, lit. 'the observation of bird-flight in divination': from Fr., or from L. *auspicium*, from *auspex* 'observer of birds'.

**auspicious** /ɔː'spɪʃəs/ ● adj. indicating a good chance of success; favourable.
– DERIVATIVES **auspiciously** adv. **auspiciousness** n.

**Aussie** /'ɒzi, 'ɒsi/ (also **Ozzie**) ● n. (pl. **-ies**) & adj. informal Australia or Australian.

**austenite** /'ɒstɪnʌɪt, 'ɔː-/ ● n. Metallurgy a relatively soft component of steel consisting of a solid solution of carbon in iron.
– DERIVATIVES **austenitic** adj.
– ORIGIN C20: named after the Engl. metallurgist Sir William Roberts-*Austen*, + **-ITE**[1].

**austere** /ɒ'stɪə, ɔː-/ ● adj. (**-er**, **-est**) **1** severe or strict in appearance or manner. **2** lacking comforts, luxuries, or adornment.
– DERIVATIVES **austerely** adv. **austerity** n.
– ORIGIN ME: via OFr. from L. *austerus*, from Gk *austēros* 'severe'.

**austral** /'ɒstr(ə)l, 'ɔː-/ ● adj. technical **1** of the southern hemisphere. **2** (**Austral**) of Australia or Australasia.
– ORIGIN C15: from L. *australis*, from *Auster* 'the south, the south wind'.

**Australasian** /ˌɒstrə'leɪʒ(ə)n, -ʃ(ə)n/ ● adj. of or relating to Australasia, a region consisting of Australia, New Zealand, and islands of the SW Pacific. ● n. a person from Australasia.

**Australian** ● n. a native or national of Australia, or a person of Australian descent. ● adj. of or relating to Australia.
– DERIVATIVES **Australianism** n.
– ORIGIN from Fr. *australien*, from L. *australis* in the phr. *Terra Australis* 'the southern land', the name of the supposed southern continent.

**Australian Rules** ● n. a form of football played on an oval field with an oval ball by teams of eighteen players.

**Australoid** /'ɒstrəlɔɪd, 'ɔː-/ ● adj. relating to or denoting the broad division of humankind represented by Australian Aboriginal peoples. ● n. an Australoid person.

**USAGE** Australoid

The term **Australoid** belongs to a set of terms introduced by 19th-century anthropologists attempting to categorize human races. Such terms are associated with outdated notions of racial types, and so are now potentially offensive and best avoided.

**Australopithecus** /ˌɒstrələʊ'pɪθɪkəs, ˌɔː-/ ● n. a genus of fossil bipedal primates with both ape-like and human characteristics, found in Pliocene and Lower Pleistocene deposits in Africa.
– DERIVATIVES **australopithecine** /-ɪsiːn/ n. & adj.
– ORIGIN mod. L., from L. *australis* (see **AUSTRAL**) + Gk *pithēkos* 'ape'.

**Austrian** ● n. a native or inhabitant of Austria, or a person of Austrian descent. ● adj. of or relating to Austria or its people.

**Austrian blind** ● n. a ruched blind extending about a

third of the way down a window.

**Austro-**[1] /ˈɒstrəʊ, ˈɔː-/ ● **comb. form** Austrian; Austrian and ...: *Austro-Hungarian.*

**Austro-**[2] /ˈɒstrəʊ, ˈɔː-/ ● **comb. form 1** Australian; Australian and ...: *Austro-Malayan.* **2** southern: *Austro-Asiatic.*
– ORIGIN from L. *australis* 'southern'.

**Austro-Asiatic** ● **adj.** relating to or denoting a phylum of languages spoken in SE Asia, including the Mon-Khmer and Munda families. ● **n.** this phylum of languages.

**Austronesian** /ˌɒstrə(ʊ)ˈniːzɪən, -ʒ(ə)n, ˌɔː-/ ● **adj.** relating to or denoting a family of languages spoken in an area extending from Madagascar in the west to the Pacific islands in the east. ● **n.** this family of languages.
– ORIGIN from Ger. *austronesisch*, based on L. *australis* (see **AUSTRAL**) + Gk *nēsos* 'island'.

**AUT** ● **abbrev.** (in the UK) Association of University Teachers.

**aut-** ● **prefix** variant spelling of **AUTO-**[1].

**autarchy** /ˈɔːtɑːki/ ● **n.** (pl. **-ies**) **1** another term for **AUTOCRACY**. **2** variant spelling of **AUTARKY**.
– DERIVATIVES **autarch** n. **autarchic** adj.

**autarky** (also **autarchy**) ● **n. 1** economic independence or self-sufficiency. **2** a state or society which is economically independent.
– DERIVATIVES **autarkic** adj.
– ORIGIN C17: from Gk *autarkeia*, from *autarkēs* 'self-sufficiency'.

**autecology** /ˌɔːtɪˈkɒlədʒi/ (also **autoecology**) ● **n.** Biology the ecological study of a particular species. Contrasted with **SYNECOLOGY**.
– DERIVATIVES **autecological** adj.

**auteur** /əʊˈtəː, ɔː-/ ● **n.** a film director who influences their films so much that they rank as their author.
– DERIVATIVES **auteurism** n. **auteurist** adj.
– ORIGIN 1960s: from Fr., lit. 'author'.

**authentic** ● **adj. 1** of undisputed origin or veracity; genuine. **2** Music (of a church mode) containing notes between the principal note or final and the note an octave higher. Compare with **PLAGAL**.
– DERIVATIVES **authentically** adv. **authenticity** /ɔːθɛnˈtɪsɪti/ n.
– ORIGIN ME: via OFr. from late L. *authenticus*, from Gk *authentikos* 'principal, genuine'.

**authenticate** ● **v.** prove or show to be authentic.
– DERIVATIVES **authentication** /-ˈkeɪʃ(ə)n/ n. **authenticator** n.

**authigenic** /ˌɔːθɪˈdʒɛnɪk/ ● **adj.** Geology (of minerals and other materials) formed in their present position. Often contrasted with **ALLOGENIC**.
– ORIGIN C19: from Gk *authigenēs* 'born on the spot' + **-IC**.

**author** ● **n. 1** a writer of a book, article, or report. **2** an originator of a plan or idea. ● **v.** be the author or the originator of.
– DERIVATIVES **authoress** n. **authorial** /ɔːˈθɔːrɪəl/ adj. **authorship** n.
– ORIGIN ME: from OFr. *autor*, from L. *auctor*, from *augere* 'increase, originate'.

**authoring** ● **n.** Computing the creation of programs and databases for computer applications such as multimedia products.

**authoritarian** /ɔːˌθɒrɪˈtɛːrɪən/ ● **adj.** favouring or enforcing strict obedience to authority at the expense of personal freedom. ● **n.** an authoritarian person.
– DERIVATIVES **authoritarianism** n.

**authoritative** /ɔːˈθɒrɪtətɪv, -ˌteɪtɪv/ ● **adj. 1** reliable because true or accurate: *an authoritative source.* **2** commanding and self-confident. **3** supported by authority.
– DERIVATIVES **authoritatively** adv. **authoritativeness** n.

**authority** ● **n.** (pl. **-ies**) **1** the power or right to give orders and enforce obedience. **2** a person or organization exerting control in a particular political or administrative sphere. **3** the power to influence others based on recognized knowledge or expertise. ➤ an authoritative person, book, or other source.
– ORIGIN ME: from OFr. *autorite*, from L. *auctoritas*, from *auctor* (see **AUTHOR**).

**authorize** (also **-ise**) ● **v.** give official permission for or approval to.
– DERIVATIVES **authorization** n.
– ORIGIN ME: from OFr. *autoriser*, from med. L. *auctorizare*, from L. *auctor* (see **AUTHOR**).

**Authorized Version** ● **n.** chiefly Brit. an English translation of the Bible made in 1611 at the order of James I and still widely used.

**autism** /ˈɔːtɪz(ə)m/ ● **n.** Psychiatry a mental condition characterized by great difficulty in communicating with others and in using language and abstract concepts.
– DERIVATIVES **autistic** adj. & n.
– ORIGIN C20: from Gk *autos* 'self' + **-ISM**.

**auto**[1] ● **n.** (pl. **-os**) informal, chiefly N. Amer. a motor car.

**auto**[2] ● **adj. & n.** short for **AUTOMATIC**.

**auto-**[1] (usu. **aut-** before a vowel) ● **comb. form 1** self: *autocrat.* **2** one's own: *autograph.* **3** automatic; spontaneous: *autoxidation.*
– ORIGIN from Gk *autos* 'self'.

**auto-**[2] ● **comb. form** relating to cars: *autocross.*
– ORIGIN C19: from **AUTOMOBILE**.

**autoantibody** ● **n.** (pl. **-ies**) Physiology an antibody produced by an organism in response to a constituent of its own tissues.

**Autobahn** /ˈɔːtə(ʊ)bɑːn, German ˈaʊtobaːn/ ● **n.** a German, Austrian, or Swiss motorway.
– ORIGIN 1930s: from Ger., from *Auto* 'motor car' + *Bahn* 'path, road'.

**autobiography** ● **n.** (pl. **-ies**) an account of a person's life written by that person.
– DERIVATIVES **autobiographer** n. **autobiographic** adj. **autobiographical** adj.

**autocatalysis** ● **n.** Chemistry catalysis of a reaction by one of its products.
– DERIVATIVES **autocatalytic** adj.

**autocephalous** /ˌɔːtə(ʊ)ˈsɛf(ə)ləs, -ˈkɛf-/ ● **adj.** (of an Eastern Christian Church) appointing its own head, not subject to the authority of an external patriarch or archbishop.
– ORIGIN C19: from Gk *autokephalos* (from *autos* 'self' + *kephalē* 'head') + **-OUS**.

**autochrome** ● **n.** an early form of colour photography using plates coated with dyed starch grains.

**autochthon** /ɔːˈtɒkθ(ə)n, -θəʊn/ ● **n.** (pl. **autochthons** or **autochthones** /-θəniːz/) an indigenous inhabitant of a place.
– ORIGIN C16: from Gk, lit. 'sprung from the earth', from *autos* 'self' + *khthōn* 'earth'.

**autochthonous** /ɔːˈtɒkθənəs/ ● **adj. 1** indigenous. **2** Geology (of a deposit or formation) formed in its present position. Often contrasted with **ALLOCHTHONOUS**.

**autoclave** /ˈɔːtə(ʊ)kleɪv/ ● **n.** a strong heated container used for chemical reactions and processes using high pressures and temperatures, e.g. steam sterilization. ● **v.** heat in an autoclave.
– ORIGIN C19: from Fr., from *auto-* 'self' + L. *clavus* 'nail' or *clavis* 'key' (so named because it is self-fastening).

**autocorrelation** ● **n.** Mathematics & Statistics correlation between the elements of a series and others from the same series separated from them by a given interval.

**autocracy** /ɔːˈtɒkrəsi/ ● **n.** (pl. **-ies**) **1** a system of government by one person with absolute power. **2** a country, state, or society governed in this way.
– ORIGIN C17: from Gk *autokrateia*, from *autokratēs*, from *autos* 'self' + *kratos* 'power'.

**autocrat** ● **n. 1** a ruler who has absolute power. **2** a domineering person.
– DERIVATIVES **autocratic** adj. **autocratically** adv.

**autocross** ● **n.** Brit. a motor racing sport in which cars are driven over courses on rough terrain or unmade roads.

**autocue** ● **n.** trademark, chiefly Brit. a device used as a television prompt in which a script is projected on to a screen visible only to the speaker or performer.

**auto-da-fé** /ˌɔːtəʊdɑːˈfeɪ/ ● **n.** (pl. **autos-da-fé** /ˌɔːtəʊz-/) the burning of a heretic by the Spanish Inquisition.
– ORIGIN C18: from Port., lit. 'act of the faith'.

**autodidact** /ˈɔːtəʊdɪdakt/ ● **n.** a self-taught person.

– DERIVATIVES **autodidactic** adj.

**autoecology** /ˌɔːtəʊɪˈkɒlədʒi/ • **n.** variant spelling of **AUTECOLOGY**.

**auto-erotic** • **adj.** of or relating to sexual excitement generated by fantasizing about or stimulating one's own body.
– DERIVATIVES **auto-eroticism** n.

**auto-exposure** • **n.** a device which sets the exposure automatically on a camera or other device.

**autofocus** • **n.** a device focusing a camera or other device automatically.
– DERIVATIVES **autofocusing** n.

**autogamy** /ɔːˈtɒgəmi/ • **n.** Biology self-fertilization. Compare with **ALLOGAMY**.
– DERIVATIVES **autogamous** adj.
– ORIGIN C19: from **AUTO-**[1] + Gk *gamos* 'marriage'.

**autogenic** /ˌɔːtə(ʊ)ˈdʒɛnɪk/ • **adj.** technical self-generated.

**autogenic training** • **n.** a form of relaxation therapy involving auto-suggestion.

**autogenous** /ɔːˈtɒdʒɪnəs/ • **adj. 1** arising from within or from a thing itself. **2** (of welding) done either without a filler or with a filler of the same metal as the pieces being welded.

**autogiro** (also **autogyro**) • **n.** (pl. **-os**) a form of aircraft with unpowered freely rotating horizontal vanes and a propeller.
– ORIGIN 1920s: from Sp., from *auto-* 'self' + *giro* 'gyration'.

**autograft** • **n.** a graft of tissue from one point to another of the same individual's body.

**autograph** • **n. 1** a celebrity's signature written for an admirer. **2** a manuscript or musical score in an author's or composer's own handwriting. **3** a person's handwriting. • **v.** write one's signature on. • **adj.** written in the author's own handwriting.
– DERIVATIVES **autographic** adj.
– ORIGIN C17: from Fr. *autographe* or late L. *autographum*, from Gk *autographon*, neut. of *autographos* 'written with one's own hand'.

**autoharp** • **n.** a kind of zither fitted with a series of sprung and padded bars which allow the playing of chords by damping selected strings.

**autoimmune** • **adj.** Medicine relating to or denoting disease caused by antibodies or lymphocytes produced against substances naturally present in the body.
– DERIVATIVES **autoimmunity** n.

**autointoxication** • **n.** Medicine poisoning by a toxin formed within the body itself.

**autologous** /ɔːˈtɒləgəs/ • **adj.** (of cells or tissues) obtained from the same individual.

**autolysis** /ɔːˈtɒlɪsɪs/ • **n.** Biology the destruction of cells or tissues by their own enzymes.
– DERIVATIVES **autolytic** adj.

**automated teller machine** • **n.** a machine that automatically provides cash and performs other banking services on insertion of a special card.

**automatic** • **adj. 1** (of a device or process) working by itself with little or no direct human control. ➤ (of a firearm) self-loading and able to fire continuously. **2** done or occurring without conscious thought. ➤ (of a penalty or legal sanction) necessary and inevitable, as a result of a fixed rule or particular set of circumstances. • **n.** an automatic machine or device.
– DERIVATIVES **automatically** adv. **automaticity** n. **automatization** (also **-isation**) n. **automatize** (also **-ise**) v.
– ORIGIN C18: from Gk *automatos* (see **AUTOMATON**) + **-IC**.

**automatic pilot** • **n. 1** a device for keeping an aircraft on a set course. **2** (in phr. **on automatic pilot**) a state of doing something out of routine or habit, without concentration or conscious thought.

**automatic writing** • **n.** writing said to be produced by a spiritual, occult, or subconscious agency.

**automation** • **n.** the use or introduction of automatic equipment in a manufacturing or other process or facility.
– DERIVATIVES **automate** v.

**automatism** /ɔːˈtɒmətɪz(ə)m/ • **n.** Psychiatry action which does not involve conscious thought or intention.
– ORIGIN C19: from Fr. *automatisme*, from *automate* 'automaton', from Gk *automatos* (see **AUTOMATON**).

**automaton** /ɔːˈtɒmət(ə)n/ • **n.** (pl. **automata** /-tə/ or **automatons**) **1** a moving mechanical device made in imitation of a human being. **2** a machine which performs a function according to a set of coded instructions.
– ORIGIN C17: via L. from Gk, neut. of *automatos* 'acting of itself', from *autos* 'self'.

**automobile** • **n.** chiefly N. Amer. a motor car.

**automotive** /ˌɔːtəˈməʊtɪv/ • **adj.** relating to motor vehicles.

**autonomic** /ˌɔːtəˈnɒmɪk/ • **adj.** Physiology relating to or denoting the part of the nervous system responsible for control of breathing, circulation, digestion, and other bodily functions not consciously directed.

**autonomy** /ɔːˈtɒnəmi/ • **n.** (pl. **-ies**) **1** the possession or right of self-government. **2** freedom of action.
– DERIVATIVES **autonomist** n. & adj. **autonomous** adj. **autonomously** adv.
– ORIGIN C17: from Gk *autonomia*, from *autonomos* 'having its own laws', from *autos* 'self' + *nomos* 'law'.

**autopilot** • **n.** short for **AUTOMATIC PILOT**.

**autopista** /ˌɔːtə(ʊ)ˈpiːstə, Spanish autoˈpista/ • **n.** a motorway in a Spanish-speaking country.
– ORIGIN 1950s: from Sp., from *auto* 'automobile' + *pista* 'track'.

**autopsy** /ˈɔːtɒpsi, ɔːˈtɒpsi/ • **n.** (pl. **-ies**) a post-mortem examination to discover the cause of death or the extent of disease.
– ORIGIN C17 (in the sense 'personal observation'): from Fr. *autopsie* or mod. L. *autopsia*, from Gk, from *autoptēs* 'eyewitness'.

**autoradiograph** (also **autoradiogram**) • **n.** a photograph produced by radiation from radioactive material in the object photographed.
– DERIVATIVES **autoradiographic** adj. **autoradiography** n.

**autorotation** • **n.** rotation of an object caused by the flow of moving air or water around it.
– DERIVATIVES **autorotate** v.

**autoroute** • **n.** a French motorway.
– ORIGIN from Fr.

**autosave** • **n.** Computing a software facility which automatically saves a user's work at regular intervals.

**autoshaping** • **n.** Psychology conditioning in which the conditioned response has not been reinforced by reward or punishment, but is a modified instinctive response to certain stimuli.

**autosome** /ˈɔːtəʃəʊm/ • **n.** Biology any chromosome that is not a sex chromosome.
– DERIVATIVES **autosomal** adj.

**autostrada** /ˈɔːtə(ʊ)ˌstrɑːdə, Italian autoˈstrada/ • **n.** (pl. **autostradas** or **autostrade** /-deɪ, Italian -de/) an Italian motorway.
– ORIGIN from Ital., from *auto* 'automobile' + *strada* 'road'.

**auto-suggestion** • **n.** the hypnotic or subconscious adoption of an idea which one has originated oneself.

**autotelic** /ˌɔːtə(ʊ)ˈtɛlɪk/ • **adj.** (of an activity or a creative work) having an end or purpose in itself.
– ORIGIN C20: from **AUTO-**[1] + Gk *telos* 'end' + **-IC**.

**autotomy** /ɔːˈtɒtəmi/ • **n.** Zoology the casting off of a part of the body (e.g. the tail of a lizard) by an animal under threat.

**autotoxin** • **n.** a substance produced by an organism which is toxic to itself.
– DERIVATIVES **autotoxic** adj.

**autotransformer** • **n.** an electrical transformer which has a single winding of which part is common to both primary and secondary circuits.

**autotransplantation** • **n.** transplantation of tissue from one site to another in the same individual.
– DERIVATIVES **autotransplant** n. **autotransplanted** adj.

**autotroph** /ˈɔːtə(ʊ)trəʊf, -trɒf/ • **n.** Biology an organism that synthesizes nutrients from simple inorganic substances. Compare with **HETEROTROPH**.

– DERIVATIVES **autotrophic** adj. **autotrophy** n.

**autoxidation** /ˌɔːtɒksɪˈdeɪʃ(ə)n/ ● n. Chemistry spontaneous oxidation of a substance in the presence of oxygen.
– DERIVATIVES **autoxidize** (also **-ise**) v.

**autumn** ● n. **1** chiefly Brit. the season after summer and before winter. **2** Astronomy the period from the autumn equinox to the winter solstice.
– DERIVATIVES **autumnal** adj.
– ORIGIN ME: from OFr. *autompne*, or later directly from L. *autumnus*.

**autumn crocus** ● n. a plant of the lily family with autumn-blooming flowers. [Genus *Colchicum*.]

**autunite** /ˈɔːtʌnʌɪt/ ● n. a yellow fluorescent mineral consisting of a phosphate of calcium and uranium.
– ORIGIN C19: from *Autun*, a town in eastern France, + **-ITE**[1].

**auxiliary** /ɔːɡˈzɪlɪəri, ɒɡ-/ ● adj. providing supplementary or additional help and support. ● n. (pl. **-ies**) an auxiliary person or thing.
– ORIGIN ME: from L. *auxiliarius*, from *auxilium* 'help'.

**auxiliary verb** ● n. Grammar a verb used in forming the tenses, moods, and voices of other verbs (in English primarily *be*, *do*, and *have*).

**auxin** /ˈɔːksɪn/ ● n. a plant growth hormone which causes the elongation of cells in shoots.
– ORIGIN 1930s: coined in Ger. from Gk *auxein* 'to increase' + **-IN**[1].

**auxotroph** /ˈɔːksətrəʊf, -trɒf/ ● n. Biology a mutant organism that requires a particular additional nutrient which the normal strain does not.
– DERIVATIVES **auxotrophic** adj.
– ORIGIN 1950s: from L. *auxilium* 'help' + Gk *trophos* 'feeder'.

**AV** ● abbrev. **1** audio-visual (teaching aids). **2** Authorized Version.

**Av** ● n. variant spelling of **AB**[1].

**avadavat** /ˈavədəvat/ (also **amadavat**) ● n. a red or green South Asian waxbill sometimes kept as a cage bird. [Genus *Amandava*: two species.]
– ORIGIN C17: named after the city of *Ahmadabad* in India.

**avail** ● v. **1** (**avail oneself of**) use or take advantage of. **2** help or benefit. ● n. (usu. in phr. **of/to no avail**) use or benefit.
– ORIGIN ME: from obs. *vail*, from OFr. *valoir*, from L. *valere* 'be strong, be of value'.

**available** ● adj. **1** able to be used or obtained. **2** not otherwise occupied; free.
– DERIVATIVES **availability** n. **availableness** n.
– ORIGIN ME (in the senses 'effectual, serviceable' and 'legally valid'): from **AVAIL** + **-ABLE**.

**avalanche** /ˈavəlɑːnʃ/ ● n. **1** a mass of snow, ice, and/or rocks falling rapidly down a mountainside. **2** an overwhelming deluge. **3** Physics a cumulative process in which an ion or electron generates further ions or electrons by collision. ● v. **1** fall in an avalanche. **2** Physics undergo a rapid increase in conductivity due to an avalanche process.
– ORIGIN C18: from Fr., alt. of Alpine dial. *lavanche*, influenced by *avaler* 'descend'.

**avant-garde** /ˌavɒ̃ˈɡɑːd/ ● adj. (in the arts) new and unusual or experimental. ● n. (**the avant-garde**) avant-garde ideas or artists.
– DERIVATIVES **avant-gardism** n. **avant-gardist** n.
– ORIGIN ME (denoting the vanguard of an army): from Fr., lit. 'vanguard'.

**Avar** /əˈvɑː/ ● n. **1** a member of an ancient nomadic people from central Asia. **2** a pastoral people of Dagestan in Russia. **3** the North Caucasian language of the modern Avars.
– ORIGIN the name in Avar.

**avarice** ● n. extreme greed for wealth or material gain.
– DERIVATIVES **avaricious** adj. **avariciously** adv. **avariciousness** n.
– ORIGIN ME: from OFr., from L. *avaritia*, from *avarus* 'greedy'.

**avascular** /əˈvaskjʊlə, eɪ-/ ● adj. Medicine characterized by or associated with a lack of blood vessels.

**avast** /əˈvɑːst/ ● exclam. Nautical stop; cease.
– ORIGIN C17: from Du. *hou'vast, houd vast* 'hold fast!'

**avatar** /ˈavətɑː/ ● n. **1** chiefly Hinduism a manifestation of a deity or released soul in bodily form on earth. **2** Computing a movable icon representing a person in cyberspace or virtual reality graphics.
– ORIGIN from Sanskrit *avatāra* 'descent'.

**avaunt** /əˈvɔːnt/ ● exclam. archaic go away.
– ORIGIN ME: from Anglo-Norman Fr. var. of OFr. *avant*, from L. *ab* 'from' + *ante* 'before'.

**Ave.** ● abbrev. Avenue.

**ave** /ˈɑːveɪ/ ● exclam. poetic/literary used to express good wishes on meeting or parting.
– ORIGIN ME: from L., 'fare well!', sing. imper. of *avere*.

**Ave Maria** /ˌɑːveɪ məˈriːə/ ● n. a prayer to the Virgin Mary used in Catholic worship; a Hail Mary.
– ORIGIN the opening words in L., lit. 'hail, Mary!'

**avenge** ● v. inflict harm in return for (an injury or wrong). ➤ inflict retribution on behalf of (a wronged person).
– DERIVATIVES **avenger** n.
– ORIGIN ME: from OFr. *avengier*, from *a-* (from L. *ad* 'to') + *vengier*, from L. *vindicare* 'vindicate'.

**avens** /ˈeɪv(ə)nz/ ● n. a plant with serrated, divided leaves and seeds bearing small hooks. [Genus *Geum*: several species.]
– ORIGIN ME: from OFr. *avence* (med. L. *avencia*).

**aventurine** /əˈvɛntʃərɪn/ ● n. **1** brownish glass containing sparkling particles of copper or gold. **2** translucent quartz or feldspar containing small reflective mineral particles.
– ORIGIN C18: from Fr., from Ital. *avventurino*, from *avventura* 'chance' (because of its accidental discovery).

**avenue** ● n. **1** a broad road or path, especially one lined with trees. **2** a means of approach.
– ORIGIN C17: from Fr., fem. past part. of *avenir* 'arrive, approach'.

**aver** /əˈvəː/ ● v. (**averred**, **averring**) formal state or assert to be the case. ➤ Law allege as a fact in support of a plea.
– ORIGIN ME: from OFr. *averer*, based on L. *ad* 'to' + *verus* 'true'.

**average** ● n. **1** the result obtained by adding several amounts together and then dividing the total by the number of amounts. **2** a usual or ordinary amount, level, or rate. **3** Law the apportionment of financial liability resulting from loss of or damage to a ship or its cargo. ● adj. **1** constituting an average. **2** of the usual or ordinary amount, level, or rate. ➤ mediocre: *a very average movie*. ● v. **1** amount to or achieve as an average. ➤ calculate or estimate the average of. **2** (**average out**) result in an even distribution.
– DERIVATIVES **averagely** adv. **averageness** n.
– ORIGIN C15: from Fr. *avarie* 'damage to ship or cargo', from Ital. *avaria*, from Arab. *'awār*; the mod. sense arose from the equitable sharing of liability for losses at sea between the owners of the vessel and of the cargo.

**avermectin** /ˌeɪvəˈmɛktɪn/ ● n. Medicine any of a group of macrocyclic anthelmintic compounds isolated from a strain of bacteria.
– ORIGIN 1970s: from mod. L. (*Streptomyces*) *averm(itilis)*, the name of the source bacterium, + *ect-* + **-IN**[1].

**averment** /əˈvəːm(ə)nt/ ● n. formal an affirmation or allegation. ➤ Law a formal statement including an offer of proof or substantiation.

**averse** ● adj. (usu. **averse to**) strongly disliking or opposed.
– ORIGIN C16: from L. *avers-*, *avertere* (see **AVERT**).

**USAGE** averse

On the confusion of **averse** with **adverse**, see **ADVERSE**.

**aversion** ● n. a strong dislike or disinclination.
– DERIVATIVES **aversive** adj.

**aversion therapy** ● n. a type of behaviour therapy designed to make patients give up a habit by causing them to associate it with an unpleasant effect.

**avert** ● v. **1** turn away (one's eyes or thoughts). **2** prevent or ward off (an undesirable occurrence).
– DERIVATIVES **avertable** adj.

– ORIGIN ME: from L. *avertere*, from *ab-* 'from' + *vertere* 'to turn'; reinforced by OFr. *avertir*.

**Aves** /'eɪviːz, 'ɑːveɪz/ • **pl. n.** Zoology the class of vertebrates which comprises the birds.
– ORIGIN L., pl. of *avis* 'bird'.

**Avesta** /ə'vɛstə/ • **n.** the sacred texts of Zoroastrianism.
– ORIGIN from Pers.

**Avestan** /ə'vɛst(ə)n/ • **adj.** relating to the Avesta. • **n.** the ancient Iranian language in which the Avesta is written.

**avgas** /'avgas/ • **n.** aircraft fuel.

**avian** /'eɪvɪən/ • **adj.** relating to birds. • **n.** a bird.
– ORIGIN C19: from L. *avis* 'bird' + **-AN**.

**aviary** /'eɪvɪəri/ • **n.** (pl. **-ies**) a large enclosure for keeping birds in.
– ORIGIN C16: from L. *aviarium*, from *avis* 'bird'.

**aviation** • **n.** the activity or business of operating and flying aircraft.
– DERIVATIVES **aviate** v.
– ORIGIN C19: from Fr., formed from L. *avis* 'bird'.

**aviator** • **n.** (fem. **aviatrix** /ˌeɪvɪ'eɪtrɪks/, pl. **-trices** /-trɪsiːz/) dated a pilot.

**aviculture** /'eɪvɪˌkʌltʃə/ • **n.** the breeding and rearing of birds.
– DERIVATIVES **avicultural** adj. **aviculturalist** n. **aviculturist** n.
– ORIGIN C19: from L. *avis* 'bird' + **CULTURE**.

**avid** /'avɪd/ • **adj.** keenly interested or enthusiastic.
– DERIVATIVES **avidly** adv.
– ORIGIN C18 (earlier (ME) as *avidity*): from Fr. *avide* or L. *avidus*, from *avere* 'crave'.

**avidin** /'avɪdɪn/ • **n.** Biochemistry a protein found in raw egg white, which combines with biotin and hinders its absorption.
– ORIGIN 1940s: from **AVID** + **-IN**[1].

**avidity** • **n. 1** keen interest or enthusiasm. **2** Biochemistry the overall strength of binding between an antibody and an antigen.

**avifauna** /'eɪvɪfɔːnə/ • **n.** Zoology the birds of a particular region, habitat, or geological period.
– DERIVATIVES **avifaunal** adj.
– ORIGIN C19: from L. *avis* 'bird' + **FAUNA**.

**avionics** /ˌeɪvɪ'ɒnɪks/ • **pl. n.** [usu. treated as sing.] electronics or electronic equipment as applied to aviation.

**avirulent** /eɪ'vɪrjʊl(ə)nt, a-/ • **adj.** (of a micro-organism) not virulent.

**avitaminosis** /eɪˌvɪtəmɪ'nəʊsɪs, -ˌvʌɪt-/ • **n.** (pl. **avitaminoses** /-siːz/) Medicine a condition resulting from a deficiency of a particular vitamin.

**avizandum** /ˌavɪ'zandəm/ • **n.** Scots Law time taken for further consideration of a judgement.
– ORIGIN C17: from med. L. *avizare* 'consider, advise'.

**avo** /'ɑːvəʊ/ • **n.** (pl. **-os**) a monetary unit of Macao, equal to one hundredth of a pataca.
– ORIGIN from Port.

**avocado** /ˌavə'kɑːdəʊ/ • **n.** (pl. **-os**) **1** a pear-shaped fruit with a rough leathery skin, smooth oily edible flesh, and a large stone. **2** the tropical evergreen tree which bears this fruit. [*Persea americana*.] **3** a light green colour like that of an avocado's flesh.
– ORIGIN C17: from Sp., alt. of *aguacate*, from Nahuatl *ahuacatl*.

**avocation** /ˌavə'keɪʃ(ə)n/ • **n.** a hobby or minor occupation.
– DERIVATIVES **avocational** adj.
– ORIGIN C17: from L. *avocatio(n-)*, from *avocare* 'call away'.

**avocet** /'avəsɛt/ • **n.** a long-legged wading bird, largely black and white, with a slender upturned bill. [Genus *Recurvirostra*: four species.]
– ORIGIN C17: from Fr. *avocette*, from Ital. *avosetta*.

**Avogadro's constant** (also **Avogadro's number**) • **n.** Chemistry the number of atoms or molecules in one mole of a substance, equal to $6.023 \times 10^{23}$.
– ORIGIN named after the Ital. physicist A. *Avogadro* (1776–1856).

**Avogadro's law** (also **Avogadro's hypothesis**) • **n.** Chemistry a law stating that equal volumes of gases at the same temperature and pressure contain equal numbers of molecules.

**avoid** • **v. 1** keep away or refrain from. ➤prevent from doing or happening. **2** Law repudiate, nullify, or render void (a decree or contract).
– DERIVATIVES **avoidable** adj. **avoidably** adv. **avoidance** n. **avoider** n.
– ORIGIN ME: from OFr. *evuider* 'clear out, get rid of', from *vuide* (see **VOID**).

**avoirdupois** /ˌavwɑːdjʊ'pwɑː, ˌavədə'pɔɪz/ • **n.** a system of weights based on a pound of 16 ounces or 7,000 grains. Compare with **TROY**.
– ORIGIN ME: from OFr. *aveir de peis* 'goods of weight', from *aveir* 'to have' (from L. *habere*) + *peis* (see **POISE**[1]).

**avouch** • **v.** archaic affirm or assert.
– DERIVATIVES **avouchment** n.
– ORIGIN C15: from OFr. *avochier*, from L. *advocare* 'summon in defence'.

**avow** • **v.** assert or confess openly.
– DERIVATIVES **avowal** n. **avowed** adj. **avowedly** adv.
– ORIGIN ME: from OFr. *avouer* 'acknowledge', from L. *advocare* (see **AVOUCH**).

**avulsion** /ə'vʌlʃ(ə)n/ • **n. 1** chiefly Medicine the action of pulling or tearing away. **2** Law the sudden separation of land from one property and its attachment to another, especially by flooding. Compare with **ALLUVION**.
– DERIVATIVES **avulse** v.
– ORIGIN C17: from L. *avulsio(n-)*, from *avellere* 'pluck from'.

**avuncular** /ə'vʌŋkjʊlə/ • **adj.** like an uncle in being kind and friendly towards a younger or less experienced person.
– ORIGIN C19: from L. *avunculus* 'maternal uncle'.

**avunculate** /ə'vʌŋkjʊlət/ • **n.** (**the avunculate**) Anthropology the special relationship in some societies between a man and his sister's son.
– ORIGIN C20: from L. *avunculus* 'maternal uncle' + **-ATE**[2].

**aw** • **exclam.** chiefly N. Amer. & Scottish used to express mild protest, entreaty, commiseration, or disapproval.

**AWACS** /'eɪwaks/ • **abbrev.** airborne warning and control system.

**await** • **v.** wait for.
– ORIGIN ME: from Anglo-Norman Fr. *awaitier*, from *a-* (from L. *ad* 'to, at') + *waitier* 'to wait'.

**awake** • **v.** (past **awoke**; past part. **awoken**) **1** stop sleeping. **2** make or become active again. • **adj. 1** not asleep. **2** (**awake to**) aware of.
– ORIGIN OE *āwæcnan*, *āwacian* (see **A-**[2], **WAKE**[1]).

**awaken** • **v. 1** stop or cause to stop sleeping. **2** rouse (a feeling).
– DERIVATIVES **awakening** n. & adj.
– ORIGIN OE *onwæcnan*, from *on* 'on' + **WAKEN**.

**award** • **v.** give or grant officially as a prize or reward. • **n.** something awarded.
– DERIVATIVES **awardee** n. **awarder** n.
– ORIGIN ME: from Anglo-Norman Fr. *awarder*, var. of OFr. *esguarder* 'consider, ordain', from *es-* (from L. *ex* 'thoroughly') + *guarder* 'watch (over)', of Gmc origin.

**aware** • **adj.** having knowledge or perception of a situation or fact.
– DERIVATIVES **awareness** n.
– ORIGIN OE *gewær*, of W. Gmc origin.

**awash** • **adj.** covered or flooded with water.

**away** • **adv. 1** to or at a distance. ➤at a specified future distance in time. **2** towards a lower level. **3** into an appropriate place for storage or safe keeping. **4** towards or into non-existence. **5** constantly, persistently, or continuously. **6** (of a sports fixture) at the opponents' ground. • **adj.** (of a sports fixture) played at the opponents' ground. • **n.** an away game.
– ORIGIN OE *onweg*, *aweg* 'on one's way' (see **A-**[2], **WAY**).

**awe** • **n.** a feeling of reverential respect mixed with fear or wonder. • **v.** inspire with awe.
– ORIGIN OE *ege* 'terror, dread, awe'.

**aweigh** • **adj.** Nautical (of an anchor) raised just clear of the seabed.

**awesome** • **adj. 1** inspiring awe. **2** informal excellent.

– DERIVATIVES **awesomely** adv. **awesomeness** n.

**awestruck** ● **adj.** filled with awe.

**awful** ● **adj. 1** very bad or unpleasant. **2** used for emphasis: *an awful lot of letters.* **3** archaic inspiring awe.
– DERIVATIVES **awfulness** n.

**awfully** ● **adv. 1** informal very or very much: *I'm awfully sorry.* **2** very badly or unpleasantly.

**awhile** ● **adv.** for a short time.

**awkward** ● **adj. 1** hard to do or deal with. **2** uneasily embarrassed. **3** not smooth or graceful.
– DERIVATIVES **awkwardly** adv. **awkwardness** n.
– ORIGIN ME (in the sense 'the wrong way round, upside down'): from dial. *awk* (from ON *afugr*) + **-WARD**.

**awl** /ɔːl/ ● **n.** a small pointed tool used for piercing holes.
– ORIGIN OE *æl*, of Gmc origin.

**awn** /ɔːn/ ● **n.** Botany a stiff bristle growing from the ear or flower of barley, rye, and grasses.
– DERIVATIVES **awned** adj.
– ORIGIN OE, from ON *ǫgn*.

**awning** ● **n.** a sheet of canvas or similar material stretched on a frame and used to shelter a shop window or doorway.
– ORIGIN C17 (orig. in naut. use): of unknown origin.

**awoke** past of **AWAKE**.

**awoken** past participle of **AWAKE**.

**AWOL** /ˈeɪwɒl/ ● **adj.** Military absent but without intent to desert.
– ORIGIN 1920s: acronym from *absent without* (*official*) *leave.*

**awry** /əˈrʌɪ/ ● **adv. & adj.** away from the appropriate or expected course or position.
– ORIGIN ME: from **A-**[2] + **WRY**.

**AWS** ● **abbrev.** Brit. automatic warning system (used on trains).

**axe** (US also **ax**) ● **n. 1** a heavy-bladed tool used for chopping wood. **2** (**the axe**) cost-cutting action, especially redundancy: *thirty staff are facing the axe.* **3** informal a guitar or (in jazz) a saxophone. ● **v. 1** end, cancel, or dismiss suddenly and ruthlessly. **2** cut or strike with an axe.
– PHRASES **have an axe to grind** have a private reason for doing something.
– ORIGIN OE *æx*, of Gmc origin.

**axe kick** ● **n.** a type of kick used in martial arts, in which the opponent's head is struck with the heel of the foot.

**axel** /ˈaks(ə)l/ ● **n.** a jump in skating with one (or more) and a half turns in the air.
– ORIGIN 1930s: named after the Norw. skater *Axel* R. Paulsen.

**axenic** /eɪˈzɛnɪk/ ● **adj.** Biology (of a culture) free from living organisms other than the species required.
– DERIVATIVES **axenically** adv.
– ORIGIN 1940s: from *a-* 'not' + *xenikos* 'alien, strange' + **-IC**.

**axes** plural form of **AXIS**[1].

**axial** /ˈaksɪəl/ ● **adj.** forming, relating to, or around an axis.
– DERIVATIVES **axially** adv.

**axil** /ˈaksɪl/ ● **n.** Botany the upper angle between a leaf stalk or branch and the stem or trunk from which it is growing.
– ORIGIN C18: from L. *axilla* (see **AXILLA**).

**axilla** /akˈsɪlə/ ● **n.** (pl. **axillae** /-liː/) **1** Anatomy an armpit, or the corresponding part in a bird or other animal. **2** Botany an axil.
– DERIVATIVES **axillary** adj.
– ORIGIN C17: from L., dimin. of *ala* 'wing'.

**axiom** /ˈaksɪəm/ ● **n. 1** an accepted statement or proposition regarded as being self-evidently true. **2** chiefly Mathematics a statement or proposition on which an abstractly defined structure is based.
– DERIVATIVES **axiomatic** adj. **axiomatically** adv.
– ORIGIN C15: from Fr. *axiome* or L. *axioma*, from Gk *axiōma*, from *axios* 'worthy'.

**axiomatize** /ˌaksɪˈɒmətʌɪz/ (also **-ise**) ● **v.** express (a theory) as a set of axioms.

**axion** /ˈaksɪɒn/ ● **n.** Physics a hypothetical subatomic particle postulated to account for the rarity of processes which break charge-parity symmetry.
– ORIGIN 1970s: from **AXIAL** + **-ON**.

**axis**[1] /ˈaksɪs/ ● **n.** (pl. **axes** /-siːz/) **1** an imaginary line about which a body rotates or with respect to which it possesses rotational symmetry. **2** an imaginary line which divides something in half, especially in the direction of its greatest length. **3** Mathematics a fixed reference line for the measurement of coordinates. **4** a straight central part in a structure to which other parts are connected. **5** Anatomy the second cervical vertebra, below the atlas at the top of the backbone. **6** (**the Axis**) the alliance between Germany and Italy in the Second World War.
– ORIGIN ME: from L., 'axle, pivot'.

**axis**[2] /ˈaksɪs/ ● **n.** (pl. same) another term for **CHITAL**.
– ORIGIN C17: from L.

**axisymmetric** /ˌaksɪsɪˈmɛtrɪk/ ● **adj.** Geometry symmetrical about an axis.

**axle** /ˈaks(ə)l/ ● **n.** a rod or spindle passing through the centre of a wheel or group of wheels.
– ORIGIN ME (orig. *axle-tree*): from ON *ǫxultré.*

**Axminster** /ˈaksmɪnstə/ ● **n.** a kind of machine-woven patterned carpet with a cut pile.
– ORIGIN C19: named after the town of *Axminster* in southern England, where such carpets are made.

**axolotl** /ˈaksəlɒt(ə)l/ ● **n.** a Mexican salamander which retains its aquatic newt-like larval form throughout life but is able to breed. [*Ambystoma mexicanum.*]
– ORIGIN C18: from Nahuatl, from *atl* 'water' + *xolotl* 'servant'.

**axon** /ˈaksɒn/ ● **n.** the long thread-like part of a nerve cell along which impulses are conducted from the cell body to other cells. Compare with **DENDRITE**.
– DERIVATIVES **axonal** adj.
– ORIGIN C19: from Gk *axōn* 'axis'.

**axoneme** /ˈaksə(ʊ)niːm/ ● **n.** Biology the central strand of a cilium or flagellum, consisting of an array of microtubules.
– DERIVATIVES **axonemal** adj.
– ORIGIN C20: from Gk *axōn* 'axis' + *nēma* 'thread'.

**axonometric** /ˌaks(ə)nə(ʊ)ˈmɛtrɪk/ ● **adj.** (of a pictorial representation) three-dimensional but without perspective.

**axoplasm** /ˈaksə(ʊ)plaz(ə)m/ ● **n.** Biology the cytoplasm of a nerve axon.
– DERIVATIVES **axoplasmic** adj.

**ay** ● **exclam. & n.** variant spelling of **AYE**[1].

**ayah** /ˈʌɪə/ ● **n.** a nanny employed by Europeans in India or another former British territory.
– ORIGIN Anglo-Ind., from Port. *aia* 'nurse', fem. of *aio* 'tutor'.

**ayahuasca** /ˌʌɪəˈwaskə/ ● **n. 1** a tropical vine of the Amazon region, noted for its hallucinogenic properties. [Genus *Banisteriopsis.*] **2** a hallucinogenic drink prepared from the bark of this.
– ORIGIN 1940s: from Latin Amer. Sp., from Quechua *ayawáskha*, from *aya* 'corpse' + *waskha* 'rope'.

**ayatollah** /ˌʌɪəˈtɒlə/ ● **n.** a high-ranking Shiite religious leader in Iran.
– ORIGIN 1950s: from Pers., from Arab. *'āyatu-llāh*, lit. 'token of God'.

**aye**[1] /ʌɪ/ (also **ay**) ● **exclam.** archaic or dialect yes. ➤(**aye aye**) Nautical a response accepting an order. ➤(in voting) I assent. ● **n.** an affirmative answer, especially in voting.
– ORIGIN C16: prob. from *I*, first person personal pronoun, expressing assent.

**aye**[2] /eɪ, ʌɪ/ ● **adv.** archaic or Scottish always; still.
– PHRASES **for aye** forever.
– ORIGIN ME: from ON *ei, ey.*

**aye-aye** /ˈʌɪʌɪ/ ● **n.** a rare nocturnal Madagascan primate related to the lemurs. [*Daubentonia madagascariensis.*]
– ORIGIN C18: from Fr., from Malagasy *aiay.*

**Aylesbury** /ˈeɪlzb(ə)ri/ ● **n.** (pl. **Aylesburys**) a domestic duck of a breed with white plumage.
– ORIGIN named after the town of *Aylesbury* in south central England, where the ducks were bred.

**Aymara** /'ʌɪmərɑː/ ● **n.** (pl. same or **Aymaras**) **1** a member of an American Indian people inhabiting the high plateau region of Bolivia and Peru near Lake Titicaca. **2** the language of this people, perhaps related to Quechua.
– ORIGIN from Bolivian Sp.

**Ayrshire** /'ɛːʃə/ ● **n.** an animal of a mainly white breed of dairy cattle.
– ORIGIN named after the former Sc. county of *Ayrshire*, where the cattle were bred.

**Ayurveda** /ˌɑːjʊə'veɪdə, -'viːdə/ ● **n.** the traditional Hindu system of medicine, which is based on the idea of balance in bodily systems and uses diet, herbal treatment, and yogic breathing.
– DERIVATIVES **Ayurvedic** adj.
– ORIGIN from Sanskrit *āyus* 'life' + *veda* '(sacred) knowledge'.

**AZ** ● **abbrev.** Arizona (in official postal use).

**azalea** /ə'zeɪlɪə/ ● **n.** a deciduous flowering shrub with clusters of brightly coloured flowers, related to rhododendrons but generally smaller. [Genus *Rhododendron*: many species.]
– ORIGIN C18: mod. L. (former genus name), from Gk, fem. of *azaleos* 'dry' (because the shrubs flourish in dry soil).

**azan** /ə'zɑːn/ ● **n.** the Muslim call to prayer made by a muezzin from the minaret of a mosque.
– ORIGIN C19: from Arab. *'aḏān* 'announcement'.

**Azande** /a'zandi/ ● **n. & adj.** see **ZANDE**.

**azarole** /'azərəʊl/ ● **n. 1** an edible Mediterranean fruit. **2** the small hawthorn-like tree bearing this fruit. [*Crataegus azarolus*.]
– ORIGIN C17: from Fr. *azerole*, from Sp. *azarolla*.

**azeotrope** /'eɪzɪətrəʊp, ə'ziːə-/ ● **n.** Chemistry a mixture of two liquids which has a constant boiling point and composition throughout distillation.
– DERIVATIVES **azeotropic** /-'trəʊpɪk, -'trɒpɪk/ adj.
– ORIGIN C20: from **A-**[1] + Gk *zein* 'to boil' + *tropos* 'turning'.

**Azerbaijani** ● **n.** (pl. **Azerbaijanis**) **1** a native or national of Azerbaijan or a person of Azerbaijani descent. **2** the Turkic language of Azerbaijan and adjacent regions. ● **adj.** of or relating to Azerbaijan or its people or their language.

**Azeri** /ə'zɛːri/ ● **n.** (pl. **Azeris**) **1** a member of a Turkic people forming the majority population of Azerbaijan, and also living in Armenia and northern Iran. **2** the Azerbaijani language. ● **adj.** relating to or denoting this people or their language.
– ORIGIN from Turk. *azerî*.

**azide** /'eɪzʌɪd/ ● **n.** Chemistry a compound containing the anion $N_3^-$ or the group $-N_3$.

**azidothymidine** /ˌeɪzɪdəʊ'θʌɪmɪdiːn, eɪˌzʌɪdəʊ-/ ● **n.** trademark for the drug **ZIDOVUDINE**.

**Azilian** /ə'zɪlɪən/ ● **adj.** Archaeology relating to or denoting an early Mesolithic culture in Europe, succeeding the Magdalenian and dated to about 11,500–9,500 years ago.
– ORIGIN C19: named after *Mas d'Azil* in the Fr. Pyrenees, where objects from this culture were found.

**azimuth** /'azɪməθ/ ● **n. 1** Astronomy the horizontal component of the direction of a celestial object from the observer, expressed as an angular distance from the north or south point of the horizon. **2** the horizontal angle or direction of a compass bearing.
– DERIVATIVES **azimuthal** /-'mjuːθ(ə)l/ adj.
– ORIGIN ME: from OFr. *azimut*, from Arab. *as-samt*, from *al* 'the' + *samt* 'way, direction'.

**azimuthal projection** /ˌazɪ'mjuːθ(ə)l/ ● **n.** a map projection in which a region of the earth is projected on to a plane tangential to the surface, usually at a pole or the equator.

**azine** /'eɪziːn/ ● **n.** Chemistry a cyclic organic compound having a ring including one or (usually) more nitrogen atoms.

**azo-** /'eɪzəʊ/ ● **prefix** Chemistry containing two adjacent nitrogen atoms between carbon atoms: *azobenzene*.
– ORIGIN from obs. *azote* 'nitrogen', from Fr., from Gk *a-* 'without' + *zōē* 'life'.

**azobenzene** /ˌeɪzəʊ'bɛnziːn/ ● **n.** Chemistry a synthetic crystalline organic compound used chiefly in dye manufacture.

**azo dye** ● **n.** Chemistry any of a large class of synthetic dyes whose molecules contain two adjacent nitrogen atoms between carbon atoms.

**azoic** /eɪ'zəʊɪk/ ● **adj.** Geology having no trace of life or organic remains.
– ORIGIN C19: from Gk *azōos* 'without life' + **-IC**.

**azonal** /eɪ'zəʊn(ə)l/ ● **adj.** (especially of soils) having no zonal organization or structure.

**azoospermia** /ˌeɪzəʊə'spəːmɪə, ə'zəʊ-/ ● **n.** Medicine absence of viable motile sperm in the semen.
– DERIVATIVES **azoospermic** adj.

**azoturia** /ˌazə(ʊ)'tjʊərɪə/ ● **n.** Medicine abnormal excess of nitrogen compounds in the urine.
– ORIGIN C19: from obs. *azote* 'nitrogen' + **-URIA**.

**AZT** ● **abbrev.** trademark azidothymidine.

**Aztec** /'aztɛk/ ● **n. 1** a member of the American Indian people dominant in Mexico before the Spanish conquest of the 16th century. **2** the extinct Uto-Aztecan language of this people, from which modern Nahuatl is descended.
– ORIGIN from Fr. *Aztèque* or Sp. *Azteca*, from Nahuatl *aztecatl* 'person of Aztlan', their legendary place of origin.

**azulejo** /ˌazjʊ'leɪhəʊ/ ● **n.** (pl. **azulejos**) a kind of glazed coloured tile traditionally used in Spanish and Portuguese buildings.
– ORIGIN from Sp., from *azul* 'blue'.

**azure** /'aʒə, -ʒj(ʊ)ə, 'eɪ-/ ● **adj.** bright blue in colour like a cloudless sky. ➤ Heraldry blue. ● **n.** a bright blue colour.
– ORIGIN ME: from OFr. *asur, azur*, from med. L. *azzurum, azolum*, from Arab. *al* 'the' + *lāzaward* (from Pers. *lāžward* 'lapis lazuli').

**azurite** /'aʒʊrʌɪt, -ʒj(ʊ)ə-/ ● **n.** a blue mineral consisting of basic copper carbonate.

**azygous** /'azɪgəs/ ● **adj.** Anatomy & Biology (of an organic structure) not existing in pairs; single.
– ORIGIN C19: from Gk *azugos*, from *a-* 'without' + *zugon* 'yoke', + **-OUS**.

# B b

**B**[1] (also **b**) ● **n.** (pl. **Bs** or **B's**) **1** the second letter of the alphabet. **2** denoting the second, second-best, or secondary item in a set. **3** Music the seventh note of the diatonic scale of C major. **4** the human blood type (in the ABO system) containing the B antigen and lacking the A.

**B**[2] ● **abbrev. 1** Belgium (international vehicle registration). **2** (in chess) bishop. **3** black (used in describing grades of pencil lead). **4** bomber (in designations of US aircraft types). ● **symb. 1** the chemical element boron. **2** Physics magnetic flux density.

**b** ● **abbrev. 1** Physics barn(s). **2** (**b.**) born. **3** Cricket bowled by. **4** Cricket bye(s).

**BA** ● **abbrev. 1** Bachelor of Arts. **2** British Airways. **3** British Association (for the Advancement of Science). **4** Buenos Aires.

**Ba** ● **symb.** the chemical element barium.

**ba** /bɑː/ ● **n.** (in ancient Egypt) the supposed soul of a person or god, which survived after death but had to be sustained with offerings of food. See also **KA**.

**baa** ● **v.** (**baas**, **baaed**, **baaing**) (of a sheep or lamb) bleat. ● **n.** the cry of a sheep or lamb.
– ORIGIN C16: imitative.

**baap** /bɑːp/ ● **n.** Indian a father.
– ORIGIN from Hindi *bāp*.

**baas** /bɑːs/ ● **n.** S. African offensive a supervisor or employer, especially a white man in charge of coloureds or blacks.
– ORIGIN Du., 'master'; cf. **BOSS**[1].

**baasie** /'bɑːsi/ ● **n.** S. African offensive a form of address to a young white male.
– ORIGIN Afrik. (from earlier Du. *baasje*), lit. 'little master'.

**Baathist** /bɑːθɪst/ (also **Ba'athist**) ● **n.** a member or supporter of the Baath Party, a pan-Arab socialist party founded in Syria in 1943. ● **adj.** of or relating to the Baath Party.
– DERIVATIVES **Baathism** n.
– ORIGIN from *Baath*, from Arab. *ba'ṯ* 'resurrection, renaissance', + **-IST**.

**baba**[1] /'bɑːbɑː/ (also **rum baba**) ● **n.** a small rich sponge cake, soaked in rum-flavoured syrup.
– ORIGIN via Fr. from Polish, lit. 'married peasant woman'.

**baba**[2] /'bɑːbɑː/ ● **n.** Indian informal **1** father or holy man. **2** a child, especially a male one.
– ORIGIN from Hindi *bābā*.

**baba ganoush** /ˌbɑːbə ga'nuːʃ/ (also **baba ghanouj** /ga'nuːʒ/) ● **n.** a thick dip made from puréed aubergines, tahini, lemon, and garlic, typical of eastern Mediterranean cuisine.
– ORIGIN from Egyptian Arab., from Arab. *bābā*, lit. 'father' + *ghannūj*, perh. a personal name.

**Babbitt** /'babɪt/ ● **n.** dated, chiefly N. Amer. a materialistic, complacent, and conformist businessman.
– DERIVATIVES **Babbittry** n.
– ORIGIN 1922: from the name George *Babbitt*, the protagonist of the novel *Babbitt* by Sinclair Lewis.

**babbitt metal** ● **n.** a soft alloy of tin, antimony, copper, and usually lead, used to line bearings.
– ORIGIN C19: named after Isaac *Babbitt*, the Amer. inventor of the lining.

**babble** ● **v. 1** talk rapidly and continuously in a foolish, excited, or incomprehensible way. ➤ reveal something secret. **2** [usu. as adj. **babbling**] (of a stream) make a continuous murmur as the water flows over stones. ● **n.** the sound of babbling. ➤ foolish, excited, or confused talk.
– DERIVATIVES **babblement** n.
– ORIGIN ME: from Mid. Low Ger. *babbelen*, or an independent Engl. formation, based on the repeated syllable *ba*, typical of a child's early speech.

**babbler** ● **n. 1** a person who babbles. **2** a thrush-like songbird with a long tail, short rounded wings, and a loud voice. [Family Timaliidae: many species.]

**babby** ● **n.** (pl. **-ies**) dialect form of **BABY**.

**babe** ● **n. 1** poetic/literary a baby. **2** informal a sexually attractive young woman.
– ORIGIN ME: prob. imitative of an infant's first attempts at speech.

**babel** /'beɪb(ə)l/ ● **n.** a confused noise made by a number of voices.
– ORIGIN C16: from the Tower of *Babel*, where, according to the biblical story, God confused the languages of the builders.

**babesiosis** /bəˌbiːzɪ'əʊsɪs/ (also **babesiasis** /ˌbɑːbɪ'zʌɪəsɪs/) ● **n.** a protozoal disease of livestock transmitted by tick bites, affecting the red blood cells and causing red or blackish urine.
– ORIGIN C20: from mod. L. *Babesia* (a genus of protozoans), from the name of the Romanian bacteriologist Victor *Babès*.

**babiche** /bə'biːʃ/ ● **n.** strips of rawhide, used by North American Indians for making fastenings, snares, etc.
– ORIGIN C19: from Canad. Fr., from Micmac *a:papi:č*.

**babirusa** /ˌbɑːbɪ'ruːsə/ ● **n.** a forest-dwelling wild pig with several upturned horn-like tusks, native to Malaysia. [*Babyrousa babyrussa*.]
– ORIGIN C17: from Malay, from *babi* 'hog' + *rusa* 'deer'.

**Babism** /'bɑːbɪz(ə)m/ ● **n.** a religion founded in 1844 by the Persian Mirza Ali Muhammad, who taught that a new prophet would follow Muhammad. See also **BAHA'I**.
– DERIVATIVES **Babi** n.
– ORIGIN C19: via Pers. from Arab. *bāb* 'intermediary', lit. 'gate' (taken as a name by the founder) + **-ISM**.

**baboon** ● **n.** a large ground-dwelling social monkey with a long doglike snout and large teeth. [Genera *Papio* and *Mandrillus*: several species.]
– ORIGIN ME (denoting a grotesque figure used in architecture): from OFr. *babuin* or med. L. *babewynus*, perh. from OFr. *baboue* 'muzzle, grimace'.

**babu** /'bɑːbuː/ ● **n.** (pl. **babus**) Indian **1** a respectful title or form of address for a man. **2** an office worker.
– ORIGIN from Hindi *bābū*, lit. 'father'.

**babul** /bə'buːl/ ● **n.** (in the Indian subcontinent) a tropical acacia introduced from Africa, used as a source of fuel and gum arabic. [*Acacia nilotica*.]
– ORIGIN C19: from Hindi *babūl*.

**babushka** /bə'bʊʃkə, 'babʊʃkə/ ● **n. 1** (in Russia) an old woman or grandmother. **2** N. Amer. a headscarf tied under the chin.
– ORIGIN Russ., 'grandmother'.

**baby** ● **n.** (pl. **-ies**) **1** a child or animal that is newly or recently born. **2** a timid or childish person. **3** informal a person with whom one is having a romantic relationship (often as a form of address). ● **adj.** comparatively small or immature of its kind. ● **v.** (**-ies**, **-ied**) pamper or be overprotective towards.
– DERIVATIVES **babyhood** n.
– PHRASES **throw the baby out with the bathwater** discard something valuable along with other things that are undesirable.
– ORIGIN ME: prob. imitative of an infant's first attempts at speech.

**baby blue** ● **n. 1** a pale shade of blue. **2** (**baby blues**) informal blue eyes.

**baby boom** ● **n.** informal a temporary marked increase in the birth rate, especially the one following the Second World War.
– DERIVATIVES **baby boomer** n.

**baby bouncer** ● **n.** Brit. a harness suspended by elastic or a spring, into which a baby is put, with its feet within reach of the floor, to exercise its legs.

**baby buggy** ● **n.** trademark, chiefly Brit. a light collapsible pushchair.

**baby bust** ● **n.** N. Amer. informal a temporary marked decrease in the birth rate.
– DERIVATIVES **baby buster** n.

**baby carriage** ● **n.** N. Amer. a pram.

**baby doll** ● **n.** a girl or woman with pretty, childlike looks. ● **adj.** denoting a style of women's clothing resembling that traditionally worn by a doll or young child.

**baby grand** ● **n.** the smallest size of grand piano.

**Babygro** ● **n.** (pl. **-os**) trademark an all-in-one stretch garment for babies.

**babyish** ● **adj.** childish; immature.
– DERIVATIVES **babyishly** adv. **babyishness** n.

**Babylon** /ˈbabɪlɒn/ ● **n.** black English, derogatory (chiefly among Rastafarians) aspects of white culture seen as degenerate or oppressive, especially the police.
– ORIGIN 1940s: by assoc. with the ancient city of *Babylon* (see **BABYLONIAN**).

**Babylonian** /ˌbabɪˈləʊnɪən/ ● **n. 1** an inhabitant of Babylon or Babylonia, an ancient city and kingdom in Mesopotamia. **2** the dialect of Akkadian spoken in ancient Babylon. ● **adj.** of or relating to Babylon or Babylonia.

**baby's breath** ● **n.** a herbaceous plant of delicate appearance which bears tiny scented pink or white flowers. [*Gypsophila paniculata*.]

**babysit** ● **v.** (**-sitting**; past and past part. **-sat**) look after a child or children while the parents are out.
– DERIVATIVES **babysitter** n.

**baby walker** ● **n.** another term for **WALKER** (sense 2).

**bacalao** /ˌbakəˈlaʊ/ ● **n.** dried or salted codfish, as used in Spanish and Latin American cookery.
– ORIGIN from Sp.

**baccalaureate** /ˌbakəˈlɔːrɪət/ ● **n. 1** an examination qualifying successful candidates for higher education. See also **INTERNATIONAL BACCALAUREATE**. **2** a university bachelor's degree.
– ORIGIN C17: from Fr. *baccalauréat* or med. L. *baccalaureatus*, from *baccalaureus* 'bachelor'.

**baccarat** /ˈbakərɑː/ ● **n.** a gambling card game in which players hold two- or three-card hands, the winning hand being that giving the highest remainder when its face value is divided by ten.
– ORIGIN C19: from Fr. *baccara*, of unknown origin.

**bacchanal** /ˈbakən(ə)l, -nal/ chiefly poetic/literary ● **n. 1** an occasion of wild and drunken revelry. **2** a priest, worshipper, or follower of Bacchus, the Greek or Roman god of wine. ● **adj.** bacchanalian.
– ORIGIN C16: from L. *bacchanalis*, from the name of the god *Bacchus*.

**Bacchanalia** /ˌbakəˈneɪlɪə/ ● **pl. n.** [also treated as sing.] **1** the Roman festival of Bacchus. **2** (**bacchanalia**) drunken revelry.
– DERIVATIVES **bacchanalian** adj.
– ORIGIN C16: from L. *bacchanalia*, neut. pl. of the adj. *bacchanalis* (see **BACCHANAL**).

**bacchant** /ˈbakənt/ ● **n.** (pl. **bacchants** or **bacchantes** /bəˈkantiːz/; fem. **bacchante** /bəˈkant, bəˈkanti/) a priest, priestess, or follower of Bacchus.
– ORIGIN C16: from Fr. *bacchante*, from L. *bacchari* 'celebrate the feast of Bacchus'.

**baccy** ● **n.** Brit. informal term for **TOBACCO**.

**bachelor** ● **n. 1** a man who is not and has never been married. **2** Zoology a male bird or mammal prevented from breeding by a dominant male. **3** a person who holds a first degree from a university or other academic institution (only in titles or set expressions). **4** historical a young knight serving under another's banner.
– DERIVATIVES **bachelorhood** n.
– ORIGIN ME: from OFr. *bacheler* 'a young man aspiring to knighthood'.

**bachelorette** ● **n.** N. Amer. a young unmarried woman.

**bachelorette party** ● **n.** N. Amer. a women-only party given for a woman who is about to get married.

**bachelor girl** ● **n.** an independent, unmarried young woman.

**bachelor party** ● **n.** N. Amer. a men-only party given for a man who is about to get married.

**bachelor's buttons** ● **pl. n.** [treated as sing. or pl.] an ornamental plant with small, button-like, double flowers. [*Achillea ptarmica* (daisy family) and *Ranunculus acris* (buttercup family).]

**Bach flower remedies** /batʃ/ ● **pl. n.** preparations of the flowers of various plants used in a system of complementary medicine intended to relieve ill health by influencing underlying emotional states.
– ORIGIN 1970s: named after the Brit. physician Edward *Bach*.

**bacilliform** /bəˈsɪlɪfɔːm/ ● **adj.** chiefly Biology rod-shaped.

**bacillus** /bəˈsɪləs/ ● **n.** (pl. **bacilli** /-lʌɪ, -liː/) a rod-shaped bacterium.
– DERIVATIVES **bacillary** adj.
– ORIGIN C19: from late L. (genus name), dimin. of L. *baculus* 'stick'.

**back** ● **n. 1** the rear surface of the human body from the shoulders to the hips. ➤ the corresponding upper surface of an animal's body. ➤ the part of a chair against which the sitter's back rests. **2** the side or part of something away from the spectator or from the direction in which it moves or faces. ➤ the side or part of an object opposed to the one that is normally seen or used. **3** a player in a team game who plays in a defensive position behind the forwards. **4** the main structure of a ship's hull or an aircraft's fuselage. ● **adv. 1** in the opposite direction from the one that one is facing or travelling towards. ➤ at a distance away. ➤ (also **back of**) N. Amer. behind. **2** so as to return to an earlier or normal position or condition. **3** in or into the past. **4** in return. ● **v. 1** give material or moral support to. ➤ bet money on (a person or animal) winning a race or contest. **2** cover the back of for support, protection, or decoration. **3** (especially in popular music) provide musical accompaniment to (a singer or musician). **4** walk or drive backwards. ➤ (of the wind) change direction anticlockwise around the points of the compass. The opposite of **VEER**[1]. ➤ Sailing put (a sail) aback in order to slow down or assist in turning through the wind. **5** (**back on/on to**) (of a building or other structure) have its back facing or adjacent to. ➤ lie behind. ● **adj. 1** of or at the back. **2** in a remote or subsidiary position. **3** from or relating to the past. **4** directed towards the rear or in a reversed course. **5** Phonetics (of a sound) articulated at the back of the mouth.
– PHRASES **at someone's back** in pursuit or support of someone. **back and forth** to and fro. **the back of beyond** a very remote or inaccessible place. **back to front** Brit. with the back at the front and the front at the back. **back water** reverse the action of the oars to slow down or stop a boat. **behind someone's back** without a person's knowledge and in an unfair way. **get** (or **put**) **someone's back up** annoy or anger someone. **put one's back into** approach (a task) with vigour. **turn one's back on** ignore; reject. **with one's back to** (or **up against**) **the wall** in a desperate situation.
– PHRASAL VERBS **back down** concede defeat. **back off** draw back from action or confrontation. **back out** withdraw from a commitment. **back up 1** Computing make a spare copy of (data or a disk). **2** (of vehicles) form into a queue due to congestion.
– DERIVATIVES **backer** n. **backless** adj.
– ORIGIN OE *bæc*, of Gmc origin.

**backache** ● **n.** prolonged pain in one's back.

**backbeat** ● **n.** Music a strong accent on one of the normally unaccented beats of the bar, used especially in jazz and popular music.

**back bench** ● **n.** (in the UK) any of the benches behind the front benches on either side of the House of Commons, occupied by members of parliament who do not

hold office.
– DERIVATIVES **back-bencher** n.

**backbiting** • n. malicious talk about an absent person.
– DERIVATIVES **backbiter** n.

**backblocks** • pl. n. Austral./NZ land in the remote and sparsely inhabited interior.

**backboard** • n. **1** a board used to support or straighten a person's back, especially after an accident. **2** Basketball an upright board behind the basket, off which the ball may rebound.

**back boiler** • n. Brit. a boiler supplying hot water, built in behind a fireplace or integral to a gas fire.

**backbone** • n. **1** the spine. **2** the chief support of a system or organization. ➤ strength of character.

**back-breaking** • adj. (especially of manual labour) physically demanding.

**back-burner** • v. US postpone action on.
– PHRASES **on the back burner** having low priority.

**backchannel** • n. **1** a secondary or covert route for the passage of information. **2** Psychology a sound or gesture made to give continuity to a conversation by a person who is listening to another.

**backchat** • n. Brit. informal rude or impudent remarks.

**backcloth** • n. Brit. another term for **BACKDROP**.

**backcomb** • v. chiefly Brit. comb (the hair) from the ends of the strands towards the scalp to make it look thicker.

**backcountry** • n. chiefly N. Amer. sparsely inhabited rural areas.

**backcourt** • n. **1** (in tennis, basketball, and other games) the part of each side of the court nearest the back wall or back boundary line. **2** the defensive players in a basketball team.

**backcross** Genetics • v. cross (a hybrid) with one of its parents or an organism with the same genetic characteristics as one of the parents. • n. an instance of or the result of this.

**backdate** • v. Brit. make (something, especially a pay increase) retrospectively valid. ➤ put an earlier date to (a document or agreement) than the actual one.

**back door** • adj. underhand; clandestine.
– PHRASES **by** (or **through**) **the back door** in a clandestine or underhand way.

**backdraught** (US **backdraft**) • n. **1** a current of air or water that flows backwards down a chimney, pipe, etc. **2** a phenomenon in which a fire that has consumed all available oxygen suddenly explodes when more oxygen is made available.
– DERIVATIVES **backdraughting** n.

**backdrop** • n. **1** a painted cloth hung at the back of a theatre stage as part of the scenery. **2** the setting or background for a scene or event.

**back-end** • adj. **1** relating to the end of a project, process, or investment. **2** Computing denoting a specialized subordinate processor or program, not directly accessed by the user.

**back-fanged** • adj. Zoology denoting a snake (such as a boomslang) in which the rear pair or pairs of teeth have grooves to conduct the venom. Compare with **FRONT-FANGED**.

**backfield** • n. American Football the area of play behind the line of scrimmage.

**backfill** • v. refill (an excavated hole) with the material dug out of it. • n. material used for backfilling.

**backfire** • v. /bak'fʌɪə/ **1** (of a vehicle or its engine) undergo a mistimed explosion in the cylinder or exhaust. **2** (of a plan or action) rebound adversely on the originator.

**backflip** • n. a backward somersault done in the air with the arms and legs stretched out straight.

**back focus** • n. Photography the distance between the back of a lens and the image of an object at infinity.

**back-formation** • n. a word that is formed from its seeming derivative, typically by removal of a suffix (e.g. *edit* from *editor*).

**backgammon** • n. **1** a board game in which two players move their pieces around twenty-four triangular points according to the throw of dice. **2** the most complete form of win in this game.
– ORIGIN C17: from **BACK** + **GAMMON**[2].

**background** • n. **1** part of a scene, picture, or description that forms a setting for the main figures, events, etc. **2** a persistent low level of radioactivity, radiation, noise, etc. present in a particular environment. **3** explanatory or contributory information or circumstances. ➤ a person's education, experience, and social circumstances. **4** Computing tasks or processes running on a computer that do not need input from the user.

**backgrounder** • n. N. Amer. an official briefing or handout giving background information.

**backhand** • n. (in tennis and other racket sports) a stroke played with the back of the hand facing in the direction of the stroke, with the arm across the body. • v. strike with a backhanded blow or stroke.

**backhanded** • adj. **1** made with the back of the hand facing in the direction of movement. **2** indirect or ambiguous: *a backhanded compliment.* • adv. with the back of the hand or with the hand turned backwards.

**backhander** • n. **1** a backhand stroke or blow. **2** Brit. informal a bribe.

**back-heel** • v. kick backwards with the heel.

**backhoe** (Brit. also **backhoe loader**) • n. a mechanical excavator which draws towards itself a bucket attached to a hinged boom.

**backing** • n. **1** support. ➤ a layer of material that forms, protects, or strengthens the back of something. **2** (especially in popular music) musical or vocal accompaniment to the main singer or soloist. **3** Phonetics the movement of the place of formation of a sound towards the back of the mouth.

**backing track** • n. a recorded musical accompaniment, especially one for a soloist to play or sing along with.

**backland** • n. **1** (also **backlands**) another term for **BACKCOUNTRY**. **2** land behind an area which is built on or otherwise developed.

**backlash** • n. **1** a strong and adverse reaction by a large number of people. **2** recoil or degree of play arising between parts of a mechanism.

**backlight** • n. illumination from behind. • v. (past **-lit**; past part. **-lit** or **lighted**) illuminate from behind.
– DERIVATIVES **backlighting** n.

**backline** • n. **1** a line marking the back of something, especially the area of play in a game. **2** Rugby the players lined out across the field behind a scrum or line-out.

**backlist** • n. a publisher's list of books published before the current season and still in print.

**backload** • n. a load transported on the return journey of a delivery truck. • v. **1** transport such a load. **2** place more charges at the later stages of (a financial agreement) than at the earlier stages.

**backlog** • n. an accumulation of work or matters needing to be dealt with.

**backlot** • n. an outdoor area in a film studio where large exterior sets are made and some outside scenes are filmed.

**backmarker** • n. Brit. a competitor who is among the last in a race.

**backpack** • n. a rucksack. • v. [usu. as noun **backpacking**] travel or hike carrying one's belongings in a rucksack.
– DERIVATIVES **backpacker** n.

**back pass** • n. Soccer a deliberate pass to one's own goalkeeper.

**back passage** • n. Brit. euphemistic a person's rectum.

**back-pedal** • v. **1** move the pedals of a bicycle backwards in order to brake. **2** hastily reverse one's previous action or opinion.

**backplane** • n. a board to which the main circuit boards of a computer may be connected, and which provides connections between them.

**back-projection** • n. the projection of a picture on to the back of a translucent screen.

**backrest** • n. a support for a person's back when they are seated.

**back room** • n. a place where secret, administrative, or

supporting work is done.

**back row** • **n.** [treated as sing. or pl.] Rugby the forwards who are in the second row in a scrum.
– DERIVATIVES **back-rower** n.

**backscatter** • **n. 1** Physics deflection of radiation or particles through an angle of 180°. **2** Photography light from a flashgun or other light source that is deflected directly into a lens. • **v.** Physics deflect (radiation or particles) through an angle of 180°.

**backscratching** • **n.** informal the reciprocal provision of help, typically in an underhand manner.

**back-seat driver** • **n.** informal a passenger in a car who gives the driver unwanted advice.
– DERIVATIVES **back-seat driving** n.

**backshift** • **n.** Grammar the changing of a present tense in direct speech to a past tense in reported speech (or a past tense to pluperfect).

**backside** • **n. 1** informal a person's buttocks or anus. **2** chiefly N. Amer. the reverse or rearward side.

**backsight** • **n. 1** the sight of a rifle or other weapon that is nearer the eye of the person aiming. **2** Surveying a sight or reading taken backwards or towards the point of starting.

**back slang** • **n.** slang in which words are spoken as though they were spelled backwards (e.g. *redraw* for *warder*).

**backslapping** • **n.** the action of offering hearty congratulations or praise. • **adj.** vigorously hearty.
– DERIVATIVES **backslapper** n.

**backslash** • **n.** a backward-sloping diagonal line (\).

**backslide** • **v.** (past **-slid**; past part. **-slid** or **-slidden**) relapse into bad ways.
– DERIVATIVES **backslider** n. **backsliding** n.

**backspace** • **n. 1** a key on a typewriter or computer keyboard used to cause the carriage or cursor to move backwards. **2** a device on a video recorder or camcorder which produces a slight backward run between shots to eliminate disturbance caused by the interruption of the scanning process. • **v.** move a typewriter carriage or computer cursor backwards.

**backspin** • **n.** a backward spin given to a moving ball, causing it to stop more quickly or rebound at a steeper angle on hitting a surface.

**back-stabbing** • **n.** the action of criticizing someone while feigning friendship. • **adj.** behaving in such a way.
– DERIVATIVES **back-stabber** n.

**backstage** • **adv.** in or to the area behind the stage in a theatre. • **adj.** of or relating to this area in a theatre.

**backstairs** • **pl. n. 1** stairs at the back or side of a building. **2** [as modifier] underhand; clandestine.

**backstay** • **n.** a stay on a sailing ship leading downwards and aft from the upper part of a mast.

**backstitch** • **n.** a method of sewing with overlapping stitches. • **v.** sew using backstitch.

**backstop** • **n. 1** a person or thing placed at the rear of something as a barrier or support. **2** Baseball a high fence or similar structure behind the home plate area. **3** Baseball a catcher. • **v.** Baseball act as backstop for.

**back straight** • **n.** Brit. the part of a racecourse that is furthest from the grandstand and parallel to the home straight.

**backstreet** • **n. 1** a minor street. **2** [as modifier] secret, especially because illegal.

**backstretch** • **n.** N. Amer. **1** another term for **BACK STRAIGHT**. **2** the area adjacent to a race course where the horses are stabled and stable employees have temporary living accommodation.

**backstroke** • **n. 1** a swimming stroke performed on the back with the arms lifted alternately out of the water in a backward circular motion and the legs extended and kicking. **2** Bell-ringing a pull of the tail end of the rope from its highest position so as to swing the bell through a full circle. Compare with **HANDSTROKE**.
– DERIVATIVES **backstroker** n.

**backswing** • **n.** Golf a backward swing of the arm or the golf club when about to hit a ball.

**backsword** • **n.** a sword with only one cutting edge.

**back talk** • **n.** informal North American term for **BACKCHAT**.

**back-to-back** • **adj. 1** chiefly Brit. (of houses) built in a terrace backing on to another terrace, with a party wall or a narrow alley between. **2** consecutive. • **adv.** (**back to back**) **1** (of two people) facing in opposite directions with their backs touching. **2** consecutively.

**back-to-nature** • **adj.** advocating or relating to reversion to a simpler way of life.

**backtrack** • **v. 1** retrace one's steps. ➤ reverse one's previous position or opinion. **2** US pursue; track.

**back-up** • **n. 1** support. ➤ a reserve. **2** Computing the procedure for backing up data. ➤ a copy made in such a way. **3** N. Amer. a traffic jam.

**back-up light** • **n.** North American term for **REVERSING LIGHT**.

**backveld** /'bakfɛlt/ • **n.** S. African remote country districts, especially when considered to be unsophisticated or conservative.
– DERIVATIVES **backvelder** n.
– ORIGIN partial translation of Afrik. *agterveld*, lit. 'back countryside'.

**backward** • **adj. 1** directed behind or to the rear. **2** having made less progress than is normal or expected. ➤ having learning difficulties. **3** [with neg.] (**backward in**) lacking the confidence to do: *he was not backward in displaying his talents.* **4** Cricket (of a fielding position) behind an imaginary line passing through the stumps at the batsman's end at right angles to the wicket. • **adv.** variant of **BACKWARDS**.
– DERIVATIVES **backwardly** adv. **backwardness** n.
– ORIGIN ME: from earlier *abackward*, from **ABACK**.

**backwardation** • **n.** Brit. Stock Exchange **1** a situation in which the spot or cash price of a commodity is higher than the forward price. **2** a situation in which the offer price for stock is lower than the bid.

**backwards** (also **backward**) • **adv. 1** in the direction of one's back. **2** back towards the starting point. **3** in reverse of the usual direction or order. ➤ towards the past. ➤ towards a worse state.
– PHRASES **backwards and forwards** to and fro. **bend** (or **fall** or **lean**) **over backwards** informal make every effort, especially to be fair or helpful. **know something backwards** be entirely familiar with something.

**backwash** • **n. 1** the motion of receding waves. **2** a backward current created by an object moving through water or air.

**backwater** • **n. 1** a part of a river not reached by the current, where the water is stagnant. **2** a place or state in which no development or progress is taking place.

**backwind** Sailing • **v.** (of a sail or vessel) deflect a flow of air into the back of (another sail or vessel). • **n.** a flow of air so deflected.

**backwoods** • **pl. n.** chiefly N. Amer. remote uncleared forest land. ➤ a remote or sparsely inhabited region, especially one considered backward or conservative.

**backwoodsman** • **n.** (pl. **-men**) **1** chiefly N. Amer. an inhabitant of backwoods. **2** Brit. informal a peer who very rarely attends the House of Lords.

**backyard** • **n. 1** Brit. a yard at the back of a house or other building. **2** N. Amer. a back garden. **3** informal the area close to where one lives, regarded with proprietorial concern.

**bacon** • **n.** cured meat from the back or sides of a pig.
– PHRASES **bring home the bacon** informal **1** supply material provision or support. **2** achieve success.
– ORIGIN ME: from OFr., from a Gmc word meaning 'ham, flitch'.

**baconer** • **n.** a pig suitable for being made into bacon and ham, typically heavier than both a porker and a cutter.

**Baconian** /beɪ'kəʊnɪən/ • **adj. 1** of or relating to the English philosopher Sir Francis Bacon (1561–1626) or his inductive method of reasoning and philosophy. **2** relating to or denoting the theory that Bacon wrote the plays attributed to Shakespeare. • **n. 1** an adherent of Baconian philosophy. **2** a supporter of the Baconian theory.

**bacteraemia** /ˌbaktə'riːmɪə/ (US **bacteremia**) • **n.** Medi-

cine the presence of bacteria in the blood.
– DERIVATIVES **bacteraemic** adj.

**bacteria** plural form of **BACTERIUM**.

**bactericide** /bak'tɪərɪsʌɪd/ ● n. a substance which kills bacteria.
– DERIVATIVES **bactericidal** adj.

**bacterio-** /bak'tɪərɪəʊ/ ● comb. form representing **BACTERIUM**.

**bacteriological** ● adj. **1** of or relating to bacteriology or bacteria. **2** relating to or denoting germ warfare.
– DERIVATIVES **bacteriologic** adj. **bacteriologically** adv.

**bacteriology** ● n. the study of bacteria.
– DERIVATIVES **bacteriologist** n.

**bacteriolysis** /bak,tɪərɪ'ɒlɪsɪs/ ● n. Biology the rupture of bacterial cells, especially by an antibody.
– DERIVATIVES **bacteriolytic** adj.

**bacteriophage** /bak'tɪərɪə(ʊ)feɪdʒ, -fɑːʒ/ ● n. Biology a kind of virus which parasitizes a bacterium by infecting it and reproducing inside it.
– ORIGIN 1920s: from **BACTERIUM** + Gk *phagein* 'eat'.

**bacteriostat** /bak'tɪərɪə(ʊ)stat/ ● n. a substance that prevents the multiplying of bacteria without destroying them.
– DERIVATIVES **bacteriostasis** n. **bacteriostatic** adj. **bacteriostatically** adv.
– ORIGIN C20: from **BACTERIUM** + Gk *statos* 'standing'.

**bacterium** /bak'tɪərɪəm/ ● n. (pl. **bacteria** /-rɪə/) a member of a large group of unicellular micro-organisms (prokaryotes) which have cell walls but lack an organized nucleus and other structures, and include numerous disease-causing forms.
– DERIVATIVES **bacterial** adj.
– ORIGIN C19: mod. L., from Gk *baktērion*, dimin. of *baktēria* 'rod, cane' (because the first ones to be discovered were rod-shaped).

**USAGE** bacterium

Bacteria, the plural form of **bacterium**, is sometimes mistakenly treated as a singular form.

**Bactrian** /'baktrɪən/ ● n. a native or inhabitant of Bactria, an ancient region and empire in central Asia. ● adj. of or relating to this region or its inhabitants.

**Bactrian camel** ● n. see **CAMEL**.

**baculovirus** /'bakjʊlə(ʊ),vʌɪrəs/ ● n. Biology a member of a family of DNA viruses infecting invertebrates.
– ORIGIN 1980s: from L. *baculum* 'rod, stick' + **VIRUS**.

**bad** ● adj. (**worse**, **worst**) **1** of poor quality or a low standard. **2** unwelcome; unpleasant. ➤severe; serious. ➤(**bad for**) harmful to. **3** offending moral standards or accepted conventions. **4** injured, ill, or diseased. **5** (of food) decayed. **6** guilty; ashamed. **7** inappropriate. **8** (**badder**, **baddest**) informal, chiefly N. Amer. good; excellent.
– PHRASES **in a bad way** ill or in trouble. **to the bad 1** to ruin. **2** in deficit. **too bad** informal indicating that something is regrettable but now beyond retrieval.
– DERIVATIVES **baddish** adj. **badness** n.
– ORIGIN ME: perh. from OE *bǣddel* 'hermaphrodite, womanish man'.

**badass** N. Amer. informal ● n. an aggressive or uncooperative person. ● adj. **1** tough; aggressive. **2** very good.

**bad blood** ● n. ill feeling.

**bad break** ● n. informal a piece of bad luck.

**bad debt** ● n. a debt that cannot be recovered.

**baddy** (also **baddie**) ● n. (pl. **-ies**) informal a villain or criminal in a book, film, etc.

**bade** /beɪd, bad/ past of **BID**².

**bad faith** ● n. intent to deceive: *the slave owners had acted in bad faith.*

**bad form** ● n. an offence against current social conventions.

**badge** ● n. **1** a small piece of metal, plastic, or cloth bearing a design or words, typically worn to identify a person or to indicate support for a cause. **2** a sign or feature revealing a quality or condition: *he converts the macho stereotype into a badge of honour.* ● v. mark with a badge.
– ORIGIN ME: of unknown origin.

**badger** ● n. a heavily built omnivorous nocturnal mammal of the weasel family, typically having a grey and black coat and a white-striped head. [*Meles meles* (Eurasia) and *Taxidea taxus* (N. America).] ● v. repeatedly and annoyingly ask (someone) to do something.
– ORIGIN C16: perh. from **BADGE**, with ref. to its distinctive head markings.

**badger-baiting** ● n. a sport in which dogs draw a badger from its sett and kill it, illegal in the UK since 1830.

**bad hair day** ● n. informal, chiefly US a day on which everything goes wrong.

**badinage** /'badɪnɑːʒ/ ● n. witty conversation.
– ORIGIN C17: from Fr., from *badiner* 'to joke'.

**badlands** ● pl. n. extensive tracts of heavily eroded, uncultivable land with little vegetation.

**badly** ● adv. (**worse**, **worst**) **1** in a bad manner. **2** severely; seriously. **3** very much.
– PHRASES **badly off** at a disadvantage, especially by being poor.

**badminton** ● n. a game with rackets in which a shuttlecock is hit back and forth across a net.
– ORIGIN named after *Badminton* in SW England, country seat of the Duke of Beaufort, where the game was first played.

**bad-mouth** ● v. informal criticize maliciously.

**bad-tempered** ● adj. easily annoyed or angered.
– DERIVATIVES **bad-temperedly** adv.

**BAe** ● abbrev. British Aerospace.

**Baedeker** /'beɪdɪkə, German 'bɛːdəkɐ/ ● n. a travel guidebook published by the firm founded by the German publisher Karl Baedeker (1801–59).

**baffle** ● v. **1** totally bewilder. **2** restrain or regulate (a fluid, a sound, etc.). ● n. a device used to restrain the flow of a fluid, gas, or loose material or to prevent the spreading of sound or light in a particular direction.
– DERIVATIVES **bafflement** n. **baffler** n. **baffling** adj. **bafflingly** adv.
– ORIGIN C16 (in the sense 'cheat, deceive'): perh. rel. to Fr. *bafouer* 'ridicule' or obs. Fr. *beffer* 'mock, deceive'.

**bafflegab** /'baf(ə)lgab/ ● n. N. Amer. informal incomprehensible or pretentious jargon.

**BAFTA** /'baftə/ ● abbrev. British Academy of Film and Television Arts.

**bafta** /'bɑːftə/ (also **baft**) ● n. coarse fabric, typically of cotton.
– ORIGIN C16: from Urdu, from Pers. *bāft* 'textile', *bāfta* 'woven'.

**bag** ● n. **1** a flexible container with an opening at the top. ➤a piece of luggage. **2** (**bags**) loose folds of skin under a person's eyes. **3** (**bags**) Brit. dated loose-fitting trousers. **4** (**bags of**) informal, chiefly Brit. plenty of. **5** the amount of game shot by a hunter. **6** (usu. **old bag**) informal an unpleasant or unattractive woman. **7** (**one's bag**) informal one's particular interest or taste. **8** Baseball a padded square marking each of the first, second, and third bases. ● v. (**bagged**, **bagging**) **1** put in a bag. **2** succeed in killing or catching (an animal). ➤succeed in securing. **3** (of clothes) form loose bulges due to wear. **4** [often as noun **bagging**] Austral. informal criticize.
– PHRASES **bag and baggage** with all one's belongings. **a bag of tricks** informal a set of ingenious plans, techniques, or resources. **bags** (or **bags I**) Brit. informal a child's expression used to make a claim to something. **in the bag** informal **1** (of something desirable) as good as secured. **2** US drunk.
– DERIVATIVES **bagful** n. (pl. **-fuls**). **bagger** n. **baggily** adv. **bagginess** n. **baggy** adj. (**-ier**, **-iest**).
– ORIGIN ME: perh. from ON *baggi*.

**Baganda** /bə'gandə/ ● pl. n. (sing. **Muganda**) an African people of the kingdom of Buganda, now forming part of Uganda.
– ORIGIN a local name; cf. Kiswahili *Waganda*.

**bagasse** /bə'gas/ ● n. the dry pulpy residue left after the extraction of juice from sugar cane.
– ORIGIN C19: from Fr., from Sp. *bagazo* 'pulp'.

**bagatelle** /,bagə'tɛl/ ● n. **1** a game in which small balls

are hit into numbered holes on a board, with pins as obstructions. **2** something trifling or negligible. **3** a short, light piece of music.
– ORIGIN C17: from Fr., from Ital. *bagatella*, perh. from *baga* 'baggage' or from a dimin. of L. *baca* 'berry'.

**bagel** /ˈbeɪɡ(ə)l/ ● **n.** a dense, ring-shaped bread roll that is simmered before baking.
– ORIGIN C20 (as *beigel*): from Yiddish *beygel*.

**baggage** ● **n. 1** personal belongings packed in suitcases for travelling. **2** past experiences or long-held opinions perceived as encumbrances: *emotional baggage*. **3** dated a cheeky or disagreeable girl or woman.
– ORIGIN ME: from OFr. *bagage* (from *baguer* 'tie up'), or *bagues* 'bundles'; perh. rel. to **BAG**.

**bag lady** ● **n.** informal a homeless woman who carries her possessions around in shopping bags.

**bagman** ● **n.** (pl. **-men**) **1** Brit. informal, dated a travelling salesman. **2** Austral. a tramp. **3** Canadian a political fund-raiser. **4** US & Austral. informal an agent who collects or distributes the proceeds of illicit activities.

**bagnio** /ˈbɑːnjəʊ, ˈbanjəʊ/ ● **n.** (pl. **-os**) **1** archaic a brothel. **2** historical (in the Far East) a prison.
– ORIGIN C16: from Ital. *bagno*, from L. *balneum* 'bath'.

**bagpipe** ● **n.** a musical instrument with reed pipes that are sounded by the pressure of wind emitted from a bag squeezed by the player's arm.
– DERIVATIVES **bagpiper** n.

**ba gua** /bɑː ˈɡwɑː/ (also **pa kua**) ● **n. 1** a Chinese religious motif incorporating the eight trigrams of the I Ching, arranged around a symbol denoting the balance of yin and yang. **2** a Chinese martial art in which movements are focused on a circle and the defence of eight points around it.
– ORIGIN from Chin. *bā* 'eight' + *guà* 'divinatory symbols'.

**baguette** /baˈɡɛt/ ● **n. 1** a long, narrow French loaf. **2** a gem, especially a diamond, cut in a long rectangular shape. **3** Architecture a small moulding, semicircular in section. **4** a slim, rectangular handbag with a short strap.
– ORIGIN C18: from Fr., from Ital. *bacchetto*, dimin. of *bacchio*, from L. *baculum* 'staff'.

**bagworm** ● **n.** an American moth, the caterpillar and flightless female of which live in a portable protective case constructed out of plant debris. [Family Psychidae.]

**bah** ● **exclam.** an expression of contempt or disagreement.
– ORIGIN C19: prob. from Fr.

**bahada** /bəˈhɑːdə/ ● **n.** variant spelling of **BAJADA**.

**Baha'i** /bɑːˈhɑːi/ (also **Bahai**) ● **n.** (pl. **Baha'is**) **1** a monotheistic religion founded in the 19th century as a development of Babism, emphasizing the essential oneness of humankind and of all religions and seeking world peace. **2** an adherent of the Baha'i faith.
– DERIVATIVES **Baha'ism** /bɑːˈhɑːɪz(ə)m/ n.
– ORIGIN Pers., from Arab. *bahā'* 'splendour'.

**Bahamian** /bəˈheɪmɪən/ ● **n.** a native or inhabitant of the Bahamas. ● **adj.** of or relating to the Bahamas or its inhabitants.

**Bahasa Indonesia** /bəˈhɑːsə/ ● **n.** the official language of Indonesia. See **INDONESIAN**.
– ORIGIN from Malay *bahasa* 'language'.

**Bahasa Malaysia** ● **n.** the official language of Malaysia. See **MALAY**.

**Bahraini** /bɑːˈreɪni/ ● **n.** a native or inhabitant of Bahrain. ● **adj.** of or relating to Bahrain or its inhabitants.

**baht** /bɑːt/ ● **n.** (pl. same) the basic monetary unit of Thailand, equal to 100 satangs.
– ORIGIN from Thai *bāt*.

**Bahutu** plural form of **HUTU**.

**bail**[1] ● **n. 1** the temporary release of an accused person awaiting trial, sometimes on condition that a sum of money is lodged to guarantee their appearance in court. **2** money paid by or for such a person as security. ● **v.** release or secure the release of (an accused person) on payment of bail.
– PHRASES **go** (or **stand**) **bail** act as surety for an accused person. **jump bail** informal fail to appear for trial after being released on bail.
– DERIVATIVES **bailable** adj.
– ORIGIN ME: from OFr., lit. 'custody, jurisdiction', from *bailler* 'take charge of', from L. *bajulare* 'bear a burden'.

**bail**[2] ● **n. 1** Cricket either of the two crosspieces bridging the stumps. **2** a bar on a typewriter or computer printer which holds the paper steady. **3** a bar separating horses in an open stable. **4** Austral./NZ a movable framework for securing the head of a cow during milking. ● **v.** Austral./NZ **1** secure (a cow) during milking. **2** confront with intent to rob. **3** detain in conversation.
– ORIGIN ME (denoting a bailey): from OFr. *baile* 'palisade, enclosure', *baillier* 'enclose'.

**bail**[3] (Brit. also **bale**) ● **v. 1** scoop water out of (a ship or boat). **2** (**bail out**) make an emergency parachute descent from an aircraft. **3** (**bail someone/thing out**) rescue someone or something from a difficulty.
– DERIVATIVES **bailer** n.
– ORIGIN C17: from obs. *bail* 'bucket', from Fr. *baille*, based on L. *bajulus* 'carrier'.

**bailee** /beɪˈliː/ ● **n.** Law a person or party to whom goods are delivered for a purpose, without transfer of ownership.

**bailey** ● **n.** (pl. **-eys**) the outer wall of a castle.
– ORIGIN ME: prob. from OFr. *baile* (see **BAIL**[2]).

**Bailey bridge** ● **n.** a temporary bridge of lattice steel designed for rapid assembly from prefabricated standard parts, used especially in military operations.
– ORIGIN Second World War: named after the Engl. engineer Sir D. *Bailey*, its designer.

**bailie** /ˈbeɪli/ ● **n.** (pl. **-ies**) chiefly historical a municipal officer and magistrate in Scotland.
– ORIGIN ME (orig. used interchangeably with **BAILIFF**): from OFr. *bailli*.

**bailiff** /ˈbeɪlɪf/ ● **n. 1** chiefly Brit. a sheriff's officer who executes writs and processes and carries out distraints and arrests. **2** Brit. the agent of a landlord. **3** N. Amer. an official in a court of law who keeps order and looks after prisoners. **4** Brit. historical the sovereign's representative in a district, especially the chief officer of a hundred. **5** the first civil officer in the Channel Islands.
– ORIGIN ME: from OFr. *baillif*, inflected form of *bailli* (see **BAILIE**), based on L. *bajulus* 'carrier, manager'.

**bailiwick** /ˈbeɪlɪwɪk/ ● **n. 1** Law the district or jurisdiction of a bailie or bailiff. **2** informal one's sphere of operations or particular area of interest.
– ORIGIN ME: from **BAILIE** + **WICK**[2].

**bailment** ● **n.** Law an act of delivering goods to a bailee.

**bailor** /beɪˈlɔː/ ● **n.** Law a person or party that entrusts goods to a bailee.

**Baily's beads** ● **pl. n.** Astronomy a string of bright points seen at the edge of the darkened moon at the beginning or end of totality in an eclipse of the sun, caused by the uneven lunar topography.
– ORIGIN C19: named after the Engl. astronomer Francis *Baily*.

**bain-marie** /ˌbanməˈriː/ ● **n.** (pl. **bains-marie** or **bain-maries** pronunc. same) a pan of hot water in which a cooking container is placed for slow cooking.
– ORIGIN C18: Fr., translation of med. L. *balneum Mariae* 'bath of Maria', translating Gk *kaminos Marias* 'furnace of *Maria*', said to be a Jewish alchemist.

**Bairam** /bʌɪˈrɑːm/ ● **n.** either of two annual Muslim festivals, **Greater Bairam** at the end of the Islamic year and **Lesser Bairam** at the end of Ramadan.
– ORIGIN from Turk. *baïram* (earlier form of *bayram*), from Pers. *bazrām*.

**bairn** /bɛːn/ ● **n.** chiefly Scottish & N. English a child.
– ORIGIN OE *bearn*, of Gmc origin; rel. to **BEAR**[1].

**bait** ● **n. 1** food used to entice fish or other animals as prey. **2** variant spelling of **BATE**[1]. ● **v. 1** deliberately annoy or taunt. **2** allow dogs to attack (a trapped or restrained animal). **3** put bait on (a hook) or in (a trap, net, or fishing area).
– PHRASES **rise to the bait** react to a provocation or temptation exactly as intended.
– ORIGIN ME: from ON *beit* 'pasture, food', *beita* 'to hunt or

chase'.

**bait-and-switch** ● **n.** N. Amer. the advertising of goods which are an apparent bargain, with the intention of substituting inferior or more expensive goods.

**baitcasting** ● **n.** fishing by throwing a bait or lure into the water on the end of a line using a rod and reel.
– DERIVATIVES **baitcaster** n.

**baiza** /'bʌɪzɑː/ ● **n.** (pl. same or **baizas**) a monetary unit of Oman, equal to one thousandth of a rial.

**baize** /beɪz/ ● **n.** a coarse felt-like woollen material that is typically green, used chiefly for covering billiard and card tables.
– ORIGIN C16: from Fr. *baies*, fem. pl. of *bai* (see **BAY**[4]), treated as a sing. noun.

**bajada** /bə'hɑːdə/ (also **bahada**) ● **n.** a broad slope of alluvial material at the foot of an escarpment.
– ORIGIN C19: from Sp., 'descent, slope'.

**Bajan** /'beɪdʒ(ə)n/ ● **adj. & n.** informal term for **BARBADIAN**.

**bajra** /'bɑːdʒrɑː/ ● **n.** (in the Indian subcontinent) pearl millet or similar grain.
– ORIGIN from Hindi *bājrā, bājrī*.

**bake** ● **v. 1** cook (food) by dry heat without direct exposure to a flame, typically in an oven. **2** (of the sun or other agency) subject to dry heat. ➤ informal be or become extremely hot in prolonged hot weather. ● **n. 1** a dish consisting of a number of ingredients mixed together and baked. **2** N. Amer. a social gathering at which baked food of a specified kind is eaten.
– ORIGIN OE *bacan*, of Gmc origin.

**baked Alaska** ● **n.** a dessert consisting of sponge cake and ice cream in a meringue covering, cooked briefly in a hot oven.

**baked beans** ● **pl. n.** baked haricot beans, typically cooked in tomato sauce and tinned.

**bakehouse** ● **n.** dated a building or area in which bread is made.

**Bakelite** /'beɪk(ə)lʌɪt/ ● **n.** trademark an early brittle form of plastic made from formaldehyde and phenol.
– ORIGIN C20: named after Leo H. *Baekeland*, the Belgian-born Amer. chemist who invented it, + **-ITE**[1].

**baker** ● **n.** a person whose trade is making and selling bread and cakes.
– PHRASES **baker's dozen** a group of thirteen. [from the former bakers' custom of adding an extra loaf to a dozen sold to a retailer, this constituting the latter's profit.]
– DERIVATIVES **bakery** n.

**Bakewell tart** ● **n.** Brit. a baked open tart consisting of a pastry case lined with jam and filled with almond sponge cake.
– ORIGIN named after the town of *Bakewell* in Derbyshire.

**baking powder** ● **n.** a mixture of sodium bicarbonate and cream of tartar, used as a raising agent in baking.

**baking soda** ● **n.** sodium bicarbonate.

**baklava** /'bɑːkləvə, 'bak-/ ● **n.** a Middle Eastern dessert made of filo pastry filled with chopped nuts and soaked in honey.
– ORIGIN from Turk.

**baksheesh** /bak'ʃiːʃ/ ● **n.** (in parts of the Middle and Far East and the Indian subcontinent) a small sum of money given as alms, a tip, or a bribe.
– ORIGIN based on Pers. *bak̲šīš*, from *bak̲šīdan* 'give'.

**balaclava** /ˌbalə'klɑːvə/ ● **n.** a close-fitting woollen hat covering the whole head and encircling the neck.
– ORIGIN C19 (worn orig. by soldiers in the Crimean War): named after the village of *Balaclava* in the Crimea.

**balafon** /'baləfɒn/ ● **n.** a large xylophone with hollow gourds as resonators, used in West African music.
– ORIGIN C18: via Fr. from Manding *bala* 'xylophone' + *fo* 'to play'.

**balalaika** /ˌbalə'lʌɪkə/ ● **n.** a Russian musical instrument like a guitar with a triangular body and typically three strings.
– ORIGIN C18: from Russ., of Tartar origin.

**balance** ● **n. 1** an even distribution of weight ensuring stability. **2** mental or emotional stability. **3** a condition in which different elements are equal or in the correct proportions. **4** Sailing the ability of a boat to stay on course without adjustment of the rudder. **5** an apparatus for weighing, especially one with a central pivot, beam, and two scales. **6** a counteracting weight or force. ➤ (also **balance wheel**) the regulating device in a clock or watch. **7** a preponderance: *the balance of opinion was that work was important.* **8** a figure representing the difference between credits and debits in an account; the amount of money held in an account. ➤ the difference between an amount due and an amount paid. ● **v. 1** be or put in a steady position. **2** offset or compare the value of (one thing) with another. ➤ [often as adj. **balanced**] establish equal or appropriate proportions of elements in: *a balanced diet.* **3** compare debits and credits in (an account) to ensure that they are equal.
– PHRASES **balance of payments** the difference in total value between payments into and out of a country over a period. **balance of power 1** a situation in which states of the world have roughly equal power. **2** the power held by a small group when larger groups are of equal strength. **balance of trade** the difference in value between a country's imports and exports. **be** (or **hang**) **in the balance** be in an uncertain or critical state. **on balance** when all factors are taken into consideration. **throw** (or **catch**) **someone off balance** cause (or find) someone to be unsteady.
– DERIVATIVES **balancer** n.
– ORIGIN ME: from OFr. *balance* (n.), *balancer* (v.), based on late L. (*libra*) *bilanx* '(balance) having two scale-pans'.

**balance sheet** ● **n.** a written statement of the assets, liabilities, and capital of a business.

**balance wheel** ● **n.** another term for **BALANCE** (see sense 6).

**balander** /bə'landə/ (also **balanda**) ● **n.** derogatory (among Australian Aboriginals) a white man.
– ORIGIN C19: from Makasarese *balanda*, from Malay *belanda* (alt. of **HOLLANDER** in the sense 'Dutchman').

**balanitis** /ˌbalə'nʌɪtɪs/ ● **n.** Medicine inflammation of the glans penis.
– ORIGIN C19: from Gk *balanos* 'glans penis' (lit. 'acorn') + **-ITIS**.

**balas ruby** /'baləs/ ● **n.** a ruby of a delicate rose-red variety.
– ORIGIN ME: from OFr. *balais*, from Arab. *balak̲š*, from Pers. *Badak̲šān*, a district of Afghanistan where it is found.

**balata** /'balətə, bə'lɑːtə/ ● **n.** a tropical American tree which bears edible fruit and produces latex. [*Manilkara bidentata*.]
– ORIGIN C17: from Carib *balatá*.

**balboa** /bal'bəʊə/ ● **n.** the basic monetary unit of Panama, equal to 100 centésimos.
– ORIGIN named after the Sp. explorer Vasco Núñez de *Balboa*.

**balbriggan** /bal'brɪg(ə)n/ ● **n.** a knitted cotton fabric, formerly used for stockings and underwear.
– ORIGIN C19: named after the town of *Balbriggan* in Ireland, where it was orig. made.

**balcony** ● **n.** (pl. **-ies**) **1** a platform enclosed by a wall or balustrade on the outside of a building. **2** the highest tier of seats in a theatre or cinema. ➤ N. Amer. the dress circle in a theatre.
– DERIVATIVES **balconied** adj.
– ORIGIN C17: from Ital. *balcone*.

**bald** ● **adj. 1** having a scalp wholly or partly lacking hair. **2** (of an animal) not covered by the usual fur, hair, or feathers. **3** (of a tyre) having the tread worn away. **4** (of language) plain; blunt.
– DERIVATIVES **balding** adj. **baldish** adj. **baldly** adv. **baldness** n.
– ORIGIN ME: prob. from an OE base meaning 'white patch'.

**baldachin** /'baldəkɪn, 'bɔːld-/ (also **baldaquin** /'bɔːldəkɪn/) ● **n.** a ceremonial canopy over an altar, throne, or doorway.
– ORIGIN C16 (denoting a rich brocade): from Ital. *baldacchino*, from *Baldacco* 'Baghdad', from where the brocade originated.

**bald eagle** ● n. a white-headed North American eagle, the national bird of the US. [*Haliaeetus leucocephalus*.]

**balderdash** /ˈbɔːldədaʃ/ ● n. senseless talk or writing.
– ORIGIN C16 (denoting a frothy liquid or an unappetizing mixture of drinks): of unknown origin.

**baldie** ● n. & adj. variant spelling of **BALDY**.

**baldmoney** /ˈbɔːldmʌni/ ● n. (pl. **-eys**) another term for **SPIGNEL**.
– ORIGIN ME (denoting the gentian; now only Scots): origin unknown.

**baldric** /ˈbɔːldrɪk/ ● n. historical a belt for a sword or other piece of equipment, worn over one shoulder and reaching down to the opposite hip.
– ORIGIN ME *baudry*, from OFr. *baudre*.

**baldy** (also **baldie**) ● n. (pl. **-ies**) informal, derogatory a bald-headed person. ● adj. chiefly Scottish & Irish bald.

**bale**[1] ● n. **1** a large wrapped or bound bundle of paper, hay, or cotton. **2** the quantity in a bale as a measure, specifically (in the US) 500 lb of cotton. ● v. make up into bales.
– DERIVATIVES **baler** n.
– ORIGIN ME: prob. from MDu., from OFr.; ult. of Gmc origin and rel. to **BALL**[1].

**bale**[2] ● n. archaic **1** evil considered as a destructive force. **2** physical or mental torment.
– ORIGIN OE *balu*, *bealu*, of Gmc origin.

**bale**[3] ● v. Brit. variant spelling of **BAIL**[3].

**baleen** /bəˈliːn/ ● n. whalebone.
– ORIGIN ME: from OFr. *baleine*, from L. *balaena* 'whale'.

**baleen whale** ● n. any of the group of whales that have plates of whalebone in the mouth for straining plankton from the water. [Suborder Mysticeti.]

**balefire** ● n. US a large open-air fire.
– ORIGIN OE: from obs. *bale* 'great fire' + **FIRE**.

**baleful** ● adj. menacing. ➤having a harmful effect.
– DERIVATIVES **balefully** adv. **balefulness** n.
– ORIGIN OE *bealufull* (see **BALE**[2], **-FUL**).

**balibuntal** /ˌbalɪˈbʌnt(ə)l/ ● n. a fine close-woven straw, used for making hats.
– ORIGIN C20: from *Baliuag* in the Philippines, where it originated, + **BUNTAL**.

**Balinese** /ˌbɑːlɪˈniːz/ ● n. (pl. same) **1** a native or inhabitant of Bali. **2** the Indonesian language of Bali. ● adj. of or relating to Bali or its people or language.

**balk** ● v. & n. chiefly US variant spelling of **BAULK**.

**Balkan** /ˈbɔːlkən/ ● adj. of or relating to the countries occupying the part of SE Europe forming a peninsula bounded by the Adriatic, Ionian, Aegean, and the Black Seas. ● n. (**the Balkans**) the Balkan countries.
– ORIGIN from Turk.

**Balkanize** /ˈbɔːlkənʌɪz, ˈbɒl-/ (also **-ise**) ● v. divide (a region or body) into smaller mutually hostile states or groups.
– DERIVATIVES **Balkanization** /-ˈzeɪʃ(ə)n/ n.
– ORIGIN 1920s: from *Balkan* Peninsula (where this was done in the late 19th and early 20th cent.) + **-IZE**.

**balky** /ˈbɔːlki, ˈbɔːki/ (Brit. also **baulky**) ● adj. (**-ier**, **-iest**) chiefly N. Amer. awkward; uncooperative.

**ball**[1] ● n. **1** a solid or hollow sphere, especially one that is kicked, thrown, or hit in a game. ➤N. Amer. a game played with a ball, especially baseball. **2** a single throw or kick of the ball in a game. ➤Cricket a delivery of the ball by the bowler to the batsman. ➤Baseball a pitch delivered outside the strike zone which the batter does not attempt to hit. ● v. **1** squeeze or form into a ball. **2** N. Amer. vulgar slang (of a man) have sexual intercourse with. **3** Brit. (of a flower) fail to open properly, decaying in the half-open bud.
– PHRASES **the ball is in your court** it is up to you to make the next move. **the ball of the foot** the rounded protuberant part of the foot at the base of the big toe. **the ball of the thumb** the rounded protuberant part of the hand at the base of the thumb. **have a lot** (or **not much**) **on the ball** US have a lot of (or not much) ability. **keep the ball rolling** maintain the momentum of an activity. **keep one's eye on** (or **take one's eye off**) **the ball** keep (or fail to keep) one's attention focused on the matter in hand. **on the ball** alert to new ideas, methods, and trends. **play ball** informal cooperate. **start** (or **get** or **set**) **the ball rolling** make a start. **the whole ball of wax** N. Amer. informal everything.
– ORIGIN ME: from ON *bǫllr*, of Gmc origin.

**ball**[2] ● n. a formal social gathering for dancing.
– PHRASES **have a ball** informal enjoy oneself greatly.
– ORIGIN C17: from Fr. *bal* 'a dance'.

**ballad** ● n. **1** a poem or song narrating a popular story in short stanzas. **2** a slow sentimental or romantic song.
– DERIVATIVES **balladeer** n. **balladry** n.
– ORIGIN C15: from OFr. *balade*, from Provençal *balada* 'dance, song to dance to'.

**ballade** /baˈlɑːd/ ● n. **1** a poem consisting of one or more triplets of stanzas with a repeated refrain and an envoy. **2** a short, lyrical piece of music, especially one for piano.
– ORIGIN ME: earlier spelling of **BALLAD**.

**ballad metre** ● n. another term for **COMMON METRE**.

**ball and chain** ● n. a heavy metal ball secured by a chain to the leg of a prisoner to prevent escape.

**ball-and-socket joint** ● n. a joint in which a partially spherical end lies in a socket, allowing movement and rotation in all directions.

**ballan wrasse** /ˈbalən/ ● n. a large wrasse of rocky shores and reefs. [*Labrus bergylta*.]
– ORIGIN C18: *ballan* from Ir. *ballán*, from *ball* 'spot'.

**ballast** /ˈbaləst/ ● n. **1** a heavy substance, such as gravel or lead, placed in the bilge of a ship to ensure its stability. ➤a substance carried in an airship or on a hot-air balloon to stabilize it. **2** gravel or coarse stone used to form the bed of a railway track or the substratum of a road. ➤a mixture of coarse and fine aggregate for making concrete. **3** a passive component used in an electric circuit to moderate changes in current. ● v. provide with ballast.
– ORIGIN C16: prob. of Low Ger. or Scand. origin.

**ball bearing** ● n. a bearing in which the parts are separated by a ring of small metal balls which reduce friction. ➤a ball used in such a bearing.

**ballboy** (or **ballgirl**) ● n. a boy (or girl) who retrieves balls that go out of play during a tennis match or baseball game.

**ball-breaker** (also **ball-buster**) ● n. informal a sexually demanding woman who destroys men's self-confidence.
– DERIVATIVES **ball-breaking** adj.

**ball clay** ● n. a fine-textured clay used in the manufacture of ceramics.

**ballcock** ● n. a valve which automatically tops up a cistern when liquid is drawn from it, especially in a flushing toilet.

**ballerina** ● n. a female ballet dancer.
– ORIGIN C18: from Ital., fem. of *ballerino* 'dancing master'.

**ballet** ● n. **1** an artistic dance form performed to music, using precise and formalized set steps and gestures. **2** a creative work of this form or the music written for it.
– DERIVATIVES **balletic** adj. **balletically** adv.
– ORIGIN C17: from Fr., from Ital. *balletto*, dimin. of *ballo* 'a dance'.

**balletomane** /ˈbalɪtəʊˌmeɪn/ ● n. a ballet enthusiast.
– DERIVATIVES **balletomania** n.

**ball float** ● n. the spherical float attached to a hinged arm in the ballcock of a water cistern.

**ball game** ● n. **1** a game played with a ball. ➤N. Amer. a baseball match. **2** informal a situation that is completely different from a previous one: *a whole new ball game*.

**ballhawk** ● n. N. Amer. informal a skilled ball player.
– DERIVATIVES **ballhawking** n.

**ballista** /bəˈlɪstə/ ● n. (pl. **ballistae** /-stiː/ or **ballistas**) a catapult used in ancient warfare for hurling large boulders.
– ORIGIN C16: from L., based on Gk *ballein* 'to throw'.

**ballistic** /bəˈlɪstɪk/ ● adj. **1** of or relating to projectiles or their flight. **2** moving under the force of gravity only.
– PHRASES **go ballistic** informal fly into a rage.
– DERIVATIVES **ballistically** adv.

**ballistic missile** ● n. a missile which is initially powered and guided but falls under gravity on to its target.

**ballistics** ● pl. n. [treated as sing.] the science of projectiles and firearms.

**ball lightning** ● **n.** a rare form of lightning in the shape of a moving luminous globe.

**ballocks** ● **pl. n.** variant spelling of **BOLLOCKS**.

**ballon** /ˈbalɔ̃/ ● **n.** (in dancing) the ability to appear effortlessly suspended while performing movements during a jump.
– ORIGIN Fr., from Ital. *ballone*, from *balla* 'ball'.

**balloon** ● **n. 1** a small rubber sac which is inflated and used as a child's toy or a decoration. ➤a rounded outline in which the words or thoughts of characters in a comic strip or cartoon are written. **2** a large bag filled with hot air or gas to make it rise in the air, typically having a basket for passengers. **3** a large rounded drinking glass, used especially for brandy. **4** Scottish informal a stupid person. ● **v. 1** swell out in a spherical shape. ➤increase rapidly. **2** Brit. lob or be lobbed high in the air.
– PHRASES **when the balloon goes up** informal when the action or trouble starts.
– DERIVATIVES **ballooning** n. **balloonist** n.
– ORIGIN C16 (orig. denoting a game played with a large inflated leather ball): from Fr. *ballon* or Ital. *ballone* 'large ball'.

**balloon angioplasty** ● **n.** Medicine surgical widening of a blood vessel by means of a balloon catheter.

**balloon catheter** ● **n.** Medicine a type of catheter incorporating a small balloon which is introduced into a blood vessel and then inflated in order to clear an obstruction or dilate a narrowed region.

**balloonfish** ● **n.** (pl. same or **-fishes**) a tropical porcupine fish which lives in shallow water and can inflate itself when threatened. [*Diodon holocanthus*.]

**balloon tyre** ● **n.** a large tyre containing air at low pressure.
– DERIVATIVES **balloon-tyred** adj.

**balloon whisk** ● **n.** a hand whisk made of loops of metal wire.

**ballot** ● **n. 1** a procedure by which people vote secretly on an issue. ➤(**the ballot**) the total number of votes cast in such a process. **2** a lottery held to decide the allocation of tickets or other things among a number of applicants. ● **v.** (**balloted**, **balloting**) **1** elicit a secret vote from (members). ➤cast one's vote. **2** allocate by drawing lots.
– ORIGIN C16 (orig. denoting a small coloured ball placed in a container to register a vote): from Ital. *ballotta*, dimin. of *balla* (see **BALL**[1]).

**ballot box** ● **n.** a sealed box into which voters put completed ballot papers.

**ballpark** chiefly N. Amer. ● **n. 1** a baseball ground. **2** informal a particular area or range. ● **adj.** informal approximate: *the ballpark figure is $400–500.*

**ballpoint pen** ● **n.** a pen with a tiny ball as its writing point.

**ballroom** ● **n.** a large room for formal dancing.

**ballroom dancing** ● **n.** formal social dancing in couples.

**balls** vulgar slang ● **pl. n. 1** testicles. **2** courage; nerve. **3** [treated as sing.] Brit. nonsense; rubbish. ● **v.** (**balls something up**) bungle something.

**balls-up** ● **n.** Brit. vulgar slang a bungled task or action.

**ballsy** ● **adj.** (**-ier**, **-iest**) informal bold and confident.
– DERIVATIVES **ballsiness** n.

**ball valve** ● **n.** a one-way valve opened and closed by pressure on a ball which fits into a cup-shaped opening.

**bally** /ˈbali/ ● **adj. & adv.** Brit. old-fashioned euphemism for **BLOODY**[2].

**ballyhoo** informal ● **n.** extravagant publicity or fuss. ● **v.** (**ballyhoos**, **ballyhooed**) chiefly N. Amer. praise or publicize extravagantly.
– ORIGIN C19: Amer. coinage of unknown origin.

**ballyrag** ● **v.** variant spelling of **BULLYRAG**.

**balm** /bɑːm/ ● **n. 1** a fragrant ointment used to heal or soothe the skin. ➤something that has a soothing or restorative effect. **2** a tree which yields a fragrant resinous substance, especially one used in medicine. [Genus *Commiphora*; numerous species.] ➤used in names of other fragrant plants, chiefly of the mint family, e.g. **lemon balm**.
– ORIGIN ME: from OFr. *basme*, from L. *balsamum* (see **BALSAM**).

**balm of Gilead** /ˈgɪlɪad/ ● **n. 1** a fragrant medicinal resin obtained from certain trees. **2** a tree that yields this. [*Commiphora gileadensis* (Arabia) and other species.]

**balmoral** /balˈmɒr(ə)l/ ● **n. 1** a round brimless hat with a cockade or ribbons attached, worn by certain Scottish regiments. **2** a heavy laced leather walking boot.
– ORIGIN C19: named after *Balmoral* Castle in Scotland.

**bal musette** /ˌbal mjuːˈzɛt, French bal myzɛt/ ● **n.** (pl. **bals musettes** pronunc. same) (in France) a dance hall with an accordion band.
– ORIGIN Fr., orig. denoting dancing outdoors to bagpipe accompaniment.

**balmy** /ˈbɑːmi/ ● **adj.** (**-ier**, **-iest**) **1** (of the weather) pleasantly warm. **2** old-fashioned spelling of **BARMY**.
– DERIVATIVES **balmily** adv. **balminess** n.

**balneology** /ˌbalnɪˈɒlədʒi/ ● **n. 1** the study of medicinal springs and the therapeutic effects of bathing in them. **2** another term for **BALNEOTHERAPY**.
– DERIVATIVES **balneological** adj. **balneologist** n.
– ORIGIN C19: from L. *balneum* 'bath' + **-LOGY**.

**balneotherapy** /ˌbalnɪə(ʊ)ˈθɛrəpi/ ● **n.** the treatment of disease by bathing in mineral springs.

**baloney** /bəˈləʊni/ (also **boloney**) ● **n. 1** informal nonsense. [said to be a corruption of **BOLOGNA**: the connection remains conjectural.] **2** North American term for **BOLOGNA**.

**balsa** /ˈbɒlsə/ ● **n. 1** (also **balsa wood**) very lightweight timber used chiefly for making models and rafts. **2** the fast-growing tropical American tree from which this wood is obtained. [*Ochroma lagopus*.]
– ORIGIN C17: from Sp., 'raft'.

**balsam** /ˈbɔːlsəm, ˈbɒl-/ ● **n. 1** an aromatic resinous substance exuded by various trees and shrubs, used as a base for certain fragrances and medical preparations. ➤a tree or shrub which yields balsam. **2** a herbaceous plant cultivated for its helmeted pink or purple flowers. [Genus *Impatiens*.]
– DERIVATIVES **balsamic** /-ˈsamɪk/ adj.
– ORIGIN OE, via L. from Gk *balsamon*.

**balsam fir** ● **n.** a North American fir tree which yields Canada balsam. [*Abies balsamea*.]

**balsamic vinegar** ● **n.** dark, sweet Italian vinegar that has been matured in wooden barrels.

**bals musettes** plural form of **BAL MUSETTE**.

**Balt** /bɔːlt, bɒlt/ ● **n. 1** a speaker of a Baltic language. **2** a native or inhabitant of one of the Baltic States of Lithuania, Latvia, and Estonia.

**Balthazar** /balˈθazə/ ● **n.** a very large wine bottle, equivalent in capacity to sixteen regular bottles.
– ORIGIN 1930s: from *Balthazar*, the name of the king of Babylon who 'made a great feast ... and drank wine before a thousand' (Dan: 5:1).

**Balti** /ˈbalti/ ● **n. 1** a native or inhabitant of Baltistan, a region in the Himalayas. **2** the Tibetan language of this people. ● **adj.** of or relating to the Baltis or their language.
– ORIGIN the name in Ladakhi dial.

**balti** /ˈbɔːlti, ˈbalti/ ● **n.** (pl. **baltis**) a type of Pakistani cuisine in which the food is cooked in a small two-handled pan known as a karahi.
– ORIGIN from Urdu *bāltī*, lit. 'pail'.

**Baltic** /ˈbɔːltɪk, ˈbɒlt-/ ● **n. 1** (**the Baltic**) an almost landlocked sea of northern Europe. ➤(also **the Baltic States**) a small group of states on the eastern shores of this sea, consisting of Latvia, Lithuania, and Estonia. **2** an Indo-European branch of languages consisting of Lithuanian, Latvian, and Old Prussian. ● **adj.** of or relating to this sea or group of languages.
– ORIGIN C16: from med. L. *Balticus*, from late L. *Balthae* 'dwellers near the Baltic Sea'.

**Baluchi** /bəˈluːtʃi/ ● **n. 1** a native or inhabitant of Baluchistan in western Asia. **2** the Iranian language of Baluchistan. ● **adj.** of or relating to this people or their language.

– ORIGIN from Pers. *Balūčī*.

**balun** /ˈbalʌn/ ● **n.** a type of electrical transformer used to connect an unbalanced circuit to a balanced one.
– ORIGIN from *bal(ance to) un(balance transformer)*.

**baluster** /ˈbaləstə/ ● **n.** a short pillar forming part of a series supporting a rail or coping.
– ORIGIN C17: from Fr. *balustre*, from Ital. *balaustro*, from *balaust(r)a* 'wild pomegranate flower' (because of the resemblance to the curving calyx tube of the flower).

**balustrade** /ˌbaləˈstreɪd/ ● **n.** a railing supported by balusters.
– DERIVATIVES **balustraded** adj.
– ORIGIN C17: from Fr., from *balustre* (see **BALUSTER**).

**bam** ● **exclam.** used to imitate the sound of a hard blow or convey the idea of something happening abruptly.

**Bambara** /bamˈbɑːrə/ ● **n.** (pl. same or **Bambaras**) **1** a member of a West African people living chiefly in Mali. **2** the Mande language of this people.

**bambino** /bamˈbiːnəʊ/ ● **n.** (pl. **bambini** /-ni/) a baby or young child.
– ORIGIN C18: Ital., dimin. of *bambo* 'silly'.

**bamboo** ● **n.** a giant woody grass with hollow jointed stems, grown chiefly in the tropics for use in furniture and implements. [*Bambusa* and other genera.]
– ORIGIN C16: from Du. *bamboes*, based on Malay *mambu*.

**bamboo rat** ● **n.** a large nocturnal burrowing rat found in the forests of SE Asia. [Genus *Rhyzomys*: several species.]

**bamboo shoot** ● **n.** a young shoot of bamboo, eaten as a vegetable.

**bamboozle** /bamˈbuːz(ə)l/ ● **v.** informal cheat or mystify.
– DERIVATIVES **bamboozler** n.
– ORIGIN C18: of unknown origin.

**ban**[1] /ban/ ● **v.** (**banned**, **banning**) officially or legally prohibit. ● **n.** an official or legal prohibition.
– ORIGIN OE *bannan* 'summon by a public proclamation', of Gmc origin; the noun is partly from OFr. *ban* 'proclamation, summons, banishment'.

**ban**[2] /bɑːn/ ● **n.** (pl. **bani** /ˈbɑːni/) a monetary unit of Romania, equal to one hundredth of a leu.
– ORIGIN from Romanian.

**banal** /bəˈnɑːl, -ˈnal/ ● **adj.** tediously unoriginal or commonplace.
– DERIVATIVES **banality** n. (pl. **-ies**). **banally** adv.
– ORIGIN C18 (orig. relating to feudal service in the sense 'compulsory', hence 'common to all'): from Fr., from *ban* (see **BAN**[1]).

**banana** ● **n.** **1** a long curved fruit which grows in clusters and has soft pulpy flesh and yellow skin when ripe. **2** (also **banana plant** or **banana tree**) the tropical and subtropical palm-like plant which bears this fruit. [Genus *Musa*: several species.]
– PHRASES **go** (or **be**) **bananas** informal become (or be) mad, angry, or excited. **top banana** informal, chiefly N. Amer. the most important person in an organization.
– ORIGIN C16: via Port. or Sp. from Mande.

**banana belt** ● **n.** N. Amer. informal a region with a comparatively warm climate.

**banana plug** ● **n.** Electronics a single-pole connector with a curved strip of metal forming a spring along its tip.

**bananaquit** /bəˈnɑːnəkwɪt/ ● **n.** a small grey and yellow songbird with a curved bill, common in the Caribbean and Central and South America. [*Coereba flaveola*.]
– ORIGIN C19: *quit* is of imitative origin.

**banana republic** ● **n.** derogatory a small state that is politically unstable as a result of the domination of its economy by a single export controlled by foreign capital.

**banana split** ● **n.** a sweet dish made with bananas cut down the middle and filled with ice cream, sauce, and nuts.

**banausic** /bəˈnɔːsɪk/ ● **adj.** formal **1** mundane. **2** relating to technical work.
– ORIGIN C19: from Gk *banausikos* 'of or for artisans'.

**Banbury cake** ● **n.** Brit. a flat pastry with a spicy currant filling.
– ORIGIN C16: named after the town of *Banbury* in Oxfordshire, where it was orig. made.

**bancassurance** /ˈbaŋkəˌʃɔːrəns/ (also **bankassurance**) ● **n.** Brit. the selling of life assurance and other insurance products by banking institutions.
– DERIVATIVES **bancassurer** n.

**banco** /ˈbaŋkəʊ/ ● **exclam.** (in baccarat and chemin de fer) expressing a player's willingness to meet the banker's whole stake single-handed.
– ORIGIN C18: via Fr. from Ital., 'bank'.

**band**[1] ● **n.** **1** a flat, thin strip or loop of material used as a fastener, for reinforcement, or as decoration. ➤a belt or strap transmitting motion between two wheels or pulleys. ➤N. Amer. Ornithology a ring of metal placed round a bird's leg to identify it. **2** a stripe, line, or elongated area of a different colour or composition from its surroundings: *a band of cloud*. **3** (especially in financial contexts) a range of values or a specified category within a series. ➤a range of frequencies or wavelengths in a spectrum: *channels in the UHF band*. ➤any of several groups into which school pupils of the same age are divided on the basis of similar ability. **4** (**bands**) a collar with two hanging strips, worn by certain lawyers, clerics, and academics as part of their formal dress. **5** archaic a bond. ● **v.** **1** surround or fit with a band. **2** mark with a stripe or stripes of a different colour. **3** allocate to a range or category.
– DERIVATIVES **bander** n. **banding** n.
– ORIGIN OE, from ON, reinforced in ME by OFr. *bande*, of Gmc origin; rel. to **BIND**.

**band**[2] ● **n.** **1** a small group of musicians and vocalists who play pop, jazz, or rock music. ➤a group of musicians who play brass, wind, or percussion instruments. **2** a group of people having a common interest or purpose or characterized by a common feature. **3** N. Amer. a herd or flock. ● **v.** form a group for a mutual purpose.
– ORIGIN ME: from OFr. *bande*, of Gmc origin; rel. to **BANNER**.

**bandage** ● **n.** a strip of woven material used to bind up a wound or to protect an injured part of the body. ● **v.** bind with a bandage.
– DERIVATIVES **bandaging** n.
– ORIGIN C16: from Fr., from *bande* (see **BAND**[1]).

**bandanna** /banˈdanə/ ● **n.** a large coloured handkerchief or neckerchief.
– ORIGIN C18: prob. via Port. from Hindi.

**B. & B.** ● **abbrev.** bed and breakfast.

**bandbox** ● **n.** a circular cardboard box for carrying hats.
– ORIGIN C17: orig. denoting a box used for carrying neckbands.

**bandeau** /ˈbandəʊ/ ● **n.** (pl. **bandeaux** /-dəʊz/) **1** a narrow band worn round the head to hold the hair in position. **2** a woman's strapless top formed from a band of fabric fitting around the bust.
– ORIGIN C18: from Fr., from OFr. *bandel*, dimin. of *bande* (see **BAND**[1]).

**banderilla** /ˌbandəˈriːjə, -rɪljə/ ● **n.** a decorated dart thrust into a bull's neck or shoulders during a bullfight.
– ORIGIN Sp., dimin. of *bandera* 'banner'.

**banderillero** /ˌbandərɪlˈjɛrəʊ, -riːˈjɛːrəʊ/ ● **n.** (pl. **-os**) a bullfighter who uses banderillas.
– ORIGIN from Sp.

**banderole** /ˈbandərəʊl/ (also **banderol**) ● **n.** **1** a long, narrow flag with a cleft end, flown at a masthead. **2** a ribbon-like stone scroll bearing an inscription.
– ORIGIN C16: from Fr., from Ital. *banderuola*, dimin. of *bandiera* 'banner'.

**bandersnatch** /ˈbandəsnatʃ/ ● **n.** a fierce mythical creature immune to bribery and capable of moving very fast.
– ORIGIN 1871: coined by Lewis Carroll in *Through the Looking Glass*.

**bandfish** ● **n.** (pl. same or **-fishes**) **1** an elongated marine fish with dorsal and often anal fins that extend the length of the body. [*Cepola rubescens* and other species.] **2** a large edible South American freshwater fish with a long trunk-like snout and no tail fins. [*Rhamphichthys rostratus*.]

**bandicoot** /ˈbandɪkuːt/ ● **n.** a mainly insectivorous mar-

supial native to Australia and New Guinea. [Family Peramelidae: several species.]
– ORIGIN C18: from Telugu *pandikokku*, lit. 'pig-rat'.

**bandicoot rat** • n. an Asian rat that is a destructive pest in many places. [*Bandicota indica* and other species.]

**bandit** • n. (pl. **bandits** or **banditti** /ban'di:ti/) **1** a violent robber or outlaw belonging to a gang. **2** military slang an enemy aircraft.
– DERIVATIVES **banditry** n.
– ORIGIN C16: from Ital. *bandito*, *bandire* 'ban'.

**bandleader** • n. a player at the head of a musical band.

**bandmaster** • n. the conductor of a musical band, especially a brass or military one.

**bandog** • n. a fighting dog bred for its strength and ferocity.
– ORIGIN ME, orig. denoting a dog kept on a chain or 'band'.

**bandolier** /ˌbandə'lɪə/ (also **bandoleer**) • n. a shoulder belt with loops or pockets for cartridges.
– ORIGIN C16: from Fr. *bandoulière*; perh. from Sp. *bandolera* (from *banda* 'sash'), or from Catalan *bandolera* (from *bandoler* 'bandit').

**bandoneon** /ban'dəʊnɪən/ • n. a type of square concertina, especially popular in Argentina.
– ORIGIN via Sp. from Ger. *Bandonion*, named after Heinrich *Band*, the Ger. musician who invented it.

**bandora** /ban'dɔ:rə/ (also **bandore** /ban'dɔ:/) • n. a kind of bass lute with a scallop-shaped body and metal strings.
– ORIGIN C16: origin uncertain; rel. to Du. *bandoor*, Sp. *bandurria*, also **BANJO**: prob. based on Gk *pandoura* 'three-stringed lute'.

**bandpass** • n. Electronics the range of frequencies which are transmitted through a filter.

**bandsaw** • n. a saw consisting of an endless moving steel belt with a serrated edge.

**bandshell** • n. chiefly N. Amer. a bandstand in the form of a large concave shell with special acoustic properties.

**bandstand** • n. a covered outdoor platform for a band to play on.

**bandura** /ban'du:rə/ • n. a Ukrainian stringed instrument resembling a large asymmetrical lute with many strings, held vertically and plucked like a zither.
– ORIGIN Ukrainian; cf. **BANDORA**.

**bandwagon** • n. **1** historical a wagon used for carrying a band in a parade or procession. **2** a particular activity or cause that has suddenly become fashionable or popular: *the company is jumping on the Green bandwagon.*

**bandwidth** • n. a range of frequencies, especially one used in telecommunications. ➤ the transmission capacity of a computer network or other telecommunication system.

**bandy**[1] • adj. (**-ier**, **-iest**) (of a person's legs) curved outwards so that the knees are wide apart.
– ORIGIN C17: perh. from obs. *bandy*, denoting a curved stick used in hockey.

**bandy**[2] • v. (**-ies**, **-ied**) (usu. **be bandied about/around**) pass on or discuss (an idea or rumour) in a casual or uninformed way.
– PHRASES **bandy words** argue pointlessly or rudely.
– ORIGIN C16 (in the sense 'pass (a ball) to and fro'): perh. from Fr. *bander* 'take sides at tennis', from *bande* (see **BAND**[2]).

**bandy-bandy** • n. (pl. **bandy-bandys**) a small mildly venomous Australian snake marked with black-and-white bands. [*Vermicella annulata*.]
– ORIGIN 1920s: from Kattah (an Aborig. lang.) *bandi bandi*.

**bane** • n. **1** a cause of great distress or annoyance: *the telephone was the bane of my life.* **2** archaic poison.
– DERIVATIVES **baneful** adj. (archaic).
– ORIGIN OE *bana*, of Gmc origin.

**baneberry** • n. (pl. **-ies**) a plant with fluffy spikes of creamy-white flowers and shiny berries. [*Actaea spicata* (herb Christopher) and other species.] ➤ the bitter, often poisonous berry of this plant.

**bang**[1] • n. **1** a sudden loud, sharp noise. ➤ a sudden painful blow. **2** (**bangs**) chiefly N. Amer. a fringe of hair cut straight across the forehead. **3** Computing, chiefly N. Amer. the character '!' • v. **1** strike or put down forcefully and noisily. ➤ make or cause to make a sudden loud noise. **2** vulgar slang (of a man) have sexual intercourse with. • adv. informal, chiefly Brit. exactly: *the train arrived bang on time.*
– PHRASES **bang for one's** (or **the**) **buck** US informal value for money. **bang goes ——** informal a plan or hope is suddenly or completely destroyed. **bang on** Brit. informal exactly right. **get a bang out of** informal, chiefly N. Amer. derive excitement or pleasure from. **with a bang 1** abruptly. **2** impressively or spectacularly.
– PHRASAL VERBS **bang away at** informal do persistently or doggedly. **bang on about** informal talk at tedious length about. **bang something out** informal **1** play music noisily and unskilfully. **2** produce something hurriedly or in great quantities. **bang someone up** Brit. informal imprison someone.
– ORIGIN C16: imitative, perh. of Scand. origin.

**bang**[2] /baŋ/ • n. variant spelling of **BHANG**.

**Bangalore torpedo** • n. a tube containing explosive used by infantry for blowing up wire entanglements or other barriers.

**banger** • n. chiefly Brit. **1** informal a sausage. **2** informal an old car. **3** a loud explosive firework.

**Bangla** /'bʌŋlə:/ • n. the Bengali language.
– ORIGIN from Bengali *bāṅglā*.

**Bangladeshi** /ˌbaŋglə'dɛʃi/ • n. (pl. same or **Bangladeshis**) a native or inhabitant of Bangladesh. • adj. of or relating to Bangladesh or its people.

**bangle** • n. a rigid ornamental band worn around the arm.
– ORIGIN C18: from Hindi *baṅglī* 'glass bracelet'.

**bangtail** • n. a horse's tail that has been cut straight across just below the level of the hocks.

**bangtail muster** • n. Austral. a count of cattle involving cutting across the tufts at the tail ends as each is counted.

**bang-up** • adj. N. Amer. informal excellent.

**bani** plural form of **BAN**[2].

**banish** • v. **1** send (someone) away, especially from a country, as an official punishment. **2** dismiss from one's mind.
– DERIVATIVES **banishment** n.
– ORIGIN ME: from OFr. *baniss-*, *banir*; ult. of Gmc origin and rel. to **BAN**[1].

**banister** /'banɪstə/ (also **bannister**) • n. the uprights and handrail at the side of a staircase. ➤ a single upright at the side of a staircase.
– ORIGIN C17: from earlier *barrister*, alt. of **BALUSTER**.

**banjax** /'bandʒaks/ • v. informal ruin or incapacitate.
– ORIGIN 1930s: orig. Anglo-Ir., of unknown origin.

**banjo** • n. (pl. **-os** or **-oes**) a stringed instrument of the guitar family, with an open-backed soundbox of vellum (or plastic) stretched over a round hoop.
– DERIVATIVES **banjoist** n.
– ORIGIN C18: orig. a black Amer. alt. of *bandore* (see **BANDORA**).

**bank**[1] • n. **1** the land alongside or sloping down to a river or lake. **2** a long, high mound or elevation. **3** a transverse slope given to a road, railway, or sports track to enable vehicles or runners to maintain speed round a curve. **4** the sideways tilt of an aircraft when turning in flight. **5** a set of similar things grouped together in rows. **6** the cushion of a pool table. • v. **1** heap or form into a mass or mound. **2** (of an aircraft or vehicle) tilt sideways in making a turn. **3** build (a road, railway, or sports track) with a bank on a bend. **4** Brit. (of a locomotive) provide additional power for (a train) in ascending an incline. **5** (of an angler) land (a fish).
– ORIGIN ME: from ON *bakki*, of Gmc origin; rel. to **BENCH**.

**bank**[2] • n. **1** a financial establishment that uses money deposited by customers for investment, pays it out when

required, makes loans at interest, and exchanges currency. ➤a site or receptacle where something may be deposited for recycling: *a paper bank*. ➤(**the bank**) the store of money or tokens held by the banker in some gambling or board games. **2** a stock of something available for use when required: *a blood bank*. ● **v. 1** deposit (money or valuables) in a bank. ➤have an account at a particular bank. **2** (**bank on**) base one's hopes or confidence on.
– PHRASES **break the bank** [usu. with neg.] informal cost more than one can afford.
– ORIGIN C15 (orig. denoting a money dealer's table): from Fr. *banque* or Ital. *banca*, from med. L. *banca*, *bancus*, of Gmc origin; rel. to **BANK**[1] and **BENCH**.

**bankable** ● **adj.** certain to bring profit and success.
– DERIVATIVES **bankability** /-əˈbɪlɪti/ n.

**bankassurance** ● **n.** variant spelling of **BANCASSURANCE**.

**bank bill** ● **n. 1** Brit. a bill of exchange drawn by one bank on another. **2** chiefly US a banknote.

**bank card** ● **n.** another term for **CHEQUE CARD**.

**bank draft** ● **n.** a cheque drawn by a bank on its own funds.

**banker**[1] ● **n. 1** a person who manages or owns a bank or group of banks. ➤the person running the table, controlling play, or acting as dealer in some gambling or board games. **2** Brit. a supposedly certain bet. ➤a result forecast identically (while other forecasts differ) in several football-pool entries on one coupon.
– ORIGIN C16: from Fr. *banquier*, from *banque* (see **BANK**[2]).

**banker**[2] ● **n.** Austral./NZ informal a river flooded to the top of its banks.

**banker's hours** ● **pl. n.** N. Amer. short working hours.

**banker's order** ● **n.** Brit. an instruction to a bank to make payments of a stated sum at regular intervals.

**bank holiday** ● **n.** Brit. a day on which banks are officially closed, kept as a public holiday.

**banking**[1] ● **n.** the business conducted or services offered by a bank.

**banking**[2] ● **n.** an embankment or artificial bank.

**banknote** ● **n.** a piece of paper money, constituting a central bank's promissory note.

**bank rate** ● **n.** another term for **BASE RATE** or **DISCOUNT RATE**.

**bankroll** chiefly N. Amer. ● **n.** a roll of banknotes. ● **v.** informal support financially.

**bankrupt** ● **adj. 1** declared in law unable to pay one's debts. **2** completely lacking in a particular good quality or value: *the cause is morally bankrupt*. ● **n.** a person judged by a court to be bankrupt. ● **v.** reduce to a bankrupt state.
– DERIVATIVES **bankruptcy** n.
– ORIGIN C16: from Ital. *banca rotta* 'broken bench'.

**banksia** /ˈbaŋksɪə/ ● **n.** an evergreen Australian shrub with flowers resembling bottlebrushes. [Genus *Banksia*.]
– ORIGIN mod. L., named after the Engl. botanist Sir Joseph *Banks*.

**banksia rose** ● **n.** a small-flowered Chinese climbing rose. [*Rosa banksiae*.]

**bank statement** ● **n.** a printed record of the transactions in and balance of a bank account.

**banner** ● **n.** a long strip of cloth bearing a slogan or design. ➤a flag on a pole used as the standard of a king, knight, or army. ● **adj.** N. Amer. excellent; outstanding.
– DERIVATIVES **bannered** adj.
– ORIGIN ME: from OFr. *baniere*, ult. of Gmc origin and rel. to **BAND**[2].

**banneret** /ˈbanərɪt/ ● **n.** historical **1** a knight who commanded his own troops in battle under his own banner. **2** a knighthood given on the battlefield for courage.
– ORIGIN ME: from OFr. *baneret*, lit. 'bannered', from *baniere* (see **BANNER**).

**bannister** ● **n.** variant spelling of **BANISTER**.

**bannock** /ˈbanək/ ● **n.** a round, flat loaf, typically unleavened, associated with Scotland and northern England.
– ORIGIN OE *bannuc*, of Celtic origin.

**banns** ● **pl. n.** a notice read out on three successive Sundays in a parish church, announcing an intended marriage and giving the opportunity for objections.
– ORIGIN ME: pl. of **BAN**[1].

**banoffi pie** /bəˈnɒfi/ (also **banoffee pie**) ● **n.** a pie or tart made with bananas, toffee, and cream.
– ORIGIN 1970s: from **BANANA** + **TOFFEE**.

**banquet** /ˈbaŋkwɪt/ ● **n.** an elaborate and formal meal for many people. ● **v.** (**banqueted**, **banqueting**) entertain with a banquet.
– DERIVATIVES **banqueter** n.
– ORIGIN C15: from Fr., dimin. of *banc* (see **BANK**[1]).

**banquette** /baŋˈkɛt/ ● **n. 1** an upholstered bench along a wall. **2** a raised step behind a rampart.
– ORIGIN C17: from Fr., from Ital. *banchetta*, dimin. of *banca* (see **BANK**[2]).

**banshee** /banˈʃiː, ˈbanʃiː/ ● **n.** (in Irish legend) a female spirit whose wailing warns of a death in a house.
– ORIGIN C17: from Ir. *bean sídhe*, from Old Ir. *ben síde* 'woman of the fairies'.

**bantam** ● **n.** a chicken of a small breed.
– ORIGIN C18: appar. named after the province of *Bantam* in Java, although the fowl is not native there.

**bantamweight** ● **n.** a weight in boxing and other sports intermediate between flyweight and featherweight.

**banteng** /ˈbantɛŋ/ ● **n.** a SE Asian forest ox that resembles the domestic cow, domesticated in Bali. [*Bos javanicus*.]
– ORIGIN C19: from Malay.

**banter** ● **n.** the playful and friendly exchange of teasing remarks. ● **v.** engage in banter.
– DERIVATIVES **banterer** n.
– ORIGIN C17: of unknown origin.

**Bantu** /banˈtuː, ˈbantuː/ ● **n.** (pl. same or **Bantus**) **1** a member of an extensive group of indigenous peoples of central and southern Africa. **2** the group of Niger–Congo languages spoken by these peoples, including Swahili, Xhosa, and Zulu.
– ORIGIN pl. (in certain Bantu langs) of *-ntu* 'person'.

**USAGE** Bantu

Bantu is a strongly offensive word in South African English, especially when used of individual people, but is still used outside South Africa to refer to the group of languages and their speakers collectively.

**banyan** /ˈbanɪən, -njən/ (also **banian**) ● **n. 1** (also **banyan tree**) an Indian fig tree, whose branches produce wide-ranging aerial roots which later become accessory trunks. [*Ficus benghalensis*.] **2** a loose flannel jacket, shirt, or gown worn in India.
– ORIGIN C16: from Port., from Gujarati *vāṇiyo* 'man of the trading caste', from Sanskrit (orig. applied by Europeans to a tree under which traders had built a pagoda).

**banzai** /banˈzʌɪ/ ● **exclam. 1** a Japanese battle cry. **2** a form of greeting used to the Japanese emperor. ● **adj.** informal fierce and reckless.
– ORIGIN Japanese, lit. 'ten thousand years (of life to you)'.

**baobab** /ˈbeɪə(ʊ)bab/ ● **n.** a short African or Australian tree with a very thick trunk and large edible fruit, living to a great age. [Genus *Adansonia*: several species.]
– ORIGIN C17: prob. from an Afr. lang.

**BAOR** ● **abbrev.** British Army of the Rhine.

**bap** ● **n.** Brit. a large, round, flattish bread roll, typically with a floury top.
– ORIGIN C16: of unknown origin.

**baptism** ● **n.** the Christian rite of sprinkling water on to a person's forehead or of immersing them in water, symbolizing purification or regeneration and admission to the Christian Church.
– PHRASES **baptism of fire** a difficult or painful new undertaking or experience.
– DERIVATIVES **baptismal** adj.
– ORIGIN ME: from OFr. *baptesme*, via eccles. L. from eccles. Gk *baptismos*, from Gk *baptizein* 'immerse, baptize'.

**baptismal name** ● **n.** a personal name given at baptism.

**baptist** ● n. **1** (**Baptist**) a member of a Protestant Christian denomination advocating baptism only of adult believers by total immersion. **2** a person who baptizes someone.

**baptistery** (also **baptistry**) ● n. (pl. **-ies**) the part of a church used for baptism. ➤(in a Baptist chapel) a sunken receptacle used for baptism by total immersion.

**baptize** (also **-ise**) ● v. **1** administer baptism to. **2** give a specified name or nickname to.
– ORIGIN ME: via OFr. from eccles. L. *baptizare*, from Gk *baptizein* 'immerse, baptize'.

**Bar.** ● abbrev. Baruch (Apocrypha) (in biblical references).

**bar[1]** ● n. **1** a long rigid piece of wood, metal, or similar material, typically used as an obstruction, fastening, or weapon. ➤a sandbank or shoal at the mouth of a harbour or an estuary. ➤Brit. a metal strip below the clasp of a medal, awarded as an additional distinction. ➤Heraldry a charge in the form of a narrow horizontal stripe across the shield. **2** a counter in a public house or cafe across which alcoholic drinks or refreshments are served. ➤a room in a public house, restaurant, or hotel in which alcohol is served. ➤an establishment where alcohol and other refreshments are served. ➤a small shop or stall serving refreshments or providing a specified service: *a snack bar.* **3** a barrier or restriction to action or advance: *a bar to promotion.* ➤a plea arresting an action or claim in a law case. **4** Music any of the short sections or measures into which a piece of music is divided, shown on a score by vertical lines across the stave. **5** (**the bar**) a partition in a court room, now usually notional, beyond which most people may not pass and at which an accused person stands. ➤Brit. a rail marking the end of each chamber in the Houses of Parliament. **6** (**the Bar**) the profession of barrister. ➤Brit. barristers collectively. ➤N. Amer. lawyers collectively. ● v. (**barred**, **barring**) **1** fasten with a bar or bars. **2** prohibit from doing something or going somewhere. ➤exclude from consideration. ➤Law prevent or delay (an action) by objection. **3** mark with bars or stripes. ● prep. chiefly Brit. except for. ➤Brit. Horse Racing except the horses indicated (used when stating the odds).
– PHRASES **bar none** with no exceptions. **be called** (or **go**) **to the Bar** Brit. be admitted as a barrister. **be called within the Bar** Brit. be appointed a Queen's Counsel. **behind bars** in prison.
– DERIVATIVES **barred** adj.
– ORIGIN ME: from OFr. *barre* (n.), *barrer* (v.), of unknown origin.

**bar[2]** ● n. a unit of pressure equivalent to a hundred thousand newtons per square metre or approximately one atmosphere.
– ORIGIN C20: from Gk *baros* 'weight'.

**bara brith** /ˌbarə ˈbrɪθ/ ● n. a traditional Welsh tea bread, made with raisins, currants, and candied peel.

**barathea** /ˌbarəˈθɪə/ ● n. a fine woollen cloth, sometimes mixed with silk or cotton, used for coats and suits.
– ORIGIN C19: of unknown origin.

**baraza** /bəˈrɑːzə/ ● n. (in East Africa) a public meeting place.
– ORIGIN from Kiswahili.

**barb[1]** ● n. **1** a sharp projection near the end of an arrow, fish hook, or similar object, which is angled away from the main point so as to make extraction difficult. ➤a barbel at the mouth of some fish. ➤one of the fine hair-like filaments growing from the shaft of a feather, forming the vane. **2** a deliberately hurtful remark. **3** a freshwater fish with barbels around the mouth, popular in aquaria. [*Barbus pentazona* and other species.]
– DERIVATIVES **barbed** adj. **barbless** adj.
– ORIGIN ME (denoting a piece of linen worn around the chin by nuns): from OFr. *barbe*, from L. *barba* 'beard'.

**barb[2]** ● n. a small horse of a hardy breed originally from North Africa.
– ORIGIN C17: from Fr. *barbe*, from Ital. *barbero* 'of Barbary'.

**Barbadian** /bɑːˈbeɪdɪən/ ● n. a native or inhabitant of Barbados. ● adj. of or relating to Barbados or its people.

**barbarian** ● n. **1** (in ancient times) a member of a people not belonging to one of the great civilizations (Greek, Roman, Christian). **2** an uncultured or brutish person. ● adj. **1** of or relating to ancient barbarians. **2** uncultured; brutish.
– ORIGIN ME: from OFr. *barbarien*, from *barbare*, or from L. *barbarus*, from Gk *barbaros* 'foreign'.

**barbaric** ● adj. **1** savagely cruel. **2** primitive; unsophisticated.
– DERIVATIVES **barbarically** adv.

**barbarism** ● n. **1** absence of culture and civilization. **2** extreme cruelty or brutality. **3** a word or expression which is badly formed according to traditional philological rules, e.g. a word formed from elements of different languages, such as *breathalyser* (English and Greek).
– DERIVATIVES **barbarity** n. **barbarization** (also **-isation**) n. **barbarize** (also **-ise**) v.

**barbarous** ● adj. **1** exceedingly brutal. **2** primitive; uncivilized.
– DERIVATIVES **barbarously** adv. **barbarousness** n.

**Barbary ape** ● n. a tailless macaque monkey that is native to NW Africa and also found on the Rock of Gibraltar. [*Macaca sylvana.*]
– ORIGIN from *Barbary*, a former name for the western part of N. Africa.

**Barbary sheep** ● n. a short-coated sheep with a long neck ruff, found in the high deserts of northern Africa. [*Ammotragus lervia.*]

**barbastelle** /ˌbɑːbəˈstɛl, ˈbɑːbəstɛl/ ● n. an Old World bat with broad ears that meet over the head. [Genus *Barbastella*: two species]
– ORIGIN C18: from Fr., from Ital. *barbastello.*

**barbecue** ● n. **1** an outdoor meal or gathering at which meat, fish, or other food is grilled on a rack over an open fire. **2** a structure for grilling food at a barbecue. ● v. (**barbecues**, **barbecued**, **barbecuing**) cook (food) on a barbecue.
– ORIGIN C17 (in the sense 'wooden framework for storing meat or fish to be dried'): from Sp. *barbacoa*, perh. from Arawak *barbacoa* 'wooden frame on posts'.

**barbecue sauce** ● n. a highly seasoned sauce containing vinegar, spices, and usually chillies.

**barbed wire** ● n. wire with clusters of short, sharp spikes set at short intervals along it, used as a defensive barrier.

**barbel** /ˈbɑːb(ə)l/ ● n. **1** a fleshy filament growing from the mouth or snout of a fish. **2** a large freshwater fish of the carp family, with barbels hanging from the mouth. [*Barbus barbus.*]
– ORIGIN ME: via OFr. from late L. *barbellus*, dimin. of *barbus* 'barbel', from *barba* 'beard'.

**barbell** /ˈbɑːbɛl/ ● n. a long metal bar to which discs of varying weights are attached at each end, used for weightlifting.
– ORIGIN C19: from BAR[1] + BELL[1].

**barber** ● n. a person who cuts men's hair and shaves or trims beards as an occupation. ● v. cut or trim (a man's hair).
– ORIGIN ME: via Anglo-Norman Fr. from OFr. *barbe* (see BARB[1]).

**barberry** ● n. (pl. **-ies**) a spiny shrub with yellow flowers and red berries. [*Berberis vulgaris* and other species.]
– ORIGIN ME: from OFr. *berberis* (see BERBERIS).

**barbershop** ● n. a popular style of close harmony singing, typically for four male voices.
– ORIGIN from the former custom of passing time in a barber's shop by harmonizing to a lute or guitar.

**barber's pole** ● n. a pole painted with spiralling red and white stripes and hung outside barbers' shops as a business sign.

**barbet** /ˈbɑːbɪt/ ● n. a brightly coloured fruit-eating songbird, chiefly tropical, that has a stout bill with tufts of bristles at the base. [Family Capitonidae: numerous species.]
– ORIGIN C16 (orig. denoting a poodle): from Fr., from *barbe* (see BARB[1]).

**barbette** /bɑːˈbɛt/ ● n. a fixed armoured housing at the

base of a gun turret on a warship or armoured vehicle.
– ORIGIN C18: from Fr., dimin. of *barbe* (see BARB[1]).

**barbican** /ˈbɑːbɪk(ə)n/ ● n. the outer defence of a city or castle, especially a double tower above a gate or drawbridge.
– ORIGIN ME: from OFr. *barbacane*; prob. based on Arab.

**barbie** ● n. (pl. **-ies**) informal, chiefly Austral./NZ a barbecue.

**Barbie doll** ● n. **1** trademark a doll representing a conventionally attractive young woman. **2** informal, chiefly N. Amer. an attractive but characterless or unintelligent young woman.

**bar billiards** ● pl. n. [treated as sing.] Brit. a form of billiards played on a small table, in which balls are struck into holes guarded by pegs.

**barbital** /ˈbɑːbɪt(ə)l/ ● n. North American term for BARBITONE.

**barbitone** /ˈbɑːbɪtəʊn/ ● n. a long-acting sedative and sleep-inducing drug of the barbiturate type.

**barbiturate** /bɑːˈbɪtjʊrət, -reɪt/ ● n. **1** any of a class of sedative drugs derived from barbituric acid. **2** Chemistry a salt or ester of barbituric acid.

**barbituric acid** /ˌbɑːbɪˈtjʊərɪk, -ˈtʃʊərɪk/ ● n. Chemistry a synthetic organic compound from which the barbiturates are derived.
– ORIGIN C19: from Fr. *barbiturique*, from Ger. *Barbitursäure*, from the given name *Barbara* + *Säure* 'acid'.

**barbola** /bɑːˈbəʊlə/ ● n. the craft of making small models of fruit or flowers from a plastic paste.
– ORIGIN 1920s: an arbitrary formation from BARBOTINE.

**barbotine** /ˈbɑːbətɪn/ ● n. slip (liquid clay) used to decorate pottery.
– ORIGIN C19: from Fr.

**Barbour** /ˈbɑːbə/ (also **Barbour jacket**) ● n. trademark a type of green waxed outdoor jacket.
– ORIGIN named after John *Barbour*, a draper in NE England.

**Barbudan** /bɑːˈbuːdən/ ● n. a native or inhabitant of Barbuda, an island in the West Indies. ● adj. of or relating to Barbuda or its inhabitants.

**barbule** /ˈbɑːbjuːl/ ● n. a minute filament projecting from the barb of a feather.
– ORIGIN C19: from L. *barbula*, dimin. of *barba* 'beard'.

**barbwire** ● n. N. Amer. barbed wire.

**barcarole** /ˈbɑːkərəʊl, ˌbɑːkəˈrəʊl/ (also **barcarolle** /-rɒl, -ˈrɒl/) ● n. a song traditionally sung by Venetian gondoliers. ➤ a musical composition in the style of such a song.
– ORIGIN C18: from Fr. *barcarolle*, from Venetian Ital. *barcarola* 'boatman's song', from *barca* 'boat'.

**barchan** /ˈbɑːk(ə)n/ ● n. a crescent-shaped shifting sand dune, as found in the deserts of Turkestan.
– ORIGIN C19: from Turkic *barkhan*.

**bar chart** (also **bar graph**) ● n. a diagram in which the numerical values of variables are represented by the height or length of lines or rectangles.

**bar code** ● n. a machine-readable code in the form of a pattern of parallel lines of varying widths, printed on and identifying a commodity for stock control.

**Barcoo** /bɑːˈkuː/ ● adj. Austral. informal of or relating to the remote inland area of Australia: *Barcoo sickness*.
– ORIGIN C19: from the name of a river (and the surrounding country) in western Queensland.

**bard**[1] ● n. **1** archaic or poetic/literary a poet, traditionally one reciting epics. ➤ (**the Bard**) Shakespeare. **2** (**Bard**) the winner of a prize for Welsh verse at an Eisteddfod.
– DERIVATIVES **bardic** adj.
– ORIGIN ME: from Sc. Gaelic *bàrd*, Ir. *bard*, Welsh *bardd*, of Celtic origin.

**bard**[2] ● n. a rasher of fat bacon placed on meat or game before roasting. ● v. cover with bards.
– ORIGIN C18: from Fr. *barde*, a transferred sense of *barde* 'armour for the breast of a warhorse'.

**bardie** /ˈbɑːdi/ (also **bardee** or **bardy**) ● n. (pl. **-ies**) Austral. the edible larva or pupa of certain beetles or moths.
– ORIGIN C19: from Nyungar (and other Aborig. langs) *bardi*.

**bardo** /ˈbɑːdəʊ/ ● n. (in Tibetan Buddhism) a state of existence between death and rebirth.
– ORIGIN Tibetan *bár-do*, from *bar* 'interval' + *do* 'two'.

**bardolatry** /bɑːˈdɒlətri/ ● n. humorous excessive admiration of Shakespeare.
– DERIVATIVES **bardolater** n.

**Bardolino** /ˌbɑːdəˈliːnəʊ/ ● n. a red wine from the Veneto region of Italy.
– ORIGIN from Ital.

**bare** ● adj. **1** (of a person or part of the body) not clothed or covered. ➤ without the appropriate or usual covering or contents. ➤ (**bare of**) without. **2** without elaboration; basic. ➤ only just sufficient: *a bare majority*. ● v. uncover (a part of the body) and expose it to view.
– PHRASES **bare one's teeth** show one's teeth, typically when angry. **with one's bare hands** without using tools or weapons.
– DERIVATIVES **barely** adv. **bareness** n.
– ORIGIN OE *bær* (n.), *barian* (v.), of Gmc origin.

**bareback** ● adj. & adv. on an unsaddled horse.

**bareboat** ● adj. (of a boat or ship) hired without a crew.

**barefaced** ● adj. shameless and undisguised: *a barefaced lie*.
– DERIVATIVES **barefacedly** adv. **barefacedness** n.

**barefoot** (also **barefooted**) ● adj. & adv. wearing nothing on the feet.

**barefoot doctor** ● n. a paramedical worker with basic medical training working in a rural district in China.

**barège** /bəˈreɪʒ/ ● n. a light, silky dress fabric resembling gauze and made from wool.
– ORIGIN Fr., named after the village of *Barèges* in SW France, where it was orig. made.

**barehanded** ● adj. & adv. with nothing in or covering one's hands.

**bareheaded** ● adj. & adv. without a covering for one's head.

**bare-knuckle** (also **bare-knuckled**) ● adj. (of a boxer or boxing match) without gloves.

**barf** informal, chiefly N. Amer. ● v. vomit. ● n. vomited food.
– ORIGIN 1960s (orig. US): of unknown origin.

**barfly** /ˈbɑːflʌɪ/ ● n. (pl. **-flies**) informal a person who spends much of their time drinking in bars.

**bargain** ● n. **1** an agreement between two or more people as to what each will do for the other. **2** a thing bought or offered for sale for a lower price than normal. ● v. **1** negotiate the terms and conditions of a transaction. **2** (**bargain for/on**) expect.
– PHRASES **drive a hard bargain** be uncompromising in making a deal. **into** (N. Amer. **in**) **the bargain** in addition.
– DERIVATIVES **bargainer** n.
– ORIGIN ME: from OFr. *bargaine* (n.), *bargaignier* (v.); prob. of Gmc origin.

**barge** ● n. **1** a long flat-bottomed boat for carrying freight on canals and rivers. ➤ a long ornamental boat used for pleasure or on ceremonial occasions. **2** a boat used by the chief officers of a warship. ● v. **1** move forcefully or roughly. ➤ (**barge in**) intrude or interrupt rudely or awkwardly. **2** convey by barge.
– ORIGIN ME: from OFr., perh. based on Gk *baris* 'Egyptian boat'.

**bargeboard** ● n. an ornamental board fixed to the gable end of a roof to hide the ends of the roof timbers.
– ORIGIN C19: from *barge-* (used in terms relating to the gable of a building), perh. from med. L. *bargus* 'gallows'.

**bargee** /bɑːˈdʒiː/ ● n. chiefly Brit. a person in charge of or working on a barge.

**bargepole** ● n. a long pole used to propel a barge and fend off obstacles.
– PHRASES **would not touch someone/thing with a bargepole** informal would refuse to have anything to do with someone or something.

**bar graph** ● n. another term for BAR CHART.

**barilla** /bəˈrɪlə/ ● n. impure alkali made from the ashes of saltwort and other plants.
– ORIGIN C17: from Sp. *barrilla*, dimin. of *barra* 'bar'.

**barite** /ˈbarʌɪt, ˈbɛː-/ ● **n.** variant spelling of **BARYTE**.

**baritone** ● **n. 1** an adult male singing voice between tenor and bass. **2** [as modifier] denoting an instrument that is second lowest in pitch in its family.
– ORIGIN C17: from Ital. *baritono*, from Gk *barutonos*, from *barus* 'heavy' + *tonos* (see **TONE**).

**barium** /ˈbɛːrɪəm/ ● **n.** the chemical element of atomic number 56, a soft white reactive metal of the alkaline earth group. (Symbol: **Ba**) ➤ Medicine a mixture of barium sulphate and water, opaque to X-rays, which is swallowed to permit radiological examination of the stomach or intestines.
– ORIGIN C19: from **BARYTA** + **-IUM**.

**bark**[1] ● **n.** the sharp explosive cry of a dog, fox, or seal. ● **v. 1** (of a dog, fox, or seal) give a bark. **2** utter (a command or question) abruptly or aggressively. ➤ US call out in order to sell or advertise something.
– PHRASES **one's bark is worse than one's bite** one is not as ferocious as one seems. **be barking up the wrong tree** informal be pursuing a mistaken line of thought or course of action.
– ORIGIN OE *beorc* (n.), *beorcan* (v.), of Gmc origin.

**bark**[2] ● **n.** the tough protective outer sheath of the trunk, branches, and twigs of a tree or woody shrub. ● **v. 1** strip the bark from. **2** scrape the skin off (one's shin) by accidentally hitting it. **3** tan or dye (leather or other materials) using the tannins found in bark.
– DERIVATIVES **-barked** adj.
– ORIGIN ME: from ON *bǫrkr*; perh. rel. to **BIRCH**.

**bark**[3] ● **n.** archaic or poetic/literary a ship or boat.
– ORIGIN ME: var. of **BARQUE**.

**bark beetle** ● **n.** a small wood-boring beetle that tunnels under the bark of trees. [Family Scolytidae: many species.]

**barkcloth** ● **n.** cloth made from the inner bark of the paper mulberry or similar tree.

**barkentine** ● **n.** US spelling of **BARQUENTINE**.

**barker** ● **n.** informal a tout at an auction or sideshow who calls out to passers-by to attract custom.

**barking** ● **adj.** Brit. informal completely mad.

**barking deer** ● **n.** another term for **MUNTJAC**.

**barley** ● **n.** a hardy cereal with coarse bristles extending from the ears, cultivated chiefly for use in brewing and stockfeed. [Genus *Hordeum*.]
– ORIGIN OE *bærlic* (adj.), from *bære*, *bere* 'barley' + *-lic* (see **-LY**[1]).

**barleycorn** ● **n.** a former unit of measurement (about a third of an inch) based on the length of a grain of barley.

**barleymow** ● **n.** Brit. archaic a stack of barley.

**barley sugar** ● **n.** an amber-coloured sweet made of boiled sugar, traditionally shaped as a twisted stick.

**barley water** ● **n.** a drink made from water and a boiled barley mixture.

**barley wine** ● **n.** a strong English ale.

**bar line** ● **n.** Music a vertical line used in a musical score to mark a division between bars.

**barm** ● **n. 1** the froth on fermenting malt liquor. **2** archaic or dialect yeast or leaven.
– ORIGIN OE *beorma*, of W. Gmc origin.

**barmaid** ● **n. 1** Brit. a woman serving behind the bar of a public house. **2** N. Amer. a waitress who serves drinks in a bar.

**barman** ● **n.** (pl. **-men**) chiefly Brit. a man serving behind the bar of a public house.

**barmbrack** ● **n.** a kind of soft, spicy bread containing dried fruit, originating in Ireland.
– ORIGIN from Ir. *bairin breac* 'speckled cake'.

**barm cake** ● **n.** N. English a soft, flattish bread roll.

**Barmecide** /ˈbɑːmɪsʌɪd/ ● **adj.** poetic/literary illusory or imaginary and therefore disappointing.
– ORIGIN C18: from Arab. *Barmakī*, the name of a prince in the *Arabian Nights' Entertainments*, who gave a beggar a feast consisting of ornate but empty dishes.

**bar mitzvah** /bɑː ˈmɪtzvə/ ● **n.** the religious initiation ceremony of a Jewish boy who has reached the age of 13. ● **v.** administer this ceremony to.
– ORIGIN from Heb. *bar miṣwāh*, lit. 'son of the commandment'.

**barmy** ● **adj.** (**-ier**, **-iest**) informal, chiefly Brit. extremely foolish.
– DERIVATIVES **barmily** adv. **barminess** n.
– ORIGIN C15 (in the sense 'frothy'): from **BARM** + **-Y**[1].

**barn**[1] ● **n. 1** a large farm building used for storage or for housing livestock. **2** N. Amer. a large shed for storing road or railway vehicles.
– ORIGIN OE *bern*, *berern*, from *bere* 'barley' + *ern*, *ærn* 'house'.

**barn**[2] (abbrev.: **b**) ● **n.** Physics a unit of area, $10^{-28}$ square metres, used especially in particle physics.
– ORIGIN 1940s: appar. from the phr. *as big as a barn door.*

**barnacle** /ˈbɑːnək(ə)l/ ● **n.** a marine crustacean with an external shell, which attaches itself permanently to underwater surfaces and feeds by using modified feathery legs as filters. [Class Cirripedia: many species.]
– DERIVATIVES **barnacled** adj.
– ORIGIN C16: from med. L. *bernaca*.

**barnacle goose** ● **n.** a goose with a white face and black neck, breeding in arctic tundra. [*Branta leucopsis*.]
– ORIGIN C18: from the former belief that the bird hatched from barnacles.

**barn burner** ● **n.** N. Amer. informal a very exciting or dramatic event, especially a sports contest.

**barn dance** ● **n. 1** an informal social gathering for country dancing. **2** a dance for a number of couples moving round a circle, typically involving changes of partner.

**barn door** ● **n. 1** the large door of a barn. **2** a hinged metal flap fitted to a spotlight to control the direction and intensity of its beam.

**barnet** /ˈbɑːnɪt/ ● **n.** Brit. informal a person's hair.
– ORIGIN C19: from rhyming sl. *barnet fair*, the name of a famous horse fair held at *Barnet*, Herts.

**barney** ● **n.** (pl. **-eys**) Brit. informal a quarrel, especially a noisy one.
– ORIGIN C19: of unknown origin.

**barn owl** ● **n.** a pale-coloured owl with a heart-shaped face, typically nesting in farm buildings. [*Tyto alba* and related species.]

**barnstorm** ● **v.** chiefly N. Amer. **1** tour rural districts giving theatrical performances, formerly often in barns. ➤ travel around giving exhibitions of flying and performing aeronautical stunts. **2** make a rapid tour as part of a political campaign.
– DERIVATIVES **barnstormer** n.

**barnstorming** ● **adj.** flamboyantly vigorous and effective.

**barnyard** ● **n.** N. Amer. a farmyard.

**baro-** /ˈbarəʊ/ ● **comb. form** relating to pressure: *barotrauma.*
– ORIGIN from Gk *baros* 'weight'.

**barograph** ● **n.** a barometer that records its readings on a moving chart.

**Barolo** /bəˈrəʊləʊ/ ● **n.** a full-bodied red wine from Barolo in NW Italy.

**barometer** ● **n. 1** an instrument measuring atmospheric pressure, used especially in forecasting the weather and determining altitude. **2** an indicator of change: *furniture is a barometer of changing tastes.*
– DERIVATIVES **barometric** adj. **barometrical** adj. **barometry** n.

**baron** ● **n. 1** a member of the lowest order of the British nobility. ➤ historical a person who held lands or property from the sovereign or a powerful overlord. **2** a powerful person in business or industry: *a press baron.*
– DERIVATIVES **baronial** /bəˈrəʊnɪəl/ adj.
– ORIGIN ME: from OFr., from med. L. *baro*, *baron-* 'man, warrior', prob. of Gmc origin.

**baronage** ● **n. 1** [treated as sing. or pl.] barons or nobles collectively. **2** an annotated list of barons or peers.

**baroness** ● **n.** the wife or widow of a baron. ➤ a woman holding the rank of baron either as a life peerage or as a hereditary rank.

**baronet** /ˈbar(ə)nɪt/ ● **n.** a member of the lowest hereditary titled British order.
– DERIVATIVES **baronetcy** n.
– ORIGIN ME: from Anglo-Latin *baronettus*, from med. L. *baro, baron-* (see **BARON**).

**baronetage** ● **n.** **1** [treated as sing. or pl.] baronets collectively. **2** an annotated list of baronets.

**baron of beef** ● **n.** Brit. a joint of beef consisting of two sirloins joined at the backbone.

**barony** ● **n.** (pl. **-ies**) **1** the rank and estates of a baron. **2** historical (in Ireland) a division of a county. **3** historical (in Scotland) a large manor or estate.

**baroque** /bəˈrɒk, -ˈrəʊk/ ● **adj.** relating to or denoting a style of European architecture, music, and art of the 17th and 18th centuries characterized by ornate detail. ➤highly ornate and extravagant in style. ● **n.** the baroque style or period.
– ORIGIN C18: from Fr. (orig. denoting a pearl of irregular shape).

**baroreceptor** ● **n.** Zoology a receptor sensitive to changes in pressure.

**barotitis** /ˌbarə(ʊ)ˈtʌɪtɪs/ ● **n.** Medicine discomfort and inflammation in the ear caused by the changes of pressure occurring during air travel.

**barotrauma** ● **n.** Medicine injury caused by a change in air pressure, affecting typically the ear or the lung.

**barouche** /bəˈruːʃ/ ● **n.** historical a four-wheeled horse-drawn carriage with a collapsible hood over the rear half.
– ORIGIN C19: from Ger. dial. *Barutsche*, from Ital. *baroccio*, based on L. *birotus* 'two-wheeled'.

**barque** /bɑːk/ ● **n.** **1** a sailing ship, typically with three masts, in which the foremast and mainmast are square-rigged and the mizzenmast is rigged fore and aft. **2** poetic/literary a boat.
– ORIGIN ME: from OFr., prob. from Provençal *barca*, from late L. *barca* 'ship's boat'.

**barquentine** /ˈbɑːk(ə)ntiːn/ (US **barkentine**) ● **n.** a sailing ship similar to a barque but with only the foremast square-rigged and the remaining masts rigged fore and aft.
– ORIGIN C17: from **BARQUE**, on the pattern of *brigantine*.

**barrack**[1] ● **v.** provide (soldiers) with accommodation.

**barrack**[2] ● **v.** **1** Brit. & Austral./NZ jeer loudly at (a performer or speaker). **2** (**barrack for**) Austral./NZ give support and encouragement to.
– ORIGIN C19: prob. from Northern Ir. dial.

**barrack-room lawyer** ● **n.** Brit. a person who makes authoritative-sounding pronouncements on subjects in which they are not qualified.

**barracks** ● **pl. n.** [often treated as sing.] a large building or group of buildings used to house soldiers.
– ORIGIN C17: *barrack* from Fr. *baraque*, from Ital. *baracca* or Sp. *barraca* 'soldier's tent'.

**barrack square** ● **n.** Brit. a drill ground near a barracks.

**barracoon** /ˌbarəˈkuːn/ ● **n.** historical an enclosure in which black slaves were temporarily confined.
– ORIGIN C19: from Sp. *barracón*, from *barraca* (see **BARRACKS**).

**barracouta** /ˌbarəˈkuːtə/ ● **n.** (pl. same or **barracoutas**) **1** a long, slender fish of southern oceans, highly valued as food. [*Thyrsites atun*.] **2** NZ a long loaf of bread.
– ORIGIN C19: alt. of **BARRACUDA**.

**barracuda** /ˌbarəˈkuːdə/ ● **n.** (pl. same or **barracudas**) a large predatory tropical marine fish with a slender body and large jaws and teeth. [Genus *Sphyraena*: several species.]
– ORIGIN C17: of unknown origin.

**barracudina** /ˌbarəkuːˈdiːnə/ ● **n.** a slender-bodied predatory fish with a long head, found in open oceans. [*Paralepis atlantica* and other species.]
– ORIGIN from Amer. Sp., dimin. of **BARRACUDA**.

**barrage** /ˈbarɑːʒ/ ● **n.** **1** a concentrated artillery bombardment over a wide area. **2** an overwhelming number of questions or complaints delivered in rapid succession. **3** Brit. an artificial barrier across a river, to prevent flooding or to aid irrigation or navigation. ● **v.** bombard with questions or complaints.
– ORIGIN C19: from Fr., from *barrer* 'to bar'.

**barrage balloon** ● **n.** a large anchored balloon, typically with netting suspended from it, serving as an obstacle to low-flying enemy aircraft.

**barramundi** /ˌbarəˈmʌndi/ ● **n.** (pl. same or **barramundis**) a large, chiefly freshwater fish of Australia and SE Asia. [*Lates calcarifer* and other species.]
– ORIGIN C19: prob. from an Aborig. lang. of Queensland.

**barranca** /bəˈraŋkə/ (also **barranco**) ● **n.** (pl. **barrancas** or **barrancos**) chiefly US a narrow, winding river gorge.
– ORIGIN C17: from Sp.

**barratry** /ˈbarətri/ ● **n.** **1** archaic fraud or gross negligence on the part of a ship's master or crew at the expense of its owners or users. **2** Law vexatious litigation or incitement to it. **3** historical trade in the sale of Church or state appointments.
– DERIVATIVES **barrator** n. **barratrous** adj.
– ORIGIN ME: from OFr. *baraterie*, from *barater* 'deceive', based on Gk *prattein* 'do, perform, manage'.

**Barr body** ● **n.** Physiology a densely staining structure in the cell nuclei of females, consisting of a condensed, inactive X chromosome and regarded as diagnostic of genetic femaleness.
– ORIGIN 1960s: named after the Canad. anatomist M. L. *Barr*.

**barre** /bɑː/ ● **n.** a horizontal bar at waist level used as a support by ballet dancers during certain exercises.
– ORIGIN from Fr.

**barré** /ˈbareɪ/ ● **n.** Music a method of playing a chord on the guitar or a similar instrument in which one finger is laid across all the strings at a particular fret.
– ORIGIN C19: Fr., lit. 'barred', past part. of *barrer*.

**barrel** ● **n.** **1** a cylindrical container bulging out in the middle, traditionally made of wooden staves enclosed by metal hoops. ➤a measure of capacity for oil and beer, equal to 36 imperial gallons for beer and 35 imperial gallons or 42 US gallons (roughly 192 litres) for oil. **2** a cylindrical tube forming part of an object such as a gun or a pen. **3** the belly and loins of a four-legged animal such as a horse. ● **v.** (**barrelled**, **barrelling**; US **barreled**, **barreling**) **1** informal, chiefly N. Amer. drive or move very fast. **2** put into a barrel or barrels.
– PHRASES **over a barrel** informal in a severely disadvantageous position. **with both barrels** informal, chiefly US with unrestrained force.
– ORIGIN ME: from OFr. *baril*, from med. L. *barriclus* 'small cask'.

**barrel-chested** ● **adj.** having a large rounded chest.

**barrel distortion** ● **n.** a type of defect in optical or electronic images in which vertical or horizontal straight lines appear as convex curves.

**barrelfish** ● **n.** (pl. same or **-fishes**) an Atlantic fish which lives chiefly in deep water when adult, and among flotsam on the surface when young. [*Schedophilus medusophagus* and *Hyperoglyphe perciforma*.]

**barrelhead** ● **n.** the flat top of a barrel.
– PHRASES **on the barrelhead** North American term for ***on the nail*** (see **NAIL**).

**barrelhouse** ● **n.** **1** N. Amer. a cheap or disreputable bar. **2** an unrestrained and unsophisticated style of jazz music.

**barrel organ** ● **n.** a small pipe organ played by turning a handle, which rotates a cylinder studded with pegs that open the valves to produce a preset tune.

**barrel roll** ● **n.** an aerobatic manoeuvre in which an aircraft follows a single turn of a spiral while rolling once about its longitudinal axis.

**barrel vault** ● **n.** Architecture a vault forming a half cylinder.
– DERIVATIVES **barrel-vaulted** adj.

**barren** ● **adj.** **1** (of land) too poor to produce much or any vegetation. ➤(of a tree or plant) not producing fruit or seed. **2** (of a female animal) unable to bear young. **3** bleak and lifeless. **4** (**barren of**) devoid of. ● **n.** (**barrens**) chiefly N. Amer. barren tracts of land.
– DERIVATIVES **barrenly** adv. **barrenness** n.

– ORIGIN ME: from OFr. *barhaine*, of unknown origin.

**barrenwort** • n. a creeping plant with cup-shaped spurred flowers and colourful foliage, formerly thought to cause infertility. [Genus *Epimedium*.]

**barrette** /baˈrɛt/ • n. a hairslide.

– ORIGIN C20: from Fr., dimin. of *barre* 'bar'.

**barricade** /ˌbarɪˈkeɪd/ • n. an improvised barrier erected to obstruct the movement of opposing forces. • v. block or defend with a barricade.

– ORIGIN C16: from Fr., from *barrique* 'cask', from Sp. *barrica*; rel. to **BARREL** (barrels often being used to build barricades).

**barrier** • n. a fence or other obstacle that prevents movement or access. ➤ an obstacle to communication, understanding, or progress: *a language barrier.*

– ORIGIN ME: from OFr. *barriere*; rel. to **BARRE**.

**barrier cream** • n. Brit. a cream used to protect the skin from damage or infection.

**barrier method** • n. a method of contraception using a device or preparation which prevents sperm from reaching an ovum.

**barrier reef** • n. a coral reef close and running parallel to the shore but separated from it by a channel of deep water.

**barring** • prep. except for; if not for.

**barrio** /ˈbarɪəʊ/ • n. (pl. **-os**) a district of a town in Spanish-speaking countries. ➤ (in the US) the Spanish-speaking quarter of a town or city.

– ORIGIN from Sp.

**barrister** (also **barrister-at-law**) • n. chiefly Brit. a person called to the bar and entitled to practise as an advocate, particularly in the higher courts. Compare with **SOLICITOR**.

– ORIGIN ME: from the noun **BAR**[1], perh. on the pattern of *minister.*

**barroom** • n. chiefly N. Amer. a room with a bar selling alcoholic drinks.

**barrow**[1] • n. Brit. a two-wheeled handcart used especially by street vendors.

– ORIGIN OE *bearwe* 'stretcher, bier', of Gmc origin; rel. to **BEAR**[1].

**barrow**[2] • n. Archaeology an ancient burial mound.

– ORIGIN OE *beorg*, of Gmc origin.

**barrow boy** • n. Brit. a boy or man who sells wares from a barrow in the street.

**barry** /ˈbɑːri/ • adj. Heraldry divided into four, six, or eight equal horizontal bars of alternating tinctures.

– ORIGIN C15: from Fr. *barré* 'barred, striped'.

**Barsac** /ˈbɑːsak, French barsak/ • n. a sweet white wine from the district of Barsac in SW France.

**bar sinister** • n. popular term for **BEND SINISTER**.

**Bart** • abbrev. Baronet.

**bar tack** • n. a stitch made to strengthen a potential weak spot in a garment or other sewn item.

– DERIVATIVES **bar-tacked** adj. **bar tacking** n.

**bartender** • n. a person serving drinks at a bar.

**barter** • v. exchange (goods or services) for other goods or services. • n. the action or system of bartering.

– DERIVATIVES **barterer** n.

– ORIGIN ME: prob. from OFr. *barater* (see **BARRATRY**).

**Bartholin's gland** /ˈbɑːtəlɪnz/ • n. Anatomy either of a pair of glands near the entrance of the vagina, which secrete a fluid that lubricates the vulva.

– DERIVATIVES **bartholinitis** n.

– ORIGIN C18: named by the Dan. anatomist Caspar *Bartholin.*

**Bartlett** /ˈbɑːtlɪt/ (also **Bartlett pear**) • n. a dessert pear of a juicy early-ripening variety.

**bar tracery** • n. Architecture tracery with strips of stone across an aperture.

**bartsia** /ˈbɑːtsɪə/ • n. a herbaceous plant of the figwort family, of which some kinds are partly parasitic on grasses. [*Odontites verna* (**red bartsia**) and other species.]

– ORIGIN mod. L. *Bartsia*, a genus named after the Prussian botanist Johann *Bartsch.*

**barwing** • n. an Asian bird of the babbler family, with barred feathers on the wings and tail. [Genus *Actinodura.*]

**barycentric** /ˌbarɪˈsɛntrɪk/ • adj. of or relating to the centre of gravity.

– DERIVATIVES **barycentre** n.

– ORIGIN C19: from Gk *barus* 'heavy' + **-CENTRIC**.

**baryon** /ˈbarɪɒn/ • n. Physics a subatomic particle with a mass equal to or greater than that of a proton, such as a nucleon or hyperon.

– DERIVATIVES **baryonic** adj.

– ORIGIN 1950s: from Gk *barus* 'heavy' + **-ON**.

**baryta** /bəˈrʌɪtə/ • n. Chemistry barium hydroxide.

**baryte** /ˈbarʌɪt, ˈbɛː-/ (also **barytes** /bəˈrʌɪtiːz/, **barite**) • n. a colourless or white mineral consisting of barium sulphate.

– ORIGIN C19: from Gk *barus* 'heavy' + var. endings based on Gk *-ites.*

**basal** /ˈbeɪs(ə)l/ • adj. forming or belonging to a base.

**basal cell carcinoma** • n. technical term for **RODENT ULCER**.

**basal ganglia** • pl. n. Anatomy a group of structures linked to the thalamus in the base of the brain and involved in coordination of movement.

**basal metabolic rate** • n. the rate at which the body uses energy while at rest to maintain vital functions such as breathing and keeping warm.

– DERIVATIVES **basal metabolism** n.

**basalt** /ˈbasɔːlt, -(ə)lt/ • n. a dark fine-grained volcanic rock composed largely of plagioclase with pyroxene and olivine.

– DERIVATIVES **basaltic** /bəˈsɔːltɪk/ adj.

– ORIGIN C17: from L. *basaltes* (var. of *basanites*), from Gk *basanitēs*, from *basanos* 'touchstone'.

**bascule bridge** /ˈbaskjuːl/ • n. a type of bridge with a section which can be raised and lowered using counterweights.

– ORIGIN C19: from Fr. (earlier *bacule*), 'see-saw', from *battre* 'to bump' + *cul* 'buttocks'.

**base**[1] • n. **1** the lowest part or edge of something, especially the part on which it rests or is supported. ➤ Architecture the part of a column between the shaft and pedestal or pavement. ➤ Botany & Zoology the end at which a part or organ is attached to the trunk or main part. **2** a conceptual structure or entity on which something draws or depends: *the town's economic base collapsed.* ➤ a foundation or starting point. **3** the main place where a person works or stays. ➤ a centre of operations for military or other activity. **4** a main or important element or ingredient to which other things are added. ➤ a substance into which a pigment is mixed to form paint. **5** Chemistry a substance capable of reacting with an acid to form a salt and water, or of accepting or neutralizing hydrogen ions. **6** Electronics the middle part of a bipolar transistor, separating the emitter from the collector. **7** Linguistics the root or stem of a word or a derivative. ➤ the uninflected form of a verb. **8** Mathematics a number used as the basis of a numeration scale. ➤ a number in terms of which other numbers are expressed as logarithms. **9** Baseball one of the four stations that must be reached in turn to score a run. • v. **1** use something as the foundation for: *the film is based on a novel.* **2** situate at a place as the centre of operations.

– PHRASES **get to first base** informal, chiefly N. Amer. achieve the first step towards one's objective. **off base** informal, chiefly N. Amer. mistaken. **touch base** informal, chiefly N. Amer. briefly make or renew contact.

– DERIVATIVES **-based** adj.

– ORIGIN ME: from OFr., from L. *basis* 'base, pedestal', from Gk.

**base**[2] • adj. **1** without moral principles; ignoble. **2** archaic denoting or befitting a person of low social class. **3** (of coins or other articles) not made of precious metal.

– DERIVATIVES **basely** adv. **baseness** n.

– ORIGIN ME (in the sense 'low, short'): from OFr. *bas*, from med. L. *bassus* 'short' (found in classical L. as a cognomen).

**baseball** • n. a ball game played chiefly in the US and Canada between two teams of nine on a diamond-shaped circuit of four bases.

**baseball cap** • n. a cotton cap with a large peak.

**baseboard** • n. North American term for **SKIRTING**.

**base dressing** • n. the application of manure or fertilizer to the earth, which is then ploughed or dug in.

**basehead** • n. US informal a habitual user of freebase or crack.

**base hit** • n. Baseball a hit that allows the batter to advance safely to a base without an error by the team in the field.

**base hospital** • n. **1** a military hospital situated away from the area of active operations during a war. **2** Austral./NZ a hospital serving a large rural area.

**base jump** • n. a parachute jump from a fixed point, e.g. a high building or promontory, rather than an aircraft. • v. [often as noun **base jumping**] perform such a jump.
– DERIVATIVES **base jumper** n.
– ORIGIN 1980s: *base* from *b*uilding, *a*ntenna-tower, *s*pan, *e*arth (denoting the types of structure used).

**baseless** • adj. without foundation in fact.
– DERIVATIVES **baselessly** adv. **baselessness** n.

**baseline** • n. **1** a minimum or starting point used for comparisons. **2** (in tennis, volleyball, etc.) the line marking each end of a court. **3** Baseball the line between bases which a runner must stay close to when running.

**baseload** • n. the permanent minimum load that a power supply system is required to deliver.

**baseman** • n. (pl. **-men**) Baseball a fielder designated to cover either first, second, or third base.

**basement** • n. **1** a room or floor which is partly or entirely below ground level. **2** Geology the oldest formation of rocks underlying a particular area.
– ORIGIN C18: prob. from archaic Du. *basement* 'foundation', perh. from Ital. *basamento* 'column base'.

**basement membrane** • n. Anatomy a thin, delicate membrane separating an epithelium from underlying tissue.

**base metal** • n. a common metal that is not considered precious, such as copper, tin, or zinc.

**basenji** /bəˈsɛndʒi/ • n. (pl. **basenjis**) a smallish hunting dog of a central African breed, which growls and yelps but does not bark.
– ORIGIN 1930s: a local word.

**base pair** • n. Biochemistry a pair of complementary bases in a double-stranded nucleic acid molecule, consisting of cytosine or adenine in one strand linked to (respectively) guanine or thymine in the other.

**base rate** • n. (in the UK) the interest rate set by the Bank of England for lending to other banks, used as the benchmark for interest rates generally.

**bases** plural form of **BASE**[1] and **BASIS**.

**bash** informal • v. **1** strike hard and violently. ➤criticize severely. **2** (**bash something out**) produce something rapidly and carelessly. • n. **1** a heavy blow. **2** a party or social event. **3** Brit. an attempt: *she'll have a bash at anything.*
– ORIGIN C17 (as v.): imitative, perh. a blend of **BANG**[1] and **SMASH**.

**basha** /ˈbaʃə/ • n. an improvised shelter for one or a few soldiers.
– ORIGIN 1920s (orig. denoting a bamboo hut with a thatched roof): Assamese.

**bashful** • adj. shy and easily embarrassed.
– DERIVATIVES **bashfully** adv. **bashfulness** n.
– ORIGIN C15: from obs. *bash* 'make or become abashed' (from **ABASH**) + **-FUL**.

**Bashkir** /baʃˈkɪə/ • n. **1** a member of a Muslim people living in the southern Urals. **2** the Turkic language of this people.
– ORIGIN via Russ. from Turkic *Başkurt.*

**basho** /ˈbaʃəʊ/ • n. (pl. same or **-os**) a sumo wrestling tournament.
– ORIGIN Japanese, from *ba* 'place' + *shō* 'victory, win'.

**BASIC** • n. a simple high-level computer programming language, formerly widely used on microcomputers.
– ORIGIN 1960s: acronym from *Beginners' All-purpose Symbolic Instruction Code.*

**basic** • adj. **1** forming an essential foundation; fundamental. **2** consisting of the minimum required or offered: *the food was good, if a bit basic.* **3** Chemistry containing or having the properties of a base; alkaline. ➤Geology relatively poor in silica: *basic lava.* ➤Metallurgy relating to or denoting steel-making processes involving lime-rich materials: *basic slag.* • n. (**basics**) the essential facts or principles of a subject or skill.

**basically** • adv. fundamentally. ➤in fact; actually.

**Basic English** • n. a simplified form of English limited to 850 selected words, intended for international communication.

**basicity** /beɪˈsɪsɪti/ • n. Chemistry the number of hydrogen atoms replaceable by a base in a particular acid.

**basic oxygen process** • n. a steel-making process in which carbon and other impurities are burned away from iron by a jet of oxygen in a retort lined with a basic refractory.

**basic wage** • n. **1** a minimum wage earned before additional payments such as overtime. **2** Austral./NZ the minimum living wage, as determined by industrial tribunal.

**basidiomycete** /bəˌsɪdɪəˈmʌɪsiːt/ • n. (pl. **basidiomycetes** /-ˈmʌɪsiːts, -mʌɪˈsiːtiːz/) Botany a fungus of a large group whose spores develop within basidia and which includes the majority of familiar mushrooms and toadstools.
– ORIGIN C19: anglicized sing. of mod. L. *Basidiomycetes* (former class name), from *basidium* (see **BASIDIUM**) + Gk *mukētes* 'fungi'.

**basidium** /bəˈsɪdɪəm/ • n. (pl. **basidia** /-dɪə/) a microscopic club-shaped spore-bearing structure produced by certain fungi.
– ORIGIN C19: mod. L., from Gk *basidion*, dimin. of *basis* (see **BASIS**).

**basil** /ˈbaz(ə)l, -zɪl/ • n. **1** an aromatic plant of the mint family, native to tropical Asia, used as a culinary herb. [*Ocimum basilicum* (**sweet basil**) and other species.] **2** (also **wild basil**) a similar European plant which grows in hedges and scrub. [*Clinopodium vulgare.*]
– ORIGIN ME: from OFr. *basile*, via med. L. from Gk *basilikon*, neut. of *basilikos* (see **BASILICA**).

**basilar** /ˈbasɪlə/ • adj. Anatomy & Zoology of or situated at the base of something, especially the skull.
– ORIGIN C16: from mod. L. *basilaris*, formed irregularly from L. *basis* (see **BASIS**).

**basilect** /ˈbasɪlɛkt, ˈbeɪsɪ-/ • n. Linguistics a less prestigious dialect or variety of a particular language. Contrasted with **ACROLECT**.
– DERIVATIVES **basilectal** /ˈlɛkt(ə)l/ adj.
– ORIGIN 1960s: from **BASIS** + *-lect* as in *dialect.*

**Basilian** /bəˈzɪlɪən/ • adj. of or relating to St Basil the Great (*c.*330–79), or the order of monks and nuns following his monastic rule. • n. a Basilian monk or nun.

**basilica** /bəˈsɪlɪkə, -ˈzɪl-/ • n. a large oblong hall or building with double colonnades and a semicircular apse, used in ancient Rome as a law court or for public assemblies. ➤a similar building used as a Christian church.
– DERIVATIVES **basilican** adj.
– ORIGIN C16: from L., lit. 'royal palace', from Gk *basilikē*, fem. of *basilikos* 'royal', from *basileus* 'king'.

**basilisk** /ˈbazɪlɪsk/ • n. **1** a mythical reptile with a lethal gaze or breath, hatched by a serpent from a cock's egg. ➤Heraldry another term for **COCKATRICE**. **2** a long, slender Central American lizard, the male of which has a crest running from the head to the tail. [*Basiliscus plumifrons.*]
– ORIGIN ME: via L. from Gk *basiliskos* 'little king, serpent', from *basileus* 'king'.

**basin** • n. **1** a large bowl or open container for washing in, preparing food, or holding liquid. **2** a broadly circular valley or natural depression on the earth's surface. ➤an area drained by a river and its tributaries. ➤an enclosed area of water where boats can be moored. **3** Geology a circumscribed rock formation where the strata dip towards the centre.
– DERIVATIVES **basinful** n. (pl. **-fuls**).
– ORIGIN ME: from OFr. *bacin*, from med. L. *bacinus*, from

*bacca* 'water container'.

**basinet** /'basɪnɪt/ ● n. historical a light, close-fitting steel helmet.
– ORIGIN ME: from OFr. *bacinet* 'little basin'.

**basipetal** /beɪ'sɪpɪt(ə)l/ ● adj. Botany (of growth or development) downwards towards the base or point of attachment. Often contrasted with **ACROPETAL**.
– DERIVATIVES **basipetally** adv.
– ORIGIN C19: from **BASIS** + L. *petere* 'seek' + **-AL**.

**basis** ● n. (pl. **bases** /-si:z/) the underlying support for an idea, argument, or process. ➤ the principles according to which an activity is carried on: *she needed coaching on a regular basis.*
– ORIGIN C16 (denoting a base or pedestal): via L. from Gk, 'stepping'; cf. **BASE**[1].

**basis point** ● n. Finance one hundredth of one per cent.

**bask** ● v. **1** lie exposed to warmth and sunlight for pleasure. **2** (**bask in**) revel in (something pleasing).
– ORIGIN ME (orig. in the sense 'bathe'); perh. rel. to ON *batha* 'bathe'.

**basket** ● n. **1** a container used to hold or carry things, made from interwoven strips of cane or wire. **2** Basketball a net fixed on a hoop used as the goal. ➤ a goal scored. **3** Finance a group or range of currencies or investments.
– DERIVATIVES **basketful** n. (pl. **-fuls**)
– ORIGIN ME: from OFr. *basket*, of unknown origin.

**basketball** ● n. a game played between two teams of five players in which goals are scored by throwing a ball through a netted hoop fixed at each end of the court.

**basket case** ● n. informal a person or thing regarded as useless or unable to cope.
– ORIGIN C20: orig. US sl. denoting a soldier who had lost all four limbs.

**Basket Maker** ● n. a member of a culture of the southwestern US, forming the early stages of the Anasazi culture.

**basketry** ● n. **1** the craft of basket-making. **2** baskets collectively.

**basket shell** ● n. a small burrowing bivalve mollusc, the left valve of which fits into the larger right valve. [Genus *Corbula*.]

**basking shark** ● n. a large shark which feeds exclusively on plankton and typically swims slowly close to the surface. [*Cetorhinus maximus*.]

**basmati rice** /bas'mɑ:ti, -z-/ ● n. a kind of long-grain Indian rice with a delicate fragrance.
– ORIGIN from Hindi *bāsmatī*, lit. 'fragrant'.

**basophil** /'beɪsə(ʊ)fɪl/ ● n. Physiology a basophilic white blood cell.

**basophilic** /ˌbeɪsə(ʊ)'fɪlɪk/ ● adj. Physiology (of a cell or its contents) readily stained with basic dyes.

**Basotho** /bə'su:tu:/ ● pl. n. (sing. **Mosotho**) the South Sotho people collectively, living chiefly in Lesotho.
– ORIGIN the name in Sesotho.

**Basque** /bask, bɑ:sk/ ● n. **1** a member of a people living in the western Pyrenees in both France and Spain. **2** the language of this people, which is thought to be unrelated to any other language.
– ORIGIN from Fr., from L. *Vasco*; cf. **GASCON**.

**basque** /bask, bɑ:sk/ ● n. a close-fitting bodice extending from the shoulders to the waist and typically having a short continuation below waist level.
– ORIGIN C19: from **BASQUE**, referring to traditional Basque dress.

**bas-relief** /'basrɪˌli:f, 'bɑ:(s)-/ ● n. Art low relief.
– ORIGIN C17 (as *basse relieve*): from Ital. *basso-rilievo* 'low relief', later altered to the Fr. form.

**bass**[1] /beɪs/ ● n. **1** the lowest adult male singing voice. **2** [as modifier] denoting the member of a family of instruments that is the lowest in pitch. ➤ informal a bass guitar or double bass. **3** the low-frequency output of a radio or audio system, corresponding to the bass in music.
– DERIVATIVES **bassist** n.
– ORIGIN ME: alt. of **BASE**[2], influenced by **BASSO**.

**bass**[2] /bas/ ● n. (pl. same or **basses**) **1** the common freshwater perch. **2** any of several fish similar to or related to this. [*Dicentrarchus labrax* (European seas) and other species. See also **SEA BASS**.]
– ORIGIN ME: alt. of dial. *barse*, of Gmc origin.

**bass**[3] /bas/ ● n. another term for **BAST**.

**bass clef** ● n. Music a clef placing F below middle C on the second-highest line of the stave.

**basset** (also **basset hound**) ● n. a sturdy hunting dog of a breed with a long body, short legs, and long, drooping ears.
– ORIGIN C17: from Fr., dimin. of *bas* 'low'.

**basset horn** ● n. an alto clarinet in F, typically with a bent mouthpiece and upturned bell.
– ORIGIN C19: from Ger., translation of Fr. *cor de bassette*, from Ital. *corno di bassetto*, from *corno* 'horn' + *di* 'of' + *bassetto* (dimin. of *basso* 'low').

**bassinet** /ˌbasɪ'nɛt/ ● n. a child's wicker cradle.
– ORIGIN C19: from Fr., dimin. of *bassin* 'basin'.

**basso** /'basəʊ/ ● n. (pl. **bassos** or **bassi** /-si/) a bass voice or vocal part.
– ORIGIN C18: Ital., 'low', from L. *bassus* 'short, low'.

**bassoon** ● n. a large bass woodwind instrument of the oboe family, played with a double reed.
– DERIVATIVES **bassoonist** n.
– ORIGIN C18: from Fr. *basson*, from Ital. *bassone*, from *basso* 'low' (see **BASSO**).

**basso profundo** /prə'fʌndəʊ/ ● n. (pl. **bassos profundos** or **bassi profundi** /-di/) a bass singer with an exceptionally low range.
– ORIGIN C19: Ital., from *basso* 'low' + *profondo* 'deep'.

**basso-relievo** /ˌbasəʊrɪ'li:vəʊ/ ● n. (pl. **-os**) Art low relief.
– ORIGIN C17: from Ital. *basso-rilievo*.

**bass viol** ● n. **1** a viola da gamba. **2** N. Amer. a double bass.

**basswood** /'baswʊd/ ● n. a North American lime tree with large leaves. [*Tilia americana*.]

**bast** /bast/ ● n. fibre obtained from plants and used for matting and cord, in particular the inner bark of a lime tree.
– ORIGIN OE *bæst*, of unknown origin.

**bastard** /'bɑ:stəd, 'bast-/ ● n. **1** archaic or derogatory an illegitimate person. **2** informal an unpleasant or despicable person. ● adj. **1** archaic or derogatory illegitimate. **2** no longer in its pure or original form.
– DERIVATIVES **bastardy** n.
– ORIGIN ME: via OFr. from med. L. *bastardus*, prob. from *bastum* 'packsaddle'; cf. OFr. *fils de bast*, lit. 'packsaddle son' (i.e. the son of a mule driver who uses a packsaddle for a pillow and is gone by morning).

**bastardize** (also **-ise**) ● v. **1** [often as adj. **bastardized**] debase by adding new elements. **2** archaic declare (someone) illegitimate.
– DERIVATIVES **bastardization** n.

**bastard wing** ● n. a group of small quill feathers on the first digit of a bird's wing.

**baste**[1] ● v. pour fat or juices over (meat) during cooking.
– DERIVATIVES **baster** n.
– ORIGIN C15: of unknown origin.

**baste**[2] ● v. Needlework tack with long, loose stitches in preparation for sewing.
– ORIGIN ME: from OFr. *bastir* 'sew lightly', ult. of Gmc origin and rel. to **BAST**.

**baste**[3] ● v. informal, dated beat soundly; thrash.
– DERIVATIVES **basting** n.
– ORIGIN C16: perh. a figurative use of **BASTE**[1].

**bastide** /ba'sti:d/ ● n. a fortified village or small town in southern France.
– ORIGIN C16: via OFr. from Provençal *bastida*.

**bastinado** /ˌbastɪ'neɪdəʊ, -'nɑ:dəʊ/ chiefly historical ● n. a form of punishment or torture that involves caning the soles of someone's feet. ● v. (**-oes**, **-oed**) punish or torture in such a way.
– ORIGIN C16: from Sp. *bastonada*, from *bastón* 'stick, cudgel', from late L. *bastum* 'stick'.

**bastion** /'bastɪən/ ● n. **1** a projecting part of a fortification allowing an increased angle of fire. **2** an institution

or person strongly maintaining particular principles, attitudes, or activities.
– ORIGIN C16: from Fr., from Ital. *bastione*, from *bastire* 'build'.

**bastnaesite** /ˈbastneɪˌsʌɪt/ • **n.** a yellow to brown mineral consisting of a fluoride and carbonate of cerium and other rare-earth metals.
– ORIGIN C19: from *Bastnäs*, the name of a district in Västmanland, Sweden, + **-ITE**[1].

**basuco** /bəˈsuːkəʊ/ • **n.** impure or low-grade cocaine.
– ORIGIN 1980s: from Colombian Sp.; perh. rel. to Sp. *bazucar* 'shake violently'.

**bat**[1] • **n. 1** an implement with a handle and a solid surface, used in sports such as cricket or baseball for hitting the ball. **2** a slab on which pottery is formed, dried, or fired. • **v.** (**batted**, **batting**) **1** (in sport) take the role of hitting rather than throwing the ball. **2** hit with the flat of one's hand. **3** (**bat around/about**) informal, chiefly N. Amer. casually discuss (an idea or proposal). **4** (**bat around/about**) informal travel widely, frequently, or casually.
– PHRASES **off one's own bat** Brit. informal at one's own instigation. **right off the bat** N. Amer. informal at the very beginning.
– ORIGIN OE *batt* 'club, stick, staff', perh. partly from OFr. *batte*, from *battre* 'to strike'.

**bat**[2] • **n. 1** a mainly nocturnal mammal capable of sustained flight, with membranous wings that extend between the fingers and limbs. [Order Chiroptera: many species.] **2** (**old bat**) informal an unattractive and unpleasant woman.
– PHRASES **have bats in the belfry** informal be eccentric or mad.
– ORIGIN C16: alt., perh. by assoc. with med. L. *batta*, *blacta*, of ME *bakke*, of Scand. origin; sense 2 is from *bat*, a sl. term for 'prostitute', or from **BATTLEAXE**.

**bat**[3] • **v.** (**batted**, **batting**) flutter (one's eyelashes).
– PHRASES **not bat** (or **without batting**) **an eyelid** (or **eye**) informal show (or showing) no surprise or concern.
– ORIGIN C19 (orig. US): from dial. and US *bat* 'to wink, blink', var. of obs. *bate* 'to flutter'.

**Batak** /ˈbatək/ • **n.** (pl. same or **Bataks**) **1** a member of a people of the northern part of Sumatra in Indonesia. **2** the Indonesian language of this people.
– ORIGIN the name in Batak.

**Batavian** historical or archaic • **n.** a member of an ancient Germanic people who inhabited the island of Betuwe, now part of the Netherlands. • **adj. 1** of or relating to this people. **2** of or relating to the people of the Netherlands. **3** of or relating to Djakarta in Indonesia (formerly the Dutch East Indies).
– ORIGIN from L. *Batavia* (from *Batavi* 'the people of Betuwe') + **-AN**.

**batch** • **n.** a quantity or consignment of goods produced at one time. ➤Computing a group of records processed as a single unit. • **v.** arrange (things) in sets or groups.
– ORIGIN C15 (in the senses 'process of baking', 'quantity produced at one baking'): based on an OE word rel. to *bacan* (see **BAKE**).

**batch file** • **n.** a computer file containing a list of instructions to be carried out in turn.

**bate**[1] (also **bait**) • **n.** Brit. informal, dated an angry mood.
– ORIGIN C19: from **BAIT** in the sense 'torment'.

**bate**[2] • **v.** Falconry (of a hawk) beat the wings in agitation and flutter off the perch.
– ORIGIN ME: from OFr. *batre* 'to beat' (see also **BATTER**[1]).

**bat-eared fox** • **n.** a small fox found in southern and East Africa, with very large ears that are used to locate insect prey. [*Otocyon megalotis*.]

**bateau** /ˈbatəʊ/ • **n.** (pl. **bateaux** /-əʊz/) a light flat-bottomed riverboat used in Canada.
– ORIGIN C18: Fr., 'boat'.

**bateau mouche** /ˌbatəʊ ˈmuːʃ, French bato muʃ/ • **n.** (pl. **bateaux mouches** pronunc. same) a type of pleasure boat used on the Seine in Paris.
– ORIGIN Fr., lit. 'fly boat', because of the boat's mobility.

**bated** • **adj.** (in phr. **with bated breath**) in great suspense.
– ORIGIN C16: from the past part. of obs. *bate* 'restrain', from **ABATE**.

**bateleur eagle** /ˈbat(ə)ləː/ • **n.** a short-tailed African eagle with mainly black plumage and a bare red face. [*Terathopius ecaudatus*.]
– ORIGIN C19: *bateleur* from Fr., lit. 'acrobat, juggler' (with ref. to the tilting motion of the bird in flight).

**Batesian mimicry** /ˈbeɪtsɪən/ • **n.** Zoology mimicry in which an animal is protected by its resemblance to one avoided by predators.
– ORIGIN C19: named after the Engl. naturalist Henry W. *Bates*.

**Bates method** • **n.** a technique intended to improve eyesight using eye exercises.
– ORIGIN 1920s: named after the Amer. ophthalmologist William H. *Bates*.

**batfish** • **n.** (pl. same or **-fishes**) **1** a sea fish with a flattened body that is round or almost triangular when viewed from above. [Family Ogcocephalidae: many species.] **2** a deep-bodied, laterally compressed sea fish of the Indo-Pacific region, resembling an angelfish. [Genus *Platax*.]

**bath**[1] /bɑːθ/ • **n.** (pl. **baths**) **1** a large tub that is filled with water for immersing and washing the body. ➤an act of immersing and washing one's body in a bath. **2** (also **baths**) a building containing a public swimming pool or washing facilities. **3** a container holding a liquid in which an object is immersed in chemical or industrial processing. • **v.** wash while immersed in a bath.
– PHRASES **take a bath** informal suffer a heavy financial loss.
– ORIGIN OE *bæth*, of Gmc origin.

**bath**[2] /baθ/ • **n.** an ancient Hebrew liquid measure equivalent to about 40 litres or 9 gallons.
– ORIGIN from Heb. *baṯ*.

**Bath bun** • **n.** Brit. a round yeast bun containing currants and topped with icing or sugar.
– ORIGIN named after the city of *Bath* in SW England, where it was orig. made.

**bath chair** • **n.** dated an invalid's wheelchair.
– ORIGIN C19: named after the city of *Bath* in SW England, frequented for its supposedly curative hot springs.

**bathe** /beɪð/ • **v. 1** wash by immersing one's body in water. ➤soak or wipe gently with liquid to clean or soothe. ➤N. Amer. wash (someone) in a bath. **2** chiefly Brit. take a swim. • **n.** a spell of swimming.
– DERIVATIVES **bather** n.
– ORIGIN OE *bathian*, of Gmc origin.

**bathhouse** • **n.** a building containing baths for communal use.

**bathing machine** • **n.** historical a wheeled hut drawn to the edge of the sea, for changing in and bathing from.

**bathing suit** (Brit. also **bathing costume**) • **n.** chiefly N. Amer. a swimming costume.

**batholith** /ˈbaθəlɪθ/ • **n.** Geology a very large igneous intrusion extending to an unknown depth in the earth's crust.
– ORIGIN C20: coined in Ger. from Gk *bathos* 'depth' + **-LITH**.

**bathos** /ˈbeɪθɒs/ • **n.** (in literature) an unintentional change in mood from the important and serious to the trivial or ridiculous.
– DERIVATIVES **bathetic** /bəˈθɛtɪk/ adj.
– ORIGIN C17: from Gk, lit. 'depth'.

**bathrobe** • **n.** a dressing gown, especially one made of towelling.

**bathroom** • **n. 1** a room containing a bath and usually also a washbasin and toilet. **2** N. Amer. a room containing a toilet.

**bath salts** • **pl. n.** a crystalline substance that is dissolved in bathwater to soften or perfume it.

**bath sponge** • **n.** a marine sponge of warm waters, the fibrous skeleton of which is used as a sponge for washing. [Genera *Spongia* and *Hippospongia*.]

**Bath stone** • **n.** a type of oolitic limestone found especially near Bath in SW England, grey to yellowish in colour and used in building and sculpture.

**bathtub** • **n.** a bath.

**bathy-** /ˈbaθi/ ● **comb. form** relating to depth: *bathysphere*.
– ORIGIN from Gk *bathus* 'deep'.

**bathyal** /ˈbaθɪəl/ ● **adj.** of or relating to the zone of the sea between the continental shelf and the abyssal zone.

**bathymeter** /bəˈθɪmɪtə/ ● **n.** an instrument used to measure the depth of water in seas or lakes.
– DERIVATIVES **bathymetric** adj. **bathymetry** n.

**bathypelagic** /ˌbaθɪpɪˈladʒɪk/ ● **adj.** Biology (of fish and other organisms) inhabiting the sea at a depth of between about 1,000 and 3,000 metres (approximately 3,300 and 9,800 ft), where it is dark and cold.

**bathyscaphe** /ˈbaθɪskaf/ ● **n.** chiefly historical a type of manned submersible vessel.
– ORIGIN 1940s: coined in Fr. from Gk *bathus* 'deep' + *skaphos* 'ship'.

**bathysphere** ● **n.** a manned spherical chamber for deep-sea observation, lowered by cable from a ship.

**batik** /ˈbatɪk, bəˈtiːk/ ● **n.** a method of producing coloured designs on textiles using wax to resist dye, originating in Java.
– ORIGIN C19: from Javanese, lit. 'painted'.

**batiste** /bəˈtiːst/ ● **n.** a fine, light linen or cotton fabric resembling cambric.
– ORIGIN C19: from Fr. (earlier *batiche*); prob. rel. to *battre* 'to beat'.

**batman** (also **batwoman**) ● **n.** (pl. **-men** or **-women**) dated (in the British armed forces) an officer's personal valet or attendant.
– ORIGIN C18 (orig. denoting an orderly in charge of the *bat horse* which carried the officer's baggage): from OFr. *bat* (from med. L. *bastum* 'packsaddle') + **MAN**.

**bat mitzvah** /bɑːt ˈmɪtzvə/ ● **n.** a religious initiation ceremony for a Jewish girl at the age of religious maturity (twelve years and one day).
– ORIGIN from Heb. *baṯ miṣwāh* 'daughter of commandment', suggested by **BAR MITZVAH**.

**baton** ● **n.** **1** a thin stick used by a conductor to direct an orchestra or choir. **2** a short stick passed from runner to runner in a relay race. **3** a stick carried and twirled by a drum major. **4** a police officer's truncheon. **5** a staff of office or authority. **6** (**batons**) one of the suits in some tarot packs, corresponding to wands in others. **7** Heraldry a narrow bend truncated at each end. **8** a short bar replacing some figures on the dial of a clock or watch.
– PHRASES **pass** (or **take up**) **the baton** hand over (or take up) a duty or responsibility.
– ORIGIN C16: from Fr. *bâton*, earlier *baston*, from late L. *bastum* 'stick'.

**baton round** ● **n.** Brit. a large rubber or plastic projectile shot from a special gun, used especially in riot control.

**Batrachia** /bəˈtreɪkɪə/ ● **pl. n.** Zoology another term for **ANURA**.
– DERIVATIVES **batrachian** n. & adj.
– ORIGIN mod. L., from Gk *batrakhos* 'frog'.

**bats** ● **adj.** informal mad.
– ORIGIN C20: from the phr. *have bats in the belfry* (see **BAT**[2]).

**batsman** ● **n.** (pl. **-men**) a player who bats in cricket.
– DERIVATIVES **batsmanship** n.

**Batswana** plural form of **TSWANA**.

**batt** /bat/ ● **n.** a piece of felted material or fibreglass used for insulation.
– ORIGIN ME (in the general sense 'lump, piece'): of unknown origin.

**battalion** /bəˈtalɪən/ ● **n.** a large body of troops, forming part of a brigade.
– ORIGIN C16: from Fr. *bataillon*, from Ital. *battaglione*, from *battaglia* 'battle', from L. (see **BATTLE**).

**battels** /ˈbat(ə)lz/ ● **pl. n.** (at Oxford University) a college account for food and accommodation expenses.
– ORIGIN C16: perh. from dial. *battle* 'nourish', 'nutritious'; prob. rel. to **BATTEN**[2].

**battement** /ˈbat(ə)mɒ̃/ ● **n.** Ballet a movement in which one leg is moved outward from the body and in again.
– ORIGIN Fr., lit. 'beating'.

**batten**[1] ● **n.** a long, flat wooden or metal strip for strengthening, stiffening, or securing something. ● **v.** strengthen, stiffen, or fasten with battens.
– PHRASES **batten down the hatches** Nautical secure a ship's tarpaulins.
– DERIVATIVES **battening** n.
– ORIGIN C15: from OFr. *batant*, pres. part. (used as n.) of *batre* 'to beat', from L. *battuere*.

**batten**[2] ● **v.** (**batten on**) thrive or prosper at the expense of.
– ORIGIN C16 (in the sense 'improve in condition, grow fat'): from ON *batna* 'get better', rel. to **BETTER**[1].

**Battenberg** ● **n.** chiefly Brit. an oblong sponge cake covered with marzipan, with a square cross section quartered with two colours of sponge.
– ORIGIN named after the town of *Battenberg* in Germany.

**batter**[1] ● **v.** strike repeatedly with hard blows. ➤subject (one's spouse, partner, or child) to repeated violence and assault.
– DERIVATIVES **batterer** n. **battering** n.
– ORIGIN ME: from OFr. *batre* 'to beat' (from L. *battuere*) + **-ER**[4].

**batter**[2] ● **n.** **1** a mixture of flour, egg, and milk or water, used for making pancakes or coating food before frying. **2** Printing a damaged area in metal type or in a block.
– ORIGIN ME: from OFr. *bateure* 'the action of beating', from *batre* 'to beat'.

**batter**[3] ● **n.** a player who bats in baseball.

**batter**[4] ● **v.** (of a wall) slope backwards from the perpendicular. ● **n.** a backwards slope in a wall.
– ORIGIN C16: of unknown origin.

**battered**[1] ● **adj.** (of food) coated in batter and fried.

**battered**[2] ● **adj.** injured by repeated blows. ➤(of a thing) damaged by age and repeated use.

**batterie** /ˌbat(ə)ˈriː/ ● **n.** Ballet the action of beating the feet or calves together during a leap.
– ORIGIN Fr., lit. 'beating'.

**batterie de cuisine** /batəˌriː də kwɪˈziːn/ ● **n.** the apparatus required for the preparation of meals.
– ORIGIN Fr., 'set of equipment for the kitchen'; cf. **BATTERY**.

**battering ram** ● **n.** a heavy object swung or rammed against a door to break it down. ➤historical a heavy beam, originally with an end in the form of a carved ram's head, used in breaching fortifications.

**battery** ● **n.** (pl. **-ies**) **1** a container consisting of one or more cells, in which chemical energy is converted into electricity and used as a source of power. **2** an extensive series, sequence, or range of things. **3** chiefly Brit. a series of small cages for the intensive rearing and housing of poultry. **4** Law the infliction of unlawful personal violence on another person, even where the contact does no physical harm. **5** (**the battery**) Baseball the pitcher and the catcher. **6** a fortified emplacement for heavy guns. ➤an artillery subunit of guns, men, and vehicles.
– ORIGIN ME: from OFr. *baterie*, from *battre* 'to strike', from L. *battuere* (in the sense 'metal articles wrought by hammering' later 'a collection of artillery', whence 'Leyden jars connected up so as to discharge simultaneously').

**batting** ● **n.** cotton wadding in sheets for use in quilts.

**battle** ● **n.** **1** a sustained fight between organized armed forces. **2** a lengthy and difficult conflict or struggle. ● **v.** fight or struggle tenaciously with an enemy or to achieve something.
– PHRASES **battle royal** (pl. **battles royal**) a fiercely contested fight or dispute. **battle stations** chiefly US the positions taken by military personnel in preparation for battle.
– DERIVATIVES **battler** n.
– ORIGIN ME: from OFr. *bataille* (n.), *bataillier* (v.), based on late L. *battualia* 'military or gladiatorial exercises', from L. *battuere* 'to beat'.

**battleaxe** ● **n.** **1** a large axe used in ancient warfare. **2** informal a formidably aggressive older woman.

**battlecruiser** ● **n.** an early 20th-century warship that was faster and more lightly armoured than a battleship.

**battledore** /ˈbat(ə)ldɔː/ ● **n.** **1** (also **battledore and shuttlecock**) a game played with a shuttlecock and

rackets, a forerunner of badminton. ➤the small racket used in this. **2** a wooden paddle-shaped implement formerly used to beat and stir washing.
– ORIGIN ME: perh. from Provençal *batedor* 'beater', from *batre* 'to beat'.

**battledress** ● n. combat dress worn by soldiers.

**battlefield** (also **battleground**) ● n. the piece of ground on which a battle is fought.

**battlement** ● n. a parapet with openings at regular intervals along the top of a wall, forming part of a fortification.
– DERIVATIVES **battlemented** adj.
– ORIGIN ME: from OFr. *bataillier* 'fortify with movable defence turrets', possibly rel. to BATTLE.

**battleship** ● n. a heavy warship with extensive armour protection and large-calibre guns.

**battue** /ba't(j)uː/ ● n. the driving of game towards hunters by beaters.
– ORIGIN C19: from Fr., fem. past part. of *battre* 'to beat'.

**batty** ● adj. (-ier, -iest) informal mad.
– DERIVATIVES **battily** adv. **battiness** n.
– ORIGIN C20: from BAT[2] + -Y[1].

**Batwa** plural form of TWA.

**batwing** ● adj. (of a sleeve) having a deep armhole and a tight cuff.

**bauble** /'bɔːb(ə)l/ ● n. **1** a small, showy trinket or decoration. ➤a decorative hollow ball hung on a Christmas tree. **2** a baton formerly used as an emblem by jesters.
– ORIGIN ME: from OFr. *baubel* 'child's toy', of unknown origin.

**baud** /bɔːd/ ● n. (pl. same or **bauds**) Computing a unit of transmission speed for electronic signals, corresponding to one information unit or event per second.
– ORIGIN 1930s: Fr., from the name of the Fr. engineer Jean M. E. *Baudot*.

**bauera** /'baʊərə/ ● n. a small evergreen shrub with pink or purple flowers, native to temperate regions of Australia. [Genus *Bauera*.]
– ORIGIN mod. L., named after the Austrian botanical draughtsmen Franz and Ferdinand *Bauer*.

**baulk** /bɔːlk, bɔːk/ (chiefly US also **balk**) ● v. (**baulk at**) **1** hesitate to accept an idea or undertaking. ➤thwart or hinder (a plan or person). **2** (of a horse) refuse to go on. ● n. **1** a roughly squared timber beam. **2** the area on a billiard table between the baulk line and the bottom cushion. **3** Baseball an illegal action made by a pitcher that may deceive a base runner. **4** a ridge left unploughed between furrows.
– ORIGIN OE *balc* (in the sense 'unploughed ridge', later 'obstacle'), from ON *bálkr* 'partition'.

**baulk line** ● n. a transverse line marked on a billiard table, extending the diameter of the D to the sides of the table.

**baulky** ● adj. British spelling of BALKY.

**bauxite** /'bɔːksʌɪt/ ● n. an amorphous clayey rock that is the chief ore of aluminium, consisting of hydrated alumina with variable proportions of iron oxides.
– DERIVATIVES **bauxitic** adj.
– ORIGIN C19: from Fr., from *Les Baux* (a village in SE France, near which it was first found) + -ITE[1].

**bavardage** /ˌbavɑː'dɑːʒ, French bavardaʒ/ ● n. rare idle gossip.
– ORIGIN Fr., from *bavarder* 'to chatter'.

**Bavarian** /bə'vɛːrɪən/ ● n. **1** a native or inhabitant of Bavaria, a region in southern Germany. **2** the dialect of German used in Bavaria. ● adj. of or relating to Bavarians or their language.

**bavarois** /ˌbavə'wɑː/ (also **bavaroise** /-'wɑːz/) ● n. a dessert containing gelatin and whipped cream.
– ORIGIN Fr., lit. 'Bavarian'.

**bawbee** /'bɔːbiː/ ● n. Scottish **1** a coin of low value. **2** a former silver coin worth three (later six) Scottish pennies.
– ORIGIN C16: from the name of the laird of Sille*bawby*, mint-master under James V.

**bawd** /bɔːd/ ● n. archaic a woman in charge of a brothel.
– ORIGIN ME: shortened from obs. *bawdstrot*, from OFr. *baudestroyt* 'procuress', from *baude* 'shameless'.

**bawdry** ● n. obscenity in speech or writing.

**bawdy** ● adj. (-ier, -iest) humorously indecent. ● n. humorously indecent talk or writing.
– DERIVATIVES **bawdily** adv. **bawdiness** n.

**bawdy house** ● n. archaic a brothel.

**bawl** ● v. **1** shout out noisily. ➤(**bawl someone out**) reprimand someone angrily. **2** weep noisily. ● n. a loud shout.
– ORIGIN ME (in the sense 'howl, bark'): imitative.

**bawn** /bɔːn/ ● n. **1** Irish & Canadian an area of grassy land near a house; a meadow. **2** Canadian a flat expanse of rocks on a beach, on which fish are spread to dry.
– ORIGIN from Ir.

**bay[1]** ● n. a broad curved inlet of the sea.
– ORIGIN ME: from OFr. *baie*, from Old Sp. *bahia*.

**bay[2]** (also **bay laurel** or **sweet bay**) ● n. an evergreen, purple-berried Mediterranean shrub, with aromatic leaves that are used in cookery. [*Laurus nobilis*.]
– ORIGIN ME (denoting the laurel berry): from OFr. *baie*, from L. *baca* 'berry'.

**bay[3]** ● n. **1** a window area that projects outwards from a wall. **2** a section of wall in the nave of a church between two buttresses or columns. **3** an area specially allocated or marked off. **4** (also **bay platform**) Brit. a short terminal platform at a railway station also having through lines.
– ORIGIN ME: from OFr. *baie*, from *baer* 'to gape', from med. L. *batare*.

**bay[4]** ● adj. (of a horse) brown with black points. ● n. a bay horse.
– ORIGIN ME: from OFr. *bai*, from L. *badius*.

**bay[5]** ● v. (of a dog) bark or howl loudly, especially in pursuit of quarry. ● n. the sound of baying.
– PHRASES **at bay** trapped or cornered. **bay for blood** demand retribution. **hold** (or **keep**) **at bay** prevent from approaching or having an effect.
– ORIGIN ME: from OFr. *(a)bai* (n.), *(a)baiier* (v.) 'bark'; imitative.

**bayadère** /ˌbʌɪə'dɛː/ ● n. a Hindu dancing girl.
– ORIGIN from Fr., from Port. *bailadeira*.

**bayberry** ● n. (pl. **-ies**) a North American shrub with aromatic leathery leaves and waxy berries. [Genus *Myrica*: several species.]

**Bayes' theorem** ● n. Statistics a theorem expressing the conditional probability of each of a set of possible causes for a given observed outcome in terms of the known probability of each cause and the conditional probability of the outcome of each cause.
– DERIVATIVES **Bayesian** adj.
– ORIGIN C19: named after the Engl. mathematician Thomas *Bayes*.

**bayonet** ● n. **1** a long blade fixed to the muzzle of a rifle for use in hand-to-hand fighting. **2** [as modifier] denoting a type of fitting for a light bulb or other appliance which is pushed into a socket and then twisted into place. ● v. (**bayoneted**, **bayoneting**) stab with a bayonet.
– ORIGIN C17 (denoting a kind of short dagger): from Fr. *baïonnette*, from *Bayonne*, the name of a town in SW France, where they were first made.

**bayou** /'bʌɪuː/ ● n. (pl. **bayous**) (in the southern US) a marshy outlet of a lake or river.
– ORIGIN C18: from Louisiana Fr., from Choctaw *bayuk*.

**bay rum** ● n. a perfume for the hair, distilled originally from rum and bayberry leaves.

**bay window** ● n. a window built to project outwards from a wall.

**baza** /'bɑːzə/ ● n. an Asian and Australasian hawk related to and resembling the cuckoo hawks of Africa. [Genus *Aviceda*: three species.]
– ORIGIN mod. L., via Hindi from Arab. *bāz*, denoting a goshawk.

**bazaar** /bə'zɑː/ ● n. **1** a market in a Middle-Eastern country. **2** a fund-raising sale of goods.
– ORIGIN C16: from Ital. *bazarro*, from Turk., from Pers. *bāzār* 'market'.

**bazoo** /bə'zuː/ ● n. US informal a person's mouth.
– ORIGIN C19: perh. from Du. *bazuin* 'trombone, trumpet'.

**bazooka** ● n. **1** a short-range tubular rocket launcher used against tanks. **2** a kazoo shaped like a trumpet.
– ORIGIN 1930s: appar. from **BAZOO** in the original sense 'kazoo'.

**bazoom** ● n. informal, chiefly N. Amer. a woman's breast.
– ORIGIN 1950s: prob. an alt. of **BOSOM**.

**BB** ● symb. **1** Brit. double-black (used in describing grades of pencil lead). **2** N. Amer. a standard size of lead pellet used in air rifles.

**BBC** ● abbrev. British Broadcasting Corporation.

**bbl.** ● abbrev. barrels (especially of oil).

**b-boy** ● n. informal, chiefly US a young man involved with hip-hop culture.
– ORIGIN 1980s: *b-* prob. from the noun **BEAT** or from **BREAK-DANCING**.

**BBQ** ● abbrev. informal a barbecue.

**BBS** ● abbrev. Computing bulletin board system.

**BC** ● abbrev. **1** before Christ (placed after a date, indicating that it is before the Christian era). **2** British Columbia (in official postal use).

**bcc** ● abbrev. blind carbon copy.

**BCD** ● abbrev. binary coded decimal.

**BCE** ● abbrev. before the Common Era (indicating dates before the Christian era, used especially by non-Christians).

**B-cell** ● n. Physiology another term for **B-LYMPHOCYTE**.

**BCG** ● abbrev. Bacillus Calmette-Guérin, an anti-tuberculosis vaccine.

**BD** ● abbrev. **1** Bachelor of Divinity. **2** Bangladesh (international vehicle registration).

**Bde** ● abbrev. Brigade.

**bdellium** /ˈdɛlɪəm/ ● n. a fragrant resin produced by a number of trees related to myrrh, used in perfumes.
– ORIGIN ME: via L. from Gk *bdellion*, of Semitic origin.

**Bdr** ● abbrev. Brit. Bombardier.

**BDS** ● abbrev. Bachelor of Dental Surgery.

**BE** ● abbrev. **1** Bachelor of Education. **2** Bachelor of Engineering. **3** bill of exchange.

**Be** ● symb. the chemical element beryllium.

**be** ● v. (sing. present **am**; **are**; **is**; pl. present **are**; 1st and 3rd sing. past **was**; 2nd sing. past and pl. past **were**; present subjunctive **be**; past subjunctive **were**; present part. **being**; past part. **been**) **1** (usu. **there is/are**) exist; be present. **2** take place. ➤ occupy a position in space. ➤ stay in the same place or condition. ➤ come; go; visit. **3** (when connecting a subject and complement) having the specified state, nature, or role. ➤ represent or signify. ● aux. v. **1** used with a present participle to form continuous tenses. **2** used with a past participle to form the passive voice. **3** used to indicate something that is due to happen. ➤ used to express obligation or necessity. ➤ used to hypothesize about something that might happen.
– PHRASES **the be-all and end-all** informal a feature of an activity that is of greater importance than any other. **not be oneself** not feel in one's usual physical or mental state. **-to-be** of the future: *his bride-to-be.*
– ORIGIN OE *bēon*, an irregular and defective verb whose full conjugation derives from several orig. distinct verbs; the forms *am* and *is* are rel. to L. *sum* and *est*.

**be-** ● prefix forming verbs: **1** all over; all round: *bespatter.* ➤ thoroughly; excessively: *bewilder.* **2** (added to intransitive verbs and to adjectives and nouns) expressing transitive action: *bemoan* | *befriend.* **3** (added to nouns) affect with: *befog.* ➤ (added to adjectives) cause to be: *befoul.* **4** (forming adjectives ending in *-ed*) having; covered with: *bejewelled.*
– ORIGIN OE, weak form of *bī* 'by'.

**beach** ● n. a pebbly or sandy shore at the edge of the sea or a lake. ● v. bring on to a beach from the water. ➤ (with reference to a whale) become or cause to become stranded on a beach.
– ORIGIN C16: perh. rel. to OE *bæce*, *bece* 'brook'.

**beachcomber** ● n. **1** a person who searches beaches for articles of value. **2** a long wave rolling in from the sea.

**beachfront** ● n. another term for **SEAFRONT**.

**beachhead** ● n. a fortified position on a beach taken by landing forces.

**Beach-la-mar** /ˌbiːtʃləˈmɑː/ ● n. variant spelling of **BISLAMA**.

**beach plum** ● n. a maritime shrub related to the plum, with edible fruit, found on the east coast of North America. [*Prunus maritima.*]

**beachside** ● adj. next to the beach.

**beachwear** ● n. clothing suitable for wearing on the beach.

**beacon** ● n. **1** a fire lit on the top of a hill as a signal. **2** a light serving as a signal for ships or aircraft. ➤ a radio transmitter signalling the position of a ship or aircraft.
– ORIGIN OE *bēacn* 'sign, portent, ensign', of W. Gmc origin.

**bead** ● n. **1** a small, rounded piece of glass, stone, plastic, etc., perforated and threaded in a string with others to make a necklace or rosary. **2** a drop of a liquid on a surface. **3** an ornamental plaster moulding resembling a string of beads. **4** a narrow moulding of circular cross section. **5** a small knob forming the foresight of a gun. **6** the reinforced inner edge of a tyre. ● v. **1** decorate or cover with beads. **2** form into a string like beads.
– PHRASES **draw** (or **get**) **a bead on** chiefly N. Amer. take aim at with a gun.
– DERIVATIVES **beaded** adj. **beading** n.
– ORIGIN OE *gebed* 'prayer', of Gmc origin; current senses derive from the use of a rosary.

**beadle** ● n. Brit. **1** a ceremonial officer of a church, college, or similar institution. **2** historical a minor parish officer dealing with petty offenders.
– ORIGIN OE *bydel* 'a person who makes a proclamation', influenced by OFr. *bedel*, ult. of Gmc origin.

**beadsman** ● n. (pl. **-men**) historical a pensioner provided for by a benefactor in return for prayers.

**beady** ● adj. (of a person's eyes) small, round, and observing things clearly.
– DERIVATIVES **beadily** adv. **beadiness** n.

**beadwork** ● n. decorative work made of beads.

**beagle** ● n. a small, short-legged hound, kept as a pet or for hunting hares. ● v. hunt with beagles.
– DERIVATIVES **beagler** n. **beagling** n.
– ORIGIN C15: perh. from OFr. *beegueule* 'open-mouthed'.

**beak**[1] ● n. **1** a bird's horny projecting jaws; a bill. ➤ a projecting jaw in some other animals. **2** a projection at the prow of an ancient warship, used to pierce the hulls of enemy ships.
– DERIVATIVES **beaked** adj. **beaky** adj.
– ORIGIN ME: from OFr. *bec*, from L. *beccus*, of Celtic origin.

**beak**[2] ● n. Brit. informal a magistrate or schoolmaster.
– ORIGIN C18: prob. from criminals' sl.

**beaked whale** ● n. a whale of a group with elongated jaws that form a beak, including the bottlenose whales. [Family Ziphiidae: several species.]

**beaker** ● n. Brit. a tall plastic cup. ➤ a lipped cylindrical glass container for laboratory use. ➤ archaic or poetic/literary a large drinking container with a wide mouth.
– ORIGIN ME: from ON *bikarr*, perh. based on Gk *bikos* 'drinking bowl'.

**Beaker folk** ● pl. n. a late Neolithic and early Bronze Age European people named after the distinctive waisted pots (**Beaker ware**) associated with their burials.

**beam** ● n. **1** a long sturdy piece of squared timber or metal used horizontally in building to support a load above. ➤ a narrow horizontal length of squared timber used for balancing exercises in gymnastics. **2** a horizontal beam supporting the deck and joining the sides of a ship. ➤ the direction of an object visible from the side of a ship when it is perpendicular to the centre line of the vessel: *there was land in sight on the port beam.* ➤ a ship's breadth at its widest point. **3** a ray or shaft of light. ➤ a directional flow of particles or radiation. ➤ a series of radio or radar signals emitted as a navigational guide. **4** a radiant smile. **5** the crossbar of a balance. **6** an oscillating shaft in a beam engine. **7** the shank of an anchor. ● v. **1** transmit (a radio signal or broadcast) in a specified direction. **2** shine brightly. **3** smile radiantly.
– PHRASES **a beam in one's eye** a fault that is greater in oneself than in the person one is finding fault with. [with

biblical allusion to Matt. 7:3.] **off beam** informal on the wrong track. **on her** (or **its**) **beam ends** (of a ship) heeled over on its side.
– ORIGIN OE *bēam* 'tree, beam', of W. Gmc origin.

**beam compass** • n. a compass for drawing large circles, consisting of a horizontal rod connected by sliding sockets to two vertical legs.

**beam engine** • n. a stationary steam engine with a large oscillating shaft that transmits the vertical movement of the pistons to a crank or pump.

**Beamer** • n. another term for BEEMER.

**beamer** • n. Cricket a ball bowled directly at a batsman's head or upper body without bouncing.

**beam sea** • n. Nautical a sea which is rolling against a ship's side approximately at right angles.

**beamy** • adj. (of a ship) broad-beamed.

**bean** • n. **1** an edible kidney-shaped seed growing in long pods on certain leguminous plants. ➤the hard seed of coffee, cocoa, and certain other plants. **2** a leguminous plant bearing beans. [*Phaseolus* and other genera: numerous species.] **3** (N. Amer. also **beans**) [with neg.] informal a very small amount or nothing at all. **4** informal, dated a person's head. • v. informal, chiefly N. Amer. hit on the head.
– PHRASES **full of beans** informal lively; in high spirits. **old bean** Brit. informal, dated a friendly form of address.
– ORIGIN OE *bēan*, of Gmc origin.

**beanbag** • n. **1** a small bag filled with dried beans and used in children's games. **2** a large cushion filled with polystyrene beads.

**bean counter** • n. informal an accountant or bureaucrat who places excessive emphasis on controlling expenditure and budgets.

**bean curd** • n. another term for TOFU.

**beanery** • n. (pl. **-ies**) N. Amer. informal a cheap restaurant.

**beanfeast** • n. Brit. informal a celebratory party with plentiful food and drink.
– ORIGIN C19: orig. denoting an annual dinner given to employees, which always featured beans and bacon.

**bean goose** • n. a grey goose with orange-yellow bill and legs, breeding in the arctic tundra of Lapland and Siberia. [*Anser fabalis*.]

**beanie** • n. (pl. **-ies**) a small close-fitting hat worn on the back of the head.
– ORIGIN 1940s: perh. from BEAN (in the sense 'head') + -IE.

**beano** • n. (pl. **-os**) Brit. informal a party.
– ORIGIN C19: abbrev. of BEANFEAST.

**beanpole** • n. informal a tall, thin person.

**bean sprouts** • pl. n. the edible sprouting seeds of certain beans.

**beanstalk** • n. the stem of a bean plant.

**bear**[1] • v. (past **bore**; past part. **borne**) **1** carry. ➤have as an attribute or visible mark. ➤(**bear oneself**) conduct oneself in a specified manner. **2** support (a weight). **3** [with neg.] manage to tolerate: *I can't bear it.* **4** give birth to (a child). ➤(of a tree or plant) produce (fruit or flowers). **5** turn and proceed in a specified direction: *bear left.*
– PHRASES **bear fruit** yield positive results. **bear someone a grudge** nurture a feeling of resentment against someone. **bear in mind** remember and take into account. **bear someone malice** (or **ill will**) wish someone harm. **bear witness** (or **testimony**) **to** testify to. **be borne in upon** come to be realized by. **bring to bear 1** muster and use to effect. **2** aim (a weapon).
– PHRASAL VERBS **bear down** (of a woman in labour) exert downwards pressure in order to push the baby out. **bear down on** approach in a purposeful or intimidating manner. **bear off** (or **away**) Sailing change course away from the wind. **bear on** be relevant to. **bear something out** support or confirm something. **bear up** remain cheerful in the face of adversity. **bear with** be patient or tolerant with.
– DERIVATIVES **bearable** adj. **bearability** n. **bearably** adv.
– ORIGIN OE *beran*, of Gmc origin.

**bear**[2] • n. **1** a large, heavy mammal which walks on the soles of its feet, having thick fur and a very short tail. [Family Ursidae: several species.] **2** Stock Exchange a person who sells shares hoping to buy them back later at a lower price. Often contrasted having BULL[1]. [said to be from a proverb warning against 'selling the bear's skin before one has caught the bear'.] **3** a brutish or ill-mannered person.
– PHRASES **like a bear with a sore head** Brit. informal very irritable. **loaded for bear** N. Amer. informal fully prepared for a confrontation or challenge.
– ORIGIN OE *bera*, of W. Gmc origin.

**bear-baiting** • n. historical a form of entertainment which involved setting dogs to attack a captive bear.

**bearberry** • n. (pl. **-ies**) a creeping dwarf shrub of the heather family, with pinkish flowers and bright red berries. [Genus *Arctostaphylos*: several species.]

**bearcat** • n. a bear-like climbing mammal, especially the red panda.

**beard** • n. **1** a growth of hair on the chin and lower cheeks of a man's face. ➤an animal's growth or marking that is likened to a beard, such as the gills of an oyster. ➤a tuft of hairs or bristles on certain plants. **2** N. Amer. informal a woman who accompanies a homosexual man as an escort to a social occasion. • v. boldly confront or challenge (someone formidable).
– DERIVATIVES **bearded** adj. **beardless** adj.
– ORIGIN OE, of W. Gmc origin.

**bearded dragon** (also **bearded lizard**) • n. a semi-arboreal Australian lizard with spiny scales and a large throat pouch bearing sharp spines. [Genus *Pogona*: several species.]

**bearded tit** • n. a small long-tailed songbird of the parrotbill family, inhabiting reed beds. [*Panurus biarmicus*.]

**bearded vulture** • n. another term for LAMMERGEIER.

**bearer** • n. **1** a person or thing that carries something. **2** a person who presents a cheque or other order to pay money. ➤[as modifier] payable to the possessor: *bearer bonds.*

**bear garden** (also **bear pit**) • n. a scene of uproar and confusion.
– ORIGIN C16, denoting a place set apart for bear-baiting.

**beargrass** • n. a North American plant with long, coarse, grass-like leaves, especially a wild yucca.

**bear hug** • n. a rough, tight embrace.

**bearing** • n. **1** a person's way of standing, moving, or behaving. **2** relation; relevance: *the case has no bearing on the issues.* **3** (**bearings**) a device in a machine that allows two parts to rotate or move in contact with each other with reduced friction. **4** the direction or position of something relative to a fixed point, normally measured in degrees and with magnetic north as zero. ➤(**one's bearings**) awareness of one's position relative to one's surroundings. **5** Heraldry a device or charge.

**bearing rein** • n. a fixed rein which causes a horse to raise its head and arch its neck.

**bearish** • adj. **1** resembling or likened to a bear. **2** Stock Exchange characterized by falling share prices. ➤inclined to sell because of an anticipated fall in prices.
– DERIVATIVES **bearishly** adv. **bearishness** n.

**bear market** • n. Stock Exchange a market in which share prices are falling, encouraging selling.

**Béarnaise sauce** /ˌbeɪəˈneɪz/ • n. a rich sauce thickened with egg yolks and flavoured with tarragon.
– ORIGIN *Béarnaise*, fem. of Fr. *béarnais* 'of *Béarn*', a region of SW France.

**bear pit** • n. another term for BEAR GARDEN.

**bear's breech** • n. a Mediterranean plant with large deep-cut leaves and tall spikes of purple-veined white flowers. [*Acanthus mollis*.]

**bear's ear** • n. another term for AURICULA.

**bear's foot** • n. a hellebore with leaves that are said to resemble a bear's foot.

**bearskin** • n. a tall cap of black fur worn ceremonially by certain troops.

**beast** • n. **1** an animal, especially a large or dangerous mammal. ➤a bovine farm animal. **2** an inhumanly cruel or depraved person.
– ORIGIN ME: from OFr. *beste*, based on L. *bestia*.

**beastie** ● n. (pl. **-ies**) Scottish or humorous a small animal or insect.

**beastly** Brit. informal ● adj. (**-ier**, **-iest**) very unpleasant. ● adv. dated to an extreme and unpleasant degree.
– DERIVATIVES **beastliness** n.

**beast of burden** ● n. an animal that is used for carrying loads.

**beast of prey** ● n. an animal, especially a mammal, that kills and eats other animals.

**beat** ● v. (past **beat**; past part. **beaten**) **1** strike (a person or an animal) repeatedly and violently so as to hurt or punish them. ➤ strike repeatedly so as to make a noise. ➤ flatten or shape (metal) by striking it repeatedly with a hammer. **2** defeat in a game or other competitive situation. ➤ surpass (a record or score). ➤ overcome (a problem). ➤ informal baffle: *it beats me how you manage it.* **3** (of the heart) pulsate. **4** (of a bird) move (the wings) up and down. **5** stir (cooking ingredients) vigorously. **6** move across (an area of land) repeatedly striking at the ground cover in order to raise game birds for shooting. **7** Sailing sail into the wind, with repeated tacking. ● n. **1** a main accent or rhythmic unit in music or poetry. ➤ a rhythm or rhythmic sound or movement. ➤ a pulsation of the heart. ➤ a periodic variation of sound or amplitude due to the combination of two sounds or other vibrations with similar but not identical frequencies. **2** the movement of a bird's wings. **3** an area allocated to a police officer and patrolled on foot. ➤ a spell of duty allocated to a police officer. ➤ a stretch of water fished by an angler. **4** a brief pause or moment of hesitation. ● adj. informal completely exhausted.
– PHRASES **beat about the bush** discuss a matter without coming to the point. **beat the bounds** historical mark parish boundaries by walking round them and striking certain points with rods. **beat the clock** perform a task within a fixed time limit. **beat a (hasty) retreat** withdraw. **beat time** indicate or follow a musical tempo with a baton or other means. **off the beaten track** in or into an isolated place. **to beat the band** informal, chiefly N. Amer. so as to surpass all competition.
– PHRASAL VERBS **beat someone down** force someone to reduce the price of something. **beat it** informal leave a place. **beat off** vulgar slang (of a man) masturbate. **beat someone/thing off** succeed in resisting an attacker or an attack. **beat someone up** assault and severely injure someone by hitting them repeatedly. **beat up on someone** North American way of saying ***beat someone up***.
– DERIVATIVES **beatable** adj. **beater** n. **beating** n.
– ORIGIN OE *bēatan*, of Gmc origin.

**beatbox** ● n. informal **1** a drum machine. **2** a radio or radio cassette player used to play loud music.

**beat generation** ● n. a movement of young people in the 1950s and early 1960s who rejected conventional society, valuing self-expression and favouring modern jazz.

**beatific** /biːəˈtɪfɪk/ ● adj. **1** feeling or expressing blissful happiness. **2** Christian Theology imparting holy bliss.
– DERIVATIVES **beatifically** adv.

**beatification** /bɪˌatɪfɪˈkeɪʃ(ə)n/ ● n. (in the Roman Catholic Church) declaration by the Pope that a dead person is in a state of bliss, constituting a first step towards canonization and permitting public veneration.

**beatify** /bɪˈatɪfʌɪ/ ● v. (**-ies**, **-ied**) (in the Roman Catholic Church) announce the beatification of.
– ORIGIN C16: from OFr. *beatifier* or eccles. L. *beatificare*, from L. *beatus* 'blessed'.

**beatitude** /bɪˈatɪtjuːd/ ● n. **1** supreme blessedness. ➤ (**the Beatitudes**) the blessings listed by Jesus in the Sermon on the Mount (Matt. 5:3–11). **2** (**His/Your Beatitude**) a title given to patriarchs in the Orthodox Church.
– ORIGIN ME: from OFr. *beatitude* or L. *beatitudo*, from *beatus* 'blessed'.

**beatnik** ● n. a young person belonging to a subculture associated with the beat generation.

**beat-up** ● adj. informal worn out by overuse.

**beau** /bəʊ/ ● n. (pl. **beaux** or **beaus** /bəʊz, bəʊ/) dated **1** a boyfriend or male admirer. **2** a dandy.
– ORIGIN C17: from Fr., lit. 'handsome'.

**Beaufort scale** /ˈbəʊfət/ ● n. a scale of wind speed ranging from 0 (calm) to 12 (hurricane).
– ORIGIN C19: named after Sir Francis *Beaufort*, the English admiral who devised it.

**beau geste** /bəʊ ˈʒɛst, French bo ʒɛst/ ● n. (pl. **beaux gestes** pronunc. same) a noble and generous act.
– ORIGIN Fr., lit. 'splendid gesture'.

**beau idéal** /ˌbəʊ iːdeɪˈal, French bo ideal/ ● n. a person or thing representing the highest possible standard of excellence in a particular respect.
– ORIGIN Fr., lit. 'ideal beauty'.

**Beaujolais** /ˈbəʊʒəleɪ, French boʒɔlɛ/ ● n. a light red wine produced in the Beaujolais district of SE France.

**Beaujolais Nouveau** /ˌbəʊʒəleɪ nuːˈvəʊ, French boʒɔlɛ nuvo/ ● n. a Beaujolais wine sold in the first year of a vintage.
– ORIGIN from **Beaujolais** + Fr. *nouveau* 'new'.

**beau monde** /bəʊ ˈmɒnd, French bo mɔ̃d/ ● n. (**the beau monde**) fashionable society.
– ORIGIN Fr., lit. 'fine world'.

**Beaune** /bəʊn/ ● n. a red burgundy wine from the region around Beaune in eastern France.

**beaut** /bjuːt/ informal, chiefly Austral./NZ ● n. an excellent or beautiful person or thing. ● adj. excellent.

**beauteous** ● adj. poetic/literary beautiful.

**beautician** ● n. a person whose job is to give facials and other beauty treatments.

**beautiful** ● adj. **1** pleasing the senses or mind aesthetically. **2** of a very high standard; excellent.
– DERIVATIVES **beautifully** adv.

**beautify** ● v. (**-ies**, **-ied**) make beautiful.
– DERIVATIVES **beautification** n. **beautifier** n.

**beauty** ● n. (pl. **-ies**) **1** a combination of qualities that delights the aesthetic senses. **2** [as modifier] denoting something intended to make someone more attractive: *beauty treatment.* **3** a beautiful woman. **4** an excellent example. ➤ an attractive feature or advantage.
– ORIGIN ME: from OFr. *beaute*, based on L. *bellus* 'beautiful, fine'.

**beauty contest** ● n. a contest in which the winner is the woman judged the most beautiful.

**beauty queen** ● n. a woman judged most beautiful in a beauty contest.

**beauty salon** (also **beauty parlour**) ● n. an establishment in which hairdressing, make-up, and similar cosmetic treatments are carried out professionally.

**beauty sleep** ● n. humorous sleep considered to be essential in keeping one looking young and attractive.

**beauty spot** ● n. **1** a place known for its beautiful scenery. **2** a small natural or artificial mole on a woman's face, considered to enhance her attractiveness.

**beaux** plural form of **beau**.

**beaux arts** /bəʊz ˈɑː, French boz aʀ/ ● pl. n. **1** fine arts. **2** (usu. **Beaux Arts**) [as modifier] relating to the classical decorative style maintained by the École des Beaux-Arts in Paris in the 19th century.
– ORIGIN from Fr. *beaux-arts*.

**beaver**[1] ● n. (pl. same or **beavers**) **1** a large semiaquatic broad-tailed rodent, noted for its habit of gnawing through trees to fell them in order to make lodges and dams. [*Castor canadensis* (N. America) and *C. fiber* (Eurasia).] ➤ the soft light brown fur of the beaver. ➤ (also **beaver hat**) chiefly historical a hat made of felted beaver fur. ➤ (also **beaver cloth**) a heavy woollen cloth resembling felted beaver fur. **2** a very hard-working person. **3** (**Beaver**) a boy aged about 6 or 7 who is an affiliated member of the Scout Association. ● v. (often **beaver away**) informal work hard.
– ORIGIN OE *beofor*, *befor*, of Gmc origin.

**beaver**[2] ● n. the lower part of the face guard of a helmet in a suit of armour.
– ORIGIN C15: from OFr. *baviere* 'bib', from *baver* 'slaver'.

**beaver**[3] ● n. **1** vulgar slang, chiefly N. Amer. a woman's genitals or pubic area. **2** Brit. informal, dated a bearded man.
– ORIGIN C20: of unknown origin.

**beaverboard** ● n. chiefly N. Amer. a kind of fibreboard.

**beaver lamb** ● n. lambskin made to look like beaver

fur.

**bebop** /ˈbiːbɒp/ ● **n.** a type of jazz originating in the 1940s and characterized by complex harmony and rhythms.
– DERIVATIVES **bebopper** n.
– ORIGIN 1940s (orig. US): imitative of the typical rhythm of this music.

**becalm** ● **v.** leave (a sailing ship) unable to move through lack of wind.

**became** past participle of **BECOME**.

**becard** /ˈbɛkəd, bəˈkɑːd/ ● **n.** a small bird of the tyrant flycatcher family, found mainly in Central and South America. [Genus *Pachyramphus*: several species.]
– ORIGIN C19: from Fr. *bécarde*, from *bec* 'beak'.

**because** ● **conj.** for the reason that; since.
– PHRASES **because of** by reason of.
– ORIGIN ME: from the phr. *by cause*, influenced by OFr. *par cause de* 'by reason of'.

**béchamel** /ˈbeɪʃəmɛl/ ● **n.** a rich white sauce made with milk infused with herbs and other flavourings.
– ORIGIN named after the Marquis Louis de *Béchamel*, who is said to have invented a similar sauce.

**bêche-de-mer** /ˌbɛʃdəˈmɛː/ ● **n.** (pl. same or **bêches-de-mer** pronunc. same) **1** a large sea cucumber which is eaten as a delicacy in China and Japan. **2** (**Bêche-de-mer**) another term for **BISLAMA**.
– ORIGIN C18: pseudo-Fr., alt. of Port. *bicho do mar*, lit. 'sea-worm'.

**beck[1]** ● **n.** N. English a stream.
– ORIGIN ME: from ON *bekkr*, of Gmc origin.

**beck[2]** ● **n.** archaic or poetic/literary a gesture requesting attention, such as a nod or wave.
– PHRASES **at someone's beck and call** always having to be ready to obey someone's orders.
– ORIGIN ME: abbreviated form of **BECKON**.

**becket** /ˈbɛkɪt/ ● **n.** a loop of rope or similar device for securing loose items on a ship.
– ORIGIN C18: of unknown origin.

**beckon** ● **v.** make a gesture to encourage or instruct someone to approach or follow. ➤summon in this way.
– ORIGIN OE *bīecnan*, *bēcnan*, of W. Gmc origin.

**become** ● **v.** (past **became**; past part. **become**) **1** begin to be. ➤develop into. ➤(of a person) qualify or be accepted as. ➤(**become of**) (in questions) happen to. **2** (of clothing) look well on. ➤be appropriate to (someone).
– ORIGIN OE *becuman* 'come to a place, come to be or do something' (see **BE-**, **COME**), of Gmc origin.

**becoming** ● **adj. 1** (of clothing) looking well on someone. **2** decorous.
– DERIVATIVES **becomingly** adv. **becomingness** n.

**becquerel** /ˈbɛkərɛl/ (abbrev.: **Bq**) ● **n.** Physics the SI unit of radioactivity, corresponding to one disintegration per second.
– ORIGIN C19: named after the Fr. physicist A-H. *Becquerel*.

**BEd** ● **abbrev.** Bachelor of Education.

**bed** ● **n. 1** a piece of furniture incorporating a mattress or other surface for sleeping or resting on. ➤a place for a patient in a hospital. ➤informal used with reference to a bed as a place for sexual activity. **2** an area of ground where flowers and plants are grown: *a flower bed*. **3** a flat base or foundation on which something rests or is supported. ➤chiefly N. Amer. the open part of a truck or cart, where goods are carried. **4** a stratum or layer of rock. **5** the bottom of the sea or a lake or river. ➤a place on the seabed where shellfish breed or are bred. ● **v.** (**bedded**, **bedding**) **1** provide with sleeping accommodation. ➤(**bed down**) settle down for the night in an improvised place. **2** informal have sexual intercourse with. **3** (**bed out**) transfer (a plant) from a pot or seed tray to the ground. **4** fix firmly; embed. ➤lay or arrange in a layer.
– PHRASES **bed of nails** a board with nails pointing out of it, as lain on by fakirs and ascetics. **a bed of roses** [usu. with neg.] a situation or activity that is comfortable or easy. **be brought to bed** archaic (of a woman) give birth to a child. **get out of bed on the wrong side** start the day in a bad mood, which continues all day long. **put something to bed** informal make a newspaper ready for press.
– DERIVATIVES **bedded** adj.
– ORIGIN OE *bed*, *bedd* (n.), *beddian* (v.), of Gmc origin.

**bedabble** /bɪˈdab(ə)l/ ● **v.** archaic stain or splash with dirty liquid or blood.

**bedad** /bɪˈdad/ ● **exclam.** Irish used to express surprise or for emphasis.
– ORIGIN C18: alt. of *by God*.

**bed and board** ● **n.** lodging and food.

**bed and breakfast** ● **n.** guest house or hotel provision consisting of sleeping accommodation and breakfast. ➤a guest house. ● **v.** (**bed-and-breakfast**) Brit. Stock Exchange sell (shares) and buy them back by agreement the next day.

**bedaub** ● **v.** poetic/literary smear or daub with a sticky substance.

**bedazzle** ● **v.** greatly impress with brilliance or skill.
– DERIVATIVES **bedazzlement** n.

**bedbug** ● **n.** a bloodsucking wingless bug which sucks the blood of sleeping humans. [*Cimex lectularius*.]

**bedchamber** ● **n.** archaic a bedroom.

**bedclothes** ● **pl. n.** coverings for a bed, such as sheets and blankets.

**beddable** /ˈbɛdəb(ə)l/ ● **adj.** informal sexually attractive or available.

**bedder** ● **n. 1** a plant suitable for use as a bedding plant. **2** Brit. informal a servant employed to clean and tidy rooms in Cambridge colleges. **3** informal a house or flat with a specified number of bedrooms: *a one-bedder*.

**bedding** ● **n. 1** bedclothes. ➤straw or similar material for animals to sleep on. **2** a base or bottom layer. **3** Geology the stratification or layering of rocks.

**bedding plant** ● **n.** an annual plant produced for planting in a bed in the spring.

**bedeck** ● **v.** decorate lavishly.

**bedeguar** /ˈbɛdɪgɑː/ ● **n.** a reddish moss-like growth on rose bushes, caused by the developing larvae of a wasp.
– ORIGIN ME: from Fr. *bédégar*, from Pers. *bād-āwar*, lit. 'wind-brought'.

**bedel** /ˈbiːd(ə)l, bɪˈdɛl/ (also **bedell**) ● **n.** (in some British universities) an official with largely ceremonial duties.
– ORIGIN ME: archaic spelling of **BEADLE**.

**bedevil** ● **v.** (**bedevilled**, **bedevilling**; US **bedeviled**, **bedeviling**) cause continual trouble to.
– DERIVATIVES **bedevilment** n.

**bedew** /bɪˈdjuː/ ● **v.** poetic/literary cover or sprinkle with drops of water.

**bedfellow** ● **n.** a person or thing that is closely connected with another.

**Bedford cord** ● **n.** a tough woven fabric with prominent ridges.
– ORIGIN C19: named after *Bedford* in central England.

**bedhead** ● **n.** Brit. an upright board or panel fixed at the head of a bed.

**bed-hop** ● **v.** informal engage in successive casual sexual affairs.
– DERIVATIVES **bed-hopper** n.

**bedight** /bɪˈdʌɪt/ ● **adj.** archaic adorned.
– ORIGIN ME: past part. of archaic *bedight* 'equip, array' (see **BE-**, **DIGHT**).

**bedim** ● **v.** (**bedimmed**, **bedimming**) poetic/literary cause to become dim.

**bedizen** /bɪˈdʌɪz(ə)n, -ˈdɪz-/ ● **v.** poetic/literary dress up or decorate gaudily.
– ORIGIN C17: from **BE-** + obs. *dizen* 'deck out'.

**bedjacket** ● **n.** a soft loose jacket worn for extra warmth when sitting up in bed.

**bed joint** ● **n.** a horizontal layer of mortar underneath a layer of masonry.

**bedlam** /ˈbɛdləm/ ● **n. 1** a scene of uproar and confusion. **2** archaic an asylum.
– ORIGIN ME: early form of *Bethlehem*, referring to the hospital of St Mary of Bethlehem in London, used as an asylum for the insane.

**bedlinen** ● **n.** sheets, pillowcases, and duvet covers.

**Bedlington terrier** /ˈbɛdlɪŋt(ə)n/ ● **n.** a terrier of a breed with a narrow head, long legs, and curly grey

hair.
– ORIGIN C19: named after the village of *Bedlington* in northern England, where the breed originated.

**bedmaker** • n. Brit. another term for BEDDER (in sense 2).

**Bedouin** /'bɛdʊɪn/ (also **Beduin**) • n. (pl. same) a nomadic Arab of the desert.
– ORIGIN from OFr. *beduin*, based on Arab. *badawī*, (pl.) *badawīn* 'dwellers in the desert', from *badw* 'desert'.

**bedpan** • n. a receptacle used by a bedridden patient for urine and faeces.

**bedplate** • n. a metal plate forming the base of a machine.

**bedpost** • n. any of the four upright supports of a bedstead.

**bedraggled** • adj. dishevelled.

**bedridden** • adj. confined to bed by sickness or old age.
– ORIGIN ME: formed irregularly from archaic *bedrid* 'bedridden person', from the base of RIDE.

**bedrock** • n. **1** solid rock underlying loose deposits such as soil or alluvium. **2** the fundamental principles on which something is based.

**bedroll** • n. chiefly N. Amer. a sleeping bag or other bedding rolled into a bundle.

**bedroom** • n. **1** a room for sleeping in. **2** [as modifier] N. Amer. denoting a dormitory town or suburb.

**Beds.** • abbrev. Bedfordshire.

**bedside** • n. the space beside a bed.
– PHRASES **bedside manner** the manner in which a doctor attends a patient.

**bedsit** (also **bedsitter** or **bed-sitting room**) • n. Brit. informal a rented room consisting of a combined bedroom and living room, with cooking facilities.

**bedskirt** • n. N. Amer. a valance for a bed.

**bedsock** • n. chiefly Brit. each of a pair of thick socks worn for extra warmth in bed.

**bedsore** • n. a sore that develops as a result of lying in bed in one position for a prolonged period.

**bedspread** • n. a decorative cloth used to cover a bed.

**bedstead** • n. the framework of a bed.

**bedstraw** • n. a herbaceous plant with small flowers and whorls of slender leaves, formerly used for stuffing mattresses. [Genus *Galium*: several species.]

**bedtime** • n. the usual time when someone goes to bed.

**Bedu** /'bɛdu:/ • n. another term for BEDOUIN.
– ORIGIN from Arab. *badw*.

**Beduin** • n. variant spelling of BEDOUIN.

**bed-warmer** • n. a long-handled metal pan filled with warm coals, formerly used for warming a bed.

**bed-wetting** • n. involuntary urination during the night.
– DERIVATIVES **bed-wetter** n.

**bee** • n. **1** (also **honeybee** or **hive bee**) a stinging social insect which collects nectar and pollen from flowers and produces wax and honey. [*Apis mellifera* and other species.] **2** an insect of a large group to which the honeybee belongs, including many solitary as well as social kinds. [Superfamily Apoidea.] **3** a meeting for communal work or amusement: *a sewing bee.*
– PHRASES **the bee's knees** informal an outstandingly good person or thing. **have a bee in one's bonnet** informal be preoccupied or obsessed with something.
– ORIGIN OE *bēo*, of Gmc origin.

**bee beetle** • n. a hairy yellowish chafer with broad black stripes, often seen on flowers. [Genus *Trichius*: several species.]

**bee bread** • n. honey or pollen used as food by bees.

**beech** • n. a large tree with smooth grey bark, glossy leaves, and hard, pale, fine-grained wood. [*Fagus sylvaticus* (Europe) and other species.]
– ORIGIN OE *bēce*, of Gmc origin.

**beechmast** • n. the angular brown nuts of the beech tree, pairs of which are enclosed in a prickly case.

**beedi** • n. (pl. **beedis**) variant spelling of BIDI.

**bee-eater** • n. a brightly coloured insectivorous bird with a downcurved bill and long central tail feathers. [*Merops apiaster* and other species.]

**beef** • n. **1** the flesh of a cow, bull, or ox, used as food. ➤(pl. **beeves** /bi:vz/ or US also **beefs**) Farming a cow, bull, or ox fattened for its meat. **2** informal flesh with well-developed muscle. ➤strength or power. ➤the substance of a matter. **3** (pl. **beefs**) informal a complaint or grievance. • v. informal **1** (**beef something up**) give something more substance or strength. **2** complain.
– DERIVATIVES **beefily** adv. **beefiness** n. **beefy** adj.
– ORIGIN ME: from OFr. *boef*, from L. *bos*, *bov-* 'ox'.

**beefalo** • n. (pl. same or **-oes**) a hybrid animal of a cross between cattle and buffalo.

**beefburger** • n. a flat round cake of minced beef, fried or grilled and typically eaten in a bun.

**beefcake** • n. informal men with well-developed muscles.

**beefeater** • n. a Yeoman Warder or Yeoman of the Guard in the Tower of London.
– ORIGIN C17 (orig. a derogatory term for a well-fed servant).

**bee fly** • n. a squat, hairy bee-like fly whose larvae are generally parasites of bees and wasps. [Family Bombyliidae: many species.]

**beefsteak** • n. a thick slice of steak, especially rump steak.

**beefsteak fungus** • n. a reddish-brown bracket fungus which resembles raw beef. [*Fistulina hepatica*.]

**beef tea** • n. Brit. a hot drink made with a beef extract.

**beef tomato** (chiefly N. Amer. also **beefsteak tomato**) • n. a tomato of a large, firm variety.

**beef Wellington** • n. a dish consisting of beef coated in pâté and wrapped in puff pastry.

**beefwood** • n. a tropical hardwood tree with close-grained red wood. [Species in several families, in particular *Casuarina equisetifolia*.]

**beehive** • n. **1** a structure in which bees are kept, typically in the form of a dome or box. **2** a woman's domed and lacquered hairstyle popular in the 1960s.
– DERIVATIVES **beehived** adj.

**bee-keeping** • n. the occupation of owning and breeding bees for their honey.
– DERIVATIVES **bee-keeper** n.

**beeline** • n. (in phr. **make a beeline for**) hurry directly to.
– ORIGIN C19: with ref. to the straight line supposedly taken instinctively by a bee when returning to the hive.

**Beelzebub** /bɪ'ɛlzɪbʌb/ • n. a name for the Devil.
– ORIGIN from late L. *Beëlzebub*, translating Heb. *ba'al zĕbūḇ* 'lord of flies', the name of a Philistine god, and Gk *Beelzeboul* 'the Devil'.

**Beemer** (also **Beamer**) • n. informal, chiefly N. Amer. a car or motorcycle manufactured by BMW.
– ORIGIN representing a pronunc. of the first two letters of *BMW*.

**been** past participle of BE.

**bee orchid** • n. an orchid with a flower that resembles a bee. [*Ophrys apifera* and related species.]

**beep** • n. a short, high-pitched sound emitted by electronic equipment or a vehicle horn. • v. produce a beep. ➤chiefly N. Amer. summon with a device that beeps.
– DERIVATIVES **beeper** n.
– ORIGIN 1920s: imitative.

**beer** • n. an alcoholic drink made from yeast-fermented malt flavoured with hops. ➤N. Amer. a drink of this type brewed by bottom fermentation. ➤used in names of certain other fermented drinks, e.g. **ginger beer**.
– PHRASES **beer and skittles** Brit. amusement or enjoyment.
– DERIVATIVES **beerily** adv. **beeriness** n. **beery** adj.
– ORIGIN OE *bēor*, of W. Gmc origin, based on monastic L. *biber* 'a drink', from L. *bibere* 'to drink'.

**beer belly** (or **beer gut**) • n. informal a man's protruding stomach, caused by excessive consumption of beer.
– DERIVATIVES **beer-bellied** adj.

**beer cellar** • n. **1** an underground room for storing beer. **2** a basement bar where beer is served.

**Beerenauslese** /'bɛ:rən,aʊslɛ:zə/ • n. a white wine of German origin or style made from selected individual

grapes picked later than the general harvest.
– ORIGIN Ger., from *Beeren* 'berries' + *aus* 'out' + *lese* 'picking'.

**beer engine** ● n. Brit. a machine that draws up beer from a barrel in a cellar.

**beer garden** ● n. a garden attached to a public house, where beer is served.

**beerhouse** ● n. Brit. historical a public house licensed to sell beer but not spirits.

**beer mat** ● n. a small cardboard mat for resting glasses on in a public house.

**beer money** ● n. informal a small amount of money allowed or earned.

**beer parlour** ● n. Canadian an establishment where beer is served.

**beestings** ● pl. n. [treated as sing.] the first milk produced by a cow or goat after giving birth.
– ORIGIN OE *bȳsting*, of W. Gmc origin.

**bee-stung** ● adj. informal (of a woman's lips) full and red.

**beeswax** ● n. **1** the wax secreted by bees to make honeycombs, used in making wood polishes and candles. **2** N. Amer. informal a person's concern: *that's none of your beeswax*. ● v. polish (furniture) with beeswax.

**beeswing** /ˈbiːzwɪŋ/ ● n. a filmy second crust on old port.

**beet** ● n. a herbaceous plant cultivated as a source of food for humans and livestock, and for processing into sugar. [*Beta vulgaris*.]
– ORIGIN OE *bēte*, of W. Gmc origin, from L. *beta*, perh. of Celtic origin.

**Beethovenian** /ˌbeɪt(h)əʊˈviːniən/ ● adj. of or relating to the work of the German composer Ludwig van Beethoven (1770–1827).

**beetle**[1] ● n. **1** an insect of a large order distinguished by having forewings modified into hard wing cases that cover and protect the hindwings and abdomen. [Order Coleoptera: many species.] **2** Brit. a dice game in which a picture of a beetle is drawn or assembled. ● v. informal make one's way hurriedly or with short, quick steps.
– ORIGIN OE *bitula*, *bitela* 'biter', from the base of *bītan* 'to bite'.

**beetle**[2] ● n. **1** a very heavy mallet. **2** a machine used for heightening the lustre of cloth by pressure from rollers. ● v. **1** ram, crush, or drive in with a beetle. **2** finish (cloth) with a beetle.
– ORIGIN OE *bētel*, of Gmc origin.

**beetle**[3] ● v. [usu. as adj. **beetling**] (especially of a person's eyebrows) project or overhang.
– DERIVATIVES **beetle-browed** adj.
– ORIGIN C16: back-form. from *beetle-browed* (ME).

**beetle-crusher** ● n. Brit. humorous a large boot, shoe, or foot.

**beetroot** ● n. chiefly Brit. **1** the edible dark-red spherical root of a variety of beet. **2** the variety of beet which produces this root. [*Beta vulgaris*.]

**beeves** plural form of BEEF (in sense 1 of the noun).

**beezer** ● adj. Brit. informal, dated excellent.
– ORIGIN 1950s: from the earlier noun *beezer*, denoting something large or impressive.

**BEF** ● abbrev. British Expeditionary Force.

**befall** ● v. (past **befell**; past part. **befallen**) poetic/literary (especially of something bad) happen to.
– ORIGIN OE *befeallan* 'to fall'.

**befit** ● v. (**befitted**, **befitting**) be appropriate for.
– DERIVATIVES **befitting** adj. **befittingly** adv.

**befog** ● v. (**befogged**, **befogging**) make confused.

**befool** ● v. archaic make a fool of.

**before** ● prep., conj., & adv. **1** during the period of time preceding. **2** in front of. ➤ in front of and required to answer to (a court of law, tribunal, or other authority). **3** in preference to; with a higher priority than.
– ORIGIN OE *beforan* (see BY, FORE), of Gmc origin.

**beforehand** ● adv. in advance.
– ORIGIN ME: prob. influenced by OFr. *avant main*.

**befoul** ● v. make dirty; pollute.

**befriend** ● v. act as or become a friend to.

**befuddle** ● v. [usu. as adj. **befuddled**] muddle or confuse.
– DERIVATIVES **befuddlement** n.

**beg** ● v. (**begged**, **begging**) **1** ask (someone) earnestly or humbly for something. ➤ ask for (something) earnestly or humbly. ➤ (**beg off**) withdraw from a promise or undertaking. **2** ask for food or money as charity. **3** (of a dog) sit up with the front paws raised expectantly in the hope of a reward.
– PHRASES **beg the question 1** (of a fact or action) invite a question or point that has not been dealt with. **2** assume the truth of an argument or proposition to be proved, without arguing it. **go begging** (of an article or opportunity) be available because unwanted by others.
– ORIGIN ME: prob. from OE *bedecian*, of Gmc origin.

**begad** /bɪˈgad/ ● exclam. archaic expressing surprise or emphasis.
– ORIGIN C16: alt. of *by God*; cf. BEDAD and GAD[2].

**began** past of BEGIN.

**begat** archaic past of BEGET.

**beget** ● v. (**begetting**; past **begot**; past part. **begotten**) archaic or poetic/literary **1** produce (a child). **2** cause.
– DERIVATIVES **begetter** n.
– ORIGIN OE *begietan* 'get, obtain by effort' (see BE-, GET).

**beggar** ● n. **1** a person who lives by begging for food or money. **2** informal a person of a specified type: *lucky beggar!* ● v. reduce to poverty.
– PHRASES **beggar belief** (or **description**) be too extraordinary to be believed or described.

**beggarly** ● adj. **1** meagre and ungenerous. **2** poverty-stricken.
– DERIVATIVES **beggarliness** n.

**beggar-my-neighbour** ● n. a card game for two players in which the object is to acquire one's opponent's cards. ● adj. (of national policy) self-aggrandizing at the expense of competitors.

**beggarticks** ● pl. n. [often treated as sing.] another term for BUR-MARIGOLD.
– ORIGIN C19 (also as *beggar's ticks*): appar. from the resemblance of the seed pods to ticks.

**beggary** ● n. a state of extreme poverty.

**begging letter** ● n. a letter asking for a gift or donation.

**begin** ● v. (**beginning**; past **began**; past part. **begun**) **1** perform or undergo the first part of (an action or activity). ➤ come into being. ➤ start speaking. ➤ (**begin with**) have as a first element. ➤ (**begin on/upon**) set to work on. ➤ (**begin at**) (of a commodity) have as its lowest price. **2** [with neg.] informal have any chance or likelihood of doing: *circuitry that Karen could not begin to comprehend*.
– DERIVATIVES **beginner** n. **beginning** n.
– ORIGIN OE *beginnan*, of Gmc origin.

**begob** /bɪˈgɒb/ ● exclam. Irish expressing amazement or emphasis.
– ORIGIN C19: alt. of *by God!*

**begone** ● exclam. archaic go away at once!

**begonia** /bɪˈgəʊnɪə/ ● n. a herbaceous plant grown for its striking foliage and for its flowers, which have brightly coloured sepals but no petals. [Genus *Begonia*.]
– ORIGIN mod. L., named after the Fr. amateur botanist Michel *Bégon*, who discovered the plant.

**begorra** /bɪˈgɒrə/ ● exclam. an exclamation of surprise traditionally attributed to the Irish.
– ORIGIN C19: alt. of *by God*.

**begot** past of BEGET.

**begotten** past participle of BEGET.

**begrime** ● v. blacken with ingrained dirt.

**begrudge** ● v. **1** envy (someone) the possession or enjoyment of. **2** give reluctantly or resentfully.
– DERIVATIVES **begrudging** adj. **begrudgingly** adv.

**beguile** ● v. **1** charm or enchant. ➤ trick into doing something. **2** archaic or poetic/literary help (time) pass pleasantly.
– DERIVATIVES **beguilement** n. **beguiler** n. **beguiling** adj. **beguilingly** adv.
– ORIGIN ME: from BE- + obs. *guile* 'to deceive' (see GUILE).

**beguine** /beɪˈgiːn/ ● n. a popular dance of Caribbean origin, similar to the foxtrot.
– ORIGIN 1930s: from W. Ind. Fr., from Fr. *béguin* 'infatu-

ation'.

**begum** /'beɪgəm/ • **n.** Indian a Muslim woman of high rank. ➤(**Begum**) the title of a married Muslim woman, equivalent to Mrs.
– ORIGIN from Urdu *begam*, from Turk. *bigim* 'princess'.

**begun** past participle of **BEGIN**.

**behalf** • **n.** (in phr. **on** (US also **in**) **behalf of** or **on someone's behalf**) **1** in the interests of a person, group, or principle. **2** as a representative of.
– ORIGIN ME: from a mixture of the earlier phrs *on his halve* and *bihalve him*, both meaning 'on his side'.

**behave** • **v. 1** act or conduct oneself in a specified way. **2** (also **behave oneself**) conduct oneself in accordance with accepted norms.
– ORIGIN ME: from **BE-** + **HAVE** in the sense 'bear (oneself) in a particular way'.

**behaved** • **adj.** conducting oneself in a specified way: *a well-behaved child.*

**behaviour** (US **behavior**) • **n.** the way in which someone behaves. ➤the way in which an animal or person responds to a situation or stimulus: *the feeding behaviour of predators.*
– ORIGIN ME: from **BEHAVE**, on the pattern of *demeanour*, and influenced by obs. *haviour* from **HAVE**.

**behavioural** (US **behavioral**) • **adj.** involving, relating to, or emphasizing behaviour.

**behaviouralism** (US **behavioralism**) • **n. 1** the methods and principles of the scientific study of animal (and human) behaviour. **2** advocacy of or adherence to a behavioural approach to social phenomena.
– DERIVATIVES **behaviouralist** n. & adj.

**behavioural science** • **n.** the scientific study of human and animal behaviour.

**behaviourism** (US **behaviorism**) • **n.** Psychology the theory that human and animal behaviour can be explained in terms of conditioning, and that psychological disorders are best treated by altering behaviour patterns.
– DERIVATIVES **behaviourist** n. & adj. **behaviouristic** adj.

**behaviour therapy** • **n.** the treatment of neurotic symptoms by training the patient's reactions to stimuli.

**behead** • **v.** cut off the head of (someone), especially as a form of execution.
– ORIGIN OE *behēafdian*; from **BE-** + *hēafod* (see **HEAD**).

**beheld** past and past participle of **BEHOLD**.

**behemoth** /bɪ'hiːmɒθ, 'biːhɪˌməʊθ/ • **n.** a huge or monstrous creature.
– ORIGIN ME: from Heb. *bĕhēmōṯ*, intensive pl. of *bĕhēmāh* 'beast'.

**behest** /bɪ'hɛst/ • **n.** (usu. **at the behest of**) poetic/literary a person's orders or command.
– ORIGIN OE *behǣs* 'a vow', from a Gmc base meaning 'bid'.

**behind** • **prep. & adv. 1** at or to the far side of. ➤hidden by. **2** further back than other members of a moving group. **3** in support of or giving guidance to. ➤guiding, controlling, or responsible for (an event or plan). **4** after the departure or death of. **5** less advanced than in achievement or development. **6** having a lower score than (another competitor). **7** late in accomplishing a task. ➤in arrears. • **n. 1** informal a person's bottom. **2** Australian Rules a kick that sends the ball over a behind line, or a touch that sends it between the inner posts, scoring one point.
– ORIGIN OE *behindan*, *bihindan*, from *bi* 'by' + *hindan* 'from behind'.

**behindhand** • **adj.** late or slow in doing something.
– ORIGIN C16: on the pattern of *beforehand*.

**behind line** • **n.** Australian Rules the line between an inner and outer goalpost.

**behold** • **v.** (past and past part. **beheld**) archaic or poetic/literary see or observe.
– DERIVATIVES **beholder** n.
– ORIGIN OE *bihaldan*, from *bi-* 'thoroughly' + *haldan* 'to hold'.

**beholden** • **adj.** (usu. **beholden to**) indebted.
– ORIGIN ME: archaic past part. of **BEHOLD**, in the otherwise unrecorded sense 'bound'.

**behoof** /bɪ'huːf/ • **n.** archaic benefit or advantage.
– ORIGIN OE *behōf*, of W. Gmc origin.

**behove** /bɪ'həʊv/ (US **behoove** /-'huːv/) • **v.** (**it behoves someone to do something**) formal it is a duty, responsibility, or appropriate response for someone to do something.
– ORIGIN OE *behōfian*, from *behōf* (see **BEHOOF**).

**beige** • **n.** a pale sandy fawn colour.
– ORIGIN C19 (denoting a usu. undyed and unbleached woollen fabric of this colour): from Fr.

**beignet** /'bɛnjeɪ/ • **n.** chiefly N. Amer. **1** a fritter. **2** a square of fried dough eaten hot sprinkled with icing sugar.
– ORIGIN Fr., from archaic *buyne* 'hump, bump'.

**being** • **n. 1** existence. ➤living; being alive. **2** the nature or essence of a person. **3** a real or imaginary living creature: *alien beings.*

**beira** /'beɪrə/ • **n.** a rare antelope found in Somalia and Ethiopia. [*Dorcatragus megalotis.*]
– ORIGIN a local name.

**beisa oryx** /'beɪzə/ • **n.** a gemsbok native to the Horn of Africa. [*Oryx gazella beisa.*]
– ORIGIN C19: from Amharic.

**Beja** /'bɛdʒə/ • **n.** (pl. same) **1** a member of a nomadic people living between the Nile and the Red Sea. **2** the Cushitic language of this people.

**bejabers** /bɪ'dʒeɪbəz/ (also **bejabbers** /-'dʒabəz/) • **exclam.** Irish expressing surprise.
– ORIGIN C19: alt. of *by Jesus.*

**bejesus** /bɪ'dʒiːzəs/ (also **bejeezus**) • **exclam.** Irish by Jesus!

**bejewelled** (US **bejeweled**) • **adj.** adorned with jewels.

**bel** • **n.** a unit of measurement used in comparing two sound intensities or electrical power levels, corresponding to an intensity ratio of 10 to 1.
– ORIGIN 1920s: named after Alexander Graham *Bell*, inventor of the telephone.

**belabour** (US **belabor**) • **v. 1** attack physically or verbally. **2** argue or discuss in excessive detail.

**belated** • **adj.** coming late or too late.
– DERIVATIVES **belatedly** adv. **belatedness** n.
– ORIGIN C17 (in the sense 'overtaken by darkness'): past part. of obs. *belate* 'delay'.

**belay** /'biːleɪ, bɪ'leɪ/ • **v. 1** fix (a rope) round a rock, pin, or other object to secure it. **2** secure (a rock climber) using a belay. **3** nautical slang stop! • **n. 1** an act of belaying. **2** a spike of rock or other object used for belaying.
– DERIVATIVES **belayer** n.
– ORIGIN C16: from **BE-** + **LAY**[1].

**belaying pin** • **n.** a fixed pin used on board ship and in rock climbing to secure a rope fastened around it.

**bel canto** /bɛl 'kantəʊ/ • **n.** a lyrical style of operatic singing using a full, rich, broad tone.
– ORIGIN C19: Ital., lit. 'fine song'.

**belch** • **v. 1** emit wind noisily from the stomach through the mouth. **2** expel (smoke or flames) forcefully out or up. • **n.** an act of belching.
– ORIGIN OE *belcettan*, prob. imitative.

**beldam** /'bɛldəm/ (also **beldame**) • **n.** archaic an old woman.
– ORIGIN ME: from OFr. *bel* 'beautiful' + **DAM**[3].

**beleaguer** • **v.** [usu. as adj. **beleaguered**] **1** lay siege to. **2** make difficulties for; harass.
– ORIGIN C16: from Du. *belegeren* 'camp round'.

**belemnite** /'bɛləmnʌɪt/ • **n.** an extinct marine cephalopod mollusc with a bullet-shaped internal shell, typically found as fossils in deposits of the Jurassic and Cretaceous periods.
– ORIGIN C17: from mod. L. *belemnites*, based on Gk *belemnon* 'dart'.

**belfry** • **n.** (pl. **-ies**) the place in a bell tower or steeple in which bells are housed.
– ORIGIN ME *berfrey*, from OFr. *berfrei*, later *belfrei*, of W. Gmc origin.

**Belgae** /'bɛldʒiː, 'bɛlgʌɪ/ • **pl. n.** an ancient Celtic people inhabiting Gaul north of the Seine and Marne Rivers.
– ORIGIN from L.

**Belgian** • **n.** a native or national of Belgium or a person of Belgian descent. • **adj.** of or relating to Belgium.

**Belgian hare** ● **n.** a rabbit of a dark red long-eared domestic breed.

**Belgian sheepdog** ● **n.** a dog of a medium-sized breed, similar in appearance to an Alsatian.

**Belgic** /'bɛldʒɪk/ ● **adj.** of or relating to the Belgae.

**Belial** /'bi:lɪəl/ ● **n.** a name for the Devil.
– ORIGIN from Heb. *bĕliyya'al* 'worthlessness'.

**belie** ● **v.** (**belying**) **1** fail to give a true notion of. **2** fail to justify (a claim or expectation).
– ORIGIN OE *belēogan* 'deceive by lying', from **BE-** + *lēogan* 'to lie'.

**belief** ● **n.** **1** an acceptance that something exists or is true, especially one without proof. ➤a firmly held opinion or conviction. ➤a religious conviction. **2** (**belief in**) trust or confidence in.
– PHRASES **beyond belief** astonishing; incredible.
– ORIGIN ME: alt. of OE *gelēafa*; cf. **BELIEVE**.

**believe** ● **v.** **1** feel sure of the truth of. ➤accept the statement of (someone) as true. ➤have religious faith. **2** (**believe in**) have faith in the truth or existence of. **3** think or suppose.
– DERIVATIVES **believability** n. **believable** adj. **believably** adv. **believer** n.
– ORIGIN OE *belȳfan*, *belēfan*, alt. of *gelēfan*, of Gmc origin.

**Belisha beacon** /bə'li:ʃə/ ● **n.** (in the UK) an orange ball containing a flashing light, mounted on a post at each end of a zebra crossing.
– ORIGIN 1930s: named after Leslie Hore-*Belisha*, Minister of Transport when the beacons were introduced.

**belittle** ● **v.** dismiss as unimportant.
– DERIVATIVES **belittlement** n. **belittler** n. **belittling** adj. **belittlingly** adv.

**Belizean** /bɛ'li:zɪən/ (also **Belizian**) ● **n.** a native or inhabitant of Belize, a country on the Caribbean coast of Central America. ● **adj.** of or relating to Belize.

**bell[1]** ● **n.** **1** a hollow object, typically made of metal and in the shape of a deep inverted cup, that sounds a clear musical note when struck. ➤the sound or stroke of a bell, used as a signal. **2** (**bells**) a musical instrument consisting of a set of metal tubes, suspended in a frame and played by being struck. **3** Nautical (preceded by a numeral) the time as indicated every half-hour of a watch by the striking of the ship's bell one to eight times: *at five bells in the forenoon of June 11.* **4** something bell-shaped, in particular the end of a trumpet. ● **v.** **1** summon or indicate with a bell. **2** flare outwards in the shape of a bell.
– PHRASES **bell the cat** take the danger of a shared enterprise upon oneself. [an allusion to a fable in which the mice suggest hanging a bell around the cat's neck to have warning of its approach.] **bells and whistles** attractive additional features or trimmings. **(as) clear** (or **sound**) **as a bell** perfectly clear (or sound). **give someone a bell** Brit. informal telephone someone. **ring a bell** informal revive a distant recollection.
– ORIGIN OE *belle*, of Gmc origin; perh. rel. to **BELL[2]**.

**bell[2]** ● **n.** the cry of a stag or buck at rutting time. ● **v.** (of a stag or buck) make this cry.
– ORIGIN OE *bellan* 'to bellow', of Gmc origin.

**belladonna** /ˌbɛlə'dɒnə/ ● **n.** deadly nightshade. ➤a drug made from this plant, containing atropine.
– ORIGIN C18: from mod. L., from Ital. *bella donna* 'fair lady', perh. from the cosmetic use of its juice to dilate the pupils.

**bellbird** ● **n.** **1** a tropical American bird of the cotinga family with a loud explosive call. [Genus *Procnias*.] **2** an Australasian songbird with ringing bell-like calls. [*Anthornis melanura* (New Zealand) and other species.]

**bell-bottoms** ● **pl. n.** trousers with a marked flare below the knee.
– DERIVATIVES **bell-bottomed** adj.

**bellboy** ● **n.** chiefly N. Amer. a porter in a hotel or club.

**bell captain** ● **n.** N. Amer. the supervisor of a group of bellboys.

**bell crank** ● **n.** an L-shaped lever with a fulcrum at the point where the two arms meet.

**bell curve** ● **n.** Mathematics a graph of a normal (Gaussian) distribution, with a large rounded peak tapering away at each end.

**belle** /bɛl/ ● **n.** a beautiful girl or woman.
– ORIGIN C17: from Fr., fem. of *beau* 'beautiful'.

**belle époque** /ˌbɛl eɪ'pɒk, French bɛl epɔk/ ● **n.** the period of settled and comfortable life preceding the First World War.
– ORIGIN Fr., 'fine period'.

**belles-lettres** /bɛl'lɛtr(ə), French bɛllɛtʀ/ ● **pl. n.** literary works written and read for their aesthetic effect.
– DERIVATIVES **belletrism** /bɛl'lɛtrɪz(ə)m/ n. **belletrist** n. **belletristic** adj.
– ORIGIN C17: from Fr., lit. 'fine letters'.

**bellflower** ● **n.** a plant with blue, purple, or white bell-shaped flowers. [Genus *Campanula*: many species.]

**bellhop** ● **n.** N. Amer. another term for **BELLBOY**.

**bellicose** /'bɛlɪkəʊs/ ● **adj.** aggressive; ready to fight.
– DERIVATIVES **bellicosity** /-'kɒsɪti/ n.
– ORIGIN ME: from L. *bellicosus*, from *bellicus* 'warlike', from *bellum* 'war'.

**belligerence** /bə'lɪdʒ(ə)r(ə)ns/ (also **belligerency**) ● **n.** aggressive or warlike behaviour.

**belligerent** ● **adj.** hostile and aggressive. ➤engaged in a war or conflict. ● **n.** a nation or person engaged in war or conflict.
– DERIVATIVES **belligerently** adv.
– ORIGIN C16: from L. *belligerant-*, *belligerare* 'wage war', from *bellum* 'war'.

**Bellini** /bə'li:ni/ ● **n.** (pl. **Bellinis**) a cocktail consisting of peach juice mixed with champagne.
– ORIGIN after the Venetian painter Giovanni *Bellini* (*c.* 1430–1516): the cocktail is said to have been invented in Venice.

**bell jar** ● **n.** a bell-shaped glass cover for use in a laboratory.

**bell metal** ● **n.** an alloy of copper and tin for making bells, with a higher tin content than in bronze.

**bellow** ● **v.** emit a loud, deep roar, typically in pain or anger. ➤shout or sing very loudly. ● **n.** a loud, deep shout or sound.
– ORIGIN ME: perh. from OE *bylgan*.

**bellows** ● **pl. n.** **1** a device with an air bag that emits a stream of air when squeezed together with two handles, used for blowing air into a fire. ➤a similar device used in a harmonium or small organ. **2** an object or device with concertinaed sides to allow it to expand and contract, such as a tube joining a lens to a camera body.
– ORIGIN ME: prob. from OE *belga*, pl. of *belig* (see **BELLY**).

**bell-ringing** ● **n.** the activity or pastime of ringing church bells or handbells.
– DERIVATIVES **bell-ringer** n.

**Bell's palsy** ● **n.** paralysis of the facial nerve causing muscular weakness in one side of the face.
– ORIGIN C19: named after the Sc. anatomist Sir Charles *Bell*, who first described it.

**bell tent** ● **n.** a cone-shaped tent supported by a central pole.

**bellwether** ● **n.** **1** the leading sheep of a flock, often with a bell on its neck. **2** a leader or indicator of something.

**belly** ● **n.** (pl. **-ies**) **1** the front part of the human trunk below the ribs, containing the stomach and bowels. ➤the stomach, especially as representing the body's need for food. ➤(also **belly pork**) a cut of pork from the underside between the legs. **2** the rounded underside of a ship or aircraft. **3** the top surface of an instrument of the violin family, over which the strings are placed. ● **v.** (**-ies**, **-ied**) swell or cause to swell or bulge.
– PHRASES **go belly up** informal go bankrupt.
– DERIVATIVES **-bellied** adj.
– ORIGIN OE *belig* 'bag', of Gmc origin.

**bellyache** informal ● **n.** a stomach pain. ● **v.** complain noisily or persistently.
– DERIVATIVES **bellyacher** n.

**belly button** ● **n.** informal a person's navel.

**belly dance** ● **n.** a style of dance originating in the Middle East, performed by women and involving undulating movements of the belly and gyration of the hips.

– DERIVATIVES **belly dancer** n. **belly dancing** n.

**bellyflop** informal • n. a dive into water, landing flat on one's front. • v. (**-flopped -flopping**) perform a bellyflop.

**bellyful** • n. (pl. **-fuls**) a sufficient amount to eat.
– PHRASES **have a** (or **one's**) **bellyful** informal have more than enough of something.

**belly laugh** • n. a loud unrestrained laugh.

**belong** • v. **1** (of a thing) be rightly placed in or assigned to a specified position. **2** (of a person) fit or be acceptable in a specified place or environment. ➤(**belong to**) be a member of. **3** (**belong to**) be the property of. ➤be the rightful possession of; be due to.
– DERIVATIVES **belonging** n. **belongingness** n.
– ORIGIN ME: from **BE-** + *long* 'belong', based on OE *gelang* 'together with'.

**belongings** • pl. n. a person's movable possessions.

**Belorussian** (also **Byelorussian**) • n. **1** a native or inhabitant of Belarus. **2** the Eastern Slavic language of Belarus. • adj. of or relating to Belarus, its people, or their language.

**beloved** • adj. dearly loved. • n. a much loved person.
– ORIGIN ME: past part. of obs. *belove* 'be pleasing', later 'love'.

**below** • prep. & adv. **1** at a lower level than. ➤[as adv.] Nautical below deck. **2** lower than (a specified amount, rate, or norm). **3** (in printed text) mentioned further down.
– PHRASES **below stairs** Brit. dated in the basement of a house as occupied by servants.
– ORIGIN ME: from **BE-** + **LOW**[1].

**below decks** (also **below deck**) • adj. & adv. in or into the space below the main deck of a ship. • n. (**belowdecks**) the space below the main deck of a ship.

**Bel Paese** /ˌbɛl pɑːˈeɪzeɪ, -zi/ • n. trademark a rich, mild, creamy white cheese of a kind originally made in Italy.
– ORIGIN Ital., lit. 'fair country'.

**belt** • n. **1** a strip of leather or other material worn round the waist to support or hold in clothes or to carry weapons. ➤a belt worn as a sign of rank or achievement, as in judo, karate, or similar sports. ➤(**the belt**) the punishment of being struck with a belt. **2** a continuous band of material used in machinery for transferring motion from one wheel to another. **3** a strip or encircling area of a specified kind: *the asteroid belt.* **4** informal a heavy blow. • v. **1** fasten or secure with a belt. **2** beat or hit very hard. ➤(**belt something out**) informal sing or play something loudly and without finesse. **3** informal rush or dash in a specified direction. **4** (**belt up**) informal be quiet.
– PHRASES **below the belt** unfair; disregarding the rules. **belt and braces** Brit. providing double security, by using more than one means to the same end. **tighten one's belt** cut one's expenditure. **under one's belt** safely or satisfactorily achieved, experienced, or acquired.
– DERIVATIVES **belted** adj. **belting** n.
– ORIGIN OE, of Gmc origin, from L. *balteus* 'girdle'.

**Beltane** /ˈbɛlteɪn/ • n. an ancient Celtic festival celebrated on May Day.
– ORIGIN ME: from Sc. Gaelic *bealltainn.*

**belted galloway** • n. an animal belonging to a variety of the galloway breed of cattle, with a broad white band across its body.

**belter** • n. informal **1** an outstanding example of something. **2** a loud, forceful singer or song.

**beltman** • n. (pl. **-men**) Austral./NZ a member of a life-saving team who swims out, wearing a belt with a line attached, to help those in difficulty.

**beltway** • n. US a ring road.

**beluga** /bəˈluːgə/ • n. (pl. same or **belugas**) **1** a small white toothed whale of Arctic coastal waters, related to the narwhal. [*Delphinapterus leucas.*] **2** a very large sturgeon occurring in the inland seas and rivers of central Eurasia, from which caviar is obtained. [*Huso huso.*]
– ORIGIN C16: from Russ. *belukha, beluga,* from *belyĭ* 'white'.

**belvedere** /ˈbɛlvɪdɪə/ • n. a summer house or other building positioned to command a fine view.
– ORIGIN C16: from Ital., lit. 'fair sight'.

**belying** present participle of **BELIE**.

**BEM** • abbrev. British Empire Medal.

**bema** /ˈbiːmə/ • n. (pl. **bemas** or **bemata**) **1** the altar part in ancient and Orthodox churches. **2** the platform from which orators spoke in ancient Athens.
– ORIGIN C17: from Gk *bēma* 'step, raised place'.

**Bemba** /ˈbɛmbə/ • n. (pl. same) **1** a member of an African people of Zambia. **2** the Bantu language of this people.
– ORIGIN the name in Bemba.

**bemire** /bɪˈmʌɪə/ • v. archaic cover or stain with mud.

**bemoan** • v. lament or express sorrow for.

**bemuse** • v. [usu. as adj. **bemused**] confuse or bewilder.
– DERIVATIVES **bemusedly** adv. **bemusement** n.
– ORIGIN C18: from **BE-** + **MUSE**[2].

**ben**[1] • n. Scottish a high mountain: *Ben Nevis.*
– ORIGIN C18: from Sc. Gaelic and Ir. *beann.*

**ben**[2] • n. (usu. in phr. **but and ben**) Scottish the inner room in a two-roomed cottage.
– ORIGIN C18: dial. var. of ME *binne* 'within', from OE *binnan.*

**bench** • n. **1** a long seat for more than one person. **2** a long, sturdy work table in a workshop or laboratory. **3** (**the bench**) the office of judge or magistrate. ➤judges or magistrates collectively. **4** a platform on which dogs are exhibited at shows. **5** (**the bench**) a seat at the side of a sports field for coaches and players not taking part in a game. • v. **1** exhibit (a dog) at a show. **2** N. Amer. withdraw (a sports player) from play.
– ORIGIN OE *benc,* of Gmc origin; rel. to **BANK**[1].

**bencher** • n. Law (in the UK) a senior member of any of the Inns of Court.

**benchmark** • n. **1** a standard or point of reference against which things may be compared or assessed. **2** a surveyor's mark cut in a wall or building and used as a reference point in measuring altitudes. • v. evaluate or check by comparison with a benchmark.

**bench press** • n. a bodybuilding and weightlifting exercise in which a lifter lies on a bench with feet on the floor and raises a weight with both arms. • v. (**bench-press**) raise (a weight) in a bench press.

**bench test** (also **bench run**) • n. a test carried out on a machine, a component, or software before it is released. • v. (**bench-test**) run a bench test on.

**bend**[1] • v. (past and past part. **bent**) **1** shape or force (something straight) into a curve or angle. ➤(of a road, river, or path) deviate from a straight line. **2** (of a person) incline the body downwards; stoop. **3** interpret or modify (a rule) to suit oneself. **4** direct (one's attention or energies) to a task. **5** Nautical attach (a sail or cable) by means of a knot. • n. **1** a curved or angled part of something. ➤a curve in a road, path, or river. **2** a kind of knot used to join two ropes together, or one rope to another object. **3** (**the bends**) [treated as sing.] decompression sickness.
– PHRASES **bend someone's ear** informal talk to someone, especially at length or when unwelcome to the listener. **bend one's elbow** N. Amer. informal drink alcohol. **round** (or US **around**) **the bend** informal mad.
– DERIVATIVES **bendable** adj. **bendiness** n. (informal). **bendy** adj. (informal).
– ORIGIN OE *bendan* 'put in bonds, tension a bow by means of a string', of Gmc origin.

**bend**[2] • n. Heraldry a broad diagonal stripe from top left to bottom right of a shield.
– ORIGIN ME: from Anglo-Norman Fr. *bande,* OFr. *bende* 'flat strip'.

**bender** • n. informal **1** a drinking bout. **2** Brit. a shelter made by covering a framework of bent branches with canvas. **3** derogatory a male homosexual.

**bendlet** • n. Heraldry a bend of half the normal width, usually borne in groups of two or three.
– ORIGIN C16: prob. from OFr. *bendel* 'little bend' + **-ET**[1].

**bend sinister** • n. Heraldry a broad diagonal stripe from top right to bottom left of a shield (a supposed sign of bastardy).

**beneath** • prep. & adv. **1** extending or directly underneath. **2** [as prep.] of lower status or worth than: *he is rather beneath her.*
– ORIGIN OE *binithan, bineothan,* from *bi* (see **BY**) + *nithan, neothan* 'below', of Gmc origin.

**benedicite** /ˌbɛnɪˈdʌɪsɪti/ ● **n.** a blessing, especially a grace said at table in religious communities.
– ORIGIN L., 'bless you!', pl. imper. from *benedicere* 'wish well'; the first word of the Latin canticle *Benedicte, omnia opera*.

**Benedictine** ● **n. 1** /ˌbɛnɪˈdɪktɪn/ a monk or nun of a Christian religious order following the rule of St Benedict. **2** /ˌbɛnɪˈdɪktiːn/ trademark a liqueur based on brandy, originally made by Benedictine monks in France. ● **adj.** /ˌbɛnɪˈdɪktɪn/ of St Benedict or the Benedictines.

**benediction** ● **n.** the utterance or bestowing of a blessing. ➤(**Benediction**) a Catholic service in which the congregation is blessed with the sacrament. ➤the state of being blessed.
– DERIVATIVES **benedictory** adj.
– ORIGIN ME: via OFr. from L. *benedictio(n-)*, from *benedicere* 'bless', from *bene* 'well' + *dicere* 'say'.

**Benedictus** /ˌbɛnɪˈdɪktəs/ ● **n.** Christian Church **1** an invocation beginning *Benedictus qui venit in nomine Domini* (Blessed is he who comes in the name of the Lord), forming a set part of the Mass. **2** a canticle beginning *Benedictus Dominus Deus* (Blessed be the Lord God), from Luke 1:68–79.
– ORIGIN L., 'blessed', past part. of *benedicere* 'bless'.

**benefaction** /ˌbɛnɪˈfakʃ(ə)n/ ● **n.** formal a donation or gift.
– ORIGIN C17: from late L. *benefactio(n-)*, from *bene facere* 'do good (to)'.

**benefactor** ● **n.** a person who gives money or other help to a person or cause.
– DERIVATIVES **benefactress** n.
– ORIGIN ME: from L., from *bene facere* 'do good (to)'.

**benefice** /ˈbɛnɪfɪs/ ● **n.** a Church office, typically that of a rector or vicar, for which property and income are provided in respect of pastoral duties.
– DERIVATIVES **beneficed** adj.
– ORIGIN ME: via OFr. from L. *beneficium* 'favour, support', from *bene facere* 'do good (to)'.

**beneficent** /bɪˈnɛfɪs(ə)nt/ ● **adj.** doing good or resulting in good.
– DERIVATIVES **beneficence** n. **beneficently** adv.
– ORIGIN C17: from L. *beneficent-*, from *bene facere* 'do good (to)'.

**beneficial** ● **adj. 1** favourable or advantageous. **2** Law of or relating to rights to the use or benefit of property, other than legal title.
– DERIVATIVES **beneficially** adv.

**beneficiary** ● **n.** (pl. **-ies**) a person who gains benefit from something, especially a trust or will.

**benefit** ● **n. 1** an advantage or profit gained from something. **2** a payment made by the state or an insurance scheme to someone entitled to receive it, e.g. an unemployed person. **3** a public performance designed to raise money for a charity. ● **v.** (**benefited** or **benefitted**, **benefiting** or **benefitting**) receive an advantage; profit.
– PHRASES **benefit of clergy 1** exemption of the English clergy and nuns from the jurisdiction of the ordinary civil courts (abolished in 1827). **2** ecclesiastical sanction or approval. **the benefit of the doubt** a concession that a person or fact must be regarded as correct, if the contrary has not been proven.
– ORIGIN ME: from OFr. *bienfet*, from L. *benefactum* 'good deed', from *bene facere* 'do good (to)'.

**benefit society** ● **n.** another term for **FRIENDLY SOCIETY**.

**benevolent** ● **adj. 1** well meaning and kindly. **2** (of an organization) serving a charitable rather than a profit-making purpose.
– DERIVATIVES **benevolence** n. **benevolently** adv.
– ORIGIN ME: from OFr. *benivolent*, from L. *bene volent-* 'well wishing', from *bene* 'well' + *velle* 'to wish'.

**BEng** ● **abbrev.** Bachelor of Engineering.

**Bengali** /bɛŋˈgɔːli/ ● **n.** (pl. **Bengalis**) **1** a native of Bengal. **2** the Indic language of Bangladesh and West Bengal, written in a script similar to the Devanagari script. ● **adj.** of or relating to Bengal, its people, or their language.
– ORIGIN from Hindi *baṅgālī*.

**Bengal light** ● **n.** a kind of firework giving off a blue flame and used for lighting or signalling.

**benighted** ● **adj. 1** in a state of intellectual or moral ignorance. **2** archaic overtaken by darkness.
– DERIVATIVES **benightedness** n.
– ORIGIN C16: past part. of archaic *benight*.

**benign** ● **adj. 1** genial and kindly. **2** favourable; not harmful. ➤Medicine (of a tumour) not malignant.
– DERIVATIVES **benignity** n. **benignly** adv.
– ORIGIN ME: from OFr. *benigne*, from L. *benignus*, prob. from *bene* 'well' + *-genus* '-born'.

**benignant** /bɪˈnɪgnənt/ ● **adj.** less common term for **BENIGN**.
– DERIVATIVES **benignancy** n. **benignantly** adv.

**benign neglect** ● **n.** non-interference which has the effect of being more beneficial than continual attention.

**Beninese** /ˌbɛnɪˈniːz/ ● **n.** a native of Benin, a country in West Africa. ● **adj.** of or relating to Benin or its people.

**benison** /ˈbɛnɪz(ə)n, -s-/ ● **n.** poetic/literary a blessing.
– ORIGIN ME: from OFr. *beneiçun*, from L. *benedictio* (see **BENEDICTION**).

**benne** /ˈbɛni/ ● **n.** US term for **SESAME**.
– ORIGIN C18: from Malay *bene*.

**bent**[1] past and past participle of **BEND**[1]. ● **adj. 1** sharply curved or having an angle. **2** informal, chiefly Brit. dishonest; corrupt. **3** Brit. informal, derogatory homosexual. **4** (**bent on**) determined to do or have. ● **n.** a natural talent or inclination.
– PHRASES **bent out of shape** N. Amer. informal angry or agitated.

**bent**[2] ● **n. 1** a stiff grass which is used for lawns and in hay grasses. [*Agrostis capillaris* and other species.] **2** Brit. archaic or dialect a heath or unenclosed pasture.
– ORIGIN ME: from OE *beonet*, of W. Gmc origin.

**Benthamism** /ˈbɛnθəmɪz(ə)m/ ● **n.** the utilitarian philosophy of Jeremy Bentham (1748–1832), which holds that the proper object of society is to secure the greatest happiness for the greatest number.
– DERIVATIVES **Benthamite** n. & adj.

**benthos** /ˈbɛnθɒs/ ● **n.** Ecology the flora and fauna found on the bottom of a sea or lake.
– DERIVATIVES **benthic** adj.
– ORIGIN C19: from Gk, 'depth of the sea'.

**bentonite** /ˈbɛntənʌɪt/ ● **n.** a kind of absorbent clay formed by breakdown of volcanic ash, used especially as a filler.
– ORIGIN C19: from the name of Fort *Benton* in Montana, US, where it is found, + **-ITE**[1].

**ben trovato** /ˌbɛn trə(ʊ)ˈvɑːtəʊ/ ● **adj.** invented but nevertheless plausible.
– ORIGIN Ital., lit. 'well found'.

**bentwood** ● **n.** wood that is artificially shaped for use in making furniture.

**Benue-Congo** /ˈbɛnweɪ/ ● **n.** a major branch of the Niger-Congo family of languages, including Efik and Fula.
– ORIGIN from the names of rivers.

**benumb** ● **v.** deprive of feeling.
– ORIGIN C15: from obs. *benome*, past part. of *benim* 'deprive', from **BE-** + OE *niman* 'take'.

**Benzedrine** /ˈbɛnzɪdriːn/ ● **n.** trademark for **AMPHETAMINE**.
– ORIGIN 1930s: from **BENZOIC ACID** and **EPHEDRINE**.

**benzene** /ˈbɛnziːn/ ● **n.** Chemistry a volatile liquid hydrocarbon present in coal tar and petroleum, having a hexagonal ring-shaped molecule which is the basis of most aromatic organic compounds. [$C_6H_6$.]
– DERIVATIVES **benzenoid** adj.
– ORIGIN C19: from **BENZOIC ACID** + **-ENE**.

**benzine** /ˈbɛnziːn/ (also **benzin** /-zɪn/) ● **n.** a mixture of liquid hydrocarbons obtained from petroleum.
– ORIGIN C19 (denoting benzene): from **BENZOIN** + **-INE**[4].

**benzodiazepine** /ˌbɛnzəʊdʌɪˈeɪzɪpiːn, -ˈazəpiːn/ ● **n.** Medicine any of a class of heterocyclic organic compounds used as tranquillizers, such as Librium and Valium.
– ORIGIN 1930s: from **BENZENE** + **DI-**[1] + **AZO-** + **EPI-** + **-INE**[4].

**benzoic acid** ● **n.** Chemistry a white crystalline compound present in benzoin and other plant resins, used as a food preservative.
– DERIVATIVES **benzoate** n.

**benzoin** /'bɛnzəʊɪn/ ● **n.** **1** (also **gum benzoin**) a fragrant gum resin obtained from certain East Asian storax trees. **2** Chemistry a crystalline aromatic ketone present in this resin.
– ORIGIN C16: from Fr. *benjoin*, based on Arab. *lubānjāwī* 'incense of Java'.

**benzol** /'bɛnzɒl/ (also **benzole** /-zəʊl/) ● **n.** crude benzene, formerly used as a fuel.

**benzopyrene** /ˌbɛnzə(ʊ)'pʌɪriːn/ ● **n.** Chemistry a polycyclic hydrocarbon which is the major carcinogen present in cigarette smoke.

**benzoquinone** /ˌbɛnzə(ʊ)'kwɪnəʊn/ ● **n.** Chemistry a yellow crystalline compound related to benzene but having two hydrogen atoms replaced by oxygen.

**benzoyl** /'bɛnzəʊʌɪl, -zəʊɪl/ ● **n.** [as modifier] Chemistry of or denoting the acyl radical $-C(O)C_6H_5$, derived from benzoic acid.

**benzyl** /'bɛnzʌɪl, -zɪl/ ● **n.** [as modifier] Chemistry of or denoting the radical $-CH_2C_6H_5$, derived from toluene.

**bequeath** /bɪ'kwiːð/ ● **v.** leave (property) to a person or other beneficiary by a will. ➤hand down or pass on.
– DERIVATIVES **bequeathal** n. **bequeather** n.
– ORIGIN OE *becwethan*, from **BE-** + *cwethan* 'say' (see **QUOTH**).

**bequest** ● **n.** the action of bequeathing. ➤something that is bequeathed.
– ORIGIN ME: from **BE-** + OE *cwis* 'speech'.

**berate** ● **v.** scold or criticize angrily.
– ORIGIN C16: from **BE-** + **RATE**[2].

**Berber** /'bəːbə/ ● **n.** **1** a member of the indigenous people of North Africa. **2** the Afro-Asiatic language of these peoples.
– ORIGIN from Arab. *barbar*, from Gk *barbaros* 'foreigner' (see **BARBARIAN**).

**berberine** /'bəːbəriːn/ ● **n.** Chemistry a bitter yellow compound of the alkaloid class, obtained from barberry and other plants.
– ORIGIN C19: from **BERBERIS** + **-INE**[4].

**berberis** /'bəːbərɪs/ ● **n.** a plant of a genus that comprises the barberries. [Genus *Berberis*.]
– ORIGIN from mod. L. and OFr., from med. L. *barbaris*.

**berceuse** /bɛː'səːz/ ● **n.** (pl. **berceuses** pronunc. same) a lullaby.
– ORIGIN Fr., from *bercer* 'to rock'.

**bereave** ● **v.** (**be bereaved**) be deprived of a close relation or friend through their death.
– DERIVATIVES **bereavement** n.
– ORIGIN OE *berēafian* (see **BE-**, **REAVE**).

**bereft** ● **adj.** deprived of something: *her room was bereft of colour.* ➤lonely and abandoned.
– ORIGIN C16: archaic past part. of **BEREAVE**.

**beret** /'bɛreɪ, -ri/ ● **n.** a round flattish cap of felt or cloth.
– ORIGIN C19: from Fr. *béret* 'Basque cap', from Old Provençal *berret*, based on late L. *birrus* 'hooded cape'.

**berg**[1] /bəːg/ ● **n.** short for **ICEBERG**.

**berg**[2] /bəːg/ ● **n.** S. African a mountain or hill.
– ORIGIN from Du.

**bergamot**[1] /'bəːgəmɒt/ ● **n.** **1** an oily substance extracted from a variety of Seville orange, used in cosmetics and as flavouring in Earl Grey tea. **2** (also **bergamot orange**) the tree bearing this fruit. **3** an aromatic North American herb of the mint family. [*Monarda didyma* and other species.]
– ORIGIN C17: named after *Bergamo* in northern Italy.

**bergamot**[2] /'bəːgəmɒt/ ● **n.** a dessert pear of a rich, sweet variety.
– ORIGIN C17: from Fr. *bergamotte*, from Ital. *bergamotta*, from Turk. *begarmudu* 'prince's pear'.

**bergenia** /bə'giːnɪə/ ● **n.** an evergreen Asian plant with large, thick leaves and typically pink, red, or purple flowers. [Genus *Bergenia*.]
– ORIGIN mod. L., named after the Ger. botanist Karl A. von *Bergen*.

**bergère** /bɛː'ʒɛː/ ● **n.** a long-seated upholstered armchair of a kind fashionable in the 18th century.
– ORIGIN Fr., lit. 'shepherdess'.

**bergschrund** /'bəːgʃrʊnd/ ● **n.** a crevasse at the head of a glacier.
– ORIGIN C19: from Ger., from *Berg* 'mountain' + *Schrund* 'crevice'.

**Bergsonian** /bəːg'səʊnɪən/ ● **adj.** of or relating to the philosophy of the French philosopher Henri Bergson (1859–1941).

**berg wind** ● **n.** S. African a hot dry northerly wind blowing from the interior to coastal districts.

**beriberi** /ˌbɛrɪ'bɛri/ ● **n.** a disease causing inflammation of the nerves and heart failure, ascribed to a deficiency of vitamin $B_1$.
– ORIGIN C18: from Sinhalese, from *beri* 'weakness'.

**Beringian** /bɛ'rɪndʒɪən/ ● **adj.** of or relating to Beringia, the region surrounding the Bering Strait, especially in the geological past when a land bridge connected Siberia and Alaska in this area.

**berk** /bəːk/ ● **n.** Brit. informal a stupid person.
– ORIGIN 1930s: abbrev. of *Berkeley* or *Berkshire Hunt*, rhyming sl. for 'cunt'.

**berkelium** /bəː'kiːlɪəm, 'bəːklɪəm/ ● **n.** the chemical element of atomic number 97, an unstable radioactive metal of the actinide series. (Symbol: **Bk**)
– ORIGIN 1949: from the University of *Berkeley* in California (where it was first made) + **-IUM**.

**Berks.** ● **abbrev.** Berkshire.

**Berliner** ● **n.** a native or citizen of Berlin.

**berm** /bəːm/ ● **n.** a raised bank or flat strip of land bordering a river, canal, or road. ➤an artificial ridge or embankment. ➤a narrow ledge, especially one between a ditch and the base of a parapet.
– ORIGIN C18 (denoting a narrow space): from Fr. *berme*.

**Bermuda grass** ● **n.** a creeping grass common in warmer parts of the world. [*Cynodon dactylon*.]

**Bermudan** /bə'mjuːd(ə)n/ ● **n.** a native or inhabitant of Bermuda. ● **adj.** of or relating to Bermuda or its people.
– DERIVATIVES **Bermudian** adj. & n.

**Bermuda rig** ● **n.** a fore-and-aft yachting rig with a tall tapering mainsail.

**Bermuda shorts** (also **Bermudas**) ● **pl. n.** casual knee-length shorts.

**berry** ● **n.** (pl. **-ies**) **1** a small roundish juicy fruit without a stone. ➤Botany any fruit that has its seeds enclosed in a fleshy pulp, for example a banana or tomato. **2** a fish egg or roe of a lobster or similar creature.
– DERIVATIVES **berried** adj. **berrying** n.
– ORIGIN OE *berie*, of Gmc origin.

**berserk** /bə'səːk, -z-/ ● **adj.** out of control; wild or frenzied. ● **n.** (also **berserker**) an ancient Norse warrior who fought with frenzy.
– ORIGIN C19: from ON *berserkr*, prob. from *birn-*, *bjorn* (see **BEAR**[2]) + *serkr* 'coat'.

**berth** ● **n.** **1** a ship's allotted place at a wharf or dock. **2** a fixed bunk on a ship or train. ● **v.** **1** moor or be moored in a berth. **2** provide a berth for (a passenger).
– PHRASES **give someone/thing a wide berth** stay well away from someone or something.
– DERIVATIVES **berthing** n.
– ORIGIN C17 (in the sense 'adequate sea room'): prob. from a naut. use of **BEAR**[1] + **-TH**[2].

**bertha** ● **n.** chiefly historical a deep collar, typically of lace, attached to the top of a low neckline.
– ORIGIN C19: from the given name *Bertha*.

**beryl** /'bɛrɪl/ ● **n.** a transparent pale green, blue, or yellow mineral consisting of a silicate of beryllium and aluminium, sometimes used as a gemstone.
– ORIGIN ME: from OFr. *beril*, via L. from Gk *bērullos*.

**berylliosis** /bəˌrɪlɪ'əʊsɪs/ ● **n.** Medicine poisoning by beryllium or beryllium compounds, especially by inhalation causing fibrosis of the lungs.

**beryllium** /bə'rɪlɪəm/ ● **n.** the chemical element of atomic number 4, a hard grey metal which is the lightest of the alkaline earth metals. (Symbol: **Be**)

**beseech** ● v. (past and past part. **besought** or **beseeched**) chiefly poetic/literary ask (someone) urgently and fervently for something.
– DERIVATIVES **beseeching** adj. **beseechingly** adv.
– ORIGIN ME: from **BE-** + OE *sēcan* (see **SEEK**).

**beset** ● v. (**besetting**; past and past part. **beset**) **1** trouble or harass persistently. ➤ surround or attack from all sides. **2** (**be beset with**) archaic be covered or studded with.
– ORIGIN OE *besettan*, from **BE-** + *settan* (see **SET**[1]).

**beside** ● prep. **1** at the side of; next to. ➤ compared with. **2** in addition to; apart from.
– PHRASES **beside oneself** distraught.
– ORIGIN OE *be sīdan* (adv.) 'by the side'.

**besides** ● prep. in addition to; apart from. ● adv. in addition; as well. ➤ used to introduce an additional idea or explanation.

**besiege** ● v. **1** surround (a place) with armed forces in order to capture it or force its surrender. ➤ crowd round oppressively. **2** (**be besieged**) be inundated by large numbers of requests or complaints.
– DERIVATIVES **besieger** n.
– ORIGIN ME: alt. of *assiege*, from OFr. *asegier*.

**besmear** ● v. poetic/literary smear or cover with.

**besmirch** /bɪˈsməːtʃ/ ● v. **1** damage (someone's reputation). **2** poetic/literary make dirty; soil.

**besom** /ˈbiːz(ə)m, ˈbɪz-/ ● n. **1** a broom made of twigs tied round a stick. **2** derogatory a woman or girl.
– ORIGIN OE *besema*, of W. Gmc origin.

**besotted** /bɪˈsɒtɪd/ ● adj. **1** strongly infatuated. **2** archaic intoxicated; drunk.
– ORIGIN C16: past part. of *besot* 'make foolishly affectionate', from **BE-** + **SOT**.

**besought** past and past participle of **BESEECH**.

**bespangle** ● v. poetic/literary adorn with something that glitters or sparkles.

**bespatter** ● v. spatter with liquid.

**bespeak** ● v. (past **bespoke**; past part. **bespoken**) **1** be evidence of. **2** order or reserve in advance. **3** archaic speak to.
– ORIGIN OE *bisprecan* 'speak out' (see **BE-**, **SPEAK**), later 'discuss, decide on'.

**bespectacled** ● adj. wearing glasses.

**bespoke** ● adj. Brit. (of goods) made to order. ➤ (of a computer program) written or adapted for a specific user or purpose.

**besprinkle** ● v. poetic/literary sprinkle with liquid, powder, etc.

**Bessemer process** ● n. a steel-making process, now largely superseded, in which carbon, silicon, and other impurities are removed from molten pig iron by oxidation in a blast of air in a special tilting retort (a **Bessemer converter**).
– ORIGIN C19: named after the Engl. engineer Sir Henry *Bessemer*, who developed it.

**best** ● adj. of the most excellent or desirable type or quality. ➤ most appropriate, advantageous, or well advised. ● adv. to the highest degree; most. ➤ to the highest standard. ➤ most suitably, appropriately, or usefully. ● n. (**the best**) that which is the most excellent or desirable. ➤ (**one's best**) the highest standard or level attainable. ➤ (in sport) a record performance. ● v. informal outwit.
– PHRASES **all the best** best wishes. **at best** taking the most optimistic view. **be for the best** be desirable in the end, although not at first seeming so. **best end** Brit. the rib end of a neck of lamb or other meat. **the best of three** (or **five** etc.) victory achieved by winning the majority of a specified odd number of games. **the best part of** most of. **best wishes** an expression of hope for someone's future happiness. **get the best of** overcome (someone). **give someone/thing best** Brit. admit the superiority of someone or something. **had best** find it most sensible or well advised to. **make the best of** derive what limited advantage one can from (something unsatisfactory). **six of the best** Brit. a caning as a punishment, traditionally with six strokes of the cane.
– ORIGIN OE *betest* (adj.), *betost* (adv.), of Gmc origin.

**best ball** ● n. Golf the better score at a hole of two or more players competing as a team.

**best boy** ● n. the assistant to the chief electrician of a film crew.

**bestial** /ˈbɛstɪəl/ ● adj. of or like a beast. ➤ savagely cruel and depraved.
– DERIVATIVES **bestialize** (also **-ise**) v. **bestially** adv.
– ORIGIN ME: via OFr. from late L. *bestialis*, from L. *bestia* 'beast'.

**bestiality** ● n. **1** savagely cruel or depraved behaviour. **2** sexual intercourse between a person and an animal.

**bestiary** /ˈbɛstɪəri/ ● n. (pl. **-ies**) a treatise on animals, especially a medieval work with a moralizing tone.
– ORIGIN C19: from med. L. *bestiarium*, from L. *bestia* 'beast'.

**bestir** ● v. (**bestirred**, **bestirring**) (**bestir oneself**) exert or rouse oneself.

**best man** ● n. a male friend or relative chosen by a bridegroom to assist him at his wedding.

**bestow** ● v. **1** confer (an honour, right, or gift). **2** archaic put (something) in a specified place.
– DERIVATIVES **bestowal** n.
– ORIGIN ME (in the sense 'use for, devote to'): from **BE-** + OE *stōw* 'place'.

**bestrew** ● v. (past part. **bestrewed** or **bestrewn**) poetic/literary scatter or lie scattered over (a surface).
– ORIGIN OE *bestrēowian* (see **BE-**, **STREW**).

**bestride** ● v. (past **bestrode**; past part. **bestridden**) span or straddle.
– ORIGIN OE *bestrīdan* (see **BE-**, **STRIDE**).

**best-seller** ● n. a book or other product that sells in very large numbers.
– DERIVATIVES **best-selling** adj.

**bet** ● v. (**betting**; past and past part. **bet** or **betted**) **1** risk a sum of money or other valued item against someone else's on the basis of the outcome of an unpredictable event such as a race or game. **2** informal used to express certainty: *he'll be surprised to see me, I'll bet.* ● n. an act of betting. ➤ a sum of money staked. ➤ informal a candidate or option offering a specified likelihood of success: *Allen looked a good bet for victory.* ➤ (**one's bet**) informal one's opinion.
– PHRASES **you bet** informal you may be sure.
– DERIVATIVES **betting** n. **bettor** (also **better**) n.
– ORIGIN C16: perh. a shortening of the obs. noun *abet* 'abetment'.

**beta** /ˈbiːtə/ ● n. **1** the second letter of the Greek alphabet (**Β**, **β**), transliterated as 'b'. ➤ [as modifier] denoting the second of a series of items or categories. ➤ Brit. a second-class mark given for a piece of work. **2** [as modifier] relating to beta decay or beta particles. **3** (also **beta coefficient**) a measure of the movement in price of a security relative to the stock market, used to indicate possible risk.
– ORIGIN via L. from Gk.

**beta blocker** ● n. any of a class of drugs which inhibit the stimulation of the adrenergic receptors responsible for increased cardiac action, used to control heart rhythm, treat angina, and reduce high blood pressure.

**beta decay** ● n. radioactive decay in which an electron is emitted.

**betaine** /ˈbiːtəiːn/ ● n. Chemistry a crystalline compound with basic properties, found in many plant juices. ➤ any compound with the zwitterionic structure represented by this.
– ORIGIN C19: from L. *beta* 'beet' (because orig. isolated from sugar beet) + **-INE**[4].

**betake** ● v. (past **betook**; past part. **betaken**) (**betake oneself to**) poetic/literary go to.

**beta particle** (also **beta ray**) ● n. Physics a fast-moving electron emitted by radioactive decay of substances (originally regarded as rays).

**beta rhythm** ● n. Physiology the normal electrical activity of the brain when conscious and alert, consisting of oscillations (**beta waves**) with a frequency of 18 to 25 hertz.

**beta test** ● n. an independent trial of machinery or software, carried out in the final stages of development (after alpha-testing). ● v. (**beta-test**) subject to a beta test.

**betatron** /ˈbiːtətrɒn/ ● n. Physics an apparatus for accelerating electrons in a circular path by magnetic induction.

– ORIGIN 1940s: from **BETA** + **-TRON**.

**betel** /ˈbiːt(ə)l/ • **n.** **1** the leaf of an Asian evergreen climbing plant, which in the East is chewed and used as a mild stimulant. **2** the plant, related to pepper, from which these leaves are taken. [*Piper betle.*]
– ORIGIN C16: via Port. from Malayalam *verrila*.

**betel nut** • **n.** the astringent seed of an areca palm, chewed with betel leaves.

**bête noire** /beɪt ˈnwɑː, bɛt, French bɛt nwaʀ/ • **n.** (pl. **bêtes noires** pronunc. same) (**one's bête noire**) a person or thing that one particularly dislikes.
– ORIGIN Fr., lit. 'black beast'.

**bethink** • **v.** (past and past part. **bethought**) (**bethink oneself**) formal come to think.

**betide** • **v.** poetic/literary happen; befall.
– ORIGIN ME: from **BE-** + obs. *tide* 'befall', from OE *tīdan* 'happen', from *tīd* (see **TIDE**).

**betimes** • **adv.** poetic/literary in good time; early.
– ORIGIN ME: from obs. *betime* (see **BY**, **TIME**).

**bêtise** /beɪˈtiːz, bɛˈtiːz, French betiz/ • **n.** a foolish or ill-timed remark or action.
– ORIGIN Fr., 'stupidity', from *bête* 'foolish'.

**betoken** • **v.** poetic/literary be a warning or sign of.
– ORIGIN OE *betācnian*, from **BE-** + *tācnian* 'signify', of Gmc origin; rel. to **TOKEN**.

**betony** /ˈbɛtəni/ • **n.** (pl. **-ies**) a plant of the mint family bearing spikes of showy purple flowers. [*Stachys officinalis.*] ➤used in names of other plants, e.g. **water betony**.
– ORIGIN ME: from OFr. *betoine*, based on L. *betonica*, perh. from the name of an Iberian tribe.

**betook** past of **BETAKE**.

**betray** • **v.** **1** act treacherously towards (one's country) by aiding the enemy. ➤be disloyal to or inform on. **2** unintentionally reveal; be evidence of: *she drew a deep breath that betrayed her indignation.*
– DERIVATIVES **betrayal** n. **betrayer** n.
– ORIGIN ME: from **BE-** + obs. *tray* 'betray', from OFr. *trair*, based on L. *tradere* 'hand over'.

**betroth** /bɪˈtrəʊð, -θ/ • **v.** [as adj. **betrothed**] formally engaged to be married. • **n.** (**one's betrothed**) the person to whom one is engaged.
– DERIVATIVES **betrothal** n.
– ORIGIN ME *betreuthe*: from **BE-** + **TRUTH**.

**better** • **adj.** **1** more desirable, satisfactory, or effective. [compar. of the adj. **GOOD**.] ➤more appropriate, advantageous, or well advised. **2** partly or fully recovered from illness or injury. [compar. of the adj. **WELL**[1].] • **adv.** more excellently or effectively. ➤to a greater degree; more. ➤more suitably or usefully. • **n.** **1** that which is better; the better one. **2** (**one's betters**) chiefly dated or humorous one's superiors in social class or ability. • **v.** improve on or surpass. ➤(**better oneself**) achieve a higher social position or status. ➤overcome or defeat (someone).
– PHRASES **better off** in a more advantageous position, especially in financial terms. **the better part of** almost all of; most of. **better than** N. Amer. more than. **the better to** —— so as to do the specified thing better. **for better or (for) worse** whether the outcome is good or bad. **get the better of** defeat or overcome. **go one better** narrowly outdo or surpass. **had better** would find it wiser to.
– ORIGIN OE *betera* (adj.), of Gmc origin.

**better half** • **n.** informal a person's spouse or partner.

**betterment** • **n.** **1** improvement. **2** Law the enhanced value of real property arising from local improvements.

**bettong** /ˈbɛtɒŋ/ • **n.** a short-nosed Australian rat-kangaroo. [Genera *Bettongia* and *Aepyprymnus.*]
– ORIGIN C19: from Dharuk.

**between** • **prep. & adv.** **1** at, into, or across the space separating (two objects, places, or points). **2** in the period separating (two points in time). **3** [as prep.] indicating a connection or relationship involving two or more parties. **4** [as prep.] by combining the resources or actions of (two or more parties).
– PHRASES **between ourselves** (or **you and me**) in confidence. (**in**) **between times** (or **whiles**) in the intervals between other actions.
– ORIGIN OE *betwēonum*, from *be* 'by' + a Gmc word rel. to **TWO**.

**betwixt** • **prep. & adv.** archaic term for **BETWEEN**.
– PHRASES **betwixt and between** informal neither one thing nor the other.
– ORIGIN OE *betwēox*, from *be* 'by' + a Gmc word rel. to **TWO**.

**beurre blanc** /bəː ˈblɒ̃, French bœʀ blɑ̃/ • **n.** a creamy sauce made with butter, onions, and vinegar or lemon juice.
– ORIGIN Fr., lit. 'white butter'.

**beurre manié** /bəː ˈmanjeɪ, French bœʀ manje/ • **n.** a mixture of flour and butter used for thickening sauces or soups.
– ORIGIN Fr., lit. 'worked butter'.

**BeV** • **abbrev.** another term for **GeV**.
– ORIGIN 1940s: from *b*illion ($10^9$) *e*lectron*v*olts.

**bevatron** /ˈbɛvətrɒn/ • **n.** a synchrotron used to accelerate protons to energies in the billion electronvolt range.
– ORIGIN 1940s: from **BeV** + **-TRON**.

**bevel** /ˈbɛv(ə)l/ • **n.** **1** (in carpentry) a surface or edge which slopes away from a horizontal or vertical surface. **2** (also **bevel square**) a tool for marking angles in carpentry and stonework. • **v.** (**bevelled**, **bevelling**; US **beveled**, **beveling**) [usu. as adj. **bevelled**] cut a bevel on.
– ORIGIN C16: from an OFr. dimin. of *baif* 'open-mouthed', from *baer* (see **BAY**[3]).

**bevel gear** • **n.** a gear working another gear at an angle to it by means of bevel wheels.

**bevel wheel** • **n.** a toothed wheel whose working face is oblique to the axis.

**beverage** /ˈbɛv(ə)rɪdʒ/ • **n.** a drink other than water.
– ORIGIN ME: from OFr. *bevrage*, based on L. *bibere* 'to drink'.

**bevvy** /ˈbɛvi/ • **n.** (pl. **-ies**) Brit. informal an alcoholic drink.
– DERIVATIVES **bevvied** adj.
– ORIGIN C19: abbrev. of **BEVERAGE**.

**bevy** /ˈbɛvi/ • **n.** (pl. **-ies**) a large group of people or things.
– ORIGIN ME: of unknown origin.

**bewail** • **v.** greatly regret or lament.
– DERIVATIVES **bewailer** n.

**beware** • **v.** be cautious and alert to risks or dangers.
– ORIGIN ME: from the phr. *be ware* (see **BE-**, **WARE**[3]).

**Bewick's swan** • **n.** a bird of the Eurasian race of the tundra swan. [*Cygnus columbianus bewickii.*]
– ORIGIN from the name of the Engl. artist and engraver Thomas *Bewick* (1753–1828).

**bewilder** • **v.** [often as adj. **bewildered**] perplex or confuse.
– DERIVATIVES **bewilderedly** adv. **bewildering** adj. **bewilderingly** adv. **bewilderment** n.
– ORIGIN C17: from **BE-** + obs. *wilder* 'lead or go astray', of unknown origin.

**bewitch** • **v.** **1** cast a spell over. **2** enchant and delight.
– DERIVATIVES **bewitcher** n. **bewitching** adj. **bewitchingly** adv. **bewitchment** n.
– ORIGIN ME: from **BE-** + **WITCH**.

**bey** /beɪ/ • **n.** (pl. **-eys**) historical the governor of a district or province in the Ottoman Empire.
– ORIGIN Turk., mod. form of *beg* 'prince, governor'.

**beyond** • **prep. & adv.** **1** at or to the further side of. ➤more extensive or extreme than. **2** happening or continuing after. **3** having reached or progressed further than (a specified level or amount). **4** to or in a degree where a specified action is impossible. ➤too advanced for. **5** [with neg.] apart from; except. • **n.** (**the beyond**) the unknown, especially in references to life after death.
– ORIGIN OE *begeondan*, from *be* 'by' + *geondan*, of Gmc origin.

**bezant** /ˈbɛz(ə)nt/ • **n.** **1** historical a gold or silver coin originally minted at Byzantium. **2** Heraldry a roundel or (i.e. a solid gold circle).
– ORIGIN ME: from OFr. *besant*, from L. *Byzantius* 'Byzantine'.

**bezel** /ˈbɛz(ə)l/ • **n.** a grooved ring holding the cover of a watch face or other instrument in position. ➤a groove holding the crystal of a watch or the stone of a gem in its

setting.
– ORIGIN C16: from OFr., of unknown origin.

**bezique** /bɪˈziːk/ ● n. a trick-taking card game for two, played with a double pack of 64 cards, including the seven to ace only in each suit. ➤ the holding of the queen of spades and the jack of diamonds in this game.
– ORIGIN C19: from Fr. *bésigue*, perh. from Pers. *bāzīgar* 'juggler' or *bāzī* 'game'.

**bezoar** /ˈbiːzɔː, ˈbɛzəʊɑː/ ● n. **1** a small stony concretion which may form in the stomachs of certain animals, formerly used as an antidote for various ailments. **2** a wild goat with flat scimitar-shaped horns, the ancestor of the domestic goat. [*Capra aegagrus*.]
– ORIGIN C15: from Fr. *bezoard*, based on Arab. *bāzahr*, from Pers. *pādzahr* 'antidote'.

**b.f.** ● abbrev. (in bookkeeping) brought forward.

**BFPO** ● abbrev. British Forces (or Field) Post Office.

**BG** ● abbrev. Bulgaria (international vehicle registration).

**BGH** ● abbrev. bovine growth hormone.

**BH** ● abbrev. Belize (international vehicle registration).
– ORIGIN from *British Honduras*.

**Bh** ● symb. the chemical element bohrium.

**Bhagwan** /bʌgˈwɑːn/ ● n. Indian God.
– ORIGIN from Hindi *bhagwān*.

**bhajan** /ˈbʌdʒ(ə)n/ ● n. Hinduism a devotional song.
– ORIGIN from Sanskrit *bhajana*.

**bhaji** /ˈbɑːdʒi/ (also **bhajia**) ● n. (pl. **bhajis**, **bhajia**) (in Indian cuisine) a small flat cake or ball of vegetables, fried in batter.
– ORIGIN from Hindi *bhājī* 'fried vegetables'.

**bhakti** /ˈbʌkti/ ● n. Hinduism devotional worship directed to one supreme deity, usually Vishnu or Shiva.
– ORIGIN from Sanskrit.

**bhang** /baŋ/ (also **bang**) ● n. the leaves and flower-tops of cannabis, used as a narcotic in India.
– ORIGIN from Hindi *bhāṅg*.

**bhangra** /ˈbɑːŋgrə/ ● n. a type of popular music combining Punjabi folk traditions with Western pop music.
– ORIGIN 1960s: from Punjabi *bhāṅgṛā*.

**bharal** /ˈbʌr(ə)l/ ● n. a Himalayan wild sheep with a bluish coat and backward-curving horns. [*Pseudois nayaur*.]
– ORIGIN C19: from Hindi.

**BHC** ● abbrev. benzene hexachloride.

**bhindi** /ˈbɪndiː/ ● n. Indian term for **OKRA**.
– ORIGIN from Hindi *bhiṇḍī*.

**Bhojpuri** /ˌbəʊdʒˈpʊəri/ ● n. a Bihari language spoken especially in western Bihar and eastern Uttar Pradesh.
– ORIGIN from the name of *Bhojpur* in Bihar.

**b.h.p.** ● abbrev. brake horsepower.

**Bhutanese** /ˌbuːtəˈniːz/ ● n. a native or inhabitant of Bhutan, a small kingdom on the slopes of the Himalayas. ● adj. of or relating to Bhutan or its people.

**Bi** ● symb. the chemical element bismuth.

**bi** /bʌɪ/ ● abbrev. informal bisexual.

**bi-** /bʌɪ/ (also **bin-** before a vowel) ● comb. form two; having two: *biathlon*. ➤ occurring twice in every one or once in every two: *bicentennial*. ➤ lasting for two: *biennial*. ➤ Chemistry (in names of compounds) containing two atoms or groups of a specified kind: *bicarbonate*.
– ORIGIN from L., 'doubly, having two'; rel. to Gk *di-* 'two'.

**bialy** /bɪˈɑːli/ ● n. (pl. **bialys**) US a flat bread roll topped with chopped onions.
– ORIGIN Yiddish, from *Białystok*, the city in Poland where such bread was orig. made.

**biannual** ● adj. occurring twice a year. Compare with **BIENNIAL**.
– DERIVATIVES **biannually** adv.

**bias** ● n. **1** inclination or prejudice for or against one thing or person. ➤ a systematic distortion of a statistical result due to a factor not allowed for in its derivation. **2** a diagonal across the grain of a fabric. **3** Bowls the irregular shape given to one side of a bowl. ➤ the oblique course taken by such a bowl. **4** Electronics a steady voltage, magnetic field, or other factor applied to a system to cause it to operate over a pre-determined range. ● v. (**biased**, **biasing** or **biassed**, **biassing**) **1** influence unfairly; prejudice. **2** Electronics give a bias to.
– ORIGIN C16 (in the sense 'oblique line'): from Fr. *biais*, from Provençal.

**bias binding** ● n. a narrow strip of fabric cut on the bias, used to bind edges or for decoration.

**bias-ply** ● adj. North American term for **CROSS-PLY**.

**biathlon** ● n. a sporting event in which the competitors combine cross-country skiing and rifle shooting.
– DERIVATIVES **biathlete** n.
– ORIGIN 1950s: from **BI-** + Gk *athlon* 'contest', on the pattern of *pentathlon*.

**biaxial** ● adj. having or relating to two axes.
– DERIVATIVES **biaxially** adv.

**bib**[1] ● n. **1** a piece of cloth or plastic fastened round a child's neck to keep its clothes clean while eating. ➤ a loose-fitting sleeveless garment worn for identification, e.g. by competitors and officials at sporting events. ➤ the part above the waist of the front of an apron or pair of dungarees. **2** a common European inshore fish of the cod family. [*Trisopterus luscus*.]
– PHRASES **one's best bib and tucker** informal one's smartest clothes. **stick** (or **poke**) **one's bib in** Austral. informal interfere.
– ORIGIN C16: prob. from **BIB**[2].

**bib**[2] ● v. (**bibbed**, **bibbing**) archaic drink (an alcoholic drink).
– DERIVATIVES **bibber** n.
– ORIGIN ME: prob. from L. *bibere* 'to drink'.

**bibb lettuce** ● n. N. Amer. a butterhead lettuce of a variety that has crisp dark green leaves.
– ORIGIN C19: named after the Amer. horticulturalist Jack *Bibb*.

**bib cock** (also **bib tap**) ● n. a tap with a bent nozzle fixed at the end of a pipe.
– ORIGIN C18: perh. from **BIB**[1] and **COCK**[1].

**bibelot** /ˈbɪbələʊ/ ● n. a small ornament or trinket.
– ORIGIN C19: from Fr., fanciful formation based on *bel* 'beautiful'.

**Bible** ● n. **1** (**the Bible**) the Christian scriptures, consisting of the Old and New Testaments. ➤ the Jewish scriptures, consisting of the Torah or Law, the Prophets, and the Hagiographa or Writings. **2** (**bible**) informal a book regarded as authoritative.
– ORIGIN ME: via OFr. from eccles. L. *biblia*, from Gk (*ta*) *biblia* '(the) books', from *biblion* 'book'.

**Bible-basher** (also **Bible-thumper**) ● n. informal a person who expounds the teachings of the Bible in an aggressively evangelical way.
– DERIVATIVES **Bible-bashing** n. & adj.

**Bible Belt** ● n. those areas of the southern and middle western US and western Canada where Protestant fundamentalism is strong.

**biblical** ● adj. of, relating to, or contained in the Bible. ➤ resembling the language or style of the Bible.
– DERIVATIVES **biblically** adv.

**biblio-** /ˈbɪblɪəʊ/ ● comb. form relating to a book or books: *bibliophile*.
– ORIGIN from Gk *biblion* 'book'.

**bibliography** /ˌbɪblɪˈɒgrəfi/ ● n. (pl. **-ies**) **1** a list of sources referred to in a particular work. ➤ a list of the books of a specific author or on a specific subject. **2** the study of books in terms of their classification, printing, and publication.
– DERIVATIVES **bibliographer** n. **bibliographic** /-əˈgrafɪk/ adj. **bibliographical** adj. **bibliographically** adv.

**bibliomancy** /ˈbɪblɪə(ʊ)mansi/ ● n. the practice of foretelling the future by interpreting a randomly chosen passage from a book, especially the Bible.

**bibliomania** ● n. passionate enthusiasm for collecting and possessing books.
– DERIVATIVES **bibliomaniac** n. & adj.

**bibliometrics** ● pl. n. [treated as sing.] statistical analysis of books or other publications.
– DERIVATIVES **bibliometric** adj.

**bibliophile** ● n. a person who collects or has a great love of books.
– DERIVATIVES **bibliophilic** adj. **bibliophily** /-ˈɒfɪli/ n.

**bibliopole** /ˈbɪblɪə(ʊ)pəʊl/ ● **n.** archaic a dealer in books.
– ORIGIN C18: via L. from Gk *bibliopōlēs*, from *biblion* 'book' + *pōlēs* 'seller'.

**bibulous** /ˈbɪbjʊləs/ ● **adj.** formal excessively fond of drinking alcohol.
– DERIVATIVES **bibulously** adv. **bibulousness** n.
– ORIGIN C17: from L. *bibulus* 'freely drinking'.

**bicameral** /bʌɪˈkam(ə)r(ə)l/ ● **adj.** (of a legislative body) having two chambers.
– DERIVATIVES **bicameralism** n.
– ORIGIN C19: from **BI-** + L. *camera* 'chamber' + **-AL**.

**bicarb** ● **n.** informal sodium bicarbonate.

**bicarbonate** /bʌɪˈkɑːbəneɪt, -nət/ ● **n. 1** Chemistry a salt containing the anion $HCO_3^-$. **2** (also **bicarbonate of soda**) sodium bicarbonate.

**bice** /bʌɪs/ ● **n.** dated a blue or blue-green pigment made from basic copper carbonate.
– ORIGIN ME: from OFr. *bis* 'dark grey'.

**bicentenary** /ˌbʌɪsɛnˈtiːnəri, -ˈtɛn-/ ● **n.** (pl. **-ies**) the two-hundredth anniversary of a significant event.
– DERIVATIVES **bicentennial** n. & adj.

**bicephalous** /bʌɪˈsɛf(ə)ləs, -ˈkɛf-/ ● **adj.** having two heads.
– ORIGIN C19: from **BI-** + Gk *kephalē* 'head' + **-OUS**.

**biceps** /ˈbʌɪsɛps/ ● **n.** (pl. same) a large muscle in the upper arm which turns the hand to face palm uppermost and flexes the arm and forearm. ➤(also **leg biceps**) a muscle in the back of the thigh which helps to flex the leg.
– ORIGIN C17: from L., 'two-headed' (because the muscle has two points of attachment).

**bichir** /ˈbɪʃɪə/ ● **n.** an elongated African freshwater fish with hard shiny scales and a series of separate fins along its back. [Genus *Polypterus*: several species.]
– ORIGIN 1960s: via Fr. from dial. Arab. *abu shīr.*

**bichon frise** /biːʃ(ə)n ˈfriːz/ ● **n.** a toy dog of a breed with a fine, curly white coat.
– ORIGIN from Fr. *barbichon* 'little water spaniel' + *frisé* 'curly-haired'.

**bicker** ● **v. 1** argue about petty and trivial matters. **2** poetic/literary (of water) flow with a gentle repetitive noise.
– DERIVATIVES **bickerer** n.
– ORIGIN ME: of unknown origin.

**bicky** (also **bikky**) ● **n.** (pl. **-ies**) informal a biscuit.

**bicolour** (US **bicolor**) ● **adj.** (also **bicoloured**) having two colours. ● **n.** a bicolour flower or breed.

**biconcave** ● **adj.** concave on both sides.

**biconvex** ● **adj.** convex on both sides.

**bicultural** ● **adj.** having or combining the cultures and customs of two nations or ethnic groups.
– DERIVATIVES **biculturalism** n.

**bicuspid** ● **adj.** having two cusps or points. ● **n.** a tooth with two cusps, especially a human premolar tooth.
– ORIGIN C19: from **BI-** + L. *cuspis, cuspid-* 'sharp point'.

**bicuspid valve** ● **n.** Anatomy the mitral valve.

**bicycle** ● **n.** a vehicle consisting of two wheels held in a frame one behind the other, propelled by pedals and steered with handlebars attached to the front wheel. ● **v.** ride a bicycle.
– DERIVATIVES **bicyclist** n.
– ORIGIN C19: from **BI-** + Gk *kuklos* 'wheel'.

**bicyclic** /bʌɪˈsʌɪklɪk, -ˈsɪk-/ ● **adj.** Chemistry having two fused rings of atoms in its molecule.

**bid**[1] ● **v.** (**bidding**; past and past part. **bid**) **1** offer (a certain price) for something, especially at an auction. ➤(**bid for**) (of a contractor) tender for (work). **2** (often **bid for**) make an effort to obtain or achieve. **3** Bridge make a statement during the auction undertaking to make (a certain number of tricks). ● **n. 1** an offer to buy something. ➤an offer to do work or supply goods at a stated price. **2** an effort to obtain or achieve. **3** Bridge an undertaking by a player in the auction to make a stated number of tricks with a stated suit as trumps.
– DERIVATIVES **bidder** n. **bidding** n.
– ORIGIN OE *bēodan* 'to offer, command', of Gmc origin.

**bid**[2] ● **v.** (**bidding**; past **bid** or **bade**; past part. **bid**) **1** utter (a greeting or farewell) to. **2** archaic command (someone) to do something.
– PHRASES **bid fair to** archaic seem likely to.
– ORIGIN OE *biddan* 'ask', of Gmc origin.

**biddable** ● **adj. 1** meekly ready to accept and follow instructions. **2** Bridge strong enough to justify a bid.
– DERIVATIVES **biddability** /-ˈbɪlɪti/ n.

**bidden** archaic or poetic/literary past participle of **BID**[2].

**biddy** ● **n.** (pl. **-ies**) informal a woman, especially an old one.
– ORIGIN C17 (orig. denoting a chicken): of unknown origin.

**bide** ● **v.** archaic or dialect remain or stay in a certain place.
– PHRASES **bide one's time** wait quietly for a good opportunity to do something.
– ORIGIN OE *bīdan*, of Gmc origin.

**bidet** ● **n.** a low oval basin used for washing one's genital and anal area.
– ORIGIN C17: from Fr., lit. 'pony'.

**bidi** /ˈbiːdiː/ (also **beedi** or **biri**) ● **n.** (pl. **bidis**) (in the Indian subcontinent) a type of cheap cigarette.
– ORIGIN from Hindi *bīḍi* 'betel plug, cigar'.

**bidirectional** ● **adj.** functioning in two directions.

**bidri** /ˈbɪdri/ ● **n.** an alloy of copper, lead, tin, and zinc, used as a ground for inlaying with gold and silver.
– ORIGIN C18: from Urdu *bidrī*, from *Bidar*, the name of a town in India.

**Biedermeier** /ˈbiːdəˌmʌɪə/ ● **adj.** denoting a 19th-century German style of furniture and decoration characterized by restraint and utilitarianism.
– ORIGIN from the name of a fictitious Ger. schoolmaster created by L. Eichrodt (1854).

**biennial** /bʌɪˈɛnɪəl/ ● **adj. 1** taking place every other year. Compare with **BIANNUAL**. **2** (of a plant) taking two years to grow from seed to fruition and die. Compare with **ANNUAL, PERENNIAL**. ● **n. 1** a biennial plant. **2** an event celebrated or taking place every two years.
– DERIVATIVES **biennially** adv.
– ORIGIN C17: from L. *biennis* (from *bi-* 'twice' + *annus* 'year') + **-AL**.

**biennium** /bʌɪˈɛnɪəm/ ● **n.** (pl. **biennia** /-nɪə/ or **bienniums**) a period of two years.

**bien pensant** /ˌbjã pɒ̃ˈsɒ̃, French bjɛ̃ pɑ̃sɑ̃/ ● **adj.** right-thinking; orthodox.
– ORIGIN Fr., lit. 'well thinking'.

**bier** /bɪə/ ● **n.** a movable platform on which a coffin or corpse is placed before burial.
– ORIGIN OE *bēr*, of Gmc origin; rel. to **BEAR**[1].

**bifacial** ● **adj.** having two faces, or two different faces.

**biff** informal ● **v.** strike (someone) roughly with the fist. ● **n.** a sharp blow with the fist.
– ORIGIN C19: prob. imitative.

**bifid** /ˈbʌɪfɪd/ ● **adj.** Botany & Zoology (of a part of a plant or animal) divided by a deep cleft or notch into two parts.
– ORIGIN C17: from L. *bifidus*, from *bi-* 'doubly' + *fidus* (from *findere* 'to split').

**bifilar** /bʌɪˈfʌɪlə/ ● **adj.** consisting of or involving two threads or wires.
– ORIGIN C19: from **BI-** + *filum* 'thread' + **-AR**[1].

**bifocal** ● **adj.** denoting a lens having two parts each with a different focal length, one for distant and one for near vision. ● **n.** (**bifocals**) a pair of glasses with bifocal lenses.

**bifurcate** ● **v.** /ˈbʌɪfəkeɪt/ divide into two branches or forks. ● **adj.** /bʌɪˈfəːkət/ forked; branched.
– DERIVATIVES **bifurcation** n.
– ORIGIN C17: from med. L. *bifurcat-, bifurcare* 'divide into two forks', from L. *bifurcus* 'two-forked'.

**big** ● **adj.** (**bigger, biggest**) **1** of considerable size, power, or extent. ➤larger than others of the same kind. ➤informal exciting great interest or popularity. **2** of considerable importance or seriousness. **3** informal, often ironic generous. **4** (**big with**) archaic advanced in pregnancy with.
– PHRASES **big money** (chiefly N. Amer. also **big bucks**) informal large amounts of money. **the big screen** informal the cinema. **give someone the big E** Brit. informal reject someone. [*E* from *elbow.*] **in a big way** informal to a great extent or

high degree. **talk big** informal talk confidently or boastfully. **think big** informal be ambitious. **too big for one's boots** informal conceited.
– DERIVATIVES **biggish** adj. **bigness** n.
– ORIGIN ME: of unknown origin.

**bigamy** ● n. the offence of marrying someone while already married to another person.
– DERIVATIVES **bigamist** n. **bigamous** adj.
– ORIGIN ME: from OFr. *bigamie*, from *bigame* 'bigamous', from late L. *bigamus*, from *bi-* 'twice' + Gk *-gamos* 'married'.

**big band** ● n. a large group of musicians playing jazz or swing music.

**big bang** ● n. **1** Astronomy the rapid expansion of matter from a state of extremely high density and temperature which according to current cosmological theories marked the origin of the universe. **2** (**Big Bang**) (in the UK) the introduction in 1986 of major changes in trading in the Stock Exchange.

**Big Brother** ● n. informal a person or organization exercising total control over people's lives.
– ORIGIN 1950s: from the name of the head of state in George Orwell's *Nineteen Eighty-four* (1949).

**big bud** ● n. a disease of blackcurrant bushes in which the buds become swollen due to the presence of mites.

**big business** ● n. large-scale financial or commercial activity.

**big cheese** ● n. informal an important person.
– ORIGIN 1920s: *cheese*, prob. via Urdu from Pers. *čīz* 'thing'.

**big crunch** ● n. Astronomy a contraction of the universe to a state of extremely high density and temperature (a hypothetical opposite of the big bang).

**big dipper** ● n. **1** Brit. a roller coaster. **2** (**the Big Dipper**) North American term for **PLOUGH** (in sense 2).

**big end** ● n. (in a piston engine) the larger end of the connecting rod, encircling the crankpin.

**bigeneric** /ˌbʌɪdʒɪˈnɛrɪk/ ● adj. Botany relating to or denoting a hybrid between two genera.

**bigeye** ● n. **1** a large migratory tuna found in warm seas. [*Thunnus obesus*.] **2** a reddish fish with large eyes which lives in the tropical Atlantic and the western Indian Ocean. [*Priacanthus arenatus*.]

**Bigfoot** ● n. (pl. **Bigfeet**) a large, hairy ape-like creature, supposedly found in NW America.

**big game** ● n. large animals hunted for sport.

**big gun** ● n. informal a powerful person.

**bigha** /ˈbiːgə/ ● n. (in the Indian subcontinent) a measure of land area varying locally from ⅓ to 1 acre (⅛ to ⅖ hectare).
– ORIGIN from Hindi *bīghā*.

**big-head** ● n. informal a conceited person.
– DERIVATIVES **big-headed** adj. **big-headedness** n.

**bighorn** ● n. (pl. same or **-horns**) a stocky brown wild sheep with large horns, found in the Rocky Mountains. [*Ovis canadensis*.]

**bight** /bʌɪt/ ● n. **1** a curve or recess in a coastline or other geographical feature. **2** a loop of rope.
– ORIGIN OE *byht* 'a bend or angle', of Gmc origin.

**big league** ● n. a top league in a professional sport, especially baseball.
– DERIVATIVES **big leaguer** n.

**big mouth** ● n. informal an indiscreet or boastful person.
– DERIVATIVES **big-mouthed** adj.

**bigot** /ˈbɪgət/ ● n. a person who is prejudiced in their views and intolerant of the opinions of others.
– DERIVATIVES **bigoted** adj. **bigotry** n.
– ORIGIN C16: from Fr., of unknown origin.

**big shot** (also **big noise**) ● n. informal an important person.

**big tent** ● n. a political party's policy of permitting and encouraging a broad spectrum of views among its members: [as modifier] *we're running a big-tent campaign.*

**big-ticket** ● adj. N. Amer. informal constituting a major expense.

**big time** ● n. (**the big time**) informal the highest or most successful level in a career.
– DERIVATIVES **big-timer** n.

**big top** ● n. the main tent in a circus.

**biguanide** /bʌɪˈgwɑːnʌɪd/ ● n. Chemistry a crystalline compound with basic properties, made by condensation of two guanidine molecules.

**big wheel** ● n. **1** a Ferris wheel. **2** North American term for **BIGWIG**.

**bigwig** ● n. informal an important person.
– ORIGIN C18: so named from the large wigs formerly worn by distinguished men.

**Bihari** /bɪˈhɑːri/ ● n. **1** a native or inhabitant of the state of Bihar in NE India. **2** a group of three closely related Indic languages spoken principally in Bihar. ● adj. of or relating to Bihar, its peoples, or their languages.

**bijou** /ˈbiːʒuː/ ● adj. small and elegant. ● n. (pl. **bijoux** pronunc. same) archaic a jewel or trinket.
– ORIGIN Fr., from Breton *bizou* 'finger-ring', from *biz* 'finger'.

**bijouterie** /biːˈʒuːt(ə)ri, French biʒutʀi/ ● n. jewellery or trinkets.
– ORIGIN Fr., from **BIJOU**.

**bike** informal ● n. a bicycle or motorcycle. ● v. ride a bicycle or motorcycle.
– DERIVATIVES **biker** n.
– ORIGIN C19: abbrev.

**bikini** ● n. (pl. **bikinis**) a women's two-piece swimsuit.
– ORIGIN 1940s: named after *Bikini*, an atoll in the western Pacific, where an atom bomb was exploded in 1946 (because of the supposed 'explosive' effect created by the garment).

**bikini briefs** ● pl. n. scanty briefs worn by women as underwear.

**bikini line** ● n. the area of skin around the edge of the bottom half of a bikini.

**bikky** ● n. (pl. **-ies**) variant spelling of **BICKY**.

**bilabial** ● adj. Phonetics denoting a speech sound formed by closure or near closure of the lips, e.g. *p*, *b*, *m*, *w*.

**bilateral** ● adj. **1** having or relating to two sides. **2** involving two parties.
– DERIVATIVES **bilaterally** adv.

**bilateral symmetry** ● n. the property of being divisible into symmetrical halves on either side of a unique plane.

**bilayer** ● n. Biochemistry a film two molecules thick, especially one formed by lipid molecules with their hydrophilic ends directed outwards.

**bilberry** ● n. (pl. **-ies**) **1** the small blue edible berry of a hardy dwarf shrub found on heathland and high ground. **2** the shrub on which these berries grow. [*Vaccinium myrtilus* and other species.]
– ORIGIN C16: prob. of Scand. origin.

**bilbo** ● n. (pl. **-os** or **-oes**) historical a sword noted for the temper and elasticity of its blade.
– ORIGIN C16: from *Bilboa*, an earlier Engl. form of *Bilbao*, the Sp. seaport noted for the manufacture of fine blades.

**bilboes** ● pl. n. an iron bar with sliding shackles, formerly used for confining a prisoner's ankles.
– ORIGIN C16: of unknown origin.

**bilby** /ˈbɪlbi/ ● n. (pl. **-ies**) a burrowing Australian bandicoot with long ears. [Genus Macrotis: two species.]
– ORIGIN C19: prob. from an Aborig. lang.

**Bildungsroman** /ˈbɪldʊŋzrəʊˌmɑːn/ ● n. a novel dealing with someone's formative years or spiritual education.
– ORIGIN Ger., from *Bildung* 'education' + *Roman* 'a novel'.

**bile** ● n. **1** a bitter greenish-brown alkaline fluid secreted by the liver and stored in the gall bladder, which aids digestion. **2** anger; irritability.
– ORIGIN C16: from Fr., from L. *bilis*.

**bile duct** ● n. the duct which conveys bile from the liver and the gall bladder to the duodenum.

**bi-level** ● adj. having or functioning on two levels.

**bilge** ● n. **1** the area on the outer surface of a ship's hull where the bottom curves to meet the vertical sides. ➤(**bilges**) the lowest internal portion of the hull. ➤(also **bilge water**) dirty water that collects inside the bilges. **2** informal nonsense; rubbish. ● v. archaic break a hole in the

bilge of (a ship).
– ORIGIN C15: prob. a var. of **BULGE**.

**bilge keel** • n. each of a pair of plates or timbers fastened under the sides of the hull of a ship to prevent rolling, and support its weight in dry dock.

**bilharzia** /bɪl'hɑːtsɪə/ • n. a chronic disease caused by infestation with blood flukes (schistosomes), endemic in parts of Africa and South America.
– ORIGIN C19: mod. L., former name of the genus *Schistosoma*, named after the Ger. physician T. *Bilharz*, who discovered the parasite.

**bilharziasis** /ˌbɪlhɑː'tsʌɪəsɪs/ • n. Medicine another term for **BILHARZIA** (the disease).

**biliary** /'bɪlɪəri/ • adj. Medicine of or relating to bile or the bile duct.

**bilinear** • adj. Mathematics **1** rare relating to or contained by two straight lines. **2** denoting a function of two variables that is linear and homogeneous in both independently.

**bilingual** • adj. speaking two languages fluently. ➤ expressed in or using two languages.
– DERIVATIVES **bilingualism** n.

**bilious** • adj. **1** affected by or associated with nausea or vomiting. ➤ (of a colour) lurid or sickly. **2** spiteful; bad-tempered. **3** Physiology of or relating to bile.
– DERIVATIVES **biliously** adv. **biliousness** n.

**bilirubin** /ˌbɪlɪ'ruːbɪn/ • n. Biochemistry an orange-yellow pigment formed in the liver by the breakdown of haemoglobin and excreted in bile.
– ORIGIN C19: from L. *bilis* 'bile' + *ruber* 'red' + **-IN**[1].

**biliverdin** /ˌbɪlɪ'vəːdɪn/ • n. Biochemistry a green pigment excreted in bile, an oxidized derivative of bilirubin.
– ORIGIN C19: from L. *bilis* 'bile' + Fr. *vert* 'green' + **-IN**[1].

**bilk** • v. informal **1** cheat or defraud. ➤ obtain (money) fraudulently. **2** archaic evade; elude.
– DERIVATIVES **bilker** n.
– ORIGIN C17 (orig. used in cribbage meaning 'spoil one's opponent's score'): perh. a var. of **BAULK**.

**Bill** • n. (**the Bill** or **the Old Bill**) [treated as sing. or pl.] Brit. informal the police.
– ORIGIN 1960s: familiar form of the given name *William*.

**bill**[1] • n. **1** a printed or written statement of the money owed for goods or services. **2** a draft of a proposed law presented to parliament for discussion. **3** a programme of entertainment at a theatre or cinema. **4** N. Amer. a banknote. **5** a poster or handbill. • v. **1** list (a person or event) in a programme. ➤ (**bill someone/thing as**) proclaim someone or something as. **2** send a bill to. ➤ charge (a sum of money).
– PHRASES **fit** (or **fill**) **the bill** be suitable for a particular purpose.
– DERIVATIVES **billable** adj. **billing** n.
– ORIGIN ME (denoting a written list or catalogue): from Anglo-Norman Fr. *bille*, prob. based on med. L. *bulla* 'seal, sealed document'.

**bill**[2] • n. **1** the beak of a bird, especially when it is slender, flattened, or weak, or belongs to a web-footed bird or a bird of the pigeon family. ➤ the muzzle of a platypus. **2** the point of an anchor fluke. **3** [in place names] a narrow promontory: *Portland Bill.* • v. (of birds, especially doves) stroke bill with bill during courtship.
– PHRASES **bill and coo** informal behave or talk in a loving and sentimental way.
– DERIVATIVES **-billed** adj.
– ORIGIN OE *bile*, of unknown origin.

**bill**[3] • n. a medieval weapon like a halberd with a hook instead of a blade.
– ORIGIN OE *bil*, of W. Gmc origin.

**billabong** • n. Austral. a branch of a river forming a backwater or stagnant pool.
– ORIGIN C19: from Wiradhuri *bilabang* (orig. as the name of the Bell River, NSW), from *billa* 'water' + *bang* 'channel that is dry except after rain'.

**billboard** • n. a hoarding.

**billet**[1] • n. a civilian house where soldiers are lodged temporarily. • v. (**billeted**, **billeting**) lodge (soldiers) in a civilian house.
– ORIGIN ME (orig. denoting a short written document, later a written order requiring a householder to lodge the bearer): from Anglo-Norman Fr. *billette*, dimin. of *bille* (see **BILL**[1]).

**billet**[2] • n. **1** a thick piece of wood. ➤ a small bar of metal for further processing. **2** Architecture each of a series of short cylindrical pieces inserted at intervals in Norman decorative mouldings. **3** Heraldry a rectangle placed vertically as a charge.
– ORIGIN ME: from OFr. *billette* and *billot*, dimins. of *bille* 'tree trunk', from med. L. *billa*, *billus* 'branch, trunk', prob. of Celtic origin.

**billet-doux** /ˌbɪlɪ'duː/ • n. (pl. **billets-doux** /-'duːz/) dated or humorous a love letter.
– ORIGIN C17: Fr., lit. 'sweet note'.

**billfish** • n. (pl. same or **-fishes**) a marlin, sailfish, spearfish, or similar fish. [Family Istiophoridae.]

**billfold** • n. N. Amer. a wallet.

**billhook** • n. a tool having a sickle-shaped blade with a sharp inner edge, used for pruning or lopping branches.

**billiards** /'bɪljədz/ • pl. n. [treated as sing.] a game played on a billiard table, for two people using three balls.
– ORIGIN C16: from Fr. *billard*, denoting both the game and the cue, dimin. of *bille* (see **BILLET**[2]).

**billiard table** • n. a smooth cloth-covered rectangular table used for billiards, snooker, and some forms of pool, with six pockets at the corners and sides into which balls are struck with cues.

**Billings method** • n. a system for finding the time of ovulation by examining cervical mucus (used as a natural form of birth control).
– ORIGIN 1960s: named after Drs John and Evelyn *Billings*, who devised the method.

**billion** • cardinal number (pl. **billions** or (with numeral or quantifying word) same) **1** the number equivalent to the product of a thousand and a million; 1,000,000,000 or $10^9$. ➤ dated, chiefly Brit. a million million (1,000,000,000,000 or $10^{12}$). **2** (**billions**) informal a very large number or amount.
– DERIVATIVES **billionth** ordinal number.
– ORIGIN C17: from Fr., from *million*, by substitution of the prefix *bi-* 'two' for the initial letters.

**billionaire** • n. a person possessing assets worth at least a billion pounds or dollars.
– ORIGIN C19: from **BILLION**, on the pattern of *millionaire*.

**bill of costs** • n. Brit. a solicitor's account of charges and expenses incurred.

**bill of exchange** • n. a written order requiring a person to make a specified payment to the signatory or to a named payee.

**bill of fare** • n. dated a menu.

**bill of goods** • n. N. Amer. a consignment of merchandise.
– PHRASES **sell someone a bill of goods** deceive someone.

**bill of health** • n. a certificate relating to the incidence of infectious disease on a ship or in a port.
– PHRASES **a clean bill of health** a declaration or confirmation of good health or condition.

**bill of indictment** • n. historical or N. Amer. a written accusation as presented to a grand jury.

**bill of lading** • n. a detailed list of a ship's cargo given by the master of the ship to the person consigning the goods.

**bill of quantities** • n. a detailed statement of work, prices, dimensions, and other details, for the erection of a building by contract.

**bill of rights** • n. a statement of rights, in particular the English constitutional settlement of 1689 and the first ten amendments to the Constitution of the US, ratified 1791.

**bill of sale** • n. a certificate of transfer of personal property, used especially where something is transferred as security for a debt.

**billon** /'bɪlən/ • n. an alloy formerly used for coinage, containing gold or silver with a predominating amount of copper or other base metal.
– ORIGIN C18: from Fr., lit. 'bronze or copper money'.

**billow** • n. **1** a large undulating mass of cloud, smoke, or steam. **2** archaic a large sea wave. • v. (of fabric) fill with air and swell outwards. ➤ (of smoke, cloud, or steam)

move or flow outward with an undulating motion.
– DERIVATIVES **billowy** adj.
– ORIGIN C16: from ON *bylgja*.

**billposter** (also **billsticker**) ● **n.** a person who pastes up advertisements on hoardings.
– DERIVATIVES **billposting** n.

**billy**[1] (also **billycan**) ● **n.** (pl. **-ies**) a tin or enamel cooking pot with a lid and folding handle, used in camping.
– ORIGIN C19: perh. from Aborig. *billa* 'water'.

**billy**[2] (also **billy club**) ● **n.** (pl. **-ies**) N. Amer. a truncheon.
– ORIGIN C19: from *Billy*, familiar form of the given name *William*.

**billycart** ● **n.** Austral. a small handcart. ➤ a go-kart.
– ORIGIN 1920s: *billy* perh. from **BILLY GOAT**; formerly such carts were sometimes pulled by a goat.

**billycock** ● **n.** historical a kind of bowler hat.
– ORIGIN C19: said to be from the name of William *Coke*, nephew of Thomas William Coke, Earl of Leicester.

**billy goat** ● **n.** a male goat.

**billy-o** ● **n.** (in phr. **like billy-o**) Brit. informal very much, hard, or strongly: *I had to run like billy-o.*
– ORIGIN C19: of unknown origin.

**bilobed** (also **bilobate**) ● **adj.** having or consisting of two lobes.

**bilocation** ● **n.** the supposed phenomenon of being in two places simultaneously.

**biltong** /ˈbɪltɒŋ, ˈbəl-/ ● **n.** chiefly S. African lean meat which is salted and dried in strips.
– ORIGIN Afrik., from Du. *bil* 'buttock' + *tong* 'tongue'.

**bimanual** ● **adj.** performed with both hands.
– DERIVATIVES **bimanually** adv.

**bimbo** ● **n.** (pl. **-os**) informal, derogatory an attractive but unintelligent or frivolous young woman.
– DERIVATIVES **bimbette** n.
– ORIGIN C20 (orig. in the sense 'fellow, chap'): from Ital., lit. 'little child'.

**bimetallic** ● **adj.** **1** made or consisting of two metals. **2** historical of or relating to bimetallism.

**bimetallism** /bʌɪˈmɛt(ə)lɪz(ə)m/ ● **n.** historical a system of allowing the unrestricted currency of two metals as legal tender at a fixed ratio to each other.
– DERIVATIVES **bimetallist** n.

**bimillenary** /ˌbʌɪmɪˈlɛnəri, -ˈliːn-, bʌɪˈmɪlənəri/ ● **adj.** of or relating to a period of two thousand years or a two-thousandth anniversary. ● **n.** (pl. **-ies**) a bimillenary period or anniversary.

**bimodal** ● **adj.** having or involving two modes, in particular (of a statistical distribution) having two maxima.

**bimonthly** ● **adj. & adv.** appearing or taking place twice a month or every two months.

**bin** Brit. ● **n.** **1** a receptacle in which to deposit rubbish. ➤ a capacious receptacle for storing a specified substance. ➤ a partitioned stand for storing bottles of wine. **2** Statistics each of a series of ranges of numerical value into which data are sorted in statistical analysis. ● **v.** **1** (**binned, binning**) throw (something) away by putting it in a bin. ➤ store (wine) in a bin. **2** Statistics group together (data) in bins.
– ORIGIN OE *bin(n)*, *binne*, of Celtic origin.

**bin-** ● **prefix** variant form of **BI-** before a vowel (as in *binaural*).

**binary** /ˈbʌɪnəri/ ● **adj.** **1** composed of, or involving two things. **2** using or denoting a system of numerical notation with two as its base, employing the digits 0 and 1. ● **n.** (pl. **-ies**) **1** the binary system of notation. **2** Astronomy a system of two stars revolving round their common centre.
– ORIGIN ME (in the sense 'duality, a pair'): from late L. *binarius*, from *bini* 'two together'.

**binary tree** ● **n.** Computing a data structure in which each record is linked to two successor records.

**binaural** /bɪˈnɔːr(ə)l, bʌɪ-/ ● **adj.** **1** of or involving both ears. **2** of or relating to sound recorded using two microphones and transmitted separately to the two ears of the listener.

**bind** ● **v.** (past and past part. **bound**) **1** tie or fasten (something) tightly together. ➤ restrain (someone) by tying their hands and feet. ➤ wrap or encircle (something) tightly. **2** hold in a united or cohesive group or mass. ➤ hold or combine with (a substance) by chemical bonding. **3** impose a legal or contractual obligation on. ➤ indenture (someone) as an apprentice. ➤ secure (a contract), typically with a sum of money. ➤ (**bind someone over**) (of a court of law) require someone to fulfil an obligation, typically by paying a sum of money as surety. **4** fix together and enclose (the pages of a book) in a cover. **5** trim (the edge of a piece of material) with a fabric strip. ➤ (**bind off**) N. Amer. cast off in knitting. **6** Logic (of a quantifier) be applied to (a given variable) so that the variable falls within its scope. **7** (of a food or medicine) make (someone) constipated. ● **n.** **1** informal an annoyance. ➤ a problematical situation. **2** a statutory constraint. **3** Music another term for **TIE**. **4** another term for **BINE**.
– ORIGIN OE *bindan*, of Gmc origin.

**binder** ● **n.** **1** a cover for holding magazines or loose sheets of paper together. **2** a reaping machine that binds grain into sheaves. **3** a bookbinder.

**bindery** ● **n.** (pl. **-ies**) a workshop or factory in which books are bound.

**bindi** /ˈbɪndiː/ ● **n.** (pl. **bindis**) a decorative mark worn in the middle of the forehead by Indian women, especially Hindus.
– ORIGIN from Hindi *bindī*.

**bindi-eye** /ˈbɪndɪʌɪ/ ● **n.** a small perennial Australian plant of the daisy family, with a bur-like fruit. [*Calotis cuneifolia*.]
– ORIGIN C20: perh. from an Aborig. lang.

**binding** ● **n.** **1** a strong covering holding the pages of a book together. **2** fabric cut or woven in a strip, used for binding the edges of a piece of material. **3** (also **ski binding**) Skiing a device fixed to a ski to grip a ski boot. ● **adj.** (of an agreement) involving a contractual obligation.

**binding energy** ● **n.** Physics the energy that holds a nucleus together, equal to the mass defect of the nucleus.

**binding post** ● **n.** Electronics a connector consisting of a threaded screw to which bare wires are attached and held in place by a nut.

**bindlestiff** /ˈbɪnd(ə)lstɪf/ ● **n.** US informal a tramp.
– ORIGIN C20: prob. from an alt. of **BUNDLE** + **STIFF**.

**bindweed** /ˈbʌɪndwiːd/ ● **n.** a twining plant with trumpet-shaped flowers, several kinds of which are invasive weeds. [*Convolvulus* and other genera: many species.]

**bine** /bʌɪn/ ● **n.** a long, flexible stem of a climbing plant, especially the hop.
– ORIGIN C19: orig. a dial. form of **BIND**.

**bin-end** ● **n.** Brit. one of the last bottles from a bin of wine.

**bing** ● **n.** chiefly Scottish a heap of ore or waste material from a mine.
– ORIGIN C16: from ON *bingr* 'heap'.

**binge** informal ● **n.** a period of excessive indulgence. ● **v.** (**bingeing** or US also **binging**) indulge in an activity, especially eating, to excess.
– DERIVATIVES **binger** n.
– ORIGIN C19: of unknown origin.

**bingo** ● **n.** a game in which players mark off randomly called numbers on printed cards, the winner being the first to mark off all their numbers. ● **exclam.** **1** a call by someone who wins a game of bingo. **2** expressing satisfaction at a sudden positive event or outcome.
– ORIGIN 1920s (as an interjection): of unknown origin.

**binnacle** /ˈbɪnək(ə)l/ ● **n.** a built-in housing for a ship's compass.
– ORIGIN C15 (as *bittacle*): from Sp. *bitácula*, *bitácora* or Port. *bitacola*, from L. *habitaculum* 'dwelling place'.

**binocular** /bɪˈnɒkjʊlə/ ● **adj.** adapted for or using both eyes.
– ORIGIN C18: from L. *bini* 'two together' + *oculus* 'eye', on the pattern of *ocular*.

**binoculars** ● **pl. n.** an optical instrument with a lens for each eye, used for viewing distant objects.

**binocular vision** ● **n.** vision using two eyes with overlapping fields of view, allowing good perception of depth.

**binomial** /bʌɪˈnəʊmɪəl/ ● **n.** **1** Mathematics an algebraic expression of the sum or the difference of two terms. **2** the two-part Latin name of a species of living organism (consisting of the genus followed by the specific epithet). **3** Grammar a noun phrase with two heads joined by a conjunction, in which the order is relatively fixed (as in *knife and fork*). ● **adj.** consisting of or relating to a binomial.
– ORIGIN C16: from Fr. *binôme* or mod. L. *binomium* (from *bi-* 'having two' + Gk *nomos* 'part, portion') + **-AL**.

**binomial distribution** ● **n.** Statistics a frequency distribution of the possible number of successful outcomes in a given number of trials in each of which there is the same probability of success.

**binomial theorem** ● **n.** a formula for finding any power of a binomial without multiplying at length.

**binominal** ● **adj.** another term for **BINOMIAL** (in sense 2).

**bint** ● **n.** Brit. informal, derogatory a girl or woman.
– ORIGIN C19: from Arab., lit. 'daughter, girl'.

**binturong** /ˈbɪntjʊrɒŋ/ ● **n.** a tree-dwelling Asian civet with a blackish coat and a muscular prehensile tail. [*Arctictis binturong*.]
– ORIGIN C19: from Malay.

**binucleate** /bʌɪˈnjuːklɪət/ ● **adj.** Biology (of a cell) having two nuclei.

**bio** informal ● **n.** (pl. **-os**) **1** biology. **2** chiefly N. Amer. a biography. ● **adj.** biological.

**bio-** /ˈbʌɪəʊ/ ● **comb. form** of or relating to life: *biosynthesis*. ➤biological; relating to biology: *biohazard*. ➤of living beings: *biogenesis*.
– ORIGIN from Gk *bios* 'human life', the sense being extended in mod. scientific usage to mean 'organic life'.

**bioaccumulate** ● **v.** (of a substance) become concentrated inside the bodies of living things.
– DERIVATIVES **bioaccumulation** n.

**bioactive** ● **adj.** (of a substance) having a biological effect.
– DERIVATIVES **bioactivity** n.

**bioassay** /ˌbʌɪəʊəˈseɪ/ ● **n.** measurement of the concentration or potency of a substance by its effect on living cells or tissues.

**bioavailability** ● **n.** Physiology the proportion of a drug or other substance which enters the circulation when introduced into the body and so is able to have an active effect.
– DERIVATIVES **bioavailable** adj.

**biocenosis** ● **n.** US spelling of **BIOCOENOSIS**.

**biocentrism** ● **n.** the view or belief that the rights and needs of humans are not more important than those of other living things.
– DERIVATIVES **biocentric** adj. **biocentrist** n.

**biochemistry** ● **n.** the branch of science concerned with the chemical and physico-chemical processes which occur within living organisms.
– DERIVATIVES **biochemical** adj. **biochemically** adv. **biochemist** n.

**biochip** ● **n.** a logical device analogous to the silicon chip, whose components are formed from biological molecules or structures.

**biocide** ● **n.** **1** a substance that is poisonous to living organisms, such as a pesticide. **2** the destruction of life.
– DERIVATIVES **biocidal** adj.

**biocircuit** ● **n.** an integrated circuit incorporating biological molecules or structures.

**bioclast** /ˈbʌɪə(ʊ)klast/ ● **n.** Geology a fragment of a shell or fossil forming part of a sedimentary rock.
– DERIVATIVES **bioclastic** adj.

**bioclimatic** ● **adj.** Ecology of or relating to the interrelation of climate and the activities and distribution of living organisms.

**biocoenosis** /ˌbʌɪə(ʊ)sɪˈnəʊsɪs/ (US **biocenosis**) ● **n.** (pl. **-noses** /-siːz/) Ecology an association of different organisms forming a closely integrated community.
– ORIGIN C19: mod. L., from **BIO-** + Gk *koinōsis* 'sharing'.

**biocompatible** ● **adj.** not harmful to living tissue.
– DERIVATIVES **biocompatibility** n.

**biocomputer** ● **n.** a computer based on circuits and components formed from biological molecules or structures. ➤the brain regarded as a computer.

**biocontrol** ● **n.** short for **BIOLOGICAL CONTROL**.

**biodata** ● **pl. n.** [treated as sing. or pl.] biographical details.

**biodegradable** ● **adj.** capable of being decomposed by bacteria or other living organisms.
– DERIVATIVES **biodegradability** n. **biodegradation** n. **biodegrade** v.

**bio-diesel** ● **n.** a biofuel intended as a substitute for diesel.

**biodiversity** ● **n.** the variety of plant and animal life in the world or in a particular habitat.

**biodynamics** ● **pl. n.** [treated as sing.] **1** the study of physical motion or dynamics in living systems. **2** a method of organic farming that incorporates certain astrological and spiritual principles and practices.
– DERIVATIVES **biodynamic** adj.

**bioelectric** ● **adj.** of or relating to electricity or electrical phenomena produced within living organisms.
– DERIVATIVES **bioelectrical** adj.

**bioenergetics** ● **pl. n.** [treated as sing.] **1** the study of the transformation of energy in living organisms. **2** a system of alternative psychotherapy based on the belief that emotional healing can be aided through resolution of bodily tension.
– DERIVATIVES **bioenergetic** adj.

**bioengineering** ● **n.** **1** another term for **GENETIC ENGINEERING**. **2** the use of artificial tissues or organs in the body. **3** the use in engineering or industry of organisms or biological processes.
– DERIVATIVES **bioengineer** n. & v.

**bioethics** ● **pl. n.** [treated as sing.] the ethics of medical and biological research.
– DERIVATIVES **bioethical** adj. **bioethicist** n.

**biofeedback** ● **n.** the use of electronic monitoring of a normally automatic bodily function in order to train someone to acquire voluntary control of that function.

**bioflavonoid** ● **n.** any of a group of compounds occurring mainly in citrus fruits and blackcurrants, sometimes regarded as vitamins.

**biofouling** ● **n.** the build-up of organisms such as barnacles and algae on underwater surfaces.

**biofuel** ● **n.** fuel derived directly from living matter.

**biogas** ● **n.** gaseous fuel, especially methane, produced by the fermentation of organic matter.

**biogenesis** /bʌɪə(ʊ)ˈdʒɛnɪsɪs/ ● **n.** **1** the synthesis of substances by living organisms. **2** historical the hypothesis that living matter arises only from other living matter.
– DERIVATIVES **biogenetic** adj.

**biogenic** /ˌbʌɪə(ʊ)ˈdʒɛnɪk/ ● **adj.** produced or brought about by living organisms.

**biogeochemical** ● **adj.** relating to the cycle in which chemical elements and simple substances are transferred between living systems and the environment.
– DERIVATIVES **biogeochemist** n. **biogeochemistry** n.

**biogeography** ● **n.** the branch of biology concerned with the geographical distribution of plants and animals.
– DERIVATIVES **biogeographer** n. **biogeographic** adj. **biogeographical** adj. **biogeographically** adv.

**biography** ● **n.** (pl. **-ies**) an account of someone's life written by someone else.
– DERIVATIVES **biographer** n. **biographic** adj. **biographical** adj. **biographically** adv.
– ORIGIN C17: from Fr. *biographie* or mod. L. *biographia*, from med. Gk, from *bios* 'life' + *-graphia* 'writing'.

**biohazard** ● **n.** a risk to human health or the environment arising from biological research.

**bioinformatics** ● **pl. n.** [treated as sing.] the science of collecting and analysing complex biological data such as genetic codes.

**biological** ● **adj.** **1** of or relating to biology or living organisms. ➤(of a detergent) containing enzymes to assist the process of cleaning. **2** (of a parent or child) related by blood; natural. **3** relating to, involving, or denoting the use of micro-organisms or toxins of biological origin as weapons of war.

– DERIVATIVES **biologically** adv.

**biological clock** ● n. an innate mechanism that controls the cyclical physiological activities of an organism.

**biological control** ● n. the control of a pest by the introduction of a natural enemy or predator.

**biologism** /bʌɪˈɒlədʒɪz(ə)m/ ● n. the interpretation of human life from a strictly biological point of view.
– DERIVATIVES **biologistic** adj.

**biology** ● n. the scientific study of living organisms. ➤ the plants and animals of a particular area. ➤ the features of a particular organism or class of organisms.
– DERIVATIVES **biologist** n.
– ORIGIN C19: coined in Ger., via Fr. from Gk *bios* 'life' + **-LOGY**.

**bioluminescence** ● n. the biochemical emission of light by living organisms such as glow-worms and deep-sea fishes.
– DERIVATIVES **bioluminescent** adj.

**biomagnetism** ● n. the interaction of living organisms with magnetic fields.

**biomass** ● n. **1** the total quantity or weight of organisms in a given area or volume. **2** organic matter used as a fuel, especially in the generation of electricity.

**biome** /ˈbʌɪəʊm/ ● n. Ecology a large naturally occurring community of flora and fauna occupying a major habitat, e.g. forest or tundra.
– ORIGIN C20: from **BIO-** + **-OME**.

**biomechanics** ● pl. n. [treated as sing.] the study of the mechanical laws relating to the movement or structure of living organisms.

**biomedical** ● adj. of or relating to both biology and medicine.
– DERIVATIVES **biomedicine** n.

**biometry** /bʌɪˈɒmɪtri/ (also **biometrics** /bʌɪə(ʊ)ˈmɛtrɪks/) ● n. the application of statistical analysis to biological data.
– DERIVATIVES **biometric** adj. **biometrical** adj. **biometrician** n.

**biomimetic** ● adj. Biochemistry relating to or denoting synthetic methods which mimic biochemical processes.

**biomorph** ● n. a decorative form or object based on or resembling a living organism. ➤ a graphical representation of an organism generated on a computer.
– DERIVATIVES **biomorphic** adj.

**bionic** ● adj. **1** relating to or denoting the use of electromechanical body parts instead of or as well as living ones. **2** informal having ordinary human powers increased by or as if by the aid of such devices.
– DERIVATIVES **bionically** adv. **bionics** pl. n.
– ORIGIN 1960s: from **BIO-**, on the pattern of *electronic*.

**bionomics** /ˌbʌɪə(ʊ)ˈnɒmɪks/ ● pl. n. [treated as sing.] the study of the behaviour and adaptation of organisms in their natural habitat; ecology.
– DERIVATIVES **bionomic** adj.
– ORIGIN C19: from **BIO-**, on the pattern of *economics*.

**biophysics** ● pl. n. [treated as sing.] the science of the application of the laws of physics to biological phenomena.
– DERIVATIVES **biophysical** adj. **biophysicist** n.

**biopic** ● n. informal a biographical film.

**biopiracy** ● n. derogatory bioprospecting, regarded as a form of exploitation of developing countries.

**biopolymer** ● n. a polymeric substance occurring in living organisms, e.g. a protein, cellulose, or DNA.

**bioprospecting** ● n. the search for plant and animal species from which medicinal drugs and other commercially valuable compounds can be obtained.
– DERIVATIVES **bioprospector** n.

**biopsy** /ˈbʌɪɒpsi/ ● n. (pl. **-ies**) an examination of tissue taken from the body, to discover the presence, cause, or extent of a disease.
– ORIGIN C19: coined in Fr. from Gk *bios* 'life' + *opsis* 'sight'.

**bioreactor** ● n. an apparatus in which a biological reaction or process is carried out, especially on an industrial scale.

**bioregion** ● n. a region defined by characteristics of the natural environment rather than by man-made divisions.
– DERIVATIVES **bioregional** adj.

**bioregionalism** ● n. the belief that human activity should be constrained by ecological or geographical boundaries rather than political ones.
– DERIVATIVES **bioregionalist** n.

**bioremediation** /ˌbʌɪə(ʊ)rɪˌmiːdiˈeɪʃ(ə)n/ ● n. the use of either naturally occurring or deliberately introduced micro-organisms to consume and break down environmental pollutants.

**biorhythm** ● n. a recurring cycle in the physiology or functioning of an organism, such as the daily cycle of sleeping and waking.
– DERIVATIVES **biorhythmic** adj.

**BIOS** /ˈbʌɪɒs/ ● n. Computing a set of computer instructions in firmware which control input and output operations.
– ORIGIN acronym from *Basic Input-Output System*.

**bioscience** ● n. any of the life sciences.
– DERIVATIVES **bioscientist** n.

**bioscope** ● n. dated, chiefly S. African a cinema or film.

**biosensor** ● n. a device which uses a living organism or biological molecules, especially enzymes or antibodies, to detect the presence of chemicals.

**biosolids** ● pl. n. organic matter recycled from sewage, especially for use in agriculture.

**biosphere** ● n. the regions of the surface and atmosphere of the earth occupied by living organisms.
– DERIVATIVES **biospheric** adj.

**biostatistics** ● pl. n. [treated as sing.] the branch of statistics concerned with data relating to living organisms.
– DERIVATIVES **biostatistical** adj. **biostatistician** n.

**biostratigraphy** /ˌbʌɪə(ʊ)strəˈtɪgrəfi/ ● n. the branch of stratigraphy concerned with fossils and their use in dating rock formations.
– DERIVATIVES **biostratigrapher** n. **biostratigraphic** adj. **biostratigraphical** adj. **biostratigraphically** adv.

**biosynthesis** ● n. the production of complex molecules within living organisms or cells.
– DERIVATIVES **biosynthetic** adj.

**biosystematics** ● pl. n. [treated as sing.] taxonomy based on the study of the genetic evolution of plant and animal populations.
– DERIVATIVES **biosystematist** n.

**biota** /bʌɪˈəʊtə/ ● n. Ecology the animal and plant life of a particular region, habitat, or geological period.
– ORIGIN C20: mod. L., from Gk *biotē* 'life'.

**biotech** ● n. short for **BIOTECHNOLOGY**.

**biotechnology** ● n. the exploitation of biological processes for industrial and other purposes, especially the genetic manipulation of micro-organisms for the production of antibiotics, hormones, etc.
– DERIVATIVES **biotechnological** adj. **biotechnologist** n.

**biotic** /bʌɪˈɒtɪk/ ● adj. of, relating to, or resulting from living things, especially in their ecological relations.
– ORIGIN C19: from Fr. *biotique*, or via late L. from Gk *biōtikos*, from *bios* 'life'.

**biotin** /ˈbʌɪətɪn/ ● n. Biochemistry a vitamin of the B complex, found in egg yolk, liver, and yeast, involved in the synthesis of fatty acids and glucose.
– ORIGIN 1930s: coined in Ger. from Gk *bios* 'life' + **-IN**[1].

**biotite** /ˈbʌɪətʌɪt/ ● n. a black, dark brown, or greenish black micaceous mineral, occurring as a constituent of many igneous and metamorphic rocks.
– ORIGIN C19: named after J.-B. *Biot* (1774–1862), Fr. mineralogist.

**biotope** /ˈbʌɪətəʊp/ ● n. Ecology the region of a habitat associated with a particular ecological community.
– ORIGIN 1920s: from Ger. *Biotop*, based on Gk *topos* 'place'.

**bioturbation** /ˌbʌɪəʊtəːˈbeɪʃ(ə)n/ ● n. Geology the disturbance of sedimentary deposits by living organisms.
– DERIVATIVES **bioturbated** adj.

**biotype** ● n. a group of organisms having an identical genetic constitution.

**bipartisan** /ˌbʌɪpɑːtɪˈzan/ ● adj. of or involving the agreement or cooperation of two political parties.

– DERIVATIVES **bipartisanship** n.

**bipartite** /bʌɪ'pɑːtʌɪt/ • **adj.** **1** involving or made by two separate parties. **2** technical consisting of two parts.

**biped** /'bʌɪpɛd/ • **n.** an animal which walks on two feet.
– DERIVATIVES **bipedal** /bʌɪ'piːd(ə)l/ adj. **bipedalism** n. **bipedality** /ˌbʌɪpiː'dalɪti/ n.
– ORIGIN C17: from L. *bipes*, *biped-* (from *bi-* 'having two' + *pes*, *ped-* 'foot').

**biphasic** /bʌɪ'feɪzɪk/ • **adj.** having two phases.

**biphenyl** /bʌɪ'fiːnʌɪl, bʌɪ'fɛnɪl/ • **n.** Chemistry an organic compound containing two phenyl groups bonded together, e.g. the PCBs.

**bipinnate** /bʌɪ'pɪneɪt/ • **adj.** Botany (of a pinnate leaf) having leaflets that are further subdivided in a pinnate arrangement.

**biplane** • **n.** an early type of aircraft with two pairs of wings, one above the other.

**bipod** /'bʌɪpɒd/ • **n.** a two-legged stand or support.

**bipolar** • **adj.** **1** having or relating to two poles or extremities. ➤(of a plant or animal species) of or occurring in both polar regions. **2** (of psychiatric illness) characterized by both manic and depressive episodes, or manic ones only. **3** (of a nerve cell) having two axons, one either side of the cell body. **4** Electronics (of a transistor or other device) using both positive and negative charge carriers.
– DERIVATIVES **bipolarity** n.

**biracial** • **adj.** concerning or containing members of two racial groups.

**biramous** /bʌɪ'reɪməs/ • **adj.** Zoology (especially of crustacean limbs and antennae) dividing to form two branches.
– ORIGIN C19: from **BI-** + **RAMUS** + **-OUS**.

**birch** • **n.** **1** a slender hardy tree which has thin, peeling, typically silver-grey or white bark and yields a hard, pale, fine-grained wood. [*Betula pendula* (**silver birch**) and related species.] **2** (**the birch**) chiefly historical a formal punishment in which a person is flogged with a bundle of birch twigs. • **v.** chiefly historical punish with the birch.
– DERIVATIVES **birchen** adj. (archaic).
– ORIGIN OE *bierce*, *birce*, of Gmc origin.

**Bircher** /'bəːtʃə/ • **n.** a member or supporter of the John Birch Society, an extreme right-wing and anti-communist American organization founded in 1958.
– ORIGIN from the name of John *Birch*, a USAF officer, killed by Chin. communists in 1945.

**bird** • **n.** **1** a warm-blooded egg-laying vertebrate animal of a class distinguished by the possession of feathers, wings, and a beak, typically able to fly. [Class Aves.] **2** informal a person of a specified kind or character: *she's a sharp old bird.* **3** Brit. informal a young woman or girlfriend.
– PHRASES **the bird has flown** the person one is looking for has escaped or left. **the birds and the bees** informal basic facts about sex and reproduction, as told to a child. **do (one's) bird** Brit. informal serve a prison sentence. [*bird* from rhyming sl. *birdlime* 'time'.] **flip someone the bird** US stick one's middle finger up at someone as a sign of contempt or anger. **(strictly) for the birds** informal not worthy of consideration. **give someone the bird** Brit. informal boo or jeer at someone. **have a bird** N. Amer. informal be very shocked or agitated.
– ORIGIN OE *brid* 'chick, fledgling', of unknown origin.

**birdbrain** • **n.** informal a stupid person.
– DERIVATIVES **birdbrained** adj.

**birdcage** • **n.** a cage for pet birds, typically made of wire or cane.

**bird cherry** • **n.** a small wild cherry tree, with bitter black fruit that is eaten by birds. [*Prunus padus.*]

**bird dog** N. Amer. • **n.** **1** a gun dog trained to retrieve birds. **2** informal a talent scout. • **v.** (**bird-dog**) informal search out or pursue with dogged determination.

**bird-eating spider** (also **bird spider**) • **n.** another term for **TARANTULA** (in sense 1).

**birder** • **n.** informal a birdwatcher.

**birdie** • **n.** (pl. **-ies**) **1** informal a little bird. **2** Golf a score of one stroke under par at a hole. • **v.** (**birdying**) Golf play (a hole) with a score of one stroke under par.
– ORIGIN C18: dimin. of **BIRD**; the golf term from US sl. *bird*, denoting any first-rate thing.

**birding** • **n.** informal birdwatching.

**birdlime** • **n.** a sticky substance spread on to twigs to trap small birds.

**bird of paradise** • **n.** **1** (pl. **birds of paradise**) a tropical Australasian bird, the male of which is noted for the beauty and brilliance of its plumage and its spectacular courtship display. [Family Paradisaeidae: many species.] **2** (also **bird of paradise flower**) a southern African plant which bears a showy flower with a long projecting tongue. [*Strelitzia regina* and related species.]

**bird of passage** • **n.** **1** dated a migratory bird. **2** a person who passes through a place without staying long.

**bird of prey** • **n.** a bird that feeds on animal flesh and typically has a hooked bill and sharp talons (e.g. an eagle, hawk, falcon, or owl); a raptor.

**bird pepper** • **n.** a tropical American capsicum pepper which is thought to be the ancestor of both sweet and chilli peppers. [*Capsicum annuum* var. *glabriusculum.*] ➤the small, red, very hot fruit of this plant.

**birdseed** • **n.** a blend of seeds for feeding pet birds.

**bird's-eye** • **n.** **1** (also **bird's-eye speedwell**) North American term for **GERMANDER SPEEDWELL**. **2** a small geometric pattern woven with a dot in the centre.

**bird's-eye chilli** • **n.** a small very hot chilli pepper.

**bird's-eye maple** • **n.** the wood of an American maple with eye-like markings, used in decorative woodwork.

**bird's-eye primrose** • **n.** a primrose with yellow-centred purple flowers. [*Primula farinosa.*]

**bird's-eye view** • **n.** a general view from above.

**bird's-foot** • **n.** (pl. **bird's-foots**) a leguminous plant bearing pods shaped like the foot of a bird. [*Ornithopus perpusillus.*]

**bird's-foot trefoil** • **n.** a small leguminous plant which has three-lobed leaves, yellow flowers streaked with red, and triple pods that resemble the feet of a bird. [*Lotus corniculatus.*]

**birdshot** • **n.** the smallest size of shot for sporting rifles or other guns.

**bird's-nest** • **n.** **1** a brownish or yellowish saprophytic flowering plant with scale-like leaves. [*Monotropa hypopitys* (**yellow bird's-nest**) and *Pterospora andromeda* (**giant bird's-nest**, N. America).] **2** a fungus with a small bowl-shaped fruiting body that opens to reveal egg-shaped organs containing the spores. [*Crucibulum laeve* and other species, family Nidulariaceae.]

**bird's-nesting** • **n.** the practice of hunting for birds' nests in order to take the eggs.

**bird's-nest orchid** • **n.** a yellowish-brown saprophytic orchid with a mass of roots resembling a bird's nest. [*Neottia nidus-avis.*]

**bird's nest soup** • **n.** (in Chinese cookery) a soup made from the dried gelatinous coating of the nests of swifts and other birds.

**birdsong** • **n.** the musical vocalizations of birds.

**birdstrike** • **n.** a collision of a bird and an aircraft.

**bird table** • **n.** Brit. a small platform or table in a garden on which food for birds is placed.

**birdwatching** • **n.** the practice of observing birds in their natural environment as a hobby.
– DERIVATIVES **birdwatcher** n.

**birdwing** • **n.** a very large boldly marked butterfly occurring in tropical Australasia. [Genus *Ornithoptera*: several species, including **Queen Alexandra's birdwing** (*O. alexandrae*), the world's largest butterfly.]

**birefringent** /ˌbʌɪrɪ'frɪn(d)ʒ(ə)nt/ • **adj.** Physics having two different refractive indices.
– DERIVATIVES **birefringence** n.

**bireme** /'bʌɪriːm/ • **n.** an ancient warship with two files of oarsmen on each side.
– ORIGIN C16: from L. *biremis*, from *bi-* 'having two' + *remus* 'oar'.

**biretta** /bɪ'rɛtə/ • **n.** a square cap with three flat projections on top, worn by Roman Catholic clergymen.
– ORIGIN C16: from Ital. *berretta* or Sp. *birreta*, based on late L. *birrus* 'hooded cape'.

**biri** • **n.** (pl. **biris**) variant spelling of **BIDI**.

**biriani** /ˌbɪrɪˈɑːni/ (also **biriyani** or **biryani**) ● **n.** an Indian dish made with highly seasoned rice and meat, fish, or vegetables.
– ORIGIN Urdu, from Pers. *biryānī*, from *biriyān* 'fried, grilled'.

**birl** /bəːl/ Scottish ● **v.** spin or whirl. ● **n.** a spin or whirl.
– ORIGIN C18: imitative.

**birlinn** /ˈbəːlɪn, ˈbɪə-/ ● **n.** a large rowing boat or barge of a kind formerly used in the Western Islands of Scotland.
– ORIGIN C16: from Sc. Gaelic.

**Birman** /ˈbəːmən/ ● **n.** a cat of a long-haired breed, typically with a cream body and dark head, tail, and legs.
– ORIGIN var. of **BURMAN**.

**biro** /ˈbʌɪrəʊ/ ● **n.** (pl. **-os**) Brit. trademark a kind of ballpoint pen.
– ORIGIN 1940s: named after László József *Biró*, Hungarian inventor of the ballpoint.

**birr** /bəː/ ● **n.** the basic monetary unit of Ethiopia, equal to 100 cents.
– ORIGIN from Amharic.

**birth** ● **n. 1** the emergence of a baby or other young from the body of its mother; the start of life as a physically separate being. **2** the beginning of something. ➤origin, descent, or ancestry: *he is of noble birth.* ● **v.** chiefly N. Amer. give birth to.
– DERIVATIVES **birthing** n.
– PHRASES **give birth** bear a child or young.
– ORIGIN ME: from ON *byrth*; rel. to **BEAR**[1].

**birth certificate** ● **n.** an official document recording a person's birth and identifying them by name, place and date of birth, and parentage.

**birth control** ● **n.** the practice of preventing unwanted pregnancies, especially by use of contraception.

**birthday** ● **n.** the annual anniversary of the day on which a person was born. ➤the day of one's birth.
– PHRASES **in one's birthday suit** humorous naked.

**Birthday Honours** ● **pl. n.** (in Britain) the titles and decorations awarded on a sovereign's official birthday.

**birthing pool** ● **n.** a large circular bath in which a woman may give birth.

**birthmark** ● **n.** a coloured mark on the body which is there from birth.

**birth mother** ● **n.** a woman who has given birth to a child, as opposed to an adoptive mother.

**birth parent** ● **n.** a biological as opposed to an adoptive parent.

**birthplace** ● **n.** the place where a person was born.

**birth rate** ● **n.** the number of live births per thousand of population per year.

**birthright** ● **n.** a particular right of possession or privilege that a person has from birth, especially as an eldest son. ➤a natural or moral right, possessed by everyone.

**birth sign** ● **n.** Astrology the zodiacal sign through which the sun is passing when a person is born.

**birthstone** ● **n.** a gemstone popularly associated with the month or astrological sign of a person's birth.

**birthwort** ● **n.** a climbing or herbaceous plant typically having heart-shaped leaves and deep-throated flowers, formerly used as an aid to childbirth and to induce abortion. [Genus *Aristolochia*.]

**biryani** ● **n.** variant spelling of **BIRIANI**.

**BIS** ● **abbrev.** Bank for International Settlements.

**bis** /bɪs/ ● **adv.** Music to be repeated.
– ORIGIN via Fr. and Ital. from L., lit. 'twice'.

**bis-** /bɪs/ ● **comb. form** Chemistry forming the names of compounds containing two groups identically substituted or coordinated: *bis(2-aminoethyl) ether.*

**biscotti** /bɪˈskɒti/ ● **pl. n.** small rectangular Italian biscuits made with nuts.
– ORIGIN from Ital.

**biscuit** ● **n. 1** Brit. a small, flat, crisp unleavened cake. ➤N. Amer. a small, soft round cake like a scone. **2** porcelain or other pottery which has been fired but not glazed. **3** a light brown colour. **4** Carpentry a small flat piece of wood used to join two larger pieces of wood together, fitting into slots in each.
– PHRASES **take the biscuit** (or chiefly N. Amer. **cake**) informal be the most remarkable or foolish of its kind.
– DERIVATIVES **biscuity** adj.
– ORIGIN ME: from OFr. *bescuit*, based on L. *bis* 'twice' + *coctus*, past part. of *coquere* 'to cook' (because biscuits were orig. cooked in a twofold process: first baked and then dried out in a slow oven).

**bisect** ● **v.** divide into two parts.
– DERIVATIVES **bisection** n. **bisector** n.
– ORIGIN C17: from **BI-** + L. *sect-*, *secare* 'to cut'.

**biserial** ● **adj.** Botany & Zoology arranged in or consisting of two series or rows.

**bisexual** ● **adj. 1** sexually attracted to both men and women. **2** Biology having characteristics of both sexes. ● **n.** a person who is sexually attracted to both men and women.
– DERIVATIVES **bisexuality** n.

**bish** ● **n.** Brit. informal, dated a mistake or blunder.
– ORIGIN 1930s: of unknown origin.

**bishop** ● **n. 1** a senior member of the Christian clergy, usually in charge of a diocese and empowered to confer holy orders. **2** (also **bishop bird**) an African weaver bird, the male of which has red, orange, yellow, or black plumage. [Genus *Euplectes*: several species.] **3** a chess piece, typically with its top shaped like a mitre, that can move in any direction along a diagonal. **4** mulled and spiced wine.
– ORIGIN OE *biscop, bisceop*, based on Gk *episkopos* 'overseer', from *epi* 'above' + *-skopos* '-looking'.

**bishopric** /ˈbɪʃəprɪk/ ● **n.** the office or rank of a bishop. ➤a diocese.
– ORIGIN OE *bisceoprīce*, from *bisceop* (see **BISHOP**) + *rīce* 'realm'.

**bishop suffragan** ● **n.** see **SUFFRAGAN**.

**Bislama** /ˈbɪʃləˌmɑː/ (also **Beach-la-mar** or **Bêche-de-mer**) ● **n.** an English-based pidgin language used as a lingua franca in Fiji and the Solomon Islands and as an official language in Vanuatu.
– ORIGIN alt. of Port. *bicho do mar* 'sea cucumber' (traded as a commodity, the word later being applied to the language of trade).

**bismillah** /bɪsˈmɪlə/ ● **exclam.** in the name of God (an invocation used by Muslims at the beginning of an undertaking).
– ORIGIN from Arab. *bi-smi-llāh(i)*, the first word of the Koran.

**bismuth** /ˈbɪzməθ/ ● **n.** the chemical element of atomic number 83, a brittle reddish-tinged grey metal. (Symbol: **Bi**)
– ORIGIN C17: from mod. L. *bisemutum*, Latinization of Ger. *Wismut*, of unknown origin.

**bison** /ˈbʌɪs(ə)n/ ● **n.** (pl. same) a humpbacked shaggy-haired wild ox. [*Bison bison* (the N. American buffalo) and *B. bonasus* (Europe, now only Poland).]
– ORIGIN ME: from L., ult. of Gmc origin.

**bisphenol A** /ˈbɪsfiːnɒl/ ● **n.** Chemistry a synthetic organic compound used in the manufacture of epoxy resins and other polymers.

**bisque**[1] /bɪsk, biːsk/ ● **n.** a rich soup made from lobster or other shellfish.
– ORIGIN Fr., 'crayfish soup'.

**bisque**[2] /bɪsk/ ● **n.** an extra turn or stroke allowed to a weaker player in croquet.
– ORIGIN C17 (orig. a term in real tennis): from Fr., of unknown ultimate origin.

**bisque**[3] /bɪsk/ ● **n.** another term for **BISCUIT** (in sense 2).

**bistable** ● **adj.** denoting an electronic circuit or device which has two stable states.

**Bisto** /ˈbɪstəʊ/ ● **n.** trademark a powder used to thicken, flavour, and colour gravy.

**bistort** /ˈbɪstɔːt/ ● **n.** a herbaceous plant with a spike of flesh-coloured flowers and a twisted root. [*Polygonum bistorta* and other species.]
– ORIGIN C16: from Fr. *bistorte* or med. L. *bistorta*, from *bis* 'twice' + *torta* (fem. past part. of *torquere* 'to twist').

**bistoury** /ˈbɪstʊri/ ● **n.** (pl. **-ies**) a surgical knife with a straight or curved narrow blade.
– ORIGIN C18: from Fr. *bistouri*, orig. *bistorie* 'dagger', of

unknown origin.

**bistre** /ˈbɪstə/ (US also **bister**) ● **n.** a brownish-yellow pigment made from the soot of burnt wood.
– ORIGIN C18: from Fr., of unknown origin.

**bistro** /ˈbiːstrəʊ, ˈbɪs-/ ● **n.** (pl. **-os**) a small, inexpensive restaurant.
– ORIGIN 1920s: Fr.; perh. rel. to *bistouille*, a northern colloq. term meaning 'bad alcohol', perh. from Russ. *bystro* 'rapidly'.

**bisulphate** (US **bisulfate**) ● **n.** Chemistry a salt of the anion $HSO_4^-$.

**bit**[1] ● **n. 1** a small piece, quantity, or extent of something. **2** informal a set of actions or ideas associated with a specific group or activity: *she did her theatrical bit.* **3** informal a girl or young woman. **4** N. Amer. informal a unit of 12½ cents (used only in even multiples).
– PHRASES **a bit** somewhat. **bit by bit** gradually. **a bit of a ——** **1** used to suggest that something is not severe or extreme: *a bit of an accident.* **2** denoting a young person or one of slight build: *you're just a bit of a girl yourself.* **a bit of all right** Brit. informal an attractive or pleasing person or thing. **bit of fluff** (or **skirt** or **stuff**) Brit. informal a woman regarded in sexual terms. **bit on the side** informal **1** a person with whom one is unfaithful to one's partner. **2** money earned outside one's normal job. **do one's bit** informal make a useful contribution. **to bits 1** into pieces. **2** informal very much; to a great degree.
– ORIGIN OE *bita* 'bite, mouthful', of Gmc origin.

**bit**[2] past of **BITE**.

**bit**[3] ● **n. 1** a metal mouthpiece attached to a bridle, used to control a horse. **2** a tool or piece for boring or drilling. ➤ the cutting or gripping part of a plane, pincers, or other tool. ➤ the part of a key that engages with the lock lever. ➤ the copper head of a soldering iron. ● **v.** put a bit into the mouth of (a horse).
– PHRASES **above** (or **behind**) **the bit** (of a horse) carrying its head too high (or with the chin tucked in) so that it evades correct contact with the bit. **get** (or **take** or **have**) **the bit between** (or N. Amer. **in**) **one's teeth** begin to tackle a problem or task in a determined way. **off the bit** (or **bridle**) (of a horse) ridden on a loose rein to allow it to gallop freely. **on the bit** (or **bridle**) (of a horse) ridden with (and calmly accepting) a light but firm contact on the mouth.
– DERIVATIVES **-bitted** adj.
– ORIGIN OE *bite* 'biting, a bite', of Gmc origin.

**bit**[4] ● **n.** Computing a unit of information expressed as either a 0 or 1 in binary notation.
– ORIGIN 1940s: blend of **BINARY** and **DIGIT**.

**bitch** ● **n. 1** a female dog, wolf, fox, or otter. **2** informal a woman whom one dislikes or considers to be malicious or unpleasant. ➤ black English a woman (used in a non-derogatory sense). **3** (**a bitch**) informal a difficult or unpleasant thing or situation. ● **v.** informal make malicious or spitefully critical comments.
– ORIGIN OE *bicce*, of Gmc origin.

**bitchery** ● **n.** informal malicious or spiteful behaviour.

**bitching** (also **bitchen**) ● **adj.** informal, chiefly US excellent. ● **adv.** extremely.

**bitchy** ● **adj.** (**-ier**, **-iest**) informal malicious or spitefully critical.
– DERIVATIVES **bitchily** adv. **bitchiness** n.

**bite** ● **v.** (past **bit**; past part. **bitten**) **1** (of a person or animal) use the teeth to cut into something. ➤ (of a snake, insect, or spider) wound with a sting, pincers, or fangs. **2** (**bite something back**) refrain with difficulty from saying something. **3** (of a tool, tyre, boot, etc.) grip or take hold on a surface. ➤ (of an object) press into a part of the body, causing pain. **4** (of an acid) corrode a surface. **5** (of a fish) take the bait or lure on the end of a fishing line into the mouth. **6** (of a policy or situation) take effect, with unpleasant consequences: *the cuts in art education were starting to bite.* ➤ informal annoy or worry: *what's biting you today?* ● **n. 1** an act or instance of biting. ➤ a piece cut off by biting. ➤ Dentistry the bringing together of the teeth in occlusion. **2** informal a quick snack. **3** a sensation of sharpness or pungency. ➤ a feeling of cold in the air or wind.
– PHRASES **be bitten by the —— bug** develop a passionate interest in a specified activity. **bite the big one** N. Amer. informal die. **bite the bullet** decide to do something difficult or unpleasant that one has been hesitating over. [from the old custom of giving wounded soldiers a bullet to bite on when undergoing surgery without anaesthetic.] **bite the dust** informal die or be killed. **bite the hand that feeds one** deliberately hurt or offend a benefactor. **bite off more than one can chew** take on a commitment one cannot fulfil. **the biter bitten** (or **bit**) indicating that someone is being treated in the same way as they have treated others. **bite one's tongue** make a desperate effort to avoid saying something. **once bitten, twice shy** an unpleasant experience induces caution. **one could have bitten one's tongue off** one profoundly regrets having said something. **put the bite on** N. Amer. & Austral./NZ informal borrow or extort money from. [1930s (orig. US): *bite*, from the sl. sense 'deception'.]
– DERIVATIVES **biter** n.
– ORIGIN OE *bītan*, of Gmc origin.

**biternate** /bʌɪˈtəːneɪt/ ● **adj.** Botany (especially of a ternate leaf) having leaflets or other parts that are further subdivided in a ternate arrangement.

**biting** ● **adj. 1** (of wind or air) painfully cold. **2** (of wit or criticism) harsh or cruel.
– DERIVATIVES **bitingly** adv.

**bitmap** Computing ● **n.** a representation in which each item corresponds to one or more bits of information, especially the information used to control the display of a computer screen. ● **v.** (**-mapped**, **-mapping**) represent as a bitmap.

**bitonal** /bʌɪˈtəʊn(ə)l/ ● **adj.** (of music) having parts in two different keys sounding together.
– DERIVATIVES **bitonality** n.

**bit part** ● **n.** a small acting role in a play or a film.

**bit rate** ● **n.** Electronics the number of bits per second that can be transmitted along a digital network.

**bitstream** /ˈbɪtstriːm/ ● **n.** Electronics a stream of data in binary form.

**bitt** ● **n.** one of a pair of posts on the deck of a ship for fastening mooring lines or cables.
– ORIGIN ME: prob. of Low Ger. origin.

**bitten** past participle of **BITE**.

**bitter** ● **adj. 1** having a sharp, pungent taste or smell; not sweet. **2** causing pain or unhappiness. ➤ feeling or showing angry hurt or resentment. ➤ (of a conflict) harsh and acrimonious. **3** (of wind or weather) intensely cold. ● **n. 1** Brit. beer that is strongly flavoured with hops and has a bitter taste. **2** (**bitters**) [treated as sing.] liquor that is flavoured with bitter plant extracts and used as an additive in cocktails.
– PHRASES **to the bitter end** to the very end, in spite of harsh difficulties.
– DERIVATIVES **bitterly** adv. **bitterness** n.
– ORIGIN OE *biter*, of Gmc origin.

**bitter apple** ● **n.** another term for **COLOCYNTH**.

**bittercress** ● **n.** a plant with small white flowers, which grows as a weed in damp soils. [Genus *Cardamine*: several species.]

**bitter lemon** ● **n.** Brit. a carbonated semi-sweet soft drink flavoured with lemons.

**bitterling** ● **n.** a small brightly coloured freshwater fish of central Europe, whose eggs develop inside mussels. [*Rhodeus amarus*.]
– ORIGIN C19: from Ger. *Bitterling*, from *bitter* 'bitter' (translating L. *amarus*) + **-LING**.

**bittern**[1] /ˈbɪtən/ ● **n.** a marshbird of the heron family with brown streaked plumage, noted for the male's deep booming call. [*Botaurus stellaris* (Eurasia), *B. lentiginosus* (N. America), and other species.]
– ORIGIN ME *bitore*, from OFr. *butor*, based on L. *butio* 'bittern' + *taurus* 'bull' (because of its call).

**bittern**[2] /ˈbɪt(ə)n/ (also **bitterns**) ● **n.** a concentrated solution of various salts remaining after the crystallization of salt from seawater.
– ORIGIN C17: prob. from **BITTER**.

**bitter orange** ● **n.** another term for **SEVILLE ORANGE**.

**bitter pit** • **n.** a disease of apples caused by calcium deficiency, characterized by sunken brown spots.

**bittersweet** • **adj. 1** sweet with a bitter aftertaste. **2** arousing pleasure tinged with sadness or pain. • **n. 1** another term for **WOODY NIGHTSHADE**. **2** a vine-like American climbing plant bearing clusters of bright orange pods. [*Celastrus scandens* and other species.]

**bitty** • **adj.** (**-ier**, **-iest**) informal **1** chiefly Brit. made up of small parts that seem unrelated. **2** [in combination] N. Amer. tiny: *a little-bitty girl.*
– DERIVATIVES **bittily** adv. **bittiness** n.

**Bitumastic** /ˌbɪtjʊˈmastɪk/ • **n.** trademark an asphaltic composition used as a protective coating.
– ORIGIN C19: blend of **BITUMEN** and **MASTIC**.

**bitumen** /ˈbɪtjʊmən/ • **n.** a black viscous mixture of hydrocarbons obtained naturally or as a residue from petroleum distillation, used for road surfacing and roofing.
– DERIVATIVES **bituminous** adj.
– ORIGIN ME (denoting naturally occurring asphalt used as mortar): from L.

**bituminize** /bɪˈtjuːmɪnʌɪz/ (also **-ise**) • **v.** convert into or treat with bitumen.
– DERIVATIVES **bituminization** n.

**bituminous coal** • **n.** black coal having a relatively high volatile content and burning with a characteristically bright smoky flame.

**bitwise** • **adj.** Computing denoting an operator in a programming language which manipulates the individual bits in a byte or word.

**bitzer** /ˈbɪtsə/ • **n.** Austral./NZ informal **1** a contraption made from previously unrelated parts. **2** a mongrel dog.
– ORIGIN 1920s: abbrev. of the phr. *bits and pieces*.

**bivalence** /bʌɪˈveɪl(ə)ns/ • **n.** Logic the existence of only two states or truth values (e.g. true and false).

**bivalent** • **adj. 1** /ˈbɪv(ə)l(ə)nt/ Biology (of homologous chromosomes) associated in pairs. **2** /bʌɪˈveɪl(ə)nt/ Chemistry another term for **DIVALENT**. • **n.** /ˈbɪv(ə)l(ə)nt/ Biology a pair of homologous chromosomes.
– ORIGIN C19: from **BI-** + L. *valent-*, *valere* 'be strong'.

**bivalve** • **n.** an aquatic mollusc which has a compressed body enclosed within two hinged shells, such as an oyster, mussel, or scallop. [Class Bivalvia.] • **adj. 1** (also **bivalved**) (of a mollusc or other aquatic invertebrate) having a hinged double shell. **2** Botany (of a fruit) having two valves.

**bivariate** /bʌɪˈvɛːrɪət/ • **adj.** Statistics involving or depending on two variates.

**bivouac** /ˈbɪvʊak, ˈbɪvwak/ • **n.** a temporary camp without tents or cover. • **v.** (**bivouacked**, **bivouacking**) stay in such a camp.
– ORIGIN C18: from Fr., prob. from Swiss Ger. *Bîwacht* 'additional guard at night'.

**bivvy** informal • **n.** (pl. **-ies**) a small tent or temporary shelter. • **v.** (**-ies**, **-ied**) use such a tent or shelter.
– ORIGIN C20: abbrev. of **BIVOUAC**.

**biweekly** • **adj. & adv.** appearing or taking place every two weeks or twice a week. • **n.** (pl. **-ies**) a periodical that appears biweekly.

**bi-wiring** • **n.** the use of two wires between an amplifier and a loudspeaker to operate the low- and high-frequency speaker circuits separately.

**biyearly** • **adj. & adv.** appearing or taking place every two years or twice a year.

**biz** • **n.** informal short for **BUSINESS**.
– ORIGIN C19 (orig. US): abbrev.

**bizarre** /bɪˈzɑː/ • **adj.** strange; unusual.
– DERIVATIVES **bizarrely** adv. **bizarreness** n.
– ORIGIN C17: from Fr., from Ital. *bizzarro* 'angry', of unknown origin.

**bizarrerie** /bɪˈzɑːrəri/ • **n.** (pl. **-ies**) a strange and unusual thing or event.
– ORIGIN C18: from Fr., from **BIZARRE**.

**bizzy** • **n.** (pl. **-ies**) variant spelling of **BUSY**.

**Bk** • **symb.** the chemical element berkelium.

**bk** • **abbrev.** book.

**BL** • **abbrev. 1** (in Scotland and Ireland) Bachelor of Law. **2** bill of lading. **3** British Library.

**blab** informal • **v.** (**blabbed**, **blabbing**) reveal secrets by indiscreet talk. • **n.** a person who blabs.
– ORIGIN ME: prob. of Gmc origin; ult. imitative.

**blabber** informal • **v.** talk indiscreetly or excessively. • **n.** a person who blabbers. ➤ indiscreet or excessive talk.

**blabbermouth** • **n.** informal a person who talks excessively or indiscreetly.

**black** • **adj. 1** of the very darkest colour due to the absence of or complete absorption of light. ➤ deeply stained with dirt. ➤ (of coffee or tea) served without milk. **2** of or relating to a human group having dark-coloured skin, especially of African or Australian Aboriginal ancestry. **3** characterized by tragedy, disaster, or despair. ➤ (of humour) presenting tragic or harrowing situations in comic terms. ➤ full of anger or hatred. **4** Brit. dated (of goods or work) not to be handled or undertaken by trade union members, as an expression of solidarity with an industrial dispute elsewhere. **5** (of a ski run) of the highest level of difficulty. **6** of or denoting the suits spades and clubs in a pack of cards. • **n. 1** black colour or pigment. ➤ black clothes or material, worn as a sign of mourning. **2** a member of a dark-skinned people, especially one of African or Australian Aboriginal ancestry. **3** (**Black**) the player of the black pieces in chess or draughts. **4** Brit. informal blackcurrant cordial. • **v. 1** make black, especially by the application of black polish, make-up, etc. **2** (**black something out**) make a room or building dark by extinguishing lights, covering windows, etc. ➤ obscure something completely. ➤ (of a television screen) go blank. **3** (**black out**) (of a person) undergo a sudden and temporary loss of consciousness. **4** Brit. dated refuse to deal with (goods or people) or undertake (work), as a form of industrial action. **5** (of a television company) decide not to broadcast a controversial programme.
– PHRASES **black someone's eye** hit someone in the eye so as to cause bruising. **in the black** not owing any money. **in someone's black books** informal in disfavour with someone. **look on the black side** informal view a situation from a pessimistic angle.
– DERIVATIVES **blackish** adj. **blackly** adv. **blackness** n.
– ORIGIN OE *blæc*, of Gmc origin.

**blackamoor** /ˈblakəmɔː, -mʊə/ • **n.** archaic a black African or a very dark-skinned person.
– ORIGIN C16: from **BLACK** + **MOOR**.

**black and tan** • **n. 1** a terrier of a breed with a black back and tan markings on face, flanks, and legs. **2** Brit. a drink composed of stout and bitter. **3** (**Black and Tans**) an armed force recruited by the British government to fight Sinn Fein in Ireland in 1921. [so named because of the khaki and black colours of their uniform.]

**black and white** • **adj. 1** consisting of or displaying images in black, white, and shades of grey rather than in colour. **2** (of a situation or debate) involving clearly defined opposing principles or issues. • **n.** US informal a police car.

**black art** • **n. 1** (also **black arts**) another term for **BLACK MAGIC**. **2** a technique or practice considered mysterious and sinister.

**blackball** • **v.** reject or vote against (a candidate applying to become a member of a private club).
– ORIGIN C18: from the practice of registering an adverse vote by placing a black ball in a ballot box.

**black bass** • **n.** a North American freshwater sporting and food fish of the sunfish family. [Genus *Micropterus*: several species.]

**black bean** • **n. 1** a cultivated variety of soy bean, used fermented in oriental cooking. **2** a Mexican variety of the French bean. **3** a leguminous Australian liana with blackish flowers. [*Kennedia nigricans*.]

**black bear** • **n.** a medium-sized forest-dwelling bear with blackish fur and a paler face. [*Ursus americanus* (America) and *Selenarctos thibetanus* (E. Asia).]

**black beetle** • **n.** Brit. informal the common cockroach.

**black belt** • **n.** a black belt worn by an expert in judo, karate, and other martial arts.

**blackberry** • **n.** (pl. **-ies**) **1** an edible soft fruit consisting of a cluster of soft purple-black drupels. **2** the prickly climbing shrub of the rose family which bears this fruit.

[*Rubus fruticosus.*] ● **v.** (**-ies**, **-ied**) [usu. as noun **blackberrying**] gather blackberries.

**black bile** ● **n.** (in medieval science and medicine) one of the four bodily humours, believed to be associated with a melancholy temperament.
– ORIGIN C18: translation of Gk *melankholia* (see **MELANCHOLY**).

**black bindweed** ● **n.** a twining weed related to the docks, with heart-shaped leaves and small white flowers. [*Fallopia convolvulus.*]

**blackbird** ● **n. 1** a thrush of which the male has all-black plumage and a yellow bill, and the female is brown. [*Turdus merula.*] **2** an American songbird with largely black plumage. [*Agelaius phoeniceus* (**red-winged blackbird**) and other species, family Icteridae.] **3** historical a black or Polynesian captive on a slave ship.

**blackboard** ● **n.** a large board with a smooth dark surface for writing on with chalk.

**black body** ● **n.** Physics a hypothetical perfect absorber and radiator of energy, with no reflecting power.

**black bottom** ● **n.** a popular American dance of the 1920s.

**black box** ● **n.** a flight recorder in an aircraft.

**blackboy** ● **n.** an Australian tree or erect shrub with long, stiff grass-like leaves. [Genus *Xanthorrhoea*: several species.]

**black bread** ● **n.** a coarse dark-coloured type of rye bread.

**blackbuck** ● **n.** a small Indian gazelle, the horned male of which has a black back and white underbelly, the female being hornless. [*Antilope cervicapra.*]

**black bulgar** ● **n.** a cup-shaped stemless black fungus which grows on the fallen trunks and branches of broad-leaved trees. [*Bulgaria inquinans.*]

**black bun** ● **n.** rich fruit cake in a pastry case, traditionally eaten in Scotland at New Year.

**blackbutt** ● **n.** a tall straight-trunked Australian eucalyptus tree, typically with fire-charred fibrous bark on the lower trunk and with pale brown wood. [*Eucalyptus pilularis.*]
– ORIGIN C19: from **BLACK** + **BUTT**[3] in the sense 'tree trunk'.

**blackcap** ● **n. 1** a warbler with a black cap in the male and a reddish-brown one in the female. [*Sylvia atricapilla.*] **2** N. Amer. the black-capped chickadee. [*Parus atricapillus.*]

**blackcock** ● **n.** (pl. same) the male of the black grouse.

**black consciousness** ● **n.** a political movement and ideology seeking to unite black people in affirming their common identity.

**blackcurrant** ● **n. 1** a small round edible black berry which grows in loose hanging clusters. **2** the widely cultivated shrub which bears this fruit. [*Ribes nigrum.*]

**black diamond** ● **n. 1** informal a lump of coal. **2** a dark, opaque form of diamond. **3** N. Amer. a difficult ski slope.

**black dog** ● **n.** informal melancholy or depression represented metaphorically: *I'm happier, but the black dog is still there.*
– ORIGIN C19: from a name used during Queen Anne's reign for a base silver coin.

**black durgon** /'də:g(ə)n/ ● **n.** a black triggerfish that occurs in tropical seas. [*Melichthys niger.*]
– ORIGIN C20: *durgon* perh. from Engl. dial. *durgan* or *durgen* 'undersized person or animal'.

**black economy** ● **n.** the part of a country's economic activity which is not recorded or taxed by its government.

**blacken** ● **v. 1** become or make black or dark. **2** damage or destroy (someone's reputation).

**black eye** ● **n.** an area of bruised skin around the eye resulting from a blow.

**black-eyed bean** (also **black-eye bean**, US **black-eyed pea**) ● **n. 1** a creamy-white edible bean with a black mark at the point where it was attached to the pod. **2** the plant which produces these beans. [*Vigna sinensis.*]

**black-eyed Susan** ● **n. 1** a slender tropical climbing plant having flowers with yellowish petals and a dark centre. [*Thunbergia alata.*] **2** a type of cultivated rudbeckia. [*Rudbeckia hirta.*]

**blackface** ● **n. 1** a sheep of a breed with a black face. **2** the make-up used by a non-black performer playing a black role.

**black-figure** ● **n.** a type of ancient Greek pottery in which figures are painted in black, details being added by incising through to the red clay background. Compare with **RED-FIGURE**.

**blackfish** ● **n.** (pl. same or **-fishes**) **1** a large, dark open-ocean fish related to the perches. [*Centrolophus niger.*] **2** a salmon just after spawning. **3** any of various other dark-coloured fish. **4** another term for **PILOT WHALE**.

**black flag** ● **n. 1** historical a pirate's ensign, featuring a white skull and crossbones on a black background. **2** historical a black flag hoisted outside a prison to announce an execution. **3** Motor Racing a black flag used to signal to a driver that he must stop at the pits as a punishment for a misdemeanour.

**blackfly** ● **n.** (pl. same or **-flies**) **1** a black or dark green aphid which is a common pest of crops and gardens. [*Aphis fabae* and other species.] **2** a small black blood-sucking fly which can transmit a number of serious diseases. [*Simulium* and other genera.]

**Blackfoot** ● **n.** (pl. same or **Blackfeet**) **1** a member of a confederacy of North American Indian peoples of the north-western plains consisting of three closely related tribes: the Blackfoot proper or Siksika, the Bloods, and the Peigan. **2** the Algonquian language of this people.

**Black Forest gateau** (N. Amer. **Black Forest cake**) ● **n.** a chocolate sponge layered with cherries and cream and topped with chocolate icing.

**Black Friar** ● **n.** a friar of the Dominican order (who wear black habits).

**black frost** ● **n.** frost which does not have a white surface.

**black game** ● **n.** [treated as pl.] black grouse regarded collectively.

**black grouse** ● **n.** (pl. same) a large grouse of which the male has glossy blue-black plumage and a lyre-shaped tail. [*Tetrao tetrix.*]

**blackguard** /'blaga:d, -gəd/ dated ● **n.** a man who behaves in a dishonourable or contemptible way. ● **v.** disparage or denounce.
– DERIVATIVES **blackguardly** adj.
– ORIGIN C16 (orig. denoting a body of servants): from **BLACK** + **GUARD**.

**black guillemot** ● **n.** a seabird of the auk family with black summer plumage and large white wing patches, breeding on the coasts of the Arctic and North Atlantic. [*Cepphus grylle.*]

**blackhead** ● **n. 1** a plug of sebum in a hair follicle, darkened by oxidation. **2** an infectious disease of turkeys producing discoloration of the head, caused by a protozoon.

**black hole** ● **n.** Astronomy a region of space having a gravitational field so intense that no matter or radiation can escape.

**black house** ● **n.** a traditional single-storeyed Scottish house built of turf or unmortared stone and roofed with turf or thatch, examples of which survive mainly in the Outer Hebrides.

**black ice** ● **n.** a transparent coating of ice on a road surface.

**blacking** ● **n.** black paste or polish, especially that used on shoes.

**blackjack** ● **n. 1** chiefly N. Amer. a gambling card game in which players try to acquire cards with a face value totalling 21 and no more. **2** a weed related to the bur-marigold, with barbed black seeds. [*Bidens pilosa.*] **3** N. Amer. a flexible lead-filled truncheon. **4** historical a pirates' black flag. **5** historical a tarred-leather container used for alcoholic liquor.

**Black Jew** ● **n.** another term for **FALASHA**.

**black kite** ● **n.** a bird of prey with dark plumage and a slightly forked tail, feeding mainly by scavenging. [*Milvus migrans.*]

**blacklead** • n. another term for **GRAPHITE**. • v. polish (metal, especially cast iron) with graphite.

**blackleg** • n. **1** Brit. derogatory a person who continues working when fellow workers are on strike. **2** a bacterial disease of cattle and sheep, causing necrosis in the leg. **3** a plant disease in which part of the stem blackens and decays. • v. (**-legged**, **-legging**) Brit. derogatory continue working when one's fellow workers are on strike.

**black letter** • n. an ornate early bold style of type.

**black light** • n. ultraviolet or infrared radiation, invisible to the eye.

**blacklist** • n. a list of people or groups regarded as unacceptable or untrustworthy. • v. put on a blacklist.

**black lung** • n. chiefly N. Amer. pneumoconiosis caused by inhalation of coal dust.

**black magic** • n. magic involving the supposed invocation of evil spirits for evil purposes.

**blackmail** • n. the action of demanding money from someone in return for not revealing discreditable information. ➤ the use of threats or unfair manipulation in an attempt to influence someone's actions. • v. subject to blackmail.
– DERIVATIVES **blackmailer** n.
– ORIGIN C16 (denoting protection money levied by Sc. chiefs): from **BLACK** + obs. *mail* 'tribute, rent', from ON *mál* 'speech, agreement'.

**Black Maria** • n. **1** informal a police vehicle for transporting prisoners. **2** a card game in which players try to avoid winning tricks containing the queen of spades or any hearts. ➤ a name for the queen of spades in this game.
– ORIGIN C19 (orig. US): said to be named after a black woman, *Maria* Lee, who kept a boarding house in Boston and helped police in escorting drunk and disorderly customers to jail.

**black mark** • n. informal a note or record of a person's misdemeanour or discreditable action.

**black market** • n. an illegal trade in officially controlled or scarce commodities.
– DERIVATIVES **black marketeer** n.

**black mass** • n. a travesty of the Roman Catholic Mass in worship of the Devil.

**black money** • n. income illegally obtained or not declared for tax purposes.

**Black Monk** • n. a member of the Benedictines (who wear black habits).

**black Muslim** • n. a member of the Nation of Islam, a black Islamic sect advocating a separate black nation.

**black nationalism** • n. the advocacy of the national civil rights of black people, especially in the US.

**blackout** • n. **1** a period when all lights must be turned out or covered to prevent them being seen by the enemy during an air raid. ➤ (**blackouts**) dark curtains put up in windows during an air raid. ➤ a sudden failure or dimming of electric lights. **2** a temporary loss of consciousness. **3** an official suppression of information: *a total news blackout.*

**Black Panther** • n. a member of a US Black Power organization.

**black powder** • n. gunpowder.

**Black Power** • n. a movement in support of rights and political power for black people.

**black pudding** • n. Brit. a black sausage containing pork, dried pig's blood, and suet.

**Black Rod** (in full **Gentleman Usher of the Black Rod**) • n. (in the UK) the chief usher of the Lord Chamberlain's department of the royal household, who is also usher to the House of Lords.

**black rot** • n. a fungal or bacterial disease of plants producing blackening, shrivelling, and rotting.

**black salsify** • n. another term for **SCORZONERA**.

**black sheep** • n. informal a member of a family or group who is regarded as a disgrace to it.

**blackshirt** • n. a member of a Fascist organization, in particular of an Italian paramilitary group before and during the Second World War.

**blacksmith** • n. a person who makes and repairs things in iron by hand. ➤ a farrier.

**black smoker** • n. Geology a geothermal vent on the seabed which ejects superheated water containing black sulphide minerals.

**black spot** • n. **1** Brit. a place marked by a particular trouble: *an accident black spot.* **2** a fungal or bacterial disease of plants, producing black blotches on the leaves.

**black stump** • n. Austral. informal a notional place regarded as the last outpost of civilization.

**black swan** • n. **1** a mainly black swan native to Australia and introduced widely elsewhere. [*Cygnus atratus.*] **2** archaic something extremely rare.

**black-tailed deer** • n. another term for **MULE DEER**.

**black tea** • n. tea of the most usual type, that is fully fermented before drying. Compare with **GREEN TEA**.

**blackthorn** • n. a thorny shrub which bears white flowers before the leaves appear, followed by astringent blue-black fruits (sloes). [*Prunus spinosa.*]

**blackthorn winter** • n. Brit. a spell of cold weather at the time in early spring when the blackthorn flowers.

**black tie** • n. men's formal evening wear.

**blacktop** • n. chiefly N. Amer. asphalt, tarmacadam, or other black material used for surfacing roads.

**black tracker** • n. Austral. an Aboriginal employed to help find people lost or hiding in the bush.

**black velvet** • n. a drink consisting of a mixture of stout and champagne.

**black water** • n. technical waste water and sewage from toilets. Compare with **GREY WATER**.

**blackwater fever** • n. a severe form of malaria in which blood cells are rapidly destroyed, resulting in dark urine.

**black widow** • n. a highly venomous American spider having a black body with red markings. [*Latrodectus mactans.*]

**blackwood** • n. a tropical hardwood tree which produces high-quality dark wood. [*Dalbergia melanoxylon* (Africa) and other species.]

**blackwork** • n. a type of embroidery done in black thread on white cloth, popular in Tudor times.

**bladder** • n. **1** a muscular membranous sac in the abdomen which receives urine from the kidneys and stores it for excretion. **2** an inflated or hollow flexible bag or chamber.
– ORIGIN OE *blǣdre*, of Gmc origin, rel. to **BLOW**[1].

**bladder campion** • n. a white-flowered campion with a swollen bladder-like calyx behind the deeply cut petals. [*Silene vulgaris.*]

**bladdered** • adj. Brit. informal extremely drunk.

**bladder fern** • n. a small, delicate fern with rounded spore cases, growing on rocks and walls. [Genus *Cystopteris*: several species.]

**bladder nut** • n. a shrub or small tree of northern temperate regions, which bears white flowers and inflated seed capsules. [Genus *Staphylea*: several species.]

**bladder senna** • n. a Mediterranean shrub of the pea family, which bears yellow flowers followed by inflated reddish pods. [*Colutea arborescens.*]

**bladderwort** /ˈbladəwəːt/ • n. an aquatic plant with small air-filled bladders which keep the plant afloat and trap tiny animals to provide nutrients. [Genus *Utricularia.*]

**bladderwrack** • n. a common brown shoreline seaweed with tough strap-like fronds containing air bladders that give buoyancy. [*Fucus vesiculosus.*]

**blade** • n. **1** the flat cutting edge of a knife or other tool or weapon. **2** the broad flat part of an oar, leaf, or other object. **3** a long narrow leaf of grass. **4** informal, dated a dashing or energetic young man. **5** a shoulder bone in a joint of meat, or the joint itself.
– DERIVATIVES **bladed** adj.
– ORIGIN OE *blæd*, of Gmc origin.

**blaeberry** /ˈbleɪb(ə)ri, -bɛri/ • n. (pl. **-ies**) Scottish and northern English term for **BILBERRY**.
– ORIGIN ME: from dial. *blae* 'blackish-blue'.

**blag** Brit. informal • n. **1** a violent robbery or raid. **2** an act of

using clever talk or lying to obtain something. ● v. (**blagged**, **blagging**) **1** steal in a violent robbery or raid. **2** obtain by clever talk or lying.
– DERIVATIVES **blagger** n.
– ORIGIN C19: perh. from Fr. *blaguer* 'tell lies'.

**blague** /blɑːg/ ● n. a joke or piece of nonsense.
– ORIGIN from Fr.

**blagueur** /bla'gəː, French blagøʀ/ ● n. a person who talks nonsense.
– ORIGIN from Fr.

**blah** informal ● used to substitute for actual words where they are felt to be too tedious or lengthy to give in full. ● n. (**the blahs**) N. Amer. depression.

**blain** /bleɪn/ ● n. rare an inflamed swelling or sore on the skin.
– ORIGIN OE *blegen*, of W. Gmc origin.

**Blairism** ● n. the policies of the British Labour statesman Tony Blair.
– DERIVATIVES **Blairite** n. & adj.

**Blakey** ● n. (pl. **-eys**) Brit. a protective metal plate fitted to the sole of a shoe or boot.
– ORIGIN C19: named after the manufacturers.

**blame** ● v. assign responsibility for a fault or wrong to. ● n. responsibility for a fault or wrong.
– PHRASES **be to blame** be responsible for a fault or wrong.
– DERIVATIVES **blameable** (US also **blamable**) adj. **blameful** adj. **blameless** adj. **blamelessly** adv. **blamelessness** n. **blameworthiness** n. **blameworthy** adj.
– ORIGIN ME: from OFr. *blamer*, *blasmer*, from pop. L. var. of eccles. L. *blasphemare*, from Gk *blasphēmein* (see **BLASPHEME**).

**blanch** /blɑːn(t)ʃ/ ● v. **1** make or become white or pale. **2** prepare (vegetables) for freezing or further cooking by immersing briefly in boiling water. ➤[often as adj. **blanched**] peel (almonds) by scalding them.
– ORIGIN ME: from OFr. *blanchir*, from *blanc* 'white', ult. of Gmc origin.

**blancmange** /blə'mɒnʒ, -'mɑːnʒ/ ● n. a sweet opaque gelatinous dessert made with flavoured cornflour and milk.
– ORIGIN ME *blancmanger*: from OFr. *blanc mangier*, from *blanc* 'white' + *mangier* 'eat'.

**blanco** /'blaŋkəʊ/ ● n. Brit. a white substance used for whitening belts and other items of military equipment. ● v. (**-oes**, **-oed**) whiten with blanco.
– ORIGIN C19: from Fr. *blanc* 'white', ult. of Gmc origin.

**bland** ● adj. lacking strong features or characteristics and therefore uninteresting. ➤(of food or drink) lacking flavour or seasoning; insipid.
– DERIVATIVES **blandly** adv. **blandness** n.
– ORIGIN ME (in the sense 'gentle in manner'): from L. *blandus* 'soft, smooth'.

**blandish** /'blandɪʃ/ ● v. archaic coax with kind words or flattery.
– ORIGIN ME: from OFr. *blandiss-*, *blandir*, from L. *blandiri*, from *blandus* 'soft, smooth'.

**blandishments** ● pl. n. flattery intended to persuade or cajole.

**blank** ● adj. **1** not marked or decorated; bare, empty, or plain. **2** not comprehending or reacting. **3** complete; absolute: *a blank refusal to discuss the issue.* **4** used euphemistically in place of an adjective regarded as obscene. ● n. **1** a space left to be filled in a document. **2** (also **blank cartridge**) a cartridge containing gunpowder but no bullet. **3** an empty space or period of time: *my mind was a total blank.* **4** an object with no mark or design on it, in particular a roughly cut disc or block intended for stamping or finishing. **5** a dash written instead of a word or letter, especially to avoid spelling out an obscene word. ● v. **1** cause to appear blank or empty. **2** N. Amer. defeat without allowing the opponent to score. **3** Brit. informal deliberately ignore (someone). **4** cut (a metal blank).
– PHRASES **draw a blank** elicit no successful response.
– DERIVATIVES **blankly** adv. **blankness** n.
– ORIGIN ME (in the sense 'white, colourless'): from OFr. *blanc* 'white', ult. of Gmc origin.

**blank cheque** ● n. **1** a cheque with the amount left for the payee to fill in. **2** an unlimited freedom of action.

**blanket** ● n. **1** a large piece of woollen material used as a covering for warmth, as on a bed. **2** a thick mass or layer of a specified material: *a blanket of cloud.* **3** Printing a rubber surface used for transferring the image in ink from the plate to the paper in offset printing. ● adj. covering all cases or instances; total: *a blanket ban on tobacco advertising.* ● v. (**blanketed**, **blanketing**) **1** cover completely with a thick layer. **2** Sailing take wind from the sails of (another craft) by passing to windward.
– PHRASES **born on the wrong side of the blanket** dated illegitimate.
– DERIVATIVES **blanketing** n.
– ORIGIN ME: via ONorth. Fr. from OFr. *blanc* 'white', ult. of Gmc origin.

**blanket bath** ● n. Brit. an all-over wash given to a person confined to bed.

**blanket bog** ● n. an extensive flat peat bog formed in cool regions of high rainfall or humidity.

**blanket finish** ● n. a very close finish in a race.

**blanket roll** ● n. N. Amer. a soldier's blanket and kit made into a roll for use on active service.

**blanket stitch** ● n. a buttonhole stitch used on the edges of a blanket or other material too thick to be hemmed.

**blanket weed** ● n. a common green freshwater alga forming mats of long filaments. [Genus *Spirogyra*.]

**blankety** (also **blankety-blank**) ● adj. & n. informal used euphemistically to replace a word considered obscene or taboo.

**blanking plate** ● n. a plate that covers an opening to protect it from moisture or dust.

**blank verse** ● n. verse without rhyme, especially that which uses iambic pentameters.

**blanquette** /blɒ̃'kɛt/ ● n. a dish consisting of white meat in a white sauce.
– ORIGIN Fr., based on *blanc* 'white'.

**blare** ● v. sound loudly and harshly. ● n. a loud, harsh sound.
– ORIGIN ME (in the sense 'roar, bellow'): from MDu. *blaren*, *bleren*, or Low Ger. *blaren*, of imitative origin.

**blarney** ● n. talk intended to be charming or flattering (often considered especially typical of Irish people).
– ORIGIN C18: named after *Blarney* Castle in Ireland, where there is a stone said to give the gift of persuasive speech to anyone who kisses it.

**blasé** /'blɑːzeɪ/ ● adj. unimpressed with or indifferent to something because of over-familiarity.
– ORIGIN C19: Fr., past part. of *blaser* 'cloy', prob. ult. of Gmc origin.

**blaspheme** /blas'fiːm/ ● v. speak irreverently about God or sacred things.
– DERIVATIVES **blasphemer** n.
– ORIGIN ME: via OFr. from eccles. L. *blasphemare* 'reproach, revile, blaspheme', from Gk *blasphēmein*, from *blasphēmos* 'evil-speaking'; cf. **BLAME**.

**blasphemy** ● n. (pl. **-ies**) profane or sacrilegious talk about God or sacred things.
– DERIVATIVES **blasphemous** adj. **blasphemously** adv.

**blast** /blɑːst/ ● n. **1** a destructive wave of highly compressed air spreading outwards from an explosion. **2** a strong gust of wind or air. ➤a strong current of air used in smelting. **3** a single loud note of a horn or whistle. **4** informal a severe reprimand. **5** N. Amer. informal an enjoyable experience or lively party. ● v. **1** blow up or break apart with explosives. **2** (**blast off**) (of a rocket or spacecraft) take off from a launching site. **3** produce loud continuous music or noise. **4** informal criticize fiercely. **5** kick or strike (a ball) hard. **6** poetic/literary (of wind) wither or shrivel (a plant). **7** strike with divine anger (used as a curse): *damn and blast this awful place!* ● exclam. Brit. informal expressing annoyance.
– PHRASES (**at**) **full blast** at maximum power or intensity.
– DERIVATIVES **blaster** n.
– ORIGIN OE *blǣst*, of Gmc origin; rel. to **BLAZE**[3].

**-blast** ● comb. form Biology denoting an embryonic cell or tissue: *erythroblast.* Compare with **-CYTE**.

– ORIGIN from Gk *blastos* 'germ, sprout'.

**blasted** ● adj. informal **1** used to express annoyance: *make your own blasted coffee!* **2** drunk.

**blast furnace** ● n. a smelting furnace in the form of a tower into which a blast of hot compressed air can be introduced, especially for smelting iron.

**blasto-** /ˈblastəʊ/ ● comb. form relating to germination: *blastoderm.*

– ORIGIN from Gk *blastos* 'germ, sprout'.

**blastocyst** ● n. Embryology a mammalian blastula in which some differentiation of cells has occurred.

**blastoderm** ● n. Embryology a blastula having the form of a disc of cells on top of the yolk.

**blastomere** /ˈblastə(ʊ)mɪə/ ● n. Embryology a cell formed by cleavage of a fertilized ovum.

**blastomycosis** /ˌblastə(ʊ)mʌɪˈkəʊsɪs/ ● n. Medicine a disease of the skin or internal organs caused by infection with parasitic fungi.

– ORIGIN from mod. L. genus name *Blastomyces.*

**blastula** /ˈblastjʊlə/ ● n. (pl. **blastulae** /-liː/ or US **blastulas**) Embryology an animal embryo at the early stage of development when it is a hollow ball of cells.

– ORIGIN C19: mod. L., from Gk *blastos* 'sprout'.

**blat** informal ● v. (**blatted**, **blatting**) **1** make a bleating sound. **2** travel quickly. ● n. a bleat or similar noise.

**blatant** /ˈbleɪt(ə)nt/ ● adj. open and unashamed; flagrant.

– DERIVATIVES **blatancy** n. **blatantly** adv.

– ORIGIN C16 (first used by Spenser in *blatant beast*, a thousand-tongued monster, then in the sense 'clamorous'): perh. alt. of Scots *blatand* 'bleating'.

**blather** /ˈblaðə/ (also **blither**) ● v. talk at length without making much sense. ● n. rambling talk with no real substance.

– ORIGIN ME (orig. Scots and north. Engl. dial.): from ON *blathra* 'talk nonsense', from *blathr* 'nonsense'.

**blatherskite** /ˈblaðəskʌɪt/ (also **bletherskate**) ● n. chiefly N. Amer. a person who talks at great length without making much sense. ➤foolish talk; nonsense.

– ORIGIN C17: from **BLATHER** + Sc. *skite* 'contemptible person'.

**blatter** ● v. informal move or strike with a clatter.

– ORIGIN C18: orig. Scots.

**blaxploitation** /ˌblaksplɔɪˈteɪʃ(ə)n/ ● n. the exploitation of black people with regard to stereotyped roles in films.

**blaze**[1] ● n. **1** a very large or fiercely burning fire. **2** a very bright light or display of colour. **3** (**blazes**) informal used as a euphemism for 'hell'. ● v. **1** burn or shine fiercely or brightly. **2** shoot repeatedly or indiscriminately.

– PHRASES **like blazes** informal very fast or forcefully.

– DERIVATIVES **blazing** adj. **blazingly** adv.

– ORIGIN OE *blæse* 'torch, bright fire', of Gmc origin.

**blaze**[2] ● n. **1** a white stripe down the face of a horse or other animal. **2** a cut made on a tree to mark a route. ● v. (**blaze a trail**) **1** mark out a path or route. **2** be the first to do something; pioneer.

– ORIGIN C17: ult. of Gmc origin; rel. to **BLAZE**[1], and prob. to **BLEMISH**.

**blaze**[3] ● v. present (news) in a prominent or sensational manner.

– ORIGIN ME (in the sense 'blow out on a trumpet'): from Mid. Low Ger. or MDu. *blāzen* 'to blow'; rel. to **BLOW**[1].

**blazer** ● n. **1** a coloured summer jacket worn by schoolchildren or sports players as part of a uniform. **2** a man's smart jacket not forming part of a suit.

**blazing star** ● n. **1** a North American plant of the daisy family with tall spikes of purple or white flowers. [Genus *Liatris.*] **2** a North American plant of the lily family bearing spikes of white flowers. [*Chamaelirium luteum.*]

**blazon** /ˈbleɪz(ə)n/ ● v. **1** display or report prominently or vividly. **2** Heraldry describe or depict (armorial bearings) in a correct heraldic manner. ● n. Heraldry a correct description of armorial bearings. ➤archaic a coat of arms.

– ORIGIN ME (denoting a shield): from OFr. *blason* 'shield', of unknown origin; verb influenced by **BLAZE**[3].

**blazonry** ● n. Heraldry the art of describing or painting heraldic devices or armorial bearings. ➤devices or bearings of this type.

**bleach** ● v. **1** cause to become white or much lighter by a chemical process or by exposure to sunlight. **2** clean or sterilize with bleach. ● n. a chemical used to bleach things and also to sterilize drains, sinks, etc.

– ORIGIN OE *blǣcan* (v.), *blǣce* (n.), from *blǣc* 'pale', of Gmc origin; rel. to **BLEAK**[1].

**bleacher** ● n. **1** a person or thing that bleaches. **2** N. Amer. a cheap bench seat in an uncovered part of a sports ground.

**bleacherite** ● n. N. Amer. a person sitting in the bleachers.

**bleaching powder** ● n. a powder containing calcium hypochlorite, used to bleach materials.

**bleak**[1] ● adj. **1** bare and exposed to the elements. ➤charmless and inhospitable; dreary. **2** (of a situation) not hopeful or encouraging.

– DERIVATIVES **bleakly** adv. **bleakness** n.

– ORIGIN OE *blāc* 'shining, white', or from ON *bleikr*; ult. of Gmc origin and rel. to **BLEACH**.

**bleak**[2] ● n. a small silvery river fish of the carp family. [*Alburnus alburnus* and other species.]

– ORIGIN C15: from ON *bleikja.*

**blear** archaic ● adj. dim, dull, or filmy. ● v. make dim; blur.

– ORIGIN ME (as v.): prob. rel. to Mid. High Ger. *blerre* 'blurred vision' and Low Ger. *blarroged* 'bleary-eyed'.

**bleary** ● adj. (-ier, -iest) (of the eyes) dull and unfocused from sleep or tiredness.

– DERIVATIVES **blearily** adv. **bleariness** n.

**bleat** ● v. **1** (of a sheep or goat) make a characteristic weak, wavering cry. **2** speak or complain in a weak or foolish way. ● n. **1** the weak, wavering cry of a sheep or goat. **2** a person's weak or foolish cry or complaint.

– DERIVATIVES **bleater** n.

– ORIGIN OE *blǣtan*, of imitative origin.

**bleb** ● n. **1** a small blister on the skin. ➤Biology a rounded outgrowth on the surface of a cell. **2** a small bubble in glass or in a fluid.

– ORIGIN C17: var. of **BLOB**.

**bleed** ● v. (past and past part. **bled**) **1** lose blood from the body as a result of injury or illness. **2** draw blood from (someone) as a former method of medical treatment. **3** (often in phr. **bleed someone dry**) informal drain of money or resources. **4** (of dye or colour) seep into an adjacent colour or area. ➤Printing (of a design) be printed so that it runs off the page after trimming. **5** allow (fluid or gas) to escape from a closed system through a valve. ● n. the action or an instance of bleeding.

– ORIGIN OE *blēdan*, of Gmc origin; rel. to **BLOOD**.

**bleeder** ● n. **1** Brit. informal a person regarded with contempt, disrespect, or pity: *lucky little bleeder!* **2** informal a haemophiliac. **3** Baseball a ground ball hit that barely passes between two infielders.

**bleeding** ● adj. Brit. informal used for emphasis, or to express annoyance.

**bleeding edge** ● n. the very forefront of technological development.

– ORIGIN after **LEADING EDGE**, **CUTTING EDGE**.

**bleeding heart** ● n. **1** informal, derogatory a person considered to be excessively soft-hearted or liberal. **2** a cultivated plant with red or partly red heart-shaped flowers. [*Dicentra cucullaria* and other species.]

**bleep** ● n. a short high-pitched sound made by an electronic device as a signal or to attract attention. ● v. **1** (of an electronic device) make a bleep. **2** (in broadcasting) censor (a word or phrase) by substituting a bleep.

– DERIVATIVES **bleeper** n.

– ORIGIN 1950s: imitative.

**blemish** ● n. **1** a small mark or flaw which spoils the appearance of something. **2** a moral defect or fault. ● v. [often as adj. **blemished**] spoil the appearance of.

– ORIGIN ME (as v.): from OFr. *ble(s)miss-*, *ble(s)mir* 'make pale, injure'; prob. of Gmc origin.

**blench**[1] /blɛn(t)ʃ/ ● v. make a sudden flinching movement out of fear or pain.

– ORIGIN OE *blencan* 'deceive', of Gmc origin.

**blench**[2] /blɛntʃ/ ● v. chiefly dialect variant spelling of

**BLANCH.**

**blend** ● v. **1** mix and combine (something) with something else. **2** form a harmonious combination or part of a whole: *a bodyguard has to blend in.* ● n. **1** a mixture of different things or people. **2** a word made up of the parts and combining the meanings of two others, for example *motel* from *motor* and *hotel.*
– ORIGIN ME: prob. of Scand. origin and rel. to ON *blanda* 'to mix'.

**blende** /blɛnd/ ● n. another term for **SPHALERITE.**
– ORIGIN C17: from Ger., from *blenden* 'deceive' (because it resembled galena but yielded no lead).

**blender** ● n. an electric device used for liquidizing, chopping, or puréeing food.

**Blenheim** /'blɛnɪm/ ● n. a dog of a small red and white breed of spaniel.
– ORIGIN C19: from the name of *Blenheim* Palace in Oxfordshire.

**Blenheim Orange** ● n. an English dessert apple of a golden or orange-red variety which ripens late in the season.

**blenny** ● n. (pl. **-ies**) a small spiny-finned fish with scaleless skin and a blunt head, typically found in shallow coastal waters. [*Blennius* and other genera, family Blennidae.]
– ORIGIN C18: from L. *blennius*, from Gk *blennos* 'mucus' (because of its mucous coating).

**blent** poetic/literary past and past participle of **BLEND.**

**bleomycin** /ˌbliːəʊ'mʌɪsɪn/ ● n. Medicine a bacterial antibiotic used to treat Hodgkin's disease and other cancers.
– ORIGIN 1960s: an arbitrary alt. of earlier *phleomycin*, a rel. antibiotic.

**blepharitis** /ˌblɛfə'rʌɪtɪs/ ● n. Medicine inflammation of the eyelid.
– ORIGIN C19: from Gk *blepharon* 'eyelid' + **-ITIS.**

**blepharoplasty** /'blɛf(ə)rə(ʊ)ˌplasti/ ● n. Medicine surgical repair or reconstruction of an eyelid.
– ORIGIN C19: from Gk *blepharon* 'eyelid' + **-PLASTY.**

**blepharospasm** /'blɛf(ə)rəʊˌspaz(ə)m/ ● n. involuntary tight closure of the eyelids.
– ORIGIN C19: from Gk *blepharon* 'eyelid' + **SPASM.**

**blesbok** /'blɛsbɒk/ ● n. an antelope with a mainly reddish-brown coat and white face, found in southwestern South Africa. [*Damaliscus dorcas phillipsi.*]
– ORIGIN C19: from Afrik., from Du. *bles* 'blaze' + *bok* 'buck'.

**bless** ● v. **1** consecrate or invoke divine favour upon (someone) by means of a religious rite. ➤ call (God) holy; praise (God). ➤ (**bless oneself**) archaic make the sign of the cross. **2** (**bless someone with**) endow someone with (a particular valued attribute); grant (health, prosperity, etc.) to someone.
– PHRASES **bless you!** said to a person who has just sneezed. [from the phr. *(may) God bless you.*]
– ORIGIN OE *blēdsian, blētsian*, based on *blōd* 'blood' (orig. perh. 'mark or consecrate with blood').

**blessed** /'blɛsɪd, blɛst/ ● adj. **1** made holy; consecrated. ➤ a title preceding the name of a dead person considered to have led a holy life, especially a person formally beatified by the Roman Catholic Church. **2** endowed with divine favour and protection. **3** informal used in mild expressions of annoyance or exasperation.
– DERIVATIVES **blessedly** adv. **blessedness** n.

**blessing** ● n. **1** God's favour and protection. ➤ a prayer asking for such favour and protection. ➤ grace said before or after a meal. **2** a beneficial thing for which one is grateful: *it's a blessing we're alive.* **3** a person's sanction or support: *he gave the plan his blessing.*
– PHRASES **a blessing in disguise** an apparent misfortune that eventually has good results.

**blest** ● adj. archaic or poetic/literary term for **BLESSED.**

**blether** /'blɛðə/ ● n. chiefly Scottish another term for **BLATHER.**

**bletherskate** /'blɛðəskeɪt/ ● n. variant spelling of **BLATHERSKITE.**

**blew** past of **BLOW**[1] and **BLOW**[3].

**blewit** /'bluːɪt/ (also **blewits**) ● n. an edible mushroom with a pale buff or lilac cap and a lilac stem. [*Lepista saeva* and other species.]
– ORIGIN C19: prob. from **BLUE**[1].

**blight** ● n. **1** a plant disease, especially one caused by fungi such as mildews, rusts, and smuts. **2** a thing that spoils or damages something. ➤ ugly or neglected urban landscape. ● v. **1** infect (plants) with blight. **2** spoil, harm, or destroy. ➤ [usu. as adj. **blighted**] subject (an urban area) to neglect.
– ORIGIN C16 (denoting inflammation of the skin): of unknown origin.

**blighter** ● n. Brit. informal a person regarded with contempt, irritation, or pity.

**Blighty** ● n. Brit. informal **1** Britain or England, as used by soldiers serving abroad in the First and Second World Wars. **2** military slang a wound suffered in the First World War, sufficiently serious to merit being shipped home to Britain.
– ORIGIN first used by soldiers in the Ind. army; Anglo-Ind. alt. of Urdu *bilāyatī, wilāyatī* 'foreign, European'.

**blimey** ● exclam. Brit. informal expressing surprise, excitement, or alarm.
– ORIGIN C19: alt. form of *(God) blind* (or *blame*) *me!*

**blimp** ● n. informal **1** (also **Colonel Blimp**) Brit. a pompous, reactionary person. **2** a small airship or barrage balloon. **3** N. Amer. an obese person. **4** a soundproof cover for a movie camera.
– DERIVATIVES **blimpish** adj.
– ORIGIN First World War (in sense 2); sense 1 derives from a character invented by the cartoonist David Low.

**blin** /blɪn/ singular form of **BLINI.**

**blind** ● adj. **1** unable to see because of injury, disease, or a congenital condition. **2** done without being able to see or without certain information. ➤ (of flying) using instruments only. **3** lacking perception, judgement, or reason. **4** concealed, closed, or blocked off. ➤ (of a corner or bend) impossible to see round. **5** (of a plant) without buds, eyes, or terminal flowers. **6** [with neg.] informal the slightest: *it didn't do a blind bit of good.* ● v. **1** cause (someone) to be unable to see. **2** deprive of understanding or judgement. ➤ (**blind someone with**) confuse or overawe someone with (something they do not understand). **3** Brit. informal, dated move very fast and dangerously. ● n. **1** a screen for a window, especially one on a roller or made of slats. ➤ Brit. an awning over a shop window. **2** something designed to conceal one's real intentions. **3** N. Amer. a hide, as used by hunters. **4** Brit. informal, dated a heavy drinking bout. ● adv. without being able to see clearly.
– PHRASES **bake something blind** bake a pastry without a filling. **(as) blind as a bat** informal having very bad eyesight. **blind drunk** informal extremely drunk. **turn a blind eye** pretend not to notice. [said to be in allusion to Nelson, who lifted a telescope to his blind eye at the Battle of Copenhagen (1801), thus not seeing the signal to 'discontinue the action'.]
– DERIVATIVES **blindly** adv. **blindness** n.
– ORIGIN OE, of Gmc origin.

**blind alley** ● n. **1** a cul-de-sac. **2** a course of action leading nowhere.

**blind date** ● n. a social engagement with a person one has not previously met, designed to have a romantic or sexual aim.

**blinder** ● n. **1** Brit. informal an excellent performance in a game or race. **2** (**blinders**) N. Amer. blinkers on a horse's bridle.

**blindfold** ● n. a piece of cloth tied around the head to cover someone's eyes. ● v. deprive of sight with a blindfold. ● adv. with a blindfold covering the eyes.
– ORIGIN C16: alt., by assoc. with **FOLD**[1], of *blindfeld*, past part. of obs. *blindfell* 'strike blind, blindfold', from OE *geblindfellan* (see **BLIND, FELL**[2]).

**blind gut** ● n. the caecum.

**blinding** ● adj. **1** (of light) very bright. **2** suddenly and overwhelmingly obvious. **3** informal (of an action) remarkably skilful and exciting. ● n. the process of covering a newly made road with grit to fill cracks. ➤ a thin bed of concrete laid before the main mass of concrete.

– DERIVATIVES **blindingly** adv.

**blind man's buff** (US also **blind man's bluff**) ● **n.** a game in which a blindfold player tries to catch others while being pushed about by them.
– ORIGIN C17: from *buff* 'a blow', from OFr. *bufe* (see **BUFFET**[2]).

**blind pig** (also **blind tiger**) ● **n.** N. Amer. informal an illegal bar.
– ORIGIN allegedly so called from the practice of charging customers to view a blind pig but giving them a drink 'free'.

**blind side** ● **n.** a direction in which a person has a poor view, especially of approaching danger. ● **v.** (**blindside**) N. Amer. **1** hit or attack on the blind side. **2** cause to be unable to perceive the truth of a situation.

**blindsight** ● **n.** Medicine a condition in which the sufferer responds to visual stimuli without consciously perceiving them.

**blind snake** ● **n.** a small burrowing insectivorous snake of a group which lacks a distinct head and has very small inefficient eyes. [Typhlopidae and other families: many species.]

**blind spot** ● **n.** **1** Anatomy the point of entry of the optic nerve on the retina, insensitive to light. **2** an area where a person's view is obstructed. ➤ an area in which a person lacks understanding or impartiality. **3** Telecommunications a point within the normal range of a transmitter where there is unusually weak reception.

**blind stamping** (also **blind tooling**) ● **n.** the impressing of a design on a book cover without the use of colour or gold leaf.

**blind stitch** ● **n.** a sewing stitch producing stitches visible on one side only.

**blind tiger** ● **n.** another term for **BLIND PIG**.

**blind trust** ● **n.** chiefly N. Amer. a trust independently administering the private business interests of a person in public office to prevent conflict of interest.

**blindworm** ● **n.** another term for **SLOW-WORM**.

**blini** /ˈblɪni, ˈbliːni/ (also **bliny** or **blinis**) ● **pl. n.** (sing. **blin**) pancakes made from buckwheat flour and served with sour cream.
– ORIGIN from Russ.

**blink** ● **v.** **1** shut and open the eyes quickly. **2** [usu. with neg.] react with surprise or disapproval: *he doesn't blink at the unsavoury aspects of his subject.* **3** (of a light) shine unsteadily or intermittently. ● **n.** **1** an act of blinking. **2** a momentary gleam of light.
– PHRASES **in the blink of an eye** (or **in a blink**) informal very quickly. **on the blink** informal (of a machine) not working properly; out of order.
– ORIGIN ME (in senses 'deceive', 'flinch', 'open the eyes after sleep'): from *blenk*, Scots var. of **BLENCH**[1].

**blinker** ● **n.** chiefly Brit. **1** (**blinkers**) a pair of small screens attached to a horse's bridle to prevent the horse seeing sideways and behind and being startled during a race. **2** a thing that prevents someone from understanding a situation fully. **3** a vehicle indicator light that flashes on and off. ● **v.** **1** put blinkers on (a horse). **2** [often as adj. **blinkered**] cause to have a narrow or limited outlook.

**blinking** ● **adj.** Brit. informal used to express annoyance.

**blinks** (also **water blinks**) ● **pl. n.** [usu. treated as sing.] a small fleshy plant with tiny white flowers, growing in damp habitats. [*Montia fontana*.]
– ORIGIN C17: from **BLINK**, with ref. to the gleaming white flowers.

**blintze** /blɪn(t)s/ ● **n.** a thin rolled pancake filled with cheese or fruit and then fried or baked.
– ORIGIN from Yiddish *blintse*, from Russ. *blinets* 'little pancake'; cf. **BLINI**.

**bliny** ● **pl. n.** variant spelling of **BLINI**.

**blip** ● **n.** **1** a very short high-pitched sound made by an electronic device. ➤ a small flashing point of light on a radar screen representing an object. **2** an unexpected, minor, and usually temporary deviation from a general trend. ● **v.** (**blipped**, **blipping**) **1** (of an electronic device) make a blip. **2** open (the throttle of a motor vehicle) momentarily.
– ORIGIN C19 (denoting a sudden rap or tap): imitative.

**blipvert** ● **n.** a television advert of a few seconds' duration.

**bliss** ● **n.** perfect happiness. ➤ a state of spiritual blessedness. ● **v.** (**bliss out** or **be blissed out**) informal be in a state of perfect happiness, oblivious to everything else.
– ORIGIN OE *blīths*, *bliss*, of Gmc origin; rel. to **BLITHE**.

**blissful** ● **adj.** extremely happy; full of joy.
– DERIVATIVES **blissfully** adv. **blissfulness** n.

**blister** ● **n.** **1** a small bubble on the skin filled with serum and typically caused by friction or burning. **2** a similar swelling, filled with air or fluid, on a surface. **3** Medicine, chiefly historical a preparation applied to the skin to form a blister. **4** Brit. informal, dated an annoying person. ● **v.** be or cause to be affected with blisters.
– ORIGIN ME: perh. from OFr. *blestre* 'swelling, pimple'.

**blister beetle** ● **n.** a beetle that, when it is alarmed, secretes a substance that causes blisters. [*Lytta* and other genera: several species.]

**blister copper** ● **n.** partly purified copper with a blistered surface formed during smelting.

**blistering** ● **adj.** **1** (of heat) intense. **2** (of criticism) very vehement. **3** (in sport) extremely fast, forceful, or impressive.
– DERIVATIVES **blisteringly** adv.

**blithe** /blʌɪð/ ● **adj.** **1** cheerfully or thoughtlessly indifferent. **2** poetic/literary happy or joyous.
– DERIVATIVES **blithely** adv. **blitheness** n. **blithesome** /-s(ə)m/ adj. (poetic/literary).
– ORIGIN OE *blīthe*, of Gmc origin; rel. to **BLISS**.

**blither** /ˈblɪðə/ ● **v. & n.** variant spelling of **BLATHER**.

**blithering** ● **adj.** informal complete; utter: *a blithering idiot.*

**BLitt** ● **abbrev.** Bachelor of Letters.
– ORIGIN from L. *Baccalaureus Litterarum*.

**blitz** ● **n.** **1** an intensive or sudden military attack. ➤ (**the Blitz**) the German air raids on Britain in 1940–1. **2** informal a sudden and concerted effort. **3** American Football a play in which one or more defensive backs charge the quarterback of the opposing team. ● **v.** **1** attack or seriously damage in a blitz. **2** succeed in overwhelming or defeating utterly. **3** American Football charge in a blitz.
– ORIGIN abbrev. of **BLITZKRIEG**.

**blitzkrieg** /ˈblɪtskriːg/ ● **n.** an intense military campaign intended to bring about a swift victory.
– ORIGIN Second World War: from Ger., lit. 'lightning war'.

**blizzard** ● **n.** a severe snowstorm with high winds.
– ORIGIN C19 (orig. US, denoting a violent blow): of unknown origin.

**bloat**[1] ● **v.** cause to swell with fluid or gas. ● **n.** a disease of livestock characterized by an accumulation of gas in the stomach.
– ORIGIN C17: from obs. *bloat* 'swollen, soft', perh. from ON *blautr* 'soft, flabby'.

**bloat**[2] ● **v.** cure (a herring) by salting and smoking it lightly.
– ORIGIN C16: rel. to *bloat herring* 'bloater', of obscure origin.

**bloated** ● **adj.** **1** swollen with fluid or gas. **2** excessively large or wealthy.

**bloater** ● **n.** a herring cured by salting and light smoking.

**blob** ● **n.** **1** a drop of a thick liquid or viscous substance. **2** an indeterminate roundish mass or shape. **3** informal a score of 0 in a game. ● **v.** splash or mark with blobs.
– DERIVATIVES **blobby** adj.
– ORIGIN ME (denoting a bubble): cf. **BLOTCH**, **BLUBBER**[1], and **PLOP**.

**bloc** ● **n.** a group of countries or political parties who have formed an alliance.
– ORIGIN C20: from Fr., lit. 'block'.

**block** ● **n.** **1** a large solid piece of hard material with flat surfaces on each side. ➤ a starting block. ➤ Printing a piece of wood or metal engraved for printing on paper or fabric. ➤ a head-shaped mould used for shaping hats or wigs. **2** chiefly Brit. a large single building subdivided into separate flats or offices. ➤ a group of buildings bounded by four streets. ➤ chiefly N. Amer. the length of one side of such

a block: *he lives a few blocks away.* **3** a large quantity or allocation of things regarded as a unit. **4** an obstacle to the normal progress or functioning of something. ➤a chock for stopping the motion of a wheel. **5** a flat area of something, especially a solid area of colour. **6** a pulley or system of pulleys mounted in a case. **7** (also **cylinder block** or **engine block**) a large metal moulding containing the cylinders of an internal-combustion engine. **8** (also **blockhole**) Cricket the spot on which a batsman rests the end of the bat while waiting to receive a ball. ●**v. 1** prevent movement or flow in. **2** impede or prevent (an action or movement). ➤(in sport) impede with one's body. ➤Cricket stop (a ball) with the bat defensively. **3** impress a design on (a book cover). **4** (**block something out/in**) mark out an outline or shade something in roughly. **5** shape (a hat) using a wooden mould.
– PHRASES **knock someone's block off** informal hit someone about the head; give someone a beating. **on the** (**auction**) **block** chiefly N. Amer. for sale at auction. **put one's head** (or **neck**) **on the block** informal put one's standing or reputation at risk by proceeding with an action.
– DERIVATIVES **blocker** n. **blocky** adj.
– ORIGIN ME (denoting a log or tree stump): from OFr. *bloc* (n.), *bloquer* (v.), from MDu. *blok*, of unknown ult. origin.

**blockade** ●**n. 1** an act of sealing off a place to prevent goods or people from entering or leaving. **2** an obstruction of a biochemical or other physiological function. ●**v.** set up a blockade of.
– PHRASES **run a blockade** (of a ship) manage to enter or leave a blockaded port.
– DERIVATIVES **blockader** n.
– ORIGIN C17: from BLOCK + -ADE[1].

**blockage** ●**n.** an obstruction which makes movement or flow difficult or impossible.

**block and tackle** ●**n.** a lifting mechanism consisting of ropes, a pulley block, and a hook.

**blockboard** ●**n.** Brit. a building material consisting of a core of wooden strips between two layers of plywood.

**blockbuster** ●**n.** informal a film or book that is a great commercial success.
– ORIGIN 1940s (denoting a huge aerial bomb): from BLOCK + BUSTER.

**blockbusting** ●**adj.** informal very successful commercially.

**block capitals** ●**pl. n.** plain capital letters.

**block diagram** ●**n.** a diagram showing the general arrangement of parts of a complex system or process.

**blockhead** ●**n.** informal a very stupid person.
– DERIVATIVES **blockheaded** adj.

**block heater** ●**n. 1** Brit. a storage heater. **2** N. Amer. a device for heating the engine block of a vehicle.

**blockhole** ●**n.** see BLOCK (sense 8).

**blockhouse** ●**n. 1** a reinforced concrete shelter used as an observation point. ➤historical a one-storeyed timber building used as a fort. **2** US a house made of squared logs.

**blocking** ●**n. 1** Psychiatry the sudden halting of the flow of thought or speech, as a symptom of schizophrenia or other mental disorder. ➤failure to recall or consider an unpleasant memory or train of thought. **2** the physical arrangement of actors on a stage or film set.

**blockish** ●**adj. 1** bulky or crude in form. **2** unintelligent; stupid.

**block letters** ●**pl. n.** block capitals.

**block mountain** ●**n.** Geology a mountain formed by natural faults in the earth's crust.

**block plane** ●**n.** a carpenter's plane with a blade set at an acute angle, used especially for planing across the end grain of wood.

**block release** ●**n.** Brit. a system of allowing employees the whole of a stated period off work for education.

**blockship** ●**n.** a ship which is moored or grounded in a channel in order to block it.

**block system** ●**n.** a system of railway signalling which divides the track into sections and allows no train to enter a section that is not completely clear.

**block vote** ●**n.** Brit. a vote proportional in power to the number of people a delegate represents, used particularly at a trade-union conference.

**bloke** ●**n.** Brit. informal a man.
– ORIGIN C19: from Shelta.

**blokeish** (also **blokish** or **blokey**) ●**adj.** Brit. informal stereotypically male in behaviour and interests.
– DERIVATIVES **blokeishness** n.

**blonde** ●**adj.** (also **blond**) (of hair) fair or pale yellow. ➤having fair hair and a light complexion. ●**n. 1** a woman with blonde hair. **2** the colour of blonde hair.
– DERIVATIVES **blondish** adj. **blondness** n.
– ORIGIN C17 (earlier as *blond*): from Fr., fem. of *blond*.

**Blood** /blʌd/ ●**n.** (pl. same or **Bloods**) a member of a North American Indian people belonging to the Blackfoot Confederacy.

**blood** ●**n. 1** the red liquid that circulates in the arteries and veins, carrying oxygen to and carbon dioxide from the tissues of the body. **2** violence involving bloodshed. **3** fiery or passionate temperament. **4** family background; descent or lineage: *she must have Irish blood.* **5** dated a fashionable and dashing young man. ●**v. 1** initiate in a particular activity. **2** Hunting smear the face of (a novice hunter) with the blood of the kill. ➤give (a hound) a first taste of blood.
– PHRASES **blood and thunder** informal unrestrained and violent action or behaviour. **one's blood is up** one is in a fighting mood. **blood, sweat, and tears** extremely hard work. **first blood 1** the first shedding of blood in a fight or (formerly) a duel. **2** the first point or advantage gained in a contest. **give blood** allow blood to be removed medically from one's body in order to be stored for use in transfusions. **have blood on one's hands** be responsible for someone's death. **in one's blood** ingrained in or fundamental to one's character. **make someone's blood boil** informal infuriate someone. **make someone's blood run cold** horrify someone. **new** (or **fresh**) **blood** new members admitted to a group. **of the blood** (**royal**) poetic/literary royal. **young blood** a younger member or members of a group.
– ORIGIN OE *blōd*, of Gmc origin.

**blood bank** ●**n.** a place where supplies of blood or plasma for transfusion are stored.

**bloodbath** ●**n.** an event in which many people are killed violently.

**blood brother** ●**n.** a man who has sworn to treat another man as a brother, typically by a ceremonial mingling of blood.

**blood count** ●**n.** a determination of the number of corpuscles in a specific volume of blood.

**blood-curdling** ●**adj.** horrifying; very frightening.

**blood donor** ●**n.** a person who gives blood.

**blood doping** (also **blood boosting**) ●**n.** the injection of oxygenated blood into an athlete before an event in an (illegal) attempt to enhance performance.

**blooded** ●**adj. 1** having blood or a temperament of a specified kind: *thin-blooded.* **2** chiefly N. Amer. (of horses or cattle) of good pedigree.

**blood feud** ●**n.** a lengthy conflict between families involving a cycle of retaliatory killings.

**bloodfin** ●**n.** a small South American freshwater fish with bright red fins, popular in aquaria. [*Aphyocharax rubripinnis.*]

**blood fluke** ●**n.** another term for SCHISTOSOME.

**blood group** ●**n.** any of the various types of human blood whose antigen characteristics determine compatibility in transfusion, especially those of the ABO system.

**blood horse** ●**n.** dated a thoroughbred horse.

**bloodhound** ●**n.** a large hound of a breed with a very keen sense of smell, used in tracking.

**blood knot** ●**n.** a type of knot used by anglers to join two fishing lines.

**bloodless** ●**adj. 1** (of a conflict) without violence or killing. **2** (of the skin) drained of colour. ➤lacking in vitality; feeble. **3** (of a person) cold or ruthless.
– DERIVATIVES **bloodlessly** adv. **bloodlessness** n.

**bloodletting** • n. **1** historical the surgical removal of some of a patient's blood for therapeutic purposes. **2** violence during a war or conflict.

**bloodline** • n. a pedigree or set of ancestors.

**bloodlust** • n. uncontrollable desire to kill.

**blood meal** • n. dried blood used for feeding animals and as a fertilizer.

**blood money** • n. **1** money paid in compensation to the family of someone who has been killed. **2** money paid to a hired killer.

**blood orange** • n. an orange of a variety with red or red-streaked flesh.

**blood poisoning** • n. a diseased state due to the presence of micro-organisms or their toxins in the blood.

**blood pressure** • n. the pressure of the blood in the circulatory system, which is closely related to the force and rate of the heartbeat and the diameter and elasticity of the arterial walls.

**blood pudding** (also **blood sausage**) • n. black pudding.

**blood relation** (also **blood relative**) • n. a person who is related to another by birth rather than by marriage.

**bloodroot** • n. **1** a North American plant with fleshy rhizomes which exude red sap when cut. [*Sanguinaria canadensis*.] **2** a lily-like Australian plant with a red edible rhizome. [*Haemodorum coccineum*.]

**bloodshed** • n. the killing or wounding of people.

**bloodshot** • adj. (of the eyes) inflamed or tinged with blood, typically as a result of tiredness.

**blood sport** • n. a sport involving the hunting, wounding, or killing of animals.

**bloodstain** • n. a mark or discoloration caused by blood.
– DERIVATIVES **bloodstained** adj.

**bloodstock** • n. [treated as sing. or pl.] thoroughbred horses considered collectively.

**bloodstone** • n. a type of green chalcedony spotted or streaked with red, used as a gemstone.

**bloodstream** • n. the blood circulating through the body of a person or animal.

**bloodsucker** • n. an animal or insect that sucks blood, especially a leech or a mosquito.
– DERIVATIVES **bloodsucking** adj.

**blood sugar** • n. the concentration of glucose in the blood.

**bloodthirsty** • adj. (**-ier**, **-iest**) eager to kill and maim.
– DERIVATIVES **bloodthirstily** adv. **bloodthirstiness** n.

**blood vessel** • n. a tubular structure carrying blood through the tissues and organs; a vein, artery, or capillary.

**bloodwood** • n. a hardwood tree with deep red wood. [*Eucalyptus gummifera* (Australia) and other species.]

**bloodworm** • n. **1** the bright red aquatic larva of a midge. **2** another term for **TUBIFEX**.

**bloody**[1] • adj. (**-ier**, **-iest**) **1** covered with or composed of blood. **2** involving much violence or cruelty. • v. (**-ies**, **-ied**) cover or stain with blood.
– DERIVATIVES **bloodily** adv. **bloodiness** n.

**bloody**[2] • adj. informal, chiefly Brit. **1** used to express anger or shock, or for emphasis. **2** dated unpleasant or perverse: *don't be too bloody to poor Nigel.*
– ORIGIN C17: from **BLOODY**[1]; perh. connected with the 'bloods' (aristocratic rowdies) of C17–18; hence the phr. *bloody drunk* (= as drunk as a blood) meant 'very drunk indeed'.

**Bloody Mary** • n. (pl. **Bloody Marys**) a drink consisting of vodka and tomato juice.

**bloody-minded** • adj. Brit. informal deliberately uncooperative.
– DERIVATIVES **bloody-mindedly** adv. **bloody-mindedness** n.

**blooey** /'bluːi/ (also **blooie**) • adv. & adj. US informal awry; amiss.
– ORIGIN 1920s: of unknown origin.

**bloom**[1] • v. **1** produce flowers; be in flower. **2** be or become very healthy. **3** coat (a lens) with a special surface layer to reduce reflection. • n. **1** a flower, especially one cultivated for its beauty. ➤the state or period of blooming: *the apple trees were in bloom.* **2** a youthful or healthy glow in a person's complexion. **3** a delicate powdery surface deposit on fruits, leaves, or stems. **4** a full bright sound in a musical recording. **5** a rapid growth of microscopic algae or cyanobacteria in water resulting in a coloured scum on the surface.
– ORIGIN ME: from ON *blóm* 'flower, blossom', *blómi* 'prosperity', *blómar* 'flowers'.

**bloom**[2] • n. a mass of iron or steel hammered or rolled into a thick bar for further working. ➤historical an unworked mass of puddled iron. • v. [usu. as noun **blooming**] make (metal) into such a mass.
– ORIGIN OE *blōma*, of unknown origin.

**bloomer**[1] • n. Brit. informal, dated a stupid mistake.
– ORIGIN C19: equivalent to *blooming error.*

**bloomer**[2] • n. Brit. a large loaf with diagonal slashes on a rounded top.
– ORIGIN 1930s: of unknown origin.

**bloomer**[3] • n. [in combination] a plant that blooms at a specified time.

**bloomers** • pl. n. **1** women's loose-fitting knee-length knickers. **2** historical women's loose-fitting trousers, gathered at the knee or ankle.
– ORIGIN C19: named after Mrs Amelia J. *Bloomer*, an Amer. social reformer who advocated a similar garment.

**bloomery** • n. (pl. **-ies**) historical a forge or mill producing blooms of wrought iron.

**blooming** • adj. Brit. informal used to express annoyance or for emphasis.

**bloop** informal, chiefly N. Amer. • v. **1** (of an electronic device) emit a short low-pitched noise. **2** make a mistake. **3** Baseball make (a hit) from a poorly hit fly ball landing just beyond the reach of the infielders. • n. **1** a short low-pitched noise emitted by an electronic device. **2** a mistake. **3** Baseball another term for **BLOOPER** (in sense 2).
– DERIVATIVES **bloopy** adj.
– ORIGIN 1920s: imitative.

**blooper** • n. informal, chiefly N. Amer. **1** an embarrassing error. **2** Baseball a poorly hit fly ball landing just beyond the reach of the infielders.

**blossom** • n. a flower or a mass of flowers on a tree or bush. ➤the state or period of flowering. • v. **1** (of a tree or bush) produce blossom. **2** mature or develop in a promising or healthy way.
– DERIVATIVES **blossomy** adj.
– ORIGIN OE *blōstm*, *blōstma* (n.), *blōstmian* (v.), of Gmc origin; rel. to **BLOOM**[1].

**blot** • n. **1** a dark mark or stain, especially one made by ink. **2** a thing that mars something that is otherwise good. **3** Biochemistry a procedure in which proteins or nucleic acids separated on a gel are transferred directly to an immobilizing medium for identification. • v. (**blotted**, **blotting**) **1** dry with an absorbent material. **2** mark, stain, or mar. **3** (**blot something out**) obscure a view. ➤obliterate or disregard a painful memory or thought. **4** Biochemistry transfer by means of a blot.
– PHRASES **blot one's copybook** Brit. tarnish one's good reputation.
– ORIGIN ME: prob. of Scand. origin and rel. to ON *blettr.*

**blotch** • n. a large irregular patch or unsightly mark. • v. cover or mark with blotches.
– DERIVATIVES **blotchiness** n. **blotchy** adj.
– ORIGIN C17: partly alt. of obs. *plotch*, influenced by **BLOT**; partly a blend of **BLOT** and **BOTCH**.

**blotter** • n. **1** a sheet or pad of blotting paper inserted into a frame and kept on a desk. **2** N. Amer. a temporary recording book, especially a police charge sheet.

**blotting paper** • n. absorbent paper used for soaking up excess ink when writing.

**blotto** • adj. informal extremely drunk.
– ORIGIN C20: from **BLOT** + **-O**.

**blouse** • n. **1** a woman's upper garment resembling a shirt. **2** a loose smock or tunic of a type worn by peasants and manual workers. **3** a type of jacket worn as part of military uniform. • v. make (a garment) hang in loose

folds.
– PHRASES **big girl's blouse** Brit. informal a weak, cowardly, or over-sensitive man.
– ORIGIN C19: from Fr., of unknown origin.

**blouson** /'blu:zɒn/ ● n. a short loose-fitting jacket, typically bloused and finishing at the waist.
– ORIGIN C20: from Fr., dimin. of BLOUSE.

**blow**[1] ● v. (past **blew**; past part. **blown**) **1** (of wind) move creating an air current. ➤be carried or driven by the wind. **2** expel air through pursed lips. ➤force air through the mouth into (an instrument) to make a sound. ➤force air through a tube into (molten glass) to create an artefact. ➤remove the contents of (an egg) by forcing air through it. **3** sound (the horn of a vehicle). **4** (of a whale) eject air and vapour through the blowhole. **5** (of an explosion) displace violently or send flying. ➤burst or burn out through pressure or overheating. ➤(of a vehicle tyre) burst suddenly while the vehicle is in motion. **6** informal spend recklessly. **7** informal completely bungle (an opportunity). ➤expose (a stratagem): *his cover was blown.* **8** (past part. **blowed**) Brit. informal damn: *'Well, blow me', he said.* **9** informal leave. **10** (of flies) lay eggs in or on. **11** informal play jazz or rock music in an unrestrained style. **12** [as adj. **blown**] breathing hard; exhausted. ● n. **1** a strong wind. **2** an act of blowing. **3** informal cannabis.
– PHRASES **blow a fuse** (or **gasket**) informal lose one's temper. **blow hot and cold** vacillate. **blow someone a kiss** kiss the tips of one's fingers then blow across them towards someone as a gesture of affection. **blow someone's mind** informal impress or otherwise affect someone very strongly. **blow one's nose** clear one's nose of mucus by blowing through it into a handkerchief. **blow one's top** (or chiefly N. Amer. **lid** or **stack**) informal lose one's temper. **blow up in one's face** (of an action) go drastically wrong with damaging effects to oneself. **blow with the wind** be incapable of maintaining a consistent course of action.
– PHRASAL VERBS **blow someone away** informal **1** kill someone using a firearm. **2** cause someone to be extremely impressed. **blow in** informal arrive casually and unannounced. **blow off** informal **1** lose one's temper and shout. **2** break wind noisily. **blow someone off** N. Amer. informal fail to keep an appointment with someone. ➤end a romantic or sexual relationship with someone. **blow something off** N. Amer. informal ignore or fail to attend something. **blow someone out** N. Amer. informal defeat someone convincingly. **blow over** (of trouble) fade away without serious consequences. **blow up 1** explode. **2** lose one's temper. **3** (of a wind or storm) begin to develop. **4** (of a scandal or dispute) emerge or become public. **5** inflate. **blow something up 1** cause something to explode. **2** inflate or enlarge something.
– ORIGIN OE *blāwan*, of Gmc origin.

**blow**[2] ● n. **1** a powerful stroke with a hand or weapon. **2** a sudden shock or disappointment.
– PHRASES **come to blows** start fighting after a disagreement.
– ORIGIN ME: of unknown origin.

**blow**[3] archaic or poetic/literary ● v. (past **blew**; past part. **blown**) produce flowers or be in flower. ● n. the state or period of flowering.
– ORIGIN OE *blōwan*, of Gmc origin; rel. to BLOOM[1] and BLOSSOM.

**blowback** ● n. a process in which gases expand or travel in a direction opposite to the usual one.

**blow-by-blow** ● adj. (of a description of an event) giving all the details in the order in which they occurred.

**blowdown** ● n. **1** N. Amer. a tree that has been blown down by the wind. **2** the removal of solids or liquids from a container or pipe using pressure.

**blow-dry** ● v. arrange (the hair) into a particular style while drying it with a hand-held dryer.
– DERIVATIVES **blow-dryer** n.

**blower** ● n. **1** a device for creating a current of air to dry or heat something. **2** informal, chiefly Brit. a telephone.

**blowfish** ● n. (pl. same or **-fishes**) a fish that is able to inflate its body when alarmed, especially a globefish.

**blowfly** ● n. (pl. **-flies**) a bluebottle or similar large fly which lays its eggs on meat and carcasses. [Family Calliphoridae.]

**blowgun** ● n. another term for BLOWPIPE.

**blowhard** ● n. N. Amer. informal a person who blusters and boasts in an unpleasant way.

**blowhole** ● n. **1** the nostril of a whale or dolphin on the top of its head. **2** a hole in ice for breathing or fishing through. **3** a vent for air or smoke in a tunnel or other structure.

**blow-in** ● n. Irish & Austral. a newcomer or recent arrival.

**blow job** ● n. vulgar slang an act of fellatio.

**blowlamp** ● n. British term for BLOWTORCH.

**blown**[1] past participle of BLOW[1]. ● adj. informal (of a vehicle) provided with a turbocharger.

**blown**[2] past participle of BLOW[3].

**blowout** ● n. **1** an occasion when a vehicle tyre bursts or an electric fuse melts. ➤an uprush of oil or gas from a well. **2** N. Amer. informal an argument or outburst of anger. **3** informal a large, lavish meal. **4** N. Amer. informal an easy victory. **5** a hollow eroded by the wind.

**blowpipe** ● n. **1** a primitive weapon consisting of a long tube through which an arrow or dart is blown. **2** a long tube by means of which molten glass is blown. ➤a tube used to intensify the heat of a flame by blowing air or other gas through it at high pressure.

**blowsy** /'blaʊzi/ (also **blowzy**) ● adj. (of a woman) coarse, untidy, and red-faced.
– DERIVATIVES **blowsily** adv. **blowsiness** n.
– ORIGIN C17: from obs. *blowze* 'beggar's female companion', of unknown origin.

**blowtorch** ● n. a portable device producing a hot flame which can be directed on to a surface, typically to burn off paint.

**blow-up** ● n. **1** an enlargement of a photograph. **2** informal an outburst of anger. ● adj. inflatable.

**blowy** ● adj. (**-ier**, **-iest**) windy or windswept.

**BLT** ● n. informal, chiefly N. Amer. a sandwich filled with bacon, lettuce, and tomato.

**blub** ● v. (**blubbed**, **blubbing**) informal sob noisily and uncontrollably.
– ORIGIN C19: abbrev. of BLUBBER[2].

**blubber**[1] ● n. the fat of sea mammals, especially whales and seals. ● adj. archaic (of a person's lips) swollen or protruding.
– DERIVATIVES **blubbery** adj.
– ORIGIN ME (denoting the foaming of the sea): perh. symbolic; cf. BLOB and BLOTCH; the adj. is an alt. of obs. *blabber* 'swollen'.

**blubber**[2] ● v. informal sob noisily and uncontrollably.
– DERIVATIVES **blubberer** n.
– ORIGIN ME: prob. symbolic; cf. BLOB and BLUBBER[1].

**bluchers** /'blu:kəz/ ● pl. n. historical strong leather half-boots or high shoes.
– ORIGIN C19: named after the Prussian general G. L. von *Blücher*.

**bludge** Austral./NZ informal ● v. live off the efforts of others. ➤cadge or scrounge. ● n. an easy job or assignment.
– ORIGIN C19: back-form. from BLUDGER.

**bludgeon** /'blʌdʒ(ə)n/ ● n. a thick stick with a heavy end, used as a weapon. ● v. **1** beat with a bludgeon. **2** bully into doing something.
– ORIGIN C18: of unknown origin.

**bludger** ● n. Austral./NZ informal a scrounger or idler: *a dole bludger.*
– ORIGIN C19 (orig. Brit. sl. denoting a pimp who robbed his prostitute's clients): abbrev. of *bludgeoner.*

**blue**[1] ● adj. (**bluer**, **bluest**) **1** of a colour intermediate between green and violet, as of the sky or sea on a sunny day. ➤(of a cat, fox, or rabbit) having fur of a smoky grey colour. **2** informal melancholy, sad, or depressed. **3** informal (of a film, joke, or story) with sexual or pornographic content. **4** Brit. informal politically conservative. **5** (of a ski run) of the second-lowest level of difficulty. ● n. **1** blue colour, pigment, or material. ➤(**the blue**) poetic/literary the sky or sea, or the unknown. ➤another term for BLUING. **2** Brit. a person who has represented Cambridge University or Oxford University in a particular sport. **3** used in

names of small butterflies with predominantly blue wings. [*Polyommatus icarus* (**common blue**) and related species.] **4** Austral./NZ informal a nickname for a red-headed person. **5** Austral./NZ informal an argument or fight. ● **v.** (**blues, blued, bluing** or **blueing**) **1** make or become blue. **2** chiefly historical wash (white clothes) with bluing.
– PHRASES **once in a blue moon** informal very rarely. [because a 'blue moon' is a phenomenon that never occurs.] **out of the blue** (or **out of a clear blue sky**) informal without warning; unexpectedly. **talk a blue streak** N. Amer. informal speak continuously and at great length.
– DERIVATIVES **blueness** n.
– ORIGIN ME: from OFr. *bleu*, ult. of Gmc origin.

**blue**[2] ● **v.** (**blues, blued, bluing** or **blueing**) Brit. informal, dated squander or spend recklessly.
– ORIGIN C19: perh. a var. of **BLOW**[1].

**blue baby** ● **n.** a baby with cyanosis, generally due to a congenital heart or circulatory defect.

**Bluebeard** ● **n.** a man who murders his wives.
– ORIGIN from the name of a fairytale character who killed several wives in turn for disobeying his order to avoid a locked room, which contained the bodies of his previous wives.

**blue beat** ● **n.** another term for **SKA**.

**bluebell** ● **n. 1** a woodland plant of the lily family, which produces clusters of blue bell-shaped flowers in spring. [*Hyacinthoides nonscripta*.] **2** Scottish term for **HAREBELL**. **3** any of various other plants with blue bell-shaped flowers. [Genera *Mertensia* (N. America) and *Wahlenbergia* (Australia and S. Africa).]

**blueberry** ● **n.** (pl. **-ies**) **1** the small blue-black berry of a North American dwarf shrub, related to the bilberry. **2** the shrub that produces this berry. [Genus *Vaccinium*: several species.]

**bluebird** ● **n.** an American songbird, the male of which has a blue head, back, and wings. [Genus *Sialia*: three species.]

**blue blood** ● **n.** noble birth.
– DERIVATIVES **blue-blooded** adj.

**blue bonnet** ● **n.** a pale grey-brown Australian parrot with a deep blue face. [*Psephotus haematogaster*.]

**blue book** ● **n. 1** (in the UK) a report bound in a blue cover and issued by Parliament or the Privy Council. **2** (in the US) an official book listing government officials.

**bluebottle** ● **n. 1** a common blowfly with a metallic-blue body. [*Calliphora vomitoria*.] **2** Austral. & S. African the Portuguese man-of-war. **3** Brit. the wild cornflower. **4** Brit. informal, dated a police officer.

**blue cheese** ● **n.** cheese containing veins of blue mould, such as Stilton and Danish Blue.

**blue-chip** ● **adj. 1** denoting companies or their shares considered to be a reliable investment, though less secure than gilt-edged stock. **2** of the highest quality.
– DERIVATIVES **blue chipper** n.
– ORIGIN C20 (orig. US): from the *blue chip* used in gambling games, which usu. has a high value.

**blue coat** ● **n.** a person wearing a blue coat or uniform, especially a US soldier of the 19th century.

**blue-collar** ● **adj.** chiefly N. Amer. of or relating to manual work or workers, particularly in industry.

**blue crane** ● **n.** a large South African crane with blue-grey plumage, the national bird of South Africa. [*Anthropoides paradisea*.]

**blue ensign** ● **n.** a blue flag with the Union Jack in the top corner next to the flagstaff, flown chiefly by British naval auxiliary vessels.

**blue-eyed boy** ● **n.** Brit. informal, chiefly derogatory a person highly regarded and treated with special favour.

**blue-eyed grass** ● **n.** a chiefly North American plant of the iris family, with small blue flowers. [Genus *Sisyrinchium*: several species.]

**blue-eyed Mary** ● **n.** a low-growing southern European plant of the borage family, with bright blue flowers. [*Omphalodes verna*.]

**bluefin** ● **n.** the commonest large tuna, which occurs worldwide in warm seas. [*Thunnus thynnus*.]

**bluefish** ● **n.** (pl. same or **-fishes**) a predatory blue-coloured marine fish, which inhabits tropical and temperate waters and is popular as a game fish. [*Pomatomus saltatrix*, the only member of the family Pomatomidae.]

**blue flag** ● **n. 1** a European award for beaches based on cleanliness and safety. **2** Motor Racing a blue flag used to indicate to a driver that there is another driver trying to lap him.

**bluegill** /ˈbluːgɪl/ ● **n.** an edible North American freshwater fish of the sunfish family, with a deep body and bluish cheeks and gill covers. [*Lepomis macrochirus*.]

**bluegrass** ● **n. 1** (also **Kentucky bluegrass**) a European meadow grass introduced into North America and grown for fodder. [*Poa pratensis* and other species.] **2** a kind of country music characterized by virtuosic playing of banjos and guitars and high-pitched close-harmony vocals.

**blue-green algae** ● **pl. n.** another term for **CYANOBACTERIA**.

**blue ground** ● **n.** another term for **KIMBERLITE**.

**bluegum** ● **n.** a eucalyptus tree with blue-green aromatic leaves and smooth bark. [Genus *Eucalyptus*: several species.]

**bluehead** ● **n.** a small wrasse of the tropical East Atlantic, the large males of which have a blue head and green body with vertical stripes. [*Thalassoma bifasciatum*.]

**blue heeler** ● **n.** Austral./NZ a cattle dog with a dark speckled body.

**blue helmet** ● **n.** a member of a United Nations peacekeeping force.

**blueing** ● **n.** variant spelling of **BLUING**.

**blueish** ● **adj.** variant spelling of **BLUISH**.

**bluejacket** ● **n.** informal a sailor in the navy.

**Blue John** ● **n.** a blue or purple banded variety of fluorite found in Derbyshire.

**blue law** ● **n.** N. Amer. a law prohibiting certain activities, such as shopping, on a Sunday.
– ORIGIN C18: in ref. to strict puritanical laws in colonial New England, orig. printed on blue paper.

**blue line** ● **n.** Ice Hockey either of the two lines running across the ice between the centre line and the goal line.

**blue metal** ● **n.** Brit. broken blue stone used for road-making.

**blue mould** ● **n.** a bluish fungus which grows on food, especially the mould producing blue cheeses. [*Penicillium* and other genera.]

**bluenose** ● **n.** informal, chiefly N. Amer. **1** (**Bluenose**) a person from Nova Scotia. **2** a priggish or puritanical person.
– DERIVATIVES **bluenosed** adj.
– ORIGIN prob. with ref. to **BLUE LAW**.

**blue note** ● **n.** Music a minor interval where a major would be expected, used especially in jazz.

**blue pencil** ● **n.** a blue pencil as traditionally used to censor a text.

**Blue Peter** ● **n.** a blue flag with a white square in the centre, raised by a ship about to leave port.

**blue-plate** ● **adj.** N. Amer. (of a restaurant meal) consisting of a full main course ordered as a single menu item.
– ORIGIN with ref. to blue plates divided into compartments, on which fixed-price restaurant meals were formerly served.

**blue pointer** ● **n.** another term for **MAKO**[1].

**blueprint** ● **n. 1** a design plan or other technical drawing. **2** something which acts as a plan, model, or template. ● **v.** N. Amer. draw up (a plan or model).
– ORIGIN C19: from the original process in which prints were composed of white lines on a blue ground or of blue lines on a white ground.

**blue riband** ● **n. 1** (also **blue ribbon**) a ribbon of blue silk given to the winner of a competition or as a mark of great distinction. ➤a badge worn by members of the Order of the Garter. **2** (**Blue Riband** or **Ribbon**) a trophy for the ship making the fastest eastward sea crossing of the Atlantic Ocean on a regular commercial voyage. ● **adj.** (**blue-ribbon**) N. Amer. **1** of the highest quality; first-class. **2** (of a jury or committee) carefully or specially selected.

**blue rinse** ● **n.** a preparation used as a rinse on grey or white hair to give it a temporary blue tint.

**blue roan** • **n.** an animal with a coat of black and white hairs evenly mixed, giving it a blue-grey hue.

**blues** • **pl. n. 1** [treated as sing. or pl.] melancholic music of black American folk origin, typically in a twelve-bar sequence. **2** (**the blues**) informal feelings of melancholy, sadness, or depression.
– DERIVATIVES **bluesy** adj.
– ORIGIN C18: from *blue devils* 'depression or delirium tremens'.

**blueschist** /'blu:ʃɪst/ • **n.** a metamorphic rock with a blue colour, formed under conditions of high pressure and low temperature.

**blue shift** • **n.** Astronomy the displacement of the spectrum to shorter wavelengths in the light coming from distant celestial objects moving towards the observer. Compare with **RED SHIFT**.

**blue-sky** • **adj.** informal not yet practicable or profitable: *blue-sky research*.

**bluestocking** • **n.** often derogatory an intellectual or literary woman.
– ORIGIN C17: in ref. to literary assemblies held in London by society ladies, where some of the men favoured less formal dress.

**bluestone** • **n. 1** a bluish or grey building stone. **2** any of the smaller dolerite stones forming the inner part of Stonehenge.

**bluet** /'blu:ɪt/ • **n.** a low-growing evergreen North American plant with milky-blue flowers. [*Hedyotis caerulea*.]
– ORIGIN C18: from Fr., dimin. of *bleu* 'blue'.

**bluethroat** • **n.** a songbird resembling the robin, of which the male has a blue throat with a red or white spot in the centre. [*Luscinia svecicus*.]

**blue tit** • **n.** a common titmouse with a blue cap, greenish-blue back, and yellow underparts. [*Parus caeruleus*.]

**bluetongue** • **n.** a viral disease of sheep, characterized by fever, lameness, and a blue, swollen mouth and tongue.

**Bluetooth** • **n.** trademark a standard for the short-range wireless interconnection of mobile phones, computers, and other electronic devices.
– ORIGIN named after the 10th-cent. Viking king Harald *Bluetooth*, who united Denmark and Norway.

**blue vinny** /'vɪni/ (also **blue vinney**) • **n.** a blue-mould skimmed-milk cheese from Dorset.
– ORIGIN from OE *fyniġ* 'mouldy, musty'.

**blue vitriol** • **n.** archaic crystalline copper sulphate.

**blue whale** • **n.** a mottled bluish-grey rorqual which is the largest living animal and reaches lengths of up to 27 m (90 ft). [*Balaenoptera musculus*.]

**bluey** • **adj.** almost or partly blue. • **n.** (pl. **-eys**) Austral./NZ informal, archaic **1** a bundle of possessions carried by a bushman. [so named because the covering was generally a blue blanket.] **2** a nickname for a red-headed person.

**bluff**[1] • **n.** an attempt to deceive someone into believing that one can or will do something. • **v.** try to deceive someone as to one's abilities or intentions.
– PHRASES **call someone's bluff 1** challenge someone to carry out a stated intention, in the expectation of being able to expose it as a pretence. **2** (in poker or brag) make an opponent show their hand in order to reveal that its value is weaker than their heavy betting suggests.
– DERIVATIVES **bluffer** n.
– ORIGIN C17 (in the sense 'blindfold, hoodwink'): from Du. *bluffen* 'brag', or *bluf* 'bragging'.

**bluff**[2] • **adj.** good-naturedly frank and direct.
– DERIVATIVES **bluffly** adv. **bluffness** n.
– ORIGIN C18 (in the sense 'surly'): figurative use of **BLUFF**[3].

**bluff**[3] • **n. 1** a steep cliff, bank, or promontory. **2** Canadian a grove or clump of trees. • **adj.** (of a cliff or a ship's bows) having a vertical or steep broad front.
– ORIGIN C17 (in naut. use): of unknown origin.

**bluing** (also **blueing**) • **n. 1** chiefly historical blue powder used to preserve the whiteness of laundry. **2** a greyish-blue finish on metal produced by heating.

**bluish** (also **blueish**) • **adj.** having a blue tinge.

**blunder** • **n.** a stupid or careless mistake. • **v. 1** make a blunder. **2** move clumsily or as if unable to see.
– DERIVATIVES **blunderer** n. **blundering** adj. **blunderingly** adv.
– ORIGIN ME: prob. of Scand. origin and rel. to **BLIND**.

**blunderbuss** • **n. 1** historical a short large-bored gun firing balls or slugs. **2** an unsubtle and imprecise action or method.
– ORIGIN C17: alt. (by assoc. with **BLUNDER**) of Du. *donderbus*, lit. 'thunder gun'.

**blunge** /blʌn(d)ʒ/ • **v.** mix (clay or other materials) with water in a revolving apparatus, for use in ceramics.
– DERIVATIVES **blunger** n.
– ORIGIN C19: blend of **BLEND** and **PLUNGE**.

**blunt** • **adj. 1** lacking a sharp edge or point. ➤having a flat or rounded end. **2** uncompromisingly forthright in manner. • **v. 1** make or become less sharp. **2** weaken or reduce the force of. • **n.** black slang a hollowed-out cigar filled with cannabis.
– DERIVATIVES **bluntly** adv. **bluntness** n.
– ORIGIN ME (in the sense 'dull, insensitive'): perh. of Scand. origin and rel. to ON *blunda* 'shut the eyes'.

**blur** • **v.** (**blurred**, **blurring**) make or become unclear or less distinct. • **n.** something that cannot be seen, heard, or recalled clearly.
– DERIVATIVES **blurry** adj. (**-ier**, **-iest**).
– ORIGIN C16 (in the sense 'smear)': perh. rel. to **BLEAR**.

**blurb** • **n.** a short description of a book, film, or other product written for promotional purposes. • **v.** informal, chiefly N. Amer. write a blurb for.
– ORIGIN C20: coined by the US humorist Gelett Burgess.

**blurt** • **v.** (usu. **blurt out**) say suddenly and without careful consideration.
– ORIGIN C16: prob. imitative.

**blush** • **v. 1** become red in the face through shyness, embarrassment, or shame. **2** poetic/literary be or become pink or pale red. • **n. 1** an instance of blushing. **2** poetic/literary a pink or pale red tinge. **3** a wine with a slight pink tint made in the manner of white wine but from red grape varieties.
– PHRASES **at first blush** at the first glimpse or impression.
– DERIVATIVES **blushing** adj. **blushingly** adv.
– ORIGIN OE *blyscan*, rel. to Du. *blozen*.

**blusher** • **n. 1** a cosmetic used to give a warm reddish tinge to the cheeks. **2** a toadstool with white flesh that turns pink when bruised or cut. [*Amanita rubescens*.]

**bluster** • **v. 1** talk in a loud, aggressive, or indignant way with little effect. **2** (of wind or rain) blow or beat fiercely and noisily. • **n.** blustering talk.
– DERIVATIVES **blusterer** n. **blustery** adj.
– ORIGIN ME: ult. imitative.

**Blu-tack** • **n.** Brit. trademark a blue sticky material used to attach paper to walls.

**B-lymphocyte** • **n.** Physiology a lymphocyte of a type not processed by the thymus gland, responsible for producing antibodies. Compare with **T-LYMPHOCYTE**.
– ORIGIN *B* for **BURSA**, referring to the organ in birds where it was first identified.

**BM** • **abbrev. 1** Bachelor of Medicine. **2** British Museum.

**BMA** • **abbrev.** British Medical Association.

**B-movie** • **n.** a low-budget film of poor quality made for use as a supporting feature in a cinema programme.

**BMR** • **abbrev.** basal metabolic rate.

**BMus** • **abbrev.** Bachelor of Music.

**BMX** • **n.** [as modifier] denoting or relating to bicycles of a robust design suitable for cross-country racing.
– ORIGIN 1970s: from *bicycle motocross*.

**Bn** • **abbrev. 1** Baron. **2** Battalion.

**bn** • **abbrev.** billion.

**BNP** • **abbrev.** British National Party.

**BO** • **abbrev.** informal body odour.

**bo**[1] • **exclam.** another term for **BOO**.

**bo**[2] • **n.** US informal used as a friendly form of address.
– ORIGIN C19: perh. an abbrev. of **BOY**.

**boa** /'bəʊə/ • **n. 1** a large snake which kills its prey by

constriction and bears live young. [*Boa constrictor* (tropical America) and other species, family Boidae.] **2** a long, thin stole of feathers or fur worn around a woman's neck, usually as part of evening dress.
– ORIGIN ME: from L., of unknown ultimate origin.

**boab** /ˈbəʊab/ • **n.** Austral. another term for BAOBAB.

**boak** /ˈbəʊk/ • **v.** variant spelling of BOKE.

**boar** • **n.** (pl. same or **boars**) **1** (also **wild boar**) a tusked wild pig from which domestic pigs are descended. [*Sus scrofa*.] **2** an uncastrated domestic male pig. **3** the full-grown male of certain other animals, especially a badger, guinea pig, or hedgehog.
– ORIGIN OE *bār*, of W. Gmc origin.

**board** • **n.** **1** a long, thin, flat piece of wood used for floors or other building purposes. ➤ **(the boards)** informal the stage of a theatre. **2** a thin, flat, rectangular piece of stiff material, e.g. a chopping board or noticeboard. ➤ the piece of equipment on which one stands in surfing, skateboarding, etc. **3** [treated as sing. or pl.] the decision-making body of an organization. **4** the provision of regular meals in return for payment or services. ➤ archaic a table set for a meal. **5** Sailing a distance covered by a vessel in a single tack. • **v.** **1** get on or into (a ship, aircraft, or other vehicle). ➤ **(be boarding)** (of an aircraft) be ready for passengers to get on. **2** live somewhere and receive meals in return for payment or services. ➤ (of a pupil) live in school during term time in return for payment. **3** (**board something up/over**) cover or seal a window or building with pieces of wood. **4** [as adj. **boarded**] made of wooden boards. **5** ride on a snowboard.
– PHRASES **go by the board** (of a plan or principle) be abandoned, rejected, or ignored. [from naut. use meaning 'fall overboard', *board* meaning the side of the ship.] **on board** on or in a ship, aircraft, or other vehicle. **take something on board** informal fully consider or assimilate a new idea or situation. **tread** (or **walk**) **the boards** informal appear on stage as an actor.
– DERIVATIVES **boarding** n.
– ORIGIN OE *bord*, of Gmc origin; reinforced in ME by OFr. *bort* 'edge, ship's side' and ON *borth* 'board, table'.

**boarder** • **n.** **1** a person who boards, in particular a pupil who lives in school during term time in return for payment. **2** a person who forces their way on to a ship in an attack.

**board foot** • **n.** (pl. **board feet**) a unit of volume for wood equal to 144 cu. in.

**board game** • **n.** a game that involves the movement of counters or other objects around a board.

**boarding house** • **n.** a private house providing food and lodging for paying guests.

**boarding kennel** • **n.** a place in which dogs are kept and looked after while their owners are away.

**boarding pass** (also **boarding card**) • **n.** a passenger's pass for boarding an aircraft.

**boarding school** • **n.** a school in which the pupils live during term time.

**Board of Green Cloth** • **n.** full form of GREEN CLOTH.

**Board of Trade** • **n.** **1** North American term for CHAMBER OF COMMERCE. **2** a now nominal British government department within the Department of Trade and Industry concerned with commerce and industry.

**boardroom** • **n.** a room in which a board of directors meets regularly.

**boardsailing** • **n.** another term for WINDSURFING.
– DERIVATIVES **boardsailor** n.

**board school** • **n.** historical an elementary school under the management of a School Board.

**boardwalk** • **n.** a wooden walkway across sand or marshy ground. ➤ N. Amer. a promenade along a beach or waterfront.

**boarfish** • **n.** (pl. same or **-fishes**) a deep-bodied fish with a protruding snout, a small mouth, small toothed scales, and a spiny dorsal fin. [*Pentaceros richardsoni*, *Capros aper*, and other species.]

**boart** • **n.** variant spelling of BORT.

**boast**[1] • **v.** **1** talk with excessive pride and self-satisfaction about oneself. **2** possess (a feature that is a source of pride). • **n.** an act of boasting.
– DERIVATIVES **boaster** n. **boastful** adj. **boastfully** adv. **boastfulness** n. **boasting** adj. **boastingly** adv.
– ORIGIN ME: of unknown origin.

**boast**[2] • **n.** (in squash) a stroke in which the ball hits a side wall before hitting the front wall.
– ORIGIN C19: perh. from Fr. *bosse*, denoting a rounded projection in the wall of a court for real tennis.

**boat** • **n.** a small vessel propelled by oars, sails, or an engine. ➤ a vessel of any size. • **v.** travel in a boat. ➤ transport in a boat.
– PHRASES **be in the same boat** informal be in the same difficult circumstances as others. **miss the boat** see MISS. **push the boat out** Brit. informal be extravagant. **rock the boat** informal disturb an existing situation.
– DERIVATIVES **boatful** n. (pl. **-fuls**). **boating** n. **boatload** n.
– ORIGIN OE *bāt*, of Gmc origin.

**boatbill** • **n.** (also **boat-billed heron**) a small Central and South American heron with a broad flattened bill and a prominent black crest. [*Cochlearius cochlearius*.]

**boat deck** • **n.** the deck from which a ship's lifeboats are launched.

**boatel** /bəʊˈtɛl/ (also **botel**) • **n.** **1** a waterside hotel with facilities for mooring boats. **2** a moored ship used as a hotel.
– ORIGIN 1950s (orig. US): blend of BOAT and HOTEL.

**boater** • **n.** **1** a flat-topped hardened straw hat with a brim. [orig. worn while boating.] **2** a person who travels in a boat.

**boathook** • **n.** a long pole with a hook and a spike at one end, used for moving boats.

**boathouse** • **n.** a shed at the edge of a river or lake used for housing boats.

**boatie** • **n.** (pl. **-ies**) informal a boating enthusiast.

**boatman** • **n.** (pl. **-men**) a person who provides transport by boat.

**boat people** • **pl. n.** refugees who have left a country by sea.

**boat race** • **n.** **1** a race between rowing crews. **2** Brit. rhyming slang a person's face.

**boatswain** /ˈbəʊs(ə)n/ (also **bo'sun** or **bosun**) • **n.** a ship's officer in charge of equipment and the crew.
– ORIGIN OE *bātswegen* (see BOAT, SWAIN).

**boatswain's chair** • **n.** a seat suspended from ropes, used for work on the body or masts of a ship or the face of a building.

**boat train** • **n.** a train scheduled to connect with the arrival or departure of a boat.

**boatyard** • **n.** a place where boats are built or stored.

**Bob** • **n.** (in phr. **Bob's your uncle**) Brit. informal an expression signifying the simplicity of completing a task.

**bob**[1] • **v.** (**bobbed**, **bobbing**) **1** make or cause to make a quick, short movement up and down. ➤ make a sudden move so as to appear or disappear. **2** curtsy briefly. • **n.** **1** a quick, short movement up and down. **2** a brief curtsy.
– PHRASES **bob and weave** (of a boxer) move rapidly up and down and from side to side as an evasive tactic. **bob for apples** try to catch floating apples with one's mouth, as a game.
– ORIGIN ME: of unknown origin.

**bob**[2] • **n.** **1** a short hairstyle hanging evenly all round. **2** a weight on a pendulum, plumb line, or kite-tail. **3** a bobsleigh. **4** a short line at or towards the end of a stanza. • **v.** (**bobbed**, **bobbing**) **1** cut (hair) in a bob. **2** ride on a bobsleigh.
– ORIGIN ME (denoting a bunch or cluster): of unknown origin.

**bob**[3] • **n.** (pl. same) Brit. informal a shilling.
– ORIGIN C18: of unknown origin.

**bob**[4] • **n.** a change of order in bell-ringing.
– ORIGIN C17: perh. connected with BOB[1].

**bobber** • **n.** **1** a person who rides on a bobsleigh. **2** a float used in angling.

**bobbin** • **n.** **1** a cylinder, cone, or reel holding thread or yarn. **2** a small bar attached to a string used for raising a

door latch.
– ORIGIN C16: from Fr. *bobine*.

**bobbinet** /ˈbɒbɪnɛt/ ● **n.** machine-made cotton net (imitating bobbin lace).

**bobbin lace** ● **n.** lace made by hand with thread wound on bobbins.

**bobble**[1] ● **n.** a small ball made of strands of wool, as used as a decoration on a hat or as forming on the surface of knitted fabric.
– DERIVATIVES **bobbly** adj.
– ORIGIN 1920s: dimin. of **BOB**[2].

**bobble**[2] /ˈbɒb(ə)l/ informal ● **v. 1** move with an irregular bouncing motion. **2** N. Amer. mishandle (a ball). ● **n. 1** an irregular bouncing motion. **2** N. Amer. a mishandling of a ball.
– ORIGIN C19: frequentative of **BOB**[1].

**bobby** ● **n.** (pl. **-ies**) Brit. informal, dated a police officer.
– ORIGIN C19: after Sir *Robert* Peel, the Brit. Prime Minister who established the Metropolitan Police.

**bobby calf** ● **n.** (pl. **-ies**) an unweaned calf slaughtered for veal.
– ORIGIN 1920s: perh. from **BOB**[2], in the sense 'small, short'.

**bobby-dazzler** ● **n.** Brit. informal, dated an excellent person or thing.
– ORIGIN C19: orig. north. Engl. dial.

**bobby pin** ● **n.** N. Amer. & Austral./NZ a sprung hairpin or small clip. ● **v.** (**bobby-pin**) fix (hair) in place with a bobby pin.
– ORIGIN 1930s: from **BOB**[2] (because orig. used with bobbed hair) + **-Y**[2].

**bobby socks** ● **pl. n.** N. Amer. socks reaching just above the ankle, worn by teenage girls in the 1940s and 1950s.
– ORIGIN cf. **BOB**[2] in the sense 'cut short'.

**bobby-soxer** ● **n.** N. Amer. informal, dated a teenage girl.

**bobcat** ● **n.** a small North American lynx with a barred and spotted coat and a short tail. [*Felis rufus*.]
– ORIGIN C19: from **BOB**[2] (with ref. to its short tail) + **CAT**[1].

**bobolink** /ˈbɒbəlɪŋk/ ● **n.** a North American songbird with a finch-like bill. [*Dolichonyx oryzivorus*.]
– ORIGIN C18 (orig. *Bob o'Lincoln, Bob Lincoln*): imitative of its call.

**bobotie** /bəˈbuːti, -ˈbʊəti/ ● **n.** a South African dish of curried minced meat baked with a savoury custard topping.
– ORIGIN Afrik., prob. of Malay or Javanese origin.

**bobskate** ● **n.** an adjustable skate for a child, consisting of two sections of double runners.

**bobsled** /ˈbɒbslɛd/ ● **n.** North American term for **BOBSLEIGH**.
– DERIVATIVES **bobsledding** n.

**bobsleigh** ● **n.** chiefly Brit. a mechanically steered and braked sledge used for racing down an ice-covered run.
– DERIVATIVES **bobsleighing** n.
– ORIGIN C19: from **BOB**[2] in the sense 'short' + **SLEIGH**.

**bobstay** ● **n.** a rope used to hold down the bowsprit of a ship and keep it steady.
– ORIGIN C18: prob. from **BOB**[1] + **STAY**[2].

**bobsy-die** /ˌbɒbzɪˈdʌɪ/ ● **n.** dialect & NZ a great deal of fuss or trouble.
– ORIGIN C19: contr. of *Bob's-a-dying*.

**bobtail** ● **n.** a docked tail of a horse or dog.
– ORIGIN C16: prob. from **BOB**[2] + **TAIL**[1].

**bobweight** ● **n.** a counterweight to a moving part in a machine.

**bobwhite** ● **n.** an American quail with mottled reddish-brown plumage, and a pale throat and eyestripe. [Genus *Colinus virginianus*.]
– ORIGIN C19: imitative of its call.

**bocage** /bəˈkɑːʒ/ ● **n. 1** (in France) pastureland divided into small hedged fields interspersed with groves of trees. **2** the modelling of plants and flowers in clay.
– ORIGIN C16: from Fr., from OFr. *boscage* (see **BOSCAGE**).

**bocce** /ˈbɒtʃeɪ, ˈbɒtʃi/ (also **boccia** /ˈbɒtʃə/) ● **n.** an Italian game similar to bowls but played on a smaller green.
– ORIGIN Ital., 'bowls', pl. of *boccia* 'ball'.

**bocconcini** /ˌbɒkɒnˈtʃiːni/ ● **pl. n.** small balls of mozzarella cheese.
– ORIGIN from Ital.

**Boche** /bɒʃ/ ● **n.** (**the Boche**) informal, dated Germans, especially German soldiers, collectively.
– ORIGIN from Fr. soldiers' sl., orig. in the sense 'rascal'; applied to Germans in World War I.

**bock** ● **n.** a strong, dark German beer.
– ORIGIN C19: via Fr. from an abbrev. of Ger. *Eimbockbier* 'beer from *Einbeck*', a town in Hanover.

**BOD** ● **abbrev.** biochemical oxygen demand.

**bod** ● **n.** informal **1** a body. **2** chiefly Brit. a person.
– ORIGIN C18: orig. Scots.

**bodach** /ˈbəʊdɑːx/ ● **n.** Scottish & Irish **1** an old man or peasant. **2** a ghost.
– ORIGIN C19 (earlier as *buddough*): from Sc. Gaelic.

**bodacious** /bəʊˈdeɪʃəs/ ● **adj.** N. Amer. informal excellent, admirable, or attractive.
– ORIGIN C19: perh. a var. of SW dial. *boldacious*, blend of **BOLD** and **AUDACIOUS**.

**bode** ● **v.** (**bode well/ill**) be a portent of a good or bad outcome.
– ORIGIN OE *bodian* 'proclaim, foretell', from *boda* 'messenger', of Gmc origin.

**bodega** /bəˈdeɪɡə/ ● **n.** a cellar or shop selling wine and food, especially in a Spanish-speaking country.
– ORIGIN C19: from Sp., via L. from Gk *apothēkē* 'storehouse': cf. **BOUTIQUE**.

**Bode's law** /ˈbəʊdz, ˈbəʊdəz/ ● **n.** Astronomy an empirical formula by which the distances of the first seven planets from the sun are roughly derived in terms of powers of two.
– ORIGIN C19: named after the Ger. astronomer Johann E. *Bode*.

**bodge** ● **v.** Brit. informal make or repair badly or clumsily.
– DERIVATIVES **bodger** n.
– ORIGIN C16: alt. of **BOTCH**.

**bodgie** ● **n.** (pl. **-ies**) Austral./NZ informal **1** historical a Teddy boy. **2** a flawed or worthless thing.
– ORIGIN prob. from ***bodger*** (see **BODGE**).

**bodhisattva** /ˌbɒdɪˈsɑːtvə/ ● **n.** (in Mahayana Buddhism) a person who is able to reach nirvana but delays doing so through compassion for suffering beings.
– ORIGIN Sanskrit, 'a person whose essence is perfect knowledge', from *bodhi* 'perfect knowledge' + *sattva* 'being, essence'.

**bodhrán** /ˈbaʊrɑːn, baʊˈrɑːn/ ● **n.** a shallow one-sided Irish drum typically played using a short stick.
– ORIGIN from Ir.

**bodh tree** ● **n.** variant of **BO TREE**.

**bodice** ● **n.** the part of a woman's dress (excluding sleeves) above the waist. ➤a woman's sleeveless undergarment, often laced at the front.
– ORIGIN C16 orig. *bodies*, pl. of **BODY**, retaining the original pronunc.

**bodice-ripper** ● **n.** informal, humorous a sexually explicit historical novel or film.
– DERIVATIVES **bodice-ripping** adj.

**bodiless** ● **adj. 1** lacking a body. **2** incorporeal; insubstantial.

**bodily** ● **adj. 1** of or concerning the body. **2** material or physical. ● **adv.** by taking hold of a person's body with force.

**bodkin** ● **n. 1** a thick, blunt needle with a large eye, used for drawing tape through a hem. ➤historical a long pin used to fasten women's hair. **2** Printing a pointed tool used for removing pieces of metal type for correction.
– ORIGIN ME: perh. of Celtic origin and rel. to Ir. *bod*, Welsh *bidog*, Sc. Gaelic *biodag* 'dagger'.

**body** ● **n.** (pl. **-ies**) **1** the physical structure, including the bones, flesh, and organs, of a person or an animal. ➤informal, dated a person. ➤the trunk apart from the head and the limbs. ➤a corpse. **2** the main or central part of something. ➤a mass or collection of something. **3** an organized group of people with a common function: *a*

*regulatory body.* **4** technical a material object. **5** a full flavour in wine. **6** fullness of a person's hair. **7** a bodysuit. ● v. (**-ies, -ied**) (**body something forth**) give material form to something abstract.
– PHRASES **in a body** as a group. **keep body and soul together** stay alive in difficult circumstances. **over my dead body** informal used to express strong opposition.
– DERIVATIVES **-bodied** adj.
– ORIGIN OE *bodig*, of unknown origin.

**body armour** ● n. clothing worn by the army and police to protect against gunfire.

**body art** ● n. **1** the practice of decorating the body by means of tattooing, piercing, etc. **2** an artistic genre in which the actual body of the artist or model is integral to the work.

**body bag** ● n. a bag used for carrying a corpse from the scene of an accident or crime.

**body blow** ● n. **1** a heavy punch to the body. **2** a severe setback.

**bodyboard** ● n. a short, light surfboard ridden in a prone position.
– DERIVATIVES **bodyboarder** n. **bodyboarding** n.

**bodybuilder** ● n. a person who strengthens and enlarges their muscles through exercise such as weightlifting.
– DERIVATIVES **bodybuilding** n.

**body-check** ● n. (especially in ice hockey) an attempt to obstruct a player by bumping into them. ● v. obstruct (a player) in such a way.

**body clock** ● n. a person's biological clock.

**body colour** ● n. opaque pigment used in painting, especially gouache.

**body corporate** ● n. formal term for **CORPORATION**.

**body double** ● n. a stand-in for a film actor during stunt or nude scenes.

**body dysmorphic disorder** ● n. a psychological disorder in which a person becomes obsessed with imaginary defects in their appearance.

**body English** ● n. N. Amer. **1** a follow-through bodily motion after throwing a ball, intended as an attempt to control the ball's trajectory. **2** another term for **BODY LANGUAGE**.
– ORIGIN from **ENGLISH** (in sense 2).

**bodyguard** ● n. a person employed to protect a rich or famous person.

**body language** ● n. the conscious and unconscious bodily movements by which feelings are communicated.

**bodyline** ● n. Cricket, historical fast short-pitched bowling on the leg side, threatening the batsman's body.

**body louse** ● n. a louse which infests the human body and is able to transmit several diseases through its bite, including typhus. [*Pediculus humanus humanus.*]

**body odour** ● n. the unpleasant smell of a person's unwashed body.

**body piercing** ● n. the decorative piercing of parts of the body other than the ear lobes.

**body politic** ● n. the people of a nation or society considered as an organized group of citizens.

**body-popping** ● n. a kind of dancing characterized by jerky robotic movements of the joints.

**body scrub** ● n. an exfoliating and cleansing cosmetic preparation applied to the skin.

**bodyshell** ● n. the frame of a motor or railway vehicle, to which the panels are attached.

**body shop** ● n. a garage where repairs to the bodywork of vehicles are carried out.

**bodysnatcher** ● n. historical a person who illicitly disinterred corpses for dissection.
– DERIVATIVES **bodysnatching** n.

**body stocking** ● n. a woman's one-piece undergarment covering the torso and legs.

**bodysuit** ● n. a woman's close-fitting stretch garment for the upper body, fastening at the crotch.

**bodysurf** ● v. surf without using a board.

**body warmer** ● n. a sleeveless padded jacket worn outdoors.

**body wave** ● n. a light permanent wave designed to give the hair body.

**bodywork** ● n. **1** the metal outer shell of a vehicle. **2** therapies in complementary medicine which involve touching or manipulating the body.
– DERIVATIVES **bodyworker** n.

**body wrap** ● n. a beauty treatment intended to result in a reduction in body measurements, involving wrapping the body in hot bandages.

**Boer** /bɔː, ˈbəʊə, bʊə/ ● n. a member of the Dutch and Huguenot population which settled in southern Africa in the late 17th century. ● adj. of or relating to the Boers.
– ORIGIN from Du. *boer* 'farmer'.

**boerbull** /ˈbʊəbʊl/ ● n. S. African a large cross-breed dog bred from the mastiff and indigenous African dogs.
– ORIGIN 1960s: from Afrik. *boerboel*, from *boer* (applied to indigenous plants and animals) + *boel*, from Du. *bul* (as in *bulhond* 'mastiff').

**boerewors** /ˈbuːrəˌvɔːs, ˈbʊ-/ ● n. S. African a traditional sausage containing coarsely ground beef and pork.
– ORIGIN Afrik., from *boere* 'Afrikaner or farmer's' + *wors* 'sausage'.

**boeuf bourguignon** /ˌbəːf ˈbɔːgɪnjɒ̃/ ● n. a dish consisting of beef stewed in red wine.
– ORIGIN Fr., lit. 'Burgundy beef'.

**boff** N. Amer. informal ● v. **1** hit or strike. **2** have sexual intercourse with. ● n. **1** a blow or punch. **2** an act of sexual intercourse.
– ORIGIN 1920s: imitative.

**boffin** ● n. informal, chiefly Brit. a person engaged in scientific or technical research.
– DERIVATIVES **boffiny** adj.
– ORIGIN Second World War: of unknown origin.

**boffo** N. Amer. informal ● adj. **1** (of a play or film) resoundingly successful. **2** (of a laugh) deep and unrestrained. ● n. (pl. **-os**) a success.
– ORIGIN 1940s: from US *boff* 'roaring success' + **-O**.

**boffola** /bɒˈfəʊlə/ ● n. N. Amer. informal a joke that elicits a hearty laugh.
– ORIGIN 1940s: extension of sl. *boff* 'hearty laugh'.

**bog** ● n. **1** an area of very soft wet muddy ground. ➤ Ecology wetland with acid, peaty soil. Compare with **FEN**[1]. **2** Brit. informal a toilet. ● v. (**bogged, bogging**) **1** (usu. **be bogged down**) cause to become stuck; hinder the progress of. **2** (**bog in**) Austral./NZ informal start a task enthusiastically. **3** (**bog off**) Brit. informal go away.
– DERIVATIVES **bogginess** n. **boggy** adj.
– ORIGIN ME: from Ir. or Sc. Gaelic *bogach*, from *bog* 'soft'.

**bog arum** ● n. an arum with heart-shaped leaves, a white spathe, and a green spadix, growing in boggy ground. [*Calla palustris.*]

**bog asphodel** ● n. a yellow-flowered marsh plant of the lily family. [*Narthecium ossifragum.*]

**bogbean** ● n. a plant of bogs and shallow water with creeping rhizomes, three-lobed leaves, and hairy flowers. [*Menyanthes trifoliata.*]

**bog cotton** ● n. another term for **COTTON GRASS**.

**bogey**[1] Golf ● n. (pl. **-eys**) a score of one stroke over par at a hole. ➤ old-fashioned term for **PAR**[1] (in sense 1). ● v. (**-eys, -eyed**) play (a hole) in one stroke over par.
– ORIGIN C19: perh. from *Bogey*, denoting the Devil (see **BOGEY**[2]).

**bogey**[2] (also **bogy**) ● n. (pl. **-eys**) **1** an evil or mischievous spirit. **2** US military slang an enemy aircraft. **3** Brit. informal a piece of nasal mucus.
– ORIGIN C19 (as a name applied to the Devil): of unknown origin.

**bogeyman** (also **bogyman**) ● n. (pl. **-men**) an evil spirit.

**boggart** /ˈbɒgət/ ● n. Scottish & N. English an evil or mischievous spirit.
– ORIGIN C16: rel. to obs. *bog* 'bugbear', **BOGGLE**, and **BOGLE**.

**boggle** ● v. informal be startled or baffled: *the mind boggles at the spectacle.* ➤ (**boggle at**) hesitate or be anxious at.
– ORIGIN C16: prob. of dial. origin and rel. to **BOGLE** and **BOGEY**[2].

**bogie** /ˈbəʊgi/ ● **n.** (pl. **-ies**) chiefly Brit. **1** an undercarriage with four or six wheels pivoted beneath the end of a railway vehicle. ➤Indian a railway carriage. **2** chiefly N. English a low truck on four small wheels.
– ORIGIN C19 (orig. in north. Engl. dial. use): of unknown origin.

**bog iron** ● **n.** an impure, porous form of limonite deposited in bogs.

**bogle** ● **n.** **1** a phantom or goblin. **2** Scottish & N. English a scarecrow.
– ORIGIN C16: of unknown origin; prob. rel. to **BOGEY**[2].

**bog moss** ● **n.** another term for **PEAT MOSS** (in sense 1).

**bog myrtle** ● **n.** a deciduous shrub of boggy places, with short upright catkins and aromatic grey-green leaves. [*Myrica gale.*]

**bog oak** ● **n.** an ancient oak tree preserved in peat, with hard black wood.

**Bogomil** /ˈbəʊgəmɪl, ˈbɒg-/ ● **n.** a member of a heretical medieval Balkan sect professing a form of Manichaeism.
– DERIVATIVES **Bogomilism** n.
– ORIGIN C19: from med. Gk *Bogomilos*, from *Bogomil*, lit. 'beloved of God', the name of the person who first spread the heresy.

**bogong** /ˈbəʊgɒŋ/ ● **n.** a large brown moth of southern Australia, formerly eaten by Aboriginals. [*Agrotis infusa.*]
– ORIGIN C19: from Aborig.

**bog rosemary** ● **n.** a pink-flowered evergreen dwarf shrub, growing in boggy soils. [Genus *Andromeda*: two species.]

**bog spavin** ● **n.** a soft swelling of the joint capsule of the hock, occurring in young horses.

**bog-standard** ● **adj.** informal, derogatory ordinary; basic.

**bogtrotter** ● **n.** informal, offensive an Irish person.

**bogus** /ˈbəʊgəs/ ● **adj.** not genuine or true.
– DERIVATIVES **bogusly** adv. **bogusness** n.
– ORIGIN C18 (orig. US, denoting a machine for making counterfeit money): of unknown origin.

**bogy** ● **n.** (pl. **-ies**) variant spelling of **BOGEY**[2].

**bogyman** ● **n.** variant spelling of **BOGEYMAN**.

**bohea** /bəʊˈhiː/ ● **n.** a low-quality black China tea from the last crop of the season.
– ORIGIN C18: named after the *Bu-yi* (*Wuyi*) hills in China.

**Bohemian** ● **n.** **1** a native or inhabitant of Bohemia, a region of the Czech Republic. **2** a socially unconventional person, especially an artist or writer. [C19: from Fr. *bohémien* 'gypsy' (because gypsies were thought to come from Bohemia).] ● **adj.** **1** of or relating to Bohemia or its people. **2** socially unconventional.
– DERIVATIVES **Bohemianism** n.

**boho** /ˈbəʊhəʊ/ ● **n.** (pl. **-os**) & **adj.** informal term for **BOHEMIAN** (in sense 2).

**bohrium** /ˈbɔːrɪəm/ ● **n.** the chemical element of atomic number 107, a very unstable element made by high-energy atomic collisions. (Symbol: **Bh**)
– ORIGIN C20: named after the Dan. physicist Niels *Bohr*.

**bohunk** /ˈbəʊhʌŋk/ ● **n.** N. Amer. informal, derogatory an immigrant from central or SE Europe.
– ORIGIN C20: appar. from **BOHEMIAN** + *-hunk*, alt. of **HUNGARIAN**.

**boil**[1] ● **v.** **1** (with reference to a liquid) reach or cause to reach the temperature at which it bubbles and turns to vapour. **2** (with reference to food) cook or be cooked by immersing in boiling water. **3** (of the sea or clouds) be turbulent and stormy. ➤(of a person or emotion) be stirred up or inflamed. ➤(**boil over**) become so excited or tense as to lose control. **4** (**boil down to**) amount to. ● **n.** **1** the act or process of boiling; boiling point. **2** Fishing a sudden rise of a fish at a fly.
– PHRASES **keep the pot boiling** maintain the momentum or interest value of something.
– ORIGIN ME: from OFr. *boillir*, from L. *bullire* 'to bubble', from *bulla* 'bubble'.

**boil**[2] ● **n.** an inflamed pus-filled swelling on the skin.
– ORIGIN OE *bȳle*, *bȳl*, of W. Gmc origin.

**boiled shirt** ● **n.** dated a dress shirt with a starched front.

**boiled sweet** ● **n.** Brit. a hard sweet made of boiled sugar.

**boiler** ● **n.** **1** a fuel-burning apparatus for heating water, especially a device providing a domestic hot-water supply or serving a central heating system. ➤a tank for generating steam in a steam engine. **2** Brit. informal a chicken suitable for cooking only by boiling.

**boilermaker** ● **n.** **1** a person who makes boilers. **2** N. Amer. a shot of whisky followed immediately by a glass of beer.

**boilerplate** ● **n.** **1** rolled steel plates for making boilers. **2** (**boilerplates**) Climbing smooth, overlapping slabs of rock. **3** chiefly N. Amer. stereotyped or clichéd writing. ➤standardized pieces of text for use as clauses in contracts or as part of a computer program.

**boiler suit** ● **n.** Brit. a one-piece suit worn as overalls for heavy manual work.

**boilie** /ˈbɔɪli/ ● **n.** (pl. **-ies**) a flavoured fishing bait, spherical in shape, used to catch carp.

**boiling** ● **adj.** at or near boiling point. ➤informal extremely hot. ● **n.** boiling point.

**boiling point** ● **n.** **1** the temperature at which a liquid boils. **2** the point at which anger or excitement breaks out into violence.

**boiling-water reactor** ● **n.** a nuclear reactor in which the coolant and moderator is water, which is boiled to produce steam.

**boing** /bɔɪŋ/ ● **exclam.** representing a reverberating sound, especially the noise of a compressed spring suddenly released.
– ORIGIN 1950s: imitative.

**boisterous** ● **adj.** **1** noisy, energetic, and cheerful. **2** (of weather or water) wild or stormy.
– DERIVATIVES **boisterously** adv. **boisterousness** n.
– ORIGIN ME (in the sense 'rough, stiff'): var. of earlier *boistuous* 'rustic, coarse, boisterous'.

**boîte** /bwʌt/ ● **n.** (pl. pronounced same) a small restaurant or nightclub.
– ORIGIN Fr., lit. 'box'.

**bok choy** /bɒk ˈtʃɔɪ/ ● **n.** US spelling of **PAK CHOI**.

**boke** /bəʊk/ (also **boak**) Scottish ● **v.** vomit. ● **n.** a spell of vomiting.
– ORIGIN ME *bolke*; rel. to **BELCH**.

**bokken** /ˈbɒk(ə)n/ ● **n.** a wooden sword used as a practice weapon in kendo.
– ORIGIN from Japanese.

**bokmakierie** /ˌbɒkməˈkɪəri/ ● **n.** (pl. **-ies**) a shrike with yellow underparts and a black band across the breast, common in southern Africa. [*Telophorus zeylonus.*]
– ORIGIN C19: from Afrik., imitative of its call.

**Bokmål** /ˈbuːkmɔːl/ ● **n.** one of two standard forms (the other being Nynorsk) of the Norwegian language, a modified form of Danish.
– ORIGIN from Norw. *bok* 'book' + *mål* 'language'.

**bolas** /ˈbəʊləs/ ● **n.** [treated as sing. or pl.] (especially in South America) a missile consisting of a number of balls connected by strong cord, thrown to entangle the limbs of cattle or other animals.
– ORIGIN C19: from Sp. and Port., pl. of *bola* 'ball'.

**bold** ● **adj.** **1** confident and daring or courageous. ➤dated audacious; impudent. **2** (of a colour or design) strong or vivid. ➤(of type) having thick strokes. ● **n.** a typeface with thick strokes.
– PHRASES **be** (or **make**) **so bold as to do something** dare to do something that might be considered audacious. (**as**) **bold as brass** confident to the point of impudence.
– DERIVATIVES **boldly** adv. **boldness** n.
– ORIGIN OE *bald*, of Gmc origin.

**boldface** ● **n.** a typeface with thick strokes.
– DERIVATIVES **boldfaced** adj.

**boldo** /ˈbɒldəʊ/ ● **n.** an evergreen Chilean tree from which an edible fruit, a dye, and a medicinal leaf infusion are obtained. [*Peumus boldus.*]
– ORIGIN C18: via Amer. Sp. from Araucanian *voldo*.

**bole**[1] • **n.** a tree trunk.
– ORIGIN ME: from ON *bolr.*

**bole**[2] • **n.** a fine reddish clay containing iron oxide, used as a ground for oil painting.
– ORIGIN ME: from late L. *bolus* (see **BOLUS**).

**bolection** /bəˈlɛkʃ(ə)n/ • **n.** Architecture a decorative moulding above or around a panel.
– ORIGIN C17: of unknown origin.

**bolero** /bəˈlɛːrəʊ/ • **n.** (pl. **-os**) **1** a Spanish dance in simple triple time. ➤ the music for such a dance. **2** /also ˈbɒlərəʊ/ a woman's short open jacket.
– ORIGIN C18: from Sp.

**boletus** /bəˈliːtəs/ (also **bolete**) • **n.** (pl. **boletuses**) a toadstool with pores rather than gills on the underside of the cap, and a thick stem. [Genus *Boletus.*]
– ORIGIN from L., from Gk *bōlitēs*, perh. from *bōlos* 'lump'.

**bolide** /ˈbəʊlʌɪd/ • **n.** a large meteor which explodes in the atmosphere.
– ORIGIN C19: from Fr., from L. *bolis, bolid-*, from Gk *bolis* 'missile'.

**bolivar** /ˌbɒlɪˈvɑː, bɒˈliːvɑː, Spanish boˈliβar/ • **n.** the basic monetary unit of Venezuela, equal to 100 centimos.
– ORIGIN named after the Venezuelan Simon *Bolívar*, who liberated Venezuela from the Spanish.

**Bolivian** /bəˈlɪvɪən/ • **n.** a native or inhabitant of Bolivia. • **adj.** of or relating to Bolivia or its inhabitants.

**boliviano** /bəˌlɪvɪˈɑːnəʊ, Spanish boliˈβjano/ • **n.** (pl. **-os**) the basic monetary unit of Bolivia, equal to 100 centavos or cents.
– ORIGIN Sp., lit. 'Bolivian'.

**boll** /bəʊl/ • **n.** the rounded seed capsule of plants such as cotton or flax.
– ORIGIN ME (orig. denoting a bubble): from MDu. *bolle* 'rounded object'; rel. to **BOWL**[1].

**bollard** /ˈbɒlɑːd, -ləd/ • **n. 1** Brit. a short post used to prevent traffic from entering an area. **2** a short post on a ship or quayside for securing a rope.
– ORIGIN ME: perh. from ON *bolr* (see **BOLE**[1]) + **-ARD**.

**bollix** vulgar slang • **v.** (usu. **bollix something up**) bungle (a task). • **pl. n.** informal spelling of **BOLLOCKS**.

**bollocking** (also **ballocking**) • **n.** Brit. vulgar slang a severe reprimand.
– DERIVATIVES **bollock** v.

**bollocks** (also **ballocks**) • **pl. n.** Brit. vulgar slang **1** the testicles. **2** [treated as sing.] nonsense; rubbish.
– ORIGIN C18: pl. of *bollock*, var. of earlier *ballock*, of Gmc origin; rel. to **BALL**[1].

**bollocky** • **adj.** Austral. informal naked.

**boll weevil** • **n.** a small weevil which feeds on the fibres of the cotton boll. [*Anthonomus grandis.*]

**bollworm** • **n.** a moth caterpillar which is a pest of cotton and other crops in North America.

**Bollywood** • **n.** informal the Indian popular film industry, based in Bombay.

**bolo** /ˈbəʊləʊ/ • **n.** (pl. **-os**) a large single-edged knife used in the Philippines.
– ORIGIN from Sp.

**bologna** /bəˈləʊnjə, bəˈlɒnjə/ • **n.** a large smoked sausage made chiefly of bacon, veal, and pork suet.
– ORIGIN named after *Bologna*, a city in northern Italy.

**bolometer** /bəˈlɒmɪtə/ • **n.** an electrical instrument for measuring radiant energy.
– DERIVATIVES **bolometric** adj.
– ORIGIN C19: from Gk *bolē* 'ray of light' + **-METER**.

**boloney** • **n.** variant spelling of **BALONEY**.

**bolo tie** • **n.** N. Amer. a tie consisting of a cord around the neck with a large ornamental fastening at the throat.
– ORIGIN alt. of *bola tie*, from its resemblance to the **BOLAS**.

**Bolshevik** /ˈbɒlʃɪvɪk/ • **n.** historical **1** a member of the majority faction of the Russian Social Democratic Party, which seized power in the Revolution of 1917. **2** a person with politically subversive or radical views. • **adj.** of, relating to, or characteristic of Bolsheviks or Bolshevism.
– DERIVATIVES **Bolshevism** n. **Bolshevist** n.
– ORIGIN Russ., from *bol'she* 'greater' (with ref. to the greater faction).

**bolshie** (also **bolshy**) Brit. informal • **adj.** deliberately combative or uncooperative. • **n.** (pl. **-ies**) (**Bolshie**) dated a Bolshevik or socialist.
– DERIVATIVES **bolshiness** n.
– ORIGIN C20: abbrev. of **BOLSHEVIK**.

**bolster**[1] /ˈbəʊlstə/ • **n. 1** a long, thick pillow. **2** a part on a vehicle or tool providing structural support or reducing friction. ➤ Building a short timber cap over a post increasing the bearing of the beams it supports. • **v.** support or strengthen.
– DERIVATIVES **bolsterer** n.
– ORIGIN OE of Gmc origin.

**bolster**[2] /ˈbəʊlstə/ • **n.** a heavy chisel used for cutting bricks.
– ORIGIN C20: of unknown origin.

**bolt**[1] • **n. 1** a long pin with a head that screws into a nut, used to fasten things together. ➤ a bar that slides into a socket to fasten a door or window. ➤ the sliding piece of the breech mechanism of a rifle. **2** a short, heavy arrow shot from a crossbow. **3** a flash of lightning across the sky. • **v.** fasten with a bolt.
– PHRASES **a bolt from** (or **out of**) **the blue** a sudden and unexpected event. **bolt upright** with the back very straight. **have shot one's bolt** informal have done everything possible but still not succeeded.
– ORIGIN OE: of unknown origin.

**bolt**[2] • **v. 1** run away suddenly. ➤ (in hunting) cause (a rabbit or fox) to run out of its burrow or hole. **2** (of a plant) grow quickly upwards and stop flowering as seeds develop. **3** eat (food) quickly.
– PHRASES **make a bolt for** try to escape by running suddenly towards.
– ORIGIN ME: from **BOLT**[1], expressing the sense 'fly like an arrow'.

**bolt**[3] • **n. 1** a roll of fabric, originally as a measure. **2** a folded edge of a piece of paper that is trimmed off to allow it to be opened.
– ORIGIN ME: transferred use of **BOLT**[1].

**bolt**[4] (also **boult**) • **v.** archaic pass through a sieve.
– ORIGIN ME: from OFr. *bulter.*

**bolt-action** • **adj.** (of a gun) having a breech which is opened by turning a bolt and sliding it back.

**bolter** • **n. 1** a person or animal that bolts or runs away. ➤ Austral. historical an escaped convict or absconder. **2** a plant that bolts.

**bolt hole** • **n.** chiefly Brit. an escape route or hiding place.

**bolt rope** • **n.** a rope sewn round the edge of a sail to prevent tearing.

**Boltzmann's constant** • **n.** Chemistry the ratio of the gas constant to Avogadro's constant, equal to $1.381 \times 10^{-23}$ joule per kelvin.
– ORIGIN named after the Austrian physicist L. *Boltzmann.*

**bolus** /ˈbəʊləs/ • **n.** (pl. **boluses**) **1** a small rounded mass of a substance, especially of food being swallowed. **2** a large pill used in veterinary medicine. ➤ Medicine a single dose of a drug given all at once.
– ORIGIN C16: via late L. from Gk *bōlos* 'clod'.

**boma** /ˈbəʊmə/ • **n.** (in eastern and southern Africa) an enclosure.
– ORIGIN from Kiswahili.

**bomb** • **n. 1** a container of explosive or incendiary material, designed to explode on impact or when detonated by a timing or remote-control device. ➤ (**the bomb**) nuclear weapons collectively. **2** (**a bomb**) Brit. informal a large sum of money. **3** informal a thing that fails badly. **4** (also **volcanic bomb**) a lump of lava thrown out by a volcano. **5** a pear-shaped weight used to anchor a fishing line to the bottom. **6** informal a cannabis cigarette. • **v. 1** attack with a bomb or bombs. **2** Brit. informal move very quickly. **3** informal fail badly.
– PHRASES **go down a bomb** Brit. informal be very well received. **go like a bomb** Brit. informal **1** be very successful. **2** move very fast.
– ORIGIN C17: from Fr. *bombe*, from Ital. *bomba*, prob. from L. *bombus* 'booming, humming', from Gk *bombos*, of imi-

tative origin.

**bombard** /bɒm'bɑːd/ • **v.** **1** attack continuously with bombs or other missiles. **2** subject to a continuous flow of questions or information. **3** Physics direct a stream of high-speed particles at (a substance). • **n.** /'bɒmbɑːd/ an early form of cannon.
– DERIVATIVES **bombardment** n.
– ORIGIN ME: from OFr. *bombarde*, prob. based on L. *bombus* (see **BOMB**).

**bombarde** /'bɒmbɑːd/ • **n.** **1** a shawm of alto pitch. **2** a powerful bass reed organ stop.
– ORIGIN ME: from OFr. (see **BOMBARD**).

**bombardier** /ˌbɒmbə'dɪə/ • **n.** **1** a rank of non-commissioned officer in certain artillery regiments, equivalent to corporal. **2** a member of a bomber crew in the US air force responsible for sighting and releasing bombs.
– ORIGIN C16: from Fr., from OFr. *bombarde* (see **BOMBARD**).

**bombardier beetle** • **n.** a beetle that discharges a puff of irritant vapour from its anus with an audible pop when alarmed. [*Brachinus crepitans* and other species.]

**bombardon** /'bɒmbɑːd(ə)n/ • **n.** a bass tuba.
– ORIGIN C19: from Ital. *bombardone*, from *bombardo* 'cannon'.

**bombast** /'bɒmbast/ • **n.** high-sounding language with little meaning.
– DERIVATIVES **bombastic** adj. **bombastically** adv.
– ORIGIN C16 (denoting cotton wool used as padding, later used figuratively): from OFr. *bombace*, from med. L. *bombax*, *bombac-*, alt. of *bombyx* 'silkworm'.

**Bombay duck** • **n.** the bummalo (fish), dried and eaten as an accompaniment with curries.
– ORIGIN C19: alt. of **BUMMALO** by assoc. with the city of *Bombay* in India, from which bummalo were exported; the reason for the use of the term *duck* is unknown.

**Bombay mix** • **n.** an Indian spiced snack consisting of lentils, peanuts, and deep-fried strands of gram flour.

**bombazine** /'bɒmbəziːn/ • **n.** a twilled dress fabric of worsted and silk or cotton.
– ORIGIN C16 (denoting raw cotton): from Fr. *bombasin*, from med. L. *bombacinum*, from *bombycinus* 'silken', based on Gk *bombux* 'silkworm'.

**bomb bay** • **n.** a compartment in the fuselage of an aircraft used to hold bombs.

**bomb disposal** • **n.** the defusing or controlled detonation of unexploded bombs.

**bombe** /bɒmb/ • **n.** a frozen dome-shaped dessert.
– ORIGIN Fr., lit. 'bomb'.

**bombé** /'bɒ̃beɪ/ • **adj.** (of furniture) rounded.
– ORIGIN C20: Fr., lit. 'swollen out'.

**bombed** • **adj.** **1** subjected to bombing. **2** informal intoxicated by drink or drugs.

**bomber** • **n.** **1** an aircraft that drops bombs. **2** a person who plants bombs, especially as a terrorist. **3** informal a large cannabis cigarette.

**bomber jacket** • **n.** a short jacket gathered at the waist and cuffs by elasticated bands and having a zip front.

**bombinate** /'bɒmbɪneɪt/ • **v.** poetic/literary buzz; hum.
– ORIGIN C19: from med. L. *bombinat-*, *bombinare* 'buzz', from L. *bombus* (see **BOMB**).

**bombing run** • **n.** the part of the flight path of a bomber which brings it into position to drop bombs.

**bombora** /bɒm'bɔːrə/ • **n.** Austral. a wave which forms over a submerged offshore reef or rock, producing a dangerous stretch of broken water.
– ORIGIN 1930s: from an Aborig. word, perh. Dharuk *bumbora*.

**bombshell** • **n.** **1** an overwhelming surprise or disappointment. **2** informal a very attractive woman. **3** dated an artillery shell.

**bombsight** • **n.** a device used in an aircraft for aiming bombs.

**bomb squad** • **n.** a division of a police force investigating the planting of terrorist bombs.

**Bon** /bɒn/ (also **O-Bon**) • **n.** a Japanese Buddhist festival held annually in August to honour the dead.
– ORIGIN from Japanese.

**bona fide** /ˌbəʊnə 'fʌɪdi/ • **adj.** genuine; real. • **adv.** chiefly Law without intention to deceive.
– ORIGIN L., lit. 'with good faith', ablative sing. of **BONA FIDES**.

**bona fides** /ˌbəʊnə 'fʌɪdiːz/ • **n.** **1** honesty and sincerity of intention. **2** [treated as pl.] informal a person's credentials.
– ORIGIN L., lit. 'good faith'.

**bonanza** /bə'nanzə/ • **n.** a source of wealth, good fortune, or profits.
– ORIGIN C19 (orig. US, with ref. to success when mining): from Sp., lit. 'fair weather, prosperity', from L. *bonus* 'good'.

**Bonapartism** /'bəʊnəpɑːtɪz(ə)m/ • **n.** attachment to or advocacy of the government and dynasty of Napoleon Bonaparte (1769–1821).
– DERIVATIVES **Bonapartist** n. & adj.

**bon appétit** /ˌbɒn apɛ'tiː, French bɔn apeti/ • **exclam.** used as a salutation to a person about to eat.
– ORIGIN Fr., lit. 'good appetite'.

**bona vacantia** /ˌbəʊnə və'kantɪə/ • **n.** Law (in the UK) goods without an apparent owner, to which the Crown may have right.
– ORIGIN L., 'ownerless goods'.

**bonbon** • **n.** a sweet.
– ORIGIN C18: from Fr., reduplication of *bon* 'good', from L. *bonus*.

**bonbonnière** /ˌbɒnbɒn'jɛː/ • **n.** a small ornamental box or jar for confectionery.
– ORIGIN from Fr.

**bonce** • **n.** Brit. informal a person's head.
– ORIGIN C19 (denoting a large marble): of unknown origin.

**bond¹** /bɒnd/ • **n.** **1** a thing used to tie or fasten things together. ➤**(bonds)** physical restraints used to hold someone prisoner. **2** a force or feeling that unites people. **3** a binding agreement, especially one which commits someone to make a payment to another. ➤a certificate issued by a government or a public company promising to repay borrowed money at a fixed rate of interest at a specified time. ➤an insurance policy held by a company, which protects against losses resulting from circumstances such as bankruptcy. **4** (also **chemical bond**) a strong force of attraction holding atoms together in a molecule. **5** Building a pattern in which bricks are laid to ensure the strength of a structure. • **v.** **1** join or be joined securely to something else. **2** establish a relationship based on shared feelings or experiences. **3** join or be joined by a chemical bond. **4** [usu. as adj. **bonding**] lay (bricks) in a strong overlapping pattern. **5** [usu. as noun **bonding**] place (dutiable goods) in bond.
– PHRASES **in bond** (of dutiable goods) stored in a bonded warehouse.
– ORIGIN ME: var. of **BAND¹**.

**bond²** /bɒnt/ • **n.** S. African an Afrikaner league or association.
– ORIGIN Afrik., 'league, fellowship'.

**bondage** • **n.** **1** the state of being a slave or serf. **2** sexual practice that involves the tying up or restraining of one partner.
– ORIGIN ME: from Anglo-Latin *bondagium*, from ME *bond* 'serf' from ON *bóndi* 'tiller of the soil', based on *búa* 'dwell'; influenced by **BOND¹**.

**bondager** • **n.** historical a person who performed services as a condition of feudal tenure.

**bonded** • **adj.** **1** joined securely together, especially by an adhesive, heat process, or pressure. **2** bound by a legal agreement. **3** (of dutiable goods) placed in bond.

**bonded warehouse** • **n.** a customs-controlled warehouse for the retention of imported goods until the duty owed is paid.

**bondi** /'bɒndʌɪ/ • **n.** Austral. a heavy Aboriginal club.
– ORIGIN prob. from Wiradhuri and Kamilaroi.

**bondieuserie** /bɒn'djəːz(ə)ri, French bɔ̃djøzʀi/ • **n.** (pl. **-ies**) a church ornament or devotional object.
– ORIGIN 1940s: from Fr., from *bon* 'good' + *Dieu* 'God'.

**bond paper** • **n.** high-quality writing paper.

**bondsman** • **n.** (pl. **-men**) **1** a person who stands surety for a bond. **2** archaic a slave or feudal serf.

**bondstone** • n. a stone or brick running through a wall to strengthen it.

**bone** • n. **1** any of the pieces of hard, whitish tissue making up the skeleton in vertebrates. ➤ (**one's bones**) one's body. **2** the calcified material of which bones consist. ➤ a thing made of a substance resembling bone, e.g. a strip of stiffening for an undergarment. **3** (in southern Africa) one of a set of carved dice or bones used by traditional healers in divination. • v. **1** remove the bones from (meat or fish) before cooking. **2** (**bone up on**) informal study (a subject) intensively.

– PHRASES **bone of contention** a source of continuing disagreement. **close to the bone** (of a remark) accurate to the point of causing discomfort. ➤ (of a joke or story) near the limit of decency. **cut** (or **pare**) **something to the bone** reduce something to the bare minimum. **have a bone to pick with someone** informal have reason to disagree or be annoyed with someone. **in one's bones** felt or believed deeply or instinctively. **make no bones about** have no hesitation in stating or dealing with (something unpleasant). **off** (or **on**) **the bone** (of meat or fish) having had the bones removed (or left in). **to the bone 1** (of a wound) so deep as to expose a bone. **2** (especially of cold) affecting a person in a penetrating way. **work one's fingers to the bone** work very hard.

– DERIVATIVES **boned** adj. **boneless** adj.

– ORIGIN OE *bān*, of Gmc origin.

**bone ash** • n. the mineral residue of calcined bones, used in making bone China and in fertilizer.

**bone china** • n. white porcelain containing bone ash.

**bone dry** • adj. extremely dry.

**bonefish** • n. (pl. same or **-fishes**) a silvery game fish of warm coastal waters. [*Albula vulpes* and other species.]

**bonehead** • n. informal a stupid person.

– DERIVATIVES **boneheaded** adj.

**bone idle** • adj. extremely idle.

– ORIGIN C19: expressing *idle through to the bone.*

**bonemeal** • n. crushed or ground bones used as a fertilizer.

**boner** • n. **1** informal a stupid mistake. **2** informal an erection of the penis. **3** NZ a farm animal with meat only suitable for use in processed products.

**boneset** • n. **1** a plant of the daisy family, bearing clusters of small white flowers and used in herbal medicine. [*Eupatorium perfoliatum.*] **2** Brit. the common comfrey, the ground-up root of which was formerly used as a 'plaster' to set broken bones.

**bone-setter** • n. historical a person who set broken or dislocated bones without being a qualified surgeon.

**boneshaker** • n. Brit. informal an old vehicle with poor suspension. ➤ an early type of bicycle without rubber tyres.

**bone spavin** • n. osteoarthritis of the hock in horses.

**boneyard** • n. informal a cemetery.

**bonfire** • n. a large open-air fire.

– ORIGIN ME (orig. denoting a fire on which bones were burnt, or for burning heretics): from **BONE** + **FIRE**.

**Bonfire Night** • n. (in the UK) 5 November, on which fireworks are displayed and effigies of Guy Fawkes burnt in memory of the Gunpowder Plot of 1605.

**bong**[1] • n. a low-pitched resonant sound. • v. make this sound.

– ORIGIN 1920s: imitative.

**bong**[2] • n. a water pipe used for smoking cannabis.

– ORIGIN 1970s: from Thai *baung*, lit. 'cylindrical wooden tube'.

**bongo**[1] /ˈbɒŋgəʊ/ • n. (pl. **-os** or **-oes**) each of a pair of small drums, held between the knees and played with the fingers.

– ORIGIN 1920s: from Latin Amer. Sp. *bongó.*

**bongo**[2] /ˈbɒŋgəʊ/ • n. (pl. same or **-os**) an African forest antelope having a chestnut coat with white stripes. [*Tragelaphus euryceros.*]

– ORIGIN C19: from Kikongo.

**bonhomie** /ˈbɒnəmiː, ˌbɒnəˈmiː/ • n. good-natured friendliness.

– DERIVATIVES **bonhomous** adj.

– ORIGIN C18: from Fr., from *bonhomme* 'good fellow'.

**bonito** /bəˈniːtəʊ/ • n. (pl. **-os**) a small tuna with dark stripes, important as a food and game fish. [*Sarda sarda* (Mediterranean), *Katsuwonus pelamis* (the skipjack, worldwide), and other species.]

– ORIGIN C16: from Sp.

**bonk** informal • v. **1** hit so as to cause a reverberating sound. **2** Brit. have sexual intercourse. • n. **1** a reverberating sound. **2** Brit. an act of sexual intercourse.

– ORIGIN 1930s: imitative.

**bonkers** • adj. informal mad; crazy.

– ORIGIN 1940s: of unknown origin.

**bon mot** /bɒn ˈməʊ/ • n. (pl. **bons mots** pronunc. same or /-məʊz/) a clever or witty remark.

– ORIGIN C18: Fr., lit. 'good word'.

**bonne bouche** /bɒn ˈbuːʃ/ • n. (pl. **bonne bouches** or **bonnes bouches** pronunc. same) an appetizing item of food eaten at the end of a meal.

– ORIGIN Fr., from *bonne*, fem. of *bon* 'good', and *bouche* 'mouth'.

**bonne femme** /bɒn ˈfam/ • adj. [postpos.] (of fish, stews, and soups) cooked in a simple way.

– ORIGIN Fr., from the phr. *à la bonne femme* 'in the manner of a good housewife'.

**bonnet** • n. **1** a woman's or child's hat tied under the chin and with a brim framing the face. **2** a soft brimless hat like a beret, worn by men and boys in Scotland. ➤ Heraldry the velvet cap within a coronet. **3** (also **war bonnet**) the ceremonial headdress of an American Indian. **4** Brit. the hinged metal canopy covering the engine of a motor vehicle. **5** a cowl on a chimney. **6** Sailing, historical an additional canvas laced to the foot of a sail.

– DERIVATIVES **bonneted** adj.

– ORIGIN ME: from OFr. *bonet*, from med. L. *abonnis* 'headgear'.

**bonnethead** • n. a small American hammerhead shark with a narrow rounded head. [*Sphyrna tiburo.*]

**bonnetmouth** • n. a small, slender fish with an extensible mouth and a long spiny dorsal fin, occurring in the tropical western Atlantic. [*Inermia vittata.*]

**bonny** (also **bonnie**) • adj. (**-ier**, **-iest**) chiefly Scottish & N. English **1** physically attractive; healthy-looking. **2** sizeable; considerable: *it's worth a bonny sum.*

– DERIVATIVES **bonnily** adv. **bonniness** n.

– ORIGIN C15: perh. rel. to OFr. *bon* 'good'.

**bonny clabber** • n. another term for **CLABBER**.

– ORIGIN C17: from Ir. *bainne clabair*, denoting thick milk for churning.

**bonobo** /ˈbɒnəbəʊ/ • n. (pl. **-os**) a chimpanzee with a black face and black hair, found in the rainforests of Zaire (Democratic Republic of Congo). [*Pan paniscus.*]

– ORIGIN 1950s: a local word.

**bonsai** /ˈbɒnsʌɪ/ • n. the art of growing ornamental, artificially dwarfed varieties of trees or shrubs.

– ORIGIN 1950s: from Japanese, from *bon* 'tray' + *sai* 'planting'.

**bonspiel** /ˈbɒnspiːl/ • n. a curling match.

– ORIGIN C16: prob. of Low Ger. origin.

**bontebok** /ˈbɒntəbɒk/ • n. (pl. same or **bonteboks**) an antelope with a reddish-brown coat and white face, found in eastern South Africa. [*Damaliscus dorcas dorcas.*]

– ORIGIN C18: from Afrik., from Du. *bont* 'pied' + *bok* 'buck'.

**bonus** • n. **1** a sum of money added seasonally to a person's wages for good performance. ➤ Brit. an extra dividend or issue paid to shareholders. **2** an extra and unexpected welcome event.

– ORIGIN C18: from L. *bonus* (masc.) 'good'.

**bonus issue** • n. Brit. an issue of additional shares to shareholders instead of a dividend.

**bon vivant** /ˌbɒ̃ viːˈvɒ̃, French bɔ̃ vivɑ̃/ • n. (pl. **bon vivants** or **bons vivants** pronunc. same) a person indulging in a sociable and luxurious lifestyle.

– ORIGIN C17: from Fr., lit. 'person living well'.

**bon viveur** /ˌbɒ̃ viːˈvəː/ • n. (pl. **bon viveurs** or **bons viveurs** pronunc. same) another term for **BON VIVANT**.

– ORIGIN C19: pseudo-Fr., from Fr. *bon* 'good' and *viveur* 'a living person'.

**bon voyage** /ˌbɒn vɔɪˈjɑːʒ, French bɔ̃ vwajaʒ/ ● **exclam.** have a good journey.
– ORIGIN C17: Fr., lit. 'good journey'.

**bonxie** /ˈbɒŋksi/ ● **n.** (pl. **-ies**) the great skua.
– ORIGIN C18: Shetland dial., from Norw. *bunksi*, from *bunke* 'dumpy body'.

**bony** ● **adj.** (**-ier**, **-iest**) **1** of, like, or containing bones. **2** so thin that the bones can be seen.
– DERIVATIVES **boniness** n.

**bony fish** ● **n.** a fish of a large class distinguished by a skeleton of bone, and comprising the majority of modern fishes. [Class Osteichthyes.]

**bonze** /bɒnz/ ● **n.** a Japanese or Chinese Buddhist religious teacher.
– ORIGIN C16: prob. from Japanese *bonzō, bonsō* 'priest'.

**bonzer** ● **adj.** Austral./NZ informal excellent.
– ORIGIN C20: perh. an alt. of **BONANZA**.

**boo** ● **exclam. 1** said suddenly to surprise someone. **2** said to show disapproval or contempt. ● **v.** (**boos**, **booed**) say 'boo' to show disapproval or contempt.
– PHRASES **wouldn't say boo to a goose** is very shy or reticent.
– ORIGIN C19: imitative of the lowing of oxen.

**booay** /ˈbuːʌɪ/ (also **booai**) ● **n.** (**the booay**) NZ remote rural districts.
– PHRASES **up the booay** informal completely wrong or astray.
– ORIGIN perh. from the place name *Puhoi* in North Auckland, New Zealand.

**boob[1]** informal ● **n. 1** Brit. an embarrassing mistake. **2** N. Amer. a stupid person. ● **v.** Brit. make an embarrassing mistake.
– ORIGIN C20: abbrev. of **BOOBY[1]**.

**boob[2]** ● **n.** informal a woman's breast.
– ORIGIN 1950s: abbrev. of **BOOBY[2]**, from dial. *bubby*; perh. rel. to Ger. dial. *Bübbi* 'teat'.

**boo-boo** ● **n.** informal a mistake.
– ORIGIN 1950s: reduplication of **BOOB[1]**.

**boobook owl** /ˈbuːbʊk/ ● **n.** a small brown Australasian owl with a characteristic double hoot. [*Ninox novaeseelandiae*.]
– ORIGIN C19: imitative of its call.

**boob tube** ● **n.** informal **1** Brit. a woman's tight-fitting strapless top. **2** N. Amer. television; a television set.

**booby[1]** ● **n.** (pl. **-ies**) **1** informal a stupid person. **2** a large tropical seabird of the gannet family, with brown, black, or white plumage and brightly coloured feet. [Genus *Sula*: several species.]
– ORIGIN C17: prob. from Sp. *bobo*, from L. *balbus* 'stammering'.

**booby[2]** ● **n.** (pl. **-ies**) informal a woman's breast.
– ORIGIN 1930s: alt. of dial. *bubby* (see **BOOB[2]**).

**booby prize** ● **n.** a prize given to the person who comes last in a contest.

**booby trap** ● **n.** an object containing a concealed explosive device designed to detonate when someone touches it. ● **v.** (**booby-trap**) place a booby trap in or on.

**boodie** /ˈbuːdi/ ● **n.** a burrowing rat-kangaroo found on islands off Western Australia. [*Bettongia lesueur*.]
– ORIGIN C19: from Nyungar *burdi*.

**boodle** ● **n.** informal money, especially that gained or spent dishonestly.
– ORIGIN C17 (denoting a pack or crowd): from Du. *boedel*, *boel* 'possessions, disorderly mass'.

**boofhead** ● **n.** informal, chiefly Austral. a fool.
– ORIGIN 1940s: prob. from *bufflehead* 'simpleton', based on obs. *buffle* 'buffalo'.

**boogaloo** /ˌbuːgəˈluː/ US ● **n.** a dance to rock-and-roll music performed with swivelling and shuffling movements of the body. ● **v.** (**boogaloos**, **boogalooed**) perform this dance.
– ORIGIN 1960s: perh. an alt. of ***boogie-woogie*** (see **BOOGIE**).

**boogie** ● **n.** (also **boogie-woogie**) (pl. **-ies**) **1** a style of blues played on the piano with a strong, fast beat. **2** informal a dance to pop or rock music. ● **v.** (**boogieing**) informal dance to pop or rock music.
– ORIGIN C20 (orig. US in the sense 'party'): of unknown origin.

**boogie board** ● **n.** a short, light surfboard ridden in a prone position.
– DERIVATIVES **boogie-boarder** n.

**boohoo** ● **exclam.** representing the sound of someone crying noisily.
– ORIGIN C19: imitative.

**boojum** /ˈbuːdʒəm/ ● **n.** an imaginary dangerous animal.
– ORIGIN 1876: nonsense word coined by Lewis Carroll in *The Hunting of the Snark*.

**book** ● **n. 1** a written or printed work consisting of pages glued or sewn together along one side and bound in covers. ➤ a main division of a literary work or of the Bible. **2** (**books**) a set of records or accounts. ➤ a bookmaker's record of bets accepted and money paid out. **3** a set of tickets, stamps, matches, etc., bound together. **4** (**the book**) the first six tricks taken by the declarer in a hand of bridge. ● **v. 1** reserve (accommodation, a ticket, etc.). ➤ (**book in**) register one's arrival at a hotel. ➤ engage (a performer or guest) for an event. ➤ (**be booked up**) have all places reserved. **2** make an official note of the details of (someone who has broken a law or rule).
– PHRASES **bring someone to book** officially call someone to account for their behaviour. **by the book** strictly according to the rules. **in someone's bad** (or **good**) **books** in disfavour (or favour) with someone. **in my book** in my opinion. **make** (or **open**) **a book** (US **make book**) take bets and pay out winnings on the outcome of a contest or other event. **on the books** contained in a list of members, employees, or clients. **People of the Book** Jews and Christians as regarded by Muslims. **suit one's book** Brit. be convenient to one. **take a leaf out of someone's book** imitate someone in a particular way. **throw the book at** informal charge or punish (someone) as severely as possible.
– DERIVATIVES **booker** n. **booking** n.
– ORIGIN OE *bōc*, *bōcian* 'to grant by charter', of Gmc origin.

**bookable** ● **adj. 1** able to be reserved. **2** Soccer (of an offence) serious enough for the offending player to be cautioned by the referee.

**bookbinder** ● **n.** a person who binds books.
– DERIVATIVES **bookbinding** n.

**bookcase** ● **n.** an open cabinet containing shelves on which to keep books.

**book club** ● **n.** a society which sells its members selected books at reduced prices.

**bookend** ● **n.** a support placed at the end of a row of books to keep them upright.

**book hand** ● **n.** a formal style of handwriting used by professional copiers of books before the invention of printing.

**bookie** ● **n.** (pl. **-ies**) informal a bookmaker.

**bookish** ● **adj. 1** devoted to reading and studying. **2** (of language) literary in style.
– DERIVATIVES **bookishly** adv. **bookishness** n.

**bookkeeping** ● **n.** the activity of keeping records of financial affairs.
– DERIVATIVES **bookkeeper** n.

**bookland** ● **n.** Brit. historical an area of common land granted by charter to a private owner.
– ORIGIN OE, from *bóc* 'charter' + **LAND**.

**book learning** ● **n.** knowledge gained from study rather than personal experience.

**booklet** ● **n.** a small, thin book with paper covers.

**booklouse** ● **n.** (pl. **booklice**) a minute insect with no or rudimentary wings, capable of causing damage to books and paper. [*Liposcelis bostrychophilus* and other species.]

**book lung** ● **n.** Zoology (in an arachnid) each of a pair of respiratory organs in the abdomen, composed of many fine leaves.

**bookmaker** ● **n.** a person whose job is to take bets, calculate odds, and pay out winnings.
– DERIVATIVES **bookmaking** n.

**bookman** • n. (pl. **-men**) archaic a literary man.
**bookmark** • n. a strip of leather or card used to mark a place in a book. ➤ Computing a record of the address of a file, Internet page, etc. enabling quick access by a user.
**bookmobile** /ˈbʊkmə,biːl/ • n. N. Amer. a mobile library.
**book of hours** • n. a book of prayers appointed for particular canonical hours or times of day, used by Roman Catholics for private devotions.
**bookplate** • n. a decorative label in the front of a book, bearing the name of its owner.
**bookrest** • n. Brit. a support for an open book on a table.
**bookshelf** • n. (pl. **-shelves**) a shelf on which books can be stored.
**bookstall** • n. a kiosk where books, magazines, etc. are sold.
**booksy** • adj. informal affectedly literary or bookish.
**book token** • n. Brit. a voucher which can be exchanged for books costing up to a specified amount.
**book value** • n. the value of a security or asset as entered in a firm's books. Often contrasted with **MARKET VALUE**.
**bookworm** • n. **1** informal a person who enjoys reading. **2** the larva of a wood-boring beetle which feeds on the paper and glue in books.
**Boolean** /ˈbuːlɪən/ • adj. denoting a system of algebraic notation used to represent logical propositions by means of the binary digits 0 (false) and 1 (true), especially in computing and electronics. • n. Computing a binary variable with these possible values.
– ORIGIN C19: from the name of the Engl. mathematician G. *Boole* + **-AN**.
**boom[1]** • n. a loud, deep, resonant sound. • v. make this sound.
– DERIVATIVES **boominess** n. **booming** adj. **boomy** adj.
– ORIGIN ME: ult. imitative; perh. from Du. *bommen* 'to hum, buzz'.
**boom[2]** • n. a period of great prosperity. • v. experience a boom: *business is booming.*
– DERIVATIVES **boomy** adj.
– ORIGIN C19: prob. from **BOOM[1]**.
**boom[3]** • n. **1** a pivoted spar to which the foot of a vessel's sail is attached. **2** a movable arm carrying a microphone or film camera. **3** a floating beam used to contain oil spills or to form a barrier across a harbour mouth.
– ORIGIN C16: from Du., 'beam, tree, pole'; rel. to **BEAM**.
**boomer** • n. **1** Austral. informal a large male kangaroo. **2** a large wave.
**boomerang** • n. a curved flat piece of wood that can be thrown so as to return to the thrower, used by Australian Aboriginals as a hunting weapon.
– ORIGIN C19: from Dharuk.
**boomslang** • n. a large, highly venomous southern African tree snake. [*Dispholidus typus*.]
– ORIGIN C18: from Afrik., from Du. *boom* 'tree' + *slang* 'snake'.
**boon** • n. **1** a thing that is helpful or beneficial. **2** archaic a favour or request.
– ORIGIN ME: from ON *bón*.
**boon companion** • n. a close friend.
– ORIGIN C16: *boon* from OFr. *bon*, from L. *bonus* 'good'.
**boondocks** /ˈbuːndɒks/ • pl. n. (**the boondocks**) N. Amer. informal rough or isolated country.
– ORIGIN 1940s: from Tagalog *bundok* 'mountain'.
**boondoggle** /ˈbuːndɒg(ə)l/ N. Amer. informal • n. an unnecessary, wasteful, or fraudulent project. • v. waste money or time on such projects.
– ORIGIN 1930s: of unknown origin.
**boong** /bʊŋ/ • n. Austral. offensive an Aboriginal.
– ORIGIN 1920s: from an Aborig. word meaning 'human being'.
**boonies** /ˈbuːnɪz/ • pl. n. short for **BOONDOCKS**.
**boor** /bʊə/ • n. a rough and bad-mannered person.
– DERIVATIVES **boorish** adj. **boorishly** adv. **boorishness** n.
– ORIGIN C16: from Low Ger. *būr* or Du. *boer* 'farmer'.
**boost** • v. help or encourage to increase or improve. • n. a source of help or encouragement.
– ORIGIN C19 (orig. US, in the sense 'push from below'): of unknown origin.
**booster** • n. **1** Medicine a dose of a vaccine increasing or renewing the effect of an earlier one. **2** the first stage of a rocket or spacecraft, used to give initial acceleration. **3** a source of help or encouragement. **4** a device for increasing electrical voltage or signal strength.
**booster seat** • n. an extra seat placed on an existing seat for a small child.
**boot[1]** • n. **1** a sturdy item of footwear covering the foot and ankle, and sometimes the lower leg. **2** informal a hard kick. **3** Brit. a space at the back of a car for carrying luggage. **4** historical an instrument of torture crushing the foot. • v. **1** kick hard. **2** (**boot someone out**) informal force someone to leave unceremoniously. **3** start (a computer) and put it into a state of readiness for operation. [from **BOOTSTRAP**.]
– PHRASES **the boot** (or N. Amer. **shoe**) **is on the other foot** the situation has reversed. **die with one's boots on** die in battle or while actively occupied. **give** (or **get**) **the boot** informal dismiss (or be dismissed) from a job. **old boot** informal an ugly or disliked old woman. **put the boot in** Brit. informal kick or attack someone when they are already on the ground. **with one's heart in one's boots** very depressed or anxious.
– DERIVATIVES **bootable** adj. **booted** adj.
– ORIGIN ME: from ON *bóti* or its source, OFr. *bote*.
**boot[2]** • n. (in phr. **to boot**) as well.
– ORIGIN OE *bōt* 'advantage, remedy', of Gmc origin.
**bootblack** • n. historical a person who polished boots and shoes.
**bootboy** • n. **1** informal a rowdy youth with close-cropped hair and heavy boots. **2** historical a boy who cleaned boots and shoes.
**boot camp** • n. chiefly N. Amer. a military training camp with very harsh discipline. ➤ a prison for young offenders, run on military lines.
**bootee** /buːˈtiː/ (also **bootie**) • n. **1** a baby's soft woollen shoe. **2** a woman's short boot.
**booth** /buːð, buːθ/ • n. **1** a small temporary structure used for selling goods or staging shows at a market or fair. **2** an enclosed compartment allowing privacy when telephoning, voting, etc.
– ORIGIN ME: from ON *buth*, based on *búa* 'dwell'.
**bootjack** • n. a device for holding a boot by the heel to ease withdrawal of one's foot.
**bootlace** • n. a cord or leather strip for lacing boots.
**bootleg** • adj. (of alcoholic drink or a recording) made or distributed illegally. • n. an illegal musical recording.
– DERIVATIVES **bootlegger** n. **bootlegging** n.
– ORIGIN C19: from the smugglers' practice of hiding bottles in their boots.
**bootless** • adj. archaic (of a task) ineffectual; useless.
– ORIGIN OE *bōtlēas* 'not able to be compensated for by payment' (see **BOOT[2]**).
**bootlicker** • n. informal an obsequious person.
– DERIVATIVES **bootlicking** n.
**boots** • n. Brit. dated a hotel employee performing menial tasks such as cleaning shoes.
– ORIGIN C18: pl. of **BOOT[1]**, used as sing.
**bootstrap** • n. **1** a loop at the back of a boot, used to pull it on. **2** Computing the action of loading a program into a computer by means of a few initial instructions which enable the introduction of the rest of the program from an input device.
– PHRASES **pull oneself up by one's bootstraps** improve one's position by one's own efforts.
**boot top** • n. the part of the hull of a ship just above the waterline.
**booty[1]** • n. valuable stolen goods.
– ORIGIN ME: from Mid. Low Ger. *būte*, *buite* 'exchange, distribution'.
**booty[2]** • n. (pl. **-ies**) N. Amer. informal a person's behind.
– ORIGIN alt. of **BODY**.
**booze** informal • n. alcoholic drink. • v. drink large quantities of alcohol.
– ORIGIN ME *bouse*, from MDu. *būsen* 'drink to excess'.
**boozer** • n. informal **1** a person who drinks large quantities

of alcohol. **2** Brit. a pub.

**booze-up** ● **n.** informal a heavy drinking session.

**boozy** ● **adj.** (**-ier**, **-iest**) informal drinking or involving large quantities of alcohol.
– DERIVATIVES **boozily** adv. **booziness** n.

**bop**[1] informal ● **n. 1** chiefly Brit. a dance to pop music. ➤ an organized social occasion with such dancing. **2** short for **BEBOP**. ● **v.** (**bopped**, **bopping**) dance to pop music.
– DERIVATIVES **bopper** n.
– ORIGIN 1940s: shortening of **BEBOP**.

**bop**[2] informal ● **v.** (**bopped**, **bopping**) hit or punch quickly. ● **n.** a quick blow or punch.
– ORIGIN 1930s (orig. US): imitative.

**bora**[1] /'bɔːrə/ ● **n.** a cold, dry NE wind blowing in the upper Adriatic.
– ORIGIN C19: dial. var. of Ital. *borea*, from L. *boreas* (see **BOREAL**).

**bora**[2] /'bɔːrə/ ● **n.** an Australian Aboriginal rite in which boys are initiated into manhood.
– ORIGIN C19: from Kamilaroi *buuru*.

**boracic** /bə'rasɪk/ ● **adj. 1** consisting of, containing, or denoting boric acid. **2** Brit. informal having no money. [from *boracic lint*, rhyming sl. for 'skint'.]
– ORIGIN C18: from med. L. *borax*, *borac-* (see **BORAX**[1]) + **-IC**.

**borage** /'bɒrɪdʒ/ ● **n.** a herbaceous plant with bright blue flowers and hairy leaves. [*Borago officinalis*.]
– ORIGIN ME: from OFr. *bourrache*, from med. L. *borrago*, perh. from Arab. *'abū ḥurāš* 'father of roughness' (referring to the leaves).

**boraginaceous** /ˌbɒrɪdʒɪ'neɪʃəs/ ● **adj.** Botany relating to or denoting plants of the borage family (Boraginaceae).

**borak** /'bɔːrak/ (also **borax**) ● **n.** Austral./NZ informal banter; ridicule.
– ORIGIN C19: orig. Austral. pidgin (expressing negation), based on Aborig. *burag* 'no, not'.

**borane** /'bɔːreɪn/ ● **n.** Chemistry any of a series of unstable compounds of boron and hydrogen.

**borate** /'bɔːreɪt/ ● **n.** Chemistry a salt in which the anion contains both boron and oxygen, as in borax.

**borax**[1] /'bɔːraks/ ● **n.** a white mineral consisting of hydrated sodium borate, found in some alkaline salt deposits and used in making glass and as a metallurgical flux.
– ORIGIN ME: from med. L., from Arab. *būraḳ*, from Pahlavi *būrak*.

**borax**[2] /'bɔːraks/ ● **n.** variant spelling of **BORAK**.

**borborygmus** /ˌbɔːbə'rɪgməs/ ● **n.** (pl. **borborygmi** /-mʌɪ/) technical a rumbling noise made by fluid and gas in the intestines.
– DERIVATIVES **borborygmic** adj.
– ORIGIN C18: mod. L., from Gk *borborugmos*.

**Bordeaux** /bɔː'dəʊ/ ● **n.** (pl. same /-'dəʊz/) a wine from Bordeaux, a district of SW France.

**Bordeaux mixture** ● **n.** a fungicidal solution for plants, containing copper sulphate and calcium oxide.
– ORIGIN C19: first used in the vineyards of the Bordeaux region of SW France.

**bordelaise** /ˌbɔːdə'leɪz/ ● **adj.** denoting or served with a sauce of red wine and onions.
– ORIGIN Fr., from (*à la*) *bordelaise* 'Bordeaux-style'.

**bordello** /bɔː'dɛləʊ/ ● **n.** (pl. **-os**) chiefly N. Amer. a brothel.
– ORIGIN C16: from Ital., prob. from OFr. *bordel*, dimin. of *borde* 'small farm, cottage', ult. of Gmc origin.

**border** ● **n. 1** a line separating two countries or other areas. ➤ (**the Border**) the boundary between Northern Ireland and the Republic of Ireland. ➤ (**the Borders**) the boundary and adjoining districts between Scotland and England. **2** a decorative band around the edge of something. ➤ a strip of ground along the edge of a lawn for planting flowers or shrubs. ● **v. 1** form a border around or along. **2** (of a country or area) be adjacent to (another). **3** (**border on**) come close to (an extreme condition).
– ORIGIN ME: from OFr. *bordeure*; ult. of Gmc origin.

**borderer** ● **n.** a person living near the border between two countries.

**borderline** ● **n.** a boundary separating two countries or areas. ● **adj.** only just acceptable in quality or as belonging to a category.

**bordure** /'bɔːdjʊə/ ● **n.** Heraldry a broad border used as a charge in a coat of arms, often as a mark of difference.
– ORIGIN ME: var. of **BORDER**.

**bore**[1] ● **v. 1** make (a hole) in something with a drill or other tool. ➤ hollow out (a gun barrel or other tube). **2** (of an athlete or racehorse) push another competitor out of the way. ● **n.** the hollow part inside a gun barrel or other tube. ➤ the diameter of this: *a small-bore rifle*.
– ORIGIN OE *borian* (v.), of Gmc origin.

**bore**[2] ● **n.** a dull and uninteresting person or activity. ● **v.** cause to feel weary and uninterested by being dull and tedious.
– DERIVATIVES **bored** adj. **boredom** n. **boring** adj. **boringly** adv. **boringness** n.
– ORIGIN C18: of unknown origin.

**bore**[3] ● **n.** a steep-fronted wave caused by the meeting of two tides or by a tide rushing up a narrow estuary.
– ORIGIN C17: perh. from ON *bára* 'wave'.

**bore**[4] past of **BEAR**[1].

**boreal** /'bɔːrɪəl/ ● **adj. 1** chiefly Ecology of the North or northern regions, adjacent to or including the Arctic. **2** (**Boreal**) Geology relating to or denoting the second climatic stage of the postglacial period in northern Europe (about 9,000 to 7,500 years ago).
– ORIGIN ME: from late L. *borealis*, from L. *Boreas*, denoting the god of the north wind, from Gk.

**-bored** ● **adj.** (of a gun) having a specified bore.

**boreen** /bɔː'riːn/ ● **n.** Irish a narrow country road.
– ORIGIN C19: from Ir. *bóithrín*, dimin. of *bóthar* 'road'.

**borehole** ● **n.** a deep, narrow hole in the ground made to locate water or oil.

**borer** ● **n. 1** a worm, mollusc, or insect which bores into plant material or rock. **2** a tool for boring.

**boric** /'bɔːrɪk/ ● **adj.** Chemistry of boron.

**boric acid** ● **n.** Chemistry a weakly acid crystalline compound derived from borax, used as a mild antiseptic. [$B(OH)_3$.]

**borlotti bean** /bɔː'lɒti/ ● **n.** a type of kidney bean with a pink speckled skin that turns brown when cooked.
– ORIGIN Ital. *borlotti*, pl. of *borlotto* 'kidney bean'.

**born** ● **adj. 1** existing as a result of birth. **2** (**born of**) existing as a result of (a situation or feeling). **3** having a natural ability to do a particular job or task: *a born engineer.* **4** (**-born**) having a specific nationality: *a German-born philosopher.*
– PHRASES **born and bred** by birth and upbringing. **in all one's born days** throughout one's life (used for emphasis). **not know one is born** not realize how easy one's life is. **I** (or **she**, etc.) **wasn't born yesterday** I am (or she, etc. is) not foolish or gullible.
– ORIGIN OE *boren*, past part. of *beran* (see **BEAR**[1]).

**born-again** ● **adj. 1** relating to or denoting a person who has converted to a personal faith in Christ. **2** newly converted to and very enthusiastic about (an idea, cause, etc.).

**borne** past participle of **BEAR**[1].

**-borne** ● **adj.** carried by the thing specified.

**Bornean** /'bɔːnɪən/ ● **n.** a native or inhabitant of Borneo. ● **adj.** of or relating to Borneo or its people.

**Bornholm disease** ● **n.** a viral infection with fever and pain in the muscles of the ribs.
– ORIGIN 1930s: named after the Dan. island of *Bornholm*, where it was first described.

**bornite** /'bɔːnʌɪt/ ● **n.** a brittle reddish-brown mineral with an iridescent purple tarnish, consisting of a sulphide of copper and iron.
– ORIGIN C19: from the name of the Austrian mineralogist Ignatius von *Born*.

**boro-** /'bɔːrəʊ/ ● **comb. form** Chemistry representing **BORON**: *borosilicate*.

**boron** /'bɔːrɒn/ ● **n.** the chemical element of atomic number 5, a non-metal which can be isolated as a brown, amorphous powder or (if pure) a black crystalline semiconductor. (Symbol: **B**)
– DERIVATIVES **boride** n.

– ORIGIN C19: from **BORAX**[1], on the pattern of *carbon* (which it resembles).

**boronia** /bəˈrəʊnɪə/ ● **n.** a sweet-scented Australian shrub, cultivated for its perfume and flowers. [Genus *Boronia*.]
– ORIGIN mod. L., named after the Ital. botanist Francesco *Borone*.

**borosilicate glass** /ˌbɔːrəʊˈsɪlɪkeɪt/ ● **n.** a low-melting glass made from a mixture of silica and boric oxide.

**borough** /ˈbʌrə/ ● **n. 1** Brit. a town (as distinct from a city) with a corporation and privileges granted by a royal charter. ➤historical a town sending representatives to Parliament. ➤an administrative division of London. **2** a municipal corporation in certain US states. ➤each of five divisions of New York City.
– ORIGIN OE *burg, burh* 'fortress, citadel', later 'fortified town', of Gmc origin, cf. **BURGH**.

**borrow** ● **v. 1** take and use (something belonging to someone else) with the intention of returning it. ➤take and use (money) from a person or bank under agreement to pay it back later. **2** Golf allow (a certain distance) when playing a shot to compensate for a slope or other irregularity. ● **n.** Golf a slope or other irregularity on a golf course.
– PHRASES **be (living) on borrowed time** be surviving against expectations. **borrow trouble** N. Amer. take needless action that may have detrimental effects.
– DERIVATIVES **borrower** n. **borrowing** n.
– ORIGIN OE *borgian*, of Gmc origin.

**borrow pit** ● **n.** a pit resulting from the excavation of material for use in embankments.

**Borsalino** /ˌbɔːsəˈliːnəʊ/ ● **n.** (pl. **-os**) trademark a man's wide-brimmed felt hat.
– ORIGIN C20: from the name of the manufacturer.

**borscht** /bɔːʃt/ (also **borsch** /bɔːʃ/) ● **n.** a Russian or Polish soup made with beetroot.
– ORIGIN from Russ. *borshch*.

**borstal** /ˈbɔːst(ə)l/ ● **n.** Brit. historical a custodial institution for young offenders.
– ORIGIN C20: named after the village of *Borstal* in southern England, where the first of these was established.

**bort** /bɔːt/ (also **boart**) ● **n.** inferior diamonds used in cutting tools.
– ORIGIN C17: from Du. *boort*.

**borzoi** /ˈbɔːzɔɪ/ ● **n.** (pl. **borzois**) a large Russian wolfhound of a breed with a narrow head and silky coat.
– ORIGIN C19: from Russ. *borzoĭ* (adj.), *borzaya* (n.), from *borzyĭ* 'swift'.

**boscage** /ˈbɒskɪdʒ/ (also **boskage**) ● **n.** a mass of trees or shrubs.
– ORIGIN ME: from OFr., ult. of Gmc origin.

**bosh** ● **n.** informal nonsense.
– ORIGIN C19: from Turk. *boş* 'empty, worthless'.

**bosky** /ˈbɒski/ ● **adj.** poetic/literary covered by trees or bushes.
– ORIGIN C16: from ME *bosk*, var. of **BUSH**[1].

**Bosnian** /ˈbɒznɪən/ ● **n.** a native or inhabitant of Bosnia. ● **adj.** of or relating to Bosnia or its people.

**bosom** ● **n. 1** a woman's breast or chest. **2** the breast as the seat of emotions: *quivering dread was settling in her bosom.* ➤a person's loving care or protection: *Bruno went home each night to the bosom of his family.* ● **adj.** (of a friend) very close.
– DERIVATIVES **-bosomed** adj. **bosomy** adj.
– ORIGIN OE *bōsm*, of W. Gmc origin.

**boson** /ˈbəʊzɒn/ ● **n.** Physics a subatomic particle, such as a photon, which has zero or integral spin.
– ORIGIN 1940s: named after the Ind. physicist S. N. *Bose* + **-ON**.

**boss**[1] informal ● **n.** a person who is in charge of an employee or organization. ● **v.** give orders in a domineering manner. ● **adj.** N. Amer. excellent.
– ORIGIN C19 (orig. US): from Du. *baas* 'master'.

**boss**[2] ● **n. 1** a stud on the centre of a shield. **2** Architecture an ornamental carving at the point where the ribs in a ceiling cross. **3** the central part of a propeller. **4** Geology a large mass of igneous rock protruding through other strata.
– ORIGIN ME: from OFr. *boce*.

**boss**[3] ● **n.** US informal a cow.
– ORIGIN C19: of unknown origin.

**bossa nova** /ˌbɒsə ˈnəʊvə/ ● **n.** a dance like the samba, originating in Brazil. ➤a piece of music for this dance.
– ORIGIN 1960s: from Port., from *bossa* 'tendency' and *nova* (fem. of *novo*) 'new'.

**boss-eyed** ● **adj.** Brit. informal cross-eyed; squinting.
– ORIGIN C19: cf. dial. *boss* 'miss, bungle'.

**bossism** ● **n.** US the controlling of a political party by party managers.

**boss-shot** ● **n.** dialect or informal a bad shot or aim.
– ORIGIN C19: from dial. *boss* 'miss, bungle'.

**bossy**[1] ● **adj.** (**-ier**, **-iest**) informal fond of giving orders; domineering.
– DERIVATIVES **bossily** adv. **bossiness** n.

**bossy**[2] ● **n.** (pl. **-ies**) N. Amer. informal a cow or calf.
– ORIGIN C19: of unknown origin.

**bossyboots** ● **n.** Brit. informal a bossy person.

**Boston** ● **n. 1** a card game resembling solo whist. **2** a variation of the waltz or the two-step.

**Boston crab** ● **n.** Wrestling a hold in which a wrestler sits astride a prone opponent and pulls upwards on the opponent's legs.

**Bostonian** ● **n.** a native or inhabitant of Boston, the state capital of Massachusetts. ● **adj.** of or relating to Boston.

**Boston ivy** ● **n.** a Virginia creeper with three-lobed leaves, cultivated for its foliage. [*Parthenocissus tricuspidata*.]

**Boston terrier** ● **n.** a small terrier of a breed originating in Massachusetts from a crossing of the bulldog and terrier.

**bosun** /ˈbəʊs(ə)n/ (also **bo'sun**) ● **n.** variant spelling of **BOATSWAIN**.

**bot**[1] ● **n.** the larva of a botfly.
– ORIGIN C16: prob. of Low Ger. origin.

**bot**[2] ● **n.** Computing an autonomous program on a network which can interact with systems or users, especially in the manner of a player in some computer games.
– ORIGIN 1980s: shortening of **ROBOT**.

**bot.** ● **abbrev. 1** botanic; botanical; botany. **2** bottle. **3** bought.

**botanical** ● **adj.** of or relating to botany. ● **n.** a substance obtained from a plant and used as an additive.
– DERIVATIVES **botanically** adv.

**botanic garden** (also **botanical garden**) ● **n.** a place where plants are grown for scientific study and display to the public.

**botanizing** (also **-ising**) ● **n.** the studying of plants in their natural habitat.
– DERIVATIVES **botanize** v.

**Botany** /ˈbɒt(ə)ni/ (also **Botany wool**) ● **n.** merino wool.
– ORIGIN C19: named after *Botany* Bay in Australia, from where the wool orig. came.

**botany** /ˈbɒt(ə)ni/ ● **n.** the scientific study of the structure, ecology, distribution, classification, and economic importance of plants. ➤the plant life of a particular region or geological period.
– DERIVATIVES **botanic** adj. **botanist** n.
– ORIGIN C17: from earlier *botanic* (from Fr. *botanique*, based on Gk *botanikos*, from *botanē* 'plant') + **-Y**[3].

**botch** informal ● **v.** carry out (a task) badly or carelessly. ● **n.** (also **botch-up**) a badly carried out task.
– DERIVATIVES **botcher** n.
– ORIGIN ME (in the sense 'repair' but orig. not implying clumsiness): of unknown origin.

**botel** ● **n.** variant spelling of **BOATEL**.

**botfly** /ˈbɒtflʌɪ/ ● **n.** (pl. **-flies**) a stout hairy-bodied fly whose larvae are internal parasites of horses and other mammals. [*Gasterophilus* and other genera.]

**both** ● **predet., det., & pron.** two people or things, regarded and identified together. ● **adv.** applying equally to each of two alternatives.
– ORIGIN ME: from ON *báthir*.

**bother** ● **v. 1** [with neg.] take the trouble to do something. **2**

worry, disturb, or upset (someone). ➤ [usu. with neg.] feel concern about or interest in. ● **n.** trouble; fuss. ➤ a cause of trouble or fuss. ● **exclam.** chiefly Brit. used to express mild irritation.
– ORIGIN C17 (as a noun in the dial. sense 'noise, chatter'): of Anglo-Ir. origin; prob. rel. to Ir. *bodhaire* 'noise', *bodhraim* 'deafen, annoy'.

**botheration** informal, dated ● **n.** bother. ● **exclam.** used to express irritation.

**bothersome** ● **adj.** annoying; troublesome.

**both ways** ● **adv. & adj.** another term for **EACH-WAY**.
– PHRASES **have it both ways** benefit from two incompatible ways of thinking or behaving.

**bothy** /'bɒθi/ (also **bothie**) ● **n.** (pl. **-ies**) (in Scotland) a small hut for farm labourers or as a mountain refuge.
– ORIGIN C18: obscurely rel. to Ir. and Sc. Gaelic *both*, *bothan*, and perh. to **BOOTH**.

**boto** ● **n.** variant spelling of **BOUTU**.

**Botox** /'baʊtɒks/ ● **n.** trademark a drug prepared from botulin, used medically to treat certain muscular conditions and cosmetically to remove wrinkles by temporarily paralysing facial muscles.
– ORIGIN from **BOTULINUM TOXIN**.

**bo tree** /bəʊ/ (also **bodh tree**) ● **n.** a fig tree native to India and SE Asia, regarded as sacred by Buddhists. [*Ficus religiosa*.]
– ORIGIN C19: representing Sinhalese *bōgaha* 'tree of knowledge' (Buddha's enlightenment having occurred beneath such a tree), from *bō* (from Sanskrit *budh* 'understand thoroughly') + *gaha* 'tree'.

**botryoidal** /ˌbɒtrɪ'ɔɪd(ə)l/ ● **adj.** (chiefly of minerals) shaped like a cluster of grapes.
– ORIGIN C18: from Gk *botruoeidēs* (from *botrus* 'bunch of grapes') + **-AL**.

**botrytis** /bə'trʌɪtɪs/ ● **n.** a greyish powdery mould deliberately cultivated on the grapes for certain wines.
– ORIGIN mod. L. (name of a genus of moulds), from Gk *botrus* 'cluster of grapes'.

**Botswanan** /bɒ'tswɑːnən/ ● **n.** a native or inhabitant of Botswana, a country of southern Africa. ● **adj.** of or relating to Botswana.

**botte** /bɒt/ ● **n.** Fencing an attack or thrust.
– ORIGIN from Fr.

**bottle** ● **n. 1** a container with a narrow neck, used for storing liquids. ➤ a large metal cylinder holding liquefied gas. ➤ a baby's feeding bottle. **2** Brit. informal one's courage or confidence. ● **v. 1** place in bottles for storage. **2** (**bottle something up**) repress or conceal feelings. **3** (**bottle out**) Brit. informal lose one's nerve and decide not to do something. **4** informal hit with a glass bottle.
– PHRASES **bottle and glass** Brit. rhyming slang arse. **hit the bottle** informal start to drink alcohol heavily.
– ORIGIN ME: from OFr. *boteille*, from med. L. *butticula*, dimin. of late L. *buttis* (see **BUTT**[4]).

**bottle bank** ● **n.** Brit. a place where used glass bottles may be deposited for recycling.

**bottle blonde** ● **adj.** (of a woman's hair) of a shade of blonde that looks dyed. ● **n.** a woman with such hair.

**bottlebrush** ● **n. 1** a cylindrical brush for cleaning inside bottles. **2** an Australian shrub or small tree with spikes of scarlet or yellow flowers resembling bottlebrushes. [Genus *Callistemon*.]

**bottle-feed** ● **v.** feed (a baby) with milk from a bottle.

**bottle green** ● **n.** dark green.

**bottle jack** ● **n.** NZ a large jack for lifting heavy objects.

**bottleneck** ● **n. 1** the neck or mouth of a bottle. **2** a narrow section of road where traffic flow is restricted. **3** a device worn on a guitarist's finger and used to produce sliding effects on the strings.

**bottlenose dolphin** (also **bottle-nosed dolphin**) ● **n.** a stout-bodied dolphin with a distinct short beak, found in tropical and temperate coastal waters. [*Tursiops truncatus*.]

**bottlenose whale** (also **bottle-nosed whale**) ● **n.** a beaked whale with a bulbous forehead. [Genus *Hyperoodon*: two species.]

**bottler** ● **n. 1** a person who bottles drinks. **2** Austral./NZ informal an admirable person or thing.

**bottlescrew** ● **n.** British term for **TURNBUCKLE**.

**bottle tree** ● **n.** an Australian tree with a swollen bottle-shaped trunk containing water. [*Adansonia gregorii* (a baobab) and *Brachychiton rupestre*.]

**bottom** ● **n. 1** the lowest point or part of something. ➤ the furthest part or point of something. ➤ (also **bottoms**) the lower half of a two-piece garment. **2** chiefly Brit. a person's buttocks. **3** archaic stamina or strength of character, especially of a horse. **4** Physics one of six flavours of quark. ● **adj.** in the lowest position. ➤ in the furthest position away in a downhill direction. ● **v. 1** (of a ship) touch the bottom of the sea. **2** (**bottom out**) (of a situation) reach the lowest point before stabilizing or improving.
– PHRASES **at bottom** fundamentally. **be at the bottom of** be the fundamental cause or origin of. **the bottom falls** (or **drops**) **out** something suddenly fails or collapses. **bottoms up!** informal said as a toast before drinking. **get to the bottom of** find an explanation for (a mystery). **you** (**can**) **bet your bottom dollar** informal, chiefly N. Amer. a particular thing is bound to happen.
– DERIVATIVES **-bottomed** adj. **bottomless** adj. **bottommost** adj.
– ORIGIN OE *botm*, of Gmc origin.

**bottom drawer** ● **n.** Brit. dated linen and other items stored by a woman in preparation for her marriage.

**bottom feeder** ● **n. 1** any marine creature that lives on the seabed and feeds by scavenging. **2** N. Amer. informal a member of a group of very low social status who survives by any means possible.

**bottom fermentation** ● **n.** the process by which lagers are fermented, proceeding at low temperature with the yeast falling to the bottom.

**bottomland** ● **n.** N. Amer. low-lying land, typically by a river.

**bottom line** ● **n.** informal **1** the final total of an account or balance sheet. **2** the fundamental and deciding factor.

**bottomry** ● **n.** dated a system of merchant insurance in which a ship is used as security against a loan to finance a voyage.
– ORIGIN C16: from **BOTTOM** (in the sense 'ship') + **-RY**.

**bottom-up** ● **adj.** proceeding from the bottom or beginning of a hierarchy or process upwards.

**botty** ● **n.** (pl. **-ies**) Brit. informal a person's bottom.

**botulin** /'bɒtjʊlɪn/ ● **n.** the bacterial toxin involved in botulism.

**botulinum toxin** /ˌbɒtjʊ'lʌɪnəm/ (also **botulinus toxin**) ● **n.** another term for **BOTULIN**.

**botulism** /'bɒtjʊlɪz(ə)m/ ● **n.** a dangerous form of food poisoning caused by a bacterium (*Clostridium botulinum*) growing on improperly sterilized foods.
– ORIGIN C19: from Ger. *Botulismus*, 'sausage poisoning', from L. *botulus* 'sausage'.

**bouclé** /'buːkleɪ/ ● **n.** yarn with a looped or curled ply.
– ORIGIN C19: Fr., lit. 'buckled, curled'.

**boudin** /'buːdã/ ● **n. 1** (pl. same) a French type of black pudding. **2** /also 'buːdɪn/ (**boudins**) Geology a series of elongated parallel sections formed by the fracturing of a sedimentary rock stratum during folding.
– ORIGIN from Fr.

**boudoir** /'buːdwɑː/ ● **n.** a woman's bedroom or small private room.
– ORIGIN C18: Fr., lit. 'sulking-place', from *bouder* 'pout, sulk'.

**bouffant** /'buːfɒ̃/ ● **adj.** (of hair) styled so as to stand out from the head in a rounded shape. ● **n.** a bouffant hairstyle.
– ORIGIN C19: from Fr., lit. 'swelling', pres. part. of *bouffer*.

**bougainvillea** /ˌbuːg(ə)n'vɪlɪə/ (also **bougainvillaea**) ● **n.** an ornamental shrubby climbing plant widely cultivated in the tropics, with brightly coloured papery bracts surrounding the flowers. [Genus *Bougainvillea*.]
– ORIGIN named after the Fr. explorer L. A. de *Bougainville*.

**bough** /baʊ/ ● **n.** a main branch of a tree.
– ORIGIN OE *bōg*, *bōh* 'bough or shoulder', of Gmc origin;

rel. to **BOW**[3].

**bought** past and past participle of **BUY**.

**boughten** /ˈbɔːt(ə)n/ archaic past participle of **BUY**. ● **adj.** dialect, chiefly N. Amer. bought rather than home-made.

**bougie** /ˈbuːʒiː/ ● **n.** (pl. **-ies**) Medicine a thin, flexible surgical instrument for exploring or dilating a passage of the body.
– ORIGIN C18: from Fr., lit. 'wax candle', from Arab. *Bijāya*, the name of an Algerian town which traded in wax.

**bouillabaisse** /ˈbuːjəˌbeɪs/ ● **n.** a rich, spicy stew or soup made with fish, originally from Provence.
– ORIGIN Fr., from mod. Provençal *bouiabaisso*.

**bouilli** /ˈbuːjiː/ ● **n.** stewed or boiled meat.
– ORIGIN Fr., 'boiled'.

**bouillon** /ˈbuːjɒ̃/ ● **n.** thin soup or stock made by stewing meat, fish, or vegetables.
– ORIGIN Fr., from *bouillir* 'to boil'.

**boulder** ● **n.** a large rock.
– DERIVATIVES **bouldery** adj.
– ORIGIN ME: shortened from earlier *boulderstone*, of Scand. origin.

**boulder clay** ● **n.** clay containing many large stones, formed by deposition from melting glaciers.

**bouldering** ● **n.** Climbing climbing on large boulders, either for practice or as a sport in its own right.

**boule**[1] /buːl/ (also **boules** pronunc. same) ● **n.** a French form of bowls, played with metal balls.
– ORIGIN C20 (orig. denoting a form of roulette): Fr., lit. 'bowl'.

**boule**[2] /ˈbuːliː/ ● **n.** a legislative body of ancient or modern Greece.
– ORIGIN from Gk *boulē* 'senate'.

**boulevard** /ˈbuːləvɑːd/ ● **n.** a wide street, typically one lined with trees.
– ORIGIN C18: Fr., 'a rampart' (later 'a promenade on the site of one'), from Ger. *Bollwerk* (see **BULWARK**).

**boulevardier** /ˌbuːləvɑːˈdjeɪ/ ● **n.** a wealthy, fashionable socialite.
– ORIGIN C19: from Fr., orig. in the sense 'person who frequents boulevards'.

**boulle** /buːl/ (also **buhl**) ● **n.** brass, tortoiseshell, or other material used for inlaying furniture.
– ORIGIN C19: from Fr. *boule*, from the name of the Fr. cabinetmaker André *Boulle*.

**boult** ● **v.** variant spelling of **BOLT**[4].

**bounce** ● **v. 1** (of an object, especially a ball) spring quickly up or away from a surface after hitting it. ➤ move or jump up and down repeatedly. **2** (of light, sound, or an electronic signal) reflect back from a surface. **3** (**bounce back**) recover well after a setback or problem. **4** move in an energetic or enthusiastic manner. **5** informal (of a cheque) be returned by a bank when there are insufficient funds in an account to meet it. **6** informal, chiefly N. Amer. dismiss from a job. **7** Brit. informal pressurize (someone) into doing something. ● **n. 1** a rebound of a ball or other object. ➤ an act of bouncing up and down. **2** exuberant self-confidence. **3** health and body in a person's hair.
– PHRASES **bounce an idea off someone** informal discuss an idea with someone in order to test or improve it.
– ORIGIN ME *bunsen* 'beat, thump', perh. imitative, or from Low Ger. *bunsen* 'beat', Du. *bons* 'a thump'.

**bouncer** ● **n. 1** a person employed by a nightclub or pub to prevent troublemakers entering or to eject them from the premises. **2** Cricket a ball bowled fast and short so as to rise high after pitching.

**bouncing** ● **adj.** (of a baby) vigorous and healthy.

**bouncing Bet** ● **n.** another term for **SOAPWORT**.

**bouncy** ● **adj.** (**-ier**, **-iest**) **1** able to bounce or making something bounce well. **2** confident and lively.
– DERIVATIVES **bouncily** adv. **bounciness** n.

**bouncy castle** ● **n.** a large inflatable structure on which children can jump and play.

**bound**[1] ● **v.** walk or run with leaping strides. ● **n.** a leaping movement towards or over something.
– ORIGIN C16: from Fr. *bond* (n.), *bondir* (v.) 'resound', later 'rebound', from late L. *bombitare*, from L. *bombus* 'humming'.

**bound**[2] ● **n. 1** a boundary. **2** a limitation or restriction. ➤ technical a limiting value. ● **v. 1** form the boundary of. **2** restrict.
– PHRASES **out of bounds 1** beyond the acceptable or permitted limits. **2** (in sport) beyond the field of play.
– ORIGIN ME: from OFr. *bodne*, from med. L. *bodina*, earlier *butina*.

**bound**[3] ● **adj.** going towards somewhere: *a train bound for Edinburgh.*
– ORIGIN ME *boun* (in the sense 'ready, dressed'), from ON *búinn*, past part. of *búa* 'get ready'.

**bound**[4] past and past participle of **BIND**. ● **adj. 1** (**-bound**) restricted or confined to or by a place or situation: *his job kept him city-bound.* **2** destined or certain to be, do, or have something. ➤ obliged to do something. **3** (**-bound**) (of a book) having a specified binding. **4** (of a grammatical element) occurring only in combination with another form.
– PHRASES **I'll be bound** I am sure.

**boundary** ● **n.** (pl. **-ies**) **1** a line marking the limits of an area. **2** Cricket a hit crossing the limits of the field, scoring four or six runs.
– ORIGIN C17: var. of dial. *bounder*, from **BOUND**[2] + **-ER**[1].

**boundary layer** ● **n.** a layer of stationary fluid (such as water or air) surrounding an immersed moving object.

**bounden** /ˈbaʊnd(ə)n/ archaic past participle of **BIND**.
– PHRASES **a** (or **one's**) **bounden duty** an obligatory responsibility.

**bounder** ● **n.** Brit. informal, dated a dishonourable man.

**boundless** ● **adj.** unlimited.
– DERIVATIVES **boundlessly** adv. **boundlessness** n.

**bounteous** ● **adj.** archaic bountiful.
– DERIVATIVES **bounteously** adv. **bounteousness** n.
– ORIGIN ME: from OFr. *bontif*, *-ive* 'benevolent' (from *bonte* 'bounty'), on the pattern of *plenteous*.

**bountiful** ● **adj. 1** abundant. **2** giving generously.
– PHRASES **Lady Bountiful** a woman who engages in ostentatious acts of charity. [C19: from the name of a character in Farquhar's *The Beaux' Stratagem* (1707).]
– DERIVATIVES **bountifully** adv.

**bounty** ● **n.** (pl. **-ies**) **1** a reward paid for killing or capturing someone. **2** historical a sum paid by the state to encourage trade. ➤ chiefly historical a sum paid by the state to enlisting army or navy recruits. **3** poetic/literary something given or occurring in generous amounts.
– ORIGIN ME: from OFr. *bonte* 'goodness', from L. *bonitas*, from *bonus* 'good'.

**bounty hunter** ● **n.** a person who pursues a criminal for a reward.

**bouquet** /bʊˈkeɪ, bəʊˈkeɪ, ˈbʊkeɪ/ ● **n. 1** a bunch of flowers. **2** the characteristic scent of a wine or perfume.
– ORIGIN C18: from Fr. (earlier 'clump of trees'), from a dial. var. of OFr. *bos* 'wood'.

**bouquet garni** /bʊˌkeɪ ˈgɑːni, bəʊˈkeɪ, ˈbʊkeɪ/ ● **n.** (pl. **bouquets garnis**) a bunch of herbs used for flavouring a stew or soup.
– ORIGIN Fr., lit. 'garnished bouquet'.

**Bourbon** /ˈbʊəb(ə)n/ ● **n. 1** US a reactionary. **2** Brit. a chocolate-flavoured biscuit with a chocolate-cream filling. **3** (also **Bourbon rose**) a long-flowering rose with a rich scent, originally from the island of Réunion (formerly Île de Bourbon). [*Rosa* × *borboniana*.]
– ORIGIN C19: from *Bourbon*, the surname of a branch of the Fr. royal family.

**bourbon** /ˈbəːb(ə)n, ˈbʊə-/ ● **n.** a kind of American whisky distilled from maize and rye.
– ORIGIN C19: named after *Bourbon* County, Kentucky, where it was first made.

**bourdon** /ˈbʊəd(ə)n/ ● **n.** Music a low-pitched stop in an organ or harmonium.
– ORIGIN ME (in the sense 'drone of a bagpipe'): from OFr., 'drone', of imitative origin.

**bourgeois** /ˈbʊəʒwɑː/ (also **bourgeoise**) /ˈbʊəʒwɑːz/ ● **adj.** of or characteristic of the middle class, especially in having materialistic values or conventional attitudes. ➤ (in Marxist contexts) capitalist. ● **n.** (pl. same) a bourgeois person.
– ORIGIN C16: from Fr., from late L. *burgus* 'castle' (in med.

L. 'fortified town'), ult. of Gmc origin and rel. to **BOROUGH**; cf. **BURGESS**.

**bourgeoisie** /ˌbʊəʒwɑːˈziː/ ● **n.** [treated as sing. or pl.] the middle class. ➤(in Marxist contexts) the capitalist class.
– ORIGIN C18: Fr., from **BOURGEOIS**.

**bourn**[1] /bɔːn, bʊən/ ● **n.** dialect a small stream.
– ORIGIN ME: S. Engl. var. of **BURN**[2].

**bourn**[2] /bɔːn, bʊən/ (also **bourne**) ● **n.** poetic/literary **1** a boundary. **2** a goal; a destination.
– ORIGIN C16: from Fr. *borne*, from OFr. *bodne* (see **BOUND**[2]).

**bourrée** /ˈbʊəreɪ/ ● **n. 1** a lively French dance like a gavotte. **2** Ballet a series of very fast little steps performed on the tips of the toes with the feet close together. ● **v.** perform a bourrée.
– ORIGIN C17: Fr., lit. 'faggot of twigs' (the dance being performed around a twig fire).

**bourse** /bʊəs, French buʀs/ ● **n.** a stock market in a non-English-speaking country, especially France.
– ORIGIN C16: from Fr., lit. 'purse', via med. L. from Gk *bursa* 'leather'.

**Boursin** /ˈbʊəsã, French buʀsɛ̃/ ● **n.** trademark a kind of soft cheese from France.
– ORIGIN from Fr.

**boustrophedon** /ˌbaʊstrəˈfiːd(ə)n, ˌbuː-/ ● **adj. & adv.** (of words) written from right to left and from left to right in alternate lines.
– ORIGIN C17: from Gk, lit. 'as an ox turns in ploughing'.

**bout** /baʊt/ ● **n. 1** a short period of intense activity. ➤an attack of illness or strong emotion. **2** a wrestling or boxing match. **3** a curve in the side of a violin or other musical instrument.
– ORIGIN C16: from dial. *bought* 'bend, loop'; prob. of Low Ger. origin.

**boutade** /buːˈtɑːd/ ● **n.** formal a sudden outburst.
– ORIGIN C17: Fr., from *bouter* 'to thrust'.

**boutique** /buːˈtiːk/ ● **n.** a small shop selling fashionable clothes.
– ORIGIN C18: from Fr., 'small shop', via L. from Gk *apothēkē* 'storehouse'.

**bouton** /ˈbuːtɒn/ ● **n.** Anatomy an enlarged part of a nerve fibre or cell where it forms a synapse with another nerve.
– ORIGIN C20: from Fr., lit. 'button'.

**boutonnière** /ˌbuːtɒnˈjɛː/ ● **n.** a spray of flowers worn in a buttonhole.
– ORIGIN C19: Fr., 'buttonhole', from *bouton* 'button'.

**boutu** /ˈbəʊtuː/ (also **boto**) ● **n.** a pink and grey river dolphin found in the Amazon and Orinoco River systems. [*Inia geoffrensis*.]
– ORIGIN local name.

**bouvier** /ˈbuːvɪeɪ/ ● **n.** a large, powerful dog of a rough-coated breed originating in Belgium.
– ORIGIN Fr., lit. 'cowherd'.

**bouzouki** /bʊˈzuːki/ ● **n.** (pl. **bouzoukis**) a long-necked Greek form of mandolin.
– ORIGIN 1950s: from mod. Gk *mpouzouki*, perh. rel. to Turk. *bozuk* 'spoilt' (with ref. to roughly made instruments).

**bovid** /ˈbəʊvɪd/ ● **n.** Zoology a mammal of the cattle family (Bovidae).
– ORIGIN C19: from mod. L. *Bovidae*, from L. *bos*, *bov-* 'ox'.

**bovine** /ˈbəʊvʌɪn/ ● **adj.** of, relating to, or resembling cattle. ● **n.** an animal of the cattle family.
– DERIVATIVES **bovinely** adv.
– ORIGIN C19: from late L. *bovinus*, from L. *bos*, *bov-* 'ox'.

**bovine spongiform encephalopathy** ● **n.** see **BSE**.

**bovver** ● **n.** Brit. informal hooliganism or trouble-making: [as modifier] *a bovver boy*.
– ORIGIN 1960s: cockney pronunc. of **BOTHER**.

**bow**[1] /bəʊ/ ● **n. 1** a knot tied with two loops and two loose ends. **2** a weapon for shooting arrows, made of a curved piece of wood joined at both ends by a taut string. **3** a partially curved rod with horsehair stretched along its length, used for playing some stringed instruments. **4** a curved stroke forming part of a letter (e.g. *b*, *p*). **5** a metal ring forming the handle of a key or pair of scissors. **6** N. Amer. a side piece or lens frame of a pair of glasses. ● **v.** play (a stringed instrument) using a bow.
– PHRASES **have** (or **add**) **another string to one's bow** Brit. have a further resource available.
– ORIGIN OE *boga* 'bend, bow, arch', of Gmc origin; rel. to **BOW**[2].

**bow**[2] /baʊ/ ● **v. 1** bend the head or upper body as a sign of respect, greeting, or shame. **2** cause to bend with age or under a heavy weight. **3** submit to pressure or demands. **4** (**bow out**) withdraw or retire from something. ● **n.** an act of bowing.
– PHRASES **bow and scrape** behave in an obsequious way. **make one's bow** make one's first formal appearance in a particular role. **take a bow** acknowledge applause by bowing.
– ORIGIN OE *būgan* 'bend, stoop', of Gmc origin; rel. to **BOW**[1].

**bow**[3] /baʊ/ (also **bows**) ● **n.** the front end of a ship.
– PHRASES **on the bow** Nautical within 45° of the point directly ahead. **a shot across the bows** a warning statement or gesture.
– ORIGIN ME: from Low Ger. *boog*, Du. *boeg*, 'shoulder or ship's bow'; rel. to **BOUGH**.

**bow compass** ● **n.** a compass with jointed legs.

**bowdlerize** /ˈbaʊdlərʌɪz/ (also **-ise**) ● **v.** remove from (a text) material regarded as improper or offensive.
– DERIVATIVES **bowdlerism** n. **bowdlerization** n.
– ORIGIN C19: from the name of Dr Thomas *Bowdler*, an American who published an expurgated edition of Shakespeare.

**bowel** /ˈbaʊəl/ ● **n. 1** the intestine. **2** (**bowels**) the deepest inner parts of something.
– ORIGIN ME: from OFr. *bouel*, from L. *botellus*, dimin. of *botulus* 'sausage'.

**bowel movement** ● **n.** an act of defecation.

**bower**[1] /ˈbaʊə/ ● **n. 1** a pleasant shady place under trees. **2** poetic/literary a summer house or country cottage. **3** poetic/literary a lady's private room. ● **v.** poetic/literary shade; enclose.
– ORIGIN OE *būr*, of Gmc origin.

**bower**[2] /ˈbaʊə/ ● **n.** an anchor carried at a ship's bow.
– ORIGIN C15: from **BOW**[3] + **-ER**[1].

**bowerbird** ● **n.** an Australasian bird noted for the male's habit of constructing an elaborate bower adorned with feathers, shells, etc. to attract the female. [Family Ptilonorhynchidae: several species.]

**bowfin** /ˈbəʊfɪn/ ● **n.** a predatory American freshwater fish with a large blunt head and a long dorsal fin, able to survive long periods out of water. [*Amia calva*.]

**bow-fronted** ● **adj.** having a convexly curved front.
– DERIVATIVES **bow front** n.

**bowhead whale** /ˈbəʊhɛd/ ● **n.** a black Arctic right whale, feeding by skimming the surface for plankton. [*Balaena mysticetus*.]

**bowie knife** /ˈbəʊi/ ● **n.** (pl. **-ies**) a long knife with a blade double-edged at the point.
– ORIGIN C19: named after the Amer. frontiersman Jim *Bowie*.

**bowl**[1] ● **n. 1** a round, deep dish or basin. ➤a rounded, concave part of an object. ➤Geography a natural basin. **2** [in names] chiefly N. Amer. a stadium for sporting or musical events. ➤an American football game played after the season between leading teams.
– DERIVATIVES **bowlful** n. (pl. **-fuls**).
– ORIGIN OE *bolle*, *bolla*, of Gmc origin; rel. to **BOLL**.

**bowl**[2] ● **n. 1** a wooden or hard rubber ball used in the game of bowls. ➤a large ball used in tenpin bowling or skittles. **2** a spell of bowling in cricket. ● **v. 1** roll (a round object) along the ground. **2** Cricket (of a bowler) propel (the ball) towards the wicket for the batsman to attempt to hit. ➤dismiss (a batsman) by knocking down the wicket with a bowled ball. **3** move rapidly and smoothly. **4** (**bowl someone over**) knock someone down. **5** (usu. **be bowled over**) informal completely overwhelm or astonish.
– DERIVATIVES **bowling** n.
– ORIGIN ME: from OFr. *boule*, from L. *bulla* 'bubble'.

**bow-legged** • adj. having legs that curve outwards at the knee.
– DERIVATIVES **bow legs** pl. n.

**bowler**[1] • n. **1** Cricket a member of the fielding side who bowls. **2** a player at bowls, tenpin bowling, or skittles.

**bowler**[2] (also **bowler hat**) • n. a man's hard felt hat with a round dome-shaped crown.
– ORIGIN C19: named after the Engl. hatter William *Bowler*.

**bowline** /ˈbəʊlɪn/ • n. **1** a rope attaching the weather side of a square sail to a ship's bow. **2** a simple knot for forming a non-slipping loop at the end of a rope.
– ORIGIN ME: from Mid. Low Ger. *bōlīne*, MDu. *boechlijne*, from *boeg* 'ship's bow' + *lijne* 'line'.

**bowling alley** • n. a long narrow track along which balls are rolled in skittles or tenpin bowling.

**bowling crease** • n. Cricket the line from behind which a bowler delivers the ball.

**bowling green** • n. an area of closely mown grass on which the game of bowls is played.

**bowls** /bəʊlz/ • pl. n. [treated as sing.] a game played with heavy wooden bowls, the object of which is to propel one's bowl as close as possible to a small white ball (the jack).

**bowman**[1] /ˈbəʊmən/ • n. (pl. **-men**) an archer.

**bowman**[2] /ˈbaʊmən/ • n. (pl. **-men**) the rower who sits nearest the bow of a boat.

**bowsaw** /ˈbəʊsɔː/ • n. a saw with a narrow blade stretched on a light curved frame.

**bowser** /ˈbaʊzə/ • n. trademark **1** a tanker used for fuelling aircraft or supplying water. **2** Austral./NZ a petrol pump.
– ORIGIN 1920s: from the name of a company of oil storage engineers.

**bowshot** /ˈbəʊʃɒt/ • n. the distance to which a bow can send an arrow.

**bowsie** /ˈbaʊziː/ • n. (pl. **-ies**) Irish a low-class or unruly person.
– ORIGIN of unknown origin.

**bowsprit** /ˈbəʊsprɪt/ • n. a spar running out from a ship's bow, to which the forestays are fastened.
– ORIGIN ME: from Mid. Low Ger. *bōgsprēt*, MDu. *boechspriet*, from *boech* 'bow' + *spriet* 'sprit'.

**Bow Street Runner** /ˈbəʊ/ • n. historical, informal a London policeman.
– ORIGIN named after *Bow Street* in London, site of the chief metropolitan magistrates' court.

**bow tie** • n. a necktie in the form of a bow.

**bow window** • n. a curved bay window.

**bow-wow** • exclam. /baʊˈwaʊ/ an imitation of a dog's bark. • n. /ˈbaʊwaʊ/ informal a dog.

**bowyer** /ˈbəʊjə/ • n. a person who makes or sells archers' bows.

**box**[1] • n. **1** a container with a flat base and sides and a lid. **2** (**the box**) informal, chiefly Brit. television. **3** historical a coachman's seat. **4** an area enclosed within straight lines on a page or computer screen, to be filled in with or containing information. **5** (**the box**) Soccer the penalty area. ➤(**the box**) Baseball the area occupied by the batter. **6** an enclosed area reserved for people in a theatre or sports ground, or for witnesses or the jury in a law court. **7** Brit. a small country house used when shooting or fishing. **8** a protective casing for part of a mechanism. ➤Brit. a shield for protecting a man's genitals in sport, especially cricket. **9** a facility at a newspaper office for receiving replies to an advertisement. ➤a facility at a post office whereby letters are kept until collected by the addressee. • v. **1** [often as adj. **boxed**] put in or provide with a box. **2** (**box someone in**) restrict someone's ability to move freely.
– PHRASES **out of one's box** Brit. informal intoxicated with alcohol or drugs.
– DERIVATIVES **boxful** n. (pl. **-fuls**). **box-like** adj.
– ORIGIN OE, prob. from late L. *buxis*, from L. *pyxis* 'boxwood box', from Gk *puxos* (see **BOX**[3]).

**box**[2] • v. fight an opponent with the fists in padded gloves as a sport. • n. a slap on the side of a person's head.
– PHRASES **box clever** Brit. informal outwit someone. **box someone's ears** slap someone on the side of the head.
– DERIVATIVES **boxing** n.
– ORIGIN ME: of unknown origin.

**box**[3] (also **box tree**) • n. a slow-growing evergreen shrub with small glossy leaves, yielding hard wood. [*Buxus sempervirens*.] ➤any of various other trees with similar foliage or wood. [*Casearia praecox* (tropical America) and other species.]
– ORIGIN OE, via L. from Gk *puxos*.

**box**[4] • v. (in phr. **box the compass**) recite the compass points in correct order.
– ORIGIN C18: perh. from Sp. *bojar* 'sail round', from Mid. Low Ger. *bōgen* 'bend', from the base of **BOW**[1].

**box beam** • n. another term for **BOX GIRDER**.

**boxboard** • n. stiff cardboard used to make boxes.

**box camera** • n. a simple box-shaped hand camera.

**box canyon** • n. N. Amer. a narrow canyon with a flat bottom and vertical walls.

**boxcar** • n. N. Amer. an enclosed railway freight wagon.

**box elder** • n. an American maple with leaves resembling those of the elder and green or purplish twigs. [*Acer negundo*.]

**Boxer** • n. a member of a fiercely nationalistic Chinese secret society which flourished in the 19th century.
– ORIGIN from **BOXER**, translating Chin. *yì hé quán*, lit. 'righteous harmony fists'.

**boxer** • n. **1** a person who boxes as a sport. **2** a medium-sized dog of a breed with a smooth brown coat and pug-like face.

**boxer shorts** • pl. n. men's underpants resembling shorts.

**boxfish** • n. (pl. same or **-fishes**) a tropical marine fish with a shell of bony plates covered in spines enclosing the body. [*Tetrosomus gibbosus* and other species.]

**box girder** • n. a hollow girder square in cross section.

**Boxing Day** • n. chiefly Brit. a public holiday on the first day (or first weekday) after Christmas Day.
– ORIGIN C19: from the former custom of giving tradespeople a Christmas box on this day.

**boxing glove** • n. a heavily padded mitten worn in boxing.

**box jellyfish** • n. a jellyfish with a box-shaped swimming bell, living in warm seas. [Class Cubozoa.]

**box junction** • n. Brit. a road area at a junction marked with a yellow grid, which a vehicle should enter only if its exit is clear.

**box kite** • n. a tailless kite in the form of a long box open at each end.

**box number** • n. a number identifying an advertisement in a newspaper, used as an address for replies.

**box office** • n. a place at a theatre, cinema, etc. where tickets are sold.

**box pew** • n. a church pew enclosed by wooden partitions.

**box pleat** • n. a pleat consisting of two parallel creases facing opposite directions and forming a raised band.

**boxroom** • n. Brit. a very small room.

**box score** • n. N. Amer. the tabulated results of a baseball game or other sporting event.

**box spanner** • n. Brit. a cylindrical spanner with a hexagonal end fitting over the head of a nut.

**box spring** • n. each of a set of vertical springs housed in a frame in a mattress.

**boxthorn** • n. a thorny shrub bearing red berries, some kinds of which are used for hedging. [Genus *Lycium*: several species.]

**box turtle** • n. a land-living turtle having a lower shell with hinged lobes that can be drawn up tightly. [Genus *Terrapene*: several species.]

**boxty** /ˈbɒksti/ • n. a type of Irish bread made using grated raw potatoes and flour.
– ORIGIN from Ir. *bacstaí*.

**boxy** • adj. (**-ier**, **-iest**) **1** squarish in shape. **2** (of a room or space) cramped.

**boy** • n. **1** a male child or youth. **2** (**boys**) informal men who mix socially or belong to a particular group. **3** dated, offen-

sive a black male servant or worker. ● **exclam.** informal used to express strong feelings: *Oh boy, that's wonderful!*
– DERIVATIVES **boyhood** n. **boyish** adj. **boyishly** adv. **boyishness** n.
– ORIGIN ME: of unknown origin.

**boyar** /bəʊˈjɑː/ ● **n.** a member of the old aristocracy in Russia, next in rank to a prince.
– ORIGIN C16: from Russ. *boyarin* 'grandee'.

**boycott** ● **v.** withdraw from commercial or social relations with, as a punishment or protest. ➤ refuse to buy or handle (goods) for this reason. ● **n.** an act of boycotting.
– ORIGIN from the name of Captain Charles C. *Boycott*, an Ir. land agent so treated in 1880 in an attempt to get rents reduced.

**boyfriend** ● **n.** a person's regular male companion in a romantic or sexual relationship.

**boyla** /ˈbɔɪlə/ ● **n.** Austral. an Aboriginal witch doctor.
– ORIGIN from Nyungar *bolya*.

**Boyle's law** ● **n.** Chemistry a law stating that the pressure of a given mass of an ideal gas is inversely proportional to its volume at a constant temperature.
– ORIGIN from the name of the Engl. scientist Robert *Boyle* (1627–91).

**boyo** ● **n.** (pl. **-os**) Welsh & Irish informal a boy or man.

**boy racer** ● **n.** informal a young man fond of driving very fast in high-powered cars.

**Boy Scout** ● **n.** old-fashioned term for **SCOUT**[1] (in sense 2).

**boysenberry** /ˈbɔɪz(ə)nˌb(ə)ri, -ˌbɛri/ ● **n.** (pl. **-ies**) **1** a large red edible blackberry-like fruit. **2** the shrubby hybrid bramble plant that bears this fruit. [*Rubus loganobaccus*.]
– ORIGIN 1930s: named after the Amer. horticulturalist Robert *Boysen*.

**boy wonder** ● **n.** an exceptionally talented young man.

**bozo** /ˈbəʊzəʊ/ ● **n.** (pl. **-os**) informal, chiefly N. Amer. a stupid or insignificant person.
– ORIGIN 1920s: of unknown origin.

**BP** ● **abbrev. 1** before the present (era). **2** blood pressure. **3** British Pharmacopoeia.

**Bp** ● **abbrev.** Bishop.

**bp** ● **abbrev. 1** Biochemistry base pair(s). **2** Finance basis point(s). **3** boiling point.

**BPC** ● **abbrev.** British Pharmaceutical Codex.

**BPH** ● **abbrev.** Medicine benign prostatic hyperplasia (or hypertrophy).

**BPhil** ● **abbrev.** Bachelor of Philosophy.

**bpi** ● **abbrev.** Computing bits per inch, used to indicate the density of data that can be stored on magnetic tape.

**bps** ● **abbrev.** Computing bits per second.

**Bq** ● **abbrev.** becquerel.

**BR** ● **abbrev. 1** Brazil (international vehicle registration). **2** (formerly) British Rail.

**Br** ● **symb.** the chemical element bromine.

**Br.** ● **abbrev. 1** British. **2** (in religious orders) Brother.

**bra** ● **n.** a woman's undergarment worn to support the breasts.
– DERIVATIVES **braless** adj.
– ORIGIN 1930s: abbrev. of **BRASSIERE**.

**braai** /ˈbrʌi/ S. African ● **n.** (pl. **braais**) short for **BRAAIVLEIS**. ● **v.** (**braaied**, **braaiing** or **braaing**) grill (meat) over an open fire.
– ORIGIN from Afrik.

**braaivleis** /ˈbrʌɪˌfleɪs/ ● **n.** S. African a picnic or barbecue where meat is grilled over an open fire.
– ORIGIN Afrik., 'grilled meat', from *braai* 'to grill' + *vleis* 'meat'.

**braata** /ˈbrɑːtə/ (also **braatas**) ● **n.** W. Indian a small amount added to a purchase in a market to encourage the customer to return.
– ORIGIN prob. from Sp. *barata* 'bargain'.

**brace** ● **n. 1** (**braces**) Brit. a pair of straps passing over the shoulders and fastening to the top of trousers at the front and back to hold them up. **2** a device supporting a weak or injured part of the body. ➤ a wire device fitted in the mouth to straighten the teeth. ➤ a strengthening piece of iron or timber in building or carpentry. **3** (also **brace and bit**) a drilling tool with a crank handle and a socket to hold a bit. **4** a rope attached to the yard of a ship for trimming the sail. **5** (pl. same) a pair of things, especially birds or mammals killed in hunting. **6** either of two connecting marks { and }, used in printing. ➤ Music a similar mark connecting staves to be performed at the same time. ● **v. 1** make stronger or firmer with wood, iron, etc. **2** press (one's body) firmly against something in order to stay balanced. **3** (**brace oneself**) prepare for something difficult or unpleasant.
– ORIGIN ME: from OFr. *bracier* 'embrace', from *brace* 'two arms', from L. *bracchia*, pl. of *bracchium* 'arm', from Gk *brakhiōn*.

**bracelet** ● **n. 1** an ornamental band or chain worn on the wrist or arm. **2** (**bracelets**) informal handcuffs.
– ORIGIN ME: from OFr., from *bras* 'arm', from L. *bracchium*.

**bracer**[1] ● **n.** informal an alcoholic drink taken to prepare one for something difficult or unpleasant.

**bracer**[2] ● **n.** a wristguard used in archery and other sports. ➤ historical a piece of armour covering the arm.
– ORIGIN ME: from OFr. *braciere*, from *bras* (see **BRACELET**).

**brachial** /ˈbreɪkɪəl/ ● **adj. 1** Anatomy of or relating to the arm or an arm-like structure. **2** Zoology denoting the upper valve of a brachiopod's shell.
– ORIGIN ME: from L. *brachialis*, from *brac(c)hium* 'arm'.

**brachiate** ● **v.** /ˈbrakɪeɪt/ (of apes) swing from branch to branch by the arms. ● **adj.** /ˈbrakɪət, ˈbreɪk-/ Biology branched. ➤ having arms.
– DERIVATIVES **brachiation** n. **brachiator** n.
– ORIGIN C18: from L. *brachium* 'arm' + **-ATE**[2].

**Brachiopoda** /ˌbrakɪəˈpəʊdə/ ● **pl. n.** Zoology a phylum of marine invertebrates that comprises the lamp shells.
– DERIVATIVES **brachiopod** /ˈbrakɪə(ʊ)pɒd/ n.
– ORIGIN mod. L., from Gk *brakhiōn* 'arm' + *pous, pod-* 'foot'.

**brachiosaurus** /ˌbrakɪə(ʊ)ˈsɔːrəs/ ● **n.** a huge herbivorous dinosaur of the late Jurassic to mid Cretaceous periods, with forelegs much longer than the hind legs. [Genus *Brachiosaurus*.]
– ORIGIN mod. L., from Gk *brakhiōn* 'arm' + *sauros* 'lizard'.

**brachistochrone** /brəˈkɪstəkrəʊn/ ● **n.** a curve between two points along which a body can move under gravity in a shorter time than for any other curve.
– ORIGIN C18: from Gk *brakhistos* 'shortest' + *khronos* 'time'.

**brachy-** /ˈbraki/ ● **comb. form** short: *brachycephalic*.
– ORIGIN from Gk *brakhus* 'short'.

**brachycephalic** /ˌbrakɪsɪˈfalɪk, -kɛˈfalɪk/ ● **adj.** having a relatively broad, short skull. Often contrasted with **DOLICHOCEPHALIC**.
– DERIVATIVES **brachycephaly** n.

**brachytherapy** /ˌbrakiˈθɛrəpi/ ● **n.** the treatment of cancer, especially prostate cancer, by the insertion of radioactive implants directly into the tissue.

**bracing** ● **adj. 1** fresh and invigorating. **2** (of a support) serving as a brace.
– DERIVATIVES **bracingly** adv. **bracingness** n.

**brack** ● **n.** Irish a cake or bun containing dried fruit.
– ORIGIN shortening of **BARMBRACK**.

**bracken** ● **n.** a tall fern with coarse lobed fronds. [*Pteridium aquilinum*.]
– ORIGIN ME: of Scand. origin.

**bracket** ● **n. 1** each of a pair of marks ( ) [ ] { } < > used to enclose words or figures and separate them from the surrounding context. **2** a category of similar people or things. **3** a right-angled support projecting from a wall, holding a shelf, lamp, etc. **4** Military the distance between two artillery shots fired either side of the target to establish range. ● **v.** (**bracketed**, **bracketing**) **1** enclose (words or figures) in brackets. ➤ Mathematics enclose (a complex expression) in brackets to denote that the whole of the expression has a particular relation to another expression. **2** place in the same category. **3** attach by means of a bracket. **4** Military establish the range of (a target) by firing preliminary shots short of and beyond it.

– ORIGIN C16: from Fr. *braguette* or Sp. *bragueta* 'codpiece, bracket, corbel', from Provençal *braga*, from L. *braca*, (pl.) *bracae* 'breeches'.

**bracket fungus** ● n. a fungus which forms shelf-like projections on the trunks of trees. [Order Aphyllophorales: many species.]

**brackish** ● adj. (of water) slightly salty, as in river estuaries. ➤ living in or requiring such water.
– DERIVATIVES **brackishness** n.
– ORIGIN C16: from obs. *brack* 'salty', from Mid. Low Ger., MDu. *brac*.

**braconid** /ˈbrakənɪd/ ● n. Entomology a small parasitic wasp of a family (Braconidae) related to the ichneumons.
– ORIGIN C19: from mod. L. *Braconidae*, formed irregularly from Gk *brakhus* 'short'.

**bract** ● n. Botany a modified leaf or scale with a flower or flower cluster in its axil.
– ORIGIN C18: from L. *bractea* 'thin plate of metal'.

**bracteate** /ˈbraktɪət, -tɪeɪt/ ● adj. having or bearing bracts. ● n. Archaeology a coin or ornament of thinly beaten precious metal.

**brad** ● n. a nail of rectangular cross section with a flat tip and a small asymmetrical head.
– ORIGIN ME: from ON *broddr* 'spike'.

**bradawl** /ˈbradɔːl/ ● n. a tool for boring holes, resembling a screwdriver.

**bradoon** /brəˈduːn/ ● n. variant spelling of **BRIDOON**.

**bradycardia** /ˌbradɪˈkɑːdɪə/ ● n. Medicine abnormally slow heart action.
– ORIGIN C19: from Gk *bradus* 'slow' + *kardia* 'heart'.

**bradykinin** /ˌbradɪˈkʌɪnɪn/ ● n. Biochemistry a compound released in the blood which causes contraction of smooth muscle and dilation of blood vessels.
– ORIGIN 1940s: from Gk *bradus* 'slow' + *kinēsis* 'motion' + **-IN**[1].

**brae** /breɪ/ ● n. Scottish a steep bank or hillside.
– ORIGIN ME: from ON *brá* 'eyelash', of Gmc origin; cf. **BROW**[1].

**Braeburn** /ˈbreɪbəːn/ ● n. a New Zealand dessert apple of a variety with crisp flesh.
– ORIGIN 1950s: from *Braeburn Orchards*, where it was first grown commercially.

**brag** ● v. (**bragged**, **bragging**) boast. ● n. **1** a simplified form of poker. **2** an act of bragging.
– DERIVATIVES **bragger** n. **bragging** adj. **braggingly** adv.
– ORIGIN ME: of unknown origin.

**braggadocio** /ˌbragəˈdəʊtʃɪəʊ/ ● n. boastful or arrogant behaviour.
– ORIGIN C16: from *Braggadocchio*, the name of a braggart in Spenser's *Faerie Queene*, from **BRAG** or **BRAGGART** + the Ital. suffix *-occio*, denoting something large.

**braggart** /ˈbragət, -ɑːt/ ● n. a person who brags.
– ORIGIN C16: from Fr. *bragard*, from *braguer* 'to brag'.

**Brahman** /ˈbrɑːmən/ ● n. (pl. **-mans**) **1** (also **Brahmin**) a member of the highest Hindu caste, that of the priesthood. **2** the ultimate reality underlying all phenomena in the Hindu scriptures. **3** US spelling of **BRAHMIN** (in sense 3).
– DERIVATIVES **Brahmanic** /-ˈmanɪk/ adj. **Brahmanical** /-ˈmanɪk(ə)l/ adj.
– ORIGIN sense 1 from Sanskrit *brāhmaṇa*; sense 2 from Sanskrit *brahman*.

**Brahmana** /ˈbrɑːmənə/ ● n. (in Hinduism) any of the lengthy commentaries on the Vedas.

**Brahmanism** /ˈbrɑːməˌnɪz(ə)m/ (also **Brahminism**) ● n. the early form of Hinduism that emerged in India (*c*.900 BC) under the influence of the Brahmans.

**brahmaputra** /ˌbrɑːməˈpuːtrə/ ● n. a chicken of a large Asian breed.
– ORIGIN C19: named after the *Brahmaputra*, a river of southern Asia.

**Brahmin** /ˈbrɑːmɪn/ ● n. **1** variant spelling of **BRAHMAN** (in sense 1). **2** US a socially or culturally superior person. **3** (also **Brahminy bull** or US **Brahman**) another term for **ZEBU**.
– DERIVATIVES **Brahminical** adj.

**Brahms and Liszt** ● adj. Brit. informal drunk.
– ORIGIN 1970s: rhyming sl. for 'pissed'.

**Brahui** /brəˈhuːi/ ● n. (pl. same) **1** a member of a pastoral people of western Pakistan. **2** the Dravidian language of this people.
– ORIGIN from Brahui.

**braid** ● n. **1** threads of silk, cotton, etc. woven into a decorative band. **2** a length of hair made up of three or more interlaced strands. ● v. **1** form a braid with three or more strands of (hair). **2** [usu. as adj. **braided**] edge or trim with braid. **3** [usu. as adj. **braided**] (of a river or stream) flow into shallow interconnected channels divided by deposited earth.
– DERIVATIVES **braiding** n.
– ORIGIN OE *bregdan* 'make a sudden movement', also 'interweave', of Gmc origin.

**brail** Sailing ● n. (**brails**) small ropes that are led from the leech of a fore-and-aft sail to pulleys on the mast for temporarily furling it. ● v. (**brail a sail up**) furl a sail by hauling on the brails.
– ORIGIN ME: from OFr. *braiel*, from med. L. *bracale* 'girdle', from *braca* 'breeches'.

**Braille** /breɪl/ ● n. a written language for the blind, in which characters are represented by patterns of raised dots. ● v. print or transcribe in Braille.
– ORIGIN C19: named after the blind Fr. educationist Louis *Braille* who developed it.

**brain** ● n. **1** an organ of soft nervous tissue contained in the skull, functioning as the coordinating centre of sensation and intellectual and nervous activity. ➤ (**brains**) the substance of an animal's brain used as food. **2** intellectual capacity. **3** (**the brains**) informal the main organizer or planner within a group. ● v. informal hit hard on the head with an object.
– PHRASES **have something on the brain** informal be obsessed with something.
– DERIVATIVES **-brained** adj.
– ORIGIN OE *brægen*, of W. Gmc origin.

**brainbox** ● n. Brit. informal a very clever person.

**braincase** ● n. the cranium.

**brainchild** ● n. (pl. **-children**) informal an idea or invention considered to be the creation of a particular person.

**brain coral** ● n. a compact coral with a convoluted surface resembling that of the brain. [*Diploria* and other genera.]

**brain death** ● n. irreversible brain damage causing the end of independent respiration.
– DERIVATIVES **brain-dead** adj.

**brain drain** ● n. informal the emigration of highly skilled or qualified people from a country.

**brainfever bird** ● n. the common hawk cuckoo of India and Sri Lanka, which has a monotonous persistent call. [*Cuculus varius*.]

**brainiac** ● n. N. Amer. informal a very intelligent person.
– ORIGIN 1950s: from the name of a superintelligent alien character of the Superman comic strip.

**brainless** ● adj. stupid; foolish.
– DERIVATIVES **brainlessly** adv. **brainlessness** n.

**brainpan** ● n. informal, chiefly N. Amer. a person's skull.

**brainpower** ● n. intellectual power or ability.

**brainstem** ● n. Anatomy the central trunk of the mammalian brain, consisting of the medulla oblongata, pons, and midbrain.

**brainstorm** ● n. **1** informal a moment or period in which one is suddenly unable to think clearly. **2** a spontaneous group discussion to produce ideas and ways of solving problems. ➤ informal, chiefly N. Amer. a sudden clever idea. ● v. [often as noun **brainstorming**] produce an idea or solution by having a spontaneous discussion.

**brain-teaser** (also **brain-twister**) ● n. informal a problem or puzzle.
– DERIVATIVES **brain-teasing** adj.

**brain trust** ● n. N. Amer. a group of experts advising a government or politician.

**brainwash** ● v. indoctrinate systemically and so completely as to effect a radical transformation of attitudes and beliefs.

**brainwave** ● **n. 1** an electrical impulse in the brain. **2** informal a sudden clever idea.

**brainy** ● **adj.** (**-ier**, **-iest**) informal intelligent.
– DERIVATIVES **brainily** adv. **braininess** n.

**braise** ● **v.** fry (food) lightly and then stew slowly in a closed container.
– ORIGIN C18: from Fr. *braiser*, from *braise* 'live coals' (in which the container was placed).

**brake**[1] ● **n.** a device for slowing or stopping a moving vehicle, typically by applying pressure to the wheels. ● **v.** slow or stop a moving vehicle using a brake.
– ORIGIN C18: of unknown origin.

**brake**[2] ● **n.** historical an open horse-drawn carriage with four wheels.
– ORIGIN C19: var. of **BREAK**[2].

**brake**[3] ● **n. 1** a toothed instrument used for crushing flax and hemp. **2** (also **brake harrow**) a heavy machine formerly used for breaking up large lumps of earth.
– ORIGIN ME: perh. rel. to **BREAK**[1].

**brake**[4] ● **n.** archaic or poetic/literary a thicket.
– ORIGIN OE *bracu* (orig. in the pl. in *fearnbraca* 'thickets of fern'), rel. to Mid. Low Ger. *brake* 'branch, stump'.

**brake**[5] ● **n.** a coarse fern of warm countries, typically with fronds divided into long segments. [Genus *Pteris*.] ➤ archaic term for **BRACKEN**.
– ORIGIN ME: perh. an abbrev. of **BRACKEN** (interpreted as pl.).

**brake**[6] archaic past of **BREAK**[1].

**brake block** ● **n.** a block of hard material pressed against the rim of a wheel to slow it down by friction.

**brake disc** ● **n.** the disc attached to the wheel in a disc brake.

**brake drum** ● **n.** a broad, short cylinder attached to a wheel, against which the brake shoes press to cause braking.

**brake horsepower** ● **n.** (pl. same) an imperial unit equal to one horsepower, used in expressing the power available at the shaft of an engine.

**brake lining** ● **n.** a layer of hard material attached to a brake shoe or pad to increase friction against the drum or disc.

**brakeman** ● **n.** (pl. **-men**) **1** (Brit. also **brakesman**) chiefly N. Amer. a railway worker responsible for a train's brakes. **2** a person in charge of the brakes in a bobsleigh.

**brake pad** ● **n.** a thin block which presses on to the disc in a disc brake.

**brake shoe** ● **n.** a long curved block which presses on to a brake drum.

**bramble** ● **n.** a prickly scrambling shrub of the rose family, especially a blackberry. ➤ chiefly Brit. the fruit of the blackberry. ● **v.** [usu. as noun **brambling**] Brit. gather blackberries.
– DERIVATIVES **brambly** adj.
– ORIGIN OE *brœmbel*, *brēmel*, of Gmc origin; rel. to **BROOM**.

**bramble shark** ● **n.** a heavy-bodied, dull-coloured shark of the tropical Atlantic, with numerous spines on the back. [*Echinorhinus brucus*.]

**brambling** /ˈbramblɪŋ/ ● **n.** a finch with a white rump, related to the chaffinch. [*Fringilla montifringilla*.]
– ORIGIN C16: perh. from or rel. to the obs. Ger. synonym *Brämling*, rel. to **BRAMBLE**.

**Bramley** (also **Bramley's seedling**) ● **n.** (pl. **-eys**) an English cooking apple of a large variety with green skin and firm flesh.
– ORIGIN C20: named after the Engl. butcher Matthew *Bramley*, in whose garden it first grew.

**bran** ● **n.** pieces of grain husk separated from flour after milling.
– ORIGIN ME: from OFr., of unknown origin.

**branch** ● **n. 1** a woody extending part of a tree which grows out from the trunk or a bough. **2** a subdivision extending from a river, road, or railway. ➤ a division of a large organization. ➤ a conceptual subdivision of a group of languages, subject, etc. ● **v. 1** (of a road or path) divide into one or more subdivisions. ➤ (of a tree or plant) bear or send out branches. **2** (**branch out**) extend one's activities or interests in a new direction.
– DERIVATIVES **branchlet** n. **branch-like** adj. **branchy** adj.
– ORIGIN ME: from OFr. *branche*, from late L. *branca* 'paw'.

**branchia** /ˈbraŋkɪə/ ● **n.** (pl. **branchiae** /-kɪiː/) the gills of fish and some invertebrates.
– DERIVATIVES **branchial** adj.
– ORIGIN C17: from L. *branchia*, (pl.) *branchiae*, from Gk *brankhia* (pl.).

**Branchiopoda** /ˌbraŋkɪəˈpəʊdə/ ● **pl. n.** Zoology a class of small aquatic crustaceans having gills on the feet, including water fleas and fairy shrimps.
– DERIVATIVES **branchiopod** /ˈbraŋkɪə(ʊ)pɒd/ n.
– ORIGIN mod. L., from Gk *brankhia* 'gills' + *pous*, *pod-* 'foot'.

**branch line** ● **n.** a secondary railway line running from a main line to a terminus.

**brand** ● **n. 1** a type of product manufactured by a company under a particular name. ➤ a particular type of something: *the Finnish brand of socialism.* **2** an identifying mark or characteristic common to the products of a particular company. **3** an identifying mark burned on livestock with a branding iron. **4** a piece of burning or smouldering wood. **5** poetic/literary a sword. ● **v. 1** mark with a branding iron. **2** mark out as having a particular shameful quality: *she was branded a liar.* **3** [usu. as adj. **branded**] assign a brand name to.
– DERIVATIVES **brander** n.
– ORIGIN OE *brand* 'burning', of Gmc origin; rel. to **BURN**[1].

**brandade** /brɒ̃ˈdɑːd/ ● **n.** a Provençal dish consisting of salt cod puréed with olive oil and milk.
– ORIGIN Fr., from mod. Provençal *brandado* 'something that has been shaken'.

**branding iron** ● **n.** a metal implement which is heated and used to brand livestock.

**brandish** ● **v.** wave or flourish as a threat or in anger or excitement.
– DERIVATIVES **brandisher** n.
– ORIGIN ME: from OFr. *brandir*, ult. of Gmc origin and rel. to **BRAND**.

**brand leader** ● **n.** the best-selling or most highly regarded product of its type.

**brandling** ● **n.** a red earthworm with rings of a brighter colour, used in compost and as bait by anglers. [*Eisenia fetida*.]

**brand name** ● **n.** a name given by the maker to a product or range of products.

**brand new** ● **adj.** completely new.
– ORIGIN C16: from **BRAND** + **NEW**, with the idea 'straight from the fire'.

**brandy** ● **n.** (pl. **-ies**) a strong alcoholic spirit distilled from wine or fermented fruit juice.
– ORIGIN C17: from earlier *brandwine*, from Du. *brandewijn*, from *branden* 'burn, distil' + *wijn* 'wine'.

**brandy-bottle** ● **n.** the common yellow water lily, having flowers that produce an alcoholic smell which attracts beetles. [*Nuphar luteum*.]

**brandy butter** ● **n.** Brit. a stiff sauce of brandy, butter, and sugar.

**brandy snap** ● **n.** a crisp rolled gingerbread wafer.

**branks** /braŋks/ ● **pl. n.** historical an instrument of punishment for a scolding woman, consisting of an iron framework for the head and a sharp metal gag for restraining the tongue.
– ORIGIN C16: origin uncertain; cf. Ger. *Pranger* 'a pillory or bit for a horse'.

**branle** /ˈbran(ə)l/ ● **n.** a 16th-century court dance of French origin.
– ORIGIN C16: from Fr., from *branler* 'shake'.

**brant** ● **n.** North American term for **BRENT GOOSE**.

**bran tub** ● **n.** Brit. a lucky dip in which items are buried in bran.

**brash**[1] ● **adj.** self-assertive in a rude, noisy, or overbearing way.
– DERIVATIVES **brashly** adv. **brashness** n.
– ORIGIN C19 (orig. dial.); perh. a form of **RASH**[1].

**brash**[2] ● n. 1 loose broken rock or ice. 2 clippings from hedges or other plants.
– ORIGIN C18: of unknown origin.

**brass** ● n. 1 a yellow alloy of copper and zinc. 2 (also **horse brass**) a flat brass ornament for the harness of a draught horse. ➤ Brit. a memorial consisting of a flat piece of inscribed brass set into the wall or floor of a church. ➤ a brass block used for stamping a design on a book binding. 3 brass wind instruments forming a band or section of an orchestra. 4 (also **top brass**) informal people in authority. 5 Brit. informal money.
– PHRASES **brassed off** Brit. informal disgruntled. **brass monkey** informal used to indicate extremely cold weather: *cold enough to freeze the balls off a brass monkey.* [from a type of brass rack or 'monkey' in which cannonballs were stored and which contracted in very cold weather, ejecting the balls.] **get down to brass tacks** informal start to consider the basic facts or practical details.
– ORIGIN OE *bræs*, of unknown origin.

**brassard** /'brasɑːd/ ● n. 1 a band or badge worn on the upper sleeve. 2 historical a piece of armour for the upper arm.
– ORIGIN C16: from Fr., from *bras* 'arm'.

**brass band** ● n. a group of musicians playing brass instruments.

**brasserie** /'brasəri/ ● n. (pl. **-ies**) a restaurant in France or in a French style, serving inexpensive food.
– ORIGIN C19: Fr., orig. 'brewery'.

**brass hat** ● n. Brit. informal a high-ranking officer in the armed forces.

**brassica** /'brasɪkə/ ● n. a plant of a genus that includes cabbage, swede, rape, and mustard. [Genus *Brassica*.]
– ORIGIN mod. L., from L. 'cabbage'.

**brassie** /'brasi, 'brɑːsi/ (also **brassy**) ● n. (pl. **-ies**) Golf, informal a number two wood.
– ORIGIN C19: so named because the wood was orig. shod with brass.

**brassiere** /'brazɪə, -s-, 'brazɪɛː/ ● n. full form of **BRA**.
– ORIGIN C20: from Fr., lit. 'bodice, child's vest'.

**brass rubbing** ● n. the action of rubbing heelball or chalk over paper laid on an engraved brass to reproduce its design.

**brassy**[1] ● adj. (**-ier**, **-iest**) 1 resembling brass in colour. 2 sounding harsh or loud like a brass instrument. 3 tastelessly showy or loud.
– DERIVATIVES **brassily** adv. **brassiness** n.

**brassy**[2] ● n. variant spelling of **BRASSIE**.

**brat** ● n. informal a badly behaved child.
– DERIVATIVES **brattish** adj. **brattishness** n. **bratty** adj.
– ORIGIN C16: perh. an abbrev. of synonymous Scots *bratchet*, from OFr. *brachet* 'hound, bitch'.

**brat pack** ● n. informal a rowdy and ostentatious group of young celebrities.
– DERIVATIVES **brat packer** n.

**brattice** /'bratɪs/ ● n. a partition or shaft lining in a coal mine.
– DERIVATIVES **bratticed** adj.
– ORIGIN ME (denoting a wooden gallery for use in a siege): from OFr. *bretesche*, from med. L. *britisca*, from OE *brittisc* 'British'.

**bratwurst** /'bratvəːst/ ● n. a type of fine German pork sausage.
– ORIGIN Ger., from *Brat* 'a spit' + *Wurst* 'sausage'.

**bravado** ● n. boldness intended to impress or intimidate.
– ORIGIN C16: from Sp. *bravada*, from *bravo* (see **BRAVE**, **-ADO**).

**brave** ● adj. showing courage. ● n. dated an American Indian warrior. ● v. endure or face (unpleasant conditions) with courage.
– DERIVATIVES **bravely** adv. **braveness** n. **bravery** n.
– ORIGIN C15: from Fr., from Ital. *bravo* 'bold' or Sp. *bravo* 'courageous, untamed, savage'.

**bravo**[1] /brɑː'vəʊ, 'brɑːvəʊ/ ● exclam. used to express approval for a performer. ● n. (pl. **-os**) a code word representing the letter B, used in radio communication.
– ORIGIN C18: from Fr., from Ital., lit. 'bold' (see **BRAVE**).

**bravo**[2] /'brɑːvəʊ/ ● n. (pl. **-os** or **-oes**) a thug or hired assassin.
– ORIGIN C16: from Ital., from *bravo* 'bold (one)' (see **BRAVE**).

**bravura** /brə'v(j)ʊərə/ ● n. 1 great skill and brilliance. 2 the display of great daring.
– ORIGIN C18: from Ital., from *bravo* 'bold'.

**braw** /brɔː/ ● adj. Scottish (of weather) fine.
– DERIVATIVES **brawly** adv.
– ORIGIN C16: var. of **BRAVE**.

**brawl** ● n. a rough or noisy fight or quarrel. ● v. take part in a brawl.
– DERIVATIVES **brawler** n.
– ORIGIN ME: perh. ult. imitative and rel. to **BRAY**[1].

**brawn** ● n. 1 physical strength as opposed to intelligence. 2 Brit. cooked meat from a pig's or calf's head, pressed with jelly.
– DERIVATIVES **brawniness** n. **brawny** adj.
– ORIGIN ME: from OFr. *braon* 'fleshy part of the leg', of Gmc origin.

**Braxton Hicks contractions** /ˌbrakstən 'hɪks/ ● pl. n. Medicine intermittent weak contractions of the uterus occurring during pregnancy.
– ORIGIN C20: named after the Engl. gynaecologist John *Braxton Hicks*.

**braxy** /'braksi/ ● n. a fatal bacterial infection of young sheep.
– ORIGIN C18: perh. from obs. *brack* 'break, rupture, flaw', from Gmc base of **BREAK**[1].

**bray**[1] ● n. the loud, harsh cry of a donkey. ● v. make such a sound.
– ORIGIN ME: from OFr. *brait* 'a shriek', *braire* 'to cry', perh. ult. of Celtic origin.

**bray**[2] ● v. archaic crush to small pieces, especially with a pestle and mortar.
– ORIGIN ME: from OFr. *breier*, of Gmc origin; rel. to **BREAK**[1].

**braze** ● v. form, fix, or join by soldering with an alloy of copper and zinc. ● n. a brazed joint.
– ORIGIN C17: from Fr. *braser* 'solder'.

**brazen** ● adj. 1 bold and shameless. 2 chiefly poetic/literary made of brass. ● v. (**brazen it out**) endure a difficult situation with apparent confidence and lack of shame.
– DERIVATIVES **brazenly** adv. **brazenness** /'breɪz(ə)nnɪs/ n.
– ORIGIN OE *bræsen* 'made of brass', from *bræs* 'brass'.

**brazier**[1] /'breɪzɪə, -ʒə/ ● n. 1 a portable heater consisting of a pan or stand holding lighted coals. 2 N. Amer. a barbecue.
– ORIGIN C17: from Fr. *brasier*, from *braise* 'hot coals'.

**brazier**[2] /'breɪzjə, -ʒə/ ● n. a worker in brass.
– DERIVATIVES **braziery** n.
– ORIGIN ME: prob. from **BRASS** + **-IER**.

**brazil** ● n. 1 (also **Brazil nut**) the large three-sided nut of a South American forest tree (*Bertholletia excelsa*). 2 (also **Brazil wood**) the hard red wood of a tropical tree (genus *Caesalpinia*) from which dye is obtained.

**Brazilian** ● n. a native or inhabitant of Brazil. ● adj. of or relating to Brazil.

**breach** ● n. 1 an act of breaking a law, agreement, or code of conduct. ➤ a break in relations. 2 a gap in a wall or barrier, especially one made by an attacking army. ● v. 1 make a breach in. 2 break (a law, agreement, or code of conduct).
– PHRASES **breach of the peace** chiefly Brit. an act of violent or noisy behaviour causing a public disturbance, considered a criminal offence. **breach of promise** the action of breaking a sworn assurance. **step into the breach** replace someone who is suddenly unable to do a job.
– ORIGIN ME: from OFr. *breche*, ult. of Gmc origin; rel. to **BREAK**[1].

**bread** ● n. 1 food made of flour, water, and yeast mixed together and baked. 2 informal money.
– PHRASES **bread and butter** a person's livelihood or main source of income. **bread and circuses** entertainment or political policies intended to keep the masses happy and docile. **break bread** celebrate the Eucharist. **cast one's bread upon the waters** do good without

expecting gratitude or reward. [with biblical allusion to Eccles. 11:1.] **know which side one's bread is buttered** informal know where one's advantage lies.
– ORIGIN OE *brēad*, of Gmc origin.

**bread-and-butter letter** • n. a letter expressing thanks for hospitality.

**breadbasket** • n. **1** a region that supplies cereals to another. **2** informal a person's stomach.

**breadboard** • n. Electronics a board for making an experimental model of an electric circuit.

**breadcrumb** • n. a small fragment of bread.
– DERIVATIVES **breadcrumbed** adj.

**breaded** • adj. (of food) coated with breadcrumbs and fried.

**breadfruit** • n. the large round starchy fruit of a tree (*Artocarpus altilis*) native to Pacific islands, used as a vegetable and to make a substitute for flour.

**breadline** • n. **1** Brit. the poorest condition in which it is acceptable to live. **2** N. Amer. a queue of people waiting to receive free food.

**bread sauce** • n. sauce made with milk and breadcrumbs, typically eaten with roast turkey.

**breadstick** • n. a crisp stick of baked dough.

**breadth** • n. **1** the distance or measurement from side to side of something. ➤ wide range: *breadth of experience*. **2** dated a piece of cloth of standard or full width.
– DERIVATIVES **breadthways** (also **breadthwise**) adv.
– ORIGIN C16: from obs. *brede* (rel. to **BROAD**), on the pattern of *length*.

**bread tree** (also **bread palm**) • n. a cycad native to tropical and southern Africa, which yields an edible sago-like starch. [Genus *Encephalartos*.]

**breadwinner** • n. a person who earns money to support their family.
– DERIVATIVES **breadwinning** n.

**break**[1] • v. (past **broke**; past part. **broken**) **1** separate or cause to separate into pieces as a result of a blow, shock, or strain. ➤ (of the amniotic fluid surrounding a fetus) be discharged when the sac is ruptured in the first stages of labour. **2** make or become inoperative. **3** interrupt (a continuity, sequence, or course). ➤ lessen the impact of (a fall). ➤ disconnect or interrupt (an electric circuit). **4** fail to observe (a law, regulation, or agreement). **5** crush the strength, spirit, or resistance of. **6** surpass (a record). **7** (of an attacking player or a military force) make a rush or dash. **8** (of the weather) change suddenly, especially after a fine spell. ➤ (of a storm) begin violently. ➤ (of dawn or a day) begin as the sun rises. ➤ (of waves) curl over and dissolve into foam. **9** (of a person's voice) falter and change tone. ➤ (of a boy's voice) change in tone and register at puberty. **10** (of news or a scandal) suddenly become public. ➤ (**break something to**) make bad news known to. **11** Phonetics (of a vowel) develop into a diphthong, under the influence of an adjacent sound. **12** (of prices on the stock exchange) fall sharply. **13** use (a banknote) to pay for something and receive change. **14** (of two boxers or wrestlers) come out of a clinch. **15** make the first stroke at the beginning of a game of billiards, pool, or snooker. **16** unfurl (a flag or sail). **17** succeed in deciphering (a code). • n. **1** an interruption or pause. ➤ Brit. an interval during the school day. ➤ a short holiday. ➤ a change of line, paragraph, or page: *a page break*. **2** a rush or dash, especially by an attacking player or team. **3** informal an opportunity or chance. **4** a gap or opening: *a break in the hedge*. **5** an instance of breaking, or the point where something is broken. **6** (also **break of serve** or **service break**) Tennis the winning of a game against an opponent's serve. **7** Snooker & Billiards a consecutive series of successful shots, scoring a specified number of points. ➤ a player's turn to make the opening shot of a game. **8** a short solo or instrumental passage in jazz or popular music.
– PHRASES **break ship** Nautical fail to rejoin one's ship after absence on leave. **break wind** release gas from the anus. **break one's back** (or **neck**) put great effort into achieving something. **break the back of** accomplish the main or hardest part of (a task). **break cover** (of game being hunted) emerge into the open. **break a leg!** theatrical slang good luck! **break of day** dawn. **break someone's serve** win a game in a tennis match against an opponent's service. **give someone a break** informal stop putting pressure on someone. **make a clean break** remove oneself completely from a situation.
– PHRASAL VERBS **break away** escape from the control or influence of a person, group, or practice. **break down 1** suddenly cease to function. **2** cease to continue; collapse. **3** lose control of one's emotions when in distress. **break in 1** force entry to a building. **2** interject. **break something in 1** accustom a horse to being ridden. **2** wear shoes until they become supple and comfortable. **break into 1** enter forcibly. **2** suddenly or unexpectedly burst forth into (laughter, song, or faster movement). **break something off** abruptly end or discontinue something. **break out 1** (of fighting or another undesirable thing) start suddenly. **2** escape. **break something out** informal open and start using something. **break out in** be suddenly affected by an unpleasant sensation or condition. **break up 1** (of a gathering or relationship) end or part. ➤ Brit. end the school term. **2** informal start laughing uncontrollably. **3** chiefly N. Amer. become upset. **break with 1** quarrel or cease relations with. **2** act in a way that is not in accordance with (a custom or tradition).
– DERIVATIVES **breakable** adj. **breakage** n.
– ORIGIN OE *brecan* (v.), of Gmc origin.

**break**[2] • n. **1** former term for **BREAKING CART**. **2** historical another term for **BRAKE**[2].
– ORIGIN C19: perh. from C16 *brake* 'cage', later 'framework'.

**breakaway** • n. **1** a divergence or secession from something established or long-standing. **2** a sudden attack or forward movement, especially in sport.

**break-dancing** • n. an energetic and acrobatic style of street dancing, developed by US blacks.
– DERIVATIVES **break-dance** v. & n. **break dancer** n.

**breakdown** • n. **1** a failure or collapse. **2** chemical or physical decomposition. **3** an explanatory analysis, especially of statistics.

**breaker** • n. **1** a heavy sea wave that breaks on the shore. **2** a person or thing that breaks. **3** a person who interrupts a conversation on a Citizens' Band radio channel, indicating that they wish to transmit a message. ➤ any CB radio user. **4** a break dancer.

**break-fall** • n. (in martial arts) a controlled fall in which most of the impact is absorbed by the arms or legs.

**breakfast** • n. a meal eaten in the morning, the first of the day. • v. eat this meal.
– PHRASES **have** (or **eat**) **someone for breakfast** informal deal with or defeat someone with contemptuous ease.
– DERIVATIVES **breakfaster** n.
– ORIGIN ME: from **BREAK**[1] + **FAST**[2].

**breakfront** • n. [usu. as modifier] a piece of furniture having the line of its front broken by a curve or angle.

**break-in** • n. an illegal forced entry in order to steal something.

**breaking and entering** • n. (in North American, and formerly also British, law) the crime of entering a building by force to commit burglary.

**breaking cart** • n. a two-wheeled carriage with a skeleton body, used for breaking in young horses.

**breakneck** • adj. dangerously or extremely fast.

**breakout** • adj. informal, chiefly US **1** suddenly and extremely popular or successful. **2** denoting a group which breaks away from a gathering for discussion.

**break point** • n. Tennis the state of a game when the player receiving service needs only one more point to win the game.

**breakthrough** • n. a sudden important development or success.

**breakthrough bleeding** • n. bleeding from the uterus occurring abnormally between menstrual periods.

**breakwater** • n. a barrier built out into the sea to protect a coast or harbour from the force of waves.

**bream**[1] • n. (pl. same) a greenish-bronze deep-bodied freshwater fish. [*Abramis brama*.] ➤ used in names of other fishes, e.g. **sea bream**.
– ORIGIN ME: from OFr. *bresme*, of Gmc origin.

**bream**[2] • v. Nautical, archaic clear (a ship's bottom) of accumulated matter by burning and scraping it.
– ORIGIN C15: prob. of Low Ger. origin and rel. to **BROOM**.

**breast** • n. **1** either of the two soft, protruding organs on the upper front of a woman's body which secrete milk after pregnancy. **2** a person's or animal's chest region. ➤ a joint of meat or poultry cut from such a part. • v. face and move forwards against or through. ➤ reach the top of (a hill).
– DERIVATIVES **-breasted** adj.
– ORIGIN OE *brēost*, of Gmc origin.

**breastbone** • n. a thin flat bone running down the centre of the chest and connecting the ribs; the sternum.

**breast drill** • n. a drill on which pressure is brought to bear by the operator's chest.

**breastfeed** • v. (past and past part. **-fed**) feed (a baby) with milk from the breast. ➤ (of a baby) feed from the breast.

**breast implant** • n. Medicine a prosthesis implanted behind or in place of a female breast in reconstructive or cosmetic surgery.

**breastpin** • n. archaic a small brooch or badge worn on the breast.

**breastplate** • n. **1** a piece of armour covering the chest. **2** a set of straps attached to the front of a saddle and passing across the horse's chest.

**breast pump** • n. a device for drawing milk from a woman's breasts by suction.

**breast shell** • n. a shallow plastic receptacle that fits over the nipple of a lactating woman to catch any milk that flows.

**breaststroke** • n. a style of swimming on one's front, in which the arms are pushed forwards and then swept back in a circular movement, while the legs are alternately tucked in and kicked out.

**breastsummer** • n. Architecture a beam across a broad opening, sustaining a superstructure.
– ORIGIN C17: from **BREAST** and **SUMMER**[2].

**breastwork** • n. a low temporary defence or parapet.

**breath** • n. **1** air taken into or expelled from the lungs. ➤ an inhalation or exhalation of air from the lungs. **2** a slight movement of air.
– PHRASES **breath of fresh air** a refreshing change. **catch one's breath 1** cease breathing momentarily in surprise or fear. **2** rest after exercise to restore normal breathing. **draw breath** breathe in. **hold one's breath** cease breathing temporarily. **out of breath** gasping for air, typically after exercise. **take breath** pause to recover normal breathing. **take someone's breath away** astonish or inspire someone with awed respect or delight. **under** (or **below**) **one's breath** in a very quiet voice. **waste one's breath** talk or give advice without effect.
– ORIGIN OE *brǣth* 'smell, scent', of Gmc origin; rel. to **BROOD**.

**breathable** • adj. **1** (of air) fit to breathe. **2** (of clothing) admitting air to the skin and allowing sweat to evaporate.

**breathalyser** (US trademark **Breathalyzer**) • n. a device used by police for measuring the amount of alcohol in a driver's breath.
– DERIVATIVES **breathalyse** (US **breathalyze**) v.
– ORIGIN 1960s: blend of **BREATH** and **ANALYSE**, + **-ER**[1].

**breathe** • v. **1** take air into the lungs and then expel it as a regular physiological process. ➤ (of a plant or invertebrate animal) respire or exchange gases. **2** (of wine) be exposed to fresh air. **3** (of material or soil) admit or emit air or moisture. **4** allow (a horse) to rest after exertion. **5** give an impression of: *the room breathed an air of hygienic efficiency.* **6** (**breathe upon**) archaic or poetic/literary tarnish or taint.
– PHRASES **breathe (freely) again** relax after being frightened or tense. **breathe down someone's neck** follow closely behind. ➤ constantly check up on someone. **breathe one's last** die. **breathe (new) life into** reinvigorate. **not breathe a word** remain silent about something secret.
– ORIGIN ME (in the sense 'exhale, steam'): from **BREATH**.

**breather** • n. **1** informal a brief pause for rest. **2** a vent or valve to release pressure or to allow air to move freely.

**breathing** • n. a sign in Greek (ʽ or ʼ) indicating the presence of an aspirate (**rough breathing**) or the absence of an aspirate (**smooth breathing**) at the beginning of a word.

**breathing space** • n. an opportunity to pause, relax, or decide what to do next.

**breathless** • adj. **1** gasping for breath, typically due to exertion. ➤ feeling or causing great excitement, fear, etc. **2** (of air) stiflingly still.
– DERIVATIVES **breathlessly** adv. **breathlessness** n.

**breathtaking** • adj. astonishing or awe-inspiring.
– DERIVATIVES **breathtakingly** adv.

**breath test** • n. a test in which a driver is made to blow into a breathalyser. • v. (**breath-test**) test with a breathalyser.

**breathy** • adj. (**-ier**, **-iest**) (of a voice) having an audible sound of breathing.
– DERIVATIVES **breathily** adv. **breathiness** n.

**breccia** /ˈbrɛtʃə, -tʃɪə/ • n. Geology rock consisting of angular fragments of stones cemented by finer calcareous material.
– DERIVATIVES **brecciate** v. **brecciation** n.
– ORIGIN C18: from Ital., lit. 'gravel', ult. rel. to **BREAK**[1].

**Brechtian** /ˈbrɛxtɪən, German brɛçtɪən/ • adj. of or relating to the work of the German dramatist Bertolt Brecht (1898–1956). • n. a follower or admirer of Brecht.

**bred** past and past participle of **BREED**.

**breech** • n. **1** the part of a cannon behind the bore. **2** the back part of a rifle or gun barrel. **3** archaic a person's buttocks.
– ORIGIN OE *brēc* 'garment covering the loins and thighs', pl. of *brōc* (of Gmc origin), interpreted as a sing. form.

**breech birth** (also **breech delivery**) • n. a delivery of a baby which is so positioned in the womb that the buttocks or feet are delivered first.

**breechblock** • n. a metal block which closes the aperture at the breech of a rifle or gun barrel.

**breechclout** • n. North American term for **LOINCLOTH**.

**breeches** • pl. n. short trousers fastened just below the knee, now chiefly worn for riding or as part of ceremonial dress. ➤ informal trousers.

**breeches buoy** • n. a lifebuoy on a rope with a canvas support resembling a pair of breeches, by means of which a person may be held and transported.

**breeching** • n. **1** a strong leather strap passing round the hindquarters of a horse harnessed to a vehicle and enabling the horse to push backwards. **2** historical a thick rope used to secure the carriages of cannon on a ship.

**breech-loader** • n. a gun designed to have ammunition inserted at the breech rather than through the muzzle.
– DERIVATIVES **breech-loading** adj.

**breed** • v. (past and past part. **bred**) **1** (of animals) mate and then produce offspring. ➤ cause (an animal) to produce offspring. **2** bring up to behave in a particular way. **3** produce or lead to: *success had bred a certain arrogance.* **4** Physics create (fissile material) by nuclear reaction. • n. **1** a distinctive stock of animals or plants within a species, typically one deliberately developed. **2** a sort or kind.
– ORIGIN OE *brēdan*, of Gmc origin; rel. to **BROOD**.

**breeder** • n. **1** a person or animal that breeds. **2** (in gay slang) a heterosexual person. **3** a nuclear reactor which creates another fissile material (plutonium-239) as a by-product of energy production by fission of uranium-238.

**breeding** • n. good manners regarded as characteristic of the aristocracy and conferred by heredity.

**breeding ground** • n. a thing that favours the development or occurrence of something.

**breeks** • pl. n. chiefly Scottish & N. English another term for **BREECHES**.

**breeze**[1] • n. **1** a gentle wind. **2** informal something easy to do. • v. informal come, go, or proceed in a casual or light-hearted manner.
– ORIGIN C16 (in sense 'NE wind'): prob. from Old Sp. and Port. *briza*.

**breeze**[2] • n. small cinders mixed with sand and cement

to make breeze blocks.
– ORIGIN C16: from Fr. *braise, brese* 'live coals'.

**breeze block** • n. Brit. a lightweight building brick made from breeze.

**breezeway** • n. N. Amer. a roofed outdoor passage, as between a house and a garage.

**breezy** • adj. (**-ier**, **-iest**) **1** pleasantly windy. **2** relaxed, informal, and cheerily brisk.
– DERIVATIVES **breezily** adv. **breeziness** n.

**bremsstrahlung** /ˈbrɛmzˌʃtrɑːlʊŋ/ • n. Physics electromagnetic radiation emitted by a charged particle on passing through the electric and magnetic fields of a nucleus.
– ORIGIN 1940s: from Ger., from *bremsen* 'to brake' + *Strahlung* 'radiation'.

**Bren gun** • n. a lightweight quick-firing machine gun used by the Allied forces in the Second World War.
– ORIGIN blend of *Brno* in the Czech Republic (where it was orig. made) and *Enfield* (where it was later made).

**brent goose** • n. a small northern goose with a mainly black head and neck. [*Branta bernicla*.]
– ORIGIN ME: of unknown origin.

**brethren** archaic plural of **BROTHER**. • pl. n. fellow Christians or members of a male religious order.

**Breton** /ˈbrɛt(ə)n/ • n. **1** a native of Brittany. **2** the Celtic language of Brittany, derived from Cornish.
– ORIGIN from OFr., 'Briton'.

**breve** • n. **1** Music a note having the time value of two semibreves, represented as a semibreve with two short bars either side, or as a square. **2** a written or printed mark (˘) indicating a short or unstressed vowel. **3** historical an authoritative letter from a pope or monarch.
– ORIGIN ME: var. of **BRIEF**: the musical term was orig. used in a series where a *long* was of greater time value than a *breve*.

**brevet** /ˈbrɛvɪt/ • n. a former type of military commission conferred especially for outstanding service, by which an officer was promoted to a higher rank without the corresponding pay. • v. (**breveted** or **brevetted**, **breveting** or **brevetting**) confer a brevet rank on.
– ORIGIN ME (denoting an official letter): from OFr. *brievet* 'little letter', dimin. of *bref*.

**breviary** /ˈbriːvɪəri/ • n. (pl. **-ies**) a book containing the service for each day, to be recited by those in orders in the Roman Catholic Church.
– ORIGIN ME: from L. *breviarium* 'summary, abridgement', from *breviare* 'abridge'.

**brevity** /ˈbrɛvɪti/ • n. **1** concise and exact use of words. **2** shortness of time.
– ORIGIN C15: from OFr. *brievete*, from L. *brevitas*, from *brevis* 'brief'.

**brew** • v. **1** make (beer) by soaking, boiling, and fermentation. **2** make (tea or coffee) by mixing it with hot water. **3** (of an unwelcome situation) begin to develop. • n. **1** a kind of beer. **2** informal a drink of tea.
– DERIVATIVES **brewer** n.
– ORIGIN OE *brēowan*, of Gmc origin.

**brewery** • n. (pl. **-ies**) a place where beer is made commercially.

**brewpub** • n. chiefly US an establishment selling beer brewed on the premises.

**brewski** • n. (pl. **-is** or **-ies**) N. Amer. informal a beer.
– ORIGIN from **BREW** + a fanciful ending.

**briar**[1] (also **brier**) • n. a prickly scrambling shrub, especially a wild rose. [*Rosa eglanteria* (**sweet briar**) and other species.]
– DERIVATIVES **briary** adj.
– ORIGIN OE *brǣr*, *brēr*, of unknown origin.

**briar**[2] (also **brier**) • n. **1** (also **briar pipe**) a tobacco pipe made from woody nodules borne by the tree heath. **2** another term for **TREE HEATH**
– ORIGIN C19: from Fr. *bruyère* 'heath, heather'.

**bribe** • v. dishonestly persuade (someone) to act in one's favour by a payment or other inducement. • n. an inducement offered in an attempt to bribe.
– DERIVATIVES **bribable** adj. **briber** n. **bribery** n.
– ORIGIN ME (in the sense 'rob, extort'): from OFr. *briber*, *brimber* 'beg', of unknown origin.

**bric-a-brac** • n. miscellaneous objects and ornaments of little value.
– ORIGIN C19: from Fr., from obs. *à bric et à brac* 'at random'.

**brick** • n. **1** a small rectangular block of fired or sun-dried clay, used in building. ➤ bricks collectively as a building material. **2** Brit. informal, dated a generous, helpful, and reliable person. • v. **1** block or enclose with a wall of bricks. **2** (**be bricking oneself**) Brit. vulgar slang be extremely worried or nervous.
– PHRASES **bricks and mortar** buildings, especially housing. **like a ton of bricks** informal with crushing weight, force, or authority.
– ORIGIN ME: from Mid. Low Ger., MDu. *bricke*, *brike*; prob. reinforced by OFr. *brique*; of unknown ultimate origin.

**brickbat** • n. **1** a piece of brick used as a missile. **2** a highly critical remark or reaction.

**brickfield** • n. an area of ground where bricks are made.

**brickfielder** • n. Austral. a hot, dry north wind, typically accompanied by dust.
– ORIGIN C19: from the name of *Brickfield* Hill, Sydney, site of a former brickworks, assoc. with dust.

**brickie** • n. (pl. **-ies**) Brit. informal a bricklayer.

**bricklayer** • n. a person whose job is to build structures with bricks.
– DERIVATIVES **bricklaying** n.

**brick red** • n. a deep brownish red.

**brickwork** • n. the bricks in a wall, house, etc.

**brickyard** • n. a place where bricks are made.

**bricolage** /ˌbrɪkəˈlɑːʒ/ • n. (pl. same or **bricolages**) **1** (in art or literature) construction or creation from a diverse range of available things. **2** a thing created in this way.
– ORIGIN from Fr.

**bricoleur** /ˌbrɪkəˈləː/ • n. a person who engages in bricolage.
– ORIGIN Fr., lit. 'handyman'.

**bridal** • adj. of or concerning a bride or a newly married couple.
– ORIGIN ME: from OE *brȳd-ealu* 'wedding feast', from *brȳd* 'bride' + *ealu* 'ale-drinking'.

**bride** • n. a woman on her wedding day or just before and after the event.
– ORIGIN OE *brȳd*, of Gmc origin.

**bridegroom** • n. a man on his wedding day or just before and after the event.
– ORIGIN OE *brȳdguma*, from *brȳd* 'bride' + *guma* 'man'; the second syllable influenced by **GROOM**.

**bride price** • n. (in tribal societies) a payment made to a bride's family by that of the groom.

**bridesmaid** • n. a girl or woman who accompanies a bride on her wedding day.

**bridewell** • n. archaic a prison or reform school for petty offenders.
– ORIGIN C16: named after *St Bride's Well* in London, near which such a building stood.

**bridge**[1] • n. **1** a structure carrying a road, path, or railway across a river, road, etc. **2** the platform on a ship from which the captain and officers direct operations. **3** the upper bony part of a person's nose. **4** an electric circuit used chiefly to measure an unknown resistance by equalizing the potentials in two parts of the circuit. **5** a partial denture supported by natural teeth on either side. **6** Music the part on a stringed instrument over which the strings are stretched. **7** Music a bridge passage or middle eight. • v. be or make a bridge over or between.
– DERIVATIVES **bridgeable** adj.
– ORIGIN OE *brycg*, of Gmc origin.

**bridge**[2] • n. a card game related to whist, played by two partnerships of two players who at the beginning of each hand bid for the right to name the trump suit, the highest bid also representing a contract to make a specified number of tricks.
– ORIGIN C19: of unknown origin.

**bridgehead** • n. a strong position secured by an army inside enemy territory from which to advance or attack.

**bridge loan** • n. North American term for **BRIDGING**

**LOAN.**

**bridge passage** • n. a transitional section in a musical composition leading to a new section or theme.

**bridge roll** • n. Brit. a small, soft bread roll with a long, thin shape.

**bridging loan** • n. chiefly Brit. a sum of money lent by a bank to cover an interval between two transactions, typically the buying of one house and the selling of another.

**bridie** • n. (pl. **-ies**) Scottish a meat pasty.
– ORIGIN perh. from obs. *bride's pie.*

**bridle** • n. **1** the headgear used to control a horse, consisting of buckled straps to which a bit and reins are attached. **2** Nautical a mooring cable. • v. **1** put a bridle on. **2** bring under control. **3** show resentment or anger.
– PHRASES **off** (or **on**) **the bridle** see **BIT**[3].
– ORIGIN OE *brīdel* (n.), *brīdlian* (v.), of Gmc origin.

**bridleway** (also **bridle path**) • n. Brit. a path or track along which horse riders have right of way.

**bridoon** /brɪˈduːn/ (also **bradoon**) • n. a snaffle bit which is frequently used in conjunction with a curb bit in a double bridle.
– ORIGIN C18: from Fr. *bridon*, from *bride* 'bridle'.

**Brie** /briː/ • n. a kind of soft, mild, creamy cheese with a firm, white skin.
– ORIGIN named after *Brie* in northern France.

**brief** • adj. **1** of short duration. **2** concise; using few words. **3** (of clothing) not covering much of the body. • n. **1** chiefly Brit. a summary of the facts and legal points in a case given to a barrister to argue in court. ➤a piece of work for a barrister. ➤US a written summary of a case, for presentation to a court. **2** informal a solicitor or barrister. **3** chiefly Brit. a set of instructions given to a person about a task. **4** a letter from the Pope on a matter of discipline. • v. instruct or inform thoroughly in preparation for a task. ➤Brit. instruct (a barrister) by brief.
– PHRASES **hold a brief for** Brit. be retained as counsel for. **hold no brief for** not support. **in brief** in short.
– DERIVATIVES **briefless** adv. (Brit. Law). **briefly** adv. **briefness** n.
– ORIGIN ME: from OFr. *brief*, from L. *brevis* 'short'; the noun is via late L. *breve* 'note, dispatch'.

**briefcase** • n. a flat rectangular case for carrying books and documents.

**briefing** • n. a meeting for giving information or instructions.

**briefs** • pl. n. short, close-fitting underpants or knickers.

**brier**[1] • n. variant spelling of **BRIAR**[1].

**brier**[2] • n. variant spelling of **BRIAR**[2].

**Brig.** • abbrev. Brigadier.

**brig**[1] • n. **1** a two-masted square-rigged ship, typically having an additional lower fore-and-aft sail on the gaff and a boom to the mainmast. **2** informal a prison, especially on a warship.
– ORIGIN C18: abbrev. of **BRIGANTINE**.

**brig**[2] • n. Scottish & N. English a bridge.
– ORIGIN from ON *bryggja.*

**brigade** • n. **1** a subdivision of an army, typically consisting of a small number of battalions and forming part of a division. **2** an organization with a quasi-military structure. **3** informal, often derogatory a group of people with a characteristic in common: *the anti-smoking brigade.*
– ORIGIN C17: from Fr., from Ital. *brigata* 'company'.

**brigade major** • n. the principal staff officer to the brigadier in command at the headquarters of a brigade.

**brigadier** • n. a rank of officer in the British army, above colonel and below major general.
– ORIGIN C17: from Fr. (see **BRIGADE**, **-IER**).

**brigadier general** • n. a rank of officer in the US army, air force, and marine corps, above colonel and below major general.

**brigalow** /ˈbrɪɡələʊ/ • n. an Australian acacia tree. [Genus *Acacia*: several species.]
– ORIGIN C19: from an Aborig. word, perh. Kamilaroi *burigal.*

**brigand** /ˈbrɪɡ(ə)nd/ • n. a member of a gang that ambushes and robs people in forests and mountains.
– DERIVATIVES **brigandage** n. **brigandry** n.
– ORIGIN ME: from OFr., from Ital. *brigante*, lit. '(person) contending', from *brigare* (see **BRIGADE**).

**brigantine** /ˈbrɪɡ(ə)ntiːn/ • n. a two-masted sailing ship with a square-rigged foremast and a mainmast rigged fore and aft.
– ORIGIN C16: from OFr., from Ital. *brigantino*, from *brigante* (see **BRIGAND**).

**bright** • adj. **1** giving out much light, or filled with light. **2** (of colour) vivid and bold. **3** intelligent and quick-witted. **4** (of sound) clear and typically high-pitched. **5** cheerfully lively. **6** (of prospects) good. • n. (**brights**) N. Amer. headlights switched to full beam.
– PHRASES **bright and early** very early in the morning. (**as**) **bright as a button** informal intelligently alert and lively. **bright-eyed and bushy-tailed** informal alert and lively. **look on the bright side** be optimistic or cheerful in spite of difficulties.
– DERIVATIVES **brighten** v. **brightish** adj. **brightly** adv. **brightness** n.
– ORIGIN OE *beorht*, of Gmc origin.

**Bright's disease** • n. a disease involving chronic inflammation of the kidneys.
– ORIGIN C19: named after the Engl. physician Richard *Bright.*

**bright spark** • n. informal, often ironic a clever or witty person.

**brightwork** • n. polished metalwork on ships or other vehicles.

**brill**[1] • n. a flatfish similar to the turbot. [*Scophthalmus rhombus.*]
– ORIGIN C15: of unknown origin.

**brill**[2] • adj. Brit. informal excellent; marvellous.

**brilliant** • adj. **1** (of light or colour) very bright or vivid. **2** exceptionally clever or talented. **3** Brit. informal excellent; marvellous. • n. a diamond of brilliant cut.
– DERIVATIVES **brilliance** (also **brilliancy**) n. **brilliantly** adv.
– ORIGIN C17: from Fr. *brillant*, from *briller* 'shine', prob. ult. from L. *beryllus* (see **BERYL**).

**brilliant cut** • n. a circular cut for gemstones in the form of two many-faceted pyramids joined at their bases, the upper one truncated near its apex.

**brilliantine** • n. **1** dated scented oil used on men's hair to make it look glossy. **2** US shiny dress fabric made from cotton and mohair or cotton and worsted.
– DERIVATIVES **brilliantined** adj.
– ORIGIN C19: from Fr. *brillantine*, from *brillant* (see **BRILLIANT**).

**brim** • n. **1** the projecting edge around the bottom of a hat. **2** the lip of a cup, bowl, etc. • v. (**brimmed**, **brimming**) [often as adj. **brimming**] fill or be full to the point of overflowing.
– DERIVATIVES **brimful** adj. **brimless** adj. **-brimmed** adj.
– ORIGIN ME (denoting the edge of a body of water): perh. rel. to Ger. *Bräme* 'trimming'.

**brimstone** /ˈbrɪmst(ə)n, -stəʊn/ • n. **1** archaic sulphur. **2** a large butterfly, the male of which is bright yellow and the female greenish-white. [*Gonepteryx rhamni.*]
– ORIGIN OE *brynstān*, prob. from *bryne* 'burning' + *stān* 'stone'.

**brimstone moth** • n. a small bright yellow moth. [*Opisthograptis luteolat.*]

**brindle** • adj. (also **brindled**) (especially of a domestic animal) brownish or tawny with streaks of other colour.
– ORIGIN C17: alt. of ME *brinded*, prob. of Scand. origin.

**brine** • n. water saturated or strongly impregnated with salt; seawater. ➤technical a strong solution of a salt or salts. • v. [often as adj. **brined**] soak in or saturate with brine.
– ORIGIN OE *brīne*, of unknown origin.

**brine shrimp** • n. a small fairy shrimp which lives in brine pools and salt lakes and is used as food for aquarium fish. [*Artemia salina.*]

**bring** • v. (past and past part. **brought**) **1** carry or accompany to a place. **2** cause to be in a particular state or condition. **3** cause someone to receive (money) as income or profit: *five novels brought him £150,000.* **4** [usu. with neg.] (**bring oneself to do something**) force oneself to do something unpleasant. **5** initiate (legal action).

– PHRASES **bring the house down** make an audience laugh or applaud very enthusiastically. **bring something to bear** exert influence or pressure. **bring something to pass** chiefly poetic/literary cause something to happen.
– PHRASAL VERBS **bring something about 1** cause something to happen. **2** cause a ship to head in a different direction. **bring someone/thing down** cause someone or something to fall over or down. ➤cause someone to lose power. **bring something forth** archaic or poetic/literary give birth to something. **bring something forward 1** [often as adj. **brought forward**] (in bookkeeping) transfer a total sum from the bottom of one page to the top of the next. **2** propose an idea for consideration. **bring someone off** vulgar slang give someone an orgasm. **bring something off** achieve something successfully. **bring someone on** encourage or help someone who is learning to develop or improve. **bring something on 1** cause something unpleasant to occur. ➤(**bring something on/upon**) be responsible for something unpleasant that happens to (someone). **2** (of the weather) promote the growth of crops. **bring someone out** encourage someone to feel more confident. **bring something out 1** produce and launch a new product or publication. **2** emphasize a feature. **bring someone round** (or US **around**) **1** restore someone to consciousness. **2** persuade someone to adopt one's own point of view. **bring someone to** restore someone to consciousness. **bring something to** cause a boat to stop, especially by turning into the wind. **bring up** (chiefly of a ship) come to a stop. **bring someone up** look after a child until it is an adult. **bring something up 1** vomit something. **2** raise a matter for discussion or consideration.
– DERIVATIVES **bringer** n.
– ORIGIN OE *bringan*, of Gmc origin.

**bring and buy sale** • n. Brit. a charity sale at which people donate things to sell and buy those brought by others.

**brinjal** /ˈbrɪndʒɔːl, -dʒɒl/ • n. Indian & S. African an aubergine.
– ORIGIN based on Port. *berinjela*, from Arab. *al-bāḏinjān* (see **AUBERGINE**).

**brink** • n. **1** the extreme edge of land before a steep slope or a body of water. **2** the verge of a state or situation, typically a bad one.
– ORIGIN ME: of Scand. origin.

**brinkmanship** /ˈbrɪŋkmənʃɪp/ (US also **brinksmanship**) • n. the pursuit of a dangerous policy to the limits of safety before stopping.

**briny** /ˈbrʌɪni/ • adj. (**-ier**, **-iest**) of salty water or the sea; salty. • n. (**the briny**) Brit. informal the sea.

**brio** /ˈbriːəʊ/ • n. vigour or vivacity.
– ORIGIN C18: from Ital.

**brioche** /briːˈɒʃ, ˈbriːɒʃ/ • n. a small round French roll made from a light sweet yeast bread.
– ORIGIN Fr., from Norman Fr. *brier*, synonym of *broyer*, lit. 'split up into small pieces'.

**briquette** /brɪˈkɛt/ (also **briquet**) • n. a block of compressed coal dust or peat used as fuel.
– ORIGIN C19: from Fr., dimin. of *brique* 'brick'.

**brisé** /ˈbriːzeɪ/ • n. Ballet a jump in which the dancer sweeps one leg into the air to the side while jumping off the other and brings both legs together in the air before landing. • adj. (of a fan) consisting entirely of pierced sticks of ivory, horn, or tortoiseshell.
– ORIGIN Fr., lit. 'broken'.

**brisk** • adj. **1** active and energetic. **2** slightly brusque.
– DERIVATIVES **brisken** v. **briskly** adv. **briskness** n.
– ORIGIN C16: prob. from Fr. *brusque* (see **BRUSQUE**).

**brisket** • n. meat from the breast of a cow.
– ORIGIN ME: perh. from ON *brjósk* 'cartilage, gristle'.

**brisling** /ˈbrɪslɪŋ, ˈbrɪz-/ • n. (pl. same or **brislings**) a sprat, especially one seasoned and smoked in Norway and sold in a can.
– ORIGIN C20: from Norw. and Dan.

**bristle** /ˈbrɪs(ə)l/ • n. a short, stiff hair on an animal's skin or a man's face. ➤a bristle, or a man-made substitute, used to make a brush. • v. **1** (of hair or fur) stand upright away from the skin, typically as a sign of anger or fear. **2** react angrily or defensively. **3** (**bristle with**) be covered with or abundant in.
– DERIVATIVES **bristly** adj.
– ORIGIN ME: from OE *byrst* (of Gmc origin) + **-LE**[1].

**bristlebird** • n. an Australian songbird with a long cocked tail and a fringe of bristles around the bill. [*Dasyornis broadbenti* and other species.]

**bristlecone pine** • n. a very long-lived shrubby pine of western North America. [*Pinus longaeva*.]

**bristletail** • n. a small primitive wingless insect which has two or three bristles at the end of the abdomen. [Orders Thysanura (with three bristles, including the silverfish) and Diplura (with two bristles).]

**bristle worm** • n. a marine annelid worm of a class including ragworms, lugworms, and fan worms, which have a segmented body with numerous bristles on the fleshy lobes of each segment. [Class Polychaeta.]

**Bristol board** • n. a type of stiff, smooth cardboard used as a drawing surface or for cutting and shaping.

**Bristol fashion** • adj. Brit. informal, dated in good order.
– ORIGIN C19: orig. in naut. use, referring to the prosperity of the Engl. city and port of Bristol, when its shipping was in good order.

**bristols** • pl. n. Brit. informal a woman's breasts.
– ORIGIN 1960s: from rhyming sl. *Bristol Cities* 'titties'.

**Brit** informal • n. a British person. • adj. British.

**Britannia** /brɪˈtanjə/ • n. the personification of Britain, usually depicted as a helmeted woman with shield and trident.
– ORIGIN the L. name for Britain.

**Britannia metal** • n. a silvery alloy consisting of tin with about 5–15 per cent antimony and usually some copper, lead, or zinc.

**Britannia silver** • n. hallmarked silver that is at least 95.8 per cent pure.

**Britannic** /brɪˈtanɪk/ • adj. dated (chiefly in names or titles) of Britain or the British Empire.

**Briticism** /ˈbrɪtɪsɪz(ə)m/ (also **Britishism** /-ʃɪz(ə)m/) • n. an idiom used in Britain but not in other English-speaking countries.

**British** • adj. **1** of or relating to Great Britain or the United Kingdom. **2** of the British Commonwealth or (formerly) the British Empire.
– DERIVATIVES **Britishness** n.
– ORIGIN OE *Brettisc*, from *Bret* 'Briton', from L. *Britto*, or its Celtic equivalent.

**Britisher** • n. informal (especially in North America) a native or inhabitant of Britain.

**British Lion** • n. see **LION** (in sense 3).

**British thermal unit** • n. a unit of heat equal to the amount of heat needed to raise 1 lb of water at maximum density through one degree Fahrenheit. [$1.055 \times 10^3$ joules.]

**Briton** • n. **1** a native or inhabitant of Great Britain, or a person of British descent. **2** one of the people of southern Britain before and during Roman times.
– ORIGIN from OFr. *Breton*, from L. *Britto*, *Britton-*, or its Celtic equivalent.

**Britpop** • n. pop music by British groups of the mid 1990s, typically influenced by the Beatles and other British groups of the 1960s.

**brittle** • adj. **1** hard but liable to break or shatter easily. **2** (of a voice) unpleasantly hard and sharp and showing signs of nervousness or instability. **3** superficial or unfeeling. • n. a brittle sweet made from nuts and set melted sugar.
– DERIVATIVES **brittlely** (or **brittly**) adv. **brittleness** n.
– ORIGIN ME, ult. of Gmc origin and rel. to OE *brēotan* 'break up'.

**brittle bone disease** • n. another term for the diseases **OSTEOGENESIS IMPERFECTA** or **OSTEOPOROSIS**.

**brittlestar** • n. a marine animal related to a starfish, with long thin flexible arms radiating from a small central disk. [*Ophiura* and other genera, class Ophiuroidea.]

**Brittonic** /brɪ'tɒnɪk/ ● **adj. & n.** variant of **BRYTHONIC**.

**BRN** ● **abbrev.** Bahrain (international vehicle registration).

**bro** /brəʊ/ ● **n.** informal short for **BROTHER**. ➤ chiefly N. Amer. a friendly greeting or form of address.

**broach**[1] ● **v.** **1** raise (a sensitive subject) for discussion. **2** pierce or open (a cask or container) to draw liquor.
– ORIGIN ME (in sense 'prick or pierce'): from OFr. *brochier*, based on L. *brocchus, broccus* 'projecting'.

**broach**[2] ● **v.** Nautical (of a ship) veer and pitch forward, presenting a side to the wind and waves and losing steerage control.
– ORIGIN C18: of unknown origin.

**broach spire** ● **n.** an octagonal church spire rising from a square tower without a parapet.

**broad** ● **adj.** **1** having a distance larger than usual from side to side; wide. ➤ of a specified distance wide. **2** large in area or scope. **3** without detail. **4** (of a hint) clear and unambiguous. **5** (of a regional accent) very noticeable and strong. **6** somewhat coarse and indecent. ● **n.** N. Amer. informal a woman.
– PHRASES **broad daylight** full daylight; day.
– DERIVATIVES **broaden** v. **broadly** adv. **broadness** n.
– ORIGIN OE *brād*, of Gmc origin.

**broadband** ● **adj.** of or using signals over a wide range of frequencies in high-capacity telecommunications.

**broad bean** ● **n.** **1** a large flat edible green bean which is usually eaten without the pod. **2** the plant which yields these beans. [*Vicia faba*.]

**broadbill** ● **n.** a small, colourful songbird of the Old World tropics, with a large head and a wide, flattened bill. [Family Eurylaimidae: numerous species.]

**broad-brush** ● **adj.** lacking in detail and finesse.

**broadcast** ● **v.** (past **broadcast**; past part. **broadcast** or **broadcasted**) **1** transmit by radio or television. **2** tell to many people. **3** scatter (seeds) rather than placing in drills or rows. ● **n.** a radio or television programme or transmission. ● **adv.** by scattering.
– DERIVATIVES **broadcaster** n.

**Broad Church** ● **n.** a tradition or group within the Anglican Church favouring a liberal interpretation of doctrine.

**broadcloth** ● **n.** clothing fabric of fine twilled wool or worsted, or plain-woven cotton.

**broad gauge** ● **n.** a railway gauge which is wider than the standard gauge of 4 ft 8½ in (1.435 m).

**broad jump** ● **n.** North American term for **LONG JUMP**.

**broadleaved** (also **broadleaf**) ● **adj.** denoting trees or herbaceous plants with relatively wide flat leaves, as opposed to conifers or grasses respectively.

**broadloom** ● **n.** carpet woven in wide widths.
– DERIVATIVES **broadloomed** adj.

**broad-minded** ● **adj.** tolerant or liberal.
– DERIVATIVES **broad-mindedly** adv. **broad-mindedness** n.

**broad money** ● **n.** Economics money in any form, including bank or other deposits as well as notes and coins.

**broad pennant** (also **broad pendant**) ● **n.** a short swallow-tailed pennant distinguishing the commodore's ship in a squadron.

**broadsheet** ● **n.** **1** a large piece of paper printed with information on one side only. **2** a newspaper with a large format, regarded as more serious than tabloids.

**broadside** ● **n.** **1** historical a firing of all the guns from one side of a warship. **2** the side of a ship above the water between the bow and quarter. **3** a strongly worded critical attack. **4** another term for **BROADSHEET** (sense 1). ● **adv.** with the side turned in a particular direction. ➤ on the side. ● **v.** N. Amer. collide with the side of (a vehicle).
– PHRASES **broadside on** sideways on.

**broadsword** ● **n.** a sword with a wide blade, used for cutting rather than thrusting.

**broadtail** ● **n.** a karakul sheep.

**broadway** ● **n.** a large open or main road.

**Brobdingnagian** /ˌbrɒbdɪŋ'nagɪən/ ● **adj.** gigantic. ● **n.** a giant.
– ORIGIN C18: from *Brobdingnag*, a land in *Gulliver's Travels* where everything is of huge size.

**brocade** ● **n.** a rich fabric woven with a raised pattern, usually with gold or silver thread. ● **v.** [usu. as adj. **brocaded**] weave with this design.
– ORIGIN C16: from Sp. and Port. *brocado*, from Ital. *broccato*, from *brocco* 'twisted thread'.

**Broca's area** /'brəʊkəz/ ● **n.** Anatomy a region of the brain concerned with the production of speech, located in the cortex of the dominant frontal lobe.
– ORIGIN C19: named after the Fr. surgeon Paul *Broca*.

**broccoli** /'brɒkəli/ ● **n.** a cultivated variety of cabbage with heads of small green or purplish flower buds, eaten as a vegetable.
– ORIGIN C17: from Ital., pl. of *broccolo* 'cabbage sprout, head'.

**broch** /brɒk, brɒx/ ● **n.** a prehistoric circular stone tower in northern Scotland.
– ORIGIN C15 (in sense 'borough or town'): alt. of **BURGH**.

**brochette** /brɒ'ʃɛt/ ● **n.** **1** a skewer or spit on which chunks of meat or fish are barbecued, grilled, or roasted. **2** a dish of meat or fish chunks cooked in such a way.
– ORIGIN Fr., dimin. of *broche* 'skewer'.

**brochure** /'brəʊʃə, brɒ'ʃʊə/ ● **n.** a small book or magazine containing pictures and information about a product or service.
– ORIGIN C18: from Fr., lit. 'something stitched', from *brocher* (see **BROACH**[1]).

**brock** ● **n.** Brit. a name for the badger.
– ORIGIN OE *brocc, broc*, of Celtic origin.

**Brocken spectre** ● **n.** a magnified shadow of an observer, typically surrounded by rainbow-like bands, thrown on to a bank of cloud in high mountain areas when the sun is low.
– ORIGIN C19: named after the *Brocken* in the Harz Mountains of Germany.

**brocket** ● **n.** a small deer with short straight antlers, found in Central and South America. [Genus *Mazama*: four species.]
– ORIGIN ME (denoting a red deer stag in its second year, with straight antlers): from Anglo-Norman Fr. *broquet*, dimin. of *broque*, var. of *broche* (see **BROOCH**).

**broderie anglaise** /ˌbrəʊd(ə)rɪ 'ɒ̃gleɪz/ ● **n.** open embroidery, typically in floral patterns, on fine white cotton or linen.
– ORIGIN C19: Fr., lit. 'Engl. embroidery'.

**brogan** /'brəʊg(ə)n/ ● **n.** a coarse stout leather shoe reaching to the ankle.
– ORIGIN C19: from Ir. *brógán*, Sc. Gaelic *brógan*, lit. 'small brogue'.

**brogue**[1] ● **n.** a strong outdoor shoe with ornamental perforated patterns in the leather. ➤ a rough shoe of untanned leather, formerly worn in Ireland and the Scottish Highlands.
– ORIGIN C16: from Sc. Gaelic and Ir. *bróg*, from ON *brók* (rel. to **BREECH**).

**brogue**[2] ● **n.** a marked accent, especially Irish or Scottish, when speaking English.
– ORIGIN C18: perh. allusively from **BROGUE**[1], referring to the rough footwear of Ir. peasants.

**broil**[1] ● **v.** chiefly N. Amer. **1** cook (meat or fish) by exposure to direct heat. **2** become very hot, especially from the sun.
– ORIGIN ME: from OFr. *bruler* 'to burn', of unknown origin.

**broil**[2] ● **n.** archaic a quarrel or a commotion.
– ORIGIN C16: from obs. *broil* 'to muddle'; cf. **EMBROIL**.

**broiler** ● **n.** **1** a young chicken suitable for roasting, grilling, or barbecuing. **2** N. Amer. a gridiron, grill, or special part of a stove for broiling meat or fish.

**broiler house** ● **n.** a building for rearing broiler chickens in close confinement.

**broke** past (and archaic past participle) of **BREAK**[1]. ● **adj.** informal having completely run out of money.
– PHRASES **go for broke** informal risk everything in an all-out effort.

**broken** past participle of **BREAK**[1]. ● **adj.** (of a language) spoken falteringly and with many mistakes, as by a foreigner.
– DERIVATIVES **brokenly** adv. **brokenness** /'brəʊk(ə)n

nɪs/ n.

**broken chord** • **n.** Music a chord in which the notes are played successively.

**broken colour** • **n.** a colour mixed or juxtaposed closely with another.

**broken-down** • **adj. 1** worn out and dilapidated. **2** not working.

**broken field** • **n.** American Football the area beyond the line of scrimmage, where the defenders are relatively scattered.

**broken-hearted** • **adj.** overwhelmed by grief or disappointment.
– DERIVATIVES **broken-heartedness** n.

**broken home** • **n.** a family in which the parents are divorced or separated.

**broken reed** • **n.** see **REED**.

**broken wind** • **n.** another term for **COPD** in horses.
– DERIVATIVES **broken-winded** adj.

**broker** • **n.** a person who buys and sells goods or assets for others. Compare with **BROKER-DEALER**. • **v.** arrange or negotiate (a deal or plan).
– DERIVATIVES **brokerage** n.
– ORIGIN ME (denoting a retailer or pedlar): from Anglo-Norman Fr. *brocour*, of unknown ultimate origin.

**broker-dealer** • **n.** (in the UK) a person combining the former functions of a broker and jobber on the Stock Exchange (now the official term on the UK Stock Exchange).

**broking** • **n.** Brit. the business or service of buying and selling goods or assets for others.

**brolga** /ˈbrɒlɡə/ • **n.** a large grey Australian crane with an elaborate courtship display. [*Grus rubicundus*.]
– ORIGIN C19: from Kamilaroi *burralga* (also found in other Aborig. langs).

**brolly** • **n.** (pl. **-ies**) Brit. informal an umbrella.

**brom-** /ˈbrəʊm/ • **comb. form** variant spelling of **BROMO-** shortened before a vowel (as in *bromide*).

**brome** /brəʊm/ • **n.** an oat-like grass which is sometimes grown for fodder or ornamental purposes. [Genus *Bromus*.]
– ORIGIN C18: from mod. L. *Bromus*, from Gk *bromos* 'oat'.

**bromeliad** /brəˈmiːlɪad/ • **n.** a plant of a tropical and subtropical American family (Bromeliaceae), typically with short stems with rosettes of stiff, spiny leaves.
– ORIGIN C19: from mod. L. *Bromelia* (a genus, named after the Swed. botanist Olaf *Bromel*), + **-AD**[1].

**bromide** /ˈbrəʊmʌɪd/ • **n. 1** Chemistry a compound of bromine with another element or group: *methyl bromide*. **2** a reproduction or piece of typesetting on bromide paper. **3** dated a sedative preparation containing potassium bromide. **4** a trite statement intended to soothe or placate.
– DERIVATIVES **bromidic** adj.

**bromide paper** • **n.** photographic printing paper coated with silver bromide emulsion.

**bromine** /ˈbrəʊmiːn/ • **n.** the chemical element of atomic number 35, a dark red toxic liquid halogen with a choking irritating smell. (Symbol: **Br**)
– ORIGIN C19: from Fr. *brome*, from Gk *brōmos* 'a stink', + **-INE**[4].

**bromo-** /ˈbrəʊməʊ/ (usu. **brom-** before a vowel) • **comb. form** Chemistry representing **BROMINE**.

**bronchi** plural form of **BRONCHUS**.

**bronchial** /ˈbrɒŋkɪəl/ • **adj.** of or relating to the bronchi or bronchioles.

**bronchial tree** • **n.** the branching system of bronchi and bronchioles, conducting air from the windpipe into the lungs.

**bronchiole** /ˈbrɒŋkɪəʊl/ • **n.** Anatomy any of the minute branches into which a bronchus divides.
– DERIVATIVES **bronchiolar** adj.
– ORIGIN C19: from mod. L. *bronchiolus, bronchiolum*, dimins of late L. *bronchia*, denoting the branches of the main bronchi.

**bronchiolitis** /ˌbrɒŋkɪəˈlʌɪtɪs/ • **n.** Medicine inflammation of the bronchioles.

**bronchitis** • **n.** inflammation of the mucous membrane in the bronchial tubes, typically with spasm of bronchial muscle and coughing.
– DERIVATIVES **bronchitic** adj. & n.

**broncho-** /ˈbrɒŋkəʊ/ • **comb. form** of or relating to the bronchi: *bronchopneumonia*.
– ORIGIN from Gk *bronkho-*, from *bronkhos* 'windpipe'.

**bronchocele** /ˈbrɒŋkə(ʊ)siːl/ • **n.** a goitre.

**bronchodilator** /ˌbrɒŋkə(ʊ)dʌɪˈleɪtə/ • **n.** Medicine a drug that causes widening of the bronchi, for example any of those taken by inhalation for the alleviation of asthma.

**bronchopneumonia** /ˌbrɒŋkə(ʊ)njuːˈməʊnɪə/ • **n.** inflammation of the lungs, arising in the bronchi or bronchioles.

**bronchoscope** • **n.** a fibre-optic cable that is passed into the windpipe in order to view the bronchi.
– DERIVATIVES **bronchoscopy** n.

**bronchus** /ˈbrɒŋkəs/ • **n.** (pl. **bronchi** /-kʌɪ/) any of the major air passages of the lungs which diverge from the windpipe.
– ORIGIN C17: from late L., from Gk *bronkhos* 'windpipe'.

**bronco** • **n.** (pl. **-os**) a wild or half-tamed horse of the western US.
– ORIGIN C19: from Sp., lit. 'rough, rude'.

**brontosaurus** /ˌbrɒntəˈsɔːrəs/ (also **brontosaur** /ˈbrɒntəsɔː/) • **n.** another term for **APATOSAURUS**.
– ORIGIN mod. L. (former genus name), from Gk *brontē* 'thunder' + *sauros* 'lizard'.

**Bronx cheer** • **n.** N. Amer. a sound of derision made by blowing through closed lips with the tongue between them.

**bronze** • **n. 1** a yellowish-brown alloy of copper with up to one-third tin. **2** a yellowish-brown colour. **3** a work of sculpture or other object made of bronze. • **v. 1** give a bronze surface to. **2** make suntanned.
– DERIVATIVES **bronzy** adj.
– ORIGIN C17 (as v.): from Fr. *bronze* (n.), *bronzer* (v.), from Ital. *bronzo*, prob. from Pers. *birinj* 'brass'.

**Bronze Age** • **n.** a prehistoric period that followed the Stone Age and preceded the Iron Age, when weapons and tools were made of bronze rather than stone.

**bronze medal** • **n.** a medal made of or coloured bronze, customarily awarded for third place in a race or competition.

**bronzewing** • **n.** an Australian pigeon with a metallic bronze band on the wing. [*Phaps chalcoptera* and related species.]

**broo** /bruː/ • **n.** Scottish informal a social security office.
– PHRASES **on the broo** claiming unemployment benefit.
– ORIGIN 1930s: alt. of **BUREAU**.

**brooch** /brəʊtʃ/ • **n.** an ornament fastened to clothing with a hinged pin and catch.
– ORIGIN ME: var. of *broach* 'skewer, bodkin', from OFr. *broche* 'spit for roasting', based on L. *brocchus, broccus* 'projecting'; cf. **BROACH**[1].

**brood** • **n. 1** a family of young animals, especially birds, produced at one hatching or birth. **2** bee or wasp larvae. • **v. 1** think deeply about something that makes one unhappy. **2** [as adj. **brooding**] appearing darkly menacing. **3** (of a bird) sit on (eggs) to hatch them. ➤(of a fish, frog, or invertebrate) hold (developing eggs) within the body. • **adj.** (of an animal) kept to be used for breeding.
– DERIVATIVES **broodingly** adv.
– ORIGIN OE *brōd*, of Gmc origin; rel. to **BREED**.

**brooder** • **n.** a heated house for chicks or piglets.

**broody** • **adj.** (**-ier, -iest**) **1** (of a hen) inclined to incubate eggs. **2** informal (of a woman) having a strong desire to have a baby. **3** thoughtful and unhappy.
– DERIVATIVES **broodily** adv. **broodiness** n.

**brook**[1] • **n.** a small stream.
– DERIVATIVES **brooklet** n.
– ORIGIN OE *brōc*, of unknown origin.

**brook**[2] • **v.** [with neg.] formal tolerate or allow (opposition).
– ORIGIN OE *brūcan* 'use, possess' or 'digest, stomach', of Gmc origin.

**brooklime** • **n.** a speedwell with smooth fleshy leaves and deep blue flowers, growing in wet areas. [*Veronica beccabunga*.]
– ORIGIN ME *broklemok*, from **BROOK**[1] + *hleomoce*, the

name of the plant in OE.

**brookweed** • n. a small white-flowered plant which grows in wet ground. [*Samolus valerandi*.]

**broom** • n. **1** a long-handled brush of bristles or twigs, used for sweeping. **2** a shrub typically having many yellow flowers, long, thin green stems, and small or few leaves. [*Cytisus scoparius* and many other species, especially in the genera *Cytisus* and *Genista*.]
– ORIGIN OE *brōm* (in sense 2), of Gmc origin; rel. to BRAMBLE.

**broomball** • n. N. Amer. a game similar to ice hockey in which players run rather than skate and use rubber brooms or broom handles to push a ball into the goal.

**broomrape** • n. a leafless parasitic plant with tubular flowers, which attaches itself to the roots of its host plant. [Genus *Orobanche*.]
– ORIGIN C16: from BROOM + L. *rapum* 'tuber'.

**broomstick** • n. the handle of a broom, on which witches are said to fly.

**Bros** /brɒs/ • pl. n. brothers (in names of companies).

**brose** /brəʊz/ • n. chiefly Scottish a kind of porridge made with oatmeal or dried peas.
– ORIGIN C17: orig. a Scots form of ME *brewis* 'broth', from OFr. *brouez*.

**broth** • n. **1** a thin soup of meat or vegetable stock, sometimes thickened with barley or other cereals. ➤meat or fish stock. **2** Microbiology a liquid nutrient medium for the culture of bacteria.
– PHRASES **a broth of a boy** Irish a very lively boy or young man.
– ORIGIN OE, of Gmc origin; rel. to BREW.

**brothel** • n. a house where men visit prostitutes.
– ORIGIN C16: from ME *brothel* 'worthless man, prostitute'.

**brothel creepers** • pl. n. informal soft-soled suede shoes.

**brother** • n. **1** a man or boy in relation to other sons and daughters of his parents. **2** a male associate or fellow member of an organization. **3** N. Amer. informal a black man. **4** something which resembles or is equivalent to another. **5** (pl. also **brethren**) Christian Church a (male) fellow Christian. ➤a member of a religious order of men. • exclam. used to express annoyance or surprise.
– DERIVATIVES **brotherliness** n. **brotherly** adj.
– ORIGIN OE *brōthor*, of Gmc origin.

**brother-german** • n. (pl. **brothers-german**) archaic a brother sharing both parents, as opposed to a half-brother or stepbrother.

**brotherhood** • n. **1** the relationship between brothers. ➤a feeling of kinship and closeness. **2** an association or community of people with a common interest, religion, or trade. ➤N. Amer. a trade union.
– ORIGIN ME: prob. from obs. *brotherred* (based on OE *-rǣden* 'condition, state'), assoc. with words ending in -HOOD and -HEAD[1].

**brother-in-law** • n. (pl. **brothers-in-law**) **1** the brother of one's wife or husband. **2** the husband of one's sister or sister-in-law.

**brougham** /ˈbruː(ə)m/ • n. historical **1** a horse-drawn carriage with a roof, four wheels, and an open driver's seat in front. **2** a motor car with an open driver's seat.
– ORIGIN C19: named after Lord *Brougham*, who designed the carriage.

**brought** past and past participle of BRING.

**brouhaha** /ˈbruːhɑːhɑː/ • n. a noisy and overexcited reaction.
– ORIGIN C19: from Fr., prob. imitative.

**brow**[1] • n. **1** a person's forehead. **2** an eyebrow. **3** the summit of a hill or pass.
– DERIVATIVES **-browed** adj.
– ORIGIN OE *brū* 'eyelash, eyebrow', of Gmc origin.

**brow**[2] • n. a ship's gangway or landing platform.
– ORIGIN C19: prob. from Norw. *bru*, from ON *brú* 'bridge'.

**browbeat** • v. (past **-beat**; past part. **-beaten**) intimidate or cajole with words or looks.
– DERIVATIVES **browbeater** n.

**brown** • adj. **1** of a colour produced by mixing red, yellow, and blue, as of dark wood or rich soil. **2** dark-skinned or suntanned. • n. **1** brown colour, pigment, or material. **2** used in names of various butterflies with mainly brown wings, e.g. **meadow brown**. • v. **1** make or become brown by cooking. **2** (**be browned off**) informal be irritated or depressed.
– PHRASES **(as) brown as a berry** very suntanned.
– DERIVATIVES **brownish** adj. **brownness** n. **browny** adj.
– ORIGIN OE *brūn*, of Gmc origin.

**brown ale** • n. Brit. dark, mild beer sold in bottles.

**brown algae** • pl. n. a large group of algae that are typically olive brown or greenish in colour, including many seaweeds. [Class Phaeophyceae.]

**brown bear** • n. a large bear with a coat colour ranging from cream to black. [*Ursus arctos*.]

**brown belt** • n. a belt of a brown colour marking a level of proficiency below that of a black belt in judo, karate, or other martial arts.

**Brown Betty** • n. chiefly N. Amer. a baked pudding made with apples or other fruit and breadcrumbs.

**brown coal** • n. another term for LIGNITE.

**brown dwarf** • n. Astronomy a celestial object intermediate in size between a giant planet and a small star, believed to emit mainly infrared radiation.

**brown fat** • n. dark-coloured adipose tissue with many blood vessels, able to provide bodily heat quite rapidly.

**brownfield** • adj. (of an urban site) having had previous development on it. Compare with GREENFIELD.

**brown goods** • pl. n. television sets, audio equipment, and similar household appliances. Compare with WHITE GOODS.

**brown holland** • n. unbleached holland linen.

**Brownian motion** /ˈbraʊnɪən/ • n. Physics the erratic random movement of microscopic particles in a fluid, as a result of continuous bombardment from molecules of the surrounding medium.
– ORIGIN C19: named after the Sc. botanist Robert *Brown*.

**Brownie** • n. (pl. **-ies**) **1** (Brit. also **Brownie Guide**) a member of the junior branch of the Guides Association, for girls aged between about 7 and 10. **2** (**brownie**) a small square of rich chocolate cake, with nuts. ➤Austral./NZ a piece of sweet currant bread. **3** (**brownie**) a benevolent elf supposedly haunting houses and doing housework secretly.
– PHRASES **brownie point** informal, humorous a notional award given for a good deed or an attempt to please.

**Browning** • n. **1** a type of water-cooled automatic machine gun. **2** a type of automatic pistol.
– ORIGIN C20: named after the Amer. designer John M. *Browning*.

**browning** • n. Brit. darkened flour for colouring gravy.

**brown-nose** N. Amer. informal • n. (also **brown-noser**) a person who acts in a grossly obsequious way. • v. curry favour with (someone) by acting in such a way.

**brownout** • n. chiefly N. Amer. a partial blackout.

**brown owl** • n. **1** another term for TAWNY OWL. **2** (**Brown Owl**) informal (in the UK) the adult leader of a group of Brownies (officially termed the Brownie Guider).

**brown rice** • n. unpolished rice with only the husk of the grain removed.

**brown rot** • n. **1** a fungal disease producing discoloration and shrivelling of apples, pears, and other fruit. **2** a fungal disease resulting in the softening and cracking of timber.

**brown sauce** • n. a commercially prepared relish containing vinegar and spices.

**Brownshirt** • n. a member of a Nazi militia founded by Hitler in 1921 and suppressed in 1934, with brown uniforms.

**brownstone** • n. N. Amer. **1** a kind of reddish-brown sandstone used for building. **2** a building faced with such sandstone.

**brown sugar** • n. unrefined or partially refined sugar.

**brown trout** • n. (pl. same) the common trout of European lakes and rivers, typically with dark spotted skin.

[*Salmo trutta.*]

**browse** /braʊz/ ● **v. 1** survey goods or text in a leisurely and casual way. ➤ Computing read or survey (data files) via a network. **2** (of an animal) feed on leaves, twigs, etc. ● **n. 1** an act of browsing. **2** vegetation eaten by animals.
– DERIVATIVES **browsable** adj.
– ORIGIN ME: from OFr. *broster*, from *brost* 'young shoot', prob. of Gmc origin.

**browser** ● **n. 1** a person or animal that browses. **2** Computing a program with an interface for displaying HTML files, used to navigate the World Wide Web.

**brrr** ● **exclam.** used to express a reaction to feeling cold.

**BRU** ● **abbrev.** Brunei (international vehicle registration).

**brucellosis** /ˌbruːsəˈləʊsɪs/ ● **n.** a bacterial disease chiefly affecting cattle and causing undulant fever in humans.
– ORIGIN 1930s: from mod. L. *Brucella*, genus name of the bacterium responsible (named after the Sc. physician Sir David *Bruce*) + **-OSIS**.

**brucite** /ˈbruːsʌɪt/ ● **n.** a white, grey, or greenish mineral consisting of hydrated magnesium hydroxide.
– ORIGIN C19: named after the Amer. mineralogist Archibald *Bruce*.

**bruise** ● **n.** an injury appearing as an area of discoloured skin on the body, caused by a blow or impact rupturing underlying blood vessels. ➤ a similar area of damage on a fruit, vegetable, or plant. ● **v. 1** inflict a bruise on. ➤ be susceptible to bruising. **2** crush or pound (food).
– ORIGIN OE *brȳsan* 'crush, injure or damage with a blow', reinforced in ME by OFr. *bruisier* 'break'.

**bruiser** ● **n.** informal, derogatory a tough, aggressive person.

**bruising** ● **adj.** (of a contest) aggressively conducted and likely to be damaging. ● **n.** bruises on the skin.

**bruit** /bruːt/ ● **v.** spread (a report or rumour) widely. ● **n. 1** archaic a report or rumour. **2** Medicine a sound, especially an abnormal one, heard through a stethoscope.
– ORIGIN ME (as n.): from OFr. *bruit* 'noise', from *bruire* 'to roar'.

**brumby** /ˈbrʌmbi/ ● **n.** (pl. **-ies**) (in Australia) a wild or unbroken horse.
– ORIGIN C19: of unknown origin.

**brume** /bruːm/ ● **n.** poetic/literary mist or fog.
– DERIVATIVES **brumous** adj.
– ORIGIN C18: from Fr., from L. *bruma* 'winter'.

**Brummagem** /ˈbrʌmədʒ(ə)m/ ● **adj.** informal of or relating to Birmingham.
– ORIGIN C17: dial. form.

**Brummie** (also **Brummy**) ● **n.** (pl. **-ies**) Brit. informal a person from Birmingham. ● **adj.** informal **1** Brit. of, from, or relating to Birmingham. **2** (**brummy**) Austral./NZ counterfeit, showy, or cheaply made.

**brunch** ● **n.** a late morning meal eaten instead of breakfast and lunch.

**Bruneian** /bruːˈnʌɪən/ ● **n.** a native or inhabitant of the sultanate of Brunei on the NW coast of Borneo. ● **adj.** of or relating to Brunei.

**brunette** /bruːˈnɛt, brʊ-/ (US also **brunet**) ● **n.** a woman or girl with dark brown hair.
– ORIGIN C16: from Fr., fem. of *brunet*, dimin. of *brun* 'brown'.

**brung** dialect past and past participle of **BRING**.

**Brunswick stew** ● **n.** US a stew of chicken and vegetables.
– ORIGIN from *Brunswick* county in Virginia, US.

**brunt** /brʌnt/ ● **n.** (usu. in phr. **bear the brunt**) the chief impact of something bad.
– ORIGIN ME (denoting a blow or attack, also the force or shock of something): of unknown origin.

**bruschetta** /brʊˈskɛtə/ ● **n.** toasted Italian bread drenched in olive oil, usually served with garlic or tomatoes.
– ORIGIN from Ital.

**brush**[1] ● **n. 1** an implement with a handle and a block of bristles, hair, or wire, used especially for cleaning, smoothing, or painting. **2** an act of brushing. **3** a slight and fleeting touch. **4** a brief encounter with something bad or unwelcome: *a brush with death*. **5** a piece of carbon or metal serving as an electrical contact with a moving part in a motor or alternator. **6** a drumstick with long wire bristles, used to make a soft hissing sound. **7** the bushy tail of a fox. **8** Austral./NZ informal girls or women regarded sexually. ● **v. 1** clean, smooth, or apply with a brush. **2** touch or push lightly and gently. **3** (**brush someone/thing off**) dismiss someone or something in an abrupt, contemptuous way. **4** (**brush up on** or **brush something up**) work to regain a previously learned skill.
– DERIVATIVES **brushless** adj. (chiefly technical) **brushy** adj.
– ORIGIN ME: noun from OFr. *broisse*; verb partly from OFr. *brosser* 'to sweep'.

**brush**[2] ● **n.** chiefly N. Amer. & Austral./NZ undergrowth, small trees, and shrubs. ➤ N. Amer. cut brushwood. ➤ Austral./NZ dense forest.
– ORIGIN ME: from OFr. *broce*, perh. based on L. *bruscum*, denoting an excrescence on a maple.

**brushback** ● **n.** Baseball a pitch aimed close to the body so that the batter must step back to avoid it.

**brush discharge** ● **n.** a broad electrical discharge from a conductor occurring when the potential difference is high but not sufficient for a spark or arc.

**brushed** ● **adj. 1** (of fabric) having a soft raised nap. **2** (of metal) finished with a non-reflective surface.

**brushtail** ● **n.** a mainly tree-dwelling nocturnal Australian marsupial with a pointed muzzle and a furred tail with a naked tip. [*Trichosurus vulpecula* and related species.]

**brush-turkey** ● **n.** a large mound-building bird resembling a turkey, found mainly in New Guinea. [Family Megapodiidae: several species.]

**brush wolf** ● **n.** North American term for **COYOTE**.

**brushwood** ● **n.** undergrowth, twigs, and small branches.

**brushwork** ● **n.** the way in which a painter uses their brush.

**brusque** /brʊsk, bruːsk/ ● **adj.** abrupt or offhand.
– DERIVATIVES **brusquely** adv. **brusqueness** n. **brusquerie** /ˈbrʊsk(ə)riː, ˈbruː-/ n. (archaic).
– ORIGIN C17: from Fr., 'lively, fierce', from Ital. *brusco* 'sour'.

**Brussels carpet** ● **n.** a carpet with a heavy woollen pile and a strong linen back.

**Brussels lace** ● **n.** an elaborate kind of lace, typically with a raised design.

**Brussels sprout** (also **Brussel sprout**) ● **n.** a vegetable consisting of the small compact bud of a variety of cabbage which bears many such buds along a tall single stem.

**brut** /bruːt, French bʀy/ ● **adj.** (of sparkling wine) very dry.
– ORIGIN Fr., lit. 'raw, rough'.

**brutal** ● **adj. 1** savagely violent. **2** without any attempt to disguise unpleasantness: *brutal honesty*.
– DERIVATIVES **brutality** /-ˈtalɪti/ n. **brutally** adv.
– ORIGIN C15 (in the sense 'relating to the lower animals'): from OFr., or from med. L. *brutalis*, from *brutus* (see **BRUTE**).

**brutalism** ● **n. 1** cruelty and savageness. **2** a stark style of functionalist architecture that makes use of steel and concrete in massive blocks.
– DERIVATIVES **brutalist** n. & adj.

**brutalize** (also **-ise**) ● **v. 1** make brutal by repeated exposure to violence. **2** treat brutally.
– DERIVATIVES **brutalization** n.

**brute** ● **n. 1** a violent or savage person or animal. ➤ informal a cruel or insensitive person. **2** an animal as opposed to a human being. ● **adj. 1** unreasoning and animal-like. **2** merely physical: *brute force*. **3** harsh or inescapable: *brute necessity*.
– DERIVATIVES **brutish** adj. **brutishly** adv. **brutishness** n.
– ORIGIN ME (as adj.): from OFr. *brut(e)*, from L. *brutus* 'dull, stupid'.

**bruxism** /ˈbrʌksɪz(ə)m/ ● **n.** Medicine involuntary habitual grinding of the teeth, typically during sleep.
– ORIGIN 1930s: from Gk *brukhein* 'gnash the teeth' +

**-ISM.**

**Brylcreem** /ˈbrɪlkriːm/ ● **n.** trademark a cream used on men's hair to give it a smooth, shiny appearance.
– DERIVATIVES **Brylcreemed** adj.

**bryology** /brʌɪˈɒlədʒi/ ● **n.** the study of mosses and liverworts.
– DERIVATIVES **bryological** adj. **bryologist** n.
– ORIGIN C19: from Gk *bruon* 'moss' + **-LOGY**.

**bryony** /ˈbrʌɪəni/ ● **n.** (pl. **-ies**) a climbing hedgerow plant with red berries. [*Bryonia dioica* (**white bryony**) and *Tamus communis* (**black bryony**).]
– ORIGIN OE, via L. from Gk *bruōnia*.

**Bryophyta** /ˌbrʌɪə(ʊ)ˈfʌɪtə/ ● **pl. n.** Botany a division of small flowerless green plants which comprises the mosses and liverworts.
– DERIVATIVES **bryophyte** n.
– ORIGIN mod. L., from Gk *bruon* 'moss' + *phuta* 'plants'.

**Bryozoa** /ˌbrʌɪəˈzəʊə/ ● **pl. n.** Zoology a phylum of sedentary aquatic invertebrates that comprises the moss animals.
– DERIVATIVES **bryozoan** n. & adj.
– ORIGIN mod. L., from Gk *bruon* 'moss' + *zōia* 'animals'.

**Brythonic** /brɪˈθɒnɪk/ (also **Brittonic**) ● **n.** the southern group of Celtic languages, consisting of Welsh, Cornish, and Breton. Compare with **GOIDELIC**. ● **adj.** denoting or relating to these languages.
– ORIGIN from Welsh *Brython* 'Britons' + **-IC**.

**BS** ● **abbrev.** **1** US Bachelor of Science. **2** Bachelor of Surgery. **3** Blessed Sacrament. **4** British Standard(s). **5** N. Amer. vulgar slang bullshit.

**BSc** ● **abbrev.** Bachelor of Science.

**BSE** ● **abbrev.** bovine spongiform encephalopathy, a fatal disease of cattle which affects the central nervous system, causing agitation and staggering, and is believed to be related to Creutzfeldt–Jakob disease in humans.

**BSI** ● **abbrev.** British Standards Institution.

**B-side** ● **n.** the less important side of a pop single.

**BSL** ● **abbrev.** British Sign Language.

**BST** ● **abbrev.** **1** bovine somatotrophin, especially as an additive in cattle feed. **2** British Summer Time.

**BT** ● **abbrev.** British Telecom.

**Bt** ● **abbrev.** Baronet.

**B2B** ● **abbrev.** business-to-business, denoting trade conducted via the Internet between businesses.

**B2C** ● **abbrev.** business-to-consumer, denoting trade conducted via the Internet between businesses and consumers.

**Btu** (also **BTU**) ● **abbrev.** British thermal unit(s).

**btw** ● **abbrev.** by the way.

**bub** ● **n.** N. Amer. informal a rude or aggressive way of addressing a boy or man.
– ORIGIN C19: from earlier *bubby* (perh. a child's form of **BROTHER**), or from Ger. *Bube* 'boy'.

**bubba** /ˈbʌbə/ ● **n.** N. Amer. informal **1** a form of address to a brother. **2** derogatory an uneducated conservative white male of the southern US.
– ORIGIN C20: alt. of **BROTHER**; cf. **BUB**.

**bubble** ● **n.** **1** a thin sphere of liquid enclosing air or another gas. ➤an air- or gas-filled spherical cavity in a liquid or a solidified liquid such as glass. **2** a transparent domed cover or enclosure. ● **v.** **1** (of a liquid) be agitated by rising bubbles of air or gas. **2** (**bubble with**) be filled with (an irrepressible positive feeling). **3** (**bubble up**) (of a feeling) intensify to the point of being expressed.
– ORIGIN ME: partly imitative, partly an alt. of **BURBLE**.

**bubble and squeak** ● **n.** Brit. a dish of cooked cabbage fried with cooked potatoes.

**bubble bath** ● **n.** fragrant liquid added to bathwater to make it foam.

**bubble car** ● **n.** a small car with a transparent domed canopy and typically three wheels.

**bubble chamber** ● **n.** Physics an apparatus in which the tracks of ionizing particles are visible as a row of bubbles in a liquid.

**bubblegum** ● **n.** **1** chewing gum that can be blown into bubbles. **2** [as modifier] chiefly N. Amer. simplistic or adolescent in style: *bubblegum pop music.*

**bubblehead** ● **n.** informal a foolish person.

**bubblejet printer** ● **n.** a form of ink-jet printer.

**bubble memory** ● **n.** Computing a type of memory in which data is stored as a pattern of magnetized regions in a thin layer of magnetic material.

**bubbler** ● **n.** Austral. & US a drinking fountain.

**bubble shell** ● **n.** a marine mollusc with a thin scroll-like shell. [Bullidae and related families: many species.]

**bubble wrap** ● **n.** (trademark in the US) plastic packaging in sheets containing numerous small air cushions.

**bubbly** ● **adj.** (**-ier**, **-iest**) **1** containing bubbles. **2** cheerful and high-spirited. ● **n.** informal champagne.

**bubinga** /bjuːˈbɪŋgə/ ● **n.** reddish-brown tropical African wood used chiefly for inlay work and veneer.

**bubo** /ˈbjuːbəʊ/ ● **n.** (pl. **-oes**) a swollen inflamed lymph node in the armpit or groin.
– DERIVATIVES **bubonic** /bjuːˈbɒnɪk/ adj.
– ORIGIN ME: from L., from Gk *boubōn* 'groin or swelling in the groin'.

**bubonic plague** ● **n.** a form of plague transmitted by rat fleas and characterized by fever, delirium, and the formation of buboes.

**buccal** /ˈbʌk(ə)l/ ● **adj.** technical of or relating to the cheek or mouth.
– ORIGIN C19: from L. *bucca* 'cheek' + **-AL**.

**buccaneer** /ˌbʌkəˈnɪə/ ● **n.** historical **1** a pirate, originally one preying on ships in the Caribbean. **2** a recklessly adventurous and unscrupulous person.
– DERIVATIVES **buccaneering** adj.
– ORIGIN C17 (orig. denoting European hunters in the Caribbean): from Fr. *boucanier*, from *boucan* 'a frame on which to cook or cure meat', from Tupi *mukem*.

**buccinator** /ˈbʌksɪneɪtə/ ● **n.** Anatomy a flat thin muscle in the wall of the cheek.
– ORIGIN C17: from L., from *buccinare* 'blow a trumpet'.

**buchu** /ˈbʌkuː/ ● **n.** **1** a heather-like South African shrub, cultivated for its essential oil and as an ornamental. [*Agathosma betulina* and other species.] **2** a diuretic drug made from buchu leaves.
– ORIGIN C18: from Khoikhoi.

**buck**[1] ● **n.** **1** the male of some animals, especially deer and antelopes. **2** S. African an antelope (of either sex). **3** a vertical jump performed by a horse, with the head lowered, back arched, and back legs thrown out behind. **4** archaic a fashionable and daring young man. ● **v.** **1** (of a horse) perform a buck. **2** oppose or resist: *buck the trend.* **3** (**buck up**) informal make or become more cheerful. ● **adj.** US military slang lowest of a particular rank.
– PHRASES **buck up one's ideas** become more serious, energetic, and hard-working.
– ORIGIN OE: partly from *buc* 'male deer', of Gmc origin; reinforced by *bucca* 'male goat'.

**buck**[2] ● **n.** informal **1** N. Amer. & Austral./NZ a dollar. **2** S. African a rand. **3** Indian a rupee.
– PHRASES **a fast buck** easily and quickly earned money.
– ORIGIN C19: of unknown origin.

**buck**[3] ● **n.** an object placed as a reminder in front of a poker player whose turn it is to deal.
– PHRASES **the buck stops here** informal the responsibility for something cannot be passed to someone else. **pass the buck** informal shift responsibility to someone else.
– ORIGIN C19: of unknown origin.

**buckaroo** /ˌbʌkəˈruː/ ● **n.** N. Amer. dated a cowboy.
– ORIGIN C19: alt. of **VAQUERO**.

**buckbean** ● **n.** another term for **BOGBEAN**.
– ORIGIN C16: from Flemish *bocks boonen* 'goat's beans'.

**buckboard** ● **n.** N. Amer. an open horse-drawn carriage with four wheels and seating that is attached to a plank between the front and rear axles.
– ORIGIN C19: from *buck* 'body of a cart' (perh. a var. of obs. *bouk* 'belly, body') + **BOARD**.

**buckeen** /bʌˈkiːn/ ● **n.** historical a poor but aspiring young man of the lower Anglo-Irish gentry.

**bucket** ● **n.** **1** a cylindrical open container with a handle, used to carry liquids. ➤a compartment on the outer edge of a waterwheel. ➤the scoop of a dredger or grain elevator, or one attached to the front of a digger or tractor. **2** (**buckets**) informal large quantities of liquid. ● **v.** (**buck-**

**eted, bucketing**) informal **1** (**bucket down**) Brit. rain heavily. **2** (of a vehicle) move quickly and jerkily.
– DERIVATIVES **bucketful** n. (pl. **-fuls**).
– ORIGIN ME: from Anglo-Norman Fr. *buquet* 'tub, pail', perh. from OE *būc* 'belly, pitcher'.

**bucket seat** ● n. a vehicle seat with a rounded back to fit one person.

**bucket shop** ● n. informal, derogatory **1** an unauthorized office speculating in stocks or currency using the funds of unwitting investors. **2** Brit. a travel agency providing cheap air tickets.

**buckeye** ● n. **1** an American tree or shrub related to the horse chestnut. [Genus *Aesculus*: several species.] ➤ the shiny brown nut of such a tree or shrub. **2** an orange and brown New World butterfly with conspicuous eyespots on the wings. [*Junonia coenia*.] **3** (**Buckeye**) US informal a native of the state of Ohio.

**buck fever** ● n. N. Amer. nervousness felt by novice hunters on first sighting game.

**buckhorn** ● n. horn of a deer used for knife handles and rifle sights.

**buckjump** Austral./NZ ● v. (of a horse) jump vertically with its head lowered, back arched, and legs drawn together. ● n. an act of buckjumping.
– DERIVATIVES **buckjumper** n.

**buckle** ● n. a flat rectangular or oval frame with a hinged pin, used for joining the ends of a belt or strap. ● v. **1** fasten or decorate with a buckle. **2** bend and give way under pressure. **3** (**buckle down**) tackle a task with determination.
– ORIGIN ME: from OFr. *bocle*, from L. *buccula* 'cheek strap of a helmet', from *bucca* 'cheek'; sense 2 is from Fr. *boucler* 'to bulge'.

**buckler** ● n. historical a small round shield held by a handle or worn on the forearm.
– ORIGIN ME: from OFr. (*escu*) *bocler*, lit. '(shield) with a boss', from *bocle* (see **BUCKLE**).

**buckler fern** ● n. a fern with deeply divided lobes and stalks covered with brown scales. [*Dryopteris dilatata* and other species.]

**Buckley's** ● n. (in phr. **have Buckley's chance**) Austral./NZ informal have little or no chance.
– ORIGIN C19: of uncertain origin.

**buckling** ● n. a smoked herring.
– ORIGIN C20: from Ger. *Bückling* 'bloater'.

**buckminsterfullerene** /ˌbʌkmɪnstəˈfʊləriːn/ ● n. Chemistry a form of carbon having molecules of 60 atoms arranged in a polyhedron resembling a geodesic sphere. See also **FULLERENE**.
– ORIGIN 1980s: named after the Amer. designer and architect Richard *Buckminster Fuller*.

**buck naked** ● adj. informal, chiefly N. Amer. completely naked.

**bucko** ● n. (pl. **-oes** or **-os**) informal, chiefly Irish a young man.

**buckra** /ˈbʌkrə/ ● n. (pl. same or **buckras**) US & W. Indian informal, chiefly derogatory a white man.
– ORIGIN C18: from Ibibio and Efik (*m*)*bakara* 'European, master'.

**buckram** /ˈbʌkrəm/ ● n. coarse linen or other cloth stiffened with paste, used as interfacing and in bookbinding.
– PHRASES **men in buckram** archaic non-existent people. [with allusion to Shakespeare's *1 Henry IV* II. iv. 210–50.]
– ORIGIN ME: from OFr. *boquerant*, perh. from *Bukhoro*, a city in Uzbekistan.

**Bucks** ● abbrev. Buckinghamshire.

**Buck's Fizz** ● n. Brit. champagne or sparkling white wine mixed with orange juice as a cocktail.
– ORIGIN 1930s: from the name *Buck's Club*, in London, and **FIZZ**.

**buckshee** /bʌkˈʃiː, ˈbʌkʃiː/ ● adj. informal, chiefly Brit. free of charge.
– ORIGIN First World War: alt. of **BAKSHEESH**.

**buckshot** ● n. coarse lead shot used in shotgun shells.

**buckskin** ● n. **1** the skin of a male deer. ➤ (**buckskins**) clothes or shoes made from buckskin. **2** thick smooth cotton or woollen fabric. **3** N. Amer. a horse of a greyish-yellow colour.
– DERIVATIVES **buckskinned** adj.

**buckthorn** ● n. a thorny shrub or small tree which bears black berries, some of which have been used medicinally as purgatives. [*Rhamnus cathartica* and other species.]

**buck-tooth** ● n. an upper tooth that projects over the lower lip.
– DERIVATIVES **buck-toothed** adj.

**buckwheat** ● n. an Asian plant of the dock family, producing starchy seeds used for fodder or milled into flour. [*Fagopyrum esculentum*.]
– ORIGIN C16: from MDu. *boecweite* 'beech wheat', its grains being shaped like beechmast.

**buckyballs** ● pl. n. Chemistry, informal spherical molecules of a fullerene, especially buckminsterfullerene.

**buckytubes** ● pl. n. Chemistry, informal cylindrical molecules of a fullerene.

**bucolic** /bjuːˈkɒlɪk/ ● adj. of or relating to rural or pastoral life. ● n. a pastoral poem.
– DERIVATIVES **bucolically** adv.
– ORIGIN C16: via L. from Gk *boukolikos*, from *boukolos* 'herdsman', from *bous* 'ox'.

**bud**[1] ● n. **1** a compact knob-like growth on a plant which develops into a leaf, flower, or shoot. **2** Biology an outgrowth from an organism that separates to form a new individual asexually. **3** Zoology a rudimentary leg or other appendage of an animal which has not yet grown, or never will grow, to full size. ● v. (**budded**, **budding**) Biology form a bud. ➤ graft a bud of (a plant) on to another plant.
– ORIGIN ME: of unknown origin.

**bud**[2] ● n. N. Amer. informal another term for **BUDDY**.

**Buddhism** /ˈbʊdɪz(ə)m/ ● n. a widespread Asian religion or philosophy, founded by Siddartha Gautama (Buddha; *c*.563–*c*.460 BC) in NE India in the 5th century BC, which teaches that elimination of the self and earthly desires is the route to enlightenment.
– DERIVATIVES **Buddhist** n. & adj. **Buddhistic** adj.

**budding** ● adj. beginning and showing signs of promise.

**buddle** ● n. a shallow container in which ore is washed.
– ORIGIN C16: of unknown origin.

**buddleia** /ˈbʌdlɪə/ ● n. a shrub with clusters of fragrant lilac, white, or yellow flowers. [*Buddleia davidii* (butterfly bush) and other species.]
– ORIGIN mod. L.: named in honour of the Engl. botanist Adam *Buddle* (died 1715).

**buddy** informal, chiefly N. Amer. ● n. (pl. **-ies**) a close friend. ➤ a working companion with whom close cooperation is required. ➤ a person who befriends and helps an Aids sufferer. ● v. (**-ies**, **-ied**) become friendly.
– ORIGIN C19: perh. an alt. of **BROTHER**, or a var. of **BUTTY**[2].

**budge** ● v. **1** [usu. with neg.] make or cause to make the slightest movement. ➤ (**budge up/over**) informal make room for another person by moving. **2** change or cause to change an opinion.
– ORIGIN C16: from Fr. *bouger* 'to stir', based on L. *bullire* 'to boil'.

**budgerigar** ● n. a small gregarious Australian parakeet which is green with a yellow head in the wild, but has been bred in a variety of colours as a pet. [*Melopsittacus undulatus*.]
– ORIGIN C19: of Aborig. origin, perh. an alt. of Kamilaroi *gijirrigaa*.

**budget** ● n. **1** an estimate of income and expenditure for a set period of time. ➤ (**Budget**) a regular estimate of national revenue and expenditure put forward by a finance minister. **2** the amount of money needed or available for a purpose. **3** archaic a quantity of written or printed material. ● v. (**budgeted**, **budgeting**) allow or provide for in a budget. ● adj. inexpensive.
– DERIVATIVES **budgetary** adj.
– ORIGIN ME (in the sense 'a pouch or wallet'): from OFr. *bougette*, dimin. of *bouge*, from L. *bulga*, of Gaulish origin; in the mid 18th cent. the Chancellor of the Exchequer, in presenting his annual statement, was said 'to open the budget'.

**budget account** ● n. Brit. an account with a bank, store, or public utility into which one makes regular payments to cover bills.

**budgie** ● n. (pl. **-ies**) informal term for **BUDGERIGAR**.

**budwood** ● n. lengths of young branches with buds prepared for grafting on to the rootstock of another plant.

**budworm** ● n. a moth caterpillar that is destructive to buds, especially of spruce and other conifers.

**Buerger's disease** /ˈbəːgəz/ ● n. a condition in which there is inflammation and thrombosis in blood vessels, typically in the legs and leading to gangrene.
– ORIGIN C20: named after the Amer. surgeon Leo *Buerger*.

**buff**[1] ● n. **1** a yellowish-beige colour. **2** a dull yellow leather with a velvety surface. **3** a cloth or pad used for polishing. ● v. polish. ➤ give (leather) a velvety finish by removing the surface of the grain. ● adj. (also **buffed**) N. Amer. informal in good physical shape; muscular.
– PHRASES **in the buff** informal naked.
– ORIGIN C16: prob. from Fr. *buffle*, from Ital. *bufalo*, from late L. *bufalus* (see **BUFFALO**).

**buff**[2] ● n. informal a person who is interested in and very knowledgeable about a particular subject.
– ORIGIN C20: from **BUFF**[1], orig. applied to fire-watchers, because of the buff uniforms worn by New York firemen.

**buffalo** ● n. (pl. same or **-oes**) **1** a heavily built wild ox with backswept horns. [*Synceros caffer* (sub-Saharan Africa) and genus *Bubalus* (India and SE Asia, four species).] **2** the North American bison. ● v. (**-oes**, **-oed**) N. Amer. informal overawe; intimidate. ➤ baffle.
– ORIGIN C16: prob. from Port. *bufalo*, from late L. *bufalus*, from earlier *bubalus*, from Gk *boubalos* 'antelope, wild ox'.

**buffalo fish** ● n. a large greyish-olive North American freshwater fish with thick lips. [Genus *Ictiobus*: several species.]

**buffalo grass** ● n. **1** a creeping grass of the North American plains. [*Buchloe dactyloides*.] **2** a grass of Australia and New Zealand. [*Stenotaphrum secundatum*.]

**Buffalo wings** ● pl. n. N. Amer. deep-fried chicken wings in a spicy sauce, served with blue cheese dressing.

**buffer**[1] ● n. **1** (**buffers**) Brit. a pair of shock-absorbing pistons projecting from a cross-beam at the end of a railway track or on a railway vehicle. **2** a person or thing that reduces a shock or forms a barrier between adversaries. **3** (also **buffer solution**) Chemistry a solution which resists changes in pH when acid or alkali is added to it. **4** Computing a temporary memory area or queue used when creating or editing text, or when transferring data. ● v. **1** lessen or moderate the impact of. **2** treat with a chemical buffer.
– ORIGIN C19: prob. from obs. *buff* (v.), imitative of the sound of a blow to a soft body.

**buffer**[2] ● n. Brit. informal an unworldly or incompetent elderly man.
– ORIGIN C18: prob. from obs. *buff* (see **BUFFER**[1]), or from dial. *buff* 'stutter, splutter'.

**buffer stock** ● n. a reserve of a commodity that can be used to offset price fluctuations.

**buffet**[1] /ˈbʊfeɪ, ˈbʌfeɪ/ ● n. **1** a meal consisting of several dishes from which guests serve themselves. **2** a room or counter in a station, hotel, etc. selling light meals or snacks. ➤ (also **buffet car**) Brit. a railway carriage selling light meals or snacks. **3** /also ˈbʌfɪt/ a piece of dining-room furniture with cupboards and open shelves for crockery.
– ORIGIN C18: from Fr., from OFr. *bufet* 'stool'.

**buffet**[2] /ˈbʌfɪt/ ● v. (**buffeted**, **buffeting**) (especially of wind or waves) strike repeatedly and violently. ● n. **1** dated a blow. **2** Aeronautics another term for **BUFFETING**.
– ORIGIN ME: from OFr. *buffeter* (v.), *buffet* (n.), dimin. of *bufe* 'a blow'.

**buffet**[3] /ˈbʌfɪt/ ● n. Scottish & N. English a low stool or hassock.
– ORIGIN ME: from OFr. *bufet*, of unknown origin.

**buffeting** ● n. Aeronautics irregular oscillation of part of an aircraft, caused by turbulence.

**bufflehead** /ˈbʌf(ə)lhɛd/ ● n. a small diving duck related to the goldeneye, with a large puffy head. [*Bucephala albeola*.]
– ORIGIN C17 (in the sense 'simpleton'): from obs. *buffle* 'buffalo' + **HEAD**.

**buffo** /ˈbʊfəʊ/ ● n. (pl. **-os**) a comic part or actor in Italian opera. ● adj. of or typical of Italian comic opera.
– ORIGIN C18: Ital., 'puff of wind, buffoon'.

**buffoon** /bəˈfuːn/ ● n. a ridiculous but amusing person.
– DERIVATIVES **buffoonery** n. **buffoonish** adj.
– ORIGIN C16: from Fr. *bouffon*, from Ital. *buffone*, from med. L. *buffo* 'clown'.

**bug** ● n. **1** Entomology an insect of a large order having piercing and sucking mouthparts, including aphids, leafhoppers, cicadas, and many other insects. [Order Hemiptera.] ➤ informal any small insect. **2** informal a harmful micro-organism. ➤ an illness caused by a micro-organism. **3** informal an enthusiasm for something: *they caught the sailing bug*. **4** a concealed miniature microphone as used for secret recording. **5** an error in a computer program or system. ● v. (**bugged**, **bugging**) **1** conceal a miniature microphone in. **2** informal annoy; bother. **3** (**bug off**) N. Amer. informal go away. **4** (**bug out**) N. Amer. informal leave quickly. **5** (**bug out**) N. Amer. informal bulge outwards.
– ORIGIN C17: of unknown origin.

**bugaboo** /ˈbʌgəbuː/ ● n. chiefly N. Amer. an object of fear.
– ORIGIN C18: prob. of Celtic origin and rel. to Welsh *bwci bo* 'bogey, the Devil', *bwci* 'hobgoblin' and Cornish *bucca*.

**bugbane** ● n. a tall plant with spikes of cream or yellow flowers and fern-like leaves, formerly used to drive away bedbugs. [*Cimifuga foetida* and related species.]

**bugbear** ● n. a cause of obsessive fear or anxiety. ➤ archaic an imaginary being invoked to frighten children.
– ORIGIN C16: prob. from obs. *bug* 'bogey' (of unknown origin) + **BEAR**[2].

**bug-eyed** ● adj. & adv. with bulging eyes.

**bugger** vulgar slang, chiefly Brit. ● n. **1** derogatory a person who commits buggery. **2** a contemptible or pitied person. ➤ an annoyingly awkward thing. ● v. **1** practise buggery with. **2** cause serious harm or trouble to. ➤ (**bugger about/around**) act stupidly or carelessly. **3** (**bugger off**) go away. ● exclam. used to express annoyance.
– PHRASES **bugger all** nothing.
– ORIGIN ME (orig. denoting a heretic): from MDu., from OFr. *bougre* 'heretic', from med. L. *Bulgarus* 'Bulgarian', particularly one belonging to the Orthodox Church.

**buggery** ● n. anal intercourse.

**Buggins's turn** ● n. Brit. informal a system by which appointments or awards are made in rotation rather than by merit.
– ORIGIN C20: from *Buggins*, used to represent a typical surname.

**buggy**[1] ● n. (pl. **-ies**) **1** a small motor vehicle with an open top. **2** a baby buggy. **3** historical a light horse-drawn vehicle for one or two people.
– ORIGIN C18: of unknown origin.

**buggy**[2] ● adj. (**-ier**, **-iest**) **1** infested with bugs. **2** N. Amer. informal mad.

**bughouse** ● n. informal, chiefly N. Amer. a mental hospital.

**bugle**[1] ● n. (also **bugle-horn**) a brass instrument like a small trumpet, traditionally used for military signals. ● v. sound a bugle.
– DERIVATIVES **bugler** n.
– ORIGIN ME (in the sense 'wild ox'): via OFr. from L. *buculus*, dimin. of *bos* 'ox'; hence *bugle-horn*, denoting the horn of an ox used to give signals.

**bugle**[2] ● n. a creeping plant with blue flowers on upright stems. [*Ajuga reptans* and other species.]
– ORIGIN ME: from late L. *bugula*.

**bugle**[3] ● n. an ornamental tube-shaped bead on clothing.
– ORIGIN C16: of unknown origin.

**bugleweed** ● n. North American term for **BUGLE**[2].

**bugloss** /ˈbjuːglɒs/ ● n. a bristly plant of the borage family, with bright blue flowers. [*Anchusa arvensis* and other species.]
– ORIGIN ME: from OFr. *buglosse* or L. *buglossus*, from Gk *bouglōssos* 'ox-tongued', from *bous* 'ox' + *glōssa* 'tongue'.

**buhl** /buːl/ ● n. variant spelling of **BOULLE**.

**build** ● v. (past and past part. **built**) **1** construct by putting parts or materials together. ➤ (**build something in/into**) incorporate something as a permanent part of. **2** increase in size or intensity over time. ➤ (**build on**) use as a basis for further development. ● n. the proportions of a person's or animal's body. ➤ the style or form of construction of something.
– DERIVATIVES **builder** n.
– ORIGIN OE *byldan*, from *bold*, *botl* 'dwelling', of Gmc origin; rel. to **BOWER**[1].

**building** ● n. **1** a structure with a roof and walls. **2** the process or trade of building houses and other structures.

**building society** ● n. Brit. a financial organization which pays interest on members' investments and lends capital for mortgages.

**build-up** ● n. **1** a gradual accumulation or increase. **2** a period of excitement and preparation before a significant event.

**built** past and past participle of **BUILD**. ● adj. of a specified physical build: *a slightly built woman.*

**built-in** ● adj. forming an integral part of a structure. ➤ inherent; innate.

**built-up** ● adj. **1** (of an area) densely covered by buildings. **2** increased in height by the addition of parts.

**bulb** ● n. **1** a rounded underground storage organ present in lilies and some other plants, consisting of a short stem surrounded by fleshy leaf bases and lying dormant over winter. **2** short for **LIGHT BULB**. **3** an expanded or rounded part at the end of something. **4** a hollow container from which air can be expelled by squeezing, used to fill a syringe, pipette, etc.
– ORIGIN ME: via L. from Gk *bolbos* 'onion, bulbous root'.

**bulbil** /'bʌlbɪl/ ● n. Botany a small bulb-like structure, especially in the axil of a leaf, which may fall to form a new plant.
– ORIGIN C19: from mod. L. *bulbillus*, dimin. of *bulbus* 'onion, bulbous root'.

**bulbous** ● adj. **1** round or bulging in shape. **2** (of a plant) growing from a bulb.

**bulbul** /'bʊlbʊl/ ● n. a tropical African and Asian songbird, typically with drab plumage. [Family Pycnonotidae: numerous species.]
– ORIGIN C17: from Pers., of imitative origin.

**Bulgar** /'bʌlgɑː/ ● n. a member of a Slavic people who settled in what is now Bulgaria in the 7th century.
– ORIGIN from med. L. *Bulgarus*, from Old Church Slavonic *Blŭgarinŭ*.

**Bulgarian** ● n. **1** a native or national of Bulgaria. **2** the Southern Slavic language spoken in Bulgaria. ● adj. of or relating to Bulgaria, its people, or their language.

**bulgar wheat** /'bʌlgə/ (also **bulgur wheat**) ● n. a cereal food made from whole wheat partially boiled then dried.
– ORIGIN 1930s: from Turk. *bulgur* 'bruised grain'.

**bulge** ● n. **1** a rounded swelling distorting a flat surface. **2** Military a piece of land projecting outwards from an otherwise regular line. **3** informal a temporary increase. ● v. swell or protrude to an unnatural extent. ➤ be full of and distended with.
– DERIVATIVES **bulging** adj. **bulgingly** adv. **bulgy** adj.
– ORIGIN ME (in the sense 'wallet or bag'): from OFr. *boulge*, from L. *bulga* (see **BUDGET**).

**bulimarexia** /bjʊˌlɪmə'rɛksɪə, bʊ-/ ● n. chiefly US another term for **BULIMIA**.
– DERIVATIVES **bulimarexic** adj. & n.

**bulimia** /bjʊ'lɪmɪə, bʊ-/ (also **bulimia nervosa**) ● n. an emotional disorder characterized by bouts of overeating, typically alternating with fasting or self-induced vomiting or purging.
– DERIVATIVES **bulimic** adj. & n.
– ORIGIN ME (as *bolisme*, later *bulimy*): mod. L., or from med. L. *bolismos*, from Gk *boulimia* 'ravenous hunger', from *bous* 'ox' + *limos* 'hunger'.

**bulk** ● n. **1** the mass or magnitude of something large. ➤ a large mass or shape. ➤ [as modifier] large in quantity: *bulk supplier.* **2** the greater part. **3** roughage in food. **4** cargo in an unpackaged mass. ● v. **1** be of great size or importance. **2** treat (a product) so that its quantity appears greater than it is. **3** combine (shares or commodities for sale).
– PHRASES **in bulk 1** (of goods) in large quantities. **2** (of a cargo or commodity) not packaged.
– ORIGIN ME: prob. from ON *búlki* 'cargo'; perh. also by alt. of obs. *bouk* 'belly, body'.

**bulk carrier** ● n. a ship that carries non-liquid cargoes in bulk.

**bulker** ● n. a bulk carrier.

**bulkhead** ● n. a barrier between separate compartments inside a ship, aircraft, etc.
– ORIGIN C15: from ON *bálkr* 'partition' + **HEAD**.

**bulk modulus** ● n. Physics the relative change in the volume of a body produced by a unit compressive or tensile stress acting uniformly over its surface.

**bulky** ● adj. (**-ier**, **-iest**) large and unwieldy.
– DERIVATIVES **bulkily** adv. **bulkiness** n.

**bull**[1] ● n. **1** an uncastrated male bovine animal. **2** a large male animal, e.g. a whale or elephant. **3** Brit. a bullseye. **4** Stock Exchange a person who buys shares hoping to sell them at a higher price later. Often contrasted with **BEAR**[2]. ● v. **1** informal move powerfully or violently. **2** (**be bulling**) (of a cow) be on heat.
– PHRASES **like a bull at a gate** acting hastily and without thought. **like a bull in a china shop** behaving clumsily in a delicate situation. **take the bull by the horns** deal decisively with a difficult or unpleasant situation.
– ORIGIN OE *bula*, from ON *boli*; cf. **BULLOCK**.

**bull**[2] ● n. a papal edict.
– ORIGIN ME: from OFr. *bulle*, from L. *bulla* 'bubble, rounded object' (in med. L. 'seal or sealed document').

**bull**[3] ● n. informal nonsense.
– ORIGIN C17: of unknown origin.

**bulla** /'bʊlə/ ● n. (pl. **bullae** /'bʊliː/) **1** Medicine a large blister or other cavity containing fluid or air. **2** Anatomy a rounded prominence. **3** a round seal attached to a papal bull.
– DERIVATIVES **bullate** adj. (Botany). **bullous** adj. (Medicine).
– ORIGIN L., lit. 'bubble'.

**bullace** /'bʊlɪs/ ● n. a thorny shrub with small purple-black fruits, of which the damson is a cultivated form. [*Prunus insititia*.]
– ORIGIN ME: from OFr. *buloce* 'sloe': of unknown origin.

**bull ant** ● n. another term for **BULLDOG ANT**.

**bull bar** ● n. a strong metal grille fitted to the front of a motor vehicle to protect against impact damage.

**bulldog** ● n. **1** a dog of a sturdy breed with a powerful protruding lower jaw, a flat wrinkled face, and a broad chest. **2** informal (at Oxford and Cambridge Universities) a proctor's assistant. ● v. (**-dogged**, **-dogging**) N. Amer. wrestle (a steer) to the ground by holding its horns and twisting its neck.
– DERIVATIVES **bulldogger** n.

**bulldog ant** ● n. a large Australian ant with large jaws and a powerful sting. [Genus *Myrmecia*.]

**bulldog bat** ● n. a long-legged fish-eating bat native to Central and South America. [*Noctilio leporinus*.]

**bulldog bond** ● n. a sterling bond issued on the UK market by a foreign borrower.

**bulldog clip** ● n. Brit. trademark a sprung metal device with two flat plates that close to hold papers together.

**bulldoze** ● v. **1** clear or destroy with a bulldozer. **2** informal intimidate or coerce.
– ORIGIN C19: from **BULL**[1] + *-doze*, alt. of the noun **DOSE**.

**bulldozer** ● n. a powerful tractor with caterpillar tracks and a broad curved blade at the front for clearing ground.

**bullet** ● n. **1** a projectile fired from a small firearm, typically metal, cylindrical and pointed. **2** (**the bullet**) informal dismissal from employment. **3** Printing a small solid circle printed before each in a list of items.
– ORIGIN C16: from Fr. *boulet*, *boulette* 'small ball', dimin. of *boule*, from L. *bulla* 'bubble'.

**bulletin** ● n. a short official statement or summary of news. ➤ a regular newsletter or report.
– ORIGIN C17: from Fr., from Ital. *bullettino*, dimin. of

*bulletta* 'passport', dimin. of *bulla* 'seal, bull'.

**bulletin board** ● n. 1 N. Amer. a noticeboard. 2 Computing a computer-based system, typically dedicated to a topic, by which users can read or download files supplied by others and add their own files.

**bullet train** ● n. a Japanese high-speed passenger train.

**bull fiddle** ● n. informal, chiefly US a double bass.

**bullfighting** ● n. the sport of baiting and killing a bull as a public spectacle.
– DERIVATIVES **bullfight** n. **bullfighter** n.

**bullfinch** ● n. a stocky finch with mainly grey and black plumage and a white rump, of which the male has a pink breast. [*Pyrrhula pyrrhula* and other species.]

**bullfrog** ● n. a very large frog with a deep booming croak. [*Rana catesbiana* (N. America) and other species elsewhere.]

**bullhead** ● n. 1 a small, mainly freshwater fish with a broad flattened head and spiny fins. [*Cottus gobio* (miller's thumb) and other species.] 2 an American freshwater catfish. [*Ictalurus nebulosus* and related species.]

**bullheaded** ● adj. determined and obstinate.
– DERIVATIVES **bullheadedly** adv. **bullheadedness** n.

**bullhorn** ● n. chiefly N. Amer. a megaphone.

**bullion** ● n. gold or silver in bulk before coining, or valued by weight.
– ORIGIN ME: from Anglo-Norman Fr., in the sense 'a mint', var. of OFr. *bouillon*, based on L. *bullire* 'to boil'.

**bullish** ● adj. 1 aggressively confident and self-assertive. 2 Stock Exchange characterized or influenced by rising share prices.
– DERIVATIVES **bullishly** adv. **bullishness** n.

**bull market** ● n. Stock Exchange a market in which share prices are rising.

**bull-nose** ● n. technical a surface or object having a rounded end.
– DERIVATIVES **bull-nosed** adj.

**bullock** ● n. a castrated male bovine animal raised for beef. ● v. Austral./NZ informal work very hard.
– ORIGIN OE *bulluc*, dimin. of *bula* (see **BULL**[1]).

**bullocky** ● n. (pl. **-ies**) Austral./NZ informal a bullock driver.

**bullpen** ● n. chiefly N. Amer. 1 an exercise area for baseball pitchers. 2 a large cell in which prisoners are held before a court hearing.

**bullring** ● n. an arena where bullfights are held.

**bullrush** ● n. variant spelling of **BULRUSH**.

**bullseye** ● n. 1 the centre of the target in sports such as archery and darts. 2 a large, hard peppermint-flavoured sweet. 3 dated a thick disc of glass forming a small window in a ship or the glass of a lamp.

**bullshit** vulgar slang ● n. nonsense. ● v. (**-shitted**, **-shitting**) talk nonsense in an attempt to deceive.
– DERIVATIVES **bullshitter** n.

**bull snake** ● n. a large constricting snake of North American plains. [*Pituophis catenifer sayi*.]

**bull terrier** ● n. a dog that is a cross-breed of bulldog and terrier.

**bull trout** ● n. a North American trout of cold rivers and lakes. [*Salvelinus confluentus*.]

**bully**[1] ● n. (pl. **-ies**) a person who deliberately intimidates or persecutes those who are weaker. ● v. (**-ies**, **-ied**) intimidate.
– ORIGIN C16 (orig. as a term of endearment, then a form of address to a male friend): prob. from MDu. *boele* 'lover'.

**bully**[2] ● adj. informal, chiefly N. Amer. excellent.
– PHRASES **bully for you!** (or **him** etc.) often ironic an expression of admiration or approval.
– ORIGIN C16 (orig. meaning 'admirable, gallant, jolly'): from **BULLY**[1].

**bully**[3] ● n. (pl. **-ies**) (also **bully off**) the start of play in field hockey, in which two opponents strike each other's sticks three times and then go for the ball. ● v. (**-ies**, **-ied**) start play in this way.
– ORIGIN C19: of unknown origin.

**bully**[4] (also **bully beef**) ● n. informal corned beef.
– ORIGIN C18: alt. of **BOUILLI**.

**bullyrag** (also **ballyrag**) ● v. (**-ragged**, **-ragging**) N. Amer. informal treat in a scolding or intimidating way.
– ORIGIN C18: of unknown origin.

**bulrush** (also **bullrush**) ● n. a reed mace, clubrush, or similar waterside plant.
– ORIGIN ME: prob. from **BULL**[1] meaning 'large, coarse'.

**bulwark** /ˈbʊlwək/ ● n. 1 a defensive wall. 2 an extension of a ship's sides above deck level.
– ORIGIN ME: from Mid. Low Ger. and MDu. *bolwerk*.

**bum**[1] ● n. Brit. informal a person's buttocks or anus.
– ORIGIN ME: of unknown origin.

**bum**[2] informal ● n. N. Amer. 1 a vagrant. 2 a lazy or worthless person. 3 a devotee of a particular activity: *a ski bum*. ● v. (**bummed**, **bumming**) 1 get by asking or begging. 2 (**bum around**) chiefly N. Amer. pass one's time idly. ● adj. bad; wrong.
– PHRASES **give someone the bum's rush** chiefly N. Amer. forcibly eject someone. **on the bum** N. Amer. vagrant.
– ORIGIN C19: prob. from **BUMMER**.

**bumbag** ● n. Brit. informal a small pouch for valuables on a belt, worn round the hips.

**bum-bailiff** ● n. historical, derogatory a bailiff who collected debts or arrested debtors.
– ORIGIN C17: from **BUM**[1], so named because of the assoc. of an approach from behind.

**bumbershoot** ● n. US informal an umbrella.
– ORIGIN alt. of **UMBRELLA** + **(PARA)CHUTE**.

**bumble** ● v. 1 act or speak in an awkward or confused manner. 2 (of an insect) buzz or hum.
– DERIVATIVES **bumbler** n.
– ORIGIN ME: from **BOOM**[1] + **-LE**[4].

**bumblebee** ● n. a large hairy bee with a loud hum, living in small colonies underground. [Genus *Bombus*: many species.]

**bumf** (also **bumph**) ● n. informal, chiefly Brit. 1 useless or tedious printed information. 2 dated toilet paper.
– ORIGIN C19: abbrev. of sl. *bum-fodder*, in the same sense.

**bumfluff** ● n. Brit. informal the first beard growth of an adolescent.

**bumiputra** /ˌbuːmɪˈpuːtrə/ ● n. (pl. same or **bumiputras**) a Malaysian of indigenous Malay origin.
– ORIGIN Malay, lit. 'son of the soil'.

**bummalo** /ˈbʌmələʊ/ ● n. (pl. same) a small elongated South Asian fish, dried as food. [*Harpodon nehereus*.]
– ORIGIN C17: perh. from Marathi *bombīl*.

**bummer** ● n. informal 1 an annoying or disappointing thing. 2 N. Amer. a vagrant or loafer.
– ORIGIN C19: perh. from Ger. *Bummler*, from *bummeln* 'stroll, loaf about'.

**bump** ● n. 1 a light blow or a jolting collision. ➤ Rowing (in races where boats make a spaced start one behind another) the point at which a boat begins to overtake or touch the boat ahead, thereby defeating it. 2 a protuberance on a level surface. ➤ a lump on a person's skull, formerly thought to indicate a particular mental faculty. 3 Aeronautics a rising air current causing an irregularity in an aircraft's motion. ● v. 1 knock or run into with a jolt. ➤ (**bump into**) meet by chance. ➤ Rowing gain a bump against. 2 move or cause to move with much jolting. 3 (**bump someone off**) informal murder someone. 4 (**bump something up**) informal make something larger or appear to be larger. 5 refuse (a passenger) a reserved place on a flight because of deliberate overbooking by the airline. 6 N. Amer. displace from a job or position.
– DERIVATIVES **bumpily** adv. **bumpiness** n. **bumpy** adj. (**-ier**, **-iest**).
– ORIGIN C16 (as v.): imitative, perh. of Scand. origin.

**bumper** ● n. 1 a horizontal bar across the front or back of a motor vehicle to reduce damage in a collision. 2 (also **bumper race**) Horse Racing a flat race for inexperienced horses intended for future steeplechases. 3 archaic a generous glass of an alcoholic drink. 4 Austral. informal a cigarette butt. ● adj. exceptionally large or successful.
– PHRASES **bumper-to-bumper** very close together.

**bumper car** ● n. a dodgem.

**bumph** ● n. variant spelling of **BUMF**.

**bumpkin** ● n. an unsophisticated country person.
– DERIVATIVES **bumpkinish** adj.
– ORIGIN C16: perh. from Du. *boomken* 'little tree' or MDu. *bommekijn* 'little barrel', denoting a dumpy person.

**bump-start** • **n. & v.** another term for **PUSH-START**.

**bumptious** • **adj.** irritatingly self-assertive or proud.
– DERIVATIVES **bumptiously** adv. **bumptiousness** n.
– ORIGIN C19: from **BUMP**, on the pattern of *fractious*.

**bum rap** • **n.** informal, chiefly N. Amer. a false charge leading to imprisonment.

**bum-rush** • **v.** US informal force or barge one's way into.

**bum steer** • **n.** N. Amer. informal a piece of false information.

**bun** • **n. 1** a small cake or bread roll. **2** a hairstyle in which the hair is drawn into a tight coil at the back of the head. **3** (**buns**) N. Amer. informal a person's buttocks.
– PHRASES **have a bun in the oven** informal be pregnant.
– ORIGIN ME: of unknown origin.

**bunch** • **n. 1** a number of things growing or fastened together. ➤informal a group of people. ➤informal, chiefly N. Amer. a lot. **2** (**bunches**) a hairstyle in which the hair is tied back into two clumps. • **v.** collect, form, or fasten into a bunch.
– PHRASES **bunch of fives** Brit. informal a punch.
– DERIVATIVES **bunchy** adj.
– ORIGIN ME: of unknown origin.

**bunch grass** • **n.** a grass that grows in clumps, especially on the North American plains. [*Schizachyrium scoparium* and other species.]

**bunco** N. Amer. informal • **n.** (pl. **-os**) a swindle or confidence trick. • **v.** (**-oes, -oed**) dated swindle or cheat.
– ORIGIN C19: perh. from Sp. *banca*, a card game.

**buncombe** • **n.** variant spelling of **BUNKUM**.

**bund** • **n.** (in India and Pakistan) an embankment or causeway.
– ORIGIN C19: via Urdu from Pers.

**bundle** • **n. 1** a collection of things or quantity of material tied or wrapped up together. ➤a set of nerve, muscle, or other fibres running in parallel close together. **2** informal a large amount of money. • **v. 1** tie or roll up in or as if in a bundle. **2** (usu. **be bundled up**) dress in many warm clothes. **3** informal push or carry forcibly. ➤(of a group) move in a disorganized way. **4** sleep fully clothed with another person, as a former local custom during courtship.
– PHRASES **a bundle of fun** (or **laughs**) informal, often ironic something extremely amusing or pleasant. **drop one's bundle** Austral./NZ informal go to pieces. **go a bundle on** [usu. with neg.] Brit. informal be very keen on.
– DERIVATIVES **bundler** n.
– ORIGIN ME: perh. orig. from OE *byndelle* 'a binding', reinforced by Low Ger. and Du. *bundel*.

**bundu** /'bʊndu:/ • **n.** S. African a distant or wilderness region.
– ORIGIN prob. from Shona *bundo* 'grasslands'.

**bunfight** • **n.** Brit. informal, humorous a grand or official tea party or other function.

**bung**[1] • **n.** a stopper for a hole in a container. • **v.** close with a bung. ➤(**bung something up**) block something up.
– ORIGIN ME: from MDu. *bonghe* (n.).

**bung**[2] Brit. informal • **v.** put or throw somewhere carelessly or casually. • **n.** a bribe.
– ORIGIN C19: symbolic; the noun sense dates from the 1950s.

**bung**[3] • **adj.** Austral./NZ informal dead, ruined, or useless.
– PHRASES **go bung** fail completely or die.
– ORIGIN C19 (orig. Austral. pidgin): from Yagara (an extinct Aborig. lang.).

**bungalow** /'bʌŋgələʊ/ • **n.** a house with only one main storey.
– ORIGIN C17: from Hindi *baṅglā* 'belonging to Bengal'.

**bungee** /'bʌndʒi/ • **n.** (also **bungee cord** or **rope**) a long nylon-cased rubber band used for securing luggage and in the sport of bungee jumping.
– ORIGIN 1930s: of unknown origin.

**bungee jumping** • **n.** the sport of leaping from a high place, secured by a bungee around the ankles.
– DERIVATIVES **bungee jump** n. **bungee jumper** n.

**bunghole** • **n.** a hole through which a cask can be filled or emptied.

**bungle** • **v.** carry out (a task) clumsily or incompetently. ➤[as adj. **bungling**] prone to making mistakes. • **n.** a mistake or failure.
– DERIVATIVES **bungler** n.
– ORIGIN C16: of unknown origin; cf. with **BUMBLE**.

**bunion** /'bʌnj(ə)n/ • **n.** a painful swelling on the first joint of the big toe.
– ORIGIN C18: ult. from OFr. *buignon*, from *buigne* 'bump on the head'.

**bunk**[1] • **n.** a narrow shelf-like bed. • **v.** chiefly N. Amer. sleep in a bunk or improvised bed in shared quarters.
– ORIGIN C18: of unknown origin; perh. rel. to **BUNKER**.

**bunk**[2] • **v.** Brit. informal abscond from school or work.
– PHRASES **do a bunk** make a hurried departure.
– ORIGIN C19: of unknown origin.

**bunk**[3] • **n.** informal, dated nonsense.
– ORIGIN C20: abbrev. of **BUNKUM**.

**bunk bed** • **n.** a piece of furniture consisting of two beds, one above the other.

**bunker** • **n. 1** a large container or compartment for storing fuel. **2** a reinforced underground shelter for use in wartime. **3** a hollow filled with sand, used as an obstacle on a golf course. • **v. 1** refuel (a ship). **2** Golf hit (the ball) into a bunker.
– ORIGIN C16 (orig. Scots, denoting a seat or bench): perh. rel. to **BUNK**[1].

**bunkhouse** • **n.** a building with basic sleeping accommodation for workers.

**bunkum** (also **buncombe**) • **n.** informal, dated nonsense.
– ORIGIN C19: named after *Buncombe* County in North Carolina, mentioned in a speech made by its congressman solely to please his constituents.

**bunk-up** • **n.** informal a helping push or pull up.

**bunny** • **n.** (pl. **-ies**) informal **1** a child's term for a rabbit. **2** (also **bunny girl**) a club hostess or waitress wearing a skimpy costume with ears and a tail. **3** Austral. a victim or dupe.
– ORIGIN C17: from dial. *bun* 'squirrel, rabbit'.

**bunny-hop** • **v.** jump forward in a crouched position. • **n.** an act of bunny-hopping.

**Bunsen burner** • **n.** a small adjustable gas burner used in laboratories.
– ORIGIN named after the Ger. chemist R. *Bunsen*.

**bunt**[1] /bʌnt/ • **n.** the baggy centre of a fishing net or a sail.
– ORIGIN C16: of unknown origin.

**bunt**[2] /bʌnt/ • **n.** a disease of wheat caused by a smut fungus, the spores of which smell of rotten fish.
– ORIGIN C17: of unknown origin.

**bunt**[3] /bʌnt/ • **v. 1** Baseball (of a batter) gently tap (a pitched ball) so that it does not roll beyond the infield. **2** butt with the head or horns. • **n.** Baseball an act of bunting a ball.
– ORIGIN C18: prob. rel. to **BUTT**[1].

**buntal** /'bʌnt(ə)l/ • **n.** the straw from a talipot palm used for making hats.
– ORIGIN C20: from Tagalog.

**bunting**[1] • **n.** any of a large group of seed-eating songbirds related to the finches, typically with brown streaked plumage and a boldly marked head. [*Emberiza* and other genera, family Emberizidae: numerous species.]
– ORIGIN ME: of unknown origin.

**bunting**[2] • **n.** flags and other colourful festive decorations.
– ORIGIN C18: of unknown origin.

**buntline** /'bʌntlʌɪn/ • **n.** a line for restraining the loose centre of a sail while it is furled.

**bunya** /'bʌnjə/ (also **bunya bunya** /'bʌnjə,bʌnjə/) • **n.** a tall Australian tree related to the monkey puzzle, bearing large cones containing edible seeds. [*Araucaria bidwillii*.]
– ORIGIN C19: from Wiradhuri (an Aborig. lang.).

**bunyip** /'bʌnjɪp/ • **n.** Austral. **1** a mythical amphibious monster said to inhabit inland waterways. **2** an impostor or pretender.
– ORIGIN from an Aborig. word.

**buoy** /bɔɪ/ ● **n.** an anchored float serving as a navigation mark, to show hazards, or for mooring. ● **v. 1** (usu. **be buoyed up**) keep afloat. **2** cause (a price) to rise to or remain high. **3** mark with a buoy.
– ORIGIN ME: prob. from MDu. *boye, boeie*, from a Gmc base meaning 'signal'.

**buoyancy aid** ● **n.** a sleeveless jacket lined with buoyant material, worn for water sports.

**buoyant** ● **adj. 1** able or tending to keep afloat. **2** cheerful and optimistic. **3** (of an economy or market) engaged in much activity.
– DERIVATIVES **buoyancy** n. **buoyantly** adv.
– ORIGIN C16: from Fr. *bouyant* or Sp. *boyante, boyar* 'to float'.

**BUPA** /'bu:pə/ ● **abbrev.** British United Provident Association, a private health insurance organization.

**BUR** ● **abbrev.** Burma (international vehicle registration).

**bur** ● **n.** see **BURR**.

**burb** ● **n.** N. Amer. informal short for **SUBURB**.

**Burberry** /'bə:b(ə)ri/ ● **n.** (pl. **-ies**) trademark a lightweight belted raincoat.
– ORIGIN C20: from *Burberrys Ltd*, the manufacturer.

**burble** ● **v. 1** make a continuous murmuring noise. **2** speak unintelligibly and at unnecessary length. **3** (of an airflow) break up into turbulence. ● **n.** continuous murmuring noise. ➤rambling speech.
– DERIVATIVES **burbler** n.
– ORIGIN ME (in the sense 'to bubble'): imitative.

**burbot** /'bə:bət/ ● **n.** an elongated bottom-dwelling fish that is the only freshwater member of the cod family. [*Lota lota*.]
– ORIGIN ME: from OFr. *borbete*, prob. from *borbe* 'mud'.

**burden** ● **n. 1** a heavy load. **2** a cause of hardship, worry, or grief. ➤the main responsibility for a task. **3** a ship's carrying capacity. **4** the main theme. ● **v. 1** (usu. **be burdened**) load heavily. **2** cause worry, hardship, or grief.
– PHRASES **burden of proof** the obligation to prove an assertion.
– DERIVATIVES **burdensome** adj.
– ORIGIN OE *byrthen*, of W. Gmc origin; rel. to **BEAR**[1].

**burdock** /'bə:dɒk/ ● **n.** a herbaceous plant of the daisy family, with large leaves and prickly flowers which cling to fur or clothing. [*Arctium pubens* and other species.]

**bureau** /'bjʊərəʊ/ ● **n.** (pl. **bureaux** or **bureaus**) **1** Brit. a writing desk with drawers and an angled top opening downwards to form a writing surface. **2** N. Amer. a chest of drawers. **3** an office for transacting particular business. **4** a government department.
– ORIGIN C17: from Fr., orig. 'baize' (covering writing desks).

**bureaucracy** /ˌbjʊ(ə)'rɒkrəsi/ ● **n.** (pl. **-ies**) **1** a system of government in which most decisions are taken by state officials rather than by elected representatives. ➤a state or organization governed according to such a system. **2** excessively complicated administrative procedure.
– DERIVATIVES **bureaucratization** (also **-isation**) n. **bureaucratize** (also **-ise**) v.
– ORIGIN C19: from Fr. *bureaucratie*, from *bureau* (see **BUREAU**).

**bureaucrat** ● **n.** a government official perceived as being overly concerned with procedural correctness.
– DERIVATIVES **bureaucratic** adj. **bureaucratically** adv.

**bureau de change** /ˌbjʊərəʊ də 'ʃɒ̃ʒ, French byʀo də ʃɑ̃ʒ/ ● **n.** (pl. **bureaux de change** pronunc. same) a place where one can exchange foreign money.
– ORIGIN 1950s: Fr., lit. 'office of exchange'.

**burette** /bjʊ'rɛt/ (US also **buret**) ● **n.** a graduated glass tube with a tap at one end, for delivering known volumes of a liquid.
– ORIGIN C19: from Fr., from *buire* 'jug'.

**burg** /bə:g/ ● **n. 1** an ancient or medieval fortress or walled town. **2** N. Amer. informal a town or city.
– ORIGIN C18: from late L. *burgus* (see **BURGESS**); sense 2 is from Ger. *Burg* 'castle, city' (rel. to **BOROUGH**).

**burgage** /'bə:gɪdʒ/ ● **n.** historical (in England and Scotland) tenure of land in a town held in return for service or annual rent.
– ORIGIN ME: from med. L. *burgagium*, from *burgus* 'fortified town', of Gmc origin.

**burgee** /bə:'dʒi:/ ● **n.** a triangular flag flown from the mast of a yacht to indicate the owner's membership of a particular sailing club.
– ORIGIN C18: perh. from Fr. *bourgeois* (see **BURGESS**) in the sense 'owner, master'.

**burgeon** /'bə:dʒ(ə)n/ ● **v.** [often as adj. **burgeoning**] grow or increase rapidly.
– ORIGIN ME: from OFr. *bourgeonner* 'put out buds', from *borjon* 'bud', based on late L. *burra* 'wool'.

**burger** ● **n.** a hamburger.

**burgess** ● **n. 1** Brit. archaic an inhabitant of a town or borough with full rights of citizenship. **2** Brit. historical a Member of Parliament for a borough, corporate town, or university. **3** (in the US and historically in the UK) a magistrate or member of the governing body of a town.
– ORIGIN ME: from Anglo-Norman Fr. *burgeis*, from late L. *burgus* 'castle, fort' (in med. L. 'fortified town'); rel. to **BOROUGH**.

**burgh** /'bʌrə/ ● **n.** archaic or Scottish a borough or chartered town.
– DERIVATIVES **burghal** /'bə:g(ə)l/ adj.
– ORIGIN ME: Scots form of **BOROUGH**.

**burgher** /'bə:gə/ ● **n. 1** archaic a citizen of a town or city. **2** historical (in southern Africa) a citizen of a Boer Republic. **3** (**Burgher**) a descendant of a Dutch or Portuguese colonist in Sri Lanka.
– ORIGIN ME: from **BURGH**, reinforced by Du. *burger*, from *burg* (see **BOROUGH**).

**burghul** /bə:'gu:l/ ● **n.** another term for **BULGAR WHEAT**.
– ORIGIN from Pers.

**burglar** ● **n.** a person who commits burglary.
– DERIVATIVES **burglarious** /-'glɛ:rɪəs/ adj. (archaic).
– ORIGIN C16: from legal Fr. *burgler* or Anglo-Latin *burgulator, burglator*; rel. to OFr. *burgier* 'pillage'.

**burglarize** (also **-ise**) ● **v.** North American term for **BURGLE**.

**burglary** ● **n.** (pl. **-ies**) illegal entry into a building with intent to commit a crime such as theft.

**burgle** ● **v.** commit burglary in (a building).
– ORIGIN C19: orig. a colloq. back-form. from **BURGLAR**.

**burgomaster** /'bə:gə(ʊ)mɑ:stə/ ● **n.** the mayor of a Dutch, Flemish, German, Austrian, or Swiss town.
– ORIGIN C16: from Du. *burgemeester*, from *burg* (see **BOROUGH**) + *meester* 'master'.

**burgoo** /bə:'gu:/ ● **n. 1** N. Amer. a stew or thick soup, typically one served at a picnic. **2** chiefly Nautical a thick porridge.
– ORIGIN from Arab. *burġul* (see **BURGHUL**).

**burgrave** /'bə:greɪv/ ● **n.** historical the governor or hereditary ruler of a German town or castle.
– ORIGIN C16: from Ger. *Burggraf*, from *Burg* (see **BOROUGH**) + *Graf* 'count, noble'.

**Burgundian** /bə:'gʌndɪən/ ● **n. 1** a native or inhabitant of Burgundy, a region of east central France. **2** a member of a Germanic people that invaded Gaul and established the kingdom of Burgundy in the 5th century AD. ● **adj.** of or relating to Burgundy or the Burgundians.

**burgundy** ● **n.** (pl. **-ies**) **1** a red wine from Burgundy, a region of east central France. **2** a deep red colour.

**burial** ● **n. 1** the burying of a dead body. ➤a funeral. **2** Archaeology a grave or the remains found in it.
– ORIGIN OE *byrgels* 'place of burial, grave', of Gmc origin; rel. to **BURY**.

**burin** /'bjʊərɪn/ ● **n. 1** a hand-held steel tool used for engraving. **2** Archaeology a flint tool with a chisel point.
– ORIGIN C17: from Fr.

**burka** /'bʊəkə/ (also **burkha**) ● **n.** a long, loose garment covering the whole body, worn in public by some Muslim women.
– ORIGIN from Urdu and Pers. *burḳa'*, from Arab. *burḳu'*.

**Burkinan** /bə:'ki:nən/ ● **n.** a native of Burkina Faso, a country in western Africa. ● **adj.** of or relating to this country or its people.

**Burkitt's lymphoma** /'bə:kɪts/ ● **n.** Medicine cancer of the lymphatic system, caused by the Epstein–Barr virus.

– ORIGIN 1960s: named after the Brit. surgeon Denis P. *Burkitt*.

**burl[1]** /bəːl/ ● **n.** **1** a lump in wool or cloth. **2** N. Amer. a rounded knotty growth on a tree.
– ORIGIN ME: from OFr. *bourle* 'tuft of wool', dimin. of *bourre* 'coarse wool', from late L. *burra* 'wool'.

**burl[2]** /bəːl/ ● **n.** Austral./NZ an attempt.
– ORIGIN C20: regional usage of **BIRL**.

**burlap** /ˈbəːlap/ ● **n.** coarse canvas woven from jute or hemp, used for sacking. ➤a similar, lighter material used in dressmaking and furnishing.
– ORIGIN C17: of unknown origin.

**burlesque** /bəːˈlɛsk/ ● **n.** **1** a comically exaggerated imitation, especially in a literary or dramatic work. ➤absurdity. **2** N. Amer. a variety show, typically including striptease. ● **v.** (**burlesques**, **burlesqued**, **burlesquing**) parody.
– DERIVATIVES **burlesquer** n.
– ORIGIN C17: from Fr., from Ital. *burlesco*, from *burla* 'mockery'.

**burly** ● **adj.** (**-ier**, **-iest**) (of a person) large and strong.
– DERIVATIVES **burliness** n.
– ORIGIN ME (in the sense 'dignified, imposing'): prob. from an unrecorded OE word meaning 'stately, fit for the bower' (see **BOWER[1]**, **-LY[1]**).

**Burman** ● **n.** (pl. **Burmans**) & **adj.** another term for **BURMESE**.

**bur-marigold** ● **n.** a plant of the daisy family, with small yellow flowers and barbed fruit which cling to passing animals. [*Bidens frondosa* and other species.]

**Burmese** ● **n.** (pl. same) **1** a member of the largest ethnic group of Burma (now Myanmar) in SE Asia. **2** a native or national of Burma. **3** the Sino-Tibetan official language of Burma. **4** (also **Burmese cat**) a cat of a short-coated breed originating in Asia. ● **adj.** of or relating to Burma, its people, or their language.

**burn[1]** ● **v.** (past and past part. **burned** or chiefly Brit. **burnt**) **1** (of a fire) flame or glow while consuming a fuel. ➤use (a fuel) as a source of heat or energy. **2** be or cause to be harmed or destroyed by fire. ➤(of the skin) become red and painful through exposure to the sun. ➤feel hot as a result of illness, injury, or emotion. **3** (**be burning with**) be entirely possessed by (a desire or emotion). **4** (**burn out**) become exhausted through overwork. **5** informal drive very fast. **6** (**burn someone up**) N. Amer. informal make someone very angry. **7** produce (a CD) by copying from an original or master copy. ● **n.** **1** an injury or area of damage caused by burning. **2** a firing of a rocket engine in flight. **3** N. Amer. & Austral./NZ an act of clearing of vegetation by burning.
– PHRASES **burn one's boats** (or **bridges**) do something which makes turning back impossible. **burn the candle at both ends** go to bed late and get up early. **burn a hole in one's pocket** (of money) tempt one to spend it quickly or extravagantly. **burn the midnight oil** work late into the night. **burn rubber** informal drive very quickly.
– ORIGIN OE *birnan* 'be on fire' and *bærnan* 'consume by fire', both from the same Gmc base.

**burn[2]** ● **n.** Scottish & N. English a small stream.
– ORIGIN OE *burna*, *burn(e)*, of Gmc origin.

**burned** ● **adj.** variant spelling of **BURNT**.

**burner** ● **n.** **1** a part of a cooker, lamp, etc. that emits a flame. **2** an apparatus for burning something.

**burnet** /ˈbəːnɪt/ ● **n.** **1** a plant of the rose family, with globular pinkish flower heads and leaves composed of many small leaflets. [Genus *Sanguisorba*: several species.] **2** a day-flying moth, typically having greenish-black wings with crimson markings. [*Zygaena* and other genera.]
– ORIGIN ME: from OFr. *brunete*, *burnete* (denoting brown cloth or a plant with brown flowers), dimin. of *brun* 'brown'.

**burnet rose** ● **n.** a small wild rose with white flowers and leaves like those of burnet. [*Rosa pimpinellifolia*.]

**burnet saxifrage** ● **n.** a slender white-flowered plant of the parsley family. [*Pimpinella saxifraga*.]

**burning** ● **adj.** **1** very deeply felt. **2** of urgent interest and importance.
– DERIVATIVES **burningly** adv.

**burning bush** ● **n.** **1** a shrub with bright red fruit or autumn foliage. **2** another term for **GAS PLANT**.
– ORIGIN C19: with biblical allusion to Exod. 3:2.

**burning glass** ● **n.** a lens for concentrating the sun's rays on an object so as to set fire to it.

**burnish** ● **v.** [usu. as adj. **burnished**] polish by rubbing. ● **n.** the shine on a polished surface.
– DERIVATIVES **burnisher** n.
– ORIGIN ME: from OFr. *burniss-*, *burnir*, var. of *brunir* 'make brown', from *brun* 'brown'.

**burnous** /bəːˈnuːs/ (US also **burnoose**) ● **n.** a long loose hooded cloak worn by Arabs.
– ORIGIN C16: Fr., from Arab. *burnus*, from Gk *birros* 'cloak'.

**burnout** ● **n.** **1** the reduction of a fuel or substance to nothing. **2** overheating of an electrical device or component. **3** physical or mental collapse.

**burnt** (also **burned**) past and past participle of **BURN[1]**.

**burnt ochre** ● **n.** a deep yellow-brown pigment made by calcining ochre.

**burnt offering** ● **n.** **1** a religious sacrifice burnt on an altar. **2** humorous burnt food.

**bur oak** ● **n.** a North American oak with large fringed acorn cups and wood formerly used in shipbuilding. [*Quercus macrocarpa*.]

**buroo** /bəˈruː/ ● **n.** variant form of **BROO**.

**burp** informal ● **v.** belch. ➤make (a baby) belch after feeding. ● **n.** a belch.
– ORIGIN 1930s: imitative.

**burpee** /ˈbəːpiː/ ● **n.** a squat thrust made from and ending in a standing position.
– ORIGIN 1930s (orig. in *Burpee test*, a test of agility in which a series of burpees were executed rapidly): named after the Amer. psychologist Royal H. *Burpee*.

**burp gun** ● **n.** US informal a lightweight sub-machine gun.

**burr** ● **n.** **1** a whirring sound. ➤a rough pronunciation of the letter *r*, as in some regional accents. **2** (also **bur**) a rough edge left on a metal object by the action of a tool. **3** (also **bur**) a small drill used in woodworking, dentistry, or surgery. **4** a siliceous rock used for millstones. ➤a whetstone. **5** (also **bur**) a prickly seed case or flower head that clings to clothing and animal fur. **6** (also **bur**) [as modifier] denoting wood containing a pattern of dense swirls in the grain. **7** the coronet of a deer's antler. ● **v.** **1** make a whirring sound. ➤speak with a burr. **2** form a rough edge on (metal).
– ORIGIN ME: prob. of Scand. origin; the accent sense is prob. imitative.

**burra** /ˈbʌrə/ ● **adj.** Indian big; important.
– ORIGIN from Hindi *baṛā* 'great, greatest'.

**Burra Din** /ˌbʌrə ˈdɪn/ ● **n.** Indian Christmas.
– ORIGIN from Hindi *baṛā* 'great' and *din* 'day'.

**burrawang** /ˈbʌrəwaŋ/ (also **burrawong**) ● **n.** **1** an Australian cycad with palm-like leaves and a sunken underground trunk. [*Macrozamia spiralis*.] **2** the poisonous nut of this tree, which becomes edible after prolonged soaking.
– ORIGIN C19: from Dharuk.

**bur-reed** ● **n.** an aquatic reed-like plant with rounded flower heads and oily seeds. [Genus *Sparganium*.]

**burrfish** ● **n.** (pl. same or **-fishes**) a porcupine fish with erect spines. [*Chilomycterus schoepfi* (western Atlantic) and related species.]

**burrito** /bʊˈriːtəʊ/ ● **n.** (pl. **-os**) a Mexican dish consisting of a tortilla rolled round a filling of minced beef or beans.
– ORIGIN Latin Amer. Sp., dimin. of Sp. *burro*, lit. 'donkey'.

**burro** /ˈbʊrəʊ/ ● **n.** (pl. **-os**) chiefly US a small donkey used as a pack animal.
– ORIGIN C19: from Sp.

**burrow** ● **n.** a hole or tunnel dug by a small animal as a dwelling. ● **v.** **1** make a burrow. ➤dig into or through something solid. **2** hide underneath or delve into something.

– DERIVATIVES **burrower** n.
– ORIGIN ME: var. of **BOROUGH**.

**bursa** /ˈbəːsə/ ● n. (pl. **bursae** /-siː/ or **bursas**) Anatomy a fluid-filled sac or cavity, especially one countering friction at a joint.
– DERIVATIVES **bursal** adj.
– ORIGIN C19: from med. L., 'bag, purse'.

**bursar** ● n. **1** chiefly Brit. a person who manages the financial affairs of a college or school. **2** Scottish a student holding a bursary.
– ORIGIN ME: from Fr. *boursier* or med. L. *bursarius*, from *bursa* (see **BURSA**).

**bursary** /ˈbəːsəri/ ● n. (pl. **-ies**) chiefly Brit. **1** a grant, especially one awarded to a student. **2** a bursar's room.
– DERIVATIVES **bursarial** /-ˈsɛːrɪəl/ adj. **bursarship** n.

**burse** /bəːs/ ● n. a flat, square, fabric-covered case in which a corporal cloth is carried to and from a church altar.
– ORIGIN C16: from Fr. *bourse* or med. L. *bursa* (see **BOURSE**, **BURSA**).

**bursitis** /bəːˈsʌɪtɪs/ ● n. Medicine inflammation of a bursa, typically in a shoulder joint.

**burst** ● v. (past and past part. **burst**) **1** break or cause to break suddenly and violently apart. **2** be very full: *the wardrobe was bursting with clothes.* ➤(**be bursting with**) feel (an irrepressible emotion or impulse). **3** move or be opened suddenly and forcibly. ➤issue suddenly and uncontrollably. **4** separate (continuous stationery) into single sheets. ● n. **1** an instance or the result of bursting. **2** a sudden brief outbreak of something violent or noisy. **3** a period of continuous effort.
– PHRASES **burst someone's bubble** shatter someone's illusions.
– ORIGIN OE *berstan*, of Gmc origin.

**burster** ● n. **1** Astronomy a cosmic source of powerful short-lived bursts of X-rays or other radiation. **2** informal a violent gale. **3** a machine which bursts continuous stationery.

**bursty** ● adj. informal or technical occurring in bursts.

**burthen** ● n. archaic form of **BURDEN**.
– DERIVATIVES **burthensome** adj.

**burton**[1] ● n. (in phr. **go for a burton**) Brit. informal be ruined, destroyed, or killed.
– ORIGIN Second World War (orig. RAF sl.): perh. referring to *Burton* ale, from Burton-upon-Trent.

**burton**[2] (also **burton-tackle**) ● n. historical a light two-block tackle for hoisting.
– ORIGIN C18: alt. of ME *Breton tackle*, a naut. term in the same sense (see **BRETON**).

**Burundian** /bʊˈrʊndiən/ ● n. a native or inhabitant of Burundi, a country in central Africa. ● adj. of or relating to Burundi or its people.

**bury** ● v. (**-ies**, **-ied**) **1** put or hide underground. ➤place (a dead body) in the earth or a tomb. **2** cause to disappear or become unnoticeable. **3** (**bury oneself**) involve oneself deeply in something.
– PHRASES **bury one's head in the sand** ignore unpleasant realities.
– ORIGIN OE *byrgan*, of W. Gmc origin; rel. to **BORROW** and **BOROUGH**.

**Buryat** /ˈbʊəyat/ ● n. **1** a member of a people living in southern Siberia, Mongolia, and northern China. **2** the language of this people, related to Mongolian. ● adj. of or relating to this people or their language.

**burying beetle** ● n. a black beetle which buries small animal carcasses to provide food for its larvae. [*Nicrophorus* and other genera.]

**bus** ● n. (pl. **buses**; US also **busses**) **1** a large motor vehicle carrying paying passengers on a fixed route. **2** Computing a distinct set of conductors within a computer system, to which pieces of equipment may be connected in parallel. ● v. (**buses** or **busses**, **bused** or **bussed**, **busing** or **bussing**) **1** transport or travel in a bus. ➤N. Amer. transport (a child of one race) to a school where another race is predominant. **2** chiefly N. Amer. clear (dirty crockery) in a restaurant or cafeteria.
– ORIGIN C19: shortening of **OMNIBUS**.

**busbar** /ˈbʌsbɑː/ ● n. a system of electrical conductors in a generating or receiving station into which power is fed for distribution.

**busboy** /ˈbʌsbɔɪ/ ● n. chiefly N. Amer. a man who clears tables in a restaurant or cafe.

**busby** /ˈbʌzbi/ ● n. (pl. **-ies**) a tall fur hat with a cloth flap hanging down on the right-hand side, worn by certain regiments of hussars and artillerymen. ➤popular term for **BEARSKIN** (the cap).
– ORIGIN C18 (denoting a bushy wig): of unknown origin.

**bush**[1] ● n. **1** a shrub or clump of shrubs with stems of moderate length. **2** (**the bush**) (in Australia and Africa) wild or uncultivated country. ➤the vegetation of such a district. ➤[as modifier] chiefly S. African uncivilized; primitive. **3** vulgar slang a woman's pubic hair. **4** historical a bunch of ivy as a vintner's sign. ● v. spread out into a thick clump.
– PHRASES **go bush** Austral. informal run wild.
– ORIGIN ME: from OFr. *bos*, *bosc*, vars of *bois* 'wood', reinforced by ON *buski*, of Gmc origin.

**bush**[2] ● n. Brit. **1** a metal lining for a round hole, especially one in which an axle revolves. **2** a sleeve that protects an electric cable where it passes through a panel.
– ORIGIN C15: from MDu. *busse*.

**bushbaby** ● n. (pl. **-ies**) a small nocturnal tree-dwelling African primate with very large eyes. [Genus *Galago*: several species.]

**bushbuck** ● n. a small antelope with a reddish-brown coat with white markings, found in southern Africa. [*Tragelaphus scriptus*.]
– ORIGIN C19: from **BUSH**[1] + **BUCK**[1], influenced by Du. *bosbok*.

**bush cricket** ● n. a mainly carnivorous insect related to the grasshoppers, with very long antennae. [Family Tettigoniidae: many species.]

**bushed** ● adj. informal **1** exhausted. **2** Austral./NZ lost in the bush. **3** Canadian & Austral./NZ mad.

**bushel** /ˈbʊʃ(ə)l/ (abbrev.: **bu.**) ● n. **1** Brit. a measure of capacity equal to 8 gallons (equivalent to 36.4 litres). **2** US a measure of capacity equal to 64 US pints (equivalent to 35.2 litres).
– DERIVATIVES **bushelful** n. (pl. **-fuls**).
– ORIGIN ME: from OFr. *boissel*, perh. of Gaulish origin.

**bush fire** ● n. a fire in scrub or a forest.

**bushido** /ˈbuːʃɪdəʊ, bʊˈʃiːdəʊ/ ● n. the code of honour and morals of the Japanese samurai.
– ORIGIN Japanese, from *bushi* 'samurai' + *dō* 'way'.

**bushing** ● n. another term for **BUSH**[2].

**bush jacket** ● n. a safari jacket.

**bush lawyer** ● n. Austral./NZ informal a person claiming legal knowledge without the qualifications to do so.

**bush league** N. Amer. ● n. a minor league of a sport, especially baseball. ● adj. (**bush-league**) informal second-rate.
– DERIVATIVES **bush-leaguer** n.

**Bushman** ● n. (pl. **-men**) **1** a member of any of several aboriginal peoples of southern Africa, especially of the Kalahari Desert. **2** old-fashioned term for **SAN** (the languages of these people). **3** (**bushman**) a person who lives or travels in the Australian bush.

**bushmaster** ● n. a very large American pit viper. [*Lachesis muta*.]
– ORIGIN C19: perh. from Du. *bosmeester*, from *bos* 'bush' + *meester* 'master'.

**bush pig** ● n. a wild pig native to the forests and savannahs of Africa and Madagascar. [*Potamochoerus porcus*.]

**bushranger** ● n. **1** US a person living far from civilization. **2** Austral./NZ historical an outlaw living in the bush.

**bush sickness** ● n. a deficiency disease of animals caused by a lack of cobalt in the soil.

**bush telegraph** ● n. a rapid informal network by which information or gossip is spread.

**bushveld** /ˈbʊʃfɛlt, -vɛlt/ ● n. (**the bushveld**) (in South Africa) an area of wild or uncultivated country.

**bushwa** /ˈbʊʃwɑː/ ● n. N. Amer. informal nonsense.
– ORIGIN 1920s: appar. a euphemism for **BULLSHIT**.

**bushwalking** ● n. chiefly Austral./NZ hiking or backpacking.
– DERIVATIVES **bushwalker** n.

**bushwhack** ● v. **1** [often as noun **bushwhacking**] N. Amer. &

Austral./NZ live or travel in the bush. **2** N. Amer. & Austral./NZ work clearing scrub and felling trees. **3** N. Amer. engage in guerrilla warfare; ambush.
– DERIVATIVES **bushwhacker** n.

**bushwhacked** • adj. exhausted.

**bushy**[1] • adj. (**-ier**, **-iest**) **1** growing thickly. **2** covered with bush or bushes.
– DERIVATIVES **bushily** adv. **bushiness** n.

**bushy**[2] • n. (pl. **-ies**) Austral./NZ informal a person who lives in the bush.

**business** • n. **1** a person's regular occupation or trade. ➤work to be done or matters to be attended to. **2** a person's concern. **3** commercial activity. ➤a commercial organization. **4** informal a matter: *the business of trying to find her mother.* **5** Theatre actions other than dialogue in a play. **6** (**the business**) informal an excellent person or thing.
– PHRASES **in business** informal able to begin something. **in the business of** engaged in or prepared to engage in. **like nobody's business** informal extraordinarily. **mind one's own business** refrain from meddling in other people's affairs. **send someone about their business** dated tell someone to go away.
– ORIGIN OE *bisignis* 'anxiety' (see **BUSY**, **-NESS**); the use 'appointed task' dates from ME.

**business card** • n. a small card printed with one's name, occupation, and business address.

**business end** • n. informal the functional part of a tool or device.

**businesslike** • adj. efficient and practical.

**businessman** (or **businesswoman**) • n. (pl. **-men** or **-women**) a person who works in commerce, especially at executive level.

**business park** • n. an area composed of company offices and light industrial premises.

**business process re-engineering** • n. the process of restructuring a company's organization and methods, especially so as to exploit the capabilities of computers.

**business studies** • pl. n. [treated as sing.] the study of economics and management.

**busk**[1] • v. **1** play music in the street for voluntary donations. **2** (**busk it**) informal improvise.
– DERIVATIVES **busker** n.
– ORIGIN C17 (in the naut. sense 'cruise about'): from obs. Fr. *busquer* 'seek'.

**busk**[2] • n. historical a stiffening strip for a corset.
– ORIGIN C16: from Fr. *busc*, from Ital. *busco* 'splinter'.

**buskin** • n. **1** historical a calf-high or knee-high boot. ➤a thick-soled laced boot worn by an ancient Athenian tragic actor to gain height. **2** (**the buskin**) the style or spirit of tragic drama.
– DERIVATIVES **buskined** adj.
– ORIGIN C16: prob. from OFr. *bouzequin*, var. of *brousequin*, from MDu. *broseken*.

**busman** • n. (pl. **-men**) a bus driver.
– PHRASES **a busman's holiday** leisure time spent doing the same thing that one does at work.

**buss** archaic or N. Amer. informal • n. a kiss. • v. kiss.
– ORIGIN C16: alt. of ME *bass* (n. and v.), prob. from Fr. *baiser*, from L. *basiare*.

**bus stop** • n. a regular stopping place on a bus route.

**bust**[1] • n. **1** a woman's breasts. **2** a sculpture of a person's head, shoulders, and chest.
– ORIGIN C17: from Fr. *buste*, from Ital. *busto*, from L. *bustum* 'tomb, sepulchral monument'.

**bust**[2] informal • v. (past and past part. **busted** or **bust**) **1** break, split, or burst. ➤(**bust up**) (of a group or couple) separate. **2** chiefly N. Amer. strike violently. **3** chiefly N. Amer. raid or search (premises). ➤arrest. **4** chiefly US demote (a soldier). • n. **1** a period of economic difficulty or depression. **2** a police raid. **3** a worthless thing. **4** chiefly N. Amer. a violent blow. • adj. **1** damaged; broken. **2** bankrupt.
– ORIGIN C18 (orig. US): var. of **BURST**.

**bustard** /ˈbʌstəd/ • n. a large, heavily built, swift-running bird of open country. [Family Otididae: several species.]
– ORIGIN C15: perh. an Anglo-Norman Fr. blend of OFr. *bistarde* and *oustarde*, both from L. *avis tarda* 'slow bird'.

**bustee** /ˈbʌstiː/ • n. Indian a slum or shanty town.
– ORIGIN from Hindi *bastī* 'dwelling'.

**buster** • n. informal **1** chiefly N. Amer. a form of address to a man or boy. **2** an impressive person or thing. **3** a violent gale.

**bustier** /ˈbʌstɪeɪ, ˈbʊst-/ • n. a close-fitting strapless top for women.
– ORIGIN 1970s: from Fr., from *buste* (see **BUST**[1]).

**bustle**[1] • v. move energetically or noisily. ➤[often as adj. **bustling**] (of a place) be full of activity. • n. excited activity and movement.
– ORIGIN ME: perh. a var. of obs. *buskle*, frequentative of *busk* 'prepare', from ON.

**bustle**[2] • n. historical a pad or frame worn under a skirt to puff it out behind.
– ORIGIN C18: of unknown origin.

**bust-up** • n. informal a serious quarrel or fight.

**busty** • adj. (**-ier**, **-iest**) informal having large breasts.
– DERIVATIVES **bustiness** n.

**busway** • n. a road or section of a road set apart exclusively for buses, typically one equipped with tracks or grooves for guiding them.

**busy** • adj. (**-ier**, **-iest**) **1** having a great deal to do. ➤chiefly N. Amer. (of a telephone line) engaged. **2** excessively detailed or decorated. • v. (**-ies**, **-ied**) (**busy oneself**) keep occupied. • n. (also **bizzy**) (pl. **-ies**) Brit. informal a police officer.
– DERIVATIVES **busily** adv. **busyness** n.
– ORIGIN OE *bisgian* (v.), *bisig* (n.).

**busybody** • n. (pl. **-ies**) a meddling or prying person.

**busy Lizzie** • n. (pl. **-ies**) Brit. an East African plant with abundant red, pink, or white flowers, grown as a house plant. [*Impatiens walleriana*.]

**busywork** • n. chiefly N. Amer. work that keeps a person busy but has little value in itself.

**but**[1] • conj. **1** nevertheless. ➤on the contrary. **2** [with neg. or in questions] other than; otherwise than. **3** [with neg.] archaic without it being the case that. • prep. except; apart from. • adv. **1** only. **2** Austral./NZ & Scottish informal though; however: *he was a nice bloke but.* • n. an objection.
– PHRASES **but for** except for. ➤if it were not for. **but then** on the other hand.
– ORIGIN OE *be-ūtan*, *būtan*, *būta* 'outside, without, except' (see **BY**, **OUT**).

**but**[2] • n. Scottish an outer room, especially in a two-roomed cottage.
– PHRASES **but and ben** see **BEN**[2].
– ORIGIN C18: from **BUT**[1] in the early sense 'outside'.

**butadiene** /ˌbjuːtəˈdʌɪiːn/ • n. Chemistry a gaseous unsaturated hydrocarbon, used in the manufacture of synthetic rubber. [$C_4H_6$.]

**butane** /ˈbjuːteɪn/ • n. Chemistry a flammable hydrocarbon gas of the alkane series, present in petroleum and natural gas and used as a fuel. [$C_4H_{10}$.]
– ORIGIN C19: from **BUTYL** + **-ANE**[2].

**butanoic acid** /ˌbjuːtəˈnəʊɪk/ • n. systematic chemical name for **BUTYRIC ACID**.
– DERIVATIVES **butanoate** n.

**butch** informal • adj. masculine in appearance or behaviour, often aggressively or ostentatiously so. • n. a mannish lesbian.
– ORIGIN 1940s: perh. an abbrev. of **BUTCHER**.

**butcher** • n. **1** a person whose trade is cutting up and selling meat in a shop. ➤a person who slaughters and cuts up animals for food. **2** N. Amer. informal a person selling refreshments, newspapers, etc. on a train or in a theatre. • v. **1** slaughter or cut up (an animal) for food. ➤kill (someone) brutally. **2** ruin deliberately or through incompetence.
– PHRASES **have** (or **take**) **a butcher's** Brit. informal have a look. [*butcher's* from *butcher's hook*, rhyming sl. for a 'look'.]
– DERIVATIVES **butchery** n.
– ORIGIN ME: from an Anglo-Norman Fr. var. of OFr.

*bochier*, from *boc* 'he-goat', prob. of the same ultimate origin as **BUCK**[1].

**butcher-bird** • n. **1** a shrike, so called from its habit of impaling prey on thorns. **2** a crow-like predacious Australasian songbird, with a heavy hook-tipped bill. [Genus *Cracticus*: several species.]

**butcher's broom** • n. a low evergreen shrub, with flat shoots that give the appearance of stiff spine-tipped leaves. [*Ruscus aculeatus*.]

**butcher's meat** (also **butcher meat**) • n. Brit. fresh uncured meat excluding game and poultry.

**Buteyko** /buːˈteɪkəʊ/ • adj. of or denoting a technique of controlled breathing claimed to alleviate asthma.
– ORIGIN 1990s: named after the Russ. physiologist Konstantin *Buteyko*.

**butler** • n. the chief manservant of a house.
– ORIGIN ME: from OFr. *bouteillier* 'cup-bearer', from *bouteille* 'bottle'.

**butt**[1] • v. **1** hit with the head or horns. **2** (**butt in**) interrupt or intrude on a conversation or activity. ➤(**butt out**) N. Amer. informal stop interfering. • n. a rough push with the head.
– ORIGIN ME: from OFr. *boter*, of Gmc origin.

**butt**[2] • n. **1** an object of criticism or ridicule. **2** an archery or shooting target or range. ➤a mound on or in front of which a target is set up for archery or shooting. ➤a grouse-shooter's stand.
– ORIGIN ME: from OFr. *but*, of unknown origin.

**butt**[3] • n. **1** (also **butt-end**) the thicker end of something, especially a tool or a weapon. ➤the square end of a plank or plate meeting the end or side of another. **2** (also **butt-end**) the stub of a cigar or a cigarette. **3** N. Amer. informal a person's bottom. **4** the trunk of a tree, especially the part just above the ground. • v. meet end to end: *the shop butted up against the row of houses.* ➤join (pieces of stone, timber, and other building materials) with the ends or sides flat against each other.
– ORIGIN ME: the noun appar. rel. to Du. *bot* 'stumpy', also to **BUTTOCK**; the verb partly from **BUTT**[2], reinforced by **ABUT**.

**butt**[4] • n. **1** a cask used for wine, ale, or water. **2** US a liquid measure equal to 126 US gallons (equivalent to 477.5 litres).
– ORIGIN ME: from OFr. *bot*, from late L. *buttis*.

**butte** /bjuːt/ • n. N. Amer. & technical an isolated hill with steep sides and a flat top.
– ORIGIN C19: from Fr., 'mound', from OFr. *but* (cf. **BUTT**[2]).

**butter** • n. a pale yellow edible fatty substance made by churning cream and used as a spread or in cooking. • v. **1** spread with butter. **2** (**butter someone up**) informal flatter someone.
– PHRASES **look as if butter wouldn't melt in one's mouth** informal appear innocent while being the opposite.
– ORIGIN OE *butere*, of W. Gmc origin, based on L. *butyrum*, from Gk *bouturon*.

**butter-and-eggs** • n. any of a number of plants having two shades of yellow in the flower, especially toadflax.

**butterball** • n. N. Amer. **1** a plump bird, especially a turkey or bufflehead. **2** informal, derogatory a fat person.

**butter bean** • n. a lima bean, especially one of a variety with large flat white seeds.

**butterbur** /ˈbʌtəbəː/ • n. a waterside plant with pale purple flowers and large soft leaves formerly used to wrap butter. [*Petasites hybridus* and related species.]

**buttercream** • n. a mixture of butter and icing sugar used as a filling or topping for a cake.

**buttercup** • n. a herbaceous plant with bright yellow cup-shaped flowers, common in grassland and as a garden weed. [Genus *Ranunculus*: many species.]

**butterfat** • n. the natural fat contained in milk and dairy products.

**butterfingers** • n. (pl. same) informal a clumsy person, especially one who fails to hold a catch.
– DERIVATIVES **butterfingered** adj.

**butterfish** • n. (pl. same or **-fishes**) any of various fishes with oily flesh or slippery skin, especially the gunnel.

**butterfly** • n. (pl. **-flies**) **1** any of a large group of nectar-feeding lepidopterous insects with two pairs of large, typically colourful wings, distinguished from moths by having clubbed or dilated antennae, holding their wings erect when at rest, and being active by day. **2** [as modifier] having a two-lobed shape resembling the spread wings of a butterfly: *a butterfly clip.* **3** a showy or frivolous person: *a social butterfly.* **4** (**butterflies**) informal a fluttering and nauseous sensation felt in the stomach when one is nervous. **5** a stroke in swimming in which both arms are raised out of the water and lifted forwards together. • v. (**-flies**, **-flied**) split (a piece of meat) almost in two and spread it out flat.
– ORIGIN OE: perh. from the cream or yellow colour of common species, or from a former belief that the insects stole butter.

**butterfly bush** • n. a buddleia cultivated for its large spikes of fragrant purplish-lilac or white flowers. [*Buddleia davidii*.]

**butterfly effect** • n. (with reference to chaos theory) the phenomenon whereby a minute localized change in a complex system can have large effects elsewhere.
– ORIGIN 1980s: from the notion that a butterfly fluttering in Rio de Janeiro could change the weather in Chicago.

**butterfly fish** • n. **1** a brightly coloured reef-dwelling fish popular in marine aquaria. [*Chaetodon* and related genera.] **2** a predatory marine fish with long venomous spines. [Genus *Pterois*.] **3** a West African freshwater fish with large pectoral fins used in leaping out of the water. [*Pantodon buchholzi*.]

**butterfly knife** • n. a long broad knife used in pairs in some forms of kung fu.

**butterfly net** • n. a fine-meshed bag supported on a frame at the end of a handle, used for catching butterflies.

**butterfly nut** • n. another term for **WING NUT**.

**butterfly valve** • n. a valve consisting of a rotating circular plate or a pair of hinged semicircular plates, mounted inside a pipe.

**butterfly weed** • n. a North American milkweed with bright orange flowers. [*Asclepias tuberosa*.]

**butterhead lettuce** • n. a class of lettuce varieties having soft leaves that grow in a loose head and are said to have the flavour of butter.

**butter icing** • n. another term for **BUTTERCREAM**.

**buttermilk** • n. **1** the slightly sour liquid left after butter has been churned, used in baking or consumed as a drink. **2** a pale yellow colour.

**butter muslin** • n. Brit. loosely woven cotton cloth, formerly used for wrapping butter.

**butternut** • n. **1** a North American walnut tree cultivated as an ornamental and also for its quality wood. [*Juglans cinerea*.] **2** the edible oily nut of this tree.

**butternut squash** • n. a winter squash of a pear-shaped variety with light yellowish-brown rind and orange flesh.

**butterscotch** • n. a brittle yellow-brown sweet made with butter and brown sugar.

**butterwort** /ˈbʌtəwəːt/ • n. a carnivorous bog plant with violet flowers and greasy yellowish-green leaves that trap and digest small insects. [Genus *Pinguicula*: several species.]
– ORIGIN C16: named from the plant's supposed ability to keep cows in milk, and so maintain the supply of butter.

**buttery**[1] • adj. containing, tasting like, or covered with butter.
– DERIVATIVES **butteriness** n.

**buttery**[2] • n. (pl. **-ies**) Brit. a room in a college where food is kept and sold to students.
– ORIGIN ME: from Anglo-Norman Fr. *boterie* 'butt-store', from OFr. *bot* (see **BUTT**[4]).

**buttie** • n. (pl. **-ies**) variant spelling of **BUTTY**[1].

**buttle** • v. humorous work as a butler.
– ORIGIN C19: back-form. from **BUTLER**.

**buttock** • n. either of the two round fleshy parts of the human body that form the bottom.
– ORIGIN OE *buttuc*, prob. from the base of **BUTT**[3] + **-OCK**.

**button** ● n. **1** a small disc or knob sewn on to a garment, either to fasten it by being pushed through a buttonhole or for decoration. **2** chiefly N. Amer. a decorative badge pinned to clothing. **3** a knob on a piece of electrical or electronic equipment which is pressed to operate it. **4** Fencing a knob fitted to the point of a foil to make it harmless. ● v. **1** fasten or be fastened with buttons. **2** (**button it**) informal stop talking. **3** (**button something up**) informal complete something satisfactorily.
– PHRASES **button one's lip** informal stop or refrain from talking. **on the button** informal, chiefly N. Amer. precisely. **push** (or **press**) **someone's buttons** informal provoke a reaction in someone.
– DERIVATIVES **-buttoned** adj. **buttonless** adj. **buttony** adj.
– ORIGIN ME: from OFr. *bouton*, of Gmc origin and rel. to **BUTT**[1].

**button-back** ● n. [as modifier] denoting a chair or sofa with a quilted back, the stitching being hidden by buttons.

**button chrysanthemum** ● n. a variety of chrysanthemum with small spherical flowers.

**button-down** ● adj. **1** (of a collar) having points which are buttoned to the garment. ➤(of a shirt) having such a collar. **2** N. Amer. (of a person) conservative or inhibited.

**buttonhole** ● n. **1** a slit made in a garment to receive a button for fastening. **2** Brit. a flower or spray worn in a lapel buttonhole. ● v. **1** informal accost and detain (a reluctant person) in conversation. **2** make buttonholes in.
– DERIVATIVES **buttonholer** n.

**buttonhole stitch** ● n. a looped stitch used for edging buttonholes or pieces of material.

**buttonhook** ● n. **1** a small hook with a long handle for fastening tight buttons (often formerly on buttoned boots). **2** American Football a play in which a pass receiver runs straight downfield and then doubles back sharply towards the line of scrimmage.

**button mushroom** ● n. a young unopened mushroom.

**button-quail** ● n. a small quail-like bird related to the rails, with only three toes. [Genus *Turnix*: several species.]

**Buttons** ● n. Brit. informal a nickname for a liveried pageboy, especially in a pantomime.
– ORIGIN C19: from the rows of buttons on his jacket.

**button-through** ● adj. Brit. (of clothing) fastened with buttons from top to bottom.

**buttonwood** ● n. **1** N. Amer. a plane tree. **2** a tropical American mangrove, used in the production of tanbark and charcoal. [*Conocarpus erectus* and *Laguncularia racemosa*.]

**buttress** /ˈbʌtrɪs/ ● n. **1** a projecting support of stone or brick built against a wall. **2** a projecting portion of a hill or mountain. ● v. support with buttresses. ➤support or strengthen: *authority was buttressed by religious belief.*
– ORIGIN ME: from OFr. (*ars*) *bouterez* 'thrusting (arch)', from *boter* (see **BUTT**[1]).

**butty**[1] (also **buttie**) ● n. (pl. **-ies**) informal, chiefly N. English a sandwich.
– ORIGIN C19: from **BUTTER** + **-Y**[2].

**butty**[2] ● n. (pl. **-ies**) Brit. **1** informal (among miners) a friend or workmate. **2** historical a middleman negotiating between the miners and mine owner. **3** (also **butty boat**) an unpowered freight barge intended to be towed.
– ORIGIN C18: prob. from **BOOTY**[1] in the phr. *play booty* 'join in sharing plunder'.

**butut** /ˈbuːtuːt/ ● n. (pl. same or **bututs**) a monetary unit of Gambia, equal to one hundredth of a dalasi.
– ORIGIN a local word.

**butyl** /ˈbjuːtʌɪl, -tɪl/ ● n. [as modifier] of or denoting an alkyl radical $-C_4H_9$, derived from butane: *butyl acetate.*

**butyl rubber** ● n. a synthetic rubber made by polymerizing isobutylene and isoprene.

**butyric acid** /bjuːˈtɪrɪk/ ● n. Chemistry a syrupy liquid organic acid present in rancid butter and in arnica oil.
– DERIVATIVES **butyrate** /ˈbjuːtɪreɪt/ n.
– ORIGIN C19: from L. *butyrum* (see **BUTTER**) + **-IC**.

**buxom** /ˈbʌks(ə)m/ ● adj. (of a woman) full-figured with large breasts.
– DERIVATIVES **buxomness** n.
– ORIGIN ME (in the sense 'compliant', later 'lively and good-tempered', influenced by the assoc. of plumpness with an easy-going nature): from the stem of OE *būgan* 'to bend' (see **BOW**[2]) + **-SOME**[1].

**buy** ● v. (**buys, buying**; past and past part. **bought**) **1** obtain in exchange for payment. ➤(**buy someone out**) pay someone to give up an ownership, interest, or share. ➤(**buy oneself out**) obtain one's release from the armed services by payment. ➤(**buy something in**) withdraw something at auction because it fails to reach the reserve price. **2** get by sacrifice or great effort. **3** informal accept the truth of. ● n. informal a purchase.
– PHRASES **buy the farm** N. Amer. informal die. **buy time** delay an event temporarily so as to have longer to improve one's own position. **have bought it** informal be killed.
– ORIGIN OE *bycgan*, of Gmc origin.

**buy-back** ● n. the buying back of goods by the original seller, especially a form of borrowing in which shares are sold with an agreement to repurchase them later.

**buyer** ● n. a person who buys. ➤a person employed to select and purchase stock for a business.
– PHRASES **a buyer's market** an economic situation in which goods or shares are plentiful and buyers can keep prices down.

**buy-in** ● n. **1** a purchase of shares by a broker after a seller has failed to deliver similar shares, the original seller being charged any difference in cost. **2** a purchase of shares in a company by managers who are not employed by it. **3** the buying back by a company of its own shares.

**buyout** ● n. the purchase of a controlling share in a company, especially by its own managers.

**buzz** ● n. **1** a low, continuous humming or murmuring sound, made by or similar to that made by an insect. ➤the sound of a buzzer or telephone. ➤informal a telephone call. **2** an atmosphere of excitement and activity. ➤informal a thrill. **3** informal a rumour. ● v. **1** make a humming sound. ➤signal with a buzzer. **2** move quickly. ➤(**buzz off**) informal go away. ➤informal (of an aircraft) fly very close to (something) at high speed. **3** have an air of excitement or purposeful activity.
– ORIGIN ME: imitative.

**buzzard** /ˈbʌzəd/ ● n. **1** a large hawklike bird of prey with broad wings and a rounded tail, typically seen soaring in wide circles. [*Buteo buteo* and other species.] **2** N. Amer. a vulture.
– ORIGIN ME: from OFr. *busard*, based on L. *buteo* 'falcon'.

**buzz bomb** ● n. informal term for **FLYING BOMB**.

**buzz cut** ● n. a very short haircut in which the hair is clipped close to the head with a razor.

**buzzer** ● n. an electrical device that makes a buzzing noise to attract attention.
– PHRASES **at the buzzer** N. Amer. at the end of a game or period of play, especially in basketball.

**buzz saw** ● n. North American term for **CIRCULAR SAW**.

**buzzword** ● n. informal a technical word or phrase that has become fashionable.

**buzzy** ● adj. informal (of a place or atmosphere) lively and exciting.

**BVM** ● abbrev. Blessed Virgin Mary.

**b/w** ● abbrev. black and white (used to describe printing, film, photographs, or television pictures).

**bwana** /ˈbwɑːnə/ ● n. (in East Africa) a boss or master (often used as a title or form of address).
– ORIGIN from Kiswahili.

**BWR** ● abbrev. boiling-water reactor.

**by** ● prep. **1** through the agency or means of. ➤indicating how something happens. **2** indicating a quantity or amount, or the size of a margin. ➤identifying a parameter. ➤expressing multiplication, especially in dimensions. **3** indicating the end of a time period. **4** near to; beside. ➤past and beyond. **5** during. **6** according to. **7** used in mild oaths. ● adv. so as to go past. ● n. (pl. **byes**) variant spelling of **BYE**[1].
– PHRASES **by and by** before long. **by the by** (or **bye**) incidentally. **by and large** on the whole. [orig. in naut. use, describing the handling of a ship both to the wind and off it.] **by oneself 1** alone. **2** unaided. **by way of** see **WAY**.

– ORIGIN OE *bī*, *bi*, *be*, of Gmc origin.

**by-** (also **bye-**) ● **prefix** subordinate; incidental; secondary: *by-election.*

**by-blow** ● **n.** Brit. dated a man's illegitimate child.

**by-catch** ● **n.** the unwanted fish and other marine creatures trapped by commercial fishing nets during fishing for a different species.

**bye**[1] ● **n. 1** the transfer of a competitor directly to the next round of a competition in the absence of an assigned opponent. **2** Cricket a run scored from a ball that passes the batsman without being hit (recorded as an extra). **3** Golf one or more holes remaining unplayed after a match has been decided.
– PHRASES **by the bye** variant spelling of ***by the by*** (see **BY**).
– ORIGIN C16 (denoting an incidental matter): from **BY**.

**bye**[2] ● **exclam.** informal goodbye.

**bye-** ● **prefix** variant spelling of **BY-**.

**bye-bye** ● **exclam.** informal goodbye.
– ORIGIN C18: child's reduplication.

**bye-byes** ● **n.** a child's word for sleep.
– ORIGIN C19: from the sound *bye-bye*, long used as a refrain in lullabies.

**by-election** ● **n.** Brit. the election of an MP in a single constituency to fill a vacancy arising during a government's term of office.

**byeline** ● **n.** variant spelling of **BYLINE** (in sense 2).

**Byelorussian** /ˌbjɛlə(ʊ)ˈrʌʃ(ə)n/ ● **adj. & n.** variant spelling of **BELORUSSIAN**.

**by-form** ● **n.** a secondary form of a word.

**bygone** ● **adj.** belonging to an earlier time.
– PHRASES **let bygones be bygones** forget past differences or offences and be reconciled.

**by-law** (also **bye-law**) ● **n. 1** Brit. a regulation made by a local authority or corporation. **2** a rule made by a company or society to control the actions of its members.
– ORIGIN ME: prob. from obs. *byrlaw* 'local law or custom', from ON *býjar*, genitive sing. of *býr* 'town', but assoc. with **BY**.

**byline** ● **n. 1** a line in a newspaper naming the writer of an article. **2** (also **byeline**) (chiefly in soccer) the part of the goal line to either side of the goal.

**byname** ● **n.** a sobriquet or nickname.

**BYOB** ● **abbrev.** bring your own bottle (used chiefly on party invitations).

**bypass** ● **n. 1** a road passing round a town to provide an alternative route for through traffic. **2** a secondary channel, pipe, or connection to allow a flow when the main one is closed or blocked. **3** a surgical operation to make an alternative passage to aid the circulation of blood. ● **v.** go past or round. ➤provide (a town) with a bypass.

**byplay** ● **n.** subsidiary action in a play or film.

**by-product** ● **n. 1** an incidental or secondary product made in the manufacture of something else. **2** an unintended but inevitable secondary result.

**byre** ● **n.** Brit. a cowshed.
– ORIGIN OE *bȳre*; perh. rel. to **BOWER**[1].

**byroad** ● **n.** a minor road.

**Byronic** /bʌɪˈrɒnɪk/ ● **adj.** characteristic of Lord Byron (1788–1824) or his poetry. ➤(of a man) alluringly dark, mysterious, and moody.

**byssinosis** /ˌbɪsɪˈnəʊsɪs/ ● **n.** a lung disease caused by prolonged inhalation of textile fibre dust.
– ORIGIN C19: from L. *byssinus* 'made of byssus' + **-OSIS**.

**byssus** /ˈbɪsəs/ ● **n.** (pl. **byssuses** or **byssi** /-sʌɪ/) **1** historical a fine textile fibre and fabric of flax. **2** Zoology a tuft of tough silky filaments by which mussels and some other bivalves adhere to rocks and other objects.
– DERIVATIVES **byssal** adj.
– ORIGIN ME: from L., from Gk *bussos*, of Semitic origin.

**bystander** ● **n.** a person who is present at an event or incident but does not take part.

**byte** /bʌɪt/ ● **n.** Computing a group of binary digits or bits (usually eight) operated on as a unit. ➤such a group as a unit of memory size.
– ORIGIN 1960s: an arbitrary formation based on **BIT**[4] and **BITE**.

**by-the-wind sailor** ● **n.** a surface-dwelling colonial marine coelenterate of the Atlantic and Mediterranean, with a disc-like float bearing a sail. [*Velella velella.*]

**bytownite** /ˈbʌɪtaʊnʌɪt/ ● **n.** a feldspar mineral present in many basic igneous rocks.
– ORIGIN C19: from *Bytown*, the former name of Ottawa, Canada.

**byway** ● **n. 1** a minor road or path. **2** a little-known area of knowledge.

**byword** ● **n. 1** a person or thing cited as a notable example or embodiment of something. **2** a word or expression summarizing a thing's characteristics or a person's principles.

**Byzantine** /bɪˈzantʌɪn, bʌɪ-/ ● **adj. 1** of or relating to Byzantium, the Byzantine Empire, or the Eastern Orthodox Church. ➤of a rich and highly decorated artistic and architectural style which developed in the Byzantine Empire and spread to Italy, Russia, and elsewhere. **2** excessively complicated and detailed. ➤characterized by deviousness or underhand methods. ● **n.** a citizen of Byzantium or the Byzantine Empire.
– DERIVATIVES **Byzantinism** /bɪˈzantɪnɪz(ə)m, bʌɪ-/ n. **Byzantinist** n.
– ORIGIN C16: from L. *Byzantinus*, from *Byzantium*, the city later called Constantinople and now Istanbul.

**C**[1] (also **c**) ● **n.** (pl. **Cs** or **C's**) **1** the third letter of the alphabet. **2** denoting the third in a set of items, categories, sizes, etc. **3** Music the first note of the diatonic scale of C major, the major scale having no sharps or flats. **4** the Roman numeral for 100. [abbrev. of L. *centum* 'hundred'.] **5** (**C**) a computer programming language originally developed for implementing the UNIX operating system. [formerly known as *B*, abbrev. of *BCPL*.]

**C**[2] ● **abbrev. 1** (**C.**) Cape (chiefly on maps). **2** Celsius or centigrade. **3** (in names of sports clubs) City. **4** (**C.**) Brit. Command Paper (second series, 1870–99). **5** (in Britain) Conservative. **6** (©) copyright. **7** Physics coulomb(s). **8** Cuba (international vehicle registration). ● **symb. 1** Physics capacitance. **2** the chemical element carbon.
– PHRASES **the Big C** informal cancer.

**c** ● **abbrev. 1** Cricket caught by. **2** cent(s). **3** centi-: *cSt (centistokes)*. **4** (**c.**) century or centuries. **5** (preceding a date or amount) circa. **6** colt. ● **symb.** Physics the speed of light in a vacuum: $E = mc^2$.

**c/-** ● **abbrev.** Austral./NZ care of (used chiefly in addresses on envelopes).

**CA** ● **abbrev. 1** California (in official postal use). **2** Scottish & Canadian chartered accountant.

**Ca** ● **symb.** the chemical element calcium.

**ca** ● **abbrev.** (preceding a date or amount) circa.

**CAA** ● **abbrev.** (in the UK) Civil Aviation Authority.

**caatinga** /ˈkɑːtɪŋɡə/ ● **n.** (in Brazil) vegetation in semi-arid country consisting of thorny shrubs and stunted trees.
– ORIGIN via Port. from Tupi, from *caá* 'natural vegetation' + *tinga* 'white'.

**CAB** ● **abbrev. 1** Citizens' Advice Bureau. **2** US Civil Aeronautics Board.

**cab**[1] ● **n. 1** (also **taxi cab**) a taxi. **2** the driver's compartment in a truck, bus, or train. **3** historical a horse-drawn vehicle for public hire.
– ORIGIN C19: abbrev. of **CABRIOLET**.

**cab**[2] ● **n.** informal a cabinet containing a speaker or speakers for a guitar amplifier.

**cabal** /kəˈbal/ ● **n. 1** a secret political clique or faction. **2** a committee of five ministers under Charles II, whose surnames happened to begin with C, A, B, A, and L.
– ORIGIN C16 (denoting the Kabbalah): from Fr. *cabale*, from med. L. *cabala* (see **KABBALAH**).

**Cabala** ● **n.** variant spelling of **KABBALAH**.

**cabaletta** /ˌkabəˈlɛtə/ ● **n.** (pl. **cabalettas** or **cabalette**) a simple aria with a repetitive rhythm. ➤ the uniformly quick final section of an aria.
– ORIGIN C19: from Ital., var. of *coboletta* 'short stanza'.

**caballero** /ˌkabəˈljɛːrəʊ/ ● **n.** (pl. **-os**) **1** a Spanish gentleman. **2** US (in the south-western states) a horseman.
– ORIGIN C19: Sp., 'gentleman, horseman', based on L. *caballus* 'horse'; cf. **CAVALIER**, **CHEVALIER**.

**cabana** /kəˈbɑːnə/ ● **n.** N. Amer. a hut, cabin, or shelter at a beach or swimming pool.
– ORIGIN C19: from Sp. *cabaña*.

**cabaret** /ˈkabəreɪ, ˌkabəˈreɪ/ ● **n.** entertainment held in a nightclub or restaurant while the audience eat or drink at tables. ➤ a nightclub or restaurant where such entertainment is performed.
– ORIGIN C17 (denoting a Fr. inn): from OFr., lit. 'wooden structure'.

**cabbage** ● **n. 1** a cultivated plant eaten as a vegetable, having thick green or purple leaves surrounding a spherical heart or head of young leaves. [*Brassica oleracea*.] **2** Brit. informal, derogatory a person whose physical or mental activity is impaired or destroyed as a result of injury or illness.
– DERIVATIVES **cabbagy** adj.
– ORIGIN ME: from OFr. (Picard) *caboche* 'head', var. of OFr. *caboce*.

**cabbage lettuce** ● **n.** a lettuce of a variety which has broad, rounded leaves forming a globular head close to the ground.

**cabbage moth** ● **n.** a brown moth whose caterpillars are pests of cabbages and related plants. [*Mamestra brassicae*.]

**cabbage palm** ● **n. 1** a Caribbean palm with edible buds that resemble a cabbage. [*Roystonea oleraceae*.] **2** an evergreen plant of warm regions, resembling a cabbage and cultivated as a greenhouse or house plant. [Genus *Cordyline*.]

**cabbage rose** ● **n.** a kind of rose with a large, round, compact double flower.

**cabbage tree** ● **n.** a cabbage palm, especially a New Zealand tree grown for its sugary sap or for ornament. [*Cordyline australis*.]

**cabbage white** ● **n.** a white butterfly whose caterpillars are pests of cabbages and related plants (see **WHITE**).

**Cabbala** ● **n.** variant spelling of **KABBALAH**.

**cabbalistic** /ˌkabəˈlɪstɪk/ ● **adj.** relating to or associated with mystical interpretation or esoteric doctrine. See also **KABBALAH**.
– DERIVATIVES **cabbalism** n. **cabbalist** n.
– ORIGIN var. of *Kabbalistic*: see **KABBALAH**.

**cabby** (also **cabbie**) ● **n.** (pl. **-ies**) informal a taxi driver.

**caber** /ˈkeɪbə/ ● **n.** a roughly trimmed tree trunk used in the Scottish Highland sport of tossing the caber.
– ORIGIN C16: from Sc. Gaelic *cabar* 'pole'.

**Cabernet Franc** /ˈkabəneɪ frɒ̃/ ● **n.** a variety of black wine grape grown chiefly in parts of the Loire Valley and NE Italy. ➤ a red wine made from this grape.
– ORIGIN from Fr.

**Cabernet Sauvignon** /ˈsəʊvɪnjɒ̃/ ● **n.** a variety of black wine grape originally from the Bordeaux area of France. ➤ a red wine made from this grape.
– ORIGIN from Fr.

**cabildo** /kəˈbɪldəʊ, Spanish kaˈβilðo/ ● **n.** (pl. **-os**) (in Spanish-speaking countries) a town council or local government council. ➤ a town hall.
– ORIGIN Sp., from late L. *capitulum* 'chapter house'.

**cabin** ● **n. 1** a private room or compartment on a ship. **2** the passenger compartment in an aircraft. **3** a small wooden shelter or house. ● **v.** (**cabined**, **cabining**) [often as adj. **cabined**] dated confine in a small place.
– ORIGIN ME: from OFr. *cabane*, from Provençal *cabana*, from late L. *capanna*, *cavanna*.

**cabin boy** ● **n.** chiefly historical a boy employed to wait on a ship's officers or passengers.

**cabin class** ● **n.** the intermediate class of accommodation on a passenger ship.

**cabin crew** ● **n.** [treated as sing. or pl.] the members of an aircraft crew who attend to passengers or cargo.

**cabin cruiser** ● **n.** a motor boat with living accommodation.

**cabinet** ● **n. 1** a cupboard with drawers or shelves for storing or displaying articles. ➤ a wooden box, container, or piece of furniture housing a radio, television set, or speaker. **2** (also **Cabinet**) (in the UK, Canada, and other

Commonwealth countries) the committee of senior ministers responsible for controlling government policy. ➤(in the US) a body of advisers to the President, composed of the heads of the executive departments of the government.
– DERIVATIVES **cabinetry** n.
– ORIGIN C16: from **CABIN** + **-ET**[1], influenced by Fr. *cabinet*; sense 2 derives from the obs. sense 'a small private room'.

**cabinetmaker** ● n. a skilled joiner who makes furniture or similar high-quality woodwork.
– DERIVATIVES **cabinetmaking** n.

**cabinet pudding** ● n. a steamed suet pudding containing dried fruit.

**cabin fever** ● n. informal, chiefly N. Amer. lassitude and irritability resulting from long confinement indoors during the winter.

**cable** ● n. **1** a thick rope of wire or hemp, typically used for construction, mooring ships, and towing vehicles. ➤the chain of a ship's anchor. ➤(also **cable moulding**) Architecture a moulding resembling twisted rope. **2** an insulated wire or wires having a protective casing and used for transmitting electricity or telecommunication signals. **3** a cablegram. **4** Nautical a length of 200 yards (182.9 m) or (in the US) 240 yards (219.4 m). ● v. **1** dated send a cablegram to. **2** provide (an area) with power lines or other equipment necessary for cable television.
– ORIGIN ME: from an Anglo-Norman Fr. var. of OFr. *chable*, from late L. *capulum* 'halter'.

**cable car** ● n. **1** a transport system, typically one on a mountainside, in which cabins are suspended on a continuous moving cable driven by a motor at one end of the route. **2** a carriage on a cable railway.

**cablegram** ● n. historical a telegraph message sent by cable.

**cable-laid** ● adj. (of rope) made of three triple strands.

**cable railway** ● n. **1** a tramway on which the unpowered cars are attached to a continuously moving cable running in a slot in the street. **2** a funicular.

**cable release** ● n. Photography a cable attached to the shutter release of a camera, allowing the photographer to open the shutter without touching the camera.

**cable stitch** ● n. a combination of knitted stitches resembling twisted rope.

**cable television** ● n. a system in which television programmes are transmitted to subscribers' sets by cable.

**cableway** ● n. a transport system in which goods are carried suspended from a continuous moving cable.

**cabochon** /'kabəʃɒn/ ● n. a gem polished but not faceted.
– ORIGIN C16: from Fr., dimin. of *caboche* 'head'.

**caboclo** /kə'bəʊkləʊ/ ● n. (pl. **-os**) (in Brazil) an American Indian. ➤a Brazilian of mixed white and Indian or Indian and black ancestry.
– ORIGIN Brazilian Port., perh. from Tupi *Kaa-boc* 'person having copper-coloured skin'.

**caboodle** ● n. (in phr. **the whole caboodle** or **the whole kit and caboodle**) informal the whole number or quantity of people or things in question.
– ORIGIN C19 (orig. US): perh. from the phr. *kit and boodle*, in the same sense.

**caboose** ● n. **1** N. Amer. a railway wagon with accommodation for the train crew, typically attached to the end of the train. **2** archaic a kitchen on a ship's deck.
– ORIGIN C18: from Du. *kabuis*, *kombuis*.

**caboshed** /kə'bɒʃt/ ● adj. [usu. postpos.] Heraldry (of the head of a stag, bull, etc.) shown full face with no neck visible.
– ORIGIN C16: from Fr. *caboché*, in the same sense.

**cabotage** /'kabətɑːʒ, -ɪdʒ/ ● n. **1** the right to operate sea, air, or other transport services within a particular territory. **2** restriction of the operation of sea, air, or other transport services within or into a particular country to that country's own transport services.
– ORIGIN C19: from Fr., from *caboter* 'sail along a coast'.

**cabriole** /'kabrɪəʊl/ ● n. Ballet a jump in which one leg is extended into the air, the other is brought up to meet it, and the dancer lands on the second foot.
– ORIGIN Fr., lit. 'light leap', from *cabrioler* (earlier *caprioler*), from Ital. *capriolare* (see **CAPRIOLE**).

**cabriole leg** ● n. a kind of curved leg characteristic of Chippendale and Queen Anne furniture.
– ORIGIN C18: so named from the resemblance to the front leg of a leaping animal (see **CABRIOLE**).

**cabriolet** /'kabrɪə(ʊ)leɪ/ ● n. **1** a car with a roof that folds down. **2** a light two-wheeled carriage with a hood, drawn by one horse.
– ORIGIN C18: from Fr., from *cabriole* (see **CABRIOLE**); so named because of the carriage's motion.

**ca'canny** /kɑː'kani/ ● n. Brit. dated a policy of deliberately limiting output at work.
– ORIGIN C19 (orig. Scots in the sense 'proceed warily'): from *ca'* (var. of the verb **CALL**) and **CANNY**.

**cacao** /kə'kɑːəʊ, -'keɪəʊ/ ● n. (pl. **-os**) **1** bean-like seeds from which cocoa, cocoa butter, and chocolate are made. **2** the small tropical American evergreen tree which bears these seeds, which are contained in large oval pods growing on the trunk. [*Theobroma cacao*.]
– ORIGIN C16: via Sp. from Nahuatl *cacaua*.

**cacciatore** /ˌkatʃə'tɔːreɪ, -ri/ (also **cacciatora** /-rə/) ● adj. [postpos.] prepared in a spicy tomato sauce with mushrooms and herbs.
– ORIGIN Ital., lit. 'hunter' (because of the use of ingredients that a hunter might have to hand).

**cachaca** /kə'ʃɑːkə/ ● n. a Brazilian white rum made from sugar cane.
– ORIGIN Brazilian Port., from Port. *cacaça* '(white) rum'.

**cachalot** /'kaʃəlɒt/ ● n. another term for **SPERM WHALE**.
– ORIGIN C18: from Fr., from Sp. and Port. *cachalote*, from *cachola* 'big head'.

**cache** /kaʃ/ ● n. **1** a hidden store of things. **2** Computing an auxiliary memory from which high-speed retrieval is possible. ● v. store in a cache.
– ORIGIN C18: from Fr., from *cacher* 'to hide'.

**cachectic** /kə'kɛktɪk/ ● adj. Medicine relating to or having the symptoms of cachexia.

**cachepot** /'kaʃpəʊ, 'kaʃpɒt/ ● n. (pl. pronounced same) an ornamental holder for a flowerpot.
– ORIGIN C19: from Fr. *cache-pot*, from *cacher* 'to hide' + *pot* 'pot'.

**cache-sexe** /'kaʃsɛks/ ● n. (pl. pronounced same) a covering for a person's genitals, typically worn by erotic dancers or tribal peoples.
– ORIGIN 1920s: from Fr., from *cacher* 'to hide' and *sexe* 'genitals'.

**cachet** /'kaʃeɪ/ ● n. **1** prestige. **2** a distinguishing mark or seal. **3** a flat capsule enclosing a dose of unpleasant-tasting medicine.
– ORIGIN C17: from Fr., from *cacher* in the sense 'to press'.

**cachexia** /kə'kɛksɪə/ ● n. Medicine weakness and wasting of the body due to severe chronic illness.
– ORIGIN C16: via late L. from Gk *kakhexia*, from *kakos* 'bad' + *hexis* 'habit'.

**cachinnate** /'kakɪneɪt/ ● v. poetic/literary laugh loudly.
– DERIVATIVES **cachinnation** n.
– ORIGIN C19 (earlier (C17) as *cachinnation*): from L. *cachinnat-*, *cachinnare* 'laugh loudly'.

**cachou** /'kaʃuː, kə'ʃuː/ ● n. (pl. **cachous**) dated a pleasant-smelling lozenge sucked to mask bad breath.
– ORIGIN C16 (in the sense 'catechu'): from Fr., from Port. *cachu*, from Malay *kacu*.

**cachucha** /kə'tʃuːtʃə/ ● n. a lively Spanish solo dance in triple time, performed with castanet accompaniment.
– ORIGIN from Sp.

**cacique** /kə'siːk/ ● n. **1** (in Latin America or the Spanish-speaking Caribbean) a native chief. **2** (in Spain or Latin America) a local political boss. **3** a gregarious tropical American bird that has black plumage with patches of red or yellow. [Genus *Cacicus*.]
– ORIGIN C16: from Sp. or Fr., from Taino.

**cack** ● n. Brit. informal excrement.
– ORIGIN OE (as *cac-* in *cachūs* 'privy'); based on L. *cacare* 'defecate'.

**cack-handed** ● adj. Brit. informal **1** inept; clumsy. **2** derogatory left-handed.
– DERIVATIVES **cack-handedly** adv. **cack-handedness** n.

**cackle** ● v. **1** (of a hen or goose) give a raucous clucking

cry. ➤make a similar sound when laughing. **2** talk inconsequentially and at length. ● **n.** a cackling sound.
– PHRASES **cut the cackle** informal stop talking aimlessly and come to the point.
– ORIGIN ME: prob. from Mid. Low Ger. *kākelen*, partly imitative, reinforced by *kāke* 'jaw, cheek'.

**cacodemon** /ˌkakə(ʊ)ˈdiːmən/ ● **n.** a malevolent spirit or person.
– ORIGIN C16: from Gk *kakodaimōn*, from *kakos* 'bad' + *daimōn* 'spirit'.

**cacodyl** /ˈkakə(ʊ)dʌɪl, -dɪl/ ● **n.** Chemistry a malodorous, toxic, spontaneously flammable liquid organic compound containing arsenic.
– ORIGIN C19: from Gk *kakōdēs* 'stinking' (from *kakos* 'bad') + **-YL**.

**cacodylic acid** /ˈkakə(ʊ)dʌɪlɪk, -dɪlɪk/ ● **n.** Chemistry a toxic crystalline acid containing arsenic, used as a herbicide.
– DERIVATIVES **cacodylate** n.

**cacoethes** /ˌkakəʊˈiːθiːz/ ● **n.** rare an urge to do something inadvisable.
– ORIGIN C16: via L. from Gk *kakoēthes* 'ill-disposed'.

**cacomistle** /ˈkakə(ʊ)ˌmɪs(ə)l/ ● **n.** a nocturnal raccoon-like animal with a dark-ringed tail, found in North and Central America. [*Bassariscus sumichrasti* (Central America).]
– ORIGIN C19: from Latin Amer. Sp. *cacomixtle*, from Nahuatl *tlacomiztli*.

**cacophony** /kəˈkɒf(ə)ni/ ● **n.** (pl. **-ies**) a harsh discordant mixture of sounds.
– DERIVATIVES **cacophonous** adj.
– ORIGIN C17: from Fr. *cacophonie*, from Gk *kakophōnia*, from *kakophōnos* 'ill-sounding'.

**cactus** ● **n.** (pl. **cacti** /-tʌɪ/ or **cactuses**) a succulent plant of a large family native to arid regions of the New World, with a thick fleshy stem which typically bears spines, lacks leaves, and has brilliantly coloured flowers. [Family Cactaceae.]
– DERIVATIVES **cactaceous** adj.
– ORIGIN C17 (in the sense 'cardoon'): from L., from Gk *kaktos* 'cardoon'.

**cacuminal** /kəˈkjuːmɪn(ə)l/ ● **adj.** Phonetics another term for **RETROFLEX**.
– ORIGIN C19: from L. *cacuminare* 'make pointed' + **-AL**.

**CAD** ● **abbrev.** computer-aided design.

**cad** ● **n.** dated or humorous a man who behaves dishonourably, especially towards a woman.
– DERIVATIVES **caddish** adj. **caddishly** adv. **caddishness** n.
– ORIGIN C18 (denoting a passenger picked up by the driver of a horse-drawn coach for personal profit): abbrev. of **CADDIE** or **CADET**.

**cadastral** /kəˈdastr(ə)l/ ● **adj.** (of a map or survey) showing the extent, value, and ownership of land, especially for taxation.
– ORIGIN C19: from Fr., from *cadastre* 'register of property'.

**cadaver** /kəˈdɑːvə, -ˈdeɪ-/ ● **n.** Medicine or poetic/literary a corpse.
– DERIVATIVES **cadaveric** adj.
– ORIGIN ME: from L., from *cadere* 'to fall'.

**cadaverous** ● **adj.** resembling a corpse in being very pale, thin, or bony.

**CADCAM** ● **abbrev.** computer-aided design, computer-aided manufacture.

**caddie** (also **caddy**) ● **n.** (pl. **-ies**) a person who carries a golfer's clubs and provides other assistance during a match. ● **v.** (**caddying**) work as a caddie.
– ORIGIN C17 (orig. Scots, denoting a gentleman who joined the army without a commission, later coming to mean 'odd-job man'): from Fr. **CADET**.

**caddis** /ˈkadɪs/ (also **caddis fly**) ● **n.** a small moth-like insect of an order having aquatic larvae that build protective cases of sticks, stones, etc. [Order Trichoptera.]
– ORIGIN C17: of unknown origin.

**caddis worm** ● **n.** the soft-bodied aquatic larva of a caddis fly, used as fishing bait.

**Caddoan** /ˈkadəʊən/ ● **n.** **1** a member of a group of American Indian peoples formerly inhabiting the Midwest. **2** the family of languages spoken by these peoples, which includes Pawnee, now all virtually extinct. ● **adj.** relating to or denoting these peoples or their languages.
– ORIGIN from Caddo (a lang. of this family) *kaduhdacu*, denoting a band belonging to this group, + **-AN**.

**caddy**[1] ● **n.** (pl. **-ies**) a small storage container.
– ORIGIN C18: from earlier *catty*, denoting a unit of weight of 1⅓ lb (0.61 kg), from Malay *kati*.

**caddy**[2] ● **n.** & **v.** variant spelling of **CADDIE**.

**cadence** /ˈkeɪd(ə)ns/ ● **n.** **1** a modulation or inflection of the voice. **2** Music a sequence of notes or chords comprising the close of a musical phrase. **3** rhythm.
– DERIVATIVES **cadenced** adj.
– ORIGIN ME: via OFr. from Ital. *cadenza*, based on L. *cadere* 'to fall'.

**cadency** ● **n.** chiefly Heraldry the status of a younger branch of a family.
– ORIGIN C17 (in the sense 'rhythm or metrical beat'): based on L. *cadent-*, *cadere* 'to fall'; the current sense is appar. by assoc. with **CADET**.

**cadential** ● **adj.** of or relating to a cadenza or cadence.

**cadenza** /kəˈdɛnzə/ ● **n.** Music a virtuoso solo passage inserted into a movement in a concerto or other work, typically near the end.
– ORIGIN C18: from Ital. (see **CADENCE**).

**cadet** ● **n.** **1** a young trainee in the armed services or police. ➤a secondary school pupil who undergoes voluntary training in the armed services. **2** formal or archaic a younger son or daughter. ➤a junior branch of a family.
– DERIVATIVES **cadetship** n.
– ORIGIN C17: from Fr., from Gascon dial. *capdet*, a dimin. based on L. *caput* 'head'.

**cadge** ● **v.** informal ask for or obtain (something to which one is not strictly entitled). ● **n.** Falconry a padded wooden frame on which hooded hawks are carried to the field.
– PHRASES **on the cadge** informal seeking to obtain something without paying for it.
– DERIVATIVES **cadger** n.
– ORIGIN C17 (in the dial. sense 'carry about'): back-form. from the noun *cadger*, denoting (in north. Engl. and Scots) an itinerant dealer; the noun is appar. an alt. of **CAGE**, perh. confused with the dial. verb *cadge* 'carry about'.

**cadi** /ˈkɑːdi, ˈkeɪdi/ (also **kadi**) ● **n.** (pl. **cadis**) (in Islamic countries) a judge.
– ORIGIN C16: from Arab. *ḳāḍī*, from *ḳaḍā* 'to judge'.

**cadmium** /ˈkadmɪəm/ ● **n.** the chemical element of atomic number 48, a silvery-white metal resembling zinc. (Symbol: **Cd**)
– ORIGIN C19: from L. *cadmia* 'calamine', so named because it is found with calamine in zinc ore.

**cadmium yellow** ● **n.** a bright yellow pigment containing cadmium sulphide.

**cadre** /ˈkɑːdə, ˈkɑːdr(ə), ˈkadri/ ● **n.** **1** a small group of people trained for a particular purpose or profession. **2** /also ˈkeɪdə/ a group of activists in a communist or other revolutionary organization.
– ORIGIN C19: from Fr., from Ital. *quadro*, from L. *quadrus* 'square'.

**caduceus** /kəˈdjuːsɪəs/ ● **n.** (pl. **caducei** /-sɪʌɪ/) an ancient Greek or Roman herald's wand, typically one with two serpents twined round it, carried by the messenger god Hermes or Mercury.
– ORIGIN L., from Doric Gk *karukeion* from Gk *kērux* 'herald'.

**caducity** /kəˈdjuːsɪti/ ● **n.** poetic/literary frailty; transitoriness.

**caducous** /kəˈdjuːkəs/ ● **adj.** chiefly Botany (of an organ or part) easily detached and shed at an early stage.
– ORIGIN C17 (in the sense 'epileptic'): from L. *caducus* 'liable to fall' (from *cadere* 'to fall') + **-OUS**.

**CAE** ● **abbrev.** computer-aided engineering.

**caecilian** /sɪˈsɪlɪən/ (also **coecilian**) ● **n.** Zoology a burrowing worm-like amphibian of a tropical order distinguished by poorly developed eyes and the lack of limbs. [Order Gymnophiona: many species.]
– ORIGIN from mod. L. *Caecilia* (genus name), from L.

*caecilia* 'slow-worm', + **-AN**.

**caecitis** /sɪ'kʌɪtɪs/ (US **cecitis**) • **n.** Medicine inflammation of the caecum.

**caecum** /'si:kəm/ (US **cecum**) • **n.** (pl. **caeca**) Anatomy a pouch connected to the junction of the small and large intestines.
- DERIVATIVES **caecal** adj.
- ORIGIN ME: from L. (*intestinum*) *caecum* 'blind (gut)', translation of Gk *tuphlon enteron*.

**Caerns.** • **abbrev.** Caernarfonshire.

**Caerphilly** /kɛ:'fɪli, kɑ:-, kə-/ • **n.** a kind of mild white cheese, originally made in Caerphilly in Wales.

**Caesar** /'si:zə/ • **n. 1** a title of Roman emperors, especially those from Augustus to Hadrian. **2** Brit. informal a Caesarean section.
- PHRASES **Caesar's wife** a person required to be above suspicion. [with ref. to Plutarch's *Caesar* (x. 6) 'I thought my wife ought not even to be under suspicion'.]
- ORIGIN ME: from L. *Caesar*, family name of the Roman statesman, Gaius Julius *Caesar*.

**Caesarean** /sɪ'zɛ:rɪən/ (also **Caesarian**) • **adj. 1** (US also **Cesarean**) of or effected by Caesarean section. **2** of or connected with Julius Caesar or the Caesars. • **n.** a Caesarean section.

**Caesarean section** • **n.** a surgical operation for delivering a child by cutting through the wall of the mother's abdomen.
- ORIGIN C17: from the story that Julius Caesar was delivered by this method.

**Caesar salad** • **n.** a salad consisting of cos lettuce and croutons served with a dressing of olive oil, lemon juice, raw egg, and Worcester sauce.
- ORIGIN named after *Caesar* Cardini, the Mexican restaurateur who invented it.

**caesium** /'si:zɪəm/ (US **cesium**) • **n.** the chemical element of atomic number 55, a soft, silvery, rare, extremely reactive metal of the alkali metal group. (Symbol: **Cs**)
- ORIGIN C19: from L. *caesius* 'greyish-blue' (because it has characteristic lines in the blue part of the spectrum).

**caesium clock** • **n.** an atomic clock that uses the vibrations of caesium atoms as a time standard.

**caesura** /sɪ'zjʊərə/ • **n.** (in Greek and Latin verse) a break between words within a metrical foot. ➤(in modern verse) a pause near the middle of a line.
- DERIVATIVES **caesural** adj.
- ORIGIN C16: from L., from *caes-*, *caedere* 'cut, hew'.

**CAF** • **abbrev.** N. Amer. cost and freight.

**cafard** /ka'fɑ:/ • **n.** melancholia.
- ORIGIN from Fr.

**cafe** /'kafeɪ, 'kafi/ • **n. 1** a small restaurant selling light meals and drinks. **2** N. Amer. a bar or nightclub.
- ORIGIN C19: from Fr. *café* 'coffee or coffee house'.

**cafe au lait** /ˌkafeɪ əʊ 'leɪ, ˌkafɪ/ • **n. 1** coffee with milk. **2** the light brown colour of this.
- ORIGIN from Fr. *café au lait*.

**cafe curtain** • **n.** a curtain covering the lower half of a window.

**cafe noir** /ˌkafeɪ 'nwɑ:, ˌkafɪ/ • **n.** black coffee.
- ORIGIN from Fr. *café noir*.

**cafe society** • **n.** the regular patrons of fashionable restaurants and nightclubs.

**cafeteria** • **n.** a self-service restaurant.
- ORIGIN C19 (orig. US): from Latin Amer. Sp. *cafetería* 'coffee shop'.

**cafetière** /ˌkaf(ə)'tjɛ:/ • **n.** a coffee pot containing a plunger with which the grounds are pushed to the bottom before the coffee is poured.
- ORIGIN C19: from Fr., from *café* 'coffee'.

**caff** • **n.** Brit. informal a cafe.

**caffeine** /'kafi:n/ • **n.** a crystalline compound of the alkaloid type which is found in tea and coffee plants and is a stimulant of the central nervous system.
- DERIVATIVES **caffeinated** adj.
- ORIGIN C19: from Fr. *caféine*, from *café* 'coffee'.

**caffè latte** /ˌkafeɪ 'lɑ:teɪ, 'lateɪ/ • **n.** a drink of frothy steamed milk with a shot of espresso coffee.
- ORIGIN Ital., lit. 'milk coffee'.

**caftan** • **n.** variant spelling of **KAFTAN**.

**cage** • **n. 1** a structure of bars or wires in which birds or other animals are confined. **2** an open framework forming the compartment in a lift. **3** a structure of crossing bars or wires designed to hold or support something. ➤Baseball a portable mesh backstop used for batting practice. • **v.** confine in or as in a cage.
- ORIGIN ME: via OFr. from L. *cavea*.

**cage bird** • **n.** a bird of a kind customarily kept in a cage.

**cagey** (also **cagy**) • **adj.** informal uncommunicative owing to caution or suspicion.
- DERIVATIVES **cagily** adv. **caginess** (also **cageyness**) n.
- ORIGIN C20 (orig. US): of unknown origin.

**cagoule** /kə'gu:l/ (also **kagoul**) • **n.** a lightweight, hooded, thigh-length waterproof jacket.
- ORIGIN 1950s: from Fr., lit. 'cowl'.

**cahier** /'kʌɪjeɪ/ • **n.** (pl. pronounced same) an exercise book or notebook.
- ORIGIN C19: from Fr.; cf. **QUIRE**.

**cahoots** /kə'hu:ts/ • **pl. n.** (in phr. **in cahoots**) informal colluding or conspiring together secretly.
- ORIGIN C19 (orig. US): of unknown origin.

**CAI** • **abbrev.** computer-assisted (or -aided) instruction.

**caiman** /'keɪmən/ (also **cayman**) • **n.** a semiaquatic tropical American reptile similar to an alligator, with a heavily armoured belly. [*Caiman sclerops* (**spectacled caiman**) and other species.]
- ORIGIN C16: from Sp. *caimán*, Port. *caimão*, from Carib *acayuman*.

**Cain** • **n.** (in phr. **raise Cain**) informal create trouble or a commotion.
- ORIGIN *Cain*, eldest son of Adam and Eve and murderer of his brother Abel (Genesis 4).

**Cainozoic** /ˌkʌɪnə'zəʊɪk/ • **adj.** variant spelling of **CENOZOIC**.

**caipirinha** /ˌkʌɪpɪ'rɪnjə/ • **n.** a Brazilian cocktail made with cachaca, lime or lemon juice, sugar, and crushed ice.
- ORIGIN Brazilian Port., from *caipira* 'yokel'.

**caique** /kʌɪ'i:k, kɑ:-/ • **n. 1** a light rowing boat used on the Bosporus. **2** a small eastern Mediterranean sailing ship.
- ORIGIN C17: from Fr. *caïque*, from Ital. *caicco*, from Turk. *kayık*.

**Cairene** /'kʌɪəri:n/ • **n.** a native or inhabitant of Cairo. • **adj.** of or relating to Cairo or its inhabitants.

**cairn** • **n. 1** a mound of rough stones built as a memorial or landmark. ➤a prehistoric burial mound made of stones. **2** (also **cairn terrier**) a small terrier of a breed with short legs, a longish body, and a shaggy coat.
- ORIGIN ME: from Sc. Gaelic *carn*.

**cairngorm** /'kɛ:ngɔ:m/ • **n.** another term for **SMOKY QUARTZ**.
- ORIGIN C18: named after the *Cairngorm* Mountains in Scotland.

**caisson** /'keɪs(ə)n, kə'su:n/ • **n. 1** a large watertight chamber in which underwater construction work may be carried out. **2** a vessel or watertight structure used as a gate across the entrance of a dry dock or basin.
- ORIGIN C17: from Fr., lit. 'large chest', from Ital. *cassone*, the spelling alt. in Fr. by assoc. with *caisse* 'case'.

**caisson disease** • **n.** another term for **DECOMPRESSION SICKNESS**.

**caitiff** /'keɪtɪf/ • **n.** archaic a contemptible or cowardly person.
- ORIGIN ME (denoting a captive or prisoner): from OFr. *caitif* 'captive', based on L. *captivus* (see **CAPTIVE**).

**cajole** /kə'dʒəʊl/ • **v.** persuade (someone) to do something by sustained coaxing or flattery.
- DERIVATIVES **cajolement** n. **cajolery** n.
- ORIGIN C17: from Fr. *cajoler*.

**Cajun** /'keɪdʒ(ə)n/ • **n.** a member of any of the communities in the bayou areas of southern Louisiana formed by descendants of French Canadians, speaking an archaic form of French. • **adj.** of or relating to the Cajuns, especially with reference to their folk music or cuisine.

– ORIGIN alt. of **ACADIAN**.

**cajuput** /ˈkadʒəpʌt/ (also **cajeput**) ● **n. 1** an aromatic medicinal oil resembling eucalyptus oil, obtained from an Australasian tree with papery bark. **2** the tree from which this oil is obtained. [*Melaleuca cajuputi*.]
– ORIGIN C18: from Malay *kayu putih*, lit. 'white tree'.

**cake** ● **n. 1** an item of soft sweet food made from baking a mixture of flour, fat, eggs, sugar, etc. **2** an item of savoury food formed into a flat round shape, and baked or fried. **3** the amount of money or assets regarded as available for sharing: *a fair slice of the education cake*. ● **v.** (of a thick or sticky substance) cover and become encrusted on.
– PHRASES **cakes and ale** dated merrymaking. **a piece of cake** informal something easily achieved. **sell like hot cakes** informal be sold quickly and in large quantities. **take the cake** see ***take the biscuit*** at **BISCUIT**.
– ORIGIN ME (denoting a small flat bread roll): of Scand. origin.

**cake flour** ● **n.** North American term for **PLAIN FLOUR**.

**cakehole** ● **n.** Brit. informal a person's mouth.

**cakewalk** ● **n. 1** informal a very easy task. **2** a strutting dance popular at the end of the 19th century, developed from an American black contest in graceful walking which had a cake as a prize. ● **v. 1** informal achieve something easily. **2** do a cakewalk.

**CAL** ● **abbrev.** computer-assisted (or -aided) learning.

**Cal** ● **abbrev.** large calorie(s).

**Cal.** ● **abbrev.** California.

**cal** ● **abbrev.** small calorie(s).

**Calabar bean** ● **n.** the poisonous seed of a tropical West African climbing plant (*Physostigma venosum*).
– ORIGIN C19: named after *Calabar* in Nigeria.

**calabash** /ˈkaləbaʃ/ ● **n. 1** (also **calabash tree**) an evergreen tropical American tree which bears fruit in the form of large woody gourds. [*Crescentia cujete*.] **2** a water container, tobacco pipe, or other object made from the dried shell of a gourd.
– ORIGIN C17: from Fr. *calebasse*, from Sp. *calabaza*, perh. from Pers. *ḵarbuz* 'melon'.

**calabaza** /ˌkaləˈbɑːzə/ ● **n.** West Indian and US term for **CALABASH**.
– ORIGIN C16: from Sp.

**calaboose** /ˌkaləˈbuːs/ ● **n.** US informal a prison.
– ORIGIN C18: from black Fr. *calabouse*, from Sp. *calabozo* 'dungeon'.

**calabrese** /ˈkaləbriːs, ˌkaləˈbriːs, -ˈbreɪsi/ ● **n.** a bright green dense-headed variety of broccoli.
– ORIGIN 1930s: from Ital., lit. 'of or from Calabria', a region of SW Italy.

**calamanco** /ˌkaləˈmaŋkəʊ/ ● **n.** (pl. **-oes**) historical a glossy woollen cloth chequered on one side only.
– ORIGIN C16: of unknown origin.

**calamander** /ˈkaləmandə/ ● **n.** another term for **COROMANDEL**.
– ORIGIN C19: from Sinhalese *kalu-madīriya*, perh. from *Coromandel ebony* (see **COROMANDEL**), changed by assoc. with Sinhalese *kaḷu* 'black'.

**calamari** /ˌkaləˈmɑːri/ (also **calamares** /ˌkaləˈmɑːreɪz/) ● **pl. n.** squid served as food.
– ORIGIN Ital., pl. of *calamaro*, from med. L. *calamarium* 'pen case', from Gk *kalamos* 'pen' (with ref. to the squid's long tapering internal shell and its ink).

**calamine** /ˈkaləmʌɪn/ ● **n.** a pink powder consisting of zinc carbonate and ferric oxide, used to make a soothing lotion or ointment.
– ORIGIN ME (referring to zinc ore): via OFr. from med. L. *calamina*, alt. of L. *cadmia*, from Gk *kadmeia* (*gē*) 'Cadmean (earth)', from *Kadmos* 'Cadmus', the name of the legendary founder of Thebes.

**calamint** /ˈkaləmɪnt/ ● **n.** an aromatic herbaceous plant or shrub with blue or lilac flowers. [Genus *Calamintha*.]
– ORIGIN ME: from OFr. *calament*, from med. L. *calamentum*, from late L. *calaminthe*, from Gk *kalaminthē*.

**calamity** ● **n.** (pl. **-ies**) an event causing great and often sudden damage or distress.
– DERIVATIVES **calamitous** adj. **calamitously** adv.
– ORIGIN ME: from OFr. *calamite*, from L. *calamitas*.

**calamus** /ˈkaləməs/ ● **n.** (pl. **calami** /-mʌɪ/) **1** another term for **SWEET FLAG**. ➤(also **calamus root**) a preparation of the aromatic root of the sweet flag. **2** Zoology the hollow lower part of the shaft of a feather.
– ORIGIN ME (denoting a reed or an aromatic plant mentioned in the Bible): from L., from Gk *kalamos*.

**calando** /kəˈlandəʊ/ ● **adv.** Music gradually decreasing in speed and volume.
– ORIGIN Ital., lit. 'slackening'.

**calandra lark** /kəˈlandrə/ ● **n.** a large lark with a stout bill and a black patch on each side of the neck. [*Melanocorypha calandra*.]
– ORIGIN C16: from OFr. *calandre*, via med. L. from Gk *kalandros*.

**calash** /kəˈlaʃ/ ● **n.** another term for **CALECHE**.

**calathea** /ˌkaləˈθɪə/ ● **n.** a tropical American plant which typically has variegated and ornamental leaves, often grown as a greenhouse or pot plant. [Genus *Calathea*: many species.]
– ORIGIN mod. L., from Gk *kalathos* 'basket'.

**calc-** ● **comb. form** (used chiefly in geological terms) of lime or calcium: *calcalkaline*.
– ORIGIN from Ger. *Kalk* 'lime', with spelling influenced by L. *calx* (see **CALX**).

**calcalkaline** /kalˈkalkəlʌɪn/ ● **adj.** Geology (chiefly of rocks) relatively rich in both calcium and alkali metals.

**calcaneus** /kalˈkeɪnɪəs/ (also **calcaneum** /-nɪəm/) ● **n.** (pl. **calcanei** /-nɪʌɪ/ or **calcanea** /-nɪə/) Anatomy the large bone forming the heel.
– ORIGIN C18: from L.

**calcareous** /kalˈkɛːrɪəs/ ● **adj. 1** containing calcium carbonate; chalky. **2** Ecology (of vegetation) occurring on chalk or limestone.
– ORIGIN C17: from L. *calcarius* (from *calx*, *calc-* 'lime') + **-EOUS**.

**calceolaria** /ˌkalsɪəˈlɛːrɪə/ ● **n.** a South American plant which is cultivated for its brightly coloured slipper- or pouch-shaped flowers. [Genus *Calceolaria*.]
– ORIGIN C18: mod. L., from L. *calceolus*, dimin. of *calceus* 'shoe'.

**calces** plural form of **CALX**.

**calci-** ● **comb. form** relating to calcium or its compounds: *calcifuge*.
– ORIGIN from L. *calx*, *calc-* 'lime'.

**calcic** /ˈkalsɪk/ ● **adj.** (chiefly of minerals) containing or relatively rich in calcium.

**calcicole** /ˈkalsɪkəʊl/ ● **n.** Botany a plant that grows best in calcareous soil.
– DERIVATIVES **calcicolous** adj.
– ORIGIN C19: from **CALCI-** + L. *colere* 'inhabit'.

**calciferol** /kalˈsɪfərɒl/ ● **n.** Biochemistry vitamin $D_2$, essential for the deposition of calcium in bones.

**calciferous** /kalˈsɪf(ə)rəs/ ● **adj.** containing or producing calcium salts, especially calcium carbonate.

**calcifuge** /ˈkalsɪfjuːdʒ/ ● **n.** Botany a plant that is not suited to calcareous soil.

**calcify** /ˈkalsɪfʌɪ/ ● **v.** (**-ies**, **-ied**) [usu. as adj. **calcified**] harden by deposition of or conversion into calcium carbonate or some other insoluble calcium compounds.
– DERIVATIVES **calcific** adj. **calcification** n.

**calcine** /ˈkalsʌɪn, -sɪn/ ● **v.** [usu. as adj. **calcined**] reduce, oxidize, or desiccate by roasting or strong heat.
– DERIVATIVES **calcination** n.
– ORIGIN ME: from med. L. *calcinare*, from late L. *calcina* 'lime', from L. *calx*, *calc-* (see **CALX**).

**calcite** /ˈkalsʌɪt/ ● **n.** a white or colourless mineral consisting of calcium carbonate.
– DERIVATIVES **calcitic** adj.
– ORIGIN C19: from Ger. *Calcit* from L. *calx*, *calc-* (see **CALX**).

**calcitonin** /ˌkalsɪˈtəʊnɪn/ ● **n.** Biochemistry a thyroid hormone that has the effect of lowering blood calcium.

**calcium** ● **n.** the chemical element of atomic number 20, a soft grey reactive metal of the alkaline earth metal group. (Symbol: **Ca**)
– ORIGIN C19: from L. *calx*, *calc-* (see **CALX**) + **-IUM**.

**calcium carbonate** • n. a white insoluble compound occurring naturally as chalk, limestone, marble, and calcite, and forming mollusc shells. [$CaCO_3$.]

**calcium hydroxide** • n. a soluble white crystalline compound commonly produced in the form of slaked lime. [$Ca(OH)_2$.]

**calcium oxide** • n. a white caustic alkaline solid commonly produced in the form of quicklime. [CaO.]

**calcrete** /ˈkalkriːt/ • n. Geology a breccia or conglomerate cemented together by calcareous material, formed in soils in semi-arid conditions.
– ORIGIN C20: from **CALC-** + a shortened form of **CONCRETE**.

**calculate** • v. **1** determine mathematically. **2** (**calculate on**) include as an essential element in one's plans. **3** intend (an action) to have a particular effect. **4** US dialect suppose.
– DERIVATIVES **calculability** n. **calculable** adj. **calculably** adv. **calculative** adj.
– ORIGIN ME: from late L. *calculat-*, *calculare* 'count', from *calculus* 'a small pebble (as used on an abacus)'.

**calculated** • adj. done with awareness of the likely consequences.
– DERIVATIVES **calculatedly** adv.

**calculating** • adj. selfishly scheming.
– DERIVATIVES **calculatingly** adv.

**calculation** • n. **1** a mathematical determination of quantity or extent. **2** an assessment of the risks or effects of a course of action.

**calculator** • n. something used for making mathematical calculations, in particular a small electronic device with a keyboard and a visual display.

**calculus** /ˈkalkjʊləs/ • n. **1** (pl. **calculuses**) (also **infinitesimal calculus**) the branch of mathematics concerned with the determination and properties of derivatives and integrals of functions, by methods based on the summation of infinitesimal differences. ➤ a particular method or system of calculation or reasoning. **2** (pl. **calculi** /-lʌɪ, -liː/) Medicine a concretion of minerals formed in the kidney, gall bladder, or other organ. ➤ another term for **TARTAR**.
– ORIGIN C17: from L., lit. 'small pebble'.

**Calcuttan** /kalˈkʌtən/ • n. a native or inhabitant of Calcutta. • adj. of or relating to Calcutta or its inhabitants.

**caldarium** /kalˈdɛːrɪəm/ • n. (pl. **caldaria** /-rɪə/) a hot room in an ancient Roman bath.
– ORIGIN from L.

**caldera** /kɒlˈdɛːrə, -ˈdɪərə/ • n. a large volcanic crater, especially one formed by a major eruption leading to the collapse of the mouth of the volcano.
– ORIGIN C17: from Sp., from late L. *caldaria* 'boiling pot'.

**caldron** • n. chiefly US variant spelling of **CAULDRON**.

**caleche** /kəˈlɛʃ/ (also **calash**) • n. historical **1** a light low-wheeled carriage with a removable folding hood. **2** a woman's hooped silk hood.
– ORIGIN C17: from Fr. *calèche*, via Ger. from Polish *kolasa*, from *koło* 'wheel'.

**Caledonian** /ˌkalɪˈdəʊnɪən/ • adj. (chiefly in names or geographical terms) of or relating to Scotland or the Scottish Highlands. • n. humorous or poetic/literary a person from Scotland.
– ORIGIN from *Caledonia*, the L. name for northern Britain, + **-AN**.

**calendar** /ˈkalɪndə/ • n. **1** a chart or series of pages showing the days, weeks, and months of a particular year. **2** a system by which the beginning, length, and subdivisions of the year are fixed. See also **JULIAN CALENDAR** and **GREGORIAN CALENDAR**. **3** a list or schedule of special days, events, etc. • v. enter in a calendar.
– DERIVATIVES **calendric** /-ˈlɛndrɪk/ adj. **calendrical** adj.
– ORIGIN ME: from OFr. *calendier*, from L. *kalendarium* 'account book', from *kalendae* (see **CALENDS**).

**calendar month** • n. see **MONTH**.

**calendar year** • n. see **YEAR** (sense 2).

**calender** /ˈkalɪndə/ • n. a machine in which cloth or paper is pressed by rollers to glaze or smooth it. • v. press in such a machine.
– ORIGIN C15: from Fr. *calendre* (n.), *calendrer* (v.).

**calends** /ˈkalɪndz/ (also **kalends**) • pl. n. the first day of the month in the ancient Roman calendar.
– ORIGIN OE (denoting an appointed time): from OFr. *calendes*, from L. *kalendae*, *calendae* 'first day of the month' (when the order of days was proclaimed).

**calendula** /kəˈlɛndjʊlə/ • n. a plant of a genus that includes the common or pot marigold. [Genus *Calendula*.]
– ORIGIN mod. L., dimin. of *calendae* (see **CALENDS**); perh. because it flowers for most of the year.

**calenture** /ˈkal(ə)ntjʊə/ • n. feverish delirium supposedly caused by the heat in the tropics.
– ORIGIN C16: from Fr., from Sp. *calentura* 'fever'.

**calf**[1] • n. (pl. **calves**) **1** a young bovine animal, especially a domestic cow or bull in its first year. **2** the young of some other large mammals, such as elephants. **3** a floating piece of ice detached from an iceberg.
– DERIVATIVES **calf-like** adj.
– ORIGIN OE *cælf*, of Gmc origin.

**calf**[2] • n. (pl. **calves**) the fleshy part at the back of a person's leg below the knee.
– ORIGIN ME: from ON *kálfi*.

**calf love** • n. another term for **PUPPY LOVE**.

**calfskin** • n. leather made from the hide or skin of a calf.

**calibrate** /ˈkalɪbreɪt/ • v. **1** mark (a gauge or instrument) with a standard scale of readings. **2** correlate the readings of (an instrument) with those of a standard. **3** adjust (experimental results) to take external factors into account or to allow comparison with other data.
– DERIVATIVES **calibration** n. **calibrator** n.
– ORIGIN C19: from **CALIBRE** + **-ATE**[3].

**calibre** /ˈkalɪbə/ (US **caliber**) • n. **1** quality of character or level of ability. ➤ the standard reached by something. **2** the internal diameter of a gun barrel. ➤ the diameter of a bullet, shell, or rocket.
– DERIVATIVES **calibred** adj.
– ORIGIN C16 (in the sense 'social standing'): from Fr., from Ital. *calibro*, perh. from Arab. *ḳālib* 'mould'.

**caliche** /kəˈliːtʃi/ • n. **1** a mineral deposit of gravel, sand, and nitrates, found in dry areas of America. **2** another term for **CALCRETE**.
– ORIGIN C19: from Latin Amer. Sp.

**calico** /ˈkalɪkəʊ/ • n. (pl. **-oes** or US also **-os**) Brit. a type of plain white or unbleached cotton cloth. ➤ N. Amer. printed cotton fabric. • adj. N. Amer. (of an animal, typically a cat) multicoloured or piebald.
– ORIGIN C16 (orig. also *calicut*): alt. of *Calicut*, a seaport in SW India where the fabric originated.

**Calif.** • abbrev. California.

**Californian** • n. a native or inhabitant of California. • adj. of or relating to California.

**California poppy** • n. an annual poppy native to western North America, cultivated for its brilliant yellow or orange flowers. [*Eschscholtzia californica*.]

**California sheepshead** • n. see **SHEEPSHEAD**.

**californium** /ˌkalɪˈfɔːnɪəm/ • n. the chemical element of atomic number 98, an unstable radioactive metal of the actinide series. (Symbol: **Cf**)
– ORIGIN 1950s: named after *California University* (where it was first made) + **-IUM**.

**caliper** /ˈkalɪpə/ (also **calliper**) • n. **1** an instrument for measuring external or internal dimensions, typically with two hinged legs and in-turned or out-turned points. **2** a motor-vehicle or bicycle brake consisting of two or more hinged components. **3** a metal support for a person's leg.
– ORIGIN C16: appar. an alt. of **CALIBRE**.

**caliph** /ˈkeɪlɪf, ˈka-/ • n. historical the chief Muslim civil and religious ruler, regarded as the successor of Muhammad.
– DERIVATIVES **caliphate** n.
– ORIGIN ME: from OFr. *caliphe*, from Arab. *ḵalīfa* 'deputy (of God)' (from the title *ḵalīfat Allāh*), or 'successor (of Muhammad)' (from the title *ḵalīfat rasūl Allāh* 'of the Messenger of God').

**calisthenics** • pl. n. US spelling of **CALLISTHENICS**.

**calix** • n. variant spelling of **CALYX**.

**calk** • n. & v. US spelling of **CAULK**.

**call** • v. **1** cry out to (someone) in order to summon them or attract their attention. ➤ telephone. **2** pay a brief visit. ➤ (**call for**) stop to collect. ➤ (**call at**) (of a train or coach) stop at (a specified station) on a particular route. **3** give a specified name; address by a specified name, title, etc. ➤ consider or describe (someone or something) as being: *he's the only person I would call a friend.* **4** fix a date or time for (a meeting, strike, or election). ➤ predict the result of (an election or a vote). **5** Computing cause the execution of (a subroutine). **6** bring (a witness) into court to give evidence. **7** dated inspire or urge to do something. **8** Bridge make (a particular bid) during the auction: *her partner called 6♠.* **9** Cricket (of an umpire) no-ball (a bowler) for throwing. • n. **1** a cry made as a summons or to attract attention. ➤ a telephone communication. **2** (**a call for**) an appeal or demand for. ➤ [usu. with neg.] a demand or need for: *there is little call for antique furniture.* **3** a vocation: *his call to be a disciple.* **4** a brief visit. **5** a shout by an official in a game indicating that the ball has gone out of play or that a rule has been breached. **6** Bridge a bid, response, or double.
– PHRASES **at call** see *on call* (sense 2). **call attention to** cause people to notice. **call collect** N. Amer. make a telephone call reversing the charges. **call something into** (or **in**) **question** cast doubt on something. **call of nature** euphemistic a need to urinate or defecate. **call the shots** (or **tune**) take the initiative in deciding how something should be done. **call someone/thing to order** ask those present at a meeting to be silent so that business may proceed. **on call 1** available to provide a professional service if necessary, but not formally on duty. **2** (of money lent) repayable on demand.
– PHRASAL VERBS **call for** require; demand. **call someone/thing down** cause someone or something to appear or occur. **call something in** require payment of a loan or promise of money. **call something off** cancel an event or agreement. **call on/upon** have recourse to. **call someone up** summon someone to serve in the army or to play in a team. **call something up** summon for use something that is stored or kept available.
– DERIVATIVES **caller** n. **calling** n.
– ORIGIN OE *ceallian*, from ON *kalla* 'summon loudly'.

**calla** /ˈkalə/ • n. **1** (also **water calla**) another term for **BOG ARUM**. **2** (usu. **calla lily**) chiefly N. Amer. another term for **ARUM LILY**.
– ORIGIN C19: mod. L.

**callaloo** /ˌkaləˈluː/ (also **callalou**) • n. **1** the spinach-like leaves of a tropical American plant, widely used in Caribbean cookery. ➤ a soup or stew made with such leaves. **2** the plant from which these leaves are obtained. [Genus *Xanthosoma*.]
– ORIGIN C18: from Amer. Sp. *calalú*.

**Callanetics** /ˌkaləˈnɛtɪks/ • pl. n. [treated as sing. or pl.] trademark a system of physical exercises based on small repeated movements.
– ORIGIN C20: named after *Callan* Pinckney, the Amer. deviser of the system.

**callback** • n. **1** chiefly N. Amer. an invitation to return for a second audition or interview. **2** a telephone call made to return one that someone has received.

**call boy** • n. a person in a theatre who summons actors when they are due on stage.

**call centre** • n. an office in which large numbers of telephone calls are handled, especially one providing the customer services functions of a large organization.

**call changes** • pl. n. Bell-ringing changes rung in response to spoken commands.

**call girl** • n. a female prostitute who accepts appointments by telephone.

**calligraph** /ˈkalɪɡrɑːf/ • v. write decoratively.

**calligraphy** • n. decorative handwriting or handwritten lettering. ➤ the art of producing this.
– DERIVATIVES **calligrapher** n. **calligraphic** adj. **calligraphist** n.
– ORIGIN C17: from Gk *kalligraphia*, from *kalligraphos* 'person who writes beautifully'.

**calling card** • n. **1** chiefly N. Amer. a visiting card or business card. **2** N. Amer. a phonecard or telephone charge card.

**calliope** /kəˈlʌɪəpi/ • n. chiefly historical an American keyboard instrument resembling an organ but with the notes produced by steam whistles.
– ORIGIN C19: from the Gk *Kalliopē*, the name of the Muse of epic poetry (lit. 'having a beautiful voice').

**calliper** /ˈkalɪpə/ • n. variant spelling of **CALIPER**.

**callipygian** /ˌkalɪˈpɪdʒɪən/ (also **callipygean**) • adj. poetic/literary having well-shaped buttocks.
– DERIVATIVES **callipygous** /ˌkalɪˈpɪdʒəs, ˌkalɪˈpʌɪdʒəs/ adj.
– ORIGIN C18: from Gk *kallipūgos*, from *kallos* 'beauty' + *pūgē* 'buttocks', + **-IAN**.

**callistemon** /ˌkalɪˈstiːmən/ • n. a plant of a genus that comprises the bottlebrushes. [Genus *Callistemon*.]
– ORIGIN mod. L., from Gk *kallos* 'beauty' + *stēmōn* 'thread or stamen'.

**callisthenics** /ˌkalɪsˈθɛnɪks/ (US **calisthenics**) • pl. n. gymnastic exercises to achieve bodily fitness and grace of movement.
– DERIVATIVES **callisthenic** adj.
– ORIGIN C19: from Gk *kallos* 'beauty' + *sthenos* 'strength' + **-ICS**.

**callitrichid** /ˌkalɪˈtrʌɪkɪd/ • n. Zoology a primate of a family (Callitrichidae) comprising the marmosets and tamarins.
– ORIGIN C18: from mod. L. *Callitrichidae*, from Gk *kallitrikhos* 'beautiful-haired'.

**call letters** • pl. n. chiefly N. Amer. a sequence of letters used by a television or radio station as an identifying code.

**call money** • n. money loaned by a bank or other institution which is repayable on demand.

**callop** /ˈkaləp/ • n. an edible deep-bodied gold and green freshwater fish found in Australia. [*Plectroplites ambiguus*.]
– ORIGIN 1920s: perh. from an Aborig. lang. of southern Australia.

**call option** • n. Stock Exchange an option to buy assets at an agreed price on or before a particular date.

**callosity** /kəˈlɒsɪti/ • n. (pl. **-ies**) technical a callus.
– ORIGIN ME: from Fr. *callosité*, from L. *callositas*, from *callosus* 'hard-skinned', from *callum*, *callus* 'hardened skin'.

**callous** • adj. insensitive and cruel. • n. variant spelling of **CALLUS**.
– DERIVATIVES **callously** adv. **callousness** n.
– ORIGIN ME: from L. *callosus* 'hard-skinned'.

**callow** • adj. (of a young person) inexperienced and immature.
– DERIVATIVES **callowly** adv. **callowness** n.
– ORIGIN OE *calu* 'bald', of W. Gmc origin, prob. from L. *calvus* 'bald', later 'unfledged'.

**call sign** (also **call signal**) • n. a message, code, or tune that is broadcast by radio to identify the broadcaster or transmitter.

**callus** /ˈkaləs/ (also **callous**) • n. **1** a thickened and hardened part of the skin or soft tissue, especially one caused by friction. ➤ Medicine the bony healing tissue which forms around the ends of broken bone. **2** Botany a hard formation of tissue, especially new tissue formed over a wound.
– DERIVATIVES **callused** adj.
– ORIGIN C16: from L. *callum*, *callus* 'hardened skin'.

**calm** • adj. **1** not showing or feeling nervousness, anger, or other emotions. **2** peaceful and undisturbed. • n. **1** the state or fact of being peaceful or tranquil. **2** (**calms**) an area of the sea without wind. • v. (often **calm down**) make or become tranquil and quiet.
– DERIVATIVES **calmly** adv. **calmness** n.
– ORIGIN ME: via one of the Romance langs from Gk *kauma* 'heat (of the day)'.

**calmative** /ˈkɑːmətɪv, ˈkal-/ • adj. (of a drug) having a sedative effect. • n. a calmative drug.

**calmodulin** /kalˈmɒdjʊlɪn/ • n. Biochemistry a protein which binds calcium and is involved in regulating a variety of activities in cells.
– ORIGIN 1970s: from *cal(cium)* + *modul(ate)* + **-IN**[1].

**calomel** /ˈkaləmɛl/ ● **n.** mercurous chloride, a white powder formerly used as a purgative. [$Hg_2Cl_2$.]
– ORIGIN C17: mod. L., perh. from Gk *kalos* 'beautiful' + *melas* 'black' (perh. because orig. obtained from a black mixture of mercury and mercuric chloride).

**Calor gas** /ˈkalə/ ● **n.** Brit. trademark liquefied butane stored under pressure in portable containers, used as a substitute for mains gas and in camping.
– ORIGIN 1930s: *Calor* from L. *calor* 'heat'.

**caloric** /kəˈlɒrɪk, ˈkalərɪk/ ● **adj.** chiefly N. Amer. or technical of or relating to heat; calorific. ● **n.** Physics a hypothetical fluid substance formerly thought to be responsible for the phenomenon of heat.
– DERIVATIVES **calorically** adv.
– ORIGIN C18: from Fr. *calorique*, from L. *calor* 'heat'.

**calorie** ● **n.** (pl. **-ies**) **1** (also **small calorie**) the energy needed to raise the temperature of 1 gram of water through 1 °C (now usually defined as 4.1868 joules). **2** (also **large calorie**) the energy needed to raise the temperature of 1 kilogram of water through 1 °C, equal to one thousand small calories and often used to measure the energy value of foods.
– ORIGIN C19: from Fr., from L. *calor* 'heat' + *-ie* (see **-Y**[3]).

**calorific** ● **adj.** chiefly Brit. relating to the amount of energy contained in food or fuel. ➤ high in calories.
– DERIVATIVES **calorifically** adv.

**calorific value** ● **n.** the energy contained in a fuel or food (now usually expressed in joules per kilogram), determined by burning a specified amount.

**calorimeter** /ˌkaləˈrɪmɪtə/ ● **n.** an apparatus for measuring the amount of heat involved in a chemical reaction or other process.
– DERIVATIVES **calorimetric** adj. **calorimetry** n.

**calotype process** /ˈkalətʌɪp/ ● **n.** historical an early photographic process in which negatives were made using paper coated with silver iodide.
– ORIGIN C19: from Gk *kalos* 'beautiful' + **TYPE**.

**calque** /kalk/ Linguistics ● **n.** another term for **LOAN TRANSLATION**. ● **v.** (**be calqued on**) be a calque of.
– ORIGIN 1930s: from Fr., lit. 'copy, tracing'.

**caltrop** /ˈkaltrəp/ (also **caltrap**) ● **n.** **1** a spiked metal ball thrown on the ground to impede wheeled vehicles or (formerly) cavalry horses. **2** a creeping plant with woody carpels that typically have hard spines. [Genus *Tribulus*.] **3** (also **water caltrop**) another term for **WATER CHESTNUT** (in sense 2).
– ORIGIN OE *calcatrippe*, from med. L. *calcatrippa*, from *calx* 'heel' or *calcare* 'to tread' + a word rel. to **TRAP**[1].

**calumet** /ˈkaljʊmɛt/ ● **n.** a North American Indian peace pipe.
– ORIGIN C17: from Fr., from late L. *calamellus* 'little reed'.

**calumniate** /kəˈlʌmnɪeɪt/ ● **v.** formal make false and defamatory statements about.
– DERIVATIVES **calumniation** n. **calumniator** n.

**calumny** /ˈkaləmni/ ● **n.** (pl. **-ies**) the making of false and defamatory statements about someone. ● **v.** (**-ies**, **-ied**) formal calumniate.
– DERIVATIVES **calumnious** /kəˈlʌmnɪəs/ adj.
– ORIGIN ME: from L. *calumnia*.

**calutron** /kəˈluːtrɒn/ ● **n.** a device that uses large electromagnets to separate uranium isotopes from uranium ore.
– ORIGIN 1940s: from *Cal(ifornia) U(niversity) (cyclo)tron*.

**Calvados** /ˈkalvədɒs/ ● **n.** apple brandy, traditionally made in the Calvados region of Normandy.

**calve** ● **v.** **1** give birth to a calf. **2** (of a mass of ice) split off from an iceberg or glacier.
– ORIGIN OE *calfian*, from *cælf* 'calf'.

**calves** plural form of **CALF**[1], **CALF**[2].

**Calvin cycle** ● **n.** another term for **DARK REACTION**.
– ORIGIN named after the Amer. biochemist Melvin *Calvin*.

**Calvinism** ● **n.** the Protestant theological system of John Calvin (1509–64) and his successors, a development of Lutheranism and centring on the doctrine of predestination.
– DERIVATIVES **Calvinist** n. **Calvinistic** adj. **Calvinistical** adj.

**calx** /kalks/ ● **n.** (pl. **calces** /ˈkalsiːz/) Chemistry, archaic a powdery metallic oxide formed when an ore or mineral has been heated.
– ORIGIN ME: from L., 'lime', prob. from Gk *khalix* 'pebble, limestone'.

**calypso** /kəˈlɪpsəʊ/ ● **n.** (pl. **-os**) a kind of West Indian music or song in syncopated African rhythm, typically with words improvised on a topical theme.
– DERIVATIVES **calypsonian** adj. & n.
– ORIGIN 1930s: of unknown origin.

**calyx** /ˈkalɪks, ˈkeɪ-/ (also **calix**) ● **n.** (pl. **calyces** /-lɪsiːz/ or **calyxes**) **1** Botany the sepals of a flower, typically forming a whorl that encloses the petals and forms a protective layer around a flower in bud. **2** Zoology a cup-like cavity or structure, in particular part of the pelvis of a mammalian kidney.
– ORIGIN C17: from L., from Gk *kalux* 'case of a bud, husk', rel. to *kaluptein* 'to hide'.

**calzone** /kalˈtsəʊneɪ, -ni/ ● **n.** (pl. **calzoni** or **calzones**) a type of pizza that is folded in half before cooking to contain a filling.
– ORIGIN Ital. dial., prob. a special use of *calzone* 'trouser leg'.

**CAM** ● **abbrev.** computer aided manufacturing.

**cam** ● **n.** **1** a projection on a rotating part in machinery, designed to make sliding contact with another part while rotating and impart reciprocal or variable motion to it. **2** short for **CAMSHAFT**.
– ORIGIN C18: from Du. *kam* 'comb', as in *kamrad* 'cog wheel'.

**camaraderie** /ˌkaməˈrɑːd(ə)ri, -riː/ ● **n.** mutual trust and friendship.
– ORIGIN C19: from Fr., from *camarade* 'comrade'.

**camarilla** /ˌkaməˈrɪl(j)ə/ ● **n.** a group of advisers to a ruler or politician, with a shared, typically nefarious, purpose.
– ORIGIN C19: from Sp., dimin. of *camara* 'chamber'.

**camas** /kəˈmas/ (also **camass** or **quamash**) ● **n.** a North American plant of the lily family, cultivated for its starlike blue or purple flowers. [Genera *Camassia* and *Zigadenus*: several species.]
– ORIGIN C19: from Chinook Jargon *kamass*.

**cambazola** /ˌkambəˈzəʊlə/ (also **cambozola**) ● **n.** trademark a type of German blue soft cheese with a rind like Camembert.
– ORIGIN blend of **CAMEMBERT** and **GORGONZOLA**.

**camber** /ˈkambə/ ● **n.** **1** a slightly convex or arched shape of a road or other horizontal surface. ➤ Brit. a tilt built into a road at a bend or curve. **2** the slight sideways inclination of the front wheels of a motor vehicle. **3** the extent of curvature of a section of an aerofoil.
– DERIVATIVES **cambered** adj.
– ORIGIN ME: from OFr. *cambre*, dial. var. of *chambre* 'arched', from L. *camurus* 'curved inwards'.

**Camberwell beauty** ● **n.** a migratory butterfly with deep purple yellow-bordered wings. [*Nymphalis antiopa*.]
– ORIGIN C19: named after *Camberwell* in London.

**cambium** /ˈkambɪəm/ ● **n.** (pl. **cambia** or **cambiums**) Botany a cellular plant tissue from which phloem, xylem, or cork grows by division.
– DERIVATIVES **cambial** adj.
– ORIGIN C16 (denoting one of the alimentary humours once supposed to nourish the body): from med. L., 'change, exchange'.

**Cambodian** ● **n.** **1** a native or national of Cambodia, or a person of Cambodian descent. **2** another term for **KHMER** (the language). ● **adj.** of or relating to Cambodia.

**Cambrian** /ˈkambrɪən/ ● **adj.** **1** (chiefly in names or geographical terms) Welsh. **2** Geology relating to or denoting the first period in the Palaeozoic era (between the Precambrian aeon and the Ordovician period, about 570 to 510 million years ago), a time when there was extensive invertebrate life.
– ORIGIN C17: from L. *Cambria* 'Wales', var. of *Cumbria*, from Welsh *Cymry* 'Welshman' or *Cymru* 'Wales'.

**cambric** /ˈkambrɪk, ˈkeɪm-/ ● **n.** a lightweight, closely woven white linen or cotton fabric.

– ORIGIN ME: from *Kamerijk*, Flemish form of *Cambrai*, a town in northern France, where it was orig. made; cf. **CHAMBRAY**.

**Cambridge blue** ● n. Brit. **1** a pale blue colour. **2** a person who has represented Cambridge University in a particular sport.

**Cambs.** ● abbrev. Cambridgeshire.

**camcorder** ● n. a portable combined video camera and video recorder.

**came**[1] past tense of **COME**.

**came**[2] ● n. each of a number of strips forming a framework for enclosing a pane of glass, especially in a leaded window.
– ORIGIN C16: of unknown origin.

**camel** ● n. **1** a large, long-necked, mainly domesticated ungulate mammal of arid country, with long slender legs, broad cushioned feet, and either one or two humps on the back. [*Camelus dromedarius* (**Arabian camel**, N. Africa and SW Asia, with one hump) and *C. ferus* (**Bactrian camel**, central Asia, two humps).] **2** a fabric made from camel hair. **3** an apparatus for raising a sunken ship, consisting of one or more watertight chests to provide buoyancy.
– ORIGIN OE, from L. *camelus*, from Gk *kamēlos*, of Semitic origin.

**camelback** ● n. a back with a hump-shaped curve on a sofa or other piece of furniture.

**camel cricket** ● n. a wingless humpbacked insect related to the grasshoppers, typically living in caves or holes. [Family Raphidophoridae: many species.]

**cameleer** /ˌkaməˈlɪə/ ● n. a person who controls or rides a camel.

**camel hair** (also **camel's hair**) ● n. **1** a fabric made from the hair of a camel. **2** fine, soft hair from a squirrel's tail, used in artists' brushes.

**camelid** /kəˈmiːlɪd, ˈkamǝlɪd/ ● n. Zoology a mammal of a family (Camelidae) comprising the camels together with the llama and its relatives.

**camellia** /kəˈmiːlɪə, -ˈmɛlɪə/ ● n. an evergreen East Asian shrub related to the tea plant, grown for its showy flowers and shiny leaves. [*Camellia japonica* and related species.]
– ORIGIN mod. L., named by Linnaeus after the C17 Moravian botanist Joseph *Kamel* (Latinized as *Camellus*).

**camelopard** /ˈkamɪlə(ʊ)pɑːd, kəˈmɛləpɑːd/ ● n. archaic a giraffe.
– ORIGIN ME: via L. from Gk *kamēlopardalis*, from *kamēlos* 'camel' + *pardalis* (see **PARD**).

**Camelot** /ˈkamɪlɒt/ ● n. a place associated with glittering romance and optimism.
– ORIGIN the place where King Arthur held his legendary court.

**camel spider** ● n. another term for **SUN SPIDER**.

**camel thorn** ● n. a spiny leguminous shrub occurring in arid country. [*Alhagi camelorum* (Middle East) and *Acacia giraffae* (southern Africa).]

**Camembert** /ˈkaməmbɛː/ ● n. a kind of rich, soft, creamy cheese with a whitish rind, originally made near Camembert in Normandy.

**cameo** /ˈkamɪəʊ/ ● n. (pl. **-os**) **1** a piece of jewellery consisting of a portrait in profile carved in relief on a background of a different colour. **2** a short piece of writing which neatly encapsulates something. **3** a small distinctive part in a play or film, played by a distinguished actor.
– ORIGIN ME: from OFr. *camahieu*, *cama(h)u*; later influenced by Ital. *cam(m)eo*, from med. L. *cammaeus*.

**cameo glass** ● n. decorative glass consisting of layers of different colours, the outermost being cut away to leave a design in relief.

**camera**[1] ● n. a device for recording visual images in the form of photographs, cinema film, or video signals.
– PHRASES **on** (or **off**) **camera** while being (or not being) filmed or televised.
– DERIVATIVES **cameraman** n.
– ORIGIN C19: from L. (see **CAMERA**[2], **CAMERA OBSCURA**).

**camera**[2] ● n. [in names] a chamber or round building.
– PHRASES **in camera** chiefly Law in private, in particular taking place in the private chambers of a judge, with the press and public excluded.
– ORIGIN C17 (denoting a council or legislative chamber): from L., 'vault, arched chamber'.

**camera lucida** /ˌkam(ə)rə ˈluːsɪdə/ ● n. an instrument in which rays of light are reflected by a prism to produce an image on a sheet of paper, from which a drawing can be made.
– ORIGIN C18: from L., 'bright chamber', on the pattern of *camera obscura*.

**camera obscura** /ɒbsˈkjʊərə/ ● n. **1** a darkened box with a convex lens or aperture for projecting the image of an external object on to a screen inside. **2** a small round building with a rotating angled mirror at the apex of the roof, projecting an image of the landscape on to a horizontal surface inside.
– ORIGIN C18: from L., 'dark chamber'.

**camera-ready** ● adj. Printing in the right form to be reproduced photographically on to a printing plate.

**Cameroonian** /ˌkaməˈruːnɪən/ ● n. a native or inhabitant of Cameroon, a country on the west coast of Africa. ● adj. of or relating to Cameroon.

**cam follower** ● n. the part of a machine in sliding or rolling contact with a rotating cam and given motion by it.

**camiknickers** ● pl. n. Brit. a woman's one-piece undergarment which combines a camisole and a pair of French knickers.

**Camisard** /ˈkamɪsɑː, ˌkamɪˈsɑː, French kamisaʀ/ ● n. a member of the French Protestant insurgents who rebelled against the persecution that followed the revocation of the Edict of Nantes.
– ORIGIN Fr., from Provençal *camisa*, from late L. *camisia* 'shirt', because of the Camisards' white shirts.

**camisole** /ˈkamɪsəʊl/ ● n. a woman's loose-fitting undergarment for the upper body.
– ORIGIN C19: from Fr., either from Ital. *camiciola*, dimin. of *camicia*, or from Sp. *camisola*, dimin. of *camisa*, both from late L. *camisia* 'shirt or nightgown'.

**camomile** ● n. variant spelling of **CHAMOMILE**.

**camouflage** /ˈkaməflɑːʒ/ ● n. **1** the disguising of military personnel and equipment by painting or covering them to make them blend in with their surroundings. ➤the clothing or materials used for such a purpose. **2** the natural colouring or form of an animal which enables it to blend in with its surroundings. ● v. hide or disguise by means of camouflage.
– ORIGIN First World War: from Fr., from *camoufler* 'to disguise'.

**camp**[1] ● n. **1** a place with temporary accommodation used by soldiers, refugees, or travelling people. ➤a complex of buildings for holiday accommodation. **2** (also **summer camp**) N. Amer. a summer holiday programme for children, offering a range of activities. **3** the supporters of a particular party or doctrine regarded collectively. **4** Brit. Archaeology a prehistoric enclosed or fortified site, especially an Iron Age hill fort. **5** S. African a fenced field or enclosed area for grazing. ➤Austral./NZ a place where livestock regularly congregate. ● v. **1** lodge temporarily, especially in a tent or caravan while on holiday. **2** Austral./NZ (of livestock) assemble together. **3** S. African divide (land) and enclose with fences.
– PHRASES **break camp** take down a tent or the tents of an encampment ready to leave.
– ORIGIN C16: from Fr. *camp*, *champ*, from Ital. *campo*, from L. *campus* 'level ground'.

**camp**[2] informal ● adj. (of a man) ostentatiously and extravagantly effeminate. ➤deliberately exaggerated and theatrical in style. ● n. camp behaviour or style. ● v. (usu. **camp it up**) (of a man) behave in a camp way.
– DERIVATIVES **campily** adv. **campiness** n. **campy** adj.
– ORIGIN C20: of unknown origin.

**campaign** ● n. **1** a series of military operations intended to achieve an objective in a particular area. **2** an organized course of action to achieve a goal. ● v. work in an organized and active way towards a goal.
– DERIVATIVES **campaigner** n.

– ORIGIN C17 (denoting a tract of open country): from Fr. *campagne*, via Ital. from late L. *campania*, from *campus* (see **CAMP**[1]).

**campanile** /ˌkampəˈniːleɪ/ ● **n.** a bell tower, especially a free-standing one.
– ORIGIN C17: from Ital., from *campana* 'bell'.

**campanology** /ˌkampəˈnɒlədʒi/ ● **n.** the art or practice of bell-ringing.
– DERIVATIVES **campanological** adj. **campanologist** n.
– ORIGIN C19: from mod. L. *campanologia*, from late L. *campana* 'bell'.

**campanula** /kamˈpanjʊlə/ ● **n.** another term for **BELLFLOWER**.
– ORIGIN mod. L., dimin. of late L. *campana* 'bell'.

**campanulate** /kamˈpanjʊlət/ ● **adj.** Botany (of a flower) bell-shaped, as in a campanula.

**Campari** /kamˈpɑːri/ ● **n.** trademark a pinkish aperitif flavoured with bitters.

**camp bed** ● **n.** Brit. a folding portable bed.

**campcraft** ● **n.** knowledge and skill required for a simple outdoor life.

**camper** ● **n. 1** a person who spends a holiday in a tent or holiday camp. **2** (also **camper van**) a large motor vehicle with living accommodation.

**campesino** /ˌkampəˈsiːnəʊ/ ● **n.** (pl. **-os** /-əʊz/) (in Spanish-speaking countries) a peasant farmer.
– ORIGIN from Sp.

**campfire** ● **n.** an open-air fire in a camp.

**camp follower** ● **n. 1** a civilian working in or attached to a military camp. **2** a person who associates with a group without being a full member of it.

**campground** ● **n.** North American term for **CAMPSITE**.

**camphor** /ˈkamfə/ ● **n.** a white volatile crystalline substance with an aromatic smell and bitter taste, occurring in certain essential oils.
– ORIGIN ME: from OFr. *camphore* or med. L. *camphora*, from Arab. *kāfūr*, via Malay from Sanskrit *karpūra*.

**camphorate** ● **v.** impregnate or treat with camphor.

**camphor tree** ● **n.** an East Asian tree, the chief natural source of camphor. [*Cinnamomum camphora*.]

**campimetry** /kamˈpɪmətri/ ● **n.** a technique for measuring or mapping the field of vision of the eye.
– ORIGIN C20: from L. *campus* (see **CAMP**[1]) + **-METRY**.

**campion** /ˈkampɪən/ ● **n.** a plant of the pink family, typically having pink or white flowers with notched petals. [Genera *Silene* and *Lychnis*.]
– ORIGIN C16: perh. rel. to **CHAMPION**, applied to a plant of this kind said to have been used for victors' garlands in ancient times.

**camp meeting** ● **n.** N. Amer. a religious meeting held in the open air or in a tent, often lasting several days.

**campo** /ˈkampəʊ/ ● **n.** (pl. **-os**) **1** (**the campo**) (in South America, especially Brazil) a grass plain with occasional stunted trees. **2** a square in an Italian or Spanish town.
– ORIGIN from Sp., Port., and Ital. *campo*, lit. 'field'.

**campsite** ● **n.** a place used for camping, especially one equipped for holidaymakers.

**campus** ● **n.** (pl. **campuses**) the grounds and buildings of a university or college. ➤ N. Amer. the grounds of a college, school, hospital, or other institution.
– ORIGIN C18 (orig. US): from L. *campus* (see **CAMP**[1]).

**campylobacter** /ˈkampɪləʊˌbaktə, ˌkampɪləʊˈbaktə/ ● **n.** a bacterium of a genus including species responsible for abortion in animals and food poisoning in humans. [Genus *Campylobacter*.]
– ORIGIN mod. L., from Gk *kampulos* 'bent' + **BACTERIUM**.

**camshaft** /ˈkamʃɑːft/ ● **n.** a shaft with one or more cams attached to it, especially one operating the valves in an internal-combustion engine.

**camwood** ● **n.** the hard red wood of the African padauk tree.
– ORIGIN C17: prob. from Temne *k'am* + **WOOD**.

**Can.** ● **abbrev.** Canada or Canadian.

**can**[1] ● **modal v.** (3rd sing. present **can**; past **could**) **1** be able to. ➤ [with neg. or in questions] used to express doubt or surprise: *he can't have finished.* ➤ used to indicate that something is typically the case: *he could be very moody.* **2** be permitted to.
– ORIGIN OE *cunnan* 'know'.

**can**[2] ● **n. 1** a cylindrical metal container, in particular one in which food or drink is hermetically sealed for storage over long periods. **2** (**the can**) N. Amer. informal prison. **3** (**the can**) N. Amer. informal the toilet. **4** (**cans**) informal headphones. ● **v.** (**canned**, **canning**) **1** preserve in a can. **2** N. Amer. informal dismiss from a job or reject as inadequate.
– PHRASES **a can of worms** a complicated matter likely to prove awkward or embarrassing. **in the can** informal on tape or film and ready to be broadcast or released.
– DERIVATIVES **canner** n.
– ORIGIN OE *canne*, either of Gmc origin or from late L. *canna*.

**Canaanite** /ˈkeɪnənʌɪt/ ● **n.** a native of inhabitant of Canaan, the biblical name for the area of ancient Palestine west of the River Jordan, the Promised Land of the Israelites.

**Canada balsam** ● **n.** a yellowish resin obtained from the balsam fir, used for mounting specimens on microscope slides.

**Canada goose** ● **n.** a common brownish-grey North American goose, introduced in Britain and elsewhere. [*Branta canadensis*.]

**Canadian** ● **n.** a native or inhabitant of Canada. ● **adj.** of or relating to Canada.
– DERIVATIVES **Canadianism** n.

**Canadian football** ● **n.** a form of football played in Canada, resembling American football.

**Canadien** /ˌkanaˈdjã, French kanadjɛ̃/ Canadian ● **n.** a French Canadian. ● **adj.** French Canadian.
– ORIGIN from Fr.

**canaille** /kaˈnʌɪ, French kanaj/ ● **n.** derogatory the common people; the masses.
– ORIGIN Fr., from Ital. *canaglia* 'pack of dogs', from *cane* 'dog'.

**canal** ● **n. 1** an artificial waterway allowing the passage of boats inland or conveying water for irrigation. **2** a tubular duct in a plant or animal conveying food, liquid, or air.
– ORIGIN ME: from OFr., alt. of *chanel* 'channel', from L. *canalis* 'pipe, groove, channel', from *canna* 'cane'.

**canalize** /ˈkan(ə)lʌɪz/ (also **-ise**) ● **v. 1** convert (a river) into a navigable canal. **2** convey through a duct or channel. **3** give a direction or purpose to.
– DERIVATIVES **canalization** n.
– ORIGIN C19: from Fr. *canaliser*, from *canal* (see **CANAL**).

**canapé** /ˈkanəpeɪ/ ● **n. 1** a small piece of bread or pastry with a savoury topping, often served with drinks. **2** a sofa, especially a decorative French antique.
– ORIGIN from Fr.

**canard** /kəˈnɑːd, ˈkanɑːd/ ● **n. 1** an unfounded rumour or story. **2** a small wing-like projection on an aircraft forward of the main wing, for extra stability or control.
– ORIGIN C19: from Fr., lit. 'duck', also 'hoax', from OFr. *caner* 'to quack'.

**Canarese** ● **n. & adj.** variant spelling of **KANARESE**.

**canary** ● **n.** (pl. **-ies**) **1** a bright yellow finch with a melodious song, popular as a cage bird. [*Serinus canaria* (Canary Islands, Azores, and Madeira) and related species in Africa.] **2** (also **canary yellow**) a bright yellow colour. **3** historical a sweet wine from the Canary Islands, similar to Madeira.
– ORIGIN C16: from Fr. *canari*, from Sp. *canario* 'canary' or 'person from the Canary Islands'.

**canary creeper** ● **n.** a South American climbing plant bearing bright yellow flowers. [*Tropaeolium peregrinum*.]

**canary grass** ● **n.** a tall grass of NW Africa and the Canary Islands, grown for its seeds which are fed to cage birds. [Genus *Phalaris*: several species.]

**canasta** /kəˈnastə/ ● **n.** a card game resembling rummy, using two packs and usually played by two pairs of partners. ➤ a meld of seven cards in this game.
– ORIGIN 1940s: from Sp. (of Uruguayan origin), lit. 'basket', based on L. *canistrum* (see **CANISTER**).

**cancan** ● **n.** a lively, high-kicking stage dance originating

in 19th-century Parisian music halls and performed by women in long skirts and petticoats.
– ORIGIN C19: from Fr., child's word for *canard* 'duck', from OFr. *caner* 'to quack'.

**cancel** • v. (**cancelled**, **cancelling**; US also **canceled**, **canceling**) **1** decide that (a planned event) will not take place. ➤annul or revoke: *his visa had been cancelled.* **2** mark or tear (a ticket or stamp) to show that it has been used or invalidated. **3** (often **cancel something out**) (of a factor or circumstance) neutralize or negate the effect of (another). **4** Mathematics delete (an equal factor) from both sides of an equation or from the numerator and denominator of a fraction. • n. **1** a mark made on a postage stamp to show that it has been used. **2** Printing a new page or section inserted in a book to replace the original text. **3** US (in music) a natural sign (♮).
– DERIVATIVES **cancellation** n. **canceller** n.
– ORIGIN ME: from OFr. *canceller*, from L. *cancellare*, from *cancelli* 'crossbars'.

**cancelbot** /ˈkansəlbɒt/ • n. Computing a program that searches for and deletes email messages originating from specified addresses.

**cancellous** /ˈkans(ə)ləs/ • adj. Anatomy (of bone tissue) having a porous, mesh-like structure, typical of the interior of mature bones.
– ORIGIN C19: from L. *cancelli* 'crossbars' + **-OUS**.

**Cancer** • n. **1** Astronomy a constellation (the Crab), said to represent a crab crushed under the foot of Hercules. **2** Astrology the fourth sign of the zodiac, which the sun enters at the northern summer solstice (about 21 June).
– DERIVATIVES **Cancerian** /-ˈsɪərɪən, -ˈsɛːrɪən/ n. & adj.
– ORIGIN from L.

**cancer** • n. **1** a disease caused by an uncontrolled division of abnormal cells in a part of the body. ➤a malignant growth or tumour resulting from such a division of cells. **2** something evil or destructive that is hard to contain or eradicate: *the cancer of racism.*
– DERIVATIVES **cancerous** adj.
– ORIGIN OE, from L., 'crab or creeping ulcer', translating Gk *karkinos*, said to have been applied to tumours because the swollen veins around them resembled the limbs of a crab.

**cancer stick** • n. informal, humorous a cigarette.

**candela** /kanˈdɛlə, -ˈdiːlə, ˈkandɪlə/ (abbrev.: **cd**) • n. Physics the SI unit of luminous intensity.
– ORIGIN 1950s: from L., 'candle'.

**candelabra tree** • n. a tree with upward-curving boughs, resembling a candelabrum. [Genus *Euphorbia* (Africa) and *Araucaria angustifolia* (S. America).]

**candelabrum** /ˌkandɪˈlɑːbrəm, -ˈleɪ-/ • n. (pl. **candelabra** /-brə/) a large branched candlestick or holder for several candles or lamps.
– ORIGIN C19: from L., from *candela* (see **CANDLE**).

**USAGE candelabrum**

Based on the Latin forms, the correct singular is **candelabrum** and the correct plural is **candelabra**, but these forms are often not observed in practice: the singular form is assumed to be **candelabra** and hence its plural is interpreted as **candelabras**.

**candid** • adj. **1** truthful and straightforward; frank. **2** (of a photograph or film) taken informally, especially without the subject's knowledge.
– DERIVATIVES **candidly** adv. **candidness** n.
– ORIGIN C17 (in the sense 'white'): from L. *candidus* cf. **CANDOUR**.

**candida** /ˈkandɪdə/ • n. a yeast-like parasitic fungus that sometimes causes thrush. [Genus *Candida*.]
– ORIGIN mod. L., fem. of L. *candidus* 'white'.

**candidate** /ˈkandɪdeɪt, -dət/ • n. **1** a person who applies for a job or is nominated for election. **2** a person taking an examination. **3** a person or thing suitable for or likely to receive a particular fate, treatment, or position.
– DERIVATIVES **candidacy** n. **candidature** n. (Brit.).
– ORIGIN C17: from L. *candidatus* 'white-robed', also denoting a candidate for office (who traditionally wore a white toga), from *candidus* 'white'.

**candidiasis** /ˌkandɪˈdʌɪəsɪs/ • n. infection with candida, especially as causing oral or vaginal thrush.

**candiru** /ˌkandɪˈruː/ • n. a minute, slender bloodsucking catfish of the Amazon region, sometimes entering the body orifices of mammals. [*Vandellia cirrhosa*.]
– ORIGIN C19: via Port. from Tupi *candirú*.

**candle** • n. **1** a cylinder of wax or tallow with a central wick which is lit to produce light as it burns. **2** (also **international candle**) Physics a unit of luminous intensity, superseded by the candela. • v. test (an egg) for freshness or fertility by holding it to the light.
– PHRASES **be unable to hold a candle to** informal be not nearly as good as. **(the game's) not worth the candle** the potential advantages to be gained from doing something do not justify the cost or trouble involved.
– DERIVATIVES **candler** n.
– ORIGIN OE *candel*, from L. *candela*, from *candere* 'be white or glisten'.

**candleberry** • n. (pl. **-ies**) a bayberry, candlenut, or other tree or shrub whose berries yield wax.

**candlefish** • n. (pl. same or **-fishes**) a small edible marine fish with oily flesh, occurring on the west coast of North America. [*Thaleichthys pacificus*.]

**candlelight** • n. dim light provided by a candle or candles.
– DERIVATIVES **candlelit** adj.

**Candlemas** /ˈkand(ə)lmas, -məs/ • n. a Christian festival held on 2 February to commemorate the purification of the Virgin Mary (after childbirth, according to Jewish law) and the presentation of Christ in the Temple.
– ORIGIN OE *Candelmæsse* (see **CANDLE**, **MASS**).

**candlenut** • n. an evergreen tree native to SE Asia and the South Pacific islands, with large seeds that yield an oil used for lighting. [*Aleurites moluccana*.]

**candlepower** • n. illuminating power expressed in candelas or candles.

**candlestick** • n. a support or holder for one or more candles.

**candlewick** • n. a thick, soft cotton fabric with a raised, tufted pattern. ➤the yarn used to make such a fabric.

**can-do** • adj. informal willing or determined to take action and achieve results: *a can-do attitude.*

**candomblé** /ˌkandɒmˈbleɪ/ • n. a Brazilian sect of the macumba cult.
– ORIGIN from Brazilian Port.

**candour** (US **candor**) • n. the quality of being open and honest.
– ORIGIN ME (in the sense 'whiteness', hence 'purity', 'lack of bias', 'honesty'): from L. *candor*.

**C & W** • abbrev. country and western (music).

**candy** • n. (pl. **-ies**) (also **sugar candy**) **1** N. Amer. sweets; confectionery. **2** chiefly Brit. sugar crystallized by repeated boiling and slow evaporation. • v. (**-ies**, **-ied**) [often as adj. **candied**] preserve (fruit) by coating and impregnating it with a sugar syrup.
– ORIGIN C17 (as v.): as n. from ME *sugar-candy*, from Fr. *sucre candi* 'crystallized sugar', from Arab. *sukkar* 'sugar' + *ḳandī* 'candied'.

**candy apple** • n. N. Amer. **1** a toffee apple. **2** (also **candy-apple red**) a bright red colour.

**candy-ass** • n. N. Amer. informal a timid, cowardly, or despicable person.
– DERIVATIVES **candy-assed** adj.

**candy cane** • n. N. Amer. a stick of striped sweet rock with a curved end, resembling a walking stick.

**candyfloss** • n. Brit. **1** a mass of pink or white fluffy spun sugar wrapped round a stick. **2** something worthless or insubstantial.

**candyman** • n. (pl. **-men**) N. Amer. informal a person who sells illegal drugs.

**candy-striped** • adj. patterned with alternating stripes of white and another colour, typically pink.
– DERIVATIVES **candy-stripe** adj. & n.

**candy-striper** • n. N. Amer. informal a female voluntary nurse in a hospital.
– ORIGIN so named because of their candy-striped uniforms.

**candytuft** • n. a plant with small heads of white, pink, or purple flowers, grown as a garden or rockery plant. [Genus *Iberis*.]
– ORIGIN C17: from *Candy* (obs. form of *Candia*, former name of Crete) + TUFT.

**cane** • n. 1 the hollow jointed stem of tall reeds, grasses, etc., especially bamboo or the slender, pliant stem of plants such as rattan. ➤ a woody stem of a raspberry or related plant. 2 a length of cane or a slender stick used as a support for plants, a walking stick, or an instrument of punishment. • v. 1 beat with a cane as a punishment. 2 Brit. informal use recklessly or without restraint.
– DERIVATIVES **caner** n.
– ORIGIN ME: from OFr., via L. from Gk *kanna*, *kannē*, of Semitic origin.

**canebrake** • n. N. Amer. a piece of ground covered with a dense growth of canes.

**caned** • adj. 1 (of furniture) made or repaired with cane. 2 Brit. informal intoxicated with drink or drugs.

**cane rat** • n. a large rat-like African rodent found in wetlands south of the Sahara. [Genus *Thryonomys*.]

**cane toad** • n. a large brown toad of tropical America, introduced elsewhere for pest control. [*Bufo marinus*.]

**Canfield** • n. chiefly N. Amer. a form of the card game patience or solitaire.
– ORIGIN C20: named after the Amer. gambler Richard A. *Canfield*.

**canid** /ˈkanɪd/ • n. Zoology a mammal of the dog family (Canidae).

**canine** /ˈkeɪnʌɪn, ˈka-/ • adj. of, relating to, or resembling a dog. • n. 1 a dog or other animal of the dog family. 2 (also **canine tooth**) a pointed tooth between the incisors and premolars, often greatly enlarged in carnivores.
– ORIGIN ME: from Fr., from L. *caninus*, from *canis* 'dog'.

**caning** • n. 1 a beating with a cane as a punishment. 2 informal a resounding defeat. 3 informal a severe reprimand.

**canister** • n. 1 a round or cylindrical container used for storing food, chemicals, rolls of film, etc. 2 historical small bullets packed in cases that fit the bore of a gun.
– ORIGIN C15 (denoting a basket): from L. *canistrum*, from Gk *kanastron* 'wicker basket', from *kanna* (see CANE).

**canker** • n. 1 a destructive fungal disease of trees that results in damage to the bark. ➤ an open lesion in plant tissue caused by infection or injury. ➤ fungal rot in parsnips, tomatoes, or other vegetables. 2 an ulcerous condition of an animal, especially an inflammation of the ear caused by a mite infestation. ➤ chiefly N. Amer. a small ulcer of the mouth or lips. • v. 1 become infected with canker. 2 [usu. as adj. **cankered**] infect with a pervasive and corrupting bitterness.
– DERIVATIVES **cankerous** adj.
– ORIGIN ME (denoting a tumour): from OFr. *chancre*, from L. *cancer* (see CANCER).

**cankerworm** • n. the caterpillar of a North American moth that feeds on the buds and leaves of trees.

**canna** /ˈkanə/ • n. a lily-like tropical American plant with bright flowers and ornamental strap-like leaves. [Genus *Canna*: several species.]
– ORIGIN from mod. L., from L. *canna* (see CANE).

**cannabinol** /ˈkanəbɪnɒl, kəˈnab-/ • n. Chemistry a crystalline compound whose derivatives, especially THC, are the active constituents of cannabis.
– DERIVATIVES **cannabinoid** n.

**cannabis** • n. 1 a dried preparation or resinous extract made from a plant, used (generally illegally) as a psychotropic drug (chiefly in cigarettes). 2 the plant from which this substance comes, also used to produce hemp fibre. [*Cannabis sativa*.]
– ORIGIN from L., from Gk *kannabis*.

**canned** • adj. 1 preserved in a sealed can. 2 informal, chiefly derogatory (of music, applause, etc.) pre-recorded.

**cannel coal** /ˈkan(ə)l/ • n. a hard, compact kind of bituminous coal.
– ORIGIN C16: perh. from north. Engl. *cannel* 'candle'.

**cannellini bean** /ˌkanəˈliːni/ • n. a kidney-shaped bean of a medium-sized creamy-white variety.
– ORIGIN Ital. *cannellini*, lit. 'small tubes'.

**cannelloni** /ˌkanəˈləʊni/ • pl. n. rolls of pasta stuffed with a meat or vegetable mixture, usually cooked in a cheese sauce.
– ORIGIN Ital., lit. 'large tubes', from *cannello* 'tube'.

**cannelure** /ˈkan(ə)ljʊə/ • n. a groove round the cylindrical part of a bullet.
– ORIGIN C18: from Fr., from *canneler* 'provide with a channel', from *canne* 'reed, cane'.

**cannery** • n. (pl. **-ies**) a factory where food is canned.

**cannibal** • n. a person who eats the flesh of other human beings. ➤ an animal that eats flesh of its own species.
– DERIVATIVES **cannibalism** n. **cannibalistic** adj. **cannibalistically** adv.
– ORIGIN C16: from Sp. *Canibales*, var. of *Caribes*, a West Indian people reputed to eat humans (see CARIB).

**cannibalize** (also **-ise**) • v. 1 use (a machine) as a source of spare parts for another, similar machine. 2 (of a company) reduce (the sales of one of its products) by introducing a similar, competing product. 3 (of an animal) eat (an animal of its own kind).
– DERIVATIVES **cannibalization** n.

**cannon** • n. 1 (pl. usu. same) a large, heavy piece of artillery formerly used in warfare. ➤ an automatic heavy gun that fires shells from an aircraft or tank. 2 Billiards & Snooker, chiefly Brit. a stroke in which the cue ball strikes two balls successively. [C19: alt. of CAROM.] 3 Engineering a heavy cylinder or hollow drum rotating independently on a shaft. • v. chiefly Brit. collide with something forcefully or at an angle. ➤ Billiards & Snooker make a cannon shot.
– ORIGIN ME: from Fr. *canon*, from Ital. *cannone* 'large tube', from *canna* (see CANE).

**cannonade** /ˌkanəˈneɪd/ • n. a period of continuous heavy gunfire. • v. discharge heavy guns continuously.
– ORIGIN C16: from Fr., from Ital. *cannonata*, from *cannone* (see CANNON).

**cannonball** • n. 1 a round metal or stone projectile fired from a cannon. 2 (also **cannonball dive**) N. Amer. a jump into water feet first with the knees clasped to the chest.

**cannon bone** • n. a long tube-shaped bone between a horse's fetlock and the knee or hock.

**cannoneer** • n. historical an artilleryman who positioned and fired a cannon.

**cannon fodder** • n. soldiers regarded merely as material to be expended in war.

**cannot** • contr. can not.

**cannula** /ˈkanjʊlə/ • n. (pl. **cannulae** /-liː/ or **cannulas**) Surgery a thin tube inserted into the body to administer medication, drain off fluid, or introduce a surgical instrument.
– ORIGIN C17: from L. 'small reed', dimin. of *canna* (see CANE).

**cannulate** • v. Surgery introduce a cannula into.
– DERIVATIVES **cannulation** n.

**canny** • adj. (**-ier**, **-iest**) 1 shrewd, especially in financial or business matters. 2 N. English & Scottish pleasant; nice.
– DERIVATIVES **cannily** adv. **canniness** n.
– ORIGIN C16 (orig. Scots): from CAN[1] (in the obs. sense 'know') + -Y[1].

**canoe** • n. a narrow keelless boat with pointed ends, propelled with a paddle. • v. (**-oes**, **-oed**, **canoeing**) travel in or paddle a canoe.
– DERIVATIVES **canoeing** n. **canoeist** n.
– ORIGIN C16: from Sp. *canoa*, from Arawak, from Carib *canaoua*.

**canoe shell** • n. a marine mollusc which has a thin shell with a wide aperture. [Family Scaphandridae.]

**canola** /kəˈnəʊlə/ • n. oilseed rape of a variety grown in North America.
– ORIGIN 1970s: from *Canada* + *-ola* (based on L. *oleum* 'oil').

**canon**[1] • n. 1 a general rule or principle by which something is judged. ➤ a Church decree or law. 2 a collection or list of sacred books accepted as genuine. ➤ the works of a particular author or artist that are recognized as genuine. ➤ a list of literary works considered to be permanently established as being of the highest quality. 3 the part of the Roman Catholic Mass containing the words of consecration. 4 Music a piece in which the same melody is begun in different parts successively, so that

the imitations overlap.
– PHRASES **in canon** Music with different parts successively beginning the same melody.
– ORIGIN OE: from L., from Gk *kanōn* 'rule', reinforced in ME by OFr. *canon*.

**canon²** ● n. **1** a member of the clergy on the staff of a cathedral, especially one who is a member of the chapter. **2** (also **canon regular** or **regular canon**) (fem. **canoness**) a member of certain orders of Roman Catholic clergy that live communally like monks or nuns.
– ORIGIN ME: from OFr. *canonie*, from L. *canonicus* (see CANONIC).

**cañon** ● n. archaic spelling of CANYON.

**canon cancrizans** /ˈkaŋkrɪˌzanz/ ● n. Music a canon in which the theme or subject is repeated backwards in the second part.
– ORIGIN C19: from CANON¹ + med. L. *cancrizans* 'walking backwards' (from *cancer* 'crab').

**canonic** /kəˈnɒnɪk/ ● adj. **1** Music in the form of a canon. **2** another term for CANONICAL.
– DERIVATIVES **canonicity** n.
– ORIGIN OE (as n.): from OFr. *canonique* or L. *canonicus* 'canonical', based on Gk *kanon* 'rule' (cf. CANON¹).

**canonical** /kəˈnɒnɪk(ə)l/ ● adj. **1** according to or ordered by canon law. **2** accepted as being accurate and authoritative. **3** of or relating to a cathedral chapter or a member of it. ● n. (**canonicals**) the prescribed official dress of the clergy.
– DERIVATIVES **canonically** adv. **canonicity** n.

**canonical hours** ● pl. n. **1** the times of daily Christian prayer appointed in the breviary, or the offices set for them (matins with lauds, prime, terce, sext, nones, vespers, and compline). **2** (in the Church of England) the time during which a marriage may lawfully be celebrated (usually between 8 a.m. and 6 p.m.).

**canonist** ● n. an expert in canon law.
– DERIVATIVES **canonistic** adj.

**canonize** (also **-ise**) ● v. **1** (in the Roman Catholic Church) officially declare (a dead person) to be a saint. **2** sanction by Church authority.
– DERIVATIVES **canonization** n.
– ORIGIN ME: from late L. *canonizare* 'admit as authoritative', from L. *canon* (see CANON¹).

**canon law** ● n. ecclesiastical law, especially that laid down by papal pronouncements.

**canon regular** ● n. see CANON².

**canonry** ● n. (pl. **-ies**) the office or benefice of a canon.

**canoodle** ● v. informal kiss and cuddle amorously.
– ORIGIN C19 (orig. US): of unknown origin.

**Canopic jar** /kəˈnəʊpɪk/ ● n. a covered urn used in ancient Egyptian burials to hold the visceral organs from an embalmed body.
– ORIGIN C19: *Canopic* from L. *Canopicus*, from *Canopus*, a town in ancient Egypt.

**canopy** ● n. (pl. **-ies**) **1** a cloth covering over a throne, bed, etc. ➤ a roof-like projection or shelter. ➤ the expanding, umbrella-like part of a parachute. **2** the transparent plastic or glass cover of an aircraft's cockpit. **3** the uppermost branches of the trees in a forest, forming a more or less continuous layer of foliage. ● v. (**-ies**, **-ied**) [usu. as adj. **canopied**] cover or provide with a canopy.
– ORIGIN ME: from med. L. *canopeum*, alt. of L. *conopeum* 'mosquito net over a bed', from Gk *kōnōpeion* 'couch with mosquito curtains', from *kōnōps* 'mosquito'.

**canorous** /kəˈnɔːrəs/ ● adj. rare melodious or resonant.
– ORIGIN C17: from L. *canorus* (from *canere* 'sing') + **-OUS**.

**canst** archaic second person singular present of CAN¹.

**Cant.** ● abbrev. Canticles (the Song of Songs) (in biblical references).

**cant¹** /kant/ ● n. **1** hypocritical and sanctimonious talk. **2** derogatory language peculiar to a specified group: *thieves' cant*. ➤ [as modifier] denoting a phrase or catchword temporarily current. ● v. dated talk hypocritically and sanctimoniously.
– ORIGIN C16 (in sense 'singing', later 'whining speech' (as of a beggar), hence 'jargon': prob. from L. *cantare* (see CHANT).

**cant²** /kant/ ● v. be or cause to be in a slanting or oblique position; tilt. ➤ (of a ship) swing round. ● n. **1** a slope or tilt. **2** a wedge-shaped block of wood remaining after the better-quality pieces have been cut off.
– ORIGIN ME (denoting an edge or brink): from Mid. Low Ger. *kant*, *kante*, MDu. *cant*, 'point, side, edge', rel. to med. L. *cantus* 'corner, side'.

**can't** ● contr. cannot.

**Cantab.** /ˈkantab/ ● abbrev. of Cambridge University.
– ORIGIN from L. *Cantabrigiensis*, from *Cantabrigia* 'Cambridge'.

**cantabile** /kanˈtɑːbɪleɪ/ ● adv. & adj. Music in a smooth singing style.
– ORIGIN Ital., lit. 'singable'.

**Cantabrigian** /ˌkantəˈbrɪdʒɪən/ ● adj. of or relating to Cambridge or Cambridge University. ● n. a member of Cambridge University.
– ORIGIN C16: from L. *Cantabrigia* 'Cambridge' + **-IAN**.

**cantal** /ˈkantɑːl/ ● n. a hard, strong cheese made chiefly in the Auvergne.
– ORIGIN named after *Cantal*, a department of Auvergne, France.

**cantaloupe** /ˈkantəluːp/ ● n. a small round melon of a variety with orange flesh and ribbed skin.
– ORIGIN C18: from Fr. *cantaloup*, from *Cantaluppi* near Rome.

**cantankerous** ● adj. bad-tempered, argumentative, and uncooperative.
– DERIVATIVES **cantankerously** adv. **cantankerousness** n.
– ORIGIN C18: of unknown origin; perh. a blend of Anglo-Irish *cant* 'auction' and *rancorous* (see RANCOUR).

**cantata** /kanˈtɑːtə/ ● n. a medium-length narrative or descriptive piece of music with vocal solos and normally a chorus and orchestra.
– ORIGIN C18: from Ital. *cantata* (*aria*) 'sung (air)', from *cantare* 'sing'.

**cant dog** ● n. another term for CANT HOOK.

**canteen** ● n. **1** a restaurant in a workplace or educational establishment. **2** Brit. a specially designed case or box containing a set of cutlery. **3** a small water bottle, as used by soldiers or campers.
– ORIGIN C18 (orig. denoting a shop selling provisions or alcohol in a barracks): from Fr. *cantine*, from Ital. *cantina* 'cellar'.

**canter** ● n. a pace of a horse between a trot and a gallop, with not less than one foot on the ground at any time. ➤ a ride on a horse at such a speed. ● v. move at this pace.
– PHRASES **in** (or **at**) **a canter** Brit. without much effort; easily.
– ORIGIN C18 (as v.): short for *Canterbury pace*, from the supposed easy pace of medieval pilgrims to Canterbury.

**canterbury** ● n. (pl. **-ies**) a low open-topped cabinet with partitions for holding music or books.

**Canterbury bell** ● n. a tall cultivated bellflower with large pale blue flowers. [*Campanula medium*.]
– ORIGIN C16: named after the bells on Canterbury pilgrims' horses.

**cantharides** /kanˈθarɪdiːz/ ● pl. n. another name for SPANISH FLY.
– ORIGIN ME: from L., pl. of *cantharis*, from Gk *kantharis*.

**cantharus** /ˈkanθ(ə)rəs/ ● n. (pl. **canthari**) (in ancient Greece and Rome) a large two-handled drinking cup.
– ORIGIN L., from Gk *kantharos*.

**cant hook** ● n. a hinged metal hook at the end of a long handle, used for gripping and rolling logs.

**canthus** /ˈkanθəs/ ● n. (pl. **canthi** /-θʌɪ/) the outer or inner corner of the eye, where the upper and lower lids meet.
– DERIVATIVES **canthic** adj.
– ORIGIN C17: from L., from Gk *kanthos*.

**canticle** /ˈkantɪk(ə)l/ ● n. a hymn or chant forming a regular part of a church service.
– ORIGIN ME: from L. *canticulum* 'little song', dimin. of *canticum*, from *canere* 'sing'.

**cantilena** /ˌkantɪˈleɪnə, -ˈliːnə/ ● n. Music the part carrying the melody in a composition.
– ORIGIN C18: from Ital., from L., 'song'.

**cantilever** /ˈkantɪliːvə/ ● **n.** a long projecting beam or girder fixed at only one end, used chiefly in bridge construction. ➤a bracket or beam projecting from a wall to support a balcony, cornice, etc. ● **v.** [usu. as adj. **cantilevered**] support by a cantilever or cantilevers.
– ORIGIN C17: of unknown origin.

**cantillate** /ˈkantɪleɪt/ ● **v.** rare chant or intone.
– DERIVATIVES **cantillation** n.
– ORIGIN C19: from L. *cantillat-*, *cantillare* 'hum', from *cantare* (see **CHANT**).

**cantina** /kanˈtiːnə/ ● **n. 1** (in a Spanish-speaking area) a bar. **2** (in Italy) a wine shop.
– ORIGIN C19: from Sp. and Ital.

**canting arms** ● **pl. n.** Heraldry arms containing an allusion to the name of the bearer.

**cantle** /ˈkant(ə)l/ ● **n.** the raised curved part at the back of a horse's saddle.
– ORIGIN ME (in the sense 'a corner'): from Anglo-Norman Fr. *cantel*, var. of OFr. *chantel*, from med. L. *cantellus*, from *cantus* 'corner, side'.

**canto** /ˈkantəʊ/ ● **n.** (pl. **-os**) one of the sections into which some long poems are divided.
– ORIGIN C16: from Ital., lit. 'song', from L. *cantus*.

**canton** ● **n. 1** /ˈkantɒn, kanˈtɒn/ a political or administrative subdivision of a country. ➤a state of the Swiss Confederation. **2** /ˈkant(ə)n/ Heraldry a square charge smaller than a quarter and positioned in the upper (usually dexter) corner of a shield.
– DERIVATIVES **cantonal** /ˈkantən(ə)l, kanˈtəʊn(ə)l/ adj.
– ORIGIN C16: from OFr., lit. 'corner', from Provençal, rel. to med. L. *cantus* (see **CANT²**).

**Cantonese** ● **n.** (pl. same) **1** a native or inhabitant of Canton (Guangzhou), a city in China. **2** a form of Chinese spoken mainly in SE China and Hong Kong. ● **adj.** of or relating to Canton or Cantonese.

**cantonment** /kanˈtɒnm(ə)nt, -ˈtuːn-/ ● **n.** a military camp, especially a permanent military station in British India.
– ORIGIN C18: from Fr. *cantonnement*, from *cantonner* 'to quarter'.

**cantor** /ˈkantɔː, -ə/ ● **n. 1** (in Jewish worship) an official who sings liturgical music and leads prayer in a synagogue. **2** (in formal Christian worship) a person who sings solo verses to which the choir or congregation respond.
– ORIGIN C16: from L., 'singer', from *canere* 'sing'.

**cantorial** ● **adj. 1** of or relating to a cantor. **2** relating to or denoting the north side of the choir in a church, on which the cantor sits. The opposite of **DECANAL**.

**cantoris** /kanˈtɔːrɪs/ ● **n.** the section of a church choir conventionally placed on the north side and taking the second or lower part in antiphonal singing. Compare with **DECANI**.
– ORIGIN C17: from L., lit. 'of the cantor' (see **CANTOR**).

**cantrail** /ˈkantreɪl/ ● **n.** Brit. a length of wood or metal supporting the roof of a railway carriage.

**cantrip** /ˈkantrɪp/ ● **n.** Scottish archaic a mischievous or playful act; a trick.
– ORIGIN C16: of unknown origin.

**cantus** /ˈkantəs/ ● **n.** the highest voice in polyphonic choral music.
– ORIGIN C16: from L.

**cantus firmus** /ˌkantəs ˈfəːməs/ ● **n.** (pl. **cantus firmi** /ˌkantuːs ˈfəːmʌɪ/) Music an existing melody used as the basis for a polyphonic composition.
– ORIGIN C19: from L., lit. 'firm song'.

**Canuck** /kəˈnʌk/ ● **n.** informal a Canadian, especially a French Canadian.
– ORIGIN appar. from *Canada*.

**canvas** ● **n.** (pl. **canvases** or **canvasses**) **1** a strong, coarse unbleached cloth used to make sails, tents, etc. and as a surface for oil painting. ➤a piece of canvas prepared for use as the surface for an oil painting. ➤(**the canvas**) the floor of a boxing or wrestling ring, having a canvas covering. **2** either of a racing boat's tapering ends, originally covered with canvas. ● **v.** (**canvassed, canvassing**; US **canvased, canvasing**) cover with canvas.
– PHRASES **under canvas 1** in a tent or tents. **2** with sails spread.
– ORIGIN ME: from ONorth. Fr. *canevas*, based on L. *cannabis* 'hemp', from Gk.

**canvasback** ● **n.** a North American diving duck related to the pochard. [*Aythya valisineria*.]

**canvass** ● **v. 1** solicit votes from (electors). ➤question (someone) in order to ascertain their opinion on something. **2** Brit. propose (an idea or plan) for discussion. ● **n.** an act of canvassing.
– DERIVATIVES **canvasser** n.
– ORIGIN C16 (in the sense 'toss in a canvas sheet' (as a sport or punishment)): from **CANVAS**.

**canyon** ● **n.** a deep gorge, especially one with a river flowing through it.
– ORIGIN C19: from Sp. *cañón* 'tube', based on L. *canna* 'reed, cane'.

**canyoning** ● **n.** the sport of jumping into a fast-flowing mountain stream and being carried downstream.

**canzone** /kanˈtsəʊneɪ, -z-/ ● **n.** (pl. **canzoni** /-ni/) **1** an Italian or Provençal song or ballad. **2** a type of lyric resembling a madrigal.
– ORIGIN C16: from Ital., 'song', from L. *cantio(n-)* 'singing', from *canere* 'sing'.

**canzonetta** /ˌkanzəˈnɛtə, ˌkantsəˈnɛtə/ ● **n.** (pl. **canzonettas** or **canzonette** /-ˈnɛteɪ/) a short, light vocal piece, especially in the Italian style of the 17th century.
– ORIGIN C16: from Ital., dimin. of *canzone* (see **CANZONE**).

**caoutchouc** /ˈkaʊtʃʊk/ ● **n.** unvulcanized natural rubber.
– ORIGIN C18: from Fr., from obs. Sp. *cauchuc*, from Quechua *kauchuk*.

**CAP** ● **abbrev.** Common Agricultural Policy.

**cap** ● **n. 1** a soft, flat hat without a brim and usually with a peak. ➤a soft, close-fitting head covering worn for a particular purpose: *a shower cap*. ➤an academic mortar board. **2** a protective lid or cover for a bottle, pen, etc. ➤Dentistry an artificial protective covering for a tooth. **3** an upper limit imposed on spending or borrowing. **4** chiefly Brit. a cap awarded to members of a sports team, especially a national team. **5** (also **Dutch cap**) Brit. informal a contraceptive diaphragm. **6** the broad upper part of the fruiting body of a mushroom or toadstool. **7** short for **PERCUSSION CAP**. ● **v.** (**capped, capping**) **1** put or form a lid or cover on. ➤put a cap on (a tooth). **2** provide a fitting climax or conclusion to. ➤follow or reply to (a story or remark) with a still better one. **3** place a limit on (prices, expenditure, etc.). **4** (**be capped**) chiefly Brit. be chosen as a member of a sports team, especially a national one. **5** Scottish & NZ confer a university degree on.
– PHRASES **cap in hand** humbly asking for a favour. **set one's cap at** (or US **for**) dated (of a woman) try to attract (a particular man) as a suitor. **to cap it all** as the final unfortunate incident in a long series.
– DERIVATIVES **capful** n. (pl. **-fuls**). **capper** n.
– ORIGIN OE *cæppe* 'hood', from late L. *cappa*, perh. from L. *caput* 'head'.

**cap.** ● **abbrev. 1** capacity. **2** capital (city). **3** capital letter.

**capability** ● **n.** (pl. **-ies**) power or ability to do something. ➤an undeveloped or unused faculty.

**capable** ● **adj. 1** (**capable of doing something**) having the ability or quality necessary to do something. ➤open to or admitting of something. **2** (of a person) competent.
– DERIVATIVES **capably** adv.
– ORIGIN C16: from Fr., from late L. *capabilis*, from L. *capere* 'take or hold'.

**capacious** ● **adj.** having a lot of space inside; roomy.
– DERIVATIVES **capaciously** adv. **capaciousness** n.
– ORIGIN C17: from L. *capax*, *capac-* 'capable' + **-IOUS**.

**capacitance** /kəˈpasɪt(ə)ns/ ● **n.** Physics ability to store electric charge, equivalent to the ratio of the change in electric charge in a system or component to the corresponding change in electric potential.
– ORIGIN C19: from **CAPACITY** + **-ANCE**.

**capacitate** ● **v. 1** formal or archaic make capable or legally competent. **2** (**be capacitated**) Physiology (of spermatozoa) undergo changes inside the female reproductive tract enabling them to penetrate and fertilize an ovum.

– DERIVATIVES **capacitation** n.

**capacitor** /kəˈpasɪtə/ ● **n.** a device used to store electric charge, consisting of one or more pairs of conductors separated by an insulator.

**capacity** ● **n.** (pl. **-ies**) **1** the maximum amount that something can contain or produce. ➤ [as modifier] fully occupying the available space: *a capacity crowd.* ➤ the total cylinder volume that is swept by the pistons in an internal-combustion engine. **2** the ability or power to do something. ➤ a person's legal competence. **3** a specified role or position. **4** dated capacitance.

– DERIVATIVES **capacitive** (also **capacitative**) adj. (chiefly Physics).

– ORIGIN ME: from Fr. *capacité*, from L. *capacitas*, from *capax, capac-* 'that can contain', from *capere* 'take or hold'.

**caparison** /kəˈparɪs(ə)n/ ● **n.** an ornamental covering spread over a horse's saddle or harness. ● **v.** (**be caparisoned**) be decked out in rich decorative coverings.

– ORIGIN C16: from obs. Fr. *caparasson*, from Sp. *caparazón* 'saddlecloth', from *capa* 'hood'.

**cape**[1] ● **n. 1** a sleeveless cloak, especially a short one. ➤ a part of a longer coat or cloak that falls loosely over the shoulders from the neckband. **2** N. Amer. the pelt from the head and neck of an animal. ● **v.** N. Amer. skin the head and neck of (an animal) to prepare a hunting trophy.

– DERIVATIVES **caped** adj.

– ORIGIN C16: from Fr., from Provençal *capa*, from late L. *cappa* 'covering for the head'.

**cape**[2] ● **n.** a headland or promontory. ➤ (**the Cape**) the Cape of Good Hope. ➤ (**the Cape**) the former Cape Province of South Africa.

– ORIGIN ME: from OFr. *cap*, from Provençal, based on L. *caput* 'head'.

**Cape doctor** ● **n.** S. African informal the strong prevailing SE wind in Western Cape Province.

**Cape Dutch** ● **n.** historical the form of Dutch spoken by the early settlers at the Cape of Good Hope, which developed into Afrikaans.

**Cape gooseberry** ● **n. 1** a soft edible yellow berry enclosed in a lantern-shaped husk. **2** the tropical South American plant which bears this fruit. [*Physalis peruviana.*]

**Cape hen** ● **n.** a petrel of southern oceans, with mainly dark brown plumage. [*Procellaria aequinoctialis.*]

**Cape jasmine** ● **n.** a fragrant Chinese gardenia with flowers that are used to perfume tea. [*Gardenia jasminioides.*]

**capelin** /ˈkeɪplɪn, ˈkap-/ (also **caplin**) ● **n.** a small fish of North Atlantic coastal waters, important as a food fish. [*Mallotus villosus.*]

– ORIGIN C17: from Fr., from Provençal *capelan*, from med. L. *cappellanus* (see **CHAPLAIN**).

**capellini** /ˌkapəˈliːniː/ ● **pl. n.** pasta in the form of very thin strands.

– ORIGIN Ital., dimin. of *capello* 'hair'.

**Cape Malay** (also **Cape Muslim**) ● **n.** (in South Africa) a member of a predominantly Afrikaans-speaking and Muslim group resident mainly in the Western Cape Province.

**Cape primrose** ● **n.** a streptocarpus.

**caper**[1] ● **v.** skip or dance about in a lively or playful way. ● **n. 1** a playful skipping movement. **2** informal an illicit or ridiculous activity or escapade.

– PHRASES **cut a caper** make a playful, skipping movement.

– DERIVATIVES **caperer** n.

– ORIGIN C16: abbrev. of **CAPRIOLE**.

**caper**[2] ● **n. 1** a cooked and pickled flower bud of a bramble-like southern European shrub, used in pickles and sauces. **2** the shrub from which these buds are taken. [*Capparis spinosa.*]

– ORIGIN ME: from Fr. *câpres* or L. *capparis*, from Gk *kapparis*; later interpreted as pl.

**capercaillie** /ˌkapəˈkeɪli/ (Scottish also **capercailzie** /-ˈkeɪlzi/) ● **n.** (pl. **-ies**) a large turkey-like grouse of mature pine forests in northern Europe. [*Tetrao urogallus.*]

– ORIGIN C16: from Sc. Gaelic *capull coille*, lit. 'horse of the wood'.

**caper spurge** ● **n.** an ornamental European spurge which has become naturalized in North America. [*Euphorbia lathyris.*]

**capeskin** ● **n.** a soft leather made from South African sheepskin.

**Capetian** /kəˈpiːʃ(ə)n/ ● **adj.** relating to or denoting a dynasty ruling France 987–1328. ● **n.** a member of this dynasty.

– ORIGIN named after Hugh *Capet*, founder of the dynasty.

**Cape Verdean** /ˈvəːdɪən/ ● **n.** a native or inhabitant of the Cape Verde Islands, a small country off the coast of Senegal. ● **adj.** of or relating to the Cape Verde Islands.

**capias** /ˈkeɪpɪəs, ˈkap-/ ● **n.** (pl. **capiases**) Law, dated a writ ordering the arrest of a named person.

– ORIGIN ME: from L. *capias* (*ad respondendum*), lit. 'you are to seize (until reply is made)'.

**capillarity** ● **n.** the tendency of a liquid in a narrow tube or pore to rise or fall as a result of surface tension.

**capillary** /kəˈpɪləri/ ● **n. 1** Anatomy any of the fine branching blood vessels that form a network between the arterioles and venules. **2** (also **capillary tube**) a tube with an internal diameter of hair-like thinness. ● **adj.** of or relating to capillaries or capillarity.

– ORIGIN C17: from L. *capillaris*, from *capillus* 'hair', influenced by OFr. *capillaire*.

**capillary action** ● **n.** another term for **CAPILLARITY**.

**capillary joint** ● **n.** a joint made between two pipes by putting their ends into a slightly larger joining piece and filling the gaps with molten solder.

**capital**[1] ● **n. 1** the most important city or town of a country or region, usually its seat of government and administrative centre. ➤ a place particularly associated with a specified activity: *the fashion capital of the world.* **2** wealth owned by a person or organization or invested, lent, or borrowed. ➤ the excess of a company's assets over its liabilities. **3** a capital letter. ● **adj. 1** (of an offence or charge) liable to the death penalty. **2** (of a letter of the alphabet) large in size and of the form used to begin sentences and names. **3** informal, dated excellent.

– PHRASES **make capital out of** use to one's own advantage. **with a capital** —— used for emphasis: *she was ugly with a capital U.*

– DERIVATIVES **capitally** adv.

– ORIGIN ME (as adj. in the sense 'relating to the head or top'): via OFr. from L. *capitalis*, from *caput* 'head'.

**capital**[2] ● **n.** Architecture the distinct, typically broader section at the head of a pillar or column.

– ORIGIN ME: from OFr. *capitel*, from late L. *capitellum* 'little head', dimin. of L. *caput*.

**capital consumption** ● **n.** Economics the total depreciation of assets in an economy in a specified period.

**capital gain** ● **n.** a profit from the sale of property or an investment.

**capital gains tax** ● **n.** a tax levied on capital gains.

**capital goods** ● **pl. n.** goods that are used in producing other goods, rather than being bought by consumers.

**capital-intensive** ● **adj.** requiring the investment of large sums of money.

**capitalism** ● **n.** an economic and political system in which a country's trade and industry are controlled by private owners for profit, rather than by the state.

– DERIVATIVES **capitalist** n. & adj. **capitalistic** adj. **capitalistically** adv.

**capitalize** (also **-ise**) ● **v. 1** (**capitalize on**) take the chance to gain advantage from. **2** provide with capital. **3** convert into capital. ➤ reckon (the value of an asset) by setting future benefits against the cost of maintenance. **4** write or print (a word or letter) in capital letters. ➤ begin (a word) with a capital letter.

– DERIVATIVES **capitalization** n.

**capital levy** ● **n.** a tax by means of which the state appropriates a fixed proportion of private wealth.

**capital punishment** ● **n.** the legally authorized killing of someone as punishment for a crime.

**capital ship** ● **n.** a large warship such as a battleship or aircraft carrier.

**capital sum** ● n. a lump sum of money payable to an insured person or paid as an initial fee or investment.

**capital territory** ● n. a territory containing the capital city of a country, as in Australia, Nigeria, and Pakistan.

**capitate** /ˈkapɪteɪt/ ● adj. Botany & Zoology ending in a distinct compact head. ● n. (also **capitate bone**) Anatomy the largest of the carpal bones, situated at the base of the palm of the hand.
– ORIGIN C17: from L. *capitatus*, from *caput*, *capit-*, 'head'.

**capitation** ● n. the payment of a fee or grant to a doctor, school, etc., the amount being determined by the number of patients, pupils, etc.
– ORIGIN C17 (denoting the counting of heads): from late L. *capitatio* 'poll tax', from *caput* 'head'.

**capitol** /ˈkapɪt(ə)l/ ● n. 1 (in the US) a building housing a legislative assembly. ➤(**the Capitol**) the seat of the US Congress in Washington DC. 2 (**the Capitol**) the temple of Jupiter on the Capitoline Hill in ancient Rome.
– ORIGIN from OFr. *capitolie*, *capitoile*, later assimilated to L. *Capitolium* (from *caput*, *capit-* 'head').

**capitular** /kəˈpɪtjʊlə/ ● adj. 1 of or relating to a cathedral chapter. 2 Anatomy & Biology of or relating to a capitulum.
– ORIGIN C16: from late L. *capitularis*, from L. *capitulum* 'small head'.

**capitulary** /kəˈpɪtjʊləri/ ● n. (pl. **-ies**) historical a royal ordinance, especially under the Merovingian dynasty.
– ORIGIN C17: from late L. *capitularius*, from L. *capitulum* in the sense 'section of a law'.

**capitulate** /kəˈpɪtjʊleɪt/ ● v. cease to resist an opponent or an unwelcome demand; surrender.
– DERIVATIVES **capitulator** n.
– ORIGIN C16 (in the sense 'parley, draw up terms'): from Fr. *capituler*, from med. L. *capitulare* 'draw up under headings', from L. *capitulum*, dimin. of *caput* 'head'.

**capitulation** ● n. 1 the action of capitulating. 2 (**capitulations**) historical an agreement or set of conditions.

**capitulum** /kəˈpɪtjʊləm/ ● n. (pl. **capitula** /-lə/) Anatomy & Biology a compact head of a structure, in particular a dense flat cluster of small flowers or florets.
– ORIGIN C18: from L., dimin. of *caput* 'head'.

**caplet** ● n. trademark a coated oral medicinal tablet.
– ORIGIN 1930s: blend of **CAPSULE** and **TABLET**.

**caplin** ● n. variant spelling of **CAPELIN**.

**cap'n** /ˈkapn/ ● n. informal contraction of **CAPTAIN**.

**capo**[1] /ˈkapəʊ/ (also **capo tasto**) ● n. (pl. **-os**) a clamp fastened across all the strings of a fretted musical instrument to raise their tuning.
– ORIGIN C19: from Ital. *capo tasto*, lit. 'head stop'.

**capo**[2] /ˈkapəʊ/ ● n. (pl. **-os**) chiefly N. Amer. the head of a crime syndicate, especially the Mafia, or a branch of one.
– ORIGIN 1950s: from Ital., from L. *caput* 'head'.

**Capo di Monte** /ˌkapəʊ dɪ ˈmɒnteɪ, ˈmɒnti/ ● n. a type of porcelain that is generally white with richly coloured rococo decoration.
– ORIGIN from the *Capo di Monte* palace near Naples.

**capoeira** /ˌkapʊˈeɪrə/ ● n. a system of physical discipline and movement originating among Brazilian slaves.
– ORIGIN from Port.

**cap of liberty** ● n. a conical cap given to Roman slaves on their emancipation and more recently used as a republican symbol.

**cap of maintenance** ● n. a cap or hat worn as a symbol of official dignity or carried in front of a sovereign on ceremonial occasions.

**capon** /ˈkeɪp(ə)n/ ● n. a castrated domestic cock fattened for eating.
– DERIVATIVES **caponize** (also **-ise**) v.
– ORIGIN OE: from OFr., based on L. *capo*, *capon-*.

**caponata** /ˌkapə(ʊ)ˈnɑːtə/ ● n. a dish of aubergines, olives, and onions seasoned with herbs.
– ORIGIN from Ital.

**caponier** /ˌkapəˈnɪə/ ● n. a covered passage across a ditch round a fort.
– ORIGIN C17: from Sp. *caponera*, lit. 'capon enclosure'.

**capot** /kəˈpɒt/ ● n. (in piquet) the winning of all twelve tricks in the hand by one player, for which a bonus is awarded. ● v. (**capotted**, **capotting**) score a capot against.
– ORIGIN C17: from Fr., perh. from a dial. var. of *chapoter* 'castrate'.

**capo tasto** /ˌkapəʊ ˈtastəʊ/ ● n. see **CAPO**[1].

**capote** /kəˈpəʊt/ ● n. N. Amer. historical a long cloak or coat with a hood.
– ORIGIN C19: from Fr., dimin. of *cape* (see **CAPE**[1]).

**cappelletti** /ˌkapəˈlɛti/ ● pl. n. small pieces of pasta folded and stuffed with meat or cheese.
– ORIGIN Ital., lit. 'little hats'.

**cappuccino** /ˌkapʊˈtʃiːnəʊ/ ● n. (pl. **-os**) coffee made with milk that has been frothed up with pressurized steam.
– ORIGIN 1940s: from Ital., lit. 'Capuchin', because its colour resembles that of a Capuchin's habit.

**capriccio** /kəˈprɪtʃɪəʊ/ ● n. (pl. **-os**) 1 a lively piece of music, especially one that is short and free in form. 2 a painting representing a fantasy or a mixture of real and imaginary features.
– ORIGIN C17 (in the sense 'caprice or capriciousness'): from Ital., lit. 'head with the hair standing on end', hence 'horror', later 'sudden start' (influenced by *capra* 'goat', assoc. with frisky movement), from *capo* 'head' + *riccio* 'hedgehog'.

**capriccioso** /kəˌprɪtʃɪˈəʊzəʊ, -səʊ/ ● adv. & adj. Music in a free and impulsive style.
– ORIGIN Ital., lit. 'capricious', from **CAPRICCIO**.

**caprice** /kəˈpriːs/ ● n. 1 a sudden and unaccountable change of mood or behaviour. 2 Music another term for **CAPRICCIO**.
– ORIGIN C17: from Fr., from Ital. **CAPRICCIO**.

**capricious** /kəˈprɪʃəs/ ● adj. given to sudden and unaccountable changes of mood or behaviour.
– DERIVATIVES **capriciously** adv. **capriciousness** n.
– ORIGIN C17: from Fr. *capricieux*, from Ital. **CAPRICCIOSO**.

**Capricorn** /ˈkaprɪkɔːn/ ● n. Astrology the tenth sign of the zodiac (the Goat), which the sun enters at the northern winter solstice (about 21 December).
– DERIVATIVES **Capricornian** n. & adj.
– ORIGIN OE, from L. *capricornus*, from *caper*, *capr-* 'goat' + *cornu* 'horn'.

**caprine** /ˈkaprʌɪn/ ● adj. relating to or resembling a goat or goats.
– ORIGIN ME: from L. *caprinus*, from *caper*, *capr-* 'goat'.

**capriole** /ˈkaprɪəʊl/ ● n. 1 a movement performed in classical riding, in which the horse leaps from the ground and kicks out with its hind legs. 2 a leap or caper in dancing, especially a cabriole.
– ORIGIN C16: from obs. Fr., from Ital. *capriola* 'leap', from *capriolo* 'roebuck', from L. *capreolus*, dimin. of *caper*, *capr-* 'goat'.

**capri pants** /kəˈpriː/ (also **capris**) ● pl. n. close-fitting tapered trousers for women.
– ORIGIN 1950s: named after the island of *Capri*.

**caproic acid** /kəˈprəʊɪk/ ● n. Chemistry a liquid fatty acid present in milk fat and coconut and palm oils.
– DERIVATIVES **caproate** n.
– ORIGIN C19: from L. *caper*, *capr-* 'goat' (because of its smell) + **-IC**.

**caprolactam** /ˌkaprə(ʊ)ˈlaktam/ ● n. Chemistry a synthetic crystalline compound which is an intermediate in nylon manufacture.
– ORIGIN 1940s: from **CAPROIC ACID** + **LACTAM**.

**caps** ● abbrev. capital letters.

**capsaicin** /kapˈseɪɪsɪn/ ● n. Chemistry a cyclic compound responsible for the pungency of capsicums.
– ORIGIN C19: alt. of *capsicine*, another substance formerly thought to have the same property.

**Capsian** /ˈkapsɪən/ ● adj. Archaeology relating to or denoting a Palaeolithic culture of North Africa and southern Europe, dated to *c.*8000–4500 BC.
– ORIGIN C20: from L. *Capsa* (now *Gafsa* in Tunisia), where objects from this culture were found, + **-IAN**.

**capsicum** /ˈkapsɪkəm/ ● n. (pl. **capsicums**) 1 the fruit of a tropical American plant, of which sweet peppers and chilli peppers are varieties. 2 the plant of the nightshade family from which such fruits come. [Genus *Capsicum*.]

– ORIGIN C16: mod. L., perh. from L. *capsa* (see **CASE²**).

**capsid¹** ● **n.** another term for **MIRID**.
– ORIGIN C19: from mod. L. *Capsidae* (former synonym of the family Miridae), from *Capsus* (genus name).

**capsid²** ● **n.** Microbiology the protein coat or shell of a virus particle.
– ORIGIN 1960s: coined in Fr. from L. *capsa* (see **CASE²**).

**capsize** ● **v.** (of a boat) be overturned in the water.
– ORIGIN C18: perh. based on Sp. *capuzar* 'sink (a ship) by the head', from *cabo* 'head' + *chapuzar* 'to dive or duck'.

**cap sleeve** ● **n.** a short sleeve which tapers to nothing under the arm.

**capstan** /'kapst(ə)n/ ● **n. 1** a broad revolving cylinder with a vertical axis used for winding a rope or cable. **2** the motor-driven spindle on a tape recorder that makes the tape travel past the head.
– ORIGIN ME: from Provençal *cabestan*, from *cabestre* 'halter', from L. *capistrum*, from *capere* 'seize'.

**capstan lathe** ● **n.** a lathe with a revolving tool holder on which several tools can be permanently mounted.

**capstone** ● **n.** a stone placed on top of a wall, tomb, or other structure.

**capsule** /'kapsjuːl, -sjʊl/ ● **n. 1** a small soluble case of gelatin containing a dose of medicine, swallowed whole. ➤a small case or container. ➤short for **SPACE CAPSULE**. **2** Anatomy a sheath or membrane that encloses an organ or other structure, such as a kidney. ➤Botany a dry fruit that releases its seeds by bursting open when ripe. ➤Botany the spore-producing structure of mosses and liverworts. **3** the foil or plastic covering the cork of a wine bottle.
– DERIVATIVES **capsular** adj. **capsulate** adj.
– ORIGIN ME: via Fr. from L. *capsula*, dimin. of *capsa* (see **CASE²**).

**capsulize** (also **-ise**) ● **v.** put (information) in compact form; summarize.

**Capt.** ● **abbrev.** Captain.

**captain** ● **n. 1** the person in command of a ship. ➤the pilot in command of a civil aircraft. ➤a rank of naval officer above commander and below commodore. **2** a rank of officer in the army and in the US and Canadian air forces, above lieutenant and below major. **3** (in the US) a police officer in charge of a precinct. **4** the leader of a team, especially in sports. ● **v.** serve as the captain of.
– DERIVATIVES **captaincy** n.
– ORIGIN ME: from OFr. *capitain* (superseding earlier *chevetaigne* 'chieftain'), from late L. *capitaneus* 'chief', from L. *caput*, *capit-* 'head'.

**captain general** ● **n.** an honorary rank of senior officer in the British army, especially in an artillery regiment.

**caption** ● **n. 1** a title or brief explanation appended to an illustration or cartoon. ➤a piece of text appearing on screen as part of a film or broadcast. **2** Law the heading of a legal document. ● **v.** provide with a caption.
– ORIGIN ME (in the sense 'seizing, capture', later 'warrant for arrest' and so 'statement of the authority issuing the warrant'): from L. *captio(n-)*, from *capere* 'take, seize'.

**captious** /'kapʃəs/ ● **adj.** formal tending to find fault or raise petty objections.
– DERIVATIVES **captiously** adv. **captiousness** n.
– ORIGIN ME: from OFr. *captieux* or L. *captiosus*, from *captio(n-)* (see **CAPTION**).

**captivate** ● **v.** attract and hold the interest and attention of; charm.
– DERIVATIVES **captivating** adj. **captivatingly** adv. **captivation** n.
– ORIGIN C16: from late L. *captivat-*, *captivare* 'take captive', from *captivus* (see **CAPTIVE**).

**captive** ● **n.** a person who has been taken prisoner or confined. ● **adj. 1** imprisoned or confined. **2** having no freedom to choose an alternative: *a captive audience*. **3** (of a facility or service) controlled by and reserved for a particular organization.
– DERIVATIVES **captivity** n.
– ORIGIN ME: from L. *captivus*, from *capere* 'seize, take'.

**captive balloon** ● **n.** a lighter-than-air balloon secured by a rope to the ground.

**captor** ● **n.** a person who imprisons or confines another.

**capture** ● **v. 1** take into one's possession or control by force. ➤(in chess and other board games) make a move that secures the removal of (an opposing piece). **2** Physics absorb (a particle). **3** record or express accurately in words or pictures. **4** cause (data) to be stored in a computer. ● **n.** the action of capturing or of being captured. ➤a person or thing that has been captured.
– DERIVATIVES **capturer** n.
– ORIGIN C16 (as n.): from Fr., from L. *captura*, from *capt-*, *capere* 'seize, take'.

**Capuchin** /'kapʊtʃɪn/ ● **n. 1** a friar belonging to a strict branch of the Franciscan order. **2** a cloak and hood formerly worn by women. **3** (**capuchin**) a South American monkey with a cowl-like cap of hair on the head. [Genus *Cebus*: four species.] **4** (**capuchin**) a pigeon of a breed with head and neck feathers resembling a cowl.
– ORIGIN C16: from obs. Fr., earlier form of *capucin*, from Ital. *cappuccino*, from *cappuccio* 'hood, cowl', from *cappa* (see **CAPE¹**).

**capybara** /ˌkapɪ'bɑːrə/ ● **n.** (pl. same or **capybaras**) a large South American rodent resembling a long-legged guinea pig. [*Hydrochaerus hydrochaeris*.]
– ORIGIN C17: from Sp. *capibara* or Port. *capivara*, from Tupi *capiuára*, from *capí* 'grass' + *uára* 'eater'.

**car** ● **n. 1** a powered road vehicle designed to carry a small number of people. **2** a railway carriage or (N. Amer.) wagon. ➤the passenger compartment of a lift, cableway, or balloon. **3** poetic/literary a chariot.
– DERIVATIVES **carful** n. (pl. **-fuls**). **carload** n.
– ORIGIN ME: from ONorth. Fr. *carre*, based on L. *carrum*, *carrus*, of Celtic origin.

**carabid** /'karəbɪd/ ● **n.** Entomology a beetle of a family (Carabidae) comprising the predatory ground beetles.
– ORIGIN C19: from mod. L *Carabidae*, from L. *carabus*, denoting a kind of crab.

**carabineer** /ˌkarəbɪ'nɪə/ (also **carabinier**) ● **n.** historical a cavalry soldier whose principal weapon was a carbine.
– ORIGIN C17: from Fr. *carabinier*, from *carabine* (see **CARBINE**).

**carabiner** ● **n.** variant spelling of **KARABINER**.

**carabiniere** /ˌkarəbɪ'njɛːri/ ● **n.** (pl. **carabinieri** pronunc. same) a member of the Italian paramilitary police.
– ORIGIN Ital., lit. 'carabineer'.

**caracal** /'karəkal/ ● **n.** a long-legged lynx-like cat with black tufted ears, native to Africa and western Asia. [*Felis caracal*.]
– ORIGIN C19: from Fr. or Sp., from Turk. *karakulak*, from *kara* 'black' + *kulak* 'ear'.

**caracara** /ˌkarə'kɑːrə/ ● **n.** (pl. same or **caracaras**) a large New World bird of prey with a bare face, feeding largely on carrion. [*Polyborus plancus* and other species.]
– ORIGIN C19: from Sp. or Port. *caracará*, from Tupi-Guarani, imitating its cry.

**caracole** /'karəkəʊl/ ● **n.** a half turn to the right or left by a horse. ● **v.** perform a caracole.
– ORIGIN C17: from Fr. *caracole*, *caracol* 'snail's shell, spiral'.

**caracul** ● **n.** variant spelling of **KARAKUL**.

**carafe** /kə'raf, -'rɑːf/ ● **n.** an open-topped glass flask typically used for serving wine in a restaurant.
– ORIGIN C18: from Fr., from Ital. *caraffa*, prob. based on Arab. *garafa* 'draw water'.

**caragana** /ˌkarə'gɑːnə/ ● **n.** a central Asian or Siberian shrub or small tree, sometimes planted as an ornamental. [Genus *Caragana*.]
– ORIGIN mod. L., of Turkic origin.

**caramba** /kə'rambə/ ● **exclam.** informal, often humorous an expression of surprise or dismay.
– ORIGIN C19: from Sp.

**carambola** /ˌkar(ə)m'bəʊlə/ ● **n. 1** a golden-yellow fruit with a star-shaped cross section; starfruit. **2** the tropical tree which bears this fruit. [*Averrhoa carambola*.]
– ORIGIN C16: from Port., prob. from Marathi *karambal*.

**caramel** /'karəm(ə)l, -mɛl/ ● **n. 1** sugar or syrup heated until it turns brown, used as a flavouring or colouring for food or drink. **2** a soft toffee made with sugar and butter that have been melted and further heated.

– DERIVATIVES **caramelization** (also **-isation**) n. **caramelize** (also **-ise**) v.
– ORIGIN C18: from Fr., from Sp. *caramelo*.

**carangid** /kəˈrandʒɪd/ ● n. Zoology a marine fish of the jack family (Carangidae), typically with a sloping forehead and two dorsal fins.
– ORIGIN C19: from mod. L. *Carangidae*, from the genus name *Caranx*.

**carapace** /ˈkarəpeɪs/ ● n. the hard upper shell of a tortoise or crustacean.
– ORIGIN C19: from Fr., from Sp. *carapacho*, of unknown origin.

**carat** /ˈkarət/ ● n. **1** a unit of weight for precious stones and pearls, equivalent to 200 milligrams. **2** (US also **karat**) a measure of the purity of gold, pure gold being 24 carats.
– ORIGIN ME: from Fr., from Ital. *carato*, from Arab. *ḳīrāṭ*, from Gk *keration* 'fruit of the carob'.

**caravan** ● n. **1** Brit. a vehicle equipped for living in, usually designed to be towed. **2** N. Amer. a covered truck. **3** historical a group of people travelling together across a desert in Asia or North Africa.
– DERIVATIVES **caravanner** n. **caravanning** n.
– ORIGIN C15: from Fr. *caravane*, from Pers. *kārwān*.

**caravanette** ● n. Brit. a motor vehicle with a rear compartment equipped for living in.

**caravanserai** /ˌkarəˈvansərʌɪ, -ri/ (US also **caravansary**) ● n. (pl. **caravanserais** or **caravansaries**) **1** historical an inn with a central courtyard for travellers in the desert regions of Asia or North Africa. **2** a group of people travelling together; a caravan.
– ORIGIN C16: from Pers. *kārwānsarāy*, from *kārwān* 'caravan' + *sarāy* 'palace'.

**caravel** /ˈkarəvɛl/ (also **carvel**) ● n. historical a small, fast Spanish or Portuguese ship of the 15th–17th centuries.
– ORIGIN C16: from Fr. *caravelle*, from Port. *caravela*, dimin. of *caravo*, via L. from Gk *karabos* 'horned beetle' or 'light ship'.

**caraway** /ˈkarəweɪ/ ● n. **1** the seeds of a plant of the parsley family, used for flavouring and as a source of oil. **2** the white-flowered Mediterranean plant which bears these seeds. [*Carum carvi*.]
– ORIGIN ME: from med. L. *carui*, from Arab. *alkarāwiyā*, prob. from Gk *karon* 'cumin'.

**carb**[1] ● n. informal short for CARBURETTOR.

**carb**[2] ● n. informal short for CARBOHYDRATE.

**carbamate** /ˈkɑːbəmeɪt/ ● n. Chemistry a salt or ester containing the anion $NH_2COO^-$ or the group $-OOCNH_2$.
– ORIGIN C19: from CARBO- + AMIDE + -ATE[1].

**carbanion** /kɑːˈbanʌɪən/ ● n. Chemistry an organic ion with a negative charge located on a carbon atom.

**carbaryl** /ˈkɑːbərɪl/ ● n. a synthetic insecticide used to protect crops and in the treatment of fleas and lice.
– ORIGIN C20: from CARBAMATE + -YL.

**carbide** /ˈkɑːbʌɪd/ ● n. Chemistry a compound of carbon with a metal or other element: *silicon carbide*.

**carbine** /ˈkɑːbʌɪn/ ● n. a light automatic rifle. ➤ historical a short rifle or musket used by cavalry.
– ORIGIN C17: from Fr. *carabine*, from *carabin* 'mounted musketeer'.

**carbo-** ● comb. form representing CARBON.

**carbocation** /ˌkɑːbə(ʊ)ˈkatʌɪən/ ● n. Chemistry another term for CARBONIUM ION.

**carbohydrate** ● n. Biochemistry any of a large group of compounds (including sugars, starch, and cellulose) which contain carbon, hydrogen, and oxygen, occur in foods and living tissues, and can be broken down to release energy in the body.

**carbolic acid** (also **carbolic**) ● n. phenol, especially when used as a disinfectant.

**car bomb** ● n. a terrorist bomb concealed in a parked car. ● v. (**car-bomb**) attack with such a bomb.
– DERIVATIVES **car bomber** n.

**carbon** ● n. **1** the chemical element of atomic number 6, a non-metal which has two main forms (diamond and graphite), occurs in impure form in charcoal, soot, and coal, and is present in all organic compounds. (Symbol: **C**) **2** a rod of carbon in an arc lamp. **3** a piece of carbon paper; a carbon copy.
– DERIVATIVES **carbonaceous** adj.
– ORIGIN C18: from Fr. *carbone*, from L. *carbo*, *carbon-* 'coal, charcoal'.

**carbonado** /ˌkɑːbəˈneɪdəʊ/ ● n. (pl. **-os**) a dark opaque diamond.
– ORIGIN C19: from Port.

**carbonara** /ˌkɑːbəˈnɑːrə/ ● adj. denoting a pasta sauce made with bacon or ham, egg, and cream.
– ORIGIN Ital., lit. 'charcoal kiln', perh. influenced by *carbonata*, a dish of charcoal-grilled salt pork.

**carbonate** /ˈkɑːbəneɪt/ ● n. a salt of the anion $CO_3^{2-}$, typically formed by reaction of carbon dioxide with bases. ● v. [usu. as adj. **carbonated**] dissolve carbon dioxide in.
– DERIVATIVES **carbonation** n.

**carbonatite** /kɑːˈbɒnətʌɪt/ ● n. Geology a lava or other igneous rock composed chiefly of carbonates.

**carbon black** ● n. a fine carbon powder used as a pigment.

**carbon copy** ● n. a copy made with carbon paper. ➤ a person or thing identical to another.

**carbon dating** ● n. the determination of the age of an organic object from the relative proportions of the isotopes carbon-12 and carbon-14 that it contains.

**carbon dioxide** ● n. a colourless, odourless gas produced by burning carbon and organic compounds and by respiration, and absorbed by plants in photosynthesis. [$CO_2$.]

**carbon disulphide** ● n. a colourless toxic flammable liquid used as a solvent. [$CS_2$.]

**carbon fibre** ● n. a material consisting of thin, strong crystalline filaments of carbon.

**carbonic** /kɑːˈbɒnɪk/ ● adj. of or relating to carbon or carbon dioxide.

**carbonic acid** ● n. a very weak acid formed when carbon dioxide dissolves in water. [$H_2CO_3$.]

**Carboniferous** /ˌkɑːbəˈnɪf(ə)rəs/ ● adj. Geology relating to or denoting the fifth period of the Palaeozoic era (between the Devonian and Permian periods, about 363 to 290 million years ago), a time when extensive coal-bearing strata were formed.

**carbonium ion** /kɑːˈbəʊnɪəm/ ● n. Chemistry an organic ion with a positive charge located on a carbon atom.
– ORIGIN C20: from CARBO-, on the pattern of *ammonium*.

**carbonize** (also **-ise**) ● v. convert into carbon, by heating or burning.
– DERIVATIVES **carbonization** n.

**carbon monoxide** ● n. a colourless, odourless toxic flammable gas formed by incomplete combustion of carbon. [CO.]

**carbonnade** /ˌkɑːbəˈnɑːd, -ˈneɪd/ ● n. a rich beef stew made with onions and beer.
– ORIGIN C17 (denoting a piece of meat or fish cooked on hot coals): from Fr., from L. *carbo*, *-onis* 'coal, charcoal'.

**carbon paper** ● n. thin paper coated with carbon, used for making copies of written or typed documents.

**carbon sink** ● n. a forest, ocean, or other natural environment viewed in terms of its ability to absorb carbon dioxide from the atmosphere.

**carbon steel** ● n. steel in which the main alloying element is carbon, and whose properties depend on the percentage of carbon present.

**carbon tax** ● n. a tax on petrol and other fossil fuels.

**carbon tetrachloride** ● n. a colourless toxic volatile liquid used as a solvent. [$CCl_4$.]

**carbonyl** /ˈkɑːbənʌɪl, -nɪl/ ● n. [as modifier] Chemistry of or denoting the divalent radical :C=O, present in aldehydes, ketones, and many other organic compounds.

**car boot sale** ● n. Brit. an outdoor sale at which people sell things, typically from the boots of their cars.

**carborundum** /ˌkɑːbəˈrʌndəm/ ● n. a very hard black solid consisting of silicon carbide, used as an abrasive.
– ORIGIN C19: blend of CARBON and CORUNDUM.

**carboxyl** /kɑːˈbɒksʌɪl, -sɪl/ ● n. [as modifier] Chemistry of or denoting the radical −COOH, present in organic acids.
– ORIGIN C19: from CARBO- + OX- + -YL.

**carboxylase** /kɑːˈbɒksɪleɪz/ ● **n.** Biochemistry an enzyme which promotes the addition of a carboxyl group to a compound.

**carboxylate** /kɑːˈbɒksɪleɪt/ Chemistry ● **n.** a salt or ester of a carboxylic acid. ● **v.** add a carboxyl group to (a compound).
– DERIVATIVES **carboxylation** n.

**carboxylic acid** /ˌkɑːbɒkˈsɪlɪk/ ● **n.** Chemistry an acid containing a carboxyl group, such as formic and acetic acids.

**carboy** ● **n.** a large globular glass bottle with a narrow neck, used for holding acids or other corrosive liquids.
– ORIGIN C18: from Pers. *ḳarāba* 'large glass flagon'.

**carbuncle** /ˈkɑːbʌŋk(ə)l/ ● **n. 1** a severe abscess or multiple boil in the skin. **2** a bright red gem, in particular a garnet cut en cabochon.
– DERIVATIVES **carbuncular** adj.
– ORIGIN ME: from OFr. *charbuncle*, from L. *carbunculus* 'small coal', from *carbo* 'coal, charcoal'.

**carburation** /ˌkɑːbjʊˈreɪʃ(ə)n/ ● **n.** the process of mixing air with a fine spray of liquid hydrocarbon fuel, as in a carburettor.

**carburettor** /ˌkɑːbjʊˈrɛtə, -bə-/ (also **carburetter**, US **carburetor**) ● **n.** a device in an internal-combustion engine for mixing air with a fine spray of liquid fuel.
– DERIVATIVES **carburetted** (US **carbureted**) adj.
– ORIGIN C19: from archaic *carburet* 'combine or charge with carbon' + **-OR**[1].

**carburize** /ˈkɑːbjʊrʌɪz, -bə-/ (also **-ise**) ● **v.** add carbon to the surface of (iron or steel) by heating with carbon.
– DERIVATIVES **carburization** n.
– ORIGIN C19: from Fr. *carbure* 'carbide' + **-IZE**.

**carcajou** /ˈkɑːkədʒuː, -ʒuː/ ● **n.** North American term for **WOLVERINE**.
– ORIGIN C18: from Canad. Fr., appar. of Algonquian origin (cf. **KINKAJOU**).

**carcass** (Brit. also **carcase**) ● **n. 1** the dead body of an animal, especially one prepared for cutting up as meat. ➤the remains of a cooked bird after all the edible parts have been removed. **2** the structural framework of a building, ship, or piece of furniture.
– ORIGIN ME: from Anglo-Norman Fr. *carcois*, var. of OFr. *charcois*; in later use from Fr. *carcasse*; of unknown ultimate origin.

**carcass meat** ● **n.** Brit. raw meat as distinct from corned or tinned meat.

**carceral** /ˈkɑːs(ə)r(ə)l/ ● **adj.** rare relating to a prison.
– ORIGIN C16: from late L. *carceralis*, from *carcer* 'prison'.

**carcinogen** /kɑːˈsɪnədʒ(ə)n/ ● **n.** a substance capable of causing cancer.

**carcinogenic** /ˌkɑːs(ɪ)nəˈdʒɛnɪk/ ● **adj.** having the potential to cause cancer.
– DERIVATIVES **carcinogenesis** n. **carcinogenicity** n.

**carcinoid** /ˈkɑːsɪnɔɪd/ ● **n.** Medicine a tumour of a type occurring especially in the appendix and sometimes secreting hormones.

**carcinoma** /ˌkɑːsɪˈnəʊmə/ ● **n.** (pl. **carcinomas** or **carcinomata** /-mətə/) a cancer arising in the epithelial tissue of the skin or of the lining of the internal organs.
– DERIVATIVES **carcinomatous** adj.
– ORIGIN C18: via L. from Gk *karkinōma*, from *karkinos* 'crab' (cf. **CANCER**).

**car coat** ● **n.** a short, square-cut style of coat designed to be worn when driving a car.

**Card.** ● **abbrev.** Cardinal.

**card**[1] ● **n. 1** thick, stiff paper or thin cardboard. **2** a piece of card for writing on, especially a postcard or greetings card. ➤a business card or visiting card. **3** a small rectangular piece of plastic containing machine-readable personal data, e.g. a credit card or cash card. **4** a playing card. ➤(**cards**) a game played with playing cards. **5** (**cards**) Brit. informal documents relating to an employee, especially for tax and national insurance, held by the employer. **6** a scorecard, in particular a list of holes on a golf course. ➤a programme of events at a race meeting. **7** Computing a circuit board that can be inserted in a computer to give extra facilities. **8** informal, dated or N. Amer. a person regarded as odd or amusing. ● **v. 1** write on a card, especially for indexing. **2** N. Amer. check the identity card of (someone), especially to verify their age.
– PHRASES **a card up one's sleeve** Brit. a plan or asset that is kept secret until it is needed. **give someone their cards** (or **get one's cards**) Brit. informal dismiss someone (or be dismissed) from employment. **hold all the cards** be in a very strong position. **on** (or N. Amer. **in**) **the cards** informal possible or likely. **play the —— card** exploit the specified issue or idea mentioned, especially for political advantage: *he saw an opportunity to play the peace card.* **play one's cards right** make the best use of one's assets and opportunities. **put** (or **lay**) **one's cards on the table** be completely open in declaring one's intentions.
– ORIGIN ME: from OFr. *carte*, from L. *carta*, *charta*, from Gk *khartēs* 'papyrus leaf'.

**card**[2] ● **v.** comb and clean (raw wool or similar material) with a sharp-toothed instrument to disentangle the fibres before spinning. ● **n.** a toothed implement or machine for this purpose.
– DERIVATIVES **carder** n.
– ORIGIN ME: from OFr. *carde*, from Provençal *carda*, from *cardar* 'tease, comb', based on L. *carere* 'to card'.

**cardamom** /ˈkɑːdəməm/ (also **cardamum**) ● **n. 1** the aromatic seeds of a plant of the ginger family, used as a spice. **2** the SE Asian plant which bears these seeds. [*Elettaria cardamomum.*]
– ORIGIN ME: from OFr. *cardamome* or L. *cardamomum*, from Gk *kardamōmon*, from *kardamon* 'cress' + *amōmon*, the name of a kind of spice plant.

**cardan joint** /ˈkɑːd(ə)n/ ● **n.** Brit. a universal joint.
– ORIGIN C20: named after Gerolamo *Cardano* (1501–76), Ital. mathematician.

**cardan shaft** /ˈkɑːd(ə)n/ ● **n.** Brit. a shaft with a universal joint at one or both ends.

**cardboard** ● **n. 1** pasteboard or stiff paper. **2** [as modifier] (of a fictional character) lacking depth and realism.

**cardboard city** ● **n.** chiefly Brit. an urban area where homeless people congregate under makeshift shelters.

**card-carrying** ● **adj.** registered as a member of a political party or trade union.

**cardia** /ˈkɑːdɪə/ ● **n.** Anatomy the upper opening of the stomach, where the oesophagus enters.
– ORIGIN C18: from Gk *kardia*.

**cardiac** /ˈkɑːdɪak/ ● **adj. 1** of or relating to the heart. **2** of or relating to the cardia of the stomach.
– ORIGIN ME: from Fr. *cardiaque* or L. *cardiacus*, from Gk *kardiakos*, from *kardia* 'heart, cardia'.

**cardigan** ● **n.** a knitted jumper fastening with buttons down the front.
– ORIGIN C19 (Crimean War): named after the 7th Earl of *Cardigan*, whose troops first wore such garments.

**cardinal** ● **n. 1** a leading dignitary of the Roman Catholic Church, nominated by and having the power to elect the Pope. **2** a deep scarlet colour like that of a cardinal's cassock. **3** an American songbird of which the male is partly or mostly red and which typically has a crest. [*Cardinalis cardinalis* and other species, subfamily Cardinalinae.] ● **adj.** of the greatest importance; fundamental.
– DERIVATIVES **cardinalate** n. **cardinally** adv. **cardinalship** n.
– ORIGIN OE, from L. *cardinalis*, from *cardo*, *cardin-* 'hinge'; sense 1 has arisen from the function of such priests as 'pivots' of church life.

**cardinal flower** ● **n.** a tall scarlet-flowered lobelia found in North America. [*Lobelia cardinalis.*]

**cardinal humour** ● **n.** see **HUMOUR** (sense 3).

**cardinality** ● **n.** (pl. **-ies**) Mathematics the number of elements in a particular set or other grouping.

**cardinal number** ● **n.** a number denoting quantity (one, two, three, etc.), as opposed to an ordinal number (first, second, third, etc.).

**cardinal point** ● **n.** each of the four main points of the compass (north, south, east, and west).

**cardinal virtue** ● **n.** each of the chief moral attributes of scholastic philosophy: justice, prudence, temperance, and fortitude.

**cardinal vowel** ● **n.** Phonetics each of a series of vowel sounds used as a standard reference point to assist in the description and classification of vowel sounds.

**card index** • n. a catalogue in which each item is entered on a separate card. • v. (**card-index**) catalogue (information) in the form of a card index.

**carding wool** • n. short-stapled pieces of wool which result from the carding process, spun and woven to make standard-quality fabrics. Compare with **COMBING WOOL**.

**cardio-** /ˈkɑːdɪəʊ/ • comb. form of or relating to the heart: *cardiograph*.
– ORIGIN from Gk *kardia* 'heart'.

**cardiogram** /ˈkɑːdɪə(ʊ)gram/ • n. a record of muscle activity within the heart made by a cardiograph.

**cardiograph** /ˈkɑːdɪə(ʊ)grɑːf/ • n. an instrument for recording heart muscle activity.
– DERIVATIVES **cardiographer** n. **cardiography** n.

**cardioid** • n. **1** Mathematics a heart-shaped curve traced by a point on the circumference of a circle as it rolls around another identical circle. **2** a directional microphone with a pattern of sensitivity of this shape. • adj. of the shape of a cardioid.
– ORIGIN C18: from Gk *kardioeidēs* 'heart-shaped', from *kardia* 'heart' + *eidos* 'form'.

**cardiology** • n. the branch of medicine concerned with diseases and abnormalities of the heart.
– DERIVATIVES **cardiological** adj. **cardiologist** n.

**cardiomegaly** /ˌkɑːdɪəʊˈmɛgəli/ • n. Medicine abnormal enlargement of the heart.
– ORIGIN 1960s: from **CARDIO-** + Gk *megas, megal-* 'great'.

**cardiomyopathy** /ˌkɑːdɪəʊmʌɪˈɒpəθi/ • n. Medicine chronic disease of the heart muscle.

**cardiopulmonary** • adj. Medicine of or relating to the heart and the lungs.

**cardiorespiratory** • adj. Medicine relating to the action of both heart and lungs.

**cardiovascular** • adj. Medicine of or relating to the heart and blood vessels.

**carditis** /kɑːˈdʌɪtɪs/ • n. Medicine inflammation of the heart.

**card key** • n. another term for **KEY CARD**.

**cardoon** /kɑːˈduːn/ • n. a tall thistle-like plant related to the globe artichoke, with edible leaves and roots. [*Cynara cardunculus*.]
– ORIGIN C17: from Fr. *cardon*, from *carde* 'edible part of an artichoke', from mod. Provençal *cardo*, based on L. *carduus, cardus* 'thistle, artichoke'.

**card sharp** (also **card sharper**) • n. a person who cheats at cards.

**card swipe** • n. an electronic reader through which a swipe card is passed.

**card table** • n. a table for playing cards on, typically having legs that fold flat for storage and a baize surface.

**card vote** • n. Brit. another term for **BLOCK VOTE**.

**cardy** (also **cardie**) • n. (pl. **-ies**) Brit. informal a cardigan.

**care** • n. **1** the provision of what is necessary for the health, welfare, maintenance, and protection of someone or something. ➤Brit. protective custody or guardianship provided for children by a local authority. **2** serious attention or consideration applied to an action or plan. ➤a feeling of or occasion for anxiety. • v. **1** feel concern or interest. ➤feel affection or liking. ➤(**care for/to do something**) like to have or be willing to do something. **2** (**care for**) look after and provide for the needs of.
– PHRASES **care of** at the address of. **take care 1** be cautious; keep oneself safe. **2** make sure of doing something. **take care of 1** keep safe and provided for. **2** deal with.
– DERIVATIVES **caring** n. & adj.
– ORIGIN OE *caru* (n.), *carian* (v.), of Gmc origin.

**careen** /kəˈriːn/ • v. **1** turn (a ship) on its side for cleaning or repair. ➤(of a ship) tilt; lean over. **2** another term for **CAREER**.
– ORIGIN C16: from Fr. *carène*, from Ital. *carena*, from L. *carina* 'a keel'.

**career** • n. an occupation undertaken for a significant period of a person's life, usually with opportunities for progress. ➤the progress through history of an institution or organization. ➤[as modifier] working with commitment in a particular profession: *a career diplomat*. ➤[as modifier] (of a woman) pursuing a profession. • v. move swiftly and in an uncontrolled way.
– ORIGIN C16 (denoting a road or racecourse): from Fr. *carrière*, from Ital. *carriera*, based on L. *carrus* 'wheeled vehicle'.

**careerist** • n. a person whose main concern is for advancement in their profession.
– DERIVATIVES **careerism** n.

**carefree** • adj. free from anxiety or responsibility.
– DERIVATIVES **carefreeness** n.

**careful** • adj. **1** taking care to avoid mishap or harm; cautious. ➤(**careful of/about**) protective of. ➤(**careful with**) prudent in the use of. **2** done with or showing thought and attention.
– DERIVATIVES **carefully** adv. **carefulness** n.
– ORIGIN OE *carful* (see **CARE, -FUL**).

**caregiver** • n. chiefly N. Amer. another term for **CARER**.
– DERIVATIVES **caregiving** n. & adj.

**care label** • n. a label giving instructions for the washing and care of a fabric or garment.

**careless** • adj. **1** not giving sufficient attention or thought to avoiding harm or mistakes. **2** (**careless of/about**) not concerned or worried about. ➤showing no interest or effort; casual.
– DERIVATIVES **carelessly** adv. **carelessness** n.
– ORIGIN OE *carlēas* 'free from care' (see **CARE, -LESS**).

**careline** • n. Brit. a telephone complaints and advice service.

**carer** • n. Brit. a family member or paid helper who regularly looks after a sick, elderly, or disabled person.

**caress** • v. touch or stroke gently or lovingly. • n. a gentle or loving touch.
– DERIVATIVES **caressing** adj. **caressingly** adv.
– ORIGIN C17: from Fr. *caresser* (v.), *caresse* (n.), from Ital. *carezza*, based on L. *carus* 'dear'.

**caret** /ˈkarət/ • n. a mark (^, ʌ) placed below a line of text to indicate a proposed insertion.
– ORIGIN C17: from L., 'is lacking'.

**caretaker** • n. **1** Brit. a person employed to look after a public building. **2** [as modifier] holding power temporarily: *he was to act as caretaker Prime Minister.* **3** chiefly N. Amer. a person employed to look after people or animals.

**careworn** • adj. tired and unhappy because of prolonged worry.

**carex** /ˈkɛːrɛks/ • n. (pl. **carices** /-rɪsiːz/) a sedge of a large genus found chiefly in temperate and cold regions. [Genus *Carex*.]
– ORIGIN mod. L., from L., 'sedge'.

**carfare** /ˈkɑːfɛː/ • n. N. Amer. the fare for travel on a bus, underground train, or similar public transport.

**cargador** /ˌkɑːgəˈdɔː/ • n. (pl. **cargadores** /ˌkɑːgəˈdɔːrɪz/) (in Spanish-speaking parts of America) a porter.
– ORIGIN C19: Sp., from *carga* 'a load'.

**cargo** • n. (pl. **-oes** or **-os**) goods carried commercially on a ship, aircraft, or truck.
– ORIGIN C17: from Sp. *cargo, carga*, from late L. *carricare, carcare* 'to load', from L. *carrus* 'wheeled vehicle'.

**cargo cult** • n. (in the Melanesian Islands) a system of beliefs based around the expected arrival of benevolent spirits in aircraft or ships bringing cargoes of food and other goods.

**cargo pants** • pl. n. loose-fitting casual cotton trousers with large patch pockets halfway down each leg.

**Carib** /ˈkarɪb/ • n. **1** a member of an indigenous South American people living mainly in coastal regions of French Guiana, Suriname, Guyana, and Venezuela. **2** the language of the Carib. **3** (also **Island Carib**) an unrelated Arawakan language, now extinct, formerly spoken in the Lesser Antilles.
– ORIGIN from Sp. *caribe*, from Haitian Creole.

**Cariban** /ˈkarɪb(ə)n/ • n. a family of South American languages including Carib, mostly extinct or nearly so. • adj. denoting the Cariban languages.

**Caribbean** /ˌkarɪˈbiːən, kəˈrɪbɪən/ • adj. of or relating to the region consisting of the Caribbean Sea, its islands (including the West Indies), and the surrounding coasts.

**USAGE** Caribbean

There are two possible pronunciations of the word **Caribbean**. The first, found in the US and the Caribbean itself, puts the stress on the **-rib-**, while the second, more familiar to most British people, puts the stress on the **-be-**.

**caribou** /'karɪbuː/ ● **n.** (pl. same) N. Amer. a reindeer.
– ORIGIN C17: from Canad. Fr., from Micmac *γalipu*, lit. 'snow-shoveller'.

**caricature** /'karɪkə,tjʊə/ ● **n.** a depiction of a person in which distinguishing characteristics are exaggerated for comic or grotesque effect. ● **v.** make a caricature of.
– DERIVATIVES **caricatural** adj. **caricaturist** n.
– ORIGIN C18: from Fr., from Ital. *caricatura*, from *caricare* 'load, exaggerate', from L. *carricare* (see CHARGE).

**CARICOM** /'karɪkɒm/ ● **abbrev.** Caribbean Community and Common Market.

**caries** /'kɛːriːz/ ● **n.** decay and crumbling of a tooth or bone.
– ORIGIN C16: from L.

**carillon** /'karɪljən, -lɒn, kə'rɪljən/ ● **n.** **1** a set of bells sounded from a keyboard or by an automatic mechanism. **2** a tune played on such bells.
– DERIVATIVES **carillonneur** /,karɪljə'nəː, -'rɪlə-, kə-/ n.
– ORIGIN C18: from Fr., from OFr. *quarregnon* 'peal of four bells', based on L. *quattuor* 'four'.

**carina** /kə'rʌɪnə, -'riː-/ ● **n.** (pl. **carinae** /-niː/ or **carinas**) **1** Zoology a keel-shaped structure, especially the ridge of a bird's breastbone to which the main flight muscles are attached. **2** Anatomy a cartilage situated at the point where the trachea (windpipe) divides into the two bronchi.
– DERIVATIVES **carinal** adj.
– ORIGIN C18: from L., 'keel'.

**carinate** /'karɪneɪt, -nət/ ● **adj.** Ornithology denoting a bird having a carina. Contrasted with RATITE.
– DERIVATIVES **carinated** adj. **carination** n.

**carioca** /,karɪ'əʊkə/ ● **n.** **1** a native of Rio de Janeiro. **2** a Brazilian dance resembling the samba.
– ORIGIN C19: from Port., from Tupi *kari'oka* 'house of the white man'.

**cariogenic** /,kɛːrɪə(ʊ)'dʒɛnɪk, ,ka-/ ● **adj.** causing tooth decay.

**cariole** ● **n.** variant spelling of CARRIOLE.

**carious** /'kɛːrɪəs/ ● **adj.** (of bones or teeth) decayed.
– ORIGIN C16: from L. *cariosus* (see CARIES).

**caritas** /'karɪtɑːs/ ● **n.** Christian love of humankind; charity.
– ORIGIN C19: from L.

**carjacking** ● **n.** chiefly N. Amer. the action of stealing a car after violently ejecting its driver.
– DERIVATIVES **carjack** v. **carjacker** n.
– ORIGIN 1990s: blend of CAR and *hijacking* (see HIJACK).

**carking** ● **adj.** archaic causing distress or worry.
– ORIGIN C16: pres. part. of ME *cark* 'worry, burden', from ONorth. Fr. *carkier*, based on late L. *carcare* (see CHARGE).

**carl** ● **n.** archaic a man of low birth. ➤Scottish a man; a fellow.
– ORIGIN OE: from ON *karl* 'man, freeman', of Gmc origin.

**Carley float** /'kɑːli/ ● **n.** a type of emergency raft carried by ships.
– ORIGIN C20: named after Horace S. *Carley*, Amer. inventor.

**carline** /'kɑːlɪn/ (also **carlin** or **carling**) ● **n.** any of the pieces of squared timber fitted fore and aft between the deck beams of a wooden ship to support the deck planking.
– ORIGIN ME (in the sense '(old) woman, witch'): from ON *karling*; the reason for naut. use of the word remains obscure.

**carline thistle** /'kɑːlɪn, -lʌɪn/ ● **n.** a spiny plant with long-lived flower heads bearing shiny straw-coloured bracts. [*Carlina vulgaris* and related species.]
– ORIGIN C16: from Fr., from med. L. *carlina*, perh. an alt. of *cardina* (from L. *carduus* 'thistle') by assoc. with *Carolus Magnus* Charlemagne.

**Carlovingian** /,kɑːlə(ʊ)'vɪndʒɪən/ ● **adj.** & **n.** another term for CAROLINGIAN.
– ORIGIN from Fr. *carlovingien*, from *Karl* 'Charles', on the pattern of *mérovingien* 'Merovingian'.

**Carlsbad plum** /'kɑːlzbad/ ● **n.** a dessert plum of a blue-black variety, often crystallized.
– ORIGIN C19: named after *Karlsbad* (now Karlovy Vary).

**Carmelite** /'kɑːməlʌɪt/ ● **n.** a friar or nun of an order founded at Mount Carmel during the Crusades. ● **adj.** of or relating to the Carmelites.

**carminative** /'kɑːmɪnətɪv, kɑː'mɪnətɪv/ Medicine ● **adj.** relieving flatulence. ● **n.** a carminative drug.
– ORIGIN ME: from OFr. *carminatif, -ive*, or med. L. *carminat-, carminare* 'heal (by incantation)' from L. *carmen* (see CHARM).

**carmine** /'kɑːmʌɪn, -mɪn/ ● **n.** a vivid crimson pigment made from cochineal.
– ORIGIN C18: from Fr. *carmin*, based on Arab. *ḳirmiz* (see KERMES).

**carnage** /'kɑːnɪdʒ/ ● **n.** the killing of a large number of people.
– ORIGIN C17: from Fr., from Ital. *carnaggio*, from med. L. *carnaticum*, from L. *caro, carn-* 'flesh'.

**carnal** /'kɑːn(ə)l/ ● **adj.** relating to physical, especially sexual, needs and activities.
– DERIVATIVES **carnality** n. **carnally** adv.
– ORIGIN ME: from Christian L. *carnalis*, from *caro, carn-* 'flesh'.

**carnal knowledge** ● **n.** dated, chiefly Law sexual intercourse.

**carnallite** /'kɑːn(ə)lʌɪt/ ● **n.** a white or reddish mineral consisting of a chloride of potassium and magnesium.
– ORIGIN C19: named after Rudolf von *Carnall*, Ger. mining engineer, + -ITE[1].

**carnassial** /kɑː'nasɪəl/ ● **adj.** Zoology denoting the large upper premolar and lower molar teeth of a carnivore, adapted for shearing flesh.
– ORIGIN C19: from Fr. *carnassier* 'carnivorous', based on L. *caro, carn-* 'flesh'.

**Carnatic** /kɑː'natɪk/ ● **adj.** of or denoting the main style of classical music in southern India, as distinct from the Hindustani music of the north.
– ORIGIN Anglicization of *Karnataka*, a state in SW India.

**carnation** ● **n.** a double-flowered cultivated variety of clove pink, with grey-green leaves and showy pink, white, or red flowers.
– ORIGIN C16 (also in sense 'flesh colour'): perh. based on a misreading of Arab. *ḳaranful* 'clove or clove pink', influenced by Fr. *carnation* 'flesh colour or rosy pink', based on L. *caro, carn-* 'flesh'.

**carnauba** /kɑː'nɔːbə, -'naʊbə/ ● **n.** **1** a NE Brazilian fan palm, the leaves of which exude a yellowish wax. [*Copernicia cerifera*.] **2** wax from this palm.
– ORIGIN C19: from Port., from Tupi.

**carnelian** /kɑː'niːlɪən/ (also **cornelian**) ● **n.** a dull red or reddish-white semi-precious variety of chalcedony.
– ORIGIN ME: from OFr. *corneline*; the prefix *car-* being suggested by L. *caro, carn-* 'flesh'.

**carnet** /'kɑːneɪ/ ● **n.** **1** a permit for a particular purpose, especially one allowing a motor vehicle to be taken across a frontier for a limited period. **2** a book of tickets for use on public transport in some countries.
– ORIGIN 1920s: from Fr., 'notebook'.

**carnival** ● **n.** **1** an annual period of public revelry involving processions, music, dancing, etc. **2** N. Amer. a travelling funfair or circus.
– DERIVATIVES **carnivalesque** adj.
– ORIGIN C16: from Ital. *carnevale, carnovale*, from med. L. *carnelevamen, carnelevarium* 'Shrovetide', from L. *caro, carn-* 'flesh' + *levare* 'put away'.

**Carnivora** /kɑː'nɪvərə/ ● **pl. n.** Zoology an order of mammals comprising the cats, dogs, bears, hyenas, weasels, civets, raccoons, and mongooses, having powerful jaws and teeth adapted for tearing and eating flesh.

**carnivore** /'kɑːnɪvɔː/ ● **n.** an animal that feeds on flesh. ➤Zoology a mammal of the order Carnivora.
– ORIGIN C19: from Fr., from L. *carnivorus* (see CARNIVOROUS).

**carnivorous** /kɑːˈnɪv(ə)rəs/ ● **adj.** (of an animal) feeding on flesh.
– DERIVATIVES **carnivorously** adv. **carnivorousness** n.
– ORIGIN C16: from L. *carnivorus*, from *caro, carn-* 'flesh' + *-vorus* (see **-VOROUS**).

**carnosaur** /ˈkɑːnəsɔː/ ● **n.** a large bipedal carnivorous dinosaur of a group including tyrannosaurus, allosaurus, and megalosaurus.
– ORIGIN 1930s: from mod. L., from L. *caro, carn-* 'flesh' + Gk *sauros* 'lizard'.

**carnotite** /ˈkɑːnətʌɪt/ ● **n.** a lemon-yellow radioactive mineral consisting of a vanadate of uranium, potassium, and other elements.
– ORIGIN C19: named after Marie Adolphe *Carnot*, Fr. inspector of mines, + **-ITE**[1].

**carny** (also **carney**) ● **adj.** (**-ier, -iest**) informal artful; sly.
– ORIGIN C19: of unknown origin.

**carob** /ˈkarəb/ ● **n. 1** the edible brownish-purple pod of an Arabian tree, from which a powder is extracted for use as a substitute for chocolate. **2** the tree which yields this pod. [*Ceratonia siliqua*.]
– ORIGIN ME from OFr. *carobe*, from med. L. *carrubia*, from Arab. *ḵarrūba*.

**carol** ● **n.** a religious song or popular hymn associated with Christmas. ● **v.** (**carolled, carolling**; US **caroled, caroling**) **1** (**go carolling**) sing carols in the streets. **2** sing or say (something) happily.
– DERIVATIVES **caroller** (US **caroler**) n. **carolling** (US **caroling**) n.
– ORIGIN ME: from OFr. *carole* (n.), *caroler* (v.), of unknown origin.

**Caroline** /ˈkarəlʌɪn/ ● **adj. 1** (also **Carolean** /-ˈliːən/) of or relating to the reigns of Charles I and II of England (1625–49; 1660–85). **2** another term for **CAROLINGIAN**.
– ORIGIN C17: from med. L. *Carolus* 'Charles'.

**Carolingian** /ˌkarəˈlɪndʒɪən/ (also **Carlovingian**) ● **adj. 1** relating to or denoting the Frankish dynasty founded by Charlemagne's father (Pepin III), which ruled in western Europe from 750 to 987. **2** denoting a minuscule script developed in France during the time of Charlemagne, on which modern lower-case letters are largely based. ● **n.** a member of the Carolingian dynasty.
– ORIGIN alt. of earlier **CARLOVINGIAN**, by assoc. with med. L. *Carolus* 'Charles'.

**Carolinian** /ˌkarəˈlɪnɪən/ ● **n.** a native or inhabitant of the US states of South or North Carolina. ● **adj. 1** of or relating to South or North Carolina. **2** denoting a forest region extending from South Ontario to South Carolina.

**carol-singing** ● **n.** the singing of carols, especially by groups going from door to door at Christmas with the object of raising money.
– DERIVATIVES **carol-singer** n.

**carom** /ˈkarəm/ chiefly N. Amer. ● **n. 1** a cannon shot in billiards or pool. **2** (also **carom billiards**) a game resembling billiards and depending on cannon shots for scoring. ● **v.** make a carom.
– ORIGIN C18: abbrev. of *carambole*, from Sp. *carambola*, appar. from *bola* 'ball'.

**carotene** /ˈkarətiːn/ ● **n.** Chemistry an orange or red plant pigment found notably in carrots and of which one form (**beta-carotene**) is important in the diet as a precursor of vitamin A.
– DERIVATIVES **carotenoid** /kəˈrɒtɪnɔɪd/ n.
– ORIGIN C19: coined in Ger. from L. *carota* 'carrot'.

**carotid** /kəˈrɒtɪd/ ● **adj.** Anatomy relating to or denoting the two main arteries carrying blood to the head and neck.
– ORIGIN C17: from Fr. *carotide* or mod. L. *carotides*, from Gk *karōtides*, pl. of *karōtis* 'drowsiness', from *karoun* 'stupefy' (because compression of these arteries was thought to cause stupor).

**carouse** /kəˈraʊz/ ● **v.** drink alcohol and enjoy oneself with others in a noisy, lively way. ● **n.** a noisy, lively drinking party.
– DERIVATIVES **carousal** n. **carouser** n. **carousing** n.
– ORIGIN C16: orig. as adv. meaning 'right out, completely' in the phr. *drink carouse*, from Ger. *gar aus trinken*.

**carousel** /ˌkarəˈsɛl, -ˈzɛl/ ● **n. 1** a merry-go-round at a fair. **2** a rotating machine or device, in particular a conveyor system for baggage collection at an airport. **3** historical an equestrian tournament among knights.
– ORIGIN C17: from Fr. *carrousel*, from Ital. *carosello*.

**carp**[1] ● **n.** (pl. same) a deep-bodied freshwater fish, often kept in ponds and sometimes farmed for food. [*Cyprinus carpio* and other species, family Cyprinidae.]
– ORIGIN ME: from OFr. *carpe*, from late L. *carpa*.

**carp**[2] ● **v.** complain or find fault continually.
– DERIVATIVES **carper** n.
– ORIGIN ME (in the sense 'talk, chatter'): from ON *karpa* 'brag'; later influenced by L. *carpere* 'pluck at, slander'.

**carpaccio** /kɑːˈpatʃɪəʊ, Italian karˈpattʃo/ ● **n.** an Italian hors d'oeuvre consisting of thin slices of raw beef or fish served with a sauce.
– ORIGIN Ital., named after the painter Vittore *Carpaccio* (from his use of red pigments, resembling raw meat).

**carpal** /ˈkɑːp(ə)l/ Anatomy & Zoology ● **adj.** of or relating to the carpus. ● **n.** a bone of the carpus.

**carpal tunnel syndrome** ● **n.** a painful condition of the hand and fingers caused by compression of a major nerve where it passes over the carpal bones.

**carpe diem** /ˌkɑːpeɪ ˈdiːɛm, ˈdʌɪɛm/ ● **exclam.** make the most of the present time.
– ORIGIN L., 'seize the day!', a quotation from Horace (*Odes* I.xi).

**carpel** /ˈkɑːp(ə)l/ ● **n.** Botany the female reproductive organ of a flower, consisting of an ovary, a stigma, and usually a style.
– DERIVATIVES **carpellary** adj.
– ORIGIN C19: from Fr. *carpelle* or mod. L. *carpellum*, from Gk *karpos* 'fruit'.

**carpenter** ● **n.** a person who makes wooden objects and structures. ● **v.** make by shaping wood.
– DERIVATIVES **carpentry** n.
– ORIGIN ME: from Anglo-Norman Fr., from OFr. *carpentier, charpentier*, from late L. *carpentarius* (*artifex*) 'carriage(-maker)', from *carpentum* 'wagon', of Gaulish origin.

**carpenter ant** ● **n.** a large ant which burrows into wood to make a nest. [Genus *Camponotus*.]

**carpenter bee** ● **n.** a large solitary black bee with purplish wings, which nests in tunnels bored in dead wood or plant stems. [Genus *Xylocopa*.]

**carpenter trousers** ● **pl. n.** loose-fitting trousers with many pockets of various sizes and loops for tools at the tops or sides of the legs.

**carpet** ● **n. 1** a floor covering made from thick woven fabric. ➤ a large rug. **2** a thick or soft expanse or layer of something. **3** used in names of geometrid moths with variegated wings. ● **v.** (**carpeted, carpeting**) **1** cover with a carpet. **2** Brit. informal reprimand severely.
– PHRASES **on the carpet** informal being severely reprimanded by someone in authority. [from *carpet* referring to the covering of the council table, before which one would be summoned for reprimand.] **sweep (a problem or difficulty) under the carpet** conceal or ignore a problem or difficulty in the hope that it will be forgotten.
– DERIVATIVES **carpeting** n.
– ORIGIN ME (denoting a thick fabric used as a cover for a table or bed): from OFr. *carpite* or med. L. *carpita*, from obs. Ital. *carpita* 'woollen counterpane', based on L. *carpere* 'pluck, pull to pieces'.

**carpet bag** ● **n.** a travelling bag of a kind originally made of carpet-like material. ● **v.** (**carpet-bag**) N. Amer. act as a carpetbagger.

**carpetbagger** ● **n.** derogatory, chiefly N. Amer. a politician who seeks election in an area where they have no local connections, originally a northerner who went to the South after the Civil War. ➤ an unscrupulous opportunist.

**carpet beetle** ● **n.** a small beetle whose larva (a woolly bear) is destructive to carpets, fabrics, etc. [Genus *Anthrenus*.]

**carpet-bomb** ● **v.** bomb (an area) intensively.
– DERIVATIVES **carpet-bombing** n.

**carpet shark** ● **n.** a small shallow-water shark of the Indo-Pacific region, typically with a conspicuous colour pattern. [Family Orectolobidae: several species.]

**carpet slipper** ● n. a soft slipper whose upper part is made of wool or thick cloth.

**carpet sweeper** ● n. a manual household implement with revolving brushes for sweeping carpets.

**carpology** /kɑːˈpɒlədʒi/ ● n. the study of fruits and seeds.
– DERIVATIVES **carpological** adj.
– ORIGIN C19: from Gk *karpos* 'fruit' + **-LOGY**.

**carpool** chiefly N. Amer. ● n. a group of people who arrange to make a journey or journeys in a single car. ● v. take part in a carpool.

**carpophore** /ˈkɑːpə(ʊ)fɔː/ ● n. Botany **1** (in a flower) an elongated axis that raises the stem of the pistil above the stamens. **2** (in a fungus) the stem of the fruiting body.
– ORIGIN C19: from Gk *karpos* 'fruit' + **-PHORE**.

**carport** ● n. a shelter for a car consisting of a roof supported on posts, built beside a house.

**carpus** /ˈkɑːpəs/ ● n. (pl. **carpi** /-pʌɪ/) the group of small bones between the main part of the forelimb and the metacarpus, forming the wrist in humans.
– ORIGIN ME: from mod. L., from Gk *karpos* 'wrist'.

**carr** ● n. Brit. fenland with neutral water. ➤Ecology wet woodland, typically dominated by alder or willow.
– ORIGIN ME: from ON *kjarr* 'brushwood', in *kjarr-mýrr* 'marsh overgrown with brushwood'.

**carrack** /ˈkarək/ ● n. a large European merchant ship of a kind operating from the 14th to the 17th century.
– ORIGIN ME: from OFr. *caraque*; perh. from Sp. *carraca*, from Arab.

**carrageen** /ˈkarəgiːn/ (also **carragheen** or **carrageen moss**) ● n. an edible red shoreline seaweed with flattened branching fronds. [*Chondrus crispus*.]
– ORIGIN C19: from Ir. *carraigín*.

**carrageenan** /ˌkarəˈgiːnən/ ● n. a carbohydrate extracted from carrageen and used as a thickening or emulsifying agent in food products.

**carrel** /ˈkar(ə)l/ ● n. **1** a small cubicle with a desk for the use of a reader in a library. **2** historical a small enclosure or study in a cloister.
– ORIGIN C16: appar. rel. to **CAROL** in the old sense 'ring'.

**carriage** ● n. **1** a four-wheeled passenger vehicle pulled by two or more horses. ➤a wheeled support for moving a heavy object such as a gun. **2** Brit. any of the separate vehicles of a passenger train. **3** Brit. the conveying of items or merchandise from one place to another. **4** a moving part of a machine that carries other parts into the required position. **5** a person's bearing or deportment.
– ORIGIN ME: from ONorth. Fr. *cariage*, from *carier* (see **CARRY**).

**carriage and pair** ● n. a carriage pulled by two horses.

**carriage bolt** ● n. N. Amer. a coach bolt.

**carriage clock** ● n. Brit. a portable clock in a rectangular case with a handle on top.

**carriage dog** ● n. archaic a Dalmatian dog.
– ORIGIN C19: because Dalmatians were formerly trained to run behind a carriage as a guard dog.

**carriage release** ● n. a function or lever which enables the carriage on a typewriter to be moved freely.

**carriage return** ● n. see **RETURN** (sense 8).

**carriage trade** ● n. N. Amer. the wealthy clientele of a business.

**carriageway** ● n. Brit. **1** each of the two sides of a dual carriageway or motorway, consisting of two or more lanes. **2** the part of a road intended for vehicles.

**carrick bend** ● n. a kind of knot used on a ship to join ropes end to end.
– ORIGIN C19: from **BEND**[2]: *carrick* perh. an alt. of **CARRACK**.

**carrier** ● n. **1** a person or thing that carries, holds, or conveys something. **2** a person or company that undertakes the professional conveyance of goods or people. **3** a person or animal that transmits a disease-causing organism to others, especially without suffering from it themselves. ➤an individual possessing a particular gene, especially as a single copy whose effect is masked by a dominant allele, so that the associated characteristic is not displayed but may be passed to offspring.

**carrier bag** ● n. Brit. a plastic or paper bag with handles, for carrying purchased goods.

**carrier pigeon** ● n. a pigeon trained to carry messages tied to its neck or leg.

**carrier wave** ● n. a high-frequency electromagnetic wave modulated in amplitude or frequency to convey a signal.

**carriole** /ˈkarɪəʊl/ (also **cariole**) ● n. **1** historical a small open horse-drawn carriage for one person. ➤a light covered cart. **2** (in Canada) a kind of sledge pulled by a horse or dogs, with space for one or more passengers.
– ORIGIN C18: from Fr., from Ital. *carriuola*, dimin. of *carro*, from L. *carrum* (see **CAR**).

**carrion** ● n. the decaying flesh of dead animals.
– ORIGIN ME: from Anglo-Norman Fr. and ONorth. Fr. *caroine*, *caroigne*, OFr. *charoigne*, based on L. *caro* 'flesh'.

**carrion beetle** ● n. a beetle that feeds on decaying animal and plant matter. [Family Silphidae: many species.]

**carrion crow** ● n. a common black crow. [*Corvus corone*.]

**carronade** /ˌkarəˈneɪd/ ● n. historical a short large-calibre cannon, chiefly in naval use.
– ORIGIN C18: from *Carron*, near Falkirk in Scotland, where this kind of cannon was first made.

**carrot** ● n. **1** a tapering orange-coloured root eaten as a vegetable. **2** a cultivated plant of the parsley family with feathery leaves, which yields this vegetable. [*Daucus carota*.] **3** an offer of something enticing as a means of persuasion (as contrasted with the 'stick' or punishment). **4** (**carrots**) informal, chiefly derogatory a nickname for a red-haired person.
– DERIVATIVES **carroty** adj.
– ORIGIN C15: from Fr. *carotte*, from L. *carota*, from Gk *karōton*.

**carry** ● v. (**-ies**, **-ied**) **1** move or transport from one place to another. ➤have on one's person wherever one goes. ➤conduct; transmit. ➤be infected with (a disease) and liable to transmit it to others. **2** support the weight of. ➤be pregnant with. ➤(**carry oneself**) stand and move in a specified way. ➤assume or accept (responsibility or blame). **3** have as a feature or consequence. **4** take or develop (an idea or activity) to a specified point. ➤propel (a missile) to a specified distance. ➤Golf & Cricket hit the ball over and beyond (a particular point). **5** (often **be carried**) approve (a proposed measure) by a majority of votes. ➤persuade to support one's policy. ➤N. Amer. gain (a state or district) in an election. **6** (of a newspaper, television station, etc.) publish or broadcast. ➤(of a retailing outlet) keep a regular stock of. **7** (of a sound or voice) be audible at a distance. ● n. (pl. **-ies**) **1** an act of carrying. ➤American Football an act of running or rushing with the ball. ➤chiefly N. Amer. the action of keeping a gun on one's person. ➤N. Amer. historical a portage for boats or supplies. **2** Finance the maintenance of an investment position in a securities market, especially with regard to the costs or profits accruing. **3** Golf the distance a ball travels before reaching the ground. **4** the range of a gun or similar weapon.
– PHRASES **carry all before one** overcome all opposition. **carry one's bat** Cricket (especially of an opening batsman) be not out at the end of one's side's completed innings. **carry the can** Brit. informal take responsibility for a mistake or misdeed. **carry the day** be victorious or successful. **carry weight** be influential or important.
– PHRASAL VERBS **be/get carried away** lose self-control. **carry away** Nautical lose (a mast or other part of a ship) through breakage. **carry forward** transfer (figures) to a new page or account. ➤keep to use or deal with at a later time. **carry off 1** take away by force. ➤(of a disease) kill (someone). **2** succeed in doing (something difficult). **carry on 1** continue an activity or task. ➤continue to move in the same direction. **2** informal behave in a specified way. **3** informal, derogatory, chiefly Brit. be engaged in a love affair. **carry out** perform (a task or planned operation). **carry over 1** extend beyond the normal or original area

of application. **2** keep to use or deal with in a new context. ➤ postpone. **carry through** bring to completion.
– ORIGIN ME: from Anglo-Norman Fr. and ONorth. Fr. *carier*, based on L. *carrus* 'wheeled vehicle'.

**carryall** ● **n.** **1** N. Amer. a large bag or case. **2** historical a light carriage. [C18: prob. from Fr. *carriole* (see **CARRIOLE**).] **3** US a large car or truck with seats facing each other along the sides.

**carrycot** ● **n.** Brit. a small portable cot for a baby.

**carry-on** ● **n.** Brit. informal **1** a display of excitement or fuss. ➤ (also **carryings-on**) questionable or improper behaviour. **2** a bag or suitcase suitable for taking on to an aircraft as hand luggage.

**carry-out** ● **n.** chiefly Scottish & US another term for **TAKEAWAY**.

**carry-over** ● **n.** something transferred or resulting from a previous situation or context.

**carse** /kɑːs/ ● **n.** Scottish fertile lowland beside a river.
– ORIGIN ME: perh. an alt. of *carrs*, pl. of **CARR**.

**carsick** ● **adj.** affected with nausea caused by the motion of a car in which one is travelling.
– DERIVATIVES **carsickness** n.

**cart** ● **n.** **1** a horse-drawn open vehicle with two or four wheels, used for carrying loads. ➤ a light two-wheeled open vehicle for driving in, pulled by a single horse. **2** a shallow open container on wheels, pulled or pushed by hand. ➤ N. Amer. a supermarket trolley. ● **v.** **1** convey or put in a cart or similar vehicle. **2** informal carry (a heavy or cumbersome object) somewhere with difficulty. ➤ convey or propel unceremoniously.
– PHRASES **in the cart** Brit. informal in trouble or difficulty. **put the cart before the horse** reverse the proper order or procedure.
– DERIVATIVES **carter** n. **cartful** n. (pl. **-fuls**). **cartload** n.
– ORIGIN ME: from ON *kartr*, prob. influenced by Anglo-Norman Fr. and ONorth. Fr. *carete*, dimin. of *carre* (see **CAR**).

**cartage** ● **n.** the conveyance of something in a cart or other vehicle.

**carte** ● **n.** variant spelling of **QUART** (in sense 2).

**carte blanche** /ˌkɑːt ˈblɑːnʃ/ ● **n.** **1** complete freedom to act as one wishes or thinks best. **2** (in piquet) a hand containing no court cards as dealt.
– ORIGIN C17: Fr., lit. 'blank paper'.

**carte de visite** /ˌkɑːt də vɪˈziːt/ ● **n.** (pl. **cartes de visite** pronunc. same) historical a card bearing a small photograph of someone.
– ORIGIN C19: Fr., 'visiting card'.

**cartel** /kɑːˈtɛl/ ● **n.** **1** an association of manufacturers or suppliers formed to maintain high prices and restrict competition. **2** chiefly historical a political coalition intended to promote a mutual interest.
– DERIVATIVES **cartelize** (also **-ise**) v.
– ORIGIN C19 (used orig. with ref. to the coalition of the Conservative and National Liberal parties in Germany (1887)): from Ger. *Kartell*, from Fr. *cartel*, from Ital. *cartello*, dimin. of *carta*, from L. *carta* (see **CARD**[1]).

**Cartesian** /kɑːˈtiːzɪən, -ʒ(ə)n/ ● **adj.** of or relating to the French philosopher René Descartes (1596–1650) and his ideas. ● **n.** a follower of Descartes.
– DERIVATIVES **Cartesianism** n.
– ORIGIN C17: from mod. L. *Cartesianus*, from *Cartesius*, Latinized form of the name *Descartes*.

**Cartesian coordinates** ● **pl. n.** coordinates which locate a point in terms of its perpendicular distance from two (or three) mutually perpendicular axes.

**Carthaginian** /kɑːθəˈdʒɪnɪən/ ● **n.** a native or inhabitant of the ancient city of Carthage on the coast of North Africa. ● **adj.** of or relating to Carthage or its people.

**carthorse** ● **n.** Brit. a large, strong horse suitable for heavy work.

**Carthusian** /kɑːˈθjuːzɪən/ ● **n.** a monk or nun of an austere contemplative order founded by St Bruno in 1084. ● **adj.** of or relating to this order.
– ORIGIN from med. L. *Carthusianus*, from *Cart(h)usia*, L. name of *Chartreuse*, near Grenoble, where the order was founded.

**cartilage** /ˈkɑːt(ɪ)lɪdʒ/ ● **n.** a firm, whitish, flexible connective tissue which is the main component of the articulating surfaces of joints and of structures such as the larynx and respiratory tract and the external ear.
– DERIVATIVES **cartilaginoid** /-ˈladʒɪnɔɪd/ adj. **cartilaginous** /-ˈladʒɪnəs/ adj.
– ORIGIN ME: from Fr., from L. *cartilago, cartilagin-*.

**cartilaginous fish** ● **n.** a fish of large class distinguished by having a skeleton of cartilage rather than bone and including the sharks, rays, and chimaeras. [Class Chondrichthyes.]

**cartogram** /ˈkɑːtəgram/ ● **n.** a map on which statistical information is shown in diagrammatic form.
– ORIGIN C19: from Fr. *cartogramme*, from *carte* 'map or card' + *-gramme* (from Gk *gramma* 'thing written').

**cartography** /kɑːˈtɒgrəfi/ ● **n.** the science or practice of drawing maps.
– DERIVATIVES **cartographer** n. **cartographic** adj. **cartographical** adj. **cartographically** adv.
– ORIGIN C19: from Fr. *cartographie*, from *carte* (see **CARD**[1]) + *-graphie* (see **-GRAPHY**).

**cartomancy** /ˈkɑːtə(ʊ)ˌmansi/ ● **n.** fortune telling involving the interpretation of playing cards.
– DERIVATIVES **cartomancer** n.
– ORIGIN C19: from Fr. *cartomancie*, from *carte* 'card' + *-mancie* (see **-MANCY**).

**carton** ● **n.** a light cardboard container.
– ORIGIN C19: from Fr., from Ital. *cartone* (see **CARTOON**).

**cartoon** ● **n.** **1** a drawing executed in an exaggerated style for humorous or satirical effect. **2** a film made from a sequence of such images, using animation techniques to produce the appearance of movement. **3** a full-size drawing made as a preliminary design for a painting or other work of art. ● **v.** represent in a cartoon.
– DERIVATIVES **cartooning** n. **cartoonish** adj. **cartoonist** n. **cartoony** adj.
– ORIGIN C16: from Ital. *cartone*, from *carta*, from L. *carta*, *charta* (see **CARD**[1]).

**cartophily** /kɑːˈtɒfɪli/ ● **n.** the collecting of picture cards, such as postcards or cigarette cards, as a hobby.
– DERIVATIVES **cartophilist** n.
– ORIGIN 1930s: from Fr. *carte* or Ital. *carta* 'card' + **-PHILY**.

**cartouche** /kɑːˈtuːʃ/ ● **n.** **1** a carved tablet or drawing representing a scroll with rolled-up ends, used ornamentally or bearing an inscription. ➤ a decorative architectural feature resembling a scroll. ➤ an ornate frame around a design or inscription. **2** Archaeology an oval or oblong enclosing a group of Egyptian hieroglyphs, typically representing the name and title of a monarch.
– ORIGIN C17: from Fr. *cartouche* (masc.), earlier *cartoche*, from Ital. *cartoccio*, from *carta*, from L. *carta, charta* (see **CARD**[1]).

**cartridge** ● **n.** **1** a container holding a spool of photographic film, a quantity of ink, or other item or substance, designed for insertion into a mechanism. **2** a casing containing a charge and a bullet or shot for small arms or an explosive charge for blasting.
– ORIGIN C16: from Fr. *cartouche* (fem.), from Ital. *cartoccio* (see **CARTOUCHE**).

**cartridge belt** ● **n.** a belt holding cartridges of ammunition.

**cartridge paper** ● **n.** thick, rough-textured paper used for drawing and for strong envelopes.
– ORIGIN C17: orig. used to make cartridge casing.

**cartwheel** ● **n.** **1** the wheel of a cart. **2** a circular sideways handspring with the arms and legs extended. ● **v.** perform cartwheels.

**cartwright** ● **n.** chiefly historical a person whose job is making carts.

**caruncle** /ˈkarəŋk(ə)l, kəˈrʌŋ-/ ● **n.** **1** Zoology a fleshy outgrowth, such as a bird's wattles or the red prominence at the inner corner of the eye. **2** Botany a coloured waxy or oily outgrowth from a seed near the micropyle.
– DERIVATIVES **caruncular** adj.
– ORIGIN C16: obs. Fr., from L. *caruncula*, from *caro, carn-* 'flesh'.

**carve** ● **v.** **1** cut into or shape (a hard material) in order to produce an object or design. ➤ produce in such a way. **2** cut (cooked meat) into slices for eating. **3** Skiing make (a

turn) by tilting one's skis on to their edges and using one's weight to bend them so that they slide into an arc. **4** (**carve something out**) develop a career, reputation, etc. through painstaking effort. **5** (**carve something up**) cut into or divide up something ruthlessly. ➤(**carve some-one up**) aggressively overtake another driver.
– DERIVATIVES **carving** n.
– ORIGIN OE *ceorfan* 'cut, carve', of W. Gmc origin.

**carvel** /ˈkɑːv(ə)l/ ● n. variant spelling of **CARAVEL**.

**carvel-built** ● adj. (of a boat) having external planks which do not overlap. Compare with **CLINKER-BUILT**.

**carven** archaic past participle of **CARVE**.

**carver** ● n. **1** a person or tool that carves. **2** Brit. the principal chair, with arms, in a set of dining chairs, intended for the person carving meat.

**carvery** ● n. (pl. **-ies**) chiefly Brit. a buffet or restaurant where cooked joints are carved as required.

**car wash** ● n. a structure through which a vehicle is driven while being washed automatically.

**caryatid** /ˌkarɪˈatɪd/ ● n. (pl. **caryatides** /-diːz/ or **caryatids**) Architecture a pillar in the form of a draped female figure, supporting an entablature.
– ORIGIN C16: via Fr. and Ital. from L. *caryatides*, from Gk *karuatides*, pl. of *karuatis* 'priestess of Artemis at Caryae', from *Karuai* (Caryae) in Laconia.

**caryophyllaceous** /ˌkarɪə(ʊ)fɪˈleɪʃəs/ ● adj. Botany of or relating to the pink family (Caryophyllaceae).
– ORIGIN C19: from mod. L. *Caryophyllaceae*, based on Gk *karuophullon* 'clove pink', + **-OUS**.

**caryopsis** /ˌkarɪˈɒpsɪs/ ● n. (pl. **caryopses** /-siːz/) Botany a dry one-seeded fruit in which the ovary wall is united with the seed coat, typical of grasses and cereals.
– ORIGIN C19: from mod. L., from Gk *karuon* 'nut' + *opsis* 'appearance'.

**Casanova** /ˌkasəˈnəʊvə, -z-/ ● n. a man notorious for seducing women.
– ORIGIN C20: from the name of the Ital. adventurer Giovanni Jacopo *Casanova* (1725–98).

**casareep** ● n. variant spelling of **CASSAREEP**.

**casbah** ● n. variant spelling of **KASBAH**.

**cascabel** /ˈkaskəb(ə)l/ ● n. a small red chilli pepper of a mild-flavoured variety.
– ORIGIN C17: from Sp., from Catalan *cascavel*, from med. L. *cascabellus* 'little bell'.

**cascade** ● n. **1** a small waterfall, especially one in a series. **2** a mass of something that falls, hangs, or occurs in copious quantities. **3** a process by which information or knowledge is passed on successively. **4** a succession of devices or stages in a process, each of which triggers or initiates the next. ● v. **1** pour downwards rapidly and in large quantities. **2** pass (information or knowledge) on to a succession of others. **3** arrange in a series or sequence.
– ORIGIN C17: from Fr., from Ital. *cascata*, from *cascare* 'to fall', based on L. *casus* (see **CASE**[1]).

**cascara** /kasˈkɑːrə/ (also **cascara sagrada** /səˈɡrɑːdə/) ● n. **1** a purgative made from the dried bark of a North American buckthorn. **2** the tree from which this bark is obtained. [*Rhamnus purshiana*.]
– ORIGIN C19: from Sp. *cáscara* (*sagrada*) '(sacred) bark'.

**case**[1] ● n. **1** an instance of a particular situation; an example of something occurring. ➤the situation affecting or relating to a particular person or thing. ➤an incident under official investigation by the police. **2** an instance of a disease, injury, or problem. ➤a person or their particular problem as a subject of medical or welfare attention. **3** a legal action, especially one that is to be decided in a court of law. ➤a set of facts or arguments supporting one side in such a legal action. ➤a legal action that has been decided and may be cited as a precedent. **4** a set of facts or arguments supporting one side of a debate or controversy. **5** Grammar any of the inflected forms of a noun, adjective, or pronoun that express the semantic relation of the word to other words in the sentence. ➤such a relation whether indicated by inflection or not.
– PHRASES **be the case** be so. **on** (or **off**) **someone's case** informal continually (or no longer) criticizing or harassing someone.
– ORIGIN ME: from OFr. *cas*, from L. *casus* 'fall', rel. to *cadere* 'to fall'.

**case**[2] ● n. **1** a container designed to hold or protect something. ➤the outer protective covering of a natural or manufactured object. **2** Brit. a suitcase. **3** a box containing twelve bottles of wine or other drink, sold as a unit. **4** Printing a partitioned container for loose metal type. ➤each of the two forms, capital or minuscule, in which a letter of the alphabet may be written or printed. ● v. **1** enclose within a case. **2** informal reconnoitre (a place) before carrying out a robbery.
– ORIGIN ME: from OFr. *casse*, *chasse* (mod. *caisse* 'trunk, chest', *châsse* 'reliquary, frame'), from L. *capsa*, rel. to *capere* 'to hold'.

**caseation** /ˌkeɪsɪˈeɪʃ(ə)n/ ● n. Medicine a form of necrosis characteristic of tuberculosis, in which diseased tissue forms a firm, dry mass like cheese.
– ORIGIN C19: from med. L. *caseatio(n-)*, from L. *caseus* 'cheese'.

**casebook** ● n. **1** Brit. a written record of cases, kept by a doctor, investigator, lawyer, etc. ➤a book containing extracts of important legal cases. **2** US a book containing a selection of source materials on a particular subject.

**case-bound** ● adj. (of a book) hardback.

**case-harden** ● v. **1** harden the surface of (a material). **2** [as adj. **case-hardened**] made callous or tough by experience.

**case history** ● n. a record of a person's background or medical history kept by a doctor or social worker.

**casein** /ˈkeɪsiːn, -sɪɪn/ ● n. the main protein present in milk and (in coagulated form) in cheese.
– ORIGIN C19: from L. *caseus* 'cheese'.

**case knife** ● n. **1** US a knife used at meals. **2** archaic a type of dagger carried in a sheath.

**case law** ● n. the law as established by the outcome of former cases.

**caseload** ● n. the number of cases with which a doctor, lawyer, or social worker is concerned at one time.

**casemate** /ˈkeɪsmeɪt/ ● n. historical **1** a small room in the thickness of the wall of a fortress, with embrasures from which guns or missiles can be fired. **2** an armoured enclosure for guns on a warship.
– ORIGIN C16: from Fr., from Ital. *casamatta*, perh. from Gk *khasma*, *khasmat-* (see **CHASM**).

**casement** ● n. a window set on a vertical hinge so that it opens like a door.
– ORIGIN ME (as an architectural term denoting a hollow moulding): from Anglo-Latin *cassimentum*, from *cassa*, from L. *capsa* (see **CASE**[2]).

**caseous** /ˈkeɪsɪəs/ ● adj. Medicine characterized by caseation.

**case-sensitive** ● adj. Computing differentiating between capital and lower-case letters.

**case-shot** ● n. historical bullets or pieces of metal in an iron case, fired from a cannon.

**case study** ● n. **1** a detailed study of the development of a particular person, group, or situation over a period of time. **2** a particular instance of something illustrating a thesis or principle.

**casework** ● n. social work directly concerned with individuals and their personal circumstances.
– DERIVATIVES **caseworker** n.

**cash**[1] ● n. money in coins or notes. ➤money in any form as an available resource. ● v. **1** give or obtain notes or coins for (a cheque or money order). **2** (**cash something in**) convert an insurance policy, savings account, etc. into money. ➤(**cash in on**) informal take advantage of or exploit (a situation). **3** (**cash up**) Brit. count and check takings at the end of a day's trading.
– PHRASES **cash down** with immediate and full payment at the time of purchase. **cash in one's chips** informal die. **cash in hand** payment in cash rather than by cheque or other means.
– DERIVATIVES **cashable** adj. **cashless** adj.
– ORIGIN C16 (denoting a box for money): from OFr. *casse* or Ital. *cassa* 'box', from L. *capsa* (see **CASE**[2]).

**cash**[2] ● n. (pl. same) historical a coin of low value from China, southern India, or SE Asia.

– ORIGIN C16: from Port. *caixa*, from Tamil *kāsu*, influenced by CASH[1].

**cash and carry** ● n. a system of wholesale trading whereby goods are paid for in full at the time of purchase and taken away by the purchaser.

**cashback** ● n. **1** a cash refund offered as an incentive to buyers. **2** a facility whereby a customer may withdraw cash when making a debit card purchase.

**cash book** ● n. a book in which receipts and payments of money are recorded.

**cash box** ● n. a lockable metal box for keeping cash in.

**cash card** ● n. Brit. a plastic card issued by a bank or building society which enables the holder to withdraw money from a cash dispenser.

**cash cow** ● n. informal a business or investment that provides a steady income or profit.

**cash crop** ● n. a crop produced for its commercial value rather than for use by the grower.
– DERIVATIVES **cash cropping** n.

**cash desk** ● n. Brit. a counter or compartment in a shop or restaurant where payments are made.

**cash dispenser** ● n. Brit. another term for AUTOMATED TELLER MACHINE.

**cashew** /ˈkaʃuː, kəˈʃuː/ ● n. **1** (also **cashew nut**) an edible kidney-shaped nut, rich in oil and protein. **2** the bushy tropical American tree that bears these nuts. [*Anacardium occidentale*.]
– ORIGIN C16: from Port., from Tupi *acajú*, *cajú*.

**cashew apple** ● n. the swollen edible fruit of the cashew tree, from which the cashew nut hangs.

**cash flow** ● n. the total amount of money passing into and out of a business, especially as affecting liquidity.

**cashier[1]** ● n. a person handling payments and receipts in a shop, bank, or business.
– ORIGIN C16: from Du. *cassier* or Fr. *caissier*, from *caisse* 'cash'.

**cashier[2]** ● v. dismiss from the armed forces because of a serious misdemeanour.
– ORIGIN C16: from Flemish *kasseren* 'disband (troops)' or 'revoke (a will)', from Fr. *casser* 'revoke, dismiss', from L. *quassare* (see QUASH).

**cashmere** ● n. fine soft wool, originally that from the Kashmir goat.
– ORIGIN C17: an early spelling of *Kashmir*.

**cash nexus** ● n. the relationship constituted by monetary transactions.

**cash on delivery** ● n. the system of paying for goods when they are delivered.

**cashpoint** ● n. Brit. another term for AUTOMATED TELLER MACHINE.

**cash ratio** ● n. **1** the ratio of the liquid assets of a company to its current liabilities. **2** the ratio of cash to deposits in a bank.

**cash register** ● n. a machine used in shops for totalling and recording the amount of each sale and storing the money received.

**casing** ● n. **1** a cover or shell that protects or encloses something. **2** the frame round a door or window.

**casino** ● n. (pl. **-os**) an establishment where gambling games are played.
– ORIGIN C18: from Ital., dimin. of *casa* 'house', from L. *casa* 'cottage'.

**cask** ● n. a large barrel-like container for the storage of liquid, especially alcoholic drinks.
– ORIGIN C16: from Fr. *casque* or Sp. *casco* 'helmet'.

**cask beer** ● n. draught beer brewed and stored in the traditional way, maturing naturally in the cask from which it is served.

**cask-conditioned** ● adj. (of beer) undergoing a secondary fermentation in the cask and not further processed before serving.

**casket** ● n. a small ornamental box or chest for holding valuable objects. ➤ Brit. a small wooden box for cremated ashes. ➤ chiefly N. Amer. a coffin.
– ORIGIN ME: perh. an Anglo-Norman Fr. form of OFr. *cassette*, dimin. of *casse* (see CASE[2]).

**casque** /kɑːsk/ ● n. **1** historical a helmet. **2** Zoology a helmet-like structure, such as that on the bill of a hornbill.
– ORIGIN C17: from Fr., from Sp. *casco*.

**Cassandra** /kəˈsandrə/ ● n. a prophet of disaster.
– ORIGIN from the name in Gk mythology of *Cassandra*, who was given the gift of prophecy by Apollo.

**cassareep** /ˈkasəriːp/ (also **casareep**) ● n. W. Indian a thick brown syrup made by boiling down the juice of grated cassava with sugar and spices.
– ORIGIN from Arawak *casiripe*.

**cassata** /kəˈsɑːtə/ ● n. Neapolitan ice cream containing candied or dried fruit and nuts.
– ORIGIN 1920s: Ital.

**cassation** /kəˈseɪʃ(ə)n/ ● n. Music an informal instrumental composition of the 18th century, similar to a divertimento and often for outdoor performance.
– ORIGIN C19: from Ger. *Kassation* 'serenade', from Ital. *cassazione*.

**cassava** /kəˈsɑːvə/ ● n. **1** a starchy tuberous root used as food in tropical countries but requiring careful preparation to remove traces of cyanide. **2** the shrubby tree from which this root is obtained, native to tropical America. [Genus *Manihot*: several species.]
– ORIGIN C16: from Taino *casávi*, *cazábbi*, influenced by Fr. *cassave*.

**Cassegrain telescope** /ˈkasɪɡreɪn/ ● n. a reflecting telescope in which light reflected from a secondary mirror passes through a hole in the primary mirror.
– ORIGIN C19: named after N. *Cassegrain*, the Fr. astronomer who devised it.

**casserole** ● n. **1** a large dish with a lid, used for cooking food slowly in an oven. **2** a kind of stew cooked slowly in an oven. ● v. cook slowly in a casserole.
– ORIGIN C18: from Fr., dimin. of *casse* 'spoon-like container', from Old Provençal *casa*, from late L. *cattia* 'ladle, pan', from Gk *kuathion*, dimin. of *kuathos* 'cup'.

**cassette** ● n. a sealed plastic unit containing a length of audio tape, videotape, film, etc. wound on a pair of spools, for insertion into a recorder, playback device, etc.
– ORIGIN C18: from Fr., dimin. of *casse* (see CASE[2]).

**cassette deck** ● n. a hi-fi unit for playing or recording audio cassettes.

**cassette player** (also **cassette recorder**) ● n. a machine for playing back or recording audio cassettes.

**cassette tape** ● n. a cassette of audio tape.

**cassia** /ˈkasɪə/ ● n. **1** a leguminous tree or plant of warm climates, producing senna and other valuable products. [Genus *Cassia*: numerous species.] **2** the aromatic bark of an East Asian tree (*Cinnamomum aromaticum*), yielding an inferior kind of cinnamon.
– ORIGIN from L., prob. orig. denoting wild cinnamon, via Gk from Heb. *qěṣīʿāh*.

**cassis[1]** /kaˈsiːs, ˈkasɪs/ (also **crème de cassis**) ● n. a syrupy blackcurrant liqueur produced mainly in Burgundy.
– ORIGIN Fr., 'blackcurrant', appar. from L. *cassia* (see CASSIA).

**cassis[2]** /kaˈsi/ ● n. a wine produced in the region of Cassis, a small town near Marseilles.

**cassiterite** /kəˈsɪtərʌɪt/ ● n. a reddish, brownish, or yellowish mineral consisting of tin dioxide.
– ORIGIN C19: from Gk *kassiteros* 'tin' + -ITE[1].

**cassock** ● n. a long garment worn by some Christian clergy and members of church choirs.
– DERIVATIVES **cassocked** adj.
– ORIGIN C16: from Fr. *casaque* 'long coat', from Ital. *casacca* 'riding coat', prob. from Turkic *kazak* 'vagabond'.

**cassoulet** /ˈkasʊleɪ/ ● n. a stew made with meat and beans.
– ORIGIN Fr., dimin. of dial. *cassolo* 'stew pan', from Old Provençal *cassa* 'pan'.

**cassowary** /ˈkasəwəri, -wɛːri/ ● n. (pl. **-ies**) a very large flightless bird related to the emu, native mainly to New Guinea. [Genus *Casuarius*: five species.]
– ORIGIN C17: from Malay *kesuari*.

**cast[1]** ● v. (past and past part. **cast**) **1** throw forcefully in a specified direction. ➤ throw so as to spread over an area. **2** cause (light or shadow) to appear on a surface. ➤ direct (one's eyes or thoughts) towards something. ➤cause to be associated with something: *journalists cast doubt on this version of events.* **3** discard. **4** shape (metal or other material) by pouring it into a mould while molten. ➤arrange and present in a specified form or style. **5** register (a vote). **6** throw the hooked and baited end of (a fishing line) out into the water. **7** cause (a magic spell) to take effect. **8** Hunting let loose (hounds) on a scent. ➤search around for a scent. ● **n.** **1** an object made by casting metal or other material. ➤(also **plaster cast**) a mould used to make such an object. ➤(also **plaster cast**) a bandage stiffened with plaster of Paris, moulded to support and protect a broken limb. **2** an act of casting something. ➤Brit. the leader of a fishing line. **3** the form, appearance, or character of something. **4** a slight squint. **5** short for WORM CAST. **6** a pellet regurgitated by a hawk or owl. **7** a wide sweep made by a dog or pack of hounds.

– PHRASAL VERBS **cast about** (or **around** or **round**) search far and wide. **be cast away** be stranded after a shipwreck. **be cast down** feel depressed. **cast off** (or **cast something off**) **1** Knitting take the stitches off the needle by looping each over the next to finish the edge. **2** set a boat or ship free from her moorings. **3** let loose a hunting hound or hawk. **4** Printing estimate the space that will be taken in print by manuscript copy. **cast on** (or **cast something on**) Knitting make the first row of a specified number of loops on the needle.

– DERIVATIVES **casting** n.

– ORIGIN ME: from ON *kasta* 'to cast or throw'.

**cast**[2] ● **n.** the actors taking part in a play or film. ● **v.** (past and past part. **cast**) assign a part to (an actor). ➤allocate parts in (a play or film).

– ORIGIN C17: a special use of CAST[1].

**castanets** ● **pl. n.** small concave pieces of wood, ivory, or plastic, joined in pairs by a cord and clicked together by the fingers as a rhythmic accompaniment to Spanish dancing.

– ORIGIN C17: from Sp. *castañeta*, dimin. of *castaña*, from L. *castanea* 'chestnut'.

**castaway** ● **n.** a person who has been shipwrecked and stranded in an isolated place.

**caste** ● **n.** **1** each of the hereditary classes of Hindu society, distinguished by relative degrees of ritual purity or pollution and of social status. **2** Entomology (in some social insects) a physically distinct kind of individual with a particular function.

– PHRASES **lose caste** descend in status.

– DERIVATIVES **casteism** n.

– ORIGIN C16: from Sp. and Port. *casta* 'lineage, breed', fem. of *casto* 'pure, unmixed', from L. *castus* 'chaste'.

**castellan** /ˈkastələn/ ● **n.** historical the governor of a castle.

– ORIGIN ME: from ONorth. Fr. *castelain*, from med. L. *castellanus*, from L. *castellum* (see CASTLE).

**castellated** /ˈkastəleɪtɪd/ ● **adj.** **1** having battlements. **2** (of a nut or other mechanical part) having grooves or slots on its upper face.

– DERIVATIVES **castellation** n.

– ORIGIN C17: from med. L. *castellatus*, from L. *castellum* (see CASTLE).

**caste mark** ● **n.** a symbol on the forehead denoting membership of a particular Hindu caste.

**caster** ● **n.** **1** a person or machine that casts. **2** Fishing a fly pupa used as bait. **3** variant spelling of CASTOR[1].

**caster sugar** (also **castor sugar**) ● **n.** Brit. finely granulated white sugar.

– ORIGIN C19: so named because it was suitable for sprinkling using a castor.

**castigate** /ˈkastɪgeɪt/ ● **v.** reprimand severely.

– DERIVATIVES **castigation** n. **castigator** n. **castigatory** adj.

– ORIGIN C17 (earlier (ME) as *castigation*): from L. *castigare* 'reprove', from *castus* 'pure, chaste'.

**Castilian** /kaˈstɪlɪən/ ● **n.** **1** a native of the central Spanish region of Castile. **2** the language of Castile, being the standard spoken and literary Spanish. ● **adj.** of or relating to Castile or Castilian.

**casting couch** ● **n.** informal used in reference to the supposed practice whereby parts in films are awarded by the director in return for sexual favours.

**casting vote** ● **n.** an extra vote used by a chairperson to decide an issue when votes on each side are equal.

– ORIGIN C17: from an obs. sense of *cast* 'turn the scale'.

**cast iron** ● **n.** **1** a hard, relatively brittle alloy of iron and carbon which can be readily cast in a mould. **2** [as modifier] firm and unchangeable: *there are no cast-iron guarantees.*

**castle** ● **n.** **1** a large building, typically of the medieval period, which is (or was formerly) fortified as a stronghold. **2** Chess, informal old-fashioned term for ROOK[2]. ● **v.** Chess move one's king from its original square two squares along the back rank towards a rook on its corner square which is simultaneously moved to the square passed over by the king.

– PHRASES **castles in the air** (or **in Spain**) visionary unattainable schemes; daydreams.

– DERIVATIVES **castled** adj.

– ORIGIN OE: from Anglo-Norman Fr. and ONorth. Fr. *castel*, from L. *castellum*, dimin. of *castrum* 'fort'.

**cast net** ● **n.** Fishing a net that is thrown out and drawn in again, as opposed to one that is set up and left.

**cast-off** ● **adj.** no longer wanted; abandoned or discarded. ● **n.** a cast-off garment.

**castor**[1] /ˈkɑːstə/ (also **caster**) ● **n.** **1** each of a set of small swivelling wheels fixed to the legs or base of a heavy piece of furniture. **2** a small container with holes in the top, used for sprinkling the contents.

– ORIGIN C17: orig. a var. of CASTER.

**castor**[2] /ˈkɑːstə/ ● **n.** a reddish-brown oily substance secreted by beavers, used in medicine and perfumes.

– ORIGIN ME (in the sense 'beaver'): from OFr. or L., from Gk *kastōr.*

**castor bean** ● **n.** the seed of the castor oil plant, containing the poisonous compound ricin.

**castor oil** ● **n.** a pale yellow purgative oil obtained from the seeds of an African shrub (*Ricinus communis*).

– ORIGIN C18: perh. so named because it succeeded CASTOR[2] in medicinal use.

**castor sugar** ● **n.** variant spelling of CASTER SUGAR.

**castrate** ● **v.** remove the testicles of (a male animal or man). ● **n.** a castrated man or male animal.

– DERIVATIVES **castration** n. **castrator** n.

– ORIGIN C16 (earlier (ME) as *castration*): from L. *castrare.*

**castrato** /kaˈstrɑːtəʊ/ ● **n.** (pl. **castrati** /-ti/) historical a male singer castrated in boyhood so as to retain a soprano or alto voice.

– ORIGIN C18: from Ital., past part. of *castrare* (see CASTRATE).

**casual** /ˈkaʒjʊəl, -zj-/ ● **adj.** **1** relaxed and unconcerned. ➤made, done, or acting without much care or thought. **2** not regular or firmly established. ➤(of a worker) employed on a temporary or irregular basis. **3** happening by chance; accidental. **4** without formality of style, manner, or procedure. ● **n.** **1** a casual worker. **2** (**casuals**) clothes or shoes suitable for everyday wear rather than formal occasions. **3** Brit. a youth belonging to a subculture characterized by the wearing of expensive casual clothing.

– DERIVATIVES **casually** adv. **casualness** n.

– ORIGIN ME: from OFr. *casuel* and L. *casualis*, from *casus* 'fall'.

**casual Friday** ● **n.** US Friday as a designated day of the week when organizations allow employees to dress more casually than on other weekdays.

**casualization** (also **-isation**) ● **n.** the replacement of a permanently employed workforce by casual workers.

– DERIVATIVES **casualize** v.

**casualty** ● **n.** (pl. **-ies**) **1** a person killed or injured in a war or accident. ➤Brit. the casualty department of a hospital. **2** (chiefly in insurance) an accident, mishap, or disaster.

– ORIGIN ME (in the sense 'chance, a chance occurrence'): from med. L. *casualitas*, from *casualis* (see CASUAL), on the pattern of words such as *penalty.*

**casualty department** (also **casualty ward**) ● **n.** Brit.

the department of a hospital providing immediate treatment for emergency cases.

**casual water** ● **n.** Golf a temporary expanse of water which is not a recognized hazard of the course and from which a player may remove a ball without penalty.

**casuarina** /ˌkasjʊəˈriːnə/ ● **n.** a tree with slender, jointed, drooping twigs bearing tiny scale-like leaves, native to Australia and SE Asia. [Genus *Casuarina*.]
– ORIGIN from mod. L. *casuarius* 'cassowary' (from the resemblance of the branches to the bird's feathers).

**casuist** /ˈkazjʊɪst, -ʒj-/ ● **n.** a person who uses clever but false reasoning.
– DERIVATIVES **casuistic** adj. **casuistical** adj. **casuistically** adv. **casuistry** n.
– ORIGIN C17: from Fr. *casuiste*, from Sp. *casuista*, from L. *casus* (see CASE[1]).

**casus belli** /ˌkeɪsəs ˈbɛlʌɪ, ˌkɑːsʊs ˈbɛli/ ● **n.** (pl. same) an act or situation provoking or justifying war.
– ORIGIN L., from *casus* (see CASE[1]) and *belli*, genitive of *bellum* 'war'.

**CAT** ● **abbrev.** **1** clear air turbulence. **2** computer-assisted testing. **3** Medicine computerized axial tomography.

**cat[1]** ● **n.** **1** a small domesticated carnivorous mammal with soft fur, a short snout, and retractile claws. [*Felis catus*.] ➤ a wild animal resembling this, in particular any member of the cat family (Felidae), which includes the lion, tiger, leopard, etc. **2** informal a malicious or spiteful woman. **3** historical short for CAT-O'-NINE-TAILS. ● **v.** (**catted, catting**) Nautical raise (an anchor) from the surface of the water to the cathead.
– PHRASES **let the cat out of the bag** informal reveal a secret carelessly or by mistake. **like a cat on a hot tin roof** (Brit. also **on hot bricks**) informal very agitated or anxious. **not have a cat in hell's chance** informal have no chance at all. **put** (or **set**) **the cat among the pigeons** Brit. say or do something likely to cause trouble or controversy. **see which way the cat jumps** informal see what direction events are taking before committing oneself.
– DERIVATIVES **catlike** adj.
– ORIGIN OE *catt, catte*, of Gmc origin.

**cat[2]** ● **n.** a catalytic converter.

**cat[3]** ● **n.** a catamaran.

**cata-** (also **cat-**) ● **prefix** **1** down; downwards: *catadromous*. **2** wrongly; badly: *catachresis*. **3** completely: *cataclysm*. **4** against; alongside: *catechize*.
– ORIGIN from Gk *kata* 'down'.

**catabolism** /kəˈtabəlɪz(ə)m/ (also **katabolism**) ● **n.** Biology the breakdown of complex molecules in living organisms to form simpler ones, together with the release of energy; destructive metabolism.
– DERIVATIVES **catabolic** /katəˈbɒlɪk/ adj.
– ORIGIN C19: from Gk *katabolē* 'throwing down'.

**catachresis** /ˌkatəˈkriːsɪs/ ● **n.** (pl. **catachreses** /-siːz/) the incorrect use of a word.
– DERIVATIVES **catachrestic** /-ˈkriːstɪk, -ˈkrɛstɪk/ adj.
– ORIGIN C16: from L., from Gk *katakhrēsis*, from *katakhrēsthai* 'misuse'.

**cataclasis** /ˌkatəˈkleɪsɪs/ ● **n.** Geology the fracture and breaking up of rock by natural processes.
– DERIVATIVES **cataclastic** /-ˈklastɪk/ adj.
– ORIGIN 1950s: from CATA- + Gk *klasis* 'breaking'.

**cataclysm** /ˈkatəˌklɪz(ə)m/ ● **n.** a violent upheaval or disaster.
– DERIVATIVES **cataclysmic** adj. **cataclysmically** adv.
– ORIGIN C17 (orig. denoting the biblical Flood): from Fr. *cataclysme*, via L. from Gk *kataklusmos* 'deluge'.

**catacomb** /ˈkatəkuːm, -kəʊm/ ● **n.** an underground cemetery consisting of a gallery with recesses for tombs.
– ORIGIN OE, from late L. *catacumbas*, the name of the subterranean cemetery of St Sebastian near Rome.

**catadioptric** /ˌkatədʌɪˈɒptrɪk/ ● **adj.** Optics denoting an optical system which involves both the reflecting and refracting of light, in order to reduce aberration.

**catadromous** /kaˈtadrəməs/ ● **adj.** Zoology (of a fish) migrating down rivers to the sea to spawn. The opposite of ANADROMOUS.
– ORIGIN C19: from CATA- + Gk *dromos* 'running', on the pattern of *anadromous*.

**catafalque** /ˈkatəfalk/ ● **n.** a decorated wooden framework to support a coffin.
– ORIGIN C17: from Fr., from Ital. *catafalco*, of unknown origin.

**Catalan** /ˈkatəlan/ ● **n.** **1** a native of Catalonia in NE Spain. **2** the Romance language of Catalonia closely related to Castilian Spanish and Provençal. ● **adj.** of or relating to Catalonia, its people, or their language.
– ORIGIN from Fr., from Sp. *catalán*, rel. to Catalan *català* 'Catalan', *Catalunya* 'Catalonia'.

**catalase** /ˈkatəleɪz/ ● **n.** Biochemistry an enzyme that promotes the reduction of hydrogen peroxide.
– ORIGIN C20: from CATALYSIS + -ASE.

**catalectic** /ˌkatəˈlɛktɪk/ ● **adj.** Prosody denoting a metrical line of verse lacking one syllable in the last foot.
– ORIGIN C16: from late L. *catalecticus*, from Gk *katalēktikos*, from *katalēgein* 'leave off'.

**catalepsy** /ˈkat(ə)lɛpsi/ ● **n.** a medical condition characterized by a trance or seizure with a loss of sensation and consciousness accompanied by rigidity of the body.
– DERIVATIVES **cataleptic** adj. & n.
– ORIGIN ME: from Fr. *catalepsie* or late L. *catalepsia*, from Gk *katalēpsis*, from *katalambanein* 'seize upon'.

**catalogue** (US also **catalog**) ● **n.** a complete list of items arranged in alphabetical or other systematic order. ➤ a publication containing details of items for sale. ➤ a series of unfortunate or bad things: *a catalogue of dismal failures*. ● **v.** (**catalogues, catalogued, cataloguing**; US also **catalogs, cataloged, cataloging**) list in a catalogue.
– DERIVATIVES **cataloguer** (US also **cataloger**) n.
– ORIGIN ME: via OFr. from late L. *catalogus*, from Gk *katalogos*, from *katalegein* 'pick out or enrol'.

**catalogue raisonné** /ˌreɪzɒˈneɪ/ ● **n.** (pl. **catalogues raisonnés** pronunc. same) a descriptive catalogue of works of art with explanations and comments.
– ORIGIN C18: Fr., 'explained catalogue'.

**Catalonian** /ˌkatəˈləʊnɪən/ ● **adj. & n.** another term for CATALAN.

**catalpa** /kəˈtalpə/ ● **n.** a tree with heart-shaped leaves, trumpet-shaped flowers, and slender seed pods, native to North America and east Asia. [Genus *Catalpa*.]
– ORIGIN from Creek.

**catalyse** /ˈkat(ə)lʌɪz/ (US **catalyze**) ● **v.** cause or accelerate (a reaction) by acting as a catalyst.
– DERIVATIVES **catalyser** n.
– ORIGIN C19: from CATALYSIS, on the pattern of *analyse*.

**catalysis** /kəˈtalɪsɪs/ ● **n.** Chemistry & Biochemistry the acceleration of a chemical reaction by a catalyst.
– DERIVATIVES **catalytic** /ˌkatəˈlɪtɪk/ adj. **catalytically** adv.
– ORIGIN C19: from mod. L., from Gk *katalusis*, from *kataluein* 'dissolve'.

**catalyst** ● **n.** a substance that increases the rate of a chemical reaction without itself undergoing any permanent chemical change. ➤ a person or thing that precipitates an event.
– ORIGIN C20: from CATALYSIS, on the pattern of *analyst*.

**catalytic converter** ● **n.** a device in the exhaust system of a motor vehicle, containing a catalyst for converting pollutant gases into less harmful ones.

**catamaran** ● **n.** a yacht or other boat with twin hulls in parallel.
– ORIGIN C17: from Tamil *kaṭṭumaram*, lit. 'tied wood'.

**catamite** /ˈkatəmʌɪt/ ● **n.** archaic a boy kept for homosexual practices.
– ORIGIN C16: from L. *catamitus*, via Etruscan from Gk *Ganumēdēs* 'Ganymede' (the name of Zeus's cup-bearer in Gk mythology).

**catamount** /ˈkatəmaʊnt/ (also **catamountain** /ˌkatəˈmaʊntɪn/) ● **n.** a medium-sized or large wild cat, especially (N. Amer.) a puma.
– ORIGIN ME (as *catamountain*): from the phr. *cat of the mountain*.

**cataphatic** /ˌkatəˈfatɪk/ ● **adj.** Theology (of knowledge of God) obtained through affirmation. The opposite of APOPHATIC.
– ORIGIN C19: from Gk *kataphatikos* 'affirmative', from

*kataphasis* 'affirmation'.

**cataphora** /kəˈtaf(ə)rə/ ● **n.** Grammar the use of a word referring to a word used later (e.g. the pronoun *he* in *he may be approaching 37, but Jeff has no plans to retire yet*). Compare with **ANAPHORA**.
– DERIVATIVES **cataphoric** /katəˈfɒrɪk/ adj. **cataphorically** adv.
– ORIGIN 1970s: from **CATA-** on the pattern of *anaphora*.

**cataplasm** /ˈkatəplaz(ə)m/ ● **n.** archaic a plaster or poultice.
– ORIGIN ME: from OFr. *cataplasme* or late L. *cataplasma*, from Gk *kataplasma*, from *kataplassein* 'plaster over'.

**cataplexy** /ˈkatəˌplɛksi/ ● **n.** a medical condition in which strong emotion or laughter causes a person to suffer sudden physical collapse though remaining conscious.
– DERIVATIVES **cataplectic** adj.
– ORIGIN C19: from Gk *kataplēxis* 'stupefaction', from *kataplessein*, from *kata-* 'down' + *plēssein* 'strike'.

**catapult** ● **n. 1** chiefly Brit. a forked stick with an elastic band fastened to the two prongs, used for shooting small stones. **2** historical a machine worked by a lever and ropes for hurling large stones or other missiles. **3** a mechanical device for launching a glider or aircraft. ● **v.** hurl or launch with or as if with a catapult. ➤ move suddenly or at great speed.
– ORIGIN C16: from Fr. *catapulte* or L. *catapulta*, from Gk *katapeltēs*, from *kata-* 'down' + *pallein* 'hurl'.

**cataract** /ˈkatərakt/ ● **n. 1** a large waterfall. **2** a medical condition in which the lens of the eye becomes progressively opaque, resulting in blurred vision.
– ORIGIN ME: from L. *cataracta* 'waterfall, floodgate', also 'portcullis', from Gk *kataraktēs* 'down-rushing'.

**catarrh** /kəˈtɑː/ ● **n.** excessive discharge of mucus in the nose or throat.
– DERIVATIVES **catarrhal** adj.
– ORIGIN C16: from Fr. *catarrhe*, from late L. *catarrhus*, from Gk *katarrhous*, from *katarrhein* 'flow down'.

**catarrhine** /ˈkatərʌɪn/ ● **adj.** Zoology relating to or denoting primates of a group distinguished by having close, downwardly directed nostrils and lacking a prehensile tail, comprising the Old World monkeys, gibbons, great apes, and humans. Compare with **PLATYRRHINE**.
– ORIGIN C19: from **CATA-** + Gk *rhis*, *rhin-* 'nose'.

**catastrophe** /kəˈtastrəfi/ ● **n. 1** an event causing great damage or suffering. **2** the denouement of a drama, especially a classical tragedy.
– DERIVATIVES **catastrophic** adj. **catastrophically** adv.
– ORIGIN C16: from L. *catastropha*, from Gk *katastrophē* 'overturning, sudden turn'.

**catastrophe theory** ● **n.** a branch of mathematics concerned with systems displaying abrupt discontinuous change.

**catastrophism** ● **n.** Geology the theory that changes in the earth's crust during geological history have resulted chiefly from sudden violent and unusual events. Often contrasted with **UNIFORMITARIANISM**.
– DERIVATIVES **catastrophist** n. & adj.

**catatonia** /ˌkatəˈtəʊnɪə/ ● **n.** Psychiatry abnormality of movement and behaviour arising from a disturbed mental state. ➤ informal a state of immobility and stupor.
– DERIVATIVES **catatonic** adj.
– ORIGIN C19: from **CATA-** + Gk *tonos* 'tone or tension'.

**catawba** /kəˈtɔːbə/ ● **n.** a North American variety of grape. ➤ a white wine made from this grape.
– ORIGIN named after the river *Catawba* in North and South Carolina.

**catbird** ● **n.** a songbird with catlike mewing calls. [*Dumetella carolinensis* (N. America) and other species.]

**catboat** ● **n.** a sailing boat with a single mast placed well forward and carrying only one sail.
– ORIGIN C19: perh. from *cat* (denoting a type of merchant ship formerly in NE England) + **BOAT**.

**cat burglar** ● **n.** a thief who enters a building by climbing to an upper storey.

**catcall** ● **n.** a shrill whistle or shout of mockery or disapproval. ● **v.** make a catcall.
– ORIGIN C17: from **CAT**[1] + **CALL**.

**catch** ● **v.** (past and past part. **caught**) **1** intercept and hold (something which has been thrown, propelled, or dropped). ➤ seize or take hold of. ➤ Cricket dismiss (a batsman) by catching the ball before it touches the ground. **2** capture (a person or animal that tries or would try to escape). **3** accidentally become entangled or trapped in something. ➤ have (a part of one's body or clothing) become entangled or trapped in something. **4** reach in time and board (a train, bus, or aircraft). ➤ reach or be in a place in time to see (a person, performance, etc.). **5** (**be caught in**) unexpectedly find oneself in (an unwelcome situation). ➤ surprise (someone) in an awkward or incriminating situation. **6** engage (a person's interest or imagination). ➤ perceive fleetingly. ➤ hear or understand (something said), especially with effort. ➤ succeed in evoking or representing. **7** strike (someone) on a part of the body. ➤ accidentally strike (a part of one's body) against something. **8** contract (an illness) through infection or contagion. **9** become ignited and start burning. ● **n. 1** an act or instance of catching. ➤ an amount of fish caught. ➤ informal a person considered desirable as a partner or spouse. **2** a device for securing something such as a door, window, or box. **3** a hidden problem or disadvantage. **4** an unevenness in a person's voice caused by emotion. **5** Music a round, typically one with words arranged to produce a humorous effect.
– PHRASES **catch one's breath 1** draw one's breath in sharply as a reaction to an emotion. **2** recover one's breath after exertion. **catch someone's eye 1** be noticed by someone. **2** attract someone's attention by making eye contact. **catch the light** shine or glint in the light. **catch sight of** suddenly notice; glimpse. **catch the sun 1** be in a sunny position. **2** Brit. become tanned or sunburnt.
– PHRASAL VERBS **catch on** informal **1** (of a practice or fashion) become popular. **2** understand what is meant or how to do something. **catch someone out** Brit. **1** detect that someone has done something wrong. **2** (often **be caught out**) put someone in a difficult situation for which they are unprepared. **catch up** (or **catch someone up**) **1** succeed in reaching a person who is ahead of one. **2** do work or other tasks which one should have done earlier. ➤ (**be/get caught up in**) become involved in. **catch up with 1** exchange news with (someone whom one has not seen for some time). **2** begin to have a damaging effect on.
– DERIVATIVES **catchable** adj.
– ORIGIN ME: from Anglo-Norman Fr. and ONorth. Fr. *cachier*, var. of OFr. *chacier*, based on L. *captare* 'try to catch'.

**catch-all** ● **n.** a term or category that includes a variety of different possibilities.

**catch-as-catch-can** ● **n. 1** archaic wrestling in which all holds are permitted. **2** [usu. as modifier] a situation of using whatever is available.

**catch crop** ● **n.** Brit. a crop grown in the space or interval between two main crops.

**catcher** ● **n.** a person or thing that catches. ➤ Baseball a fielder positioned to catch pitches not hit by the batter.

**catchfly** ● **n.** (pl. **-flies**) a campion or related plant with a sticky stem. [*Silene*, *Lychnis*, and other genera.]

**catching** ● **adj.** informal (of a disease) infectious.

**catch-light** ● **n.** a gleam of reflected light in the eye of a person in a photograph.

**catchline** ● **n.** Brit. **1** a short, eye-catching headline or title. **2** an advertising slogan.

**catchment** (also **catchment area**) ● **n. 1** the area from which a hospital's patients or a school's pupils are drawn. **2** the area from which rainfall flows into a river, lake, or reservoir.

**catchpenny** ● **adj.** having a cheap superficial attractiveness designed to encourage quick sales.

**catchphrase** ● **n.** a well-known sentence or phrase.

**catch-22** ● **n.** a difficult situation from which there is no escape because it involves mutually conflicting or dependent conditions.
– ORIGIN 1970s: title of a novel by Joseph Heller (1961).

**catchup** /ˈkatʃʌp/ ● **n.** variant spelling of **KETCHUP**.

**catchweight** • **n.** chiefly historical unrestricted weight, as a weight category in sport.

**catchword** • **n.** **1** a popular word or phrase encapsulating a particular concept. **2** a word printed or placed so as to attract attention. ➤Printing the first word of a page given at the foot of the previous one.

**catchy** • **adj.** (**-ier**, **-iest**) (of a tune or phrase) instantly appealing and memorable.
– DERIVATIVES **catchily** adv. **catchiness** n.

**catechesis** /ˌkatɪˈkiːsɪs/ • **n.** religious instruction given in preparation for Christian baptism or confirmation.
– ORIGIN C18: via eccles. L. from Gk *katēkhēsis* 'oral instruction'.

**catechetical** /ˌkatɪˈkɛtɪk(ə)l/ • **adj.** **1** of or relating to catechesis. **2** denoting religious teaching by means of questions and answers.
– DERIVATIVES **catechetic** adj. **catechetically** adv. **catechetics** pl. n.
– ORIGIN C17: from eccles. Gk *katēkhētikos*, from *katēkhētēs* 'catechist', from *katēkhein* (see CATECHIZE).

**catechin** /ˈkatɪtʃɪn/ • **n.** Chemistry a crystalline organic compound which is the major constituent of catechu.

**catechism** /ˈkatɪkɪz(ə)m/ • **n.** a summary of the principles of Christian religion in the form of questions and answers, used for teaching.
– DERIVATIVES **catechismal** adj.
– ORIGIN C16: from eccles. L. *catechismus*, from eccles. Gk, from *katēkhizein* (see CATECHIZE).

**catechist** • **n.** a Christian teacher, especially one using a catechism.
– ORIGIN C16: via eccles. L. from eccles. Gk *katēkhistēs*, from *katēkhein* (see CATECHIZE).

**catechize** (also **-ise**) • **v.** instruct by means of question and answer, especially by using a catechism.
– DERIVATIVES **catechizer** n.
– ORIGIN ME: via late L. from eccles. Gk *katēkhizein*, from *katēkhein* 'instruct orally, make hear'.

**catechol** /ˈkatɪtʃɒl, -kɒl/ • **n.** Chemistry a crystalline organic compound obtained by distilling catechu.
– ORIGIN C19: from CATECHU + -OL.

**catecholamine** /ˌkatɪˈkəʊləmiːn/ • **n.** Biochemistry any of a class of aromatic amines including neurotransmitters such as adrenalin and dopamine.

**catechu** /ˈkatɪtʃuː/ • **n.** a vegetable extract containing tannin, chiefly obtained from an Indian acacia tree and used for tanning and dyeing.
– ORIGIN C17: mod. L., from Malay *kacu*.

**catechumen** /ˌkatɪˈkjuːmɛn/ • **n.** a Christian preparing for baptism or confirmation.
– ORIGIN ME: via eccles. L. from Gk *katēkhoumenos* 'being instructed', pres. part. of *katēkhein* (see CATECHIZE).

**categorical** • **adj.** unambiguously explicit and direct.
– DERIVATIVES **categoric** adj. **categorically** adv.
– ORIGIN C16: from late L. *categoricus* (from Gk *katēgorikos*, from *katēgoria*: see CATEGORY) + -AL.

**categorical imperative** • **n.** Philosophy (in Kantian ethics) an unconditional and binding moral obligation which is not dependent on a person's inclination or purpose.

**categorize** (also **-ise**) • **v.** place in a particular category; classify.
– DERIVATIVES **categorization** n.

**category** • **n.** (pl. **-ies**) **1** a class or division of people or things having particular shared characteristics. **2** Philosophy each of a possibly exhaustive set of classes among which all things might be distributed. ➤an a priori conception applied by the mind to sense impressions.
– DERIVATIVES **categorial** adj.
– ORIGIN ME: from Fr. *catégorie* or late L. *categoria*, from Gk *katēgoria* 'statement, accusation', from *katēgoros* 'accuser'.

**catena** /kəˈtiːnə/ • **n.** (pl. **catenae** /-niː/ or **catenas**) a chain or connected series, especially a series of texts written by early Christian theologians.
– ORIGIN C17: from L., 'chain'.

**catenary** /kəˈtiːnəri/ • **n.** (pl. **-ies**) a curve formed by a chain hanging freely from two points on the same horizontal level. ➤a chain forming such a curve. • **adj.** of, involving, or denoting a catenary.
– ORIGIN C18: from L. *catenarius* 'relating to a chain', from *catena* 'chain'.

**catenated** /ˈkatɪneɪtɪd/ • **adj.** connected in a chain or series.
– DERIVATIVES **catenation** n.
– ORIGIN C19: past part. of *catenate*, from L. *catenat-*, *catenare*, 'chain, fetter'.

**catenative** /kəˈtiːnətɪv/ • **adj.** Grammar denoting a verb that governs a non-finite form of another verb, e.g. *like* in *I like swimming*.
– ORIGIN C20: from L. *catena* 'chain' + -ATIVE.

**catenoid** /ˈkatənɔɪd/ • **n.** Geometry the surface generated by rotating a catenary about its axis of symmetry.
– ORIGIN C19: from L. *catena* 'chain' + -OID.

**cater** • **v.** chiefly Brit. **1** provide food and drink at a social event. **2** (**cater for/to**) provide with what is needed or required. ➤(**cater for**) take into account or make allowances for. ➤(**cater to**) satisfy (a need or demand).
– DERIVATIVES **caterer** n. **catering** n.
– ORIGIN C16: from obs. *cater* 'caterer', from OFr. *acateor* 'buyer', from *acater* 'buy'.

**cateran** /ˈkat(ə)r(ə)n/ • **n.** historical a warrior or raider from the Scottish Highlands.
– ORIGIN ME (orig. denoting the peasantry as fighters): from Sc. Gaelic *ceathairne* 'peasantry'.

**cater-cornered** /ˈkeɪtəˌkɔːnəd/ (also **cater-corner**, **catty-cornered**, **kitty-corner**) • **adj. & adv.** N. Amer. situated diagonally opposite.
– ORIGIN C19: from dial. *cater* 'diagonally', from *cater* denoting the four on dice, from Fr. *quatre* 'four', from L. *quattuor*.

**caterpillar** • **n.** **1** the larva of a butterfly or moth. **2** (also **caterpillar track** or **tread**) trademark an articulated steel band passing round the wheels of a vehicle for travel on rough ground.
– ORIGIN ME: perh. from a var. of OFr. *chatepelose*, lit. 'hairy cat', influenced by obs. *piller* 'ravager'.

**caterwaul** /ˈkatəwɔːl/ • **v.** make a shrill howling or wailing noise. • **n.** such a noise.
– DERIVATIVES **caterwauling** n. & adj.
– ORIGIN ME: from CAT[1] + imitative WAUL.

**catfish** • **n.** (pl. same or **-fishes**) a freshwater or marine fish with whisker-like barbels round the mouth, typically bottom-dwelling. [Order Siluriformes: many species.]

**cat flap** • **n.** a small hinged flap through which a cat may enter or leave a building.

**catgut** • **n.** a material used for the strings of musical instruments and for surgical sutures, made of the dried twisted intestines of sheep or horses (but not cats).
– ORIGIN C16: the assoc. with CAT[1] remains unexplained.

**Cath.** • **abbrev.** **1** Cathedral. **2** Catholic.

**Cathar** /ˈkaθɑː/ • **n.** (pl. **Cathars** or **Cathari** /-ri/) a member of a heretical medieval Christian sect which sought to achieve great spiritual purity.
– DERIVATIVES **Catharism** n. **Catharist** n. & adj.
– ORIGIN C17: from med. L. *Cathari* (pl.), from Gk *katharoi* 'the pure'.

**catharsis** /kəˈθɑːsɪs/ • **n.** **1** the process of releasing pent-up emotions, for example through drama. **2** Medicine, rare purgation.
– DERIVATIVES **cathartic** adj. & n. **cathartically** adv.
– ORIGIN C19: from Gk *katharsis*, from *kathairein* 'cleanse', from *katharos* 'pure'.

**cathead** • **n.** a horizontal beam at each side of a ship's bow, used for raising and carrying an anchor.

**cathectic** /kəˈθɛktɪk/ • **adj.** Psychoanalysis of or relating to cathexis.

**cathedral** • **n.** the principal church of a diocese.
– ORIGIN ME (as adj., in *cathedral church* 'the church which contains the bishop's throne'): from late L. *cathedralis*, from L. *cathedra* 'seat', from Gk *kathedra*.

**Catherine wheel** • **n.** **1** Brit. a firework in the form of a spinning coil. **2** Heraldry a wheel with curved spikes projecting around the circumference.
– ORIGIN C16: named after St *Catherine*, with ref. to her martyrdom on a spiked wheel.

**catheter** /ˈkaθɪtə/ • **n.** Medicine a flexible tube inserted

through a narrow opening into a body cavity, particularly the bladder, for removing fluid.
– DERIVATIVES **catheterization** (also **-isation**) n. **catheterize** (also **-ise**) v.
– ORIGIN C17: from late L., from Gk *kathetēr*, from *kathienai* 'send or let down'.

**cathetometer** /ˌkaθɪˈtɒmɪtə/ ● n. a telescope mounted on a graduated scale, used for measurement of small vertical distances.
– ORIGIN C19: from L. *cathetus* (from Gk *kathetos* 'perpendicular line', from *kathienai* 'send or let down') + **-METER**.

**cathexis** /kəˈθɛksɪs/ ● n. Psychoanalysis the undesirable concentration of mental energy in one direction.
– ORIGIN 1920s: from Gk *kathexis* 'retention', translating Ger. *Libidobesetzung*, coined by Freud.

**cathode** /ˈkaθəʊd/ ● n. a negatively charged electrode. The opposite of **ANODE**.
– DERIVATIVES **cathodal** adj. **cathodic** /kəˈθɒdɪk/ adj.
– ORIGIN C19: from Gk *kathodos* 'way down', from *kata-* 'down'+ *hodos* 'way'.

**cathode ray** ● n. a beam of electrons emitted from the cathode of a high-vacuum tube.

**cathode ray tube** ● n. a high-vacuum tube in which cathode rays produce a luminous image on a fluorescent screen.

**cathodic protection** ● n. protection of a metal structure from corrosion under water by making it act as an electrical cathode.

**cathodoluminescence** /ˌkaθədə(ʊ),luːmɪˈnɛs(ə)ns/ ● n. Physics luminescence excited by the impact of an electron beam.

**catholic** ● adj. **1** including a wide variety of things. **2** (**Catholic**) of the Roman Catholic faith. ➤ of or including all Christians. ➤ of or relating to the historic doctrine and practice of the Western Church. ● n. (**Catholic**) a member of the Roman Catholic Church.
– DERIVATIVES **Catholicism** n. **catholicity** n. **Catholicize** (also **-ise**) v. **catholicly** adv.
– ORIGIN ME: from OFr. *catholique* or late L. *catholicus*, from Gk *katholikos* 'universal', from *kata* 'in respect of' + *holos* 'whole'.

**Catholicos** /kəˈθɒlɪkɒs/ ● n. (pl. **Catholicoses** /kəˌθɒlɪˈkəʊsiːz/ or **Catholicoi** /kəˈθɒlɪkɔɪ/) the Patriarch of the Armenian or the Nestorian Church.
– ORIGIN C17: from med. Gk *katholikos* (see **CATHOLIC**).

**cathouse** ● n. informal, chiefly N. Amer. a brothel.

**cat ice** ● n. thin ice from under which the water has receded.

**cation** /ˈkatʌɪən/ ● n. Chemistry a positively charged ion. The opposite of **ANION**.
– DERIVATIVES **cationic** /katʌɪˈɒnɪk/ adj.
– ORIGIN C19: from **CATA-** or from **CATHODE**, + **ION**.

**catkin** ● n. a downy, hanging, wind-pollinated flowering spike of trees such as willow and hazel.
– ORIGIN C16: from obs. Du. *katteken* 'kitten'.

**cat ladder** ● n. a ladder used for working on a sloping roof, with a hook at one end.

**catlick** ● n. a perfunctory wash.

**catlinite** /ˈkatlɪnʌɪt/ ● n. a red clay of the Upper Missouri region, the sacred pipe-stone of the American Indians.
– ORIGIN C19: from the name of an Amer. artist George *Catlin*, + **-ITE**[1].

**catmint** ● n. a plant with downy leaves, purple-spotted white flowers, and a pungent smell attractive to cats. [*Nepeta cataria* and related species.]

**catnap** ● n. a short sleep during the day. ● v. (**-napped, -napping**) have a catnap.

**catnip** ● n. another term for **CATMINT**.
– ORIGIN C18 (orig. US): from **CAT**[1] + *nip*, var. of dial. *nep*, *nept*, from med. L. *nepta*, from L. *nepeta* 'catmint'.

**cat-o'-nine-tails** ● n. historical a rope whip with nine knotted cords, used for flogging.

**catoptric** /kaˈtɒptrɪk/ ● adj. Physics of or relating to a mirror or reflection.
– DERIVATIVES **catoptrics** pl. n.
– ORIGIN C18: from Gk *katoptrikos*, from *katoptron* 'mirror'.

**cat's cradle** ● n. a child's game in which patterns are constructed in a loop of string held between the fingers of each hand.

**cat's ear** (also **cat's ears**) ● n. a plant with yellow flowers and rosettes of leaves, resembling the dandelion. [Genus *Hypochaeris*.]

**cat's eye** ● n. **1** a semi-precious stone, especially chalcedony, with a chatoyant lustre. **2** (**catseye**) Brit. trademark a light-reflecting stud set in a series into a road to mark traffic lanes or the edge of the carriageway.

**cat's foot** ● n. a small white-flowered creeping plant of the daisy family, with soft white hairs on the stems and leaves. [*Antennaria dioica*.]

**cat shark** ● n. a small bottom-dwelling shark that has catlike eyes and small dorsal fins set well back. [*Apristurus* and other genera.]

**cat's meow** ● n. (**the cat's meow**) chiefly N. Amer. another term for ***the cat's whiskers*** (see **CAT'S WHISKER**).

**cat's paw** ● n. a person who is used by another to carry out an unpleasant or dangerous task.

**cat's pyjamas** ● n. (**the cat's pyjamas**) chiefly N. Amer. another term for ***the cat's whiskers*** (see **CAT'S WHISKER**).

**cat's tail** (also **cattail**) ● n. a reed mace or other plant with long thin parts suggestive of cats' tails.

**catsuit** ● n. chiefly Brit. a woman's close-fitting one-piece garment with trouser legs.

**catsup** /ˈkatsəp/ ● n. US another term for **KETCHUP**.

**cat's whisker** ● n. a fine adjustable wire in a crystal radio receiver.
– PHRASES **the cat's whiskers** informal an excellent person or thing.

**cattery** ● n. (pl. **-ies**) a boarding or breeding establishment for cats.

**cattish** ● adj. another term for **CATTY**.
– DERIVATIVES **cattishly** adv. **cattishness** n.

**cattle** ● pl. n. large ruminant animals with horns and cloven hoofs, chiefly domesticated for meat or milk or as beasts of burden; cows and oxen. [*Bos taurus* and other species, family Bovidae.]
– ORIGIN ME: from Anglo-Norman Fr. *catel*, var. of OFr. *chatel* (see **CHATTEL**).

**cattle cake** ● n. Brit. concentrated food for cattle in a compressed flat form.

**cattle call** ● n. N. Amer. informal an open audition for parts in a play or film.

**cattle egret** ● n. a small egret which normally feeds around grazing cattle and game herds. [*Bubulcus ibis*.]

**cattle grid** (N. Amer. **cattle guard**) ● n. a metal grid covering a ditch, allowing vehicles and pedestrians to cross but not animals.

**cattleya** /ˈkatlɪə/ ● n. a tropical American orchid with brightly coloured showy flowers and thick leaves. [Genus *Cattleya*.]
– ORIGIN C19: mod. L., named after William *Cattley*, Engl. patron of botany.

**cat train** ● n. N. Amer. a crawler tractor pulling a train of sleighs across snow or ice.
– ORIGIN *cat* from **CATERPILLAR**.

**catty** ● adj. (**-ier, -iest**) **1** spiteful. **2** of or relating to cats; catlike.
– DERIVATIVES **cattily** adv. **cattiness** n.

**catty-cornered** ● adj. see **CATER-CORNERED**.

**CATV** ● abbrev. community antenna television (cable television).

**catwalk** ● n. **1** a narrow walkway or open bridge, especially in an industrial installation. **2** a platform extending into an auditorium, along which models walk to display clothes.

**caubeen** /kɔːˈbiːn/ ● n. Irish a hat or beret.
– ORIGIN C19: Ir., lit. 'old hat', from *cáibín* 'little cape', dimin. of *cába* 'cape'.

**Caucasian** /kɔːˈkeɪzɪən, -ʒ(ə)n/ ● adj. **1** relating to or denoting a broad division of humankind covering peoples from Europe, western Asia, and parts of India and North

Africa. ➤white-skinned; of European origin. **2** of or relating to the region of the Caucasus in SE Europe. ● **n.** a Caucasian person.

**Caucasoid** /ˈkɔːkəsɔɪd/ ● **adj.** of or relating to the Caucasian division of humankind. ● **n.** a Caucasian.

**USAGE** Caucasoid

The term **Caucasoid** belongs to a set of terms introduced by 19th-century anthropologists attempting to categorize human races. Such terms are associated with outdated notions of racial types, and so are now potentially offensive and best avoided.

**caucus** /ˈkɔːkəs/ ● **n.** (pl. **caucuses**) **1** a meeting of the members of a legislative body who belong to a particular political party, to select candidates or decide policy. **2** a group of people with shared concerns within a larger organization. ● **v.** (**caucused**, **caucusing**) chiefly N. Amer. hold or form a caucus.
– ORIGIN C18: perh. from Algonquian *cau'-cau'-as'u* 'adviser'.

**caudal** /ˈkɔːd(ə)l/ ● **adj.** of or like a tail. ➤at or near the tail or the posterior part of the body.
– DERIVATIVES **caudally** adv.
– ORIGIN C17: from mod. L. *caudalis*, from L. *cauda* 'tail'.

**caudal fin** ● **n.** Zoology another term for **TAIL FIN**.

**Caudata** /kɔːˈdeɪtə/ ● **pl. n.** Zoology another term for **URODELA**.
– ORIGIN mod. L., from L. *cauda* 'tail'.

**caudate** /ˈkɔːdeɪt/ ● **adj.** Anatomy relating to or denoting the upper of the two grey nuclei of the corpus striatum in the cerebrum of the brain.
– ORIGIN C17: from med. L. *caudatus*, from *cauda* 'tail'.

**caudillo** /kaʊˈdiːjəʊ, -ˈdiːljəʊ/ ● **n.** (pl. **-os**) (in Spanish-speaking countries) a military or political leader.
– ORIGIN Sp., from late L. *capitellum*, dimin. of *caput* 'head'.

**caught** past and past participle of **CATCH**.

**caul** /kɔːl/ ● **n. 1** the amniotic membrane enclosing a fetus. ➤part of this membrane occasionally found on a child's head at birth, thought to bring good luck. **2** historical a woman's close-fitting indoor headdress or hairnet. **3** Anatomy the omentum.
– ORIGIN ME: perh. from OFr. *cale* 'head covering'.

**cauldron** (also **caldron**) ● **n. 1** a large metal pot, used for cooking over an open fire. **2** a situation characterized by instability and strong emotions.
– ORIGIN ME: from Anglo-Norman Fr. *caudron*, based on L. *caldarium*, *calidarium* 'cooking-pot', from *calidus* 'hot'.

**cauliflower** ● **n.** a cabbage of a variety which bears a large immature flower head of small creamy-white flower buds, eaten as a vegetable.
– ORIGIN C16: from obs. Fr. *chou fleuri* 'flowered cabbage', prob. from Ital. *cavolfiore* or mod. L. *cauliflora*.

**cauliflower cheese** ● **n.** Brit. a savoury dish of cauliflower in a cheese sauce.

**cauliflower ear** ● **n.** a person's ear that has become thickened or deformed as a result of repeated blows.

**caulk** /kɔːk/ (US also **calk**) ● **n.** a waterproof filler and sealant, used in building work and repairs. ● **v. 1** seal with caulk. **2** make (a boat or its seams) watertight.
– DERIVATIVES **caulker** n.
– ORIGIN ME (in the sense 'copulate', used of birds): from ONorth. Fr. *cauquer*, *caukier*, var. of *cauchier* 'tread, press with force', from L. *calcare* 'tread', from *calx*, *calc-* 'heel'.

**causal** ● **adj.** of, relating to, or acting as a cause.
– DERIVATIVES **causally** adv.
– ORIGIN ME: from late L. *causalis*, from L. *causa* 'cause'.

**causalgia** /kɔːˈzaldʒə/ ● **n.** severe burning pain in a limb caused by injury to a peripheral nerve.
– ORIGIN C19: from Gk *kausos* 'heat, fever' + **-ALGIA**.

**causality** ● **n. 1** the relationship between cause and effect. **2** the principle that everything has a cause.

**causation** ● **n. 1** the action of causing something. **2** the relationship between cause and effect.

**causative** ● **adj. 1** acting as a cause. **2** Grammar expressing causation.
– ORIGIN ME: from OFr. *causatif*, *-ive*, or late L. *causativus*, from *causare* 'to cause'.

**cause** ● **n. 1** a person or thing that gives rise to an action, phenomenon, or condition. ➤reasonable grounds for a belief or action. **2** a principle or movement which one is prepared to defend or advocate. ➤something deserving of support. **3** a matter to be resolved in a court of law. ➤an individual's case offered at law. ● **v.** be the cause of; make happen.
– PHRASES **cause and effect** the principle of causation. **cause of action** Law a fact or facts that enable a person to bring an action against another. **make common cause** unite in order to achieve a shared aim.
– DERIVATIVES **causeless** adj. **causer** n.
– ORIGIN ME: from OFr., from L. *causa* (n.), *causare* (v.).

**'cause** ● **conj.** informal because.

**cause célèbre** /ˌkɔːz sɛˈlɛbr(ə), French koz selɛbʀ/ ● **n.** (pl. **causes célèbres** pronunc. same) a controversial issue that attracts a great deal of public attention.
– ORIGIN C18: Fr., lit. 'famous case'.

**causerie** /ˈkəʊzəri, French kozʀi/ ● **n.** (pl. **-ies** pronunc. same) an informal article or talk.
– ORIGIN Fr., from *causer* 'to talk'.

**causeway** ● **n.** a raised road or track across low or wet ground.
– DERIVATIVES **causewayed** adj.
– ORIGIN ME: from **CAUSEY** + **WAY**.

**causey** /ˈkɔːzi, -si/ ● **n.** (pl. **-eys**) archaic or dialect term for **CAUSEWAY**.
– ORIGIN ME: from Anglo-Norman Fr. *causee*, based on L. *calx* 'lime, limestone' (used for paving roads).

**caustic** /ˈkɔːstɪk, ˈkɒst-/ ● **adj. 1** able to burn or corrode organic tissue by chemical action. **2** scathingly sarcastic. **3** Physics formed by the intersection of reflected or refracted parallel rays from a curved surface. ● **n. 1** a caustic substance. **2** Physics a caustic surface or curve.
– DERIVATIVES **caustically** adv. **causticity** n.
– ORIGIN ME: via L. from Gk *kaustikos*, from *kaustos* 'combustible', from *kaiein* 'to burn'.

**caustic potash** ● **n.** potassium hydroxide.

**caustic soda** ● **n.** sodium hydroxide.

**cauterize** /ˈkɔːtərʌɪz/ (also **-ise**) ● **v.** burn the skin or flesh of (a wound) to stop bleeding or prevent infection.
– DERIVATIVES **cauterization** n.
– ORIGIN ME: from OFr. *cauteriser*, from late L. *cauterizare*, from Gk *kautēriazein*, from *kautērion* 'branding iron', from *kaien* 'to burn'.

**cautery** /ˈkɔːt(ə)ri/ ● **n.** (pl. **-ies**) Medicine **1** an instrument or caustic substance used for cauterizing. **2** the action of cauterizing.
– ORIGIN ME: via L. from Gk *kautērion* (see **CAUTERIZE**).

**caution** ● **n. 1** care taken to avoid danger or mistakes. **2** chiefly Brit. an official or legal warning given to someone who has committed a minor offence but has not been charged. **3** informal, dated an amusing or surprising person. ● **v. 1** say something as a warning. ➤(**caution against**) warn or advise against. **2** chiefly Brit. issue an official or legal warning to. ➤(of a police officer) advise (someone) of their legal rights when arresting them.
– PHRASES **throw caution to the wind** act in a reckless manner.
– ORIGIN ME: from L. *cautio(n-)*, from *cavere* 'take heed'.

**cautionary** ● **adj.** serving as a warning.

**cautious** ● **adj.** careful to avoid potential problems or dangers.
– DERIVATIVES **cautiously** adv. **cautiousness** n.

**cava** /ˈkɑːvə/ ● **n.** a Spanish sparkling wine made in the same way as champagne.
– ORIGIN from Sp.

**cavalcade** /ˌkav(ə)lˈkeɪd, ˈkav(ə)lkeɪd/ ● **n.** a procession of people walking, on horseback, or riding in vehicles.
– ORIGIN C16 (denoting a ride or raid on horseback): from Fr., from Ital. *cavalcata*, from *cavalcare* 'to ride', based on L. *caballus* 'horse'.

**cavalier** ● **n. 1** (**Cavalier**) historical a supporter of King Charles I in the English Civil War. **2** archaic or poetic/literary a gallant. **3** archaic a cavalryman. ● **adj.** showing a lack of proper concern.

– DERIVATIVES **cavalierly** adv.
– ORIGIN C16: from Fr., from Ital. *cavaliere*, based on L. *caballus* 'horse'.

**cavalry** ● n. (pl. **-ies**) [usu. treated as pl.] historical soldiers who fought on horseback. ➤ modern soldiers who fight in armoured vehicles.
– DERIVATIVES **cavalryman** n. (pl. **-men**).
– ORIGIN C16: from Fr. *cavallerie*, from Ital. *cavalleria*, from *cavallo* 'horse', from L. *caballus*.

**cavalry twill** ● n. strong woollen twill of a khaki or light brown colour.

**cavatina** /ˌkavəˈtiːnə/ ● n. (pl. **cavatine**) Music a simple operatic aria or lyrical instrumental piece without repeated sections.
– ORIGIN C19: from Ital.

**cave¹** /keɪv/ ● n. a large natural underground chamber. ● v. **1** explore caves as a sport. **2** (**cave in**) (US **cave**) (of a roof or walls) subside or collapse.
– DERIVATIVES **caver** n. **caving** n.
– ORIGIN ME: from OFr., from L. *cava*, from *cavus* 'hollow'.

**cave²** /ˈkeɪvi/ ● exclam. Brit. school slang, dated look out!
– PHRASES **keep cave** act as lookout.
– ORIGIN L., imper. of *cavere* 'beware'.

**caveat** /ˈkavɪat, ˈkeɪ-/ ● n. a warning or proviso of specific stipulations, conditions, or limitations.
– ORIGIN C16: from L., lit. 'let a person beware'.

**caveat emptor** /ˈɛmptɔː/ ● n. the principle that the buyer is responsible for checking the quality and suitability of goods before purchase.
– ORIGIN L., 'let the buyer beware'.

**caveman** (also **cavewoman**) ● n. (pl. **-men** or **-women**) a prehistoric person who lived in caves.

**cavern** /ˈkav(ə)n/ ● n. **1** a large cave, or chamber in a cave. **2** a vast, dark space.
– DERIVATIVES **cavernous** adj. **cavernously** adv.
– ORIGIN ME: from OFr. *caverne* or from L. *caverna*, from *cavus* 'hollow'.

**caviar** /ˈkavɪɑː, ˌkavɪˈɑː/ (also **caviare**) ● n. the pickled roe of sturgeon or other large fish, eaten as a delicacy.
– ORIGIN C16: from Ital. *caviale* (earlier *caviaro*) or Fr. *caviar*, prob. from med. Gk *khaviari*.

**cavil** /ˈkav(ə)l/ ● v. (**cavilled**, **cavilling**; US **caviled**, **caviling**) make petty or unnecessary objections. ● n. an objection of this kind.
– DERIVATIVES **caviller** n.
– ORIGIN C16: from Fr. *caviller*, from L. *cavillari*, from *cavilla* 'mockery'.

**cavitation** /ˌkavɪˈteɪʃ(ə)n/ ● n. Physics **1** the formation of an empty space within a solid object or body. **2** the formation of bubbles in a liquid.

**cavity** ● n. (pl. **-ies**) an empty space within a solid object. ➤ a decayed part of a tooth.
– DERIVATIVES **cavitary** adj.
– ORIGIN C16: from Fr. *cavité* or late L. *cavitas*, from L. *cavus* 'hollow'.

**cavity wall** ● n. a wall formed from two thicknesses of bricks with a space between them.

**cavort** ● v. prance around excitedly or self-indulgently.
– ORIGIN C18 (orig. US): perh. an alt. of **CURVET**.

**cavy** /ˈkeɪvi/ ● n. (pl. **-ies**) a guinea pig or related South American rodent. [Family Caviidae: numerous species.]
– ORIGIN C18: from mod. L. *cavia*, from Galibi *cabiai*.

**caw** ● n. the harsh cry of a rook, crow, or similar bird. ● v. utter a caw.
– ORIGIN C16: imitative.

**cay** /keɪ, kiː/ ● n. (in Spanish America) a low bank or reef of coral, rock, or sand.
– ORIGIN C17: from Sp. *cayo* 'shoal, reef', from Fr. *quai* 'quay'.

**cayenne** /keɪˈɛn/ (also **cayenne pepper**) ● n. a pungent, hot-tasting red powder prepared from dried chillies.
– ORIGIN C18: from Tupi *kyynha*, *quiynha*, later assoc. with *Cayenne* in French Guiana.

**cayman** ● n. variant spelling of **CAIMAN**.

**Cayuga** /ˈkeɪjuːgə, ˈkʌɪ-/ ● n. (pl. same or **Cayugas**) **1** a member of an American Indian people formerly inhabiting part of New York State. **2** the extinct Iroquoian language of this people.
– ORIGIN from an Iroquoian place name.

**Cayuse** /ˈkʌɪjuːs/ ● n. (pl. same or **Cayuses**) **1** a member of an American Indian people of Washington State and Oregon. **2** the extinct Penutian language of this people. **3** (**cayuse**) an American Indian pony.
– ORIGIN the name in Chinook Jargon.

**CB** ● abbrev. **1** Citizens' Band. **2** (in the UK) Companion of the Order of the Bath.

**CBC** ● abbrev. Canadian Broadcasting Corporation.

**CBE** ● abbrev. (in the UK) Commander of the Order of the British Empire.

**CBI** ● abbrev. Confederation of British Industry.

**CBS** ● abbrev. (in the US) Columbia Broadcasting System.

**CC** ● abbrev. **1** Brit. City Council. **2** Companion of the Order of Canada. **3** Brit. County Council. **4** Brit. County Councillor. **5** Cricket Club.

**cc** (also **c.c.**) ● abbrev. **1** carbon copy (an indication that a duplicate has been or should be sent to another person). **2** cubic centimetre(s).

**CCD** ● abbrev. Electronics charge-coupled device.

**CCTV** ● abbrev. closed-circuit television.

**CD** ● abbrev. **1** civil defence. **2** compact disc. **3** corps diplomatique.

**Cd** ● symb. the chemical element cadmium.

**Cd.** ● abbrev. (in the UK) Command Paper (third series, 1900–18).

**cd** ● abbrev. candela.

**CDC** ● abbrev. **1** (in the US) Centers for Disease Control. **2** Commonwealth Development Corporation.

**CD-I** ● abbrev. compact disc (interactive).

**CDN** ● abbrev. Canada (international vehicle registration).

**cDNA** ● abbrev. complementary DNA.

**Cdr** ● abbrev. (in the navy or air force) Commander.

**Cdre** ● abbrev. Commodore.

**CD-ROM** ● n. a compact disc used in a computer as a read-only device for displaying data.
– ORIGIN 1980s: acronym from *compact disc read-only memory*.

**CDT** ● abbrev. **1** Central Daylight Time. **2** craft, design, and technology (as a subject taught in schools in the UK).

**CDV** ● abbrev. compact disc video.

**CE** ● abbrev. **1** Church of England. **2** civil engineer. **3** Common Era.

**Ce** ● symb. the chemical element cerium.

**ceanothus** /ˌsiːəˈnəʊθəs/ ● n. a shrub with dense clusters of small blue flowers, native to North America. [Genus *Ceanothus*.]
– ORIGIN mod. L., from Gk *keanōthos*, a kind of thistle.

**cease** ● v. come or bring to an end; stop.
– PHRASES **without cease** without stopping.
– ORIGIN ME: from OFr. *cesser*, from L. *cessare*, from *cedere* 'to yield'.

**ceasefire** ● n. a temporary suspension of fighting.

**ceaseless** ● adj. constant and unending.
– DERIVATIVES **ceaselessly** adv.

**cebid** /ˈsiːbɪd/ ● n. Zoology a primate of a family (Cebidae) that includes most of the New World monkeys.
– ORIGIN C19: from mod. L. *Cebidae*, from the genus name *Cebus*.

**cecitis** ● n. US spelling of **CAECITIS**.

**cecropia** /sɪˈkrəʊpɪə/ ● n. **1** a fast-growing tropical American tree. [Genus *Cecropia*.] **2** (also **cecropia moth**) a very large reddish-brown North American silk moth. [*Platysamia cecropia*.]
– ORIGIN C19: mod. L., from the name *Cecrops*, a king of Attica.

**cecum** ● n. (pl. **ceca**) US spelling of **CAECUM**.

**cedar** ● n. a tall, elegant coniferous tree yielding typically fragrant, durable wood. [*Cedrus libani* (**cedar of Lebanon**) and other species in the genera *Cedrus* and *Thuja*.]

– DERIVATIVES **cedarn** adj. (poetic/literary).
– ORIGIN OE, from OFr. *cedre* or L. *cedrus*, from Gk *kedros*.

**cede** /siːd/ ● v. give up (power or territory).
– ORIGIN C16: from Fr. *céder* or L. *cedere* 'to yield'.

**cedi** /'siːdi/ ● n. (pl. same or **cedis**) the basic monetary unit of Ghana, equal to 100 pesewas.
– ORIGIN of Ghanaian origin, perh. an alt. of SHILLING.

**cedilla** /sɪ'dɪlə/ ● n. a mark (¸) written under the letter *c*, especially in French, to show that it is pronounced like an *s* rather than a *k* (e.g. *façade*). ➤ a similar mark under *s* in Turkish and other languages.
– ORIGIN C16: from obs. Sp., earlier form of *zedilla*, dimin. of *zeda* (the letter Z), from Gk *zēta*.

**ceiba** /'sʌɪbə/ ● n. a very tall tropical American tree from which kapok is obtained. [*Ceiba pentandra*.]
– ORIGIN via Sp. from Taino, lit. 'giant tree'.

**ceil** /siːl/ ● v. archaic line or plaster the roof of (a building).
– ORIGIN ME: perh. rel. to L. *celare*, Fr. *céler* 'conceal'.

**ceilidh** /'keɪli/ ● n. a social event with Scottish or Irish folk music and singing, traditional dancing, and storytelling.
– ORIGIN C19: from Sc. Gaelic *ceilidh* and Ir. *céilidhe* (earlier form of *céilí*), from Old Ir. *céilide* 'visit, visiting', from *céile* 'companion'.

**ceiling** ● n. **1** the upper interior surface of a room. **2** an upper limit set on prices, wages, etc. **3** the maximum altitude that an aircraft can reach. ➤ the altitude of the base of a cloud layer. **4** the inside planking of a ship's bottom and sides.
– ORIGIN ME: from CEIL + -ING[1].

**cel** /sɛl/ ● n. a transparent sheet of celluloid or similar film material, used in the production of cartoons.
– ORIGIN C20: abbrev. of CELLULOID.

**celadon** /'sɛlədɒn/ ● n. a willow-green colour. ➤ a grey-green glaze used in pottery.
– ORIGIN C18: from Fr. *céladon*, a colour named after the hero in d'Urfé's pastoral romance *L'Astrée* (1607–27).

**celandine** /'sɛləndʌɪn/ ● n. **1** (also **lesser celandine**) a common plant of the buttercup family, which produces yellow flowers in the early spring. [*Ranunculus ficaria*.] **2** (**greater celandine**) a yellow-flowered plant of the poppy family, with toxic sap. [*Chelidonium majus*.]
– ORIGIN ME, from OFr. *celidoine*, from med. L. *celidonia*, based on Gk *khelidōn* 'swallow' (the flowering of the plant being assoc. with the arrival of swallows).

**-cele** (also **-coele**) ● comb. form Medicine denoting a swelling or hernia in a specified part: *hydrocele*.
– ORIGIN from Gk *kēlē* 'tumour'.

**celeb** /sɪ'lɛb/ ● n. informal a celebrity.
– ORIGIN C20 (orig. US): abbrev.

**Celebra** ● n. trademark a synthetic drug used in the management of arthritic pain.
– ORIGIN an invented word.

**celebrant** /'sɛlɪbr(ə)nt/ ● n. **1** a person who performs a rite, especially a priest at the Eucharist. **2** a person who celebrates something.
– ORIGIN C19: from Fr. *célébrant* or L. *celebrant-*, *celebrare* (see CELEBRATE).

**celebrate** ● v. **1** mark (a significant time or event) with an enjoyable activity. ➤ engage in festivities. **2** perform (a religious ceremony), in particular officiate at (the Eucharist). **3** honour or praise publicly.
– DERIVATIVES **celebration** n. **celebrator** n. **celebratory** adj.
– ORIGIN ME: from L. *celebrat-*, *celebrare* 'celebrate', from *celeber*, *celebr-* 'frequented or honoured'.

**celebrity** ● n. (pl. **-ies**) **1** a famous person. **2** the state of being famous.
– ORIGIN ME (in the sense 'solemn ceremony'): from OFr. *celebrite* or L. *celebritas*, from *celeber*, *celebr-* 'frequented or honoured'.

**celeriac** /sɪ'lɛrɪak/ ● n. celery of a variety which forms a large swollen turnip-like root.
– ORIGIN C18: from CELERY + an arbitrary use of -AC.

**celerity** /sɪ'lɛrɪti/ ● n. archaic or poetic/literary swiftness of movement.
– ORIGIN C15: from OFr. *celerite*, from L. *celeritas*, from *celer* 'swift'.

**celery** ● n. a cultivated plant of the parsley family, with closely packed succulent leaf stalks that are eaten raw or cooked. [*Apium graveolens* var. *dulce*.]
– ORIGIN C17: from Fr. *céleri*, from Ital. dial. *selleri*, based on Gk *selinon* 'parsley'.

**celery pine** (also **celery-top pine**) ● n. a slow-growing Australasian tree with shoots that resemble celery leaves. [Genus *Phyllocladus*.]

**celery salt** ● n. a mixture of salt and ground celery seed used for seasoning.

**celesta** /sɪ'lɛstə/ (also **celeste** /sɪ'lɛst/) ● n. a small keyboard instrument in which felted hammers strike a row of steel plates suspended over wooden resonators, giving an ethereal bell-like sound.
– ORIGIN C19: pseudo-Latin, based on Fr. *céleste* 'heavenly'.

**celestial** ● adj. **1** positioned in or relating to the sky or outer space. **2** belonging or relating to heaven.
– DERIVATIVES **celestially** adv.
– ORIGIN ME: via OFr. from med. L. *caelestialis*, from L. *caelestis*, from *caelum* 'heaven'.

**celestial equator** ● n. the projection into space of the earth's equator.

**celestial latitude** ● n. Astronomy the angular distance of a point north or south of the ecliptic.

**celestial longitude** ● n. Astronomy the angular distance of a point east of the First Point of Aries, measured along the ecliptic.

**celestial mechanics** ● pl. n. [treated as sing.] the branch of astronomy concerned with the calculation of the motions of celestial objects such as planets.

**celestial navigation** ● n. navigation using the sun, moon, and stars.

**celestial pole** ● n. Astronomy the point on the celestial sphere directly above either of the earth's geographic poles, around which the stars appear to rotate.

**celestial sphere** ● n. an imaginary sphere of which the observer is the centre and on which all celestial objects are considered to lie.

**celiac** ● n. US spelling of COELIAC.

**celibate** /'sɛlɪbət/ ● adj. **1** abstaining from marriage and sexual relations for religious reasons. **2** having or involving no sexual relations. ● n. a person who is celibate.
– DERIVATIVES **celibacy** n.
– ORIGIN C19: from *celibacy* (C17, from Fr. *célibat* or L. *caelibatus* 'unmarried state') + -ATE[2].

**cell** ● n. **1** a small room in which a prisoner is locked up or in which a monk or nun sleeps. ➤ a small compartment in a larger structure such as a honeycomb. ➤ historical a small monastery dependent on a larger one. **2** Biology the smallest structural and functional unit of an organism, typically microscopic, consisting of cytoplasm and a nucleus enclosed in a membrane. **3** a small group forming a nucleus of political activity. **4** a device containing electrodes immersed in an electrolyte, used for current generation or electrolysis. ➤ a unit in a device for converting chemical energy or light into electricity.
– DERIVATIVES **-celled** adj.
– ORIGIN OE, from OFr. *celle* or L. *cella* 'storeroom or chamber'.

**cella** /'kɛlə/ ● n. (pl. **cellae** /-liː/) the inner area of an ancient temple.
– ORIGIN from L.

**cellar** ● n. a storage space or room below ground level in a house. ➤ a stock of wine. ● v. store in a cellar.
– ORIGIN ME: from OFr. *celier*, from late L. *cellarium* 'storehouse', from *cella* 'storeroom or chamber'.

**cellarage** ● n. **1** cellars collectively. **2** money charged for the use of a cellar or storehouse.

**cellarer** /'sɛlərə/ ● n. **1** the person in a monastery who is responsible for provisions and catering. **2** a cellarman.

**cellaret** /ˌsɛlə'rɛt/ (US also **cellarette**) ● n. historical a cabinet or sideboard for keeping alcoholic drinks and glasses in a dining room.

**cellarman** ● n. (pl. **-men**) Brit. a person in charge of a wine cellar.

**cell-mediated** • **adj.** Physiology (of immunity) involving the action of white blood cells. Often contrasted with **HUMORAL**.

**cello** /ˈtʃɛləʊ/ • **n.** (pl. **-os**) a bass instrument of the violin family, held upright on the floor between the legs of the seated player.
– DERIVATIVES **cellist** n.
– ORIGIN C19: shortening (perh. earlier in Ger.) of **VIOLONCELLO**.

**cellophane** /ˈsɛləfeɪn/ • **n.** trademark a thin transparent wrapping material made from viscose.
– ORIGIN C20: from **CELLULOSE** + *-phane*, from *diaphane*, a kind of semi-transparent woven silk (from med. L. *diaphanus* 'diaphanous').

**cellphone** • **n.** another term for **MOBILE PHONE**.

**cellular** /ˈsɛljʊlə/ • **adj. 1** of, relating to, or consisting of living cells. **2** denoting or relating to a mobile telephone system that uses a number of short-range radio stations. **3** (of fabric) knitted so as to form holes or hollows that trap air and provide extra insulation. **4** consisting of small compartments or rooms.
– DERIVATIVES **cellularity** n.
– ORIGIN C18: from Fr. *cellulaire*, from mod. L. *cellularis*, from *cellula* 'little chamber', dimin. of *cella*.

**cellulase** /ˈsɛljʊleɪz/ • **n.** Biochemistry an enzyme that converts cellulose into glucose or a disaccharide.

**cellulite** /ˈsɛljʊlʌɪt/ • **n.** persistent subcutaneous fat causing dimpling of the skin.
– ORIGIN 1960s: from Fr., from *cellule* 'small cell'.

**cellulitis** • **n.** Medicine inflammation of subcutaneous connective tissue.

**celluloid** • **n.** a transparent flammable plastic made in sheets from camphor and nitrocellulose, formerly used for cinematographic film. ➤the cinema as a genre.
– ORIGIN C19: from **CELLULOSE** + **-OID**.

**cellulose** /ˈsɛljʊləʊz, -s/ • **n. 1** an insoluble substance which is a polysaccharide derived from glucose and is the main constituent of plant cell walls and of vegetable fibres such as cotton. **2** paint or lacquer consisting principally of cellulose acetate or nitrate in solution.
– DERIVATIVES **cellulosic** adj.
– ORIGIN C19: from Fr., from *cellule* 'small cell' + **-OSE**².

**cellulose acetate** • **n.** Chemistry a non-flammable polymer made by acetylating cellulose, used as the basis of artificial fibres and plastic.

**cellulose nitrate** • **n.** nitrocellulose.

**Celsius** /ˈsɛlsɪəs/ • **adj.** [postpos. when used with a numeral] of or denoting a scale of temperature on which water freezes at 0° and boils at 100°.
– ORIGIN from the name of the Swed. astronomer Anders *Celsius* (1701–44).

**Celt** /kɛlt, s-/ • **n. 1** a member of a group of peoples inhabiting much of Europe and Asia Minor in pre-Roman times. **2** a native of a modern nation or region in which a Celtic language is (or was until recently) spoken.
– ORIGIN from L. *Celtae* (pl.), from Gk *Keltoi*.

**celt** /sɛlt/ • **n.** Archaeology a prehistoric stone or metal implement with a bevelled cutting edge.
– ORIGIN C18: from med. L. *celtis* 'chisel'.

**Celtiberian** /ˌkɛltɪˈbɪərɪən, -tʌɪ-, ˌsɛlt-/ • **n.** another term for **IBERIAN** (in sense 3).

**Celtic** /ˈkɛltɪk, ˈs-/ • **n.** a group of languages including Irish, Scottish Gaelic, Welsh, Breton, Manx, and Cornish. • **adj.** of or relating to this language group or to the Celts.
– DERIVATIVES **Celticism** /-sɪz(ə)m/ n.
– ORIGIN C16: from L. *Celticus* (from *Celtae* 'Celts'), or from Fr. *Celtique* (from *Celte* 'Breton').

**Celtic Church** • **n.** the early Christian Church in the British Isles.

**Celtic cross** • **n.** a Latin cross with a circle round the centre.

**Celtic fringe** • **n.** the Highland Scots, Irish, Welsh, and Cornish or their land, in relation to the rest of Britain.

**Celtic harp** • **n.** another term for **CLARSACH**.

**cembalo** /ˈtʃɛmbələʊ/ • **n.** (pl. **-os**) another term for **HARPSICHORD**.
– DERIVATIVES **cembalist** n.
– ORIGIN C19: from Ital., shortening of *clavicembalo*, from med. L. *clavicymbalum*, from L. *clavis* 'key' + *cymbalum* 'cymbal'.

**cement** • **n. 1** a powdery substance made by calcining lime and clay, used in making mortar and concrete. **2** a soft glue that hardens on setting. **3** (also **cementum**) Anatomy a thin layer of bony material that fixes teeth to the jaw. **4** Geology the material which binds particles together in sedimentary rock. • **v.** fix with cement; bind together.
– DERIVATIVES **cementer** n. **cementitious** adj.
– ORIGIN ME: from OFr. *ciment* (n.), *cimenter* (v.), from L. *caementum* 'quarry stone', from *caedere* 'hew'.

**cementation** /ˌsiːmɛnˈteɪʃ(ə)n/ • **n. 1** the binding together of particles or other things by cement. **2** Metallurgy a process of heating iron in contact with charcoal to make steel.

**cementite** /sɪˈmɛntʌɪt/ • **n.** Metallurgy a hard, brittle iron carbide present in cast iron and most steels.
– ORIGIN C19: from **CEMENT** + **-ITE**¹.

**cement mixer** • **n.** a machine with a revolving drum used for mixing cement with sand, gravel, and water to make concrete.

**cemetery** • **n.** (pl. **-ies**) a large burial ground.
– ORIGIN ME: via late L. from Gk *koimētērion* 'dormitory', from *koiman* 'put to sleep'.

**cenacle** /ˈsɛnək(ə)l/ • **n. 1** a discussion group or literary clique. **2** the room in which the Last Supper was held.
– ORIGIN ME: from OFr. *cenacle*, from L. *cenaculum*, from *cena* 'dinner'.

**CEng** • **abbrev.** (in the UK) chartered engineer.

**cenobite** • **n.** variant spelling of **COENOBITE**.

**cenotaph** /ˈsɛnətɑːf, -taf/ • **n.** a monument to someone buried elsewhere, especially a war memorial.
– ORIGIN C17: from Fr. *cénotaphe*, from late L. *cenotaphium*, from Gk *kenos* 'empty' + *taphos* 'tomb'.

**Cenozoic** /ˌsiːnəˈzəʊɪk/ (also **Cainozoic**) • **adj.** Geology relating to or denoting the era following the Mesozoic era (from about 65 million years ago to the present).
– ORIGIN C19: from Gk *kainos* 'new' + *zōion* 'animal' + **-IC**.

**cense** /sɛns/ • **v.** ritually perfume with burning incense.
– ORIGIN ME: from OFr. *encenser*.

**censer** • **n.** a container in which incense is burnt.
– ORIGIN ME: from OFr. *censier*, from *encensier*, from *encens* (see **INCENSE**¹).

**censor** • **n. 1** an official who examines material that is to be published and suppresses parts considered offensive or a threat to security. ➤Psychoanalysis an aspect of the superego which prevents certain ideas and memories from emerging into consciousness. **2** (in ancient Rome) a magistrate who held censuses and supervised public morals. • **v.** examine (a book, film, etc.) officially and suppress unacceptable parts of it.
– DERIVATIVES **censorial** adj. **censorship** n.
– ORIGIN C16: from L., from *censere* 'assess'.

**censorious** /sɛnˈsɔːrɪəs/ • **adj.** severely critical.
– DERIVATIVES **censoriously** adv. **censoriousness** n.
– ORIGIN C16: from L. *censorius* (from *censor* 'magistrate') + **-IOUS**.

**censure** /ˈsɛnʃə/ • **v.** express severe disapproval of; formally reprove. • **n.** formal disapproval.
– DERIVATIVES **censurable** adj.
– ORIGIN ME: from OFr. *censurer* (v.), *censure* (n.), from L. *censura* 'judgement, assessment', from *censere* 'assess'.

**census** • **n.** (pl. **censuses**) an official count or survey of a population.
– ORIGIN C17 (denoting a poll tax): from L., from *censere* 'assess'.

**cent** • **n. 1** a monetary unit equal to one hundredth of a dollar or other decimal currency unit. **2** Music one hundredth of a semitone.
– ORIGIN ME (in the sense 'a hundred'): from Fr. *cent*, Ital. *cento*, or L. *centum* 'hundred'.

**cent.** • **abbrev.** century.

**centas** /ˈsɛntas/ • **n.** (pl. same) a monetary unit of Lithuania, equal to one hundredth of a litas.

– ORIGIN from Lithuanian.

**centaur** /ˈsɛntɔː/ ● n. Greek Mythology a creature with the head, arms, and torso of a man and the body and legs of a horse.
– ORIGIN via L. from Gk *kentauros*, the Gk name for a Thessalonian tribe of expert horsemen.

**centaury** /ˈsɛntɔːri/ ● n. (pl. **-ies**) a plant of the gentian family, typically having pink flowers. [*Centaurium minus* and other species.]
– ORIGIN ME: from late L. *centaurea*, based on Gk *kentauros* 'centaur'.

**centavo** /sɛnˈtɑːvəʊ/ ● n. (pl. **-os**) a monetary unit of Portugal, Mexico, Brazil, and certain other countries, equal to one hundredth of the basic unit.
– ORIGIN Sp. and Port., from L. *centum* 'a hundred'.

**centenarian** /ˌsɛntɪˈnɛːrɪən/ ● n. a person a hundred or more years old. ● adj. a hundred or more years old.

**centenary** /sɛnˈtiːnəri, -ˈtɛn-/ ● n. (pl. **-ies**) chiefly Brit. the hundredth anniversary of a significant event.
– ORIGIN C17: from L. *centenarius* 'containing a hundred', based on L. *centum* 'a hundred'.

**centennial** /sɛnˈtɛnɪəl/ ● adj. of or relating to a hundredth anniversary. ● n. a hundredth anniversary.
– ORIGIN C18: from L. *centum* 'a hundred', on the pattern of *biennial*.

**center** etc. ● n. US spelling of **CENTRE** etc.

**centering** ● n. US spelling of **CENTRING**.

**centesimal** /sɛnˈtɛsɪm(ə)l/ ● adj. of or relating to division into hundredths.
– DERIVATIVES **centesimally** adv.
– ORIGIN C19: from L. *centesimus* 'hundredth', from *centum* 'a hundred'.

**centesimo** /tʃɛnˈtɛsɪməʊ/ ● n. (pl. **-os**) a monetary unit of Italy (used only in calculations), worth one hundredth of a lira.
– ORIGIN from Ital.

**centésimo** /sɛnˈtɛsɪməʊ, Spanish senˈtesimo, θen-/ ● n. (pl. **-os**) a monetary unit of Uruguay and Panama, equal to one hundredth of the basic unit.
– ORIGIN from Sp.

**centi-** ● comb. form **1** one hundredth: *centilitre*. **2** hundred: *centipede*.
– ORIGIN from L. *centum* 'hundred'.

**centigrade** ● adj. [postpos. when used with a numeral] of or denoting a scale of a hundred degrees, in particular the Celsius scale of temperature.
– ORIGIN C19: from Fr., from L. *centum* 'a hundred' + *gradus* 'step'.

**centigram** (also **centigramme**) (abbrev.: **cg**) ● n. a metric unit of mass equal to one hundredth of a gram.

**centile** /ˈsɛntʌɪl/ ● n. another term for **PERCENTILE**.

**centilitre** (US **centiliter**) (abbrev.: **cl**) ● n. a metric unit of capacity equal to one hundredth of a litre.

**centime** /ˈsɒ̃tiːm, French sɑ̃tim/ ● n. a monetary unit of France, Belgium, Switzerland, and certain other countries, equal to one hundredth of a franc or other decimal currency unit.
– ORIGIN Fr., from L. *centesimus* 'hundredth', from *centum* 'a hundred'.

**centimetre** (US **centimeter**) (abbrev.: **cm**) ● n. a metric unit of length equal to one hundredth of a metre.

**centimo** /ˈsɛntɪməʊ, Spanish ˈθentimo, ˈsen-/ ● n. (pl. **-os**) a monetary unit of Spain and a number of Latin American countries, equal to one hundredth of the basic unit.
– ORIGIN from Sp.

**centimorgan** /ˈsɛntɪˌmɔːg(ə)n/ ● n. Genetics a unit of distance between two gene loci on a chromosome, one centimorgan indicating a one per cent chance that two genes will be separated by crossing over.
– ORIGIN C20: from *centi-* (denoting a factor of one hundredth) + the name of the Amer. zoologist T. H. *Morgan*.

**centipede** /ˈsɛntɪpiːd/ ● n. a predatory arthropod with a flattened, elongated body composed of many segments, most of which bear a pair of legs. [Class Chilopoda: many species.]
– ORIGIN C17: from Fr. *centipède* or L. *centipeda*, from *centum* 'a hundred' + *pes, ped-* 'foot'.

**cento** /ˈsɛntəʊ/ ● n. (pl. **-os**) rare a literary work made up of quotations from other authors.
– ORIGIN C17: L., lit. 'patchwork garment'.

**centra** plural form of **CENTRUM**.

**central** ● adj. **1** in or near the centre of something. **2** most important; principal.
– DERIVATIVES **centrality** n. **centrally** adv.
– ORIGIN C17: from Fr., or from L. *centralis*, from *centrum* (see **CENTRE**).

**Central American** ● adj. of or relating to the countries of Guatemala, Belize, Honduras, El Salvador, Nicaragua, Costa Rica, and Panama, in the southernmost part of North America. ● n. a native or inhabitant of a Central American country.

**central bank** ● n. a national bank that provides financial and banking services for its country's government and commercial banking system, and issues currency.

**central heating** ● n. a system for warming a building by heating water or air in one place and circulating it through pipes and radiators or vents.

**centralize** (also **-ise**) ● v. [often as adj. **centralized**] concentrate (control or power) under a single authority.
– DERIVATIVES **centralism** n. **centralist** n. & adj. **centralization** n.

**central nervous system** ● n. Anatomy the complex of nerve tissues that controls the activities of the body, in vertebrates comprising the brain and spinal cord.

**central processing unit** (also **central processor**) ● n. Computing the part of a computer in which operations are controlled and executed.

**central reservation** ● n. Brit. the strip of land between the carriageways of a motorway or other major road.

**centre** (US **center**) ● n. **1** a point in the middle of something that is equally distant from all of its sides, ends, or surfaces. ➤ the middle player in some team games. ➤ (in some team games) a kick, hit, or throw of the ball from the side to the middle of field. **2** a place or group of buildings where a specified activity is concentrated. ➤ a point to or from which an activity or process is directed. ● v. **1** place in the centre. ➤ (in some team games) kick, hit, or throw (the ball) from the side to the middle of field. ➤ chiefly N. Amer. play as the middle player in some team games. **2** (**centre on/around**) have as a major concern or theme. ➤ (**be centred in**) occur mainly in or around.
– DERIVATIVES **centremost** adj.
– ORIGIN ME: from OFr., or from L. *centrum*, from Gk *kentron* 'sharp point, stationary point of a pair of compasses', rel. to *kentein* 'to prick'.

**centre back** ● n. Soccer a defender who plays in the middle of the field.

**centre bit** ● n. a drill bit with a central point and side cutters.

**centreboard** (US **centerboard**) ● n. a pivoted board that can be lowered through the keel of a sailing boat to reduce sideways movement.

**centreboarder** ● n. a sailing boat with a centreboard.

**centred** (US **centered**) ● adj. **1** (**-centred**) taking a specified subject as the most important element: *a child-centred school*. **2** chiefly US (of a person) well balanced and confident.
– DERIVATIVES **centredness** n.

**centrefield** (US **centerfield**) ● n. Baseball the central part of the outfield.
– DERIVATIVES **centrefielder** n.

**centrefire** ● adj. (of a gun cartridge) having the primer in the centre of the base.

**centrefold** (US **centerfold**) ● n. the two middle pages of a magazine.

**centre forward** ● n. Soccer & Hockey an attacker who plays in the middle of the field.

**centre half** ● n. Soccer another term for **CENTRE BACK**.

**centre of curvature** ● n. Mathematics the centre of a circle which passes through a curve at a given point and has the same tangent and curvature at that point.

**centre of gravity** ● n. the point from which the weight of a body may be considered to act (in uniform gravity the same as the centre of mass).

**centre of mass** • n. a point representing the mean position of all the matter in a body.

**centre of pressure** • n. Physics a point on a surface through which the resultant force due to pressure passes.

**centrepiece** • n. an item serving as a central or principal ornament or display.

**centre punch** • n. a punch with a conical point for making an indentation in a surface.

**centre spread** • n. the two facing middle pages of a newspaper or magazine.

**centre stage** • n. the centre of a stage. ➤ the most prominent position. • adv. in or towards this position.

**centric** • adj. **1** in or at the centre; central. **2** Botany (of a diatom) radially symmetrical. Compare with **PENNATE**.
– DERIVATIVES **centrical** adj. **centricity** /-'trɪsɪti/ n.

**-centric** • comb. form **1** having a specified centre: *geocentric*. **2** originating from a specified viewpoint: *Eurocentric*.
– DERIVATIVES **-centricity** comb. form in corresponding nouns.
– ORIGIN from Gk *kentrikos*, on the pattern of words such as (*con*)*centric*.

**centrifugal** /ˌsɛntrɪ'fjuːg(ə)l, sɛn'trɪfjʊg(ə)l/ • adj. Physics moving away from a centre.
– DERIVATIVES **centrifugally** adv.
– ORIGIN C18: from mod. L. *centrifugus*, from L. *centrum* (see **CENTRE**) + *-fugus* 'fleeing' (from *fugere* 'flee').

**centrifugal force** • n. Physics a force, arising from the body's inertia, which appears to act on a body moving in a circular path and is directed away from the centre around which the body is moving.

**centrifugal pump** • n. a pump that uses an impeller to move water or other fluids.

**centrifuge** /'sɛntrɪfjuːdʒ/ • n. a machine with a rapidly rotating container that applies centrifugal force to its contents, used chiefly to separate liquids from solids. • v. subject to the action of a centrifuge.
– DERIVATIVES **centrifugation** /-fjʊ'geɪʃ(ə)n/ n.

**centring** (US **centering**) • n. **1** the action or process of placing in the centre. **2** Architecture framing used to support an arch or dome under construction.

**centriole** /'sɛntrɪəʊl/ • n. Biology each of a pair of minute cylindrical structures near the nucleus in animal cells, involved in the development of spindle fibres in cell division.
– ORIGIN C19: from mod. L. *centriolum*, dimin. of *centrum* (see **CENTRE**).

**centripetal** /ˌsɛntrɪ'piːt(ə)l, sɛn'trɪpɪt(ə)l/ • adj. Physics moving towards a centre.
– DERIVATIVES **centripetally** adv.
– ORIGIN C18: from mod. L. *centripetus*, from L. *centrum* (see **CENTRE**) + *-petus* 'seeking' (from *petere* 'seek').

**centripetal force** • n. Physics a force which acts on a body moving in a circular path and is directed towards the centre around which the body is moving.

**centrist** • n. a person having moderate political views or policies.
– DERIVATIVES **centrism** n.

**centroid** • n. Mathematics the centre of mass of a geometric object of uniform density.

**centromere** /'sɛntrə(ʊ)mɪə/ • n. Biology the point on a chromosome by which it is attached to a spindle fibre during cell division.
– DERIVATIVES **centromeric** adj.
– ORIGIN 1920s: from L. *centrum* (see **CENTRE**) + Gk *meros* 'part'.

**centrosome** /'sɛntrəsəʊm/ • n. Biology a structure near the nucleus of a cell which contains the centrioles and from which the spindle fibres develop in cell division.
– ORIGIN C19: from L. *centrum* (see **CENTRE**) + Gk *sōma* 'body'.

**centrum** /'sɛntrəm/ • n. (pl. **centrums** or **centra** /-trə/) Anatomy the solid central part of a vertebra.
– ORIGIN C19: from L.

**centuple** /'sɛntjʊp(ə)l/ • v. multiply by a hundred.
– ORIGIN C17: from Fr., or from eccles. L. *centuplus*, alt. of L. *centuplex*, from L. *centum* 'hundred'.

**centurion** /sɛn'tjʊərɪən/ • n. the commander of a century in the ancient Roman army.
– ORIGIN ME: from L. *centurio(n-)*, from *centuria* (see **CENTURY**).

**century** • n. (pl. **-ies**) **1** a period of one hundred years, in particular each of a number of such periods from the date of the birth of Christ. **2** a batsman's score of a hundred runs in cricket. **3** a company of a hundred men in the ancient Roman army. ➤ an electoral division of ancient Rome.
– DERIVATIVES **centurial** adj.
– ORIGIN ME: from L. *centuria*, from *centum* 'hundred'.

**century plant** • n. a large agave which produces a very tall flowering stem after many years of growth and then dies. [*Agave americana*.]

**CEO** • abbrev. chief executive officer.

**cep** /sɛp/ • n. an edible mushroom with a smooth brown cap and pores rather than gills. [*Boletus edulis*.]
– ORIGIN C19: from Fr. *cèpe*, from Gascon *cep* 'tree trunk, mushroom', from L. *cippus* 'stake'.

**cephalic** /sɪ'falɪk, kɛ-/ • adj. of, in, or relating to the head.
– ORIGIN ME: from OFr. *cephalique*, from L. *cephalicus*, from Gk *kephalikos*, from *kephalē* 'head'.

**-cephalic** • comb. form (used in medical terms) -headed: *leptocephalic*.

**cephalic index** • n. Anthropology the ratio of the maximum breadth of a skull to its maximum length.

**cephalization** /ˌsɛfəlʌɪ'zeɪʃ(ə)n, ˌkɛf-/ • n. Zoology the concentration of sense organs in a head and brain (either in evolution or the development of an embryo).

**cephalo-** /'sɛfələʊ, 'kɛf-/ • comb. form relating to the head or skull: *cephalometry*.
– ORIGIN from Gk *kephalē* 'head'.

**Cephalochordata** /ˌsɛfələ(ʊ)kɔː'deɪtə, ˌkɛ-/ • pl. n. Zoology a subphylum of marine invertebrates that comprises the lancelets.
– DERIVATIVES **cephalochordate** /ˌsɛfələ(ʊ)'kɔːdeɪt, ˌkɛ-/ n. & adj.
– ORIGIN mod. L., from **CEPHALO-** + Gk *chorda* 'cord'.

**cephalometry** /ˌsɛfə'lɒmɪtri, ˌkɛf-/ • n. Medicine measurement and study of the proportions of the head and face, especially during development.
– DERIVATIVES **cephalometric** adj.

**cephalon** /'sɛfəlɒn, 'kɛf-/ • n. Zoology (in some arthropods, especially trilobites) the region of the head, composed of fused segments.
– ORIGIN C19: from Gk *kephalē* 'head'.

**Cephalopoda** /ˌsɛfələ'pəʊdə, ˌkɛ-/ • pl. n. Zoology a large class of active predatory molluscs comprising octopuses, squids, and cuttlefish.
– DERIVATIVES **cephalopod** /'sɛf(ə)lə(ʊ)pɒd, 'kɛ-/ n.
– ORIGIN mod. L., from Gk *kephalē* 'head' + *pous, pod-* 'foot'.

**cephalosporin** /ˌsɛfələ(ʊ)'spɔːrɪn, ˌkɛ-/ • n. any of a group of semi-synthetic antibiotics resembling penicillin.
– ORIGIN 1950s: from mod. L. *Cephalosporium* (the genus providing moulds for this) + **-IN**[1].

**cephalothorax** /ˌsɛf(ə)ləʊ'θɔːraks, ˌkɛf-/ • n. (pl. **-thoraces** /-'θɔːrəsiːz/ or **-thoraxes**) Zoology the fused head and thorax of spiders and other chelicerate arthropods.

**-cephalous** • comb. form equivalent to **-CEPHALIC**.

**cepheid** /'siːfɪɪd, 'sɛ-/ • n. Astronomy a star whose brightness varies on a regular cycle whose frequency is related to its luminosity, so allowing estimation of its distance from the earth.
– ORIGIN C20: from the name of the variable star *Delta Cephei*, which typifies this class.

**ceramic** /sɪ'ramɪk/ • adj. **1** made of clay that is permanently hardened by heat. **2** of or relating to ceramics. • n. (**ceramics**) **1** ceramic articles. ➤ [usu. treated as sing.] the art of making ceramics. **2** clay used in this way. ➤ any non-metallic solid which remains hard when heated.
– DERIVATIVES **ceramicist** n.
– ORIGIN C19: from Gk *keramikos*, from *keramos* 'pottery'.

**ceramic hob** • **n.** an electric cooker hob made of ceramic, with heating elements fixed to its underside.

**cerastium** /sɪˈrastɪəm/ • **n.** (pl. **cerastiums**) a plant of a genus that includes chickweed and snow-in-summer. [Genus *Cerastium*.]
– ORIGIN mod. L., from Gk *kerastēs* 'horned' (with ref. to the shape of many seed capsules) + **-IUM**.

**ceratite** /ˈsɛrətʌɪt, ˈsɪər-/ • **n.** Palaeontology an ammonoid fossil of a type with partly frilled and partly lobed suture lines.
– ORIGIN C19: from mod. L. *Ceratites* (from Gk *keras, kerat-* 'horn') + **-ITE**[1].

**ceratopsian** /ˌsɛrəˈtɒpsɪən, ˌkɛr-/ • **n.** Palaeontology a gregarious quadrupedal herbivorous dinosaur of a group including triceratops, with a bony frill protecting the neck.
– ORIGIN C20: from mod. L. *Ceratopsia* (pl., from Gk *keras, kerat-* 'horn' + *ops* 'face') + **-AN**.

**cercaria** /səːˈkɛːrɪə/ • **n.** (pl. **cercariae** /-iiː/) Zoology a free-swimming larval stage in which a parasitic fluke passes from an intermediate host (typically a snail) to another host.
– ORIGIN C19: mod. L., formed irregularly from Gk *kerkos* 'tail'.

**cercopithecine** /ˌsəːkə(ʊ)ˈpɪθɪsiːn/ • **adj.** Zoology relating to or denoting monkeys of a subfamily (Cercopithecinae) that includes the macaques, mangabeys, baboons, and guenons.
– ORIGIN based on Gk *kerkopithēkos* 'long-tailed monkey', from *kerkos* 'tail' + *pithēkos* 'ape'.

**cercopithecoid** /ˌsəːkə(ʊ)ˈpɪθɪkɔɪd/ • **adj.** Zoology relating to or denoting primates of a family (Cercopithecidae) that includes all Old World monkeys.

**cercus** /ˈsəːkəs/ • **n.** (pl. **cerci** /-kʌɪ/) Zoology either of a pair of small appendages at the end of the abdomen of some insects and other arthropods.
– ORIGIN C19: from mod. L., from Gk *kerkos* 'tail'.

**cere** /sɪə/ • **n.** Ornithology a waxy fleshy covering at the base of the upper beak in some birds.
– ORIGIN C15: from L. *cera* 'wax'.

**cereal** • **n.** **1** a grain used for food, for example wheat, maize, or rye. ➤a grass producing such grain, grown as an agricultural crop. **2** a breakfast food made from a cereal grain or grains.
– ORIGIN C19 (as adj.): from L. *cerealis*, from *Ceres*, the name of the Roman goddess of agriculture.

**cerebellum** /ˌsɛrɪˈbɛləm/ • **n.** (pl. **cerebellums** or **cerebella**) Anatomy the part of the brain at the back of the skull, which coordinates and regulates muscular activity.
– DERIVATIVES **cerebellar** adj.
– ORIGIN C16: from L., dimin. of **CEREBRUM**.

**cerebral** /ˈsɛrɪbr(ə)l/ • **adj.** **1** of the cerebrum of the brain. ➤intellectual rather than emotional or physical. **2** Phonetics another term for **RETROFLEX**.
– DERIVATIVES **cerebrally** adv.
– ORIGIN C19: from L. *cerebrum* 'brain' + **-AL**.

**cerebral palsy** • **n.** a condition marked by impaired muscle coordination and spastic paralysis, caused by damage to the brain before or at birth.

**cerebration** /ˌsɛrɪˈbreɪʃ(ə)n/ • **n.** the working of the brain; thinking.
– DERIVATIVES **cerebrate** v.

**cerebro-** • **comb. form** of or relating to the brain: *cerebrospinal.*
– ORIGIN from L. *cerebrum* 'brain'.

**cerebroside** /ˈsɛrɪbrə(ʊ)sʌɪd/ • **n.** Biochemistry any of a group of complex lipids present in the sheaths of nerve fibres.
– ORIGIN C19: from L. *cerebrum* 'brain' + **-OSE**[2] + **-IDE**.

**cerebrospinal** /ˌsɛrɪbrə(ʊ)ˈspʌɪn(ə)l/ • **adj.** Anatomy of or relating to the brain and spine.

**cerebrospinal fluid** • **n.** Anatomy clear watery fluid which fills the space between the arachnoid membrane and the pia mater.

**cerebrovascular** /ˌsɛrɪbrə(ʊ)ˈvaskjʊlə/ • **adj.** Anatomy of or relating to the brain and its blood vessels.

**cerebrum** /ˈsɛrɪbrəm/ • **n.** (pl. **cerebra** /-brə/) Anatomy the principal part of the brain, located in the front area of the skull and consisting of left and right hemispheres.
– ORIGIN C17: from L., 'brain'.

**cerecloth** /ˈsɪəklɒθ/ • **n.** historical waxed cloth, used especially for wrapping a corpse.
– ORIGIN ME: from earlier *cered cloth*, from *cere* 'to wax', from L. *cerare*, from *cera* 'wax'.

**cerement** /ˈsɪəm(ə)nt/ • **n.** (**cerements**) historical waxed cloth for wrapping a corpse.
– ORIGIN C17: from *cere* (see **CERECLOTH**).

**ceremonial** • **adj.** **1** relating to or used for ceremonies. **2** (of a post or role) involving only nominal authority or power. • **n.** another term for **CEREMONY**.
– DERIVATIVES **ceremonialism** n. **ceremonialist** n. **ceremonially** adv.

**ceremonious** • **adj.** relating or appropriate to grand and formal occasions.
– DERIVATIVES **ceremoniously** adv. **ceremoniousness** n.
– ORIGIN C16: from Fr. *cérémonieux* or late L. *caerimoniosus*, from L. *caerimonia* (see **CEREMONY**).

**ceremony** • **n.** (pl. **-ies**) **1** a formal religious or public occasion, typically celebrating a particular event, achievement, or anniversary. ➤an act or series of acts performed according to a traditional or prescribed form. **2** the ritual procedures observed at such occasions: *the new Queen was proclaimed with due ceremony.*
– PHRASES **stand on ceremony** observe formalities. **without ceremony** without formality or politeness.
– ORIGIN ME: from OFr. *ceremonie* or L. *caerimonia* 'religious worship', (pl.) 'ritual observances'.

**Cerenkov radiation** • **n.** variant spelling of **CHERENKOV RADIATION**.

**cereology** /ˌsɪərɪˈɒlədʒi/ • **n.** the study or investigation of crop circles.
– DERIVATIVES **cereologist** n.
– ORIGIN C20: from *Ceres* (see **CEREAL**) + **-LOGY**.

**ceresin** /ˈsɛrɪsɪn/ • **n.** a hard whitish paraffin wax used with or instead of beeswax.
– ORIGIN C19: from mod. L. *ceres* (from L. *cera* 'wax') + **-IN**[1].

**cerise** /sɛˈriːs, -z/ • **n.** a light, clear red colour.
– ORIGIN C19: from Fr., lit. 'cherry'.

**cerium** /ˈsɪərɪəm/ • **n.** the chemical element of atomic number 58, a silvery-white metal of the lanthanide series. (Symbol: **Ce**)
– ORIGIN C19: named after the asteroid *Ceres*, discovered shortly before.

**cermet** /ˈsəːmɛt/ • **n.** any of a class of heat-resistant materials made of ceramic and sintered metal.
– ORIGIN 1950s: blend of **CERAMIC** and **METAL**.

**CERN** /səːn/ • **abbrev.** Conseil Européen pour la Recherche Nucléaire, former title of the European Organization for Nuclear Research.

**cero** /ˈsɪərəʊ/ • **n.** (pl. same or **-os**) a large food fish of the mackerel family, found in the tropical western Atlantic. [*Scomberomorus regalis.*]
– ORIGIN C19: from Sp. *sierra* 'saw or sawfish'.

**cero-** /ˈsɪərəʊ/ • **comb. form** of or relating to wax: *ceroplastic.*
– ORIGIN from L. *cera* or Gk *kēros* 'wax'.

**ceroplastic** • **adj.** of or relating to modelling in wax.

**cert** • **n.** Brit. informal **1** an event regarded as inevitable. **2** a competitor, candidate, etc. regarded as certain to win.
– ORIGIN C19: abbrev. of **CERTAINTY**.

**cert.** • **abbrev.** **1** certificate. **2** certified.

**certain** /ˈsəːt(ə)n, -tɪn/ • **adj.** **1** able to be firmly relied on to happen or be the case. **2** completely convinced of something. **3** specific but not explicitly named or stated: *certain problems.* ➤not known to the reader or hearer: *a certain Mr Percy.* • **pron.** (**certain of**) some but not all.
– PHRASES **for certain** without any doubt. **make certain** take action to ensure that something happens. ➤establish whether something is definitely correct.
– ORIGIN ME: from OFr., based on L. *certus* 'settled, sure'.

**certainly** • **adv.** definitely; undoubtedly. ➤yes; by all means.

**certainty** • **n.** (pl. **-ies**) **1** the quality or state of being

certain. **2** a true fact or an event that is definitely going to take place.
– PHRASES **for a certainty** beyond the possibility of doubt.
– ORIGIN ME: from OFr. *certainete*, from *certain* (see **CERTAIN**).

**CertEd** ● **abbrev.** (in the UK) Certificate in Education.

**certifiable** ● **adj.** able or needing to be certified.

**certificate** ● **n.** /sə'tɪfɪkət/ **1** an official document attesting or recording a particular fact or event, a level of achievement, the fulfilment of a legal requirement, etc. **2** an official classification awarded to a cinema film by a board of censors, indicating its suitability for a particular age group. ● **v.** /sə'tɪfɪkeɪt/ provide with or attest in an official document.
– DERIVATIVES **certification** n.
– ORIGIN ME: from Fr. *certificat* or med. L. *certificat-*, *certificare* (see **CERTIFY**).

**certified cheque** ● **n.** a cheque which is guaranteed by a bank.

**certified mail** ● **n.** North American term for **RECORDED DELIVERY**.

**certified stock** ● **n.** plants or plant material certified as being free from certain diseases and pests.

**certify** ● **v.** (**-ies**, **-ied**) **1** formally attest or confirm. **2** officially recognize as possessing certain qualifications or meeting certain standards. **3** officially declare insane.
– ORIGIN ME: from OFr. *certifier*, from late L. *certificare*, from L. *certus* 'certain'.

**certiorari** /ˌsəːtɪə(ʊ)'rɑːri/ ● **n.** Law a writ by which a higher court reviews a case tried in a lower court.
– ORIGIN ME: from Law L., 'to be informed', a phr. orig. occurring at the start of the writ, from *certiorare* 'inform', from *certior*, compar. of *certus* 'certain'.

**certitude** /'səːtɪtjuːd/ ● **n.** a feeling of absolute certainty. ➤something considered with certainty to be true.
– ORIGIN ME: from late L. *certitudo*, from *certus* 'certain'.

**cerulean** /sɪ'ruːlɪən/ ● **adj.** deep blue in colour like a clear sky.
– ORIGIN C17: from L. *caeruleus*, from *caelum* 'sky'.

**cerumen** /sɪ'ruːmən/ ● **n.** technical term for **EARWAX**.
– ORIGIN C17: mod. L., from L. *cera* 'wax'.

**ceruse** /'sɪəruːs, sɪ'ruːs/ ● **n.** archaic term for **WHITE LEAD**.
– ORIGIN ME: via OFr. from L. *cerussa*, perh. from Gk *kēros* 'wax'.

**cervelat** /'səːvəlɑː, -lat/ ● **n.** a kind of smoked pork sausage.
– ORIGIN C17: from obs. Fr., earlier form of *cervelas*, from Ital. *cervellata*.

**cervical** /'səːvɪk(ə)l, səː'vʌɪk(ə)l/ ● **adj.** Anatomy **1** of or relating to the cervix. **2** of or relating to the neck.
– ORIGIN C17: from Fr., or from mod. L. *cervicalis*, from L. *cervix*, *cervic-* 'neck'.

**cervical smear** ● **n.** Brit. a specimen of cellular material from the cervix spread on a microscope slide for examination for cancerous cells.

**cervicitis** /ˌsəːvɪ'sʌɪtɪs/ ● **n.** Medicine inflammation of the cervix.

**cervid** /'səːvɪd/ ● **n.** Zoology a mammal of the deer family (Cervidae).
– ORIGIN C19: from mod. L. *Cervidae*, from L. *cervus* 'deer'.

**cervix** /'səːvɪks/ ● **n.** (pl. **cervices** /-siːz/) **1** the narrow neck-like passage forming the lower end of the womb. **2** technical the neck.
– ORIGIN C18: from L.

**Cesarean** (also **Cesarian**) ● **adj. & n.** US spelling of **CAESAREAN**.

**cesium** ● **n.** US spelling of **CAESIUM**.

**cess**[1] /sɛs/ (also **sess**) ● **n.** (in Scotland, Ireland, and India) a tax or levy.
– ORIGIN C15: shortened from the obs. noun *assess* 'assessment'.

**cess**[2] /sɛs/ ● **n.** (in phr. **bad cess to**) chiefly Irish a curse on.
– ORIGIN C19 (orig. Anglo-Ir.): perh. from **CESS**[1].

**cessation** /sɛ'seɪʃ(ə)n/ ● **n.** the fact or process of ceasing.
– ORIGIN ME: from L. *cessatio(n-)*, from *cessare* 'cease'.

**cesser** /'sɛsə/ ● **n.** Law termination or cessation, especially of a period of tenure or legal liability.
– ORIGIN C16: from OFr. *cesser* 'cease', used as n.

**cession** /'sɛʃ(ə)n/ ● **n.** the formal giving up of rights, property, or territory by a state.
– ORIGIN ME; from L. *cessio(n-)*, from *cedere* 'cede'.

**cesspit** ● **n.** a pit for the disposal of liquid waste and sewage.
– ORIGIN C19: from *cess* (the supposed base of **CESSPOOL**) + **PIT**[1].

**cesspool** ● **n.** an underground container for the temporary storage of liquid waste and sewage.
– ORIGIN C17 (denoting a trap under a drain to catch solids): prob. an alt., influenced by **POOL**[1], of archaic *suspiral* 'vent, water pipe, settling tank', from OFr. *souspirail* 'air hole', based on L. *sub-* 'from below' + *spirare* 'breathe'.

**c'est la vie** /ˌseɪ lɑː 'viː, French sɛ la vi/ ● **exclam.** that's life.
– ORIGIN from Fr.

**Cestoda** /sɛs'təʊdə/ (also **Cestoidea**) ● **pl. n.** Zoology a class of parasitic flatworms comprising the tapeworms.
– DERIVATIVES **cestode** /'sɛstəʊd/ n.
– ORIGIN mod. L., from L. *cestus*, from Gk *kestos*, lit. 'stitched', used as a noun in the sense 'girdle'.

**CET** ● **abbrev.** Central European Time.

**Cetacea** /sɪ'teɪʃə/ ● **pl. n.** Zoology an order of marine mammals comprising the whales, dolphins, and porpoises.
– DERIVATIVES **cetacean** n. & adj.
– ORIGIN mod. L., from L. *cetus*, from Gk *kētos* 'whale'.

**cetane** /'siːteɪn/ ● **n.** Chemistry a colourless liquid hydrocarbon of the alkane series, present in petroleum spirit. [$C_{16}H_{34}$.]
– ORIGIN C19: from L. *cetus* 'whale' (because rel. compounds were first derived from spermaceti) + **-ANE**[2].

**ceteris paribus** /ˌkeɪtərɪs 'parɪbʊs, ˌsɛt-, ˌsiːt-/ ● **adv.** other things being equal.
– ORIGIN C17: mod. L.

**ceviche** /sɛ'viːtʃeɪ/ (also **seviche**) ● **n.** a South American dish of marinaded raw fish or seafood.
– ORIGIN from Latin Amer. Sp.

**Ceylon moss** ● **n.** a red seaweed of the Indian subcontinent, the main source of agar. [*Gracilaria lichenoides*.]

**CF** ● **abbrev.** **1** (in the UK) Chaplain to the Forces. **2** cystic fibrosis.

**Cf** ● **symb.** the chemical element californium.

**cf.** ● **abbrev.** compare with.
– ORIGIN from L. *confer* 'compare'.

**c.f.** ● **abbrev.** carried forward (referring to figures transferred to a new page or account).

**CFA** (also **CFA franc**) ● **n.** the basic monetary unit of Cameroon, Congo, Gabon, and the Central African Republic, equal to 100 centimes.
– ORIGIN *CFA* from Fr. *Communauté Financière Africaine* 'African Financial Community'.

**CFC** ● **abbrev.** Chemistry chlorofluorocarbon, any of a class of synthetic compounds of carbon, hydrogen, chlorine, and fluorine formerly used as refrigerants and aerosol propellants and known to be harmful to the ozone layer.

**CFE** ● **abbrev.** (in the UK) College of Further Education.

**CFS** ● **abbrev.** chronic fatigue syndrome.

**CG** ● **abbrev.** Democratic Republic of Congo (international vehicle registration).

**cg** ● **abbrev.** centigram(s).

**CGS** ● **abbrev.** (in the UK) Chief of the General Staff.

**cgs** ● **abbrev.** centimetre-gram-second (denoting a system of measurement using these as basic units).

**CGT** ● **abbrev.** capital gains tax.

**CH** ● **abbrev.** **1** (in the UK) Companion of Honour. **2** Switzerland (international vehicle registration). [from Fr. *Confédération Helvétique* 'Swiss Confederation'.]

**ch.** ● **abbrev.** **1** chapter. **2** (of a horse) chestnut in colour. **3** church.

**cha** • **n.** variant spelling of CHAR³.

**chaat** /tʃɑːt/ • **n.** an Indian dish of boiled vegetables or raw fruit, with spices.
– ORIGIN from Hindi *cāṭ*.

**chabazite** /ˈkabəzʌɪt/ • **n.** a colourless, pink, or yellow zeolite mineral.
– ORIGIN C19: from Fr. *chabazie*, from Gk *khabazie*, a misreading of *khalazie*, vocative form of *khalazios* 'hailstone' (from *khalaza* 'hail', because of its form and colour), + -ITE¹.

**Chablis** /ˈʃabliː/ • **n.** a dry white burgundy wine from Chablis in eastern France.

**cha-cha** /ˈtʃɑːtʃɑː/ • **n.** a ballroom dance with small steps and swaying hip movements, performed to a Latin American rhythm. • **v.** (**cha-chas**, **cha-chaed** /-tʃɑːd/ or **cha-cha'd**, **cha-chaing** /-tʃɑː(r)ɪŋ/) dance the cha-cha.
– ORIGIN 1950s: Latin Amer. Sp.

**chacham** /ˈxɑːxəm/ • **n.** variant spelling of HAHAM.

**chacma baboon** /ˈtʃakmə/ • **n.** a dark grey baboon inhabiting savannah in southern Africa. [*Papio ursinus*.]
– ORIGIN C19: from Khoikhoi.

**chaconne** /ʃəˈkɒn/ • **n.** Music **1** a composition in a series of varying sections in slow triple time. **2** a stately dance performed to such music.
– ORIGIN C17: from Fr., from Sp. *chacona*.

**chacun à son goût** /ˌʃakəːn a sɒn ˈguː, French ʃakœ̃ a sɔ̃ gu/ • **exclam.** each to their own taste.
– ORIGIN from Fr.

**chad** • **n.** a small piece of waste paper produced by punching a hole in punched card or tape.
– ORIGIN 1950s: of unknown origin.

**Chadian** /ˈtʃadɪən/ • **n.** a native or inhabitant of Chad in central Africa. • **adj.** of or relating to Chad or Chadians.

**Chadic** /ˈtʃadɪk/ • **n.** a group of Afro-Asiatic languages spoken in the region of Lake Chad in north central Africa, of which the most important is Hausa. • **adj.** of or relating to this group of languages.

**chador** /ˈtʃɑːdɔː, ˈtʃɑːdə, ˈtʃʌdə/ (also **chadar** or **chuddar**) • **n.** a large piece of dark-coloured cloth that is wrapped around the head and upper body leaving only the face exposed, worn by Muslim women.
– ORIGIN C17: from Urdu *chādar*, *chaddar*, from Pers. *čādar* 'sheet or veil'.

**chaebol** /ˈtʃeɪbɒl/ • **n.** (pl. same or **chaebols**) (in the Republic of Korea) a large family-owned business conglomerate.
– ORIGIN 1980s: Korean, lit. 'money clan'.

**chaeta** /ˈkiːtə/ • **n.** (pl. **chaetae** /-tiː/) Zoology a stiff bristle made of chitin, especially in an annelid worm.
– ORIGIN C19: mod. L., from Gk *khaitē* 'long hair'.

**Chaetognatha** /ˌkiːtəgˈnaθə, -ˈneɪθə/ • **pl. n.** Zoology a small phylum of marine invertebrates that comprises the arrow worms.
– DERIVATIVES **chaetognath** n.
– ORIGIN mod. L., from Gk *khaitē* 'long hair' + *gnathos* 'jaw'.

**chafe** /tʃeɪf/ • **v. 1** make or become sore by rubbing. ➤ (of an object) rub abrasively against another. **2** rub (a part of the body) to restore warmth or sensation. **3** become annoyed or impatient because of a restriction or inconvenience. • **n. 1** wear or damage caused by rubbing. **2** archaic a state of annoyance.
– ORIGIN ME: from OFr. *chaufer* 'make hot', based on L. *calefacere*, from *calere* 'be hot' + *facere* 'make'.

**chafer** /ˈtʃeɪfə/ • **n.** a large flying beetle of a group within the scarab family including many kinds destructive to plants, such as the cockchafer and June bug.
– ORIGIN OE *ceafor*, *cefer*, of Gmc origin.

**chaff¹** /tʃɑːf, tʃaf/ • **n. 1** the husks of grain or other seed separated by winnowing or threshing. ➤ chopped hay and straw used as fodder. **2** strips of metal foil released in the air to obstruct radar detection.
– PHRASES **separate** (or **sort**) **the wheat from the chaff** distinguish valuable people or things from worthless ones.
– DERIVATIVES **chaffy** adj.
– ORIGIN OE *cæf*, *ceaf*, prob. from a Gmc base meaning 'gnaw'; rel. to CHAFER.

**chaff²** /tʃɑːf, tʃaf/ • **n.** light-hearted joking. • **v.** tease.
– ORIGIN C19: perh. from CHAFE.

**chaffer** /ˈtʃafə/ • **v.** haggle. • **n.** archaic haggling.
– DERIVATIVES **chafferer** n.
– ORIGIN ME (in the sense 'trade or trading'): from OE *cēap* 'a bargain' + *faru* 'journey'.

**chaffinch** • **n.** a common finch, the male of which has a bluish head, pink underparts, and dark wings with a white flash. [*Fringilla coelebs*.]
– ORIGIN OE *ceaffinc* 'chaff finch'.

**chaffweed** /ˈtʃafwiːd/ • **n.** a tiny pimpernel with pink or white flowers. [*Anagallis minima*.]
– ORIGIN C16: prob. from CHAFE + WEED.

**chafing dish** • **n. 1** a cooking pot with an outer pan of hot water, used for keeping food warm. **2** a metal pan with a spirit lamp, used for cooking at table.

**Chagas' disease** /ˈtʃɑːgəsɪz/ • **n.** a disease caused by trypanosomes transmitted by bloodsucking bugs, endemic in South America and causing damage to the heart and central nervous system.
– ORIGIN C20: named after Carlos *Chagas*, the Brazilian physician who first described it.

**chagrin** /ˈʃagrɪn/ • **n.** annoyance or shame at having failed. • **v.** (**be chagrined**) feel annoyed or ashamed.
– ORIGIN C17 (in the sense 'melancholy'): from Fr. *chagrin* (n.), lit. 'rough skin, shagreen', *chagriner* (v.).

**chai** /tʃʌɪ/ • **n.** Indian tea made by boiling tea leaves with milk, sugar, and cardamoms.
– ORIGIN a term in various Ind. langs.

**chain** • **n. 1** a connected flexible series of metal links used for fastening, pulling, etc., or in jewellery. ➤ a restricting force or factor. **2** a sequence of items of the same type forming a line. ➤ a series of connected elements. ➤ a group of hotels or shops owned by the same company. ➤ a part of a molecule consisting of a number of atoms bonded together in a linear sequence. **3** a jointed measuring line consisting of linked metal rods. ➤ the length of this (66 ft). **4** (**chains**) a structure projecting horizontally from a sailing ship's sides abreast of the masts, used to widen the basis for the shrouds. • **v.** fasten, secure, or confine with a chain.
– ORIGIN ME: from OFr. *chaine*, *chaeine*, from L. *catena* 'a chain'.

**chain drive** • **n.** a mechanism in which power is transmitted from an engine to the wheels of a vehicle or a boat's propeller by means of an endless chain.
– DERIVATIVES **chain-driven** adj.

**chaîné** /ˈʃeneɪ/ • **n.** (pl. **chaînés** pronunc. same) Ballet a sequence of fast turns from one foot to the other, executed in a straight line.
– ORIGIN Fr., lit. 'linked'.

**chain gang** • **n.** a group of convicts chained together while working outside the prison.

**chain gear** • **n.** a gear transmitting motion by means of a moving endless chain, as typically used in bicycles.

**chain letter** • **n.** one of a sequence of letters, each recipient in the sequence being requested to send copies to a specific number of other people.

**chain-link** • **adj.** made of wire in a diamond-shaped mesh.

**chain mail** • **n.** historical armour made of small metal rings linked together.

**chainplate** • **n.** a strong link or plate on a sailing ship's side, to which the shrouds are secured.

**chain reaction** • **n. 1** a chemical or other reaction in which the products themselves promote or spread the reaction, especially a self-sustaining nuclear fission process spread by neutrons. **2** a series of events, each caused by the previous one.

**chainsaw** • **n.** a mechanical power-driven saw with teeth set on a chain moving around the edge of a blade.

**chain shot** • **n.** historical pairs of cannonballs or half balls joined by a chain, fired from cannons in sea battles.

**chain-smoke** • **v.** smoke continually, typically by lighting a cigarette from the stub of the last one smoked.
– DERIVATIVES **chain-smoker** n.

**chain stitch** • **n.** an ornamental embroidery or crochet stitch resembling a chain.

**chain store** ● **n.** one of a series of shops owned by one firm and selling the same goods.

**chain wheel** ● **n.** a wheel transmitting power by means of a chain fitted to its edges.

**chair** ● **n. 1** a separate seat for one person, typically with a back and four legs. **2** the person in charge of a meeting or an organization (used as a neutral alternative to chairman or chairwoman). ➤an official position of authority, especially on a board of directors. **3** a professorship. **4** (**the chair**) US short for **ELECTRIC CHAIR**. **5** chiefly Brit. a metal socket holding a rail in place on a railway sleeper. ● **v. 1** act as chairperson of. **2** Brit. carry (someone) aloft in a chair or in a sitting position to celebrate a victory.
– ORIGIN ME: from OFr. *chaiere* (mod. *chaire* 'bishop's throne', *chaise* 'chair'), from L. *cathedra* 'seat', from Gk *kathedra*; cf. **CATHEDRAL**.

**chairlift** ● **n. 1** a series of chairs hung from a moving cable, used for carrying passengers up and down a mountain. **2** a device for carrying people in wheelchairs from one floor of a building to another.

**chairman** (or **chairwoman**) ● **n.** (pl. **-men** or **-women**) a person in charge of a meeting, committee, company, or other organization.
– DERIVATIVES **chairmanship** n.

**chairperson** ● **n.** a chairman or chairwoman (used as a neutral alternative).

**chaise** /ʃeɪz/ ● **n. 1** chiefly historical a horse-drawn carriage for one or two people, especially one with an open top and two wheels. ➤another term for **POST-CHAISE**. **2** US term for **CHAISE LONGUE**.
– ORIGIN C17: from Fr., var. of *chaire* (see **CHAIR**).

**chaise longue** /ˈlɒŋg/ (US also **chaise lounge**) ● **n.** (pl. **chaises longues** pronunc. same) **1** a sofa with a backrest at only one end. **2** N. Amer. a sunbed or other chair with a lengthened seat for reclining on.
– ORIGIN C19: Fr., lit. 'long chair'.

**chakra** /ˈtʃʌkrə/ ● **n.** (in Indian thought) each of the centres of spiritual power in the human body, usually considered to be seven in number.
– ORIGIN from Sanskrit *cakra* 'wheel or circle'.

**chalaza** /kəˈleɪzə/ ● **n.** (pl. **chalazae** /-ziː/) Zoology (in a bird's egg) each of two twisted membranous strips joining the yolk to the ends of the shell.
– DERIVATIVES **chalazal** adj.
– ORIGIN C18: mod. L., from Gk *khalaza* 'small knot'.

**Chalcedonian** /ˌkalsɪˈdəʊnɪən/ ● **adj.** of or relating to the ecumenical council of the Christian Church, held at Chalcedon in ancient Bithynia in 451, which affirmed the dual but united nature of Christ as god and man.

**chalcedony** /kalˈsɛdəni/ ● **n.** (pl. **-ies**) quartz occurring in a microcrystalline form such as onyx and agate.
– DERIVATIVES **chalcedonic** /ˌkalsɪˈdɒnɪk/ adj.
– ORIGIN ME: from L. *calcedonius*, *chalcedonius*, from Gk *khalkēdōn*.

**chalcid** /ˈkalsɪd/ ● **n.** Entomology a minute parasitic wasp of a large group (superfamily Chalcidoidea) typically having a metallic colouration.
– ORIGIN C19: from mod. L. *Chalcis* (genus name), from Gk *khalkos* 'copper, brass', + **-ID**[3].

**Chalcolithic** /ˌkalkə(ʊ)ˈlɪθɪk/ ● **adj.** Archaeology relating to or denoting a period in the 4th and 3rd millennia BC, during which some weapons and tools were made of copper.
– ORIGIN C20: from Gk *khalkos* 'copper' + *lithos* 'stone' + **-IC**.

**chalcopyrite** /ˌkalkə(ʊ)ˈpʌɪrʌɪt/ ● **n.** a yellow mineral consisting of a sulphide of copper and iron, the principal ore of copper.
– ORIGIN C19: from mod. L. *chalcopyrites*, from Gk *khalkos* 'copper' + *puritēs* (see **PYRITES**).

**Chaldean** ● **n. 1** a member of a people who lived in Chaldea, an ancient country in what is now southern Iraq. **2** the Semitic language of the ancient Chaldeans. ➤a language related to Aramaic and spoken in parts of Iraq. **3** a member of a Syrian Uniate Church based mainly in Iran and Iraq. ● **adj. 1** of or relating to ancient Chaldea or its people or language. **2** of or relating to the East Syrian Uniate Church.

**Chaldee** /kalˈdiː, ˈkaldiː/ ● **n. 1** the language of the ancient Chaldeans. ➤dated the Aramaic language as used in some books of the Old Testament. **2** a Chaldean.
– ORIGIN from L. *Chaldaei* 'Chaldeans'.

**chalet** /ˈʃaleɪ/ ● **n. 1** a wooden house with overhanging eaves, typically found in the Swiss Alps. **2** a small wooden cabin used by holidaymakers, typically one in a holiday camp.
– ORIGIN C18: from Swiss Fr., dimin. of OFr. *chasel* 'farmstead'.

**chalice** ● **n. 1** historical a goblet. **2** the wine cup used in the Christian Eucharist.
– ORIGIN ME: via OFr. from L. *calix*, *calic-* 'cup'.

**chalicothere** /ˈkalɪkəˌθɪə/ ● **n.** a horse-like fossil mammal of the late Tertiary period, with stout claws instead of hooves.
– ORIGIN C20: from mod. L. *Chalicotherium* (genus name), from Gk *khalix*, *khalik-* 'gravel' + *thērion* 'wild animal'.

**chalk** ● **n.** a white soft earthy limestone formed from the skeletal remains of sea creatures. ➤a similar substance (calcium sulphate), made into white or coloured sticks and used for drawing or writing. ● **v. 1** draw or write with chalk. ➤rub the tip of (a snooker cue) with chalk. **2** Brit. charge (drinks bought in a pub or bar) to a person's account. **3** (**chalk something up**) achieve something noteworthy.
– PHRASES **as different as chalk and cheese** Brit. fundamentally different or incompatible. **by a long chalk** Brit. by far. **chalk and talk** Brit. teaching by traditional methods focusing on the blackboard. **not by a long chalk** Brit. not at all. [with ref. to the chalk used for marking up scores in competitive games.]
– DERIVATIVES **chalkiness** n. **chalky** adj. (**-ier**, **-iest**).
– ORIGIN OE *cealc*, from L. *calx* (see **CALX**).

**chalkboard** ● **n.** North American term for **BLACKBOARD**.

**chalk-stripe** ● **adj.** (of a garment or material) having a pattern of thin white stripes on a dark background.
– DERIVATIVES **chalk-striped** adj.

**challah** /ˈhɑːlə, xɑːˈlɑː/ ● **n.** (pl. **challahs** or **chalot(h)** /xɑːˈlɒt/) a plaited loaf of white leavened bread, traditionally baked to celebrate the Jewish sabbath.
– ORIGIN 1920s: from Heb. *ḥallah*.

**challenge** ● **n. 1** a call to someone to participate in a contest or fight to decide who is superior. ➤a demanding task or situation. ➤an attempt to win a sporting contest. **2** a call to prove or justify something. **3** Medicine exposure of the immune system to pathogenic organisms or antigens. ● **v. 1** dispute the truth or validity of. ➤Law object to (a jury member). ➤(of a sentry) call on (someone) to prove their identity. **2** invite (someone) to engage in a contest. ➤compete with. ➤[usu. as adj. **challenging**] test the abilities of. **3** Medicine expose (the immune system) to pathogenic organisms or antigens.
– DERIVATIVES **challengeable** adj. **challenger** n. **challengingly** adv.
– ORIGIN ME: from OFr. *chalenge* (n.), *chalenger* (v.), from L. *calumnia* 'calumny', *calumniari* 'calumniate'.

**challenged** ● **adj. 1** euphemistic suffering from impairment or disability in a specified respect: *physically challenged*. **2** humorous lacking or deficient in a specified respect: *vertically challenged*.

**challis** /ˈʃalɪs, ˈʃali/ ● **n.** a lightweight soft clothing fabric made from silk and worsted.
– ORIGIN C19: origin uncertain.

**chalone** /ˈkaləʊn, ˈkeɪ-/ ● **n.** Biochemistry a substance secreted like a hormone but having the effect of inhibiting a physiological process.
– ORIGIN C20: from Gk *khalōn*, *khalaein* 'slacken', on the pattern of *hormone*.

**chalumeau** /ˈʃalʊməʊ/ ● **n.** (pl. **chalumeaux** pronunc. same) **1** a reed instrument of the early 18th century from which the clarinet was developed. **2** (also **chalumeau register**) the lowest octave of the clarinet's range.
– ORIGIN C18: from Fr., from L. *calamellus* 'little reed'.

**chalybeate** /kəˈlɪbɪət/ ● **adj.** of or denoting natural mineral springs containing iron salts.
– ORIGIN C17: from mod. L. *chalybeatus*, from L. *chalybs*,

from Gk *khalups, khalub-* 'steel'.

**Cham** /tʃam/ ● **n.** (pl. same or **Chams**) **1** a member of an indigenous people of Vietnam and Cambodia, whose culture is strongly influenced by that of India. **2** the Austronesian language of this people.

**chamaeleon** ● **n.** variant spelling of **CHAMELEON**.

**chamaephyte** /ˈkamɪfʌɪt/ ● **n.** Botany a woody plant whose resting buds are on or near the ground.
– ORIGIN C20: from Gk *khamai* 'on the ground' + **-PHYTE**.

**chamber** ● **n. 1** a large room used for formal or public events. **2** one of the houses of a parliament. **3** (**chambers**) Law, Brit. rooms used by a barrister or barristers, especially in the Inns of Court. ➤Law a judge's room used for official proceedings not required to be held in open court. **4** poetic/literary or archaic a private room, especially a bedroom. **5** an enclosed space or cavity. ➤the part of a gun bore that contains the charge. **6** [as modifier] Music of or for a small group of instruments: *a chamber orchestra.*
– DERIVATIVES **chambered** adj.
– ORIGIN ME: from OFr. *chambre*, from L. *camera* 'vault, arched chamber', from Gk *kamara* 'object with an arched cover'.

**chamberlain** /ˈtʃeɪmbəlɪn/ ● **n.** historical **1** an officer who managed the household of a monarch or noble. **2** Brit. an officer who received revenue on behalf of a corporation or public body.
– DERIVATIVES **chamberlainship** n.
– ORIGIN ME (denoting a servant in a bedchamber): via OFr. from Old Saxon *kamera*, from L. *camera* (see **CHAMBER**).

**chambermaid** ● **n.** a woman who cleans bedrooms and bathrooms in a hotel.

**chamber music** ● **n.** instrumental music played by a small ensemble, such as a string quartet, with one player to a part.

**Chamber of Commerce** ● **n.** a local association to promote and protect the interests of the business community.

**Chamber of Deputies** ● **n.** the lower legislative assembly in some parliaments.

**chamber of horrors** ● **n.** a place of entertainment containing instruments or scenes of torture or execution.
– ORIGIN C19: from the name given to a room in Madame Tussaud's waxwork exhibition.

**chamber organ** ● **n.** a movable pipe organ for playing in a small concert hall, chapel, or private house.

**chamber pot** ● **n.** a bowl kept in a bedroom and used as a toilet.

**Chambertin** /ˈʃɒ̃bəːtã/ ● **n.** a dry red burgundy wine of high quality from Gevrey Chambertin in eastern France.

**chambray** /ˈʃambreɪ/ ● **n.** a linen-finished gingham cloth with a white weft and a coloured warp, producing a mottled appearance.
– ORIGIN C19 (orig. US): formed irregularly from *Cambrai* (see **CAMBRIC**).

**chambré** /ˈʃɒmbreɪ, ˈʃɒ̃-/ ● **adj.** (of red wine) at room temperature.
– ORIGIN 1950s: Fr., past part. of *chambrer* 'bring to room temperature', from *chambre* (see **CHAMBER**).

**chameleon** /kəˈmiːlɪən/ (also **chamaeleon**) ● **n.** a small slow-moving lizard with a prehensile tail, long extensible tongue, protruding eyes, and the ability to change colour. [*Chamaeleo* and other genera, family Chamaeleonidae: numerous species.]
– DERIVATIVES **chameleonic** adj.
– ORIGIN ME: via L. *chamaeleon* from Gk *khamaileōn*, from *khamai* 'on the ground' + *leōn* 'lion'.

**chametz** /hɑːˈmɛts, ˈxɑːmɛts/ (also **chometz**) ● **n.** Judaism leaven or food mixed with leaven, prohibited during Passover.
– ORIGIN C19: from Heb. *ḥāmēṣ*.

**chamfer** /ˈtʃamfə/ Carpentry ● **v.** cut away (a right-angled edge or corner) to make a symmetrical sloping edge. ● **n.** a chamfered edge or corner.
– ORIGIN C16 (in the sense 'flute or furrow'): back-form. from *chamfering*, from Fr. *chamfrain*, from *chant* (see **CANT**²) + *fraint* 'broken'.

**chamise** /shəˈmiːz/ ● **n.** an evergreen shrub with small narrow leaves, common in the chaparral of California. [*Adenostoma fasciculatum.*]
– ORIGIN C19: from Mex. Sp. *chamiso.*

**chamois** ● **n. 1** /ˈʃamwɑː/ (pl. same /-wɑːz/) an agile goat-antelope with short hooked horns, found in mountainous areas of southern Europe. [Genus *Rupicapra*: two species.] **2** /ˈʃami, ˈʃamwɑː/ (pl. same /-mɪz, -wɑːz/) (also **chamois leather**) soft pliable leather made from the skin of sheep, goats, or deer.
– ORIGIN C16: from Fr.

**chamomile** /ˈkaməmʌɪl/ (also **camomile**) ● **n.** an aromatic plant of the daisy family, with white and yellow flowers. [*Chamaemelum nobile* (**sweet chamomile**) and other species.]
– ORIGIN ME: from OFr. *camomille*, from late L. *chamomilla*, from Gk *khamaimēlon* 'earth-apple' (because of the apple-like smell of its flowers).

**Chamorro** /tʃəˈmɒrəʊ/ ● **n.** (pl. same or **-os**) **1** a member of the indigenous people of Guam. **2** the Austronesian language of this people.

**champ**¹ ● **v. 1** munch enthusiastically or noisily. ➤(of a horse) make a noisy biting or chewing action. **2** fret impatiently.
– PHRASES **champ** (or **chafe**) **at the bit** be restlessly impatient to start doing something.
– ORIGIN ME: prob. imitative.

**champ**² ● **n.** informal a champion.

**champagne** /ʃamˈpeɪn/ ● **n.** a white sparkling wine from Champagne, a region in NE France.

**champagne socialist** ● **n.** Brit. derogatory a person who espouses socialist ideals while enjoying a wealthy and luxurious lifestyle.
– DERIVATIVES **champagne socialism** n.

**champaign** /ˈtʃampeɪn/ ● **n.** poetic/literary open level countryside.
– ORIGIN ME: from OFr. *champagne*, from late L. *campania*, based on L. *campus* 'level ground'.

**champak** /ˈtʃʌmpək, ˈtʃam-/ ● **n.** an Asian evergreen tree bearing fragrant orange flowers, sacred to Hindus and Buddhists. [*Michelia champaca.*]
– ORIGIN from Sanskrit *campaka.*

**champers** ● **n.** informal, chiefly Brit. champagne.

**champerty** /ˈtʃampəːti/ ● **n.** Law an illegal agreement in which a person with no previous interest in a lawsuit finances it with a view to sharing the disputed property if the suit succeeds.
– DERIVATIVES **champertous** adj.
– ORIGIN ME: from Anglo-Norman Fr. *champartie*, from OFr. *champart* 'feudal lord's share of produce', from L. *campus* 'field' + *pars* 'part'.

**champignon** /tʃamˈpɪnjən/ (also **fairy ring champignon**) ● **n.** a small edible mushroom with a light brown cap, growing in short grass and often forming fairy rings. [*Marasmius oreades.*]
– ORIGIN C16: from Fr., dimin. of OFr. *champagne* (see **CHAMPAIGN**).

**champion** ● **n. 1** a person who has surpassed all rivals in a sporting contest or other competition. **2** a defender of a cause or person. ➤historical a knight who fought in single combat on behalf of the monarch. ● **v.** support the cause of. ● **adj.** Brit. informal or dialect excellent. ● **adv.** Brit. informal or dialect very well.
– ORIGIN ME: from OFr., from med. L. *campio(n-)* 'fighter', from L. *campus* (see **CAMP**¹).

**Champion of England** ● **n.** (in the UK) a hereditary official who offers to defend the monarch's title to the throne at coronations.

**championship** ● **n. 1** a sporting contest for the position of champion. **2** the vigorous defence of a person or cause.

**champlevé** /ˌʃam(p)ləˈveɪ, ʃɒ̃ˈləveɪ/ ● **n.** enamelwork in which hollows made in a metal surface are filled with coloured enamels.
– ORIGIN Fr., from *champ* 'field' + *levé* 'raised'.

**chana** /ˈtʃʌnə/ (also **channa**) ● **n.** Indian chickpeas.
– ORIGIN from Hindi *canā.*

**chance** ● **n. 1** a possibility of something happening.

**2** (**chances**) the probability of something happening. **3** an opportunity. **4** the occurrence of events in the absence of any obvious design or cause: *he met his brother by chance*. ● **v. 1** do something by accident. ➤(**chance upon/on/across**) find or see by accident. **2** informal risk.
– PHRASES **by any chance** possibly. **chance one's arm** (or **luck**) Brit. informal risk doing something. **on the** (**off**) **chance** just in case. **stand a chance** [usu. with neg.] have a prospect of success or survival. **take a chance** (or **chances**) expose oneself to the risk of danger or failure. ➤(**take a chance on**) risk trusting. **take one's chance** do something risky with the hope of success.
– ORIGIN ME: from OFr. *cheance*, from *cheoir* 'fall, befall', based on L. *cadere*.

**chancel** /ˈtʃɑːns(ə)l/ ● **n.** the part of a church near the altar, reserved for the clergy and choir, and typically separated from the nave by steps or a screen.
– ORIGIN ME: from OFr., from L. *cancelli* 'crossbars'.

**chancellery** /ˈtʃɑːns(ə)l(ə)ri, -slәri/ ● **n.** (pl. **-ies**) **1** the position, office, or department of a chancellor. **2** chiefly US an office attached to an embassy or consulate.

**chancellor** ● **n.** a senior state or legal official of various kinds. ➤(**Chancellor**) the head of the government in some European countries, e.g. Germany. ➤chiefly Brit. the non-resident honorary head of a university. ➤US the presiding judge of a chancery court. ➤(in the UK) an officer of an order of knighthood who seals commissions.
– DERIVATIVES **chancellorship** n.
– ORIGIN OE from OFr. *cancelier*, from late L. *cancellarius* 'porter, secretary' (orig. a court official stationed at the grating separating public from judges), from *cancelli* 'crossbars'.

**Chancellor of the Duchy of Lancaster** ● **n.** (in the UK) a member of the government legally representing the Crown as Duke of Lancaster, typically a cabinet minister employed on non-departmental work.

**Chancellor of the Exchequer** ● **n.** the finance minister of the United Kingdom.

**chance-medley** ● **n.** Law, rare the killing of a person accidentally in self-defence in a fight.
– ORIGIN C15: from Anglo-Norman Fr. *chance medlee*, lit. 'mixed chance'.

**chancer** ● **n.** informal a person who exploits any opportunity to the utmost.

**chancery** ● **n.** (pl. **-ies**) **1** (**Chancery** or **Chancery Division**) Law (in the UK) the Lord Chancellor's court, a division of the High Court of Justice. **2** US a court of equity. ➤equity. **3** chiefly Brit. an office attached to an embassy or consulate. **4** a public record office.
– ORIGIN ME: contr. of **CHANCELLERY**.

**chancre** /ˈʃaŋkә/ ● **n.** Medicine a painless ulcer, particularly one developing on the genitals in venereal disease.
– ORIGIN C16: from Fr., from L. *cancer* 'creeping ulcer'.

**chancroid** /ˈʃaŋkrɔɪd/ ● **n.** a venereal infection causing ulceration of the lymph nodes in the groin.

**chancy** ● **adj.** (**-ier**, **-iest**) informal uncertain; risky.
– DERIVATIVES **chancily** adv. **chanciness** n.

**chandelier** /ˌʃandәˈlɪә/ ● **n.** a large decorative hanging light with branches for several light bulbs or candles.
– ORIGIN C18: from Fr., from *chandelle* 'candle'.

**chandler** /ˈtʃɑːndlә/ ● **n. 1** (also **ship chandler**) a dealer in supplies and equipment for ships and boats. **2** historical a dealer in household items such as oil and groceries.
– DERIVATIVES **chandlery** n.
– ORIGIN ME (denoting a candlemaker or candle seller): from OFr. *chandelier*, from *chandelle* (see **CHANDELIER**).

**change** ● **v. 1** make or become different. ➤(of the moon) arrive at a fresh phase; become new. **2** take or use another instead of. ➤move from one to (another): *she had to change trains*. ➤(**change over**) move from one system or situation to another. ➤remove (something dirty or faulty) and replace it with another of the same kind. ➤engage a different gear in a motor vehicle. **3** exchange (a sum of money) for the same sum in a different currency or denomination. ● **n. 1** the action of changing. ➤an instance of becoming different. ➤(**the change** or **the change of life**) informal the menopause. **2** a clean garment or garments as a replacement for something one is wearing. **3** coins as opposed to banknotes. ➤money given in exchange for the same sum in larger units. ➤money returned to someone as the balance of the sum paid. **4** an order in which a peal of bells can be rung.
– PHRASES **change colour** blanch or flush. **change hands** (of a business or building) pass to a different owner. ➤(of money or a marketable commodity) pass to another person in the course of a business transaction. **a change of air** a different climate, typically as means of improving one's health. **change step** alter one's step so that the opposite leg is the one that marks time when marching. **change one's tune** express a very different opinion or behave in a very different way. **for a change** contrary to how things usually happen or in order to introduce variety. **get no change out of** Brit. informal fail to get information or a desired reaction from. **ring the changes** vary the ways of doing something. [with allusion to the different orders in which a peal of bells may be rung.]
– DERIVATIVES **changeful** adj. **changeless** adj. **changelessly** adv. **changelessness** n. **changer** n.
– ORIGIN ME: from OFr. *change* (n.), *changer* (v.), from late L. *cambiare*, from L. *cambire* 'barter'.

**changeable** ● **adj. 1** liable to unpredictable variation. **2** able to be changed or exchanged.
– DERIVATIVES **changeability** n. **changeableness** n. **changeably** adv.

**changeling** ● **n.** a child believed to have been secretly substituted by fairies for the parents' real child in infancy.

**changement de pieds** /ˌʃɒ̃(d)ʒmɒ̃ dә ˈpjeɪ/ (also **changement**) ● **n.** (pl. **changements de pieds** pronunc. same) Ballet a leap during which a dancer changes the position of the feet.
– ORIGIN C19: Fr.

**changeover** ● **n.** a change from one system or situation to another.

**change-ringing** ● **n.** the ringing of sets of church bells or handbells in a constantly varying order.
– DERIVATIVES **change-ringer** n.

**change-up** ● **n.** Baseball an unexpectedly slow pitch designed to throw off the batter's timing.

**channa** /ˈtʃʌnә/ ● **n.** variant spelling of **CHANA**.

**channel** ● **n. 1** a length of water wider than a strait, joining two larger areas of water, especially two seas. ➤(**the Channel**) the English Channel. ➤a navigable passage in a stretch of water otherwise unsafe for vessels. **2** Biology a tubular passage or duct for liquid. **3** an electric circuit which acts as a path for a signal. **4** a band of frequencies used in radio and television transmission, especially as used by a particular station. **5** a medium for communication or the passage of information. ● **v.** (**channelled**, **channelling**; US **channeled**, **channeling**) **1** direct towards a particular end. ➤cause to pass along or through a specified route or medium. **2** [usu. as adj. **channelled**] form channels or grooves in.
– ORIGIN ME: from OFr. *chanel*, from L. *canalis* 'pipe, groove, channel', from *canna* (see **CANE**); cf. **CANAL**.

**channel-hop** ● **v.** informal **1** change frequently from one television channel to another, using a remote control device. **2** make frequent or brief trips across the English Channel and back to Britain.
– DERIVATIVES **channel-hopper** n.

**channelize** (also **-ise**) ● **v.** chiefly N. Amer. another term for **CHANNEL** (in sense 1).

**channel-surf** ● **v.** informal, chiefly N. Amer. another term for **CHANNEL-HOP** (in sense 1).

**chanson** /ˈʃɒ̃sɒ̃, French ʃɑ̃sɔ̃/ ● **n.** a French song.
– ORIGIN Fr., from L. *cantio(n-)* 'singing', from *canere* 'sing'.

**chanson de geste** /ˌʃɒ̃sɒ̃ dә ˈʒɛst, French ʃɑ̃sɔ̃dә ʒɛst/ ● **n.** (pl. **chansons de geste** pronunc. same) a French historical verse romance of the Middle Ages.
– ORIGIN Fr., lit. 'song of heroic deeds', from *chanson* (see **CHANSON**) and *geste* from L. *gesta* 'actions, exploits'.

**chant** ● **n. 1** a repeated rhythmic phrase, typically one shouted or sung in unison by a crowd. **2** a monotonous or

repetitive song, typically an incantation or part of a ritual. **3** Music a short musical passage in two or more phrases used for singing unmetrical words; a psalm or canticle sung to such music. ● **v.** say or shout repeatedly in a sing-song tone. ➤ sing or intone (a psalm, canticle, or sacred text).
– ORIGIN ME: from OFr. *chanter* 'sing', from L. *cantare*, frequentative of *canere* 'sing'.

**chanter** ● **n.** Music the pipe of a bagpipe with finger holes, on which the melody is played.

**chanterelle** /ˈtʃɑːntərɛl, ˌtʃɑːntəˈrɛl/ ● **n.** an edible woodland mushroom which has a yellow funnel-shaped cap and a faint smell of apricots. [*Cantharellus cibarius*.]
– ORIGIN C18: from Fr., from mod. L. *cantharellus*, dimin. of *cantharus*, from Gk *kantharos*, denoting a kind of drinking container.

**chanteuse** /ʃɑːnˈtəːz, French ʃɑ̃tøz/ ● **n.** a female singer of popular songs.
– ORIGIN Fr., from *chanter* 'sing'.

**chanticleer** /ˈtʃɑːntɪˌklɪə/ ● **n.** poetic/literary a name given to a domestic cock, especially in fairy tales.
– ORIGIN ME: from OFr. *Chantecler*, the name of the cock in the fable *Reynard the Fox*, from *chanter* (see **CHANT**) + *cler* 'clear'.

**Chantilly cream** /ʃanˈtɪli/ ● **n.** sweetened or flavoured whipped cream.
– ORIGIN C19: named after *Chantilly*, a town near Paris, where it originated.

**Chantilly lace** ● **n.** a delicate kind of bobbin lace.

**chantry** /ˈtʃɑːntri/ ● **n.** (pl. **-ies**) a chapel, altar, or other part of a church endowed for the celebration of masses for the donor's soul.
– ORIGIN ME: from OFr. *chanterie*, from *chanter* 'to sing'.

**chanty** /ˈʃanti/ ● **n.** (pl. **-ies**) variant spelling of **SHANTY**[2].

**Chanukkah** ● **n.** variant spelling of **HANUKKAH**.

**chaology** /keɪˈɒlədʒi/ ● **n.** Physics the study of chaotic systems.
– DERIVATIVES **chaologist** n.

**chaos** /ˈkeɪɒs/ ● **n.** **1** complete disorder and confusion. ➤ Physics behaviour so unpredictable as to appear random, owing to great sensitivity to small changes in conditions. **2** the formless matter supposed to have existed before the creation of the universe.
– DERIVATIVES **chaotic** adj. **chaotically** adv.
– ORIGIN C15 (denoting a gaping void): via Fr. and L. from Gk *khaos* 'vast chasm, void'.

**chap**[1] ● **v.** (**chapped**, **chapping**) (of the skin) crack and become sore, typically through exposure to cold weather. ➤ [usu. as adj. **chapped**] (of the wind or cold) cause (skin) to crack in this way. ● **n.** a chapped area.
– ORIGIN ME: of unknown origin.

**chap**[2] ● **n.** informal, chiefly Brit. a man or a boy.
– ORIGIN C16 (denoting a buyer or customer): abbrev. of **CHAPMAN**.

**chap**[3] ● **n.** the lower jaw or half of the cheek, especially that of a pig used as food.
– ORIGIN C16: of unknown origin; cf. **CHOPS**.

**chap.** ● **abbrev.** chapter.

**chaparajos** /ˌʃapəˈreɪhəʊs, ˌtʃ-/ (also **chaparejos**) ● **pl. n.** N. Amer. leather trousers without a seat, worn by a cowboy over ordinary trousers to protect the legs.
– ORIGIN C19: from Mex. Sp. *chaparreras*, from *chaparra* (with ref. to protection from thorny vegetation: see **CHAPARRAL**).

**chaparral** /ˌʃapəˈral, ˌtʃ-/ ● **n.** N. Amer. vegetation consisting chiefly of tangled shrubs and thorny bushes.
– ORIGIN C19: from Sp., from *chaparra* 'dwarf evergreen oak'.

**chapatti** /tʃəˈpɑːti, -ˈpati/ ● **n.** (pl. **chapattis**) (in Indian cookery) a thin pancake of unleavened wholemeal bread cooked on a griddle.
– ORIGIN from Hindi *capātī*, from *capānā* 'roll out'.

**chapbook** ● **n.** historical a small pamphlet containing tales, ballads, or tracts, sold by pedlars.
– ORIGIN C19: from **CHAPMAN** + **BOOK**.

**chape** /tʃeɪp/ ● **n.** **1** historical the metal point of a scabbard. **2** the metal pin of a buckle.
– ORIGIN ME: from OFr., lit. 'cape, hood', from late L. *cappa* 'cap'.

**chapeau** /ˈʃapəʊ/ ● **n.** (pl. **chapeaux**) Heraldry a hat or cap, typically a red one with an ermine lining, on which the crests of some peers are borne.
– ORIGIN C15: from Fr., from L. *cappellum*, dimin. of *cappa* 'cap'.

**chapel** ● **n.** **1** a small building for Christian worship, typically one attached to an institution or private house. ➤ a part of a large church or cathedral with its own altar and dedication. ➤ Brit. a place of worship for Nonconformist congregations. **2** Brit. the members or branch of a print or newspaper trade union at a particular place of work.
– ORIGIN ME: from OFr. *chapele*, from med. L. *cappella*, dimin. of *cappa* 'cap or cape' (the first chapel being a sanctuary in which St Martin's cloak was preserved).

**chapel of ease** ● **n.** an Anglican chapel situated for the convenience of parishioners living a long distance from the parish church.

**chapel of rest** ● **n.** Brit. an undertaker's mortuary.

**chapelry** ● **n.** (pl. **-ies**) a district served by an Anglican chapel.

**chaperone** /ˈʃapərəʊn/ (also **chaperon** /ˈʃapərɒn/) ● **n.** dated an older woman responsible for the decorous behaviour of a young unmarried girl at social occasions. ● **v.** accompany and look after.
– DERIVATIVES **chaperonage** /ˈʃap(ə)r(ə)ˌnɪdʒ/ n.
– ORIGIN ME (denoting a hood or cap): from Fr., fem. of *chaperon* 'hood', dimin. of *chape* (see **CHAPE**).

**chaperonin** /ˌʃapəˈrəʊnɪn/ ● **n.** Biochemistry a protein that aids the formation of other protein molecules in living cells.

**chap-fallen** ● **adj.** archaic with one's lower jaw hanging due to extreme exhaustion or dejection.

**chaplain** ● **n.** a member of the clergy attached to a private chapel, institution, regiment, etc.
– DERIVATIVES **chaplaincy** n.
– ORIGIN ME: from OFr. *chapelain*, from med. L. *cappellanus*, orig. denoting a custodian of the cloak of St Martin, from *cappella* (see **CHAPEL**).

**chaplet** /ˈtʃaplɪt/ ● **n.** **1** a circlet for a person's head. **2** a string of 55 beads (one third of the rosary number) for counting prayers. **3** a metal support for the core of a hollow casting mould.
– DERIVATIVES **chapleted** adj.
– ORIGIN ME: from OFr. *chapelet*, dimin. of *chapel* 'hat', based on late L. *cappa* 'cap'.

**Chaplinesque** /tʃaplɪnˈɛsk/ ● **adj.** resembling or characteristic of the style of comedy of the English film actor and director Charlie Chaplin (1889–1977).

**chapman** ● **n.** (pl. **-men**) archaic a pedlar.
– ORIGIN OE *cēapman*, from *cēap* 'bargaining, trade' (see **CHEAP**) + **MAN**.

**chappal** /ˈtʃap(ə)l/ ● **n.** Indian a sandal.
– ORIGIN from Hindi *cappal*.

**chaps** ● **pl. n.** short for **CHAPARAJOS**.

**chaptalization** /ˌtʃaptəlʌɪˈzeɪʃ(ə)n/ (also **-isation**) ● **n.** (in winemaking) the correction or improvement of must by the addition of calcium carbonate or sugar.
– DERIVATIVES **chaptalize** (also **-ise**) v.
– ORIGIN C19: from the name of Jean A. *Chaptal*, the Fr. chemist who invented the process.

**chapter** ● **n.** **1** a main division of a book. ➤ an Act of Parliament numbered as part of a session's proceedings. **2** a particular period in history or in a person's life. **3** the governing body of a cathedral or other religious community, or of a knightly order. **4** chiefly N. Amer. a local branch of a society.
– PHRASES **chapter and verse** an exact reference or authority. **a chapter of accidents** a series of unfortunate events.
– ORIGIN ME: from OFr. *chapitre*, from L. *capitulum*, dimin. of *caput* 'head'.

**Chapter 11** ● **n.** (in the US) protection from creditors given to a company in financial difficulties for a limited period to allow it to reorganize.

– ORIGIN with allusion to chapter 11 of the US bankruptcy code.

**chapter house** ● **n.** a building used for the meetings of a chapter. ➤US a place where a college fraternity or sorority meets.

**char**[1] /tʃɑː/ ● **v.** (**charred**, **charring**) partially burn so as to blacken the surface. ● **n.** charred material.
– ORIGIN C17: appar. a back-form. from CHARCOAL.

**char**[2] /tʃɑː/ Brit. informal ● **n.** a charwoman. ● **v.** (**charred**, **charring**) work as a charwoman.

**char**[3] /tʃɑː/ (also **cha** /tʃɑː/ or **chai** /tʃʌɪ/) ● **n.** Brit. informal tea.
– ORIGIN C16 (as *cha*): from Chin. (Mandarin dial.) *chá*.

**char**[4] ● **n.** variant spelling of CHARR.

**charabanc** /ˈʃarəbaŋ/ ● **n.** Brit. an early form of bus.
– ORIGIN C19: from Fr. *char-à-bancs* 'carriage with benches'.

**characin** /ˈkarəsɪn/ ● **n.** a small freshwater fish of a tropical family (Characidae) including the piranhas and tetras. [Family Characidae.]
– ORIGIN C19: from mod. L. *Characinus* (genus name), from Gk *kharax* 'pointed stake'.

**character** ● **n.** **1** the mental and moral qualities distinctive to an individual. ➤strength and originality in a person's nature. ➤a person's good reputation. **2** the distinctive nature of something. **3** a person in a novel, play, or film. ➤a part played by an actor. **4** informal an interesting, eccentric, or amusing person. **5** a printed or written letter or symbol. ➤Computing a symbol representing a letter or number. **6** chiefly Biology a characteristic, especially one that assists in the identification of a species. ● **v.** archaic inscribe or write (something). ➤describe.
– DERIVATIVES **characterful** adj. **characterfully** adv. **characterless** adj.
– ORIGIN ME (in the sense 'distinctive mark', later 'feature or trait'): from OFr. *caractere*, via L. from Gk *kharaktēr* 'a stamping tool'.

**character actor** ● **n.** an actor who specializes in playing eccentric or unusual people rather than leading roles.

**characteristic** ● **adj.** typical of a particular person, place, or thing. ● **n.** **1** a feature or quality typical of a person, place, or thing. **2** Mathematics the whole number or integral part of a logarithm.
– DERIVATIVES **characteristically** adv.

**characteristic curve** ● **n.** a graph showing the relationship between two variable but interdependent quantities.

**characteristic radiation** ● **n.** radiation consisting of wavelengths which are peculiar to the element which emits them.

**characterize** (also **-ise**) ● **v.** **1** describe the distinctive character of. **2** (of a feature or quality) be characteristic of.
– DERIVATIVES **characterization** n.

**character recognition** ● **n.** the identification by electronic means of printed or written characters.

**charade** /ʃəˈrɑːd/ ● **n.** **1** an absurd pretence intended to create a pleasant impression. **2** (**charades**) [treated as sing.] a game of guessing a word or phrase from a written or acted clue given for each syllable and for the whole item.
– ORIGIN C18: from Fr., from mod. Provençal *charrado* 'conversation'.

**charango** /tʃəˈraŋgəʊ/ ● **n.** (pl. **-os**) a small Andean guitar, traditionally made from an armadillo shell.
– ORIGIN 1920s: from Latin Amer. Sp.

**charas** /ˈtʃɑːrəs/ ● **n.** cannabis resin.
– ORIGIN from Hindi *caras*.

**charbroil** ● **v.** [usu. as adj. **charbroiled**] N. Amer. grill (food, especially meat) on a rack over charcoal.

**charcoal** ● **n.** **1** a porous black form of carbon obtained as a residue when wood or other organic matter is heated in the absence of air. ➤a stick of this used for drawing. **2** a dark grey colour.
– ORIGIN ME: prob. rel. to COAL in the early sense 'charcoal'.

**charcuterie** /ʃɑːˈkuːt(ə)ri/ ● **n.** (pl. **-ies**) **1** cold cooked meats collectively. **2** a shop selling such meats.
– ORIGIN Fr., from obs. *char* (earlier form of *chair*) 'flesh' + *cuite* 'cooked'.

**chard** /tʃɑːd/ ● **n.** (also **Swiss chard**) a beet of a variety with edible broad white leaf stalks and green blades.
– ORIGIN C17: from Fr. *carde*, perh. influenced by *chardon* 'thistle'.

**Chardonnay** /ˈʃɑːdəneɪ/ ● **n.** a variety of white wine grape used for making champagne and other wines. ➤a wine made from this grape.
– ORIGIN from Fr.

**charentais** /ˈʃarənteɪ/ ● **n.** a melon of a small variety with a pale green rind and orange flesh.
– ORIGIN Fr., lit. 'from the Charentes region'.

**charge** ● **v.** **1** demand (an amount) as a price for a service rendered or goods supplied. **2** accuse (someone) of something, especially an offence under law. **3** entrust with a task. **4** store electrical energy in (a battery or battery-operated device). **5** technical or formal load or fill (a container, gun, etc.) to the full or proper extent. ➤fill with a quality or emotion: *the air was charged with menace.* **6** rush forward in attack. ➤move quickly and with impetus. **7** Heraldry place a charge on. ● **n.** **1** a price asked. ➤a financial liability or commitment. **2** a formal accusation made against a prisoner brought to trial. **3** responsibility for care or control. ➤a person or thing entrusted to someone's care. **4** the property of matter that is responsible for electrical phenomena, existing in a positive or negative form. ➤the quantity of this carried by a body. ➤energy stored chemically in a battery for conversion into electricity. **5** a quantity of explosive to be detonated in order to fire a gun or similar weapon. **6** a headlong rush forward, typically in attack. **7** an official instruction given by a judge to a jury regarding points of law. **8** Heraldry a device or bearing placed on a shield or crest.
– PHRASES **press** (or **prefer**) **charges** accuse someone formally of a crime so that they can be brought to trial. **put someone on a charge** Brit. charge someone with a specified offence.
– DERIVATIVES **chargeable** adj. **charged** adj.
– ORIGIN ME, from OFr. *charger* (v.), *charge* (n.), from late L. *carricare, carcare* 'to load', from L. *carrus* 'wheeled vehicle'.

**charge account** ● **n.** an account to which goods and services may be charged on credit.

**charge-cap** ● **v.** [often as noun **charge-capping**] Brit. (of a government) subject (a local authority) to an upper limit on the charges it may levy on the public for services.

**charge card** ● **n.** a credit card for use with an account which must be paid in full when a statement is issued.

**charge carrier** ● **n.** an electron, ion, etc. which carries electric charge in a conductor or semiconductor.

**charge-coupled device** ● **n.** a high-speed semiconductor device used chiefly in image detection.

**chargé d'affaires** /ˌʃɑːʒeɪ daˈfɛː, French ʃarʒe dafɛʀ/ (also **chargé**) ● **n.** (pl. **chargés** pronunc. same) an ambassador's deputy. ➤a state's diplomatic representative in a minor country.
– ORIGIN C18: Fr., '(a person) in charge of affairs'.

**chargehand** ● **n.** Brit. a worker with supervisory duties ranking below a foreman.

**charge nurse** ● **n.** Brit. a nurse in charge of a ward in a hospital.

**charger**[1] ● **n.** **1** a device for charging a battery or battery-powered equipment. **2** a horse ridden by a knight or cavalryman.

**charger**[2] ● **n.** archaic a large flat dish.
– ORIGIN ME: from Anglo-Norman Fr. *chargeour*, from *chargier* 'to load', from late L. *carricare, carcare* (see CHARGE).

**chargrill** ● **v.** [usu. as adj. **chargrilled**] grill (food, typically meat or fish) quickly at a very high heat.
– ORIGIN C20: on the pattern of *charbroil*.

**chariot** ● **n.** **1** a two-wheeled vehicle drawn by horses, used in ancient warfare and racing. **2** historical a four-wheeled carriage with back seats and a coachman's seat. **3** poetic/literary a stately or triumphal carriage. ● **v.** poetic/

literary convey in or as in a chariot.
– DERIVATIVES **charioteer** n.
– ORIGIN ME: from OFr., augmentative of *char* 'cart', based on L. *carrus* 'wheeled vehicle'.

**charisma** /kə'rɪzmə/ • **n. 1** compelling attractiveness or charm that can inspire devotion. **2** (pl. **charismata** /kə'rɪzmətə/) a divinely conferred power or talent.
– ORIGIN C17: via eccles. L. from Gk *kharisma*, from *kharis* 'favour, grace'.

**charismatic** • **adj. 1** having charisma. **2** of or relating to the charismatic movement. ➤(of a power or talent) divinely conferred. • **n.** an adherent of the charismatic movement. ➤a person who claims divine inspiration.
– DERIVATIVES **charismatically** adv.

**charismatic movement** • **n.** a fundamentalist movement within the Roman Catholic, Anglican, and other Christian Churches that emphasizes talents held to be conferred by the Holy Spirit.

**charitable** • **adj. 1** of or relating to the assistance of those in need. ➤officially recognized as a charity. ➤generous in giving to those in need. **2** tolerant in judging others.
– DERIVATIVES **charitableness** n. **charitably** adv.

**charity** • **n.** (pl. **-ies**) **1** an organization set up to provide help and raise money for those in need. **2** the voluntary giving of money to those in need. ➤help or money given in this way. **3** tolerance in judging others. **4** archaic love of humankind, typically in a Christian context.
– ORIGIN OE: from OFr. *charite*, from L. *caritas*, from *carus* 'dear'.

**charivari** /ˌʃɑːrɪ'vɑːri/ (chiefly US also **shivaree**) • **n.** (pl. **charivaris**) **1** chiefly historical a cacophonous mock serenade, performed by a group of people to mock an unpopular person or to celebrate a marriage. **2** a series of discordant noises.
– ORIGIN C17: from Fr.

**charkha** /'tʃəːkə/ (also **charka**) • **n.** (in the Indian subcontinent) a domestic spinning wheel used chiefly for cotton.
– ORIGIN from Urdu *charḵa* 'spinning wheel', from Pers.

**charlady** • **n.** (pl. **-ies**) Brit. a charwoman.

**charlatan** /'ʃɑːlət(ə)n/ • **n.** a person falsely claiming to have a special knowledge or skill.
– DERIVATIVES **charlatanism** n. **charlatanry** n.
– ORIGIN C17 (denoting an itinerant seller of supposed remedies): from Fr., from Ital. *ciarlatano*, from *ciarlare* 'to babble'.

**Charles's law** • **n.** Chemistry a law stating that the volume of an ideal gas at constant pressure is directly proportional to the absolute temperature.
– ORIGIN C19: named after the Fr. physicist Jacques A. C. *Charles*.

**charleston** • **n.** a lively dance of the 1920s which involved turning the knees inwards and kicking out the lower legs.
– ORIGIN 1920s: named after the city of *Charleston* in South Carolina, US.

**charley horse** • **n.** N. Amer. informal a cramp or feeling of stiffness in a limb.
– ORIGIN C19: of unknown origin.

**charlie** • **n.** (pl. **-ies**) **1** Brit. informal a fool. **2** (**charlies**) Brit. informal, dated a woman's breasts. **3** informal cocaine. **4** a code word representing the letter C, used in radio communication.
– ORIGIN C19: dimin. of the male given name *Charles*.

**charlock** /'tʃɑːlɒk/ • **n.** a wild mustard with yellow flowers. [*Sinapis arvensis*.]
– ORIGIN OE *cerlic, cyrlic*; of unknown origin.

**charlotte** • **n.** a pudding made of stewed fruit with a casing or covering of bread, sponge cake, biscuits, or breadcrumbs.
– ORIGIN Fr., from the female given name *Charlotte*.

**charlotte russe** /'ruːs/ • **n.** a pudding consisting of custard enclosed in sponge cake or a casing of sponge fingers.
– ORIGIN Fr., lit. 'Russian charlotte'.

**charm** • **n. 1** the power or quality of delighting, attracting, or fascinating others. ➤an attractive characteristic or feature. **2** a small ornament worn on a necklace or bracelet. **3** an object, act, or saying believed to have magic power. **4** Physics one of six flavours of quark. • **v. 1** delight greatly. ➤use one's charm in order to influence someone. **2** control or achieve by or as if by magic.
– DERIVATIVES **charmer** n. **charmless** adj. **charmlessly** adv. **charmlessness** n.
– ORIGIN ME: from OFr. *charme* (n.), *charmer* (v.), from L. *carmen* 'song, verse, incantation'.

**charmed** • **adj.** (of a person's life) unusually lucky as though protected by magic. • **exclam.** dated expressing polite pleasure at an introduction: *charmed, I'm sure.*

**charmeuse** /ʃɑː'məːz/ • **n.** a soft smooth silky dress fabric.
– ORIGIN C20: from Fr., fem. of *charmeur* 'charmer'.

**charming** • **adj. 1** delightful; attractive. **2** very polite, friendly, and likeable. • **exclam.** used as an ironic expression of displeasure or disapproval.
– DERIVATIVES **charmingly** adv.

**charm offensive** • **n.** a campaign of flattery, friendliness, and cajolement designed to achieve the support of others.

**charm school** • **n.** a school where young women are taught social graces such as deportment and etiquette.

**charnel house** • **n.** historical a building or vault in which corpses or bones are piled.
– ORIGIN C16: from ME *charnel* 'burying place', from OFr., from med. L. *carnale*, from late L. *carnalis* 'relating to flesh', from *caro, carn-* 'flesh'.

**Charolais** /'ʃarə(ʊ)leɪ/ • **n.** (pl. same) an animal of a breed of large white beef cattle.
– ORIGIN C19: named after the *Monts du Charollais*, hills in eastern France where the breed originated.

**charophyte** /'kɑːrə(ʊ)ˌfʌɪt, 'karə(ʊ)-, 'tʃarə(ʊ)-/ • **n.** Botany a plant of a division (Charophyta) that includes the stoneworts.
– ORIGIN mod. L. *Charophyta*, from *Chara* (genus name) + *phuta* 'plants'.

**charpoy** /'tʃɑːpɔɪ/ • **n.** Indian a light bedstead.
– ORIGIN C17: from Urdu *cārpāī* 'four-legged', from Pers.

**charr** /tʃɑː/ (also **char**) • **n.** (pl. same) a trout-like northern freshwater or marine fish. [Genus *Salvelinus*: several species.]
– ORIGIN C17: perh. of Celtic origin.

**charro** /'tʃɑːrəʊ/ • **n.** (pl. **-os**) a Mexican cowboy.
– ORIGIN Mex. Sp., from Sp., lit. 'rustic'.

**chart** • **n. 1** a sheet of information in the form of a table, graph, or diagram. ➤(**the charts**) a weekly listing of the current best-selling pop records. **2** a geographical map, especially one used for navigation by sea or air. • **v. 1** make a map of. ➤plot (a course) on a chart. **2** (of a record) sell enough copies to enter the charts at a particular position.
– ORIGIN C16: from Fr. *charte*, from L. *charta* (see CARD[1]).

**charter** • **n. 1** a written grant by a sovereign or legislature, by which a body such as a university is created or its rights and privileges defined. **2** a written constitution or description of an organization's functions. **3** (in the UK) a written statement of the rights of a specified group of people: *the patient's charter.* **4** the hiring of an aircraft, ship, or motor vehicle. • **v. 1** [usu. as adj. **chartered**] grant a charter to (a city, university, etc.). **2** hire (an aircraft, ship, or motor vehicle).
– DERIVATIVES **charterer** n.
– ORIGIN ME: from OFr. *chartre*, from L. *chartula*, dimin. of *charta* (see CARD[1]).

**chartered** • **adj.** Brit. (of an accountant, engineer, librarian, etc.) qualified as a member of a professional body that has a royal charter.

**charter flight** • **n.** a flight by an aircraft chartered for a specific journey, not part of an airline's regular schedule.

**charter member** • **n.** chiefly N. Amer. an original or founding member of a society or organization.

**charter party** • **n.** a deed between a shipowner and a merchant for the hire of a ship and the delivery of cargo.
– ORIGIN ME: from Fr. *charte partie*, from med. L. *charta*

*partita* 'divided charter'.

**charter school** ● **n.** (in North America) a publicly funded independent school established by teachers, parents, or community groups under the terms of a charter with a local or national authority.

**Chartism** ● **n.** a UK parliamentary reform movement of 1837–48, the principles of which were set out in a manifesto called *The People's Charter.*
– DERIVATIVES **Chartist** n. & adj.

**chartreuse** /ʃɑːˈtrəːz/ ● **n. 1** a pale green or yellow liqueur made from brandy and aromatic herbs. **2** a pale green or yellow colour. **3** a dish of fruit set in jelly.
– ORIGIN named after *La Grande Chartreuse*, the Carthusian monastery near Grenoble where the liqueur was first made.

**charwoman** ● **n.** (pl. **-women**) Brit. dated a woman employed as a cleaner in a house or office.
– ORIGIN C16: from obs. *char* or *chare* 'a chore' (obscurely rel. to **CHORE**) + **WOMAN**.

**chary** /ˈtʃɛːri/ ● **adj.** (**-ier**, **-iest**) cautiously or suspiciously reluctant: *leaders are chary of major reform.*
– DERIVATIVES **charily** adv.
– ORIGIN OE *cearig* 'sorrowful, anxious', of W. Gmc origin; rel. to **CARE**.

**Chas** ● **abbrev.** Charles.

**chase**[1] ● **v. 1** pursue in order to catch or catch up with. **2** rush or cause to go in a specified direction. **3** try to obtain (something owed or required). ➤make further investigation of (an unresolved matter). ● **n. 1** an act of chasing. **2** (**the chase**) hunting as a sport. ➤Brit. (in place names) an area of unenclosed land formerly reserved for hunting: *Cannock Chase.*
– PHRASES **give chase** go in pursuit. **go and chase oneself** informal go away.
– ORIGIN ME: from OFr. *chacier* (v.), *chace* (n.), based on L. *captare* 'continue to take', from *capere* 'take'.

**chase**[2] ● **v.** [usu. as adj. **chased**] decorate (metal) by engraving or inlaying.
– ORIGIN ME: appar. from earlier *enchase*, from OFr. *enchasser* (see **ENCHASE**).

**chase**[3] ● **n.** (in letterpress printing) a metal frame for holding the composed type and blocks being printed at one time.
– ORIGIN C16: from Fr. *châsse*, from L. *capsa* (see **CASE**[2]).

**chase**[4] ● **n. 1** the part of a gun enclosing the bore. **2** a groove or furrow cut in the face of a wall or other surface to receive a pipe.
– ORIGIN C17: from Fr. *chas* 'enclosed space'.

**chaser** ● **n. 1** a person or thing that chases. **2** a horse for steeplechasing. **3** informal a strong alcoholic drink taken after a weaker one.

**Chasid** /ˈxasɪd/ ● **n.** variant spelling of **HASID**.

**Chasidism** /ˈxasɪdɪz(ə)m/ ● **n.** variant spelling of **HASIDISM**.

**chasm** /ˈkaz(ə)m/ ● **n. 1** a deep fissure. **2** a profound difference between people, viewpoints, feelings, etc.
– DERIVATIVES **chasmic** adj. (rare).
– ORIGIN C16: from L. *chasma*, from Gk *khasma* 'gaping hollow'.

**chasse** /ʃas/ ● **n.** a liqueur drunk after coffee.
– ORIGIN Fr., abbrev. of *chasse-café*, lit. 'chase-coffee'.

**chassé** /ˈʃaseɪ/ ● **n.** a gliding step in dancing in which one foot displaces the other. ● **v.** (**chasséd**, **chasséing**) make such a step.
– ORIGIN Fr., lit. 'chased'.

**Chasselas** /ˈʃas(ə)lɑː/ ● **n.** a variety of white grape, grown for wine or for eating. ➤a wine made from this grape.
– ORIGIN named after a village near Mâcon, France.

**chasseur** /ʃaˈsəː, French ʃasœʀ/ ● **n.** (pl. pronounced same) historical a soldier equipped and trained for rapid movement, especially in the French army.
– ORIGIN C18: Fr., lit. 'huntsman', from *chasser* 'to chase'.

**chasseur sauce** ● **n.** a rich, dark sauce with wine and mushrooms, typically served with poultry or game.

**Chassid** /ˈxasɪd/ ● **n.** variant spelling of **HASID**.

**Chassidism** /ˈxasɪˌdɪz(ə)m/ ● **n.** variant spelling of **HASIDISM**.

**chassis** /ˈʃasi, -iː/ ● **n.** (pl. same /-sɪz/) **1** the base frame of a motor vehicle, carriage, or other wheeled conveyance. **2** the outer structural framework of a piece of audio, radio, or computer equipment.
– ORIGIN C20: from Fr. *châssis* 'frame', based on L. *capsa* (see **CASE**[2]).

**chaste** ● **adj. 1** abstaining from extramarital, or from all, sexual intercourse. **2** without unnecessary ornamentation.
– DERIVATIVES **chastely** adv. **chasteness** n. **chastity** n.
– ORIGIN ME: from OFr., from L. *castus*.

**chasten** /ˈtʃeɪs(ə)n/ ● **v. 1** (of a reproof or misfortune) have a restraining or demoralizing effect on. **2** archaic (especially of God) discipline; punish.
– DERIVATIVES **chastener** n.
– ORIGIN C16: from an obs. verb *chaste*, from OFr. *chastier*, from L. *castigare* 'castigate', from *castus* 'chaste'.

**chaste tree** ● **n.** an ornamental shrub with blue or white flowers. [*Vitex agnus-castus.*]
– ORIGIN C16: so named because of its assoc. with chastity in sacrifices to Ceres (the Roman goddess of agriculture).

**chastise** ● **v.** reprimand severely. ➤dated punish, especially by beating.
– DERIVATIVES **chastisement** n. **chastiser** n.
– ORIGIN ME: appar. formed irregularly from the obs. verb *chaste* (see **CHASTEN**).

**chastity belt** ● **n.** historical a garment or device designed to prevent the woman wearing it from having sexual intercourse.

**chasuble** /ˈtʃazjʊb(ə)l/ ● **n.** an ornate sleeveless outer vestment worn by a priest when celebrating Mass.
– ORIGIN ME: from OFr. *chesible*, later *chasuble*, from late L. *casubla*, alt. of L. *casula* 'hooded cloak or little cottage', dimin. of *casa* 'house'.

**chat**[1] ● **v.** (**chatted**, **chatting**) talk in a friendly and informal way. ➤(**chat someone up**) informal engage someone in flirtatious conversation. ● **n.** an informal conversation.
– ORIGIN ME: shortening of **CHATTER**.

**chat**[2] ● **n.** used in names of various songbirds with harsh, chattering calls, e.g. **stonechat**.
– ORIGIN C17: prob. imitative of their calls.

**chateau** /ˈʃatəʊ, French ʃato/ ● **n.** (pl. **chateaux** pronunc. same or /-təʊz/) a large French country house or castle.
– ORIGIN C18: Fr., from OFr. *chastel* (see **CASTLE**).

**chateaubriand** /ˌʃatəʊˈbriːɒ̃/ ● **n.** a thick fillet of beef steak.
– ORIGIN C19: named after the Fr. writer and statesman François-René, Vicomte de *Chateaubriand*, whose chef is said to have created the dish.

**chatelaine** /ˈʃatəleɪn/ ● **n. 1** dated a woman in charge of a large house. **2** historical a set of short chains attached to a woman's belt, used for carrying keys or other items.
– ORIGIN C19: from Fr. *châtelaine*, fem. of *châtelain* 'castellan', ult. rel. to **CASTLE**.

**chatline** ● **n.** a telephone service which allows conversation among a number of separate callers.

**chatoyant** /ʃəˈtɔɪənt/ ● **adj.** (of a gem, especially when cut en cabochon) showing a band of bright lustre caused by reflection from inclusions in the stone.
– DERIVATIVES **chatoyance** n. **chatoyancy** n.
– ORIGIN C18: Fr., pres. part. of *chatoyer* 'to shimmer'.

**chat room** ● **n.** an area on the Internet or other computer network where users can communicate, typically one dedicated to a particular topic.

**chat show** ● **n.** Brit. a television or radio programme in which celebrities are invited to talk informally about various topics.

**chattel** /ˈtʃat(ə)l/ ● **n.** (in general use) a personal possession. ➤Law an item of property other than freehold land, including tangible goods (**chattels personal**) and leasehold interests (**chattels real**). See also **GOODS AND CHATTELS**.
– ORIGIN ME: from OFr. *chatel*, from med. L. *capitale*, from L. *capitalis*, from *caput* 'head'; cf. **CAPITAL**[1] and **CATTLE**.

**chattel mortgage** ● n. N. Amer. a mortgage on a movable item of property.

**chatter** ● v. **1** talk rapidly or incessantly about trivial matters. **2** (of a person's teeth) click repeatedly together from cold or fear. ● n. **1** incessant trivial talk. **2** a series of short quick high-pitched sounds.
– PHRASES **the chattering classes** derogatory educated or intellectual people considered as a social group given to the expression of liberal opinions.
– DERIVATIVES **chatterer** n. **chattery** adj.
– ORIGIN ME: imitative.

**chatterbot** ● n. a computer program designed to interact with people by simulating human conversation.

**chatterbox** ● n. informal a person who chatters.

**chatty** ● adj. (**-ier**, **-iest**) **1** fond of chatting. **2** (of a conversation, letter, etc.) informal and lively.
– DERIVATIVES **chattily** adv. **chattiness** n.

**Chaucerian** /tʃɔːˈsɪərɪən/ ● adj. of or relating to Geoffrey Chaucer (c.1342–1400) or his writing. ● n. a student or admirer of Chaucer.

**chauffeur** ● n. a person employed to drive a car. ● v. drive (a car or a passenger in a car) as a chauffeur.
– DERIVATIVES **chauffeuse** n. (rare).
– ORIGIN C19: from Fr., lit. 'stoker' (by assoc. with steam engines).

**chaulmoogra** /tʃɔːlˈmuːgrə/ ● n. a tropical Asian evergreen tree whose seeds yield an oil used medically and as a preservative. [*Hydnocarpus kurzii*.]
– ORIGIN C19: from Bengali *cāul-mugrā*.

**chausses** /ʃəʊs/ ● pl. n. historical close-fitting coverings for the legs and feet, in particular those forming part of a knight's armour.
– ORIGIN C15: Fr., lit. 'clothing for the legs'.

**chautauqua** /tʃɔːˈtɔːkwə, ʃ-/ ● n. N. Amer. an institution that formerly provided popular adult education courses and entertainment.
– ORIGIN C19: named after *Chautauqua*, a county in New York State, where such an institution was first set up.

**chauvinism** /ˈʃəʊv(ɪ)nɪz(ə)m/ ● n. **1** exaggerated or aggressive patriotism. **2** excessive or prejudiced support or loyalty for one's own cause, group, or sex.
– DERIVATIVES **chauvinist** n. & adj. **chauvinistic** adj. **chauvinistically** adv.
– ORIGIN C19: named after Nicolas *Chauvin*, a Napoleonic veteran noted for his extreme patriotism.

**chawl** /tʃɔːl/ ● n. (in the Indian subcontinent) a large lodging house, offering cheap, basic accommodation.
– ORIGIN from Marathi *cāḷ*, denoting a long narrow building.

**chayote** /ˈtʃeɪəʊti/ ● n. **1** a succulent green pear-shaped tropical fruit resembling a cucumber in flavour. **2** the tropical American vine which yields this fruit, also producing an edible yam-like tuberous root. [*Sechium edule*.]
– ORIGIN C19: from Sp., from Nahuatl *chayotli*.

**ChB** ● abbrev. Bachelor of Surgery.
– ORIGIN from L. *Chirurgiae Baccalaureus*.

**CHD** ● abbrev. coronary heart disease.

**cheap** ● adj. **1** low in price. ➤ charging low prices. ➤ inexpensive because of inferior quality. **2** of little worth because achieved in a discreditable way requiring little effort: *her moment of cheap triumph.* ➤ contemptible. **3** N. Amer. informal miserly. ● adv. at or for a low price.
– PHRASES **on the cheap** informal at a low cost.
– DERIVATIVES **cheapish** adj. **cheaply** adv. **cheapness** n.
– ORIGIN C15: from an obs. phr. *good cheap* 'a good bargain', from OE *cēap* 'bargaining, trade', based on L. *caupo* 'small trader, innkeeper'.

**cheapen** ● v. **1** reduce the price of. **2** degrade.

**cheapjack** ● adj. chiefly N. Amer. of inferior quality. ● n. a seller of cheap inferior goods, typically one at a fair or market.

**cheapskate** ● n. informal a miserly person.
– ORIGIN C19 (orig. US): from CHEAP + SKATE[3].

**cheat** ● v. **1** act dishonestly or unfairly in order to gain an advantage. ➤ deprive of something by deceitful or unfair means. **2** avoid (something undesirable) by luck or skill: *she cheated death in a spectacular crash.* ● n. **1** a person who cheats. **2** an act of cheating.
– ORIGIN ME: shortening of ESCHEAT.

**cheater** ● n. chiefly N. Amer. **1** a person who cheats. **2** (**cheaters**) informal, dated a pair of glasses or sunglasses.

**cheat grass** ● n. chiefly N. Amer. a tough wild grass which sometimes grows as a weed among cereal crops and in pasture. [*Bromus tectorum* and other species.]
– ORIGIN C18: a local word for various wild plants, perh. from their resemblance to the cereals among which they grew.

**Chechen** /ˈtʃɛtʃɛn/ ● n. (pl. same or **Chechens**) **1** a member of the largely Muslim people inhabiting Chechnya, an autonomous republic in SW Russia. **2** the North Caucasian language of this people.

**check**[1] ● v. **1** examine the accuracy, quality, or condition of. ➤ verify or establish to one's satisfaction. **2** stop or slow the progress of. ➤ Ice Hockey hamper or neutralize (an opponent) with one's body or stick. ➤ (of a hound) pause to make sure of or regain a scent. ➤ (of a trained hawk) abandon the intended quarry and fly after other prey. **3** Chess move a piece or pawn to a square where it attacks (the opposing king). **4** (in poker) choose not to make a bet when called upon, allowing another player to do so instead. ● n. **1** an examination to check accuracy, quality, or condition. **2** an act of checking progress. ➤ a means of control or restraint. ➤ a temporary loss of the scent in hunting. ➤ Falconry a false stoop when a hawk abandons its intended quarry and pursues other prey. **3** a part of a piano which catches the hammer and prevents it retouching the strings. **4** Chess an act of checking the opposing king. **5** N. Amer. the bill in a restaurant. **6** (also **baggage/luggage check**) a token of identification for left luggage. **7** a counter used as a stake in a gambling game. **8** (also **check mark**) North American term for TICK[1] (in sense 1). **9** a crack or flaw in timber. ● exclam. **1** informal, chiefly N. Amer. expressing assent or agreement. **2** Chess used by a player to announce that the opponent's king has been placed in check.
– PHRASES **in check 1** under control. **2** Chess (of a king) directly attacked by an opponent's piece or pawn. **keep a check on** monitor.
– PHRASAL VERBS **check in** (or **check someone in**) arrive and register at a hotel or airport. **check something in** have one's baggage weighed and consigned to the hold of an aircraft. **check into** register one's arrival at (a hotel). **check something off** mark an item on a list to show that it has been dealt with. **check on** verify, ascertain, or monitor the state or condition of. **check out 1** settle one's hotel bill before leaving. **2** N. Amer. informal die. **check someone/thing out 1** establish the truth or inform oneself about someone or something. **2** (**check something out**) chiefly N. Amer. enter the price of goods in a supermarket into a cash machine. **check up on** investigate to establish the truth about or accuracy of.
– DERIVATIVES **checkable** adj.
– ORIGIN ME: the noun and exclamation from OFr. *eschec*, from med. L. *scaccus*, via Arab. from Pers. *šāh* 'king'; the verb from OFr. *eschequier* 'play chess, put in check'.

**check**[2] ● n. a pattern of small squares. ● adj. (also **checked**) having such a pattern.
– ORIGIN ME: prob. from CHEQUER.

**check**[3] ● n. US spelling of CHEQUE.

**checkbox** ● n. Computing a small area on a computer screen which, when selected by the user, shows that a particular feature has been enabled.

**checker**[1] ● n. **1** a person or thing that checks. **2** US a cashier in a supermarket.

**checker**[2] ● n. & v. US spelling of CHEQUER.

**checkerberry** ● n. (pl. **-ies**) **1** a creeping evergreen North American shrub with spiny scented leaves and waxy white flowers. [*Gaultheria procumbens*.] **2** the edible red fruit of this plant.
– ORIGIN C18: from *checkers* or *chequers* 'berries of the service tree' (so named from their colour) + BERRY.

**checkerboard** ● n. US spelling of CHEQUERBOARD.

**checking account** (Canadian **chequing account**) ● n. N. Amer. a current account at a bank.
– ORIGIN 1920s: from CHECK[3].

**checklist** • n. a list of items required, things to be done, or points to be considered.

**check mark** • n. another term for CHECK[1] (in sense 8).

**checkmate** • n. **1** Chess a position of check from which a king cannot escape. **2** a final defeat or deadlock. • v. **1** Chess put into checkmate. **2** defeat or frustrate totally.
– ORIGIN ME: from OFr. *eschec mat*, from Arab. *šāh māta*, from Pers. *šāh māt* 'the king is dead'.

**checkout** • n. a point at which goods are paid for in a supermarket or similar store.

**checkpoint** • n. a barrier or manned entrance, typically at a border, where security checks are carried out on travellers.

**check rein** • n. a bearing rein.

**checkroom** • n. N. Amer. a room where coats, luggage, etc. may be temporarily deposited for a fee.

**checksum** • n. a digit representing the sum of the correct digits in a piece of data, against which comparisons can be made to detect errors.

**check-up** • n. a thorough medical or dental examination to detect any problems.

**check valve** • n. a valve that closes to prevent backward flow of liquid.

**Cheddar** • n. a kind of firm smooth yellow, white, or orange cheese, originally made in Cheddar in SW England.

**cheder** /'xɛdə/ (also **heder**) • n. (pl. **chedarim** /-'dɑːrɪm/, **cheders**) a school for Jewish children in which Hebrew and religious knowledge are taught.
– ORIGIN C19: from Heb. *ḥeder* 'room'.

**cheechako** /tʃiː'tʃɑːkəʊ/ • n. (pl. **-os**) N. Amer. informal a person newly arrived in the mining districts of Alaska or NW Canada.
– ORIGIN C19: Chinook Jargon, 'newcomer'.

**cheek** • n. **1** either side of the face below the eye. **2** either of the buttocks. **3** either of two side pieces or parts arranged in lateral pairs in a structure. **4** impertinence; audacity. • v. speak impertinently to.
– PHRASES **cheek by jowl** close together. **cheek to cheek** (of two people dancing) with their heads close together in an intimate and romantic way. **turn the other cheek** refrain from retaliating after an attack or insult. [with biblical allusion to Matt. 5:39.]
– DERIVATIVES **-cheeked** adj.
– ORIGIN OE *cē(a)ce*, *cēoce* 'cheek, jaw', of W. Gmc origin.

**cheekbone** • n. the bone below the eye.

**cheekpiece** • n. **1** a smooth block fitted to the stock of a rifle or shotgun and resting against the face when aiming from the shoulder. **2** either of the two straps of a horse's bridle joining the bit and the headpiece.

**cheeky** • adj. (**-ier**, **-iest**) impudent or irreverent.
– DERIVATIVES **cheekily** adv. **cheekiness** n.

**cheep** • n. **1** a shrill squeaky cry made by a young bird. **2** [with neg.] informal the slightest sound: *there hasn't been a cheep from anybody.* • v. make a cheep.
– ORIGIN C16 (orig. Scots): imitative.

**cheer** • v. **1** shout in praise or encouragement. ➤ praise or encourage with shouts. **2** give comfort or support to. ➤ (**cheer someone up** or **cheer up**) make someone or become less miserable. • n. **1** a shout of encouragement, praise, or joy. **2** (also **good cheer**) cheerfulness; optimism. **3** food and drink provided for a festive occasion.
– PHRASES **three cheers** three successive hurrahs expressing appreciation or congratulation.
– ORIGIN ME (in the sense 'face', hence 'expression, mood', later 'a good mood'): from OFr. *chiere* 'face', from late L. *cara*, from Gk *kara* 'head'.

**cheerful** • adj. **1** noticeably happy and optimistic. **2** causing happiness because pleasant.
– DERIVATIVES **cheerfully** adv. **cheerfulness** n.

**cheerio** • exclam. Brit. informal goodbye.

**cheerleader** • n. a member of a team of girls who perform organized cheering, chanting, and dancing in support of a sports team at matches in the US and elsewhere.

**cheerless** • adj. gloomy; depressing.
– DERIVATIVES **cheerlessly** adv. **cheerlessness** n.

**cheerly** • adv. archaic heartily (used as a cry of encouragement among sailors).

**cheers** • exclam. informal expressing good wishes before drinking or (Brit.) on parting. ➤ chiefly Brit. expressing gratitude or acknowledgement.

**cheery** • adj. (**-ier**, **-iest**) happy and optimistic.
– DERIVATIVES **cheerily** adv. **cheeriness** n.

**cheese**[1] • n. **1** a food made from the pressed curds of milk, having a texture either firm and elastic or soft and semi-liquid. **2** Brit. a conserve having the consistency of soft cheese: *lemon cheese.*
– PHRASES **hard cheese** Brit. informal, dated used to express sympathy over a petty matter.
– ORIGIN OE *cēse*, *cȳse*, of W. Gmc origin; from L. *caseus*.

**cheese**[2] • v. (usu. **be cheesed off**) Brit. informal exasperate, frustrate, or bore.
– ORIGIN C19: of unknown origin.

**cheeseboard** • n. **1** a board on which cheese is served and cut. **2** a selection of cheeses served as a course of a meal.

**cheeseburger** • n. a beefburger with a slice of cheese on it, served in a bread roll.

**cheesecake** • n. **1** a kind of rich sweet tart made with cream and soft cheese on a biscuit base, typically topped with fruit. **2** informal images portraying women according to a stereotypical ideal of sexual attractiveness.

**cheesecloth** • n. thin, loosely woven, unsized cotton cloth, used typically for light clothing and in preparing or protecting food.

**cheese head** • n. Brit. a type of screw head with vertical sides and a slightly domed top.

**cheese-paring** • adj. very careful or mean with money. • n. meanness.

**cheese plant** • n. see **SWISS CHEESE PLANT**.

**cheese straw** • n. a thin strip of cheese-flavoured pastry, eaten as a snack.

**cheesewood** • n. a small tropical evergreen tree with white flowers and yellowish-orange fruit. [*Pittosporum undulatum* (Australia), *P. viridifolium* (South Africa), and other species.]

**cheesy** • adj. (**-ier**, **-iest**) **1** like cheese in taste, smell, or consistency. **2** informal cheap, unpleasant, or blatantly inauthentic.
– DERIVATIVES **cheesiness** n.

**cheetah** /'tʃiːtə/ • n. a large swift-running spotted cat found in Africa and parts of Asia. [*Acinonyx jubatus.*]
– ORIGIN C18: from Hindi *cītā*, perh. from Sanskrit *citraka* 'leopard'.

**chef** • n. a professional cook, typically the chief cook in a restaurant or hotel.
– ORIGIN C19: Fr., lit. 'head'.

**chef d'école** /ˌʃɛf deɪ'kɒl, French ʃɛ dekɔl/ • n. (pl. **chefs d'école** pronunc. same) the initiator or leader of a school or style of music, painting, or literature.
– ORIGIN C19: Fr., 'head of school'.

**chef-d'œuvre** /ʃeɪ 'dəːvr(ə), French ʃɛ dœvʀ/ • n. (pl. **chefs-d'œuvre** pronunc. same) a masterpiece.
– ORIGIN Fr., 'chief work'.

**cheiro-** • comb. form variant spelling of **CHIRO-**.

**Chekhovian** /tʃɛ'kəʊvɪən/ • adj. of, relating to, or characteristic of the work of the Russian dramatist Anton Chekhov (1860–1904).

**chela**[1] /'kiːlə/ • n. (pl. **chelae** /-liː/) Zoology a pincer-like claw, especially of a crab or other crustacean.
– ORIGIN C17: mod. L., from L. *chele* or Gk *khēlē* 'claw'.

**chela**[2] /'tʃeɪlə/ • n. a follower and pupil of a guru.
– ORIGIN from Hindi *celā*.

**chelate** /'kiːleɪt/ • n. Chemistry a compound containing an organic ligand bonded to a central metal atom at two or more points. • adj. Zoology (of an appendage) bearing chelae. • v. Chemistry form a chelate with.
– DERIVATIVES **chelation** n. **chelator** n.

**chelicera** /kə'lɪs(ə)rə/ • n. (pl. **chelicerae** /-riː/) Zoology either of a pair of appendages in front of the mouth in arachnids and some other arthropods, usually modified as pincer-like claws.
– DERIVATIVES **cheliceral** adj.

– ORIGIN C19: mod. L., from Gk *khēlē* 'claw' + *keras* 'horn'.

**Chelicerata** /kəˌlɪsəˈreɪtə/ ● **pl. n.** Zoology a large subphylum of arthropods which possess chelicerae, comprising the arachnids, sea spiders, and horseshoe crabs.
– DERIVATIVES **chelicerate** /kəˈlɪsəreɪt, -(ə)rət/ n. & adj.

**Chelsea boot** ● **n.** an elastic-sided boot with a pointed toe.
– ORIGIN named after *Chelsea*, a district of London.

**Chelsea bun** ● **n.** Brit. a flat, spiral-shaped currant bun sprinkled with sugar.

**Chelsea pensioner** ● **n.** (in the UK) an inmate of the Chelsea Royal Hospital for old or disabled soldiers.

**Chelsea ware** ● **n.** a type of soft-paste porcelain made at Chelsea in London in the 18th century.

**chemi-** ● **comb. form** representing **CHEMICAL**. See also **CHEMO-**.

**chemical** ● **adj.** of or relating to chemistry or chemicals. ➤relating to or denoting the use of poison gas or other chemicals as weapons of war. ● **n.** a distinct compound or substance, especially one which has been artificially prepared or purified.
– DERIVATIVES **chemically** adv.
– ORIGIN C16: from Fr. *chimique* or mod. L. *chimicus*, *chymicus*, from med. L. *alchymicus*, from *alchimia* (see **ALCHEMY**).

**chemical bond** ● **n.** see **BOND**[1] (sense 4).

**chemical compound** ● **n.** see **COMPOUND**[1].

**chemical engineering** ● **n.** the branch of engineering concerned with the design and operation of industrial chemical plants.
– DERIVATIVES **chemical engineer** n.

**chemical formula** ● **n.** see **FORMULA** (sense 1).

**chemico-** ● **comb. form** representing **CHEMICAL**.

**chemiluminescence** ● **n.** the emission of light during a chemical reaction which does not produce significant quantities of heat.
– DERIVATIVES **chemiluminescent** adj.

**chemin de fer** /ʃəˌmã də ˈfɛː, French ʃ(ə)mɛ̃ d(ə) fɛʀ/ ● **n.** a card game which is a variety of baccarat.
– ORIGIN C19: Fr., lit. 'railway'.

**chemise** /ʃəˈmiːz/ ● **n.** **1** a dress hanging straight from the shoulders, popular in the 1920s. **2** a woman's loose-fitting undergarment or nightdress.
– ORIGIN ME: from OFr., from late L. *camisia* 'shirt or nightgown'.

**chemisorption** /ˌkɛmɪˈsɔːpʃ(ə)n, -ˈzɔːp-/ ● **n.** Chemistry adsorption in which the adsorbed substance is held by chemical bonds.
– DERIVATIVES **chemisorbed** adj.

**chemist** ● **n.** **1** Brit. a shop where medicinal drugs are dispensed and sold, and in which toiletries and other medical goods can be purchased. ➤a person who is authorized to dispense such medicinal drugs. **2** a person engaged in chemical research or experiments.
– ORIGIN ME: from Fr. *chimiste*, from mod. L. *chimista*, from *alchimista* 'alchemist', from *alchimia* (see **ALCHEMY**).

**chemistry** ● **n.** (pl. **-ies**) **1** the branch of science concerned with the properties and interactions of the substances of which matter is composed. **2** the chemical properties of a substance or body. **3** the emotional or psychological interaction between two people, especially when experienced as a powerful mutual attraction.

**chemo-** ● **comb. form** representing **CHEMICAL**. See also **CHEMI-**.

**chemoautotroph** /ˌkiːməʊˈɔːtətrəʊf, -trɒf, ˌkɛm-/ ● **n.** Biology an organism which derives energy from the oxidation of inorganic compounds.
– DERIVATIVES **chemoautotrophic** /-ˈtrəʊfɪk, -ˈtrɒfɪk/ adj. **chemoautotrophy** /-ˈtrəʊfi, -ˈtrɒfi/ n.

**chemoreceptor** /ˈkiːməʊrɪˌsɛptə, ˌkɛm-/ ● **n.** Physiology a sensory cell or organ responsive to chemical stimuli.
– DERIVATIVES **chemoreception** n.

**chemosynthesis** /ˌkiːmə(ʊ)ˈsɪnθɪsɪs, ˌkɛm-/ ● **n.** Biology the metabolic synthesis of organic compounds by living organisms using energy derived from reactions involving inorganic chemicals.
– DERIVATIVES **chemosynthetic** adj.

**chemotaxis** /ˌkiːmə(ʊ)ˈtaksɪs, ˌkɛm-/ ● **n.** Biology movement of an organism in response to the changing concentration of a particular substance.
– DERIVATIVES **chemotactic** adj.

**chemotherapy** /ˌkiːmə(ʊ)ˈθɛrəpi, ˌkɛm-/ ● **n.** the treatment of disease, especially cancer, by the use of chemical substances.
– DERIVATIVES **chemotherapist** n.

**chemurgy** /ˈkɛməːdʒi/ ● **n.** N. Amer. the chemical and industrial use of organic raw materials.
– DERIVATIVES **chemurgic** adj.
– ORIGIN 1930s: from **CHEMO-**, on the pattern of *metallurgy*.

**chenille** /ʃəˈniːl/ ● **n.** a tufty velvety cord or yarn, used for trimming furniture and made into carpets or clothing.
– ORIGIN C18: from Fr., lit. 'hairy caterpillar'.

**cheongsam** /tʃɪɒŋˈsam, tʃɒŋ-/ ● **n.** a straight, close-fitting silk dress with a high neck and slit skirt, worn by Chinese and Indonesian women.
– ORIGIN Chin. (Cantonese dial.).

**cheque** (US **check**) ● **n.** an order to a bank to pay a stated sum from the drawer's account, written on a specially printed form.
– ORIGIN C18 (orig. denoting a counterfoil, or a form with a counterfoil): var. of **CHECK**[1], in the sense 'device for checking the amount of an item'.

**chequebook journalism** ● **n.** the payment of a large amount of money to acquire the exclusive right to publish a person's story in a newspaper.

**cheque card** ● **n.** Brit. a card issued by a bank to guarantee the honouring of cheques up to a stated amount.

**chequer** (US **checker**) ● **n.** **1** (**chequers**) a pattern of alternately coloured squares. **2** (**checkers**) [treated as sing.] N. Amer. the game of draughts. ➤(**checker**) a piece used in this game. ● **v.** **1** (usu. **be chequered**) divide into or mark with chequers. **2** [as adj. **chequered**] marked by periods of fluctuating fortune: *a chequered career.*
– ORIGIN ME (in the sense 'chessboard', giving rise to *chequered* meaning 'marked like a chessboard'): from **EXCHEQUER**.

**chequerboard** (US **checkerboard**) ● **n.** a board for playing checkers and similar games, having a regular chequered pattern, typically in black and white.

**chequered flag** ● **n.** Motor Racing a flag with a black-and-white chequered pattern, displayed to drivers at the end of a race.

**Cheremis** /ˈtʃɛrəmɪs/ ● **n.** former term for the Mari language (see **MARI**).

**Cherenkov radiation** /tʃəˈrɛŋkɒf/ (also **Cerenkov radiation**) ● **n.** Physics electromagnetic radiation emitted by particles moving in a medium at speeds faster than that of light in the same medium.
– ORIGIN C20: named after the Soviet physicist Pavel *Cherenkov.*

**cherimoya** /ˌtʃɛrɪˈmɔɪə/ (also **chirimoya**) ● **n.** a green-skinned custard apple produced by an Andean tree (*Annona cherimola*).
– ORIGIN C18: from Sp., from Quechua, from *chiri* 'cold or refreshing' + *muya* 'circle'.

**cherish** ● **v.** **1** protect and care for lovingly. **2** nurture (a hope or ambition).
– ORIGIN ME: from OFr. *cheriss-*, lengthened stem of *cherir*, from *cher* 'dear', from L. *carus*.

**Cherkess** /tʃəˈkɛs/ ● **n.** another term for **CIRCASSIAN**.

**chernozem** /ˈtʃəːnəzɛm/ ● **n.** a fertile black soil rich in humus, typical of temperate grassland.
– ORIGIN C19: from Russ., from *chërnyĭ* 'black' + *zemlya* 'earth'.

**Cherokee** /ˌtʃɛrəˈkiː/ ● **n.** (pl. same or **Cherokees**) **1** a member of an American Indian people formerly inhabiting much of the southern US. **2** the Iroquoian language of this people.
– ORIGIN from obs. Cherokee *tsaraki*, earlier form of *tsaliki*.

**Cherokee rose** ● **n.** a climbing Chinese rose with fragrant white flowers, which has become naturalized in the southern US. [*Rosa laevigata*.]

**cheroot** /ʃəˈruːt/ ● **n.** a cigar with both ends open.
– ORIGIN C17: from Fr. *cheroute*, from Tamil *curuṭṭu* 'roll of tobacco'.

**cherry** ● **n.** (pl. **-ies**) **1** a small, soft round stone fruit that is typically bright or dark red. **2** the tree that bears such fruit. [*Prunus avium* (**wild cherry**), *P. cerasus* (**sour cherry**), and other species and varieties.] **3** a bright deep red colour. **4** (**one's cherry**) informal one's virginity.
– PHRASES **a bite at the cherry** an attempt or opportunity. **a bowl of cherries** [with neg.] a very pleasant situation. **the cherry on the cake** a desirable thing providing the finishing touch to something already good.
– ORIGIN ME: from ONorth. Fr. *cherise* (taken as pl.), from med. L. *ceresia*, based on Gk *kerasos* 'cherry tree, cherry'.

**cherry brandy** ● **n.** a sweet, dark red cherry-flavoured liqueur made with brandy in which cherries have been steeped, or with crushed cherry stones.

**cherry laurel** ● **n.** an evergreen shrub or small tree with leathery leaves, white flowers, and cherry-like fruits, native to the Balkans. [*Prunus laurocerasus*.]

**cherry-pick** ● **v.** selectively choose (the best things or people) from those available.

**cherry picker** ● **n.** informal **1** a hydraulic crane with a railed platform for raising and lowering people. **2** a person who cherry-picks.

**cherry pie** ● **n.** a garden heliotrope with fragrant blue flowers. [*Heliotropium arborescens*.]

**cherry plum** ● **n. 1** a SW Asian shrub or small tree with white flowers and small red and yellow edible fruit. [*Prunus cerasifera*.] **2** the fruit of this tree.

**cherry tomato** ● **n.** a miniature tomato with a strong flavour.

**chert** /tʃəːt/ ● **n.** a hard, dark, opaque rock composed of silica (chalcedony) with an amorphous or microscopically fine-grained texture.
– DERIVATIVES **cherty** adj.
– ORIGIN C17 (orig. dial.): of unknown origin.

**cherub** ● **n. 1** (pl. **cherubim** or **cherubs**) a winged angelic being described in biblical tradition as attending on God, conventionally represented as a chubby child with wings. **2** (pl. **cherubs**) a beautiful or innocent-looking child.
– DERIVATIVES **cherubic** adj. **cherubically** adv.
– ORIGIN OE *cherubin*, ult. (via L. and Gk) from Heb. *kĕrūḇ*, pl. *kĕrūḇīm*.

**chervil** /ˈtʃəːvɪl/ ● **n.** a plant of the parsley family, with delicate fern-like leaves which are used as a culinary herb. [*Anthriscus cerefolium*.]
– ORIGIN OE, from L. *chaerephylla*, from Gk *khairephullon*.

**Ches.** ● **abbrev.** Cheshire.

**Cheshire** /ˈtʃɛʃə/ ● **n.** a kind of firm crumbly cheese, originally made in Cheshire.

**Cheshire cat** ● **n.** a cat depicted with a broad fixed grin, as popularized through Lewis Carroll's *Alice's Adventures in Wonderland* (1865).
– ORIGIN C18: of unknown origin, but it is said that *Cheshire* cheeses used to be marked with the face of a smiling cat.

**chess** ● **n.** a board game of strategic skill for two players, the object of which is to put the opponent's king under a direct attack, leading to checkmate.
– ORIGIN ME: from OFr. *esches*, pl. of *eschec* (see **CHECK**[1]).

**chessboard** ● **n.** a square board divided into sixty-four alternating dark and light squares, used for playing chess or draughts.

**chessman** ● **n.** (pl. **-men**) a solid figure used as a chess piece.

**chest** ● **n. 1** the front surface of a person's or animal's body between the neck and the stomach. ➤ the whole of a person's upper trunk. **2** a large strong box for storage or transport. **3** Brit. the treasury or financial resources of an institution. ● **v.** Soccer propel (the ball) by means of one's chest.
– PHRASES **get something off one's chest** informal say something that one has wanted to say for a long time. **keep** (or **play**) **one's cards close to one's chest** (or N. Amer. **vest**) informal be extremely secretive about one's intentions.
– DERIVATIVES **-chested** adj.
– ORIGIN OE *cest*, *cyst*, based on Gk *kistē* 'box'.

**chesterfield** ● **n. 1** a sofa with padded arms and back of the same height and curved outwards at the top. **2** a man's plain straight overcoat, typically with a velvet collar.
– ORIGIN C19: named after an Earl of *Chesterfield*.

**chestnut** ● **n. 1** a glossy hard brown nut which develops within a bristly case and can be roasted and eaten. **2** (also **chestnut tree**, **sweet chestnut**, or **Spanish chestnut**) the large tree that produces these nuts. [*Castanea sativa*.] ➤ used in names of similar nuts, and trees and plants that produce them, e.g. **horse chestnut**, **water chestnut**. **3** a deep reddish-brown colour. **4** a horse of a reddish-brown or yellowish-brown colour. **5** a small horny patch on the inside of a horse's leg.
– PHRASES **an old chestnut** a joke, story, or subject that has become uninteresting through constant repetition.
– ORIGIN C16: from OE *chesten* (from OFr. *chastaine*, via L. from Gk *kastanea*) + **NUT**.

**chest of drawers** ● **n.** a piece of furniture used for storage, consisting of an upright frame into which drawers are fitted.

**chest voice** ● **n.** the lowest register of the voice in singing or speaking.

**chesty** ● **adj.** informal **1** Brit. having a lot of catarrh in the lungs. **2** (of a woman) having large or prominent breasts. **3** N. Amer. conceited and arrogant.
– DERIVATIVES **chestily** adv. **chestiness** n.

**Chetnik** /ˈtʃɛtnɪk/ ● **n.** a member of a Slavic nationalist guerrilla force in the Balkans, especially during the Second World War.
– ORIGIN C20: from Serbo-Croat *četnik*, from *četa* 'band, troop'.

**chetrum** /ˈtʃɛtruːm/ ● **n.** (pl. same or **chetrums**) a monetary unit of Bhutan, equal to one hundredth of a ngultrum.
– ORIGIN from Dzongkha.

**cheval glass** /ʃəˈval/ (also **cheval mirror**) ● **n.** a tall mirror fitted at its middle to an upright frame so that it can be tilted.
– ORIGIN C19: *cheval* from Fr., in the sense 'frame'.

**chevalier** /ˌʃɛvəˈlɪə/ ● **n.** historical a knight. ➤ a member of certain orders of knighthood or of modern French orders such as the Legion of Honour.
– ORIGIN ME: from OFr., from med. L. *caballarius*, from L. *caballus* 'horse'.

**chevet** /ʃəˈveɪ/ ● **n.** Architecture an apse with an ambulatory giving access behind the high altar to a series of chapels set in bays.
– ORIGIN C19: from Fr., lit. 'pillow'.

**Cheviot** /ˈtʃɛvɪət, ˈtʃiːv-/ ● **n. 1** a large sheep of a breed with short thick wool. **2** (**cheviot**) the wool or tweed cloth obtained from this breed.
– ORIGIN from the *Cheviot* Hills in northern England and Scotland.

**chèvre** /ʃɛvr(ə), French ʃɛvʀ/ ● **n.** French cheese made with goat's milk.
– ORIGIN 1960s: Fr., lit. 'goat, she-goat'.

**chevron** ● **n.** a V-shaped line or stripe, especially one on the sleeve of a uniform indicating rank or length of service. ➤ Heraldry an ordinary in the form of a broad inverted V-shape.
– ORIGIN ME: from OFr., based on L. *caper* 'goat'; cf. L. *capreoli* (dimin. of *caper*) used to mean 'pair of rafters'.

**chevrotain** /ˈʃɛvrəteɪn/ ● **n.** a small deer-like mammal with small tusks, found in tropical rainforests. [Genera *Tragulus* (Asia) and *Hyemoschus* (Africa): four species.]
– ORIGIN C18: from Fr., dimin. of OFr. *chevrot*, dimin. of *chèvre* 'goat'.

**chew** ● **v. 1** bite and work (food) in the mouth to make it easier to swallow. **2** (**chew something over**) discuss or consider something at length. **3** (**chew someone out**) N. Amer. informal reprimand someone severely. ● **n.** an instance

of chewing. ➤ a thing, especially a sweet, for chewing.
– PHRASES **chew the fat** (or **rag**) informal chat in a leisurely way.
– DERIVATIVES **chewable** adj. **chewer** n. **chewiness** n. **chewy** adj.
– ORIGIN OE *cēowan*, of W. Gmc origin.

**chewing gum** ● n. flavoured gum for chewing.

**Cheyenne** /ʃʌɪ'an/ ● n. (pl. same or **Cheyennes**) **1** a member of an American Indian people formerly living between the Missouri and Arkansas Rivers. **2** the Algonquian language of this people.
– ORIGIN Canad. Fr., from Dakota *šahíyena*, from *šaia* 'speak incoherently'.

**Cheyne-Stokes breathing** /tʃeɪn/ ● n. Medicine an abnormal cyclical pattern of breathing in which the rate gradually decreases to a complete stop and then increases again.
– ORIGIN C19: named after the physicians John *Cheyne* and William *Stokes*.

**chez** /ʃeɪ/ ● prep. chiefly humorous at the home of.
– ORIGIN C18: Fr., from OFr. *chiese*, from L. *casa* 'cottage'.

**chi**[1] /kʌɪ/ ● n. the twenty-second letter of the Greek alphabet (Χ, χ), transliterated as 'kh' or 'ch'.
– PHRASES **chi-square test** a statistical method assessing the goodness of fit between a set of observed values and those expected theoretically.
– ORIGIN from Gk.

**chi**[2] /kiː/ (also **qi** or **ki**) ● n. the circulating life force whose existence and properties are the basis of much Chinese philosophy and medicine.
– ORIGIN from Chin. *qì*, lit. 'air, breath'.

**Chianina** /ˌkɪə'niːnə/ ● n. an animal of a very large white breed of cattle, kept for its lean meat.
– ORIGIN from Ital.

**Chianti** /kɪ'anti/ ● n. (pl. **Chiantis**) a dry red Italian wine produced in Tuscany.
– ORIGIN named after the *Chianti* Mountains, Italy.

**chiaroscuro** /kɪˌɑːrə'skʊərəʊ/ ● n. the treatment of light and shade in drawing and painting.
– ORIGIN C17: from Ital., from *chiaro* 'clear, bright' + *oscuro* 'dark, obscure'.

**chiasma** /kʌɪ'azmə, kɪ-/ ● n. (pl. **chiasmata** /-tə/) **1** (also **optic chiasma**) Anatomy the X-shaped structure formed at the point below the brain where the two optic nerves cross over each other. **2** Biology a point at which paired chromosomes remain in contact during the first metaphase of meiosis.
– ORIGIN C19: mod. L., from Gk *chiasma* 'crosspiece, cross-shaped mark', from *khiazein* 'mark with the letter chi'.

**chiasmus** /kʌɪ'azməs, kɪ-/ ● n. the inversion in a second phrase or clause of the order of words in the first.
– DERIVATIVES **chiastic** adj.
– ORIGIN C17 (in the sense 'crosswise arrangement'): mod. L., from Gk *khiasmos*, from *khiazein* (see **CHIASMA**).

**chiastolite** /kʌɪ'astəlʌɪt, kɪ-/ ● n. a variety of the mineral andalusite containing dark carbonaceous inclusions giving a cross-shaped appearance.
– ORIGIN C19: from Gk *khiastos* 'arranged crosswise' + **-LITE**.

**Chibcha** /'tʃɪbtʃə/ ● n. (pl. same) **1** a member of a native people of Colombia whose ancient civilization was destroyed by Europeans. **2** the extinct Chibchan language of this people.
– ORIGIN Amer. Sp., from Chibcha *zipa* 'chief'.

**Chibchan** /'tʃɪbtʃ(ə)n/ ● n. a language family of Colombia and Central America, most members of which are now extinct or nearly so. ● adj. of or relating to Chibchan.

**chibouk** /tʃɪ'buːk/ (also **chibouque**) ● n. a long Turkish tobacco pipe.
– ORIGIN C19: Fr. *chibouque*, from Turk. *çubuk*, lit. 'tube'.

**chic** /ʃiːk/ ● adj. (**-er**, **-est**) elegantly and stylishly fashionable. ● n. stylishness and elegance.
– DERIVATIVES **chicly** adv.
– ORIGIN C19: from Fr., prob. from Ger. *Schick* 'skill'.

**chicane** /ʃɪ'keɪn/ ● n. **1** a sharp double bend created to form an obstacle on a motor-racing track. **2** dated (in card games) a hand without cards of one particular suit; a void. **3** archaic chicanery. ● v. archaic employ chicanery.
– ORIGIN C17: from Fr. *chicane* (n.), *chicaner* (v.) 'quibble'.

**chicanery** ● n. the use of trickery to achieve one's purpose.

**Chicano** /tʃɪ'kɑːnəʊ, ʃɪ-, -'keɪn-/ ● n. (fem. **Chicana**) (pl. **-os** or **-as**) chiefly US a North American of Mexican origin or descent.
– ORIGIN Mex. Sp., alt. of Sp. *mejicano* (masc.) 'Mexican'.

**chicha** /'tʃɪtʃə/ ● n. (in South and Central America) a kind of beer made typically from maize.
– ORIGIN Amer. Sp., from Kuna.

**Chichewa** /tʃɪ'tʃeɪwə/ ● n. another term for **NYANJA** (the language).

**chichi** /'ʃiːʃiː/ ● adj. attempting stylish elegance but achieving only an over-elaborate affectedness.
– ORIGIN C20: from Fr., of imitative origin.

**Chichimec** /ˌtʃiːtʃɪ'mɛk/ ● n. (pl. same or **Chichimecs**) **1** a member of a group of native peoples, including the Toltecs and the Aztecs, formerly dominant in central Mexico. **2** a Uto-Aztecan language of these peoples.
– ORIGIN Sp., from Nahuatl.

**chick**[1] ● n. **1** a young bird, especially one newly hatched. ➤ a newly hatched young domestic fowl. **2** informal a young woman.
– ORIGIN ME: abbrev. of **CHICKEN**.

**chick**[2] ● n. (in the Indian subcontinent) a bamboo screen for a doorway.
– ORIGIN from Urdu *chik*, from Pers. *čigh*.

**chickabiddy** ● n. (pl. **-ies**) informal an affectionate form of address for a small child or a loved one.

**chickadee** ● n. North American term for **TIT**[1].
– ORIGIN C19: imitative of its call.

**chickaree** ● n. a squirrel with red fur, found in the coniferous forests of North America. [Genus *Tamiasciurus*: three species.]
– ORIGIN C19: imitative of its call.

**Chickasaw** /'tʃɪkəsɔː/ ● n. (pl. same or **Chickasaws**) **1** a member of an American Indian people formerly resident in Mississippi and Alabama. **2** the Muskogean language of this people.
– ORIGIN the name in Chickasaw.

**chicken** ● n. **1** a domestic fowl kept for its eggs or meat, especially a young one. **2** a coward. **3** informal a game in which the first person to lose their nerve and withdraw from a dangerous situation is the loser. ● adj. informal cowardly. ● v. (**chicken out**) informal be too scared to do something.
– PHRASES **chicken-and-egg** denoting a situation in which each of two things appears to be necessary to the other. [from the question 'What came first, the chicken or the egg?'] **like a headless chicken** informal frenziedly.
– ORIGIN OE *cīcen*, *cȳcen*, of Gmc origin; prob. rel. to **COCK**[1].

**chicken à la king** ● n. cooked breast of chicken in a cream sauce with mushrooms and peppers.
– ORIGIN said to be named after E. Clark *King*, proprietor of a New York hotel.

**chicken-breasted** ● adj. pigeon-chested.

**chicken brick** ● n. Brit. an earthenware container for roasting a chicken in its own juices.

**chicken feed** ● n. informal a paltry sum of money.

**chicken-fried steak** ● n. US a thin piece of beef which is lightly battered and fried until crisp.

**chickenpox** ● n. an infectious disease causing a mild fever and a rash of itchy inflamed pimples, caused by the herpes zoster virus; varicella.
– ORIGIN C18: prob. so named because of its mildness, as compared to smallpox.

**chickenshit** informal, chiefly N. Amer. ● adj. worthless or contemptible. ● n. a worthless or contemptible person.

**chicken wire** ● n. light wire netting with a hexagonal mesh.

**chickpea** ● n. **1** a round yellowish seed which is a pulse of major importance as food. **2** the leguminous plant which bears these seeds. [*Cicer arietinum*.]
– ORIGIN C18 (earlier as *chiche-pease*): from ME *chiche* (from OFr. *chiche*, *cice*, from L. *cicer* 'chickpea') + **PEASE**.

**chickweed** ● **n.** a small white-flowered plant, often growing as a garden weed. [*Stellaria media* and numerous related species.]

**chicle** /ˈtʃɪk(ə)l, -kli/ ● **n.** the milky latex of the sapodilla tree, used to make chewing gum. ➤another term for **SAPODILLA**.
– ORIGIN via Latin Amer. Sp., from Nahuatl *tzictli*.

**chicory** /ˈtʃɪk(ə)ri/ ● **n.** (pl. **-ies**) **1** a blue-flowered Mediterranean plant of the daisy family, cultivated for its edible salad leaves and its carrot-shaped root, which is used as an additive to or substitute for coffee. [*Cichorium intybus*.] **2** North American term for **ENDIVE**.
– ORIGIN ME: from obs. Fr. *cicorée* (earlier form of *chicorée*) 'endive', via L. from Gk *kikhorion*.

**chide** /tʃʌɪd/ ● **v.** (past **chided** or **chid** /tʃɪd/; past part. **chided** or archaic **chidden** /ˈtʃɪd(ə)n/) scold or rebuke.
– DERIVATIVES **chider** n. **chiding** adj. **chidingly** adv.
– ORIGIN OE *cīdan*, of unknown origin.

**chief** ● **n. 1** a leader or ruler of a people. ➤the head of an organization. **2** Heraldry an ordinary consisting of a broad horizontal band across the top of the shield. ➤the upper third of the field. ● **adj. 1** having the highest rank or authority. **2** most important: *the chief reason*.
– DERIVATIVES **chiefdom** n.
– ORIGIN ME: from OFr. *chief*, *chef*, based on L. *caput* 'head'.

**chief constable** ● **n.** Brit. the head of the police force of a county or other region.

**chief inspector** ● **n.** Brit. a police officer ranking above inspector and below superintendent.

**chiefly** ● **adv.** mainly; especially. ➤mostly.

**chief master sergeant** ● **n.** a rank of non-commissioned officer in the US air force, above senior master sergeant and below chief warrant officer.

**chief of staff** ● **n.** the senior staff officer of a service, command, or formation.

**chief petty officer** ● **n.** a rank of non-commissioned officer in a navy, above petty officer and below warrant officer or senior chief petty officer.

**chieftain** ● **n.** the leader of a people or clan.
– DERIVATIVES **chieftaincy** /-si/ n. (pl. **-ies**). **chieftainship** n.
– ORIGIN ME and OFr. *chevetaine*, from late L. *capitaneus* (see **CAPTAIN**); the spelling was assimilated to **CHIEF**.

**chief technician** ● **n.** a rank of non-commissioned officer in the RAF, above sergeant and below flight sergeant.

**chief warrant officer** ● **n.** a rank in the US armed forces, above warrant officer and below the lowest-ranking commissioned officer.

**chiffchaff** ● **n.** a common warbler with drab plumage and a repetitive call. [*Phylloscopus collybita*.]
– ORIGIN C18: imitative of its call.

**chiffon** ● **n.** a light, transparent fabric typically made of silk or nylon.
– ORIGIN C18 (orig. pl., denoting trimmings on a woman's dress): from Fr., from *chiffe* 'rag'.

**chiffonade** /ˌʃɪfəˈnɑːd/ (also **chiffonnade**) ● **n.** (pl. same) a preparation of shredded or finely cut leaf vegetables, used as a garnish for soup.
– ORIGIN Fr., from *chiffonner* 'to crumple'.

**chiffonier** /ˌʃɪfəˈnɪə/ ● **n. 1** Brit. a low cupboard either used as a sideboard or with a raised bookshelf on top. **2** N. Amer. a tall chest of drawers.
– ORIGIN C18: from Fr. *chiffonnier*, *chiffonnière*, lit. 'rag-picker', also denoting a chest of drawers for oddments.

**chifforobe** /ˈʃɪfərəʊb/ ● **n.** US a piece of furniture with drawers on one side and hanging space on the other.
– ORIGIN C20: blend of **CHIFFONIER** and **WARDROBE**.

**chigger** /ˈtʃɪɡə, ˈdʒ-/ (also **jigger**) ● **n. 1** a tropical flea, the female of which burrows and lays eggs beneath the host's skin, causing painful sores. [*Tunga penetrans*.] **2** N. Amer. a harvest mite.
– ORIGIN C18: var. of **CHIGOE**.

**chignon** /ˈʃiːnjɒ̃/ ● **n.** a knot or coil of hair arranged on the back of a woman's head.
– ORIGIN C18: from Fr., orig. 'nape of the neck'.

**chigoe** /ˈtʃɪɡəʊ/ ● **n.** another term for **CHIGGER** (in sense 1).
– ORIGIN C17: from Fr. *chique*, from a W. Afr. lang.

**chihuahua** /tʃɪˈwɑːwə/ ● **n.** a very small dog of a smooth-haired large-eyed breed originating in Mexico.
– ORIGIN C19: named after *Chihuahua* in northern Mexico.

**chikungunya** /ˌtʃɪk(ə)nˈɡʌnjə/ ● **n.** a viral disease resembling dengue, transmitted by mosquitoes and endemic in East Africa and parts of Asia.
– ORIGIN 1950s: a local Afr. word.

**chilblain** ● **n.** a painful, itching swelling on a hand or foot caused by poor circulation in the skin when exposed to cold.
– DERIVATIVES **chilblained** adj.

**child** ● **n.** (pl. **children**) **1** a young human being below the age of full physical development. ➤a son or daughter of any age. **2** derogatory an immature or irresponsible person. **3** (**children**) archaic the descendants of a family or people.
– PHRASES **child's play** a task which is easily accomplished. **with child** archaic pregnant.
– DERIVATIVES **childhood** n. **childless** adj. **childlessness** n.
– ORIGIN OE *cild*, of Gmc origin.

**childbearing** ● **n.** the process of giving birth to children.

**childbed** ● **n.** archaic term for **CHILDBIRTH**.

**child benefit** ● **n.** (in the UK) regular payment by the state to the parents of a child up to a certain age.

**childbirth** ● **n.** the action of giving birth to a child.

**childcare** ● **n.** the care of children, especially by a crèche, nursery, etc. while the parents are working.

**child-centred** ● **adj.** giving priority to the interests and needs of children.

**Childe** /tʃʌɪld/ ● **n.** archaic a youth of noble birth.
– ORIGIN OE, var. of **CHILD**.

**Childermas** /ˈtʃɪldəmas/ ● **n.** archaic the feast of the Holy Innocents, 28 December.
– ORIGIN OE *cildramæsse*, from *cildra* 'of children' + *mæsse* (see **MASS**).

**childish** ● **adj.** of, like, or appropriate to a child. ➤silly and immature.
– DERIVATIVES **childishly** adv. **childishness** n.

**childlike** ● **adj.** (of an adult) having the good qualities, such as innocence, associated with a child.

**childminder** ● **n.** Brit. a person who looks after children in their own house for payment.

**childproof** ● **adj.** designed to prevent children from injuring themselves or doing damage.

**children** plural form of **CHILD**.

**chile** ● **n.** variant spelling of **CHILLI**.

**Chilean** /ˈtʃɪliən/ ● **n.** a native or inhabitant of Chile. ● **adj.** of or relating to Chile.

**Chile pine** ● **n.** another term for **MONKEY PUZZLE**.

**chile relleno** /ˌtʃɪlɪ rɛˈljeɪnəʊ/ ● **n.** (pl. **chiles rellenos**) (in Mexican cuisine) a stuffed chilli pepper, typically battered and deep-fried.
– ORIGIN Sp., 'stuffed chilli'.

**chili** ● **n.** (pl. **chilies**) US spelling of **CHILLI**.

**chiliarch** /ˈkɪlɪɑːk/ ● **n.** historical (in ancient Greece) a commander of a thousand men.
– ORIGIN C16: via late L. from Gk *khiliarkhēs*, from *khilioi* 'thousand'.

**chiliast** /ˈkɪlɪast/ ● **n.** another term for **MILLENARIAN**.
– DERIVATIVES **chiliasm** n. **chiliastic** adj.
– ORIGIN C16: via late L. from Gk *khiliastēs*, from *khilias* 'a thousand years', from *khilioi* 'thousand'.

**chill** ● **n. 1** an unpleasant feeling of coldness. **2** a feverish cold. **3** a metal mould designed to aid cooling of metal during casting. ● **v. 1** make cold. ➤cool (food or drink) in a refrigerator. **2** horrify or frighten. **3** (usu. **chill out**) informal calm down and relax. ● **adj.** chilly.
– DERIVATIVES **chilling** adj. **chillingly** adv. **chillness** n. **chillsome** adj. (poetic/literary).
– ORIGIN OE *cele*, *ciele* 'cold, coldness', of Gmc origin; rel. to **COLD**.

**chill-cast** • v. Metallurgy rapidly solidify (cast metal) by contact with a cooled metal mould in order to produce a hard, dense surface.

**chiller** • n. **1** a cold cabinet or refrigerator for keeping stored food a few degrees above freezing point. **2** short for SPINE-CHILLER.

**chill factor** • n. a quantity expressing the perceived lowering of the air temperature caused by the wind.

**chilli** /ˈtʃɪli/ (also **chilli pepper**, **chile**, US **chili**) • n. (pl. **chillies**, **chiles**, or US **chilies**) **1** a small hot-tasting pod of a variety of capsicum, used in sauces, relishes, and spice powders. **2** short for CHILLI POWDER or CHILLI CON CARNE.
– ORIGIN C17: from Sp. *chile*, from Nahuatl *chilli*.

**chilli con carne** /kɒn ˈkɑːneɪ, -ni/ • n. a stew of minced beef and beans flavoured with chilli powder.
– ORIGIN from Sp. *chile con carne*, lit. 'chilli pepper with meat'.

**chilli powder** • n. a hot-tasting mixture of ground dried red chillies and other spices.

**chillum** /ˈtʃɪləm/ • n. (pl. **chillums**) **1** a hookah. **2** a pipe used for smoking cannabis.
– ORIGIN from Hindi *cilam*.

**chilly** • adj. (**-ier**, **-iest**) **1** unpleasantly cold. **2** unfriendly.
– DERIVATIVES **chilliness** n.

**Chilopoda** /ˌkʌɪləˈpəʊdə/ • pl. n. Zoology a class of myriapod arthropods which comprises the centipedes.
– DERIVATIVES **chilopod** /ˈkʌɪləpɒd/ n.
– ORIGIN mod. L., from Gk *kheilos* 'lip' + *pous, pod-* 'foot'.

**chimaera** • n. variant spelling of CHIMERA.

**chime**[1] • n. **1** a bell or a metal bar or tube tuned and used in a set to produce melodious ringing sounds when struck. ➤a sound made by such an instrument. **2** Bell-ringing a stroke of the clapper against one or both sides of a scarcely moving bell. • v. **1** (of a bell or clock) make chimes. **2** (**chime with**) be in agreement with. **3** (**chime in**) interject a remark.
– DERIVATIVES **chimer** n.
– ORIGIN ME (in the senses 'cymbal' and 'ring out'): prob. from OE *cimbal* (see CYMBAL), later interpreted as *chime bell*.

**chime**[2] (also **chimb**) • n. the projecting rim at the end of a cask.
– ORIGIN ME: prob. from an OE word rel. to Du. *kim* and Ger. *Kimme*; cf. CHINE[3].

**chimera** /kʌɪˈmɪərə, kɪ-/ (also **chimaera**) • n. **1** Greek Mythology a fire-breathing female monster with a lion's head, a goat's body, and a serpent's tail. **2** something hoped for but illusory or impossible to achieve. **3** Biology an organism containing a mixture of genetically different tissues, formed by processes such as fusion of early embryos, grafting, or mutation. **4** (**chimaera**) a long-tailed cartilaginous marine fish with an erect spine before the first dorsal fin. [*Chimaera* and other genera, family Chimaeridae.]
– DERIVATIVES **chimeric** /-ˈmɛrɪk/ adj. **chimerical** adj. **chimerically** adv.
– ORIGIN ME: via L. from Gk *khimaira* 'she-goat or chimera'.

**chimichanga** /ˌtʃɪmɪˈtʃaŋgə/ • n. a tortilla rolled round a savoury filling and deep-fried.
– ORIGIN Mex. Sp., lit. 'trinket'.

**chimney** • n. (pl. **-eys**) **1** a vertical pipe which conducts smoke and gases up from a fire or furnace. ➤a chimney stack. **2** a glass tube protecting the flame of a lamp. **3** a very steep narrow cleft by which a rock face may be climbed.
– ORIGIN ME: from OFr. *cheminee*, from late L. *caminata*, perh. from *camera caminata* 'room with a fireplace', from L. *caminus* 'forge, furnace', from Gk *kaminos* 'oven'.

**chimney breast** • n. a part of an interior wall that projects to surround a chimney.

**chimney corner** • n. a warm seat within an old-fashioned fireplace.

**chimney piece** • n. Brit. a mantelpiece.

**chimney pot** • n. an earthenware or metal pipe at the top of a chimney.

**chimney stack** • n. the part of a chimney that projects above a roof.

**chimney sweep** • n. a person whose job is cleaning out the soot from chimneys.

**chimonanthus** /ˌkʌɪmə(ʊ)ˈnanθəs/ • n. a shrub of a Chinese genus including the wintersweet. [Genus *Chimonanthus*.]
– ORIGIN mod. L., from Gk *kheimōn* 'winter' + *anthos* 'flower'.

**chimp** • n. informal term for CHIMPANZEE.

**chimpanzee** • n. an anthropoid ape with large ears, mainly black coloration, and lighter skin on the face, native to west and central Africa. [*Pan troglodytes* and *P. paniscus* (the bonobo or **pygmy chimpanzee**).]
– ORIGIN C18: from Fr. *chimpanzé*, from Kikongo.

**Chimu** /tʃiːˈmuː/ • n. (pl. same or **Chimus**) **1** a member of a native people of Peru that developed the most important civilization before the Incas. **2** the extinct language of this people.
– ORIGIN from Sp.

**Chin** /tʃɪn/ • n. **1** a member of a people of SW Burma (Myanmar) and neighbouring parts of India and Bangladesh. **2** the Tibeto-Burman language of this people.
– ORIGIN from Burmese, 'hill man'.

**chin** • n. the protruding part of the face below the mouth, formed by the apex of the lower jaw. • v. **1** informal hit or punch on the chin. **2** draw one's body up so that one's chin is level with (a horizontal bar), as an exercise.
– PHRASES **keep one's chin up** informal remain cheerful in difficult circumstances. **take it on the chin** informal accept misfortune stoically.
– DERIVATIVES **-chinned** adj.
– ORIGIN OE *cin, cinn*, of Gmc origin.

**china** • n. **1** a fine white or translucent vitrified ceramic material. ➤household tableware or other objects made from china. **2** Brit. informal a friend. [from rhyming sl. *china plate* 'mate'.]
– ORIGIN C16: from Pers. *chīnī* 'relating to China'.

**China aster** • n. a Chinese plant of the daisy family, cultivated for its bright showy flowers. [*Callistephus chinensis*.]

**chinaberry** • n. (pl. **-ies**) **1** a tall tree bearing fragrant lilac flowers and yellow berries, native to Asia and Australasia. [*Melia azedarach*.] **2** the fruit of this tree.

**china blue** • n. a pale greyish blue.

**china clay** • n. another term for KAOLIN.

**chinagraph pencil** • n. Brit. a waxy pencil used to write on china, glass, or other hard surfaces.

**Chinaman** • n. (pl. **-men**) **1** chiefly archaic or derogatory a native of China. **2** Cricket a ball that spins from off to leg, bowled by a left-handed bowler to a right-handed batsman.

**China rose** • n. **1** a Chinese rose from which various garden rose varieties have been derived. [*Rosa chinensis*.] **2** a shrubby tropical hibiscus cultivated for its large showy flowers. [*Hibiscus rosa-sinensis*.]

**china stone** • n. partly kaolinized granite containing plagioclase feldspar, which is ground and mixed with kaolin to make porcelain.

**China syndrome** • n. a hypothetical sequence of events following the meltdown of a nuclear reactor, in which the core melts through its containment structure and deep into the earth.
– ORIGIN 1970s: so named because China is on the opposite side of the earth from a reactor in the US.

**China tea** • n. tea made from a small-leaved type of tea plant grown in China, typically flavoured by smoke curing or the addition of flower petals.

**Chinatown** • n. a district of a non-Chinese town in which the population is predominantly of Chinese origin.

**chinch bug** /tʃɪn(t)ʃ/ • n. a plant-eating ground bug that forms large swarms on grasses and rushes. [*Blissus leucopterus* (America) and *Ischnodemus sabuleti* (Europe).]
– ORIGIN C17 (in the sense 'bedbug'): from Sp. *chinche*, from L. *cimex, cimic-*.

**chincherinchee** /ˌtʃɪntʃərɪnˈtʃiː/ • n. a white-flowered

South African lily. [*Ornithogalum thyrsoides*.]
– ORIGIN C20: imitative of the squeaky sound made by rubbing its stalks together.

**chinchilla** /tʃɪn'tʃɪlə/ ● n. **1** a small South American rodent with soft grey fur and a long bushy tail. [Genus *Chinchilla*: two species.] **2** a cat or rabbit of a breed with silver-grey or grey fur. **3** the highly valued fur of the chinchilla, or of the chinchilla rabbit.
– ORIGIN C17: from Sp., from Aymara or Quechua.

**chin-chin** ● exclam. Brit. informal, dated a toast made before drinking.
– ORIGIN C18: representing a pronunc. of Chin. *qing qing*.

**Chindit** /'tʃɪndɪt/ ● n. a member of the Allied forces behind the Japanese lines in Burma (now Myanmar) in 1943–5.
– ORIGIN Second World War: from Burmese *chinthé*, a mythical creature.

**chine**[1] /tʃʌɪn/ ● n. **1** the backbone of an animal as it appears in a joint of meat. ➤ a joint of meat containing all or part of this. **2** a mountain ridge. ● v. cut (meat) across or along the backbone.
– ORIGIN ME: from OFr. *eschine*, based on a blend of L. *spina* 'spine' and a Gmc word meaning 'narrow piece', rel. to SHIN.

**chine**[2] /tʃʌɪn/ ● n. (in the Isle of Wight or Dorset) a deep narrow ravine.
– ORIGIN OE *cinu* 'cleft, chink', of Gmc origin; rel. to CHINK[1].

**chine**[3] /tʃʌɪn/ ● n. the angle where the strakes of the bottom of a boat or ship meet the side.
– ORIGIN ME: var. of CHIME[2].

**Chinese** ● n. (pl. same) **1** the language of China. **2** a native or national of China, or a person of Chinese descent. ● adj. of or relating to China, its people or their language. ➤ belonging to the dominant ethnic group of China (the Han).

**Chinese box** ● n. each of a nest of boxes.

**Chinese burn** ● n. informal a burning sensation inflicted on a person by placing both hands on their arm and then twisting it.

**Chinese cabbage** ● n. another term for CHINESE LEAVES.

**Chinese chequers** (US **Chinese checkers**) ● pl. n. [usu. treated as sing.] a board game for two to six players who attempt to move marbles or counters from one corner to the opposite one on a star-shaped board.

**Chinese fire drill** ● n. N. Amer. informal a state of disorder or confusion.

**Chinese gooseberry** ● n. former term for KIWI FRUIT.

**Chinese lantern** ● n. **1** a collapsible paper lantern. **2** a plant with globular orange fruits enclosed in an orange-red papery calyx. [*Physalis alkekengi*.]

**Chinese layering** ● n. another term for AIR LAYERING.

**Chinese leaves** (also **Chinese cabbage**) ● pl. n. an oriental variety of cabbage which does not form a firm heart. [*Brassica chinensis* (pak choi) and *B. pekinenis* (pe tsai).]

**Chinese puzzle** ● n. an intricate puzzle consisting of many interlocking pieces.

**Chinese red** ● n. a vivid orange-red.

**Chinese wall** ● n. an insurmountable barrier, especially to the passage of information.

**Chinese whispers** ● pl. n. [treated as sing.] a game in which a message is distorted by being passed around in a whisper.

**Chinese white** ● n. white pigment consisting of zinc oxide.

**ching** ● n. an abrupt high-pitched ringing sound.

**Chink** ● n. informal, offensive a Chinese person.

**chink**[1] ● n. **1** a narrow opening or crack. **2** a beam of light admitted by a chink.
– ORIGIN C16: rel. to CHINE[2].

**chink**[2] ● v. make a light, high-pitched ringing sound, as of glasses or coins striking together. ● n. a high-pitched ringing sound.
– ORIGIN C16: imitative.

**chinkapin** ● n. variant spelling of CHINQUAPIN.

**chinkara** /tʃɪŋ'kɑːrə/ ● n. (pl. same) the Indian gazelle. [*Gazella bennettii*.]
– ORIGIN C19: from Hindi *cikārā*, from Sanskrit *chikkāra*.

**Chinky** ● n. (pl. **-ies**) informal **1** offensive a Chinese person. **2** a Chinese restaurant.

**chinless** ● adj. **1** lacking a well-defined chin. **2** informal lacking strength of character.

**chin music** ● n. informal, chiefly US idle chatter.

**chino** /'tʃiːnəʊ/ ● n. (pl. **-os**) **1** a cotton twill fabric, typically khaki-coloured. **2** (**chinos**) casual trousers made from such fabric.
– ORIGIN 1940s: from Latin Amer. Sp., lit. 'toasted' (referring to the typical colour).

**Chino-** /'tʃʌɪnəʊ/ ● comb. form equivalent to SINO-.

**chinoiserie** /ʃɪn'wɑːzəri/ ● n. (pl. **-ies**) the use of Chinese motifs and techniques in Western art, furniture, and architecture. ➤ objects or decorations in this style.
– ORIGIN C19: from Fr., from *chinois* 'Chinese'.

**Chinook** /tʃɪ'nuːk, -'nʊk, ʃɪ-/ ● n. (pl. same or **Chinooks**) **1** a member of an American Indian people originally inhabiting the region around the Columbia River in Oregon. **2** the extinct Penutian language of this people.
– ORIGIN from Salish *tsinúk*.

**chinook** /tʃɪ'nuːk, -nʊk, ʃɪ-/ ● n. **1** (also **chinook wind**) a warm, dry wind which blows down the east side of the Rocky Mountains at the end of winter. **2** (also **chinook salmon**) a large North Pacific salmon which is an important commercial food fish. [*Oncorhynchus tshawytscha*.]

**Chinook Jargon** ● n. an extinct pidgin composed of elements from Chinook, Nootka, English, French, and other languages, formerly used in the Pacific North-West of North America.

**chinquapin** /'tʃɪŋkəpɪn/ (also **chinkapin**) ● n. **1** a North American chestnut tree. [*Castanea pumila* and other species.] **2** the edible nut of this tree.
– ORIGIN C17: from Virginia Algonquian.

**chinstrap** ● n. a strap attached to a hat, helmet, etc., to keep it in place by fitting under the wearer's chin.

**chintz** ● n. printed multicoloured cotton fabric with a glazed finish, used especially for curtains and upholstery.
– ORIGIN C17 (as *chints*, pl. of *chint*, denoting a stained or painted calico cloth imported from India): from Hindi *chīṃṭ* 'spattering, stain'.

**chintzy** ● adj. (**-ier**, **-iest**) **1** decorated with or resembling chintz. **2** gaudy and tasteless. **3** N. Amer. informal miserly.
– DERIVATIVES **chintzily** adv. **chintziness** n.

**chin-up** ● n. chiefly N. Amer. another term for PULL-UP.

**chinwag** Brit. informal ● n. a chat. ● v. (**-wagged**, **-wagging**) have a chat.

**chionodoxa** /ˌkʌɪənə'dɒksə/ ● n. a bulbous plant of the lily family, with early blooming blue flowers. [Genus *Chionodoxa*.]
– ORIGIN mod. L., from Gk *khiōn* 'snow' + *doxa* 'glory'.

**chip** ● n. **1** a small, thin piece removed in the course of chopping, cutting, or breaking a hard material. ➤ a blemish left by the removal of such a piece. ➤ Brit. wood or woody fibre split into thin strips and used for weaving hats or baskets. **2** chiefly Brit. a long rectangular piece of deep-fried potato. ➤ (also **potato chip**) chiefly N. Amer. a potato crisp. **3** short for MICROCHIP. **4** a counter used in certain gambling games to represent money. **5** (in football or golf) a short lofted kick or shot. ● v. (**chipped**, **chipping**) **1** cut or break (a chip) from a hard material. ➤ (of a hard material or object) break at the edge or on the surface. **2** (**chip away**) gradually and relentlessly make something smaller or weaker: *rivals may chip away at one's profits.* **3** (**chip in**) contribute one's share of a joint activity. ➤ Brit. informal make an interjection. **4** [usu. as adj. **chipped**] Brit. cut (a potato) into chips. **5** (in football or golf) strike (the ball) to produce a short lofted shot or pass.
– PHRASES **a chip off the old block** informal someone who resembles their parent in character. **a chip on one's shoulder** informal a deeply ingrained grievance. **have had**

**one's chips** Brit. informal be dead or out of contention. **when the chips are down** informal when a very serious situation arises.
– ORIGIN ME: rel. to OE *forcippian* 'cut off'.

**chipboard** ● n. material made in rigid sheets from compressed wood chips and resin and used for furniture and in buildings.

**Chipewyan** /ˌtʃɪpəˈwʌɪən/ ● n. (pl. same or **Chipewyans**) **1** a member of a Dene people of NW Canada. Compare with **CHIPPEWA**. **2** the Athabaskan language of this people.
– ORIGIN from Cree, lit. '(wearing) pointed-skin (garments)'.

**chipmunk** ● n. a burrowing ground squirrel with cheek pouches and light and dark stripes running down the body, found in North America and northern Eurasia. [Genus *Tamias*: many species.]
– ORIGIN C19: from Ojibwa.

**chipolata** ● n. Brit. a small thin sausage.
– ORIGIN C19: from Fr., from Ital. *cipollata* 'a dish of onions', from *cipolla* 'onion'.

**chipotle** /tʃɪˈpəʊtleɪ/ ● n. a smoked hot chilli pepper which is used in Mexican cooking.
– ORIGIN Mex. Sp., from Nahuatl.

**Chippendale** /ˈtʃɪp(ə)ndeɪl/ ● adj. (of furniture) designed by or in the style of Thomas Chippendale (1718–79), neoclassical with elements of French rococo and chinoiserie.

**chipper**[1] ● adj. informal cheerful and lively.
– ORIGIN C19: perh. from north. Engl. dial. *kipper* 'lively'.

**chipper**[2] ● n. **1** a thing that turns something into chips. **2** Irish informal a fish-and-chip shop.

**Chippewa** /ˈtʃɪpəwɔː, -wɑː/ (also **Chippeway** /-weɪ/) ● n. (pl. same) chiefly N. Amer. another term for **OJIBWA**. Compare with **CHIPEWYAN**.
– ORIGIN alt. of **OJIBWA**.

**chipping** ● n. Brit. a small fragment of stone, wood, or similar material.

**chippy** informal ● n. (also **chippie**) (pl. **-ies**) **1** Brit. a fish-and-chip shop. **2** Brit. a carpenter. **3** N. Amer. a prostitute. ● adj. touchy and irritable.

**chiral** /ˈkʌɪr(ə)l/ ● adj. Chemistry (of a molecule) not able to be superimposed on its mirror image.
– DERIVATIVES **chirality** n.
– ORIGIN C19: from Gk *kheir* 'hand' + **-AL**.

**chi-rho** ● n. a monogram of chi (X) and rho (P) as the first two letters of Greek *Khristos* Christ.

**chirimoya** /ˌtʃɪrɪˈmɔɪə/ ● n. variant spelling of **CHERIMOYA**.

**chiro-** /ˈkʌɪrəʊ/ (also **cheiro-**) ● comb. form of the hand or hands: *chiromancy*.
– ORIGIN from Gk *kheir* 'hand'.

**chirography** /kʌɪˈrɒgrəfi/ ● n. handwriting, especially as distinct from typography.
– DERIVATIVES **chirographic** adj.

**chiromancy** /ˈkʌɪrə(ʊ)mansi/ ● n. the prediction of a person's future from the lines on the palms of their hands; palmistry.

**chironomid** /kʌɪˈrɒnəmɪd/ ● n. Entomology an insect of a family (Chironomidae) which comprises the non-biting midges.
– ORIGIN C19: from mod. L. *Chironomus* (genus name), from Gk *kheironomos* 'pantomime dancer'.

**chiropody** ● n. the treatment of the feet and their ailments.
– DERIVATIVES **chiropodist** n.
– ORIGIN C19: from **CHIRO-** + Gk *pous, pod-* 'foot'.

**chiropractic** /ˌkʌɪrə(ʊ)ˈpraktɪk/ ● n. a system of complementary medicine based on the diagnosis and manipulative treatment of misalignments of the joints, especially those of the spinal column.
– DERIVATIVES **chiropractor** n.
– ORIGIN C19: from **CHIRO-** + Gk *praktikos* 'practical'.

**Chiroptera** /kʌɪˈrɒpt(ə)rə/ ● pl. n. Zoology an order of mammals that comprises the bats.
– DERIVATIVES **chiropteran** n. & adj.
– ORIGIN mod. L., from **CHIRO-** + Gk *pteron* 'wing'.

**chirp** ● v. **1** (of a small bird or a grasshopper) utter a short, sharp, high-pitched sound. **2** say something in a lively and cheerful way. ● n. a chirping sound.
– DERIVATIVES **chirper** n.
– ORIGIN ME: imitative.

**chirpy** ● adj. (**-ier**, **-iest**) informal cheerful and lively.
– DERIVATIVES **chirpily** adv. **chirpiness** n.

**chirr** /tʃəː/ (also **churr**) ● v. (especially of an insect) make a prolonged low trilling sound. ● n. a low trilling sound.
– ORIGIN C17: imitative.

**chirrup** ● v. (**chirruped**, **chirruping**) (of a small bird) make repeated short high-pitched sounds. ● n. a chirruping sound.
– DERIVATIVES **chirrupy** adj.
– ORIGIN C16: alt. of **CHIRP**.

**chiru** /ˈtʃɪruː/ ● n. (pl. same) a sandy-coloured Tibetan gazelle with black horns. [*Pantholops hodgsoni*.]
– ORIGIN C19: prob. from Tibetan.

**chisel** /ˈtʃɪz(ə)l/ ● n. a long-bladed hand tool with a bevelled cutting edge, struck with a hammer or mallet to cut or shape wood, stone, or metal. ● v. (**chiselled**, **chiselling**; US **chiseled**, **chiseling**) **1** cut or shape with a chisel. **2** [as adj. **chiselled**] (of a man's facial features) strongly and clearly defined. **3** informal, chiefly N. Amer. cheat or swindle out of something.
– DERIVATIVES **chiseller** n.
– ORIGIN ME: from ONorth. Fr., based on L. *cis-* (as in late L. *cisorium*), var. of *caes-*, *caedere* 'to cut'.

**chit**[1] ● n. derogatory an impudent or arrogant young woman: *a chit of a girl*.
– ORIGIN ME (denoting a whelp, cub, or kitten): perh. rel. to dial. *chit* 'sprout'.

**chit**[2] ● n. a short official note, memorandum, or voucher, typically recording a sum owed.
– ORIGIN C18: Anglo-Ind., from Hindi *ciṭṭhī* 'note, pass'.

**chit**[3] ● v. (**chitted**, **chitting**) induce (a potato) to sprout by placing it in a cool light place.
– ORIGIN C17: from dial. *chit* 'a shoot, sprout'.

**chital** /ˈtʃiːt(ə)l/ ● n. a deer that has lyre-shaped antlers and a fawn coat with white spots, native to India and Sri Lanka. [*Cervus axis*.]
– ORIGIN C19: from Hindi *cītal*, from Sanskrit *citrala* 'spotted'.

**chitarrone** /ˌkɪtəˈrəʊneɪ, -ni/ ● n. a very large lute similar to a theorbo, used in Italy in the late 16th and early 17th centuries.
– ORIGIN Ital., lit. 'large guitar'.

**chit-chat** informal ● n. inconsequential conversation. ● v. talk about trivial matters.
– ORIGIN C17: reduplication of **CHAT**[1].

**chitin** /ˈkʌɪtɪn/ ● n. Biochemistry a fibrous carbohydrate which forms the exoskeleton of arthropods and the cell walls of fungi.
– DERIVATIVES **chitinous** adj.
– ORIGIN C19: from Fr. *chitine*, from Gk *khitōn* (see **CHITON**).

**chiton** /ˈkʌɪtɒn, -t(ə)n/ ● n. **1** a long woollen tunic worn in ancient Greece. **2** a marine mollusc that has an oval flattened body with a shell of overlapping plates. [*Chiton* and other genera, class Polyplacophora.]
– ORIGIN from Gk *khitōn* 'tunic'.

**chitter** ● v. **1** make a twittering or chattering sound. **2** Scottish & dialect shiver with cold.
– ORIGIN ME: imitative; cf. **CHATTER**.

**chitterlings** /ˈtʃɪtəlɪŋz/ ● pl. n. the smaller intestines of a pig, cooked for food.
– ORIGIN ME: perh. rel. to synonymous Ger. *Kutteln*.

**chitty** ● n. (pl. **-ies**) Brit. informal term for **CHIT**[2].

**chivalry** ● n. **1** the medieval knightly system with its religious, moral, and social code. **2** archaic knights, noblemen, and horsemen collectively. **3** the combination of qualities expected of an ideal knight, especially courage, honour, courtesy, justice, and a readiness to help the weak. ➤courteous behaviour, especially that of a man towards women.
– DERIVATIVES **chivalric** adj. **chivalrous** adj. **chivalrously** adv.
– ORIGIN ME: from OFr. *chevalerie*, from med. L.

*caballerius*, for late L. *caballarius* (see **CHEVALIER**).

**chives** ● **pl. n.** a small plant related to the onion, with long tubular leaves used as a culinary herb. [*Allium schoenoprasum*.]
– ORIGIN ME: from OFr., var. of *cive*, from L. *cepa* 'onion'.

**chivvy** (also **chivy**) ● **v.** (**-ies**, **-ied**) tell repeatedly to do something.
– ORIGIN C18: orig. a noun denoting a hunting cry, prob. from the ballad *Chevy Chase*, celebrating a skirmish on the Sc. border.

**Chladni patterns** /ˈkladni/ ● **pl. n.** the patterns formed when a sand-covered surface is made to vibrate.
– ORIGIN C19: named after Ger. physicist Ernst *Chladni*.

**chlamydia** /kləˈmɪdɪə/ ● **n.** (pl. same or **chlamydiae** /-dɪiː/) a very small parasitic bacterium which, like a virus, requires the biochemical mechanisms of another cell in order to reproduce. [Genus *Chlamydia*, order Chlamydiales.]
– DERIVATIVES **chlamydial** adj.
– ORIGIN 1960s: mod. L., from Gk *khlamus, khlamud-* 'cloak'.

**chlamydomonas** /ˌklamɪdəˈməʊnəs/ ● **n.** Biology a common single-celled green alga living in water and moist soil. [Genus *Chlamydomonas*.]
– ORIGIN C19: mod. L., from Gk *khlamus, khlamud-* 'cloak' + *monas* (see **MONAD**).

**chlamydospore** /ˈklamɪdə(ʊ)spɔː/ ● **n.** Botany (in certain fungi) a thick-walled hyphal cell which functions like a spore.
– ORIGIN C19: from Gk *khlamus, khlamud-* 'cloak' + **SPORE**.

**chlamys** /ˈklamɪs/ ● **n.** a short cloak worn by men in ancient Greece.
– ORIGIN C17: from Gk *khlamus*.

**chloasma** /kləʊˈazmə/ ● **n.** Medicine a temporary condition, typically caused by hormones, in which large brown patches form on the skin.
– ORIGIN C19: from Gk *khloazein* 'become green'.

**chlor-** ● **comb. form** variant spelling of **CHLORO-** before a vowel: *chloracne*.

**chloracne** /klɔːˈrakni/ ● **n.** Medicine a skin disease resembling severe acne, caused by exposure to chlorinated chemicals.

**chloral** /ˈklɔːral/ ● **n.** Chemistry a viscous liquid made by chlorinating acetaldehyde and used as a sedative in the form of a crystalline hydrate.
– ORIGIN C19: from Fr., blend of *chlore* 'chlorine' and *alcool* 'alcohol'.

**chloramine** /ˈklɔːrəmiːn/ ● **n.** Chemistry any of a group of antiseptics and disinfectants which are sulphonamide derivatives containing chlorine bonded to nitrogen.

**chloramphenicol** /ˌklɔːramˈfɛnɪkɒl/ ● **n.** Medicine a bacterial antibiotic used against serious infections such as typhoid fever.
– ORIGIN 1940s: from **CHLOR-** + *am(ide)* + **PHENO-** + *ni(tro-)* + *(gly)col*.

**chlordane** /ˈklɔːdeɪn/ ● **n.** a toxic, viscous, synthetic compound used as an insecticide.
– ORIGIN 1940s: from **CHLOR-** + *(in)dene* + **-ANE**².

**chlordiazepoxide** /ˌklɔːdʌɪazɪˈpɒksʌɪd/ ● **n.** Medicine a tranquillizer used chiefly to treat anxiety and alcoholism.
– ORIGIN 1960s: from **CHLOR-** + *diazo-* + **EPOXIDE**.

**chlorella** /kləˈrɛlə/ ● **n.** Biology a common single-celled green alga, responsible for turning stagnant water an opaque green. [Genus *Chlorella*.]
– ORIGIN mod. L., dimin. of Gk *khlōros* 'green'.

**chlorhexidine** /klɔːˈhɛksɪdiːn/ ● **n.** a synthetic compound used as a mild antiseptic.
– ORIGIN C20: from **CHLOR-** + *hex(ane)* + *-id(e)* + *(am)ine*.

**chloric acid** /ˈklɔːrɪk/ ● **n.** Chemistry a colourless liquid acid with strong oxidizing properties. [$HClO_3$.]
– DERIVATIVES **chlorate** n.

**chloride** /ˈklɔːrʌɪd/ ● **n.** Chemistry a compound of chlorine with another element or group: *sodium chloride*.

**chlorinate** /ˈklɔːrɪneɪt, ˈklɒ-/ ● **v.** impregnate or treat with chlorine.
– DERIVATIVES **chlorination** n. **chlorinator** n.

**chlorine** /ˈklɔːriːn/ ● **n.** the chemical element of atomic number 17, a toxic, irritant, pale green gas of the halogen group. (Symbol: **Cl**)
– ORIGIN C19: from Gk *khlōros* 'green' + **-INE**⁴.

**chlorite**¹ /ˈklɔːrʌɪt/ ● **n.** a dark green mineral found in many rocks, consisting of an aluminosilicate of magnesium and iron.
– ORIGIN C18: via L. from Gk *khlōritis*, a green precious stone.

**chlorite**² /ˈklɔːrʌɪt/ ● **n.** Chemistry a salt of chlorous acid, containing the anion $ClO_2^-$.

**chloro-** ● **comb. form 1** Biology & Mineralogy green: *chlorophyll*. **2** Chemistry representing **CHLORINE**: *chloroquine*.

**chlorofluorocarbon** /ˌklɔːrə(ʊ)ˌflʊərə(ʊ)ˈkɑːb(ə)n, -ˌflɔː-/ ● **n.** see **CFC**.

**chloroform** ● **n.** a volatile sweet-smelling liquid used as a solvent and formerly as a general anaesthetic. [$CHCl_3$.] ● **v.** make unconscious with this substance.
– ORIGIN C19: from **CHLORO-** + *form-* from **FORMIC ACID**.

**chloromelanite** /ˌklɔːrə(ʊ)ˈmɛlənʌɪt, ˌklɒ-/ ● **n.** a greenish-black variety of jadeite rich in iron.

**chlorophyll** /ˈklɔːrəfɪl, ˈklɒ-/ ● **n.** a green pigment which is responsible for the absorption of light by plants to provide energy for photosynthesis.
– DERIVATIVES **chlorophyllous** adj.
– ORIGIN C19: coined in Fr. from Gk *khlōros* 'green' + *phullon* 'leaf'.

**Chlorophyta** /ˈklɔːrə(ʊ)ˌfʌɪtə, ˈklɒ-/ ● **pl. n.** Botany a division of lower plants that comprises the green algae.
– DERIVATIVES **chlorophyte** n.
– ORIGIN mod. L., from Gk *khlōros* 'green' + *phuton* 'plant'.

**chloroplast** /ˈklɔːrə(ʊ)plast, -plɑːst, ˈklɒ-/ ● **n.** Botany a structure in green plant cells which contains chlorophyll and in which photosynthesis takes place.
– ORIGIN C19: from Gk *khlōros* 'green' + *plastos* 'formed'.

**chloroquine** /ˈklɔːrə(ʊ)kwiːn, ˈklɒ-/ ● **n.** Medicine a synthetic drug related to quinoline, chiefly used against malaria.

**chlorosis** /klɒˈrəʊsɪs/ ● **n. 1** Botany loss of the normal green coloration of leaves, caused by mineral deficiency, disease, or lack of light. **2** Medicine anaemia caused by iron deficiency, causing a pale, faintly greenish complexion.
– DERIVATIVES **chlorotic** adj.

**chlorous acid** /ˈklɔːrəs/ ● **n.** Chemistry a weak acid with oxidizing properties, formed when chlorine dioxide dissolves in water. [$HClO_2$.]

**chlorpromazine** /klɔːˈprəʊməzɪn, -ziːn/ ● **n.** Medicine a synthetic drug used as a tranquillizer, sedative, and anti-emetic.
– ORIGIN 1950s: from **CHLORO-** + *prom(eth)azine*.

**ChM** ● **abbrev.** Master of Surgery.
– ORIGIN from L. *Chirurgiae Magister*.

**chocaholic** ● **n.** variant spelling of **CHOCOHOLIC**.

**chocho** /ˈtʃəʊtʃəʊ/ ● **n.** (pl. **-os**) West Indian term for **CHOKO**.

**choc ice** ● **n.** Brit. a small block of ice cream with a thin coating of chocolate.

**chock** ● **n. 1** a wedge or block placed against a wheel or rounded object to prevent it from moving or to support it. **2** a ring with a gap at the top, through which a rope or line is run. ● **v.** support or make fast with a chock.
– ORIGIN ME: prob. from ONorth. Fr. var. of OFr. *çouche*, *çoche* 'block, log', of unknown ultimate origin.

**chocka** ● **adj.** Brit. short for **CHOCK-A-BLOCK**.

**chock-a-block** ● **adj.** informal crammed full.
– ORIGIN C19 (orig. in naut. use, with ref. to tackle having the two blocks run close together): from *chock* (in **CHOCK-FULL**) and **BLOCK**.

**chocker** ● **adj.** informal **1** Brit. tired of or disgusted with something. **2** chiefly Austral./NZ full.

**chock-full** ● **adj.** informal filled to overflowing.
– ORIGIN ME: of unknown origin; later assoc. with **CHOCK**.

**chockstone** ● **n.** Climbing a stone that has become wedged in a vertical cleft.

**chocoholic** (also **chocaholic**) ● **n.** informal a person who is very fond of chocolate.

**chocolate** ● **n. 1** a food made from roasted and ground cacao seeds, typically sweetened and eaten as confectionery. ➤a sweet covered with chocolate. **2** a drink made by mixing milk or water with chocolate. **3** a deep brown colour.
– DERIVATIVES **chocolatey** (also **chocolaty**) adj.
– ORIGIN C17: from Fr. *chocolat* or Sp. *chocolate*, from Nahuatl *chocolatl*, influenced by unrelated *cacaua-atl* 'drink made from cacao'.

**chocolate-box** ● **adj.** (of a view or picture) pretty in a trite, conventional way.

**chocolate spot** ● **n.** a fungal disease of field and broad beans, characterized by dark brown spots.

**chocolatier** /ˌtʃɒkəˈlatɪə, French ʃɔkɔlatje/ ● **n.** (pl. pronounced same) a maker or seller of chocolate.
– ORIGIN C19: from Fr.

**Choctaw** /ˈtʃɒktɔː/ ● **n.** (pl. same or **Choctaws**) **1** a member of an American Indian people now living mainly in Mississippi. **2** the Muskogean language of this people. **3** (in skating) a step from one edge of a skate to the other edge of the other skate in the opposite direction.
– ORIGIN from Choctaw *čahta*.

**choice** ● **n. 1** an act of choosing. ➤the right or ability to choose. **2** a range from which to choose. ➤something chosen. ● **adj. 1** (especially of food) of very good quality. **2** (of language) rude and abusive.
– DERIVATIVES **choicely** adv. **choiceness** n.
– ORIGIN ME: from OFr. *chois*, from *choisir* 'choose', of Gmc origin and rel. to **CHOOSE**.

**choir** ● **n. 1** an organized group of singers, especially one that takes part in church services. **2** a group of instruments of one family playing together. **3** the part of a cathedral or large church between the altar and the nave, used by the choir and clergy.
– ORIGIN ME *quer*, *quere*, from OFr. *quer*, from L. *chorus* (see **CHORUS**).

**choirboy** (or **choirgirl**) ● **n.** a boy (or girl) who sings in a church or cathedral choir.

**choir organ** ● **n.** a separate division of many large organs, played using a third manual (keyboard).

**choisya** /ˈtʃɔɪzɪə/ ● **n.** an evergreen Mexican shrub with sweet-scented white flowers, grown as an ornamental. [*Choisya ternata*.]
– ORIGIN named after the Swiss botanist Jacques D. *Choisy*.

**choke**[1] ● **v. 1** prevent from breathing by constricting or obstructing the throat or depriving of air. ➤have trouble breathing in such a way. **2** fill (a space) so as to make movement difficult or impossible. **3** make speechless with strong emotion. **4** enrich the fuel mixture in (a petrol engine) by reducing the intake of air. ● **n. 1** a valve in the carburettor of a petrol engine used to reduce the amount of air in the fuel mixture. **2** a narrowed part of a shotgun bore serving to restrict the spread of the shot. **3** an inductance coil used to smooth the variations of an alternating current or to alter its phase.
– ORIGIN ME: from OE *āceōcian* (v.), from *cēoce* (see **CHEEK**).

**choke**[2] ● **n.** the inedible mass of silky fibres at the centre of a globe artichoke.
– ORIGIN C17: prob. a confusion of the ending of *artichoke* with **CHOKE**[1].

**chokeberry** ● **n.** a North American shrub with white flowers, bitter scarlet berries, and red autumn foliage. [Genus *Aronia*.]

**choke chain** ● **n.** a chain formed into a loop by passing one end through a ring on the other, placed round a dog's neck to exert control.

**choke cherry** ● **n.** a North American cherry with astringent fruit which is edible when cooked. [*Prunus virginiana*.]

**choke-damp** ● **n.** choking or suffocating gas, typically carbon dioxide, that is found in mines and other underground spaces.

**chokehold** ● **n.** a tight grip round a person's neck, used to restrain them by restricting their breathing.

**choker** ● **n. 1** a close-fitting necklace or ornamental neckband. ➤a clerical or other high collar. **2** N. Amer. a cable looped round a log to drag it.

**chokey** (also **choky**) ● **n.** (pl. **-eys** or **-ies**) Brit. informal, dated prison.
– ORIGIN C17: Anglo-Ind., from Hindi *caukī* 'customs or toll house, police station'; influenced by **CHOKE**[1].

**choko** /ˈtʃəʊkəʊ/ ● **n.** (pl. **-os**) Austral./NZ the fruit of the chayote, eaten as a vegetable.
– ORIGIN C18: from Sp. *chocho*, from a Brazilian Indian word.

**chokra** /ˈtʃəʊkrə/ ● **n.** chiefly derogatory (in the Indian subcontinent) a boy, especially one employed as a servant.
– ORIGIN from Hindi *chokrā*.

**choky**[1] ● **adj.** (**-ier**, **-iest**) **1** having or causing difficulty in breathing. **2** breathless with emotion.

**choky**[2] ● **n.** variant spelling of **CHOKEY**.

**chola** /ˈtʃəʊlə/ ● **n.** fem. of **CHOLO**.

**cholangiography** /ˌkɒlandʒɪˈɒgrəfi/ ● **n.** Medicine X-ray examination of the bile ducts, used to locate and identify an obstruction.
– DERIVATIVES **cholangiogram** n.
– ORIGIN 1930s: coined in Sp. from Gk *khole* 'bile' + *angeion* 'vessel' + *-graphia* (see **-GRAPHY**).

**chole-** /ˈkɒli/ (also **chol-** before a vowel) ● **comb. form** Medicine & Chemistry relating to bile or the bile ducts: *cholesterol*.
– ORIGIN from Gk *kholē* 'gall, bile'.

**cholecalciferol** /ˌkɒlɪkalˈsɪf(ə)rɒl/ ● **n.** Biochemistry vitamin $D_3$, a compound essential for the deposition of calcium in bones and formed in the skin by the action of sunlight on dehydrocholesterol.

**cholecyst-** /ˈkɒlɪsɪst/ ● **comb. form** relating to the gall bladder: *cholecystectomy*.
– ORIGIN from mod. L. *cholecystis* 'gall bladder'.

**cholecystectomy** ● **n.** (pl. **-ies**) surgical removal of the gall bladder.

**cholelithiasis** /ˌkɒlɪlɪˈθʌɪəsɪs/ ● **n.** Medicine the formation of gallstones.

**cholent** /ˈtʃɒl(ə)nt, ˈʃɒ-/ ● **n.** a Jewish Sabbath dish of slowly baked meat and vegetables.
– ORIGIN from Yiddish *tsholnt*.

**choler** /ˈkɒlə/ ● **n. 1** (in medieval science and medicine) one of the four bodily humours, identified with bile, believed to be associated with a peevish or irascible temperament. **2** archaic or poetic/literary anger or irascibility.
– ORIGIN ME: from OFr. *colere*, from L. *cholera* 'diarrhoea' (from Gk *kholera*), which in late L. acquired the senses 'bile or anger', from Gk *kholē* 'bile'.

**cholera** /ˈkɒlərə/ ● **n. 1** an infectious and often fatal bacterial disease of the small intestine, typically contracted from infected water supplies and causing severe vomiting and diarrhoea. **2** (usu. **chicken cholera**) an infectious form of pasteurellosis affecting fowls.
– ORIGIN ME: from L. (see **CHOLER**).

**choleric** /ˈkɒlərɪk/ ● **adj. 1** bad-tempered or irritable. **2** (in medieval belief) influenced by or predominating in choler.
– DERIVATIVES **cholerically** adv.

**cholesterol** /kəˈlɛstərɒl/ ● **n.** a compound which is present in most body tissues and is important in metabolism, and of which high concentrations in the blood are thought to promote atherosclerosis.
– ORIGIN C19: from Gk *kholē* 'bile' + *stereos* 'stiff' + **-OL**.

**choli** /ˈtʃəʊli/ ● **n.** (pl. **cholis**) a short-sleeved bodice worn under a sari by Indian women.
– ORIGIN from Hindi *colī*.

**choliamb** /ˈkəʊlɪam(b)/ ● **n.** Prosody another term for **SCAZON**.
– DERIVATIVES **choliambic** /ˌkəʊlɪˈambɪk/ adj.
– ORIGIN C19: via late L. from Gk *khōliambos*, from *khōlos* 'lame' + *iambos* (see **IAMBUS**).

**cholic acid** /ˈkəʊlɪk, ˈkɒl-/ ● **n.** Biochemistry a compound whose salts are present in bile, produced by oxidation of cholesterol.
– ORIGIN C19: from Gk *kholikos*, from *kholē* 'bile'.

**choline** /ˈkəʊliːn, -lɪn/ ● **n.** Biochemistry a strongly basic

compound important in the synthesis and transport of lipids in the body.
– ORIGIN C19: coined in Ger. from Gk *kholē* 'bile'.

**cholinergic** /ˌkəʊlɪˈnəːdʒɪk/ ● **adj.** Physiology relating to or denoting nerve cells in which acetylcholine acts as a neurotransmitter.
– ORIGIN 1930s: from **CHOLINE** + Gk *ergon* 'work' + **-IC**.

**cholinesterase** /ˌkəʊlɪˈnɛstəreɪz/ ● **n.** Biochemistry an enzyme which breaks down esters of choline.

**cholla** /ˈtʃɔɪə/ ● **n.** a cactus with a cylindrical stem, native to Mexico and the south-western US. [Genus *Opuntia*.]
– ORIGIN C19: Mex. Sp. use of Sp. *cholla* 'skull, head'.

**cholo** /ˈtʃəʊləʊ/ ● **n.** (fem. **chola**) (pl. **-os** or **-as**) **1** a Latin American with Indian blood; a mestizo. **2** US derogatory a lower-class Mexican, especially in an urban area.
– ORIGIN C19: Amer. Sp., from *Chololián* (now *Cholula*), in Mexico.

**chometz** /hɔːˈmɛts, ˈxɔːmɛts/ ● **n.** variant spelling of **CHAMETZ**.

**chomp** ● **v.** munch or chew noisily or vigorously.
– ORIGIN C17: imitative.

**Chomskyan** /ˈtʃɒmskiən/ (also **Chomskian**) ● **adj.** of or relating to the American theoretical linguist Noam Chomsky (b. 1928). ● **n.** a follower of Chomsky.

**chondrite** /ˈkɒndrʌɪt/ ● **n.** a stony meteorite containing small mineral granules (chondrules).
– DERIVATIVES **chondritic** adj.
– ORIGIN C19: from Gk *khondros* 'granule' + **-ITE**[1].

**chondro-** /ˈkɒndrə(ʊ)/ ● **comb. form** of or relating to cartilage: *chondrocyte*.
– ORIGIN from Gk *khondros* 'grain or cartilage'.

**chondrocyte** /ˈkɒndrə(ʊ)sʌɪt/ ● **n.** Biology a cell which has secreted the matrix of cartilage and become embedded in it.

**chondroitin** /kɒnˈdrəʊɪtɪn/ ● **n.** Biochemistry a substance which is the major constituent of cartilage and other connective tissue.

**chondrule** /ˈkɒndruːl/ ● **n.** a spheroidal mineral grain present in large numbers in some stony meteorites.

**chook** /tʃʊk/ (also **chookie**) ● **n.** informal, chiefly Austral./NZ **1** a chicken or fowl. **2** derogatory an older woman.
– ORIGIN 1920s: prob. from Engl. dial. *chuck* 'chicken', of imitative origin.

**choose** ● **v.** (past **chose**; past part. **chosen**) **1** pick out as being the best of two or more alternatives. **2** decide on a course of action.
– DERIVATIVES **chooser** n.
– ORIGIN OE *cēosan*, of Gmc origin.

**choosy** ● **adj.** (**-ier**, **-iest**) informal overly fastidious in making a choice.
– DERIVATIVES **choosily** adv. **choosiness** n.

**chop**[1] ● **v.** (**chopped**, **chopping**) **1** cut with repeated sharp, heavy blows of an axe or knife. ➤strike with a short, heavy blow. **2** ruthlessly abolish or reduce in size. ● **n. 1** a downward cutting blow or movement. **2** (**the chop**) Brit. informal dismissal, cancellation, or killing. **3** a thick slice of meat, especially pork or lamb, adjacent to and usually including a rib. **4** N. Amer. crushed or ground grain used as animal feed. **5** a broken motion of waves.
– PHRASES **chop logic** argue in a tiresomely pedantic way. [C16: from a dial. use of *chop* meaning 'bandy words'.]
– ORIGIN ME: var. of **CHAP**[1].

**chop**[2] ● **v.** (**chopped**, **chopping**) (in phr. **chop and change**) Brit. informal change one's opinions or behaviour repeatedly and abruptly.
– ORIGIN ME (in the sense 'barter, exchange'): perh. rel. to OE *cēap* 'bargaining, trade'; cf. *chap-* in **CHAPMAN**.

**chop**[3] ● **n.** Brit. archaic a trademark or brand of goods.
– PHRASES **not much chop** informal, chiefly Austral./NZ unsatisfactory.
– ORIGIN C19: from Hindi *chāp* 'stamp, brand'.

**chop-chop** ● **adv. & exclam.** quickly.
– ORIGIN C19: pidgin Engl., based on Chin. dial. *kuài-kuài*; cf. **CHOPSTICK**.

**chophouse** ● **n.** a restaurant specializing in meat chops.

**chopper** ● **n. 1** Brit. a short axe with a large blade. ➤a machine for chopping. **2** a device for regularly interrupting a current or beam. **3** (**choppers**) informal teeth. **4** informal a helicopter. **5** informal a type of motorcycle with high handlebars. **6** vulgar slang a man's penis.

**choppy** ● **adj.** (**-ier**, **-iest**) (of the sea) having many small waves.
– DERIVATIVES **choppily** adv. **choppiness** n.

**chops** ● **pl. n.** informal **1** a person's or animal's mouth, jaws, or cheeks. **2** the technical skill of a jazz or rock musician.
– PHRASES **bust one's chops** N. Amer. informal exert oneself. **bust someone's chops** N. Amer. informal nag or criticize someone.
– ORIGIN ME: var. of **CHAP**[3].

**chopsocky** /ˈtʃɒpsɒki/ ● **n.** N. Amer. informal kung fu or a similar martial art, especially as depicted in violent action films.
– ORIGIN 1970s: humorous, perh. suggested by **CHOP SUEY**.

**chopstick** ● **n.** each of a pair of small, thin, tapered sticks held in one hand and used as eating utensils by the Chinese and Japanese.
– ORIGIN C17: pidgin Engl., from *chop* 'quick' + **STICK**[1], translating Chin. dial. *kuàizi*, lit. 'nimble ones'.

**chop suey** /tʃɒpˈsuːi/ ● **n.** a Chinese-style dish of meat stewed and fried with bean sprouts, bamboo shoots, and onions, and served with rice.
– ORIGIN C19: from Chin. *tsaâp suì* 'mixed bits'.

**choral** ● **adj.** of, for, or sung by a choir or chorus.
– DERIVATIVES **chorally** adv.
– ORIGIN C16: from med. L. *choralis*, from L. *chorus* (see **CHORUS**).

**chorale** ● **n. 1** a simple, stately hymn tune, or a composition consisting of a harmonized version of one. **2** chiefly US a choir or choral society.
– ORIGIN C19: from Ger. *Choral(gesang)*, translating med. L. *cantus choralis*.

**chord**[1] ● **n.** a group of notes (usually three or more) sounded together in harmony. ● **v.** [usu. as noun **chording**] play, sing, or arrange notes in chords.
– DERIVATIVES **chordal** adj.
– ORIGIN ME *cord*, from **ACCORD**; the spelling changed due to confusion with **CHORD**[2].

**chord**[2] ● **n. 1** a straight line joining the ends of an arc. **2** Aeronautics the width of an aerofoil from leading to trailing edge. **3** Engineering each of the two principal members of a truss. **4** Anatomy variant spelling of **CORD**. **5** poetic/literary a string on a harp or other instrument.
– PHRASES **strike** (or **touch**) **a chord** affect or stir someone's emotions.
– ORIGIN C16: a later spelling (influenced by L. *chorda* 'rope') of **CORD**.

**Chordata** /kɔːˈdeɪtə/ ● **pl. n.** Zoology a large phylum of animals including the vertebrates together with the sea squirts and lancelets, distinguished by possessing a notochord.
– DERIVATIVES **chordate** /ˈkɔːdeɪt/ n. & adj.
– ORIGIN mod. L., from L. *chorda* (see **CHORD**[2]), on the pattern of words such as *Vertebrata* (see **VERTEBRATE**).

**chordotonal** /ˌkɔːdə(ʊ)ˈtəʊn(ə)l/ ● **adj.** Entomology denoting sense organs responsive to mechanical and sound vibrations.

**chore** ● **n.** a routine or tedious task, especially a household one.
– ORIGIN C18 (orig. dial. and US): var. of obs. *char* or *chare* (see **CHARWOMAN**).

**chorea** /kɒˈrɪə/ ● **n.** Medicine a neurological disorder characterized by jerky involuntary movements affecting especially the shoulders, hips, and face.
– ORIGIN C17: via L. from Gk *khoreia* 'dancing in unison', from *khoros* 'chorus'.

**choreograph** /ˈkɒrɪəgrɑːf/ ● **v.** compose the sequence of steps and moves for (a ballet or other dance performance).
– DERIVATIVES **choreographer** n.

**choreography** /ˌkɒrɪˈɒgrəfi/ ● **n.** the sequence of steps and movements in dance, especially ballet. ➤the practice of designing such sequences.

– DERIVATIVES **choreographic** adj. **choreographically** adv.
– ORIGIN C18 (in the sense 'written notation of dancing'): from Gk *khoreia* 'dancing in unison' (from *khoros* 'chorus') + **-GRAPHY**.

**choreology** /ˌkɒrɪˈɒlədʒi/ ● **n.** the notation of dance movement.
– DERIVATIVES **choreologist** n.

**choriambus** /ˌkɒrɪˈambəs/ ● **n.** (pl. **choriambi** /-bʌɪ/) a metrical foot consisting of two short (or unstressed) syllables between two long (or stressed) ones.
– DERIVATIVES **choriambic** adj.
– ORIGIN C18: via late L. from Gk *khoriambos*, from *khoreios* 'of the dance' + *iambos* (see **IAMBUS**).

**choric** /ˈkɒrɪk, ˈkɔːrɪk/ ● **adj.** of or resembling a chorus in drama or recitation.

**chorine** /ˈkɔːriːn/ ● **n.** a chorus girl.

**chorio-** /ˈkɔːrɪəʊ/ ● **comb. form** representing **CHORION** or **CHOROID**.

**chorioallantoic** /ˌkɔːrɪəʊˌalənˈtəʊɪk, ˌkɒrɪəʊ-/ ● **adj.** Embryology relating to or denoting fused chorionic and allantoic membranes around a fetus.

**choriocarcinoma** /ˌkɔːrɪə(ʊ)ˌkɑːsɪˈnəʊmə, ˈkɒrɪəʊ-/ ● **n.** (pl. **choriocarcinomas** or **choriocarcinomata** /-mətə/) Medicine a malignant tumour of the uterus originating in the fetal chorion.

**chorion** /ˈkɔːrɪən/ ● **n.** Embryology the outermost membrane surrounding the embryo of a reptile, bird, or mammal.
– DERIVATIVES **chorionic** adj.
– ORIGIN C16: from Gk *khorion*.

**chorister** ● **n.** **1** a member of a choir, especially a choirboy or choirgirl. **2** US a person who leads the singing of a church choir or congregation.
– ORIGIN ME *queristre*, from an Anglo-Norman Fr. var. of OFr. *cueriste*, from *quer* (see **CHOIR**), assoc. with obs. *chorist* 'member of a choir or chorus'.

**chorizo** /tʃəˈriːzəʊ, Spanish tʃoˈriθo, -ˈriso/ ● **n.** (pl. **-os**) a spicy Spanish pork sausage.
– ORIGIN from Sp.

**chorography** /kɔːˈrɒgrəfi/ ● **n.** chiefly historical the systematic description and mapping of regions or districts.
– DERIVATIVES **chorographer** n. **chorographic** adj.
– ORIGIN C16: via L. from Gk *khōrographia*, from *khōra* or *khōros* 'region'.

**choroid** /ˈkɔːrɔɪd, ˈkɒr-/ ● **adj.** resembling the chorion, particularly in containing many blood vessels. ● **n.** (also **choroid coat**) the pigmented vascular layer of the eyeball between the retina and the sclera.
– DERIVATIVES **choroidal** adj.
– ORIGIN C17: from Gk *khoroeidēs*, from *khorion* (see **CHORION**).

**choroid plexus** /ˈkɔːrɔɪd, ˈkɒr-/ ● **n.** (pl. same or **plexuses**) a network of blood vessels in each ventricle of the brain, producing the cerebrospinal fluid.

**choropleth map** /ˈkɒrə(ʊ)plɛθ/ ● **n.** a map which uses shading, colouring, or symbols to show the average values of a particular quantity in different areas.
– ORIGIN 1930s: from Gk *khōra* 'region' + *plēthos* 'multitude'.

**chorten** /ˈtʃɔːt(ə)n/ ● **n.** a Buddhist shrine.
– ORIGIN from Tibetan.

**chortle** ● **v.** laugh in a gleeful way. ● **n.** a gleeful laugh.
– ORIGIN 1871: coined by Lewis Carroll in *Through the Looking Glass*; prob. a blend of **CHUCKLE** and **SNORT**.

**chorus** ● **n.** (pl. **choruses**) **1** a large group of singers, especially one performing with an orchestra. **2** a piece of choral music, especially one forming part of an opera or oratorio. **3** a part of a song which is repeated after each verse. **4** (in ancient Greek tragedy) a group of performers who comment on the main action, typically speaking and moving together. **5** a simultaneous utterance by many people. **6** a character who speaks the prologue and other linking parts of the play, especially in Elizabethan drama. **7** a device used with an amplified musical instrument to give the impression that more than one instrument is being played. ● **v.** (**chorused**, **chorusing**) (of a group of people) say the same thing at the same time.
– ORIGIN C16: from L., from Gk *khoros*.

**chorus girl** ● **n.** a young woman who sings or dances in the chorus of a musical.

**chose** past of **CHOOSE**.

**chosen** past participle of **CHOOSE**.

**chota** /ˈtʃəʊtə/ ● **adj.** Indian small or unimportant.
– ORIGIN from Hindi *choṭā*.

**choucroute** /ˈʃuːkruːt/ ● **n.** sauerkraut.
– ORIGIN Fr., from Ger. dial. *Surkrut* 'sauerkraut', influenced by Fr. *chou* 'cabbage'.

**chough** /tʃʌf/ ● **n.** **1** a black bird of the crow family with a red or yellow downcurved bill, typically frequenting mountains and sea cliffs. [*Pyrrhocorax pyrrhocorax* and other species.] **2** (**white-winged chough**) a black and white Australian songbird. [*Corcorax melanorhamphos.*]
– ORIGIN ME: prob. imitative.

**choux pastry** /ʃuː/ ● **n.** very light pastry made with egg, typically used for eclairs and profiteroles.
– ORIGIN C19: from *choux* or *chou*, denoting a round cream-filled pastry, from Fr. *chou* (pl. *choux*) 'cabbage, rosette'.

**chow** /tʃaʊ/ ● **n.** **1** informal, chiefly N. Amer. food. **2** (also **chow chow**) a dog of a sturdy Chinese breed with a tail curled over its back, a bluish-black tongue, and typically a dense thick coat. ● **v.** (**chow down**) N. Amer. informal eat.
– ORIGIN C19: shortened from **CHOW CHOW**.

**chow chow** ● **n.** **1** another term for **CHOW** (in sense 2). **2** a Chinese preserve of ginger, orange peel, and other ingredients, in syrup. **3** a mixed vegetable pickle.
– ORIGIN C18: pidgin Engl., of unknown ult. origin.

**chowder** ● **n.** a rich soup typically containing fish, clams, or corn with potatoes and onions.
– ORIGIN C18: perh. from Fr. *chaudière* 'stew pot', rel. to ONorth. Fr. *caudron* (see **CAULDRON**).

**chowderhead** ● **n.** N. Amer. informal a stupid person.
– DERIVATIVES **chowderheaded** adj.
– ORIGIN C19: prob. a var. of obs. *jolter-head* 'thick-headed person'.

**chowhound** ● **n.** US informal a greedy person.

**chowk** /tʃaʊk/ ● **n.** (in the Indian subcontinent) an open market area at the junction of two roads.
– ORIGIN from Hindi *cauk*.

**chowkidar** /ˈtʃəʊkɪˌdɑː/ ● **n.** (in the Indian subcontinent) a watchman or gatekeeper.
– ORIGIN from Urdu *caukīdār*, from *caukī* 'toll house' + *-dār* 'keeper'.

**chow mein** /tʃaʊ ˈmeɪn/ ● **n.** a Chinese-style dish of fried noodles with shredded meat or seafood and vegetables.
– ORIGIN C19: from Chin. *chǎo miàn* 'stir-fried noodles'.

**CHP** ● **abbrev.** combined heat and power.

**Chr.** ● **abbrev.** Chronicles (in biblical references).

**chrestomathy** /krɛˈstɒməθi/ ● **n.** (pl. **-ies**) formal a selection of passages used to help in learning a language.
– ORIGIN C19: from Gk *khrēstomatheia*, from *khrēstos* 'useful' + *-matheia* 'learning'.

**chrism** /ˈkrɪz(ə)m/ ● **n.** a consecrated oil used for anointing in the Catholic, Orthodox, and Anglican Churches.
– ORIGIN OE, from med. L. *crisma*, eccles. L. *chrisma*, from Gk *khrisma* 'anointing', from *khriein* 'anoint'.

**chrisom** /ˈkrɪz(ə)m/ (also **chrisom-cloth**) ● **n.** historical a white robe put on a child at baptism, and used as its shroud if it died within the month.
– ORIGIN ME: alt. of **CHRISM**, representing a popular pronunc.

**Christ** ● **n.** the title, also treated as a name, given to Jesus. ● **exclam.** an oath used to express irritation, dismay, or surprise.
– DERIVATIVES **Christhood** n. **Christlike** adj. **Christly** adj.
– ORIGIN OE *Crīst*, from L. *Christus*, from Gk *Khristos*, noun use of an adjective meaning 'anointed', from *khriein* 'anoint', translating Heb. *māšīaḥ* 'Messiah'.

**Christadelphian** /ˌkrɪstəˈdɛlfɪən/ ● **n.** a member of a Christian sect claiming to return to the beliefs and practices of the earliest disciples and expecting a second coming of Christ. ● **adj.** of or adhering to this sect.
– ORIGIN from late Gk *Khristadelphos* 'in brotherhood with Christ' (from Gk *Khristos* 'Christ' + *adelphos* 'brother') + **-IAN**.

**christen** ● v. **1** name (a baby) at baptism as a sign of admission to a Christian Church. **2** informal use for the first time.
– DERIVATIVES **christener** n. **christening** n.
– ORIGIN OE *crīstnian* 'make Christian', from *crīsten* 'Christian', from L. *Christianus*, from *Christus* 'Christ'.

**Christendom** ● n. dated the worldwide body or society of Christians.

**Christian** /ˈkrɪstɪən, -tʃ(ə)n/ ● adj. **1** of, relating to, or professing Christianity or its teachings. **2** informal having qualities associated with Christians, e.g. kindness or fairness. ● n. a person who has received Christian baptism or is a believer in Christianity.
– DERIVATIVES **Christianization** (also **-isation**) n. **Christianize** (also **-ise**) v. **Christianly** adv.
– ORIGIN ME: from L. *Christianus*, from *Christus* 'Christ'.

**Christian era** ● n. the era beginning with the traditional date of Christ's birth.

**Christianity** ● n. the religion based on the person and teachings of Jesus Christ; its beliefs and practices.

**Christian name** ● n. a forename, especially one given at baptism.

**Christian Science** ● n. the beliefs and practices of the Church of Christ Scientist, a Christian sect holding that only God and the mind have ultimate reality.
– DERIVATIVES **Christian Scientist** n.

**Christingle** /ˈkrɪstɪŋg(ə)l/ ● n. a lighted candle symbolizing Christ, held by children at Advent services.
– ORIGIN 1950s: prob. from Ger. dial. *Christkindl* 'Christ-child, Christmas gift'.

**Christmas** ● n. (pl. **Christmases**) **1** (also **Christmas Day**) the annual Christian festival celebrating Christ's birth, held on 25 December. **2** the period immediately before and after this.
– DERIVATIVES **Christmassy** adj.
– ORIGIN OE *Crīstes mæsse* (see **CHRIST**, **MASS**).

**Christmas box** ● n. Brit. a present given at Christmas to tradespeople and employees.

**Christmas cactus** ● n. a succulent South American plant with red, pink, or white flowers, grown as a house plant. [*Schlumbergera bridgesii*.]
– ORIGIN so named because it flowers at about the northern midwinter.

**Christmas cake** ● n. Brit. a rich fruit cake covered with marzipan and icing, eaten at Christmas.

**Christmas pudding** ● n. Brit. a rich boiled pudding eaten at Christmas, made with flour, suet, and dried fruit.

**Christmas rose** ● n. a small white-flowered winter-blooming hellebore. [*Helleborus niger*.]

**Christmas tree** ● n. an evergreen or artificial tree decorated with lights and ornaments at Christmas.

**Christo-** ● comb. form of or relating to Christ: *Christocentric*.

**Christocentric** ● adj. having Christ as its centre.

**Christology** ● n. the branch of Christian theology relating to Christ.
– DERIVATIVES **Christological** adj. **Christologically** adv.

**christophine** /ˈkrɪstəfiːn/ (also **christophene**) ● n. another term for **CHAYOTE** (in sense 1).
– ORIGIN prob. based on the Fr. given name *Christophe*.

**Christ's thorn** ● n. a thorny shrub, popularly held to have formed Christ's crown of thorns. [*Ziziphus spina-christi* (Mediterranean region) and other species.]

**chroma** /ˈkrəʊmə/ ● n. purity or intensity of colour.
– ORIGIN C19: from Gk *khrōma* 'colour'.

**chromakey** /ˈkrəʊməkiː/ ● n. a digital technique by which a block of a particular colour in a video image can be replaced by another colour or image. ● v. (**-eys**, **-eyed**) manipulate using chromakey.

**chromate** /ˈkrəʊmeɪt/ ● n. Chemistry a salt in which the anion contains both chromium and oxygen.

**chromatic** ● adj. **1** Music relating to or using notes not belonging to the diatonic scale of the key of a passage. ➤(of a scale) ascending or descending by semitones. **2** of, relating to, or produced by colour.
– DERIVATIVES **chromatically** adv. **chromaticism** n.
– ORIGIN C17: from Fr. *chromatique* or L. *chromaticus*, from Gk *khrōmatikos*, from *khrōma*, *khrōmat-* 'colour, chromatic scale'.

**chromatic aberration** ● n. Optics the effect produced by the refraction of different wavelengths of light through slightly different angles, resulting in a failure to focus.

**chromaticity** /ˌkrəʊməˈtɪsɪti/ ● n. the quality of colour, independent of brightness.

**chromatid** /ˈkrəʊmətɪd/ ● n. Biology each of the two thread-like strands into which a chromosome divides during cell division.
– ORIGIN C20: from Gk *khrōma*, *khrōmat-* 'colour' + **-ID**².

**chromatin** /ˈkrəʊmətɪn/ ● n. Biology the material of which non-bacterial chromosomes are composed, consisting of protein, RNA, and DNA.
– ORIGIN C19: from Gk *khrōma*, *khrōmat-* 'colour'.

**chromato-** /ˈkrəʊmətəʊ/ (also **chromo-**) ● comb. form colour; of or in colours: *chromatopsia*.
– ORIGIN from Gk *khrōma*, *khrōmat-* 'colour'.

**chromatography** /ˌkrəʊməˈtɒgrəfi/ ● n. Chemistry a technique for the separation of a mixture by passing it in solution or suspension through a medium in which the components move at different rates.
– DERIVATIVES **chromatogram** n. **chromatograph** n. **chromatographic** adj.
– ORIGIN 1930s: from **CHROMATO-** + **-GRAPHY** (early separations being displayed as a number of coloured bands or spots).

**chromatopsia** /ˌkrəʊməˈtɒpsɪə/ ● n. Medicine abnormally coloured vision.
– ORIGIN C19: from **CHROMATO-** + Gk *-opsia* 'seeing'.

**chrome** ● n. **1** chromium plate as a decorative or protective finish. **2** [as modifier] denoting compounds or alloys of chromium: *chrome steel*.
– DERIVATIVES **chromed** adj.
– ORIGIN C19: from Fr., from Gk *khrōma* 'colour' (some chromium compounds having brilliant colours).

**chrome leather** ● n. leather tanned with chromium salts.

**chrome yellow** ● n. a bright yellow pigment made from lead chromate.

**chromide** ● n. a small orange or green deep-bodied cichlid fish of India and Sri Lanka. [Genus *Etroplus*: two species.]
– ORIGIN 1930s: from mod. L. *Chromides* (former order name), formed irregularly from *Chromis* (genus name), from L. *chromis* 'sea fish'.

**chrominance** /ˈkrəʊmɪnəns/ ● n. the colorimetric difference between a given colour in a television picture and a standard colour of equal luminance.
– ORIGIN 1950s: from Gk *khrōma* 'colour', on the pattern of *luminance*.

**chromite** /ˈkrəʊmʌɪt/ ● n. the main ore of chromium, a brownish-black oxide of chromium and iron.

**chromium** ● n. the chemical element of atomic number 24, a hard white metal used in stainless steel and other alloys. (Symbol: **Cr**)
– DERIVATIVES **chromic** adj. **chromous** adj.
– ORIGIN C19: from **CHROME** + **-IUM**.

**chromium plate** ● n. metallic chromium electroplated on to an object as a decorative or protective coating.

**chromo** /ˈkrəʊməʊ/ ● n. (pl. **-os**) N. Amer. shortened form of **CHROMOLITHOGRAPH**.

**chromo-**¹ /ˈkrəʊməʊ/ ● comb. form Chemistry representing **CHROMIUM**.

**chromo-**² /ˈkrəʊməʊ/ ● comb. form variant spelling of **CHROMATO-**.

**chromodynamics** ● pl. n. see **QUANTUM CHROMODYNAMICS**.

**chromogenic** ● adj. **1** involving the production of colour or pigments. **2** Photography denoting a modern process of developing film which uses couplers to produce black-and-white images of very high definition.

**chromolithograph** historical ● n. a coloured picture printed by lithography. ● v. produce (a coloured picture) by lithography.
– DERIVATIVES **chromolithographer** n. **chromolitho-**

**graphic** adj. **chromolithography** n.

**chromoly** /ˈkrəʊmɒli/ • n. steel containing chromium and molybdenum, used to make strong, lightweight components such as bicycle frames.
– ORIGIN 1980s: blend of **CHROMIUM** and **MOLYBDENUM**.

**chromoplast** /ˈkrəʊməplast, -plɑːst/ • n. Botany a coloured plastid other than a chloroplast, typically containing a yellow or orange pigment.
– ORIGIN C19: from **CHROMO-**² + Gk *plastos* 'formed'.

**chromosome** • n. Biology a thread-like structure of nucleic acids and protein found in the nuclei of most living cells, carrying genetic information in the form of genes.
– DERIVATIVES **chromosomal** adj.
– ORIGIN C19: coined in Ger. from Gk *khrōma* 'colour' + *sōma* 'body'.

**chromosphere** • n. a reddish gaseous layer immediately above the photosphere of the sun or another star.
– DERIVATIVES **chromospheric** adj.
– ORIGIN C19: from **CHROMO-**² + **SPHERE**.

**Chron.** • abbrev. Chronicles (in biblical references).

**chronic** • adj. **1** (of an illness or problem) persisting for a long time. **2** having a persistent illness or bad habit. **3** Brit. informal very bad.
– DERIVATIVES **chronically** adv. **chronicity** n.
– ORIGIN ME: from Fr. *chronique*, via L. from Gk *khronikos* 'of time', from *khronos* 'time'.

**chronic fatigue syndrome** • n. a medical condition of unknown cause, with fever, aching, and prolonged tiredness and depression.

**chronicle** • n. a written account of important or historical events in the order of their occurrence. • v. record (a series of events) in a factual and detailed way.
– DERIVATIVES **chronicler** n.
– ORIGIN ME: from Anglo-Norman Fr. *cronicle*, var. of OFr. *cronique*, via L. from Gk *khronika* 'annals', from *khronikos* (see **CHRONIC**).

**chrono-** /ˈkrɒnəʊ/ • comb. form relating to time: *chronometry*.
– ORIGIN from Gk *khronos* 'time'.

**chronobiology** • n. the branch of biology concerned with cyclical physiological phenomena.
– DERIVATIVES **chronobiologist** n.

**chronograph** • n. an instrument for recording time with great accuracy.
– DERIVATIVES **chronographic** adj.

**chronology** /krəˈnɒlədʒi/ • n. (pl. **-ies**) **1** the study of records to establish the dates of past events. **2** the arrangement of events or dates in the order of their occurrence.
– DERIVATIVES **chronological** adj. **chronologically** adv. **chronologist** n.
– ORIGIN C16: from mod. L. *chronologia*, from Gk *khronos* 'time' + *-logia* (see **-LOGY**).

**chronometer** /krəˈnɒmɪtə/ • n. an instrument for measuring time accurately in spite of motion or variations in temperature, humidity, and air pressure.

**chronometry** • n. the science of accurate time measurement.
– DERIVATIVES **chronometric** adj. **chronometrical** adj. **chronometrically** adv.

**chronotherapy** • n. the treatment of an illness or disorder by administering a drug at a time of day believed to be in harmony with the body's natural rhythms.

**chrysalid** /ˈkrɪs(ə)lɪd/ • n. another term for **CHRYSALIS**.
– ORIGIN C18: from L. *chrysal(l)is, chrysal(l)id-* (see **CHRYSALIS**).

**chrysalis** /ˈkrɪs(ə)lɪs/ • n. (pl. **chrysalises**) a quiescent insect pupa, especially of a butterfly or moth. ➤ the hard outer case enclosing this.
– ORIGIN C17: from L. *chrysal(l)is, chrysal(l)id-*, from Gk *khrusallis*, from *khrusos* 'gold' (because of the metallic sheen of some pupae).

**chrysanthemum** /krɪˈsanθɪməm, -z-/ • n. (pl. **chrysanthemums**) a plant of the daisy family with brightly coloured ornamental flowers. [Genera *Chrysanthemum* or (most cultivated species) *Dendranthema*.]
– ORIGIN from L., from Gk *khrusanthemon*, from *khrusos* 'gold' + *anthemon* 'flower'.

**chryselephantine** /ˌkrɪsɛlɪˈfantʌɪn/ • adj. (of ancient Greek sculpture) overlaid with gold and ivory.
– ORIGIN C19: from Gk *khruselephantinos*, from *khrusos* 'gold' + *elephas, elephant-* 'elephant' or 'ivory'.

**chrysoberyl** /ˌkrɪsə(ʊ)ˈbɛrɪl/ • n. a greenish or yellowish-green mineral consisting of an oxide of beryllium and aluminium.
– ORIGIN C17: from L. *chrysoberyllus*, from Gk *khrusos* 'gold' + *bērullos* 'beryl'.

**chrysocolla** /ˌkrɪsə(ʊ)ˈkɒlə/ • n. a greenish-blue mineral consisting of hydrated copper silicate.
– ORIGIN C16: from L., from Gk *khrusokolla*, denoting a mineral used in ancient times for soldering gold.

**chrysolite** /ˈkrɪsəlʌɪt/ • n. a yellowish-green or brownish variety of olivine, used as a gemstone.
– ORIGIN ME: from OFr. *crisolite*, from med. L. *crisolitus*, from L. *chrysolithus*, based on Gk *khrusos* 'gold' + *lithos* 'stone'.

**chrysoprase** /ˈkrɪsə(ʊ)preɪz/ • n. an apple-green variety of chalcedony containing nickel.
– ORIGIN ME: from OFr. *crisopace*, via L. from Gk *khrusoprasos*, from *khrusos* 'gold' + *prason* 'leek'.

**chrysotile** /ˈkrɪsə(ʊ)tʌɪl/ • n. a fibrous form of the mineral serpentine.
– ORIGIN C19: from Gk *khrusos* 'gold' + *tilos* 'fibre'.

**chthonic** /ˈ(k)θɒnɪk/ (also **chthonian** /ˈ(k)θəʊnɪən/) • adj. of, belonging to, or inhabiting the underworld.
– ORIGIN C19: from Gk *khthōn* 'earth' + **-IC**.

**chub** • n. a thick-bodied river fish with a grey-green back and white underparts. [*Leuciscus cephalus*.]
– ORIGIN ME: of unknown origin.

**Chubb** • n. trademark a lock with a device for fixing the bolt immovably to prevent it from being picked.
– ORIGIN C19: after the London locksmith Charles *Chubb*.

**chubby** • adj. (**-ier, -iest**) plump and rounded.
– DERIVATIVES **chubbily** adv. **chubbiness** n.
– ORIGIN C17: from **CHUB**.

**chuck**¹ informal • v. **1** throw carelessly or casually. ➤ (**chuck something out**) throw something away. **2** (usu. **chuck something in**) give up. **3** (**chuck up**) vomit. • n. (**the chuck**) Brit. a dismissal or rejection.
– PHRASES **chuck it down** rain heavily.
– DERIVATIVES **chucker** n.
– ORIGIN C17: from **CHUCK**².

**chuck**² • v. touch playfully under the chin. • n. a playful touch under the chin.
– ORIGIN C17: prob. from OFr. *chuquer*, later *choquer* 'to knock, bump'.

**chuck**³ • n. **1** a device for holding a workpiece in a lathe or a tool in a drill. **2** a cut of beef extending from the neck to the ribs.
– ORIGIN C17, as a var. of **CHOCK**; see also **CHUNK**¹.

**chuck**⁴ • n. N. English used as a familiar form of address.
– ORIGIN C16: alt. of **CHICK**¹.

**chuckhole** • n. N. Amer. a hole or rut in a road.

**chuckle** • v. laugh quietly or inwardly. • n. a quiet or suppressed laugh.
– DERIVATIVES **chuckler** n.
– ORIGIN C16: from *chuck* meaning 'to cluck' in ME.

**chucklehead** • n. informal a stupid person.
– DERIVATIVES **chuckleheaded** adj.
– ORIGIN C18: from *chuckle* 'big and clumsy', prob. rel. to **CHUCK**³ (see sense 2).

**chuck wagon** • n. N. Amer. a wagon with cooking facilities providing food on a ranch or by a roadside.
– ORIGIN C19: *chuck*, colloq. in the sense 'food, provisions'.

**chuckwalla** /ˈtʃʌkwɒlə/ • n. a large dark-bodied lizard of the south-western US and Mexico. [*Sauromalus obesus*.]
– ORIGIN C19: from Mex. Sp. *chacahuala*, from Amer. Ind.

**chuddar** • n. variant spelling of **CHADOR**.

**chufa** /ˈtʃuːfə/ • n. **1** a sedge which yields an edible tuber, cultivated in some marshy regions of Spain and Italy. [*Cyperus esculentus* var. *sativus*.] **2** the tuber of this plant,

which may be roasted or made into flour or juice.
– ORIGIN C19: from Sp.

**chuff** ● **v.** (of a steam engine) move with a regular sharp puffing sound.
– ORIGIN C20: imitative.

**chuffed** ● **adj.** Brit. informal very pleased.
– ORIGIN 1950s: from dial. *chuff* 'plump or pleased'.

**chug**[1] ● **v.** (**chugged**, **chugging**) emit a series of regular muffled explosive sounds, as of an engine running slowly. ● **n.** a sound of this type.
– ORIGIN C19: imitative.

**chug**[2] ● **v.** (**chugged**, **chugging**) N. Amer. informal consume (a drink) in large gulps without pausing.
– ORIGIN 1980s: imitative.

**chukar** /'tʃʊkɑː/ (also **chukor**) ● **n.** a partridge similar to the red-legged partridge, but with a call like a domestic hen. [Genus *Alectoris*: two species.]
– ORIGIN C19: from Sanskrit *cakora*.

**Chukchi** /'tʃʊktʃiː/ (also **Chukchee**) ● **n.** (pl. same or **Chukchis**) **1** a member of an indigenous people of extreme NE Siberia. **2** the language of this people, belonging to a small family also including Koryak.
– ORIGIN from Russ.

**chukka** /'tʃʌkə/ (US also **chukker**) ● **n.** each of a number of periods (typically six, of 7½ minutes each) into which play in a game of polo is divided.
– ORIGIN C19: from Hindi *cakkar*, from Sanskrit *cakra* 'circle or wheel'.

**chum**[1] informal ● **n.** dated a close friend. ● **v.** (**chummed**, **chumming**) **1** (**chum up**) form a friendship with someone. **2** Scottish accompany (someone) somewhere.
– DERIVATIVES **chummily** adv. **chumminess** n. **chummy** adj.
– ORIGIN C17: prob. short for *chamber-fellow*; cf. COMRADE and CRONY.

**chum**[2] chiefly N. Amer. ● **n.** chopped fish and other material used as bait. ➤ the remains of fish, especially after oil has been expressed. ● **v.** fish using chum as bait.
– ORIGIN C19: of unknown origin.

**chum**[3] ● **n.** (pl. same or **chums**) a large North Pacific salmon that is commercially important as a food fish. [*Oncorhynchus keta*.]
– ORIGIN C20: from Chinook Jargon *tzum* (*samun*), lit. 'spotted (salmon)'.

**Chumash** /'tʃuːmaʃ/ ● **n.** (pl. same or **Chumashes**) **1** a member of an American Indian people of coastal parts of southern California. **2** the extinct Hokan language of this people.

**chumble** ● **v.** dialect nibble; chew.
– ORIGIN C19: prob. imitative.

**chump** ● **n.** **1** informal, dated a foolish person. **2** Brit. the thick end of something, especially a loin of lamb or mutton.
– PHRASES **off one's chump** Brit. informal, dated mad.
– ORIGIN C18: prob. a blend of CHUNK[1] and LUMP[1] or STUMP.

**chump change** ● **n.** N. Amer. informal a very small amount of money.
– ORIGIN 1960s: orig. black Engl.

**chunder** informal, chiefly Austral./NZ ● **v.** vomit. ● **n.** vomit.
– ORIGIN 1950s: prob. from rhyming sl. *Chunder Loo* 'spew', from the name of a cartoon character *Chunder Loo of Akim Foo* in advertisements in the Sydney *Bulletin*.

**chunk**[1] ● **n.** a thick, solid piece. ➤ a large amount. ● **v.** N. Amer. divide into chunks.
– ORIGIN C17: appar. an alt. of CHUCK[3].

**chunk**[2] ● **v.** make a muffled, metallic sound.
– ORIGIN C19: imitative.

**chunky** ● **adj.** (**-ier**, **-iest**) **1** (of a person) short and sturdy. ➤ bulky; thick. **2** containing chunks.
– DERIVATIVES **chunkily** adv. **chunkiness** n.

**chunter** ● **v.** Brit. informal **1** chatter or grumble monotonously. **2** move slowly and noisily.
– ORIGIN C17: prob. imitative.

**chuppah** /'xʊpə/ (also **chuppa**) ● **n.** (pl. **chuppot** /'xʊpəʊt/) a canopy beneath which Jewish marriage ceremonies are performed.
– ORIGIN C19: from Heb. *ḥuppāh* 'cover, canopy'.

**church** ● **n.** **1** a building used for public Christian worship. **2** (**Church**) a particular Christian organization with its own distinctive doctrines. **3** institutionalized religion as a political or social force. ● **v.** archaic take (a woman who has recently given birth) to church for a service of thanksgiving.
– ORIGIN OE *cir(i)ce*, *cyr(i)ce*, based on med. Gk *kurikon*, from Gk *kuriakon* (*dōma*) 'Lord's (house)', from *kurios* 'master or lord'.

**Church Commissioners** ● **pl. n.** a body managing the finances of the Church of England.

**churchman** (or **churchwoman**) ● **n.** (pl. **-men** or **-women**) a member of the Christian clergy or of a Church.

**Church Militant** ● **n.** the body of living Christian believers, regarded as striving to combat evil on earth.
– ORIGIN C16: contrasted with the *Church Triumphant* in heaven.

**Church of England** ● **n.** the English branch of the Western Christian Church, which combines Catholic and Protestant traditions, rejects the Pope's authority, and has the monarch as its titular head.

**Church of Scotland** ● **n.** the national (Presbyterian) Christian Church in Scotland.

**church school** ● **n.** (in the UK) a school founded by or associated with the Church of England. ➤ (in the US) a private school supported by a Church.

**Church Slavonic** ● **n.** the liturgical language used in the Orthodox Church in Russia, Serbia, and some other countries.

**churchwarden** ● **n.** **1** either of two elected lay representatives in an Anglican parish. ➤ US a church administrator. **2** Brit. a long-stemmed clay pipe.

**churchy** ● **adj.** **1** excessively pious. **2** resembling a church.
– DERIVATIVES **churchiness** n.

**churchyard** ● **n.** an enclosed area surrounding a church, especially as used for burials.

**churchyard beetle** ● **n.** a flightless black beetle which lives in damp dark places and emits a foul smell when alarmed. [*Blaps mucronata*.]

**churidars** /'tʃʊrɪdɑːz/ ● **pl. n.** tight trousers worn by people from the Indian subcontinent.
– ORIGIN from Hindi *cūrīdār* 'having a series of gathered rows' (the trousers traditionally being worn too long and tucked up).

**churinga** /tʃʌ'rɪŋgə/ ● **n.** (pl. same or **churingas**) (among Australian Aboriginals) a sacred amulet or other object.
– ORIGIN C19: from Aranda, lit. 'object from the dreaming'.

**churl** ● **n.** **1** an impolite and mean-spirited person. ➤ archaic a miser. **2** archaic a peasant.
– ORIGIN OE *ceorl*, of W. Gmc origin; rel. to CARL.

**churlish** ● **adj.** rude, mean-spirited, and surly.
– DERIVATIVES **churlishly** adv. **churlishness** n.

**churn** ● **n.** **1** a machine for making butter by agitating milk or cream. **2** Brit. a large metal milk can. ● **v.** **1** agitate (milk or cream) in a churn to produce butter. **2** move (liquid) about vigorously. **3** (**churn something out**) produce something mechanically in large quantities. **4** [as adj. **churned up**] upset or nervous.
– ORIGIN OE *cyrin*, of Gmc origin.

**churr** ● **v.** & **n.** variant spelling of CHIRR.

**churrasco** /tʃʊ'raskəʊ/ ● **n.** a South American dish of steak barbecued over a wood or charcoal fire.
– ORIGIN Latin Amer. Sp., prob. from Sp. dial. *churrascar* 'to burn', rel. to Sp. *soccarar* 'to scorch'.

**Churrigueresque** /ˌtʃʊərɪgə'rɛsk/ ● **adj.** Architecture of or relating to the lavishly ornamented late Spanish baroque style.
– ORIGIN C19: from the name of the C17 Sp. architect José Benito de *Churriguera*.

**chute**[1] (also **shoot**) ● **n.** a sloping channel or slide for conveying things to a lower level. ➤ a water slide into a swimming pool.
– ORIGIN C19: from Fr., 'fall' (of water or rocks); influenced by SHOOT.

**chute**[2] ● **n.** informal **1** a parachute. **2** Sailing a spinnaker.
– DERIVATIVES **chutist** n.

**chutney** ● **n.** (pl. **-eys**) a spicy condiment made of fruits or vegetables with vinegar, spices, and sugar.
– ORIGIN C19: from Hindi *caṭnī*.

**chutzpah** /ˈxʊtspə, ˈhʊ-/ ● **n.** informal shameless audacity.
– ORIGIN C19: Yiddish, from Aramaic *ḥu ṣpā*.

**Chuvash** /ˈtʃuːvɑːʃ/ ● **n.** (pl. same) **1** a member of a people living in Chuvashia, an autonomous republic in Russia. **2** the Turkic language of this people.

**chyle** /kʌɪl/ ● **n.** Physiology a milky fluid which drains from the small intestine into the lymphatic system during digestion.
– DERIVATIVES **chylous** adj.
– ORIGIN ME: from late L. *chylus*, from Gk *khūlos* 'juice'.

**chyme** /kʌɪm/ ● **n.** Physiology the fluid which passes from the stomach to the small intestine, consisting of gastric juices and partly digested food.
– DERIVATIVES **chymous** adj.
– ORIGIN ME: from late L. *chymus*, from Gk *khūmos* 'juice'.

**chymotrypsin** /ˌkʌɪmə(ʊ)ˈtrɪpsɪn/ ● **n.** a pancreatic enzyme which breaks down proteins in the small intestine.

**chypre** /ʃiːpr(ə)/ ● **n.** a heavy perfume made from sandalwood.
– ORIGIN C19: from Fr., lit. 'Cyprus', perh. where it was first made.

**CI** ● **abbrev.** **1** Channel Islands. **2** Ivory Coast (international vehicle registration). [from Fr. *Côte d'Ivoire*.]

**Ci** ● **abbrev.** curie.

**CIA** ● **abbrev.** Central Intelligence Agency.

**ciabatta** /tʃəˈbɑːtə/ ● **n.** a flattish, open-textured Italian bread, made with olive oil.
– ORIGIN Ital., lit. 'slipper' (from its shape).

**ciao** /tʃaʊ/ ● **exclam.** informal used as a greeting at meeting or parting.
– ORIGIN 1920s: Ital., dial. alt. of *schiavo* '(I am your) slave'.

**ciborium** /sɪˈbɔːrɪəm/ ● **n.** (pl. **ciboria** /-rɪə/) **1** a receptacle with an arched cover, used to hold the Eucharist. **2** a canopy over an altar in a church, standing on four pillars.
– ORIGIN C16: via med. L. from Gk *kibōrion* 'seed vessel of the water lily or a cup made from it'.

**cicada** /sɪˈkɑːdə/ ● **n.** a large bug with long transparent wings, the males of which make a loud shrill droning noise after dark. [Family Cicadidae: many species.]
– ORIGIN ME: from L. *cicada*, *cicala*.

**cicatrix** /ˈsɪkətrɪks/ (also **cicatrice** /ˈsɪkətrɪs/) ● **n.** (pl. **cicatrices** /-ˈtrʌɪsiːz/) **1** a scar. **2** Botany a mark on a stem left after a leaf or other part has become detached.
– DERIVATIVES **cicatricial** /sɪkəˈtrɪʃ(ə)l/ adj.
– ORIGIN ME: from L. *cicatrix* or OFr. *cicatrice*.

**cicatrize** /ˈsɪkətrʌɪz/ (also **-ise**) ● **v.** heal by scar formation.
– DERIVATIVES **cicatrization** n.

**cicely** /ˈsɪsɪli/ (also **sweet cicely**) ● **n.** (pl. **-ies**) an aromatic white-flowered plant of the parsley family, with fern-like leaves. [*Myrrhis odorata* (Europe), *Osmorhiza claytoni* (N. America), and other species.]
– ORIGIN C16: from L. *seselis*, from Gk; influenced by the given name *Cicely*.

**cicerone** /ˌtʃɪtʃəˈrəʊni, ˌsɪs-/ ● **n.** (pl. **ciceroni** pronunc. same) a guide who gives information to sightseers.
– ORIGIN C18: from Ital., from L. *Cicero*, *Ciceron-* (see **CICERONIAN**), appar. alluding to the guides' learning.

**Ciceronian** /ˌsɪsəˈrəʊnɪən/ ● **adj.** **1** characteristic of the work and thought of Cicero (106–43 BC), a writer and orator of Ancient Rome. **2** (of speech or writing) in an eloquent and rhythmic style.

**cichlid** /ˈsɪklɪd/ ● **n.** Zoology a perch-like freshwater fish of a large tropical family (Cichlidae).
– ORIGIN C19: from mod. L. *Cichlidae*, from Gk *kikhlē*, denoting a kind of fish.

**cicisbeo** /ˌtʃɪtʃɪzˈbeɪəʊ/ ● **n.** (pl. **cicisbei** or **cicisbeos**) a married woman's male companion or lover.
– ORIGIN C18: Ital., of unknown origin.

**CID** ● **abbrev.** (in the UK) Criminal Investigation Department.

**-cide** ● **comb. form** **1** denoting a person or substance that kills: *insecticide*. **2** denoting an act of killing: *suicide*. See word-formation panel.
– DERIVATIVES **-cidal** comb. form in corresponding adjectives. **-cidally** comb. form in corresponding adverbs.
– ORIGIN via Fr.; sense 1 from L. *-cida*; sense 2 from L. *-cidium*, both from *caedere* 'kill'.

**cider** ● **n.** Brit. an alcoholic drink made from fermented apple juice. ➤(also **apple cider**) N. Amer. a cloudy unfermented drink made from crushed apples.
– ORIGIN ME: from OFr. *sidre*, via eccles. L. from eccles. Gk *sikera*, from Heb. *šēkār* 'strong drink'.

**ci-devant** /ˌsiːdəˈvɒ̃, French sidvɑ̃/ ● **adj.** former.
– ORIGIN Fr., 'heretofore'.

**c.i.f.** ● **abbrev.** cost, insurance, freight (as included in a price).

**cigar** ● **n.** a cylinder of tobacco rolled in tobacco leaves for smoking.
– PHRASES **close but no cigar** N. Amer. informal almost but not quite successful.
– ORIGIN C18: from Fr. *cigare*, or from Sp. *cigarro*, prob. from Mayan *sik'ar* 'smoking'.

**cigarette** (US also **cigaret**) ● **n.** a thin cylinder of finely cut tobacco rolled in paper for smoking.
– ORIGIN C19: from Fr., dimin. of *cigare* (see **CIGAR**).

**cigarette card** ● **n.** Brit. a small collectable card with a picture on it, formerly included in packets of cigarettes.

**cigarette pants** ● **pl. n.** women's trousers with straight, very narrow legs.

**cigarette paper** ● **n.** a piece of thin paper with a gummed edge for rolling around tobacco to make a cigarette.

**cigarillo** /ˌsɪgəˈrɪləʊ/ ● **n.** (pl. **-os**) a small cigar.
– ORIGIN C19: from Sp., dimin. of *cigarro* (see **CIGAR**).

**ciggy** ● **n.** (pl. **-ies**) informal a cigarette.

**ciguatera** /ˌsɪgwəˈtɛːrə/ ● **n.** poisoning caused by eating tropical marine fish that carry a toxic dinoflagellate.
– ORIGIN C19: from Amer. Sp., from *cigua* 'sea snail'.

**cilantro** /sɪˈlantrəʊ/ ● **n.** (especially in Mexican cookery) coriander.
– ORIGIN 1920s: from Sp., from L. *coliandrum* 'coriander'.

**cilia** plural form of **CILIUM**.

**ciliary** /ˈsɪlɪəri/ ● **adj.** **1** Biology of, relating to, or involving cilia. **2** Anatomy of or relating to the eyelashes or eyelids.

**ciliary body** ● **n.** Anatomy the part of the eye that connects the iris to the choroid.

**ciliate** /ˈsɪlɪeɪt/ ● **n.** Zoology a single-celled animal of a phylum (Ciliophora) distinguished by the possession of cilia. ● **adj.** **1** Zoology bearing cilia. **2** Botany having a fringe of hairs.
– DERIVATIVES **ciliated** adj. **ciliation** n.

**cilice** /ˈsɪlɪs/ ● **n.** haircloth.
– ORIGIN C16: from Fr., from L. *cilicium*, from Gk *kilikion*, from *Kilikia*, the Gk name for *Cilicia*, an ancient region of SE Asia Minor (because the cloth was made of Cicilian goats' hair).

**cilium** /ˈsɪlɪəm/ ● **n.** (pl. **cilia** /-lɪə/) **1** Biology a short microscopic hair-like vibrating structure, occurring in large numbers on the surface of certain cells. **2** Anatomy an eyelash.
– ORIGIN C18: from L.

**cill** ● **n.** chiefly Building variant spelling of **SILL**.

**cimbalom** /ˈsɪmb(ə)l(ə)m/ ● **n.** a large Hungarian dulcimer.
– ORIGIN C19: from Hungarian, from Ital. *cembalo*, *cimbalo*, from L. *cymbalum* (see **CYMBAL**).

**cimetidine** /sʌɪˈmɛtɪdiːn/ ● **n.** Medicine an antihistamine drug used to treat stomach acidity and peptic ulcers.
– ORIGIN 1970s: from *ci-* (alt. of *cy-* in *cyano-*) + *met(hyl)* + **-IDE** + **-INE**[4].

**C.-in-C.** ● **abbrev.** Commander-in-Chief.

**cinch** ● **n.** **1** informal an extremely easy task. ➤a certainty. **2** chiefly N. Amer. a girth for a Western saddle or pack, used in Mexico and the western US. ● **v.** chiefly N. Amer. secure with a belt. ➤fix (a saddle) securely by means of a girth.

## Word *Formation*

**-cide** 'killing', from Latin *caedere* 'to kill'

➤ **-cide** words in current use (full entries and definitions to be found in this dictionary):

**1.** with the meaning 'the killing of another':

| | | |
|---|---|---|
| deicide | the killing of a god | L. *deus* 'god' |
| filicide | the killing of one's son or daughter | L. *filius* 'son', *filia* 'daughter' |
| fratricide | the killing of one's brother or sister | L. *frater* 'brother' |
| genocide | the killing of a large number of people within a single population | Gk *genos* 'race' |
| homicide | the killing of a person; murder | L. *homo*, *homin-* 'man' |
| infanticide | the killing of a baby | based on INFANT |
| matricide | the killing of one's mother | L. *mater*, *matr-* 'mother' |
| parricide | the killing of a parent or near relation | associated with L. *pater* 'father' and *parens* 'parent' |
| patricide | the killing of one's father | L. *pater*, *patr-* 'father' |
| regicide | the killing of a king | L. *rex*, *reg-* 'king' |
| siblicide | the killing of siblings in animal groups | based on SIBLING |
| suicide | the intentional killing of oneself | L. *sui* 'of oneself' |
| tyrannicide | the killing of a tyrant | L. *tyrannus* 'tyrant' |
| uxoricide | the killing of one's wife | L. *uxor* 'wife' |

**2.** with the meaning 'a substance used to destroy plant or animal life':

| | | |
|---|---|---|
| acaricide | a substance used to kill mites or ticks | Gk *akari* 'mite, tick' |
| bactericide | a substance used to destroy bacteria | based on BACTERIA |
| biocide | a substance used to kill living organisms; a pesticide | Gk *bios* 'life' |
| fungicide | a substance used to destroy fungi | based on FUNGI |
| germicide | a substance used to kill germs | based on GERM |
| herbicide | a substance used to destroy vegetation | L. *herba* 'green crops, grass' |
| pesticide | a substance used to kill pests | based on PEST |
| spermicide | a contraceptive that kills spermatozoa | based on SPERM |
| vermicide | a substance used to kill worms | L. *vermis* 'worm' |

Many of the words in the first list have a long history in English: ***homicide***, for example, is first recorded in the late 14th century, while ***fratricide*** makes its appearance in the mid 15th century. In earlier uses the sense was frequently also 'a person who kills . . .'. This sense is less common in modern use, though it survives in certain words, e.g. ***suicide***: '*suicides used to be interred with a stake through the body*'.

The words in the second list are more recent: the vast majority were not used before the late 19th century or early 20th century. The word ***spermicide***, for example, does not enter the language until around 1930.

Many **-cide** words are formed with a connecting -i- (i.e. **-icide**), as in ***pesticide*** and ***spermicide***. These are formed by analogy with early formations from Latin or via French, in which the -i- belongs to the first element, as in ***homicide*** (the -i- in Latin *homo, homin-*).

– ORIGIN C19: from Sp. *cincha* 'girth'.

**cinchona** /sɪŋˈkəʊnə/ ● **n.** a medicinal drug containing quinine and related compounds, made from the dried bark of various South American trees.
– ORIGIN C18: mod. L. (genus name), named after the Countess of *Chinchón*, who brought the drug to Spain.

**cincture** /ˈsɪŋktʃə/ ● **n. 1** poetic/literary a girdle or belt. **2** Architecture a ring at either end of a column shaft.
– ORIGIN C16: from L. *cinctura*, from *cinct-*, *cingere* 'encircle'.

**cinder** ● **n.** a piece of burnt coal or wood that has stopped giving off flames but still has combustible matter in it.
– DERIVATIVES **cindery** adj.
– ORIGIN OE *sinder* 'slag', of Gmc origin (cf. **SINTER**); influenced by Fr. *cendre* (from L. *cinis* 'ashes').

**cinder block** ● **n.** North American term for **BREEZE BLOCK**.

**cinder cone** ● **n.** a cone formed round a volcanic vent by fragments of lava from eruptions.

**cine** ● **adj.** cinematographic.

**cine-** ● **comb. form** representing ***cinematographic*** (see **CINEMATOGRAPHY**).

**cineaste** /ˈsɪnɪast/ (also **cineast**) ● **n.** an enthusiast of the cinema.
– ORIGIN 1920s: from Fr. *cinéaste*, from *ciné* (from *cinéma*).

**cinema** ● **n.** chiefly Brit. **1** a theatre where films are shown. **2** the production of films as an art or industry.
– ORIGIN C20: from Fr. *cinéma*, abbrev. of *cinématographe* (see **CINEMATOGRAPH**).

**cinema organ** ● **n.** Music an organ with extra stops and special effects, originally accompanying silent films.

**cinematheque** /ˌsɪnɪməˈtɛk/ ● **n. 1** a film library or archive. **2** a small cinema.
– ORIGIN 1960s: from Fr. *cinémathèque*, from *cinéma* 'cinema', on the pattern of *bibliothèque* 'library'.

**cinematic** ● **adj.** of, relating to, or characteristic of the cinema.
– DERIVATIVES **cinematically** adv.

**cinematograph** /ˌsɪnɪˈmatəgrɑːf/ (also **kinematograph**) ● **n.** historical, chiefly Brit. an apparatus for showing films.
– ORIGIN C19: from Fr. *cinématographe*, from Gk *kinēma*, *kinēmat-* 'movement', from *kinein* 'to move'.

**cinematography** /ˌsɪnɪməˈtɒgrəfi/ ● **n.** the art of photography and camerawork in film-making.
– DERIVATIVES **cinematographer** n. **cinematographic** adj. **cinematographically** adv.

**cinéma-vérité** /ˌsɪnɪməˈvɛrɪteɪ, French sinemaveʀite/ ● **n.** a style of film-making characterized by realistic films avoiding artistic effect.
– ORIGIN Fr., lit. 'cinema truth'.

**cinephile** ● **n.** an enthusiast of the cinema.

**cineplex** ● **n.** trademark, chiefly N. Amer. a multiplex cinema.

**cineraria** /ˌsɪnəˈrɛːrɪə/ ● **n.** a plant of the daisy family, cultivated as a winter-flowering pot plant. [Genus *Pericallis* (formerly *Cineraria*).]
– ORIGIN mod. L., fem. of L. *cinerarius* 'of ashes' (because of the ash-coloured down on the leaves).

**cinerarium** /ˌsɪnəˈrɛːrɪəm/ ● **n.** (pl. **cinerariums**) a place where a cinerary urn is kept.
– ORIGIN C19: from late L., neut. of *cinerarius* 'of ashes'.

**cinerary urn** /ˈsɪnərəri/ ● **n.** an urn for holding a person's ashes after cremation.
– ORIGIN C18: *cinerary* from L. *cinerarius* 'of ashes'.

**cinereous** /sɪˈnɪərɪəs/ ● **adj.** ash-grey.
– ORIGIN ME: from L. *cinereus* 'similar to ashes' (from *cinis*, *ciner-* 'ashes') + **-ous**.

**Cingalese** /ˌsɪŋgəˈliːz/ ● **n.** & **adj.** archaic spelling of **Sinhalese**.
– ORIGIN C16: from Fr. *Cinghalais*, from Sanskrit *Siṃhala*.

**cingulum** /ˈsɪŋgjʊləm/ ● **n.** (pl. **cingula** /-lə/) Anatomy **1** a curved bundle of nerve fibres in the brain. **2** a ridge of enamel on the crown of a tooth.
– DERIVATIVES **cingulate** adj.
– ORIGIN C19: from L., 'belt', from *cingere* 'gird'.

**cinnabar** /ˈsɪnəbɑː/ ● **n.** **1** a bright red mineral consisting of mercury sulphide. **2** (also **cinnabar moth**) a day-flying moth with black and red wings. [*Tyria jacobaeae*.]
– ORIGIN ME: from L. *cinnabaris*, from Gk *kinnabari*, of oriental origin.

**cinnamon** ● **n.** **1** an aromatic spice made from the dried and rolled bark of a SE Asian tree. **2** the tree which yields this spice. [*Cinnamomum zeylanicum* and related species.] **3** a yellowish-brown colour resembling cinnamon.
– ORIGIN ME: from OFr. *cinnamome* (from Gk *kinnamōmon*), and L. *cinnamon*, both from a Semitic lang. and perh. based on Malay.

**cinque** /sɪŋk/ (also **cinq**) ● **n.** **1** the five on dice. **2** (**cinques**) Bell-ringing a system of change-ringing using eleven bells, with five pairs changing places each time.
– ORIGIN ME: from OFr. *cinc*, *cink*, from L. *quinque* 'five'.

**cinquecento** /ˌtʃɪŋkwɪˈtʃɛntəʊ/ ● **n.** the 16th century as a period of Italian art and literature with a reversion to classical forms.
– ORIGIN Ital., lit. '500' (shortened from *milcinquecento* '1500') used with ref. to the years 1500–99.

**cinquefoil** /ˈsɪŋkfɔɪl/ ● **n.** **1** a herbaceous plant of the rose family, with compound leaves of five leaflets and five-petalled yellow flowers. [Genus *Potentilla*.] **2** Art an ornamental design of five lobes arranged in a circle.
– ORIGIN ME: from L. *quinquefolium*, from *quinque* 'five' + *folium* 'leaf'.

**Cinzano** /tʃɪnˈzɑːnəʊ/ ● **n.** trademark an Italian vermouth.

**CIO** ● **abbrev.** Congress of Industrial Organizations.

**cion** ● **n.** US variant spelling of **scion** (in sense 1).

**cipher**[1] /ˈsʌɪfə/ (also **cypher**) ● **n.** **1** a code. ➤a key to a code. **2** dated a zero. **3** an unimportant person or thing. **4** a monogram. ● **v.** **1** encode (a message). **2** archaic do arithmetic.
– ORIGIN ME: from OFr. *cifre*, based on Arab. *ṣifr* 'zero'.

**cipher**[2] ● **n.** a continuous sounding of an organ pipe, caused by a defect. ● **v.** (of an organ pipe) sound continuously.
– ORIGIN C18: perh. from **cipher**[1].

**cipolin** /ˈsɪpəlɪn/ ● **n.** an Italian marble with veins of talc, mica, or quartz, showing white and green streaks.
– ORIGIN C18: from Fr., from Ital. *cipollino*, from *cipolla* 'onion' (because the veins of other minerals resemble those of onion skin).

**circa** /ˈsəːkə/ ● **prep.** approximately.
– ORIGIN C19: L.

**circadian** /səːˈkeɪdɪən/ ● **adj.** (of biological processes) recurring naturally on a twenty-four-hour cycle.
– ORIGIN 1950s: formed irregularly from L. *circa* 'about' + *dies* 'day'.

**Circassian** /səːˈkasɪən/ ● **n.** **1** a member of a group of mainly Sunni Muslim peoples of the NW Caucasus. **2** either of two North Caucasian languages of this people, Adyghe and Kabardian. ● **adj.** relating to or denoting the Circassians.
– ORIGIN from *Circassia*, Latinized form of Russ. *Cherkes*, denoting a district in the northern Caucasus.

**circinate** /ˈsəːsɪnət, -eɪt/ ● **adj.** **1** Botany rolled up with the tip in the centre. **2** Medicine circular.
– ORIGIN C19: from L. *circinat-*, *circinare* 'make round'.

**circle** ● **n.** **1** a round plane figure whose boundary consists of points equidistant from the centre. ➤a group of people or things forming a circle. **2** a curved upper tier of seats in a theatre. **3** a group of people with a shared profession, interests, or acquaintances. ● **v.** move or be situated all the way around. ➤draw a line around.
– PHRASES **circle the wagons** N. Amer. informal unite in defence of something. [with ref. to the defensive position of a wagon train under attack.] **come** (or **turn**) **full circle** return to a past position or situation. **go** (or **run**) **round in circles** informal do something for a long time without achieving anything.
– ORIGIN OE, from OFr. *cercle*, from L. *circulus* 'small ring', dimin. of *circus* 'ring'.

**circlet** ● **n.** **1** an ornamental circular band worn on the head. **2** a small circular arrangement or object.

**circlip** /ˈsəːklɪp/ ● **n.** Brit. a metal ring sprung into a slot in a bar to hold something in place.
– ORIGIN C20: blend of **circle** or **circular** and **clip**[1].

**circs** ● **pl. n.** Brit. informal circumstances.

**circuit** ● **n.** **1** a roughly circular line, route, or movement. **2** Brit. a track used for motor racing, horse racing, or athletics. **3** a system of electrical conductors and components forming a complete path around which an electric current can flow. **4** an established series of sporting events or entertainments. **5** a series of athletic exercises performed in one training session. **6** a regular journey by a judge around a district to hear court cases. **7** a group of Methodist Churches forming an administrative unit. **8** a chain of theatres or cinemas under a single management. ● **v.** move all the way around.
– ORIGIN ME: via OFr. from L. *circuitus*, from *circuire*, var. of *circumire* 'go round'.

**circuit board** ● **n.** a thin rigid board containing an electric circuit.

**circuit-breaker** ● **n.** an automatic safety device for stopping the flow of current in an electric circuit.

**circuitous** /səːˈkjuːɪtəs/ ● **adj.** (of a route) longer than the most direct way.
– DERIVATIVES **circuitously** adv. **circuitousness** n.

**circuitry** ● **n.** (pl. **-ies**) electric circuits collectively.

**circular** ● **adj.** **1** having the form of a circle. **2** Logic (of an argument) already containing an assumption of what is to be proved. **3** (of a letter or advertisement) for distribution to a large number of people. ● **n.** a circular letter or advertisement.
– DERIVATIVES **circularity** n. **circularly** adv.

**circular breathing** ● **n.** a technique of inhaling through the nose while blowing air through the lips, used especially by players of wind instruments.

**circularize** (also **-ise**) ● **v.** **1** distribute a large number of letters, leaflets, etc. to. **2** make circular.
– DERIVATIVES **circularization** n.

**circular polarization** ● **n.** Physics polarization in which either the electric or the magnetic vector of the light rotates in a circle perpendicular to the path of propagation.

**circular saw** ● n. a power saw with a rapidly rotating toothed disc.

**circulate** ● v. 1 move or cause to move continuously or freely through a closed area. ➤move around a social function and talk to many people. 2 pass or cause to pass from place to place or person to person.
– DERIVATIVES **circulative** adj. **circulator** n.
– ORIGIN C15 (as an alchemical term meaning 'distil something, allowing condensed vapour to return to the original liquid'): from L. *circulat-*, *circulare* 'move in a circular path', from *circulus* (see CIRCLE).

**circulating library** ● n. historical a small library with books lent for a fee.

**circulating medium** ● n. a commodity used in commercial exchange, especially coins or gold.

**circulation** ● n. 1 movement to and fro or around something. ➤the continuous motion by which blood travels through the body. 2 the public availability or knowledge of something. 3 the number of copies sold of a newspaper or magazine.
– PHRASES **in** (or **out of**) **circulation** 1 available (or unavailable) for general use. 2 (of a person) seen (or not seen) in public.
– DERIVATIVES **circulatory** adj.

**circum-** /'sə:kəm/ ● prefix about; around (functioning within the word as an adverb as in *circumambulate*, or as a preposition as in *circumpolar*).
– ORIGIN from L. *circum* 'round'.

**circumambient** /ˌsə:kəm'ambɪənt/ ● adj. chiefly poetic/literary surrounding.
– DERIVATIVES **circumambience** n. **circumambiency** n.

**circumambulate** /ˌsə:kəm'ambjʊleɪt/ ● v. formal walk all the way round.
– DERIVATIVES **circumambulation** n. **circumambulatory** adj.

**circumcircle** ● n. Geometry a circle touching all the vertices of a triangle or polygon.

**circumcise** /'sə:kəmsʌɪz/ ● v. 1 cut off the foreskin of (a young boy or man) as a Jewish or Islamic rite, or as a medical treatment. 2 cut off the clitoris, and sometimes the labia, of (a girl or young woman) as a traditional practice in some cultures.
– ORIGIN ME: from OFr. *circonciser*, or from L. *circumcis-*, *circumcidere* 'cut around'.

**circumcision** ● n. 1 the action or practice of circumcising. 2 (**Circumcision**) (in church use) the feast of the Circumcision of Christ, 1 January.

**circumference** /sə'kʌmf(ə)r(ə)ns/ ● n. 1 the enclosing boundary of a circle. 2 the distance around something.
– DERIVATIVES **circumferential** adj. **circumferentially** adv.
– ORIGIN ME: from OFr. *circonference*, from L. *circumferentia*, from *circum* 'around' + *ferre* 'carry'.

**circumflex** /'sə:kəmflɛks/ ● n. a mark (ˆ) placed over a vowel in some languages to indicate contraction, length, or another quality. ● adj. Anatomy curved.
– ORIGIN C16: from L. *circumflexus* (from *circum* 'around' + *flectere* 'to bend'), translating Gk *perispōmenos* 'drawn around'.

**circumfluent** /sə:'kʌmflʊənt/ ● adj. flowing round; surrounding.
– DERIVATIVES **circumfluence** n.
– ORIGIN C16: from L. *circumfluent-*, *circumfluere* 'flow around'.

**circumfuse** /ˌsə:kəm'fju:z/ ● v. archaic pour (a liquid) so as to surround something with it.
– ORIGIN C16: from L. *circumfus-*, *circumfundere* 'pour around'.

**circumjacent** /ˌsə:kəm'dʒeɪs(ə)nt/ ● adj. archaic surrounding.
– ORIGIN C15: from L. *circumjacent-*, *circumjacere* 'lie round about, border upon'.

**circumlocution** /ˌsə:kəmlə'kju:ʃ(ə)n/ ● n. the use of many words where fewer would do.
– DERIVATIVES **circumlocutory** /-'lɒkjʊt(ə)ri/ adj.
– ORIGIN ME: from L. *circumlocutio(n-)* (translating Gk *periphrasis*), from *circum* 'around' + *locutio(n-)* from *loqui* 'speak'.

**circumlunar** ● adj. moving or situated around the moon.

**circumnavigate** ● v. sail all the way around.
– DERIVATIVES **circumnavigation** n. **circumnavigator** n.

**circumpolar** /sə:kəm'pəʊlə/ ● adj. 1 situated or occurring around one of the earth's poles. 2 Astronomy (of a star) above the horizon at all times in a given latitude.

**circumscribe** ● v. 1 restrict; limit. 2 Geometry draw (a figure) round another, touching it at points but not cutting it. Compare with INSCRIBE.
– DERIVATIVES **circumscriber** n. **circumscription** n.
– ORIGIN ME: from L. *circumscribere*, from *circum* 'around' + *scribere* 'write'.

**circumsolar** /ˌsə:kəm'səʊlə/ ● adj. moving or situated around the sun.

**circumspect** ● adj. cautious or prudent.
– DERIVATIVES **circumspection** n. **circumspectly** adv.
– ORIGIN ME: from L. *circumspectus*, from *circumspicere* 'look around'.

**circumstance** ● n. 1 a fact or condition connected with or relevant to an event or action. 2 (**circumstances**) one's state of financial or material welfare.
– PHRASES **under** (or **in**) **the circumstances** given the difficult nature of the situation. **under** (or **in**) **no circumstances** never.
– DERIVATIVES **circumstanced** adj.
– ORIGIN ME: from OFr. *circonstance* or L. *circumstantia*, from *circumstare* 'encircle, encompass'.

**circumstantial** ● adj. 1 (of evidence or a legal case) pointing indirectly towards someone's guilt. 2 (of a description) containing full details.
– DERIVATIVES **circumstantiality** n. **circumstantially** adv.

**circumterrestrial** ● adj. moving or situated around the earth.

**circumvallate** /ˌsə:kəm'valeɪt/ ● v. poetic/literary surround with or as if with a rampart. ● adj. 1 poetic/literary surrounded or surrounding as if by a rampart. 2 Anatomy denoting papillae near the back of the tongue, surrounded by taste receptors.
– ORIGIN C17: from L. *circumvallat-*, *circumvallare* 'surround with a rampart'.

**circumvent** /sə:kəm'vɛnt/ ● v. 1 find a way around (an obstacle). 2 archaic outwit.
– DERIVATIVES **circumvention** n.
– ORIGIN ME: from L. *cirumvent-*, *circumvenire* 'skirt around'.

**circumvolution** /ˌsə:kəmvə'lu:ʃ(ə)n/ ● n. a winding movement of one thing round another.
– ORIGIN ME: from L. *circumvolut-*, *circumvolvere* 'roll around'.

**circus** ● n. (pl. **circuses**) 1 a travelling company of acrobats, trained animals, and clowns, giving performances typically in a large tent. 2 (in ancient Rome) a rounded sporting arena lined with tiers of seats. 3 informal a scene of lively activity. 4 [Brit.] a rounded open space in a town where several streets converge: *Piccadilly Circus*.
– ORIGIN ME: from L., 'ring or circus'.

**ciré** /'si:reɪ/ ● n. fabric with a shiny surface obtained by waxing and heating.
– ORIGIN 1920s: Fr., lit. 'waxed'.

**cire perdue** /ˌsɪə pə:'dju:/ ● n. a method of casting bronze using a clay core and a wax coating placed in a mould; the wax is melted in the mould and bronze poured into the space left, producing a hollow bronze figure when the core is discarded.
– ORIGIN Fr., 'lost wax'.

**cirl bunting** /sə:l/ ● n. a bunting related to the yellowhammer, the male having a distinctive facial pattern and a black throat. [*Emberiza cirlus*.]
– ORIGIN C18: *cirl* from Ital. *cirlo*, prob. from *zirlare* 'whistle as a thrush'.

**cirque** /sə:k/ ● n. 1 Geology a steep-sided hollow at the head of a valley or on a mountainside. 2 poetic/literary a ring, circlet, or circle.
– ORIGIN C17: from Fr., from L. *circus*.

**cirrhosis** /sɪ'rəʊsɪs/ ● n. a chronic liver disease marked by degeneration of cells, inflammation, and thickening of

tissue.
– DERIVATIVES **cirrhotic** /sɪˈrɒtɪk/ adj.
– ORIGIN C19: mod. L., from Gk *kirrhos* 'tawny' (the colour of the liver in many cases).

**cirriped** /ˌsɪrɪˈpiːdɪə/ (also **cirripede**) ● **n.** Zoology a crustacean of a class (Cirripedia) that comprises the barnacles.
– ORIGIN mod. L. *Cirripedia*, from L. *cirrus* 'a curl' (because of the form of the legs) + *pes, ped-* 'foot'.

**cirrocumulus** /ˌsɪrəʊˈkjuːmjʊləs/ ● **n.** cloud forming a broken layer of small fleecy clouds at high altitude.

**cirrostratus** /ˌsɪrəʊˈstrɑːtəs, -ˈstreɪtəs/ ● **n.** cloud forming a thin, uniform semi-translucent layer at high altitude.

**cirrus** /ˈsɪrəs/ ● **n.** (pl. **cirri** /-rʌɪ/) **1** cloud forming wispy filamentous tufted streaks at high altitude. **2** Zoology a slender tendril or hair-like filament, e.g. the appendage of a barnacle or the barbel of a fish. ➤ Botany a tendril.
– ORIGIN C18: from L., lit. 'a curl'.

**CIS** ● **abbrev.** Commonwealth of Independent States.

**cis-** ● **prefix 1** on this side of: *cislunar.* ➤ historical on the side nearer to Rome: *cisalpine.* **2** closer to the present: *cis-Elizabethan.* **3** Chemistry (usu. ***cis-***) denoting molecules in which two particular atoms or groups lie on the same side of a given plane, in particular denoting an isomer in which substituents at opposite ends of a carbon–carbon double bond are on the same side of the bond: cis-*1,2-dichloroethene.*
– ORIGIN from L. *cis.*

**cisalpine** /sɪsˈalpʌɪn/ ● **adj.** on the southern side of the Alps.
– ORIGIN C16: from L. *cisalpinus.*

**cisatlantic** /sɪsətˈlantɪk/ ● **adj.** on this side of the Atlantic.

**cisco** /ˈsɪskəʊ/ ● **n.** (pl. **-oes**) a northern freshwater whitefish, important as a food fish. [Genus *Coregonus*, several species.]
– ORIGIN C19: of unknown origin.

**cislunar** /sɪsˈluːnə/ ● **adj.** between the earth and the moon.

**cisplatin** /sɪsˈplatɪn/ ● **n.** Medicine a compound of platinum used in cancer chemotherapy.
– ORIGIN C20: from **CIS-** + **PLATINUM**.

**cispontine** /sɪsˈpɒntʌɪn/ ● **adj.** archaic on the north side of the Thames bridges in London.
– ORIGIN C19: from **CIS-** + L. *pons, pont-* 'bridge'.

**cissing** /ˈsɪsɪŋ/ ● **n.** cracking in a top coat of paint.
– ORIGIN C19: of unknown origin.

**cissy** ● **n. & adj.** variant spelling of **SISSY**.

**cist**[1] /sɪst/ (also **kist**) ● **n.** Archaeology a coffin or burial chamber made from stone or a hollowed tree.
– ORIGIN Welsh, lit. 'chest'.

**cist**[2] /sɪst/ ● **n.** (in ancient Greece) a box for sacred utensils.
– ORIGIN C19: from L. *cista*, from Gk *kistē* 'box'.

**Cistercian** /sɪˈstəːʃ(ə)n/ ● **n.** a monk or nun of an order that is a stricter branch of the Benedictines. ● **adj.** of or relating to this order.
– ORIGIN from Fr. *cistercien*, from *Cistercium*, the L. name of *Citeaux* near Dijon in France, where the order was founded.

**cistern** ● **n. 1** a water storage tank, especially as part of a flushing toilet. **2** an underground reservoir for rainwater.
– ORIGIN ME: from OFr. *cisterne*, from L. *cisterna*, from *cista* (see **CIST**[2]).

**cistron** /ˈsɪstrɒn/ ● **n.** Biochemistry a section of a DNA or RNA molecule that codes for a specific polypeptide in protein synthesis.
– ORIGIN 1950s: from **CIS-** + **TRANS-** (because of the possibility of two genes being on the same or different chromosomes) + **-ON**.

**cistus** /ˈsɪstəs/ ● **n.** a shrub with large white or red flowers, the twigs of which yield ladanum. [Genus *Cistus.*]
– ORIGIN mod. L., from Gk *kistos.*

**citadel** /ˈsɪtəd(ə)l, -dɛl/ ● **n. 1** a fortress protecting or dominating a city. **2** a meeting hall of the Salvation Army.
– ORIGIN C16: from Fr. *citadelle*, or from Ital. *cittadella*, based on L. *civitas* (see **CITY**).

**citation** /sʌɪˈteɪʃ(ə)n/ ● **n. 1** a quotation from or reference to a book or author. **2** a mention of a praiseworthy act in an official report. ➤ a note accompanying an award, giving reasons for it. **3** Law a reference to a former case, used as guidance or in support of an argument. **4** Law, chiefly N. Amer. a summons.

**cite** /sʌɪt/ ● **v. 1** quote (a book or author) as evidence for an argument. **2** praise for a courageous act in an official dispatch. **3** Law summon to appear in a law court.
– DERIVATIVES **citable** adj.
– ORIGIN ME: from OFr. *citer*, from L. *citare*, from *ciere, cire* 'to call'.

**CITES** /ˈsʌɪtiːz/ ● **abbrev.** Convention on International Trade in Endangered Species.

**citified** (also **cityfied**) ● **adj.** chiefly derogatory characteristic of or adjusted to a city.

**citizen** ● **n. 1** a legally recognized subject or national of a state or commonwealth. **2** an inhabitant of a town or city.
– DERIVATIVES **citizenry** n. **citizenship** n.
– ORIGIN ME: from Anglo-Norman Fr. *citezein*, alt. of OFr. *citeain*, based on L. *civitas* (see **CITY**).

**Citizens' Advice Bureau** ● **n.** (in the UK) an office providing free advice on civil matters.

**citizen's arrest** ● **n.** an arrest by an ordinary person without a warrant, allowable in certain cases.

**Citizens' Band** ● **n.** a range of radio frequencies which are allocated for local communication by private individuals.

**Citizen's Charter** ● **n.** a document setting out the rights of citizens, especially a British government document of 1991, guaranteeing citizens the right of redress where a public service fails to meet certain standards.

**citole** /sɪˈtəʊl/ ● **n.** a lute-like medieval stringed instrument, forerunner of the cittern.
– ORIGIN ME: from OFr., based on L. *cithara* (see **CITTERN**).

**citral** /ˈsɪtral/ ● **n.** Chemistry a fragrant liquid occurring in citrus and lemon grass oils and used in flavourings and perfumes.

**citric** ● **adj.** derived from or related to citrus fruit.
– ORIGIN C18: from L. *citrus* 'citron tree' + **-IC**.

**citric acid** ● **n.** Chemistry a sharp-tasting crystalline acid present in the juice of lemons and other sour fruits, used commercially as a flavouring and setting agent.
– DERIVATIVES **citrate** n.

**citrine** /ˈsɪtrɪn/ ● **n.** a glassy yellow variety of quartz.
– ORIGIN ME: from OFr. *citrin* 'lemon-coloured', from med. L. *citrinus*, from L. *citrus* 'citron tree'.

**citron** /ˈsɪtr(ə)n/ ● **n. 1** a shrubby Asian tree bearing large lemon-like fruits with thick fragrant peel. [*Citrus medica.*] **2** the fruit of this tree.
– ORIGIN C16: from Fr., from L. *citrus* 'citron tree', on the pattern of *limon* 'lemon'.

**citronella** ● **n. 1** a fragrant natural oil used as an insect repellent and in perfume. **2** the South Asian grass from which this oil is obtained. [*Cymbopogon nardus.*]
– ORIGIN C19: mod. L., from **CITRON** + the dimin. suffix *-ella.*

**citrus** ● **n.** (pl. **citruses**) **1** a tree of a genus that includes citron, lemon, lime, orange, and grapefruit. [Genus *Citrus.*] **2** (also **citrus fruit**) a fruit from such a tree.
– DERIVATIVES **citrous** adj. **citrusy** adj.
– ORIGIN L., 'citron tree, thuja'.

**cittern** /ˈsɪt(ə)n/ ● **n.** a lute-like stringed instrument with a flattened back and wire strings, used in 16th- and 17th-century Europe.
– ORIGIN C16: from L. *cithara*, from Gk *kithara*, denoting a kind of harp; the spelling being influenced by **GITTERN**.

**city** ● **n.** (pl. **-ies**) **1** a large town, in particular (Brit.) a town created a city by charter and containing a cathedral. ➤ N. Amer. a municipal centre incorporated by the state or province. **2** (**the City**) the part of London governed by

the Lord Mayor and the Corporation. ➤ the financial and commercial institutions in this part of London.
– DERIVATIVES **cityward** adj. & adv. **citywards** adv.
– ORIGIN ME (orig. denoting a town): from OFr. *cite*, from L. *civitas*, from *civis* 'citizen'.

**City Company** ● n. (in the UK) a corporation descended from an ancient trade guild of London.

**city desk** ● n. Brit. the department of a newspaper dealing with business news. ➤ N. Amer. the department of a newspaper dealing with local news.

**city farm** ● n. chiefly Brit. a farm in an urban area, used for educational purposes.

**city father** ● n. a person concerned with the administration of a city.

**cityfied** ● adj. variant spelling of **CITIFIED**.

**city hall** ● n. [treated as sing.] N. Amer. municipal offices or officers collectively.

**city manager** ● n. N. Amer. an official directing the administration of a city.

**cityscape** ● n. a city landscape.

**city slicker** ● n. a person with the sophisticated tastes or values associated with city dwellers.

**city state** ● n. a city and surrounding territory that forms an independent state.

**City Technology College** ● n. (in the UK) a type of secondary school set up to teach technology and science in inner-city areas.

**civet** /ˈsɪvɪt/ ● n. **1** a slender nocturnal cat with a barred and spotted coat, native to Africa and Asia. [*Viverra civetta* (Africa), and other species.] **2** a strong musky perfume obtained from the scent glands of the civet.
– ORIGIN C16: from Fr. *civette*, ult. from Arab. *zabād*.

**civic** ● adj. of or relating to a city or town. ● n. informal (in South Africa) an elected, community-based body concerned with local government in a black township.
– DERIVATIVES **civically** adv.
– ORIGIN C16: from Fr. *civique* or L. *civicus*, from *civis* 'citizen'.

**civic centre** ● n. **1** the area of a town where municipal offices are situated. **2** a building containing municipal offices.

**civics** ● pl. n. [treated as sing.] the study of the rights and duties of citizenship.

**civil** ● adj. **1** of or relating to ordinary citizens, as distinct from military or ecclesiastical matters. **2** Law non-criminal: *a civil court.* **3** courteous and polite. **4** (of time measurement) fixed by custom or law, not natural or astronomical.
– DERIVATIVES **civilly** adv.
– ORIGIN ME: via OFr. from L. *civilis*, from *civis* 'citizen'.

**civil commotion** ● n. English Law a riot.

**civil defence** ● n. the organization and training of civilians for their protection during and after attacks in wartime.

**civil disobedience** ● n. the refusal to comply with certain laws or to pay taxes, as a political protest.

**civil engineer** ● n. an engineer who designs roads, bridges, dams, etc.
– DERIVATIVES **civil engineering** n.

**civilian** ● n. a person not in the armed services or the police force. ● adj. of, denoting, or relating to a civilian.
– DERIVATIVES **civilianization** (also **-isation**) n. **civilianize** (also **-ise**) v.
– ORIGIN ME (denoting a practitioner of civil law): from OFr. *civilien*, in the phr. *droit civilien* 'civil law'.

**civility** ● n. (pl. **-ies**) politeness and courtesy. ➤ (**civilities**) polite remarks used in formal conversation.

**civilization** (also **-isation**) ● n. **1** an advanced stage or system of human social development. ➤ the process of achieving this. **2** a civilized nation or region.

**civilize** (also **-ise**) ● v. **1** [usu. as adj. **civilized**] bring to an advanced stage of social development. **2** [as adj. **civilized**] polite and good-mannered.
– DERIVATIVES **civilizable** adj. **civilizer** n.

**civil law** ● n. **1** law concerned with ordinary citizens, rather than criminal, military, or religious affairs. **2** the system of law predominant on the European continent, influenced by that of ancient Rome.

**civil liberty** ● n. freedom of action and speech subject to laws established for the good of the community. ➤ (**civil liberties**) one's rights to this.
– DERIVATIVES **civil libertarian** n.

**Civil List** ● n. (in the UK) an annual allowance voted by Parliament for the royal family's household expenses.

**civil marriage** ● n. a marriage without religious ceremony.

**civil parish** ● n. see **PARISH** (in sense 2).

**civil rights** ● pl. n. the rights of citizens to political and social freedom and equality.

**civil servant** ● n. a member of the civil service.

**civil service** ● n. the permanent professional branches of state administration, excluding military and judicial branches and elected politicians.

**civil war** ● n. a war between citizens of the same country.

**civil wrong** ● n. Law an infringement of a person's rights.

**civil year** ● n. see **YEAR** (sense 2).

**civvy** ● n. (pl. **-ies**) informal **1** a civilian. **2** (**civvies**) civilian clothes, as opposed to uniform.
– PHRASES **Civvy Street** Brit. informal civilian life.

**CJ** ● abbrev. Chief Justice.

**CJD** ● abbrev. Creutzfeldt–Jakob disease.

**CL** ● abbrev. **1** chemiluminescence. **2** Sri Lanka (international vehicle registration). [from *Ceylon*.]

**Cl** ● symb. the chemical element chlorine.

**cl** ● abbrev. centilitre.

**clabber** chiefly US ● n. milk that has clotted on souring. ● v. curdle or cause to curdle.
– ORIGIN C19: shortening of **BONNY CLABBER**.

**clack** ● v. **1** make or cause to make a sharp sound as of a hard object striking another. **2** archaic chatter loudly. ● n. **1** a clacking sound. **2** archaic loud chatter.
– DERIVATIVES **clacker** n.
– ORIGIN ME: imitative.

**clacket** /ˈklakɪt/ ● v. (**clacketed**, **clacketing**) make a series of clacks.
– ORIGIN C16: from Fr. *claquet*, from *claquer* 'to clack'.

**clad**[1] archaic or poetic past participle of **CLOTHE**. ● adj. **1** clothed. **2** provided with cladding.

**clad**[2] ● v. (**cladding**; past and past part. **cladded** or **clad**) cover with cladding.
– ORIGIN C16 (in the sense 'clothe'): appar. from **CLAD**[1].

**Claddagh ring** /ˈkladə/ ● n. a ring in the form of two hands clasping a heart, given in Ireland as a token of love.
– ORIGIN from the name of a small fishing village on the edge of Galway city.

**cladding** ● n. a covering or coating on a structure or material.

**clade** /kleɪd/ ● n. Biology a group of organisms comprising all the evolutionary descendants of a common ancestor.
– ORIGIN 1950s: from Gk *klados* 'branch'.

**cladistics** /kləˈdɪstɪks/ ● pl. n. [treated as sing.] Biology a method of classification of animals and plants into groups based on characteristics which originated in a common evolutionary ancestor.
– DERIVATIVES **cladism** /ˈkladɪz(ə)m/ n. **cladistic** adj.

**clado-** /ˈkleɪdəʊ, ˈkladəʊ/ ● comb. form relating to a branch or branching: *cladogram.*
– ORIGIN from Gk *klados* 'branch or shoot'.

**Cladocera** /kləˈdɒs(ə)rə/ ● pl. n. Zoology an order of minute branchiopod crustaceans which includes the water fleas.
– DERIVATIVES **cladoceran** n. & adj.
– ORIGIN mod. L., from Gk *klados* 'branch or root' + *keras* 'horn' (because of the branched antennae).

**cladode** /ˈkleɪdəʊd/ ● n. Botany a flattened leaf-like stem.
– ORIGIN C19: from Gk *kladōdēs* 'with many shoots'.

**cladogenesis** /ˌkleɪdə(ʊ)ˈdʒɛnɪsɪs, ˈkladə(ʊ)-/ ● n. Biology the formation of a new group of organisms by evolutionary divergence from an ancestral form.
– DERIVATIVES **cladogenetic** adj.

**cladogram** /ˈkleɪdə(ʊ)gram, ˈkladə(ʊ)-/ • **n.** Biology a branching diagram showing the cladistic relationship between species.

**claggy** • **adj.** Brit. dialect tending to form sticky lumps.
– ORIGIN C16: perh. of Scand. origin; cf. Dan. *klag* 'sticky mud'.

**claim** • **v. 1** assert that something is the case. **2** demand as one's property or earnings. ➤request (money) under the terms of an insurance policy. **3** call for (someone's attention). **4** cause the loss of (someone's life). • **n. 1** an assertion of the truth of something. ➤(also **statement of claim**) a statement of the novel features in a patent. **2** a demand for something considered one's due. ➤a request for compensation under the terms of an insurance policy. **3** (also **mining claim**) a piece of land allotted to or taken by someone in order to be mined.
– DERIVATIVES **claimable** adj. **claimant** n.
– ORIGIN ME: from OFr. *claime* (n.), *clamer* (v.), from L. *clamare* 'call out'.

**claimer** • **n.** Horse Racing **1** (N. Amer. also **claiming race**) a race in which every horse may be claimed by a buyer for a predetermined price related to the weight that the horse carries. **2** a jockey claiming a weight allowance in a race.

**claim jumper** • **n.** N. Amer. a person who appropriates a mining claim already taken by another.

**clairaudience** /klɛːrˈɔːdɪəns/ • **n.** the supposed faculty of perceiving, as if by hearing, what is inaudible.
– DERIVATIVES **clairaudient** adj. & n.
– ORIGIN C19: from Fr. *clair* 'clear' + **AUDIENCE**.

**clairvoyance** • **n.** the supposed faculty of perceiving events in the future or beyond normal sensory contact.
– ORIGIN C19: from Fr., from *clair* 'clear' + *voir* 'to see'.

**clairvoyant** • **n.** a person claiming to have clairvoyance. • **adj.** having clairvoyance.
– DERIVATIVES **clairvoyantly** adv.
– ORIGIN C17: from Fr., from *clair* 'clear' + *voyant* 'seeing'.

**clam**[1] • **n.** a large marine bivalve mollusc with shells of equal size, several kinds of which are edible. [*Mya arenaria* (**softshell clam**), *Venus mercenaria* (**hardshell clam**, both N. America), *Tridacna gigas* (**giant clam**, Indo-Pacific), and many other species.] • **v.** (**clammed**, **clamming**) **1** chiefly N. Amer. dig for or collect clams. **2** (**clam up**) informal abruptly stop talking.
– ORIGIN C16: appar. from earlier *clam* 'a clamp', from OE *clam, clamm* 'a bond or bondage', of Gmc origin; rel. to **CLAMP**[1].

**clam**[2] • **n.** US informal a dollar.
– ORIGIN 1930s: of unknown origin.

**clamant** /ˈkleɪm(ə)nt, ˈklam-/ • **adj.** forcing itself urgently on the attention.
– DERIVATIVES **clamantly** adv.
– ORIGIN C17: from L. *clamant-*, *clamare* 'cry out'.

**clambake** • **n.** N. Amer. a social gathering outdoors, especially for eating seafood.

**clamber** • **v.** climb or move in an awkward and laborious way. • **n.** an act of clambering.
– ORIGIN ME: prob. from *clamb*, obs. past tense of **CLIMB**.

**clamdiggers** • **pl. n.** close-fitting calf-length trousers for women.

**clammy** • **adj.** (**-ier**, **-iest**) unpleasantly damp and sticky or slimy. ➤(of air) cold and damp.
– DERIVATIVES **clammily** adv. **clamminess** n.
– ORIGIN ME: from dial. *clam* 'to be sticky or adhere', of Gmc origin; rel. to **CLAY**.

**clamour** (US **clamor**) • **n.** a loud and confused noise, especially of vehement shouting. ➤a vehement protest or demand. • **v.** (of a group) make a clamour.
– DERIVATIVES **clamorous** adj. **clamorously** adv. **clamorousness** n.
– ORIGIN ME: via OFr. from L. *clamor*, from *clamare* 'cry out'.

**clamp**[1] • **n. 1** a brace, band, or clasp for strengthening or holding things together. **2** an electric circuit maintaining the voltage limits of a signal at prescribed levels. • **v. 1** fasten in place or together with a clamp. ➤hold tightly against another thing. ➤fit a wheel clamp to (an illegally parked car). **2** (**clamp down**) suppress or prevent something. **3** maintain the voltage limits of (an electrical signal) at prescribed values.
– DERIVATIVES **clamper** n.
– ORIGIN ME: prob. of Du. or Low Ger. origin and rel. to **CLAM**[1].

**clamp**[2] • **n.** Brit. **1** a heap of potatoes or other root vegetables stored under straw or earth. **2** a three-sided structure used to store silage.
– ORIGIN C16 (denoting a pile of bricks for firing): prob. from Du. *klamp* 'heap'; rel. to **CLUMP**.

**clampdown** • **n.** informal a concerted attempt to suppress something.

**clan** • **n. 1** a group of close-knit and interrelated families, especially in the Scottish Highlands. **2** a group with a strong common interest.
– ORIGIN ME: from Sc. Gaelic *clann* 'offspring, family', from Old Ir. *cland*, from L. *planta* 'sprout'.

**clandestine** /klanˈdɛstɪn, ˈklandɛstɪn/ • **adj.** surreptitious.
– DERIVATIVES **clandestinely** adv. **clandestinity** n.
– ORIGIN C16: from Fr. *clandestin* or L. *clandestinus*, from *clam* 'secretly'.

**clang** • **n.** a loud, resonant metallic sound. • **v.** make or cause to make a clang.
– ORIGIN C16: imitative, influenced by L. *clangere* 'resound'.

**clanger** • **n.** informal, chiefly Brit. a mistake.

**clangour** /ˈklaŋgə/ (US **clangor**) • **n.** a continuous clanging sound.
– DERIVATIVES **clangorous** adj. **clangorously** adv.
– ORIGIN C16: from L. *clangor*, from *clangere* 'resound'.

**clank** • **n.** a loud, sharp sound as of pieces of metal being struck together. • **v.** make or cause to make a clank.
– DERIVATIVES **clanking** adj. **clankingly** adv.
– ORIGIN ME: imitative.

**clannish** • **adj.** tending to exclude others outside the group.
– DERIVATIVES **clannishly** adv. **clannishness** n.

**clanship** • **n.** the system of clan membership or loyalty.

**clansman** • **n.** (pl. **-men**) a male member of a clan.

**clap**[1] • **v.** (**clapped**, **clapping**) **1** strike the palms of (one's hands) together repeatedly, especially to applaud. **2** slap encouragingly on the back. **3** place (a hand) briefly over one's face as a gesture of dismay or regret. **4** (of a bird) flap (its wings) audibly. **5** (**clap something on**) abruptly impose a restrictive or punitive measure on. • **n. 1** an act of clapping. **2** an explosive sound, especially of thunder.
– PHRASES **clap someone in jail** (or **irons**) put someone in prison (or in chains).
– ORIGIN OE *clappan* 'throb, beat', of imitative origin.

**clap**[2] • **n.** informal a venereal disease, especially gonorrhoea.
– ORIGIN C16: from OFr. *clapoir* 'venereal bubo'.

**clapboard** /ˈklapbɔːd, ˈklabəd/ • **n.** chiefly N. Amer. one of a series of long planks of wood with edges horizontally overlapping, covering the outer walls of buildings.
– DERIVATIVES **clapboarded** adj.
– ORIGIN C16: partial translation of Low Ger. *klappholt* 'barrel stave', from *klappen* 'to crack' + *holt* 'wood'.

**clapped-out** • **adj.** informal, chiefly Brit. worn out from age or heavy use.

**clapper** • **n.** the tongue or striker of a bell.
– PHRASES **like the clappers** Brit. informal very fast or hard.

**clapperboard** • **n.** a device of hinged boards that are struck together before filming to synchronize the starting of picture and sound machinery.

**clapper bridge** • **n.** a simple bridge consisting of planks or stone slabs laid across a series of rocks.

**claptrap** • **n.** nonsense.
– ORIGIN C18 (denoting something designed to elicit applause): from **CLAP**[1] + **TRAP**[1].

**claque** /klak, klɑːk/ • **n.** a group of people hired to applaud or heckle a performer.
– ORIGIN C19: Fr., from *claquer* 'to clap'.

**claqueur** /klaˈkəː, klɑː-/ • **n.** a member of a claque.

**clarabella** /ˌklarəˈbɛlə/ • **n.** an organ stop with the qual-

ity of a flute.
– ORIGIN C19: from the fem. forms of L. *clarus* 'clear' and *bellus* 'pretty'.

**clarence** ● **n.** historical a closed four-wheeled horse-drawn carriage, seating four inside and two outside.
– ORIGIN C19: named in honour of the Duke of *Clarence*, later William IV.

**claret** /ˈklarət/ ● **n. 1** a red wine, especially from Bordeaux. **2** a deep purplish red colour.
– ORIGIN ME: from OFr. (*vin*) *claret* and med. L. *claratum* (*vinum*) 'clarified (wine)', from L. *clarus* 'clear'.

**clarify** /ˈklarɪfʌɪ/ ● **v.** (**-ies**, **-ied**) **1** make more comprehensible. **2** [usu. as adj. **clarified**] melt (butter) to separate out the impurities.
– DERIVATIVES **clarification** n. **clarificatory** adj. **clarifier** n.
– ORIGIN ME: from OFr. *clarifier*, from late L. *clarificare*, from L. *clarus* 'clear'.

**clarinet** ● **n.** a woodwind instrument with a single-reed mouthpiece, a cylindrical tube of dark wood with a flared end, and holes stopped by keys.
– DERIVATIVES **clarinettist** (US **clarinetist**) n.
– ORIGIN C18: from Fr. *clarinette*, dimin. of *clarine*, denoting a kind of bell; rel. to **CLARION**.

**clarion** /ˈklarɪən/ ● **n.** chiefly historical a shrill narrow-tubed war trumpet. ● **adj.** loud and clear.
– PHRASES **clarion call** a strongly expressed demand for action.
– ORIGIN ME: from med. L. *clario(n-)*, from L. *clarus* 'clear'.

**clarity** ● **n. 1** the state or quality of being clear, distinct, and easily perceived or understood. **2** the quality of transparency or purity: *the crystal clarity of water.*
– ORIGIN ME (in the sense 'glory, divine splendour'): from L. *claritas*, from *clarus* 'clear'.

**clarkia** /ˈklɑːkɪə/ ● **n.** a North American plant with showy white, pink, or purple flowers. [Genus *Clarkia*.]
– ORIGIN mod. L., named after the US explorer, William *Clark*, who discovered it.

**clarsach** /ˈklɑːrsəx, ˈklɑːsək/ ● **n.** a small harp with wire strings, used in the folk and early music of Scotland and Ireland.
– ORIGIN C15: from Sc. Gaelic, perh. based on *clar* 'table, board'.

**clart** /klɑːt/ (also **clarts**) ● **n.** Scottish & N. English sticky mud; filth.
– DERIVATIVES **clarty** adj.
– ORIGIN C17 (as a verb in the sense 'smear, plaster'): of unknown origin.

**clary** /ˈklɛːri/ ● **n.** an aromatic plant of the mint family, used as a culinary and medicinal herb. [*Salvia sclarea* (S. Europe) and related species.]
– ORIGIN ME: from obs. Fr. *clarie.*

**clash** ● **v. 1** (of two opposing groups) come abruptly into violent conflict. ➤have a forceful disagreement. **2** be incompatible. **3** (of colours) appear discordant when placed together. **4** (of dates or events) occur inconveniently at the same time. **5** strike (cymbals) together, producing a loud discordant sound. ● **n.** an instance of clashing.
– DERIVATIVES **clasher** n.
– ORIGIN C16: imitative.

**clasp** ● **v. 1** grasp tightly with one's hand. ➤place (one's arms) around something so as to hold it tightly. ➤hold tightly. ➤press (one's hands) together with the fingers interlaced. **2** fasten with a clasp. ● **n. 1** a small device with interlocking parts used for fastening things together. **2** an inscribed silver bar on a medal ribbon. **3** an act of clasping.
– PHRASES **clasp hands** shake hands with fervour or affection.
– ORIGIN ME: of unknown origin.

**claspers** ● **pl. n.** Zoology a pair of appendages under the abdomen of a male shark or ray, or at the end of the abdomen of a male insect, used to hold the female during copulation.
– ORIGIN C19: from **CLASP**.

**clasp knife** ● **n.** a knife with a blade that folds into the handle.

**class** ● **n. 1** a set or category of things having some property in common and differentiated from others by kind or quality. ➤Biology a principal taxonomic grouping that ranks above order and below phylum or division, such as Mammalia or Insecta. ➤Brit. a division of candidates according to merit in a university examination. **2** a system that divides members of a society into sets based on perceived social or economic status. ➤such a set. **3** a group of students or pupils who are taught together. ➤a lesson. ➤N. Amer. all of the college or school students of a particular year. **4** informal impressive stylishness in appearance or behaviour. ● **v.** assign or regard as belonging to a particular category. ● **adj.** informal showing stylish excellence: *he's a class player.*
– PHRASES **class act** informal, chiefly N. Amer. a person or thing displaying impressive and stylish excellence.
– ORIGIN C16: from L. *classis* 'a division of the Roman people, a grade, or a class of pupils'.

**class action** ● **n.** Law, chiefly N. Amer. a law suit filed or defended by an individual acting on behalf of a group.

**class consciousness** ● **n.** awareness of one's place in a system of social class, especially (in Marxist terms) as it relates to the class struggle.
– DERIVATIVES **class-conscious** adj.

**classic** ● **adj. 1** judged over a period of time to be of the highest quality. ➤(of a garment) of a simple, elegant style not greatly subject to changes in fashion. **2** remarkably typical: *the classic symptoms of flu.* ● **n. 1** a work of art of recognized and established value: *his books have become classics.* **2** (**Classics**) the study of ancient Greek and Latin literature, philosophy, and history. ➤(**the classics**) the works of ancient Greek and Latin writers and philosophers. **3** (**Classic**) a major sports tournament or competition, especially in golf or tennis.
– ORIGIN C17: from Fr. *classique* or L. *classicus* 'belonging to a class or division', later 'of the highest class'.

**classical** ● **adj. 1** of or relating to ancient Greek or Latin literature, art, or culture. ➤(of art or architecture) influenced by ancient Greek or Roman forms or principles. **2** (of a form of art or a language) representing an exemplary standard within a traditional and long-established form or style. ➤(of music) of traditional and long-established form or style or (more specifically) written in the European tradition during a period lasting approximately from 1750 to 1830, when forms such as the symphony were standardized. **3** of or relating to the first significant period of an area of study: *classical Marxism.* **4** Physics relating to or based upon concepts and theories which preceded the theories of relativity and quantum mechanics; Newtonian.
– DERIVATIVES **classicalism** n. **classicality** n. **classically** adv.

**classicism** ● **n.** the following of ancient Greek or Roman principles and style in art and literature, generally associated with harmony, restraint, and adherence to recognized standards of form and craftsmanship.

**classicist** ● **n. 1** a person who studies Classics. **2** a follower of classicism.

**classicize** (also **-ise**) ● **v.** [usu. as adj. **classicizing**] imitate a classical style: *the classicizing strains in Guercino's art.*

**Classico** /ˈklasɪkəʊ/ ● **adj.** [postpos.] (in the classification of Italian wines) denoting a wine produced in the region from which the type takes its name: *Chianti Classico.*
– ORIGIN from Ital. *classico* 'classic, traditional, genuine'.

**classic race** ● **n.** (in the UK) each of the five main flat races of the horse-racing season.

**classification** ● **n. 1** the action or process of classifying. **2** a category into which something is put.
– DERIVATIVES **classificatory** adj.

**classified** ● **adj. 1** (of newspaper or magazine advertisements) organized in categories according to what is being advertised. **2** (of information or documents) designated as officially secret. **3** Brit. (of a road) assigned to a category according to its importance within the overall system of road numbering. ● **n.** (**classifieds**) classified advertisements.

**classify** ● **v.** (**-ies**, **-ied**) **1** arrange (a group) in classes or

categories according to shared qualities or characteristics. ➤assign (someone or something) to a particular class or category. **2** designate (documents or information) as officially secret or to which only authorized people may have access.
– DERIVATIVES **classifiable** adj. **classifier** n. **classifying** adj.
– ORIGIN C18: back-form. from CLASSIFICATION, from Fr., from *classe* 'class', from L. *classis* 'division'.

**classism** ● n. prejudice against or in favour of people belonging to a particular social class.
– DERIVATIVES **classist** adj. & n.

**classless** ● adj. **1** (of a society) not divided into social classes. **2** not showing characteristics of a particular social class: *a classless accent.*
– DERIVATIVES **classlessness** n.

**classmate** ● n. a fellow member of one's school class.

**classroom** ● n. a room in which a class of pupils or students is taught.

**class struggle** ● n. (in Marxist ideology) the conflict of interests between the workers and the ruling class in a capitalist society.

**classy** ● adj. (**-ier**, **-iest**) informal stylish and sophisticated.
– DERIVATIVES **classily** adv. **classiness** n.

**clast** /klast/ ● n. Geology a constituent fragment of a clastic rock.
– ORIGIN C20: back-form. from CLASTIC.

**clastic** ● adj. Geology denoting rocks composed of broken pieces of older rocks.
– ORIGIN C19: from Fr. *clastique*, from Gk *klastos* 'broken in pieces'.

**clathrate** /'klaθreɪt/ ● n. Chemistry a compound in which molecules of one component are physically trapped within the crystal structure of another.
– ORIGIN 1940s: from L. *clathratus*, from *clathri* 'lattice-bars'.

**clatter** ● n. a loud rattling sound as of hard objects falling or striking each other. ● v. make or cause to make a clatter. ➤fall or move with a clatter.
– ORIGIN OE (as v.), of imitative origin.

**claudication** /ˌklɔːdɪ'keɪʃ(ə)n/ ● n. Medicine **1** limping. **2** (also **intermittent claudication**) a condition in which cramping pain in the leg is induced by exercise, typically caused by obstruction of the arteries.
– ORIGIN ME: from L. *claudicatio(n-)*, from *claudicare* 'to limp', from *claudus* 'lame'.

**clause** ● n. **1** a unit of grammatical organization next below the sentence in rank, and in traditional grammar said to consist of a subject and predicate. **2** a particular and separate article, stipulation, or proviso in a treaty, bill, or contract.
– DERIVATIVES **clausal** adj.
– ORIGIN ME: via OFr. *clause*, based on L. *claus-*, *claudere* 'shut, close'.

**claustral** /'klɔːstr(ə)l/ ● adj. **1** of or relating to a cloister or religious house. **2** poetic/literary enveloping; confining.
– ORIGIN ME: from late L. *claustralis*, from L. *claustrum* (see CLOISTER).

**claustration** /klɔː'streɪʃ(ə)n/ ● n. poetic/literary confinement as if in a cloister.
– ORIGIN C19: from L. *claustrum* 'lock, bolt' + -ATION.

**claustrophobia** /klɔːstrə'fəʊbɪə/ ● n. extreme or irrational fear of confined places.
– DERIVATIVES **claustrophobe** n.
– ORIGIN C19: mod. L., from L. *claustrum* 'lock, bolt' + -PHOBIA.

**claustrophobic** ● adj. suffering from claustrophobia. ➤(of a place or situation) inducing claustrophobia. ● n. a claustrophobic person.
– DERIVATIVES **claustrophobically** adv.

**clavate** /'kleɪveɪt/ ● adj. Botany & Zoology club-shaped; thicker at the apex than the base.
– ORIGIN C17: from mod. L. *clavatus*, from L. *clava* 'club'.

**clave**[1] /kleɪv, klɑːv/ ● n. one of a pair of hardwood sticks used in music to make a hollow sound when struck together.
– ORIGIN 1920s: from Latin Amer. Sp., from Sp. *clave* 'keystone', from L. *clavis* 'key'.

**clave**[2] archaic past of CLEAVE[2].

**clavichord** /'klavɪkɔːd/ ● n. a small, rectangular keyboard instrument with a soft tone.
– ORIGIN ME: from med. L. *clavichordium*, from L. *clavis* 'key' + *chorda* 'string'.

**clavicle** /'klavɪk(ə)l/ ● n. Anatomy technical term for COLLARBONE.
– DERIVATIVES **clavicular** /klə'vɪkjʊlə/ adj.
– ORIGIN C17: from L. *clavicula* 'small key', dimin. of *clavis* (because of its shape).

**clavier** /'klavɪə, klə'vɪə/ ● n. Music a keyboard instrument.
– ORIGIN C18: from Ger. *Klavier*, from Fr. *clavier*, from med. L. *claviarius* 'key-bearer', from L. *clavis* 'key'.

**claviform** /'klavɪfɔːm/ ● adj. another term for CLAVATE.
– ORIGIN C19: from L. *clava* 'club' + -IFORM.

**claw** ● n. **1** a curved, pointed horny nail on each digit of the foot in birds, lizards, and some mammals. ➤either of a pair of small hooked appendages on an insect's foot. **2** the pincer of a crab, scorpion, or other arthropod. **3** a mechanical device resembling a claw, used for gripping or lifting. ● v. **1** (usu. **claw at**) scratch or tear at with the claws or fingernails. ➤clutch at with the hands. ➤(**claw something away**) try desperately to move something with the hands. **2** (**claw one's way**) haul oneself forward with one's hands. **3** (**claw something back**) regain or recover money, power, etc. laboriously or harshly. **4** (of a sailing ship) beat to windward.
– PHRASES **get one's claws into** informal have a controlling influence over.
– DERIVATIVES **-clawed** adj. **clawless** adj.
– ORIGIN OE *clawu* (n.), *clawian* (v.), of W. Gmc origin.

**clawback** ● n. an act of retrieving money already paid out, typically by a government using taxation.

**claw hammer** ● n. a hammer with one side of the head split and curved, used for extracting nails.

**clay** ● n. **1** a stiff, sticky fine-grained impermeable earth that can be moulded when wet and baked to make bricks and pottery. **2** poetic/literary the substance of the human body: *this lifeless clay.*
– DERIVATIVES **clayey** adj. **clayish** adj.
– ORIGIN OE *clǣg*, of W. Gmc origin; rel. to CLEAVE[2] and CLIMB.

**claymore** ● n. **1** historical a type of two-edged or single-edged broadsword used in Scotland. **2** a type of anti-personnel mine.
– ORIGIN C18: from Sc. Gaelic *claidheamh* 'sword' + *mór* 'great'.

**claypan** ● n. Austral. a shallow depression or hollow in the ground with an impermeable clay base, which holds water after rain.

**clay pigeon** ● n. a saucer-shaped piece of baked clay or other material thrown up in the air from a trap as a target for shooting.

**clay pipe** ● n. a tobacco pipe made of hardened clay.

**-cle** ● suffix forming nouns such as *article*, *particle*, which were originally diminutives.
– ORIGIN via Fr. from L. *-culus*, *-cula*, *-culum*.

**clean** ● adj. **1** free from dirt, pollutants, or harmful substances. ➤attentive to personal hygiene. **2** morally pure. ➤not obscene: *good clean fun.* ➤showing or having no record of offences or crimes. ➤played or done according to the rules. **3** free from irregularities; smooth; well defined. ➤(of timber) free from knots. **4** (of an action) smoothly and skilfully done. **5** (of a taste, sound, or smell) distinctive and fresh. ● adv. **1** so as to be free from dirt. **2** informal completely: *I clean forgot her birthday.* ● v. **1** make clean; make free of mess. **2** (**clean someone out**) informal use up or take all someone's money or resources. ➤(**clean something out**) strip a place of and steal all its contents. **3** (**clean up**) informal make a substantial gain or profit. ● n. chiefly Brit. an act of cleaning.
– PHRASES **clean someone's clock** N. Amer. informal beat physically or decisively defeat someone. **a clean sheet** (or **slate**) an absence of existing restraints or commitments. ➤(**keep a clean sheet**) (in a soccer match) prevent the opposing side from scoring. **come clean** informal

fully confess something. **keep one's hands clean** remain uninvolved in an immoral or illegal act. **make a clean breast of it** fully confess one's mistakes or wrongdoings. **make a clean job of something** informal do something thoroughly. **make a clean sweep 1** remove all unwanted people or things ready to start afresh. **2** win all of a group of related sporting contests.
– DERIVATIVES **cleanable** adj. **cleaning** n. **cleanish** adj. **cleanness** n.
– ORIGIN OE *clǣne*, of W. Gmc origin.

**clean and jerk** • n. a weightlifting exercise in which a weight is raised above the head following an initial lift to shoulder level.

**clean-cut** • adj. **1** sharply outlined. **2** (of a person) clean and neat.

**cleaner** • n. a person or thing that cleans. ➤ (**the cleaners**) a shop where clothes and fabrics are dry-cleaned.
– PHRASES **take someone to the cleaners** informal **1** unscrupulously take a large portion of someone's money or resources. **2** inflict a crushing defeat on someone.

**cleaner fish** • n. a small fish that removes parasites from the skin, gills, and mouth of larger fishes. [*Labroides dimidiatus* and other species.]

**cleanly** /ˈkliːnli/ • adv. in a clean manner. • adj. /ˈklɛnli/ (**-ier, -iest**) archaic habitually clean.
– DERIVATIVES **cleanliness** n.

**clean room** • n. an environment free from dust and other contaminants, used chiefly for the manufacture of electronic components.

**cleanse** • v. **1** make thoroughly clean. **2** archaic (in biblical translations) cure (a leper). • n. an act of cleansing.
– DERIVATIVES **cleanser** n. **cleansing** adj.
– ORIGIN OE *clǣnsian* (v.), from *clǣne* (see **CLEAN**).

**clean-shaven** • adj. (of a man) without a beard or moustache.

**cleansing department** • n. Brit. a local government department that collects refuse.

**cleanskin** • n. another term for **CLEARSKIN**.

**clean-up** • n. **1** an act of making a place clean or restoring order. **2** (also **cleanup**) Baseball the fourth position in a team's batting order, usually reserved for a strong batter whose hits are likely to enable any runner who is on base to score.

**clear** • adj. **1** easy to perceive or understand. ➤ leaving or feeling no doubt. **2** transparent; unclouded. ➤ free of mist; having good visibility. ➤ (of a person's skin) free from blemishes. ➤ (of a colour) pure and intense. **3** free of any obstructions or unwanted objects. ➤ (of a period of time) free of any commitments. **4** free from disease, contamination, or guilt. **5** (**clear of**) not touching; away from: *the lorry had one wheel clear of the ground.* **6** complete: *seven clear days' notice.* ➤ (of a sum of money) net. • adv. **1** so as to be out of the way of, away from, or uncluttered by. **2** with clarity: *I heard the message loud and clear.* • v. **1** make or become clear. ➤ cause people to leave (a building or place). ➤ chiefly Soccer send (the ball) away from the area near one's goal. ➤ discharge (a debt). **2** get past or over (something) safely or without touching it. **3** show or declare officially to be innocent. **4** give official approval or authorization to or for. ➤ (of a person or goods) satisfy the necessary requirements to pass through (customs). ➤ (with reference to a cheque) pass or cause to pass through a clearing house so that the money goes into the payee's account. **5** earn or gain (an amount of money) as a net profit. **6** (of a person's face or expression) assume a happier or less confused aspect.
– PHRASES **clear the air 1** make the air less sultry. **2** defuse or clarify a tense situation by frank discussion. **clear the decks** prepare for something by dealing beforehand with anything that might hinder progress. **clear one's lines** chiefly Rugby make a kick sending the ball well upfield from near one's own goal line. **in clear** not in code. **in the clear** no longer in danger or suspected of something. **out of a clear sky** as a complete surprise.
– PHRASAL VERBS **clear away** remove the remains of a meal from the table. **clear off** informal go away. **clear out** informal leave quickly. **clear something out** empty something. **clear up 1** (of an illness or other medical condition) become cured. **2** (of the weather) become brighter; stop raining. **clear something up 1** (also **clear up**) tidy something up by removing unwanted items. **2** solve or explain something. **3** cure an illness or other medical condition.
– DERIVATIVES **clearable** adj. **clearness** n.
– ORIGIN ME: from OFr. *cler*, from L. *clarus*.

**clearance** • n. **1** the action or process of clearing or of being dispersed. **2** (in soccer and other games) a kick or hit that sends the ball out of a defensive zone. **3** Snooker the potting of all the balls remaining on the table in a single break. **4** official authorization for something to proceed or take place. **5** clear space allowed for a thing to move past or under another.

**clearcole** /ˈklɪəkəʊl/ • n. historical a mixture of size and whiting or white lead, formerly used as a primer for distemper.
– ORIGIN C19: from Fr. *claire colle* 'clear glue'.

**clear-cut** • adj. **1** sharply defined; easy to perceive or understand. **2** (of an area) from which every tree has been cut down and removed. • v. cut down and remove every tree from (an area).

**clearer** • n. **1** a person or thing that clears away obstructions. **2** Brit. a clearing bank.

**clear-fell** • v. another term for **CLEAR-CUT**.

**clearing** • n. an open space in a forest.

**clearing bank** • n. Brit. a bank which is a member of a clearing house.

**clearing house** • n. **1** a bankers' establishment where cheques and bills from member banks are exchanged, so that only the balances need be paid in cash. **2** an agency which collects and distributes something, especially information.

**clearly** • adv. **1** with clarity. **2** obviously; without doubt.

**clear-sighted** • adj. thinking clearly; perspicacious.

**clearskin** (also **cleanskin**) • n. Austral./NZ **1** an unbranded animal. **2** informal a person without a police record.

**clearstory** • n. (pl. **-ies**) US spelling of **CLERESTORY**.

**clearway** • n. Brit. a main road other than a motorway on which vehicles are not permitted to stop.

**clearwing** • n. a day-flying moth with mainly transparent wings, resembling a wasp or bee. [Family Sesiidae: many species.]

**cleat** /kliːt/ • n. **1** a T-shaped or similar projection to which a rope may be attached. **2** a projecting wedge on a spar, tool, etc., to prevent slippage. ➤ one of a number of projections on the sole of a boot, to increase its grip.
– DERIVATIVES **cleated** adj.
– ORIGIN ME: of W. Gmc origin; rel. to **CLOT** and **CLOUT**.

**cleavage** • n. **1** a sharp division; a split. **2** the cleft between a woman's breasts. **3** Biology cell division, especially of a fertilized egg cell. **4** the splitting of rocks or crystals in a preferred plane or direction.

**cleave**[1] • v. (past **clove** or **cleft** or **cleaved**; past part. **cloven** or **cleft** or **cleaved**) **1** split or sever along a natural grain or line. ➤ split (a molecule) by breaking a particular chemical bond. ➤ Biology (of a cell) divide. **2** make a way through: *they watched a coot cleave the smooth water.*
– DERIVATIVES **cleavable** adj.
– ORIGIN OE *clēofan*, of Gmc origin.

**cleave**[2] • v. (**cleave to**) poetic/literary **1** stick fast to. **2** become strongly involved with or emotionally attached to.
– ORIGIN OE *cleofian*, *clifian*, *clīfan*, of W. Gmc origin; rel. to **CLAY** and **CLIMB**.

**cleaver** • n. a tool with a heavy broad blade, used for chopping meat.

**cleavers** • pl. n. [treated as sing. or pl.] another term for **GOOSEGRASS**.
– ORIGIN OE *clīfe*, rel. to **CLEAVE**[2].

**clef** • n. Music any of several symbols placed at the left-hand end of a stave, indicating the pitch of the notes written on the stave.
– ORIGIN C16: from Fr., from L. *clavis* 'key'.

**cleft**[1] past participle of **CLEAVE**[1]. ● **adj.** split, divided, or partially divided into two.
– PHRASES **be** (or **be caught**) **in a cleft stick** chiefly Brit. be in a situation in which any action one takes will have adverse consequences.

**cleft**[2] ● **n.** **1** a fissure or split in rock or the ground. **2** an indentation or deep hollow in a person's forehead or chin, or between two parts of the body.
– ORIGIN ME *clift*: of Gmc origin; rel. to **CLEAVE**[1] and alt. by assoc. with **CLEFT**[1].

**cleft lip** ● **n.** a congenital split in the upper lip on one or both sides of the centre, often associated with a cleft palate.

**cleft palate** ● **n.** a congenital split in the roof of the mouth.

**cleft sentence** ● **n.** Grammar a sentence in which an element is emphasized by being put in a separate clause, with the use of an empty introductory word such as *it* or *that*, e.g. *it was today that I saw him*.

**cleg** /klɛg/ ● **n.** Brit. another term for **HORSEFLY**.
– ORIGIN ME: from ON *kleggi*.

**cleistogamy** /klʌɪˈstɒgəmi/ ● **n.** Botany self-fertilization that occurs within a permanently closed flower.
– DERIVATIVES **cleistogamous** adj.
– ORIGIN C19: from Gk *kleistos* 'closed' + *gamos* 'marriage'.

**clematis** /ˈklɛmətɪs, kləˈmeɪtɪs/ ● **n.** an ornamental climbing plant of the buttercup family which bears white, pink, or purple flowers and feathery seeds. [Genus *Clematis*.]
– ORIGIN L. (also denoting the periwinkle), from Gk *klēmatis*, from *klēma* 'vine branch'.

**clement** ● **adj.** **1** (of weather) mild. **2** merciful.
– DERIVATIVES **clemency** n.
– ORIGIN ME: from L. *clemens, clement-*.

**clementine** /ˈklɛm(ə)ntʌɪn, -tiːn/ ● **n.** a tangerine of a deep orange-red North African variety which is grown around the Mediterranean and in South Africa.
– ORIGIN 1920s: from Fr. *clémentine*, from the male given name *Clément*.

**clenbuterol** /klɛnˈbjuːtərɒl/ ● **n.** Medicine a synthetic drug used to treat respiratory diseases, also used illegally by athletes to enhance performance.
– ORIGIN 1970s: from *c(h)l(oro-)* + *(ph)en(yl)* + *but(yl)* + *er* + **-OL**.

**clench** ● **v.** **1** (with reference to one's fist or teeth) close or press together tightly, in response to stress or anger. ➤ (with reference to a set of muscles) contract or cause to contract sharply. **2** grasp tightly with the hands or between the teeth. ● **n.** the action or state of clenching or being clenched.
– DERIVATIVES **clenched** adj.
– ORIGIN OE (in the sense of *clinch* 'fix securely'): of Gmc origin; rel. to **CLING**.

**clepsydra** /ˈklɛpsɪdrə/ ● **n.** (pl. **clepsydras** or **clepsydrae** /-driː/) an ancient time-measuring device worked by a flow of water.
– ORIGIN ME: via L. from Gk *klepsudra*, based on *kleptein* 'steal' + *hudōr* 'water'.

**clerestory** /ˈklɪəˌstɔːri/ (US also **clearstory**) ● **n.** (pl. **-ies**) **1** the upper part of the nave, choir, and transepts of a large church, containing a series of windows and admitting light to the central parts of the building. **2** a raised section of roof running down the centre of a railway carriage, with small windows or ventilators.
– ORIGIN ME: from **CLEAR** + **STOREY**.

**clerestory window** ● **n.** a window with no crosspiece dividing the light.

**clergy** /ˈkləːdʒi/ ● **n.** (pl. **-ies**) [usu. treated as pl.] the body of people ordained for religious duties in the Christian Church.
– ORIGIN ME: from OFr., based on eccles. L. *clericus* (see **CLERIC**).

**clergyman** (or **clergywoman**) ● **n.** (pl. **-men** or **-women**) a priest or minister of a Christian church.

**cleric** ● **n.** a priest or religious leader.
– ORIGIN C17 (earlier (C15) as *clerical*): from eccles. L. *clericus* 'clergyman', from Gk *klērikos* 'belonging to the Christian clergy', from *klēros* 'lot, heritage' (Acts 1:26).

**clerical** ● **adj.** **1** concerned with or relating to the routine work of an office clerk. **2** of or relating to the clergy.
– DERIVATIVES **clericalism** n. **clericalist** n. **clerically** adv.

**clerical collar** ● **n.** a stiff upright white collar which fastens at the back, worn by the clergy in some churches.

**clerical error** ● **n.** a mistake made in copying or writing out a document.

**clerihew** /ˈklɛrɪhjuː/ ● **n.** a short comic or nonsensical verse, typically in two rhyming couplets with lines of unequal length and referring to a famous person.
– ORIGIN 1920s: named after Edmund *Clerihew* Bentley, the Engl. writer who invented it.

**clerisy** /ˈklɛrɪsi/ ● **n.** [usu. treated as pl.] a distinct class of learned or literary people.
– ORIGIN C19: appar. influenced by Ger. *Klerisei*, based on Gk *klēros* (see **CLERIC**).

**clerk** ● **n.** **1** a person employed in an office or bank to keep records or accounts and to undertake other routine administrative duties. **2** an official in charge of the records of a local council or court. ➤ a senior official in Parliament. ➤ a lay officer of a cathedral, church, or chapel. **3** (also **desk clerk**) N. Amer. a receptionist in a hotel. ➤ an assistant in a shop; a sales clerk. **4** (also **clerk in holy orders**) formal a member of the clergy. ● **v.** N. Amer. work as a clerk.
– PHRASES **Clerk of the Closet** (in the UK) the sovereign's principal chaplain. **clerk of the course** an official who assists the judges in horse racing or motor racing. **clerk of** (**the**) **works** Brit. a person who oversees building work in progress.
– DERIVATIVES **clerkess** n. (chiefly Scottish). **clerkish** adj. **clerkly** adj. **clerkship** n.
– ORIGIN OE *cleric, clerc*, from eccles. L. *clericus* (see **CLERIC**); reinforced by OFr. *clerc*, from the same source.

**Cleveland bay** ● **n.** a bay horse of a strong breed originating in the north of England, formerly popular as carriage horses.

**clever** ● **adj.** (**-er**, **-est**) **1** quick to understand, learn, and devise or apply ideas. ➤ skilful; adroit. **2** [with neg.] Brit. informal healthy; well: *I didn't feel too clever*.
– PHRASES **too clever by half** informal annoyingly proud of one's cleverness, and bound to overreach oneself.
– DERIVATIVES **cleverly** adv. **cleverness** n.
– ORIGIN ME (in the sense 'quick to catch hold', later 'manually skilful', then 'possessing mental agility'): perh. of Du. or Low Ger. origin, and rel. to **CLEAVE**[2].

**clever-clever** ● **adj.** derogatory seeking to appear clever.

**clever clogs** ● **n.** another term for **CLEVER DICK**.

**clever Dick** ● **n.** informal, chiefly Brit. a person who is irritatingly and ostentatiously knowledgeable or intelligent.

**clevis** /ˈklɛvɪs/ ● **n.** a U-shaped or forked metal connector within which another part can be fastened by means of a bolt or pin.
– ORIGIN C16: perh. rel. to **CLEAVE**[1].

**clew** /kluː/ ● **n.** **1** the lower or after corner of a sail. **2** (**clews**) Nautical the cords by which a hammock is suspended. **3** archaic a ball of thread. **4** archaic variant of **CLUE**. ● **v.** (**clew a sail up/down**) draw a sail up or let it down by the clews when preparing for furling or when unfurling.
– ORIGIN OE *cliwen, cleowen* (denoting a rounded mass, also a ball of thread), of Gmc origin; cf. **CLUE**.

**clianthus** /klʌɪˈanθəs, klɪ-/ ● **n.** an Australasian leguminous plant which bears drooping clusters of large scarlet flowers. [Genus *Clianthus*.]
– ORIGIN mod. L., appar. from Gk *kleos, klei-* 'glory' + *anthos* 'flower'.

**cliché** /ˈkliːʃeɪ/ (also **cliche**) ● **n.** **1** a hackneyed or overused phrase or opinion. ➤ a very predictable or unoriginal thing or person. **2** Printing, chiefly Brit. a stereotype or electrotype.
– ORIGIN C19: Fr., past part. (used as n.) of *clicher* 'to stereotype'.

**clichéd** (also **cliché'd** or **cliched**) ● **adj.** showing a lack of originality; hackneyed or overused.

**click** • n. a short, sharp sound as of two metallic or plastic objects coming smartly into contact. ➤ a speech sound produced by sudden withdrawal of the tongue from the soft palate, front teeth, or back teeth and hard palate, occurring in some southern African and other languages. ➤ Computing an act of pressing one of the buttons on a mouse. • v. 1 make or cause to make a click. ➤ move or become secured with such a sound: *it clicked into place.* ➤ Computing press (one of the buttons on a mouse). 2 informal become suddenly clear and understandable. ➤ become friendly and compatible.
– DERIVATIVES **clickable** adj. **clicker** n. **clicky** adj.
– ORIGIN C16 (as v.): imitative.

**click beetle** • n. a long, narrow beetle which can spring up with a click as a means of startling predators and escaping. [Family Elateridae.]

**click-clack** • n. a repeated clicking sound as of shoe heels on a hard surface. • v. move with a click-clack.

**client** • n. 1 a person using the services of a professional person or organization. 2 Computing (in a network) a computer or workstation that obtains information and applications from a server. ➤ (also **client application** or **program**) a program that obtains a service provided by another program. 3 (in ancient Rome) a plebeian under the protection of a patrician. ➤ archaic a dependant; a hanger-on.
– DERIVATIVES **clientship** n.
– ORIGIN ME (orig. denoting a person under the protection and patronage of another): from L. *cliens*, *client-*, var. of *cluent-*, *cluere* 'hear or obey'.

**clientele** /ˌkliːɒnˈtɛl/ • n. [treated as sing. or pl.] clients collectively. ➤ the customers of a shop, restaurant, etc.
– ORIGIN C16: via Fr. from L. *clientela* 'clientship', from *cliens*, *client-* (see **CLIENT**).

**clientelism** /ˌkliːɒnˈtɛlɪz(ə)m/ (also **clientism** /ˈklʌɪəntɪz(ə)m/) • n. a social order which depends on relations of patronage, especially one that is exploitative of these relations.
– DERIVATIVES **clientelistic** adj.

**Clifden nonpareil** • n. a large moth of mostly subdued coloration, with a pale blue band on the underwing. [*Catocala fraxini.*]
– ORIGIN C18: from *Clifden* (now *Cliveden*), a village in Buckinghamshire, England, and **NONPAREIL**.

**cliff** • n. a steep rock face, especially at the edge of the sea.
– DERIVATIVES **cliffy** adj.
– ORIGIN OE *clif*, of Gmc origin.

**cliffhanger** • n. a dramatic story or climactic ending that leaves an audience in suspense.
– DERIVATIVES **cliffhanging** adj.

**climacteric** /klʌɪˈmakt(ə)rɪk, ˌklʌɪmakˈtɛrɪk/ • n. 1 a critical period or event. 2 Medicine the period of life when fertility is in decline; (in women) the menopause. 3 Botany the ripening period while still on the tree of certain fruits such as apples, involving increased metabolism. • adj. 1 having extreme and far-reaching implications or results; critical. 2 Medicine & Botany occurring at, characteristic of, or undergoing a climacteric.
– ORIGIN C16: from Fr. *climactérique* or via L. from Gk *klimaktērikos*, from *klimaktēr* 'critical period', from *klimax* 'ladder, climax'.

**climactic** /klʌɪˈmaktɪk/ • adj. forming an exciting climax.
– DERIVATIVES **climactically** adv.
– ORIGIN C19: formed irregularly from **CLIMAX** + **-IC**, prob. influenced by **CLIMACTERIC**.

**climate** • n. 1 the general weather conditions prevailing in an area over a long period. 2 a prevailing trend or public attitude.
– DERIVATIVES **climatic** adj. **climatical** adj. **climatically** adv. **climatology** n. **climatological** adj. **climatologically** adv.
– ORIGIN ME (orig. denoting a zone of the earth between two lines of latitude, later a region considered with ref. to its atmospheric conditions): from OFr. *climat* or late L. *clima*, *climat-*, from Gk *klima* 'slope, zone'.

**climate control** • n. another term for **AIR CONDITIONING**.

**climax** • n. 1 the most intense, exciting, or important point of something. 2 an orgasm. 3 Rhetoric a sequence of propositions or ideas in order of increasing importance, force, or effectiveness of expression. 4 Ecology the final stage in a succession in a given environment, at which a plant community reaches a state of equilibrium. • v. reach or bring to a climax.
– ORIGIN C16 (in rhetoric): from late L., from Gk *klimax* 'ladder, climax'.

**climb** • v. 1 go or come up to a higher position. ➤ go up mountains as a sport. ➤ slope or lead up. ➤ (of a plant) grow up (a supporting structure) by clinging to or twining round it. 2 move with effort into or out of a confined space. 3 increase in scale, value, or power. 4 (**climb down**) withdraw from a position taken up in argument or negotiation. • n. 1 an instance of climbing; an ascent. 2 a recognized route up a mountain or cliff.
– PHRASES **be climbing the walls** informal feel frustrated, helpless, and trapped.
– DERIVATIVES **climbable** adj. **climber** n. **climbing** n.
– ORIGIN OE *climban*, of W. Gmc origin; rel. to **CLAY** and **CLEAVE**[2].

**climbdown** • n. a withdrawal from a position taken up in argument or negotiation.

**climbing frame** • n. Brit. a structure of joined bars for children to climb on.

**climbing irons** • pl. n. a set of spikes attached to boots for climbing trees or ice slopes.

**climbing perch** • n. a small edible freshwater fish which is able to breathe air and move over land, native to Africa and Asia. [*Anabas testudinens* and other species.]

**climbing wall** • n. a wall simulating a rock face, used for climbing practice.

**clime** /klʌɪm/ • n. chiefly poetic/literary a region considered with reference to its climate: *jetting off to sunnier climes.*
– ORIGIN ME: from late L. *clima* (see **CLIMATE**).

**clinch** • v. 1 conclusively settle (a contract or contest). 2 secure (a nail or rivet) by driving the point sideways when it has penetrated. 3 (of two people) grapple at close quarters. ➤ come together in an embrace. 4 fasten (a rope or angling line) with a clinch knot. • n. 1 a struggle or scuffle at close quarters. ➤ an embrace. 2 (also **clinch knot**) a knot used to fasten ropes or angling lines, using a half hitch with the end seized back on its own part.
– ORIGIN C16: var. of **CLENCH**.

**clincher** • n. informal a fact, argument, or event that settles a matter conclusively.

**cline** /klʌɪn/ • n. a continuum with an infinite number of gradations from one extreme to the other. ➤ Biology a gradation in one or more characteristics within a species or other taxon, especially between different populations.
– DERIVATIVES **clinal** adj.
– ORIGIN 1930s: from Gk *klinein* 'to slope'.

**cling** • v. (past and past part. **clung**) (**cling to/on to**) 1 hold on tightly to. ➤ adhere or stick to. 2 remain persistently faithful to: *she clung to her convictions.* 3 be emotionally dependent on. • n. (also **cling peach**) a clingstone peach.
– DERIVATIVES **clinger** n. **clinginess** n. **clinging** adj. **clingy** adj. (**-ier**, **-iest**).
– ORIGIN OE *clingan* 'stick together', of Gmc origin; rel. to **CLENCH**.

**cling film** • n. Brit. a thin transparent plastic film that adheres to surfaces and to itself, used as a wrapping or covering for food.

**clingfish** • n. (pl. same or **-fishes**) a small fish with a sucker for attachment to rocks and other surfaces. [*Lepadogaster lepadogaster* and other species.]

**clingstone** • n. a peach or nectarine of a variety in which the flesh adheres to the stone. Contrasted with **FREESTONE**.

**clinic** • n. 1 a place where specialized medical treatment or advice is given. 2 a gathering at a hospital bedside for the teaching of medicine or surgery. 3 chiefly N. Amer. a conference or short course on a particular subject: *a drum*

*clinic.*
– ORIGIN C19 (earlier (C18) as *clinical*): from Fr. *clinique*, from Gk *klinikē* (*tekhnē*) 'bedside (art)', from *klinē* 'bed'.

**clinical** ● **adj. 1** relating to the observation and treatment of patients (rather than theoretical or laboratory studies). ➤(of a disease or condition) causing observable and recognizable symptoms. **2** efficient and coldly detached. ➤(of a place) bare, functional, and clean.
– DERIVATIVES **clinically** adv.

**clinical death** ● **n.** death as judged by the medical observation of the cessation of respiration and the beating of the heart.

**clinical psychology** ● **n.** the branch of psychology concerned with the assessment and treatment of mental illness.
– DERIVATIVES **clinical psychologist** n.

**clinician** ● **n.** a doctor having direct contact with and responsibility for treating patients, rather than one involved with theoretical or laboratory studies.

**clink**[1] ● **n.** a sharp ringing sound, such as that made when metal or glass are struck. ● **v.** make or cause to make a clink.
– ORIGIN ME (as v.): prob. from MDu. *klinken*.

**clink**[2] ● **n.** informal prison.
– ORIGIN C16 (orig. denoting a prison in Southwark, London): of unknown origin.

**clinker**[1] ● **n. 1** the stony residue from burnt coal or from a furnace. **2** a brick with a vitrified surface.
– ORIGIN C17: from obs. Du. *klinckaerd* (earlier form of *klinker*), from *klinken* 'to clink'.

**clinker**[2] ● **n.** informal **1** N. Amer. something that is unsatisfactory; a failure. ➤a wrong musical note. **2** Brit. dated something or someone excellent or outstanding.
– ORIGIN C17: from **CLINK**[1] + **-ER**[1].

**clinker-built** ● **adj.** (of a boat) having external planks which overlap downwards and are secured with clinched nails. Compare with **CARVEL-BUILT**.
– ORIGIN C18: *clinker* from *clink* (north. Engl. var. of **CLINCH**).

**clinometer** /klʌɪˈnɒmɪtə, klɪ-/ ● **n.** Surveying an instrument used for measuring the angle or elevation of slopes.
– ORIGIN C19: from Gk *klinein* 'to slope' + **-METER**.

**clint** ● **n.** a block forming part of a natural limestone pavement.
– ORIGIN ME: of Scand. origin.

**cliometrics** /ˌklʌɪə(ʊ)ˈmɛtrɪks/ ● **pl. n.** [treated as sing.] a technique for the interpretation of economic history, based on the statistical analysis of numerical data from population censuses, parish registers, etc.
– DERIVATIVES **cliometric** adj. **cliometrician** n.
– ORIGIN 1960s (orig. US): from *Clio*, the Muse of history in Gk and Roman mythology, on the pattern of words such as *econometrics*.

**clip**[1] ● **n. 1** a flexible or spring-loaded device for holding an object or objects together or in place. **2** a piece of jewellery fastened by a clip. **3** a metal holder containing cartridges for an automatic firearm. ● **v.** (**clipped**, **clipping**) fasten or be fastened with a clip or clips.
– ORIGIN OE *clyppan* (v.), of W. Gmc origin.

**clip**[2] ● **v.** (**clipped**, **clipping**) **1** cut, trim, or excise with shears or scissors. ➤trim the hair or wool of (an animal). **2** strike smartly or with a glancing blow. **3** informal, chiefly N. Amer. swindle or rob. **4** informal, chiefly US move quickly in a specified direction. **5** Electronics truncate the amplitude of (a signal) above or below predetermined levels. ● **n. 1** an act of clipping. ➤a short sequence taken from a film or broadcast. ➤the quantity of wool clipped from a sheep or flock. **2** informal a smart or glancing blow. **3** informal a rapid or specified speed.
– PHRASES **clip the wings of** trim the feathers of (a bird) to disable it from flight. ➤hamper the aspirations of.
– DERIVATIVES **clipping** n.
– ORIGIN ME: from ON *klippa*, prob. imitative.

**clip art** ● **n.** pre-drawn pictures and symbols provided with word-processing software and drawing packages.

**clipboard** ● **n. 1** a small board with a spring clip at the top, used for holding papers and providing support for writing. **2** Computing a temporary storage area where text or other data cut or copied from a file is kept until it is pasted into another file.

**clip-clop** ● **n.** the sound of a horse's hoofs beating on a hard surface. ● **v.** move with a clip-clop.

**clip joint** ● **n.** informal a nightclub or bar that charges exorbitant prices.

**clip-on** ● **adj.** attached by a clip so as to be easy to fasten or remove.

**clipped** ● **adj.** (of speech) having short, sharp vowel sounds and clear pronunciation.

**clipper** ● **n. 1** (**clippers**) an instrument for clipping. **2** a fast sailing ship, especially one of 19th-century design with concave bows and raked masts.

**clippie** ● **n.** (pl. **-ies**) Brit. informal a bus conductress.

**clique** /kliːk/ ● **n.** a small group of people who spend time together and do not readily allow others to join them.
– DERIVATIVES **cliquey** adj. (**-ier**, **-iest**). **cliquish** adj. **cliquishness** n.
– ORIGIN C18: from Fr., from OFr. *cliquer* 'make a noise'.

**CLit** ● **abbrev.** (in the UK) Companion of Literature.

**clitic** /ˈklɪtɪk/ ● **n.** Grammar an unstressed word that normally occurs only in combination with another word, for example *'m* in *I'm*.
– DERIVATIVES **cliticization** /ˌklɪtɪkʌɪˈzeɪʃ(ə)n/ (also **-isation**) n.
– ORIGIN 1940s: from (*en*)*clitic* and (*pro*)*clitic*.

**clitoridectomy** /ˌklɪt(ə)rɪˈdɛktəmi/ ● **n.** (pl. **-ies**) excision of the clitoris; female circumcision.

**clitoris** /ˈklɪt(ə)rɪs/ ● **n.** a small sensitive and erectile part of the female genitals at the anterior end of the vulva.
– DERIVATIVES **clitoral** adj.
– ORIGIN C17: mod. L., from Gk *kleitoris*.

**clivia** /ˈklʌɪvɪə/ ● **n.** a southern African plant of the lily family, with dark green strap-like leaves and trumpet-shaped orange, red, or yellow flowers. [Genus *Clivia*.]
– ORIGIN mod. L., from *Clive*, maiden name of Charlotte, Duchess of Northumberland (1787–1866).

**Cllr** ● **abbrev.** (in the UK) Councillor.

**cloaca** /kləʊˈeɪkə/ ● **n.** (pl. **cloacae** /-siː, -kiː/) **1** Zoology a common cavity at the end of the digestive tract for the release of both excretory and genital products in vertebrates (except most mammals) and certain invertebrates. **2** archaic a sewer.
– DERIVATIVES **cloacal** adj.
– ORIGIN C16: from L., rel. to *cluere* 'cleanse'.

**cloak** ● **n. 1** an overgarment that hangs loosely from the shoulders over the arms to the knees or ankles. **2** something that hides or covers: *a cloak of secrecy.* **3** (**cloaks**) Brit. a cloakroom. ● **v.** dress or hide in a cloak.
– ORIGIN ME: from OFr. *cloke*, dial. var. of *cloche* 'bell, cloak', from med. L. *clocca* 'bell'.

**cloak-and-dagger** ● **adj.** involving intrigue and secrecy.

**cloakroom** ● **n. 1** a room in a public building where outdoor clothes and bags may be left. **2** Brit. a room that contains a toilet or toilets.

**clobber**[1] ● **n.** Brit. informal clothing and personal belongings.
– ORIGIN C19: of unknown origin.

**clobber**[2] ● **v.** informal **1** hit hard. **2** defeat heavily.
– ORIGIN Second World War: of unknown origin.

**clobber**[3] ● **v.** add enamelled decoration to (porcelain).
– ORIGIN C19: of unknown origin.

**cloche** /klɒʃ, kləʊʃ/ ● **n. 1** a small translucent cover for protecting or forcing outdoor plants. **2** (also **cloche hat**) a woman's close-fitting, bell-shaped hat.
– ORIGIN C19: from Fr., lit. 'bell' (see **CLOAK**).

**clock**[1] ● **n. 1** an instrument that measures and indicates the time by means of a dial or a digital display. ➤informal a measuring device resembling a clock, such as a speedometer. **2** Brit. the downy spherical seed head of a dandelion. **3** Brit. informal a person's face. ● **v.** informal **1** attain or register (a specified time, distance, or speed). ➤achieve (a victory). **2** (**clock in/out** or Brit. **on/off**) register by means of an automatic recording clock one's arrival at or

departure from work. **3** Brit. informal see or watch. **4** informal, chiefly Brit. hit on the head. **5** Brit. informal illegally wind back the milometer of (a car).
– PHRASES **round** (or **around**) **the clock** all day and all night. **turn** (or **put**) **back the clock** return to the past or to a previous way of doing things.
– DERIVATIVES **clocker** n.
– ORIGIN ME: from Mid. Low Ger. and MDu. *klocke*, based on med. L. *clocca* 'bell'.

**clock²** ● **n.** an ornamental pattern woven or embroidered on the side of a stocking or sock near the ankle.
– ORIGIN C16: of unknown origin.

**clock golf** ● **n.** a lawn game in which the players putt to a hole in the centre of a circle from successive points on its circumference.

**clock radio** ● **n.** a combined bedside radio and alarm clock.

**clock speed** ● **n.** the operating speed of a computer or its microprocessor, expressed in cycles per second (megahertz).

**clock tower** ● **n.** a tower, especially that of a church or civic building, displaying a large clock.

**clock-watch** ● **v.** take care not to work more than the hours prescribed.
– DERIVATIVES **clock-watcher** n. **clock-watching** n.

**clockwise** ● **adv. & adj.** in a curve corresponding in direction to the movement of the hands of a clock.

**clockwork** ● **n.** a mechanism with a spring and toothed gearwheels, used to drive a mechanical clock, toy, or other device.
– PHRASES **like clockwork** very smoothly and easily.

**clod** ● **n. 1** a lump of earth or clay. **2** informal a stupid person. **3** Brit. a coarse cut of meat from the lower neck of an ox.
– ORIGIN ME: var. of CLOT.

**cloddish** ● **adj.** foolish, awkward, or clumsy.
– DERIVATIVES **cloddishly** adv. **cloddishness** n.

**clodhopper** ● **n.** informal **1** a large, heavy shoe. **2** a foolish, awkward, or clumsy person.
– DERIVATIVES **clodhopping** adj.

**clodpole** ● **n.** dated, informal a foolish or clumsy person.

**clog** ● **n. 1** a shoe with a thick wooden sole. **2** an encumbrance. ● **v.** (**clogged**, **clogging**) (often **clog up**) block or become blocked with something thick or sticky.
– ORIGIN ME (in the sense 'block of wood to impede an animal's movement'): of unknown origin.

**clog dance** ● **n.** a traditional dance for which clogs are worn.
– DERIVATIVES **clog dancer** n. **clog dancing** n.

**clogger** ● **n. 1** a person who makes clogs. **2** Brit. informal a footballer who habitually fouls when tackling someone.

**clogging** ● **n.** N. Amer. clog dancing.

**cloggy** ● **adj.** (**-ier**, **-iest**) thick, lumpy, or sticky.

**cloisonné** /'klwɑːzɒneɪ, -'zɒneɪ/ ● **n.** enamel work in which different colours are separated by strips of flattened wire placed edgeways on a metal backing.
– ORIGIN C19: Fr., lit. 'partitioned', past part. of *cloisonner*, from *cloison* 'a partition or division'.

**cloister** /'klɔɪstə/ ● **n. 1** a covered, and typically colonnaded, passage round an open court in a convent, monastery, college, or cathedral. **2** a convent or monastery. ➤(**the cloister**) monastic life. ● **v.** seclude or shut up in a convent or monastery.
– DERIVATIVES **cloistral** adj.
– ORIGIN ME (in the sense 'place of religious seclusion'): from OFr. *cloistre*, from L. *claustrum*, *clostrum* 'lock, enclosed place', from *claudere*, 'to close'.

**cloistered** ● **adj. 1** having or enclosed by a cloister. **2** sheltered from the outside world: *a cloistered upbringing*.

**clomiphene** /'kləʊmɪfiːn/ ● **n.** Medicine a synthetic non-steroidal drug used to treat infertility in women by stimulating ovulation.
– ORIGIN C20: from *chlo(ro-)* + *(a)mi(ne)* + *phen(yl)*.

**clomp** ● **v.** walk with a heavy tread. ● **n.** the sound of a heavy tread.
– ORIGIN C19: imitative; cf. CLUMP.

**clompy** ● **adj.** variant spelling of CLUMPY (in sense 1).

**clone** ● **n. 1** Biology an organism or cell, or a group of organisms or cells, produced asexually from one ancestor to which they are genetically identical. **2** a person or thing regarded as identical with another; a copy or double. **3** informal (within gay culture) a homosexual man who adopts an exaggeratedly macho appearance. ● **v. 1** propagate (an organism or cell) as a clone. ➤Biochemistry replicate (a fragment of DNA placed in an organism). **2** make an identical copy of. **3** illegally copy the security codes from (a mobile phone) to others as a way of obtaining free calls.
– DERIVATIVES **clonal** adj.
– ORIGIN C20: from Gk *klōn* 'twig'.

**clonk** ● **n.** a sound made by an abrupt and heavy impact. ● **v. 1** move with or make a clonk. **2** informal hit.
– DERIVATIVES **clonky** adj.

**clonus** /'kləʊnəs/ ● **n.** Medicine muscular spasm involving repeated, often rhythmic, contractions.
– DERIVATIVES **clonic** adj.
– ORIGIN C19: from Gk *klonos* 'turmoil'.

**clop** ● **n.** a sound made by a horse's hooves on a hard surface. ● **v.** (**clopped**, **clopping**) move with such a sound.

**cloqué** /'kləʊkeɪ/ ● **n.** a fabric with an irregularly raised or embossed surface.
– ORIGIN Fr., lit. 'blistered'.

**close¹** /kləʊs/ ● **adj. 1** only a short distance away or apart in space or time. ➤dense: *close print*. ➤(**close to**) very near to (being or doing something). **2** denoting someone who is part of a person's immediate family, typically a parent or sibling. ➤(of a connection or resemblance) strong. **3** (of a relationship or the people conducting it) very affectionate or intimate. **4** (of observation or examination) done in a careful and thorough way. **5** (of information) carefully guarded: *a close secret*. ➤(of a person) not willing to give away money or information. **6** uncomfortably humid or airless. **7** Phonetics another term for HIGH (sense 7). ● **adv.** so as to be very near; with very little space between. ● **n. 1** Brit. a residential street without through access. **2** Brit. the precinct surrounding a cathedral. **3** Scottish an entry from the street to a common stairway or to a court at the back of a building.
– PHRASES **close-fisted** unwilling to spend money; mean. **close-knit** (of a group of people) united or bound together by strong relationships and common interests. **close-mouthed** reticent; discreet. **at** (or **from**) **close quarters** (or **range**) close to or from a position close to someone or something. **close-run** (of a contest or objective) won or lost by a very small margin. **close shave** (also **close call**) informal a narrow escape from danger or disaster.
– DERIVATIVES **closely** adv. **closeness** n. **closish** adj.
– ORIGIN ME: from OFr. *clos*, from L. *clausum* 'enclosure' and *clausus* 'closed' (past part. of *claudere*).

**close²** /kləʊz/ ● **v. 1** move so as to cover an opening. **2** (also **close something up**) bring two parts of (something) together. ➤grow or cause to grow smaller; make or become blocked: *she felt her throat close up*. **3** (**close on/in on/up on**) gradually get nearer to or surround. ➤(**close with**) come near, especially so as to engage with (an enemy force). ➤(**close in**) (of days) get successively shorter with the approach of the winter solstice. **4** (**close around/over**) encircle and hold. **5** make (an electric circuit) continuous. **6** bring or come to an end. ➤finish speaking or writing. ➤ (often **close down/up**) (of a business or other organization) cease to be open to the public or in operation. ➤bring (a transaction or arrangement) to a conclusion. ➤(**close something out**) N. Amer. bring something to an end. ● **n. 1** the end of an event or of a period of time or activity. **2** the shutting of a door.
– DERIVATIVES **closable** adj. **closer** n. **closing** adj.
– ORIGIN ME: from OFr. *clos-*, stem of *clore*, from L. *claudere* 'to shut'.

**closed** ● **adj. 1** not open or allowing access. **2** not communicating with or influenced by others. **3** Mathematics (of a set) having the property that the result of a specified operation on any element of the set is itself a member of the set. **4** Geometry (of a curve or figure) formed from a

single unbroken line. **5** Phonetics (of a syllable) ending in a consonant.
– PHRASES **behind closed doors** taking place secretly. **a closed book** a subject or person about which one knows nothing.

**closed caption** chiefly N. Amer. • **n.** one of a series of subtitles to a television programme, accessible through a decoder. • **v.** (**closed-caption**) [usu. as noun **closed-captioning**] provide (a programme) with such captions.
– DERIVATIVES **closed-captioned** adj.

**closed-circuit television** • **n.** a television system in which the video signals are transmitted from one or more cameras by cable to a restricted set of monitors.

**closed-end** • **adj. 1** having a predetermined and fixed extent. **2** N. Amer. denoting an investment trust or company that issues a fixed number of shares.

**closed season** • **n.** chiefly N. Amer. another term for **CLOSE SEASON**.

**closed shop** • **n.** a place of work where all employees must belong to an agreed trade union.

**close harmony** • **n.** Music harmony in which the notes of the chord are close together, typically in vocal music.

**close-hauled** • **adj. & adv.** Sailing with the sails hauled aft to sail close to the wind.

**close season** • **n.** (also chiefly N. Amer. **closed season**) **1** a period between specified dates when fishing or the killing of particular game is officially forbidden. **2** Brit. a part of the year when a particular sport is not played.

**close-stool** • **n.** historical a covered chamber pot enclosed in a wooden stool.

**closet** • **n. 1** chiefly N. Amer. a tall cupboard or wardrobe. **2** a small room. **3** archaic a toilet. **4** (**the closet**) (especially with reference to homosexuality) a state of secrecy or concealment. **5** [as modifier] secret; covert: *a closet socialist.* • **v.** (**closeted**, **closeting**) shut away in private conference or study. ➤ [as adj. **closeted**] keeping something, especially the fact of being homosexual, secret.
– ORIGIN ME: from OFr., dimin. of *clos* (see **CLOSE**[1]).

**closet play** (also **closet drama**) • **n.** a play to be read rather than acted.

**close-up** • **n.** a photograph or film sequence taken at close range and showing the subject on a large scale.

**closing order** • **n.** English Law an order by a local authority prohibiting the use of premises for specified purposes.

**clostridium** /klɒˈstrɪdɪəm/ • **n.** (pl. **clostridia** /-dɪə/) Biology an anaerobic bacterium of a large genus that includes many pathogenic species, e.g. those causing tetanus and botulism.
– DERIVATIVES **clostridial** adj.
– ORIGIN mod. L., based on Gk *klōstēr* 'spindle'.

**closure** • **n. 1** an act or process of closing something. **2** a device that closes or seals something. **3** (in a legislative assembly) a procedure for ending a debate and taking a vote. • **v.** apply the closure to (a debate or speaker) in a legislative assembly.
– ORIGIN ME: from OFr., from late L. *clausura*, from *claus-*, *claudere* 'to close'.

**clot** • **n. 1** a thick mass of coagulated liquid, especially blood, or of material stuck together. **2** Brit. informal a foolish or clumsy person. • **v.** (**clotted**, **clotting**) form or cause to form into clots. ➤ cover with sticky matter.
– ORIGIN OE *clott*, *clot*, of Gmc origin.

**clotbur** /ˈklɒtbəː/ • **n.** a plant of the daisy family with burred fruits, native to tropical America. [*Xanthium spinosum.*]
– ORIGIN C16: from dial. *clote* 'burdock' + **BUR**.

**cloth** • **n.** (pl. **cloths**) **1** woven, knitted, or felted fabric made from a soft fibre such as wool or cotton. **2** a piece of cloth for a particular purpose. **3** (**the cloth**) the clergy; the clerical profession.
– ORIGIN OE *clāth*, of unknown origin.

**cloth cap** • **n.** Brit. a man's flat woollen cap with a peak. ➤ [as modifier] relating to or associated with the working class: *Labour's traditional cloth-cap image.*

**clothe** • **v.** (past and past part. **clothed** or archaic or poetic/literary **clad**) (often **be clothed in**) put clothes on; dress. ➤ provide (someone) with clothes.
– ORIGIN OE (only recorded in the past part. *geclāded*), from *clāth* (see **CLOTH**).

**cloth-eared** • **adj.** Brit. informal, derogatory unable to hear or understand clearly.

**clothes** • **pl. n.** items worn to cover the body.
– ORIGIN OE *clāthas*, pl. of *clāth* (see **CLOTH**).

**clothes horse** • **n. 1** a frame on which washed clothes are hung to dry. **2** informal a person who wears or models fashionable clothes.

**clothes line** • **n.** a rope or wire on which washed clothes are hung to dry.

**clothes moth** • **n.** a small drab moth whose larvae can be destructive to textile fibres. [*Tineola bisselliella* and related species.]

**clothes peg** (also N. Amer. **clothespin**) • **n.** Brit. a clip or forked device for securing clothes to a clothes line.

**clothier** /ˈkləʊðɪə/ • **n.** a person who makes or sells clothes or cloth.
– ORIGIN ME *clother*, from **CLOTH**; the change in the ending was due to assoc. with **-IER**.

**clothing** • **n.** clothes collectively.

**cloth of gold** • **n.** fabric made of wool or silk interwoven with gold threads.

**clotted cream** • **n.** chiefly Brit. thick cream obtained by heating milk slowly and then allowing it to cool while the cream content rises to the top in coagulated lumps.

**clotting factor** • **n.** Physiology any of a number of substances in blood plasma which are involved in the clotting process, such as factor VIII.

**cloture** /ˈkləʊtjʊə/ • **n. & v.** US term for **CLOSURE** (in sense 3 of the n. and as a v.).
– ORIGIN C19: from Fr. *clôture*, from OFr. *closure*.

**clou** /kluː/ • **n.** the chief attraction, point of greatest interest, or central idea of a thing.
– ORIGIN Fr., lit. 'nail'.

**cloud** • **n. 1** a visible mass of condensed watery vapour floating in the atmosphere, typically high above the general level of the ground. ➤ an indistinct or billowing mass of smoke, dust, or something consisting of numerous particles. ➤ an opaque patch within a transparent substance. **2** an oppressive burden of gloom or anxiety. • **v. 1** (usu. **cloud over**) (of the sky) become full of clouds. **2** make or become less clear or transparent. **3** (of someone's face or eyes) become expressive of sadness, anxiety, or anger. **4** make unclear or uncertain.
– PHRASES **in** (or **with one's head in**) **the clouds** full of idealistic dreams; out of touch with reality. **on cloud nine** (or **seven**) extremely happy. [with ref. to a ten-part classification of clouds in which 'nine' was next to the highest.] **under a cloud** under suspicion or discredited.
– DERIVATIVES **cloudiness** n. **cloudless** adj. **cloudlessly** adv. **cloudlet** n. **cloudy** adj. (**-ier**, **-iest**).
– ORIGIN OE *clūd* 'mass of rock or earth'; prob. rel. to **CLOT**.

**cloud base** • **n.** the level or altitude of the lowest part of a general mass of clouds.

**cloudberry** • **n.** (pl. **-ies**) a dwarf bramble with white flowers and edible orange fruit, growing on high, open land. [*Rubus chamaemorus.*]
– ORIGIN C16: appar. from the noun **CLOUD** in the obs. sense 'hill' + **BERRY**.

**cloudburst** • **n.** a sudden violent rainstorm.

**cloud chamber** • **n.** Physics an apparatus in which the tracks of ionizing particles are visible as condensation trails in gas supersaturated with water vapour.

**cloud cover** • **n.** a mass of cloud covering all or most of the sky.

**cloud cuckoo land** • **n.** a state of unrealistic or absurdly over-optimistic fantasy.
– ORIGIN C19: translation of Gk *Nephelokokkugia*, the name of a city built by the birds in Aristophanes' comedy *Birds*, from *nephelē* 'cloud' + *kokkux* 'cuckoo'.

**clouded leopard** • **n.** a large spotted cat found in forests in SE Asia. [*Neofelis nebulosa.*]

**clouded yellow** • **n.** a migratory butterfly which has

yellowish wings with black margins. [*Colias croceus* and related species.]

**cloud street** ● n. a line of cumulus clouds formed parallel to the wind direction.

**clough** /klʌf/ ● n. N. English a steep valley or ravine.
– ORIGIN OE *clōh* (recorded in place names), of Gmc origin.

**clout** ● n. **1** informal a heavy blow. **2** informal influence or power. **3** archaic a piece of cloth or clothing. **4** Archery a large target placed flat on the ground with a flag marking its centre and used in long-distance shooting. **5** (also **clout nail**) a nail with a large, flat head, used especially in securing roofing felt. ● v. **1** informal hit hard. **2** archaic mend with a patch.
– ORIGIN OE *clūt* (in the sense 'a patch or metal plate'); rel. to **CLEAT** and **CLOT**.

**clove**[1] ● n. **1** the dried flower bud of a tropical tree, used as a pungent aromatic spice. ➤(**oil of cloves**) aromatic analgesic oil extracted from these buds and used medicinally, especially for the relief of dental pain. **2** the Indonesian tree from which these buds are obtained. [*Syzygium aromaticum* (also called *Eugenia caryophyllus*).] **3** (also **clove pink** or **clove gillyflower**) a clove-scented pink which is the original type from which the carnation and other double pinks have been bred. [*Dianthus caryophyllus*.]
– ORIGIN ME: from OFr. *clou de girofle*, lit. 'nail of gillyflower' (from its shape), **GILLYFLOWER** being orig. the name of the spice and later applied to the similarly scented pink.

**clove**[2] ● n. any of the small bulbs making up a compound bulb of garlic, shallot, etc.
– ORIGIN OE *clufu*, of Gmc origin, corresp. to the base of **CLEAVE**[1].

**clove**[3] past of **CLEAVE**[1].

**clove hitch** ● n. a knot by which a rope is secured by passing it twice round a spar or another rope that it crosses at right angles in such a way that both ends pass under the loop of rope at the front.
– ORIGIN C18: *clove*, past tense of **CLEAVE**[1] (because the rope appears as separate parallel lines at the back of the knot).

**cloven** past participle of **CLEAVE**[1].

**cloven hoof** (also **cloven foot**) ● n. the divided hoof or foot of ruminants such as cattle, sheep, goats, antelopes, and deer.
– DERIVATIVES **cloven-hoofed** adj.

**clover** ● n. a herbaceous leguminous plant with dense white or red globular flower heads and leaves which are typically three-lobed. [Genus *Trifolium*: many species.]
– PHRASES **in clover** in ease and luxury.
– ORIGIN OE *clāfre*, of Gmc origin.

**cloverleaf** ● n. chiefly N. Amer. a junction of roads intersecting at different levels and forming the pattern of a four-leaved clover.

**Clovis** /ˈkləʊvɪs/ ● n. [as modifier] Archaeology denoting a Palaeo-Indian culture of Central and North America, dated to about 11,500–11,000 years ago and earlier.
– ORIGIN named after *Clovis* in New Mexico.

**clown** ● n. **1** a comic entertainer, especially one in a circus, wearing a traditional costume and exaggerated make-up. **2** a playful, extrovert person. **3** archaic an unsophisticated country person. ● v. act comically or playfully.
– DERIVATIVES **clownish** adj. **clownishly** adv. **clownishness** n.
– ORIGIN C16: perh. of Low Ger. origin.

**clownfish** ● n. (pl. same or **-fishes**) a small, brightly coloured tropical fish that lives in close association with sea anemones. [*Amphiprion percula* and other species.]

**cloy** ● v. [usu. as adj. **cloying**] disgust or sicken with an excess of sweetness, richness, or sentiment.
– DERIVATIVES **cloyingly** adv.
– ORIGIN ME: shortening of obs. *accloy* 'stop up, choke', from OFr. *encloyer* 'drive a nail into'.

**clozapine** /ˈkləʊzəpiːn/ ● n. Medicine a sedative drug of the benzodiazepine group, used to treat schizophrenia.
– ORIGIN C20: from *c(h)lo(ro)-* + elements of **BENZODIAZEPINE**.

**cloze test** /kləʊz/ ● n. a procedure in which a subject is asked to supply words that have been removed from a passage as a test of their ability to comprehend text.
– ORIGIN 1950s: *cloze* representing a spoken abbrev. of **CLOSURE**.

**club**[1] ● n. **1** an association dedicated to a particular interest or activity. ➤an organization constituted to play matches in a particular sport. **2** an organization offering members social amenities, meals, and temporary residence. **3** a nightclub with dance music. ● v. (**clubbed**, **clubbing**) **1** (**club together**) combine with others to do something, especially to collect a sum of money. **2** informal go out to nightclubs.
– PHRASES **in the pudding club** Brit. informal pregnant.
– DERIVATIVES **clubber** n. **clubbing** n.
– ORIGIN C17: formed obscurely from **CLUB**[2].

**club**[2] ● n. **1** a heavy stick with a thick end, used as a weapon. **2** (also **golf club**) a club used to hit the ball in golf, with a heavy wooden or metal head on a slender shaft. **3** (**clubs**) one of the four suits in a conventional pack of playing cards, denoted by a black trefoil. ➤a card of such a suit. ● v. (**clubbed**, **clubbing**) beat with a club or similar implement.
– ORIGIN ME: from ON *clubba*, var. of *klumba*; rel. to **CLUMP**.

**clubbable** ● adj. suitable for membership of a club because of one's sociability or popularity.
– DERIVATIVES **clubbability** n.

**clubby** ● adj. (**-ier**, **-iest**) informal friendly and sociable with fellow members of a group or organization but not with outsiders.

**club car** ● n. chiefly N. Amer. a railway carriage equipped with a lounge and other amenities.

**club class** ● n. Brit. the intermediate class of seating on an aircraft, designed especially for business travellers.

**club foot** ● n. **1** a deformed foot which is twisted so that the sole cannot be placed flat on the ground. **2** a woodland toadstool having a stem with a swollen woolly base. [*Clitocybe clavipes*.]
– DERIVATIVES **club-footed** adj.

**clubhouse** ● n. a building having a bar and other facilities for the members of a club.

**clubmoss** ● n. a low-growing flowerless plant belonging to a group of pteridophytes resembling large mosses. [Class Lycopsida: many species.]

**clubroot** ● n. a fungal disease of cabbages, turnips, etc. in which the root becomes swollen and distorted.

**clubrush** ● n. a tall rush-like water plant, used for weaving. [*Scirpus lacustris* and other species.]

**club sandwich** ● n. a sandwich consisting typically of chicken and bacon, tomato, and lettuce, layered between three slices of bread.

**club soda** ● n. trademark North American term for **SODA** (in sense 1).

**cluck** ● n. **1** the characteristic short, guttural sound made by a hen. **2** N. Amer. informal a silly or foolish person. ● v. **1** (of a hen) make a cluck. **2** (**cluck over/around**) express fussy concern about.
– DERIVATIVES **clucky** adj.
– ORIGIN C15: imitative.

**clue** ● n. a fact or piece of evidence serving to reveal a hidden truth or solve a problem. ● v. (**clues**, **clued**, **clueing**) (**clue someone in**) informal inform someone about a particular matter.
– PHRASES **not have a clue** informal know nothing about something or about how to do something.
– ORIGIN ME (orig. 'a ball of thread', hence one used to guide a person out of a labyrinth): var. of **CLEW**.

**clued-up** (also chiefly N. Amer. **clued-in**) ● adj. informal well informed about a particular subject.

**clueless** ● adj. informal having no knowledge, understanding, or ability.
– DERIVATIVES **cluelessly** adv. **cluelessness** n.

**Clumber spaniel** /ˈklʌmbə/ ● n. a spaniel of a slow, heavily built breed.
– ORIGIN C19: from the name of *Clumber* Park, Nottinghamshire.

**clump** ● n. **1** a small group of trees or plants growing closely together. ➤a compacted mass or lump of something. ➤Physiology an agglutinated mass of blood cells or bacteria, especially as an indicator of the presence of an antibody to them. **2** a thick extra sole on a boot or shoe. **3** another term for **CLOMP**. ● v. **1** form into a clump or mass. **2** another term for **CLOMP**.
– ORIGIN ME (denoting a heap or lump): partly imitative; rel. to **CLUB**[2].

**clumpy** ● adj. (**-ier**, **-iest**) **1** (also **clompy**) (of shoes or boots) heavy and inelegant. **2** forming or showing a tendency to form clumps.

**clumsy** ● adj. (**-ier**, **-iest**) awkward in movement or performance. ➤tactless. ➤unwieldy.
– DERIVATIVES **clumsily** adv. **clumsiness** n.
– ORIGIN C16: from obs. *clumse* 'make or be numb', prob. of Scand. origin.

**clunch** ● n. Brit. soft limestone capable of being easily worked.
– ORIGIN C19: perh. from dial. *clunch* 'lumpy, thickset'.

**clung** past and past participle of **CLING**.

**Cluniac** /'klu:nɪak/ ● n. a monk of a reformed Benedictine monastic order founded at Cluny in eastern France.

**clunk** ● n. **1** a dull, heavy sound such as that made by thick pieces of metal striking together. **2** US informal a stupid or foolish person. ● v. move with or make a clunk.
– ORIGIN C18 (orig. Scots): imitative; cf. **CLANK**, **CLINK**[1], and **CLONK**.

**clunker** ● n. N. Amer. informal **1** a dilapidated vehicle or machine. **2** a thing that is totally unsuccessful.

**clunky** ● adj. (**-ier**, **-iest**) informal **1** chiefly N. Amer. solid, heavy, and old-fashioned. ➤(of shoes) clumpy. **2** making a clunking sound.

**clupeoid** /'klu:pɪɔɪd/ ● adj. Zoology relating to or denoting fish of an order (Clupeiformes) including the herrings and anchovies.
– ORIGIN C19: from mod. L. *Clupeoidei* (a suborder), from L. *clupea*, the name of a river fish.

**cluster** ● n. **1** a group of similar things positioned or occurring closely together. **2** a natural subgroup of a population, used for statistical sampling or analysis. **3** Chemistry a group of atoms of the same element, typically a metal, bonded closely together in a molecule. ● v. **1** form a cluster. **2** Statistics (of data points) have similar numerical values.
– DERIVATIVES **clustered** adj.
– ORIGIN OE *clyster*; prob. rel. to **CLOT**.

**cluster bean** ● n. another term for **GUAR**.

**cluster bomb** ● n. a bomb which releases a number of projectiles on impact.

**cluster fly** ● n. a fly which forms clusters in buildings before overwintering. [*Pollenia rudis* and *Thaumatomyia notata*.]

**cluster pine** ● n. another term for **MARITIME PINE**.

**clutch**[1] ● v. grasp tightly. ● n. **1** a tight grasp. **2** (**clutches**) power; control: *she was about to fall into his clutches.* **3** a mechanism for connecting and disconnecting the engine and the transmission system in a vehicle, or the working parts of any machine.
– ORIGIN ME (in the sense 'bend, crook'): var. of obs. *clitch* 'close the hand', from OE *clyccan* 'crook, clench', of Gmc origin.

**clutch**[2] ● n. **1** a group of eggs fertilized at the same time, laid in a single session and (in birds) incubated together. ➤a brood of chicks. **2** a small group of people or things.
– ORIGIN C18: prob. a southern var. of north. Engl. dial. *cletch*, rel. to ME *cleck* 'to hatch', from ON *klekja*.

**clutch bag** ● n. a slim, flat handbag without handles or a strap.

**clutter** ● n. things lying about untidily. ➤an untidy state. ● v. cover or fill with clutter.
– ORIGIN ME: var. of dial. *clotter* 'to clot', influenced by **CLUSTER** and **CLATTER**.

**Clydesdale** ● n. **1** a horse of a heavy, powerful breed, used for pulling heavy loads. **2** a dog of a small breed of terrier.
– ORIGIN from the name of the river *Clyde* in Scotland, in the area of which they were orig. bred.

**clypeus** /'klɪpɪəs/ ● n. (pl. **clypei** /-pɪʌɪ/) Entomology a broad plate at the front of an insect's head.
– DERIVATIVES **clypeal** adj.
– ORIGIN C19: from L., lit. 'round shield'.

**clyster** /'klɪstə/ ● n. archaic term for **ENEMA**.
– ORIGIN ME: from OFr. *clystere* or L. *clyster*, from Gk *klustēr* 'syringe'.

**CM** ● abbrev. **1** command module. **2** common metre. **3** Member of the Order of Canada.

**Cm** ● symb. the chemical element curium.

**Cm.** ● abbrev. (in the UK) Command Paper (sixth series, 1986–).

**cm** ● abbrev. centimetre(s).

**Cmd.** ● abbrev. (in the UK) Command Paper (fourth series, 1918–56).

**Cmdr** ● abbrev. Commander.

**Cmdre** ● abbrev. Commodore.

**CMEA** ● abbrev. Council for Mutual Economic Assistance.

**CMG** ● abbrev. (in the UK) Companion (of the Order) of St Michael and St George.

**Cmnd.** ● abbrev. (in the UK) Command Paper (fifth series, 1956–86).

**CMOS** ● n. Electronics a technology for making low-power integrated circuits. ➤a chip based on such technology.
– ORIGIN 1980s: from *Complementary Metal Oxide Semiconductor.*

**CMSgt** ● abbrev. Chief Master Sergeant.

**CMV** ● abbrev. cytomegalovirus.

**CNAA** ● abbrev. Council for National Academic Awards.

**CND** ● abbrev. Campaign for Nuclear Disarmament.

**cnemial crest** /'(k)ni:mɪəl/ ● n. Zoology (in the legs of many mammals, birds, and dinosaurs) a ridge at the front of the head of the tibia or tibiotarsus to which the main extensor muscle of the thigh is attached.
– ORIGIN C19: from Gk *knēmē* 'tibia' + **-AL**.

**CNG** ● abbrev. compressed natural gas.

**Cnidaria** /(k)nʌɪ'dɛ:rɪə/ ● pl. n. Zoology a phylum of aquatic invertebrate animals that comprises the coelenterates.
– DERIVATIVES **cnidarian** n. & adj.
– ORIGIN mod. L., from Gk *knidē* 'nettle'.

**CNN** ● abbrev. Cable News Network.

**CNS** ● abbrev. central nervous system.

**CO** ● abbrev. **1** Colombia (international vehicle registration). **2** Colorado (in official postal use). **3** Commanding Officer. **4** conscientious objector.

**Co** ● symb. the chemical element cobalt.

**Co.** ● abbrev. **1** company. **2** county.

**c/o** ● abbrev. care of.

**co-** /kəʊ/ ● prefix **1** (forming nouns) joint; mutual; common: *co-driver.* **2** (forming adjectives) jointly; mutually: *coequal.* **3** (forming verbs) together with another or others: *co-produce.* **4** Mathematics of the complement of an angle: *cosine.* ➤the complement of: *co-latitude.*
– ORIGIN from L., orig. a form of **COM-**.

**coacervate** /kəʊ'asəveɪt/ ● n. Chemistry a colloid-rich viscous liquid phase which may separate from a colloidal solution on addition of a third component.
– ORIGIN C20: back-form. from *coacervation*, based on L. *cum* '(together) with' + *acervus* 'heap'.

**coach**[1] ● n. **1** chiefly Brit. a comfortably equipped single-decker bus used for longer journeys. **2** a railway carriage. **3** [as modifier] N. Amer. denoting economy-class seating in an aircraft or train. **4** a closed horse-drawn carriage. ● v. travel or convey by coach.
– ORIGIN C16: from Fr. *coche*, from Hungarian *kocsi* (*szekér*) '(wagon) from *Kocs*', a town in Hungary.

**coach**[2] ● n. **1** an instructor or trainer in sport. **2** a tutor who gives private or specialized teaching. **3** Austral. a docile cow or bullock used as a decoy to attract wild cattle. ● v. train or teach as a coach.
– ORIGIN C18: figuratively from **COACH**[1].

**coach bolt** ● n. Brit. a large bolt with a round head, used chiefly for fixing wooden panels to masonry or to one another.

**coach-built** • **adj.** Brit. (of a vehicle) having specially or individually built bodywork.
– DERIVATIVES **coachbuilder** n.

**coach house** • **n.** a building formerly used for the storage of coaches.

**coaching inn** • **n.** historical an inn along a route followed by horse-drawn coaches, at which horses could be changed.

**coachload** • **n.** a group of people travelling in a coach.

**coachman** • **n.** (pl. **-men**) a driver of a horse-drawn carriage.

**coachroof** • **n.** a raised part of the cabin roof of a yacht.

**coachwhip** • **n. 1** a harmless North American snake, whose scales form a pattern said to resemble a braided whip. [*Masticophis flagellum.*] **2** Austral. the whipbird.

**coachwood** • **n.** a slender tree of the rainforests of Australia and New Guinea, with close-grained timber that is used for cabinetmaking and veneers. [*Ceratopetalum apetalum.*]

**coachwork** • **n.** the bodywork of a road or railway vehicle.

**coadjutor** /kəʊ'adʒʊtə/ • **n.** a bishop appointed to assist and often to succeed a diocesan bishop.
– ORIGIN ME: via OFr. from late L. *coadjutor*, from *co-* + *adjutor* 'assistant'.

**coagulant** /kəʊ'agjʊlənt/ • **n.** a substance that causes coagulation.

**coagulase** /kəʊ'agjʊleɪz, -s/ • **n.** Biochemistry a bacterial enzyme which brings about the coagulation of blood or plasma and is produced by disease-causing forms of staphylococcus.

**coagulate** /kəʊ'agjʊleɪt/ • **v.** (of a fluid, especially blood) change to a solid or semi-solid state.
– DERIVATIVES **coagulable** adj. **coagulation** n. **coagulative** adj. **coagulator** n.
– ORIGIN ME: from L. *coagulat-*, *coagulare* 'curdle'.

**coagulum** /kəʊ'agjʊləm/ • **n.** (pl. **coagula** /-lə/) a mass of coagulated matter.
– ORIGIN C16 (denoting a coagulant): from L., lit. 'rennet'.

**coal** • **n.** a combustible black rock consisting mainly of carbonized plant matter and used as fuel. ➤ Brit. a piece of coal. • **v.** provide with or extract coal.
– PHRASES **coals to Newcastle** something supplied to a place where it is already plentiful. **haul someone over the coals** reprimand someone severely.
– DERIVATIVES **coaly** adj.
– ORIGIN OE *col* (in the senses 'glowing ember' and 'charred remnant'), of Gmc origin.

**coaler** • **n. 1** a ship that transports coal. **2** a large mechanized structure for loading coal.

**coalesce** /ˌkəʊə'lɛs/ • **v.** come or bring together to form one mass or whole.
– DERIVATIVES **coalescence** n. **coalescent** adj.
– ORIGIN C16: from L. *coalescere*, from *co-* + *alescere* 'grow up'.

**coalface** • **n.** an exposed surface of coal in a mine.
– PHRASES **at the coalface** engaged in work at an active rather than theoretical level in a particular field.

**coalfield** • **n.** an extensive area containing a number of underground coal strata.

**coalfish** • **n.** (pl. same or **-fishes**) another term for **SAITHE**.

**coal gas** • **n.** a mixture of gases (chiefly hydrogen, methane, and carbon monoxide) obtained by distilling coal and formerly used for lighting and heating.

**coalition** /ˌkəʊə'lɪʃ(ə)n/ • **n.** a temporary alliance, especially of political parties forming a government.
– DERIVATIVES **coalitionist** n.
– ORIGIN C17 (in the sense 'fusion'): from med. L. *coalitio(n-)*, from L. *coalescere* (see **COALESCE**).

**coal measures** • **pl. n.** Geology a series of strata of the Carboniferous period, including coal seams.

**Coalport** • **n.** a kind of porcelain produced at Coalport in Shropshire, England, from the late 18th century.

**coal tar** • **n.** a thick black liquid produced by distilling bituminous coal, containing organic chemicals including benzene, naphthalene, phenols, and aniline.

**coal tit** (also **cole tit**) • **n.** a small titmouse with a grey back, black cap and throat, and white cheeks. [*Parus ater.*]

**coaming** /'kəʊmɪŋ/ (also **coamings**) • **n.** a raised border round the cockpit or hatch of a yacht or other boat to keep out water.
– ORIGIN C17: of unknown origin.

**coaptation** /ˌkəʊap'teɪʃ(ə)n/ • **n. 1** the adaptation of things or people to each other. **2** Medicine the drawing together of the separated tissue in a wound or fracture.
– ORIGIN C16: from late L. *coaptatio(n-)*, from *coaptare* (from *aptus* 'apt').

**coarctate** /kəʊ'ɑːkteɪt/ • **adj.** chiefly Anatomy & Biology compressed; contracted.
– ORIGIN ME: from L. *coarctat-*, *coarctare* 'press or draw together'.

**coarctation** • **n.** Medicine congenital narrowing of a short section of the aorta.

**coarse** • **adj. 1** rough or harsh in texture; unrefined. ➤ consisting of large grains or particles. **2** (of a person's features) not elegantly formed or proportioned. **3** (of a person or their speech) rude or vulgar. **4** Brit. relating to the sport of angling for coarse fish.
– DERIVATIVES **coarsely** adv. **coarseness** n. **coarsish** adj.
– ORIGIN ME (in the sense 'ordinary or inferior'): origin uncertain; perh. rel. to **COURSE**.

**coarse fish** • **n.** (pl. same) Brit. any freshwater fish other than salmon and trout. Compare with **GAME FISH**.

**coarsen** • **v.** make or become coarse.

**coast** • **n. 1** the part of the land adjoining or near the sea. **2** the easy movement of a vehicle without the use of power. • **v. 1** move easily without using power. ➤ act or make progress with little effort: *they coasted to victory.* **2** sail along the coast.
– PHRASES **the coast is clear** there is no danger of being observed or caught.
– DERIVATIVES **coastal** adj. **coastwise** adj. & adv.
– ORIGIN ME (in the sense 'side of the body'), from OFr. *coste* (n.), *costeier* (v.), from L. *costa* 'rib, flank, side'.

**coaster** • **n. 1** a ship carrying cargo along the coast from port to port. **2** a small mat for a glass. **3** N. Amer. a toboggan. **4** short for **ROLLER COASTER**.

**coastguard** • **n.** a person or organization that keeps watch over coastal waters to assist people or ships in danger and to prevent smuggling.

**coastland** • **n.** an expanse of land near the sea.

**coastline** • **n.** a length of coast: *a rugged coastline.*

**coat** • **n. 1** a full-length outer garment with sleeves. ➤ a man's jacket. **2** an animal's covering of fur or hair. **3** an enclosing or covering layer or structure. **4** a single application of paint or similar material. • **v.** provide with or form a layer or covering.
– DERIVATIVES **-coated** adj.
– ORIGIN ME: from OFr. *cote*, of unknown origin.

**coat armour** • **n.** heraldic arms.

**coat check** • **n.** N. Amer. a cloakroom with an attendant.
– DERIVATIVES **coat-checker** n.

**coat dress** • **n.** a woman's tailored dress that resembles a coat.

**coati** /kəʊ'ɑːti/ • **n.** (pl. **coatis**) a raccoon-like animal found in Central and South America, with a long flexible snout and a ringed tail. [Genera *Nasua* and *Nasuella*: three or four species.]
– ORIGIN C17: from Sp. and Port., from Tupi *kua'ti*, from *cua* 'belt' + *tim* 'nose'.

**coatimundi** /kəʊˌɑːtɪ'mʌndi/ • **n.** (pl. **coatimundis**) another term for **COATI**.
– ORIGIN C17: from Port., from Tupi *kuatimu'ne*, from *kua'ti* (see **COATI**) + *mu'ne* 'snare or trick'.

**coating** • **n.** a thin layer or covering of something.

**coat of arms** • **n.** the distinctive heraldic bearings or shield of a person, family, corporation, or country.

**coat of mail** • **n.** historical a jacket composed of metal rings or plates, serving as armour.

**coatroom** ● **n.** N. Amer. a cloakroom.

**coat-tail** ● **n.** each of the flaps formed by the back of a tailcoat.

**co-author** ● **n.** a joint author. ● **v.** be a joint author of.

**coax**[1] /kəʊks/ ● **v.** persuade (someone) gradually or by flattery to do something. ➤use such persuasion to obtain (something). ➤manipulate (something) carefully into a particular situation or position.
– DERIVATIVES **coaxer** n. **coaxing** adj. **coaxingly** adv.
– ORIGIN C16 (in the sense 'pet, fondle'): from obs. *cokes* 'simpleton', of unknown origin.

**coax**[2] /'kəʊaks/ ● **n.** informal coaxial cable.

**coaxial** /kəʊ'aksɪəl/ ● **adj. 1** having a common axis. **2** (of a cable or line) transmitting by means of two concentric conductors separated by an insulator.
– DERIVATIVES **coaxially** adv.

**cob**[1] ● **n. 1** Brit. a loaf of bread. **2** short for **CORNCOB**. **3** (also **cobnut**) a hazelnut or filbert. ➤a hazel or filbert bush. **4** a powerfully built, short-legged horse. **5** a male swan. **6** a roundish lump of coal.
– ORIGIN ME (denoting a strong man or leader): of unknown origin.

**cob**[2] ● **n.** Brit. a mixture of compressed clay and straw used, especially formerly, for building walls.
– ORIGIN C17: of unknown origin.

**cobalamin** /kə(ʊ)'baləmɪn/ ● **n.** Biochemistry any of a group of cobalt-containing substances including cyanocobalamin (vitamin $B_{12}$).
– ORIGIN 1950s: blend of **COBALT** and **VITAMIN**.

**cobalt** /'kəʊbɔːlt, -ɒlt/ ● **n.** the chemical element of atomic number 27, a hard silvery-white magnetic metal. (Symbol: **Co**)
– DERIVATIVES **cobaltic** /kə(ʊ)'bɔːltɪk, -'bɒlt-/ adj. **cobaltous** /kə(ʊ)'bɔːltəs, -'bɒlt-/ adj.
– ORIGIN C17: from Ger. *Kobalt* 'imp, demon' (from the belief that cobalt was harmful to the ores with which it occurred).

**cobalt blue** ● **n.** a deep blue pigment containing cobalt and aluminium oxides.

**cobber** ● **n.** Austral./NZ informal a companion or friend.
– ORIGIN C19: perh. rel. to Engl. dial. *cob* 'take a liking to'.

**cobble**[1] ● **n.** (also **cobblestone**) a small round stone used to cover road surfaces.
– DERIVATIVES **cobbled** adj.
– ORIGIN ME: from **COB**[1] + **-LE**[2].

**cobble**[2] ● **v. 1** (**cobble something together**) roughly assemble something from available parts or elements. **2** dated repair (shoes).
– ORIGIN C15: back-form. from **COBBLER**.

**cobbler** ● **n. 1** a person whose job is mending shoes. **2** an iced drink made with wine or sherry, sugar, and lemon. **3** chiefly N. Amer. a fruit pie with a rich, cake-like crust. **4** (**cobblers**) Brit. informal a man's testicles. [from rhyming sl. *cobbler's awls* 'balls'.] ➤nonsense.
– ORIGIN ME: of unknown origin.

**cobby** ● **adj.** (of a horse or other animal) stocky.
– ORIGIN C17: from **COB**[1] + **-Y**[1].

**co-belligerent** ● **n.** any of two or more nations engaged in war as allies.
– DERIVATIVES **co-belligerence** n.

**cobia** /'kəʊbɪə/ ● **n.** (pl. same) a large edible game fish living in the open ocean. [*Rachycentron canadum*.]
– ORIGIN C19: of unknown origin.

**coble** /'kəʊb(ə)l/ ● **n.** a flat-bottomed fishing boat of a type used in Scotland and NE England.
– ORIGIN OE, perh. of Celtic origin.

**COBOL** /'kəʊbɒl/ ● **n.** a computer programming language designed for use in commerce.
– ORIGIN 1960s: from *co(mmon) b(usiness) o(riented) l(anguage)*.

**cobra** /'kəʊbrə, 'kɒbrə/ ● **n.** a highly venomous African or Asian snake that spreads the skin of its neck into a hood when disturbed. [*Naja naja* (**spectacled cobra**), *N. haje* (**Egyptian cobra**), and other species.]
– ORIGIN C17: from Port. *cobra de capello*, lit. 'snake with hood'.

**cobweb** ● **n.** a spider's web, especially an old or dusty one.
– DERIVATIVES **cobwebbed** adj. **cobwebby** adj.
– ORIGIN ME *coppeweb*, from obs. *coppe* 'spider' + **WEB**.

**coca** /'kəʊkə/ ● **n. 1** a tropical American shrub grown for its leaves, which are the source of cocaine. [*Erythroxylum coca*.] **2** the dried leaves of this shrub mixed with lime and chewed as a stimulant by the native people of western South America.
– ORIGIN C16: from Sp., from Aymara *kuka* or Quechua *koka*.

**cocaine** /kə(ʊ)'keɪn/ ● **n.** an addictive drug derived from coca or prepared synthetically, used as an illegal stimulant and sometimes medicinally as a local anaesthetic.
– ORIGIN C19: from **COCA** + **-INE**[4].

**coccidia** /kɒk'sɪdɪə/ ● **pl. n.** Biology parasitic protozoans of a group responsible for toxoplasmosis and other diseases. [Suborder Eimeriorina.]
– DERIVATIVES **coccidian** adj. & n. **coccidiosis** n.
– ORIGIN C19: from mod. L. (former order name), from Gk *kokkis*, dimin. of *kokkos* 'berry'.

**coccidioidomycosis** /kɒkˌsɪdɪˌɔɪdəʊmʌɪ'kəʊsɪs/ ● **n.** a serious fungal disease of the lungs and other tissues, endemic in the warmer, arid regions of America.
– ORIGIN 1930s: from mod. L. *Coccidioides* (genus name of the fungus) + **MYCOSIS**.

**coccolith** /'kɒkəlɪθ/ ● **n.** Biology a minute rounded calcareous platelet, numbers of which form the spherical shells of coccolithophores.
– ORIGIN C19: from Gk *kokkos* 'grain or berry' + *lithos* 'stone'.

**coccolithophore** /ˌkɒkə(ʊ)'lɪθəfɔː/ ● **n.** Biology a single-celled planktonic flagellate that secretes a calcareous shell. [Order Coccolithophorida.]
– DERIVATIVES **coccolithophorid** n. & adj.

**coccus** /'kɒkəs/ ● **n.** (pl. **cocci** /'kɒk(s)ʌɪ, 'kɒk(s)iː/) Biology any spherical or roughly spherical bacterium.
– DERIVATIVES **coccal** adj. **coccoid** adj.
– ORIGIN C18 (denoting a scale insect): mod. L., from Gk *kokkos* 'berry'.

**coccyx** /'kɒksɪks/ ● **n.** (pl. **coccyges** /-ɪdʒiːz/ or **coccyxes**) a small triangular bone at the base of the spinal column in humans and some apes, formed of fused vestigial vertebrae.
– DERIVATIVES **coccygeal** /kɒk'sɪdʒɪəl/ adj.
– ORIGIN C16: via L. from Gk *kokkux* 'cuckoo' (because the shape of the human bone resembles the cuckoo's bill).

**cochineal** /ˌkɒtʃɪ'niːl, 'kɒtʃɪniːl/ ● **n. 1** a scarlet dye used for colouring food, made from the crushed dried bodies of a female scale insect. **2** (**cochineal insect**) the scale insect that is used for cochineal, native to Mexico and formerly widely cultivated on cacti. [*Dactylopius coccus*.]
– ORIGIN C16: from Fr. *cochenille* or Sp. *cochinilla*, from L. *coccinus* 'scarlet'.

**cochlea** /'kɒklɪə/ ● **n.** (pl. **cochleae** /-klɪiː/) the spiral cavity of the inner ear containing the organ of Corti, which produces nerve impulses in response to sound vibrations.
– DERIVATIVES **cochlear** adj.
– ORIGIN C16: from L., 'snail shell or screw'.

**cock**[1] ● **n. 1** a male bird, especially of a domestic fowl. ➤used in names of birds, especially game birds, e.g. **snowcock**. ➤Brit. a male lobster, crab, or salmon. ➤Brit. informal a friendly form of address among men. **2** vulgar slang a man's penis. **3** Brit. informal nonsense. **4** a firing lever in a gun which can be raised to be released by the trigger. **5** a stopcock. ● **v. 1** tilt (something) in a particular direction. ➤bend a (limb or joint) at an angle. **2** raise the cock of (a gun) in order to make it ready for firing. **3** (**cock something up**) Brit. informal spoil or ruin something.
– PHRASES **at full cock** (of a gun) with the cock lifted to the position at which the trigger will act. **cock one's ear** (of a dog) raise its ears to an erect position. **cock one's eye** glance in a quizzical or knowing manner with a raised eyebrow. **cock of the walk** someone who dominates others within a group.
– ORIGIN OE *cocc*, from med. L. *coccus*; reinforced in ME by

OFr. *coq*.

**cock**[2] ● n. dated a small pile of hay or other material, with vertical sides and a rounded top. ● v. archaic pile (hay or other material) into a cock.
– ORIGIN ME: perh. of Scand. origin.

**cockabully** /ˈkɒkəbʊli/ ● n. (pl. **-ies**) NZ a small blunt-nosed freshwater fish related to the sleepers. [Genus *Gobiomorphus*.]
– ORIGIN C19: from Maori *kokopu*.

**cockade** /kɒˈkeɪd/ ● n. a rosette or knot of ribbons worn in a hat as a badge of office or as part of a livery.
– DERIVATIVES **cockaded** adj.
– ORIGIN C17: from Fr. *cocarde*, orig. in *bonnet à la coquarde*, from the fem. of obs. *coquard* 'saucy'.

**cock-a-doodle-doo** ● exclam. used to represent the sound made by a cock when it crows.

**cock-a-hoop** ● adj. extremely pleased.
– ORIGIN C17: from the phr. *set cock a hoop*, of unknown origin, appar. denoting the action of turning on a tap and allowing liquor to flow.

**cock-a-leekie** ● n. a soup traditionally made in Scotland with chicken and leeks.

**cockalorum** /ˌkɒkəˈlɔːrəm/ ● n. (pl. **cockalorums**) informal, dated a self-important man.
– ORIGIN C18: an arbitrary formation from **COCK**[1].

**cockamamie** /ˈkɒkəˌmeɪmi/ (also **cockamamy**) ● adj. informal, chiefly N. Amer. ridiculous; nonsensical.
– ORIGIN 1940s (orig. denoting a design left by a transfer): prob. an alt. of **DECALCOMANIA**.

**cock and bull story** ● n. informal a ridiculous and implausible story.

**cockatiel** /ˌkɒkəˈtiːl/ ● n. a slender long-crested Australian parrot related to the cockatoos, with a mainly grey body and a yellow and orange face. [*Nymphicus hollandicus*.]
– ORIGIN C19: from Du. *kaketielje*, prob. a dimin. of *kaketoe* 'cockatoo'.

**cockatoo** /ˌkɒkəˈtuː/ ● n. a parrot with an erectile crest, found in Australia, eastern Indonesia, and neighbouring islands. [Family Cacatuidae: numerous species.]
– ORIGIN C17: from Du. *kaketoe*, from Malay *kakatua*.

**cockatrice** /ˈkɒkətrʌɪs, -trɪs/ ● n. another term for **BASILISK** (in sense 1). ➤ Heraldry a mythical animal depicted as a two-legged dragon (or wyvern) with a cock's head.
– ORIGIN ME: from OFr. *cocatris*, from L. *calcatrix* 'tracker', translating Gk *ikhneumōn* (see **ICHNEUMON**).

**cockboat** ● n. a small boat towed behind a larger vessel.
– ORIGIN ME: from obs. *cock* 'small boat' (from OFr. *coque*, based on L. *caudex*, *codex* 'block of wood') + **BOAT**.

**cockchafer** /ˈkɒkˌtʃeɪfə/ ● n. a large brown dusk-flying beetle which is a destructive plant pest. [*Melolontha melolontha*.]
– ORIGIN C18: from **COCK**[1] (expressing size) + **CHAFER**.

**cockcrow** ● n. poetic/literary dawn.

**cocked hat** ● n. a brimless triangular hat pointed at the front, back, and top. ➤ historical a hat with a wide brim permanently turned up towards the crown.
– PHRASES **knock something into a cocked hat** utterly defeat or outdo something.

**cockerel** ● n. a young domestic cock.
– ORIGIN ME: dimin. of **COCK**[1].

**cocker spaniel** ● n. a small spaniel of a breed with a silky coat.
– ORIGIN C19: from **COCK**[1] + **-ER**[1] (because the dog was bred to flush game birds such as woodcock).

**cock-eyed** ● adj. informal **1** crooked or askew; not level. ➤ absurd; impractical. **2** having a squint.

**cockfighting** ● n. the sport (illegal in the UK and some other countries) of setting two cocks to fight each other.
– DERIVATIVES **cockfight** n.

**cockle**[1] ● n. **1** an edible burrowing bivalve mollusc with a strong ribbed shell. [Genus *Cardium*.] **2** (also **cockleshell**) poetic/literary a small shallow boat.
– PHRASES **warm the cockles of one's heart** give one a comforting feeling of contentment.
– DERIVATIVES **cockler** n. **cockling** n.
– ORIGIN ME: from OFr. *coquille* 'shell', based on Gk *konkhulion*, from *konkhē* 'conch'.

**cockle**[2] ● v. wrinkle or pucker.
– ORIGIN C16: from Fr. *coquiller* 'blister (bread in cooking)', from *coquille* (see **COCKLE**[1]).

**cocklebur** ● n. a plant of the daisy family with broad leaves and burred fruits, native to tropical America. [*Xanthium strumarium*.]
– ORIGIN C19: from **COCKLE**[2] + **BUR**.

**cockney** /ˈkɒkni/ ● n. (pl. **-eys**) **1** a native of the East End of London, traditionally one born within hearing of Bow Bells. ➤ the dialect or accent typical of such people. **2** Austral. a young snapper (fish).
– DERIVATIVES **cockneyism** n.
– ORIGIN ME (denoting a pampered child, later a town-dweller regarded as affected or puny): origin uncertain; appar. not rel. to ME *cokeney* 'cock's egg'.

**cock-of-the-rock** ● n. (pl. **cocks-of-the-rock**) a crested cotinga found in the tropical forests of South America, the male of which has brilliant orange or red plumage. [Genus *Rupicola*: two species.]

**cockpit** ● n. **1** a compartment for the pilot and crew in an aircraft or spacecraft. ➤ the driver's compartment in a racing car. **2** a place where cockfights are held. **3** a place where a battle or other conflict takes place.
– ORIGIN C16: from **COCK**[1] + **PIT**[1]; sense 1 derives from a C18 naut. use denoting an area in the aft lower deck where the wounded were taken, later coming to mean 'the pit' or well from which a yacht was steered'.

**cockroach** /ˈkɒkrəʊtʃ/ ● n. a beetle-like scavenging insect with long antennae and legs, some kinds of which are household pests. [*Blatta orientalis* and other species, suborder Blattodea.]
– ORIGIN C17 (as *cacaroch*): from Sp. *cucaracha*.

**cockscomb** ● n. **1** the crest or comb of a domestic cock. **2** (also **coxcomb**) a tropical plant with a crest of tiny yellow, orange, or red flowers, grown as a pot plant. [*Celosia cristata*.] **3** a brightly coloured orchid related to the coralroots, native to southern North America. [Genus *Hexalectris*.]

**cocksfoot** ● n. chiefly Brit. a pasture grass with broad leaves and green or purplish flowering spikes. [*Dactylis glomerata*.]

**cockshy** /ˈkɒkʃʌɪ/ ● n. (pl. **-ies**) Brit. dated a target for throwing sticks or stones at as a game.
– ORIGIN from the original use of a replica of a cockerel as a target.

**cocksman** ● n. (pl. **-men**) US vulgar slang a man who is reputed to be extremely virile or sexually accomplished.
– DERIVATIVES **cocksmanship** n.

**cockspur thorn** ● n. a North American hawthorn which is widely planted for its rich orange autumn foliage. [*Crataegus crus-galli*.]

**cocksure** ● adj. presumptuously or arrogantly confident.
– DERIVATIVES **cocksurely** adv. **cocksureness** n.
– ORIGIN C16: from archaic *cock* (a euphemism for *God*) + **SURE**; later assoc. with **COCK**[1].

**cocktail** ● n. **1** an alcoholic drink consisting of a spirit mixed with other ingredients, such as fruit juice. ➤ [as modifier] relating to or associated with cocktail drinking or formal social occasions: *a cocktail dress*. ➤ a dish consisting of small pieces of food, typically served as an hors d'oeuvre: *a prawn cocktail*. **2** a mixture of diverse substances or factors, especially when dangerous or unpleasant: *a potent cocktail of tranquillizers*.
– ORIGIN C17: from **COCK**[1] + **TAIL**[1]; earlier denoting a horse with a docked tail, later a racehorse which was not a thoroughbred (through having a cock-tailed horse in its pedigree).

**cock-up** ● n. Brit. informal something done badly or inefficiently.

**cocky**[1] ● adj. (**-ier**, **-iest**) conceited in a bold or cheeky way.
– DERIVATIVES **cockily** adv. **cockiness** n.
– ORIGIN C16 (in the sense 'lecherous'): from **COCK**[1] + **-Y**[1].

**cocky**[2] ● n. (pl. **-ies**) Austral./NZ informal a cockatoo.

**coco** ● n. (pl. **-os**) **1** coconut. **2** W. Indian the root of the

taro.
– ORIGIN C16: from Sp. and Port., lit. 'grinning face' (because of the appearance of the base of the coconut).

**cocoa** ● n. a powder made from roasted and ground cacao seeds. ➤a hot drink made from such a powder mixed with milk or water.
– ORIGIN C18: alt. of **CACAO**.

**cocoa bean** ● n. a cacao seed.

**cocoa butter** ● n. a fatty substance obtained from cocoa beans, used in making confectionery and cosmetics.

**cocoanut** ● n. old-fashioned spelling of **COCONUT**.

**cocobolo** /ˌkəʊkə(ʊ)ˈbəʊləʊ/ ● n. (pl. **-os**) a tropical American tree with hard reddish wood. [*Dalbergia retusa*.]
– ORIGIN C19: via Sp. from Arawak *kakabali*.

**coco de mer** /ˌkəʊkəʊdəˈmɛː/ ● n. a tall palm tree native to the Seychelles, having an immense nut in a hard woody shell. [*Lodoicea maldivica*.]
– ORIGIN C19: from Fr. *coco-de-mer*, lit. 'coco from the sea' (because the tree was first known from nuts found floating in the sea).

**coconut** ● n. **1** the large oval brown seed of a tropical palm, consisting of a hard woody husk surrounded by fibre, lined with edible white flesh and containing a clear liquid (**coconut milk**). ➤the flesh of a coconut, often shredded and used as food. **2** (also **coconut palm** or **tree**) the tall palm tree that yields this nut, and also other products such as copra and coir. [*Cocos nucifera*.]

**coconut butter** ● n. a solid fat obtained from the flesh of the coconut, and used in the manufacture of soap, candles, ointment, etc.

**coconut ice** ● n. Brit. a sweet made from sugar and desiccated coconut.

**coconut shy** ● n. Brit. a fairground sideshow where balls are thrown at coconuts in an attempt to knock them off stands.

**cocoon** /kəˈkuːn/ ● n. **1** a silky case spun by the larvae of many insects for protection as pupae. ➤something that envelops, especially in a protective or comforting way. **2** a covering that prevents the corrosion of metal equipment. ● v. **1** wrap in a cocoon. **2** N. Amer. retreat from the stressful conditions of public life.
– DERIVATIVES **cocooner** n.
– ORIGIN C17: from Fr. *cocon*, from med. Provençal *coucoun* 'eggshell, cocoon', dimin. of *coca* 'shell'.

**cocotte** /kɒˈkɒt/ ● n. **1** (usu. in phr. **en cocotte**) a small casserole in which individual portions of food can be cooked and served. [C20: from Fr. *cocasse*, from L. *cucuma* 'cooking container'.] **2** dated a fashionable prostitute. [C19: Fr., from a child's name for a hen.]

**COD** ● abbrev. **1** cash on delivery. **2** N. Amer. collect on delivery.

**cod**[1] (also **codfish**) ● n. (pl. same) a large marine fish with a small barbel on the chin, important as a food fish. [*Gadus morhua* (N. Atlantic) and other species, family Gadidae.]
– ORIGIN ME: perh. the same word as OE *cod(d)* 'bag', because of the fish's appearance.

**cod**[2] Brit. informal ● adj. not authentic; fake: *a cod Mittel-European accent.* ● n. a joke or hoax. ● v. (**codded**, **codding**) play a joke on.
– ORIGIN C19: perh. from sl. *cod* 'a fool'.

**cod**[3] ● n. Brit. informal, dated nonsense.
– ORIGIN 1960s: abbrev. of **CODSWALLOP**.

**coda** /ˈkəʊdə/ ● n. Music **1** the concluding passage of a piece or movement, typically forming an addition to the basic structure. **2** a concluding event, remark, or section.
– ORIGIN C18: Ital., from L. *cauda* 'tail'.

**coddle** ● v. **1** treat in an indulgent or overprotective way. **2** cook (an egg) in water below boiling point.
– DERIVATIVES **coddler** n.
– ORIGIN C16: origin uncertain; sense 1 is prob. a dial. var. of obs. *caudle* 'administer invalids' gruel'.

**code** ● n. **1** a system of words, figures, or symbols used to represent others, especially for the purposes of secrecy. ➤a sequence of numbers dialled to connect a telephone with the exchange of the telephone being called. **2** Computing program instructions. **3** a systematic collection of laws or statutes: *the penal code.* ➤a set of conventions governing behaviour or activity in a particular sphere. ● v. **1** convert into a code. ➤assign a code to for purposes of classification or identification. **2** (**code for**) Biochemistry be the genetic code for (an amino acid or protein). ➤be the genetic determiner of (a characteristic).
– DERIVATIVES **coder** n. **coding** n. & adj.
– ORIGIN ME (orig. denoting a systematic collection of statutes made by one of the later Roman emperors): via OFr. from L. *codex*, *codic-* (see **CODEX**).

**codec** /ˈkəʊdɛk/ ● n. Electronics a microchip that compresses data to enable faster transmission or decompresses received data.
– ORIGIN 1960s: blend of ***coder*** and ***decoder***.

**codeine** /ˈkəʊdiːn, -dɪiːn/ ● n. Medicine a sleep-inducing and analgesic drug derived from morphine.
– ORIGIN C19: from Gk *kōdeia* 'poppy head' + **-INE**[4].

**codependency** ● n. excessive emotional or psychological reliance on a partner, typically one with an illness or addiction who requires support.
– DERIVATIVES **codependence** n. **codependent** adj. & n.

**codex** /ˈkəʊdɛks/ ● n. (pl. **codices** /ˈkəʊdɪsiːz, ˈkɒd-/ or **codexes**) **1** an ancient manuscript text in book form. **2** an official list of medicines, chemicals, etc.
– ORIGIN C16 (denoting a collection of statutes): from L., lit. 'block of wood', later denoting a block split into tablets for writing on, hence a book.

**codfish** ● n. (pl. same or **-fishes**) another term for **COD**[1].

**codger** ● n. informal, derogatory an elderly man.
– ORIGIN C18: perh. a var. of *cadger* (see **CADGE**).

**codicil** /ˈkɒdɪsɪl, ˈkəʊ-/ ● n. an addition or supplement that explains, modifies, or revokes a will or part of one.
– DERIVATIVES **codicillary** /ˌkɒdɪˈsɪləri/ adj.
– ORIGIN ME: from L. *codicillus*, dimin. of *codex* (see **CODEX**).

**codicology** /ˌkəʊdɪˈkɒlədʒi/ ● n. the study of manuscripts and their interrelationships.
– DERIVATIVES **codicological** adj. **codicologically** adv.
– ORIGIN 1950s: from Fr. *codicologie*, from L. *codex* (see **CODEX**).

**codify** /ˈkəʊdɪfʌɪ/ ● v. (**-ies**, **-ied**) organize (procedures or rules) into a system or code.
– DERIVATIVES **codification** n. **codifier** n.

**codling**[1] ● n. an immature cod.

**codling**[2] ● n. any of several varieties of cooking apple having a long tapering shape.
– ORIGIN ME: from Anglo-Norman Fr. *quer de lion* 'lion-heart'.

**codling moth** ● n. a small greyish moth whose larvae feed on apples. [*Cydia pomonella*.]

**cod liver oil** ● n. oil pressed from the fresh liver of cod, which is rich in vitamins D and A.

**codomain** /ˈkəʊdə(ʊ)meɪn/ ● n. Mathematics a set that includes all the possible values of a given function.

**codon** /ˈkəʊdɒn/ ● n. Biochemistry a sequence of three nucleotides which together form a unit of genetic code in a DNA or RNA molecule.
– ORIGIN 1960s: from **CODE** + **-ON**.

**codpiece** ● n. a pouch to cover the genitals on a pair of man's breeches, worn in the 15th and 16th centuries.
– ORIGIN from earlier *cod* 'scrotum' (from OE *codd* 'bag, pod') + **PIECE**.

**codswallop** ● n. Brit. informal nonsense.
– ORIGIN 1960s: origin uncertain, but perh. named after Hiram *Codd*, who invented a bottle for fizzy drinks (1875).

**coecilian** ● n. variant spelling of **CAECILIAN**.

**co-ed** /ˈkəʊɛd, kəʊˈɛd/ informal ● n. N. Amer. dated a female student at a co-educational institution. ● adj. co-educational.

**co-education** ● n. the education of pupils of both sexes together.
– DERIVATIVES **co-educational** adj.

**coefficient** /ˌkəʊɪˈfɪʃ(ə)nt/ ● n. **1** Mathematics a numerical or constant quantity placed before and multiplying the variable in an algebraic expression (e.g. *4* in $4x^y$). **2** Physics

a multiplier or factor that measures some property.
– ORIGIN C17: from mod. L. *coefficient-*, from *com-* 'together' + *efficient-* (see **EFFICIENT**).

**coelacanth** /ˈsiːləkanθ/ ● **n.** a large bony marine fish with a three-lobed tail fin and fleshy pectoral fins, known only from fossils until one was found alive in 1938. [*Latimeria chalumnae*.]
– ORIGIN C19: from mod. L. *Coelacanthus* (genus name), from Gk *koilos* 'hollow' + *akantha* 'spine' (because its fins have hollow spines).

**-coele** ● **comb. form** variant spelling of **-CELE**.

**coelenterate** /siːˈlɛnt(ə)rət, -reɪt/ ● **n.** Zoology an aquatic invertebrate animal, typically having a tube- or cup-shaped body with a single opening ringed with tentacles, belonging to a phylum (Cnidaria, formerly Coelenterata) that includes jellyfishes, corals, and sea anemones.
– ORIGIN C19: from mod. L. *Coelenterata*, from Gk *koilos* 'hollow' + *enteron* 'intestine'.

**coeliac** /ˈsiːlɪak/ (US **celiac**) ● **adj.** Anatomy & Medicine of or relating to the abdomen.
– ORIGIN C17: from L. *coeliacus*, from Gk *koiliakos*, from *koilia* 'belly'.

**coeliac disease** ● **n.** a disease in which chronic failure to digest food is triggered by hypersensitivity of the small intestine to gluten.

**coelom** /ˈsiːləm/ ● **n.** (pl. **-oms** or **-omata** /-ˈləʊmətə/) Zoology the principal body cavity in most animals, located between the intestinal canal and the body wall.
– DERIVATIVES **coelomate** adj. & n. **coelomic** /səˈlɒmɪk/ adj.
– ORIGIN C19: from Gk *koilōma* 'cavity'.

**coelurosaur** /sɪˈljʊərəsɔː/ ● **n.** a small slender bipedal carnivorous dinosaur with long forelimbs, believed to be an evolutionary ancestor of birds.
– ORIGIN 1950s: from Gk *koilos* 'hollow' + *oura* 'tail' + *sauros* 'lizard'.

**coenobite** /ˈsiːnəbʌɪt/ (also **cenobite**) ● **n.** a member of a monastic community.
– DERIVATIVES **coenobitic** /-ˈbɪtɪk/ adj. **coenobitical** adj.
– ORIGIN ME: from OFr. *cenobite* or eccles. L. *coenobita*, via late L. from Gk *koinobion* 'convent'.

**coenocyte** /ˈsiːnəʊsʌɪt/ ● **n.** Botany a body of algal or fungal cytoplasm containing several nuclei, enclosed in a single membrane.
– DERIVATIVES **coenocytic** /-ˈsɪtɪk/ adj.
– ORIGIN C20: from Gk *koinos* 'common' + **-CYTE**.

**coenzyme** /ˈkəʊˌɛnzʌɪm/ ● **n.** Biochemistry a non-protein compound that is necessary for the functioning of an enzyme.

**coequal** ● **adj.** having the same rank or importance. ● **n.** a person or thing equal with another.
– DERIVATIVES **coequality** /kəʊɪˈkwɒlɪti/ n.

**coerce** /kəʊˈəːs/ ● **v.** persuade (an unwilling person) to do something by using force or threats.
– DERIVATIVES **coercible** adj. **coercion** n. **coercive** adj.
– ORIGIN ME: from L. *coercere* 'restrain', from *co-* 'jointly, together' + *arcere* 'restrain'.

**coercivity** /ˌkəʊəˈsɪvɪti/ ● **n.** Physics the resistance of a magnetic material to changes in magnetization, equivalent to the field intensity necessary to demagnetize the fully magnetized material.

**coeval** /kəʊˈiːv(ə)l/ ● **adj.** having the same age or date of origin; contemporary. ● **n.** a person of roughly the same age as oneself; a contemporary.
– DERIVATIVES **coevality** n. **coevally** adv.
– ORIGIN C17: from late L. *coaevus*, from *co-* 'jointly, in common' + L. *aevum* 'age'.

**coexist** ● **v.** exist at the same time or in the same place. ➤ exist in harmony.
– DERIVATIVES **coexistence** n. **coexistent** adj.

**coextensive** ● **adj.** extending over the same area, extent, or time.

**cofactor** ● **n.** Biochemistry a substance whose presence is essential for the activity of an enzyme.

**C. of E.** ● **abbrev.** Church of England.

**coffee** ● **n. 1** a hot drink made from the roasted and ground bean-like seeds of a tropical shrub. ➤ the processed, roasted, and ground seeds used to make this drink. **2** the shrub which yields these seeds. [Genus *Coffea*: several species.]
– ORIGIN C16: from Turk. *kahveh*, from Arab. *ḳahwa*.

**coffee morning** ● **n.** Brit. a morning social gathering at which coffee is served.

**coffee table** ● **n.** a small, low table.

**coffee-table book** ● **n.** a large, lavishly illustrated book, especially one intended only for casual reading.

**coffer** ● **n. 1** a small chest for holding valuables. ➤ (**coffers**) the funds or financial reserves of an institution. **2** a decorative sunken panel in a ceiling. ● **v.** [usu. as adj. **coffered**] decorate with a coffer or coffers.
– ORIGIN ME: from OFr. *coffre* 'chest', via L. from Gk *kophinos* 'basket'.

**cofferdam** ● **n.** a watertight enclosure pumped dry to permit construction work below the waterline, as when building bridges or repairing a ship.

**coffin** ● **n.** a long, narrow box in which a dead body is buried or cremated. ● **v.** (**coffined**, **coffining**) place in a coffin.
– ORIGIN ME: from OFr. *cofin* 'little basket', from L. *cophinus* (see **COFFER**).

**coffin bone** ● **n.** the terminal bone in a horse's hoof (the distal phalanx).

**coffle** /ˈkɒf(ə)l/ ● **n.** a line of animals or slaves fastened or driven along together.
– ORIGIN C18: from Arab. *ḳāfila* 'caravan'.

**coffret** /ˈkɒfrɪt/ ● **n.** a small container.
– ORIGIN C15: from OFr., 'small chest', dimin. of *coffre* (see **COFFER**).

**cog**[1] ● **n.** a wheel or bar with a series of projections on its edge, which transfers motion by engaging with projections on another wheel or bar. ➤ each of such a series of projections.
– DERIVATIVES **cogged** adj.
– ORIGIN ME: prob. of Scand. origin.

**cog**[2] ● **n.** a broadly built medieval ship with a rounded prow and stern.
– ORIGIN ME: rel. to MDu. *kogge*, OFr. *cogue*.

**cogeneration** ● **n.** the generation of electricity and useful heat jointly, especially the utilization of the steam left over from electricity generation for heating.

**cogent** /ˈkəʊdʒ(ə)nt/ ● **adj.** (of an argument or case) clear, logical, and convincing.
– DERIVATIVES **cogency** n. **cogently** adv.
– ORIGIN C17: from L. *cogent-*, *cogere* 'compel'.

**cogitate** /ˈkɒdʒɪteɪt/ ● **v.** formal meditate or reflect.
– DERIVATIVES **cogitation** n. **cogitative** adj. **cogitator** n.
– ORIGIN C16 (earlier (ME) as *cogitation*): from L. *cogitat-*, *cogitare* 'to consider'.

**cogito** /ˈkəʊgɪtəʊ, -dʒɪ-/ ● **n.** Philosophy the principle establishing the existence of a being from the fact of its thinking or awareness.
– ORIGIN L., as in Descartes' formula (1641) *cogito, ergo sum* 'I think, therefore I am'.

**cognac** /ˈkɒnjak/ ● **n.** a high-quality brandy, strictly speaking that distilled in Cognac in western France.

**cognate** /ˈkɒgneɪt/ ● **adj. 1** Linguistics (of a word) having the same linguistic derivation as another (e.g. English *father*, German *Vater*, Latin *pater*). **2** formal related; connected. ➤ related to or descended from a common ancestor. Compare with **AGNATE**. ● **n. 1** Linguistics a cognate word. **2** Law a blood relative.
– DERIVATIVES **cognately** adv. **cognateness** n.
– ORIGIN C17: from L. *cognatus*, from *co-* 'together with' + *natus* 'born'.

**cognition** /kɒgˈnɪʃ(ə)n/ ● **n.** the mental action or process of acquiring knowledge through thought, experience, and the senses. ➤ a perception, sensation, or intuition resulting from this.
– DERIVATIVES **cognitional** adj.
– ORIGIN ME: from L. *cognitio(-)*, from *cognoscere* 'get to know'.

**cognitive** /ˈkɒgnɪtɪv/ ● **adj.** of or relating to cognition.
– DERIVATIVES **cognitively** adv.

**cognitive dissonance** • n. Psychology the state of having inconsistent thoughts, beliefs, or attitudes.

**cognitive science** • n. the study of thought, learning, and mental organization.
– DERIVATIVES **cognitive scientist** n.

**cognitive therapy** • n. a type of psychotherapy in which negative patterns of thought about the self and the world are challenged.

**cognizable** /ˈkɒ(g)nɪzəb(ə)l/ (also **-isable**) • adj. **1** formal perceptible; clearly identifiable. **2** Law within the jurisdiction of a court.

**cognizance** /ˈkɒ(g)nɪz(ə)ns/ (also **cognisance**) • n. **1** formal knowledge or awareness. ➤ Law the action of taking judicial notice. **2** Heraldry a distinctive device or mark, especially as formerly worn by retainers of a noble house.
– PHRASES **take cognizance of** formal attend to; take account of.
– DERIVATIVES **cognizant** adj. **cognize** (also **-ise**) v.
– ORIGIN ME *conisance*, from OFr. *conoisance*, based on L. *cognoscere* 'get to know'.

**cognomen** /kɒgˈnəʊmən/ • n. an extra personal name given to an ancient Roman citizen, functioning rather like a nickname and often passed down from father to son.
– ORIGIN L., from *co-* 'together with' + *gnomen*, *nomen* 'name'.

**cognoscenti** /ˌkɒnjəˈʃɛnti/ • pl. n. people who are considered to be especially well informed about a particular subject.
– ORIGIN C18: Ital., lit. 'people who know', from L. *cognoscent-*, *cognoscere* 'to get to know'.

**cohabit** • v. (**cohabited**, **cohabiting**) **1** live together and have a sexual relationship without being married. **2** coexist.
– DERIVATIVES **cohabitant** n. **cohabitation** /-ˈteɪʃ(ə)n/ n. **cohabitee** /-ˈtiː/ n. **cohabiter** n.
– ORIGIN C16 (earlier (ME) as *cohabitation*): from L. *cohabitare*, from *co-* 'together' + *habitare* 'dwell'.

**cohen** • n. variant spelling of **KOHEN**.

**cohere** /kə(ʊ)ˈhɪə/ • v. **1** hold firmly together; form a whole. **2** (of an argument or theory) be logically consistent.
– ORIGIN C16: from L. *cohaerere*, from *co-* 'together' + *haerere* 'to stick'.

**coherent** • adj. **1** (of an argument or theory) logical and consistent. ➤ able to speak clearly and logically. **2** holding together to form a whole. **3** Physics (of waves) having a constant phase relationship.
– DERIVATIVES **coherence** n. **coherency** n. (rare). **coherently** adv.

**coherer** /kə(ʊ)ˈhɪːrə/ • n. an early form of radio detector consisting of a glass tube filled with metal filings.

**cohesion** /kə(ʊ)ˈhiːʒ(ə)n/ • n. the action or fact of forming a united whole. ➤ Physics the sticking together of particles of the same substance.
– ORIGIN C17: from L. *cohaes-*, *cohaerere* (see **COHERE**).

**cohesive** • adj. characterized by or causing cohesion.
– DERIVATIVES **cohesively** adv. **cohesiveness** n.

**coho** /ˈkəʊhəʊ/ (also **cohoe**) • n. (pl. same, **-os**, or **-oes**) a deep-bodied North Pacific salmon with small black spots. [*Oncorhynchus kisutch*.]
– ORIGIN C19: prob. from Salish.

**cohort** /ˈkəʊhɔːt/ • n. **1** [treated as sing. or pl.] an ancient Roman military unit, comprising six centuries, equal to one tenth of a legion. **2** [treated as sing. or pl.] a group of people banded together or treated as a group. **3** derogatory, chiefly N. Amer. a supporter or companion.
– ORIGIN ME: from OFr. *cohorte*, or from L. *cohors*, *cohort-* 'yard, retinue'.

**cohosh** /kəˈhɒʃ/ • n. a North American plant with medicinal properties. [*Cimicifuga racemosa* (**black cohosh**) and other species.]
– ORIGIN C18: from Eastern Abnaki.

**cohune** /kəˈhuːn/ • n. a Central American palm whose nut is a valuable source of oil. [*Orbignya cohune*.]
– ORIGIN C18: from Miskito.

**coif** /kɔɪf/ • n. **1** a woman's close-fitting cap, worn under a veil by nuns. ➤ historical a protective metal skullcap worn under armour. **2** /also kwɑːf/ informal, chiefly N. Amer. short for **COIFFURE**. • v. /kwɑːf, kwɒf/ (**coiffed**, **coiffing**; US also **coifed**, **coifing**) style or arrange (someone's hair).
– ORIGIN ME: from OFr. *coife* 'headdress', from late L. *cofia* 'helmet'.

**coiffeur** /kwɑːˈfəː, kwɒ-/ • n. (fem. **coiffeuse** /kwɑːˈfəːz, kwɒ-/) a hairdresser.
– ORIGIN C19: Fr., from *coiffer* 'arrange the hair'.

**coiffure** /kwɑːˈfjʊə, kwɒ-/ • n. a person's hairstyle.
– DERIVATIVES **coiffured** adj.

**coign** /kɔɪn/ • n. a projecting corner or angle of a wall.
– PHRASES **coign of vantage** a favourable position for observation or action.
– ORIGIN ME: var. of **COIN**.

**coil**[1] • n. **1** a length of something wound in a joined sequence of concentric rings. **2** an intrauterine contraceptive device in the form of a coil. **3** an electrical device consisting of a coiled wire, for converting the level of a voltage, producing a magnetic field, or adding inductance to a circuit. • v. arrange or form into a coil.
– ORIGIN C16: from OFr. *coillir*, from L. *colligere* (see **COLLECT**[1]).

**coil**[2] • n. archaic or dialect a confusion or turmoil.
– ORIGIN C16: of unknown origin.

**coin** • n. **1** a flat disc or piece of metal with an official stamp, used as money. ➤ money in the form of coins. **2** (**coins**) one of the suits in some tarot packs, corresponding to pentacles in others. • v. **1** make (coins) by stamping metal. ➤ Brit. informal earn (large amounts of money) quickly and easily: *the company was coining it in.* **2** invent or devise (a new word or phrase).
– PHRASES **pay someone back in their own coin** retaliate by similar behaviour. **to coin a phrase** said when introducing a new expression or a variation on a familiar one.
– DERIVATIVES **coiner** n.
– ORIGIN ME: from OFr. *coin* 'wedge, corner, die', *coigner* 'to mint', from L. *cuneus* 'wedge'.

**coinage** • n. **1** coins collectively. ➤ the action or process of producing coins. ➤ a system or type of coins in use. **2** the invention of a new word or phrase. ➤ a newly invented word or phrase.

**coincide** /ˌkəʊɪnˈsʌɪd/ • v. **1** occur at the same time or place. **2** correspond in nature; tally. ➤ be in agreement.
– ORIGIN C18: from med. L. *coincidere*, from *co-* 'together with' + *incidere* 'fall upon or into'.

**coincidence** • n. **1** a remarkable concurrence of events or circumstances without apparent causal connection. **2** correspondence in nature or in time of occurrence. **3** Physics the presence of ionizing particles or other objects in two or more detectors simultaneously, or of two or more signals simultaneously in a circuit.
– DERIVATIVES **coincidental** adj. **coincidentally** adv.

**coincident** • adj. **1** occurring together in space or time. **2** in agreement or harmony.
– DERIVATIVES **coincidently** adv.

**coin-op** • n. a machine operated by the insertion of coins.

**Cointreau** /ˈkwʌntrəʊ/ • n. trademark a colourless orange-flavoured liqueur.
– ORIGIN named after the *Cointreau* family, liqueur producers based in Angers, France.

**coir** /ˈkɔɪə/ • n. fibre from the outer husk of the coconut, used in potting compost and for making ropes and matting.
– ORIGIN C16: from Malayalam *kayaṟu* 'cord, coir'.

**coition** /kəʊˈɪʃ(ə)n/ • n. another term for **COITUS**.
– ORIGIN C16: from L. *coitio(n-)*, from *coire* 'go together'.

**coitus** /ˈkəʊɪtəs/ • n. technical sexual intercourse.
– DERIVATIVES **coital** adj.
– ORIGIN C19: from L., from *coire* 'go together'.

**coitus interruptus** /ˌɪntəˈrʌptəs/ • n. sexual intercourse in which the penis is withdrawn before ejaculation.

**cojones** /kəˈhəʊneɪz/ • pl. n. informal, chiefly N. Amer. **1** a man's testicles. **2** courage; guts.
– ORIGIN from Sp.

**coke**[1] • n. a solid fuel made by heating coal in the ab-

sence of air so that the volatile components are driven off. ➤carbon residue left after the incomplete combustion or distillation of petrol or other fuels. ● **v.** [usu. as noun **coking**] convert (coal) into coke.
– ORIGIN ME (in the sense 'charcoal'): of unknown origin.

**coke**[2] ● **n.** informal term for **COCAINE**.

**Col.** ● **abbrev. 1** Colonel. **2** the Epistle to the Colossians (in biblical references).

**col** ● **n. 1** the lowest point of a ridge or saddle between two peaks. **2** Meteorology a region of slightly elevated pressure between two anticyclones.
– ORIGIN C19: from Fr., lit. 'neck', from L. *collum*.

**col-** ● **prefix** variant spelling of **COM-** assimilated before *l* (as in *collocate, collude*).

**cola** ● **n. 1** a brown carbonated drink that is flavoured with an extract of cola nuts, or with a similar flavouring. **2** (also **kola**) a small evergreen African tree cultivated in the tropics, whose seed (the **cola nut**) contains caffeine. [*Cola acuminata* and related species.]
– ORIGIN from Temne *k'ola* 'cola nut'.

**colander** /'kʌləndə, 'kɒl-/ ● **n.** a perforated bowl used to strain off liquid from food.
– ORIGIN ME: based on L. *colare* 'to strain'.

**co-latitude** ● **n.** Astronomy the difference between a given latitude and 90°.

**colcannon** /kɒl'kanən/ ● **n.** an Irish and Scottish dish of cabbage and potatoes boiled and mashed together.
– ORIGIN C18: from **COLE** + an uncertain second element.

**colchicine** /'kɒltʃɪsiːn, 'kɒlk-/ ● **n.** Chemistry a yellow compound present in the corms of colchicums, used to relieve pain in cases of gout.

**colchicum** /'kɒltʃɪkəm, 'kɒlk-/ ● **n.** (pl. **colchicums**) a plant of a genus that includes the autumn crocuses. [Genus *Colchicum*.] ➤the dried corm or seed of meadow saffron, which is used medicinally.
– ORIGIN from L., from Gk *kolkhikon* 'of Colchis', an ancient region east of the Black Sea, alluding to the skills as a poisoner of Medea of Colchis in classical mythology.

**cold** ● **adj. 1** of or at a low or relatively low temperature. **2** lacking affection or warmth of feeling; unemotional. ➤not affected by emotion; objective. ➤(of a colour) containing pale blue or grey and giving no impression of warmth. **3** (of a scent or trail) no longer fresh and easy to follow: *the trail went cold.* ➤(in children's games) far from finding or guessing what is sought. **4** without preparation or rehearsal; unawares. **5** informal unconscious: *she was out cold.* ● **n. 1** a low temperature; cold weather; a cold environment. **2** a common infection in which the mucous membrane of the nose and throat becomes inflamed, causing running at the nose and sneezing.
– PHRASES **catch a cold** informal encounter trouble or difficulties. **cold comfort** poor or inadequate consolation. **cold feet** loss of nerve or confidence. **the cold light of day** the objective realities of a situation. **the cold shoulder** a show of intentional unfriendliness; rejection. **in cold blood** without feeling or mercy. **leave someone cold** fail to interest or excite someone. **out in the cold** ignored; neglected.
– DERIVATIVES **coldish** adj. **coldly** adv. **coldness** n.
– ORIGIN OE *cald*, of Gmc origin; rel. to L. *gelu* 'frost'.

**cold-blooded** ● **adj. 1** denoting animals whose body temperature varies with that of the environment (e.g. reptiles and fish); poikilothermic. **2** without emotion; deliberately cruel.
– DERIVATIVES **cold-bloodedly** adv. **cold-bloodedness** n.

**cold-call** ● **v.** [usu. as noun **cold-calling**] make an unsolicited visit or telephone call to (someone), in an attempt to sell goods or services.

**cold cathode** ● **n.** Electronics a cathode that emits electrons without being heated.

**cold chisel** ● **n.** a toughened chisel used for cutting metal.

**cold cream** ● **n.** a cosmetic preparation used for cleansing and softening the skin.

**cold cuts** ● **pl. n.** slices of cold cooked meats.

**cold frame** ● **n.** a frame with a glass top in which small plants are grown and protected without artificial heat.

**cold fusion** ● **n.** nuclear fusion supposedly occurring at or close to room temperature.

**cold-hearted** ● **adj.** lacking affection or warmth; unfeeling.
– DERIVATIVES **cold-heartedly** adv. **cold-heartedness** n.

**cold-rolled** ● **adj.** (of metal) having been rolled into sheets while cold, resulting in a smooth, hard finish.
– DERIVATIVES **cold-rolling** n.

**cold-short** ● **adj.** (of a metal) brittle in its cold state.
– ORIGIN C17: from Swed. *kallskör*, from *kall* 'cold' + *skör* 'brittle', later assoc. with **SHORT** in the same sense.

**cold sore** ● **n.** an inflamed blister in or near the mouth, caused by infection with the herpes simplex virus.

**cold storage** ● **n.** the keeping of something in a refrigerator or other cold place for preservation.

**cold store** ● **n.** a large refrigerated room for preserving food stocks at very low temperatures.

**cold sweat** ● **n.** a state of sweating induced by nervousness or illness.

**cold turkey** informal ● **n.** the abrupt and complete cessation of taking a drug to which one is addicted. ➤withdrawal symptoms, typically sweating and nausea, caused by this. ● **adv.** chiefly N. Amer. in a sudden and abrupt manner.

**cold war** ● **n.** (**the cold war**) a state of political hostility existing between the Soviet bloc countries and the Western powers after the Second World War.

**cold wave** ● **n. 1** a spell of cold weather over a wide area. **2** a kind of permanent wave for the hair created by applying chemicals at room temperature.

**cole** ● **n.** chiefly archaic a brassica, especially cabbage, kale, or rape.
– ORIGIN OE *cāwel*, *caul*, from L. *caulis* 'stem, cabbage'; cf. **KALE**.

**colectomy** /kə(ʊ)'lɛktəmi/ ● **n.** (pl. **-ies**) surgical removal of all or part of the colon.

**Coleoptera** /ˌkɒlɪ'ɒpt(ə)rə/ ● **pl. n.** Entomology an order of insects that comprises the beetles (including weevils), forming the largest order of animals on the earth.
– DERIVATIVES **coleopteran** n. & adj. **coleopterous** adj.
– ORIGIN mod. L., from Gk *koleopteros*, from *koleos* 'sheath' + *pteron* 'wing'.

**coleopterist** /ˌkɒlɪ'ɒptərɪst/ ● **n.** a person who studies or collects beetles.

**coleoptile** /ˌkɒlɪ'ɒptʌɪl/ ● **n.** Botany a sheath protecting a young shoot tip in a grass or cereal.
– ORIGIN C19: from Gk *koleon* 'sheath' + *ptilon* 'feather'.

**coleorhiza** /ˌkɒlɪə(ʊ)'rʌɪzə/ ● **n.** (pl. **coleorhizae** /-'rʌɪziː/) Botany a sheath protecting the root of a germinating grass or cereal grain.
– ORIGIN C19: from *koleos* 'sheath' + *rhiza* 'root'.

**coleslaw** ● **n.** a salad dish of shredded raw cabbage, carrots, and other vegetables mixed with mayonnaise.
– ORIGIN C18: from Du. *koolsla*, from *kool* 'cabbage' + *sla* (see **SLAW**).

**cole tit** ● **n.** variant spelling of **COAL TIT**.

**coleus** /'kəʊlɪəs/ ● **n.** a tropical SE Asian plant of the mint family, with brightly coloured variegated leaves. [Genus *Solenostemon* (formerly *Coleus*).]
– ORIGIN mod. L., from Gk *koleos* 'sheath' (because the stamens are joined together, resembling a sheath).

**coley** /'kəʊli/ ● **n.** (pl. same or **-eys**) another term for **SAITHE**.
– ORIGIN 1960s: perh. from **COALFISH**.

**colic** ● **n.** severe pain in the abdomen caused by wind or obstruction in the intestines.
– DERIVATIVES **colicky** adj.
– ORIGIN ME: from OFr. *colique*, from late L. *colicus*, from *colon* (see **COLON**[2]).

**coliform** /'kɒlɪfɔːm/ ● **adj.** Biology belonging to a group of rod-shaped bacteria typified by *E. coli*.
– ORIGIN C20: from mod. L. *coli* 'of the colon' + **-IFORM**.

**coliseum** /ˌkɒlɪ'siːəm/ (also **colosseum**) ● **n.** [in names] a large theatre, cinema, or stadium.
– ORIGIN C19: from med. L., alt. of L. *Colosseum* (the name given to the vast amphitheatre of ancient Rome), neut. of *colosseus* 'gigantic'.

**colitis** /kə'lʌɪtɪs/ ● **n.** Medicine inflammation of the lining of the colon.

**collaborate** /kə'labəreɪt/ ● **v. 1** work jointly on an activity or project. **2** cooperate traitorously with an enemy.
– DERIVATIVES **collaboration** n. **collaborationist** n. & adj. **collaborative** adj. **collaboratively** adv. **collaborator** n.
– ORIGIN C19: from L. *collaborat-*, *collaborare* 'work together'.

**collage** /'kɒlɑːʒ, kə'lɑːʒ/ ● **n. 1** a form of art in which various materials such as photographs and pieces of paper or fabric are arranged and stuck to a backing. **2** a combination or collection of various things.
– DERIVATIVES **collagist** n.
– ORIGIN C20: from Fr., lit. 'gluing'.

**collagen** /'kɒlədʒ(ə)n/ ● **n.** Biochemistry the main structural protein found in animal connective tissue, yielding gelatin when boiled.
– ORIGIN C19: from Fr. *collagène*, from Gk *kolla* 'glue' + Fr. *-gène* (see **-GEN**).

**collapsar** /kə'lapsɑː/ ● **n.** Astronomy an old star that has collapsed under its own gravity to form a white dwarf, neutron star, or black hole.
– ORIGIN C20: from **COLLAPSE**, on the pattern of words such as *pulsar*.

**collapse** ● **v. 1** (of a structure) suddenly fall down or give way. ➤ [usu. as adj. **collapsed**] (of a lung or blood vessel) fall inwards and become flat and empty. **2** (of a person) fall down as a result of physical breakdown. **3** fail suddenly and completely. ● **n. 1** an instance of a structure collapsing. **2** a sudden failure or breakdown.
– ORIGIN C17: from medical L. *collaps-*, *collabi*, from *col-* 'together' + *labi* 'to slip'.

**collapsible** ● **adj.** able to be folded down.
– DERIVATIVES **collapsibility** n.

**collar** ● **n. 1** a band of material around the neck of a shirt or other garment, either upright or turned over. **2** a band put around the neck of a domestic animal, used to restrain or control. **3** a connecting band or pipe in a piece of machinery. **4** Brit. a piece of meat rolled up and tied. ➤ a cut of bacon taken from the neck of a pig. ● **v.** informal seize or apprehend (someone).
– DERIVATIVES **collared** adj. **collarless** adj.
– ORIGIN ME: from OFr. *colier*, from L. *collare* 'band for the neck', from *collum* 'neck'.

**collarbone** ● **n.** either of the pair of bones joining the breastbone to the shoulder blades; the clavicle.

**collard** /'kɒlɑːd/ ● **n.** chiefly dialect or N. Amer. a cabbage of a variety that does not develop a heart.
– ORIGIN C18: reduced form of archaic *colewort*, in the same sense, from **COLE** + **WORT**.

**collared dove** ● **n.** a grey-brown dove with a narrow black band on the neck. [*Streptopelia decaocto.*]

**collate** /kɒ'leɪt/ ● **v. 1** collect and combine (texts or information). ➤ compare and analyse (two or more sources of information). ➤ Printing verify the number and order of (the sheets of a book). **2** appoint (a clergyman) to a benefice.
– DERIVATIVES **collator** n.

**collateral** /kɒ'lat(ə)r(ə)l/ ● **n. 1** something pledged as security for repayment of a loan. **2** a person descended from the same ancestor as another but through a different line. ● **adj. 1** descended from the same stock but by a different line. **2** additional but subordinate; secondary. **3** situated side by side; parallel: *collateral veins.*
– DERIVATIVES **collaterality** n. **collaterally** adv.
– ORIGIN ME: from med. L. *collateralis*, from *col-* 'together with' + *lateralis* (from *latus*, *later-* 'side').

**collateral damage** ● **n.** inadvertent casualties and destruction in civilian areas caused by military operations.

**collateralize** (also **-ise**) ● **v.** provide something as collateral for (a loan).

**collation** /kə'leɪʃ(ə)n/ ● **n. 1** the action of collating. **2** a light informal meal. ➤ (in the Roman Catholic Church) a light meal allowed during a fast.
– ORIGIN ME: via OFr. from L. *collatio(n-)*, from *conferre* (see **CONFER**); sense 2 from a text entitled *Collationes Patrum in Scetica Eremo Commorantium*, from which a reading would be given in Benedictine communities prior to a light meal.

**colleague** ● **n.** a person with whom one works in a profession or business.
– ORIGIN C16: from Fr. *collègue*, from L. *collega* 'partner in office'.

**collect**[1] /kə'lɛkt/ ● **v. 1** bring or gather together. ➤ systematically seek and acquire (items of a particular kind) as a hobby. **2** call for and take away; fetch. ➤ call for and receive (something) as a right or due. **3** (**collect oneself**) regain control of oneself, typically after a shock. **4** archaic conclude; infer. **5** Austral./NZ informal collide with. ● **adv. & adj.** N. Amer. (with reference to a telephone call) to be paid for by the person receiving it.
– ORIGIN ME: from OFr. *collecter* or med. L. *collectare*, from L. *collect-*, *colligere* 'gather together'.

**collect**[2] /'kɒlɛkt, -lɪkt/ ● **n.** (in church use) a short prayer, especially one assigned to a particular day or season.
– ORIGIN ME: from OFr. *collecte*, from L. *collecta* 'gathering', fem. past part. of *colligere* 'gather together'.

**collectable** /kə'lɛktəb(ə)l/ (also **collectible**) ● **adj. 1** worth collecting; of interest to a collector. **2** able to be collected. ● **n.** an item valued and sought by collectors.
– DERIVATIVES **collectability** /-'bɪlɪti/ n.

**collected** ● **adj. 1** not perturbed or distracted. **2** (of works) brought together in one volume or edition.

**collection** ● **n. 1** the action or process of collecting. ➤ a regular removal of mail for dispatch or of refuse for disposal. ➤ an instance of collecting money, as in a church service. **2** a group of things collected or accumulated. **3** (**collections**) Brit. college examinations held at the beginning or end of a term, especially at Oxford University.

**collective** ● **adj.** done by or belonging to all the members of a group. ➤ taken as a whole; aggregate. ● **n.** a cooperative enterprise. ➤ a collective farm.
– DERIVATIVES **collectively** adv. **collectiveness** n. **collectivity** n.

**collective bargaining** ● **n.** negotiation of wages and other conditions of employment by an organized body of employees.

**collective farm** ● **n.** a jointly operated amalgamation of several smallholdings, especially one owned by the state.

**collective noun** ● **n.** Grammar a count noun that denotes a group of individuals (e.g. *assembly, family, crew*).

**collective unconscious** ● **n.** (in Jungian psychology) the part of the unconscious mind which is derived from ancestral memory and experience and is common to all humankind, as distinct from the individual's unconscious.

**collectivism** ● **n. 1** the practice or principle of giving the group priority over each individual in it. **2** the ownership of land and the means of production by the people or the state.
– DERIVATIVES **collectivist** adj. & n. **collectivization** (also **-isation**) n. **collectivize** (also **-ise**) v.

**collector** /kə'lɛktə/ ● **n. 1** a person who collects things of a specified type, professionally or as a hobby. **2** an official who is responsible for collecting money owed. **3** Electronics the region in a bipolar transistor that absorbs charge carriers.

**colleen** /kɒ'liːn, 'kɒliːn/ ● **n.** Irish a girl or young woman.
– ORIGIN C19: from Ir. *cailín*, dimin. of *caile* 'countrywoman'.

**college** ● **n. 1** an educational establishment providing higher education or specialized professional or vocational training. ➤ (in Britain) any of the independent institutions into which some universities are separated. **2** an organized group of professional people with particular aims, duties, and privileges.
– ORIGIN ME: from OFr., from L. *collegium* 'partnership', from *collega* (see **COLLEAGUE**).

**College of Arms** ● **n.** (in the UK) a corporation which officially records and grants armorial bearings.

**college of education** ● **n.** an institution where schoolteachers are trained.

**collegial** /kə'liːdʒɪəl, -dʒ(ə)l/ ● **adj. 1** another term for

**COLLEGIATE** (in sense 1). **2** relating to or involving shared responsibility.
– DERIVATIVES **collegiality** n.

**collegian** /kəˈliːdʒɪən, -dʒ(ə)n/ ● n. a member of a college.

**collegiate** /kəˈliːdʒ(ɪ)ət/ ● adj. **1** belonging to, relating to, or appropriate for a college or for college students. **2** (of a university) composed of different colleges.

**collegiate church** ● n. a church endowed for a chapter of canons but without a bishop's see. ➤ US & Scottish a church or group of churches established under two or more pastors.

**collegium** /kəˈliːdʒɪəm/ ● n. (pl. **collegia** /kəˈliːdʒɪə, -dʒə/) **1** (in full **collegium musicum**) (pl. **collegia musica**) a society of amateur musicians, especially one attached to a German or US university. **2** historical an administrative board in Russia.
– ORIGIN C19: from L., lit. 'association'.

**col legno** /kɒl ˈlɛnjəʊ/ ● adv. Music (with reference to a bowed instrument) played by hitting the strings with the back of the bow.
– ORIGIN Ital., 'with the wood (of the bow)'.

**collenchyma** /kəˈlɛŋkɪmə/ ● n. Botany tissue strengthened by the thickening of cell walls, as in young shoots.
– ORIGIN C19: from Gk *kolla* 'glue' + *enkhuma* 'infusion'.

**Colles' fracture** /ˈkɒlɪs/ ● n. Medicine a fracture of the radius in the wrist with a characteristic backward displacement of the hand.
– ORIGIN C19: named after the Ir. surgeon Abraham *Colles*.

**collet** /ˈkɒlɪt/ ● n. **1** a segmented band put round a shaft and tightened so as to grip it. **2** a small collar in a clock to which the inner end of a balance spring is attached. **3** a flange or socket for setting a gem in jewellery.
– ORIGIN ME: from OFr., dimin. of *col* 'neck', from L. *collum*.

**colliculus** /kəˈlɪkjʊləs/ ● n. (pl. **colliculi** /-lʌɪ, -liː/) Anatomy any of a number of small swellings in the roof of the midbrain, involved in vision and hearing.
– DERIVATIVES **collicular** adj.
– ORIGIN C19: from L., dimin. of *collis* 'hill'.

**collide** ● v. **1** hit by accident when moving. **2** come into conflict or opposition.
– ORIGIN C17: from L. *collidere*, from *col-* 'together' + *laedere* 'to strike'.

**collider** ● n. Physics an accelerator in which two beams of particles are made to collide.

**collie** ● n. (pl. **-ies**) a sheepdog of a breed having a long, pointed nose and thick long hair.
– ORIGIN C17: perh. from **COAL** (the breed orig. being black).

**collier** /ˈkɒlɪə/ ● n. chiefly Brit. **1** a coal miner. **2** a ship carrying coal.
– ORIGIN ME: from **COAL** + **-IER**.

**colliery** ● n. (pl. **-ies**) a coal mine and the buildings and equipment associated with it.

**colligative** /kəˈlɪgətɪv/ ● adj. Chemistry of or relating to the binding together of molecules.
– ORIGIN C20: from L. *colligat-*, *colligare* 'bind together'.

**collimate** /ˈkɒlɪmeɪt/ ● v. **1** make (rays of light or particles) accurately parallel. **2** accurately set the alignment of (an optical or other system).
– DERIVATIVES **collimation** n. **collimator** n.
– ORIGIN C19: from L. *collimare*, an erroneous reading of *collineare* 'align or aim'.

**collinear** /kɒˈlɪnɪə/ ● adj. Geometry (of points) lying in the same straight line.
– DERIVATIVES **collinearity** n.

**collision** ● n. an instance of colliding.
– DERIVATIVES **collisional** adj.
– ORIGIN ME: from late L. *collisio(n-)*, from L. *collidere* (see **COLLIDE**).

**collocation** ● n. **1** Linguistics the habitual juxtaposition of a particular word with another word or words with a frequency greater than chance. **2** the action of placing things together according to some system or order.
– DERIVATIVES **collocate** v.
– ORIGIN ME: from L. *collocatio(n-)*, from *collocare* 'place together'.

**collodion** /kəˈləʊdɪən/ ● n. a syrupy solution of nitrocellulose in a mixture of alcohol and ether, used for coating things, chiefly in surgery and in a former photographic process.
– ORIGIN C19: from Gk *kollōdēs* 'glue-like'.

**collogue** /kɒˈləʊg/ ● v. (**collogues**, **collogued**, **colloguing**) archaic talk confidentially.
– ORIGIN C17: prob. an alt. of obs. *colleague* 'conspire', by assoc. with L. *colloqui* 'to converse'.

**colloid** /ˈkɒlɔɪd/ ● n. a homogeneous non-crystalline substance consisting of large molecules or ultramicroscopic particles of one substance dispersed in a second substance, as in gels, sols, and emulsions. ➤ Anatomy & Medicine a substance of gelatinous consistency.
– DERIVATIVES **colloidal** adj.
– ORIGIN C19: from Gk *kolla* 'glue' + **-OID**.

**collop** /ˈkɒləp/ ● n. dialect & N. Amer. a slice of meat.
– ORIGIN ME: of Scand. origin.

**colloquial** /kəˈləʊkwɪəl/ ● adj. (of language) used in ordinary or familiar conversation; not formal or literary.
– DERIVATIVES **colloquially** adv.
– ORIGIN C18: from L. *colloquium* 'conversation' + **-AL**.

**colloquialism** ● n. a colloquial word or phrase.

**colloquium** /kəˈləʊkwɪəm/ ● n. (pl. **colloquiums** or **colloquia** /-kwɪə/) an academic conference or seminar.
– ORIGIN C16 (denoting a conversation or dialogue): from L., from *colloqui* 'to converse'.

**colloquy** /ˈkɒləkwi/ ● n. (pl. **-ies**) **1** a formal conference or conversation. **2** a gathering for discussion of theological questions.
– ORIGIN ME: from L. *colloquium* 'conversation'.

**collotype** /ˈkɒlətʌɪp/ ● n. a process for making high-quality prints using a sheet of light-sensitive gelatin.
– ORIGIN C19: from Gk *kolla* 'glue' + **TYPE**.

**collude** /kəˈl(j)uːd/ ● v. come to a secret understanding; conspire.
– DERIVATIVES **colluder** n.
– ORIGIN C16: from L. *colludere* 'have a secret agreement', from *col-* 'together' + *ludere* 'to play'.

**collusion** ● n. secret or illegal cooperation in order to cheat or deceive others.
– DERIVATIVES **collusive** adj. **collusively** adv.
– ORIGIN ME: from L. *collusio(n-)*, from *colludere* (see **COLLUDE**).

**collyrium** /kəˈlɪrɪəm/ ● n. (pl. **collyria** /-rɪə/) a kind of dark eyeshadow, used especially in Eastern countries.
– ORIGIN ME: L., from Gk *kollurion* 'poultice'.

**collywobbles** ● pl. n. informal, chiefly humorous stomach pain or queasiness. ➤ intense anxiety.
– ORIGIN C19: fanciful form from **COLIC** and **WOBBLE**.

**Colo.** ● abbrev. Colorado.

**colobus** /ˈkɒləbəs/ ● n. (pl. same) a slender leaf-eating African monkey with silky fur. [Genera *Colobus* and *Procolobus*: several species.]
– DERIVATIVES **colobine** n.
– ORIGIN mod. L., from Gk *kolobos* 'curtailed' (with ref. to its shortened thumbs).

**colocynth** /ˈkɒləsɪnθ/ ● n. a tropical climbing plant with pulpy fruit which yield a bitter purgative drug. [*Citrullus colocynthis*.]
– ORIGIN C16: via L. from Gk *kolokunthis*.

**cologne** /kəˈləʊn/ ● n. eau de cologne or similarly scented toilet water.

**Colombian** /kəˈlɒmbɪən/ ● n. a native or inhabitant of Colombia. ● adj. of or relating to Colombia or its people.

**colon**[1] /ˈkəʊlən/ ● n. **1** a punctuation mark (:) used to precede a list of items, a quotation, or an expansion or explanation. **2** this mark used in various technical and formulaic contexts, for example a statement of proportion between two numbers.
– ORIGIN C16: via L. from Gk *kōlon* 'limb, clause'.

**colon**[2] /ˈkəʊlən, -lɒn/ ● n. Anatomy the main part of the large intestine, which passes from the caecum to the rectum.
– ORIGIN ME: via L. from Gk *kolon*.

**colón** /kɒ'lɒn/ ● **n.** (pl. **colones** /-'lɒnɛz/) the basic monetary unit of Costa Rica and El Salvador, equal to 100 centimos in Costa Rica and 100 centavos in El Salvador.
– ORIGIN from Cristóbal *Colón*, the Sp. name of Christopher Columbus.

**colonel** /'kəːn(ə)l/ ● **n.** a rank of officer in the army and in the US air force, above a lieutenant colonel and below a brigadier or brigadier general.
– DERIVATIVES **colonelcy** n. (pl. **-ies**).
– ORIGIN C16: from obs. Fr. *coronel*, from Ital. *colonnello* 'column of soldiers'.

**colonial** ● **adj.** **1** of, relating to, or characteristic of a colony or colonies. **2** (of architecture or furniture) in the style of the period of the British colonies in America before independence. **3** (of animals or plants) living in colonies. ● **n.** a person who lives in a colony.
– DERIVATIVES **colonially** adv.

**colonialism** ● **n.** the policy or practice of acquiring political control over another country, occupying it with settlers, and exploiting it economically.
– DERIVATIVES **colonialist** n. & adj.

**colonic** /kə'lɒnɪk/ ● **adj.** Anatomy of, relating to, or affecting the colon.

**colonic irrigation** ● **n.** the practice of inserting water via the anus to flush out the colon, used as a therapeutic treatment.

**colonist** ● **n.** a settler in or inhabitant of a colony.

**colonize** (also **-ise**) ● **v.** **1** establish a colony in (a place). ➤establish control over (the indigenous people of a colony). **2** appropriate (a place or domain) for one's own use. **3** Ecology (of a plant or animal) establish itself in (an area).
– DERIVATIVES **colonization** n. **colonizer** n.

**colonnade** /ˌkɒlə'neɪd/ ● **n.** a row of evenly spaced columns supporting a roof or other structure.
– DERIVATIVES **colonnaded** adj.
– ORIGIN C18: from Fr., from *colonne* 'column', from L. *columna*.

**colonoscopy** /ˌkəʊlə'nɒskəpɪ/ ● **n.** (pl. **-ies**) Medicine examination of the colon with a fibre-optic instrument inserted through the anus.

**colony** ● **n.** (pl. **-ies**) **1** a country or area under the political control of another country and occupied by settlers from that country. ➤(**the colonies**) all the foreign places formerly under British political control. ➤(**the colonies**) the thirteen areas on the east coast of North America that gained independence and founded the United States of America. **2** a group of people of one nationality or race living in a foreign place. ➤a group of people separated by occupation or interest: *a nudist colony.* **3** Biology a community of animals or plants of one kind living close together or forming a physically connected structure.
– ORIGIN ME: from L. *colonia* 'settlement, farm', from *colonus* 'settler, farmer', from *colere* 'cultivate'.

**colophon** /'kɒləf(ə)n/ ● **n.** **1** a publisher's emblem or imprint. **2** historical a statement at the end of a book giving information about its authorship and printing.
– ORIGIN C17: via late L. from Gk *kolophōn* 'summit or finishing touch'.

**colophony** /kə'lɒfəni, 'kɒləˌfəʊni/ ● **n.** another term for **ROSIN**.
– ORIGIN ME: from L. *colophonia* (*resina*) '(resin) from *Colophon*', a town in Lydia, Asia Minor.

**color** ● **n.** & **v.** US spelling of **COLOUR**.

**Coloradan** /ˌkɒlə'rɑːd(ə)n/ ● **n.** a native or inhabitant of the US state of Colorado. ● **adj.** of or relating to Colorado.

**Colorado beetle** ● **n.** a yellow- and black-striped beetle, native to America, whose larvae are highly destructive to potato plants. [*Leptinotarsa decemlineata.*]

**coloration** (also **colouration**) ● **n.** **1** arrangement or scheme of colour; colouring. **2** the character or tone of something, especially musical expression.
– ORIGIN C17: from late L. *coloratio(n-)*, from *colorare* 'to colour'.

**coloratura** /ˌkɒlərə'tjʊərə/ ● **n.** elaborate ornamentation of a vocal melody. ➤a soprano skilled in such singing.
– ORIGIN Ital., lit. 'colouring'.

**colorectal** /ˌkəʊləʊ'rɛkt(ə)l/ ● **adj.** relating to or affecting the colon and the rectum.

**colorific** /ˌkʌlə'rɪfɪk, ˌkɒl-/ ● **adj.** rare having much colour.

**colorimeter** /ˌkʌlə'rɪmɪtə, ˌkɒl-/ ● **n.** an instrument for measuring the intensity of colour.
– DERIVATIVES **colorimetric** adj. **colorimetry** n.

**colossal** ● **adj.** **1** extremely large. ➤Sculpture (of a statue) at least twice life size. **2** Architecture (of an order) having more than one storey of columns.
– DERIVATIVES **colossally** adv.
– ORIGIN C18: from Fr., from *colosse*, from L. *colossus* (see **COLOSSUS**).

**colosseum** ● **n.** variant spelling of **COLISEUM**.

**colossus** /kə'lɒsəs/ ● **n.** (pl. **colossi** /-sʌɪ/ or **colossuses**) a person or thing of enormous size, in particular a statue that is much bigger than life size.
– ORIGIN ME: via L. from Gk *kolossos* (applied by Herodotus to the statues of Egyptian temples).

**colostomy** /kə'lɒstəmi/ ● **n.** (pl. **-ies**) a surgical operation in which the colon is shortened to remove a damaged part and the cut end diverted to an opening in the abdominal wall.
– ORIGIN C19: from **COLON**[2] + Gk *stoma* 'mouth'.

**colostrum** /kə'lɒstrəm/ ● **n.** the first secretion from the mammary glands after giving birth, rich in antibodies.
– ORIGIN C16: from L.

**colour** (US **color**) ● **n.** **1** the property possessed by an object of producing different sensations on the eye as a result of the way it reflects or emits light. ➤one, or any mixture, of the constituents into which light can be separated in a spectrum or rainbow. ➤the use of all colours, not only black and white, in photography or television. ➤Heraldry any of the major conventional colours used in coats of arms (gules, vert, sable, azure, purpure). ➤Snooker any of the balls other than the white cue ball and the reds. **2** pigmentation of the skin, especially as an indication of someone's race. **3** redness of the complexion, as indicating health or an emotion such as anger. **4** interest, excitement, and vitality: *a town full of colour and character.* **5** (**colours**) chiefly Brit. an item of a particular colour worn to identify or distinguish, in particular the clothes worn by a jockey or the members of sports team. ➤a badge or cap awarded to a pupil representing a school in sport. ➤the flag of a regiment or ship. **6** Physics a property of quarks which can take three values designated blue, green, and red. ● **v.** **1** give a colour to. **2** show embarrassment by becoming red; blush. **3** influence, especially in a negative way; distort: *the experiences had coloured her whole existence.*
– PHRASES **sail under false colours** disguise one's true nature or intentions. **show one's true colours** reveal one's real character or intentions, especially when these are disreputable. **under colour of** under the pretext of.
– ORIGIN ME: from OFr. *colour* (n.), *colourer* (v.), from L. *color* (n.), *colorare* (v.).

**colourable** (US **colorable**) ● **adj.** **1** apparently correct or justified. ➤counterfeit. **2** capable of being coloured.

**colourant** (US **colorant**) ● **n.** a dye or pigment used to colour something.

**colouration** ● **n.** variant spelling of **COLORATION**.

**colour-blind** ● **adj.** unable to distinguish certain colours.
– DERIVATIVES **colour blindness** n.

**colour code** ● **n.** a system of marking things with different colours as a means of identification. ● **v.** (**colour-code**) mark using a colour code.

**coloured** (US **colored**) ● **adj.** **1** having a colour or colours. **2** (also **Coloured**) wholly or partly of non-white descent (now usually offensive, except in South African use). ➤S. African of mixed ethnic origin. ● **n.** **1** (also **Coloured**) dated or offensive a person who is wholly or partly of non-white descent. ➤S. African an Afrikaans- or English-speaking person of mixed descent. **2** (**coloureds**) clothes, sheets, etc. that are any colour but white.

**colour-fast** ● **adj.** dyed in colours that will not fade or be

washed out.
– DERIVATIVES **colour fastness** n.

**colourful** (US **colorful**) • adj. **1** having many or varied colours. **2** lively and exciting. ➤(of language) vulgar or rude.
– DERIVATIVES **colourfully** adv. **colourfulness** n.

**colouring** (US **coloring**) • n. **1** the process or art of applying colour. **2** visual appearance with regard to colour. ➤the natural hues of a person's skin, hair, and eyes. **3** a substance used to colour something, especially food.

**colourist** (US **colorist**) • n. an artist or designer who uses colour in a special or skilful way.

**colouristic** (US **coloristic**) • adj. **1** showing or relating to a special use of colour. **2** having or showing a variety of musical expression.
– DERIVATIVES **colouristically** adv.

**colourless** (US **colorless**) • adj. **1** without colour. **2** lacking character or interest; dull.
– DERIVATIVES **colourlessly** adv.

**colour scheme** • n. an arrangement or combination of colours.

**colour sergeant** • n. a rank of non-commissioned officer in the Royal Marines, above sergeant and below warrant officer.
– ORIGIN with ref. to the sergeant's responsibility for carrying one of the regiment's colours in a guard of honour.

**colour supplement** • n. Brit. a magazine printed in colour and issued with a newspaper.

**colour temperature** • n. another term for **EFFECTIVE TEMPERATURE**.

**colourway** (US **colorway**) • n. any of a range of combinations of colours in which something is available.

**colporteur** /ˈkɒl,pɔːtə, ˌkɒlpɔːˈtəː/ • n. a person who sells or distributes books, newspapers, or religious material.
– DERIVATIVES **colportage** /ˈkɒl,pɔːtɪdʒ/ n.
– ORIGIN C18: Fr., from *colporter*, prob. an alt. of *comporter*, from L. *comportare* 'carry with one'.

**colposcope** /ˈkɒlpəskəʊp/ • n. a surgical instrument used to examine the vagina and the cervix of the womb.
– DERIVATIVES **colposcopy** /kɒlˈpɒskəpi/ n.
– ORIGIN C20: from Gk *kolpos* 'womb' + **-SCOPE**.

**colt** /kəʊlt/ • n. **1** a young uncastrated male horse, in particular one less than four years old. **2** a member of a junior sports team.
– ORIGIN OE; perh. rel. to Swed. *kult*, applied to boys or half-grown animals.

**colter** • n. US spelling of **COULTER**.

**coltish** • adj. energetic but awkward in one's movements or behaviour.
– DERIVATIVES **coltishly** adv. **coltishness** n.

**coltsfoot** • n. (pl. **coltsfoots**) a plant of the daisy family, with yellow flowers and large leaves. [*Tussilago farfara*.]

**colubrid** /ˈkɒljʊbrɪd/ • n. Zoology a snake of a very large family (Colubridae) which includes the majority of harmless species, such as grass snakes.

**colubrine** /ˈkɒljʊbrʌɪn/ • adj. of or resembling a snake.
– ORIGIN C16: from L. *colubrinus*, from *coluber* 'snake'.

**colugo** /kəˈluːgəʊ/ • n. (pl. **-os**) another term for **FLYING LEMUR**.
– ORIGIN C18: of unknown origin.

**columbarium** /ˌkɒl(ə)mˈbɛːrɪəm/ • n. (pl. **columbaria**) a room or building with niches for funeral urns to be stored.
– ORIGIN C18: from L., lit. 'pigeon house'.

**columbine** /ˈkɒl(ə)mbʌɪn/ • n. a plant with long-spurred, typically purplish-blue flowers. [*Aquilegia vulgaris* and related species.]
– ORIGIN ME: from OFr. *colombine*, ult. from L. *columba* 'dove' (from the supposed resemblance of the flower to a cluster of five doves).

**columbite** /kəˈlʌmbʌɪt/ • n. a black mineral consisting of an oxide of iron, manganese, niobium, and tantalum.
– ORIGIN C19: from **COLUMBIUM** + **-ITE**[1].

**columbium** /kəˈlʌmbɪəm/ • n. old-fashioned term for **NIOBIUM**.
– ORIGIN C19: mod. L., from *Columbia*, a poetic name for America from the name of Christopher *Columbus*.

**columella** /ˌkɒljʊˈmɛlə/ • n. (pl. **columellae** /-liː/) **1** Zoology the central pillar or axis of a spiral structure such as a shell. **2** Botany the axis of the spore-producing body of some lower plants.
– DERIVATIVES **columellar** adj.
– ORIGIN C16: from L., 'small column'.

**column** • n. **1** an upright pillar supporting an arch or other structure or standing alone as a monument. ➤an upright shaft used for controlling a machine. **2** a vertical division of a page or text. ➤a regular section of a newspaper or magazine on a particular subject or by a particular person. **3** a line of people or vehicles moving in the same direction. ➤Military a narrow-fronted deep formation of troops in successive lines.
– DERIVATIVES **columnar** adj. **columned** adj.
– ORIGIN ME: partly from OFr. *columpne*, reinforced by its source, L. *columna* 'pillar'.

**columnated** /ˈkɒl(ə)mneɪtɪd/ • adj. supported on or having columns.

**columnist** /ˈkɒl(ə)m(n)ɪst/ • n. a journalist who writes a column in a newspaper or magazine.

**colure** /kəˈljʊə/ • n. Astronomy either of two great circles intersecting at right angles at the celestial poles and passing through the ecliptic at either the equinoxes or the solstices.
– ORIGIN ME: from late L. *coluri* (pl.), from Gk *kolourai* (*grammai*) 'truncated (lines)', so named because the lower part is permanently cut off from view.

**coly** /ˈkəʊli/ • n. (pl. **-ies**) another term for **MOUSEBIRD**.
– ORIGIN C19: from mod. L. *Colius*, from Gk *kolios*, denoting a type of woodpecker.

**colza** /ˈkɒlzə/ • n. another term for **RAPE**[2].
– ORIGIN C18: from Walloon Fr. *kolza*, from Low Ger. *kōlsāt*, Du. *koolzaad*, from *kool* 'cole' + *zaad* 'seed'.

**COM** • abbrev. computer output on microfilm or microfiche.

**com-** (also **co-**, **col-**, **con-**, or **cor-**) • prefix with; together; jointly; altogether: *combine*.
– ORIGIN from L. *cum* 'with'.

**coma**[1] /ˈkəʊmə/ • n. a state of prolonged deep unconsciousness, caused especially by severe injury or illness.
– ORIGIN C17: mod. L., from Gk *kōma* 'deep sleep'.

**coma**[2] /ˈkəʊmə/ • n. (pl. **comae** /-miː/) **1** Astronomy a diffuse cloud of gas and dust surrounding the nucleus of a comet. **2** Optics aberration which causes an off-axis image to be flared like a comet.
– ORIGIN C17: via L. from Gk *komē* 'hair of the head'.

**Comanche** /kəˈmantʃi/ • n. (pl. same or **Comanches**) **1** a member of an American Indian people of the south-western US. **2** the Uto-Aztecan language of this people.
– ORIGIN Sp., from Comanche.

**comatose** /ˈkəʊmətəʊs, -z/ • adj. of or in a state of coma. ➤humorous extremely tired or lethargic.

**comb** • n. **1** an article with a row of narrow teeth, used for untangling or arranging the hair. ➤a short curved comb worn by women to hold the hair in place. **2** a device for separating and dressing textile fibres. ➤Austral./NZ the lower, fixed cutting piece of a sheep-shearing machine. **3** the red fleshy crest on the head of a domestic fowl, especially a cock. **4** a honeycomb. • v. **1** untangle or arrange (the hair) by drawing a comb through it. **2** prepare (wool, flax, or cotton) for manufacture with a comb. **3** search carefully and systematically.
– ORIGIN OE *camb*, of Gmc origin.

**combat** • n. fighting, especially between armed forces. • v. (**combated** or **combatted**, **combating** or **combatting**) **1** take action to reduce or prevent (something bad or undesirable). **2** archaic engage in a fight with.
– ORIGIN C16: from Fr. *combattre*, from late L. *combattere*, from *com-* 'together with' + *battere*, var. of L. *batuere* 'to fight'.

**combatant** /ˈkɒmbət(ə)nt, ˈkʌm-/ • n. a person or nation engaged in fighting during a war. • adj. engaged in fighting during a war.

**combat fatigue** • n. **1** more recent term for **SHELL**

**SHOCK**. **2** (**combat fatigues**) uniform worn by soldiers in combat.

**combative** /'kɒmbətɪv, 'kʌm-/ ● **adj.** ready or eager to fight or argue.
– DERIVATIVES **combatively** adv. **combativeness** n.

**combat trousers** ● **pl. n.** loose trousers with large patch pockets halfway down each leg, typically made of hard-wearing cotton.

**comb-back** ● **n.** a high-backed Windsor chair with a straight top rail.

**combe** /ku:m/ (also **coomb** or **coombe**) ● **n.** Brit. a short valley or hollow on a hillside or coastline, especially in southern England. ➤ Geology a dry valley in a limestone or chalk escarpment.
– ORIGIN OE *cumb*, of Celtic origin, rel. to **CWM**.

**comber**[1] /'kəʊmə/ ● **n. 1** a long curling sea wave. **2** a person or machine that combs cotton or wool.

**comber**[2] /'kɒmbə/ ● **n.** a small coastal sea bass. [*Serranus cabrilla*.]
– ORIGIN C18: of unknown origin.

**combi** ● **n.** a machine or appliance with two or more functions.

**combination** ● **n. 1** the action of combining two or more different things. **2** a union in which the component elements are individually distinct. **3** Mathematics a group of things chosen from a larger number without regard to their arrangement. **4** a sequence of numbers or letters used to open a combination lock. **5** (**combinations**) dated a single undergarment covering the body and legs.
– DERIVATIVES **combinational** adj. **combinative** adj. **combinatory** adj.

**combination lock** ● **n.** a lock that is opened by rotating a set of dials, marked with letters or numbers, to show a specific sequence.

**combination therapy** ● **n.** treatment in which a patient is given two or more drugs for one disease.

**combinatorial** /ˌkɒmbɪnə'tɔːrɪəl/ ● **adj.** Mathematics of or relating to combinations of items.
– DERIVATIVES **combinatorially** adv. **combinatorics** pl. n.

**combine**[1] ● **v.** /kəm'bʌɪn/ unite; merge. ➤ Chemistry unite to form a compound. ● **n.** /'kɒmbʌɪn/ a group of people or companies acting together for a commercial purpose.
– DERIVATIVES **combinable** adj. **combiner** n.
– ORIGIN ME: from OFr. *combiner* or late L. *combinare* 'join two by two', from *com-* 'together' + L. *bini* 'two together'.

**combine**[2] /'kɒmbʌɪn/ ● **v.** harvest (a crop) with a combine harvester. ● **n.** a combine harvester.

**combine harvester** ● **n.** a machine that reaps, threshes, and cleans a cereal crop in one operation.

**combing wool** ● **n.** long-stapled wool with straight, parallel fibres, suitable for combing and making into high-quality fabrics. Compare with **CARDING WOOL**.

**combining form** ● **n.** Grammar a form of a word normally used in compounds in combination with another element to form a word (e.g. *bio-* 'life' in *biology*).

**comb jelly** ● **n.** a marine animal with a jellyfish-like body bearing rows of fused cilia for propulsion. [Phylum Ctenophora.]

**combo** ● **n.** (pl. **-os**) informal **1** a small jazz, rock, or pop band. **2** chiefly N. Amer. a combination. ➤ a guitar amplifier with an integral speaker rather than a separate one.

**combust** /kəm'bʌst/ ● **v.** consume or be consumed by fire.
– DERIVATIVES **combustible** adj. & n.
– ORIGIN C15 (earlier (ME) as *combustion*): from obs. *combust* 'burnt', from L. *combust-*, *comburere* 'burn up'.

**combustion** ● **n.** the process of burning. ➤ Chemistry rapid chemical combination with oxygen, involving the production of heat and light.
– DERIVATIVES **combustive** adj.

**combustion chamber** ● **n.** an enclosed space in which combustion takes place, especially in an engine or furnace.

**come** ● **v.** (past **came**; past part. **come**) **1** move or travel towards or into a place thought of as near or familiar to the speaker. ➤ arrive. ➤ (of a thing) reach or extend to a specified point. ➤ join in a specified activity: *do you want to come fishing?* ➤ (**come along/on**) make progress; develop. ➤ [as adj. **coming**] likely to be important or successful in the future: *a coming man.* ➤ said to correct, reassure, or urge on someone. **2** occur; happen. ➤ (**come across** or chiefly Brit. **over** or US **off**) give a specified impression. **3** occupy or achieve a specified position in space, order, or priority: *she came second.* **4** pass into a specified state, especially one of separation: *his shirt had come undone.* ➤ (**come to/into**) reach or be brought to a specified situation. **5** be sold or available in a specified form. **6** informal have an orgasm. ● **prep.** informal when a specified time is reached or event happens. ● **n.** informal semen ejaculated at an orgasm.
– PHRASES **come again?** informal used to ask someone to repeat or explain something they have said. **come off it** informal said when vigorously expressing disbelief. **come the ——** informal play the part of; behave like: *don't come the innocent with me.* **come to nothing** have no significant or successful result. **come to pass** poetic/literary happen. **come to that** informal in fact. **come to think of it** on reflection. **come what may** no matter what happens. **have it coming (to one)** informal be due for retribution. **how come?** informal said when asking how or why something happened. **not know if one is coming or going** informal be confused, especially through being very busy. **to come** in the future.
– PHRASAL VERBS **come about 1** happen; take place. **2** (of a ship) change direction. **come across 1** meet or find by chance. **2** informal hand over what is wanted. **come around** see *come round*. **come at** launch oneself at; attack. **come away** be left with a specified feeling or result. **come back** chiefly N. Amer. reply or respond, especially vigorously. **come before** be dealt with by (a judge or court). **come by** manage to acquire or obtain. **come down on 1** criticize or punish harshly. **2** reach a decision or recommendation in favour of one side or another. **come down to** be dependent on (a factor). **come for** launch oneself at in order to attack. **come forward** volunteer for a task or to give evidence. **come from** originate in; have as a source or place of birth. **come in 1** have a useful role or function. **2** (of money) be earned or received regularly. **3** join others in speaking or playing music. **4** (of the tide) rise; advance to high tide. **come in for** receive (a reaction), typically a negative one. **come into** inherit (money or property). **come of 1** result from. **2** be descended from. **come off 1** succeed; be accomplished. ➤ fare in a specified way. **2** become detached. **3** Brit. informal have an orgasm. **come on 1** (of a state or condition) start to arrive or happen. **2** (also **come upon**) meet or find by chance. **3** said to encourage or correct someone or hurry them up. **come on to** informal make sexual advances towards. **come out 1** (of a fact) emerge; become known. ➤ happen as a result. ➤ (of a photograph) be produced satisfactorily or in a specified way. ➤ (of the result of a calculation or measurement) emerge at a specified figure. ➤ (of patience or a similar card game) be played to a finish with all cards dealt with. **2** (of a book or other work) be released or published. **3** declare oneself as being for or against something. **4** achieve a specified placing in an examination or contest. ➤ acquit oneself in a specified way. **5** (of a stain) be removed or able to be removed. **6** Brit. go on strike. **7** informal openly declare that one is homosexual. **8** Brit. dated (of a young upper-class woman) make one's debut in society. **come out in** Brit. (of a person's skin) break out in (spots or a similar condition). **come out with** say in a sudden, rude, or incautious way. **come over 1** (of a feeling) begin to affect. ➤ Brit. informal suddenly start to feel a specified way. **2** change to another side or point of view. **come round** chiefly Brit. (chiefly US also **come around**) **1** recover consciousness. **2** be converted to another person's opinion. **3** (of a date or regular occurrence) recur; be imminent again. **come through 1** succeed in surviving or dealing with. **2** (of a message) be sent and received. ➤ (of an official decree) be processed and notified. **come to 1** recover consciousness. **2** (of an expense) reach in total; amount to. **3** (of a ship) come to a stop. **come under 1** be classified as or among. **2** be subject to. **come up** (of a situation or problem) occur or present itself, especially

unexpectedly. ➤(of a time or event) approach or draw near. **come up against** be faced with or opposed by. **come up with** produce (something), especially when pressured or challenged. **come upon 1** attack by surprise. **2** see ***come on*** (sense 2).
– ORIGIN OE *cuman*, of Gmc origin.

**come-along** ● **n.** N. Amer. informal a hand-operated winch.

**comeback** ● **n. 1** a return to prominence or fashionability. **2** informal a quick reply to a critical remark. ➤opportunity to seek redress.

**comedian** ● **n.** (fem. **comedienne**) an entertainer whose act is designed to arouse laughter. ➤a comic playwright.

**comedo** /ˈkɒmɪdəʊ, kəˈmiːdəʊ/ ● **n.** (pl. **comedones** /-ˈdəʊniːz/) technical term for **BLACKHEAD** (in sense 1).
– ORIGIN C19: from L., lit. 'glutton' (a former name for parasitic worms, later referring to worm-like matter squeezed from a blackhead).

**comedogenic** /ˌkɒmɪdə(ʊ)ˈdʒɛnɪk/ ● **adj.** tending to block the pores of the skin and thereby cause blackheads.

**comedown** ● **n.** informal **1** a loss of status or importance. **2** a feeling of disappointment or depression. ➤a lessening of the sensations generated by a narcotic drug as its effects wear off.

**comedy** ● **n.** (pl. **-ies**) **1** entertainment consisting of jokes and sketches intended to make an audience laugh. ➤a film, play, or programme intended to arouse laughter. **2** a play with a humorous or satirical tone, in which the characters ultimately triumph over adversity.
– DERIVATIVES **comedic** /kəˈmiːdɪk, -ˈmɛ-/ adj.
– ORIGIN ME: from OFr. *comedie*, via L. from Gk *kōmōidia*, based on *kōmos* 'revel' + *aoidos* 'singer'.

**comedy of manners** ● **n.** a play, novel, or film that gives a satirical portrayal of behaviour in a particular social group.

**come-hither** ● **adj.** informal flirtatious or coquettish: *a come-hither look.*

**comely** /ˈkʌmli/ ● **adj.** (**-ier**, **-iest**) **1** archaic or humorous (typically of a woman) pleasant to look at; attractive. **2** archaic agreeable; suitable.
– DERIVATIVES **comeliness** n.
– ORIGIN ME: prob. shortened from *becomely* 'fitting, becoming', from **BECOME**.

**come-on** ● **n.** informal **1** a gesture or remark intended to attract someone sexually. **2** a marketing ploy, such as a free or cheap offer.

**comer** ● **n. 1** [with adj.] a person who arrives. **2** N. Amer. informal a person or thing likely to succeed.

**comestible** /kəˈmɛstɪb(ə)l/ formal or humorous ● **n.** an item of food. ● **adj.** edible.
– ORIGIN C15: from OFr., from med. L. *comestibilis*, from L. *comest-*, *comedere* 'eat up'.

**comet** /ˈkɒmɪt/ ● **n.** a celestial object which consists of a nucleus of ice and dust and, when near the sun, a diffuse tail, and typically follows a highly eccentric orbit around the sun.
– DERIVATIVES **cometary** adj.
– ORIGIN OE, from L. *cometa*, from Gk *komētēs* 'long-haired (star)', from *komē* 'hair'; reinforced by OFr. *comete*.

**comeuppance** ● **n.** informal a punishment or fate that someone deserves.

**comfit** /ˈkʌmfɪt/ ● **n.** archaic a sweet consisting of a nut, seed, or other centre coated in sugar.
– ORIGIN ME: from OFr. *confit*, from L. *confect-*, *conficere* (see **CONFECT**).

**comfort** ● **n. 1** a state of physical ease and freedom from pain or constraint. ➤(**comforts**) things that contribute to comfort. ➤prosperity and a pleasant lifestyle. **2** consolation for grief or anxiety. ➤a person or thing that gives such consolation. **3** US dialect a warm quilt. ● **v.** cause to feel less unhappy; console.
– DERIVATIVES **comforting** adj. **comfortingly** adv. **comfortless** adj.
– ORIGIN ME: from OFr. *confort* (n.), *conforter* (v.), from late L. *confortare* 'strengthen'.

**comfortable** ● **adj. 1** providing or enjoying physical comfort. ➤relaxed and free from constraint. **2** free from financial worry. **3** (of a victory) with a wide margin. ● **n.** US dialect a warm quilt.
– DERIVATIVES **comfortableness** n. **comfortably** adv.

**comforter** ● **n. 1** a person or thing that provides consolation. ➤Brit. a baby's dummy. **2** dated a woollen scarf. **3** N. Amer. a warm quilt.

**comfort station** ● **n.** N. Amer. euphemistic a public toilet.

**comfrey** /ˈkʌmfri/ ● **n.** (pl. **-eys**) a plant with large hairy leaves and clusters of purplish or white bell-shaped flowers. [*Symphytum officinale* and related species.]
– ORIGIN ME: from Anglo-Norman Fr. *cumfirie*, based on L. *conferva*, from *confervere* 'heal' (referring to the plant's medicinal use).

**comfy** ● **adj.** (**-ier**, **-iest**) informal comfortable.
– DERIVATIVES **comfily** adv. **comfiness** n.

**comic** ● **adj.** causing or meant to cause laughter. ➤relating to or in the style of comedy. ● **n. 1** a comedian. **2** a children's periodical containing comic strips. ➤(**comics**) N. Amer. comic strips.
– ORIGIN C16: via L. from Gk *kōmikos*, from *kōmos* 'revel'.

**comical** ● **adj.** amusing.
– DERIVATIVES **comicality** n. (archaic). **comically** adv.

**Comice** /ˈkɒmɪs/ ● **n.** a large yellow dessert pear of a late-fruiting variety that is cultivated commercially.
– ORIGIN C19: from Fr., lit. 'association, cooperative', referring to the *Comice Horticole* of Angers, France.

**comic opera** ● **n.** an opera that portrays humorous situations and characters, with much spoken dialogue.

**comic relief** ● **n.** humorous content in a dramatic or literary work which offsets more serious portions.

**comic strip** ● **n.** a sequence of drawings in boxes that tell an amusing story.

**COMINT** ● **abbrev.** communications intelligence.

**comital** /ˈkɒmɪt(ə)l/ ● **adj.** chiefly historical of or relating to a count or earl.
– ORIGIN C19: from med. L. *comitalis*, from *comes*, *comit-* 'a count'.

**comity** /ˈkɒmɪti/ ● **n.** (pl. **-ies**) **1** an association of nations for their mutual benefit. ➤(also **comity of nations**) the mutual recognition by nations of the laws and customs of others. **2** formal courtesy and considerate behaviour towards others.
– ORIGIN C16: from L. *comitas*, from *comis* 'courteous'.

**comm** (also **comms**) ● **n.** communication, especially to and from a computer.

**comma** ● **n. 1** a punctuation mark (,) indicating a pause between parts of a sentence or separating items in a list. **2** Music a minute interval or difference of pitch. **3** a widespread butterfly that has orange and brown wings and a white comma-shaped mark on the underside of the hindwing. [*Polygonia c-album.*]
– ORIGIN C16: via L. from Gk *komma* 'piece cut off, short clause', from *koptein* 'cut'.

**command** ● **v. 1** give an authoritative or peremptory order. ➤Military be in charge of (a unit). ➤[as adj. **commanding**] indicating or expressing authority; imposing. ➤[as adj. **commanding**] possessing or giving superior strength: *a commanding lead.* ➤archaic control or restrain (oneself or one's feelings). **2** dominate (a strategic position) from a superior height. **3** be in a position to receive (something such as respect). ● **n. 1** an authoritative order. ➤authority, especially over armed forces: *the officer in command.* ➤a group of officers exercising control over a particular group or operation. ➤a body of troops or a district under the control of a particular officer. **2** the ability to use or control something: *his command of English.* **3** Computing an instruction causing a computer to perform one of its basic functions.
– DERIVATIVES **commandingly** adv.
– ORIGIN ME: from OFr. *comander*, from late L. *commandare*, from *com-* (expressing intensive force) + *mandare* 'commit, command'.

**commandant** /ˌkɒmənˈdant, ˈkɒmənˌdant, -dɑːnt/ ● **n.** an officer in charge of a particular force or institution.

**command economy** ● **n.** another term for **PLANNED ECONOMY**.

**commandeer** /ˌkɒmənˈdɪə/ ● **v.** officially take possession or control of for military purposes. ➤seize for one's own purposes.

– ORIGIN C19: from Afrik. *kommandeer*, from Du. *commanderen*, from Fr. *commander* 'command'.

**commander** ● n. **1** a person in authority, especially in a military context. ➤a rank of naval officer, above lieutenant commander and below captain. ➤an officer in charge of a Metropolitan Police district in London. **2** a member of a higher class in some orders of knighthood.

– DERIVATIVES **commandership** n.

**commander-in-chief** ● n. (pl. **commanders-in-chief**) an officer in charge of all of the armed forces of a country, or a major subdivision of them.

**Commander of the Faithful** ● n. one of the titles of a caliph.

**command language** ● n. Computing a source language composed chiefly of a set of commands or operators, used especially for communicating with the operating system of a computer.

**commandment** ● n. a divine rule, especially one of the Ten Commandments.

**command module** ● n. the detachable control compartment of a manned spacecraft.

**commando** ● n. (pl. **-os**) a soldier specially trained for carrying out raids. ➤a unit of such troops.

– ORIGIN C18: from Port. (earlier form of *comando*), from *commandar* 'to command'.

**commando knife** ● n. a long, slender knife suitable for hand-to-hand combat.

**Command Paper** ● n. (in the UK) a document laid before Parliament by order of the Crown, though in practice by the government.

**command performance** ● n. a presentation of a play, concert, or film at the request of royalty.

**comme ci, comme ça** /kɒm ˌsiː kɒm ˈsɑː, French kɔm si kɔm sa/ ● adv. neither very good nor very bad.

– ORIGIN Fr., lit. 'like this, like that'.

**commedia dell'arte** /kɒˈmeɪdɪə dɛlˈɑːteɪ, Italian komˈmɛdja delˈlarte/ ● n. an improvised kind of popular comedy in Italian theatres in the 16th–18th centuries, based on stock characters.

– ORIGIN Ital., 'comedy of art'.

**comme il faut** /ˌkɒm iːl ˈfəʊ, French kɔm il fo/ ● adj. correct in behaviour or etiquette.

– ORIGIN Fr., lit. 'as is necessary'.

**commemorate** ● v. honour the memory of as a mark of respect, especially with a ceremony or memorial.

– DERIVATIVES **commemoration** n. **commemorative** adj. **commemorator** n.

– ORIGIN C16 (earlier (ME) as *commemoration*): from L. *commemorat-*, *commemorare* 'bring to remembrance'.

**commence** ● v. begin.

– ORIGIN ME: from OFr. *commencier*, *comencier*, based on L. *com-* (expressing intensive force) + *initiare* 'begin'.

**commencement** ● n. **1** the beginning of something. **2** N. Amer. a ceremony in which degrees or diplomas are conferred.

**commend** ● v. **1** praise formally or officially. **2** present as suitable or good; recommend. **3** (**commend someone/thing to**) archaic or formal entrust someone or something to. ➤pass on someone's good wishes to.

– DERIVATIVES **commendation** n. **commendatory** adj.

– ORIGIN ME: from L. *commendare*, from *com-* (expressing intensive force) + *mandare* 'commit, entrust'.

**commendable** ● adj. deserving praise.

– DERIVATIVES **commendably** adv.

**commensal** /kəˈmɛns(ə)l/ Biology ● adj. relating to or denoting an association between two organisms in which one benefits and the other derives neither benefit nor harm. ● n. a commensal organism, such as many bacteria.

– DERIVATIVES **commensalism** n. **commensality** /kɒmənˈsalɪti/ n.

– ORIGIN C19: from med. L. *commensalis*, from *com-* 'sharing' + *mensa* 'a table'.

**commensurable** /kəˈmɛnʃ(ə)rəb(ə)l, -sjə-/ ● adj. **1** measurable by the same standard. **2** (**commensurable to**) proportionate to. **3** Mathematics (of numbers) in a ratio equal to a ratio of integers.

– DERIVATIVES **commensurability** n. **commensurably** adv.

– ORIGIN C16: from late L. *commensurabilis*, from *com-* 'together' + *mensurabilis*, from *mensurare* 'to measure'.

**commensurate** /kəˈmɛnʃ(ə)rət, -sjə-/ ● adj. corresponding in size or degree; in proportion.

– DERIVATIVES **commensurately** adv.

– ORIGIN C17: from late L. *commensuratus*, from *com-* 'together' + *mensurat-*, *mensurare* 'to measure'.

**comment** ● n. **1** a remark expressing an opinion or reaction. ➤discussion, especially of a critical nature, of an issue or event. ➤an explanatory note in a book or other written text. **2** archaic a written explanation or commentary. ● v. express an opinion or reaction.

– DERIVATIVES **commenter** n.

– ORIGIN ME: from L. *commentum* 'contrivance' (in late L. also 'interpretation'), neut. past part. of *comminisci* 'devise'.

**commentary** ● n. (pl. **-ies**) **1** the expression of opinions or offering of explanations about an event or situation. ➤a set of explanatory or critical notes on a text. **2** a descriptive spoken account (especially on radio or television) of a sports match or other event as it happens.

**commentate** ● v. provide a commentary on a sports match or other event.

**commentator** ● n. **1** a person who comments on events or texts, especially in the media. **2** a person who provides a commentary on a sports match or other event.

**commerce** ● n. **1** the activity of buying and selling, especially on a large scale. **2** dated social dealings between people. **3** archaic sexual intercourse.

– ORIGIN C16: from Fr., or from L. *commercium* 'trade, trading', based on *merx*, *merc-* 'merchandise'.

**commercial** ● adj. **1** concerned with or engaged in commerce. **2** making or intended to make a profit. **3** (of television or radio) funded by the revenue from broadcast advertisements. **4** (of chemicals) supplied in bulk and not of the highest purity. ● n. **1** a television or radio advertisement. **2** Brit. dated a travelling sales representative.

– DERIVATIVES **commerciality** n. **commercially** adv.

**commercial art** ● n. art used in advertising and selling.

**commercial bank** ● n. a bank that offers services to the general public and to companies.

**commercial bill** ● n. a bill of exchange issued by a commercial organization to raise money for short-term needs.

**commercial break** ● n. an interruption in a radio or television broadcast for advertisements.

**commercialism** ● n. emphasis on the maximizing of profit.

**commercialize** (also **-ise**) ● v. manage or exploit in a way designed to make a profit.

– DERIVATIVES **commercialization** n.

**commercial paper** ● n. short-term unsecured promissory notes issued by companies.

**commercial traveller** ● n. Brit. dated a travelling sales representative.

**commercial vehicle** ● n. a vehicle used for carrying goods or fare-paying passengers.

**commère** /ˈkɒmɛː/ ● n. Brit. a female compère.

**Commie** ● n. (pl. **-ies**) informal, derogatory a communist.

**commination** /ˌkɒmɪˈneɪʃ(ə)n/ ● n. the action of threatening divine vengeance. ➤the recital of divine threats against sinners in the Anglican Liturgy for Ash Wednesday.

– ORIGIN ME: from L. *comminatio(n-)*, from *comminari*, from *com-* (expressing intensive force) + *minari* 'threaten'.

**comminatory** /ˈkɒmɪnəˌt(ə)ri/ ● adj. rare threatening, punitive, or vengeful.

**commingle** /kɒˈmɪŋg(ə)l/ ● v. poetic/literary mix; blend.

**comminuted** /ˈkɒmɪnjuːtɪd/ ● adj. **1** technical reduced to minute particles or fragments. **2** Medicine (of a fracture) producing multiple bone splinters.

– DERIVATIVES **comminution** n.

– ORIGIN C17 (earlier (C16) as *comminution*): past part. of *comminute*, from L. *comminut-*, *comminuere* 'break into pieces'.

**commis chef** /'kɒmi/ ● **n.** (pl. same /'kɒmi, 'kɒmɪz/) a junior chef.
– ORIGIN 1930s: from Fr., 'deputy, clerk'.

**commiserate** /kə'mɪzəreɪt/ ● **v.** express sympathy or pity; sympathize.
– DERIVATIVES **commiseration** n. **commiserative** adj.
– ORIGIN C16: from L. *commiserat-*, *commiserari*, from *com-* 'with' + *miserari* 'to lament'.

**commissaire** /ˌkɒmɪ'sɛː, French kɔmisɛʀ/ ● **n. 1** a senior police officer in France. **2** an official at a cycle race or other sporting event.
– ORIGIN C18: from Fr. from med. L. *commissarius* (see **COMMISSARY**).

**commissar** /ˌkɒmɪ'sɑː/ ● **n.** a Communist official, especially in Soviet Russia or China, responsible for political education. ➤ a head of a government department in the Soviet Union before 1946.
– ORIGIN C20: from Russ. *komissar*, from Fr. *commissaire*.

**commissariat** /ˌkɒmɪ'sɛːrɪət/ ● **n. 1** chiefly Military a department for the supply of food and equipment. **2** a government department of the Soviet Union before 1946.
– ORIGIN C16: from Fr. *commissariat*, reinforced by med. L. *commissariatus*, both from med. L. *commissarius* (see **COMMISSARY**).

**commissary** /'kɒmɪs(ə)ri/ ● **n.** (pl. **-ies**) **1** a deputy or delegate. ➤ a representative or deputy of a bishop. **2** N. Amer. a restaurant or food store in a military base or other institution.
– DERIVATIVES **commissarial** /-'sɛːrɪəl/ adj.
– ORIGIN ME: from med. L. *commissarius* 'person in charge', from L. *commiss-*, *committere* (see **COMMIT**).

**commission** ● **n. 1** an instruction or command. ➤ an order for something, especially a work of art, to be produced specially. ➤ archaic the authority to perform a task. **2** a group of people given official authority to do something. **3** a sum paid to an agent in a commercial transaction. **4** a warrant conferring the rank of military officer. **5** the action of committing a crime or offence. ● **v. 1** order or authorize the production of. ➤ order or authorize (someone) to do or produce something. **2** bring into working order. **3** appoint to the rank of military officer.
– PHRASES **in** (or **out of**) **commission** in (or not in) use or working order.
– ORIGIN ME: via OFr. from L. *commissio(n-)*, from *committere* (see **COMMIT**).

**commissionaire** /kəˌmɪʃə'nɛː/ ● **n.** chiefly Brit. a uniformed door attendant at a hotel, theatre, or other building.
– ORIGIN C17: from Fr., from med. L. *commissarius* (see **COMMISSARY**).

**commissioner** ● **n.** a person appointed to a role on or by a commission. ➤ a representative of the supreme authority in an area. ➤ the head of the Metropolitan Police in London. ➤ N. Amer. a person appointed to regulate a particular sport.

**commissioner for oaths** ● **n.** Brit. a solicitor authorized to administer an oath to a person making an affidavit.

**commission of the peace** ● **n.** Brit., chiefly historical the Justices of the Peace in a particular jurisdiction considered collectively.

**commissure** /'kɒmɪsjʊə/ ● **n.** Anatomy **1** a seam between two bones. **2** a band of nerve tissue connecting the hemispheres of the brain, the two sides of the spinal cord, etc. **3** the line where the upper and lower lips or eyelids meet.
– DERIVATIVES **commissural** /ˌkɒmɪ'sjʊər(ə)l/ adj.
– ORIGIN ME: from L. *commissura* 'junction', from *committere* (see **COMMIT**).

**commit** ● **v.** (**committed**, **committing**) **1** perpetrate or carry out (a mistake, crime, or immoral act). **2** pledge or bind to a course, policy, or use. ➤ [often as adj. **committed**] dedicate to a cause: *a committed Christian*. ➤ (**be committed**) be in a long-term emotional relationship. **3** transfer for safe keeping or permanent preservation. ➤ send to prison or psychiatric hospital, or for trial in a higher court. ➤ refer (a parliamentary or legislative bill) to a committee.
– DERIVATIVES **committable** adj. **committer** n.
– ORIGIN ME: from L. *committere* 'join, entrust' (in med. L. 'put into custody'), from *com-* 'with' + *mittere* 'put or send'.

**commitment** ● **n. 1** the state or quality of being dedicated to a cause or policy. ➤ a pledge or undertaking. **2** an engagement or obligation that restricts freedom of action.

**committal** ● **n. 1** the sending of someone to prison or psychiatric hospital, or for trial. **2** the burial of a corpse.

**committee** /kə'mɪti/ ● **n. 1** [treated as sing. or pl.] a group of people appointed for a specific function by a larger group. ➤ a committee appointed by Parliament to consider proposed legislation. ➤ (**Committee of the whole House**) the whole House of Commons when sitting as a committee. **2** /ˌkɒmɪ'tiː/ Law, Brit. a person entrusted with the charge of another person or another person's property. ➤ chiefly US a person who has been judicially committed to the charge of another because of insanity or mental retardation.

**committee stage** ● **n.** Brit. the third of five stages of a bill's progress through Parliament, when it may be debated and amended.

**commix** /kɒ'mɪks/ ● **v.** archaic mix; mingle.
– DERIVATIVES **commixture** n.

**commode** ● **n. 1** a piece of furniture containing a concealed chamber pot. ➤ N. Amer. a toilet. **2** a chest of drawers or chiffonier of a decorative type popular in the 18th century. **3** N. Amer. historical a movable washstand.
– ORIGIN C18: from Fr., lit. 'convenient, suitable'.

**commodify** /kə'mɒdɪfʌɪ/ ● **v.** (**-ies**, **-ied**) turn into or treat as a mere commodity.
– DERIVATIVES **commodification** n.

**commodious** /kə'məʊdɪəs/ ● **adj. 1** formal roomy and comfortable. **2** archaic convenient.
– DERIVATIVES **commodiously** adv. **commodiousness** n.
– ORIGIN ME: from Fr. *commodieux* or med. L. *commodiosus*, based on L. *commodus* 'convenient'.

**commodity** /kə'mɒdɪti/ ● **n.** (pl. **-ies**) **1** a raw material or primary agricultural product that can be bought and sold. **2** something useful or valuable.
– DERIVATIVES **commoditize** (also **-ise**) v.
– ORIGIN ME: from OFr. *commodite* or L. *commoditas*, from *commodus* (see **COMMODIOUS**).

**commodore** /'kɒmədɔː/ ● **n.** a naval rank above captain and below rear admiral, generally given temporarily to an officer commanding a squadron or division of a fleet. ➤ the president of a yacht club. ➤ the senior captain of a shipping line.
– ORIGIN C17: prob. from Du. *komandeur*, from Fr. *commandeur* 'commander'.

**common** ● **adj.** (**-er**, **-est**) **1** occurring, found, or done often; not rare. ➤ without special rank or position; ordinary. ➤ (of a quality) of a sort to be generally expected: *common decency*. ➤ of the most familiar type. **2** showing a lack of taste and refinement supposedly typical of the lower classes; vulgar. **3** shared by two or more people or things. ➤ belonging to or affecting the whole of a community: *common land*. ➤ Mathematics belonging to two or more quantities. **4** Grammar of or denoting a noun that refers to individuals of either sex (e.g. *teacher*) or belongs to a gender conventionally regarded as masculine or feminine. **5** Prosody (of a syllable) able to be either short or long. **6** Law (of a crime) of lesser importance. ● **n. 1** a piece of open land for public use. **2** Brit. informal common sense. **3** a form of Christian service used for each of a group of occasions. **4** (also **right of common**) English Law a person's right over another's land, e.g. for pasturage or mineral extraction.
– PHRASES **common ground** views shared by each of two or more differing parties. **common or garden** Brit. informal of the usual or ordinary type. **in common** in joint use or possession; shared. **in common with** in the same way as. **out of the common** Brit. rarely occurring; unusual.
– DERIVATIVES **commonness** n.

– ORIGIN ME: from OFr. *comun*, from L. *communis*.

**commonable** • **adj.** Brit., chiefly historical (of land) allowed to be jointly used or owned. ➤(of an animal) allowed to be pastured on public land.

**commonage** • **n. 1** chiefly Brit. the right of pasturing animals on common land. ➤land held in common. **2** the common people; the commonalty.

**commonality** • **n.** (pl. **-ies**) **1** the state of sharing features or attributes. ➤a shared feature or attribute. **2** (**the commonality**) another term for **COMMONALTY**.

**commonalty** /'kɒmən(ə)lti/ • **n.** [treated as pl.] (**the commonalty**) chiefly historical people without special rank or position, usually viewed as an estate of the realm.
– ORIGIN ME: from OFr. *comunalte*, from med. L. *communalitas*, from L. *communis* (see **COMMON**).

**common carrier** • **n. 1** a person or company undertaking to transport any goods or passengers on regular routes at agreed rates. **2** N. Amer. a company providing public telecommunications facilities.

**common chord** • **n.** Music a triad containing a root, a major or minor third, and a perfect fifth.

**common denominator** • **n. 1** Mathematics a common multiple of the denominators of several fractions. **2** a feature shared by all members of a group.

**Common Entrance** • **n.** Brit. an examination taken, usually at 13, by pupils wishing to enter public schools.

**commoner** • **n. 1** one of the ordinary or common people, as opposed to the aristocracy or to royalty. **2** a person who has the right of common. **3** (at some British universities) an undergraduate without a scholarship.

**Common Era** • **n.** another term for **CHRISTIAN ERA**.

**commonhold** • **n.** Brit. a proposed system of freehold tenure of a unit within a multi-occupancy building, but with shared responsibility for common services.

**common jury** • **n.** Brit. historical a jury for which no qualification of property or social standing was required. Compare with **SPECIAL JURY**.

**common law** • **n. 1** the part of English law that is derived from custom and judicial precedent rather than statutes. ➤the body of English law as adopted and adapted by the different states of the US. **2** [as modifier] denoting a partner in a marriage recognized in some jurisdictions (excluding the UK) as valid by common law, though not brought about by a civil or ecclesiastical ceremony. ➤denoting a partner in a relationship in which a man and woman cohabit for a period long enough to suggest stability.

**common logarithm** • **n.** a logarithm to the base 10.

**commonly** • **adv.** very often; frequently.

**common market** • **n.** a group of countries imposing few or no duties on trade with one another and a common tariff on trade with other countries. ➤(**the Common Market**) a name for the European Economic Community or European Union, used especially in the 1960s and 1970s.

**common metre** • **n.** a metrical pattern for hymns in which the stanzas have four lines containing eight and six syllables alternately.

**common noun** • **n.** Grammar a noun denoting a class of objects or a concept as opposed to a particular individual. Often contrasted with **PROPER NOUN**.

**commonplace** • **adj.** not unusual; ordinary. ➤not interesting or original; trite. • **n. 1** a usual or ordinary thing. ➤a trite saying or topic; a platitude. **2** passage copied into a commonplace book.
– DERIVATIVES **commonplaceness** n.
– ORIGIN C16: translation of L. *locus communis*, rendering Gk *koinos topos* 'general theme'.

**commonplace book** • **n.** a book into which notable extracts from other works are copied for personal use.

**common room** • **n.** chiefly Brit. a room in an educational institution for use of students or staff outside teaching hours.

**commons** • **pl. n. 1** (**the Commons**) short for **HOUSE OF COMMONS**. ➤historical the common people regarded as a part of a political system. **2** [treated as sing.] land or resources belonging to or affecting the whole of a community. **3** archaic provisions shared in common; rations.
– PHRASES **short commons** insufficient allocation of food.

**common seal** • **n.** an official seal of a corporate body.

**common sense** • **n.** good sense and sound judgement in practical matters.
– DERIVATIVES **commonsensical** adj.

**Common Serjeant** • **n.** a circuit judge of the Central Criminal Court with duties in the City of London.

**common stock** (also **common stocks**) • **pl. n.** N. Amer. ordinary shares.

**common time** • **n.** Music a rhythmic pattern in which there are two or four beats, especially four crotchets, in a bar.

**commonweal** /'kɒmənwi:l/ • **n.** (**the commonweal**) archaic the welfare of the public.

**commonwealth** • **n. 1** an independent state or community, especially a democratic republic. ➤a self-governing unit voluntarily grouped with the US, such as Puerto Rico. ➤a formal title of certain US states. ➤the title of the federated Australian states. ➤(**the Commonwealth**) the republican period of government in Britain between the execution of Charles I in 1649 and the Restoration of Charles II in 1660. **2** (**the Commonwealth**) (in full **the Commonwealth of Nations**) an international association consisting of the UK together with states that were previously part of the British Empire, and dependencies. **3** (**the commonwealth**) archaic the general good.

**commotion** • **n. 1** a state of confused and noisy disturbance. **2** civil insurrection.
– ORIGIN ME: from L. *commotio(n-)*, from *com-* 'altogether' + *motio* (see **MOTION**).

**communal** /'kɒmjʊn(ə)l, kə'mju:-/ • **adj. 1** shared or done by all members of a community. ➤involving the sharing of work and property: *communal living*. **2** (of conflict) between different communities, especially those having different religions or ethnic origins.
– DERIVATIVES **communality** n. **communalization** (also **-isation**) n. **communalize** (also **-ise**) v. **communally** adv.
– ORIGIN C19: from Fr., from late L. *communalis*, from *communis* (see **COMMON**).

**communalism** • **n. 1** a principle of political organization based on federated communes. ➤the principle or practice of living together communally. **2** allegiance to one's own ethnic group rather than to the wider society.
– DERIVATIVES **communalist** adj. & n. **communalistic** adj.

**communard** /'kɒmjʊnɑ:d/ • **n. 1** a member of a commune. **2** (**Communard**) historical a supporter of the Paris Commune.

**commune**[1] /'kɒmju:n/ • **n. 1** a group of people living together and sharing possessions and responsibilities. ➤a communal settlement in a communist country. **2** the smallest French territorial division for administrative purposes. **3** (**the Commune**) the group which seized the municipal government of Paris in the French Revolution and played a leading part in the Reign of Terror. ➤the municipal government organized on communalistic principles elected in Paris in 1871.
– ORIGIN C17: from Fr., from med. L. *communia*, neut. pl. of L. *communis* (see **COMMON**).

**commune**[2] /kə'mju:n/ • **v.** (**commune with**) share one's intimate thoughts or feelings with. ➤feel in close spiritual contact with.
– ORIGIN ME: from OFr. *comuner* 'to share', from *comun* (see **COMMON**).

**communicable** • **adj.** (especially of a disease) able to be communicated to others.
– DERIVATIVES **communicability** n. **communicably** adv.

**communicant** • **n. 1** a person who receives Holy Communion. **2** archaic a person who imparts information.

**communicate** • **v. 1** share or exchange information or ideas. ➤convey (an emotion or feeling) in a non-verbal way. ➤pass on (an infectious disease). ➤transmit (heat or motion). **2** [often as adj. **communicating**] (of two rooms) have a common connecting door. **3** receive Holy Communion.
– DERIVATIVES **communicator** n. **communicatory** adj.

– ORIGIN C16 (earlier (ME) as *communication*): from L. *communicat-*, *communicare* 'share', from *communis* (see **COMMON**).

**communication** • n. **1** the action of communicating. ➤a letter or message containing information or news. ➤social contact. **2** (**communications**) the means of sending or receiving information, such as telephone lines or computers. ➤the means of travelling or of transporting goods, such as roads or railways.
– PHRASES **line of communications** the connections between an army in the field and its bases.
– DERIVATIVES **communicational** adj.

**communication cord** • n. Brit. a cord or chain which a train passenger may pull in an emergency, causing the train to brake.

**communications satellite** • n. a satellite placed in orbit round the earth in order to relay television, radio, and telephone signals.

**communicative** • adj. **1** willing, eager, or able to talk or impart information. **2** relating to the conveyance or exchange of information.
– DERIVATIVES **communicatively** adv.

**communion** • n. **1** the sharing or exchanging of intimate thoughts and feelings. **2** (also **Holy Communion**) the service of Christian worship at which bread and wine are consecrated and shared; the Eucharist. **3** a relationship of recognition and acceptance between Christian Churches or denominations. ➤a group of Christian Churches or communities which recognize one another's ministries or that of a central authority.
– ORIGIN ME: from L. *communio(n-)*, from *communis* (see **COMMON**).

**communion of saints** • n. a fellowship between Christians living and dead.

**communiqué** /kə'mju:nɪkeɪ/ • n. an official announcement or statement, especially one made to the media.
– ORIGIN C19: from Fr., past part. of *communiquer* 'communicate'.

**communism** • n. a theory or system of social organization in which all property is vested in the community and each person contributes and receives according to their ability and needs. ➤a theory or system of this kind derived from Marxism and established in the Soviet Union, China, and elsewhere.
– DERIVATIVES **communist** n. & adj. **communistic** adj.
– ORIGIN C19: from Fr. *communisme*, from *commun* (see **COMMON**).

**communitarianism** /kə,mju:nɪ'tɛ:rɪənɪz(ə)m/ • n. **1** a system of social organization based on small self-governing communities. **2** an ideology which emphasizes the responsibility of the individual to the community and the social importance of the family unit.
– DERIVATIVES **communitarian** adj. & n.

**community** • n. (pl. **-ies**) **1** a group of people living together in one place, especially one practising common ownership. ➤a place considered together with its inhabitants: *a rural community.* ➤(**the community**) the people of an area or country considered collectively; society. **2** a group of people having a religion, race, or profession in common: *the scientific community.* **3** the condition of having certain attitudes and interests in common. ➤joint ownership or liability. **4** Ecology a group of interdependent plants or animals growing or living together.
– ORIGIN ME: from OFr. *comunete*, reinforced by its source, L. *communitas*, from *communis* (see **COMMON**).

**community care** • n. long-term care for the mentally ill, the elderly, and people with disabilities provided within the community rather than in hospitals or institutions.

**community centre** • n. a place providing educational or recreational activities for a neighbourhood.

**community charge** • n. (in the UK) a tax levied locally on every adult in a community, replaced in 1993 by the council tax; the poll tax.

**community chest** • n. a fund for charitable activities among the people in a particular area.

**community home** • n. Brit. a centre for housing young offenders and other young people in need of custodial care.

**community service** • n. unpaid work, intended to be of social use, that an offender is required to do instead of going to prison.

**community singing** • n. singing by a large crowd.

**communize** /'kɒmjʊnʌɪz/ (also **-ise**) • v. rare organize on communist principles.
– DERIVATIVES **communization** n.

**commutate** /'kɒmjʊteɪt/ • v. regulate or reverse the direction of (an alternating electric current), especially to make it a direct current.
– ORIGIN C19: from L. *commutat-*, *commutare* (see **COMMUTE**).

**commutation** • n. **1** the action or process of commuting a judicial sentence or a legal obligation or entitlement. **2** the process of commutating an electric current. **3** Mathematics the property of having a commutative relation.

**commutative** /kə'mju:tətɪv, 'kɒmjʊ,tətɪv/ • adj. Mathematics involving the condition that a group of quantities connected by operators gives the same result whatever the order of the quantities involved, e.g. $a \times b = b \times a$.

**commutator** /'kɒmjʊ,teɪtə/ • n. **1** an attachment, connected with the armature of a motor or dynamo, through which electrical connection is made and which ensures the current flows as direct current. **2** a device for reversing the direction of flow of electric current.

**commute** • v. **1** travel some distance between one's home and place of work on a regular basis. **2** reduce (a judicial sentence, especially a sentence of death) to a less severe one. ➤change one kind of payment or obligation for (another). ➤replace (an annuity or other series of payments) with a single payment. **3** Mathematics (of two operations or quantities) have a commutative relation.
– DERIVATIVES **commutable** adj. **commuter** n.
– ORIGIN ME: from L. *commutare*, from *com-* 'altogether' + *mutare* 'to change'; sense 1 derives from *commutation ticket*, the US term for a season ticket (because the daily fare is commuted to a single payment).

**Comoran** /'kɒmərən/ • n. a native or inhabitant of the Comoros, a country consisting of a group of islands to the north of Madagascar. • adj. of or relating to the Comoros.

**comp** • abbrev. informal **1** Brit. a competition. **2** Brit. a comprehensive school. **3** Brit. a compositor. **4** a composition. **5** a compilation. **6** N. Amer. a complimentary ticket or voucher. **7** N. Amer. compensation. **8** a musical accompaniment. • v. **1** play (music) as an accompaniment, especially in jazz or blues. **2** [as noun **comping**] Brit. informal the practice of entering competitions. **3** N. Amer. give away as part of a promotion. • adj. N. Amer. complimentary; free.
– DERIVATIVES **comper** n. (Brit. informal).

**compact**[1] • adj. /kəm'pakt/ **1** closely and neatly packed together; dense. ➤having all the necessary components or features neatly fitted into a small space. **2** (**compact of**) archaic composed or made up of. • v. /kəm'pakt/ exert force on to make more dense; compress. ➤archaic form by pressing the component parts firmly together. • n. /'kɒmpakt/ a small flat case containing face powder, a mirror, and a powder puff.
– DERIVATIVES **compaction** n. **compactly** adv. **compactness** n. **compactor** n.
– ORIGIN ME: from L. *compact-*, *compingere*, from *com-* 'together' + *pangere* 'fasten'.

**compact**[2] /'kɒmpakt/ • n. a formal agreement or contract between two or more parties. • v. make or enter into (a formal agreement).
– ORIGIN C16: from L. *compact-*, *compacisci*, from *com-* 'with' + *pacisci* 'make a covenant'; cf. **PACT**.

**compact disc** • n. a small plastic disc on which music or other digital information is stored in the form of a pattern of metal-coated pits from which it can be read using laser light reflected off the disc.

**compadre** /kɒm'pɑ:dreɪ/ • n. (pl. **compadres**) informal, chiefly N. Amer. a friend or companion.
– ORIGIN Sp., lit. 'godfather'.

**compand** /kɒm'pand/ • v. reduce the signal-to-noise

ratio of (a signal) using a compander.

**compander** (also **compandor**) ● **n.** a device that improves the signal-to-noise ratio of an electrical signal by compressing the range of amplitudes of the signal before transmission, and then expanding it on reproduction or reception.
– ORIGIN 1930s: blend of **COMPRESSOR** and *expander*.

**companion**[1] ● **n.** **1** a person with whom one spends time or travels. ➤a person employed to live with and assist someone old or unwell. **2** each of a pair of things intended to complement or match each other. ➤Brit. dated a piece of equipment containing several objects used in a particular activity. **3** (**Companion**) a member of the lowest grade of certain orders of knighthood. ● **v.** formal accompany.
– DERIVATIVES **companionship** n.
– ORIGIN ME: from OFr. *compaignon*, lit. 'one who breaks bread with another', based on L. *com-* 'together with' + *panis* 'bread'.

**companion**[2] ● **n.** Nautical **1** a covering over the hatchway leading to a companionway. ➤archaic a raised frame with windows to allow light into the decks below. **2** short for **COMPANIONWAY**.
– ORIGIN C18: from obs. Du. *kompanje* (earlier form of *kampanje*) 'quarterdeck'.

**companionable** ● **adj.** friendly and sociable.
– DERIVATIVES **companionableness** n. **companionably** adv.
– ORIGIN C17: alt. of obs. *companiable*, influenced by **COMPANION**[1].

**companionate** /kəmˈpanjənət/ ● **adj.** formal (of a marriage or relationship) between partners or spouses as equal companions.

**companion-in-arms** ● **n.** a fellow soldier.

**companion ladder** ● **n.** another term for **COMPANIONWAY**.

**Companion of Honour** ● **n.** a member of an order of knighthood founded in 1917.

**Companion of Literature** ● **n.** a holder of an honour awarded by the Royal Society of Literature.

**companion set** ● **n.** Brit. a collection of fireside implements on a stand.

**companionway** ● **n.** a set of steps leading from a ship's deck down to a cabin or lower deck.

**company** ● **n.** (pl. **-ies**) **1** a commercial business. **2** the fact or condition of being with another or others. ➤a person as a source of friendship and entertainment: *she is excellent company.* ➤a visitor or visitors: *I'm expecting company.* **3** a number of individuals gathered together. ➤a body of soldiers, especially the smallest subdivision of an infantry battalion. ➤a group of actors, singers, or dancers who perform together. ➤Brit. a group of Guides. ● **v.** (**-ies**, **-ied**) archaic or poetic/literary associate with or accompany.
– PHRASES **in company with** together with. **keep** (or archaic **bear**) **someone company** spend time with someone to prevent them feeling lonely or bored. **keep company with** associate with habitually.
– ORIGIN ME: from OFr. *compainie*; rel. to *compaignon* (see **COMPANION**[1]).

**company car** ● **n.** a car provided by a firm for the business and private use of an employee.

**company officer** ● **n.** an army officer serving within an infantry company.

**company sergeant major** ● **n.** the highest-ranking non-commissioned officer of an infantry company.

**comparable** /ˈkɒmp(ə)rəb(ə)l/ ● **adj.** able to be likened to another; similar. ➤of equivalent quality.
– DERIVATIVES **comparability** n. **comparably** adv.

**comparatist** /kəmˈparətɪst/ ● **n.** a person who carries out comparative study, especially of language or literature.

**comparative** /kəmˈparətɪv/ ● **adj.** **1** measured or judged by comparison; relative. **2** involving comparison between two or more subjects or branches of science: *comparative religion.* **3** Grammar (of an adjective or adverb) expressing a higher degree of a quality, but not the highest possible (e.g. *braver*; *more fiercely*). Contrasted with **POSITIVE**, **SUPERLATIVE**.

**comparative advantage** ● **n.** Economics the ability of an individual or group to carry out a particular economic activity more efficiently than another activity.

**comparative linguistics** ● **pl. n.** [treated as sing.] the study of similarities and differences between languages, in particular the comparison of related languages with a view to reconstructing forms in their lost parent languages.

**comparatively** ● **adv.** to a moderate degree as compared to something else; relatively.

**comparator** /kəmˈparətə/ ● **n.** a device for comparing something measurable with a reference or standard. ➤something used as a standard for comparison.

**compare** ● **v.** **1** (often **compare something to/with**) estimate, measure, or note the similarity or dissimilarity between. ➤(**compare something to**) point out or describe the resemblances of something with; liken to. ➤(usu. **compare with**) be similar to or have a specified relationship with another thing or person: *salaries compare favourably with those of other professions.* **2** Grammar form the comparative and superlative degrees of (an adjective or an adverb).
– PHRASES **beyond** (or **without**) **compare** surpassing all others of the same kind. **compare notes** exchange ideas or information about a particular subject.
– ORIGIN ME: from OFr. *comparer*, from L. *comparare*, from *compar* 'like, equal'.

**comparison** ● **n.** **1** the action of comparing. ➤the quality of being similar or equivalent. **2** Grammar the formation of the comparative and superlative forms of adjectives and adverbs.
– PHRASES **beyond comparison** another way of saying ***beyond compare*** (see **COMPARE**).
– ORIGIN ME: from OFr. *comparesoun*, from L. *comparatio(n-)*, from *comparare* (see **COMPARE**).

**compartment** ● **n.** **1** a separate section of a structure or container. ➤a division of a railway carriage marked by partitions. **2** Heraldry a grassy mound or other support depicted below a shield. ● **v.** divide into compartments.
– DERIVATIVES **compartmental** adj. **compartmentally** adv. **compartmentation** n.
– ORIGIN C16: from Fr. *compartiment*, based on late L. *compartiri* 'divide'.

**compartmentalize** (also **-ise**) ● **v.** divide into categories or sections.
– DERIVATIVES **compartmentalism** n. **compartmentalization** n.

**compass** ● **n.** **1** an instrument containing a magnetized pointer which shows the direction of magnetic north and bearings from it. **2** (also **compasses**) an instrument for drawing circles and arcs and measuring distances between points, consisting of two arms linked by a movable joint. **3** range or scope. ● **v.** archaic **1** circle or surround. **2** contrive to accomplish.
– ORIGIN ME: from OFr. *compas* (n.), *compasser* (v.), based on L. *com-* 'together' + *passus* 'a step or pace'.

**compass card** ● **n.** a circular rotating card showing the thirty-two principal bearings, forming the indicator of a magnetic compass.

**compassion** ● **n.** sympathetic pity and concern for the sufferings or misfortunes of others.
– ORIGIN ME: via OFr. from eccles. L. *compassio(n-)*, from *compati* 'suffer with'.

**compassionate** ● **adj.** feeling or showing compassion.
– DERIVATIVES **compassionately** adv.

**compassionate leave** ● **n.** a period of absence from work granted as the result of particular personal circumstances, especially the death of a close relative.

**compassion fatigue** ● **n.** indifference to charitable appeals on behalf of those who are suffering, experienced as a result of the frequency of such appeals.

**compass rose** ● **n.** a graduated circle printed on a map or chart from which bearings can be taken.

**compass saw** ● **n.** a handsaw with a narrow blade for cutting curves.

**compass window** ● **n.** a bay window with a semicircular curve.

**compatible** ● **adj.** **1** able to exist or be used together without problems or conflict. ➤(of two people) able to have a harmonious relationship; well suited. **2** (usu. **compatible with**) consistent or in keeping.
– DERIVATIVES **compatibility** n. **compatibly** adv.
– ORIGIN ME: from Fr., from med. L. *compatibilis*, from *compati* 'suffer with'.

**compatriot** /kəm'patrɪət, -'peɪt-/ ● **n.** a fellow citizen or national of a country.
– ORIGIN C16: from Fr. *compatriote*, based on late L. *com-* 'together with' + *patriota* (see **PATRIOT**).

**compeer** /kəm'pɪə/ ● **n.** **1** formal a person of equal rank, status, or ability. **2** archaic a companion or associate.
– ORIGIN ME: from OFr. *comper*, from *com-* 'with' + *per*, from L. *par* 'equal' (cf. **PEER**[2]).

**compel** ● **v.** (**compelled**, **compelling**) **1** force or oblige to do something. ➤bring about by force or pressure. ➤poetic/literary force to move in a particular direction. **2** [as adj. **compelling**] powerfully evoking attention or admiration.
– DERIVATIVES **compellingly** adv.
– ORIGIN ME: from L. *compellere*, from *com-* 'together' + *pellere* 'drive'.

**compellable** ● **adj.** Law (of a witness) able to be made to attend court or give evidence.

**compendious** ● **adj.** formal presenting the essential facts in a comprehensive but concise way.
– DERIVATIVES **compendiously** adv. **compendiousness** n.
– ORIGIN ME: from OFr. *compendieux*, from L. *compendiosus* 'advantageous, brief', from *compendium* 'profit, saving, abbreviation'.

**compendium** ● **n.** (pl. **compendiums** or **compendia** /-dɪə/) **1** a collection of concise but detailed information about a particular subject. **2** a collection of similar items. **3** a package of stationery for writing letters.
– ORIGIN C16: from L., 'profit, saving' (lit. 'what is weighed together'), from *compendere* 'weigh together'.

**compensable** /kəm'pɛnsəb(ə)l/ ● **adj.** (of a loss or hardship) for which compensation can be obtained.

**compensate** ● **v.** **1** give something to reduce or balance the bad effect of loss, suffering, or injury. **2** (**compensate for**) make up for (something undesirable) by exerting an opposite force or effect.
– DERIVATIVES **compensative** adj. **compensator** n. **compensatory** adj.
– ORIGIN C17 (earlier (ME) as *compensation*), in the sense 'counterbalance': from L. *compensat-*, *compensare* 'weigh against'.

**compensation** ● **n.** **1** something awarded to compensate for loss, suffering, or injury. ➤something that compensates for an undesirable state of affairs. ➤the action or process of compensating. **2** chiefly N. Amer. money received as salary or wages.
– DERIVATIVES **compensational** adj.

**compensation pendulum** ● **n.** Physics a pendulum constructed from metals with differing coefficients of expansion in order to neutralize the effects of temperature variation.

**compère** /'kɒmpɛː/ Brit. ● **n.** a person who introduces the acts in a variety show. ● **v.** act as a compère for.
– ORIGIN C20: Fr., lit. 'godfather'.

**compete** ● **v.** strive to gain or win something by defeating or establishing superiority over others.
– ORIGIN C17 (earlier (C16) as *competitor*): from L. *competere*, from *com-* 'together' + *petere* 'aim at, seek'.

**competence** (also **competency**) ● **n.** **1** the quality or extent of being competent. **2** Linguistics a person's subconscious knowledge of the rules governing the formation of speech in their first language. Often contrasted with **PERFORMANCE**. **3** dated an income large enough to live on.

**competent** ● **adj.** having the necessary ability or knowledge to do something successfully. ➤(of a person) efficient and capable. ➤(of a court or other body) having legal authority to deal with a particular matter.
– DERIVATIVES **competently** adv.
– ORIGIN ME (in the sense 'suitable, adequate'): from L. *competent-*, *competere* in the sense 'be fit or proper' (see **COMPETE**).

**competition** ● **n.** **1** the activity or condition of competing against others. ➤Ecology interaction between species or organisms which share a limited environmental resource. **2** an event or contest in which people compete. ➤the person or people with whom one is competing.

**competitive** ● **adj.** **1** relating to or characterized by competition. ➤strongly desiring to be more successful than others. **2** as good as or better than others of a comparable nature.
– DERIVATIVES **competitively** adv. **competitiveness** n.

**competitor** ● **n.** **1** a person who takes part in a sporting contest. **2** an organization engaged in commercial or economic competition with others.

**compilation** ● **n.** **1** the action or process of compiling something. **2** a thing, especially a book or record, compiled from different sources.

**compile** ● **v.** **1** produce (a collection) by assembling material from other sources. ➤accumulate (a specified score). **2** Computing convert (a program) into a lower-level form in which the program can be executed.
– DERIVATIVES **compiler** n.
– ORIGIN ME: from OFr. *compiler* or its apparent source, L. *compilare* 'plunder or plagiarize'.

**complacent** /kəm'pleɪs(ə)nt/ ● **adj.** smug and uncritically satisfied with oneself or one's achievements.
– DERIVATIVES **complacency** (also **complacence**) n. **complacently** adv.
– ORIGIN C17 (earlier (ME) as *complacence*), in the sense 'pleasant': from L. *complacent-*, *complacere* 'to please'.

**USAGE** complacent

The words **complacent** and **complaisant** are sometimes confused: **complacent** means 'smug and self-satisfied', whereas **complaisant** means 'willing to please'.

**complain** ● **v.** **1** express dissatisfaction or annoyance. **2** (**complain of**) state that one is suffering from (a symptom of illness).
– DERIVATIVES **complainer** n. **complaining** adj. **complainingly** adv.
– ORIGIN ME: from OFr. *complaindre*, from med. L. *complangere* 'bewail', from L. *com-* (expressing intensive force) + *plangere* 'to lament'.

**complainant** ● **n.** Law a plaintiff in certain lawsuits.

**complaint** ● **n.** **1** an act or the action of complaining. ➤a reason for dissatisfaction. ➤Law the plaintiff's reasons for proceeding in a civil action. **2** an illness or medical condition, especially a relatively minor one.

**complaisant** /kəm'pleɪz(ə)nt/ ● **adj.** willing to please others or to accept their behaviour without protest.
– DERIVATIVES **complaisance** n.
– ORIGIN C17: Fr., from *complaire* 'acquiesce in order to please', from L. *complacere* 'to please'.

**USAGE** complaisant

On the confusion of **complaisant** with **complacent**, see **COMPLACENT**.

**compleat** ● **adj.** & **v.** archaic spelling of **COMPLETE**.

**complected** /kəm'plɛktɪd/ ● **adj.** N. Amer. having a specified complexion.

**complement** ● **n.** /'kɒmplɪm(ə)nt/ **1** a thing that contributes extra features to something else so as to enhance or improve it. **2** the number or quantity that makes something complete. **3** Grammar a word, phrase, or clause governed by a verb that completes the meaning of the predicate. ➤an adjective or noun that has the same reference as either the subject or object (as *mad* in *he is mad* or *he drove her mad*). **4** Physiology protein present in blood plasma which combines with an antigen–antibody complex to bring about the destruction of foreign cells. **5** Geometry the amount by which a given angle is less than 90°. ● **v.** /'kɒmplɪmɛnt/ serve as a complement to.
– PHRASES **in her complement** Heraldry (of the moon) depicted as full.
– DERIVATIVES **complemental** adj.
– ORIGIN ME (in the sense 'completion'): from L. *complementum*, from *complere* (see **COMPLETE**).

**USAGE complement**

**Complement** and **compliment** (together with related words such as **complementary** and **complimentary**) are frequently confused. **Complement** means 'add to in a way that enhances or improves', while **compliment** means 'politely congratulate or praise'.

**complementarity** ● **n.** (pl. **-ies**) **1** a situation in which two or more different things enhance each other or form a balanced whole. **2** Physics the concept that two contrasted theories may be able to explain a set of phenomena, although each separately only accounts for some aspects.

**complementary** ● **adj. 1** combining in such a way as to form a complete whole or enhance each other. **2** of or relating to complementary medicine.
– DERIVATIVES **complementarily** adv. **complementariness** n.

**complementary angle** ● **n.** either of two angles whose sum is 90°.

**complementary colour** ● **n.** a colour that combined with a given colour makes white or black.

**complementary distribution** ● **n.** the occurrence of phenomena such as speech sounds in mutually exclusive contexts.

**complementary DNA** ● **n.** synthetic DNA in which the sequence of bases is complementary to that of a given example of DNA.

**complementary medicine** ● **n.** medical therapy that falls beyond the scope of scientific medicine but may be used alongside it in the treatment of disease and ill health, e.g. acupuncture and osteopathy.

**complementation** ● **n. 1** the action of complementing. **2** Grammar all the clause constituents that are governed by a verb. **3** Genetics the phenomenon by which the effects of two different non-allelic mutations in a gene are partly or entirely cancelled out when they occur together.

**complete** ● **adj. 1** having all the necessary or appropriate parts; entire. ➤(**complete with**) having as an additional part or feature. **2** having run its full course; finished. **3** to the greatest extent or degree; total: *a complete surprise.* **4** (also **compleat**) chiefly humorous skilled at every aspect of an activity; consummate. ● **v. 1** finish making or doing. ➤Brit. conclude the sale of a property. **2** provide with the items necessary to make (something) complete. ➤write the required information on (a form).
– DERIVATIVES **completeness** n.
– ORIGIN ME: from OFr. *complet*, or L. *complet-*, *complere* 'fill up, finish, fulfil', from *com-* (expressing intensive force) + *plere* 'fill'.

**completely** ● **adv.** totally; utterly.

**completion** ● **n.** the action or state of completing or being completed. ➤Brit. the final stage in the sale of a property, at which point it legally changes ownership.

**completist** ● **n.** an obsessive fan who wants to own everything produced by a particular person or group.

**complex** ● **adj. 1** consisting of many different and connected parts. **2** not easy to analyse or understand; complicated or intricate. **3** Mathematics (of a number) containing both a real and an imaginary part. ● **n. 1** a group of similar buildings or facilities on the same site. ➤an interlinked system; a network. **2** Psychoanalysis a related group of repressed or partly repressed emotionally significant ideas which lead to abnormal mental states or behaviour. ➤informal a feeling of disproportionate anxiety about something. **3** Chemistry an ion or molecule in which one or more groups are linked to a metal atom by coordinate bonds. ● **v.** Chemistry form or cause to form a complex with another.
– DERIVATIVES **complexation** n. (Chemistry). **complexity** n. **complexly** adv.
– ORIGIN C17 (as n.): from L. *complexus*, from *complectere* 'embrace, comprise', later assoc. with *complexus* 'plaited'; the adjective is partly via Fr. *complexe*.

**complexion** ● **n. 1** the natural tone and texture of the skin of a person's face. **2** the general aspect or character of something.
– DERIVATIVES **-complexioned** adj.
– ORIGIN ME (denoting temperament or constitution as determined by combination of the bodily humours): via OFr. from L. *complexio(n-)* 'combination', from *complectere* 'embrace, comprise'.

**complex sentence** ● **n.** a sentence containing a subordinate clause or clauses.

**compliance** /kəm'plʌɪəns/ ● **n. 1** the action or fact of being compliant. **2** Physics the capacity of a material or object of yielding when subjected to an applied force.

**compliant** ● **adj. 1** disposed to agree with others or obey rules, especially to an excessive degree; acquiescent. **2** meeting or in accordance with rules or standards. **3** Physics & Medicine having the property of compliance.
– DERIVATIVES **compliantly** adv.

**complicate** /'kɒmplɪkeɪt/ ● **v. 1** make more complicated. **2** Medicine introduce complications in (an existing condition).
– ORIGIN C17 (in the sense 'combine, entangle, intertwine'): from L. *complicat-*, *complicare* 'fold together'.

**complicated** ● **adj. 1** consisting of many interconnecting parts or elements; intricate. ➤involving many different and confusing aspects. **2** Medicine involving complications.
– DERIVATIVES **complicatedly** adv.

**complication** ● **n. 1** a circumstance that complicates something; a difficulty. ➤an involved or confused condition or state. **2** Medicine a secondary disease or condition aggravating an already existing one.

**complicit** /kəm'plɪsɪt/ ● **adj.** involved with others in an unlawful activity; having complicity.

**complicity** ● **n.** the fact or condition of being involved with others in an unlawful activity.
– ORIGIN C17: from ME *complice* 'an associate', from OFr., from late L. *complex*, *complic-* 'allied', from L. *complicare* 'fold together'; cf. ACCOMPLICE.

**compliment** ● **n.** /'kɒmplɪm(ə)nt/ a polite expression of praise or admiration. ➤(**compliments**) congratulations or praise expressed to someone. ➤(**compliments**) formal greetings, especially when sent as a message. ● **v.** /'kɒmplɪmɛnt/ **1** politely congratulate or praise (someone). **2** (**compliment someone with**) archaic present someone with (something) as a mark of courtesy.
– PHRASES **return the compliment** give a compliment in return for another. ➤retaliate or respond in kind. **with the compliments of someone** given without charge; free.
– ORIGIN C17: from Fr. *compliment* (n.), *complimenter* (v.), from Ital. *complimento* 'fulfilment of the requirements of courtesy', from L. *complementum* 'completion, fulfilment'.

**USAGE compliment**

On the confusion of **compliment** with **complement**, see COMPLEMENT.

**complimentary** ● **adj. 1** expressing a compliment; praising or approving. **2** given or supplied free of charge.

**compliments slip** ● **n.** Brit. a small piece of paper printed with a company's name and address, sent out with goods or information in place of a covering letter.

**compline** /'kɒmplɪn, -ʌɪn/ ● **n.** a service of evening prayers forming part of the Divine Office of the Western Christian Church, traditionally said before retiring for the night.
– ORIGIN ME: from OFr. *complie*, fem. past part. of *complir*, from L. *complere* (see COMPLETE).

**comply** /kəm'plʌɪ/ ● **v.** (**-ies**, **-ied**) **1** act in accordance with a wish or command. **2** meet specified standards.
– ORIGIN C16 (in sense 'fulfil, accomplish', later 'fulfil the requirements of courtesy'): from Ital. *complire*, Catalan *complir*, Sp. *cumplir*, from L. *complere* (see COMPLETE); cf. COMPLIMENT.

**compo** ● **n.** (pl. **-os**) **1** a composite material. **2** (also **compo rations**) Brit. a supply of food designed to last a specified number of man-days and made up of various tinned items carried in a large pack.

**component** /kəm'pəʊnənt/ ● **n. 1** a part or element of a larger whole, especially a part of a machine or vehicle. **2**

Physics each of two or more forces, velocities, or other vectors acting in different directions which are together equivalent to a given vector. ● **adj.** constituting part of a larger whole; constituent.
– ORIGIN C17: from L. *component-*, *componere* 'put together'; cf. COMPOUND[1].

**componential analysis** /ˌkɒmpəˈnɛnʃ(ə)l/ ● **n.** Linguistics the analysis of the meaning of a word or other linguistic unit into discrete semantic components.

**compony** /kɒmˈpɒni/ ● **adj.** Heraldry divided into a single row of squares in alternating tinctures.
– ORIGIN C16: from Fr. *componé*, from OFr. *compondre*, from L. *componere* 'put together'.

**comport**[1] /kəmˈpɔːt/ ● **v. 1** (**comport oneself**) formal conduct oneself; behave. **2** (**comport with**) archaic accord with; agree with.
– ORIGIN ME (in the sense 'tolerate'): from L. *comportare*, from *com-* 'together' + *portare* 'carry, bear'.

**comport**[2] /ˈkɒmpɔːt/ ● **n.** another term for COMPOTE (in sense 2).
– ORIGIN C19: appar. an abbrev. of Fr. *comportier*.

**comportment** ● **n.** formal behaviour or bearing.

**compose** ● **v. 1** write or create (a work of art, especially music or poetry). ➤ order or arrange in order to form an artistic whole. **2** (of elements) constitute or make up (a whole). **3** [often as adj. **composed**] calm or settle (one's features or thoughts). **4** prepare (a text) for printing by setting up the characters to be printed. **5** archaic settle (a dispute).
– DERIVATIVES **composedly** adv.
– ORIGIN ME: from OFr. *composer*, from L. *componere* (see COMPONENT), but influenced by L. *compositus* 'composed' and OFr. *poser* 'to place'.

**composer** ● **n.** a person who writes music.

**composite** /ˈkɒmpəzɪt/ ● **adj. 1** made up of various parts or elements. ➤ (of a constructional material) made up of recognizable constituents. **2** (**Composite**) relating to or denoting a classical order of architecture consisting of elements of the Ionic and Corinthian orders. **3** /usu. ˈkɒmpəzʌɪt/ Botany relating to or denoting plants of the family Compositae, which have composite flower heads consisting of numerous florets and include daisies, dandelions, thistles, and chrysanthemums. **4** Mathematics (of an integer) being the product of two or more factors greater than unity; not prime. ● **n. 1** a thing made up of several parts or elements. ➤ a composite constructional material. ➤ /ˈkɒmpəzʌɪt/ a motion for debate composed of two or more related resolutions. **2** /usu. ˈkɒmpəzʌɪt/ Botany a plant of the daisy family (Compositae). ● **v.** [usu. as noun **compositing**] combine (two or more images) to make a single picture, especially electronically.
– DERIVATIVES **compositely** adv. **compositeness** n.
– ORIGIN ME: via Fr. from L. *composit-*, *componere* 'put together'.

**composition** ● **n. 1** the way in which a whole or mixture is made up; ingredients or constituents. ➤ a thing composed of various elements. ➤ a compound artificial substance. **2** a work of music, literature, or art. **3** the action of composing. **4** archaic mental constitution; character. **5** a legal agreement to pay a sum in lieu of a larger debt or other obligation. **6** Mathematics the successive application of functions to a variable. **7** Physics the process of finding the resultant of a number of forces.
– DERIVATIVES **compositional** adj. **compositionally** adv.

**compositor** /kəmˈpɒzɪtə/ ● **n.** a person who arranges type for printing or keys text into a composing machine.
– ORIGIN ME (in sense 'arbiter'): from Anglo-Norman Fr. *compositour*, from L. *compositor*, from *composit-*, *componere* (see COMPOSE).

**compos mentis** /ˌkɒmpɒs ˈmɛntɪs/ ● **adj.** having full control of one's mind.
– ORIGIN C17: L.

**compost** ● **n.** decayed organic material used as a fertilizer for growing plants. ➤ a mixture of compost with loam soil used as a growing medium. ● **v.** make into or treat with compost.
– ORIGIN ME: from OFr. *composte*, from L. *composita*, *compositum* 'something put together', fem. and neut. past part. of *componere*.

**compost heap** (N. Amer. also **compost pile**) ● **n.** a pile of garden and kitchen refuse which decomposes to produce compost.

**composure** ● **n.** the state or feeling of being calm and composed.

**compote** /ˈkɒmpəʊt, -ɒt/ ● **n. 1** fruit preserved or cooked in syrup. **2** a bowl-shaped dessert dish with a stem.
– ORIGIN C17: from Fr., from OFr. *composte* (see COMPOST).

**compound**[1] ● **n.** /ˈkɒmpaʊnd/ a thing composed of two or more separate elements. ➤ Chemistry a substance formed from two or more elements chemically united in fixed proportions. ➤ a word made up of two or more existing words. ● **adj.** /ˈkɒmpaʊnd/ made up or consisting of several parts or elements. ➤ (of interest) payable on both capital and the accumulated interest. Compare with SIMPLE. ➤ Biology (of a leaf, flower, or eye) consisting of two or more simple parts or individuals in combination. ● **v.** /kəmˈpaʊnd/ **1** make up (a composite whole); constitute. ➤ mix or combine (ingredients or constituents). ➤ reckon (interest) on previously accumulated interest. **2** make (something bad) worse. **3** Law forbear from prosecuting (a felony) in exchange for money or other consideration. ➤ settle (a debt or other matter) in this way.
– DERIVATIVES **compoundable** adj. **compounder** n.
– ORIGIN ME *compoune* (v.), from OFr. *compoun-*, *compondre*, from L. *componere* 'put together'; the final *-d* was added on the pattern of *expound* and *propound*.

**compound**[2] /ˈkɒmpaʊnd/ ● **n.** a large open area enclosed by a fence, e.g. around a factory or within a prison. ➤ S. African an area containing single-sex living quarters for migrant workers, especially miners. ➤ another term for POUND[3].
– ORIGIN C17: from Port. *campon* or Du. *kampoeng*, from Malay *kampong* 'enclosure, hamlet'; cf. KAMPONG.

**compound eye** ● **n.** an eye consisting of an array of numerous small visual units, as found in insects and crustaceans. Contrasted with SIMPLE EYE.

**compound fracture** ● **n.** an injury in which a broken bone pierces the skin.

**compound interval** ● **n.** Music an interval greater than an octave.

**compound sentence** ● **n.** a sentence with more than one subject or predicate.

**compound time** ● **n.** Music musical rhythm or metre in which each beat in a bar is subdivided into three smaller units, so having the value of a dotted note. Compare with SIMPLE TIME.

**comprador** /ˌkɒmprəˈdɔː/ (also **compradore**) ● **n.** a person who acts as an agent for foreign businesses.
– ORIGIN C17: from Port., 'buyer'.

**comprehend** /ˌkɒmprɪˈhɛnd/ ● **v. 1** grasp mentally; understand. **2** formal include, comprise, or encompass.
– ORIGIN ME: from OFr. *comprehender*, or L. *comprehendere*, from *com-* 'together' + *prehendere* 'grasp'.

**comprehensible** ● **adj.** able to be understood; intelligible.
– DERIVATIVES **comprehensibility** n. **comprehensibly** adv.

**comprehension** ● **n. 1** the action or capability of understanding. ➤ Brit. the school exercise of answering questions on a set text to test understanding. **2** archaic inclusion. ➤ historical the proposed inclusion of Nonconformists within the Established Church of England.

**comprehensive** ● **adj. 1** including or dealing with all or nearly all aspects of something. ➤ of large content or scope; wide-ranging. ➤ (of a victory or defeat) by a large margin. ➤ (of motor-vehicle insurance) providing cover for most risks, including damage to the policyholder's own vehicle. **2** Brit. denoting a system of secondary education in which children of all abilities from a particular area are educated in one school. **3** archaic of or relating to understanding. ● **n.** Brit. a comprehensive school.
– DERIVATIVES **comprehensively** adv. **comprehensiveness** n.

**compress** ● v. /kəmˈprɛs/ flatten by pressure; squeeze into less space. ➤ [as adj. **compressed**] chiefly Biology having a narrow shape as if flattened, especially sideways. ➤ squeeze or press (two things) together. ● n. /ˈkɒmprɛs/ a pad of absorbent material pressed on to part of the body to relieve inflammation or stop bleeding.
– DERIVATIVES **compressibility** /-ˈbɪlɪti/ n. **compressible** /kəmˈprɛsɪb(ə)l/ adj. **compressive** /kəmˈprɛsɪv/ adj.
– ORIGIN ME: from OFr. *compresser* or late L. *compressare*, frequentative of L. *compress-*, *comprimere*.

**compressed air** ● n. air that is at more than atmospheric pressure.

**compression** ● n. **1** the action of compressing or being compressed. **2** the reduction in volume (causing an increase in pressure) of the fuel mixture in an internal-combustion engine before ignition.
– DERIVATIVES **compressional** adj.

**compression ratio** ● n. the ratio of the maximum to minimum volume in the cylinder of an internal-combustion engine.

**compressive strength** ● n. the resistance of a material to breaking under compression. Compare with TENSILE STRENGTH.

**compressor** ● n. **1** an instrument or device for compressing something. ➤ a machine used to supply air or other gas at increased pressure. **2** an electrical device which reduces the dynamic range of a sound signal.

**comprise** ● v. consist of; be made up of. ➤ (also **be comprised of**) make up; constitute.
– ORIGIN ME: from Fr., 'comprised', fem. past part. of *comprendre* (see COMPREHEND).

**USAGE** comprise

According to traditional usage, **comprise** means 'consist of' and should not be used to mean 'constitute or make up (a whole)'. However, a passive use of **comprise** is fast becoming part of standard English: this use (as in *the country is comprised of twenty states*) is more or less synonymous with the traditional active sense (as in *the country comprises twenty states*).

**compromise** ● n. **1** an agreement reached by each side making concessions. ➤ an intermediate state between conflicting opinions. **2** the expedient acceptance of standards that are lower than is desirable. ● v. **1** settle a dispute by mutual concession. **2** expediently accept standards that are lower than is desirable. **3** bring into disrepute or danger by indiscreet or reckless behaviour. ➤ [as adj. **compromising**] revealing an embarrassing or incriminating secret: *a compromising situation*.
– DERIVATIVES **compromiser** n.
– ORIGIN ME: from OFr. *compromis*, from late L. *compromiss-*, *compromittere*, from *com-* 'together' + *promittere* (see PROMISE).

**compte rendu** /ˌkɔ̃t rɑ̃ˈdjuː, French kɔ̃t ʀɑ̃dy/ ● n. (pl. **comptes rendus** pronunc. same) a formal report or review.
– ORIGIN C19: Fr., lit. 'account rendered'.

**Compton effect** ● n. Physics an increase in wavelength of X-rays or gamma rays that occurs when they are scattered.
– ORIGIN C20: named after the Amer. physicist A. H. *Compton*.

**comptroller** /kənˈtrəʊlə, kɒmp-/ ● n. a controller (used in the title of some financial officers).
– ORIGIN C15: var. of *controller* (see CONTROL), by assoc. with Fr. *compte* 'calculation' or its source, late L. *computus*.

**compulsion** ● n. **1** the action or state of compelling or being compelled; constraint. **2** an irresistible urge to behave in a certain way, especially against one's conscious wishes.

**compulsive** ● adj. **1** resulting from or acting on an irresistible urge or compulsion. **2** irresistibly interesting or exciting; compelling.
– DERIVATIVES **compulsively** adv. **compulsiveness** n.

**compulsory** ● adj. required by law or a rule; obligatory. ➤ involving or exercising compulsion; coercive.
– DERIVATIVES **compulsorily** adv. **compulsoriness** n.

**compulsory purchase** ● n. Brit. the officially enforced purchase of privately owned land or property for public use.

**compunction** ● n. a feeling of guilt or moral scruple that prevents or follows the doing of something bad.
– DERIVATIVES **compunctious** adj. **compunctiously** adv.
– ORIGIN ME: from OFr. *componction*, from eccles. L. *compunctio(n-)*, from L. *compungere* 'prick sharply'.

**compurgation** /ˌkɒmpəːˈgeɪʃ(ə)n/ ● n. Law, historical acquittal from a charge or accusation obtained by statements of innocence given by witnesses under oath.
– ORIGIN C17: from med. L. *compurgatio(n-)*, from L. *compurgare*, from *com-* (expressing intensive force) + *purgare* 'purify'.

**compurgator** /ˈkɒmpəːgeɪtə/ ● n. Law, historical a sworn witness to the innocence or good character of an accused person.

**computation** ● n. **1** the action of mathematical calculation. **2** the use of computers, especially as a subject of research or study.
– DERIVATIVES **computational** adj. **computationally** adv.

**computational linguistics** ● pl. n. [treated as sing.] the branch of linguistics in which the techniques of computer science are applied to the analysis and synthesis of language and speech.

**compute** ● v. **1** reckon or calculate (a figure or amount). **2** [with neg.] informal seem reasonable; make sense.
– DERIVATIVES **computability** n. **computable** adj.
– ORIGIN C17: from Fr. *computer* or L. *computare*, from *com-* 'together' + *putare* 'to settle (an account)'.

**computer** ● n. an electronic device which is capable of receiving information (data) and performing a sequence of logical operations in accordance with a predetermined but variable set of procedural instructions (program) to produce a result in the form of information or signals.

**computerate** /kəmˈpjuːtərət/ ● adj. informal another term for COMPUTER-LITERATE.

**computer dating** ● n. the use of computer databases to identify potentially compatible partners for people.

**computer game** ● n. a game played using a computer, especially a video game.

**computerize** (also **-ise**) ● v. [often as adj. **computerized**] convert to a system or form which is controlled, stored, or processed by computer.
– DERIVATIVES **computerization** n.

**computer-literate** ● adj. having sufficient knowledge and skill to be able to use computers.
– DERIVATIVES **computer literacy** n.

**computer science** ● n. the study of the principles and use of computers.

**computing** ● n. the use or operation of computers.

**comrade** ● n. (among men) a companion who shares one's activities or is a fellow member of an organization. ➤ (also **comrade-in-arms**) a fellow soldier or serviceman. ➤ a fellow socialist or communist.
– DERIVATIVES **comradely** adj. **comradeship** n.
– ORIGIN C16 (orig. also *camerade*): from Fr. *camerade*, *camarade*, from Sp. *camarada* 'room-mate'.

**Comsat** ● n. trademark a communications satellite.

**Con** ● abbrev. Brit. **1** Conservative (as a political affiliation). **2** constable (as part of a police officer's title).

**con**[1] informal ● v. (**conned**, **conning**) deceive (someone) into doing or believing something by lying to them. ● n. a deception of this kind.
– ORIGIN C19 (orig. US): abbrev. of CONFIDENCE, as in *confidence trick*.

**con**[2] ● n. (usu. in phr. **pros and cons**) a disadvantage of or argument against something.
– ORIGIN C16: from L. *contra* 'against'.

**con**[3] ● n. informal a convict.

**con**[4] (US also **conn**) Nautical ● v. (**conned**, **conning**) direct the steering of (a ship). ● n. (**the con**) the action or post of conning a ship.
– ORIGIN C17: appar. a weakened form of obs. *cond* 'conduct, guide', from OFr. *conduire*.

**con**[5] ● v. (**conned**, **conning**) archaic study attentively or learn by heart (a piece of writing).
– ORIGIN ME *cunne*, *conne*, *con*, vars of CAN[1].

**con-** • prefix variant spelling of **COM-** assimilated before *c, d, f, g, j, n, q, s, t, v,* and sometimes before vowels (as in *concord, condescend, confide,* etc.).

**conacre** /'kɒneɪkə/ • n. (in Ireland) the letting by a tenant of small portions of land for crops or grazing.
– ORIGIN C19: from **CORN**[1] + **ACRE**.

**con amore** /ˌkɒn a'mɔːreɪ/ • adv. Music with tenderness.
– ORIGIN Ital., 'with love'.

**conation** /kə'neɪʃ(ə)n/ • n. Philosophy & Psychology desire or will to perform an action; volition.
– DERIVATIVES **conative** adj.
– ORIGIN C17 (denoting an attempt or endeavour): from L. *conatio(n-)*, from *conari* 'to try'.

**con brio** /kɒn 'briːəʊ/ • adv. Music with vigour.
– ORIGIN from Ital.

**concatenate** /kən'katɪneɪt/ • v. formal or technical link together in a chain or series.
– DERIVATIVES **concatenation** n.
– ORIGIN C15 (as adj.): from late L. *concatenat-*, *concatenare* 'link together'.

**concave** /'kɒnkeɪv/ • adj. having an outline or surface that curves inwards like the interior of a circle or sphere. Compare with **CONVEX**.
– DERIVATIVES **concavely** adv. **concavity** n.
– ORIGIN ME: from L. *concavus*, from *con-* 'together' + *cavus* 'hollow'.

**conceal** • v. not allow to be seen; hide. ➤keep secret; prevent from being known.
– DERIVATIVES **concealment** n.
– ORIGIN ME: from OFr. *conceler*, from L. *concelare*, from *con-* 'completely' + *celare* 'hide'.

**concealer** • n. a flesh-toned cosmetic used to cover spots and blemishes.

**concede** • v. **1** finally admit or agree that something is true. ➤admit (defeat) in a match or contest. **2** surrender or yield (a possession, advantage, or right). ➤fail to prevent an opponent scoring (a goal or point).
– DERIVATIVES **conceder** n.
– ORIGIN C15: from Fr. *concéder* or L. *concedere*, from *con-* 'completely' + *cedere* 'yield'.

**conceit** • n. **1** excessive pride in oneself. **2** an elaborate metaphor or artistic effect. ➤a fanciful notion.
– ORIGIN ME: from **CONCEIVE**, on the pattern of *deceive, deceit*.

**conceited** • adj. excessively proud of oneself.
– DERIVATIVES **conceitedly** adv. **conceitedness** n.

**conceivable** • adj. capable of being imagined or understood.
– DERIVATIVES **conceivability** n. **conceivably** adv.

**conceive** • v. **1** become pregnant with (a child). **2** devise in the mind; imagine.
– ORIGIN ME: from OFr. *concevoir*, from L. *concipere*, from *com-* 'together' + *capere* 'take'.

**concelebrate** /kɒn'sɛlɪbreɪt/ • v. Christian Church officiate jointly at (a Mass).
– DERIVATIVES **concelebrant** n. **concelebration** n.
– ORIGIN C19: from L. *concelebrat-*, *concelebrare* 'celebrate together'.

**concentrate** • v. **1** focus all one's attention or mental effort on. ➤(**concentrate on**) do (one particular thing) above all others. **2** gather together in numbers or a mass at one point. **3** increase the strength of (a solution). • n. a concentrated form of something, especially food.
– DERIVATIVES **concentrated** adj. **concentratedly** adv. **concentrative** adj. **concentrator** n.
– ORIGIN C17 (in the sense 'bring towards a centre'): Latinized form of **CONCENTRE**, or from Fr. *concentrer* 'to concentrate'.

**concentration** • n. **1** the action or power of concentrating. **2** a close gathering of people or things. **3** the relative amount of a particular substance contained within a solution or mixture.

**concentration camp** • n. a camp for detaining political prisoners, especially in Nazi Germany.

**concentre** (US **concenter**) • v. concentrate in a small space. ➤collect at a common centre.
– ORIGIN C16: from Fr. *concentrer*, from L. *con-* 'together' + *centrum* 'centre'.

**concentric** • adj. of or denoting circles, arcs, or other shapes which share the same centre.
– DERIVATIVES **concentrically** adv. **concentricity** n.
– ORIGIN ME: from OFr. *concentrique* or med. L. *concentricus*, from *con-* 'together' + *centrum* 'centre'.

**concept** • n. **1** an abstract idea. ➤an idea to help sell or publicize a commodity. **2** Philosophy an idea or mental picture of a group or class of objects, formed by combining all their aspects.
– ORIGIN C16: from L. *conceptum* 'something conceived', from L. *concept-*, *concipere* (see **CONCEIVE**).

**concept album** • n. a rock album featuring songs expressing a particular theme.

**conception** • n. **1** the action of conceiving a child or of one being conceived. ➤the devising of a plan or idea. **2** the way in which something is perceived. ➤a concept. ➤ability to imagine or understand.
– DERIVATIVES **conceptional** adj.
– ORIGIN ME: via OFr. from L. *conceptio(n-)*, from *concipere* (see **CONCEIVE**).

**conceptual** • adj. of, relating to, or based on mental concepts.
– DERIVATIVES **conceptually** adv.

**conceptualism** • n. Philosophy the theory that universals can be said to exist, but only as concepts in the mind.
– DERIVATIVES **conceptualist** n.

**conceptualize** (also **-ise**) • v. form a concept or idea of.
– DERIVATIVES **conceptualization** n.

**conceptus** /kən'sɛptəs/ • n. (pl. **conceptuses**) technical the embryo during the early stages of pregnancy.
– ORIGIN C18: from L., 'conception, embryo', from *concept-*, *concipere* 'conceive'.

**concern** • v. **1** relate to; be about. ➤affect or involve. **2** worry (someone). • n. **1** worry; anxiety. **2** a matter of interest or importance. **3** a business. **4** informal, dated a complicated or awkward thing.
– PHRASES **as** (or **so**) **far as —— is concerned** as regards the interests or case of ——. **have no concern with** have nothing to do with. **to whom it may concern** used to address a reader whose identity is unknown.
– ORIGIN ME: from Fr. *concerner* or late L. *concernere* (in med. L. 'be relevant to'), from *con-* (expressing intensive force) + *cernere* 'sift, discern'.

**concerned** • adj. worried; anxious.
– DERIVATIVES **concernedly** adv.

**concerning** • prep. about.

**concernment** • n. archaic importance. ➤a matter of interest or importance.

**concert** • n. /'kɒnsət/ **1** a musical performance given in public, typically of several compositions. **2** formal agreement; harmony. ➤Law joint action, especially in committing a crime. • v. /kən'səːt/ formal arrange by mutual agreement or coordination.
– PHRASES **in concert 1** acting jointly. **2** giving a live public performance.
– ORIGIN C16: from Fr. *concerter*, from Ital. *concertare* 'harmonize'; the noun is from Fr. *concert*.

**concertante** /ˌkɒntʃə'tanteɪ, -'tanti/ • adj. **1** denoting a piece of music containing one or more solo parts, of less prominence than in a concerto. **2** chiefly historical denoting prominent instrumental parts throughout a piece of music.
– ORIGIN Ital., 'harmonizing'.

**concerted** • adj. **1** jointly arranged or carried out. ➤done with great effort. **2** (of music) arranged in several parts of equal importance.

**concert grand** • n. the largest size of grand piano, used for concerts.

**concertina** /ˌkɒnsə'tiːnə/ • n. **1** a small musical instrument played by stretching and squeezing a central bellows between the hands to blow air over reeds, each note being sounded by a button. **2** [as modifier] opening or closing in multiple folds. • v. (**concertinas**, **concertinaed** or **concertina'd**, **concertinaing**) extend or compress in folds like those of a concertina.

**concertino** /ˌkɒntʃə'tiːnəʊ/ • n. (pl. **-os**) **1** a simple or

short concerto. **2** a solo instrument playing with an orchestra.
– ORIGIN C18: Ital., dimin. of *concerto* (see **CONCERTO**).

**concertmaster** • **n.** chiefly N. Amer. the leading first-violin player in some orchestras.

**concerto** /kən'tʃəːtəʊ, -'tʃɛːtəʊ/ • **n.** (pl. **concertos** or **concerti**) a musical composition for a solo instrument accompanied by an orchestra.
– ORIGIN C18: Ital., from *concertare* 'harmonize'.

**concerto grosso** /'grɒsəʊ/ • **n.** (pl. **concerti grossi** /-si/) a musical composition for a group of solo instruments accompanied by an orchestra.
– ORIGIN C18: Ital., lit. 'big concerto'.

**concert overture** • **n.** a piece of music in the style of an overture but intended for independent performance.

**concert party** • **n.** a group of performers giving variety concerts.

**concert performance** • **n.** Brit. a performance of a piece of music written for an opera or ballet without the accompanying dramatic action.

**concert pitch** • **n. 1** Music a standard for the tuning of musical instruments, in which the note A above middle C has a frequency of 440 Hz. **2** a state of readiness and keenness.

**concession** • **n. 1** a thing that is conceded. ➤a gesture made in recognition of a demand or prevailing standard. **2** a reduction in price for a certain category of person. **3** the right to use land or other property for a specified purpose. ➤a commercial operation set up within the premises of a larger concern.
– DERIVATIVES **concessional** adj. **concessionary** adj.
– ORIGIN ME: from L. *concessio(n-)*, from *concedere* (see **CONCEDE**).

**concessionaire** /kən,sɛʃə'nɛː/ (also **concessionnaire**) • **n.** the holder of a concession or grant, especially for the use of land or trading rights.
– ORIGIN C19: from Fr. *concessionnaire*, from L. *concessio* (see **CONCESSION**).

**concessive** • **adj. 1** of, characterized by, or tending to concession. **2** Grammar (of a preposition or conjunction) introducing a phrase or clause denoting a circumstance which might be expected to preclude the action of the main clause, but does not (e.g. *in spite of*, *although*).

**conch** /kɒŋk, kɒn(t)ʃ/ • **n.** (pl. **conchs** /kɒŋks/ or **conches** /'kɒntʃɪz/) **1** a tropical marine mollusc with a robust spiral shell which may bear long projections and have a flared lip. [*Strombus* and other genera: many species.] **2** Architecture the roof of a semicircular apse. **3** another term for **CONCHA**.
– ORIGIN ME: from L. *concha* 'shellfish, shell', from Gk *konkhē* 'mussel, cockle, or shell-like cavity'.

**concha** /'kɒŋkə/ • **n.** (pl. **conchae** /-kiː/) Anatomy & Zoology a part resembling a spiral shell, in particular the depression in the external ear leading to its central opening.
– ORIGIN C16: from L. (see **CONCH**).

**conchie** /'kɒnʃi/ • **n.** (pl. **-ies**) Brit. informal, derogatory a conscientious objector.

**conchoidal** /kɒŋ'kɔɪd(ə)l/ • **adj.** chiefly Mineralogy denoting a type of fracture in a solid which results in a smooth rounded surface resembling a scallop shell.

**conchology** /kɒŋ'kɒlədʒi/ • **n.** the scientific study or collection of mollusc shells.
– DERIVATIVES **conchological** adj. **conchologist** n.

**concierge** /'kɒnsɪɛːʒ/ • **n. 1** (especially in France) a resident caretaker of a block of flats or small hotel. **2** a hotel employee who assists guests by booking tours, making theatre and restaurant reservations, etc.
– ORIGIN C16: Fr., prob. based on L. *conservus* 'fellow slave'.

**conciliar** /kən'sɪlɪə/ • **adj.** of or relating to a council, especially an ecclesiastical one.
– ORIGIN C17: from med. L. *consiliarius* 'counsellor', from L. *concilium* (see **COUNCIL**).

**conciliate** /kən'sɪlɪeɪt/ • **v. 1** placate; pacify. ➤act as a mediator. ➤formal reconcile. **2** archaic gain (esteem or goodwill).
– DERIVATIVES **conciliation** n. **conciliative** adj. **conciliator** n. **conciliatoriness** n. **conciliatory** adj.
– ORIGIN C16: from L. *conciliat-*, *conciliare* 'combine, gain', from *concilium* (see **COUNCIL**).

**concinnity** /kən'sɪnɪti/ • **n.** rare elegance or neatness of literary or artistic style.
– ORIGIN C16: from L. *concinnitas*, from *concinnus* 'skilfully put together'.

**concise** • **adj.** giving a lot of information clearly and in few words.
– DERIVATIVES **concisely** adv. **conciseness** n. **concision** n.
– ORIGIN C16 (earlier (ME) as *concision*): from Fr. *concis* or L. *concisus*, past part. of *concidere* 'cut up, cut down'.

**conclave** /'kɒŋkleɪv/ • **n. 1** a private meeting. **2** (in the Roman Catholic Church) the assembly of cardinals for the election of a pope.
– ORIGIN ME: via Fr. from L. *conclave* 'lockable room', from *con-* 'with' + *clavis* 'key'.

**conclude** • **v. 1** bring or come to an end. ➤formally settle or arrange (a treaty or agreement). **2** arrive at a judgement or opinion by reasoning. **3** US dated decide to do.
– ORIGIN ME (in the sense 'convince'): from L. *conclus-*, *concludere*, from *con-* 'completely' + *claudere* 'to shut'.

**conclusion** • **n. 1** the end or finish of something. ➤the summing-up of an argument or text. ➤the settling of a treaty or agreement. **2** a judgement or decision reached by reasoning. ➤Logic a proposition that is reached from given premises.
– PHRASES **jump to conclusions** make a hasty judgement before considering all the facts. **try conclusions with** formal engage in a trial of skill or argument with.

**conclusive** • **adj.** (of evidence or argument) decisive or convincing.
– DERIVATIVES **conclusively** adv. **conclusiveness** n.

**concoct** /kən'kɒkt/ • **v.** make (a dish or meal) by combining ingredients. ➤create or devise (a story or plan).
– DERIVATIVES **concocter** n. **concoction** n.
– ORIGIN C16: from L. *concoct-*, *concoquere* 'cook together'.

**concomitance** /kən'kɒmɪt(ə)ns/ • **n.** (also **concomitancy**) **1** the fact of existing or occurring with something else. **2** Theology the doctrine that the body and blood of Christ are each present in the bread and wine of the Eucharist.
– ORIGIN C16: from med. L. *concomitantia*, from *concomitant-*, *concomitari* 'accompany'.

**concomitant** /kən'kɒmɪt(ə)nt/ formal • **adj.** naturally accompanying or associated. • **n.** a concomitant phenomenon.
– DERIVATIVES **concomitantly** adv.

**concord** • **n. 1** formal agreement; harmony. ➤a treaty. **2** Grammar agreement between words in gender, number, case, or person. **3** Music a chord that is pleasing or satisfactory in itself.
– ORIGIN ME: from OFr. *concorde*, from L. *concordia*, from *concors* 'of one mind'.

**concordance** /kən'kɔːd(ə)ns/ • **n. 1** an alphabetical list of the important words in a text, usually with citations of the passages concerned. **2** formal agreement. **3** Medicine the inheritance by two related individuals of the same genetic characteristic.
– ORIGIN ME: from OFr., from med. L. *concordantia*, from L. *concordant-*, *concordare* 'agree on'.

**concordant** • **adj. 1** in agreement; consistent. **2** Medicine (of twins) inheriting the same genetic characteristic. **3** Music in harmony.
– DERIVATIVES **concordantly** adv.

**concordat** /kən'kɔːdat/ • **n.** an agreement or treaty, especially one between the Vatican and a secular government.
– ORIGIN C17: from Fr., or from L. *concordatum* 'something agreed upon'.

**concours** /'kɒ̃kʊə/ (also **concours d'élégance** /,dɛleɪ'gɒ̃s/) • **n.** (pl. same) an exhibition of vintage or classic motor vehicles, with prizes awarded to those in the best condition.
– ORIGIN Fr., 'contest (of elegance)'.

**concourse** • **n. 1** a large open central area inside or in front of a public building. **2** formal a crowd or assembly. ➤the action of coming together.

– ORIGIN ME: from OFr. *concours*, from L. *concursus*, from *concurs-*, *concurrere* (see **CONCUR**).

**concrescence** /kən'krɛs(ə)ns/ ● **n.** Biology the coalescence or growing together of separate parts.
– DERIVATIVES **concrescent** adj.
– ORIGIN C17: from **CON-** + *-crescence*, on the pattern of words such as *excrescence*.

**concrete** ● **adj.** /'kɒŋkriːt/ existing in a material or physical form. ➤ specific; definite. ➤ (of a noun) denoting a material object as opposed to an abstract quality, state, or action. ● **n.** a building material made from a mixture of gravel, sand, cement, and water, forming a stone-like mass on hardening. ● **v. 1** /'kɒŋkriːt/ cover or fix solidly with concrete. **2** /kən'kriːt/ archaic solidify. ➤ make real.
– DERIVATIVES **concretely** adv. **concreteness** n.
– ORIGIN ME: from Fr. *concret* or L. *concretus*, past part. of *concrescere* 'grow together'.

**concrete jungle** ● **n.** an area with a high density of large, unattractive, modern buildings.

**concrete mixer** ● **n.** a cement mixer.

**concrete music** ● **n.** another term for **MUSIQUE CONCRÈTE**.

**concrete poetry** ● **n.** poetry in which part of the meaning is conveyed visually, using patterns of words or letters.

**concretion** ● **n.** a hard solid mass formed by accumulation of matter.
– DERIVATIVES **concretionary** adj.
– ORIGIN C16: from L. *concretio(n-)*, from *concrescere* 'grow together'.

**concretize** /'kɒŋkrɪtʌɪz/ (also **-ise**) ● **v.** make concrete instead of abstract.
– DERIVATIVES **concretization** n.

**concubinage** /kɒn'kjuːbɪnɪdʒ/ ● **n.** chiefly historical the practice of keeping or the state of being a concubine.

**concubine** /'kɒŋkjʊbʌɪn/ ● **n. 1** chiefly historical (in polygamous societies) a woman who lives with a man but has lower status than his wife or wives. **2** archaic a mistress.
– DERIVATIVES **concubinary** /kən'kjuːbɪn(ə)ri/ adj.
– ORIGIN ME: from OFr., from L. *concubina*, from *con-* 'with' + *cubare* 'to lie'.

**concupiscence** /kən'kjuːpɪs(ə)ns/ ● **n.** formal lust.
– DERIVATIVES **concupiscent** adj.
– ORIGIN ME: via OFr. from late L. *concupiscentia*, from L. *concupiscent-*, *concupiscere* 'begin to desire'.

**concur** ● **v.** (**concurred**, **concurring**) **1** (often **concur with**) agree. **2** happen at the same time.
– ORIGIN ME: from L. *concurrere* 'run together, assemble in crowds'.

**concurrent** ● **adj. 1** existing or happening at the same time. **2** Mathematics (of three or more lines) meeting at or tending towards one point.
– DERIVATIVES **concurrence** n. **concurrently** adv.

**concussion** ● **n. 1** temporary unconsciousness or confusion caused by a blow on the head. **2** a violent shock as from a heavy blow.
– DERIVATIVES **concuss** v. **concussive** adj.
– ORIGIN ME: from L. *concussio(n-)*, from *concutere* 'dash together, shake'.

**condemn** ● **v. 1** express complete disapproval of. **2** (usu. **condemn someone to**) sentence to a punishment, especially death. ➤ force (someone) to endure something unpleasant. ➤ prove the guilt of. **3** officially declare to be unfit for use.
– DERIVATIVES **condemnable** adj. **condemnation** n. **condemnatory** adj.
– ORIGIN ME: from OFr. *condemner*, from L. *condemnare*, from *con-* (expressing intensive force) + *damnare* (see **DAMN**).

**condemned cell** ● **n.** Brit. historical a cell for a prisoner who was condemned to death.

**condensate** /'kɒnd(ə)nseɪt/ ● **n.** technical a substance produced by condensation.

**condensation** ● **n. 1** water from humid air collecting as droplets on a cold surface. **2** the conversion of a vapour or gas to a liquid. **3** Chemistry a reaction in which two molecules combine to form a larger molecule, producing a small molecule such as $H_2O$ as a by-product. **4** a concise version of something.

**condense** ● **v. 1** make denser or more concentrated. ➤ [usu. as adj. **condensed**] thicken (a liquid) by heating it to reduce the water content. ➤ express (a piece of writing or speech) in fewer words; make concise. **2** change from a gas or vapour to a liquid.
– DERIVATIVES **condensable** adj.
– ORIGIN ME: from OFr. *condenser* or L. *condensare*, from *condensus* 'very thick'.

**condensed milk** ● **n.** milk that has been thickened by evaporation and sweetened.

**condenser** ● **n. 1** an apparatus for condensing vapour. **2** a lens or system of lenses for collecting and directing light. **3** another term for **CAPACITOR**.

**condescend** ● **v.** show that one feels superior. ➤ do something despite regarding it as below one's dignity: *he condescended to see me at my hotel.*
– DERIVATIVES **condescending** adj. **condescendingly** adv. **condescension** n.
– ORIGIN ME (in the sense 'give way, defer'): from OFr. *condescendre*, from eccles. L. *condescendere*, from *con-* 'together' + *descendere* 'descend'.

**condign** /kən'dʌɪn/ ● **adj.** formal (of punishment) fitting and deserved.
– DERIVATIVES **condignly** adv.
– ORIGIN ME: from OFr. *condigne*, from L. *condignus*, from *con-* 'altogether' + *dignus* 'worthy'.

**condiment** ● **n.** a substance such as salt or pepper, used to flavour food.
– ORIGIN ME: from L. *condimentum*, from *condire* 'to pickle'.

**condition** ● **n. 1** the state of something or someone, with regard to appearance, fitness, or working order. ➤ an illness or medical problem. ➤ archaic social position. **2** (**conditions**) circumstances affecting the functioning or existence of something. **3** a state of affairs that must exist before something else is possible. **4** US an unsatisfactory grade indicating that a student must pass an examination within a stated time to receive a course credit. ● **v. 1** have a significant influence on. ➤ train or accustom to behave in a certain way. ➤ [as adj. **conditioned**] relating to or denoting automatic responses established by training to an ordinarily neutral stimulus. **2** bring into the desired state for use. ➤ [often as adj. **conditioned**] make fit and healthy. **3** apply conditioner to (the hair). **4** set prior requirements on (something) before it can occur. **5** US give (a student) a condition.
– PHRASES **in** (or **out of**) **condition** in a fit (or unfit) physical state. **on condition that** with the stipulation that.
– ORIGIN ME: from OFr. *condicion* (n.), *condicionner* (v.), from L. *condicio(n-)* 'agreement', from *condicere* 'agree upon', from *con-* 'with' + *dicere* 'say'.

**conditional** ● **adj. 1** subject to one or more conditions being met. **2** Grammar expressing a condition. ● **n. 1** Grammar & Philosophy a conditional clause or conjunction. **2** Grammar the conditional mood of a verb, for example *should* in *if I should die.*
– DERIVATIVES **conditionality** n. **conditionally** adv.

**conditional discharge** ● **n.** an order made by a criminal court whereby an offender will not be sentenced for an offence unless a further offence is committed within a stated period.

**conditioner** ● **n.** a thing used to improve the condition of something, especially a liquid applied to the hair after shampooing.

**condo** /'kɒndəʊ/ ● **n.** (pl. **-os**) N. Amer. informal short for **CONDOMINIUM** (in sense 2).

**condole** /kən'dəʊl/ ● **v.** (**condole with**) express sympathy for.
– ORIGIN C16: from Christian L. *condolere*, from *con-* 'with' + *dolere* 'grieve, suffer'.

**condolence** ● **n.** an expression of sympathy, especially on the occasion of a death.

**condom** ● **n.** a thin rubber sheath worn on the penis during sexual intercourse as a contraceptive or to protect against infection.
– ORIGIN C18: of unknown origin.

**condominium** /ˌkɒndəˈmɪnɪəm/ • n. (pl. **condominiums**) **1** the joint control of a state's affairs by other states. **2** N. Amer. a building or complex containing a number of individually owned flats or houses. ➤each of the flats or houses in such a building.
– ORIGIN C18: mod. L., from *con-* 'together with' + *dominium* (see **DOMINION**).

**condone** /kənˈdəʊn/ • v. **1** [usu. with neg.] accept or forgive (behaviour considered wrong or offensive). **2** approve or sanction, especially reluctantly.
– DERIVATIVES **condonation** /ˌkɒndəˈneɪʃ(ə)n/ n. **condoner** n.
– ORIGIN C19 (earlier (C17) as *condonation*): from L. *condonare* 'refrain from punishing'.

**condor** • n. a very large American vulture with a bare head and mainly black plumage. [*Vultur gryphus* (**Andean condor**, S. America), and *Gymnogyps californianus* (**California condor**, endangered).]
– ORIGIN C17: from Sp. *cóndor*, from Quechua *kuntur*.

**condottiere** /ˌkɒndɒˈtjɛːreɪ, -ri/ • n. (pl. **condottieri** pronunc. same) historical (in Italy) a leader or member of a troop of mercenaries.
– ORIGIN Ital., from *condotto* 'troop under contract'.

**conduce** • v. (**conduce to**) formal help to bring about.
– ORIGIN ME: from L. *conducere* (see **CONDUCT**).

**conducive** • adj. (**conducive to**) contributing or helping towards.

**conduct** • n. /ˈkɒndʌkt/ **1** the manner in which a person behaves. **2** the directing or managing of something. • v. /kənˈdʌkt/ **1** organize and carry out. ➤direct the performance of (a piece of music or an orchestra or choir). ➤guide to or around a place. **2** Physics transmit by conduction. **3** (**conduct oneself**) behave in a specified way.
– DERIVATIVES **conductible** /kənˈdʌktɪb(ə)l/ adj.
– ORIGIN ME (as *conduit*): from OFr. *conduit* (n.), *conduire* (v.), from L. *conduct-*, *conducere* 'bring together'; cf. **CONDUIT**.

**conductance** • n. the degree to which a material conducts electricity.

**conduction** • n. **1** the transmission of heat through a medium from a region of higher temperature to a region of lower temperature. **2** the transmission of electricity or sound through a medium. **3** the conveying of fluid through a channel.
– DERIVATIVES **conductive** adj. **conductively** adv.

**conductive education** • n. Brit. a system of training for people with motor disorders, aiming to reduce dependence on artificial aids.

**conductivity** • n. (pl. **-ies**) the degree to which a specified material conducts electricity or heat.

**conductor** • n. **1** a person who conducts an orchestra or choir. **2** a person who collects fares on a bus. ➤N. Amer. a guard on a train. **3** Physics a material or device that conducts heat or electricity.
– DERIVATIVES **conductorship** n. **conductress** n.

**conductor rail** • n. a rail transmitting current to an electric train or other vehicle.

**conduct sheet** • n. a military form recording someone's offences and punishments.

**conductus** /kənˈdʌktəs/ • n. (pl. **conducti** /-tʌɪ/) a musical setting of a metrical Latin text, of the 12th or 13th century.
– ORIGIN from med. L., from L. *conducere* (see **CONDUCT**).

**conduit** /ˈkɒndɪt, -jʊɪt/ • n. **1** a channel for conveying water or other fluid. **2** a tube or trough protecting electric wiring.
– ORIGIN ME: from OFr., from med. L. *conductus*, from L. *conducere* (see **CONDUCT**).

**condylarth** /ˈkɒndɪlɑːθ/ • n. Palaeontology a fossil herbivorous mammal, ancestral to the ungulates.
– ORIGIN C19: from mod. L. *Condylarthra* (name of an order), from Gk *kondulos* 'knuckle' + *arthron* 'joint'.

**condyle** /ˈkɒndɪl, -dʌɪl/ • n. Anatomy a rounded protuberance at the end of some bones, forming an articulation with another bone.
– DERIVATIVES **condylar** adj. **condyloid** adj.
– ORIGIN C17: from Fr., from L. *condylus*, from Gk *kondulos* 'knuckle'.

**condyloma** /ˌkɒndɪˈləʊmə/ • n. (pl. **condylomas** or **condylomata** /-mətə/) Medicine a raised growth on the skin resembling a wart, typically in the genital region, caused by viral infection or syphilis.
– DERIVATIVES **condylomatous** adj.
– ORIGIN ME: via L. from Gk *kondulōma* 'callous lump', from *kondulos* 'knuckle'.

**cone** • n. **1** an object which tapers from a circular or roughly circular base to a point. ➤(also **traffic cone**) a plastic cone-shaped object used to separate off sections of a road. ➤a cone-shaped wafer container in which ice cream is served. ➤the peak of a volcano. **2** the cone-shaped dry fruit of a conifer, formed of a tight array of overlapping scales on a central axis. **3** Anatomy one of two types of light-sensitive cell present in the retina of the eye, responding to bright light and responsible for sharpness of vision and colour perception. Compare with **ROD** (in sense 6). • v. (**cone something off**) Brit. separate off part of a road with traffic cones.
– DERIVATIVES **coned** adj.
– ORIGIN ME: from Fr. *cône*, via L. from Gk *kōnos*.

**coneflower** • n. a North American plant of the daisy family with cone-shaped flowers. [*Rudbeckia*, *Echinacea*, and other genera.]

**cone shell** • n. a predatory marine mollusc with a conical shell. [Genus *Conus*: numerous species.]

**coney** /ˈkəʊni/ (also **cony**) • n. (pl. **-eys**) **1** Brit. & Heraldry a rabbit. **2** a small grouper (fish) of the tropical western Atlantic. [*Epinephelus fulvus*.]
– ORIGIN ME: from OFr. *conin*, from L. *cuniculus*.

**confab** informal • n. an informal private conversation or discussion. • v. (**confabbed**, **confabbing**) engage in such conversation.

**confabulate** /kənˈfabjʊleɪt/ • v. **1** formal converse. **2** Psychiatry fabricate imaginary experiences as compensation for loss of memory.
– DERIVATIVES **confabulation** n. **confabulatory** adj.
– ORIGIN C17 (earlier (ME) as *confabulation*): from L. *confabulat-*, *confabulari* 'chat together'.

**confect** /kənˈfɛkt/ • v. make (something elaborate or dainty).
– ORIGIN ME: from L. *confect-*, *conficere* 'put together'.

**confection** • n. **1** an elaborate sweet dish or delicacy. **2** an elaborate article of women's dress. **3** the action of mixing or compounding something.

**confectioner** • n. a person who makes or sells confectionery.

**confectioner's custard** • n. thick sweet custard used as a filling for cakes and pastries.

**confectioner's sugar** • n. US term for **ICING SUGAR**.

**confectionery** • n. (pl. **-ies**) sweets and chocolates collectively.

**confederacy** • n. (pl. **-ies**) **1** a league or alliance, especially of confederate states. ➤(**the Confederacy**) the Confederate states of the US. **2** a league formed for an unlawful purpose.

**confederal** • adj. relating to or denoting a confederation.

**confederate** • adj. /kənˈfɛd(ə)rət/ joined by an agreement or treaty. ➤(**Confederate**) denoting the southern states which separated from the US in 1860–1. • n. /kənˈfɛd(ə)rət/ an accomplice or fellow worker. • v. /kənˈfɛdəreɪt/ [usu. as adj. **confederated**] bring into an alliance.
– ORIGIN ME: from late (eccles.) L. *confoederatus*, from *con-* 'together' + *foederatus* (see **FEDERATE**).

**confederation** • n. **1** an alliance of a number of parties or groups. ➤a more or less permanent union of states with some political power vested in a central authority. **2** the action of confederating or state of being confederated.

**confer** /kənˈfəː/ • v. (**conferred**, **conferring**) **1** grant (a title, degree, benefit, or right). **2** have discussions.
– DERIVATIVES **conferment** n. **conferrable** adj. **conferral** n.
– ORIGIN ME: from L. *conferre*, from *con-* 'together' + *ferre* 'bring'.

**conferee** ● n. **1** a person who attends a conference. **2** a person on whom something is conferred.

**Conference** ● n. a dessert pear of a firm-fleshed variety.
– ORIGIN C19: appar. named after the National Pear Conference of 1885.

**conference** ● n. **1** a formal meeting of people with a shared interest, typically taking place over several days. ➤a linking of several telephones or computers, so that each user may communicate with the others simultaneously. **2** an association in commerce for regulation or exchange of information. ➤a league of sports teams or clubs. **3** the governing body of Methodist and other Christian Churches. ● v. [usu. as noun **conferencing**] take part in a conference.
– PHRASES **in conference** in a meeting.
– ORIGIN C16: from Fr. *conférence* or med. L. *conferentia*, from L. *conferre* (see **CONFER**).

**confess** ● v. **1** admit to a crime or wrongdoing. ➤acknowledge reluctantly: *I must confess that I was surprised.* **2** declare one's sins formally to a priest. ➤(of a priest) hear the confession of.
– ORIGIN ME: from OFr. *confesser*, from L. *confess-*, *confiteri* 'acknowledge'.

**confessant** ● n. a person who confesses to a priest.

**confessedly** ● adv. by one's own admission.

**confession** ● n. **1** a formal statement admitting to a crime. ➤a reluctant acknowledgement. **2** a formal admission of one's sins privately to a priest. **3** (also **confession of faith**) a statement setting out essential religious doctrine. ➤the religious body or Church sharing a confession of faith.
– DERIVATIVES **confessionary** adj.

**confessional** ● n. **1** an enclosed stall in a church, divided by a screen, in which a priest sits to hear confessions. **2** a confession. ● adj. **1** (of speech or writing) in which a person reveals or admits to private thoughts or incidents in their past. **2** of or relating to religious confession. **3** of or relating to confessions of faith.

**confessor** ● n. **1** a priest who hears confessions. **2** a person who makes a confession. **3** a person who avows religious faith in the face of opposition.

**confetti** ● n. small pieces of coloured paper traditionally thrown over a bride and groom after a marriage ceremony.
– ORIGIN C19 (orig. denoting real or imitation sweets thrown during Italian carnivals): from Ital.

**confidant** /ˈkɒnfɪdant, ˌkɒnfɪˈdant, -dɑːnt/ ● n. (fem. **confidante** pronunc. same) a person in whom one confides.
– ORIGIN C17: alt. of **CONFIDENT** (as a noun in the same sense), prob. to represent the pronunc. of Fr. *confidente* 'having full trust'.

**confide** /kənˈfʌɪd/ ● v. **1** (often **confide in**) tell someone about a secret or private matter in confidence. **2** (**confide something to**) dated entrust something to the care of.
– DERIVATIVES **confiding** adj. **confidingly** adv.
– ORIGIN ME: from L. *confidere* 'have full trust'.

**confidence** ● n. **1** the belief that one can have faith in or rely on someone or something. ➤a feeling of self-assurance arising from an appreciation of one's own abilities. **2** the telling of private matters or secrets with mutual trust. ➤a secret or private matter told to someone under a condition of trust.
– PHRASES **in someone's confidence** in a position of trust with someone. **take someone into one's confidence** tell someone one's secrets.
– ORIGIN ME: from L. *confidentia*, from *confidere* (see **CONFIDENT**).

**confidence interval** ● n. Statistics a range of values so defined that there is a specified probability that the value of a parameter lies within it.

**confidence man** ● n. dated a confidence trickster.

**confidence trick** (N. Amer. also **confidence game**) ● n. an act of cheating or tricking someone by persuading them to believe something that is not true.
– DERIVATIVES **confidence trickster** n.

**confident** ● adj. **1** feeling confidence in oneself. **2** feeling certainty about something. ● n. archaic a confidant.
– DERIVATIVES **confidently** adv.

**confidential** ● adj. **1** intended to be kept secret. **2** entrusted with private information: *a confidential secretary.*
– DERIVATIVES **confidentiality** n. **confidentially** adv.

**configuration** /kənˌfɪgəˈreɪʃ(ə)n, -gjʊ-/ ● n. **1** an arrangement of parts or elements in a particular form or figure. ➤Chemistry the fixed three-dimensional relationship of the atoms in a molecule. **2** Psychology another term for **GESTALT**.
– DERIVATIVES **configurational** adj.

**configure** ● v. (often **be configured**) arrange in a particular configuration. ➤Computing arrange or order (a computer system) so as to fit it for a designated task.
– DERIVATIVES **configurable** adj.
– ORIGIN ME: from L. *configurare* 'shape after a pattern', from *con-* 'together' + *figurare* 'to shape' (from *figura* 'shape or figure').

**confine** ● v. /kənˈfʌɪn/ (**confine someone/thing to**) keep or restrict someone or something within certain limits of (space, scope, or time). ➤(**be confined to**) be unable to leave (one's bed, home, etc.) due to illness or disability. ➤(**be confined**) dated (of a woman) remain in bed for a period before, during, and after giving birth. ● n. /ˈkɒnfʌɪn/ (**confines**) limits or boundaries.
– DERIVATIVES **confinement** n.
– ORIGIN ME (as n.): from Fr. *confins* (pl. n.), from L. *confinia*, from *confinis* 'bordering', from *con-* 'together' + *finis* 'end, limit' (pl. *fines* 'territory'); the verb is from Fr. *confiner*, based on L. *confinis*.

**confined** ● adj. (of a space) enclosed; cramped.

**confirm** ● v. **1** establish the truth or correctness of. ➤state with assurance that something is true. ➤(**confirm someone in**) reinforce someone in (an opinion or feeling). **2** make (a provisional arrangement) definite. ➤declare formally to be appointed to a post. **3** (usu. **be confirmed**) administer the religious rite of confirmation to.
– DERIVATIVES **confirmative** adj. **confirmatory** adj.
– ORIGIN ME: from OFr. *confermer*, from L. *confirmare*, from *con-* 'together' + *firmare* 'strengthen' (from *firmus* 'firm').

**confirmand** /ˈkɒnfəmand/ ● n. a person about to undergo the religious rite of confirmation.

**confirmation** ● n. **1** the action of confirming or state of being confirmed. **2** (in the Christian Church) the rite at which a baptized person affirms Christian belief and is admitted as a full member of the Church. **3** the Jewish ceremony of bar mitzvah.

**confirmed** ● adj. firmly established in a habit, belief, or way of life: *a confirmed bachelor.*

**confiscate** /ˈkɒnfɪskeɪt/ ● v. take or seize (property) with authority. ➤appropriate to the public treasury as a penalty.
– DERIVATIVES **confiscation** n. **confiscator** n. **confiscatory** adj.
– ORIGIN C16: from L. *confiscat-*, *confiscare* 'put away in a chest, consign to the public treasury', based on *con-* 'together' + *fiscus* 'chest, treasury'.

**confit** /ˈkɒnfi/ ● n. duck or other meat cooked very slowly in its own fat.
– ORIGIN Fr., 'conserved', from *confire* 'prepare'.

**conflab** ● n. & v. informal another term for **CONFAB**.

**conflagration** /ˌkɒnfləˈgreɪʃ(ə)n/ ● n. an extensive and destructive fire.
– ORIGIN C15: from L. *conflagratio(n-)*, from *conflagrare*, from *con-* (expressing intensive force) + *flagrare* 'to blaze'.

**conflate** ● v. combine into one.
– DERIVATIVES **conflation** n.
– ORIGIN ME (in the sense 'fuse or melt down metal'): from L. *conflat-*, *conflare* 'kindle, fuse', from *con-* 'together' + *flare* 'to blow'.

**conflict** ● n. /ˈkɒnflɪkt/ a serious disagreement or argument. ➤a prolonged armed struggle. ➤an incompatibility between opinions, principles, etc. ● v. /kənˈflɪkt/ [often as adj. **conflicting**] be incompatible or at variance with.

– DERIVATIVES **conflictual** adj.
– ORIGIN ME: from L. *conflict-*, *confligere* 'strike together, fight', from *con-* 'together' + *fligere* 'to strike'; the noun is via L. *conflictus* 'a contest'.

**confluence** /ˈkɒnflʊəns/ ● n. **1** the junction of two rivers. **2** an act or process of merging.
– DERIVATIVES **confluent** adj.
– ORIGIN ME: from late L. *confluentia*, from L. *confluere* 'flow together', from *con-* 'together' + *fluere* 'to flow'.

**conflux** /ˈkɒnflʌks/ ● n. another term for **CONFLUENCE**.
– ORIGIN C17: from late L. *confluxus*, from *con-* 'together' + *fluxus* (see **FLUX**).

**confocal** /kɒnˈfəʊk(ə)l/ ● adj. having a common focus.

**conform** ● v. **1** comply with rules, standards, or laws. ➤ behave according to social convention. **2** be similar in form or type.
– ORIGIN ME: from OFr. *conformer*, from L. *conformare*, from *con-* 'together' + *formare* 'to form'.

**conformable** ● adj. (usu. **conformable to**) **1** disposed or accustomed to conform. **2** similar in nature; consistent. **3** Geology (of strata) deposited in a continuous sequence, and having the same direction of stratification.
– DERIVATIVES **conformability** n. **conformably** adv.

**conformal** ● adj. (of a map) preserving the correct angles between directions within small areas, though distorting distances.
– DERIVATIVES **conformally** adv.
– ORIGIN C17 (in the sense 'conformable'): from late L. *conformalis*, from *con-* 'together' + *formalis* 'formal'.

**conformance** ● n. another term for **CONFORMITY**.

**conformation** ● n. the shape or structure of something. ➤ Chemistry any of the spatial arrangements which the atoms in a molecule may adopt, especially by rotation about individual single bonds.
– DERIVATIVES **conformational** adj.
– ORIGIN C16: from L. *conformatio(n-)*, from *conformare* (see **CONFORM**).

**conformer** ● n. Chemistry a form of a compound having a particular molecular conformation.
– ORIGIN 1960s: blend of *conformational* (see **CONFORMATION**) and **ISOMER**.

**conformist** ● n. a person who conforms to social convention. ➤ Brit., chiefly historical a person who conforms to the practices of the Church of England. ● adj. conforming to accepted behaviour or established practices.
– DERIVATIVES **conformism** n.

**conformity** ● n. **1** compliance with conventions, rules, or laws. ➤ Brit., chiefly historical compliance with the practices of the Church of England. **2** similarity in form or type.

**confound** ● v. **1** surprise or confuse. ➤ prove wrong. ➤ defeat (a plan, aim, or hope). **2** (often **be confounded with**) mix up with something else. ● exclam. (**confound it!**) dated used to express annoyance.
– ORIGIN ME: from OFr. *confondre*, from L. *confundere* 'pour together, mix up'; cf. **CONFUSE**.

**confounded** ● adj. informal, dated used for emphasis to express annoyance: *a confounded nuisance.*
– DERIVATIVES **confoundedly** adv.

**confraternity** ● n. (pl. **-ies**) a brotherhood, especially with a religious or charitable purpose.
– ORIGIN ME: from OFr. *confraternite*, from med. L. *confraternitas*, from *confrater* (see **CONFRÈRE**).

**confrère** /ˈkɒnfrɛː/ ● n. a fellow member of a profession.
– ORIGIN C18: Fr., from med. L. *confrater*, from *con-* 'together with' + *frater* 'brother'.

**confront** ● v. **1** stand or meet face to face with hostile intent. **2** (of a problem) present itself to (someone). ➤ face up to and deal with (a problem). ➤ compel to face or consider something.
– DERIVATIVES **confrontation** n. **confrontational** adj.
– ORIGIN C16: from Fr. *confronter*, from med. L. *confrontare*, from L. *con-* 'with' + *frons, front-* 'face'.

**Confucian** /kənˈfjuːʃ(ə)n/ ● adj. of or relating to Confucius or Confucianism. ● n. an adherent of Confucianism.

**Confucianism** /kənˈfjuːʃənɪz(ə)m/ ● n. a system of philosophical and ethical teachings founded by the Chinese philosopher Confucius (551–479 BC).
– DERIVATIVES **Confucianist** n. & adj.

**confuse** ● v. **1** cause to become bewildered or perplexed. **2** make less easy to understand. ➤ identify wrongly.
– DERIVATIVES **confusability** n. **confusable** adj. **confusing** adj. **confusingly** adv.
– ORIGIN ME: from OFr. *confus*, from L. *confusus*, past part. of *confundere* (see **CONFOUND**).

**confused** ● adj. **1** bewildered. **2** lacking order and so difficult to understand or distinguish.
– DERIVATIVES **confusedly** adv.

**confusion** ● n. **1** uncertainty. ➤ a situation of panic. ➤ a disorderly jumble. **2** the state of being bewildered. ➤ the mistaking of one person or thing for another.

**confute** ● v. formal prove to be wrong.
– DERIVATIVES **confutation** n.
– ORIGIN C16 (earlier (ME) as *confutation*): from L. *confutare* 'restrain, answer conclusively', from *con-* 'altogether' + the base of *refutare* 'refute'.

**conga** /ˈkɒŋgə/ ● n. **1** a Latin American dance of African origin, typically with several people in a line, one behind the other. **2** (also **conga drum**) a tall, narrow drum beaten with the hands. ● v. (**congas**, **congaed** or **conga'd**, **congaing**) perform the conga.
– ORIGIN 1930s: from Latin Amer. Sp., from Sp., fem. of *congo* 'Congolese'.

**congé** /ˈkɔ̃ʒeɪ/ ● n. an unceremonious dismissal or rejection.
– ORIGIN ME: from OFr. *congie*, from L. *commeatus* 'leave of absence', from *commeare* 'go and come'.

**congeal** /kənˈdʒiːl/ ● v. become semi-solid, especially on cooling.
– DERIVATIVES **congealable** adj. **congealment** n. (archaic). **congelation** /ˌkɒndʒəˈleɪʃ(ə)n/ n.
– ORIGIN ME: from OFr. *congeler*, from L. *congelare*, from *con-* 'together' + *gelare* 'freeze' (from *gelu* 'frost').

**congener** /ˈkɒndʒɪnə, kənˈdʒiːnə/ ● n. **1** a person or thing of the same kind as another. ➤ an animal or plant of the same genus as another. **2** a minor chemical constituent, especially one giving a distinctive character to a wine or spirit.
– DERIVATIVES **congeneric** /ˌkɒndʒɪˈnɛrɪk/ adj. **congenerous** /kənˈdʒɛn(ə)rəs/ adj.
– ORIGIN C18: from L., from *con-* 'together with' + *genus, gener-* 'race, stock'.

**congenial** /kənˈdʒiːnɪəl/ ● adj. pleasant because of qualities or interests similar to one's own. ➤ suited to one's taste or inclination.
– DERIVATIVES **congeniality** n. **congenially** adv.

**congenital** /kənˈdʒɛnɪt(ə)l/ ● adj. (especially of a disease or abnormality) present from birth. ➤ having a particular trait from birth or by established habit.
– DERIVATIVES **congenitally** adv.
– ORIGIN C18: from L. *congenitus*, from *con-* 'together' + *genitus* (past part. of *gignere* 'beget') + **-AL**.

**conger** /ˈkɒŋgə/ (also **conger eel**) ● n. a large edible predatory eel of shallow coastal waters. [*Conger conger* (Europe), *C. oceanica* (America), and other species.]
– ORIGIN ME: from OFr. *congre*, via L. from Gk *gongros*.

**congeries** /kɒnˈdʒɪəriːz, -ɪz/ ● n. (pl. same) a disorderly collection.
– ORIGIN C16: from L. *congeries* 'heap, pile', from *congerere* 'heap up'.

**congested** ● adj. so crowded as to hinder freedom of movement. ➤ (of a part of the body) abnormally full of blood. ➤ (of the respiratory tract) blocked with mucus.
– DERIVATIVES **congestion** n.
– ORIGIN ME (as *congest*): from L. *congest-*, *congerere* 'heap up', from *con-* 'together' + *gerere* 'bring'.

**congestive** ● adj. Medicine involving or produced by congestion.

**congius** /ˈkɒndʒɪəs/ ● n. (pl. **congii** /ˈkɒndʒɪʌɪ/) an ancient Roman liquid measure of one eighth of an amphora, equal to about 6 imperial pints.
– ORIGIN from L.

**conglobulate** /kɒnˈglɒbjʊleɪt/ ● v. rare join closely together.
– ORIGIN C18: from L. *globulus* 'globule', on the pattern of

earlier *conglobate* 'make into a ball'.

**conglomerate** • n. /kən'glɒm(ə)rət/ **1** something consisting of a number of different and distinct things. ➤ a large corporation formed by the merging of separate firms. **2** Geology a coarse-grained sedimentary rock composed of rounded fragments cemented together. • adj. /kən'glɒm(ə)rət/ relating to a conglomerate. • v. /kən'glɒməreɪt/ gather into or form a conglomerate.
– DERIVATIVES **conglomeration** n.
– ORIGIN ME: from L. *conglomerat-*, *conglomerare*, from *con-* 'together' + *glomus*, *glomer-* 'ball'.

**Congolese** /ˌkɒŋgə'liːz/ • n. (pl. same) **1** a native or inhabitant of the Congo or the Democratic Republic of Congo (formerly Zaire). **2** any of the Bantu languages spoken in the Congo region. • adj. of or relating to the Congo or the Democratic Republic of Congo.

**congrats** • pl. n. informal congratulations.

**congratulate** • v. express pleasure at the happiness or good fortune of. ➤ praise for an achievement. ➤ (**congratulate oneself**) feel pride or satisfaction.
– DERIVATIVES **congratulator** n. **congratulatory** adj.
– ORIGIN C16: from L. *congratulat-*, *congratulari* 'congratulate', from *con-* 'with' + *gratulari* 'show joy' (from *gratus* 'pleasing').

**congratulation** • n. **1** (**congratulations**) praise or good wishes on a special occasion. **2** the action of congratulating.

**congregant** /'kɒŋgrɪg(ə)nt/ • n. a member of a congregation.

**congregate** • v. gather into a crowd or mass.
– ORIGIN ME: from L. *congregat-*, *congregare* 'collect (into a flock), unite', from *con-* 'together' + *gregare* (from *grex*, *greg-* 'a flock').

**congregation** • n. **1** a group of people assembled for religious worship. ➤ a group of people obeying a common religious rule. **2** a gathering or collection of people or things. ➤ the action of congregating. **3** (in the Roman Catholic Church) a permanent committee of the College of Cardinals. ➤ Brit. (in some universities) a general assembly of resident senior members.

**congregational** • adj. **1** of or relating to a congregation. **2** (**Congregational**) of or adhering to Congregationalism.

**Congregationalism** • n. a system of organization among Christian churches whereby individual churches are largely self-governing.
– DERIVATIVES **Congregationalist** n. & adj.

**congress** • n. **1** a formal meeting or series of meetings between delegates. **2** (**Congress**) a national legislative body, especially that of the US. **3** a society or organization. **4** the action of coming together.
– DERIVATIVES **congressional** adj.
– ORIGIN ME: from L. *congressus*, from *congredi* 'meet', from *con-* 'together' + *gradi* 'walk'.

**congressman** (or **congresswoman**) • n. (pl. **-men** or **-women**) a male (or female) member of the US Congress.

**congruent** /'kɒŋgrʊənt/ • adj. **1** in agreement or harmony. **2** Geometry (of figures) identical in form.
– DERIVATIVES **congruence** n. **congruency** n. **congruently** adv.
– ORIGIN ME: from L. *congruent-*, *congruere* 'agree, meet together', from *con-* 'together' + *ruere* 'fall or rush'.

**congruous** /'kɒŋgrʊəs/ • adj. in agreement or harmony.
– DERIVATIVES **congruity** /-'gruːɪti/ n. **congruously** adv.

**conic** /'kɒnɪk/ chiefly Mathematics • adj. of a cone. • n. short for **CONIC SECTION**.
– ORIGIN C16: from mod. L. *conicus*, from Gk *kōnikos*, from *kōnos* 'cone'.

**conical** • adj. shaped like a cone.
– DERIVATIVES **conically** adv.

**conical projection** • n. a map projection in which an area of the earth is projected on to a cone.

**conic section** • n. the figure of a circle, ellipse, parabola, or hyperbola formed by the intersection of a plane and a circular cone.

**conidium** /kəʊ'nɪdɪəm/ • n. (pl. **conidia** /-dɪə/) Botany a spore produced asexually by various fungi at the tip of a specialized hypha.
– ORIGIN C19: mod. L., from Gk *konis* 'dust' + the dimin. suffix *-idium*.

**conifer** /'kɒnɪfə, 'kəʊn-/ • n. a tree bearing cones and evergreen needle-like or scale-like leaves, e.g. a pine, fir, or cypress. [Order Coniferales.]
– DERIVATIVES **coniferous** adj.
– ORIGIN C19: from L., lit. 'cone-bearing', from *conus* (see **CONE**).

**coniine** /'kəʊniiːn/ • n. Chemistry a volatile poisonous compound found in hemlock and other plants.
– ORIGIN C19: from L. *conium* (from Gk *kōneion* 'hemlock') + **-INE**[4].

**conjecture** /kən'dʒɛktʃə/ • n. **1** an opinion or conclusion based on incomplete information. ➤ an unproven mathematical or scientific theorem. **2** (in textual criticism) the suggestion of a reading not present in the original source. • v. **1** form a conjecture. **2** (in textual criticism) propose (a reading).
– DERIVATIVES **conjecturable** adj. **conjectural** adj. **conjecturally** adv.
– ORIGIN ME: from OFr., or from L. *conjectura*, from *conicere* 'put together in thought', from *con-* 'together' + *jacere* 'throw'.

**conjoin** • v. formal join; combine.
– ORIGIN ME: from OFr. *conjoindre*, from L. *conjungere*, from *con-* 'together' + *jungere* 'to join'.

**conjoined twins** • pl. n. technical term for **SIAMESE TWINS**.

**conjoint** • adj. combining all people or things involved.
– DERIVATIVES **conjointly** adv.

**conjugal** /'kɒndʒʊg(ə)l/ • adj. of or relating to marriage or the relationship between husband and wife.
– DERIVATIVES **conjugality** n. **conjugally** adv.
– ORIGIN C16: from L. *conjugalis*, from *conjux*, *conjug-* 'spouse', from *con-* 'together'+ *jugum* 'a yoke'.

**conjugal rights** • pl. n. the rights, especially to sexual relations, regarded as exercisable in law by each partner in a marriage.

**conjugate** • v. /'kɒndʒʊgeɪt/ **1** Grammar give the different forms of (a verb). **2** Biology (of bacteria or unicellular organisms) become temporarily united in order to exchange genetic material. ➤ (of gametes) fuse. **3** Chemistry be combined with or joined to reversibly. • adj. /'kɒndʒʊgət/ **1** Chemistry (of an acid or base) related by loss or gain of a proton. **2** Mathematics joined in a reciprocal relation, especially having the same real parts and equal magnitudes but opposite signs of imaginary parts. **3** Geometry (of angles) adding up to 360°. **4** Biology (of gametes) fused. • n. /'kɒndʒʊgət/ **1** chiefly Biochemistry a conjugated substance. **2** a conjugate mathematical value or entity.
– DERIVATIVES **conjugacy** n. **conjugation** n. **conjugational** adj.
– ORIGIN C15 (as adj.): from L. *conjugat-*, *conjugare* 'yoke together', from *con-* 'together' + *jugum* 'yoke'.

**conjunct** • adj. /kən'dʒʌŋ(k)t/ **1** joined together, combined, or associated. **2** Music of or relating to the movement of a melody between adjacent notes of the scale. • n. /'kɒndʒʌŋ(k)t/ **1** each of two or more joined or associated things. **2** Logic each of the terms of a conjunctive proposition. **3** Grammar an adverbial joining two sentences or clauses (e.g. *however*).
– ORIGIN ME: from L. *conjunctus*, past part. of *conjungere* (see **CONJOIN**).

**conjunction** • n. **1** Grammar a word used to connect clauses or sentences or to coordinate words in the same clause (e.g. *and*, *if*). **2** an instance of two or more events occurring at the same point in time or space. ➤ Astronomy & Astrology an alignment of two planets so that they appear to be in the same place in the sky.
– PHRASES **in conjunction** together.
– DERIVATIVES **conjunctional** adj.

**conjunctiva** /ˌkɒndʒʌŋ(k)'tʌɪvə, kən'dʒʌŋ(k)tɪvə/ • n. Anatomy the mucous membrane that covers the front of the eye and lines the inside of the eyelids.
– DERIVATIVES **conjunctival** adj.
– ORIGIN ME: from med. L. (*membrana*) *conjunctiva* 'con-

junctive (membrane)', from late L. *conjunctivus*, from *conjungere* (see **CONJOIN**).

**conjunctive** ● adj. of, relating to, or forming a conjunction. ➤ involving the combination or co-occurrence of two or more things. ● n. Grammar a conjunction.
– DERIVATIVES **conjunctively** adv.

**conjunctivitis** /kənˌdʒʌŋ(k)tɪ'vʌɪtɪs/ ● n. Medicine inflammation of the conjunctiva.

**conjuncture** ● n. **1** a combination of events. **2** a state of affairs.

**conjure** /'kʌndʒə/ ● v. **1** (usu. **conjure up**) cause to appear as if by magic. ➤ call to the mind. ➤ call upon (a spirit) to appear by means of a magic ritual. **2** /kən'dʒʊə/ archaic implore to do something.
– PHRASES **a name to conjure with** a name of great importance within a particular field.
– DERIVATIVES **conjuration** /ˌkʌndʒə'reɪʃ(ə)n, ˌkɒn dʒʊ(ə)-/ n. **conjuring** n.
– ORIGIN ME: from OFr. *conjurer* 'to plot or exorcize', from L. *conjurare* 'band together by an oath, conspire' (in med. L. 'invoke'), from *con-* 'together' + *jurare* 'swear'.

**conjuror** (also **conjurer**) ● n. a performer of conjuring tricks.

**conk**[1] ● v. (**conk out**) informal **1** (of a machine) break down. **2** faint or go to sleep. ➤ die.
– ORIGIN First World War: of unknown origin.

**conk**[2] informal ● n. Brit. a person's nose. ➤ dated a person's head. ● v. chiefly N. Amer. hit on the head.
– ORIGIN C19: perh. an alt. of **CONCH**.

**conker** ● n. Brit. the hard shiny dark brown nut of a horse chestnut tree. ➤ (**conkers**) [treated as sing.] a children's game in which each has a conker on a string and tries to break another's with it.
– ORIGIN C19 (a dial. word denoting a snail shell, with which the game was orig. played): perh. from **CONCH**, but assoc. with **CONQUER**.

**con man** ● n. informal a man who cheats others using confidence tricks.

**con moto** /kɒn 'məʊtəʊ/ ● adv. Music with movement.
– ORIGIN from Ital.

**Conn.** ● abbrev. Connecticut.

**conn** ● v. US spelling of **CON**[4].

**connate** /'kɒneɪt/ ● adj. **1** innate. **2** Biology (of parts) united so as to form a single part. **3** Geology (of water) trapped in sedimentary rock during its deposition.
– ORIGIN C17: from late L. *connatus*, past part. of *connasci*, from *con-* 'together' + *nasci* 'be born'.

**connatural** ● adj. innate.
– DERIVATIVES **connaturally** adv.
– ORIGIN C16: from late L. *connaturalis*, from *con-* 'together'+ L. *naturalis* 'natural'.

**connect** ● v. **1** bring together so as to establish a link. ➤ be related in some respect. ➤ join together so as to provide access and communication. ➤ put into contact by telephone. **2** (of a train, bus, etc.) arrive at its destination just before another departs so that passengers can transfer. **3** informal (of a blow) hit the intended target.
– DERIVATIVES **connectable** adj. **connectedly** adv. **connectedness** n. **connector** n.
– ORIGIN ME: from L. *connectere*, from *con-* 'together' + *nectere* 'bind'.

**Connecticutter** /kə'nɛtɪkʌtə/ ● n. a native or inhabitant of the US state of Connecticut.

**connecting rod** ● n. the rod connecting the piston and the crankpin in an engine or pump.

**connection** (Brit. also **connexion**) ● n. **1** a link or relationship between people or things. **2** an opportunity for catching a connecting train, bus, etc. **3** (**connections**) people with whom one has contact. **4** informal, chiefly N. Amer. a supplier of narcotics. **5** chiefly historical an association of Methodist churches.
– PHRASES **in connection with** concerning. **in this** (or **that**) **connection** with reference to this (or that).
– DERIVATIVES **connectional** adj.

**connectionism** ● n. a theory of cognition which regards the brain as a massive interactive network with multiple connections between nodes.

**connective** ● adj. connecting. ● n. **1** Grammar a word or phrase linking other linguistic units. **2** Anatomy a bundle of nerve fibres connecting two nerve centres or ganglia, especially in invertebrates.

**connective tissue** ● n. Anatomy tissue that connects, supports, binds, or separates other tissues or organs, including cartilaginous, fatty, and elastic tissues.

**connectivity** ● n. the state or extent of being connected. ➤ Computing capacity for the interconnection of platforms, systems, and applications.

**connexion** ● n. variant spelling of **CONNECTION**.

**conning tower** /'kɒnɪŋ/ ● n. the superstructure of a submarine, containing the periscope.

**conniption** /kə'nɪpʃ(ə)n/ ● n. N. Amer. informal a fit of rage or hysterics.
– ORIGIN C19: prob. an invented word.

**connive** /kə'nʌɪv/ ● v. (**connive at/in**) secretly allow (a wrongdoing). ➤ [often as adj. **conniving**] conspire.
– DERIVATIVES **connivance** n. **conniver** n.
– ORIGIN C17: from Fr. *conniver* or L. *connivere* 'shut the eyes (to)', from *con-* 'together' + an unrecorded word rel. to *nictare* 'to wink'.

**connoisseur** /ˌkɒnə'səː/ ● n. an expert judge in matters of taste.
– DERIVATIVES **connoisseurship** n.
– ORIGIN C18: from obs. Fr., from *conoistre* 'know'.

**connotation** /kɒnə'teɪʃ(ə)n/ ● n. an idea or feeling which a word invokes in addition to its primary meaning. ➤ Philosophy the abstract meaning of a term, determining which objects or concepts it applies to.
– ORIGIN C16: from med. L. *connotatio(n-)*, from *connotare* (see **CONNOTE**).

**connote** /kə'nəʊt/ ● v. (of a word) imply or suggest. ➤ imply as a consequence or condition.
– DERIVATIVES **connotative** /'kɒnəteɪtɪv, kə'nəʊtətɪv/ adj.
– ORIGIN C17: from med. L. *connotare* 'mark in addition', from *con-* 'together with' + *notare* 'to note'.

**connubial** /kə'njuːbɪəl/ ● adj. poetic/literary conjugal.
– DERIVATIVES **connubiality** n. **connubially** adv.
– ORIGIN C17: from L. *connubialis*, from *connubium* 'marriage', from *con-* 'with' + *nubere* 'marry'.

**conodont** /'kəʊnədɒnt/ ● n. Palaeontology an extinct marine invertebrate with a long worm-like body and numerous small teeth. ➤ (also **conodont element**) a tooth of such an animal, often found as a fossil.
– ORIGIN C19: from mod. L. *Conodonta* (name of a class), from Gk *kōnos* 'cone' + *odous, odont-* 'tooth'.

**conoid** /'kəʊnɔɪd/ ● adj. (also **conoidal**) chiefly Zoology approximately conical in shape. ● n. a conoid object.

**conquer** ● v. **1** overcome and take control of by military force. **2** successfully overcome (a problem). **3** climb (a mountain) successfully.
– DERIVATIVES **conquerable** adj. **conqueror** n.
– ORIGIN ME: from OFr. *conquerre*, based on L. *conquirere* 'gain, win', from *con-* (expressing completion) + *quaerere* 'seek'.

**conquest** ● n. **1** the action of conquering. ➤ a territory gained in such a way. **2** a person whose affection or favour has been won.
– PHRASES **make a conquest of** win the affections of.
– ORIGIN ME: from OFr. *conquest(e)*, based on L. *conquirere* (see **CONQUER**).

**conquistador** /kɒn'kwɪstədɔː, -'kɪst-/ ● n. (pl. **conquistadores** /-'dɔːreɪz/ or **conquistadors**) a conqueror, especially a Spanish conqueror of Mexico or Peru in the 16th century.
– ORIGIN C19: from Sp.

**con rod** ● n. Brit. informal term for **CONNECTING ROD**.

**Cons.** ● abbrev. Conservative.

**consanguineous** /ˌkɒnsaŋ'gwɪnɪəs/ ● adj. relating to or denoting people descended from the same ancestor.
– DERIVATIVES **consanguine** adj. **consanguinity** n.
– ORIGIN C17: from L. *consanguineus* 'of the same blood' (from *con-* 'together' + *sanguis* 'blood') + **-OUS**.

**conscience** ● n. a person's moral sense of right and wrong.
– PHRASES **in (all) conscience** in fairness. **on one's conscience** causing feelings of guilt.

– DERIVATIVES **conscienceless** adj.
– ORIGIN ME: via OFr. from L. *conscientia*, from *conscient-*, *conscire* 'be privy to', from *con-* 'with' + *scire* 'know'.

**conscience clause** ● n. chiefly N. Amer. a clause in a law providing for exemption or other allowances on the grounds of moral or religious conscience.

**conscience money** ● n. money paid due to feelings of guilt.

**conscientious** /ˌkɒnʃɪˈɛnʃəs/ ● adj. **1** wishing to do what is right. **2** relating to a person's conscience.
– DERIVATIVES **conscientiously** adv. **conscientiousness** n.
– ORIGIN C17: from Fr. *consciencieux*, from med. L. *conscientiosus*, from L. *conscientia* (see CONSCIENCE).

**conscientious objector** ● n. a person who for reasons of conscience objects to serving in the armed forces.
– DERIVATIVES **conscientious objection** n.

**conscious** ● adj. **1** aware of and responding to one's surroundings. **2** (usu. **conscious of**) having knowledge of something. ➤[in combination] concerned about a matter: *security-conscious*. **3** deliberate.
– DERIVATIVES **consciously** adv.
– ORIGIN C16: from L. *conscius* 'knowing with others or in oneself' (from *conscire* 'be privy to') + **-ous**.

**consciousness** ● n. **1** the state of being conscious. ➤the fact of awareness by the mind of itself and the world. **2** one's awareness or perception of something.

**conscript** ● v. /kənˈskrɪpt/ enlist compulsorily, typically into the armed services. ● n. /ˈkɒnskrɪpt/ a conscripted person.
– DERIVATIVES **conscription** n.
– ORIGIN C18 (earlier (ME) as *conscription*): from Fr. *conscrit*, from L. *conscriptus*, past part. of *conscribere* 'enrol'.

**consecrate** /ˈkɒnsɪkreɪt/ ● v. (usu. **be consecrated**) **1** make or declare sacred. ➤(in Christian belief) make (bread or wine) into the body and blood of Christ. **2** ordain to a sacred office, typically that of bishop.
– DERIVATIVES **consecration** n. **consecrator** n. **consecratory** adj.
– ORIGIN ME: from L. *consecrat-*, *consecrare* 'dedicate, devote as sacred', from *con-* (expressing intensive force) + *sacrare* 'dedicate', from *sacer* 'sacred'.

**consecutive** /kənˈsɛkjʊtɪv/ ● adj. **1** following continuously. ➤in sequence. **2** Grammar expressing consequence or result. **3** Music denoting intervals of the same kind occurring in succession between two parts or voices.
– DERIVATIVES **consecutively** adv. **consecutiveness** n.
– ORIGIN C17: from Fr. *consécutif*, *-ive*, from med. L. *consecutivus*, from L. *consecut-*, *consequi* 'follow closely'.

**consensual** /kənˈsɛnsjʊəl, -ʃʊəl/ ● adj. relating to or involving consent or consensus.
– DERIVATIVES **consensually** adv.

**consensus** /kənˈsɛnsəs/ ● n. general agreement.
– ORIGIN C17: from L., 'agreement', from *consens-*, *consentire* 'agree'.

**consensus sequence** ● n. Biochemistry a sequence of DNA having similar structure and function in different organisms.

**consent** ● n. permission. ● v. give permission. ➤agree to do something.
– PHRASES **informed consent** permission granted in the knowledge of the possible consequences.
– ORIGIN ME: from OFr. *consente* (n.), *consentir* (v.), from L. *consentire*, from *con-* 'together' + *sentire* 'feel'.

**consentient** /kənˈsɛnʃ(ə)nt/ ● adj. archaic in agreement.

**consenting adult** ● n. an adult who willingly agrees to engage in a sexual act.

**consequence** ● n. **1** a result or effect. **2** [usu. with neg.] importance or relevance. ➤dated social distinction. **3** (**consequences**) [treated as sing.] a game in which a narrative is made up by the players in turn, each ignorant of what has already been contributed.
– PHRASES **in consequence** as a result. **take** (or **bear**) **the consequences** accept responsibility for negative results or effects.
– ORIGIN ME: via OFr. from L. *consequentia*, from *consequent-*, *consequi* 'follow closely'.

**consequent** ● adj. **1** following as a consequence. ➤archaic logically consistent. **2** Geology (of a stream or valley) having a direction or character determined by the original slope of the land before erosion. ● n. **1** Logic the second part of a conditional proposition, whose truth is stated to be implied by that of the antecedent. **2** Music the second or imitating voice or part in a canon.
– DERIVATIVES **consequential** adj. **consequentiality** n. **consequentially** adv. **consequently** adv.

**consequentialism** ● n. Philosophy the doctrine that the morality of an action is to be judged solely by its consequences.
– DERIVATIVES **consequentialist** adj. & n.

**conservancy** /kənˈsəːv(ə)nsi/ ● n. (pl. **-ies**) **1** a body concerned with the preservation of natural resources. **2** a commission controlling a port, river, or catchment area. **3** conservation.
– ORIGIN C18: alt. of obs. *conservacy*, from Anglo-Norman Fr. *conservacie*, via Anglo-Latin from L. *conservatio* (see CONSERVATION).

**conservation** ● n. **1** preservation or restoration of the natural environment and wildlife. ➤preservation and repair of archaeological, historical, and cultural sites and artefacts. **2** careful use of a resource. **3** Physics the principle by which the total value of a quantity remains constant in a system which is not subject to external influence.
– DERIVATIVES **conservational** adj. **conservationist** n.
– ORIGIN ME: from L. *conservatio(n-)*, from *conservare* (see CONSERVE).

**conservative** ● adj. **1** averse to change or innovation and holding traditional values. ➤(of dress or taste) sober and conventional. **2** (in a political context) favouring free enterprise, private ownership, and socially conservative ideas. ➤(**Conservative**) of or relating to a Conservative Party. **3** (of an estimate) purposely low for the sake of caution. **4** (of surgery or medical treatment) intended to control rather than eliminate a condition, and preserve existing tissue. ● n. **1** a conservative person. **2** (**Conservative**) a supporter or member of a Conservative Party.
– DERIVATIVES **conservatism** n. **conservatively** adv. **conservativeness** n.

**Conservative Judaism** ● n. a form of Judaism seeking to preserve Jewish tradition and ritual but with a more flexible approach than Orthodox Judaism.

**conservatoire** /kənˈsəːvətwɑː/ ● n. a college for the study of classical music or other arts.
– ORIGIN C18: Fr., from Ital. *conservatorio*.

**conservator** /ˈkɒnsəˌveɪtə, kənˈsəːvətə/ ● n. a person involved in conservation.

**conservatorium** /kənˌsəːvəˈtɔːrɪəm/ ● n. (pl. **conservatoriums** or **conservatoria**) Australian term for CONSERVATOIRE.
– ORIGIN C19: from Ger. *Conservatorium* and mod. L.

**conservatory** ● n. (pl. **-ies**) **1** Brit. a room with a glass roof and walls, attached to a house and used as a sun lounge or for growing delicate plants. **2** chiefly N. Amer. another term for CONSERVATOIRE.
– ORIGIN C16: from late L. *conservatorium*, from *conservare* (see CONSERVE).

**conserve** /kənˈsəːv/ ● v. **1** protect from harm or destruction. ➤prevent the wasteful overuse of. ➤preserve (food, typically fruit) with sugar. **2** Physics maintain (a quantity) at a constant overall total. ● n. /also ˈkɒnsəːv/ jam.
– ORIGIN ME: from OFr. *conserver* (v.), *conserve* (n.), from L. *conservare* 'to preserve', from *con-* 'together' + *servare* 'to keep'.

**consider** ● v. **1** think carefully about. ➤believe to be. ➤take into account when making a judgement. **2** look attentively at.
– PHRASES **all things considered** taking everything into account.
– ORIGIN ME: from OFr. *considerer*, from L. *considerare* 'examine', perh. based on *sidus*, *sider-* 'star'.

**considerable** ● adj. **1** notably large. **2** having merit or distinction.
– DERIVATIVES **considerably** adv.

**considerate** ● adj. **1** careful not to harm or inconvenience others. **2** archaic careful.
– DERIVATIVES **considerately** adv. **considerateness** n.

**consideration** ● n. **1** careful thought. ➤a fact taken into account when making a decision. **2** thoughtfulness towards others. **3** a payment or reward. ➤Law anything given or promised by one party in exchange for the promise or undertaking of another. **4** archaic importance.
– PHRASES **in consideration of** in return for. **take into consideration** take into account. **under consideration** being considered.

**considering** ● prep. & conj. taking into consideration. ● adv. informal taking everything into account.

**consign** /kən'sʌɪn/ ● v. deliver to someone's custody. ➤send (goods) by a public carrier. ➤(**consign someone/thing to**) put someone or something in (a place) in order to be rid of them.
– DERIVATIVES **consignee** n. **consignor** n.
– ORIGIN ME: from Fr. *consigner* or L. *consignare* 'mark with a seal'.

**consignment** ● n. a batch of goods consigned.

**consilience** /kən'sɪlɪəns/ ● n. concurrence between the approaches to a topic of different academic subjects, especially science and the humanities.
– DERIVATIVES **consilient** adj.
– ORIGIN from **CON-** + L. *-silient-*, *-siliens* 'jumping' (as in *resilient-* **RESILIENT**), after **CONCURRENT**.

**consist** ● v. /kən'sɪst/ **1** (**consist of**) be composed of. ➤(**consist in**) have as an essential feature. **2** (**consist with**) archaic be consistent with. ● n. /'kɒnsɪst/ Railways the set of vehicles forming a complete train.
– ORIGIN ME: from L. *consistere* 'stand firm or still, exist', from *con-* 'together' + *sistere* 'stand (still)'.

**consistency** (also **consistence**) ● n. (pl. **-ies**) **1** the state of being consistent. **2** the thickness or viscosity of a substance.

**consistent** ● adj. **1** unchanging over time. **2** (usu. **consistent with**) congruous or in agreement. **3** not containing any logical contradictions.
– DERIVATIVES **consistently** adv.
– ORIGIN C16 (in the sense 'consisting or composed of'): from L. *consistent-*, *consistere* (see **CONSIST**).

**consistory** /kən'sɪst(ə)ri/ ● n. (pl. **-ies**) **1** (in the Roman Catholic Church) the council of cardinals, with or without the Pope. **2** (also **consistory court**) (in the Church of England) a court presided over by a bishop, for the administration of ecclesiastical law in a diocese. **3** (in other Churches) a local administrative body.
– DERIVATIVES **consistorial** /ˌkɒnsɪ'stɔːrɪəl/ adj.
– ORIGIN ME: from Anglo-Norman Fr. *consistorie*, from late L. *consistorium*, from *consistere* (see **CONSIST**).

**consociation** ● n. **1** a political system formed by the cooperation of different social groups on the basis of shared power. ➤dated close association or fellowship. **2** Ecology a small climax community of plants having a characteristic dominant species.
– DERIVATIVES **consociational** adj. **consociationalism** n.
– ORIGIN C16: from L. *consociatio(n-)*, from *consociare*, from *con-* 'together' + *sociare* 'to associate' (from *socius* 'fellow').

**consolation** /ˌkɒnsə'leɪʃ(ə)n/ ● n. comfort received by someone after a loss or disappointment. ➤a source of such comfort.
– DERIVATIVES **consolatory** /kən'sɒlət(ə)ri, -'səʊl-/ adj.
– ORIGIN ME: via OFr. from L. *consolatio(n-)*, from *consolari* (see **CONSOLE[1]**).

**consolation prize** ● n. a prize given to a competitor who just fails to win.

**console[1]** /kən'səʊl/ ● v. give consolation to.
– DERIVATIVES **consolable** adj. **consoler** n. **consoling** adj. **consolingly** adv.
– ORIGIN C17 (orig. *consolate*): from Fr. *consoler*, from L. *consolari*, from *con-* 'with' + *solari* 'soothe'.

**console[2]** /'kɒnsəʊl/ ● n. **1** a panel or unit accommodating a set of controls. ➤a cabinet for television or radio equipment. ➤(also **games console**) a small machine for playing computerized video games. ➤the cabinet or enclosure containing the keyboards, stops, etc. of an organ. **2** an ornamented bracket or corbel.
– ORIGIN C17: from Fr., perh. from *consolider*, from L. *consolidare* (see **CONSOLIDATE**).

**console table** ● n. a table top supported by ornamented brackets against a wall.

**consolidate** /kən'sɒlɪdeɪt/ ● v. **1** make stronger or more solid. **2** combine into a single unit.
– DERIVATIVES **consolidation** n. **consolidator** n.
– ORIGIN C16: from L. *consolidare*, from *con-* 'together' + *solidare* 'make firm' (from *solidus* 'solid').

**Consols** /'kɒns(ə)lz/ ● pl. n. British government securities without redemption date and with fixed annual interest.
– ORIGIN C18: contr. of *consolidated annuities*.

**consommé** /kən'sɒmeɪ/ ● n. a clear soup made with concentrated stock.
– ORIGIN Fr., past part. of *consommer* 'consume or consummate', from L. *consummare* (see **CONSUMMATE**).

**consonance** /'kɒns(ə)nəns/ ● n. **1** agreement or compatibility. **2** the recurrence of similar-sounding consonants, especially in prosody. **3** Music a harmonious combination of notes.
– ORIGIN ME: from OFr., or from L. *consonantia*, from *consonant-*, *consonare* (see **CONSONANT**).

**consonant** /'kɒns(ə)nənt/ ● n. a speech sound in which the breath is at least partly obstructed and which can be combined with a vowel to form a syllable. ➤a letter representing such a sound. ● adj. **1** denoting or relating to a consonant. **2** (**consonant with**) in agreement or harmony with. **3** Music making a harmonious interval or chord.
– DERIVATIVES **consonantal** adj. **consonantly** adv.
– ORIGIN ME: via OFr. from L. *consonare* 'sound together', from *con-* 'with' + *sonare* 'to sound' (from *sonus* 'sound').

**con sordino** /ˌkɒn sɔː'diːnəʊ/ ● adv. Music using a mute.
– ORIGIN from Ital.

**consort[1]** ● n. /'kɒnsɔːt/ **1** a wife, husband, or companion, in particular the spouse of a monarch. **2** a ship sailing in company with another. ● v. /kən'sɔːt/ **1** (**consort with**) habitually associate with. **2** (**consort with/to**) archaic agree or be in harmony with.
– ORIGIN ME: via Fr. from L. *consors* 'sharing, partner', from *con-* 'together with' + *sors*, *sort-* 'lot, destiny'.

**consort[2]** /'kɒnsɔːt/ ● n. a small group of musicians performing together, typically playing Renaissance music.
– ORIGIN C16: earlier form of **CONCERT**.

**consortium** /kən'sɔːtɪəm/ ● n. (pl. **consortia** /-tɪə/ or **consortiums**) **1** an association, typically of several companies. **2** Law the right of association and companionship with one's spouse.
– ORIGIN C19: from L., from *consors* (see **CONSORT[1]**).

**conspecific** /kɒnspə'sɪfɪk/ Biology ● adj. belonging to the same species. ● n. a member of the same species.
– DERIVATIVES **conspecificity** n.

**conspectus** /kən'spɛktəs/ ● n. a summary or overview of a subject.
– ORIGIN C19: from L., past part. (used as n.) of *conspicere* (see **CONSPICUOUS**).

**conspicuous** /kən'spɪkjʊəs/ ● adj. clearly visible. ➤attracting notice or attention.
– PHRASES **conspicuous by one's absence** obviously not present where one should be.
– DERIVATIVES **conspicuity** n. **conspicuously** adv. **conspicuousness** n.
– ORIGIN C16: from L. *conspicuus* (from *conspicere* 'look at attentively', from *con-* (expressing intensive force) + *spicere* 'look at') + **-OUS**.

**conspiracist** ● n. a supporter of a conspiracy theory.

**conspiracy** ● n. (pl. **-ies**) a secret plan by a group to do something unlawful or harmful. ➤the action of conspiring.
– PHRASES **a conspiracy of silence** an agreement to say nothing.
– ORIGIN ME: from Anglo-Norman Fr. *conspiracie*, alt. of OFr. *conspiration*, based on L. *conspirare* (see **CONSPIRE**).

**conspiracy theory** ● **n.** a belief that some covert but influential organization is responsible for an unexplained event.

**conspire** ● **v.** make secret plans jointly to commit an unlawful or harmful act. ➤(of circumstances) seem to be acting together, especially with unfortunate results.
– DERIVATIVES **conspirator** n. **conspiratorial** adj. **conspiratorially** adv.
– ORIGIN ME: from OFr. *conspirer*, from L. *conspirare* 'agree, plot', from *con-* 'together with' + *spirare* 'breathe'.

**Const.** ● **abbrev.** constable.

**constable** /'kʌnstəb(ə)l, 'kɒn-/ ● **n. 1** Brit. a police officer. ➤(also **police constable**) a police officer of the lowest rank. **2** the governor of a royal castle. ➤historical the highest-ranking official in a royal household.
– ORIGIN ME: from OFr. *conestable*, from late L. *comes stabuli* 'count (head officer) of the stable'.

**constabulary** /kən'stabjʊləri/ ● **n.** (pl. **-ies**) chiefly Brit. a police force.
– ORIGIN C15: from med. L. *constabularia (dignitas)* '(rank) of constable', from *constabulus*, based on L. *comes stabuli* (see **CONSTABLE**).

**constant** ● **adj. 1** occurring continuously. **2** remaining the same. ➤faithful and dependable. ● **n.** an unchanging situation. ➤Mathematics a component of a relationship between variables that does not change its value. ➤Physics a number expressing a relation or property which remains the same in all circumstances, or for the same substance under the same conditions.
– DERIVATIVES **constancy** n. **constantly** adv.
– ORIGIN ME: from OFr., from L. *constant-*, *constare* 'stand firm', from *con-* 'with' + *stare* 'stand'.

**constantan** /'kɒnst(ə)ntan/ ● **n.** a copper–nickel alloy used in electrical work for its high resistance.

**constative** /'kɒnstətɪv, kən'steɪtɪv/ Linguistics ● **adj.** denoting a statement declaring something to be the case. ● **n.** a constative speech act or sentence.
– ORIGIN C20: from L. *constat-*, *constare* 'establish' + **-IVE**.

**constellation** ● **n. 1** a group of stars forming a recognized pattern and typically named after a mythological or other figure. **2** a group of associated people or things.
– DERIVATIVES **constellate** v. (poetic/literary).
– ORIGIN ME: via OFr. from late L. *constellatio(n-)*, based on L. *stella* 'star'.

**consternate** /'kɒnstəneɪt/ ● **v.** fill with anxiety.
– ORIGIN C17: from L. *consternat-*, *consternare* 'terrify, prostrate'.

**consternation** ● **n.** anxiety or dismay.

**constipate** /'kɒnstɪpeɪt/ ● **v.** (usu. **be constipated**) affect with constipation.
– ORIGIN C16: from L. *constipat-*, *constipare* 'crowd or press together', from *con-* 'together' + *stipare* 'press, cram'.

**constipation** ● **n.** a difficulty in emptying the bowels, associated with hardened faeces.

**constituency** /kən'stɪtjʊənsi/ ● **n.** (pl. **-ies**) **1** a body of voters in a specified area who elect a representative to a legislative body. ➤chiefly Brit. the area represented in this way. **2** a body of customers or supporters.

**constituent** ● **adj. 1** being a part of a whole. **2** having the power to appoint or elect. ➤able to make or change a political constitution. ● **n. 1** a member of a constituency. **2** a component part.
– ORIGIN C15: from L. *constituent-* (partly via Fr. *constituant*), *constituere* (see **CONSTITUTE**).

**constitute** /'kɒnstɪtjuːt/ ● **v. 1** be (a part) of a whole. ➤be or be equivalent to. **2** (usu. **be constituted**) establish by law.
– ORIGIN ME: from L. *constitut-*, *constituere* 'establish, appoint', from *con-* 'together' + *statuere* 'set up'.

**constitution** ● **n. 1** a body of fundamental principles or established precedents according to which a state or organization is governed. ➤historical a decree, ordinance, or law. **2** the composition or forming of something. **3** a person's physical or mental state.

**constitutional** ● **adj. 1** of, relating to, or in accordance with a constitution. **2** of or relating to a person's physical or mental state. ● **n.** dated a walk taken regularly to maintain good health.
– DERIVATIVES **constitutionality** n. **constitutionally** adv.

**constitutionalism** ● **n.** constitutional government. ➤adherence to such a system.
– DERIVATIVES **constitutionalist** n.

**constitutionalize** (also **-ise**) ● **v.** N. Amer. make subject to the provisions of a country's constitution.

**constitutive** ● **adj. 1** having the power to establish something. **2** forming a constituent of something.
– DERIVATIVES **constitutively** adv.

**constrain** ● **v.** compel or force towards a course of action. ➤archaic bring about by compulsion. ➤[as adj. **constrained**] appearing forced. ➤severely restrict the scope, extent, or activity of. ➤poetic/literary imprison.
– DERIVATIVES **constrainedly** adv.
– ORIGIN ME: from OFr. *constraindre*, from L. *constringere* 'bind tightly together'.

**constraint** ● **n. 1** a limitation or restriction. **2** stiffness of manner and inhibition.

**constrict** ● **v.** make or become narrower, especially by encircling pressure. ➤(of a snake) coil round (prey) in order to asphyxiate it.
– DERIVATIVES **constriction** n. **constrictive** adj.
– ORIGIN C18 (earlier (ME) as *constriction*): from L. *constrict-*, *constringere* (see **CONSTRAIN**).

**constrictor** ● **n. 1** a snake that kills by constricting its prey, such as a boa or python. **2** Anatomy a muscle whose contraction narrows a vessel or passage.

**construct** ● **v.** /kən'strʌkt/ **1** build or erect. **2** form (a theory) from various conceptual elements. **3** Grammar form (a sentence) according to grammatical rules. **4** Geometry draw or delineate (a geometrical figure). ● **n.** /'kɒnstrʌkt/ **1** an idea or theory. **2** Linguistics a group of words forming a phrase. **3** a thing constructed.
– DERIVATIVES **constructor** n.
– ORIGIN ME: from L. *construct-*, *construere* 'heap together, build', from *con-* 'together' + *struere* 'pile, build'.

**construction** ● **n. 1** the action or process of constructing. ➤the industry of erecting buildings. **2** an interpretation or explanation.
– DERIVATIVES **constructional** adj. **constructionally** adv.

**constructionism** ● **n.** another term for **CONSTRUCTIVISM**.

**constructionist** ● **n. 1** another term for ***constructivist*** (see **CONSTRUCTIVISM**). **2** US a person who puts a particular interpretation upon a legal document.

**constructive** ● **adj. 1** serving a useful purpose. **2** Law not stated explicitly. **3** of or relating to construction.
– DERIVATIVES **constructively** adv. **constructiveness** n.

**constructive dismissal** ● **n.** the changing of an employee's job with the aim of forcing resignation.

**constructivism** ● **n.** Art a style in which mechanical objects are combined into abstract mobile forms.
– DERIVATIVES **constructivist** n.

**construe** ● **v.** (**construes**, **construed**, **construing**) (often **be construed**) interpret in a particular way. ➤dated analyse the construction of (a text, sentence, or word). ➤dated translate word for word.
– DERIVATIVES **construable** adj. **construal** n.
– ORIGIN ME: from L. *construere* (see **CONSTRUCT**).

**consubstantial** ● **adj.** (especially of the three persons of the Trinity in Christian theology) of the same substance.
– DERIVATIVES **consubstantiality** n.
– ORIGIN ME: from eccles. L. *consubstantialis* (translating Gk *homoousios* 'of one substance'), from *con-* 'with' + *substantialis* (see **SUBSTANTIAL**).

**consubstantiation** /ˌkɒnsəbstanʃɪ'eɪʃ(ə)n, -sɪ-/ ● **n.** Christian Theology the doctrine that the substance of the bread and wine coexists with the body and blood of Christ in the Eucharist. Compare with **TRANSUBSTANTIATION**.

**consuetude** /'kɒnswɪtjuːd/ ● **n.** chiefly Scottish a custom, especially one with legal force.
– DERIVATIVES **consuetudinary** /-'tjuːdɪn(ə)ri/ adj.
– ORIGIN ME: from OFr., or from L. *consuetudo* (see **CUSTOM**).

**consul** /'kɒns(ə)l/ ● **n. 1** a state official living in a foreign

city and protecting the state's citizens and interests there. **2** (in ancient Rome) one of the two annually elected chief magistrates who ruled the republic. ➤any of the three chief magistrates of the first French republic (1799–1804).
– DERIVATIVES **consular** /'kɒnsjʊlə/ adj. **consulship** n.
– ORIGIN ME: from L., rel. to *consulere* 'take counsel'.

**consulate** ● n. **1** the place where a consul works. **2** historical the period of office of a Roman consul. ➤the system of government by consuls in ancient Rome. **3** (**the Consulate**) the government of the first French republic by consuls.

**consult** ● v. seek information or advice from (someone, especially an expert or professional). ➤seek permission or approval from. ➤[as adj. **consulting**] engaged in the business of giving advice to others in the same field: *a consulting engineer.*
– DERIVATIVES **consultation** n. **consultative** adj. **consultee** n.
– ORIGIN C16 (earlier (ME) as *consultation*): from Fr. *consulter*, from L. *consultare*, frequentative of *consulere* 'take counsel'.

**consultancy** ● n. (pl. **-ies**) a professional practice giving expert advice in a particular field.

**consultant** ● n. **1** a person who provides expert advice professionally. **2** Brit. a hospital doctor of senior rank.

**consumable** ● adj. intended to be used up and then replaced. ● n. a consumable commodity.

**consume** ● v. **1** eat, drink, or ingest. **2** buy (goods or services) for personal use. ➤use up. **3** (especially of a fire) completely destroy. **4** (usu. **be consumed**) (of a feeling) absorb all of the attention and energy of.
– DERIVATIVES **consumer** n. **consuming** adj. **consumingly** adv.
– ORIGIN ME: from L. *consumere*, from *con-* 'altogether' + *sumere* 'take up'.

**consumer durable** ● n. a product expected to have a long useful life.

**consumerism** ● n. **1** the protection or promotion of the interests of consumers. **2** the preoccupation of society with the acquisition of goods.
– DERIVATIVES **consumerist** adj. & n. **consumeristic** adj.

**consummate** ● v. /'kɒnsəmeɪt, -sjʊ-/**1** make (a marriage or relationship) complete by having sexual intercourse. **2** complete (a transaction). ● adj. /kən'sʌmət, 'kɒnsʌmət/ showing great skill and flair.
– DERIVATIVES **consummately** adv. **consummation** n. **consummator** n.
– ORIGIN ME: from L. *consummat-*, *consummare* 'bring to completion', from *con-* 'altogether' + *summa* 'sum total', fem. of *summus* 'highest, supreme'.

**consumption** ● n. **1** the action or process of consuming. ➤an amount consumed. **2** dated a wasting disease, especially tuberculosis.
– DERIVATIVES **consumptive** adj. & n. (dated). **consumptively** adv. (dated).
– ORIGIN ME: from L. *consumptio(n-)*, from *consumere* (see CONSUME).

**cont.** ● abbrev. **1** contents. **2** continued.

**contact** ● n. /'kɒntakt/ **1** the state or condition of physical touching. ➤the state or condition of communicating or meeting. ➤[as modifier] caused by or operating through physical touch: *contact dermatitis.* **2** a connection for the passage of an electric current from one thing to another. **3** (**contacts**) contact lenses. **4** a communication or relationship. ➤a person who may be asked for information or assistance. **5** a person who has associated with a patient with a contagious disease. ● v. /'kɒntakt, kən'takt/ get in touch or communication with.
– DERIVATIVES **contactable** adj.
– ORIGIN C17: from L. *contactus*, from *contact-*, *contingere* 'touch, grasp, border on', from *con-* 'together with' + *tangere* 'to touch'.

**contact clause** ● n. Grammar a relative clause appended without a relative pronoun to the noun phrase that governs it, as in *the man I saw yesterday.*

**contactee** ● n. a person who claims to have been contacted by alien beings.

**contact flight** (also **contact flying**) ● n. navigation of an aircraft by the observation of landmarks.

**contact lens** ● n. a thin plastic lens placed directly on the surface of the eye to correct visual defects.

**contact print** ● n. a photographic print made by placing a negative directly on to sensitized paper, glass, or film and illuminating it. ● v. (**contact-print**) make a photograph from (a negative) in this way.

**contact sheet** ● n. a sheet of contact prints.

**contact sport** ● n. a sport in which the participants necessarily come into bodily contact with one another.

**contagion** /kən'teɪdʒ(ə)n/ ● n. the communication of disease from one person to another by close contact. ➤dated a disease spread in such a way.
– ORIGIN ME: from L. *contagio(n-)*, from *con-* 'together with' + the base of *tangere* 'to touch'.

**contagious** ● adj. **1** (of a disease) spread by direct or indirect contact of people or organisms. ➤having a contagious disease. **2** (of an emotion, attitude, etc.) likely to spread to and affect others.
– DERIVATIVES **contagiously** adv. **contagiousness** n.

**contagious abortion** ● n. a type of brucellosis which causes spontaneous abortion in cattle.

**contain** ● v. **1** have or hold within. **2** control or restrain. ➤prevent (a problem) from becoming worse. **3** (of a number) be divisible by (a factor) without a remainder.
– DERIVATIVES **containable** adj.
– ORIGIN ME: from OFr. *contenir*, from L. *continere*, from *con-* 'altogether' + *tenere* 'to hold'.

**container** ● n. an object for holding or transporting something. ➤a large standard-sized metal box for the transport of goods by road, rail, sea, or air.

**containerize** (also **-ise**) ● v. [usu. as adj. **containerized**] pack into or transport by container.
– DERIVATIVES **containerization** n.

**containment** ● n. the action of keeping something harmful under control. ➤the action of preventing the expansion of a hostile country or influence.

**contaminate** ● v. make impure by exposure to or addition of a poisonous or polluting substance.
– DERIVATIVES **contaminant** n. **contamination** n. **contaminator** n.
– ORIGIN ME: from L. *contaminat-*, *contaminare* 'make impure', from *contamen* 'contact, pollution', from *con-* 'together with' + the base of *tangere* 'to touch'.

**contango** /kən'taŋgəʊ/ ● n. Brit. Stock Exchange the normal situation in which the spot or cash price of a commodity is lower than the forward price. ➤historical a percentage paid by a buyer of stock to postpone transfer to a future settling day.
– ORIGIN C19: prob. an arbitrary formation on the pattern of Latin verbs ending in *-o* in the first person sing., perh. with the idea 'I make contingent' (see CONTINGENT).

**Conté** /'kɒnteɪ/ ● n. a kind of hard grease-free crayon used for artwork.
– ORIGIN C19: named after the Fr. inventor Nicolas J. *Conté.*

**conte** /kɒnt, French kɔ̃t/ ● n. a short story as a form of literary composition. ➤a medieval narrative tale.
– ORIGIN Fr., based on L. *computare* 'reckon, sum up'.

**contemn** /kən'tɛm/ ● v. archaic treat or regard with contempt.
– DERIVATIVES **contemner** /-'tɛmə, -'tɛmnə/ n.
– ORIGIN ME: from L. *contemnere*, from *con-* (expressing intensive force) + *temnere* 'despise'.

**contemplate** /'kɒntɛmpleɪt, -təm-/ ● v. look at thoughtfully. ➤think about. ➤think profoundly and at length. ➤have as a probable intention.
– DERIVATIVES **contemplator** n.
– ORIGIN C16: from L. *contemplat-*, *contemplari* 'survey, observe, contemplate', based on *templum* 'place for observation'.

**contemplation** ● n. **1** the action of contemplating. **2** religious meditation. ➤(in Christian spirituality) a form of prayer in which a person seeks a direct experience of the divine.

**contemplative** /kən'tɛmplətɪv/ ● adj. expressing or involving contemplation. ● n. a person whose life is de-

voted to prayer, especially in a monastery or convent.
– DERIVATIVES **contemplatively** adv.

**contemporaneous** /kənˌtɛmpəˈreɪnɪəs, kɒn-/ ● **adj.** existing at or occurring in the same period of time.
– DERIVATIVES **contemporaneity** n. **contemporaneously** adv. **contemporaneousness** n.
– ORIGIN C17: from L., from *con-* 'together with' + *temporaneus* (from *tempus, tempor-* 'time') + **-OUS**.

**contemporary** /kənˈtɛmp(ə)r(ər)i/ ● **adj. 1** living, occurring, or originating at the same time. **2** belonging to or occurring in the present. ➤modern in style or design. ● **n.** (pl. **-ies**) a person or thing existing at the same time as another. ➤a person of roughly the same age as another.
– DERIVATIVES **contemporarily** adv. **contemporariness** n.
– ORIGIN C17: from med. L. *contemporarius*, from *con-* 'together with' + *tempus, tempor-* 'time' (on the pattern of L. *contemporaneus* and late L. *contemporalis*).

**contempt** ● **n. 1** the feeling that a person or a thing is worthless or beneath consideration. **2** (also **contempt of court**) the offence of being disobedient to or disrespectful of a court of law.
– PHRASES **beneath contempt** utterly worthless or despicable. **hold someone in contempt** judge someone to be in contempt of court. **hold someone/thing in contempt** despise someone or something.
– ORIGIN ME: from L. *contemptus*, from *contemnere* (see **CONTEMN**).

**contemptible** ● **adj.** deserving contempt.
– DERIVATIVES **contemptibly** adv.

**contemptuous** ● **adj.** showing contempt.
– DERIVATIVES **contemptuously** adv. **contemptuousness** n.

**contend** ● **v. 1** (**contend with/against**) struggle to surmount (a difficulty). ➤(**contend for**) engage in a struggle or campaign to achieve. **2** assert.
– DERIVATIVES **contender** n.
– ORIGIN ME: from OFr. *contendre* or L. *contendere*, from *con-* 'with' + *tendere* 'stretch, strive'.

**content**[1] /kənˈtɛnt/ ● **adj.** in a state of peaceful happiness or satisfaction. ● **v.** satisfy. ➤(**content oneself with**) accept as adequate despite wanting more or better. ● **n. 1** a state of satisfaction. **2** a member of the British House of Lords who votes for a motion.
– PHRASES **to one's heart's content** to the full extent of one's desires.
– DERIVATIVES **contented** adj. **contentedly** adv. **contentedness** n. **contentment** n.
– ORIGIN ME: via OFr. from L. *contentus* 'satisfied', past part. of *continere* (see **CONTAIN**).

**content**[2] /ˈkɒntɛnt/ ● **n. 1** (**contents**) the things that are contained in something. ➤(**contents** or **table of contents**) a list of chapters or sections at the front of a book or periodical. **2** the material dealt with in a speech, literary work, etc. as distinct from its form or style.
– DERIVATIVES **contentless** adj.
– ORIGIN ME: from med. L. *contentum* (pl. *contenta* 'things contained'), neut. past part. of *continere* (see **CONTAIN**).

**contention** ● **n. 1** heated disagreement. **2** an assertion.
– PHRASES **in contention** having a good chance of success in a contest.
– ORIGIN ME: from L. *contentio(n-)*, from *contendere* (see **CONTEND**).

**contentious** ● **adj.** causing or likely to cause disagreement or controversy. ➤Law of, relating to, or involving differences between contending parties. ➤given to provoking argument.
– DERIVATIVES **contentiously** adv. **contentiousness** n.
– ORIGIN ME: from OFr. *contentieux*, from L. *contentiosus*, from *content-*, *contendere* 'strive'.

**conterminous** /kɒnˈtəːmɪnəs/ ● **adj. 1** sharing a common boundary. **2** having the same area, context, or meaning.
– DERIVATIVES **conterminously** adv.
– ORIGIN C17: from L. *conterminus* (from *con-* 'with' + *terminus* 'boundary') + **-OUS**.

**contessa** /kɒnˈtɛsə/ ● **n.** an Italian countess.
– ORIGIN Ital., from late L. *comitissa*, fem. of *comes* (see **COUNT**[2])

**contest** ● **n.** /ˈkɒntɛst/ an event in which people compete for supremacy. ➤a dispute or conflict. ● **v.** /kənˈtɛst/ **1** compete to attain (a position of power). ➤take part in (a competition or election). **2** challenge or dispute.
– PHRASES **no contest 1** chiefly US another term for **NOLO CONTENDERE**. **2** a decision to declare a boxing match invalid on the grounds that one or both of the boxers are not making serious efforts. ➤a competition or comparison of which the outcome is a foregone conclusion.
– DERIVATIVES **contestable** adj. **contester** n.
– ORIGIN C16 (as v. 'swear to, attest'): from L. *contestari* 'call upon to witness, initiate an action (by calling witnesses)', from *con-* 'together' + *testare* 'to witness'.

**contestant** ● **n.** a person who takes part in a contest.

**contestation** ● **n.** formal the action or process of disputing or arguing.
– ORIGIN C16: from L. *contestatio(n-)*, from *contestari* (see **CONTEST**); reinforced by Fr. *contestation*.

**context** /ˈkɒntɛkst/ ● **n.** the circumstances that form the setting for an event, statement, or idea, and in terms of which it can be fully understood. ➤the parts that immediately precede and follow a word or passage and clarify its meaning.
– DERIVATIVES **contextual** adj. **contextualization** (also **-isation**) n. **contextualize** (also **-ise**) v. **contextually** adv.
– ORIGIN ME (denoting the construction of a text): from L. *contextus*, from *con-* 'together' + *texere* 'to weave'.

**contextualism** ● **n.** Philosophy a doctrine which emphasizes the importance of the context of enquiry in a particular question.
– DERIVATIVES **contextualist** n.

**contiguity** /ˌkɒntɪˈgjuːɪti/ ● **n. 1** the state of being contiguous with something. **2** Psychology the sequential occurrence or proximity of stimulus and response, causing their association in the mind.

**contiguous** /kənˈtɪgjʊəs/ ● **adj.** sharing a common border. ➤next or together in sequence.
– DERIVATIVES **contiguously** adv.
– ORIGIN C16: from L. *contiguus* 'touching', from *contingere* (see **CONTINGENT**), + **-OUS**.

**continent**[1] ● **n. 1** any of the world's main continuous expanses of land (Europe, Asia, Africa, North and South America, Australia, Antarctica). **2** (also **the Continent**) the mainland of Europe as distinct from the British Isles.
– ORIGIN C16: from L. *terra continens* 'continuous land'.

**continent**[2] ● **adj. 1** able to control movements of the bowels and bladder. **2** exercising self-restraint, especially sexually.
– DERIVATIVES **continence** n. **continently** adv.
– ORIGIN ME: from L. *continent-*, *continere* (see **CONTAIN**).

**continental** ● **adj. 1** forming or belonging to a continent. **2** (also **Continental**) coming from or characteristic of mainland Europe. ● **n.** an inhabitant of mainland Europe.
– DERIVATIVES **continentally** adv.

**continental breakfast** ● **n.** a light breakfast of coffee and bread rolls with butter and jam.

**continental climate** ● **n.** a relatively dry climate with very hot summers and very cold winters, characteristic of the central parts of Asia and North America.

**continental day** ● **n.** Brit. a school day lasting from early morning to early afternoon.

**continental drift** ● **n.** the gradual movement of the continents across the earth's surface through geological time.

**continental quilt** ● **n.** British term for **DUVET**.

**continental shelf** ● **n.** an area of seabed around a large land mass where the sea is relatively shallow.

**contingency** /kənˈtɪndʒ(ə)nsi/ ● **n.** (pl. **-ies**) **1** a future event or circumstance which is possible but cannot be predicted with certainty. ➤a provision for such an event or circumstance. **2** the absence of certainty in events. **3** Philosophy the absence of necessity.

**contingency table** • n. Statistics a table showing the distribution of one variable in rows and another in columns, used to study the correlation between the two.

**contingent** /kən'tɪndʒ(ə)nt/ • adj. **1** subject to chance. ➤(**contingent on/upon**) dependent on. ➤(of losses, liabilities, etc.) that can be anticipated to arise if a particular event occurs. **2** Philosophy true by virtue of the way things in fact are and not by logical necessity. • n. a group of people within a larger group. ➤a body of troops or police sent to join a larger force.
– DERIVATIVES **contingently** adv.
– ORIGIN ME: from L. *contingere* 'befall', from *con-* 'together with' + *tangere* 'to touch'.

**continual** • adj. constantly or frequently occurring.
– DERIVATIVES **continually** adv.
– ORIGIN ME: from OFr. *continuel*, from *continuer* 'continue', from L. *continuare*, from *continuus* (see **CONTINUOUS**).

**continuance** • n. **1** formal the state of continuing. ➤the time for which a situation or action lasts. **2** US Law a postponement or adjournment.

**continuant** • n. **1** Phonetics a consonant which is sounded with the vocal tract only partly closed, allowing the breath to pass through and the sound to be prolonged (as with *f, l, m, n, r, s, v*). **2** Philosophy & Psychology a thing that retains its identity even though its states and relations may change. • adj. relating to or denoting a continuant.
– ORIGIN C17: from Fr., from *continuer*, reinforced by L. *continuant-*, *continuare* 'continue', from *continuus* (see **CONTINUOUS**).

**continuation** • n. **1** the action of continuing or state of being continued. **2** a part that is attached to and is an extension of something else.

**continuative** /kən'tɪnjʊətɪv/ Linguistics • adj. (of a word or phrase) having the function of moving a discourse or conversation forward. • n. a word or phrase of this type (e.g. *yes, well, as I was saying*).
– ORIGIN C16: from late L. *continuativus*, from *continuat-*, *continuare* (see **CONTINUE**).

**continue** • v. (**continues**, **continued**, **continuing**) **1** persist in an activity or process. ➤remain in existence, operation, or a specified state. **2** carry on with. ➤carry on travelling in the same direction. **3** recommence or resume. **4** US Law postpone or adjourn (a legal proceeding).
– DERIVATIVES **continuator** n. **continuer** n.
– ORIGIN ME: from OFr. *continuer*, from L. *continuare*, from *continuus* (see **CONTINUOUS**).

**continuing education** • n. education provided for adults after they have left the formal education system.

**continuity** /ˌkɒntɪ'nju:ɪti/ • n. (pl. **-ies**) **1** the unbroken and consistent existence or operation of something. ➤a connection or line of development with no sharp breaks. **2** the maintenance of continuous action and self-consistent detail in the scenes of a film or broadcast. **3** the linking of broadcast items by a spoken commentary.

**continuo** /kən'tɪnjʊəʊ/ (also **basso continuo**) • n. (pl. **-os**) (in baroque music) an accompanying part which includes a bass line and harmonies, typically played on a keyboard instrument.
– ORIGIN C18: Ital. *basso continuo* 'continuous bass'.

**continuous** • adj. **1** without interruption. ➤forming a series with no exceptions or reversals. ➤Mathematics (of a function) of which the graph is a smooth unbroken curve. **2** Grammar another term for **PROGRESSIVE** (in sense 4).
– DERIVATIVES **continuously** adv. **continuousness** n.
– ORIGIN C17: from L. *continuus* 'uninterrupted', from *continere* 'hang together' (from *con-* 'together with' + *tenere* 'hold') + **-OUS**.

**continuous assessment** • n. Brit. the evaluation of a pupil's progress throughout a course of study, as distinct from by examination.

**continuous creation** • n. the creation of matter as a continuing process throughout time, especially as postulated in steady-state theories of the universe.

**continuous stationery** • n. Brit. a long continuous strip of paper that is usually perforated to form sheets.

**continuum** • n. (pl. **continua**) a continuous sequence in which adjacent elements are not perceptibly different from each other, but the extremes are quite distinct.
– ORIGIN C17: from L., neut. of *continuus* (see **CONTINUOUS**).

**contort** /kən'tɔ:t/ • v. twist or bend out of its normal shape.
– DERIVATIVES **contortion** n.
– ORIGIN ME: from L. *contort-*, *contorquere* 'twist round, brandish', from *con-* 'together' + *torquere* 'twist'.

**contortionist** • n. an entertainer who twists and bends their body into strange and unnatural positions.

**contour** • n. **1** an outline, especially one representing or bounding the shape or form of something. ➤(also **contour line**) a line on a map joining points of equal height above or below sea level. ➤a line joining points on a diagram at which some property has the same value. **2** a way in which something varies, especially the pitch of music or the pattern of tones in an utterance. • v. **1** mould into a specific shape. **2** [usu. as adj. **contoured**] mark (a map or diagram) with contours. **3** (of a road or railway) follow the outline of (a topographical feature).
– ORIGIN C17: from Fr., from Ital. *contorno*, from *contornare* 'draw in outline', from *con-* 'together'+ *tornare* 'to turn'.

**contour feather** • n. any of the mainly small feathers which form the outline of an adult bird's plumage.

**contour ploughing** • n. ploughing along the contours of the land in order to minimize soil erosion.

**contra** /'kɒntrə/ • n. a member of a US-supported guerrilla force in Nicaragua which opposed the left-wing Sandinista government 1979–90.
– ORIGIN abbrev. of Sp. *contrarevolucionario* 'counter-revolutionary'.

**contra-** /'kɒntrə/ • prefix **1** against; opposite: *contraception*. **2** Music (of instruments or organ stops) pitched an octave below: *contrabass*.
– ORIGIN from L. *contra* 'against'.

**contraband** /'kɒntrəband/ • n. goods that have been imported or exported illegally. ➤trade in smuggled goods. ➤(also **contraband of war**) goods forbidden to be supplied by neutrals to those engaged in war. • adj. imported or exported illegally. ➤relating to traffic in illegal goods.
– DERIVATIVES **contrabandist** n.
– ORIGIN C16: from Sp. *contrabanda*, from Ital. *contrabando*, from *contra-* 'against' + *bando* 'proclamation, ban'.

**contrabass** • n. another term for **DOUBLE BASS**. • adj. denoting a musical instrument with a range an octave lower than the normal bass range.
– ORIGIN C18: from Ital. *contrabasso*, from *contra-* 'pitched an octave below' + *basso* (see **BASS**[1]).

**contrabassoon** • n. another term for **DOUBLE BASSOON**.

**contraception** • n. the use of artificial methods or other techniques to prevent pregnancy.

**contraceptive** • adj. serving to prevent pregnancy. ➤of or relating to contraception. • n. a contraceptive device or drug.

**contract** • n. /'kɒntrakt/ **1** a written or spoken agreement intended to be enforceable by law. **2** informal an arrangement for someone to be killed by a hired assassin. **3** Bridge the declarer's undertaking to win the number of tricks bid with a stated suit as trumps. • v. /kən'trakt/ **1** decrease in size, number, or range. **2** (of a muscle) become shorter and tighter in order to effect movement of part of the body. **3** shorten (a word or phrase) by combination or elision. **4** enter into a formal and legally binding agreement. ➤(**contract in/into**) Brit. choose to be involved in. ➤(**contract out**) Brit. choose to withdraw from or not become involved in. ➤(**contract something out**) arrange for work to be done by another organization. **5** catch or develop (a disease). **6** become liable to pay (a debt).
– DERIVATIVES **contractive** adj. **contractual** adj. **contractually** adv.
– ORIGIN ME: via OFr. from L. *contractus*, from *contract-*, *contrahere* 'draw together, tighten'.

**contractable** • adj. (of a disease) able to be caught.

**contract bridge** ● n. the standard form of the card game bridge, in which only tricks bid and won count towards the game.

**contractible** ● adj. able to be shrunk or capable of contracting.

**contractile** /kən'traktʌɪl/ ● adj. Biology & Physiology capable of or producing contraction.
– DERIVATIVES **contractility** n.

**contraction** ● n. **1** the process of contracting. **2** a shortening of the uterine muscles occurring at intervals before and during childbirth. **3** a word or group of words resulting from contracting an original form.

**contract note** ● n. a certificate confirming the terms of a sale of specified assets or securities.

**contractor** ● n. a person who undertakes a contract to provide materials or labour for a job.

**contractorization** (also **-isation**) ● n. Brit. the provision of a public service by an external contractor.
– DERIVATIVES **contractorize** v.

**contractural** ● adj. **1** Medicine relating to or involving contracture. **2** another term for ***contractual*** (see **CONTRACT**). [formed by erroneous insertion of *-r-*.]

**contracture** /kən'traktʃə/ ● n. Medicine a condition of shortening and hardening of muscles, tendons, or other tissue, often leading to deformity and rigidity of joints.
– ORIGIN C17: from Fr., or from L. *contractura*, from L. *contract-*, *contrahere* 'draw together'.

**contradict** ● v. deny the truth of (a statement) by asserting the opposite. ➤assert the opposite of a statement made by (someone).
– DERIVATIVES **contradictor** n.
– ORIGIN C16: from L. *contradict-*, *contradicere* 'speak against'.

**contradiction** ● n. a combination of statements, ideas, or features which are opposed to one another. ➤the statement of a position opposite to one already made.
– PHRASES **contradiction in terms** a statement or group of words associating incompatible objects or ideas.

**contradictory** ● adj. mutually opposed or inconsistent. ➤containing inconsistent elements. ➤Logic (of two propositions) so related that one and only one must be true. Compare with **CONTRARY**.
– DERIVATIVES **contradictorily** adv. **contradictoriness** n.

**contradistinction** ● n. distinction made by contrasting the different qualities of two things.

**contrafactive** ● adj. Linguistics denoting a verb that assigns to its object the status of not being true, e.g. *pretend* and *wish*. Contrasted with **FACTIVE**, **NON-FACTIVE**.

**contrafactual** /kɒntrə'faktʃʊəl, -tjʊəl/ ● adj. another term for **COUNTERFACTUAL**.

**contraflow** ● n. Brit. a temporary arrangement where traffic on a road is transferred from its usual side to share the other half of the carriageway with traffic moving in the opposite direction.

**contrail** /'kɒntreɪl/ ● n. chiefly N. Amer. another term for **VAPOUR TRAIL**.
– ORIGIN 1940s: abbrev. of *condensation trail*.

**contraindicate** ● v. (usu. **be contraindicated**) Medicine (of a condition or circumstance) suggest or indicate that (a particular technique or drug) should not be used.
– DERIVATIVES **contraindication** n.

**contralateral** /ˌkɒntrə'lat(ə)r(ə)l/ ● adj. Medicine relating to or denoting the side of the body opposite to that on which a particular structure or condition occurs.

**contralto** /kən'traltəʊ/ ● n. (pl. **-os**) the lowest female singing voice.
– ORIGIN C18: Ital.

**contra mundum** /ˌkɒntrə 'mʌndəm/ ● adv. defying or opposing everyone else.
– ORIGIN L., 'against the world'.

**contraposition** ● n. Logic conversion of a proposition from *all A is B* to *all not-B is not-A*.
– DERIVATIVES **contrapositive** adj. & n.
– ORIGIN C16: from late L. *contrapositio(n-)*, from *contraponere* 'place against'.

**contrapposto** /ˌkɒntrə'pɒstəʊ/ ● n. (pl. **contrapposti** /-ti/) Sculpture an asymmetrical arrangement of the human figure in which the line of the arms and shoulders contrasts with, while balancing, that of the hips and legs.
– ORIGIN Ital., past part. of *contrapporre*, from L. *contraponere* 'place against'.

**contra proferentem** /ˌkɒntrə prɒfə'rɛntɛm/ ● adv. Law (of the interpretation of a contract) against the party which proposes or adduces the contract or a condition in the contract.
– ORIGIN L., 'against (the person) mentioning'.

**contraption** ● n. a machine or device that appears strange or unnecessarily complicated.
– ORIGIN C19: perh. from **CONTRIVE** (on the pattern of pairs such as *conceive*, *conception*), by assoc. with **TRAP**[1].

**contrapuntal** /ˌkɒntrə'pʌnt(ə)l/ ● adj. Music of or in counterpoint.
– DERIVATIVES **contrapuntally** adv. **contrapuntist** n.
– ORIGIN C19: from Ital. *contrapunto* (see **COUNTERPOINT**) + **-AL**.

**contrarian** /kən'trɛːrɪən/ ● n. a person who opposes or rejects popular opinion, especially in stock exchange dealing.
– DERIVATIVES **contrarianism** n.

**contrariety** /ˌkɒntrə'rʌɪəti/ ● n. **1** Logic contrary opposition. **2** opposition or inconsistency between two things.
– ORIGIN ME: from OFr. *contrariete*, from late L. *contrarietas*, from *contrarius* (see **CONTRARY**).

**contrariwise** /kən'trɛːrɪwʌɪz, 'kɒntrərɪˌwʌɪz/ ● adv. in the opposite way. ➤on the other hand.

**contrary** /'kɒntrəri/ ● adj. **1** (often **contrary to**) opposite in nature, direction, or meaning. **2** (of two or more statements, beliefs, etc.) opposed to one another. ➤Logic (of two propositions) so related that one or neither but not both must be true. Compare with **CONTRADICTORY**. **3** /kən'trɛːri/ perversely inclined to do the opposite of what is expected or desired. ● n. (pl. **-ies**) (**the contrary**) the opposite.
– PHRASES **on** (or **quite**) **the contrary** used to intensify a denial of what has just been implied or stated. **to the contrary** with the opposite meaning or implication.
– DERIVATIVES **contrarily** /'kɒntrərɪli, kən'trɛːrɪli/ adv. **contrariness** /'kɒntrərɪnɪs, kən'trɛːrɪnɪs/ n.
– ORIGIN ME: from Anglo-Norman Fr. *contrarie*, from L. *contrarius*, from *contra* 'against'.

**contrast** ● n. /'kɒntrɑːst/ **1** the state of being strikingly different from something else in juxtaposition or close association. **2** the degree of difference between tones in a television picture, photograph, etc. **3** enhancement of the apparent brightness or clarity of a design provided by the juxtaposition of different colours or textures. **4** a thing or person noticeably different from another. ● v. /kən'trɑːst/ differ strikingly. ➤compare so as to emphasize differences.
– DERIVATIVES **contrasting** adj. **contrastingly** adv. **contrastive** adj.
– ORIGIN C17: from Fr. *contraste* (n.), *contraster* (v.), via Ital. from med. L. *contrastare*, from L. *contra-* 'against' + *stare* 'stand'.

**contrast medium** ● n. Medicine a substance introduced into a part of the body in order to improve the visibility of internal structure during radiography.

**contrasty** ● adj. informal (of a photograph, film, etc.) showing a high degree of contrast.

**contra-suggestible** ● adj. tending to respond to a suggestion by believing or doing the contrary.

**contrate wheel** /'kɒntreɪt/ ● n. another term for **CROWN WHEEL**.
– ORIGIN C17: *contrate* (a rare adj. meaning 'opposed, contrary') from med. L. *contrata* 'lying opposite'.

**contravene** /ˌkɒntrə'viːn/ ● v. offend against the prohibition or order of (a law, treaty, etc.). ➤conflict with (a right, principle, etc.), especially to its detriment.
– DERIVATIVES **contravener** n. **contravention** n.
– ORIGIN C16: from late L. *contravenire*, from L. *contra-* 'against' + *venire* 'come'.

**contredanse** /'kɒntrədɑːns, -dɒ̃s/ ● n. (pl. same) a French form of country dance, originating in the 18th century and related to the quadrille. ➤a piece of music for such a dance.

– ORIGIN Fr., alt. of COUNTRY DANCE, by assoc. with *contre* 'against, opposite'.

**contre-jour** /ˈkɒ̃trəˌʒʊə, French kɔ̃trəʒuʀ/ ● **adj. & adv.** Photography having or involving the sun or other light source behind the subject.

– ORIGIN C20: Fr., from *contre* 'against' + *jour* 'daylight'.

**contretemps** /ˈkɒntrətɒ̃/ ● **n.** (pl. same /-tɒ̃z/) a minor dispute or disagreement.

– ORIGIN C17 (orig. 'motion out of time', denoting a thrust in fencing made at an inopportune moment): Fr., from *contre-* 'against' + *temps* 'time'.

**contribute** /kənˈtrɪbjuːt, ˈkɒntrɪbjuːt/ ● **v.** give in order to help achieve or provide something. ➤(**contribute to**) help to cause or bring about.

– DERIVATIVES **contribution** n. **contributive** /kənˈtrɪb-/ adj. **contributor** n.

– ORIGIN C16 (earlier (ME) as *contribution*): from L. *contribut-*, *contribuere* 'bring together, add', from *con-* 'with' + *tribuere* 'bestow'.

**USAGE** contribute

The first pronunciation, which puts the stress on **-tri-**, is held to be the only correct one, despite the fact that the alternative, with the stress on **con-**, is older.

**contributory** ● **adj. 1** playing a part in bringing something about. **2** (of a pension or insurance scheme) operated by means of a fund into which people pay. ● **n.** (pl. **-ies**) Brit. Law a person liable to contribute towards the payment of a wound-up company's debts.

**contributory negligence** ● **n.** Law failure of an injured party to act prudently, considered to be a contributory factor in the injury suffered.

**con trick** ● **n.** informal term for CONFIDENCE TRICK.

**contrite** /kənˈtrʌɪt, ˈkɒntrʌɪt/ ● **adj.** feeling or expressing remorse.

– DERIVATIVES **contritely** adv. **contriteness** n.

– ORIGIN ME: from OFr. *contrit*, from L. *contritus*, past part. of *conterere* 'grind down, wear away'.

**contrition** ● **n.** the state of feeling contrite. ➤(in the Roman Catholic Church) the repentance of past sins during or after confession.

**contrivance** ● **n. 1** the action of contriving something. **2** an ingenious device or scheme.

**contrive** /kənˈtrʌɪv/ ● **v. 1** devise or plan using skill and artifice. **2** manage to do something foolish.

– DERIVATIVES **contrivable** adj. **contriver** n.

– ORIGIN ME: from OFr. *contreuve-*, stressed stem of *controver* 'imagine, invent', from med. L. *contropare* 'compare'.

**contrived** ● **adj.** deliberately created rather than arising spontaneously.

**control** ● **n. 1** the power to influence people's behaviour or the course of events. ➤the restriction of an activity, tendency, or phenomenon. **2** a device by which a machine is regulated. **3** the place where something is verified or from which an activity is directed. **4** Bridge a high card that will prevent the opponents from establishing a particular suit. **5** a person or thing used as a standard of comparison for checking the results of a survey or experiment. **6** a member of an intelligence organization who personally directs the activities of a spy. ● **v.** (**controlled**, **controlling**) **1** have control or command of. ➤regulate. **2** [as adj. **controlled**] (of a drug) restricted by law in respect of use and possession. **3** (**control for**) take into account (an extraneous factor that might affect the results of an experiment).

– PHRASES **in control** able to direct a situation, person, or activity. **out of control** no longer possible to manage. **under control** (of a danger or emergency) being dealt with or contained successfully.

– DERIVATIVES **controllability** n. **controllable** adj. **controllably** adv. **controller** n. **controllership** n.

– ORIGIN ME (in the sense 'verify accounts'): from Anglo-Norman Fr. *contreroller* 'keep a copy of a roll of accounts', from med. L. *contrarotulare*, from *contrarotulus* 'copy of a roll', from *contra-* 'against' + *rotulus* 'a roll'.

**control character** ● **n.** Computing a character that does not represent a printable character but serves to initiate a particular action.

**control key** ● **n.** Computing a key which alters the function of another key if they are pressed at the same time.

**controlling interest** ● **n.** the holding by one person or group of a majority of the stock of a business.

**control rod** ● **n.** a rod of a neutron-absorbing substance used to vary the output power of a nuclear reactor.

**control tower** ● **n.** a tall building at an airport from which the movements of air traffic are controlled.

**controversial** ● **adj.** causing or likely to cause controversy.

– DERIVATIVES **controversialist** n. **controversially** adv.

**controversy** /ˈkɒntrəvəːsi, kənˈtrɒvəsi/ ● **n.** (pl. **-ies**) disagreement, typically when prolonged and public.

– ORIGIN ME: from L. *controversia*, from *controversus* 'turned against, disputed'.

**USAGE** controversy

The second pronunciation, putting the stress on **-trov-**, is widely held to be incorrect in standard English.

**controvert** ● **v.** deny the truth of.

– DERIVATIVES **controvertible** adj.

– ORIGIN C16: from L. *controversus* (see CONTROVERSY).

**contumacious** /ˌkɒntjʊˈmeɪʃəs/ ● **adj.** archaic or Law stubbornly or wilfully disobedient to authority.

– DERIVATIVES **contumaciously** adv. **contumacy** n.

– ORIGIN C16: from L. *contumax*, *contumac-* (perh. from *con-* 'with' + *tumere* 'to swell') + -IOUS.

**contumely** /ˈkɒntjuːmɪli, -tjuːmli/ ● **n.** (pl. **-ies**) archaic insolent or insulting language or treatment.

– DERIVATIVES **contumelious** /ˌkɒntjʊˈmiːlɪəs/ adj. **contumeliously** adv.

– ORIGIN ME: from OFr. *contumelie*, from L. *contumelia*, perh. from *con-* 'with' + *tumere* 'to swell'.

**contusion** /kənˈtjuːʒ(ə)n/ ● **n.** Medicine a bruise.

– DERIVATIVES **contuse** v.

– ORIGIN ME: from Fr., from L. *contusio(n-)*, from *contundere*, from *con-* 'together' + *tundere* 'to beat, thump'.

**conundrum** /kəˈnʌndrəm/ ● **n.** (pl. **conundrums**) a confusing and difficult problem or question. ➤a riddle.

– ORIGIN C16 (in the sense 'a crank or pedant'): of unknown origin.

**conurbation** /ˌkɒnəˈbeɪʃ(ə)n/ ● **n.** an extended urban area, typically consisting of several towns merging with the suburbs of a central city.

– ORIGIN C20: from CON- + L. *urbs*, *urb-* 'city' + -ATION.

**conure** /ˈkɒnjʊə/ ● **n.** a Central and South American parakeet, typically green with patches of other colours. [*Aratinga*, *Pyrrhura*, and other genera.]

– ORIGIN C19: from mod. L. *conurus* (former genus name), from Gk *kōnos* 'cone' + *oura* 'tail'.

**conus** /ˈkəʊnəs/ ● **n.** (pl. **coni** /-nʌɪ/) Anatomy **1** (also **conus arteriosus** /ɑːˌtɪərɪˈəʊsəs/) the upper front part of the right ventricle of the heart. **2** (also **conus medullaris** /ˌmɛdəˈlɑːrɪs/) the conical lower extremity of the spinal cord.

– ORIGIN C19: from L., lit. 'cone'.

**convalesce** /ˌkɒnvəˈlɛs/ ● **v.** gradually recover one's health after an illness or medical treatment.

– ORIGIN C15: from L. *convalescere*, from *con-* 'altogether' + *valescere* 'grow strong'.

**convalescent** ● **adj.** recovering from an illness or medical treatment. ● **n.** a convalescent person.

– DERIVATIVES **convalescence** n.

**convection** ● **n.** transference of mass or heat within a fluid caused by the tendency of warmer and less dense material to rise.

– DERIVATIVES **convect** v. **convectional** adj. **convective** adj.

– ORIGIN C19: from late L. *convectio(n-)*, from L. *convehere*, from *con-* 'together' + *vehere* 'carry'.

**convector** ● **n.** a heating appliance that circulates warm air by convection.

**convenance** /ˈkɒnvəˌnɑːns/ (also **convenances**) ● **n.** archaic conventional propriety.

– ORIGIN Fr., from *convenir* 'be fitting', from L. *convenire* (see **CONVENE**).

**convene** /kən'vi:n/ ● **v.** call people together for (a meeting). ➤ assemble for a common purpose.
– DERIVATIVES **convenable** adj.
– ORIGIN ME: from L. *convenire* 'assemble, agree, fit', from *con-* 'together' + *venire* 'come'.

**convener** (also **convenor**) ● **n. 1** a person who convenes meetings of a committee. **2** Brit. a senior trade union official at a workplace.

**convenience** ● **n. 1** freedom from effort or difficulty. ➤ a useful or helpful device or situation. **2** Brit. a public toilet.
– PHRASES **at one's convenience** when or where it suits one. **at one's earliest convenience** as soon as one can without difficulty.
– DERIVATIVES **conveniency** n. (rare).
– ORIGIN ME: from L. *convenientia*, from *convenient-*, *convenire* (see **CONVENE**).

**convenience food** ● **n.** a food that has been pre-prepared commercially and so requires little preparation by the consumer.

**convenience store** ● **n.** chiefly N. Amer. a small local shop with extended opening hours.

**convenient** ● **adj.** fitting in well with a person's needs, activities, and plans.
– DERIVATIVES **conveniently** adv.
– ORIGIN ME: from L. *convenient-*, *convenire* (see **CONVENE**).

**convenor** ● **n.** variant spelling of **CONVENER**.

**convent** ● **n.** a Christian community under monastic vows, especially one of nuns. ➤ (also **convent school**) a school attached to and run by a convent.
– ORIGIN ME: from OFr., from L. *conventus* 'assembly, company', from *convenire* (see **CONVENE**).

**conventicle** /kən'vɛntɪk(ə)l/ ● **n.** historical a secret or unlawful religious meeting, typically of nonconformists.
– ORIGIN ME: from L. *conventiculum* '(place of) assembly', dimin. of *conventus* 'assembly, company', from *convenire* (see **CONVENE**).

**convention** ● **n. 1** a way in which something is usually done. ➤ socially acceptable behaviour. **2** an agreement between states, especially one less formal than a treaty. **3** a large meeting, especially of members of a political party or a particular profession. ➤ N. Amer. an assembly of the delegates of a political party to select candidates for office. ➤ a body set up by agreement to deal with a particular issue. ➤ historical a meeting of Parliament without a summons from the sovereign. **4** Bridge a bid or system of bidding by which the bidder tries to convey specific information about the hand to their partner.
– ORIGIN ME: via OFr. from L. *conventio(n-)* 'meeting, covenant', from *convenire* (see **CONVENE**).

**conventional** ● **adj. 1** based on or in accordance with convention. ➤ overly concerned with convention. **2** (of weapons or power) non-nuclear. **3** Bridge (of a bid) intended to convey a particular meaning according to an agreed convention. Often contrasted with **NATURAL**.
– DERIVATIVES **conventionalism** n. **conventionalist** n. **conventionality** n. **conventionalize** (also **-ise**) v. **conventionally** adv.

**conventioneer** ● **n.** N. Amer. a person attending a convention.

**conventual** /kən'vɛntʃʊəl/ ● **adj.** relating or belonging to a convent. ➤ relating to the less strict order of the Franciscans, living in large convents. ● **n.** a person who lives in or is a member of a convent.
– ORIGIN ME: from med. L. *conventualis*, from L. *conventus* (see **CONVENT**).

**converge** /kən'və:dʒ/ ● **v. 1** come together from different directions so as eventually to meet. ➤ (**converge on/upon**) come from different directions and meet at. **2** Mathematics (of a series) approximate in the sum of its terms towards a definite limit.
– ORIGIN C17: from late L. *convergere*, from *con-* 'together' + L. *vergere* 'incline'.

**convergent** ● **adj. 1** converging. **2** Biology (of unrelated animals and plants) showing a tendency to evolve superficially similar characteristics under similar environmental conditions. **3** (of thought) tending to follow well-established patterns.
– DERIVATIVES **convergence** n. **convergency** n.

**conversant** ● **adj.** familiar with or knowledgeable about something.
– DERIVATIVES **conversance** n. **conversancy** n.
– ORIGIN ME: from OFr., pres. part. of *converser* (see **CONVERSE[1]**).

**conversation** ● **n.** an informal spoken exchange of news and ideas between two or more people.
– DERIVATIVES **conversational** adj. **conversationally** adv.

**conversationalist** ● **n.** a person who is good at or fond of engaging in conversation.

**conversation piece** ● **n. 1** a type of genre painting in which a group of figures are posed in a landscape or domestic setting. **2** an object whose unusual quality makes it a topic of conversation.

**conversazione** /ˌkɒnvəsatsɪ'əʊneɪ/ ● **n.** (pl. **conversaziones** or **conversazioni** pronunc. same) a scholarly social gathering held for discussion of literature and the arts.
– ORIGIN Ital., from L. *conversatio*, from *conversari* (see **CONVERSE[1]**).

**converse[1]** ● **v.** /kən'və:s/ engage in conversation. ● **n.** /'kɒnvə:s/ archaic conversation.
– DERIVATIVES **converser** n.
– ORIGIN ME (in the sense 'live among, be familiar with'): from OFr. *converser*, from L. *conversari* 'keep company (with)', from *con-* 'with' + *versare*, frequentative of *vertere* 'to turn'.

**converse[2]** /'kɒnvə:s/ ● **n.** a situation, object, or statement that is the opposite of another. ➤ Mathematics a theorem whose hypothesis and conclusion are the conclusion and hypothesis of another. ● **adj.** opposite.
– DERIVATIVES **conversely** adv.
– ORIGIN ME: from L. *conversus* 'turned about', past part. of *convertere* (see **CONVERT**).

**conversion** ● **n. 1** the process or action of converting or of being converted. **2** Brit. a building that has been converted to a new purpose. **3** Law the changing of real property into personalty, or of joint into separate property, or vice versa. **4** Psychiatry the manifestation of a mental disturbance as a physical disorder or disease. **5** Rugby & American Football the action of converting a try, touchdown, or down. **6** Law the action of wrongfully dealing with goods in a manner inconsistent with the owner's rights.
– ORIGIN ME: via OFr. from L. *conversio(n-)*, from *convers-*, *convertere* (see **CONVERT**).

**conversion factor** ● **n. 1** an arithmetical multiplier for converting a quantity expressed in one set of units into an equivalent expressed in another. **2** Economics the manufacturing cost of a product relative to the cost of raw materials.

**convert** ● **v.** /kən'və:t/ **1** change or cause to change in form, character, or function. ➤ change (money, stocks, or units in which a quantity is expressed) into others of a different kind. ➤ adapt (a building) to make it suitable for a new purpose. **2** change one's religious faith or other beliefs. **3** Logic transpose the subject and predicate of (a proposition) according to certain rules to form a new proposition by inference. **4** Rugby score extra points after (a try) by a successful kick at goal. ➤ American Football make an extra score after (a touchdown) by kicking a goal or running another play into the end zone. ➤ American Football advance the ball far enough after (a down) to get another try for a first down. ● **n.** /'kɒnvə:t/ a person who has changed their religious faith or other beliefs.
– PHRASES **convert something to one's own use** Law wrongfully make use of another's property.
– ORIGIN ME: from OFr. *convertir*, based on L. *convertere* 'turn about'.

**converter** (also **convertor**) ● **n. 1** a person or thing that converts something. **2** a retort used in steel-making.

**converter reactor** ● **n.** a nuclear reactor that converts fertile material into fissile material.

**convertible** ● **adj. 1** able to be converted. ➤ (of currency) able to be converted into other forms, especially into gold or US dollars. ➤ (of a bond or stock) able to be converted

into ordinary or preference shares. **2** (of a car) having a folding or detachable roof. **3** Logic (of terms) synonymous. ● **n. 1** a convertible car. **2** a convertible bond or stock.
– DERIVATIVES **convertibility** n.

**convex** /ˈkɒnvɛks/ ● **adj.** having an outline or surface curved like the exterior of a circle or sphere. Compare with **CONCAVE**.
– DERIVATIVES **convexity** n. **convexly** adv.
– ORIGIN C16: from L. *convexus* 'vaulted, arched'.

**convey** /kənˈveɪ/ ● **v. 1** transport or carry to a place. **2** communicate (an idea, impression, or feeling). **3** Law transfer the title to (property).
– DERIVATIVES **conveyable** adj. **conveyor** (also **conveyer**) n.
– ORIGIN ME (in the sense 'escort'; cf. **CONVOY**): from OFr. *conveier*, from med. L. *conviare*, from *con-* 'together' + L. *via* 'way'.

**conveyance** ● **n. 1** the action or process of conveying. **2** formal or humorous a vehicle. **3** the legal process of transferring property from one owner to another.
– DERIVATIVES **conveyancer** n. **conveyancing** n.

**conveyor belt** ● **n.** a continuous moving band of fabric, rubber, or metal used for transporting objects from one place to another.

**convict** ● **v.** /kənˈvɪkt/ declare to be guilty of a criminal offence by the verdict of a jury or the decision of a judge in a court of law. ● **n.** /ˈkɒnvɪkt/ a person convicted of a criminal offence and serving a sentence of imprisonment.
– ORIGIN ME: from L. *convict-*, *convincere* (see **CONVINCE**).

**conviction** ● **n. 1** an instance of being convicted. ➤the action or process of convicting someone. **2** a firmly held belief or opinion. ➤the quality of showing that one is firmly convinced of something.

**convince** ● **v.** cause to believe firmly in the truth of something. ➤persuade to do something. ➤[as adj. **convinced**] firm in one's belief with regard to a particular cause: *a convinced pacifist.*
– DERIVATIVES **convincer** n. **convincible** adj.
– ORIGIN C16: from L. *convincere*, from *con-* 'with' + *vincere* 'conquer'; cf. **CONVICT**.

**convincing** ● **adj. 1** able to convince. **2** (of a victory or a winner) leaving no margin of doubt.
– DERIVATIVES **convincingly** adv.

**convivial** /kənˈvɪvɪəl/ ● **adj.** (of an atmosphere or event) friendly, lively, and enjoyable. ➤cheerful and sociable.
– DERIVATIVES **conviviality** n. **convivially** adv.
– ORIGIN C17 (in the sense 'fit for a feast'): from L. *convivialis*, from *convivium* 'a feast'.

**convocation** /ˌkɒnvəˈkeɪʃ(ə)n/ ● **n. 1** (in the Church of England) a representative assembly of clergy of the province of Canterbury or York. ➤Brit. a legislative or deliberative assembly of a university. ➤N. Amer. a formal ceremony for the conferment of university awards. **2** the action of convoking a large formal assembly.
– DERIVATIVES **convocational** adj.
– ORIGIN ME: from L. *convocatio(n-)*, from *convocare* (see **CONVOKE**).

**convoke** /kənˈvəʊk/ ● **v.** formal call together (an assembly or meeting).
– ORIGIN C16: from L. *convocare.*

**convoluted** /ˌkɒnvəˈl(j)uːtɪd/ ● **adj. 1** (especially of an argument, story, or sentence) extremely complex. **2** chiefly technical intricately folded, twisted, or coiled.
– DERIVATIVES **convolutedly** adv.

**convolution** ● **n. 1** a coil or twist. ➤a sinuous fold in the surface of the brain. ➤the state of being or process of becoming coiled or twisted. **2** a thing that is complicated and hard to follow.
– DERIVATIVES **convolutional** adj.
– ORIGIN C16: from med. L. *convolutio(n-)*, from *convolvere* (see **CONVOLVE**).

**convolve** /kənˈvɒlv/ ● **v.** rare roll or coil together.
– ORIGIN C16 (in the sense 'enclose in folds'): from L. *convolvere* 'roll together'.

**convolvulus** /kənˈvɒlvjʊləs/ ● **n.** (pl. **convolvuluses**) a twining plant with trumpet-shaped flowers, some kinds of which are invasive weeds; bindweed. [Genus *Convolvulus.*]
– ORIGIN L., 'bindweed', from *convolvere* (see **CONVOLVE**).

**convoy** /ˈkɒnvɔɪ/ ● **n.** a group of ships or vehicles travelling together and accompanied by armed troops or warships for protection. ● **v.** (of a warship or armed troops) accompany (a group of ships or vehicles) for protection.
– PHRASES **in convoy** (of travelling vehicles) as a group.
– ORIGIN ME (orig. Scots, in the senses 'convey', 'conduct', and 'act as escort'): from Fr. *convoyer*, from med. L. *conviare* (see **CONVEY**).

**convulsant** ● **adj.** (chiefly of drugs) producing convulsions. ● **n.** a convulsant drug.
– ORIGIN C19: from Fr., from *convulser*, from L. *convuls-*, *convellere* (see **CONVULSE**).

**convulse** /kənˈvʌls/ ● **v.** suffer convulsions. ➤(usu. **be convulsed**) (of an emotion, laughter, or physical stimulus) cause to make sudden, violent, uncontrollable movements.
– DERIVATIVES **convulsive** adj. **convulsively** adv.
– ORIGIN C17: from L. *convuls-*, *convellere* 'pull violently, wrench'.

**convulsion** ● **n. 1** a sudden, violent, irregular movement of the body caused by involuntary contraction of muscles. **2** (**convulsions**) uncontrollable laughter. **3** a violent social or natural upheaval.

**cony** ● **n.** (pl. **-ies**) variant spelling of **CONEY**.

**coo**[1] ● **v.** (**coos**, **cooed**) **1** (of a pigeon or dove) make a soft murmuring sound. **2** (of a person) speak in a soft gentle voice. ● **n.** a cooing sound.
– ORIGIN C17: imitative.

**coo**[2] ● **exclam.** Brit. informal used to express surprise.
– ORIGIN C20: imitative.

**cooee** informal ● **exclam.** used to attract attention. ● **v.** (**cooees**, **cooeed**, **cooeeing**) make such a call.
– PHRASES **within cooee** Austral./NZ within reach.
– ORIGIN C18: imitative of a signal used by Austral. Aboriginals and copied by settlers.

**cook** ● **v. 1** prepare (food) by mixing, combining, and heating the ingredients. ➤(of food) be heated so as to reach an edible state. **2** informal alter dishonestly. ➤(**cook something up**) concoct a story, excuse, or plan, especially an ingenious or devious one. **3** (**be cooking**) informal be happening or planned. **4** N. Amer. informal perform or proceed vigorously or very well. ● **n.** a person who cooks, especially as a job.
– PHRASES **cook someone's goose** informal spoil someone's plans.
– DERIVATIVES **cookable** adj. **cooking** n.
– ORIGIN OE *cōc* (n.), from pop. L. *cocus*, from L. *coquus.*

**cookbook** ● **n.** a cookery book.

**cook-chill** ● **adj.** Brit. relating to or denoting a procedure whereby food is cooked and refrigerated by the manufacturer ready for reheating by the consumer.

**cooker** ● **n.** Brit. **1** an appliance for cooking food, typically consisting of an oven, hob, and grill. **2** informal an apple or other fruit more suitable for cooking than for eating raw.

**cookery** ● **n.** (pl. **-ies**) **1** the practice or skill of preparing and cooking food. **2** N. Amer. a kitchen.

**cookhouse** ● **n.** a building used for cooking, especially on a ranch, military camp, etc.

**cookie** ● **n.** (pl. **-ies**) **1** N. Amer. a sweet biscuit. **2** informal a person of a specified kind: *she's a tough cookie.* **3** Scottish a plain bun. **4** Computing a packet of data sent by an Internet server to a browser and used to identify the user or track their access to the server.
– PHRASES **the way the cookie crumbles** informal, chiefly N. Amer. the way things turn out, especially when undesirable.
– ORIGIN C18: from Du. *koekje* 'little cake', dimin. of *koek.*

**cookie cutter** ● **n.** N. Amer. **1** a device with sharp edges for cutting biscuit dough into a particular shape. **2** [as modifier] denoting something mass-produced or lacking any distinguishing characteristics.

**cookout** ● **n.** N. Amer. a party or gathering where a meal is cooked and eaten outdoors.

**Cook's tour** ● **n.** informal a rapid tour of many places.
– ORIGIN C20: from the name of the Engl. travel agent

Thomas *Cook*.

**cooktop** • **n.** N. Amer. a cooking unit with hot plates or burners, built into or fixed on the top of a cabinet or other surface.

**cookware** • **n.** pots, pans, or dishes in which food can be cooked.

**cool** • **adj. 1** of or at a fairly low temperature. ➤(especially of clothing) keeping one from becoming too hot. **2** unfriendly or unenthusiastic. ➤free from anxiety or excitement. **3** (of jazz, especially modern jazz) restrained and relaxed. **4** informal fashionably attractive or impressive. ➤excellent. **5** (**a cool ——**) informal used to emphasize a specified large amount of money. • **n.** (**the cool**) a fairly low temperature, or a place or time characterized by this. • **v.** become or cause to become cool.
– PHRASES **keep** (or **lose**) **one's cool** informal maintain (or fail to maintain) a calm and controlled attitude.
– DERIVATIVES **-cooled** adj. **coolish** adj. **coolly** adv. **coolness** n.
– ORIGIN OE *cōl* (n.), *cōlian* (v.), of Gmc origin; rel. to **COLD**.

**coolant** • **n.** a fluid used to cool an engine, nuclear reactor, or other device.
– ORIGIN 1930s: from **COOL**, on the pattern of *lubricant*.

**cooler** • **n. 1** a device or container for keeping things cool. ➤N. Amer. a refrigerator. **2** a long drink, especially a mixture of wine, fruit juice, and soda water. **3** (**the cooler**) informal prison or a prison cell.

**Cooley's anaemia** /ˈkuːlɪz/ • **n.** another term for **THALASSAEMIA**.
– ORIGIN 1930s: named after the Amer. paediatrician Thomas B. *Cooley*.

**coolibah** /ˈkuːlɪbɑː/ • **n.** a North Australian gum tree which typically grows near watercourses and yields very strong, hard wood. [*Eucalyptus microtheca*.]
– ORIGIN C19: from Kamilaroi (and related langs) *gulubaa*.

**coolie** /ˈkuːli/ • **n.** (pl. **-ies**) **1** dated an unskilled native labourer in India, China, and some other Asian countries. **2** offensive a person from the Indian subcontinent or of Indian descent.
– ORIGIN C17: from Hindi and Telugu *kūlī* 'day-labourer', prob. assoc. with Urdu *ḳulī* 'slave'.

**coolie hat** • **n.** a broad conical hat as worn by labourers in some Asian countries.

**cooling-off period** • **n. 1** an interval during which the parties in a dispute can try to settle their differences before taking further action. **2** an interval after a sale contract is agreed during which the purchaser can decide to cancel without loss.

**cooling tower** • **n.** a tall, open-topped, cylindrical concrete tower, used for cooling water or condensing steam from an industrial process.

**coolth** /kuːlθ/ • **n. 1** pleasantly low temperature. **2** informal articles, activities, or people perceived as fashionable.

**coombe** (also **coomb**) • **n.** variant spelling of **COMBE**.

**coon** • **n. 1** N. Amer. short for **RACCOON**. **2** informal, offensive a black person. [sl. use of sense 1, from an earlier sense '(sly) fellow'.]

**cooncan** /ˈkuːnkan/ • **n.** a card game for two players, originally from Mexico, similar to rummy.
– ORIGIN C19: prob. from Sp. *con quién* 'with whom?'

**coonhound** • **n.** a dog of a black-and-tan American breed, used to hunt raccoons.

**coop** • **n. 1** a cage or pen for confining poultry. **2** Brit. a basket used in catching fish. • **v.** (usu. **be cooped up**) confine in a small space.
– ORIGIN ME *cowpe*, based on L. *cupa*; cf. **COOPER**.

**co-op** /ˈkəʊɒp/ • **n.** informal a cooperative organization.

**cooper** • **n.** a maker or repairer of casks and barrels. • **v.** make or repair (a cask or barrel).
– DERIVATIVES **cooperage** n. **coopery** n.
– ORIGIN ME *cowper*, from MDu., Mid. Low Ger. *kūper*, from *kūpe* 'tub, vat', based on L. *cupa*.

**cooperate** /kəʊˈɒpəreɪt/ (also **co-operate**) • **v.** work jointly towards the same end. ➤assist someone or comply with their requests.
– DERIVATIVES **cooperant** n. **cooperator** n.
– ORIGIN C16: from eccles. L. *cooperat-*, *cooperari* 'work together'.

**cooperation** (also **co-operation**) • **n. 1** the action or process of cooperating. **2** Economics the formation and operation of cooperatives.

**cooperative** (also **co-operative**) • **adj. 1** involving cooperation. **2** willing to be of assistance. **3** (of a farm, business, etc.) owned and run jointly by its members, with profits or benefits shared among them. • **n.** a cooperative organization.
– DERIVATIVES **cooperatively** adv. **cooperativeness** n.

**Cooper pair** • **n.** Physics a loosely bound pair of electrons with opposite spins, held to be responsible for superconductivity.
– ORIGIN 1960s: named after the Amer. physicist Leon N. *Cooper*.

**co-opt** • **v. 1** appoint to membership of a committee or other body by invitation of the existing members. **2** divert to a role different from the usual or original one. **3** adopt (an idea or policy) for one's own use.
– DERIVATIVES **co-optation** n. **co-option** n. **co-optive** adj.
– ORIGIN C17: from L. *cooptare*, from *co-* 'together' + *optare* 'choose'.

**coordinate** (also **co-ordinate**) • **v.** /kəʊˈɔːdɪneɪt/ **1** bring the different elements of (a complex activity or organization) into a harmonious or efficient relationship. **2** negotiate with others in order to work together effectively. **3** match or harmonize attractively. **4** Chemistry form a coordinate bond to. • **adj.** /kəʊˈɔːdɪnət/ **1** equal in rank or importance. ➤Grammar (of parts of a compound sentence) equal in rank and fulfilling identical functions. **2** Chemistry denoting a covalent bond in which one atom provides both the shared electrons. • **n.** /kəʊˈɔːdɪnət/ **1** Mathematics each of a group of numbers used to indicate the position of a point, line, or plane. **2** (**coordinates**) matching items of clothing.
– DERIVATIVES **coordinative** adj. **coordinator** n.
– ORIGIN C17: from **co-** + L. *ordinare* (from *ordo* 'order').

**coordinating conjunction** • **n.** a conjunction placed between words, phrases, clauses, or sentences of equal rank, e.g. *and*, *but*, *or*. Contrasted with **SUBORDINATING CONJUNCTION**.

**coordination** (also **co-ordination**) • **n. 1** the action or process of coordinating. ➤the ability to move different parts of the body smoothly and at the same time. **2** Chemistry the linking of atoms by coordinate bonds.

**coot** • **n. 1** (pl. same) an aquatic bird of the rail family with black plumage and a white bill that extends back on to the forehead as a horny shield. [*Fulica atra* and related species.] **2** (usu. **old coot**) informal a stupid or eccentric person, typically an old man.
– ORIGIN ME: prob. of Du. or Low Ger. origin.

**cooter** • **n.** a North American river turtle with yellow stripes on the head. [*Pseudemys concinna* and related species.]
– ORIGIN C19: of unknown origin.

**cootie** /ˈkuːti/ • **n.** N. Amer. informal a body louse.
– ORIGIN First World War: perh. from Malay *kutu*, denoting a parasitic biting insect.

**co-own** • **v.** own jointly.
– DERIVATIVES **co-owner** n. **co-ownership** n.

**cop**[1] informal • **n.** a police officer. • **v.** (**copped**, **copping**) **1** catch or arrest (an offender). **2** incur (something unwelcome). **3** US obtain (an illegal drug). **4** N. Amer. strike (an attitude or pose). **5** (**cop off**) have a sexual encounter. **6** (**cop out**) avoid doing something that one ought to do. **7** (**cop to**) US accept or admit to.
– PHRASES **cop hold of** Brit. take hold of. **cop it** Brit. **1** get into trouble. **2** be killed. **cop a plea** N. Amer. engage in plea bargaining. **not much cop** Brit. not very good.
– ORIGIN C18 (as v.): perh. from obs. *cap* 'arrest', from OFr. *caper* 'seize', from L. *capere*.

**cop**[2] • **n.** a conical mass of thread wound on to a spindle.
– ORIGIN C18: possibly from OE *cop* 'summit, top'.

**copacetic** /ˌkəʊpəˈsɛtɪk, -ˈsiːt-/ • **adj.** N. Amer. informal in excellent order.

– ORIGIN C20: of unknown origin.

**copal** /ˈkəʊp(ə)l/ ● **n.** resin from any of a number of tropical trees, used to make varnish.
– ORIGIN C16: via Sp. from Nahuatl *copalli* 'incense'.

**coparcener** /kəʊˈpɑːs(ə)nə/ ● **n.** English Law a person who shares equally with others in the inheritance of an undivided estate or in the rights to it (in the UK now as equitable interests).
– DERIVATIVES **coparcenary** n.
– ORIGIN ME: from **co-** + *parcener*, legal term for **PARTNER**).

**co-partner** ● **n.** a partner or associate, especially an equal partner in a business.
– DERIVATIVES **co-partnership** n.

**COPD** ● **abbrev.** Medicine chronic obstructive pulmonary disease, involving constriction of the airways and difficulty or discomfort in breathing.

**cope**[1] ● **v.** deal effectively with something difficult.
– DERIVATIVES **coper** n.
– ORIGIN ME (in the sense 'meet in battle, come to blows'): from OFr. *coper, colper*, from *cop, colp* 'a blow', via L. from Gk *kolaphos* 'a blow with the fist'.

**cope**[2] ● **n.** a long, loose cloak worn by a priest or bishop on ceremonial occasions. ● **v.** [usu. as adj. **coped**] (in building) cover (a joint or structure) with a coping.
– ORIGIN ME: from med. L. *capa*, var. of late L. *cappa* (see **CAP** and **CAPE**[1]).

**copeck** ● **n.** variant spelling of **KOPEK**.

**Copepoda** /ˌkəʊpɪˈpəʊdə/ ● **pl. n.** Zoology a large class of small aquatic crustaceans, many of which occur in plankton.
– DERIVATIVES **copepod** /ˈkəʊpɪpɒd/ n.
– ORIGIN mod. L., from Gk *kōpē* 'handle, oar' + *pous, pod-* 'foot' (because of their paddle-like feet).

**Copernican** /kəˈpəːnɪk(ə)n/ ● **adj.** of or relating to the Polish astronomer Nicolaus Copernicus (1473–1543) or to the Copernican system.

**Copernican system** /kəˈpəːnɪk(ə)n/ (also **Copernican theory**) ● **n.** Astronomy the theory proposed by Nicolaus Copernicus that the sun is the centre of the solar system, with the planets (including the earth) orbiting round it. Compare with **PTOLEMAIC SYSTEM**.

**copiable** ● **adj.** able to be copied, especially legitimately.

**copier** ● **n.** a machine that makes exact copies of something.

**co-pilot** ● **n.** a second pilot in an aircraft.

**coping** ● **n.** the top, typically sloping, course of a brick or stone wall.
– ORIGIN C16: from **COPE**[2], orig. meaning 'dress in a cope', hence 'to cover'.

**coping saw** ● **n.** a saw with a very narrow blade stretched across a D-shaped frame, used for cutting curves in wood.
– ORIGIN 1920s: *coping* from **COPE**[2], used to describe likeness to a vault, arch, canopy, etc.

**coping stone** ● **n.** a flat stone forming part of a coping.

**copious** ● **adj.** abundant; plentiful.
– DERIVATIVES **copiously** adv. **copiousness** n.
– ORIGIN ME: from OFr. *copieux* or L. *copiosus*, from *copia* 'plenty'.

**copita** /kəˈpiːtə/ ● **n.** a slim stemmed glass that narrows slightly towards the top, used for sherry.
– ORIGIN C19: from Sp., dimin. of *copa* 'cup', from pop. L. *cuppa* (see **CUP**).

**coplanar** /kəʊˈpleɪnə/ ● **adj.** Geometry in the same plane.
– DERIVATIVES **coplanarity** n.

**copolymer** /kəʊˈpɒlɪmə/ ● **n.** Chemistry a polymer made by reaction of two different monomers, with units of more than one kind.
– DERIVATIVES **copolymerization** (also **-isation**) n. **copolymerize** (also **-ise**) v.

**cop-out** ● **n.** informal an instance of avoiding a commitment or responsibility.

**copper**[1] ● **n. 1** a red-brown metal, the chemical element of atomic number 29, which is a good conductor of electricity and heat and is used for electrical wiring and as a component of brass and bronze. (Symbol: **Cu**) **2** (**coppers**) Brit. coins of low value made of copper or bronze. **3** Brit. dated a large copper or iron container for boiling laundry. **4** a reddish-brown colour. **5** a small butterfly with bright reddish-brown wings. [*Lycaena phlaeas* (**small copper**) and related species.] ● **v.** cover or coat with copper.
– DERIVATIVES **coppery** adj.
– ORIGIN OE *copor, coper*, based on late L. *cuprum*, from L. *cyprium aes* 'Cyprus metal' (so named because Cyprus was the chief source).

**copper**[2] ● **n.** Brit. informal a police officer.
– ORIGIN C19: from **COP**[1] + **-ER**[1].

**copperas** /ˈkɒp(ə)rəs/ ● **n.** green crystals of hydrated ferrous sulphate, especially as an industrial product.
– ORIGIN ME *coperose*, from OFr. *couperose*, from med. L. *cuperosa*, lit. 'flower of copper', from late L. *cuprum* (see **COPPER**[1]) + *rosa* 'rose', translating Gk *khalkanthon*.

**copper beech** ● **n.** a beech tree of a variety with purplish-brown leaves.

**copper-bottomed** ● **adj.** Brit. thoroughly reliable.
– ORIGIN from earlier usage referring to the copper sheathing of the bottom of a ship.

**copperhead** ● **n.** a venomous snake with reddish-brown coloration. [*Agkistrodon contortrix* (N. America) and *Austrelaps superbus* (Australia).]

**copperplate** ● **n. 1** a polished copper plate with a design engraved or etched into it. **2** a style of neat, round handwriting, usually slanted and looped. [the copybooks for this were orig. printed from copperplates.] ● **adj.** of or in copperplate writing.

**copper pyrites** ● **n.** another term for **CHALCOPYRITE**.

**coppersmith** ● **n. 1** a person who makes things out of copper. **2** (also **coppersmith barbet**) the crimson-breasted barbet of SE Asia, which has a red breast band, a streaked belly, and a repetitive metallic call. [*Megalaima hemacephala*.]

**copper sulphate** ● **n.** a blue crystalline solid used in electroplating and as a fungicide.

**coppice** ● **n.** an area of woodland in which the trees or shrubs are periodically cut back to ground level to stimulate growth and provide wood. ● **v.** cut back (a tree or shrub) in this way.
– ORIGIN ME: from OFr. *copeiz*, based on med. L. *colpus* (see **COPE**[1]); cf. **COPSE**.

**copra** /ˈkɒprə/ ● **n.** dried coconut kernels, from which oil is obtained.
– ORIGIN C16: via Port. and Sp. from Malayalam *koppara* 'coconut'.

**co-precipitation** ● **n.** Chemistry the simultaneous precipitation of more than one compound from a solution.
– DERIVATIVES **co-precipitate** v.

**copro-** ● **comb. form** of or relating to dung or faeces: *coprophagous*.
– ORIGIN from Gk *kopros* 'dung'.

**coprocessor** ● **n.** Computing a microprocessor designed to supplement the capabilities of the primary processor.

**co-produce** ● **v.** produce (a theatrical work or a radio or television programme) jointly.
– DERIVATIVES **co-producer** n. **co-production** n.

**coprolalia** /ˌkɒprə(ʊ)ˈleɪlɪə/ ● **n.** Psychiatry the involuntary and repetitive use of obscene language, as a symptom of mental illness or organic brain disease.
– ORIGIN C19: from Gk *kopros* 'dung' + *lalia* 'speech, chatter'.

**coprolite** /ˈkɒprə(ʊ)lʌɪt/ ● **n.** Palaeontology a piece of fossilized dung.

**coprophagy** /kɒˈprɒfədʒi/ (also **coprophagia** /ˌkɒprə(ʊ)ˈfeɪdʒɪə/) ● **n.** Zoology the eating of faeces.
– DERIVATIVES **coprophagic** adj. **coprophagous** adj.

**coprophilia** /ˌkɒprə(ʊ)ˈfɪlɪə/ ● **n.** abnormal interest and pleasure in faeces and defecation.

**copse** ● **n.** a small group of trees.
– ORIGIN C16: shortened form of **COPPICE**.

**cop shop** ● **n.** informal a police station.

**Copt** /kɒpt/ ● **n. 1** a native Egyptian in the Hellenistic and Roman periods. **2** a member of the Coptic Church,

the native Christian Church in Egypt.
– ORIGIN from Fr. *Copte* or mod. L. *Coptus*, from Arab. *al-ḳibṭ, al-ḳubṭ* 'Copts', from Coptic *Gyptios*, from Gk *Aiguptios* 'Egyptian'.

**Coptic** • n. the language of the Copts, which survives only in the Coptic Church. • adj. of or relating to the Copts or their language.

**copula** /ˈkɒpjʊlə/ • n. Logic & Grammar a connecting word, in particular a form of the verb *be* connecting a subject and complement.
– DERIVATIVES **copular** adj.
– ORIGIN C17: from L., 'connection, linking of words', from *co-* 'together' + *apere* 'fasten'.

**copulate** /ˈkɒpjʊleɪt/ • v. have sexual intercourse.
– DERIVATIVES **copulation** n. **copulatory** adj.
– ORIGIN ME: from L. *copulat-*, *copulare* 'fasten together', from *copula* (see COPULA).

**copulative** • adj. 1 Grammar (of a word) connecting words or clauses linked in sense. ➤connecting a subject and predicate. 2 of or relating to sexual intercourse.
– DERIVATIVES **copulatively** adv.

**copy** • n. (pl. **-ies**) 1 a thing made to be similar or identical to another. 2 a single specimen of a particular book, record, etc. 3 matter to be printed. ➤material for a newspaper or magazine article. • v. (**-ies**, **-ied**) make a copy of. ➤imitate the behaviour or style of.
– ORIGIN ME: from OFr. *copie* (n.), *copier* (v.), from L. *copia* 'abundance' (in med. L. 'transcript', from such phrs as *copiam describendi facere* 'give permission to transcribe').

**copybook** • n. a book containing models of handwriting for learners to imitate. • adj. exactly in accordance with established standards.

**copycat** • n. informal 1 a person who copies another, especially slavishly. 2 [as modifier] denoting an action, typically a crime, carried out in imitation of another.

**copy-edit** • v. edit (text) by checking its consistency and accuracy.
– DERIVATIVES **copy editor** n.

**copyhold** • n. Brit. historical tenure of land based on manorial records.

**copyholder** • n. 1 Brit. historical a person who held land in copyhold. 2 a clasp or stand for holding sheets of text while it is keyed or typed.

**copyist** • n. 1 a person who makes copies. 2 a person who imitates the styles of others, especially in art.

**copyleft** • n. Computing an agreement allowing software to be used, modified, and distributed freely on condition that a notice to this effect is included with it.
– DERIVATIVES **copylefted** adj.
– ORIGIN 1980s: after COPYRIGHT.

**copyread** • v. read and edit (text) for a newspaper, magazine, or book.
– DERIVATIVES **copyreader** n.

**copyright** • n. the exclusive legal right, given to the originator or their assignee for a fixed number of years, to publish, perform, film, or record literary, artistic, or musical material, and to authorize others to do the same. • v. secure copyright for (such material).

**copyright library** • n. a library entitled to a free copy of each book published in the UK.

**copy typist** • n. a person whose job is to type transcripts of written drafts.

**copywriter** • n. a person who writes the text of advertisements or publicity material.
– DERIVATIVES **copywriting** n.

**coq au vin** /ˌkɒk əʊ ˈvã/ • n. a casserole of chicken pieces cooked in red wine.
– ORIGIN Fr., lit. 'cock in wine'.

**coquette** /kɒˈkɛt/ • n. 1 a woman who flirts. 2 a crested Central and South American hummingbird. [*Lophornis* and other genera.]
– DERIVATIVES **coquetry** n. **coquettish** adj. **coquettishly** adv. **coquettishness** n.
– ORIGIN C17: Fr., fem. of *coquet* 'wanton', dimin. of *coq* 'cock'.

**coquina** /kɒˈkiːnə/ • n. 1 a soft limestone of broken shells, used in road-making in the Caribbean and Florida. 2 a small American bivalve mollusc with a wedge-shaped shell. [*Donax variabilis* and related species.]
– ORIGIN C19: from Sp., lit. 'cockle', based on L. *concha* (see CONCH).

**coquito** /kɒˈkiːtəʊ/ • n. (pl. **-os**) a thick-trunked Chilean palm tree which yields large amounts of sweet sap and fibre. [*Jubaea chilensis*.]
– ORIGIN C19: from Sp., dimin. of *coco* 'coconut'.

**Cor.** • abbrev. 1 US coroner. 2 Epistle to the Corinthians (in biblical references).

**cor** • exclam. Brit. informal expressing surprise, excitement, admiration, or alarm.
– ORIGIN 1930s: alt. of GOD.

**cor-** • prefix variant spelling of COM- assimilated before *r* (as in *corrode*, *corrugate*).

**Cora** /ˈkɔːrə/ • n. 1 a member of an American Indian people of western Mexico. 2 the Uto-Aztecan language of this people.

**coracle** /ˈkɒrək(ə)l/ • n. (especially in Wales and Ireland) a small, round boat made of wickerwork covered with a watertight material, propelled with a paddle.
– ORIGIN C16: from Welsh *corwgl*, *cwrwgl*, rel. to Sc. Gaelic and Ir. *curach* 'small boat'; cf. CURRACH.

**coracoid** /ˈkɒrəkɔɪd/ • n. (also **coracoid process**) Anatomy a short projection from the shoulder blade in mammals, to which part of the biceps is attached.
– ORIGIN C18: from mod. L. *coracoides*, from Gk *korakoeidēs* 'raven-like', from *korax* 'raven' (because of the resemblance to a raven's beak).

**coral** • n. 1 a hard stony substance secreted by certain colonial marine animals as an external skeleton, typically forming large reefs. ➤precious red coral, used in jewellery. 2 the pinkish-red colour of red coral. 3 an anthozoan of a large group including those that form coral reefs, secreting a calcareous, horny, or soft skeleton. [Orders Scleractinia or Madreporaria (the reef-forming **stony corals**), Alcyonacea (**soft corals**), and Gorgonacea (**horny corals**).] 3 the edible unfertilized roe of a lobster or scallop, reddening when cooked.
– DERIVATIVES **coralloid** adj. (chiefly Biology & Zoology).
– ORIGIN ME: via OFr. from L. *corallum*, from Gk *korallion*, *kouralion*.

**coralberry** • n. (pl. **-ies**) an evergreen North American shrub of the honeysuckle family, which has fragrant white flowers followed by deep red berries. [*Symphoricarpos orbiculatus*.]

**coral fungus** • n. a fungus which produces a fruiting body composed of upright branching finger-like projections which resemble coral. [Genus *Clavulina*.]

**Corallian** /kɒˈralɪən/ • adj. Geology relating to or denoting an age in the Upper Jurassic period when extensive coral-derived limestone deposits were laid down.
– ORIGIN from L. *corallium* 'coral' + -AN.

**coralline** /ˈkɒrəlʌɪn/ • adj. 1 derived or formed from coral. 2 of the pinkish-red colour of red coral. 3 resembling coral. • n. a branching reddish seaweed with a calcareous jointed stem. [*Corallina officinalis* and other species.]
– ORIGIN C16: the adjective from Fr. *corallin* or late L. *corallinus*, the noun from Ital. *corallina*, dimin. of *corallo* 'coral', both based on L. *corallum* 'coral'.

**corallita** /ˌkɒrəˈliːtə/ (also **coralita**) • n. a pink-flowered climbing vine native to Mexico and the Caribbean, grown as an ornamental. [*Antigonon leptopus*.]
– ORIGIN C19: from Amer. Sp. *coralito*, dimin. of Sp. *coral* 'coral'.

**corallite** /ˈkɒrəlʌɪt/ • n. Palaeontology the cup-like calcareous skeleton of a single coral polyp. ➤a fossil coral.

**coralroot** • n. 1 a leafless saprophytic orchid with inconspicuous flowers. [Genus *Corallorhiza*: several species.] ➤another term for COCKSCOMB (in sense 3). 2 (also **coralroot bittercress**) a woodland plant with purple flowers and bud-like swellings at the base of the stem. [*Cardamine bulbifera*.]

**coral snake** • n. a brightly banded venomous snake of the cobra family. [*Micrurus* and other genera: numerous species.]

**coral spot** • n. a common fungal disease of trees and shrubs, causing minute pink or dark red cushion-like growths.

**coral tree** • n. a tropical or subtropical thorny shrub or tree with showy red or orange flowers that are pollinated by birds. [Genus *Erythrina*.]

**cor anglais** /kɔːr ˈɑːŋgleɪ, ˈɒŋgleɪ/ • n. (pl. **cors anglais** pronunc. same) an alto woodwind instrument of the oboe family, having a bulbous bell and sounding a fifth lower than the oboe.
– ORIGIN C19: Fr., lit. 'English horn'.

**corbel** /ˈkɔːb(ə)l/ • n. a projection jutting out from a wall to support a structure above it. • v. (**corbelled, corbelling**; US **corbeled, corbeling**) [often as adj. **corbelled**] support on corbels.
– ORIGIN ME: from OFr., dimin. of *corp* 'crow', from L. *corvus* 'raven'.

**corbel table** • n. a projecting course of bricks or stones resting on corbels.

**corbicula** /kɔːˈbɪkjʊlə/ • n. (pl. **corbiculae** /-liː/) Entomology another term for **POLLEN BASKET**.
– ORIGIN C19: from late L.

**corbie** /ˈkɔːbi/ • n. (pl. **-ies**) Scottish a raven, crow, or rook.
– ORIGIN ME: from OFr. *corb*, var. of *corp* (see **CORBEL**).

**cord** • n. **1** long thin string or rope made from several twisted strands. ➤a length of such material. **2** an anatomical structure resembling a cord (e.g. the spinal cord). **3** an electric flex. **4** corduroy. ➤(**cords**) corduroy trousers. **5** a measure of cut wood (usually 128 cu. ft, 3.62 cubic metres). • v. [usu. as adj. **corded**] attach a cord to.
– DERIVATIVES **cording** n. **cord-like** adj.
– ORIGIN ME: from OFr. *corde*, from L. *chorda*, from Gk *khordē* 'gut, string of a musical instrument'.

**cordage** • n. cords or ropes, especially in a ship's rigging.

**cordate** /ˈkɔːdeɪt/ • adj. Botany & Zoology heart-shaped.
– ORIGIN C17 (in the sense 'wise'): from L. *cordatus* 'wise' (in mod. L. 'heart-shaped'), from *cor, cord-* 'heart'.

**corded** • adj. **1** (of cloth) ribbed. **2** (of a muscle) tensed and standing out. **3** equipped with a cord or flex.

**Cordelier** /ˌkɔːdəˈlɪə/ • n. a Franciscan Observant.
– ORIGIN ME: from OFr., from *cordelle* 'small rope', dimin. of *corde* (see **CORD**), from the knotted cord worn by the Cordeliers around the waist.

**cordgrass** • n. a coarse wiry coastal grass which is sometimes used to stabilize mudflats. [Genus *Spartina*.]

**cordial** • adj. **1** warm and friendly. **2** strongly felt: *cordial loathing*. • n. **1** Brit. a sweet fruit-flavoured drink, sold as a concentrate. **2** chiefly N. Amer. another term for **LIQUEUR**. **3** a pleasant-tasting medicine.
– DERIVATIVES **cordiality** n. **cordially** adv.
– ORIGIN ME: from med. L. *cordialis*, from L. *cor, cord-* 'heart'.

**cordierite** /ˈkɔːdɪərʌɪt/ • n. a dark blue mineral consisting of an aluminosilicate of magnesium and iron.
– ORIGIN C19: named after the Fr. geologist Pierre L. A. *Cordier*.

**cordillera** /ˌkɔːdɪˈljɛːrə/ • n. a system or group of parallel mountain ranges together with the intervening plateaux and other features, especially in the Andes or the Rocky Mountains.
– ORIGIN C18: from Sp., from *cordilla*, dimin. of *cuerda* 'cord', from L. *chorda* (see **CORD**).

**cordite** • n. a smokeless explosive made from nitrocellulose, nitroglycerine, and petroleum jelly.
– ORIGIN C19: from **CORD** (because of its appearance) + **-ITE**[1].

**cordless** • adj. (of an electrical appliance or telephone) working without connection to a mains supply or central unit.

**cordoba** /ˈkɔːdəbə/ • n. the basic monetary unit of Nicaragua, equal to 100 centavos.
– ORIGIN named after F. Fernández de *Córdoba*, a C16 Sp. governor of Nicaragua.

**cordon** /ˈkɔːd(ə)n/ • n. **1** a line or circle of police, soldiers, or guards preventing access to or from an area or building. **2** a fruit tree trained to grow as a single stem. **3** Architecture another term for **STRING COURSE**. • v. (**cordon something off**) prevent access to or from an area by means of a cordon.
– ORIGIN ME: from Ital. *cordone*, augmentative of *corda*, and Fr. *cordon*, dimin. of *corde*, both from L. *chorda* (see **CORD**).

**cordon bleu** /ˌkɔːdɒ̃ ˈbləː/ • adj. Cookery of the highest class. • n. **1** (pl. **cordons bleus** (pronounced same)) a cook of the highest class. **2** (**cordon-bleu**) (pl. **cordon-bleus**) an African waxbill popular as a cage bird, the male of which has a blue face, breast, and tail. [Genus *Uraeginthus*.]
– ORIGIN C18: Fr., lit. 'blue ribbon' (once signifying the highest order of chivalry in the reign of the Bourbon kings).

**cordon sanitaire** /ˌkɔːdɒ̃ sanɪˈtɛː/ • n. (pl. **cordons sanitaires** pronunc. same) **1** a guarded line preventing anyone from leaving an area infected by a disease. **2** a measure designed to prevent communication or the spread of undesirable influences.
– ORIGIN C19: Fr., lit. 'sanitary line'.

**cordovan** /ˈkɔːdəv(ə)n/ • n. a kind of soft leather made originally from goatskin and now from horsehide.
– ORIGIN C16: from Sp. *cordován*, former spelling of *cordobán* 'of Cordoba' (a city in southern Spain).

**corduroy** /ˈkɔːdərɔɪ, -djʊ-/ • n. a thick cotton fabric with velvety ribs.
– ORIGIN C18: prob. from **CORD** + *duroy*, denoting a former kind of lightweight worsted.

**corduroy road** • n. historical a road made of tree trunks laid across a swamp.

**cordwainer** /ˈkɔːdweɪnə/ • n. Brit. archaic a shoemaker (still used in the names of guilds).
– ORIGIN ME: from Anglo-Norman Fr. *cordewaner*, from OFr. *cordewan* (see **CORDOVAN**).

**cordwood** • n. wood cut into cords or uniform lengths.

**CORE** • abbrev. (in the US) Congress of Racial Equality.

**core** • n. **1** the tough central part of various fruits, containing the seeds. **2** the central or most important part. ➤the dense metallic or rocky central region of a planet. ➤the central part of a nuclear reactor, which contains the fissile material. ➤a piece of soft iron forming the centre of an electromagnet or an induction coil. **3** an internal mould filling a space to be left hollow in a casting. **4** Archaeology a piece of flint from which flakes or blades have been removed. **5** a cylindrical sample of rock, ice, or other material obtained by boring with a hollow drill. • v. remove the core from (a fruit).
– PHRASES **to the core** to the depths of one's being.
– DERIVATIVES **corer** n.
– ORIGIN ME: of unknown origin.

**core dump** • n. Computing a dump of the contents of main memory, carried out typically as an aid to debugging.

**coreferential** /ˌkəʊrɛfəˈrɛnʃ(ə)l/ • adj. Linguistics (of two elements or units) having the same reference.
– DERIVATIVES **coreference** n.

**co-religionist** (also **coreligionist**) • n. an adherent of the same religion as another person.

**corella** /kəˈrɛlə/ • n. a white Australasian cockatoo with some pink feathers on the face and bare blue skin around the eye. [*Cacatua sanguinea* (**little corella**) and other species.]
– ORIGIN C19: from Wiradhuri.

**coreopsis** /ˌkɒrɪˈɒpsɪs/ • n. a plant of the daisy family, cultivated for its rayed, typically yellow, flowers. [Genus *Coreopsis*.]
– ORIGIN mod. L., from Gk *koris* 'bug' + *opsis* 'appearance' (because of the shape of the seed).

**co-respondent** (also **corespondent**) • n. a person cited in a divorce case as having committed adultery with the respondent.

**core time** • n. Brit. the central part of the working day in a flexitime system, when an employee must be present.

**corf** /kɔːf/ • n. (pl. **corves**) Brit. a wagon or large basket, formerly used for bringing coal out of a mine.
– ORIGIN ME: from Mid. Low Ger. and MDu. *korf*, from L. *corbis* 'basket'.

**corgi** (also **Welsh corgi**) • n. (pl. **corgis**) a dog of a short-

legged breed with a foxlike head.
– ORIGIN 1920s: from Welsh, from *cor* 'dwarf' + *ci* 'dog'.

**coriaceous** /ˌkɒrɪˈeɪʃəs/ ● **adj.** technical resembling or having the texture of leather.
– ORIGIN C17: from late L. *coriaceus* (from L. *corium* 'leather') + **-OUS**.

**coriander** /ˌkɒrɪˈandə/ ● **n.** an aromatic Mediterranean plant of the parsley family, the leaves and seeds of which are used as culinary herbs. [*Coriandrum sativum*.]
– ORIGIN ME: from OFr. *coriandre*, from L. *coriandrum*, from Gk *koriannon*.

**Corinthian** /kəˈrɪnθɪən/ ● **adj. 1** belonging or relating to Corinth, a city in southern Greece and a city state in ancient Greece. **2** relating to or denoting the most ornate of the classical orders of architecture, characterized by flared capitals with rows of acanthus leaves. **3** involving the highest standards of amateur sportsmanship. ● **n. 1** a native or inhabitant of Corinth. **2** the Corinthian order of architecture. **3** historical a wealthy amateur of sport.

**Coriolis effect** /ˌkɒrɪˈəʊlɪs/ ● **n.** Physics an effect whereby a mass moving in a rotating system experiences a force perpendicular to the direction of motion and to the axis of rotation (influencing, for example, the formation of cyclonic weather systems).
– ORIGIN C20: named after the Fr. engineer Gaspard *Coriolis*.

**corium** /ˈkɔːrɪəm/ ● **n.** chiefly Zoology another term for **DERMIS**.
– ORIGIN C19: from L., 'skin'.

**cork** ● **n. 1** the buoyant, light brown substance obtained from the outer layer of the bark of the cork oak. **2** a bottle stopper made of cork. **3** a piece of cork used as a float for a fishing line or net. **4** Botany a protective layer of dead cells immediately below the bark of woody plants. ● **v.** (often **be corked**) **1** close or seal (a bottle) with a cork. ➤ [as adj. **corked**] (of wine) spoilt by tannin from the cork. **2** Baseball illicitly hollow out (a bat) and fill it with cork to make it lighter.
– DERIVATIVES **cork-like** adj.
– ORIGIN ME: from Du. and Low Ger. *kork*, from Sp. *alcorque* 'cork-soled sandal', from Arab. *al-* 'the' and (prob.) Sp. Arab. *ḳurḳ, ḳorḳ*, based on L. *quercus* 'oak, cork oak'.

**corkage** ● **n.** a charge made by a restaurant or hotel for serving wine that has been brought in by a customer.

**corker** ● **n.** informal an excellent person or thing.
– DERIVATIVES **corking** adj.

**cork oak** ● **n.** an evergreen Mediterranean oak, the outer layer of the bark of which is the source of cork. [*Quercus suber*.]

**corkscrew** ● **n.** a device for pulling corks from bottles, consisting of a spiral metal rod that is inserted into the cork, and a handle. ● **v.** move or twist in a spiral.

**corkwood** ● **n.** a small tree yielding light porous wood. [*Leitneria floridana* (America) or *Entelea arborescens* (New Zealand).]

**corky** ● **adj.** (**-ier, -iest**) **1** cork-like. **2** (of wine) corked.

**corm** ● **n.** a rounded underground storage organ present in plants such as crocuses and cyclamens, consisting of a swollen stem base covered with scale leaves.
– DERIVATIVES **cormlet** n.
– ORIGIN C19: from mod. L. *cormus*, from Gk *kormos* 'trunk stripped of its boughs'.

**cormorant** /ˈkɔːm(ə)r(ə)nt/ ● **n.** a large diving seabird with a long neck, long hooked bill, short legs, and mainly black plumage. [*Phalacrocorax carbo* and other species.]
– ORIGIN ME: from OFr. *cormaran*, from med. L. *corvus marinus* 'sea-raven'; the final *-t* is on the pattern of words such as *peasant*.

**corn**[1] ● **n. 1** chiefly Brit. the chief cereal crop of a district, especially (in England) wheat or (in Scotland) oats. ➤ informal the grain of any cereal, especially as fed to livestock. ➤ N. Amer. & Austral./NZ maize. **2** informal something banal or sentimental. ● **v.** [as adj. **corned**] preserved with salt or brine.
– ORIGIN OE, of Gmc origin.

**corn**[2] ● **n.** a small, painful area of thickened skin on the foot, especially on the toes, caused by pressure.
– ORIGIN ME: via Anglo-Norman Fr. from L. *cornu* 'horn'.

**cornball** ● **adj.** N. Amer. informal trite and sentimental.

**cornbrash** ● **n.** Geology an earthy fossiliferous limestone occurring widely in England in a thin formation of Jurassic age.
– ORIGIN C19: from **CORN**[1] + **BRASH**[2].

**cornbread** ● **n.** a type of bread made from maize meal.

**corn bunting** ● **n.** a large thickset bunting with brown streaked plumage, inhabiting open grassland and arable land. [*Miliaria calandra*.]

**corn circle** ● **n.** another term for **CROP CIRCLE**.

**corncob** ● **n.** the central cylindrical woody part of the maize ear to which the grains are attached.

**corncockle** ● **n.** a pink-flowered Mediterranean plant which became a cornfield weed in Britain but is now rare. [*Agrostemma githago*.]
– ORIGIN C18: from **CORN**[1] + *cockle* (from OE *coccul* 'corncockle', perh. via L. from Gk *kokkos* 'berry').

**corncrake** ● **n.** a secretive crake inhabiting coarse grasslands, with mainly brown streaked plumage and a distinctive double rasping call. [*Crex crex*.]

**corn crib** ● **n.** N. Amer. a bin or ventilated building for storing maize.

**corn dog** ● **n.** N. Amer. a hot dog covered in maize-flour batter, fried, and served on a stick.

**corn dolly** ● **n.** Brit. a symbolic or decorative model of a human figure, made of plaited straw.

**cornea** /ˈkɔːnɪə/ ● **n.** the transparent layer forming the front of the eye.
– DERIVATIVES **corneal** adj.
– ORIGIN ME: from med. L. *cornea tela* 'horny tissue', from L. *cornu* 'horn'.

**corned beef** ● **n. 1** Brit. beef preserved in brine, chopped and pressed and sold in tins. **2** N. Amer. beef brisket cured in brine and boiled, typically served cold.

**cornel** /ˈkɔːn(ə)l/ ● **n.** a dogwood, especially of a dwarf variety. [*Cornus suecica* and other species.]
– ORIGIN ME (denoting the wood of the cornelian cherry): from OFr. *corneille*, from L. *cornus*.

**cornelian** /kɔːˈniːlɪən/ ● **n.** variant spelling of **CARNELIAN**.

**cornelian cherry** ● **n. 1** a flowering shrub or small tree of the dogwood family, cultivated as an ornamental. [*Cornus mas*.] **2** the edible oval red berry of this plant.
– ORIGIN C17: *cornelian* from **CORNEL** + **-IAN**.

**corneous** /ˈkɔːnɪəs/ ● **adj.** formal horn-like; horny.
– ORIGIN C17: from L. *corneus* (from *cornu* 'horn') + **-OUS**.

**corner** ● **n. 1** a place or angle where two or more sides or edges meet. ➤ a place where two streets meet. **2** Brit. a triangular cut from the hind end of a side of bacon. **3** a secluded or remote region or area. **4** a difficult or awkward position. **5** a position in which one dominates the supply of a particular commodity. **6** (also **corner kick**) Soccer a free kick taken by the attacking side from a corner of the field after the ball has been sent over the byline by a defender. ➤ a similar free hit in field hockey. **7** Boxing & Wrestling each of the diagonally opposite ends of the ring, where a contestant rests between rounds. ➤ a contestant's supporters or seconds. ● **v. 1** force into a place or situation from which it is hard to escape. **2** control (a market) by dominating the supply of a particular commodity. **3** go round a bend in a road.
– PHRASES **(just) around the corner** very near. **fight one's corner** defend one's position or interests. **in someone's corner** supporting and encouraging someone.
– DERIVATIVES **-cornered** adj.
– ORIGIN ME: from Anglo-Norman Fr., based on L. *cornu* 'horn, tip, corner'.

**cornerback** ● **n.** American Football a defensive back positioned to the outside of the linebackers.

**corner boy** ● **n.** chiefly Irish a disreputable man or youth who spends his time loitering on the street.

**cornerman** ● **n.** (pl. **-men**) a person whose job is to assist a boxer or wrestler at the corner between rounds.

**corner shop** ● **n.** Brit. a small shop selling groceries and general goods in a mainly residential area.

**cornerstone** • n. **1** a stone that forms the base of a corner of a building, joining two walls. **2** an important quality or feature on which something is based.

**cornerwise** • adv. at an angle of 45°; diagonally.

**cornet¹** /ˈkɔːnɪt/ • n. **1** a brass instrument resembling a trumpet but shorter and wider. **2** Brit. a cone-shaped wafer for holding ice cream.
– DERIVATIVES **cornetist** /kɔːˈnɛtɪst/ (also **cornettist**) n.
– ORIGIN ME (orig. denoting a wind instrument made of a horn): from OFr., dimin. of a var. of L. *cornu* 'horn'.

**cornet²** /ˈkɔːnɪt/ • n. (formerly) the fifth grade of commissioned officer in a cavalry troop, who carried the colours. ➤(in some British cavalry regiments) an officer of the rank of second lieutenant.
– DERIVATIVES **cornetcy** n. (pl. **-ies**).
– ORIGIN C16 (earlier denoting the pennant of a cavalry troop): from Fr. *cornette*, dimin. of *corne* (orig. a collective term), based on L. *cornua* 'horns'.

**cornetfish** • n. (pl. same or **-fishes**) an elongated tropical marine fish with a long, narrow snout and a whip-like extension to the tail. [Genus *Fistularia*: several species.]

**cornetto** /kɔːˈnɛtəʊ/ (also **cornett** /ˈkɔːnɪt, kɔːˈnɛt/) • n. (pl. **cornetti** or **cornetts**) a former woodwind instrument with finger holes and a cup-shaped mouthpiece.
– ORIGIN C19: from Ital., dimin. of *corno* 'horn', from L. *cornu*.

**corn exchange** • n. (in the UK) a building where corn is or was traded.

**corn-fed** • adj. **1** fed on grain, especially maize. **2** US informal provincial; unsophisticated.

**cornflakes** • pl. n. a breakfast cereal consisting of toasted flakes made from maize flour.

**cornflour** • n. Brit. finely ground maize flour, used for thickening sauces.

**cornflower** • n. a slender plant related to the knapweeds, with flowers that are typically a deep, vivid blue. [*Centaurea cyaneus* and related species.]

**cornice** /ˈkɔːnɪs/ • n. **1** an ornamental moulding round the wall of a room just below the ceiling. ➤a horizontal moulded projection crowning a building or structure, especially the uppermost member of the entablature of an order, surmounting the frieze. **2** an overhanging mass of hardened snow at the edge of a mountain precipice.
– DERIVATIVES **corniced** adj. **cornicing** n.
– ORIGIN C16: from Fr. *corniche*, from Ital. *cornice*, perh. from L. *cornix* 'crow' (cf. CORBEL), but influenced by Gk *korōnis* 'coping stone'.

**corniche** /ˈkɔːnɪʃ, kɔːˈniːʃ/ • n. a road cut into the edge of a cliff, especially one running along a coast.
– ORIGIN C19: from Fr. (see CORNICE).

**Cornish** • adj. of or relating to Cornwall, or its people or language. • n. the ancient Celtic language of Cornwall, belonging to the Brythonic branch of the Celtic language group.
– DERIVATIVES **Cornishman** n. (pl. **-men**). **Cornishwoman** n. (pl. **-women**).

**Cornish pasty** • n. Brit. a pasty containing seasoned meat and vegetables, especially potato.

**corn marigold** • n. a daisy-like yellow-flowered plant, formerly a common weed of cornfields. [*Chrysanthemum segetum*.]

**cornmeal** • n. meal made from corn, especially (in the US) maize flour or (in Scotland) oatmeal.

**corn oil** • n. an oil obtained from the germ of maize, used in cookery and salad dressings.

**corn pone** N. Amer. • n. unleavened maize bread. • adj. rustic; unsophisticated.

**cornrows** • pl. n. (especially among black people) a style of braiding and plaiting the hair in narrow strips to form geometric patterns on the scalp.

**corn salad** • n. another term for LAMB'S LETTUCE.

**corn snake** • n. a long North American rat snake with a spear-shaped mark between the eyes. [*Elaphe guttata*.]
– ORIGIN C17: so named because often found in cornfields.

**corn snow** • n. chiefly N. Amer. snow with a rough granular surface resulting from alternate thawing and freezing.
– ORIGIN from *corn* in the dial. sense 'granule'.

**cornstarch** • n. North American term for CORNFLOUR.

**cornstone** • n. a mottled red and green limestone.

**cornu** /ˈkɔːnjuː/ • n. (pl. **cornua** /ˈ-njʊə/) Anatomy **1** a horn-shaped projection of the thyroid cartilage or of certain bones. **2** either of the two lateral cavities of the womb, into which the Fallopian tubes pass. **3** each of three elongated parts of the lateral ventricles of the brain.
– DERIVATIVES **cornual** adj.
– ORIGIN C17: from L., 'horn'.

**cornucopia** /ˌkɔːnjʊˈkəʊpɪə/ • n. **1** a symbol of plenty consisting of a goat's horn overflowing with flowers, fruit, and corn. **2** an abundant supply of good things.
– DERIVATIVES **cornucopian** adj.
– ORIGIN C16: from late L., from L. *cornu copiae* 'horn of plenty' (a mythical horn able to provide whatever is desired).

**corny** • adj. (**-ier**, **-iest**) informal trite or mawkishly sentimental.
– DERIVATIVES **cornily** adv. **corniness** n.
– ORIGIN 1930s: from an earlier sense 'rustic, appealing to country folk'.

**corolla** /kəˈrɒlə/ • n. Botany the petals of a flower, typically forming a whorl within the sepals and enclosing the reproductive organs.
– ORIGIN C17: from L., dimin. of *corona* 'wreath, crown'.

**corollary** /kəˈrɒləri/ • n. (pl. **-ies**) **1** Logic a proposition that follows from (and is often appended to) one already proved. **2** a direct consequence or result. • adj. **1** Logic forming a corollary. **2** associated; supplementary.
– ORIGIN ME: from L. *corollarium* 'money paid for a garland or chaplet; gratuity' (in late L. 'deduction'), from *corolla* (see COROLLA).

**coromandel** /ˌkɒrəˈmand(ə)l/ • n. **1** (also **coromandel wood** or **coromandel ebony**) a fine-grained, greyish-brown ebony streaked with black, used in furniture. **2** the Sri Lankan tree yielding this wood. [*Diospyros quaesita*.] • adj. denoting a form of oriental lacquerware with intaglio designs.
– ORIGIN from the *Coromandel* Coast, the southern part of India's east coast, from which oriental lacquerware was orig. trans-shipped.

**corona¹** /kəˈrəʊnə/ • n. (pl. **coronae** /-niː/) **1** Astronomy the rarefied gaseous envelope of the sun or a star. ➤(also **corona discharge**) Physics the glow around a conductor at high potential. ➤a small circle of light seen round the sun or moon. **2** Anatomy a crown or crown-like structure. **3** Botany the trumpet-shaped central part of a daffodil or narcissus flower. **4** a circular chandelier in a church. **5** Architecture a part of a cornice having a broad vertical face.
– ORIGIN C16: from L., 'wreath, crown'.

**corona²** /kəˈrəʊnə/ • n. a long, straight-sided cigar.
– ORIGIN C19: from Sp. *La Corona*, lit. 'the crown', orig. a proprietary name.

**coronach** /ˈkɒrənək, -x/ • n. (in Scotland or Ireland) a funeral song.
– ORIGIN C16: from Sc. Gaelic *corranach* (Ir. *coranach*), from *comh-* 'together' + *rànach* 'outcry'.

**coronagraph** • n. an instrument that blocks out light emitted by the sun's actual surface so that the corona can be observed.

**coronal¹** /kəˈrəʊn(ə)l, ˈkɒr(ə)n(ə)l/ • adj. **1** of or relating to the crown or corona of something. **2** Anatomy of or in the coronal plane. **3** Phonetics (of a consonant) formed by raising the tip or blade of the tongue towards the hard palate. • n. Phonetics a coronal consonant.

**coronal²** /ˈkɒr(ə)n(ə)l/ • n. a garland or wreath for the head. ➤archaic a coronet.
– ORIGIN ME: appar. from Anglo-Norman Fr., from *corune* (see CROWN).

**coronal bone** • n. former term for FRONTAL BONE.

**coronal plane** • n. Anatomy an imaginary plane dividing the body into dorsal and ventral parts.

**coronal suture** • n. Anatomy the transverse suture in the skull separating the frontal bone from the parietal bones.

**coronary** • adj. Anatomy **1** relating to or denoting the arteries which surround and supply the heart. **2** relating to

or denoting a structure encircling a part of the body. ● **n.** (pl. **-ies**) short for **CORONARY THROMBOSIS**.
– ORIGIN C17: from L. *coronarius*, from *corona* 'wreath, crown'.

**coronary thrombosis** ● **n.** a blockage of the flow of blood to the heart, caused by a blood clot in a coronary artery.

**coronation** ● **n.** the ceremony of crowning a sovereign or a sovereign's consort.
– ORIGIN ME: via OFr. from med. L. *coronatio(n-)*, from *coronare* 'to crown', from *corona* (see **CROWN**).

**coronation chicken** ● **n.** a cold dish of cooked chicken served in a sauce flavoured with apricots and curry powder.
– ORIGIN so named because the dish was created for the coronation of Queen Elizabeth II in 1953.

**coronavirus** /kəˈrəʊnəˌvʌɪrəs/ ● **n.** Medicine any of a group of RNA viruses that cause a variety of diseases in humans and other animals.

**coroner** /ˈkɒr(ə)nə/ ● **n.** **1** an official who holds inquests into violent, sudden, or suspicious deaths, and (in Britain) inquiries into cases of treasure trove. **2** historical an official responsible for safeguarding the private property of the Crown.
– DERIVATIVES **coronership** n. **coronial** adj.
– ORIGIN ME: from Anglo-Norman Fr. *coruner*, from *corune* (see **CROWN**); reflecting the L. title *custos placitorum coronae* 'guardian of the pleas of the Crown'.

**coronet** /ˈkɒr(ə)nɪt/ ● **n.** **1** a small or simple crown, especially as worn by lesser royalty and nobles. ➤ a circular decoration for the head. **2** a ring of bone at the base of a deer's antler. **3** the band of tissue containing the horn-producing cells from which a horse's hoof grows.
– DERIVATIVES **coroneted** adj.
– ORIGIN ME: from OFr. *coronete*, dimin. of *corone* (see **CROWN**).

**coronoid process** ● **n.** Anatomy **1** a flattened triangular projection above the angle of the jaw where the temporalis muscle is attached. **2** a projection from the front of the ulna.
– ORIGIN C18: *coronoid* from Gk *korōnē* (denoting something hooked) + **-OID**.

**Corp.** ● **abbrev.** **1** (**Corp**) informal Corporal. **2** N. Amer. Corporation.

**corpora** plural form of **CORPUS**.

**corporal**[1] ● **n.** **1** a rank of non-commissioned officer in the army, above lance corporal or private first class and below sergeant. **2** (also **ship's corporal**) Brit. historical a petty officer who attended solely to police matters, under the master-at-arms. **3** North American term for **FALLFISH**.
– ORIGIN C16: from Fr., obs. var. of *caporal*, from Ital. *caporale*, prob. based on L. *corpus*, *corpor-* 'body (of troops)'.

**corporal**[2] ● **adj.** of or relating to the human body.
– DERIVATIVES **corporally** adv.
– ORIGIN ME: via OFr. from L. *corporalis*, from *corpus*, *corpor-* 'body'.

**corporal**[3] ● **n.** a cloth on which the chalice and paten are placed during the celebration of the Eucharist.
– ORIGIN ME: from med. L. *corporale (pallium)* 'body (cloth)', from L. *corpus*, *corpor-* 'body'.

**corporality** ● **n.** rare material or corporeal existence.

**corporal punishment** ● **n.** physical punishment, such as caning or flogging.

**corporate** ● **adj.** **1** of or relating to a large company or group. **2** Law (of a large company or group) authorized to act as a single entity and recognized as such in law. **3** of or shared by all the members of a group. ● **n.** a corporate company or group.
– DERIVATIVES **corporately** adv.
– ORIGIN C15: from L. *corporat-*, *corporare* 'form into a body', from *corpus*, *corpor-* 'body'.

**corporate raider** ● **n.** a financier who makes a practice of making hostile takeover bids for companies.

**corporate state** ● **n.** a state governed by representatives of trades, professions, or industries rather than of geographical areas.

**corporation** ● **n.** **1** a large company or group of companies authorized to act as a single entity and recognized as such in law. **2** Brit. a group of people elected to govern a city, town, or borough. **3** humorous, dated a paunch.
– ORIGIN ME: from late L. *corporatio(n-)*, from L. *corporare* (see **CORPORATE**).

**corporation tax** ● **n.** tax levied on companies' profits.

**corporatism** ● **n.** the control of a state or organization by large interest groups.
– DERIVATIVES **corporatist** adj. & n.

**corporative** ● **adj.** relating to or denoting a state, typically a fascist one, organized into corporations representing employers and workers in various spheres.
– DERIVATIVES **corporativism** n. **corporativist** adj. & n.

**corporatize** (also **-ise**) ● **v.** convert (a state organization) into an independent commercial company.

**corporeal** /kɔːˈpɔːrɪəl/ ● **adj.** **1** of or relating to a person's body, especially as opposed to their spirit. ➤ having a body. **2** Law consisting of material objects.
– DERIVATIVES **corporeality** /-ˈalɪti/ n. **corporeally** adv.
– ORIGIN ME: from late L. *corporealis*, from L. *corporeus* 'bodily, physical', from *corpus*, *corpor-* 'body'.

**corporeity** /ˌkɔːpəˈriːɪti, -ˈreɪɪti/ ● **n.** rare the quality of having a physical body or existence.

**corposant** /ˈkɔːpəzant/ ● **n.** archaic an appearance of St Elmo's fire on a ship.
– ORIGIN C16: from Old Sp., Port., and Ital. *corpo santo* 'holy body'.

**corps** /kɔː/ ● **n.** (pl. **corps** /kɔːz/) a main subdivision of an army in the field, consisting of two or more divisions. ➤ a branch of an army assigned to a particular kind of work. ➤ a body of people engaged in a particular activity.
– ORIGIN C16: from Fr., from L. *corpus* 'body'.

**corps de ballet** /ˌkɔː də ˈbaleɪ/ ● **n.** [treated as sing. or pl.] the members of a ballet company who dance together as a group. ➤ the lowest rank of dancers in a ballet company.
– ORIGIN C19: Fr.

**corpse** ● **n.** a dead body, especially of a human. ● **v.** theatrical slang spoil a piece of acting by forgetting one's lines or laughing uncontrollably.
– ORIGIN ME: alt. of **CORSE** by assoc. with L. *corpus*.

**corpse-candle** ● **n.** a lambent flame seen just above the ground in a churchyard or over a grave, superstitiously regarded as an omen of death.

**corpulent** /ˈkɔːpjʊl(ə)nt/ ● **adj.** (of a person) fat.
– DERIVATIVES **corpulence** n. **corpulency** n.
– ORIGIN ME: from L. *corpulentus*, from *corpus* 'body'.

**cor pulmonale** /ˌkɔː pʌlməˈnɑːli, -eɪli/ ● **n.** Medicine abnormal enlargement of the right side of the heart as a result of disease of the lungs or the pulmonary blood vessels.
– ORIGIN C19: from L. *cor* 'heart' and mod. L. *pulmonalis* (from L. *pulmo(n-)* 'lung').

**corpus** /ˈkɔːpəs/ ● **n.** (pl. **corpora** or **corpuses**) **1** a body or collection of written texts. ➤ a collection of written or spoken material in machine-readable form. **2** Anatomy the main body or mass of a structure. ➤ the central part of the stomach, between the fundus and the antrum.
– ORIGIN ME: from L., lit. 'body'.

**corpus callosum** /kəˈləʊsəm/ ● **n.** (pl. **corpora callosa** /-sə/) Anatomy a broad band of nerve fibres joining the two hemispheres of the brain.
– ORIGIN C18: from **CORPUS** and L. *callosum*, neut. of *callosus* 'tough'.

**corpus cavernosum** /ˌkavəˈnəʊsəm/ ● **n.** (pl. **corpora cavernosa** /-sə/) Anatomy either of two masses of erectile tissue forming the bulk of the penis and the clitoris.
– ORIGIN from **CORPUS** and L. *cavernosum*, neut. of *cavernosus* 'containing hollows'.

**Corpus Christi** /ˌkɔːpəs ˈkrɪsti/ ● **n.** a feast commemorating the institution of the Eucharist, observed on the Thursday after Trinity Sunday.
– ORIGIN L., lit. 'body of Christ'.

**corpuscle** /ˈkɔːpʌs(ə)l/ ● **n.** **1** Biology a minute body or cell in an organism, especially a red or white blood cell. **2** historical a minute particle regarded as the basic constituent of matter or light.
– DERIVATIVES **corpuscular** /kɔːˈpʌskjʊlə/ adj.

– ORIGIN C17: from L. *corpusculum* 'small body', dimin. of *corpus*.

**corpus delicti** /dɪˈlɪktʌɪ/ ● **n.** Law the facts and circumstances constituting a breach of a law.
– ORIGIN L., lit. 'body of offence'.

**corpus luteum** /ˈluːtɪəm/ ● **n.** (pl. **corpora lutea** /ˈluːtɪə/) Anatomy a hormone-secreting structure that develops in an ovary after an ovum has been discharged but degenerates after a few days unless pregnancy has begun.
– ORIGIN C18: from **CORPUS** and L. *luteum*, neut. of *luteus* 'yellow'.

**corpus spongiosum** /ˌspʌndʒɪˈəʊsəm/ ● **n.** (pl. **corpora spongiosa** /-sə/) Anatomy a mass of erectile tissue alongside the corpora cavernosa of the penis and terminating in the glans.
– ORIGIN from **CORPUS** and L. *spongiosum*, neut. of *spongiosus* 'porous'.

**corpus striatum** /strʌɪˈeɪtəm/ ● **n.** (pl. **corpora striata** /-tə/) Anatomy part of the basal ganglia of the brain, comprising the caudate and lentiform nuclei.
– ORIGIN from **CORPUS** and L. *striatum*, neut. of *striatus* 'grooved'.

**corral** /kəˈrɑːl/ ● **n.** N. Amer. **1** a pen for livestock on a farm or ranch. **2** historical a defensive enclosure of wagons in an encampment. ● **v.** (**corralled**, **corralling**) **1** chiefly N. Amer. put or keep (livestock) in a corral. ➤gather (a group) together. **2** N. Amer. historical form (wagons) into a corral.
– ORIGIN C16: from Sp. and Old Port. (now *curral*), perh. based on L. *currere* 'to run'; cf. **KRAAL**.

**correct** ● **adj. 1** free from error; true; right. ➤chiefly N. Amer. conforming to a particular political or ideological orthodoxy: *environmentally correct.* **2** conforming to accepted social standards. ● **v.** put right. ➤mark the errors in (a text). ➤adjust (an instrument) to function accurately or accord with a standard. ➤adjust (a numerical result or reading) to allow for departure from standard conditions.
– DERIVATIVES **correctable** adj. **correctly** adv. **correctness** n. **corrector** n.
– ORIGIN ME (as v.; the adj. is via Fr.): from L. *correct-*, *corrigere*, 'make straight, amend', from *cor-* 'together' + *regere* 'guide'.

**correction** ● **n. 1** the action or process of correcting something. ➤a change that rectifies an error or inaccuracy. ➤a quantity adjusting a numerical result to allow for a departure from standard conditions. **2** N. Amer. or dated punishment, especially that of criminals in prison.
– DERIVATIVES **correctional** adj. (chiefly N. Amer.).

**correction fluid** ● **n.** an opaque liquid painted over a typed or written error to allow for the insertion of the correct character.

**correctitude** /kəˈrɛktɪtjuːd/ ● **n.** correctness, especially conscious correctness in one's behaviour.

**corrective** ● **adj.** designed to correct or counteract something undesirable. ● **n.** a corrective measure.
– DERIVATIVES **correctively** adv.

**correlate** /ˈkɒrəleɪt, -rɪ-/ ● **v.** have a relationship or connection in which one thing affects or depends on another. ➤establish a correlation between. ● **n.** each of two or more related or complementary things.
– ORIGIN C17: back-form. from **CORRELATION** and **CORRELATIVE**.

**correlation** ● **n. 1** a mutual relationship or connection. ➤the process of correlating two or more things. **2** Statistics interdependence of variable quantities.
– DERIVATIVES **correlational** adj.
– ORIGIN C16: from med. L. *correlatio(n-)*, from *cor-* 'together' + *relatio* (see **RELATION**).

**correlation coefficient** ● **n.** Statistics a number between +1 and −1 calculated so as to represent the linear interdependence of two variables or sets of data. (Symbol: **r**.)

**correlative** /kəˈrɛlətɪv/ ● **adj. 1** having a correlation. **2** Grammar (of words such as *neither* and *nor*) corresponding to each other and regularly used together. ● **n.** a correlative word or concept.
– DERIVATIVES **correlatively** adv. **correlativity** n.
– ORIGIN C16: from med. L. *correlativus*, from *cor-* 'together' + late L. *relativus* 'having reference or relation' (see **RELATE**).

**correspond** ● **v. 1** have a close similarity; match or agree almost exactly. ➤be analogous or equivalent. **2** communicate by exchanging letters.
– DERIVATIVES **corresponding** adj. **correspondingly** adv.
– ORIGIN ME: from OFr. *correspondre*, from med. L. *correspondere*, from *cor-* 'together' + L. *respondere* (see **RESPOND**).

**correspondence** ● **n. 1** the action or fact of corresponding. **2** letters sent or received.

**correspondence course** ● **n.** a course of study in which student and tutors communicate by post.

**correspondence principle** ● **n.** Physics the principle that states that for very large quantum numbers the laws of quantum theory merge with those of classical physics.

**correspondence theory** ● **n.** Philosophy the theory that states that the definition or criterion of truth is that true propositions correspond to the facts.

**correspondent** ● **n. 1** a person who writes letters, especially on a regular basis. **2** a journalist reporting on a particular subject or from a particular country. ● **adj.** corresponding.

**corresponding member** ● **n.** an honorary member of a learned society who has no voice in the society's affairs.

**corrida** /kɒˈriːdə/ ● **n.** a bullfight.
– ORIGIN C19: from Sp. *corrida de toros* 'running of bulls'.

**corridor** ● **n. 1** a long passage from which doors lead into rooms. ➤Brit. a passage along the side of a railway carriage giving access to compartments. **2** a belt of land linking two other areas or following a road or river.
– PHRASES **the corridors of power** the senior levels of government or administration.
– ORIGIN C16: from Fr., from Ital. *corridore*, alt. (by assoc. with *corridore* 'runner') of *corridoio* 'running-place', from *correre* 'to run', from L. *currere*.

**corrie** /ˈkɒri/ ● **n.** (pl. **-ies**) a cirque, especially one in the mountains of Scotland.
– ORIGIN C16: from Sc. Gaelic and Ir. *coire* 'cauldron, hollow'.

**corrigendum** /ˌkɒrɪˈdʒɛndəm/ ● **n.** (pl. **corrigenda** /-də/) a thing to be corrected, especially an error in a book.
– ORIGIN C19: L., neut. gerundive of *corrigere* (see **CORRECT**).

**corrigible** /ˈkɒrɪdʒɪb(ə)l/ ● **adj.** capable of being corrected or reformed.
– DERIVATIVES **corrigibility** n.
– ORIGIN ME: via Fr. from med. L. *corrigibilis*, from L. *corrigere* 'to correct'.

**corroborate** /kəˈrɒbəreɪt/ ● **v.** confirm or give support to (a statement or theory).
– DERIVATIVES **corroboration** n. **corroborative** adj. **corroborator** n. **corroboratory** adj.
– ORIGIN C16 (earlier (ME) as *corroboration* in the sense 'strengthening'): from L. *corroborat-*, *corroborare*, from *cor-* 'together' + *roborare*, from *robur* 'strength'.

**corroboree** /kəˈrɒbəri/ ● **n.** an Australian Aboriginal dance ceremony in the form of a sacred ritual or informal gathering.
– ORIGIN from Dharuk *garaabara*, denoting a style of dancing.

**corrode** /kəˈrəʊd/ ● **v.** destroy or damage (metal or other hard material) slowly by chemical action. ➤be destroyed or damaged in this way. ➤gradually weaken or erode.
– DERIVATIVES **corrodible** adj. **corrosion** n.
– ORIGIN ME: from L. *corrodere*, from *cor-* (expressing intensive force) + *rodere* 'gnaw'.

**corrody** /ˈkɒrədi/ ● **n.** (pl. **-ies**) historical a pension or provision for maintenance.
– ORIGIN ME: from Anglo-Norman Fr. *corodie*, from a Romance word meaning 'preparation'.

**corrosive** ● **adj.** tending to cause corrosion. ● **n.** a corrosive substance.
– DERIVATIVES **corrosively** adv. **corrosiveness** n.

**corrugate** /ˈkɒrʊɡeɪt/ ● **v.** contract into wrinkles or folds.
– ORIGIN ME: from L. *corrugat-*, *corrugare* 'to wrinkle', from *cor-* (expressing intensive force) + *rugare* (from *ruga* 'a wrinkle').

**corrugated** ● **adj.** shaped into alternate ridges and grooves.
– DERIVATIVES **corrugation** n.

**corrugated paper** ● **n.** packaging material made from layers of thick paper, the top layer of which is corrugated for added strength and rigidity.

**corrupt** ● **adj. 1** willing to act dishonestly in return for money or personal gain. ➤evil or morally depraved. **2** (of a text or a computer database or program) made unreliable by errors or alterations. **3** archaic rotten or putrid. ● **v. 1** cause to become corrupt. **2** debase by making errors. **3** archaic infect; contaminate.
– DERIVATIVES **corrupter** n. **corruptibility** n. **corruptible** adj. **corruption** n. **corruptive** adj. **corruptly** adv.
– ORIGIN ME: from L. *corrupt-*, *corrumpere* 'mar, bribe, destroy', from *cor-* 'altogether' + *rumpere* 'to break'.

**corsac fox** /ˈkɔːsak/ ● **n.** a russet-grey fox found on the steppes of central Asia. [*Vulpes corsac.*]
– ORIGIN C19: *corsac* from Russ. *korsak*, from Turkic *karsak*.

**corsage** /kɔːˈsɑːʒ, ˈkɔːsɑːʒ/ ● **n. 1** a spray of flowers worn pinned to a woman's clothes. **2** the upper part of a woman's dress.
– ORIGIN C19: Fr., from OFr. *cors* 'body', from L. *corpus*.

**corsair** /kɔːˈsɛː, ˈkɔːsɛː/ ● **n.** archaic a pirate. ➤historical a privateer, especially one operating along the southern shore of the Mediterranean.
– ORIGIN C16: from Fr. *corsaire*, from med. L. *cursarius*, from *cursus* 'a raid, plunder', special use of L. *cursus* 'course', from *currere* 'to run'.

**corse** /kɔːs/ ● **n.** archaic a corpse.
– ORIGIN ME: from OFr. *cors* 'body', from L. *corpus*; cf. **CORPSE**.

**corselet** ● **n. 1** /ˈkɔːs(ə)lɪt/ historical a piece of armour covering the trunk. **2** variant spelling of **CORSELETTE**.
– ORIGIN C15: from OFr. *corslet*, dimin. of *cors* 'body'.

**corselette** /ˌkɔːs(ə)ˈlɛt, ˈkɔːs(ə)lɛt/ (also **corselet**) ● **n.** a woman's garment combining corset and brassiere.

**corset** ● **n.** a woman's tightly fitting undergarment extending from below the chest to the hips, formerly worn to shape the figure. ➤a similar garment worn to support a weak or injured back. ➤historical a tightly fitting laced or stiffened outer bodice or dress.
– DERIVATIVES **corseted** adj. **corsetry** n.
– ORIGIN ME: from OFr., dimin. of *cors* 'body', from L. *corpus*.

**corsetière** /ˌkɔːsɪˈtjɛː, ˈkɔːsɪtjɛː/ ● **n.** a woman who makes or fits corsets.

**Corsican** ● **n. 1** a native of Corsica. **2** the language of Corsica, which originated as a dialect of Italian. ● **adj.** of or relating to Corsica or its language.

**cortège** /kɔːˈteɪʒ, -ˈtɛʒ/ ● **n. 1** a solemn procession, especially for a funeral. **2** a person's entourage or retinue.
– ORIGIN C17: from Fr., from Ital. *corteggio*, from *corteggiare* 'attend court', from *corte* 'court', from L. *cohors*, *cohort-* 'retinue'.

**Cortes** /ˈkɔːtɛs, -z, Spanish ˈkortes/ ● **n.** the legislative assembly of Spain and formerly of Portugal.
– ORIGIN Sp. and Port., pl. of *corte* 'court', from L. *cohors*, *cohort-* 'retinue'.

**cortex** /ˈkɔːtɛks/ ● **n.** (pl. **cortices** /-tɪˌsiːz/) **1** Anatomy the outer layer of an organ or structure, such as a kidney or adrenal gland. ➤(also **cerebral cortex**) the outer, folded layer of the cerebrum, which plays an important role in consciousness. **2** Botany an outer layer of tissue immediately below the epidermis of a stem or root.
– DERIVATIVES **cortical** adj.
– ORIGIN ME: from L., lit. 'bark'.

**corticate** /ˈkɔːtɪkeɪt/ ● **adj.** Botany having a cortex, bark, or rind.
– DERIVATIVES **cortication** n.

**cortico-** ● **comb. form** representing **CORTEX**, used especially with reference to the adrenal and cerebral cortices.

**corticosteroid** /ˌkɔːtɪkəʊˈstɪərɔɪd, -ˈstɛrɔɪd/ ● **n.** Biochemistry any of a group of steroid hormones produced in the adrenal cortex.

**corticosterone** /ˌkɔːtɪkəʊˈstɛrəʊn/ ● **n.** Biochemistry a hormone secreted by the adrenal cortex, one of the glucocorticoids.

**corticotrophin** /ˌkɔːtɪkə(ʊ)ˈtrəʊfɪn/ (also **corticotropin** /-pɪn/) ● **n.** Biochemistry another term for **ADRENOCORTICOTROPHIC HORMONE**.

**cortisol** /ˈkɔːtɪsɒl/ ● **n.** Biochemistry another term for **HYDROCORTISONE**.

**cortisone** /ˈkɔːtɪzəʊn/ ● **n.** Biochemistry a hormone produced by the adrenal cortex or made synthetically, used as an anti-inflammatory and anti-allergy agent.
– ORIGIN 1940s: from elements of its chemical name *17-hydroxy-11-dehydrocorticosterone.*

**corundum** /kəˈrʌndəm/ ● **n.** extremely hard crystallized alumina, used as an abrasive.
– ORIGIN C18: from Tamil *kuruntam* and Telugu *kuruvindam*.

**coruscate** /ˈkɒrəskeɪt/ ● **v.** poetic/literary (of light) flash or sparkle.
– DERIVATIVES **coruscant** adj. **coruscation** n.
– ORIGIN C18: from L. *coruscat-*, *coruscare* 'glitter'.

**corvée** /ˈkɔːveɪ/ ● **n. 1** historical a day's unpaid labour owed by a vassal to his feudal lord. **2** forced labour exacted in lieu of taxes.
– ORIGIN ME: from OFr., based on L. *corrogare* 'ask for, collect'.

**corves** plural form of **CORF**.

**corvette** /kɔːˈvɛt/ ● **n.** a small warship designed for convoy escort duty. ➤historical a flush-decked sailing warship with one tier of guns.
– ORIGIN C17: from Fr., from Du. *korf*, denoting a kind of ship, + the dimin. suffix *-ette*.

**corvid** /ˈkɔːvɪd/ ● **n.** Ornithology a bird of the crow family (Corvidae); a crow.
– ORIGIN C20: from mod. L. *Corvidae*, from L. *corvus* 'raven'.

**corvine** /ˈkɔːvʌɪn/ ● **adj.** of or like a raven or crow, especially in colour.
– ORIGIN C17: from L. *corvinus*, from *corvus* 'raven'.

**corybantic** /ˌkɒrɪˈbantɪk/ ● **adj.** wild; frenzied.
– ORIGIN C17: from *Corybantes*, L. name of the priests of Cybele, a Phrygian goddess of nature who performed wild dances, from Gk *Korubantes* + **-IC**.

**corydalis** /kəˈrɪdəlɪs/ ● **n.** a herbaceous plant with spurred tubular flowers. [*Corydalis lutea* (**yellow corydalis**) and related species.]
– ORIGIN mod. L., from Gk *korudallis* 'crested lark', alluding to a similarity between the flower and the bird's spur.

**corymb** /ˈkɒrɪmb/ ● **n.** Botany a flower cluster whose lower stalks are proportionally longer so that the flowers form a flat or slightly convex head.
– DERIVATIVES **corymbose** adj.
– ORIGIN C18: from Fr. *corymbe* or L. *corymbus*, from Gk *korumbos* 'cluster'.

**corynebacterium** /ˌkɒrɪnɪbakˈtɪərɪəm, kəˌrɪn-/ ● **n.** (pl. **corynebacteria** /-rɪə/) a bacterium of a genus including the causative agent of diphtheria. [Genus *Corynebacterium.*]
– ORIGIN mod. L., from Gk *korunē* 'club' + **BACTERIUM**.

**coryphée** /ˈkɒrɪfeɪ/ ● **n.** a leading dancer in a corps de ballet.
– ORIGIN Fr., via L. from Gk *koruphaios* 'leader of a chorus', from *koruphē* 'head'.

**coryza** /kəˈrʌɪzə/ ● **n.** Medicine catarrhal inflammation of the mucous membrane in the nose, as caused by a cold.
– ORIGIN C16: from L., from Gk *koruza* 'nasal mucus'.

**cos**[1] /kɒs/ ● **n.** a variety of lettuce with crisp narrow leaves that form a tall head.
– ORIGIN C17: named after the Aegean island of *Cos*, where it originated.

**cos**[2] /kɒz, kɒs/ ● **abbrev.** cosine.

**cos**[3] /kɒz, kəz/ (also **'cos** or **coz**) ● **conj.** informal short for

**BECAUSE.**

**Cosa Nostra** /ˌkəʊzə ˈnɒstrə/ ● **n.** a US criminal organization resembling and related to the Mafia.
– ORIGIN Ital., lit. 'our affair'.

**cosec** /ˈkəʊsɛk/ ● **abbrev.** cosecant.

**cosecant** /kəʊˈsiːk(ə)nt, -ˈsɛk-/ ● **n.** Mathematics the ratio of the hypotenuse (in a right-angled triangle) to the side opposite an acute angle; the reciprocal of sine.
– ORIGIN C18: from mod. L. *cosecant-*, from **co-** + L. *secant-*, *secare* 'to cut'; cf. **SECANT**.

**coset** /ˈkəʊsɛt/ ● **n.** Mathematics a set composed of all the products obtained by multiplying each element of a subgroup in turn by one particular element of the group containing the subgroup.

**cosh**[1] Brit. ● **n.** a thick heavy stick or bar used as a weapon. ● **v.** hit on the head with a cosh.
– ORIGIN C19: of unknown origin.

**cosh**[2] /kɒʃ, kɒsˈeɪtʃ/ ● **abbrev.** Mathematics hyperbolic cosine.
– ORIGIN from **cos**[2] + *-h* for *hyperbolic*; cf. **COTH**.

**COSHH** ● **abbrev.** Brit. control of substances hazardous for health.

**co-signatory** ● **n.** a person or state signing a treaty or other document jointly with others.

**cosine** /ˈkəʊsʌɪn/ ● **n.** Mathematics the trigonometric function that is equal to the ratio of the side adjacent to an acute angle (in a right-angled triangle) to the hypotenuse.

**cosmetic** ● **adj.** **1** relating to treatment intended to improve a person's appearance. **2** affecting only the appearance of something. ● **n.** (**cosmetics**) cosmetic preparations, especially for the face.
– DERIVATIVES **cosmetically** adv.
– ORIGIN C17: from Fr. *cosmétique*, from Gk *kosmētikos*, from *kosmein* 'arrange or adorn', from *kosmos* 'order or adornment'.

**cosmetician** /ˌkɒzməˈtɪʃ(ə)n/ ● **n.** N. Amer. a person who sells or applies cosmetics as an occupation.

**cosmetology** /ˌkɒzmɪˈtɒlədʒi/ ● **n.** the professional application of cosmetic preparations and techniques.
– DERIVATIVES **cosmetological** adj. **cosmetologist** n.

**cosmic** ● **adj.** of or relating to the universe or cosmos, especially as distinct from the earth.
– DERIVATIVES **cosmical** adj. **cosmically** adv.

**cosmic dust** ● **n.** small particles of matter distributed throughout space.

**cosmic radiation** ● **n.** radiation consisting of cosmic rays.

**cosmic ray** ● **n.** a highly energetic atomic nucleus or other particle travelling through space at a speed approaching that of light.

**cosmic string** ● **n.** see **STRING** (in sense 7).

**cosmo-** /ˈkɒzməʊ/ ● **comb. form** of or relating to the world or the universe: *cosmography.*
– ORIGIN from Gk *kosmos* 'order, world'.

**cosmogenesis** /ˌkɒzmə(ʊ)ˈdʒɛnɪsɪs/ ● **n.** the origin or evolution of the universe.
– DERIVATIVES **cosmogenetic** adj. **cosmogenic** adj.

**cosmogony** /kɒzˈmɒgəni/ ● **n.** (pl. **-ies**) the branch of science concerned with the origin of the universe, especially the solar system.
– DERIVATIVES **cosmogonic** /-məˈgɒnɪk/ adj. **cosmogonical** /-məˈgɒnɪk(ə)l/ adj. **cosmogonist** n.
– ORIGIN C17: from Gk *kosmogonia*, from *kosmos* 'order or world' + *-gonia* '-begetting'.

**cosmography** ● **n.** (pl. **-ies**) **1** the branch of science which deals with the general features of the universe, including the earth. **2** a description or representation of the universe or the earth.
– DERIVATIVES **cosmographer** n. **cosmographic** adj. **cosmographical** adj.

**cosmological constant** ● **n.** Physics an arbitrary constant in the field equations of general relativity.

**cosmology** ● **n.** (pl. **-ies**) the science of the origin and development of the universe. ➤ an account or theory of the origin of the universe.
– DERIVATIVES **cosmological** adj. **cosmologist** n.

**cosmonaut** ● **n.** a Russian astronaut.
– ORIGIN 1950s: from **COSMOS**[1], on the pattern of *astronaut* and Russ. *kosmonavt*.

**cosmopolis** /kɒzˈmɒp(ə)lɪs/ ● **n.** a city inhabited by people from many different countries.
– ORIGIN C19: from Gk *kosmos* 'world' + *polis* 'city'.

**cosmopolitan** /ˌkɒzməˈpɒlɪt(ə)n/ ● **adj.** **1** familiar with or representative of many different countries and cultures. ➤ having an exciting and glamorous character associated with travel and a mixture of cultures. **2** (of a plant or animal) found all over the world. ● **n.** a cosmopolitan person, plant, or animal.
– DERIVATIVES **cosmopolitanism** n. **cosmopolitanize** (also **-ise**) v.
– ORIGIN C17 (as n.): from **COSMOPOLITE** + **-AN**.

**cosmopolite** /kɒzˈmɒp(ə)lʌɪt/ ● **n.** a cosmopolitan person.
– ORIGIN C17: from Fr., from Gk *kosmopolitēs*, from *kosmos* 'world' + *politēs* 'citizen'.

**cosmos**[1] ● **n.** the universe seen as a well-ordered whole.
– ORIGIN ME: from Gk *kosmos* 'order or world'.

**cosmos**[2] ● **n.** an ornamental plant of the daisy family, which bears single dahlia-like flowers and is native to Mexico and warm regions of America. [Genus *Cosmos*.]
– ORIGIN from Gk *kosmos* in the sense 'ornament'.

**Cossack** /ˈkɒsak/ ● **n.** a member of a people of southern Russia, Ukraine, and Siberia, noted for their horsemanship and military skill. ➤ a member of a Cossack military unit.
– ORIGIN from Russ. *kazak* from Turkic, 'vagabond, nomad'; later influenced by Fr. *Cosaque* (cf. **KAZAKH**).

**cosset** ● **v.** (**cosseted**, **cosseting**) care for and protect in an overindulgent way.
– ORIGIN C16 (as n. denoting a lamb brought up by hand, later a spoiled child): prob. from Anglo-Norman Fr. *coscet* 'cottager', from OE *cotsǣta* 'cottar'.

**cossie** (also **cozzie**) ● **n.** (pl. **-ies**) informal a swimming costume or a pair of swimming trunks.

**cost** ● **v.** (past and past part. **cost**) **1** require the payment of (a specified sum) in order to be bought or obtained. ➤ cause or require the expenditure or loss of. ➤ informal be expensive for: *it'll cost you.* **2** (past and past part. **costed**) estimate the price or cost of. ● **n.** the amount that something costs. ➤ the effort or loss necessary to achieve something. ➤ (**costs**) legal expenses, especially those allowed in favour of the winning party or against the losing party in a suit.
– PHRASES **at all costs** (or **at any cost**) regardless of the price or the effort needed. **at cost** at cost price. **cost someone dear** (or **dearly**) involve someone in a serious loss or a heavy penalty. **to someone's cost** with loss or disadvantage to someone.
– ORIGIN ME: from OFr. *coust* (n.), *couster* (v.), based on L. *constare* 'stand firm, stand at a price'.

**costa** ● **n.** (pl. **costae** /ˈkɒstiː/) **1** Botany & Zoology a rib, midrib, or rib-like structure. **2** Entomology the main vein running along the leading edge of an insect's wing.
– DERIVATIVES **costal** adj.
– ORIGIN C19: from L.

**cost accounting** ● **n.** the recording of all the costs incurred in a business in a way that can be used to improve its management.
– DERIVATIVES **cost accountant** n.

**co-star** ● **n.** a performer appearing with another or others of equal importance. ● **v.** appear in a production as a co-star. ➤ (of a production) include as a co-star.

**Costard** /ˈkɒstəd, ˈkʌst-/ ● **n.** Brit. a cooking apple of a large ribbed variety.
– ORIGIN ME: from Anglo-Norman Fr., from *coste* 'rib', from L. *costa*.

**Costa Rican** /ˈriːkən/ ● **n.** a native of inhabitant of Costa Rica, a republic in Central America. ● **adj.** of or relating to Costa Rica.

**costate** /ˈkɒsteɪt/ ● **adj.** Botany & Zoology ribbed; possessing a costa.

**cost-benefit** ● **adj.** relating to a process that assesses the relation between the cost of an undertaking and the value of the resulting benefits: *a cost-benefit analysis.*

**cost-effective** ● **adj.** effective or productive in relation

to its cost.
– DERIVATIVES **cost-effectively** adv. **cost-effectiveness** n.

**cost-efficient** • adj. another term for **COST-EFFECTIVE**.
– DERIVATIVES **cost-efficiency** n.

**coster** • n. Brit. short for **COSTERMONGER**.

**costermonger** /ˈkɒstəmʌŋgə/ • n. Brit. dated a person who sells goods, especially fruit and vegetables, from a handcart in the street.
– ORIGIN C16 (denoting an apple seller): from **COSTARD** + **-MONGER**.

**costing** • n. the estimated cost of producing or undertaking something.

**costive** /ˈkɒstɪv/ • adj. constipated.
– DERIVATIVES **costively** adv. **costiveness** n.
– ORIGIN ME: via OFr. from L. *constipare* (see **CONSTIPATE**).

**costly** • adj. (**-ier**, **-iest**) **1** expensive. **2** causing suffering, loss, or disadvantage.
– DERIVATIVES **costliness** n.

**costmary** /ˈkɒstmɛːri/ • n. (pl. **-ies**) an aromatic plant of the daisy family, formerly used in medicine and for flavouring ale prior to the use of hops. [*Balsamita major*.]
– ORIGIN ME: from obs. *cost* (via L. from Gk *kostos*, via Arab. from Sanskrit *kuṣṭha*, denoting an aromatic plant) + *Mary*, the mother of Christ.

**cost-of-carry** • n. Finance the difference between the cost and the financial benefit of holding a particular asset for a specified period.

**cost of living** • n. the level of prices relating to a range of everyday items.

**cost-of-living index** • n. another term for **RETAIL PRICE INDEX**.

**cost-plus** • adj. denoting a method of pricing something in which a fixed profit factor is added to the costs.

**cost price** • n. the price at which goods are bought by a retailer.

**cost-push** • adj. relating to or denoting inflation caused by increased labour or raw material costs.

**costume** • n. a set of clothes in a style typical of a particular country or historical period. ➤a set of clothes worn by an actor or performer for a role. ➤Brit. dated a woman's matching jacket and skirt. • v. dress in a particular set of clothes.
– ORIGIN C18: from Fr., from Ital. *costume* 'custom, fashion, habit', from L. *consuetudo* (see **CUSTOM**).

**costume drama** • n. a television or cinema production set in a historical period.

**costume jewellery** • n. jewellery made with inexpensive materials or imitation gems.

**costumier** /kɒˈstjuːmɪə/ (US also **costumer** /-mə/) • n. a maker or supplier of theatrical or fancy-dress costumes.
– ORIGIN C19: Fr., from *costumer* (see **COSTUME**).

**cosy** (US **cozy**) • adj. (**-ier**, **-iest**) **1** comfortable, warm, and secure. **2** not seeking or offering challenge or difficulty. ➤informal, derogatory (of a transaction or arrangement) beneficial to all those involved and possibly somewhat unscrupulous. • n. (pl. **-ies**) **1** a cover to keep a teapot or a boiled egg hot. **2** Brit. a canopied corner seat for two. • v. (**-ies**, **-ied**) informal make (someone) feel cosy. ➤(**cosy up to**) snuggle up to or ingratiate oneself with.
– DERIVATIVES **cosily** adv. **cosiness** n.
– ORIGIN C18 (orig. Scots): of unknown origin.

**cot**[1] • n. Brit. a small bed with high barred sides for a baby or very young child. ➤a plain narrow bed. ➤N. Amer. a camp bed. ➤Nautical a bed resembling a hammock hung from deck beams, formerly used by officers.
– ORIGIN C17: from Hindi *khāṭ* 'bedstead, hammock'.

**cot**[2] • n. **1** a small shelter for livestock. **2** archaic a small, simple cottage.
– ORIGIN OE, of Gmc origin; rel. to **COTE**.

**cot**[3] • abbrev. Mathematics cotangent.

**cotangent** /kəʊˈtandʒ(ə)nt/ • n. Mathematics (in a right-angled triangle) the ratio of the side (other than the hypotenuse) adjacent to a particular acute angle to the side opposite the angle.

**cot death** • n. Brit. the unexplained death of a baby in its sleep.

**cote** • n. a shelter for mammals or birds, especially pigeons.
– ORIGIN OE (in the sense 'cottage'), of Gmc origin; rel. to **COT**[2].

**coterie** /ˈkəʊt(ə)ri/ • n. (pl. **-ies**) a small exclusive group of people with shared interests or tastes.
– ORIGIN C18: from Fr., based on Mid. Low Ger. *kote* 'cote'.

**coterminous** /kəʊˈtəːmɪnəs/ • adj. having the same boundaries or extent.
– ORIGIN C18: alt. of **CONTERMINOUS**.

**coth** /kɒθ, kɒtˈeɪtʃ/ • abbrev. hyperbolic cotangent.
– ORIGIN from **COT**[3] + *-h* for *hyperbolic*.

**co-tidal line** • n. a line on a map connecting points at which a tidal level, especially high tide, occurs simultaneously.

**cotillion** /kəˈtɪljən/ • n. **1** an 18th-century French dance based on the contredanse. ➤US a quadrille. **2** US a formal ball, especially one at which debutantes are presented.
– ORIGIN C18: from Fr. *cotillon*, lit. 'petticoat dance', dimin. of *cotte*, from OFr. *cote*.

**cotinga** /kəˈtɪŋgə/ • n. a perching bird found in the forests of Central and South America, the male of which is typically brilliantly coloured. [*Cotinga* and other genera: numerous species.]
– ORIGIN via Fr. from Tupi *cutinga*.

**cotoneaster** /kəˌtəʊnɪˈastə/ • n. a small-leaved shrub of the rose family, cultivated as a hedging plant or for its bright red berries. [Genus *Cotoneaster*.]
– ORIGIN C18: mod. L., from L. *cotoneum* (see **QUINCE**) + **-ASTER**.

**Cotswold** /ˈkɒtswəʊld/ • n. **1** a sheep of a breed with fine wool, often used to produce cross-bred lambs. **2** Double Gloucester cheese containing chives and onions.
– ORIGIN from the *Cotswold* Hills in central England.

**cotta** /ˈkɒtə/ • n. a short garment resembling a surplice, worn typically by Catholic priests and servers.
– ORIGIN C19: from Ital.; rel. to **COAT**.

**cottage** • n. **1** a small simple house, typically one in the country. **2** informal (in the context of casual homosexual encounters) a public toilet. • v. [usu. as noun **cottaging**] informal perform homosexual acts in a public toilet.
– DERIVATIVES **cottagey** adj.
– ORIGIN ME: from Anglo-Norman Fr. *cotage* and Anglo-Latin *cotagium*, from **COT**[2] or **COTE**.

**cottage cheese** • n. soft, lumpy white cheese made from the curds of skimmed milk.

**cottage garden** • n. an informal garden stocked typically with colourful flowering plants.

**cottage hospital** • n. Brit. a small local hospital.

**cottage industry** • n. a business or manufacturing activity carried on in people's homes.

**cottage loaf** • n. Brit. a loaf made from two round pieces of dough, the smaller on top of the larger.

**cottage pie** • n. Brit. a dish of minced meat topped with browned mashed potato.

**cottager** • n. a person living in a cottage.

**cottar** /ˈkɒtə/ (also **cotter**) • n. historical (in Scotland and Ireland) a farm labourer or tenant occupying a cottage in return for labour.
– ORIGIN OE, from **COT**[2] + **-AR**[4].

**cotter pin** • n. a metal pin used to fasten two parts of a mechanism together. ➤a split pin that is opened out after being passed through a hole.
– ORIGIN C17: of unknown origin.

**cottier** /ˈkɒtɪə/ • n. **1** Brit. archaic a rural labourer living in a cottage. **2** historical an Irish peasant holding land by cottier tenure.
– ORIGIN ME: from OFr. *cotier*, ult. of Gmc origin and rel. to **COT**[2].

**cottier tenure** • n. historical (in Ireland) the letting of land in small portions direct to the labourers, at a rent fixed by competition.

**cottise** /ˈkɒtɪs/ (also **cotise**) • n. Heraldry a narrow band adjacent and parallel to an ordinary such as a bend or chevron.
– DERIVATIVES **cottised** adj.

– ORIGIN C16: from Fr. *cotice* 'leather thong'.

**cotton** • n. **1** a soft white fibrous substance which surrounds the seeds of the cotton plant and is used as textile fibre and thread for sewing. **2** (also **cotton batting**) N. Amer. cotton wool. **3** (also **cotton plant**) the tropical and subtropical plant commercially grown for this product. [Genus *Gossypium*.] • v. informal **1** (**cotton on**) begin to understand. **2** (**cotton to**) N. Amer. have a liking for.
– DERIVATIVES **cottony** adj.
– ORIGIN ME: from OFr. *coton*, from Arab. *ḳuṭn*.

**cotton bud** • n. Brit. a small wad of cotton wool on a short thin stick, used for cosmetic purposes or cleaning the ears.

**cotton cake** • n. compressed cotton seed, used as food for cattle.

**cotton candy** • n. N. Amer. candyfloss.

**cotton grass** • n. a sedge producing tufts of long white silky hairs which aid in the dispersal of the seeds. [Genus *Eriophorum*.]

**cotton lavender** • n. a small aromatic shrubby plant of the daisy family, with silvery or greenish lavender-like foliage and yellow button flowers. [Genus *Santolina*: several species.]

**cottonmouth** (also **cottonmouth moccasin**) • n. a large, dangerous semiaquatic pit viper of the south-eastern US, which opens its mouth wide to display the white interior when threatening. [*Agkistrodon piscivorus*.]

**cotton-picking** • adj. N. Amer. informal used for emphasis: *just a cotton-picking minute!*

**cotton spinner** • n. a dark sea cucumber of shallow seas which ejects long sticky threads when disturbed. [*Holothuria forskali*.]

**cotton stainer** • n. a North American bug which feeds on cotton bolls, causing reddish staining. [*Dysdercus suturellus* and related species.]

**cotton swab** • n. N. Amer. a cotton bud.

**cottontail** • n. an American rabbit which has a speckled brownish coat and a white underside to the tail. [Genus *Sylvilagus*.]

**cotton waste** • n. scraps of waste cotton yarn used to clean machinery.

**cottonweed** • n. a yellow-flowered aromatic plant of the daisy family, with silvery felted leaves and stems. [*Otanthus maritimus*.]

**cottonwood** • n. **1** a North American poplar with seeds covered in white cottony hairs. [*Populus deltoides* and other species.] **2** a downy-leaved Australasian shrub. [*Pomaderris phylicifolia* (a buckthorn) and *Bedfordia salicina* (daisy family).]

**cotton wool** • n. **1** Brit. fluffy wadding of a kind originally made from raw cotton, used especially for cleaning the skin or bathing wounds. **2** US raw cotton.
– PHRASES **wrap someone in cotton wool** be overprotective towards someone.

**cottony-cushion scale** • n. an Australian scale insect with a large fluted cottony egg sac, infesting citrus trees. [*Icerya purchasi*.]

**cotyledon** /ˌkɒtɪˈliːd(ə)n/ • n. **1** Botany an embryonic leaf in seed-bearing plants, one or more of which are the first leaves to appear from a germinating seed. **2** a succulent plant of the stonecrop family. [Genus *Cotyledon*.]
– DERIVATIVES **cotyledonary** adj.
– ORIGIN C16: from L., 'navelwort', from Gk *kotulēdōn* 'cup-shaped cavity'.

**coucal** /ˈkuːk(ə)l, ˈkʊkɑːl/ • n. a large, ungainly ground-dwelling bird of the cuckoo family. [Genera *Centropus* and *Coua*: numerous species.]
– ORIGIN C19: from Fr., perh. a blend of *coucou* 'cuckoo' and *alouette* 'lark'.

**couch**[1] /kaʊtʃ/ • n. a long upholstered piece of furniture for several people to sit on. ➤a reclining seat with a headrest at one end on which a psychoanalyst's subject or doctor's patient lies while undergoing treatment. • v. **1** (usu. **be couched in**) express in language of a specified style. **2** poetic/literary lie down. **3** archaic lower (a spear) to the position for attack. **4** chiefly historical treat (a cataract) by pushing the lens of the eye downwards and backwards, out of line with the pupil. **5** (in embroidery) fix (a thread) to a fabric by stitching it down flat with another thread.
– ORIGIN ME: from OFr. *couche* (n.), *coucher* (v.), from L. *collocare* (see **COLLOCATION**).

**couch**[2] /kaʊtʃ, kuːtʃ/ (also **couch grass**) • n. a coarse grass with long creeping roots. [*Elymus repens* and other species.]
– ORIGIN C16: var. of **QUITCH**.

**couchant** /ˈkaʊtʃ(ə)nt/ • adj. [usu. postpos.] Heraldry (of an animal) lying with the body resting on the legs and the head raised.
– ORIGIN ME: Fr., 'lying', pres. part. of *coucher* (see **COUCH**[1]).

**couchette** /kuːˈʃɛt/ • n. a railway carriage with seats convertible into sleeping berths. ➤a berth in such a carriage.
– ORIGIN 1920s: Fr., dimin. of *couche* 'a couch'.

**couch potato** • n. informal a person who spends a great deal of time watching television.

**coudé** /kuːˈdeɪ/ • adj. denoting a telescope in which the rays are bent to a focus at a fixed point off the axis.
– ORIGIN C19: Fr., lit. 'bent at right angles'.

**cougar** /ˈkuːɡə/ • n. North American term for **PUMA**.
– ORIGIN C18: from Fr. *couguar*, abbrev. of mod. L. *cuguarcarana*, from Guarani *guaçuarana*.

**cough** • v. **1** expel air from the lungs with a sudden sharp sound. **2** (of an engine) make a sudden harsh noise, especially as a sign of malfunction. **3** (**cough up**) informal give something, especially money, reluctantly. ➤Brit. informal reveal information; confess. • n. an act or sound of coughing. ➤a condition of the respiratory organs causing coughing.
– DERIVATIVES **cougher** n.
– ORIGIN ME: of imitative origin.

**cough drop** (also **cough sweet**) • n. a medicated lozenge sucked to relieve a cough.

**cough mixture** • n. Brit. liquid medicine taken to relieve a cough.

**could** • modal v. past of **CAN**[1]. ➤used in making suggestions or polite requests: *could I use the phone?*

**couldn't** • contr. could not.

**coulee** /ˈkuːli/ • n. N. Amer. a deep ravine.
– ORIGIN C19: from Fr. *coulée* '(lava) flow'.

**coulibiac** /ˌkuːlɪˈbjak/ (also **koulibiac**) • n. a Russian fish or meat pie.
– ORIGIN from Russ. *kulebyaka*.

**coulis** /ˈkuːli/ • n. (pl. same) a thin fruit or vegetable purée, used as a sauce.
– ORIGIN Fr., from *couler* 'to flow'.

**coulisse** /kuːˈliːs/ • n. a flat piece of scenery at the side of the stage in a theatre. ➤(**the coulisses**) the wings.
– ORIGIN C19: Fr., fem. of *coulis* 'sliding'.

**couloir** /ˈkuːlwɑː/ • n. a steep, narrow gully on a mountainside.
– ORIGIN C19: Fr., 'gully, corridor'.

**coulomb** /ˈkuːlɒm/ (abbrev.: **C**) • n. Physics the SI unit of electric charge, equal to the quantity of electricity conveyed in one second by a current of one ampere.
– ORIGIN C19: named after the Fr. military engineer Charles-Augustin de *Coulomb*.

**Coulomb's law** /ˈkuːlɒmz/ • n. Physics a law stating that like electric charges repel and opposite charges attract, with a force proportional to the product of the charges and inversely proportional to the square of the distance between them.

**coulter** /ˈkəʊltə/ (US **colter**) • n. a vertical cutting blade fixed in front of a ploughshare. ➤the part of a seed drill that makes the furrow for the seed.
– ORIGIN OE, from L. *culter* 'knife or ploughshare'.

**coumarin** /ˈkuːmərɪn/ • n. Chemistry a vanilla-scented organic compound found in many plants.
– ORIGIN C19: from Fr. *coumarine*, from *coumarou*, via Port. and Sp. from Tupi *cumarú* 'tonka bean'.

**coumarone** /ˈkuːmərəʊn/ • n. Chemistry an organic compound present in coal tar, used to make thermoplastic resins for paints and varnishes.

– ORIGIN C19: from **COUMARIN** + **-ONE**.

**council** ● **n.** **1** a formally constituted advisory, deliberative, or administrative body. ➤a body elected to manage the affairs of a city, county, or district. **2** [as modifier] Brit. denoting housing provided by a local council.
– ORIGIN OE: from Anglo-Norman Fr. *cuncile*, from L. *concilium* 'convocation, assembly'; cf. **COUNSEL**.

**councillor** (US also **councilor**) ● **n.** a member of a council.
– DERIVATIVES **councillorship** n.

**councilman** (or **councilwoman**) ● **n.** (pl. **-men** or **-women**) chiefly US a councillor.

**council of war** ● **n.** a gathering of military officers in wartime. ➤a meeting held to plan a response to an emergency.

**council tax** ● **n.** a tax levied on households by local authorities in the UK, based on the estimated value of a property.

**counsel** ● **n.** **1** advice, especially that given formally. ➤archaic consultation. **2** (pl. same) a barrister or other legal adviser conducting a case. ● **v.** (**counselled**, **counselling**; US **counseled**, **counseling**) **1** give advice to. ➤recommend (a course of action). **2** [often as noun **counselling**] give professional help and advice to (someone) to resolve personal, social, or psychological problems.
– PHRASES **a counsel of despair** an action to be taken when all else fails. **a counsel of perfection** advice that is ideal but not feasible. **keep one's own counsel** not confide in others. **take counsel** discuss a problem.
– ORIGIN ME: via OFr. *counseil* (n.), *conseiller* (v.), from L. *consilium* 'consultation, advice', rel. to *consulere* (see **CONSULT**); cf. **COUNCIL**.

**counsellor** (US **counselor**) ● **n.** **1** a person trained to give guidance on personal, social, or psychological problems. **2** a senior officer in the diplomatic service. **3** (also **counselor-at-law**) US & Irish a barrister.

**Counsellor of State** ● **n.** (in the UK) a temporary regent during a sovereign's absence.

**count**[1] ● **v.** **1** determine the total number of. **2** recite numbers in ascending order. ➤(**count down**) recite or display numbers backwards to zero to indicate remaining time, especially before the launch of a rocket. **3** (**count someone out**) complete a count of ten seconds over a fallen boxer to indicate defeat. **4** (**count something out**) take out items one by one, keeping a note of how many one takes. **5** (**count something out**) Brit. procure the adjournment of the House of Commons when fewer than forty members are present. **6** take into account; include. ➤(**count someone in** or **out**) include (or not include) someone in a planned activity. **7** regard or be regarded as possessing a quality or fulfilling a role: *people she had counted as her friends.* **8** matter: *it was the critics that counted.* **9** (**count on/upon**) rely on. ● **n.** **1** an act of counting. ➤the total determined by counting. ➤a referee's count of up to ten seconds when a boxer is knocked down. **2** a point for discussion or consideration. ➤Law a separate charge in an indictment. **3** the measure of the fineness of a yarn or woven fabric.
– PHRASES **count one's blessings** be grateful for what one has. **count the cost** calculate the consequences of a careless or foolish action. **count the days** (or **hours**) be impatient for time to pass. **keep** (or **lose**) **count** take note of (or forget) the number or amount when counting. **out** (or N. Amer. also **down**) **for the count** Boxing defeated by being knocked to the ground and unable to rise within ten seconds.
– DERIVATIVES **countable** adj.
– ORIGIN ME (as n.): from OFr. *counte* (n.), *counter* (v.), from L. *computare* (see **COMPUTE**).

**count**[2] ● **n.** a foreign nobleman whose rank corresponds to that of an earl.
– DERIVATIVES **countship** n.
– ORIGIN ME: from OFr. *conte*, from L. *comes*, *comit-* 'companion, overseer, attendant'.

**countback** ● **n.** a method of deciding the winner of a tied game or competition by awarding it to the contestant with the better score in the later part.

**countdown** ● **n.** **1** an act of counting down to zero, especially before the launching of a rocket. **2** the final moments before a significant event. **3** a digital display that counts down.

**countenance** /'kaʊnt(ə)nəns, -tɪn-/ ● **n.** **1** a person's face or facial expression. **2** formal support or approval. ● **v.** admit as acceptable or possible.
– PHRASES **keep one's countenance** maintain one's composure. **keep someone in countenance** help someone to remain calm and confident. **out of countenance** disconcerted or unpleasantly surprised.
– ORIGIN ME: from OFr. *contenance* 'bearing, behaviour', from *contenir* (see **CONTAIN**).

**counter**[1] ● **n.** **1** a long flat-topped fitment across which business is conducted in a shop or food and drinks are served. ➤N. Amer. a worktop. **2** a small disc used in board games for keeping the score or as a place marker. ➤a token representing a coin. **3** a factor used to give one party an advantage in negotiations. **4** a person or thing that counts something. ➤Physics an apparatus used for counting individual ionizing particles or events.
– PHRASES **over the counter** by ordinary retail purchase, with no need for a prescription or licence. ➤(of share transactions) taking place outside the stock exchange system. **under the counter** (or **table**) (with reference to goods bought or sold) surreptitiously and illegally.
– ORIGIN ME (in sense 2): from OFr. *conteor*, from med. L. *computatorium*, from L. *computare* (see **COMPUTE**).

**counter**[2] ● **v.** **1** speak or act in opposition or response to. **2** Boxing give a return blow while parrying. ● **adv.** (**counter to**) in the opposite direction to or in conflict with. ● **adj.** responding to something of the same kind, especially in opposition: *argument and counter argument.* ● **n.** **1** an act or speech which counters something else. **2** Boxing a counterpunch. **3** the curved part of the stern of a ship projecting aft above the waterline. **4** Printing the white space enclosed by a letter such as *O* or *c*.
– ORIGIN ME: from OFr. *contre*, from L. *contra* 'against'.

**counter**[3] ● **n.** the back part of a shoe or boot, enclosing the heel.
– ORIGIN C19: abbrev. of *counterfort* 'buttress', from Fr. *contrefort*.

**counter-** ● **prefix** denoting opposition, retaliation, or rivalry: *counter-attack.* ➤denoting movement or effect in the opposite direction: *counterpoise.* ➤denoting correspondence, duplication, or substitution: *counterpart.*
– ORIGIN from Anglo-Norman Fr. *countre-*, OFr. *contre*, from L. *contra* 'against'.

**counteract** ● **v.** act against (something) in order to reduce its force or neutralize it.
– DERIVATIVES **counteraction** n. **counteractive** adj.

**counter-attack** ● **n.** an attack made in response to one by an enemy or opponent. ● **v.** attack in response.
– DERIVATIVES **counter-attacker** n.

**counter-attraction** ● **n.** a rival attraction.

**counterbalance** ● **n.** /'kaʊntə,bal(ə)ns/ **1** a weight that balances another. **2** a factor having the opposite effect to that of another, preventing it from exercising a disproportionate influence. ● **v.** /,kaʊntə'bal(ə)ns/ be a counterbalance to.

**counterblast** ● **n.** a strongly worded reply to someone else's views.

**counterbore** ● **n.** **1** a drilled hole which has a wider section at the top. **2** a drill whose bit has a uniform smaller diameter near the tip, for drilling counterbores. ● **v.** drill a counterbore in.

**counterchange** ● **v.** poetic/literary chequer with contrasting colours. ➤Heraldry interchange the tinctures of (a charge) with that of a divided field. ● **n.** **1** change that is opposite in effect to a previous change. **2** patterning in which a dark motif on a light ground alternates with the same motif light on a dark ground.

**counterclaim** ● **n.** a claim made to rebut a previous claim. ➤Law a claim made by a defendant against the plaintiff. ● **v.** chiefly Law make a counterclaim.

**counterclockwise** ● **adv.** & **adj.** North American term for **ANTICLOCKWISE**.

**counterculture** ● **n.** a way of life and set of attitudes at variance with the prevailing social norm.

**counter-espionage** • **n.** activities designed to prevent or thwart spying by an enemy.

**counterfactual** Philosophy • **adj.** relating to or expressing what has not happened or is not the case. • **n.** a counterfactual conditional statement (e.g. *If kangaroos had no tails, they would topple over*).

**counterfeit** • **adj.** made in exact imitation of something valuable with the intention to deceive or defraud. ➤ archaic pretended; sham. • **n.** a forgery. • **v.** imitate fraudulently. ➤ poetic/literary resemble closely.
– DERIVATIVES **counterfeiter** n.
– ORIGIN ME (as v.): from Anglo-Norman Fr. *countrefeter*, from OFr. *contrefait*, *contrefaire*, from L. *contra-* 'in opposition' + *facere* 'make'.

**counterfoil** • **n.** chiefly Brit. the part of a cheque, ticket, etc. that is kept as a record by the person issuing it.

**counter-insurgency** • **n.** military or political action taken against guerrillas or revolutionaries.

**counter-intelligence** • **n.** counter-espionage.

**counter-intuitive** • **adj.** contrary to intuition or to common-sense expectation.
– DERIVATIVES **counter-intuitively** adv.

**countermand** /ˌkaʊntəˈmɑːnd/ • **v.** revoke (an order). ➤ declare (voting) invalid.
– ORIGIN ME: from OFr. *contremander* (v.), *contremand* (n.), from med. L. *contramandare*, from L. *contra-* 'against' + *mandare* 'to order'.

**countermeasure** • **n.** an action taken to counteract a danger or threat.

**counterpane** • **n.** dated a bedspread.
– ORIGIN C17: alt. of COUNTERPOINT, based on med. L. *culcitra puncta* 'quilted mattress'.

**counterpart** • **n.** **1** a person or thing that corresponds to or has the same function as another. **2** Law each of two copies of a legal document.

**counterpoint** • **n.** **1** Music the technique of setting, writing, or playing a melody or melodies in conjunction with another, according to fixed rules. ➤ a melody played in conjunction with another. **2** an idea or theme contrasting with the main element. • **v.** **1** Music add counterpoint to (a melody). **2** emphasize by contrast. **3** compensate for.
– ORIGIN ME: from OFr. *contrepoint*, from med. L. *contrapunctum* in sense '(song) marked over against (the original melody)'.

**counterpoise** • **n.** a factor or force that balances or neutralizes another. ➤ archaic a state of equilibrium. ➤ a counterbalancing weight. • **v.** have an opposing and balancing effect on. ➤ bring into contrast.
– ORIGIN ME: from OFr. *contrepois* from *contre* 'against' + *pois* from L. *pensum* 'weight'; cf. POISE[1].

**counterpose** • **v.** set against or in opposition to.
– DERIVATIVES **counterposition** n.

**counterproductive** • **adj.** having the opposite of the desired effect.

**counterpunch** Boxing • **n.** a punch thrown in return for one received. • **v.** throw a counterpunch.
– DERIVATIVES **counterpuncher** n.

**Counter-Reformation** • **n.** the reform of the Church of Rome in the 16th and 17th centuries which was stimulated by the Protestant Reformation.

**counter-revolution** • **n.** a revolution opposing a former one or reversing its results.
– DERIVATIVES **counter-revolutionary** adj. & n.

**counterrotate** • **v.** rotate in opposite directions, especially about the same axis.
– DERIVATIVES **counterrotation** n.

**counterscarp** • **n.** the outer wall of a ditch in a fortification.

**countershading** • **n.** Zoology protective coloration used by some animals in which parts normally in shadow are light and those exposed to the sky are dark.
– DERIVATIVES **countershaded** adj.

**countershaft** • **n.** a machine driveshaft that transmits motion from the main shaft to where it is required.

**countersign** • **v.** add a signature to (a document already signed by another person). • **n.** archaic a signal or password given in reply to a soldier on guard.
– DERIVATIVES **countersignature** n.

**countersink** • **v.** (past and past part. **-sunk**) enlarge and bevel the rim of (a drilled hole) so that a screw or bolt can be inserted flush with the surface. ➤ drive (a screw or bolt) into such a hole.

**countertenor** • **n.** Music the highest male adult singing voice.

**countertop** • **n.** N. Amer. a worktop.

**countertrade** • **n.** international trade by exchange of goods rather than by currency purchase.

**counter-transference** • **n.** Psychoanalysis the emotional reaction of the analyst to the subject's contribution.

**countervail** /ˌkaʊntəˈveɪl/ • **v.** [usu. as adj. **countervailing**] offset the effect of (something) by countering it with something of equal force.
– ORIGIN ME: from Anglo-Norman Fr. *contrevaloir*, from L. *contra valere* 'be of worth against'.

**countervailing duty** • **n.** an import tax imposed on certain goods in order to prevent dumping or counter export subsidies.

**countervalue** • **n.** Brit. an equivalent or equal, especially in military strategy.

**counterweight** • **n.** a counterbalancing weight.

**countess** • **n.** the wife or widow of a count or earl. ➤ a woman holding the rank of count or earl.

**countian** • **n.** US an inhabitant of a specified county.

**counting** • **prep.** taking account of; including: *there were three of us, or four counting the baby.*

**counting house** • **n.** historical a place where the accounts and money of a person or company were kept.

**countless** • **adj.** too many to be counted; very many.

**count noun** • **n.** Grammar a noun that can form a plural and, in the singular, can be used with the indefinite article (e.g. *books*, *a book*). Contrasted with MASS NOUN.

**Count Palatine** • **n.** historical a feudal lord having royal authority within a region of a kingdom. ➤ a high official of the Holy Roman Empire with royal authority within his domain.

**countrified** (also **countryfied**) • **adj.** characteristic of the country, especially in being unsophisticated.

**country** • **n.** (pl. **-ies**) **1** a nation with its own government, occupying a particular territory. **2** districts outside large urban areas. **3** an area or region with regard to its physical features: *a tract of wild country.*
– PHRASES **across country** not keeping to roads. **go to the country** Brit. dissolve Parliament and hold a general election. **line of country** Brit. a subject in which a person is skilled or knowledgeable.
– ORIGIN ME: from OFr. *cuntree*, from med. L. *contrata* (*terra*) '(land) lying opposite', from L. *contra* 'against, opposite'.

**country and western** • **n.** country music.

**country club** • **n.** a club with sporting and social facilities, set in a rural area.

**country cousin** • **n.** an unsophisticated and provincial person.

**country dance** • **n.** a traditional type of social English dance, in particular one performed by couples facing each other in long lines.

**countryfied** • **adj.** variant spelling of COUNTRIFIED.

**country house** • **n.** a large house in the country, typically the seat of a wealthy or aristocratic family.

**countryman** (or **countrywoman**) • **n.** (pl. **-men** or **-women**) **1** a person living or born in the country. **2** a person from the same country as someone else: *my fellow countryman.*

**country mile** • **n.** informal a very long way.

**country music** • **n.** a form of popular music originating in the rural southern US, characteristically featuring guitar and pedal steel guitar.

**country rock**[1] • **n.** Geology the rock which encloses a mineral deposit, igneous intrusion, or other feature.

**country rock**[2] • **n.** a type of popular music that is a blend of rock and country music.

**countryside** • **n.** the land and scenery of a rural area.

**countrywide** • **adj.** & **adv.** extending throughout a nation.

**county** ● n. (pl. **-ies**) **1** a territorial division of some countries, forming the chief unit of local administration. ➤US a political and administrative division of a state. **2** [as modifier] Brit. of or denoting aristocratic people with an ancestral home in a particular county.
– ORIGIN ME: from OFr. *conte*, from L. *comitatus*, from *comes*, *comit-* (see **COUNT**[2]).

**county borough** ● n. (in England, Wales, and Northern Ireland) a large town formerly having the administrative status of a county.

**county commissioner** ● n. Brit. a justice of the peace on the commission of the peace of a county.

**county corporate** ● n. Brit. historical a city or town ranking as an administrative county.

**county council** ● n. (in the UK) the elected governing body of an administrative county.
– DERIVATIVES **county councillor** n.

**county court** ● n. (in England and Wales) a judicial court for civil cases. ➤US a court for civil and criminal cases.

**County Palatine** ● n. historical (in England and Ireland) a county in which royal privileges and exclusive rights of jurisdiction were held by its earl or lord.

**county town** (N. Amer. **county seat**) ● n. the town that is the administrative capital of a county.

**coup** /kuː/ ● n. (pl. **coups** /kuːz/) **1** (also **coup d'état**) a sudden violent seizure of power from a government. **2** an unexpected and notably successful act. **3** Billiards a direct pocketing of the cue ball, which is a foul stroke. **4** historical (among North American Indians) an act of touching an enemy, as a deed of bravery.
– ORIGIN C18: from Fr., from med. L. *colpus* (see **COPE**[1]).

**coup de foudre** /ˌkuː də ˈfuːdr(ə), French ku də fudʀ/ ● n. (pl. **coups de foudre** pronunc. same) a sudden unforeseen event, especially love at first sight.
– ORIGIN Fr., lit. 'stroke of lightning'.

**coup de grâce** /ˌkuː də ˈgrɑːs, French ku də gʀas/ ● n. (pl. **coups de grâce** pronunc. same) a final blow or shot given to kill a wounded person or animal.
– ORIGIN Fr., lit. 'stroke of grace'.

**coup de main** /ˌkuː də ˈmã, French ku də mɛ̃/ ● n. (pl. **coups de main** pronunc. same) a sudden surprise attack.
– ORIGIN Fr., lit. 'stroke of hand'.

**coup de maître** /ˌkuː də ˈmɛːtr(ə), French ku də mɛtʀ/ ● n. (pl. **coups de maître** pronunc. same) a master stroke.
– ORIGIN from Fr.

**coup d'état** /ˌkuː deɪˈtɑː, French ku deta/ ● n. (pl. **coups d'état** pronunc. same) see **COUP** (sense 1).
– ORIGIN Fr., lit. 'blow of state'.

**coup de théâtre** /ˌkuː də teɪˈɑːtr(ə), French ku də teɑtʀ/ ● n. (pl. **coups de théâtre** pronunc. same) **1** a dramatically sudden action or turn of events, especially in a play. **2** a successful theatrical production.
– ORIGIN Fr., lit. 'blow of theatre'.

**coup d'œil** /kuː ˈdəːɪ, French ku dœj/ ● n. (pl. **coups d'œil** pronunc. same) a comprehensive glance.
– ORIGIN Fr., lit. 'stroke of eye'.

**coupe** /kuːp/ ● n. **1** a shallow glass or glass dish, typically with a stem, in which desserts or champagne are served. **2** a dessert served in such a dish.
– ORIGIN Fr., 'goblet'.

**coupé** /ˈkuːpeɪ/ (also **coupe** /kuːp/) ● n. **1** a car with a fixed roof, two doors, and a sloping rear. **2** historical a four-wheeled enclosed carriage for two passengers and a driver.
– ORIGIN C19: from Fr. *carrosse coupé*, lit. 'cut carriage'.

**couped** /kuːpt/ ● adj. Heraldry cut off or truncated in a straight line.
– ORIGIN C16: from Fr. *couper* 'to cut' + **-ED**[2].

**couple** ● n. **1** two individuals of the same sort considered together. **2** informal an indefinite small number. **3** [treated as sing. or pl.] two people who are married or otherwise closely associated romantically or sexually. **4** Mechanics a pair of equal and parallel forces acting in opposite directions, and tending to cause rotation about an axis perpendicular to the plane containing them. ● v. **1** join to form a pair. ➤(often **be coupled to/with**) combine. ➤connect (a railway vehicle or a piece of equipment) to another. **2** have sexual intercourse.
– DERIVATIVES **coupledom** n.
– ORIGIN ME: from OFr. *cople* (n.), *copler* (v.), from L. *copula* (n.), *copulare* (v.), from *co-* 'together' + *apere* 'fasten'; cf. **COPULA** and **COPULATE**.

**coupler** ● n. **1** something that connects or couples two things. **2** Photography a compound in a developer or an emulsion which combines with the products of development to form an insoluble dye, part of the image. **3** (also **acoustic coupler**) a modem which interconverts digital signals from a computer and audible sound signals for transmission over telephone lines.

**couplet** ● n. a pair of successive lines of verse, typically rhyming and of the same length.
– ORIGIN C16: from Fr., dimin. of *couple*, from OFr. *cople* (see **COUPLE**).

**coupling** ● n. a device for coupling railway vehicles or parts of machinery together.

**coupling constant** ● n. Physics a constant representing the strength of the interaction between a particle and a field.

**coupling rod** ● n. a rod which couples the driving wheels of a locomotive, enabling them to act as a unit.

**coupon** ● n. **1** a voucher entitling the holder to a discount on a product or a quantity of something rationed. **2** a detachable portion of a bond which is given up in return for a payment of interest. ➤the nominal rate of interest on a fixed-interest security. **3** a detachable form used to send for a purchase or information or to enter a competition. **4** Scottish & Irish a person's face.
– ORIGIN C19: from Fr., lit. 'piece cut off', from *couper* 'cut'.

**coupon-clipper** ● n. N. Amer. informal a person with a large number of interest-bearing bonds.

**courage** ● n. the ability to do something that frightens one. ➤strength in the face of pain or grief.
– PHRASES **have the courage of one's convictions** act on one's beliefs despite danger or disapproval. **take courage** make an effort to do something that frightens one. **take one's courage in both hands** nerve oneself to do something that frightens one.
– ORIGIN ME: from OFr. *corage*, from L. *cor* 'heart'.

**courageous** ● adj. having courage; brave.
– DERIVATIVES **courageously** adv. **courageousness** n.

**courant** /kʊˈrant/ ● adj. Heraldry represented as running.
– ORIGIN C17: Fr., 'running', pres. part. of *courir*.

**courante** /kʊˈrɒt, -ˈrɑːnt/ ● n. a rapid gliding dance in quick triple time.
– ORIGIN C16: Fr., lit. 'running', fem. pres. part. of *courir*.

**courbette** /kʊəˈbɛt/ ● n. (in classical riding) a movement in which the horse performs a series of jumps on the hind legs without the forelegs touching the ground.
– ORIGIN C17: Fr., from Ital. *corvetta* 'little curve' based on L. *curvus* 'curved'.

**courgette** /kʊəˈʒɛt/ ● n. Brit. a variety of marrow harvested and eaten at an early stage of growth.
– ORIGIN 1930s: from Fr., dimin. of *courge* 'gourd', from L. *cucurbita*.

**courier** /ˈkʊrɪə/ ● n. **1** a messenger who transports goods or documents. **2** a person employed to guide and assist a group of tourists. ● v. send or transport by courier.
– ORIGIN ME: orig. from OFr. *coreor*; later from Fr. *courier* (now *courrier*), from Ital. *corriere*; based on L. *currere* 'to run'.

**course** ● n. **1** the route or direction followed by a ship, aircraft, road, or river. **2** the way in which something progresses or develops. ➤a procedure adopted to deal with a situation. **3** a dish forming one of the successive parts of a meal. **4** a series of lectures or lessons in a particular subject. ➤Medicine a series of repeated treatments or doses of medication. **5** an area of land prepared for racing, golf, or another sport. **6** Architecture a continuous horizontal layer of brick or stone. **7** Bell-ringing a series of changes which brings the bells back to their original order, or the changes of a particular bell. **8** a sail on the lowest yards of a square-rigged ship. ● v. **1** (of liquid)

flow. **2** [often as noun **coursing**] pursue (game, especially hares) with greyhounds using sight rather than scent.
– PHRASES **the course of nature** normal and expected events or processes. **in (the) course of 1** undergoing (the specified process). **2** during (the specified period). **of course** as expected. ➤used to give or emphasize agreement or permission. ➤admittedly. **on** (or **off**) **course** following (or not following) the intended route. **run** (or **take**) **its course** complete its natural development without interference.
– ORIGIN ME: from OFr. *cours*, from L. *cursus*, from *curs-*, *currere* 'run'.

**coursebook** ● n. Brit. a textbook designed for use on a particular course of study.

**courser**[1] ● n. poetic/literary a swift horse.
– ORIGIN ME: from OFr. *corsier*, based on L. *cursus* (see **COURSE**).

**courser**[2] ● n. a fast-running plover-like bird found in open country in Africa and Asia. [*Cursorius cursor* (**cream-coloured courser**) and other species.]
– ORIGIN C18: from mod. L. *Cursorius* 'adapted for running', from L. *cursor* 'runner'.

**courser**[3] ● n. a person who goes coursing with greyhounds.

**courseware** ● n. computer programs or other material designed for use in an educational or training course.

**coursework** ● n. work done during a course of study, typically counting towards a final mark.

**court** ● n. **1** (also **court of law**) a body of people before whom judicial cases are heard. ➤the place where they meet. **2** a quadrangular area marked out for ball games such as tennis. ➤a quadrangle surrounded by a building or group of buildings. **3** the establishment, retinue, and courtiers of a sovereign. **4** the qualified members of a company or a corporation. ● v. **1** dated be involved with romantically, typically with the intention of marrying. ➤(of a male bird or other animal) try to attract (a mate). **2** attempt to win the support or favour of. ➤go to great lengths to win (favourable attention). **3** risk incurring (misfortune) because of the way one behaves.
– PHRASES **out of court** before a legal hearing can take place. **pay court to** pay flattering attention to.
– ORIGIN ME: from OFr. *cort*, from L. *cohors*, *cohort-* 'yard or retinue'; the verb is influenced by Old Ital. *corteare*, OFr. *courtoyer*.

**court bouillon** /kɔːt ˈbuːjɒn/ ● n. a stock made from wine and vegetables, typically used in fish dishes.
– ORIGIN Fr., from *court* 'short' and **BOUILLON**.

**court card** ● n. Brit. a playing card that is a king, queen, or jack of a suit.
– ORIGIN C17: alt. of C16 *coat card*, from the decorative dress of the figures depicted.

**court circular** ● n. Brit. a daily report of the activities and public engagements of royal family members.

**court cupboard** ● n. a 16th- or 17th-century sideboard for displaying plate and other ornaments, usually having three open shelves.

**courteous** /ˈkəːtjəs/ ● adj. polite, respectful, and considerate.
– DERIVATIVES **courteously** adv. **courteousness** n..
– ORIGIN ME (meaning 'having manners fit for a royal court'): from OFr. *corteis*, based on L. *cohors* (see **COURT**).

**courtesan** /ˌkɔːtɪˈzan, ˈkɔːtɪ-/ ● n. a prostitute, especially one with wealthy or upper-class clients.
– ORIGIN C16: from Fr. *courtisane*, from obs. Ital. *cortigiana*, fem. of *cortigiano* 'courtier'.

**courtesy** /ˈkəːtɪsi/ ● n. (pl. **-ies**) **1** courteous behaviour. ➤a polite speech or action, especially one required by convention. **2** archaic a curtsy.
– PHRASES **(by) courtesy of** given or allowed by.

**courtesy light** ● n. a small light in a car that is automatically switched on when one of the doors is opened.

**courtesy title** ● n. a title given to someone, especially the son or daughter of a peer, that has no legal validity.

**courthouse** ● n. **1** a building in which a judicial court is held. **2** US a building containing the administrative offices of a county.

**courtier** /ˈkɔːtɪə/ ● n. a companion or adviser to a king or queen.
– ORIGIN ME: via Anglo-Norman Fr. from OFr. *cortoyer* 'be present at court', from *cort* (see **COURT**).

**courtly** ● adj. (**-ier**, **-iest**) very polite and refined.
– DERIVATIVES **courtliness** n.

**courtly love** ● n. a highly conventionalized medieval tradition of love between a knight and a married noblewoman.

**court martial** ● n. (pl. **courts martial** or **court martials**) a judicial court for trying members of the armed services accused of offences against military law. ● v. (**court-martial**) (**-martialled**, **-martialling**; US **-martialed**, **-martialing**) try by court martial.

**Court of Appeal** ● n. (in England and Wales) a court of law that hears appeals against judgements from the Crown Courts, High Court, and County Courts. ➤(**court of appeals**) US a court of law in a federal circuit or state to which appeals are taken.

**Court of Claims** ● n. US a federal court in which claims against the government are adjudicated.

**court of first instance** ● n. a court in which legal proceedings are begun or first heard.

**court of record** ● n. a court whose proceedings are recorded and available as evidence of fact.

**court of review** ● n. a court before which sentences previously imposed come for revision.

**Court of St James's** ● n. the British sovereign's court.

**Court of Session** ● n. the supreme civil court in Scotland.

**court of summary jurisdiction** ● n. Brit. a court, especially a magistrate's court, that tries summary offences without a jury.

**court order** ● n. a direction issued by a court or a judge requiring a person to do or not do something.

**court plaster** ● n. historical adhesive sticking plaster made of silk or other cloth.
– ORIGIN C18: so named because it was formerly used by ladies at court for beauty spots.

**court roll** ● n. Brit. historical the record kept by a manorial court of rent paid and property held by tenants.

**courtroom** ● n. the room or building in which a court of law meets.

**courtship** ● n. **1** a period of courting, especially with a view to marriage. ➤the courting behaviour of male birds and other animals. **2** the process of courting favour or support.

**court shoe** ● n. Brit. a woman's plain, lightweight shoe that has a low-cut upper and no fastening.

**court tennis** ● n. N. Amer. real tennis.

**courtyard** ● n. an open area enclosed by walls or buildings, especially in a castle or large house.

**couscous** /ˈkʊskʊs, ˈkuːskuːs/ ● n. a North African dish of steamed or soaked semolina, usually served with spicy meat or vegetables.
– ORIGIN C17: from Fr., from Arab. *kuskus*, from *kaskasa* 'to pound', prob. of Berber origin.

**cousin** ● n. **1** (also **first cousin**) a child of one's uncle or aunt. **2** a person of a kindred people or nation. **3** historical a title formerly used by a sovereign in addressing another sovereign or a noble of their own country.
– PHRASES **first cousin once removed 1** a child of one's first cousin. **2** one's parent's first cousin. **first cousin twice removed 1** a grandchild of one's first cousin. **2** one's grandparent's first cousin. **second cousin** a child of one's parent's first cousin. **second cousin once removed 1** a child of one's second cousin. **2** one's parent's second cousin. **third cousin** a child of one's parent's second cousin.
– DERIVATIVES **cousinhood** n. **cousinly** adj. **cousinship** n.
– ORIGIN ME: from OFr. *cosin*, from L. *consobrinus* 'mother's sister's child', from *con-* 'with' + *sobrinus* 'second cousin' (from *soror* 'sister').

**cousin-german** ● n. (pl. **cousins-german**) old-fashioned term for **COUSIN**.

– ORIGIN ME: from Fr. *cousin germain* (see **GERMAN**).

**couth** /kuːθ/ ● **adj.** humorous refined and well mannered.
– ORIGIN C19: back-form. from **UNCOUTH**.

**couthy** /ˈkuːθi/ (also **couthie**) ● **adj.** Scottish (of a person) warm and friendly. ➤(of a place) cosy and comfortable.
– ORIGIN C18: appar. from OE *cūth* 'known' + **-Y**[1] (also **-IE**).

**couture** /kuːˈtjʊə/ ● **n.** the design and manufacture of fashionable clothes to a client's specific requirements. ➤clothes of this type.
– ORIGIN 1920s: Fr., 'sewing, dressmaking'.

**couturier** /kuːˈtjʊərɪeɪ/ ● **n.** (fem. **couturière** /kuːˈtjʊərɪɛː/) a person who makes and sells couture clothes.

**couvade** /kuːˈvɑːd/ ● **n.** the custom in some cultures in which a man takes to his bed and goes through certain rituals when his child is being born.
– ORIGIN C19: Fr., from *couver* 'to hatch', from L. *cubare* 'lie down'.

**couvert** /kuːˈvɛː/ ● **n.** another term for **COVER** (in sense 7).
– ORIGIN C18: Fr., past part. of *couvrir* 'to cover'.

**couverture** /ˈkuːvətjʊə/ ● **n.** chocolate with extra cocoa butter to give a high gloss, used to cover sweets and cakes.
– ORIGIN 1930s: Fr., lit. 'covering', from *couvrir* 'to cover'.

**covalent** /kəʊˈveɪl(ə)nt/ ● **adj.** Chemistry relating to or denoting chemical bonds formed by the sharing of electrons between atoms. Often contrasted with **IONIC**.
– DERIVATIVES **covalence** n. **covalency** n. **covalently** adv.

**covariance** /kəʊˈvɛːrɪəns/ ● **n. 1** Mathematics the property of a function of retaining its form when the variables are linearly transformed. **2** Statistics the mean value of the product of the deviations of two variates from their respective means.

**covariant** ● **adj.** Mathematics changing in such a way that mathematical interrelations with another simultaneously changing quantity remains unchanged.

**covariation** ● **n.** Mathematics correlated variation.

**cove**[1] ● **n. 1** a small sheltered bay. **2** Architecture a concave arch or arched moulding, especially one formed at the junction of a wall with a ceiling. ● **v.** [usu. as adj. **coved**] Architecture fit with a cove.
– DERIVATIVES **coving** n.
– ORIGIN OE *cofa* 'chamber, cave', of Gmc origin.

**cove**[2] ● **n.** Brit. informal, dated a man.
– ORIGIN C16: perh. from Romany *kova* 'thing or person'.

**covelline** /kəʊˈvɛlʌɪn/ ● **n.** another term for **COVELLITE**.

**covellite** /kəʊˈvɛlʌɪt/ ● **n.** a blue mineral consisting of copper sulphide.
– ORIGIN C19: named after the Ital. chemist Nicolò *Covelli*.

**coven** /ˈkʌv(ə)n/ ● **n.** a group of witches who meet regularly.
– ORIGIN C17: var. of **COVIN**.

**covenant** /ˈkʌv(ə)nənt/ ● **n. 1** a solemn agreement. ➤Theology an agreement held to be the basis of a relationship of commitment with God. **2** a contract by which one undertakes to make regular payments to a charity. ● **v.** agree or pay by covenant.
– DERIVATIVES **covenantal** adj. **covenantor** n.
– ORIGIN ME: from OFr., pres. part. of *covenir* 'agree', from L. *convenire* (see **CONVENE**).

**Covenanter** /ˈkʌv(ə)nəntə/ ● **n.** an adherent of the National Covenant or of the Solemn League and Covenant in 17th-century Scotland, in support of Presbyterianism.

**cover** ● **v. 1** put something on top of or in front of (something) in order to protect or conceal it. **2** extend over (an area). **3** deal with (a subject). ➤(of a rule or law) apply to. **4** travel (a specified distance). **5** (of money) be enough to pay (a cost). ➤(of insurance) protect against a liability, loss, or accident. ➤(**cover oneself**) take precautions against future blame or liability. **6** (**cover up**) try to hide or deny the fact of (a wrongful action). ➤(**cover for**) temporarily take over the job or role of. **7** aim a gun at. ➤protect (an exposed person) by shooting at the enemy. ➤(in team games) take up a position ready to defend against (an opponent). ➤Baseball be in position at (a base) ready to catch the ball. **8** Bridge play a higher card on (a high card). **9** record or perform a cover version of (a song). **10** (of a male animal, especially a stallion) copulate with (a female animal). ● **n. 1** something that covers or protects. ➤a thick protective outer part or page of a book or magazine. ➤(**the covers**) bedclothes. **2** physical shelter: *they ran for cover.* ➤vegetation used as a shelter by hunted animals. **3** military support for someone in danger. **4** a means of concealing an illegal or secret activity. ➤an identity adopted by a spy to conceal their true activities. **5** Ecology the amount of ground covered by a vertical projection of the vegetation. **6** Brit. protection by insurance. **7** a place setting at a table in a restaurant. **8** Cricket short for **COVER POINT**. ➤(**the covers**) an area of the field consisting of cover point and extra cover. **9** (also **cover version**) a recording or performance of a song previously recorded by a different artist.
– PHRASES **break cover** suddenly leave a place of shelter when being hunted or pursued. **cover one's back** informal take steps to avoid attack or criticism. **cover one's tracks** conceal evidence of one's actions. **cover the waterfront** N. Amer. informal cover every aspect of something. **from cover to cover** from beginning to end of a book or magazine. **take cover** take shelter from an attack. **under cover** under a roof or other shelter. **under cover of** concealed by. ➤while pretending to do something. **under separate cover** in a separate envelope.
– DERIVATIVES **coverable** adj. **covering** n.
– ORIGIN ME: from OFr. *covrir*, from L. *cooperire*, from *co-* + *operire* 'to cover'; sense 7 of the noun from Fr. *couvert*.

**coverage** ● **n.** the extent to which something is covered.

**coverall** ● **n.** (also **coveralls**) a full-length protective outer garment.

**cover charge** ● **n.** a fee paid for admission to a restaurant, bar, or club.

**cover crop** ● **n.** a crop grown to protect and enrich the soil.

**covering letter** (N. Amer. **cover letter**) ● **n.** a letter explaining the contents of an accompanying enclosure.

**coverlet** ● **n.** a bedspread.
– ORIGIN ME: from Anglo-Norman Fr. *covrelet*, from OFr. *covrir* 'to cover' + *lit* 'bed'.

**cover note** ● **n.** Brit. a temporary certificate showing that a person has a current insurance policy.

**cover point** ● **n.** Cricket a fielding position a little in front of the batsman on the off side and halfway to the boundary.

**coverslip** ● **n.** a thin piece of glass used to cover and protect a specimen on a microscope slide.

**covert** ● **adj.** /ˈkʌvət, ˈkəʊvəːt/ not openly acknowledged or displayed. ● **n.** /ˈkʌvət, ˈkʌvə/ **1** a thicket in which game can hide. **2** Ornithology a feather covering the base of a main flight or tail feather of a bird.
– DERIVATIVES **covertly** adv. **covertness** n.
– ORIGIN ME: from OFr., 'covered', past part. of *covrir* (see **COVER**).

**covert coat** ● **n.** Brit. a short, light overcoat worn for shooting or other outdoor sports.

**coverture** /ˈkʌvətjʊə/ ● **n.** poetic/literary protective or concealing covering.
– ORIGIN ME: from OFr., from *covrir* 'to cover'.

**cover-up** ● **n.** an attempt to conceal the truth about a mistake or crime.

**covet** /ˈkʌvɪt/ ● **v.** (**coveted**, **coveting**) yearn to possess (something belonging to someone else).
– DERIVATIVES **covetable** adj. **covetous** adj. **covetously** adv. **covetousness** n.
– ORIGIN ME: from OFr. *cuveitier*, based on L. *cupiditas* (see **CUPIDITY**).

**covey** /ˈkʌvi/ ● **n.** (pl. **-eys**) a small flock of birds, especially partridge.
– ORIGIN ME: from OFr. *covee*, fem. past part. of *cover*, from L. *cubare* 'lie down'.

**covin** /ˈkʌvɪn/ ● **n.** archaic fraud; deception.
– ORIGIN ME (denoting a company or band): from OFr.,

from med. L. *convenium*, from L. *convenire* (see **CONVENE**).

**cow**[1] ● **n. 1** a fully grown female animal of a domesticated breed of ox. ➤(in farming) an animal of this type which has borne more than one calf. Compare with **HEIFER**. ➤the female of certain other large animals, e.g. elephant, rhinoceros, or whale. **2** informal, derogatory a woman. ➤Austral./NZ an unpleasant person or thing.
– PHRASES **have a cow** N. Amer. informal become angry or excited. **till the cows come home** informal for an indefinitely long time.
– ORIGIN OE *cū*, of Gmc origin.

**cow**[2] ● **v.** (usu. **be cowed**) cause (someone) to submit to one's wishes by intimidation.
– ORIGIN C16: prob. from ON *kúga* 'oppress'.

**coward** ● **n.** a person contemptibly lacking in courage.
– DERIVATIVES **cowardice** n. **cowardliness** n. **cowardly** adj.
– ORIGIN ME: from OFr. *couard*, based on L. *cauda* 'tail', perh. with ref. to an animal with its tail between its legs.

**cowbane** ● **n.** a tall poisonous plant of the parsley family, growing in wet habitats. [*Cicuta virosa* and related species.]

**cowbell** ● **n.** a bell hung round a cow's neck.

**cowberry** ● **n.** (pl. **-ies**) a low-growing evergreen northern shrub, bearing dark red berries. [*Vaccinium vitis-idaea*.] ➤the berry of this plant.

**cowbird** ● **n.** an American songbird with dark plumage, most kinds of which lay their eggs in other birds' nests. [*Molothrus ater* (**brown-headed cowbird**) and related species.]

**cowboy** ● **n. 1** a man on horseback who herds cattle, especially in the western US. **2** informal an unscrupulous or unqualified tradesman.

**cowcatcher** ● **n.** a metal frame at the front of a locomotive for pushing aside obstacles on the line.

**cower** ● **v.** crouch down in fear.
– ORIGIN ME: from Mid. Low Ger. *kūren* 'lie in wait'.

**cowfish** ● **n.** (pl. same or **-fishes**) a boxfish with horn-like spines on its head. [*Lactoria diaphana* and other species.]

**cowherd** ● **n.** a person who tends grazing cattle.
– ORIGIN OE, from **cow**[1] + obs. *herd* 'herdsman'.

**cowhide** ● **n.** leather made from the hide of a cow.

**cowl** ● **n. 1** a large loose hood forming part of a monk's habit. **2** a hood-shaped covering for a chimney or ventilation shaft. ➤another term for **COWLING**.
– DERIVATIVES **cowled** adj.
– ORIGIN OE *cugele*, *cūle*, from eccles. L. *cucullа*, from L. *cucullus*.

**cowlick** ● **n.** a lock of hair hanging over the forehead.

**cowling** ● **n.** a removable cover for a vehicle or aircraft engine.

**cowl neck** ● **n.** a neckline on a woman's garment that hangs in draped folds.

**cow parsley** ● **n.** a hedgerow plant of the parsley family with fern-like leaves and large, lacy heads of tiny white flowers. [*Anthriscus sylvestris*.]

**cow parsnip** ● **n.** another term for **HOGWEED**.

**cowpat** ● **n.** a flat, round piece of cow dung.

**cowpea** ● **n.** a tropical leguminous plant cultivated for its edible pods and seeds. [*Vigna unguiculata*.] ➤the seed of this plant as food.

**Cowper's gland** ● **n.** Anatomy either of a pair of small glands at the base of the penis which secrete a constituent of seminal fluid.
– ORIGIN C18: named after the Engl. anatomist William *Cowper*.

**cowpoke** ● **n.** N. Amer. informal a cowboy.

**cowpox** ● **n.** a viral disease of cows' udders which can be contracted by humans and resembles mild smallpox.

**cowpuncher** ● **n.** N. Amer. informal a cowboy.

**cowrie** /'kaʊ(ə)ri/ (also **cowry**) ● **n.** (pl. **-ies**) a marine gastropod mollusc with a smooth, domed shell with a long, narrow opening. [Genus *Cypraea*: numerous species.]
– ORIGIN C17: from Hindi *kauṛī*.

**co-write** ● **v.** write together with another person.
– DERIVATIVES **co-writer** n.

**cowshed** ● **n.** a farm building in which cattle are kept when not at pasture, or in which they are milked.

**cowslip** ● **n.** a wild primula with clusters of drooping fragrant yellow flowers in spring. [*Primula veris*.] ➤North American term for **MARSH MARIGOLD**.
– ORIGIN OE *cūslyppe*, from *cū* 'cow' + *slipa*, *slyppe* 'slime'.

**cow wheat** ● **n.** a partly parasitic plant with yellowish flowers. [*Melampyrum pratense* and related species.]

**Cox** (in full **Cox's orange pippin**) ● **n.** an English eating apple of a variety with a red-tinged green skin.
– ORIGIN C19: named after the Engl. fruit grower R. *Cox*.

**cox** ● **n.** a coxswain. ● **v.** act as a coxswain for.
– DERIVATIVES **coxless** adj.

**coxa** /'kɒksə/ ● **n.** (pl. **coxae** /-siː/) Anatomy the hip bone or hip joint. ➤Entomology the first or basal segment of the leg of an insect.
– DERIVATIVES **coxal** adj.
– ORIGIN C17: from L., 'hip'.

**coxcomb** /'kɒkskəʊm/ ● **n. 1** archaic a vain and conceited man; a dandy. **2** variant spelling of **COCKSCOMB**.
– DERIVATIVES **coxcombry** /-kəmri/ n.
– ORIGIN C16: var. of **COCKSCOMB**.

**Coxsackie virus** /kɒk'saki, kʊk-/ ● **n.** Medicine an enterovirus of a group causing various respiratory, neurological, and muscular diseases.
– ORIGIN 1940s: named after *Coxsackie*, New York State, where the first cases were diagnosed.

**coxswain** /'kɒks(ə)n/ ● **n.** the steersman of a boat. ➤the senior petty officer in a small ship or submarine in the Royal Navy.
– DERIVATIVES **coxswainship** n.
– ORIGIN ME: from obs. *cock* (see **COCKBOAT**) + **SWAIN**.

**Coy** ● **abbrev.** chiefly Military Company.

**coy** ● **adj.** (**coyer**, **coyest**) pretending shyness or modesty. ➤reluctant to give details about something sensitive.
– DERIVATIVES **coyly** adv. **coyness** n.
– ORIGIN ME (in the sense 'quiet, still'): from OFr. *coi*, *quei*, from L. *quietus* (see **QUIET**).

**coyote** /'kɔɪəʊt, kɔɪ'əʊti/ ● **n.** (pl. same or **coyotes**) a wolf-like wild dog native to North America. [*Canis latrans*.]
– ORIGIN C18: from Mex. Sp., from Nahuatl *coyotl*.

**coypu** /'kɔɪpuː/ ● **n.** (pl. **coypus**) a large semiaquatic beaver-like South American rodent, farmed for its fur (nutria). [*Myocastor coypus*.]
– ORIGIN C18: from Araucanian.

**coz** /kʌz/ ● **n.** informal, archaic or N. Amer. cousin.

**cozen** /'kʌz(ə)n/ ● **v.** poetic/literary trick or deceive.
– DERIVATIVES **cozenage** n. **cozener** n.
– ORIGIN C16: perh. from obs. Ital. *cozzonare* 'to cheat'.

**cozy** ● **adj.** US spelling of **COSY**.

**cozzie** ● **n.** (pl. **-ies**) variant spelling of **COSSIE**.

**CP** ● **abbrev. 1** cerebral palsy. **2** Finance commercial paper. **3** Communist Party.

**cp.** ● **abbrev.** compare.

**CPA** ● **abbrev.** N. Amer. certified public accountant.

**CPI** ● **abbrev.** (in the US) consumer price index.

**Cpl** ● **abbrev.** Corporal.

**CPO** ● **abbrev.** Chief Petty Officer.

**CPR** ● **abbrev.** cardiopulmonary resuscitation.

**CPS** ● **abbrev.** (in the UK) Crown Prosecution Service.

**cps** (also **c.p.s.**) ● **abbrev. 1** Computing characters per second. **2** cycles per second.

**CPU** ● **abbrev.** Computing central processing unit.

**CPVC** ● **abbrev.** chlorinated polyvinyl chloride.

**CR** ● **abbrev. 1** Community of the Resurrection. **2** Costa Rica (international vehicle registration).

**Cr**[1] ● **symb.** the chemical element chromium.

**Cr**[2] ● **abbrev. 1** Councillor. **2** credit.

**crab**[1] ● **n. 1** a crustacean, found chiefly on seashores, with a broad carapace, stalked eyes, and five pairs of legs, the first of which are modified as pincers. [Order Decapoda: many species.] **2** (**crabs**) informal an infestation

of crab lice. **3** a machine with pincer-like arms for picking up heavy weights. ● v. **1** move sideways or obliquely. **2** fish for crabs.
– PHRASES **catch a crab** Rowing make a faulty stroke.
– DERIVATIVES **crabber** n. **crablike** adj. & adv.
– ORIGIN OE *crabba*, of Gmc origin.

**crab²** ● v. (**crabbed**, **crabbing**) informal grumble.
– ORIGIN C16 (referring to hawks, meaning 'claw or fight each other'): from Low Ger. *krabben*; rel. to CRAB¹.

**crab apple** ● n. **1** a small, sour kind of apple. **2** (also **crab tree**) a small tree bearing such apples. [*Malus sylvestris* and other species.]
– ORIGIN ME: perh. an alt. of Scots and north. Engl. *scrab*.

**crabbed** ● adj. **1** (of writing) hard to read or understand. **2** crabby.
– DERIVATIVES **crabbedly** adv. **crabbedness** n.
– ORIGIN ME: from CRAB¹, because of the crab's sideways gait and habit of snapping.

**crabby** ● adj. (**-ier**, **-iest**) bad-tempered; morose.
– DERIVATIVES **crabbily** adv. **crabbiness** n.

**crabgrass** ● n. N. Amer. a creeping grass that can become a serious weed. [*Digitaria sanguinalis* and other species.]

**crab louse** ● n. a louse that infests human body hair. [*Phthirus pubis*.]

**crabmeat** ● n. the flesh of a crab as food.

**crab spider** ● n. a spider with long front legs that moves with a crablike sideways motion. [Family Thomisidae: many species.]

**crab stick** ● n. a stick of mixed compressed fish pieces flavoured with crab.

**crabwise** ● adv. & adj. (of movement) sideways, especially in an awkward way.

**crack** ● n. **1** a narrow opening between two parts of something which has split or been broken. **2** a sudden sharp or explosive noise. ➤ a sharp blow. **3** informal a joke or jibe. ➤ Scottish & N. English a conversation. **4** informal, chiefly Irish enjoyable entertainment; a good time. **5** informal an attempt to do something. **6** (also **crack cocaine**) a potent hard crystalline form of cocaine broken into small pieces. ● v. **1** break or cause to break with little or no separation of the parts. **2** give way under pressure or strain. ➤ (**crack up**) informal suffer an emotional breakdown under pressure. ➤ (**crack up**) informal burst into laughter. **3** make or cause to make a sudden sharp or explosive sound. ➤ hit hard. **4** (of a person's voice) suddenly change in pitch, especially through strain. **5** (**crack down on**) informal take severe measures against. **6** (**crack on**) informal proceed or progress quickly. **7** informal solve, interpret, or decipher. ➤ break into (a safe). **8** decompose (hydrocarbons) by heat and pressure to produce lighter hydrocarbons. ● adj. very good or skilful.
– PHRASES **crack a crib** Brit. archaic, informal break into a house. **crack of dawn** daybreak. **crack of doom** a thunder peal announcing the Day of Judgement. **crack of the whip** Brit. informal a chance to try or participate in something. **cracked up to be** [with neg.] informal asserted to be: *acting is not as glamorous as it's cracked up to be.* **get cracking** informal act quickly and energetically.
– DERIVATIVES **cracky** adj.
– ORIGIN OE *cracian* 'make an explosive noise'; of Gmc origin.

**crackbrained** ● adj. informal extremely foolish.

**crackdown** ● n. a series of severe measures against undesirable or illegal behaviour.

**cracked** ● adj. **1** having cracks. **2** informal crazy.

**cracked wheat** ● n. grains of wheat that have been crushed into small pieces.

**cracker** ● n. **1** a decorated paper cylinder which, when pulled apart, makes a sharp noise and releases a small toy or other novelty. **2** a firework exploding with a crack. **3** a thin dry biscuit, typically eaten with cheese. **4** Brit. informal a fine example of something. **5** an installation for cracking hydrocarbons.

**cracker-barrel** ● adj. N. Amer. simple and unsophisticated.
– ORIGIN C19: with ref. to the barrels of soda crackers formerly found in country stores.

**crackerjack** informal, chiefly N. Amer. ● adj. exceptionally good. ● n. an exceptionally good person or thing.
– ORIGIN C19: fanciful formation from CRACK or CRACKER.

**crackers** ● adj. informal, chiefly Brit. insane; crazy.

**cracking** ● adj. Brit. informal excellent. ➤ fast and exciting: *a cracking pace.*

**crackle** ● v. make a rapid succession of slight cracking noises. ● n. **1** a cracking sound of this type. **2** a pattern of minute surface cracks.
– DERIVATIVES **crackly** adj.
– ORIGIN ME: from CRACK + -LE⁴.

**crackling** ● n. the crisp fatty skin of roast pork.

**cracknel** /ˈkrakn(ə)l/ ● n. **1** a light, crisp, savoury biscuit. **2** a brittle sweet made from set melted sugar.
– ORIGIN ME: alt. of OFr. *craquelin*, from MDu. *krākelinc*, from *krāken* 'to crack'.

**crackpot** informal ● n. an eccentric or foolish person. ● adj. eccentric; impractical.

**cracksman** ● n. (pl. **-men**) informal, dated a safe-breaker.

**crack willow** ● n. a large willow of damp or riverside habitats, with long glossy leaves and brittle branches. [*Salix fragilis*.]

**-cracy** ● comb. form denoting a particular form of government or rule: *democracy*. See word-formation panel.
– ORIGIN from Fr. *-cratie*, via med. L. from Gk *-kratia* 'power, rule'.

**cradle** ● n. **1** a baby's bed or cot, especially one mounted on rockers. **2** a supporting framework resembling this, in particular for a boat under repair or for workers on the side of high building. ● v. **1** hold gently and protectively. **2** place in a cradle.
– DERIVATIVES **cradling** n.
– ORIGIN OE *cradol*, of uncertain origin.

**cradle cap** ● n. a skin condition in babies in which there are areas of yellowish or brownish scales on the top of the head.

**cradle-snatcher** ● n. derogatory a person who marries or has a sexual relationship with a much younger person.

**craft** ● n. **1** an activity involving skill in making things by hand. ➤ (**crafts**) things made by hand. ➤ skill in carrying out one's work. ➤ the members of a skilled profession. **2** cunning. **3** (pl. same) a boat or ship. ➤ an aircraft or spaceship. ● v. exercise skill in making (something).
– DERIVATIVES **crafter** n. **craftwork** n. **craftworker** n.
– ORIGIN OE *cræft* 'strength, skill', of Gmc origin; sense 3 perh. with ref. to vessels requiring skill to handle.

**craftsman** (or **craftswoman**) ● n. (pl. **-men** or **-women**) **1** a worker skilled in a particular craft. **2** (**Craftsman**) a qualified private soldier in the Royal Electrical and Mechanical Engineers.
– DERIVATIVES **craftsmanship** n.

**crafty** ● adj. (**-ier**, **-iest**) **1** cunning or deceitful. **2** informal of or relating to the making of objects by hand.
– DERIVATIVES **craftily** adv. **craftiness** n.
– ORIGIN OE *cræftig* 'strong, powerful' (see CRAFT, -Y¹).

**crag** ● n. **1** a steep or rugged cliff or rock face. **2** Geology a shelly sandstone occurring in eastern England.
– ORIGIN ME: of Celtic origin.

**craggy** ● adj. (**-ier**, **-iest**) **1** having many crags. ➤ (of a rock face) rough and uneven. **2** (of a man's face) attractively rugged and rough-textured.
– DERIVATIVES **craggily** adv. **cragginess** n.

**cragsman** ● n. (pl. **-men**) a skilled rock climber.

**crake** ● n. a bird of the rail family with a short bill, such as the corncrake.
– ORIGIN ME: from ON *kráka*, *krákr*, of imitative origin.

**cram** ● v. (**crammed**, **cramming**) **1** force too many (people or things) into a room or container. ➤ fill to the point of overflowing. **2** study intensively just before an examination.
– ORIGIN OE *crammian*, of Gmc origin.

**crambo** ● n. a game in which a player gives a word or line of verse to which other players must find a rhyme.
– ORIGIN C17: from earlier *crambe* 'cabbage', appar. from L. *crambe repetita* 'cabbage served up again', applied by the

## Word *Formation*

**-cracy** 'government or rule', from Greek *kratia* 'power, rule'

The words ***democracy*** and ***aristocracy*** have their origins in Greek: ***democracy*** (*dēmos* 'the people') referred to direct rule through assembly by the citizens of the ancient Greek city states, while ***aristocracy*** (*aristos* 'best') referred to rule by the best—those best qualified to rule by education or social position. In English these words (adopted in the 15th/16th century) have acquired somewhat different, though clearly related, meanings: the chief sense in the current use of ***aristocracy***, for example, is 'the highest social class, comprising people of noble birth with hereditary titles'.

➤ Other **-cracy** words used in Greek and adopted into English include:

| | | |
|---|---|---|
| ochlocracy | mob rule | Gk *okhlos* 'mob' |
| plutocracy | government by the wealthy | Gk *ploutos* 'wealth' |
| theocracy | government by priests (as God's representatives) | Gk *theos* 'God' |

➤ Further **-cracy** words in English:

| | | |
|---|---|---|
| autocracy | government by one person with absolute power | Gk *autos* 'self' |
| bureaucracy | a system of government by state officials | Fr. *bureau* 'baize' (alluding to the baize covering a desk) |
| gerontocracy | government by old people | Gk *gerōn*, *geront-* 'old man' |
| mediocracy | a dominant class of mediocre people | L. *mediocris* 'middling' |
| meritocracy | government by those selected on merit | based on MERIT |

The presence in original Greek elements of the letter -o- (in *dēmos*, *aristos*, etc.) has given rise to the insertion of -o- in some English formations, even where this is superfluous, as in ***meritocracy*** (where, strictly speaking, the logical formation is ***meritcracy***).

➤ Related words:

**-cratic** forming adjectives, eg. ***aristocratic*** 'relating to the aristocracy'

Roman satirist Juvenal to distasteful repetition.

**cram-full** ● **adj.** very full; packed.

**crammer** ● **n.** Brit. a college or school that prepares pupils intensively for a particular examination.

**cramp** ● **n. 1** painful involuntary contraction of a muscle or muscles, typically caused by fatigue or strain. ➤(**cramps**) N. Amer. abdominal pain caused by menstruation. **2** a tool, typically shaped like a capital G, for clamping two objects together. ➤(also **cramp-iron**) a metal bar with bent ends for holding masonry together. ● **v. 1** restrict or inhibit the development of. **2** fasten with a cramp or cramps. **3** suffer from cramp.
– PHRASES **cramp someone's style** informal prevent a person from acting freely or naturally.
– ORIGIN ME: from Mid. Low Ger. and MDu. *krampe*; sense 1 of the noun is via OFr. *crampe*.

**cramp balls** ● **pl. n.** a fungus which produces a shiny spherical black fruiting body on dead wood. [*Daldinia concentrica*.]
– ORIGIN so named because it was once believed to be a charm against cramp.

**cramped** ● **adj. 1** uncomfortably small or crowded. **2** (of handwriting) small and difficult to read.

**crampon** /ˈkrampɒn, -pən/ ● **n.** a metal plate with spikes fixed to a boot for climbing on ice or rock.
– ORIGIN ME (in the sense 'grappling hook'): from OFr., of Gmc origin.

**cran** ● **n.** historical a measure of fresh herrings, equivalent to 37½ gallons.
– ORIGIN C18: from Sc. Gaelic *crann*.

**cranberry** ● **n.** (pl. **-ies**) **1** a small red acid berry used in cooking. **2** an evergreen dwarf shrub which yields this fruit. [*Vaccinium oxycoccos* (Europe), *V. macrocarpon* (N. America), and other species.]
– ORIGIN C17: from Ger. *Kranbeere* or Low Ger. *kranebeere* 'crane-berry'.

**crane**[1] ● **n.** a large, tall machine used for moving heavy objects by suspending them from a projecting arm. ➤a moving platform supporting a camera. ● **v. 1** stretch out (one's neck) in order to see something. **2** move (an object) by means of a crane.
– DERIVATIVES **cranage** n.
– ORIGIN ME: figuratively from **CRANE**[2].

**crane**[2] ● **n.** a tall, long-legged, long-necked bird, typically with white or grey plumage and tail plumes. [*Grus grus* (**common crane**, Eurasia) and related species, family Gruidae.]
– ORIGIN OE, of Gmc origin.

**crane fly** ● **n.** a slender two-winged fly with very long legs; a daddy-long-legs. [*Tipula maxima* and related species, family Tipulidae.]

**cranesbill** ● **n.** a herbaceous plant with lobed leaves and typically purple or violet five-petalled flowers. [*Geranium pratense* (**meadow cranesbill**) and related species.]
– ORIGIN C16: so named because of the long spur on the fruit, thought to resemble a crane's beak.

**cranial** /ˈkreɪnɪəl/ ● **adj.** Anatomy of or relating to the skull or cranium.

**cranial index** ● **n.** another term for **CEPHALIC INDEX**.

**cranial nerves** ● **pl. n.** Anatomy the twelve pairs of nerves which arise directly from the brain and pass through separate apertures in the skull.

**craniate** /ˈkreɪnɪət/ ● **adj.** Zoology relating to or denoting animals that possess a skull.
– ORIGIN C19: from mod. L. *craniatus*, from med. L. *cranium*.

**cranio-** /ˈkreɪnɪəʊ/ ● **comb. form** relating to the cranium: *craniotomy*.

**craniology** /ˌkreɪnɪˈɒlədʒi/ ● **n.** historical the scientific study of the shape and size of the human skull.
– DERIVATIVES **craniological** adj. **craniologist** n.

**craniometry** /ˌkreɪnɪˈɒmɪtri/ ● **n.** the measurement of the dimensions of skulls.
– DERIVATIVES **craniometric** adj.

**craniosacral therapy** /ˌkreɪnɪəʊˈseɪkr(ə)l, -ˈsak-/ ● **n.** a system of alternative medicine intended to relieve pain and tension by gentle manipulations of the skull.

**craniotomy** /ˌkreɪnɪˈɒtəmi/ ● **n.** surgical removal of a portion of the skull.

**cranium** /ˈkreɪnɪəm/ ● **n.** (pl. **craniums** or **crania** /-nɪə/) Anatomy the skull, especially the part enclosing the brain.
– ORIGIN ME: via med. L. from Gk *kranion*.

**crank**[1] ● **v.** **1** turn a crankshaft or handle, especially in order to start an engine. **2** (**crank up**) informal increase the intensity of. **3** (**crank out**) informal, derogatory produce regularly and routinely. **4** give a bend to (a shaft or bar). **5** informal inject a narcotic drug. ● **n.** a part of an axle or shaft bent out at right angles, for converting reciprocal to circular motion and vice versa.
– ORIGIN OE *cranc*, rel. to *crincan* (see **CRINGE**).

**crank**[2] ● **n.** **1** a person with eccentric or obsessive views. ➤N. Amer. a bad-tempered person. **2** poetic/literary a fanciful turn of speech.
– ORIGIN back-form. from **CRANKY**; sense 2 is perh. from a base meaning 'bent together, curled up', shared by **CRANK**[1].

**crank**[3] ● **adj.** Nautical, archaic (of a sailing ship) liable to heel over.
– ORIGIN C17: perh. from dial. *crank* 'weak, shaky'.

**crankcase** ● **n.** a case or covering enclosing a crankshaft.

**crankpin** ● **n.** a pin by which a connecting rod is attached to a crank.

**crankshaft** ● **n.** a shaft driven by a crank.

**cranky** ● **adj.** (**-ier, -iest**) informal **1** eccentric, odd. ➤chiefly N. Amer. ill-tempered; irritable. **2** (of a machine) working erratically.
– DERIVATIVES **crankily** adv. **crankiness** n.
– ORIGIN C18 (in the sense 'sickly, in poor health'): perh. ult. from Du. or Ger. *krank* 'sick'.

**crannog** /ˈkranəg/ ● **n.** an ancient Scottish or Irish fortified dwelling constructed in a lake or marsh.
– ORIGIN C17: from Ir. *crannóg*, Sc. Gaelic *crannag*, from *crann* 'tree, beam'.

**cranny** ● **n.** (pl. **-ies**) a small, narrow space or opening.
– DERIVATIVES **crannied** adj.
– ORIGIN ME: from OFr. *crane* 'notched', from *cran*, from pop. L. *crena* 'notch'.

**crap**[1] vulgar slang ● **n.** **1** nonsense; rubbish. **2** excrement. ➤an act of defecation. ● **v.** (**crapped, crapping**) defecate. ● **adj.** extremely poor in quality.
– DERIVATIVES **crappy** adj.
– ORIGIN ME, in sense 'chaff': rel. to Du. *krappe*, from *krappen* 'pluck or cut off', and perh. also to OFr. *crappe* 'siftings', Anglo-Latin *crappa* 'chaff'.

**crap**[2] N. Amer. ● **n.** a losing throw in craps. ● **v.** (**crap out**) informal make a losing throw at craps. ➤give up; fail.

**crape** ● **n.** **1** variant spelling of **CRÊPE**. **2** black silk, formerly used for mourning clothes.
– DERIVATIVES **crapy** adj.
– ORIGIN C16: from Fr. *crêpe* (see **CRÊPE**).

**crape fern** ● **n.** a tall New Zealand fern with dark green fronds. [*Leptopteris superba*.]

**crape hair** ● **n.** Brit. artificial hair used by actors, chiefly for false beards and moustaches.

**crape myrtle** (also **crepe myrtle**) ● **n.** an ornamental Chinese shrub or small tree with pink, white, or purplish crinkled petals. [*Lagerstroemia indica*.]

**crap game** ● **n.** N. Amer. a game of craps.

**crapper** ● **n.** vulgar slang a toilet.

**crappie** ● **n.** (pl. **-ies**) a North American freshwater fish, the male of which builds a nest and guards the eggs and young. [Genus *Pomoxis*: several species.]
– ORIGIN C19: of unknown origin.

**craps** ● **pl. n.** [treated as sing.] a North American gambling game played with two dice, in which 7 or 11 is a winning throw, 2, 3, or 12 is a losing throw.
– ORIGIN C19: perh. from **CRAB**[1] or *crab's eyes*, denoting a throw of two ones.

**crapshoot** ● **n.** N. Amer. a game of craps.

**crapulent** /ˈkrapjʊl(ə)nt/ ● **adj.** poetic/literary of or relating to the drinking of alcohol or drunkenness.
– DERIVATIVES **crapulence** n. **crapulous** adj.
– ORIGIN C17: from late L. *crapulentus* 'very drunk', from L. *crapula* 'inebriation'.

**craquelure** /ˈkrakljʊə, krakˈljʊə/ ● **n.** a network of fine cracks in the paint or varnish of a painting.
– ORIGIN C20: Fr., from *craqueler* 'to crackle'.

**crash**[1] ● **v.** **1** collide violently with an obstacle or another vehicle. ➤(of an aircraft) fall from the sky and violently hit the land or sea. **2** informal (of a company's shares) fall suddenly and disastrously in value. ➤Computing fail suddenly. **3** (also **crash out**) informal fall deeply asleep. **4** move with force, speed, and sudden loud noise. ➤make a sudden loud, deep noise. **5** informal gatecrash (a party). ● **n.** **1** an instance of crashing. **2** a sudden loud discordant noise. ● **adj.** done rapidly and involving a concentrated effort: *a crash course in Italian.*
– ORIGIN ME: imitative, perh. partly suggested by **CRAZE** and **DASH**.

**crash**[2] ● **n.** dated a coarse plain linen, woollen, or cotton fabric.
– ORIGIN C19: from Russ. *krashenina* 'dyed coarse linen'.

**crash-dive** ● **v.** **1** (of a submarine) dive rapidly to a deeper level in an emergency. **2** (of an aircraft) plunge steeply downwards into a crash. ● **n.** (**crash dive**) a steep dive of this kind.

**crash helmet** ● **n.** a helmet worn by a motorcyclist to protect the head in case of a crash.

**crashing** ● **adj.** informal complete; total: *a crashing bore.*
– DERIVATIVES **crashingly** adv.

**crash-land** ● **v.** land roughly in an emergency.

**crash pad** ● **n.** informal a place to sleep, especially for emergency use.

**crash-test** ● **v.** deliberately crash (a new vehicle) under controlled conditions in order to evaluate and improve its ability to withstand impact. ● **n.** (**crash test**) a test of this kind.

**crashworthiness** ● **n.** the degree to which a vehicle will protect its occupants from the effects of an accident.

**crasis** /ˈkreɪsɪs/ ● **n.** (pl. **crases** /-siːz/) Phonetics a contraction of two adjacent vowels into one long vowel or diphthong.
– ORIGIN C16: from Gk *krasis* 'mixture'.

**crass** ● **adj.** showing a grossly insensitive lack of intelligence.
– DERIVATIVES **crassitude** n. **crassly** adv. **crassness** n.
– ORIGIN C15 (in the sense 'dense or coarse'): from L. *crassus* 'solid, thick'.

**-crat** ● **comb. form** denoting a member or supporter of a particular form of government or rule: *plutocrat.*
– ORIGIN from Fr. *-crate*, from adjectives ending in *-cratique* (see **-CRATIC**).

**crate** ● **n.** **1** a slatted wooden case used for transporting goods. ➤a square container divided into small individual units for holding bottles. **2** informal, dated an old and dilapidated vehicle. ● **v.** pack in a crate for transportation.
– DERIVATIVES **crateful** n. (pl. **-fuls**).
– ORIGIN ME: perh. rel. to Du. *krat* 'tailboard of a wagon'.

**crater** ● **n.** **1** a large bowl-shaped cavity, especially one caused by an explosion or impact or forming the mouth of a volcano. **2** a large bowl used in ancient Greece for mixing wine. ● **v.** form a crater or craters in.
– ORIGIN C17: via L. from Gk *kratēr* 'mixing-bowl'.

**-cratic** ● **comb. form** relating to a particular kind of government or rule: *democratic.*
– DERIVATIVES **-cratically** comb. form in corresponding adverbs.
– ORIGIN from Fr. *-cratique*, from *-cratie* (see **-CRACY**).

**craton** /ˈkratɒn/ ● **n.** Geology a large stable block of the earth's crust forming the nucleus of a continent.
– DERIVATIVES **cratonic** adj.
– ORIGIN 1930s: alt. of *kratogen* in the same sense, from Gk *kratos* 'strength'.

**cravat** ● **n.** a short, wide strip of fabric worn by men round the neck and tucked inside an open-necked shirt.
– DERIVATIVES **cravatted** adj.
– ORIGIN C17: from Fr. *cravate*, from *Cravate* 'Croat', be-

cause of the scarf worn by Croatian mercenaries.

**crave** ● v. **1** feel a powerful desire for. **2** dated ask for: *I must crave your indulgence.*
– DERIVATIVES **craver** n. **craving** n.
– ORIGIN OE *crafian* (in the sense 'demand, claim as a right'), of Gmc origin.

**craven** ● adj. contemptibly lacking in courage; cowardly. ● n. archaic a cowardly person.
– DERIVATIVES **cravenly** adv. **cravenness** n.
– ORIGIN ME *cravant* 'defeated', perh. via Anglo-Norman Fr. from OFr. *cravanter* 'crush, overwhelm', based on L. *crepare* 'burst'.

**craw** ● n. dated the crop of a bird or insect.
– PHRASES **stick in one's craw** see STICK².
– ORIGIN ME: rel. to MDu. *crāghe* or Mid. Low Ger. *krage* 'neck, throat'.

**crawdad** /ˈkrɔːdad/ ● n. N. Amer. a freshwater crayfish.
– ORIGIN C20: fanciful alt. of CRAWFISH.

**crawfish** ● n. (pl. same or **-fishes**) **1** another term for SPINY LOBSTER. **2** chiefly N. Amer. a freshwater crayfish. ● v. US informal retreat from a position.
– ORIGIN C17: var. of CRAYFISH.

**crawl** ● v. **1** move forward on the hands and knees or by dragging the body close to the ground. ➤(of an insect or small animal) move slowly along a surface. ➤move at an unusually slow pace. **2** informal behave obsequiously or ingratiatingly. **3** (**be crawling with**) be unpleasantly covered or crowded with: *the place was crawling with soldiers.* ➤feel an unpleasant sensation resembling something moving over the skin. ● n. **1** an act of crawling. ➤a slow rate of movement. **2** a swimming stroke involving alternate overarm movements and rapid kicks of the legs.
– DERIVATIVES **crawling** adj. **crawlingly** adv. **crawly** adj.
– ORIGIN ME: possibly rel. to Swed. *kravla* and Dan. *kravle.*

**crawler** ● n. **1** a person or thing that crawls. ➤a vehicle moving on an endless caterpillar track. **2** Computing a program that searches the Internet in order to create an index of data.

**crayfish** ● n. (pl. same or **-fishes**) **1** a nocturnal freshwater crustacean resembling a lobster. [*Astacus* (Europe), *Cambarus* (N. America), and other genera.] **2** another term for SPINY LOBSTER.
– ORIGIN ME: from OFr. *crevice*, rel. to Ger. *Krebs* 'crab'.

**crayon** ● n. a pencil or stick of coloured chalk or wax, used for drawing. ● v. draw with a crayon or crayons.
– ORIGIN C17: from Fr., from *craie* 'chalk'.

**craze** ● n. a widespread but short-lived enthusiasm for something. ● v. **1** [usu. as adj. **crazed**] make or become wildly insane: *a crazed killer.* **2** (usu. **be crazed**) produce a network of fine cracks on (a surface).
– DERIVATIVES **crazing** n.
– ORIGIN ME (in the sense 'break, shatter, produce cracks'): perh. of Scand. origin.

**crazy** informal ● adj. (**-ier**, **-iest**) **1** insane or unbalanced, especially as manifested in wild or aggressive behaviour. **2** extremely enthusiastic about something. **3** appearing absurdly out of place or unlikely: *the monument leant at a crazy angle.* **4** archaic full of cracks or flaws. ● n. (pl. **-ies**) chiefly N. Amer. an insane person.
– PHRASES **like crazy** to a great degree.
– DERIVATIVES **crazily** adv. **craziness** n.

**crazy bone** ● n. US term for FUNNY BONE.

**crazy paving** ● n. Brit. paving made of irregular pieces of flat stone.

**CRC** ● abbrev. **1** (in printing) camera-ready copy. **2** (in computing) cyclic redundancy check or code.

**creak** ● v. **1** make a harsh high-pitched sound when being moved or when pressure is applied. **2** show weakness or frailty under strain. ● n. a creaking sound.
– DERIVATIVES **creaking** adj. **creakingly** adv. **creaky** adj.
– ORIGIN ME (in the sense 'croak'): imitative.

**cream** ● n. **1** the thick white or pale yellow fatty liquid which rises to the top when milk is left to stand. ➤a sauce, soup, dessert, or other food containing cream or having the consistency of cream. **2** a thick liquid or semi-solid cosmetic or medical preparation. **3** the very best of a group of people or things: *the cream of American society.* **4** a very pale yellow or off-white colour. ● v. **1** work (butter) to form a smooth soft paste. ➤mash (a cooked vegetable) and mix with milk or cream. ➤add cream to (coffee). **2** (**cream off**) take away (the best part of a group of people or things). **3** rub a cosmetic cream into (the skin). **4** informal, chiefly N. Amer. defeat heavily. ➤hit or beat.
– DERIVATIVES **creamily** adv. **creaminess** n. **creamy** adj.
– ORIGIN ME: from OFr. *cresme*, from a blend of late L. *cramum* and eccles. L. *chrisma* (see CHRISM).

**cream cheese** ● n. soft, rich cheese made from unskimmed milk and cream.

**cream cracker** ● n. Brit. a dry unsweetened biscuit eaten chiefly with cheese.

**creamer** ● n. **1** a cream or milk substitute for adding to coffee or tea. **2** N. Amer. a jug for cream. **3** historical a flat dish for skimming the cream off milk. ➤a machine for separating cream from milk.

**creamery** ● n. (pl. **-ies**) a factory that produces butter and cheese.

**cream puff** ● n. **1** a cake made of puff pastry filled with cream. **2** informal a weak or ineffectual person.

**cream sherry** ● n. a full-bodied mellow sweet sherry.

**cream soda** ● n. a carbonated vanilla-flavoured soft drink.

**cream tea** ● n. Brit. an afternoon meal consisting of tea to drink with scones, jam, and cream.

**creamware** ● n. glazed earthenware pottery of a rich cream colour.

**creance** /ˈkriːəns/ ● n. Falconry a long fine cord attached to a hawk's leash to prevent escape during training.
– ORIGIN C15: from Fr. *créance*, lit. 'faith'.

**crease** ● n. **1** a line or ridge produced on paper or cloth by folding, pressing, or crushing. ➤a wrinkle or furrow in the skin, especially of the face. **2** Cricket any of a number of lines marked on the pitch at specified places. ● v. **1** make a crease in. **2** (of a bullet) graze. **3** Brit. informal hit or punch hard. **4** (**crease up**) Brit. informal burst out or cause to burst out laughing.
– ORIGIN C16: prob. a var. of CREST.

**create** ● v. **1** bring into existence. **2** invest with a title of nobility. **3** Brit. informal make a fuss; complain.
– ORIGIN ME: from L. *creat-*, *creare* 'produce'.

**creatine** /ˈkriːətiːn/ ● n. Biochemistry a compound formed in protein metabolism and involved in the supply of energy for muscular contraction.
– ORIGIN C19: formed irregularly from Gk *kreas* 'meat' + -INE⁴.

**creatinine** /krɪˈatɪniːn/ ● n. Biochemistry a compound produced by metabolism of creatine and excreted in the urine.

**creation** ● n. **1** the action or process of creating. ➤a thing which has been made or invented, especially something showing artistic talent. **2** (**the Creation**) the creating of the universe, especially when regarded as an act of God. ➤the universe.

**creationism** ● n. the belief that the universe and living organisms originated from specific acts of divine creation.
– DERIVATIVES **creationist** n. & adj.

**creation science** ● n. the reinterpretation of scientific knowledge in accord with belief in the literal truth of the Bible.

**creative** ● adj. relating to or involving the use of imagination or original ideas in order to create something. ● n. a person engaged in creative work.
– DERIVATIVES **creatively** adv. **creativeness** n. **creativity** n.

**creative accountancy** (also **creative accounting**) ● n. informal the exploitation of loopholes in financial regulation to gain advantage or to present figures in a misleadingly favourable light.

**creator** ● n. a person or thing that creates. ➤(**the Creator**) God.

**creature** ● n. **1** an animal, as distinct from a human being. ➤an animal or person. ➤archaic anything living or

existing. **2** a person or organization considered to be under the complete control of another.
– DERIVATIVES **creaturely** adj.
– ORIGIN ME (in the sense 'something created'): via OFr. from late L. *creatura*, from *creare* (see **CREATE**).

**creature comforts** ● pl. n. material comforts that contribute to physical ease and well-being, such as good food and accommodation.

**crèche** /krɛʃ, kreɪʃ/ ● n. **1** Brit. a nursery where babies and young children are cared for during the working day. **2** N. Amer. a representation of the nativity scene.
– ORIGIN C18: Fr., ult. of Gmc origin and rel. to **CRIB**.

**cred** ● n. informal short for **CREDIBILITY** (in sense 2).

**credal** /ˈkriːd(ə)l/ (also **creedal**) ● adj. of or relating to a creed.

**credence** /ˈkriːd(ə)ns/ ● n. **1** belief in or acceptance of something as true. ➤ the likelihood of something being true; plausibility. **2** a small side table, shelf, or niche in a church for holding the elements of the Eucharist before they are consecrated.
– ORIGIN ME: via OFr. from med. L. *credentia*, from L. *credent-*, *credere* 'believe'.

**credential** /krɪˈdɛnʃ(ə)l/ ● n. **1** a qualification, achievement, etc., especially when used to indicate suitability. **2** a letter of introduction given by a government to an ambassador before a new posting.
– ORIGIN ME (as an adj.): from med. L. *credentialis*, from *credentia* (see **CREDENCE**).

**credenza** /krɪˈdɛnzə/ ● n. a sideboard or cupboard.
– ORIGIN C19: Ital., from med. L. *credentia* (see **CREDENCE**).

**credibility** ● n. **1** the quality of being credible. **2** (also **street credibility**) acceptability among young fashionable urban people.

**credibility gap** ● n. an apparent difference between what is said or promised and what happens or is true.

**credible** ● adj. able to be believed; convincing.
– DERIVATIVES **credibly** adv.
– ORIGIN ME: from L. *credibilis*, from *credere* 'believe'.

**credit** ● n. **1** the ability of a customer to obtain goods or services before payment, based on the trust that payment will be made in the future. ➤ money lent or made available under such an arrangement. **2** an entry in an account recording a sum received. **3** public acknowledgement or praise given for an achievement or quality. ➤ a source of pride. **4** (also **credit title**) an item in a list displayed at the beginning or end of a film or programme, acknowledging a contributor's role. **5** chiefly N. Amer. the acknowledgement of a student's completion of a course or activity that counts towards a degree or diploma. ➤ Brit. a grade above a pass in an examination. **6** archaic credibility. ➤ good reputation. ● v. (**credited**, **crediting**) **1** publicly acknowledge someone as a participant in the production of (something published or broadcast). ➤ (**credit someone with**) ascribe (an achievement or good quality) to someone. **2** add (an amount of money) to an account. **3** believe (something surprising or unlikely).
– PHRASES **be in credit** (of an account) have money in it. **do someone credit** make someone worthy of praise or respect. **have something to one's credit** have achieved something notable. **on credit** with an arrangement to pay later.
– ORIGIN C16: from Fr. *crédit*, prob. via Ital. *credito* from L. *creditum*, neut. past part. of *credere* 'believe, trust'.

**creditable** ● adj. deserving public acknowledgement and praise but not necessarily outstanding or successful.
– DERIVATIVES **creditability** n. **creditably** adv.

**credit card** ● n. a small plastic card issued by a bank or building society, allowing the holder to make purchases on credit.

**creditor** ● n. a person or company to whom money is owing.

**credit title** ● n. see **CREDIT** (sense 4).

**credit transfer** ● n. Brit. a direct payment of money from one bank account to another.

**credit union** ● n. a non-profit-making money cooperative whose members can borrow from pooled deposits at low interest rates.

**creditworthy** ● adj. considered suitable to receive commercial credit.
– DERIVATIVES **creditworthiness** n.

**credo** /ˈkriːdəʊ, ˈkreɪ-/ ● n. (pl. **-os**) **1** a statement of a person's beliefs or aims. **2** (**Credo**) a creed of the Christian Church in Latin. ➤ (**Credo**) a musical setting of the Nicene Creed.
– ORIGIN ME: L., 'I believe'; cf. **CREED**.

**credulous** /ˈkrɛdjʊləs/ ● adj. having or showing too great a readiness to believe things.
– DERIVATIVES **credulity** /krɪˈdjuːlɪti/ n. **credulously** adv. **credulousness** n.
– ORIGIN C16: from L. *credulus* (from *credere* 'believe') + **-OUS**.

**Cree** /kriː/ ● n. (pl. same or **Crees**) **1** a member of an American Indian people living in central Canada. **2** the Algonquian language of this people.
– ORIGIN from Canad. Fr. *Cris*, abbrev. of *Cristinaux*, from Algonquian.

**creed** ● n. **1** a system of religious belief; a faith. ➤ a formal statement of Christian beliefs. **2** a credo.
– ORIGIN OE, from L. **CREDO**.

**creedal** ● adj. variant spelling of **CREDAL**.

**Creek** /kriːk/ ● n. (pl. same) **1** a member of a confederacy of American Indian peoples of the south-eastern US in the 16th to 19th centuries. **2** the Muskogean language spoken by these peoples.
– ORIGIN from **CREEK**, because they lived beside the waterways of the flatlands of Georgia and Alabama.

**creek** ● n. a narrow, sheltered waterway such as an inlet in a shoreline or channel in a marsh. ➤ N. Amer. & Austral./NZ a stream or minor tributary of a river.
– PHRASES **up the creek** informal **1** in severe difficulty or trouble. **2** Brit. stupid or misguided.
– ORIGIN ME: from OFr. *crique* or from ON *kriki* 'nook'.

**creel** ● n. **1** a large basket for carrying fish. **2** a rack holding bobbins or spools when spinning.
– ORIGIN ME; orig. Scots and north. Engl.: of unknown origin.

**creep** ● v. (past and past part. **crept** /krɛpt/) **1** move slowly and carefully, especially in order to avoid being heard or noticed. ➤ move or progress very slowly and steadily. ➤ (of a plant) grow along the ground or other surface by extending stems or branches. **2** (of a plastic solid) undergo gradual deformation under stress. **3** (**creep to**) informal behave obsequiously towards. ● n. **1** informal a contemptible person, especially one who behaves obsequiously in the hope of advancement. **2** very slow, steady movement or progress. ➤ gradual deformation of a plastic solid under stress. **3** Brit. an opening in a hedge or wall for an animal to pass through. ➤ a feeding enclosure for young animals, with a long narrow entrance.
– PHRASES **give someone the creeps** informal induce a feeling of revulsion or fear in someone. **make one's flesh creep** cause one to feel revulsion and have a sensation like that of something crawling over the skin.
– DERIVATIVES **creeper** n. **creeping** adj.
– ORIGIN OE *crēopan*, of Gmc origin.

**creeping Jenny** ● n. a trailing evergreen plant with round glossy leaves and yellow flowers, growing in damp places. [*Lysimachia nummularia*.]

**creeping Jesus** ● n. Brit. informal a person who is obsequious or hypocritically pious.

**creepy** ● adj. (**-ier**, **-iest**) informal causing an unpleasant feeling of fear or unease.
– DERIVATIVES **creepily** adv. **creepiness** n.

**creepy-crawly** informal ● n. (pl. **-ies**) a spider, worm, or other small flightless creature, especially when considered unpleasant or frightening. ● adj. creepy.

**creese** ● n. archaic spelling of **KRIS**.

**cremaster** /krɪˈmastə/ ● n. **1** Anatomy the muscle of the spermatic cord, by which the testicle can be partially raised. **2** Entomology the hook-like tip of a butterfly pupa.
– ORIGIN C17: from Gk *kremastēr*, from *krema-* 'hang'.

**cremate** ● v. dispose of (a dead person's body) by burning it to ashes.

– DERIVATIVES **cremation** n. **cremator** n.
– ORIGIN C19 (earlier (C17) as *cremation*): from L. *cremare* 'burn'.
**crematorium** /ˌkrɛməˈtɔːrɪəm/ ● n. (pl. **crematoria** or **crematoriums**) a building where the dead are cremated.
– ORIGIN C19: mod. L., from *cremare* 'burn'.
**crematory** /ˈkrɛmət(ə)ri/ ● adj. of or relating to cremation. ● n. (pl. **-ies**) North American term for **CREMATORIUM**.
**crème anglaise** /ˌkrɛm ɒ̃ˈgleɪz/ ● n. a rich egg custard.
– ORIGIN Fr., lit. 'English cream'.
**crème brûlée** /ˌkrɛm bruːˈleɪ/ ● n. (pl. **crèmes brûlées** pronunc. same or **crème brûlées** /-ˈleɪz/) a dessert of custard topped with caramelized sugar.
– ORIGIN Fr., lit. 'burnt cream'.
**crème caramel** /krɛm ˌkarəˈmɛl, ˈkarəmɛl/ ● n. (pl. **crèmes caramel** pronunc. same or **crème caramels**) a custard dessert made with whipped cream and eggs and topped with caramel.
– ORIGIN from Fr.
**crème de cassis** /ˌkrɛm də kaˈsiːs/ ● n. see **CASSIS**[1].
**crème de la crème** /ˌkrɛm də la ˈkrɛm, French kʀɛm də la kʀɛm/ ● n. the best person or thing of a particular kind.
– ORIGIN Fr., lit. 'cream of the cream'.
**crème de menthe** /ˌkrɛm də ˈmɒnθ, ˈmɒ̃t/ ● n. a green peppermint-flavoured liqueur.
– ORIGIN Fr., lit. 'cream of mint'.
**crème fraiche** /krɛm ˈfrɛʃ/ ● n. a type of thick cream made from double cream with the addition of buttermilk, sour cream, or yogurt.
– ORIGIN from Fr. *crème fraîche*, lit. 'fresh cream'.
**crenate** /ˈkriːneɪt/ ● adj. Botany & Zoology having a round-toothed or scalloped edge.
– DERIVATIVES **crenated** adj. **crenation** n.
– ORIGIN C18: from mod. L. *crenatus*, from pop. L. *crena* 'notch'.
**crenel** /ˈkrɛn(ə)l/ (also **crenelle** /krɪˈnɛl/) ● n. an indentation in the battlements of a building.
– ORIGIN C15: from OFr., based on pop. L. *crena* 'notch'.
**crenellate** /ˈkrɛn(ə)leɪt/ (also **crenelate**) ● v. [usu. as adj. **crenellated**] chiefly historical provide with battlements.
**crenellations** ● pl. n. battlements.
**crenulate** /ˈkrɛnjʊleɪt/ ● adj. technical having a finely scalloped or notched outline or edge.
– DERIVATIVES **crenulated** adj. **crenulation** n.
– ORIGIN C18: from mod. L. *crenulatus*, from *crenula*, dimin. of *crena* 'notch'.
**creodont** /ˈkriːədɒnt/ ● n. a fossil carnivorous mammal of the early Tertiary period, ancestral to modern carnivores.
– ORIGIN C19: from mod. L. *Creodonta* (name of an order), from Gk *kreas* 'flesh' + *odous, odont-* 'tooth'.
**Creole** /ˈkriːəʊl/ (also **creole**) ● n. **1** a person of mixed European and black descent. **2** a descendant of European settlers in the Caribbean or Central or South America. **3** a white descendant of French settlers in Louisiana. **4** a mother tongue formed from the contact of a European language with a local language (especially African languages spoken by slaves in the West Indies). ● adj. of or relating to a Creole or Creoles.
– ORIGIN from Fr. *créole, criole*, from Sp. *criollo*, prob. from Port. *crioulo* 'black person born in Brazil'.
**creolize** /ˈkriːə(ʊ)lʌɪz, ˈkrɪɒl-/ (also **-ise**) ● v. transform (a language) into a Creole.
– DERIVATIVES **creolization** /-ˈzeɪʃ(ə)n/ n.
**creosol** /ˈkriːəsɒl/ ● n. Chemistry a colourless liquid which is the chief constituent of wood-tar creosote.
– ORIGIN C19: from **CREOSOTE** + **-OL**.
**creosote** ● n. **1** a dark brown oil containing various phenols and other compounds distilled from coal tar, used as a wood preservative. **2** a colourless, pungent, oily liquid distilled from wood tar and used as an antiseptic. ● v. treat with creosote.
– ORIGIN C19: coined in Ger. from Gk *kreas* 'flesh' + *sōtēr* 'preserver', with ref. to its antiseptic properties.
**creosote bush** ● n. a common shrub of arid parts of Mexico and the western US, whose leaves yield a pungent antiseptic. [*Larrea tridentata*.]
**crêpe** /kreɪp/ (also **crape**) ● n. **1** a light, thin fabric with a wrinkled surface. **2** (also **crêpe rubber**) hard-wearing wrinkled rubber, used especially for the soles of shoes. **3** /also krɛp/ a thin pancake.
– DERIVATIVES **crêpey** (also **crêpy**) adj.
– ORIGIN C18: Fr., from OFr. *crespe* 'curled, frizzed'.
**crêpe de Chine** /də ˈʃiːn/ ● n. a fine crêpe of silk or similar fabric.
– ORIGIN C19: Fr., lit. 'crêpe of China'.
**crepe myrtle** ● n. variant spelling of **CRAPE MYRTLE**.
**crêpe paper** ● n. thin, crinkled paper used chiefly for making decorations.
**crêpe Suzette** ● n. (pl. **crêpes Suzette** pronunc. same) a thin dessert pancake flamed and served in alcohol.
**crépinette** /ˌkreɪpɪˈnɛt, French kʀepinɛt/ ● n. a flat sausage consisting of minced meat and savoury stuffing wrapped in pieces of pork caul.
– ORIGIN Fr., dimin. of *crêpine* 'caul'.
**crepitate** /ˈkrɛpɪteɪt/ ● v. make a crackling sound.
– DERIVATIVES **crepitant** adj. **crepitation** n.
– ORIGIN C17 from L. *crepitat-*, *crepitare*, from *crepare* 'to rattle'.
**crepitus** /ˈkrɛpɪtəs/ ● n. Medicine a grating sound or sensation produced by friction between bone and cartilage or the fractured parts of a bone. ➤ the production of rattling sounds in the lungs.
– ORIGIN C19: from L., from *crepare* 'rattle'.
**crépon** /ˈkreɪpɒn/ ● n. a fabric resembling crêpe, but heavier and with a more pronounced crinkled effect.
– ORIGIN C19: Fr.
**crept** past and past participle of **CREEP**.
**crepuscular** /krɪˈpʌskjʊlə, krɛ-/ ● adj. of, resembling, or relating to twilight.
– ORIGIN C17: from L. *crepusculum* 'twilight' + **-AR**[1].
**Cres.** ● abbrev. crescent.
**cresc.** (also **cres.**) ● abbrev. Music crescendo.
**crescendo** /krɪˈʃɛndəʊ/ ● n. **1** (pl. **crescendos** or **crescendi** /-di/) a gradual increase in loudness in a piece of music. **2** the loudest or climactic point. ● adv. & adj. Music with a gradual increase in loudness. ● v. (**-oes**, **-oed**) increase in loudness or intensity.
– ORIGIN C18: Ital., pres. part. of *crescere* 'to increase'.
**crescent** /ˈkrɛz(ə)nt, -s-/ ● n. **1** the curved sickle shape of the waxing or waning moon. **2** a thing which has the shape of a single curve, especially when broad in the centre and tapering to a point at each end. ➤ chiefly Brit. a street or terrace of houses forming an arc. **3** (**the Crescent**) chiefly historical the political power of Islam or of the Ottoman Empire. ● adj. **1** having the shape of a crescent: *a crescent moon.* **2** poetic/literary growing, increasing, or developing.
– DERIVATIVES **crescentic** /-ˈsɛntɪk/ adj.
– ORIGIN ME *cressant*, from OFr. *creissant*, from L. *crescere* 'grow'; sense 3 is from the crescent-shaped emblem of Islam or Turkey.
**cresol** /ˈkriːsɒl/ ● n. Chemistry each of three isomeric crystalline compounds present in coal-tar creosote.
– ORIGIN C19: from **CREOSOTE** + **-OL**.
**cress** ● n. a plant of the cabbage family with small white flowers and pungent leaves. [*Barbarea* and other genera.] ➤ young sprouts of garden cress eaten in salads.
– ORIGIN OE *cresse, cærse*, of W. Gmc origin.
**cresset** /ˈkrɛsɪt/ ● n. historical a metal container of oil, grease, wood, or coal set alight for illumination and typically mounted on a pole.
– ORIGIN ME: from OFr., from *craisse*, var. of *graisse* 'oil, grease'.
**crest** ● n. **1** a comb or tuft of feathers, fur, or skin on the head of a bird or other animal. ➤ a plume of feathers on a helmet. **2** the top of a ridge, wave, etc. ➤ Anatomy a ridge along the surface of a bone. **3** a distinctive heraldic device representing a family or corporate body, displayed above the shield of a coat of arms or separately. ● v. reach the top of. ➤ (of a wave) form a curling foamy top. ➤ (**be crested with**) have attached at the top.

– PHRASES **on the crest of a wave** at a very successful point.
– DERIVATIVES **crested** adj. **crestless** adj.
– ORIGIN ME: from OFr. *creste*, from L. *crista* 'tuft, plume'.

**crestfallen** ● **adj.** sad and disappointed.
– ORIGIN C16: orig. with ref. to an animal with a fallen or drooping crest.

**crestfish** ● **n.** (pl. same or **-fishes**) a very elongated silvery marine fish with a long crimson dorsal fin. [*Lophotus lacepedei.*]

**cresting** ● **n.** an ornamental decoration at the top of a roof or wall.

**cresyl** /'kri:sʌɪl, -sɪl/ ● **n.** [as modifier] Chemistry of or denoting a radical derived from a cresol.

**Cretaceous** /krɪ'teɪʃəs/ ● **adj.** Geology relating to or denoting the last period of the Mesozoic era (between the Jurassic and Tertiary periods, about 146 to 65 million years ago), a time when the first flowering plants appeared and at the end of which dinosaurs, ammonites, and many other organisms died out.
– ORIGIN C17: from L. *cretaceus* (from *creta* 'chalk') + **-OUS**.

**Cretan** /'kri:tən/ ● **n.** an inhabitant or native of the Greek island of Crete. ● **adj.** of or relating to Crete or its inhabitants.

**cretic** /'kri:tɪk/ ● **n.** Prosody a metrical foot containing one short or unstressed syllable between two long or stressed ones.
– ORIGIN C16: from L. *Creticus*, from Gk *Krētikos* 'of Crete'.

**cretin** /'krɛtɪn/ ● **n. 1** a stupid person. **2** Medicine, dated a person who is deformed and mentally handicapped because of congenital thyroid deficiency.
– DERIVATIVES **cretinism** n. **cretinous** adj.
– ORIGIN C18: from Fr. *crétin*, from Swiss Fr. *crestin* 'Christian', appar. used to convey a reminder that handicapped people are human.

**cretonne** /krɛ'tɒn, 'krɛtɒn/ ● **n.** a heavy cotton fabric, typically with a floral pattern, used for upholstery.
– ORIGIN C19: from Fr.

**Creutzfeldt–Jakob disease** /ˌkrɔɪtsfɛlt'jakɒb/ ● **n.** a fatal degenerative disease affecting nerve cells in the brain, believed to be caused by a prion.
– PHRASES **new variant Creutzfeldt–Jakob disease** a form of the disease characterized by an early age of onset and possibly linked to BSE.
– ORIGIN 1930s: named after the Ger. neurologists H. G. *Creutzfeldt* and A. *Jakob*.

**crevasse** /krɪ'vas/ ● **n.** a deep open crack in a glacier or ice field.
– ORIGIN C19: from Fr., from OFr. *crevace* (see **CREVICE**).

**crevice** /'krɛvɪs/ ● **n.** a narrow opening or fissure, especially in a rock or wall.
– ORIGIN ME: from OFr. *crevace*, from *crever* 'to burst', from L. *crepare* 'to rattle, crack'.

**crew**[1] ● **n.** [treated as sing. or pl.] **1** a group of people who work on and operate a ship, boat, aircraft, or train. ➤ such a group other than the officers. **2** informal, often derogatory a group of people. ● **v.** provide with a crew. ➤ act as a member of a crew.
– DERIVATIVES **crewman** n. (pl. **-men**).
– ORIGIN ME, in sense 'band of soldiers': from OFr. *creue* 'augmentation, increase', fem. past part. of *croistre* 'grow', from L. *crescere*.

**crew**[2] past of **CROW**[2].

**crew cut** ● **n.** a very short haircut for men and boys.
– ORIGIN 1940s: appar. first adopted by boat crews of Harvard and Yale universities.

**crewel** /'kru:əl/ ● **n.** a thin, loosely twisted, worsted yarn used for tapestry and embroidery.
– ORIGIN C15: of unknown origin.

**crew neck** ● **n.** a close-fitting round neckline.
– DERIVATIVES **crew-necked** adj.

**crib** ● **n. 1** chiefly N. Amer. a child's bed with barred or latticed sides; a cot. ➤ a manger. ➤ Brit. a model of the Nativity of Christ. **2** informal a translation of a text for use by students, especially in a surreptitious way. ➤ a thing that has been plagiarized. **3** informal, chiefly N. Amer. an apartment or house. **4** short for **CRIBBAGE**. ➤ the cards discarded by the players at cribbage. **5** (also **cribwork**) a heavy timber framework used in foundations. **6** Austral./NZ a snack. ● **v.** (**cribbed, cribbing**) **1** informal copy illicitly or without acknowledgement. ➤ archaic steal. **2** archaic restrain. **3** Brit. dated grumble.
– DERIVATIVES **cribber** n.
– ORIGIN OE, of Gmc origin.

**cribbage** ● **n.** a card game for two players, in which the objective is to play so that the pip value of one's cards played reaches exactly 15 or 31.
– ORIGIN C17: rel. to **CRIB**.

**crib-biting** ● **n.** a repetitive habit of some horses involving biting and chewing of wood in the stable.

**crib death** ● **n.** North American term for **COT DEATH**.

**cribellum** /krɪ'bɛləm/ ● **n.** (pl. **cribella** /-lə/) Zoology (in some spiders) an additional spinning organ with numerous fine pores, situated in front of the spinnerets.
– DERIVATIVES **cribellate** adj.
– ORIGIN C19: from late L., dimin. of *cribrum* 'sieve'.

**cribo** /'kri:bəʊ, 'krʌɪbəʊ/ ● **n.** (pl. **-os**) another term for **INDIGO SNAKE**.
– ORIGIN C19: of unknown origin.

**cribriform** /'krɪbrɪfɔ:m/ ● **adj.** Anatomy pierced by numerous small holes.
– ORIGIN C18: from L. *cribrum* 'sieve' + **-IFORM**.

**cribwork** ● **n.** see **CRIB** (sense 5).

**crick** ● **n.** a painful stiff feeling in the neck or back. ● **v.** twist or strain (one's neck or back), causing painful stiffness.
– ORIGIN ME: of unknown origin.

**cricket**[1] ● **n.** an open-air game played on a large grass field with bat and ball between teams of eleven players, the batsmen attempting to score runs by hitting the ball and running between the wickets.
– PHRASES **not cricket** Brit. informal contrary to traditional standards of fairness or rectitude.
– DERIVATIVES **cricketer** n. **cricketing** adj.
– ORIGIN C16: of unknown origin.

**cricket**[2] ● **n.** an insect related to the grasshoppers but with shorter legs, of which the male produces a characteristic musical chirping sound. [Family Gryllidae: many species.] ➤ used in names of similar insects of related families, e.g. **bush cricket**.
– ORIGIN ME: from OFr. *criquet*, from *criquer* 'to crackle', of imitative origin.

**cricoid** /'krʌɪkɔɪd/ ● **n.** (also **cricoid cartilage**) Anatomy the ring-shaped cartilage of the larynx.
– ORIGIN C18: from mod. L. *cricoides* 'ring-shaped'.

**cri de cœur** /ˌkri: də 'kə:, French kʀi də kœʀ/ ● **n.** (pl. **cris de cœur** pronunc. same) a passionate appeal or complaint.
– ORIGIN Fr., 'cry from the heart'.

**cried** past and past participle of **CRY**.

**crier** ● **n.** an officer who makes public announcements in a court of justice.

**crikey** ● **exclam.** Brit. informal an expression of surprise.
– ORIGIN C19: euphemism for **CHRIST**.

**crim** ● **n. & adj.** informal, chiefly Austral./NZ short for **CRIMINAL**.

**crime** ● **n. 1** an action which constitutes a serious offence against an individual or the state and is punishable by law. ➤ such actions collectively: *the victims of crime.* **2** informal a shameful or deplorable action or state of affairs.
– ORIGIN ME (in the sense 'sin'): via OFr. from L. *crimen* 'judgement, offence', based on *cernere* 'to judge'.

**Crimean** /krʌɪ'mi:ən/ ● **adj.** of or relating to the Crimea, a peninsula of Ukraine between the Sea of Azov and the Black Sea.

**crime passionnel** /ˌkri:m pasjə'nɛl/ ● **n.** (pl. **crimes passionnels** pronunc. same) a crime committed in a fit of sexual jealousy.
– ORIGIN Fr., 'crime of passion'.

**criminal** ● **n.** a person who has committed a crime. ● **adj. 1** of, relating to, or constituting a crime. **2** informal deplorable and shocking.
– DERIVATIVES **criminality** /-'nalɪti/ n. **criminalization** (also **-isation**) n. **criminalize** (also **-ise**) v.

**criminally** adv.
– ORIGIN ME: from late L. *criminalis*, from L. *crimen*, *crimin-* (see **CRIME**).

**criminal conversation** ● **n.** Law, historical adultery.

**criminalistics** ● **pl. n.** [treated as sing.] another term for *forensics* (see **FORENSIC**).

**criminal law** ● **n.** a system of law concerned with the punishment of offenders.

**criminal libel** ● **n.** Law a malicious defamatory statement in a permanent form, rendering the maker liable to criminal prosecution.

**criminogenic** /ˌkrɪmɪnəˈdʒɛnɪk/ ● **adj.** causing or likely to cause criminal behaviour.

**criminology** /ˌkrɪmɪˈnɒlədʒi/ ● **n.** the scientific study of crime and criminals.
– DERIVATIVES **criminological** adj. **criminologist** n.

**crimp** ● **v. 1** compress into small folds or ridges. ➤ connect by squeezing together. ➤ [often as adj. **crimped**] make waves in (hair) with a hot iron. **2** N. Amer. informal have a limiting or adverse effect on. ● **n. 1** a curl, wave, or folded or compressed edge. **2** a small connecting piece for crimping wires or lines together.
– PHRASES **put a crimp in** N. Amer. informal have an adverse effect on.
– DERIVATIVES **crimpy** adj.
– ORIGIN OE *gecrympan*, of Gmc origin.

**crimper** ● **n. 1** a person or thing that crimps. **2** informal a hairdresser.

**crimplene** /ˈkrɪmpliːn/ ● **n.** trademark a synthetic crease-resistant fibre and fabric.
– ORIGIN 1950s: prob. from **CRIMP** + a shortened form of **TERYLENE**.

**crimson** /ˈkrɪmz(ə)n/ ● **n.** a rich deep red colour. ● **v.** become flushed, especially through embarrassment.
– ORIGIN ME: from obs. Fr. *cramoisin* or Old Sp. *cremesin*, based on Arab. *ḳirmizī*, from *ḳirmiz* (see **KERMES**).

**cringe** /krɪn(d)ʒ/ ● **v.** (**cringing**) **1** bend one's head and body in fear or apprehension or in a servile manner. **2** experience an inward shiver of embarrassment or disgust. ● **n.** an act of cringing.
– DERIVATIVES **cringer** n.
– ORIGIN ME *crenge*, *crenche*, rel. to OE *cringan*, *crincan* 'bend, yield, fall in battle', of Gmc origin and rel. to **CRANK**[1].

**cringeworthy** ● **adj.** informal causing embarrassment.

**cringle** ● **n.** Sailing a ring of rope containing a thimble, for another rope to pass through.
– ORIGIN C17: from Low Ger. *kringel*, dimin. of *kring* 'ring'.

**crinkle** ● **v.** form or cause to form small creases or wrinkles. ● **n.** a small crease or wrinkle.
– DERIVATIVES **crinkly** adj.
– ORIGIN ME: rel. to OE *crincan* (see **CRINGE**).

**crinkum-crankum** /krɪŋkəmˈkraŋkəm/ ● **n.** archaic elaborate decoration or detail.
– ORIGIN C17: fanciful reduplication of **CRANK**[1] or **CRANK**[2].

**crinoid** /ˈkrɪnɔɪd, ˈkrʌɪnɔɪd/ ● **n.** Zoology an echinoderm of a class (Crinoidea) that comprises the sea lilies and feather stars.
– DERIVATIVES **crinoidal** /-ˈnɔɪd(ə)l/ adj.
– ORIGIN mod. L. *Crinoidea*, from Gk *krinoeidēs* 'lily-like', from *krinon* 'lily'.

**crinoline** /ˈkrɪn(ə)lɪn/ ● **n. 1** historical a stiffened or hooped petticoat worn to make a long skirt stand out. **2** a stiff fabric made of horsehair and cotton or linen thread, used for stiffening petticoats or as a lining.
– ORIGIN C19: from Fr., formed irregularly from L. *crinis* 'hair' + *linum* 'thread'.

**criollo** /krɪˈɒləʊ, -ɒljəʊ/ (also **Criollo**) ● **n.** (pl. **-os**) **1** a person from Spanish South or Central America, especially one of pure Spanish descent. **2** (also **criollo tree**) a cacao tree of a variety producing thin-shelled beans of high quality.
– ORIGIN C19: Sp., lit. 'native to the locality' (see **CREOLE**).

**cripes** /krʌɪps/ ● **exclam.** dated, informal used as a euphemism for Christ.

**cripple** ● **n.** archaic or offensive a person who is unable to walk or move properly through disability or injury. ● **v.** (usu. **be crippled**) make unable to move or walk properly. ➤ cause severe and disabling damage to.
– DERIVATIVES **crippledom** n. **crippler** n.
– ORIGIN OE: from two words, *crypel* and *crēopel*, both of Gmc origin and rel. to **CREEP**.

**crisis** ● **n.** (pl. **crises**) **1** a time of intense difficulty or danger. **2** the turning point of a disease when an important change takes place, indicating either recovery or death.
– ORIGIN ME: medical L., from Gk *krisis* 'decision', from *krinein* 'decide'.

**crisp** ● **adj. 1** firm, dry, and brittle, especially in a way considered pleasing. ➤ (of hair) having tight curls, giving an impression of rigidity. **2** (of the weather) cool, fresh, and invigorating. **3** (of a way of speaking) briskly decisive and matter-of-fact. ● **n.** (also **potato crisp**) Brit. a wafer-thin slice of potato fried until crisp and eaten as a snack. ● **v. 1** give (food) a crisp surface by placing it in an oven or grill. **2** archaic curl into short, stiff, wavy folds or crinkles.
– PHRASES **burn to a crisp** burn so as to leave only a charred remnant.
– DERIVATIVES **crispiness** n. **crisply** adv. **crispness** n. **crispy** adj. (**-ier**, **-iest**).
– ORIGIN OE: from L. *crispus* 'curled'.

**crispate** ● **adj.** Botany having a wavy or curly edge.
– ORIGIN C19: from L. *crispatus*, past part. of *crispare* 'to curl'.

**crispbread** ● **n.** a thin crisp biscuit made from crushed rye or wheat.

**crisper** ● **n.** a compartment at the bottom of a refrigerator for storing fruit and vegetables.

**criss-cross** ● **n.** a pattern of intersecting straight lines or paths. ● **adj.** (of a pattern) containing a number of intersecting straight lines or paths. ● **v. 1** form a criss-cross pattern on (a place). **2** move or travel around (a place) by going back and forth repeatedly.
– ORIGIN C17 (denoting a figure of a cross preceding the alphabet in a hornbook): from *Christ-cross*, later treated as a reduplication of **CROSS**.

**crista** /ˈkrɪstə/ ● **n.** (pl. **cristae** /-tiː/) **1** Anatomy & Zoology a ridge or crest. **2** Biology an infolding of the inner membrane of a mitochondrion.
– DERIVATIVES **cristate** adj.
– ORIGIN C19: from L., 'tuft, plume, crest'.

**cristobalite** /krɪˈstəʊbəlʌɪt/ ● **n.** a form of silica which is the main component of opal.
– ORIGIN C19: named after *Cerro San Cristóbal* in Mexico, where it was discovered.

**criterion** /krʌɪˈtɪərɪən/ ● **n.** (pl. **criteria** /-rɪə/) a principle or standard by which something may be judged or decided.
– DERIVATIVES **criterial** adj.
– ORIGIN C17: from Gk *kritērion* 'means of judging', from *kritēs* (see **CRITIC**).

**USAGE criterion**

The singular form is **criterion** and the plural form is **criteria**. It is a common mistake to use **criteria** as if it were a singular, as in *a further criteria needs to be considered.*

**critic** ● **n. 1** a person who expresses an unfavourable opinion of something. **2** a person who judges the merits of literary, artistic, or musical works, especially one who does so professionally.
– ORIGIN C16: from L. *criticus*, from Gk *kritikos*, from *kritēs* 'a judge'.

**critical** ● **adj. 1** expressing adverse or disapproving comments or judgements. **2** expressing or involving an analysis of the merits and faults of a work of literature, music, or art. **3** (of a situation or problem) at a point of crisis. ➤ extremely ill and at risk of death. ➤ having a decisive importance in the success or failure of something. **4** Mathematics & Physics relating to or denoting a point of transition from one state to another. **5** (of a nuclear reactor or fuel) maintaining a self-sustaining chain reaction.
– DERIVATIVES **criticality** n. **critically** adv. **criticalness** n.

**critical angle** • **n.** Optics the angle of incidence beyond which rays of light passing through a denser medium to the surface of a less dense medium are no longer refracted but totally reflected.

**critical apparatus** • **n.** see **APPARATUS** (sense 3).

**critical damping** • **n.** Physics damping just sufficient to prevent oscillations.

**critical mass** • **n. 1** Physics the minimum amount of fissile material needed to maintain a nuclear chain reaction. **2** the minimum size or amount of resources required to start or maintain a venture.

**critical path** • **n.** the sequence of stages determining the minimum time needed for a complex operation.

**critical point** • **n. 1** Chemistry a set of conditions at which both the liquid and gas phases of a substance have the same density, and are therefore indistinguishable. **2** Mathematics US term for **STATIONARY POINT**.

**critical pressure** • **n.** Chemistry the pressure of a gas or vapour in its critical state.

**critical state** • **n.** Chemistry the state of a substance when it is at the critical point.

**critical temperature** • **n.** Chemistry the temperature of a gas in its critical state, above which it cannot be liquefied by pressure alone.

**criticism** • **n. 1** the expression of disapproval of someone or something based on perceived faults or mistakes. **2** the critical assessment of a literary or artistic work.

**criticize** (also **-ise**) • **v. 1** indicate the faults of in a disapproving way. **2** form and express a critical assessment of (a literary or artistic work).
– DERIVATIVES **criticizable** adj. **criticizer** n.

**critique** /krɪ'ti:k/ • **n.** a detailed analysis and assessment. • **v.** (**critiques**, **critiqued**, **critiquing**) evaluate in a detailed and analytical way.
– ORIGIN C17: from Fr., based on Gk *kritikē tekhnē* 'critical art'.

**critter** • **n.** informal or dialect, chiefly N. Amer. a living creature.
– ORIGIN C19: var. of **CREATURE**.

**croak** • **n.** a characteristic deep hoarse sound made by a frog or a crow. • **v. 1** (of a frog or crow) utter a croak. **2** informal die. **3** archaic prophesy evil or misfortune.
– DERIVATIVES **croakily** adv. **croaky** adj. (**-ier**, **-iest**).
– ORIGIN ME: imitative.

**croaker** • **n.** a person or animal that croaks. ➤ another term for **DRUM**[2].

**Croatian** /krəʊ'eɪʃ(ə)n/ • **n.** (also **Croat** /'krəʊat/) **1** a native or national of Croatia, or a person of Croatian descent. **2** the Southern Slavic language of the Croats, almost identical to Serbian but written in the Roman alphabet. • **adj.** of or relating to Croatia, its people, or their language.

**crochet** /'krəʊʃeɪ, -ʃi/ • **n.** a handicraft in which yarn is made up into a patterned fabric by means of a hooked needle. ➤ fabric or items made in this way. • **v.** (**crocheted** /-ʃeɪd/, **crocheting** /-ʃeɪɪŋ/) make (a garment or piece of fabric) in this way.
– DERIVATIVES **crocheter** /'krəʊʃeɪə/ n.
– ORIGIN C19: from Fr., dimin. of *croc* 'hook'.

**croci** plural form of **CROCUS**.

**crocidolite** /krə(ʊ)'sɪdəlʌɪt/ • **n.** a fibrous blue or green mineral consisting of a silicate of iron and sodium.
– ORIGIN C19: from Gk *krokis*, *krokid-* 'nap of cloth' + **-LITE**.

**crock**[1] informal • **n.** an old person considered to be feeble and useless. ➤ Brit. an old and worn-out vehicle. • **v. 1** Brit. cause an injury to. **2** [as adj. **crocked**] N. Amer. drunk.
– ORIGIN ME (orig. denoting an old ewe, later an old or broken-down horse): perh. from Flemish, and prob. rel. to **CRACK**.

**crock**[2] • **n. 1** an earthenware pot or jar. ➤ a broken piece of earthenware. ➤ a plate, cup, or other item of crockery. **2** (also vulgar slang **crock of shit**) chiefly N. Amer. something considered to be complete nonsense.
– ORIGIN OE *croc*, *crocca*, of Gmc origin.

**crockery** • **n.** plates, dishes, cups, and similar items made of earthenware or china.
– ORIGIN C18: from obs. *crocker* 'potter', from **CROCK**[2].

**crocket** /'krɒkɪt/ • **n.** (in Gothic architecture) a small carved ornament on the inclined side of a pinnacle or gable.
– ORIGIN ME: from ONorth. Fr., var. of OFr. *crochet* (see **CROTCHET**).

**crocodile** • **n. 1** a large predatory semiaquatic reptile with long jaws, long tail, short legs, and a horny textured skin. [*Crocodylus* and other genera.] **2** leather made from crocodile skin, used especially to make bags and shoes. **3** Brit. informal a line of schoolchildren walking in pairs.
– ORIGIN ME *cocodrille*, *cokadrill*, from OFr. *cocodrille*, via med. L. from L. *crocodilus*, from Gk *krokodilos* 'worm of the stones'.

**crocodile clip** • **n.** chiefly Brit. a sprung metal clip with long, serrated jaws, used to connect an electric cable temporarily to a battery or other component.

**crocodile tears** • **pl. n.** tears or expressions of sorrow that are insincere.
– ORIGIN C16: said to be so named from a belief that crocodiles wept while devouring or luring their prey.

**crocodilian** /ˌkrɒkə'dɪlɪən/ • **n.** Zoology a reptile of the order Crocodylia, comprising the crocodiles, alligators, caimans, and gharial.

**crocus** /'krəʊkəs/ • **n.** (pl. **crocuses** or **croci** /-kʌɪ, -ki:/) a small spring-flowering plant of the iris family, which grows from a corm and bears bright yellow, purple, or white flowers. [Genus *Crocus*.]
– ORIGIN ME: via L. from Gk *krokos*, of Semitic origin.

**Croesus** /'kri:səs/ • **n.** a person of great wealth.
– ORIGIN C17: from the name of a famously wealthy king of Lydia *c.* 560–546 BC.

**croft** Brit. • **n. 1** a small rented farm, especially in Scotland, having a right of pasturage held in common with other such farms. **2** a small enclosed field, typically attached to a house. • **v.** farm (land) as a croft or crofts.
– DERIVATIVES **crofter** n. **crofting** n.
– ORIGIN OE: of unknown origin.

**Crohn's disease** /'krəʊnz/ • **n.** a chronic inflammatory disease of the intestines, especially the colon and ileum, associated with ulcers and fistulae.
– ORIGIN 1930s: named after the Amer. pathologist Burrill B. *Crohn*.

**croissant** /'krwasɒ̃, French krwasɑ̃/ • **n.** a French crescent-shaped roll made of sweet flaky pastry, eaten for breakfast.
– ORIGIN C19: Fr. (see **CRESCENT**).

**Cro-Magnon** /krəʊ'manjɒ̃, -'magnən/ • **n.** [as modifier] denoting the earliest form of modern human in Europe, appearing *c.*35,000 years ago and associated with the Aurignacian flint industry.
– ORIGIN the name of a hill in the Dordogne, France.

**crombec** /'krɒmbɛk/ • **n.** a small African warbler with a very short tail. [Genus *Sylvietta*: several species.]
– ORIGIN C20: from Fr., from Du. *krom* 'crooked' + *bek* 'beak'.

**cromlech** /'krɒmlɛk/ • **n. 1** (in Wales) a megalithic tomb consisting of a large flat stone laid on upright ones; a dolmen. **2** (in Brittany) a circle of standing stones.
– ORIGIN Welsh, from *crom*, fem. of *crwm* 'arched' + *llech* 'flat stone' (sense 1); sense 2 via Fr. from Breton *krommlec'h*.

**crone** • **n.** an ugly old woman.
– ORIGIN ME: via MDu. *croonje*, *caroonje* 'carcass, old ewe' from ONorth. Fr. *caroigne* (see **CARRION**).

**croning** • **n.** (especially among feminists in the US and Australasia) a celebration or ceremony to honour older women.
– ORIGIN blend of **CRONE** + *crowning* from **CROWN**.

**cronk** • **adj.** Austral./NZ informal, dated unfit, unsound, or fraudulent.
– ORIGIN C19: prob. rel. to **CRANK**[3].

**crony** /'krəʊni/ • **n.** (pl. **-ies**) informal, often derogatory a close friend or companion.
– ORIGIN C17 (orig. Cambridge university sl.): from Gk *khronios* 'long-lasting' (here used to mean 'contemporary'); cf. **CHUM**[1].

**cronyism** (also **croneyism**) • **n.** derogatory the improper appointment of friends and associates to positions of authority.

**crook** ● **n.** **1** a shepherd's hooked staff. ➤a bishop's crozier. **2** a bend, especially at the elbow in a person's arm. **3** informal a person who is dishonest or a criminal. ● **v.** bend (something, especially a finger as a signal). ● **adj.** Austral./NZ informal bad, unsound, or unwell. ➤dishonest; illegal.
– DERIVATIVES **crookery** n.
– ORIGIN ME: from ON *krókr* 'hook'.

**crookback** ● **n.** archaic a person with a hunchback.
– DERIVATIVES **crookbacked** adj.

**crooked** /'krʊkɪd/ ● **adj.** **1** bent or twisted out of shape or position. **2** informal dishonest or illegal. **3** Austral./NZ informal annoyed; exasperated.
– DERIVATIVES **crookedly** adv. **crookedness** n.

**croon** ● **v.** hum, sing, or speak in a soft, low voice. ● **n.** a soft, low voice or tone.
– DERIVATIVES **crooner** n.
– ORIGIN C15 (orig. Scots and north. Engl.): from Mid. Low Ger. and MDu. *krōnen* 'groan, lament'.

**crop** ● **n.** **1** a plant cultivated on a large scale for food or other use, especially a cereal, fruit, or vegetable. ➤an amount of a crop harvested at one time. **2** an amount of related people or things appearing at one time: *the current crop of politicians.* **3** a hairstyle in which the hair is cut very short. **4** a riding crop or hunting crop. **5** a pouch in a bird's gullet where food is stored or prepared for digestion. **6** the entire tanned hide of an animal. ● **v.** (**cropped**, **cropping**) **1** cut (something, especially a person's hair) very short. ➤(of an animal) bite off and eat the tops of (plants). ➤trim off the edges of (a photograph). **2** harvest (a crop) from an area. ➤sow or plant (land) with plants that will produce a crop. ➤(of land or a plant) yield a harvest. **3** (**crop up**) appear or occur unexpectedly. **4** (**crop out**) (of rock) appear or be exposed at the surface of the earth.
– ORIGIN OE, of Gmc origin.

**crop circle** ● **n.** an area of standing crops which has been flattened in the form of a circle or more complex pattern by an unexplained agency.

**crop dusting** ● **n.** the spraying of powdered insecticide or fertilizer on crops, especially from the air.

**crop-eared** ● **adj.** historical **1** having the tops of the ears cut off. **2** (especially of a Roundhead in the English Civil War) having the hair cut very short.

**crop-over** ● **n.** a West Indian celebration marking the end of the sugar-cane harvest.

**cropper** ● **n.** **1** a plant which yields a specified crop. **2** a machine or person that cuts or trims something. **3** chiefly US a person who raises a crop, especially as a sharecropper.
– PHRASES **come a cropper** informal fall heavily. ➤suffer a defeat or disaster.

**crop top** (also **cropped top**) ● **n.** a woman's casual garment for the upper body, cut short so that it reveals the stomach.

**croquembouche** /ˌkrɒkɒm'buːʃ/ ● **n.** a decorative dessert consisting of choux pastry and crystallized fruit arranged in a cone and held together by a caramel sauce.
– ORIGIN Fr., lit. 'crunch in the mouth'.

**croque-monsieur** /ˌkrɒk mə'sjəː/ ● **n.** a fried or grilled cheese and ham sandwich.
– ORIGIN Fr., lit. 'bite (a) man'.

**croquet** /'krəʊkeɪ, -ki/ ● **n.** a game played on a lawn, in which wooden balls are driven through a series of square-topped hoops by means of mallets. ➤an act of croqueting a ball. ● **v.** (**croqueted** /-keɪd/, **croqueting** /-keɪɪŋ/) drive away (an opponent's ball) by holding one's own ball against it and striking one's own.
– ORIGIN C19: perh. a dial. form of Fr. *crochet* 'hook'.

**croquette** /krə(ʊ)'kɛt/ ● **n.** a small ball or roll of vegetables, minced meat, or fish, fried in breadcrumbs.
– ORIGIN Fr., from *croquer* 'to crunch'.

**crore** /krɔː/ ● **cardinal number** Indian ten million; one hundred lakhs.
– ORIGIN from Hindi *karoṛ*, based on Sanskrit *koṭi* 'ten millions'.

**crosier** /'krəʊzɪə, -ʒə/ ● **n.** variant spelling of CROZIER.

**cross** ● **n.** **1** a mark, object, or figure formed by two short intersecting lines or pieces (+ or ×). **2** an upright post with a transverse bar, as used in antiquity for crucifixion. ➤(**the Cross**) the cross on which Christ was crucified. ➤a cross-shaped decoration awarded for personal valour or indicating rank in some orders of knighthood. **3** a thing that is unavoidable and has to be endured: *she's just a cross we have to bear.* **4** an animal or plant resulting from cross-breeding; a hybrid. ➤(**a cross between**) a mixture or compromise of two things. **5** (in soccer) a pass of the ball across the field towards the centre close to one's opponents' goal. **6** (in boxing) a blow given with a crosswise movement of the fist. ● **v.** **1** go or extend across or to the other side of (a path, obstacle, or area). ➤(**cross over**) (of an artist) begin to appeal to a wider audience. **2** pass in an opposite or different direction; intersect. ➤place crosswise: *Michele crossed her arms.* **3** draw a line or lines across; mark with a cross. ➤Brit. mark or annotate (a cheque), typically with a pair of parallel lines, to indicate that it must be paid into a named bank account. ➤(**cross something off**) delete an item on a list. ➤(**cross something out/through**) delete a word or phrase by drawing a line through it. **4** (**cross oneself**) make the sign of the cross in front of one's chest as a sign of Christian reverence or to invoke divine protection. **5** Soccer pass (the ball) across the field towards the centre when attacking. **6** cause (an animal of one species, breed, or variety) to interbreed with one of another. ➤cross-fertilize (a plant). **7** oppose or stand in the way of. ● **adj.** annoyed.
– PHRASES **at cross purposes** misunderstanding or having different aims from one another. **cross one's fingers** put one finger across another as a sign of hoping for good luck. **cross the floor** Brit. join the opposing side in Parliament. **cross my heart** (**and hope to die**) used to emphasize the truthfulness and sincerity of what one is saying. **cross someone's palm with silver** often humorous pay someone for a favour or service, especially having one's fortune told. **cross swords** have an argument or dispute. **crossed line** a telephone connection that has been wrongly made with the result that another call can be heard. **get one's wires** (or **lines**) **crossed** have a misunderstanding.
– DERIVATIVES **crosser** n. **crossly** adv. **crossness** n.
– ORIGIN OE: from ON *kross*, from Old Ir. *cros*, from L. *crux.*

**cross-** ● **comb. form** **1** denoting movement or position across: *cross-channel.* ➤denoting interaction: *cross-pollinate.* ➤passing from side to side; transverse: *cross-piece.* **2** describing the form of a cross: *crossbones.*

**crossbar** ● **n.** a horizontal bar, in particular one between the two upright posts of a football goal or between the handlebars and saddle on a bicycle.

**cross-bedding** ● **n.** Geology layering within a stratum and at an angle to the main bedding plane.

**cross bench** ● **n.** a seat in the House of Lords occupied by a member who is independent of any political party.
– DERIVATIVES **cross-bencher** n.

**crossbill** ● **n.** a thickset finch with a crossed bill adapted for extracting seeds from the cones of conifers. [*Loxia curvirostra* and related species.]

**crossbow** ● **n.** a medieval bow of a kind fixed across a wooden support, having a groove for the bolt and a mechanism for drawing and releasing the string.
– DERIVATIVES **crossbowman** n. (pl. **-men**).

**cross-breed** ● **n.** an animal or plant produced by mating or hybridizing two different species, breeds, or varieties. ● **v.** breed or cause to breed in this way.

**cross-check** ● **v.** **1** verify (figures or information) by using an alternative source or method. **2** Ice Hockey obstruct (an opponent) illegally with the stick held horizontally in both hands. ● **n.** an instance of cross-checking figures or information.

**cross-correlate** ● **v.** compare (a sequence of data) against another.
– DERIVATIVES **cross-correlation** n.

**cross-country** ● **adj.** **1** across fields or countryside, as opposed to on roads or tracks: *cross-country running.* **2** across a region or country, in particular not keeping to main or direct routes. • n. the sport of cross-country running, riding, skiing, or motoring.

**cross cousin** • n. each of two cousins who are children of a brother and sister.

**cross-current** • n. **1** a current in a river or sea which flows across another. **2** a process or tendency which is in conflict with another.

**cross-cut** • v. **1** cut (wood or stone) across its main grain or axis. **2** alternate (one sequence) with another when editing a film. • n. an instance of cross-cutting. • adj. (of a file) having two sets of grooves crossing each other diagonally.

**cross-cut saw** • n. a saw with a handle at each end, used by two people for cutting across the grain of timber.

**cross-dating** • n. Archaeology the dating of objects by correlation with the chronology of another culture or site.

**cross-dress** • v. wear clothing typical of the opposite sex.

– DERIVATIVES **cross-dresser** n.

**crosse** /krɒs/ • n. the stick used in women's field lacrosse.

– ORIGIN C19: from Fr., from OFr. *croce* 'bishop's crook'.

**cross-examine** • v. question (a witness called by the other party) in a court of law to check or extend testimony already given.

– DERIVATIVES **cross-examination** n. **cross-examiner** n.

**cross-eyed** • adj. having one or both eyes turned inwards towards the nose, either temporarily or as a permanent condition (convergent strabismus).

**cross-fade** • v. (in sound or film editing) make a picture or sound appear or be heard gradually as another disappears or becomes silent. • n. an act or instance of cross-fading.

**cross-fertilize** (also **-ise**) • v. **1** fertilize (a plant) using pollen from another plant of the same species. **2** stimulate the development of with an exchange of ideas or information.

– DERIVATIVES **cross-fertilization** n.

**crossfire** • n. gunfire from two or more directions passing through the same area.

**crossflow** • n. a type of engine cylinder head where the intake ports are on the opposite side of the engine from the exhaust ports.

**cross-grain** • adj. running across the regular grain in timber.

**cross-grained** • adj. **1** (of timber) having a cross-grain. **2** stubbornly contrary or bad-tempered.

**cross hairs** • pl. n. a pair of fine wires crossing at right angles at the focus of an optical instrument or gunsight.

**cross-hatch** • v. shade (an area) with intersecting sets of parallel lines.

– DERIVATIVES **cross-hatching** n.

**cross head** • n. **1** a bar or block between the piston rod and connecting rod in a steam engine. **2** a screw with an indented cross shape in its head. **3** a paragraph heading printed across a column in the body of a newspaper article.

**cross index** • n. a note or cross reference which refers the reader to other material. • v. index (something) under another heading as a cross reference.

**cross infection** • n. the transfer of infection, especially to a hospital patient with a different infection or between different species of animal or plant.

**crossing** • n. **1** a place where things, especially roads or railway lines, cross. ➤ Architecture the intersection of a church nave and the transepts. **2** a place at which one may safely cross something, especially a street.

**crossing over** • n. Genetics the exchange of genes between homologous chromosomes, resulting in a mixture of parental characteristics in offspring.

**cross-legged** • adj. & adv. (of a seated person) with the legs crossed at the ankles and the knees bent outwards.

**cross link** • n. a transverse link, especially between chains of atoms in a polymeric molecule. • v. (**cross-link**) connect by a series of transverse links.

– DERIVATIVES **cross-linkage** n.

**crossmatch** • v. Medicine test the compatibility of (a donor's and a recipient's blood or tissue).

**cross member** • n. a transverse structural piece which adds support to a motor-vehicle chassis or other construction.

**crossopterygian** /ˌkrɒsɒptəˈrɪdʒɪən/ • n. Zoology a fish of the subclass Crossopterygia (of which the only living example is the coelacanth), distinguished by having fleshy, lobed fins.

– ORIGIN C19: from mod. L. *Crossopterygia*, from Gk *krossos* 'tassel' + *pterux*, *pterug-* 'fin'.

**crossover** • n. **1** a point or place of crossing from one side to the other. **2** the process of producing work or achieving success in a new field or style, especially in popular music.

**cross ownership** • n. the ownership by one corporation of different companies with related interests or commercial aims.

**crosspatch** • n. informal a bad-tempered person.

– ORIGIN C18: from CROSS + obs. *patch* 'fool, clown', perh. from Ital. *pazzo* 'madman'.

**crosspiece** • n. a beam or bar fixed or placed across something else.

**cross-platform** • adj. Computing able to be used on different types of computers or with different software packages.

**cross-ply** • adj. Brit. (of a tyre) having fabric layers with their threads running diagonally, crosswise to each other.

**cross-pollinate** • v. pollinate (a flower or plant) with pollen from another flower or plant.

– DERIVATIVES **cross-pollination** n.

**cross product** • n. another term for **VECTOR PRODUCT**.

**cross-question** • v. question in great detail.

**cross-rate** • n. an exchange rate between two currencies computed by reference to a third currency, usually the US dollar.

**cross reference** • n. a reference to another text or part of a text, typically given in order to elaborate on a point. • v. (**cross-reference**) provide with cross references.

– DERIVATIVES **cross-refer** v.

**cross-rhythm** • n. Music a rhythm used simultaneously with another rhythm or rhythms.

**crossroads** • n. **1** an intersection of two or more roads. **2** (**crossroad**) N. Amer. a road that crosses a main road or joins two main roads.

**cross section** • n. **1** a surface or shape exposed by making a straight cut through something, especially at right angles to an axis. **2** a typical or representative sample of a larger group. **3** Physics a quantity having the dimensions of an area which expresses the probability of a given interaction between particles. • v. (**cross-section**) make a cross section of.

– DERIVATIVES **cross-sectional** adj.

**cross-sell** • v. sell (a different product or service) to an existing customer.

**cross stitch** Needlework • n. a stitch formed of two stitches crossing each other. • v. (**cross-stitch**) sew or embroider using such stitches.

**cross-subsidize** (also **-ise**) • v. subsidize (a business or activity) out of the profits of another business or activity.

– DERIVATIVES **cross-subsidization** n. **cross-subsidy** n.

**crosstalk** • n. **1** unwanted transfer of signals between communication channels. **2** witty conversation.

**cross tie** • n. US a railway sleeper.

**cross-train** • v. **1** learn another skill, especially one related to one's current job. **2** [as noun **cross-training**] training in two or more sports in order to improve fitness and performance.

**crosstrees** • pl. n. a pair of horizontal struts attached to a sailing ship's mast to spread the rigging, especially at the head of a topmast.

**cross-voting** • n. voting for a party one does not belong to, or for more than one party.

**crosswalk** ● n. N. Amer. & Austral. a pedestrian crossing.

**crossways** ● adv. another term for **CROSSWISE**.

**crosswind** ● n. a wind blowing across one's direction of travel.

**crosswise** ● adv. **1** in the form of a cross. **2** diagonally; transversely.

**crossword** ● n. a puzzle consisting of a grid of squares and blanks into which words crossing vertically and horizontally are written according to clues.

**crosswort** /'krɒswəːt/ ● n. a yellow-flowered plant related to the bedstraws, with leaves arranged in a cross or whorl of four. [*Cruciata laevipes*.]

**crostini** /krɒ'stiːni/ ● pl. n. small pieces of toasted or fried bread served with a topping as a starter or canapé.
– ORIGIN Ital., pl. of *crostino* 'little crust'.

**crotal** ● n. variant spelling of **CROTTLE**.

**crotale** /'krəʊt(ə)l/ ● n. a small tuned cymbal.
– ORIGIN 1930s: Fr.

**crotch** ● n. **1** the part of the human body between the legs where they join the torso. **2** a fork in a tree, road, or river.
– DERIVATIVES **crotched** adj. **crotchless** adj.
– ORIGIN C16: perh. rel. to OFr. *croche* 'shepherd's crook', based on ON *krókr* 'hook'; partly also a var. of **CRUTCH**.

**crotchet** /'krɒtʃɪt/ ● n. **1** Music, chiefly Brit. a musical note having the time value of a quarter of a semibreve or half a minim, represented by a large solid dot with a plain stem. **2** a perverse or unfounded belief or notion.
– ORIGIN ME (in the sense 'hook'): from OFr. *crochet*, dimin. of *croc*, from ON *krókr*.

**crotchety** ● adj. irritable.
– DERIVATIVES **crotchetiness** n.
– ORIGIN C19: from sense 2 of **CROTCHET** + **-Y**[1].

**croton** /'krəʊt(ə)n/ ● n. **1** a strong-scented tree, shrub, or herbaceous plant, native to tropical and warm regions. [Genus *Croton*.] **2** a small evergreen tree or shrub of the Indo-Pacific region, with colourful foliage. [Genus *Codiaeum*.]
– ORIGIN mod. L., from Gk *krotōn* 'sheep tick' (from the shape of the seeds of the croton in sense 1).

**crottle** /'krɒt(ə)l/ (also **crotal**) ● n. a common lichen found on rocks, used in Scotland to make a dye for making tweed. [*Parmelia saxatilis* and other species.]
– ORIGIN C18: from Sc. Gaelic and Ir. *crotal*, *crotan*.

**crouch** ● v. adopt a position where the knees are bent and the upper body is brought forward and down. ➤ (**crouch over**) bend over so as to be close to. ● n. a crouching stance or posture.
– ORIGIN ME: perh. from OFr. *crochir* 'be bent', from *croche* (see **CROTCH**).

**croup**[1] /kruːp/ ● n. inflammation of the larynx and trachea in children, associated with infection and causing breathing difficulties.
– DERIVATIVES **croupy** adj.
– ORIGIN C18: from dial. *croup* 'to croak', of imitative origin.

**croup**[2] /kruːp/ ● n. the rump or hindquarters of a horse.
– ORIGIN ME: from OFr. *croupe*, ult. of Gmc origin and rel. to **CROP**.

**croupade** /krʊ'peɪd/ ● n. a movement performed in classical riding, in which the horse leaps from the ground with its legs tucked under its body.
– ORIGIN C17: Fr., from Ital. *groppata*, from *groppa* 'croup'.

**croupier** /'kruːpɪə, -pɪeɪ/ ● n. **1** the person in charge of a gaming table, gathering in and paying out money or tokens. **2** historical the assistant chairman at a public dinner.
– ORIGIN C18 (denoting a person standing behind a gambler to give advice): Fr., from OFr. *cropier* 'pillion rider', rel. to OFr. *croupe* (see **CROUP**[2]).

**croustade** /krʊ'stɑːd/ ● n. a crisp piece of bread or pastry hollowed to receive a savoury filling.
– ORIGIN Fr., from OFr. *crouste* or Ital. *crostata* 'tart'.

**croute** /kruːt/ ● n. a piece of toasted bread on which savoury snacks can be served.
– ORIGIN Fr. *croûte* (see **CRUST**).

**crouton** /'kruːtɒn/ ● n. a small piece of fried or toasted bread served with soup or used as a garnish.
– ORIGIN from Fr. *croûton*, from *croûte* (see **CRUST**).

**Crow** ● n. (pl. same or **Crows**) **1** a member of an American Indian people inhabiting eastern Montana. **2** the Siouan language of this people.
– ORIGIN suggested by Fr. *gens de corbeaux*, translating Siouan *apsáaloke* 'crow people'.

**crow**[1] ● n. **1** a large perching bird with mostly glossy black plumage, a heavy bill, and a raucous voice. [*Corvus corone* (**carrion crow**), and related species, family Corvidae.] **2** informal an old or ugly woman.
– PHRASES **as the crow flies** in a straight line across country. **eat crow** N. Amer. informal be humiliated by having to admit one's defeats or mistakes.
– ORIGIN OE *crāwe*, of W. Gmc origin; rel. to **CROW**[2].

**crow**[2] ● v. (past **crowed** or **crew**) **1** (of a cock) utter its characteristic loud cry. **2** express great pride or triumph, especially in a tone of gloating satisfaction. ● n. **1** the cry of a cock. **2** a sound expressing great pride or triumph.
– ORIGIN OE *crāwan*, of W. Gmc origin, rel. to **CROW**[1]; ult. imitative.

**crowbar** ● n. an iron bar with a flattened end, used as a lever. ● v. (**-barred**, **-barring**) strike or open with a crowbar.

**crowberry** ● n. (pl. **-ies**) **1** a creeping heather-like dwarf shrub with small leaves and black berries. [*Empetrum nigrum*.] **2** the edible but flavourless black berry of this plant.

**crowd** ● n. a large number of people gathered together. ➤ a large audience, especially at a sporting event. ➤ informal, often derogatory a group of people with a common interest. ● v. **1** [often as adj. **crowded**] (of a number of people) fill (a space) almost completely, leaving little or no room for movement. ➤ move or come together as a crowd. **2** move too close to: *don't crowd her, she needs air.* **3** (**crowd someone/thing out**) exclude by taking the place of someone or something.
– DERIVATIVES **crowdedness** n.
– ORIGIN OE *crūdan* 'press, hasten', of Gmc origin.

**crowdie** /'kraʊdi/ (also **crowdy**) ● n. a soft Scottish cheese made from buttermilk or sour milk.
– ORIGIN C19: from **CRUD** + **-IE**.

**crowd-puller** ● n. informal an event or person that attracts a large audience.
– DERIVATIVES **crowd-pulling** adj.

**crowfoot** ● n. a plant related to the buttercups, typically aquatic and with lobed or divided leaves and white or yellow flowers. [*Ranunculus aquatilis* (**water crowfoot**) and related species.]

**crow hop** ● n. a short jump with both feet together. ➤ N. Amer. a jump by a horse with its back arched and its legs stiffened.

**crown** ● n. **1** a circular ornamental headdress worn by a monarch as a symbol of authority. ➤ (**the Crown**) the monarchy or reigning monarch. ➤ a wreath of leaves or flowers, especially that worn as an emblem of victory in ancient Greece or Rome. **2** an award or distinction gained by a victory or achievement, especially in sport. **3** the top or highest part. ➤ the top part of a person's head or a hat. ➤ the upper branching part of a tree or other plant. ➤ the upper part of a cut gem, above the girdle. **4** the part of a tooth projecting from the gum. ➤ an artificial replacement or covering for the upper part of a tooth. **5** a British coin with a face value of five shillings or 25 pence, now minted only for commemorative purposes. **6** (in full **metric crown**) a paper size, 384 × 504 mm. ➤ (in full **crown octavo**) a book size, 186 × 123 mm. ➤ (in full **crown quarto**) a book size, 246 × 189 mm. ● v. **1** ceremonially place a crown on the head of (someone) to invest them as a monarch. ➤ declare to be the best, especially at a sport: *he was crowned world champion.* ➤ (in draughts) promote (a piece) to king by placing another on top of it. **2** rest on or form the top of. **3** be the triumphant culmination of (an effort or endeavour). **4** fit a crown to (a tooth). **5** informal hit on the head. **6** (of a baby's head

during labour) fully appear in the vaginal opening prior to emerging.
– ORIGIN ME: from Anglo-Norman Fr. *corune* (n.), *coruner* (v.), OFr. *corone*, *coroner*, from L. *corona* 'wreath, chaplet'.

**crown and anchor** • n. a gambling game played with three dice each bearing a crown, an anchor, and the four card suits.

**Crown attorney** • n. Canadian term for **CROWN PROSECUTOR**.

**crown cap** • n. another term for **CROWN CORK**.

**Crown Colony** • n. a British colony whose legislature and administration is controlled by the Crown, represented by a governor.

**crown cork** • n. a metal bottle cap with a crimped edge.

**Crown Court** • n. (in England and Wales) a court of criminal jurisdiction, which deals with serious offences and appeals referred from the magistrates' courts.

**Crown Derby** • n. a kind of soft-paste porcelain made at Derby and often marked with a crown above the letter 'D'.

**crowned head** • n. a king or queen.

**crown gall** • n. a large tumour-like gall on the roots or lower trunk of a tree, caused by a bacterium.

**crown glass** • n. glass made without lead or iron, originally in a circular sheet, and used as optical glass.

**crown green** • n. Brit. a kind of bowling green which rises slightly towards the middle.

**crown imperial** • n. an Asian fritillary (plant) with a cluster of bell-like flowers at the top of a tall, largely bare stem. [*Fritillaria imperialis*.]

**Crown jewels** • pl. n. the crown and other ornaments and jewellery worn or carried by the sovereign on certain state occasions.

**crown moulding** • n. US term for **CORNICE** (in sense 1).

**Crown Office** • n. an office of the Supreme Court responsible for listing cases to be tried in the High Court.

**crown of thorns** • n. **1** a large spiky starfish of the tropical Indo-Pacific, feeding on coral. [*Acanthaster planci*.] **2** a thorny shrub. [*Euphorbia milii* (Madagascar, a popular house plant), and other species.]

**Crown prince** • n. (in some countries) a male heir to a throne.

**Crown princess** • n. the wife of a Crown prince. ➤(in some countries) a female heir to a throne.

**Crown prosecutor** • n. (in England, Wales, and Canada) a lawyer who acts for the Crown, especially a prosecutor in a criminal court.

**crown saw** • n. another term for **HOLE SAW**.

**crown wheel** • n. a gearwheel or cogwheel with teeth that project from the face of the wheel at right angles, used especially in the gears of motor vehicles.

**crow's foot** • n. (pl. **feet**) **1** a branching wrinkle at the outer corner of a person's eye. **2** a mark, symbol, or design formed of lines diverging from a point. **3** historical a military caltrop.

**crow's-nest** • n. a platform at the masthead of a vessel for a lookout to watch from.

**croze** /krəʊz/ • n. **1** a groove at the end of a cask or barrel to receive the edge of the head. **2** a cooper's tool for making such grooves.
– ORIGIN C17: perh. from Fr. *creux*, *creuse* 'hollow'.

**crozier** /'krəʊzɪə/ (also **crosier**) • n. **1** a hooked staff carried by a bishop as a symbol of pastoral office. **2** the curled top of a young fern.
– ORIGIN ME: from OFr. *croisier* 'cross-bearer', reinforced by OFr. *crocier* 'bearer of a bishop's crook'.

**CRT** • abbrev. cathode ray tube.

**cru** /kruː, French kʀy/ • n. (pl. **crus** pronunc. same) (in France) a vineyard or group of vineyards, especially one of recognized superior quality. See also **GRAND CRU**, **PREMIER CRU**.
– ORIGIN Fr., from *crû*, lit. 'growth', past part. of *croître*.

**cruces** plural form of **CRUX**.

**crucial** /'kruːʃ(ə)l/ • adj. **1** decisive or critical, especially in the success or failure of something. **2** informal excellent.
– DERIVATIVES **cruciality** /-ʃɪ'alɪti/ n. **crucially** adv.
– ORIGIN C18 (in the sense 'cross-shaped'): from Fr., from L. *crux*, *cruc-* 'cross'; the sense 'decisive' arose from the L. phr. *instantia crucis* 'crucial instance', with ref. to a *crux* or finger-post marking a fork at a crossroad.

**crucian carp** /'kruːʃ(ə)n/ • n. a small carp of still or slow-moving waters, farmed in eastern Europe. [*Carassius carassius*.]
– ORIGIN C18: from Low Ger. *karusse*, *karutze*, perh. based on L. *coracinus*, from Gk *korax* 'raven', also denoting a black fish found in the Nile.

**cruciate** /'kruːʃɪət, -eɪt/ • adj. Anatomy & Botany cross-shaped.
– ORIGIN C19: from L. *cruciatus*, from *crux*, *cruc-* 'cross'.

**cruciate ligament** • n. Anatomy either of a pair of ligaments in the knee which cross each other and connect the femur to the tibia.

**crucible** /'kruːsɪb(ə)l/ • n. **1** a container in which metals or other substances may be melted or subjected to very high temperatures. **2** a situation of severe trial, or in which different elements interact to produce something new.
– ORIGIN ME: from med. L. *crucibulum* 'night lamp, crucible', from L. *crux*, *cruc-* 'cross'.

**crucifer** /'kruːsɪfə/ • n. **1** Botany a cruciferous plant. **2** a person carrying a cross or crucifix in a procession.
– ORIGIN C16: from Christian L., from L. *crux*, *cruc-* 'cross'.

**cruciferous** /kruː'sɪf(ə)rəs/ • adj. Botany relating to or denoting plants of the cabbage family (Cruciferae), with four equal petals arranged in a cross.
– ORIGIN C19: from mod. L. *Cruciferae*, from L. *crux*, *cruc-* 'cross' + *-fer* 'bearing' + **-OUS**.

**crucifix** /'kruːsɪfɪks/ • n. a representation of a cross with a figure of Christ on it.
– ORIGIN ME: via OFr. from eccles. L. *crucifixus*, from L. *cruci fixus* 'fixed to a cross'.

**cruciform** /'kruːsɪfɔːm/ • adj. having the shape of a cross.
– ORIGIN C17: from L. *crux*, *cruc-* 'cross' + **-IFORM**.

**crucify** /'kruːsɪfʌɪ/ • v. (**-ies**, **-ied**) **1** put (someone) to death by nailing or binding them to a cross. **2** criticize severely and unrelentingly. ➤cause anguish to.
– DERIVATIVES **crucifier** n. **crucifixion** n.
– ORIGIN ME: from OFr. *crucifier*, from late L. *crucifigere*, from L. *crux*, *cruc-* 'cross' + *figere* 'fix'.

**cruck** /krʌk/ • n. Brit. either of a pair of curved timbers extending to the ground in the roof framework of a type of medieval house.
– ORIGIN C16: var. of **CROOK**.

**crud** • n. informal **1** an unpleasantly dirty or messy substance. **2** nonsense.
– DERIVATIVES **cruddy** adj.
– ORIGIN ME: var. of **CURD** (the original sense).

**crude** • adj. **1** in a natural or raw state; not yet processed or refined. **2** Statistics (of figures) not adjusted or corrected. ➤(of an estimate or guess) likely to be only approximately accurate. **3** constructed or carried out in a rudimentary or makeshift way. **4** offensively coarse or rude, especially in relation to sexual matters. • n. natural mineral oil.
– DERIVATIVES **crudely** adv. **crudeness** n. **crudity** n.
– ORIGIN ME: from L. *crudus* 'raw, rough'.

**crudités** /'kruːdɪteɪ/ • pl. n. mixed raw vegetables served as an hors d'oeuvre, typically with a sauce into which they may be dipped.
– ORIGIN pl. of Fr. *crudité* 'rawness, crudity'.

**cruel** • adj. (**crueller**, **cruellest** or **crueler**, **cruelest**) disregarding or taking pleasure in the pain or suffering of others. ➤causing pain or suffering.
– DERIVATIVES **cruelly** adv.
– ORIGIN ME: via OFr. from L. *crudelis*, rel. to *crudus* (see **CRUDE**).

**cruelty** • n. (pl. **-ies**) cruel behaviour or attitudes. ➤Law behaviour which causes physical or mental harm to another, whether intentionally or not.

**cruelty-free** • adj. (of cosmetics) manufactured or developed by methods which do not involve cruelty to animals.

**cruet** /ˈkruːɪt/ • n. **1** a small container for salt, pepper, oil, or vinegar for use at a dining table. ➤(also **cruet stand**) Brit. a stand holding such containers. **2** (in church use) a small container for the wine or water to be used in the celebration of the Eucharist.
– ORIGIN ME: from Anglo-Norman Fr., dimin. of OFr. *crue* 'pot', from Old Saxon *krūka*; rel. to **CROCK²**.

**cruise** • v. **1** sail, travel, or move slowly around without a precise destination, especially for pleasure. ➤travel smoothly at a moderate or economical speed. **2** achieve an objective with ease: *Millwall cruised to a 2-0 win.*. **3** informal wander about in search of a sexual partner. • n. an instance of cruising. ➤a voyage on a ship taken as a holiday and usually calling in at several places.
– ORIGIN C17: prob. from Du. *kruisen* 'to cross'.

**cruise control** • n. a device in a motor vehicle which can be switched on to maintain a selected constant speed without the use of the accelerator pedal.

**cruise missile** • n. a low-flying missile which is guided to its target by an on-board computer.

**cruiser** • n. **1** a relatively fast warship larger than a destroyer and less heavily armed than a battleship. **2** a yacht or motor boat with passenger accommodation, designed for leisure use. **3** N. Amer. a police patrol car.

**cruiserweight** • n. chiefly Brit. another term for **LIGHT HEAVYWEIGHT**.

**cruller** /ˈkrʌlə/ • n. N. Amer. a small cake made of rich dough twisted or curled and fried in deep fat.
– ORIGIN C19: from Du. *kruller*, from *krullen* 'to curl'.

**crumb** • n. **1** a small fragment of bread, cake, or biscuit. ➤the soft inner part of a loaf of bread. **2** informal, chiefly N. Amer. an objectionable or contemptible person. • v. [often as adj. **crumbed**] cover (food) with breadcrumbs.
– ORIGIN OE *cruma*, of Gmc origin; the final *-b* was added in the 16th cent., perh. from **CRUMBLE**.

**crumble** • v. break or fall apart into small fragments, especially as part of a gradual process of deterioration. ➤cause (something, especially food) to crumble. • n. Brit. a pudding made with fruit and a topping of flour and fat rubbed to the texture of breadcrumbs.
– ORIGIN ME: prob. from an OE word rel. to **CRUMB**.

**crumbly** • adj. (**-ier**, **-iest**) easily crumbling. • n. (pl. **-ies**) informal, humorous an old person.
– DERIVATIVES **crumbliness** n.

**crumbs** • exclam. Brit. informal used to express dismay or surprise.
– ORIGIN C19: euphemism for *Christ*.

**crumby** • adj. (**-ier**, **-iest**) **1** resembling or covered in crumbs. **2** variant spelling of **CRUMMY**.

**crumhorn** • n. variant spelling of **KRUMMHORN**.

**crummy** (also **crumby**) • adj. (**-ier**, **-iest**) informal bad, unpleasant, or of poor quality.
– DERIVATIVES **crummily** adv. **crumminess** n.
– ORIGIN var. of **CRUMBY**.

**crump** • n. a loud thudding sound, especially one made by an exploding bomb or shell.
– ORIGIN C17: imitative.

**crumpet** • n. **1** a thick, flat, savoury cake with a soft, porous texture, made from a yeast mixture cooked on a griddle and eaten toasted and buttered. **2** Brit. informal women regarded as objects of sexual desire. **3** Brit. archaic, informal a person's head.
– ORIGIN C17: of unknown origin.

**crumple** • v. **1** crush or become crushed so as to become creased and wrinkled. **2** suddenly lose force, effectiveness, or composure. • n. a crushed fold, crease, or wrinkle.
– DERIVATIVES **crumply** adj.
– ORIGIN ME: from obs. *crump* 'make or become curved', from OE *crump* 'bent, crooked', of W. Gmc origin.

**crumple zone** • n. a part of a motor vehicle, especially the extreme front and rear, designed to crumple easily in a crash and absorb the main force of an impact.

**crunch** • v. **1** crush (a hard or brittle foodstuff) with the teeth, making a marked grinding sound. **2** make or move with such a sound. • n. **1** a crunching sound. **2** (**the crunch**) informal the crucial point of a situation. **3** a sit-up.
– ORIGIN C19: var. of C17 *cranch* (prob. imitative), assoc. with **CRUSH** and **MUNCH**.

**cruncher** • n. informal **1** a crucial or difficult point or question. **2** a computer, system, or person able to perform operations of great complexity or size. See also **NUMBER CRUNCHER**.

**crunchy** • adj. (**-ier**, **-iest**) **1** making a crunching noise when bitten or crushed. **2** N. Amer. informal politically liberal and environmentally aware.
– DERIVATIVES **crunchily** adv. **crunchiness** n.

**crupper** /ˈkrʌpə/ • n. a strap buckled to the back of a saddle and looped under the horse's tail to prevent the saddle or harness from slipping forward.
– ORIGIN ME: from OFr. *cropiere*, rel. to *croupe* (see **CROUP²**).

**crura cerebri** plural form of **CRUS CEREBRI**.

**crural** /ˈkrʊər(ə)l/ • adj. Anatomy & Zoology of or relating to the leg or the thigh. ➤of or relating to the crura cerebri.
– ORIGIN C16: from L. *cruralis*, from *crus*, *crur-* 'leg'.

**crusade** /kruːˈseɪd/ • n. **1** any of a series of medieval military expeditions made by Europeans to recover the Holy Land from the Muslims. ➤a war instigated for alleged religious ends. **2** an energetic organized campaign with a political, social, or religious aim: *a crusade against crime*. • v. [often as adj. **crusading**] lead or take part in a crusade.
– DERIVATIVES **crusader** n.
– ORIGIN C16: from Fr. *croisade*, alt. (influenced by Sp. *cruzado*) of earlier *croisée*, lit. 'the state of being marked with the cross', based on L. *crux*, *cruc-* 'cross'.

**crus cerebri** /krʊs ˈsɛrɪbrʌɪ/ • n. (pl. **crura cerebri**) Anatomy either of two symmetrical tracts of nerve fibres at the base of the midbrain, linking the pons and the cerebral hemispheres.
– ORIGIN C18: from L., lit. 'leg of the brain'.

**cruse** /kruːz/ • n. archaic an earthenware pot or jar.
– ORIGIN OE *crūse*, of Gmc origin.

**crush** • v. **1** deform, pulverize, or force inwards by compressing forcefully. ➤crease or crumple (cloth or paper). **2** violently subdue (opposition or a rebellion). **3** cause to feel overwhelming disappointment or embarrassment. • n. **1** a crowd of people pressed closely together. **2** informal an intense infatuation. **3** a drink made from the juice of pressed fruit. **4** (also **crush pen**) a fenced passage with one narrow end used for handling cattle or sheep.
– DERIVATIVES **crushable** adj. **crusher** n. **crushing** adj. **crushingly** adv.
– ORIGIN ME: from OFr. *cruissir*, 'gnash (teeth) or crack', of unknown origin.

**crush bar** • n. Brit. a bar in a theatre or opera house that sells drinks in the interval.

**crush barrier** • n. Brit. a barrier, especially a temporary one, for restraining a crowd.

**crushed velvet** • n. velvet which has its nap pointing in different directions in irregular patches.

**crush zone** • n. another term for **CRUMPLE ZONE**.

**crust** • n. **1** the tough outer part of a loaf of bread. ➤a hard, dry scrap of bread. **2** a hardened layer, coating, or deposit on something soft. ➤a layer of pastry covering a pie. **3** the outermost layer of rock of which a planet consists, especially the part of the earth above the mantle. **4** a deposit of tartrates and other substances formed in wine aged in the bottle, especially port. **5** informal a living or livelihood: *earning a crust*. • v. [often as adj. **crusted**] form into or cover with a crust: *crusted port*.
– DERIVATIVES **crustal** adj. (Geology).
– ORIGIN ME: from OFr. *crouste*, from L. *crusta* 'rind, shell, crust'.

**Crustacea** /krʌˈsteɪʃ(ə)/ • pl. n. Zoology a large group of mainly aquatic arthropods including crabs, lobsters, shrimps, woodlice, and barnacles.
– DERIVATIVES **crustacean** n. & adj. **crustaceous** adj.

– ORIGIN mod. L., from *crusta* (see **CRUST**).

**crustose** /'krʌstəʊs/ ● **adj.** Botany (of a lichen or alga) forming or resembling a crust.

– ORIGIN C19: from L. *crustosus*, from *crusta* (see **CRUST**).

**crusty** ● **adj.** (**-ier, -iest**) **1** having or consisting of a crust. **2** (of an old person) conservative and easily irritated. ● **n.** (also **crustie**) (pl. **-ies**) informal a young person of a subculture characterized by a shabby appearance, a nomadic lifestyle, and a rejection of conventional values.

– DERIVATIVES **crustily** adv. **crustiness** n.

**crutch** ● **n. 1** a long stick with a crosspiece at the top, used as a support by a lame person. **2** something used for support or reassurance. **3** the crotch of the body or a garment.

– ORIGIN OE *crycc*, *cryc*, of Gmc origin.

**crux** /krʌks/ ● **n.** (pl. **cruxes** or **cruces** /'kru:si:z/) (**the crux**) the decisive or most important point at issue. ➤ a particular point of difficulty.

– ORIGIN C17: from L., lit. 'cross'.

**cry** ● **v.** (**-ies, -ied**) **1** shed tears. **2** shout or scream loudly. ➤ (of a hawker) proclaim (wares) for sale in the street. **3** (of a bird or other animal) make a loud characteristic call. **4** (**cry out for**) demand as a self-evident requirement or solution. **5** (**cry off**) informal go back on a promise or fail to keep to an arrangement. **6** (**cry someone/thing up** or **down**) dated disparage (or praise) someone or something. ● **n.** (pl. **-ies**) **1** a spell of weeping. **2** a loud shout or scream. ➤ an urgent appeal, entreaty, or demand. **3** a distinctive call of a bird or other animal.

– PHRASES **cry for the moon** ask for what is unattainable or impossible. **cry stinking fish** Brit. informal disparage one's own efforts or products. **for crying out loud** informal used to express irritation or impatience.

– ORIGIN ME: from OFr. *crier* (v.), *cri* (n.), from L. *quiritare* 'raise a public outcry', lit. 'call on the *Quirites* (Roman citizens) for help'.

**crybaby** ● **n.** (pl. **-ies**) a person, especially a child, who sheds tears frequently or readily.

**cryer** ● **n.** archaic spelling of **CRIER**.

**crying** ● **adj.** very great: *it would be a crying shame.*

**cryo-** /'krʌɪəʊ/ ● **comb. form** involving or producing cold, especially extreme cold: *cryosurgery.*

– ORIGIN from Gk *kruos* 'frost'.

**cryobiology** ● **n.** the branch of biology which deals with the properties of organisms at low temperatures.

– DERIVATIVES **cryobiological** adj. **cryobiologist** n.

**cryogen** /'krʌɪə(ʊ)dʒ(ə)n/ ● **n.** a substance used to produce very low temperatures.

**cryogenics** /ˌkrʌɪə(ʊ)'dʒɛnɪks/ ● **pl. n.** [treated as sing.] the branch of physics concerned with the production and effects of very low temperatures. ➤ another term for **CRYONICS**.

– DERIVATIVES **cryogenic** adj.

**cryolite** /'krʌɪəlʌɪt/ ● **n.** a white or colourless mineral consisting of a fluoride of sodium and aluminium.

**cryonics** /krʌɪ'ɒnɪks/ ● **pl. n.** [treated as sing.] the deep-freezing of the bodies of people who have died of an incurable disease, in the hope of a future cure.

– DERIVATIVES **cryonic** adj.

– ORIGIN 1960s: contr. of **CRYOGENICS**.

**cryoprecipitate** /ˌkrʌɪəʊprɪ'sɪpɪtət/ ● **n.** chiefly Biochemistry a substance precipitated from a solution, especially from the blood, at low temperatures.

**cryoprotectant** ● **n.** Physiology a substance that prevents the freezing of tissues, or prevents damage to cells during freezing.

**cryostat** /'krʌɪə(ʊ)stat/ ● **n. 1** an apparatus for maintaining a very low temperature. **2** a cold chamber in which frozen tissue is divided with a microtome.

**cryosurgery** ● **n.** surgery using the local application of intense cold to destroy unwanted tissue.

**crypt** ● **n. 1** an underground room or vault beneath a church, used as a chapel or burial place. **2** Anatomy a small tubular gland, pit, or recess.

– ORIGIN ME (in the sense 'cavern'): from L. *crypta*, from Gk *kruptē* 'a vault', from *kruptos* 'hidden'.

**cryptanalysis** ● **n.** the art or process of deciphering coded messages without being told the key.

– DERIVATIVES **cryptanalyst** n. **cryptanalytic** adj. **cryptanalytical** adj.

**cryptic** ● **adj. 1** mysterious or obscure in meaning. ➤ (of a crossword) having difficult clues which indicate the solutions indirectly. **2** Zoology (of coloration etc.) serving to camouflage an animal in its natural environment.

– DERIVATIVES **cryptically** adv.

– ORIGIN C17: from late L. *crypticus*, from Gk *kruptikos*, from *kruptos* 'hidden'.

**crypto-** /'krɪptəʊ/ ● **comb. form** concealed; secret: *cryptogram.*

– ORIGIN from Gk *kruptos* 'hidden'.

**cryptobiont** /ˌkrɪptəʊ'bʌɪɒnt/ ● **n.** Biology an organism capable of cryptobiosis.

**cryptobiosis** /ˌkrɪptə(ʊ)bʌɪ'əʊsɪs/ ● **n.** Biology a physiological state in which metabolic activity is reduced to an undetectable level without disappearing altogether.

– DERIVATIVES **cryptobiotic** adj.

**cryptococcosis** /ˌkrɪptə(ʊ)kə'kəʊsɪs/ ● **n.** Medicine infestation with a yeast-like fungus, resulting in tumours in the lungs.

– DERIVATIVES **cryptococcal** adj.

– ORIGIN 1930s: from mod. L. *Cryptococcus* (genus name of the fungus) + **-OSIS**.

**cryptocrystalline** ● **adj.** having a crystalline structure visible only when magnified.

**cryptogam** /'krɪptə(ʊ)gam/ ● **n.** Botany, dated a plant with no true flowers or seeds, such as a fern, moss, liverwort, lichen, alga, or fungus.

– DERIVATIVES **cryptogamous** adj.

– ORIGIN C19: from Fr. *cryptogame*, from mod. L. *cryptogamae* (*plantae*) from Gk *kruptos* 'hidden' + *gamos* 'marriage' (because the means of reproduction was not apparent).

**cryptogamic** ● **adj. 1** Botany relating to or denoting cryptogams. **2** Ecology relating to or denoting a fragile black surface layer of cyanobacteria, mosses, and lichens.

**cryptogenic** /ˌkrɪptəʊ'dʒɛnɪk/ ● **adj.** (of a disease) of obscure or uncertain origin.

**cryptogram** /'krɪptə(ʊ)gram/ ● **n.** a text written in code.

**cryptography** ● **n.** the art of writing or solving codes.

– DERIVATIVES **cryptographer** n. **cryptographic** adj. **cryptographically** adv.

**cryptology** ● **n.** the study of codes, or the art of writing and solving them.

– DERIVATIVES **cryptological** adj. **cryptologist** n.

**cryptomeria** /ˌkrɪptə(ʊ)'mɪərɪə/ ● **n.** a tall conical coniferous tree with long, curved leaves and short cones, native to China and Japan. [*Cryptomeria japonica*.]

– ORIGIN mod. L., from **CRYPTO-** + Gk *meros* 'part' (because the seeds are concealed by scales).

**cryptonym** /'krɪptənɪm/ ● **n.** a code name.

– DERIVATIVES **cryptonymous** adj.

– ORIGIN C19: from **CRYPTO-** + Gk *onoma* 'name'.

**cryptorchid** /ˌkrɪp'tɔ:kɪd/ ● **n.** Medicine a person suffering from cryptorchidism.

**cryptorchidism** ● **n.** Medicine a condition in which one or both of the testes fail to descend from the abdomen into the scrotum.

– ORIGIN C19: from **CRYPTO-** + Gk *orkhis*, *orkhid-* 'testicle' + **-ISM**.

**cryptosporidiosis** ● **n.** an intestinal disease caused by infection with cryptosporidium, causing diarrhoea and vomiting.

**cryptosporidium** /ˌkrɪptə(ʊ)spɒ'rɪdɪəm/ ● **n.** a parasitic coccidian protozoan found in the intestinal tract of many vertebrates, where it sometimes causes disease.

– ORIGIN C20: from **CRYPTO-** + mod. L. *sporidium* 'small spore'.

**cryptozoology** ● **n.** the search for animals whose existence is disputed or unsubstantiated, such as the Loch Ness monster.

– DERIVATIVES **cryptozoological** adj. **cryptozoologist** n.

**crystal** ● **n. 1** a piece of a homogeneous solid substance having a natural geometrically regular form with symmetrically arranged plane faces. ➤ Chemistry any solid consisting of a symmetrical, ordered, three-dimensional

aggregation of atoms or molecules. ➤a clear transparent mineral, especially quartz. **2** (also **crystal glass**) highly transparent glass with a high refractive index. ➤the glass over a watch face. **3** [as modifier] clear and transparent: *the crystal waters of the lake.*
– ORIGIN OE (denoting ice or a mineral resembling it), from OFr. *cristal*, from L. *crystallum*, from Gk *krustallos* 'ice, crystal'.

**crystal axis** • n. each of three axes used to define the edges of the unit cell of a crystal.

**crystal ball** • n. a solid globe of glass or rock crystal, used by fortune tellers and clairvoyants for crystal-gazing.

**crystal class** • n. each of thirty-two categories of crystals classified according to the possible combinations of symmetry elements possessed by the crystal lattice.

**crystal-gazing** • n. looking intently into a crystal ball with the aim of seeing images relating to future or distant events.

**crystal lattice** • n. the symmetrical three-dimensional arrangement of atoms inside a crystal.

**crystalline** /ˈkrɪst(ə)lʌɪn/ • adj. **1** having the structure and form of a crystal. **2** poetic/literary very clear.
– DERIVATIVES **crystallinity** n.

**crystalline lens** • n. the lens of the eye.

**crystallite** /ˈkrɪst(ə)lʌɪt/ • n. an individual perfect crystal or region of regular crystalline structure in the substance of a material. ➤a very small crystal.

**crystallize** (also **-ise**) • v. **1** form or cause to form crystals. ➤[as adj. **crystallized**] (of fruit or petals) coated and impregnated with sugar. **2** make or become definite and clear. **3** Finance convert or be converted from a floating charge into a fixed charge.
– DERIVATIVES **crystallizable** adj. **crystallization** n.

**crystallography** /ˌkrɪstəˈlɒgrəfi/ • n. the branch of science concerned with the structure and properties of crystals.
– DERIVATIVES **crystallographer** n. **crystallographic** adj. **crystallographically** adv.

**crystalloid** • adj. resembling a crystal in shape or structure. • n. **1** Botany a small crystal-like mass of protein in a plant cell. **2** Chemistry a substance that, when dissolved, forms a true solution rather than a colloid and is able to pass through a semipermeable membrane.

**crystal meth** • n. see METH.

**crystal set** • n. a simple early form of radio receiver with a crystal touching a metal wire as the rectifier and lacking an amplifier or loudspeaker, necessitating headphones or an earphone.

**crystal system** • n. each of seven categories of crystals (cubic, tetragonal, orthorhombic, trigonal, hexagonal, monoclinic, and triclinic) classified according to the possible relations of the crystal axes.

**CS** • abbrev. Brit. **1** chartered surveyor. **2** Civil Service. **3** Court of Session.

**Cs** • symb. the chemical element caesium.

**c/s** • abbrev. cycles per second.

**CSA** • abbrev. Child Support Agency.

**csardas** /ˈtʃɑːdaʃ, ˈzɑːdəs/ (also **czardas**) • n. (pl. same) a Hungarian dance with a slow introduction and a fast, wild finish.
– ORIGIN C19: from Hungarian *csárdás*, from *csárda* 'inn'.

**CSE** • abbrev. Certificate of Secondary Education.

**CS gas** • n. a powerful form of tear gas used particularly in the control of riots.
– ORIGIN 1960s: from the initials of the Amer. chemists Ben B. *Corson* and Roger W. *Stoughton*.

**CSM** • abbrev. Company Sergeant Major.

**CST** • abbrev. Central Standard Time.

**CT** • abbrev. **1** computerized (or computed) tomography. **2** Connecticut (in official postal use).

**ct** • abbrev. **1** carat. **2** cent.

**CTC** • abbrev. City Technology College.

**ctenidium** /tɪˈnɪdɪəm/ • n. (pl. **ctenidia** /-dɪə/) Zoology a comb-like respiratory organ in a mollusc.
– ORIGIN C19; mod. L., from Gk *ktenidion*, dimin. of *kteis*, *kten-* 'comb'.

**ctenoid** /ˈtiːnɔɪd/ • adj. Zoology (of fish scales) having many tiny projections on the edge like the teeth of a comb, as in many bony fishes. Compare with GANOID and PLACOID.
– ORIGIN C19: from Gk *kteis*, *kten-* 'comb' + **-OID**.

**Ctenophora** /tiːˈnɒfərə, tɛ-/ • pl. n. Zoology a small phylum of aquatic invertebrates that comprises the comb jellies.
– DERIVATIVES **ctenophore** /ˈtiːnəfɔː, ˈtɛ-/ n.
– ORIGIN mod. L., from Gk *kteis*, *kten-* 'comb' + *pherein* 'to bear'.

**CTS** • abbrev. carpal tunnel syndrome.

**CU** • abbrev. Christian Union.

**Cu** • symb. the chemical element copper.
– ORIGIN from late L. *cuprum*.

**cu.** • abbrev. cubic.

**cuadrilla** /kwɒˈdriːljə, -ˈdriːjə/ • n. a matador's team.
– ORIGIN C19: Sp.

**cuatro** /ˈkwatrəʊ/ • n. (pl. **-os**) a small guitar, typically with four or five single or paired strings, used in Latin American and Caribbean folk music.
– ORIGIN Latin Amer. Sp., lit. 'four'.

**cub** • n. **1** the young of a fox, bear, lion, or other carnivorous mammal. ➤archaic a young man. **2** (**Cubs**) a junior branch of the Scout Association, for boys aged about 8 to 11. ➤(also **Cub Scout**) a member of this organization. • v. (**cubbed**, **cubbing**) **1** give birth to cubs. **2** hunt fox cubs.
– ORIGIN C16: of unknown origin.

**cubage** • n. cubic content or capacity.

**Cuban** /ˈkjuːbən/ • n. a native or inhabitant of Cuba. • adj. of or relating to Cuba.

**Cuban heel** • n. a moderately high straight-sided heel on a shoe or boot.

**cubature** /ˈkjuːbətʃə/ • n. the determination of the volume of a solid.

**cubby** • n. (pl. **-ies**) chiefly N. Amer. a cubbyhole.

**cubbyhole** • n. a small enclosed space or room.
– ORIGIN C17 (orig. Scots, denoting a straw basket): rel. to dial. *cub* 'stall, pen, hutch', of Low Ger. origin.

**cube** • n. **1** a symmetrical three-dimensional shape contained by six equal squares. **2** Mathematics the product of a number multiplied by its square, represented by a superscript figure 3. • v. **1** Mathematics raise (a number or value) to its cube. **2** cut (food) into small cubes.
– ORIGIN C16: from OFr., or via L. from Gk *kubos*.

**cubeb** /ˈkjuːbɛb/ • n. **1** a tropical shrub of the pepper family, which bears pungent berries. [*Piper cubeba* (Asia) and other species.] **2** the dried unripe berries of this shrub, used medicinally and to flavour cigarettes.
– ORIGIN ME: from OFr. *cubebe*, from Sp. Arab. *kubēba*, from Arab. *kubāba*.

**cube root** • n. the number which produces a given number when cubed.

**cubic** /ˈkjuːbɪk/ • adj. **1** having the shape of a cube. ➤denoting a crystal system with three equal axes at right angles. **2** denoting a unit of measurement equal to the volume of a cube whose side is one of the linear unit specified: *a cubic metre.* **3** involving the cube (and no higher power) of a quantity or variable.
– DERIVATIVES **cubical** adj. **cubically** adv.

**cubicle** • n. a small partitioned-off area of a room.
– ORIGIN ME (in the sense 'bedroom'): from L. *cubiculum*, from *cubare* 'lie down'.

**cubiform** • adj. technical cube-shaped.

**cubism** • n. an early 20th-century style of painting in which perspective with a single viewpoint was abandoned and use was made of simple geometric shapes and interlocking planes.
– DERIVATIVES **cubist** n. & adj.

**cubit** /ˈkjuːbɪt/ • n. an ancient measure of length, approximately equal to the length of a forearm.
– ORIGIN ME: from L. *cubitum* 'elbow, forearm, cubit'.

**cubital** /ˈkjuːbɪt(ə)l/ • adj. **1** Anatomy of the forearm or the elbow. **2** Entomology of the cubitus.
– ORIGIN ME: from L. *cubitalis*, from *cubitus* 'cubit'.

**cuboid** /ˈkjuːbɔɪd/ • adj. more or less cubic in shape. • n.

**1** Geometry a solid which has six rectangular faces at right angles to each other. **2** (also **cuboid bone**) Anatomy a squat tarsal bone on the outer side of the foot, articulating with the heel bone and the fourth and fifth metatarsals.
– DERIVATIVES **cuboidal** adj.

**cub reporter** • n. informal a young or inexperienced newspaper reporter.

**cucking-stool** /ˈkʌkɪŋstuːl/ • n. historical a chair to which disorderly women were tied and then ducked into water or subjected to public ridicule as a punishment.
– ORIGIN ME: from obs. *cuck* 'defecate' (because a stool containing a chamber pot was often used).

**cuckold** /ˈkʌk(ə)ld/ • n. the husband of an adulteress regarded as an object of derision. • v. make (a married man) a cuckold.
– DERIVATIVES **cuckoldry** n.
– ORIGIN OE, from OFr. *cucuault*, from *cucu* 'cuckoo' (from the cuckoo's habit of laying its egg in another bird's nest).

**cuckoo** • n. a grey or brown bird known for the far-carrying two-note call of the male and for the habit of laying its eggs in the nests of small songbirds. [*Cuculus canorus*.] ➤ used in names of other birds of the same family (Cuculidae). • adj. informal crazy.
– ORIGIN ME: from OFr. *cucu*, imitative of its call.

**cuckoo bee** • n. a parasitic bee which lays its eggs in the nest of another kind of bee. [*Nomada*, *Psithyrus*, and other genera.]

**cuckoo clock** • n. a clock with a mechanical cuckoo that pops out on the hour making a sound like a cuckoo's call.

**cuckooflower** • n. a spring-flowering plant with pale lilac flowers, growing in damp habitats. [*Cardamine pratensis*.]
– ORIGIN C16: so named because it flowers at the time of year when the cuckoo is first heard calling.

**cuckoo pint** • n. the common wild arum with a pale spathe and a purple or green spadix followed by bright red berries. [*Arum maculatum*.]
– ORIGIN ME: from earlier *cuckoo-pintle*, from PINTLE in the obs. sense 'penis' (because of the shape of the spadix).

**cuckoo spit** • n. whitish froth found in compact masses on leaves and plant stems, exuded by the larvae of froghoppers.

**cuckoo wasp** • n. a ruby-tail or other wasp which lays its eggs in the nest of a bee or other wasp.

**cucumber** • n. **1** a long, green-skinned fruit with watery flesh, eaten raw in salads. **2** the widely cultivated climbing plant of the gourd family which yields this fruit, originally native to the Chinese Himalayan region. [*Cucumis sativus*.]
– PHRASES **(as) cool as a cucumber** very cool or calm.
– ORIGIN ME: from OFr. *cocombre*, *coucombre*, from L. *cucumis*, *cucumer-*.

**cucurbit** /kjʊˈkəːbɪt/ • n. chiefly N. Amer. a plant of the gourd family (Cucurbitaceae), which includes melon, pumpkin, squash, and cucumber.
– DERIVATIVES **cucurbitaceous** adj.
– ORIGIN ME: from OFr. *cucurbite*, from L. *cucurbita*.

**cud** • n. partly digested food returned from the first stomach of ruminants to the mouth for further chewing.
– PHRASES **chew the cud** think or talk reflectively.
– ORIGIN OE *cwidu*, *cudu*, of Gmc origin.

**cuddle** • v. hold close in one's arms as a way of showing love or affection. ➤ (often **cuddle up to**) lie or sit close and snug. • n. a prolonged and affectionate hug.
– DERIVATIVES **cuddlesome** adj.
– ORIGIN C16: of unknown origin.

**cuddly** • adj. (**-ier**, **-iest**) pleasantly soft or plump.

**cuddy** • n. (pl. **-ies**) chiefly Scottish **1** a donkey. **2** a stupid person.
– ORIGIN C18: perh. a familiar form of the name *Cuthbert*.

**cudgel** /ˈkʌdʒ(ə)l/ • n. a short thick stick used as a weapon. • v. (**cudgelled**, **cudgelling**; US **cudgeled**, **cudgeling**) beat with a cudgel.
– PHRASES **cudgel one's brain** think hard about a problem. **take up cudgels** start to defend or support someone or something strongly.
– ORIGIN OE *cycgel*, of unknown origin.

**cudweed** • n. a plant of the daisy family, with hairy or downy leaves and inconspicuous flowers. [Genera *Gnaphalium* and *Filago*.]

**cue**[1] • n. **1** a signal to an actor or other performer to enter or to begin their speech or performance. ➤ a signal or prompt for action. **2** Psychology a feature of something perceived that is used in the brain's interpretation of the perception. **3** a facility for playing through an audio or video recording very rapidly until a desired starting point is reached. • v. (**cues**, **cued**, **cueing** or **cuing**) **1** give a cue to or for. ➤ act as a prompt or reminder. **2** set a piece of audio or video equipment in readiness to play (a particular part of a recording).
– PHRASES **on cue** at the correct moment.
– ORIGIN C16: of unknown origin.

**cue**[2] • n. a long tapering wooden rod for striking the ball in snooker, billiards, etc. • v. (**cues**, **cued**, **cueing** or **cuing**) use a cue to strike the ball.
– DERIVATIVES **cueist** n. (rare).
– ORIGIN C18 (denoting a long plait or pigtail): var. of QUEUE.

**cue ball** • n. the ball, usually a white one, that is to be struck with the cue in snooker, billiards, etc.

**cue bid** • n. Bridge a bid intended to give specific information about the content of the hand to the bidder's partner rather than to advance the auction.

**cueca** /ˈkwɛkə/ • n. a lively South American dance.
– ORIGIN C20: Amer. Sp.

**cue card** • n. a card held beside a camera for a television broadcaster to read from while appearing to look into the camera.

**cuesta** /ˈkwɛstə/ • n. Geology a ridge formed by inclined strata, with a gentle slope on one side and a steep slope on the other.
– ORIGIN C19: from Sp., 'slope'.

**cuff**[1] • n. **1** the end part of a sleeve, where the material of the sleeve is turned back or a separate band is sewn on. ➤ chiefly N. Amer. a trouser turn-up. **2** (**cuffs**) informal handcuffs. **3** an inflatable bag wrapped round the arm when blood pressure is measured. • v. informal secure with handcuffs.
– PHRASES **off the cuff** informal without preparation. [as if from impromptu notes made on one's shirt cuffs.]
– DERIVATIVES **cuffed** adj.
– ORIGIN ME (denoting a glove or mitten): of unknown origin.

**cuff**[2] • v. strike with an open hand, especially on the head. • n. a blow given with an open hand.
– ORIGIN C16: of unknown origin.

**cufflink** • n. a device for fastening together the sides of a shirt cuff, passed through a hole in each side of the cuff.

**Cufic** • n. & adj. variant spelling of KUFIC.

**cui bono?** /kwiː ˈbɒnəʊ, ˈbəʊ-/ • exclam. who stands to gain (i.e. from a crime, and so might have been responsible for it)?
– ORIGIN L., 'to whom (is it) a benefit?'

**cuirass** /kwɪˈras/ • n. **1** historical a piece of armour consisting of breastplate and backplate fastened together. **2** Medicine an artificial ventilator which encloses the body and forces air in and out of the lungs.
– ORIGIN ME: from OFr. *cuirace*, based on late L. *coriaceus*, from *corium* 'leather'.

**cuirassier** /ˌkwɪrəˈsɪə, French kɥirasje/ • n. historical a cavalry soldier wearing a cuirass.
– ORIGIN C16: Fr.

**cuisine** /kwɪˈziːn/ • n. a style or method of cooking, especially as characteristic of a particular country or region. ➤ food cooked in a certain way.
– ORIGIN C18: Fr., lit. 'kitchen'.

**cuisse** /kwɪs/ (also **cuish** /kwɪʃ/) • n. historical a piece of armour for the thigh.
– ORIGIN ME (orig. in pl.): from OFr. *cuisseaux*, pl. of *cuissel*, from late L. *coxale*, from *coxa* 'hip'.

**culch** • n. variant spelling of CULTCH.

**culchie** /ˈkʌl(t)ʃi/ • n. (pl. **-ies**) Irish derogatory a country bumpkin.

– ORIGIN 1950s: appar. an alt. of *Kiltimagh* (Ir. *Coillte Mach*), a country town in County Mayo.

**Culdee** /kʌl'di:/ ● n. a monk of the Celtic Church, living as a recluse usually in a group of thirteen (on the analogy of Christ and his Apostles).
– ORIGIN ME: from med. L. *culdeus*, alt. of *kelledei*, from Old Ir. *céle dé*, lit. 'companion of God'.

**cul-de-sac** /'kʌldə,sak, 'kʊl-/ ● n. (pl. **culs-de-sac** pronunc. same) a street or passage closed at one end.
– ORIGIN C18 (orig. in anatomy): Fr., lit. 'bottom of a sack'.

**-cule** ● suffix forming nouns such as *molecule, reticule*, which were originally diminutives.
– ORIGIN from Fr. *-cule* or L. *-culus, -cula, -culum*.

**culex** /'kju:lɛks/ ● n. (pl. **culices** /-lɪsi:z/) a mosquito of a genus which does not transmit malaria.
– DERIVATIVES **culicine** /'kju:lɪsʌɪn, -si:n/ adj. & n.
– ORIGIN L., 'gnat'.

**culinary** ● adj. of or for cooking.
– DERIVATIVES **culinarily** adv.
– ORIGIN C17: from L. *culinarius*, from *culina* 'kitchen'.

**cull** ● v. **1** reduce the population of (a wild animal) by selective slaughter. ➤ send (an unwanted farm animal) to be slaughtered. **2** select from a large quantity; obtain from a variety of sources. ● n. a selective slaughter of wild animals. ➤ a livestock animal selected for killing.
– DERIVATIVES **culler** n.
– ORIGIN ME: from OFr. *coillier*, based on L. *colligere* (see **COLLECT**[1]).

**cullet** /'kʌlɪt/ ● n. recycled broken or waste glass used in glass-making.
– ORIGIN C19: var. of **COLLET**.

**cully** /'kʌli/ ● n. (pl. **-ies**) informal, archaic a friendly form of address for a man.
– ORIGIN C17 (denoting a person who is imposed upon): of unknown origin.

**Culm** /kʌlm/ ● n. Geology a series of Carboniferous strata in SW England, mainly shale and limestone with some thin coal seams. ➤ (**culm**) archaic coal dust or slack.
– ORIGIN ME: prob. rel. to **COAL**.

**culm** /kʌlm/ ● n. the hollow stem of a grass or cereal plant, especially that bearing the flower.
– ORIGIN C17: from L. *culmus* 'stalk'.

**culminant** ● adj. at or forming the top or highest point.

**culminate** /'kʌlmɪneɪt/ ● v. **1** (usu. **culminate in**) reach or be a climax or point of highest development. **2** archaic or Astrology (of a celestial body) reach or be at the meridian.
– DERIVATIVES **culmination** n.
– ORIGIN C17: from late L. *culminat-*, *culminare*, from L. *culmen* 'summit'.

**culottes** /kju:'lɒt(s)/ ● pl. n. women's knee-length trousers, cut with very full legs to resemble a skirt.
– ORIGIN C19: Fr., 'knee breeches', dimin. of *cul* 'rump'.

**culpable** ● adj. deserving blame.
– DERIVATIVES **culpability** n. **culpably** adv.
– ORIGIN ME: from OFr. *coupable, culpable*, from L. *culpabilis*, from *culpare* 'to blame', from *culpa* 'fault, blame'.

**culpable homicide** ● n. Law (in some jurisdictions) an act which has resulted in a person's death but is held not to amount to murder.

**culprit** ● n. a person who is responsible for a crime or other misdeed.
– ORIGIN C17: orig. in the judicial formula *Culprit, how will you be tried?*, perh. from a misinterpretation of the written abbrev. *cul. prist* for Anglo-Norman Fr. *Culpable: prest d'averrer notre bille* '(You are) guilty: (We are) ready to prove our indictment'.

**cult** ● n. **1** a system of religious devotion directed towards a particular figure or object. ➤ a relatively small religious group regarded by others as strange or as imposing excessive control over members. **2** something popular or fashionable among a particular section of society.
– DERIVATIVES **cultic** adj. **cultish** adj. **cultishness** n. **cultism** n. **cultist** n.
– ORIGIN C17: from Fr. *culte* or L. *cultus* 'worship'.

**cultch** /kʌltʃ/ (also **culch**) ● n. the mass of stones, broken shells, and grit of which an oyster bed is formed.
– ORIGIN C17: of unknown origin.

**cultigen** /'kʌltɪdʒ(ə)n/ ● n. Botany a plant species or variety known only in cultivation, especially one with no known wild ancestor.
– ORIGIN C20: from *cultivated* + **-GEN**.

**cultivar** /'kʌltɪvɑ:/ ● n. Botany a plant variety that has been produced in cultivation by selective breeding.
– ORIGIN 1920s: blend of **CULTIVATE** and **VARIETY**.

**cultivate** ● v. **1** prepare and use (land) for crops or gardening. ➤ raise or grow (plants), especially on a large scale for commercial purposes. **2** Biology grow or maintain (living cells or tissue) in culture. **3** try to acquire or develop (a quality or skill). ➤ try to win the friendship or favour of. **4** [as adj. **cultivated**] refined and well educated.
– DERIVATIVES **cultivable** adj. **cultivatable** adj. **cultivation** n.
– ORIGIN C17: from med. L. *cultivat-*, *cultivare*, from *cultiva (terra)* 'arable (land)', from *colere* 'cultivate, inhabit'.

**cultivator** ● n. a person or thing that cultivates something. ➤ a mechanical implement for breaking up the ground.

**cultural** ● adj. **1** of or relating to the culture of a society. **2** of or relating to the arts and to intellectual achievements.
– DERIVATIVES **culturally** adv.

**cultural anthropology** ● n. see **SOCIAL ANTHROPOLOGY**.

**cultural attaché** ● n. an embassy official whose function is to promote cultural relations between his or her own country and that to which he or she is accredited.

**culture** ● n. **1** the arts and other manifestations of human intellectual achievement regarded collectively. ➤ a refined understanding or appreciation of this. **2** the customs, institutions, and achievements of a particular nation, people, or group. **3** Biology the cultivation of bacteria, tissue cells, etc. in an artificial medium containing nutrients. ➤ a preparation of cells obtained in such a way. ➤ the cultivation of plants. **4** [in combination] denoting cultivation or husbandry: *aviculture*. See word-formation panel. ● v. Biology maintain (tissue cells, bacteria, etc.) in conditions suitable for growth.
– ORIGIN C17 (denoting a cultivated piece of land): the noun from Fr. *culture* or directly from L. *cultura* 'growing, cultivation'; the verb from obs. Fr. *culturer* or med. L. *culturare*, both based on L. *colere* (see **CULTIVATE**).

**cultured** ● adj. **1** refined and well educated. **2** (of a pearl) formed round a foreign body inserted into an oyster.

**culture shock** ● n. the feeling of disorientation experienced when suddenly subjected to an unfamiliar culture or way of life.

**culture vulture** ● n. informal a person who is very interested in the arts.

**cultus** /'kʌltəs/ ● n. technical a system or variety of religious worship.
– ORIGIN C19: L. (see **CULT**).

**culverin** /'kʌlv(ə)rɪn/ ● n. **1** a 16th- or 17th- century cannon with a relatively long barrel for its bore. **2** a kind of handgun of the 15th and 16th centuries.
– ORIGIN C15: from OFr. *coulevrine*, from *couleuvre* 'snake'.

**culvert** /'kʌlvət/ ● n. a tunnel carrying a stream or open drain under a road or railway.
– ORIGIN C18: of unknown origin.

**cum**[1] /kʌm/ ● prep. combined with; also used as: *a study-cum-bedroom*.
– ORIGIN C19: L.

**cum**[2] /kʌm/ ● n. informal variant spelling of **COME**.

**cumber** /'kʌmbə/ ● v. dated hamper, hinder, or obstruct. ● n. archaic a hindrance, obstruction, or burden.
– ORIGIN ME (in the sense 'overthrow, destroy'): prob. from **ENCUMBER**.

**Cumberland sauce** ● n. a piquant sauce made from redcurrant jelly, served with game and cold meats.

**Cumberland sausage** ● n. Brit. a type of coarse sausage traditionally made in a continuous strip and cooked as a spiral.

## Word *Formation*

**-culture** 'cultivation or husbandry, especially of a specified animal or plant'

➤ **-culture** words in current use (full entries and definitions to be found in this dictionary):

| | | |
|---|---|---|
| agriculture | farming | L. *ager, agri-* 'field' |
| apiculture | bee-keeping | L. *apis* 'bee' |
| aviculture | rearing of birds | L. *avis* 'bird' |
| floriculture | cultivation of flowers | L. *flos, flor-* 'flower' |
| horticulture | gardening | L. *hortus* 'garden' |
| mariculture | cultivation of sea fish or other marine life | L. *mare, mari-* 'sea' |
| pisciculture | breeding of fish | L. *piscis* 'fish' |
| pomiculture | fruit-growing | L. *pomum* 'apple, fruit' |
| sericulture | cultivation of silk and silkworms | L. *sericum* 'silk' |
| silviculture | cultivation of trees | L. *silva* 'wood' |
| viniculture | less common term for VITICULTURE | L. *vinum* 'wine' |
| viticulture | cultivation of grapevines | L. *vitis* 'vine' |

➤ Archaic or less common **-culture** words:

| | | |
|---|---|---|
| boviculture | cattle-rearing | L. *bos, bov-* 'ox' |
| caniculture | breeding of dogs | L. *canis* 'dog' |
| demoniculture | demon worship | based on DEMON |
| domiculture | housekeeping | L. *domus* 'house' |
| menticulture | cultivation of the mind | L. *mens, ment-* 'mind' |
| olericulture | cultivation of vegetables | L. *oleri-, olus* 'pot-herb' |
| ostreiculture | breeding of oysters | L. *ostreum* 'oyster' |
| urbiculture | development of cities and towns | L. *urbs, urb-* 'city' |

Most **-culture** words were first used in English in the 19th century, though a few, notably ***agriculture*** and ***horticulture***, are recorded earlier (17th century).

**cumbersome** ● **adj. 1** difficult to carry or use through size; unwieldy. **2** slow or complicated and therefore inefficient.
– DERIVATIVES **cumbersomely** adv. **cumbersomeness** n.

**cumbia** /ˈkʊmbɪə/ ● **n.** a kind of dance music of Colombian origin, similar to salsa.
– ORIGIN 1940s: from Colombian Sp.

**cumbrous** /ˈkʌmbrəs/ ● **adj.** poetic/literary cumbersome.
– DERIVATIVES **cumbrously** adv. **cumbrousness** n.

**cum dividend** ● **adv.** (of share purchases) with a dividend about to be paid.

**cum grano salis** /kʌm ˌɡrɑːnəʊ ˈsɑːlɪs/ ● **adv.** with a pinch of salt.
– ORIGIN from L.

**cumin** /ˈkʌmɪn/ (also **cummin**) ● **n. 1** the aromatic seeds of a plant of the parsley family, used as a spice, especially in curry powder. **2** the plant which bears this fruit, occurring from the Mediterranean to central Asia. [*Cuminum cyminum*.]
– ORIGIN OE *cymen*, OFr. *cumon, comin*, from L. *cuminum*, from Gk *kuminon*, prob. of Semitic origin.

**cummerbund** /ˈkʌməbʌnd/ ● **n.** a sash worn around the waist, especially as part of a man's formal evening suit.
– ORIGIN C17: from Urdu and Pers. *kamar-band*.

**cumquat** ● **n.** variant spelling of **KUMQUAT**.

**cumulate** ● **v.** /ˈkjuːmjʊleɪt/ **1** accumulate or be accumulated. **2** [as adj. **cumulated**] Chemistry denoting two double bonds attached to the same carbon atom. ● **n.** /ˈkjuːmjʊlət/ Geology an igneous rock formed by gravitational settling of particles in a magma.
– DERIVATIVES **cumulation** n.
– ORIGIN C16 (in the sense 'gather in a heap'): from L. *cumulat- cumulare*, from *cumulus* 'a heap'.

**cumulative** ● **adj.** increasing or increased in quantity or degree by successive additions.
– DERIVATIVES **cumulatively** adv. **cumulativeness** n.

**cumulative error** ● **n.** Statistics an error that increases with the size of the sample revealing it.

**cumulative preference share** ● **n.** a preference share whose annual fixed-rate dividend, if it cannot be paid in any year, accrues until it can.

**cumulative voting** ● **n.** a system of voting in an election in which each voter is allowed as many votes as there are candidates.

**cumulonimbus** /ˌkjuːmjʊləʊˈnɪmbəs/ ● **n.** (pl. **cumulonimbi** /-bʌɪ/) Meteorology cloud forming a towering mass with a flat base at fairly low altitude and often a flat top, as in thunderstorms.

**cumulus** /ˈkjuːmjʊləs/ ● **n.** (pl. **cumuli** /-lʌɪ, -liː/) Meteorology cloud forming rounded masses heaped on each other above a flat base at fairly low altitude.
– ORIGIN C17: from L., 'heap'.

**Cuna** ● **n.** variant spelling of **KUNA**.

**cuneate** /ˈkjuːnɪət/ ● **adj.** chiefly Anatomy & Botany wedge-shaped.
– ORIGIN C19: from L. *cuneus* 'wedge' + **-ATE**².

**cuneiform** /ˈkjuːnɪfɔːm, kjuːˈneɪɪfɔːm/ ● **adj. 1** denoting or relating to the wedge-shaped characters used in the ancient writing systems of Mesopotamia, Persia, and Ugarit. **2** chiefly Biology wedge-shaped. ➤Anatomy denoting three bones of the tarsus between the navicular bone and the metatarsals. ● **n.** cuneiform writing.
– ORIGIN C17: from Fr. *cunéiforme* or mod. L. *cuneiformis*, from L. *cuneus* 'wedge'.

**cunjevoi** /ˈkʌndʒɪvɔɪ/ ● **n. 1** a tall Australian plant of the arum family, with edible corms. [*Alocasia macrorrhiza*.] **2** an Australian sea squirt used as fishing bait. [*Pyura praeputialis*.]
– ORIGIN C19: of Aborig. origin.

**cunner** /ˈkʌnə/ ● **n.** an edible greenish-grey wrasse (fish) which lives along the Atlantic coast of North America. [*Tautogolabrus adspersus*.]
– ORIGIN C17: perh. assoc. with archaic *conder*, denoting a lookout who alerts the crew of fishing boats to the direction taken by shoals of herring.

**cunnilingus** /ˌkʌnɪˈlɪŋɡəs/ ● **n.** stimulation of the female genitals using the tongue or lips.
– ORIGIN C19: from L., from *cunnus* 'vulva' + *lingere* 'lick'.

**cunning** ● **adj. 1** skilled in achieving one's ends by deceit or evasion. **2** ingenious. **3** N. Amer. attractive; charming. ● **n. 1** craftiness. **2** ingenuity.
– DERIVATIVES **cunningly** adv. **cunningness** n.
– ORIGIN ME (in the sense '(possessing) erudition or skill'):

perh. from ON *kunnandi* 'knowledge', from *kunna* 'know' (rel. to **CAN**[1]), or perh. from ME *cunne*, an obs. var. of **CAN**[1].

**cunt** ● n. vulgar slang **1** a woman's genitals. **2** an unpleasant or stupid person.
– ORIGIN ME: of Gmc origin.

**cup** ● n. **1** a small bowl-shaped container for drinking from. ➤(in church use) a chalice used at the Eucharist. ➤a cup-shaped trophy, usually made of gold or silver and having a stem and two handles, awarded as a prize in a sports contest. ➤(**cups**) one of the suits in a tarot pack. **2** chiefly N. Amer. a measure of capacity used in cookery, equal to half a US pint (0.237 litre). **3** either of the two parts of a bra shaped to contain or support one breast. **4** Golf the hole on a putting green or the metal container in it. **5** a long mixed drink made from wine or cider and fruit juice. ● v. (**cupped**, **cupping**) **1** form (one's hand or hands) into the curved shape of a cup. ➤place the curved hand or hands around. **2** Medicine historical bleed (someone) by using a glass in which a partial vacuum is formed by heating.
– PHRASES **in one's cups** informal drunk. **not one's cup of tea** informal not what one likes or is interested in.
– DERIVATIVES **cupful** n. (pl. **-fuls**).
– ORIGIN OE: from pop. L. *cuppa*, prob. from L. *cupa* 'tub'.

**cup-and-ring** ● adj. denoting marks cut in megalithic monuments consisting of a circular depression surrounded by concentric rings.

**cup-bearer** ● n. historical or poetic/literary a person who serves wine, especially in a royal or noble household.

**cupboard** ● n. a piece of furniture or small recess with a door and usually shelves, used for storage.
– PHRASES **cupboard love** affection that is feigned so as to obtain something.
– ORIGIN ME (denoting a table or sideboard on which cups, plates, etc. were displayed).

**cupcake** ● n. **1** a small iced cake baked in a cup-shaped foil or paper container. **2** US informal a weak or effeminate man.

**cupel** /'kju:p(ə)l/ ● n. a shallow, porous container in which gold or silver can be refined or assayed by melting with a blast of hot air which oxidizes lead or other base metals. ● v. (**cupelled**, **cupelling**; US **cupeled**, **cupeling**) assay or refine (a metal) in a cupel.
– DERIVATIVES **cupellation** n.
– ORIGIN C17: from Fr. *coupelle*, dimin. of *coupe* 'goblet'.

**Cup Final** ● n. the final match in a sports competition in which the winners are awarded a cup.

**cupidity** /kju:'pɪdɪti/ ● n. greed for money or possessions.
– ORIGIN ME: from OFr. *cupidite* or L. *cupiditas*, from *cupidus* 'desirous', from *cupere* 'to desire'.

**Cupid's bow** ● n. a pronounced double curve at the top edge of a person's upper lip, resembling the shape of the bow carried by the Roman god of love Cupid.

**cupid's dart** ● n. a herbaceous plant of the daisy family, with white, blue, or lilac flowers. [*Catananche caerulea*.]

**cupola** /'kju:pələ/ ● n. **1** a rounded dome forming or adorning a roof or ceiling. **2** a gun turret. **3** (also **cupola furnace**) a cylindrical furnace for refining metals.
– DERIVATIVES **cupolaed** /-ləd/ adj.
– ORIGIN C16: Ital., from late L. *cupula* 'small cask or burying vault', dimin. of *cupa* 'cask'.

**cuppa** ● n. Brit. informal a cup of tea.

**cupr-** ● comb. form variant spelling of **CUPRO-** shortened before a vowel (as in *cuprammonium*).

**cuprammonium** /,kju:prə'məʊnɪəm/ ● n. [as modifier] Chemistry of or denoting a complex ion containing copper bonded to ammonia, solutions of which are deep blue in colour and able to dissolve cellulose.

**cupreous** /'kju:prɪəs/ ● adj. of or like copper.
– ORIGIN C17: from late L. *cupreus* (from *cuprum* 'copper') + **-OUS**.

**cupric** /'kju:prɪk/ ● adj. Chemistry of copper with a valency of two; of copper(II).

**cuprite** /'kju:prʌɪt/ ● n. a dark red or brownish black mineral consisting of cuprous oxide.

**cupro** /'k(j)u:prəʊ/ ● n. a type of rayon made by dissolving cotton cellulose with cuprammonium salts and spinning the resulting solution into filaments.
– ORIGIN an invented word, prob. from **CUPRAMMONIUM**.

**cupro-** /'kju:prəʊ/ (also **cupr-**) ● comb. form of or relating to copper: *cupro-nickel.*
– ORIGIN from late L. *cuprum*.

**cupro-nickel** ● n. an alloy of copper and nickel, especially in the proportions 3:1 as used in 'silver' coins.

**cuprous** /'kju:prəs/ ● adj. Chemistry of copper with a valency of one; of copper(I).

**cup-tied** ● adj. Brit. (of a soccer player) ineligible to play for one's club in a cup competition as a result of having played for another club in an earlier round.

**cupule** /'kju:pju:l/ ● n. Botany & Zoology a cup-shaped organ, structure, or receptacle in a plant or animal.
– ORIGIN ME: from late L. *cupula* (see **CUPOLA**).

**cur** /kə:/ ● n. **1** an aggressive dog, especially a mongrel. **2** informal a despicable man.
– ORIGIN ME: prob. orig. in *cur-dog*, perh. from ON *kurr* 'grumbling'.

**curaçao** /,kjʊərə'səʊ/ ● n. (pl. **-os**) a liqueur flavoured with the peel of bitter oranges.
– ORIGIN C19: named after *Curaçao*, the Caribbean island where the oranges are grown.

**curandero** /,kjʊərən'dɛ:rəʊ, Spanish kuran'ðero/ ● n. (fem. **curandera** /-'dɛ:rə, Spanish -'ðera/) (pl. **-os** or **-as**) (in Spain and Latin America) a healer who uses folk remedies.
– ORIGIN Sp., from *curar* 'to cure', from L. *curare*.

**curare** /kjʊ'rɑ:ri/ ● n. a paralysing poison obtained from the bark and stems of some South American plants and traditionally used by Indian peoples as an arrow poison.
– ORIGIN C18: from a Carib word, partly via Sp. and Port.

**curassow** /'kjʊərəsəʊ/ ● n. a large crested pheasant-like bird of the guan family, found in tropical American forests. [Genus *Crax*: several species.]
– ORIGIN C17: anglicized form of *Curaçao* (see **CURAÇAO**).

**curate**[1] /'kjʊərət/ ● n. (also **assistant curate**) a member of the clergy engaged as assistant to a parish priest. ➤archaic a minister with pastoral responsibility.
– PHRASES **curate's egg** Brit. something that is partly good and partly bad. [from a cartoon in *Punch* (1895) depicting a meek curate who, given a stale egg when dining with the bishop, assures his host that 'parts of it are excellent'.]
– DERIVATIVES **curacy** n. (pl. **-ies**).
– ORIGIN ME: from med. L. *curatus*, from L. *cura* 'care'.

**curate**[2] /kjʊ(ə)'reɪt/ ● v. select, organize, and look after the items in (a collection or exhibition).
– DERIVATIVES **curation** n.
– ORIGIN C19: back-form. from **CURATOR**.

**curate-in-charge** ● n. another term for **PRIEST-IN-CHARGE**.

**curative** ● adj. able to cure disease. ● n. a curative medicine or agent.
– DERIVATIVES **curatively** adv.

**curator** ● n. a keeper or custodian of a museum or other collection.
– DERIVATIVES **curatorial** adj. **curatorship** n.
– ORIGIN ME (denoting a pastor or a guardian of a minor): from OFr. *curateur* or, in later use, directly from L. *curator*, from *curare* (see **CURE**).

**curb** ● n. **1** a check or restraint. ➤(also **curb bit**) a type of bit with a strap or chain attached which passes under a horse's lower jaw, used as a check. **2** US variant spelling of **KERB**. **3** a swelling on the back of a horse's hock, caused by spraining a ligament. ● v. keep in check.
– ORIGIN C15: from OFr. *courber* 'bend, bow', from L. *curvare* (see **CURVE**).

**curb roof** ● n. the shallow upper slopes of a mansard roof. ➤Brit. a mansard roof.

**curbstone** ● n. US spelling of **KERBSTONE**.

**curculio** /kə:'kju:lɪəʊ/ ● n. (pl. **-os**) chiefly N. Amer. a weevil which is a pest of fruit trees. [*Conotrachelus nenuphar* (the **plum curculio**), and other species.]
– ORIGIN C18: mod. L., 'corn weevil'.

**curcuma** /'kə:kjʊmə/ ● n. a tropical Asian plant of a

genus that includes turmeric and other species yielding spices, dyes, and medicinal products. [Genus *Curcuma*.]
– ORIGIN mod. L., from Arab. *kurkum* 'saffron', from Sanskrit *kuṅkuma*.

**curd** ● n. **1** (also **curds**) a soft, white substance formed when milk coagulates, used as the basis for cheese. ➤a fatty substance found between the flakes of poached salmon. **2** the edible head of a cauliflower or similar plant.
– DERIVATIVES **curdy** adj.
– ORIGIN ME: of unknown origin.

**curd cheese** ● n. chiefly Brit. a mild, soft, smooth cheese made from skimmed milk curd.

**curdle** ● v. separate or cause to separate into curds or lumps.
– PHRASES **make one's blood curdle** fill one with horror.
– DERIVATIVES **curdler** n.
– ORIGIN C16: frequentative of obs. *curd* 'congeal'.

**cure** ● v. **1** relieve of the symptoms of a disease or condition. ➤end (a disease, condition, or problem) by treatment or remedial action. **2** preserve (meat, fish, tobacco, or an animal skin) by salting, drying, or smoking. ➤harden (rubber, plastic, concrete, etc.) after manufacture by a chemical process such as vulcanization. ● n. **1** a substance, treatment, or remedy that cures a disease, condition, or problem. ➤restoration to health. **2** the process of curing meat, fish, rubber, etc. **3** a Christian minister's pastoral charge or area of responsibility for spiritual ministry. ➤a parish.
– DERIVATIVES **curability** n. **curable** adj. **curer** n.
– ORIGIN ME (in the senses 'care, concern, responsibility'): from OFr. *curer* (v.), *cure* (n.), both from L. *curare* 'take care of', from *cura* 'care'.

**curé** /'kjʊəreɪ, French kyʀe/ ● n. a parish priest in a French-speaking country.
– ORIGIN Fr., from med. L. *curatus* (see **CURATE**[1]).

**cure-all** ● n. a remedy that will supposedly cure any ailment or problem.

**curettage** /kjʊə'rɛtɪdʒ, ˌkjʊərɪ'tɑːʒ/ ● n. Surgery the use of a curette, especially on the lining of the uterus. See **DILATATION AND CURETTAGE**.
– ORIGIN C19: from Fr., from **CURETTE**.

**curette** /kjʊə'rɛt/ ● n. a small surgical instrument used to remove material by a scraping action, especially from the uterus. ● v. clean or scrape with a curette.
– ORIGIN C18: from Fr., from *curer* 'cleanse'.

**curfew** /'kəːfjuː/ ● n. a regulation requiring people to remain indoors between specified hours, typically at night. ➤the time designated as the beginning of such a restriction.
– ORIGIN ME (denoting a regulation requiring fires to be extinguished at a fixed hour in the evening): from OFr. *cuevrefeu*, from *cuvrir* 'to cover' + *feu* 'fire'.

**Curia** /'kjʊərɪə/ ● n. the papal court at the Vatican, by which the Roman Catholic Church is governed.
– DERIVATIVES **Curial** adj.
– ORIGIN C19: from L. *curia*, denoting a division of an ancient Roman tribe, (by extension) the senate of cities other than Rome, and later a feudal or Roman Catholic court of justice.

**curie** /'kjʊəri/ (abbrev.: **Ci**) ● n. (pl. **-ies**) a unit of radioactivity, corresponding to $3.7 \times 10^{10}$ disintegrations per second. ➤the quantity of radioactive substance that has this amount of activity.
– ORIGIN C20: named after the Fr. physicists Pierre and Marie *Curie*.

**curio** /'kjʊərɪəʊ/ ● n. (pl. **-os**) a rare, unusual, or intriguing object.
– ORIGIN C19: abbrev. of **CURIOSITY**.

**curiosa** /ˌkjʊərɪ'əʊsə/ ● pl. n. curiosities, especially erotica or pornography.
– ORIGIN C19: from L., neut. pl. of *curiosus* (see **CURIOUS**).

**curiosity** ● n. (pl. **-ies**) **1** a strong desire to know or learn something. **2** a unusual or interesting object or fact.

**curious** ● adj. **1** eager to know or learn something. **2** strange; unusual. ➤euphemistic erotic or pornographic.
– DERIVATIVES **curiously** adv. **curiousness** n.
– ORIGIN ME: from OFr. *curios*, from L. *curiosus* 'careful', from *cura* 'care'.

**curium** /'kjʊərɪəm/ ● n. the chemical element of atomic number 96, an artificially made radioactive metal of the actinide series. (Symbol: **Cm**)
– ORIGIN 1940s: from the name of Marie and Pierre *Curie* (see **CURIE**).

**curl** ● v. **1** form or cause to form a curved or spiral shape. **2** move or cause to move in a spiral or curved course. **3** (in weight training) lift (a weight) using only the hands, wrists, and forearms. **4** play at the game of curling. ● n. **1** something in the shape of a spiral or coil, especially a lock of hair. **2** a curling movement. **3** a weightlifting exercise involving movement of only the hands, wrists, and forearms. **4** Mathematics a function giving a measure of the rotation of a vector field.
– PHRASES **make someone's hair curl** informal shock or horrify someone.
– DERIVATIVES **curly** adj. (**-ier**, **-iest**).
– ORIGIN ME: from obs. *crulle* 'curly', from MDu. *krul*.

**curler** ● n. **1** a roller or clasp around which a lock of hair is wrapped to curl it. **2** a player in the game of curling.

**curlew** /'kəːl(j)uː/ ● n. (pl. same or **curlews**) a large wading bird of the sandpiper family, with a long downcurved bill and brown streaked plumage. [*Numenius arquata* and other species.]
– ORIGIN ME: from OFr. *courlieu*, alt. (by assoc. with *courliu* 'courier') of imitative *courlis*.

**curlicue** /'kəːlɪkjuː/ ● n. a decorative curl or twist in calligraphy or in the design of an object.
– ORIGIN C19: from ***curly*** (see **CURL**) + **CUE**[2] (in the sense 'pigtail'), or *-cue* representing the letter *q*.

**curling** ● n. a game played on ice, especially in Scotland and Canada, in which large circular flat stones are slid across the surface towards a mark.

**curling tongs** (also **curling iron**) ● pl. n. a device incorporating a heated rod around which hair can be wound so as to curl it.

**curly endive** ● n. see **ENDIVE**.

**curmudgeon** /kəː'mʌdʒ(ə)n/ ● n. a bad-tempered or surly person.
– DERIVATIVES **curmudgeonliness** n. **curmudgeonly** adj.
– ORIGIN C16: of unknown origin.

**currach** /'kʌrə(x)/ (also **curragh**) ● n. Irish and Scottish term for **CORACLE**.
– ORIGIN ME: from Ir. and Sc. Gaelic *curach* 'small boat'.

**curragh** /'kʌrə(x)/ ● n. (in Ireland and the Isle of Man) a stretch of marshy waste ground.
– ORIGIN C17: from Ir. *currach* 'marsh', Manx *curragh* 'bog, fen'.

**currant** ● n. **1** a small dried fruit made from a small seedless variety of grape, used in cookery. **2** used in names of various small edible berries and the shrubs which produce them, e.g. **blackcurrant**, **white currant**.
– ORIGIN ME *raisons of Corauntz*, translating Anglo-Norman Fr. *raisins de Corauntz* 'grapes of Corinth' (the original source).

**currawong** /'kʌrəwɒŋ/ ● n. a crow-like Australian songbird with mainly black or grey plumage, a robust straight bill, and a resonant call. [Genus *Strepera*: three species.]
– ORIGIN 1920s: from an Aborig. word.

**currency** ● n. (pl. **-ies**) **1** a system of money in general use in a particular country. **2** the fact or quality of being current. ➤the time during which something is current.

**current** ● adj. happening or being used or done now. ➤in common or general use. ● n. **1** a body of water or air moving in a definite direction through a surrounding body of water or air in which there is less movement. **2** a flow of electricity which results from the ordered directional movement of electrically charged particles. ➤a quantity representing the rate of flow of electric charge, usually measured in amperes.
– ORIGIN ME (in the sense 'running, flowing'): from OFr. *corant* 'running', from *courre* 'run', from L. *currere* 'run'.

**current account** ● n. Brit. an account with a bank or building society from which money may be withdrawn without notice.

**current assets** ● pl. n. cash and other assets that are expected to be converted to cash within a year. Compare with **FIXED ASSETS**.

**current liabilities** ● pl. n. amounts due to be paid to creditors within twelve months.

**currently** ● adv. at the present time.

**curricle** /ˈkʌrɪk(ə)l/ ● n. historical a light, open, two-wheeled carriage pulled by two horses side by side.
– ORIGIN C18: from L. *curriculum* 'course, racing chariot'.

**curriculum** /kʌˈrɪkjʊləm/ ● n. (pl. **curricula** or **curriculums**) the subjects comprising a course of study in a school or college.
– DERIVATIVES **curricular** adj.
– ORIGIN C19: from L. (see **CURRICLE**).

**curriculum vitae** /ˈviːtʌɪ, ˈvʌɪtiː/ ● n. (pl. **curricula vitae**) a brief account of a person's education, qualifications, and previous occupations, typically sent with a job application.
– ORIGIN C20: L., 'course of life'.

**currier** /ˈkʌrɪə/ ● n. a person who curries leather.
– ORIGIN ME: from OFr. *corier*, from L. *coriarius*, from *corium* 'leather'.

**currish** /ˈkəːrɪʃ/ ● adj. like a cur, especially in being bad-tempered.
– DERIVATIVES **currishly** adv. **currishness** n.

**curry**[1] ● n. (pl. **-ies**) a dish of meat, vegetables, etc., cooked in an Indian-style sauce of strong spices. ● v. (**-ies**, **-ied**) [usu. as adj. **curried**] prepare or flavour with such a sauce.
– ORIGIN C16: from Tamil *kaṟi*.

**curry**[2] ● v. (**-ies**, **-ied**) **1** chiefly N. Amer. groom (a horse) with a curry-comb. **2** historical treat (tanned leather) to improve its properties.
– PHRASES **curry favour** ingratiate oneself through obsequious behaviour. [alt. of ME *curry favel*, from the name (*Favel*) of a horse in a C14 Fr. romance who became a symbol of cunning and duplicity; hence 'to rub down Favel' meant to use cunning.]
– ORIGIN ME: from OFr. *correier*, ult. of Gmc origin.

**curry-comb** ● n. a hand-held device with serrated ridges, used for grooming horses.

**curry leaf** ● n. a shrub or small tree native to India and Sri Lanka, the leaves of which are widely used in Indian cooking. [*Murraya koenigii*.]

**curry plant** ● n. a small shrubby plant with narrow silver-grey leaves, small yellow flowers, and a strong smell of curry. [*Helichrysum angustifolium*.]

**curry powder** ● n. a mixture of finely ground spices, such as turmeric and coriander, used for making curry.

**curse** ● n. **1** a solemn appeal to a supernatural power to inflict harm on someone or something. ➤ a cause of harm or misery. **2** an offensive word or phrase used to express anger or annoyance. ● v. **1** use a curse against. ➤ (**be cursed with**) be afflicted with. **2** utter or address with expletives.
– DERIVATIVES **curser** n.
– ORIGIN OE, of unknown origin.

**cursed** /ˈkəːsɪd, kəːst/ ● adj. informal, dated used to express annoyance or irritation.
– DERIVATIVES **cursedly** adv. **cursedness** n.

**cursillo** /kəːˈsiːjəʊ, -ˈsiːljəʊ/ ● n. (pl. **-os**) a short informal spiritual retreat by a group of Roman Catholics, especially in Spain or Latin America.
– ORIGIN 1950s: Sp., 'little course'.

**cursive** /ˈkəːsɪv/ ● adj. written with the characters joined. ● n. writing with such a style.
– DERIVATIVES **cursively** adv.
– ORIGIN C18: from med. L. *cursivus*, from L. *curs-*, *currere* 'run'.

**cursor** ● n. **1** a movable indicator on a computer screen identifying the point that will be affected by input from the user. **2** chiefly historical the transparent slide engraved with a hairline used to locate points on a slide rule.
– ORIGIN ME (denoting a runner): from L., 'runner', from *curs-* (see **CURSIVE**).

**cursorial** /kəːˈsɔːrɪəl/ ● adj. Zoology having limbs adapted for running.

**cursory** /ˈkəːs(ə)ri/ ● adj. hasty and therefore not thorough.
– DERIVATIVES **cursorily** adv. **cursoriness** n.
– ORIGIN C17: from L. *cursorius* 'of a runner', from *cursor* (see **CURSOR**).

**curst** ● adj. archaic spelling of **CURSED**.

**curt** ● adj. rudely brief.
– DERIVATIVES **curtly** adv. **curtness** n.
– ORIGIN ME (in the sense 'short, shortened'): from L. *curtus* 'cut short, abridged'.

**curtail** /kəːˈteɪl/ ● v. reduce in extent or quantity.
– DERIVATIVES **curtailment** n.
– ORIGIN C15: from obs. *curtal* 'horse with a docked tail', from Fr. *courtault*, from *court* 'short', from L. *curtus*; the change in the ending was due to assoc. with **TAIL**[1].

**curtain** ● n. **1** a piece of material suspended at the top to form a screen, typically movable sideways and found as one of a pair at a window. ➤ (**the curtain**) a screen of heavy cloth or other material that can be raised or lowered at the front of a stage. ➤ a raising or lowering of such a screen at the beginning or end of an act or scene. **2** (**curtains**) informal a disastrous outcome. ● v. [often as adj. **curtained**] provide with a curtain or curtains. ➤ conceal with or as with a curtain.
– ORIGIN ME: from OFr. *cortine*, from late L. *cortina*, translation of Gk *aulaia*, from *aulē* 'court'.

**curtain call** ● n. the appearance of one or more performers on stage after a performance to acknowledge the audience's applause.

**curtain fire** (also chiefly US **curtain of fire**) ● n. Brit. rapid, continuous artillery or machine-gun fire on a designated line or area.

**curtain lecture** ● n. dated a wife's private reprimand to her husband.
– ORIGIN C17: orig. a reprimand given behind bed curtains.

**curtain-raiser** ● n. an entertainment or other event happening just before a longer or more important one.
– ORIGIN C19: orig. used in the theatre to denote a short opening piece performed before a play.

**curtain wall** ● n. **1** a fortified wall around a medieval castle, typically one linking towers together. **2** a wall which encloses the space within a building but does not support the roof.

**curtal** /ˈkəːt(ə)l/ ● n. a dulcian or bassoon of the late 16th to early 18th century.
– ORIGIN C15 (denoting a short-barrelled cannon): from Fr. *courtault*, from *court* 'short' + the pejorative suffix *-ault*.

**curtana** /kəːˈtɑːnə, -ˈteɪnə/ ● n. the unpointed sword carried in front of English sovereigns at their coronation to represent mercy.
– ORIGIN ME: from Anglo-Latin *curtana* (*spatha*) 'shortened (sword)', from OFr. *cortain*, the name of the sword belonging to Charlemagne's paladin Roland (the point of which was damaged), from *cort* 'short', from L. *curtus* 'cut short'.

**curtilage** /ˈkəːt(ɪ)lɪdʒ/ ● n. an area of land attached to a house and forming one enclosure with it.
– ORIGIN ME: from Anglo-Norman Fr., var. of OFr. *courtillage*, from *courtil* 'small court', from *cort* 'court'.

**curtsy** (also **curtsey**) ● n. (pl. **-ies** or **-eys**) a woman's or girl's formal greeting made by bending the knees with one foot in front of the other. ● v. (**-ies**, **-ied** or **-eys**, **-eyed**) perform a curtsy.
– ORIGIN C16: var. of **COURTESY**.

**curule** /ˈkjʊəruːl/ ● adj. denoting or relating to the authority exercised by the senior magistrates in ancient Rome, chiefly the consul and praetor, who were entitled to use the *sella curulis* (a kind of folding chair).
– ORIGIN C17: from L. *curulis*, from *currus* 'chariot' (in which the chief magistrate was conveyed to the seat of office).

**curvaceous** /kəːˈveɪʃəs/ ● adj. (especially of a woman or a woman's figure) having an attractively curved shape.
– DERIVATIVES **curvaceousness** n.

**curvature** /ˈkəːvətʃə/ ● n. the fact of being curved or the degree to which something is curved. ➤ Geometry the degree to which a curve deviates from a straight line, or a curved surface deviates from a plane.

**curve** • **n.** a line or outline which gradually deviates from being straight for some or all of its length. ➤a line on a graph (whether straight or curved) showing how one quantity varies with respect to another. ➤(also **curve ball**) Baseball a delivery in which the pitcher causes the ball to deviate from a straight path by imparting spin. • **v.** form or cause to form a curve.
– ORIGIN ME: from L. *curvare* 'to bend', from *curvus* 'bent'.

**curvet** /kəːˈvɛt/ • **n.** a graceful or energetic leap. • **v.** (**curvetted**, **curvetting** or **curveted**, **curveting**) (of a horse) perform a courbette.
– ORIGIN C16: from Ital. *corvetta*, dimin. of *corva*, earlier form of *curva* 'a curve', from L. *curvus* 'bent'.

**curvilinear** /ˌkəːvɪˈlɪnɪə/ • **adj.** contained by or consisting of a curved line or lines.
– DERIVATIVES **curvilinearly** adv.
– ORIGIN C18: from L. *curvus* 'bent, curved', on the pattern of *rectilinear*.

**curvy** • **adj.** (**-ier**, **-iest**) having many curves. ➤informal (especially of a woman's figure) shapely and voluptuous.
– DERIVATIVES **curviness** n.

**cuscus** /ˈkʌskʌs/ • **n.** a tree-dwelling marsupial with a prehensile tail, native to New Guinea and northern Australia. [*Spilocuscus maculatus* (**spotted cuscus**) and other species.]
– ORIGIN C17: via Fr. and Du. from a local name in the Molucca Islands.

**cusec** /ˈkjuːsɛk/ • **n.** a unit of flow (especially of water) equal to one cubic foot per second.

**cushat** /ˈkʌʃət/ • **n.** dialect, chiefly Scottish a wood pigeon.
– ORIGIN OE, of unknown origin.

**cushaw** /kʊˈʃɔː, ˈkuːʃɔː/ • **n.** US a large winter squash of a variety with a curved neck.
– ORIGIN C16: of unknown origin.

**cush-cush** /ˈkʊʃkʊʃ/ • **n.** a tropical American yam which produces a number of edible tubers on each plant. [*Dioscorea trifida*.]
– ORIGIN C19: perh. ult. of Afr. origin.

**Cushing's disease** • **n.** Cushing's syndrome as caused by a tumour of the pituitary gland.

**Cushing's syndrome** • **n.** Medicine a metabolic disorder caused by overproduction of corticosteroid hormones by the adrenal cortex and often involving obesity and high blood pressure.
– ORIGIN 1930s: named after the Amer. surgeon Harvey W. *Cushing*.

**cushion** • **n. 1** a bag of cloth stuffed with a mass of soft material, used as a comfortable support for sitting or leaning on. **2** something providing support or protection against impact. ➤the elastic lining of the sides of a billiard table, from which the ball rebounds. • **v. 1** soften the effect of an impact on. **2** mitigate the adverse effects of.
– DERIVATIVES **cushioned** adj. **cushiony** adj.
– ORIGIN ME: from OFr. *cuissin*, based on a L. word meaning 'cushion for the hip', from *coxa* 'hip, thigh'.

**cushion star** • **n.** a small starfish with a broad body and very short blunt arms. [*Asterina gibbosa* and other species.]

**Cushitic** /kʊˈʃɪtɪk/ • **n.** a group of East African languages of the Afro-Asiatic family spoken mainly in Ethiopia and Somalia. • **adj.** of or relating to this group of languages.
– ORIGIN C20: from *Cush*, the name of part of ancient Nubia, + **-ITIC**.

**cushy** • **adj.** (**-ier**, **-iest**) informal **1** (of a task or situation) undemanding, easy, or secure. **2** N. Amer. (of furniture) comfortable.
– DERIVATIVES **cushiness** n.
– ORIGIN First World War (orig. Anglo-Ind.): from Urdu *k͟hushī* 'pleasure'.

**cusk** /kʌsk/ • **n.** another term for **TORSK**.
– ORIGIN C17: of unknown origin.

**cusk-eel** • **n.** a small eel-like marine fish with a tapering body and a pointed tail. [Family Ophidiidae: many species.]

**cusp** /kʌsp/ • **n. 1** each of the pointed ends of a crescent, especially of the moon. ➤Architecture a projecting point between small arcs in Gothic tracery. **2** a cone-shaped prominence on the surface of a tooth, especially of a molar or premolar. **3** Mathematics a point at which the direction of a curve is abruptly reversed. **4** Astrology the initial point of an astrological sign or house. ➤a point of transition between two different states: *those on the cusp of adulthood.* **5** Anatomy a pocket or fold in the wall of the heart or a major blood vessel, forming part of a valve.
– DERIVATIVES **cuspate** adj. **cusped** adj. **cusping** n.
– ORIGIN C16: from L. *cuspis* 'point or apex'.

**cuspid** • **n.** a tooth with a single cusp or point; a canine tooth.
– DERIVATIVES **cuspidate** adj.
– ORIGIN C18: from L. *cuspis*, *cuspid-* 'point or apex'.

**cuspidor** /ˈkʌspɪdɔː/ • **n.** N. Amer. a spittoon.
– ORIGIN C18: from Port., 'spitter'.

**cuss** informal • **n. 1** an annoying or stubborn person or animal. **2** another term for **CURSE** (in sense 2). • **v.** another term for **CURSE** (in sense 2).

**cussed** /ˈkʌsɪd/ • **adj.** informal awkward; annoying.
– DERIVATIVES **cussedly** adv. **cussedness** n.
– ORIGIN C19 (orig. US): var. of **CURSED**.

**custard** • **n.** a dessert or sweet sauce made with milk and eggs and thickened with cornflour, or milk and a proprietary powder.
– ORIGIN ME *crustarde*, *custarde* (denoting an open pie containing meat or fruit in a sauce thickened with eggs), from OFr. *crouste* (see **CRUST**).

**custard apple** • **n. 1** a large fleshy tropical fruit with a sweet yellow pulp. **2** the tree which bears this fruit, native to Central and South America. [Genus *Annona*: several species.]

**custard marrow** • **n.** a summer squash which has flattened round fruits with scalloped edges.

**custard pie** • **n.** an open pie containing cold set custard. ➤a pie of this type, or a flat container of foam, used for throwing in someone's face in slapstick comedy.

**custody** /ˈkʌstədi/ • **n. 1** the protective care or guardianship of someone or something. ➤Law parental responsibility, especially as allocated to one of two divorcing parents. **2** imprisonment.
– DERIVATIVES **custodial** /kʌˈstəʊdɪəl/ adj. **custodian** n. **custodianship** n.
– ORIGIN ME: from L. *custodia*, from *custos* 'guardian'.

**custom** • **n. 1** a traditional and widely accepted way of behaving or doing something that is specific to a particular society, place, or time. ➤Law established usage having the force of law or right. **2** chiefly Brit. regular dealings with a shop or business by customers.
– ORIGIN ME: from OFr. *coustume*, based on L. *consuetudo*, from *consuetus*, past part. of *consuescere* 'accustom'.

**customal** /ˈkʌstəm(ə)l/ • **n.** variant spelling of **CUSTUMAL**.

**customary** • **adj.** in accordance with custom; usual. ➤Law established by or based on custom rather than common law or statute. • **n.** (pl. **-ies**) historical another term for **CUSTUMAL**.
– DERIVATIVES **customarily** adv. **customariness** n.

**custom-built** • **adj.** made to a particular customer's order.

**customer** • **n. 1** a person who buys goods or services from a shop or business. **2** a person or thing of a specified kind that one has to deal with: *he's a tough customer.*

**custom house** (also **customs house**) • **n.** chiefly historical the office at a port or frontier where customs duty is collected.

**customize** (also **-ise**) • **v.** modify to suit a particular individual or task.

**custom-made** • **adj.** another term for **CUSTOM-BUILT**.

**customs** • **pl. n.** the official department that administers and collects the duties levied by a government on imported goods. ➤(also **customs duties**) the duties levied by a government on imported goods.
– ORIGIN ME: orig. in the sing., denoting a customary due paid to a ruler, later duty levied on goods on their way to

market.

**customs union** ● **n.** a group of states that have agreed to charge the same import duties as each other and usually to allow free trade between themselves.

**custos rotulorum** /ˌkʌstɒs ˌrəʊtjʊˈlɔːrəm/ ● **n.** (pl. **custodes rotulorum** /kʌˈstəʊdiːz/) (in England and Wales) the principal Justice of the Peace of a county, who has nominal custody of the records of the commission of the peace.
– ORIGIN from L.

**custumal** /ˈkʌstjʊm(ə)l/ (also **customal**) ● **n.** historical a written account of the customs of a manor or local community.
– ORIGIN C16: from med. L. *custumale* 'customs book'.

**cut** ● **v.** (**cutting**; past and past part. **cut**) **1** make an opening, incision, or wound in (something) with a sharp tool or object. **2** remove (something) from something larger by using a sharp implement. **3** divide into pieces with a knife or other sharp implement. ➤(**cut something down**) cause something to fall by cutting through at the base. **4** make or form by using a sharp tool to remove material. ➤[often as adj. **cut**] make or design (a garment) in a particular way: *an impeccably cut suit.* **5** reduce the length of by using a sharp implement. **6** reduce the amount or quantity of. ➤Computing delete (part of a text). ➤end or interrupt the provision of (a supply). ➤(**cut something off**) block the usual means of access to a place. ➤chiefly N. Amer. absent oneself deliberately from: *Rod was cutting class.* **7** (of a line) cross or intersect (another line). **8** stop filming or recording. ➤move to another shot in a film. ➤make (a film) into a coherent whole by removing or reordering parts. **9** make (a sound recording). **10** divide a pack of playing cards by lifting a portion from the top. **11** strike or kick (a ball) quickly and abruptly. ➤Golf slice (the ball). ➤Cricket hit (the ball) to the off side with the bat held almost horizontally; play such a stroke against (the bowler). ➤Cricket (of the ball) turn sharply on pitching. **12** chiefly N. Amer. adulterate (a drug) or dilute (alcohol) by mixing it with another substance: *speed cut with rat poison.* **13** (**cut it**) informal, chiefly N. Amer. come up to expectations. [shortened form of the idiom *cut the mustard.*] ● **n. 1** an act of cutting. ➤a reduction in amount or size. **2** a result of cutting: *a cut on his jaw.* ➤a piece of meat cut from a carcass. ➤informal a share of profits. ➤a version of a film after editing: *the director's cut.* **3** the way or style in which a garment or the hair is cut: *the elegant cut of his jacket.*
– PHRASES **be cut out for** (or **to be**) [usu. with neg.] informal have exactly the right qualities for a particular role. **a cut above** informal noticeably superior to. **cut and dried** (of a situation) completely settled. [C18: orig. used to distinguish the herbs of herbalists' shops from growing herbs.] **cut and run** informal make a speedy departure from a difficult situation rather than deal with it. [orig. a naut. phr., meaning 'cut the anchor cable because of an emergency and make sail immediately'.] **cut and thrust** a difficult or competitive atmosphere or environment: *the cut and thrust of political debate.* [orig. a fencing phr.] **cut both ways** (of a point or statement) serve both sides of an argument. ➤(of an action or process) have both good and bad effects. **cut corners** undertake something perfunctorily so as to save time or money. **cut a dash** be stylish or impressive in one's dress or behaviour. **cut someone dead** completely ignore someone. **cut from the same cloth** of the same nature. **cut in line** US jump the queue. **cut it out** informal stop it. **cut the mustard** informal reach the required standard. **cut no ice** informal have no influence or effect. **cut a** (or **the**) **rug** informal, chiefly N. Amer. dance, especially in an energetic or accomplished way. **cut one's teeth** acquire initial practice or experience of a particular sphere of activity. **cut a tooth** (of a baby) have a tooth appear through the gum. **cut to the chase** N. Amer. informal come to the point. **cut up rough** Brit. informal behave in an aggressive or awkward way. **make** (or **miss**) **the cut** Golf reach (or fail to reach) a required score, thus avoiding (or ensuring) elimination from the last two rounds of a four-round tournament.
– PHRASAL VERBS **cut in 1** interrupt. **2** pull in too closely in front of another vehicle. **3** (of a motor or other device) begin operating, especially when triggered automatically. **cut someone in** informal include someone in a deal and give them a share of the profits. **cut someone off 1** break the connection during a telephone call. **2** deprive someone of a supply of power, water, etc. **3** disinherit someone. **cut out 1** (of an engine) suddenly stop operating. **2** N. Amer. informal leave quickly. **cut someone out** exclude someone. **cut up 1** N. Amer. informal behave in a mischievous or unruly manner. **2** informal (of a horse race) have a particular selection of runners. **cut someone up 1** informal (of a driver) overtake someone and pull in too closely. **2** informal, chiefly N. Amer. criticize someone severely.
– ORIGIN ME (prob. existing, although not recorded, in OE); prob. of Gmc origin.

**cut and paste** ● **n.** a process used in assembling text on a word processor or computer, in which items are removed from one part and inserted elsewhere. ● **v.** move (an item of text) using such a technique.

**cutaneous** /kjuːˈteɪnɪəs/ ● **adj.** of, relating to, or affecting the skin.
– ORIGIN C16: from mod. L. *cutaneus* (from L. *cutis* 'skin') + **-OUS**.

**cutaway** ● **adj. 1** denoting a coat or jacket with the front cut away below the waist. **2** denoting a diagram or drawing with some external parts left out to reveal the interior. ● **n.** a shot in a film which is of a different subject from those to which it is joined in editing.

**cutback** ● **n.** a reduction, especially in expenditure.

**cute** ● **adj. 1** endearingly pretty. ➤N. Amer. informal sexually attractive. **2** informal, chiefly N. Amer. clever; shrewd.
– DERIVATIVES **cutely** adv. **cuteness** n.
– ORIGIN C18: shortening of **ACUTE**.

**cutesy** ● **adj.** informal cute to a sentimental or mawkish extent.

**cut glass** ● **n.** glass that has been ornamented by having patterns cut into it by grinding and polishing.

**cuticle** /ˈkjuːtɪk(ə)l/ ● **n. 1** Botany & Zoology a protective layer covering the epidermis of a plant or of an insect or other invertebrate. **2** Anatomy the epidermis of the body. ➤dead skin at the base of a fingernail or toenail. ➤the outer cellular layer of a hair.
– DERIVATIVES **cuticular** /-ˈtɪkjʊlə/ adj.
– ORIGIN C15: from L. *cuticula*, dimin. of *cutis* 'skin'.

**cutie** ● **n.** (pl. **-ies**) informal an attractive or endearing person.

**cutin** /ˈkjuːtɪn/ ● **n.** Biochemistry a waxy water-repellent substance in the cuticle of plants.
– ORIGIN C19: from **CUTIS** + **-IN**[1].

**cut-in** ● **n.** a shot in a film that is edited into another shot or scene.

**cutis** /ˈkjuːtɪs/ ● **n.** Anatomy the true skin or dermis.
– ORIGIN C17: from L., 'skin'.

**cutlass** /ˈkʌtləs/ ● **n.** a short sword with a slightly curved blade, formerly used by sailors.
– ORIGIN C16: from Fr. *coutelas*, based on L. *cultellus* (see **CUTLER**).

**cutler** ● **n.** a person who makes or sells cutlery.
– ORIGIN ME: from OFr. *coutelier*, from *coutel* 'knife', from L. *cultellus*, dimin. of *culter* 'knife, ploughshare'.

**cutlery** ● **n.** knives, forks, and spoons used for eating or serving food.

**cutlet** ● **n.** a portion of meat, especially a lamb or veal chop from just behind the neck served grilled or fried. ➤a flat croquette of minced meat, nuts, or pulses.
– ORIGIN C18: from Fr. *côtelette*, earlier *costelette*, dimin. of *coste* 'rib'.

**cutline** ● **n. 1** N. Amer. the caption to a photograph or other illustration. **2** (in squash) the line above which a served ball must strike the front wall.

**cut-off** ● **n. 1** a point or level marking a designated limit. **2** a device for producing an interruption in flow of a power or fuel supply. ➤a sudden drop in amplification or responsiveness of an electric device at a certain frequency. **3** (**cut-offs**) shorts made by cutting off the legs of a pair of jeans. **4** chiefly N. Amer. a short cut.

**cut-out** ● **n. 1** a shape cut out of board or another material. **2** a hole cut in something for decoration or to allow the insertion of something else. **3** a device that automatically breaks an electric circuit for safety.

**cutover** ● n. a rapid transition from one phase of a project to another.

**cut-price** (chiefly N. Amer. also **cut-rate**) ● adj. for sale at a reduced price; cheap.

**cutpurse** ● n. archaic term for **PICKPOCKET**.
– ORIGIN ME: with ref. to stealing by cutting purses suspended from a waistband.

**cutter** ● n. **1** a person or thing that cuts. **2** a light, fast coastal patrol boat. ➤ a ship's boat used for carrying light stores or passengers. ➤ historical a small fore-and-aft rigged sailing boat with one mast, more than one headsail, and a running bowsprit, used as a fast auxiliary. ➤ a yacht with one mainsail and two foresails. **3** Cricket & Baseball a ball that deviates sharply on pitching. **4** a pig heavier than a porker but lighter than a baconer.

**cut-throat** ● n. **1** dated a murderer or other violent criminal. **2** (also **cut-throat trout**) a trout of western North America, with red or orange markings under the jaw. [*Salmo clarki*.] ● adj. **1** ruthless and intense. **2** (of some card games) played by three rather than four players.

**cut-throat razor** ● n. Brit. a razor with a long blade which folds like a penknife.

**cutting** ● n. **1** a piece cut off from something. ➤ Brit. an article or other piece cut from a newspaper. ➤ a piece cut from a plant for propagation. **2** an open passage excavated through higher ground for a railway, road, or canal. ● adj. **1** capable of cutting. **2** (of a remark) hurtful.
– DERIVATIVES **cuttingly** adv.

**cutting edge** ● n. the latest or most advanced stage; the forefront. ● adj. (**cutting-edge**) innovative; pioneering.

**cuttle** ● n. a cuttlefish.
– ORIGIN OE *cudele* 'cuttlefish', of Gmc origin; rel. to *codd* 'bag', with ref. to its ink bag.

**cuttlebone** ● n. the flattened internal skeleton of the cuttlefish, used as a dietary supplement for cage birds and for making casts for precious metal items.

**cuttlefish** ● n. (pl. same or **-fishes**) a swimming marine mollusc that resembles a broad-bodied squid, having eight arms and two long tentacles that are used for grabbing prey. [*Sepia* and other genera, order Sepioidea.]

**cut up** ● adj. informal very distressed. ● n. (**cut-up**) a film or sound recording made by cutting and editing material from pre-existing recordings.

**cutwater** ● n. **1** the forward edge of a ship's prow. **2** a wedge-shaped projection on the pier of a bridge.

**cutwork** ● n. embroidery or lace with parts cut out and the edges oversewn or filled with needlework designs.

**cutworm** ● n. a moth caterpillar that lives in the soil and eats through the stems of young plants at ground level.

**cuvée** /'kju:veɪ, French kyve/ ● n. a type, blend, or batch of wine, especially champagne.
– ORIGIN C19: Fr., 'vatful'.

**cuvette** /kju:'vɛt/ ● n. a straight-sided container for holding liquid samples in a spectrophotometer etc.
– ORIGIN C18: from Fr., dimin. of *cuve* 'cask'.

**CV** ● abbrev. curriculum vitae.

**cv** ● abbrev. cultivated variety.

**CVO** ● abbrev. (in the UK) Commander of the Royal Victorian Order.

**CVS** ● abbrev. chorionic villus sampling, a test made in early pregnancy to detect fetal abnormalities.

**CVT** ● abbrev. continuously variable transmission.

**cwm** /kʊm/ ● n. a cirque, especially in the Welsh mountains.
– ORIGIN C19: Welsh; rel. to **COMBE**.

**CWO** ● abbrev. Chief Warrant Officer.

**c.w.o.** ● abbrev. cash with order.

**cwt.** ● abbrev. hundredweight.
– ORIGIN from L. *centum* 'a hundred'.

**CY** ● abbrev. Cyprus (international vehicle registration).

**-cy** ● suffix **1** denoting state or condition: *bankruptcy*. **2** denoting rank or status: *baronetcy*.
– ORIGIN from L. *-cia*, *-tia* and Gk *-k(e)ia*, *-t(e)ia*.

**cyan** /'sʌɪən/ ● n. a greenish-blue colour which is one of the primary subtractive colours, complementary to red.
– ORIGIN C19: from Gk *kuaneos* 'dark blue'.

**cyanamide** /sʌɪ'anəmʌɪd/ ● n. Chemistry a weakly acidic crystalline compound produced in ammonia manufacture. ➤ a salt of this, containing the anion $CN_2^{2-}$.
– ORIGIN C19: blend of **CYANOGEN** and **AMIDE**.

**cyanic acid** ● n. Chemistry a colourless, poisonous, volatile, strongly acidic liquid. [HOCN.]
– DERIVATIVES **cyanate** n.
– ORIGIN C19: from **CYANOGEN**.

**cyanide** /'sʌɪənʌɪd/ ● n. Chemistry a salt or ester of hydrocyanic acid, examples of which are extremely toxic.
– ORIGIN C19: from **CYANOGEN** + **-IDE**.

**cyano-** ● comb. form **1** relating to the colour blue: *cyanosis*. **2** representing **CYANIDE**: *cyanogenic*.
– ORIGIN from Gk *kuan(e)os* 'dark blue'.

**cyanoacrylate** /ˌsʌɪənəʊ'akrɪleɪt/ ● n. Chemistry any of a class of compounds which are cyanide derivatives of acrylates, used to make quick-setting adhesives.

**cyanobacteria** /ˌsʌɪənəʊbak'tɪərɪə/ ● pl. n. (sing. **cyanobacterium**) Biology micro-organisms of a division (Cyanobacteria) comprising the blue-green algae, related to bacteria but capable of photosynthesis.
– ORIGIN mod. L., from Gk *kuaneos* 'dark blue' + **BACTERIUM**.

**cyanocobalamin** /ˌsʌɪənə(ʊ)kə'baləmɪn/ ● n. vitamin $B_{12}$, a cobalt-containing vitamin derived from liver, fish, and eggs, a deficiency of which can cause pernicious anaemia.
– ORIGIN 1950s: from **CYANO-** and *cobalamin* (blend of **COBALT** and **VITAMIN**).

**cyanogen** /sʌɪ'anədʒ(ə)n/ ● n. a flammable poisonous gas made by oxidizing hydrogen cyanide. [$C_2N_2$.]
– ORIGIN C19: from Fr. *cyanogène*, from Gk *kuanos* 'dark blue mineral' + *-gène* (see **-GEN**), so named because it is rel. to Prussian blue.

**cyanogenic** /ˌsʌɪənə'dʒɛnɪk/ (also **cyanogenetic**) ● adj. Botany capable of producing cyanides.

**cyanohydrin** /ˌsʌɪənə(ʊ)'hʌɪdrɪn/ ● n. Chemistry an organic compound containing a carbon atom linked to both cyanide and hydroxyl groups.

**cyanophyte** /'sʌɪənə(ʊ)fʌɪt/ ● n. Biology a micro-organism of the division Cyanobacteria.

**cyanosis** /ˌsʌɪə'nəʊsɪs/ ● n. Medicine a bluish discoloration of the skin due to poor circulation or inadequate oxygenation of the blood.
– DERIVATIVES **cyanotic** adj.
– ORIGIN C19: mod. L., from Gk *kuanōsis* 'blueness'.

**cyathium** /sʌɪ'aθɪəm/ ● n. (pl. **cyathia** /-ɪə/) Botany the inflorescence of a spurge, a cup-shaped structure of bracts enclosing several greatly reduced male flowers and a single female flower.
– ORIGIN C19: mod. L., from Gk *kuathion*, dimin. of *kuathos* 'cup'.

**cyber-** /'sʌɪbə/ ● comb. form relating to information technology, the Internet, and virtual reality: *cyberspace*.
– ORIGIN back-form. from **CYBERNETICS**.

**cybernetics** ● pl. n. [treated as sing.] the science of communications and automatic control systems in both machines and living things.
– DERIVATIVES **cybernetic** adj. **cybernetician** n. **cyberneticist** n.
– ORIGIN 1940s: from Gk *kubernētēs* 'steersman'.

**cyberphobia** ● n. extreme or irrational fear of computers or technology.
– DERIVATIVES **cyberphobe** n. **cyberphobic** adj. & n.

**cyberpunk** ● n. **1** a genre of science fiction set in a lawless subculture of an oppressive society dominated by computer technology. **2** a person who accesses computer networks illegally.

**cyberspace** ● n. the notional environment in which communication over computer networks occurs.

**cybersquatting** ● n. the practice of registering names, especially well-known company or brand names, as Internet domains, in the hope of reselling them at a profit.
– DERIVATIVES **cybersquatter** n.

**cyborg** /'sʌɪbɔːg/ ● n. a fictional or hypothetical person whose physical abilities are extended beyond human limitations by mechanical elements built into the body.

– ORIGIN 1960s: blend of **CYBER-** and **ORGANISM**.

**cycad** /'sʌɪkad/ ● **n.** a tall, cone-bearing, palm-like plant of tropical and subtropical regions. [Genus *Cycas*, class Cycadopsida: several species.]
– ORIGIN C19: from mod. L. *Cycas*, *Cycad-*, from supposed Gk *kukas*, scribal error for *koikas*, pl. of *koix* 'Egyptian palm'.

**Cycladic** /sɪ'kladɪk, sʌɪ-/ ● **adj. 1** of or relating to the Cyclades, a group of Greek islands in the southern Aegean. **2** Archaeology denoting a Bronze Age civilization that flourished in the Cyclades, dated to *c.*3000–1050 BC.

**cyclamate** /'sɪkləmeɪt, 'sʌɪk-/ ● **n.** Chemistry a salt of a synthetic organic acid, formerly used as an artificial sweetener.
– ORIGIN 1950s: contr. of *cyclohexylsulphamate*.

**cyclamen** /'sɪkləmən/ ● **n.** (pl. same or **cyclamens**) a plant of the primrose family, having pink, red, or white flowers with backward-curving petals. [Genus *Cyclamen*: several species.]
– ORIGIN mod. L., from L. *cyclaminos*, from Gk *kuklaminos*, perh. from *kuklos* 'circle', with ref. to its bulbous roots.

**cycle** ● **n. 1** a series of events that are regularly repeated in the same order. ➤ the period of time taken to complete a single such series. **2** one complete sequence of changes associated with a recurring phenomenon such as an alternating current, wave, etc. **3** Ecology the movement of a simple substance through the soil, rocks, water, atmosphere, and living organisms of the earth: *the carbon cycle*. **4** a series of musical or literary works composed around a particular theme. **5** a bicycle. ● **v. 1** ride a bicycle. **2** move in or follow a cycle of events.
– DERIVATIVES **cycling** n. **cyclist** n.
– ORIGIN ME: from OFr., from late L. *cyclus*, from Gk *kuklos* 'circle'.

**cyclic** /'sʌɪklɪk, 'sɪk-/ ● **adj. 1** occurring in cycles. **2** having the form of a circle or closed ring. ➤ Chemistry having a molecular structure containing one or more closed rings of atoms.
– DERIVATIVES **cyclical** adj. **cyclically** adv.

**cyclic redundancy check** (also **cyclic redundancy code**) ● **n.** Computing a code added to data in order to detect errors occurring during transmission, storage, or retrieval.

**cyclin** /'sʌɪklɪn/ ● **n.** Biochemistry a protein which is thought to initiate certain processes of mitosis.

**cyclize** /'sʌɪklʌɪz/ (also **-ise**) ● **v.** Chemistry undergo or cause to undergo a reaction in which one part of a molecule becomes linked to another to form a closed ring.
– DERIVATIVES **cyclization** n.

**cyclo-** /'sʌɪkləʊ/ ● **comb. form 1** circular: *cyclorama*. **2** relating to a cycle or cycling: *cyclo-cross*. **3** cyclic: *cycloalkane*.
– ORIGIN from Gk *kuklos* 'circle', or directly from **CYCLE** or **CYCLIC**.

**cycloalkane** ● **n.** Chemistry a hydrocarbon with a molecule containing a ring of carbon atoms joined by single bonds.

**cyclo-cross** ● **n.** cross-country racing on bicycles.

**cyclohexane** ● **n.** Chemistry a volatile cyclic hydrocarbon obtained from petroleum, used as a solvent. [$C_6H_{12}$]

**cyclohexyl** /ˌsʌɪklə(ʊ)'hɛksʌɪl, -sɪl/ ● **n.** [as modifier] Chemistry of or denoting the radical $-C_6H_{11}$, derived from cyclohexane.

**cycloid** /'sʌɪklɔɪd/ ● **n.** Mathematics a curve (resembling a series of arches) traced by a point on a circle being rolled along a straight line.
– DERIVATIVES **cycloidal** adj.
– ORIGIN C17: from Gk *kukloeidēs* 'circular'.

**cyclometer** /sʌɪ'klɒmɪtə/ ● **n. 1** an instrument for measuring circular arcs. **2** an instrument attached to a bicycle for measuring distance.

**cyclone** /'sʌɪkləʊn/ ● **n.** Meteorology a system of winds rotating inwards to an area of low barometric pressure; a depression. ➤ another term for **TROPICAL STORM**.
– DERIVATIVES **cyclonic** adj. **cyclonically** adv.
– ORIGIN C19: prob. from Gk *kuklōma* 'wheel, coil of a snake'.

**cyclopean** /ˌsʌɪklə'piːən, sʌɪ'kləʊpɪən/ (also **cyclopian**) ● **adj. 1** of or resembling a Cyclops, especially in size. **2** denoting a type of ancient masonry made with massive irregular blocks.

**cyclopedia** /sʌɪklə(ʊ)'piːdɪə/ (also **cyclopaedia**) ● **n.** archaic (except in book titles) an encyclopedia.
– DERIVATIVES **cyclopedic** adj.

**Cyclops** /'sʌɪklɒps/ ● **n. 1** (pl. **Cyclops**, **Cyclopses**, or **Cyclopes** /sʌɪ'kləpiːz/) Greek Mythology a member of a race of savage one-eyed giants. **2** (**cyclops**) a minute predatory freshwater crustacean which has a cylindrical body with a single central eye. [*Cyclops* and other genera, order Cyclopoida.]
– ORIGIN via L. from Gk *Kuklōps*, lit. 'round-eyed'.

**cyclorama** /ˌsʌɪklə'rɑːmə/ ● **n. 1** a panoramic scene set on the inside of a cylindrical surface, to be viewed by a central spectator. **2** a cloth stretched tight in an arc around the back of a stage set, often used to represent the sky.
– DERIVATIVES **cycloramic** /-'ramɪk/ adj.

**cyclosporin** /ˌsʌɪklə(ʊ)'spɔːrɪn/ (also **cyclosporin A**, **cyclosporine**) ● **n.** Medicine an immunosuppressive drug obtained from a fungus, used to prevent the rejection of grafts and transplants.
– ORIGIN 1970s: from **CYCLO-** + *-sporin* (from L. *spora* 'spore') + **-IN**[1].

**cyclostome** /'sʌɪklə(ʊ)stəʊm/ ● **n.** Zoology an eel-like jawless vertebrate with a round sucking mouth, such as a lamprey or hagfish.
– ORIGIN C19: from **CYCLO-** + Gk *stoma* 'mouth'.

**cyclostyle** /'sʌɪklə(ʊ)stʌɪl/ ● **n.** an early device for duplicating handwriting, in which a pen with a small toothed wheel makes a stencil in a sheet of waxed paper. ● **v.** [usu. as adj. **cyclostyled**] duplicate with a cyclostyle.

**cyclothymia** /ˌsʌɪklə(ʊ)'θʌɪmɪə/ ● **n.** Psychiatry, dated manic-depressive tendency.
– DERIVATIVES **cyclothymic** adj.
– ORIGIN 1920s: from **CYCLO-** + Gk *thumos* 'temper'.

**cyclotron** /'sʌɪklətrɒn/ ● **n.** Physics an apparatus in which charged atomic and subatomic particles are accelerated by an alternating electric field while following an outward spiral or circular path in a magnetic field.

**cyder** ● **n.** archaic spelling of **CIDER**.

**cygnet** /'sɪgnɪt/ ● **n.** a young swan.
– ORIGIN ME: from Anglo-Norman Fr. *cignet*, dimin. of OFr. *cigne* 'swan', based on L. *cycnus*, from Gk *kuknos*.

**cylinder** /'sɪlɪndə/ ● **n. 1** a three-dimensional shape with straight parallel sides and a circular or oval cross section. **2** a piston chamber in a steam or internal-combustion engine. **3** a cylindrical container for liquefied gas under pressure. **4** a rotating metal roller in a printing press.
– DERIVATIVES **cylindric** /sə'lɪndrɪk/ adj. **cylindrical** adj. **cylindrically** adv.
– ORIGIN C16: from L. *cylindrus*, from Gk *kulindros* 'roller'.

**cylinder block** ● **n.** see **BLOCK** (sense 7).

**cylinder head** ● **n.** the end cover of a cylinder in an internal-combustion engine, against which the piston compresses the cylinder's contents.

**cylinder seal** ● **n.** Archaeology a small barrel-shaped stone object bearing an incised design or cuneiform inscription, used chiefly as a seal in ancient Mesopotamia.

**cymbal** /'sɪmb(ə)l/ ● **n.** a musical instrument consisting of a slightly concave round brass plate which is either struck against another one or struck with a stick.
– DERIVATIVES **cymbalist** n.
– ORIGIN OE, from L. *cymbalum*, from Gk *kumbalon*, from *kumbē* 'cup'; readopted in ME from OFr. *cymbale*.

**cymbidium** /sɪm'bɪdɪəm/ ● **n.** (pl. **cymbidiums**) a tropical orchid with long narrow leaves and arching stems bearing several flowers, growing chiefly as an epiphyte from Asia to Australasia. [Genus *Cymbidium*.]
– ORIGIN mod. L., from Gk *kumbē* 'cup'.

**cyme** /sʌɪm/ ● **n.** Botany a flower cluster with a central stem bearing a single terminal flower that develops first, the other flowers in the cluster developing as terminal buds of lateral stems. Compare with **RACEME**.

– DERIVATIVES **cymose** adj.
– ORIGIN C18 (denoting the unopened head of a plant): from Fr., lit. 'summit', from a pop. var. of L. *cyma*.

**Cymric** /ˈkɪmrɪk/ • **adj.** Welsh in language or culture. • **n.** the Welsh language.
– ORIGIN C19: from Welsh *Cymru* 'Wales', *Cymry* 'the Welsh', + **-IC**.

**cynic** /ˈsɪnɪk/ • **n. 1** a person who believes that people are motivated purely by self-interest. ➤a sceptic. **2** (**Cynic**) a member of a school of ancient Greek philosophers founded by Antisthenes, characterized by an ostentatious contempt for wealth and pleasure.
– DERIVATIVES **cynicism** n.
– ORIGIN C16: from L. *cynicus*, from Gk *kunikos*; prob. orig. from *Kunosarges*, the name of a gymnasium where Antisthenes taught, but popularly taken to mean 'dog-like, churlish', *kuōn, kun-*, 'dog' becoming a nickname for a Cynic.

**cynical** • **adj. 1** believing that people are motivated purely by self-interest. ➤sceptical. ➤contemptuous; mocking. **2** concerned only with one's own interests and disregarding accepted standards to achieve them: *a cynical foul.*
– DERIVATIVES **cynically** adv.

**cynodont** /ˈsʌɪnə(ʊ)dɒnt/ • **n.** a fossil carnivorous mammal-like reptile of the late Permian and Triassic periods, with well-developed specialized teeth.
– ORIGIN C19: from Gk *kuōn, kun-* 'dog' + *odous, odont-* 'tooth'.

**cynosure** /ˈsɪnəzjʊə, ˈsʌɪn-, -sjʊə/ • **n.** a person or thing that is the centre of attention or admiration.
– ORIGIN C16 (orig. denoting the constellation Ursa Minor, or the pole star which it contains): from Fr., or from L. *cynosura*, from Gk *kunosoura* 'dog's tail' (also 'Ursa Minor').

**cyphel** /ˈsʌɪf(ə)l/ (also **mossy cyphel**) • **n.** a mountain plant of the pink family, which forms cushion-like mounds and bears small greenish flowers. [*Minuartia sedoides.*]
– ORIGIN ME (denoting the houseleek): appar. from Gk *kuphella* 'hollows of the ears'.

**cypher** • **n.** variant spelling of **CIPHER**[1].

**cypherpunk** • **n.** a person who uses encryption when accessing a computer network in order to ensure privacy, especially from government authorities.
– ORIGIN 1990s: on the pattern of *cyberpunk*.

**cy-pres** /siː ˈpreɪ/ • **adv. & adj.** Law as near as possible to the testator's or donor's intentions when these cannot be precisely followed.
– ORIGIN C19: from a late Anglo-Norman Fr. var. of Fr. *si près* 'so near'.

**cypress** • **n.** an evergreen coniferous tree with flattened shoots bearing small scale-like leaves, whose dark foliage is sometimes associated with mourning. [*Cupressus sempervirens* (southern Europe) and other species, family Cupressaceae.]
– ORIGIN ME: from OFr. *cipres*, from late L. *cypressus*, from Gk *kuparissos*.

**cyprinid** /ˈsɪprɪnɪd/ • **n.** Zoology a fish of the carp family (Cyprinidae).
– ORIGIN C19: from mod. L. *Cyprinidae* based on Gk *kuprinos* 'carp'.

**Cypriot** • **n. 1** a native or national of Cyprus. **2** the dialect of Greek used in Cyprus. • **adj.** of or relating to Cyprus or its people or the Greek dialect used there.
– ORIGIN from Gk *Kupriōtes*, from *Kupros* 'Cyprus'.

**cypripedium** /ˌsɪprɪˈpiːdɪəm/ • **n.** (pl. **cypripediums**) an orchid of a genus which comprises the lady's slippers. [Genus *Cypripedium.*]
– ORIGIN mod. L., from Gk *Kupris* 'Aphrodite' + *pedilon* 'slipper'.

**cypsela** /ˈsɪpsɪlə/ • **n.** (pl. **cypselae** /-liː/) Botany a dry single-seeded fruit formed from a double ovary of which only one develops into a seed, as in the daisy family.
– ORIGIN C19: mod. L., from Gk *kupselē* 'hollow vessel'.

**Cyrenaic** /ˌsʌɪərɪˈneɪɪk/ • **adj.** of or denoting the hedonistic school of philosophy founded *c.*400 BC by Aristippus the Elder of Cyrene. • **n.** a follower of this school of philosophy.
– DERIVATIVES **Cyrenaicism** n.

**Cyrillic** /sɪˈrɪlɪk/ • **adj.** denoting the alphabet used by many Slavic peoples, chiefly those with a historical allegiance to the Orthodox Church; now used especially for Russian and Bulgarian. • **n.** the Cyrillic alphabet.
– ORIGIN C19: named after the C9 Gk missionary St *Cyril*, its reputed inventor.

**cyst** /sɪst/ • **n. 1** Biology a thin-walled hollow organ or cavity in an animal or plant, containing a liquid secretion. **2** Medicine a membranous sac or cavity of abnormal character in the body, containing fluid. **3** a tough protective capsule enclosing the larva of a parasitic worm or the resting stage of an organism.
– ORIGIN C18: from late L. *cystis*, from Gk *kustis* 'bladder'.

**cystectomy** /sɪsˈtɛktəmi/ • **n.** (pl. **-ies**) **1** a surgical operation to remove the urinary bladder. **2** a surgical operation to remove an abnormal cyst.

**cysteine** /ˈsɪstɪiːn, -tɪɪn, -teɪn, -tiːn/ • **n.** Biochemistry a sulphur-containing amino acid which occurs in keratins and other proteins.
– ORIGIN C19: from **CYSTINE** + *-eine* (var. of **-INE**[4]).

**cystic** • **adj. 1** chiefly Medicine of, relating to, or characterized by cysts. **2** Zoology (of a parasite or other organism) enclosed in a cyst. **3** of or relating to the urinary bladder or the gall bladder.

**cystic fibrosis** • **n.** a hereditary disorder which affects the exocrine glands, and results in the production of abnormally thick mucus, leading to the blockage of the pancreatic ducts, intestines, and bronchi.

**cystine** /ˈsɪstiːn, -tɪn/ • **n.** Biochemistry an oxidized dimeric form of cysteine.
– ORIGIN C19: from Gk *kustis* 'bladder' (because it was first isolated from urinary calculi) + **-INE**[4].

**cystitis** /sɪˈstʌɪtɪs/ • **n.** Medicine inflammation of the urinary bladder, typically caused by infection and accompanied by frequent painful urination.

**cysto-** /ˈsɪstəʊ/ • **comb. form** of or relating to the urinary bladder: *cystotomy.*
– ORIGIN from Gk *kustis* 'bladder'.

**cystoscope** /ˈsɪstəskəʊp/ • **n.** Medicine an instrument inserted into the urethra for examining the urinary bladder.
– DERIVATIVES **cystoscopic** adj. **cystoscopy** n.

**cystotomy** /sɪˈstɒtəmi/ • **n.** (pl. **-ies**) a surgical incision into the urinary bladder.

**-cyte** • **comb. form** Biology denoting a mature cell: *lymphocyte.* Compare with **-BLAST**.
– ORIGIN from Gk *kutos* 'vessel'.

**cytidine** /ˈsʌɪtɪdiːn/ • **n.** Biochemistry a nucleoside consisting of cytosine combined with ribose.

**cytisus** /sʌɪˈtɪsəs, ˈsɪtɪsəs/ • **n.** a shrub of a large genus which includes many brooms. [Genus *Cytisus.*]
– ORIGIN mod. L., from Gk *kutisos*.

**cyto-** /ˈsʌɪtəʊ/ • **comb. form** Biology of a cell or cells: *cytology.*
– ORIGIN from Gk *kutos* 'vessel'.

**cytoarchitectonics** /ˌsʌɪtəʊˌɑːkɪtɛkˈtɒnɪks/ • **pl. n.** [treated as sing. or pl.] another term for **CYTOARCHITECTURE**.
– DERIVATIVES **cytoarchitectonic** adj.

**cytoarchitecture** /ˌsʌɪtəʊˈɑːkɪtɛktʃə/ • **n.** Anatomy the arrangement of cells in a tissue.
– DERIVATIVES **cytoarchitectural** adj. **cytoarchitecturally** adv.

**cytochrome** • **n.** Biochemistry any of a number of compounds consisting of haem bonded to a protein, involved in cellular respiration.

**cytogenetics** /ˌsʌɪtəʊdʒəˈnɛtɪks/ • **pl. n.** [treated as sing.] Biology the study of inheritance in relation to the structure and function of chromosomes.
– DERIVATIVES **cytogenetic** adj. **cytogenetical** adj. **cytogenetically** adv. **cytogeneticist** n.

**cytokine** /ˈsʌɪtə(ʊ)kʌɪn/ • **n.** Physiology a substance, such as interferon and interleukin, which is secreted by the immune system and has an effect on other cells.

**cytokinesis** /ˌsʌɪtə(ʊ)kʌɪˈniːsɪs/ • **n.** Biology the cytoplasmic division of a cell into two daughter cells at the end of mitosis or meiosis.

**cytology** /sʌɪˈtɒlədʒi/ • **n.** the branch of biology concerned with the structure and function of plant and animal cells.
– DERIVATIVES **cytological** adj. **cytologically** adv. **cytologist** n.

**cytolysis** /sʌɪˈtɒlɪsɪs/ • **n.** Biology the dissolution or disruption of cells, especially by an external agent.
– DERIVATIVES **cytolytic** adj.

**cytomegalic** /ˌsʌɪtə(ʊ)mɪˈɡalɪk/ • **adj.** Medicine (of disease) characterized by enlarged cells.

**cytomegalovirus** /ˌsʌɪtə(ʊ)ˈmɛɡ(ə)lə(ʊ)ˌvʌɪrəs/ • **n.** Medicine a kind of herpesvirus which usually produces very mild symptoms in an infected person but may cause severe neurological damage in people with weakened immune systems and in the newborn.

**cytoplasm** /ˈsʌɪtə(ʊ)plaz(ə)m/ • **n.** Biology the material or protoplasm within a living cell, excluding the nucleus.
– DERIVATIVES **cytoplasmic** adj.

**cytosine** /ˈsʌɪtəsiːn/ • **n.** Biochemistry a compound found in living tissue as a constituent base of DNA.

**cytoskeleton** • **n.** Biology a microscopic network of protein filaments and tubules in the cytoplasm of many living cells, giving them shape and coherence.
– DERIVATIVES **cytoskeletal** adj.

**cytosol** /ˈsʌɪtə(ʊ)sɒl/ • **n.** Biology the aqueous component of the cytoplasm of a cell.
– DERIVATIVES **cytosolic** adj.

**cytotoxic** • **adj.** toxic to living cells.
– DERIVATIVES **cytotoxicity** n.

**czar etc.** • **n.** variant spelling of **TSAR** etc.

**czardas** • **n.** variant spelling of **CSARDAS**.

**Czech** /tʃɛk/ • **n. 1** a native or national of the Czech Republic or (formerly) Czechoslovakia, or a person of Czech descent. **2** the Western Slavic language spoken in the Czech Republic, closely related to Slovak. • **adj.** of or relating to the Czechs or their language.
– ORIGIN Polish spelling of Czech *Čech*.

**Czechoslovak** /-ˈsləʊvak/ (also **Czechoslovakian**) • **n.** a native or national of the former country of Czechoslovakia, now divided between the Czech Republic and Slovakia. • **adj.** of or relating to Czechoslovaks or the former country of Czechoslovakia.

# D d

**D**[1] (also **d**) ● **n.** (pl. **Ds** or **D's**) **1** the fourth letter of the alphabet. **2** denoting the fourth in a set of items, categories, sizes, etc. **3** Music the second note of the diatonic scale of C major. **4** the Roman numeral for 500. [understood as half of CIↃ, an earlier form of M (= 1,000).]

**D**[2] ● **abbrev.** **1** (in the US) Democrat or Democratic. **2** depth (in the sense of the dimension of an object from front to back). **3** Chemistry dextrorotatory. **4** (with a numeral) dimension(s) or dimensional. **5** (in tables of sports results) drawn. **6** Germany (international vehicle registration). [from Ger. *Deutschland*.] ● **symb.** **1** Physics electric flux density. **2** Chemistry the hydrogen isotope deuterium.

**d** ● **abbrev.** **1** (in genealogies) daughter. **2** day(s). **3** deci-. **4** (in travel timetables) departs. **5** (**d.**) died (used to indicate a date of death). **6** Brit. penny or pence (of pre-decimal currency). [from L. *denarius* 'penny'.] **7** Chemistry denoting electrons and orbitals possessing two units of angular momentum. [*d* from *diffuse*, orig. applied to lines in atomic spectra.] ● **symb.** **1** Mathematics diameter. **2** Mathematics denoting a small increment in a given variable.

**'d** ● **contr.** **1** had. **2** would.

**DA** ● **abbrev.** **1** US district attorney. **2** informal duck's arse.

**D/A** ● **abbrev.** Electronics digital to analogue.

**da** ● **abbrev.** deca-.

**dab**[1] ● **v.** (**dabbed**, **dabbing**) press against (something) lightly several times with a piece of absorbent material. ➤ apply (a substance) with light quick strokes. ● **n.** **1** a small amount: *she put a dab of perfume behind her ears.* ➤ a brief application of a piece of absorbent material to a surface. **2** (**dabs**) Brit. informal fingerprints.
– ORIGIN ME: symbolic of a light striking movement; cf. **DABBLE** and **DIB**.

**dab**[2] ● **n.** a small, commercially important flatfish found chiefly in the North Atlantic. [*Limanda limanda* and other species.]
– ORIGIN ME: of unknown origin.

**dabber** ● **n.** a rounded pad used in printing to apply ink to a surface.

**dabble** ● **v.** **1** move (one's hands or feet) around gently in water. ➤ (of a duck or other water bird) move the bill around in shallow water while feeding. **2** (often **dabble in**) take part in an activity in a casual or superficial way.
– DERIVATIVES **dabbler** n.
– ORIGIN C16: from obs. Du. *dabbelen*, or a frequentative of **DAB**[1].

**dabbling duck** ● **n.** a duck which typically feeds by dabbling and upending in fresh water, such as the mallard or teal.

**dabchick** ● **n.** a small grebe, especially the little grebe.
– ORIGIN C16 (as *dapchick* or *dopchick*): the first element is perh. rel. to **DIP** and **DEEP**.

**dab hand** ● **n.** Brit. informal a person who is an expert at a particular activity.
– ORIGIN C19: of unknown origin.

**DAC** ● **abbrev.** Electronics digital to analogue converter.

**da capo** /dɑː ˈkɑːpəʊ/ ● **adv. & adj.** Music repeat or repeated from the beginning. Compare with **DAL SEGNO**.
– ORIGIN Ital., lit. 'from the head'.

**dace** /deɪs/ ● **n.** (pl. same) a freshwater fish related to the carp, typically living in running water. [*Leuciscus leuciscus* and other species.]
– ORIGIN ME: from OFr. *dars* (see **DART**).

**dacha** /ˈdatʃə/ (also **datcha**) ● **n.** a country house or cottage in Russia, typically used as a second or holiday home.
– ORIGIN Russ., orig. 'grant (of land)'.

**dachshund** /ˈdakshʊnd, -s(ə)nd/ ● **n.** a dog of a very short-legged, long-bodied breed.
– ORIGIN C19: from Ger., lit. 'badger dog' (the breed being orig. used to dig badgers out of their setts).

**dacite** /ˈdeɪsʌɪt/ ● **n.** Geology a volcanic rock resembling andesite but containing free quartz.
– DERIVATIVES **dacitic** adj.
– ORIGIN C18: from the name of the ancient Roman province of *Dacia* in SE Europe (as the rock was first found in the Carpathian Mountains) + **-ITE**[1].

**dacoit** /dəˈkɔɪt/ ● **n.** a member of a band of armed robbers in India or Burma (Myanmar).
– DERIVATIVES **dacoity** n. (pl. **-ies**).
– ORIGIN from Hindi *ḍakait*, from *ḍakaitī* 'robbery by a gang'.

**dactyl** /ˈdaktɪl/ ● **n.** Prosody a metrical foot consisting of one stressed syllable followed by two unstressed syllables or (in Greek and Latin) one long syllable followed by two short syllables. See word-formation panel.
– ORIGIN ME: via L. from Gk *daktulos*, lit. 'finger' (the three bones of the finger corresp. to the three syllables).

## Word *Formation*

**-dactyl** from Greek *daktulos* 'finger, toe'

➤ Used alone, **dactyl** is a technical term in prosody. However, the literal meaning of the Greek root *daktulos* 'finger' forms part of a number of technical (chiefly zoological) terms in English:

| | | |
|---|---|---|
| artiodactyl | a mammal belonging to the order of even-toed ungulates, as ruminants, camels, and pigs | Gk *artios* 'even' |
| monodactyl | having only one finger or toe on each hand or foot | Gk *monos* 'one' |
| pentadactyl | having five toes or fingers | Gk *pente* 'five' |
| perissodactyl | a mammal belonging to the order of odd-toed ungulates, as horses and rhinoceroses | Gk *perissos* 'uneven' |
| polydactyl | having more than five fingers or toes on each hand or foot | Gk *polu-* 'many' |
| pterodactyl | a type of fossil warm-blooded flying reptile | Gk *pteron* 'wing' |
| tetradactyl | having four toes or fingers | Gk *tettares* 'four' |
| tridactyl | having three toes or fingers | Gk *treis* 'three' |
| zygodactyl | (of a bird) having two toes pointing forward and two backward | based on ZYGO- |

**dactylic** Prosody ● **adj.** of or using dactyls. ● **n.** (**dactylics**) dactylic verse.

**dactylic hexameter** ● **n.** Prosody a hexameter consisting of five dactyls and either a spondee or trochee, in which any of the first four dactyls, and sometimes the fifth, may be replaced by a spondee.

**dad** ● **n.** informal one's father.
– ORIGIN C16: perh. imitative of a young child's first syllables *da, da*.

**Dada** /ˈdɑːdɑː/ ● **n.** an early 20th-century international movement in art, literature, music, and film, repudiating and mocking artistic and social conventions and emphasizing the illogical and absurd.
– DERIVATIVES **Dadaism** n. **Dadaist** n. & adj. **Dadaistic** adj.
– ORIGIN Fr., lit. 'hobby horse', the title of a review which appeared in Zurich in 1916.

**dada**[1] /ˈdadə/ ● **n.** informal one's father.
– ORIGIN C17: perh. imitative of a young child's first syllables (see **DAD**).

**dada**[2] /ˈdɑːdɑː/ ● **n.** Indian an older brother or male cousin. ➤a respectful form of address for any familiar older male.
– ORIGIN from Hindi *dādā*.

**daddy** ● **n.** (pl. **-ies**) informal one's father.

**daddy-long-legs** ● **n.** informal **1** Brit. a crane fly. **2** N. Amer. a harvestman.

**dado** /ˈdeɪdəʊ/ ● **n.** (pl. **-os**) **1** the lower part of the wall of a room, when decorated differently from the upper part. **2** N. Amer. a groove cut in the face of a board, into which the edge of another board is fixed. **3** Architecture the cube of a pedestal between the base and the cornice.
– ORIGIN C17: from Ital., lit. 'dice or cube'.

**dado rail** ● **n.** a waist-high moulding round the wall of a room.

**daemon**[1] /ˈdiːmən/ (also **daimon**) ● **n.** **1** (in ancient Greek belief) a divinity or supernatural being of a nature between gods and humans. ➤an inner or attendant spirit or inspiring force. **2** archaic spelling of **DEMON**[1].
– DERIVATIVES **daemonic** adj.
– ORIGIN C16: common spelling of **DEMON**[1] until the 19th cent.

**daemon**[2] /ˈdiːmən/ (also **demon**) ● **n.** Computing a background process that handles requests for services such as print spooling, and is dormant when not required.
– ORIGIN 1980s: perh. from *d(isk) a(nd) e(xecution) mon(itor)* or from *de(vice) mon(itor)*, or merely a transferred use of **DEMON**[1].

**daffodil** ● **n.** a bulbous plant bearing bright yellow flowers with a long trumpet-shaped centre. [*Narcissus pseudonarcissus* and related species.]
– ORIGIN C16: from ME *affodill*, from med. L. *affodilus*, var. of L. *asphodilus* (see **ASPHODEL**).

**daffodil yellow** ● **n.** a shade of pale yellow.

**daffy** ● **adj.** (**-ier**, **-iest**) informal silly; mildly eccentric.
– DERIVATIVES **daffiness** n.
– ORIGIN C19: from north. Engl. dial. *daff* 'simpleton' + **-Y**[1]; perh. rel. to **DAFT**.

**daft** ● **adj.** informal, chiefly Brit. **1** silly; foolish. **2** (**daft about**) infatuated with.
– ORIGIN OE *gedæfte* 'mild, meek', of Gmc origin.

**dag**[1] Austral./NZ ● **n.** a lock of wool matted with dung hanging from the hindquarters of a sheep. ● **v.** (**dagged**, **dagging**) cut dags from (a sheep).
– PHRASES **rattle one's dags** informal hurry up.
– ORIGIN ME (denoting a hanging pointed part of something): possibly rel. to **TAG**[1].

**dag**[2] ● **n.** Austral./NZ informal a socially conservative person.
– ORIGIN C19 (orig. denoting an eccentric person): transferred use of Engl. dial. meaning 'a challenge'.

**Dagestanian** /ˌdagɪˈstɑːnɪən, -ˈstanɪən/ ● **n.** **1** a native or inhabitant of Dagestan, an autonomous republic in SW Russia. **2** the family of North Caucasian languages spoken in Dagestan. ● **adj.** of or relating to Dagestan, its inhabitants, or their language.

**dagga** /ˈdaxə/ ● **n.** chiefly S. African cannabis.
– ORIGIN C17: from Afrik., from Khoikhoi *dachab*.

**dagger** ● **n.** **1** a short knife with a pointed and edged blade, used as a weapon. **2** Printing another term for **OBELUS**.
– PHRASES **at daggers drawn** in bitter enmity. **look daggers at** glare angrily or venomously at.
– ORIGIN ME: perh. from obs. *dag* 'pierce', influenced by OFr. *dague* 'long dagger'.

**daggerboard** ● **n.** a kind of centreboard which slides vertically through the keel of a sailing boat.

**daggy** ● **adj.** (**-ier**, **-iest**) Austral./NZ informal **1** (especially of clothes) scruffy. **2** not stylish; unfashionable.

**dago** /ˈdeɪgəʊ/ ● **n.** (pl. **-os** or **-oes**) informal, offensive a Spanish, Portuguese, or Italian-speaking person.
– ORIGIN C19: from the Sp. given name *Diego* (equivalent to *James*).

**daguerreotype** /dəˈgɛrətʌɪp/ (also **daguerrotype**) ● **n.** a photograph taken by an early photographic process employing an iodine-sensitized silvered plate and mercury vapour.
– ORIGIN C19: from Fr. *daguerréotype*, named after L.-J.-M. *Daguerre*, its Fr. inventor.

**Dagwood** ● **n.** N. Amer. a thick sandwich with a variety of different fillings.
– ORIGIN named after *Dagwood* Bumstead, a comic-strip character who made and ate this type of sandwich.

**dah** /dɑː/ ● **n.** (in the Morse system) another term for **DASH**.
– ORIGIN Second World War: imitative.

**dahabeeyah** /ˌdɑːhəˈbiːjə/ ● **n.** a large passenger boat used on the Nile, typically with lateen sails.
– ORIGIN C19: from Arab., lit. 'golden', denoting the gilded state barge formerly used by the Muslim rulers of Egypt.

**dahi** /ˈdəhiː/ ● **n.** Indian term for **YOGURT**.
– ORIGIN from Hindi *dahī* 'curds'.

**dahlia** /ˈdeɪlɪə/ ● **n.** a tuberous-rooted Mexican plant of the daisy family, cultivated for its brightly coloured single or double flowers. [Genus *Dahlia*.]
– ORIGIN mod. L., named in honour of the Swed. botanist Andreas *Dahl*.

**daikon** /ˈdʌɪk(ə)n, -kɒn/ ● **n.** another term for **MOOLI**.
– ORIGIN Japanese, from *dai* 'large' + *kon* 'root'.

**Dáil** /dɔɪl, Irish dɑːlʲ/ (in full **Dáil Éireann** /ˈɛːr(ə)n, Irish ˈeːrʲən/) ● **n.** the lower House of Parliament in the Republic of Ireland, composed of 166 members.
– ORIGIN Ir., 'assembly (of Ireland)'.

**daily** ● **adj.** done, produced, or occurring every day or every weekday. ● **adv.** every day. ● **n.** (pl. **-ies**) informal **1** a newspaper published every day except Sunday. **2** (also **daily help**) Brit. dated a daily charwoman. **3** (**dailies**) the first prints from cinematographic takes; the rushes.

**daily double** ● **n.** Horse Racing a single bet on the winners of two named races in a day.

**daily dozen** ● **n.** informal, dated regular exercises, especially those done first thing in the morning.

**daimon** /ˈdʌɪməʊn/ ● **n.** variant spelling of **DAEMON**[1].
– DERIVATIVES **daimonic** /-ˈməʊnɪk, -ˈmɒnɪk/ adj.

**daimyo** /ˈdʌɪmɪəʊ, ˈdʌɪmjəʊ/ (also **daimio**) ● **n.** (pl. **-os**) (in feudal Japan) one of the great lords who were vassals of the shogun.
– ORIGIN Japanese, from *dai* 'great' + *myō* 'name'.

**dainty** ● **adj.** (**-ier**, **-iest**) **1** delicately small and pretty. ➤delicate and graceful in build or movement. **2** fastidious, typically concerning food. ● **n.** (pl. **-ies**) a delicacy.
– DERIVATIVES **daintily** adv. **daintiness** n.
– ORIGIN ME (as n.): from OFr. *daintie, deintie* 'choice morsel, pleasure', from L. *dignitas* 'worthiness or beauty', from *dignus* 'worthy'.

**daiquiri** /ˈdʌɪkɪri, ˈdak-/ ● **n.** (pl. **daiquiris**) a cocktail containing rum and lime juice.
– ORIGIN named after *Daiquiri*, a rum-producing district in Cuba.

**dairy** ● **n.** (pl. **-ies**) a building or room for the storage, processing, and distribution of milk and milk products. ● **adj.** containing or made from milk. ➤concerned with or involved in the production of milk.
– DERIVATIVES **dairying** n.
– ORIGIN ME *deierie*, from *deie* 'dairymaid' (in OE *dǣge* 'female servant'), of Gmc origin; rel. to **DOUGH**.

**dairymaid** ● **n.** archaic a woman employed in a dairy.

**dairyman** ● **n.** (pl. **-men**) a man who is employed in a dairy or who sells dairy products.

**dais** /ˈdeɪɪs, deɪs/ ● **n.** a low platform for a lectern or throne.
– ORIGIN ME (orig. denoting a raised table for distinguished guests): from OFr. *deis*, from L. *discus* 'disc or dish' (later 'table').

**daisy** ● **n.** (pl. **-ies**) a small grassland plant with composite flowers having a yellow disc and white rays. [*Bellis perennis*.] ➤used in names of other plants of the same family, e.g. **Michaelmas daisy**.
– PHRASES **pushing up (the) daisies** informal dead and buried.
– ORIGIN OE *dæges ēage* 'day's eye' (because the flower opens in the morning and closes at night).

**daisy chain** ● **n. 1** a string of daisies threaded together by their stems. **2** a string of associated people or things. ● **v.** (**daisy-chain**) Computing connect (several devices) together in a linear series.
– DERIVATIVES **daisy-chainable** adj.

**daisy-cutter** ● **n.** (in cricket and baseball) a ball hit or bowled so as to roll along the ground.

**daisy wheel** ● **n.** a device used as a printer in word processors and typewriters, consisting of a disc of spokes extending radially from a central hub, each terminating in a printing character.

**Dak.** ● **abbrev.** Dakota.

**Dakota** /dəˈkəʊtə/ ● **n.** (pl. same or **Dakotas**) **1** a member of a North American Indian people of the northern Mississippi valley and the surrounding plains. **2** the Siouan language of this people.
– ORIGIN the name in Dakota, lit. 'allies'.

**Dakotan** /dəˈkəʊt(ə)n/ ● **n.** a native or inhabitant of the US states of North or South Dakota. ● **adj.** of or relating to North or South Dakota.

**daks** ● **pl. n.** Austral. informal trousers.
– ORIGIN a proprietary name.

**dal**[1] ● **abbrev.** decalitre(s).

**dal**[2] ● **n.** variant spelling of **DHAL**.

**Dalai Lama** /ˌdalʌɪ ˈlɑːmə/ ● **n.** the spiritual head of Tibetan Buddhism and, until the establishment of Chinese communist rule, the spiritual and temporal ruler of Tibet.
– ORIGIN from Tibetan, lit. 'ocean monk', so named because he is regarded as 'the ocean of compassion'.

**dalasi** /dɑːˈlɑːsiː/ ● **n.** (pl. same or **dalasis**) the basic monetary unit of Gambia, equal to 100 butut.
– ORIGIN a local word.

**dale** ● **n.** a valley, especially in northern England.
– ORIGIN OE *dæl*, of Gmc origin; rel. to **DELL**.

**Dalesman** ● **n.** (pl. **-men**) an inhabitant of the Yorkshire Dales in northern England.

**Daliesque** /dɑːlɪˈɛsk/ ● **adj.** resembling or characteristic of the work of the Spanish painter Salvador Dali (1904–89), especially in being surrealistic.

**Dalit** /ˈdɑːlɪt/ ● **n.** (in the traditional Indian caste system) a member of the lowest caste. See also **UNTOUCHABLE**, **SCHEDULED CASTE**.
– ORIGIN via Hindi from Sanskrit *dalita* 'oppressed'.

**dally** ● **v.** (**-ies**, **-ied**) **1** act or move slowly. **2** (**dally with**) have a casual romantic or sexual liaison with. ➤show a casual interest in.
– DERIVATIVES **dalliance** n.
– ORIGIN ME: from OFr. *dalier* 'to chat'.

**Dalmatian** ● **n. 1** a dog of a large, white short-haired breed with dark spots. **2** a native or inhabitant of Dalmatia, a region in Croatia.
– ORIGIN C16: the dog is believed to have originated in Dalmatia in the 18th cent.

**dalmatic** /dalˈmatɪk/ ● **n.** a wide-sleeved long, loose vestment open at the sides, worn by deacons and bishops, and by monarchs at their coronation.
– ORIGIN ME: from OFr. *dalmatique* or late L. *dalmatica*, from *dalmatica* (*vestis*) '(robe) of (white) Dalmatian wool', from *Dalmaticus* 'of Dalmatia'.

**Dalradian** /dalˈreɪdɪən/ ● **adj.** Geology relating to or denoting a series of late Precambrian rocks in Scotland and Ireland.
– ORIGIN C19: from *Dalrad-*, alt. form of *Dalriada*, an ancient Gaelic kingdom in northern Ireland, + **-IAN**.

**dal segno** /dal ˈsɛnjəʊ/ ● **adv. & adj.** Music repeat or repeated from the point marked by a sign. Compare with **DA CAPO**.
– ORIGIN Ital., 'from the sign'.

**dalton** /ˈdɔːlt(ə)n/ ● **n.** Chemistry a unit used in expressing the molecular weight of proteins, equivalent to atomic mass unit.
– ORIGIN 1930s: named after the Engl. chemist John *Dalton*.

**daltonism** ● **n.** another term for **PROTANOPIA**, a form of colour blindness.
– ORIGIN C19: from the name of J. *Dalton* (see **DALTON**) + **-ISM**.

**dam**[1] ● **n. 1** a barrier constructed to hold back water and raise its level, forming a reservoir or preventing flooding. ➤a barrier of branches in a stream, constructed by a beaver to provide a deep pool and a lodge. **2** chiefly N. Amer. a rubber sheet used to keep saliva from the teeth during dental operations. ● **v.** (**dammed**, **damming**) build a dam across. ➤hold back or obstruct.
– ORIGIN ME: from Mid. Low Ger. or MDu.; rel. to OE *fordemman* 'close up'.

**dam**[2] ● **n.** the female parent of an animal, especially a mammal.
– ORIGIN ME: alt. of **DAME**.

**dam**[3] ● **abbrev.** decametre(s).

**damage** ● **n. 1** physical harm impairing the value, usefulness, or normal function of something. ➤unwelcome and detrimental effects. **2** (**damages**) a sum of money claimed or awarded in compensation for a loss or injury. ● **v.** inflict damage on.
– PHRASES **what's the damage?** informal, humorous what does it cost?
– DERIVATIVES **damaging** adj. **damagingly** adv.
– ORIGIN ME: from OFr., from *dam*, *damne* 'loss or damage', from L. *damnum* 'loss or hurt'; cf. **DAMN**.

**damaged goods** ● **pl. n.** a person regarded as inadequate or impaired in some way.

**damage feasant** /ˈfiːz(ə)nt/ English Law ● **n.** damage done on one person's land by animals or goods of another, justifying the landowner in retaining them until compensated. ● **adv.** on grounds of damage caused to land or property.
– ORIGIN C16: from OFr. *damage fesant* 'doing damage'.

**damar** /ˈdamə/ ● **n.** variant spelling of **DAMMAR**.

**Damara** /dəˈmɑːrə/ ● **n.** (pl. same or **Damaras**) a member of a people inhabiting mountainous parts of Namibia and speaking the Nama language.
– ORIGIN the name in Nama.

**Damascene** /ˈdaməsiːn, ˌdaməˈsiːn/ ● **adj. 1** of or relating to the city of Damascus, the capital of Syria. ➤of, relating to, or resembling the conversion of St Paul on the road to Damascus. **2** historical of or relating to Damascus steel or its manufacture. **3** relating to or denoting a process of inlaying a metal object with gold or silver decoration. ● **n.** a native or inhabitant of Damascus.

**damascened** /ˈdaməsiːnd, ˌdaməˈsiːnd/ ● **adj. 1** (of iron or steel) given a wavy pattern by hammer-welding and repeated heating and forging. **2** (of a metal object) inlaid with gold or silver.

**Damascus steel** /dəˈmɑːskəs, -ˈmaskəs/ ● **n.** historical damascened steel, used chiefly for knife and sword blades.

**damask** /ˈdaməsk/ ● **n. 1** a figured, lustrous fabric, with a pattern visible on both sides. ➤a tablecloth made of damask. **2** (also **damask steel**) historical another term for **DAMASCUS STEEL**. ● **adj.** poetic/literary of the colour of a damask rose. ● **v.** poetic/literary decorate with or as if with a variegated pattern.
– ORIGIN ME: from *Damaske*, early form of the name of *Damascus*, the city in Syria where the fabric was first produced.

**damask rose** ● **n.** a sweet-scented rose of an old variety, having pink or light red velvety petals which are used to make attar. [*Rosa damascena*.]

**dame** • n. **1** (**Dame**) (in the UK) the title given to a woman with the rank of Knight Commander or holder of the Grand Cross in the Orders of Chivalry. **2** archaic or humorous an elderly or mature woman. ➤ N. Amer. informal a woman. ➤ (also **pantomime dame**) Brit. a comic middle-aged female character in pantomime, typically played by a man.
– ORIGIN ME: via OFr. from L. *domina* 'mistress'.

**dame school** • n. historical a small primary school run by elderly women.

**damfool** informal, dated • adj. thoroughly foolish. • n. a foolish person.

**dammar** /'damə/ (also **damar**) • n. resin obtained from various mainly Indo-Malaysian trees, used to make varnish.
– ORIGIN C17: from Malay *damar* 'resin'.

**damn** /dam/ • v. **1** (**be damned**) (in Christian belief) be condemned by God to suffer eternal punishment in hell. ➤ be doomed to misfortune or failure. **2** condemn, especially publicly. **3** curse. • exclam. informal expressing anger or frustration. • adj. informal used to emphasize one's anger or frustration: *turn that damn thing off!*
– PHRASES **as near as damn it** as close to being accurate as makes no difference. **damn all** Brit. informal nothing. **damn with faint praise** praise so unenthusiastically as to imply condemnation. **I'm** (or **I'll be**) **damned if** informal used to express a strong negative: *I'm damned if I know.* **not be worth a damn** informal have no value. **well I'll be** (or **I'm**) **damned** informal used to express surprise.
– ORIGIN ME: from OFr. *dam(p)ner*, from L. *dam(p)nare* 'inflict loss on', from *damnum* 'loss, damage'.

**damna** /'damnə/ plural form of DAMNUM.

**damnable** /'damnəb(ə)l/ • adj. **1** very bad or unpleasant. **2** worthy of divine condemnation.
– DERIVATIVES **damnably** adv.

**damnation** /dam'neɪʃ(ə)n/ • n. condemnation to eternal punishment in hell. • exclam. expressing anger or frustration.

**damnatory** /'damnə,t(ə)ri/ • adj. conveying or causing censure or damnation.

**damned** /damd/ • adj. informal used to emphasize one's anger or frustration. ➤ (**damnedest**) used to emphasize the surprising nature of something.
– PHRASES **do** (or **try**) **one's damnedest** do (or try) one's utmost.

**damnify** /'damnɪfʌɪ/ • v. (**-ies**, **-ied**) English Law, rare cause injury to.
– DERIVATIVES **damnification** n.
– ORIGIN C16: from OFr. *damnefier*, *dam(p)nifier*, from late L. *damnificare* 'injure, condemn', from L. *damnificus* 'hurtful', from *damnus* 'loss, damage'.

**damning** • adj. strongly suggestive of guilt or error.
– DERIVATIVES **damningly** adv.

**damnum** /'damnəm/ • n. (pl. **damna**) Law a loss.
– ORIGIN L., 'hurt, harm, or damage'.

**damp** • adj. slightly wet. • n. **1** moisture in the air, on a surface, or in a solid, typically with detrimental or unpleasant effects. ➤ (**damps**) archaic damp air or atmosphere. **2** archaic a check or discouragement. • v. **1** make damp. **2** control or restrain (a feeling or a situation). **3** make (a fire) burn less strongly by reducing its air supply. **4** reduce or stop the vibration of (the strings of a musical instrument). ➤ Physics progressively reduce the amplitude of (an oscillation or vibration).
– DERIVATIVES **dampish** adj. **damply** adv. **dampness** n.
– ORIGIN ME (in the sense 'noxious inhalation'): of W. Gmc origin.

**damp course** (also **damp-proof course**) • n. a layer of waterproof material in the wall of a building near the ground, to prevent rising damp.

**dampen** • v. **1** make damp. **2** make less strong or intense. ➤ reduce the amplitude of (a sound source).
– DERIVATIVES **dampener** n.

**damper** • n. **1** Music a pad silencing a piano string except when removed by means of a pedal or by the note being struck. **2** a device for reducing vibration or oscillation. **3** a movable metal plate in a flue or chimney, used to regulate the draught and so control the rate of combustion. **4** chiefly Austral./NZ an unleavened loaf or cake of flour and water baked in wood ashes. [in the sense 'something that takes the edge off the appetite'.]
– PHRASES **put a** (or **the**) **damper on** have a subduing or inhibiting effect on.

**damping** • n. **1** a reduction in the amplitude of a vibration or oscillation. ➤ a mechanism for bringing about such a reduction. **2** (**damping off**) the death of young seedlings as a result of a fungal infection in damp conditions.

**damp-proof** • adj. impervious to damp. • v. make impervious to damp by using a damp course.

**damp squib** • n. Brit. something much less impressive than expected.

**damsel** /'damz(ə)l/ • n. archaic or poetic/literary a young unmarried woman.
– ORIGIN ME: from OFr. *dameisele*, *damisele*, based on L. *domina* 'mistress'.

**damsel bug** • n. a slender long-legged predatory bug. [Family Nabidae: many species.]

**damselfish** • n. (pl. same or **-fishes**) a small brightly coloured tropical fish living near coral reefs. [*Chromis chromis* and other species.]

**damselfly** • n. (pl. **-flies**) a slender insect related to the dragonflies, typically resting with the wings folded back along the body. [Suborder Zygoptera: many species.]

**damson** /'damz(ə)n/ • n. **1** a small purple-black plumlike fruit. **2** (also **damson tree**) the small tree which bears this fruit, probably derived from the bullace. [*Prunus domestica* subsp. *insititia*.]
– ORIGIN ME *damascene*, from L. *damascenum* (*prunum*) '(plum) of Damascus'.

**damson cheese** • n. a solid preserve of damsons and sugar.

**Dan.** • abbrev. Daniel (in biblical references).

**dan**[1] • n. any of ten degrees of advanced proficiency in judo or karate. ➤ a person who has achieved a dan.
– ORIGIN 1940s: from Japanese.

**dan**[2] (also **dan buoy**) • n. a small temporary marker buoy with a lightweight flagpole.
– ORIGIN C17: of unknown origin.

**Danakil** /'danəkɪl, də'nɑːk(ə)l/ • n. another term for AFAR.
– ORIGIN from Arab. *danākil*, pl. of *dankalī*.

**dance** • v. **1** move rhythmically to music, typically following a set sequence of steps. ➤ perform (a particular dance or a role in a ballet). **2** move in a quick and light or lively way. ➤ (of someone's eyes) sparkle with pleasure or excitement. • n. **1** a series of steps and movements that match the speed and rhythm of a piece of music. **2** a social gathering at which people dance. **3** (also **dance music**) music for dancing to, especially in a nightclub.
– PHRASES **dance attendance on** do one's utmost to please someone. **dance to someone's tune** comply with someone's demands and wishes. **lead someone a merry dance** Brit. cause someone a great deal of trouble or worry.
– DERIVATIVES **danceable** adj. **dancer** n. **dancing** n.
– ORIGIN ME: from OFr. *dancer*, *dance*, of unknown origin.

**dance band** • n. a band that plays music suitable for dancing to, especially swing.

**dance floor** • n. an area of floor in a nightclub, disco, or restaurant reserved for dancing.

**dance hall** • n. a large public hall or building where people pay to enter and dance.

**dance of death** • n. a medieval allegorical representation in which a personified Death leads all to the grave.

**dancercise** (also **-ize**) • n. a system of aerobic exercise using dance movements.

**dancetté** /'dansəteɪ/ (also **dancetty**) • adj. Heraldry having large, deep zigzag indentations.
– ORIGIN C17: alt. of Fr. *denché*, based on L. *dens*, *dent-* 'tooth'.

**dancing girl** • n. a female professional dancer, especially a member of a chorus in a musical.

**D and C** • **abbrev.** dilatation and curettage.

**dandelion** • **n.** a widely distributed weed of the daisy family, with large bright yellow flowers followed by globular heads of seeds with downy tufts. [*Taraxacum officinale* and related species.]
– ORIGIN ME: from Fr. *dent-de-lion* 'lion's tooth' (because of the jagged shape of the leaves).

**dandelion clock** • **n.** see CLOCK[1] (sense 2).

**dander[1]** • **n.** (in phr. **get/have one's dander up**) informal lose one's temper.
– ORIGIN C19: of unknown origin.

**dander[2]** • **n.** skin flakes in an animal's fur.
– ORIGIN C18: rel. to DANDRUFF.

**dander[3]** chiefly Scottish • **n.** a stroll. • **v.** stroll.
– ORIGIN C16: perh. rel. to dial. *dadder* 'quake' and *daddle* 'dawdle'.

**Dandie Dinmont** /ˌdandɪ ˈdɪnmənt/ • **n.** a terrier of a breed from the Scottish Borders, with short legs, a long body, and a rough coat.
– ORIGIN C19: named after a character in Sir Walter Scott's *Guy Mannering* who owned a special breed of terriers.

**dandified** • **adj.** **1** (of a man) showing excessive concern about his appearance. **2** self-consciously elaborate: *dandified prose.*

**dandiprat** • **n.** archaic, informal a young or insignificant person.
– ORIGIN C16 (denoting a coin worth three halfpence): of unknown origin.

**dandle** • **v.** move (a baby or young child) up and down in a playful or affectionate way.
– ORIGIN C16: of unknown origin.

**dandruff** • **n.** small pieces of dead skin among a person's hair.
– DERIVATIVES **dandruffy** adj.
– ORIGIN C16: the first element is unknown; the second (*-ruff*) is perh. rel. to ME *rove* 'scurfy condition of the skin'.

**dandy** • **n.** (pl. **-ies**) **1** a man unduly concerned with a stylish and fashionable appearance. **2** informal, dated an excellent thing of its kind. • **adj.** (**-ier**, **-iest**) informal, chiefly N. Amer. excellent.
– DERIVATIVES **dandiacal** adj. (dated or humorous). **dandyish** adj. **dandyism** n.
– ORIGIN C18: perh. a shortened form of C17 *Jack-a-dandy* 'conceited fellow' (*Dandy* was a familiar form of the given name *Andrew*).

**dandy brush** • **n.** a coarse brush used for grooming a horse.

**Dane** • **n.** a native or national of Denmark, or a person of Danish descent.
– ORIGIN OE *Dene*.

**Danegeld** /ˈdeɪngɛld/ • **n.** a land tax levied in Anglo-Saxon England to raise funds for protection against Danish invaders. ➤ taxes collected for national defence by the Norman kings until 1162.
– ORIGIN OE, from ON *Danir* 'Danes' + *gjald* 'payment'.

**dang** • **adj.**, **exclam.**, & **v.** informal, chiefly N. Amer. euphemism for DAMN.

**danger** • **n.** **1** the possibility of suffering harm or injury. ➤ a cause of harm or injury. **2** the possibility of something unwelcome or unpleasant: *there was no danger of the champagne running out.*
– ORIGIN ME (in the sense 'jurisdiction or power', 'power to harm'): from OFr. *dangier*, based on L. *dominus* 'lord'.

**danger list** • **n.** Brit. a list of those who are dangerously ill in a hospital.

**danger money** (N. Amer. **danger pay**) • **n.** extra payment for working under dangerous conditions.

**dangerous** • **adj.** able or likely to cause harm or injury. ➤ likely to cause problems or difficulties.
– DERIVATIVES **dangerously** adv. **dangerousness** n.

**dangle** • **v.** hang or cause to hang so as to swing freely.
– PHRASES **keep someone dangling** keep someone in an uncertain position.
– DERIVATIVES **dangler** n. **dangly** adj.
– ORIGIN C16: symbolic of something loose and pendulous.

**dangling participle** • **n.** Grammar a participle intended to modify a noun which is not actually present in the text (e.g. *arriving* in *arriving at the station, the sun came out*), regarded as a mistake in standard English.

**danio** /ˈdanɪəʊ/ • **n.** (pl. **-os**) a small, brightly coloured freshwater fish of the Indian subcontinent and SE Asia. [Genera *Danio* and *Brachydanio*: several species.]
– ORIGIN mod. L. (genus name).

**Danish** /ˈdeɪnɪʃ/ • **adj.** of or relating to Denmark or its people or language. • **n.** the Scandinavian language spoken in Denmark.
– ORIGIN OE *Denisc*, of Gmc origin.

**Danish blue** • **n.** a soft, salty, strong-flavoured white cheese with blue veins.

**Danish oil** • **n.** a mixture of tung oil and other vegetable oils, used to treat wood.

**Danish pastry** • **n.** a cake of sweetened yeast pastry with toppings or fillings of icing, fruit, or nuts.

**dank** • **adj.** damp, cold, and musty.
– DERIVATIVES **dankly** adv. **dankness** n.
– ORIGIN ME: prob. of Scand. origin and rel. to Swed. *dank* 'marshy spot'.

**Dano-Norwegian** /ˌdeɪnəʊnɔːˈwiːdʒ(ə)n/ • **n.** another term for BOKMÅL.

**danse macabre** /ˌdɑːns məˈkɑːbr(ə)/ • **n.** another term for DANCE OF DEATH.
– ORIGIN from Fr.

**danseur** /dɑ̃ˈsəː/ (or **danseuse** /dɑ̃ˈsəːz/) • **n.** a male (or female) ballet dancer.
– ORIGIN Fr., from *danser* 'to dance'.

**danseur noble** /dɑ̃ˌsəː ˈnɒbl(ə)/ • **n.** a principal male ballet dancer, especially one who is particularly suited by bearing or physique to princely roles.
– ORIGIN Fr., lit. 'noble dancer'.

**Dantean** /ˈdantɪən, danˈtiːən/ • **adj.** of or reminiscent of the work of the Italian poet Dante (1265–1321), especially his vision of hell in *The Divine Comedy*. • **n.** an admirer of Dante or his work.
– DERIVATIVES **Dantesque** /ˌdantɪˈɛsk/ adj.

**Danubian** /daˈnjuːbɪən/ • **adj.** of, relating to, or bordering on the Danube, a river flowing from SW Germany to the Black Sea.

**dap** • **v.** (**dapped**, **dapping**) fish by letting the fly (but not the line) bob lightly on the water. • **n.** **1** a fishing fly used in this way. **2** dialect a rubber-soled shoe.
– ORIGIN C17: symbolic of a flicking movement, similar to DAB[1].

**daphne** /ˈdafni/ • **n.** a small, typically evergreen shrub with sweet-scented flowers. [Genus *Daphne*.]
– ORIGIN ME (denoting the laurel or bay tree): from Gk *daphnē*, from the name of *Daphne*, a nymph in Gk mythology who was turned into a laurel bush.

**daphnia** /ˈdafnɪə/ • **n.** (pl. same) a minute semi-transparent freshwater crustacean with long antennae and prominent eyes. [Genus *Daphnia*.]
– ORIGIN mod. L., from Gk *Daphnē*, from the name of the nymph *Daphne* (see DAPHNE).

**dapper** • **adj.** (of a man) neat and trim in dress and appearance.
– DERIVATIVES **dapperly** adv. **dapperness** n.
– ORIGIN ME: prob. from a Mid. Low Ger. or MDu. word meaning 'strong, stout'.

**dapple** • **v.** (usu. **be dappled**) mark with spots or rounded patches. • **n.** **1** a patch of colour or light. **2** an animal whose coat is dappled.
– ORIGIN C16 (as adj.): perh. rel. to ON *depill* 'spot'.

**dapple grey** • **adj.** (of a horse) grey or white with darker ring-like markings. • **n.** a horse of this type.

**dapsone** /ˈdapsəʊn/ • **n.** Medicine a sulphur-containing drug used to treat leprosy.
– ORIGIN 1950s: from elements of the systematic name *dipara-aminophenyl sulphone*.

**darbies** /ˈdɑːbɪz/ • **pl. n.** Brit. archaic, informal handcuffs.
– ORIGIN C17: allusive use of *Father Darby's bands*, an agreement which put debtors in the power of money-lenders.

**Darby and Joan** • **n.** chiefly Brit. a devoted old married

couple.
– ORIGIN C18: from a poem (1735) in the *Gentleman's Magazine*.

**Darby and Joan club** • n. Brit. a club for senior citizens.

**Dard** /dɑːd/ • n. **1** a member of a group of peoples inhabiting eastern Afghanistan, northern Pakistan, and Kashmir. **2** the Indic languages spoken by these people.
– DERIVATIVES **Dardic** n. & adj.
– ORIGIN the name in Dard.

**dare** • v. (3rd sing. present usu. **dare** before an expressed or implied infinitive without 'to') **1** have the courage to do something. ➤(**how dare you**) used to express indignation. ➤(**don't you dare**) used to order someone threateningly not to do something. **2** defy or challenge to do something. **3** poetic/literary take the risk of. • n. a challenge, especially to prove courage.
– PHRASES **I dare say** (or **daresay**) it is probable.
– DERIVATIVES **darer** n.
– ORIGIN OE *durran*, of Gmc origin.

**daredevil** • n. a person who enjoys doing dangerous things.
– DERIVATIVES **daredevilry** n.

**darg** /dɑːg/ • n. dialect or Austral./NZ a fixed amount of work.
– ORIGIN ME: alt. of north. Engl. dial. *daywork* 'a day's work'.

**dargah** /ˈdɑːgə/ • n. the tomb or shrine of a Muslim holy man.
– ORIGIN from Urdu, from Pers.

**Dari** /ˈdɑːriː/ • n. the form of Persian spoken in Afghanistan.

**daring** • adj. adventurous or audaciously bold. • n. adventurous courage.
– DERIVATIVES **daringly** adv.

**dariole** /ˈdarɪəʊl/ • n. (in French cooking) a small, round mould in which an individual dish is cooked and served.
– ORIGIN ME: from OFr.

**Darjeeling** /dɑːˈdʒiːlɪŋ/ • n. a high-quality tea grown in the mountains of northern India.
– ORIGIN from *Darjeeling*, a hill station in W. Bengal.

**dark** • adj. **1** with little or no light. **2** of a deep or sombre colour. ➤(of skin, hair, or eyes) brown or black. ➤(of a person) having such skin, hair, or eyes. **3** mysterious: *a dark secret.* ➤(**darkest**) humorous (of a region) most remote, inaccessible, or uncivilized. ➤archaic ignorant. **4** characterized by unhappiness or unpleasantness: *the dark days of the war.* ➤(of an expression) angry. ➤evil; sinister: *dark deeds.* • n. **1** (**the dark**) the absence of light. ➤a dark colour or shade. **2** nightfall.
– PHRASES **in the dark** in a state of ignorance. **keep something dark** keep something secret. **a shot** (or **stab**) **in the dark** a mere guess.
– DERIVATIVES **darkish** adj. **darkly** adv. **darkness** n. **darksome** adj. (poetic/literary).
– ORIGIN OE *deorc*, of Gmc origin.

**Dark Ages** • pl. n. **1** the period in Europe between the fall of the Roman Empire and the Middle Ages, *c.*500–1100 AD, judged to have been a time of relative unenlightenment. **2** Archaeology a period in ancient Greece from the end of the Bronze Age until the historical period, in which there was no building and the art of writing was apparently lost.

**dark chocolate** • n. plain chocolate.

**dark current** • n. the residual electric current flowing in a photoelectric device when there is no illumination.

**darken** • v. **1** make or become dark or darker. ➤(of something unpleasant) cast a shadow over; spoil. **2** make or become unhappy or angry. ➤(of someone's eyes or expression) show anger.
– PHRASES **never darken someone's door** keep away from someone's home.
– DERIVATIVES **darkener** n.

**dark horse** • n. a person about whom little is known, especially one with unexpected abilities.
– ORIGIN C19: orig. racing sl.

**darkie** (also **darky**) • n. (pl. **-ies**) informal, offensive a black person.

**darkling** • adj. poetic/literary of or relating to growing darkness.

**dark matter** • n. Astronomy (in some cosmological theories) non-luminous material postulated to exist in space.

**dark night of the soul** • n. a period of spiritual desolation suffered by a mystic in which all sense of consolation is removed.
– ORIGIN C19: translating Sp. *noche oscura* (St John of the Cross).

**dark reaction** • n. Biochemistry (in photosynthesis) the cycle of reactions involving the fixation of carbon dioxide and its reduction to carbohydrate, which does not require the presence of light.

**darkroom** • n. a room for developing photographs, from which normal light is excluded.

**darky** • n. variant spelling of **DARKIE**.

**darling** • n. used as an affectionate form of address. ➤a lovable or endearing person. ➤a favourite of a certain group: *the darling of Labour's left wing.* • adj. beloved. ➤pretty; charming.
– ORIGIN OE *dēorling* (see **DEAR**, **-LING**).

**darn**[1] • v. mend (knitted material or a hole in this) by interweaving yarn across it with a needle. ➤embroider with a large running stitch. • n. a place in a garment that has been darned.
– DERIVATIVES **darning** n.
– ORIGIN C17: perh. from dial. *dern* 'to hide', from OE *diernan*, of W. Gmc origin.

**darn**[2] (US also **durn**) • v., adj., & exclam. informal euphemism for **DAMN**.

**darned** (US also **durned**) • adj. informal euphemism for **DAMNED**.

**darnel** /ˈdɑːn(ə)l/ • n. a ryegrass, formerly a common weed of cereals. [*Lolium temulentum* and other species.]
– ORIGIN ME: of unknown origin; appar. rel. to Fr. (Walloon dial.) *darnelle*.

**darner** • n. **1** a darning needle. **2** N. Amer. a large slender-bodied dragonfly. [Family Aeshnidae: many species.]

**darning needle** • n. **1** a long sewing needle with a large eye, used in darning. **2** N. Amer. another term for **DARNER** (in sense 2).

**darshan** /ˈdɑːʃ(ə)n/ • n. Hinduism an opportunity of seeing a holy person or the image of a deity.
– ORIGIN via Hindi from Sanskrit *darśana* 'sight or seeing'.

**dart** • n. **1** a small pointed missile thrown or fired as a weapon. ➤a small pointed missile with a flight, used in the game of darts. **2** an act of moving suddenly and rapidly. **3** a tapered tuck in a garment. • v. **1** move suddenly or rapidly. **2** archaic throw or shoot (a missile).
– ORIGIN ME: from OFr., accusative of *darz*, *dars*, from a W. Gmc word meaning 'spear, lance'.

**dartboard** • n. a circular board marked with numbered segments, used as a target in the game of darts.

**darter** • n. **1** a long-necked bird which spears fish with its long pointed bill. [Genus *Anhinga*.] **2** a small North American freshwater fish. [Genera *Etheostoma* and *Percina*.] **3** a broad-bodied dragonfly which darts out to grab prey. [Libellulidae and other families.]

**Dartmoor pony** • n. a pony of a small hardy breed with a long shaggy coat in winter.

**darts** • pl. n. [usu. treated as sing.] an indoor game in which darts are thrown at a dartboard to score points.

**Darwinism** • n. the theory of the evolution of species by natural selection, advanced by the English natural historian Charles Darwin (1809–82).
– DERIVATIVES **Darwinian** n. & adj. **Darwinist** n. & adj.

**Dasein** /ˈdɑːzʌɪn/ • n. Philosophy **1** (in Hegelianism) existence or determinate being. **2** (in existentialism) human existence.
– ORIGIN C19: Ger., from *dasein* 'exist'.

**dash** • v. **1** run or travel in a great hurry. **2** strike or fling with great force. **3** destroy or frustrate (hopes or expectations). **4** (**dash something off**) write something hurriedly and without much thought. • exclam. Brit. informal used to express mild annoyance. • n. **1** an act of dashing. ➤chiefly N. Amer. a sprint. **2** a small quantity of a substance,

added to something else. ➤a small amount of a particular quality adding distinctiveness to something. **3** a horizontal stroke in writing, marking a pause or to represent omitted letters or words. ➤the longer signal of the two used in Morse code. ➤Music a short vertical mark placed above or beneath a note to indicate that it is to be performed staccato. **4** panache. **5** short for **DASHBOARD**.
– ORIGIN ME: prob. symbolic of forceful movement.

**dashboard** ● **n.** **1** the panel of instruments and controls facing the driver of a vehicle. **2** historical a board of wood or leather in front of a carriage, to keep out mud.

**dashed** ● **adj.** Brit. informal, dated used for emphasis: *it's a dashed shame.*

**dasheen** /da'ʃiːn/ ● **n.** another term for **TARO**.
– ORIGIN C19 (orig. W. Ind.): of unknown origin.

**dasher** ● **n.** **1** informal a flamboyant or stylish person. **2** a plunger for agitating cream in a churn.

**dashiki** /'dɑːʃɪki/ ● **n.** (pl. **dashikis**) a loose, brightly coloured shirt, originally from West Africa.
– ORIGIN from Yoruba or Hausa.

**dashing** ● **adj.** (of a man) attractive in a romantic, adventurous way. ➤stylish.
– DERIVATIVES **dashingly** adv.

**dashpot** ● **n.** a device for damping shock or vibration.

**dassie** /'dasi/ ● **n.** (pl. **-ies**) S. African **1** a rock hyrax. **2** a silvery fish with dark fins and a black spot on the tail. [*Diplodus sargus*.]
– ORIGIN C18: from Afrik., from S. Afr. Du. *dasje*, dimin. of Du. *das* 'badger'.

**dastard** /'dastəd, 'dɑː-/ ● **n.** dated or humorous a dishonourable or despicable person.
– ORIGIN ME: prob. from *dazed*, influenced by *dotard* and *bastard*.

**dastardly** ● **adj.** dated or humorous wicked and cruel.
– DERIVATIVES **dastardliness** n.

**dastur** /də'stʊə/ (also **dastoor**) ● **n.** Indian a chief priest of the Parsees.
– ORIGIN Pers., from Old Pers. *dastōbār*.

**dasyure** /'dasɪjʊə/ ● **n.** another term for **QUOLL**.
– ORIGIN C19: from Fr., from mod. L. *dasyurus*, from Gk *dasus* 'rough, hairy' + *oura* 'tail'.

**DAT** ● **abbrev.** digital audiotape.

**data** /'deɪtə/ ● **n.** **1** facts and statistics used for reference or analysis. ➤Philosophy things known or assumed as facts, making the basis of reasoning. **2** the quantities, characters, or symbols on which operations are performed by a computer.
– ORIGIN C17: from L., pl. of **DATUM**.

**USAGE** data

In Latin, **data** is the plural of **datum** and, historically and in specialized scientific fields, it is also treated as a plural in English. In modern non-scientific use, however, it is often treated as a mass noun, similar to a word like **information**, which cannot normally have a plural and which takes a singular verb. Sentences such as *data was collected over a number of years* are now widely accepted in standard English.

**databank** ● **n.** Computing a large repository of data, sometimes formed from more than one database.

**database** ● **n.** a structured set of data held in a computer.

**datable** (also **dateable**) ● **adj.** able to be dated to a particular time.

**data capture** ● **n.** Computing the action of gathering data from an automatic device, control system, or sensor.

**data processing** ● **n.** a series of operations on data, especially by a computer, to retrieve, transform, or classify information.
– DERIVATIVES **data processor** n.

**data protection** ● **n.** Brit. legal control over access to and use of data stored in computers.

**datcha** /'datʃə/ ● **n.** variant spelling of **DACHA**.

**date**[1] ● **n.** **1** the day of the month or year as specified by a number. **2** a day or year when a given event occurred or will occur. ➤(**dates**) the years of a person's birth and death or of the beginning and end of a period or event. ➤the period of time to which something belongs. **3** informal a social or romantic appointment. **4** a musical or theatrical performance, especially as part of a tour. ● **v.** **1** establish or ascertain the date of. ➤mark with a date. ➤have existed since. **2** [often as adj. **dated**] appear or cause to appear old-fashioned. **3** informal, chiefly N. Amer. go on a date with.
– PHRASES **to date** until now.
– DERIVATIVES **dateless** adj.
– ORIGIN ME: via OFr. from med. L. *data*, fem. past part. of *dare* 'give'; from the L. formula used in dating letters, *data (epistola)* '(letter) given or delivered'.

**date**[2] ● **n.** **1** a sweet, dark brown, oval fruit with a hard stone, usually eaten dried. **2** (also **date palm**) a tall palm tree which bears clusters of this fruit, native to western Asia and North Africa. [*Phoenix dactylifera*.]
– ORIGIN ME: from OFr., via L. from Gk *daktulos* 'finger' (because of the finger-like shape of its leaves).

**dateable** ● **adj.** variant spelling of **DATABLE**.

**datebook** ● **n.** N. Amer. an engagement diary.

**Date Line** (also **International Date Line**) ● **n.** an imaginary North–South line through the Pacific Ocean, chiefly along the meridian furthest from Greenwich, to the east of which the date is a day earlier than it is to the west.

**date line** ● **n.** a line at the head of a dispatch or special article in a newspaper showing the date and place of writing.

**date rape** ● **n.** rape by a person with whom the victim has gone on a date.

**date stamp** ● **n.** a stamped mark indicating a date. ➤an adjustable stamp used to make such a mark. ● **v.** (**date-stamp**) mark with a date stamp.

**dating agency** ● **n.** a service which arranges introductions for people seeking romantic partners or friends.

**dative** /'deɪtɪv/ Grammar ● **adj.** (in Latin, Greek, German, etc.) denoting a case of nouns and pronouns indicating an indirect object or recipient. ● **n.** a dative noun, pronoun, etc.
– ORIGIN ME: from L. *(casus) dativus* '(case) of giving', from *dat-*, *dare* 'give'.

**datum** /'deɪtəm/ ● **n.** (pl. **data**) See also **DATA**. **1** a piece of information. **2** an assumption or premise from which inferences may be drawn. See **SENSE DATUM**. **3** a fixed starting point of a scale or operation.
– ORIGIN C18: from L., lit. 'something given'.

**datum line** (also **datum level**) ● **n.** a standard of comparison or point of reference. ➤Surveying an assumed surface used as a reference for the measurement of heights and depths.

**datura** /də'tjʊərə/ ● **n.** a shrubby North American plant of a genus including the thorn apple. [Genus *Datura*.]
– ORIGIN mod. L., from Hindi *dhatūrā*.

**daub** /dɔːb/ ● **v.** coat or smear with a thick substance carelessly or liberally. ➤spread (a thick substance) on a surface in such a way. ● **n.** **1** plaster, clay, etc., especially when mixed with straw and applied to laths or wattles to form a wall. **2** a patch or smear of a thick substance. **3** a painting executed without much skill.
– DERIVATIVES **dauber** n.
– ORIGIN ME: from OFr. *dauber*, from L. *dealbare* 'whiten, whitewash', based on *albus* 'white'.

**daube** /dəʊb/ ● **n.** a stew of meat, typically beef, braised in wine.
– ORIGIN Fr.; cf. Ital. *addobbo* 'seasoning'.

**daughter** ● **n.** **1** a girl or woman in relation to her parents. ➤a female descendant. **2** a woman considered as the product of a particular influence or environment. **3** Physics a nuclide formed by the radioactive decay of another.
– DERIVATIVES **daughterhood** n. **daughterly** adj.
– ORIGIN OE *dohtor*, of Gmc origin.

**daughter cell** ● **n.** Biology a cell formed by the division or budding of another.

**daughter-in-law** ● **n.** (pl. **daughters-in-law**) the wife of one's son.

**daunt** /dɔːnt/ ● **v.** (usu. **be daunted**) cause to feel intimidated or apprehensive.

– DERIVATIVES **daunting** adj. **dauntingly** adv.
– ORIGIN ME: from OFr. *danter*, from L. *domitare*, frequentative of *domare* 'to tame'.

**dauntless** • adj. fearless and determined.
– DERIVATIVES **dauntlessly** adv. **dauntlessness** n.

**dauphin** /'dɔːfɪn, 'dəʊfã, French dofɛ̃/ • n. historical the eldest son of the King of France.
– ORIGIN Fr., from the family name of the lords of the Dauphiné, ult. a nickname meaning 'dolphin'.

**dauphinois** /ˌdəʊfɪ'nwʌ/ (also **dauphinoise** /-'nwʌz/) • adj. (of potatoes) sliced and baked in milk, typically with a topping of cheese.
– ORIGIN Fr., 'from the province of Dauphiné'.

**daven** /'dɑːv(ə)n/ • v. (**davened**, **davening**) (in Judaism) recite the prescribed liturgical prayers.
– ORIGIN from Yiddish.

**davenport** /'dav(ə)npɔːt/ • n. **1** Brit. an ornamental writing desk with drawers and a sloping surface for writing. **2** N. Amer. a large heavily upholstered sofa or sofa bed.
– ORIGIN sense 1 is named after Captain *Davenport*, for whom a desk of this type was made in the late C18; sense 2 is prob. from a manufacturer's name.

**davit** /'davɪt, 'deɪv-/ • n. a small crane on a ship, especially one of a pair for lowering a lifeboat.
– ORIGIN C15: from OFr. *daviot*, dimin. of *david*, denoting a kind of carpenter's tool.

**Davy Jones's locker** • n. informal the bottom of the sea, especially regarded as the grave of those who drowned.
– ORIGIN from C18 naut. sl. *Davy Jones*, denoting the evil spirit of the sea.

**Davy lamp** • n. historical a miner's portable safety lamp with the flame enclosed by wire gauze to reduce the risk of a gas explosion.
– ORIGIN named after the Engl. chemist Sir Humphry *Davy* (1778–1829), who invented it.

**dawdle** • v. waste time. ➤ move slowly and idly.
– DERIVATIVES **dawdler** n.
– ORIGIN C17: rel. to dial. *daddle*, *doddle* 'dally'.

**dawn** • n. **1** the first appearance of light in the sky before sunrise. **2** the beginning of something. • v. **1** (of a day) begin. **2** come into existence. ➤ (often **dawn on**) become evident or understood.
– ORIGIN C15 (as v.): back-form. from DAWNING.

**dawn chorus** • n. the singing of a large number of birds before dawn each day.

**dawning** • n. **1** poetic/literary dawn. **2** the beginning or first appearance of something.
– ORIGIN ME: alt. of earlier *dawing*, from OE *dagian* 'to dawn', of Gmc origin; rel. to DAY.

**dawn redwood** • n. a coniferous tree with deciduous needles, known only as a fossil until it was found growing in SW China in 1941. [*Metasequoia glyptostroboides*.]

**day** • n. **1** a twenty-four-hour period as a unit of time, reckoned from one midnight to the next and corresponding to a rotation of the earth on its axis. ➤ the time between sunrise and sunset. ➤ Astronomy a single rotation of a planet in relation to its primary. **2** a particular period of the past. ➤ (**the day**) the present time. ➤ (**days**) a particular period in a person's life: *my student days*. ➤ (**one's day**) the successful or influential period of a person's life. • adj. working or done during the day.
– PHRASES **all in a day's work** part of someone's normal routine. **any day** informal at any time. ➤ under any circumstances. **call it a day** decide to stop doing something. **day and night** all the time. **day by day** gradually and steadily. **day in, day out** continuously or repeatedly over a long period. **day of reckoning** a testing time when the degree of one's success or failure will be revealed. [with allusion to Judgement Day.] **one day** (or **some day** or **one of these days**) at some time in the future. **one of those days** a day when things go badly. **that will be the day** informal that is very unlikely. **these days** at present.
– ORIGIN OE *dæg*, of Gmc origin; rel. to Ger. *Tag*.

**Dayak** /'dʌɪak/ (also **Dyak**) • n. (pl. same or **Dayaks**) **1** a member of a group of indigenous peoples inhabiting parts of Borneo, including the Iban (or **Sea Dayak**) of the north and the **Land Dayak** of the south-west. **2** the Austronesian languages spoken by these peoples.
– ORIGIN Malay, lit. 'up-country'.

**dayan** /dɑ'jɑːn/ (also **Dayan**) • n. (pl. **dayanim** /dɑ'jɑːnɪm/) Judaism a senior rabbi, especially one who acts as a religious judge.
– ORIGIN from Heb. *dayyān*, from *dān* 'to judge'.

**daybed** • n. a bed for daytime rest. ➤ N. Amer. a couch that can be made into a bed.

**daybook** • n. **1** an account book in which a day's transactions are entered for later transfer to a ledger. **2** N. Amer. a diary.

**day boy** (or **day girl**) • n. Brit. a boy (or girl) who lives at home but attends a boarding school.

**daybreak** • n. dawn.

**day care** • n. daytime care for people who cannot be fully independent. ➤ (**daycare**) N. Amer. a day centre.

**day centre** (also **day-care centre**) • n. a place providing care and recreation facilities for those who cannot be fully independent.

**day-dawn** • n. poetic/literary daybreak.

**daydream** • n. a series of pleasant thoughts that distract one's attention from the present. • v. indulge in a daydream.
– DERIVATIVES **daydreamer** n.

**day flower** • n. a plant with short-lived blue flowers, found in warm climates. [Genus *Commelina*.]

**Day-Glo** • n. trademark fluorescent paint or other colouring.

**day labourer** • n. an unskilled labourer paid by the day.

**daylight** • n. **1** the natural light of the day. ➤ dawn. **2** visible distance between one person or thing and another. **3** (**daylights**) used to emphasize the severity of an action: *he beat the living daylights out of them*.
– PHRASES **see daylight** begin to understand something.

**daylight robbery** • n. Brit. informal blatant overcharging.

**daylight saving time** (also **daylight time**) • n. chiefly N. Amer. another term for SUMMER TIME.

**day lily** • n. a lily which bears large yellow, red, or orange flowers, each lasting only one day. [Genus *Hemerocallis*.]

**Day of Atonement** • n. another term for YOM KIPPUR.

**day off** • n. (pl. **days off**) a day's holiday from work or school.

**Day of Judgement** • n. another term for JUDGEMENT DAY.

**day of rest** • n. a day set aside from normal activity, typically Sunday on religious grounds.

**day out** • n. (pl. **days out**) Brit. an outing for a day.

**daypack** • n. chiefly N. Amer. a small rucksack.

**day release** • n. Brit. a system of allowing employees days off work to go on educational courses.

**day return** • n. Brit. a ticket at a reduced rate for a return journey on public transport in one day.

**day room** • n. a communal room in an institution, used during the day.

**daysack** • n. Brit. a small rucksack.

**day school** • n. **1** a non-residential fee-paying school. **2** a short educational course.

**dayside** • n. Astronomy the side of a planet that is facing its primary star.

**Days of Awe** • pl. n. another term for HIGH HOLIDAYS.

**day surgery** • n. minor surgery that does not require an overnight stay in hospital.

**daytime** • n. the time between sunrise and sunset.

**day-to-day** • adj. **1** happening regularly every day. ➤ ordinary. **2** short-term. • n. an ordinary, everyday routine. • adv. on a daily basis.

**day trading** • n. a form of share dealing in which individuals buy and sell shares over the Internet over a period of a single day's trading, with the intention of profiting from small price fluctuations.
– DERIVATIVES **day trader** n.

**day trip** • n. a journey or outing completed in one day.
– DERIVATIVES **day tripper** n.

**daywear** • n. casual clothing suitable for informal or everyday occasions.

**daywork** • n. casual work paid for on a daily basis.

– DERIVATIVES **dayworker** n.

**daze** ● v. (usu. **be dazed**) make unable to think or react properly. ● n. a state of stunned confusion.
– DERIVATIVES **dazedly** /-zɪdli/ adv.
– ORIGIN ME: back-form. from *dazed* (adj.), from ON *dasathr* 'weary'.

**dazzle** ● v. **1** (of a bright light) blind temporarily. **2** overwhelm with an impressive quality. ● n. blinding brightness.
– DERIVATIVES **dazzlement** n. **dazzler** n.
– ORIGIN C15: frequentative of **DAZE**.

**dazzling** ● adj. **1** very bright. **2** very impressive.
– DERIVATIVES **dazzlingly** adv.

**Db** ● symb. the chemical element dubnium.

**dB** ● abbrev. decibel(s).

**DBE** ● abbrev. (in the UK) Dame Commander of the Order of the British Empire.

**DBS** ● abbrev. **1** direct broadcasting by satellite. **2** direct-broadcast satellite.

**dbx** ● n. trademark electronic circuitry designed to increase the dynamic range of reproduced sound.
– ORIGIN 1970s: from **DB** + *x* (representing *expander*).

**DC** ● abbrev. **1** Music da capo. **2** direct current. **3** District of Columbia. **4** District Commissioner.

**DCB** ● abbrev. (in the UK) Dame Commander of the Order of the Bath.

**DCC** ● abbrev. digital compact cassette.

**DCL** ● abbrev. (in the UK) Doctor of Civil Law.

**DCM** ● abbrev. (in the UK) Distinguished Conduct Medal.

**DCMG** ● abbrev. (in the UK) Dame Commander of the Order of St Michael and St George.

**DCVO** ● abbrev. (in the UK) Dame Commander of the Royal Victorian Order.

**DD** ● abbrev. Doctor of Divinity.

**D-Day** ● n. **1** the day (6 June 1944) in the Second World War on which Allied forces invaded northern France. **2** the day on which something important is to begin.
– ORIGIN from *D* for *day* + **DAY**.

**DDE** ● n. Computing a standard allowing data to be shared between different programs.
– ORIGIN 1980s: abbrev. of *Dynamic Data Exchange*.

**DDI** ● abbrev. **1** dideoxyinosine. **2** divisional detective inspector.

**DDos** ● abbrev. distributed denial of service, denoting the intentional paralysing of a computer network by flooding it with data sent simultaneously from many individual computers.

**DDR** ● abbrev. historical German Democratic Republic.
– ORIGIN abbrev. of Ger. *Deutsche Demokratische Republik*.

**DDT** ● abbrev. dichlorodiphenyltrichloroethane, a synthetic organic compound used as an insecticide but now banned in many countries.

**DE** ● abbrev. **1** Delaware (in official postal use). **2** (in the UK) Department of Employment.

**de-** ● prefix **1** (forming verbs and their derivatives) down; away: *descend* | *deduct*. ➤ completely: *denude*. **2** (added to verbs and their derivatives) denoting removal or reversal: *de-ice*. **3** denoting formation from: *deverbal*.
– ORIGIN from L. *de* 'off, from'; sense 2 via OFr. *des-* from L. *dis-*.

**deaccession** /ˌdiːək'sɛʃ(ə)n/ ● v. officially remove (an item) from a library, museum, or art gallery in order to sell it. ● n. the disposal of items in this way.

**deacon** /'diːk(ə)n/ ● n. **1** (in Catholic, Anglican, and Orthodox Churches) an ordained minister of an order ranking below that of priest. ➤ (in some Protestant Churches) a lay officer assisting a minister. **2** (in the early Church) an appointed minister of charity. ● v. appoint or ordain as a deacon.
– DERIVATIVES **deaconship** n.
– ORIGIN OE *diacon*, via eccles. L. from Gk *diakonos* 'servant' (in eccles. Gk 'Christian minister').

**deaconess** /ˌdiːkə'nɛs, 'diːk(ə)nɪs/ ● n. (in the early Church and some modern Churches) a woman with duties similar to those of a deacon.

**deactivate** ● v. make (technical equipment or a virus) inactive by disconnecting or destroying it.
– DERIVATIVES **deactivation** n. **deactivator** n.

**dead** ● adj. **1** no longer alive. ➤ devoid of living things. **2** (of a part of the body) numb. ➤ lacking emotion, sympathy, or sensitivity. **3** no longer relevant or important. **4** lacking activity or excitement. ➤ (of sound or a colour) dull. **5** (of equipment) not functioning. ➤ (of a glass or bottle) empty or no longer in use. ➤ (of the ball in a game) out of play. **6** complete; absolute: *dead silence*. ● adv. absolutely. ➤ exactly. ➤ straight; directly. ➤ Brit. informal very.
– PHRASES **dead and buried** over; finished. **dead in the water** (of a ship) unable to move. ➤ unable to function effectively. **the dead of night** the quietest, darkest part of the night. **the dead of winter** the coldest part of winter. **dead on one's feet** informal extremely tired. **dead to the world** informal fast asleep. **from the dead** from a state of death. **wouldn't be seen** (or **caught**) **dead in** (or **with**, **at**, etc.) informal have a strong dislike for.
– DERIVATIVES **deadness** n.
– ORIGIN OE *dēad*, of Gmc origin: rel. to Ger. *tot*, also to **DIE**[1].

**dead-ball line** ● n. **1** Rugby a line behind the goal line, beyond which the ball is out of play. **2** Soccer the byline.

**deadbeat** ● adj. **1** (**dead beat**) informal completely exhausted. **2** (of a mechanism) without recoil. ● n. informal **1** an idle or feckless person. **2** N. Amer. a person who tries to evade paying debts.

**deadbolt** ● n. a bolt engaged by turning a knob or key, rather than by spring action.

**dead centre** ● n. the position of a crank when it is in line with the connecting rod and not exerting torque.

**dead duck** ● n. informal an unsuccessful or useless person or thing.
– ORIGIN from the old saying 'never waste powder on a dead duck'.

**deaden** ● v. **1** make (a noise or sensation) less strong or intense. ➤ make insensitive. **2** deprive of force or vitality.
– DERIVATIVES **deadener** n. **deadening** adj.

**dead end** ● n. an end of a road or passage from which no exit is possible.

**deadeye** ● n. **1** Sailing a circular wooden block with a groove round the circumference to take a lanyard, used singly or in pairs to tighten a shroud. **2** informal, chiefly N. Amer. an expert marksman.

**deadfall** ● n. N. Amer. **1** a trap consisting of a heavy weight positioned to fall on an animal. **2** a mass of fallen trees and brush.

**dead hand** ● n. an undesirable persisting influence.

**deadhead** ● n. **1** chiefly Brit. a faded flower head. **2** informal a boring person. **3** chiefly N. Amer. a person with a free ticket. **4** a partially submerged log. ● v. **1** chiefly Brit. remove dead flower heads from (a plant). **2** N. Amer. informal drive or travel in an empty vehicle.

**dead heat** ● n. a race in which two or more competitors are exactly level. ● v. (**dead-heat**) run a dead heat.

**dead leg** ● n. an injury caused by a numbing blow to a person's upper leg. ● v. (**dead-leg**) informal give (someone) a dead leg.

**dead letter** ● n. **1** a law or treaty which has not been repealed but is defunct in practice. **2** a letter that has not been delivered or claimed.

**dead letter box** ● n. a place where messages can be left and collected without the sender and recipient meeting.

**dead lift** ● n. Weightlifting a lift made from a standing position, without the use of a bench.

**deadlight** ● n. **1** a protective cover fitted over a porthole or window on a ship. **2** US a skylight designed not to be opened.

**deadline** ● n. **1** the latest time or date by which something should be completed. **2** historical a line drawn around a prison beyond which prisoners were liable to be shot.

**dead load** ● n. the weight of a structure or vehicle, excluding that of passengers or goods.

**deadlock** ● n. **1** a situation in which no progress can be made. **2** Brit. a lock operated by a key, as distinct from a spring lock. ● v. **1** cause to come to a deadlock. **2** Brit. secure with a deadlock.

**dead loss** ● n. an unproductive or useless venture, person, or thing.

**deadly** ● adj. (**-ier, -iest**) **1** causing or able to cause death. ➤(of a voice, glance, etc.) filled with hate. **2** extremely accurate or effective. **3** informal extremely boring. **4** complete: *she was in deadly earnest.* ● adv. **1** in a way that resembles or suggests death. **2** extremely.
– DERIVATIVES **deadliness** n.

**deadly nightshade** ● n. a poisonous bushy plant with drooping purple flowers and black cherry-like fruit. [*Atropa belladonna.*]

**deadly sin** ● n. (in Christian tradition) a sin regarded as leading to damnation. See ***the seven deadly sins*** at **SEVEN**.

**dead man** ● n. **1** informal a bottle after the contents have been drunk. **2** (usu. **deadman**) an object secured to the ground to provide anchorage or leverage.

**dead man's fingers** ● pl. n. **1** a colonial soft coral with spongy lobes resembling the fingers of a corpse. [*Alcyonium digitatum.*] **2** a fungus that produces clumps of dull black fruiting bodies. [*Xylaria polymorpha.*] **3** informal the divisions of a lobster's or crab's gills.

**dead man's handle** (also **dead man's pedal**) ● n. (especially in a train) a safety lever which shuts off power when not held in place by the driver.

**dead march** ● n. a slow, solemn piece of music suitable for a funeral procession.

**dead-nettle** ● n. a plant of the mint family, with leaves that resemble those of a nettle without stinging hairs. [*Lamium album* and other species.]

**deadpan** ● adj. impassive or expressionless. ● adv. in a deadpan manner. ● v. (**-panned**, **-panning**) say something amusing while affecting a serious manner.

**dead reckoning** ● n. the process of calculating one's position, especially at sea, by estimating the direction and distance travelled.

**dead ringer** ● n. a person or thing closely resembling another.

**deadrise** ● n. the vertical distance between a line horizontal to the keel of a boat and its chine.

**dead set** ● n. see **SET**[2] (sense 2).

**dead shot** ● n. an extremely accurate marksman or markswoman.

**deadstock** ● n. the machinery used on a farm, as opposed to the livestock.

**dead time** ● n. Physics the period after the recording of a particle or pulse when a detector is unable to record another.

**dead water** ● n. still water without any current.

**deadweight** ● n. **1** the weight of an inert person or thing. ➤the total weight of cargo, stores, etc. which a ship can carry. ➤Farming animals sold by the estimated weight of saleable meat that they will yield. **2** Economics losses incurred because of the inefficient allocation of resources. ➤a debt not covered by assets.

**dead wood** ● n. useless or unproductive people or things.

**deaf** ● adj. without hearing or having impaired hearing. ➤(**deaf to**) unwilling to listen or respond to.
– PHRASES **fall on deaf ears** be ignored. **turn a deaf ear** refuse to listen or respond.
– DERIVATIVES **deafness** n.
– ORIGIN OE *dēaf*, of Gmc origin.

**deaf aid** ● n. Brit. a hearing aid.

**deaf-blind** ● adj. having severely impaired hearing and vision.

**deafen** ● v. cause to become deaf. ➤[as adj. **deafening**] extremely loud. ➤(**deafen someone to**) (of a sound) cause someone to be unaware of (other sounds).
– DERIVATIVES **deafeningly** adv.

**deaf mute** ● n. a person who is deaf and unable to speak.

**USAGE deaf mute**

In modern use **deaf mute** has acquired offensive connotations. It is advisable to avoid it in favour of other terms such as **profoundly deaf**.

**deal**[1] ● v. (past and past part. **dealt**) **1** distribute (cards) to players for a game or round. ➤(**deal someone in**) include a new player in a card game. **2** (**deal something out**) distribute or apportion something. **3** take part in commercial trading of a commodity. ➤informal buy and sell illegal drugs. ➤(**deal with**) have relations with in a commercial context. **4** (**deal with**) take measures concerning. ➤cope with. ➤have as a subject. **5** inflict (a blow) on. ● n. **1** an agreement entered into by two or more parties for their mutual benefit. ➤a particular form of treatment: *working mothers get a bad deal.* **2** the process of dealing cards in a card game.
– PHRASES **a big deal** informal [usu. with neg.] an important thing. ➤(**big deal**) used ironically to express contempt for something regarded as unimpressive. **a raw deal** informal unfair or harsh treatment. **a deal of** a large amount of. **a good** (or **great**) **deal** a large amount. ➤to a considerable extent: *a good deal better.* **a square deal** a fair bargain or treatment. **it's a deal** informal used to express assent to an agreement.
– DERIVATIVES **dealing** n.
– ORIGIN OE *dǣlan* 'divide', 'participate', of Gmc origin; rel. to **DOLE**[1].

**deal**[2] ● n. fir or pine wood (as a building material).
– ORIGIN ME: from Mid. Low Ger. and MDu. *dele* 'plank'.

**dealer** ● n. **1** a person who buys and sells goods. ➤a person who buys and sells shares or other financial assets as a principal (rather than as a broker or agent). **2** a player who deals cards in a card game.
– DERIVATIVES **dealership** n.

**dealfish** ● n. (pl. same or **-fishes**) a long slender silvery marine fish with a dorsal fin running the length of the body. [*Trachipterus arcticus.*]
– ORIGIN C19: from **DEAL**[2] in the sense 'board' (with ref. to its shape) + **FISH**[1].

**dealt** past participle of **DEAL**[1].

**deamination** /diːamɪˈneɪʃ(ə)n/ ● n. Biochemistry the removal of an amino group from an amino acid or other compound.
– DERIVATIVES **deaminated** adj.

**dean**[1] ● n. **1** the head of the chapter of a cathedral or collegiate church. ➤(also **rural dean**) Brit. a member of the clergy exercising supervision over a group of parochial clergy within a division of an archdeaconry. **2** the head of a university faculty or department or of a medical school. ➤a college official with a disciplinary role.
– DERIVATIVES **deanery** n.
– ORIGIN ME: from OFr. *deien*, from late L. *decanus* 'chief of a group of ten', from *decem* 'ten'; cf. **DOYEN**.

**dean**[2] ● n. variant spelling of **DENE**[1].

**dear** ● adj. **1** regarded with deep affection. ➤endearing; sweet. ➤used in the polite introduction to a letter. **2** expensive. ● n. used as an affectionate form of address. ➤an endearing person. ● adv. at a high cost. ● exclam. used in expressions of surprise, dismay, or sympathy.
– DERIVATIVES **dearness** n.
– ORIGIN OE *dēore*, of Gmc origin.

**dearest** ● adj. **1** most loved or cherished. **2** most expensive. ● n. used as an affectionate form of address.

**dearie** ● n. (pl. **-ies**) informal, chiefly Brit. used as a friendly or condescending form of address.

**Dear John letter** (also **Dear John**) ● n. informal a letter from a woman to a man, ending a personal relationship.

**dearly** ● adv. **1** very much. **2** at great cost.

**dearth** /dəːθ/ ● n. a scarcity or lack of something.
– ORIGIN ME *derthe* (see **DEAR**, **-TH**[2]).

**death** ● n. **1** the action or fact of dying or being killed. ➤an instance of a person or an animal dying. **2** the state of being dead. ➤(**Death**) the personification of the power that destroys life, often represented as a skeleton or an old man holding a scythe. **3** the destruction or end of something.

– PHRASES **as sure as death** quite certain. **at death's door** so ill that one may die. **be the death of someone** cause someone's death. **be in at the death** be present when a hunted animal is caught and killed. ➤be present when something fails or ends. **catch one's death (of cold)** informal catch a severe cold. **die a** (or **the**) **death** fail utterly or come to an end. **do someone to death** kill someone. **do something to death** repeat something so frequently that it becomes tedious. **like death warmed up** (or N. Amer. **over**) informal extremely tired or ill. **put someone to death** execute someone. **to death** until dead. ➤used to emphasize the extreme nature of a feeling or action: *I'm sick to death of you.*

– DERIVATIVES **deathless** adj. **deathlessness** n. **deathlike** adj.

– ORIGIN OE *dēath*, of Gmc origin; rel. to **DIE**[1].

**death adder** ● n. a venomous Australian snake with a thin worm-like tail that it uses to lure prey. [*Acanthophis antarcticus* and related species.]

**deathbed** ● n. the bed where someone is dying or has died.

**death camp** ● n. a prison camp, especially for political prisoners or prisoners of war, in which many die.

**death cap** ● n. a deadly poisonous toadstool with a pale olive-green cap and white gills, growing in broadleaved woodland. [*Amanita phalloides.*]

**death cell** ● n. a cell occupied by a prisoner condemned to death.

**death certificate** ● n. an official statement, signed by a doctor, of the cause, date, and place of a person's death.

**death duty** ● n. (in the UK) a tax levied on property after the owner's death. Now called **INHERITANCE TAX**.

**death futures** ● pl. n. US informal life insurance policies of terminally ill people, purchased by a third party as a form of short-term investment.

**death grant** ● n. historical (in the UK) a state grant towards funeral expenses.

**death knell** ● n. **1** the tolling of a bell to mark someone's death. **2** an event that heralds the end of something.

**deathly** ● adj. (**-ier**, **-iest**) resembling or suggestive of death. ➤archaic or poetic/literary of, relating to, or causing death.

**death mask** ● n. a plaster cast of a dead person's face, used to make a mask or model.

**death penalty** ● n. punishment by death.

**death rate** ● n. the number of deaths per one thousand people per year.

**death rattle** ● n. a gurgling sound in a dying person's throat.

**death row** ● n. a prison block or section for those sentenced to death.

**death's head** ● n. a human skull as a symbol of mortality.

**death's head hawkmoth** ● n. a large dark hawkmoth with a skull-like marking on the thorax and a very large caterpillar. [*Acherontia atropos.*]

**death tax** ● n. US term for **INHERITANCE TAX**.

**death toll** ● n. the number of deaths resulting from a particular cause.

**death trap** ● n. a thing that is potentially very dangerous.

**death warrant** ● n. an order for the execution of a condemned person.

**death-watch beetle** ● n. a small beetle whose larvae bore into and damage dead wood and structural timbers, making a sound like a watch ticking which was formerly believed to portend death. [*Xestobium rufovillosum.*]

**death wish** ● n. an unconscious desire for one's own or another's death.

**deb** ● n. informal short for **DEBUTANTE**.

**debacle** /deɪˈbɑːk(ə)l/ ● n. an utter failure or disaster.

– ORIGIN C19: from Fr. *débâcle*, from *débâcler* 'unleash', from *dé-* 'un-' + *bâcler* 'to bar' (from L. *baculum* 'staff').

**debag** /diːˈbag/ ● v. (**debagged**, **debagging**) Brit. informal remove the trousers of as a joke or punishment.

**debar** ● v. (**debarred**, **debarring**) exclude or prohibit from doing something.

– DERIVATIVES **debarment** n.

– ORIGIN ME: from Fr. *débarrer*, from OFr. *desbarrer* 'remove the bars from', from *des-* (expressing reversal) + *barrer* 'to bar'.

**debark**[1] ● v. leave a ship or aircraft.

– DERIVATIVES **debarkation** n.

– ORIGIN C17: from Fr. *débarquer.*

**debark**[2] ● v. remove (the bark) from a tree.

**debase** /dɪˈbeɪs/ ● v. **1** lower the quality, value, or character of. **2** historical lower the value of (coinage) by reducing the content of precious metal.

– DERIVATIVES **debasement** n. **debaser** n.

– ORIGIN C16: from **DE-** + the obs. v. *base* (cf. **ABASE**), expressing the notion 'bring down completely'.

**debatable** ● adj. open to discussion or argument.

– DERIVATIVES **debatably** adv.

**debate** ● n. a formal discussion in a public meeting or legislative assembly. ➤an argument, especially one involving many people. ● v. discuss or argue about. ➤consider; ponder.

– PHRASES **under debate** being discussed or disputed.

– DERIVATIVES **debater** n.

– ORIGIN ME: via OFr. from L. *dis-* (expressing reversal) + *battere* 'to fight'.

**debauch** /dɪˈbɔːtʃ/ ● v. destroy the moral purity of. ● n. a bout of excessive indulgence in sensual pleasures.

– DERIVATIVES **debauched** adj. **debaucher** n.

– ORIGIN C16: from Fr. *débaucher* (v.) 'turn away from one's duty', from OFr. *desbaucher*, of uncertain ultimate origin.

**debauchee** /ˌdɪbɔːˈtʃiː, -ˈʃiː/ ● n. a person given to debauchery.

**debauchery** ● n. excessive indulgence in sensual pleasures.

**debeak** ● v. remove the upper part of the beak of (a bird) to prevent it injuring other birds.

**debenture** /dɪˈbɛntʃə/ ● n. Brit. a long-term security yielding a fixed rate of interest, issued by a company and secured against assets. ➤(also **debenture bond**) N. Amer. an unsecured loan certificate issued by a company.

– ORIGIN ME: from L. *debentur* 'are owing' (from *debere* 'owe'), used as the first word of a certificate recording a debt.

**debilitate** /dɪˈbɪlɪteɪt/ ● v. [often as adj. **debilitating**] make very weak and infirm.

– DERIVATIVES **debilitatingly** adv. **debilitation** n. **debilitative** adj. **debility** n.

– ORIGIN C16: from L. *debilitat-*, *debilitare* 'weaken', from *debilitas*, from *debilis* 'weak'.

**debit** ● n. an entry in an account recording a sum owed. ➤a payment made or owed. ● v. (**debited**, **debiting**) (of a bank) remove (money) from a customer's account.

– ORIGIN ME: from Fr. *débit*, from L. *debitum* (see **DEBT**).

**debit card** ● n. a card allowing the holder to transfer money electronically from one bank account to another when making a purchase.

**debonair** ● adj. (of a man) confident, stylish, and charming.

– DERIVATIVES **debonairly** adv.

– ORIGIN ME: from OFr. *debonaire*, from *de bon aire* 'of good disposition'.

**debouch** /dɪˈbaʊtʃ, -ˈbuːʃ/ ● v. emerge from a confined space into a wide, open area.

– DERIVATIVES **debouchment** n.

– ORIGIN C18: from Fr. *déboucher*, from *dé-* (expressing removal) + *bouche* 'mouth' (from L. *bucca* 'cheek').

**debridement** /deɪˈbriːdmɒ̃, dɪˈbriːdm(ə)nt/ ● n. Medicine the removal of damaged tissue or foreign objects from a wound.

– ORIGIN C19: from Fr., from *débrider*, lit. 'unbridle', based on *bride* 'bridle' (of Gmc origin).

**debrief** ● v. question (someone, typically a soldier or spy) about a completed mission or undertaking.

– DERIVATIVES **debriefer** n. **debriefing** n.

**debris** /ˈdɛbriː, ˈdeɪbriː/ ● n. scattered rubbish or remains. ➤loose natural material, e.g. broken rocks.

– ORIGIN C18: from Fr. *débris*, from obs. *débriser* 'break down'.

**debruise** /dɪ'bru:z/ ● **v.** Heraldry partly obscure (another charge).

**debt** ● **n.** **1** money or services owed or due. **2** the state of owing money: *they are in debt.* ➤ a feeling of obligation or gratitude for a favour.

– PHRASES **be in someone's debt** owe gratitude to someone for a favour.

– ORIGIN ME *dette*: from OFr., based on L. *debitum* 'something owed', past part. of *debere* 'owe'.

**debt collector** ● **n.** a person who collects debts for creditors.

**debt of honour** ● **n.** a debt that is not legally recoverable, especially a sum lost in gambling.

**debtor** ● **n.** a person who owes money.

**debug** ● **v.** (**debugged**, **debugging**) **1** remove errors from (computer hardware or software). **2** detect and remove concealed microphones from. **3** N. Amer. remove insects from.

**debugger** ● **n.** a computer program for debugging other programs.

**debunk** ● **v.** **1** expose the falseness of (an idea or belief). **2** reduce the inflated reputation of (someone).

– DERIVATIVES **debunker** n.

**deburr** /di:'bə:/ (also **debur**) ● **v.** (**deburred**, **deburring**) neaten and smooth the rough edges or ridges of.

**debus** /di:'bʌs/ ● **v.** (**debussed**, **debussing**) Brit., chiefly military slang unload (something) or alight from a motor vehicle.

**debut** /'deɪbju:, -bu:/ ● **n.** a person's first appearance in a capacity or role. ➤ dated the first appearance of a debutante in society. ➤ [as modifier] denoting the first recording or publication of a singer or writer. ● **v.** make a debut.

– ORIGIN C18: from Fr. *début*, from *débuter* 'lead off'.

**debutant** /'dɛbju:tɒ̃, 'deɪ-/ ● **n.** a person making a debut.

**debutante** /'dɛbjʊtɑ:nt, 'deɪ-/ ● **n.** a young upper-class woman making her debut. ➤ a female debutant.

**debye** /də'bʌɪ/ ● **n.** Chemistry a unit of measurement used to express electric dipole moments of molecules, equal to $3.336 \times 10^{-30}$ coulomb metre.

– ORIGIN C20: named after the Dutch-born US physicist Peter *Debye*.

**Dec.** ● **abbrev.** December.

**dec.** ● **abbrev.** **1** deceased. **2** Cricket declared.

**deca-** /'dɛkə/ (also **dec-** before a vowel) ● **comb. form** ten; having ten: *decahedron.*

– ORIGIN from Gk *deka* 'ten'.

**decade** /'dɛkeɪd, dɪ'keɪd/ ● **n.** **1** a period of ten years. **2** a set or group of ten. ➤ a range of electrical resistances or other quantities spanning from one to ten times a base value.

– DERIVATIVES **decadal** adj.

– ORIGIN ME: via OFr. and late L. from Gk *deka* 'ten'.

**USAGE** decade

The second pronunciation, with the stress on **-cade** (sounds like **decayed**), is disapproved of by some traditionalists. However, it is now widely regarded as a standard alternative.

**decadence** /'dɛkəd(ə)ns/ ● **n.** **1** the process, period, or manifestation of moral or cultural decline. **2** luxurious self-indulgence.

– ORIGIN C16: from Fr. *décadence*, from med. L. *decadentia*; rel. to **DECAY**.

**decadent** ● **adj.** **1** characterized by or reflecting a state of moral or cultural decline. **2** luxuriously self-indulgent. ● **n.** a decadent person.

– DERIVATIVES **decadently** adv.

**decaf** /'di:kaf/ ● **n.** informal (trademark in the UK) decaffeinated coffee.

**decaffeinate** /di:'kafɪneɪt/ ● **v.** [usu. as adj. **decaffeinated**] remove most or all of the caffeine from (coffee or tea).

– DERIVATIVES **decaffeination** n.

**decagon** /'dɛkəg(ə)n/ ● **n.** a plane figure with ten straight sides and angles.

– DERIVATIVES **decagonal** adj.

– ORIGIN C17: via med. L. from Gk *dekagōnon*, neut. of *dekagōnos* 'ten-angled'.

**decahedron** /ˌdɛkə'hi:dr(ə)n, -'hɛd-/ ● **n.** (pl. **decahedra** or **decahedrons**) a solid figure with ten plane faces.

– DERIVATIVES **decahedral** adj.

– ORIGIN C19: from **DECA-** + **-HEDRON**.

**decal** /'di:kal/ ● **n.** chiefly N. Amer. a design on prepared paper for transferring on to glass, porcelain, etc.

– ORIGIN 1950s: abbrev. of **DECALCOMANIA**.

**decalcified** ● **adj.** (of rock or bone) containing a reduced quantity of calcium salts.

– DERIVATIVES **decalcification** n. **decalcifier** n.

**decalcomania** /dɪˌkalkə(ʊ)'meɪnɪə/ ● **n.** the process of transferring designs from prepared paper on to glass or porcelain.

– ORIGIN C19: from Fr. *décalcomanie*, from *décalquer* 'transfer a tracing' + *-manie* '-mania' (with ref. to the enthusiasm for the process in the 1860s).

**decalitre** (US **decaliter**, **dekaliter**) (abbrev.: **dal**; US also **dkl**) ● **n.** a metric unit of capacity, equal to 10 litres.

**Decalogue** /'dɛkəlɒg/ ● **n.** the Ten Commandments.

– ORIGIN ME: via Fr. and eccles. L. from Gk *dekalogos* (*biblos*) '(book of) the Ten Commandments', from *hoi deka logoi* 'the Ten Commandments'.

**decametre** (US **decameter**, **dekameter**) (abbrev.: **dam**; US also **dkm**) ● **n.** a metric unit of length, equal to 10 metres.

– DERIVATIVES **decametric** adj.

**decamp** ● **v.** **1** depart suddenly or secretly. **2** archaic break up or leave a military camp.

– DERIVATIVES **decampment** n.

– ORIGIN C17: from Fr. *décamper*, from *dé-* (expressing removal) + *camp* 'camp'.

**decanal** /dɪ'keɪn(ə)l, 'dɛk(ə)n(ə)l/ ● **adj.** **1** of or relating to a dean or deanery. **2** relating to or denoting the south side of the choir of a church, on which the dean sits. The opposite of **CANTORIAL**.

– ORIGIN C18: from med. L. *decanalis*, from late L. *decanus* (see **DEAN**[1]).

**decane** /'dɛkeɪn/ ● **n.** Chemistry a liquid hydrocarbon of the alkane series, present in petroleum spirit. [$C_{10}H_{22}$.]

– ORIGIN C19: from **DECA-** 'ten' (denoting ten carbon atoms) + **-ANE**[2].

**decani** /dɪ'keɪnʌɪ/ ● **n.** the section of a church choir conventionally placed on the south side and taking the first or higher part in antiphonal singing. The opposite of **CANTORIS**.

– ORIGIN C18: from L., lit. 'of the dean' (see **DEAN**[1]).

**decant** /dɪ'kant/ ● **v.** gradually pour from one container into another, typically in order to separate the liquid from the sediment.

– ORIGIN C17: from med. L. *decanthare*, from L. *de-* 'away from' + *canthus* 'edge, rim'.

**decanter** ● **n.** a stoppered glass container into which wine or spirit is decanted.

**decapitate** /dɪ'kapɪteɪt/ ● **v.** cut off the head of.

– DERIVATIVES **decapitation** n. **decapitator** n.

– ORIGIN C17: from late L. *decapitat-*, *decapitare* 'to decapitate', from *de-* + *caput*, *capit-* 'head'.

**Decapoda** /ˌdɛkə'pəʊdə/ ● **pl. n.** Zoology an order of crustaceans with five pairs of walking legs, including shrimps, crabs, and lobsters.

– DERIVATIVES **decapod** /'dɛkəpɒd/ n. & adj.

– ORIGIN mod. L., from **DECA-** + Gk *pous*, *pod-* 'foot'.

**decarbonize** (also **-ise**) ● **v.** remove carbon or carbonaceous deposits from.

– DERIVATIVES **decarbonization** n. **decarbonizer** n.

**decarboxylase** /ˌdi:kɑ:'bɒksɪleɪz/ ● **n.** Biochemistry an enzyme that catalyses the decarboxylation of a particular organic molecule.

**decarboxylate** /ˌdi:kɑ:'bɒksɪleɪt/ ● **v.** Chemistry eliminate a carboxylic acid group from (an organic compound).

– DERIVATIVES **decarboxylation** n.

**decarburize** /di:'kɑ:bjʊrʌɪz/ (also **-ise**) ● **v.** Metallurgy remove carbon from (iron or steel).

– DERIVATIVES **decarburization** n.

**decastyle** /ˈdɛkəstʌɪl/ ● **adj.** Architecture (of a temple or portico) having ten columns.
– ORIGIN C18: from Gk *dekastulos*, from *deka* 'ten' + *stulos* 'column'.

**decasyllabic** /ˌdɛkəsɪˈlabɪk/ ● **adj.** Prosody (of a metrical line) consisting of ten syllables.

**decathlon** /dɪˈkaθlɒn, -lən/ ● **n.** an athletic event in which each competitor takes part in the same ten events.
– DERIVATIVES **decathlete** n.
– ORIGIN C20: from **DECA-** + Gk *athlon* 'contest'.

**decay** ● **v. 1** rot or cause to rot through the action of bacteria and fungi; decompose. ➤deteriorate; decline in quality or vigour. **2** Physics (of a radioactive substance, particle, etc.) undergo change to a different form by emitting radiation. ● **n. 1** the state or process of decaying. **2** rotten matter or tissue.
– ORIGIN ME: from OFr. *decair*, based on L. *decidere* 'fall down or off', from *de-* 'from' + *cadere* 'fall'.

**decease** ● **n.** formal or Law death. ● **v.** archaic die.
– ORIGIN ME: from OFr. *deces*, from L. *decessus* 'death', past part. of *decedere* 'to die'.

**deceased** formal or Law ● **n.** (**the deceased**) the recently dead person in question. ● **adj.** recently dead.

**decedent** /dɪˈsiːd(ə)nt/ ● **n.** US Law a deceased person.
– ORIGIN C16: from L. *decedent-*, *decedere* (see **DECEASE**).

**deceit** ● **n.** the action or practice of deceiving. ➤a deceitful act or statement.
– ORIGIN ME: from OFr., past part. of *deceveir* 'deceive'.

**deceitful** ● **adj.** acting to deceive others.
– DERIVATIVES **deceitfully** adv. **deceitfulness** n.

**deceive** ● **v.** deliberately mislead or misrepresent the truth to. ➤(of a thing) give a mistaken impression: *the area may seem to offer nothing of interest, but don't be deceived.*
– DERIVATIVES **deceivable** adj. **deceiver** n.
– ORIGIN ME: from OFr. *deceivre*, from L. *decipere* 'ensnare, cheat'.

**decelerate** /diːˈsɛləreɪt/ ● **v.** begin to move more slowly.
– DERIVATIVES **deceleration** n. **decelerator** n.
– ORIGIN C19: from **DE-** + **ACCELERATE**.

**December** ● **n.** the twelfth month of the year.
– ORIGIN ME: from L., from *decem* 'ten' (being orig. the tenth month of the Roman year).

**decency** ● **n.** (pl. **-ies**) **1** decent behaviour. **2** (**decencies**) things required for a reasonable standard of living.

**decennial** /dɪˈsɛnɪəl/ ● **adj.** lasting for or recurring every ten years.
– DERIVATIVES **decennially** adv.
– ORIGIN C17: from L. *decennis* (from *decem* 'ten' + *annus* 'year'), + **-AL**.

**decent** ● **adj. 1** conforming with generally accepted standards of morality or respectability. **2** of an acceptable or appropriate standard; satisfactory. ➤Brit. informal obliging or generous: *that's very decent of you.*
– DERIVATIVES **decently** adv.
– ORIGIN C16: from L. *decent-*, *decere* 'to be fit'.

**decentralize** (also **-ise**) ● **v.** [often as adj. **decentralized**] transfer (authority) from central to local government. ➤disperse or divide (a large organization) into smaller separate units.
– DERIVATIVES **decentralist** n. & adj. **decentralization** n.

**decentre** (US **decenter**) ● **v.** displace from the centre or from a central position.

**deception** ● **n.** the action of deceiving. ➤a thing that deceives.
– ORIGIN ME: from late L. *deceptio(n-)*, from *decipere* 'deceive'.

**deceptive** ● **adj.** giving an appearance or impression different from the true one; misleading.
– DERIVATIVES **deceptively** adv. **deceptiveness** n.

**decerebrate** /diːˈsɛrɪbreɪt/ ● **adj.** Biology having had the cerebrum removed.
– DERIVATIVES **decerebration** n.

**deci-** ● **comb. form** one tenth: *decilitre*.
– ORIGIN from L. *decimus* 'tenth'.

**decibel** /ˈdɛsɪbɛl/ (abbrev.: **dB**) ● **n.** a unit of measurement expressing the intensity of a sound or the power of an electrical signal, equal to one tenth of a bel.

**decide** ● **v.** come to or cause to come to a resolution in the mind as a result of consideration. ➤resolve or settle (an issue or contest).
– DERIVATIVES **decidable** adj. **deciding** adj.
– ORIGIN ME: from Fr. *décider*, from L. *decidere* 'determine', from *de-* 'off' + *caedere* 'cut'.

**decided** ● **adj.** definite; unquestionable: *a decided improvement.* ➤(of a person) having clear opinions; resolute.
– DERIVATIVES **decidedly** adv. **decidedness** n.

**decider** ● **n.** a contest that settles the outcome of a series of contests.

**decidua** /dɪˈsɪdjʊə/ ● **n.** Physiology a thick layer of modified mucous membrane which lines the uterus during pregnancy and is shed with the afterbirth.
– DERIVATIVES **decidual** adj.
– ORIGIN C18: from mod. L. *decidua* (*membrana*), lit. 'falling off (membrane)'.

**deciduous** /dɪˈsɪdjʊəs/ ● **adj. 1** (of a tree or shrub) shedding its leaves annually. Often contrasted with **EVERGREEN**. **2** denoting the milk teeth of a mammal, which are shed after a time.
– DERIVATIVES **deciduously** adv. **deciduousness** n.
– ORIGIN C17: from L. *deciduus* (from *decidere* 'fall down or off') + **-OUS**.

**decile** /ˈdɛsʌɪl/ ● **n.** Statistics each of ten equal groups into which a population can be divided according to the distribution of values of a particular variable.
– ORIGIN C17: from Fr. *décile*, from L. *decem* 'ten'.

**decilitre** (US **-liter**) (abbrev.: **dl**) ● **n.** a metric unit of capacity, equal to one tenth of a litre.

**decimal** ● **adj.** relating to or denoting a system of numbers and arithmetic based on the number ten, tenth parts, and powers of ten. ● **n.** a fraction whose denominator is a power of ten and whose numerator is expressed by figures placed to the right of a decimal point. ➤a system of decimal numerical notation.
– DERIVATIVES **decimalization** (also **-isation**) n. **decimalize** (also **-ise**) v. **decimally** adv.
– ORIGIN C17: from mod. L. *decimalis* (adj.), from L. *decimus* 'tenth'.

**decimal place** ● **n.** the position of a digit to the right of a decimal point.

**decimal point** ● **n.** a full point or dot placed after the figure representing units in a decimal fraction.

**decimate** /ˈdɛsɪmeɪt/ ● **v. 1** kill or destroy a large proportion of. ➤drastically reduce the strength of. **2** (in ancient Rome) kill one in every ten of (a group of soldiers) as a punishment for the mutiny of the whole group.
– DERIVATIVES **decimation** n. **decimator** n.
– ORIGIN ME: from L. *decimat-*, *decimare* 'take as a tenth', from *decimus* 'tenth'.

**USAGE decimate**

The earliest sense of **decimate**, 'kill one in every ten of', has been more or less totally superseded by the more general sense 'kill or destroy (a large proportion of)'. Some traditionalists argue that this later sense is incorrect, but it is clear that this is now part of standard English.

**decimetre** (US **-meter**) (abbrev.: **dm**) ● **n.** a metric unit of length, equal to one tenth of a metre.
– DERIVATIVES **decimetric** adj.

**decipher** /dɪˈsʌɪfə/ ● **v.** convert from code into normal language. ➤succeed in understanding or interpreting (something obscure or unclear).
– DERIVATIVES **decipherable** adj. **decipherment** n.

**decision** ● **n. 1** a conclusion or resolution reached after consideration. ➤the action or process of deciding. **2** the quality of being decisive; resoluteness.
– ORIGIN ME: from L. *decisio(n-)*, from *decidere* (see **DECIDE**).

**decision theory** ● **n.** the mathematical study of strategies for optimal decision-making between options involving different risks or expectations of gain or loss depending on the outcome. Compare with **GAME THEORY.**

**decisive** • adj. acting to settle an issue quickly and effectively. ➤ tending or able to make decisions quickly.
– DERIVATIVES **decisively** adv. **decisiveness** n.

**deck** • n. 1 a floor of a ship, especially the upper, open level. ➤ a similar floor or platform, as in a bus or car park. ➤ (**the deck**) informal the ground or floor: *there was a big thud when I hit the deck.* 2 a component or unit in sound-reproduction equipment that incorporates a playing or recording mechanism for discs or tapes. 3 chiefly N. Amer. a pack of cards. ➤ N. Amer. informal a packet of narcotics. • v. 1 (usu. **be decked out**) decorate or dress brightly or festively. 2 informal knock to the ground with a punch.
– DERIVATIVES **-decked** adj.
– ORIGIN ME (orig. denoting a canvas covering, especially on a ship, later a solid surface serving as roof and floor): from MDu. *dec* 'covering, roof', *dekken* 'to cover'.

**deckchair** • n. a folding chair with a frame of wood and a suspended seat of canvas.

**-decker** • comb. form having a specified number of decks or layers: *double-decker.*

**deckhand** • n. a member of a ship's crew whose duties include cleaning, mooring, and cargo handling.

**deckhead** • n. the underside of the deck of a ship.

**decking** • n. material used in making a deck.

**deckle** /ˈdɛk(ə)l/ • n. a continuous belt on either side in a papermaking machine, used for controlling the size of paper produced.
– ORIGIN C18: from Ger. *Deckel*, dimin. of *Decke* 'covering'.

**deckle edge** • n. the rough uncut edge of a sheet of paper, formed by a deckle.
– DERIVATIVES **deckle-edged** adj.

**declaim** • v. utter or deliver words or a speech in a rhetorical or impassioned way.
– DERIVATIVES **declaimer** n. **declamatory** adj.
– ORIGIN ME: from Fr. *déclamer* or L. *declamare*, from *de-* (expressing thoroughness) + *clamare* 'to shout'.

**declamation** • n. the action or art of declaiming. ➤ a rhetorical exercise or set speech.

**declarant** /dɪˈklɛːr(ə)nt/ • n. chiefly Law a person or party who makes a formal declaration.

**declaration** • n. 1 a formal or explicit statement or announcement. ➤ (also **declaration of the poll**) Brit. a public official announcement of the votes cast for candidates in an election. ➤ Law a plaintiff's statement of claims in proceedings. 2 Law an affirmation made instead of taking an oath. 3 an act or instance of declaring.

**declarative** /dɪˈklarətɪv/ • adj. of the nature of or making a declaration. ➤ Grammar (of a sentence or phrase) taking the form of a simple statement.
– DERIVATIVES **declaratively** adv.

**declare** • v. 1 announce solemnly or officially; make clearly known. ➤ (**declare for/against**) openly align oneself for or against (a party or position). 2 (**declare oneself**) reveal one's intentions or identity. ➤ express feelings of love to someone. 3 announce oneself as a candidate for an election. 4 acknowledge possession of (taxable income or dutiable goods). 5 Cricket close an innings voluntarily before all the wickets have fallen. 6 announce that one holds (certain combinations of cards) in a card game.
– DERIVATIVES **declarable** adj. **declaratory** adj. **declared** adj. **declaredly** adv.
– ORIGIN ME: from L. *declarare*, from *de-* 'thoroughly' + *clarare* 'make clear' (from *clarus* 'clear').

**declarer** • n. Bridge the player whose bid establishes the suit of the contract.

**déclassé** /deɪˈklaseɪ/ (also **déclassée**) • adj. having fallen in social status: *his parents were poor and déclassé.*
– ORIGIN C19: Fr., past part. of *déclasser.*

**declassify** • v. (-ies, -ied) (often **be declassified**) officially declare (information or documents) to be no longer secret.
– DERIVATIVES **declassification** n.

**declension** /dɪˈklɛnʃ(ə)n/ • n. 1 the variation of the form of a noun, pronoun, or adjective, by which its grammatical case, number, and gender are identified. ➤ the class to which a noun or adjective is assigned according to this variation. 2 poetic/literary a condition of decline or moral deterioration.
– DERIVATIVES **declensional** adj.
– ORIGIN ME *declinson*, from OFr. *declinaison*, from *decliner* 'to decline'.

**declination** /ˌdɛklɪˈneɪʃ(ə)n/ • n. 1 Astronomy the angular distance of a point north or south of the celestial equator. ➤ the angular deviation of a compass needle from true north. 2 US formal refusal.
– DERIVATIVES **declinational** adj.

**decline** • v. 1 become smaller, fewer, or less; decrease. ➤ diminish in strength or quality; deteriorate. 2 politely refuse: *the company declined to comment.* 3 (especially of the sun) move downwards. 4 Grammar state the forms of (a noun, pronoun, or adjective) corresponding to cases, number, and gender. • n. 1 a gradual and continuous loss of strength, numbers, or value. 2 archaic a disease in which the bodily strength gradually fails, especially tuberculosis.
– DERIVATIVES **declinable** adj. **decliner** n. **declining** adj.
– ORIGIN ME: from OFr. *decliner*, from L. *declinare* 'bend down, turn aside', from *de-* 'down' + *clinare* 'to bend'.

**declivity** /dɪˈklɪvɪti/ • n. (pl. **-ies**) a downward slope.
– DERIVATIVES **declivitous** adj.
– ORIGIN C17: from L. *declivitas*, from *declivis* 'sloping down', from *de-* 'down' + *clivus* 'a slope'.

**declutch** • v. disengage the clutch of a motor vehicle.

**decoct** /dɪˈkɒkt/ • v. archaic extract the essence from (something) by heating or boiling it.
– ORIGIN ME: from L. *decoct-*, *decoquere* 'boil down', from *de-* 'down' + *coquere* 'cook'.

**decoction** • n. a liquor containing the concentrated essence of a substance, produced as a result of heating or boiling, especially as used in medicinal and herbal preparations.

**decode** • v. convert (a coded message) into intelligible language. ➤ convert (audio or video signals), in particular from digital to analogue.
– DERIVATIVES **decodable** adj. **decoder** n.

**decoke** /diːˈkəʊk/ • v. Brit. informal remove carbon or carbonaceous material from.

**decollement** /deɪˈkɒlmɔ̃/ • n. Geology a process in which some strata become partly detached from those underneath and slide over them, causing folding and deformation.
– ORIGIN C19: from Fr., from *décoller* 'unstick'.

**décolletage** /ˌdeɪkɒlˈtɑːʒ/ • n. a low neckline on a woman's dress or top.
– ORIGIN C19: Fr., from *décolleter* 'expose the neck'.

**décolleté** /deɪˈkɒlteɪ/ • adj. (also **décolletée**) having a low neckline. • n. a décolletage.
– ORIGIN C19: Fr., past part. of *décolleter* 'expose the neck'.

**decolonize** (also **-ise**) • v. withdraw from (a colony), leaving it independent.
– DERIVATIVES **decolonization** n.

**decolorize** (also **decolourize** or **-ise**) • v. remove the colour from.
– DERIVATIVES **decolorization** n.

**decommission** • v. 1 take (a ship) out of service. 2 dismantle and make safe (a nuclear reactor or weapon).

**decompensation** • n. Medicine the failure of an organ (especially the liver or heart) to compensate for the functional overload resulting from disease.
– DERIVATIVES **decompensated** adj.

**decompose** • v. 1 (of organic matter) decay; become rotten. 2 break down or cause to break down into component elements. 3 Mathematics express (a number or function) as a combination of simpler components.
– DERIVATIVES **decomposable** adj. **decomposer** n. **decomposition** n.

**decompress** /ˌdiːkəmˈprɛs/ • v. 1 expand (compressed computer data) to its normal size. 2 subject (a diver) to decompression. 3 N. Amer. informal calm down and relax.
– DERIVATIVES **decompressor** n.

**decompression** • n. 1 reduction in air pressure. ➤ a gradual reduction of air pressure on a person who has been experiencing high pressure while diving. **2** the process of expanding computer data to its normal size.

**decompression chamber** • n. a small room in which the air pressure can be varied, used to allow deep-sea divers to adjust to normal air pressure.

**decompression sickness** • n. a condition that results when too rapid decompression causes nitrogen bubbles to form in the tissues of the body, characterized by pain in the muscles and joints, cramp, numbness, nausea, and paralysis.

**decondition** • v. **1** [usu. as adj. **deconditioned**] cause to lose fitness or muscle tone. **2** Psychiatry reform or reverse (a person's behaviour), especially in the treatment of phobia.
– DERIVATIVES **deconditioning** n.

**decongest** • v. relieve the congestion of.
– DERIVATIVES **decongestion** n.

**decongestant** • adj. (chiefly of a medicine) used to relieve nasal congestion. • n. a decongestant medicine.

**deconsecrate** • v. transfer (a building) from sacred to secular use.
– DERIVATIVES **deconsecration** n.

**deconstruct** /ˌdiːk(ə)nˈstrʌkt/ • v. **1** analyse (a text, conceptual system, etc.) by deconstruction. **2** dismantle and expose the workings of: *social forms will have to be deconstructed before socialism can develop.*
– DERIVATIVES **deconstructive** adj.

**deconstruction** • n. a method of critical analysis of philosophical and literary language which emphasizes the internal workings of language and conceptual systems, the relational quality of meaning, and the assumptions implicit in forms of expression.
– DERIVATIVES **deconstructionism** n. **deconstructionist** adj. & n.

**decontaminate** • v. remove dangerous substances from.
– DERIVATIVES **decontamination** n.

**decontextualize** (also **-ise**) • v. consider in isolation from its context.
– DERIVATIVES **decontextualization** n.

**decontrol** • v. (**decontrolled**, **decontrolling**) release (a commodity, market, etc.) from controls or restrictions. • n. the action of decontrolling.

**deconvolution** • n. a process of resolving something mathematically or conceptually into its constituent parts.

**decor** /ˈdeɪkɔː, ˈdɛ-/ • n. **1** the furnishing and decoration of a room. **2** stage scenery.
– ORIGIN C19: from Fr. *décor*, from *décorer*, from L. *decorare* (see DECORATE).

**decorate** • v. **1** add ornament to. ➤ apply paint or wallpaper to. **2** confer an award or medal on.
– ORIGIN C16: from L. *decoratus* 'embellished', from *decus, decor-* 'honour or embellishment'.

**Decorated** • adj. denoting a stage of English Gothic church architecture typical of the 14th century, characterized by geometrical, curvilinear, and reticulated tracery.

**decoration** • n. **1** the process or art of decorating. **2** ornamentation. ➤ a thing that serves as an ornament. **3** a medal or award conferred as an honour.

**Decoration Day** • n. US another term for MEMORIAL DAY.

**decorative** /ˈdɛk(ə)rətɪv/ • adj. serving to make something look more attractive; ornamental. ➤ relating to decoration.
– DERIVATIVES **decoratively** adv. **decorativeness** n.

**decorator** • n. a person who decorates. ➤ chiefly Brit. a person whose job is to decorate the interior of buildings by painting the walls or hanging wallpaper.

**decorous** /ˈdɛk(ə)rəs/ • adj. in keeping with good taste and propriety; polite and restrained.
– DERIVATIVES **decorously** adv. **decorousness** n.
– ORIGIN C17: from L. *decorus* 'seemly' + **-ous**.

**decorticate** /diːˈkɔːtɪkeɪt/ • v. **1** [often as adj. **decorticated**] technical remove the bark, rind, or husk from. **2** remove the cortex from (an organ).
– DERIVATIVES **decortication** n.
– ORIGIN C17: from L. *decorticat-*, *decorticare* 'to strip of bark'.

**decorum** /dɪˈkɔːrəm/ • n. behaviour in keeping with good taste and propriety. ➤ prescribed behaviour; etiquette.
– ORIGIN C16: from L., neut. of the adjective *decorus* 'seemly'.

**découpage** /ˌdeɪkuːˈpɑːʒ, dɪˈkuːpɑːʒ, ˈdɛkuːpɑːʒ/ • n. the decoration of the surface of an object with paper cut-outs.
– ORIGIN 1960s: Fr., from *découper* 'cut out'.

**decouple** • v. separate or disengage one thing from another.

**decoy** • n. /ˈdiːkɔɪ, dɪˈkɔɪ/ **1** a bird or mammal, or an imitation of one, used to lure game. **2** a person or thing used to mislead or lure someone into a trap. **3** a pond from which narrow netted channels lead, into which wild duck may be enticed for capture. • v. /dɪˈkɔɪ, ˈdiːkɔɪ/ lure by means of a decoy.
– ORIGIN C16 (earlier as *coy*): from Du. *de kooi* 'the decoy', from MDu. *de kouw* 'the cage', from L. *cavea* 'cage'.

**decrease** • v. /dɪˈkriːs/ make or become smaller or fewer in size, amount, intensity, or degree. • n. /ˈdiːkriːs/ an instance or example of decreasing. ➤ the action or process of decreasing.
– DERIVATIVES **decreasing** adj. **decreasingly** adv.
– ORIGIN ME: from OFr. *decreis* (n.), *decreistre* (v.), based on L. *decrescere*, from *de-* 'down' + *crescere* 'grow'.

**decree** • n. an official order issued by a ruler or authority that has the force of law. ➤ a judgement or decision of certain law courts. • v. (**decrees**, **decreed**, **decreeing**) order by decree: *the government decreed a ban on contact with the guerrillas.*
– ORIGIN ME: from OFr. *decre*, *decret*, from L. *decretum* 'something decided', from *decernere* 'decide'.

**decree absolute** • n. (pl. **decrees absolute**) English Law a final order by a court of law which officially ends a marriage.

**decree nisi** • n. (pl. **decrees nisi**) English Law an order by a court of law that states the date on which a marriage will end, unless a good reason to prevent a divorce is produced.
– ORIGIN C19: L. *nisi* 'unless'.

**decrement** /ˈdɛkrɪm(ə)nt/ • n. **1** a reduction or diminution. **2** Physics the ratio of the amplitudes in successive cycles of a damped oscillation. • v. chiefly Computing cause a discrete reduction in (a numerical quantity).
– ORIGIN C17: from L. *decrementum* 'diminution', from *decrescere* 'to decrease'.

**decrepit** /dɪˈkrɛpɪt/ • adj. elderly and infirm. ➤ worn out or ruined because of age or neglect.
– DERIVATIVES **decrepitude** n.
– ORIGIN ME: from L. *decrepitus*, from *de-* 'down' + *crepitus*, past part. of *crepare* 'rattle, creak'.

**decrepitate** /dɪˈkrɛpɪteɪt/ • v. technical (of a solid) disintegrate audibly when heated.
– DERIVATIVES **decrepitation** n.
– ORIGIN C17: from **DE-** + L. *crepitat-*, *crepitare* 'to crackle', frequentative of *crepare* (see DECREPIT).

**decrescendo** /ˌdiːkrɪˈʃɛndəʊ/ • adv. & adj. another term for DIMINUENDO.
– ORIGIN C19: Ital., lit. 'decreasing'.

**decrescent** /dɪˈkrɛs(ə)nt/ • adj. (of the moon) waning.
– ORIGIN C17: from L. *decrescent-*, *decrescere* (see DECREASE).

**decretal** /dɪˈkriːt(ə)l/ • n. a papal decree concerning a point of canon law. • adj. of the nature of a decree.
– ORIGIN ME: from late L. *decretale*, neut. of *decretalis* (adj.), from L. *decret-*, *decernere* 'to decide'.

**decriminalize** (also **-ise**) • v. cease to treat as illegal.
– DERIVATIVES **decriminalization** n.

**decry** /dɪˈkrʌɪ/ • v. (**-ies**, **-ied**) publicly denounce.
– DERIVATIVES **decrier** n.
– ORIGIN C17 (in the sense 'decrease the value of coins by royal proclamation'): from **DE-** + **CRY**, on the pattern of Fr. *décrier* 'cry down'.

**decrypt** /diːˈkrɪpt/ ● v. make (a coded or unclear message) intelligible.
– DERIVATIVES **decryption** n.
– ORIGIN 1930s: from **DE-** + *crypt* as in *encrypt*.

**decubitus** /dɪˈkjuːbɪtəs/ ● n. chiefly Medicine the posture adopted by a person who is lying down.
– ORIGIN C19: mod. L., from L. *decumbere* 'lie down'.

**decumbent** /dɪˈkʌmb(ə)nt/ ● adj. Botany (of a plant stem) lying along the ground, with the extremity upturned.
– ORIGIN C18: from L. *decumbent-*, *decumbere* 'lie down'.

**decurrent** /dɪˈkʌr(ə)nt/ ● adj. Botany extending down the stem below the point of attachment. ➤(of a tree) having several roughly equal branches.
– ORIGIN C18: from L. *decurrent-*, *decurrere* 'to run down'.

**decurved** ● adj. Biology (especially of a bird's bill) curved downwards.

**decussate** technical ● v. /dɪˈkʌseɪt, ˈdɛkəseɪt/ (of two or more things) cross or intersect. ● adj. /dɪˈkʌsət/ shaped like an X. ➤Botany (of leaves) arranged in opposite pairs.
– DERIVATIVES **decussation** n.
– ORIGIN C17: from L. *decussatus*, past part. of *decussare* 'divide crosswise', from *decussis* (describing the figure X, i.e. the Roman numeral for the number 10), from *decem* 'ten'.

**decyl** /ˈdɪsʌɪl, -sɪl/ ● n. [as modifier] Chemistry of or denoting an alkyl radical $-C_{10}H_{21}$, derived from decane.

**dedendum** /dɪˈdɛndəm/ ● n. Engineering the radial distance from the pitch circle of a cogwheel or wormwheel to the bottom of the tooth space or groove. Compare with **ADDENDUM**.
– ORIGIN C20: from L., 'thing that can be surrendered', neut. gerundive of *dedere*.

**dedicate** ● v. **1** devote to a particular subject, task, or purpose: *Joan has dedicated her life to animals.* **2** address (a book) to a particular person, as a sign of respect or affection. ➤ceremonially assign (a church or other building) to a deity or saint.
– DERIVATIVES **dedicatee** n. **dedicator** n. **dedicatory** adj.
– ORIGIN ME: from L. *dedicat-*, *dedicare* 'to devote or consecrate'.

**dedicated** ● adj. **1** devoted to a task or purpose. **2** exclusively assigned or allocated for a particular purpose: *a dedicated high-speed rail link.*
– DERIVATIVES **dedicatedly** adv.

**dedication** ● n. **1** the quality of being dedicated. **2** the action of dedicating. ➤an inscription dedicating a building. ➤the words with which a book is dedicated.

**deduce** ● v. **1** arrive at (a fact or a conclusion) by reasoning. **2** archaic trace the course or derivation of.
– DERIVATIVES **deducible** adj.
– ORIGIN ME: from L. *deducere*, from *de-* 'down' + *ducere* 'lead'.

**deduct** ● v. subtract or take away from a total.
– ORIGIN ME: from L. *deduct-*, *deducere* 'to take or lead away'.

**deductible** ● adj. able to be deducted, especially from taxable income. ● n. chiefly N. Amer. the part of an insurance claim to be paid by the insured; an excess.
– DERIVATIVES **deductibility** n.

**deduction** ● n. **1** the action of deducting: *paid without deduction of tax.* ➤an amount that is or may be deducted. **2** the inference of particular instances by reference to a general law or principle. Often contrasted with **INDUCTION**. ➤a conclusion that has been deduced.
– DERIVATIVES **deductive** adj. **deductively** adv.

**deed** ● n. **1** an action that is performed intentionally or consciously. **2** (usu. **deeds**) a legal document, especially one relating to property ownership or legal rights. ● v. N. Amer. convey or transfer by legal deed.
– ORIGIN OE *dēd*, *dǣd*, of Gmc origin.

**deed of covenant** ● n. Brit. an agreement to pay a regular amount of money, particularly when this enables the recipient (typically a charity) to reclaim any tax paid by the donor on the amount.

**deed poll** ● n. English Law a legal deed made and executed by one party only, especially to formalize a change of a person's name.
– ORIGIN C16: so named because the parchment was 'polled' or cut even, not indented as in the case of a deed made by two parties.

**deejay** ● n. informal a disc jockey.
– ORIGIN 1950s: representing the pron. of the initials *DJ*.

**deem** ● v. formal regard or consider in a specified way: *the event was deemed a great success.*
– ORIGIN OE *dēman*, of Gmc origin.

**deemster** /ˈdiːmstə/ ● n. a judge (of whom there are two) in the Isle of Man judiciary.
– ORIGIN ME: from **DEEM** + **-STER**.

**de-energize** (also **-ise**) ● v. disconnect (an electric circuit) from a power supply.

**deep** ● adj. **1** extending far down or in from the top or surface. ➤extending a specified distance from the top, surface, or outer edge. ➤Cricket (of a fielding position) relatively distant from the batsman. ➤(in ball games) to or from a position far down or across the field. **2** very intense, profound, or extreme. ➤difficult to understand. **3** (of sound) low in pitch and full in tone; not shrill. **4** (of colour) dark and intense. ● n. **1** (**the deep**) poetic/literary the sea. **2** (usu. **deeps**) a deep part of something, especially the sea. ➤(**the deep**) Cricket the part of the field distant from the batsman. ● adv. far down or in; deeply. ➤(in sport) distant from the batsman or forward line of one's team.
– PHRASES **go off** (or **go in off**) **the deep end** informal give way immediately to an emotional or irrational outburst. **in deep water** informal in trouble or difficulty. **jump** (or **be thrown**) **in at the deep end** informal face a difficult problem or undertaking with little experience.
– DERIVATIVES **deeply** adv. **deepness** n.
– ORIGIN OE *dēop* (adj.), *dīope*, *dēope* (adv.), of Gmc origin; rel. to **DIP**.

**deep-bodied** ● adj. (of an animal, especially a fish) having a body which is deeper (from back to belly) than it is wide.

**deep-discount** ● adj. denoting financial securities carrying a low rate of interest and issued at a discount to their redemption value, so mainly providing capital gain rather than income. ➤N. Amer. heavily discounted.

**deep-dish** ● adj. chiefly N. Amer. **1** (of a pie or pizza) baked in a deep dish. **2** informal extreme or thoroughgoing: *deep-dish conservatism.*

**deep-dyed** ● adj. informal thoroughgoing; complete.

**deepen** ● v. make or become deep or deeper.

**deep freeze** ● n. (also **deep freezer**) a freezer. ● v. (**deep-freeze**) store in or freeze using a deep freeze.

**deep-fry** ● v. [usu. as adj. **deep-fried**] fry (food) in an amount of fat or oil sufficient to cover it completely.

**deep-rooted** ● adj. firmly established.
– DERIVATIVES **deep-rootedness** n.

**deep-seated** ● adj. firmly established.

**deep-set** ● adj. embedded or positioned firmly or deeply.

**deep-six** ● v. N. Amer. informal get rid of; destroy utterly.
– ORIGIN 1920s (as *the deep six* 'the grave'): perh. from the custom of burial at sea at a depth of six fathoms.

**deep space** ● n. another term for **OUTER SPACE**.

**deep structure** ● n. (in transformational grammar) the underlying logical relationships of the elements of a phrase or sentence. Contrasted with **SURFACE STRUCTURE**.

**deep-vein thrombosis** ● n. thrombosis in a vein lying deep below the skin, especially in the legs.

**deer** ● n. (pl. same) a hoofed grazing or browsing animal, with branched bony antlers that are shed annually (and typically born only by the male). [Family Cervidae: many species.]
– ORIGIN OE *dēor*, also orig. denoting any quadruped, used in the phr. *small deer* meaning 'small creatures collectively'; of Gmc origin.

**deer fly** ● n. **1** a bloodsucking louse fly which is a parasite of deer. [*Lipoptena cervi*.] **2** a bloodsucking horsefly which attacks large mammals and can transmit various diseases. [Genus *Chrysops*.]

**deergrass** ● n. a small sedge related to cotton grass, growing in tufts on wet moors and bogs. [*Trichophorum cespitosum* (or *Scirpus cespitosus*).]

**deerhound** • **n.** a large dog of a rough-haired breed, resembling the greyhound.

**deer mouse** • **n.** a mainly nocturnal mouse found in North and Central America. [*Peromyscus maniculatus* and related species.]

**deerskin** • **n.** leather made from the skin of a deer.

**deerstalker** • **n. 1** a soft cloth cap, originally worn for hunting, with peaks in front and behind and ear flaps which can be tied together over the top. **2** a person who stalks deer.

**de-escalate** • **v.** reduce the intensity of (a conflict or crisis).
– DERIVATIVES **de-escalation** n.

**def** • **adj.** chiefly black slang excellent.
– ORIGIN 1980s: prob. an alt. of **DEATH** (used in Jamaican Engl. as an intensifier), or shortened from **DEFINITIVE** or **DEFINITE**.

**deface** • **v.** spoil the surface or appearance of.
– DERIVATIVES **defacement** n. **defacer** n.
– ORIGIN ME: from OFr. *desfacier.*

**de facto** /deɪ ˈfaktəʊ, diː/ • **adv.** in fact, whether by right or not. Often contrasted with **DE JURE**. • **adj.** existing in fact: *a de facto one-party system.*
– ORIGIN L., lit. 'of fact'.

**defalcate** /ˈdiːfalˌkeɪt/ • **v.** formal embezzle (funds).
– DERIVATIVES **defalcation** n. **defalcator** n.
– ORIGIN C16 (in the sense 'deduct, subtract'): from med. L. *defalcat-*, *defalcare* 'to lop'.

**defame** • **v.** damage the good reputation of.
– DERIVATIVES **defamation** n. **defamatory** adj. **defamer** n.
– ORIGIN ME: from OFr. *diffamer*, from L. *diffamare* 'spread evil report', from *dis-* (expressing removal) + *fama* 'report'.

**defang** • **v.** render harmless or ineffectual.

**default** • **n. 1** failure to fulfil an obligation, especially to repay a loan or appear in a law court. **2** a pre-selected option adopted by a computer program or other mechanism when no alternative is specified. • **v. 1** fail to fulfil an obligation, especially to repay a loan or to appear in a law court: *some had defaulted on student loans.* ➤ declare (a party) in default and give judgement against that party. **2** (**default to**) revert automatically to (a pre-selected option).
– PHRASES **by default** because of a lack of opposition or positive action: *he became an actor by default.* **go by default** be decided in favour of one party because of lack of opposition by the other party. **in default** guilty of default. **in default of** in the absence of.
– ORIGIN ME: from OFr. *defaut*, from *defaillir* 'to fail', based on L. *fallere* 'disappoint, deceive'.

**defaulter** • **n.** a person who defaults. ➤ chiefly Brit. a member of the armed forces guilty of a military offence.

**defeasance** /dɪˈfiːz(ə)ns/ • **n.** Law the action or process of rendering something null and void.
– ORIGIN ME: from OFr., from *defaire*, *desfaire* (see **DEFEAT**).

**defeasible** /dɪˈfiːzɪb(ə)l/ • **adj.** chiefly Law & Philosophy open in principle to revision, valid objection, forfeiture, or annulment.
– DERIVATIVES **defeasibility** n. **defeasibly** adv.

**defeat** • **v. 1** win a victory over. **2** prevent (an aim) from being achieved: *this defeats the object of the exercise.* ➤ thwart or frustrate. ➤ Law render null and void. • **n.** an instance of defeating or being defeated.
– DERIVATIVES **defeated** adj. **defeatedly** adv.
– ORIGIN ME: from OFr. *desfait* 'undone', past part. of *desfaire*, from med. L. *disfacere* 'undo'.

**defeatist** • **n.** a person who gives in to failure too readily. • **adj.** showing ready acceptance of failure.
– DERIVATIVES **defeatism** n.

**defecate** /ˈdɛfɪkeɪt, ˈdiːf-/ • **v.** discharge faeces from the body.
– DERIVATIVES **defecation** n. **defecator** n. **defecatory** adj.
– ORIGIN ME (orig. in the sense 'clear of dregs, purify'): from L. *defaecat-*, *defaecare*, from *de-* + *faex*, *faec-* 'dregs'.

**defect**[1] • **n.** /ˈdiːfɛkt, dɪˈfɛkt/ a shortcoming, imperfection, or lack.
– ORIGIN ME: from L. *defectus*, past part. of *deficere* 'desert or fail', from *de-* (expressing reversal) + *facere* 'do'.

**defect**[2] /dɪˈfɛkt/ • **v.** abandon one's country or cause in favour of an opposing one.
– DERIVATIVES **defection** n. **defector** n.
– ORIGIN C16: from L. *defect-* 'failed', from *deficere* (see **DEFECT**[1]).

**defective** • **adj. 1** imperfect or faulty. **2** lacking or deficient: *dystrophin is commonly defective in muscle tissue.*
– DERIVATIVES **defectively** adv. **defectiveness** n.

**defence** (US **defense**) • **n. 1** the action of defending from or resisting attack. ➤ military measures or resources for protecting a country. ➤ (**defences**) fortifications against attack. **2** the case presented by or on behalf of the party being accused or sued in a lawsuit. ➤ (usu. **the defence**) [treated as sing. or pl.] the counsel for the defendant in a lawsuit. **3** attempted justification or vindication: *he spoke in defence of a disciplined approach.* **4** (in sport) the action or role of defending one's goal or wicket against the opposition. ➤ (**the defence**) the players in a team who perform this role.
– DERIVATIVES **defenceless** (US **defenseless**) adj. **defencelessness** (US **defenselessness**) n.

**defence mechanism** • **n.** an automatic reaction of the body against disease-causing organisms. ➤ a mental process initiated, typically unconsciously, to avoid conscious conflict or anxiety.

**defend** • **v. 1** resist an attack on; protect from harm or danger. **2** conduct the case for (the party being accused or sued) in a lawsuit. **3** attempt to justify. **4** compete to retain (a title or seat). **5** (in sport) protect one's goal or wicket rather than attempt to score against one's opponents.
– DERIVATIVES **defendable** adj. **defender** n.
– ORIGIN ME: from OFr. *defendre*, from L. *defendere*, from *de-* 'off' + *-fendere* 'to strike'.

**defendant** • **n.** an individual, company, or institution sued or accused in a court of law. Compare with **PLAINTIFF**.

**defenestration** • **n.** formal or humorous the action of throwing someone out of a window.
– DERIVATIVES **defenestrate** v.
– ORIGIN C17: from mod. L. *defenestratio(n-)*, from *de-* + L. *fenestra* 'window'.

**defense** • **n.** US spelling of **DEFENCE**.

**defensible** • **adj. 1** justifiable by argument. **2** able to be defended or protected.
– DERIVATIVES **defensibility** n. **defensibly** adv.

**defensive** • **adj. 1** used or intended to defend or protect. ➤ (in sport) relating to or intended as defence. **2** very anxious to challenge or avoid criticism.
– PHRASES **on the defensive** expecting or resisting criticism or attack.
– DERIVATIVES **defensively** adv. **defensiveness** n.

**defer**[1] /dɪˈfəː/ • **v.** (**deferred**, **deferring**) put off to a later time; postpone. ➤ Law (of a judge) postpone (a sentence) for a period of up to six months from conviction. ➤ US historical postpone the conscription of.
– DERIVATIVES **deferment** n. **deferrable** adj. **deferral** n.
– ORIGIN ME: from OFr. *differer* 'defer or differ', from L. *differre*, from *dis-* 'apart' + *ferre* 'bring, carry'.

**defer**[2] /dɪˈfəː/ • **v.** (**deferred**, **deferring**) (**defer to**) submit humbly to: *he deferred to Tim's superior knowledge.*
– DERIVATIVES **deferrer** n.
– ORIGIN ME: from OFr. *deferer*, from L. *deferre* 'carry away, refer', from *de-* 'away from' + *ferre* 'bring, carry'.

**deference** • **n.** humble submission and respect.

**deferential** • **adj.** showing deference; respectful.
– DERIVATIVES **deferentially** adv.

**defervescence** /ˌdɪfəˈvɛs(ə)ns/ • **n.** Medicine the abatement of a fever.
– DERIVATIVES **defervesce** v.
– ORIGIN C18: from L. *defervescent-*, *defervescere* 'to cease to boil'.

**defiance** • **n.** open resistance; bold disobedience.
– DERIVATIVES **defiant** adj. **defiantly** adv.

– ORIGIN ME: from OFr., from *defier* 'defy'.

**defibrillation** /ˌdiːfɪbrɪˈleɪʃ(ə)n/ ● **n.** Medicine the stopping of fibrillation of the heart by administering a controlled electric shock, to allow restoration of the normal rhythm.
– DERIVATIVES **defibrillate** v. **defibrillator** n.

**deficiency** ● **n.** (pl. **-ies**) a lack or shortage. ➤ a failing or shortcoming.

**deficiency disease** ● **n.** a disease caused by the lack of some essential element in the diet, usually a particular vitamin or mineral.

**deficient** /dɪˈfɪʃ(ə)nt/ ● **adj.** not having enough of a specified quality or ingredient: *this diet is deficient in vitamin B.* ➤ insufficient or inadequate.
– ORIGIN C16: from L. *deficient-*, *deficere* (see **DEFECT**[1]).

**deficit** /ˈdɛfɪsɪt, ˈdiː-/ ● **n. 1** the amount by which something, especially a sum of money, falls short. ➤ an excess of expenditure or liabilities over income or assets in a given period. **2** technical a deficiency or failing, especially in a neurological or psychological function.
– ORIGIN C18: via Fr. from L. *deficit* 'it is lacking', from *deficere* (see **DEFECT**[1]).

**deficit spending** ● **n.** government spending, in excess of revenue, of funds raised by borrowing rather than from taxation.

**defilade** /ˌdɛfɪˈleɪd/ ● **n.** Military the protection of a position, vehicle, or troops against enemy observation or gunfire.
– ORIGIN C19: from Fr. *défiler* 'protect from the enemy' + **-ADE**[1].

**defile**[1] /dɪˈfʌɪl/ ● **v.** sully, mar, or spoil. ➤ desecrate or profane (something sacred). ➤ archaic violate the chastity of (a woman).
– DERIVATIVES **defilement** n. **defiler** n.
– ORIGIN ME: alt. of obs. *defoul*, from OFr. *defouler* 'trample down', influenced by obs. *befile* 'befoul, defile'.

**defile**[2] /dɪˈfʌɪl/ ● **n.** /also ˈdiːfʌɪl/ a steep-sided narrow gorge or passage (originally one requiring troops to march in single file). ● **v.** archaic (of troops) march in single file.
– ORIGIN C17: from Fr. *défilé* (n.), *défiler* (v.), from *dé* 'away from' + *file* 'column, file'.

**define** ● **v. 1** state or describe exactly the nature, scope, or meaning of. ➤ give the meaning of (a word or phrase). **2** mark out the limits of.
– DERIVATIVES **definable** adj. **definer** n.
– ORIGIN ME: from OFr. *definer*, from a var. of L. *definire*, from *de-* (expressing completion) + *finire* 'finish'.

**definite** ● **adj. 1** clearly stated or decided; not vague or doubtful. ➤ (of a person) certain or sure about something. **2** clearly true or real. **3** having exact and discernible physical limits.
– DERIVATIVES **definiteness** n.
– ORIGIN C16: from L. *definitus* 'defined, set within limits', past part. of *definire* (see **DEFINE**).

**definite article** ● **n.** Grammar a determiner (*the* in English) that introduces a noun phrase and implies that the thing mentioned has already been mentioned, or is common knowledge, or is about to be defined.

**definite integral** ● **n.** Mathematics an integral expressed as the difference between values at specified upper and lower limits of the independent variable.

**definitely** ● **adv.** without doubt (used for emphasis).

**definition** ● **n. 1** a formal statement of the exact meaning of a word. ➤ an exact description of the nature, scope, or meaning of something. ➤ the action or process of defining. **2** the degree of distinctness in outline of an object or image.
– PHRASES **by definition** by its very nature; intrinsically.
– DERIVATIVES **definitional** adj.

**definitive** ● **adj. 1** (of a conclusion or agreement) done or reached decisively and with authority. ➤ (of a book or other text) the most authoritative of its kind. **2** (of a postage stamp) for general use, not special or commemorative. ● **n.** a definitive postage stamp.
– DERIVATIVES **definitively** adv.
– ORIGIN ME: from OFr. *definitif, -ive*, from L. *definitivus*, from *definit-*, *definire* (see **DEFINE**).

**deflagration** ● **n.** Chemistry the action of heating a substance until it burns away rapidly.
– DERIVATIVES **deflagrate** v. **deflagrator** n.
– ORIGIN C17: from L. *deflagratio(n-)*, from *deflagrare* 'burn up', from *de-* 'away, thoroughly' + *flagrare* 'to burn'.

**deflate** ● **v. 1** let air or gas out of (a tyre, balloon, or similar object). ➤ be emptied of air or gas. **2** [usu. as adj. **deflated**] cause to feel suddenly dispirited. **3** Economics reduce price levels in (an economy).
– DERIVATIVES **deflator** n.
– ORIGIN C19: from **DE-** + *-flate* (as in *inflate*).

**deflation** ● **n. 1** the action or process of deflating or being deflated. **2** Economics reduction of the general level of prices in an economy. **3** Geology the removal of particles of rock, sand, etc. by the wind.
– DERIVATIVES **deflationary** adj. **deflationist** n. & adj.

**deflect** ● **v.** deviate or cause to deviate from a straight course.
– DERIVATIVES **deflective** adj. **deflector** n.
– ORIGIN C16: from L. *deflectere*, from *de-* + *flectere* 'to bend'.

**deflection** (also **deflexion**) ● **n.** the action or process of deflecting or being deflected. ➤ the amount by which something is deflected.

**deflexed** ● **adj.** technical curving downwards or backwards.

**deflocculate** /diːˈflɒkjʊleɪt/ ● **v.** Chemistry break up (a suspended substance) into finer particles, producing a dispersion.
– DERIVATIVES **deflocculation** n.

**defloration** /ˌdiːflɔːˈreɪʃ(ə)n/ ● **n.** dated or poetic/literary the taking of a woman's virginity.
– ORIGIN ME: from late L. *defloratio(n-)*, from *deflorare* (see **DEFLOWER**).

**deflower** ● **v. 1** dated or poetic/literary deprive (a woman) of her virginity. **2** strip of flowers.
– ORIGIN ME: from OFr. *desflourer*, from a var. of late L. *deflorare*, from *de-* + L. *flos, flor-* 'a flower'.

**defoliant** ● **n.** a chemical that removes the leaves from trees and plants, often used in warfare.

**defoliate** /diːˈfəʊlɪeɪt/ ● **v.** remove leaves or foliage from (a plant or area).
– DERIVATIVES **defoliation** n. **defoliator** n.
– ORIGIN C18: from late L. *defoliat-*, *defoliare* 'to strip of leaves', from *de-* + *folium* 'leaf'.

**deforest** ● **v.** clear of forest or trees.
– DERIVATIVES **deforestation** n.

**deform** ● **v.** [often as adj. **deformed**] distort the shape or form of; make or become misshapen.
– DERIVATIVES **deformable** adj. **deformation** n.
– ORIGIN ME: from OFr. *desformer*, via med. L. from L. *deformare*, from *de-* + *forma* 'a shape'.

**deformity** ● **n.** (pl. **-ies**) a deformed part, especially of the body. ➤ the state of being deformed: *spinal deformity.*

**defragment** /ˌdiːfragˈmɛnt/ ● **v.** Computing reduce the fragmentation of (a file) by concatenating parts stored in separate locations.
– DERIVATIVES **defragmentation** n. **defragmenter** n.

**defraud** ● **v.** illegally obtain money from (someone) by deception.
– DERIVATIVES **defrauder** n.
– ORIGIN ME: from OFr. *defrauder* or L. *defraudare*, from *de-* + *fraudare* 'to cheat'.

**defray** /dɪˈfreɪ/ ● **v.** provide money to pay (a cost).
– DERIVATIVES **defrayable** adj. **defrayal** n. **defrayment** n.
– ORIGIN ME: from Fr. *défrayer*, from *dé-* + obs. *frai* 'cost, expenses'.

**defrock** ● **v.** deprive (a person in holy orders) of ecclesiastical status.

**defrost** ● **v. 1** make or become free of accumulated ice. **2** thaw (frozen food).
– DERIVATIVES **defroster** n.

**deft** ● **adj.** quick and neatly skilful.
– DERIVATIVES **deftly** adv. **deftness** n.
– ORIGIN ME: var. of **DAFT**, in the obs. sense 'meek'.

**defunct** /dɪˈfʌŋ(k)t/ ● **adj.** no longer existing or functioning.

– ORIGIN C16: from L. *defunctus* 'dead', past part. of *defungi* 'carry out, finish'.

**defuse** • v. **1** remove the fuse from (an explosive device) in order to prevent it from exploding. **2** reduce the danger or tension in (a difficult situation).

**defy** • v. (**-ies**, **-ied**) **1** openly resist or refuse to obey. **2** challenge to do or prove something: *he glowered at her, defying her to mock him.* ➤ archaic challenge to combat.
– DERIVATIVES **defier** n.
– ORIGIN ME: from OFr. *desfier*, based on L. *dis-* (expressing reversal) + *fidus* 'faithful'.

**deg.** • abbrev. degree(s).

**dégagé** /deɪˈgɑːʒeɪ, -ˈgaʒeɪ/ • adj. unconcerned or unconstrained.
– ORIGIN C17: Fr., past part. of *dégager* 'set free'.

**degauss** /diːˈgaʊs/ • v. Physics remove unwanted magnetism from.
– DERIVATIVES **degausser** n.
– ORIGIN C20: from **DE-** + the name of the C19 Ger. physicist Karl Friedrich *Gauss*.

**degenerate** • adj. /dɪˈdʒɛn(ə)rət/ **1** having lost the physical or moral qualities considered normal and desirable; showing evidence of decline. **2** Physics relating to or denoting a quantized energy level corresponding to more than one state. ➤ denoting matter at such high density (e.g. in neutron stars) that quantum effects are dominant. • n. /dɪˈdʒɛn(ə)rət/ a morally degenerate person. • v. /dɪˈdʒɛnəreɪt/ decline or deteriorate physically or morally.
– DERIVATIVES **degeneracy** n. **degenerately** adv.
– ORIGIN C15: from L. *degeneratus* 'no longer of its kind', from *degenerare*, from *degener* 'debased', from *de-* + *genus, gener-* 'race, kind'.

**degeneration** • n. the state or process of being or becoming degenerate; decline or deterioration.

**degenerative** • adj. (of a disease or symptom) characterized by progressive deterioration and loss of function.

**deglaze** • v. dilute meat sediments in (a pan) in order to make a gravy or sauce: *deglaze the pan with the wine.*
– ORIGIN C19: from Fr. *déglacer*.

**deglutition** /ˌdiːgluːˈtɪʃ(ə)n/ • n. technical the action or process of swallowing.
– DERIVATIVES **deglutitive** adj.
– ORIGIN C17: from Fr. *déglutition* or mod. L. *deglutitio(n-)*, from *deglutire* 'swallow down'.

**degradation** /ˌdɛgrəˈdeɪʃ(ə)n/ • n. **1** the condition or process of degrading or being degraded. **2** Geology the wearing down of rock by disintegration.

**degrade** • v. **1** cause to suffer a severe loss of dignity or respect; demean. ➤ lower the character or quality of. ➤ archaic reduce to a lower rank, especially as a punishment. **2** cause to break down or deteriorate chemically. ➤ Physics reduce (energy) to a less readily convertible form.
– DERIVATIVES **degradability** n. **degradable** adj. **degradative** adj. **degrader** n.
– ORIGIN ME: from OFr. *degrader*, from eccles. L. *degradare*, from *de-* 'down' + L. *gradus* 'grade'.

**degrading** • adj. causing a loss of self-respect; humiliating.

**degree** • n. **1** the amount, level, or extent to which something happens or is present. **2** a unit of measurement of angles, equivalent to one ninetieth of a right angle. (Symbol: °) **3** a unit in any of various scales of temperature, intensity, or hardness. (Symbol: °) **4** a stage in a scale or series, in particular: ➤ each of a set of grades (usually three) used to classify burns according to their severity. ➤ chiefly N. Amer. a legal grade of crime, especially murder. ➤ a step in direct genealogical descent: *second-degree relatives.* ➤ Music a position in a musical scale, counting upwards from the tonic or fundamental note. **5** an academic rank conferred by a college or university after examination or after completion of a course, or conferred as an honour. **6** archaic social or official rank.
– PHRASES **by degrees** a little at a time; gradually. **to a degree** to some extent. ➤ dated to a considerable extent.
– ORIGIN ME: from OFr., based on L. *de-* 'down' + *gradus* 'grade'.

**degree of freedom** • n. technical each of a set of independent ways in which a system can change, in particular any of the directions in which motion is possible.

**degressive** /dɪˈgrɛsɪv/ • adj. reducing by gradual amounts. ➤ (of taxation) at successively lower rates on lower amounts.
– ORIGIN C20: from L. *degress-* 'descended' + **-IVE**.

**degu** /ˈdeɪguː/ • n. a rat-like South American rodent with a long silky coat. [Genus *Octodon*.]
– ORIGIN C19: from Amer. Sp., from S. Amer. Ind. *deuñ*.

**degust** /dɪˈgʌst/ • v. rare taste (food or drink).
– DERIVATIVES **degustation** n.
– ORIGIN C17: from L. *degustare*, from *de-* 'completely' + *gustare* 'to taste'.

**de haut en bas** /də ˌəʊt ɒ̃ ˈbɑː, French də ot ɑ̃ ba/ • adv. & adj. in a condescending or superior manner.
– ORIGIN Fr., 'from above to below'.

**dehisce** /dɪˈhɪs/ • v. technical (of a pod or seed vessel, or of a cut or wound) gape or burst open.
– DERIVATIVES **dehiscence** n. **dehiscent** adj.
– ORIGIN C17: from L. *dehiscere*, from *de-* 'away' + *hiscere* 'begin to gape'.

**dehors** /dəˈɔː, dəˈhɔː/ • prep. Law not including or outside the scope of.
– ORIGIN C18: from OFr. usage as prep.

**dehumanize** (also **-ise**) • v. deprive of positive human qualities.
– DERIVATIVES **dehumanization** n.

**dehumidify** • v. (**-ies**, **-ied**) remove moisture from (the air or a gas).
– DERIVATIVES **dehumidification** n. **dehumidifier** n.

**dehydrate** /diːˈhʌɪdreɪt, -hʌɪˈdreɪt/ • v. [often as adj. **dehydrated**] lose or cause to lose a large amount of water. ➤ remove water from (food) in order to preserve it.
– DERIVATIVES **dehydration** n. **dehydrator** n.
– ORIGIN C19: from **DE-** + Gk *hudros, hudr-* 'water'.

**dehydrocholesterol** /diːˌhʌɪdrə(ʊ)kəˈlɛstərɒl/ • n. Biochemistry a compound present in the skin, which is converted to cholecalciferol (vitamin $D_3$) by ultraviolet light.
– ORIGIN 1930s: from *dehydro-* 'that has lost hydrogen' + **CHOLESTEROL**.

**dehydrogenase** /ˌdiːhʌɪˈdrɒdʒəneɪz/ • n. Biochemistry an enzyme that brings about the removal of hydrogen atoms from a molecule.

**dehydrogenate** • v. Chemistry remove a hydrogen atom or atoms from.
– DERIVATIVES **dehydrogenation** n.

**de-ice** • v. remove ice from.
– DERIVATIVES **de-icer** n.

**deicide** /ˈdeɪɪsʌɪd, ˈdiːɪ-/ • n. the killing of a god. ➤ a person who kills a god.
– ORIGIN C17: from eccles. L. *deicida*, or directly from L. *deus* 'god' + **-CIDE**.

**deictic** /ˈdeɪktɪk, ˈdʌɪktɪk/ • adj. Linguistics of or denoting a word or expression whose meaning is dependent on the context in which it is used (such as *here*, or *next week*).
– DERIVATIVES **deictically** adv.
– ORIGIN C19: from Gk *deiktikos, deiktos* 'capable of proof', from *deiknunai* 'to show'.

**deify** /ˈdeɪɪfʌɪ, ˈdiːɪ-/ • v. (**-ies**, **-ied**) make into or worship as a god.
– DERIVATIVES **deification** n.
– ORIGIN ME: from OFr. *deifier*, from eccles. L. *deificare*, from *deus* 'god'.

**deign** /deɪn/ • v. do something that one considers to be beneath one's dignity: *she did not deign to answer.*
– ORIGIN ME: from OFr. *degnier*, from L. *dignare, dignari* 'deem worthy', from *dignus* 'worthy'.

**de-index** • v. end the indexation to inflation of (pensions or other benefits).

**deindustrialization** (also **-isation**) • n. decline in industrial activity in a region or economy.
– DERIVATIVES **deindustrialize** v.

**deinonychus** /dʌɪˈnɒnɪkəs/ • n. a dromaeosaurid dinosaur of the mid Cretaceous period, growing up to 3.3 m (11 ft) in length.

– ORIGIN mod. L., from Gk *deinos* 'terrible' + *onux, onukh-* 'claw'.

**deionize** /diːˈʌɪənʌɪz/ (also **-ise**) ● **v.** [usu. as adj. **deionized**] remove the ions or ionic constituents from.
– DERIVATIVES **deionization** n. **deionizer** n.

**deism** /ˈdeɪɪz(ə)m, ˈdiːɪ-/ ● **n.** belief in the existence of a supreme being, specifically of a creator who does not intervene in the universe. Compare with **THEISM**.
– DERIVATIVES **deist** n. **deistic** adj. **deistical** adj.
– ORIGIN C17: from L. *deus* 'god' + **-ISM**.

**deity** /ˈdeɪɪti, ˈdiːɪ-/ ● **n.** (pl. **-ies**) **1** a god or goddess (especially in a polytheistic religion). ➤(**the Deity**) the creator and supreme being. **2** divine status, quality, or nature.
– ORIGIN ME: from OFr. *deite*, from eccles. L. *deitas*, from *deus* 'god'.

**deixis** /ˈdeɪksɪs, ˈdʌɪksɪs/ ● **n.** Linguistics the function or use of deictic words or forms.
– ORIGIN 1940s: from Gk, lit. 'reference', from *deiknunai* 'to show'.

**déjà vu** /deɪʒɑː ˈvuː, French deʒa vy/ ● **n.** a feeling of having already experienced the present situation.
– ORIGIN C20: Fr., lit. 'already seen'.

**deject** ● **v.** [usu. as adj. **dejected**] make sad or dispirited.
– DERIVATIVES **dejectedly** adv. **dejection** n.
– ORIGIN ME: from L. *deject-* 'thrown down', from *deicere*, from *de-* 'down' + *jacere* 'to throw'.

**de jure** /deɪ ˈjʊəreɪ, diː ˈdʒʊəri/ ● **adv.** rightfully; by right. Often contrasted with **DE FACTO**. ● **adj.** rightful.
– ORIGIN L., lit. 'of law'.

**dekaliter** ● **n.** US variant spelling of **DECALITRE**.

**dekameter** ● **n.** US variant spelling of **DECAMETRE**.

**deke** /diːk/ Ice Hockey ● **n.** a deceptive movement that induces an opponent to move out of position. ● **v.** draw (a player) out of position in this way.
– ORIGIN 1960s: shortened form of **DECOY**.

**dekko** /ˈdɛkəʊ/ ● **n.** Brit. informal a quick look or glance.
– ORIGIN C19 (orig. used by the Brit. army in India): from Hindi *dekho* 'look!', imper. of *dekhnā*.

**Del.** ● **abbrev.** Delaware.

**delaminate** /diːˈlamɪneɪt/ ● **v.** divide or become divided into layers.
– ORIGIN C19: from **DE-** + L. *lamina* 'thin plate' + **-ATE**³.

**delate** /dɪˈleɪt/ ● **v.** archaic **1** report (an offence). **2** inform against.
– DERIVATIVES **delation** n. **delator** n.
– ORIGIN C15: from L. *delat-* 'referred, carried away', from *deferre* (see **DEFER**²).

**Delaware** /ˈdɛləwɛː/ ● **n.** (pl. same or **Delawares**) **1** a member of an American Indian people formerly inhabiting the Delaware River valley of New Jersey and eastern Pennsylvania. **2** either of two Algonquian languages, both now extinct, spoken by this people.

**Delawarean** /dɛləˈwɛːrɪən/ ● **n.** a native or inhabitant of the US state of Delaware. ● **adj.** of or relating to Delaware.

**delay** ● **v.** **1** become or cause to become late or slow. **2** postpone or defer. ● **n.** a period of time by which something is late or postponed.
– DERIVATIVES **delayer** n.
– ORIGIN ME: from OFr. *delayer* (v.).

**dele** /ˈdiːli/ ● **n.** a proofreader's sign (₰) indicating matter to be deleted. ● **v.** (**deled**, **deleing**) delete or mark for deletion.
– ORIGIN L., 'blot out! efface!', imper. of *delere*.

**delectable** ● **adj.** (of food or drink) delicious. ➤chiefly humorous lovely; delightful.
– DERIVATIVES **delectability** n. **delectably** adv.

**delectation** /ˌdiːlɛkˈteɪʃ(ə)n/ ● **n.** formal, chiefly humorous pleasure and delight.
– ORIGIN ME: via OFr. from L. *delectatio(n-)*, from *delectare* (see **DELIGHT**).

**delegacy** /ˈdɛlɪgəsi/ ● **n.** (pl. **-ies**) [treated as sing. or pl.] a body of delegates; a committee or delegation.

**delegate** ● **n.** /ˈdɛlɪgət/ a person sent or authorized to represent others, in particular a representative sent to a conference. ➤a member of a committee. ● **v.** /ˈdɛlɪgeɪt/ entrust (a task or responsibility) to another person. ➤authorize (someone) to act as a representative or on one's behalf: *Edward was delegated to meet new arrivals.*
– DERIVATIVES **delegable** /ˈdɛlɪgəb(ə)l/ adj. **delegator** n.
– ORIGIN ME: from L. *delegatus* 'sent on a commission', from *delegare*, from *de-* 'down' + *legare* 'depute'.

**delegation** ● **n.** [treated as sing. or pl.] **1** a body of delegates; a deputation. **2** the action or process of delegating or being delegated.

**delete** ● **v.** **1** remove or erase (text). **2** remove (a product) from the catalogue of those available for purchase.
– DERIVATIVES **deletion** n.
– ORIGIN ME (in the sense 'destroy'): from L. *delet-*, *delere* 'to blot out'.

**deleterious** /ˌdɛlɪˈtɪərɪəs/ ● **adj.** causing harm or damage.
– DERIVATIVES **deleteriously** adv.
– ORIGIN C17: via med. L. from Gk *dēlētērios* 'noxious' + **-OUS**.

**delft** /dɛlft/ ● **n.** English or Dutch tin-glazed earthenware, typically decorated by hand in blue on a white background.
– DERIVATIVES **delftware** n.
– ORIGIN C17: from the name of the town of *Delft* in the Netherlands, where the pottery originated.

**deli** ● **n.** (pl. **delis**) informal short for **DELICATESSEN**.

**Delian** /ˈdiːlɪən/ ● **adj.** of or relating to Delos, an island in the Aegean Sea considered to be sacred to Apollo in classical times. ● **n.** a native or inhabitant of Delos.

**deliberate** ● **adj.** /dɪˈlɪb(ə)rət/ **1** done consciously and intentionally. ➤fully considered; not impulsive. **2** done or acting in a careful and unhurried way. ● **v.** /dɪˈlɪbəreɪt/ engage in long and careful consideration.
– DERIVATIVES **deliberately** adv. **deliberateness** n. **deliberator** n.
– ORIGIN ME: from L. *deliberat-*, *deliberare* 'consider carefully'.

**deliberation** ● **n.** **1** long and careful consideration. **2** slow and careful movement or thought.

**deliberative** ● **adj.** relating to or involving consideration or discussion: *a deliberative assembly.*

**delicacy** ● **n.** (pl. **-ies**) **1** fineness or intricacy of texture or structure. **2** susceptibility to illness or adverse conditions; fragility. **3** discretion and tact: *treat this matter with the utmost delicacy.* **4** a choice or expensive food.

**delicate** ● **adj.** **1** very fine in texture or structure; of intricate workmanship or quality. ➤(of food or drink) subtly and pleasantly flavoured. **2** easily broken or damaged; fragile. ➤susceptible to illness or adverse conditions. **3** requiring sensitive or careful handling. ➤skilful; deft. ● **n.** (**delicates**) garments made from delicate fabric.
– PHRASES **in a delicate condition** archaic, euphemistic pregnant.
– DERIVATIVES **delicately** adv. **delicateness** n.
– ORIGIN ME (in the sense 'delightful, charming'): from Fr. *délicat* or L. *delicatus*, of unknown origin.

**delicatessen** /ˌdɛlɪkəˈtɛs(ə)n/ ● **n.** a shop selling cooked meats, cheeses, and unusual or foreign prepared foods.
– ORIGIN C19: from Ger. *Delikatessen* or Du. *delicatessen*, from Fr. *délicatesse* 'delicateness'.

**delicious** ● **adj.** **1** highly pleasant to the taste. **2** delightful: *a delicious irony.*
– DERIVATIVES **deliciously** adv. **deliciousness** n.
– ORIGIN ME: via OFr. from late L. *deliciosus*, from L. *deliciae* (pl.) 'delight, pleasure'.

**delict** /dɪˈlɪkt, ˈdiːlɪkt/ ● **n.** Law a violation of the law; a tort.
– ORIGIN ME: from L. *delictum* 'something showing fault', neut. past part. of *delinquere* (see **DELINQUENT**).

**delight** ● **v.** please greatly. ➤(**delight in**) take great pleasure in. ● **n.** great pleasure. ➤a cause or source of great pleasure.
– DERIVATIVES **delighted** adj. **delightedly** adv.
– ORIGIN ME: from OFr. *delitier* (v.), *delit* (n.), from L. *delectare* 'to charm', frequentative of *delicere*.

**delightful** ● **adj.** causing delight; charming.
– DERIVATIVES **delightfully** adv. **delightfulness** n.

**delimit** /dɪˈlɪmɪt/ ● v. (**delimited**, **delimiting**) determine the limits or boundaries of.
– DERIVATIVES **delimitation** n. **delimiter** n.

**delineate** /dɪˈlɪnɪeɪt/ ● v. describe or indicate precisely. ➤trace the outline of (a border or boundary).
– DERIVATIVES **delineation** /-ˈeɪʃ(ə)n/ n. **delineator** n.
– ORIGIN C16: from L. *delineat-*, *delineare* 'to outline'.

**delinquency** ● n. (pl. **-ies**) **1** minor crime, especially that committed by young people. **2** formal neglect of one's duty. **3** chiefly US a failure to pay an outstanding debt.

**delinquent** /dɪˈlɪŋkw(ə)nt/ ● adj. **1** (typically with reference to young people) showing or characterized by a tendency to commit crime. **2** formal failing in one's duty. **3** chiefly N. Amer. in arrears: *delinquent accounts.* ● n. a delinquent person.
– DERIVATIVES **delinquently** adv.
– ORIGIN C15: from L. *delinquent-*, *delinquere* 'to offend'.

**deliquesce** /ˌdɛlɪˈkwɛs/ ● v. **1** (of organic matter) become liquid, typically during decomposition. **2** Chemistry (of a solid) become liquid by absorbing moisture from the air.
– DERIVATIVES **deliquescence** n. **deliquescent** adj.
– ORIGIN C18: from L. *deliquescere* 'dissolve'.

**delirious** ● adj. **1** suffering from delirium. **2** in a state of wild excitement or ecstasy.
– DERIVATIVES **deliriously** adv.

**delirium** /dɪˈlɪrɪəm/ ● n. an acutely disturbed state of mind characterized by restlessness, illusions, and incoherence of thought and speech, occurring in fever, intoxication, and other disorders.
– ORIGIN C16: from L., from *delirare* 'deviate, be deranged' (lit. 'deviate from the furrow'), from *de-* 'away' + *lira* 'ridge between furrows'.

**delirium tremens** /ˈtriːmɛnz, ˈtrɛ-/ ● n. a psychotic condition typical of withdrawal in chronic alcoholics, involving tremors, hallucinations, anxiety, and disorientation.
– ORIGIN C19: from L., 'trembling delirium'.

**delist** ● v. remove from a list, in particular remove (a security) from the official register of a stock exchange.

**deliver** ● v. **1** bring and hand over (a letter or goods) to the appropriate recipient. ➤formally hand over (someone). ➤Law acknowledge that one intends to be bound by (a deed), either explicitly by declaration or implicitly by formal handover. **2** provide (something promised or expected). **3** save or set free: *deliver us from the nightmare of junk paper.* **4** state or present in a formal manner: *he will deliver a lecture on endangered species.* **5** assist in the birth of. ➤(also **be delivered of**) give birth to. **6** launch or aim (a blow or attack).
– DERIVATIVES **deliverable** adj. & n. **deliverer** n.
– ORIGIN ME: from OFr. *delivrer*, based on L. *de-* 'away' + *liberare* 'set free'.

**deliverance** ● n. **1** the process of being rescued or set free. **2** a formal or authoritative utterance.

**delivery** ● n. (pl. **-ies**) **1** the action of delivering something, especially letters or goods. ➤a regular or scheduled occasion for this. ➤Law the acknowledgement by the maker of a deed that they intend to be bound by it. **2** the process of giving birth. **3** an act of throwing or bowling a ball, especially a cricket ball. ➤the style or manner of such an action. **4** the manner or style of giving a speech.
– PHRASES **take delivery of** receive at one's address (something purchased).

**dell** ● n. poetic/literary a small valley.
– ORIGIN OE, of Gmc origin; rel. to **DALE**.

**delocalize** (also **-ise**) ● v. detach or remove from a particular location.
– DERIVATIVES **delocalization** n.

**Delphic** /ˈdɛlfɪk/ (also **Delphian** /-fɪən/) ● adj. **1** of or relating to the ancient Greek oracle at Delphi. **2** deliberately obscure or ambiguous: *Foster has been criticized for his Delphic utterances.*

**delphinium** /dɛlˈfɪnɪəm/ ● n. (pl. **delphiniums**) a popular garden plant bearing tall spikes of blue flowers. [Genus *Delphinium*.]
– ORIGIN mod. L., from Gk *delphinion* 'larkspur', from *delphin* 'dolphin' (because of the shape of the spur, thought to resemble a dolphin's back).

**delta**[1] ● n. **1** the fourth letter of the Greek alphabet (Δ, δ), transliterated as 'd'. ➤[as modifier] denoting the fourth in a series of items or categories. ➤ Brit. a fourth-class mark given for a piece of work. **2** a code word representing the letter D, used in radio communication. ● symb. Mathematics variation of a variable or quantity.
– ORIGIN Gk, from Phoenician *daleth*.

**delta**[2] ● n. a triangular tract of sediment deposited at the mouth of a river, typically where it diverges into several outlets.
– DERIVATIVES **deltaic** adj.
– ORIGIN C16: orig. *the Delta* (of the River Nile), from the shape of the Gk letter (see **DELTA**[1]).

**delta rays** ● pl. n. Physics rays of low penetrative power consisting of slow electrons or other particles ejected from atoms by the impact of ionizing radiation.

**delta rhythm** ● n. electrical activity of the brain typical of sleep, consisting of oscillations (**delta waves**) with a frequency of 1 to 8 Hz.

**delta-v** ● n. informal acceleration.
– ORIGIN C20: from **DELTA**[1] (as a mathematical symbol denoting variation) + *v* for *velocity.*

**delta wing** ● n. the single triangular swept-back wing on some aircraft.

**deltiologist** /ˌdɛltɪˈɒlədʒɪst/ ● n. a person who collects postcards as a hobby.
– DERIVATIVES **deltiology** n.
– ORIGIN 1940s: from Gk *deltion* (dimin. of *deltos* 'writing tablet') + **-LOGIST**.

**deltoid** /ˈdɛltɔɪd/ ● adj. technical **1** triangular. **2** denoting a thick triangular muscle covering the shoulder joint and used for raising the arm away from the body. ● n. a deltoid muscle, or one of the three parts of a deltoid muscle.
– ORIGIN C18: from Fr. *deltoïde*, or via mod. L. from Gk *deltoeidēs*.

**delude** /dɪˈl(j)uːd/ ● v. impose a misleading belief upon.
– DERIVATIVES **deluded** adj. **deludedly** adv. **deluder** n.
– ORIGIN ME: from L. *deludere* 'to mock', from *de-* + *ludere* 'to play'.

**deluge** /ˈdɛljuːdʒ/ ● n. **1** a severe flood. ➤a very heavy fall of rain. **2** a great quantity of something arriving at the same time: *a deluge of complaints.* ● v. **1** inundate; overwhelm. **2** flood.
– ORIGIN ME: from OFr., var. of *diluve*, from L. *diluvium*, from *diluere* 'wash away'.

**delusion** ● n. **1** an idiosyncratic belief or impression that is not in accordance with a generally accepted reality. **2** the action of deluding or being deluded.
– DERIVATIVES **delusional** adj. **delusive** adj. **delusory** adj.

**de luxe** /dɪ ˈlʌks, ˈlʊks/ ● adj. luxurious or sumptuous; of a superior kind.
– ORIGIN C19: Fr., lit. 'of luxury'.

**delve** ● v. **1** reach inside a receptacle and search for something. **2** research intensively into something.
– DERIVATIVES **delver** n.
– ORIGIN OE *delfan* 'dig', of W. Gmc origin.

**Dem.** ● abbrev. US Democrat.

**demagnetize** (also **-ise**) ● v. remove magnetic properties from.
– DERIVATIVES **demagnetization** n. **demagnetizer** n.

**demagogue** /ˈdɛməgɒg/ ● n. **1** a political leader who seeks support by appealing to popular desires and prejudices rather than by using rational argument. **2** (in ancient Greece and Rome) an orator who espoused the cause of the common people.
– DERIVATIVES **demagogic** /-ˈgɒgɪk/ adj. **demagoguery** /-ˈgɒg(ə)ri/ n. **demagogy** n.
– ORIGIN C17: from Gk *dēmagōgos*, from *dēmos* 'the people' + *agōgos* 'leading'.

**demand** ● n. **1** an insistent and peremptory request, made as of right. ➤(**demands**) pressing requirements. **2** Economics the desire of purchasers, consumers, etc. for a particular commodity or service: *a recent slump in demand.* ● v. ask authoritatively or brusquely. ➤insist on having. ➤require; need.

– PHRASES **in demand** sought after. **on demand** as soon as or whenever required.
– DERIVATIVES **demander** n.
– ORIGIN ME: from OFr. *demande* (n.), *demander* (v.), from L. *demandare* 'hand over, entrust'.

**demand feeding** • n. the practice of feeding a baby when it cries for a feed rather than at set times.

**demanding** • adj. requiring much skill or effort: *a demanding job.*
– DERIVATIVES **demandingly** adv.

**demarcation** (also **demarkation**) • n. the action of fixing boundaries or limits. ➤a dividing line.
– DERIVATIVES **demarcate** v. **demarcator** n.
– ORIGIN C18: from Sp. *demarcación* (from *demarcar* 'mark the bounds of'), orig. used with ref. to the line dividing the New World between the Spanish and Portuguese, laid down by the Pope in 1493.

**démarche** /deɪˈmɑːʃ/ • n. a political step or initiative.
– ORIGIN C17: Fr., from *démarcher* 'take steps'.

**demark** /diːˈmɑːk/ • v. set the boundaries or limits of.
– ORIGIN C19: from DEMARCATION.

**demassify** /diːˈmasɪfʌɪ/ • v. (**-ies**, **-ied**) divide or break up into component parts.
– DERIVATIVES **demassification** n.

**dematerialize** (also **-ise**) • v. make or become no longer physically present, or spiritual rather than physical.
– DERIVATIVES **dematerialization** n.

**deme** /diːm/ • n. **1** a political division in ancient or modern Greece. **2** Biology a subdivision of a population consisting of closely related plants or animals.
– ORIGIN from Gk *dēmos* 'people'.

**demean**[1] /dɪˈmiːn/ • v. cause to suffer a severe loss of dignity or respect. ➤(**demean oneself**) do something that is beneath one's dignity.
– DERIVATIVES **demeaning** adj.
– ORIGIN C17: from DE- + the adj. MEAN[2], on the pattern of *debase.*

**demean**[2] /dɪˈmiːn/ • v. (**demean oneself**) archaic conduct oneself.
– ORIGIN ME: from OFr. *demener* 'to lead'.

**demeanour** (US **demeanor**) • n. outward behaviour or bearing.
– ORIGIN C15: from DEMEAN[2], prob. influenced by obs. *havour* 'behaviour'.

**demented** • adj. **1** suffering from dementia. **2** informal wild and irrational.
– DERIVATIVES **dementedly** adv. **dementedness** n.
– ORIGIN C17: past part. of earlier *dement* 'drive mad': from Fr. *dément* or L. *demens, dement-* 'insane'.

**démenti** /deɪˈmɒ̃ti/ • n. an official denial of a published statement.
– ORIGIN Fr., from *démentir* 'contradict or accuse of lying'.

**dementia** /dɪˈmɛnʃə/ • n. Medicine a chronic or persistent mental disorder marked by memory failures, personality changes, and impaired reasoning.
– ORIGIN C18: from L., from *demens, dement-* 'out of one's mind'.

**dementia praecox** /ˈpriːkɒks/ • n. archaic term for SCHIZOPHRENIA.
– ORIGIN L., lit. 'early insanity'.

**demerara sugar** /ˌdɛməˈrɛːrə, -ˈrɑːrə/ • n. light brown cane sugar coming originally and chiefly from the region of Demerara in Guyana.

**demerge** • v. Brit. separate (a company) from another with which it was merged.
– DERIVATIVES **demerger** n.

**demerit** • n. **1** a feature or fact deserving censure. **2** N. Amer. a mark awarded against someone for a fault or offence.
– DERIVATIVES **demeritorious** /-ˈtɔːrɪəs/ adj.

**demersal** /dɪˈməːs(ə)l/ • adj. (of fish) living close to the seabed.
– ORIGIN C19: from L. *demersus* (past part. of *demergere* 'submerge, sink') + -AL.

**demesne** /dɪˈmeɪn, dɪˈmiːn/ • n. historical **1** land attached to a manor and retained by the owner for their own use. ➤archaic a domain. **2** Law possession of real property in one's own right.
– ORIGIN ME: from OFr. *demeine* 'belonging to a lord', from L. *dominicus*, from *dominus* 'lord, master'.

**demi-** • prefix **1** half: *demisemiquaver.* **2** partially; in an inferior degree: *demigod.*
– ORIGIN via Fr. from med. L. *dimedius* 'half', from earlier *dimidius.*

**demi-glace** /ˈdɛmɪglas/ (also **demi-glaze**) • n. a rich, glossy, brown sauce, typically flavoured with wine and served with meat.
– ORIGIN Fr., lit. 'half glaze'.

**demigod** (or **demigoddess**) • n. a being with partial or lesser divine status.

**demijohn** • n. a bulbous narrow-necked bottle holding from 3 to 10 gallons of liquid.
– ORIGIN C18: prob. an alt. of Fr. *dame-jeanne* 'Lady Jane', assoc. with DEMI- and the given name *John.*

**demilitarize** (also **-ise**) • v. [usu. as adj. **demilitarized**] remove all military forces from: *a demilitarized zone.*
– DERIVATIVES **demilitarization** n.

**demilune** /ˈdɛmɪluːn/ • n. a crescent or half-circle, or a thing of this shape.
– ORIGIN C18: from Fr. *demi-lune*, lit. 'half-moon'.

**demi-mondaine** /ˈdɛmɪmɒnˌdeɪn, French dəmimɔ̃dɛn/ • n. a woman considered to belong to the demi-monde.
– ORIGIN from Fr.

**demi-monde** /ˌdɛmɪˈmɒnd/ • n. a group considered to be on the fringes of respectable society.
– ORIGIN C19: Fr. (orig. with ref. to C19 France and the class of women considered morally dubious), lit. 'half-world'.

**demineralize** (also **-ise**) • v. remove salts or minerals from.
– DERIVATIVES **demineralization** n.

**demi-pension** /ˌdɛmɪˈpɒ̃sjɒ̃, French dəmipɑ̃sjɔ̃/ • n. hotel accommodation with bed, breakfast, and one main meal per day.
– ORIGIN Fr., lit. 'half board'.

**demise** /dɪˈmʌɪz/ • n. **1** the end or failure of something. **2** a person's death. **3** Law the transfer of property or a title by demising. • v. Law convey or grant by will or lease.
– ORIGIN ME: from Anglo-Norman Fr., past part. (used as n.) of OFr. *desmettre* 'dismiss'.

**demi-sec** /dɛmɪˈsɛk, French dəmisɛk/ • adj. (of wine) medium dry.
– ORIGIN Fr., lit. 'half-dry'.

**demisemiquaver** /ˌdɛmɪˈsɛmɪˌkweɪvə/ • n. Music, chiefly Brit. a note having the time value of half a semiquaver.

**demist** /diːˈmɪst/ • v. Brit. clear condensation from.
– DERIVATIVES **demister** n.

**demit** /dɪˈmɪt/ • v. (**demitted**, **demitting**) archaic resign from (a position).
– DERIVATIVES **demission** n.
– ORIGIN C16: from Fr. *démettre*, from *dé-* 'away from' + *mettre* 'put'.

**demitasse** /ˈdɛmɪtas/ • n. a small coffee cup.
– ORIGIN C19: from Fr., lit. 'half-cup'.

**demiurge** /ˈdiːmɪəːdʒ, ˈdɛm-/ • n. **1** (in Platonic philosophy) the creator of the world. **2** (in Gnosticism) a heavenly being subordinate to the supreme being, considered to control the material world.
– DERIVATIVES **demiurgic** /-ˈəːdʒɪk/ adj. **demiurgical** adj.
– ORIGIN C17: via eccles. L. from Gk *dēmiourgos* 'craftsman', from *dēmios* 'public' + *-ergos* 'working'.

**demo** informal • n. (pl. **-os**) **1** short for DEMONSTRATION. **2** a demonstration recording or piece of software. • v. (**-os**, **-oed**) give a demonstration of.

**demob** /diːˈmɒb/ Brit. informal • v. (**demobbed**, **demobbing**) demobilize. • n. demobilization.

**demobilize** /diːˈməʊbɪlʌɪz/ (also **-ise**) • v. (usu. **be demobilized**) take (troops) out of active service.
– DERIVATIVES **demobilization** n.

**democracy** /dɪˈmɒkrəsi/ • n. (pl. **-ies**) a form of government in which the people have a voice in the exercise of power, typically through elected representatives. ➤a state governed in such a way. ➤control of a group by the

majority of its members.
– ORIGIN C16: from Fr. *démocratie*, via late L. from Gk *dēmokratia*, from *dēmos* 'the people' + *-kratia* 'power, rule'.

**democrat** ● n. **1** a supporter of democracy. **2** (**Democrat**) (in the US) a member of the Democratic Party.
– ORIGIN C18 (orig. denoting an opponent of the aristocrats in the French Revolution of 1790): from Fr. *démocrate*, on the pattern of *aristocrate* 'aristocrat'.

**democratic** ● adj. **1** of, relating to, or supporting democracy. ➤ egalitarian. **2** (**Democratic**) (in the US) of or relating to the Democratic Party.
– DERIVATIVES **democratically** adv.

**democratize** (also **-ise**) ● v. introduce a democratic system or democratic principles to.
– DERIVATIVES **democratization** n.

**démodé** /deɪˈməʊdeɪ/ ● adj. out of fashion.
– ORIGIN Fr., past part. of *démoder* 'go out of fashion'.

**demodectic mange** /ˌdiːmə(ʊ)ˈdɛktɪk/ ● n. a form of mange tending to affect chiefly the head and foreparts.
– ORIGIN C19: from mod. L. *Demodex* (genus name of a mite, from Gk *dēmos* 'fat' + *dēx* 'woodworm') + **-IC**.

**demodulate** ● v. Electronics extract (a modulating signal) from its carrier.
– DERIVATIVES **demodulation** n. **demodulator** n.

**demography** /dɪˈmɒgrəfi/ ● n. the study of the structure of human populations using statistics relating to births, deaths, wealth, disease, etc.
– DERIVATIVES **demographer** n. **demographic** /ˌdɛməˈgrafɪk/ adj. **demographical** adj. **demographically** adv. **demographics** pl. n.
– ORIGIN C19: from Gk *dēmos* 'the people' + **-GRAPHY**.

**Demoi** plural form of **DEMOS**.

**demoiselle** /ˌdɛmwɑːˈzɛl/ ● n. archaic or poetic/literary a young woman.
– ORIGIN C16: from Fr., from OFr. *dameisele* 'damsel'.

**demoiselle crane** ● n. a small crane, breeding in SE Europe and central Asia. [*Anthropoides virgo.*]

**demolish** /dɪˈmɒlɪʃ/ ● v. **1** pull or knock down (a building). **2** comprehensively refute or defeat. **3** humorous eat up (food) quickly.
– DERIVATIVES **demolisher** n.
– ORIGIN C16: from Fr. *démoliss-*, lengthened stem of *démolir*, from L. *demoliri*, from *de-* (expressing reversal) + *moliri* 'construct'.

**demolition**/ˌdɛməˈlɪʃ(ə)n/ ● n. the action or process of demolishing or being demolished.
– ORIGIN C16: via Fr. from L. *demolitio(n-)*, from *demoliri* (see **DEMOLISH**).

**demon**[1] ● n. **1** an evil spirit or devil. ➤ often humorous an evil or destructive person or thing: *I was a little demon, I can tell you.* **2** [as modifier] denoting a person forceful or skilful in a specified role: *a demon cook.* **3** another term for **DAEMON**[1].
– PHRASES **like a demon** in a very forceful, fierce, or skilful way.
– ORIGIN ME: from med. L., from L. *daemon* (or its dimin. *daemonium*), from Gk *daimōn* 'deity, genius'.

**demon**[2] ● n. Austral./NZ informal a police officer.
– ORIGIN C19: appar. from Van *Diemen*'s Land, an early name for Tasmania.

**demon**[3] ● n. variant spelling of **DAEMON**[2].

**demonetize** /diːˈmʌnɪtʌɪz, -mɒn-/ (also **-ise**) ● v. deprive a coin or precious metal of its status as money.
– DERIVATIVES **demonetization** n.
– ORIGIN C19: from Fr. *démonétiser*, from *dé-* (expressing reversal) + L. *moneta* 'money'.

**demoniac** /dɪˈməʊnɪak/ ● adj. demonic. ● n. a person supposedly possessed by an evil spirit.
– DERIVATIVES **demoniacal** adj. **demoniacally** adv.
– ORIGIN ME: from OFr. *demoniaque*, from eccles. L. *daemoniacus*, from *daemonium* (see **DEMON**[1]).

**demonic** /dɪˈmɒnɪk/ ● adj. of, resembling, or characteristic of demons or evil spirits.
– DERIVATIVES **demonically** adv.

**demonism** /ˈdiːmənɪz(ə)m/ ● n. **1** belief in the power of demons. **2** demonic action or behaviour.

**demonize** (also **-ise**) ● v. portray as wicked and threatening.
– DERIVATIVES **demonization** n.

**demono-** /ˈdiːmənəʊ/ ● comb. form of or relating to demons: *demonolatry.*

**demonolatry** /ˌdiːməˈnɒlətri/ ● n. the worship of demons.

**demonology** ● n. the study of demons or demonism.
– DERIVATIVES **demonological** adj. **demonologist** n.

**demonstrable** /dɪˈmɒnstrəb(ə)l, ˈdɛmən-/ ● adj. clearly apparent or capable of being logically proved.
– DERIVATIVES **demonstrability** n. **demonstrably** adv.
– ORIGIN ME: from L. *demonstrabilis.*

**demonstrate** ● v. **1** clearly show the existence or truth of. ➤ give a practical exhibition and explanation of. **2** take part in a public demonstration.
– DERIVATIVES **demonstrator** n.
– ORIGIN C16: from L. *demonstrat-*, *demonstrare* 'point out'.

**demonstration** ● n. **1** the action of demonstrating something. **2** a public meeting or march expressing protest or other opinion on an issue.

**demonstrative** /dɪˈmɒnstrətɪv/ ● adj. **1** tending to show affectionate or other feelings openly. **2** serving to demonstrate something. **3** Grammar (of a determiner or pronoun) indicating the person or thing referred to (e.g. *this, that, those*). ● n. Grammar a demonstrative determiner or pronoun.
– DERIVATIVES **demonstratively** adv. **demonstrativeness** n.

**demoralize** (also **-ise**) ● v. **1** cause to lose confidence or hope. **2** archaic corrupt the morals of.
– DERIVATIVES **demoralization** n. **demoralized** adj. **demoralizing** adj. **demoralizingly** adv.
– ORIGIN C18: from Fr. *démoraliser* (a word of the Fr. Revolution).

**Demos** /ˈdiːmɒs/ ● n. (pl. **Demoi** /ˈdiː-mɔɪ/) the common people of an ancient Greek state.
– ORIGIN from Gk *dēmos.*

**demote** ● v. give a lower rank or less senior position to, often as a punishment.
– DERIVATIVES **demotion** n.
– ORIGIN C19: from **DE-** + a shortened form of **PROMOTE**.

**demotic** /dɪˈmɒtɪk/ ● adj. **1** denoting or relating to the kind of language used by ordinary people; colloquial. **2** denoting or relating to the form of modern Greek used in everyday speech and writing. Compare with **KATHAREVOUSA**. **3** denoting a simplified, cursive form of ancient Egyptian script. Compare with **HIERATIC**. ● n. demotic speech, language, or writing.
– ORIGIN C19: from Gk *dēmotikos*, from *dēmotēs* 'one of the people', from *dēmos* 'the people'.

**demotivate** ● v. make less eager to work or study.
– DERIVATIVES **demotivation** n.

**demountable** ● adj. able to be dismantled or removed and readily reassembled or repositioned.
– DERIVATIVES **demount** v.

**demulcent** /dɪˈmʌls(ə)nt/ ● adj. Medicine relieving inflammation or irritation.
– ORIGIN C18: from L. *demulcent-*, *demulcere* 'to stroke caressingly', from *de-* 'away' + *mulcere* 'soothe'.

**demur** /dɪˈməː/ ● v. (**demurred**, **demurring**) raise doubts or objections; show reluctance. ● n. the action of demurring: *they accepted this ruling without demur.*
– DERIVATIVES **demurral** n.
– ORIGIN ME: from OFr. *demourer* (v.), *demeure* (n.), based on L. *de-* 'away, completely' + *morari* 'delay'.

**demure** /dɪˈmjʊə/ ● adj. (**-er**, **-est**) (of a woman) reserved, modest, and shy.
– DERIVATIVES **demurely** adv. **demureness** n.
– ORIGIN ME: perh. from OFr. *demoure*, past part. of *demourer* (see **DEMUR**); influenced by OFr. *mur* 'grave'.

**demurrage** /dɪˈmʌrɪdʒ/ ● n. Law a charge payable to the owner of a chartered ship in respect of delay in loading or discharging.

**demurrer** /dɪˈməːrə/ ● n. Law a pleading that an opponent's point is irrelevant.
– ORIGIN C16: from Anglo-Norman Fr. (infin. used as n.), from OFr. *demourer* (see **DEMUR**).

**demutualize** /diːˈmjuːtʃʊəlʌɪz, -tjʊə-/ (also **-ise**) • **v.** change (a mutual organization such as a building society) to one of a different kind.
– DERIVATIVES **demutualization** n.

**demy** /dɪˈmʌɪ/ • **n. 1** a paper size, 564 × 444 mm. **2** (also **demy octavo**) a book size, 216 × 138 mm. **3** (also **demy quarto**) a book size, 276 × 219 mm.
– ORIGIN ME: from **DEMI-**, or its source, Fr. *demi* 'half'.

**demyelinate** /diːˈmʌɪəlɪneɪt/ • **v.** Medicine cause the loss of myelin in (nerve tissue).
– DERIVATIVES **demyelination** n.

**demystify** • **v.** (**-ies**, **-ied**) make (a subject) easier to understand.
– DERIVATIVES **demystification** n.

**demythologize** (also **-ise**) • **v.** reinterpret (a subject) so that it is free of mythical elements.

**den** • **n. 1** a wild animal's lair or habitation. **2** informal a person's private room. **3** a place where people meet secretly or illicitly: *an opium den.* • **v.** (**denned**, **denning**) (of an animal) live in or retreat to a den.
– ORIGIN OE *denn*, of Gmc origin.

**denar** /ˈdiːnə/ • **n.** the basic monetary unit of Macedonia.
– ORIGIN based on L. *denarius*; cf. **DINAR**.

**denarius** /dɪˈnɛːrɪəs, dɪˈnɑːrɪəs/ • **n.** (pl. **denarii** /-rɪʌɪ, -rɪiː/) an ancient Roman silver coin, originally worth ten asses. ➤ an ancient Roman gold coin worth 25 silver denarii.
– ORIGIN L., lit. 'containing ten', from *deni* 'in tens'.

**denary** /ˈdiːn(ə)ri/ • **adj.** relating to or based on the number ten.

**denationalize** (also **-ise**) • **v. 1** transfer from public to private ownership. **2** deprive of nationality or national characteristics.
– DERIVATIVES **denationalization** n.

**denaturalize** (also **-ise**) • **v. 1** make unnatural. **2** deprive of citizenship of a country.
– DERIVATIVES **denaturalization** n.

**denature** /diːˈneɪtʃə/ • **v. 1** take away or alter the natural qualities of. **2** make (alcohol) unfit for drinking by adding toxic or foul-tasting substances.
– DERIVATIVES **denaturant** n. **denaturation** n.

**dendrimer** /ˈdɛndrɪmə/ • **n.** Chemistry a synthetic polymer with a branching, tree-like structure.

**dendrite** /ˈdɛndrʌɪt/ • **n. 1** a short extension of a nerve cell conducting impulses to the cell body. **2** a crystalline mass with a branching, tree-like structure. ➤ a natural tree-like marking on a rock or mineral.
– DERIVATIVES **dendritic** /dɛnˈdrɪtɪk/ adj. **dendritically** adv.
– ORIGIN C18: from Fr., from Gk *dendritēs* 'tree-like'.

**dendro-** /ˈdɛndrəʊ/ • **comb. form** of or relating to a tree or trees: *dendrology.*
– ORIGIN from Gk *dendron* 'tree'.

**dendrochronology** • **n.** a technique of dating based on the investigation of annual growth rings in tree trunks.
– DERIVATIVES **dendrochronological** adj. **dendrochronologist** n.

**dendrogram** /ˈdɛndrə(ʊ)gram/ • **n.** a tree diagram.

**dendroid** /ˈdɛndrɔɪd/ • **adj.** Biology tree-shaped; branching. • **n.** Palaeontology a graptolite of a type that formed much-branched colonies.

**dendrology** /dɛnˈdrɒlədʒi/ • **n.** the scientific study of trees.
– DERIVATIVES **dendrological** adj. **dendrologist** n.

**dendron** /ˈdɛndrɒn/ • **n.** another term for **DENDRITE** (in sense 1).
– ORIGIN C19: from **DENDRITE**, on the pattern of words such as *axon*.

**Dene** /ˈdɛneɪ, ˈdɛni/ • **n.** (pl. same) **1** a member of a group of American Indian peoples of the Canadian North-West and Alaska. **2** any of the Athabaskan languages of these peoples.
– ORIGIN from Fr. *Déné*, from an Athabaskan word meaning 'people'.

**dene**[1] /diːn/ (also **dean**) • **n.** [usu. in place names] Brit. a deep, narrow, wooded valley.
– ORIGIN OE *denu*, of Gmc origin; rel. to **DEN**.

**dene**[2] /diːn/ • **n.** dialect a bare sandy tract or low sandhill by the sea.
– ORIGIN ME: perh. of Gmc origin and rel. to **DUNE**.

**denervate** /diːˈnəːveɪt/ • **v.** Medicine cut off the nerve supply from.
– DERIVATIVES **denervation** n.

**dengue** /ˈdɛŋgi/ (also **dengue fever**) • **n.** a debilitating tropical viral disease transmitted by mosquitoes, causing sudden fever and acute pains in the joints.
– ORIGIN C19: from W. Ind. Sp., from Kiswahili *dinga*, influenced by Sp. *dengue* 'fastidiousness' (with ref. to the dislike of movement by affected patients).

**deniable** • **adj.** able to be denied.
– DERIVATIVES **deniability** n. **deniably** adv.

**denial** • **n. 1** the action of denying something. **2** Psychology refusal to acknowledge an unacceptable truth or emotion, used as a defence mechanism.

**denier**[1] /ˈdɛnɪə/ • **n. 1** a unit by which the fineness of yarn is measured, equal to the weight in grams of 9,000 metres of the yarn. **2** a former French coin equal to one twelfth of a sou.
– ORIGIN ME (in sense 2): via OFr. from L. *denarius* (see **DENARIUS**).

**denier**[2] /dɪˈnʌɪə/ • **n.** a person who denies something.

**denigrate** /ˈdɛnɪgreɪt/ • **v.** criticize unfairly; disparage.
– DERIVATIVES **denigration** n. **denigrator** n. **denigratory** /-ˈgreɪt(ə)ri/ adj.
– ORIGIN ME (in the sense 'blacken, make dark'): from L. *denigrat-*, *denigrare*, from *de-* 'away, completely' + *nigare* (from *niger* 'black').

**denim** • **n.** a hard-wearing cotton twill fabric, typically blue. ➤ (**denims**) jeans or other clothes made of such fabric.
– ORIGIN C17 (as *serge denim*): from Fr. *serge de Nîmes*, denoting serge from the manufacturing town of *Nîmes*.

**denitrify** /diːˈnʌɪtrɪfʌɪ/ • **v.** (**-ies**, **-ied**) remove the nitrates or nitrites from (soil, water, etc.) by chemical reduction.
– DERIVATIVES **denitrification** n.

**denizen** /ˈdɛnɪz(ə)n/ • **n. 1** formal or humorous an inhabitant or occupant: *denizens of field and forest.* **2** Brit. historical a foreigner allowed certain rights in their adopted country.
– DERIVATIVES **denizenship** n.
– ORIGIN ME *deynseyn*, via Anglo-Norman Fr. from OFr. *deinz* 'within' + *-ein* (from L. *-aneus* '-aneous'); influenced by **CITIZEN**.

**denominal** /dɪˈnɒmɪnəl/ • **adj.** (of a word) derived from a noun.
– ORIGIN 1930s: from **DE-** + **NOMINAL**.

**denominate** /dɪˈnɒmɪneɪt/ • **v. 1** formal call; name. **2** (**be denominated**) (of sums of money) be expressed in a specified monetary unit.
– ORIGIN ME: from L. *denominat-*, *denominare*, from *de-* 'away, formally' + *nominare* 'to name'.

**denomination** • **n. 1** a recognized autonomous branch of a church or religion. **2** the face value of a banknote, coin, or postage stamp. ➤ the rank of a playing card. **3** formal a name or designation.

**denominational** • **adj.** of or relating to a particular religious denomination.
– DERIVATIVES **denominationalism** n.

**denominator** • **n.** Mathematics the number below the line in a vulgar fraction; a divisor.
– ORIGIN C16: from Fr. *dénominateur* or med. L. *denominator*.

**de nos jours** /ˌdə nəʊ ˈʒʊə, French də no ʒuʀ/ • **adj.** [postpos.] contemporary.
– ORIGIN Fr., 'of our days'.

**denote** /dɪˈnəʊt/ • **v.** be a sign of; indicate. ➤ stand as a name or symbol for.
– DERIVATIVES **denotation** n. **denotational** adj. **denotative** /-tətɪv/ adj.
– ORIGIN C16: from Fr. *dénoter* or L. *denotare*, from *de-* 'away, thoroughly' + *notare* 'observe, note'.

**denouement** /deɪˈnuːmɒ̃/ • **n.** the final part of a play, film, etc. in which matters are explained or resolved.

– ORIGIN C18: Fr. *dénouement*, from *dénouer* 'unknot'.

**denounce** ● v. publicly declare to be wrong or evil.
– DERIVATIVES **denouncement** n. **denouncer** n.
– ORIGIN ME: from OFr. *denoncier*, from L. *denuntiare*, based on *nuntius* 'messenger'.

**de novo** /deɪ 'nəʊvəʊ, diː/ ● adv. & adj. starting from the beginning; anew.
– ORIGIN L., lit. 'from new'.

**dense** ● adj. **1** closely compacted in substance. ➤ crowded closely together. **2** informal (of a person) stupid.
– DERIVATIVES **densely** adv. **denseness** n. **densification** n. **densify** v.
– ORIGIN ME: from L. *densus*.

**densitometer** /ˌdɛnsɪ'tɒmɪtə/ ● n. **1** an instrument for measuring the photographic density of an image. **2** a device for measuring the optical density of a material.
– DERIVATIVES **densitometric** adj. **densitometrically** adv. **densitometry** n.

**density** ● n. (pl. **-ies**) the degree of compactness of a substance. ➤ the opacity of a photographic image. ➤ the quantity of people or things in a given area or space.
– ORIGIN C17: from Fr. *densité* or L. *densitas*, from *densus* 'dense'.

**dent** ● n. a slight hollow in a hard even surface made by a blow or pressure. ● v. **1** mark with a dent. **2** have an adverse effect on.
– ORIGIN ME: var. of **DINT**.

**dental** ● adj. **1** of or relating to the teeth or dentistry. **2** Phonetics (of a consonant) pronounced with the tip of the tongue against the upper front teeth (as *th*) or the alveolar ridge (as *n, d, t*).
– DERIVATIVES **dentalize** (also **-ise**) v. **dentally** adv.
– ORIGIN C16: from late L. *dentalis*, from L. *dens, dent-* 'tooth'.

**dentalium** /dɛn'teɪlɪəm/ ● n. tusk shells used as ornaments or money.
– ORIGIN mod. L., from late L. *dentalis*.

**dental surgeon** ● n. a dentist.

**dental technician** ● n. a person who makes and repairs artificial teeth.

**dentary** /'dɛnt(ə)ri/ ● n. (pl. **-ies**) Zoology the bone of the lower jaw which bears the teeth.
– ORIGIN C19: from late L. *dentarius*.

**dentate** /'dɛnteɪt/ ● adj. Botany & Zoology having a tooth-like or serrated edge.
– ORIGIN ME: from L. *dentatus*.

**dentelle** /dɛn'tɛl/ ● n. (pl. pronounced same) ornamental tooling used in bookbinding, resembling lace edging.
– ORIGIN C19: from Fr., 'lace'.

**denticle** /'dɛntɪk(ə)l/ ● n. Zoology a small tooth or tooth-like projection.
– ORIGIN ME: from L. *denticulus*, dimin. of *dens, dent-* 'tooth'.

**denticulate** /dɛn'tɪkjʊlət/ ● adj. having small teeth or tooth-like projections.
– DERIVATIVES **denticulated** adj.

**dentifrice** /'dɛntɪfrɪs/ ● n. a paste or powder for cleaning the teeth.
– ORIGIN ME: from Fr., from L. *dentifricium*, from *dens, dent-* 'tooth' + *fricare* 'to rub'.

**dentil** /'dɛntɪl/ ● n. Architecture one of a series of small tooth-like rectangular blocks used as a decoration under the moulding of a cornice.
– ORIGIN C16: from Ital. *dentello* or obs. Fr. *dentille*, dimin. of *dent* 'tooth'.

**dentine** /'dɛntiːn/ (US **dentin** /-tɪn/) ● n. hard dense bony tissue forming the bulk of a tooth.
– DERIVATIVES **dentinal** /'dɛntɪn(ə)l/ adj.
– ORIGIN C19: from L. *dens, dent-* 'tooth' + **-INE**[4].

**dentist** ● n. a person who is qualified to treat the diseases and conditions that affect the teeth and gums.
– DERIVATIVES **dentistry** n.
– ORIGIN C18: from Fr. *dentiste*, from *dent* 'tooth'.

**dentition** /dɛn'tɪʃ(ə)n/ ● n. the arrangement or condition of the teeth in a particular species or individual.
– ORIGIN C16: from L. *dentitio(n-)*, from *dentire* 'teethe'.

**denture** /'dɛntʃə/ ● n. a removable plate or frame holding one or more artificial teeth.
– DERIVATIVES **denturist** n.
– ORIGIN C19: from Fr.

**denuclearize** (also **-ise**) ● v. remove nuclear weapons from.
– DERIVATIVES **denuclearization** n.

**denude** ● v. (often **be denuded of**) strip of covering or possessions; make bare.
– DERIVATIVES **denudation** n.
– ORIGIN ME: from L. *denudare*, from *de-* 'completely' + *nudare* 'to bare'.

**denumerable** /dɪ'njuːm(ə)rəb(ə)l/ ● adj. Mathematics able to be counted by correspondence with the set of integers.
– DERIVATIVES **denumerability** n. **denumerably** adv.
– ORIGIN C20: from late L. *denumerare* 'count out'.

**denunciation** /dɪˌnʌnsɪ'eɪʃ(ə)n/ ● n. the action of denouncing someone or something.
– DERIVATIVES **denunciator** n. **denunciatory** adj.
– ORIGIN ME: from L. *denuntiatio(n-)*, from *denuntiare* (see **DENOUNCE**).

**deny** /dɪ'nʌɪ/ ● v. (**-ies**, **-ied**) **1** refuse to admit the truth or existence of. **2** refuse to give (something requested or desired) to (someone). ➤ archaic refuse access to. ➤ (**deny oneself**) go without.
– ORIGIN ME: from OFr. *deni-, deneier*, from L. *denegare*, from *de-* 'formally' + *negare* 'say no'.

**deoch an doris** /ˌdɒx (ə)n 'dɒrɪs, dɒk/ (also **doch an dorris**) ● n. Scottish & Irish a final drink taken before parting.
– ORIGIN C17: from Sc. Gaelic *deoch an doruis* 'drink at the door'.

**deodar** /'diːə(ʊ)dɑː/ ● n. a tall cedar with drooping branches, native to the Himalayas. [*Cedrus deodara*.]
– ORIGIN C19: from Hindi *deodār*, from Sanskrit *devadāru* 'divine tree'.

**deodorant** /dɪ'əʊd(ə)r(ə)nt/ ● n. a substance which removes or conceals unpleasant bodily odours.
– ORIGIN C19: from **DE-** + L. *odor* 'smell' + **-ANT**.

**deodorize** (also **-ise**) ● v. remove or conceal an unpleasant smell in.
– DERIVATIVES **deodorization** n. **deodorizer** n.

**deontic** /dɪ'ɒntɪk/ ● adj. Philosophy of or relating to duty and obligation as ethical concepts.
– ORIGIN C20: from Gk *deont-* 'being right' (from *dei* 'it is right') + **-IC**.

**deontology** /ˌdiːɒn'tɒlədʒi/ ● n. Philosophy the study of the nature of duty and obligation.
– DERIVATIVES **deontological** adj. **deontologist** n.

**Deo volente** /ˌdeɪəʊ vɒ'lɛnteɪ/ ● adv. God willing; if nothing prevents it.
– ORIGIN from L.

**deoxygenate** /diː'ɒksɪdʒəneɪt/ ● v. remove oxygen from.
– DERIVATIVES **deoxygenation** n.

**deoxyribonucleic acid** /dɪˌɒksɪrʌɪbəʊnjuː'kleɪɪk/ ● n. see **DNA**.
– ORIGIN 1930s: from a blend of **DEOXYRIBOSE** and **NUCLEIC ACID**.

**deoxyribose** /dɪˌɒksɪ'rʌɪbəʊz, -s/ ● n. Biochemistry a sugar derived from ribose by replacement of a hydroxyl group by hydrogen.
– ORIGIN 1930s: from **DE-** (expressing reduction) + **OXY-**[2] + **RIBOSE**.

**dep.** ● abbrev. **1** departs. **2** deputy.

**depart** ● v. **1** leave, especially in order to start a journey. **2** (**depart from**) deviate from (a course of action).
– PHRASES **depart this life** archaic die.
– ORIGIN ME: from OFr. *departir*, based on L. *dispertire* 'to divide'.

**departed** ● adj. deceased.

**department** ● n. **1** a division of a large organization or building, dealing with a specific area of activity. **2** an administrative district in France and other countries. **3** (**one's department**) informal an area of special expertise or responsibility. ➤ informal a specified aspect or quality: *he was a bit lacking in the height department.*
– DERIVATIVES **departmental** adj. **departmentalism** n.

**departmentalization** (also **-isation**) n. **departmentalize** (also **-ise**) v. **departmentally** adv.
– ORIGIN ME: from OFr. *departement*, from *departir* (see **DEPART**).

**department store** ● n. a large shop stocking many varieties of goods in different departments.

**departure** ● n. **1** the action of departing. **2** Nautical the amount of a ship's change of longitude.
– ORIGIN ME: from OFr. *departeure*.

**depasture** ● v. Brit. put to graze on pasture.
– DERIVATIVES **depasturage** n.

**depauperate** /dɪˈpɔːp(ə)rət/ ● adj. Biology lacking in numbers or variety of species. ➤ imperfectly developed.
– ORIGIN ME (in the sense 'impoverished'): from med. L. *depauperat-*, *depauperare*, from *de-* 'completely' + *pauperare* 'make poor'.

**depend** ● v. **1** (**depend on**) be controlled or determined by. **2** (**depend on**) rely on. **3** archaic or poetic/literary hang down.
– PHRASES **depending on** according to.
– ORIGIN ME: from OFr. *dependre*, from L. *dependere*, from *de-* 'down' + *pendere* 'hang'.

**dependable** ● adj. trustworthy and reliable.
– DERIVATIVES **dependability** n. **dependably** adv.

**dependant** (also **dependent**) ● n. a person who relies on another, especially a family member, for financial support.

**dependency** ● n. (pl. **-ies**) **1** a country or province controlled by another. **2** the state of being dependent.

**dependent** ● adj. **1** (**dependent on**) contingent on or determined by. **2** relying on someone or something for financial or other support. ➤ (**dependent on**) unable to do without: *dependent on drugs*. **3** Grammar subordinate to another clause, phrase, or word. ● n. variant spelling of **DEPENDANT**.
– DERIVATIVES **dependence** n. **dependently** adv.
– ORIGIN ME *dependant* 'hanging down', from OFr., pres. part. of *dependre* (see **DEPEND**).

**dependent variable** ● n. Mathematics a variable (often denoted by *y*) whose value depends on that of another.

**depersonalize** (also **-ise**) ● v. divest of human characteristics or individuality.
– DERIVATIVES **depersonalization** n.

**depict** /dɪˈpɪkt/ ● v. represent by a drawing, painting, or other art form. ➤ portray in words.
– DERIVATIVES **depicter** n. **depiction** n.
– ORIGIN ME: from L. *depict-*, *depingere*, from *de-* 'completely' + *pingere* 'to paint'.

**depigment** /diːˈpɪgm(ə)nt/ ● v. [usu. as adj. **depigmented**] reduce or remove the pigmentation of (the skin).
– DERIVATIVES **depigmentation** n.

**depilate** /ˈdɛpɪleɪt/ ● v. remove the hair from.
– DERIVATIVES **depilation** n. **depilator** n.
– ORIGIN C16: from L. *depilat-*, *depilare*, from *de-* (expressing removal) + *pilare* (from *pilus* 'hair').

**depilatory** /dɪˈpɪlət(ə)ri/ ● adj. used to remove unwanted hair. ● n. (pl. **-ies**) a depilatory cream or lotion.

**deplane** ● v. chiefly N. Amer. disembark from an aircraft.

**deplete** /dɪˈpliːt/ ● v. reduce the number or quantity of: *fish stocks are severely depleted*. ➤ exhaust.
– DERIVATIVES **depletion** n.
– ORIGIN C19: from L. *deplet-*, *deplere* 'empty out', from *de-* (expressing reversal) + *plere* 'fill'.

**depleted uranium** ● n. uranium from which most of the fissile isotope uranium-235 has been removed.

**deplorable** /dɪˈplɔːrəb(ə)l/ ● adj. deserving strong condemnation; shockingly bad.
– DERIVATIVES **deplorably** adv.

**deplore** /dɪˈplɔː/ ● v. feel or express strong disapproval of.
– DERIVATIVES **deploring** adj. **deploringly** adv.
– ORIGIN C16 (in the sense 'weep for, regret deeply'): from Fr. *déplorer* or Ital. *deplorare*, from L. *deplorare*, from *de-* 'away, thoroughly' + *plorare* 'bewail'.

**deploy** /dɪˈplɔɪ/ ● v. bring or move into position for military action. ➤ bring into effective action.
– DERIVATIVES **deployment** n.
– ORIGIN C18: from Fr. *déployer*, from L. *displicare* and late L. *deplicare* 'unfold or explain'.

**deplume** ● v. deprive of feathers.

**depolarize** /diːˈpəʊlərʌɪz/ (also **-ise**) ● v. Physics reduce or remove the polarization of.
– DERIVATIVES **depolarization** n.

**depoliticize** (also **-ise**) ● v. remove from political activity or influence.
– DERIVATIVES **depoliticization** n.

**depolymerize** /diːˈpɒlɪmərʌɪz/ (also **-ise**) ● v. Chemistry break (a polymer) down into smaller units.
– DERIVATIVES **depolymerization** n.

**deponent** /dɪˈpəʊnənt/ ● adj. Grammar denoting verbs which are passive or middle in form but active in meaning. ● n. Law a person who makes a deposition or affidavit under oath.
– ORIGIN ME: from L. *deponent-*, *deponere* 'lay aside, put down'

**depopulate** ● v. substantially reduce the population of (an area).
– DERIVATIVES **depopulation** n.

**deport** ● v. **1** expel (a foreigner or immigrant) from a country. **2** (**deport oneself**) archaic conduct oneself in a specified manner.
– DERIVATIVES **deportable** adj. **deportation** n. **deportee** n.
– ORIGIN C16: from Fr. *déporter*, from L. *deportare*, from *de-* 'away' + *portare* 'carry'.

**deportment** ● n. **1** chiefly Brit. the way a person stands and walks, particularly as an element of etiquette. **2** chiefly N. Amer. a person's behaviour or manners.

**depose** ● v. **1** remove from office suddenly and forcefully. **2** Law testify to or give (evidence) on oath, especially in writing.
– ORIGIN ME: from OFr. *deposer*, from L. *deponere* (see **DEPONENT**), but influenced by L. *depositus* and OFr. *poser* 'to place'.

**deposit** ● n. **1** a sum of money placed in a bank or other account. **2** a sum payable as a first instalment or as a pledge. ➤ a returnable sum paid to cover possible loss or damage. **3** a layer or body of accumulated matter. **4** the action of depositing something. ● v. (**deposited**, **depositing**) **1** put or set down in a specific place. ➤ lay down naturally as a layer or covering. **2** store or entrust with someone for safe keeping. ➤ pay as a deposit.
– PHRASES **lose one's deposit** (of a candidate in a UK parliamentary election) receive less than a certain proportion of the votes (thereby forfeiting a statutory financial deposit).
– DERIVATIVES **depositor** n.
– ORIGIN C16: from L. *depositum* (n.), med. L. *depositare* (v.), both from L. *deposit-*, *deponere* 'lay aside'.

**deposit account** ● n. chiefly Brit. a bank account that pays interest and may not usually be drawn on without notice.

**depositary** (also **depository**) ● n. (pl. **-ies**) a person to whom something is lodged in trust.

**deposition** /ˌdɛpəˈzɪʃ(ə)n, diː-/ ● n. **1** the action of deposing a monarch. **2** Law the process of giving sworn evidence. ➤ a statement to be used as evidence. **3** the action of depositing something. **4** (**the Deposition**) the taking down of the body of Christ from the Cross.
– ORIGIN ME: from L. *depositio(n-)*, from *deponere* (see **DEPOSIT**).

**depository** ● n. (pl. **-ies**) **1** a place where things are stored. **2** variant spelling of **DEPOSITARY**.

**depot** /ˈdɛpəʊ/ ● n. **1** a place for the storage of large quantities of a commodity. **2** a place where buses, trains, or other vehicles are housed and maintained. ➤ N. Amer. a railway or bus station. **3** the headquarters of a regiment.
– ORIGIN C18 (in the sense 'act of depositing'): from Fr. *dépôt*, from L. *depositum* (see **DEPOSIT**).

**depower** ● v. Sailing adjust (a sail) so that the wind no longer fills it.

**deprave** /dɪˈpreɪv/ ● v. lead away from what is natural or right; corrupt.
– DERIVATIVES **depravation** n. **depravity** /dɪˈpravɪti/ n.

– ORIGIN ME (in the sense 'pervert in meaning or intention'): from OFr. *depraver* or L. *depravare*, from *de-* 'down, thoroughly' + *pravus* 'crooked, perverse'.

**depraved** • adj. morally corrupt.

**deprecate** /'dɛprɪkeɪt/ • v. **1** express disapproval of. **2** another term for DEPRECIATE (in sense 2).
– DERIVATIVES **deprecating** adj. **deprecatingly** adv. **deprecation** n. **deprecative** /'dɛprɪkətɪv/ adj. **deprecator** n. **deprecatory** adj.
– ORIGIN C17 (earlier (ME) as *deprecation* in the sense 'a prayer to ward off evil'): from L. *deprecat-*, *deprecari*, from *de-* (expressing reversal) + *precari* 'pray'.

**depreciate** /dɪ'priːʃɪeɪt, -sɪ-/ • v. **1** diminish in value over a period of time. ➤ reduce the recorded value of (an asset) over a predetermined period. **2** disparage or belittle.
– DERIVATIVES **depreciation** n. **depreciatory** /dɪ'priːʃ(ɪ)ət(ə)ri/ adj.
– ORIGIN ME: from late L. *depreciat-*, *depreciare* 'lower in price, undervalue', from L. *de-* 'down' + *pretium* 'price'.

**depredation** /ˌdɛprɪ'deɪʃ(ə)n/ • n. (usu. **depredations**) an act of attacking or plundering.
– ORIGIN C15: from Fr. *déprédation*, from late L. *depraedatio(n-)*, from *depraedari* 'to plunder'.

**depredator** /'dɛprɪdeɪtə/ • n. archaic a person or thing that makes depredations.

**depress** • v. **1** cause to feel utterly dispirited or dejected. **2** reduce the level of activity in (a system). **3** push or pull down into a lower position.
– DERIVATIVES **depressed** adj. **depressible** adj. **depressing** adj. **depressingly** adv.
– ORIGIN ME: from OFr. *depresser*, from late L. *depressare*, frequentative of *deprimere* 'press down'.

**depressant** • adj. reducing functional or nervous activity. • n. a depressant drug or other agent.

**depression** • n. **1** severe despondency and dejection, especially when long-lasting. **2** a long and severe recession in an economy or market. ➤ (**the Depression** or **the Great Depression**) the financial and industrial slump of 1929 and subsequent years. **3** the action of depressing something. ➤ a sunken place or hollow. **4** Meteorology a cyclonic weather system.
– ORIGIN ME: from L. *depressio(n-)*, from *deprimere* (see DEPRESS).

**depressive** • adj. tending to causing depression. • n. a person who tends to suffer from depression.

**depressor** • n. **1** Anatomy a muscle whose contraction pulls down a part of the body. **2** Physiology a nerve whose stimulation results in a lowering of blood pressure. **3** an instrument for pressing something down.

**depressurize** (also **-ise**) • v. release the pressure inside (a compartment or container).
– DERIVATIVES **depressurization** n.

**deprivation** /dɛprɪ'veɪʃ(ə)n/ • n. **1** the damaging lack of basic material benefits. ➤ the lack or denial of something considered essential. **2** archaic the action of depriving someone of office.

**deprive** /dɪ'prʌɪv/ • v. **1** deny (a person or place) the possession or use of something. **2** archaic depose (someone, especially a clergyman) from office.
– DERIVATIVES **deprival** n. **deprived** adj.
– ORIGIN ME: from OFr. *depriver*, from med. L. *deprivare*, from *de-* 'away, completely' + *privare* (see PRIVATE).

**de profundis** /ˌdeɪ prə'fʊndɪs/ • adv. expressing one's deepest feelings. • n. a heartfelt appeal.
– ORIGIN L., 'from the depths', the opening words of Psalm 130.

**deprogramme** (US **deprogram**) • v. (**deprogrammed**, **deprogramming**; US **deprogramed**, **deprograming**) release from brainwashing or indoctrination.

**Dept** • abbrev. Department.

**depth** • n. **1** the distance from the top or surface to the bottom of something or to a specified point within it. ➤ distance from the front to the back of something. ➤ the apparent existence of three dimensions in a two-dimensional representation. **2** complexity and profundity of thought. ➤ comprehensiveness of study or detail: *third-year courses go into more depth.* ➤ creditable intensity of emotion. **3** (**the depths**) the deepest or lowest part of something.
– PHRASES **hidden depths** previously unnoticed qualities. **in depth** in great detail; comprehensively and thoroughly. **out of one's depth 1** in water too deep to stand in. **2** in a situation beyond one's capabilities.
– ORIGIN ME: from DEEP + -TH², on the pattern of pairs such as *long*, *length*.

**depth charge** • n. an explosive charge designed to explode under water at a preset depth, used for attacking submarines.

**depthless** • adj. **1** unfathomably deep. **2** shallow and superficial.
– DERIVATIVES **depthlessly** adv.

**depth of field** • n. (in photography) the distance between the nearest and the furthest objects giving a focused image.

**depth psychology** • n. the psychoanalytic study of unconscious mental processes and motives.

**deputation** • n. a group of people who undertake a mission on behalf of a larger group.

**depute** • v. /dɪ'pjuːt/ appoint (someone) to perform a task for which one is responsible. ➤ delegate (authority or a task). • n. /'dɛpjuːt/ Scottish a person appointed to act in an official capacity or as a representative.
– ORIGIN ME: via OFr. from L. *deputare* 'consider to be, assign', from *de-* 'away'+ *putare* 'think over, consider'.

**deputize** /'dɛpjʊtʌɪz/ • v. temporarily act or speak on behalf of someone else. ➤ N. Amer. make (someone) a deputy.

**deputy** • n. (pl. **-ies**) **1** a person appointed to undertake the duties of a superior in the superior's absence. **2** a parliamentary representative in certain countries. **3** Brit. a coal mine official responsible for safety.
– PHRASES **by deputy** historical by proxy.
– DERIVATIVES **deputyship** n.
– ORIGIN ME: from OFr. *depute*, from late L. *deputatus*, past part. of *deputare* (see DEPUTE).

**deracinate** /dɪ'rasɪneɪt/ • v. **1** tear up by the roots. **2** [as adj. **deracinated**] displaced from one's environment.
– DERIVATIVES **deracination** n.
– ORIGIN C16: from Fr. *déraciner*, from *dé-* (expressing removal) + *racine* 'root'.

**derail** • v. cause (a train) to leave the tracks.
– DERIVATIVES **derailment** n.
– ORIGIN C19: from Fr. *dérailler*.

**derailleur** /dɪ'reɪl(j)ə/ • n. a bicycle gear which works by lifting the chain from one sprocket wheel to another.
– ORIGIN 1930s: from Fr., from *dérailler* 'derail'.

**derange** • v. **1** [usu. as adj. **deranged**] cause to become insane. **2** throw into disorder. **3** archaic intrude on; interrupt.
– DERIVATIVES **derangement** n.
– ORIGIN C18: from Fr. *déranger*, from OFr. *desrengier*, lit. 'move from orderly rows'.

**derate** • v. reduce the rating of (a component or device).

**Derby¹** /'dɑːbi/ • n. (pl. **-ies**) **1** an annual flat race at Epsom in Surrey for three-year-old horses, founded in 1780 by the 12th Earl of Derby. ➤ [in names] a similar race or other important sporting contest. **2** (**derby**; also **local derby**) a sports match between two rival teams from the same area. **3** (**derby**) N. Amer. a bowler hat. **4** a boot or shoe having the eyelet tabs stitched on top of the vamp.

**Derby²** /'dɑːbi/ • n. a hard pressed cheese made from skimmed milk.
– ORIGIN from *Derbyshire* in England, where it is made.

**derecognize** (also **-ise**) • v. withdraw recognition of.
– DERIVATIVES **derecognition** n.

**dereference** /diː'rɛfərəns/ • v. Computing obtain the address of a data item held in another location from (a pointer).

**deregister** • v. remove from a register.
– DERIVATIVES **deregistration** n.

**deregulate** • v. remove regulations or restrictions from.
– DERIVATIVES **deregulation** n. **deregulatory** adj.

**derelict** • adj. **1** in a very poor condition as a result of

## Word *Formation*

**-derm** (also **-derma** and **-dermy**) from Greek *derma, dermat-* 'skin'

| | | |
|---|---|---|
| ectoderm | the outermost layer of cells or tissue of an embryo | Gk *ektos* 'outside' |
| endoderm | the innermost layer of cells or tissue of an embryo | Gk *endon* 'within' |
| epidermis | the surface part of the skin of an animal | Gk *epi* 'upon' |
| hypodermic | relating to the region immediately beneath the skin (also, a needle used to inject beneath the skin) | Gk *hupo* 'under' |
| mesoderm | the middle layer of cells or tissue of an embryo | Gk *mesos* 'middle' |
| ostracoderm | an early fossil fish with a heavily armoured body | Gk *ostrakon* 'shell' |
| pachyderm | a large mammal with thick skin (e.g. an elephant) | Gk *pakhus* 'thick' |
| pyoderma | a skin infection with pus formation | Gk *puon* 'pus' |
| scleroderma | the hardening and contraction of the skin and connective tissue | Gk *sklēros* 'hard' |
| taxidermy | the preparation and stuffing of animal skins | Gk *taxis* 'arrangement' |
| xeroderma | a disease characterized by dryness of the skin | Gk *xēros* 'dry' |

The prefix **dermato-** is also derived from Greek, and gives rise to such English words as ***dermatology***, ***dermatitis***, and ***dermatomycosis***.

disuse and neglect. **2** chiefly N. Amer. shamefully negligent. ● **n. 1** a destitute person. **2** a ship or other piece of property abandoned by its owner.
– ORIGIN C17: from L. *derelict-, derelinquere* 'abandon', from *de-* 'completely' + *relinquere* 'forsake'.

**dereliction** ● **n. 1** the state of having been abandoned and become dilapidated. **2** (usu. **dereliction of duty**) shameful failure to fulfil one's obligations.

**derepress** /ˌdiːrɪˈprɛs/ ● **v.** Biochemistry & Genetics activate from an inoperative or latent state.
– DERIVATIVES **derepression** n.

**derestrict** ● **v.** remove restrictions from.
– DERIVATIVES **derestriction** n.

**deride** /dɪˈrʌɪd/ ● **v.** express contempt for; ridicule.
– DERIVATIVES **derider** n.
– ORIGIN C16: from L. *deridere* 'scoff at'.

**de-rig** ● **v.** dismantle the rigging of.

**de rigueur** /ˌdə rɪˈgəː/ ● **adj.** required by etiquette or current fashion.
– ORIGIN C19: Fr., lit. 'in strictness'.

**derision** /dɪˈrɪʒ(ə)n/ ● **n.** contemptuous ridicule or mockery.
– DERIVATIVES **derisible** /dɪˈrɪzɪb(ə)l/ adj.
– ORIGIN ME: via OFr. from late L. *derisio(n-)*, from *deridere* 'scoff at'.

**derisive** /dɪˈrʌɪsɪv, -z-/ ● **adj.** expressing contempt or ridicule.
– DERIVATIVES **derisively** adv. **derisiveness** n.

**derisory** /dɪˈrʌɪs(ə)ri, -z-/ ● **adj. 1** ridiculously small or inadequate. **2** another term for DERISIVE.

**derivation** ● **n. 1** the deriving of something from a source or origin. **2** the formation of a word from another word or from a root in the same or another language.
– DERIVATIVES **derivational** adj.

**derivative** /dɪˈrɪvətɪv/ ● **adj. 1** chiefly derogatory imitative of the work of another artist, writer, etc. **2** (of a financial product) having a value deriving from an underlying variable asset. ● **n. 1** something which is derived from another source. **2** Finance (often **derivatives**) a derivative future, option, or other financial product. **3** Mathematics an expression representing the rate of change of a function with respect to an independent variable.
– DERIVATIVES **derivatively** adv.
– ORIGIN ME: from Fr. *dérivatif, -ive*, from L. *derivativus*, from *derivare* (see DERIVE).

**derive** /dɪˈrʌɪv/ ● **v. 1** (**derive something from**) obtain something from (a specified source). ➤base something on a modification of: *Marx derived his philosophy of history from Hegel.* ➤Mathematics obtain a function or equation from another, especially by differentiation. **2** (**derive from**) have as a root or origin; originate from.
– DERIVATIVES **derivable** adj.
– ORIGIN ME (in the sense 'draw a fluid through or into a channel'): from OFr. *deriver* or L. *derivare*, from *de-* 'down, away' + *rivus* 'brook, stream'.

**derm** /dəːm/ ● **n.** another term for DERMIS.

**derma** /ˈdəːmə/ ● **n.** another term for DERMIS.
– ORIGIN C18: mod. L., from Gk 'skin'.

**dermabrasion** /ˌdəːməˈbreɪʒ(ə)n/ ● **n.** (in cosmetic surgery) the removal of superficial layers of skin with an abrasive tool.
– ORIGIN 1950s: from Gk *derma* 'skin' + ABRASION.

**dermatitis** /ˌdəːməˈtʌɪtɪs/ ● **n.** inflammation of the skin as a result of irritation by or allergic reaction to an external agent.
– ORIGIN C19: from Gk *derma, dermat-* 'skin' + -ITIS.

**dermato-** /ˈdəːmətəʊ/ ● **comb. form** of or relating to the skin: *dermatomycosis*. See word-formation panel.

**dermatoglyphics** /ˌdəːmətə(ʊ)ˈglɪfɪks/ ● **pl. n.** [treated as sing.] the study of skin markings or patterns on fingers, hands, and feet, especially in criminology.
– DERIVATIVES **dermatoglyph** n. **dermatoglyphic** adj. **dermatoglyphically** adv.

**dermatology** /ˌdəːməˈtɒlədʒi/ ● **n.** the branch of medicine concerned with skin disorders.
– DERIVATIVES **dermatological** adj. **dermatologically** adv. **dermatologist** n.

**dermatomycosis** /ˌdəːmətə(ʊ)mʌɪˈkəʊsɪs/ ● **n.** (pl. **dermatomycoses** /-siːz/) a fungal infection of the skin.

**dermatomyositis** /ˌdəːmətə(ʊ)mʌɪə(ʊ)ˈsʌɪtɪs/ ● **n.** Medicine inflammation of the skin and underlying muscle tissue.

**dermatophyte** /ˈdəːmətə(ʊ)fʌɪt/ ● **n.** a pathogenic fungus that grows on skin and other body surfaces, causing ringworm and related diseases.
– DERIVATIVES **dermatophytic** adj. **dermatophytosis** n.

**dermatosis** /ˌdəːməˈtəʊsɪs/ ● **n.** (pl. **dermatoses** /-siːz/) a disease of the skin, especially one that does not cause inflammation.

**dermestid** /dəːˈmɛstɪd/ ● **n.** Entomology a small beetle of a family (Dermestidae) including many kinds destructive to materials such as hides and wool.
– ORIGIN C19: from mod. L. *Dermestidae*, from the genus name *Dermestes*, from Gk *derma* 'skin' + *esthiein* 'eat'.

**dermis** /ˈdəːmɪs/ ● **n.** technical the skin. ➤Anatomy the thick layer of living tissue below the epidermis, containing blood capillaries, nerve endings, sweat glands, hair follicles, and other structures.
– DERIVATIVES **dermal** adj.
– ORIGIN C19: mod. L., suggested by *epidermis*.

**dermoid cyst** ● **n.** Medicine an abnormal growth containing epidermis, hair follicles, and sebaceous glands, derived from residual embryonic cells.

**dernier cri** /dəːnjeɪ ˈkriː/ ● **n.** the very latest fashion.
– ORIGIN C19: Fr., lit. 'last cry'.

**derogate** /ˈdɛrəgeɪt/ ● **v.** formal **1** (**derogate from**) detract from. **2** (**derogate from**) deviate from: *one country*

*derogated from the Rome Convention.* **3** disparage.
– DERIVATIVES **derogation** n. **derogative** adj.
– ORIGIN ME: from L. *derogat-, derogare* 'abrogate', from *de-* 'aside, away' + *rogare* 'ask'.

**derogatory** /dɪˈrɒɡət(ə)ri/ ● **adj.** showing a critical or disrespectful attitude.
– DERIVATIVES **derogatorily** adv.

**derrick** /ˈdɛrɪk/ ● **n. 1** a kind of crane with a movable pivoted arm. **2** the framework over an oil well, holding the drilling machinery.
– ORIGIN C17 (denoting a hangman, also the gallows): from *Derrick*, the surname of a London hangman.

**derrière** /ˌdɛrɪˈɛː/ ● **n.** euphemistic or humorous a person's buttocks.
– ORIGIN C18: Fr., lit. 'behind'.

**derring-do** /ˌdɛrɪŋˈduː/ ● **n.** dated or humorous action displaying heroic courage.
– ORIGIN C16: from ME *dorryng do* 'daring to do', misprinted as *derrynge do* and misinterpreted by Spenser; later popularized by Scott.

**derringer** /ˈdɛrɪn(d)ʒə/ ● **n.** a small pistol with a large bore, effective at close range.
– ORIGIN C19: named after the Amer. gunsmith Henry *Deringer.*

**derris** /ˈdɛrɪs/ ● **n.** an insecticide containing rotenone, made from the powdered roots of a tropical plant.
– ORIGIN C19: mod. L. (genus name of the plant), from Gk, 'leather covering' (referring to the plant's pods).

**derry** ● **n.** (in phr. **have a derry on**) Austral./NZ informal be prejudiced against.
– ORIGIN C19: appar. from the song refrain *derry down.*

**derv** (also **DERV**) ● **n.** Brit. diesel oil for motor vehicles.
– ORIGIN 1940s: acronym from *diesel-engined road-vehicle.*

**dervish** /ˈdəːvɪʃ/ ● **n.** a member of a Muslim fraternity vowed to poverty and known for their wild rituals.
– ORIGIN from Turk. *derviş*, from Pers. *darvīš* 'poor'.

**desacralize** /diːˈsakrəlʌɪz/ (also **-ise**) ● **v.** remove the religious or sacred status or significance from.
– DERIVATIVES **desacralization** n.

**desalinate** /diːˈsalɪneɪt/ ● **v.** remove salt from (seawater).
– DERIVATIVES **desalination** n. **desalinator** n.

**desalinize** ● **v.** US term for **DESALINATE**.
– DERIVATIVES **desalinization** n.

**desalt** ● **v.** another term for **DESALINATE**.

**desaparecido** /ˌdɛzəparəˈsiːdəʊ, Spanish desapareˈsido, -ˈθido/ ● **n.** (pl. **-os**) a person who has disappeared, presumed killed by soldiers or police.
– ORIGIN 1970s: Sp. (first used in Argentina), lit. 'disappeared'.

**desaturate** ● **v.** make less saturated or unsaturated.
– DERIVATIVES **desaturation** n.

**descale** ● **v.** remove deposits of scale from.
– DERIVATIVES **descaler** n.

**descant** ● **n.** /ˈdɛskant/ **1** Music an independent treble melody sung or played above a basic melody. ➤ archaic or poetic/literary a melodious song. **2** a discourse on a theme or subject. ● **v.** /dɪˈskant, dɛ-/ talk tediously or at length.
– ORIGIN ME: from OFr. *deschant*, from med. L. *discantus* 'part song, refrain'.

**descant recorder** ● **n.** the most common size of recorder, with a range of two octaves above the C above middle C.

**descend** ● **v. 1** move downwards. ➤ (of a road or flight of steps) slope or lead down. **2** Music become lower in pitch. **3** (**descend on**) make a sudden attack on or unwelcome visit to. **4** (**be descended from**) be a blood relative of (an ancestor). ➤ pass by inheritance.
– DERIVATIVES **descendent** adj.
– ORIGIN ME: from OFr. *descendre*, from L. *descendere*, from *de-* 'down' + *scandere* 'to climb'.

**descendant** ● **n.** a person, animal, etc. that is descended from a particular ancestor.

**descender** ● **n.** a part of a letter that extends below the line (as in *g* and *p*).

**descendeur** /dɪˈsɛndə/ ● **n.** Climbing a piece of metal around which a rope is passed to slow descent during abseiling.
– ORIGIN C20: from Fr., lit. 'descender'.

**descendible** ● **adj.** Law (of property) able to be inherited by a descendant.

**descent** ● **n. 1** the action of descending. ➤ a downward slope. **2** a person's origin or nationality: *the settlers were of Cornish descent.* ➤ transmission by inheritance. **3** (**descent on**) a sudden violent attack.
– ORIGIN ME: from OFr. *descente*, from *descendre* (see **DESCEND**).

**descramble** ● **v.** restore (a signal) to intelligible form.
– DERIVATIVES **descrambler** n.

**describe** ● **v. 1** give a detailed account in words of. **2** mark out or draw (a geometrical figure).
– DERIVATIVES **describable** adj. **describer** n.
– ORIGIN ME: from L. *descript-, describere*, from *de-* 'down' + *scribere* 'write'.

**description** ● **n. 1** a spoken or written account of a person, object, or event. ➤ the process of describing. **2** a sort, kind, or class: *people of any description.*
– PHRASES **beyond description** to a great and astonishing extent. **defy description** be so remarkable as to be impossible to describe.

**descriptive** ● **adj. 1** serving or seeking to describe. **2** describing or classifying without expressing judgement.
– DERIVATIVES **descriptively** adv. **descriptiveness** n.

**descriptivism** ● **n.** Philosophy the doctrine that the meanings of terms are purely descriptive.
– DERIVATIVES **descriptivist** n. & adj.

**descriptor** ● **n.** an element or term that serves to describe, identify, or index something.

**descry** /dɪˈskrʌɪ/ ● **v.** (**-ies**, **-ied**) poetic/literary catch sight of.
– ORIGIN ME: perh. confused with obs. *descry* 'describe', var. of obs. *descrive* 'perceive'.

**desecrate** /ˈdɛsɪkreɪt/ ● **v.** treat (a sacred place or thing) with violent disrespect.
– DERIVATIVES **desecration** n. **desecrator** n.
– ORIGIN C17: from **DE-** (expressing reversal) + a shortened form of **CONSECRATE**.

**deseed** ● **v.** remove the seeds from.
– DERIVATIVES **deseeder** n.

**desegregate** ● **v.** end a policy of racial segregation in.
– DERIVATIVES **desegregation** n.

**deselect** ● **v. 1** Brit. reject the candidature of (an existing MP). **2** Computing turn off (a feature) on a list of options.
– DERIVATIVES **deselection** n.

**desensitize** (also **-ise**) ● **v. 1** make less sensitive. **2** make indifferent to cruelty or suffering.
– DERIVATIVES **desensitization** n. **desensitizer** n.

**desert**[1] /dɪˈzəːt/ ● **v. 1** callously or treacherously abandon. **2** [usu. as adj. **deserted**] leave (a place), causing it to appear empty. **3** illegally run away from military service.
– DERIVATIVES **desertion** n.
– ORIGIN ME: from OFr. *deserter*, from late L. *desertare*, from L. *desertus* (see **DESERT**[2]).

**desert**[2] /ˈdɛzət/ ● **n. 1** a waterless, desolate area of land with little or no vegetation, typically covered with sand. **2** a situation or area considered dull and uninteresting: *a cultural desert.* ● **adj.** like a desert; uninhabited and desolate.
– ORIGIN ME: via OFr. from late L. *desertum* 'something left waste', neut. past part. of *deserere* 'leave, forsake'.

**desert**[3] /dɪˈzəːt/ ● **n.** (usu. **deserts**) a person's worthiness or entitlement to reward or punishment.
– PHRASES **get** (or **receive**) **one's just deserts** receive the appropriate reward or (more usually) punishment.
– ORIGIN ME: via OFr. from *deservir* (see **DESERVE**).

**desert boot** ● **n.** a lightweight boot with the upper made from suede.

**deserter** ● **n.** a member of the armed forces who deserts.

**desertification** /dɛˌzəːtɪfɪˈkeɪʃ(ə)n/ ● **n.** the process by which fertile land becomes desert.

**desert pavement** ● **n.** Geology a hard surface layer of cemented rock fragments from which fine material has been removed by the wind in arid regions.

**desert rat** • **n.** informal a soldier of the 7th British armoured division (with the jerboa as a badge) in the North African desert campaign of 1941–2.

**desert rose** • **n. 1** a flower-like aggregate of mineral crystals, occurring in arid areas. **2** a succulent plant with pink tubular flowers and toxic milky sap, native to East Africa and Arabia. [*Adenium obesum*.] **3** a dense Australian shrub with pinkish-lilac flowers. [*Gossypium sturtianum*.]

**desert varnish** • **n.** Geology a dark hard film of oxides formed on exposed rock surfaces in arid regions.

**deserve** • **v.** do something or show qualities worthy of (a reward or punishment as appropriate).
– DERIVATIVES **deserved** adj. **deservedly** adv.
– ORIGIN ME: from OFr. *deservir*, from L. *deservire* 'serve well or zealously'.

**deserving** • **adj.** worthy of favourable treatment or assistance.
– DERIVATIVES **deservingly** adv. **deservingness** n.

**desex** • **v. 1** deprive of sexual qualities. **2** castrate or spay.

**desexualize** (also **-ise**) • **v.** deprive of sexual character.
– DERIVATIVES **desexualization** n.

**déshabillé** /ˌdɛzaˈbiːjeɪ/ (also **dishabille**) • **n.** the state of being only partly or scantily clothed.
– ORIGIN Fr., 'undressed'.

**desiccant** • **n.** a hygroscopic substance used as a drying agent.

**desiccate** /ˈdɛsɪkeɪt/ • **v.** remove the moisture from.
– DERIVATIVES **desiccation** n. **desiccative** adj.
– ORIGIN C16: from L. *desiccat-*, *desiccare* 'make thoroughly dry'.

**desiccator** • **n.** an apparatus holding a drying agent for removing or keeping moisture from specimens.

**desiderate** /dɪˈzɪdəreɪt, -ˈsɪd-/ • **v.** archaic feel a keen desire for (something lacking).
– ORIGIN C17: from L. *desiderat-*, *desiderare* 'to desire', perh. from *de-* 'down' + *sidus, sider-* 'star'.

**desideratum** /dɪˌzɪdəˈrɑːtəm, -ˈreɪtəm, -ˌsɪd-/ • **n.** (pl. **desiderata** /-tə/) something that is needed or wanted.
– ORIGIN C17: from L., 'something desired', neut. past part. of *desiderare* (see **DESIDERATE**).

**design** • **n. 1** a plan or drawing produced to show the look and function or workings of something before it is built or made. ➤ the art or action of conceiving of and producing such a plan or drawing. ➤ purpose or planning that exists behind an action or object. **2** a decorative pattern. • **v.** decide upon the look and functioning of (something), especially by making a detailed drawing of it. ➤ do or plan (something) with a specific purpose in mind.
– PHRASES **by design** as a result of a plan; intentionally. **have designs on** aim to obtain, especially in an underhand way.
– ORIGIN ME (as a verb in the sense 'to designate'): from L. *designare*, reinforced by Fr. *désigner*.

**designate** • **v.** /ˈdɛzɪgneɪt/ give a specified position or status to: *he was designated as prime minister.* • **adj.** /ˈdɛzɪgnət/ [postpos.] appointed to an office or position but not yet installed: *the Director designate.*
– DERIVATIVES **designator** n.
– ORIGIN C17: from L. *designare* (see **DESIGN**).

**designated driver** • **n.** N. Amer. a person who abstains from alcohol at a social gathering so as to be fit to drive others home.

**designated hitter** • **n.** Baseball a non-fielding player named to bat instead of the pitcher.

**designation** • **n.** the choosing and naming of someone or something to have a specified position or status. ➤ an official title or description.

**designedly** • **adv.** deliberately in order to produce a specific effect.

**designer** • **n.** a person who designs things. ➤ [as modifier] made by a famous and prestigious fashion designer: *designer clothing.*

**designer drug** • **n.** chiefly N. Amer. a synthetic analogue of an illegal drug, devised to circumvent drug laws.

**designing** • **adj.** acting in a calculating, deceitful way.

**desirable** • **adj.** wished for as being attractive, useful, or necessary. ➤ (of a person) arousing sexual desire. • **n.** a desirable person or thing.
– DERIVATIVES **desirability** n. **desirableness** n. **desirably** adv.
– ORIGIN ME: from OFr., suggested by L. *desiderabilis*, from *desiderare* (see **DESIDERATE**).

**desire** • **n.** a strong feeling of wanting to have something or wishing for something to happen. ➤ strong sexual feeling or appetite. • **v.** strongly wish for or want. ➤ want sexually. ➤ archaic request or entreat.
– DERIVATIVES **desirous** adj.
– ORIGIN ME: from OFr. *desir* (n.), *desirer* (v.), from L. *desiderare* (see **DESIDERATE**).

**desist** /dɪˈzɪst, dɪˈsɪst/ • **v.** cease; abstain.
– ORIGIN ME: from OFr. *desister*, from L. *desistere*, from *de-* 'down from' + *sistere* 'to stop'.

**desk** • **n. 1** a piece of furniture with a flat or sloped surface and typically with drawers, at which one can read, write, or do other work. **2** Music a position in an orchestra at which two players share a music stand. **3** a counter in a hotel, bank, airport, etc. **4** a specified section of a news organization.
– ORIGIN ME: from med. L. *desca*, prob. based on Provençal *desca* 'basket' or Ital. *desco* 'table, butcher's block', both based on L. *discus* (see **DISCUS**).

**deskill** • **v.** reduce the level of skill required to carry out (a job).

**desk job** • **n.** a clerical or administrative job.

**desktop** • **n. 1** the working surface of a desk. **2** a microcomputer suitable for use at an ordinary desk. **3** the working area of a computer screen regarded as representing a notional desktop.

**desktop publishing** • **n.** the production of high-quality printed matter by means of a printer linked to a desktop computer.

**desman** /ˈdɛzmən/ • **n.** a small semiaquatic mammal related to the mole. [*Desmana moschata* (Russia) and *Galemys pyrenaicus* (the Pyrenees).]
– ORIGIN C18: via Fr. and Ger. from Swed. *desman-råtta* 'muskrat', from *desman* 'musk'.

**desmid** /ˈdɛzmɪd/ • **n.** Biology a single-celled freshwater alga which appears to be composed of two rigid cells with a shared nucleus. [Family Desmidiaceae.]
– ORIGIN C19: from mod. L. *Desmidium* (genus name), from Gk *desmos* 'band, chain' (because the algae are often found united in chains or masses).

**desolate** • **adj.** /ˈdɛs(ə)lət/ giving an impression of bleak and dismal emptiness. ➤ utterly wretched and unhappy. • **v.** /ˈdɛsəleɪt/ make desolate.
– DERIVATIVES **desolately** adv. **desolateness** n. **desolation** n. **desolator** n.
– ORIGIN ME: from L. *desolat-*, *desolare* 'abandon', from *de-* 'thoroughly' + *solus* 'alone'.

**desorb** /diːˈsɔːb/ • **v.** Chemistry cause the release of (an adsorbed substance) from a surface.
– DERIVATIVES **desorbent** adj. & n. **desorber** n. **desorption** n.
– ORIGIN 1920s: orig. as *desorption* (from *de-* 'away' + *adsorption*).

**despair** • **n.** the complete loss or absence of hope. • **v.** lose or be without hope.
– PHRASES **be the despair of** be the cause of despair in (someone else).
– DERIVATIVES **despairing** adj. **despairingly** adv.
– ORIGIN ME: via Anglo-Norman Fr. from OFr. *desespeir* (n.), *desperer* (v.), from L. *desperare*, from *de-* 'down from' + *sperare* 'to hope'.

**despatch** • **v. & n.** variant spelling of **DISPATCH**.

**desperado** /ˌdɛspəˈrɑːdəʊ/ • **n.** (pl. **-oes** or **-os**) dated a desperate or reckless criminal.
– DERIVATIVES **desperadoism** n.
– ORIGIN C17: pseudo-Sp. alt. of the obs. n. *desperate*.

**desperate** • **adj. 1** feeling, showing, or involving des-

pair. ➤tried in despair or when everything else has failed. **2** extremely bad or serious: *a desperate shortage.* **3** having a great need or desire for something. **4** violent or dangerous: *a desperate criminal.*
– DERIVATIVES **desperately** adv. **desperateness** n.
– ORIGIN ME: from L. *desperatus* 'deprived of hope', past part. of *desperare* (see **DESPAIR**).

**desperation** ● n. a state of despair, especially as resulting in rash or extreme behaviour.

**despicable** /dɪ'spɪkəb(ə)l, 'dɛspɪk-/ ● adj. deserving hatred and contempt.
– DERIVATIVES **despicably** adv.
– ORIGIN C16: from late L. *despicabilis*, from *despicari* 'look down on'.

**despise** /dɪ'spʌɪz/ ● v. feel contempt or repugnance for.
– DERIVATIVES **despiser** n.
– ORIGIN ME: from OFr. *despire*, from L. *despicere*, from *de-* 'down' + *specere* 'look at'.

**despite** /dɪ'spʌɪt/ ● prep. without being affected by; in spite of. ● n. archaic or poetic/literary **1** outrage; injury. **2** contempt; disdain.
– PHRASES **despite** (or **in despite**) **of** archaic in spite of. **despite oneself** without intending to or expecting to.
– DERIVATIVES **despiteful** adj. (archaic or poetic/literary).
– ORIGIN ME: from OFr. *despit* (n.), from L. *despectus* 'looking down on', past part. of *despicere* (see **DESPISE**).

**despoil** /dɪ'spɔɪl/ ● v. steal valuable or attractive possessions from (a place).
– DERIVATIVES **despoiler** n. **despoilment** n. **despoliation** /dɪˌspəʊlɪ'eɪʃ(ə)n/ n.
– ORIGIN ME: from OFr. *despoillier*, from L. *despoliare* 'rob, plunder' (from *spolia* 'spoil').

**despond** /dɪ'spɒnd/ ● v. archaic become dejected and lose confidence.
– ORIGIN C17: from L. *despondere* 'give up, abandon', from *de-* 'away' + *spondere* 'to promise'.

**despondent** ● adj. in low spirits from loss of hope or courage.
– DERIVATIVES **despondence** n. **despondency** n. **despondently** adv.

**despot** /'dɛspɒt/ ● n. a ruler who exercises absolute power, especially in a cruel or oppressive way.
– DERIVATIVES **despotic** adj. **despotically** adv. **despotism** n.
– ORIGIN C16: from Fr. *despote*, via med. L. from Gk *despotēs*, 'master, absolute ruler'.

**desquamate** /'dɛskwəmeɪt/ ● v. (of a layer of cells) come off in scales or flakes.
– DERIVATIVES **desquamation** n. **desquamative** /-'skwamətɪv/ adj.
– ORIGIN C18 (earlier (ME) as *desquamation*): from L. *desquamat-*, *desquamare* 'remove the scales from'.

**des res** /dɛz 'rɛz/ ● n. Brit. informal a desirable residence.
– ORIGIN 1980s: abbrev.

**dessert** /dɪ'zəːt/ ● n. the sweet course eaten at the end of a meal.
– ORIGIN C16: from Fr., past part. of *desservir* 'clear the table'.

**dessertspoon** ● n. a spoon used for dessert, smaller than a tablespoon and larger than a teaspoon.
– DERIVATIVES **dessertspoonful** n. (pl. **-fuls**).

**dessert wine** ● n. a sweet wine drunk with or following dessert.

**destabilize** (also **-ise**) ● v. upset the stability of.
– DERIVATIVES **destabilization** n.

**destination** ● n. the place to which someone or something is going or being sent.

**destine** /'dɛstɪn/ ● v. (**be destined**) be intended or chosen for a particular purpose or end.
– ORIGIN ME (in the sense 'predetermine, decree'): from OFr. *destiner*, from L. *destinare*, 'make firm, establish'.

**destiny** ● n. (pl. **-ies**) the events that will necessarily happen to a particular person in the future. ➤the hidden power believed to control this; fate.
– ORIGIN ME: from OFr. *destinee*, from L. *destinata*, fem. past part. of *destinare* 'make firm, establish'.

**destitute** /'dɛstɪtjuːt/ ● adj. **1** extremely poor and lacking the means to provide for oneself. **2** (**destitute of**) not having.
– DERIVATIVES **destitution** n.
– ORIGIN ME (in the sense 'deserted, abandoned, empty'): from L. *destitut-*, *destituere* 'forsake'.

**destock** ● v. Brit. reduce the quantity of stock held in a shop.

**de-stress** ● v. relax after a period of work or tension.

**destrier** /'dɛstrɪə, dɛ'striːə/ ● n. a medieval knight's warhorse.
– ORIGIN ME: from OFr., based on L. *dextera* 'the right hand', from *dexter* 'on the right' (because the squire led the knight's horse with his right hand).

**destroy** ● v. **1** put an end to the existence of (something) by damaging or attacking it. ➤ruin emotionally or spiritually. **2** kill (an animal) by humane means.
– ORIGIN ME: from OFr. *destruire*, based on L. *destruct-*, *destruere*, from *de-* (expressing reversal) + *struere* 'build'.

**destroyer** ● n. **1** someone or something that destroys. **2** a small fast warship equipped for a defensive role against submarines and aircraft.

**destroying angel** ● n. a deadly poisonous white toadstool which grows in woodland. [*Amanita virosa*.]

**destruct** ● v. cause the destruction of.
– DERIVATIVES **destructor** n.
– ORIGIN 1950s (orig. US): back-form. from **DESTRUCTION**.

**destructible** ● adj. able to be destroyed.
– DERIVATIVES **destructibility** n.
– ORIGIN C18 (earlier in *indestructible*): from Fr., from late L. *destructibilis*.

**destruction** ● n. the action or process of causing so much damage to something that it no longer exists or cannot be repaired. ➤a cause of someone's ruin.
– ORIGIN ME: from L. *destructio(n-)*, from *destruere* (see **DESTROY**).

**destructive** ● adj. **1** causing destruction. **2** tending to refute or disparage; negative and unhelpful.
– DERIVATIVES **destructively** adv. **destructiveness** n.

**desuetude** /dɪ'sjuːɪtjuːd, 'dɛswɪ-/ ● n. formal a state of disuse.
– ORIGIN C17 (in the sense 'cessation'): from Fr., from L. *desuetudo*, from *desuet-*, *desuescere* 'make unaccustomed', from *de-* (expressing reversal) + *suescere* 'be accustomed'.

**desulphurize** (also **-ise**, US **desulfurize**) ● v. remove sulphur from.
– DERIVATIVES **desulphurization** n. **desulphurizer** n.

**desultory** /'dɛs(ə)lt(ə)ri, -z-/ ● adj. lacking purpose or enthusiasm.
– DERIVATIVES **desultorily** adv. **desultoriness** n.
– ORIGIN C16 (lit. 'skipping about'): from L. *desultorius* 'superficial' (lit. 'relating to a vaulter'), from *desultor* 'vaulter', from the verb *desilire*.

**desuperheater** ● n. a container for reducing the temperature of steam to make it less superheated.

**desynchronize** (also **-ise**) ● v. disturb the synchronization of.
– DERIVATIVES **desynchronization** n.

**detach** ● v. **1** disengage (something) and remove it. ➤(**detach oneself from**) leave or separate oneself from (a group or place). **2** (**be detached**) Military be sent on a separate mission.
– DERIVATIVES **detachability** n. **detachable** adj.
– ORIGIN C16 (in the sense 'discharge a gun'): from Fr. *détacher*, from *des-* (expressing reversal) + *attacher* 'attach'.

**detached** ● adj. **1** separate or disconnected. ➤(of a house) not joined to another on either side. **2** aloof and objective. **3** denoting a retina that has become separated from the underlying choroid tissue at the back of the eye, causing loss of vision in the affected area.
– DERIVATIVES **detachedly** adv.

**detachment** ● n. **1** the state of being objective or aloof. **2** Military a group of troops, ships, etc. sent away on a separate mission. **3** the action or process of detaching.

**detail** ● n. **1** a small individual feature, fact, or item. ➤a small part of a picture reproduced separately for close study. **2** a small detachment of troops or police officers given a special duty. ➤a special duty assigned to such a

detachment. ● v. **1** describe item by item; give the full particulars of. **2** assign to undertake a particular task.
– PHRASES **go into detail** give a full account of something. **in detail** as regards every feature or aspect; fully.
– ORIGIN C17: from Fr. *détail* (n.), *détailler* (v.), from *dé-* (expressing separation) + *tailler* 'to cut'.

**detailed** ● adj. including many details. ➤showing attention to detail.

**detailing** ● n. small decorative features on a building, garment, or work of art.

**detain** ● v. **1** keep (someone) from proceeding by holding them back or making claims on their attention. **2** keep (someone) in official custody.
– DERIVATIVES **detainment** n.
– ORIGIN ME (in the sense 'be afflicted with sickness or infirmity'): from OFr. *detenir*, from a var. of L. *detinere*, from *de-* 'away, aside' + *tenere* 'to hold'.

**detainee** /ˌdɪteɪˈniː, ˌdiː-/ ● n. a person held in custody, especially for political reasons.

**detainer** ● n. Law **1** the action of detaining or withholding property. **2** an order authorizing the continued detention of a person in custody. **3** a person who detains.

**detect** ● v. **1** discover or identify the presence or existence of. **2** discover or investigate (a crime or its perpetrators). **3** discern (something intangible or barely perceptible).
– DERIVATIVES **detectable** adj. **detectably** adv. **detection** n.
– ORIGIN ME: from L. *detect-*, *detegere* 'uncover' from *de-* (expressing reversal) + *tegere* 'to cover'.

**detective** ● n. a person, especially a police officer, whose occupation is to investigate crimes.

**detector** ● n. a device designed to detect the presence of a particular object or substance and to emit a signal in response.

**detectorist** ● n. a person who uses a metal detector for a hobby.

**detent** /dɪˈtɛnt/ ● n. a catch in a machine which prevents motion until released. ➤(in a clock) a catch that regulates striking.
– ORIGIN C17: from Fr. *détente*, from OFr. *destente*, from *destendre* 'slacken'.

**détente** /deɪˈtɑːnt/ ● n. the easing of hostility or strained relations between countries.
– ORIGIN C20: Fr., 'loosening, relaxation'.

**detention** ● n. **1** the action or state of detaining or being detained. **2** the punishment of being kept in school after hours.
– ORIGIN ME: from late L. *detentio(n-)*, from L. *detinere* (see **DETAIN**).

**detention centre** ● n. an institution where people, in particular refugees and people awaiting trial, are detained for short periods.

**deter** /dɪˈtəː/ ● v. (**deterred**, **deterring**) discourage (someone) from doing something by instilling fear of the consequences. ➤prevent the occurrence of.
– ORIGIN C16: from L. *deterrere*, from *de-* 'away from' + *terrere* 'frighten'.

**detergent** ● n. a soluble cleansing agent which combines with impurities and dirt to make them more soluble. ● adj. of or relating to detergents or their action.
– DERIVATIVES **detergence** n. **detergency** n.
– ORIGIN C17 (as adj.): from L. *detergent-*, *detergere*, 'wipe away'.

**deteriorate** /dɪˈtɪərɪəreɪt/ ● v. become progressively worse.
– DERIVATIVES **deterioration** n. **deteriorative** adj.
– ORIGIN C16: from late L. *deteriorat-*, *deteriorare*, from L. *deterior* 'worse'.

**determinable** ● adj. **1** able to be determined. **2** Law capable of being brought to an end under given conditions.

**determinant** /dɪˈtəːmɪnənt/ ● n. **1** a factor which determines the nature or outcome of something. **2** Biology a gene determining the character and development of particular cells in an organism. **3** Mathematics a quantity obtained by the addition of products of the elements of a square matrix according to a given rule. ● adj. serving to determine or decide something.

**determinate** /dɪˈtəːmɪnət/ ● adj. **1** having exact and discernible limits or form. **2** Botany (of a flowering shoot) having the main axis ending in a flower, as in a cyme.
– DERIVATIVES **determinacy** n. **determinately** adv. **determinateness** n.

**determination** ● n. **1** the quality of being determined; firmness of purpose. **2** the process of determining something. ➤Law the settlement of a dispute by the authoritative decision of a judge or arbitrator. ➤Law a judicial decision or sentence. **3** Law the cessation of an estate or interest. **4** archaic a tendency to move in a fixed direction.

**determinative** /dɪˈtəːmɪnətɪv/ ● adj. chiefly Law serving to define, qualify, or direct. ● n. Grammar another term for **DETERMINER**.

**determine** /dɪˈtəːmɪn/ ● v. **1** cause to occur in a particular way; be the decisive factor in. **2** firmly decide: *she determined to tackle Stephen the next day.* **3** ascertain or establish by research or calculation. **4** Mathematics specify the value, position, or form of (a mathematical or geometrical object) uniquely. **5** Law, archaic bring or come to an end.
– ORIGIN ME: from OFr. *determiner*, from L. *determinare* 'limit, fix', from *de-* 'completely' + *terminare* 'terminate'.

**determined** ● adj. having firmness of purpose; resolute.
– DERIVATIVES **determinedly** adv. **determinedness** n.

**determiner** ● n. **1** a person or thing that determines something. **2** Grammar a modifying word that determines the kind of reference a noun or noun group has, for example *a*, *the*, *every*.

**determinism** ● n. Philosophy the doctrine that all events and actions are ultimately determined by causes regarded as external to the will.
– DERIVATIVES **determinist** n. & adj. **deterministic** adj. **deterministically** adv.

**deterrent** /dɪˈtɛr(ə)nt/ ● n. a thing that deters or is intended to deter someone from doing something. ● adj. able or intended to deter.
– DERIVATIVES **deterrence** n.

**detest** ● v. dislike intensely.
– DERIVATIVES **detester** n.
– ORIGIN C15: from L. *detestari*, from *de-* 'down' + *testari* 'witness, call upon to witness' (from *testis* 'a witness').

**detestable** ● adj. deserving intense dislike.
– DERIVATIVES **detestably** adv.

**detestation** /ˌdiːtɛˈsteɪʃ(ə)n/ ● n. intense dislike. ➤archaic a detested person or thing.

**dethrone** ● v. remove (a monarch) from power. ➤remove from a position of authority or dominance.
– DERIVATIVES **dethronement** n.

**detinue** /ˈdɛtɪnjuː/ ● n. Law the crime of wrongful detention of goods or personal possessions.
– ORIGIN ME: from OFr. *detenue*, past part. (used as n.) of *detenir* 'detain'.

**detonate** /ˈdɛtəneɪt/ ● v. explode or cause to explode.
– DERIVATIVES **detonation** n. **detonative** adj.
– ORIGIN C18: from L. *detonat-*, *detonare*, from *de-* 'down' + *tonare* 'to thunder'.

**detonator** ● n. a device or small sensitive charge used to detonate an explosive. ➤Brit. another term for **FOG SIGNAL**.

**detour** ● n. a roundabout route taken to avoid something or to visit somewhere along the way. ● v. take a detour.
– ORIGIN C18: from Fr. *détour* 'change of direction', from *détourner* 'turn away'.

**detox** informal ● n. /ˈdiːtɒks/ detoxification. ● v. /diːˈtɒks/ detoxify.

**detoxicate** /diːˈtɒksɪkeɪt/ ● v. another term for **DETOXIFY**.
– DERIVATIVES **detoxication** n.

**detoxify** /diːˈtɒksɪfʌɪ/ ● v. (**-ies**, **-ied**) **1** remove toxic substances or qualities from. **2** abstain or help to abstain from drink and drugs until the bloodstream is free of toxins.
– DERIVATIVES **detoxification** n. **detoxifier** n.
– ORIGIN C20: from **DE-** + L. *toxicum* 'poison' + **-FY**.

**detract** ● **v.** (**detract from**) reduce or take away the worth or value of (a quality or achievement) so as to make it seem less impressive.
– DERIVATIVES **detraction** n. **detractive** adj.
– ORIGIN ME: from L. *detract-*, *detrahere* 'draw away'.

**detractor** ● **n.** a person who disparages someone or something.

**detrain** ● **v.** leave a train, or cause or assist to leave a train.
– DERIVATIVES **detrainment** n.

**detribalize** (also **-ise**) ● **v.** [usu. as adj. **detribalized**] remove from a traditional tribal social structure.
– DERIVATIVES **detribalization** n.

**detriment** /ˈdɛtrɪm(ə)nt/ ● **n.** (often in phr. **to the detriment of**) the state of being harmed or damaged.
– ORIGIN ME (in the sense 'loss sustained by damage'): from OFr., from L. *detrimentum*, from *detri-*, *deterere* 'wear away'.

**detrimental** ● **adj.** tending to cause harm.
– DERIVATIVES **detrimentally** adv.

**detrition** /dɪˈtrɪʃ(ə)n/ ● **n.** rare the action of wearing away by friction.
– ORIGIN C17: from med. L. *detritio(n-)*, from *detri-*, *deterere* 'wear away'.

**detritivore** /dɪˈtrɪtɪvɔː/ ● **n.** Zoology an animal which feeds on dead organic material, especially plant detritus.
– DERIVATIVES **detritivorous** /ˌdɛtrɪˈtɪv(ə)rəs/ adj.
– ORIGIN 1960s: from **DETRITUS** + *-vore* 'eating' (see **-VOROUS**).

**detritus** /dɪˈtrʌɪtəs/ ● **n.** waste or debris, in particular organic matter produced by decomposition or loose matter produced by erosion.
– DERIVATIVES **detrital** adj.
– ORIGIN C18 (in the sense 'detrition'): from Fr. *détritus*, from L. *detritus*, from *deterere* 'wear away'.

**de trop** /də ˈtrəʊ, French də tʀo/ ● **adj.** not wanted; unwelcome.
– ORIGIN C18: Fr., lit. 'excessive'.

**detrusor** /dɪˈtruːsə/ ● **n.** Anatomy a muscle which forms a layer of the wall of the bladder.
– ORIGIN C18: mod. L., from L. *detrus-*, *detrudere* 'thrust down'.

**detumescence** /ˌdiːtjʊˈmɛs(ə)ns/ ● **n.** the process of subsiding from a state of tension, swelling, or sexual arousal.
– DERIVATIVES **detumesce** v. **detumescent** adj.
– ORIGIN C17: from L. *detumescent-*, *detumescere*, from *de-* 'down, away'+ *tumescere* 'to swell'.

**detune** ● **v. 1** cause (a musical instrument) to become out of tune. **2** change the frequency of (an oscillatory system such as a laser) away from a state of resonance. **3** [usu. as adj. **detuned**] reduce the performance of (a motor vehicle or engine) by adjustment.

**deuce**[1] /djuːs/ ● **n. 1** chiefly N. Amer. a thing representing, or represented by, the number two, in particular the two on dice or playing cards. **2** Tennis the score of 40 all in a game, at which each player needs two consecutive points to win the game.
– ORIGIN C15: from OFr. *deus* 'two', from L. *duos*.

**deuce**[2] /djuːs/ ● **n.** (**the deuce**) informal used as a euphemism for 'devil' in exclamations or for emphasis.
– ORIGIN C17: from Low Ger. *duus*, prob. of the same origin as **DEUCE**[1] (two aces at dice being the worst throw).

**deuced** /ˈdjuːsɪd, djuːst/ ● **adj.** informal used for emphasis, especially to express disapproval or frustration.
– DERIVATIVES **deucedly** adv.

**deus ex machina** /ˌdeɪʊs ɛks ˈmakɪnə, ˌdiːəs ɛks məˈʃiːnə/ ● **n.** an unexpected power or event saving a seemingly hopeless situation, especially as a narrative device in a play or novel.
– ORIGIN C17: mod. L., translation of Gk *theos ek mēkhanēs*, 'god from the machinery' (with ref. to the actors representing gods suspended above the stage in ancient Greek theatre, who brought about the denouement of the play by their intervention).

**Deut.** ● **abbrev.** Deuteronomy (in biblical references).

**deuteragonist** /ˌdjuːtəˈragənɪst/ ● **n.** the person second in importance to the protagonist in a drama.
– ORIGIN C19: from Gk *deuteragōnistēs*, from *deuteros* 'second' + *agōnistēs* 'actor'.

**deuteranope** /ˈdjuːt(ə)rəˌnəʊp/ ● **n.** a person suffering from deuteranopia.

**deuteranopia** /ˌdjuːt(ə)rəˈnəʊpɪə/ ● **n.** colour blindness resulting from insensitivity to green light, causing confusion of greens, reds, and yellows. Compare with **PROTANOPIA**, **TRITANOPIA**.
– ORIGIN C20: from **DEUTERO-** 'second' (green being regarded as the second component of colour vision) + **AN-**[1] + **-OPIA**.

**deuterated** /ˈdjuːtəreɪtɪd/ (also **deuteriated** /djuːˈtɪərɪeɪtɪd/) ● **adj.** Chemistry (of a compound) in which the ordinary isotope of hydrogen has been replaced with deuterium.
– DERIVATIVES **deuteration** n.

**deuteric** /ˈdjuːtərɪk/ ● **adj.** Geology relating to or denoting alteration of the minerals of an igneous rock during the later stages of consolidation.
– ORIGIN C20: from **DEUTERO-** + **-IC**.

**deuterium** /djuːˈtɪərɪəm/ ● **n.** Chemistry a stable isotope of hydrogen with a mass approximately twice that of the usual isotope. (Symbol: **D**)
– ORIGIN 1930s: mod. L., from Gk *deuteros* 'second'.

**deutero-** /ˈdjuːtərəʊ/ ● **comb. form** second: *deuteranopia*. ➤ secondary: *deuterocanonical*.
– ORIGIN from Gk *deuteros* 'second'.

**deuterocanonical** /ˌdjuːtərəʊkəˈnɒnɪk(ə)l/ ● **adj.** (of sacred books or literary works) forming a secondary canon.

**deuteron** /ˈdjuːtərɒn/ ● **n.** the nucleus of a deuterium atom, consisting of a proton and a neutron.

**Deutschmark** /ˈdɔɪtʃmɑːk/ (also **Deutsche Mark** /ˈdɔɪtʃə mɑːk, German ˌdɔytʃə ˈmark/) ● **n.** the basic monetary unit of Germany, equal to 100 pfennig.
– ORIGIN from Ger. *deutsche Mark* 'German mark'.

**deutzia** /ˈdjuːtsɪə, ˈdɔɪt-/ ● **n.** an ornamental shrub with white or pinkish flowers, native to Asia and Central America. [Genus *Deutzia*.]
– ORIGIN mod. L., named after the C18 Du. patron of botany Johann van der *Deutz*.

**deva** /ˈdeɪvə/ ● **n.** a member of a class of divine beings in the Vedic period, which in Indian religion are benevolent and in Zoroastrianism are evil. Compare with **ASURA**.
– ORIGIN from Sanskrit, lit. 'shining one'.

**devadasi** /ˌdeɪvəˈdɑːsi/ ● **n.** (pl. **devadasis**) a female dancer in a Hindu temple.
– ORIGIN from Sanskrit *devadāsī*, lit. 'female servant of a god'.

**devalue** ● **v.** (**devalues**, **devalued**, **devaluing**) reduce or underestimate the worth or importance of. ➤ Economics reduce the official value of (a currency) in relation to other currencies.
– DERIVATIVES **devaluation** n.

**Devanagari** /ˌdeɪvəˈnɑːg(ə)ri, dɛv-/ ● **n.** the alphabet used for Sanskrit, Hindi, and other Indian languages.
– ORIGIN from Sanskrit, lit. 'divine town script', from *deva* 'god' + *nāgarī*, an earlier name of the script.

**devastate** /ˈdɛvəsteɪt/ ● **v. 1** destroy or ruin. **2** cause (someone) severe and overwhelming shock or grief.
– DERIVATIVES **devastation** n. **devastator** n.
– ORIGIN C17 (earlier (ME) as *devastation*): from L. *devastat-*, *devastare*, from *de-* 'thoroughly' + *vastare* 'lay waste'.

**devastating** ● **adj. 1** highly destructive or damaging. ➤ causing severe shock or grief. **2** informal extremely impressive, effective, or attractive.
– DERIVATIVES **devastatingly** adv.

**develop** ● **v.** (**developed**, **developing**) **1** grow or cause to grow and become larger or more advanced. **2** convert (land) to a new purpose, especially by constructing buildings. **3** start to exist, experience, or possess: *I developed an interest in law.* **4** treat (a photographic film) with chemicals to make a visible image. **5** Chess bring (a piece) into play from its initial position on a player's back rank.
– DERIVATIVES **developable** adj. **developer** n.
– ORIGIN C17 (in the sense 'unfold, unfurl'): from Fr. *développer*, based on L. *dis-* 'un-' + a second element of

unknown origin found also in **ENVELOP**.

**developing country** • **n.** a poor agricultural country that is seeking to become more advanced economically and socially.

**development** • **n. 1** the process of developing or being developed. ➤a specified state of growth or advancement. **2** a new product or idea. **3** an event constituting a new stage in a changing situation. **4** an area of land with new buildings on it: *a major housing development.*
– DERIVATIVES **developmental** adj. **developmentally** adv.

**développé** /ˌdeɪv(ə)lɒˈpeɪ/ • **n.** (pl. **développés** pronunc. same) Ballet a movement in which one leg is raised and then kept in a fully extended position.

**deverbal** /diːˈvəːb(ə)l/ • **adj.** (of a noun or adjective) derived from a verb. • **n.** a deverbal noun or adjective.

**devi** /ˈdeɪvi/ • **n.** Indian a goddess.
– ORIGIN from Sanskrit.

**deviant** • **adj.** diverging from usual or accepted standards, especially in social or sexual behaviour. • **n.** a deviant person or thing.
– DERIVATIVES **deviance** n. **deviancy** n.
– ORIGIN ME: from late L. *deviant-*, *deviare* (see **DEVIATE**).

**deviate** • **v.** /ˈdiːvɪeɪt/ diverge from an established course or from usual or accepted standards. • **n. & adj.** /ˈdiːvɪət/ old-fashioned term for **DEVIANT**.
– DERIVATIVES **deviator** n.
– ORIGIN C16 (as adj. in the sense 'remote'): from late L. *deviat-*, *deviare* 'turn out of the way', from L. *de-* 'away from' + *via* 'way'.

**deviation** • **n. 1** the action of deviating. **2** Statistics the amount by which a single measurement differs from a fixed value such as the mean. **3** the deflection of a ship's compass needle caused by iron in the ship.
– DERIVATIVES **deviationism** n. **deviationist** n.

**device** • **n. 1** a thing made or adapted for a particular purpose, especially a mechanical or electronic contrivance. **2** a plan, scheme, or trick. ➤a turn of phrase intended to produce a particular effect. **3** a drawing or design. ➤an emblematic or heraldic design. **4** archaic design or look: *works of strange device.*
– PHRASES **leave someone to their own devices** leave someone to do as they wish without supervision.
– ORIGIN ME (in sense 'desire or intention'): from OFr. *devis*, based on L. *divis-*, *dividere* 'to divide'.

**devil** • **n. 1** (usu. **the Devil**) (in Christian and Jewish belief) the supreme spirit of evil; Satan. ➤an evil spirit; a demon. **2** a very wicked or cruel person. ➤a mischievously clever or self-willed person. **3** (**the devil**) fighting spirit; wildness: *he was born with the devil in him.* **4** (**the devil**) a thing that is very difficult or awkward to do or deal with. **5** informal a person with specified characteristics: *the poor devil.* **6** (**the devil**) expressing surprise or annoyance in various questions or exclamations. **7** an instrument or machine used for tearing or other destructive work. **8** informal, dated a junior assistant of a barrister or other professional. See also **PRINTER'S DEVIL**. • **v.** (**devilled**, **devilling**; US **deviled**, **deviling**) **1** informal, dated act as a junior assistant for a barrister or other professional. **2** N. Amer. harass or worry.
– PHRASES **be a devil!** informal said when encouraging someone to do something that they are hesitating to do. **between the devil and the deep blue sea** caught in a dilemma. **devil-may-care** cheerful and reckless. **the devil's dozen** thirteen. **the devil's in the detail** the details of a matter are its most problematic aspect. **the devil to pay** serious trouble to be dealt with. **like the devil** with great speed or energy. **play the devil with** have a damaging or disruptive effect on. **speak** (or **talk**) **of the devil** said when a person appears just after being mentioned. [from the superstition that the devil will appear if his name is spoken.]
– ORIGIN OE *dēofol*, via late L. from Gk *diabolos* 'accuser, slanderer' (used in the Septuagint to translate Heb. *śāṭān* 'Satan'), from *diaballein* 'to slander'.

**devilfish** • **n.** (pl. same or **-fishes**) any of a number of marine creatures perceived as having a sinister appearance, in particular a devil ray, a stonefish, or an octopus or squid.

**devilish** • **adj.** of, like, or appropriate to a devil in evil and cruelty. ➤mischievous and rakish. ➤very difficult to deal with or use. • **adv.** informal, dated very; extremely.
– DERIVATIVES **devilishly** adv. **devilishness** n.

**devilled** • **adj.** (of food) cooked with hot seasoning.

**devilment** • **n.** reckless mischief; wild spirits.

**devil ray** • **n.** a manta or other large long-tailed ray with a fleshy horn-like projection on each side of the mouth. [Family Mobulidae, several species.]

**devilry** • **n.** wicked activity. ➤reckless mischief. ➤black magic; dealings with the devil.

**devil's advocate** • **n. 1** a person who expresses a contentious opinion in order to provoke debate or test the strength of the opposing arguments. **2** historical a person appointed by the Roman Catholic Church to challenge a proposed beatification or canonization, or the verification of a miracle.

**devil's bit** • **n. 1** (also **devil's bit scabious**) a blue-flowered scabious with a short rootstock (said in folklore to have been bitten off by the devil). [*Succisa pratensis*] **2** N. Amer. a blazing star. [*Chamaelirium luteum.*]

**devil's claw** • **n.** a plant whose seed pods bear claw-like hooks which can harm livestock. [Genus *Proboscidea* (warmer parts of America) and *Harpagophytum procumbens* (southern Africa).]

**devil's club** • **n.** a very spiny straggling shrub of western North America. [*Oplopanax horridus.*]

**devil's coach-horse** • **n.** Brit. a large black predatory rove beetle which raises its hind end and opens its jaws threateningly when disturbed. [*Staphylinus olens.*]

**devil's darning needle** • **n.** N. Amer. another term for **DARNER** (in sense 2).

**devil's food cake** • **n.** chiefly N. Amer. a rich chocolate cake.

**devil's grip** • **n.** informal term for **BORNHOLM DISEASE**.

**devils on horseback** • **pl. n.** chiefly Brit. a savoury snack of prunes individually wrapped in slices of bacon.

**devil's paintbrush** • **n.** N. Amer. the European orange hawkweed, which has become naturalized in North America. [*Hieracium aurantiacum.*]

**devil's walking stick** • **n.** a prickly angelica tree native to the eastern US. [*Aralia spinosa.*]

**deviltry** • **n.** archaic variant of **DEVILRY**.

**devious** /ˈdiːvɪəs/ • **adj. 1** skilfully using underhand tactics to achieve goals. **2** (of a route or journey) longer and less direct than the most straightforward way.
– DERIVATIVES **deviously** adv. **deviousness** n.
– ORIGIN C16 (in sense 'remote', later 'departing from the direct route'): from L. *devius* (from *de-* 'away from' + *via* 'way') + **-ous**.

**devise** /dɪˈvʌɪz/ • **v. 1** plan or invent (a complex procedure or mechanism). **2** Law leave (real property) to someone by the terms of a will. • **n.** Law a clause in a will leaving real property to someone.
– DERIVATIVES **devisable** adj. **devisee** n. **deviser** n. **devisor** n.
– ORIGIN ME: from OFr. *deviser*, from L. *divis-*, *dividere* (see **DIVIDE**); the noun is a var. of **DEVICE**.

**devitalize** (also **-ise**) • **v.** [usu. as adj. **devitalized**] deprive of strength and vigour.
– DERIVATIVES **devitalization** n.

**devitrify** • **v.** (**-ies**, **-ied**) make or become hard, opaque, and crystalline.
– DERIVATIVES **devitrification** n.

**devoice** • **v.** Phonetics make (a vowel or voiced consonant) voiceless.

**devoid** /dɪˈvɔɪd/ • **adj.** (**devoid of**) entirely lacking or free from.
– ORIGIN ME: past part. of obs. *devoid* 'cast out', from OFr. *devoidier.*

**devoir** /dəˈvwɑː/ • **n.** archaic a person's duty. ➤(**pay one's devoirs**) pay one's respects formally.
– ORIGIN ME: from OFr. *deveir*, from L. *debere* 'owe', influenced by Fr. *devoir.*

**devolution** /ˌdiːvəˈluːʃ(ə)n, dɛv-/ • **n. 1** the devolving of power by central government to local or regional administration. **2** formal descent or degeneration to a lower or

worse state. **3** Law the legal transfer of property from one owner to another. **4** Biology evolutionary degeneration.
– DERIVATIVES **devolutionary** adj. **devolutionist** n.

**devolve** /dɪ'vɒlv/ ● **v. 1** transfer or delegate (power) to a lower level, especially from central government to local or regional administration. **2** (**devolve on/upon/to**) (of duties or responsibility) pass to (a body or person at a lower level). **3** Law (of property) be transferred from one owner to (another), especially by inheritance. **4** (**devolve into**) formal degenerate or be split into.
– DERIVATIVES **devolvement** n.
– ORIGIN ME (in the sense 'roll down'): from L. *devolvere*, from *de-* 'down' + *volvere* 'to roll'.

**Devonian** /dɛ'vəʊnɪən, dɪ-/ ● **adj. 1** of or relating to the English county of Devon. **2** Geology relating to or denoting the fourth period of the Palaeozoic era (between the Silurian and Carboniferous periods, about 409 to 363 million years ago), a time when the first amphibians appeared. ● **n.** a native or inhabitant of Devon.

**devoré** /də'vɔːreɪ/ ● **n.** a velvet fabric with a pattern formed by burning the pile away with acid.
– ORIGIN from Fr. *dévoré*, lit. 'devoured', past part. of *dévorer*.

**devote** ● **v. 1** (**devote something to**) give time or resources to (a person or activity). **2** archaic invoke or pronounce a curse upon.
– ORIGIN C16 (in the sense 'dedicate formally, consecrate'): from L. *devot-*, *devovere*, from *de-* 'formally' + *vovere* 'to vow'.

**devoted** ● **adj.** very loving or loyal.
– DERIVATIVES **devotedly** adv. **devotedness** n.

**devotee** /ˌdɛvə(ʊ)'tiː/ ● **n. 1** a person who is very interested in and enthusiastic about someone or something. **2** a follower of a particular religion or god.

**devotion** ● **n. 1** love, loyalty, or enthusiasm for a person or activity. **2** religious worship or observance. ➤(**devotions**) prayers or religious observances.
– DERIVATIVES **devotional** adj.

**devour** /dɪ'vaʊə/ ● **v. 1** eat (food or prey) hungrily or quickly. ➤(of fire or a similar force) consume destructively. **2** read quickly and eagerly. **3** (**be devoured**) be totally absorbed by a powerful feeling.
– DERIVATIVES **devourer** n. **devouring** adj. **devouringly** adv.
– ORIGIN ME: from OFr. *devorer*, from L. *devorare*, from *de-* 'down' + *vorare* 'to swallow'.

**devout** /dɪ'vaʊt/ ● **adj. 1** having or showing deep religious feeling or commitment. **2** earnest; sincere: *my devout hope.*
– DERIVATIVES **devoutly** adv. **devoutness** n.
– ORIGIN ME: from OFr. *devot*, from L. *devotus* 'devoted' from *devovere* (see **DEVOTE**).

**DEW** ● **abbrev.** distant early warning.

**dew** ● **n.** tiny drops of water that form on cool surfaces at night, when atmospheric vapour condenses. ➤beaded or glistening liquid resembling dew. ● **v.** wet with a beaded or glistening liquid.
– ORIGIN OE *dēaw*, of Gmc origin.

**dewan** /dɪ'wɑːn/ ● **n.** variant spelling of **DIWAN**.

**dewar** /'djuːə/ ● **n.** a double-walled flask of metal or silvered glass with a vacuum between the walls, used to hold liquids at well below ambient temperature.
– ORIGIN C19: named after the Sc. physicist Sir James *Dewar*.

**dewater** ● **v.** drain (a waterlogged or flooded area). ➤remove water from (sediment or waste materials).

**dewberry** ● **n.** (pl. **-ies**) **1** a trailing bramble with soft prickles and edible blue-black fruit with a dewy white bloom. [*Rubus caesius* (Europe) and other species.] **2** the fruit of this plant.

**dewclaw** ● **n.** a rudimentary inner toe present in some dogs. ➤a false hoof on an animal such as a deer, which is formed by its rudimentary side toes.

**dewdrop** ● **n.** a drop of dew.

**Dewey decimal classification** ● **n.** an internationally applied decimal system of library classification which uses a three-figure code from 000 to 999 to represent the major branches of knowledge, with finer classifications made by adding figures after a decimal point.
– ORIGIN C19: named after the Amer. librarian Melvil *Dewey*.

**dewfall** ● **n.** poetic/literary the time of evening when dew begins to form.

**dewlap** ● **n.** a fold of loose skin hanging from the neck or throat of an animal or bird, especially that present in many cattle.
– ORIGIN ME: from **DEW** and **LAP**[1], perh. influenced by a Scand. word (cf. Dan. *doglæp*).

**deworm** ● **v.** treat (an animal) to free it of worms.
– DERIVATIVES **dewormer** n.

**dew point** ● **n.** the atmospheric temperature below which water droplets begin to condense and dew can form.

**dew pond** ● **n.** Brit. a shallow pond, especially an artificial one, on downs where the water supply from springs or surface drainage is inadequate.

**dew worm** ● **n.** N. Amer. an earthworm, in particular one used as fishing bait.
– ORIGIN OE *deaw-wyrm* 'ringworm'.

**dewy** ● **adj.** (**-ier**, **-iest**) **1** wet with dew. **2** (of a person's skin) appearing soft and lustrous.
– DERIVATIVES **dewily** adv. **dewiness** n.

**dewy-eyed** ● **adj.** having eyes that are moist with tears (taken as indicating nostalgia, naivety, or sentimentality).

**dex** ● **n.** informal short for **DEXEDRINE**.

**Dexedrine** /'dɛksədriːn, -drɪn/ ● **n.** trademark a form of amphetamine.
– ORIGIN 1940s: prob. from **DEXTRO-**, on the pattern of *Benzedrine*.

**dexter**[1] /'dɛkstə/ ● **adj.** archaic & Heraldry on or towards the right-hand side (in a coat of arms, from the bearer's point of view, i.e. the left as it is depicted). The opposite of **SINISTER**.
– ORIGIN C16: from L., 'on the right'.

**dexter**[2] /'dɛkstə/ ● **n.** an animal of a small, hardy breed of Irish cattle.
– ORIGIN C19: said to have been named after the breeder.

**dexterity** /dɛk'stɛrɪti/ ● **n.** skill in performing tasks, especially with the hands.
– ORIGIN C16: from Fr. *dextérité*, from L. *dexteritas*, from *dexter* 'on the right'.

**dexterous** /'dɛkst(ə)rəs/ (also **dextrous**) ● **adj.** showing or having dexterity; adroit.
– DERIVATIVES **dexterously** adv. **dexterousness** n.

**dextral** /'dɛkstr(ə)l/ ● **adj. 1** of or on the right side or the right hand. The opposite of **SINISTRAL**. ➤right-handed. **2** Geology relating to or denoting a strike-slip fault in which the motion of the block on the further side of the fault is towards the right. **3** Zoology (of a spiral mollusc shell) with whorls rising to the right and coiling anticlockwise. ● **n.** a right-handed person.
– DERIVATIVES **dextrality** /-'stralɪti/ n. **dextrally** adv.
– ORIGIN C17: from med. L. *dextralis*, from L. *dextra* 'the right hand', from *dexter* 'on the right'.

**dextran** /'dɛkstran/ ● **n.** Chemistry a carbohydrate gum formed by the fermentation of sugars, used to make a substitute for blood plasma.
– ORIGIN C19: from **DEXTRO-** + **-AN**.

**dextrin** /'dɛkstrɪn/ ● **n.** a soluble gummy substance obtained by hydrolysis of starch, used as a thickening agent and in adhesives and dietary supplements.
– ORIGIN C19: from **DEXTRO-** + **-IN**[1].

**dextro-** ● **comb. form** on or to the right: *dextrorotatory.*
– ORIGIN from L. *dexter*, *dextr-* 'right'.

**dextrorotatory** /ˌdɛkstrəʊ'rəʊtət(ə)ri/ ● **adj.** Chemistry (of a compound) having the property of rotating the plane of a polarized light ray to the right, i.e. clockwise facing the oncoming radiation. The opposite of **LAEVOROTATORY**.
– DERIVATIVES **dextrorotation** n.

**dextrose** /'dɛkstrəʊz, -s/ ● **n.** Chemistry the dextrorotatory form of glucose (and the predominant naturally occurring form).

**dextrous** ● **adj.** variant spelling of **DEXTEROUS**.

**DF** ● **abbrev. 1** Defender of the Faith. [from L. *Defensor*

*Fidei.*] **2** direction-finder.

**DFC** ● **abbrev.** (in the UK) Distinguished Flying Cross.

**DFE** ● **abbrev.** Department for Education.

**Dfl** ● **abbrev.** Dutch florins.

**DFM** ● **abbrev.** (in the UK) Distinguished Flying Medal.

**DG** ● **abbrev. 1** by the grace of God. [L. *Dei gratia.*] **2** thanks be to God. [L. *Deo gratias.*] **3** director general.

**DH** ● **abbrev.** Baseball designated hitter.

**dhal** /dɑːl/ (also **dal**) ● **n.** (in Indian cookery) split pulses.
– ORIGIN from Hindi *dāl.*

**dhamma** /'dɑːmə, 'dʌmə/ ● **n.** another term for **DHARMA**, especially among Theravada Buddhists.
– ORIGIN Pali, from Sanskrit *dharma.*

**dhansak** /'dʌnsɑːk/ ● **n.** an Indian dish of meat or vegetables cooked with lentils and coriander.
– ORIGIN from Gujarati.

**dharma** /'dɑːmə, 'dəːmə/ ● **n.** (in Indian religion) the eternal law of the cosmos, inherent in the very nature of things.
– ORIGIN Sanskrit, lit. 'decree or custom'.

**dharmashala** /'dɑːmə,ʃɑːlə/ (also **dharmsala**) ● **n.** (in the Indian subcontinent) a building devoted to religious or charitable purposes, especially a rest house for travellers.
– ORIGIN from Sanskrit *dharmaśālā.*

**dharna** /'dəːnə, -ɑː/ ● **n.** Indian a mode of compelling payment or compliance, by sitting at the debtor's or offender's door without eating until the demand is complied with. ➤ a peaceful demonstration.
– ORIGIN from Hindi *dharnā* 'sitting in restraint, placing'.

**Dharuk** /'dʌrʊk/ ● **n.** an extinct Aboriginal language of the area around Sydney.

**dhikr** /'dɪkʌr/ ● **n.** Islam a form of devotion, associated chiefly with Sufism, in which the worshipper is absorbed in the rhythmic repetition of the name of God or his attributes.

**dhobi** /'dəʊbi/ ● **n.** (pl. **dhobis**) (in the Indian subcontinent) a person whose occupation is washing clothes.
– ORIGIN from Hindi *dhobī,* from *dhob* 'washing'.

**dhobi itch** ● **n.** informal itching inflammation of the skin, especially in the groin region, suffered in the tropics, typically caused by ringworm infection or by allergic dermatitis.

**dhol** /dəʊl/ ● **n.** a large, typically two-headed drum used in the Indian subcontinent.
– ORIGIN from Hindi *ḍhol.*

**dholak** /'dəʊlək/ ● **n.** a dhol, especially a small one.
– ORIGIN from Hindi *ḍholak.*

**dhole** /dəʊl/ ● **n.** an Asian wild dog with a sandy coat and a black bushy tail, living in packs. [*Cuon alpinus.*]
– ORIGIN C19: of unknown origin.

**dhoti** /'dəʊti/ ● **n.** (pl. **dhotis**) a loincloth worn by male Hindus.
– ORIGIN from Hindi *dhotī.*

**dhow** /daʊ/ ● **n.** a lateen-rigged ship with one or two masts, used chiefly in the Arabian region.
– ORIGIN C18: from Arab. *dāwa,* prob. rel. to Marathi *dāw.*

**DHSS** ● **abbrev.** Brit. historical Department of Health and Social Security.

**DHT** ● **abbrev.** dihydrotestosterone.

**dhurrie** /'dʌri/ ● **n.** (pl. **-ies**) a heavy cotton rug of Indian origin.
– ORIGIN from Hindi *darī.*

**dhyana** /dɪ'ɑːnə/ ● **n.** (in Hindu and Buddhist practice) profound meditation which is the penultimate stage of yoga.
– ORIGIN from Sanskrit *dhyāna.*

**DI** ● **abbrev. 1** Defence Intelligence. **2** direct injection.

**di-**[1] /dʌɪ, di/ ● **comb. form** twice; two-; double: *dichromatic.* ➤ Chemistry containing two atoms, molecules, or groups of a specified kind: *dioxide.*
– ORIGIN from Gk *dis* 'twice'.

**di-**[2] /di, dʌɪ/ ● **prefix** variant spelling of **DIS-** shortened before *l, m, n, r, s* (followed by a consonant), and *v;* also often shortened before *g,* and sometimes before *j.*
– ORIGIN from L.

**di-**[3] /dʌɪ/ ● **prefix** variant spelling of **DIA-** shortened before a vowel (as in *dielectric*).

**dia.** ● **abbrev.** diameter.

**dia-** (also **di-** before a vowel) ● **prefix 1** through; across: *diaphanous.* **2** apart: *diakinesis.*
– ORIGIN from Gk *dia* 'through'.

**diabase** /'dʌɪəbeɪs/ ● **n.** Geology another term for **DOLERITE.**
– ORIGIN C19: from Fr., formed irregularly as if from *di-* 'two' + *base* 'base', but perh. assoc. later with Gk *diabasis* 'transition'.

**diabetes** /,dʌɪə'biːtiːz/ ● **n.** a disorder of the metabolism causing excessive thirst and the production of large amounts of urine.
– ORIGIN C16: via L. from Gk, lit. 'siphon', from *diabainein* 'go through'.

**diabetes insipidus** /ɪn'sɪpɪdəs/ ● **n.** a rare form of diabetes caused by a deficiency of the pituitary hormone vasopressin, which regulates kidney function.
– ORIGIN C19: from **DIABETES** + L. *insipidus* 'insipid'.

**diabetes mellitus** /mɪ'lʌɪtəs/ ● **n.** the commonest form of diabetes, caused by a deficiency of the pancreatic hormone insulin, which results in a failure to metabolize sugars and starch.
– ORIGIN C19: from **DIABETES** + L. *mellitus* 'sweet'.

**diabetic** ● **adj.** having or relating to diabetes. ● **n.** a person suffering from diabetes.

**diablerie** /dɪ'ɑːbləri/ ● **n.** reckless mischief; charismatic wildness. ➤ archaic sorcery supposedly assisted by the devil.
– ORIGIN C18: from Fr., from *diable,* from eccles. L. *diabolus* 'devil'.

**diabolical** ● **adj. 1** (also **diabolic**) characteristic of or associated with the Devil: *diabolical cunning.* **2** informal disgracefully bad or unpleasant.
– DERIVATIVES **diabolically** adv.
– ORIGIN ME: from OFr. *diabolique* or eccles. L. *diabolicus,* from *diabolus* 'devil'.

**diabolism** /dʌɪ'abəlɪz(ə)m/ ● **n.** worship of the Devil.
– DERIVATIVES **diabolist** n.
– ORIGIN C17: from eccles. L. *diabolus* or Gk *diabolos* 'devil' + **-ISM.**

**diabolo** /dɪ'abələʊ, dʌɪ-/ ● **n.** (pl. **-os**) a game in which a two-headed top is thrown up and caught with a string stretched between two sticks. ➤ the top used in this game.
– ORIGIN C20: from Ital., from eccles. L. *diabolus* 'devil'.

**diacetylmorphine** /dʌɪ,asɪtʌɪl'mɔːfiːn/ ● **n.** technical term for **HEROIN.**

**diachronic** /,dʌɪə'krɒnɪk/ ● **adj.** concerned with the way in which something, especially language, has developed through time. Often contrasted with **SYNCHRONIC.**
– DERIVATIVES **diachroneity** /,dʌɪəkrə'niːɪti, -'neɪɪti/ n. **diachronically** adv. **diachronistic** /dʌɪ,akrə'nɪstɪk/ adj. **diachrony** /dʌɪ'akrəni/ n.
– ORIGIN C19: from **DIA-** + Gk *khronos* 'time' + **-IC.**

**diachronism** /dʌɪ'akrənɪz(ə)m/ ● **n.** Geology the occurrence of a feature or phenomenon in different geological periods.
– DERIVATIVES **diachronous** adj. **diachronously** adv.

**diaconal** /dʌɪ'ak(ə)n(ə)l/ ● **adj.** relating to a deacon or deacons.
– ORIGIN C17: from eccles. L. *diaconalis,* from *diaconus* (see **DEACON**).

**diaconate** /dʌɪ'akəneɪt, -ət/ ● **n.** the office of deacon. ➤ a body of deacons collectively.
– ORIGIN C18: from eccles. L. *diaconatus,* from *diaconus* (see **DEACON**).

**diacritic** /,dʌɪə'krɪtɪk/ ● **n.** a sign such as an accent written above or below a letter to indicate a difference in pronunciation from the same letter when unmarked. ● **adj.** (of a mark or sign) indicating a difference in pronunciation.
– DERIVATIVES **diacritical** adj. **diacritically** adv.
– ORIGIN C17: from Gk *diakritikos,* from *diakrinein* 'distinguish'.

**diadelphous** /,dʌɪə'dɛlfəs/ ● **adj.** Botany (of stamens) united by their filaments so as to form two groups.

– ORIGIN C19: from **DI-**[1] + Gk *adelphos* 'brother' + **-OUS**.

**diadem** /ˈdʌɪədɛm/ ● **n.** a jewelled crown or headband worn as a symbol of sovereignty.
– DERIVATIVES **diademed** adj.
– ORIGIN ME: from OFr. *diademe*, via L. from Gk *diadēma*, from *diadein* 'bind round'.

**diaeresis** /dʌɪˈɪərɪsɪs, -ˈɛr-/ (US **dieresis**) ● **n.** (pl. **diaereses** /-siːz/) **1** a mark (¨) placed over a vowel to indicate that it is sounded separately, as in *naïve, Brontë*. ➤ the division of a sound into two syllables, especially by sounding a diphthong as two vowels. **2** Prosody a natural rhythmic break in a line of verse where the end of a metrical foot coincides with the end of a phrase.
– ORIGIN C16: via L. from Gk *diairesis* 'separation', from *diairein* 'take apart'.

**diagenesis** /ˌdʌɪəˈdʒɛnɪsɪs/ ● **n.** Geology the physical and chemical changes occurring during the conversion of sediment to sedimentary rock.
– DERIVATIVES **diagenetic** adj. **diagenetically** adv.

**diagnose** /ˈdʌɪəgnəʊz, -ˈnəʊz/ ● **v.** make a diagnosis of (an illness or other problem). ➤ identify the medical condition of (someone): *she was diagnosed as having epilepsy.*
– DERIVATIVES **diagnosable** adj.

**diagnosis** /ˌdʌɪəgˈnəʊsɪs/ ● **n.** (pl. **diagnoses** /-siːz/) **1** the identification of the nature of an illness or other problem by examination of the symptoms. **2** the distinctive characterization in precise terms of a genus, species, or phenomenon.
– ORIGIN C17: mod. L., from Gk, from *diagignōskein* 'distinguish, discern'.

**diagnostic** /dʌɪəgˈnɒstɪk/ ● **adj. 1** concerned with the diagnosis of illness or other problems. ➤ (of a symptom) distinctive, and so indicating the nature of an illness. **2** characteristic of a particular species, genus, or phenomenon. ● **n. 1** a distinctive symptom or characteristic. **2** (**diagnostics**) [treated as sing. or pl.] the practice or techniques of diagnosis. **3** Computing a program or routine that helps a user to identify errors.
– DERIVATIVES **diagnostically** adv. **diagnostician** /-nɒˈstɪʃ(ə)n/ n.

**diagonal** /dʌɪˈag(ə)n(ə)l/ ● **adj.** denoting a straight line joining opposite corners of a rectangle, square, or other figure. ➤ (of a line) straight and at an angle; slanting. ➤ Mathematics denoting a matrix with non-zero elements only on the diagonal running from the upper left to the lower right. ● **n.** a diagonal line.
– DERIVATIVES **diagonally** adv.
– ORIGIN C16: from L. *diagonalis*, from Gk *diagōnios* 'from angle to angle', from *dia* 'through' + *gōnia* 'angle'.

**diagram** /ˈdʌɪəgram/ ● **n. 1** a simplified drawing showing the appearance or structure of something. **2** Brit. a graphical schedule for operating railway stock to provide a desired service. ● **v.** (**diagrammed**, **diagramming**; US **diagramed**, **diagraming**) **1** represent in graphic form. **2** Brit. schedule the operations of (a locomotive or train) according to a diagram.
– DERIVATIVES **diagrammatic** /-grəˈmatɪk/ adj. **diagrammatically** adv.
– ORIGIN C17: from L. *diagramma*, from Gk, from *diagraphein* 'mark out by lines'.

**diakinesis** /ˌdʌɪəkʌɪˈniːsɪs/ ● **n.** (pl. **diakineses** /-siːz/) Biology the final stage of the prophase of meiosis, following diplotene, when the separation of homologous chromosomes is complete and crossing over has occurred.
– ORIGIN C20: from **DIA-** + Gk *kinēsis* 'motion'.

**dial** ● **n. 1** a disc marked to show the time on a clock or indicate a reading or measurement by means of a pointer. ➤ a disc with numbered holes on a telephone, turned to make a call. ➤ a disc turned to select a setting on a radio, cooker, etc. **2** Brit. informal a person's face. ● **v.** (**dialled**, **dialling**; US **dialed**, **dialing**) call (a telephone number) by turning a dial or using a keypad. ➤ indicate or regulate by means of a dial.
– ORIGIN ME: from med. L. *diale* 'clock dial', based on L. *dies* 'day'.

**dialect** /ˈdʌɪəlɛkt/ ● **n. 1** a form of a language which is peculiar to a specific region or social group. **2** Computing a particular version of a programming language.
– DERIVATIVES **dialectal** /-ˈlɛkt(ə)l/ adj.
– ORIGIN C16 (denoting the art of investigating the truth of opinions): from Fr. *dialecte*, or via L. from Gk *dialektos* 'discourse, way of speaking', from *dialegesthai* (see **DIALOGUE**).

**dialectic** /ˌdʌɪəˈlɛktɪk/ Philosophy ● **n.** (also **dialectics**) [usu. treated as sing.] **1** the art of investigating or discussing the truth of opinions. **2** enquiry into metaphysical contradictions and their solutions. **3** the existence or action of opposing social forces, concepts, etc. ● **adj.** of or relating to dialectic or dialectics; dialectical.
– ORIGIN ME: from OFr. *dialectique* or L. *dialectica*, from Gk *dialektikē* (*tekhnē*) '(art) of debate', from *dialegesthai* (see **DIALOGUE**).

**dialectical** ● **adj. 1** relating to the logical discussion of ideas and opinions. **2** concerned with or acting through opposing forces.
– DERIVATIVES **dialectically** adv.

**dialectical materialism** ● **n.** the Marxist theory that political and historical events result from the conflict of social forces (as caused by material needs) and are interpretable as a series of contradictions and their solutions.
– DERIVATIVES **dialectical materialist** n. & adj.

**dialectician** /ˌdʌɪəlɛkˈtɪʃ(ə)n/ ● **n.** a person skilled in philosophical debate.

**dialectology** /ˌdʌɪəlɛkˈtɒlədʒi/ ● **n.** the branch of linguistics concerned with the study of dialects.
– DERIVATIVES **dialectological** /-təˈlɒdʒɪk(ə)l/ adj. **dialectologist** n.

**dialler** (also **dialer**) ● **n.** a device or piece of software for calling telephone numbers automatically.

**dialling code** ● **n.** Brit. a sequence of numbers dialled to connect a telephone to an exchange in another area or country.

**dialling tone** (N. Amer. **dial tone**) ● **n.** a sound produced by a telephone that indicates that a caller may start to dial.

**dialog box** (Brit. also **dialogue box**) ● **n.** Computing a small area on screen in which the user is prompted to provide information or select commands.

**dialogic** /ˌdʌɪəˈlɒdʒɪk/ ● **adj.** relating to or in the form of dialogue.
– DERIVATIVES **dialogical** adj.

**dialogism** /dʌɪˈalədʒɪz(ə)m/ ● **n.** the use in a text of different tones or viewpoints, whose interaction or contradiction are important to the text's interpretation.

**dialogue** (US also **dialog**) ● **n.** conversation between two or more people as a feature of a book, play, or film. ➤ discussion directed towards exploration of a subject or resolution of a problem. ● **v.** chiefly N. Amer. take part in dialogue. ➤ provide (a film or play) with dialogue.
– ORIGIN ME: from OFr. *dialoge*, via L. from Gk *dialogos*, from *dialegesthai* 'converse with', from *dia* 'through' + *legein* 'speak'.

**dial tone** ● **n.** North American term for **DIALLING TONE**.

**dialysate** /dʌɪˈalɪzeɪt/ (US also **dialyzate**) ● **n.** the part of a mixture which passes through the membrane in dialysis, or a solution containing this.

**dialyse** /ˈdʌɪəlʌɪz/ (US **dialyze**) ● **v.** purify (a mixture) or treat (a patient) by means of dialysis.

**dialysis** /dʌɪˈalɪsɪs/ ● **n.** (pl. **dialyses** /-siːz/) **1** Chemistry the separation of particles in a liquid on the basis of differences in their ability to pass through a membrane. **2** Medicine the clinical purification of blood by this technique, as a substitute for the normal function of the kidney.
– DERIVATIVES **dialytic** adj.
– ORIGIN C19: via L. from Gk *dialusis*, from *dialuein* 'split, separate'.

**diamagnetic** ● **adj.** Physics tending to become magnetized in a direction at 180° to the applied magnetic field.
– DERIVATIVES **diamagnet** n. **diamagnetically** adv. **diamagnetism** n.

**diamanté** /dɪəˈmɒnteɪ/ ● **adj.** decorated with artificial jewels. ● **n.** fabric or costume jewellery decorated with artificial jewels.

– ORIGIN C20: Fr., lit. 'set with diamonds'.

**diamantiferous** /ˌdʌɪəmən'tɪf(ə)rəs/ • **adj.** (of a region or rock formation) producing or yielding diamonds.

**diamantine** /ˌdʌɪə'mantɪn, -iːn/ • **adj.** made from or resembling diamonds.

– ORIGIN C16: from Fr. *diamantin*, from *diamant* 'diamond'.

**diameter** /dʌɪ'amɪtə/ • **n. 1** a straight line passing from side to side through the centre of a body or figure, especially a circle or sphere. ➤a transverse measurement of something; width or thickness. **2** a unit of linear measurement of magnifying power.

– DERIVATIVES **diametral** adj.

– ORIGIN ME: from OFr. *diametre*, via L. from Gk *diametros* (*grammē*) '(line) measuring across'.

**diametrical** /ˌdʌɪə'mɛtrɪk(ə)l/ • **adj. 1** (of opposites) complete; absolute: *he's the diametrical opposite of Gabriel.* **2** of or along a diameter.

– DERIVATIVES **diametric** adj. **diametrically** adv.

**diamine** /dʌɪ'eɪmiːn, dʌɪ'am-, 'dʌɪəmiːn/ • **n.** Chemistry a compound whose molecule contains two amino groups, especially when not part of amide groups.

**diamond** • **n. 1** a precious stone consisting of a clear and colourless crystalline form of pure carbon, the hardest naturally occurring substance. **2** a figure with four straight sides of equal length forming two opposite acute angles and two opposite obtuse angles; a rhombus. **3** (**diamonds**) one of the four suits in a conventional pack of playing cards, denoted by a red figure of such a shape. ➤a card of this suit. **4** a baseball field. **5** a railway crossing in which two tracks cross over each other at an acute angle.

– PHRASES **diamond in the rough** North American term for **ROUGH DIAMOND**.

– DERIVATIVES **diamondiferous** /-'dɪf(ə)rəs/ adj.

– ORIGIN ME: from OFr. *diamant*, from med. L. *diamas*, *diamant-*, var. of L. *adamans* (see **ADAMANT**).

**diamondback** • **n. 1** a large, common North American rattlesnake with diamond-shaped markings. [Genus *Crotalus*: two species.] **2** (also **diamondback terrapin**) see **TERRAPIN** (in sense 1).

**diamond-bird** • **n.** Austral. a pardalote, which typically has rows of small white spots on the dark parts of its plumage.

**diamond-cut** • **adj. 1** cut with facets like a diamond. **2** cut into the shape of a diamond.

**diamond jubilee** • **n.** the sixtieth anniversary of a notable event.

**diamond wedding** • **n.** the sixtieth anniversary of a wedding.

**diamorphine** /dʌɪ'mɔːfiːn/ • **n.** short for **DIACETYLMORPHINE** (heroin).

**diana** /dʌɪ'anə/ • **n.** a North American fritillary (butterfly), the male of which is orange and black and the female blue and black. [*Speyeria diana.*]

– ORIGIN mod. L.; assoc. with *Diana*, the Roman goddess of the moon, because of the silvery crescents on the wings.

**Diana monkey** • **n.** a West African monkey that has a black face with a white crescent on the forehead. [*Cercopithecus diana.*]

– ORIGIN C19: named after the Roman moon goddess *Diana*.

**Dianetics** /ˌdʌɪə'nɛtɪks/ • **pl. n.** [treated as sing.] a system developed by the founder of the Church of Scientology, L. Ron Hubbard, which aims to relieve psychosomatic disorder by cleansing the mind of harmful mental images.

– ORIGIN 1950s: from Gk *dianoētikos* 'relating to thought' + **-ICS**.

**dianthus** /dʌɪ'anθəs/ • **n.** (pl. **dianthuses**) a flowering plant of a genus that includes the pinks and carnations. [Genus *Dianthus.*]

– ORIGIN from Gk *Dios* 'of Zeus' + *anthos* 'flower'.

**diapason** /ˌdʌɪə'peɪs(ə)n, -z-/ • **n. 1** (also **open diapason** or **stopped diapason**) an organ stop sounding a main register of flue pipes, typically of eight-foot pitch. **2** a grand swelling burst of harmony.

– ORIGIN ME (denoting the interval of an octave): via L. from Gk *dia pasōn* (*khordōn*) 'through all (notes)'.

**diapause** /'dʌɪəpɔːz/ • **n.** Zoology a period of suspended development in an organism.

**diaper** /'dʌɪəpə/ • **n. 1** N. Amer. a baby's nappy. **2** a linen or cotton fabric woven in a repeating pattern of small diamonds. ➤a repeating geometrical or floral pattern. • **v. 1** N. Amer. put a nappy on (a baby). **2** decorate with a repeating geometrical or floral pattern.

– ORIGIN ME (denoting a costly fabric): from OFr. *diapre*, from med. L. *diasprum*, from med. Gk *diaspros* (adj.), from *dia* 'across' + *aspros* 'white'.

**diaphanous** /dʌɪ'af(ə)nəs/ • **adj.** (of fabric) light, delicate, and translucent.

– ORIGIN C17: from med. L. *diaphanus*, from Gk *diaphanēs*, from *dia* 'through' + *phainein* 'to show'.

**diaphone** /'dʌɪəfəʊn/ • **n.** a low-pitched fog signal operated by compressed air.

**diaphoretic** /ˌdʌɪəfə'rɛtɪk/ • **adj.** Medicine (chiefly of a drug) inducing perspiration. ➤(of a person) sweating heavily.

– DERIVATIVES **diaphoresis** n.

– ORIGIN ME: via late L. from Gk *diaphorētikos*, from *diaphorein* 'sweat out'.

**diaphragm** /'dʌɪəfram/ • **n. 1** a dome-shaped muscular partition separating the thorax from the abdomen in mammals. **2** a thin sheet of material forming a partition. ➤a taut flexible membrane in mechanical or acoustic systems. **3** a thin contraceptive cap fitting over the cervix. **4** a device for varying the effective aperture of the lens in a camera or other optical system.

– DERIVATIVES **diaphragmatic** adj.

– ORIGIN ME: from late L. *diaphragma*, from Gk, from *dia* 'through, apart' + *phragma* 'a fence'.

**diaphragm pump** • **n.** a pump using a flexible diaphragm in place of a piston.

**diaphysis** /dʌɪ'afɪsɪs/ • **n.** (pl. **diaphyses** /-siːz/) Anatomy the shaft or central part of a long bone. Compare with **EPIPHYSIS**.

– ORIGIN C19: from Gk *diaphusis* 'growing through'.

**diapir** /'dʌɪəpɪə/ • **n.** Geology a domed rock formation in which a core of rock has moved upward to pierce the overlying strata.

– DERIVATIVES **diapiric** adj. **diapirism** n.

– ORIGIN C20: from Gk *diapeirainein* 'pierce through'.

**diapositive** /ˌdʌɪə'pɒzɪtɪv/ • **n.** a positive photographic slide or transparency.

**diapsid** /dʌɪ'apsɪd/ • **n.** Zoology a reptile of a large group having two temporal openings in the skull, including the lizards, snakes, crocodiles, dinosaurs, and pterosaurs.

– ORIGIN C20: from mod. L. *Diapsida* (name of a subclass), from **DI-**[1] + Gk *apsis*, *apsid-* 'arch'.

**diarchy** /'dʌɪɑːki/ (also **dyarchy**) • **n.** (pl. **-ies**) government by two independent authorities.

– DERIVATIVES **diarchal** adj. **diarchic** adj.

– ORIGIN C19: from **DI-**[1] + Gk *arkhia* 'rule', on the pattern of *monarchy*.

**diarist** • **n.** a person who writes a diary.

– DERIVATIVES **diaristic** adj.

**diarize** (also **-ise**) • **v.** archaic keep a record of events in a diary.

**diarrhoea** /ˌdʌɪə'rɪə/ (US **diarrhea**) • **n.** a condition in which faeces are discharged from the bowels frequently and in a liquid form.

– DERIVATIVES **diarrhoeal** adj. **diarrhoeic** adj.

– ORIGIN ME: via late L. from Gk *diarrhoia*, from *diarrhein* 'flow through'.

**diary** • **n.** (pl. **-ies**) a book in which one keeps a daily record of events and experiences. ➤a book with spaces for each day of the year in which to note appointments.

– ORIGIN C16: from L. *diarium*, from *dies* 'day'.

**diaspora** /dʌɪ'asp(ə)rə/ • **n.** (**the diaspora**) the dispersion of the Jews beyond Israel. ➤Jews living outside Israel.

– ORIGIN Gk (orig. in the Septuagint, Deut. 28:25), from *diaspeirein* 'disperse'.

**diaspore** /'dʌɪəspɔː/ • **n.** Botany a spore, seed, or other structure that functions in plant dispersal; a propagule.

**diastase** /'dʌɪəsteɪz/ • **n.** Biochemistry another term for **AMYLASE**.

– ORIGIN C19: from Gk *diastasis* 'separation'.

**diastema** /ˌdʌɪəˈstiːmə, dʌɪˈastɪmə/ ● n. (pl. **diastemata**) **1** Zoology a space separating teeth of different functions, especially that between the biting teeth and grinding teeth in rodents and ungulates. **2** a gap between a person's two upper front teeth.
– ORIGIN C19: via late L. from Gk *diastēma* 'space between'.

**diastereoisomer** /ˌdʌɪəstɛrɪəʊˈʌɪsəmə/ ● n. Chemistry each of a pair of stereoisomeric compounds that are not mirror images of one another.
– DERIVATIVES **diastereoisomeric** adj.

**diastole** /dʌɪˈastəli/ ● n. Physiology the phase of the heartbeat when the heart muscle relaxes and allows the chambers to fill with blood. Often contrasted with **SYSTOLE**.
– DERIVATIVES **diastolic** adj.
– ORIGIN C16: via late L. from Gk, 'separation, expansion'.

**diathermy** /ˈdʌɪəˌθəːmi/ ● n. a medical and surgical technique involving the production of heat in a part of the body by high-frequency electric currents.
– ORIGIN C20: from **DIA-** + Gk *thermon* 'heat'.

**diathesis** /dʌɪˈaθəsɪs/ ● n. **1** Medicine a tendency to suffer from a particular medical condition. **2** Linguistics the set of syntactic patterns with which a verb or other word is most typically associated.
– ORIGIN C17: mod. L., from Gk, 'disposition'.

**diatom** /ˈdʌɪətəm/ ● n. Biology a single-celled alga which has a cell wall of silica. [Class Bacillariophyceae.]
– DERIVATIVES **diatomaceous** adj.
– ORIGIN C19: from mod. L. *Diatoma* (genus name), from Gk *diatomos* 'cut in two'.

**diatomaceous earth** /ˌdʌɪətəˈmeɪʃəs/ ● n. a soft, crumbly, porous sedimentary deposit formed from the fossil remains of diatoms.

**diatomic** /ˌdʌɪəˈtɒmɪk/ ● adj. Chemistry consisting of two atoms.

**diatomite** /dʌɪˈatəmʌɪt/ ● n. Geology a fine-grained sedimentary rock formed from consolidated diatomaceous earth.

**diatonic** /ˌdʌɪəˈtɒnɪk/ ● adj. Music involving only notes proper to the prevailing key without chromatic alteration.
– ORIGIN C17: from Fr. *diatonique*, or via late L. from Gk *diatonikos* 'at intervals of a tone'.

**diatreme** /ˈdʌɪətriːm/ ● n. Geology a long vertical pipe or plug formed when gas-filled magma forced its way up through overlying strata.
– ORIGIN C20: from **DIA-** + Gk *trēma* 'perforation'.

**diatribe** /ˈdʌɪətrʌɪb/ ● n. a forceful and bitter verbal attack.
– ORIGIN C16: from Fr., via L. from Gk *diatribē* 'spending of time, discourse'.

**diazepam** /dʌɪˈazɪpam, -ˈeɪz-/ ● n. a tranquillizing muscle-relaxant drug used chiefly to relieve anxiety. Also called **VALIUM** (trademark).
– ORIGIN 1960s: blend of **BENZODIAZEPINE** and **AMIDE**.

**diazo** /dʌɪˈazəʊ, -ˈeɪzəʊ/ (also **diazotype**) ● n. a copying or colouring process using a diazo compound decomposed by ultraviolet light.

**diazo compound** ● n. Chemistry an organic compound containing two nitrogen atoms bonded together, especially a diazonium compound.
– ORIGIN C19: *diazo* from **DIAZONIUM**.

**diazonium** /ˌdʌɪəˈzəʊnɪəm/ ● n. [as modifier] Chemistry of or denoting an organic cation containing two nitrogen atoms bonded together, present in many synthetic dyes.
– ORIGIN C19: coined in Ger. from *diazo-* (indicating the presence of two nitrogen atoms) + the suffix *-onium* (from **AMMONIUM**).

**dib** ● v. (**dibbed**, **dibbing**) another term for **DAP**.
– ORIGIN C17: rel to **DAB**[1].

**dibasic** /dʌɪˈbeɪsɪk/ ● adj. Chemistry (of an acid) having two replaceable hydrogen atoms.

**dibatag** /ˈdɪbətag/ ● n. a gazelle that stands on its hind legs to browse, found in semi-desert regions of Somalia and Ethiopia. [*Ammodorcas clarkei*.]
– ORIGIN C19: from Somali.

**dibber** ● n. Brit. another term for **DIBBLE**.

**dibble** ● n. a pointed hand tool for making holes in the ground for seeds or young plants. ● v. dig or plant with a dibble.
– ORIGIN ME: appar. rel. to **DIB** (also used in this sense in dial.).

**dibbler** ● n. a marsupial mouse of SW Australia, now endangered. [*Parantechinus apicalis*.]

**dibs** ● pl. n. informal **1** (often in phr. **have first dibs**) N. Amer. the right to share or choose something. **2** money.
– ORIGIN C18 (denoting pebbles used in a children's game): from earlier *dib-stones*, perh. from **DIB**.

**dice** ● n. (pl. same; sing. also **die**) **1** a small cube with faces bearing from one to six spots, used in games of chance. See also **DIE**[2]. ➤ a game played with dice. **2** small cubes of food. ● v. **1** [often as noun **dicing**] play or gamble with dice. **2** [often as adj. **diced**] cut (food) into small cubes.
– PHRASES **dice with death** take serious risks. **no dice** informal, chiefly N. Amer. used to refuse a request or indicate no chance of success.
– DERIVATIVES **dicer** n.
– ORIGIN ME: from OFr. *des*, pl. of *de* (see **DIE**[2]).

> **USAGE dice**
> Historically, **dice** is the plural of **die**, but in modern standard English **dice** is used as both the singular and the plural.

**dicentra** /dʌɪˈsɛntrə/ ● n. a herbaceous plant of a genus with drooping clusters of flowers and including bleeding heart. [Genus *Dicentra*.]
– ORIGIN mod. L., from Gk *dikentros*, from *di-* 'two' + *kentron* 'spur, sharp point'.

**dicentric** /dʌɪˈsɛntrɪk/ ● adj. Genetics (of a chromosome) having two centromeres.

**dicey** ● adj. (**-ier**, **-iest**) informal unpredictable and potentially dangerous.

**dichogamy** /dʌɪˈkɒgəmi/ ● n. Botany the ripening of the stamens and pistils of a flower at different times, so that self-fertilization is prevented. Compare with **HOMOGAMY** (in sense 4).
– DERIVATIVES **dichogamous** adj.
– ORIGIN C19: from Gk *dikho-* 'apart, in two' + *gamos* 'marriage'.

**dichotic** /dʌɪˈkɒtɪk/ ● adj. involving the simultaneous stimulation of the right and left ear by different sounds.
– ORIGIN C20: from Gk *dikho-* 'apart' + *ous, ōt-* 'ear' + **-IC**.

**dichotomize** /dʌɪˈkɒtəmʌɪz, dɪ-/ (also **-ise**) ● v. regard or represent as divided or opposed.

**dichotomy** /dʌɪˈkɒtəmi, dɪ-/ ● n. (pl. **-ies**) **1** a division or contrast between two things that are opposed or entirely different. **2** Botany repeated branching into two equal parts.
– DERIVATIVES **dichotomous** adj. **dichotomously** adv.
– ORIGIN C16: via mod. L. from Gk *dikhotomia*, from *dikho-* 'in two, apart' + *-tomia* (see **-TOMY**).

**dichroic** /dʌɪˈkrəʊɪk/ ● adj. (of a crystal) showing different colours when viewed from different directions or in light of differing polarization.
– DERIVATIVES **dichroism** n.
– ORIGIN C19: from Gk *dikhroos* (from *di-* 'twice' + *khrōs* 'colour') + **-IC**.

**dichromate** /dʌɪˈkrəʊmeɪt/ ● n. Chemistry a salt, typically red or orange, containing the anion $Cr_2O_7^{2-}$.

**dichromatism** /dʌɪˈkrəʊmətɪz(ə)m/ ● n. **1** the occurrence of two different kinds of colouring, especially in an animal species. **2** colour blindness in which only two of the three primary colours can be discerned.
– DERIVATIVES **dichromatic** adj.

**dick**[1] ● n. **1** vulgar slang a man's penis. **2** Brit. vulgar slang a stupid or contemptible person. **3** [with neg.] N. Amer. informal anything at all: *you don't know dick about it!* ● v. (usu. **dick around/about**) informal meddle or fool around.
– ORIGIN C16 (in the general sense 'fellow'): familiar form of the given name *Richard*.

**dick**[2] ● n. informal, dated, chiefly N. Amer. a detective.
– ORIGIN C20: perh. an arbitrary shortening of **DETECTIVE**, or from obs. sl. *dick* 'look', from Romany.

**dickcissel** /dɪkˈsɪs(ə)l, ˈdɪksɪs(ə)l/ ● n. a sparrow-like North American songbird with a black-and-white throat

and bright yellow breast. [*Spiza americana*.]
– ORIGIN C19: imitative of its call.

**dickens** /ˈdɪkɪnz/ ● n. informal used for emphasis, or to express annoyance or surprise when asking questions: *what the dickens is going on?*
– ORIGIN C16: a euphemism for 'devil', prob. a use of the surname *Dickens*.

**Dickensian** /dɪˈkɛnzɪən/ ● adj. reminiscent of the novels of Charles Dickens, especially in terms of the poverty and squalor that they portray.

**dicker** ● v. **1** engage in petty argument or bargaining. **2** toy or fiddle with something.
– DERIVATIVES **dickerer** n.
– ORIGIN C19 (orig. US): perh. from obs. *dicker* 'set of ten (hides)', used as a unit of trade, based on L. *decem* 'ten'.

**dickhead** ● n. vulgar slang a stupid, irritating, or ridiculous man.

**dicky**[1] (also **dickey**) ● n. (pl. **-ies** or **-eys**) informal **1** a false shirt front. **2** dated, chiefly Brit. a folding outside seat at the back of a vehicle. ➤a driver's seat in a carriage.
– ORIGIN C18 (denoting a petticoat): each sense prob. has a different origin; perh. partly from *Dicky*, familiar form of *Richard*.

**dicky**[2] ● adj. (**-ier**, **-iest**) Brit. informal not strong, healthy, or functioning reliably.
– ORIGIN C18: perh. from the given name *Dick*, in the old saying *as queer as Dick's hatband*.

**dicky bird** ● n. informal a child's word for a bird.
– PHRASES **not a dicky bird** not a word; nothing at all.

**dicky bow** ● n. informal a bow tie.

**dicot** /ˈdʌɪkɒt/ ● n. short for DICOTYLEDON.

**dicotyledon** /ˌdʌɪkɒtɪˈliːd(ə)n/ ● n. Botany a plant with an embryo bearing two cotyledons, such plants constituting the larger (Dicotyledoneae) of the two classes of flowering species. Compare with MONOCOTYLEDON.
– DERIVATIVES **dicotyledonous** adj.

**dicrotic** /dʌɪˈkrɒtɪk/ ● adj. Medicine denoting a pulse in which a double beat is detectable for each beat of the heart.
– ORIGIN C19: from Gk *dikrotos* 'beating twice' + -IC.

**dicta** plural form of DICTUM.

**Dictaphone** /ˈdɪktəfəʊn/ ● n. trademark a small cassette recorder used to record speech for transcription at a later time.

**dictate** ● v. /dɪkˈteɪt/ **1** state or order authoritatively. ➤control or decisively affect; determine. **2** say or read aloud (words to be typed or written down). ● n. /ˈdɪkteɪt/ an order or principle that must be obeyed.
– DERIVATIVES **dictation** n.
– ORIGIN C16: from L. *dictat-*, *dictare*.

**dictator** ● n. **1** a ruler with total power over a country. ➤an autocratic person. **2** (in ancient Rome) a chief magistrate with absolute power, appointed in an emergency.
– DERIVATIVES **dictatorial** adj. **dictatorially** adv.

**dictatorship** ● n. **1** government by a dictator. **2** a country governed by a dictator.

**diction** ● n. **1** the choice and use of words in speech or writing. **2** the style of enunciation in speaking or singing.
– ORIGIN C16: from L. *dictio(n-)*, from *dicere* 'to say'.

**dictionary** ● n. (pl. **-ies**) a book that lists the words of a language in alphabetical order and gives their meaning, or their equivalent in a different language.
– ORIGIN C16: from med. L. *dictionarium* (*manuale*) or *dictionarius* (*liber*) 'manual or book of words', from L. *dictio* (see DICTION).

**dictum** /ˈdɪktəm/ ● n. (pl. **dicta** /-tə/ or **dictums**) a formal pronouncement from an authoritative source. ➤a short statement that expresses a general truth or principle. ➤Law short for OBITER DICTUM.
– ORIGIN C16: from L., lit. 'something said', neut. past part. of *dicere*.

**Dictyoptera** /ˌdɪktɪˈɒptərə/ ● pl. n. Entomology an order of insects that comprises the cockroaches and mantises.
– DERIVATIVES **dictyopteran** n. & adj.
– ORIGIN mod. L., from Gk *diktuon* 'net' + *pteron* 'wing'.

**dicynodont** /dʌɪˈsɪnədɒnt/ ● n. a fossil herbivorous mammal-like reptile of the late Permian and Triassic periods, with beaked jaws and no teeth apart from two tusks in the upper jaw of the male.
– ORIGIN C19: from mod. L. *Dicynodontia*, from Gk *di-* 'two' + *kuōn* 'dog' + *odous, odont-* 'tooth'.

**did** past of DO[1].

**didactic** /dɪˈdaktɪk, dʌɪ-/ ● adj. intended to teach, in particular having moral instruction as an ulterior motive. ➤in the manner of a teacher; patronizing or hectoring.
– DERIVATIVES **didactically** adv. **didacticism** n.
– ORIGIN C17: from Gk *didaktikos*, from *didaskein* 'teach'.

**didanosine** /dɪˈdanəʊsiːn/ ● n. Medicine another term for DIDEOXYINOSINE.

**diddicoy** ● n. variant spelling of DIDICOI.

**diddle** ● v. informal **1** cheat or swindle. **2** chiefly N. Amer. pass time aimlessly or unproductively. **3** vulgar slang, chiefly N. Amer. have sexual intercourse with.
– DERIVATIVES **diddler** n.
– ORIGIN C19: prob. from the name of Jeremy *Diddler*, a character in the farce *Raising the Wind* (1803) who constantly borrowed small sums of money.

**diddly-squat** /ˈdɪdlɪˌskwɒt/ (also **doodly-squat**) ● pron. [usu. with neg.] N. Amer. informal anything at all.
– ORIGIN C20: prob. from US sl. *doodle* 'excrement' + SQUAT in the sense 'defecate'.

**diddums** /ˈdɪdəmz/ ● exclam. Brit. informal used to express commiseration to a child.
– ORIGIN C19: from *did 'em*, i.e. 'did they?' (tease you, do that to you, etc.).

**diddy**[1] ● n. (pl. **-ies**) Brit. informal a fool.
– ORIGIN C18: alt. of TITTY.

**diddy**[2] ● adj. Brit. informal little.
– ORIGIN prob. a child's corruption of LITTLE.

**dideoxyinosine** /ˌdʌɪdɪɒksɪˈɪnəʊsiːn/ ● n. Medicine a drug used in the treatment of Aids, especially in combination with zidovudine.
– ORIGIN 1970s: from DI-[1] + *deoxy-* (in the sense 'that has lost oxygen') + INOSINE.

**didgeridoo** /ˌdɪdʒ(ə)rɪˈduː/ ● n. an Australian Aboriginal wind instrument in the form of a long wooden tube, which is blown to produce a deep resonant sound.
– ORIGIN from an Aborig. lang. of Arnhem Land.

**didicoi** /ˈdɪdɪkɔɪ/ (also **diddicoy**) ● n. (pl. **didicois**) dialect a gypsy or itinerant tinker.
– ORIGIN C19: perh. an alt. of Romany *dik akei* 'look here'.

**didn't** ● contr. did not.

**dido** /ˈdʌɪdəʊ/ ● n. (pl. **-oes** or **-os**) (in phr. **cut (up) didoes**) N. Amer. informal perform mischievous tricks or deeds.
– ORIGIN C19: of unknown origin.

**didst** archaic second person singular past of DO[1].

**didymium** /dɪˈdɪmɪəm/ ● n. Chemistry a mixture containing the rare-earth elements praseodymium and neodymium, used to colour glass for optical filters.
– ORIGIN C19: from Gk *didumos* 'twin' + *-ium*.

**die**[1] ● v. (**dying**) **1** stop living. ➤(**die out**) become extinct. ➤be forgotten: *her name will never die.* ➤(often **die away/down**) become less loud or strong. **2** informal used to emphasize strong feelings of desire, embarrassment, shock, etc.: *I nearly died when I saw them.* ➤(**be dying for/to do something**) be very eager for something.
– PHRASES **die hard** disappear or change very slowly. **never say die** said to encourage someone not to give up hope. **to die for** informal extremely good or desirable.
– ORIGIN ME: from ON *deyja*, of Gmc origin; rel. to DEAD.

**die**[2] ● n. **1** singular form of DICE. **2** (pl. **dies**) a device for cutting or moulding metal or for stamping a design on coins or medals. **3** (pl. **dies**) Architecture the cubic part of a pedestal between the base and the cornice; a dado or plinth.
– PHRASES **the die is cast** an event has happened or a decision has been taken that cannot be changed. **(as) straight as a die 1** completely straight. **2** entirely open and honest.
– ORIGIN ME: from OFr. *de*, from L. *datum* 'something given or played', neut. past part. of *dare*.

**USAGE die**

In modern standard English, the singular **die** (rather than **dice**) for sense 1 is relatively uncommon. **Dice** is widely used for both the singular and the plural.

**dieback** • **n.** a condition in which a tree or shrub begins to die from the tip of its leaves or roots backwards.

**die-cast** • **adj.** (of a metal object) formed by pouring molten metal into a reusable mould. • **v.** [usu. as noun **die-casting**] make (a metal object) in this way.

**dieffenbachia** /ˌdiːf(ə)nˈbakɪə/ • **n.** a plant of a genus that includes dumb cane and its relatives. [Genus *Dieffenbachia*.]
– ORIGIN mod. L., named after the Ger. horticulturalist Ernst *Dieffenbach*.

**diegesis** /ˌdʌɪəˈdʒiːsɪs/ • **n.** (pl. **diegeses** /-siːz/) formal a narrative or plot.
– DERIVATIVES **diegetic** /-ˈdʒɛtɪk/ adj.
– ORIGIN C19: from Gk *diēgēsis* 'narrative'.

**diehard** • **n.** a person who strongly opposes change or who continues to support something in spite of opposition.

**diel** /ˈdiːl/ • **adj.** Biology denoting or involving a period of twenty-four hours.
– ORIGIN 1930s: from L. *dies* 'day' + *-(a)l* (see **-AL**).

**dieldrin** /ˈdiːldrɪn/ • **n.** an insecticide made by the oxidation of aldrin, now largely banned.
– ORIGIN 1940s: from the name of the Ger. chemist Otto *Diels* + **ALDRIN**.

**dielectric** /ˌdʌɪɪˈlɛktrɪk/ Physics • **adj.** having the property of transmitting electric force without conduction; insulating. • **n.** an insulator.
– DERIVATIVES **dielectrically** adv.
– ORIGIN C19: from **DI-**[3] + **ELECTRIC**.

**dielectric constant** • **n.** Physics a quantity measuring the ability of a substance to store electrical energy in an electric field.

**diencephalon** /ˌdʌɪɛnˈsɛf(ə)lɒn, -ˈkɛf-/ • **n.** Anatomy the caudal (posterior) part of the forebrain, containing the epithalamus, thalamus, hypothalamus, and ventral thalamus and the third ventricle. Compare with **TELENCEPHALON**.
– DERIVATIVES **diencephalic** adj.
– ORIGIN C19: from **DI-**[3] + **ENCEPHALON**.

**diene** /ˈdʌɪiːn/ • **n.** Chemistry an unsaturated hydrocarbon containing two double bonds between carbon atoms.
– ORIGIN C20: from **DI-**[1] + **-ENE**.

**dieresis** • **n.** US spelling of **DIAERESIS**.

**diesel** /ˈdiːz(ə)l/ • **n.** **1** an internal-combustion engine in which heat produced by the compression of air in the cylinder is used to ignite the fuel. **2** a heavy petroleum fraction used as fuel in diesel engines.
– DERIVATIVES **dieselize** (also **-ise**) v.
– ORIGIN C19: named after the Ger. engineer Rudolf *Diesel*.

**diesel-electric** • **adj.** denoting or relating to a locomotive driven by the electric current produced by a diesel-engined generator. • **n.** a locomotive of this type.

**diesel-hydraulic** • **adj.** denoting or relating to a locomotive driven by a hydraulic transmission system powered by a diesel engine. • **n.** a locomotive of this type.

**die-sinker** • **n.** a person who engraves dies used to stamp designs on coins or medals.
– DERIVATIVES **die-sinking** n.

**Dies Irae** /ˌdiːeɪz ˈɪərʌɪ, ˈɪəreɪ/ • **n.** a Latin hymn sung in a Mass for the dead.
– ORIGIN L., 'day of wrath' (the opening words of the hymn).

**dies non** /ˌdiːeɪz ˈnɒn/ • **n.** (pl. same) a day on which no legal business can be done, or which does not count for legal or other purposes.
– ORIGIN L., short for *dies non juridicus* 'non-judicial day'.

**die-stamping** • **n.** a method of embossing paper or another surface using a die.

**diestock** • **n.** a hand tool used in the cutting of external screw threads.

**diestrus** • **n.** US spelling of **DIOESTRUS**.

**diet**[1] • **n.** **1** the kinds of food that a person, animal, or community habitually eats. **2** a special course of food to which a person restricts themselves to lose weight or for medical reasons. ➤[as modifier] (of food or drink) with reduced fat or sugar content. • **v.** (**dieted**, **dieting**) restrict oneself to a special diet to lose weight.
– DERIVATIVES **dietary** adj. **dieter** n.
– ORIGIN ME: from OFr. *diete* (n.), *dieter* (v.), via L. from Gk *diaita* 'a way of life'.

**diet**[2] • **n.** **1** a legislative assembly in certain countries. ➤historical a regular meeting of the states of a confederation. **2** Scots Law a meeting or session of a court.
– ORIGIN ME: from med. L. *dieta* 'day's work, wages'.

**dietetic** /ˌdʌɪəˈtɛtɪk/ • **adj.** concerned with diet and nutrition.
– DERIVATIVES **dietetically** adv.

**dietetics** • **pl. n.** [treated as sing.] the branch of knowledge concerned with the diet and its effects on health.

**dietitian** /dʌɪəˈtɪʃ(ə)n/ (also **dietician**) • **n.** an expert on diet and nutrition.

**dif-** • **prefix** variant spelling of **DIS-** assimilated before *f* (as in *diffraction*, *diffuse*).
– ORIGIN from L., var. of **DIS-**.

**differ** • **v.** **1** be unlike or dissimilar. **2** disagree.
– PHRASES **agree to differ** amicably stop arguing about something because agreement will clearly not be reached. **beg to differ** politely disagree.
– ORIGIN ME: from OFr. *differer* 'differ, defer', from L. *different-*, *differre*, from *dis-* 'from, away' + *ferre* 'bring, carry'; cf. **DEFER**[1].

**difference** • **n.** **1** a way in which people or things are different. ➤the state or condition of being different. **2** the remainder left after subtraction of one value from another. **3** a disagreement, quarrel, or dispute. **4** Heraldry an alteration in a coat of arms to distinguish members or branches of a family. • **v.** Heraldry alter (a coat of arms) to distinguish members or branches of a family.
– PHRASES **with a difference** having a new or unusual feature or treatment.
– ORIGIN ME: via OFr. from L. *differentia*, from L. *different-* (see **DIFFER**).

**different** • **adj.** **1** not the same as another or each other; unlike in nature, form, or quality. **2** informal novel and unusual. **3** distinct; separate.
– DERIVATIVES **differently** adv. **differentness** n.
– ORIGIN ME: via OFr. from L. *different-*, *differre* (see **DIFFER**).

**USAGE different**

There is little difference in sense between **different from**, **different to**, and **different than**, and all have been used by respected writers. **Different from** is traditionally held to be the correct collocation, and is by far the commonest in written evidence; **different than**, which is often criticized, is largely restricted to North America.

**differentia** /ˌdɪfəˈrɛnʃɪə/ • **n.** (pl. **differentiae** /-ʃɪiː/) a distinguishing mark or characteristic. ➤chiefly Philosophy an attribute that distinguishes a species of thing from other species of the same genus.
– ORIGIN C17: from L. (see **DIFFERENCE**).

**differentiable** /ˌdɪfəˈrɛnʃɪəb(ə)l/ • **adj.** able to be differentiated.
– DERIVATIVES **differentiability** n.

**differential** /ˌdɪfəˈrɛnʃ(ə)l/ chiefly technical • **adj.** **1** of, constituting, or depending on a difference; differing or varying according to circumstances or relevant factors. **2** Mathematics relating to infinitesimal differences or to the derivatives of functions. • **n.** **1** a difference. ➤Brit. a difference in wages between industries or between categories of employees in the same industry. ➤Mathematics an infinitesimal difference between successive values of a variable. **2** a gear allowing a vehicle's driven wheels to revolve at different speeds in cornering.
– DERIVATIVES **differentially** adv.

**differential calculus** • **n.** Mathematics the part of calculus concerned with the derivatives of functions.

**differential coefficient** • **n.** Mathematics another term for **DERIVATIVE**.

**differential equation** • **n.** an equation involving derivatives of a function or functions.

**differentiate** /ˌdɪfəˈrɛnʃɪeɪt/ • **v. 1** recognize or identify as different; distinguish. ➤cause to appear different or distinct. **2** technical make or become different in the process of growth or development. **3** Mathematics transform (a function) into its derivative.
– DERIVATIVES **differentiation** n. **differentiator** n.

**differently abled** • **adj.** euphemistic, chiefly N. Amer. disabled.

**difficult** • **adj. 1** needing much effort or skill to accomplish, deal with, or understand. **2** (of a person) not easy to please or satisfy; awkward.
– DERIVATIVES **difficultly** adv. (rare). **difficultness** n.
– ORIGIN ME: back-form. from DIFFICULTY.

**difficulty** • **n.** (pl. **-ies**) **1** the state or condition of being difficult. **2** a difficult or dangerous situation or circumstance; a problem.
– ORIGIN ME: from L. *difficultas*, from *dis-* (expressing reversal) + *facultas* 'ability, opportunity'.

**diffident** • **adj.** modest or shy because of a lack of self-confidence.
– DERIVATIVES **diffidence** n. **diffidently** adv.
– ORIGIN ME: from L. *diffident-*, *diffidere* 'fail to trust'.

**diffract** /dɪˈfrakt/ • **v.** Physics cause to undergo diffraction.
– DERIVATIVES **diffractive** adj. **diffractively** adv.
– ORIGIN C19: from L. *diffract-*, *diffringere* 'break in pieces'.

**diffraction** • **n.** Physics the process by which a beam of light or other system of waves is spread out as a result of passing through a narrow aperture or across an edge.

**diffraction grating** • **n.** a plate of glass or metal ruled with very close parallel lines, producing a spectrum by diffraction and interference of light.

**diffractometer** /ˌdɪfrakˈtɒmɪtə/ • **n.** an instrument for detecting and measuring diffracted radiation, especially in crystallography.

**diffuse** • **v.** /dɪˈfjuːz/ spread or cause to spread over a wide area. ➤Physics intermingle with another substance by movement of particles. • **adj.** /dɪˈfjuːs/ **1** spread out over a large area; not concentrated. ➤(of disease) not localized in the body. **2** lacking clarity or conciseness.
– DERIVATIVES **diffusely** /dɪˈfjuːsli/ adv. **diffuseness** /dɪˈfjuːsnɪs/ n. **diffuser** (also **diffusor**) n. **diffusible** adj.
– ORIGIN ME: from L. *diffus-*, *diffundere* 'pour out'; the adj. is via Fr. *diffus* or L. *diffusus* 'extensive'.

**diffusion** • **n.** the action or process of diffusing. ➤Anthropology the dissemination of elements of culture to another region or people.
– DERIVATIVES **diffusionism** n. **diffusionist** adj. & n. **diffusive** adj.

**diffusivity** /ˌdɪfjuːˈsɪvɪti/ • **n.** (pl. **-ies**) Physics a measure of the capability of a substance or energy to be diffused or to allow something to pass by diffusion.

**dig** • **v.** (**digging**; past and past part. **dug**) **1** break up and move earth with a tool or with hands, paws, etc. ➤make (a hole) by digging. ➤extract from the ground by digging. ➤(**dig in**) begin eating heartily. ➤(**dig in**) (of a soldier) protect oneself by making a trench or similar ground defence. **2** poke or jab sharply. **3** search, rummage, or investigate. ➤(**dig something out/up**) bring out or uncover something hidden. **4** excavate (an archaeological site). **5** informal, dated like, appreciate, or understand. • **n. 1** an act or spell of digging. **2** an archaeological excavation. **3** a sharp push or poke. **4** informal a remark intended to mock or criticize. **5** (**digs**) informal, chiefly Brit. lodgings.
– PHRASES **dig up dirt** informal discover and reveal damaging information about someone. **dig oneself into a hole** get oneself into an awkward or restrictive situation. **dig in one's heels** resist stubbornly; refuse to give in.
– ORIGIN ME: perh. from OE *dīc* 'ditch'.

**Digambara** /dɪˈgʌmbərə/ • **n.** a member of one of two principal sects of Jainism, who reject property ownership and usually do not wear clothes. See also SVETAMBARA.
– ORIGIN from Sanskrit *Digāmbara*, lit. 'sky-clad'.

**digamma** /dʌɪˈgamə/ • **n.** the sixth letter of the early Greek alphabet (Ϝ, ϝ), probably pronounced as 'w'.
– ORIGIN C17: via L. from Gk, from *di-* 'twice' + GAMMA (because of the shape of the letter, resembling gamma (Γ) with an extra stroke).

**digastric muscle** /dʌɪˈgastrɪk/ • **n.** Anatomy each of a pair of muscles which run under the jaw and act to open it.
– ORIGIN C17: from mod. L. *digastricus*, from *di-* 'twice' + Gk *gastēr* 'belly' (because the muscle has two fleshy parts or 'bellies' connected by a tendon).

**digenean** /ˌdʌɪdʒɪˈniːən, dʌɪˈdʒɛnɪən/ • **adj.** Zoology relating to or denoting parasitic flukes which need from two to four hosts to complete their life cycle. Compare with MONOGENEAN.
– ORIGIN 1960s: from the mod. L. name of the subclass *Digenea* (from Gk *di-* 'twice' + *genea* 'generation, race') + -AN.

**digerati** /ˌdɪdʒəˈrɑːtiː/ • **pl. n.** informal people with expertise or professional involvement in information technology.
– ORIGIN 1990s: blend of DIGITAL and LITERATI.

**digest** • **v.** /dʌɪˈdʒɛst, dɪ-/ **1** break down (food) in the stomach and intestines into substances that can be used by the body. **2** Chemistry treat (a substance) with heat, enzymes, or a solvent in order to break it down. **3** understand or assimilate (information) by reflection. **4** arrange in a systematic or convenient order, especially by reduction. • **n.** /ˈdʌɪdʒɛst/ **1** a compilation or summary of material or information. ➤a methodical summary of a body of laws. ➤(**the Digest**) the compendium of Roman law compiled in the reign of Justinian. **2** Chemistry a substance or mixture obtained by digestion.
– DERIVATIVES **digestibility** n. **digestible** adj.
– ORIGIN ME: from L. *digest-*, *digerere* 'distribute, dissolve, digest'; the n. is from L. *digesta* 'matters methodically arranged'.

**digester** • **n.** Chemistry a container in which substances are treated with heat, enzymes, or a solvent in order to promote decomposition or extract essential components.

**digestif** /dʌɪˈdʒɛstɪf, ˌdiːʒɛˈstiːf/ • **n.** a drink, especially an alcoholic one, taken before or after a meal in order to aid the digestion.
– ORIGIN Fr., lit. 'digestive'.

**digestion** • **n.** the process of digesting. ➤a person's capacity to digest food.

**digestive** • **adj.** of or relating to the process of digesting food. ➤(of food or medicine) aiding or promoting the process of digestion. • **n. 1** a food or medicine that aids or promotes the digestion of food. **2** Brit. a round semi-sweet biscuit made of wholemeal flour.
– DERIVATIVES **digestively** adv.
– ORIGIN ME: from OFr. *digestif*, *-ive* or L. *digestivus*, from *digest-*, *digerere* (see DIGEST).

**digger** • **n. 1** a person, animal, or large machine that digs earth. **2** (**Digger**) a member of a group of radical dissenters formed as an offshoot of the Levellers, believing in a form of agrarian communism. **3** Austral./NZ informal a friendly form of address for a man.

**digger wasp** • **n.** a solitary wasp which excavates a burrow, filling it with paralysed insects or spiders for its larvae to feed on. [Families Sphecidae and Pompilidae: many species.]

**diggings** • **pl. n. 1** a site such as a mine or goldfield that has been excavated. ➤material that has been dug from the ground. **2** Brit. informal, dated lodgings.

**dight** /dʌɪt/ • **adj.** archaic clothed or equipped. • **v. 1** poetic/literary make ready; prepare. **2** Scottish & N. English wipe clean or dry.
– ORIGIN ME: past part. of archaic *dight* 'order, deal with', based on L. *dictare* 'dictate'.

**digit** /ˈdɪdʒɪt/ • **n. 1** any of the numerals from 0 to 9, especially when forming part of a number. **2** a finger or thumb. ➤Zoology a finger, thumb, or toe.
– ORIGIN ME: from L. *digitus* 'finger, toe'.

**digital** • **adj. 1** relating to or using signals or information represented as digits using discrete values of a physical quantity such as voltage or magnetic polarization. Com-

pare with **ANALOGUE.** ➤(of a clock or watch) showing the time by means of displayed digits rather than hands or a pointer. **2** of or relating to a finger or fingers.
– DERIVATIVES **digitally** adv.

**digital audiotape** ● n. magnetic tape used to make digital recordings.

**digital divide** ● n. the gulf between those who have ready access to computers and the Internet and those who do not.

**digitalin** /ˌdɪdʒɪˈteɪlɪn/ ● n. a drug containing the active constituents of digitalis.

**digitalis** /ˌdɪdʒɪˈteɪlɪs/ ● n. a drug prepared from foxglove leaves, containing substances that stimulate the heart muscle.
– ORIGIN C18: from the mod. L. genus name of the foxglove, from *digitalis* (*herba*) '(plant) relating to the finger', suggested by Ger. *Fingerhut* 'thimble or foxglove'.

**digitalize**[1] (also **-ise**) ● v. another term for **DIGITIZE.**
– DERIVATIVES **digitalization** n.

**digitalize**[2] (also **-ise**) ● v. Medicine administer digitalis or digoxin to (a patient with a heart complaint).
– DERIVATIVES **digitalization** n.

**digitate** /ˈdɪdʒɪtət, -eɪt/ ● adj. shaped like a spread hand.

**digitation** ● n. **1** Zoology & Botany a finger-like protuberance. **2** Computing the conversion of data to digital form.

**digitigrade** /ˈdɪdʒɪtɪˌgreɪd/ ● adj. Zoology (of a mammal) walking on its toes and not touching the ground with its heels, as a dog, cat, or rodent. Compare with **PLANTIGRADE.**
– ORIGIN C19: from L. *digitus* 'finger, toe' + *-gradus* '-walking'.

**digitize** (also **-ise**) ● v. [usu. as adj. **digitized**] convert (pictures or sound) into a digital form that can be processed by a computer.
– DERIVATIVES **digitization** n. **digitizer** n.

**digitoxin** /ˌdɪdʒɪˈtɒksɪn/ ● n. Chemistry a compound with similar properties to digoxin and found with it in the foxglove and other plants.

**diglossia** /dʌɪˈglɒsɪə/ ● n. Linguistics a situation in which two languages (or two varieties of the same language) are used under different conditions within a community, often by the same speakers.
– DERIVATIVES **diglossic** adj.
– ORIGIN 1950s: from Gk *diglōssos* 'bilingual', on the pattern of Fr. *diglossie.*

**dignified** ● adj. having or showing dignity.
– DERIVATIVES **dignifiedly** adv.

**dignify** ● v. (**-ies, -ied**) make (something) seem worthy and impressive. ➤give an impressive name to (someone or something unworthy of it).
– ORIGIN ME: from OFr. *dignefier*, from late L. *dignificare*, from L. *dignus* 'worthy'.

**dignitary** /ˈdɪgnɪt(ə)ri/ ● n. (pl. **-ies**) a person holding high rank or office.

**dignity** ● n. (pl. **-ies**) **1** the state or quality of being worthy of honour or respect. **2** a composed or serious manner or style. ➤a sense of pride in oneself.
– PHRASES **stand on one's dignity** insist on being treated with due respect.
– ORIGIN ME: from OFr. *dignete*, from L. *dignitas*, from *dignus* 'worthy'.

**digoxin** /dɪˈdʒɒksɪn/ ● n. Chemistry a poisonous compound present in the foxglove and other plants, used as a cardiac stimulant.
– ORIGIN 1930s: contr. of **DIGITOXIN.**

**digraph** /ˈdʌɪgrɑːf/ ● n. **1** a combination of two letters representing one sound, as in *ph* and *ey.* **2** Printing a ligature.
– DERIVATIVES **digraphic** adj.

**digress** /dʌɪˈgrɛs/ ● v. leave the main subject temporarily in speech or writing.
– DERIVATIVES **digresser** n. **digression** n. **digressive** adj. **digressively** adv. **digressiveness** n.
– ORIGIN C16: from L. *digress-*, *digredi* 'step away', from *di-* 'aside' + *gradi* 'to walk'.

**dihedral** /dʌɪˈhiːdr(ə)l/ ● adj. having or contained by two plane faces. ● n. **1** an angle formed by two plane faces. **2** Aeronautics upward inclination of an aircraft's wing. **3** N. Amer., Climbing a place where two planes of rock meet at an angle of between 60° and 120°.
– ORIGIN C18: from **DI-**[1] + *-hedral* (see **-HEDRON**).

**dihybrid** /dʌɪˈhʌɪbrɪd/ ● n. Genetics a hybrid that is heterozygous for alleles of two different genes.

**dihydric** /dʌɪˈhʌɪdrɪk/ ● adj. Chemistry (of an alcohol) containing two hydroxyl groups.

**dihydrotestosterone** /dʌɪˌhʌɪdrəʊtɛsˈtɒstərəʊn/ ● n. Biochemistry a male sex hormone which is the active form of testosterone.
– ORIGIN 1950s: from *dihydro-* (in the sense 'containing two hydrogen atoms in the molecule') + **TESTOSTERONE.**

**dik-dik** /ˈdɪkdɪk/ ● n. a dwarf antelope found on the dry savannah of Africa. [Genus *Madoqua*: several species.]
– ORIGIN C19: a local word in East Africa, imitative of its call.

**dike**[1] ● n. variant spelling of **DYKE**[1].

**dike**[2] ● n. variant spelling of **DYKE**[2].

**diktat** /ˈdɪktat/ ● n. an order or decree imposed by someone in power without popular consent.
– ORIGIN 1930s: from Ger.

**DIL** ● abbrev. Electronics dual in-line (package).

**dilapidate** /dɪˈlapɪdeɪt/ ● v. archaic cause to fall into disrepair or ruin.
– ORIGIN C16 (in the sense 'waste, squander'): from L. *dilapidat-*, *dilapidare* 'demolish, squander', lit. 'scatter as if throwing stones'.

**dilapidated** ● adj. (of a building or object) in a state of disrepair or ruin as a result of age or neglect.

**dilapidation** ● n. **1** the state or process of falling into decay or being in disrepair. **2** (**dilapidations**) repairs required during or at the end of a tenancy or lease. ➤(in church use) a sum charged against an incumbent for wear and tear during a tenancy.

**dilatancy** /dʌɪˈleɪt(ə)nsi, dɪ-/ ● n. Chemistry the phenomenon exhibited by some fluids, sols, and gels in which they become more viscous when stress is applied.

**dilatation** /ˌdʌɪleɪˈteɪʃ(ə)n, dɪ-, -lə-/ ● n. chiefly Medicine & Physiology the action of dilating a vessel or opening or the process of becoming dilated. ➤a dilated part of a hollow organ or vessel.

**dilatation and curettage** ● n. Medicine a surgical procedure involving dilatation of the cervix and curettage of the uterus, performed after a miscarriage or for the removal of cysts or tumours.

**dilate** /dʌɪˈleɪt, dɪ-/ ● v. **1** become or make wider, larger, or more open. **2** (**dilate on**) speak or write at length on.
– DERIVATIVES **dilatable** adj. **dilation** n.
– ORIGIN ME: from OFr. *dilater*, from L. *dilatare* 'spread out'.

**dilator** ● n. **1** (also **dilator muscle**) Anatomy a muscle whose contraction dilates an organ or aperture, such as the pupil of the eye. **2** a surgical instrument for dilating a tube or cavity in the body. ➤a vasodilatory drug.

**dilatory** /ˈdɪlət(ə)ri/ ● adj. **1** slow to act. **2** intended to cause delay.
– DERIVATIVES **dilatorily** adv. **dilatoriness** n.
– ORIGIN ME: from late L. *dilatorius* 'delaying', from L. *dilator* 'delayer', from *dilat-*, *differre* 'defer'.

**dildo** ● n. (pl. **-os** or **-oes**) an object shaped like an erect penis used for sexual stimulation.
– ORIGIN C16: of unknown origin.

**dilemma** /dɪˈlɛmə, dʌɪ-/ ● n. **1** a situation in which a difficult choice has to be made between two or more alternatives. ➤informal a difficult situation or problem. **2** Logic an argument forcing an opponent to choose either of two unfavourable alternatives.
– ORIGIN C16: via L. from Gk *dilēmma*, from *di-* 'twice' + *lēmma* 'premise'.

**dilettante** /ˌdɪlɪˈtanteɪ, -ti/ ● n. (pl. **dilettanti** /-ti/ or **dilettantes**) **1** a person who cultivates an area of interest, such as the arts, without real commitment or knowledge. **2** archaic a person with an amateur interest in the arts.
– DERIVATIVES **dilettantish** adj. **dilettantism** n.
– ORIGIN C18: from Ital., 'person loving the arts'.

**diligence**[1] /ˈdɪlɪdʒ(ə)ns/ ● n. careful and persistent work or effort.

**diligence**[2] /ˈdɪlɪdʒ(ə)ns/ • **n.** historical a public stagecoach.
– ORIGIN C17: from Fr., shortened from *carrosse de diligence* 'coach of speed'.
**diligent** • **adj.** careful and conscientious in one's work or duties.
– DERIVATIVES **diligently** adv.
– ORIGIN ME: via OFr. from L. *diligens, diligent-* 'assiduous', from *diligere* 'love, take delight in'.
**dill**[1] (also **dill weed**) • **n.** an aromatic culinary and medicinal herb of the parsley family, with yellow flowers. [*Anethum graveolens*.]
– ORIGIN OE *dile, dyle*, of unknown origin.
**dill**[2] • **n.** Austral./NZ informal a naive or foolish person.
– ORIGIN 1940s: appar. a back-form. from **DILLY**[2].
**dill pickle** • **n.** pickled cucumber flavoured with dill.
**dill water** • **n.** an extract distilled from dill, used to relieve flatulence.
**dilly**[1] • **n.** (pl. **-ies**) N. Amer. informal an excellent example.
– ORIGIN C19: alt. of the first syllable of **DELIGHTFUL** or **DELICIOUS**.
**dilly**[2] • **adj.** (**-ier**, **-iest**) Austral./NZ informal, dated odd or foolish.
– ORIGIN C19: perh. a blend of **DAFT** and **SILLY**.
**dillybag** • **n.** Austral. a bag or basket of traditional Aboriginal design, made from woven grass or fibre.
– ORIGIN from an Aborig. word meaning 'coarse grass or reeds' + **BAG**.
**dilly-dally** • **v.** (**-ies**, **-ied**) informal dawdle or vacillate.
– ORIGIN C17: reduplication of **DALLY**.
**dilophosaurus** /dʌɪˌləʊfə(ʊ)ˈsɔːrəs/ • **n.** a large bipedal dinosaur of the early Jurassic period, with two long crests on the head.
– ORIGIN mod. L., from Gk *dilophos* 'two-crested' + *sauros* 'lizard'.
**diluent** /ˈdɪljʊənt/ technical • **n.** a substance used to dilute something. • **adj.** acting to cause dilution.
– ORIGIN C18: from L. *diluent-*, *diluere* 'dissolve'.
**dilute** /dʌɪˈl(j)uːt, dɪ-/ • **v.** **1** make (a liquid) thinner or weaker by adding water or another solvent. **2** make weaker or less forceful by modifying or adding other elements. • **adj.** /also ˈdʌɪ-/ (of a liquid) diluted. ➤ Chemistry (of a solution) having a relatively low concentration of solute.
– DERIVATIVES **diluter** n. **dilution** n. **dilutive** adj.
– ORIGIN C16: from L. *dilut-*, *diluere* 'wash away, dissolve'.
**diluvial** /dʌɪˈl(j)uːvɪəl, dɪ-/ (also **diluvian**) • **adj.** of or relating to a flood or floods, especially the biblical Flood.
– ORIGIN C17: from late L. *diluvialis*, from *diluvium* 'deluge'.
**dim** • **adj.** (**dimmer**, **dimmest**) **1** (of a light or illuminated object) not shining brightly or clearly. ➤ made difficult to see by darkness, shade, or distance. ➤ (of the eyes) not able to see clearly. **2** not clearly recalled or formulated in the mind. **3** informal stupid or slow to understand. • **v.** (**dimmed**, **dimming**) make or become dim. ➤ N. Amer. dip (a vehicle's headlights).
– PHRASES **take a dim view of** regard with disapproval.
– DERIVATIVES **dimly** adv. **dimmish** adj. **dimness** n.
– ORIGIN OE *dim, dimm*, of Gmc origin.
**dim.** • **abbrev.** diminuendo.
**dime** /dʌɪm/ • **n.** N. Amer. a ten-cent coin. ➤ informal a small amount of money.
– PHRASES **a dime a dozen** informal very common and of little value. **drop a** (or **the**) **dime on** informal inform on. **on a dime** informal within a small area or short distance.
– ORIGIN ME (orig. denoting a tithe or tenth part): from OFr. *disme*, from L. *decima pars* 'tenth part'.
**dime novel** • **n.** N. Amer. dated a cheap, popular novel.
**dimension** /dɪˈmɛnʃ(ə)n, dʌɪ-/ • **n.** **1** a measurable extent, such as length, breadth, or height. ➤ Physics an expression for a derived physical quantity in terms of fundamental quantities such as mass, length, or time, raised to the appropriate power (acceleration, for example, having the dimension of *length* × *time*$^{-2}$). **2** an aspect or feature: *water can add a new dimension to your garden*. • **v.** cut or shape to particular dimensions. ➤ [usu. as adj. **dimensioned**] mark (a diagram) with dimensions.
– DERIVATIVES **-dimensional** adj. **dimensionless** adj.
– ORIGIN ME: via OFr. from L. *dimensio(n-)*, from *dimetiri* 'measure out'.
**dimer** /ˈdʌɪmə/ • **n.** Chemistry a molecule or molecular complex consisting of two identical molecules linked together.
– DERIVATIVES **dimeric** adj.
– ORIGIN 1930s: from **DI-**[1], on the pattern of *polymer*.
**dimerize** /ˈdʌɪmərʌɪz/ (also **-ise**) • **v.** Chemistry combine with a similar molecule to form a dimer.
– DERIVATIVES **dimerization** n.
**dimerous** /ˈdɪm(ə)rəs/ • **adj.** Botany & Zoology having parts arranged in groups of two. ➤ consisting of two joints or parts.
– ORIGIN C19: from mod. L. *dimerus* + **-OUS**.
**dime store** • **n.** N. Amer. a shop selling cheap merchandise (originally one where the maximum price was a dime). ➤ [as modifier] cheap and inferior.
**dimeter** /ˈdɪmɪtə/ • **n.** Prosody a line of verse consisting of two metrical feet.
– ORIGIN C16: via late L. from Gk *dimetros* 'of two measures'.
**dimethyl sulphoxide** /dʌɪˌmiːθʌɪl sʌlˈfɒksʌɪd, -ˌmɛθ-, -θɪl/ (US **dimethyl sulfoxide**) • **n.** Chemistry a colourless liquid used as a solvent, especially for medicines applied to the skin (which it readily penetrates).
**dimetrodon** /dʌɪˈmiːtrədɒn/ • **n.** a large fossil carnivorous mammal-like reptile of the Permian period, with long spines on its back supporting a sail-like crest.
– ORIGIN mod. L., from *di-* 'twice' + Gk *metron* 'measure' + *odous, odont-* 'tooth' (taken in the sense 'two long teeth').
**dimidiate** /dɪˈmɪdɪeɪt/ • **v.** Heraldry (of a coat of arms or a charge) adjoin (another) so that only half of each is visible. ➤ [as adj. **dimidiated**] (of a charge) having only one half depicted.
– ORIGIN C16: from L. *dimidiat-*, *dimidiare* 'halve'.
**diminish** • **v.** **1** make or become less. **2** [as adj. **diminished**] Music denoting an interval which is one semitone less than the corresponding minor or perfect interval.
– PHRASES (**the law of**) **diminishing returns** the principle that as expenditure or investment increases each further increase produces a proportionately smaller return.
– DERIVATIVES **diminishable** adj.
– ORIGIN ME: blend of archaic *minish* 'diminish' (based on L. *minutia* 'smallness') and obs. *diminue* 'speak disparagingly' (based on L. *deminuere* 'lessen'.
**diminished responsibility** • **n.** English Law an unbalanced mental state which is recognized as grounds to reduce a charge of murder to that of manslaughter.
**diminuendo** /dɪˌmɪnjʊˈɛndəʊ/ Music • **adv. & adj.** with a decrease in loudness. • **v.** (**-os**, **-oed**) decrease in loudness or intensity.
– ORIGIN Ital., lit. 'diminishing'.
**diminution** /ˌdɪmɪˈnjuːʃ(ə)n/ • **n.** **1** a reduction. **2** Music the shortening of the time values of notes in a melodic part.
**diminutive** /dɪˈmɪnjʊtɪv/ • **adj.** **1** extremely or unusually small. **2** (of a word, name, or suffix) implying smallness, either actual or as an expression of affection or scorn (e.g. *teeny, -let*). • **n.** **1** a shortened form of a name, typically used informally. **2** Heraldry a charge of the same form as an ordinary but of lesser size or width.
– DERIVATIVES **diminutively** adv. **diminutiveness** n.
– ORIGIN ME: from OFr. *diminutif, -ive*, from late L. *diminutivus*, from L. *deminut-*, *deminuere* 'lessen'.
**dimissory** /ˈdɪmɪs(ə)ri/ • **adj.** (in the Christian Church) denoting formal permission from a bishop for a person from one diocese to be ordained in another.
– ORIGIN ME (as pl. n.): from late L. *dimissorius*, from *dimiss-*, *dimittere* 'send away'.
**dimity** /ˈdɪmɪti/ • **n.** a hard-wearing cotton fabric woven with stripes or checks.
– ORIGIN ME: from Ital. *dimito* or med. L. *dimitum*, from Gk *dimitos*, from *di-* 'twice' + *mitos* 'warp thread'.
**dimmer** • **n.** **1** (also **dimmer switch**) a device for vary-

ing the brightness of an electric light. **2** US a dipped headlight.

**dimorphic** /dʌɪˈmɔːfɪk/ ● **adj.** chiefly Biology occurring in or representing two distinct forms.
– DERIVATIVES **dimorphism** n.
– ORIGIN C19: from Gk *dimorphos* (from *di-* 'twice' + *morphē* 'form') + **-IC**.

**dimple** ● **n.** a small depression in the flesh, either permanent or forming in the cheeks when one smiles. ● **v.** produce a dimple or dimples in the surface of. ➤ [usu. as adj. **dimpled**] form or show a dimple or dimples.
– DERIVATIVES **dimply** adj.
– ORIGIN ME: of Gmc origin.

**dim sum** /dɪm ˈsʌm/ (also **dim sim** /ˈsɪm/) ● **n.** a Chinese dish of small steamed or fried savoury dumplings containing various fillings.
– ORIGIN from Chin. (Cantonese dial.) *tim sam*, from *tim* 'dot' and *sam* 'heart'.

**dimwit** ● **n.** informal a stupid or silly person.
– DERIVATIVES **dim-witted** adj. **dim-wittedly** adv. **dim-wittedness** n.

**DIN** ● **n.** any of a series of technical standards originating in Germany and used internationally, especially to designate electrical connections and film speeds.
– ORIGIN C20: acronym from *Deutsche Industrie-Norm* 'German Industrial Standard'.

**din** ● **n.** a loud, unpleasant, and prolonged noise. ● **v.** (**dinned**, **dinning**) **1** (**din something into**) instil information into (someone) by constant repetition. **2** make a din.
– ORIGIN OE *dyne*, *dynn* (n.), *dynian* (v.), of Gmc origin.

**dinar** /ˈdiːnɑː/ ● **n. 1** the basic monetary unit of the states of Yugoslavia, equal to 100 paras. **2** the basic monetary unit of certain countries of the Middle East and North Africa, equal to 1,000 fils in Jordan, Bahrain, and Iraq, 1,000 dirhams in Libya, 100 centimes in Algeria, and 10 pounds in the Sudan. **3** a monetary unit of Iran, equal to one hundredth of a rial.
– ORIGIN from Arab. and Pers. *dīnār*, Turk. and Serbo-Croat *dinar*, via late Gk from L. *denarius* (see **DENARIUS**).

**dine** ● **v. 1** eat dinner. **2** (**dine out on**) regularly entertain friends with (a humorous or interesting anecdote).
– ORIGIN ME: from OFr. *disner*, prob. from *desjëuner* 'to break fast'.

**diner** ● **n. 1** a person who dines. **2** a dining car on a train. **3** N. Amer. a small roadside restaurant, originally one designed to resemble a dining car.

**dinero** /dɪˈnɛːrəʊ/ ● **n.** N. Amer. informal money.
– ORIGIN Sp., 'coin, money'.

**dinette** /dʌɪˈnɛt/ ● **n. 1** a small room or part of a room used for eating meals. **2** N. Amer. a set of table and chairs for such an area.
– ORIGIN 1930s: formed irregularly from **DINE** + **-ETTE**.

**ding**[1] ● **v.** make the metallic ringing sound of a bell.

**ding**[2] ● **n. 1** N. Amer. informal a mark or dent on the bodywork of a car or other vehicle. **2** Scottish or dialect a blow on the head. ● **v. 1** informal, chiefly N. Amer. dent or hit. **2** (**ding into**) Scottish bump into.
– ORIGIN ME: prob. of Scand. origin.

**ding-a-ling** ● **n. 1** the ringing sound of a bell. **2** N. Amer. informal an eccentric or stupid person.

**Ding an sich** /ˌdɪŋ an ˈzɪx, German ˌdɪŋ an ˈzɪç/ ● **n.** (in Kant's philosophy) a thing as it is in itself, not mediated through perception by the senses or conceptualization, and therefore unknowable.
– ORIGIN from Ger.

**dingbat** /ˈdɪŋbat/ ● **n.** informal **1** N. Amer. & Austral./NZ a stupid or eccentric person. **2** (**dingbats**) Austral./NZ delusions or feelings of unease, particularly those induced by delirium tremens. **3** a typographical device other than a letter or numeral, used to signal divisions in text or to replace letters in a euphemistically presented vulgar word.
– ORIGIN C19: origin uncertain; perh. based on **DING**[2].

**ding-dong** ● **n.** informal **1** Brit. a fierce argument or fight. **2** N. Amer. a silly or foolish person. ● **adv. & adj. 1** with the simple alternate chimes of a bell. **2** [as adj.] Brit. informal (of a contest) evenly matched and intensely waged.

**dinger** /ˈdɪŋə/ ● **n. 1** US informal something outstanding of its kind. **2** Baseball a home run.
– ORIGIN C19: shortening of **HUMDINGER**.

**dinghy** /ˈdɪŋgi, ˈdɪŋi/ ● **n.** (pl. **-ies**) **1** a small boat for recreation or racing, especially an open boat with a mast and sails. **2** a small inflatable rubber boat.
– ORIGIN C19 (denoting a rowing boat in India): from Hindi *ḍiṅgī*.

**dingle** ● **n.** poetic/literary or dialect a deep wooded valley.
– ORIGIN ME (denoting a deep abyss): of unknown origin.

**dingo** /ˈdɪŋgəʊ/ ● **n.** (pl. **-oes** or **-os**) **1** a wild or semi-domesticated Australian dog with a sandy-coloured coat. [*Canis dingo*.] **2** Austral. informal a cowardly or treacherous person.
– ORIGIN C18: from Dharuk *din-gu* 'domesticated dingo'.

**dingus** /ˈdɪŋəs/ ● **n.** (pl. **dinguses**) N. Amer. & S. African informal a thing one cannot or does not wish to name specifically.
– ORIGIN C19: via Afrik. from Du. *ding* 'thing'.

**dingy** /ˈdɪn(d)ʒi/ ● **adj.** (**-ier**, **-iest**) gloomy and drab.
– DERIVATIVES **dingily** adv. **dinginess** n.
– ORIGIN C18: perh. based on OE *dynge* 'dung'.

**dining car** ● **n.** a railway carriage equipped as a restaurant.

**dining room** ● **n.** a room in a house or hotel in which meals are eaten.

**dink** chiefly Tennis ● **n.** a drop shot. ● **v.** hit (the ball) with a drop shot.
– ORIGIN 1930s: symbolic of the light action.

**Dinka** /ˈdɪŋkə/ ● **n.** (pl. same or **Dinkas**) **1** a member of a Sudanese people of the Nile basin. **2** the Nilotic language of this people.
– ORIGIN from the local word *Jieng* 'people'.

**dinkum** /ˈdɪŋkəm/ (also **fair dinkum**) Austral./NZ informal ● **adj.** genuine. ● **adv.** [often in questions] really.
– ORIGIN C19: of unknown origin.

**dinkum oil** ● **n.** Austral./NZ informal the honest truth.

**dinky**[1] ● **adj.** (**-ier**, **-iest**) informal **1** Brit. small and neat in an attractive way. **2** N. Amer. disappointingly small; insignificant.
– ORIGIN C18: from Scots and north. Engl. dial. *dink* 'neat, trim'.

**dinky**[2] ● **n.** (pl. **-ies**) informal a partner in a well-off working couple with no children.
– ORIGIN 1980s: acronym from *double income, no kids*.

**dinky-di** /ˌdɪŋkiˈdʌɪ/ ● **adj.** Austral./NZ informal variant of **DINKUM**.

**dinner** ● **n.** the main meal of the day, taken either around midday or in the evening. ➤ a formal evening meal, typically one in honour of a person or event.
– ORIGIN ME: from OFr. *disner* (see **DINE**).

**dinner jacket** ● **n.** a man's short jacket without tails, typically a black one, worn with a bow tie for formal evening occasions.

**dinner lady** ● **n.** Brit. a woman who serves meals and supervises children at mealtimes in a school.

**dinner theatre** ● **n.** N. Amer. a theatre in which a meal is included in the price of a ticket.

**dinoflagellate** /ˌdʌɪnə(ʊ)ˈfladʒələɪt/ ● **n.** Biology a single-celled aquatic organism with two flagella, occurring in large numbers in marine plankton. [Division Dinophyta.]
– ORIGIN C19 (as adj.): from mod. L. *Dinoflagellata*, from Gk *dinos* 'whirling' + L. *flagellum* (see **FLAGELLUM**).

**dinosaur** /ˈdʌɪnəsɔː/ ● **n. 1** a Mesozoic fossil reptile of a diverse group including large bipedal and quadrupedal forms such as tyrannosaurus, brachiosaurus, triceratops, etc. **2** a person or thing that is outdated or has become obsolete because of failure to adapt.
– DERIVATIVES **dinosaurian** adj. & n.
– ORIGIN C19: from mod. L. *dinosaurus*, from Gk *deinos* 'terrible' + *sauros* 'lizard'.

**dint** ● **n. 1** an impression or hollow in a surface. **2** archaic a blow or stroke. ● **v.** mark with dints.
– PHRASES **by dint of** by means of.
– ORIGIN OE *dynt*, reinforced in ME by the rel. ON word *dyntr*; of unknown ultimate origin; cf. **DENT**.

**diocesan** /dʌɪˈɒsɪs(ə)n/ ● **adj.** of or concerning a diocese. ● **n.** the bishop of a diocese.

**diocese** /ˈdʌɪəsɪs/ ● **n.** (pl. **dioceses** /ˈdʌɪəsiːz, -siːzɪz/) a district under the pastoral care of a bishop in the Christian Church.
– ORIGIN ME: from OFr. *diocise*, from late L. *diocesis*, from L. *dioecesis* 'governor's jurisdiction, diocese'.

**diode** /ˈdʌɪəʊd/ ● **n.** Electronics **1** a semiconductor device with two terminals, typically allowing the flow of current in one direction only. **2** a thermionic valve with two electrodes.
– ORIGIN C20: from **DI-**[1] + a shortened form of **ELECTRODE**.

**dioecious** /dʌɪˈiːʃəs/ ● **adj.** Biology (of a plant or invertebrate animal) having the male and female reproductive organs in separate individuals. Compare with **MONOECIOUS**.
– DERIVATIVES **dioecy** n.
– ORIGIN C18: from mod. L. *Dioecia* (a class in Linnaeus's sexual system), from **DI-**[1] + Gk *-oikos* 'house'.

**dioestrus** /dʌɪˈiːstrəs/ (US **diestrus**) ● **n.** Zoology (in most female mammals) a period of sexual inactivity between recurrent periods of oestrus.

**diol** /ˈdʌɪɒl/ ● **n.** Chemistry an alcohol containing two hydroxyl groups in its molecule.

**Dionysiac** /ˌdʌɪəˈnɪzɪak/ (also **Dionysian** /-zɪən/) ● **adj. 1** Greek Mythology of or relating to the god Dionysus. **2** of or relating to the sensual, spontaneous, and emotional aspects of human nature. Compare with **APOLLONIAN**.

**Diophantine equation** /ˌdʌɪəˈfantɪn, -tʌɪn/ ● **n.** Mathematics a polynomial equation with integral coefficients for which integral solutions are required.
– ORIGIN C18: named after the C3 Gk mathematician *Diophantus*.

**diopside** /dʌɪˈɒpsʌɪd/ ● **n.** a pale green to white silicate mineral occurring in many metamorphic and igneous rocks.
– ORIGIN C19: from Fr., formed irregularly from **DI-**[3] + Gk *opsis* 'aspect', later interpreted as from Gk *diopsis* 'a view through'.

**dioptre** /dʌɪˈɒptə/ (US **diopter**) ● **n.** a unit of refractive power, which is equal to the reciprocal of the focal length (in metres) of a given lens.
– ORIGIN C16 (orig. denoting an alidade, later a form of theodolite): from Fr., from L. *dioptra*, from Gk, from *di-* 'through' + *optos* 'visible'.

**dioptric** /dʌɪˈɒptrɪk/ ● **adj.** of or relating to the refraction of light, especially in the organs of sight or in devices which aid or improve the vision.
– ORIGIN C17: from Gk *dioptrikos*, from *dioptra*, a kind of theodolite (see **DIOPTRE**).

**dioptrics** ● **pl. n.** [treated as sing.] the branch of optics concerned with refraction.

**diorama** /ˌdʌɪəˈrɑːmə/ ● **n. 1** a model representing a scene with three-dimensional figures. ➤ a miniature film set used for special effects or animation. **2** chiefly historical a scenic painting, viewed through a peephole, in which changes in colour and direction of illumination simulate changes in the weather and time of day.
– ORIGIN C19: Fr., from **DIA-**, on the pattern of *panorama*.

**diorite** /ˈdʌɪərʌɪt/ ● **n.** Geology a speckled, coarse-grained igneous rock consisting typically of plagioclase, feldspar, and hornblende.
– DERIVATIVES **dioritic** adj.
– ORIGIN C19: Fr., formed irregularly from Gk *diorizein* 'distinguish' + **-ITE**[1].

**diosgenin** /dʌɪˈɒsdʒənɪn/ ● **n.** Chemistry a steroid compound obtained from Mexican yams and used in the synthesis of steroid hormones.
– ORIGIN 1930s: from *dios-* (from the mod. L. genus name *Dioscorea*) + *genin*, denoting steroids that occur as the non-sugar part of certain glycosides.

**dioxane** /dʌɪˈɒkseɪn/ (also **dioxan** /-an/) ● **n.** Chemistry a colourless toxic heterocyclic compound used as an organic solvent.

**dioxide** /dʌɪˈɒksʌɪd/ ● **n.** Chemistry an oxide containing two atoms of oxygen in its molecule or empirical formula.

**dioxin** /dʌɪˈɒksɪn/ ● **n.** a highly toxic organic compound produced as a by-product in some manufacturing processes.

**DIP** ● **abbrev. 1** Computing document image processing. **2** Electronics dual in-line package.

**Dip.** ● **abbrev.** diploma.

**dip** ● **v.** (**dipped**, **dipping**) **1** (**dip something in/into**) put or let something down quickly or briefly in or into (liquid). ➤ make (a candle) by immersing a wick repeatedly in hot wax. **2** sink, drop, or slope downwards. ➤ (of a level or amount) temporarily become lower or smaller. ➤ lower or move downwards. ➤ Brit. lower the beam of (a vehicle's headlights). **3** (**dip into**) put a hand or implement into (a bag or container) in order to take something out. **4** (**dip into**) spend from or make use of (one's financial resources). **5** (**dip out**) Austral./NZ informal fail. ● **n. 1** an act of dipping, especially a brief swim. **2** a thick sauce in which pieces of food are dipped before eating. **3** a brief downward slope followed by an upward one. ➤ an instance of dropping briefly before rising again. **4** the angle made with the horizontal at any point by the earth's magnetic field. ➤ Geology the angle a stratum makes with the horizontal. ➤ Astronomy & Surveying the apparent depression of the horizon from the line of observation, due to the curvature of the earth. **5** N. Amer. informal a stupid or foolish person.
– ORIGIN OE *dyppan*, of Gmc origin; rel. to **DEEP**.

**DipAD** ● **abbrev.** (in the UK) Diploma in Art and Design.

**DipEd** ● **abbrev.** (in the UK) Diploma in Education.

**dipeptide** /dʌɪˈpɛptʌɪd/ ● **n.** Biochemistry a peptide composed of two amino-acid residues.

**DipHE** ● **abbrev.** (in the UK) Diploma of Higher Education.

**diphenhydramine** /ˌdʌɪfɛnˈhʌɪdrəmiːn/ ● **n.** Medicine an antihistamine compound used for the symptomatic relief of allergies.

**diphtheria** /dɪpˈθɪərɪə, dɪf-/ ● **n.** a serious bacterial disease causing inflammation of the mucous membranes and formation of a false membrane in the throat which hinders breathing and swallowing.
– DERIVATIVES **diphtherial** adj. **diphtheritic** /-θəˈrɪtɪk/ adj. **diphtheroid** adj.
– ORIGIN C19: mod. L., from Fr. *diphthérie*, from Gk *diphthera* 'skin, hide'.

**diphthong** /ˈdɪfθɒŋ/ ● **n.** a sound formed by the combination of two vowels in a single syllable, in which the sound begins as one vowel and moves towards another (as in *coin*). ➤ a digraph representing the sound of a diphthong or single vowel (as in *feat*). ➤ a ligature (such as *œ*).
– DERIVATIVES **diphthongal** /-ˈθɒŋg(ə)l/ adj. **diphthongization** (also **-isation**) n. **diphthongize** (also **-ise**) v.
– ORIGIN ME: from Fr. *diphtongue*, via late L. from Gk *diphthongos*, from *di-* 'twice' + *phthongos* 'sound'.

**diphycercal** /ˌdɪfɪˈsəːk(ə)l/ ● **adj.** Zoology (of a fish's tail) approximately symmetrical and with the vertebral column continuing to the tip.
– ORIGIN C19: from Gk *diphu-* 'of double form' + *kerkos* 'tail' + **-AL**.

**diplegia** /dʌɪˈpliːdʒə/ ● **n.** Medicine paralysis of corresponding parts on both sides of the body, typically affecting the legs more severely than the arms.

**diplo-** ● **comb. form 1** double: *diplococcus*. **2** diploid: *diplotene*.
– ORIGIN from Gk *diplous* 'double'.

**diplococcus** /ˌdɪplə(ʊ)ˈkɒkəs/ ● **n.** (pl. **diplococci** /-k(s)ʌɪ, -k(s)iː/) a bacterium that occurs as pairs of cocci, e.g. pneumococcus.

**diplodocus** /dɪˈplɒdəkəs, ˌdɪplə(ʊ)ˈdəʊkəs/ ● **n.** a huge herbivorous dinosaur of the late Jurassic period, with a long slender neck and tail.
– ORIGIN mod. L., from **DIPLO-** + Gk *dokos* 'wooden beam'.

**diploid** /ˈdɪplɔɪd/ ● **adj.** Genetics (of a cell or nucleus) containing two complete sets of chromosomes, one from each parent. Compare with **HAPLOID**.
– DERIVATIVES **diploidy** n.
– ORIGIN C19: from Gk *diplous* 'double' + **-OID**.

**diploma** ● **n. 1** a certificate awarded by an educational establishment for passing an examination or completing a course of study. **2** historical an official document or

charter.
– ORIGIN C17: via L. from Gk *diplōma* 'folded paper'.

**diplomacy** • n. **1** the profession, activity, or skill of managing international relations. **2** skill and tact in dealing with people.
– ORIGIN C18: from Fr. *diplomatie*, from *diplomatique* 'diplomatic', on the pattern of *aristocratie* 'aristocracy'.

**diplomat** • n. an official representing a country abroad.

**diplomate** /ˈdɪpləmeɪt/ • n. chiefly US a holder of a diploma, especially a doctor certified as a specialist by a board of examiners.

**diplomatic** • adj. **1** of or concerning diplomacy. **2** tactful. **3** (of an edition or copy) exactly reproducing the original.
– DERIVATIVES **diplomatically** adv.

**diplomatic bag** • n. chiefly Brit. a container in which official mail is sent to or from an embassy, which is not subject to customs inspection.

**diplomatic corps** • n. the body of diplomats representing other countries in a particular state.

**diplomatic immunity** • n. the privilege of exemption from certain laws and taxes granted to diplomats by the state in which they are working.

**diplomatic pouch** • n. US term for **DIPLOMATIC BAG**.

**diplomatist** • n. old-fashioned term for **DIPLOMAT**.

**diplopia** /dɪˈpləʊpɪə/ • n. technical term for **DOUBLE VISION**.

**Diplopoda** /ˌdɪpləˈpəʊdə/ • pl. n. Zoology a class of myriapod arthropods that comprises the millipedes.
– DERIVATIVES **diplopod** /ˈdɪpləpɒd/ n.
– ORIGIN mod. L., from Gk *diploos* 'double' + *pous, pod-* 'foot'.

**diplotene** /ˈdɪplətiːn/ • n. Biology the fourth stage of the prophase of meiosis, following pachytene, during which the paired chromosomes begin to separate.
– ORIGIN 1920s: from **DIPLO-** + Gk *tainia* 'band'.

**dip net** • n. chiefly N. Amer. a small fishing net with a long handle.

**dipole** /ˈdʌɪpəʊl/ • n. **1** Physics a pair of equal and oppositely charged or magnetized poles separated by a distance. **2** an aerial consisting of a horizontal metal rod with a connecting wire at its centre.
– DERIVATIVES **dipolar** adj.

**dipole moment** • n. Physics & Chemistry the mathematical product of the separation of the ends of a dipole and the magnitude of the charges.

**dip pen** • n. a pen that has to be dipped in ink.

**dipper** • n. **1** a stocky, short-tailed songbird frequenting fast-flowing streams and able to dive or walk under water to feed. [*Cinclus cinclus* and related species.] **2** a ladle or scoop. **3** archaic, informal a Baptist or Anabaptist.

**dippy** • adj. (**-ier, -iest**) informal foolish or eccentric.
– ORIGIN C20: of unknown origin.

**dipshit** • n. vulgar slang, chiefly N. Amer. a contemptible or inept person.
– ORIGIN 1970s: perh. a blend of **DIPPY** and **SHIT**.

**dip slope** • n. Geology the gentler slope of a cuesta, following the underlying strata. Often contrasted with **SCARP SLOPE**.

**dipso** • n. (pl. **-os**) informal an alcoholic.

**dipsomania** /ˌdɪpsə(ʊ)ˈmeɪnɪə/ • n. alcoholism, specifically in a form characterized by intermittent bouts of craving for alcohol.
– DERIVATIVES **dipsomaniac** n.
– ORIGIN C19: from Gk *dipso-* (from *dipsa* 'thirst') + **-MANIA**.

**dipstick** • n. **1** a graduated rod for measuring the depth of a liquid, especially oil in a vehicle's engine. **2** informal a stupid or inept person.

**DIP switch** • n. Computing an arrangement of switches in a dual in-line package used to select the operating mode of a device such as a printer.

**Diptera** /ˈdɪpt(ə)rə/ • pl. n. Entomology a large order of insects that comprises the two-winged or true flies, which have the hindwings reduced to form balancing organs (halteres).
– DERIVATIVES **dipteran** n. & adj.
– ORIGIN mod. L., from Gk *diptera*, neut. pl. of *dipteros* 'two-winged'.

**dipteral** /ˈdɪpt(ə)r(ə)l/ • adj. Architecture having a double peristyle.
– ORIGIN C19: from L. *dipteros* (from Gk, from *di-* 'twice' + *pteron* 'wing') + **-AL**.

**dipterist** /ˈdɪpt(ə)rɪst/ • n. a person who studies or collects flies.
– ORIGIN C19: from **DIPTERA** + **-IST**.

**dipterocarp** /ˈdɪpt(ə)rə(ʊ),kɑːp/ • n. a tall forest tree of a large, mainly SE Asian family (Dipterocarpaceae).
– ORIGIN C19: from mod. L. *Dipterocarpus* (genus name), from Gk *dipteros* 'two-winged' + *karpos* 'fruit'.

**dipterous** /ˈdɪpt(ə)rəs/ • adj. **1** Entomology of or relating to flies of the order Diptera. **2** Botany having two wing-like appendages.

**diptych** /ˈdɪptɪk/ • n. **1** a painting, especially an altarpiece, on two hinged wooden panels which may be closed like a book. **2** an ancient writing tablet consisting of two hinged leaves with waxed inner sides.
– ORIGIN C17: via late L. from late Gk *diptukha* 'pair of writing tablets', neut. pl. of Gk *diptukhos* 'folded in two'.

**dire** • adj. **1** extremely serious or urgent. **2** informal of a very poor quality.
– DERIVATIVES **direly** adv. **direness** n.
– ORIGIN C16: from L. *dirus* 'fearful, threatening'.

**direct** /dɪˈrɛkt, dʌɪ-/ • adj. **1** going from one place to another without changing direction or stopping. ➤ Astronomy & Astrology (of apparent planetary motion) proceeding from west to east in accord with actual motion. **2** straightforward; frank. ➤ clear; unambiguous. **3** without intervening factors or intermediaries: *the complications are a direct result of bacteria spreading.* ➤ (of descent) proceeding in continuous succession from parent to child. ➤ Soccer denoting a free kick from which a goal may be scored without another player touching the ball. **4** perpendicular to a surface. • adv. in a direct way or by a direct route. • v. **1** control the operations of. ➤ supervise and control (a film, play, or other production). **2** aim (something) in a particular direction. ➤ tell or show (someone) the way. **3** give an order or authoritative instruction to.
– DERIVATIVES **directness** n.
– ORIGIN ME: from L. *directus*, past part. of *dirigere*, from *di-* 'distinctly' or *de-* 'down' + *regere* 'put straight'.

**direct action** • n. the use of strikes, demonstrations, or other public forms of protest rather than negotiation to achieve one's demands.

**direct current** (abbrev.: **DC**) • n. an electric current flowing in one direction only. Compare with **ALTERNATING CURRENT**.

**direct debit** • n. Brit. an arrangement made with a bank that allows a third party to transfer money from a person's account on agreed dates.

**direct dialling** • n. the facility of making a telephone call without connection by the operator.

**direct-drive** • adj. denoting or relating to mechanical parts driven directly by a motor, without a belt or other device to transmit power.

**direct-grant school** • n. historical (in the UK) a fee-paying school that received government funds in return for the admission of some non-paying pupils.

**direct injection** • n. (in diesel engines) the use of a pump to spray fuel into the cylinder at high pressure, without the use of compressed air.

**direction** /dɪˈrɛkʃ(ə)n, dʌɪ-/ • n. **1** a course along which someone or something moves, or which must be taken to reach a destination. ➤ a point to or from which a person or thing moves or faces. ➤ a trend or tendency. **2** the action of directing or managing people. ➤ (**directions**) instructions on how to reach a destination or about how to do something.
– DERIVATIVES **directionless** adj.

**directional** • adj. **1** relating to or indicating the direction in which someone or something is facing or moving. **2** having a particular direction of motion, progression, or orientation.
– DERIVATIVES **directionality** /-ˈnalɪti/ n. **directionally**

adv.

**direction-finder** ● n. a system of aerials for locating the source of radio signals, used as an aid to navigation.

**directive** ● n. an official or authoritative instruction. ● adj. involving the direction of operations.
– ORIGIN ME (as adj.): from med. L. *directivus*, from *direct-*, *dirigere* (see DIRECT).

**directly** ● adv. 1 in a direct manner. ➤ immediately. ➤ dated soon. 2 exactly in a specified position. ● conj. Brit. as soon as.

**direct mail** ● n. unsolicited commercial literature mailed to prospective customers.
– DERIVATIVES **direct mailing** n.

**direct marketing** ● n. the business of selling products or services directly to the customer, e.g. by telephone selling.

**direct object** ● n. a noun phrase denoting a person or thing that is the recipient of the action of a transitive verb, for example *the dog* in *Jeremy fed the dog*.

**Directoire** /dɪ'rɛktwɑː, French diʀɛktwaʀ/ ● adj. of or relating to a neoclassical decorative style prevalent during the French Directory.
– ORIGIN from Fr.

**Directoire drawers** (also **Directoire knickers**) ● pl. n. Brit. historical straight, full, knee-length knickers.

**director** ● n. 1 a person who is in charge of an activity, department, or organization. 2 a member of the managing board of a business. 3 a person who directs a film, play, etc.
– DERIVATIVES **directorial** adj. **directorship** n. **directress** (also **directrice**) n.

**directorate** ● n. [treated as sing. or pl.] 1 the board of directors of a company. 2 a section of a government department in charge of a particular activity.

**director-general** ● n. (pl. **directors-general**) chiefly Brit. the chief executive of a large organization.

**directory** ● n. (pl. **-ies**) 1 a book listing individuals or organizations alphabetically or thematically with details such as addresses and telephone numbers. ➤ Computing a file consisting solely of a set of other files. 2 chiefly historical a book of directions for the conduct of Christian worship, especially in Presbyterian and Roman Catholic Churches. 3 (**the Directory**) the revolutionary government in France 1795–9.

**directory enquiries** (N. Amer. **directory assistance**) ● pl. n. a telephone service used to find out someone's telephone number.

**direct proportion** (also **direct ratio**) ● n. the relation between quantities whose ratio is constant.

**directrix** /dɪ'rɛktrɪks, dʌɪ-/ ● n. (pl. **directrices** /-trɪsiːz/) Geometry a fixed line used in describing a curve or surface.
– ORIGIN C18: from med. L., lit. 'directress'.

**direct speech** ● n. the reporting of speech by repeating the actual words of a speaker, for example *'I'm going', she said*. Contrasted with REPORTED SPEECH.

**direct tax** ● n. a tax, such as income tax, which is levied on the income or profits of the person who pays it.

**direful** ● adj. archaic or poetic/literary extremely bad.
– DERIVATIVES **direfully** adv.

**dirge** /dəːdʒ/ ● n. 1 a lament for the dead, especially one forming part of a funeral rite. 2 a mournful song, piece of music, or sound.
– DERIVATIVES **dirgeful** adj.
– ORIGIN ME: from L. *dirige!* 'direct!', the first word of an antiphon (Ps. 5:8) used in the Latin Office for the Dead.

**dirham** /'dɪər(h)əm/ ● n. 1 the basic monetary unit of Morocco and the United Arab Emirates, equal to 100 centimes in Morocco and 100 fils in the United Arab Emirates. 2 a monetary unit of Libya and Qatar, equal to one thousandth of a dinar in Libya and one hundredth of a riyal in Qatar.
– ORIGIN from Arab., from Gk *drakhmē* (see DRACHMA).

**dirigible** /'dɪrɪdʒɪb(ə)l/ ● n. an airship. ● adj. capable of being steered or guided.
– ORIGIN C16: from L. *dirigere* 'to direct' + -IBLE.

**dirigisme** /'dɪrɪʒɪz(ə)m/ ● n. state control of economic and social matters.
– DERIVATIVES **dirigiste** adj.
– ORIGIN 1950s: from Fr., from *diriger* 'to direct'.

**diriment impediment** /'dɪrɪm(ə)nt/ ● n. (in ecclesiastical law) a factor which invalidates a marriage, such as the existence of a prior marriage.
– ORIGIN C19: *diriment* from L. *diriment-*, *dirimere* 'interrupt'.

**dirk** /dəːk/ ● n. a short dagger of a kind formerly carried by Scottish Highlanders.
– ORIGIN C16: of unknown origin.

**dirndl** /'dəːnd(ə)l/ ● n. 1 (also **dirndl skirt**) a full, wide skirt with a tight waistband. 2 a woman's dress in the style of Alpine peasant costume, with a dirndl skirt and a close-fitting bodice.
– ORIGIN 1930s: from Ger. dial., dimin. of *Dirne* 'girl'.

**dirt** ● n. 1 a substance, such as mud, that causes uncleanliness. ➤ informal excrement: *dog dirt*. 2 loose soil or earth. 3 informal scandalous or sordid information or material.
– PHRASES **do someone dirt** informal harm someone's reputation maliciously. **eat dirt** informal suffer insults or humiliation.
– ORIGIN ME: from ON *drit* 'excrement'.

**dirt bike** ● n. a motorcycle designed for use on rough terrain, especially in scrambling.

**dirt cheap** ● adv. & adj. informal extremely cheap.

**dirt farmer** ● n. N. Amer. a farmer who ekes out a living from poor land, typically unaided by hired labour.
– DERIVATIVES **dirt farm** n.

**dirt poor** ● adv. & adj. extremely poor.

**dirt track** ● n. a course made of rolled cinders for motorcycle racing or of earth for flat racing.
– DERIVATIVES **dirt tracker** n.

**dirty** ● adj. (**-ier**, **-iest**) 1 covered or marked with an unclean substance. 2 lewd; obscene. 3 dishonest; dishonourable. 4 (of weather) rough, stormy, and unpleasant. 5 (of a nuclear weapon) producing considerable radioactive fallout. ● adv. Brit. informal very: *a dirty great stone*. ● v. (**-ies**, **-ied**) make dirty.
– PHRASES **do the dirty on** Brit. informal cheat or betray. **get one's hands dirty** (or **dirty one's hands**) do manual, menial, or other hard work. **play dirty** informal act in a dishonest or unfair way.
– DERIVATIVES **dirtily** adv. **dirtiness** n.

**dirty look** ● n. informal a look expressing disapproval, disgust, or anger.

**dirty old man** ● n. informal an older man who is sexually interested in younger women or girls.

**dirty weekend** ● n. Brit. informal a weekend spent away, especially in secret, with a lover.

**dirty word** ● n. 1 an offensive or indecent word. 2 something regarded with dislike or disapproval.

**dirty work** ● n. unpleasant or dishonest activities that are delegated to someone else.

**dis** /dɪs/ informal, chiefly US ● v. (also **diss**) (**dissed**, **dissing**) speak disrespectfully to. ● n. disrespectful talk.

**dis-** /dɪs/ ● prefix 1 expressing negation: *disadvantage*. 2 denoting reversal or absence of an action or state: *diseconomy*. 3 denoting removal, separation, or expulsion: *disbud* | *disbar*. 4 expressing completeness or intensification of an action: *disgruntled*.
– ORIGIN from L., sometimes via OFr. *des-*.

**disability** ● n. (pl. **-ies**) 1 a physical or mental condition that limits a person's movements, senses, or activities. 2 a disadvantage or handicap, especially one imposed or recognized by the law.

**disable** ● v. 1 (of a disease, injury, or accident) limit (someone) in their movements, senses, or activities. 2 put out of action.
– DERIVATIVES **disablement** n.

**disabled** ● adj. (of a person) having a physical or mental disability. ➤ designed for or relating to disabled people: *disabled access*.

**disabuse** /ˌdɪsə'bjuːz/ ● v. (usu. **disabuse someone of**) persuade (someone) that an idea or belief is mistaken.

**disaccharide** /dʌɪ'sakərʌɪd/ ● n. Chemistry any of a class of sugars whose molecules contain two monosaccharide residues.

**disaccord** • n. rare lack of agreement or harmony.

**disadvantage** • n. an unfavourable circumstance or condition. • v. put in an unfavourable position. ➤ [as adj. **disadvantaged**] in socially or economically deprived circumstances.

**disadvantageous** • adj. involving or creating unfavourable circumstances.
– DERIVATIVES **disadvantageously** adv.

**disaffected** • adj. dissatisfied with those in authority and no longer willing to support them.
– DERIVATIVES **disaffectedly** adv. **disaffection** n.
– ORIGIN C17: past part. of *disaffect*, orig. in the sense 'dislike or disorder'.

**disaffiliate** /ˌdɪsəˈfɪlɪeɪt/ • v. (of a group or organization) end its affiliation with (a subsidiary group). ➤ (of a subsidiary group) end its affiliation.
– DERIVATIVES **disaffiliation** n.

**disaffirm** • v. Law reverse (a previous decision). ➤ repudiate (a settlement).
– DERIVATIVES **disaffirmation** n.

**disafforest** /ˌdɪsəˈfɒrɪst/ • v. **1** another term for DEFOREST. **2** English Law, historical reduce (a district) from the legal status of forest to that of ordinary land.
– DERIVATIVES **disafforestation** n. **disafforestment** n.

**disaggregate** /dɪsˈagrɪgeɪt/ • v. separate into component parts.
– DERIVATIVES **disaggregation** n.

**disagree** • v. (**disagrees**, **disagreed**, **disagreeing**) **1** have a different opinion. **2** (**disagree with**) be inconsistent with. ➤ affect adversely: *the sea crossing disagreed with her.*
– DERIVATIVES **disagreement** n.

**disagreeable** • adj. unpleasant. ➤ unfriendly and bad-tempered.
– DERIVATIVES **disagreeableness** n. **disagreeably** adv.

**disallow** • v. refuse to declare valid.
– DERIVATIVES **disallowance** n.

**disambiguate** • v. remove uncertainty of meaning from.
– DERIVATIVES **disambiguation** n.

**disamenity** /ˌdɪsəˈmiːnɪti, -ˈmɛnɪti/ • n. (pl. **-ies**) unpleasant quality or character.

**disappear** • v. cease to be visible. ➤ cease to exist or be in use. ➤ (of a person) go missing or (in coded political language) be killed.
– DERIVATIVES **disappearance** n.
– ORIGIN ME: from DIS- + APPEAR, on the pattern of Fr. *disparaître.*

**disapply** • v. (**-ies**, **-ied**) treat as inapplicable.
– DERIVATIVES **disapplication** n.

**disappoint** • v. fail to fulfil the hopes or expectations of. ➤ prevent (hopes or expectations) from being realized.
– DERIVATIVES **disappointing** adj. **disappointingly** adv. **disappointment** n.
– ORIGIN ME (in the sense 'deprive of a position'): from OFr. *desappointer.*

**disappointed** • adj. sad or displeased because one's hopes or expectations have not been fulfilled.
– DERIVATIVES **disappointedly** adv.

**disapprobation** /dɪsˌaprəˈbeɪʃ(ə)n/ • n. strong disapproval, especially on moral grounds.

**disapprove** • v. (often **disapprove of**) have or express an unfavourable opinion. ➤ officially refuse to agree to.
– DERIVATIVES **disapproval** n. **disapprover** n. **disapprovingly** adj. **disapprovingly** adv.

**disarm** • v. **1** take a weapon or weapons away from. ➤ (of a country or force) give up or reduce its armed forces or weapons. ➤ remove the fuse from (a bomb). **2** deprive of the power to hurt. ➤ [often as adj. **disarming**] allay the hostility or suspicions of. • n. Fencing an act of disarming an opponent.
– DERIVATIVES **disarmer** n. **disarmingly** adv.

**disarmament** /dɪsˈɑːməm(ə)nt/ • n. the reduction or withdrawal of military forces and weapons.

**disarrange** • v. make untidy or disordered.
– DERIVATIVES **disarrangement** n.

**disarray** • n. a state of disorganization or untidiness. • v. make disorganized or untidy.

**disarticulate** • v. **1** separate (bones) at the joints. **2** break up and disrupt the logic of (an argument or opinion).
– DERIVATIVES **disarticulation** n.

**disassemble** • v. **1** take to pieces. **2** Computing translate (a program) from machine code into a symbolic language.
– DERIVATIVES **disassembler** n. **disassembly** n.

**disassociate** • v. another term for DISSOCIATE.
– DERIVATIVES **disassociation** n.

**disaster** • n. **1** a sudden accident or a natural catastrophe that causes great damage or loss of life. **2** an event or fact leading to ruin or failure.
– ORIGIN C16: from Ital. *disastro* 'ill-starred event', based on L. *astrum* 'star'.

**disastrous** • adj. **1** causing great damage. **2** informal highly unsuccessful.
– DERIVATIVES **disastrously** adv.

**disavow** • v. deny any responsibility or support for.
– DERIVATIVES **disavowal** n.

**disband** • v. (with reference to an organized group) break up or cause to break up.
– DERIVATIVES **disbandment** n.
– ORIGIN C16: from obs. Fr. *desbander.*

**disbar** • v. (**disbarred**, **disbarring**) **1** expel (a barrister) from the Bar. **2** exclude from something.
– DERIVATIVES **disbarment** n.

**disbelief** • n. inability or refusal to accept that something is true or real. ➤ lack of faith.

**disbelieve** • v. be unable to believe. ➤ have no religious faith.
– DERIVATIVES **disbeliever** n. **disbelieving** adj. **disbelievingly** adv.

**disbenefit** • n. Brit. a disadvantage.

**disbud** • v. (**disbudded**, **disbudding**) remove superfluous or unwanted buds from.

**disburden** • v. relieve of a burden or responsibility.

**disburse** /dɪsˈbəːs/ • v. pay out (money from a fund).
– DERIVATIVES **disbursal** n. **disbursement** n. **disburser** n.
– ORIGIN C16: from OFr. *desbourser*, from *des-* (expressing removal) + *bourse* 'purse'.

**disc** (US also **disk**) • n. **1** a flat, thin, round object. **2** (**disk**) an information storage device for a computer comprising a rotatable disc on which data is stored either magnetically or optically (as on a CD-ROM). **3** dated a gramophone record. **4** (**discs**) one of the suits in some tarot packs, corresponding to coins in others. **5** (also **intervertebral disc**) a layer of cartilage separating adjacent vertebrae in the spine. **6** Botany the central part of the flower of a daisy or other composite plant, consisting of a close-packed cluster of tubular florets.
– ORIGIN C17: from Fr. *disque* or L. *discus* (see DISCUS).

**discalced** /dɪsˈkalst/ • adj. denoting or belonging to one of several strict orders of Catholic friars or nuns who go barefoot or are shod only in sandals.
– ORIGIN C17: var. of earlier *discalceated*, influenced by Fr. *déchaux*, from L. *discalceatus* 'unshod'.

**discard** • v. /dɪˈskɑːd/ **1** get rid of as no longer useful or desirable. **2** (in bridge, whist, and similar card games) play (a card that is neither of the suit led nor a trump), when one is unable to follow suit. • n. /ˈdɪskɑːd/ a discarded item, especially a card in bridge or whist.
– DERIVATIVES **discardable** /dɪsˈkɑːdəb(ə)l/ adj.
– ORIGIN C16: from DIS- + CARD[1].

**discarnate** /dɪsˈkɑːnət/ • adj. not having a physical body.
– ORIGIN C19: from DIS- + L. *caro, carn-* 'flesh' or late L. *carnatus* 'fleshy'.

**disc brake** • n. a type of vehicle brake employing the friction of pads against a disc attached to the wheel.

**disc camera** • n. a camera in which the images are formed on a disc, rather than on film.

**discern** /dɪˈsəːn/ • v. recognize or find out. ➤ distinguish with difficulty by sight or with the other senses.

– DERIVATIVES **discerner** n. **discernible** adj. **discernibly** adv.
– ORIGIN ME: via OFr. from L. *discernere*, from *dis-* 'apart' + *cernere* 'to separate'.

**discerning** • **adj.** having or showing good judgement.
– DERIVATIVES **discerningly** adv. **discernment** n.

**discerption** /dɪ'səːpʃ(ə)n/ • **n.** archaic the action of pulling something apart.
– DERIVATIVES **discerptibility** n. **discerptible** adj.
– ORIGIN C17: from late L. *discerptio(n-)*, from L. *discerpere* 'pluck to pieces'.

**discharge** • **v.** /dɪs'tʃɑːdʒ/ **1** allow to go, especially from hospital. ➤dismiss from a job. ➤release from the custody or restraint of the law. **2** emit or send out (a liquid, gas, or other substance). ➤Physics release or neutralize the electric charge of (an electric field, battery, or other object). ➤fire (a gun or missile). ➤unload (goods or passengers) from a ship. **3** do all that is required to fulfil (a responsibility) or perform (a duty). ➤release from a contract or obligation. ➤Law relieve (a bankrupt) of residual liability. **4** Law (of a judge or court) cancel (an order of a court). • **n.** /'dɪstʃɑːdʒ, dɪs'tʃɑːdʒ/ **1** the action of discharging. **2** a substance that has been discharged. ➤a flow of electricity through air or other gas, especially when accompanied by emission of light.
– DERIVATIVES **dischargeable** adj. **discharger** n.
– ORIGIN ME: from OFr. *descharger*, from late L. *discarricare* 'unload', from *dis-* (expressing reversal) + *carricare* (see CHARGE).

**discharge tube** • **n.** a gas-filled tube in which light emission is induced by exciting the gas molecules by means of an electric field.

**disc harrow** • **n.** a harrow with cutting edges consisting of a row of concave discs set at an oblique angle.

**disciple** /dɪ'sʌɪp(ə)l/ • **n.** **1** a personal follower of Christ during his life, especially one of the twelve Apostles. **2** a follower or pupil of a teacher, leader, or philosophy.
– DERIVATIVES **discipleship** n. **discipular** /dɪ'sɪpjʊlə/ adj.
– ORIGIN OE, from L. *discipulus* 'learner', from *discere* 'learn'; reinforced by OFr. *deciple*.

**disciplinarian** • **n.** a person who believes in or practises firm discipline.

**discipline** /'dɪsɪplɪn/ • **n.** **1** the practice of training people to obey rules or a code of behaviour. ➤controlled behaviour resulting from such training. **2** a branch of knowledge, especially one studied in higher education. • **v.** **1** train in obedience or self-control by punishment or imposing rules. ➤[as adj. **disciplined**] showing a controlled form of behaviour. **2** punish or rebuke formally for an offence.
– DERIVATIVES **disciplinable** adj. **disciplinal** /ˌdɪsɪ'plʌɪn(ə)l, 'dɪsɪˌplɪn(ə)l/ adj. **disciplinary** adj.
– ORIGIN ME (in the sense 'mortification by scourging oneself'): via OFr. from L. *disciplina* 'instruction, knowledge', from *discipulus* (see DISCIPLE).

**disc jockey** • **n.** a person who introduces and plays recorded popular music, especially on radio or at a disco.

**disclaim** • **v.** **1** refuse to acknowledge. **2** Law renounce a legal claim to (a property or title).
– ORIGIN ME: from Anglo-Norman Fr. *desclamer*, from *des-* (expressing reversal) + *clamer* (see CLAIM).

**disclaimer** • **n.** **1** a statement disclaiming something, especially responsibility. **2** Law an act of repudiating another's claim or renouncing one's own.

**disclose** • **v.** make (secret or new information) known. ➤expose to view.
– DERIVATIVES **discloser** n. **disclosure** n.
– ORIGIN ME: from OFr. *desclos-*, stem of *desclore*, based on L. *claudere* 'to close'.

**disco** • **n.** (pl. **-os**) informal **1** a club or party at which people dance to pop music. **2** (also **disco music**) soul-influenced, melodic pop music with a regular bass beat, intended for dancing to.

**discobolus** /dɪ'skɒbələs/ • **n.** (pl. **discoboli** /-lʌɪ/) a discus-thrower in ancient Greece.
– ORIGIN C18: via L. from Gk *diskobolos*, from *diskos* 'discus' + *-bolos* '-throwing'.

**discography** /dɪ'skɒgrəfi/ • **n.** (pl. **-ies**) **1** a descriptive catalogue of musical recordings, particularly those of a particular performer or composer. **2** the study of musical recordings and compilation of descriptive catalogues.
– DERIVATIVES **discographer** n.

**discoid** /'dɪskɔɪd/ • **adj.** technical shaped like a disc.
– DERIVATIVES **discoidal** adj.

**discolour** (US **discolor**) • **v.** become or cause to become a different, less attractive colour.
– DERIVATIVES **discoloration** (also **discolouration**) n.

**discombobulate** /ˌdɪskəm'bɒbjʊleɪt/ • **v.** humorous, chiefly N. Amer. disconcert or confuse.
– ORIGIN C19: prob. based on DISCOMPOSE or DISCOMFIT.

**discomfit** /dɪs'kʌmfɪt/ • **v.** (**discomfited**, **discomfiting**) make uneasy or embarrassed.
– DERIVATIVES **discomfiture** n.
– ORIGIN ME (in the sense 'defeat in battle'): from OFr. *desconfit*, past part. of *desconfire*, based on L. *dis-* (expressing reversal) + *conficere* (see CONFECT).

**discomfort** • **n.** **1** slight pain. **2** slight anxiety or embarrassment. • **v.** cause discomfort to.
– ORIGIN ME (as a verb in the sense 'dishearten, distress'): from OFr. *desconforter* (v.), *desconfort* (n.), from *des-* (expressing reversal) + *conforter* (see COMFORT).

**discommode** /ˌdɪskə'məʊd/ • **v.** formal cause trouble or inconvenience to.
– DERIVATIVES **discommodious** adj. **discommodity** n.
– ORIGIN C18: from obs. Fr. *discommoder*, var. of *incommoder* (see INCOMMODE).

**discompose** • **v.** [often as adj. **discomposed**] disturb or agitate.
– DERIVATIVES **discomposure** n.

**disconcert** /ˌdɪskən'səːt/ • **v.** disturb the composure of.
– DERIVATIVES **disconcerted** adj. **disconcertedly** adv. **disconcerting** adj. **disconcertingly** adv. **disconcertion** n. **disconcertment** n. (rare).
– ORIGIN C17 (in the sense 'upset the progress of'): from obs. Fr. *desconcerter*, from *des-* (expressing reversal) + *concerter* 'bring together'.

**disconfirm** • **v.** show that (a belief or hypothesis) is not or may not be true.
– DERIVATIVES **disconfirmation** /ˌdɪskɒnfə'meɪʃ(ə)n/ n. **disconfirmatory** adj.

**disconformity** • **n.** (pl. **-ies**) **1** lack of conformity. **2** Geology a break in a sequence of strata which does not involve a difference of inclination on each side of the break.

**disconnect** • **v.** break the connection of or between. ➤put (an electrical device) out of action by detaching it from a power supply.
– DERIVATIVES **disconnection** (also **disconnexion**) n.

**disconnected** • **adj.** (of speech, writing, or thought) lacking a logical sequence.
– DERIVATIVES **disconnectedly** adv. **disconnectedness** n.

**disconsolate** /dɪs'kɒns(ə)lət/ • **adj.** very unhappy and unable to be comforted.
– DERIVATIVES **disconsolately** adv. **disconsolateness** n. **disconsolation** n.
– ORIGIN ME: from med. L. *disconsolatus*, from *dis-* (expressing reversal) + L. *consolat-*, *consolari* 'to console'.

**discontent** • **n.** lack of contentment or satisfaction. ➤a person who is dissatisfied.
– DERIVATIVES **discontented** adj. **discontentedly** adv. **discontentedness** n. **discontentment** n.

**discontinue** • **v.** (**discontinues**, **discontinued**, **discontinuing**) stop doing, providing, or making.
– DERIVATIVES **discontinuance** n. **discontinuation** n.

**discontinuous** • **adj.** having intervals or gaps; not continuous.
– DERIVATIVES **discontinuity** n. **discontinuously** adv.

**discord** • **n.** /'dɪskɔːd/ **1** lack of agreement or harmony. **2** Music lack of harmony between notes sounding together. ➤a chord which is regarded as displeasing or requiring resolution by another. ➤any interval except unison, an octave, a perfect fifth or fourth, a major or minor third and sixth, or their octaves. • **v.** /dɪs'kɔːd/ archaic disagree.
– DERIVATIVES **discordance** n. **discordancy** n. **discordant** adj. **discordantly** adv.
– ORIGIN ME: from OFr. *descord* (n.), *descorder* (v.), from L.

*discordare*, from *discors* 'discordant', from *dis-* (expressing negation) + *cor, cord-* 'heart'.

**discotheque** /ˈdɪskətɛk/ ● **n.** another term for **DISCO** (in sense 1).
– ORIGIN 1950s: from Fr. *discothèque*, orig. 'record library', on the pattern of *bibliothèque* 'library'.

**discount** ● **n.** /ˈdɪskaʊnt/ a deduction from the usual cost of something. ➤ Finance a percentage deducted from the face value of a bill of exchange or promissory note when it changes hands before the due date. ● **v.** /dɪsˈkaʊnt/ **1** deduct a discount from (the usual price of something). ➤ reduce (a product or service) in price. ➤ Finance buy or sell (a bill of exchange) before its due date at less than its maturity value. **2** disregard as lacking credibility or significance.
– DERIVATIVES **discountable** /dɪʃˈkaʊntəb(ə)l/ adj. **discounter** /dɪsˈkaʊntə/ n.
– ORIGIN C17: from obs. Fr. *descompte* (n.), *descompter* (v.), or (in commercial contexts) from Ital. *(di)scontare*, based on L. *dis-* (expressing reversal) + *computare* (see **COMPUTE**).

**discounted cash flow** ● **n.** Finance a method of assessing investments taking into account the expected accumulation of interest.

**discountenance** ● **v. 1** refuse to approve of. **2** disturb the composure of.

**discount house** ● **n. 1** Brit. a company that discounts bills of exchange. **2** N. Amer. another term for **DISCOUNT STORE**.

**discount rate** ● **n.** Finance **1** the minimum interest rate set by the US Federal Reserve (and some other national banks) for lending to other banks. **2** a rate used for discounting bills of exchange.

**discount store** ● **n.** a shop that sells goods at less than the normal retail price.

**discourage** ● **v. 1** cause a loss of confidence or enthusiasm in. **2** prevent or seek to prevent by showing disapproval or creating difficulties. ➤ (**discourage someone from**) persuade someone against (an action).
– DERIVATIVES **discouragement** n. **discouraging** adj. **discouragingly** adv.
– ORIGIN ME: from OFr. *descouragier*, from *des-* (expressing reversal) + *corage* 'courage'.

**discourse** ● **n.** /ˈdɪskɔːs, -ˈkɔːs/ written or spoken communication or debate. ➤ a formal discussion of a topic in speech or writing. ➤ Linguistics a text or conversation. ● **v.** /dɪsˈkɔːs/ speak or write authoritatively about a topic. ➤ engage in conversation.
– ORIGIN ME (denoting the process of reasoning): from OFr. *discours*, from L. *discursus* 'running to and fro' (in med. L. 'argument'), from *discurrere* 'run away'.

**discourse marker** ● **n.** Grammar a word or phrase whose function is to organize discourse into segments, for example *I mean*.

**discourteous** ● **adj.** rude and lacking consideration for others.
– DERIVATIVES **discourteously** adv. **discourteousness** n. **discourtesy** n. (pl. **-ies**).

**discover** ● **v. 1** find unexpectedly or in the course of a search. ➤ become aware of (a fact or situation). ➤ be the first to find or observe (a place, substance, or scientific phenomenon). **2** archaic divulge (a secret). ➤ display (a quality or feeling).
– DERIVATIVES **discoverable** adj. **discoverer** n.
– ORIGIN ME: from OFr. *descovrir*, from late L. *discooperire*, from L. *dis-* (expressing reversal) + *cooperire* (see **COVER**).

**discovered check** ● **n.** Chess a check which results when a player moves a piece or pawn so as to put the opponent's king in check from another piece.

**discovery** ● **n.** (pl. **-ies**) **1** the action or process of discovering or being discovered. ➤ a person or thing discovered. **2** Law the compulsory disclosure, by a party to an action, of relevant documents referred to by the other party.

**discredit** ● **v.** (**discredited**, **discrediting**) harm the good reputation of. ➤ cause (an idea or piece of evidence) to seem false or unreliable. ● **n.** loss or lack of reputation.
– DERIVATIVES **discreditable** adj. **discreditably** adv.

**discreet** /dɪˈskriːt/ ● **adj.** (**-er**, **-est**) **1** careful and prudent in one's speech or actions, especially so as to avoid giving offence or attracting attention. **2** unobtrusive.
– DERIVATIVES **discreetly** adv. **discreetness** n.
– ORIGIN ME: from OFr. *discret*, from L. *discretus* 'separate', past part. of *discernere* 'discern', the sense arising from late L. *discretio* (see **DISCRETION**).

**USAGE** discreet

The words **discrete** and **discreet** are often confused. **Discrete** means 'separate' (*a discrete unit*), while **discreet** means 'careful and prudent'. Around 10 per cent of citations in the British National Corpus for **discrete** are misspellings for **discreet**.

**discrepancy** /dɪsˈkrɛp(ə)nsi/ ● **n.** (pl. **-ies**) an illogical or surprising lack of compatibility or similarity between two or more facts.
– DERIVATIVES **discrepant** adj.
– ORIGIN C17: from L. *discrepantia*, from *discrepare* 'be discordant'.

**discrete** /dɪˈskriːt/ ● **adj.** individually separate and distinct.
– DERIVATIVES **discretely** adv. **discreteness** n.
– ORIGIN ME: from L. *discretus* 'separate'; cf. **DISCREET**.

**discretion** ● **n. 1** the quality of being discreet. **2** the freedom to decide what should be done in a particular situation.
– DERIVATIVES **discretionary** adj.
– ORIGIN ME (in the sense 'discernment'): via OFr. from L. *discretio(n-)* 'separation' (in late L. 'discernment'), from *discernere* (see **DISCERN**).

**discretionary income** ● **n.** income remaining after deduction of taxes, social security charges, and basic living costs. Compare with **DISPOSABLE INCOME**.

**discriminable** /dɪˈskrɪmɪnəb(ə)l/ ● **adj.** able to be discriminated; distinguishable.
– DERIVATIVES **discriminability** n. **discriminably** adv.

**discriminant** /dɪˈskrɪmɪnənt/ ● **n.** a distinguishing feature or characteristic.

**discriminate** /dɪˈskrɪmɪneɪt/ ● **v. 1** recognize a distinction. ➤ perceive or constitute the difference in or between. **2** (usu. **discriminate against**) make an unjust distinction in the treatment of different categories of people, especially on the grounds of race, sex, or age.
– DERIVATIVES **discriminately** adv. **discriminative** adj.
– ORIGIN C17: from L. *discriminat-*, *discriminare* 'distinguish between'.

**discriminating** ● **adj.** having or showing good taste or judgement.
– DERIVATIVES **discriminatingly** adv.

**discrimination** ● **n. 1** the action of discriminating against people. **2** recognition and understanding of the difference between one thing and another. ➤ good judgement or taste. **3** Electronics the selection of a signal having a required characteristic by means of a discriminator.

**discriminator** ● **n. 1** a distinguishing characteristic. **2** Electronics a device which only produces an output when the input exceeds a fixed value. ➤ a circuit which converts a frequency-modulated signal into an amplitude-modulated one.

**discriminatory** /dɪˈskrɪmɪnɪˌt(ə)ri, dɪˌskrɪmɪˈneɪt(ə)ri/ ● **adj.** showing discrimination or prejudice.

**discursive** /dɪsˈkəːsɪv/ ● **adj. 1** digressing from subject to subject. **2** of or relating to discourse or modes of discourse. **3** Philosophy, archaic proceeding by argument or reasoning rather than by intuition.
– DERIVATIVES **discursively** adv. **discursiveness** n.
– ORIGIN C16: from med. L. *discursivus*, from L. *discurs-*, *discurrere* (see **DISCOURSE**).

**discus** /ˈdɪskəs/ ● **n.** (pl. **discuses**) **1** a heavy thick-centred disc thrown by an athlete, in ancient Greek games or in modern field events. **2** a small colourful South American freshwater fish with a rounded laterally compressed body. [Genus *Symphysodon*: several species.]
– ORIGIN via L. from Gk *diskos*.

**discuss** • v. talk about so as to reach a decision. ➤ talk or write about (a topic) in detail.
– DERIVATIVES **discussable** adj. **discussant** n. **discusser** n. **discussion** n.
– ORIGIN ME (in the sense 'dispel, disperse', also 'examine by argument'): from L. *discuss-*, *discutere* 'dash to pieces', later 'investigate', from *dis-* 'apart' + *quatere* 'shake'.

**disdain** • n. the feeling that someone or something is unworthy of one's consideration or respect. • v. consider or reject with disdain.
– DERIVATIVES **disdainful** adj. **disdainfully** adv. **disdainfulness** n.
– ORIGIN ME: from OFr. *desdeign* (n.), *desdeignier* (v.), based on L. *dedignari*, from *de-* (expressing reversal) + *dignari* 'consider worthy'.

**disease** • n. **1** a disorder of structure or function in a human, animal, or plant, especially one that produces specific symptoms or that affects a specific part. **2** a quality, habit, or disposition that adversely affects a person or group: *the British disease of self-deprecation.*
– DERIVATIVES **diseased** adj.
– ORIGIN ME (in the sense 'lack of ease; inconvenience'): from OFr. *desaise* 'lack of ease'.

**diseconomy** • n. (pl. **-ies**) Economics an economic disadvantage such as an increase in cost arising from an increase in the size of an organization.

**disembark** • v. leave a ship, aircraft, or train.
– DERIVATIVES **disembarkation** n.

**disembarrass** • v. (**disembarrass oneself of/from**) free oneself of (a burden or nuisance).
– DERIVATIVES **disembarrassment** n.

**disembodied** • adj. separated from or existing without the body. ➤ (of a sound) lacking any obvious physical source.
– DERIVATIVES **disembodiment** n. **disembody** v.

**disembogue** /ˌdɪsɪm'bəʊg, ˌdɪsɛm-/ • v. (**disembogues, disembogued, disemboguing**) poetic/literary (of a river or stream) flow or pour out into.
– ORIGIN C16: from Sp. *desembocar*, from *des-* (expressing reversal) + *embocar* 'run into a creek or strait'.

**disembowel** /ˌdɪsɪm'baʊəl, ˌdɪsɛm-/ • v. (**disembowelled, disembowelling**; US **disemboweled, disemboweling**) cut open and remove the internal organs of.
– DERIVATIVES **disembowelment** n.

**disempower** • v. make less powerful or confident.
– DERIVATIVES **disempowerment** n.

**disenchant** • v. make disillusioned.
– DERIVATIVES **disenchanting** adj. **disenchantingly** adv. **disenchantment** n.
– ORIGIN C16: from Fr. *désenchanter*, from *dés-* (expressing reversal) + *enchanter* (see **ENCHANT**).

**disencumber** • v. free from an encumbrance.

**disendow** • v. deprive of an endowment, in particular deprive (a Church) of the property and funds that it receives from the state.
– DERIVATIVES **disendowment** n.

**disenfranchise** /ˌdɪsɪn'fran(t)ʃʌɪz, ˌdɪsɛn-/ (also **disfranchise**) • v. deprive of the right to vote. ➤ deprive of a right or privilege.
– DERIVATIVES **disenfranchisement** n.

**disengage** /ˌdɪsɪn'geɪdʒ, ˌdɪsɛn-/ • v. **1** separate, release, or detach. ➤ [as adj. **disengaged**] emotionally detached; uninvolved. **2** remove (troops) from an area of conflict. **3** Fencing pass the point of one's sword over or under the opponent's sword to change the line of attack. • n. Fencing a disengaging movement.
– DERIVATIVES **disengagement** n.

**disentailment** • n. Law the action of freeing property from entail.
– DERIVATIVES **disentail** v.

**disentangle** • v. free from entanglement; untwist. ➤ remove knots or tangles from (wool, rope, or hair).
– DERIVATIVES **disentanglement** n.

**disenthral** /ˌdɪsɪn'θrɔːl, ˌdɪsɛn-/ (US **disenthrall**) • v. (**disenthralled, disenthralling**) poetic/literary set free.

**disentitle** • v. deprive of an entitlement.
– DERIVATIVES **disentitlement** n.

**disequilibrium** /dɪsiːkwɪ'lɪbrɪəm, ˌdɪsɛk-/ • n. a loss or lack of equilibrium, especially in relation to supply, demand, and prices.

**disestablish** • v. deprive (an organization, especially a national Church) of its official status.
– DERIVATIVES **disestablishment** n.

**disesteem** dated • n. low esteem. • v. have a low opinion of.

**diseuse** /diː'zəːz/ • n. a female artiste entertaining with spoken monologues.
– ORIGIN Fr., lit. 'talker'.

**disfavour** (US **disfavor**) • n. disapproval or dislike. • v. regard or treat with disfavour.

**disfellowship** • n. exclusion from fellowship, especially as a form of discipline in some Protestant and Mormon Churches.

**disfigure** • v. spoil the appearance of.
– DERIVATIVES **disfiguration** n. **disfigurement** n.
– ORIGIN ME: from OFr. *desfigurer*, based on L. *figura* 'figure'.

**disfranchise** • v. another term for **DISENFRANCHISE**.

**disgorge** • v. **1** discharge; cause to pour out. ➤ bring up or vomit (food). ➤ yield or give up (funds, especially when dishonestly acquired). **2** remove the sediment from (a sparkling wine) after fermentation.
– DERIVATIVES **disgorgement** n.
– ORIGIN C15: from OFr. *desgorger*, from *des-* (expressing removal) + *gorge* 'throat'.

**disgorger** • n. Fishing a device for extracting a hook from a fish's throat.

**disgrace** • n. loss of reputation as the result of a dishonourable action. ➤ a person or thing regarded as shameful and unacceptable. • v. bring disgrace on. ➤ cause to fall from favour or a position of power or honour.
– ORIGIN C16: via Fr. from Ital. *disgrazia* (n.), *disgraziare* (v.).

**disgraceful** • adj. shockingly unacceptable.
– DERIVATIVES **disgracefully** adv.

**disgruntled** • adj. angry or dissatisfied.
– DERIVATIVES **disgruntlement** n.
– ORIGIN C17: from **DIS-** + dial. *gruntle* 'utter little grunts'.

**disguise** • v. alter the appearance, sound, taste, or smell of so as to conceal the identity. ➤ conceal the nature or existence of (a feeling or situation). • n. a means of disguising one's identity. ➤ the state of being disguised.
– ORIGIN ME (meaning 'change one's usual style of dress'): from OFr. *desguisier*.

**disgust** • n. strong revulsion or profound indignation. • v. cause disgust in.
– DERIVATIVES **disgusted** adj. **disgustedly** adv. **disgusting** adj. **disgustingly** adv. **disgustingness** n.
– ORIGIN C16: from early mod. Fr. *desgoust* or Ital. *disgusto*, from L. *dis-* (expressing reversal) + *gustus* 'taste'.

**disgustful** • adj. dated disgusting.

**dish** • n. **1** a shallow, typically flat-bottomed container for cooking or serving food. ➤ (**the dishes**) all the items that have been used in the preparation, serving, and eating of a meal. ➤ a shallow, concave receptacle: *a soap dish.* ➤ (also **dish aerial**) a bowl-shaped radio aerial. **2** a particular variety or preparation of food served as part of a meal. **3** informal a sexually attractive person. **4** (**the dish**) informal information which is not generally known or available. **5** concavity of a spoked wheel resulting from a difference in spoke tension. • v. **1** (**dish something out/up**) put food on to a plate or plates before a meal. ➤ (**dish something out**) dispense something in a casual or indiscriminate way. **2** informal, chiefly Brit. utterly destroy or defeat. **3** N. Amer. informal gossip. **4** [usu. as adj. **dished**] make slightly concave.
– PHRASES **dish the dirt** informal reveal or spread scandal or gossip.
– DERIVATIVES **dishful** n. (pl. **-fuls**).
– ORIGIN OE *disc* 'plate, bowl', based on L. *discus* (see **DISCUS**).

**dishabille** /ˌdɪsa'biːl, -'biː/ • n. variant spelling of **DÉSHABILLÉ**.

**disharmony** • n. lack of harmony.

– DERIVATIVES **disharmonious** adj. **disharmoniously** adv.

**dishcloth** • **n.** a cloth for washing dishes.

**dishcloth gourd** • **n.** North American term for **LOOFAH**.

**dishdasha** /ˈdɪʃˌdaʃə/ (also **dishdash**) • **n.** a long robe with long sleeves, worn by men from Arabia.
– ORIGIN C19: from Arab. *dišdāša*.

**dishearten** • **v.** cause to lose determination or confidence.
– DERIVATIVES **disheartening** adj. **dishearteningly** adv. **disheartenment** n.

**dishevelled** /dɪˈʃɛv(ə)ld/ (US **disheveled**) • **adj.** (of a person's hair, clothes, or appearance) untidy.
– DERIVATIVES **dishevel** (**dishevelled**, **dishevelling**; US **disheveled**, **disheveling**) v. **dishevelment** n.
– ORIGIN ME (orig. in the sense 'having the hair uncovered'): from obs. *dishevely*, from OFr. *deschevele*, past part. of *descheveler* (based on *chevel* 'hair', from L. *capillus*).

**dishonest** • **adj.** not honest, trustworthy, or sincere.
– DERIVATIVES **dishonestly** adv. **dishonesty** n.

**dishonour** (US **dishonor**) • **n.** a state of shame or disgrace. • **v. 1** bring dishonour to. ➤ archaic rape (a woman). **2** fail to honour (an agreement, cheque, etc.).

**dishonourable** (US **dishonorable**) • **adj.** bringing shame or disgrace.
– DERIVATIVES **dishonourableness** n. **dishonourably** adv.

**dishonourable discharge** • **n.** dismissal from the armed forces as a result of criminal or morally unacceptable actions.

**dishrag** • **n.** a dishcloth.

**dishwasher** • **n. 1** a machine for washing dishes automatically. **2** a person employed to wash dishes.

**dishwater** • **n.** water in which dishes have been washed.

**dishy** • **adj.** (**-ier**, **-iest**) informal **1** chiefly Brit. sexually attractive. **2** N. Amer. scandalous or gossipy.

**disillusion** /ˌdɪsɪˈl(j)uːʒ(ə)n/ • **n.** the disappointing loss of a belief or an ideal. • **v.** cause to experience this.
– DERIVATIVES **disillusioned** adj. **disillusionment** n.

**disincarnate** /ˌdɪsɪŋˈkɑːnət/ • **adj.** another term for **DISCARNATE**.

**disincentive** • **n.** a factor that discourages a particular action.

**disinclination** • **n.** a reluctance or unwillingness to do something.

**disinclined** • **adj.** reluctant; unwilling.

**disincorporate** • **v.** dissolve (a corporate body).

**disinfect** • **v.** make clean and free from infection, especially by the use of a chemical disinfectant.
– DERIVATIVES **disinfection** n.

**disinfectant** • **n.** a chemical liquid that destroys bacteria. • **adj.** causing disinfection.

**disinfest** • **v.** rid of infesting vermin.
– DERIVATIVES **disinfestation** n.

**disinflation** • **n.** Economics reduction in the rate of inflation.
– DERIVATIVES **disinflationary** adj.

**disinformation** • **n.** information which is intended to mislead.
– ORIGIN 1950s: formed on the pattern of Russ. *dezinformatsiya*.

**disingenuous** /ˌdɪsɪnˈdʒɛnjʊəs/ • **adj.** not candid or sincere, especially in pretending that one knows less about something than one really does.
– DERIVATIVES **disingenuously** adv. **disingenuousness** n.

**disinherit** • **v.** (**disinherited**, **disinheriting**) dispossess of or bar from an inheritance.
– DERIVATIVES **disinheritance** n.
– ORIGIN ME (superseding earlier *disherit*): from **DIS-** + *inherit* in the obs. sense 'make someone an heir'.

**disinhibit** • **v.** (**disinhibited**, **disinhibiting**) make less inhibited.
– DERIVATIVES **disinhibition** n.

**disintegrate** /dɪsˈɪntɪɡreɪt/ • **v. 1** break up into small parts as a result of impact or decay. **2** lose strength or cohesion. **3** Physics undergo or cause to undergo disintegration at a subatomic level.
– DERIVATIVES **disintegrative** adj. **disintegrator** n.

**disintegration** • **n. 1** the process of disintegrating. **2** Physics a process in which a nucleus or other subatomic particle emits a smaller particle or divides into smaller particles.

**disinter** /ˌdɪsɪnˈtəː/ • **v.** (**disinterred**, **disinterring**) dig up (something that has been buried).
– DERIVATIVES **disinterment** n.

**disinterest** • **n. 1** impartiality. **2** lack of interest.

**disinterested** • **adj. 1** not influenced by considerations of personal advantage; impartial. **2** having or feeling no interest or concern.
– DERIVATIVES **disinterestedly** adv. **disinterestedness** n.
– ORIGIN C17: past part. of the rare verb *disinterest* 'rid of interest'.

**USAGE disinterested**

According to traditional guidelines, it is a mistake to use **disinterested** to mean 'not interested'. In fact, the earliest recorded use is for this sense, and today this use is widespread (accounting for around 20 per cent of uses on the British National Corpus for **disinterested**).

**disintermediation** • **n.** Economics reduction in the use of intermediaries between producers and consumers, e.g. by involvement in the securities market directly rather than through a bank.

**disinvent** • **v.** undo the invention of.

**disinvest** • **v.** withdraw or reduce an investment.
– DERIVATIVES **disinvestment** n.

**disinvite** • **v.** withdraw or cancel an invitation to.

**disjecta membra** /dɪsˌdʒɛktə ˈmɛmbrə/ • **pl. n.** scattered fragments, especially of written work.
– ORIGIN L., alt. of *disjecti membra poetae* (used by Horace) 'limbs of a dismembered poet'.

**disjoin** • **v.** separate or disunite.

**disjoint** • **v. 1** disturb the cohesion or organization of. **2** dated take apart at the joints. • **adj.** Mathematics (of sets) having no elements in common.

**disjointed** • **adj.** lacking a coherent sequence or connection.
– DERIVATIVES **disjointedly** adv. **disjointedness** n.

**disjunct** /ˈdɪsdʒʌŋ(k)t/ • **n. 1** Logic each of the terms of a disjunctive proposition. **2** Grammar another term for **SENTENCE ADVERB**. • **adj.** disjoined and distinct from one another.
– ORIGIN ME: from L. *disjunct-*, *disjungere* 'disjoin, separate'.

**disjunction** • **n. 1** a lack of correspondence or consistency. **2** Logic the relation of two distinct alternatives, or a statement expressing this.

**disjunctive** • **adj. 1** lacking connection. **2** Grammar (of a conjunction) expressing a choice between two mutually exclusive possibilities, for example *or* in *she asked if he was going or staying*. **3** Logic (of a proposition) expressing alternatives. • **n. 1** Grammar a disjunctive conjunction. **2** Logic a disjunctive proposition.
– DERIVATIVES **disjunctively** adv.

**disjuncture** • **n.** a separation or disconnection.

**disk** • **n.** variant spelling in the US and in computing contexts of **DISC**.
– DERIVATIVES **diskless** adj.

**disk drive** • **n.** a device which allows a computer to read from and write on to computer disks.

**diskette** • **n.** another term for **FLOPPY**.

**dislike** • **v.** feel distaste for or hostility towards. • **n.** a feeling of dislike. ➤ a thing that is disliked.
– DERIVATIVES **dislikable** (also **dislikeable**) adj. **disliker** n.

**dislocate** /ˈdɪsləkeɪt/ • **v. 1** disturb the normal arrangement or position of (a joint in the body). **2** disturb the organization of; disrupt.

**dislocation** /ˌdɪslə(ʊ)ˈkeɪʃ(ə)n/ • **n. 1** the process or state of dislocating or being dislocated. **2** Crystallography a displacement of part of a crystal lattice structure.

**dislodge** ● v. remove from an established or fixed position.
– DERIVATIVES **dislodgeable** adj. **dislodgement** n.

**disloyal** ● adj. not loyal or faithful.
– DERIVATIVES **disloyally** adv. **disloyalty** n.

**dismal** /ˈdɪzm(ə)l/ ● adj. **1** causing or demonstrating a mood of gloom or depression; dreary. **2** informal pitifully or disgracefully bad: *a dismal performance.*
– PHRASES **the dismal science** humorous economics.
– DERIVATIVES **dismally** adv. **dismalness** n.
– ORIGIN ME: from earlier *dismals*, the two days in each month which in medieval times were believed to be unlucky, from Anglo-Norman Fr. *dis mal*, from med. L. *dies mali* 'evil days'.

**dismantle** ● v. take to pieces.
– DERIVATIVES **dismantlement** n. **dismantler** n.
– ORIGIN C16 (in the sense 'destroy the defensive capability of (a fortification)'): from OFr. *desmanteler*, from *des-* (expressing reversal) + *manteler* 'fortify'.

**dismast** ● v. break or force down the mast or masts of (a ship).

**dismay** ● n. consternation and distress. ● v. cause to feel dismay.
– ORIGIN ME: from OFr., based on L. *dis-* (expressing negation) + the Gmc base of **MAY**[1].

**dismember** /dɪsˈmɛmbə/ ● v. **1** tear or cut the limbs from. **2** partition or divide up (a territory or organization).
– DERIVATIVES **dismembered** adj. **dismemberment** n.
– ORIGIN ME: from OFr. *desmembrer*, based on L. *dis-* 'apart' + *membrum* 'limb'.

**dismiss** ● v. **1** order or allow to leave; send away. **2** discharge from employment. **3** Law refuse further hearing to (a case). **4** Cricket end the innings of (a batsman or side). **5** treat as being unworthy of serious consideration.
– DERIVATIVES **dismissal** n. **dismissible** adj.
– ORIGIN ME: from med. L. *dismiss-*, var. of L. *dimiss-*, *dimittere* 'send away'.

**dismissive** ● adj. feeling or showing that something is unworthy of serious consideration.
– DERIVATIVES **dismissively** adv. **dismissiveness** n.

**dismount** ● v. **1** alight from a horse or bicycle. **2** remove (something) from its support. **3** Computing make (a disk or disk drive) unavailable for use.
– ORIGIN C16: from **DIS-** + **MOUNT**[1], prob. on the pattern of OFr. *desmonter*, med. L. *dismontare.*

**disobedient** ● adj. failing or refusing to be obedient.
– DERIVATIVES **disobedience** n. **disobediently** adv.

**disobey** ● v. fail or refuse to obey.
– DERIVATIVES **disobeyer** n.

**disoblige** ● v. offend (someone) by not acting in accordance with their wishes.
– DERIVATIVES **disobliging** adj.

**disomy** /dʌɪˈsəʊmi/ ● n. Genetics the condition of having a chromosome represented twice in a chromosomal complement.
– DERIVATIVES **disomic** adj.
– ORIGIN C20: from **DI-**[1] + **-SOME**[3] + **-Y**[3].

**disorder** ● n. **1** a lack of order; a confused or untidy state. **2** the disruption of peaceful and law-abiding behaviour. **3** Medicine a disruption of normal physical or mental functions: *a skin disorder.* ● v. [usu. as adj. **disordered**] bring disorder to.
– ORIGIN C15: alt., influenced by **ORDER**, of earlier *disordain*, from OFr. *desordener*, ult. based on L. *ordinare* 'ordain'.

**disorderly** ● adj. **1** lacking organization; untidy. **2** involving or contributing to a breakdown of peaceful and law-abiding behaviour.
– DERIVATIVES **disorderliness** n.

**disorderly conduct** ● n. Law unruly behaviour constituting a minor offence.

**disorderly house** ● n. Law or archaic a brothel.

**disorganized** (also **-ised**) ● adj. **1** not properly planned and controlled. **2** (of a person) inefficient.
– DERIVATIVES **disorganization** n.

**disorient** /dɪsˈɔːrɪɛnt/ ● v. chiefly N. Amer. another term for **DISORIENTATE.**

**disorientate** ● v. cause (someone) to lose their sense of direction or feel confused.
– DERIVATIVES **disorientated** adj. **disorientation** n.

**disown** ● v. refuse to acknowledge or maintain any connection with.
– DERIVATIVES **disowner** n. **disownment** n.

**disparage** /dɪˈsparɪdʒ/ ● v. represent as being of little worth; scorn.
– DERIVATIVES **disparagement** n. **disparaging** adj. **disparagingly** adv.
– ORIGIN ME (in the sense 'marry someone of unequal rank', also 'bring discredit on'): from OFr. *desparagier* 'marry someone of unequal rank', based on L. *par* 'equal'.

**disparate** /ˈdɪsp(ə)rət/ ● adj. essentially different in kind; not able to be compared. ● n. (**disparates**) things so different that there is no basis for comparison between them.
– DERIVATIVES **disparately** adv. **disparateness** n.
– ORIGIN ME: from L. *disparatus*, *disparare* 'separate'; influenced in sense by L. *dispar* 'unequal'.

**disparity** ● n. (pl. **-ies**) a great difference.
– ORIGIN C16: from Fr. *disparité*, from late L. *disparitas*, based on L. *paritas* 'parity'.

**dispassionate** ● adj. not influenced by strong emotion; rational and impartial.
– DERIVATIVES **dispassion** n. **dispassionately** adv. **dispassionateness** n.

**dispatch** (also **despatch**) ● v. **1** send off promptly to a destination or for a purpose. **2** deal with (a task or problem) quickly and efficiently. **3** kill. ● n. **1** an instance of dispatching. **2** an official report on the latest situation in state or military affairs. ➤a report sent in from abroad by a journalist. **3** promptness and efficiency: *he should proceed with dispatch.*
– DERIVATIVES **dispatcher** n.
– ORIGIN C16: from Ital. *dispacciare* or Sp. *despachar* 'expedite'.

**dispatch box** ● n. **1** (also **dispatch case**) a container for state or military dispatches. **2** (**the Dispatch Box**) a box in the House of Commons next to which ministers stand when speaking.

**dispatch rider** ● n. a messenger who delivers urgent business documents or military dispatches by motor cycle or (formerly) on horseback.

**dispel** /dɪˈspɛl/ ● v. (**dispelled**, **dispelling**) make (a doubt, feeling, or belief) disappear.
– DERIVATIVES **dispeller** n.
– ORIGIN ME: from L. *dispellere* 'drive apart'.

**dispensable** ● adj. **1** able to be replaced or done without. **2** (of a law or other rule) able to be relaxed in special cases.
– DERIVATIVES **dispensability** n.

**dispensary** /dɪˈspɛns(ə)ri/ ● n. (pl. **-ies**) **1** a room where medicines are prepared and provided. **2** a clinic provided by public or charitable funds.

**dispensation** ● n. **1** the action of dispensing. **2** exemption from a rule or usual requirement. **3** a religious or political system prevailing at a particular time: *the Mosaic dispensation.* **4** archaic an act of divine providence.
– DERIVATIVES **dispensational** adj.

**dispensationalism** ● n. Christian Theology belief in a system of historical progression, as revealed in the Bible, consisting of a series of stages in God's self-revelation and plan of salvation.
– DERIVATIVES **dispensationalist** n.

**dispense** /dɪˈspɛns/ ● v. **1** distribute to a number of people. ➤(of a machine or container) supply or release (a product). **2** (of a chemist) supply (medicine) according to a doctor's prescription. **3** (**dispense with**) get rid of or manage without. **4** grant (someone) an exemption from a religious obligation.
– DERIVATIVES **dispenser** n.
– ORIGIN ME: via OFr. from L. *dispensare* 'continue to weigh out or disburse', from *dispendere*, based on *pendere* 'weigh'.

**dispensing chemist** ● n. Brit. a chemist who is qualified to make up, advise on, and dispense medicine.

**dispensing optician** ● n. an optician who is qualified to prescribe and dispense as well as to make glasses and contact lenses.

**dispersant** ● n. a liquid or gas used to disperse small particles in a medium.

**disperse** /dɪˈspəːs/ ● v. **1** go or distribute in different directions or over a wide area. **2** thin out and eventually disappear. **3** Physics divide (light) into constituents of different wavelengths. ● adj. Chemistry denoting a phase dispersed in another phase, as in a colloid.
– DERIVATIVES **dispersal** n. **disperser** n. **dispersible** adj. **dispersive** adj.
– ORIGIN ME: from L. *dispers-*, *dispergere* 'scatter widely'.

**dispersion** ● n. **1** the action, process, or state of dispersing or being dispersed. **2** (**the dispersion**) another term for DIASPORA. **3** a mixture of one substance dispersed in another medium. **4** Physics the separation of white light into colours or of any radiation according to wavelength. **5** Statistics the extent to which values of a variable differ from a fixed value such as the mean.

**dispirit** /dɪˈspɪrɪt/ ● v. cause to lose enthusiasm or hope.
– DERIVATIVES **dispiritedly** adv. **dispiritedness** n. **dispiriting** adj. **dispiritingly** adv.

**displace** ● v. **1** shift (something) from its proper or usual position. **2** take the place, position, or role of; oust. **3** [often as adj. **displaced**] (especially of war, persecution, or natural disaster) force (someone) to leave their home: *displaced persons.*

**displacement** ● n. **1** the action or process of displacing. **2** the amount by which a thing is moved from a position. **3** the volume or weight of water that would fill the volume displaced by a floating ship, used as a measure of the ship's size. **4** the volume swept by a reciprocating system, as in a pump or engine. **5** Physics the component of an electric field due to free separated charges, regardless of any polarizing effects. **6** Psychoanalysis the unconscious transfer of an intense emotion from one object to another.

**displacement activity** ● n. Psychology an irrelevant activity that is engaged upon when a conflict between antagonistic urges cannot be resolved (e.g. head-scratching when confused).

**displacement pump** ● n. a pump in which liquid is moved out of the pump chamber by a moving surface or by the introduction of compressed air or gas.

**display** ● v. **1** place (something) prominently so that it may readily be seen. **2** show (data or an image) on a computer, television or cinema screen. **3** give a conspicuous demonstration of (a quality, emotion, or skill). **4** (of a male animal) engage in a specialized pattern of behaviour intended to attract a mate. ● n. **1** an instance of displaying or being displayed. **2** a collection of objects being displayed. **3** an electronic device for the visual presentation of data.
– DERIVATIVES **displayer** n.
– ORIGIN ME (in the sense 'unfurl, unfold'): from OFr. *despleier*, from L. *displicare* 'scatter, disperse' (in med. L. 'unfold').

**display case** (also **display cabinet**) ● n. a case, made all or partly of glass, for displaying items in a shop or museum for observation or inspection.

**displayed** ● adj. Heraldry (of a bird of prey) depicted with the wings extended.

**display type** ● n. large, bold, or eye-catching type used for headings or advertisements.

**displease** ● v. annoy or upset.
– DERIVATIVES **displeased** adj. **displeasing** adj. **displeasingly** adv.

**displeasure** ● n. a feeling of annoyance or dissatisfaction. ● v. archaic annoy; displease.

**disport** ● v. (**disport oneself**) enjoy oneself unrestrainedly; frolic. ● n. archaic recreation; amusement. ➤a pastime or sport.
– ORIGIN ME: from OFr. *desporter* 'carry away' (from L. *portare*).

**disposable** ● adj. **1** (of an article) intended to be used once and then thrown away. ➤(of a person or idea) able to be dispensed with; easily dismissed. **2** (chiefly of financial assets) readily available for the owner's use as required. ● n. a disposable article.
– DERIVATIVES **disposability** n.

**disposable income** ● n. income remaining after deduction of taxes and social security charges, available to be spent or saved as one wishes. Compare with DISCRETIONARY INCOME.

**disposal** ● n. **1** the action or process of disposing. **2** the sale of assets. **3** N. Amer. informal a waste disposal unit.
– PHRASES **at one's disposal** available for one to use whenever or however one wishes. **at someone's disposal** ready to assist the person concerned in any way they wish.

**dispose** ● v. **1** (**dispose of**) get rid of. **2** arrange in a particular position. **3** incline (someone) towards a particular activity or frame of mind. **4** archaic or poetic/literary determine the course of events: *man proposes, but God disposes.*
– DERIVATIVES **disposer** n.
– ORIGIN ME: from OFr. *disposer*, from L. *disponere* 'arrange', influenced by *dispositus* 'arranged' and OFr. *poser* 'to place'.

**disposed** ● adj. **1** inclined or willing to do or feel something: *he was not disposed to take the hint.* **2** having a specified attitude to or towards: *he is favourably disposed towards the proposals.*

**disposition** ● n. **1** a person's inherent qualities of mind and character. ➤an inclination or tendency. **2** the action or result of arranging people or things in a particular way. ➤(**dispositions**) the stationing of troops ready for military action. **3** Law the action of distributing or transferring property or money to someone, in particular by bequest. **4** the power to deal with something as one pleases. ➤archaic the determination of events, especially by divine power.

**dispositive** /dɪsˈpɒzətɪv/ ● adj. relating to or bringing about the settlement of an issue or the disposition of property.

**dispossess** ● v. **1** deprive of land or property. ➤[as pl. n. **the dispossessed**] people who have been dispossessed. **2** (in sport) deprive (a player) of the ball.
– DERIVATIVES **dispossession** n.

**dispraise** ● n. rare censure; criticism. ● v. archaic censure or criticize.
– ORIGIN ME: from OFr. *despreisier*, based on late L. *depreciare* (see DEPRECIATE).

**disproof** ● n. action or evidence that proves something to be untrue.

**disproportion** ● n. a lack of proportion.
– DERIVATIVES **disproportional** adj. **disproportionality** n. **disproportionally** adv.

**disproportionate**[1] /ˌdɪsprəˈpɔːʃ(ə)nət/ ● adj. too large or too small in comparison with something else.
– DERIVATIVES **disproportionately** adv. **disproportionateness** n.

**disproportionate**[2] /ˌdɪsprəˈpɔːʃ(ə)neɪt/ ● v. Chemistry undergo disproportionation.

**disproportionation** ● n. Chemistry a reaction in which a substance is simultaneously oxidized and reduced, giving two different products.

**disprove** ● v. prove to be false.
– DERIVATIVES **disprovable** adj.

**disputable** ● adj. open to question or debate.
– DERIVATIVES **disputably** adv.

**disputation** ● n. debate or argument.
– DERIVATIVES **disputative** adj.
– ORIGIN ME: from L. *disputatio(n-)*, from *disputare* (see DISPUTE).

**disputatious** ● adj. **1** fond of argument. **2** (of an argument or situation) motivated by or causing strong opinions.
– DERIVATIVES **disputatiously** adv. **disputatiousness** n.

**dispute** ● v. /dɪˈspjuːt/ **1** argue about (something). ➤question whether (a statement or alleged fact) is true or valid. **2** contend for. **3** resist (a military landing or

advance). ● **n.** /dɪ'spjuːt, 'dɪspjuːt/ a disagreement or argument. ➤a disagreement between management and employees that leads to industrial action.
– DERIVATIVES **disputant** n. **disputer** n.
– ORIGIN ME: via OFr. from L. *disputare* 'to estimate' (in late L. 'to dispute').

**disqualify** ● **v.** (**-ies, -ied**) pronounce (someone) ineligible for an office or activity because of an offence or infringement. ➤(of a feature or characteristic) make (someone) unsuitable for an office or activity.
– DERIVATIVES **disqualification** n.

**disquiet** ● **n.** a feeling of anxiety. ● **v.** [usu. as adj. **disquieted**] make (someone) anxious.
– DERIVATIVES **disquieting** adj. **disquietingly** adv. **disquietude** n.

**disquisition** /ˌdɪskwɪ'zɪʃ(ə)n/ ● **n.** a piece of long or complex discourse.
– DERIVATIVES **disquisitional** adj. (archaic).
– ORIGIN C15: via Fr. from L. *disquisitio(n-)* 'investigation', based on *quaerere* 'seek'.

**disrate** /dɪs'reɪt/ ● **v.** reduce (a sailor) to a lower rank.

**disregard** ● **v.** pay no attention to; ignore. ● **n.** the action or state of disregarding or being disregarded.

**disrelish** archaic ● **n.** a feeling of dislike or distaste. ● **v.** regard with dislike or distaste.

**disremember** ● **v.** US dialect fail to remember.

**disrepair** ● **n.** a poor condition due to neglect.

**disreputable** ● **adj.** not respectable in appearance or character; sleazy or shabby.
– DERIVATIVES **disreputableness** n. **disreputably** adv.

**disrepute** /ˌdɪsrɪ'pjuːt/ ● **n.** the state of being discredited.

**disrespect** ● **n.** lack of respect or courtesy. ● **v.** informal, chiefly N. Amer. show a lack of respect for; insult.
– DERIVATIVES **disrespectful** adj. **disrespectfully** adv.

**disrobe** ● **v. 1** take off one's clothes; undress. **2** take off official regalia or vestments.

**disrupt** ● **v. 1** disturb or interrupt. **2** drastically alter or destroy the structure of.
– DERIVATIVES **disrupter** (also **disruptor**) n. **disruption** n. **disruptive** adj. **disruptively** adv. **disruptiveness** n.
– ORIGIN ME: from L. *disrupt-*, *disrumpere* 'break apart'.

**diss** ● **v.** variant spelling of **DIS**.

**dissatisfaction** ● **n.** lack of satisfaction.

**dissatisfied** ● **adj.** not content or happy.
– DERIVATIVES **dissatisfiedly** adv.

**dissatisfy** ● **v.** (**-ies, -ied**) fail to satisfy or give pleasure to.
– DERIVATIVES **dissatisfaction** n.

**dissaving** ● **n.** chiefly N. Amer. the action of spending more than one has earned in a given period. ➤(**dissavings**) the excess amount spent.
– DERIVATIVES **dissaver** n.

**dissect** /dʌɪ'sɛkt, dɪ-/ ● **v. 1** methodically cut up (a body, part, or plant) in order to study its internal parts. **2** analyse in minute detail.
– DERIVATIVES **dissection** n. **dissector** n.
– ORIGIN C16: from L. *dissect-*, *dissecare* 'cut up'.

**dissected** ● **adj. 1** Botany (of a leaf) divided into many deep lobes. **2** Geology (of a plateau or upland) divided by a number of deep valleys.

**dissemble** /dɪ'sɛmb(ə)l/ ● **v.** hide or disguise one's true motives or feelings.
– DERIVATIVES **dissemblance** n. **dissembler** n.
– ORIGIN ME: alt. (suggested by **SEMBLANCE**) of obs. *dissimule*, via OFr. from L. *dissimulare* 'disguise, conceal'.

**disseminate** /dɪ'sɛmɪneɪt/ ● **v.** spread widely.
– DERIVATIVES **dissemination** n. **disseminator** n.
– ORIGIN ME: from L. *disseminat-*, *disseminare* 'scatter', from *dis-* 'abroad' + *semen, semin-* 'seed'.

**disseminule** /dɪ'sɛmɪnjuːl/ ● **n.** Botany a part of a plant that serves to propagate it, such as a seed or a fruit.
– ORIGIN C20: formed irregularly from *dissemination* (see **DISSEMINATE**) + **-ULE**.

**dissension** /dɪ'sɛnʃ(ə)n/ ● **n.** disagreement that leads to discord.
– ORIGIN ME: via OFr. from L. *dissensio(n-)*, from *dissentire* (see **DISSENT**).

**dissensus** /dɪ'sɛnsəs/ ● **n.** widespread dissent.
– ORIGIN 1960s: from **DIS-** + a shortened form of **CONSENSUS**, or from L. *dissensus* 'disagreement'.

**dissent** /dɪ'sɛnt/ ● **v.** express disagreement with a prevailing view or official decision. ➤disagree with the doctrine of an established or orthodox Church. ● **n.** the holding or expression of a dissenting view.
– ORIGIN ME: from L. *dissentire* 'differ in sentiment'.

**dissenter** ● **n.** a person who dissents. ➤(**Dissenter**) Brit. historical a member of a non-established Church; a Nonconformist.

**dissentient** /dɪ'sɛnʃɪənt, -ʃ(ə)nt/ ● **adj.** in opposition to a majority or official opinion. ● **n.** a dissentient person.
– ORIGIN C17: from L. *dissentient-*, *dissentire* 'differ in opinion'.

**dissepiment** /dɪ'sɛpɪm(ə)nt/ ● **n.** Botany & Zoology a partition in a part or organ; a septum.
– ORIGIN C18: from L. *dissaepimentum*, from *dissaepire* 'make separate'.

**dissertation** /ˌdɪsə'teɪʃ(ə)n/ ● **n.** a long essay, especially one written for a university degree or diploma.
– DERIVATIVES **dissertational** adj.
– ORIGIN C17 (in the sense 'discussion, debate'): from L. *dissertatio(n-)*, from *dissertare* 'continue to discuss'.

**disservice** ● **n.** a harmful action.

**dissever** /dɪ(s)'sɛvə/ ● **v.** divide or sever.
– DERIVATIVES **disseverance** n. **disseverment** n.
– ORIGIN ME: from OFr. *dessevrer*, from late L. *disseparare*, from *dis-* (expressing intensive force) + L. *separare* 'to separate'.

**dissident** /'dɪsɪd(ə)nt/ ● **n.** a person who opposes official policy. ● **adj.** in opposition to official policy.
– DERIVATIVES **dissidence** n.
– ORIGIN C16: from L. *dissident-*, *dissidere* 'sit apart, disagree'.

**dissimilar** ● **adj.** not similar; different.
– DERIVATIVES **dissimilarity** n. **dissimilarly** adv.

**dissimilate** /dɪ'sɪmɪleɪt/ ● **v.** Linguistics change (a sound in a word) to another when the word originally had identical sounds near each other (e.g. in *taper*, which derives from *papyrus*, the *p* is dissimilated to *t*).
– DERIVATIVES **dissimilation** n. **dissimilatory** /dɪ'sɪmɪlət(ə)ri/ adj.
– ORIGIN C19: from **DIS-** + L. *similis* 'like, similar', on the pattern of *assimilate*.

**dissimilitude** /ˌdɪsɪ'mɪlɪtjuːd/ ● **n.** formal dissimilarity or diversity.
– ORIGIN ME: from L. *dissimilitudo*, from *dissimilis* 'unlike'.

**dissimulate** /dɪ'sɪmjʊleɪt/ ● **v.** hide or disguise one's thoughts or feelings.
– DERIVATIVES **dissimulation** n. **dissimulator** n.
– ORIGIN ME: from L. *dissimulat-*, *dissimulare* 'to conceal'.

**dissipate** /'dɪsɪpeɪt/ ● **v. 1** be dispelled or dispersed, or cause to be so. **2** waste (money, energy, or resources). **3** Physics cause (energy) to be lost through its conversion into heat.
– DERIVATIVES **dissipative** adj. **dissipator** (also **dissipater**) n.
– ORIGIN ME: from L. *dissipat-*, *dissipare* 'scatter'.

**dissipated** ● **adj.** overindulgent in sensual pleasures.

**dissipation** ● **n. 1** dissipated living. **2** the action of dissipating something.

**dissociable** ● **adj.** able to be dissociated; separable.

**dissociate** /dɪ'səʊʃɪeɪt, -sɪ-/ ● **v. 1** disconnect or separate. **2** Psychiatry cause (a component of mental activity) to undergo dissociation. **3** Chemistry undergo or cause to undergo dissociation.
– DERIVATIVES **dissociative** adj.
– ORIGIN C16: from L. *dissociat-*, *dissociare* 'separate'.

**dissociation** /dɪˌsəʊʃɪ'eɪʃ(ə)n, -sɪ-/ ● **n. 1** the action or process of disconnecting or separating. **2** Psychiatry separation of normally related mental processes, resulting in one group functioning independently from the rest and leading to disorders such as multiple personality. **3** Chemistry the splitting of a molecule into smaller molecules, atoms, or ions, especially by a reversible process.

**dissoluble** • **adj.** able to be dissolved, loosened, or disconnected.
– DERIVATIVES **dissolubility** n.
– ORIGIN C16: from L. *dissolubilis*, from *dissolvere* (see **DISSOLVE**).

**dissolute** /ˈdɪsəluːt/ • **adj.** overindulgent in sensual pleasures.
– DERIVATIVES **dissolutely** adv. **dissoluteness** n.
– ORIGIN ME: from L. *dissolutus* 'disconnected, loose', from *dissolvere* (see **DISSOLVE**).

**dissolution** • **n.** **1** the closing down of an assembly, partnership, or official body. **2** the action or process of dissolving or being dissolved. **3** disintegration; decomposition. **4** archaic death. **5** debauched living; dissipation.
– ORIGIN ME: from L. *dissolutio(n-)*, from *dissolvere* (see **DISSOLVE**).

**dissolve** • **v.** **1** (with reference to a solid) become or cause to become incorporated into a liquid so as to form a solution. **2** (with reference to an assembly or body) close down, dismiss, or annul. ➤(of something abstract) disappear. **3** (**dissolve into/to**) (of an image or scene in a film) gradually blend into another. **4** (**dissolve into/in**) subside uncontrollably into (an expression of strong feelings). • **n.** (with reference to an image or scene in a film) an instance of dissolving.
– DERIVATIVES **dissolvable** adj.
– ORIGIN ME: from L. *dissolvere*, from *dis-* 'apart' + *solvere* 'loosen or solve'.

**dissolvent** • **n.** a substance or agent that dissolves something.

**dissonant** • **adj.** **1** Music lacking harmony. **2** unsuitable in combination; clashing.
– DERIVATIVES **dissonance** n. **dissonantly** adv.
– ORIGIN ME: from OFr., or from L. *dissonant-*, *dissonare* 'be discordant', from *dis-* 'apart' + *sonare* 'to sound'.

**dissuade** /dɪˈsweɪd/ • **v.** (**dissuade someone from**) advise someone against; persuade someone not to do something.
– DERIVATIVES **dissuader** n. **dissuasion** n. **dissuasive** adj.
– ORIGIN C15: from L. *dissuadere*, from *dis-* (expressing reversal) + *suadere* 'advise, persuade'.

**dissyllable** /dɪˈsɪləb(ə)l/ • **n.** variant spelling of **DISYLLABLE**.
– DERIVATIVES **dissyllabic** adj.

**dissymmetry** • **n.** (pl. **-ies**) **1** lack of symmetry. **2** the symmetrical relation of mirror images, as between the left and right hands.
– DERIVATIVES **dissymmetric** adj. **dissymmetrical** adj.

**distaff** /ˈdɪstɑːf/ • **n.** **1** a stick or spindle on to which wool or flax is wound for spinning. **2** [as modifier] denoting or concerning women: *a family tree on the distaff side*. Compare with **SPEAR** (in sense 3).
– ORIGIN OE *distæf*: the first element is appar. rel. to Mid. Low Ger. *dise*, *disene* 'distaff, bunch of flax'; the second is **STAFF**[1].

**distal** /ˈdɪst(ə)l/ • **adj.** chiefly Anatomy situated away from the centre of the body or an area or from the point of attachment. The opposite of **PROXIMAL**.
– DERIVATIVES **distally** adv.
– ORIGIN C19: from **DISTANT**, on the pattern of words such as *dorsal*.

**distance** • **n.** **1** the length of the space between two points. **2** the condition of being far off; remoteness. ➤a far-off point or place. **3** the full length or time of a race or other contest. ➤Brit. Horse Racing a space of more than twenty lengths between two finishers in a race. ➤Brit. a length of 240 yards from the winning post on a racecourse. ➤N. Amer. Horse Racing the distance from the winning post which a horse must have reached when the winner finishes in order to qualify for a subsequent heat. **4** an interval of time or relation. **5** aloofness or reserve. • **v.** **1** make distant. ➤(often **distance oneself from**) dissociate or separate. **2** N. Amer. Horse Racing beat (a horse) by a distance.
– PHRASES **go the distance** last or continue to participate until the scheduled end of a contest. **keep one's distance** stay far away. ➤maintain one's reserve.
– ORIGIN ME (in the sense 'discord, debate'): from OFr. or from L. *distantia*, from *distant-*, *distare* (see **DISTANT**).

**distance learning** • **n.** a method of studying in which lectures are broadcast and lessons are conducted by correspondence.

**distance runner** • **n.** an athlete who competes in long- or middle-distance races.

**distant** • **adj.** **1** far away in space or time. ➤at a specified distance: *the town lay half a mile distant*. ➤(of a sound) faint or vague because far away. **2** remote or far apart in resemblance or relationship. ➤(of a person) not closely related: *a distant cousin*. **3** (of a person) cool or reserved. **4** remote; abstracted: *a distant look*.
– DERIVATIVES **distantly** adv.
– ORIGIN ME: from L. *distant-*, *distare* 'stand apart'.

**distantiate** /dɪˈstanʃɪeɪt/ • **v.** set or keep at a distance emotionally or intellectually.
– DERIVATIVES **distantiation** n.
– ORIGIN 1940s: based on L. *distantia* 'distance'.

**distant signal** • **n.** a railway signal giving a warning of the condition of the next home signal.

**distaste** • **n.** dislike or aversion.
– DERIVATIVES **distasteful** adj. **distastefully** adv. **distastefulness** n.
– ORIGIN C16: from **DIS-** + **TASTE**, on the pattern of early mod. Fr. *desgout*, Ital. *disgusto*; cf. **DISGUST**.

**distemper**[1] /dɪˈstɛmpə/ • **n.** a kind of paint having a base of glue or size instead of oil, used on walls. ➤a method of mural and poster painting using this. • **v.** [often as adj. **distempered**] paint with distemper.
– ORIGIN ME (orig. as a verb in the senses 'dilute' and 'steep'): from OFr. *destremper* or late L. *distemperare* 'soak'.

**distemper**[2] /dɪˈstɛmpə/ • **n.** **1** a viral disease of some animals, especially dogs, causing fever, coughing, and catarrh. **2** archaic political disorder.
– ORIGIN C16 (orig. in the sense 'bad temper', later 'illness'): from ME *distemper* 'upset, derange', from late L. *distemperare* 'soak, mix in the wrong proportions'.

**distend** /dɪˈstɛnd/ • **v.** swell or cause to swell because of pressure from inside.
– DERIVATIVES **distended** adj. **distensibility** n. **distensible** adj. **distension** n.
– ORIGIN ME: from L. *distendere*, from *dis-* 'apart' + *tendere* 'to stretch'.

**distich** /ˈdɪstɪk/ • **n.** Prosody a pair of verse lines; a couplet.
– ORIGIN C16: via L. from Gk *distikhon* (*metron*) '(measure) of two lines', neut. of *distikhos*, from *di-* 'twice' + *stikhos* 'line'.

**distichous** /ˈdɪstɪkəs/ • **adj.** Botany arranged alternately in two opposite vertical rows.
– DERIVATIVES **distichously** adv.
– ORIGIN C18: via L. from Gk *distikhos* (see **DISTICH**) + **-OUS**.

**distil** /dɪˈstɪl/ (US **distill**) • **v.** (**distilled**, **distilling**) **1** purify (a liquid) by heating it so that it vaporizes, then cooling and condensing the vapour and collecting the resulting liquid. ➤make (spirits) in this way. ➤extract a volatile component of (a substance) by heating, often with a solvent. **2** extract the essential meaning of.
– DERIVATIVES **distillate** n. **distillation** n. **distillatory** adj.
– ORIGIN ME: from L. *distillare*, var. of *destillare*, from *de-* 'down, away' + *stillare* (from *stilla* 'a drop').

**distiller** • **n.** a person or company that manufactures spirits.

**distillery** • **n.** (pl. **-ies**) a place where spirits are manufactured.

**distinct** • **adj.** **1** recognizably different in nature; individual or separate. **2** readily distinguishable by the senses.
– DERIVATIVES **distinctly** adv. **distinctness** n.
– ORIGIN ME: from L. *distinctus* 'separated, distinguished', from *distinguere* (see **DISTINGUISH**).

**distinction** • **n.** **1** a marked difference or contrast. ➤the action of distinguishing. **2** excellence that serves to mark someone or something out from others. ➤special honour or recognition. ➤an examination grade denoting excellence.

**distinctive** ● adj. individually characteristic; distinct from others of its kind.
– DERIVATIVES **distinctively** adv. **distinctiveness** n.

**distingué** /dɪˈstaŋgeɪ/ ● adj. (fem. **distinguée** pronunc. same) distinguished.
– ORIGIN from Fr.

**distinguish** /dɪˈstɪŋgwɪʃ/ ● v. **1** recognize, show, or treat as different. ➤(**distinguish between**) perceive or point out a difference between. ➤[often as adj. **distinguishing**] be an identifying characteristic of. **2** manage to discern (something barely perceptible). **3** (**distinguish oneself**) make oneself worthy of respect.
– DERIVATIVES **distinguishable** adj.
– ORIGIN C16: formed irregularly from Fr. *distinguer* or L. *distinguere*, from *dis-* 'apart' + *stinguere* 'put out'.

**distinguished** ● adj. **1** noble and dignified in appearance. **2** successful and commanding great respect.

**distort** /dɪˈstɔːt/ ● v. **1** pull or twist out of shape. **2** give a misrepresentative account or impression of. **3** change the form of (an electrical signal or sound wave) during transmission or amplification.
– DERIVATIVES **distorted** adj. **distortedly** adv. **distortedness** n. **distortion** n. **distortional** adj. **distortionless** adj.
– ORIGIN C15: from L. *distort-*, *distorquere* 'twist apart'.

**distract** /dɪˈstrakt/ ● v. prevent (someone) from giving their full attention to something. ➤divert (attention) from something.
– DERIVATIVES **distracted** adj. **distractedly** adv. **distracting** adj. **distractingly** adv.
– ORIGIN ME: from L. *distract-*, *distrahere* 'draw apart'.

**distraction** ● n. **1** a thing that diverts someone's attention. **2** a thing offering recreation or entertainment. **3** an agitated mental state: *her air of distraction.*
– PHRASES **to distraction** almost to a state of madness: *she loved him to distraction.*

**distractor** ● n. **1** a person or thing that distracts. **2** an incorrect option in a multiple-choice question.

**distrain** /dɪˈstreɪn/ ● v. Law impose distraint on.
– DERIVATIVES **distrainer** n. **distrainment** n.
– ORIGIN ME: from OFr. *destreindre*, from L. *distringere* 'stretch apart'.

**distraint** /dɪˈstreɪnt/ ● n. Law the seizure of someone's property in order to obtain payment of rent or other money owed.

**distrait** /dɪˈstreɪ, ˈdɪstreɪ/ ● adj. (fem. **distraite** /-ˈstreɪt/) distracted; absent-minded.
– ORIGIN C18: Fr., from OFr. *destrait*, past part. of *destraire* 'distract'.

**distraught** /dɪˈstrɔːt/ ● adj. very worried and upset.
– ORIGIN ME: alt. of the obs. adj. *distract* (from L. *distractus* 'pulled apart').

**distress** ● n. **1** extreme anxiety or suffering. **2** the state of a ship or aircraft when in danger or difficulty. **3** Medicine a state of physical strain, especially difficulty in breathing. **4** Law another term for DISTRAINT. ● v. **1** cause distress to. **2** give (furniture, leather, etc.) simulated marks of age and wear.
– DERIVATIVES **distressed** adj. **distressful** adj. **distressing** adj. **distressingly** adv.
– ORIGIN ME: from OFr. *destresce* (n.), *destrecier* (v.), based on L. *distringere* 'stretch apart'.

**distress warrant** ● n. Law a warrant authorizing distraint.

**distributary** /dɪˈstrɪbjʊt(ə)ri/ ● n. (pl. **-ies**) a branch of a river that does not return to the main stream after leaving it (as in a delta).

**distribute** /dɪˈstrɪbjuːt, ˈdɪstrɪbjuːt/ ● v. **1** hand or share out to a number of recipients. **2** (**be distributed**) be spread over an area. **3** supply (goods) to retailers. **4** Logic use (a term) to include every individual of the class to which it refers.
– DERIVATIVES **distributable** adj. **distribution** n. **distributional** adj.
– ORIGIN ME: from L. *distribut-*, *distribuere* 'divide up'.

**distributed system** ● n. Computing a number of independent computers linked by a network.

**distributive** /dɪˈstrɪbjʊtɪv/ ● adj. **1** of or relating to the processes of distribution or things that are distributed. **2** Grammar (of a determiner or pronoun) referring to each individual of a class, not to the class collectively, e.g. *each*, *either*. **3** Mathematics involving the condition that an operation performed on two or more quantities already combined by another operation gives the same result as when it is performed on each quantity individually and the products then combined, e.g. $a \times (b + c) = ab + ac$.
– DERIVATIVES **distributively** adv.

**distributor** /dɪˈstrɪbjʊtə/ ● n. **1** an agent who supplies goods to retailers. **2** a device in a petrol engine for passing electric current to each spark plug in turn.

**district** ● n. **1** an area or part of a town or region. **2** Brit. a division of a county or region that elects its own councillors. ● v. N. Amer. divide into areas.
– ORIGIN C17: from Fr., from med. L. *districtus* '(territory of) jurisdiction', from L. *distringere* 'draw apart'.

**district attorney** ● n. (in the US) a public official who acts as prosecutor for the state or the federal government in court in a particular district.

**district auditor** ● n. (in the UK) a civil servant responsible for auditing the accounts of local authorities.

**district court** ● n. (in the US) the federal or state court of first instance.

**district nurse** ● n. (in the UK) a nurse who visits and treats patients in their homes, operating within a particular district.

**distrust** ● n. lack of trust. ● v. have little trust in; regard with suspicion.
– DERIVATIVES **distruster** n. **distrustful** adj. **distrustfully** adv.

**disturb** ● v. **1** interfere with the normal arrangement or functioning of. **2** interrupt the sleep, relaxation, or privacy of. **3** cause to feel anxious.
– DERIVATIVES **disturber** n. **disturbing** adj. **disturbingly** adv.
– ORIGIN ME: from OFr. *destourber*, from L. *disturbare*, from *dis-* 'utterly' + *turbare* 'disturb'.

**disturbance** ● n. **1** the action of disturbing or the process of being disturbed. **2** a breakdown of peaceful behaviour; a riot. **3** Law interference with rights or property; molestation.

**disturbed** ● adj. suffering from emotional or psychological problems.

**disubstituted** /dʌɪˈsʌbstɪtjuːtɪd/ ● adj. Chemistry (of a molecule) having two substituent groups.

**disulfiram** /dʌɪˈsʌlfɪram/ ● n. Medicine a synthetic compound used in the treatment of alcoholism, causing unpleasant after-effects after the drinking of alcohol.
– ORIGIN 1940s: blend of DI-[1], *sulfide* (see SULPHIDE), and *thiuram*, a radical (from THIO- + UREA + AMIDE).

**disunion** ● n. the breaking of or a lack of union; separation.

**disunited** ● adj. lacking unity.
– DERIVATIVES **disunity** n.

**disuse** /dɪsˈjuːs/ ● n. the state of not being used; neglect.
– DERIVATIVES **disused** adj.

**disutility** /ˌdɪsjuːˈtɪlɪti/ ● n. Economics the adverse qualities associated with a particular activity or process.

**disyllable** /dʌɪˈsɪləb(ə)l, ˈdʌɪsɪl-/ (also **dissyllable** /dɪˈsɪləb(ə)l/) ● n. Prosody a word or metrical foot consisting of two syllables.
– DERIVATIVES **disyllabic** /ˌdʌɪsɪˈlabɪk/ adj.
– ORIGIN C16: alt. (influenced by SYLLABLE) of Fr. *disyllabe*, via L. from Gk *disullabos* 'of two syllables'.

**dit** ● n. (in the Morse system) another term for DOT[1].
– ORIGIN Second World War: imitative.

**ditch** ● n. a narrow channel dug to hold or carry water. ● v. **1** provide with a ditch. **2** (with reference to an aircraft) bring or come down in a forced landing on the sea. ➤US derail (a train). **3** informal get rid of; give up. ➤N. Amer. informal play truant from (school).
– DERIVATIVES **ditcher** n. **ditching** n.
– ORIGIN OE *dīc*, of Gmc origin; rel. to DYKE[1].

**diterpene** /dʌɪˈtəːpiːn/ ● **n.** Chemistry any of a group of terpenes with unsaturated molecules based on a unit with the formula $C_{20}H_{32}$.
– DERIVATIVES **diterpenoid** adj. & n.

**ditheism** /ˈdʌɪθiːɪz(ə)m/ ● **n.** a belief in two gods, especially as independent and opposed principles of good and evil.
– DERIVATIVES **ditheist** n.

**dither** ● **v. 1** be indecisive. **2** Computing display or print (a colour image) without sharp edges so that it appears to contain extra colours. ● **n.** informal **1** a state of dithering. **2** a state of agitation.
– DERIVATIVES **ditherer** n. **dithery** adj.
– ORIGIN C17 (in the dial. sense 'tremble, quiver'): var. of dial. *didder*; rel. to **DODDER**[1].

**dithionite** /dʌɪˈθʌɪənʌɪt/ ● **n.** Chemistry a salt containing the anion $S_2O_4^{2-}$.
– ORIGIN C20: from **DI-**[1] + Gk *theion* 'sulphur' + **-ITE**[1].

**dithyramb** /ˈdɪθɪram(b)/ ● **n.** a wildly ecstatic choral hymn of ancient Greece, especially one dedicated to the god Dionysus. ➤ a passionate or inflated speech, poem, or text.
– DERIVATIVES **dithyrambic** adj.
– ORIGIN C17: via L. from Gk *dithurambos*.

**ditransitive** /dʌɪˈtransɪtɪv, -ˈtrɑː-, -nz-/ ● **adj.** Grammar denoting a verb that takes two objects, for example *give* as in *I gave her the book*.

**ditsy** ● **adj.** variant spelling of **DITZY**.

**dittany** /ˈdɪtəni/ ● **n. 1** an aromatic, shrubby plant of the mint family with white woolly leaves and pink flowers. [*Origanum dictamnus* (Crete and Greece) and other species.] **2** another term for **GAS PLANT**.
– ORIGIN ME: from OFr. *ditain* or med. L. *ditaneum*, from L. *dictamnus, dictamnum*, from Gk *diktamnon*, perh. from *Diktē*, the name of a mountain in Crete.

**ditto** ● **n. 1** the same thing again (used in lists and often indicated by a ditto mark under the word or figure to be repeated). **2** (also **ditto mark**) a symbol consisting of two apostrophes („) representing a repetition.
– ORIGIN C17: from Tuscan dial., var. of Ital. *detto* 'said', from L. *dictus* 'said'.

**ditty** ● **n.** (pl. **-ies**) a short simple song.
– ORIGIN ME: from OFr. *dite* 'composition', from L. *dictatum* 'something dictated', from *dictare* 'to dictate'.

**ditty bag** (also **ditty box**) ● **n.** a receptacle for odds and ends, especially one used by sailors or fishermen.
– ORIGIN C19: of unknown origin.

**ditz** ● **n.** N. Amer. informal a scatterbrained person.
– ORIGIN 1970s: back-form. from **DITZY**.

**ditzy** (also **ditsy**) ● **adj.** N. Amer. informal silly or scatterbrained.
– DERIVATIVES **ditziness** n.
– ORIGIN 1970s: of unknown origin.

**diuresis** /ˌdʌɪjʊ(ə)ˈriːsɪs/ ● **n.** Medicine increased or excessive production of urine.
– ORIGIN C17: mod. L., from **DI-**[3] + Gk *ourēsis* 'urination'.

**diuretic** /ˌdʌɪjʊ(ə)ˈrɛtɪk/ Medicine ● **adj.** causing increased passing of urine. ● **n.** a diuretic drug.
– ORIGIN ME: from OFr. *diuretique*, or via late L. from Gk *diourētikos*, from *diourein* 'urinate'.

**diurnal** /dʌɪˈəːn(ə)l/ ● **adj. 1** of or during the daytime. **2** daily; of each day: *diurnal rhythms*.
– DERIVATIVES **diurnally** adv.
– ORIGIN ME: from late L. *diurnalis*, from L. *diurnus* 'daily', from *dies* 'day'.

**Div.** ● **abbrev.** Division.

**div** ● **abbrev.** divergence (in mathematical equations).

**diva** /ˈdiːvə/ ● **n.** a celebrated female opera singer.
– ORIGIN C19: via Ital. from L., lit. 'goddess'.

**divagate** /ˈdʌɪvəgeɪt/ ● **v.** poetic/literary stray; digress.
– DERIVATIVES **divagation** n.
– ORIGIN C16: from L. *divagat-, divagari* 'wander about'.

**divalent** /dʌɪˈveɪl(ə)nt/ ● **adj.** Chemistry having a valency of two.

**Divali** ● **n.** variant spelling of **DIWALI**.

**divan** /dɪˈvan, dʌɪˈvan, ˈdʌɪvan/ ● **n. 1** a bed consisting of a base and mattress but no footboard or headboard. **2** a long, low sofa without a back or arms. **3** historical a legislative body, council chamber, or court of justice in the Ottoman Empire or elsewhere in the Middle East.
– ORIGIN C16 (in sense 3): via Fr. or Ital. from Turk. *dīvān*, from Pers. *dīwān* 'anthology, register, court, or bench'.

**divaricate** /dʌɪˈvarɪkeɪt, dɪ-/ ● **v.** stretch or spread apart; diverge widely. ● **adj.** Botany (of a branch) coming off the stem almost at a right angle.
– DERIVATIVES **divarication** n.
– ORIGIN C17: from L. *divaricat-, divaricare* 'stretch apart'.

**dive** ● **v.** (past and past part. **dived**; US also **dove** /dəʊv/) **1** plunge head first and with arms outstretched into water. **2** go to a deeper level in water. ➤ swim under water using breathing equipment. **3** plunge steeply downwards through the air. ➤ move quickly or suddenly in a downward direction or under cover. ➤ Soccer deliberately fall when challenged in order to deceive the referee into awarding a foul. **4** (of prices or profits) drop suddenly. ● **n. 1** an act or instance of diving. **2** informal a disreputable nightclub or bar.
– DERIVATIVES **diving** n.
– ORIGIN OE *dūfan* 'dive, sink' and *dȳfan* 'immerse', of Gmc origin; rel. to **DEEP** and **DIP**.

**dive-bomb** ● **v.** bomb (a target) while diving steeply downwards in an aircraft.
– DERIVATIVES **dive-bomber** n.

**diver** ● **n. 1** a person who dives under water as a sport or as part of their work. **2** a large diving waterbird with a sleek black or grey head, a straight pointed bill, and a wailing call. [*Gavia immer* (**great northern diver** or **common loon**) and related species, family Gaviidae.]

**diverge** /dʌɪˈvəːdʒ, dɪ-/ ● **v. 1** (of a road, route, or line) separate and go in a different direction. **2** (of an opinion or approach) differ. **3** (**diverge from**) depart from (a set course or standard). **4** Mathematics (of a series) increase without limit as more of its terms are added.
– DERIVATIVES **divergence** n. **divergency** n.
– ORIGIN C17: from med. L. *divergere*, from L. *dis-* 'in two ways' + *vergere* 'to turn or incline'.

**divergent** ● **adj. 1** diverging. **2** (of thought) using a variety of premises and avoiding common assumptions in making deductions.
– DERIVATIVES **divergently** adv. **diverging** adj.

**divers** /ˈdʌɪvəz/ ● **adj.** archaic or poetic/literary of varying types; several.
– ORIGIN ME: via OFr. from L. *diversus* 'diverse', from *divertere* (see **DIVERT**).

**diverse** /dʌɪˈvəːs, ˈdʌɪvəːs/ ● **adj.** widely varied.
– DERIVATIVES **diversely** adv.
– ORIGIN ME: var. of **DIVERS**.

**diversify** /dʌɪˈvəːsɪfʌɪ, dɪ-/ ● **v.** (**-ies**, **-ied**) make or become more diverse. ➤ (of a company) enlarge or vary its range of products or field of operation.
– DERIVATIVES **diversification** n.

**diversion** /dʌɪˈvəːʃ(ə)n, dɪ-/ ● **n. 1** an instance of diverting. **2** Brit. an alternative route for use by traffic when the usual road is temporarily closed. **3** something intended to distract someone's attention: *a raid was carried out to create a diversion*. **4** a recreation or pastime.
– DERIVATIVES **diversionary** adj.

**diversity** /dʌɪˈvəːsɪti, dɪ-/ ● **n.** (pl. **-ies**) the state of being diverse. ➤ a diverse range; a variety: *a diversity of views*.

**divert** /dʌɪˈvəːt, dɪ-/ ● **v. 1** cause to change course or take a different route. **2** reallocate (a resource) to a different purpose. **3** draw the attention of; distract or entertain.
– DERIVATIVES **diverting** adj. **divertingly** adv.
– ORIGIN ME: via Fr. from L. *divers-, divertere*, from *di-* 'aside' + *vertere* 'to turn'.

**diverticula** plural form of **DIVERTICULUM**.

**diverticular** /ˌdʌɪvəˈtɪkjʊlə/ ● **adj.** Medicine of or relating to diverticula.

**diverticular disease** ● **n.** a condition in which muscle spasm in the colon (lower intestine) in the presence of diverticula causes abdominal pain and disturbance of bowel function without inflammation.

**diverticulitis** /ˌdʌɪvətɪkjʊˈlʌɪtɪs/ ● **n.** Medicine inflammation of a diverticulum, especially in the colon, causing pain and disturbance of bowel function. Compare with **DIVERTICULOSIS**.

**diverticulosis** /ˌdʌɪvətɪkjʊˈləʊsɪs/ ● **n.** Medicine a condition in which diverticula are present in the intestine without signs of inflammation. Compare with **DIVERTICULITIS**.

**diverticulum** /ˌdʌɪvəˈtɪkjʊləm/ ● **n.** (pl. **diverticula** /-lə/) Anatomy & Zoology **1** a blind tube leading from a cavity or passage. **2** Medicine an abnormal sac or pouch formed at a weak point in the wall of the alimentary tract.
– ORIGIN C19: from med. L., var. of L. *deverticulum* 'byway', from *devertere* 'turn down or aside'.

**divertimento** /dɪˌvəːtɪˈmɛntəʊ, -ˌvɛːt-/ ● **n.** (pl. **divertimenti** /-ti/ or **divertimentos**) Music a light and entertaining composition, typically in the form of a suite for chamber orchestra.
– ORIGIN C18: Ital., lit. 'diversion'.

**divertissement** /dɪˈvəːtɪsmənt, ˌdiːvɛːˈtiːsmɒ̃/ ● **n. 1** a minor entertainment or diversion. **2** Ballet a short discrete dance within a ballet, intended to display a dancer's technical skill.
– ORIGIN C18 (denoting a short ballet): Fr., from *divertiss-*, *divertir*, from L. *divertere* 'turn in separate ways'.

**Dives** /ˈdʌɪviːz/ ● **n.** poetic/literary a typical or hypothetical rich man.
– ORIGIN ME: from late L., used in the Vulgate translation of the Bible (Luke 16).

**divest** /dʌɪˈvɛst, dɪ-/ ● **v.** (**divest someone/thing of**) **1** deprive or dispossess someone or something of. **2** free or rid of.
– ORIGIN C17: alt. of *devest*, from OFr. *desvestir*, from *des-* (expressing removal) + L. *vestire* (from *vestis* 'garment').

**divestiture** (also **divesture**) ● **n.** another term for **DIVESTMENT**.

**divestment** ● **n.** the action or process of selling off subsidiary business interests or investments.

**divi** ● **n.** (pl. **divis**) variant spelling of **DIVVY**[1].

**divide** ● **v. 1** separate or be separated into parts. ➤(usu. **divide something between**) distribute or share out. ➤form a boundary between. **2** disagree or cause to disagree. **3** Mathematics find how many times (a number) contains another: *36 divided by 2 equals 18.* ➤(of a number) be susceptible of division without a remainder. ● **n. 1** an instance of dividing or being divided. **2** chiefly US a ridge or line of high ground forming the division between two valleys or river systems.
– PHRASES **divide and rule** (or **conquer**) maintain control over subordinates or opponents by encouraging dissent between them so that they do not unite in opposition.
– DERIVATIVES **divided** adj.
– ORIGIN ME: from L. *divis-*, *dividere* 'force apart, remove'.

**divided highway** ● **n.** N. Amer. a dual carriageway.

**divided skirt** ● **n.** a pair of culottes.

**dividend** /ˈdɪvɪdɛnd/ ● **n. 1** a sum of money that is divided among a number of people, such as the part of a company's profits paid to its shareholders or the winnings from a football pool. ➤an individual's share of this money. **2** (**dividends**) a benefit from an action or policy: *the policy would pay dividends in the future.* **3** Mathematics a number to be divided by another number.
– ORIGIN C15: from Anglo-Norman Fr. *dividende*, from L. *dividendum* 'something to be divided', from *dividere* (see **DIVIDE**).

**dividend cover** ● **n.** the ratio of a company's net profits to the total sum allotted in dividends to ordinary shareholders.

**divider** ● **n. 1** (also **room divider**) a screen or piece of furniture that divides a room into two parts. **2** (**dividers**) a measuring compass, especially one with a screw for making fine adjustments.

**divi-divi** /ˈdɪvɪˌdɪvi/ ● **n.** (pl. **divi-divis**) **1** a small tropical American leguminous tree bearing curled pods. [*Caesalpinia coriaria*.] **2** these pods, used as a source of tannin.
– ORIGIN C19: via Amer. Sp. from Carib.

**divination** /ˌdɪvɪˈneɪʃ(ə)n/ ● **n.** the practice of divining or seeking knowledge by supernatural means.
– DERIVATIVES **divinatory** adj.

**divine**[1] ● **adj.** (**-er**, **-est**) **1** of, from, or like God or a god. ➤devoted to God; sacred. **2** informal excellent; delightful. ● **n. 1** dated a cleric or theologian. **2** (**the Divine**) providence or God.
– DERIVATIVES **divinely** adv. **divineness** n.
– ORIGIN ME: via OFr. from L. *divinus*, from *divus* 'godlike' (rel. to *deus* 'god').

**divine**[2] ● **v. 1** discover by guesswork or intuition. **2** have supernatural or magical insight into (the future). **3** discover (water) by dowsing.
– DERIVATIVES **diviner** n.
– ORIGIN ME: from OFr. *deviner* 'predict', from L. *divinare*, from *divinus* (see **DIVINE**[1]).

**divine right of kings** ● **n.** the doctrine that kings derive their authority from God, not from their subjects.

**divine service** ● **n.** public Christian worship.

**diving beetle** ● **n.** a predatory water beetle which stores air under its wing cases for swimming underwater. [Family Dytiscidae: numerous species.]

**diving bell** ● **n.** an open-bottomed chamber supplied with air, in which a person can be let down under water.

**diving board** ● **n.** an elevated board projecting over a swimming pool or other body of water, from which people dive or jump in.

**diving duck** ● **n.** a duck which typically feeds by diving underwater, such as a pochard or goldeneye.

**diving suit** ● **n.** a watertight suit, typically with a helmet and an air supply, worn for working or exploring deep under water.

**divining rod** ● **n.** a stick or rod used for dowsing.

**divinity** /dɪˈvɪnɪti/ ● **n.** (pl. **-ies**) **1** the state or quality of being divine. **2** a divine being; a god or goddess. **3** (**the Divinity**) God. **4** the study of religion; theology.

**divinize** /ˈdɪvɪnʌɪz/ (also **-ise**) ● **v.** make divine; deify.

**divisi** /dɪˈviːsi/ ● **adv. & adj.** (with reference to a section of musicians) divided into two or more groups each playing a different part: *violas divisi.*
– ORIGIN Ital., lit. 'divided' (pl.), from *dividere* 'to divide'.

**divisible** /dɪˈvɪzɪb(ə)l/ ● **adj.** capable of being divided. ➤Mathematics (of a number) containing another number a number of times without a remainder.
– DERIVATIVES **divisibility** n.

**division** ● **n. 1** the action or process of dividing or being divided. **2** the separation of members of a legislative body into groups to vote for or against a bill. **3** the action of splitting the roots of a perennial plant into parts to be replanted separately, as a means of propagation. **4** the process of dividing one number by another. ➤Mathematics the process of dividing a matrix, vector, or other quantity by another under specific rules to obtain a quotient. **5** each of the parts into which something is divided. ➤a major unit or section of an organization. ➤a number of teams or competitors grouped together in a sport for competitive purposes. ➤Botany a principal taxonomic category that ranks above class and below kingdom, equivalent to the phylum in zoology. ➤Zoology any subsidiary category between major levels of classification. **6** a partition that divides two groups or things.
– PHRASES **division of labour** the assignment of different parts of a manufacturing process or task to different people in order to improve efficiency.
– DERIVATIVES **divisional** adj. **divisionally** adv.

**divisionalize** /dɪˈvɪʒ(ə)n(ə)lʌɪz/ (also **-ise**) ● **v.** [usu. as adj. **divisionalized**] subdivide (an organization) into a number of separate divisions.
– DERIVATIVES **divisionalization** n.

**division bell** ● **n.** a bell rung in the British Parliament to announce an imminent division.

**divisionism** ● **n.** another term for **POINTILLISM**.

**division sign** ● **n.** the sign ÷, placed between two numbers showing that the first is to be divided by the second, as in $6 \div 3 = 2$.

**divisive** /dɪˈvʌɪsɪv/ ● **adj.** causing disagreement or hostility.
– DERIVATIVES **divisively** adv. **divisiveness** n.

– ORIGIN C16: from late L. *divisivus*, from L. *dividere* (see **DIVIDE**).

**divisor** /dɪˈvʌɪzə/ • **n.** Mathematics a number by which another number is to be divided. ➤a number that divides into another without a remainder.

**divorce** • **n.** the legal dissolution of a marriage. ➤a legal decree dissolving a marriage. • **v. 1** legally dissolve one's marriage with. **2** detach or dissociate: *religion cannot be divorced from morality.*
– DERIVATIVES **divorcement** n.
– ORIGIN ME: from OFr. *divorce*, from L. *divortium*, based on *divertere* (see **DIVERT**).

**divorcee** /ˌdɪvɔːˈsiː/ • **n.** (US masc. **divorcé**, fem. **divorcée** /-ˈseɪ/) a divorced person.
– ORIGIN C19: from Fr. *divorcé(e)* 'divorced man (or woman)'.

**divot** /ˈdɪvət/ • **n. 1** a piece of turf cut out of the ground by a golf club in making a stroke. ➤a small hole made in this way. **2** chiefly Scottish a piece of turf, as formerly used for roofing cottages.
– ORIGIN C16: of unknown origin.

**divulge** /dʌɪˈvʌldʒ, dɪ-/ • **v.** make known.
– DERIVATIVES **divulgation** n. **divulgence** n.
– ORIGIN ME: from L. *divulgare*, from *di-* 'widely' + *vulgare* 'publish' (from *vulgus* 'common people').

**divvy**[1] informal • **n.** (also **divi**) (pl. **-ies**) Brit. a dividend or share, especially of profits earned by a cooperative. • **v.** (**-ies**, **-ied**) share out.

**divvy**[2] • **n.** (pl. **-ies**) Brit. informal a foolish or stupid person.
– ORIGIN 1970s: of unknown origin.

**Diwali** /dɪˈwɑːli/ (also **Divali**) • **n.** a Hindu festival with lights, held in October and November to celebrate the end of the monsoon.
– ORIGIN from Hindi *dīvālī*, from Sanskrit *dīpāvali* 'row of lights'.

**diwan** /dɪˈwɑːn/ (also **dewan**) • **n. 1** (in Islamic societies) a central finance department, chief administrative office, or regional governing body. **2** a chief treasury official, finance minister, or Prime Minister in some Indian states.
– ORIGIN Urdu, from Pers. *dīwān* 'fiscal register'; cf. **DIVAN**.

**Dixie** • **n.** an informal name for the Southern states of the US.
– PHRASES **whistle Dixie** US informal engage in unrealistic fantasies; waste one's time.
– ORIGIN C19: of unknown origin.

**dixie** • **n.** (pl. **-ies**) a large iron cooking pot used especially by campers or soldiers.
– ORIGIN C20: from Hindi *degcī* 'cooking pot', from Pers. *degča*, dimin. of *deg* 'pot'.

**Dixieland** • **n.** a kind of jazz with a strong two-beat rhythm and collective improvisation, which originated in New Orleans in the early 20th century.

**DIY** • **n.** chiefly Brit. the activity of decorating and making fixtures and repairs in the home oneself rather than employing a professional.
– DERIVATIVES **DIY'er** n.
– ORIGIN 1950s: abbrev. of **DO-IT-YOURSELF**.

**dizygotic** /ˌdʌɪzʌɪˈgɒtɪk/ • **adj.** (of twins) derived from two separate ova, and so not identical.

**dizygous** /dʌɪˈzʌɪgəs/ • **adj.** another term for **DIZYGOTIC**.

**dizzy** • **adj.** (**-ier**, **-iest**) **1** having a sensation of spinning around and losing one's balance. **2** informal (of a woman) silly but attractive. • **v.** (**-ies**, **-ied**) [usu. as adj. **dizzying**] make (someone) feel unsteady, confused, or amazed: *the dizzying rate of change.*
– PHRASES **the dizzy heights** informal a position of great importance in a particular field.
– DERIVATIVES **dizzily** adv. **dizziness** n.
– ORIGIN OE *dysig* 'foolish', of W. Gmc origin.

**DJ**[1] • **n.** a disc jockey. ➤a person who uses samples of recorded music to make techno or rap music.

**DJ**[2] • **abbrev.** Brit. dinner jacket.

**djellaba** /ˈdʒɛləbə/ (also **djellabah** or **jellaba**) • **n.** a loose hooded woollen cloak of a kind traditionally worn by Arabs.
– ORIGIN C19: from Moroccan Arab. *jellāba*, *jellābiyya*.

**Djiboutian** /dʒɪˈbuːtiən/ (also **Jibutian**) • **n.** a native or inhabitant of the country of Djibouti on the NE coast of Africa. • **adj.** of or relating to Djibouti.

**djinn** • **n.** variant spelling of **JINN**.

**DK** • **abbrev.** Denmark (international vehicle registration).

**dkl** • **abbrev.** US dekaliter(s).

**dkm** • **abbrev.** US dekameter(s).

**DL** • **abbrev. 1** Deputy Lieutenant. **2** N. Amer. (with reference to sports players) disabled list.

**dl** • **abbrev.** decilitre(s).

**D-layer** • **n.** the lowest layer of the ionosphere, able to reflect low-frequency radio waves.
– ORIGIN 1930s: from an arbitrary use of the letter *D*.

**DLitt** • **abbrev.** Doctor of Letters.
– ORIGIN from L. *Doctor Litterarum*.

**DLL** • **abbrev.** Computing dynamic linked library.

**D-lock** • **n.** a mechanism used to secure a bicycle or motorbike when parked, consisting of a solid metal U-shaped bar and crosspiece.

**DM** (also **D-mark**) • **abbrev.** Deutschmark.

**dm** • **abbrev.** decimetre(s).

**DMA** • **abbrev.** Computing direct memory access.

**DMD** • **abbrev.** Duchenne muscular dystrophy.

**DMs** • **abbrev.** Dr Martens (shoes or boots).

**DMSO** • **abbrev.** Chemistry dimethyl sulphoxide.

**dmu** • **abbrev.** Brit. diesel multiple unit.

**DMus** • **abbrev.** Doctor of Music.

**DMV** • **abbrev.** (in the US) Department of Motor Vehicles.

**DMZ** • **abbrev.** N. Amer. demilitarized zone.

**DNA** • **n.** Biochemistry deoxyribonucleic acid, a substance present in nearly all living organisms as the carrier of genetic information, and typically consisting of a very long double-stranded chain of sugar and phosphate groups cross-linked by pairs of organic bases.

**DNA fingerprinting** (also **DNA profiling**) • **n.** another term for **GENETIC FINGERPRINTING**.

**DNase** /ˌdiːɛnˈeɪz/ • **n.** Biochemistry an enzyme which breaks down DNA into smaller molecules.
– ORIGIN 1940s: from **DNA** + **-ASE**.

**DNA virus** • **n.** a virus in which the genetic information is stored in the form of DNA (as opposed to RNA).

**DNB** • **abbrev.** Dictionary of National Biography.

**D notice** • **n.** Brit. a government notice issued to news editors requiring them not to publicize certain information for reasons of national security.
– ORIGIN Second World War: *D* for *defence*.

**do**[1] • **v.** (**does**; past **did**; past part. **done**) **1** perform or carry out (an action). ➤work on (something) to bring it to completion or to a required state. ➤make, produce, or provide. ➤work at for a living or take as one's subject of study. ➤informal regularly take (a narcotic drug). **2** achieve or complete (a specified target). ➤informal visit as a tourist. ➤informal spend (a specified period of time) in a particular occupation or in prison. ➤(**be/have done with**) give up concern for; have finished with. **3** act or progress in a specified way. ➤have a specified result or effect on. **4** be suitable or acceptable. **5** informal beat up or kill. ➤swindle. **6** (usu. **be/get done for**) Brit. informal prosecute; convict. • **aux. v. 1** used before a verb in questions and negative statements. **2** used to refer back to a verb already mentioned. **3** used in negative or positive commands, or to give emphasis to a positive verb. **4** used with inversion of a subject and verb when an adverbial phrase begins a clause for emphasis. • **n.** (pl. **dos** or **do's**) informal, chiefly Brit. a party or other social event.
– PHRASES **be** (or **have**) **to do with** be concerned or connected with. **do one's head in** Brit. informal make one extremely angry or agitated. **do or die** persist, even if death is the result. **dos and don'ts** rules of behaviour. **that does it!** informal indicating that one will not tolerate something any longer.
– PHRASAL VERBS **do away with** informal put an end to; remove or kill. **do by** treat or deal with in a specified way:

*she did well by them.* **do someone down** Brit. informal criticize someone. **do for 1** informal defeat, ruin, or kill. **2** suffice for. **do something** (or **nothing**) **for** informal enhance (or detract from) the appearance or quality of. **do someone in** informal **1** kill someone. **2** (usu. **be done in**) informal tire someone out. **do someone out of** informal deprive someone of (something) in an underhand or unfair way. **do something out** Brit. informal decorate or furnish a room or building in a particular way. **do someone/thing over** Brit. informal beat up or ransack. **be done up** be dressed elaborately or impressively. **do something up 1** fasten, wrap, or arrange something. **2** informal renovate or redecorate a room or building. **do with 1** (**can/could do with**) would find useful or would like to have or do: *I could do with a cup of coffee.* **2** (**can't/won't be doing with**) Brit. be unwilling to tolerate.
– DERIVATIVES **doable** adj. (informal). **doer** n.
– ORIGIN OE *dōn*, of Gmc origin.

**do²** • n. variant spelling of **DOH¹**.

**do.** • abbrev. ditto.

**DOA** • abbrev. dead on arrival.

**dob** • v. (**dobbed**, **dobbing**) Austral./NZ informal inform on.
– ORIGIN 1950s: figurative use of dial. *dob* 'put down abruptly', later 'throw something at a target'.

**dobbin** • n. a pet name for a draught horse or a farm horse.
– ORIGIN C16: familiar form of the given name *Robert*.

**dobby** • n. (pl. **-ies**) a mechanism attached to a loom for weaving small patterns.
– ORIGIN C19: perh. an application of the given name *Dobbie*, from *Dob* (alt. of the given name *Rob*); the usage is prob. an extension of the earlier sense 'benevolent elf' (who performed household tasks secretly).

**dobby weave** • n. a style of patterned weave consisting of small geometric devices repeated frequently.

**dobe** /'dəʊbi/ • n. US informal short for **ADOBE**.

**Dobermann** /'dəʊbəmən/ (also **Dobermann pinscher** /'pɪnʃə/, chiefly N. Amer. also **Doberman**) • n. a large dog of a German breed with powerful jaws and a smooth coat, typically black with tan markings.
– ORIGIN C20: from the name of the Ger. dog-breeder Ludwig *Dobermann* (+ Ger. *Pinscher* 'terrier').

**dobra** /'dɒbrə/ • n. the basic monetary unit of São Tomé and Principe, equal to 100 centavos.
– ORIGIN from Port. *dóbra* 'doubloon'.

**dobro** /'dɒbrəʊ/ • n. (pl. **-os**) trademark a type of acoustic guitar with steel resonating discs inside the body under the bridge.
– ORIGIN 1950s: from *Do(pěra) Bro(thers)*, the Czech-Amer. inventors of the instrument.

**dobsonfly** /'dɒbs(ə)nflʌɪ/ • n. (pl. **-flies**) a large grey North American winged insect related to the alderflies, whose aquatic larva (the hellgrammite) is used as fishing bait. [*Corydalis cornutus* and other species.]
– ORIGIN C20: of unknown origin.

**Dobsonian** /dɒb'səʊnɪən/ • adj. denoting or relating to a low-cost Newtonian reflecting telescope with large aperture and short focal length.
– ORIGIN C20: from the name of John *Dobson*, Amer. amateur astronomer, + **-IAN**.

**doc** • abbrev. informal **1** doctor. **2** Computing document.

**docent** /'dəʊs(ə)nt/ • n. **1** (in certain US and European universities and colleges) a member of the teaching staff immediately below professorial rank. **2** a person who acts as a guide in a museum, art gallery, or zoo.
– ORIGIN C19: via Ger. from L. *docent-*, *docere* 'teach'.

**Docetism** /də'si:tɪz(ə)m, 'dəʊsɪˌtɪz(ə)m/ • n. the doctrine that Christ's body was not human (being either a phantasm or of real but celestial substance) and that therefore his sufferings were only apparent.
– DERIVATIVES **Docetist** n.
– ORIGIN C19: from med. L. *Docetae* (the name, based on Gk *dokein* 'seem', given to a group of 2nd-cent. Christian heretics) + **-ISM**.

**doch an dorris** • n. variant spelling of **DEOCH AN DORIS**.

**docile** /'dəʊsʌɪl/ • adj. ready to accept control or instruction; submissive.
– DERIVATIVES **docilely** adv. **docility** n.
– ORIGIN C15 (in the sense 'apt or willing to learn'): from L. *docilis*, from *docere* 'teach'.

**dock¹** • n. **1** an enclosed area of water in a port for the loading, unloading, and repair of ships. ➤ N. Amer. a group of piers where a ship or boat may moor for loading and unloading. **2** (also **loading dock**) a platform for loading trucks or goods trains. • v. **1** (with reference to a ship) come or bring into a dock. **2** (of a spacecraft) join with a space station or another spacecraft in space. **3** attach (a piece of equipment) to another.
– PHRASES **in dock** Brit. informal out of action; indisposed.
– ORIGIN ME: from MDu., Mid. Low Ger. *docke*, of unknown origin.

**dock²** • n. the enclosure in a criminal court where a defendant stands or sits.
– ORIGIN C16: prob. orig. sl. and rel. to Flemish *dok* 'chicken coop, rabbit hutch', of unknown origin.

**dock³** • n. a coarse weed of temperate regions, with inconspicuous greenish or reddish flowers, and leaves that are popularly used to relieve nettle stings. [Genus *Rumex*.]
– ORIGIN OE *docce*, of Gmc origin.

**dock⁴** • v. **1** deduct (money or a point in a score). **2** cut short (an animal's tail). • n. the solid bony or fleshy part of an animal's tail. ➤ the stump left after a tail has been docked.
– ORIGIN ME (orig. in sense 'the solid part of an animal's tail'): perh. rel. to Frisian *dok* 'bunch, ball (of string)' and Ger. *Docke* 'doll'.

**dockage** • n. accommodation or berthing of ships in docks.

**docker** • n. a person employed in a port to load and unload ships.

**docket** • n. **1** Brit. a document accompanying a consignment of goods that lists its contents, certifies payment of duty, or entitles the holder to delivery. **2** N. Amer. a list of cases for trial or people having cases pending. • v. (**docketed**, **docketing**) **1** mark (a consignment or package) with a document listing the contents. **2** N. Amer. enter (a case or suit) on to a list of those due to be heard.
– ORIGIN C15 (orig. denoting a short abstract or summary): perh. from **DOCK⁴**.

**docking station** • n. a device to which a portable computer is connected so that it can be used like a desktop computer.

**dockland** • n. (also **docklands**) the area containing a city's docks.

**dockominium** /ˌdɒkə'mɪnɪəm/ • n. (pl. **dockominiums**) US a waterfront condominium with a private mooring. ➤ a privately owned landing stage at a marina.
– ORIGIN 1980s: from **DOCK¹**, on the pattern of *condominium*.

**dockside** • n. the area immediately adjacent to a dock.

**dockyard** • n. an area with docks and equipment for repairing and maintaining ships.

**doctor** • n. **1** a person who is qualified to practise medicine. ➤ N. Amer. a qualified dentist or veterinary surgeon. **2** (**Doctor**) a person who holds the highest university degree. **3** an artificial fishing fly. **4** Austral./NZ informal a cook on board a ship or in a camp or station. **5** a cool onshore breeze that blows regularly in a particular warm location. • v. **1** adulterate, tamper with, or falsify. **2** informal practise medicine. **3** Brit. remove the sexual organs of (an animal) so that it cannot reproduce. **4** repair (a machine).
– PHRASES **go for the doctor** Austral./NZ informal make an all-out effort. **what the doctor ordered** informal something beneficial or desirable.
– DERIVATIVES **doctoring** n. **doctorly** adj.
– ORIGIN ME (in the senses 'learned person' and 'Doctor of the Church'): via OFr. from L. *doctor* 'teacher'.

**doctoral** /'dɒkt(ə)r(ə)l/ • adj. relating to a doctorate.

**doctorate** /'dɒkt(ə)rət/ • n. the highest degree awarded by a university faculty or other approved educational organization.

**Doctor of Philosophy** • n. a person holding a doctorate in any faculty except law, medicine, or sometimes theology.

**Doctor of the Church** ● n. one of the early Christian theologians regarded as especially authoritative in the Western Church (particularly St Augustine of Hippo, St Jerome, St Ambrose, and St Gregory the Great) or later so designated by the Pope (e.g. St Thomas Aquinas, St Teresa of Ávila).

**doctrinaire** /ˌdɒktrɪˈnɛː/ ● adj. seeking to impose a doctrine without questions or considerations. ● n. a doctrinaire person.
– DERIVATIVES **doctrinairism** n.
– ORIGIN C19: from Fr., from *doctrine* (see **DOCTRINE**).

**doctrine** /ˈdɒktrɪn/ ● n. a set of beliefs or principles held and taught by a Church, political party, or other group.
– DERIVATIVES **doctrinal** adj. **doctrinally** adv.
– ORIGIN ME: from OFr., from L. *doctrina* 'teaching, learning', from *doctor* 'teacher', from *docere* 'teach'.

**docudrama** /ˈdɒkjʊˌdrɑːmə/ ● n. a dramatized film based on real events and incorporating documentary features.

**document** ● n. /ˈdɒkjʊm(ə)nt/ a piece of written, printed, or electronic matter that provides information or evidence or that serves as an official record. ● v. /ˈdɒkjʊmɛnt/ record in written, photographic, or other form.
– DERIVATIVES **documentable** adj. **documental** /-ˈmɛnt(ə)l/ adj.
– ORIGIN ME: from OFr., from L. *documentum* 'lesson, proof' (in med. L. 'written instruction, official paper'), from *docere* 'teach'.

**documentalist** ● n. a person engaged in keeping records and providing information.

**documentarian** /ˌdɒkjʊmɛnˈtɛːrɪən/ ● n. **1** (also **documentarist**) a photographer specializing in producing a factual record. **2** a director or producer of documentaries. **3** an expert analyst of historical documents.

**documentary** ● adj. **1** consisting of documents, photographs, and other material providing a factual account. **2** using film, photographs, and sound recordings of real events. ● n. (pl. **-ies**) a documentary film or television or radio programme.

**documentation** ● n. **1** the documents required in the provision of information or evidence. **2** written specifications or instructions. **3** the process of classifying and annotating texts, photographs, etc.

**documentative** /ˌdɒkjʊˈmɛntətɪv/ ● adj. employing or providing documentation.

**docusoap** ● n. a documentary following people in a particular occupation or location over a period of time.

**docutainment** /ˌdɒkjʊˈteɪnmənt/ ● n. N. Amer. entertainment that incorporates documentary features, intended both to inform and entertain.

**DOD** ● abbrev. (in the US) Department of Defense.

**dodder**[1] ● v. be slow and unsteady.
– DERIVATIVES **dodderer** n. **doddering** adj. **doddery** adj.
– ORIGIN C17: var. of obs. dial. *dadder*; rel. to **DITHER**.

**dodder**[2] ● n. a parasitic climbing plant of the convolvulus family, with leafless stems that are attached to the host plant by means of suckers. [Genus *Cuscuta*.]
– ORIGIN ME: rel. to Mid. Low Ger. *doder*, *dodder*, Mid. High Ger. *toter*.

**doddle** ● n. Brit. informal a very easy task.
– ORIGIN 1930s: perh. from dial. *doddle* 'toddle', of unknown origin.

**dodeca-** /ˈdəʊdɛkə/ ● comb. form twelve; having twelve: *dodecahedron*.
– ORIGIN from Gk.

**dodecagon** /dəʊˈdɛkəg(ə)n/ ● n. a plane figure with twelve straight sides and angles.
– ORIGIN C17: from Gk *dōdekagōnon*, neut. (used as a noun) of *dōdekagōnos* 'twelve-angled'.

**dodecahedron** /ˌdəʊdɛkəˈhiːdr(ə)n, -ˈhɛd-/ ● n. (pl. **dodecahedra** /-drə/ or **dodecahedrons**) a three-dimensional shape having twelve plane faces, in particular a regular solid figure with twelve equal pentagonal faces.
– DERIVATIVES **dodecahedral** adj.
– ORIGIN C16: from Gk *dōdekaedron*, neut. (used as a noun) of *dōdekaedros* 'twelve-faced'.

**dodecaphonic** /ˌdəʊdɛkəˈfɒnɪk/ ● adj. Music another term for **TWELVE-NOTE**.

**dodge** ● v. **1** avoid by a sudden quick movement. ➤ move quickly to one side or out of the way. ➤ cunningly avoid doing or paying. **2** [often as noun **dodging**] Photography expose (one area of a print) less than the rest during processing or enlarging. **3** (of a bell in change-ringing) move one place contrary to the normal sequence, and then back again in the following round. ● n. **1** an act or instance of dodging. **2** informal a cunning trick, especially one used to avoid something.
– ORIGIN C16 (in the senses 'dither' and 'haggle'): of unknown origin.

**dodgeball** ● n. N. Amer. a game in which a team of players forms a circle and tries to hit its opponents with a large ball.

**dodgem** (also **dodgem car**) ● n. a small electrically powered car driven within an enclosure at a funfair, with the aim of bumping other such cars and avoiding being bumped by them.
– ORIGIN 1920s: US proprietary name (as *Dodg'em*), from the phr. *dodge them*.

**dodger** ● n. **1** informal a person who evades something that is required of them: *a tax dodger*. **2** Nautical a canvas screen on a ship giving protection from spray. **3** US & Austral. a small handbill or leaflet. **4** Austral. informal bread.

**dodgy** ● adj. (**-ier**, **-iest**) Brit. informal **1** dishonest. **2** risky; dangerous. **3** not good or reliable.

**dodo** /ˈdəʊdəʊ/ ● n. (pl. **-os** or **-oes**) a large extinct flightless bird found on Mauritius until the end of the 17th century. [*Raphus cucullatus*.]
– PHRASES **as dead as a dodo** utterly dead or finished.
– ORIGIN C17: from Port. *doudo* 'simpleton' (because the birds were tame and easy to catch); cf. **DOTTEREL**.

**DoE** ● abbrev. (in the UK) Department of the Environment.

**doe** ● n. **1** a female roe or fallow deer or reindeer. **2** a female hare, rabbit, rat, ferret, or kangaroo.
– ORIGIN OE *dā* of unknown origin.

**doe-eyed** ● adj. having large gentle dark eyes.

**does** third person singular present of **DO**[1].

**doeskin** /ˈdəʊskɪn/ ● n. **1** leather made from the skin of a doe fallow deer. **2** a fine satin-weave woollen cloth resembling this.

**doesn't** ● contr. does not.

**doest** archaic second person singular present of **DO**[1].

**doeth** archaic third person singular present of **DO**[1].

**doff** ● v. remove (an item of clothing, especially a hat).
– ORIGIN ME: contr. of *do off*; cf. **DON**[2].

**dog** ● n. **1** a domesticated carnivorous mammal probably descended from the wolf, with a barking or howling voice, an acute sense of smell, and non-retractile claws. [*Canis familiaris*.] ➤ a wild animal resembling this, in particular any member of the dog family (Canidae), which includes the wolf, fox, coyote, jackal, and other species. ➤ the male of such an animal. ➤ (**the dogs**) Brit. informal greyhound racing. **2** informal a contemptible man. ➤ dated a person of a specified kind: *you lucky dog!* ➤ (usu. in phr. **turn dog on**) Austral./NZ informal an informer or a traitor. ➤ informal, chiefly N. Amer. a thing of poor quality; a failure. **3** informal, derogatory an unattractive woman. **4** used in names of dogfishes, e.g. **spur-dog**. **5** a mechanical device for gripping. **6** (**dogs**) N. Amer. informal feet. ● v. (**dogged**, **dogging**) **1** follow closely and persistently. **2** (of a problem) cause continual trouble for. **3** (**dog it**) informal, chiefly N. Amer. act lazily. **4** grip with a mechanical device.
– PHRASES **a dog in the manger** a person who prevents others from having things that they do not need themselves. [alluding to the fable of the dog that lay in a manger to prevent the ox and horse from eating the hay.] **a dog's age** N. Amer. informal a very long time. **a dog's dinner** (or **breakfast**) Brit. informal a mess. **a dog's life** an unhappy and oppressed existence. **go to the dogs** informal deteriorate badly. **not a dog's chance** no chance at all. **put on the dog** N. Amer. informal behave in a pretentious or ostentatious way.
– DERIVATIVES **dogdom** n. **doggish** adj.

– ORIGIN OE *docga*, of unknown origin.

**dog-and-pony show** • n. N. Amer. an elaborate and ostentatious presentation or event.

**dogbane** /ˈdɒgbeɪn/ • n. a shrubby North American plant, typically having bell-shaped flowers and reputed to be poisonous to dogs. [Genus *Apocynum*.]

**dogberry** • n. (pl. **-ies**) informal **1** a fruit of poor eating quality from a dogwood, rowan, or other tree or shrub. **2** a dogwood.

**dog cart** • n. a two-wheeled cart for driving in, with cross seats back to back, originally incorporating a box under the seat for sportsmen's dogs.

**dog clutch** • n. a device for coupling two shafts in order to transmit motion, one part having teeth which engage with slots in another.

**dog collar** • n. **1** a collar for a dog. **2** informal a clerical collar.

**dog days** • pl. n. chiefly poetic/literary the hottest period of the year (reckoned in antiquity from the heliacal rising of Sirius, the Dog Star).

**doge** /dəʊdʒ/ • n. historical the chief magistrate of Venice or Genoa.
– ORIGIN C16: from Fr., from Venetian Ital. *doze*, based on L. *dux, duc-* 'leader'.

**dog-eared** • adj. having worn or battered corners.

**dog-end** • n. informal **1** a cigarette end. **2** the last and least pleasing part of something.

**dog face** • n. **1** an American butterfly with a marking on the forewing resembling a dog's face. [Genus *Zerene*: several species.] **2** (**dogface**) US informal, dated a soldier, especially an infantryman.

**dogfight** • n. **1** a close combat between military aircraft. **2** a ferocious struggle or fight.
– DERIVATIVES **dogfighter** n. **dogfighting** n.

**dogfish** • n. (pl. same or **-fishes**) a small bottom-dwelling shark with a long tail. [*Scyliorhinus canicula* and other species.]

**dogged** /ˈdɒgɪd/ • adj. tenacious; grimly persistent.
– DERIVATIVES **doggedly** adv. **doggedness** n.

**dogger**[1] • n. historical a two-masted bluff-bowed Dutch fishing boat.
– ORIGIN ME: from MDu.

**dogger**[2] • n. Geology a large spherical concretion in sedimentary rock.
– ORIGIN C17 (orig. dial. denoting a kind of ironstone): perh. from **DOG**.

**doggerel** /ˈdɒg(ə)r(ə)l/ • n. comic verse composed in irregular rhythm. ➤ badly written verse or words.
– ORIGIN ME (as adj.): appar. from **DOG** (used contemptuously) + **-REL**.

**doggie** • n. variant spelling of **DOGGY**.

**doggo** • adv. (in phr. **lie doggo**) Brit. informal, dated remain motionless and quiet to escape detection.
– ORIGIN C19: of obscure origin.

**doggone** /ˈdɒgɒn/ N. Amer. informal • adj. damned. • v. damn (used to express surprise or irritation).
– ORIGIN C19: prob. from *dog on it*, euphemism for *God damn it*.

**doggy** • adj. **1** of or like a dog. **2** fond of dogs. • n. (also **doggie**) (pl. **-ies**) a child's word for a dog.
– DERIVATIVES **dogginess** n.

**doggy bag** • n. a bag used to take home leftover food from a restaurant, supposedly for one's dog.

**doggy-paddle** • n. an elementary swimming stroke resembling that of a dog. • v. swim using this stroke.

**doghouse** • n. **1** N. Amer. a dog's kennel. **2** Sailing a raised standing area at the after end of a yacht's coachroof.
– PHRASES **in the doghouse** informal in disgrace or disfavour.

**dogie** /ˈdəʊgi/ • n. (pl. **-ies**) N. Amer. a motherless or neglected calf.
– ORIGIN C19: of unknown origin.

**dog Latin** • n. a debased form of Latin.

**dog-leg** • n. **1** a sharp bend. **2** Golf a hole where the fairway has a bend.

**dogma** /ˈdɒgmə/ • n. a principle or set of principles laid down by an authority as incontrovertible.
– ORIGIN C16: via late L. from Gk *dogma* 'opinion', from *dokein* 'seem good, think'.

**dogman** • n. (pl. **-men**) Austral./NZ a person directing the operator of a crane while sitting on the crane's load.

**dogmatic** /dɒgˈmatɪk/ • adj. inclined to impose dogma; firmly asserting personal opinions as true.
– DERIVATIVES **dogmatically** adv. **dogmatism** n. **dogmatist** n.
– ORIGIN C17: via late L. from Gk *dogmatikos*, from *dogma, dogmat-* (see **DOGMA**).

**dogmatics** • pl. n. [treated as sing.] a system of dogma, especially one laid down by the Roman Catholic Church.

**dogmatize** /ˈdɒgmətʌɪz/ (also **-ise**) • v. represent as an incontrovertible truth.

**do-gooder** • n. a well-meaning but unrealistic or interfering person.
– DERIVATIVES **do-goodery** n. **do-goodism** n.

**dog-paddle** • n. & v. chiefly N. Amer. another term for **DOGGY-PADDLE**.

**Dogrib** /ˈdɒgrɪb/ • n. **1** a member of a Dene people of NW Canada. **2** the Athabaskan language of this people.
– ORIGIN translation of Dogrib *Thlingchadinne* 'dog's flank', from the legend that their common ancestor was a dog.

**dog rose** • n. a delicately scented wild rose with pink or white flowers, commonly growing in hedgerows. [*Rosa canina* and other species.]

**dogsbody** • n. (pl. **-ies**) Brit. informal a person who is given boring, menial tasks.

**dogshore** • n. each of two blocks of timber positioned on each side of a ship on a slipway to prevent it sliding.

**dog sled** • n. a sled pulled by dogs.

**dog's mercury** • n. a plant of the spurge family, with hairy stems and small green flowers, occurring as a dominant plant of old woodland. [*Mercurialis perennis*.]
– ORIGIN C16: translating mod. L. *Mercurialis canina* (former taxonomic name).

**dogstail** • n. a fodder grass with spiky flower heads. [Genus *Cynosurus*: several species.]

**Dog Star** • n. Sirius, the brightest star in the sky.
– ORIGIN translating Gk *kuon* or L. *canicula* 'small dog'; so named as it appears to follow at the heels of Orion (the hunter).

**dog's-tooth violet** • n. a plant of the lily family with speckled leaves and pinkish-purple flowers with backward-curving pointed petals. [*Erythronium dens-canis* and related species.]

**dog tag** • n. **1** a metal tag attached to a dog's collar, giving its name and owner's address. **2** informal, chiefly N. Amer. a soldier's metal identity tag.

**dog-tired** • adj. extremely tired.

**dog-tooth** • n. **1** Architecture a small pointed moulding forming one of a series radiating like petals from a raised centre. **2** (also **dogstooth**) a small check pattern with notched corners suggestive of a canine tooth.

**dogtrot** • n. a gentle easy trot.

**dog violet** • n. a scentless wild violet with purple or lilac flowers. [*Viola riviniana* and other species.]

**dogwatch** • n. either of two short watches on a ship (4–6 or 6–8 p.m.).

**dog whelk** • n. a predatory marine mollusc found on the shore or in shallow waters. [*Nucella* and other genera.]

**dogwood** • n. a flowering shrub or small tree with red stems, colourful berries, and hard wood. [*Cornus sanguinea* and related species.]
– ORIGIN so named because the wood was formerly used to make 'dogs' (i.e. skewers).

**DoH** • abbrev. (in the UK) Department of Health.

**doh**[1] /dəʊ/ (also **do**) • n. Music (in tonic sol-fa) the first and eighth note of a major scale. ➤ the note C in the fixed-doh system.
– ORIGIN C18: from Ital. *do*, an arbitrarily chosen syllable.

**doh**[2] /dəː/ • exclam. informal used to comment on a foolish action.

**doily** /ˈdɔɪli/ • n. (pl. **-ies**) a small ornamental mat made of lace or paper, put on a plate under sweet food.
– ORIGIN C17 (orig. denoting a woollen material for sum-

mer wear): from *Doiley* or *Doyley*, the name of a C17 London draper.

**doing** ● n. **1** (also **doings**) the activities in which someone engages. ➤[treated as sing. or pl.] informal, chiefly Brit. things whose name one has forgotten. **2** (**doings**) informal excrement. **3** informal a beating or scolding. **4** activity or effort: *it would take some doing to calm him down.*

**doit** /dɔɪt/ ● n. archaic a very small amount of money.
– ORIGIN C16: from Mid. Low Ger. *doyt*, MDu. *duit*, of unknown origin.

**do-it-yourself** ● n. full form of **DIY**.

**dojo** /ˈdəʊdʒəʊ/ ● n. (pl. **-os**) a place in which judo and other martial arts are practised.
– ORIGIN Japanese, from *dō* 'way, pursuit' + *jō* 'a place'.

**dol.** ● abbrev. dollar(s).

**Dolby** /ˈdɒlbi, ˈdəʊl-/ ● n. trademark **1** an electronic noise-reduction system used in tape recording. **2** an electronic system providing stereophonic sound for cinemas and televisions.
– ORIGIN 1960s: named after the Amer. engineer Ray M. *Dolby*.

**dolce** /ˈdɒltʃeɪ/ ● adv. & adj. Music sweetly and softly.
– ORIGIN Ital., lit. 'sweet'.

**dolce far niente** /ˌdɒltʃeɪ fɑː nɪˈɛnteɪ/ ● n. pleasant idleness.
– ORIGIN Ital., 'sweet doing nothing'.

**Dolcelatte** /ˌdɒltʃəˈlɑːteɪ, -ˈlati/ ● n. trademark a kind of soft creamy blue-veined cheese from Italy.
– ORIGIN Ital., lit. 'sweet milk'.

**dolce vita** /ˌdɒltʃeɪ ˈviːtə/ ● n. a life of pleasure and luxury.
– ORIGIN Ital., lit. 'sweet life'.

**doldrums** /ˈdɒldrəmz/ ● pl. n. (**the doldrums**) **1** a state of stagnation or depression. **2** an equatorial region of the Atlantic Ocean with calms, sudden storms, and light unpredictable winds.
– ORIGIN C18 (as *doldrum* 'dull, sluggish person'): perh. from **DULL**.

**dole**[1] ● n. **1** (often in phr. **on the dole**) Brit. informal benefit paid by the state to the unemployed. ➤dated a charitable gift. **2** poetic/literary a person's lot or destiny. ● v. (**dole something out**) distribute something.
– ORIGIN OE *dāl* 'division, portion, or share', of Gmc origin; rel. to **DEAL**[1].

**dole**[2] ● n. archaic or poetic/literary sorrow; mourning.
– ORIGIN ME: from OFr. *doel* 'mourning', from pop. L. *dolus*, from L. *dolere* 'grieve'.

**doleful** ● adj. **1** sorrowful. **2** causing grief or misfortune.
– DERIVATIVES **dolefully** adv. **dolefulness** n.

**dolerite** /ˈdɒlərʌɪt/ ● n. Geology a dark, medium-grained igneous rock typically occurring in dykes and sills.
– ORIGIN C19: from Fr. *dolérite*, from Gk *doleros* 'deceptive' (because it resembles diorite).

**doli capax** /ˌdɒlɪ ˈkapaks/ ● adj. Law capable of intending to commit a crime, especially through being ten years old or more.
– ORIGIN L., 'capable of evil'.

**dolichocephalic** /ˌdɒlɪkə(ʊ)sɪˈfalɪk, -kɛˈfalɪk-/ ● adj. Anatomy having a relatively long skull. Often contrasted with **BRACHYCEPHALIC**.
– DERIVATIVES **dolichocephaly** n.
– ORIGIN C19: from Gk *dolikhos* 'long' + **-CEPHALIC**.

**doli incapax** /ɪnˈkapaks/ ● adj. Law incapable of intending to commit a crime, especially through being under ten years old.
– ORIGIN L., lit. 'incapable of evil'.

**doline** /dɒˈliːn/ (also **dolina** /dɒˈliːnə/) ● n. Geology a hollow or basin in a karstic region.
– ORIGIN C19: via Ger. from Slovene *dolina* 'valley'.

**doll**[1] ● n. **1** a small model of a human figure, used as a child's toy. **2** informal an attractive young woman or (in the US) man. ● v. (**doll someone up**) informal dress someone smartly and attractively.
– ORIGIN C16 (denoting a mistress): familiar form of the given name *Dorothy*.

**doll**[2] Brit. Horse Racing ● n. a temporary barrier on a race course or gallop. ● v. close off with a barrier.
– ORIGIN 1940s: perh. a var. of archaic *dool* 'boundary marker'.

**dollar** ● n. the basic monetary unit of the US, Canada, Australia, and certain countries in the Pacific, Caribbean, SE Asia, Africa, and South America.
– ORIGIN from early Flemish or Low Ger. *daler*, from Ger. *T(h)aler*, short for *Joachimsthaler*, a coin from the silver-mine of *Joachimsthal* ('Joachim's valley'), now *Jáchymov* in the Czech Republic.

**dollarbird** ● n. the eastern broad-billed roller of Asia and Australasia, with a conspicuous white coin-like mark on the wing. [*Eyrystomus orientalis*.]

**dollar diplomacy** ● n. the use of a country's financial power to extend its international influence.

**dollarization** (also **-sation**) ● n. **1** the process of aligning a country's currency with the US dollar. **2** the dominating effect of the US on a country's economy.

**dollar sign** (also **dollar mark**) ● n. the sign $, representing a dollar.

**dollop** ● n. informal a shapeless mass or lump, especially of soft food. ● v. (**dolloped**, **dolloping**) add or serve out in large shapeless quantities.
– ORIGIN C16 (denoting a clump of grass or weeds in a field): perh. of Scand. origin.

**doll's house** (N. Amer. also **dollhouse**) ● n. a miniature toy house for dolls.

**dolly** ● n. (pl. **-ies**) **1** a child's word for a doll. **2** informal, dated an attractive and stylish young woman. **3** a small platform on wheels for holding heavy objects, typically film cameras. **4** Cricket, informal an easy catch. **5** historical a short wooden pole for stirring clothes in a washtub. ● v. (**-ies**, **-ied**) (of a film camera) be moved on a dolly.

**dolly bird** ● n. Brit. informal, dated an attractive but unintelligent young woman.

**dolly mixtures** ● pl. n. Brit. a mixture of small variously shaped and coloured sweets.

**dolly tub** ● n. historical a washtub.

**Dolly Varden** /ˈvɑːd(ə)n/ ● n. **1** a large hat with a floral trimming and one drooping side, formerly worn by women. **2** a brightly spotted edible charr (fish) of western North America. [*Salvelinus malma*.]
– ORIGIN C19: from the name of a character in Dickens's *Barnaby Rudge*, who wore a similar hat.

**dolma** /ˈdɒlmə/ ● n. (pl. **dolmas** or **dolmades** /-ˈmɑːðɛz/) a Greek and Turkish delicacy of spiced rice and meat wrapped in vine or cabbage leaves.
– ORIGIN from mod. Gk *ntolmas* or its source, Turk. *dolma*, from *dolmak* 'fill, be filled'.

**dolman** /ˈdɒlmən/ ● n. a long Turkish robe open in front. ➤a woman's loose cloak with cape-like sleeves.
– ORIGIN C16: based on Turk. *dolama*, *dolaman*.

**dolman sleeve** ● n. a loose sleeve cut in one piece with the body of a garment.

**dolmen** /ˈdɒlmɛn/ ● n. a megalithic tomb with a large flat stone laid on upright ones.
– ORIGIN C19: from Fr., perh. via Breton from Cornish *tolmen* 'hole of a stone'.

**dolomite** /ˈdɒləmʌɪt/ ● n. a mineral or sedimentary rock consisting chiefly of a carbonate of calcium and magnesium.
– DERIVATIVES **dolomitic** adj.
– ORIGIN C18: from Fr., from the name of the Fr. geologist *Dolomieu* + **-ITE**[1].

**dolorous** /ˈdɒl(ə)rəs/ ● adj. poetic/literary feeling great sorrow or distress.
– DERIVATIVES **dolorously** adv.
– ORIGIN ME: from OFr. *doleros*, from late L. *dolorosus*, from L. *dolor* 'pain, grief'.

**dolostone** /ˈdɒləstəʊn/ ● n. Geology rock consisting of dolomite.

**dolour** /ˈdɒlə/ (US **dolor**) ● n. poetic/literary a state of great sorrow or distress.
– ORIGIN ME: via OFr. from L. *dolor* 'pain, grief'.

**dolphin** ● n. **1** a small gregarious and intelligent toothed whale with a beak-like snout and a curved fin on the back. [Families Delphinidae (marine) and Platanistidae

(**river dolphins**): many species.] **2** (also **dolphinfish**) another term for **DORADO** (in sense 1). **3** a bollard, pile, or buoy for mooring. **4** a structure protecting the pier of a bridge.
– ORIGIN ME: from OFr. *dauphin*, from Provençal *dalfin*, from L. *delphinus*, from Gk *delphin*.

**dolphinarium** /ˌdɒlfɪˈnɛːrɪəm/ ● n. (pl. **dolphinariums** or **dolphinaria**) an aquarium in which dolphins are kept and trained for public entertainment.

**dolt** /dəʊlt/ ● n. a stupid person.
– DERIVATIVES **doltish** adj. **doltishly** adv. **doltishness** n.
– ORIGIN C16: perh. a var. of *dulled*, past part. of **DULL**.

**Dom** /dɒm/ ● n. **1** a title prefixed to the names of some Roman Catholic dignitaries and Benedictine and Carthusian monks. **2** Portuguese form of **DON**[1] (in sense 2).
– ORIGIN from L. *dominus* 'master'.

**-dom** ● suffix forming nouns: **1** denoting a state or condition: *freedom*. **2** denoting rank or status: *earldom*. **3** denoting a domain: *fiefdom*. **4** denoting a class of people or attitudes associated with them: *officialdom*.
– ORIGIN OE *-dōm*, orig. meaning 'decree, judgement'.

**domain** /də(ʊ)ˈmeɪn/ ● n. **1** an area owned or controlled by a ruler or government. ➤a sphere of activity or knowledge. **2** Physics a discrete region of magnetism in ferromagnetic material. **3** Computing a distinct subset of the Internet with addresses sharing a common suffix. **4** Mathematics the possible values of the independent variable or variables of a function.
– DERIVATIVES **domanial** /dəˈmeɪnɪəl/ adj.
– ORIGIN ME: from Fr. *domaine*, alt. (by assoc. with L. *dominus* 'lord') of OFr. *demeine* (see **DEMESNE**).

**domaine** /dəˈmeɪn/ ● n. a vineyard.
– ORIGIN 1960s: from Fr., lit. 'estate' (see **DOMAIN**).

**dome** ● n. **1** a rounded vault forming the roof of a building or structure. ➤the revolving openable hemispherical roof of an observatory. **2** the rounded summit of a hill or mountain. ➤Geology a rounded uplifted landform or underground structure. **3** informal the top of the head. **4** poetic/literary a stately building. ● v. [often as noun **doming**] form a rounded shape; swell out.
– DERIVATIVES **domed** adj. **dome-like** adj.
– ORIGIN C16: from Fr. *dôme*, from Ital. *duomo* 'cathedral, dome', from L. *domus* 'house'.

**Domesday Book** /ˈduːmzdeɪ/ ● n. a comprehensive record of the extent, value, ownership, and liabilities of land in England, made in 1086 by order of William I.
– ORIGIN ME: var. of **DOOMSDAY**, because the book was regarded as a final authority.

**domestic** ● adj. **1** of or relating to a home or family affairs or relations. ➤of or for use in the home. **2** (of a person) fond of family life and running a home. **3** (of an animal) tame and kept by humans. **4** existing or occurring within a country. ● n. **1** (also **domestic worker** or **domestic help**) a person who is employed to do domestic tasks. **2** informal a violent quarrel between family members. **3** N. Amer. a product not made abroad.
– DERIVATIVES **domestically** adv.
– ORIGIN ME: from Fr. *domestique*, from L. *domesticus*, from *domus* 'house'.

**domesticate** ● v. **1** tame (an animal) and keep it as a pet or for farm produce. ➤humorous accustom (someone) to home life and domestic tasks. **2** cultivate (a plant) for food.
– DERIVATIVES **domesticable** adj. **domestication** n.

**domesticity** ● n. home or family life.

**domestic science** ● n. dated home economics.

**domical** /ˈdəʊmɪk(ə)l/ ● adj. domed.

**domicile** /ˈdɒmɪsʌɪl, -sɪl/ (also **domicil** /-sɪl/) ● n. formal or Law **1** the country in which a person has permanent residence. ➤chiefly N. Amer. a person's home. **2** the place at which a company or other body is registered. ● v. (**be domiciled**) formal or Law treat a specified country as a permanent home. ➤chiefly N. Amer. reside; be based.
– ORIGIN ME: via OFr. from L. *domicilium* 'dwelling', from *domus* 'home'.

**domiciliary** /ˌdɒmɪˈsɪlɪəri/ ● adj. concerned with or occurring in someone's home.

**dominance** ● n. **1** power and influence over others. **2** Genetics the phenomenon whereby one allelic form of a gene is expressed to the exclusion of the other. **3** Ecology the predominance of one or more species in a plant or animal community.
– DERIVATIVES **dominancy** n.

**dominant** ● adj. **1** most important, powerful, or influential. **2** (of a high place or object) overlooking others. **3** Genetics relating to or denoting heritable characteristics which are controlled by genes that are expressed in offspring even when inherited from only one parent. Often contrasted with **RECESSIVE**. **4** Ecology denoting the predominant species in a plant or animal community. ● n. Genetics **1** a dominant trait or gene. **2** Ecology a dominant species in a community. **3** Music the fifth note of the diatonic scale of any key, considered in relation to the key of the tonic.
– DERIVATIVES **dominantly** adv.

**dominate** /ˈdɒmɪneɪt/ ● v. **1** have a commanding or controlling influence over. **2** (of something tall or high) overlook.
– DERIVATIVES **domination** n. **dominator** n.
– ORIGIN C17 (earlier (ME) as *domination*): from L. *dominat-*, *dominari* 'rule, govern', from *dominus* 'lord, master'.

**dominatrix** /ˌdɒmɪˈneɪtrɪks/ ● n. (pl. **dominatrices** /-trɪsiːz/ or **dominatrixes**) a dominating woman, especially in sadomasochistic practices.
– ORIGIN C16: from L., fem. of *dominator*, from *dominat-*, *dominari* (see **DOMINATE**).

**domineer** /ˌdɒmɪˈnɪə/ ● v. [usu. as adj. **domineering**] behave in an arrogant and overbearing way.
– DERIVATIVES **domineeringly** adv.
– ORIGIN C16: from Du. *dominieren*, from Fr. *dominer*, from L. *dominari* (see **DOMINATE**).

**dominical** /dəˈmɪnɪk(ə)l/ ● adj. **1** of Sunday as the Lord's day. **2** of Jesus Christ as the lord.
– ORIGIN ME: from late L. *dominicalis*, from L. *dominicus*, from *dominus* 'lord, master'.

**dominical letter** ● n. any of the seven letters A–G used in Church calendars to indicate the date (1–7 January) of the first Sunday in the year.

**Dominican**[1] /dəˈmɪnɪk(ə)n/ ● n. a member of the Roman Catholic order of preaching friars founded by St Dominic, or of a similar religious order for women. ● adj. of or relating to St Dominic or the Dominicans.

**Dominican**[2] /dəˈmɪnɪk(ə)n/ ● n. a native or national of the Dominican Republic in the Caribbean. ● adj. of or relating to the Dominican Republic.

**Dominican**[3] /ˌdɒmɪˈniːk(ə)n, dəˈmɪnɪk(ə)n/ ● n. a native or national of the Caribbean island of Dominica. ● adj. of or relating to the island of Dominica.

**dominie** /ˈdɒmɪni/ ● n. (pl. **-ies**) **1** Scottish a schoolmaster. **2** chiefly US a pastor or clergyman.
– ORIGIN C17: alt. of L. *domine!* (vocative) 'master!, sir!', from *dominus* 'lord'.

**dominion** ● n. **1** sovereignty; control. **2** the territory of a sovereign or government. ➤(**Dominion**) historical a self-governing territory of the British Commonwealth.
– ORIGIN ME: via OFr. from med. L. *dominio(n-)*, from L. *dominium*, from *dominus* 'lord, master'.

**domino** /ˈdɒmɪnəʊ/ ● n. (pl. **-oes**) **1** any of 28 small oblong pieces marked with 0–6 pips in each half. ➤(**dominoes**) [treated as sing.] the game played with such pieces, each player in turn trying to lay down a domino with a value matching that of a piece at either end of the line already formed. **2** historical a loose cloak, worn with a mask for the upper part of the face at masquerades.
– ORIGIN C17: from Fr., denoting a hood worn by priests in winter, prob. based on L. *dominus* 'lord, master'.

**domino effect** ● n. the effect of the domino theory.

**domino theory** ● n. the theory that a political event in one country will cause similar events in neighbouring countries, like a row of falling dominoes.

**dom palm** ● n. variant spelling of **DOUM PALM**.

**don**[1] ● n. **1** a university teacher, especially a senior member of a college at Oxford or Cambridge. **2** (**Don**) a Spanish title prefixed to a male forename. ➤N. Amer. informal a high-ranking member of the Mafia.

– ORIGIN C16: from Sp., from L. *dominus* 'lord, master'.

**don**[2] ● v. (**donned**, **donning**) put on (an item of clothing).
– ORIGIN ME: contr. of *do on*; cf. DOFF.

**donate** ● v. **1** give (money or goods) for a good cause. **2** allow the removal of (blood or an organ) from one's body for transfusion or transplantation. **3** Chemistry & Physics provide or contribute (electrons or protons).
– DERIVATIVES **donator** n.

**donation** ● n. something that is given to a charity, especially a sum of money.
– ORIGIN ME: via OFr. from L. *donatio(n-)*, from *donare* 'give', based on *donum* 'gift'.

**Donatist** /'dəʊnətɪst/ ● n. a member of a schismatic Christian group in North Africa who held that only those living a blameless life belonged in the Church.
– DERIVATIVES **Donatism** n.
– ORIGIN from the group's leader *Donatus* (died *c.*355).

**donative** /'dəʊnətɪv/ rare ● n. a donation. ● adj. given as a donation. ➤ historical (of a benefice) given directly, not presentative.

**done** past participle of DO[1]. ● adj. **1** (of food) cooked thoroughly. **2** no longer happening or existing. **3** informal socially acceptable: *the done thing.* ● exclam. (in response to an offer) accepted.
– PHRASES **done for** informal in serious trouble. **done in** informal extremely tired.

**donee** /dəʊ'ni:/ ● n. a person who receives a gift. ➤ Law a person who is given a power of appointment.

**doner kebab** /'dɒnə, 'dəʊnə/ ● n. a Turkish dish consisting of spiced lamb cooked on a spit and served in slices, typically in pitta bread.
– ORIGIN from Turk. *döner kebap*, from *döner* 'rotating' and *kebap* 'roast meat'.

**dong**[1] ● v. **1** (of a bell) make a deep resonant sound. **2** Austral./NZ informal hit or punch. ● n. **1** a deep resonant sound. **2** Austral./NZ informal a punch. **3** vulgar slang a man's penis.

**dong**[2] ● n. the basic monetary unit of Vietnam, equal to 100 xu.
– ORIGIN from Vietnamese *dông* 'coin'.

**donga** /'dɒŋgə/ ● n. **1** S. African & Austral./NZ a dry watercourse. **2** Austral. a makeshift shelter.
– ORIGIN from Xhosa and Zulu *udonga*.

**dongle** /'dɒŋg(ə)l/ ● n. Computing an electronic device which must be attached to a computer in order for protected software to be used.
– ORIGIN 1980s: an arbitrary formation.

**donjon** /'dɒndʒ(ə)n, 'dʌn-/ ● n. the great tower or innermost keep of a castle.
– ORIGIN ME: var. of DUNGEON.

**Don Juan** /dɒn 'dʒʊən, 'hwɑ:n/ ● n. a seducer of women.
– ORIGIN C19: from the name of a legendary Sp. nobleman of dissolute life.

**donkey** ● n. (pl. **-eys**) **1** a domesticated hoofed mammal of the horse family with long ears and a braying call, used as a beast of burden. [*Equus asinus*.] **2** informal a foolish person. **3** (also **donkey stool**) a low stool astride which an artist sits. **4** a children's card game.
– PHRASES **donkey's years** informal a very long time. **talk the hind leg off a donkey** Brit. informal talk incessantly.
– ORIGIN C18: perh. from DUN[1], or from the given name *Duncan*.

**donkey derby** ● n. a race between competitors riding donkeys.

**donkey engine** ● n. a small auxiliary engine.

**donkey jacket** ● n. Brit. a heavy jacket with a patch of waterproof leather or plastic across the shoulders.

**donkeyman** ● n. (pl. **-men**) a man working in a ship's engine room.

**donkey work** ● n. informal the laborious part of a job.

**donna** /'dɒnə/ ● n. an Italian, Spanish, or Portuguese lady. ➤ (**Donna**) a courtesy title prefixed to the forename of such a lady.
– ORIGIN C17: from Ital., from L. *domina* 'mistress', fem. of *dominus* 'lord, master'; cf. DON[1].

**donnée** /'dɒneɪ/ (also **donné**) ● n. **1** a subject or theme of a narrative. **2** a basic fact or assumption.
– ORIGIN Fr., 'given'.

**donnish** ● adj. resembling or likened to a college don, particularly in having a pedantic manner.
– DERIVATIVES **donnishly** adv. **donnishness** n.

**donnybrook** /'dɒnɪbrʊk/ ● n. N. Amer. & Austral./NZ a heated argument.
– ORIGIN C19: from the name of a suburb of Dublin, Ireland, formerly famous for its annual fair.

**donor** /'dəʊnə, -nɔ:/ ● n. **1** a person who donates something. **2** Chemistry an atom or molecule that provides a pair of electrons in forming a coordinate bond. **3** Physics an impurity atom in a semiconductor which contributes conducting electrons to the material.
– ORIGIN ME: from OFr. *doneur*, from L. *donator*, from *donare* 'give'.

**donor card** ● n. a card carried to indicate consent to the use of one's organs for transplant surgery in the event of one's death.

**don't** ● contr. do not.

**donut** ● n. US spelling of DOUGHNUT.

**doodah** /'du:dɑ:/ (N. Amer. **doodad** /'du:dad/) ● n. informal an object that the speaker cannot name precisely.
– PHRASES **all of a doodah** very agitated.
– ORIGIN C20: perh. from the refrain of the song *Camptown Races*.

**doodle** ● v. scribble absent-mindedly. ● n. a drawing made absent-mindedly.
– DERIVATIVES **doodler** n.
– ORIGIN C17 (orig. as n. denoting a fool): from Low Ger. *dudeltopf, dudeldopp* 'simpleton'.

**doodlebug** ● n. informal **1** N. Amer. the larva of an ant lion. **2** US a divining rod. **3** Brit. informal term for **V-1**. **4** a small car or other vehicle.
– ORIGIN C19: from C17 *doodle* 'ninny' + BUG.

**doodly-squat** ● n. another term for DIDDLY-SQUAT.

**doo-doo** ● n. a child's word for excrement.

**doofus** /'du:fʌs/ (also **dufus**) ● n. (pl. **doofuses**) N. Amer. informal a stupid person.
– ORIGIN 1960s: perh. an alt. of GOOFUS, or from Scots *doof* 'dolt'.

**doohickey** /'du:hɪki/ ● n. (pl. **-eys**) N. Amer. informal a small object or gadget, especially one whose name the speaker cannot recall.
– ORIGIN C20: blend of *doodad* (see DOODAH) and HICKEY.

**doolally** /du:'lali/ ● adj. informal temporarily insane.
– ORIGIN C20: orig. *doolally tap*, Ind. army sl., from *Deolali* (a town near Bombay) + Urdu *tap* 'fever'.

**doom** ● n. death, destruction, or another terrible fate. ➤ archaic (in Christian belief) the Last Judgement. ● v. (usu. **be doomed to**) condemn to certain destruction, death, or failure.
– DERIVATIVES **doomily** adv. **doomy** adj.
– ORIGIN OE *dōm* 'statute, judgement', of Gmc origin, from a base meaning 'to put in place'; rel. to DO[1].

**doomsayer** ● n. a person who predicts disaster.
– DERIVATIVES **doomsaying** n.

**doomsday** ● n. the last day of the world's existence. ➤ (in religious belief) the day of the Last Judgement.

**doomster** ● n. a doomsayer.

**Doona** /'du:nə/ ● n. Austral. trademark a quilt or duvet.
– ORIGIN 1970s: perh. from Swed. *dun* (see DOWN[2]).

**door** ● n. a hinged, sliding, or revolving barrier at the entrance to a building, room, or vehicle, or in the framework of a cupboard. ➤ used to refer to a house: *he lived two doors away.*
– PHRASES **lay something at someone's door** blame someone for something. **out of doors** in or into the open air.
– DERIVATIVES **-doored** adj.
– ORIGIN OE *duru, dor*, of Gmc origin.

**doorbell** ● n. a bell in a building which can be rung by visitors arriving outside.

**do-or-die** ● adj. showing or requiring a determination not to compromise or be deterred.

**door frame** (also **doorcase**) ● n. the frame into which a door is fitted.

**door furniture** ● n. the handles, lock, and other fixtures on a door.

**door head** ● n. the upper part of a door frame.

**doorkeeper** ● n. a person on duty at the entrance to a building.

**doorknob** ● n. a door handle that is roundish in shape.

**doorknock** ● n. Austral./NZ a campaign of house visits to collect for a charity or appeal for a cause.

**doorman** ● n. (pl. **-men**) a man who is on duty at the entrance to a large building.

**doormat** ● n. **1** a mat placed in a doorway for wiping the shoes. **2** informal a submissive person.

**doornail** ● n. a stud in a door.
– PHRASES **(as) dead as a doornail** quite dead.

**doorpost** ● n. an upright part of a door frame.

**doorstep** ● n. **1** a step leading up to the outer door of a house. **2** Brit. informal a thick sandwich or slice. ● v. (**-stepped**, **-stepping**) Brit. informal **1** (of a journalist) wait uninvited outside the home of (someone) for an interview or photograph. **2** go from door to door selling or canvassing.
– PHRASES **on one's** (or **the**) **doorstep** very close by.

**doorstop** (also **doorstopper**) ● n. a fixed or heavy object that keeps a door open or in place.

**doorway** ● n. an entrance with a door.

**dooryard** ● n. N. Amer. a yard or garden by the door of a house.

**doo-wop** /'du:wɒp/ ● n. a style of pop music involving close harmony vocals and nonsense phrases, originating in the 1950s.
– ORIGIN imitative.

**doozy** /'du:zi/ (also **doozie**) ● n. (pl. **-ies**) informal, chiefly N. Amer. something outstanding or unique of its kind.
– ORIGIN C20: of unknown origin.

**dop** /dɒp/ ● n. (pl. **dops** or **doppe** /'dɒpə/) S. African **1** a rounded or spherical container. **2** (**dops/doppe**) grape skins, especially when left after winemaking. ➤ cheap liquor, especially brandy made from such grape skins.
– ORIGIN S. Afr. Du., 'shell, husk'.

**dopa** /'dəʊpə/ ● n. Biochemistry a compound which is present in nerve tissue as a precursor of dopamine (especially as the laevorotatory form **l-dopa**) and is used to treat Parkinsonism.
– ORIGIN C20: from Ger., acronym from the systematic name *dihydroxyphenylalanine*.

**dopamine** /'dəʊpəmi:n/ ● n. Biochemistry a compound present in the body as a neurotransmitter and as a precursor of other substances including adrenalin.
– ORIGIN 1950s: blend of **DOPA** and **AMINE**.

**dopant** /'dəʊp(ə)nt/ ● n. Electronics a substance used to produce a desired electrical characteristic in a semiconductor.
– ORIGIN 1960s: from **DOPE** + **-ANT**.

**dope** ● n. **1** informal an illegal drug, especially cannabis or (US) heroin. ➤ a drug used to enhance the performance of an athlete, racehorse, or greyhound. **2** informal a stupid person. **3** informal information. **4** a varnish used to strengthen the fabric surface of model aircraft. ➤ a lubricant. ➤ a substance added to petrol to increase its effectiveness. ● v. **1** administer dope to (a racehorse, greyhound, or athlete). ➤ (**be doped up**) informal be heavily under the influence of drugs. **2** cover with varnish or other thick liquid. **3** Electronics add an impurity to (a semiconductor) to produce a desired electrical characteristic. **4** (**dope something out**) informal, dated work something out. ● adj. black slang very good.
– DERIVATIVES **doper** n.
– ORIGIN C19 (in the sense 'thick liquid'): from Du. *doop* 'sauce', from *doopen* 'to dip, mix'.

**dopester** /'dəʊpstə/ ● n. N. Amer. informal a person who supplies information, especially on sport or politics.

**dopey** (also **dopy**) ● adj. (**-ier**, **-iest**) informal **1** stupefied by sleep or a drug. **2** idiotic.
– DERIVATIVES **dopily** adv. **dopiness** n.

**dopiaza** /'dəʊpɪɑ:ʒə/ ● n. an Indian dish consisting of meat in an onion sauce.
– ORIGIN from Hindi *do* 'two' + *pyāz* 'onion'.

**doppelgänger** /'dɒp(ə)l,gɛŋə, -,gaŋə/ ● n. an apparition or double of a living person.
– ORIGIN C19: from Ger., lit. 'double-goer'.

**Dopper** /'dɒpə/ ● n. (in South Africa) a member of the Gereformeerde Kerk, a strictly orthodox Calvinistic denomination.
– ORIGIN Afrik., of unknown origin.

**Doppler effect** (also **Doppler shift**) ● n. Physics an increase (or decrease) in the frequency of sound, light, or other waves as the source and observer move towards (or away from) each other.
– ORIGIN C19: named after the Austrian physicist Johann Christian *Doppler*.

**dopy** ● adj. variant spelling of **DOPEY**.

**dorado** /də'rɑ:dəʊ/ ● n. (pl. **-os**) **1** a large edible fish of warm seas, with silver and bright blue or green coloration. [*Coryphaena hippurus*.] **2** a South American freshwater game fish with a golden body and red fins. [*Salminus maxillosus*.]
– ORIGIN C17: from Sp., lit. 'gilded'.

**do-rag** ● n. US black slang a scarf or cloth worn to protect one's hairstyle.
– ORIGIN C20: from **HAIRDO**.

**dor beetle** /dɔ:/ ● n. a large black dung beetle that makes a droning sound in flight. [*Geotrupes stercorarius* and other species.]
– ORIGIN OE: prob. imitative.

**dorcas gazelle** /'dɔ:kəs/ ● n. a small gazelle found on semi-desert plains in North Africa and western Asia. [*Gazella dorcas*.]
– ORIGIN C19: from Gk *dorkas* 'gazelle'.

**Dorian** /'dɔ:rɪən/ ● n. a member of a people speaking the Doric dialect of Greek, thought to have entered Greece from the north *c.*1100 BC. ● adj. of or relating to this people or to Doris in central Greece.
– ORIGIN via L. from Gk *Dōrios* 'of Doris' + **-IAN**.

**Dorian mode** ● n. Music the mode represented by the natural diatonic scale D–D (containing a minor 3rd and minor 7th).

**Doric** /'dɒrɪk/ ● adj. **1** relating to or denoting a classical order of architecture characterized by a plain, sturdy column and a thick square abacus resting on a rounded moulding. **2** relating to or denoting the ancient Greek dialect of the Dorians. **3** archaic (of a dialect) broad. ● n. **1** the Doric order of architecture. **2** the ancient Greek dialect of the Dorians. **3** a broad dialect, especially that spoken in the north-east of Scotland.

**dork** ● n. informal **1** a socially inept person. **2** N. Amer. vulgar slang a man's penis.
– ORIGIN 1960s: perh. a var. of **DIRK**, influenced by **DICK**[1].

**dorm** ● n. informal a dormitory.

**dormant** ● adj. **1** (of an animal) in or as if in a deep sleep. ➤ Heraldry (of an animal) lying with its head on its paws. **2** (of a plant or bud) alive but not growing. **3** (of a volcano) temporarily inactive. **4** (of a disease) causing no symptoms but liable to recur.
– DERIVATIVES **dormancy** n.
– ORIGIN ME: from OFr., 'sleeping', pres. part. of *dormir*, from L. *dormire* 'to sleep'.

**dormer** (also **dormer window**) ● n. a window that projects vertically from a sloping roof.
– ORIGIN C16 (denoting a dormitory or bedroom window): from OFr. *dormeor* 'dormitory', from *dormir* 'to sleep'.

**Dormition** /dɔ:'mɪʃ(ə)n/ ● n. (in the Orthodox Church) the passing of the Virgin Mary from earthly life. ➤ the feast in honour of this on 15 August.
– ORIGIN C15: from Fr., from L. *dormitio(n-)* 'falling asleep', from *dormire* 'to sleep'.

**dormitory** /'dɔ:mɪt(ə)ri/ ● n. (pl. **-ies**) **1** a bedroom for a number of people in a school or institution. ➤ N. Amer. a college hall of residence. **2** [as modifier] denoting a small town or suburb from which people travel to work in a nearby city.
– ORIGIN ME: from L. *dormitorium*, neut. (used as n.) of *dormitorius*, from *dormire* 'to sleep'.

**Dormobile** /'dɔ:məbi:l/ ● n. Brit. trademark a motor vehicle that is fitted out as a caravan.

**dormouse** ● **n.** (pl. **dormice**) an agile mouse-like rodent with a bushy tail. [*Muscardinus avellanarius* and other species, family Gliridae.]
– ORIGIN ME: of unknown origin, but assoc. with Fr. *dormir* or L. *dormire* 'to sleep'.

**dormy** /ˈdɔːmi/ ● **adj.** Golf (of a player) ahead by as many holes as there are holes left to play: *dormy two.*
– ORIGIN C19: of unknown origin.

**dorp** /dɔːp/ ● **n.** S. African a small rural town or village.
– ORIGIN Du., 'village' (see **THORP**).

**dorsal** /ˈdɔːs(ə)l/ ● **adj.** Anatomy, Zoology, & Botany of, on, or relating to the upper side or back. Compare with **VENTRAL.**
– DERIVATIVES **dorsally** adv.
– ORIGIN ME: from late L. *dorsalis*, from L. *dorsum* 'back'.

**dorsal fin** ● **n.** Zoology an unpaired fin on the back of a fish or whale.

**Dorset Down** ● **n.** a sheep of a breed with a brown face and legs.

**Dorset Horn** ● **n.** a sheep of a breed with a white face and horns.

**dorsi-** ● **comb. form** towards or on the back: *dorsiventral.*
– ORIGIN from L. *dorsum* 'back'.

**dorsiflex** /ˈdɔːsɪflɛks/ ● **v.** Physiology bend (something) towards its upper surface.
– DERIVATIVES **dorsiflexion** n.

**dorsiventral** /ˌdɔːsɪˈvɛntr(ə)l/ ● **adj.** chiefly Botany **1** having dissimilar dorsal and ventral surfaces. **2** another term for **DORSOVENTRAL.**
– DERIVATIVES **dorsiventrality** n. **dorsiventrally** adv.

**dorso-** ● **comb. form** relating to the back: *dorsoventral.*
– ORIGIN from L. *dorsum* 'back'.

**dorsolateral** /ˌdɔːsə(ʊ)ˈlat(ə)r(ə)l/ ● **adj.** Anatomy & Biology of or relating to the dorsal and lateral surfaces.
– DERIVATIVES **dorsolaterally** adv.

**dorsoventral** /ˌdɔːsə(ʊ)ˈvɛntr(ə)l/ ● **adj.** Anatomy & Biology extending along or denoting an axis joining the dorsal and ventral surfaces. ➤ of or relating to these surfaces.
– DERIVATIVES **dorsoventrally** adv.

**dorsum** /ˈdɔːsəm/ ● **n.** (pl. **dorsa**) Anatomy & Zoology the dorsal part of an organism or structure.
– ORIGIN C18 (denoting a long hill or ridge): from L., 'back'.

**dory**[1] /ˈdɔːri/ ● **n.** (pl. **-ies**) a deep-bodied marine fish with a large mouth. [Families Zeidae and Oreosomatidae: several species, including the John Dory.]
– ORIGIN ME: from Fr. *dorée*, fem. past part. of *dorer* 'gild', based on L. *aurum* 'gold'.

**dory**[2] /ˈdɔːri/ ● **n.** (pl. **-ies**) a small flat-bottomed rowing boat with a high bow and stern.
– ORIGIN C18: perh. from Miskito *dóri* 'dugout'.

**doryphore** /ˈdɒrɪfɔː/ ● **n.** rare a pedantic and persistent critic.
– ORIGIN 1950s: from Fr., lit. 'Colorado beetle', from Gk *doruphoros* 'spear-carrier'.

**DOS** ● **abbrev.** Computing disk operating system.

**dosa** /ˈdəʊsə/ ● **n.** (pl. **dosas** or **dosai** /ˈdəʊsʌɪ/) (in Indian cooking) a pancake made from rice flour.
– ORIGIN from Tamil *tōcai.*

**dos-à-dos** /ˌdəʊzəˈdəʊ/ ● **adj.** (of two books) bound together with a shared central board and facing in opposite directions. ● **n.** (pl. same) a seat or carriage in which the occupants sit back to back.
– ORIGIN Fr., 'back to back'.

**dosage** ● **n.** the size of a dose of medicine or radiation.

**dose** ● **n. 1** a quantity of a medicine or drug taken at one time. ➤ an amount of ionizing radiation received or absorbed at one time. **2** informal a venereal infection. **3** informal a quantity of something necessary but unpleasant. ● **v. 1** administer a dose to. **2** adulterate or blend (a substance) with another.
– PHRASES **like a dose of salts** Brit. informal very fast and efficiently. [from the use of Epsom salts as an aperient.]
– ORIGIN ME: from Fr., via late L. from Gk *dosis* 'gift', from *didonai* 'give'.

**dose equivalent** ● **n.** an estimate of the biological effect of a dose of ionizing radiation, expressed in sieverts.

**dosh** ● **n.** Brit. informal money.
– ORIGIN 1950s: of unknown origin.

**do-si-do** /ˌdəʊzɪˈdəʊ, -sɪ-/ (also **do-se-do**) ● **n.** (pl. **-os**) (in country dancing) a figure in which two dancers pass round each other back to back and return to their original positions.
– ORIGIN 1920s: alt. of **DOS-À-DOS.**

**dosimeter** /dəʊˈsɪmɪtə/ (also **dosemeter** /ˈdəʊsmiːtə/) ● **n.** a device used to measure an absorbed dose of ionizing radiation.
– DERIVATIVES **dosimetric** adj. **dosimetry** n.

**doss** Brit. informal ● **v. 1** sleep in rough accommodation or on an improvised bed. **2** spend time idly. ● **n. 1** archaic a bed in a cheap lodging house. **2** an easy task giving time for idling.
– DERIVATIVES **dosser** n.
– ORIGIN C18: perh. based on L. *dorsum* 'back'.

**dossal** /ˈdɒs(ə)l/ ● **n.** an ornamental cloth hung behind an altar in a church or at the sides of a chancel.
– ORIGIN C17: from med. L. *dossale*, from late L. *dorsalis* (see **DORSAL**).

**dosshouse** ● **n.** Brit. informal a cheap lodging house for homeless people.

**dossier** /ˈdɒsɪə, -ɪeɪ, -jeɪ/ ● **n.** a collection of documents about a person or subject.
– ORIGIN C19: from Fr., denoting a bundle of papers with a label on the back, from *dos* 'back', based on L. *dorsum.*

**dost** /dʌst/ archaic second person singular present of **DO**[1].

**DoT** ● **abbrev. 1** (in the UK and Canada) Department of Transport. **2** (in the US) Department of Transportation.

**dot**[1] ● **n.** a small round mark or spot. ➤ Music a dot used to denote the lengthening of a note or rest by half, or to indicate staccato. ➤ the shorter signal of the two used in Morse code. ● **v.** (**dotted**, **dotting**) **1** mark with a dot or dots. **2** scatter or be scattered over (an area). **3** Brit. informal hit (someone).
– PHRASES **dot the i's and cross the t's** informal ensure that all details are correct. **on the dot** informal exactly on time. **the year dot** Brit. informal a very long time ago.
– DERIVATIVES **dotter** n.
– ORIGIN OE *dott* 'head of a boil'; perh. influenced by Du. *dot* 'a knot'.

**dot**[2] ● **n.** archaic a dowry from which only the interest or annual income was available to the husband.
– ORIGIN from Fr., from L. *dos, dot-* (see **DOWER**).

**dotage** /ˈdəʊtɪdʒ/ ● **n.** the period of life in which a person is old and weak.
– ORIGIN ME: from **DOTE** + **-AGE.**

**dotard** /ˈdəʊtəd/ ● **n.** an old person, especially one who is weak or senile.

**dot-com** ● **n.** a company that conducts its business on the Internet.
– ORIGIN from 'com' in an Internet address, indicating a commercial site.

**dote** ● **v. 1** (**dote on/upon**) be extremely and uncritically fond of. **2** archaic be silly or feeble-minded, especially as a result of old age.
– DERIVATIVES **doter** n. **doting** adj. **dotingly** adv.
– ORIGIN ME: of uncertain origin; rel. to MDu. *doten* 'be silly'.

**doth** /dʌθ/ archaic third person singular present of **DO**[1].

**dotish** ● **adj.** archaic or W. Indian stupid or silly.
– ORIGIN C16: from obs. *dote* 'folly' + **-ISH**[1].

**dot matrix** ● **n.** a grid of dots which are filled selectively to produce an image on a screen or paper.

**dot product** ● **n.** another term for **SCALAR PRODUCT.**

**dotted line** ● **n.** a line of dots or dashes, especially as a space for a signature on a contract.

**dotterel** /ˈdɒt(ə)r(ə)l/ ● **n.** a small migratory plover which breeds in northern mountains and tundra. [*Eudromias morinellus.*] ➤ chiefly Austral./NZ used in names of other small plovers.
– ORIGIN ME: from **DOTE** (with ref. to the birds' tameness) + **-REL**; cf. **DODO.**

**dottle** /ˈdɒt(ə)l/ ● **n.** a remnant of tobacco left in a pipe

after smoking.
– ORIGIN ME (denoting a plug for a barrel): from **DOT**[1] + **-LE**[1].

**dotty** ● adj. (**-ier, -iest**) informal, chiefly Brit. **1** slightly mad or eccentric. **2** (**dotty about**) infatuated with.
– DERIVATIVES **dottily** adv. **dottiness** n.
– ORIGIN C19: perh. from obs. *dote* 'simpleton, fool'.

**double** ● adj. **1** consisting of two equal, identical, or similar parts or things. ➤designed to be used by two people. ➤having two different roles or interpretations. ➤(of a domino) having the same number of pips on each half. **2** having twice the usual size, quantity, or strength. ➤(of a flower) having more than one circle of petals. **3** Music lower in pitch by an octave. ● predet. twice as much or as many. ● adv. at or to twice the amount or extent. ● n. **1** a thing which is twice as large as usual or is made up of two parts. **2** Brit. two sporting victories or championships in the same season, event, etc. **3** a system of betting in which the winnings from the first bet are transferred to a second. **4** Bridge a call that increases the penalty points for the defenders if the declarer fails to make the contract. **5** Darts a hit on the ring enclosed by the two outer circles of a dartboard, scoring double. **6** a person who looks exactly like another. **7** (**doubles**) a game involving sides made up of two players. **8** Bell-ringing a system of change-ringing using five bells, with two pairs changing places each time. ● pron. an amount twice as large as usual. ● v. **1** make or become double. ➤(**double up**) use the winnings from a bet as stake for another bet. ➤(**double up**) share a room. **2** fold or bend over on itself. ➤(**double up**) bend over or curl up, typically with pain or mirth. ➤(usu. **double back**) go back in the direction one has come. **3** (**double (up) as**) be used in or play another, different role. **4** Music add the same note in a higher or lower octave to (a note). **5** Bridge call a double. **6** Snooker pot (a ball) by making it rebound off a cushion.
– PHRASES **at** (or **on**) **the double** very fast. **double or nothing** (or Brit. **quits**) a gamble to decide whether a debt should be doubled or cancelled.
– DERIVATIVES **doubleness** n. **doubler** n. **doubly** adv.
– ORIGIN ME: via OFr. from L. *duplus* (see **DUPLE**).

**double acrostic** ● n. an acrostic using the first and last letters of each line.

**double act** ● n. a performance involving two people.

**double agent** ● n. an agent who pretends to act as a spy for one country while in fact acting for its enemy.

**double axe** ● n. an axe with two blades.

**double-bank** ● v. chiefly Brit. arrange in two similar or parallel lines.

**double bar** ● n. a pair of closely spaced lines marking the end of a piece of music.

**double-barrelled** ● adj. **1** (of a gun) having two barrels. **2** Brit. (of a surname) having two parts joined by a hyphen.

**double bass** ● n. the largest and lowest-pitched instrument of the violin family.

**double bassoon** ● n. a bassoon that is larger and longer than usual and an octave lower in pitch.

**double bill** ● n. a programme of entertainment with two main items.

**double bind** ● n. a dilemma.

**double-blind** ● adj. denoting a test or trial in which information which may influence the behaviour of the tester or subject is withheld.

**double bluff** ● n. an action or statement intended to appear as a bluff, but which is in fact genuine.

**double boiler** ● n. a saucepan with a detachable upper compartment heated by boiling water in the lower one.

**double bond** ● n. a chemical bond in which two pairs of electrons are shared between two atoms.

**double-book** ● v. inadvertently reserve (something) for two different customers at the same time.

**double-breasted** ● adj. (of a jacket or coat) having a large overlap at the front and two rows of buttons.

**double-check** ● v. check again.

**double chin** ● n. a roll of flesh below a person's chin.
– DERIVATIVES **double-chinned** adj.

**double concerto** ● n. a concerto for two solo instruments.

**double cream** ● n. Brit. thick cream containing a high proportion of milk fat.

**double-cross** ● v. deceive or betray (a person one is supposedly helping). ● n. an act of double-crossing.
– DERIVATIVES **double-crosser** n.

**double dagger** (also **double obelus, double obelisk**) ● n. a symbol (‡) used to introduce an annotation.

**double-dealing** ● n. deceitful behaviour. ● adj. acting deceitfully.
– DERIVATIVES **double-dealer** n.

**double-decker** ● n. something, especially a bus, with two levels.

**double-declutch** ● v. Brit. release and re-engage the clutch of a vehicle twice when changing gear.

**double decomposition** ● n. Chemistry a reaction in which two compounds exchange ions.

**double-density** ● adj. Computing (of a disk) having twice the basic capacity.

**double-dip** ● v. N. Amer. informal illicitly obtain an income from two different sources.

**double Dutch** ● n. **1** Brit. informal incomprehensible language. **2** N. Amer. a jumping game played with two skipping ropes swung in opposite directions.

**double-dyed** ● adj. thoroughly imbued with a particular quality: *a double-dyed Liberal.*

**double eagle** ● n. **1** a representation of a two-headed eagle. **2** US historical a gold coin worth twenty dollars. **3** Golf a score of three strokes under par.

**double-edged** ● adj. **1** (of a knife or sword) having two cutting edges. **2** having two contradictory aspects or possible outcomes.

**double-ender** ● n. a boat in which stern and bow are similarly tapered.

**double entendre** /ˌduːb(ə)l ɒ̃ˈtɒ̃dr(ə)/ ● n. (pl. **double entendres** pronunc. same) a word or phrase open to two interpretations, one of which is usually indecent.
– ORIGIN C17: from obs. Fr. (now *double entente*), 'double understanding'.

**double-entry** ● adj. denoting a system of bookkeeping in which each transaction is entered as a debit in one account and a credit in another.

**double exposure** ● n. the repeated exposure of a photographic plate or film.

**double-faced** ● adj. **1** deceitful. **2** (of a fabric) finished on both sides.

**double fault** ● n. Tennis an instance of two consecutive faults in serving, counting as a point against the server. ● v. (**double-fault**) serve a double fault.

**double feature** ● n. a cinema programme with two films.

**double figures** ● pl. n. a number between 10 and 99.

**double first** ● n. Brit. a university degree with first-class honours in two subjects or examinations.

**double flat** ● n. a sign (𝄫) placed before a musical note to indicate that it is to be lowered two semitones. ➤a note so marked or lowered.

**double-fronted** ● adj. (of a house) with principal windows either side of the front door.

**double glazing** ● n. windows having two layers of glass with a space between them, designed to reduce heat loss and exclude noise.
– DERIVATIVES **double-glaze** v.

**Double Gloucester** ● n. a hard cheese originally made in Gloucestershire.
– ORIGIN so named because the curd is milled twice.

**double-header** ● n. **1** a train pulled by two locomotives. **2** chiefly N. Amer. a sporting event in which two games are played in succession at the same venue.
– DERIVATIVES **double-headed** adj.

**double helix** ● n. a pair of parallel helices intertwined about a common axis, especially that in the structure of DNA.

**double indemnity** ● n. chiefly N. Amer. provision for payment of double the face amount of an insurance policy under certain conditions.

**double jeopardy** • **n.** Law the prosecution of a person twice for the same offence.

**double-jointed** • **adj.** (of a person) having unusually flexible joints.
– DERIVATIVES **double-jointedness** n.

**double knitting** • **n.** a grade of yarn of medium thickness, used in hand knitting.

**double napoleon** • **n.** historical a gold forty-franc French coin.

**double negative** • **n.** Grammar **1** a negative statement containing two negative elements (e.g. *didn't say nothing*), regarded as incorrect in standard English. **2** a positive statement in which two negative elements are used to produce the positive force, e.g. *there is not nothing to worry about!*

**double obelus** (also **double obelisk**) • **n.** another term for **DOUBLE DAGGER**.

**double-park** • **v.** park (a vehicle) alongside one that is already parked.

**double play** • **n.** Baseball a defensive play in which two runners are put out.

**double pneumonia** • **n.** pneumonia affecting both lungs.

**double quick** • **adj. & adv.** informal very quick or quickly.

**double reed** • **n.** Music a reed with two slightly separated blades, used for playing a wind instrument such as an oboe or bassoon.

**double refraction** • **n.** Physics division of a single incident light ray into two separate rays in an anisotropic medium.

**double rhyme** • **n.** a rhyme involving two syllables in each rhyming line.

**double salt** • **n.** Chemistry a salt composed of two simple salts but with a different crystal structure from either.

**double saucepan** • **n.** Brit. a double boiler.

**double sharp** • **n.** a sign (𝄪) placed before a musical note to indicate that it is to be raised two semitones. ➤a note so marked or raised.

**doublespeak** • **n.** deliberately ambiguous or obscure language.
– ORIGIN 1949: coined by George Orwell (see **DOUBLETHINK**).

**double standard** • **n.** a rule or principle applied unfairly in different ways to different people.

**double star** • **n.** two stars actually or apparently very close together.

**double-stopping** • **n.** the sounding of two strings at once on a violin or similar instrument.
– DERIVATIVES **double stop** n.

**doublet** • **n.** **1** a man's short close-fitting padded jacket, commonly worn from the 14th to the 17th century. **2** a pair of similar things, in particular either of two words having the same derivation but different meanings, for example *fashion* and *faction*. **3** technical a pair of similar things, e.g. lines in a spectrum. **4** (**doublets**) the same number on two dice thrown at once.
– ORIGIN ME: from OFr., 'something folded', from *double* 'double'.

**double take** • **n.** a delayed reaction to something unexpected, immediately after one's first reaction.

**doubletalk** • **n.** chiefly N. Amer. doublespeak.

**double-team** • **v.** N. Amer. (in ball games) block (an opponent) with two players.

**doublethink** • **n.** the acceptance of contrary opinions or beliefs at the same time.
– ORIGIN 1949: coined by George Orwell in his novel *Nineteen Eighty-Four.*

**double time** • **n.** **1** a rate of pay equal to double the standard rate. **2** Military a regulation running pace. **3** Music a rhythm twice as fast as an earlier one.

**doubleton** /ˈdʌb(ə)lt(ə)n/ • **n.** (in card games) a pair of cards which are the only cards of their suit in a hand.
– ORIGIN C20: from **DOUBLE**, on the pattern of *singleton.*

**double tonguing** • **n.** Music the use of two alternating movements of the tongue in playing rapid passages on a wind instrument.

**double top** • **n.** Darts a score of double twenty.

**double vision** • **n.** the perception of two overlapping images of a single scene.

**double whammy** • **n.** informal a twofold blow or setback.

**double-wide** • **n.** N. Amer. a semi-permanent mobile home consisting of two connected units.

**doubloon** /dʌˈbluːn/ • **n.** historical a Spanish gold coin.
– ORIGIN from Fr. *doublon* or its source, Sp. *doblón*, from *doble* 'double' (because the coin was worth double the value of a pistole).

**doublure** /duːbˈljʊə/ • **n.** an ornamental lining, especially of leather, in a book cover.
– ORIGIN Fr., 'lining', from *doubler* 'to line'.

**doubt** • **n.** a feeling of uncertainty or lack of conviction. • **v.** **1** feel uncertain about. ➤question the truth or fact of. ➤disbelieve (someone). **2** Brit. archaic be afraid.
– PHRASES **beyond doubt** allowing no uncertainty. **in doubt 1** open to question. **2** feeling uncertain. **no doubt 1** certainly. **2** probably.
– DERIVATIVES **doubtable** adj. **doubter** n. **doubting** adj. **doubtingly** adv.
– ORIGIN ME: from OFr. *doute* (n.), *douter* (v.), from L. *dubitare* 'hesitate', from *dubius* (see **DUBIOUS**).

**doubtful** • **adj.** **1** uncertain. **2** not known with certainty. ➤improbable. ➤not established as genuine.
– DERIVATIVES **doubtfully** adv. **doubtfulness** n.

**doubting Thomas** • **n.** a person who refuses to believe something without proof.
– ORIGIN C17: with biblical allusion to the apostle Thomas (John 20: 24–29).

**doubtless** • **adv.** very probably.
– DERIVATIVES **doubtlessly** adv.

**douce** /duːs/ • **adj.** chiefly Scottish sober, gentle, and sedate.
– ORIGIN ME: from OFr. *dous*, *douce*, from L. *dulcis* 'sweet'.

**douceur** /duːˈsəː, French dusœʀ/ • **n.** a bribe.
– ORIGIN Fr., lit. 'sweetness'.

**douche** /duːʃ/ • **n.** a shower of water. ➤a jet of liquid applied to part of the body for cleansing or medicinal purposes. ➤a device for washing out the vagina as a contraceptive measure. • **v.** spray or shower with water. ➤use a contraceptive douche.
– ORIGIN C18: via Fr. from Ital. *doccia* 'conduit pipe'.

**douc langur** /duːk/ (also **douc monkey**) • **n.** a langur with black, white, and orange fur, native to the tropical rainforests of SE Asia. [*Pygathrix nemaeus.*]
– ORIGIN C18: via Fr. from Vietnamese.

**dough** • **n.** **1** a thick, malleable mixture of flour and liquid, for baking into bread or pastry. **2** informal money.
– DERIVATIVES **doughiness** n. **doughy** adj. (**-ier, -iest**).
– ORIGIN OE *dāg*, of Gmc origin.

**doughboy** • **n.** **1** a boiled or deep-fried dumpling. **2** US informal (especially in the First World War) a United States infantryman.

**doughnut** (also US **donut**) • **n.** **1** a small fried cake or ring of sweetened dough. **2** a ring-shaped object.

**doughty** /ˈdaʊti/ • **adj.** (**-ier, -iest**) archaic or humorous brave and resolute.
– DERIVATIVES **doughtily** adv. **doughtiness** n.
– ORIGIN OE *dohtig*, var. of *dyhtig*, of Gmc origin.

**Douglas fir** • **n.** a tall, slender conifer native to western North America. [*Pseudotsuga menziesii.*]
– ORIGIN C19: named after the Sc. botanist and explorer David *Douglas.*

**doula** /ˈduːlə/ • **n.** a woman giving support, help, and advice to another woman during pregnancy and during and after the birth.
– ORIGIN mod. Gk, from Gk *doulē* 'female slave'.

**doum palm** /duːm/ (also **dom palm**) • **n.** an Egyptian palm tree producing edible fruit and a vegetable ivory substitute. [*Hyphaene thebaica.*]
– ORIGIN C18: from Arab. *dawm*, *dūm*.

**dour** /ˈdʊə, ˈdaʊə/ • **adj.** very severe, stern, or gloomy.
– DERIVATIVES **dourly** adv. **dourness** n.
– ORIGIN ME (orig. Scots): prob. from Sc. Gaelic *dúr* 'dull, obstinate, stupid', perh. from L. *durus* 'hard'.

**dourocouli** /ˌdʊərʊ'ku:li/ ● **n.** (pl. **dourocoulis**) a large-eyed chiefly nocturnal monkey found in South America. [Genus *Aotus*: two or more species.]
– ORIGIN C19: prob. a S. Amer. Ind. name.

**douse** /daʊs/ (also **dowse**) ● **v. 1** drench with liquid. **2** extinguish (a fire or light). **3** Sailing lower (a sail) quickly.
– ORIGIN C17: perh. imitative, influenced by **SOUSE**, or perh. from dial. *douse* 'strike, beat', from MDu. and Low Ger. *dossen*.

**dout** /daʊt/ (also **dowt**) chiefly Scottish ● **v.** extinguish (a fire or light). ● **n.** a cigarette end.
– ORIGIN C16 (as v.): contr. of *do out*.

**dove**[1] /dʌv/ ● **n. 1** a stocky seed- or fruit-eating bird with a small head, short legs, and a cooing voice, similar to but generally smaller and more delicate than a pigeon. [Family Columbidae: many species.] **2** a person who advocates peaceful or conciliatory policies. **3** (**Dove**) (in Christian art and poetry) the Holy Spirit.
– DERIVATIVES **dovelike** adj. **dovish** adj.
– ORIGIN ME: from ON *dúfa*.

**dove**[2] /dəʊv/ chiefly N. Amer. past of **DIVE**.

**dovecote** /'dʌvkɒt/ (also **dovecot**) ● **n.** a shelter with nest holes for domesticated pigeons.

**dove grey** ● **n.** light grey.

**dovekie** /'dʌvki/ ● **n.** chiefly N. Amer. another term for **LITTLE AUK**.
– ORIGIN C19: from a Scots dimin. of **DOVE**[1].

**Dover sole** ● **n.** a marine flatfish which is highly valued as food. [*Solea solea* (Europe) and *Microstomus pacificus* (eastern Pacific).]

**dove's-foot cranesbill** ● **n.** a cranesbill with white downy hairs on the leaves, spreading stems, and leaves that resemble a bird's foot. [*Geranium molle*.]

**dove shell** ● **n.** a small mollusc with a robust shell, occurring in tropical and subtropical seas. [*Pyrene* and other genera.]

**dovetail** ● **n.** a joint formed by one or more tapered tenons which interlock with corresponding mortises. ● **v. 1** join together by means of a dovetail. **2** fit together easily or conveniently.

**dove tree** ● **n.** a slender deciduous Chinese tree with flowers that bear large white bracts resembling doves' wings. [*Davidia involucrata*.]

**dowager** /'daʊədʒə/ ● **n. 1** a widow with a title or property derived from her late husband. **2** informal a dignified elderly woman.
– ORIGIN C16: from OFr. *douagiere*, from *douage* 'dower', from *douer* 'endow', from L. *dotare* (see **DOWER**).

**dowager's hump** ● **n.** forward curvature of the spine resulting in a stoop.

**dowd** /daʊd/ ● **n.** a dowdy person.
– ORIGIN ME: of unknown origin.

**dowdy** ● **adj.** (**-ier**, **-iest**) (especially of a woman) unfashionable and dull in appearance.
– DERIVATIVES **dowdily** adv. **dowdiness** n.

**dowel** /'daʊəl/ ● **n.** a headless peg used for holding together components. ● **v.** (**dowelled**, **dowelling**; US **doweled**, **doweling**) fasten with a dowel.
– ORIGIN ME: perh. from Mid. Low Ger. *dovel*.

**dowelling** (US **doweling**) ● **n.** cylindrical rods for cutting into dowels.

**dower** /'daʊə/ ● **n. 1** a widow's share for life of her husband's estate. **2** archaic a dowry. ● **v.** archaic give a dowry to.
– ORIGIN ME: from OFr. *douaire*, from med. L. *dotarium*, from L. *dotare* 'endow', from *dos*, *dot-* 'dowry'; rel. to *dare* 'give'.

**dower house** ● **n.** Brit. a house intended for a widow, typically one on her late husband's estate.

**dowitcher** /'daʊɪtʃə/ ● **n.** a large North American sandpiper with a long straight bill. [Genus *Limnodromus*: two species.]
– ORIGIN C19: from Iroquoian.

**Dow Jones index** /daʊ'dʒəʊnz/ (also **Dow Jones average**) ● **n.** an index of figures indicating the relative price of shares on the New York Stock Exchange.
– ORIGIN from the name of the Amer. financial news agency *Dow Jones & Co, Inc.*

**down**[1] ● **adv. 1** towards or in a lower place or position. ➤to or at a place perceived as lower. ➤away from the north. ➤Brit. away from the capital or major city. ➤Brit. away from a university, especially Oxford or Cambridge. ➤so as to lie flush or flat. **2** to or at a lower level or value. ➤to a smaller amount or size, or a simpler or more basic state. ➤from an earlier to a later point in time or order. **3** in or into a weaker or worse position, mood, or condition. ➤(of a computer system) out of action. **4** (**down with** ——) expressing strong dislike. **5** in or into writing. ➤on or on to a list, schedule, or record. **6** (with reference to partial payment of a sum of money) made initially or on the spot. **7** (of sailing) with the current or the wind. ➤(of a ship's helm) moved round to leeward. **8** American Football (of the ball or a player in possession) not in play. ● **prep. 1** from a higher to a lower point of. **2** at a point further along the course of. ➤along the course or extent of. **3** throughout (a period of time). **4** informal at or to (a place). ● **adj. 1** directed or moving towards a lower place or position. ➤denoting trains travelling away from the main terminus. **2** unhappy. **3** (of a computer system) out of action. **4** US black slang supporting or going along with. ➤following the latest fashion. **5** Physics denoting a flavour of quark having a charge of −⅓. ● **v.** informal **1** knock or bring to the ground. **2** consume (a drink). **3** (of a golfer) sink (a putt). ● **n. 1** American Football a chance for a team to advance the ball, ending when the ball-carrier is tackled or the ball becomes out of play. **2** (**downs**) informal unwelcome events. **3** informal a period of unhappiness.
– PHRASES **be** (or **have a**) **down on** informal feel hostile towards. **be down to 1** be attributable to (a factor). ➤be the responsibility of. **2** be left with only (the specified amount). **down in the mouth** informal unhappy. **down on one's luck** informal having a period of bad luck. **down tools** Brit. informal stop work. **have** (or **put**) **someone/thing down as** judge someone or something to be (a particular type).
– ORIGIN OE *dūn*, *dūne*, shortened from *adūne* 'downward', from the phr. *of dūne* 'off the hill' (see **DOWN**[3]).

**down**[2] ● **n. 1** soft fine feathers forming the covering of a young bird or an insulating layer below the contour feathers of an adult bird, used for stuffing cushions and quilts. **2** fine soft hair on a person's skin. ➤short soft hairs on leaves, fruit, or seeds.
– ORIGIN ME: from ON *dúnn*.

**down**[3] ● **n. 1** a gently rolling hill. ➤(**the Downs**) ridges of undulating chalk and limestone hills in southern England. **2** (**the Downs**) a stretch of sea off the east coast of Kent.
– ORIGIN OE *dūn* 'hill', perh. ult. of Celtic origin and rel. to Old Ir. *dún* and obs. Welsh *din* 'fort'.

**down-and-dirty** ● **adj.** informal, chiefly N. Amer. **1** highly competitive or unprincipled. **2** explicit.

**down and out** ● **adj. 1** destitute. **2** (of a boxer) knocked down and unable to continue fighting. ● **n.** (**down-and-out**) a destitute person.

**down at heel** ● **adj.** chiefly Brit. **1** (of a shoe) with the heel worn down. **2** shabby or impoverished.

**downbeat** ● **adj. 1** pessimistic; gloomy. **2** understated. ● **n.** Music an accented beat, usually the first of the bar.

**downcast** ● **adj. 1** (of eyes) looking downwards. **2** (of a person) feeling despondent. ● **n.** a shaft dug in a mine for ventilation.

**downcomer** ● **n.** a pipe for the downward transport of water or gas from the top of a furnace or boiler.

**downconverter** ● **n.** Electronics a device that converts a signal to a lower frequency.
– DERIVATIVES **downconversion** n.

**downdraught** ● **n.** a downward current of air.

**downer** ● **n.** informal **1** a depressant or tranquillizing drug. **2** something dispiriting or depressing.

**downfall** ● **n.** a loss of power, prosperity, or status.

**downfield** ● **adv. 1** chiefly N. Amer. another term for **UPFIELD** (in sense 1). **2** Physics in a direction corresponding to decreasing field strength.

**downforce** ● **n.** a force pressing a moving vehicle down towards the ground, giving increased stability.

**downgrade** ● v. reduce to a lower grade, rank, or level of importance. ● n. **1** an instance of downgrading. **2** chiefly N. Amer. a downward gradient.

**downhearted** ● adj. discouraged; dejected.
– DERIVATIVES **downheartedly** adv. **downheartedness** n.

**downhill** ● adv. & adj. /daʊn'hɪl/ **1** towards the bottom of a slope. **2** into a steadily worsening situation. ● n. /'daʊnhɪl/ **1** a downward slope. **2** Skiing a downhill race.
– DERIVATIVES **downhiller** n. (Skiing).

**down-home** ● adj. chiefly N. Amer. unpretentious; homely.

**downland** ● n. gently rolling hill country.

**downlink** ● n. a telecommunications link for signals coming to the earth from a satellite, spacecraft, or aircraft.

**download** Computing ● v. copy (data) from one computer system to another or to a disk. ● n. the act or process of downloading.
– DERIVATIVES **downloadable** adj.

**downmarket** ● adj. & adv. chiefly Brit. towards or relating to the cheaper or less prestigious sector of the market.

**downmost** ● adj. & adv. chiefly Brit. the furthest down.

**down payment** ● n. an initial payment made when buying on credit.

**downpipe** ● n. Brit. a pipe to carry rainwater from a roof to a drain or to ground level.

**downplay** ● v. make (something) appear less important than it really is.

**downpour** ● n. a heavy fall of rain.

**downright** ● adj. **1** utter; complete: *it's a downright disgrace.* **2** so direct in manner as to be blunt. ● adv. to an extreme degree; thoroughly: *he was downright rude.*
– DERIVATIVES **downrightness** n.

**downriver** ● adv. & adj. towards or situated at a point nearer the mouth of a river.

**downscale** N. Amer. ● v. reduce in size, scale, or extent. ● adj. at the lower end of a scale; downmarket.

**downshift** chiefly N. Amer. ● v. **1** change to a lower gear. **2** change one's lifestyle to one that is less stressful. ● n. an instance of downshifting.

**downside** ● n. the negative aspect of something.

**downsize** ● v. chiefly N. Amer. make (something) smaller. ➤ (of a company) shed staff.

**downslope** ● n. a downward slope. ● adv. & adj. at or towards a lower point on a slope.

**downspout** ● n. North American term for DOWNPIPE.

**Down's syndrome** ● n. Medicine a congenital disorder causing intellectual impairment and physical abnormalities including short stature and a broad facial profile.
– ORIGIN 1960s: named after the C19 Engl. physician John L. H. *Down.*

**USAGE** Down's syndrome

Of relatively recent coinage, **Down's syndrome** is the accepted term in modern use, and former terms such as **mongol** and **mongolism**, which are likely to cause offence, should be avoided.

**downstage** ● adj. & adv. at or towards the front of a stage.

**downstairs** ● adv. & adj. down a flight of stairs; on or to a lower floor. ● n. the ground floor or lower floors of a building.

**downstate** US ● adj. & adv. of, in, or to a part of a state remote from its large cities. ● n. such an area.
– DERIVATIVES **downstater** n.

**downstream** ● adv. & adj. situated or moving in the direction in which a stream or river flows.

**downstroke** ● n. a stroke made downwards.

**downswing** ● n. **1** another term for DOWNTURN. **2** Golf the downward movement of a club when the player is about to hit the ball.

**downthrow** ● v. (past **-threw**; past part. **-thrown**) Geology displace downwards.

**down time** ● n. time during which a computer or other machine is out of action.

**down-to-earth** ● adj. practical and realistic.
– DERIVATIVES **down-to-earthness** n.

**downtown** chiefly N. Amer. ● adj. & adv. of, in, or towards the central area or main business area of a city. ● n. such an area of a city.
– DERIVATIVES **downtowner** n.

**downtrodden** ● adj. oppressed or treated badly by people in power.

**downturn** ● n. a decline in economic or other activity. ● v. [usu. as adj. **downturned**] turn downwards.

**down under** informal ● adv. in or to Australia or New Zealand. ● n. Australia and New Zealand.

**downward** ● adv. (also **downwards**) towards a lower point or level. ● adj. moving or leading towards a lower point or level.
– DERIVATIVES **downwardly** adv.

**downwarp** /'daʊnwɔːp/ ● n. Geology a broad depression of the earth's surface.

**downwash** ● n. the downward deflection of an airstream by a wing or rotor blade.

**downwelling** ● n. the downward movement of fluid.

**downwind** ● adv. & adj. in the direction in which the wind is blowing.

**downy** ● adj. (**-ier, -iest**) **1** covered with fine soft hair or feathers. ➤ soft and fluffy. **2** informal shrewd.
– DERIVATIVES **downily** adv. **downiness** n.

**dowry** /'daʊ(ə)ri/ ● n. (pl. **-ies**) property or money brought by a bride to her husband on their marriage.
– ORIGIN ME (denoting a widow's life interest in her husband's estate): from Anglo-Norman Fr. *dowarie*, from med. L. *dotarium* (see DOWER).

**dowse**[1] /daʊz/ ● v. [usu. as noun **dowsing**] search for underground water or minerals by observing the motion of a pointer, supposedly in response to unseen influences.
– DERIVATIVES **dowser** n.
– ORIGIN C17: of unknown origin.

**dowse**[2] ● v. variant spelling of DOUSE.

**doxastic** /dɒk'sastɪk/ ● adj. Philosophy of or relating to an individual's beliefs.
– ORIGIN C18: from Gk *doxastikos* 'conjectural'.

**doxology** /dɒk'sɒlədʒi/ ● n. (pl. **-ies**) a liturgical formula of praise to God.
– DERIVATIVES **doxological** adj.
– ORIGIN C17: via med. L. from Gk *doxologia*, from *doxa* 'appearance, glory' + *-logia* (see -LOGY).

**doxorubicin** /ˌdɒksəʊ'ruːbɪsɪn/ ● n. Medicine a bacterial antibiotic used to treat leukaemia and other forms of cancer.
– ORIGIN 1970s: from *deoxy-* (in the sense 'that has lost oxygen') + L. *rubus* 'red' + -MYCIN.

**doxy** /'dɒksi/ ● n. (pl. **-ies**) archaic a lover or mistress. ➤ a prostitute.
– ORIGIN C16: of unknown origin.

**doyen** /'dɔɪən, 'dwɑːjã/ ● n. (fem. **doyenne** /'dɔɪɛn, dɔɪ'ɛn, dwʌ'jɛn/) the most respected or prominent person in a particular field.
– ORIGIN C17: via Fr. from OFr. *deien* (see DEAN[1]).

**doz.** ● abbrev. dozen.

**doze** ● v. sleep lightly. ● n. a short light sleep.
– ORIGIN C17 (in the sense 'stupefy, bewilder, or make drowsy'): perh. rel. to Dan. *døse* 'make drowsy'.

**dozen** ● n. **1** (pl. same) a group or set of twelve. **2** (**the dozens**) a ritual exchange of insults among black Americans.
– PHRASES **talk nineteen to the dozen** Brit. talk incessantly.
– DERIVATIVES **dozenth** adj.
– ORIGIN ME: from OFr. *dozeine*, based on L. *duodecim* 'twelve'.

**dozer** ● n. informal short for BULLDOZER.

**dozy** ● adj. (**-ier, -iest**) feeling drowsy and lazy. ➤ Brit. informal not alert; stupid.
– DERIVATIVES **dozily** adv. **doziness** n.

**DP** ● abbrev. **1** data processing. **2** displaced person.

**dpc** ● abbrev. damp-proof course.

**DPhil** ● abbrev. Doctor of Philosophy.

**dpi** ● abbrev. Computing dots per inch.

**dpm** ● abbrev. damp-proof membrane.

**DPP** ● **abbrev.** (in the UK) Director of Public Prosecutions.

**DPT** ● **abbrev.** Medicine diphtheria, pertussis (whooping cough), and tetanus.

**Dr** ● **abbrev. 1** debit. [formerly representing *debtor*.] **2** (as a title) Doctor. **3** (in street names) Drive.

**dr.** ● **abbrev. 1** drachm(s). **2** drachma(s). **3** dram(s).

**drab**[1] ● **adj.** (**drabber, drabbest**) drearily dull. ● **n.** a dull light brown colour.
– DERIVATIVES **drably** adv. **drabness** n.
– ORIGIN C16 (denoting undyed cloth): prob. from OFr. *drap* (see **DRAPE**).

**drab**[2] ● **n.** archaic **1** a slovenly woman. **2** a prostitute.
– ORIGIN C16: perh. rel. to Low Ger. *drabbe* 'mire' and Du. *drab* 'dregs'.

**drabble** ● **v.** archaic make wet and dirty in muddy water.
– ORIGIN ME: from Low Ger. *drabbelen* 'paddle in water or mire'.

**drachm** /dram/ ● **n.** historical a unit of weight equivalent to 60 grains or one eighth of an ounce. ➤ (also **fluid drachm**) a liquid measure equivalent to 60 minims or one eighth of a fluid ounce.
– ORIGIN ME (denoting the ancient Gk drachma): from OFr. *dragme* or late L. *dragma*.

**drachma** /ˈdrakmə/ ● **n.** (pl. **drachmas** or **drachmae** /-miː/) the basic monetary unit of Greece. ➤ a silver coin of ancient Greece.
– ORIGIN via L. from Gk *drakhmē*, an Attic weight and coin.

**drack** /drak/ Austral. informal ● **adj.** unattractive or unwelcome; dreary. ● **n.** an unattractive woman.
– ORIGIN said to be from the 1930s film *Dracula's Daughter*, but possibly rel. to sl. *dreck* 'rubbish', from Yiddish *drek* 'filth, dregs'.

**draconian** /drəˈkəʊnɪən, dreɪ-/ ● **adj.** (of laws) excessively harsh and severe.
– DERIVATIVES **draconic** /-ˈkɒnɪk/ adj.
– ORIGIN C19: from *Draco*, name of an ancient Athenian legislator, + **-IAN**.

**draff** /draf/ ● **n.** poetic/literary dregs or refuse.
– ORIGIN ME: perh. rel. to Ger. *Treber, Träber* 'husks, grains', and to **DRIVEL**.

**draft** ● **n. 1** a preliminary version of a piece of writing. ➤ a plan or sketch. **2** a written order to pay a specified sum. **3** (**the draft**) chiefly US compulsory recruitment for military service. ➤ N. Amer. a procedure whereby sports players are made available for selection or reselection by the teams in a league. **4** US spelling of **DRAUGHT**. ● **v. 1** prepare a preliminary version of (a text). **2** select (a person or group) and bring them somewhere for a certain purpose. ➤ US conscript for military service.
– DERIVATIVES **drafter** n.
– ORIGIN C16: phonetic spelling of **DRAUGHT**.

**draftee** ● **n.** chiefly US a person conscripted for military service.

**draftsman** ● **n.** (pl. **-men**) **1** a person who drafts legal documents. **2** chiefly N. Amer. variant spelling of **DRAUGHTSMAN**.

**drafty** ● **adj.** US spelling of **DRAUGHTY**.

**drag** ● **v.** (**dragged, dragging**) **1** pull along forcefully, roughly, or with difficulty. ➤ take (someone) somewhere, despite their reluctance. ➤ move (an image) across a computer screen using a mouse. ➤ trail along the ground. ➤ (**drag at**) catch hold of and pull. ➤ search the bottom of (a body of water) with grapnels or nets. **2** (**drag something up**) informal deliberately mention something unwelcome. **3** (of time) pass slowly and tediously. ➤ (**drag something out**) protract something unnecessarily. **4** (**drag on**) informal inhale the smoke from (a cigarette). **5** (**drag someone up**) Brit. dated bring up a child badly. ● **n. 1** the action of dragging. **2** the longitudinal retarding force exerted by air or other fluid surrounding a moving object. **3** informal a boring or tiresome person or thing. **4** informal an act of inhaling smoke from a cigarette. **5** women's clothing worn by a man: *men in drag*. **6** short for **DRAG RACE**. **7** informal, chiefly N. Amer. a street or road: *the main drag*. **8** historical a private vehicle like a stagecoach, drawn by four horses. **9** an apparatus for dredging or for recovering objects from the bottom of water. **10** historical a harrow used for breaking up the surface of land. **11** archaic an iron shoe applied as a brake to a wheel. **12** N. Amer. informal influence over other people. **13** a strong-smelling lure drawn before hounds as a substitute for a fox. **14** Music (in drumming) a basic pattern consisting of a stroke preceded by two grace notes played with the other stick.
– PHRASES **drag one's feet 1** walk slowly and wearily or with difficulty. **2** be deliberately slow or reluctant to act.
– ORIGIN ME: from OE *dragan* or ON *draga* 'to draw'.

**dragée** /ˈdrɑːʒeɪ/ ● **n. 1** a sweet consisting of a centre covered with a coating, such as a sugared almond. **2** a small silver ball for decorating a cake.
– ORIGIN C17: Fr., from OFr. *dragie* (see **DREDGE**[2]).

**dragger** ● **n.** N. Amer. a fishing boat that uses a dragnet.

**draggle** ● **v. 1** make dirty or wet. ➤ hang untidily. **2** archaic trail behind others.
– ORIGIN C16: dimin. and frequentative of **DRAG**.

**draggy** ● **adj.** (**-ier, -iest**) informal dreary; tedious.

**drag hound** ● **n.** a hound used to hunt with a drag.

**dragline** ● **n. 1** a large excavator with a bucket pulled in by a wire cable. **2** a line of silk produced by a spider and acting as a safety line.

**dragnet** ● **n. 1** a net drawn through water or across ground to trap fish or game. **2** a systematic search for criminals or criminal activity.

**dragoman** /ˈdragə(ʊ)mən/ ● **n.** (pl. **dragomans** or **dragomen**) an interpreter or guide in a country speaking Arabic, Turkish, or Persian.
– ORIGIN ME: from obs. Fr., from Ital. *dragomanno*, from med. Gk *dragoumanos*, from Arab. *tarjumān* 'interpreter'.

**dragon** ● **n. 1** a mythical monster like a giant reptile, typically with wings and claws and able to breathe out fire. ➤ used in names of various lizards, e.g. **Komodo dragon**. **2** derogatory a fierce and intimidating woman.
– PHRASES **chase the dragon** informal smoke heroin.
– ORIGIN ME: from OFr., via L. from Gk *drakōn* 'serpent'.

**dragon boat** ● **n.** a boat of a traditional Chinese design resembling a dragon, propelled with paddles by a large crew.

**dragonet** /ˈdrag(ə)nɪt/ ● **n.** a small marine fish of which the male is brightly coloured. [*Callionymus lyra* and other species.]
– ORIGIN ME (denoting a small dragon): from OFr., dimin. of *dragon* 'dragon'.

**dragonfish** ● **n.** (pl. same or **-fishes**) a long, slender deep-sea fish with fang-like teeth, a barbel on the chin, and luminous organs. [Families Stomiatidae and Idiacanthidae: numerous species.]

**dragonfly** ● **n.** (pl. **-flies**) a fast-flying long-bodied predatory insect with two pairs of large transparent wings (spread out sideways at rest) and voracious aquatic larvae. [Suborder Anisoptera: many species.]

**dragonnade** /ˌdragəˈneɪd/ ● **n.** historical a form of persecution involving quartering troops on a population.
– ORIGIN C18: from Fr., from *dragon* (see **DRAGOON**).

**dragon's blood** ● **n.** a red gum or powder from the fruit of certain palm trees or from the stem of the dragon tree.

**dragon ship** ● **n.** a Viking longship ornamented with a beaked prow.

**dragon tree** ● **n.** a slow-growing palm-like tree native to the Canary Islands, yielding dragon's blood. [*Dracaena draco*.]

**dragoon** /drəˈguːn/ ● **n. 1** a member of any of several British cavalry regiments. ➤ historical a mounted infantryman armed with a carbine. **2** a variety of pigeon. ● **v.** coerce into doing something.
– ORIGIN C17 (denoting a kind of carbine or musket, thought of as breathing fire): from Fr. *dragon* 'dragon'.

**drag queen** ● **n.** a man who ostentatiously dresses up in women's clothes.

**drag race** ● **n.** a race between two cars over a short distance as a test of acceleration.
– DERIVATIVES **drag racer** n. **drag racing** n.

**dragster** ● n. a car built or modified to take part in drag races.

**drail** /dreɪl/ ● n. Fishing a weighted fish hook and line for dragging below the surface.
– ORIGIN C16 (denoting part of a plough): from the obs. v. *drail*, an alt. of **TRAIL**.

**drain** ● v. **1** cause the water or other liquid in (something) to run out, leaving it empty or dry. ➤(of liquid) run off or out. ➤(of a river) carry off the superfluous water from (an area). ➤become dry as liquid runs off. ➤drink the entire contents of. **2** deprive of strength or vitality. ➤cause to be lost or used up. **3** Golf, informal hole (a putt). ● n. **1** a channel or pipe carrying off surplus liquid, especially rainwater or liquid waste. **2** a thing that uses up a particular resource. ➤the continuous loss of a resource: *the drain of talented staff.*
– PHRASES **go down the drain** informal be totally wasted. **laugh like a drain** Brit. informal laugh raucously.
– ORIGIN OE *drēahnian, drēhnian* 'strain (liquid)', of Gmc origin; rel. to **DRY**.

**drainage** ● n. **1** the action or process of draining something. **2** a system of drains.

**drainboard** ● n. North American term for **DRAINING BOARD**.

**drainer** ● n. **1** a rack used to hold crockery while it drains. **2** a draining board.

**draining board** ● n. Brit. a sloping grooved board or surface on which crockery is left to drain into an adjacent sink.

**drainpipe** ● n. **1** a pipe for carrying off rainwater or liquid refuse from a building. **2** (**drainpipes** or **drainpipe trousers**) trousers with very narrow legs.

**Draize test** ● n. a pharmacological test in which a potentially harmful substance is introduced into the eye or on to the skin of a laboratory animal.
– ORIGIN 1970s: named after the Amer. pharmacologist John H. *Draize.*

**drake**[1] ● n. a male duck.
– ORIGIN ME: of W. Gmc origin.

**drake**[2] ● n. Fishing a kind of natural or artificial mayfly.
– ORIGIN OE *draca*, from L. *draco* 'dragon'.

**Drake equation** ● n. Astronomy a formula giving an estimate of the likelihood of discovering intelligent extraterrestrial life in the galaxy.
– ORIGIN 1960s: named after the Amer. astronomer Frank *Drake*, who formulated it.

**Dralon** /ˈdreɪlɒn/ ● n. trademark, chiefly Brit. a synthetic textile made from acrylic fibre.
– ORIGIN 1950s: on the pattern of *nylon.*

**DRAM** ● abbrev. Electronics dynamic random-access memory.

**dram**[1] /dram/ ● n. **1** chiefly Scottish a small drink of spirits. **2** another term for **DRACHM**.
– ORIGIN ME: from OFr. *drame, dragme* or med. L. *drama, dragma* (see **DRACHM**).

**dram**[2] /drɑːm/ ● n. the basic monetary unit of Armenia, equal to 100 luma.

**drama** ● n. **1** a play. ➤plays as a genre or literary style. **2** an exciting or emotional series of events.
– ORIGIN C16: via late L. from Gk *drama*, from *dran* 'do, act'.

**dramatic** ● adj. **1** of or relating to drama. **2** sudden and striking: *a dramatic increase.* ➤exciting or impressive. ➤intended to create an effect; theatrical.
– DERIVATIVES **dramatically** adv.

**dramatics** ● pl. n. **1** [treated as sing. or pl.] the study or practice of acting in and producing plays. **2** theatrically exaggerated or overemotional behaviour.

**dramatis personae** /ˌdramətɪs pəːˈsəʊnʌɪ, -niː/ ● pl. n. the characters of a play, novel, or narrative.
– ORIGIN C18: from L., lit. 'persons of the drama'.

**dramatist** ● n. a person who writes plays.

**dramatize** (also **-ise**) ● v. **1** present (a novel, event, etc.) as a play. **2** exaggerate the excitement or seriousness of.
– DERIVATIVES **dramatization** /-ˈzeɪʃ(ə)n/ n.

**dramaturge** /ˈdramətəːdʒ/ (also **dramaturg**) ● n. **1** a dramatist. **2** a literary editor on the staff of a theatre who liaises with authors and edits texts.
– ORIGIN C19: via Fr. and Ger. from Gk *dramatourgos*, from *drama, dramat-* 'drama' + *-ergos* 'worker'.

**dramaturgy** /ˈdraməˌtəːdʒi/ ● n. the theory and practice of dramatic composition.
– DERIVATIVES **dramaturgic** adj. **dramaturgical** adj. **dramaturgically** adv.

**Drambuie** /dramˈbuːi, -ˈbjʊi/ ● n. trademark a sweet Scotch whisky liqueur.
– ORIGIN from Sc. Gaelic *dram buidheach* 'satisfying drink'.

**drank** past of **DRINK**.

**drape** ● v. arrange (cloth or clothing) loosely on or round something. ➤adorn or wrap loosely with folds of cloth. ● n. **1** (**drapes**) long curtains. **2** the way in which a garment or fabric hangs. **3** a cloth for covering a patient's body when a surgical operation is being performed.
– ORIGIN C17: back-form. from **DRAPERY**, influenced by Fr. *draper* 'to drape'.

**draper** ● n. Brit. dated a person who sells textile fabrics.
– ORIGIN ME: from OFr. *drapier*, from *drap* 'cloth'.

**drapery** ● n. (pl. **-ies**) cloth, curtains, or clothing hanging in loose folds.
– ORIGIN ME: from OFr. *draperie*, from *drap* 'cloth'.

**drastic** /ˈdrastɪk, ˈdrɑː-/ ● adj. having a strong or far-reaching effect.
– DERIVATIVES **drastically** adv.
– ORIGIN C17: from Gk *drastikos*, from *dran* 'do'.

**drat** ● exclam. used to express mild annoyance.
– DERIVATIVES **dratted** adj.
– ORIGIN C19: shortening of *od rat*, euphemism for *God rot.*

**draught** /drɑːft/ (US **draft**) ● n. **1** a current of cool air in a room or confined space. **2** a single act of drinking or inhaling. ➤poetic/literary or archaic a quantity of a liquid with medicinal properties: *a sleeping draught.* **3** the depth of water needed to float a particular ship: *her shallow draught.* **4** the drawing in of a fishing net. ➤a catch of fish. ● v. variant spelling of **DRAFT**. ● adj. **1** denoting beer served from a cask rather than from a bottle or can. **2** denoting an animal used for pulling heavy loads.
– PHRASES **on draught** (of beer) ready to be drawn from a cask.
– ORIGIN ME (in the sense 'drawing, pulling'): from ON *dráttr*, of Gmc origin; cf. **DRAFT**.

**draughtboard** ● n. Brit. a square chequered board of sixty-four small squares, used for playing draughts.

**draughtproof** ● adj. sealed so as to keep out draughts. ● v. make (a building, window, etc.) draughtproof.

**draughts** ● n. Brit. a game played on a chequered board by two players, who each start with twelve disc-shaped pieces and move them diagonally with the aim of capturing all the opponent's pieces.
– ORIGIN ME: from **DRAUGHT**; rel. to obs. *draught* in the sense 'move' (in chess).

**draughtsman** (or **draughtswoman**) ● n. (pl. **-men** or **-women**) **1** a person who makes detailed technical plans or drawings. ➤an artist skilled in drawing. **2** variant spelling of **DRAFTSMAN**.
– DERIVATIVES **draughtsmanship** n.

**draughty** (US **drafty**) ● adj. (**-ier, -iest**) cold and uncomfortable because of draughts of air.
– DERIVATIVES **draughtily** adv. **draughtiness** n.

**Dravidian** /drəˈvɪdɪən/ ● n. **1** a family of languages spoken in southern India and Sri Lanka, including Tamil and Kannada. **2** a member of any of the peoples speaking these languages. ● adj. relating to or denoting this family of languages or its speakers.
– ORIGIN from Sanskrit *drāviḍa* 'relating to the Tamils' (from *Dravida* 'Tamil') + **-IAN**.

**draw** ● v. (past **drew**; past part. **drawn**) **1** produce (a picture or diagram) by making lines and marks on paper. ➤trace or produce (a line) on a surface. **2** pull or drag (a vehicle) so as to make it follow behind. ➤pull or move (something) in a specified direction. ➤pull (curtains) shut or open. **3** arrive at a specified stage or point in time: *the campaign drew to a close.* **4** extract from a container or receptacle: *he drew his gun.* ➤(**draw from**) obtain from (a particular source). ➤(**draw on**) use as a resource: *Sue has a lot of experience to draw on.* ➤Bridge cause to be played. **5** take in (a breath). ➤(**draw on**) suck smoke from (a cigarette or pipe). ➤(of a chimney or fire) allow air to flow in and upwards freely, so that a fire can burn. **6** be the cause of (a specified response). ➤attract to come to a place or an event. ➤induce to reveal or do something: *he refused to be drawn on what would happen.* ➤direct or attract (someone's attention). ➤reach (a conclusion) by deduction or inference. ➤formulate or perceive (a comparison or distinction). **7** finish (a contest or game) with an even score. **8** Bowls cause (a bowl) to travel in a curve to the desired point. ➤Golf hit (the ball) so that it travels slightly to the left (for a left-handed player, the right). **9** make (wire) by pulling metal through successively smaller holes. **10** (of a ship) require (a specified depth of water) to float in. **11** (of a sail) be filled with wind. **12** historical disembowel. **13** Hunting search (cover) for game. ● **n. 1** an act of selecting names randomly, to decide winners in a lottery, opponents in a sporting contest, etc. **2** a game or match that ends with the scores even. ➤Cricket a game which is left incomplete for lack of time. Compare with **TIE**. **3** a person or thing that is very attractive or interesting: *the big city was a powerful draw to youngsters.* **4** an act of inhaling smoke from a cigarette. ➤informal cannabis. **5** Golf a shot which draws the ball.

– PHRASES **draw blood** cause someone to bleed, especially in the course of a fight. **draw someone's fire** attract hostile criticism away from a more important target. **draw the line at** set a limit of what one is willing to do or accept.

– PHRASAL VERBS **draw back** choose not to do something that one was expected to do. **draw in** (of successive days) become shorter or (of nights) start earlier, because of the changing seasons. **draw on** (of a period of time) pass by and approach its end. **draw out** (of successive days) become longer because of the changing seasons. **draw someone out** gently or subtly persuade someone to be more talkative. **draw something out** make something last longer. **draw up** come to a halt. **draw something up** prepare a plan or document in detail.

– ORIGIN OE *dragan*, of Gmc origin; rel. to **DRAUGHT**.

**drawback** ● **n. 1** a disadvantage or problem. **2** (also **duty drawback**) excise or import duty remitted on goods exported.

**drawbar** ● **n. 1** a bar on a vehicle to which something can be attached to pull it or be pulled. **2** a bar in a structure that can be pulled out to free something.

**drawbridge** ● **n.** a bridge, typically over a castle moat, which is hinged at one end so that it can be raised.

**drawcard** ● **n.** informal an attractive quality or feature.

**drawcord** ● **n.** another term for **DRAWSTRING**.

**drawdown** ● **n. 1** a reduction in the quantity of something. **2** an act of drawing on available loan facilities.

**drawee** /drɔː(r)ˈiː/ ● **n.** the person or organization who has to pay a draft or bill.

**drawer** ● **n. 1** /drɔː/ a lidless box-like storage compartment made to slide horizontally in and out of a desk or chest. **2** (**drawers**) /drɔːz/ dated or humorous knickers or underpants. **3** /ˈdrɔː(r)ə/ a person who draws something. ➤the person who writes a cheque.

**drawing** ● **n.** a picture or diagram made with a pencil, pen, or crayon rather than paint, especially one drawn in monochrome. ➤the art or skill of making such pictures.

**drawing board** ● **n.** a large flat board on which paper can be spread for artists or designers to work on.

– PHRASES **back to the drawing board** a plan has failed and a new one is needed.

**drawing pin** ● **n.** Brit. a short flat-headed pin for fastening paper to a surface.

**drawing room** ● **n.** a room in a large private house in which guests can be received and entertained.

– ORIGIN C17: abbrev. of *withdrawing-room* 'a room to withdraw to'.

**drawknife** ● **n.** (pl. **-knives**) a knife with a handle at right angles at each end of the blade, for removing wood from a surface.

**drawl** ● **v.** speak in a slow, lazy way with prolonged vowel sounds. ● **n.** a drawling accent.

– DERIVATIVES **drawler** n. **drawly** adj.

– ORIGIN C16: prob. orig. sl., from Low Ger. or Du. *dralen* 'delay, linger'.

**drawn** past participle of **DRAW**. ● **adj.** looking strained from illness or exhaustion: *Cathy was pale and drawn.*

**drawn butter** ● **n.** N. Amer. melted butter.

**drawn-out** ● **adj.** lasting longer than is necessary.

**drawn work** (also **drawn-thread-work**) ● **n.** ornamental work on fabric done by drawing out threads, usually with additional needlework.

**draw reins** ● **n.** reins that are attached to a horse's saddle or girth and pass through the bit rings to the rider's hands.

**draw sheet** ● **n.** a sheet that can be taken from under a patient or invalid without disturbing the bedclothes.

**drawstring** ● **n.** a string in the seam of a garment or bag, which can be pulled to tighten or close it.

**dray** ● **n.** a low truck or cart without sides, for delivering barrels or other heavy loads. ➤Austral./NZ a two-wheeled cart.

– ORIGIN ME: perh. from OE *dræge* 'dragnet', rel. to *dragan* 'to pull' (see **DRAW**).

**dread** ● **v. 1** anticipate with great apprehension or fear. **2** archaic regard with great awe. ● **n. 1** great fear or apprehension. **2** a sudden take-off of a flock of birds. **3** (**dreads**) informal dreadlocks. ● **adj. 1** greatly feared; dreadful. **2** archaic regarded with awe.

– DERIVATIVES **dreaded** adj.

– ORIGIN OE *ādrǣdan*, *ondrǣdan*, of W. Gmc origin.

**dreadful** ● **adj. 1** extremely bad or serious. **2** used for emphasis: *you're a dreadful flirt.*

– DERIVATIVES **dreadfully** adv. **dreadfulness** n.

**dreadlocks** ● **pl. n.** a Rastafarian hairstyle in which the hair is twisted into tight braids or ringlets.

– DERIVATIVES **dreadlocked** adj.

**dreadnought** /ˈdrɛdnɔːt/ ● **n. 1** historical a type of battleship of the early 20th century, equipped entirely with large-calibre guns. [named after Britain's HMS *Dreadnought*, completed 1906.] **2** archaic a fearless person. **3** archaic a heavy overcoat for stormy weather.

**dream** ● **n. 1** a series of thoughts, images, and sensations occurring in a person's mind during sleep. ➤a state of mind in which someone is not fully aware of their surroundings: *he walked around in a dream.* **2** a cherished ambition or ideal; a fantasy. ➤informal someone or something perceived as wonderful or perfect. ● **v.** (past and past part. **dreamed** /drɛmt, driːmd/ or **dreamt** /drɛmt/) **1** experience dreams during sleep. **2** indulge in daydreams or fantasies. ➤(**dream up**) imagine or invent. **3** [with neg.] contemplate the possibility of: *I never dreamed anyone would take offence.*

– PHRASES **like a dream** informal very easily or successfully.

– DERIVATIVES **dreamer** n. **dreamful** adj. (poetic/literary). **dreamless** adj. **dreamlike** adj.

– ORIGIN ME: of Gmc origin.

**dreamboat** ● **n.** informal a very attractive person, especially a man.

**dreamcatcher** ● **n.** a small hoop containing a decorated horsehair mesh, believed by American Indians to give its owner good dreams.

**dreamland** ● **n.** sleep regarded as a world of dreams. ➤an unrealistically ideal world.

**dreamscape** ● **n.** a scene with the strangeness or mystery characteristic of dreams.

**dreamtime** ● **n.** another term for **ALCHERINGA**.

**dreamwork** ● **n.** Psychoanalysis the supposed alteration of the content of dreams by the unconscious, in order to conceal their meaning.

**dreamy** ● **adj.** (**-ier**, **-iest**) **1** dreamlike; pleasantly distracting or unreal. **2** given to daydreaming.

– DERIVATIVES **dreamily** adv. **dreaminess** n.

**drear** /drɪə/ ● **adj.** poetic/literary dreary.

**dreary** ● **adj.** (**-ier**, **-iest**) dull, bleak, and depressing.

– DERIVATIVES **drearily** adv. **dreariness** n.

– ORIGIN OE *drēorig* 'gory, cruel, melancholy', from *drēor* 'gore', of Gmc origin; rel. to **DROWSY**, and prob. to **DRIZZLE**.

**dreck** /drɛk/ (also **drek**) • n. informal rubbish.
– DERIVATIVES **dreckish** adj. **drecky** adj.
– ORIGIN C20: from Yiddish *drek* 'filth, dregs'.

**dredge**[1] • v. **1** clean out the bed of (a harbour, river, etc.) with a dredge. ➤ bring up or remove with a dredge. **2** (**dredge something up**) bring something unwelcome and forgotten or obscure to people's attention. • n. an apparatus for bringing up objects or mud from a river or seabed by scooping or dragging.
– DERIVATIVES **dredger** n.
– ORIGIN C15 (orig. in *dredge-boat*): perh. rel. to MDu. *dregghe* 'grappling hook'.

**dredge**[2] • v. sprinkle (food) with sugar or other powdered substance.
– ORIGIN C16: from obs. *dredge* 'sweetmeat, mixture of spices', from OFr. *dragie*, perh. via L. from Gk *tragēmata* 'spices'.

**dree** /driː/ • v. (**drees, dreed, dreeing**) Scottish or archaic endure (something burdensome or painful).
– PHRASES **dree one's weird** submit to one's destiny.
– ORIGIN OE *drēogan*, of Gmc origin.

**dregs** • n. **1** the remnants of a liquid left in a container, together with any sediment. **2** the most worthless parts: *the dregs of society.*
– DERIVATIVES **dreggy** adj.
– ORIGIN ME: prob. of Scand. origin.

**dreich** /driːx/ (also **driech**) • adj. Scottish dreary; bleak.
– ORIGIN ME (in the sense 'patient, long-suffering'): of Gmc origin.

**dreidel** /'dreɪd(ə)l/ (also **dreidl**) • n. N. Amer. a small four-sided spinning top with a Hebrew letter on each side, used by Jews in gambling games, especially at Hanukkah.
– ORIGIN 1930s: from Yiddish *dreydl*; rel. to Ger. *drehen* 'to turn'.

**drek** • n. variant spelling of **DRECK**.

**drench** • v. **1** wet thoroughly; soak. ➤ [often as adj. **drenched**] cover liberally with something: *a sun-drenched clearing.* **2** forcibly administer a liquid medicine to (an animal). • n. a dose of medicine administered to an animal. ➤ archaic a draught of medicine or poison.
– ORIGIN OE *drencan* 'force to drink', *drenc* 'a drink or draught', of Gmc origin; rel. to **DRINK**.

**Dresden china** /'drɛzd(ə)n/ • n. porcelain ware with elaborate decoration and delicate colourings, made originally at Dresden in Germany.

**dress** • v. **1** put on one's clothes. ➤ put clothes on (someone). ➤ wear clothes in a particular way or of a particular type: *she dresses well.* ➤ put on clothes appropriate for a formal occasion. ➤ (**dress up**) dress in smart or formal clothes, or in a special costume. **2** decorate in an artistic or attractive way. ➤ arrange or style (the hair). **3** clean, treat, or apply a dressing to (a wound). **4** clean and prepare (food) for cooking or eating. ➤ add a dressing to (a salad). **5** apply fertilizer to. **6** treat the surface of (leather or fabric) during manufacture. **7** smooth the surface of (stone). **8** Military draw up (troops) in the proper alignment. **9** make (an artificial fly) for use in fishing. **10** (**dress someone down**) informal reprimand someone. • n. **1** a one-piece garment for a woman or girl that covers the body and extends down over the legs. **2** clothing of a specified kind for men or women. ➤ [as modifier] denoting ceremonial clothing or uniform: *a dress suit.*
– PHRASES **dressed overall** (of a ship) decorated with a continuous line of flags from bow to stern. **dressed to kill** informal wearing glamorous clothes intended to create a striking impression.
– ORIGIN ME: from OFr. *dresser* 'arrange, prepare', based on L. *directus* 'direct, straight'.

**dressage** /'drɛsɑː(d)ʒ/ • n. the art of riding and training horses so as to develop obedience, flexibility, and balance.
– ORIGIN 1930s: from Fr., lit. 'training', from *dresser* 'to train'.

**dress circle** • n. the first level of seats above the ground floor in a theatre.

**dress coat** • n. a coat with long tails at the back, worn by men on very formal occasions.

**dress-down Friday** • n. another term for **CASUAL FRIDAY**.

**dresser**[1] • n. a sideboard with shelves above for storing and displaying crockery. ➤ N. Amer. a dressing table or chest of drawers.
– ORIGIN ME (denoting a sideboard or table on which food was prepared).

**dresser**[2] • n. **1** a person who dresses in a specified way: *a snappy dresser.* **2** a person who looks after theatrical costumes. **3** a person who dresses something. ➤ Brit. a person who assists a surgeon during operations.

**dressing** • n. **1** (also **salad dressing**) a sauce for salads, usually consisting of oil and vinegar with herbs or other flavourings. **2** N. Amer. stuffing. **3** a piece of material placed on a wound to protect it. **4** size or stiffening used in the finishing of fabrics. **5** a fertilizer spread over or ploughed into land.

**dressing case** • n. a case used for toiletries.

**dressing gown** • n. a long loose robe worn after getting out of bed or bathing.

**dressing room** • n. a room in which actors or sports players change clothes. ➤ a small room attached to a bedroom, containing clothes.

**dressing station** • n. a place for giving emergency treatment to troops injured in battle.

**dressing table** • n. a table with a mirror and drawers, used while dressing or applying make-up.

**dressmaker** • n. a person who makes women's clothes.
– DERIVATIVES **dressmaking** n.

**dress parade** • n. a military parade in full dress uniform.

**dress rehearsal** • n. a final rehearsal in which everything is done as it would be in a real performance.

**dress sense** • n. a good instinct for selecting garments.

**dress shield** (also **dress preserver**) • n. a piece of waterproof material in the armpit of a dress to protect it from perspiration.

**dress shirt** • n. a man's white shirt worn with a bow tie and a dinner jacket on formal occasions. ➤ N. Amer. a shirt suitable for wearing with a tie.

**dressy** • adj. (**-ier, -iest**) (of clothes) suitable for a smart or formal occasion.
– DERIVATIVES **dressily** adv. **dressiness** n.

**drew** past of **DRAW**.

**drey** /dreɪ/ • n. (pl. **-eys**) a squirrel's nest of twigs in a tree.
– ORIGIN C17: of unknown origin.

**dribble** • v. **1** (of a liquid) fall slowly in drops or a thin stream. ➤ allow saliva to run from the mouth. **2** (in soccer and hockey) take (the ball) forward past opponents with slight touches of the feet or the stick, or (in basketball) by continuous bouncing. • n. **1** a thin stream of liquid. ➤ saliva running from the mouth. **2** (in soccer, hockey, and basketball) an act of dribbling.
– DERIVATIVES **dribbler** n. **dribbly** adj.
– ORIGIN C16: frequentative of obs. *drib*, var. of **DRIP**.

**driblet** • n. **1** a thin stream or small drop of liquid. **2** a small or insignificant amount.
– ORIGIN C16: from obs. *drib* (see **DRIBBLE**) + **-LET**.

**dribs and drabs** • pl. n. (in phr. **in dribs and drabs**) informal in small scattered or sporadic amounts.
– ORIGIN C19: from obs. *drib* (see **DRIBBLE**) and *drab* (by reduplication).

**driech** • adj. variant spelling of **DREICH**.

**dried** past and past participle of **DRY**.

**drier**[1] • adj. compar. of **DRY**.

**drier**[2] • n. variant spelling of **DRYER**.

**drift** • v. **1** be carried slowly by a current of air or water. **2** walk slowly or casually. ➤ move aimlessly or involuntarily into a certain situation or condition: *Lewis and his father drifted apart.* **3** (chiefly of snow) be blown into heaps by the wind. • n. **1** a continuous slow movement from one place to another. ➤ deviation from an intended or expected course because of currents or winds. ➤ Motor

Racing a controlled skid, used in taking bends at high speeds. ➤Brit. historical an act of driving cattle or sheep. **2** the general intention or meaning of someone's remarks: *he didn't understand much Greek, but he got her drift.* **3** a large mass of snow or other material piled up by the wind. ➤Geology deposits left by retreating ice sheets. **4** a state of inaction or indecision. **5** Mining a passage following a mineral vein or coal seam. **6** S. African a ford.
– DERIVATIVES **drifty** adj.
– ORIGIN ME: orig. from ON *drift* 'snowdrift, something driven'; in later use from MDu. *drift* 'course, current', rel. to **DRIVE**.

**drifter** ● n. **1** a person who is continually moving from place to place, without any fixed home or job. **2** a fishing boat equipped with a drift net.

**driftfish** ● n. (pl. same or **-fishes**) a slender-bodied fish found in the deeper parts of warm seas. [Family Nomeidae.]

**drift ice** ● n. detached pieces of ice drifting with the wind or ocean currents.

**drift net** ● n. a large fishing net, kept upright by weights at the bottom and floats at the top and allowed to drift in the sea.
– DERIVATIVES **drift netter** n. **drift netting** n.

**drift pin** ● n. a steel pin driven into a hole in a piece of metal to enlarge or align the hole.

**driftwood** ● n. pieces of wood floating on the sea or washed ashore.

**drill**[1] ● n. **1** a tool or machine with a rotating or reciprocating cutting tip, used for boring holes. **2** training in military exercises. ➤instruction by means of repeated exercises. ➤(**the drill**) informal the correct or recognized procedure. **3** a predatory mollusc that bores into the shells of other molluscs. [*Urosalpinx cinerea* (**oyster drill**, America) and other species.] ● v. **1** bore (a hole) in something with a drill. ➤sink a borehole. **2** subject to military training or other intensive instruction. **3** informal hit (something) so that it travels fast in a straight line.
– DERIVATIVES **driller** n.
– ORIGIN C17: from MDu. *drillen* 'bore, turn in a circle'.

**drill**[2] ● n. a machine which makes small furrows, sows seed in them, and then covers the sown seed. ➤a small furrow made by such a machine. ● v. sow with a drill.
– ORIGIN C18: perh. from **DRILL**[1].

**drill**[3] ● n. a West African baboon with a naked blue or purple rump. [*Mandrillus leucophaeus*.]
– ORIGIN C17: prob. a local word; cf. **MANDRILL**.

**drill**[4] ● n. a coarse twilled cotton or linen fabric.
– ORIGIN C18: abbrev. of earlier *drilling*, from Ger. *Drillich*, from L. *trilix* 'triple-twilled', from *tri-* 'three' + *licium* 'thread'.

**drilling rig** ● n. a large structure with equipment for drilling an oil well.

**drill sergeant** ● n. a non-commissioned officer who trains soldiers in military parade exercises.

**drill stem** ● n. a rotating rod or cylinder used in drilling.

**drill string** ● n. a series of coupled lengths of pipe or casing occupying a borehole.

**drily** /ˈdrʌɪli/ (also **dryly**) ● adv. **1** in a matter-of-fact or ironically humorous way. **2** in a dry way or condition.

**drink** ● v. (past **drank**; past part. **drunk**) **1** take (a liquid) into the mouth and swallow. ➤consume alcohol, especially to excess. ➤(**drink up**) consume the rest of a drink. **2** (**drink something in**) watch or listen eagerly to something. **3** absorb (moisture). ● n. **1** a liquid consumed as refreshment or nourishment. ➤a quantity of liquid swallowed at one go. **2** the habitual or excessive consumption of alcohol. **3** (**the drink**) informal the sea.
– PHRASES **drink deep** take a large draught or draughts of something. **drink someone's health** (or **drink to someone**) express good wishes for someone by raising one's glass and drinking a small amount. **drink someone under the table** informal consume as much alcohol as one's drinking companion without becoming as drunk. **I'll drink to that** expressing agreement or approval. **in drink** when intoxicated.
– DERIVATIVES **drinkable** adj.
– ORIGIN OE *drincan* (v.), *drinc* (n.), of Gmc origin.

**drink-driving** ● n. Brit. the crime of driving a vehicle with an excess of alcohol in the blood.
– DERIVATIVES **drink-driver** n.

**drinker** ● n. **1** a person who drinks. **2** a large brownish moth, the caterpillar of which is noted for drinking dew. [*Euthrix potatoria*.] **3** a container from which an animal can drink.

**drinking chocolate** ● n. a mixture of cocoa powder, milk solids, and sugar, added to hot water to make a chocolate drink.

**drinking fountain** ● n. a device producing a small jet of water for drinking.

**drinking song** ● n. a hearty or bawdy song sung by a group while drinking alcohol.

**drip** ● v. (**dripped**, **dripping**) let fall small drops of liquid. ➤fall in small drops. ● n. **1** a small drop of a liquid. **2** Medicine an apparatus which slowly passes fluid, nutrients, or drugs into a patient's body intravenously. **3** informal a weak and ineffectual person. **4** Architecture a projection on a moulding or cornice, channelled to prevent rain from running down the wall below.
– ORIGIN OE *dryppan*, *drȳpen*, of Gmc origin; rel. to **DROP**.

**drip-dry** ● v. (of fabric or a garment) become dry without forming creases when hung up after washing. ● adj. capable of drip-drying.

**drip feed** ● n. a device for introducing fluid drop by drop into a system. ● v. (**drip-feed**) introduce (fluid) drop by drop. ➤supply (a patient) with fluid through a drip.

**dripping** ● n. **1** Brit. fat that has melted and dripped from roasting meat. **2** (**drippings**) chiefly N. Amer. wax, fat, or other liquid produced from something by the effect of heat. ● adj. extremely wet.

**drippy** ● adj. (**-ier**, **-iest**) **1** informal weak, ineffectual, or sloppily sentimental. **2** tending to drip.
– DERIVATIVES **drippily** adv. **drippiness** n.

**dripstone** ● n. **1** Architecture a moulding over a door or window which deflects rain. **2** Geology rock deposited by precipitation from dripping water, e.g. as stalactites and stalagmites.

**drive** ● v. (past **drove**; past part. **driven**) **1** operate and control the direction and speed of a motor vehicle. ➤convey in a car. **2** propel or carry along by force in a specified direction. ➤provide the energy to keep (an engine or machine) in motion. ➤(in ball games) hit or kick (the ball) hard. **3** bore (a tunnel). **4** urge or force to move in a specified direction. **5** (usu. **be driven**) compel to act in a particular way: *he was driven by ambition.* ● n. **1** a trip or journey in a car. **2** (also **driveway**) a short private road leading to a house. **3** an innate, biologically determined urge. ➤determination and ambition. **4** an organized effort to achieve a particular purpose: *a recruitment drive.* ➤Brit. a large organized gathering to play whist or another game. **5** the transmission of power to machinery or to the wheels of a vehicle. ➤Computing short for **DISK DRIVE**. **6** an act of driving a ball. **7** an act of driving animals.
– PHRASES **what someone is driving at** the point that someone is attempting to make.
– DERIVATIVES **drivability** (also **driveability**) n. **drivable** (also **driveable**) adj.
– ORIGIN OE *drīfan*, of Gmc origin.

**drive-by** ● adj. chiefly N. Amer. denoting a shooting carried out from a passing vehicle.

**drive-in** ● adj. chiefly N. Amer. denoting a cinema, restaurant, etc. that one can visit without leaving one's car.

**drivel** /ˈdrɪv(ə)l/ ● n. nonsense. ● v. (**drivelled**, **drivelling**; US **driveled**, **driveling**) **1** talk nonsense. **2** archaic let saliva or mucus flow from the mouth or nose.
– DERIVATIVES **driveller** (US **driveler**) n.
– ORIGIN OE *dreflian*, of uncertain origin; perh. rel. to **DRAFF**.

**driveline** /ˈdrʌɪvlʌɪn/ ● n. another term for **DRIVETRAIN**.

**driven** past participle of **DRIVE**.

**driver** ● n. **1** a person or thing that drives something. **2** a flat-faced golf club used for driving.
– PHRASES **in the driver's seat** in control.

## Word *Formation*

**-drome** from Greek *dromos* 'running, course'

➤ A number of seemingly unrelated English words are formed using the element **-drome**:

| | | |
|---|---|---|
| aerodrome | a small airport (also used earlier (1890s) in the sense 'aeroplane') | Gk *aēr* 'air' |
| hippodrome | (in the ancient world) a course for chariot races; in modern use, in names of theatres and concert halls | Gk *hippos* 'horse' |
| loxodrome | an imaginary line cutting all meridians at the same angle, used in navigation | Gk *loxos* 'oblique' |
| palindrome | a sequence of letters that reads the same backwards as forwards | Gk *palin* 'back again' |
| prodrome | an early symptom of illness | Gk *pro* 'before' |
| syndrome | a group of symptoms occurring together | Gk *sun-* 'together' |
| velodrome | a steeply banked cycle-racing track | Fr. *vélo* 'bicycle' |

The term ***dromedary***, denoting the Arabian (or one-humped) camel, is also related etymologically, deriving from Latin *dromedarius (camelus)* 'swift-running camel', based on Greek *dromas* 'runner'.

– DERIVATIVES **driverless** adj.

**driver ant** ● n. another term for **ARMY ANT**.

**driveshaft** ● n. a rotating shaft which transmits torque in an engine.

**drive-through** ● adj. chiefly N. Amer. denoting a restaurant or other facility in which one can be served without leaving one's car.

**drivetrain** ● n. the system in a motor vehicle which connects the transmission to the drive axles.

**driveway** ● n. see **DRIVE** (sense 2).

**driving** ● adj. **1** having a strong and controlling influence: *she was the driving force behind the plan.* **2** being blown by the wind with great force: *driving rain.*
– PHRASES **in the driving seat** in control.

**driving range** ● n. an area where golfers can practise drives.

**drizzle** ● n. **1** light rain falling in very fine drops. **2** Cookery a thin stream of a liquid ingredient trickled over something. ● v. **1** (**it drizzles**, **it is drizzling**, etc.) rain lightly. **2** Cookery apply (an ingredient) as a drizzle.
– DERIVATIVES **drizzly** adj.
– ORIGIN C16: prob. based on OE *drēosan* 'to fall', of Gmc origin; prob. rel. to **DREARY**.

**drogue** /drəʊg/ ● n. a device, typically conical or funnel-shaped, towed behind a boat, aircraft, etc., especially to reduce speed or improve stability.
– ORIGIN C18 (orig. a whaling term denoting a board attached to a harpoon line, used to slow down or mark the position of a whale): perh. rel. to **DRAG**.

**drogue parachute** ● n. a small parachute used as a brake or to pull out a larger parachute.

**droid** /drɔɪd/ ● n. **1** (in science fiction) a robot. **2** Computing a program which automatically collects information from remote systems.
– ORIGIN 1970s: shortening of **ANDROID**.

**droit** /drɔɪt/ ● n. Law, historical a right or due.
– ORIGIN ME: from OFr., based on L. *directus* 'straight, right, direct'.

**droit de seigneur** /ˌdrwʌ də sɛnˈjəː/ ● n. the alleged right of a medieval feudal lord to have sexual intercourse with a vassal's bride on her wedding night.
– ORIGIN Fr., lit. 'lord's right'.

**droll** /drəʊl/ ● adj. amusing in a strange or quaint way. ● n. archaic a jester; a buffoon.
– DERIVATIVES **drollery** n. **drollness** n. **drolly** /ˈdrəʊlli/ adv.
– ORIGIN C17: from Fr. *drôle*, perh. from MDu. *drolle* 'imp, goblin'.

**dromaeosaur** /ˈdrəʊmɪə(ʊ)sɔː/ ● n. a carnivorous bipedal dinosaur of a group including deinonychus and the velociraptors.
– DERIVATIVES **dromaeosaurid** n.
– ORIGIN 1970s: from mod. L. *Dromaeosauridae* (name of a family), based on Gk *dromaios* 'swift-running' + *sauros* 'lizard'.

**-drome** ● comb. form **1** denoting a place for running or racing: *velodrome.* **2** denoting something that proceeds in a certain way: *palindrome.* See word-formation panel.
– ORIGIN from Gk *dromos* (see **DROMOS**).

**dromedary** /ˈdrɒmɪd(ə)ri, ˈdrʌm-/ ● n. (pl. **-ies**) an Arabian camel (with one hump), especially one of a breed trained for riding or racing.
– ORIGIN ME: from OFr. *dromedaire* or late L. *dromedarius (camelus)* 'swift camel', based on Gk *dromas, dromad-* 'runner'.

**dromos** /ˈdrɒmɒs/ ● n. (pl. **dromoi** /-mɔɪ/) an avenue or passage leading into an ancient Greek temple or tomb.
– ORIGIN Gk; rel. to *dramein* 'to run'.

**drone** ● v. make a continuous low humming sound. ➤ speak tediously and at length: *Jim droned on for an hour.* ● n. **1** a low continuous humming sound. ➤ a pipe (especially in a set of bagpipes) or string used to sound a continuous note of low pitch. **2** a male bee which does no work in a colony but can fertilize a queen. ➤ an idler. **3** a remote-controlled pilotless aircraft.
– ORIGIN OE *drān, drǣn* 'male bee', from a W. Gmc verb meaning 'resound, boom'.

**drone fly** ● n. a hoverfly resembling a honeybee. [*Eristalis tenax*.]

**drongo** /ˈdrɒŋgəʊ/ ● n. (pl. **-os** or **-oes**) **1** a long-tailed, crested songbird with glossy black plumage, found in Africa, southern Asia, and Australia. [Family Dicruridae: several species.] **2** informal, chiefly Austral./NZ a stupid or incompetent person.
– ORIGIN C19: from Malagasy; sense 2 is said to be from the name of a very unsuccessful Austral. racehorse of the 1920s.

**droob** /druːb/ ● n. Austral. informal an unprepossessing or contemptible person.
– ORIGIN 1930s: perh. rel. to **DROOP**.

**drool** ● v. **1** drop saliva uncontrollably from the mouth. **2** informal make an excessive show of pleasure or desire: *enthusiasts drooled over old cars.* ● n. saliva falling from the mouth.
– ORIGIN C19: contr. of **DRIVEL**.

**droop** ● v. bend or hang downwards limply. ➤ sag down from weariness or dejection. ● n. an act or instance of drooping.
– DERIVATIVES **droopily** adv. **droopiness** n. **droopy** adj. (**-ier**, **-iest**).
– ORIGIN ME: from ON *drúpa* 'hang the head'; rel. to **DRIP** and **DROP**.

**drop** ● v. (**dropped**, **dropping**) **1** fall or cause to fall vertically. ➤ deliver by parachute. **2** (of an animal) give birth to. **3** sink to or towards the ground. ➤ informal collapse from exhaustion. **4** make or become lower, weaker, or less. **5** abandon or discontinue: *the charges against him were dropped.* ➤ discard or exclude. **6** set down or unload

(a passenger or goods). ➤ place without ceremony: *drop it in the post.* ➤ mention in passing, especially in order to impress. **7** lose (a point, a match, etc.). **8** Bridge be forced to play (a relatively high card) as a loser. **9** [usu. as adj. **dropped**] Rugby score by a drop kick. **10** informal take (a drug) orally. ● **n. 1** a small round or pear-shaped portion of liquid. ➤ (**drops**) liquid medication applied in very small amounts. **2** [usu. with neg.] a drink of alcohol. **3** an instance of falling or dropping. ➤ an abrupt fall or slope. **4** informal a delivery. ➤ US a letter box. **5** a sweet or lozenge: *a chocolate drop.* **6** a pendant earring. **7** a drop cloth. **8** the trapdoor on a gallows, through which the victim fell.
– PHRASES **at the drop of a hat** informal without delay or good reason. **drop one's aitches** omit the 'h' sound from the beginning of words. **drop asleep** fall gently asleep. **drop the ball** N. Amer. informal make a mistake. **drop a brick** Brit. informal make an indiscreet or embarrassing remark. **drop a clanger** Brit. informal make an embarrassing or foolish mistake. **drop a curtsy** Brit. make a curtsy. **drop dead** die suddenly and unexpectedly. **drop one's guard** abandon one's habitual defensive or watchful stance. **drop a hint** let fall a hint, as if casually or unconsciously. **a drop in the ocean** (or **in a bucket**) a very small amount compared with what is needed or expected. **drop someone a line** send someone an informal note or letter. **drop a stitch** let a stitch fall off the end of a knitting needle. **have the drop on** informal have the advantage over.
– PHRASAL VERBS **drop back/behind** fall back or get left behind. **drop by/in** visit informally and briefly. **drop off** fall asleep, especially without intending to. **drop out 1** cease to participate. **2** abandon a course of study. **3** pursue an alternative lifestyle. **4** Rugby restart play with a drop kick.
– DERIVATIVES **droppable** adj.
– ORIGIN OE *dropa* (n.), *droppian* (v.), of Gmc origin; rel. to **DRIP** and **DROOP**.

**drop capital** ● **n.** a large opening capital letter occupying more than the depth of one line.

**drop cloth** ● **n. 1** (also **drop curtain**) a curtain or painted cloth lowered vertically on to a theatre stage. **2** N. Amer. a dust sheet.

**drop-dead** ● **adj.** informal used to emphasize attractiveness: *drop-dead gorgeous.*

**drop-forged** ● **adj.** made by forcing hot metal into or through a die with a drop hammer.
– DERIVATIVES **drop-forging** n.

**drop goal** ● **n.** Rugby a goal scored by drop-kicking the ball over the crossbar.

**drop hammer** ● **n.** a large heavy weight allowed to drop, used in drop-forging and piledriving.

**drop handlebars** ● **pl. n.** handlebars with the handles bent below the rest of the bar, used especially on racing cycles.

**drophead** ● **n.** Brit. a convertible car.

**drop initial** ● **n.** another term for **DROP CAPITAL**.

**drop kick** ● **n. 1** a kick made by dropping the ball and kicking it as it bounces. **2** (chiefly in martial arts) a flying kick made while dropping to the ground. ● **v.** (**drop-kick**) kick using a drop kick.

**droplet** ● **n.** a very small drop of a liquid.

**drop-off** ● **n. 1** a decline or decrease. **2** chiefly N. Amer. a sheer downward slope.

**dropout** ● **n. 1** a person who has dropped out of society or a course of study. **2** Rugby the restarting of play with a drop kick. **3** a momentary loss of recorded audio signal or an error in reading data.

**dropper** ● **n. 1** a short glass tube with a rubber bulb at one end, for measuring out drops of liquid. **2** Austral./NZ & S. African a light vertical stave in a fence. **3** Fishing a subsidiary line or loop of filament attached to a main line.

**droppings** ● **pl. n.** the excrement of animals.

**drop scene** ● **n. 1** a drop curtain used as part of stage scenery. **2** the last scene of a play.

**drop scone** ● **n.** a small thick pancake made by dropping batter on to a heated surface.

**dropseed** ● **n.** a grass that readily drops its seeds. [Genus *Sporobolus*: several species.]

**drop shot** ● **n.** (in tennis or squash) a softly hit shot, usually with backspin, which drops abruptly to the ground.

**drop shoulder** ● **n.** a style of shoulder on a garment cut with the seam positioned on the upper arm rather than the shoulder.

**dropsy**[1] /ˈdrɒpsi/ ● **n.** (pl. **-ies**) old-fashioned or less technical term for **OEDEMA**.
– DERIVATIVES **dropsical** adj.
– ORIGIN ME: shortening of obs. *hydropsy*, via OFr. and L. from Gk *hudrōps*, from *hudōr* 'water'.

**dropsy**[2] /ˈdrɒpsi/ ● **n.** (pl. **-ies**) Brit. informal a tip or bribe.
– ORIGIN 1930s: elaborated form of sl. *drop* 'a bribe'.

**drop tank** ● **n.** an external fuel tank on an aircraft which can be jettisoned when empty.

**drop test** ● **n.** a test of the strength of an object, in which it is dropped under standard conditions or a set weight is dropped on it from a given height.
– DERIVATIVES **drop-testing** n.

**drop-top** ● **n.** another term for **DROPHEAD**.

**drop waist** ● **n.** a style of waistline with the seam positioned at the hips rather than the waist.

**dropwort** ● **n. 1** a grassland plant with small white flowers and divided leaves. [*Filipendula vulgaris*.] **2** (**water dropwort**) a poisonous plant of the parsley family, which grows in wet habitats. [*Oenanthe crocata* (Europe) and other species.]
– ORIGIN ME: named from the small drop-like fibrous tubers on its roots.

**drop zone** ● **n.** a designated area into which troops or supplies are dropped by parachute.

**drosera** /ˈdrɒs(ə)rə/ ● **n.** a sundew (insectivorous plant). [Genus *Drosera*.]
– ORIGIN mod. L., from Gk *droseros* 'dewy'.

**droshky** /ˈdrɒʃki/ ● **n.** (pl. **-ies**) a low four-wheeled open carriage of a kind formerly used in Russia.
– ORIGIN C19: from Russ. *drozhki*, dimin. of *drogi* 'wagon'.

**drosophila** /drɒˈsɒfɪlə/ ● **n.** a genus of fruit flies used extensively in genetic research.
– ORIGIN mod. L., from Gk *drosos* 'dew, moisture' + *philos* 'loving'.

**dross** ● **n. 1** rubbish. **2** scum on the surface of molten metal.
– DERIVATIVES **drossy** adj.
– ORIGIN OE *drōs*; rel. to Du. *droesem* and Ger. *Drusen* 'dregs, lees'.

**drought** /draʊt/ ● **n.** a prolonged period of abnormally low rainfall; a shortage of water. ➤ archaic thirst.
– DERIVATIVES **droughtiness** n. **droughty** adj.
– ORIGIN OE *drūgath* 'dryness', of Gmc origin; rel. to **DRY**.

**drouth** /draʊθ/ ● **n.** dialect or poetic/literary form of **DROUGHT**.
– DERIVATIVES **drouthy** adj.

**drove**[1] past of **DRIVE**.

**drove**[2] ● **n.** a flock of animals being driven. ➤ a large number of people doing the same thing: *tourists arrived in droves.* ● **v.** [usu. as noun **droving**] historical drive (livestock) to market.
– DERIVATIVES **drover** n.
– ORIGIN OE *drāf*, rel. to *drīfan* 'to drive'.

**drove road** ● **n.** an ancient roadway along which cattle were driven to market.

**drown** ● **v. 1** die or kill through submersion in water. **2** submerge or flood (an area). **3** (usu. **drown something out**) make inaudible by being much louder.
– PHRASES **drown one's sorrows** forget one's problems by getting drunk.
– ORIGIN ME (orig. northern): rel. to ON *drukkna* 'to be drowned', also to **DRINK**.

**drowse** /draʊz/ ● **v.** be half asleep; doze. ➤ archaic make sleepy. ● **n.** an instance of drowsing. ➤ a state of drowsiness.
– ORIGIN C16: back-form. from **DROWSY**.

**drowsy** ● **adj.** (**-ier**, **-iest**) sleepy and lethargic.
– DERIVATIVES **drowsily** adv. **drowsiness** n.
– ORIGIN C15: prob. from the stem of OE *drūsian* 'be lan-

guid or slow', of Gmc origin; rel. to **DREARY**.

**drub** • v. (**drubbed**, **drubbing**) **1** hit or beat repeatedly. **2** informal defeat thoroughly.
– DERIVATIVES **drubbing** n.
– ORIGIN C17 (orig. with ref. to the punishment of bastinado): prob. from Arab. *ḍaraba* 'to beat, bastinado'.

**drudge** • n. a person made to do hard, menial, or dull work. • v. archaic do such work.
– DERIVATIVES **drudgery** n.
– ORIGIN ME: of unknown origin; perh. rel. to **DRAG**.

**drug** • n. a medicine or other substance which has a marked physiological effect when taken into the body. ➤a substance with narcotic or stimulant effects. • v. (**drugged**, **drugging**) administer a drug to, in order to induce stupor or insensibility.
– ORIGIN ME: from OFr. *drogue*, perh. from MDu. *droge vate*, lit. 'dry vats', referring to the contents.

**drugget** /ˈdrʌɡɪt/ • n. a floor covering made of a coarse woven fabric.
– ORIGIN C16: from Fr. *droguet*, from *drogue* in the sense 'poor-quality article'.

**druggist** • n. chiefly N. Amer. a pharmacist or retailer of medicinal drugs.

**druggy** informal • adj. caused by or involving drugs. • n. (also **druggie**) (pl. **-ies**) a drug addict.

**drugstore** • n. N. Amer. a pharmacy which also sells toiletries and other articles.

**Druid** /ˈdruːɪd/ • n. a priest, magician, or soothsayer in the ancient Celtic religion. ➤a member of a present-day group claiming to be derived from this religion.
– DERIVATIVES **Druidic** adj. **Druidical** adj. **Druidism** n.
– ORIGIN from L. *druidae*, *druides* (pl.), from Gaulish; rel. to Ir. *draoidh* 'magician, sorcerer'.

**drum**[1] • n. **1** a percussion instrument sounded by being struck with sticks or the hands, typically cylindrical, barrel-shaped, or bowl-shaped with a taut membrane over one or both ends. ➤a sound made by or resembling that of a drum. **2** historical a military drummer. **3** a cylindrical object or part, especially a container: *an oil drum*. ➤Architecture the circular vertical wall supporting a dome. **4** Brit. informal a house or flat. ➤Austral./NZ informal a brothel. **5** a tea party of a kind popular in the late 18th and early 19th century. **6** Austral./NZ informal a piece of reliable inside information. **7** Austral./NZ dated a tramp's bundle of belongings. • v. (**drummed**, **drumming**) **1** play on a drum. ➤make or cause to make a continuous rhythmic noise. **2** (**drum something into**) drive a lesson into (someone) by constant repetition. **3** (**drum someone out**) expel or dismiss someone with ignominy. **4** (**drum something up**) attempt to obtain something by canvassing or soliciting: *they drummed up support*. **5** Austral./NZ informal, dated give (someone) reliable information or a warning.
– PHRASES **beat** (or **bang**) **the drum of** (or **for**) be ostentatiously in support of.
– ORIGIN ME: from MDu. or Low Ger. *tromme*, of imitative origin.

**drum**[2] (also **drumfish**) • n. (pl. same or **drums**) a coastal or estuarine fish that makes a drumming sound by vibrating its swim bladder. [Family Sciaenidae: many species.]

**drum and bass** • n. a type of dance music characterized by bare instrumentation consisting largely of electronic drums and bass.

**drumbeat** • n. a stroke or pattern of strokes on a drum.

**drumfire** • n. heavy continuous rapid artillery fire.

**drumhead** • n. **1** the membrane or skin of a drum. **2** a winter cabbage of a flat-topped variety. **3** chiefly historical the circular top of a ship's capstan. • adj. denoting a summary trial, as carried out by an army in the field.

**drum kit** • n. a set of drums, cymbals, and other percussion instruments.

**drumlin** /ˈdrʌmlɪn/ • n. Geology an oval mound or small hill consisting of compacted boulder clay moulded by glacial action.
– ORIGIN C19: prob. from *drum* 'long narrow hill' (from Sc. Gaelic and Ir. *druim* 'ridge') + *-lin* (from **-LING**).

**drum major** • n. **1** a non-commissioned officer commanding regimental drummers. **2** the male leader of a marching band, who twirls a baton.

**drum majorette** • n. the female leader of a marching band, who twirls a baton. ➤a female member of such a band.

**drummer** • n. **1** a person who plays a drum or drums. **2** informal, chiefly N. Amer. a travelling sales representative. **3** Brit. informal, dated a thief or burglar.

**drum pad** • n. an electronic device with pads which imitate the sounds of a drum kit when struck.

**drum roll** • n. a rapid succession of drumbeats, typically used to introduce an announcement or event.

**drumstick** • n. **1** a stick used for beating a drum. **2** the lower joint of the leg of a cooked fowl.

**drunk** past part. of **DRINK**. • adj. affected by alcohol to the extent of losing control of one's faculties or behaviour. • n. **1** a person who is drunk or who habitually drinks to excess. **2** informal a drinking bout.
– PHRASES **drunk and disorderly** creating a public disturbance under the influence of alcohol.

**drunkard** • n. a person who is habitually drunk.
– ORIGIN ME: from Mid. Low Ger. *drunkert*.

**drunken** • adj. drunk, especially habitually or frequently. ➤caused by or showing the effects of drink.
– DERIVATIVES **drunkenly** adv. **drunkenness** n.
– ORIGIN OE, archaic past part. of **DRINK**.

**drupe** /druːp/ • n. **1** Botany a fleshy fruit with thin skin and a central stone, e.g. a plum or olive. **2** a small marine mollusc with a thick knobbly shell. [Genus *Drupa*.]
– DERIVATIVES **drupaceous** adj. (Botany).
– ORIGIN C18: from L. *drupa* 'overripe olive'.

**drupel** /ˈdruːp(ə)l/ (also **drupelet**) • n. Botany any of the small individual drupes forming a fleshy aggregate fruit such as a raspberry.
– ORIGIN C19: from mod. L. *drupella*, dimin. of *drupa* (see **DRUPE**).

**druse** /druːz/ • n. **1** Geology a rock cavity lined with a crust of projecting crystals. **2** Botany a rounded cluster of calcium oxalate crystals found in some plant cells.
– DERIVATIVES **drusy** adj. (Geology).
– ORIGIN C19: via Fr. from Ger. *Druse* 'weathered ore'.

**druther** /ˈdrʌðə/ N. Amer. informal • n. (usu. **one's druthers**) a person's preference in a matter. • adv. rather.
– ORIGIN C19: from a US regional pronunc. of *I'd rather*.

**Druze** /druːz/ (also **Druse**) • n. (pl. same, **Druzes**, or **Druses**) a member of a political and religious sect of Islamic origin, living chiefly in Lebanon and Syria.
– ORIGIN from Fr., from Arab. *durūz* (pl.), from the name of one of their founders, Muhammad ibn Ismail *al-Darazī* (died 1019).

**dry** • adj. (**drier**, **driest**) **1** free from moisture or liquid. ➤not yielding water, oil, or milk: *a dry well*. ➤without grease or other moisturizer or lubricator: *dry hair*. **2** (of information, writing, etc.) dully factual. ➤unemotional or undemonstrative. ➤(of humour) subtle and expressed in a matter-of-fact way. **3** prohibiting the sale or consumption of alcoholic drink. ➤no longer drinking alcohol. **4** (of wine) not sweet. • v. (**-ies**, **-ied**) **1** become or cause to become dry. ➤[usu. as adj. **dried**] preserve by evaporating the moisture from: *dried milk*. **2** (**dry up**) (of a supply or flow) decrease and stop. **3** theatrical slang forget one's lines. ➤(**dry up**) informal cease talking. **4** (**dry out**) informal overcome alcoholism. • n. (pl. **dries** or **drys**) **1** (**the dry**) chiefly Austral. the dry season, or a tract of waterless country. **2** Brit. a Conservative politician (especially in the 1980s) in favour of strict monetarist policies. **3** US a person in favour of the prohibition of alcohol.
– PHRASES **come up dry** N. Amer. informal be unsuccessful.
– DERIVATIVES **dryish** adj. **dryness** n.
– ORIGIN OE *drȳge* (adj.), *drȳgan* (v.), of Gmc origin.

**dryad** /ˈdrʌɪəd, -ad/ • n. **1** (in folklore and Greek mythology) a nymph inhabiting a tree or wood. **2** a dark brown butterfly with prominent bluish eyespots. [*Minois dryas*.]
– ORIGIN via OFr. and L. from Gk *druas*, *druad-*, from *drus* 'tree'.

**dryas** /ˈdrʌɪəs/ • n. **1** a plant of a genus that comprises the mountain avens. [Genus *Dryas*.] **2** (**Dryas**) Geology a

cold stage at the end of the glacial period in northern Europe, in which such plants were abundant.
– ORIGIN mod. L., from Gk *druas* (see **DRYAD**); so named because the plant's leaves resemble those of an oak.

**dry bulb** • **n.** an ordinary exposed thermometer bulb, as used in conjunction with a wet bulb.

**dry cell** (also **dry battery**) • **n.** an electric cell (or battery) in which the electrolyte is absorbed in a solid to form a paste.

**dry-clean** • **v.** clean (a garment) with an organic solvent.
– DERIVATIVES **dry-cleaner** n.

**dry cough** • **n.** a cough not producing phlegm.

**dry-cure** • **v.** cure (meat or fish) with salt rather than in liquid.

**dry dock** • **n.** a dock which can be drained of water to allow repair of a ship's hull. • **v.** (**dry-dock**) place in a dry dock.

**dryer** (also **drier**) • **n. 1** a machine or device for drying something, especially the hair or laundry. **2** a substance mixed with oil paint or ink to promote drying.

**dry fly** • **n.** an artificial fishing fly which floats lightly on the water.

**dry-fry** • **v.** fry in a pan without fat or oil.

**dry goods** • **pl. n. 1** solid commodities traded in bulk, e.g. tea or sugar. **2** chiefly N. Amer. drapery and haberdashery.

**dry ice** • **n.** solid carbon dioxide. ➤ white mist produced with this as a theatrical effect.

**drying oil** • **n.** an oil that thickens or hardens in air, used in mixing paint.

**dry lease** • **n.** an arrangement for the hire of an aircraft without the provision of a flight crew.

**dryly** • **adv.** variant spelling of **DRILY**.

**dry measure** • **n.** a measure of volume for dry goods.

**dry milk** • **n.** US dried milk.

**dry mounting** • **n.** Photography a process in which a print is bonded to a mount using shellac in a hot press.

**Dryopithecus** /ˌdrʌɪə'pɪθɪkəs/ • **n.** a genus of anthropoid apes of the middle Miocene to early Pliocene periods, including the supposed common ancestor of gorillas, chimpanzees, and humans.
– DERIVATIVES **dryopithecine** /-siːn/ n. & adj.
– ORIGIN mod. L., from Gk *drus* 'tree' + *pithēkos* 'ape'.

**dry plate** • **n.** Photography a glass plate coated with a light-sensitive gelatin-based emulsion.

**dry point** • **n.** a needle for engraving on a bare copper plate without acid. ➤ an engraving so produced.

**dry rot** • **n.** a fungus causing decay of wood in poorly ventilated conditions. [*Serpula lacrymans*.]

**dry run** • **n.** informal a rehearsal of a performance or procedure.

**dry-salt** • **v.** another term for **DRY-CURE**.

**dry-salter** • **n.** Brit. historical a dealer in dyes, gums, and drugs, and sometimes also in preserved foodstuffs.

**dry-shod** • **adj. & adv.** without wetting one's shoes.

**dry sink** • **n.** N. Amer. an antique kitchen cabinet with an inset basin.

**dry slope** (also **dry-ski slope**) • **n.** an artificial ski slope.

**drystone** • **adj.** Brit. (of a stone wall) built without using mortar.

**drysuit** • **n.** a waterproof rubber suit for water sports, under which warm clothes can be worn.

**dry valley** • **n.** a valley containing no permanent surface stream.

**drywall** • **n.** N. Amer. plasterboard.

**DS** • **abbrev. 1** Music dal segno. **2** Military directing staff. **3** document signed.

**DSC** • **abbrev.** (in the UK) Distinguished Service Cross.

**DSc** • **abbrev.** Doctor of Science.

**DSL** • **abbrev.** digital subscriber line, a technology for the high-speed transmission of digital information over standard telephone lines.

**DSM** • **abbrev.** (in the UK) Distinguished Service Medal.

**DSO** • **abbrev.** (in the UK) Distinguished Service Order.

**DSP** • **abbrev. 1** died without issue. [from L. *decessit sine prole*.] **2** digital signal processor or processing.

**DSS** • **abbrev. 1** decision support system. **2** (in the UK) Department of Social Security.

**DTI** • **abbrev.** (in the UK) Department of Trade and Industry.

**DTP** • **abbrev.** desktop publishing.

**DTp** • **abbrev.** (in the UK) Department of Transport.

**DTs** • **pl. n.** informal delirium tremens.

**dual** • **adj. 1** consisting of two parts, elements, or aspects. ➤ Grammar denoting an inflection that refers to exactly two people or things. **2** (often **dual to**) Mathematics related to another theorem or expression by the interchange of terms, such as 'point' and 'line'. • **n. 1** Grammar a dual inflection. **2** Mathematics a theorem or expression that is dual to another. • **v.** (**dualled**, **dualling**) Brit. convert (a road) into a dual carriageway.
– DERIVATIVES **duality** n. **dualize** (also **-ise**) v. **dually** adv.
– ORIGIN ME: from L. *dualis*, from *duo* 'two'.

**dual carriageway** • **n.** Brit. a road consisting of two or more lanes in each direction and with a dividing strip separating the two directions.

**dual in-line package** • **n.** Electronics a package for an integrated circuit consisting of a rectangular sealed unit with two parallel rows of downward-pointing pins.

**dualism** • **n. 1** the division of something conceptually into two opposed or contrasted aspects, such as good and evil or mind and matter. **2** duality.
– DERIVATIVES **dualist** n. & adj. **dualistic** adj. **dualistically** adv.

**dual-use** • **adj.** chiefly US (of technology or equipment) suitable for both civilian and military purposes.

**dub**[1] • **v.** (**dubbed**, **dubbing**) **1** give an unofficial name or nickname to. **2** knight (someone) by the ritual touching of the shoulder with a sword. **3** dress (an artificial fishing fly) with fur or wool. **4** smear (leather) with grease.
– ORIGIN OE: from OFr. *adober* 'equip with armour'.

**dub**[2] • **v.** (**dubbed**, **dubbing**) **1** provide (a film) with a soundtrack in a different language from the original. ➤ add (sound effects or music) to a film or a recording. **2** make a copy of (a recording). ➤ transfer (a recording) from one medium to another. ➤ combine (two or more sound recordings) into one soundtrack. • **n. 1** an instance of dubbing sound effects or music. **2** a style of popular music originating from the remixing of recorded music (especially reggae).
– DERIVATIVES **dubby** adj.
– ORIGIN 1920s: abbrev. of **DOUBLE**.

**dub**[3] informal • **n.** chiefly US an inexperienced or unskilful person. • **v.** (**dubbed**, **dubbing**) Golf misplay (a shot).
– ORIGIN C19: perh. from **DUB**[1] in the obs. technical sense 'make blunt'.

**dubbin** /'dʌbɪn/ Brit. • **n.** prepared grease used for softening and waterproofing leather. • **v.** (**dubbined**, **dubbining**) apply dubbin to (leather).
– ORIGIN C19: alt. of *dubbing*, pres. part. of **DUB**[1] (sense 4).

**dubbing** • **n.** material used for the bodies of artificial fishing flies, especially fur or wool on waxed silk.
– ORIGIN C17: from **DUB**[1] + **-ING**[1].

**dubiety** /djuː'bʌɪɪti/ • **n.** formal uncertainty.
– ORIGIN C18: from late L. *dubietas*, from L. *dubium* 'a doubt'.

**dubious** /'djuːbɪəs/ • **adj. 1** hesitating or doubting. **2** not to be relied upon. ➤ of questionable value.
– DERIVATIVES **dubiously** adv. **dubiousness** n.
– ORIGIN C16: from L. *dubiosus*, from *dubium* 'a doubt', neut. of *dubius* 'doubtful'.

**dubitable** /'djuːbɪtəb(ə)l/ • **adj.** rare open to doubt.
– DERIVATIVES **dubitability** n.
– ORIGIN C17: from L. *dubitabilis*, from *dubitare* 'to doubt'.

**dubitation** /ˌdjuːbɪ'teɪʃ(ə)n/ • **n.** formal doubt; hesitation.
– DERIVATIVES **dubitative** adj.
– ORIGIN ME: from L. *dubitatio(n-)*, from *dubitare* 'to doubt'.

**Dublin Bay prawn** • **n.** another term for **NORWAY LOB-**

**STER.** ➤(**Dublin Bay prawns**) scampi.

**dubnium** /'dʌbnɪəm/ ● **n.** the chemical element of atomic number 105, a very unstable element made by high-energy atomic collisions. (Symbol: **Db**)
– ORIGIN 1990s: mod. L., from *Dubna* in Russia, site of the Joint Nuclear Institute.

**Dubonnet** /d(j)uː'bɒneɪ/ ● **n.** trademark a sweet French red wine.
– ORIGIN from the name of a family of Fr. wine merchants.

**ducal** /'djuːk(ə)l/ ● **adj.** of, like, or relating to a duke or dukedom.
– ORIGIN C15: from OFr., from *duc* 'duke'.

**ducat** /'dʌkət/ ● **n. 1** a gold coin formerly current in most European countries. ➤(**ducats**) informal money. **2** informal, chiefly N. Amer. a ticket.
– ORIGIN from Ital. *ducato*, orig. referring to a silver coin minted by the Duke of Apulia in 1190: from med. L. *ducatus* (see **DUCHY**).

**Duchenne muscular dystrophy** /duː'ʃɛn/ ● **n.** a severe form of muscular dystrophy caused by a genetic defect and usually affecting boys.
– ORIGIN C19: named after the Fr. neurologist G. B. A. *Duchenne*.

**duchess** ● **n. 1** the wife or widow of a duke. ➤a woman holding a rank equivalent to duke in her own right. **2** Brit. informal (especially among cockney men) an affectionate form of address for a girl or woman.
– ORIGIN ME: via OFr. from med. L. *ducissa*, from L. *dux*, *duc-* (see **DUKE**).

**duchesse** /duː'ʃɛs, 'dʌtʃɪs, -ɛs/ ● **n. 1** (also **duchesse satin**) a soft, heavy, glossy kind of satin. **2** a chaise longue resembling two armchairs linked by a stool. **3** a dressing table with a pivoting mirror.
– ORIGIN C18: from Fr., lit. 'duchess'.

**duchesse lace** ● **n.** a kind of Brussels pillow lace with bold floral patterns worked in a fine thread.

**duchesse potatoes** ● **pl. n.** mashed potatoes mixed with egg yolk, piped into small shapes and baked.

**duchy** /'dʌtʃi/ ● **n.** (pl. **-ies**) the territory of a duke or duchess.
– ORIGIN ME: from OFr. *duche*, from med. L. *ducatus*, from L. *dux*, *duc-* (see **DUKE**).

**duck**[1] ● **n.** (pl. same or **ducks**) **1** a waterbird with a broad blunt bill, short legs, webbed feet, and a waddling gait, some kinds of which are domesticated. [Family Anatidae: many species.] ➤the female of such a bird. Contrasted with **DRAKE**[1]. **2** a pure white, thin-shelled bivalve mollusc found off the Atlantic coasts of America. [Genus *Anatina*.]
– PHRASES **get** (or **have**) **one's ducks in a row** N. Amer. informal get (or have) everything organized. **like water off a duck's back** referring to a hurtful remark which has no effect. **take to something like a duck to water** take to something very readily.
– ORIGIN OE *duce*, from the Gmc base of **DUCK**[2] (expressing the notion of 'diving bird').

**duck**[2] ● **v. 1** lower the head or body quickly to avoid a blow or missile or so as not to be seen. ➤avoid (a blow or missile) by ducking. ➤informal evade (an unwelcome duty). **2** push (someone) under water. **3** Bridge refrain from playing a winning card on a particular trick for tactical reasons. ● **n.** a quick lowering of the head.
– PHRASES **duck and dive** use one's ingenuity to deal with or evade a situation.
– DERIVATIVES **ducker** n.
– ORIGIN ME: of Gmc origin; rel. to **DUCK**[1].

**duck**[3] ● **n.** Cricket a batsman's score of nought.
– PHRASES **break one's duck** Cricket score the first run of one's innings.
– ORIGIN C19: short for *duck's egg*, used for the figure 0.

**duck**[4] (also **ducks**) ● **n.** Brit. informal dear (used as an affectionate form of address).
– ORIGIN C16: from **DUCK**[1].

**duck**[5] ● **n.** a strong untwilled linen or cotton fabric, used chiefly for work clothes and sails. ➤(**ducks**) trousers made from such a fabric.
– ORIGIN C17: from MDu. *doek* 'linen'.

**duckbill** ● **n.** an animal with jaws resembling a duck's bill, e.g. a platypus.

**duck-billed dinosaur** ● **n.** another term for **HADROSAUR**.

**duck-billed platypus** ● **n.** see **PLATYPUS**.

**duckboards** ● **pl. n.** wooden slats joined together to form a path over muddy ground.

**ducking stool** ● **n.** historical a chair fastened to the end of a pole, used to plunge offenders into a pond or river as a punishment.

**duckling** ● **n.** a young duck.

**duck mussel** ● **n.** a freshwater mussel found in rivers with sandy or gravelly beds. [*Anodonta anatina*.]

**duckpin** ● **n.** US a short squat bowling pin.

**ducks and drakes** ● **n.** a game of throwing flat stones so that they skim along the surface of water.
– PHRASES **play ducks and drakes with** treat frivolously.
– ORIGIN C16: from the movement of the stone over the water.

**duck's arse** (US **duck's ass**) ● **n.** informal a man's hairstyle in which the hair is slicked back on both sides and tapered at the nape.

**duck soup** ● **n.** N. Amer. informal an easy task.

**duckwalk** ● **v.** walk in a squatting posture.

**duckweed** ● **n.** a tiny aquatic flowering plant that floats in large quantities on still water. [*Lemna* and other genera, family Lemnaceae.]

**ducky** informal ● **n.** (pl. **-ies**) Brit. dear (used as a form of address). ● **adj.** chiefly N. Amer. delightful.
– ORIGIN C19: from **DUCK**[4].

**duct** ● **n.** a tube or passageway in a building or machine for air, cables, etc. ➤a vessel in the body for conveying lymph or glandular secretions. ➤a vessel in a plant for conveying water, sap, or air. ● **v.** (usu. **be ducted**) convey through a duct.
– DERIVATIVES **ducting** n.
– ORIGIN C17 (in the sense 'course' or 'direction'): from L. *ductus* 'leading, aqueduct' from *duct-*, *ducere* 'lead'.

**ductile** /'dʌktʌɪl/ ● **adj. 1** (of a metal) able to be drawn out into a thin wire. **2** able to be deformed without losing toughness.
– DERIVATIVES **ductility** n.
– ORIGIN ME: from L. *ductilis*, from *duct-*, *ducere* 'to lead'.

**ductless** ● **adj.** Anatomy denoting a gland that secretes directly into the bloodstream, such as an endocrine gland.

**duct tape** ● **n.** N. Amer. strong cloth-backed waterproof adhesive tape.
– ORIGIN 1970s: orig. used for repairing leaks in ducted ventilation and heating systems.

**ductule** /'dʌktjuːl/ ● **n.** Anatomy a minute duct.
– DERIVATIVES **ductular** adj.

**ductus** /'dʌktəs/ ● **n.** (pl. **ducti**) Anatomy a duct.
– ORIGIN C17: from L., lit. 'leading'.

**dud** informal ● **n. 1** a thing that fails to work properly. ➤an ineffectual person. **2** (**duds**) clothes. ● **adj.** failing to work or meet a standard.
– ORIGIN ME: of unknown origin.

**dude** /d(j)uːd/ N. Amer. informal ● **n. 1** a man. **2** a dandy. ● **v.** (**dude up**) dress up elaborately.
– DERIVATIVES **dudish** adj.
– ORIGIN C19: prob. from Ger. dial. *Dude* 'fool'.

**dude ranch** ● **n.** (in the western US) a cattle ranch converted to a holiday centre for tourists.

**dudgeon** /'dʌdʒ(ə)n/ ● **n.** deep resentment.
– ORIGIN C16: of unknown origin.

**due** ● **adj. 1** expected at, planned for, or required by a certain time. ➤(of a person) at a point where something is owed or merited. ➤required as a legal or moral obligation. **2** proper; appropriate. ● **n. 1** (**one's due/dues**) a person's right. **2** (**dues**) fees. ● **adv.** (with reference to a point of the compass) directly.
– PHRASES **due to 1** caused by. **2** because of. **give someone their due** be fair to someone. **in due course** at the appropriate time. **pay one's dues** fulfil one's obligations.
– ORIGIN ME: from OFr. *deu* 'owed', based on L. *debitus*

'owed', from *debere* 'owe'.

**USAGE due**

**Due to** in the sense 'because of' has been condemned as incorrect on the grounds that **due** is an adjective and should not be used in a prepositional phrase. However, the prepositional use is now common in all types of literature and is regarded as part of standard English.

**duel** • **n.** chiefly historical a pre-arranged contest with deadly weapons between two people to settle a point of honour. ➤(in modern use) a contest between two parties. • **v.** (**duelled**, **duelling**; US **dueled**, **dueling**) fight a duel.
– DERIVATIVES **dueller** (US **dueler**) n. **duellist** (US **duelist**) n.
– ORIGIN C15: from L. *duellum*, archaic and literary form of *bellum* 'war', used in med. L. with the meaning 'combat between two persons', influenced by *dualis* 'of two'.

**duende** /duːˈɛndeɪ/ • **n. 1** passion. **2** an evil spirit.
– ORIGIN 1920s: from Sp., contr. of *duen de casa*, from *dueño de casa* 'owner of the house'.

**duenna** /duːˈɛnə/ • **n.** an older woman acting as a governess and chaperone to girls in a Spanish family.
– ORIGIN C17: earlier form of Sp. *dueña*, from L. *domina* 'lady, mistress'.

**due process** (also **due process of law**) • **n.** fair treatment through the normal judicial system.

**duet** • **n.** a performance by two singers, instrumentalists, or dancers. ➤a musical composition for two performers. • **v.** (**duetted**, **duetting**) perform a duet.
– DERIVATIVES **duettist** n.
– ORIGIN C18: from Ital. *duetto*, dimin. of *duo* 'duet'.

**duff**[1] • **n.** a flour pudding boiled or steamed in a cloth bag.
– ORIGIN C19: north. Engl. form of **DOUGH**.

**duff**[2] • **adj.** Brit. informal worthless or false. • **n.** N. Amer. & Scottish decaying vegetable matter covering the ground under trees.
– ORIGIN C18 (denoting something worthless): of unknown origin.

**duff**[3] • **v.** informal **1** (**duff someone up**) Brit. beat someone up. **2** Austral. steal and alter brands on (cattle). **3** Golf mishit (a shot).
– ORIGIN sense 1 (1960s) of uncertain origin; senses 2 and 3 (both C19) prob. back-forms. from **DUFFER**[2] and **DUFFER**[1] respectively.

**duff**[4] • **n.** N. Amer. informal a person's buttocks.
– ORIGIN C19: of unknown origin.

**duff**[5] • **n.** (in phr. **up the duff**) Brit. informal pregnant.
– ORIGIN 1940s (orig. Austral.): perh. rel. to **DUFF**[1].

**duffel** (also **duffle**) • **n. 1** a coarse woollen cloth with a thick nap. **2** N. Amer. sporting or camping equipment.
– ORIGIN C17: from *Duffel*, the name of a town in Belgium where the cloth was orig. made.

**duffel bag** • **n.** a cylindrical canvas bag closed by a drawstring.
– ORIGIN C20 (orig. US): from sense 2 of **DUFFEL**.

**duffel coat** • **n.** a hooded coat made of duffel, typically fastened with toggles.

**duffer**[1] • **n.** informal **1** an incompetent or stupid person. **2** Austral./NZ an unproductive mine.
– ORIGIN C19: from Scots *dowfart* 'stupid person'.

**duffer**[2] • **n.** Austral. informal a person who steals and alters the brands on cattle.
– ORIGIN C19 (orig. thieves' sl. for 'someone who sells trashy articles as valuable'): of unknown origin.

**dufus** • **n.** variant spelling of **DOOFUS**.

**dug**[1] past and past participle of **DIG**.

**dug**[2] • **n.** the udder, teat, or nipple of a female animal. ➤archaic a woman's breast.
– ORIGIN C16: perh. of ON origin.

**dugite** /ˈdjuːgʌɪt/ • **n.** a highly venomous snake of SW Australia. [*Pseudonaja affinis*.]
– ORIGIN C19: from Nyungar *dukayj*.

**dugong** /ˈduːgɒŋ, ˈdjuː-/ • **n.** (pl. same or **dugongs**) a sea cow found in the Indian Ocean, distinguished from the manatees by its forked tail. [*Dugong dugon*.]
– ORIGIN C19: based on Malay *duyong*.

**dugout** • **n. 1** a trench that is roofed over as a shelter for troops. ➤an underground air-raid or nuclear shelter. ➤a low shelter at the side of a sports field for a team's coaches and substitutes. **2** (also **dugout canoe**) a canoe made from a hollowed tree trunk.

**duh** • **exclam.** another way of saying **DOH**[2].

**DUI** • **abbrev.** US driving under the influence (of drugs or alcohol).

**duiker** /ˈdʌɪkə/ • **n.** (pl. same or **duikers**) **1** a small African antelope, typically with a tuft of hair between the horns. [*Sylvicapra grimmia* and other species.] **2** S. African a cormorant.
– ORIGIN C18: from S. Afr. Du., from Du., lit. 'diver', from the antelope's habit of plunging through bushes when pursued.

**du jour** /d(j)uː ˈʒʊə, French dy ʒuʀ/ • **adj.** [postpos.] informal referring to something that is enjoying great but probably short-lived popularity.
– ORIGIN Fr., lit. 'of the day'.

**duke** • **n. 1** a male holding the highest hereditary title in the British and certain other peerages. **2** chiefly historical (in parts of Europe) a male ruler of a small independent state. **3** (**dukes**) informal the fists.
– PHRASES **duke it out** N. Amer. informal fight it out.
– DERIVATIVES **dukedom** n.
– ORIGIN OE, from OFr. *duc*, from L. *dux*, *duc-* 'leader', rel. to *ducere* 'to lead'; sense 3 is from rhyming sl. *Duke of Yorks* 'forks' (= fingers).

**Duke of Argyll's tea tree** • **n.** see **TEA TREE** (sense 2).

**DUKW** /dʌk/ • **n.** an amphibious transport vehicle, especially as used by the Allies during the Second World War.
– ORIGIN an official designation, being a combination of factory-applied letters referring to features of the vehicle.

**dulcamara** /ˌdʌlkəˈmɛːrə/ • **n.** an extract of woody nightshade, used in homeopathy especially for treating skin diseases and chest complaints.
– ORIGIN C16: from med. L. (used as a specific epithet in *Solanum dulcamara*), from L. *dulcis* 'sweet' + *amara* 'bitter'.

**dulcet** /ˈdʌlsɪt/ • **adj.** (of a sound) sweet and soothing.
– ORIGIN ME *doucet*, from OFr. *doucet*, dimin. of *doux*, from L. *dulcis* 'sweet'.

**dulcian** /ˈdʌlsɪən/ • **n. 1** an early type of bassoon made in one piece. **2** an organ stop, typically with 8-foot funnel-shaped flue pipes or 8- or 16-foot reed pipes.
– ORIGIN C19: from Ger. *Dulzian*, or a var. of **DULCIANA**.

**dulciana** /ˌdʌlsɪˈɑːnə/ • **n.** an organ stop, typically with small conical open metal pipes.
– ORIGIN C18: via med. L. from L. *dulcis* 'sweet'.

**dulcify** /ˈdʌlsɪfʌɪ/ • **v.** (**-ies**, **-ied**) poetic/literary **1** sweeten. **2** calm or soothe.
– DERIVATIVES **dulcification** n.
– ORIGIN C16: from L. *dulcificare*.

**dulcimer** /ˈdʌlsɪmə/ • **n.** a musical instrument with a sounding board or box over which strings of graduated length are stretched, played by striking the strings with hand-held hammers.
– ORIGIN C15: from OFr. *doulcemer*, prob. from L. *dulce melos* 'sweet melody'.

**dulcitone** /ˈdʌlsɪtəʊn/ • **n.** a musical keyboard instrument, superseded by the celesta, in which a series of steel tuning forks are struck by hammers.
– ORIGIN C19: from L. *dulcis* 'sweet' + *tonus* 'tone'.

**dulia** /djʊˈlʌɪə/ • **n.** (in Roman Catholic theology) the reverence accorded to saints and angels. Compare with **LATRIA**.
– ORIGIN ME: via med. L. from Gk *douleia* 'servitude', from *doulos* 'slave'.

**dull** • **adj. 1** lacking interest or excitement. **2** lacking brightness or sheen. ➤(of the weather) overcast. **3** slow to understand. ➤slow-moving. **4** indistinctly felt or heard. • **v.** make or become dull.
– DERIVATIVES **dullish** adj. **dullness** (also **dulness**) n. **dully** /ˈdʌlˌli/ adv.
– ORIGIN OE *dol* 'stupid', of Gmc origin.

**dullard** /ˈdʌləd/ ● n. a slow or stupid person.
– ORIGIN ME: from MDu. *dullaert*, from *dul* 'dull'.

**dulse** /dʌls/ ● n. a dark red edible seaweed with flattened branching fronds. [*Rhodymenia palmata*.]
– ORIGIN C17: from Ir. and Sc. Gaelic *duileasg*.

**duly** ● adv. in accordance with what is required or appropriate. ➤as might be expected.

**dum** /dʌm/ ● adj. Indian cooked with steam.
– ORIGIN from Hindi *dam*.

**Duma** /ˈduːmə/ ● n. a legislative body in the ruling assembly of Russia and of some other republics of the former USSR.
– ORIGIN from Russ.

**dumb** ● adj. **1** unable to speak, normally because of congenital deafness. ➤(of animals) unable to speak as a natural state. ➤temporarily unable or unwilling to speak. **2** informal, chiefly N. Amer. stupid. **3** (of a computer terminal) having no independent processing capability. ● v. **1** (**dumb something down**) N. Amer. informal reduce the intellectual content of something. ➤(**dumb down**) become less intellectually challenging. **2** poetic/literary silence.
– DERIVATIVES **dumbly** adv. **dumbness** n.
– ORIGIN OE, of Gmc origin.

USAGE dumb

In the sense meaning 'not able to speak', **dumb** has been overwhelmed by the sense 'stupid' to such an extent that the use of the first sense is now almost certain to cause offence. Alternatives such as **speech-impaired** should be used instead.

**dumb-bell** ● n. **1** a short bar with a weight at each end, used typically in pairs for exercise or muscle-building. **2** informal a stupid person.
– ORIGIN C18: orig. denoting an object similar to that used to ring a church bell (but without the bell, so 'dumb').

**dumb cane** ● n. a thick-stemmed Caribbean plant with a poisonous sap that swells the tongue and destroys the power of speech. [*Dieffenbachia seguine*.]

**dumbfound** (also **dumfound**) ● v. (usu. **be dumbfounded**) astonish greatly.
– ORIGIN C17: blend of DUMB and CONFOUND.

**dumbo** ● n. (pl. **-os**) informal a stupid person.
– ORIGIN 1950s (orig. US): from DUMB + **-O**, popularized by the cartoon film *Dumbo*.

**dumb piano** ● n. a dummy piano keyboard for exercising the fingers.

**dumbshow** ● n. gestures used to convey something without speech. ➤(especially in English drama of the 16th and 17th centuries) a part of a play acted in mime.

**dumbsize** ● v. informal, chiefly US (of a company) reduce staff numbers to inefficiently low levels.

**dumbstruck** ● adj. so shocked or surprised as to be unable to speak.

**dumb waiter** ● n. **1** a small lift for carrying food and crockery between floors. **2** Brit. a movable table, typically with revolving shelves, used in a dining room.

**dumdum** (also **dumdum bullet**) ● n. a kind of soft-nosed bullet that expands on impact and inflicts laceration.
– ORIGIN C19: from *Dum Dum*, name of a town and arsenal near Calcutta, India, where they were first produced.

**dum-dum** ● n. informal a stupid person.
– ORIGIN 1970s (orig. US): reduplication of DUMB.

**dumfound** ● v. variant spelling of DUMBFOUND.

**dummy** ● n. (pl. **-ies**) **1** a model or replica of a human being. **2** an object designed to resemble and serve as a substitute for the real one. ➤Brit. a rubber or plastic teat for a baby to suck on. **3** (chiefly in rugby and soccer) a feigned pass or kick. **4** Bridge the declarer's partner, whose cards are exposed on the table after the opening lead and played by the declarer. ➤(in whist) an imaginary fourth player. **5** informal, chiefly N. Amer. a stupid person. ● v. (**-ies**, **-ied**) **1** (chiefly in rugby and soccer) feign a pass or kick. **2** (**dummy up**) N. Amer. informal keep quiet.
– PHRASES **sell someone a dummy** (chiefly in rugby and soccer) deceive an opponent by feigning a pass or kick.
– ORIGIN C16 (orig. 'a person who cannot speak', later 'an imaginary fourth player in whist'): from DUMB + **-Y**[1].

**dummy run** ● n. a practice or trial.

**dump** ● n. **1** a site for depositing rubbish or waste. ➤a heap of rubbish left at a dump. ➤informal an unpleasant or dreary place. **2** Computing an act of dumping stored data. ● v. **1** deposit or dispose of (rubbish or something unwanted). ➤put down firmly and carelessly. ➤informal desert (someone). ➤send (goods unsaleable in the home market) to a foreign market for sale at a low price. **2** Computing copy (stored data) to a different location, especially so as to protect against loss. ➤print out the contents of (a store). **3** (**dump on**) N. Amer. informal treat badly or criticize harshly.
– PHRASES **take a dump** N. Amer. informal defecate.
– ORIGIN ME (orig. in the sense 'fall suddenly'): in later use partly imitative; cf. THUMP.

**dumper** ● n. **1** a person or thing that dumps something. **2** (also **dumper truck**) Brit. a truck with a body that tilts or opens at the back for unloading. **3** Austral./NZ a large wave that hurls a swimmer or surfer on to the beach.

**dumpling** ● n. **1** a small savoury ball of dough (usually made with suet) which may be boiled in water or a stew. **2** a pudding consisting of apple or other fruit enclosed in a sweet dough and baked.
– ORIGIN C17: appar. from the rare adjective *dump* 'of the consistency of dough', although *dumpling* is recorded much earlier.

**dumps** ● pl. n. (in phr. (**down**) **in the dumps**) informal depressed or unhappy.
– ORIGIN C16 (orig. sing. in the sense 'a dazed or puzzled state'): prob. a figurative use of MDu. *domp* 'haze, mist'.

**dumpster** ● n. N. Amer. a rubbish skip.
– ORIGIN 1930s: orig. *Dempster Dumpster*, proprietary name (based on DUMP) given by the Amer. manufacturers, Dempster Brothers of Tennessee.

**dump truck** ● n. N. Amer. a dumper truck.

**dumpy** ● adj. (**-ier**, **-iest**) short and stout.
– DERIVATIVES **dumpily** adv. **dumpiness** n.
– ORIGIN C18: from DUMPLING + **-Y**[1].

**dun**[1] ● adj. of a dull greyish-brown colour. ● n. **1** a dull greyish-brown colour. **2** a horse with a sandy coat, black mane, tail, and lower legs, and a dark dorsal stripe. **3** a sub-adult mayfly with drab, opaque wings, or a fishing fly imitating this.
– ORIGIN OE *dun*, *dunn*, of Gmc origin; prob. rel. to DUSK.

**dun**[2] ● v. (**dunned**, **dunning**) (usu. **be dunned**) make persistent demands on for payment of a debt. ● n. archaic a debt collector or an insistent creditor.
– ORIGIN C17 (as n.): perh. from obs. *Dunkirk privateer* (with connotations of piratical demands), or from the name of a Joe *Dun*, a well-known bailiff.

**dun**[3] ● n. Archaeology (often in place names) a stone-built fortified settlement in Scotland or Ireland, of a kind built from the late Iron Age to the early Middle Ages.
– ORIGIN C18: from Ir. *dún*, Sc. Gaelic *dùn* 'hill or hill fort'.

**dunam** /ˈdʊnəm/ ● n. a measure of land area used in parts of the Middle East, including Israel (where it is equal to about 900 square metres).
– ORIGIN from mod. Heb. *dûnām* or Arab. *dūnum*, from Turk. *dönüm*, from *dönmek* 'go round'.

**dunce** ● n. a person who is slow at learning.
– ORIGIN C16: orig. an epithet for a follower of the C13 Sc. theologian John *Duns* Scotus, whose followers were ridiculed by humanists as enemies of learning.

**dunce's cap** (N. Amer. also **dunce cap**) ● n. a paper cone formerly put on the head of a dunce at school as a mark of disgrace.

**Dundee cake** ● n. chiefly Brit. a rich fruit cake, decorated with almonds.

**dunderhead** ● n. informal a stupid person.
– DERIVATIVES **dunderheaded** adj.
– ORIGIN C17: cf. obs. Scots *dunder*, *dunner* 'resounding noise'; rel. to DIN.

**dune** ● n. a mound or ridge of sand or other loose sediment formed by the wind, especially on the sea coast or in a desert.
– ORIGIN C18: from Fr., from MDu. *dūne*; rel. to OE *dūn* 'hill' (see DOWN[3]).

**dung** ● **n.** manure. ● **v.** (of an animal) defecate.
– ORIGIN OE, of Gmc origin.

**dungaree** /ˌdʌŋɡəˈriː/ ● **n. 1** (**dungarees**) trousers with a bib held up by straps over the shoulders, made of denim or a similar material and worn for work or leisure. **2** a kind of coarse Indian calico.
– ORIGIN C17: from Hindi *duṅgrī*.

**dung beetle** ● **n.** a beetle whose larvae feed on dung, especially a scarab.

**dungeon** ● **n. 1** a strong underground prison cell, especially in a castle. **2** archaic term for **DONJON**. ● **v.** poetic/literary imprison in a dungeon.
– ORIGIN ME: from OFr. (perh. orig. with the sense 'lord's tower'), based on L. *dominus* 'lord'.

**dung fly** ● **n.** a hairy fly that lays its eggs in fresh dung. [*Scathophaga stercoraria* and other species.]

**dunghill** ● **n.** a heap of dung or refuse, especially in a farmyard.

**dungworm** ● **n.** an earthworm found in dung or compost, used by anglers as bait.

**dunite** /ˈdʌnʌɪt/ ● **n.** Geology a green to brownish coarse-grained igneous rock consisting largely of olivine.
– ORIGIN C19: from the name of *Dun* Mountain, New Zealand, + **-ITE**[1].

**dunk** ● **v. 1** dip (bread or other food) into a drink or soup before eating it. ➤ immerse in water. **2** Basketball score a field goal by shooting the ball down through the basket with the hands above the rim. ● **n.** Basketball a goal scored by dunking.
– DERIVATIVES **dunker** n.
– ORIGIN C20: from Pennsylvanian Ger. *dunke* 'dip', from Ger. *tunken* 'dip or plunge'.

**dunlin** /ˈdʌnlɪn/ ● **n.** (pl. same or **dunlins**) a common migratory sandpiper with a downcurved bill and (in winter) greyish-brown upper parts. [*Calidris alpina*.]
– ORIGIN C16: prob. from **DUN**[1] + **-LING**.

**dunnage** /ˈdʌnɪdʒ/ ● **n. 1** loose wood, matting, or similar material used to keep a cargo in position in a ship's hold. **2** informal baggage.
– ORIGIN ME: of unknown origin.

**dunnart** /ˈdʌnɑːt/ ● **n.** a mouse-like insectivorous marsupial with a pointed snout and prominent eyes, found in Australia and New Guinea. [*Sminthopsis murina* and related species.]
– ORIGIN 1920s: from Nyungar *danart*.

**dunnock** /ˈdʌnək/ ● **n.** a small songbird of the accentor family, with a dark grey head and a reddish-brown back. [*Prunella modularis*.]
– ORIGIN ME: appar. from **DUN**[1] + **-OCK**.

**dunny** /ˈdʌni/ ● **n.** (pl. **-ies**) Austral./NZ informal a toilet.
– ORIGIN C19 (in the sense 'dung'): from dial. *dunnekin* 'privy', prob. from **DUNG** + archaic sl. *ken* 'house'.

**dunt** /dʌnt/ chiefly N. Amer. & Scottish ● **v.** bump into or hit heavily. ● **n.** a dull-sounding blow.
– ORIGIN ME: perh. a var. of **DINT**.

**duo** ● **n.** (pl. **-os**) **1** a pair of people or things, especially in music or entertainment. **2** Music a duet.
– ORIGIN C16: via Ital. from L. *duo* 'two'.

**duo-** ● **comb. form** two; having two: *duopoly*.
– ORIGIN from L.

**duodecimal** /ˌdjuːə(ʊ)ˈdɛsɪm(ə)l/ ● **adj.** relating to or denoting a system of counting or numerical notation that has twelve as a base.
– DERIVATIVES **duodecimally** adv.
– ORIGIN C17: from L. *duodecimus* 'twelfth' + **-AL**.

**duodecimo** /ˌdjuːə(ʊ)ˈdɛsɪməʊ/ ● **n.** (pl. **-os**) a size of book in which each leaf is one twelfth of the size of the printing sheet.
– ORIGIN C17: from L. (*in*) *duodecimo* 'in a twelfth'.

**duodenum** /ˌdjuːəˈdiːnəm/ ● **n.** (pl. **duodenums** or **duodena** /-ˈdiːnə/) Anatomy the first part of the small intestine immediately beyond the stomach.
– DERIVATIVES **duodenal** adj. **duodenitis** /-ˈnʌɪtɪs/ n.
– ORIGIN ME: from med. L., from *duodeni* 'in twelves', its length being equivalent to the breadth of approximately twelve fingers.

**duologue** /ˈdjʊəlɒɡ/ ● **n.** a play or part of a play with speaking roles for only two actors.
– ORIGIN C18: from **DUO-**, on the pattern of *monologue*.

**duomo** /ˈdwəʊməʊ/ ● **n.** (pl. **-os**) an Italian cathedral.
– ORIGIN Ital., lit. 'dome'.

**duopoly** /djʊˈɒpəli/ ● **n.** (pl. **-ies**) a situation in which two suppliers dominate a market.
– DERIVATIVES **duopolistic** adj.
– ORIGIN 1920s: from **DUO-**, on the pattern of *monopoly*.

**duotone** /ˈdjuːətəʊn/ ● **n.** a half-tone illustration made from a single original with two colours at different screen angles.

**dupatta** /dʊˈpʌtə/ ● **n.** a length of material worn as a head covering by women from the Indian subcontinent.
– ORIGIN from Hindi *dupaṭṭā*.

**dupe** ● **v.** deceive; trick. ● **n.** a victim of deception.
– DERIVATIVES **dupable** adj. **duper** n. **dupery** n.
– ORIGIN C17: from Fr. dial. *dupe* 'hoopoe', from the bird's supposedly stupid appearance.

**dupion** /ˈdjuːpɪən/ ● **n.** a rough slubbed silk fabric woven from the threads of double cocoons.
– ORIGIN C19 (in the sense 'double cocoon'): from Fr. *doupion*, from Ital. *doppione*, from *doppio* 'double'.

**duple** /ˈdjuːp(ə)l/ ● **adj.** Music (of rhythm) based on two main beats to the bar.
– ORIGIN C16: from L. *duplus*, from *duo* 'two'.

**duplet** /ˈdjuːplɪt/ ● **n.** a set of two things, especially a pair of equal musical notes to be performed in the time of three.
– ORIGIN C17: from L. *duplus* 'duple', on the pattern of *doublet*.

**duplex** /ˈdjuːplɛks/ ● **n. 1** N. Amer. a residential building divided into two apartments. **2** chiefly N. Amer. & Austral. a semi-detached house. **3** Biochemistry a double-stranded polynucleotide molecule. ● **adj. 1** having two parts. **2** (of a printer) capable of printing on both sides of the paper. **3** (of a communications system, computer circuit, etc.) allowing the transmission of two signals simultaneously in opposite directions.
– ORIGIN C16 (as adj.): from L. *duplex*, *duplic-*, from *duo* 'two' + *plicare* 'to fold'.

**duplicate** ● **adj.** /ˈdjuːplɪkət/ **1** exactly like something else. **2** having two corresponding parts. **3** twice the number or quantity. ● **n.** /ˈdjuːplɪkət/ one of two or more identical things. ● **v.** /ˈdjuːplɪkeɪt/ make or be an exact copy of. ➤ multiply by two. ➤ do again unnecessarily.
– DERIVATIVES **duplicable** adj. **duplication** n.
– ORIGIN ME: from L. *duplicat-*, *duplicare* 'double', from *duplic-* (see **DUPLEX**).

**duplicate bridge** ● **n.** a competitive form of bridge in which the same hands are played successively by different partnerships.

**duplicator** ● **n.** a machine for copying something.

**duplicitous** ● **adj. 1** deceitful. **2** Law (of a charge or plea) containing more than one allegation.

**duplicity** /djuːˈplɪsɪti, djʊ-/ ● **n. 1** deceitfulness. **2** archaic the quality of being double.
– ORIGIN ME: from OFr. *duplicite* or late L. *duplicitas*, from L. *duplic-* (see **DUPLEX**).

**duppy** /ˈdʌpi/ ● **n.** (pl. **-ies**) W. Indian a malevolent spirit or ghost.
– ORIGIN C18: prob. of W. Afr. origin.

**Dupuytren's contracture** /djʊˈpwiːtrəns/ ● **n.** Medicine fixed forward curvature of one or more fingers, caused by a growth of fibrous tissue.
– ORIGIN C19: named after the Fr. surgeon Baron Guillaume *Dupuytren*.

**durable** ● **adj. 1** hard-wearing. **2** (of goods) not for immediate consumption and so able to be kept.
– DERIVATIVES **durability** n. **durableness** n. **durably** adv.
– ORIGIN ME (in the sense 'steadfast'): via OFr. from L. *durabilis*, from *durare* (see **DURATION**).

**Duralumin** /djʊˈraljʊmɪn/ ● **n.** trademark a hard, light alloy of aluminium with copper and other elements.
– ORIGIN C20: perh. from L. *durus* 'hard' + **ALUMINIUM**, but prob. influenced by *Düren*, the name of the Ger. town where the alloy was first produced.

**dura mater** /ˌdjʊərə ˈmeɪtə/ ● **n.** Anatomy the tough outermost membrane enveloping the brain and spinal cord.

– DERIVATIVES **dural** adj.
– ORIGIN C19: from med. L., lit. 'hard mother', translation of Arab. *al-'umm al-jāfiya* 'coarse mother'.

**duramen** /djʊ'reɪmɛn/ ● **n.** Botany the heartwood of a tree.
– ORIGIN C19: from L., lit. 'hardness'.

**durance** ● **n.** archaic imprisonment.
– ORIGIN ME (in the sense 'continuance'): from OFr., from *durer* 'to last', from L. *durare*.

**duration** ● **n.** the time during which something continues.
– PHRASES **for the duration** informal for a very long time.
– DERIVATIVES **durational** adj.
– ORIGIN ME: via OFr. from med. L. *duratio(n-)*, from *durare* 'to last', from *durus* 'hard'.

**durative** /'djʊərətɪv/ ● **adj.** Grammar of or denoting continuing action. Contrasted with **PUNCTUAL**.

**durbar** /'də:bɑ:/ ● **n.** historical **1** the court of an Indian ruler. **2** a public reception held by an Indian prince or a British governor or viceroy in India.
– ORIGIN Urdu, from Pers. *darbār* 'court'.

**durchkomponiert** /ˌdʊəx'kɒmpɒnɪət, German ˌdʊrç kɔmpo'ni:rt/ ● **adj.** Music (of a song) having different music for each verse.
– ORIGIN from Ger., from *durch* 'through' + *komponiert* 'composed' (because the music is different throughout).

**duress** /djʊ(ə)'rɛs, 'djʊərɛs/ ● **n.** threats, violence, etc. used to coerce a person into doing something. ➤ Law constraint illegally exercised to force someone to perform an act.
– ORIGIN ME (in the sense 'harshness, cruel treatment'): via OFr. from L. *duritia*, from *durus* 'hard'.

**Durex** ● **n.** (pl. same) Brit. trademark a contraceptive sheath.
– ORIGIN 1930s: name invented by the manufacturers, prob. based on L. *durare* 'to last'.

**durian** /'dʊərɪən/ ● **n. 1** an oval spiny tropical fruit containing a creamy pulp with a fetid smell but agreeable taste. **2** (also **durian tree**) the large Malaysian tree that bears this fruit. [*Durio zibethinus*.]
– ORIGIN C16: from Malay *durian*, from *duri* 'thorn'.

**duricrust** /'djʊərɪkrʌst/ ● **n.** Geology a hard mineral crust formed at or near the surface of soil in semi-arid regions by the evaporation of groundwater.
– ORIGIN 1920s: from L. *durus* 'hard' + **CRUST**.

**during** ● **prep.** throughout the course or duration of. ➤ at a particular point in the course of.
– ORIGIN ME: pres. part. of the obs. verb *dure* 'last, endure, extend', via OFr. from L. *durare* (see **DURATION**).

**durmast oak** /'də:mɑ:st/ ● **n.** another term for **SESSILE OAK**.
– ORIGIN C18: *durmast* perh. orig. an error for *dunmast*, from **DUN**[1] + **MAST**[2].

**durn** ● **v., exclam., adj., & adv.** US dialect form of **DARN**[2].

**durned** ● **adj. & adv.** US dialect form of **DARNED**.

**durra** /'dʊrə, 'dʊərə/ ● **n.** sorghum of the principal variety grown from NE Africa to India.
– ORIGIN C18: from Arab. *ḍura, ḍurra*.

**durst** archaic or regional past of **DARE**.

**durum wheat** /'djʊərəm/ ● **n.** a kind of hard wheat grown in arid regions, yielding flour that is used to make pasta. [*Triticum durum*.]
– ORIGIN C20: from L., neut. of *durus* 'hard'.

**durzi** /'də:zi/ ● **n.** (pl. **durzis**) Indian a tailor.
– ORIGIN Urdu, from Pers. *darzī*, from *darz* 'sewing'.

**dusk** ● **n.** the darker stage of twilight. ● **v.** poetic/literary grow dark.
– ORIGIN OE *dox* 'dark, swarthy' and *doxian* 'darken in colour', of Gmc origin; cf. **DUN**[1].

**dusky** ● **adj.** (**-ier**, **-iest**) darkish in colour. ➤ euphemistic, dated or poetic/literary (of a person) black; dark-skinned.
– DERIVATIVES **duskily** adv. **duskiness** n.

**Dussehra** /'dʌʃərə/ ● **n.** the tenth and final day of the Hindu festival of Navaratri.
– ORIGIN from Hindi *daśahrā*, from Sanskrit *daśaharā*.

**dust** ● **n. 1** fine, dry powder consisting of tiny particles of earth or waste matter. ➤ any material in the form of tiny particles: *coal dust*. ➤ poetic/literary a dead person's remains. **2** an act of dusting. ● **v. 1** remove dust from the surface of. ➤ (**dust something down/off**) bring something out for use again after a long period of neglect. **2** (usu. **be dusted**) cover lightly with a powdered substance. **3** US informal beat up or kill.
– PHRASES **dust and ashes** a feeling of great disappointment. **the dust settles** things quieten down. **eat someone's dust** N. Amer. informal fall far behind someone in a competitive situation. **leave someone/thing in the dust** surpass someone or something easily. **not see someone for dust** find that a person has made a hasty departure. **kick up a dust** (or US **kick up dust**) informal create a disturbance.
– DERIVATIVES **dustless** adj.
– ORIGIN OE *dūst*, of Gmc origin.

**dust bath** ● **n.** a bird's rolling in dust to clean its feathers.

**dustbin** ● **n.** Brit. a large container for household refuse.

**dust bowl** ● **n.** an area where vegetation has been lost and soil reduced to dust and eroded, especially as a consequence of drought or unsuitable farming practice.

**dust bunny** ● **n.** N. Amer. informal a ball of dust and fluff.

**dustcart** ● **n.** Brit. a vehicle used for collecting household refuse.

**dustcoat** ● **n.** another term for **DUSTER** (in sense 2).

**dust cover** ● **n.** a dust jacket or dust sheet.

**dust devil** ● **n.** a small whirlwind or air vortex over land, visible as a column of dust and debris.

**duster** ● **n. 1** Brit. a cloth for dusting furniture. **2** (also **duster coat**) chiefly N. Amer. a woman's loose, lightweight coat without buttons, of a style originally worn when travelling in an open car.

**dusting powder** ● **n.** powder for dusting over something, especially talcum powder.

**dust jacket** ● **n.** a removable paper cover on a book.

**dustman** ● **n.** (pl. **-men**) Brit. a man employed to remove household refuse from dustbins.

**dustpan** ● **n.** a flat hand-held receptacle into which dust and waste can be swept.

**dust sheet** ● **n.** Brit. a large sheet for covering furniture to protect it from dust or while decorating.

**dust shot** ● **n.** the smallest size of gunshot.

**dust storm** ● **n.** a strong, turbulent wind which carries clouds of fine dust and sand over a large area.

**dust-up** ● **n.** informal a fight or quarrel.

**dusty** ● **adj.** (**-ier**, **-iest**) **1** covered with or resembling dust. **2** staid and uninteresting.
– PHRASES **a dusty answer** Brit. a curt and unhelpful reply.
– DERIVATIVES **dustily** adv. **dustiness** n.

**dusty miller** ● **n.** a plant of the daisy family with whitish or greyish foliage. [*Artemisia stellerana* (N. America), *Senecio cineraria* (Mediterranean), and other species.]
– ORIGIN C19: named from the fine powder on the flowers and leaves.

**Dutch** ● **adj.** of or relating to the Netherlands, its people, or their language. ● **n. 1** the West Germanic language of the Netherlands. **2** S. African derogatory Afrikaans.
– PHRASES **go Dutch** share the cost of a meal equally.
– ORIGIN from MDu. *dutsch* 'Dutch, Netherlandish, German'.

**dutch** ● **n.** (usu. **one's old dutch**) Brit. informal (especially among cockneys) one's wife.
– ORIGIN C19: abbrev. of **DUCHESS**.

**Dutch auction** ● **n.** a method of selling in which the price is reduced until a buyer is found.

**Dutch barn** ● **n.** Brit. a farm building comprising a curved roof set on an open frame, used to cover hay.

**Dutch cap** ● **n. 1** a woman's lace cap with triangular flaps on each side, worn as part of Dutch traditional dress. **2** see **CAP** (sense 5).

**Dutch courage** ● **n.** confidence gained from drinking alcohol.

**Dutch door** ● **n.** N. Amer. a stable door.

**Dutch elm disease** ● **n.** a fungal disease of elm trees, spread by bark beetles.

**Dutch hoe** ● **n.** a hoe used with a pushing action just under the surface of the soil.

**Dutchman** (or **Dutchwoman**) • **n.** (pl. **-men** or **-women**) a native or national of the Netherlands.
– PHRASES **I'm a Dutchman** Brit. an expression of disbelief.

**Dutchman's breeches** • **n.** a plant with pale yellow spurred flowers suggesting pairs of breeches. [*Dicentra spectabilis* and related species.]

**Dutchman's pipe** • **n.** a vigorous climbing vine with hooked tubular flowers. [*Aristolochia durior.*]

**Dutch metal** • **n.** an alloy of copper and zinc used in imitation of gold leaf.

**Dutch oven** • **n. 1** a covered earthenware or cast-iron container for cooking casseroles. **2** chiefly historical a large metal box serving as a simple oven, heated by being placed under or next to hot coals.

**Dutch tile** • **n.** a kind of glazed white tile painted with traditional Dutch motifs in blue or brown.

**Dutch uncle** • **n.** informal, chiefly N. Amer. a person giving firm but benevolent advice.

**duteous** /'dju:tɪəs/ • **adj.** archaic dutiful.
– DERIVATIVES **duteously** adv. **duteousness** n.
– ORIGIN C16: from DUTY, on the pattern of words such as *bounteous.*

**duty** • **n.** (pl. **-ies**) **1** a moral or legal obligation. **2** a task required as part of one's job. ➤(**duties**) performance of prescribed church services by a priest or minister. **3** a payment levied on the import, export, manufacture, or sale of goods. ➤Brit. a payment levied on the transfer of property, for licences, and for the legal recognition of documents. **4** technical the measure of an engine's effectiveness in units of work done per unit of fuel.
– PHRASES **do duty as** (or **for**) serve or act as a substitute for. **on** (or **off**) **duty** engaged (or not engaged) in one's regular work.
– DERIVATIVES **dutiable** adj. **dutiful** adj. **dutifully** adv. **dutifulness** n.
– ORIGIN ME: from Anglo-Norman Fr. *duete*, from OFr. *deu* (see DUE).

**duty drawback** • **n.** see DRAWBACK (sense 2).

**duty-free** • **adj. & adv.** exempt from payment of duty.

**duty-paid** • **adj.** on which the duty has been met.

**duumvir** /dju:'ʌmvə/ • **n.** (in ancient Rome) each of two magistrates or officials holding a joint office.
– ORIGIN L., from *duum virum* 'of the two men'.

**duumvirate** /dju:'ʌmvɪrət/ • **n.** a coalition of two people having joint authority.
– ORIGIN C17: from L. *duumviratus.*

**duvet** /'d(j)u:veɪ/ • **n.** chiefly Brit. a soft thick quilt used instead of an upper sheet and blankets.
– ORIGIN C18: from Fr., lit. 'down' (see DOWN[2]).

**duvet day** • **n.** informal an unscheduled extra day's leave from work, taken to alleviate stress or pressure and sanctioned by one's employer.

**dux** /dʌks/ • **n.** (pl. **duces**) chiefly Scottish the top pupil in a school or class.
– ORIGIN C18: from L., 'leader'.

**duxelles** /'dʌks(ə)lz, dʊk'sɛl/ • **n.** a stuffing made from chopped mushrooms, onions, shallots, and parsley.
– ORIGIN named after the Marquis *d'Uxelles*, a C17 Fr. nobleman.

**DV** • **abbrev.** Deo volente.

**DVD** • **abbrev.** digital versatile disc (formerly digital videodisc).

**DVLA** • **abbrev.** Driver and Vehicle Licensing Agency.

**dwaal** /dwɑ:l/ • **n.** S. African informal a dreamy, dazed, or absent-minded state.
– ORIGIN from Afrik.

**dwale** /dweɪl/ • **n.** archaic deadly nightshade.
– ORIGIN ME: prob. of Scand. origin.

**dwam** /dwɑ:m/ • **n.** chiefly Scottish a dreamy or semi-conscious state.
– ORIGIN C16: from the Gmc base of DWELL.

**dwarf** • **n.** (pl. **dwarfs** or **dwarves**) **1** a member of a mythical race of short, stocky human-like creatures, skilled in mining and metalworking. **2** an abnormally small person. ➤[as modifier] denoting an animal or plant that is much smaller than is usual for its type or species. **3** (also **dwarf star**) Astronomy a star of relatively small size and low luminosity. • **v.** cause to seem small in comparison. ➤stunt the growth of.
– DERIVATIVES **dwarfish** adj.
– ORIGIN OE *dweorg, dweorh*, of Gmc origin.

**dwarfism** • **n.** (in medical or technical contexts) unusually low stature or small size.

**dweeb** • **n.** informal, chiefly N. Amer. a boring, studious, or socially inept person.
– DERIVATIVES **dweebish** adj. **dweeby** adj.
– ORIGIN 1980s: perh. a blend of DWARF and *feeb* 'a feeble-minded person'.

**dwell** • **v.** (past and past part. **dwelt** or **dwelled**) **1** formal live in or at a place. **2** (**dwell on/upon**) think, speak, or write at length about. • **n.** technical a slight regular pause in the motion of a machine.
– DERIVATIVES **dweller** n.
– ORIGIN OE *dwellan* 'lead astray, delay' (in ME 'remain in a place'), of Gmc origin.

**dwelling** (also **dwelling place**) • **n.** formal a house or other place of residence.

**dwelling house** • **n.** Law a house used as a residence and not for business purposes.

**dwindle** • **v.** diminish gradually.
– ORIGIN C16: frequentative of Scots and dial. *dwine* 'fade away', from OE *dwīnan*, of Gmc origin.

**dwt** • **abbrev. 1** deadweight tonnage. **2** pennyweight.

**DY** • **abbrev.** Benin (international vehicle registration).
– ORIGIN from *Dahomey*, name for Benin until 1975.

**Dy** • **symb.** the chemical element dysprosium.

**dyad** /'dʌɪad/ • **n.** technical something that consists of two elements or parts. ➤Mathematics an operator which is a combination of two vectors.
– DERIVATIVES **dyadic** adj.
– ORIGIN C17: from late L. *dyas, dyad-*, from Gk *duas*, from *duo* 'two'.

**Dyak** /'dʌɪak/ • **n. & adj.** variant spelling of DAYAK.

**dyarchy** • **n.** (pl. **-ies**) variant spelling of DIARCHY.

**dybbuk** /'dɪbʊk/ • **n.** (pl. **dybbuks** or **dybbukim** /-kɪm/) (in Jewish folklore) a malevolent wandering spirit that possesses the body of a living person until exorcized.
– ORIGIN from Yiddish *dibek*, from Heb. *dibbūq*, from *dāḇaq* 'cling'.

**dye** • **n.** a natural or synthetic substance used to colour something. • **v.** (**dyeing**) colour with dye.
– PHRASES **dyed in the wool** unchanging in a particular belief. [with allusion to the fact that yarn was dyed when raw, producing a more even and permanent colour.]
– DERIVATIVES **dyeable** adj. **dyer** n.
– ORIGIN OE *dēag* (n.), *dēagian* (v.).

**dye laser** • **n.** a tunable laser using the fluorescence of an organic dye.

**dyeline** • **n.** a print made by the diazo process.

**dyer's greenweed** • **n.** a bushy yellow-flowered leguminous plant, formerly used to make a yellow or green dye. [*Genista tinctoria.*]

**dyer's oak** • **n.** another term for VALONIA.

**dyer's rocket** • **n.** another term for WELD[2].

**dyestuff** • **n.** a substance used as or yielding a dye.

**dying** present participle of DIE[1]. • **adj.** relating to or at the time of death.
– PHRASES **to one's dying day** for the rest of one's life.

**dyke**[1] (also **dike**) • **n. 1** an embankment built to prevent flooding from the sea. ➤an earthwork serving as a boundary or defence: *Offa's Dyke.* **2** a ditch or watercourse. **3** Geology an intrusion of igneous rock cutting across existing strata. Compare with SILL. • **v.** [often as adj. **dyked**] provide (land) with a dyke to prevent flooding.
– ORIGIN ME: from ON *dík*, rel. to DITCH.

**dyke**[2] (also **dike**) • **n.** informal a lesbian.
– DERIVATIVES **dykey** adj.
– ORIGIN 1940s (earlier as *bulldyke*): of unknown origin.

**dyn** • **abbrev.** dyne.

**dynamic** /dʌɪ'namɪk/ • **adj. 1** (of a process or system) characterized by constant change or activity. ➤full of energy and new ideas. **2** Physics of or relating to forces pro-

ducing motion. Often contrasted with **STATIC**. **3** Linguistics (of a verb) expressing an action, activity, event, or process. Contrasted with **STATIVE**. **4** Electronics (of a memory device) needing to be refreshed by the periodic application of a voltage. **5** Music relating to the volume of sound produced by an instrument or voice. ● **n.** **1** an energizing or motive force. **2** Music another term for **DYNAMICS** (in sense 3).
– DERIVATIVES **dynamical** adj. **dynamically** adv.
– ORIGIN C19: from Fr. *dynamique*, from Gk *dunamikos*, from *dunamis* 'power'.

**dynamic equilibrium** ● **n.** a state of balance between continuing processes.

**dynamic range** ● **n.** the range of sound intensity that occurs in a piece of music or that can be satisfactorily handled by a piece of equipment.

**dynamics** ● **pl. n.** **1** [treated as sing.] the branch of mechanics concerned with the motion of bodies under the action of forces. Compare with **KINEMATICS**, **STATICS**. **2** the forces which stimulate development or change within a system or process. **3** Music the varying levels of volume of sound in a musical performance.
– DERIVATIVES **dynamicist** n.

**dynamic viscosity** ● **n.** a quantity measuring the force needed to overcome internal friction in a fluid.

**dynamism** ● **n.** **1** the quality of being dynamic. **2** Philosophy, chiefly historical the theory that phenomena can be explained by an immanent force.
– DERIVATIVES **dynamist** n. **dynamization** (also **-isation**) n. **dynamize** (also **-ise**) v.

**dynamite** ● **n.** **1** a high explosive consisting of nitroglycerine mixed with an absorbent material. **2** informal an extremely impressive or potentially dangerous person or thing. ● **v.** blow up with dynamite.
– DERIVATIVES **dynamiter** n.
– ORIGIN C19: from Gk *dunamis* 'power' + **-ITE**[1].

**dynamo** ● **n.** (pl. **-os**) chiefly Brit. a machine for converting mechanical energy into electrical energy by rotating conducting coils in a magnetic field.
– ORIGIN C19: abbrev. of *dynamo-electric machine*, from Gk *dunamis* 'power'.

**dynamometer** /ˌdʌɪnəˈmɒmɪtə/ ● **n.** an instrument which measures the power output of an engine.

**dynast** /ˈdɪnəst, ˈdʌɪnəst, -nast/ ● **n.** a member of a dynasty, especially a hereditary ruler.
– ORIGIN C17: via L. from Gk *dunastēs*, from *dunasthai* 'be able'.

**dynasty** /ˈdɪnəsti/ ● **n.** (pl. **-ies**) a line of hereditary rulers. ➤ a succession of powerful or prominent people from the same family.
– DERIVATIVES **dynastic** adj. **dynastically** adv.
– ORIGIN ME: from Fr. *dynastie*, or via late L. from Gk *dunasteia* 'lordship', from *dunastēs* (see **DYNAST**).

**dyne** /dʌɪn/ ● **n.** Physics a unit of force that, acting on a mass of one gram, increases its velocity by one centimetre per second every second along the direction in which it acts.
– ORIGIN C19: from Fr., from Gk *dunamis* 'force, power'.

**dyno** ● **n.** (pl. **-os**) **1** short for **DYNAMOMETER**. **2** Climbing a rapid move across a rock face in order to reach a hold.

**dynode** /ˈdʌɪnəʊd/ ● **n.** Electronics an intermediate electrode which emits additional electrons in a photomultiplier or similar amplifying device.
– ORIGIN 1930s: from Gk *dunamis* 'power' + **-ODE**[2].

**dys-** /dɪs/ ● **comb. form** bad; difficult (used especially in medical terms): *dyspepsia*.
– ORIGIN from Gk *dus-*.

**dysarthria** /dɪsˈɑːθrɪə/ ● **n.** Medicine unclear articulation of speech that is otherwise linguistically normal.
– ORIGIN C19: from **DYS-** + Gk *arthron* 'joint or articulation'.

**dyscalculia** /ˌdɪskalˈkjuːlɪə/ ● **n.** Psychiatry severe difficulty in making arithmetical calculations, as a result of brain disorder.

**dyscrasia** /dɪsˈkreɪzɪə/ ● **n.** Medicine an abnormal or disordered physiological state.
– DERIVATIVES **dyscrasic** adj.
– ORIGIN ME: via late L. from Gk *duskrasia* 'bad combination'.

**dysentery** /ˈdɪs(ə)nt(ə)ri/ ● **n.** infection of the intestines with bacteria or protozoans, resulting in severe diarrhoea with blood and mucus in the faeces.
– DERIVATIVES **dysenteric** /-ˈtɛrɪk/ adj.
– ORIGIN ME: from OFr. *dissenterie*, or via L. from Gk *dusenteria*, from *dusenteros* 'afflicted in the bowels'.

**dysfunctional** ● **adj.** **1** not operating normally or properly. **2** unable to deal adequately with normal social relations.
– DERIVATIVES **dysfunction** n. **dysfunctionally** adv.

**dysgenic** /dɪsˈdʒɛnɪk/ ● **adj.** exerting a detrimental effect on later generations.

**dysgraphia** /dɪsˈgrafɪə/ ● **n.** Psychiatry inability to write coherently, as a symptom of brain disease or damage.
– DERIVATIVES **dysgraphic** adj.
– ORIGIN 1930s: from **DYS-** + Gk *-graphia* 'writing'.

**dyskinesia** /ˌdɪskɪˈniːzɪə, -kʌɪ-/ ● **n.** Medicine abnormality or impairment of voluntary movement.
– ORIGIN C18: from **DYS-** + Gk *kinēsis* 'motion'.

**dyslexia** /dɪsˈlɛksɪə/ ● **n.** a disorder involving difficulty in learning to read or interpret words, letters, and other symbols. Compare with **ALEXIA**.
– DERIVATIVES **dyslectic** adj. & n. **dyslexic** adj. & n.
– ORIGIN C19: Ger. *Dyslexie* from **DYS-** + Gk *lexis* 'speech' (appar. by confusion of Gk *legein* 'to speak' and L. *legere* 'to read').

**dysmenorrhoea** /ˌdɪsmɛnəˈriːə/ (US **dysmenorrhea**) ● **n.** Medicine painful menstruation.

**dyspepsia** /dɪsˈpɛpsɪə/ ● **n.** indigestion.
– ORIGIN C18: via L. from Gk *duspepsia*, from *duspeptos* 'difficult to digest'.

**dyspeptic** ● **adj.** of or relating to dyspepsia or the resulting irritableness. ● **n.** a dyspeptic person.

**dysphagia** /dɪsˈfeɪdʒɪə/ ● **n.** Medicine difficulty in swallowing, as a symptom of disease.
– ORIGIN C18: from **DYS-** + Gk *phagia* 'eating'.

**dysphasia** /dɪsˈfeɪzɪə/ ● **n.** Psychiatry language disorder marked by deficiency in the generation of speech, due to brain disease or damage.
– DERIVATIVES **dysphasic** adj.
– ORIGIN C19: from Gk *dusphatos* 'hard to utter'.

**dysphemism** /ˈdɪsfɪmɪz(ə)m/ ● **n.** a derogatory or unpleasant term used instead of a pleasant or neutral one.

**dysphonia** /dɪsˈfəʊnɪə/ ● **n.** Medicine difficulty in speaking due to a physical disorder of the mouth, tongue, throat, or vocal cords.
– ORIGIN C18: from **DYS-** + L. *phonia* from Gk, from *phōnē* 'sound, voice'.

**dysphoria** /dɪsˈfɔːrɪə/ ● **n.** Psychiatry a state of unease or general dissatisfaction.
– DERIVATIVES **dysphoric** adj. & n.
– ORIGIN C19: from Gk *dusphoria*, from *dusphoros* 'hard to bear'.

**dysplasia** /dɪsˈpleɪzɪə/ ● **n.** Medicine the enlargement of an organ or tissue by the proliferation of abnormal cells.
– DERIVATIVES **dysplastic** adj.
– ORIGIN 1930s: from **DYS-** + Gk *plasis* 'formation'.

**dyspnoea** /dɪspˈniːə/ (US **dyspnea**) ● **n.** Medicine laboured breathing.
– DERIVATIVES **dyspnoeic** adj.
– ORIGIN C17: via L. from Gk *duspnoia*, from *dus-* 'difficult' + *pnoē* 'breathing'.

**dyspraxia** /dɪsˈpraksɪə/ ● **n.** a developmental disorder of the brain in childhood causing difficulty in activities requiring coordination and movement.
– ORIGIN C20: from Gk *dus-* 'bad or difficult' + *praxis* 'action'.

**dysprosium** /dɪsˈprəʊzɪəm/ ● **n.** the chemical element of atomic number 66, a soft silvery-white metal of the lanthanide series. (Symbol: **Dy**)
– ORIGIN C19: from Gk *dusprositos* 'hard to get at' + **-IUM**.

**dysrhythmia** /dɪsˈrɪðmɪə/ ● **n.** Medicine abnormality in a physiological rhythm, especially of the brain or heart.
– DERIVATIVES **dysrhythmic** adj. **dysrhythmical** adj.

**dysthymia** /dɪsˈθʌɪmɪə/ ● **n.** Psychiatry persistent mild depression.

– DERIVATIVES **dysthymic** adj. & n.
– ORIGIN C19: from Gk *dusthumia*.

**dystocia** /dɪs'təʊʃə/ ● **n.** Medicine difficulty in giving birth.
– ORIGIN C18: from Gk *dustokia*, from *dus-* 'difficult' + *tokos* 'childbirth'.

**dystonia** /dɪs'təʊnɪə/ ● **n.** Medicine a state of abnormal muscle tone resulting in muscular spasm and abnormal posture.
– DERIVATIVES **dystonic** adj.

**dystopia** /dɪs'təʊpɪə/ ● **n.** an imaginary place or society in which everything is bad.
– DERIVATIVES **dystopian** adj. & n.
– ORIGIN C18: from **DYS-** + **UTOPIA**.

**dystrophic** /dɪs'trəʊfɪk, -'trɒfɪk/ ● **adj. 1** Medicine affected by or relating to dystrophy, especially muscular dystrophy. **2** Ecology (of a body of water) having brown acidic water that is poor in oxygen, owing to high levels of dissolved humus.
– ORIGIN C19: from Gk *dus-* 'bad' + *-trophia* 'nourishment' + **-IC**.

**dystrophin** /dɪs'trəʊfɪn/ ● **n.** Biochemistry a protein found in skeletal muscle, which is absent in sufferers from muscular dystrophy.

**dystrophy** /'dɪstrəfi/ ● **n.** Medicine a disorder in which an organ or tissue of the body wastes away. See also **MUSCULAR DYSTROPHY**.
– ORIGIN C19: from mod. L. *dystrophia*, from Gk *dus-* 'bad' + *-trophia* 'nourishment'.

**dysuria** /dɪs'jʊərɪə/ ● **n.** Medicine painful or difficult urination.
– ORIGIN ME: via late L. from Gk *dusouria*, from *dus-* 'difficult' + *ouron* 'urine'.

**DZ** ● **abbrev. 1** Algeria (international vehicle registration). [from Arab. *Djazir.*] **2** drop zone.

**dzo** /ʒəʊ, zəʊ/ (also **dzho** or **zho**) ● **n.** (pl. same or **-os**) a hybrid of a cow and a yak.
– ORIGIN C19: from Tibetan *mdso*.

**Dzongkha** /'zɒŋkə/ ● **n.** the official language of Bhutan, closely related to Tibetan.

**E**[1] (also **e**) ● n. (pl. **Es** or **E's**) **1** the fifth letter of the alphabet. **2** denoting the fifth in a set. **3** Music the third note of the diatonic scale of C major.

**E**[2] ● abbrev. **1** East or Eastern. **2** informal the drug Ecstasy or a tablet of Ecstasy. **3** denoting products, in particular food additives, which comply with EU regulations. See also **E-NUMBER**. **4** exa- ($10^{18}$). **5** Spain (international vehicle registration). [from Sp. *España*.] ● symb. Physics **1** electric field strength. **2** energy.

**e** ● symb. **1** (also $e^-$) Chemistry an electron. **2** (**e**) Mathematics the transcendental number that is the base of Napierian or natural logarithms, approximately equal to 2.71828.

**e-**[1] ● prefix variant spelling of **EX-**[1] (as in *elect*, *emit*).

**e-**[2] ● prefix denoting the use of electronic data transfer, especially through the Internet: *e-cash*.
– ORIGIN from **ELECTRONIC**, on the pattern of *email*.

**ea.** ● abbrev. each.

**each** ● det. & pron. every one of two or more people or things, regarded and identified separately. ● adv. to, for, or by every one of a group.
– PHRASES **each and every** every single.
– ORIGIN OE *ǣlc*, based on a W. Gmc phr. meaning 'ever alike' (see **AYE**[2], **ALIKE**).

**each other** ● pron. the other one or ones.

**each-way** ● adj. & adv. Brit. (of a bet) backing a horse or other competitor either to win or to finish in the first three.

**eager** ● adj. strongly wanting to do or have. ➤ keenly expectant or interested.
– DERIVATIVES **eagerly** adv. **eagerness** n.
– ORIGIN ME (also in the sense 'pungent, sour'): from OFr. *aigre* 'keen', from L. *acer, acr-* 'sharp, pungent'.

**eagle** ● n. **1** a large bird of prey with a massive hooked bill and long broad wings, renowned for its keen sight and powerful soaring flight. [*Aquila* and other genera.] **2** Golf a score of two strokes under par at a hole. **3** US a former gold coin worth ten dollars. ● v. Golf play (a hole) in two strokes under par.
– DERIVATIVES **eaglet** n.
– ORIGIN ME: from OFr. *aigle*, from L. *aquila*. The golf term was suggested by **BIRDIE**.

**eagle eye** ● n. a close watch.
– DERIVATIVES **eagle-eyed** adj.

**eagle owl** ● n. a very large owl with ear tufts and a deep hoot. [*Bubo bubo* (Eurasia) and related species.]

**eagle ray** ● n. a large ray with long pointed pectoral fins, a long tail, and a distinct head. [Genera *Myliobatis* and *Aetobatus*; several species.]

**eagre** /ˈeɪgə, ˈiː-/ ● n. dialect term for **BORE**[3].
– ORIGIN C17: of unknown origin.

**EAK** ● abbrev. Kenya (international vehicle registration).
– ORIGIN from *East Africa Kenya*.

**-ean** ● suffix forming adjectives and nouns such as *Antipodean*.
– ORIGIN from L. *-aeus, -eus* or Gk *-aios, -eios*, + **-AN**.

**ear**[1] ● n. **1** the organ of hearing and balance in humans and other vertebrates, especially the external part of this. ➤ (in other animals) an organ sensitive to sound. **2** an ability to recognize and appreciate sounds. **3** willingness to listen and pay attention: *a sympathetic ear*.
– PHRASES **be all ears** informal be listening attentively. **one's ears are burning** one is subconsciously aware of being talked about. **have someone's ear** have access to and influence with someone. **have** (or **keep**) **an ear to the ground** be well informed about events and trends. **be out on one's ear** informal be dismissed ignominiously. **up to one's ears in** informal very busy with.
– DERIVATIVES **-eared** adj. **earless** adj.
– ORIGIN OE *ēare*, of Gmc origin.

**ear**[2] ● n. the seed-bearing head or spike of a cereal plant.
– ORIGIN OE *ēar*, of Gmc origin.

**earache** ● n. pain inside the ear.

**earbashing** ● n. informal a lengthy and reproachful speech.
– DERIVATIVES **earbasher** n.

**eardrum** ● n. the membrane of the middle ear, which vibrates in response to sound waves.

**eared seal** ● n. see **SEAL**[2].

**earful** ● n. informal a prolonged reprimand.

**earhole** ● n. the external opening of the ear.

**earl** ● n. a British nobleman ranking above a viscount and below a marquess.
– DERIVATIVES **earldom** n.
– ORIGIN OE *eorl*, of Gmc origin.

**Earl Grey** ● n. a kind of China tea flavoured with bergamot.
– ORIGIN prob. named after the 2nd *Earl Grey* (1764–1845), said to have been given the recipe by a Chin. mandarin.

**Earl Marshal** ● n. (in the UK) the officer presiding over the College of Arms, with ceremonial duties on various royal occasions.

**ear lobe** ● n. a soft, rounded fleshy part hanging from the lower margin of the ear.

**Earl Palatine** ● n. historical an earl having royal authority within his country or domain.

**early** ● adj. (**-ier**, **-iest**) & adv. **1** before the usual or expected time. **2** of, at, or near the beginning of a particular time, period, or sequence. ● n. (**earlies**) **1** potatoes ready to be harvested before the main crop. **2** informal early shifts.
– PHRASES **at the earliest** not before the time or date specified. **early bird** humorous a person who rises or arrives early. **early** (or **earlier**) **on** at an early (or earlier) stage. **it's** (or **these are**) **early days** informal, chiefly Brit. it is too soon to be sure how a situation will develop.
– DERIVATIVES **earliness** n.
– ORIGIN OE (as adv.) *ǣrlīce* (see **ERE**, **-LY**[2]), influenced by ON *árliga*.

**early closing** ● n. Brit. the practice of shutting business premises on a particular afternoon every week.

**Early English** ● adj. denoting a style of English Gothic architecture typical of the late 12th and 13th centuries, characterized by pointed arches and simple lancet windows.

**early music** ● n. medieval, Renaissance, and early baroque music, especially as revived and played on period instruments.

**earmark** ● n. a mark on the ear of a domesticated animal indicating ownership or identity. ➤ an identifying feature. ● v. **1** (usu. **be earmarked**) designate for a particular purpose. **2** mark (an animal) with an earmark.

**earmuffs** ● pl. n. a pair of soft fabric coverings, connected by a band, worn over the ears to protect them from cold or noise.

**earn** ● v. obtain (money) in return for labour or services. ➤ (of capital invested) gain (money) as interest or profit. ➤ gain as the reward for hard work or merit.
– ORIGIN OE *earnian*, of W. Gmc origin.

**earned income** ● n. money derived from paid work as opposed to profit from investments.

**earned run** ● n. Baseball a run that is not the result of an error or passed ball.

**earner** • n. a person or thing earning money or income of a specified kind or level: *high earners.*

**earnest**[1] /'ə:nɪst/ • adj. intensely serious.
– PHRASES **in earnest** to a greater extent or more intensely than before. ➤ sincere and serious in intention.
– DERIVATIVES **earnestly** adv. **earnestness** n.
– ORIGIN OE *eornoste* (adj.), *eornost* (n.), of Gmc origin.

**earnest**[2] /'ə:nɪst/ • n. a sign or promise of what is to come.
– ORIGIN ME *ernes*, lit. 'instalment paid to confirm a contract', based on OFr. *erres*, from L. *arra*, shortened form of *arrabo* 'a pledge'.

**earnest money** • n. chiefly US money paid to confirm a contract.

**earnings** • pl. n. money or income earned.

**earphone** • n. an electrical device worn on the ear to receive radio or telephone communications or to listen to a radio or tape recorder.

**earpiece** • n. the part of a telephone, radio receiver, or other aural device that is applied to the ear during use.

**ear-piercing** • adj. loud and shrill. • n. the piercing of the lobes or edges of the ears to allow the wearing of earrings.

**earplug** • n. a piece of wax, cotton wool, etc., placed in the ear as protection against noise, water, or cold air.

**earring** • n. a piece of jewellery worn on the lobe or edge of the ear.

**earshot** • n. the range or distance over which one can hear or be heard.

**ear-splitting** • adj. extremely loud.

**earth** • n. **1** (also **Earth**) the planet on which we live, the third planet of the solar system in order of distance from the sun. **2** the substance of the land surface; soil. ➤ one of the four elements in ancient and medieval philosophy and in astrology. ➤ used in names of stable, dense, non-volatile inorganic substances, e.g. **fuller's earth**. ➤ poetic/literary the substance of the human body: *earth to earth, ashes to ashes.* **3** Brit. electrical connection to the ground, regarded as having zero electrical potential. **4** the underground lair of a badger or fox. • v. **1** Brit. connect (an electrical device) to earth. **2** Hunting (of a fox) run to its earth.
– PHRASES **bring** (or **come**) **back** (**down**) **to earth** cause to return (or return) to reality. **the earth** chiefly Brit. a very large amount: *her hat cost the earth.* **go to earth** go into hiding. **on earth** used for emphasis: *what on earth are you doing?*
– DERIVATIVES **earthward** adj. & adv. **earthwards** adv.
– ORIGIN OE *eorthe*, of Gmc origin.

**earthbound** • adj. **1** confined to the earth or earthly things. **2** moving towards the earth.

**earth closet** • n. Brit. a basic type of toilet with dry earth used to cover excrement.

**earthen** • adj. **1** made of compressed earth. **2** (of a pot) made of baked or fired clay.

**earthenware** • n. pottery made of fired clay.

**earthling** • n. (in science fiction) an inhabitant of the earth.

**earthly** • adj. **1** of or relating to the earth or human life on the earth. ➤ material; worldly. **2** [with neg.] informal used for emphasis: *there was no earthly reason to rush.*
– PHRASES **not stand** (or **have**) **an earthly** Brit. informal have no chance at all.
– DERIVATIVES **earthliness** n.

**earth mother** • n. (in mythology and primitive religion) a goddess symbolizing fertility and the source of life.

**earthnut** • n. a plant of the parsley family with an edible roundish tuber. [*Conopodium majus.*] ➤ the almond-flavoured tuber of this plant.

**earthquake** • n. a sudden violent shaking of the ground as a result of movements within the earth's crust.

**earth science** • n. the branch of science concerned with the physical constitution of the earth and its atmosphere. ➤ (**earth sciences**) the various branches of this subject, e.g. geology.

**earth-shattering** • adj. informal very important or shocking.
– DERIVATIVES **earth-shatteringly** adv.

**earthshine** • n. Astronomy the glow caused by sunlight reflected by the earth, especially on the darker portion of a crescent moon.

**earthstar** • n. a brownish woodland fungus with a spherical fruiting body surrounded by a fleshy star-shaped structure. [*Geastrum* and other genera.]

**earthwork** • n. a large artificial bank of soil, especially one made as a defence in ancient times.

**earthworm** • n. a burrowing annelid worm that lives in the soil. [*Lumbricus* and other genera, family Lumbricidae.]

**earthy** • adj. (**-ier**, **-iest**) **1** resembling or suggestive of soil. **2** direct and uninhibited, especially about sexual subjects or bodily functions.
– DERIVATIVES **earthily** adv. **earthiness** n.

**ear trumpet** • n. a trumpet-shaped device formerly used as a hearing aid.

**ear tuft** • n. each of a pair of tufts of longer feathers on the top of the head of some owls.

**earwax** • n. the protective yellow waxy substance secreted in the passage of the outer ear.

**earwig** • n. a small elongated insect with a pair of terminal appendages that resemble pincers. [Order Dermaptera: many species.] • v. (**earwigged**, **earwigging**) informal eavesdrop.
– ORIGIN OE *ēarwicga*, from *ēare* 'ear' + *wicga* 'earwig' (prob. rel. to *wiggle*); the insect was once thought to crawl into the human ear.

**ease** • n. absence of difficulty or effort. ➤ freedom from worries or problems. • v. **1** make or become less serious or severe. ➤ facilitate. **2** move carefully or gradually. ➤ (**ease something away/down/off**) Nautical slacken a rope or sail slowly or gently. **3** (of share prices, interest rates, etc.) decrease in value or amount.
– PHRASES **at** (**one's**) **ease** relaxed. ➤ (**at ease**) Military in a relaxed attitude with the feet apart and the hands behind the back.
– DERIVATIVES **easeful** adj. (poetic/literary). **easer** n.
– ORIGIN ME: from OFr. *aise*, based on L. *adjacens*, *adjacere* 'lie close by'.

**easel** /'i:z(ə)l/ • n. a wooden frame for holding an artist's work in progress.
– ORIGIN C16: from Du. *ezel* 'ass'.

**easement** /'i:zm(ə)nt/ • n. **1** Law a right to cross or otherwise use another's land for a specified purpose. **2** poetic/literary comfort or peace.

**easily** • adv. **1** without difficulty or effort. ➤ more quickly or frequently than is usual. **2** without doubt. ➤ very probably.

**east** • n. (usu. **the east**) **1** the direction towards the point of the horizon where the sun rises at the equinoxes, on the right-hand side of a person facing north. **2** the eastern part of a country, region, or town. ➤ (**the East**) the regions or countries lying to the east of Europe, especially China, Japan, and India. ➤ (**the East**) historical the former communist states of eastern Europe. • adj. **1** lying towards, near, or facing the east. **2** (of a wind) blowing from the east. • adv. to or towards the east.
– DERIVATIVES **eastbound** adj. & adv.
– ORIGIN OE *ēast-*, of Gmc origin.

**East Coast Fever** • n. a feverish tick-borne disease of cattle, prevalent mostly in Africa and usually fatal.

**East Ender** • n. an inhabitant of the part of London east of the City.

**Easter** • n. the festival of the Christian Church celebrating the resurrection of Christ, held (in the Western Church) on the first Sunday after the first full moon following the northern spring equinox.
– ORIGIN OE *ēastre*, of Gmc origin and rel. to EAST; perh. from *Ēastre*, the name of a goddess assoc. with spring.

**Easter bunny** • n. an imaginary rabbit said to bring gifts to children at Easter.

**Easter Day** (also **Easter Sunday**) • n. the day on which the festival of Easter is celebrated.

**Easter egg** • n. an artificial chocolate egg or decorated hard-boiled egg given at Easter, especially to children.

**easterly** • adj. & adv. **1** in an eastward position or direction. **2** (of a wind) blowing from the east. • n. a wind blowing from the east.

**eastern** • adj. **1** situated in, directed towards, or facing the east. **2** (**Eastern**) coming from or characteristic of the regions to the east of Europe.
– DERIVATIVES **easternmost** adj.

**Eastern Church** (also **Eastern Orthodox Church**) • n. another name for **ORTHODOX CHURCH**. ➤ any of the Christian Churches originating in eastern Europe and the Middle East.

**easterner** • n. a native or inhabitant of the east of a particular region or country.

**Easter Sepulchre** • n. a recess in certain medieval churches for keeping the Eucharistic elements from Good Friday until the Easter festivities.

**Eastertide** • n. the Easter period.

**East Germanic** • n. the extinct eastern group of Germanic languages, including Gothic. • adj. of or relating to this group of languages.

**East Indiaman** • n. historical a trading ship belonging to the East India Company.

**East Indian** • adj. of or relating to the islands of SE Asia or (archaic) the whole of SE Asia to the east of and including India.

**easting** • n. **1** distance travelled or measured eastward, especially at sea. **2** a figure or line representing eastward distance on a map.

**east-north-east** • n. the direction or compass point midway between east and north-east.

**east-south-east** • n. the direction or compass point midway between east and south-east.

**eastward** • adj. in an easterly direction. • adv. (also **eastwards**) towards the east. • n. (**the eastward**) the direction or region to the east.
– DERIVATIVES **eastwardly** adj. & adv.

**easy** • adj. (**-ier**, **-iest**) **1** achieved without great effort; presenting few difficulties. ➤ free from worry or problems. **2** informal, derogatory (of a woman) very receptive to sexual advances. **3** lacking anxiety or awkwardness. • exclam. be careful!
– PHRASES **easy on the eye** (or **ear**) informal pleasant to look at (or listen to). **go** (or **be**) **easy on** informal refrain from being harsh with or critical of. **of easy virtue** dated or humorous (of a woman) sexually promiscuous. **stand easy!** Military used to instruct soldiers standing at ease that they may relax their attitude further. **take it easy** make little effort; rest.
– DERIVATIVES **easiness** n.
– ORIGIN ME: from OFr. *aisie*, past part. of *aisier* (see **EASE**).

**easy chair** • n. a large, comfortable chair, typically an armchair.

**easy-going** • adj. relaxed and tolerant.

**easy listening** • n. popular music that is tuneful and undemanding.

**easy money** • n. **1** money obtained by dubious means or for little work. **2** money available at relatively low interest.

**easy-peasy** • adj. Brit. informal very easy.
– ORIGIN 1970s: reduplication of **EASY**.

**easy street** • n. informal a state of financial comfort or security.

**EAT** • abbrev. Tanzania (international vehicle registration).
– ORIGIN from *East Africa Tanzania*.

**eat** • v. (past **ate** /ɛt, eɪt/; past part. **eaten**) **1** put (food) into the mouth and chew and swallow it. ➤ (**eat out** or **in**) have a meal in a restaurant (or at home). **2** (**eat something away** or **eat away at/into**) erode or destroy something gradually. ➤ (**eat something up**) use resources in very large quantities. ➤ (**eat someone up**) dominate someone's thoughts completely. • n. (**eats**) informal light food or snacks.
– PHRASES **eat one's heart out** suffer from excessive longing, especially for something unattainable. **eat like a bird** (or **a horse**) informal eat very little (or a lot). **eat one's words** retract what one has said, especially in a humiliated way. **I'll eat my hat** informal said to indicate that one thinks something is extremely unlikely to happen. **what's eating you** (or **him** etc.)**?** informal what is worrying or annoying you (or him etc.)?
– DERIVATIVES **eater** n.
– ORIGIN OE *etan*, of Gmc origin.

**eatable** • adj. fit to be consumed as food. • n. (**eatables**) items of food.

**eatery** • n. (pl. **-ies**) informal a restaurant or cafe.

**eating apple** • n. an apple suitable for eating raw.

**EAU** • abbrev. Uganda (international vehicle registration).
– ORIGIN from *East Africa Uganda*.

**eau de cologne** /ˌəʊ də kəˈləʊn/ • n. (pl. **eaux de cologne** pronunc. same) a toilet water with a strong scent.
– ORIGIN C19: Fr., lit. 'water of Cologne'.

**eau de Nil** /ˌəʊ də ˈniːl/ • n. a pale greenish colour.
– ORIGIN C19: from Fr. *eau-de-Nil*, lit. 'water of the Nile'.

**eau de toilette** /ˌəʊ də twɑːˈlɛt/ • n. (pl. **eaux de toilette** pronunc. same) a dilute form of perfume.
– ORIGIN C20: Fr., 'toilet water'.

**eau de vie** /ˌəʊ də ˈviː/ • n. (pl. **eaux de vie** pronunc. same) brandy.
– ORIGIN from Fr. *eau-de-vie*, lit. 'water of life'.

**eaves** • pl. n. the part of a roof that meets or overhangs the walls of a building.
– ORIGIN OE *efes* (sing.); of Gmc origin; prob. rel. to **OVER**.

**eavesdrop** • v. (**eavesdropped**, **eavesdropping**) secretly listen to a conversation.
– DERIVATIVES **eavesdropper** n.
– ORIGIN C17: back-form. from *eavesdropper* (ME), from the obs. noun *eavesdrop* 'the ground on to which water drips from the eaves', prob. from ON *upsardropi*.

**eavestrough** • n. Canadian a gutter fixed beneath the edge of a roof.

**ebb** • n. the movement of the tide out to sea. • v. **1** (of tidewater) move away from the land; recede. Compare with **FLOW**. **2** (often **ebb away**) (of an emotion or quality) gradually lessen or reduce.
– PHRASES **at a low ebb** in a poor state.
– ORIGIN OE *ebba* (n.), *ebbian* (v.), of W. Gmc origin; ult. rel. to **OF**.

**EBD** • abbrev. emotional and behavioural difficulties (or disorder).

**E-boat** • n. a German torpedo boat used in the Second World War.
– ORIGIN from *E-* for *enemy* + **BOAT**.

**Ebola fever** /iːˈbəʊlə, əˈbəʊlə/ • n. an infectious and generally fatal viral disease marked by fever and severe internal bleeding.
– ORIGIN 1976: named after a river in Zaire (Democratic Republic of Congo).

**ebon** /ˈɛb(ə)n/ • n. poetic/literary very dark in colour; ebony.

**Ebonics** /ɛˈbɒnɪks/ • pl. n. [treated as sing.] American black English regarded as a language in its own right rather than as a dialect of standard English.
– ORIGIN blend of **EBONY** and **PHONICS**.

**ebonite** • n. another term for **VULCANITE**.

**ebonize** (also **-ise**) • v. [usu. as adj. **ebonized**] make (furniture) look like ebony.

**ebony** /ˈɛb(ə)ni/ • n. **1** heavy blackish or very dark brown wood from a tree of tropical and warm regions. **2** the tree which produces this wood. [*Diospyros ebenum* (India and Sri Lanka) and other species.] **3** a very dark brown or black colour.
– ORIGIN ME: from earlier *ebon* (via OFr. and L. from Gk *ebenos* 'ebony tree'), perh. on the pattern of *ivory*.

**e-book** • n. an electronic version of a printed book which can be read on a personal computer or handheld device designed specifically for this purpose.

**EBRD** • abbrev. European Bank for Reconstruction and Development.

**ebullient** /ɪˈbʌljənt, -ˈbʊl-/ • adj. **1** cheerful and full of energy. **2** archaic (of liquid) boiling or turbulent.

– DERIVATIVES **ebullience** n. **ebulliently** adv.
– ORIGIN C16: from L. *ebullient-*, *ebullire* 'boil up'.

**ebullition** /ˌɛbəˈlɪʃ(ə)n, -bʊ-/ • **n.** technical or archaic **1** the action of bubbling or boiling. **2** a sudden outburst of emotion or violence.
– ORIGIN ME: from late L. *ebullitio(n-)*, from *ebullire* (see **EBULLIENT**).

**EBV** • **abbrev.** Epstein-Barr virus.

**EC** • **abbrev. 1** East Central (London postal district). **2** Ecuador (international vehicle registration). **3** European Commission. **4** European Community. **5** executive committee.

**ecad** /ˈiːkad/ • **n.** Ecology an organism that is modified by its environment.
– ORIGIN C20: from Gk *oikos* 'house' + **-AD**[1].

**écarté** • **n. 1** /eɪˈkɑːteɪ/ a card game for two players, in which thirty-two cards are used and certain cards may be discarded in exchange for others. **2** /ˌeɪkɑːˈteɪ/ Ballet a position in which the dancer extends one leg in the air to the side with the arm of the same side raised above the head and the other arm extended to the side.
– ORIGIN C19: Fr., past part. of *écarter* 'discard, throw out'.

**e-cash** • **n.** electronic financial transactions conducted in cyberspace via computer networks.

**ECB** • **abbrev.** (in the UK) English Cricket Board.

**ecbolic** /ɛkˈbɒlɪk/ • **adj.** Medicine inducing contractions of the uterus leading to expulsion of a fetus.
– ORIGIN C18: from Gk *ekbolē* 'expulsion' + **-IC**.

**Ecce Homo** /ˌɛkeɪ ˈhɒməʊ, ˈhəʊməʊ/ • **n.** Art a painting of Christ wearing the crown of thorns.
– ORIGIN L., 'behold the man', the words of Pontius Pilate to the Jews after Jesus was crowned with thorns (John 19:5).

**eccentric** /ɪkˈsɛntrɪk, ɛk-/ • **adj. 1** unconventional and slightly strange. **2** technical not placed centrally or not having its axis placed centrally. ➤(of an orbit) not circular, especially to a marked degree. • **n. 1** an eccentric person. **2** a cam or other part mounted eccentrically on a revolving shaft in order to transform rotation into backward-and-forward motion.
– DERIVATIVES **eccentrically** adv. **eccentricity** n.
– ORIGIN ME: via late L. from Gk *ekkentros*, from *ek* 'out of' + *kentron* 'centre'.

**ecchymosis** /ˌɛkɪˈməʊsɪs/ • **n.** (pl. **ecchymoses** /-siːz/) Medicine a discoloration of the skin resulting from bleeding underneath, typically caused by bruising.
– ORIGIN C16: mod. L., from Gk *ekkhumōsis* 'escape of blood'.

**Eccles.** • **abbrev.** Ecclesiastes (in biblical references).

**Eccles cake** • **n.** Brit. a round flat cake of sweetened pastry filled with currants.
– ORIGIN named after the town of *Eccles* near Manchester.

**ecclesial** /ɪˈkliːzɪ(ə)l/ • **adj.** formal relating to or constituting a Church or denomination.
– ORIGIN C17: via OFr. from Gk *ekklēsia* (see **ECCLESIASTICAL**).

**ecclesiarch** /ɪkˈliːzɪɑːk/ • **n.** archaic a ruler of a Church.
– ORIGIN C18: from Gk *ekklēsia* 'church' + *arkhos* 'leader'.

**ecclesiastic** formal • **n.** a priest or clergyman. • **adj.** another term for **ECCLESIASTICAL**.

**ecclesiastical** • **adj.** of or relating to the Christian Church or its clergy.
– DERIVATIVES **ecclesiastically** adv.
– ORIGIN ME: from Fr. *ecclésiastique*, or via late L. from Gk *ekklēsiastikos*, from *ekklēsiastēs* 'member of an assembly', from *ekklēsia* 'assembly, church'.

**ecclesiasticism** • **n.** adherence or over-attention to details of Church practice.

**ecclesiology** /ɪˌkliːzɪˈɒlədʒi/ • **n. 1** the study of churches. **2** theology as applied to the nature and structure of the Christian Church.
– DERIVATIVES **ecclesiological** adj. **ecclesiologist** n.

**Ecclus** • **abbrev.** Ecclesiasticus (in biblical references).

**eccrine** /ˈɛkrʌɪn, -krɪn/ • **adj.** Physiology relating to or denoting multicellular glands which do not lose cytoplasm in their secretions, especially the sweat glands.
– ORIGIN 1930s: from Gk *ekkrinein* 'secrete'.

**ecdysiast** /ɛkˈdɪzɪast/ • **n.** humorous a striptease performer.
– ORIGIN 1940s: from Gk *ekdusis* 'shedding', on the pattern of *enthusiast*.

**ecdysis** /ˈɛkdɪsɪs, ɛkˈdʌɪsɪs/ • **n.** Zoology the process of shedding the old skin (in reptiles) or casting off the outer cuticle (in insects and other arthropods).
– DERIVATIVES **ecdysial** /ɛkˈdɪzɪəl/ adj.
– ORIGIN C19: from Gk *ekdusis* 'shedding'.

**ecdysone** /ˈɛkdɪsəʊn, ɛkˈdʌɪsəʊn/ • **n.** Biochemistry a steroid hormone that controls moulting in insects and other arthropods.
– ORIGIN 1950s: from Gk *ekdusis* 'shedding' + **-ONE**.

**ECG** • **abbrev.** electrocardiogram or electrocardiograph.

**echelon** /ˈɛʃəlɒn, ˈeɪʃ-/ • **n. 1** a level or rank in an organization, profession, or society. **2** Military a formation of troops, ships, aircraft, or vehicles in parallel rows with the end of each row projecting further than the one in front. • **v.** Military arrange in an echelon formation.
– ORIGIN C18: from Fr. *échelon*, from *échelle* 'ladder'.

**echeveria** /ˌɛtʃɪˈvɪərɪə/ • **n.** a succulent plant with rosettes of fleshy colourful leaves, native to warm regions of America. [Genus *Echeveria*.]
– ORIGIN mod. L., named after the Mex. illustrator Anastasio *Echeveri* or *Echeverría*.

**echidna** /ɪˈkɪdnə/ • **n.** a spiny insectivorous egg-laying mammal with a long snout and claws, native to Australia and New Guinea. [*Tachyglossus aculeatus* and *Zaglossus bruijni*.]
– ORIGIN C19: mod. L., from Gk *ekhidna* 'viper'; cf. *ekhinos* 'sea urchin, hedgehog'.

**echinacea** /ˌɛkɪˈneɪsɪə/ • **n.** a North American plant of the daisy family, whose flowers have a raised cone-like centre which appears to consist of soft spines. [Genus *Echinacea*: several species.]
– ORIGIN mod. L., from Gk *ekhinos* 'hedgehog'.

**Echinodermata** /ɪˌkʌɪnə(ʊ)dəˈmɑːtə, ˌɛkɪn-, -ˈdəːmətə/ • **pl. n.** Zoology a phylum of marine invertebrates which includes starfishes, sea urchins, brittlestars, crinoids, and sea cucumbers.
– DERIVATIVES **echinoderm** /ɪˈkʌɪnə(ʊ)dəːm, ˈɛkɪn-/ n.
– ORIGIN mod. L., from Gk *ekhinos* 'hedgehog, sea urchin' + *derma* 'skin'.

**Echinoidea** /ˌɛkɪˈnɔɪdɪə/ • **pl. n.** Zoology a class of echinoderms that comprises the sea urchins.
– DERIVATIVES **echinoid** /ˈɛkɪnɔɪd/ n. & adj.
– ORIGIN mod. L., from *Echinus* (genus name), from Gk *ekhinos* (see **ECHINUS**).

**echinus** /ɪˈkʌɪnəs/ • **n.** Architecture a rounded moulding below an abacus on a Doric or Ionic capital.
– ORIGIN ME: via L. from Gk *ekhinos* 'hedgehog, sea urchin'.

**echo** • **n.** (pl. **-oes**) **1** a sound caused by the reflection of sound waves from a surface back to the listener. **2** a reflected radio or radar beam. **3** Linguistics the repetition of one speaker's utterance by another. **4** something suggestive of or parallel to something else. **5** Bridge a play by a defender of a higher card in a suit followed by a lower one in a subsequent trick, used as a signal to request a further lead of that suit by their partner. **6** a code word representing the letter E, used in radio communication. • **v.** (**-oes, -oed**) **1** (of a sound) reverberate or be repeated after the original sound has stopped. **2** have a continued significance or influence. **3** repeat (someone's words or opinions).
– DERIVATIVES **echoer** n. **echoey** adj. **echoless** adj.
– ORIGIN ME: from OFr. or L., from Gk *ēkhō*, rel. to *ēkhē* 'a sound'.

**echocardiography** /ˌɛkəʊkɑːdɪˈɒgrəfi/ • **n.** Medicine the use of ultrasound waves to investigate the action of the heart.
– DERIVATIVES **echocardiogram** n. **echocardiograph** n. **echocardiographic** adj.

**echo chamber** • **n.** an enclosed space for producing reverberation of sound.

**echogram** • **n.** a recording of depth or distance under water made by an echo sounder.

**echograph** • **n.** an instrument for recording echograms.

**echoic** /ɛˈkəʊɪk/ ● **adj.** **1** of or like an echo. **2** Linguistics representing a sound by imitation; onomatopoeic.
– DERIVATIVES **echoically** adv.

**echolalia** /ˌɛkəʊˈleɪlɪə/ ● **n.** **1** Psychiatry meaningless repetition of another person's spoken words as a symptom of psychiatric disorder. **2** repetition of speech by a child learning to talk.
– ORIGIN C19: mod. L., from Gk *ēkhō* 'echo' + *lalia* 'speech'.

**echolocation** /ˈɛkə(ʊ)lə(ʊ),keɪʃ(ə)n/ ● **n.** the location of objects by reflected sound, in particular as used by animals such as dolphins and bats.

**echopraxia** /ˌɛkəʊˈpraksɪə/ ● **n.** Psychiatry meaningless repetition or imitation of the movements of others as a symptom of psychiatric disorder.
– ORIGIN C20: mod. L., from Gk *ēkhō* 'echo' + *praxis* 'action'.

**echo sounder** ● **n.** a device for determining the depth of the seabed or detecting objects in water by measuring the time taken for echoes to return to the listener.
– DERIVATIVES **echo-sounding** n.

**echovirus** (also **ECHO virus**) ● **n.** Medicine any of a group of enteroviruses which can cause respiratory infections and a mild form of meningitis.
– ORIGIN 1950s: *echo* is acronym from *enteric cytopathogenic human orphan*, because the virus was not orig. assignable to any known disease.

**echt** /ɛxt/ ● **adj.** authentic and typical.
– ORIGIN from Ger.

**eclair** /eɪˈklɛː, ɪ-/ ● **n.** a small, soft cake of choux pastry filled with cream and topped with chocolate icing.
– ORIGIN C19: from Fr. *éclair*, lit. 'lightning'.

**éclaircissement** /ˌeɪklɛːˈsiːsmɒ̃/ ● **n.** an explanation or clarification of something obscure or puzzling.
– ORIGIN Fr., from *éclaircir* 'clear up'.

**eclampsia** /ɪˈklam(p)sɪə/ ● **n.** Medicine a condition in which one or more convulsions occur in a pregnant woman suffering from high blood pressure, often followed by coma and posing a threat to the health of mother and baby.
– DERIVATIVES **eclamptic** adj.
– ORIGIN C19: mod. L., from Fr. *éclampsie*, from Gk *eklampsis* 'sudden development'.

**éclat** /eɪˈklɑː/ ● **n.** brilliant display or effect. ➤social distinction or conspicuous success.
– ORIGIN C17: from Fr., from *éclater* 'burst out'.

**eclectic** /ɪˈklɛktɪk/ ● **adj.** **1** deriving ideas or style from a broad and diverse range of sources. **2** (**Eclectic**) denoting or belonging to a class of ancient philosophers who selected doctrines from various schools of thought. ● **n.** an eclectic person.
– DERIVATIVES **eclectically** adv. **eclecticism** n.
– ORIGIN C17: from Gk *eklektikos*, from *eklegein* 'pick out'.

**eclipse** /ɪˈklɪps/ ● **n.** **1** an obscuring of the light from one celestial body by the passage of another between it and the observer or between it and its source of illumination. ➤an instance of being eclipsed by another person or thing. **2** Ornithology a phase during which the distinctive markings of a bird (especially a male duck) are obscured by moulting of the breeding plumage. ● **v.** **1** (of a celestial body) obscure the light from or to (another body). **2** deprive of significance, power, or prominence.
– ORIGIN ME: from OFr. *e(s)clipse* (n.), *eclipser* (v.), via L. from Gk *ekleipsis*, from *ekleipein* 'fail to appear, be eclipsed'.

**eclipsing binary** ● **n.** Astronomy a binary star whose brightness varies periodically as the two components pass one in front of the other.

**ecliptic** /ɪˈklɪptɪk/ Astronomy ● **n.** a great circle on the celestial sphere representing the sun's apparent path during the year, so called because lunar and solar eclipses can only occur when the moon crosses it. ● **adj.** of eclipses or the ecliptic.
– ORIGIN ME: via L. from Gk *ekleiptikos*, from *ekleipein* (see **ECLIPSE**).

**eclogite** /ˈɛklɒdʒʌɪt/ ● **n.** Geology a metamorphic rock containing granular minerals, typically garnet and pyroxene.
– ORIGIN C19: from Fr., from Gk *eklogē* 'selection' + **-ITE**[1].

**eclogue** /ˈɛklɒg/ ● **n.** a short pastoral poem, especially one in the form of a dialogue.
– ORIGIN ME: via L. from Gk *eklogē* 'selection'.

**eclose** /ɪˈkləʊz/ ● **v.** Entomology (of an insect) emerge as an adult from the pupa or as a larva from the egg.
– DERIVATIVES **eclosion** n.
– ORIGIN C19 (as *eclosion*): from Fr. *éclore* 'to hatch'.

**ECM** ● **abbrev.** electronic countermeasures.

**eco-** /ˈiːkəʊ, ˈɛkəʊ/ ● **comb. form** representing **ECOLOGY**.

**ecocide** ● **n.** destruction of the natural environment, especially when wilfully done.

**eco-friendly** ● **adj.** not harmful to the environment.

**eco-labelling** ● **n.** the use of labels to identify products conforming to recognized environmental standards.
– DERIVATIVES **eco-label** n.

**E. coli** /ˈkəʊlʌɪ/ ● **n.** the bacterium *Escherichia coli*, commonly found in the intestines of humans and other animals, some strains of which can cause severe food poisoning.

**ecology** /ɪˈkɒlədʒi, ɛ-/ ● **n.** the branch of biology concerned with the relations of organisms to one another and to their physical surroundings.
– DERIVATIVES **ecological** adj. **ecologically** adv. **ecologist** n.
– ORIGIN C19 (orig. as *oecology*): from Gk *oikos* 'house' + **-LOGY**.

**e-commerce** ● **n.** commercial transactions conducted electronically on the Internet.

**econometrics** /ɪˌkɒnəˈmɛtrɪks/ ● **pl. n.** [treated as sing.] the branch of economics concerned with the use of mathematical methods (especially statistics) in describing economic systems.
– DERIVATIVES **econometric** adj. **econometrical** adj. **econometrician** n. **econometrist** n.
– ORIGIN 1930s: from **ECONOMY**, on the pattern of words such as *biometrics*.

**economic** /ˌiːkəˈnɒmɪk, ɛk-/ ● **adj.** **1** of or relating to economics or the economy. **2** justified in terms of profitability.
– ORIGIN ME: via OFr. and L. from Gk *oikonomikos*, from *oikonomia* (see **ECONOMY**).

**economical** ● **adj.** giving good value or return in relation to the resources or money expended. ➤sparing in the use of resources or money.
– PHRASES **economical with the truth** euphemistic lying or deliberately withholding information.

**economically** ● **adv.** **1** in a way that relates to economics or finance. **2** in an economical way.

**economic good** ● **n.** Economics a product or service which can command a price when sold.

**economic rent** ● **n.** Economics the extra amount earned by a resource (e.g. land, capital, or labour) by virtue of its present use.

**economics** ● **pl. n.** [often treated as sing.] the branch of knowledge concerned with the production, consumption, and transfer of wealth.

**economism** /ɪˈkɒnəmɪz(ə)m/ ● **n.** belief in the primacy of economic causes or factors.

**economist** ● **n.** an expert in economics.

**economize** (also **-ise**) ● **v.** spend less; be economical.
– DERIVATIVES **economization** n. **economizer** n.

**economy** ● **n.** (pl. **-ies**) **1** the state of a country or region in terms of the production and consumption of goods and services and the supply of money. ➤a country or region having a particular economy: *a free-market economy*. **2** careful management of available resources. ➤[as modifier] offering good value for money: *an economy pack of soap flakes*. ➤a financial saving. **3** (also **economy class**) the cheapest class of air or rail travel.
– PHRASES **economy of scale** a proportionate saving in costs gained by an increased level of production. **economy of scope** a proportionate saving gained by producing two or more distinct goods, when the cost of doing so is less than that of producing each separately.
– ORIGIN C15: from Fr. *économie*, or via L. from Gk

*oikonomia* 'household management', based on *oikos* 'house' + *nemein* 'manage'.

**economy-class syndrome** ● **n.** deep-vein thrombosis said to be caused by periods of prolonged immobility on long-haul flights.

**écorché** /ˌɛkɔːˈʃeɪ/ ● **n.** (pl. pronounced same) a painting or sculpture of a human figure with the skin removed to display the musculature.
– ORIGIN Fr., lit. 'flayed'.

**ecosphere** ● **n.** a region in which life exists or could exist; the biosphere.

**ecossaise** /ˌɛkɒˈseɪz/ ● **n.** (pl. pronounced same) an energetic country dance in duple time.
– ORIGIN C19: from Fr., fem. of *écossais* 'Scottish'.

**ecosystem** ● **n.** Ecology a biological community of interacting organisms and their physical environment.

**ecotone** /ˈiːkə(ʊ)təʊn, ˈɛk-/ ● **n.** Ecology a region of transition between two biological communities.
– DERIVATIVES **ecotonal** adj.
– ORIGIN from **ECO-** + Gk *tonos* 'tension'.

**ecotourism** ● **n.** tourism directed towards unspoiled natural environments and intended to support conservation efforts.
– DERIVATIVES **ecotour** n. & v. **ecotourist** n.

**ecotype** ● **n.** Botany & Zoology a distinct form or race of a plant or animal species occupying a particular habitat.

**eco-warrior** ● **n.** a person actively involved in preventing damage to the environment.

**ecru** /ˈeɪkruː, ɛˈkruː/ ● **n.** the light fawn colour of unbleached linen.
– ORIGIN C19: from Fr. *écru* 'unbleached'.

**ECSC** ● **abbrev.** European Coal and Steel Community.

**ecstasy** /ˈɛkstəsi/ ● **n.** (pl. **-ies**) **1** an overwhelming feeling of great happiness or joyful excitement. **2** an emotional or religious frenzy or trancelike state. **3** (**Ecstasy**) an illegal amphetamine-based synthetic drug with euphoric effects.
– ORIGIN ME: from OFr. *extasie*, via late L. from Gk *ekstasis* 'standing outside oneself'.

**ecstatic** /ɪkˈstatɪk, ɛk-/ ● **adj.** feeling or characterized by ecstasy. ● **n.** a person subject to mystical experiences.
– DERIVATIVES **ecstatically** adv.

**ECT** ● **abbrev.** electroconvulsive therapy.

**ecto-** ● **comb. form** outer; external: *ectoparasite*.
– ORIGIN from Gk *ektos* 'outside'.

**ectoderm** /ˈɛktə(ʊ)dəːm/ ● **n.** Zoology & Embryology the outermost layer of cells or tissue of an embryo, or the parts derived from this (e.g. the epidermis).
– DERIVATIVES **ectodermal** adj.
– ORIGIN C19: from **ECTO-** + Gk *derma* 'skin'.

**ectogenesis** /ˌɛktə(ʊ)ˈdʒɛnɪsɪs/ ● **n.** (chiefly in science fiction) the development of embryos in artificial conditions outside the womb.
– DERIVATIVES **ectogene** n. **ectogenetic** adj. **ectogenetically** adv.

**ectomorph** /ˈɛktə(ʊ)mɔːf/ ● **n.** Physiology a person with a lean and delicate build of body. Compare with **ENDOMORPH** and **MESOMORPH**.
– DERIVATIVES **ectomorphic** adj. **ectomorphy** n.
– ORIGIN 1940s: *ecto-* from *ectodermal* (being the layer of the embryo giving rise to physical characteristics which predominate) + **-MORPH**.

**-ectomy** ● **comb. form** denoting surgical removal of a specified part of the body: *appendectomy*.
– ORIGIN from Gk *ektomē* 'excision'.

**ectoparasite** /ˌɛktəʊˈparəsʌɪt/ ● **n.** Biology a parasite, such as a flea, that lives on the outside of its host. Compare with **ENDOPARASITE**.
– DERIVATIVES **ectoparasitic** adj.

**ectopic** /ɛkˈtɒpɪk/ ● **adj.** Medicine in an abnormal place or position.
– ORIGIN C19: from mod. L. *ectopia* 'presence of tissue, cells, etc. in an abnormal place' (from Gk *ektopos* 'out of place') + **-IC**.

**ectopic pregnancy** ● **n.** a pregnancy in which the fetus develops outside the womb, typically in a Fallopian tube.

**ectoplasm** /ˈɛktə(ʊ)plaz(ə)m/ ● **n. 1** Biology, dated the more viscous, clear outer layer of the cytoplasm in amoeboid cells. Compare with **ENDOPLASM**. **2** a viscous substance that supposedly exudes from the body of a medium during a spiritualistic trance and forms the material for the manifestation of spirits.
– DERIVATIVES **ectoplasmic** adj.

**Ectoprocta** /ˌɛktə(ʊ)ˈprɒktə/ ● **pl. n.** Zoology another term for **BRYOZOA**.
– DERIVATIVES **ectoproct** n.
– ORIGIN mod. L., from *ektos* 'outside or external' + *prōktos* 'anus'.

**ectotherm** /ˈɛktəʊθəːm/ ● **n.** Zoology an animal that is dependent on external sources of body heat.
– DERIVATIVES **ectothermic** adj. **ectothermy** n.

**ectropion** /ɛkˈtrəʊpɪən/ ● **n.** Medicine a condition, typically a consequence of advanced age, in which the eyelid is turned outwards away from the eyeball.
– ORIGIN C17: from Gk, from *ek-* 'out' + *trepein* 'to turn'.

**ecu** /ˈɛkjuː, ˈiː-, ˈeɪ-, -kuː/ (also **ECU**) ● **n.** (pl. same or **ecus**) former term for **EURO**.
– ORIGIN acronym from *European currency unit*.

**Ecuadorean** /ɛkwəˈdɔːrɪən, Spanish ekwaˈðorian/ (also **Ecuadorian**) ● **n.** a native or inhabitant of Ecuador. ● **adj.** of or relating to Ecuador.

**ecumenical** /ˌiːkjʊˈmɛnɪk(ə)l, ɛk-/ ● **adj.** representing a number of different Christian Churches. ➤ promoting or relating to unity among the world's Christian Churches.
– DERIVATIVES **ecumenically** adv.
– ORIGIN C16: via late L. from Gk *oikoumenikos* from *oikoumenē* 'the (inhabited) earth'.

**Ecumenical Patriarch** ● **n.** a title of the Orthodox Patriarch of Constantinople.

**ecumenism** /ɪˈkjuːmənɪz(ə)m/ ● **n.** the principle or aim of promoting unity among the world's Christian Churches.

**eczema** /ˈɛksɪmə, ˈɛkzɪmə/ ● **n.** a medical condition in which patches of skin become rough and inflamed with blisters which cause itching and bleeding.
– DERIVATIVES **eczematous** /ɛkˈziːmətəs, ɛkˈzɛm-/ adj.
– ORIGIN C18: mod. L., from Gk *ekzema*, from *ekzein* 'boil over, break out'.

**ed.** ● **abbrev. 1** edited by. **2** edition. **3** editor.

**-ed**[1] ● **suffix** forming adjectives: **1** (added to nouns) having; possessing; affected by: *talented*. **2** from phrases consisting of adjective and noun: *bad-tempered*.
– ORIGIN OE *-ede*.

**-ed**[2] ● **suffix** forming: **1** the past tense and past participle of weak verbs: *landed*. **2** participial adjectives: *wounded*.
– ORIGIN OE *-ed*, *-ad*, *-od*.

**edacious** /ɪˈdeɪʃəs/ ● **adj.** rare of or given to eating.
– DERIVATIVES **edacity** n.
– ORIGIN C19: from L. *edax*, *edac-* (from *edere* 'eat') + **-IOUS**.

**Edam** /ˈiːdam/ ● **n.** a round Dutch cheese, typically pale yellow with a red wax coating, traditionally made at Edam in the Netherlands.

**edaphic** /ɪˈdafɪk/ ● **adj.** Ecology of, produced by, or influenced by the soil.
– ORIGIN C19: coined in Ger. from Gk *edaphos* 'floor' + **-IC**.

**Edda** /ˈɛdə/ ● **n.** either of two 13th-century Icelandic books, the **Elder** or **Poetic Edda** (a collection of Old Norse poems on Norse legends) and the **Younger** or **Prose Edda** (a handbook to Icelandic poetry).
– ORIGIN either from the name of a character in the ON poem *Rigsthul*, or from ON *óthr* 'poetry'.

**eddo** /ˈɛdəʊ/ ● **n.** (pl. **-oes**) a taro corm or plant of a West Indian variety with many edible cormlets.
– ORIGIN C17: of W. Afr. origin.

**eddy** ● **n.** (pl. **-ies**) a circular movement of water causing a small whirlpool. ● **v.** (**-ies**, **-ied**) (of water, air, or smoke) move in a circular way.
– ORIGIN ME: prob. from the Gmc base of the OE prefix *ed-* 'again, back'.

**eddy current** ● **n.** a localized electric current induced in a conductor by a varying magnetic field.

**edelweiss** /ˈeɪd(ə)lvʌɪs/ ● **n.** a mountain plant which

has woolly white bracts around its small flowers and downy grey-green leaves. [*Leontopodium alpinum*.]
– ORIGIN C19: from Ger., from *edel* 'noble' + *weiss* 'white'.

**edema** ● **n.** US spelling of **OEDEMA**.

**Eden** /'i:d(ə)n/ ● **n.** **1** (also **Garden of Eden**) the place where Adam and Eve lived in the biblical account of the Creation. **2** a place or state of unspoilt happiness or beauty.
– ORIGIN from late L. (Vulgate), Gk *Ēdēn* (Septuagint), and Heb. *'Ēḏen*; perh. ult. from Sumerian *eden* 'plain, desert', but prob. rel. to Heb. *'ēḏen* 'delight'.

**edentate** /'i:dənteɪt/ ● **n.** Zoology a mammal of an order distinguished by the lack of incisor and canine teeth, including the anteaters, sloths, and armadillos. [Order Xenarthra (or Edentata).]
– ORIGIN C19: from L. *edentat-*, *edentare* 'make toothless'.

**edentulous** /ɪ'dɛntjʊləs/ ● **adj.** Medicine & Zoology lacking teeth.
– ORIGIN C18: from L. *edentulus*.

**edge** ● **n.** **1** the outside limit of an object, area, or surface. ➤ an area next to a steep drop. **2** the sharpened side of a blade. **3** an intense or striking quality. ➤ a quality or factor which gives superiority over close rivals. **4** the line along which two surfaces of a solid meet. ● **v.** **1** provide with a border or edge. **2** move carefully or furtively. **3** (usu. **edge out**) informal defeat by a small margin. **4** give an intense or sharp quality to. **5** Cricket strike (the ball) with the edge of the bat. **6** ski with one's weight on the edges of one's skis.
– PHRASES **on edge** tense, nervous, or irritable. **set someone's teeth on edge** (of a sound or taste) cause intense discomfort or irritation to someone.
– DERIVATIVES **-edged** adj. **edgeless** adj. **edger** n.
– ORIGIN OE *ecg* 'sharpened side of a blade', of Gmc origin.

**edge tool** ● **n.** a handworked or machine-operated cutting tool.

**edgeways** (also **edgewise**) ● **adv.** with the edge uppermost or towards the viewer.
– PHRASES **get a word in edgeways** [usu. with neg.] manage to contribute to a conversation with a voluble person.

**edging** ● **n.** something forming an edge or border.

**edgy** ● **adj.** (**-ier**, **-iest**) tense, nervous, or irritable.
– DERIVATIVES **edgily** adv. **edginess** n.

**edh** /ɛð/ ● **n.** variant spelling of **ETH**.

**EDI** ● **abbrev.** electronic data interchange.

**edible** /'ɛdɪb(ə)l/ ● **adj.** fit to be eaten. ● **n.** (**edibles**) items of food.
– DERIVATIVES **edibility** n.
– ORIGIN C16: from late L. *edibilis*, from L. *edere* 'eat'.

**edible dormouse** ● **n.** another term for **FAT DORMOUSE**.

**edible snail** ● **n.** a large snail which is widely collected or cultured for food, occurring chiefly in southern Europe. [*Helix pomatia*.]

**edict** /'i:dɪkt/ ● **n.** an official order or proclamation.
– DERIVATIVES **edictal** /ɪ'dɪkt(ə)l/ adj.
– ORIGIN ME: from L. *edictum* 'something proclaimed', neut. past part. of *edicere*, from *e-* (var. of *ex-*) 'out' + *dicere* 'say, tell'.

**edifice** /'ɛdɪfɪs/ ● **n.** **1** a building, especially a large, imposing one. **2** a complex system of beliefs.
– ORIGIN ME: via OFr. from L. *aedificium*, from *aedis* 'dwelling' + *facere* 'make'.

**edify** /'ɛdɪfʌɪ/ ● **v.** (**-ies**, **-ied**) formal instruct or improve morally or intellectually.
– DERIVATIVES **edification** n. **edifying** adj. **edifyingly** adv.
– ORIGIN ME: from OFr. *edifier*, from L. *aedificare* 'build', from *aedis* 'dwelling' + *facere* 'make' (cf. **EDIFICE**).

**edit** ● **v.** (**edited**, **editing**) prepare (written material) for publication by correcting, condensing, or otherwise modifying it. ➤ prepare and arrange material for (a recording or broadcast). ➤ be editor of (a newspaper or magazine). ➤ (**edit something out**) remove material in preparing a recording or broadcast. ● **n.** a change or correction made as a result of editing.
– DERIVATIVES **editable** adj.
– ORIGIN C18: partly a back-form. from **EDITOR**, reinforced by Fr. *éditer* 'to edit'.

**edition** ● **n.** a particular form or version of a published text. ➤ the total number of copies of a book, newspaper, etc. issued at one time. ➤ a particular version or instance of a regular programme or broadcast.
– ORIGIN ME: from Fr. *édition*, from L. *editio(n-)*, from *edere* 'put out'.

**editio princeps** /ɪˌdɪʃɪəʊ 'prɪnsɛps/ ● **n.** (pl. **editiones principes** /ɪˌdɪʃɪˌəʊni:z 'prɪnsɪpi:z/) the first printed edition of a book.
– ORIGIN L., from *editio(n-)* 'edition' and *princeps* 'chief'.

**editor** ● **n.** **1** a person who is in charge of a newspaper, magazine, or multi-author book. **2** a person who commissions or prepares written or recorded material. **3** a computer program enabling the user to alter or rearrange online text.
– DERIVATIVES **editorship** n.
– ORIGIN C17: from L., 'producer (of games), publisher', from *edit-*, *edere* 'put out'.

**editorial** ● **adj.** of or relating to the commissioning or preparing of material for publication. ● **n.** a newspaper article giving an opinion on a topical issue.
– DERIVATIVES **editorialist** n. **editorially** adv.

**editorialize** (also **-ise**) ● **v.** (of a newspaper or editor) express opinions rather than just report news.

**editress** (also **editrix**) ● **n.** dated or humorous a female editor.

**edit suite** ● **n.** a room containing equipment for electronically editing video-recorded material.

**-edly** ● **suffix** (forming adverbs) in a manner characterized by the action expressed by the formative verb: *repeatedly*.

**Edo** /'ɛdəʊ/ ● **n.** (pl. same or **-os**) **1** a member of a people inhabiting the district of Benin in Nigeria. **2** the Benue-Congo language of this people.
– ORIGIN the name of Benin City in Edo.

**Edomite** /'i:dəmʌɪt/ ● **n.** a member of an ancient people living in Edom, south of the Dead Sea, in biblical times, traditionally believed to be descended from Esau.

**EDP** ● **abbrev.** electronic data processing.

**EDT** ● **abbrev.** Eastern Daylight Time.

**EDTA** ● **abbrev.** Chemistry ethylenediamine tetra-acetic acid, an organic acid which is a strong chelating agent.

**educate** /'ɛdjʊkeɪt/ ● **v.** give intellectual, moral, and social instruction to. ➤ train or give information on a particular subject.
– DERIVATIVES **educability** n. **educable** adj. **educative** adj. **educator** n.
– ORIGIN ME: from L. *educat-*, *educare* 'lead out', rel. to *educere* (see **EDUCE**).

**educated guess** ● **n.** a guess based on knowledge and experience.

**education** ● **n.** **1** the process of educating or being educated. ➤ the theory and practice of teaching. ➤ information about or training in a particular subject. **2** (**an education**) informal an enlightening experience.
– DERIVATIVES **educational** adj. **educationalist** n. **educationally** adv. **educationist** n.

**educe** /ɪ'dju:s/ ● **v.** formal **1** bring out or develop (something latent or potential). **2** infer from data.
– DERIVATIVES **educible** adj. **eduction** n.
– ORIGIN ME: from L. *educere* 'lead out'.

**edulcorate** /ɪ'dʌlkəreɪt/ ● **v.** rare make more acceptable or palatable.
– DERIVATIVES **edulcoration** n.
– ORIGIN C17: from med. L. *edulcorat-*, *edulcorare* 'sweeten'.

**edutainment** /ˌɛdjʊ'teɪnm(ə)nt/ ● **n.** entertainment, especially computer games, with an educational aspect.

**Edw.** ● **abbrev.** Edward.

**Edwardian** /ɛd'wɔ:dɪən/ ● **adj.** relating to or characteristic of the reign of King Edward VII. ● **n.** a person who lived during this period.

**Edwardiana** /ɛdˌwɔ:dɪ'ɑ:nə/ ● **pl. n.** articles, especially collectors' items, from the reign of Edward VII.

**ee** ● **exclam.** northern English form of **OH**[1].

**-ee** ● **suffix** forming nouns: **1** denoting the person affected

directly or indirectly by the action of the formative verb: *employee.* **2** denoting a person described as or concerned with: *absentee.* **3** denoting an object of relatively smaller size: *bootee.*
– ORIGIN from Anglo-Norman Fr. *-é*, from L. *-atus* (past participial ending); some forms are anglicized mod. Fr. nouns (e.g. *refugee* from *réfugié*).

**EEC** • abbrev. European Economic Community.

**EEG** • abbrev. electroencephalogram or electroencephalograph.

**eejit** /ˈiːdʒɪt/ • n. informal Irish and Scottish form of IDIOT.

**eek** • exclam. informal used to express alarm or surprise.

**eel** • n. a snake-like fish with a slender elongated body and poorly developed fins, proverbial for its slipperiness. [*Anguilla anguilla* (Europe) and related species, order Anguilliformes.] ➤ used in names of unrelated fishes that resemble the true eels, e.g. **electric eel**.
– DERIVATIVES **eel-like** adj. **eely** adj.
– ORIGIN OE *ǣl*, of Gmc origin.

**eelgrass** • n. **1** a marine plant with long ribbon-like leaves. [*Zostera marina.*] **2** a submerged aquatic plant with narrow, grass-like leaves. [Genus *Valisneria.*]

**eelpout** /ˈiːlpaʊt/ • n. a small broad-headed sea fish with an elongated body and the dorsal and anal fins continuous with the tail. [Family Zoarcidae: numerous species.]

**eelworm** • n. a nematode, especially a small soil nematode that can become a serious pest of crops and ornamental plants.

**e'en** /iːn/ • adv. poetic/literary form of EVEN¹.

**-een** • suffix Irish forming diminutive nouns such as *colleen.*
– ORIGIN from the Ir. dimin. suffix *-ín.*

**eensy** /ˈiːnsi/ (also **eensy-weensy**) • adj. informal tiny.

**EEPROM** • n. Computing a read-only memory whose contents can be erased and reprogrammed using a pulsed voltage.
– ORIGIN acronym from *electrically erasable programmable ROM.*

**e'er** /ɛː/ • adv. poetic/literary form of EVER.

**-eer** • suffix **1** (forming nouns) denoting a person concerned with or engaged in an activity: *auctioneer.* **2** (forming verbs) denoting concern or involvement with an activity: *electioneer.*
– ORIGIN from Fr. *-ier*, from L. *-arius*; verbs are often back-forms (e.g. *electioneer* from *electioneering*).

**eerie** /ˈɪəri/ • adj. (**-ier**, **-iest**) strange and frightening.
– DERIVATIVES **eerily** adv. **eeriness** n.
– ORIGIN ME (orig. north. Engl. and Scots in the sense 'fearful'): prob. from OE *earg* 'cowardly', of Gmc origin.

**ef-** • prefix variant spelling of EX-¹ assimilated before *f* (as in *efface, effloresce*).

**EFA** • abbrev. essential fatty acid.

**eff** • n. & v. Brit. used as a euphemism for 'fuck'.
– PHRASES **eff and blind** informal swear. [*blind* from its use in expletives such as *blind me* (see BLIMEY).]
– DERIVATIVES **effing** adj. & adv.

**effable** /ˈɛfəb(ə)l/ • adj. rare able to be described in words.
– ORIGIN C17: from L. *effabilis*, from *effari* 'utter'.

**efface** /ɪˈfeɪs/ • v. **1** erase (a mark) from a surface. **2** (**efface oneself**) make oneself appear insignificant or inconspicuous.
– DERIVATIVES **effacement** n.
– ORIGIN C15 (in the sense 'pardon or be absolved from (an offence)'): from Fr. *effacer*, from *e-* (from L. *ex-* 'away from') + *face* 'face'.

**effect** • n. **1** a change which is a result or consequence of an action or other cause. ➤ the extent to which something succeeds or is operative. **2** (often in phr. **to that effect**) general sense or meaning. **3** the state of being or becoming operative: *the law came into effect.* **4** (**effects**) the lighting, sound, or scenery used in a play or film. **5** (**effects**) personal belongings. **6** Physics a physical phenomenon, typically named after its discoverer: *the Renner effect.* • v. cause to happen; bring about.
– PHRASES **for effect** in order to impress people. **in effect** in practice, even if not formally acknowledged.
– ORIGIN ME: from OFr., or from L. *effectus*, from *effect-*, *efficere* 'accomplish'.

**USAGE** effect

On the confusion of **effect** with **affect**, see AFFECT¹.

**effective** • adj. **1** producing a desired or intended result. **2** (of a law or policy) operative. **3** existing in fact, though not formally acknowledged as such. • n. a soldier fit and available for service.
– DERIVATIVES **effectively** adv. **effectiveness** n. **effectivity** n.

**effective demand** • n. Economics the level of demand that represents a real intention to purchase by people with the means to pay.

**effective temperature** • n. Physics the temperature of an object calculated from the radiation it emits, assuming black-body behaviour.

**effector** • n. Biology an organ or cell that acts in response to a stimulus.

**effectual** /ɪˈfɛktʃʊəl, -tjʊəl/ • adj. **1** effective. **2** Law (of a legal document) valid or binding.
– DERIVATIVES **effectuality** n. **effectually** adv. **effectualness** n.

**effectuate** /ɪˈfɛktʃʊeɪt, -tjʊ-/ • v. formal put into force or operation.
– DERIVATIVES **effectuation** n.

**effeminate** /ɪˈfɛmɪnət/ • adj. derogatory (of a man) having characteristics regarded as typical of a woman.
– DERIVATIVES **effeminacy** n. **effeminately** adv.
– ORIGIN ME: from L. *effeminat-*, *effeminare* 'make feminine'.

**effendi** /ɛˈfɛndi/ • n. (pl. **effendis**) a man of high education or social standing in an eastern Mediterranean or Arab country.
– ORIGIN C17: from Turk. *efendi*, from mod. Gk *aphentēs*, from Gk *authentēs* 'lord, master'.

**efferent** /ˈɛf(ə)r(ə)nt/ Physiology • adj. relating to or denoting the conduction of nerve impulses or blood outwards or away from something. The opposite of AFFERENT. • n. an efferent nerve fibre or blood vessel.
– ORIGIN C19: from L. *efferent-*, *efferre* 'carry out'.

**effervescent** • adj. **1** (of a liquid) giving off bubbles; fizzy. **2** vivacious and enthusiastic.
– DERIVATIVES **effervesce** v. **effervescence** n.
– ORIGIN C17: from L. *effervescent-*, *effervescere* 'boil up'.

**effete** /ɪˈfiːt/ • adj. **1** affected, over-refined, and ineffectual. **2** no longer capable of effective action.
– DERIVATIVES **effetely** adv. **effeteness** n.
– ORIGIN C17: from L. *effetus* 'worn out by bearing young'; rel. to FETUS.

**efficacious** /ˌɛfɪˈkeɪʃəs/ • adj. formal effective.
– DERIVATIVES **efficaciously** adv. **efficaciousness** n. **efficacy** /ˈɛfɪkəsi/ n.
– ORIGIN C16: from L. *efficax*, *efficac-* (from *efficere* 'accomplish') + **-IOUS**.

**efficiency** • n. (pl. **-ies**) **1** the state or quality of being efficient. **2** technical the ratio of the useful work performed by a machine or in a process to the total energy expended or heat taken in.

**efficient** • adj. working productively with minimum wasted effort or expense.
– DERIVATIVES **efficiently** adv.
– ORIGIN ME: from L. *efficient-*, *efficere* (see EFFECT).

**efficient cause** • n. Philosophy an agent that brings a thing into being or initiates a change.

**effigy** /ˈɛfɪdʒi/ • n. (pl. **-ies**) a sculpture or model of a person.
– ORIGIN C16: from L. *effigies*, from *effingere* 'to fashion (artistically)'.

**effleurage** /ˌɛfləːˈrɑːʒ/ • n. a form of massage involving a repeated circular stroking movement made with the palm of the hand.
– ORIGIN C19: from Fr., from *effleurer* 'skim the surface, stroke lightly'.

**effloresce** /ˌɛfləˈrɛs/ • v. **1** (of a substance) lose moisture and turn to a fine powder on exposure to air. **2** (of salts) come to the surface of brickwork or other material and

crystallize. ➤(of a surface) become covered with salt particles. **3** reach an optimum stage of development.
– DERIVATIVES **efflorescence** n. **efflorescent** adj.
– ORIGIN C18: from L. *efflorescere*, from *e-* (var. of *ex-*) 'out' + *florescere* 'begin to bloom'.

**effluence** /ˈɛflʊəns/ ● **n. 1** a substance that flows out. **2** the action of flowing out.
– ORIGIN ME: from med. L. *effluentia*, from L. *effluent-*, *effluere* 'flow out'.

**effluent** ● **n.** liquid waste or sewage discharged into a river or the sea.

**effluvium** /ɪˈfluːvɪəm/ ● **n.** (pl. **effluvia** /-vɪə/) an unpleasant or harmful odour or discharge.
– ORIGIN C17: from L., from *effluere* 'flow out'.

**efflux** /ˈɛflʌks/ ● **n.** technical the flowing out of a substance or particle.
– ORIGIN C16: from med. L. *effluxus*, from *effluere* 'flow out'.

**effluxion** /ɪˈflʌkʃ(ə)n/ ● **n. 1** Law the passing of time. **2** archaic the action of flowing out.

**effort** ● **n. 1** a vigorous or determined attempt. ➤strenuous physical or mental exertion. **2** technical a force exerted by a machine or in a process.
– DERIVATIVES **effortful** adj. **effortfully** adv.
– ORIGIN C15: from Fr., from OFr. *esforcier*, based on L. *ex-* 'out' + *fortis* 'strong'.

**effortless** ● **adj.** requiring no effort. ➤achieved with admirable ease.
– DERIVATIVES **effortlessly** adv. **effortlessness** n.

**effrontery** /ɪˈfrʌnt(ə)ri/ ● **n.** insolence or impertinence.
– ORIGIN C17: from Fr. *effronterie*, based on late L. *effrons*, *effront-* 'shameless, barefaced', from *ex-* 'out' + *frons* 'forehead'.

**effulgent** /ɪˈfʌldʒ(ə)nt/ ● **adj.** poetic/literary shining brightly.
– DERIVATIVES **effulgence** n. **effulgently** adv.
– ORIGIN C18: from L. *effulgent-*, *effulgere* 'shine brightly'.

**effusion** ● **n. 1** an instance of giving off a liquid, light, or smell. **2** Medicine an escape of fluid into a body cavity. **3** an instance of unrestrained speech or writing.
– DERIVATIVES **effuse** v.
– ORIGIN ME: from L. *effusio(n-)*, from *effus-*, *effundere* 'pour out'.

**effusive** ● **adj. 1** expressing gratitude, pleasure, or approval in an unrestrained manner. **2** Geology relating to or denoting igneous rocks poured out as lava and later solidified.
– DERIVATIVES **effusively** adv. **effusiveness** n.

**Efik** /ˈɛfɪk/ ● **n.** (pl. same) **1** a member of a people of southern Nigeria. **2** the Benue-Congo language of this people.
– ORIGIN the name in Efik.

**EFL** ● **abbrev.** English as a foreign language.

**eft** /ɛft/ ● **n.** dialect a newt. ➤Zoology the juvenile stage of a newt.
– ORIGIN OE *efeta*, of unknown origin; cf. **NEWT**.

**EFTA** ● **abbrev.** European Free Trade Association.

**EFTPOS** /ˈɛftpɒz/ ● **abbrev.** electronic funds transfer at point of sale.

**e.g.** ● **abbrev.** for example.
– ORIGIN from L. *exempli gratia* 'for the sake of example'.

**egad** /ɪˈgad/ ● **exclam.** archaic expressing surprise, anger, or affirmation.
– ORIGIN C17: representing earlier *A God*.

**egalitarian** /ɪˌgalɪˈtɛːrɪən/ ● **adj.** believing in or based on the principle that all people are equal and deserve equal rights and opportunities. ● **n.** an egalitarian person.
– DERIVATIVES **egalitarianism** n.
– ORIGIN C19: from Fr. *égalitaire*, from *égal* 'equal', from L. *aequalis* (see **EQUAL**).

**egg**[1] ● **n. 1** an oval or round object laid by a female bird, reptile, fish, or invertebrate and containing an ovum which if fertilized can develop into a new organism. ➤an infertile egg, typically of the domestic hen, used for food. **2** Biology the female reproductive cell in animals and plants; an ovum. **3** informal, dated a person of a specified kind: *a thoroughly bad egg*. **4** Architecture a decorative oval moulding, used alternately with triangular figures.
– PHRASES **kill the goose that lays the golden eggs** destroy a reliable and valuable source of income. [with allusion to one of Aesop's fables.] **with egg on one's face** informal appearing foolish or ridiculous.
– DERIVATIVES **eggless** adj. **eggy** adj.
– ORIGIN ME (superseding earlier *ey*, from OE *ǣg*): from ON.

**egg**[2] ● **v.** (**egg someone on**) urge or encourage someone to do something foolish or risky.
– ORIGIN ME: from ON *eggja* 'incite'.

**eggar** /ˈɛgə/ ● **n.** a large brownish moth which is often active during the day. [*Lasiocampa quercus* (**oak eggar**) and other species.]
– ORIGIN C18: prob. from **EGG**[1] (from the shape of the moth's cocoons) + **-ER**[1].

**egg-bound** ● **adj.** (of a hen) unable through weakness or disease to expel its eggs.

**egg cream** ● **n.** US a drink consisting of milk and soda water, flavoured with syrup.

**egg custard** ● **n.** a custard made with milk and eggs, typically sweetened and baked.

**egghead** ● **n.** informal a very academic or studious person.

**egg-nog** (Brit. also **egg-flip**) ● **n.** a drink consisting of wine or other alcohol mixed with beaten egg and milk.

**eggplant** ● **n.** chiefly N. Amer. another term for **AUBERGINE**.

**egg roll** ● **n.** N. Amer. a Chinese-style snack similar to a spring roll, encased in a dough made with egg and deep-fried.

**eggs and bacon** ● **n.** any of a number of plants with yellow flowers marked with orange, red, or brown, supposedly suggestive of eggs and bacon, especially bird's-foot trefoil.

**eggs Benedict** ● **pl. n.** a dish consisting of poached eggs and sliced ham on toast, covered with hollandaise sauce.

**eggshell** ● **n. 1** the thin, hard, fragile outer layer of an egg. **2** [as modifier] (of china) extremely thin and delicate. **3** [as modifier] denoting an oil-based paint that dries with a slight sheen.

**egg timer** ● **n.** a device, traditionally a small hourglass, for timing the cooking of a boiled egg.

**egg tooth** ● **n.** a hard white protuberance on the beak or jaw of an embryo bird or reptile, used for breaking out of the shell.

**egg white** ● **n.** the clear, viscous substance round the yolk of an egg that turns white when cooked or beaten.

**eglantine** /ˈɛgləntʌɪn/ ● **n.** another term for **SWEETBRIAR**.
– ORIGIN ME: from OFr. *eglantine*, from Provençal *aiglentina*, based on L. *acus* 'needle' or *aculeus* 'prickle'.

**EGM** ● **abbrev.** extraordinary general meeting.

**ego** /ˈiːgəʊ, ˈɛ-/ ● **n.** (pl. **-os**) **1** a person's sense of self-esteem or self-importance. **2** Psychoanalysis the part of the mind that mediates between the conscious and the unconscious and is responsible for reality testing and a sense of personal identity. Compare with **ID** and **SUPEREGO**. **3** Philosophy (in metaphysics) a conscious thinking subject.
– DERIVATIVES **egoless** adj.
– ORIGIN C19: from L., lit. 'I'.

**egocentric** /ˌɛgə(ʊ)ˈsɛntrɪk, iː-/ ● **adj. 1** self-centred. **2** centred in or arising from a person's own individual existence or perspective. ● **n.** an egocentric person.
– DERIVATIVES **egocentrically** adv. **egocentricity** n. **egocentrism** n.

**ego-ideal** ● **n.** Psychoanalysis (in Freudian theory) the part of the mind which imposes on itself concepts of ideal behaviour developed from parental and social standards.

**egoism** /ˈɛgəʊɪz(ə)m, ˈiː-/ ● **n. 1** Ethics an ethical theory that treats self-interest as the foundation of morality. **2** another term for **EGOTISM**.
– DERIVATIVES **egoist** n. **egoistic** adj. **egoistical** adj. **egoistically** adv.

**egomania** /ɛgə(ʊ)ˈmeɪnɪə, iː-/ ● **n.** obsessive egotism.
– DERIVATIVES **egomaniac** n. **egomaniacal** adj.

**egotism** /ˈɛɡətɪz(ə)m, ˈiː-/ ● **n.** the quality of being excessively conceited or absorbed in oneself.
– DERIVATIVES **egotist** n. **egotistic** adj. **egotistical** adj. **egotistically** adv. **egotize** (also **-ise**) v.

**ego trip** ● **n.** informal something done to increase one's sense of self-importance.

**egregious** /ɪˈɡriːdʒəs/ ● **adj. 1** outstandingly bad; shocking. **2** archaic remarkably good.
– DERIVATIVES **egregiously** adv. **egregiousness** n.
– ORIGIN C16: from L. *egregius* 'illustrious', lit. 'standing out from the flock', from *ex-* 'out' + *grex, greg-* 'flock'.

**egress** /ˈiːɡrɛs/ ● **n.** formal the action of going out of or leaving a place. ➤a way out. ● **v.** chiefly US go out of or leave (a place).
– DERIVATIVES **egression** n.
– ORIGIN C16: from L. *egress-*, *egredi* 'go out'.

**egret** /ˈiːɡrɪt, ˈɛ-/ ● **n.** a heron with mainly white plumage, having long plumes in the breeding season. [Genus *Egretta* (and *Bubulcus*): several species.]
– ORIGIN ME: from OFr. *aigrette*, from Provençal *aigreta*, from the Gmc base of **HERON**.

**Egyptian** ● **n. 1** a native of ancient or modern Egypt, or a person of Egyptian descent. **2** the Afro-Asiatic language used in ancient Egypt, represented in its oldest stages by hieroglyphic inscriptions. ● **adj.** of or relating to Egypt or its people or language.
– DERIVATIVES **Egyptianization** (also **-isation**) n. **Egyptianize** (also **-ise**) v.

**Egyptian cobra** ● **n.** a large African cobra with a thick body and large head. [*Naja haje*.]

**Egyptology** /ˌiːdʒɪpˈtɒlədʒi/ ● **n.** the study of the language, history, and culture of ancient Egypt.
– DERIVATIVES **Egyptological** adj. **Egyptologist** n.

**eh** ● **exclam.** expressing enquiry or surprise.

**eicosapentaenoic acid** /ˌʌɪkɒsəˌpɛntiːˈnəʊɪk/ ● **n.** Chemistry a polyunsaturated fatty acid found especially in fish oils.
– ORIGIN C20: from Gk *eicosa-* 'twenty' (the number of carbon atoms in the molecule) + **PENTA-** 'five' (the number of unsaturated bonds) + **-ENE** + *-oic* on the pattern of *methanoic*.

**Eid** /iːd/ (also **Id**) ● **n. 1** (in full **Eid ul-Fitr** /ˌiːdʊlˈfɪtrə/) the Muslim festival marking the end of the fast of Ramadan. **2** (in full **Eid ul-Adha** /ˌiːdʊlˈɑːdə/) the festival marking the culmination of the annual pilgrimage to Mecca.
– ORIGIN from Arab. *ʿīd* 'feast', from Aramaic.

**eider** /ˈʌɪdə/ ● **n.** (pl. same or **eiders**) **1** (also **eider duck**) a northern sea duck of which the male is mainly black-and-white and the female brown. [*Somateria mollissima* and related species.] **2** (also **eider down**) small, soft feathers from the breast of the female eider duck.
– ORIGIN C17: from Icelandic *æthur*, from ON *æthr*.

**eiderdown** ● **n.** chiefly Brit. a quilt filled with down (originally from the eider) or some other soft material.

**eidetic** /ʌɪˈdɛtɪk/ ● **adj.** Psychology relating to or denoting mental images having unusual vividness and detail, as if actually visible.
– DERIVATIVES **eidetically** adv.
– ORIGIN 1920s: coined in Ger. from Gk *eidētikos*, from *eidos* 'form'.

**eidolon** /ʌɪˈdəʊlɒn/ ● **n.** (pl. **eidolons** or **eidola** /-lə/) **1** a spectre or phantom. **2** an idealized person or thing.
– ORIGIN C19: from Gk *eidōlon*, from *eidos* 'form'.

**eidos** /ˈʌɪdɒs/ ● **n.** Anthropology the distinctive expression of the character of a culture or social group.
– ORIGIN 1930s: from Gk, lit. 'form, type, or idea', partly in contrast to **ETHOS**.

**eigen-** /ˈʌɪɡ(ə)n/ ● **comb. form** Mathematics & Physics proper; characteristic: *eigenfunction*.
– ORIGIN from Ger. *eigen* 'own'.

**eigenfrequency** ● **n.** (pl. **-ies**) Mathematics & Physics one of the natural resonant frequencies of a system.

**eigenfunction** ● **n.** Mathematics & Physics each of a set of independent functions which are the solutions to a given differential equation.

**eigenvalue** ● **n.** Mathematics & Physics a value of a parameter for which a differential equation has a non-zero solution (an eigenfunction) under given conditions.

**eigenvector** ● **n.** Mathematics & Physics a vector which when operated on by a given operator gives a scalar multiple of itself.

**eight** ● **cardinal number 1** equivalent to the product of two and four; one more than seven, or two less than ten; 8. (Roman numeral: **viii** or **VIII**.) **2** an eight-oared rowing boat or its crew.
– PHRASES **have one over the eight** Brit. informal have one drink too many.
– DERIVATIVES **eightfold** adj. & adv.
– ORIGIN OE *ehta*, *eahta*, of Gmc origin.

**eight ball** ● **n.** chiefly N. Amer. a variety of the game of pool.
– PHRASES **behind the eight ball** informal at a disadvantage.

**eighteen** ● **cardinal number** equivalent to the product of two and nine; one more than seventeen, or eight more than ten; 18. (Roman numeral: **xviii** or **XVIII**.)
– DERIVATIVES **eighteenth** ordinal number.
– ORIGIN OE *e(a)htatēne* (see **EIGHT**, **-TEEN**).

**eighteenmo** ● **n.** (pl. **-os**) another term for **OCTODECIMO**.

**eighth** ● **ordinal number** constituting number eight in a sequence; 8th.
– DERIVATIVES **eighthly** adv.

**eighth note** ● **n.** Music, chiefly N. Amer. a quaver.

**eights** ● **pl. n.** a race for eight-oared rowing boats.

**eightsome reel** ● **n.** a lively Scottish dance for eight people.

**8vo** ● **abbrev.** octavo.

**eighty** ● **cardinal number** (pl. **-ies**) equivalent to the product of eight and ten; ten less than ninety; 80. (Roman numeral: **lxxx** or **LXXX**.)
– DERIVATIVES **eightieth** ordinal number. **eightyfold** adj. & adv.
– ORIGIN OE *hunde(a)htatig*, from *hund* (of uncertain origin) + *e(a)hta* 'eight' + *-tig* (see **-TY²**).

**eina** /ˈeɪnɑː/ S. African ● **exclam.** used as an expression of pain or distress. ● **n.** pain or trouble.
– ORIGIN Afrik., perh. from Khoikhoi *llé* + *llná* or Nama *llei*.

**einkorn** /ˈʌɪnkɔːn/ ● **n.** an old kind of wheat with small bearded ears and spikelets that each contain one slender grain, now rarely grown. [*Triticum monococcum*.]
– ORIGIN C20: from Ger., from *ein* 'one' + *Korn* 'seed'.

**Einstein** /ˈʌɪnstʌɪn/ ● **n.** informal a genius.
– ORIGIN from the name of the German-born physicist Albert *Einstein* (1879–1955).

**einsteinium** /ʌɪnˈstʌɪnɪəm/ ● **n.** the chemical element of atomic number 99, an artificially made radioactive metal of the actinide series. (Symbol: **Es**)

**eirenic** /ʌɪˈrɛnɪk, -ˈriː-/ (also **irenic**) ● **adj.** formal aiming or aimed at peace.
– DERIVATIVES **eirenical** adj.
– ORIGIN C19: from Gk *eirēnikos*, from *eirēnē* 'peace'.

**eisteddfod** /ʌɪˈstɛdvəd, Welsh ʌɪˈstɛðvɒd/ ● **n.** (pl. **eisteddfods** or **eisteddfodau** /-ˈvɒdʌɪ/) a competitive festival of music and poetry in Wales.
– DERIVATIVES **eisteddfodic** /-ˈvɒdɪk/ adj.
– ORIGIN Welsh, lit. 'session', from *eistedd* 'sit'.

**Eiswein** /ˈʌɪsvʌɪn/ ● **n.** (pl. **Eisweine** /-nə/ or **Eisweins**) wine made from ripe grapes picked while covered with frost.
– ORIGIN from Ger., from *Eis* 'ice' + *Wein* 'wine'.

**either** /ˈʌɪðə, ˈiː-/ ● **conj. & adv. 1** used before the first of two (or occasionally more) alternatives specified (the other being introduced by 'or'). **2** [adv., with neg.] used to indicate a similarity or link with a statement just made. ➤moreover. ● **det. & pron.** one or the other of two people or things. ➤each of two.
– ORIGIN OE *ǣgther*, contracted form of *ǣg(e)hwæther*, of Gmc origin; ult. rel. to **AYE²** and **WHETHER**.

**eiusdem generis** ● **adj.** variant spelling of **EJUSDEM GENERIS**.

**ejaculate** ● **v.** /ɪˈdʒakjʊleɪt/ **1** (of a man or male animal) eject semen from the body at the moment of sexual climax. **2** dated say something quickly and suddenly. ● **n.** /ɪˈdʒakjʊlət/ semen that has been ejaculated.

– DERIVATIVES **ejaculation** n. **ejaculator** n. **ejaculatory** /ɪˈdʒakjʊlət(ə)ri/ adj.
– ORIGIN C16: from L. *ejaculat-*, *ejaculari* 'dart out', ult. from *iacere* 'to throw'.

**eject** ● v. force or throw out violently or suddenly. ➤(of a pilot) escape from an aircraft by means of an ejection seat. ➤compel (someone) to leave a place.
– DERIVATIVES **ejection** n. **ejector** n.
– ORIGIN ME: from L. *eject-*, *eicere* 'throw out', from *e-* (var. of *ex-*) 'out' + *jacere* 'to throw'.

**ejecta** /ɪˈdʒɛktə/ ● pl. n. [often treated as sing.] chiefly Geology & Astronomy material that is forced or thrown out, especially as a result of volcanic eruption or meteoritic impact.
– ORIGIN C19: from L., 'things thrown out', neut. pl. of *ejectus*, from *eicere* (see EJECT).

**ejection seat** (also **ejector seat**) ● n. an aircraft seat that can propel its occupant from the craft in an emergency.

**ejective** /ɪˈdʒɛktɪv/ Phonetics ● adj. denoting a type of consonant in some languages (e.g. Hausa) produced by sudden release of pressure from the glottis. ● n. an ejective consonant.

**ejectment** ● n. Law, chiefly historical the eviction of a tenant from property. ➤the process whereby an evicted tenant seeks to recover possession and damages.

**ejido** /ɛˈhiːdəʊ/ ● n. (pl. **-os**) (in Mexico) a piece of land farmed communally under a system supported by the state.
– ORIGIN Mex. Sp., from Sp.

**ejusdem generis** /eɪˌ(j)ʊsdɛm ˈdʒɛnɛrɪs/ (also **eiusdem generis**) ● adj. & adv. Law of or as the same kind.
– ORIGIN from L.

**eke**[1] /iːk/ ● v. (**eke something out**) make something last longer by using or consuming it frugally. ➤manage to make a living with difficulty: *eke out a living.*
– ORIGIN OE *ēacian*, *ēcan* (in the sense 'increase'), of Gmc origin.

**eke**[2] /iːk/ ● adv. archaic term for ALSO.
– ORIGIN OE, of Gmc origin.

**El** ● n. (**the El**) (in the US) an elevated railway, especially that in Chicago.

**-el** ● suffix variant spelling of -LE[2].

**elaborate** ● adj. /ɪˈlab(ə)rət/ involving many carefully arranged parts; detailed and complicated. ● v. /ɪˈlabəreɪt/ **1** develop or present in further detail. ➤(often **elaborate on**) add more detail to something already said. **2** Biology (of a natural agency) produce (a substance) from its elements or simpler constituents.
– DERIVATIVES **elaborately** adv. **elaborateness** n. **elaboration** n. **elaborative** adj. **elaborator** n.
– ORIGIN C16 (earlier (ME) as *elaboration*): from L. *elaborat-*, *elaborare* 'work out'.

**elaichi** /ɪˈlʌɪtʃi/ ● n. Indian term for CARDAMOM.
– ORIGIN from Hindi *ilāycī*.

**Elamite** ● n. **1** a native or inhabitant of ancient Elam (now SW Iran). **2** the agglutinative language of Elam.

**elan** /eɪˈlɒ̃, eɪˈlan/ ● n. energy, style, and enthusiasm.
– ORIGIN C19: from Fr. *élan*, from *élancer* 'to dart'.

**eland** /ˈiːlənd/ ● n. a spiral-horned African antelope, the largest of the antelopes. [*Tragelaphus oryx* and *T. derbianus*.]
– ORIGIN C18: via Afrik. from Du., 'elk'.

**elapse** ● v. (of time) pass.
– ORIGIN C16: from L. *elaps-*, *elabi* 'slip away'.

**elasmobranch** /ɪˈlazmə(ʊ)braŋk/ ● n. Zoology a cartilaginous fish of a group (subclass Elasmobranchii) that comprises the sharks, rays, and skates.
– ORIGIN C19: from mod. L. *Elasmobranchii*, from Gk *elasmos* 'beaten metal' + *brankhia* 'gills'.

**elasmosaur** /ɪˈlazmə(ʊ)sɔː/ ● n. a Cretaceous plesiosaur with a long neck shaped like that of a swan.
– ORIGIN C19: from mod. L. *Elasmosaurus*, from Gk *elasmos* 'beaten metal' + *sauros* 'lizard'.

**elastane** /ɪˈlasteɪn/ ● n. an elastic polyurethane material, used for close-fitting clothing.

**elastase** /ɪˈlasteɪz/ ● n. Biochemistry a pancreatic enzyme which digests elastin.

**elastic** /ɪˈlastɪk/ ● adj. **1** able to resume normal shape spontaneously after being stretched or squeezed. **2** flexible and adaptable: *the definition is elastic.* ➤Economics (of demand or supply) sensitive to changes in price or income. **3** Physics (of a collision) involving no decrease of kinetic energy. ● n. cord, tape, or fabric which returns to its original length or shape after being stretched.
– DERIVATIVES **elastically** adv. **elasticity** /ɛlaˈstɪsɪti, iː-, ɪ-/ n. **elasticize** (also **-ise**) v.
– ORIGIN C17: from mod. L. *elasticus*, from Gk *elastikos* 'propulsive'.

**elasticated** ● adj. chiefly Brit. (of a garment or material) made elastic by the insertion of rubber thread or tape.

**elastic band** ● n. a rubber band.

**elastic limit** ● n. Physics the maximum extent to which a solid can be stretched without permanent alteration of size or shape.

**elastic modulus** ● n. Physics the ratio of the force exerted upon a substance or body to the resultant deformation.

**elastin** /ɪˈlastɪn/ ● n. Biochemistry an elastic, fibrous glycoprotein found in connective tissue.

**elastomer** /ɪˈlastəmə/ ● n. a natural or synthetic polymer having elastic properties, e.g. rubber.
– DERIVATIVES **elastomeric** adj.

**Elastoplast** /ɪˈlastəplast, -plɑːst/ ● n. trademark adhesive sticking plaster for covering cuts and wounds.

**elate** /ɪˈleɪt/ ● v. [usu. as adj. **elated**] make ecstatically happy. ● adj. archaic in high spirits; exultant or proud.
– DERIVATIVES **elatedly** adv. **elatedness** n. **elation** n.
– ORIGIN ME (as adj.): from L. *elat-*, *efferre* 'to raise'.

**E-layer** ● n. a layer of the ionosphere able to reflect medium-frequency radio waves.
– ORIGIN 1930s: arbitrary use of the letter *E*.

**elbow** ● n. **1** the joint between the forearm and the upper arm. **2** a piece of piping or something similar bent through an angle. ● v. **1** strike with one's elbow. ➤(often **elbow one's way**) move by pushing past people with one's elbows. **2** informal summarily reject or dismiss.
– PHRASES **give someone the elbow** informal summarily reject or dismiss someone. **up to one's elbows in** informal deeply involved in.
– ORIGIN OE *elboga*, *elnboga*, of Gmc origin; cf. ELL, BOW[1].

**elbow grease** ● n. informal hard physical work, especially vigorous polishing or cleaning.

**elbow room** ● n. informal adequate space to move or work in.

**eld** /ɛld/ ● n. poetic/literary old age. ➤former times; the past.
– ORIGIN OE *ieldu*, *eldu*, of Gmc origin; rel. to ELDER[1] and OLD.

**elder**[1] ● adj. (of one or more out of a group of people) of a greater age. ● n. **1** (**one's elder**) a person of greater age than one. **2** a leader or senior figure in a tribe. **3** an official in the early Christian Church, or of various Protestant Churches and sects.
– DERIVATIVES **eldership** n.
– ORIGIN OE *ieldra*, *eldra*, of Gmc origin; rel. to ELD and OLD.

**elder**[2] ● n. a small tree or shrub with white flowers and bluish-black or red berries. [*Sambucus nigra* and related species.] ➤used in names of other plants resembling this, e.g. **ground elder**.
– ORIGIN OE *ellærn*; rel. to Mid. Low Ger. *ellern*, *elderne*.

**elderberry** ● n. the berry of the elder, used for making jelly or wine. ➤an elder tree or shrub.

**Elder Brother** ● n. (pl. **Elder Brethren**) each of the thirteen senior Trinity Brethren.

**elderflower** ● n. the flower of the elder, used to make wines and cordials.

**elder hand** ● n. (in card games for two players) the first player dealt to.

**elderly** ● adj. old or ageing.
– DERIVATIVES **elderliness** n.

**elder statesman** ● n. an experienced and respected politician or other public figure.

**eldest** ● adj. (of one out of a group of people) oldest.

– ORIGIN OE *ieldest, eldest,* of Gmc origin; rel. to **ELD** and **OLD.**

**eldest hand** ● **n.** (in card games for three or more players) the first player dealt to.

**El Dorado** /ˌɛl dəˈrɑːdəʊ/ (also **eldorado**) ● **n.** (pl. **-os**) a place of great abundance and wealth.
– ORIGIN Sp., lit. 'the gilded one', the name of a country or city formerly believed to exist in South America.

**eldritch** /ˈɛl(d)rɪtʃ/ ● **adj.** weird and sinister or ghostly.
– ORIGIN C16 (orig. Scots): perh. rel. to **ELF.**

**Eleatic** /ˌɛlɪˈatɪk/ ● **adj.** of or relating to the ancient Greek city of Elea in SW Italy, home to a 5th-century school of philosophers that included Xenophanes, Parmenides, and Zeno. ● **n.** an Eleatic philosopher.

**elecampane** /ˌɛlɪkamˈpeɪn/ ● **n.** a plant with yellow daisy-like flowers and bitter aromatic roots that are used in herbal medicine. [*Inula helenium.*]
– ORIGIN ME: from med. L. *enula* 'elecampane' + *campana* (prob. meaning 'of the fields').

**elect** /ɪˈlɛkt/ ● **v. 1** choose (someone) to hold a position, especially public office, by voting. **2** opt for or choose to do something. **3** Christian Theology (of God) choose (someone) in preference to others for salvation. ● **adj. 1** chosen or singled out. ➤ Christian Theology chosen by God for salvation. **2** [postpos.] elected to a position but not yet in office: *the President Elect.*
– DERIVATIVES **electable** adj.
– ORIGIN ME: from L. *elect-, eligere* 'pick out'.

**election** ● **n. 1** a formal procedure whereby a person is elected, especially to a political office. **2** the action or fact of electing or being elected.

**electioneer** ● **v.** [usu. as noun **electioneering**] campaign to be elected to public office. ● **n.** a campaigning politician during an election.

**elective** ● **adj. 1** relating to or appointed by election. **2** (of a course of study) chosen by the student rather than compulsory. ➤ (of surgical or medical treatment) chosen by the patient rather than urgently necessary. ● **n.** chiefly N. Amer. an optional course of study.
– DERIVATIVES **electively** adv.

**elector** ● **n. 1** a person who has the right to vote in an election. ➤ (in the US) a member of the electoral college. **2** historical a German prince entitled to take part in the election of the Holy Roman Emperor.
– DERIVATIVES **electorship** n.

**electoral** ● **adj.** of or relating to elections or electors.
– DERIVATIVES **electorally** adv.

**electoral college** ● **n.** a body of electors chosen or appointed by a larger group. ➤ (in the US) a body of people representing the states of the US, who formally cast votes for the election of the President and Vice-President.

**electoral roll** (also **electoral register**) ● **n.** an official list of the people in a district who are entitled to vote in an election.

**electorate** /ɪˈlɛkt(ə)rət/ ● **n. 1** [treated as sing. or pl.] all the people in a country or area who are entitled to vote in an election. **2** Austral./NZ the area represented by one Member of Parliament. **3** historical the office or territories of a German elector.

**Electra complex** ● **n.** Psychoanalysis old-fashioned term for the Oedipus complex as manifested in young girls.
– ORIGIN C20: named after *Electra* in Gk mythology, who persuaded her brother to kill their mother in revenge for the murder of their father.

**electress** /ɪˈlɛktrɪs/ ● **n.** historical the wife of a German elector.

**electret** /ɪˈlɛktrɪt/ ● **n.** Physics a permanently polarized piece of dielectric material, analogous to a permanent magnet.
– ORIGIN C19: blend of **ELECTRICITY** and **MAGNET.**

**electric** /ɪˈlɛktrɪk/ ● **adj. 1** of, worked by, or producing electricity. **2** thrillingly exciting: *the atmosphere was electric.* ● **n. 1** (**electrics**) Brit. the system of electric wiring and parts in a house or vehicle. **2** an electric train or other vehicle.
– DERIVATIVES **electrically** adv.
– ORIGIN C17: from mod. L. *electricus,* from L. *electrum* 'amber', from Gk *ēlektron* (because rubbing amber causes electrostatic phenomena).

**electrical** ● **adj.** concerned with, operating by, or producing electricity. ● **n.** (**electricals**) electrical equipment or circuitry.

**electric-arc furnace** ● **n.** a furnace using an electric arc as a heat source, especially for steel-making.

**electric blanket** ● **n.** an electrically wired blanket used for heating a bed.

**electric blue** ● **n.** a steely or brilliant light blue.

**electric chair** ● **n.** a chair in which convicted criminals are executed by electrocution.

**electric eel** ● **n.** a large eel-like freshwater fish of South America, using pulses of electricity to kill prey, assist in navigation, and for defence. [*Electrophorus electricus.*]

**electric eye** ● **n.** informal a photoelectric cell operating a relay when the beam of light illuminating it is obscured.

**electric fence** ● **n.** a fence through which an electric current can be passed, giving an electric shock to any person or animal touching it.

**electric guitar** ● **n.** a guitar with a built-in pickup or pickups which convert sound vibrations into electrical signals for amplification.

**electrician** ● **n.** a person who installs and maintains electrical equipment.

**electricity** /ˌɪlɛkˈtrɪsɪti, ˌɛl-, ˌiːl-/ ● **n. 1** a form of energy resulting from the existence of charged particles (such as electrons or protons), either statically as an accumulation of charge or dynamically as a current. **2** the supply of electric current to a building for heating, lighting, etc. **3** thrilling excitement.

**electric ray** ● **n.** a sluggish bottom-dwelling marine ray that can produce an electric shock for the capture of prey and for defence. [*Torpedo* and other genera: many species.]

**electric shock** ● **n.** a sudden discharge of electricity through a part of the body.

**electric storm** ● **n.** a thunderstorm or other violent disturbance of the electrical condition of the atmosphere.

**electrify** /ɪˈlɛktrɪfʌɪ/ ● **v.** (**-ies, -ied**) **1** charge with electricity. **2** convert to the use of electrical power. **3** [often as adj. **electrifying**] cause a sense of thrilling excitement in.
– DERIVATIVES **electrification** n. **electrifier** n.

**electro** /ɪˈlɛktrəʊ/ ● **n.** (pl. **-os**) **1** short for **ELECTROTYPE** or **ELECTROPLATE. 2** a style of dance music with a fast beat and synthesized backing track.

**electro-** ● **comb. form** of, involving, or caused by electricity: *electroconvulsive.*

**electro-acoustic** ● **adj. 1** involving the interconversion of electrical and acoustic energy. **2** denoting a guitar with both a pickup and a reverberating hollow body.

**electrocardiography** /ɪˌlɛktrəʊˌkɑːdɪˈɒgrəfi/ ● **n.** the measurement and recording of electrical activity in the heart using electrodes placed on the skin.
– DERIVATIVES **electrocardiogram** n. **electrocardiograph** n. **electrocardiographic** adj.

**electrocautery** /ɪˌlɛktrəʊˈkɔːtəri/ ● **n.** cautery using an electrically heated instrument.

**electrochemistry** ● **n.** the branch of chemistry concerned with the relations between electrical and chemical phenomena.
– DERIVATIVES **electrochemical** adj. **electrochemically** adv. **electrochemist** n.

**electrochromism** /ɪˌlɛktrə(ʊ)ˈkrəʊmɪz(ə)m/ ● **n.** the property of changing colour when placed in an electric field.
– DERIVATIVES **electrochromic** adj.

**electroconvulsive** ● **adj.** relating to or denoting the treatment of mental illness by applying electric shocks to the brain.

**electrocorticogram** /ɪˌlɛktrə(ʊ)ˈkɔːtɪkə(ʊ)gram/ ● **n.** Physiology a record of the electrical activity of the brain made directly using electrodes.

**electrocute** ● **v.** (often **be electrocuted**) injure or kill by electric shock.

– DERIVATIVES **electrocution** n.
– ORIGIN C19: from **ELECTRO-**, on the pattern of *execute*.

**electrode** /ɪˈlɛktrəʊd/ ● n. a conductor through which electricity enters or leaves something.
– ORIGIN C19: from **ELECTRIC** + Gk *hodos* 'way', on the pattern of *anode* and *cathode*.

**electrodermal** /ɪˌlɛktrə(ʊ)ˈdəːməl/ ● adj. relating to or denoting measurement of the electrical conductivity of the skin.

**electrodynamics** ● pl. n. [usu. treated as sing.] the branch of mechanics concerned with the interaction of electric currents with magnetic or electric fields.
– DERIVATIVES **electrodynamic** adj.

**electroencephalography** /ɪˌlɛktrəʊɪnˌsɛfəˈlɒgrəfi, -ˌkɛf-/ ● n. the measurement and recording of electrical activity in different parts of the brain.
– DERIVATIVES **electroencephalogram** n. **electroencephalograph** n.

**electrojet** ● n. an intense electric current occurring in the lower ionosphere in the region of strong auroral displays.

**electroless** /ɪˈlɛktrəʊlɪs/ ● adj. denoting nickel plating using chemical rather than electrical means.

**electroluminescence** /ɪˌlɛktrəʊluːmɪˈnɛs(ə)ns/ ● n. luminescence produced by the application of a voltage.
– DERIVATIVES **electroluminescent** adj.

**electrolyse** /ɪˈlɛktrəlʌɪz/ (US **electrolyze**) ● v. subject to electrolysis.
– DERIVATIVES **electrolyser** n.

**electrolysis** /ˌɪlɛkˈtrɒlɪsɪs, ˌɛl-/ ● n. **1** Chemistry chemical decomposition produced by passing an electric current through a conducting liquid. **2** the removal of hair roots or small blemishes on the skin by the application of heat using an electric current.
– DERIVATIVES **electrolytic** /ɪˌlɛktrə(ʊ)ˈlɪtɪk/ adj. **electrolytical** adj. **electrolytically** adv.

**electrolyte** /ɪˈlɛktrəlʌɪt/ ● n. **1** a liquid or gel which contains ions and can be decomposed by electrolysis, e.g. that present in a battery. **2** Physiology the ionic constituents of cells, blood, etc.
– ORIGIN C19: from **ELECTRO-** + Gk *lutos* 'released' (from *luein* 'loosen').

**electromagnet** ● n. Physics a soft metal core made into a magnet by the passage of electric current through a surrounding coil.

**electromagnetic** ● adj. of or relating to the interrelation of electric currents or fields and magnetic fields.
– DERIVATIVES **electromagnetically** adv. **electromagnetism** n.

**electromagnetic radiation** ● n. Physics a kind of radiation including visible light, radio waves, gamma rays, and X-rays, in which electric and magnetic fields vary simultaneously.

**electromechanical** /ɪˌlɛktrəʊmɪˈkanɪk(ə)l/ ● adj. relating to or denoting a mechanical device which is electrically operated.

**electrometer** /ˌɪlɛkˈtrɒmɪtə/ ● n. Physics an instrument for measuring electrical potential without drawing any current from the circuit.
– DERIVATIVES **electrometric** adj. **electrometry** n.

**electromotive** /ɪˌlɛktrəˈməʊtɪv/ ● adj. Physics tending to produce an electric current.

**electromotive force** ● n. Physics a difference in potential that tends to give rise to an electric current.

**electromyography** /ɪˌlɛktrə(ʊ)mʌɪˈɒgrəfi/ ● n. the recording of the electrical activity of muscle tissue by means of electrodes.
– DERIVATIVES **electromyogram** n. **electromyograph** n. **electromyographic** adj. **electromyographically** adv.

**electron** /ɪˈlɛktrɒn/ ● n. Physics a stable negatively charged subatomic particle with a mass 1,836 times less than that of the proton, found in all atoms and acting as the primary carrier of electricity in solids.
– ORIGIN C19: from **ELECTRIC** + **-ON**.

**electronegative** ● adj. **1** Physics electrically negative. **2** Chemistry (of an element) tending to acquire electrons and form negative ions in chemical reactions.
– DERIVATIVES **electronegativity** n.

**electron gun** ● n. Physics a device for producing a narrow stream of electrons from a heated cathode.

**electronic** ● adj. **1** having components such as microchips and transistors that control and direct electric currents. **2** (of music) produced by electronic instruments. **3** of or relating to electrons or electronics. **4** carried out using a computer, especially over a network: *electronic shopping*.
– DERIVATIVES **electronically** adv.
– ORIGIN C20: from **ELECTRON** + **-IC**.

**electronic flash** ● n. Photography a flash from a gas-discharge tube.

**electronic mail** ● n. another term for **EMAIL**.

**electronic publishing** ● n. the issuing of texts in machine-readable form rather than on paper.

**electronics** ● pl. n. **1** [usu. treated as sing.] the branch of physics and technology concerned with the behaviour and movement of electrons, especially in semiconductors and gases. **2** [treated as pl.] circuits or devices using transistors, microchips, etc.

**electron microscope** ● n. Physics a microscope with high magnification and resolution, employing electron beams in place of light.

**electron optics** ● pl. n. [treated as sing.] the branch of physics concerned with the behaviour of electrons in magnetic and electric fields.

**electron spin resonance** ● n. Physics a spectroscopic method of locating electrons within the molecules of a paramagnetic substance.

**electron tube** ● n. Physics an evacuated or gas-filled tube in which a current of electrons flows between electrodes.

**electronvolt** ● n. Physics a unit of energy equal to the work done on an electron in accelerating it through a potential difference of one volt.

**electro-optics** ● pl. n. [treated as sing.] the branch of science concerned with the effect of electric fields on light and optics.
– DERIVATIVES **electro-optic** adj. **electro-optical** adj.

**electrophilic** /ɪˌlɛktrə(ʊ)ˈfɪlɪk/ ● adj. Chemistry having a tendency to attract or acquire electrons. Often contrasted with **NUCLEOPHILIC**.
– DERIVATIVES **electrophile** n.

**electrophoresis** /ɪˌlɛktrə(ʊ)fəˈriːsɪs/ ● n. Physics & Chemistry the movement of charged particles in a fluid or gel under the influence of an electric field.
– DERIVATIVES **electrophorese** v. **electrophoretic** adj. **electrophoretically** adv.
– ORIGIN C20: from **ELECTRO-** + Gk *phorēsis* 'being carried'.

**electrophorus** /ˌɪlɛkˈtrɒf(ə)rəs, ɛl-/ ● n. Physics a device for repeatedly generating static electricity by induction.
– ORIGIN C18: from **ELECTRO-** + Gk *-phoros* 'bearing'.

**electrophysiology** /ɪˌlɛktrəʊfɪzɪˈɒlədʒi/ ● n. the branch of physiology concerned with electrical phenomena such as nerve impulses.
– DERIVATIVES **electrophysiological** adj. **electrophysiologically** adv. **electrophysiologist** n.

**electroplate** /ɪˈlɛktrə(ʊ)pleɪt, ɪˌlɛktrə(ʊ)ˈpleɪt/ ● v. [usu. as noun **electroplating**] coat (a metal object) by electrolytic deposition with another metal. ● n. electroplated articles.
– DERIVATIVES **electroplater** n.

**electropolish** /ɪˈlɛktrəʊˌpɒlɪʃ/ ● v. give a shiny surface to (metal) using electrolysis.

**electroporation** /ɪˌlɛktrə(ʊ)pəˈreɪʃ(ə)n/ ● n. Biology the process of introducing DNA or chromosomes into cells using an electrical pulse to open the pores in the cell membranes briefly.
– DERIVATIVES **electroporate** v.

**electropositive** ● adj. **1** Physics electrically positive. **2** Chemistry (of an element) tending to lose electrons and form positive ions in chemical reactions.

**electroreception** ● n. the detection by an aquatic animal of electric fields or currents.
– DERIVATIVES **electroreceptor** n.

**electroscope** • n. Physics an instrument for detecting and measuring electric charge, especially as an indication of the ionization of air by radioactivity.
– DERIVATIVES **electroscopic** adj.

**electroshock** • adj. another term for **ELECTROCONVULSIVE**.

**electrostatic** • adj. Physics of or relating to stationary electric charges or fields as opposed to electric currents.
– DERIVATIVES **electrostatics** pl. n.
– ORIGIN C19: from **ELECTRO-** + **STATIC**, on the pattern of *hydrostatic*.

**electrosurgery** • n. surgery using a high-frequency electric current to cut tissue.
– DERIVATIVES **electrosurgical** adj.

**electrotechnology** • n. the technological application of electricity.
– DERIVATIVES **electrotechnic** adj. **electrotechnical** adj. **electrotechnics** pl. n.

**electrotherapy** • n. the use of electric currents passed through the body to treat paralysis and other disorders.
– DERIVATIVES **electrotherapeutic** adj. **electrotherapeutical** adj. **electrotherapist** n.

**electrothermal** • adj. Physics of or relating to heat derived from electricity.

**electrotype** • v. [often as noun **electrotyping**] copy by the electrolytic deposition of copper on a mould. • n. a copy made in such a way.
– DERIVATIVES **electrotyper** n.

**electrovalent** /ɪˌlɛktrə(ʊ)ˈveɪl(ə)nt/ • adj. Chemistry (of bonding) ionic.
– DERIVATIVES **electrovalence** n. **electrovalency** n.
– ORIGIN 1920s: from **ELECTRO-** + *-valent*, on the pattern of *trivalent*.

**electroweak** • adj. Physics relating to or denoting electromagnetic and weak interactions regarded as manifestations of the same interaction.

**electrum** /ɪˈlɛktrəm/ • n. an alloy of gold with at least 20 per cent of silver, used for jewellery.
– ORIGIN ME: via L. from Gk *ēlektron* 'amber, electrum'.

**electuary** /ɪˈlɛktjʊ(ə)ri/ • n. (pl. **-ies**) archaic a medicinal substance mixed with honey or another sweet substance.
– ORIGIN ME: from late L. *electuarium*, prob. from Gk *ekleikton*, from *ekleikhein* 'lick up'.

**eleemosynary** /ˌɛliiːˈmɒsɪnəri, -ˈmɒz-/ • adj. formal charitable.
– ORIGIN C16: from med. L. *eleemosynarius*, from late L. *eleemosyna* 'alms', from Gk *eleēmosunē* (see **ALMS**).

**elegant** • adj. **1** graceful and stylish. **2** pleasingly ingenious and simple.
– DERIVATIVES **elegance** n. **elegantly** adv.
– ORIGIN C15: from Fr., or from L. *elegans*, *elegant-*, rel. to *eligere* (see **ELECT**).

**elegiac** /ˌɛlɪˈdʒʌɪək/ • adj. of, relating to, or characteristic of an elegy. ➤wistfully mournful. • n. (**elegiacs**) verses in an elegiac metre.
– DERIVATIVES **elegiacally** adv.

**elegiac couplet** • n. a pair of lines consisting of a dactylic hexameter and a pentameter, used especially in Greek and Latin verse.

**elegize** /ˈɛlɪdʒʌɪz/ (also **-ise**) • v. write elegiacally.
– DERIVATIVES **elegist** n.

**elegy** /ˈɛlɪdʒi/ • n. (pl. **-ies**) **1** a mournful poem, typically a lament for the dead. **2** (in Greek and Latin verse) a poem written in elegiac couplets.
– ORIGIN C16: from Fr. *élégie*, or via L., from Gk *elegeia*, from *elegos* 'mournful poem'.

**element** • n. **1** a basic constituent part. ➤an aspect: *an element of danger.* ➤a group of a particular kind within a larger group: *right-wing elements.* **2** (also **chemical element**) each of more than one hundred substances that cannot be chemically interconverted or broken down, each consisting of atoms with the same atomic number. **3** any of the four substances (earth, water, air, and fire) regarded as the fundamental constituents of the world in ancient and medieval philosophy. **4** (**the elements**) the weather, especially bad weather. **5** one's natural or preferred environment: *she was in her element.* **6** a part in an electric device consisting of a wire through which an electric current is passed to provide heat.
– ORIGIN ME: via OFr. from L. *elementum* 'principle, rudiment'.

**elemental** /ˌɛlɪˈmɛnt(ə)l/ • adj. **1** fundamental. **2** concerned with chemical elements. ➤denoting uncombined chemical elements: *elemental sulphur.* **3** (of action or emotion) basic and primitive. • n. a supernatural entity or force thought to be physically manifested by occult means.
– DERIVATIVES **elementalism** n.

**elementary** • adj. **1** of or relating to the most rudimentary aspects of a subject; introductory. ➤simple. **2** not decomposable into elements or other primary constituents.
– DERIVATIVES **elementarily** adv. **elementariness** n.

**elementary school** • n. a primary school, especially (N. Amer.) for the first six or eight grades.

**elemi** /ˈɛləmi/ • n. an oleoresin obtained from certain tropical trees and used in varnishes, ointments, and aromatherapy.
– ORIGIN C16: perh. from Arab. *al-lāmī*.

**elenchus** /ɪˈlɛŋkəs/ • n. (pl. **elenchi** /-kʌɪ/) Logic a logical refutation, especially the Socratic method of eliciting truth by question and answer.
– ORIGIN C17: via L. from Gk *elenkhos*.

**elephant** • n. (pl. same or **elephants**) a very large plant-eating mammal with a prehensile trunk, long curved ivory tusks, and large ears. [*Loxodonta africana* (**African elephant**, Africa) and *Elephas maximus* (**Indian elephant**, southern Asia).]
– DERIVATIVES **elephantoid** /ˌɛlɪˈfantɔɪd/ adj.
– ORIGIN ME: from OFr. *elefant*, via L. from Gk *elephas*, *elephant-* 'ivory, elephant'.

**elephant bird** • n. an aepyornis or related extinct giant bird.

**elephant grass** • n. a very tall robust tropical African grass. [*Pennisetum purpureum*.]

**elephantiasis** /ˌɛlɪf(ə)nˈtʌɪəsɪs/ • n. Medicine a condition in which a limb becomes grossly enlarged due to obstruction of the lymphatic vessels, especially by nematode parasites.
– ORIGIN C16: via L. from Gk, from *elephas*, *elephant-* 'elephant' + **-IASIS**.

**elephantine** /ɛlɪˈfantʌɪn/ • adj. of, resembling, or characteristic of an elephant, especially in being large or clumsy.

**elephant seal** • n. a large seal that breeds on the west coast of North America and around Antarctica, the male of which has a very thick neck and an inflatable snout. [Genus *Mirounga*: two species.]

**elephant shrew** • n. a small insectivorous African mammal with a long mobile snout, long hindlimbs, and a rat-like tail. [Family Macroscelididae: many species.]

**Eleusinian mysteries** /ˌɛljuːˈsɪnɪən/ • pl. n. the annual rites performed by the ancient Greeks at the village of Eleusis near Athens in honour of Demeter and Persephone.

**elevate** /ˈɛlɪveɪt/ • v. lift to a higher position. ➤raise to a higher level or status. ➤(of a priest) hold up (a consecrated host or chalice) for adoration. ➤Military raise the axis of (a piece of artillery) to increase its range.
– DERIVATIVES **elevated** adj. **elevatory** adj.
– ORIGIN ME: from L. *elevat-*, *elevare* 'to raise'.

**elevation** • n. **1** the action or fact of elevating or being elevated. **2** height above a given level, especially sea level. ➤the angle of something with the horizontal. **3** Ballet the ability of a dancer to attain height in jumps. **4** a particular side of a building. ➤a scale drawing showing the vertical projection of one side of a building.
– DERIVATIVES **elevational** adj.

**elevator** • n. **1** North American term for **LIFT** (in sense 1). **2** a hinged flap on the tailplane of an aircraft, used to control pitch. **3** a muscle whose contraction raises a part of the body. **4** a machine consisting of an endless belt with scoops attached, used for raising grain. ➤N. Amer. a tall building used for storing grain.

**eleven** ● cardinal number **1** equivalent to the sum of six and five; one more than ten; 11. (Roman numeral: **xi** or **XI**.) **2** a sports team of eleven players: *the first eleven.*
– DERIVATIVES **elevenfold** adj. & adv.
– ORIGIN OE *endleofon*, from the base of ONE + a second element (prob. expressing the sense 'left over') occurring also in TWELVE; of Gmc origin.

**eleven-plus** ● n. chiefly historical (in the UK) an examination taken at the age of 11–12 to determine the type of secondary school a child should enter.

**elevenses** ● pl. n. Brit. informal a break for light refreshments taken at about eleven o'clock in the morning.

**eleventh** ● ordinal number constituting number eleven in a sequence; 11th.
– PHRASES **the eleventh hour** the latest possible moment.

**ELF** ● abbrev. extremely low frequency.

**elf** ● n. (pl. **elves**) a supernatural creature of folk tales, represented as a small, delicate human figure with pointed ears and a capricious nature.
– DERIVATIVES **elfish** adj. **elven** adj. (poetic/literary). **elvish** adj.
– ORIGIN OE, of Gmc origin.

**elf cup** ● n. a fungus of decaying wood, producing small groups of shallow short-stemmed cups with a scarlet interior. [*Sarcoscypha coccinea.*]

**elfin** ● adj. of or resembling an elf.

**elf-locks** ● pl. n. a tangled mass of hair.

**elf owl** ● n. a tiny owl that nests in cacti and trees in the southern US and Mexico. [*Micrathene whitneyi.*]

**elicit** /ɪ'lɪsɪt/ ● v. (**elicited**, **eliciting**) **1** evoke or draw out (a response or answer). **2** archaic draw forth into existence.
– DERIVATIVES **elicitation** n. **elicitor** n.
– ORIGIN C17: from L. *elicit-*, *elicere* 'to draw out by trickery'.

**elide** /ɪ'lʌɪd/ ● v. **1** [often as adj. **elided**] omit (a sound or syllable) when speaking. **2** join together; merge.
– ORIGIN C16: from L. *elidere* 'crush out'.

**eligible** /'ɛlɪdʒɪb(ə)l/ ● adj. **1** (often **eligible for/to do something**) satisfying the appropriate conditions. **2** desirable as a spouse: *an eligible bachelor.*
– DERIVATIVES **eligibility** n. **eligibly** adv.
– ORIGIN ME: via Fr. from late L. *eligibilis*, from L. *eligere* (see ELECT).

**eliminate** /ɪ'lɪmɪneɪt/ ● v. **1** completely remove or get rid of. ➤reject or exclude from consideration or further participation. **2** Chemistry generate (a simple substance) as a product in the course of a reaction involving larger molecules.
– DERIVATIVES **eliminable** adj. **elimination** n. **eliminator** n. **eliminatory** adj.
– ORIGIN C16: from L. *eliminat-*, *eliminare* 'to turn out of doors'.

**ELINT** /ɪ'lɪnt/ ● n. covert intelligence-gathering by electronic means.
– ORIGIN 1960s: blend of ELECTRONIC and INTELLIGENCE.

**ELISA** /ɪ'lʌɪzə/ ● n. Biochemistry enzyme-linked immunosorbent assay, an immunological assay technique making use of an enzyme bonded to a particular antibody or antigen.

**elision** /ɪ'lɪʒ(ə)n/ ● n. **1** the omission of a sound or syllable in speech. **2** the process of joining or merging things.
– ORIGIN C16: from late L. *elisio(n-)*, from L. *elidere* 'crush out'.

**elite** /eɪ'liːt, ɪ-/ ● n. **1** a group of people considered to be superior in a particular society or organization. **2** a size of letter in typewriting, with 12 characters to the inch (about 4.7 to the centimetre).
– ORIGIN C18: from Fr. *élite* 'selection, choice'.

**elitism** ● n. **1** the belief that a society or system should be run by an elite. **2** the superior attitude or behaviour associated with an elite.
– DERIVATIVES **elitist** adj. & n.

**elixir** /ɪ'lɪksə, -sɪə/ ● n. a magical or medicinal potion, especially (in former times) either one supposedly able to change metals into gold or (also called **elixir of life**) supposedly able to prolong life indefinitely.
– ORIGIN ME: via med. L. from Arab. *al-'iksīr*, from *al* 'the' + *'iksīr* from Gk *xērion* 'powder for drying wounds'.

**Elizabethan** /ɪˌlɪzə'biːθ(ə)n/ ● adj. of, relating to, or characteristic of the reign of Queen Elizabeth I. ● n. a person, especially a writer, of the Elizabethan age.

**elk** /ɛlk/ ● n. (pl. same or **elks**) a large northern deer with palmate antlers and a growth of skin hanging from the neck. Called MOOSE in North America. [*Alces alces.*] ➤North American term for WAPITI.
– ORIGIN C15: prob. from OE *elh*, *eolh*, with substitution of *k* for *h*.

**elkhound** ● n. a large hunting dog of a Scandinavian breed with a shaggy grey coat.

**ell** ● n. a former measure of length used mainly for textiles, normally 45 inches in England and 37 inches in Scotland.
– ORIGIN OE *eln*; from an Indo-Eur. root shared by L. *ulna* (see ULNA); the measure was orig. linked to the length of the human arm or forearm.

**ellagic acid** /ɛ'ladʒɪk/ ● n. Chemistry a compound extracted from oak galls and some fruits and nuts, able to retard the growth of cancer cells to some extent.
– ORIGIN C19: from Fr. *ellagique* (an anagram of *galle* 'gall nut' + *-ique*), thus avoiding the form *gallique*, already in use.

**ellipse** /ɪ'lɪps/ ● n. a regular oval shape, traced by a point moving in a plane so that the sum of its distances from two other points (the foci) is constant, or resulting when a cone is cut by an oblique plane which does not intersect the base.
– ORIGIN C17: via Fr. from L. *ellipsis* (see ELLIPSIS).

**ellipsis** /ɪ'lɪpsɪs/ ● n. (pl. **ellipses** /-siːz/) the omission of words from speech or writing. ➤a set of dots indicating such an omission.
– ORIGIN C16: via L. from Gk *elleipsis*, from *elleipein* 'leave out'.

**ellipsoid** /ɪ'lɪpsɔɪd/ ● n. a three-dimensional figure symmetrical about each of three perpendicular axes, whose plane sections normal to one axis are circles and all the other plane sections are ellipses.
– DERIVATIVES **ellipsoidal** adj.

**elliptic** ● adj. of, relating to, or having the form of an ellipse.
– DERIVATIVES **ellipticity** n.

**elliptical** ● adj. **1** another term for ELLIPTIC. **2** (of speech or text) using or involving ellipsis, especially so as to be difficult to understand.
– DERIVATIVES **elliptically** adv.

**elm** ● n. a tall deciduous tree with rough serrated leaves. [*Ulmus procera* (**English elm**), *U. americana* (N. America), and related species.]
– DERIVATIVES **elmy** adj.
– ORIGIN OE, of Gmc origin.

**El Niño** /ɛl 'niːnjəʊ/ ● n. (pl. **-os**) an irregularly occurring and complex series of climatic changes affecting the equatorial Pacific region and beyond every few years, characterized by the appearance of unusually warm, nutrient-poor water off northern Peru and Ecuador.
– ORIGIN Sp., lit. 'the (Christ) child', because of its occurrence around Christmas time.

**elocution** /ˌɛlə'kjuːʃ(ə)n/ ● n. the skill of clear and expressive speech, especially of distinct pronunciation and articulation. ➤a particular style of speaking.
– DERIVATIVES **elocutionary** adj. **elocutionist** n.
– ORIGIN ME: from L. *elocutio(n-)*, from *eloqui* (see ELOQUENCE).

**Elohim** /ɛ'ləʊhɪm, 'ɛləʊhiːm/ ● n. a name for God used in the Hebrew Bible.
– ORIGIN from Heb. *'ĕlōhīm* (pl.).

**elongate** /'iːlɒŋgeɪt/ ● v. [usu. as adj. **elongated**] make or become longer. ● adj. chiefly Biology long; elongated.
– ORIGIN ME (in the sense 'move away'): from late L. *elongat-*, *elongare* 'to place at a distance'.

**elongation** ● n. **1** the lengthening of something. **2** Astronomy the angular separation of a planet from the sun or of a satellite from a planet.
– ORIGIN ME: from late L. *elongatio(n-)*, from *elongare* (see ELONGATE).

**elope** • v. run away secretly in order to get married.
– DERIVATIVES **elopement** n. **eloper** n.
– ORIGIN C16 (in the sense 'abscond, run away'): from Anglo-Norman Fr. *aloper*.

**eloquence** /ˈɛləkwəns/ • n. fluent or persuasive speaking or writing.
– ORIGIN ME: via OFr. from L. *eloquentia*, from *eloqui* 'speak out'.

**eloquent** • adj. **1** showing eloquence. **2** clearly expressive: *the bus journey alone is eloquent of class inequality.*
– DERIVATIVES **eloquently** adv.

**Elsan** /ˈɛlsan/ • n. Brit. trademark a type of transportable chemical toilet.
– ORIGIN 1930s: appar. from the initials of *Ephraim Louis* Jackson (its manufacturer) and **SANITATION**.

**else** • adv. **1** in addition; besides. **2** different; instead.
– PHRASES **or else** used to introduce the second of two alternatives. ➤ in circumstances different from those mentioned. ➤ used as a threat or warning.
– ORIGIN OE *elles*, of Gmc origin.

**elsewhere** • adv. in, at, or to some other place or other places. • pron. some other place.
– ORIGIN OE *elles hwǣr* (see **ELSE**, **WHERE**).

**ELT** • abbrev. English language teaching.

**eluate** /ˈɛljuːət, -eɪt/ • n. Chemistry a solution obtained by elution.
– ORIGIN 1930s: from L. *eluere* 'wash out' + **-ATE**[1].

**elucidate** /ɪˈl(j)uːsɪdeɪt/ • v. make clear; explain.
– DERIVATIVES **elucidation** n. **elucidative** adj. **elucidator** n. **elucidatory** adj.
– ORIGIN C16: from late L. *elucidat-*, *elucidare* 'to make clear'.

**elude** /ɪˈl(j)uːd/ • v. **1** evade or escape from, typically in a skilful or cunning way. **2** fail to be attained or understood by; baffle.
– DERIVATIVES **elusion** n.
– ORIGIN C16: from L. *eludere*, from *e-* 'out, away from' + *ludere* 'to play'.

**Elul** /ˈiːlʌl, ˈɛlʌl/ • n. (in the Jewish calendar) the twelfth month of the civil and sixth of the religious year, usually coinciding with parts of August and September.
– ORIGIN from Heb. *'ĕlūl*.

**elusive** • adj. difficult to find, catch, or achieve.
– DERIVATIVES **elusively** adv. **elusiveness** n.
– ORIGIN C18: from L. *elus-*, *eludere* 'elude' + **-IVE**.

**elute** /ɪˈl(j)uːt/ • v. Chemistry remove (an adsorbed substance) by washing with a solvent, especially in chromatography.
– DERIVATIVES **elution** n.
– ORIGIN 1920s: from L. *elut-*, *eluere* 'to wash out'.

**elutriate** /ɪˈl(j)uːtrɪeɪt/ • v. Chemistry separate (particles in a mixture) by suspension in an upward flow of liquid or gas.
– DERIVATIVES **elutriation** n.
– ORIGIN C18: from L. *elutriat-*, *elutriare* 'to wash out'.

**elver** /ˈɛlvə/ • n. a young eel, especially when undergoing mass migration upriver from the sea.
– ORIGIN C17: var. of dial. *eel-fare* 'the passage of young eels up a river', from **EEL** + **FARE** in its original sense 'a journey'.

**elves** plural form of **ELF**.

**Elysian** /ɪˈlɪzɪən/ • adj. of or relating to Elysium or the Elysian Fields, the place in Greek mythology where heroes were conveyed after death. ➤ of or like paradise.

**elytron** /ˈɛlɪtrɒn/ • n. (pl. **elytra** /-trə/) Entomology each of the two wing cases of a beetle.
– ORIGIN C18: from Gk *elutron* 'sheath'.

**em** • n. Printing a unit for measuring the width of printed matter, equal to the height of the type size being used. ➤ a unit of measurement equal to twelve points.
– ORIGIN C18: the letter *M*, since it is approx. this width.

**em-** /ɪm, ɛm/ • prefix variant spelling of **EN-**[1], **EN-**[2] assimilated before *b*, *p* (as in *emblazon*, *emplacement*).

**emaciated** /ɪˈmeɪsɪeɪt, ɪˈmeɪʃ-/ • adj. abnormally thin and weak.
– DERIVATIVES **emaciation** n.
– ORIGIN C17: from L. *emaciat-*, *emaciare* 'to make thin'.

**email** • n. the system of sending messages by electronic means from one computer user to one or more recipients via a network. • v. mail or send using email.
– DERIVATIVES **emailer** n.
– ORIGIN C20: abbrev. of *electronic mail*.

**emalangeni** plural form of **LILANGENI**.

**emanate** /ˈɛməneɪt/ • v. issue or spread out from a source. ➤ give out or emit.
– ORIGIN C18 (earlier (C16) as *emanation*): from L. *emanat-*, *emanare* 'to flow out'.

**emanation** • n. **1** something which emanates or is produced from a source. **2** (in various mystical traditions) a being or force which is a manifestation of God. **3** the action or process of emanating.

**emancipate** /ɪˈmansɪpeɪt/ • v. set free, especially from legal, social, or political restrictions. ➤ free from slavery. ➤ Law set (a child) free from the authority of its father or parents.
– DERIVATIVES **emancipation** n. **emancipator** n. **emancipatory** adj.
– ORIGIN C17: from L. *emancipat-*, *emancipare* 'to transfer as property', from *e-* 'out' + *mancipium* 'slave'.

**emasculate** /ɪˈmaskjʊleɪt/ • v. **1** make weaker or less effective. **2** [usu. as adj. **emasculated**] deprive (a man) of his male role or identity. **3** Botany remove the male parts (anthers) from (a flower).
– DERIVATIVES **emasculation** n. **emasculator** n. **emasculatory** /-lət(ə)ri/ adj.
– ORIGIN C17: from L. *emasculat-*, *emasculare* 'to castrate'.

**embalm** /ɪmˈbɑːm, ɛm-/ • v. **1** [often as noun **embalming**] preserve (a corpse) from decay, originally with spices and now usually by injection of a preservative. **2** archaic give a pleasant fragrance to.
– DERIVATIVES **embalmer** n. **embalmment** n.
– ORIGIN ME: from OFr. *embaumer*, from *em-* 'in' + *baume* 'balm', var. of *basme* (see **BALM**).

**embank** • v. protect or provide with an embankment.

**embankment** • n. **1** a wall or bank built to prevent flooding by a river. **2** a bank of earth or stone built to carry a road or railway over an area of low ground.

**embargo** /ɛmˈbɑːɡəʊ, ɪm-/ • n. (pl. **-oes**) **1** an official ban, especially on trade or other commercial activity with a particular country. ➤ archaic a stoppage or impediment. **2** historical an order of a state forbidding foreign ships to enter, or any ships to leave, its ports. • v. (**-oes**, **-oed**) **1** impose an embargo on. **2** archaic seize (a ship or goods) for state service.
– ORIGIN C17: from Sp., from *embargar* 'arrest'.

**embark** • v. **1** go on board a ship or aircraft. **2** (**embark on/upon**) begin (a new project or course of action).
– DERIVATIVES **embarkation** n.
– ORIGIN C16: from Fr. *embarquer*, from *em-* 'in' + *barque* 'bark, ship'.

**embarras de richesses** /ɒmbaˌrɑː də riːˈʃɛs/ (also **embarras de choix** /ˈʃwɑː/) • n. more options or resources than one knows what to do with.
– ORIGIN Fr., 'embarrassment of riches (or choice)'.

**embarrass** /ɪmˈbarəs, ɛm-/ • v. **1** cause to feel awkward, self-conscious, or ashamed. ➤ (**be embarrassed**) be caused financial difficulties. **2** archaic hamper or impede.
– DERIVATIVES **embarrassed** adj. **embarrassedly** adv. **embarrassing** adj. **embarrassingly** adv. **embarrassment** n.
– ORIGIN C17: from Fr. *embarrasser*, from Sp. *embarazar*, prob. from Port. *embaraçar* (from *baraço* 'halter').

**embassage** /ˈɛmbəsɪdʒ/ • n. archaic **1** the business or message of an envoy. **2** a deputation.
– ORIGIN C15: from OFr. *ambasse* 'message or embassy' + **-AGE**.

**embassy** • n. (pl. **-ies**) **1** the official residence or offices of an ambassador. **2** chiefly historical a deputation or mission sent by one state to another.
– ORIGIN C16: from OFr. *ambasse*, based on L. *ambactus* 'servant'; cf. **AMBASSADOR**.

**embattle** • v. archaic **1** make ready for battle. **2** fortify (a building) against attack.
– ORIGIN ME: from OFr. *embataillier*.

**embattled** • adj. **1** prepared for battle. **2** fortified; having battlements. **3** [postpos.] Heraldry divided or edged by a line of square notches like battlements in outline. **4** beset by problems or difficulties.

**embay** ● v. **1** force (a boat) into a bay. **2** chiefly Geology enclose in a recess or hollow. **3** [as adj. **embayed**] formed into bays.

**embayment** ● n. a recess in a coastline forming a bay.

**embed** (also **imbed**) ● v. (**embedded**, **embedding**) **1** fix or become fixed firmly and deeply in the surrounding mass. **2** implant (an idea or feeling). **3** Computing incorporate within the body of a file or document.
– DERIVATIVES **embedment** n.

**embellish** ● v. **1** adorn; decorate. **2** add extra details to (a story or account) for interest.
– DERIVATIVES **embellisher** n. **embellishment** n.
– ORIGIN ME: from OFr. *embelliss-*, from *embellir*, based on *bel* 'handsome', from L. *bellus*.

**ember** /'ɛmbə/ ● n. a small piece of burning or glowing material in a dying fire.
– ORIGIN OE *ǣmyrge*, of Gmc origin.

**Ember day** ● n. any of a number of days reserved for fasting and prayer in the Western Christian Church.
– ORIGIN OE *ymbren*, perh. an alt. of *ymbryne* 'period', from *ymb* 'about' + *ryne* 'course'.

**embezzle** ● v. steal or misappropriate (money placed in one's trust or under one's control).
– DERIVATIVES **embezzlement** n. **embezzler** n.
– ORIGIN ME (in the sense 'steal'): from Anglo-Norman Fr. *embesiler*, from *besiler*, of unknown ultimate origin.

**embitter** ● v. [usu. as adj. **embittered**] make bitter or resentful.
– DERIVATIVES **embitterment** n.

**emblazon** /ɪm'bleɪz(ə)n, ɛm-/ ● v. **1** (usu. **be emblazoned**) conspicuously display (a design) on something. ➤depict (a heraldic device) on something. **2** archaic celebrate or extol publicly.
– DERIVATIVES **emblazonment** n.

**emblem** /'ɛmbləm/ ● n. a heraldic device or symbolic object as a distinctive badge of a nation, organization, or family. ➤a symbol or symbolic representation.
– DERIVATIVES **emblematic** adj. **emblematical** adj. **emblematically** adv.
– ORIGIN C16: from L. *emblema* 'inlaid work, raised ornament', from Gk *emblēma* 'insertion'.

**emblematize** /ɛm'blɛmətʌɪz/ (also **-ise**) ● v. formal serve as an emblem of.

**embody** /ɪm'bɒdi, ɛm-/ ● v. (**-ies**, **-ied**) **1** give a tangible or visible form to (an idea or quality). **2** include or contain as a constituent part.
– DERIVATIVES **embodiment** n.

**embolden** ● v. **1** cause to have courage or confidence. **2** (of typeface) make bold.

**embolectomy** /ˌɛmbə'lɛktəmi/ ● n. (pl. **-ies**) surgical removal of an embolus.

**embolism** /'ɛmbəlɪz(ə)m/ ● n. Medicine obstruction of an artery, typically by a clot of blood or an air bubble.
– ORIGIN C19: via late L. from Gk *embolismos*, from *emballein* 'insert'.

**embolization** /ˌɛmbəlʌɪ'zeɪʃ(ə)n/ (also **-isation**) ● n. Medicine the formation of an embolus.

**embolus** /'ɛmbələs/ ● n. (pl. **emboli** /-lʌɪ, iː/) a blood clot, air bubble, piece of fatty deposit, or other object obstructing a blood vessel.
– DERIVATIVES **embolic** adj.
– ORIGIN C17 (denoting the plunger of a syringe): from L., lit. 'piston', from Gk *embolos* 'peg, stopper'.

**embonpoint** /ˌɒmbɒ̃'pwã/ ● n. plumpness or fleshiness, especially with reference to a woman's bosom.
– ORIGIN C17: from Fr. *en bon point* 'in good condition'.

**emboss** ● v. [usu. as adj. **embossed**] carve a design in relief on (a surface).
– DERIVATIVES **embosser** n.
– ORIGIN ME: from the OFr. base of obs. Fr. *embosser*, from *em-* 'into' + *boce* 'protuberance'.

**embouchure** /ˌɒmbʊ'ʃʊə/ ● n. **1** Music the way in which a player applies the mouth and tongue in playing a brass or wind instrument. **2** archaic the mouth of a river.
– ORIGIN C18: Fr., from *s'emboucher*, from *emboucher* 'put in or to the mouth'.

**embourgeoisement** /ɒ̃'bʊəʒwɑːzmɒ̃, French ɑ̃buʀʒwazmɑ̃/ ● n. the process of becoming bourgeois or middle class.
– ORIGIN 1930s: Fr., from *embourgeoiser* 'become or make bourgeois'.

**embower** /ɪm'baʊə, ɛm-/ ● v. poetic/literary surround or enclose.

**embrace** ● v. **1** hold closely in one's arms, especially as a sign of affection. **2** include or contain. **3** accept or support (a belief or change) willingly. ● n. an act of embracing.
– DERIVATIVES **embraceable** adj. **embracement** n. **embracer** n.
– ORIGIN ME: from OFr. *embracer*, based on L. *in-* 'in' + *bracchium* 'arm'.

**embrasure** /ɪm'breɪʒə, ɛm-/ ● n. **1** an opening in a wall or parapet, used for shooting through. **2** an opening or recess around a window or door forming an enlargement of the area from the inside.
– DERIVATIVES **embrasured** adj.
– ORIGIN C18: from Fr., from obs. *embraser* 'widen an opening', of unknown ultimate origin.

**embrittle** ● v. make or become brittle.
– DERIVATIVES **embrittlement** n.

**embrocation** /ˌɛmbrə'keɪʃ(ə)n/ ● n. a liquid medication rubbed on the body to relieve pain from sprains and strains.
– ORIGIN ME: from med. L. *embrocatio(n-)*, from *embrocare*, based on Gk *embrokhē* 'lotion'.

**embroider** ● v. **1** sew decorative needlework patterns on. **2** add fictitious or exaggerated details to.
– DERIVATIVES **embroiderer** n.
– ORIGIN ME: from Anglo-Norman Fr. *enbrouder*.

**embroidery** ● n. (pl. **-ies**) **1** the art or pastime of embroidering. **2** embroidered cloth.

**embroil** ● v. [often as adj. **embroiled**] involve deeply in a conflict or difficult situation. ➤archaic bring into a state of confusion or disorder.
– DERIVATIVES **embroilment** n.
– ORIGIN C17: from Fr. *embrouiller* 'to muddle'.

**embryo** /'ɛmbrɪəʊ/ ● n. (pl. **-os**) **1** an unborn or unhatched offspring in the process of development, especially an unborn human in the first eight weeks from conception. Compare with **FETUS**. **2** Botany the part of a seed which develops into a new plant.
– PHRASES **in embryo** at a rudimentary stage.
– DERIVATIVES **embryonal** /'ɛmbrɪən(ə)l/ adj.
– ORIGIN ME: via late L. from Gk *embruon* 'fetus', from *em-* 'into' + *bruein* 'grow'.

**embryogenesis** /ˌɛmbrɪə(ʊ)'dʒɛnɪsɪs/ ● n. Biology the formation and development of an embryo.
– DERIVATIVES **embryogenic** adj. **embryogeny** n.

**embryology** /ˌɛmbrɪ'ɒlədʒi/ ● n. the branch of biology and medicine concerned with the study of embryos.
– DERIVATIVES **embryologic** adj. **embryological** adj. **embryologist** n.

**embryonic** /ˌɛmbrɪ'ɒnɪk/ ● adj. **1** of or relating to an embryo. **2** in or at a rudimentary stage.
– DERIVATIVES **embryonically** adv.

**emcee** /ɛm'siː/ N. Amer. informal ● n. a master of ceremonies. ● v. (**emcees**, **emceed**, **emceeing**) act as a master of ceremonies for or at.
– ORIGIN 1930s: representing the pron. of **MC**.

**-eme** ● suffix Linguistics forming nouns denoting minimal linguistic units that are in systemic contrast with one other: *phoneme*.
– ORIGIN abstracted from **PHONEME**.

**emend** /ɪ'mɛnd/ ● v. correct and revise (a text).
– DERIVATIVES **emendation** n.
– ORIGIN ME: from L. *emendare*, from *e-* 'out of' + *menda* 'a fault'; cf. **AMEND**.

**emerald** ● n. **1** a bright green precious stone consisting of a chromium-rich variety of beryl. **2** a bright green colour. **3** (also **emerald moth**) a slender-bodied green moth. [*Geometra papilionaria* (**large emerald**) and other species.]

– ORIGIN ME: from OFr. *e(s)meraud*, ult. via L. from Gk *(s)maragdos*, via Prakrit from Semitic (cf. Heb. *bāreqeṯ*, from *bāraq* 'flash, sparkle').

**emerge** /ɪˈməːdʒ/ ● **v.** **1** become gradually visible or apparent. ➤(of facts) become known. **2** recover from or survive a difficult period. **3** (of an insect) break out from an egg, cocoon, or pupal case.
– DERIVATIVES **emergence** n. **emerging** adj.
– ORIGIN C16: from L. *emergere*, from *e-* 'out, forth' + *mergere* 'to dip'.

**emergency** ● **n.** (pl. **-ies**) **1** a serious, unexpected, and potentially dangerous situation requiring immediate action. ➤[as modifier] arising from or used in an emergency: *an emergency exit.* **2** N. Amer. the casualty department in a hospital. **3** Austral./NZ dated (in sport) a reserve player or runner.
– ORIGIN C17: from med. L. *emergentia*, from L. *emergere* (see **EMERGE**).

**emergent** ● **adj.** **1** in the process of coming into being; emerging. **2** Philosophy (of a property) arising as an effect of complex causes and not analysable simply as the sum of their effects. **3** denoting water plants with leaves and flowers that appear above the water surface. ● **n.** Philosophy an emergent property.

**emeritus** /ɪˈmɛrɪtəs, iː-/ ● **adj.** having retired but allowed to retain a title as an honour: *emeritus professor of microbiology.*
– ORIGIN C18: from L., past part. of *emereri* 'earn one's discharge by service'.

**emersion** ● **n.** **1** the process or state of emerging, especially from water. **2** Astronomy the reappearance of a celestial body after eclipse or occultation.

**emery** /ˈɛm(ə)ri/ ● **n.** a greyish-black form of corundum containing iron oxide, used in powdered form as an abrasive.
– ORIGIN C15: from Fr. *émeri*, from OFr. *esmeri*, from Ital. *smeriglio*, based on Gk *smuris* 'polishing powder'.

**emery board** ● **n.** a strip of thin wood or card coated with emery or another abrasive and used as a nail file.

**emesis** /ˈɛmɪsɪs/ ● **n.** technical vomiting.
– ORIGIN C19: from Gk, from *emein* 'to vomit'.

**emetic** /ɪˈmɛtɪk/ ● **adj.** (of a substance) causing vomiting. ● **n.** an emetic medicine or other substance.
– ORIGIN C17: from Gk *emetikos*, from *emein* 'to vomit'.

**EMF** ● **abbrev.** **1** electromagnetic field(s). **2** (**emf**) electromotive force. **3** European Monetary Fund.

**EMG** ● **abbrev.** electromyogram or electromyography.

**-emia** ● **comb. form** US spelling of **-AEMIA**.

**emigrant** ● **n.** a person who leaves their own country in order to settle permanently in another.

**emigrate** /ˈɛmɪgreɪt/ ● **v.** leave one's own country in order to settle permanently in another.
– DERIVATIVES **emigration** n.
– ORIGIN C18: from L. *emigrat-*, *emigrare* 'to emigrate'.

**émigré** /ˈɛmɪgreɪ/ ● **n.** a person who has emigrated, especially for political reasons.
– ORIGIN C18 (orig. denoting a person escaping the French Revolution): Fr., past part. of *émigrer* 'emigrate'.

**eminence** /ˈɛmɪnəns/ ● **n.** **1** acknowledged superiority within a particular sphere. **2** an important or distinguished person. ➤(**His/Your Eminence**) a title given to a Roman Catholic cardinal. **3** formal or poetic/literary a piece of rising ground. **4** Anatomy a slight projection from the surface of the body.
– ORIGIN ME: from L. *eminentia*, from *eminere* 'jut, project'.

**éminence grise** /ˌɛmɪnɒs ˈgriːz/ ● **n.** (pl. **éminences grises** pronunc. same) a person who exercises power or influence without holding an official position.
– ORIGIN 1930s: Fr., lit 'grey eminence'; the term was orig. applied to Cardinal Richelieu's grey-cloaked private secretary, Père Joseph (1577–1638).

**eminent** ● **adj.** **1** respected; distinguished. **2** notable; outstanding: *his eminent suitability for studio work.*
– DERIVATIVES **eminently** adv.

**eminent domain** ● **n.** Law the right of a government or its agent to expropriate private property for public use, with payment of compensation.

**emir** /ɛˈmɪə/ (also **amir**) ● **n.** a title of various Muslim (mainly Arab) rulers. ➤historical a Muslim (usually Arab) military commander or local chief.
– ORIGIN C16 (denoting a male descendant of Muhammad): from Fr. *émir*, from Arab. *'amīr* (see **AMIR**).

**emirate** /ˈɛmɪrət/ ● **n.** the rank, lands, or reign of an emir.

**emissary** /ˈɛmɪs(ə)ri/ ● **n.** (pl. **-ies**) a person sent as a diplomatic representative on a special mission.
– ORIGIN C17: from L. *emissarius* 'scout, spy', from *emittere* (see **EMIT**).

**emission** /ɪˈmɪʃ(ə)n/ ● **n.** the action of emitting something, especially heat, light, gas, or radiation. ➤a substance which is emitted.
– ORIGIN ME (in the sense 'emanation'): from L. *emissio(n-)*, from *emiss-*, *emittere* (see **EMIT**).

**emissive** ● **adj.** having the power to radiate or emit.
– DERIVATIVES **emissivity** n.

**emit** ● **v.** (**emitted**, **emitting**) **1** discharge; send forth or give out. **2** make (a sound).
– ORIGIN C17: from L. *emittere*, from *e-* 'out of' + *mittere* 'send'.

**emitter** ● **n.** **1** a thing which emits. **2** Electronics the region in a bipolar transistor that produces carriers of current.

**Emmental** /ˈɛməntɑːl/ (also **Emmenthal**) ● **n.** a kind of hard Swiss cheese with holes in it, similar to Gruyère.
– ORIGIN from Ger. *Emmentaler*, from *Emmental*, the name of a valley in Switzerland where the cheese was orig. made.

**emmer** /ˈɛmə/ ● **n.** an old kind of wheat with bearded ears and spikelets that each contain two grains, now grown mainly for fodder and breakfast cereals. [*Triticum dicoccum*.]
– ORIGIN C20: from Ger., from Old High Ger. *amer* (see **SPELT**²).

**emmet** /ˈɛmɪt/ ● **n.** dialect an ant.
– ORIGIN OE *ǣmete* (see **ANT**).

**Emmy** ● **n.** (pl. **Emmys**) (in the US) a statuette awarded annually to an outstanding television programme or performer.
– ORIGIN 1940s: said to be from *Immy*, short for *image orthicon tube* (a kind of television camera tube).

**emollient** /ɪˈmɒlɪənt/ ● **adj.** **1** having the quality of softening or soothing the skin. **2** attempting to avoid confrontation or anger; soothing or calming. ● **n.** an emollient preparation.
– DERIVATIVES **emollience** n.
– ORIGIN C17: from L. *emollient-*, *emollire* 'to make soft'.

**emolument** /ɪˈmɒljʊm(ə)nt, ɛ-/ ● **n.** formal a salary, fee, or benefit from employment or office.
– ORIGIN ME: from L. *emolumentum*, orig. prob. 'payment for grinding corn', from *emolere* 'grind up'.

**emote** /ɪˈməʊt/ ● **v.** portray emotion theatrically.
– DERIVATIVES **emoter** n.
– ORIGIN C20: back-form. from **EMOTION**.

**emoticon** /ɪˈməʊtɪkɒn, -ˈmɒtɪ-/ ● **n.** a representation of a facial expression such as a smile or frown, formed with keyboard characters and used in electronic communications to convey the writer's feelings.
– ORIGIN 1990s: blend of **EMOTION** and **ICON**.

**emotion** ● **n.** a strong feeling, such as joy, anger, or sadness. ➤instinctive or intuitive feeling as distinguished from reasoning or knowledge.
– DERIVATIVES **emotionless** adj.
– ORIGIN C16 (denoting a public disturbance): from Fr. *émotion*, from *émouvoir* 'excite', based on L. *emovere*, from *e-* 'out' + *movere* 'move'.

**emotional** ● **adj.** of or relating to emotions. ➤arousing or showing intense feeling: *an emotional speech.*
– DERIVATIVES **emotionalism** n. **emotionalist** n. & adj. **emotionality** n. **emotionalize** (also **-ise**) v. **emotionally** adv.

**emotive** ● **adj.** arousing intense feeling.
– DERIVATIVES **emotively** adv. **emotiveness** n. **emotivity** /ˌiːməʊˈtɪvɪti/ n.

**empanada** /ˌɛmpəˈnɑːdə/ ● **n.** a pastry turnover filled with savoury ingredients and baked or fried, typical of

South American cooking.
– ORIGIN Sp., fem. past part. of *empanar* 'roll in pastry', based on L. *panis* 'bread'.

**empanel** • v. variant spelling of **IMPANEL**.
– DERIVATIVES **empanelment** n.

**empathize** (also **-ise**) • v. understand and share the feelings of another.

**empathy** /ˈɛmpəθi/ • n. the ability to empathize.
– DERIVATIVES **empathetic** adj. **empathetically** adv. **empathic** /ɛmˈpaθɪk/ adj. **empathically** adv.
– ORIGIN C20: from Gk *empatheia* (from *em-* 'in' + *pathos* 'feeling') translating Ger. *Einfühlung*.

**empennage** /ɛmˈpɛnɪdʒ/ • n. Aeronautics an arrangement of stabilizing surfaces at the tail of an aircraft.
– ORIGIN C20: from Fr., from *empenner* 'to feather an arrow', from *em-* 'in' + *penne* 'a feather'.

**emperor** • n. **1** the ruler of an empire. **2** in names of certain large, strikingly marked butterflies, e.g. **purple emperor**.
– DERIVATIVES **emperorship** n.
– ORIGIN ME: from OFr. *emperere*, from L. *imperator* 'military commander', from *imperare* 'to command'.

**emperor moth** • n. a large moth of the silk moth family, with eyespots on all four wings. [*Saturnia pavonia* and related species.]

**emperor penguin** • n. the largest kind of penguin, which breeds in the Antarctic and has a yellow patch on each side of the head. [*Aptenodytes forsteri*.]

**emphasis** /ˈɛmfəsɪs/ • n. (pl. **emphases** /-siːz/) **1** special importance, value, or prominence given to something. **2** stress laid on a word or words in speaking.
– ORIGIN C16: via L. from Gk, orig. 'appearance, show', later denoting a figure of speech in which more is implied than is said, from *emphainein* 'exhibit'.

**emphasize** (also **-ise**) • v. **1** give emphasis to. **2** make more clearly defined: *a jacket which emphasized her hips*.

**emphatic** • adj. showing or giving emphasis. ➤definite and clear: *the answer was an emphatic 'yes'*.
– DERIVATIVES **emphatically** adv.

**emphysema** /ˌɛmfɪˈsiːmə/ • n. Medicine **1** (also **pulmonary emphysema**) a condition in which the air sacs of the lungs are damaged and enlarged, causing breathlessness. **2** a condition in which air is abnormally present within the body tissues.
– ORIGIN C17: via late L. from Gk *emphusēma*, from *emphusan* 'puff up'.

**empire** • n. **1** an extensive group of states ruled over by a single monarch, an oligarchy, or a sovereign state. **2** supreme political power: *his dream of empire in Asia Minor*. **3** a large commercial organization under the control of one person or group. • adj. **(Empire)** denoting a neoclassical style of furniture and dress fashionable chiefly during the First Empire (1804–15) in France.
– ORIGIN ME: via OFr. from L. *imperium*, rel. to *imperare* (see **EMPEROR**).

**empire line** • n. a style of women's clothing characterized by a waistline cut just under the bust and typically a low neckline, first popular during the First Empire.

**empiric** /ɛmˈpɪrɪk, ɪm-/ • adj. another term for **EMPIRICAL**. • n. archaic **1** a scientist who relies solely on observation and experiment. **2** a quack doctor.
– ORIGIN ME: via L. from Gk *empeirikos*, from *empeiria* 'experience'.

**empirical** • adj. based on, concerned with, or verifiable by observation or experience rather than theory or pure logic.
– DERIVATIVES **empirically** adv.

**empirical formula** • n. Chemistry a formula giving the proportions of the elements present in a compound but not the actual numbers or arrangement of atoms.

**empiricism** /ɛmˈpɪrɪsɪz(ə)m/ • n. Philosophy the theory that all knowledge is derived from sense-experience.
– DERIVATIVES **empiricist** n. & adj.

**emplacement** • n. **1** a structure or platform where a gun is placed for firing. **2** chiefly Geology the process or state of setting something in place.

**emplane** (also **enplane**) • v. go or put on board an aircraft.

**employ** • v. **1** give work to (someone) and pay them for it. ➤keep occupied. **2** make use of. • n. the state of being employed; employment: *in the employ of a wine merchant*.
– DERIVATIVES **employability** n. **employable** adj.
– ORIGIN ME: from OFr. *employer*, based on L. *implicari*, from *implicare* (see **IMPLY**).

**employee** • n. a person employed for wages or salary.

**employer** • n. a person that employs people.

**employment** • n. **1** the action or condition of employing. **2** a person's work or profession.

**emporium** /ɛmˈpɔːrɪəm, ɪm-/ • n. (pl. **emporia** /-rɪə/ or **emporiums**) a large store selling a wide variety of goods.
– ORIGIN C16: from L., from Gk *emporion*, from *emporos* 'merchant'.

**empower** • v. give authority or power to; authorize. ➤give strength and confidence to.
– DERIVATIVES **empowerment** n.

**empress** /ˈɛmprɪs/ • n. a female emperor. ➤the wife or widow of an emperor.
– ORIGIN ME: from OFr. *emperesse*, fem. of *emperere* (see **EMPEROR**).

**empty** • adj. (**-ier**, **-iest**) **1** containing nothing; not filled or occupied. ➤Mathematics (of a set) containing no members or elements. **2** (of words or a gesture) lacking sincerity. **3** having no value or purpose. • v. (**-ies**, **-ied**) **1** make or become empty. ➤discharge (the contents) from a container. **2** (of a river) discharge itself into the sea or a lake. • n. (pl. **-ies**) informal a bottle or glass left empty of its contents.
– PHRASES **be running on empty** have exhausted all of one's resources.
– DERIVATIVES **emptily** adv. **emptiness** n.
– ORIGIN OE *ǣmtig*, *ǣmetig* 'at leisure, empty', from *ǣmetta* 'leisure'.

**empty-handed** • adj. having failed to obtain or achieve what one wanted.

**empty-headed** • adj. unintelligent and foolish.

**empty nester** • n. informal, chiefly N. Amer. a parent whose children have grown up and left home.

**empyema** /ˌɛmpʌɪˈiːmə/ • n. Medicine the collection of pus in a body cavity, especially in the pleural cavity.
– ORIGIN ME: via late L. from Gk *empuēma*, from *empuein* 'suppurate'.

**empyrean** /ˌɛmpʌɪˈriːən, -pɪ-, ɛmˈpɪrɪən/ • adj. of or relating to heaven. • n. (**the empyrean**) the highest part of heaven, thought by the ancients to be the realm of pure fire. ➤poetic/literary the visible heavens; the sky.
– DERIVATIVES **empyreal** /ˌɛmpʌɪˈriːəl, -pɪ-, ɛmˈpɪrɪəl/ adj.
– ORIGIN ME: via med. L. from Gk *empurios*, from *en-* 'in' + *pur* 'fire'.

**em rule** /ˈɛm ruːl/ • n. Brit. a long dash used in punctuation, roughly the width of the letter *M*.

**EMS** • abbrev. European Monetary System.

**EMU** • abbrev. Economic and Monetary Union.

**emu**[1] • n. a large flightless fast-running Australian bird resembling the ostrich, with shaggy grey or brown plumage, bare blue skin on the head and neck, and three-toed feet. [*Dromaius novaehollandiae*.]
– ORIGIN C17 (orig. denoting the cassowary, later the greater rhea): from Port. *ema*.

**emu**[2] • abbrev. Brit. **1** electric multiple unit. **2** electromagnetic unit(s).

**emulate** /ˈɛmjʊleɪt/ • v. attempt to match or surpass, typically by imitation.
– DERIVATIVES **emulation** n. **emulative** adj. **emulator** n.
– ORIGIN C16: from L. *aemulat-*, *aemulari* 'to rival or equal'.

**emulous** /ˈɛmjʊləs/ • adj. formal seeking to emulate.
– DERIVATIVES **emulously** adv.
– ORIGIN ME: from L. *aemulus* 'rival'.

**emulsifier** • n. a substance that stabilizes an emulsion, in particular an additive used to stabilize processed foods.

**emulsify** /ɪ'mʌlsɪfʌɪ/ ● v. (**-ies**, **-ied**) make into or become an emulsion.
– DERIVATIVES **emulsifiable** adj. **emulsification** n.

**emulsion** /ɪ'mʌlʃ(ə)n/ ● n. **1** a fine dispersion of minute droplets of one liquid in another in which it is not soluble or miscible. **2** a type of paint consisting of pigment bound in a synthetic resin which forms an emulsion with water. **3** a light-sensitive coating for photographic films and plates, containing crystals of a silver compound dispersed in a medium such as gelatin.
– DERIVATIVES **emulsive** adj.
– ORIGIN C17 (denoting a milky liquid made by crushing almonds in water): from mod. L. *emulsio(n-)*, from *emulgere* 'milk out'.

**en** ● n. Printing a unit of measurement equal to half an em and approximately the average width of typeset characters.
– ORIGIN C18: the letter *N*, since it is approx. this width.

**en-**[1] (also **em-**) ● prefix **1** (added to nouns) forming verbs meaning 'put into or on': *engulf.* **2** (added to nouns and adjectives) forming verbs (often with the suffix *-en*) meaning 'bring into the condition of': *enliven.* **3** (added to verbs) in; into; on: *ensnare.* ➤as an intensifier: *entangle.*
– ORIGIN from Fr., from L. *in-*.

**en-**[2] (also **em-**) ● prefix within; inside: *enthusiasm.*
– ORIGIN from Gk.

**-en**[1] ● suffix forming verbs: **1** (from adjectives) denoting the development or intensification of a state: *widen.* **2** from nouns (such as *strengthen* from *strength*).
– ORIGIN OE *-nian*, of Gmc origin.

**-en**[2] ● suffix (also **-n**) forming adjectives from nouns: **1** made or consisting of: *earthen.* **2** resembling: *golden.*
– ORIGIN OE, of Gmc origin.

**-en**[3] (also **-n**) ● suffix forming past participles of strong verbs: **1** as a regular inflection: *spoken.* **2** as an adjective: *mistaken.*
– ORIGIN OE, of Gmc origin.

**-en**[4] ● suffix forming the plural of a few nouns such as *children, oxen.*
– ORIGIN ME reduction of the earlier suffix *-an.*

**-en**[5] ● suffix forming diminutives of nouns (such as *chicken*).
– ORIGIN OE, of Gmc origin.

**-en**[6] ● suffix **1** forming feminine nouns such as *vixen.* **2** forming abstract nouns such as *burden.*
– ORIGIN OE, of Gmc origin.

**enable** ● v. **1** provide with the ability or means to do something. **2** make possible.
– DERIVATIVES **enablement** n. **enabler** n.
– ORIGIN ME: from **EN-**[1], **IN-**[2], + **ABLE**.

**enabling act** ● n. Law a statute empowering a person or body to take certain action, especially to make regulations.

**enact** ● v. **1** make (a bill or other proposal) law. **2** put into practice. **3** act out (a role or play).
– DERIVATIVES **enactable** adj. **enaction** n. **enactor** n.
– ORIGIN ME: from **EN-**[1], **IN-**[2], + **ACT**.

**enactment** ● n. **1** the process of enacting. **2** a law that has been passed.
– DERIVATIVES **enactive** adj.

**enamel** ● n. **1** an opaque or semi-transparent glassy substance applied to metallic or other hard surfaces for ornament or as a protective coating. **2** the hard glossy substance that covers the crown of a tooth. **3** a paint that dries to give a smooth, hard coat. ● v. (**enamelled**, **enamelling**; US **enameled**, **enameling**) [usu. as adj. **enamelled**] coat or decorate with enamel.
– DERIVATIVES **enameller** n. **enamelware** n. **enamelwork** n.
– ORIGIN ME: from Anglo-Norman Fr. *enamailler*, from *en-* 'in, on' + *amail* 'enamel'.

**enamour** /ɪ'namə, ɛ-/ (US **enamor**) ● v. (**be enamoured of/with/by**) be filled with love or admiration for.
– ORIGIN ME: from OFr. *enamourer*, from *en-* 'in' + *amour* 'love'.

**enanthema** /ˌɛnən'θiːmə/ ● n. Medicine an ulcer or eruption occurring on a mucus-secreting surface such as the inside of the mouth.
– ORIGIN C19: from **EN-**[2] + a shortened form of **EXANTHEMA**.

**enantiomer** /ɪ'nantɪə(ʊ)mə, ɛ-/ ● n. Chemistry each of a pair of molecules that are mirror images of each other.
– DERIVATIVES **enantiomeric** adj. **enantiomerically** adv.
– ORIGIN 1930s: from Gk *enantios* 'opposite' + **-MER**.

**enantiomorph** /ɪ'nantɪə(ʊ)mɔːf, ɛ-/ ● n. each of two crystalline or other geometrical forms which are mirror images of each other.
– DERIVATIVES **enantiomorphic** adj. **enantiomorphism** n. **enantiomorphous** adj.
– ORIGIN C19: from Gk *enantios* 'opposite' + **-MORPH**.

**enation** /ɪ'neɪʃ(ə)n/ ● n. Botany an outgrowth from the surface of a leaf or other part of a plant.
– ORIGIN C19: from L. *enatio(n-)*, from *enasci* 'issue forth'.

**en bloc** /ɒ̃ 'blɒk/ ● adv. all together or all at the same time.
– ORIGIN C19: Fr.

**en brosse** /ɒ̃ 'brɒs/ ● adj. [postpos.] (of hair) cut in a short and bristly style.
– ORIGIN Fr., 'in the form of a brush'.

**enc.** ● abbrev. **1** enclosed. **2** enclosure.

**encamp** ● v. settle in or establish a camp.

**encampment** ● n. **1** a place where a camp is set up. **2** a prehistoric enclosed or fortified site, especially an Iron Age hill fort. **3** the process of setting up a camp.

**encapsulate** /ɪn'kapsjʊleɪt, ɛn-/ ● v. **1** enclose in or as if in a capsule. **2** express concisely and succinctly. **3** Computing enclose in a set of codes which allow transfer across networks.
– DERIVATIVES **encapsulation** n.
– ORIGIN C19: from **EN-**[1], **IN-**[2] + L. *capsula* (see **CAPSULE**).

**encase** (also **incase**) ● v. enclose or cover in a case or close-fitting surround.
– DERIVATIVES **encasement** n.

**encash** ● v. Brit. convert (a cheque, bond, etc.) into money.
– DERIVATIVES **encashable** adj. **encashment** n.

**encaustic** /ɛn'kɔːstɪk/ ● adj. (in painting and ceramics) decorated by burning in colours as an inlay, especially using coloured clays or pigments mixed with hot wax. ● n. the art or process of encaustic painting.
– ORIGIN C16: via L. from Gk *enkaustikos*, from *enkaiein* 'burn in'.

**-ence** ● suffix forming nouns: **1** denoting a quality: *impertinence.* **2** denoting an action or its result: *reference.*
– ORIGIN from Fr. *-ence*, from L. *-entia, -antia.*

**enceinte**[1] /ɒ̃'sãt/ ● n. archaic an enclosure or wall of a fortified place.
– ORIGIN C18: from Fr., from L. *incincta*, fem. past part. of *incingere* 'gird in'.

**enceinte**[2] /ɒ̃'sãt/ ● adj. archaic pregnant.
– ORIGIN C17: from Fr.

**encephalic** /ˌɛnsɪ'falɪk, ɛn'kɛf(ə)lɪk/ ● adj. Anatomy relating to or situated in the brain.
– ORIGIN C19: from Gk *enkephalos* 'brain' (from *en-* 'in' + *kephalē* 'head') + **-IC**.

**encephalitis** /ɛnˌsɛfə'lʌɪtɪs, -ˌkɛfə-/ ● n. inflammation of the brain.
– DERIVATIVES **encephalitic** adj.

**encephalitis lethargica** /lɪ'θɑːdʒɪkə/ ● n. a form of encephalitis caused by a virus and characterized by headache and drowsiness leading to coma.

**encephalization** (also **-isation**) ● n. Zoology an evolutionary increase in the complexity or relative size of the brain.

**encephalo-** /ɛn'sɛf(ə)ləʊ, -'kɛf-/ ● comb. form of or relating to the brain: *encephalopathy.*
– ORIGIN from Gk *enkephalos.*

**encephalography** /ɛnˌsɛfə'lɒgrəfi, -ˌkɛfə-/ ● n. Medicine any of various techniques for recording the structure or electrical activity of the brain.
– DERIVATIVES **encephalogram** /ɛn'sɛf(ə)lə(ʊ)gram, -'kɛf-/ n. **encephalograph** n. **encephalographic** adj.

**encephalomyelitis** /ɛnˌsɛf(ə)ləʊmʌɪə'lʌɪtɪs, -ˌkɛf-/ ● n. Medicine inflammation of the brain and spinal cord, typically due to acute viral infection.

**encephalon** /ɛnˈsɛfəlɒn, -ˈkɛf-/ ● **n.** Anatomy the brain.
– ORIGIN C18: from Gk *enkephalon* 'what is inside the head', from *en-* 'inside' + *kephalē* 'head'.

**encephalopathy** /ɛnˌsɛfəˈlɒpəθi, -ˌkɛf-/ ● **n.** (pl. **-ies**) Medicine a disease in which the functioning of the brain is affected, especially by viral infection or toxins in the blood.

**enchaînement** /ɒ̃ˈʃɛnmɒ̃/ ● **n.** (pl. pronounced same) Ballet a linked sequence of steps or movements constituting a phrase.
– ORIGIN C19: Fr., 'chaining together'.

**enchant** ● **v.** **1** delight; charm. **2** [often as adj. **enchanted**] put under a spell: *an enchanted garden.*
– DERIVATIVES **enchantedly** adv. **enchanter** n. **enchanting** adj. **enchantingly** adv. **enchantment** n. **enchantress** n.
– ORIGIN ME: from Fr. *enchanter*, from L. *incantare*, from *in-* 'in' + *cantare* 'sing'.

**enchanter's nightshade** ● **n.** a woodland plant with small white flowers and fruit with hooked bristles. [*Circaea lutetiana.*]
– ORIGIN C16: believed by early botanists to be the herb used by Circe to charm Odysseus' companions.

**enchase** /ɪnˈtʃeɪs, ɛn-/ ● **v.** another term for **CHASE**[2].
– ORIGIN ME: from OFr. *enchasser* 'set gems, encase'.

**enchilada** /ˌɛntʃɪˈlɑːdə/ ● **n.** a tortilla filled with meat or cheese and served with chilli sauce.
– PHRASES **the big enchilada** N. Amer. informal a person or thing of great importance. **the whole enchilada** N. Amer. informal the whole situation; everything.
– ORIGIN Latin Amer. Sp., fem. past part. of *enchilar* 'season with chilli'.

**enchiridion** /ˌɛnkʌɪˈrɪdɪən/ ● **n.** (pl. **enchiridions** or **enchiridia** /-dɪə/) formal a handbook containing essential information on a subject.
– ORIGIN ME: via late L. from Gk *enkheiridion*, from *en-* 'within' + *kheir* 'hand' + the dimin. suffix *-idion.*

**encipher** ● **v.** convert into a coded form.
– DERIVATIVES **encipherment** n.

**encircle** ● **v.** form a circle around; surround.
– DERIVATIVES **encirclement** n.

**encl.** ● **abbrev.** enclosed or enclosure.

**en clair** /ɒ̃ ˈklɛː/ ● **adj. & adv.** in ordinary language, rather than in code or cipher.
– ORIGIN Fr., lit. 'in clear'.

**enclave** /ˈɛnkleɪv/ ● **n.** **1** a portion of territory surrounded by a larger territory whose inhabitants are culturally or ethnically distinct. Compare with **EXCLAVE**. **2** a group that is different in character from those surrounding it: *a male enclave.*
– ORIGIN C19: from Fr., from OFr. *enclaver* 'enclose, dovetail', based on L. *clavis* 'key'.

**enclitic** /ɪnˈklɪtɪk, ɛn-/ Linguistics ● **n.** a word pronounced with so little emphasis that it is shortened and forms part of the preceding word, for example *n't* in *can't*. Compare with **PROCLITIC**. ● **adj.** denoting or relating to such a word.
– DERIVATIVES **enclitically** adv.
– ORIGIN C17: via late L. from Gk *enklitikos*, from *enklinein* 'lean on'.

**enclose** (also **inclose**) ● **v.** **1** surround or close off on all sides. **2** historical fence in (common land) so as to make it private property. **3** place in an envelope together with a letter.
– ORIGIN ME: from OFr. *enclos*, past part. of *enclore*, based on L. *includere* 'shut in'.

**enclosure** /ɪnˈkləʊʒə, ɛn-/ (also **inclosure**) ● **n.** **1** an area that is sealed off by a barrier. ➤ Brit. a section of a racecourse or stadium allocated to a particular group: *the members' enclosure.* **2** the process or policy of enclosing wasteland or common land so as to make it private property, as carried out in much of Britain in the 18th and early 19th centuries. **3** a document or object placed in an envelope together with a letter.

**encode** ● **v.** convert into a coded form.
– DERIVATIVES **encoder** n.

**encomiast** /ɛnˈkəʊmɪast/ ● **n.** formal a person who publicly praises or flatters someone else.
– DERIVATIVES **encomiastic** adj.
– ORIGIN C17: from Gk *enkōmiastēs*, from *enkōmiazein* 'to praise'.

**encomium** /ɛnˈkəʊmɪəm/ ● **n.** (pl. **encomiums** or **encomia**) formal a speech or piece of writing expressing praise.
– ORIGIN C16: L., from Gk *enkōmion* 'eulogy'.

**encompass** /ɪnˈkʌmpəs, ɛn-/ ● **v.** **1** surround and have or hold within. **2** include comprehensively. **3** archaic cause to take place.
– DERIVATIVES **encompassment** n.

**encopresis** /ˌɛnkəʊˈpriːsɪs/ ● **n.** Medicine involuntary defecation, especially associated with emotional or psychiatric disorder.

**encore** /ˈɒŋkɔː/ ● **n.** a repeated or additional performance of an item at the end of a concert, as called for by an audience. ● **exclam.** again! (as called by an audience at the end of a concert) ● **v.** call for (an encore). ➤ demand an encore from (a performer).
– ORIGIN C18: Fr., lit. 'still, again'.

**encounter** ● **v.** unexpectedly meet or be faced with. ● **n.** **1** an unexpected or casual meeting. **2** a confrontation or unpleasant struggle.
– ORIGIN ME: from OFr. *encontrer* (v.), *encontre* (n.), based on L. *in-* 'in' + *contra* 'against'.

**encourage** ● **v.** give support, confidence, or hope to. ➤ help or stimulate the development of.
– DERIVATIVES **encouragement** n. **encourager** n. **encouraging** adj. **encouragingly** adv.
– ORIGIN ME: from Fr. *encourager*, from *en-* 'in' + *corage* 'courage'.

**encroach** ● **v.** (**encroach on/upon**) gradually and steadily intrude on (a person's territory, rights, etc.). ➤ advance gradually beyond expected or acceptable limits.
– DERIVATIVES **encroacher** n. **encroachment** n.
– ORIGIN ME (in the sense 'seize'): from OFr. *encrochier* 'seize, fasten upon', from *en-* 'in, on' + *crochier* (from *croc* 'hook').

**en croute** /ɒ̃ ˈkruːt/ ● **adj. & adv.** in a pastry crust.
– ORIGIN Fr. *en croûte.*

**encrust** /ɪnˈkrʌst, ɛn-/ (also **incrust**) ● **v.** [usu. as adj. **encrusted**] cover with a hard crust.
– DERIVATIVES **encrustation** n.
– ORIGIN C17: from Fr. *incruster* or *encroûter*, both from L. *incrustare*, from *in-* 'into' + *crusta* 'a crust'.

**encrypt** /ɛnˈkrɪpt/ ● **v.** convert into code.
– DERIVATIVES **encryption** n.
– ORIGIN 1950s: from **EN-**[1] + Gk *kruptos* 'hidden'.

**enculturation** (also **inculturation**) ● **n.** the gradual acquisition of the norms of a culture or group.

**encumber** /ɪnˈkʌmbə, ɛn-/ ● **v.** impede or burden.
– ORIGIN ME: from OFr. *encombrer* 'block up', from *en-* 'in' + *combre* 'river barrage'.

**encumbrance** ● **n.** **1** a burden or impediment. **2** Law a mortgage or other charge on property or assets.

**-ency** ● **suffix** forming nouns: **1** denoting a quality: *efficiency.* **2** denoting a state: *presidency.*
– ORIGIN from L. *-entia* (cf. **-ENCE**).

**encyclical** /ɛnˈsɪklɪk(ə)l, ɪn-, -ˈsʌɪk-/ ● **n.** a letter sent by the pope to all bishops of the Roman Catholic Church.
– ORIGIN C17: via late L. from Gk *enkuklios* 'circular, general'.

**encyclopedia** /ɛnˌsʌɪkləˈ(ʊ)ˈpiːdɪə, ɪn-/ (also **encyclopaedia**) ● **n.** a book or set of books giving information on many subjects or on many aspects of one subject, typically arranged alphabetically.
– ORIGIN C16: mod. L., from pseudo-Gk *enkuklopaideia* for *enkuklios paideia* 'all-round education'.

**encyclopedic** /ɛnˌsʌɪklə(ʊ)ˈpiːdɪk, ɪn-/ (also **encyclopaedic**) ● **adj.** **1** comprehensive: *an encyclopedic knowledge of food.* **2** of or relating to encyclopedias or information suitable for an encyclopedia.

**encyclopedism** (also **encyclopaedism**) ● **n.** comprehensive learning or knowledge.

**encyclopedist** (also **encyclopaedist**) ● **n.** a person who writes, edits, or contributes to an encyclopedia.

**encyst** /ɪn'sɪst, ɛn-/ ● v. Zoology enclose or become enclosed in a cyst.
– DERIVATIVES **encystation** n. **encystment** n.

**end** ● n. **1** a final part of something. ➤a termination of a state or situation. **2** the furthest or most extreme part of something. ➤a small piece that is left after use. **3** a part or share of an activity. **4** a place linked to another by a telephone call, letter, or journey. **5** the part of a sports field or court defended by one team or player. **6** a goal or desired result. **7** Bowls & Curling a session of play in one particular direction across the playing area. **8** American Football a lineman positioned nearest the sideline. ● v. come or bring to an end; finish.
– PHRASES **at the end of the day** informal, chiefly Brit. when everything is taken into consideration. **be the end** informal be the limit of what one can tolerate. **end it all** commit suicide. **the end of the road** (or **line**) the point beyond which progress or survival cannot continue. **the end of one's tether** (or N. Amer. **rope**) having no patience or energy left. **end on** situated on or viewed from the end. **end to end** in a row with the ends touching or close together. **get** (or **have**) **one's end away** Brit. vulgar slang have sexual intercourse. **in the end** eventually. **keep** (or **hold**) **one's end up** informal perform well in a difficult or competitive situation. **make** (**both**) **ends meet** earn just enough money to live on. **never** (or **not**) **hear the end of** be continually reminded of. **no end** informal very much. **no end of** informal a vast number or amount of. **on end 1** continuing without stopping. **2** in an upright position. **the sharp end** informal the most challenging and risky part of an activity. **a —— to end all ——s** informal the most impressive or successful of its kind: *a party to end all parties.*
– ORIGIN OE *ende* (n.), *endian* (v.), of Gmc origin.

**-end** ● suffix denoting a person or thing to be treated in a specified way: *dividend* | *reverend.*
– ORIGIN from L. *-endus*, gerundive ending.

**endanger** ● v. put at risk or in danger.
– DERIVATIVES **endangerment** n.

**endangered** ● adj. at risk, especially of extinction.

**endarterectomy** /ˌɛndɑːtə'rɛktəmi/ ● n. (pl. **-ies**) surgical removal of part of the inner lining of an artery, together with any obstructive deposits.
– ORIGIN C20: from **ENDO-** + **ARTERY** + **-ECTOMY**.

**endarteritis** /ˌɛndɑːtə'rʌɪtɪs/ ● n. Medicine inflammation of the inner lining of an artery.

**endear** /ɪn'dɪə, ɛn-/ ● v. cause to be loved or liked.

**endearing** ● adj. inspiring love or affection.
– DERIVATIVES **endearingly** adv.

**endearment** ● n. love or affection. ➤a word or phrase expressing this.

**endeavour** /ɪn'dɛvə, ɛn-/ (US **endeavor**) ● v. try hard to do or achieve something. ● n. **1** an act of endeavouring; an enterprise. **2** earnest and industrious effort.
– ORIGIN ME: from the phr. *put oneself in devoir* 'do one's utmost' (see **DEVOIR**).

**endemic** /ɛn'dɛmɪk/ ● adj. **1** (of a disease or condition) regularly found among particular people or in a certain area. **2** (of a plant or animal) native or restricted to a certain area. ● n. an endemic plant or animal.
– DERIVATIVES **endemically** adv. **endemicity** /ˌɛndɪ'mɪsɪti/ n. **endemism** /'ɛndɪmɪz(ə)m/ n.
– ORIGIN C17: from Fr. *endémique* or mod. L. *endemicus*, from Gk *endēmios* 'native'.

**endgame** ● n. the final stage of a game such as chess or bridge, when few pieces or cards remain.

**end grain** ● n. the grain of wood seen when it is cut across the growth rings.

**ending** ● n. an end or final part. ➤the final part of a word, constituting a grammatical inflection or formative element.

**endite** /'ɛndʌɪt/ ● n. Zoology an inwardly directed lobe on a limb segment of an arthropod.
– ORIGIN C19: from **ENDO-** + **-ITE**[1].

**endive** /'ɛndʌɪv, -dɪv/ ● n. **1** an edible Mediterranean plant, the bitter leaves of which may be blanched and used in salads. [*Cichorium endivia.*] **2** (also **Belgian endive**) N. Amer. a chicory crown.
– ORIGIN ME (also denoting the sowthistle): via OFr. from med. L. *endivia*, based on Gk *entubon.*

**endless** ● adj. **1** having or seeming to have no end or limit. **2** innumerable. **3** (of a belt, chain, or tape) having the ends joined to allow for continuous action.
– DERIVATIVES **endlessly** adv. **endlessness** n.

**endmember** ● n. Geology a mineral or rock representing one end of a series having a range of composition.

**endmost** ● adj. nearest to the end.

**endnote** ● n. a note printed at the end of a book or section of a book.

**endo-** ● comb. form internal; within: *endoderm.*
– ORIGIN from Gk *endon* 'within'.

**endocardial** /ˌɛndə(ʊ)'kɑːdɪəl/ ● adj. Anatomy & Medicine **1** of or relating to the endocardium. **2** inside the heart.

**endocarditis** /ˌɛndəʊkɑː'dʌɪtɪs/ ● n. Medicine inflammation of the endocardium.
– DERIVATIVES **endocarditic** adj.

**endocardium** /ˌɛndəʊ'kɑːdɪəm/ ● n. the thin, smooth membrane which lines the chambers of the heart and forms the surface of the valves.
– ORIGIN C19: mod. L., from **ENDO-** + Gk *kardia* 'heart'.

**endocarp** /'ɛndə(ʊ)kɑːp/ ● n. Botany the innermost layer of the pericarp which surrounds a seed in a fruit.
– DERIVATIVES **endocarpic** adj.

**endocentric** /ˌɛndəʊ'sɛntrɪk/ ● adj. Linguistics denoting or being a construction in which the whole has the same syntactic function as the head, for example *big black dogs.* Contrasted with **EXOCENTRIC**.

**endocrine** /'ɛndə(ʊ)krʌɪn, -krɪn/ ● adj. Physiology of or denoting glands which secrete hormones or other products directly into the blood.
– ORIGIN C20: from **ENDO-** + Gk *krinein* 'sift'.

**endocrinology** /ˌɛndəʊkrɪ'nɒlədʒi/ ● n. the branch of physiology and medicine concerned with endocrine glands and hormones.
– DERIVATIVES **endocrinological** adj. **endocrinologist** n.

**endocytosis** /ˌɛndəʊsʌɪ'təʊsɪs/ ● n. Biology the taking in of matter by a living cell by enclosing it in a vacuole.
– DERIVATIVES **endocytotic** adj.

**endoderm** /'ɛndə(ʊ)dəːm/ ● n. Zoology & Embryology the innermost layer of cells or tissue of an embryo, or the parts derived from this (e.g. the lining of the gut).
– DERIVATIVES **endodermal** adj.
– ORIGIN C19: from **ENDO-** + Gk *derma* 'skin'.

**endogamy** /ɛn'dɒgəmi/ ● n. **1** Anthropology the custom of marrying only within the limits of a community, clan, or tribe. Compare with **EXOGAMY**. **2** Biology inbreeding or self-pollination.
– DERIVATIVES **endogamous** adj.
– ORIGIN C19: from **ENDO-** + Gk *gamos* 'marriage'.

**endogenic** /ˌɛndəʊ'dʒɛnɪk/ ● adj. Geology formed or occurring beneath the surface of the earth. Often contrasted with **EXOGENIC**.

**endogenous** /ɛn'dɒdʒɪnəs, ɪn-/ ● adj. technical of or relating to an internal cause or origin. Often contrasted with **EXOGENOUS**.
– DERIVATIVES **endogenously** adv.

**endolymph** /'ɛndə(ʊ)lɪmf/ ● n. Anatomy the fluid in the membranous labyrinth of the ear.

**endometriosis** /ˌɛndə(ʊ)miːtrɪ'əʊsɪs/ ● n. Medicine a condition resulting from the appearance of endometrial tissue outside the womb, causing pelvic pain.

**endometrium** /ˌɛndə(ʊ)'miːtrɪəm/ ● n. Anatomy the mucous membrane lining the womb.
– DERIVATIVES **endometrial** adj.
– ORIGIN C19: mod. L., from **ENDO-** + Gk *mētra* 'womb'.

**endomorph** /'ɛndə(ʊ)mɔːf/ ● n. Physiology a person with a soft round build of body and a high proportion of fat tissue. Compare with **ECTOMORPH** and **MESOMORPH**.
– DERIVATIVES **endomorphic** adj. **endomorphy** n.
– ORIGIN 1940s: *endo-* from *endodermal* (the endoderm being the layer of the embryo giving rise to these physical characteristics) + **-MORPH**.

**endoparasite** ● n. Biology a parasite, such as a tapeworm, that lives inside its host. Compare with **ECTOPARASITE**.

– DERIVATIVES **endoparasitic** adj.

**endophyte** /ˈɛndəʊfʌɪt/ ● **n.** Botany a plant, especially a fungus, which lives inside another plant.

– DERIVATIVES **endophytic** adj.

**endoplasm** /ˈɛndə(ʊ)plaz(ə)m/ ● **n.** Biology, dated the more fluid, granular inner layer of the cytoplasm in amoeboid cells. Compare with **ECTOPLASM** (in sense 1).

**endoplasmic reticulum** /ˌɛndəʊˈplazmɪk/ ● **n.** Biology a network of membranous tubules within the cytoplasm of a eukaryotic cell, continuous with the nuclear membrane.

**endorphin** /ɛnˈdɔːfɪn/ ● **n.** Biochemistry any of a group of hormones secreted within the brain and nervous system and activating the body's opiate receptors, causing an analgesic effect.

– ORIGIN 1970s: blend of **ENDOGENOUS** and **MORPHINE**.

**endorse** /ɪnˈdɔːs, ɛn-/ (US & Law also **indorse**) ● **v. 1** declare one's public approval of. **2** sign (a cheque or bill of exchange) on the back to specify another as the payee or to accept responsibility for paying it. ➤(usu. **be endorsed on**) write (a comment) on a document. **3** Brit. enter an endorsement on (a driving licence).

– DERIVATIVES **endorsable** adj. **endorsee** n. **endorser** n.

– ORIGIN C15: from med. L. *indorsare*, from L. *in-* 'in, on' + *dorsum* 'back'.

**endorsement** (chiefly US also **indorsement**) ● **n. 1** an act of endorsing someone or something. **2** (in the UK) a note on a driving licence recording the penalty points incurred for a driving offence. **3** a clause in an insurance policy detailing an exemption from or change in cover. **4** the action of endorsing a cheque or bill of exchange.

**endoscope** /ˈɛndəskəʊp/ ● **n.** Medicine an instrument which can be introduced into the body to view its internal parts.

– DERIVATIVES **endoscopic** adj. **endoscopically** adv. **endoscopist** n. **endoscopy** n.

**endoskeleton** ● **n.** Zoology an internal skeleton, such as that of vertebrates. Compare with **EXOSKELETON**.

– DERIVATIVES **endoskeletal** adj.

**endosperm** ● **n.** Botany the part of a seed which acts as a food store for the developing plant embryo.

**endothelium** /ˌɛndə(ʊ)ˈθiːlɪəm/ ● **n.** the layer of cells lining the blood vessels, heart, and other organs and cavities of the body, and formed from the embryonic mesoderm. Compare with **EPITHELIUM**.

– DERIVATIVES **endothelial** adj.

– ORIGIN C19: mod. L., from **ENDO-** + Gk *thēlē* 'nipple'.

**endotherm** /ˈɛndə(ʊ)θəːm/ ● **n.** Zoology an animal that is dependent on the internal generation of heat.

– DERIVATIVES **endothermy** n.

**endothermic** ● **adj. 1** Chemistry (of a reaction) accompanied by the absorption of heat. The opposite of **EXOTHERMIC**. **2** Zoology (of an animal) dependent on the internal generation of heat.

**endotoxin** /ˈɛndəʊˌtɒksɪn/ ● **n.** Microbiology a toxin present inside a bacterial cell and released when the cell disintegrates. Compare with **EXOTOXIN**.

**endow** /ɪnˈdaʊ, ɛn-/ ● **v. 1** give or bequeath an income or property to. ➤establish (a university post, annual prize, etc.) by donating funds. **2** (usu. **be endowed with**) provide with a quality, ability, or asset.

– DERIVATIVES **endower** n.

– ORIGIN ME: from legal Anglo-Norman Fr. *endouer*, from *en-* 'in, towards' + OFr. *douer* 'give as a gift' (from L. *dotare*: see **DOWER**).

**endowment** ● **n. 1** the action of endowing. ➤an income or form of property endowed. **2** a quality or ability with which a person is endowed. **3** [as modifier] denoting a form of life insurance involving payment of a fixed sum to the insured person on a specified date, or to their estate should they die before this date.

**endowment mortgage** ● **n.** Brit. a mortgage linked to an endowment insurance policy which is intended to repay the capital sum on maturity.

**endpaper** ● **n.** a leaf of paper at the beginning or end of a book, especially that fixed to the inside of the cover.

**endplay** ● **n.** Bridge a way of playing in the last few tricks which forces an opponent to make a disadvantageous lead.

**end point** ● **n.** Chemistry the point in a titration at which a reaction is complete, often marked by a colour change.

**end run** ● **n. 1** American Football an attempt by the ball-carrier to run around the end of the defensive line. **2** N. Amer. an evasive tactic. ● **v.** (**end-run**) N. Amer. evade.

**end standard** ● **n.** a standard of length in the form of a metal bar or block whose end faces are the standard distance apart.

**end-stopped** ● **adj.** (of verse) having a pause at the end of each line.

**endue** /ɪnˈdjuː, ɛn-/ (also **indue**) ● **v.** (**endues**, **endued**, **enduing**) poetic/literary endow with a quality or ability.

– ORIGIN ME: from OFr. *enduire*, partly from L. *inducere* (see **INDUCE**), reinforced by the sense of L. *induere* 'put on clothes'.

**endure** /ɪnˈdjʊə, ɛn-/ ● **v. 1** suffer (something painful and prolonged) patiently. ➤tolerate. **2** remain in existence.

– DERIVATIVES **endurable** adj. **endurance** n. **enduring** adj. **enduringly** adv.

– ORIGIN ME: from OFr. *endurer*, from L. *indurare* 'harden'.

**enduro** /ɪnˈdjʊərəʊ, ɛn-/ ● **n.** (pl. **-os**) a long-distance race for motor vehicles or bicycles over rough terrain, designed to test endurance.

**end-user** ● **n.** the person who uses a particular product.

**endways** (also **endwise**) ● **adv. 1** with its end facing upwards, forwards, or towards the viewer. **2** end to end.

**end zone** ● **n.** American Football the rectangular area at the end of the field into which the ball must be carried or passed to score a touchdown.

**ENE** ● **abbrev.** east-north-east.

**-ene** ● **suffix 1** denoting an inhabitant: *Nazarene*. **2** Chemistry forming names of unsaturated hydrocarbons containing a double bond: *benzene*.

– ORIGIN from Gk *-ēnos*.

**enema** /ˈɛnɪmə/ ● **n.** (pl. **enemas** or **enemata** /ɪˈnɛmətə/) a procedure in which fluid is injected into the rectum, typically to expel its contents.

– ORIGIN ME: via late L. from Gk, from *enienai* 'send or put in'.

**enemy** ● **n.** (pl. **-ies**) a person who is actively opposed or hostile to someone or something. ➤(**the enemy**) [treated as sing. or pl.] a hostile nation or its armed forces in time of war.

– ORIGIN ME: from OFr. *enemi*, from L. *inimicus*, from *in-* 'not' + *amicus* 'friend'.

**energetic** /ˌɛnəˈdʒɛtɪk/ ● **adj. 1** showing or involving great energy or activity. **2** Physics of or relating to energy.

– DERIVATIVES **energetically** adv.

– ORIGIN C17 (in the sense 'powerfully effective'): from Gk *energētikos*, from *energein* 'operate, work in or upon'.

**energetics** ● **pl. n.** the properties or behaviour of something in terms of energy.

**energumen** /ˌɛnəˈgjuːmən/ ● **n.** archaic a person believed to be possessed by the devil or a spirit.

– ORIGIN C18: via late L. from Gk *energoumenos*, passive part. of *energein* 'work in or upon'.

**energy** ● **n.** (pl. **-ies**) **1** the strength and vitality required for sustained activity. ➤(**energies**) a person's physical and mental powers as applied to a particular activity. **2** power derived from physical or chemical resources to provide light and heat or to work machines. **3** Physics the property of matter and radiation which is manifest as a capacity to perform work.

– DERIVATIVES **energize** (also **-ise**) v.

– ORIGIN C16: from Fr. *énergie*, or via late L. from Gk *energeia*, from *en-* 'in, within' + *ergon* 'work'.

**energy audit** ● **n.** an assessment of the energy needs and efficiency of a building or buildings.

**enervate** /ˈɛnəveɪt/ ● **v.** cause to feel drained of energy.

– DERIVATIVES **enervation** n.

– ORIGIN C17 (earlier (ME) as *enervation*): from L. *enervat-*, *enervare* 'weaken (by extraction of the sinews)'.

**en face** /ɒ̃ ˈfas/ ● **adv. & adj.** facing forwards.

– ORIGIN from Fr.

**en famille** /ɒ̃ fa'miː/ ● **adv.** with one's family. ➤ as or like a family; informally.
– ORIGIN Fr., lit. 'in family'.

**enfant gâté** /ˌɒ̃fɒ̃ 'gateɪ/ ● **n.** dated a person who is excessively flattered or indulged.
– ORIGIN Fr., lit. 'spoilt child'.

**enfant terrible** /ˌɒ̃fɒ̃ tɛ'riːbl(ə)/ ● **n.** (pl. **enfants terribles** pronunc. same) a person who behaves in an unconventional or controversial way.
– ORIGIN Fr., lit. 'terrible child'.

**enfeeble** ● **v.** weaken.
– DERIVATIVES **enfeeblement** n.
– ORIGIN ME: from OFr. *enfeblir*.

**enfeoff** /ɪn'fiːf, -'fɛf, ɛn-/ ● **v.** (under the feudal system) give freehold property or land in exchange for a pledge of service.
– DERIVATIVES **enfeoffment** n.
– ORIGIN ME: from Anglo-Norman Fr. *enfeoffer*, from OFr. *en-* 'in' + *fief* 'fief'; cf. FEOFFMENT.

**en fête** /ɒ̃ 'fɛt/ ● **adv. & adj.** holding or prepared for a celebration.
– ORIGIN Fr., 'in festival'.

**enfilade** /ˌɛnfɪ'leɪd/ ● **n. 1** a volley of gunfire directed along a line from end to end. **2** a suite of rooms with doorways in line with each other. ● **v.** direct an enfilade at.
– ORIGIN C18 (denoting a military post commanding the length of a line): from Fr., from *enfiler* 'thread on a string'.

**enfleurage** /ˌɒ̃flə'rɑːʒ/ ● **n.** the extraction of essential oils and perfumes from flowers.
– ORIGIN C19: Fr., from *enfleurer* 'saturate with the perfume from flowers'.

**enfold** /ɪn'fəʊld, ɛn-/ ● **v.** surround; envelop.

**enforce** ● **v.** compel compliance with (a law, rule, or obligation). ➤ cause to happen by necessity or force.
– DERIVATIVES **enforceability** n. **enforceable** adj. **enforced** adj. **enforcedly** adv. **enforcement** n. **enforcer** n.
– ORIGIN ME: from OFr. *enforcir*, *enforcier*, based on L. *in-* 'in' + *fortis* 'strong'.

**enforcement notice** ● **n.** English Law an official notification to remedy a breach of planning legislation.

**enfranchise** /ɪn'fran(t)ʃʌɪz, ɛn-/ ● **v. 1** give the right to vote to. **2** historical free (a slave).
– DERIVATIVES **enfranchisement** n.
– ORIGIN ME: from OFr. *enfranchiss-*, *enfranchir*, from *en-* (expressing a change of state) + *franc*, *franche* 'free'.

**ENG** ● **abbrev.** electronic news-gathering.

**engage** ● **v. 1** attract or involve (someone's interest or attention). **2** chiefly Brit. employ or hire. ➤ enter into a contract to do. **3** (**engage in/with**) participate or become involved in. ➤ enter into combat with. ➤ (of fencers or swordsmen) bring (weapons) together preparatory to fighting. **4** (with reference to a part of a machine or engine) move or cause to move into position so as to come into operation.
– ORIGIN ME (orig. in the sense 'pawn or pledge something'): from Fr. *engager*, ult. from the base of GAGE[1].

**engagé** /ˌɒ̃ga'ʒeɪ/ ● **adj.** (of a writer or artist) morally committed to a particular cause.
– ORIGIN Fr., past part. of *engager* (see ENGAGE).

**engaged** ● **adj. 1** busy; occupied. ➤ Brit. (of a telephone line) unavailable because already in use. **2** having formally agreed to marry. **3** Architecture (of a column) attached to or partly let into a wall.

**engagement** ● **n. 1** a formal agreement to get married. **2** an appointment. **3** the action of engaging or being engaged. **4** a fight or battle between armed forces.

**engaging** ● **adj.** charming and attractive.
– DERIVATIVES **engagingly** adv. **engagingness** n.

**engender** /ɪn'dʒɛndə, ɛn-/ ● **v. 1** give rise to. **2** archaic beget (offspring).
– ORIGIN ME: from OFr. *engendrer*, from L. *ingenerare*, from *in-* 'in' + *generare* 'beget'.

**engine** ● **n. 1** a machine with moving parts that converts power into motion. ➤ historical a mechanical device or instrument, especially one used in warfare. **2** (also **railway engine**) a locomotive.
– DERIVATIVES **-engined** adj. **engineless** adj.
– ORIGIN ME (orig. in the sense 'ingenuity, cunning'): from OFr. *engin*, from L. *ingenium* 'talent, device', from *in-* 'in' + *gignere* 'beget'; cf. INGENIOUS.

**engine block** ● **n.** see BLOCK (sense 7).

**engineer** ● **n. 1** a person qualified in engineering. **2** a person who maintains or controls an engine or machine. **3** a skilful contriver. ● **v. 1** design and build. **2** contrive to bring about. **3** modify (an organism) by manipulating its genetic material.
– ORIGIN ME: from OFr. *engigneor*, from med. L. *ingeniator*, from *ingeniare* 'contrive', from L. *ingenium* (see ENGINE).

**engineering** ● **n.** the branch of science and technology concerned with the design, building, and use of engines, machines, and structures.

**engineering brick** ● **n.** a strong, dense brick made of semi-vitreous material.

**engineering science** (also **engineering sciences**) ● **n.** the parts of science concerned with the physical and mathematical basis of engineering and machine technology.

**engine room** ● **n.** a room containing engines, especially in a ship.

**engirdle** (also **engird**) ● **v.** poetic/literary encircle.

**English** ● **n. 1** the language of England, now used in many varieties throughout the world. **2** N. Amer. (in pool or billiards) spin or side given to a ball. ● **adj.** of or relating to England or its people or language.
– DERIVATIVES **Englishness** n.
– ORIGIN OE *Englisc* (see ANGLE, -ISH[1]).

**English bond** ● **n.** Building a bond used in brickwork consisting of alternate courses of stretchers and headers.

**English breakfast** ● **n.** a substantial breakfast including hot cooked food such as bacon and eggs.

**English horn** ● **n.** chiefly N. Amer. another term for COR ANGLAIS.

**Englishman** (or **Englishwoman**) ● **n.** (pl. **-men** or **-women**) a native or national of England, or a person of English descent.

**English muffin** ● **n.** North American term for MUFFIN (in sense 1).

**English mustard** ● **n.** a kind of mustard with a very hot taste.

**English rose** ● **n.** an attractive English girl with a delicate, fair-skinned complexion.

**English setter** ● **n.** a setter of a breed with a long white or partly white coat.

**engorge** /ɪn'gɔːdʒ, ɛn-/ ● **v.** swell or cause to swell with blood, water, etc.
– DERIVATIVES **engorgement** n.
– ORIGIN C15 (in the sense 'gorge oneself'): from OFr. *engorgier* 'feed to excess', from *en-* 'into' + *gorge* 'throat'.

**engraft** (also **ingraft**) ● **v.** another term for GRAFT[1].
– DERIVATIVES **engraftment** n.

**engrailed** ● **adj.** chiefly Heraldry having semicircular indentations along the edge. Compare with INVECTED.

**engrain** ● **v.** variant spelling of INGRAIN.

**engrained** ● **adj.** variant spelling of INGRAINED.

**engram** /'ɛngram/ ● **n.** a hypothetical permanent change in the brain accounting for the existence of memory.
– DERIVATIVES **engrammatic** adj.
– ORIGIN C20: from Ger. *Engramm*, from Gk *en-* 'within' + *gramma* 'letter of the alphabet'.

**engrave** ● **v. 1** cut or carve (a text or design) on a hard surface. ➤ cut or carve a text or design on. ➤ cut (a design) as lines on a metal plate for printing. **2** (**be engraved on** or **in**) be permanently fixed in (one's memory or mind).
– DERIVATIVES **engraver** n. **engraving** n.
– ORIGIN C15: from EN-[1], IN-[2] + GRAVE[3], influenced by obs. Fr. *engraver*.

**engross** /ɪn'grəʊs, ɛn-/ ● **v. 1** [often as adj. **engrossed**] absorb all the attention of. ➤ archaic monopolize. **2** Law produce (a legal document) in its final or definitive form.
– ORIGIN ME: sense 1 is from OFr. *en gros*, from med. L. *in*

*grosso* 'wholesale'; sense 2 is from Anglo-Norman Fr. *engrosser*, med. L. *ingrossare* (from OFr. *grosse*, med. L. *grossa* 'large writing').

**engrossment** • n. Law the final version of a legal document, eventually becoming the original deed.

**engulf** • v. (of a natural force) sweep over so as to completely surround or cover.
– DERIVATIVES **engulfment** n.

**enhance** /ɪn'hɑːns, -hans, ɛn-/ • v. improve the quality, value, or extent of.
– DERIVATIVES **enhancement** n. **enhancer** n.
– ORIGIN ME (orig. in the sense 'elevate'): from Anglo-Norman Fr. *enhauncer*, based on L. *in-* (expressing intensive force) + *altus* 'high'.

**enharmonic** /ˌɛnhɑː'mɒnɪk/ • adj. Music of or relating to notes which are the same in pitch (in modern tuning) though bearing different names (e.g. F sharp and G flat). ➤of or having intervals smaller than a semitone (e.g. between notes such as F sharp and G flat, in systems of tuning which distinguish them).
– DERIVATIVES **enharmonically** adv.
– ORIGIN C17: via late L. from Gk *enarmonikos*, from *en-* 'in' + *harmonia* 'harmony'.

**enigma** /ɪ'nɪgmə/ • n. a mysterious or puzzling person or thing.
– DERIVATIVES **enigmatic** adj. **enigmatical** adj. **enigmatically** adv.
– ORIGIN C16: via L. from Gk *ainigma* 'riddle'.

**enjambement** /ɪn'dʒam(b)m(ə)nt, ɛn-, ɒ̃'ʒɒ̃bmɒ̃/ (also **enjambment**) • n. (in verse) the continuation of a sentence without a pause beyond the end of a line, couplet, or stanza.
– DERIVATIVES **enjambed** adj.
– ORIGIN C19: Fr., from *enjamber* 'stride over, go beyond'.

**enjoin** • v. instruct or urge to do something. ➤(**enjoin someone from**) Law prohibit someone from performing (an action) by issuing an injunction.
– DERIVATIVES **enjoinment** n.
– ORIGIN ME: from OFr. *enjoindre*, from L. *injungere* 'join, attach, impose'.

**enjoy** • v. **1** take pleasure in. **2** possess and benefit from.
– DERIVATIVES **enjoyability** n. **enjoyable** adj. **enjoyableness** n. **enjoyably** adv. **enjoyer** n. **enjoyment** n.
– ORIGIN ME: from OFr. *enjoier* 'give joy to' or *enjoïr* 'enjoy', both based on L. *gaudere* 'rejoice'.

**enkephalin** /ɛn'kɛf(ə)lɪn/ • n. Biochemistry either of two compounds which occur naturally in the brain and are related to the endorphins.
– ORIGIN 1970s: from Gk *enkephalos* 'brain' + **-IN**[1].

**enlarge** • v. **1** make or become bigger. **2** (**enlarge on/upon**) speak or write about in greater detail.
– ORIGIN ME: from OFr. *enlarger*.

**enlargement** • n. the action or state of enlarging or being enlarged. ➤a photograph that is larger than the original negative or than an earlier print.

**enlarger** • n. Photography an apparatus for enlarging or reducing negatives or positives.

**enlighten** • v. give greater knowledge and understanding to. ➤give spiritual insight to. ➤[as adj. **enlightened**] rational, tolerant, and well-informed.
– DERIVATIVES **enlightener** n.
– ORIGIN ME (in the sense 'make luminous'): in early use from OE *inlīhtan* 'to shine'; later from **EN-**[1], **IN-**[2] + **LIGHTEN**[2] or the noun **LIGHT**[1].

**enlightenment** • n. **1** the action of enlightening or the state of being enlightened. ➤the attainment of spiritual insight, in particular (in Buddhism) that awareness which frees a person from the cycle of rebirth. **2** (**the Enlightenment**) a European intellectual movement of the late 17th and 18th centuries emphasizing reason and individualism rather than tradition.

**enlist** • v. enrol or be enrolled in the armed services. ➤engage (a person or their help).
– DERIVATIVES **enlister** n. **enlistment** n.

**enlisted man** • n. US a member of the armed forces below the rank of officer.

**enliven** • v. make more entertaining or interesting. ➤make more cheerful or animated.
– DERIVATIVES **enlivener** n. **enlivenment** n.
– ORIGIN C17 (in the sense 'give life to'): from C16 *enlive*, *inlive* (in the same sense).

**en masse** /ɒ̃ 'mas/ • adv. all together.
– ORIGIN C18: Fr., 'in a mass'.

**enmesh** • v. (usu. **be enmeshed in**) entangle.
– DERIVATIVES **enmeshment** n.

**enmity** • n. (pl. **-ies**) the state of being an enemy; hostility.
– ORIGIN ME: from OFr. *enemi(s)tie*, based on L. *inimicus* (see **ENEMY**).

**ennead** /'ɛnɪad/ • n. rare a group or set of nine.
– ORIGIN C16: from Gk *enneas*, *ennead-*, from *ennea* 'nine'.

**ennoble** • v. give a noble rank or title to. ➤give greater dignity to; elevate.
– DERIVATIVES **ennoblement** n.
– ORIGIN C15: from Fr. *ennoblir*.

**ennui** /ɒn'wiː/ • n. listlessness and dissatisfaction arising from boredom.
– ORIGIN C18: Fr., from L. *in odio(n-)*, from *mihi in odio est* 'it is hateful to me'; cf. **ANNOY**.

**enology** • n. US spelling of **OENOLOGY**.

**enormity** • n. (pl. **-ies**) **1** (**the enormity of**) the large scale or extreme seriousness of (something bad). ➤(in neutral use) great size or scale. **2** a grave crime or sin.
– ORIGIN ME (orig. in the sense 'deviation from rectitude'): via OFr. from L. *enormitas*, from *enormis*, from *e-* 'out of' + *norma* 'pattern, standard'.

**USAGE enormity**

In its earliest sense **enormity** meant 'a crime' and some argue that it should therefore continue to be used only of contexts in which a negative moral judgement is implied. Nevertheless, in modern English **enormity** is increasingly used neutrally, as a synonym for **hugeness**, and the use is now broadly accepted in standard English.

**enormous** • adj. very large.
– DERIVATIVES **enormously** adv. **enormousness** n.

**enosis** /ɪ'nəʊsɪs, 'ɛnəsɪs/ • n. the political union of Cyprus and Greece, as an aim or ideal of certain Greeks and Cypriots.
– ORIGIN 1920s: from mod. Gk *henōsis*, from *hena* 'one'.

**enough** • det. & pron. as much or as many as is necessary or desirable. • adv. **1** to the required degree or extent. **2** to a moderate degree.
– PHRASES **enough is enough** no more will be tolerated. **enough said** all is understood and there is no need to say more.
– ORIGIN OE *genōg*, of Gmc origin.

**en papillote** /ɒ̃ 'papɪjɒt/ • adj. & adv. (of food) cooked and served in a paper wrapper.
– ORIGIN from Fr.

**en passant** /ɒ̃ pa'sɑːnt, 'pasɒ̃/ • adv. by the way.
– PHRASES **en passant rule** (or **law**) Chess the rule that a pawn making a first move of two squares instead of one may nevertheless be immediately captured by an opposing pawn on the fifth rank.
– ORIGIN C17: Fr., lit. 'in passing'.

**en pension** /ɒ̃ 'pɒ̃sjɒ̃/ • adv. as a boarder or lodger.
– ORIGIN Fr. (see **PENSION**[2]).

**enplane** • v. variant spelling of **EMPLANE**.

**en pointe** • adj. & adv. Ballet on the tips of the toes. See **POINTE**.
– ORIGIN from Fr.

**en poste** /ɒ̃ pɒst/ • adv. in an official diplomatic position at a particular place.
– ORIGIN from Fr.

**en primeur** /ˌɒ̃ prɪ'məː, French ɑ̃ pʀimœʀ/ • adj. & adv. (of wine) newly produced and made available.
– ORIGIN Fr., lit. 'as being new'.

**enprint** /'ɛnprɪnt/ • n. Brit. a standard-sized photographic print made by printing the whole of a negative to a moderate enlargement.
– ORIGIN C20: from *enlarged print*.

**en prise** /ɒ̃ 'priːz/ • adj. Chess (of a piece or pawn) in a position to be taken.

– ORIGIN C19: Fr.

**enquire** ● v. ask for information. ➤(**enquire after**) ask about the health and well-being of. ➤(**enquire into**) investigate. ➤[as adj. **enquiring**] (of a look) suggesting that information is sought.
– DERIVATIVES **enquirer** n. **enquiringly** adv.
– ORIGIN ME *enquere*, from OFr. *enquerre*, based on L. *inquirere* (based on *quaerere* 'seek').

**enquiry** ● n. (pl. **-ies**) an act of asking for information. ➤an official investigation.

**enquiry agent** ● n. Brit. a private detective.

**enrage** ● v. (usu. **be enraged**) make very angry.
– ORIGIN C15: from Fr. *enrager*.

**enrapture** ● v. give intense pleasure to.
– DERIVATIVES **enrapt** adj.

**enrich** ● v. **1** improve the quality or value of. **2** [usu. as adj. **enriched**] increase the proportion of a particular isotope in (an element), especially that of the fissile isotope U-235 in uranium. **3** make wealthy or wealthier.
– DERIVATIVES **enrichment** n.
– ORIGIN ME: from OFr. *enrichir*.

**enrobe** ● v. formal dress in a robe or vestment.

**enrol** /ɪn'rəʊl, ɛn-/ (US **enroll**) ● v. (**enrolled**, **enrolling**) officially register as a member or student. ➤recruit. ➤Law historical enter (a deed or other document) among the rolls of a court of justice.
– DERIVATIVES **enrollee** n.
– ORIGIN ME: from OFr. *enroller*, from *en-* 'in' + *rolle* 'a roll' (names being orig. written on a roll of parchment).

**enrolment** (US **enrollment**) ● n. the action of enrolling or being enrolled. ➤N. Amer. the number of people enrolled, typically at a school or college.

**en route** /ɒn 'ru:t/ ● adv. on the way.
– ORIGIN C18: Fr. (see **ROUTE**).

**en rule** /'ɛn ru:l/ ● n. Brit. a short dash, the width of an en, used in punctuation.

**ensconce** /ɪn'skɒns, ɛn-/ ● v. (often **ensconce oneself**) establish in a comfortable, safe, or secret place.
– ORIGIN C16 (in the senses 'fortify' and 'shelter within or behind a fortification'): from **EN-**[1], **IN-**[2] + **SCONCE**[2].

**ensemble** /ɒn'sɒmb(ə)l/ ● n. **1** a group of musicians, actors, or dancers who perform together. ➤a scene or passage written for performance by a whole cast, choir, or group of instruments. **2** a group of items viewed as a whole. ➤a set of clothes worn together.
– ORIGIN ME: from Fr., based on L. *insimul*, from *in-* 'in' + *simul* 'at the same time'.

**enshrine** ● v. (usu. **be enshrined**) **1** place (a revered or precious object) in an appropriate receptacle. **2** preserve (a right, tradition, or idea) in a form that ensures it will be respected.
– DERIVATIVES **enshrinement** n.

**enshroud** /ɪn'ʃraʊd, ɛn-/ ● v. poetic/literary envelop completely and hide from view.

**ensiform** /'ɛnsɪfɔ:m/ ● adj. chiefly Botany long and narrow with sharp edges and a pointed tip.
– ORIGIN C16: from L. *ensis* 'sword' + **-FORM**.

**ensiform cartilage** ● n. another term for **XIPHOID PROCESS**.

**ensign** /'ɛnsʌɪn/ ● n. **1** a flag, especially a military or naval one indicating nationality. **2** the lowest rank of commissioned officer in the US and some other navies, above chief warrant officer and below lieutenant. ➤historical the lowest rank of commissioned infantry officer in the British army. **3** historical a standard-bearer.
– ORIGIN ME: from OFr. *enseigne*, from L. *insignia* (see **INSIGNIA**).

**ensilage** /'ɛnsɪlɪdʒ, ɛn'sʌɪlɪdʒ/ ● n. another term for **SILAGE**. ● v. another term for **ENSILE**.
– ORIGIN C19: from Fr., from *ensiler* (see **ENSILE**).

**ensile** /ɛn'sʌɪl/ ● v. put (grass or another crop) into a silo.
– ORIGIN C19: from Fr. *ensiler*, from Sp. *ensilar*.

**enslave** ● v. make a slave. ➤cause to lose freedom of choice or action.
– DERIVATIVES **enslavement** n. **enslaver** n.
– ORIGIN C17 (in the sense 'make subject to a superstition, habit, etc.'): from **EN-**[1], **IN-**[2] + **SLAVE**.

**ensnare** ● v. catch in or as in a trap.
– DERIVATIVES **ensnarement** n.

**ensorcell** /ɪn'sɔ:s(ə)l, ɛn-/ (US also **ensorcel**) ● v. (**ensorcelled**, **ensorcelling**; US **ensorceled**, **ensorceling**) poetic/literary enchant; fascinate.
– DERIVATIVES **ensorcellment** n.
– ORIGIN C16: from OFr. *ensorceler*, alt. of *ensorcerer*, from *sorcier* 'sorcerer'.

**enstatite** /'ɛnstətʌɪt/ ● n. a translucent mineral consisting of magnesium silicate, found in igneous rocks and some meteorites.
– ORIGIN C19: from Gk *enstatēs* 'adversary' (because of its refractory nature) + **-ITE**[1].

**ensue** ● v. (**ensues**, **ensued**, **ensuing**) happen or occur afterwards or as a result.
– ORIGIN ME: from OFr. *ensivre*, from L. *insequi*, based on *sequi* 'follow'.

**en suite** /ɒn 'swi:t/ ● adj. & adv. Brit. (of a bathroom) immediately adjoining a bedroom and forming a single unit. ➤(of a bedroom) having such a bathroom.
– ORIGIN C18 (in the sense 'in agreement'): from Fr., lit. 'in sequence'.

**ensure** /ɪn'ʃʊə, ɛn-/ ● v. make certain that (something) will occur or be so. ➤(**ensure against**) make sure that (a problem) does not occur.
– ORIGIN ME: from Anglo-Norman Fr. *enseurer*. alt. of OFr. *aseurer*, earlier form of *assurer* (see **ASSURE**).

**ENT** ● abbrev. ear, nose, and throat (as a department in a hospital).

**-ent** ● suffix **1** (forming adjectives) denoting an occurrence of action: *refluent*. ➤denoting a state: *convenient*. **2** (forming nouns) denoting an agent: *coefficient*.
– ORIGIN from Fr., or from the L. pres. participial verb stem *-ent-* (see also **-ANT**).

**entablature** /ɛn'tablətʃə, ɪn-/ ● n. Architecture the upper part of a classical building supported by columns or a colonnade, comprising the architrave, frieze, and cornice.
– ORIGIN C17: from Ital. *intavolatura* 'boarding'.

**entablement** /ɛn'teɪb(ə)lm(ə)nt, ɪn-/ ● n. Architecture a platform supporting a statue, above the dado and base.
– ORIGIN C17 (in the sense 'entablature'): from Fr., based on *table* 'table'.

**entail** ● v. **1** involve as an inevitable part or consequence. **2** Law settle the inheritance of (property) over a number of generations so that ownership remains within a particular family. ● n. Law an instance of entailing property. ➤an entailed estate.
– DERIVATIVES **entailment** n.
– ORIGIN ME: from **EN-**[1], **IN-**[2] + OFr. *taille* (see **TAIL**[2]).

**entangle** ● v. (usu. **be entangled in/with**) **1** cause to become tangled. **2** involve in complicated circumstances.
– DERIVATIVES **entanglement** n.

**entasis** /'ɛntəsɪs/ ● n. (pl. **entases**) Architecture a slight convex curve in the shaft of a column, introduced to correct the visual illusion of concavity produced by a straight shaft.
– ORIGIN C17: mod. L., from Gk, from *enteinein* 'to stretch or strain'.

**entelechy** /ɛn'tɛləki, ɪn-/ ● n. (pl. **-ies**) Philosophy **1** the realization of potential. **2** the supposed vital principle that guides the development and functioning of an organism or other system.
– ORIGIN ME: via late L. from Gk *entelekheia* (used by Aristotle), from *en-* 'within' + *telos* 'end, perfection' + *ekhein* 'be in a certain state'.

**entente** /ɒn'tɒnt, ɒ̃'tɒ̃t/ (also **entente cordiale** /ˌkɔ:dɪ'ɑ:l/) ● n. a friendly understanding or informal alliance between states or factions. ➤(**the Entente Cordiale**) the understanding between Britain and France reached in 1904, forming the basis of Anglo-French cooperation in the First World War.
– ORIGIN C19: Fr. *entente* (*cordiale*) '(friendly) understanding'.

**enter** ● v. **1** come or go into. ➤penetrate. ➤(**enter on/upon**) Law (as a legal entitlement) go freely into (prop-

erty) as or as if the owner. **2** (often **enter into**) begin to be involved in. ➤(**enter on/upon**) begin (an activity or job). ➤join (an institution or profession). ➤register as a competitor or participant in. ➤register to participate in a competition or examination. ➤(**enter into**) undertake to bind oneself by (an agreement) **3** record (information) in a book, computer, etc. ➤Law submit (a statement) in an official capacity, usually in a court of law.
– ORIGIN ME: from OFr. *entrer*, from L. *intrare*, from *intra* 'within'.

**enteral** /'ɛntər(ə)l/ ● **adj.** Medicine (chiefly of nutrition) involving or passing through the intestine. Often contrasted with **PARENTERAL**.
– DERIVATIVES **enterally** adv.
– ORIGIN C20: from Gk *enteron* 'intestine' + **-AL**, partly as a back-form. from **PARENTERAL**.

**enteric** /ɛn'tɛrɪk/ ● **adj.** of, relating to, or occurring in the intestines.
– ORIGIN C19: from Gk *enterikos*, from *enteron* 'intestine'.

**enteric fever** ● **n.** another term for **TYPHOID** or **PARATYPHOID**.

**enteritis** /ˌɛntə'rʌɪtɪs/ ● **n.** Medicine inflammation of the intestine, especially the small intestine, usually accompanied by diarrhoea.

**entero-** ● **comb. form** of or relating to the intestine: *enterovirus*.
– ORIGIN from Gk *enteron*.

**enterococcus** /ˌɛntərəʊ'kɒk(ə)s/ ● **n.** (pl. **enterococci** /-'kɒk(s)ʌɪ, -k(s)iː/) a streptococcus that occurs naturally in the intestine but can cause infection elsewhere in the body.

**enteropathy** /ˌɛntə'rɒpəθi/ ● **n.** (pl. **-ies**) Medicine a disease of the intestine, especially the small intestine.

**enterostomy** /ˌɛntə'rɒstəmi/ ● **n.** (pl. **-ies**) a surgical operation in which the small intestine is diverted to an artificial opening, usually in the abdominal wall.

**enterotoxin** /ˌɛntərəʊ'tɒksɪn/ ● **n.** Medicine a toxin produced in or affecting the intestines.

**enterovirus** /'ɛntərəʊˌvʌɪrəs/ ● **n.** Medicine any of a group of RNA viruses (e.g. those causing polio and hepatitis A) which occur chiefly in the gastrointestinal tract.

**enterprise** ● **n. 1** a project or undertaking, especially a bold one. ➤bold resourcefulness. **2** a business or company.
– DERIVATIVES **enterpriser** n.
– ORIGIN ME: from OFr., 'something undertaken', fem. past part. (used as n.) of *entreprendre*, based on L. *prendere*, *prehendere* 'to take'.

**enterprise zone** ● **n.** an area in which tax concessions or other state incentives are offered to encourage business investment.

**enterprising** ● **adj.** showing initiative and resourcefulness.
– DERIVATIVES **enterprisingly** adv.

**entertain** ● **v. 1** provide with amusement or enjoyment. ➤show hospitality to. **2** give attention or consideration to.
– DERIVATIVES **entertaining** adj. **entertainingly** adv. **entertainment** n.
– ORIGIN ME (orig. in the sense 'maintain, continue', later 'treat in a certain way'): from Fr. *entretenir*, based on L. *inter* 'among' + *tenere* 'to hold'.

**entertainer** ● **n.** a person, such as a singer or comedian, whose job is to entertain others.

**enthalpy** /'ɛnθ(ə)lpi, ɛn'θalpi/ ● **n.** Physics a thermodynamic quantity equivalent to the total heat content of a system.
– ORIGIN 1920s: from Gk *enthalpein* (v.), from *en-* 'within' + *thalpein* 'to heat'.

**enthral** /ɪn'θrɔːl, ɛn-/ (US **enthrall**) ● **v.** (**enthralled**, **enthralling**) **1** (usu. **be enthralled**) capture the fascinated attention of. **2** (also **inthrall**) archaic enslave.
– DERIVATIVES **enthralment** (US **enthrallment**) n.
– ORIGIN ME: from **EN-**[1], **IN-**[2] + **THRALL**.

**enthrone** ● **v.** install (a monarch or bishop) on a throne with due ceremony. ➤treat with honour and respect.
– DERIVATIVES **enthronement** n.

**enthuse** /ɪn'θjuːz, ɛn-/ ● **v.** be or make enthusiastic.

**enthusiasm** ● **n. 1** intense enjoyment, interest, or approval. ➤an object of such feelings. **2** archaic, derogatory religious fervour supposedly resulting directly from divine inspiration.
– ORIGIN C17: from Fr. *enthousiasme*, or via late L. from Gk *enthousiasmos*, from *enthous* 'possessed by a god' (based on *theos* 'god').

**enthusiast** ● **n. 1** a person who is full of enthusiasm for something. **2** archaic, derogatory a person of intense and visionary Christian views.
– DERIVATIVES **enthusiastic** adj. **enthusiastically** adv.

**enthymeme** /'ɛnθɪmiːm/ ● **n.** Logic an argument in which one premise is not explicitly stated.
– ORIGIN C16: via L. from Gk *enthumēma*, from *enthumeisthai* 'consider'.

**entice** /ɪn'tʌɪs, ɛn-/ ● **v.** attract by offering pleasure or advantage.
– DERIVATIVES **enticement** n. **enticer** n. **enticing** adj. **enticingly** adv.
– ORIGIN ME: from OFr. *enticier*, prob. from a base meaning 'set on fire', based on an alt. of L. *titio* 'firebrand'.

**entire** /ɪn'tʌɪə, ɛn-/ ● **adj. 1** with no part left out; whole. **2** (of a male horse) not castrated. **3** Botany (of a leaf) without indentations or division into leaflets. **4** without qualification; absolute.
– ORIGIN ME: from OFr. *entier*, based on L. *integer* 'untouched, whole', from *in-* 'not' + *tangere* 'to touch'.

**entirely** ● **adv.** completely. ➤solely.

**entirety** ● **n.** (**the entirety**) the whole.
– PHRASES **in its entirety** as a whole.

**entisol** /'ɛntɪsɒl/ ● **n.** Soil Science a mineral soil that has not yet differentiated into distinct horizons.
– ORIGIN C20: from **ENTIRE** + **-SOL**.

**entitle** ● **v. 1** give a right to. **2** give a title to (a book, play, etc.).
– DERIVATIVES **entitlement** n.
– ORIGIN ME: via OFr. from late L. *intitulare*, from *in-* 'in' + L. *titulus* 'title'.

**entity** /'ɛntɪti/ ● **n.** (pl. **-ies**) a thing with distinct and independent existence.
– DERIVATIVES **entitative** adj. (chiefly Philosophy).
– ORIGIN C15: from Fr. *entité* or med. L. *entitas*, from late L. *ens*, *ent-* 'being'.

**entomb** ● **v. 1** place in a tomb. **2** bury in or under.
– DERIVATIVES **entombment** n.
– ORIGIN ME: from OFr. *entomber*.

**entomo-** /'ɛntəməʊ/ ● **comb. form** of an insect; of or relating to insects: *entomophagous*.
– ORIGIN from Gk *entomon*, neut. (denoting an insect) of *entomos* 'cut up, segmented'.

**entomology** /ˌɛntə'mɒlədʒi/ ● **n.** the branch of zoology concerned with the study of insects.
– DERIVATIVES **entomological** adj. **entomologist** n.
– ORIGIN C18: from Fr. *entomologie* or mod. L. *entomologia*, from Gk *entomon* (denoting an insect) + *-logia* (see **-LOGY**).

**entomophilous** /ˌɛntə'mɒfɪləs/ ● **adj.** Botany pollinated by insects.
– DERIVATIVES **entomophily** n.

**Entoprocta** /ˌɛntə(ʊ)'prɒktə/ ● **pl. n.** Zoology a small phylum of sedentary aquatic invertebrates with a rounded body on a long stalk, bearing a ring of tentacles for filtering food from the water.
– DERIVATIVES **entoproct** n.
– ORIGIN mod. L., from Gk *entos* 'within' + *prōktos* 'anus', the anus being within the ring of tentacles.

**entoptic** /ɪn'tɒptɪk, ɛn-/ ● **adj.** (of visual images) occurring or originating inside the eye.
– ORIGIN C19: from Gk *entos* 'within' + **OPTIC**.

**entourage** /'ɒntʊrɑːʒ, ˌɒntʊ(ə)'rɑːʒ/ ● **n.** a group of people attending or surrounding an important person.
– ORIGIN C19: Fr., from *entourer* 'to surround'.

**entr'acte** /'ɒntrakt, 'ɒ̃-/ ● **n.** an interval between two acts of a play or opera. ➤a piece of music or a dance performed during such an interval.
– ORIGIN C19: Fr. (earlier form of *entracte*), from *entre* 'between' + *acte* 'act'.

**entrails** • **pl. n.** a person's or animal's intestines or internal organs.
– ORIGIN ME: from OFr. *entrailles*, from med. L. *intralia*, alt. of L. *interanea* 'internal things', based on *inter* 'among'.

**entrain**[1] /ɪn'treɪn, ɛn-/ • **v.** board or put on board a train.

**entrain**[2] /ɪn'treɪn, ɛn-/ • **v. 1** (of a current or fluid) incorporate and sweep along in its flow. **2** bring about as a consequence. **3** Biology cause to fall into synchronism with a rhythmic phenomenon.
– DERIVATIVES **entrainment** n.
– ORIGIN C16: from Fr. *entraîner*, from *en-* 'in' + *traîner* 'to drag'.

**entrain**[3] /ɒ̃'trã/ • **n.** enthusiasm or animation.
– ORIGIN Fr., from the phr. *être en train* 'be in the process of, be in action'.

**entrammel** /ɪn'tram(ə)l, ɛn-/ • **v.** (**entrammelled**, **entrammelling**; US **entrammeled**, **entrammeling**) poetic/literary entangle.

**entrance**[1] /'ɛntr(ə)ns/ • **n. 1** an opening allowing access. **2** an act of entering. **3** the right, means, or opportunity to enter.
– ORIGIN C15: from OFr., from *entrer* 'enter'.

**entrance**[2] /ɪn'trɑːns, ɛn-/ • **v.** (usu. **be entranced**) fill with wonder and delight. ➤cast a spell on.
– DERIVATIVES **entrancement** n. **entrancing** adj. **entrancingly** adv.

**entrant** • **n.** a person who enters something.
– ORIGIN C17: from Fr., lit. 'entering', pres. part. of *entrer* (see **ENTER**).

**entrap** • **v.** (**entrapped**, **entrapping**) catch in or as in a trap. ➤(of a police officer) deceive (someone) into committing a crime in order to secure their prosecution.
– DERIVATIVES **entrapment** n.
– ORIGIN C16: from OFr. *entraper*.

**en travesti** /ɒ̃ ˌtravɛ'stiː/ • **adv. & adj.** dressed as a member of the opposite sex, especially for a theatrical role.
– ORIGIN Fr., lit. '(dressed) in disguise'.

**entreat** • **v. 1** ask (someone) earnestly or anxiously. ➤ask earnestly or anxiously for. **2** archaic treat in a specified manner.
– DERIVATIVES **entreating** adj. **entreatingly** adv. **entreaty** n. (pl. **-ies**).
– ORIGIN ME: from OFr. *entraitier*, based on *traitier* 'to treat', from L. *tractare* 'to handle'.

**entrechat** /'ɒ̃trəʃɑː/ • **n.** Ballet a vertical jump during which the dancer repeatedly crosses the feet and beats them together.
– ORIGIN Fr., from Ital. (*capriola*) *intrecciata* 'complicated (caper)'.

**entrecôte** /'ɒntrəkəʊt/ • **n.** a boned steak cut off the sirloin.
– ORIGIN Fr., from *entre* 'between' + *côte* 'rib'.

**entrée** /'ɒntreɪ/ • **n. 1** the main course of a meal. ➤Brit. a dish served between the fish and meat courses at a formal dinner. **2** right of entry.
– ORIGIN C18 (denoting a piece of instrumental music forming the first part of a suite): Fr., fem. past part. of *entrer* (see **ENTRY**).

**entremets** /ˌɒntrə'meɪ/ • **n.** a light dish served between two courses of a formal meal.
– ORIGIN Fr., from *entre* 'between' + *mets* 'dish'.

**entrench** (also **intrench**) • **v. 1** (usu. **be entrenched**) establish so firmly that change is difficult. ➤apply extra legal safeguards to (a constitutional right guaranteed by legislation). **2** establish (a military force, camp, etc.) in trenches or other fortified positions.
– DERIVATIVES **entrenchment** n.

**entre nous** /ˌɒ̃trə 'nuː/ • **adv.** between ourselves.
– ORIGIN from Fr.

**entrepôt** /'ɒntrəpəʊ/ • **n.** a port or other place which acts as a centre for import and export.
– ORIGIN C18: Fr., from *entreposer* 'to store'.

**entrepreneur** /ˌɒntrəprə'nəː/ • **n.** a person who sets up a business or businesses, taking on greater than normal financial risks in order to do so.
– DERIVATIVES **entrepreneurial** /-'n(j)əːrɪəl, -'njʊərɪəl/ adj. **entrepreneurialism** n. **entrepreneurially** adv. **entrepreneurism** n. **entrepreneurship** n.
– ORIGIN C19 (denoting the director of a musical institution): from Fr., from *entreprendre* (see **ENTERPRISE**).

**entresol** /'ɒntrəsɒl/ • **n.** a mezzanine floor.
– ORIGIN C18: Fr., from Sp. *entresuelo*, from *entre* 'between' + *suelo* 'storey'.

**entropion** /ɪn'trəʊpɪən, ɛn-/ • **n.** Medicine a condition in which the eyelid is rolled inward against the eyeball.
– ORIGIN C19: from **EN-**[2], on the pattern of *ectropion*.

**entropy** /'ɛntrəpi/ • **n. 1** Physics a thermodynamic quantity representing the unavailability of a system's thermal energy for conversion into mechanical work, often interpreted as the degree of disorder or randomness in the system. **2** (in information theory) a logarithmic measure of the rate of transfer of information in a particular message or language.
– DERIVATIVES **entropic** /-'trɒpɪk/ adj. **entropically** adv.
– ORIGIN C19: from **EN-**[2] + Gk *tropē* 'transformation'.

**entrust** • **v.** assign a responsibility to. ➤put into someone's care.
– DERIVATIVES **entrustment** n.

**entry** • **n.** (pl. **-ies**) **1** an act or the action of entering. **2** a place of entrance. ➤dialect a passage between buildings. **3** the right, means, or opportunity to enter. ➤(also **entry into possession**) Law the action of taking up the legal right to property. ➤Bridge a card providing an opportunity to transfer the lead to a particular hand. **4** an item entered in a list, account book, reference book, etc. **5** an entrant to a competition. ➤the number of entrants in a race or competition. **6** the forward part of a ship's hull below the waterline, considered in terms of breadth or narrowness.
– ORIGIN ME: from OFr. *entree*, based on L. *intrata*, fem. past part. of *intrare* (see **ENTER**).

**entryism** • **n.** the infiltration of a political party by members of another group, to subvert its policies or objectives.
– DERIVATIVES **entryist** n.

**entry-level** • **adj.** suitable for a beginner or first-time user.

**entry permit** • **n.** an official document that authorizes a foreign citizen to enter a country.

**entryphone** • **n.** Brit. trademark a type of intercom at the entrance to a building by which visitors may identify themselves before the door is unlocked.

**entryway** • **n.** N. Amer. an entrance.

**entwine** • **v.** wind or twist together.
– DERIVATIVES **entwinement** n.

**enucleate** /ɪ'njuːklɪeɪt/ • **v. 1** Biology remove the nucleus from (a cell). **2** surgically remove (an eyeball or other structure) from its surrounding capsule. • **adj.** Biology lacking a nucleus.
– DERIVATIVES **enucleation** n.
– ORIGIN C16 (in the sense 'clarify, explain'): from L. *enucleat-*, *enucleare* 'extract'.

**E-number** • **n.** Brit. a code number preceded by the letter E, denoting food additives numbered in accordance with EU directives.

**enumerable** /ɪ'njuːm(ə)rəb(ə)l/ • **adj.** Mathematics able to be counted by one-to-one correspondence with the set of positive integers.

**enumerate** /ɪ'njuːməreɪt/ • **v. 1** mention one by one. **2** formal establish the number of.
– DERIVATIVES **enumeration** n. **enumerative** adj.
– ORIGIN C17: from L. *enumerat-*, *enumerare* 'count out'.

**enumerator** • **n.** a person employed in taking a census of the population.

**enunciate** /ɪ'nʌnsɪeɪt/ • **v. 1** say or pronounce clearly. **2** set out precisely or definitely.
– DERIVATIVES **enunciation** n. **enunciative** adj. **enunciator** n.
– ORIGIN C17 (earlier (C16) as *enunciation*): from L. *enuntiat-*, *enuntiare* 'announce clearly'.

**enure** /ɪ'njʊə/ • **v. 1** (**enure for/to**) Law (of a right or other advantage) belong or be available to. **2** variant spelling of **INURE**.

**enuresis** /ˌɛnjʊə'riːsɪs/ • **n.** Medicine involuntary urin-

ation, especially by children at night.
– DERIVATIVES **enuretic** adj. & n.
– ORIGIN C19: mod. L., from Gk *enourein* 'urinate in'.

**enurn** ● v. place or bury (ashes) in an urn.

**envelop** /ɪn'vɛləp, ɛn-/ ● v. (**enveloped**, **enveloping**) wrap up, cover, or surround completely.
– DERIVATIVES **envelopment** n.
– ORIGIN ME: from OFr. *envoluper*, from *en-* 'in' + a second element of unknown origin (also found in **DEVELOP**).

**envelope** /'ɛnvələʊp, 'ɒn-/ ● n. **1** a flat paper container with a sealable flap, used to enclose a letter or document. **2** a covering or containing structure or layer. **3** Electronics a curve joining the successive peaks of a modulated wave. **4** Mathematics a curve or surface tangent to each of a family of curves or surfaces.
– PHRASES **push the** (**edge of the**) **envelope** informal approach or extend the limits of what is possible. [orig. aviation sl., relating to graphs of aerodynamic performance.]
– ORIGIN C16 (in the sense 'enveloping layer'): from Fr. *enveloppe*, from *envelopper* 'envelop'.

**envenom** (also **envenomate**) ● v. Zoology & Medicine poison by biting or stinging.
– DERIVATIVES **envenomation** n.

**enviable** /'ɛnvɪəb(ə)l/ ● adj. arousing or likely to arouse envy.
– DERIVATIVES **enviably** adv.

**envious** ● adj. feeling or showing envy.
– DERIVATIVES **enviously** adv.

**environ** /ɪn'vʌɪrən, ɛn-/ ● v. formal surround; enclose.
– ORIGIN ME: from OFr. *environer*, from *environ* 'surroundings', from *en* 'in' + *viron* 'circuit'.

**environment** ● n. **1** the surroundings or conditions in which a person, animal, or plant lives or operates. ➤Computing the overall structure within which a user, computer, or program operates. **2** (**the environment**) the natural world, especially as affected by human activity.
– DERIVATIVES **environmental** adj. **environmentally** adv.

**environmental audit** ● n. an assessment of the extent to which an organization is observing practices which seek to minimize harm to the environment.

**environmentalist** ● n. **1** a person who is concerned with or advocates the protection of the environment. **2** a person who considers that environment has the primary influence on the development of a person or group.
– DERIVATIVES **environmentalism** n.

**environs** ● pl. n. the surrounding area or district.
– ORIGIN C17: from Fr., pl. of *environ* (see **ENVIRON**).

**envisage** /ɪn'vɪzɪdʒ, ɛn-/ ● v. regard or conceive of as a possibility. ➤form a mental picture of.
– ORIGIN C19: from Fr. *envisager*, from *en-* 'in' + *visage* 'face'.

**envision** ● v. visualize.

**envoi** /'ɛnvɔɪ/ (also **envoy**) ● n. **1** a short stanza concluding a ballade. **2** archaic an author's concluding words.
– ORIGIN ME: from OFr. *envoi*, from *envoyer* (see **ENVOY**).

**envoy** /'ɛnvɔɪ/ ● n. **1** a messenger or representative, especially one on a diplomatic mission. **2** (also **envoy extraordinary**) a minister plenipotentiary, ranking below ambassador and above chargé d'affaires.
– ORIGIN C17: from Fr. *envoyé*, past part. of *envoyer* 'send'.

**envy** ● n. (pl. **-ies**) discontented or resentful longing aroused by another's possessions, qualities, or luck. ➤(**the envy of**) a person or thing that inspires such a feeling. ● v. (**-ies**, **-ied**) feel envy of.
– DERIVATIVES **envier** n.
– ORIGIN ME (also in the sense 'hostility'): from OFr. *envie* (n.), *envier* (v.), from L. *invidia*, from *invidere* 'regard maliciously', from *in-* 'into' + *videre* 'to see'.

**enwrap** (also **inwrap**) ● v. (**enwrapped**, **enwrapping**) wrap; envelop.

**Enzed** /ɛn'zɛd/ ● n. Austral./NZ informal New Zealand or a New Zealander.
– DERIVATIVES **Enzedder** n.
– ORIGIN representing a pronunc. of the initials *NZ*.

**enzootic** /ˌɛnzəʊ'ɒtɪk/ ● adj. (of a disease) regularly affecting animals in a particular district or at a particular season.
– ORIGIN C19: from **EN-**[2] + Gk *zōion* 'animal' + **-IC**.

**enzyme** /'ɛnzʌɪm/ ● n. Biochemistry a substance produced by a living organism and acting as a catalyst to promote a specific biochemical reaction.
– DERIVATIVES **enzymatic** adj. **enzymic** adj. **enzymological** adj. **enzymologist** n. **enzymology** n.
– ORIGIN C19: Ger. *Enzym*, from mod. Gk *enzumos* 'leavened'.

**EOC** ● abbrev. (in the UK) Equal Opportunities Commission.

**Eocene** /'iːə(ʊ)siːn/ ● adj. Geology relating to or denoting the second epoch of the Tertiary period (between the Palaeocene and Oligocene epochs, 56.5 to 35.4 million years ago), a time when the first horses, bats, and whales appeared.
– ORIGIN C19: from Gk *ēōs* 'dawn' + *kainos* 'new'.

**eohippus** /ˌiːəʊ'hɪpəs/ ● n. (pl. **eohippuses**) former term for **HYRACOTHERIUM**.
– ORIGIN C19: from Gk *ēōs* 'dawn' + *hippos* 'horse'.

**eo ipso** /ˌeɪəʊ 'ɪpsəʊ/ ● adv. formal thereby.
– ORIGIN L., ablative of *id ipsum* 'the thing itself'.

**eolian** ● adj. US spelling of **AEOLIAN**.

**eolith** /'iːə(ʊ)lɪθ/ ● n. Archaeology a roughly chipped flint found in Tertiary strata, originally thought to be an early artefact but probably of natural origin.
– ORIGIN C19: from Gk *ēōs* 'dawn' + *lithos* 'stone'.

**eon** ● n. US and technical spelling of **AEON**.

**eosin** /'iːə(ʊ)sɪn/ ● n. a red fluorescent dye that is a bromine derivative of fluorescein.
– ORIGIN C19: from Gk *ēōs* 'dawn' + **-IN**[1].

**eosinophil** /ˌiːə(ʊ)'sɪnəfɪl/ ● n. Physiology a white blood cell containing granules that are readily stained by eosin.
– DERIVATIVES **eosinophilic** adj.

**eosinophilia** /ˌiːə(ʊ)ˌsɪnə'fɪlɪə/ ● n. Medicine an increase in the number of eosinophils in the blood.

**EOT** ● abbrev. **1** Computing end of tape. **2** Telecommunications end of transmission.

**-eous** ● suffix (forming adjectives) resembling; displaying the nature of: *aqueous*.
– ORIGIN from the L. suffix *-eus* + **-OUS**.

**EP** ● abbrev. **1** electroplate. **2** European Parliament. **3** extended-play (of a record or compact disc). **4** extreme pressure (used in grading lubricants).

**Ep.** ● abbrev. Epistle.

**ep-** /ɛp, ɪp, iːp/ ● prefix variant spelling of **EPI-** shortened before a vowel or *h* (as in *eparch*, *ephod*).

**e.p.** ● abbrev. Chess en passant.

**EPA** ● abbrev. (in the US) Environmental Protection Agency.

**epact** /'iːpakt/ ● n. the number of days by which the solar year exceeds the lunar year.
– ORIGIN C16: from Fr. *épacte*, via late L. from Gk *epaktai* (*hēmerai*) 'intercalated (days)'.

**eparch** /'ɛpɑːk/ ● n. the chief bishop of an eparchy.
– ORIGIN C17: from Gk *eparkhos*, from *epi* 'above' + *arkhos* 'ruler'.

**eparchy** /'ɛpɑːki/ ● n. (pl. **-ies**) a province of the Orthodox Church.
– ORIGIN C18: from Gk *eparkhia*, from *eparkhos* (see **EPARCH**).

**épater** /eɪ'pateɪ, French epate/ ● v. (in phr. **épater les bourgeois**) shock people regarded as conventional or complacent.
– ORIGIN from Fr.

**epaulette** /'ɛpəlɛt, -pɔːl-, ˌɛpə'lɛt/ (US also **epaulet**) ● n. an ornamental shoulder piece on a military uniform.
– ORIGIN C18: from Fr. *épaulette*, dimin. of *épaule* 'shoulder'.

**epaxial** /ɛ'paksɪəl/ ● adj. Anatomy & Zoology situated on the dorsal side of an axis.

**épée** /'eɪpeɪ, 'ɛp-/ ● n. a sharp-pointed duelling sword, used, with the end blunted, in fencing.
– DERIVATIVES **épéeist** n.
– ORIGIN C19: Fr., 'sword'.

**epenthesis** /ɛ'pɛnθɪsɪs/ ● n. (pl. **epentheses** /-siːz/) the insertion of a sound or an unetymological letter within a word, e.g. the *b* in *thimble*.

– DERIVATIVES **epenthetic** adj.
– ORIGIN C16: via late L. from Gk, from *epentithenai* 'insert'.

**epergne** /ɪˈpəːn/ ● n. an ornamental centrepiece for a dining table, holding fruit or flowers.
– ORIGIN C18: perh. an alt. form of Fr. *épargne* 'economy'.

**epexegesis** /ɛˌpɛksɪˈdʒiːsɪs/ ● n. (pl. **epexegeses** /-siːz/) the addition of words to clarify meaning.
– DERIVATIVES **epexegetic** /-ˈdʒɛtɪk/ adj. **epexegetical** adj. **epexegetically** adv.
– ORIGIN C16: from Gk *epexēgēsis*.

**Eph.** ● abbrev. Epistle to the Ephesians (in biblical references).

**ephebe** /ɛˈfiːb, ɪ-, ˈɛfiːb/ ● n. (in ancient Greece) a young man of 18–20 years undergoing military training.
– DERIVATIVES **ephebic** adj.
– ORIGIN via L. from Gk *ephēbos*, from *epi* 'near to' + *hēbē* 'early manhood'.

**ephedra** /ɛˈfɛdrə/ ● n. an evergreen trailing or climbing shrub of warm arid regions, some kinds of which are a source of the drug ephedrine. [Genus *Ephedra*.]
– ORIGIN mod. L., from L., 'equisetum' (which it resembles).

**ephedrine** /ˈɛfədriːn/ ● n. Medicine an alkaloid drug which causes constriction of the blood vessels and widening of the bronchial passages and is used to relieve asthma and hay fever.
– ORIGIN C19: from **EPHEDRA** + **-INE**[4].

**ephemera** /ɪˈfɛm(ə)rə, -ˈfiːm-/ ● pl. n. items of short-lived interest or usefulness.
– DERIVATIVES **ephemerist** n.
– ORIGIN C16 (orig. (as sing. n.) denoting a plant said to last only one day, or an insect with a short lifespan): pl. of *ephemeron*, from Gk, neut. of *ephēmeros* 'lasting only a day'.

**ephemeral** ● adj. lasting or living for a very short time. ➤(chiefly of plants) having a very short life cycle.
– DERIVATIVES **ephemerality** n. **ephemerally** adv. **ephemeralness** n.

**ephemeris** /ɪˈfɛm(ə)rɪs, -ˈfiːm-/ ● n. (pl. **ephemerides** /ˌɛfɪˈmɛrɪdiːz/) Astronomy & Astrology a table of the calculated positions of a celestial object at regular intervals throughout a period.
– ORIGIN C16: from L., from Gk *ephēmeros* 'lasting only a day'.

**ephemeris time** ● n. time on a scale defined by the orbital period rather than the axial rotation of the earth.

**Ephemeroptera** /ɪˌfɛməˈrɒptərə, -ˌfiːm-/ ● pl. n. Entomology an order of insects that comprises the mayflies.
– DERIVATIVES **ephemeropteran** n. & adj.
– ORIGIN mod. L., from *Ephemera* (genus name) + *pteron* 'wing'.

**ephod** /ˈiːfɒd, ˈɛfɒd/ ● n. (in ancient Israel) a sleeveless garment worn by Jewish priests.
– ORIGIN ME: from Heb. *'ēpōḏ*.

**ephor** /ˈɛfɔː/ ● n. (in ancient Greece) one of five senior Spartan magistrates.
– DERIVATIVES **ephorate** n.
– ORIGIN from Gk *ephoros* 'overseer'.

**epi-** (also **ep-**) ● prefix **1** upon: *epigraph*. **2** above: *epicotyl*. **3** in addition: *epiphenomenon*.
– ORIGIN from Gk *epi* 'upon, near to, in addition'.

**epiblast** /ˈɛpɪblast/ ● n. Embryology the outermost layer of an embryo before it differentiates into ectoderm and mesoderm.

**epic** ● n. a long poem narrating the deeds of heroic or legendary figures or the past history of a nation. ➤a long film, book, or other work portraying heroic deeds or covering an extended period of time. ● adj. of, relating to, or characteristic of an epic or epics.
– DERIVATIVES **epical** adj. **epically** adv.
– ORIGIN C16 (as adj.): via L. from Gk *epikos*, from *epos* 'word, song'.

**epicanthic fold** ● n. a fold of skin from the upper eyelid covering the inner angle of the eye, typical in many peoples of eastern Asia.

**epicardium** /ˌɛpɪˈkɑːdɪəm/ ● n. Anatomy a serous membrane that forms the innermost layer of the pericardium.
– DERIVATIVES **epicardial** adj.
– ORIGIN C19: from **EPI-** + Gk *kardia* 'heart', on the pattern of *pericardium*.

**epicedium** /ˌɛpɪˈsiːdɪəm/ ● n. (pl. **epicedia** /-dɪə/) formal a funeral ode.
– DERIVATIVES **epicedian** adj.
– ORIGIN C16: from L., from Gk *epikēdeion*, neut. of *epokēdeios* 'of a funeral'.

**epicene** /ˈɛpɪsiːn/ ● adj. **1** having characteristics of both sexes or no characteristics of either sex. **2** effete. ● n. an epicene person.
– ORIGIN ME: via late L. from Gk *epikoinos* (based on *koinos* 'common').

**epicentre** (US **epicenter**) ● n. the point on the earth's surface vertically above the focus of an earthquake.
– DERIVATIVES **epicentral** adj.
– ORIGIN C19: from Gk *epikentros* 'situated on a centre'.

**epicondyle** /ˌɛpɪˈkɒndɪl/ ● n. Anatomy a protuberance on the condyle of a long bone, especially the humerus.
– DERIVATIVES **epicondylar** adj.
– ORIGIN C19: from Fr. *épicondyle*, mod. L. *epicondylus*.

**epicondylitis** /ˌɛpɪkɒndɪˈlʌɪtɪs/ ● n. Medicine inflammation of tendons surrounding an epicondyle.

**epicontinental** ● adj. denoting those areas of sea or ocean overlying the continental shelf.

**epicotyl** /ˌɛpɪˈkɒtɪl/ ● n. Botany the region of an embryo or seedling stem above the cotyledon.

**epicritic** /ˌɛpɪˈkrɪtɪk/ ● adj. Physiology relating to or denoting sensory nerve fibres in the skin which are capable of fine discrimination of touch or temperature stimuli.
– ORIGIN C20: from Gk *epikritikos* 'giving judgement over' + **-IC**.

**epicure** /ˈɛpɪkjʊə/ ● n. a person who takes particular pleasure in fine food and drink.
– DERIVATIVES **epicurism** n.
– ORIGIN ME: via med. L. from Gk *Epikouros* 'Epicurus' (see **EPICUREAN**).

**Epicurean** /ˌɛpɪkjʊ(ə)ˈriːən/ ● n. **1** a disciple or student of the Greek philosopher Epicurus (341–270 BC), who taught that pleasure, particularly mental pleasure, was the highest good. **2** (**epicurean**) an epicure. ● adj. **1** of or concerning Epicurus or his ideas. **2** (**epicurean**) relating to or suitable for an epicure.
– DERIVATIVES **Epicureanism** n.

**epicycle** /ˈɛpɪˌsʌɪk(ə)l/ ● n. Geometry a small circle whose centre moves round the circumference of a larger one.
– DERIVATIVES **epicyclic** adj.
– ORIGIN ME: from OFr., or via late L. from Gk *epikuklos*.

**epicycloid** /ˌɛpɪˈsʌɪklɔɪd/ ● n. Mathematics a curve traced by a point on the circumference of a circle rolling on the exterior of another circle.
– DERIVATIVES **epicycloidal** adj.

**epideictic** /ˌɛpɪˈdeɪktɪk, -ˈdʌɪktɪk/ ● adj. formal characterized by or designed to display rhetorical or oratorical skill.
– ORIGIN C18: from Gk *epideiktikos*.

**epidemic** ● n. a widespread occurrence of an infectious disease in a community at a particular time. ➤a sudden, widespread occurrence of an undesirable phenomenon. ● adj. relating to or of the nature of an epidemic.
– ORIGIN C17 (as adj.): from Fr. *épidémique*, from *épidémie*, via late L. from Gk *epidēmia* 'prevalence of disease'.

**epidemiology** /ˌɛpɪdiːmɪˈɒlədʒi/ ● n. the branch of medicine concerned with the incidence and distribution of diseases and other factors relating to health.
– DERIVATIVES **epidemiological** adj. **epidemiologist** n.
– ORIGIN C19: from Gk *epidēmia* 'prevalence of disease' + **-LOGY**.

**epidermis** /ˌɛpɪˈdəːmɪs/ ● n. **1** Zoology & Anatomy the surface epithelium of the skin of an animal, overlying the dermis. **2** Botany the outer layer of tissue in a plant.
– DERIVATIVES **epidermal** adj. **epidermic** adj. **epidermoid** adj.
– ORIGIN C17: via late L. from Gk, from *epi* 'upon' + *derma* 'skin'.

**epidiascope** /ˌɛpɪˈdʌɪəskəʊp/ ● n. an optical projector capable of giving images of both opaque and transparent objects.

**epididymis** /ˌɛpɪˈdɪdɪmɪs/ ● **n.** (pl. **epididymides** /ˌɛpɪdɪˈdɪmɪdiːz/) Anatomy a highly convoluted duct behind the testis, along which sperm passes to the vas deferens.
– DERIVATIVES **epididymal** adj.
– ORIGIN C17: from Gk *epididumis*, from *epi* 'upon' + *didumos* 'testicle'.

**epidote** /ˈɛpɪdəʊt/ ● **n.** a lustrous yellow-green mineral consisting of a silicate of calcium, aluminium, and iron.
– ORIGIN C19: from Fr. *épidote*, from Gk *epididonai* 'give additionally' (because of the length of the crystals).

**epidural** /ˌɛpɪˈdjʊər(ə)l/ Anatomy & Medicine ● **adj.** on or around the dura mater of the spinal cord. ● **n.** an anaesthetic introduced into the space around the dura mater, used especially in childbirth.

**epifauna** ● **n.** Ecology animals living on the bed of a body of water or on other submerged surfaces. Compare with **INFAUNA**.
– DERIVATIVES **epifaunal** adj.

**epigastrium** /ˌɛpɪˈgastrɪəm/ ● **n.** (pl. **epigastria** /-rɪə/) Anatomy the part of the upper abdomen immediately over the stomach.
– DERIVATIVES **epigastric** adj.
– ORIGIN C17: via late L. from Gk *epigastrion*, neut. of *epigastrios* 'over the belly'.

**epigeal** /ˌɛpɪˈdʒiːəl/ ● **adj.** Botany growing or occurring above the ground surface. Compare with **HYPOGEAL**.
– ORIGIN C19: from Gk *epigeios* + **-AL**.

**epigene** /ˈɛpɪdʒiːn/ ● **adj.** Geology taking place or produced on the surface of the earth.
– ORIGIN C19: from Fr. *épigène*, from Gk *epigenēs*, from *epi* 'upon' + *genēs* (see **-GEN**).

**epigenesis** /ˌɛpɪˈdʒɛnɪsɪs/ ● **n.** Biology the progressive development of an embryo from an undifferentiated egg cell.

**epigenetic** /ˌɛpɪdʒɪˈnɛtɪk/ ● **adj.** **1** Biology resulting from external rather than genetic influences. **2** Biology of or relating to epigenesis. **3** Geology formed later than the surrounding or underlying rocks.
– DERIVATIVES **epigenetically** adv. **epigeneticist** n.

**epiglottis** /ˌɛpɪˈglɒtɪs/ ● **n.** a flap of cartilage at the root of the tongue, which is depressed during swallowing to cover the opening of the windpipe.
– DERIVATIVES **epiglottal** adj. **epiglottic** adj.
– ORIGIN ME: from Gk *epiglōttis*, from *epi* 'upon, near to' + *glōtta* 'tongue'.

**epigone** /ˈɛpɪgəʊn/ ● **n.** (pl. **epigones** or **epigoni** /ɪˈpɪgənʌɪ, ɛ-/) a less distinguished follower or imitator.
– ORIGIN C18: pl. from Fr. *épigones* and L. *epigoni*, from Gk *epigonoi* 'those born afterwards'.

**epigram** /ˈɛpɪgram/ ● **n.** a concise and witty saying or remark. ➤ a short witty poem.
– DERIVATIVES **epigrammatic** adj. **epigrammatically** adv. **epigrammatist** n. **epigrammatize** (also **-ise**) v.
– ORIGIN ME: from Fr. *épigramme*, or L. *epigramma*, from Gk, from *epi* 'upon, in addition' + *gramma* (see **-GRAM**[1]).

**epigraph** /ˈɛpɪgrɑːf/ ● **n.** **1** an inscription on a building, statue, or coin. **2** a short quotation or saying at the beginning of a book or chapter, intended to suggest its theme.
– ORIGIN C16: from Gk *epigraphē*, from *epigraphein* 'write on'.

**epigraphy** /ɪˈpɪgrəfi, ɛ-/ ● **n.** the study and interpretation of ancient inscriptions.
– DERIVATIVES **epigrapher** n. **epigraphic** adj. **epigraphical** adj. **epigraphically** adv. **epigraphist** n.

**epigynous** /ɪˈpɪdʒɪnəs, ɛ-/ ● **adj.** Botany (of a plant or flower) having the ovary enclosed in the receptacle, with the stamens and other floral parts situated above. Compare with **HYPOGYNOUS** and **PERIGYNOUS**.
– DERIVATIVES **epigyny** n.

**epilation** /ˌɛpɪˈleɪʃ(ə)n/ ● **n.** the removal of hair by the roots.
– DERIVATIVES **epilate** v. **epilator** n.
– ORIGIN C19: from Fr. *épiler*, from *é-* (expressing removal) + L. *pilus* 'strand of hair'.

**epilepsy** /ˈɛpɪlɛpsi/ ● **n.** a neurological disorder marked by sudden recurrent episodes of sensory disturbance, loss of consciousness, or convulsions.
– DERIVATIVES **epileptic** adj. & n.
– ORIGIN C16: from Fr. *épilepsie*, or via late L. from Gk *epilēpsia*, from *epilambanein* 'seize, attack'.

**epilimnion** /ˌɛpɪˈlɪmnɪən/ ● **n.** (pl. **epilimnia** /-nɪə/) the upper layer of water in a stratified lake. Compare with **HYPOLIMNION**.
– ORIGIN C20: from **EPI-** + Gk *limnion* (dimin. of *limnē* 'lake').

**epilogue** /ˈɛpɪlɒg/ (US also **epilog**) ● **n.** a section or speech at the end of a book or play serving as a comment on or a conclusion to what has happened.
– ORIGIN ME: from Fr. *épilogue*, via L. from Gk *epilogos*, from *epi* 'in addition' + *logos* 'speech'.

**epimer** /ˈɛpɪmə/ ● **n.** Chemistry each of two isomers with different configurations of atoms about one of several asymmetric carbon atoms present.
– DERIVATIVES **epimeric** /-ˈmɛrɪk/ adj. **epimerism** /ɪˈpɪm-, ɛ-/ n.

**epimerize** /ɪˈpɪmərʌɪz, ɛ-/ (also **-ise**) ● **v.** Chemistry convert from one epimeric form into the other.

**epinephrine** /ˌɛpɪˈnɛfrɪn, -riːn/ ● **n.** Biochemistry the hormone adrenalin.
– ORIGIN C19: from **EPI-** + Gk *nephros* 'kidney' + **-INE**[4].

**epinician** /ˌɛpɪˈnɪsɪən/ ● **adj.** denoting an ancient Greek lyric poem celebrating a victory.
– ORIGIN C17: from Gk *epinikion*, neut. (used as n.) of *epinikios* 'relating to victory', + **-AN**.

**epiphany** /ɪˈpɪf(ə)ni, ɛ-/ ● **n.** (pl. **-ies**) **1** (**Epiphany**) the manifestation of Christ to the Gentiles as represented by the Magi (Matthew 2: 1-12). ➤ the festival commemorating this on 6 January. **2** a moment of sudden and great revelation.
– DERIVATIVES **epiphanic** /ɛpɪˈfanɪk/ adj.
– ORIGIN ME: from Gk *epiphainein* 'reveal'; sense 1 is via OFr. *epiphanie* and eccles. L. *epiphania*.

**epiphenomenon** /ˌɛpɪfəˈnɒmɪnən/ ● **n.** (pl. **epiphenomena** /-nə/) **1** Medicine a secondary symptom, occurring simultaneously with a disease or condition but not directly related to it. **2** a mental state regarded as a by-product of brain activity.
– DERIVATIVES **epiphenomenal** adj.

**epiphora** /ɪˈpɪf(ə)rə/ ● **n.** **1** Medicine excessive watering of the eye. **2** Rhetoric another term for **EPISTROPHE**.
– ORIGIN C16: via L. from Gk *epi* 'upon' + *pherein* 'to carry'.

**epiphysis** /ɪˈpɪfɪsɪs, ɛ-/ ● **n.** (pl. **epiphyses**) Anatomy the end part of a long bone, initially growing separately from the shaft. Compare with **DIAPHYSIS**.
– ORIGIN C17: mod. L., from Gk *epiphusis*, from *epi-* 'in addition' + *phusis* 'growth'.

**epiphyte** /ˈɛpɪfʌɪt/ ● **n.** Botany a plant that grows non-parasitically on a tree or other plant.
– DERIVATIVES **epiphytal** /-ˈfʌɪt(ə)l/ adj. **epiphytic** /-ˈfɪtɪk/ adj.
– ORIGIN C19: from **EPI-** + Gk *phuton* 'plant'.

**EPIRB** ● **abbrev.** emergency position-indicating radio beacon.

**episcopacy** /ɪˈpɪskəpəsi, ɛ-/ ● **n.** (pl. **-ies**) government of a Church by bishops. ➤ (**the episcopacy**) the bishops of a region or church collectively.
– ORIGIN C17: from eccles. L. *episcopatus* 'episcopate'.

**episcopal** /ɪˈpɪskəp(ə)l, ɛ-/ ● **adj.** of a bishop or bishops. ➤ (of a Church) governed by or having bishops.
– DERIVATIVES **episcopalism** n. **episcopally** adv.
– ORIGIN ME: from Fr. *épiscopal* or eccles. L. *episcopalis*, from *episcopus* 'bishop', from Gk *episkopos* (see **BISHOP**).

**Episcopal Church** ● **n.** the Anglican Church in Scotland and the US.

**episcopalian** /ɪˌpɪskəˈpeɪlɪən, ɛ-/ ● **adj.** of or advocating episcopacy. ➤ of or belonging to an episcopal or (**Episcopalian**) the Episcopal Church. ● **n.** an adherent of episcopacy. ➤ (**Episcopalian**) a member of the Episcopal Church.
– DERIVATIVES **episcopalianism** n.

**episcopate** /ɪˈpɪskəpət, ɛ-/ ● **n.** the office or term of office of a bishop. ➤ (**the episcopate**) the bishops of a church or region collectively.

**episcope** /ˈɛpɪskəʊp/ ● **n.** an optical projector which gives images of opaque objects.

**episematic** /ˌɛpɪsɪˈmatɪk/ ● **adj.** Zoology (of coloration or markings) serving to help recognition by animals of the same species.
– ORIGIN C19: from **EPI-** + Gk *sēma* 'sign' + **-ATIC**.

**episiotomy** /ɪˌpɪsɪˈɒtəmi, ɛ-/ ● **n.** (pl. **-ies**) a surgical cut made at the opening of the vagina during childbirth, to aid a difficult delivery.
– ORIGIN C19: from Gk *epision* 'pubic region' + **-TOMY**.

**episode** ● **n.** an event or a group of events occurring as part of a sequence. ➤each of the separate instalments into which a serialized story or radio or television programme is divided. ➤Music a passage containing distinct material or introducing a new subject. ➤a section between two choric songs in Greek tragedy.
– ORIGIN C17: from Gk *epeisodion*, neut. of *epeisodios* 'coming in besides'.

**episodic** /ˌɛpɪˈsɒdɪk/ ● **adj. 1** occurring as or presented in episodes. **2** occurring at irregular intervals.
– DERIVATIVES **episodically** adv.

**episome** /ˈɛpɪsəʊm/ ● **n.** Microbiology a genetic element inside some bacterial cells that can replicate independently of the host.

**epistasis** /ɪˈpɪstəsɪs/ ● **n.** Genetics the suppression by a gene of the effect of another gene.
– DERIVATIVES **epistatic** /ˌɛpɪˈstatɪk/ adj.
– ORIGIN C19: from Gk, lit. 'stoppage'.

**epistaxis** /ˌɛpɪˈstaksɪs/ ● **n.** Medicine bleeding from the nose.
– ORIGIN C18: mod. L., from Gk, from *epistazein* 'bleed from the nose'.

**epistemology** /ɪˌpɪstɪˈmɒlədʒi, ɛ-/ ● **n.** Philosophy the theory of knowledge, especially with regard to its methods, validity, and scope.
– DERIVATIVES **epistemic** adj. **epistemically** adv. **epistemological** adj. **epistemologically** adv. **epistemologist** n.
– ORIGIN C19: from Gk *epistēmē* 'knowledge'.

**epistle** /ɪˈpɪs(ə)l/ ● **n.** formal or humorous a letter. ➤(**Epistle**) a book of the New Testament in the form of a letter from an Apostle.
– ORIGIN OE, via L. from Gk *epistolē*, from *epistellein* 'send news'.

**epistolary** /ɪˈpɪst(ə)ˌləri/ ● **adj.** relating to or denoting the writing of letters or literary works in the form of letters.

**epistrophe** /ɪˈpɪstrəfi, ɛ-/ ● **n.** the repetition of a word at the end of successive clauses or sentences.
– ORIGIN C16: from Gk *epistrophē*, from *epistrephein* 'turn around'.

**epistyle** /ˈɛpɪstʌɪl/ ● **n.** Architecture an architrave.
– ORIGIN C16: from Fr. *épistyle* or via L., from Gk *epistulion*, from *epi* 'upon' + *stulos* 'pillar'.

**epitaph** /ˈɛpɪtɑːf, -taf/ ● **n.** words written in memory of a person who has died, especially as an inscription on a tombstone.
– ORIGIN ME: from OFr. *epitaphe*, via L. from Gk *epitaphion* 'funeral oration', neut. of *ephitaphios* 'over or at a tomb'.

**epitaxy** /ˈɛpɪtaksi/ ● **n.** Crystallography the growth of crystals on a crystalline substrate that determines their orientation.
– DERIVATIVES **epitaxial** adj.
– ORIGIN 1930s: from Fr. *épitaxie*, from Gk *epi* 'upon' + *taxis* 'arrangement'.

**epithalamium** /ˌɛpɪθəˈleɪmɪəm/ ● **n.** (pl. **epithalamiums** or **epithalamia**) a song or poem celebrating a marriage.
– DERIVATIVES **epithalamic** /-ˈlamɪk/ adj.
– ORIGIN C16: via L. from Gk *epithalamion*, from *epi* 'upon' + *thalamos* 'bridal chamber'.

**epithelium** /ˌɛpɪˈθiːlɪəm/ ● **n.** (pl. **epithelia** /-lɪə/) Anatomy the thin tissue forming the outer layer of the body's surface and lining the alimentary canal and other hollow structures, especially that part derived from the embryonic ectoderm and endoderm. Compare with **ENDOTHELIUM**.
– DERIVATIVES **epithelial** adj.
– ORIGIN C18: mod. L., from **EPI-** + Gk *thēlē* 'teat'.

**epithet** /ˈɛpɪθɛt/ ● **n.** an adjective or phrase expressing a quality or attribute of the person or thing mentioned.
– DERIVATIVES **epithetic** adj. **epithetical** adj. **epithetically** adv.
– ORIGIN C16: from Fr. *épithète*, or via L. from Gk *epitheton*, neut. of *epithetos* 'attributed', from *epitithenai* 'add'.

**epitome** /ɪˈpɪtəmi, ɛ-/ ● **n. 1** (**the epitome of**) a person or thing that is a perfect example of a quality or type. **2** a summary of a written work.
– DERIVATIVES **epitomist** n.
– ORIGIN C16: via L. from Gk *epitomē*, from *epitemnein* 'abridge'.

**epitomize** (also **-ise**) ● **v. 1** be a perfect example of. **2** archaic summarize (a written work).
– DERIVATIVES **epitomization** n.

**epitope** /ˈɛpɪtəʊp/ ● **n.** Biochemistry the part of an antigen molecule to which an antibody attaches itself.
– ORIGIN 1960s: from **EPI-** + Gk *topos* 'place'.

**epizoic** /ˌɛpɪˈzəʊɪk/ ● **adj.** Biology living non-parasitically on the exterior of a living animal.
– DERIVATIVES **epizoite** /ɛpɪˈzəʊʌɪt/ n.
– ORIGIN C19: from **EPI-** + Gk *zōion* 'animal' + **-IC**.

**epizootic** /ˌɛpɪzəʊˈɒtɪk/ ● **adj.** (of a disease) temporarily prevalent and widespread in an animal population. ● **n.** an outbreak of such a disease.
– ORIGIN C18: from Fr. *épizootique*, from *épizootie*, from Gk *epi* 'upon' + *zōion* 'animal'.

**e pluribus unum** /eɪ ˌplʊərɪbʊs ˈjuːnʊm/ ● **n.** one out of many (the motto of the US).
– ORIGIN from L.

**EPNS** ● **abbrev.** electroplated nickel silver.

**EPO** ● **abbrev. 1** erythropoietin (used especially when isolated as a drug). **2** European Patent Office.

**epoch** /ˈiːpɒk, ˈɛpɒk/ ● **n.** a period of time marked by particular events or characteristics. ➤Geology a division of time that is a subdivision of a period and is itself subdivided into ages, corresponding to a series. ➤Astronomy an arbitrarily fixed date relative to which planetary or stellar measurements are expressed.
– DERIVATIVES **epochal** adj.
– ORIGIN C17 (in the L. form *epocha*): from mod. L. *epocha*, from Gk *epokhē* 'stoppage, fixed point of time', from *epekhein* 'stop, take up a position'.

**epoch-making** ● **adj.** significant; historic.

**epode** /ˈɛpəʊd/ ● **n. 1** a form of lyric poem written in couplets, in which a long line is followed by a shorter one. **2** the third section of an ancient Greek choral ode, or of one division of such an ode.
– ORIGIN C17: from Fr. *épode*, or via L. *epodos*, from Gk *epōidos*, from *epi* 'upon' + *ōidē* (see **ODE**).

**eponym** /ˈɛpənɪm/ ● **n.** a word or name derived from the name of a person. ➤a person after whom a discovery, invention, place, etc. is named.
– DERIVATIVES **eponymous** adj.
– ORIGIN C19: from Gk *epōnumos* 'given as a name, giving one's name to someone or something', from *epi* 'upon' + *onoma* 'name'.

**EPOS** /ˈiːpɒz, ˈiːpɒs/ ● **abbrev.** electronic point of sale.

**epoxide** /ɪˈpɒksʌɪd/ ● **n.** Chemistry an organic compound whose molecule contains a three-membered ring involving an oxygen atom and two carbon atoms.
– ORIGIN 1930s: from **EPI-** + **OXIDE**.

**epoxy** /ɪˈpɒksi, ɛ-/ ● **n.** (pl. **-ies**) (also **epoxy resin**) an adhesive, plastic, paint, etc. made from a class of synthetic polymers containing epoxide groups. ● **v.** (**-ies**, **-ied**) glue using an epoxy.
– ORIGIN C20: from **EPI-** + **OXY-**[2].

**EPROM** /ˈiːprɒm/ ● **n.** Electronics a read-only memory whose contents can be erased by ultraviolet light or other means and reprogrammed using a pulsed voltage.
– ORIGIN 1970s: acronym from *erasable programmable ROM*.

**eps** ● **abbrev.** earnings per share.

**epsilon** /ˈɛpsɪlɒn, ɛpˈsʌɪlɒn/ ● **n.** the fifth letter of the Greek alphabet (Ε, ε), transliterated as 'e'. ➤[as modifier] denoting the fifth in a series of items or categories.

– ORIGIN Gk, 'bare or simple E', from *psilos* 'bare'.

**Epsom salts** ● pl. n. crystals of hydrated magnesium sulphate used as a purgative.
– ORIGIN C18: named after the town of Epsom in Surrey, where the salts were first found occurring naturally.

**EPSRC** ● abbrev. (in the UK) Engineering and Physical Sciences Research Council.

**Epstein–Barr virus** (abbrev.: **EBV**) ● n. Medicine a herpesvirus causing glandular fever and associated with certain cancers.
– ORIGIN 1960s: named after Brit. and Ir. virologists Michael A. *Epstein* and Y. M. *Barr*.

**epyllion** /ɪˈpɪlɪən, ɛ-/ ● n. (pl. **epyllia**) a narrative poem resembling an epic but of shorter extent.
– ORIGIN C19: from Gk *epullion*, dimin. of *epos* 'word, song', from *eipein* 'say'.

**equable** /ˈɛkwəb(ə)l/ ● adj. **1** calm and even-tempered. **2** not varying or fluctuating greatly.
– DERIVATIVES **equability** n. **equably** adv.
– ORIGIN C17 (in the sense 'fair, equitable'): from L. *aequabilis*, from *aequare* (see **EQUATE**).

**equal** ● adj. **1** being the same in quantity, size, degree, value, or status. ➤ evenly or fairly balanced: *an equal contest*. **2** (**equal to something**) having the ability or resources to meet a challenge. ● n. a person or thing that is equal to another. ● v. (**equalled**, **equalling**; US **equaled**, **equaling**) be equal or equivalent to. ➤ match or rival.
– ORIGIN ME: from L. *aequalis*, from *aequus* 'even, level, equal'.

**equalitarian** /ɪˌkwɒlɪˈtɛːrɪən, iː-/ ● n. another term for **EGALITARIAN**.
– DERIVATIVES **equalitarianism** n.

**equality** ● n. **1** the state of being equal. **2** Mathematics a symbolic expression of the fact that two quantities are equal; an equation.
– ORIGIN ME: via OFr. from L. *aequalitas*, from *aequalis* (see **EQUAL**).

**equalize** (also **-ise**) ● v. make or become equal. ➤ level the score in a match by scoring a goal.
– DERIVATIVES **equalization** n.
– ORIGIN C16: from **EQUAL** + **-IZE**, partly suggested by Fr. *égaliser*.

**equalizer** (also **-iser**) ● n. **1** a thing that has an equalizing effect. ➤ a goal that levels the score in a match. **2** N. Amer. informal a weapon, especially a gun. **3** Electronics a passive network designed to modify a frequency response, especially to compensate for distortion.

**equally** ● adv. **1** in an equal manner. **2** in amounts or parts that are equal. **3** to an equal degree.

**equals sign** (also **equal sign**) ● n. the symbol =.

**equal temperament** ● n. see **TEMPERAMENT** (sense 2).

**equanimity** /ˌɛkwəˈnɪmɪti, iː-/ ● n. calmness; composure.
– DERIVATIVES **equanimous** /ɪˈkwanɪməs, iː-/ adj.
– ORIGIN C17: from L. *aequanimitas*, from *aequus* 'equal' + *animus* 'mind'.

**equant** /ˈiːkwənt/ ● n. Astronomy, historical (in the Ptolemaic system) an imaginary circle that reconciles the planetary movements with the hypothesis of uniform circular motion. ● adj. **1** Astronomy, historical relating to or denoting an equant. **2** Geology (of a crystal or particle) having its different diameters approximately equal.
– ORIGIN C16: from L. *aequant-*, *aequare* 'make equal'.

**equate** /ɪˈkweɪt/ ● v. consider (one thing) as equal or equivalent to another. ➤ (**equate to/with**) be the same as or equivalent to. ➤ cause to be equal.
– DERIVATIVES **equatable** adj.
– ORIGIN ME: from L. *aequat-*, *aequare* 'make level or equal', from *aequus* (see **EQUAL**).

**equation** /ɪˈkweɪʒ(ə)n/ ● n. **1** the process of equating one thing with another. **2** Mathematics a statement that the values of two mathematical expressions are equal (indicated by the sign =). **3** Chemistry a symbolic representation of the changes which occur in a chemical reaction, expressed in terms of the formulae of the molecules or other species involved.
– PHRASES **equation of the first** (or **second** etc.) **order** Mathematics an equation involving only the first derivative, second derivative, etc.
– ORIGIN ME: from L. *aequatio(n-)*, from *aequare* (see **EQUATE**).

**equation of state** ● n. Chemistry an equation showing the relationship between the values of the pressure, volume, and temperature of a quantity of a particular substance.

**equation of time** ● n. the difference between mean solar time (as shown by clocks) and apparent time (indicated by sundials), which varies with the time of year.

**equator** /ɪˈkweɪtə/ ● n. a line notionally drawn on the earth equidistant from the poles, dividing the earth into northern and southern hemispheres and constituting the parallel of latitude 0°. ➤ Astronomy short for **CELESTIAL EQUATOR**.
– ORIGIN ME: from med. L. *aequator*, in the phr. *circulus aequator diei et noctis* 'circle equalizing day and night', from L. *aequare* (see **EQUATE**).

**equatorial** /ˌɛkwəˈtɔːrɪəl/ ● adj. of, at, or near the equator.
– DERIVATIVES **equatorially** adv.

**Equatorial Guinean** /ˈgɪnɪən/ ● n. a native or inhabitant of the West African country of Equatorial Guinea. ● adj. of or relating to Equatorial Guinea or its people.

**equatorial mount** (also **equatorial mounting**) ● n. Astronomy a telescope mounting with one axis aligned to the celestial pole, which allows the movement of celestial objects to be followed by motion about this axis alone. Compare with **ALTAZIMUTH** (in sense 1).

**equatorial telescope** ● n. an astronomical telescope on an equatorial mount.

**equerry** /ɪˈkwɛri, ˈɛkwəri/ ● n. (pl. **-ies**) **1** an officer of the British royal household who attends members of the royal family. **2** historical an officer of the household of a prince or noble who had charge over the stables.
– ORIGIN C16 (formerly also as *esquiry*): from OFr. *esquierie* 'company of squires, prince's stables', from OFr. *esquier* 'esquire', perh. assoc. with L. *equus* 'horse'.

**eques** /ˈɛkweɪz/ singular form of **EQUITES**.

**equestrian** /ɪˈkwɛstrɪən, ɛ-/ ● adj. **1** of or relating to horse riding. **2** depicting or representing a person on horseback. ● n. (fem. **equestrienne** /ɪˌkwɛstrɪˈɛn/) a person on horseback.
– ORIGIN C17: from L. *equester* 'belonging to a horseman' (from *eques* 'horseman, knight', from *equus* 'horse') + **-IAN**.

**equestrianism** ● n. the skill or sport of horse riding.

**equi-** /ˈiːkwi, ˈɛkwi-/ ● comb. form equal; equally: *equidistant*.
– ORIGIN from L. *aequi-*, from *aequus* 'equal'.

**equiangular** ● adj. having equal angles.

**equiangular spiral** ● n. Geometry a spiral such that the angle between the tangent and the radius vector is the same for all points of the spiral.

**equid** /ˈɛkwɪd/ ● n. Zoology a mammal of the horse family (Equidae).
– ORIGIN C19: from mod. L. *Equidae*, from L. *equus* 'horse'.

**equidistant** ● adj. at equal distances.
– DERIVATIVES **equidistance** n. **equidistantly** adv.

**equifinal** /ˌɛkwɪˈfʌɪn(ə)l/ ● adj. having the same end or result.
– DERIVATIVES **equifinality** n. **equifinally** adv.

**equilateral** /ˌiːkwɪˈlat(ə)r(ə)l, ˌɛkwɪ-/ ● adj. having all its sides of the same length.
– ORIGIN C16: from Fr. *équilatéral* or late L. *aequilateralis*, from *aequilaterus* 'equal-sided' (based on L. *latus, later-* 'side').

**equilibrate** /ˌiːkwɪˈlʌɪbreɪt, ɪˈkwɪlɪ-, iːˈkwɪlɪ-/ ● v. bring into, attain, or maintain a state of equilibrium.
– DERIVATIVES **equilibration** n.
– ORIGIN C17: from late L. *aequilibrat-*, *aequilibrare* 'cause to balance', from *aequi-* 'equally' + *libra* 'balance'.

**equilibrist** /ɪˈkwɪlɪbrɪst, iːˈkwɪlɪ-, ˌiːkwɪˈlɪb-, ˌɛkwɪ-/ ● n. chiefly archaic an acrobat, especially a tightrope walker.
– ORIGIN C18: from **EQUILIBRIUM** + **-IST**.

**equilibrium** /ˌiːkwɪˈlɪbrɪəm, ˌɛkwɪ-/ ● n. (pl. **equilibria** /-rɪə/) **1** a state in which opposing forces or influences are balanced. ➤the state of being physically balanced. **2** a calm state of mind. **3** Chemistry a state in which a process and its reverse are occurring at equal rates so that no overall change is taking place. **4** Economics a situation in which supply and demand are matched and prices stable.
– DERIVATIVES **equilibrial** adj.
– ORIGIN C17: from L. *aequilibrium*, from *aequi-* 'equal' + *libra* 'balance'.

**equine** /ˈiːkwʌɪn, ˈɛ-/ ● adj. of, relating to, or affecting horses or other members of the horse family. ➤resembling a horse. ● n. a horse or other member of the horse family.
– ORIGIN C18: from L. *equinus*, from *equus* 'horse'.

**equinoctial** /ˌiːkwɪˈnɒkʃ(ə)l, ˌɛkwɪ-/ ● adj. **1** of, relating to, or at the time of the equinox. **2** at or near the equator. ● n. (also **equinoctial line**) another term for **CELESTIAL EQUATOR**.

**equinoctial point** ● n. either of two points at which the ecliptic cuts the celestial equator.

**equinoctial year** ● n. another term for **SOLAR YEAR**.

**equinox** /ˈiːkwɪnɒks, ˌɛkwɪ-/ ● n. the time or date (twice each year, about 22 September and 20 March) at which the sun crosses the celestial equator, when day and night are of equal length. ➤another term for **EQUINOCTIAL POINT**.
– ORIGIN ME: from OFr. *equinoxe* or L. *aequinoctium*, from *aequi-* 'equal' + *nox, noct-* 'night'.

**equip** ● v. (**equipped**, **equipping**) **1** supply with the items needed for a particular purpose. **2** prepare (someone) mentally for a particular situation or task.
– DERIVATIVES **equipper** n.
– ORIGIN C16: from Fr. *équiper*, prob. from ON *skipa* 'to man (a ship)', from *skip* 'ship'.

**equipage** /ˈɛkwɪpɪdʒ/ ● n. **1** archaic equipment. **2** historical a carriage and horses with attendants.
– ORIGIN C16 (denoting the crew of a ship): from Fr. *équipage*, from *équiper* 'equip'.

**equipartition** /ˌiːkwɪpɑːˈtɪʃ(ə)n/ (also **equipartition of energy**) ● n. Physics the principle that the kinetic energy of a system is equally distributed among its various degrees of freedom.
– DERIVATIVES **equipartitioned** adj.

**equipment** ● n. **1** the items needed for a particular purpose. **2** the process of supplying these items.
– ORIGIN C18: from Fr. *équipement*, from *équiper* 'equip'.

**equipoise** /ˈɛkwɪpɔɪz, ˈiːkwɪ-/ ● n. balance of forces or interests. ➤a counterbalance or balancing force. ● v. balance or counterbalance (something).
– ORIGIN C17: from **EQUI-** + the noun **POISE**[1], replacing the phr. *equal poise*.

**equipollent** /ˌiːkwɪˈpɒl(ə)nt, ˌɛkwɪ-/ archaic ● adj. equal in power, effect, or significance. ● n. an equipollent thing.
– DERIVATIVES **equipollence** n. **equipollency** n.
– ORIGIN ME: from OFr. *equipolent*, from L. *aequipollent-* 'of equal value', from *aequi-* 'equally' + *pollere* 'be strong'.

**equipotent** /ˌiːkwɪˈpəʊt(ə)nt, ˌɛkwɪ-/ ● adj. (chiefly of chemicals and medicines) having equal potencies.

**equipotential** ● adj. Physics (of a surface or line) composed of points all at the same potential. ● n. an equipotential line or surface.

**equiprobable** ● adj. Mathematics & Logic (of two or more things) equally probable.
– DERIVATIVES **equiprobability** n.

**equisetum** /ˌɛkwɪˈsiːtəm/ ● n. (pl. **equiseta** /-tə/ or **equisetums**) Botany a plant of a genus that comprises the horsetails. [Genus *Equisetum*.]
– ORIGIN mod. L., from L. *equus* 'horse' + *saeta* 'bristle'.

**equitable** /ˈɛkwɪtəb(ə)l/ ● adj. **1** fair and impartial. **2** Law valid in equity as distinct from law.
– DERIVATIVES **equitability** n. **equitableness** n. **equitably** adv.
– ORIGIN C16: from Fr. *équitable*, from *équité* (see **EQUITY**).

**equitant** /ˈɛkwɪt(ə)nt/ ● adj. Botany (of a leaf) having its base folded and partly enclosing the leaf next above it, as in an iris.
– ORIGIN C18: from L. *equitant-*, *equitare* 'ride a horse'.

**equitation** /ˌɛkwɪˈteɪʃ(ə)n/ ● n. formal the art and practice of horse riding.
– ORIGIN C16: from Fr. *équitation* or L. *equitatio(n-)*, from *equitare* 'ride a horse', from *eques, equit-* 'horseman' (from *equus* 'horse').

**equites** /ˈɛkwɪteɪz/ ● pl. n. (sing. **eques**) (in ancient Rome) a class of citizens originally forming the cavalry of the Roman army, who later came to acquire considerable wealth and political importance.
– ORIGIN L., pl. of *eques* 'horseman'.

**equity** /ˈɛkwɪti/ ● n. (pl. **-ies**) **1** the quality of being fair and impartial. **2** Law a branch of law that developed alongside common law in order to remedy some of its defects in fairness and justice. **3** (**Equity**) a trade union for professional actors. **4** the value of the shares issued by a company. ➤(**equities**) stocks and shares that carry no fixed interest. **5** the value of a mortgaged property after deduction of charges against it.
– ORIGIN ME: from OFr. *equité*, from L. *aequitas*, from *aequus* 'equal'.

**equity of redemption** ● n. Law the right of a mortgagor over the mortgaged property, especially the right to redeem the property on payment of the principal, interest, and costs.

**equivalence class** ● n. Mathematics & Logic the class of all members of a set that are in a given equivalence relation.

**equivalence relation** ● n. Mathematics & Logic a relation between elements of a set which is reflexive, symmetric, and transitive and which defines exclusive classes whose members bear the relation to each other and not to those in other classes.

**equivalent** /ɪˈkwɪv(ə)l(ə)nt/ ● adj. **1** equal in value, amount, function, meaning, etc. ➤(**equivalent to**) having the same or a similar effect as. **2** Mathematics belonging to the same equivalence class. ● n. **1** a person or thing that is equivalent to another. **2** (also **equivalent weight**) Chemistry the mass of a particular substance that can combine with or displace one gram of hydrogen or eight grams of oxygen, used in expressing combining powers of elements.
– DERIVATIVES **equivalence** n. **equivalency** n. **equivalently** adv.
– ORIGIN ME: via OFr. from late L. *aequivalent-*, *aequivalere* 'be of equal worth'.

**equivocal** /ɪˈkwɪvək(ə)l/ ● adj. unclear in meaning or intention; ambiguous.
– DERIVATIVES **equivocality** n. **equivocally** adv. **equivocalness** n.
– ORIGIN C16: from late L. *aequivocus*, from L. *aequus* 'equally' + *vocare* 'to call'.

**equivocate** /ɪˈkwɪvəkeɪt/ ● v. use ambiguous or evasive language.
– DERIVATIVES **equivocation** n. **equivocator** n. **equivocatory** adj.
– ORIGIN ME: from late L. *aequivocat-*, *aequivocare* 'call by the same name', from *aequivocus* (see **EQUIVOCAL**).

**equivoque** /ˈiːkwɪvəʊk, ˈɛkwɪ-/ (also **equivoke**) ● n. an ambiguous expression or pun. ➤ambiguity.
– ORIGIN ME: from OFr. *equivoque* or late L. *aequivocus* (see **EQUIVOCAL**).

**ER** ● abbrev. **1** N. Amer. emergency room. **2** King Edward. [from L. *Edwardus Rex*.] **3** Queen Elizabeth. [from L. *Elizabetha Regina*.]

**Er** ● symb. the chemical element erbium.

**er** ● exclam. expressing hesitation.
– ORIGIN C19: natural utterance.

**-er**[1] ● suffix **1** denoting a person, animal, or thing that performs a specified action or activity: *farmer*. **2** denoting a person or thing that has a specified attribute or form: *two-wheeler*. **3** denoting a person concerned with a specified thing or subject: *milliner*. **4** denoting a person belonging to a specified place or group: *city-dweller*.
– ORIGIN OE *-ere*, of Gmc origin.

**-er**[2] ● suffix forming the comparative of adjectives (as in *bigger*) and adverbs (as in *faster*).
– ORIGIN OE suffix *-ra* (adjectival), *-or* (adverbial), of Gmc

origin.

**-er**[3] ● **suffix** forming nouns used informally, usually by distortion of the root word: *footer.*

– ORIGIN prob. an extended use of **-ER**[1]; orig. Rugby School sl., later adopted at Oxford University.

**-er**[4] ● **suffix** forming frequentative verbs such as *patter.*

– ORIGIN OE *-erian, -rian*, of Gmc origin.

**-er**[5] ● **suffix** forming nouns: **1** such as *sampler.* Compare with **-AR**[1]. [ending corresponding to L. *-aris.*] ➤ such as *butler, danger.* [ending corresponding to L. *-arius, -arium.*] ➤ such as *border.* [ending corresponding (via OFr. *-eure*) to L. *-atura.*] ➤ such as *laver.* See **LAVER**[2]. [ending corresponding (via OFr. *-eor*) to L. *-atorium.*] **2** equivalent to **-OR**[1].

– ORIGIN via OFr. or Anglo-Norman Fr. (see above).

**-er**[6] ● **suffix** chiefly Law (forming nouns) denoting verbal action or a document effecting such action: *disclaimer.*

– ORIGIN from Anglo-Norman Fr. (infin. ending).

**era** /'ɪərə/ ● **n.** a long and distinct period of history. ➤ Geology a major division of time that is a subdivision of an aeon and is itself subdivided into periods.

– ORIGIN C17: from late L. *aera*, denoting a number used as a basis of reckoning, an epoch from which time is reckoned, pl. of *aes, aer-* 'money, counter'.

**eradicate** /ɪ'radɪkeɪt/ ● **v.** remove or destroy completely.

– DERIVATIVES **eradicable** adj. **eradicant** n. **eradication** n. **eradicator** n.

– ORIGIN ME: from L. *eradicat-, eradicare* 'tear up by the roots'.

**eradicated** ● **adj.** [postpos.] Heraldry (of a tree or plant) depicted with the roots exposed.

**erase** /ɪ'reɪz/ ● **v.** rub out or obliterate; remove all traces of.

– DERIVATIVES **erasable** adj. **erasure** n.

– ORIGIN C16 (orig. as a heraldic term meaning 'represent the head or limb of an animal with a jagged edge'): from L. *eras-, eradere* 'scrape away'.

**erased** ● **adj.** [postpos.] Heraldry (of a head or limb) depicted as cut off in a jagged line.

**eraser** ● **n.** a piece of rubber or plastic used to rub out something written.

**Erastianism** /ɪ'rastɪə,nɪz(ə)m/ ● **n.** the doctrine that the state should have supremacy over the Church in ecclesiastical matters (wrongly attributed to the C16 Swiss theologian Thomas Lieber Erastus).

– DERIVATIVES **Erastian** n. & adj.

**erbium** /'ə:bɪəm/ ● **n.** the chemical element of atomic number 68, a soft silvery-white metal of the lanthanide series. (Symbol: **Er**)

– ORIGIN C19: mod. L., from *Ytterby* (see **YTTERBIUM**).

**ere** /ɛ:/ ● **prep. & conj.** poetic/literary or archaic before (in time).

– ORIGIN OE *ǣr*, of Gmc origin.

**erect** ● **adj.** rigidly upright or straight. ➤ (of the penis, clitoris, or nipples) enlarged and rigid, especially in sexual excitement. ➤ (of hair) standing up from the skin. ● **v.** construct (a building, wall, etc.). ➤ create or establish (a theory or system).

– DERIVATIVES **erectable** adj. **erectly** adv. **erectness** n. **erector** n.

– ORIGIN ME: from L. *erect-, erigere* 'set up'.

**erectile** /ɪ'rɛktʌɪl/ ● **adj.** able to become erect. ➤ denoting tissues which are capable of becoming temporarily engorged with blood, particularly those of the penis or other sexual organs. ➤ relating to this process.

**erection** ● **n. 1** the action of erecting. **2** a building or other upright structure. **3** an erect state of the penis.

**E-region** ● **n.** another term for **E-LAYER**.

**eremite** /'ɛrɪmʌɪt/ ● **n.** a Christian hermit.

– DERIVATIVES **eremitic** adj. **eremitical** adj.

– ORIGIN ME: from OFr. *eremite* from late L. *eremita* (see **HERMIT**).

**erethism** /'ɛrɪθɪz(ə)m/ ● **n. 1** excessive sensitivity to stimulation of a part of the body, especially the sexual organs. **2** a state of abnormal mental excitement or irritation.

– ORIGIN C19: from Fr. *éréthisme*, from Gk *erethismos*, from *erethizein* 'irritate'.

**erewhile** /ɛ:'wʌɪl/ ● **adv.** archaic a while before; some time ago.

– ORIGIN ME: from **ERE** + **WHILE**.

**erg**[1] /ə:g/ ● **n.** Physics a unit of work or energy, equal to the work done by a force of one dyne when its point of application moves one centimetre in the direction of action of the force.

– ORIGIN C19: from Gk *ergon* 'work'.

**erg**[2] /ə:g/ ● **n.** (pl. **ergs** or **areg** /'ɑ:rɛg/) an area of shifting sand dunes in the Sahara.

– ORIGIN C19: from Fr., from Arab. *'irk, 'erg.*

**ergative** /'ə:gətɪv/ Grammar ● **adj. 1** (in some languages, e.g. Basque) relating to or denoting a case of nouns that identifies the doer of an action as the object rather than the subject of a verb. **2** (in English) denoting verbs which can be used both transitively and intransitively to describe the same action, with the object in the former case being the subject in the latter, as in *I boiled the kettle* and *the kettle boiled.* Compare with **INCHOATIVE**. ● **n.** an ergative word or the ergative case.

– DERIVATIVES **ergativity** n.

– ORIGIN 1950s: from Gk *ergatēs* 'worker' (from *ergon* 'work') + **-IVE**.

**ergo** /'ə:gəʊ/ ● **adv.** therefore.

– ORIGIN from L.

**ergocalciferol** /,ə:gə(ʊ)kal'sɪfərɒl/ ● **n.** Biochemistry another term for **CALCIFEROL** (vitamin $D_2$).

– ORIGIN 1950s: blend of **ERGOT** and **CALCIFEROL**.

**ergodic** /ə:'gɒdɪk/ ● **adj.** Mathematics denoting systems or processes which, given sufficient time, include or impinge on all points in a given space.

– DERIVATIVES **ergodicity** n.

– ORIGIN C20: from Ger. *ergoden*, from Gk *ergon* 'work' + *hodos* 'way' + **-IC**.

**ergometer** /ə:'gɒmɪtə/ ● **n.** an apparatus which measures work or energy expended during a period of physical exercise.

**ergonomics** /,ə:gə'nɒmɪks/ ● **pl. n.** [treated as sing.] the study of people's efficiency in their working environment.

– DERIVATIVES **ergonomic** adj. **ergonomist** n.

– ORIGIN 1950s: from Gk *ergon* 'work', on the pattern of *economics.*

**ergosphere** /'ə:gəʊsfɪə/ ● **n.** Astronomy a postulated region round a black hole, from which energy could escape.

**ergosterol** /ə:'gɒstərɒl/ ● **n.** a compound present in many fungi which is converted to vitamin $D_2$ when irradiated with ultraviolet light.

– ORIGIN C20: from **ERGOT**, on the pattern of *cholesterol.*

**ergot** /'ə:gɒt/ ● **n. 1** a fungal disease of rye and other cereals, forming black elongated fruiting bodies which are a source of various medicinal alkaloids. **2** a small horny protuberance on the back of a horse's fetlock.

– ORIGIN C17: from Fr., from OFr. *argot* 'cock's spur' (because of the appearance produced by the disease).

**ergotamine** /ə:'gɒtəmi:n/ ● **n.** Medicine an ergot alkaloid that causes constriction of blood vessels and is used to treat migraine.

**ergotism** /'ə:gətɪz(ə)m/ ● **n.** poisoning produced by eating food affected by ergot, typically resulting in headache, vomiting, diarrhoea, and gangrene of the fingers and toes.

**erhu** /ə:'hu:/ (also **erh hu**) ● **n.** a Chinese two-stringed musical instrument held in the lap and played with a bow.

– ORIGIN C20: from Chin. *èr* 'two' + *hú* 'bowed instrument'.

**erica** /'ɛrɪkə/ ● **n.** a plant of a large genus including the heaths. [Genus *Erica.*]

– ORIGIN mod. L., from Gk *ereikē.*

**ericaceous** /,ɛrɪ'keɪʃəs/ ● **adj.** Botany **1** relating to or denoting plants of the heather family (Ericaceae). **2** (of compost) suitable for heathers and other lime-hating plants.

– ORIGIN C19: from mod. L. *Ericaceae* (pl.), from the genus name *Erica* (see **ERICA**).

**erigeron** /ɪ'rɪdʒərɒn, ɛ-/ ● **n.** a herbaceous plant of the daisy family. [Genus *Erigeron.*]

– ORIGIN mod. L., from L., 'groundsel' (the original sense

in Engl.), from Gk *ērigerōn*, from *ēri* 'early' + *gerōn* 'old man' (because the plant flowers early in the year, and some species bear grey down).

**Erin** /'ɛrɪn, 'ɪərɪn/ ● **n.** archaic or poetic/literary Ireland.
– ORIGIN from Ir. *Ériu, Éirinn.*

**Erinys** /ɛ'rɪnɪs/ ● **n.** (pl. **Erinyes** /ɛ'rɪnɪiːz/) (in Greek mythology) a Fury.
– ORIGIN from Gk.

**eristic** /ɛ'rɪstɪk/ formal ● **adj.** of or characterized by debate or argument. ➤(of an argument or arguer) aiming at winning rather than at reaching the truth. ● **n.** a person given to debate or argument. ➤the art or practice or debate or argument.
– DERIVATIVES **eristically** adv.
– ORIGIN C17: from Gk *eristikos*, from *erizein* 'to wrangle', from *eris* 'strife'.

**Eritrean** /ˌɛrɪ'treɪən/ ● **n.** a native or inhabitant of the independent state of Eritrea in NE Africa. ● **adj.** of or relating to Eritrea or its inhabitants.

**erk** /əːk/ ● **n.** Brit. informal a male member of the RAF of the lowest rank.
– ORIGIN 1920s: of unknown origin.

**Erlenmeyer flask** /'əːlənˌmʌɪə/ ● **n.** a conical flat-bottomed laboratory flask with a narrow neck.
– ORIGIN C19: named after the Ger. chemist Emil *Erlenmeyer.*

**erl-king** /'əːlkɪŋ/ ● **n.** (in Germanic mythology) a bearded giant or goblin believed to lure little children to the land of death.
– ORIGIN C18: from Ger. *Erlkönig* 'alder-king', a mistranslation of Dan. *ellerkonge* 'king of the elves'.

**ERM** ● **abbrev.** Exchange Rate Mechanism.

**ermine** /'əːmɪn/ ● **n.** (pl. same or **ermines**) **1** a stoat. ➤the white winter fur of the stoat, used for trimming the ceremonial robes of judges or peers. ➤Heraldry fur represented as black spots on a white ground, as a heraldic tincture. **2** a stout-bodied moth that has cream or white wings with black spots, and a very hairy caterpillar. [Genus *Spilosoma*: several species.]
– DERIVATIVES **ermined** adj.
– ORIGIN ME: from OFr. *hermine*, prob. from med. L. (*mus*) *Armenius* 'Armenian (mouse)'.

**ermines** /'əːmɪnz/ ● **n.** Heraldry fur resembling ermine but with white spots on a black ground.
– ORIGIN C16: perh. from OFr. *hermines*, pl. of *herminet*, dimin. of *hermine* 'ermine'.

**erminois** /ˌəːmɪ'nɔɪz/ ● **n.** Heraldry fur resembling ermine but with black spots on a gold ground.
– ORIGIN C16: from OFr., from *hermine* 'ermine'.

**-ern** ● **suffix** forming adjectives such as *northern.*
– ORIGIN OE *-erne*, of Gmc origin.

**erne** /əːn/ ● **n.** poetic/literary the sea eagle.
– ORIGIN OE *earn* 'eagle', of Gmc origin.

**Ernie** /'əːni/ ● **n.** (in the UK) the computer that randomly selects the prize-winning numbers of Premium Bonds.
– ORIGIN 1950s: acronym from *electronic random number indicator equipment.*

**erode** /ɪ'rəʊd/ ● **v.** (with reference to the action of wind, water, etc. on the land) gradually wear or be worn away. ➤gradually destroy (an abstract quality or state). ➤Medicine (of a disease) gradually destroy (bodily tissue).
– DERIVATIVES **erodible** adj.
– ORIGIN C17: from Fr. *éroder* or L. *erodere*, from *e-* (var. of *ex-*) 'out, away' + *rodere* 'gnaw'.

**erogenous** /ɪ'rɒdʒɪnəs, ɛ-/ ● **adj.** (of a part of the body) sensitive to sexual stimulation.
– ORIGIN C19: from **Eros** + **-genous**.

**Eros** /'ɪərɒs/ ● **n.** **1** sexual love or desire. **2** (in Freudian theory) the life instinct. Often contrasted with **Thanatos**. **3** (in Jungian psychology) the principle of personal relatedness in human activities, associated with the anima. Often contrasted with **Logos**.
– ORIGIN L. from Gk *erōs*, lit. 'sexual love' (also the name of the god of love in Gk mythology).

**erosion** /ɪ'rəʊʒ(ə)n/ ● **n.** **1** the process or result of eroding or being eroded. **2** Medicine a place where surface tissue has been gradually destroyed.
– DERIVATIVES **erosional** adj. **erosive** adj.

**erotic** /ɪ'rɒtɪk/ ● **adj.** of, relating to, or tending to arouse sexual desire or excitement.
– DERIVATIVES **erotically** adv.
– ORIGIN C17: from Fr. *érotique*, from Gk *erōtikos*, from *erōs, erōt-* 'sexual love'.

**erotica** ● **pl. n.** [treated as sing. or pl.] erotic literature or art.
– ORIGIN C19: from Gk *erōtika*, neut. pl. of *erōtikos* (see **erotic**).

**eroticism** ● **n.** **1** the quality or character or being erotic. **2** sexual desire or excitement.

**eroticize** (also **-ise**) ● **v.** give erotic qualities to.
– DERIVATIVES **eroticization** n.

**erotism** /'ɛrətɪz(ə)m/ ● **n.** sexual desire or excitement.
– ORIGIN C19: from Gk *erōs, erōt-* 'sexual love' + **-ism**.

**eroto-** /ɪ'rɒtəʊ/ ● **comb. form** relating to eroticism: *erotomania.*
– ORIGIN from Gk *erōs, erōt-* 'sexual love'.

**erotogenic** /ɪˌrɒtə'dʒɛnɪk/ (also **erotogenous** /ˌɛrə'tɒdʒɪnəs/) ● **adj.** another term for **erogenous**.

**erotology** /ˌɛrə'tɒlədʒi/ ● **n.** the study of sexual love and behaviour.

**erotomania** /ɪˌrɒtə(ʊ)'meɪnɪə/ ● **n.** **1** excessive sexual desire. **2** Psychiatry a delusion in which a person (typically a woman) believes that another person (typically of higher social status) is in love with them.
– DERIVATIVES **erotomaniac** n.

**err** /əː/ ● **v.** be mistaken or incorrect. ➤[often as adj. **erring**] do wrong.
– PHRASES **err on the right side** act so that the least harmful of possible errors is the most likely to occur. **err on the side of** display more rather than less of (a specified quality) in one's actions.
– ORIGIN ME: from OFr. *errer*, from L. *errare* 'to stray'.

**errand** ● **n.** a short journey made to deliver or collect something, especially on someone else's behalf.
– PHRASES **errand of mercy** a journey or mission carried out to help someone in difficulty or danger.
– ORIGIN OE *ǣrende* 'message, mission', of Gmc origin.

**errant** /'ɛr(ə)nt/ ● **adj.** **1** chiefly formal or humorous erring or straying from the accepted course or standards. **2** archaic or poetic/literary travelling in search of adventure. See also **knight errant**. **3** Zoology (of a polychaete worm) of a predatory kind that moves about actively and is not confined to a tube or burrow.
– DERIVATIVES **errancy** n. **errantry** n.
– ORIGIN ME: sense 1 from L. *errant-, errare* 'err'; sense 2 from OFr. *errant* 'travelling', pres. part. of *errer*, from late L. *iterare* 'go on a journey', from *iter* 'journey'.

**erratic** /ɪ'ratɪk/ ● **adj.** not even or regular in pattern or movement. ● **n.** (also **erratic block** or **boulder**) Geology a large rock that differs from the surrounding rock, brought from a distance by glacial action.
– DERIVATIVES **erratically** adv. **erraticism** n.
– ORIGIN ME: from OFr. *erratique*, from L. *erraticus*, from *errare* 'to stray, err'.

**erratum** /ɛ'rɑːtəm, -reɪt-/ ● **n.** (pl. **errata**) an error in printing or writing. ➤(**errata**) a list of corrected errors appended to a publication.
– ORIGIN C16: from L., 'error', neut. past part. of *errare* 'err'.

**erroneous** /ɪ'rəʊnɪəs, ɛ-/ ● **adj.** wrong; incorrect.
– DERIVATIVES **erroneously** adv. **erroneousness** n.
– ORIGIN ME: from L. *erroneus* (from *erro(n-)* 'vagabond', from *errare* 'to stray, err') + **-ous**.

**error** ● **n.** **1** a mistake. **2** the state of being wrong in conduct or judgement. **3** technical a measure of the estimated difference between the observed or calculated value of a quantity and its true value.
– PHRASES **see the error of one's ways** acknowledge one's wrongdoing.
– DERIVATIVES **errorless** adj.
– ORIGIN ME: via OFr. from L. *error*, from *errare* 'to stray, err'.

**error bar** ● **n.** Mathematics a line through a point on a graph, parallel to one of the axes, which represents the uncertainty or error of the corresponding coordinate of the point.

**-ers** ● **suffix** forming colloquial nouns and adjectives (such

as *preggers* for *pregnant*).
– ORIGIN extension of **-ER**[3].

**ersatz** /ˈəːsats, ˈɛː-/ ● **adj.** (of a product) made or used as an inferior substitute for something else. ➤not real or genuine: *ersatz emotion.*
– ORIGIN C19: from Ger., lit. 'replacement'.

**Erse** /əːs/ ● **n.** the Scottish or Irish Gaelic language.
– ORIGIN early Scots form of **IRISH**.

**erst** /əːst/ ● **adv.** archaic long ago; formerly.
– ORIGIN OE *ǣrest*, superlative of *ǣr* (see **ERE**).

**erstwhile** ● **adj.** former. ● **adv.** archaic formerly.

**Ertebølle** /ˈɛːtəˌbəːlə/ ● **n.** Archaeology a late Mesolithic culture in the western Baltic (4th millennium BC).
– ORIGIN named after *Ertebølle* in Jutland, Denmark.

**erubescent** /ˌɛrʊˈbɛs(ə)nt/ ● **adj.** rare reddening; blushing.
– ORIGIN C18: from L. *erubescent-*, *erubescere* 'redden'.

**erucic acid** /ɪˈruːsɪk/ ● **n.** Chemistry a fatty acid present in mustard and rape seeds.
– ORIGIN C19: *erucic* from L. *eruca* 'rocket' (denoting the plant) + **-IC**.

**eructation** /ˌiːrʌkˈteɪʃ(ə)n, ɪ-, ɛ-/ ● **n.** formal a belch.
– ORIGIN ME: from L. *eructatio(n-)*, from *eructare*, from *e-* (var. of *ex-*) 'out' + *ructare* 'belch'.

**erudite** /ˈɛrʊdʌɪt/ ● **adj.** having or showing knowledge or learning.
– DERIVATIVES **eruditely** adv. **erudition** n.
– ORIGIN ME: from L. *eruditus*, from *erudire* 'instruct, train' (based on *rudis* 'rude, untrained').

**erupt** ● **v. 1** (of a volcano) forcefully eject lava, rocks, ash, or gases. **2** break out suddenly: *fierce fighting erupted.* **3** (**erupt in**) give vent to (feelings) in a sudden and noisy way: *they erupted in fits of laughter.* **4** (of a spot, rash, etc.) suddenly appear on the skin. ➤(of the skin) suddenly develop spots, a rash, etc. **5** (of a tooth) break through the gums.
– DERIVATIVES **eruptive** adj.
– ORIGIN C17: from L. *erupt-*, *erumpere* 'break out'.

**eruption** ● **n.** an act or instance or erupting. ➤a spot or rash appearing suddenly on the skin.

**eruv** /ˈɛrʊv/ ● **n.** (pl. usu. **eruvim** /ˈɛrʊvɪm/) Judaism an enclosed urban area in which activities normally forbidden in public on the Sabbath are allowed to take place (the boundary wire symbolically extending the private domain of a Jewish household).
– ORIGIN from Heb. *ʿērūḇ*, from a base meaning 'mixture'.

**-ery** (also **-ry**) ● **suffix** forming nouns: **1** denoting a class or kind: *greenery.* **2** denoting an occupation, a state or condition, or behaviour: *archery* | *bravery.* ➤with depreciatory reference: *tomfoolery.* **3** denoting a place set aside for an activity or a grouping of things, animals, etc.: *rookery.*
– ORIGIN from Fr. *-erie*, based on L. *-arius* and *-ator.*

**eryngium** /ɪˈrɪndʒɪəm/ ● **n.** (pl. **eryngiums**) sea holly or a related plant. [Genus *Eryngium.*]
– ORIGIN C16: mod. L., from L. *eryngion*, from a dimin. of Gk *ērungos.*

**eryngo** /ɪˈrɪŋgəʊ/ ● **n.** (pl. **-os** or **-oes**) another term for **SEA HOLLY** or **ERYNGIUM**.
– ORIGIN C16: from Ital. and Sp. *eringio*, from L. *eryngion* (see **ERYNGIUM**).

**erysipelas** /ˌɛrɪˈsɪpɪləs/ ● **n.** Medicine a skin disease caused by a streptococcus and characterized by large raised red patches on the face and legs.
– ORIGIN ME: via L. from Gk *erusipelas*; perh. rel. to *eruthros* 'red' and *pella* 'skin'.

**erysipeloid** /ˌɛrɪˈsɪpəlɔɪd/ ● **n.** Medicine a bacterial dermatitis of the hands, occurring mainly among handlers of meat and fish products.

**erythema** /ˌɛrɪˈθiːmə/ ● **n.** Medicine superficial reddening of the skin caused by dilatation of the blood capillaries, as a result of injury or irritation.
– DERIVATIVES **erythemal** adj. **erythematous** adj.
– ORIGIN C18: from Gk *eruthēma*, from *eruthainein* 'be red', from *eruthros* 'red'.

**erythrism** /ˈɛrɪθrɪz(ə)m/ ● **n.** Zoology a congenital condition of abnormal redness in an animal's fur, plumage, or skin.
– ORIGIN C19: from Gk *eruthros* 'red' + **-ISM**.

**erythro-** ● **comb. form** red (used commonly in zoological and medical terms): *erythrocyte.*
– ORIGIN from Gk *eruthros* 'red'.

**erythroblast** /ɪˈrɪθrə(ʊ)blast/ ● **n.** Physiology an immature erythrocyte, containing a nucleus.
– DERIVATIVES **erythroblastic** adj.

**erythroblastosis** /ɪˌrɪθrə(ʊ)blasˈtəʊsɪs/ ● **n.** Medicine the abnormal presence of erythroblasts in the blood.

**erythrocyte** /ɪˈrɪθrə(ʊ)sʌɪt/ ● **n.** a red blood cell (typically a biconcave disc without a nucleus) that contains the pigment haemoglobin and transports oxygen and carbon dioxide to and from the tissues.
– DERIVATIVES **erythrocytic** adj.

**erythrogenic** /ɪˌrɪθrə(ʊ)ˈdʒɛnɪk/ ● **adj.** Medicine (of a bacterial toxin) causing inflammation and reddening of the skin.

**erythroid** /ˈɛrɪθrɔɪd/ ● **adj.** Physiology of or relating to erythrocytes.

**erythroleukaemia** /ɪˌrɪθrə(ʊ)luːˈkiːmɪə/ (US **erythroleukemia**) ● **n.** Medicine a rare and acute form of leukaemia in which there is proliferation of immature red and white blood cells.

**erythromycin** /ɪˌrɪθrə(ʊ)ˈmʌɪsɪn/ ● **n.** Medicine an antibiotic obtained from a streptomycete bacterium (*Streptomyces erythreus*).
– ORIGIN 1950s: from elements of the mod. L. taxonomic name (see above) + **-IN**[1].

**erythronium** /ˌɛrɪˈθrəʊnɪəm/ ● **n.** (pl. **erythroniums** or **erythronia** /-ɪə/) a plant of a genus which includes dog's-tooth violet. [Genus *Erythronium.*]
– ORIGIN mod. L., from Gk (*saturion*) *eruthronion* 'red-flowered (orchid)'.

**erythropoiesis** /ɪˌrɪθrə(ʊ)pɔɪˈiːsɪs/ ● **n.** Physiology the production of red blood cells.
– DERIVATIVES **erythropoietic** adj.

**erythropoietin** /ɪˌrɪθrə(ʊ)pɔɪˈɛtɪn/ ● **n.** Biochemistry a hormone secreted by the kidneys that increases the rate of production of red blood cells in response to falling levels of oxygen in the tissues.

**ES** ● **abbrev.** El Salvador (international vehicle registration).

**Es** ● **symb.** the chemical element einsteinium.

**-es**[1] ● **suffix 1** forming plurals of nouns ending in sibilant sounds: *kisses.* **2** forming plurals of certain nouns ending in *-o*: *potatoes.*
– ORIGIN var. of **-S**[1].

**-es**[2] ● **suffix** forming the third person singular of the present tense: **1** in verbs ending in sibilant sounds: *pushes.* **2** in verbs ending in *-o* (but not *-oo*): *goes.*
– ORIGIN var. of **-S**[2].

**ESA** ● **abbrev. 1** (in the UK) Environmentally Sensitive Area. **2** European Space Agency.

**ESC** ● **abbrev.** Economic and Social Committee.

**escadrille** /ˌɛskəˈdrɪl/ ● **n.** a French squadron of aircraft.
– ORIGIN Fr., lit. 'flotilla, flight'.

**escalade** /ˌɛskəˈleɪd/ ● **n.** historical the scaling of fortified walls using ladders, as a form of military attack.
– ORIGIN C16: from Fr., or from Sp. *escalada*, *escalado*, from med. L. *scalare* 'to scale, climb', from L. *scala* 'ladder'.

**escalate** /ˈɛskəleɪt/ ● **v. 1** increase rapidly. **2** become or cause to become more intense or serious.
– DERIVATIVES **escalation** n.
– ORIGIN 1920s (in the sense 'travel on an escalator'): back-form. from **ESCALATOR**.

**escalator** ● **n.** a moving staircase consisting of a circulating belt of steps driven by a motor.
– ORIGIN C20 (orig. US, as a trade name): from *escalade* 'climb a wall by ladder' (from the noun **ESCALADE**), on the pattern of *elevator.*

**escalator clause** (also **escalation clause**) ● **n.** a clause in a contract that allows for a rise in wages or prices under certain conditions.

**escallonia** /ˌɛskəˈləʊnɪə/ ● **n.** an evergreen South American shrub with pink or white flowers. [Genus *Escallonia.*]

E

– ORIGIN mod. L., named after the C18 Sp. traveller *Escallon*, who discovered the plants.

**escallop** /ɪˈskaləp, ɛ-, -ˈskɒl-/ ● **n.** **1** variant spelling of ESCALOPE. **2** another term for SCALLOP (in sense 2). **3** Heraldry a scallop shell as a charge. ● **v.** (**escalloped**, **escalloping**) another term for SCALLOP (in sense 3).
– ORIGIN C15: from OFr. *escalope* 'shell'.

**escalope** /ɪˈskaləp, ɛ-, -ˈskɒl-, ˈɛskələʊp/ ● **n.** a thin slice of coated and fried meat, especially veal.
– ORIGIN Fr.; cf. ESCALLOP and SCALLOP.

**escapade** /ˈɛskəpeɪd, ˌɛskəˈpeɪd/ ● **n.** an incident involving daring and adventure.
– ORIGIN C17 (in the sense 'an escape'): from Fr., from Provençal or Sp., from *escapar* 'to escape'.

**escape** ● **v.** **1** break free from confinement or control. ➤(of a gas, liquid, or heat) leak from a container. **2** elude or get free from (someone). **3** succeed in eluding (something dangerous or undesirable): *the baby narrowly escaped death.* ● **n.** **1** an act of escaping. **2** a means of escaping. **3** (also **escape key**) Computing a key on a computer keyboard which interrupts the current operation or converts subsequent characters to a control sequence. **4** a garden plant or pet animal that has gone wild and (in plants) become naturalized.
– DERIVATIVES **escapable** adj. **escapee** n. **escaper** n.
– ORIGIN ME: from OFr. *eschaper*, based on med. L. *ex-* 'out' + *cappa* 'cloak'.

**escape clause** ● **n.** a clause in a contract which specifies the conditions under which one party can be freed from an obligation.

**escapement** /ɪˈskeɪpm(ə)nt, ɛ-/ ● **n.** **1** a mechanism in a clock or watch that connects and regulates the motive power. **2** a mechanism in a typewriter that shifts the carriage a small fixed amount to the left after a key is pressed and released. **3** the part of the mechanism in a piano that enables the hammer to fall back as soon as it has struck the string.
– ORIGIN C18: from Fr. *échappement*, from *échapper* 'to escape'.

**escape road** ● **n.** chiefly Brit. a slip road on a bend in a racing circuit or on a steep hill, into which a driver can turn if unable to negotiate a bend or slope safely.

**escape velocity** ● **n.** the lowest velocity which a body must have in order to escape the gravitational attraction of a particular planet or other object.

**escape wheel** ● **n.** a toothed wheel in the escapement of a watch or clock.

**escapism** ● **n.** the process of seeking distraction from reality by engaging in entertainment or fantasy.
– DERIVATIVES **escapist** n. & adj.

**escapologist** /ˌɛskəˈpɒlədʒɪst/ ● **n.** an entertainer who specializes in breaking free from ropes, handcuffs, and chains.
– DERIVATIVES **escapology** n.

**escargot** /ɛˈskɑːɡəʊ, ɪ-/ ● **n.** an edible snail.
– ORIGIN Fr., from OFr. *escargol*, from Provençal *escaragol*.

**escarole** /ˈɛskərəʊl/ ● **n.** N. Amer. an endive of a variety with broad undivided leaves.
– ORIGIN C20: from Fr., from Ital. *scar(i)ola*, based on L. *esca* 'food'.

**escarpment** /ɪˈskɑːpm(ə)nt, ɛ-/ ● **n.** a long, steep slope at the edge of a plateau or separating areas of land at different heights.
– ORIGIN C19: from Fr. *escarpement*, *escarpe* 'scarp', from Ital. *scarpa* 'slope'.

**-esce** ● **suffix** forming verbs, often denoting the initiation of action: *effervesce*.
– ORIGIN from or suggested by L. verbs ending in *-escere*.

**-escent** ● **suffix** forming adjectives denoting a developing state or action: *coalescent*.
– DERIVATIVES **-escence** suffix forming corresponding nouns.
– ORIGIN from Fr., or from L. *-escent-* (pres. participial stem of verbs ending in *-escere*).

**eschar** /ˈɛskɑː/ ● **n.** Medicine a dry, dark scab caused by a burn, bite, etc.
– ORIGIN ME: from Fr. *eschare* or late L. *eschara* 'scar or scab', from Gk (see also SCAR).

**eschatology** /ˌɛskəˈtɒlədʒi/ ● **n.** the part of theology concerned with death, judgement, and destiny.
– DERIVATIVES **eschatological** adj. **eschatologist** n.
– ORIGIN C19: from Gk *eskhatos* 'last' + -LOGY.

**eschaton** /ˈɛskətɒn/ ● **n.** Theology the final event in the divine plan; the end of the world.
– ORIGIN 1930s: from Gk *eskhaton*, neut. of *eskhatos* 'last'.

**escheat** /ɪsˈtʃiːt, ɛs-/ chiefly historical ● **n.** the reversion of property to the state, or (in feudal law) to a lord, on the owner's dying without legal heirs. ● **v.** revert or cause to be reverted as an escheat.
– ORIGIN ME: from OFr. *eschete*, based on L. *excidere* 'fall away', from *ex-* 'out of, from' + *cadere* 'to fall'.

**eschew** /ɪsˈtʃuː, ɛs-/ ● **v.** abstain from.
– DERIVATIVES **eschewal** n.
– ORIGIN ME: from OFr. *eschiver*, ult. of Gmc origin; rel. to SHY[1].

**eschscholzia** /ɪsˈʃɒlzɪə, ɛʃˈʃɒlzɪə/ (also **eschscholtzia** /-tsɪə/) ● **n.** a North American poppy with bright yellow, orange, or red flowers. [Genus *Eschscholzia*: several species, in particular the California poppy.]
– ORIGIN mod. L., named in honour of the Russian-born botanist Johann Friedrich von *Eschscholtz*.

**escolar** /ˌɛskəˈlɑː/ ● **n.** a large, elongated predatory marine fish. [Family Gempylidae: several species.]
– ORIGIN C19: from Sp., lit. 'scholar', so named because the ringed markings around the eyes resemble spectacles.

**escort** ● **n.** /ˈɛskɔːt/ **1** a person or vehicle (or group of these) accompanying another to provide protection or as a mark of rank. **2** a person who is hired or formally requested to accompany a member of the opposite sex to a social event. ● **v.** /ɪˈskɔːt, ɛ-/ accompany as an escort.
– ORIGIN C16: from Fr. *escorte* (n.), *escorter* (v.), from Ital. *scorta*, fem. past part. of *scorgere* 'to conduct, guide', based on L. *ex-* 'out of' + *corrigere* (see CORRECT).

**escritoire** /ˌɛskriːˈtwɑː/ ● **n.** a small writing desk with drawers and compartments.
– ORIGIN C16: from Fr., from med. L. *scriptorium* (see SCRIPTORIUM).

**escrow** /ɪˈskrəʊ, ɛ-/ Law ● **n.** a bond, deed, deposit, etc. kept in the custody of a third party, taking effect or made available only when a specified condition has been fulfilled. ➤the state of being kept in this way. ● **v.** chiefly N. Amer. place in escrow.
– ORIGIN C16: from OFr. *escroe* 'scrap, scroll', from med. L. *scroda*, of Gmc origin; rel. to SHRED.

**escudo** /ɛˈsk(j)uːdəʊ, ɛˈʃk-/ ● **n.** (pl. **-os**) the basic monetary unit of Portugal and Cape Verde, equal to 100 centavos.
– ORIGIN Sp. and Port., from L. *scutum* 'shield'.

**esculent** /ˈɛskjʊlənt/ formal ● **adj.** fit to be eaten. ● **n.** an esculent thing.
– ORIGIN C17: from L. *esculentus*, from *esca* 'food', from *esse* 'eat'.

**escutcheon** /ɪˈskʌtʃ(ə)n, ɛ-/ ● **n.** **1** a shield or emblem bearing a coat of arms. **2** (also **escutcheon plate**) a flat piece of metal framing a keyhole, door handle, or light switch.
– PHRASES **a blot on one's escutcheon** a stain on one's reputation or character. **escutcheon of pretence** a small shield within a coat of arms, bearing another coat or device to which the bearer has a claim.
– DERIVATIVES **escutcheoned** adj.
– ORIGIN C15: from Anglo-Norman Fr. *escuchon*, based on L. *scutum* 'shield'.

**Esd.** ● **abbrev.** Esdras (in biblical references).

**ESE** ● **abbrev.** east-south-east.

**-ese** ● **suffix** forming adjectives and nouns: **1** denoting an inhabitant or language of a country or city: *Taiwanese*. **2** often derogatory (especially with reference to language) denoting character or style: *journalese*.
– ORIGIN from OFr. *-eis*, based on L. *-ensis*.

**eserine** /ˈɛsəriːn/ ● **n.** Chemistry another term for PHYSOSTIGMINE.
– ORIGIN C19: from Fr. *ésérine*, from Efik *esere*.

**esker** /ˈɛskə/ ● **n.** Geology a long winding ridge of gravel and other sediment, deposited by meltwater from a re-

treating glacier or ice sheet.
– ORIGIN C19: from Ir. *eiscir.*

**Eskimo** ● **n.** (pl. same or **-os**) **1** a member of an indigenous people inhabiting northern Canada, Alaska, Greenland, and eastern Siberia. **2** either of the two main languages of this people (Inuit and Yupik), comprising a major division of the Eskimo-Aleut family. ● **adj.** of or relating to the Eskimos or their languages.
– ORIGIN an Algonquian word, perh. in the sense 'people speaking a different language'.

**USAGE** Eskimo

In recent years, the word **Eskimo** has come to be regarded by some as offensive: the peoples inhabiting the regions from NW Canada to western Greenland prefer to call themselves **Inuit**. The term **Eskimo**, however, continues to be the only term which can be properly understood as applying to the people as a whole and is still widely used in anthropological and archaeological contexts.

**Eskimo-Aleut** ● **n.** the family of languages comprising Inuit, Yupik, and Aleut. ● **adj.** of or relating to this family of languages.

**Eskimo curlew** ● **n.** a small New World curlew with a striped head, formerly common in the arctic tundra but now close to extinction. [*Numenius borealis.*]

**Eskimo roll** ● **n.** a complete rollover in canoeing, from upright to capsized to upright.

**ESL** ● **abbrev.** English as a second language.

**ESN** ● **abbrev.** **1** dated educationally subnormal. **2** electronic serial number.

**ESOL** ● **abbrev.** English for speakers of other languages.

**esophagus** etc. ● **n.** US spelling of **OESOPHAGUS** etc.

**esoteric** /ˌɛsəˈtɛrɪk, ˌiːsə-/ ● **adj.** intended for or understood by only a small number of people with a specialized knowledge or interest. The opposite of **EXOTERIC**.
– DERIVATIVES **esoterically** adv. **esotericism** n. **esotericist** n.
– ORIGIN C17: from Gk *esōterikos*, from *esōterō*, compar. of *esō* 'within', from *es, eis* 'into'.

**esoterica** /ˌɛsəˈtɛrɪkə, ˌiːsə-/ ● **pl. n.** [treated as sing. or pl.] esoteric subjects or publications.
– ORIGIN C20: from Gk *esōterika*, neut. pl. of *esōterikos* 'esoteric'.

**ESP** ● **abbrev.** extrasensory perception.

**esp.** ● **abbrev.** especially.

**espada** /ɛˈspɑːdə/ ● **n.** (pl. same) a scabbardfish, especially as caught for food in Madeira and elsewhere.
– ORIGIN via Port. from Sp., from L. *spatha* 'sword'.

**espadrille** /ˈɛspədrɪl, ˌɛspəˈdrɪl/ ● **n.** a light canvas shoe with a plaited fibre sole.
– ORIGIN C19: from Fr., from Provençal *espardi(l)hos*, from *espart* 'esparto', from L. *spartum* (see **ESPARTO**).

**espalier** /ɪˈspaljə, ɛ-/ ● **n.** a fruit tree or ornamental shrub whose branches are trained to grow flat against a wall. ● **v.** train (a tree or shrub) in such a way.
– ORIGIN C17: from Fr., from Ital. *spalliera*, from *spalla* 'shoulder', from L. *spatula* (see **SPATULA**), in late L. 'shoulder blade'.

**esparto** /ɛˈspɑːtəʊ, ɪ-/ (also **esparto grass**) ● **n.** (pl. **-os**) a coarse grass native to Spain and North Africa, used to make ropes, wickerwork, and paper. [*Stipa tenacissima.*]
– ORIGIN C19: from Sp., via L. from Gk *sparton* 'rope'.

**especial** /ɪˈspɛʃ(ə)l, ɛ-/ ● **adj.** **1** notable; special. **2** for or belonging chiefly to one person or thing.
– ORIGIN ME: via OFr. from L. *specialis* 'special', from *species* (see **SPECIES**).

**especially** ● **adv.** **1** in particular. **2** to a great extent; very much.

**Esperanto** /ˌɛspəˈrantəʊ/ ● **n.** an artificial language devised in 1887 as an international medium of communication, based on roots from the chief European languages.
– DERIVATIVES **Esperantist** n.
– ORIGIN from the name *Dr Esperanto*, used as a pen name by the inventor of the language, Polish physician Ludwik L. Zamenhof; the literal sense is 'one who hopes' (based on L. *sperare* 'to hope').

**espial** /ɪˈspʌɪ(ə)l, ɛ-/ ● **n.** archaic the action or an instance of catching sight of something or of being seen.
– ORIGIN ME: from OFr. *espiaille*, from *espier* 'espy'.

**espionage** /ˈɛspɪənɑːʒ, -ɪdʒ/ ● **n.** the practice of spying or of using spies.
– ORIGIN C18: from Fr. *espionnage*, from *espionner* 'to spy', from *espion* 'a spy'.

**esplanade** /ˌɛspləˈneɪd, -ˈnɑːd/ ● **n.** a long, open, level area, typically beside the sea, along which people may promenade. ➤an open, level space separating a fortress from a town.
– ORIGIN C16: from Fr., from Ital. *spianata*, from L. *explanatus* 'levelled', from *explanare* (see **EXPLAIN**).

**espousal** /ɪˈspaʊz(ə)l, ɛ-/ ● **n.** **1** the action of espousing. **2** archaic a marriage or engagement.

**espouse** /ɪˈspaʊz, ɛ-/ ● **v.** **1** adopt or support (a cause, belief, or way of life). **2** archaic marry. ➤(**be espoused to**) be engaged to.
– DERIVATIVES **espouser** n.
– ORIGIN ME: from OFr. *espouser*, from L. *sponsare*, from *sponsus* 'betrothed', past part. of *spondere.*

**espressivo** /ˌɛsprɛˈsiːvəʊ/ ● **adv. & adj.** Music with expression of feeling.
– ORIGIN Ital., from L. *expressus* 'distinctly presented'.

**espresso** /ɛˈsprɛsəʊ/ (also **expresso**) ● **n.** (pl. **-os**) strong black coffee made by forcing steam through ground coffee beans.
– ORIGIN 1940s: from Ital. *(caffè) espresso*, lit. 'pressed out (coffee)'.

**esprit** /ɛˈspriː, French ɛspʀi/ ● **n.** liveliness.
– ORIGIN Fr., from L. *spiritus* 'spirit'.

**esprit de corps** /ɛˌspriː dəˈkɔː, French ɛspʀi də kɔʀ/ ● **n.** a feeling of pride, fellowship, and loyalty uniting the members of a particular group.
– ORIGIN Fr., lit. 'spirit of the body'.

**espy** /ɪˈspʌɪ, ɛ-/ ● **v.** (**-ies**, **-ied**) poetic/literary catch sight of.
– ORIGIN ME: from OFr. *espier*, ult. of Gmc origin.

**Esq.** ● **abbrev.** Esquire.

**-esque** ● **suffix** (forming adjectives) in the style of; resembling: *Dantesque.*
– ORIGIN from Fr., via Ital. *-esco* from med. L. *-iscus.*

**Esquimau** ● **n.** (pl. **Esquimaux**) archaic spelling of **ESKIMO**.

**esquire** /ɪˈskwʌɪə, ɛ-/ (abbrev.: **esq.**) ● **n.** **1** (**Esquire**) Brit. a polite title appended to a man's name when no other title is used, especially in a letter. ➤N. Amer. a title appended to a lawyer's surname. **2** historical a young nobleman who, in training for knighthood, acted as an attendant to a knight. ➤an officer in the service of a king or nobleman. ➤a landed proprietor or country squire.
– ORIGIN ME: from OFr. *esquier*, from L. *scutarius* 'shield-bearer', from *scutum* 'shield'.

**ESR** ● **abbrev.** Physics electron spin resonance.

**ESRC** ● **abbrev.** (in the UK) Economic and Social Research Council.

**-ess**[1] ● **suffix** forming nouns denoting female gender: *abbess.*
– ORIGIN from Fr. *-esse*, via late L. from Gk *-issa.*

**USAGE** -ess

In modern English, there are few new words coined with the suffix **-ess**. Many existing feminine forms (e.g. **poetess**, **authoress**) are likely to be regarded as old-fashioned or sexist and avoided in favour of the 'neutral' base form (e.g. **poet**, **author**).

**-ess**[2] ● **suffix** forming abstract nouns from adjectives, such as *largess.*
– ORIGIN ME via Fr. *-esse* from L. *-itia.*

**essay** ● **n.** /ˈɛseɪ/ **1** a piece of writing on a particular subject. **2** formal an attempt or effort. **3** a trial design of a postage stamp. ● **v.** /ɛˈseɪ/ formal attempt.
– DERIVATIVES **essayist** n. **essayistic** adj.
– ORIGIN C15 (in the sense 'test the quality of'): alt. of **ASSAY**, by assoc. with OFr. *essayer*, based on late L. *exagium* 'weighing'; the noun (C16) is from OFr. *essai* 'trial'.

**esse** /ˈɛsi/ ● **n.** Philosophy essential nature or essence.

– ORIGIN L., 'to be'.

**essence** • n. **1** the intrinsic nature of something; the quality which determines something's character. ➤ Philosophy a property or group of properties of something without which it would not exist or be what it is. **2** an extract or concentrate obtained from a plant or other substance and used for flavouring or scent.
– PHRASES **in essence** basically; fundamentally. **of the essence** critically important.
– ORIGIN ME: via OFr. from L. *essentia*, from *esse* 'be'.

**Essene** /ˈɛsiːn/ • n. a member of an ancient Jewish ascetic sect of the 2nd century BC–2nd century AD in Palestine.
– ORIGIN from L. *Esseni* (pl.), from Gk *Essēnoi*, perh. from Aramaic.

**essential** /ɪˈsɛnʃ(ə)l/ • adj. **1** fundamental; central. **2** absolutely necessary; extremely important. **3** (of an amino acid or fatty acid) required for normal growth but not synthesized in the body and therefore necessary in the diet. **4** Medicine (of a disease) with no known external stimulus or cause; idiopathic. • n. (**essentials**) **1** the fundamental elements. **2** things that are absolutely necessary.
– DERIVATIVES **essentiality** n. **essentially** adv. **essentialness** n.
– ORIGIN ME (in the sense 'in the highest degree'): from late L. *essentialis*, from L. *essentia* (see ESSENCE).

**essentialism** • n. Philosophy a belief that things have a set of characteristics which make them what they are; the doctrine that essence is prior to existence.
– DERIVATIVES **essentialist** n. & adj.

**essential oil** • n. a natural oil extracted from a plant, used especially in aromatherapy or in making perfume.

**EST** • abbrev. Eastern Standard Time.

**est** /ɛst/ • n. a system aimed at developing a person's potential through intensive group awareness and training sessions.
– ORIGIN 1970s (orig. US): acronym from *Erhard Seminars Training*, from the name of Werner *Erhard*, the Amer. businessman who devised the technique.

**est.** • abbrev. **1** established. **2** estimated.

**-est**[1] • suffix forming the superlative of adjectives (such as *shortest*) and of adverbs (such as *soonest*).
– ORIGIN OE *-ost-*, *-ust-*, *-ast-*.

**-est**[2] (also **-st**) • suffix archaic forming the second person singular of verbs: *goest*.
– ORIGIN OE *-est*, *-ast*, *-st*.

**establish** • v. **1** set up on a firm or permanent basis. **2** initiate or bring about. **3** (**be established**) be settled or accepted in a particular place or role. **4** (of a plant) take root and grow. **5** show to be true or certain by determining the facts. **6** Bridge ensure that one's remaining cards in (a suit) will be winners (if not trumped) by playing off the high cards in that suit. **7** [as adj. **established**] recognized by the state as the national Church or religion.
– DERIVATIVES **establisher** n.
– ORIGIN ME (recorded earlier as *stablish*): from OFr. *establiss-*, lengthened stem of *establir*, from L. *stabilire* 'make firm', from *stabilis* (adj.) 'stable'.

**establishment** • n. **1** the action of establishing or being established. **2** a business organization, public institution, or household. **3** (**the Establishment**) a group in a society exercising power and influence over matters of policy, opinion, or taste, and seen as resisting change.

**establishmentarian** /ɪˌstablɪʃm(ə)nˈtɛːrɪən/ • adj. advocating or relating to the principle of an established Church. • n. a person advocating this.
– DERIVATIVES **establishmentarianism** n.

**estaminet** /ɛˈstamɪneɪ, French ɛstamine/ • n. a small cafe selling alcoholic drinks.
– ORIGIN Fr., from Walloon *staminé* 'byre', from *stamo* 'a pole for tethering a cow', prob. from Ger. *Stamm* 'stem'.

**estancia** /ɛˈstansɪə/ • n. a cattle ranch in Latin America or the southern US.
– ORIGIN C17: from Sp., lit. 'station'.

**estate** • n. **1** a property consisting of a large house and extensive grounds. **2** Brit. an area of land and modern buildings developed for residential, industrial, or commercial purposes. **3** a property where crops such as coffee or rubber are cultivated or where wine is produced. **4** a person's money and property in its entirety at the time of their death. **5** (also **estate of the realm**) a class or order forming part of the body politic, in particular (in Britain) one of the three groups constituting Parliament, now the Lords spiritual (the heads of the Church), the Lords temporal (the peerage), and the Commons (also known as **the three estates**). **6** archaic or poetic/literary a particular state, period, or condition in life. **7** Brit. short for ESTATE CAR.
– ORIGIN ME: from OFr. *estat*, from L. *status* 'state, condition', from *stare* 'to stand'.

**estate agency** • n. chiefly Brit. a business that sells and rents out buildings and land for clients.
– DERIVATIVES **estate agent** n.

**estate car** • n. Brit. a car incorporating a large carrying area behind the seats, accessed by a door at the rear.

**estate duty** • n. Brit. a former death duty levied on property, now incorporated in inheritance tax.

**esteem** • n. respect and admiration. • v. **1** (usu. **be esteemed**) respect and admire. **2** formal consider; deem.
– ORIGIN ME: from OFr. *estime* (n.), *estimer* (v.), from L. *aestimare* 'to estimate'.

**ester** /ˈɛstə/ • n. Chemistry an organic compound made by replacing the hydrogen of an acid by an alkyl or other organic group.
– DERIVATIVES **esterify** /ɛˈstɛrɪfʌɪ/ v. (**-ies**, **-ied**).
– ORIGIN C19: from Ger., prob. from a blend of *Essig* 'vinegar' and *Äther* 'ether'.

**esterase** /ˈɛstəreɪz/ • n. Biochemistry an enzyme which breaks down particular esters into acids and alcohols or phenols.

**Esth.** • abbrev. Esther (in biblical references).

**esthetic** etc. • adj. US spelling of AESTHETIC etc.

**Estima** /ɛˈstiːmə/ • n. a Dutch potato of a yellow-fleshed variety.

**estimable** /ˈɛstɪməb(ə)l/ • adj. worthy of great respect.
– DERIVATIVES **estimably** adv.

**estimate** • n. /ˈɛstɪmət/ **1** an approximate calculation or judgement. ➤ a written statement indicating the likely price that will be charged for specified work. **2** a judgement or appraisal. • v. /ˈɛstɪmeɪt/ form an estimate of.
– DERIVATIVES **estimation** n. **estimative** /-mətɪv/ adj. **estimator** n.
– ORIGIN ME: from L. *aestimat-*, *aestimare* 'determine, appraise'.

**estival** • adj. US spelling of AESTIVAL.

**estivation** • n. US spelling of AESTIVATION.

**estoile** /ɪˈstɔɪl, ɛ-/ • n. Heraldry a star with (usually six) wavy points or rays.
– ORIGIN C16: via OFr. from L. *stella* 'star'.

**Estonian** • n. **1** a native or national of Estonia, or a person of Estonian descent. **2** the Finno-Ugric language of Estonia. • adj. of or relating to Estonia or its people or language.

**estop** /ɪˈstɒp/ • v. (**estopped**, **estopping**) Law bar or preclude by estoppel.
– ORIGIN ME: from OFr. *estopper* 'stop up, impede'.

**estoppel** /ɪˈstɒp(ə)l/ • n. Law the principle which precludes a person from asserting something contrary to what is implied by a previous action or statement of that person or by a previous pertinent judicial determination.
– ORIGIN C16: from OFr. *estouppail* 'bung', from *estopper* (see ESTOP).

**estovers** /ɪˈstəʊvəz, ɛ-/ • pl. n. (usu. **common/right of estovers**) Brit., chiefly historical the right to take wood for fuel, repairs, or other necessary purpose from land which one does not own, especially land of which one is the tenant or lessee.
– ORIGIN C15: from Anglo-Norman Fr. *estover* 'be necessary', based on L. *est opus* 'it is necessary'.

**estradiol** • n. US spelling of OESTRADIOL.

**estrange** /ɪˈstreɪn(d)ʒ, ɛ-/ • v. **1** cause to feel less close or friendly; alienate. **2** [as adj. **estranged**] (of a husband or wife) no longer living with their spouse.

– DERIVATIVES **estrangement** n.
– ORIGIN C15: from OFr. *estranger*, from L. *extraneare* 'treat as a stranger'.

**estreat** /ɪ'striːt, ɛ-/ Law, chiefly historical • v. enforce the forfeit of (a surety for bail or other recognizance). • n. a copy of a court record for use in estreating.
– DERIVATIVES **estreatment** n.
– ORIGIN ME: from OFr. *estraite*, fem. past part. of *estraire*, from L. *extrahere* (see **EXTRACT**).

**estrogen** etc. • n. US spelling of **OESTROGEN** etc.

**estrus** etc. • n. US spelling of **OESTRUS** etc.

**estuary** /'ɛstjʊ(ə)ri/ • n. (pl. **-ies**) the tidal mouth of a large river.
– DERIVATIVES **estuarial** adj. **estuarine** /-rʌɪn/ adj.
– ORIGIN C16: from L. *aestuarium* 'tidal part of a shore', from *aestus* 'tide'.

**Estuary English** • n. (in the UK) a type of accent identified as spreading outwards from London and containing features of both received pronunciation and London speech.

**estufa** /ɛ'stuːfə/ • n. **1** a heated chamber in which Madeira wine is stored and matured. **2** US an underground chamber in which a fire is kept alight, used as a place of assembly by Pueblo Indians.
– ORIGIN C19: from Sp., prob. based on Gk *tuphos* 'steam or smoke'.

**e.s.u.** • abbrev. electrostatic unit(s).

**esurient** /ɪ'sjʊərɪənt, ɛ-/ • adj. rare hungry or greedy.
– DERIVATIVES **esuriently** adv.
– ORIGIN C17: from L. *esurient-*, *esurire* 'be hungry'.

**ET** • abbrev. **1** (in North America) Eastern time. **2** Egypt (international vehicle registration). **3** extraterrestrial.

**-et[1]** • suffix forming nouns which were originally diminutives: *baronet*.
– ORIGIN from OFr. *-et*, *-ete*.

**-et[2]** (also **-ete**) • suffix forming nouns such as *comet*, and often denoting people: *athlete*.
– ORIGIN from Gk *-ētēs*.

**ETA** /ˌiːtiː'eɪ/ • abbrev. estimated time of arrival.

**eta** /'iːtə/ • n. the seventh letter of the Greek alphabet (Η, η), transliterated as 'e' or 'ē'.
– ORIGIN from Gk *ēta*.

**etagere** /ˌɛtə'ʒɛː/ • n. (pl. same or **etageres**) a piece of furniture with a number of open shelves.
– ORIGIN Fr. *étagère*, from *étage* 'shelf'.

**e-tailer** • n. a retailer selling goods via electronic transactions on the Internet.

**et al.** /ɛt 'al/ • abbrev. and others.
– ORIGIN from L. *et alii*.

**etalon** /'ɛtəlɒn/ • n. Physics a device consisting of two reflecting plates, for producing interfering light beams.
– ORIGIN C20: from Fr. *étalon*, lit. 'standard of measurement'.

**etc.** • abbrev. et cetera.

**et cetera** /ɛt'sɛt(ə)rə, ɪt-/ (also **etcetera**) • adv. and other similar things; and so on. • n. (**etceteras**) unspecified extra items.
– ORIGIN L., from *et* 'and' and *cetera* 'the rest' (neut. pl. of *ceterus* 'left over').

**etch** • v. **1** engrave (metal, glass, or stone) by coating it with a protective layer, drawing on it with a needle, and then covering it with acid to attack the parts the needle has exposed. **2** (of an acid or other solvent) corrode or eat away the surface of. **3** cut or carve (a text or design) on a surface. ➤carve with a text or design. **4** cause to be clearly defined: *the outline of the town was etched against the sky.*
– DERIVATIVES **etcher** n.
– ORIGIN C17: from Du. *etsen*, from Ger. *ätzen*; rel. to **EAT**.

**etchant** /'ɛtʃ(ə)nt/ • n. an acid or corrosive chemical used in etching; a mordant.

**etching** • n. **1** the art or process of etching. **2** a print produced by the process of etching.

**-ete** • suffix variant spelling of **-ET[2]** (as in *athlete*).

**eternal** /ɪ'təːn(ə)l, iː-/ • adj. **1** lasting or existing forever. ➤informal tediously lengthy or persistent. **2** valid for all time; essentially unchanging: *eternal truths*. **3** (**the Eternal**) used to refer to an everlasting or universal spirit, as represented by God.
– PHRASES **the Eternal City** the city of Rome. **eternal triangle** a relationship between three people involving sexual rivalry.
– DERIVATIVES **eternality** /ɪˌtəː'nalɪti, iː-/ n. **eternalize** (also **-ise**) v. **eternally** adv. **eternalness** n.
– ORIGIN ME: via OFr. from late L. *aeternalis*, from L. *aeternus*, from *aevum* 'age'.

**eternity** • n. (pl. **-ies**) infinite or unending time. ➤Theology endless life after death. ➤(**an eternity**) informal an undesirably long period of time.

**eternity ring** • n. a ring given as a symbol of lasting affection, typically set with an unbroken circle of gems.

**Etesian wind** /ɪ'tiːʒɪən, ɪ'tiːz-, ɪ'tiːʒ(ə)n/ • n. another term for **MELTEMI**.
– ORIGIN C17: *Etesian* from L. *etesius* 'annual' + **-AN**.

**ETH** • abbrev. Ethiopia (international vehicle registration).

**eth** /ɛð/ (also **edh**) • n. an Old English letter, ð or Ð, representing the dental fricatives /ð/ and /θ/, eventually superseded by the digraph *th*.
– ORIGIN from Dan. *edh*, perh. representing the sound of the letter.

**-eth[1]** • suffix variant spelling of **-TH[1]** (as in *fiftieth*).

**-eth[2]** (also **-th**) • suffix archaic forming the third person singular of the present tense of verbs: *doeth*.
– ORIGIN OE *-eth*, *-ath*, *-th*.

**ethanal** /'ɛθ(ə)nal/ • n. systematic chemical name for **ACETALDEHYDE**.
– ORIGIN C19: blend of **ETHANE** and **ALDEHYDE**.

**ethanamide** /ɪ'θanəmʌɪd/ • n. systematic chemical name for **ACETAMIDE**.

**ethane** /'iːθeɪn, 'ɛθ-/ • n. Chemistry a flammable hydrocarbon gas of the alkane series, present in petroleum and natural gas. [$C_2H_6$.]
– ORIGIN C19: from **ETHER** + **-ANE[2]**.

**ethanediol** /'iːθeɪnˌdʌɪɒl, 'ɛθ-/ • n. systematic chemical name for **ETHYLENE GLYCOL**.

**ethanoic acid** /ˌɛθə'nəʊɪk/ • n. systematic chemical name for **ACETIC ACID**.
– DERIVATIVES **ethanoate** n.

**ethanol** /'ɛθənɒl/ • n. systematic chemical name for **ETHYL ALCOHOL** (see **ALCOHOL**).

**ethene** /'ɛθiːn/ • n. systematic chemical name for **ETHYLENE**.
– ORIGIN C19: from **ETHER** + **-ENE**.

**ether** /'iːθə/ • n. **1** (also **diethyl ether**) a pleasant-smelling, volatile, highly flammable liquid used as an anaesthetic and as a solvent. **2** Chemistry any organic compound with an oxygen atom linking two alkyl groups. **3** (also **aether**) chiefly poetic/literary the clear sky; the upper regions of air beyond the clouds. **4** (also **aether**) Physics, historical a substance formerly postulated to permeate all space and to transmit light.
– DERIVATIVES **etheric** /iː'θɛrɪk, 'iːθ(ə)rɪk/ adj.
– ORIGIN ME: from OFr., or via L. from Gk *aithēr* 'upper air', from the base of *aithein* 'burn, shine'.

**ethereal** /ɪ'θɪərɪəl/ (also **etherial**) • adj. **1** extremely delicate and light in a way that seems not to be of this world. **2** Chemistry (of a solution) having diethyl ether as a solvent.
– DERIVATIVES **ethereality** n. **etherealize** (also **-ise**) v. **ethereally** adv.
– ORIGIN C16: via L. from Gk *aitherios* (from *aithēr* 'ether') + **-AL**.

**etherize** (also **-ise**) • v. historical anaesthetize with ether.
– DERIVATIVES **etherization** n.

**Ethernet** /'iːθənɛt/ • n. Computing a system for connecting a number of computer systems to form a local area network.
– ORIGIN 1970s: blend of **ETHER** and **NETWORK**.

**ethic** /'ɛθɪk/ • n. a set of moral principles.
– ORIGIN ME: from OFr. *éthique*, from L. *ethice*, from Gk (*hē*) *ēthikē* (*tekhnē*) '(the science of) morals', based on *ēthos* (see **ETHOS**).

**ethical** • adj. **1** of or relating to moral principles or the

branch of knowledge concerned with these. **2** morally correct. **3** (of a medicine) available only on prescription.
– DERIVATIVES **ethicality** n. **ethically** adv.

**ethics** • pl. n. **1** [usu. treated as pl.] the moral principles governing or influencing conduct. **2** [usu. treated as sing.] the branch of knowledge concerned with moral principles.
– DERIVATIVES **ethicist** n.

**Ethiopian** • n. a native or national of Ethiopia, or a person of Ethiopian descent. • adj. **1** of or relating to Ethiopia or its people. **2** Zoology relating to or denoting a zoogeographical region comprising sub-Saharan Africa, the Arabian peninsula, and (usually) Madagascar.

**Ethiopic** /ˌiːθɪˈɒpɪk/ • n. another term for **GE'EZ**. • adj. of, in, or relating to Ge'ez.

**ethmoid** /ˈɛθmɔɪd/ • n. Anatomy a square bone at the root of the nose, forming part of the cranium, and having many perforations through which the olfactory nerves pass to the nose.
– DERIVATIVES **ethmoidal** adj.
– ORIGIN C18: from Gk *ēthmoeidēs*, from *ēthmos* 'a sieve'.

**ethnic** • adj. **1** of or relating to a group of people having a common national or cultural tradition. **2** denoting origin by birth or descent rather than by present nationality: *ethnic Albanians*. **3** characteristic of or belonging to a non-Western cultural tradition: *ethnic dresses*. **4** archaic heathen. • n. chiefly N. Amer. a member of an ethnic minority.
– DERIVATIVES **ethnically** adv. **ethnicity** n.
– ORIGIN ME (denoting a person not of the Christian or Jewish faith): via eccles. L. from Gk *ethnikos* 'heathen', from *ethnos* 'nation'.

**ethnic cleansing** • n. the mass expulsion or killing of members of one ethnic or religious group in an area by those of another.

**ethnic minority** • n. a subgroup within a community which differs ethnically from the main population.

**ethno-** /ˈɛθnəʊ/ • comb. form ethnic; ethnological: *ethnocentric*.
– ORIGIN from Gk *ethnos* 'nation'.

**ethnocentric** • adj. evaluating other cultures according to preconceptions originating in one's own culture.
– DERIVATIVES **ethnocentrically** adv. **ethnocentricity** n. **ethnocentrism** n.

**ethnocultural** • adj. of or relating to a particular ethnic group.

**ethnography** /ɛθˈnɒɡrəfi/ • n. the scientific description of peoples and cultures with reference to their particular customs and characteristics.
– DERIVATIVES **ethnographer** n. **ethnographic** adj. **ethnographical** adj. **ethnographically** adv.

**ethnology** /ɛθˈnɒlədʒi/ • n. the study of the characteristics of different peoples and the differences and relationships between them.
– DERIVATIVES **ethnologic** /-nəˈlɒdʒɪk/ adj. **ethnological** adj. **ethnologically** adv. **ethnologist** n.

**ethnomusicology** • n. the study of the music of different cultures.
– DERIVATIVES **ethnomusicologic** adj. **ethnomusicological** adj. **ethnomusicologist** n.

**ethology** /iːˈθɒlədʒi/ • n. **1** the science of animal behaviour. **2** the study of human behaviour and social organization from a biological perspective.
– DERIVATIVES **ethological** adj. **ethologist** n.
– ORIGIN C19: via L. from Gk *ēthologia*, from *ēthos* (see **ETHOS**).

**ethos** /ˈiːθɒs/ • n. the characteristic spirit of a culture, era, or community as manifested in its attitudes and aspirations.
– ORIGIN C19: from mod. L., from Gk *ēthos* 'nature, disposition', (pl.) 'customs'.

**ethyl** /ˈɛθʌɪl, -θɪl, ˈiː-/ • n. [as modifier] Chemistry of or denoting the alkyl radical $-C_2H_5$, derived from ethane.
– ORIGIN C19: from Ger., from *Äther* 'ether' + **-YL**.

**ethyl acetate** • n. Chemistry a colourless volatile liquid with a fruity smell, used as a plastics solvent and in flavourings and perfumes.

**ethyl alcohol** • n. another term for **ALCOHOL** (in sense 1).

**ethylene** /ˈɛθɪliːn, -θ(ə)l-/ • n. Chemistry a flammable hydrocarbon gas of the alkene series, occurring in natural gas and coal gas. [$C_2H_4$.]

**ethylene glycol** • n. Chemistry a colourless viscous hygroscopic liquid used in antifreeze and in wood preservatives.

**ethyne** /ˈiːθʌɪn, ˈɛθ-/ • n. systematic chemical name for **ACETYLENE**.

**-etic** • suffix forming adjectives and nouns, such as *pathetic, peripatetic*.
– ORIGIN from Gk *-ĕtikos* or *-ētikos*.

**etiolated** /ˈiːtɪəˌleɪtɪd/ • adj. (of a plant) pale and weak due to a lack of light.
– DERIVATIVES **etiolation** n.
– ORIGIN C18: from *etiolate* (from Fr. *étioler*, from Norman Fr. *étieuler* 'grow into haulm').

**etiology** • n. US spelling of **AETIOLOGY**.

**etiquette** /ˈɛtɪkɛt, ɛtɪˈkɛt/ • n. the customary code of polite behaviour in a society.
– ORIGIN C18: from Fr. *étiquette* 'list of ceremonial observances of a court', also 'label, etiquette', from OFr. *estiquette* (see **TICKET**).

**Eton collar** • n. a broad, stiff white collar worn over the collar of a jacket or coat.

**Etonian** /iːˈtəʊnɪən/ • n. a pupil of Eton College, a boys' public school in southern England. • adj. relating to or typical of Eton College.

**Eton jacket** • n. a short black waist-length jacket that is pointed at the back, formerly worn by pupils of Eton College.

**étouffée** /ˌeɪtuːˈfeɪ/ • n. US a spicy Cajun stew made with vegetables and seafood.
– ORIGIN Fr., past part. of *étouffer* 'stifle, suffocate, choke'.

**etrier** /ˈeɪtrɪeɪ/ • n. Climbing a short rope ladder with a few rungs of wood or metal.
– ORIGIN 1950s: from Fr. *étrier* 'stirrup'.

**Etrurian** /ɪˈtrʊərɪən/ • n. & adj. another term for **ETRUSCAN**.

**Etruscan** /ɪˈtrʌsk(ə)n/ • n. **1** a native of Etruria, an ancient state of western Italy that was at its height *c.*500 BC. **2** the language of Etruria, written in an alphabet derived from Greek. • adj. of or relating to Etruria, its people, or their language.
– ORIGIN from L. *Etruscus* + **-AN**.

**et seq.** (also **et seqq.**) • adv. and what follows (used in page references).
– ORIGIN from L. *et sequens* 'and the following'.

**-ette** • suffix forming nouns: **1** denoting small size: *kitchenette*. **2** denoting an imitation or substitute: *leatherette*. **3** denoting female gender: *suffragette*.
– ORIGIN from OFr. *-ette*, fem. of **-ET**[1].

**étude** /ˈeɪtjuːd, eɪˈtjuːd/ • n. a short musical composition or exercise.
– ORIGIN C19: from Fr., lit. 'study'.

**etui** /ɛˈtwiː/ • n. (pl. **etuis**) dated a small ornamental case for holding needles, cosmetics, and other articles.
– ORIGIN C17: from Fr. *étui*, from OFr. *estui* 'prison'; cf. **TWEEZERS**.

**-etum** • suffix (forming nouns) denoting a collection of trees or other plants: *arboretum*.
– ORIGIN from L.

**etymology** /ˌɛtɪˈmɒlədʒi/ • n. (pl. **-ies**) an account of the origins and the developments in meaning of a word.
– DERIVATIVES **etymological** adj. **etymologically** adv. **etymologist** n. **etymologize** (also **-ise**) v.
– ORIGIN ME: from OFr. *ethimologie*, via L. from Gk *etumologia*, from *etumologos* 'student of etymology', from *etumon*, neut. sing. of *etumos* 'true'.

**etymon** /ˈɛtɪmɒn/ • n. (pl. **etymons** or **etyma**) a word or morpheme from which a later word is derived.
– ORIGIN C16: via L. from Gk *etumon* (see **ETYMOLOGY**).

**EU** • abbrev. European Union.

**Eu** • symb. the chemical element europium.

**eu-** • comb. form well; easily: *eupeptic*.
– ORIGIN from Gk *eu* 'well', from *eus* 'good'.

**eubacteria** /ˌjuːbakˈtɪərɪə/ • pl. n. Biology a large group of

bacteria with simple cells and rigid cell walls, comprising the 'true' bacteria and cyanobacteria as distinct from archaea.
– DERIVATIVES **eubacterial** adj.
– ORIGIN C20: from mod. L *Eubacterium* (genus name), from **EU-** (in sense 'normal') + **BACTERIUM**.

**eucalyptus** /ˌjuːkəˈlɪptəs/ (also **eucalypt**) ● n. (pl. **eucalyptuses** or **eucalypti** /-tʌɪ/) a fast-growing evergreen Australasian tree valued for its wood, oil, gum, and resin. [Genus *Eucalyptus*: numerous species.] ➤ the oil from eucalyptus leaves, chiefly used for its medicinal properties.
– ORIGIN mod. L., from Gk *eu* 'well' + *kaluptos* 'covered', because the unopened flower is protected by a cap.

**eucaryote** ● n. variant spelling of **EUKARYOTE**.

**Eucharist** /ˈjuːk(ə)rɪst/ ● n. the Christian service, ceremony, or sacrament commemorating the Last Supper, in which bread and wine are consecrated and consumed. ➤ the consecrated elements, especially the bread.
– DERIVATIVES **Eucharistic** adj. **Eucharistical** adj.
– ORIGIN ME: from OFr. *eucariste*, based on eccles. Gk *eukharistia* 'thanksgiving', from Gk *eukharistos* 'grateful', from *eu* 'well' + *kharizesthai* 'offer graciously' (from *kharis* 'grace').

**euchre** /ˈjuːkə/ ● n. a North American card game for two to four players, played with the thirty-two highest cards, the aim being to win at least three of the five tricks played. ● v. **1** (in euchre) prevent (another player) from taking three tricks. **2** N. Amer. informal deceive or outwit. **3** (**be euchred**) Austral. informal be exhausted or ruined.
– ORIGIN C19: from Ger. dial. *Jucker(spiel)*.

**Euclidean** /juːˈklɪdɪən/ ● adj. of or relating to the ancient Greek mathematician Euclid and his system of geometry.

**eucryphia** /juːˈkrɪfɪə/ ● n. a shrub or small tree with glossy dark green leaves and large white flowers, native to Australia and South America. [Genus *Eucryphia*.]
– ORIGIN mod. L., from Gk *eu* 'well' + *-kruphos* 'hidden' (with ref. to its joined sepals).

**eudaemonic** /ˌjuːdɪˈmɒnɪk/ (also **eudemonic**) ● adj. formal conducive to happiness.
– ORIGIN C19: from Gk *eudaimonikos*, from *eudaimōn* (see **EUDAEMONISM**).

**eudaemonism** /juːˈdiːmənɪz(ə)m/ (also **eudemonism**) ● n. a system of ethics that bases moral value on the likelihood of actions producing happiness.
– DERIVATIVES **eudaemonist** n. **eudaemonistic** adj.
– ORIGIN C19: from Gk *eudaimonismos* 'system of happiness', from *eudaimōn* 'happy', from *eu* 'well' + *daimōn* 'guardian spirit'.

**eudiometer** /ˌjuːdɪˈɒmɪtə/ ● n. Chemistry a graduated glass tube in which mixtures of gases can be made to react by an electric spark, used to measure changes in volume during chemical reactions.
– DERIVATIVES **eudiometric** adj. **eudiometrical** adj. **eudiometry** n.
– ORIGIN C18 (denoting an instrument used to measure amounts of oxygen, thought to be greater in fine weather): from Gk *eudios* 'clear, fine' (weather), from *eu* 'well' + *dios* 'heavenly'.

**eugenics** /juːˈdʒɛnɪks/ ● pl. n. [treated as sing.] the science of using controlled breeding to increase the occurrence of desirable heritable characteristics in a population.
– DERIVATIVES **eugenic** adj. **eugenically** adv. **eugenicist** n. & adj. **eugenist** n. & adj.
– ORIGIN C19: from **EU-** + **-GEN** + **-ICS**.

**eugenol** /ˈjuːdʒɪnɒl/ ● n. Chemistry a colourless or pale yellow liquid compound present in oil of cloves and used in perfumery.
– ORIGIN C19: from *Eugenia* (genus name of the tree from which oil of cloves is obtained, named in honour of Prince *Eugene* of Savoy) + **-OL**.

**euglena** /juːˈgliːnə/ ● n. Biology a single-celled freshwater flagellate organism, sometimes forming a green scum on stagnant water. [Genus *Euglena*.]
– DERIVATIVES **euglenoid** n. & adj.
– ORIGIN mod. L., from **EU-** + Gk *glēnē* 'eyeball, socket of joint'.

**euhedral** /juːˈhiːdr(ə)l/ ● adj. Geology (of a mineral crystal) having faces corresponding to its regular crystal form, not constrained by adjacent minerals.

**eukaryote** /juːˈkarɪəʊt/ (also **eucaryote**) ● n. Biology an organism consisting of a cell or cells in which the genetic material is DNA in the form of chromosomes contained within a distinct nucleus (that is, all living organisms other than the eubacteria and archaea). Compare with **PROKARYOTE**.
– DERIVATIVES **eukaryotic** adj.
– ORIGIN 1960s: from **EU-** + **KARYO-** + *-ote* as in *zygote*.

**eulachon** /ˈjuːləkɒn/ ● n. (pl. same) another term for **CANDLEFISH**.
– ORIGIN C19: from Lower Chinook.

**eulogium** /juːˈləʊdʒɪəm/ ● n. (pl. **eulogia** /-dʒɪə/ or **eulogiums**) another term for **EULOGY**.
– ORIGIN C17: from med. L., 'praise'.

**eulogize** /ˈjuːlədʒʌɪz/ (also **-ise**) ● v. praise highly.
– DERIVATIVES **eulogist** n. **eulogistic** adj. **eulogistically** adv.

**eulogy** /ˈjuːlədʒi/ ● n. (pl. **-ies**) a speech or piece of writing that praises someone highly.
– ORIGIN ME: from med. L. *eulogium*, *eulogia* (from Gk *eulogia* 'praise'), appar. influenced by L. *elogium* 'inscription on a tomb' (from Gk *elegia* 'elegy').

**eunuch** /ˈjuːnək/ ● n. a man who has been castrated.
– ORIGIN OE, via L. from Gk *eunoukhos*, lit. 'bedroom guard', from *eunē* 'bed' + a second element rel. to *ekhein* 'to hold'.

**eunuchoid** /ˈjuːnəkɔɪd/ ● adj. chiefly Medicine having reduced or indeterminate sexual characteristics.
– DERIVATIVES **eunuchoidism** n.

**euonymus** /juːˈɒnɪməs/ ● n. a shrub or small tree noted for its autumn colours and bright fruit. [Genus *Euonymus*: numerous species.]
– ORIGIN mod. L. (named by Linnaeus), from L. *euonymos*, from Gk *euōnumos* 'having an auspicious or honoured name', from *eus* 'good' + *onoma* 'name'.

**eupeptic** /juːˈpɛptɪk/ ● adj. of or having good digestion.
– ORIGIN C17: from Gk *eupeptos*, from *eu* 'well, easily' + *peptein* 'to digest'.

**euphausiid** /juːˈfɔːzɪɪd/ ● n. Zoology a shrimp-like planktonic crustacean of an order (Euphausiaceae) which includes krill.
– ORIGIN C19: from mod. L. *Euphausia* (genus name, from Gk *eu* 'well' + *phainein* 'to show' + *ousia* 'substance') + **-ID**[3].

**euphemism** /ˈjuːfəmɪz(ə)m/ ● n. a mild or less direct word substituted for one that is harsh or blunt when referring to something unpleasant or embarrassing.
– DERIVATIVES **euphemistic** adj. **euphemistically** adv. **euphemize** (also **-ise**) v.
– ORIGIN C16: from Gk *euphēmismos*, from *euphēmizein* 'use auspicious words', from *eu* 'well' + *phēmē* 'speaking'.

**euphonious** /juːˈfəʊnɪəs/ ● adj. sounding pleasant.
– DERIVATIVES **euphoniously** adv.

**euphonium** /juːˈfəʊnɪəm/ ● n. a valved brass musical instrument of tenor pitch, resembling a small tuba.
– ORIGIN C19: from Gk *euphōnos* 'having a pleasing sound' + **-IUM**.

**euphony** /ˈjuːf(ə)ni/ ● n. (pl. **-ies**) **1** the quality of being pleasing to the ear. **2** the tendency to make phonetic change for ease of pronunciation.
– DERIVATIVES **euphonic** adj. **euphonize** (also **-ise**) v.
– ORIGIN ME: from Fr. *euphonie*, via late L. from Gk *euphōnia*, from *euphōnos* 'well sounding' (based on *phōnē* 'sound').

**euphorbia** /juːˈfɔːbɪə/ ● n. a plant of a genus that comprises the spurges. [Genus *Euphorbia*.]
– ORIGIN ME: from L. *euphorbea*, named after *Euphorbus*, Gk physician to the reputed discoverer of the plant, Juba II of Mauretania.

**euphoria** /juːˈfɔːrɪə/ ● n. a feeling of intense happiness.
– DERIVATIVES **euphoric** adj. **euphorically** adv.
– ORIGIN C17: mod. L., from Gk, from *euphoros* 'borne well, healthy', from *eu* 'well' + *pherein* 'to bear'.

**euphoriant** ● adj. producing a feeling of euphoria. ● n. a euphoriant drug.

**euphrasia** /juːˈfreɪzɪə/ • **n.** eyebright or a related plant, especially as a herbal or homeopathic remedy for eye problems. [Genus *Euphrasia*.]
– ORIGIN C18: via med. L. from Gk, lit. 'cheerfulness'.

**euphuism** /ˈjuːfjʊɪz(ə)m/ • **n.** formal an artificial, highly elaborate way of writing or speaking.
– DERIVATIVES **euphuist** n. **euphuistic** adj. **euphuistically** adv.
– ORIGIN C16: with ref. to the high-flown style of John Lyly's prose romance *Euphues*.

**Eurasian** • **adj. 1** of mixed European (or European-American) and Asian parentage. **2** of or relating to Eurasia. • **n.** a person of Eurasian parentage.

**Euratom** /ˌjʊ(ə)ˈratəm/ • **abbrev.** European Atomic Energy Community.

**eureka** /ˌjʊ(ə)ˈriːkə/ • **exclam.** a cry of joy or satisfaction when one finds or discovers something. • **n.** an alloy of copper and nickel used for electrical filament and resistance wire.
– ORIGIN C17: from Gk *heurēka* 'I have found it', said to have been uttered by Archimedes when he hit upon a method of determining the purity of gold.

**eurhythmic** /jʊ(ə)ˈrɪðmɪk/ • **adj.** rare in or relating to harmonious proportion.
– ORIGIN C19: based on Gk *euruthmia* 'proportion' + **-IC**.

**eurhythmics** (also **eurhythmy**; US also **eurythmics**, **eurythmy**) • **pl. n.** [treated as sing.] a system of rhythmical physical movements to music used to teach musical understanding or for therapeutic purposes.
– ORIGIN C20: from **EU-** + **RHYTHM** + **-ICS**.

**Euro** /ˈjʊərəʊ/ • **adj.** informal European, especially concerned with the European Union. • **n.** (**euro**) the single European currency, introduced in the European Union in 1999.

**Euro-** • **comb. form** European; European and ... ➤relating to Europe or the European Union: *a Euro-MP.*

**Eurobond** • **n.** an international bond issued in Europe or elsewhere outside the country in whose currency its value is stated.

**Eurocentric** • **adj.** implicitly regarding European culture as pre-eminent.
– DERIVATIVES **Eurocentricity** n. **Eurocentrism** n.

**Eurocommunism** • **n.** a European form of communism which advocates the preservation of many elements of Western liberal democracy.
– DERIVATIVES **Eurocommunist** adj. & n.

**Eurocrat** • **n.** informal, chiefly derogatory a bureaucrat in the administration of the European Union.

**Eurocurrency** • **n. 1** a form of money held or traded outside the country in whose currency its value is stated. **2** a single currency for use by the member states of the European Union.

**Eurodollar** • **n.** a US dollar held in Europe or elsewhere outside the US.

**Euroland** • **n.** the economic region formed by those member countries of the European Union that have adopted the euro.

**Euromarket** • **n. 1** a financial market which deals with Eurocurrencies. **2** the European Union regarded as a single commercial or financial market.

**Euro-MP** • **n.** a member of the European Parliament.

**European** • **n.** a native or inhabitant of Europe. ➤a person who is white or of European parentage. • **adj.** of or relating to Europe or the European Union.
– DERIVATIVES **Europeanism** n. **Europeanization** (also **-isation**) n. **Europeanize** (also **-ise**) v.

**European plan** • **n.** N. Amer. a system of charging for a hotel room only, without meals.

**European Union** • **n.** an economic and political association of certain European countries as a unit with internal free trade and common external tariffs.

**europium** /jʊ(ə)rˈəʊpɪəm/ • **n.** the chemical element of atomic number 63, a soft silvery-white metal of the lanthanide series. (Symbol: **Eu**)
– ORIGIN C20: mod. L., based on *Europe*.

**Euro-sceptic** • **n.** a person who is opposed to increasing the powers of the European Union.
– DERIVATIVES **Euro-scepticism** n.

**Eurostar** • **n.** trademark the high-speed passenger rail service that links London with various European cities via the Channel Tunnel.

**Eurotrash** • **n.** informal rich European socialites, especially those living or working in the United States.

**Eurozone** • **n.** another term for **EUROLAND**.

**eury-** • **comb. form** denoting a wide variety or range of something specified: *eurytopic.*
– ORIGIN from Gk *eurus* 'wide'.

**euryhaline** /ˌjʊərɪˈheɪlʌɪn, -ˈheɪliːn/ • **adj.** Ecology able to tolerate a wide range of salinity. Often contrasted with **STENOHALINE**.
– ORIGIN C19: from Gk *eurus* 'wide' + *halinos* 'of salt'.

**eurypterid** /ˌjʊ(ə)ˈrɪptərɪd/ • **n.** a giant fossil marine arthropod of a group occurring in the Palaeozoic era, resembling large scorpions.
– ORIGIN C19: from mod. L. *Eurypterus* (genus name), from **EURY-** + Gk *pteron* 'wing' + **-ID**[3].

**eurythermal** /ˌjʊərɪˈθəːm(ə)l/ • **adj.** Ecology able to tolerate a wide range of temperature. Often contrasted with **STENOTHERMAL**.

**eurythmics** (also **eurythmy**) • **pl. n.** US spelling of **EURHYTHMICS**.

**Euskara** /ˈjuːskərə/ • **n.** the Basque language.
– ORIGIN the name in Basque.

**eusocial** /juːˈsəʊʃ(ə)l/ • **adj.** Zoology denoting social organisms (e.g. the honeybee) in which a single female or caste produces the offspring and non-reproductive individuals cooperate in caring for the young.
– DERIVATIVES **eusociality** n.

**Eustachian tube** /juːˈsteɪʃ(ə)n/ • **n.** Anatomy a narrow passage leading from the pharynx to the cavity of the middle ear, permitting the equalization of pressure on each side of the eardrum.
– ORIGIN C18: named after the C16 Ital. anatomist Bartolomeo *Eustachio*.

**eustasy** /ˈjuːstəsi/ • **n.** a change of sea level throughout the world, caused typically by movements of parts of the earth's crust or melting of glaciers.
– DERIVATIVES **eustatic** adj.
– ORIGIN 1940s: back-form. from *eustatic*, coined in Ger. from Gk *eu* 'well' + *statikos* 'static'.

**eutectic** /juːˈtɛktɪk/ • **adj.** Chemistry (of a mixture of two substances) having a distinct melting point which is lower than the melting points of the separate constituents.
– ORIGIN C19: from Gk *eutēktos* 'easily melting'.

**eutectic point** • **n.** Chemistry the temperature at which a particular eutectic mixture freezes or melts.

**euthanasia** /ˌjuːθəˈneɪzɪə/ • **n.** the painless killing of a patient suffering from an incurable disease or in an irreversible coma.
– ORIGIN C17: from Gk, from *eu* 'well' + *thanatos* 'death'.

**euthanize** /ˈjuːθənʌɪz/ (also **-ise**) • **v.** N. Amer. put (an animal) to death humanely.

**Eutheria** /juːˈθɪərɪə/ • **pl. n.** Zoology a major group of mammals that comprises the placentals. Compare with **METATHERIA**.
– DERIVATIVES **eutherian** n. & adj.
– ORIGIN mod. L., from **EU-** + Gk *thēria*, pl. of *thērion* 'wild beast'.

**euthyroid** /juːˈθʌɪrɔɪd/ • **adj.** Medicine having a normally functioning thyroid gland.

**eutrophic** /juːˈtrəʊfɪk, -ˈtrɒfɪk/ • **adj.** Ecology (of a body of water) rich in nutrients and so supporting a dense plant population, the decomposition of which kills animal life by depriving it of oxygen.
– DERIVATIVES **eutrophicate** v. **eutrophication** n.
– ORIGIN C18: from Gk *eutrophia*, from *eu* 'well' + *trephein* 'nourish'.

**eV** • **abbrev.** electronvolt(s).

**EVA** • **abbrev. 1** ethyl vinyl acetate. **2** (in space) extravehicular activity.

**evacuant** /ɪˈvakjʊənt/ • **adj.** (of a medicine or treatment) acting to induce some kind of bodily discharge. • **n.** an evacuant medicine.

**evacuate** /ɪˈvakjʊeɪt/ ● **v. 1** remove from a place of danger to a safer place. ➤ leave (a dangerous place). **2** technical remove air, water, or other contents from (a container). ➤ empty (the bowels or another bodily organ).
– DERIVATIVES **evacuation** n.
– ORIGIN ME: from L. *evacuat-*, *evacuare*, from *e-* (var. of *ex-*) 'out of' + *vacuus* 'empty'.

**evacuative** ● **n. & adj.** another term for **EVACUANT**.

**evacuee** ● **n.** a person evacuated from a place of danger.

**evade** ● **v. 1** escape or avoid, especially by guile or trickery. ➤ avoid giving a direct answer to (a question). **2** escape paying (tax or duty), especially by illegitimate presentation of one's finances. ➤ defeat the intention of (a law or rule), especially while complying with its letter.
– DERIVATIVES **evadable** adj. **evader** n.
– ORIGIN C15: from Fr. *évader*, from L. *evadere* from *e-* (var. of *ex-*) 'out of' + *vadere* 'go'.

**evaginate** /ɪˈvadʒɪneɪt/ ● **v.** Biology & Physiology turn (a tubular or pouch-shaped organ or structure) inside out.
– DERIVATIVES **evagination** n.
– ORIGIN C17: from L. *evaginat-*, *evaginare* 'unsheath'.

**evaluate** ● **v. 1** form an idea of the amount, number, or value of; assess. **2** Mathematics find a numerical expression or equivalent for (an equation, formula, or function).
– DERIVATIVES **evaluation** n. **evaluative** adj. **evaluator** n.
– ORIGIN C19: back-form. from *evaluation*, from Fr. *évaluer*, from *es-* (from L. *ex-*) 'out, from' + OFr. *value* 'value'.

**evanescent** ● **adj. 1** chiefly poetic/literary quickly fading from sight, memory, or existence. **2** Physics denoting a field or wave which extends into a region where it cannot propagate and whose amplitude therefore decreases with distance.
– DERIVATIVES **evanesce** v. **evanescence** n. **evanescently** adv.
– ORIGIN C18: from L. *evanescent-*, *evanescere* 'disappear'.

**evangel** /ɪˈvan(d)ʒɛl, -(d)ʒ(ə)l/ ● **n. 1** archaic the Christian gospel. ➤ any of the four Gospels. **2** North American term for **EVANGELIST**.
– ORIGIN ME: from OFr. *evangile*, via eccles. L. from Gk *euangelion* 'good news', from *euangelos* 'bringing good news', from *eu-* 'well' + *angelein* 'announce'.

**evangelical** ● **adj. 1** of or according to the teaching of the gospel or the Christian religion. ➤ of or denoting a tradition within Protestant Christianity emphasizing the authority of the Bible, personal conversion, and the doctrine of salvation by faith in the Atonement. **2** fervent in advocating something. ● **n.** a member of the evangelical tradition in the Christian Church.
– DERIVATIVES **evangelic** adj. **evangelicalism** n. **evangelically** adv.

**evangelist** ● **n. 1** a person who seeks to convert others to the Christian faith, especially by public preaching. **2** the writer of one of the four Gospels (Matthew, Mark, Luke, or John). **3** a zealous advocate of something.
– DERIVATIVES **evangelism** n. **evangelistic** adj.

**evangelize** (also **-ise**) ● **v.** convert or seek to convert (someone) to Christianity. ➤ preach the gospel.
– DERIVATIVES **evangelization** n. **evangelizer** n.

**evaporate** /ɪˈvapəreɪt/ ● **v. 1** turn from liquid into vapour. **2** (of something abstract) cease to exist.
– DERIVATIVES **evaporable** adj. **evaporation** n. **evaporative** adj. **evaporator** n.
– ORIGIN ME: from L. *evaporat-*, *evaporare*, from *e-* (var. of *ex-*) 'out of' + *vapor* 'steam, vapour'.

**evaporated milk** ● **n.** thick sweetened milk that has had some of the liquid removed by evaporation.

**evaporating dish** ● **n.** Chemistry a small ceramic dish in which liquids are heated over a flame so that they evaporate, leaving a solid residue.

**evaporite** /ɪˈvapərʌɪt/ ● **n.** Geology a natural salt or mineral deposit left after the evaporation of a body of water.

**evapotranspiration** /ɪˌvapəʊtranspɪˈreɪʃ(ə)n/ ● **n.** the process by which water is transferred from the land to the atmosphere by evaporation from the soil and other surfaces and by transpiration from plants.

**evasion** ● **n.** the action or an instance of evading.

**evasive** ● **adj.** tending to avoid commitment or self-revelation. ➤ directed towards avoidance or escape.
– DERIVATIVES **evasively** adv. **evasiveness** n.

**eve** ● **n. 1** the day or period of time immediately before an event or occasion. ➤ the evening or day before a religious festival. **2** chiefly poetic/literary evening.
– ORIGIN ME: short form of **EVEN**[2].

**evection** /ɪˈvɛkʃ(ə)n/ ● **n.** Astronomy regular variation in the eccentricity of the moon's orbit around the earth, caused mainly by the sun's attraction.
– ORIGIN C17 (in the sense 'elevation, exaltation'): from L. *evectio(n-)*, from *evehere* 'carry out or up'.

**Even** /eɪˈvɛn/ ● **n.** (pl. same) **1** a member of an indigenous people living in the Kamchatka peninsula of eastern Siberia. **2** the Tungusic language of this people.

**even**[1] ● **adj. 1** flat and smooth; level. ➤ having little variation in quality; regular. **2** equal in number, amount, or value. **3** equally balanced: *the match was fairly even.* **4** (of a person's temper or disposition) equable; calm. **5** (of a number) divisible by two without a remainder. ● **v.** (often **even out/up**) make or become even. ● **adv.** used for emphasis: *he knows even less than I do.*
– PHRASES **even as** at the very same time as. **an even break** informal a fair chance. **even if** despite the possibility or fact that. **even now** (or **then**) **1** now (or then) as well as before. **2** in spite of what has (or had) happened. **3** at this (or that) very moment. **even so** nevertheless. **even though** despite the fact that. **of even date** Law or formal of the same date. **on an even keel** not listing or tilting to one side.
– DERIVATIVES **evenly** adv. **evenness** n.
– ORIGIN OE *efen* (adj.), *efne* (adv.), of Gmc origin.

**even**[2] ● **n.** archaic or poetic/literary evening.
– ORIGIN OE *ǣfen*, of Gmc origin.

**even-aged** ● **adj.** Forestry (of woodland) composed of trees of approximately the same age.

**even-handed** ● **adj.** fair and impartial.
– DERIVATIVES **even-handedly** adv. **even-handedness** n.

**evening** ● **n.** the period of time at the end of the day, between late afternoon and bedtime. ● **adv.** (**evenings**) informal in the evening; every evening.
– ORIGIN OE *ǣfnung*, from *ǣfnian* 'approach evening', from *ǣfen* (see **EVEN**[2]).

**evening primrose** ● **n.** a plant with pale yellow flowers that open in the evening, whose seeds are used for a medicinal oil. [Genus *Oenothera*: numerous species.]

**evening star** ● **n.** (**the evening star**) the planet Venus, seen shining in the western sky after sunset.

**Evenki** /eɪˈvɛnki/ ● **n.** (pl. same or **Evenkis**) **1** a member of an indigenous people of northern Siberia. **2** the Tungusic language of this people.

**even money** ● **n.** (in betting) odds offering an equal chance of winning or losing, with the amount won being the same as the stake.

**evens** ● **pl. n.** Brit. another term for **EVEN MONEY**.

**evensong** ● **n.** (especially in the Anglican Church) a service of evening prayers, psalms, and canticles.

**even-steven** (also **even-stevens**) ● **adj. & adv.** informal fair and equal in competition or distribution of resources.

**event** ● **n. 1** a thing that happens or takes place. ➤ a public or social occasion. **2** each of several contests making up a sports competition. **3** Physics a single occurrence of a process, e.g. the ionization of one atom.
– PHRASES **in any event** (or **at all events**) whatever happens or may have happened. **in the event 1** as it turned out. **2** (**in the event of/that**) if the specified thing happens.
– DERIVATIVES **eventless** adj. **eventlessness** n.
– ORIGIN C16: from L. *eventus*, from *evenire* 'result, happen'.

**eventer** ● **n.** Brit. a horse or rider that takes part in eventing.

**eventful** ● **adj.** marked by interesting or exciting events.
– DERIVATIVES **eventfully** adv. **eventfulness** n.

**event horizon** ● **n.** Astronomy a notional boundary around a black hole beyond which no light or other radiation can escape.

**eventide** ● **n.** archaic or poetic/literary evening.

**eventing** ● **n.** an equestrian sport in which competitors must take part in each of several contests, usually cross-country, dressage, and showjumping.

**eventual** /ɪˈvɛn(t)ʃʊəl/ ● **adj.** occurring at the end of or resulting from a process or period of time.
– DERIVATIVES **eventually** adv.
– ORIGIN C17 (in the sense 'relating to an event or events'): from L. *eventus* (see **EVENT**), on the pattern of *actual*.

**eventuality** ● **n.** (pl. **-ies**) a possible event or outcome.

**eventuate** /ɪˈvɛn(t)ʃʊeɪt, -tjʊ-/ ● **v.** formal occur as a result. ➤(**eventuate in**) lead to as a result.
– DERIVATIVES **eventuation** n.
– ORIGIN C18 (orig. US): from **EVENT**, on the pattern of *actuate*.

**ever** ● **adv. 1** [usu. with neg. or in questions] at any time. ➤used in comparisons for emphasis. **2** always. **3** increasingly; constantly. **4** used for emphasis in questions expressing astonishment or outrage.
– PHRASES **ever and anon** archaic occasionally. **ever since** throughout the period since. **ever so** (or **such**) Brit. informal very; very much.
– ORIGIN OE *ǣfre*, of unknown origin.

**evergreen** ● **adj. 1** (of a plant) retaining green leaves throughout the year. Often contrasted with **DECIDUOUS**. **2** having an enduring freshness, success, or popularity. ● **n.** an evergreen plant.

**evergreen oak** ● **n.** another term for **HOLM OAK**.

**everlasting** ● **adj.** lasting forever or a very long time. ● **n.** a helichrysum or similar flower that retains its shape and colour after being dried.
– DERIVATIVES **everlastingly** adv. **everlastingness** n.

**evermore** ● **adv.** archaic or poetic/literary always; forever.

**evert** /ɪˈvəːt/ ● **v.** Biology & Physiology turn (a structure or organ) outwards or inside out.
– DERIVATIVES **eversible** adj. **eversion** n.
– ORIGIN C16 (in the sense 'upset, overthrow'): from L. *evertere*, from *e-* (var. of *ex-*) 'out' + *vertere* 'to turn'.

**every** ● **det. 1** used to refer to all the individual members of a set without exception. ➤all possible; the utmost. **2** used to indicate something happening at specified intervals.
– PHRASES **every bit as** (in comparisons) quite as. **every now and again** (or **every so often**) occasionally. **every other** each alternate in a series. **every which way** informal in all directions. ➤by all available means.
– ORIGIN OE *ǣfre ǣlc* (see **EVER**, **EACH**).

**everybody** ● **pron.** every person.

**everyday** ● **adj. 1** daily. **2** commonplace.

**Everyman** ● **n.** an ordinary or typical human being.

**everyone** ● **pron.** every person.

**every one** ● **pron.** each one.

**everyplace** ● **adv.** N. Amer. informal everywhere.

**everything** ● **pron. 1** all things, or all the things of a group or class. ➤all things of importance. ➤the most important thing or aspect: *money isn't everything.* **2** the current situation; life in general.

**everywhere** ● **adv.** in or to all places. ➤very common or widely distributed.

**evict** ● **v.** expel (someone) from a property, especially with the support of the law.
– DERIVATIVES **eviction** n. **evictor** n.
– ORIGIN ME (in the sense 'recover property by legal process'): from L. *evict-*, *evincere* 'overcome, defeat'.

**evidence** ● **n.** information indicating whether a belief or proposition is true or valid. ➤Law information used to establish facts in a legal investigation or admissible as testimony in a law court. ➤signs; indications. ● **v.** be or show evidence of.
– PHRASES **in evidence** noticeable; conspicuous. **turn King's** (or **Queen's** or US **state's**) **evidence** Law (of a criminal) give information in court against one's partners in order to receive a less severe punishment.
– ORIGIN ME: via OFr. from L. *evidentia*, from *evident-* (see **EVIDENT**).

**evident** ● **adj.** plain or obvious; clear.
– DERIVATIVES **evidently** adv.
– ORIGIN ME: from OFr., or from L. *evidens*, *evident-* 'obvious to the eye or mind', from *e-* (var. of *ex-*) 'out' + *videre* 'to see'.

**evidential** /ˌɛvɪˈdɛnʃ(ə)l/ ● **adj.** formal of or providing evidence.
– DERIVATIVES **evidentiality** n. **evidentially** adv.

**evidentiary** /ˌɛvɪˈdɛnʃ(ə)ri/ ● **adj.** chiefly US Law another term for **EVIDENTIAL**.

**evil** ● **adj. 1** profoundly immoral and malevolent. ➤embodying or associated with the forces of the devil. ➤harmful or tending to harm. **2** extremely unpleasant: *an evil smell.* ● **n.** profound wickedness and depravity, especially when regarded as a supernatural force. ➤something harmful or undesirable: *social evils.*
– PHRASES **the evil eye** a gaze or stare superstitiously believed to cause material harm. **the Evil One** archaic the Devil. **speak evil of** slander.
– DERIVATIVES **evilly** adv. **evilness** n.
– ORIGIN OE *yfel*, of Gmc origin.

**evil-doer** ● **n.** a person who commits evil deeds.
– DERIVATIVES **evil-doing** n.

**evince** /ɪˈvɪns/ ● **v.** formal reveal the presence of; indicate (a quality or feeling).
– ORIGIN C16 (in the sense 'prove by argument or evidence'): from L. *evincere* (see **EVICT**).

**eviscerate** /ɪˈvɪsəreɪt/ ● **v.** formal disembowel.
– DERIVATIVES **evisceration** n.
– ORIGIN C16: from L. *eviscerat-*, *eviscerare*, from *e-* (var. of *ex-*) 'out' + *viscera* 'internal organs'.

**eviternity** /ˌiːvɪˈtəːnɪti/ ● **n.** archaic or poetic/literary eternal existence; everlasting duration.
– DERIVATIVES **eviternal** adj.
– ORIGIN C16: from L. *aeviternus* 'eternal' + **-ITY**.

**evocative** /ɪˈvɒkətɪv/ ● **adj.** evoking strong images, memories, or feelings.
– DERIVATIVES **evocatively** adv. **evocativeness** n.

**evoke** /ɪˈvəʊk/ ● **v. 1** bring or recall to the conscious mind. **2** elicit (a response). **3** invoke (a spirit or deity).
– DERIVATIVES **evocation** n. **evoker** n.
– ORIGIN C17 (earlier (ME) as *evocation*): from L. *evocat-*, *evocare*, from *e-* (var. of *ex-*) 'out of, from' + *vocare* 'to call'.

**evolute** /ˈiːvəl(j)uːt, ˈɛv-/ ● **n.** Mathematics a curve which is the locus of the centres of curvature of another curve (its involute). ● **adj.** Zoology & Botany rolled outwards at the edges.
– ORIGIN C18: from L. *evolutus*, past part. of *evolvere* (see **EVOLVE**).

**evolution** /ˌiːvəˈluːʃ(ə)n, ˈɛv-/ ● **n. 1** the process by which different kinds of living organism are believed to have developed from earlier forms, especially by natural selection. **2** gradual development. **3** Chemistry the giving off of a gaseous product, or of heat. **4** a pattern of movements or manoeuvres. **5** Mathematics, dated the extraction of a root from a given quantity.
– DERIVATIVES **evolutional** adj. **evolutionally** adv. **evolutionarily** adv. **evolutionary** adj. **evolutive** adj.
– ORIGIN C17: from L. *evolutio(n-)* 'unrolling', from *evolvere* (see **EVOLVE**).

**evolutionist** ● **n.** a person who believes in the theories of evolution and natural selection.
– DERIVATIVES **evolutionism** n.

**evolve** ● **v. 1** develop gradually. **2** (of an organism or biological feature) develop over successive generations by evolution. **3** Chemistry give off (gas or heat).
– DERIVATIVES **evolvable** adj. **evolvement** n.
– ORIGIN C17 (in the sense 'make more complex, develop'): from L. *evolvere*, from *e-* (var. of *ex-*) 'out of' + *volvere* 'to roll'.

**evzone** /ˈɛvzəʊn/ ● **n.** a kilted soldier belonging to a select Greek infantry regiment.
– ORIGIN C19: from mod. Gk *euzōnos*, from Gk, 'dressed for exercise' (from *eu-* 'fine' + *zōnē* 'belt').

**Ewe** /ˈeɪweɪ/ ● **n.** (pl. same) **1** a member of a West African people of Ghana, Togo, and Benin. **2** the Kwa language of this people.
– ORIGIN the name in Ewe.

**ewe** /juː/ ● **n.** a female sheep.

– ORIGIN OE *eowu*, of Gmc origin.

**ewe neck** ● **n.** a horse's neck of which the upper outline curves inwards instead of outwards.
– DERIVATIVES **ewe-necked** adj.

**ewer** /'juːə/ ● **n.** a large jug with a wide mouth.
– ORIGIN ME: from Anglo-Norman Fr. *ewer*, var. of OFr. *aiguiere*, based on L. *aquarius* 'of water'.

**Ex.** ● **abbrev.** Exodus (in biblical references).

**ex**[1] ● **prep. 1** (of goods) sold direct from. **2** without; excluding.
– ORIGIN C19: from L., 'out of'.

**ex**[2] ● **n.** informal a former husband, wife, or partner in a relationship.

**ex-**[1] (also **e-**; **ef-** before *f*) ● **prefix 1** out: *exclude*. **2** upward: *extol*. **3** thoroughly: *excruciate*. **4** denoting removal or release: *excommunicate*. **5** forming verbs which denote inducement of a state: *exasperate*. **6** denoting a former state: *ex-husband*.
– ORIGIN from L. *ex* 'out of'.

**ex-**[2] ● **prefix** out: *exodus*.
– ORIGIN from Gk *ex* 'out of'.

**exa-** ● **comb. form** denoting a factor of $10^{18}$: *exajoule*.
– ORIGIN from *(h)exa-* (see **HEXA-**), based on the supposed analogy of *tera-* and *tetra-*.

**exacerbate** /ɪɡ'zasəbeɪt, ɛk'sas-/ ● **v.** make (something bad) worse.
– DERIVATIVES **exacerbation** n.
– ORIGIN C17: from L. *exacerbat-*, *exacerbare* 'make harsh'; *exacerbation* (ME) orig. meant 'provocation to anger'.

**exact** ● **adj.** not approximated in any way; precise. ➤accurate or correct in all details: *an exact replica*. ➤tending to be accurate and careful about minor details. ● **v. 1** demand and obtain (something) from someone. **2** inflict (revenge) on someone.
– DERIVATIVES **exactable** adj. **exactitude** n. **exactness** n. **exactor** n.
– ORIGIN ME (as v.): from L. *exact-*, *exigere* 'complete, ascertain, enforce'; the adj. reflects L. *exactus* 'precise'.

**exacta** /ɪɡ'zaktə/ ● **n.** N. Amer. another term for **PERFECTA**.
– ORIGIN 1960s: from Amer. Sp. *quiniela exacta* 'exact quinella'.

**exacting** ● **adj.** making great demands on one's endurance or skill.
– DERIVATIVES **exactingly** adv. **exactingness** n.

**exaction** ● **n.** formal the action or an act of exacting something, especially a payment. ➤a sum of money exacted.

**exactly** ● **adv. 1** in exact terms. **2** used to confirm or agree with what has just been said.

**exaggerate** /ɪɡ'zadʒəreɪt, ɛɡ-/ ● **v.** represent (something) as being larger or better than it really is. ➤[as adj. **exaggerated**] enlarged or altered beyond normal proportions.
– DERIVATIVES **exaggeratedly** adv. **exaggeration** n. **exaggerative** adj. **exaggerator** n.
– ORIGIN C16: from L. *exaggerat-*, *exaggerare* 'heap up'.

**exalt** /ɪɡ'zɔːlt, ɛɡ-/ ● **v. 1** praise or regard highly. **2** raise to a higher rank or position. ➤make noble in character; dignify.
– ORIGIN ME: from L. *exaltare*, from *ex-* 'out, upward' + *altus* 'high'.

**exaltation** ● **n. 1** extreme happiness. **2** the action of exalting.

**exalté** /ɪɡ'zɔːlteɪ/ dated or poetic/literary ● **n.** a person who is elated or impassioned. ● **adj.** inspiring or stimulating.
– ORIGIN C19: Fr., 'lifted up', past part. of *exalter*.

**exalted** ● **adj. 1** at a high level. **2** (of an idea) noble; lofty. **3** extremely happy.
– DERIVATIVES **exaltedly** adv. **exaltedness** n.

**exam** ● **n. 1** short for **EXAMINATION** (in sense 2). **2** N. Amer. a medical test of a specified kind.

**examen** /ɛɡ'zeɪmɛn/ (also **examen de conscience**) ● **n.** a formal examination of the soul or conscience, made usually daily by Jesuits and some other Roman Catholics.
– ORIGIN C17: from L., 'examination' (lit. 'tongue of a balance'), from *exigere* 'weigh accurately'.

**examination** ● **n. 1** a detailed inspection or investigation. ➤the action of examining. **2** a formal test of knowledge or proficiency in a subject or skill. **3** Law the formal questioning of a defendant or witness in court.

**examination-in-chief** ● **n.** Law the questioning of a witness by the party which has called that witness to give evidence, in order to support their case.

**examine** ● **v. 1** inspect closely to determine the nature or condition of; investigate thoroughly. **2** test the knowledge or proficiency of. **3** Law formally question (a defendant or witness) in court.
– DERIVATIVES **examinable** adj. **examinee** n. **examiner** n.
– ORIGIN ME: from OFr. *examiner*, from L. *examinare* 'weigh, test', from *examen* (see **EXAMEN**).

**example** ● **n. 1** a thing characteristic of its kind or illustrating a general rule. ➤a written problem or exercise designed to illustrate a rule. **2** a person or thing regarded in terms of their fitness to be imitated: *parents should set an example*. ● **v.** (**be exampled**) be exemplified.
– PHRASES **for example** by way of illustration. **make an example of** punish as a warning or deterrent to others.
– ORIGIN ME: from OFr., from L. *exemplum*, from *eximere* 'take out'; cf. **SAMPLE**.

**ex ante** /ɛks 'anti/ ● **adj. & adv.** based on forecasts rather than actual results.
– ORIGIN mod. L., from L. *ex* 'from, out of' + *ante* 'before'.

**exanthema** /ɪk'sanθɪmə, ˌɛksan'θiːmə/ ● **n.** (pl. **exanthemata**) Medicine a skin rash accompanying a disease or fever.
– DERIVATIVES **exanthematic** adj. **exanthematous** adj.
– ORIGIN C17: via late L. from Gk *exanthēma* 'eruption', from *ex-* 'out' + *antheein* 'to blossom'.

**exarch** /'ɛksɑːk/ ● **n. 1** (in the Orthodox Church) a bishop lower in rank than a patriarch and having jurisdiction wider than the metropolitan of a diocese. **2** historical a governor of a distant province under the Byzantine emperors.
– ORIGIN C16: via eccles. L. from Gk *exarkhos*, from *ex-* 'out of' + *arkhos* 'ruler'.

**exarchate** /'ɛksɑːkeɪt/ ● **n.** historical a Byzantine province governed by an exarch.

**exasperate** /ɪɡ'zasp(ə)reɪt, ɛɡ-/ ● **v.** irritate intensely.
– DERIVATIVES **exasperated** adj. **exasperatedly** adv. **exasperating** adj. **exasperatingly** adv. **exasperation** n.
– ORIGIN C16: from L. *exasperat-*, *exasperare* 'irritate to anger'.

**ex cathedra** /ˌɛks kə'θiːdrə/ ● **adv. & adj.** with the full authority of office (especially that of the Pope, implying infallibility as defined in Roman Catholic doctrine).
– ORIGIN L., 'from the (teacher's) chair'.

**excavate** /'ɛkskəveɪt/ ● **v. 1** make (a hole or channel) by digging. ➤extract (material) from the ground by digging. **2** carefully remove earth from (an area) in order to find buried remains.
– DERIVATIVES **excavation** n. **excavator** n.
– ORIGIN C16: from L. *excavat-*, *excavare* 'hollow out'.

**exceed** ● **v.** be greater in number or size than. ➤go beyond what is allowed or stipulated by (a set limit, especially of one's authority). ➤surpass.
– ORIGIN ME (in the sense 'go over (a boundary or specified point)'): from OFr. *exceder*, from L. *excedere*, from *ex-* 'out' + *cedere* 'go'.

**exceeding** archaic or poetic/literary ● **adj.** very great. ● **adv.** exceedingly.

**exceedingly** ● **adv. 1** extremely. **2** archaic to a great extent.

**excel** /ɪk'sɛl, ɛk-/ ● **v.** (**excelled**, **excelling**) be exceptionally good at an activity or subject. ➤(**excel oneself**) perform exceptionally well.
– ORIGIN ME: from L. *excellere*, from *ex-* 'out, beyond' + *celsus* 'lofty'.

**excellence** ● **n.** the quality of being excellent. ➤archaic an outstanding feature or quality.

**excellency** ● **n.** (pl. **-ies**) **1** (**His**, **Your**, etc. **Excellency**) a title or form of address for certain high officials of state, especially ambassadors, or of the Roman Catholic

Church. **2** archaic an outstanding feature or quality.

**excellent** ● **adj.** extremely good; outstanding.
– DERIVATIVES **excellently** adv.
– ORIGIN ME (in the general sense 'outstanding' in either a good or bad way): from OFr., from L. *excellent-*, *excellere* (see **EXCEL**).

**excelsior** /ɛk'sɛlsɪɔː/ ● **n. 1** used in the names of hotels and products to indicate superior quality. **2** N. Amer. softwood shavings used for packing fragile goods or stuffing furniture.
– ORIGIN C18 (as exclam.): from L., compar. of *excelsus*, from *ex-* 'out, beyond' + *celsus* 'lofty'.

**excentric** /ɪk'sɛntrɪk, ɛk-/ ● **adj.** chiefly Biology not placed centrally or arranged symmetrically about a centre.
– DERIVATIVES **excentrically** adv.

**except** ● **prep.** not including; other than. ● **conj. 1** used before a statement that forms an exception to one just made. **2** archaic unless. ● **v.** [often as postpos. adj. **excepted**] specify as not included: *present company excepted.*
– ORIGIN ME: from L. *except-*, *excipere* 'take out'.

**excepting** ● **prep.** except for; apart from.

**exception** ● **n.** a person or thing that is excepted or that does not follow a rule. ➤the action or state of excepting or being excepted.
– PHRASES **take exception to** object strongly to; be offended by.

**exceptionable** ● **adj.** formal open to objection; causing disapproval or offence.

**exceptional** ● **adj.** unusual; not typical. ➤unusually good. ● **n.** an item in a company's accounts arising from its normal activity but much larger or smaller than usual.
– DERIVATIVES **exceptionality** n. **exceptionally** adv.

**excerpt** ● **n.** /'ɛksəːpt/ a short extract from a film or piece of music or writing. ● **v.** /ɪk'səːpt, ɛk-/ take (a short extract) from a text.
– DERIVATIVES **excerptible** adj. **excerption** n.
– ORIGIN C16 (as v.): from L. *excerpt-*, *excerpere* 'pluck out'.

**excess** /ɪk'sɛs, ɛk-, 'ɛksɛs/ ● **n. 1** an amount that is more than necessary, permitted, or desirable. ➤(often in phr. **in/to excess**) the action of exceeding a permitted or proper limit. ➤the amount by which one quantity or number exceeds another. **2** lack of moderation, especially in eating or drinking. ➤(**excesses**) outrageous or immoderate behaviour. **3** Brit. a part of an insurance claim to be paid by the insured. ● **adj.** /usu. 'ɛksɛs/ **1** exceeding a prescribed or desirable amount. **2** Brit. required as extra payment.
– PHRASES **in excess of** more than; exceeding.
– ORIGIN ME: via OFr. from L. *excessus*, from *excedere* (see **EXCEED**).

**excess baggage** ● **n.** luggage weighing more than the limit allowed on an aircraft, liable to an extra charge.

**excessive** ● **adj.** more than is necessary, normal, or desirable.
– DERIVATIVES **excessively** adv. **excessiveness** n.

**exchange** ● **v.** give something and receive something else, especially of the same kind, in return. ● **n. 1** an act or the action of exchanging. **2** a short conversation or argument. **3** the giving of money for its equivalent in the currency of another country. ➤a system or market in which commercial transactions involving currency, shares, etc. can be carried out within or between countries. **4** a building or institution used for the trading of commodities. **5** Chess a move or short sequence of moves in which both players capture material of comparable value. **6** a set of equipment that connects telephone lines during a call.
– DERIVATIVES **exchangeability** n. **exchangeable** adj. **exchanger** n.
– ORIGIN ME: from OFr. *eschange* (n.), *eschangier* (v.), based on *changer* (see **CHANGE**).

**exchange rate** ● **n.** the value of one currency for the purpose of conversion to another.

**exchequer** /ɪks'tʃɛkə, ɛks-/ ● **n. 1** a royal or national treasury. **2** (**Exchequer**) Brit. the account at the Bank of England into which tax receipts and other public monies are paid. ➤historical the former government office in charge of national revenue.
– ORIGIN ME: from OFr. *eschequier*, from med. L. *scaccarium* 'chessboard', from *scaccus* (see **CHECK**[1]); mod. senses derive from the chequered tablecloth on which accounts were kept by means of counters.

**excimer** /'ɛksɪmə/ ● **n.** Chemistry an unstable excited molecule which is formed by the combination of two smaller molecules and rapidly dissociates with emission of radiation.
– ORIGIN 1960s: blend of ***excited*** and **DIMER**.

**excipient** /ɛk'sɪpɪənt/ ● **n.** an inactive substance that serves as the vehicle or medium for a drug or other active substance.
– ORIGIN C18 (as adj. in the sense 'that takes exception'): from L. *excipient-*, *excipere* 'take out'.

**excise**[1] /'ɛksʌɪz/ ● **n.** a tax levied on certain goods and commodities and on licences granted for certain activities. ● **v.** [usu. as adj. **excised**] charge excise on (goods).
– ORIGIN C15: from MDu. *excijs*, *accijs*, perh. based on L. *accensare* 'to tax'; rel. to **CENSUS**.

**excise**[2] /ɪk'sʌɪz, ɛk-/ ● **v. 1** cut out surgically. **2** remove (a section) from a text or piece of music.
– DERIVATIVES **excision** n.
– ORIGIN C16: from L. *excis-*, *excidere* 'cut out'.

**exciseman** ● **n.** (pl. **-men**) Brit. historical an official who collected excise duty and prevented smuggling.

**excitable** ● **adj. 1** easily excited. **2** (of tissue or a cell) responsive to stimulation.
– DERIVATIVES **excitability** n. **excitably** adv.

**excitant** /'ɛksɪt(ə)nt, ɪk'sʌɪt(ə)nt, ɛk-/ ● **n.** Biology a substance which elicits an active physiological or behavioural response.

**excite** ● **v. 1** cause strong feelings of enthusiasm and eagerness in. ➤arouse (someone) sexually. **2** give rise to (a feeling or reaction). **3** produce a state of increased energy or activity in (a physical or biological system).
– DERIVATIVES **excitation** n. (chiefly technical). **excitative** adj. (rare). **excitatory** adj. (chiefly Physiology). **excited** adj. **excitedly** adv. **excitement** n. **exciter** n. **exciting** adj. **excitingly** adv. **excitingness** n.
– ORIGIN ME (in the sense 'incite someone to do something'): from OFr. *exciter* or L. *excitare*, frequentative of *exciere* 'call out'.

**exciton** /'ɛksɪtɒn, ɪk'sʌɪ-, ɛk-/ ● **n.** Physics a mobile concentration of energy in a crystal formed by an excited electron and an associated hole.

**exclaim** ● **v.** cry out suddenly, especially in surprise, anger, or pain.
– DERIVATIVES **exclamation** n. **exclamatory** adj.
– ORIGIN C16 (ME as *exclamation*): from Fr. *exclamer* or L. *exclamare*, from *ex-* 'out' + *clamare* 'to shout'.

**exclamation mark** (N. Amer. **exclamation point**) ● **n.** a punctuation mark (!) indicating an exclamation.

**exclave** /'ɛkskleɪv/ ● **n.** a portion of territory of one state completely surrounded by territory of another or others. Compare with **ENCLAVE**.
– ORIGIN C19: from **EX-**[1] + **ENCLAVE**.

**exclosure** /ɪk'skləʊʒə, ɛk-/ ● **n.** Forestry an area from which unwanted animals are excluded.

**exclude** ● **v.** deny access to; keep out. ➤rule out. ➤prevent the occurrence of. ➤expel (a pupil) from a school.
– PHRASES **law** (or **principle**) **of the excluded middle** Logic the principle that one (and one only) of two contradictory propositions must be true.
– DERIVATIVES **excludable** adj. **excluder** n.
– ORIGIN ME: from L. *exclus-*, *excludere*, from *ex-* 'out' + *claudere* 'to shut'.

**excluding** ● **prep.** not taking into account; except.

**exclusion** ● **n. 1** the process or state of excluding or being excluded. **2** an item or eventuality specifically not covered by an insurance policy or other contract.
– DERIVATIVES **exclusionary** adj.

**exclusionist** ● **adj.** acting to exclude someone from a place, group, or privilege. ● **n.** a person favouring the exclusion of another person or group.

**exclusion order** ● **n.** Brit. an official order excluding a person from a particular place, especially to prevent a crime being committed.

**exclusive** ● **adj.** **1** excluding or not admitting other things. ➤unable to exist or be true if something else exists or is true: *mutually exclusive options.* ➤(of terms) excluding all but what is specified. **2** restricted to the person, group, or area concerned. ➤not published or broadcast elsewhere. **3** high-class and expensive; select. **4** (**exclusive of**) not including. ● **n.** an exclusive story or broadcast.
– DERIVATIVES **exclusively** adv. **exclusiveness** n. **exclusivity** n.
– ORIGIN C15: from med. L. *exclusivus*, from L. *excludere* (see EXCLUDE).

**Exclusive Brethren** ● **pl. n.** the more rigorous of two principal divisions of the Plymouth Brethren (the other is the Open Brethren).

**exclusivism** ● **n.** the action or policy of excluding a person or group from a place, group, or privilege.
– DERIVATIVES **exclusivist** adj. & n.

**excogitate** /ɪks'kɒdʒɪteɪt, ɛks-/ ● **v.** formal think out, plan, or devise.
– DERIVATIVES **excogitation** n.
– ORIGIN C16: from L. *excogitat-*, *excogitare*, from *ex-* 'out' + *cogitare* 'think'.

**excommunicant** /ˌɛkskə'mju:nɪk(ə)nt/ ● **n.** an excommunicated person.

**excommunicate** ● **v.** /ˌɛkskə'mju:nɪkeɪt/ officially exclude from participation in the sacraments and services of the Christian Church. ● **adj.** /ˌɛkskə'mju:nɪkət/ excommunicated. ● **n.** /ˌɛkskə'mju:nɪkət/ an excommunicated person.
– DERIVATIVES **excommunication** n. **excommunicative** adj. **excommunicator** n. **excommunicatory** adj.
– ORIGIN ME: from eccles. L. *excommunicat-*, *excommunicare*, from *ex-* 'out' + L. *communis* 'common to all'.

**ex-con** ● **n.** informal an ex-convict.

**excoriate** /ɪk'skɔ:rɪeɪt, ɛks-/ ● **v.** **1** chiefly Medicine damage or remove part of the surface of (the skin). **2** formal censure or criticize severely.
– DERIVATIVES **excoriation** n.
– ORIGIN ME: from L. *excoriat-*, *excoriare* 'to skin', from *ex-* 'out, from' + *corium* 'skin, hide'.

**excrement** /'ɛkskrɪm(ə)nt/ ● **n.** faeces.
– DERIVATIVES **excremental** adj.
– ORIGIN C16: from Fr. *excrément* or L. *excrementum*, from *excernere* (see EXCRETE).

**excrescence** /ɪk'skrɛs(ə)ns, ɛks-/ ● **n.** an abnormal outgrowth on a body or plant. ➤an unattractive or superfluous addition or feature.
– DERIVATIVES **excrescent** adj.
– ORIGIN ME: from L. *excrescentia*, from *excrescere* 'grow out'.

**excreta** /ɪk'skri:tə, ɛk-/ ● **n.** [treated as sing. or pl.] waste discharged from the body, especially faeces and urine.
– ORIGIN C19: from L., neut. pl. of *excretus*, past part. of *excernere* (see EXCRETE).

**excrete** /ɪk'skri:t, ɛk-/ ● **v.** (of a living organism) separate and expel as waste (a substance, especially a product of metabolism).
– DERIVATIVES **excreter** n. **excretion** n. **excretive** adj. **excretory** adj.
– ORIGIN C17: from L. *excret-*, *excernere* 'sift out'.

**excruciate** /ɪk'skru:ʃɪeɪt, ɛk-/ ● **v.** rare torment physically or mentally.
– DERIVATIVES **excruciation** n.
– ORIGIN C16: from L. *excruciat-*, *excruciare* 'torment' (based on *crux*, *cruc-* 'a cross').

**excruciating** ● **adj.** **1** intensely painful. **2** very embarrassing, awkward, or tedious.
– DERIVATIVES **excruciatingly** adv.

**exculpate** /'ɛkskʌlpeɪt/ ● **v.** formal show or declare to be not guilty of wrongdoing.
– DERIVATIVES **exculpation** n. **exculpatory** adj.
– ORIGIN C17: from med. L. *exculpat-*, *exculpare* 'free from blame', from *ex-* 'out, from' + L. *culpa* 'blame'.

**excurrent** ● **adj.** chiefly Zoology (of a vessel or opening) conveying fluid outwards. The opposite of INCURRENT.
– ORIGIN C17: from L. *excurrent-*, *excurrere* 'run out'.

**excursion** ● **n.** **1** a short journey or trip, especially one taken for leisure. **2** technical a movement along a path or through an angle. ➤a deviation from a regular pattern, path, or level of operation. **3** archaic a digression.
– DERIVATIVES **excursionist** n.
– ORIGIN C16: from L. *excursio(n-)*, from *excurrere* 'run out'.

**excursive** ● **adj.** formal tending to digress.
– DERIVATIVES **excursively** adv. **excursiveness** n.
– ORIGIN C17: from L. *excurs-*, *excurrere* 'digress, run out'.

**excursus** /ɪk'skə:səs, ɛk-/ ● **n.** (pl. same or **excursuses**) a detailed discussion of a particular point in a book, usually in an appendix. ➤a digression in a written text.
– ORIGIN C19: from L., 'excursion', from *excurrere* 'run out'.

**excuse** ● **v.** /ɪk'skju:z, ɛk-/ **1** seek or serve to justify (a fault or offence); mitigate. ➤forgive (a fault or offence, or a person committing one). **2** release from a duty or requirement. ➤(used in polite formulas) allow (someone) to leave a room or gathering. ➤(**excuse oneself**) say politely that one is leaving. ● **n.** /ɪk'skju:s, ɛk-/ **1** a defence or justification of a fault or offence. **2** something said to conceal the real reason for an action. **3** (**an excuse for**) informal a poor or inadequate example of.
– PHRASES **excuse me** a polite apology for an interruption, lack of ceremony, etc. ➤chiefly N. Amer. used to ask someone to repeat what they have just said.
– DERIVATIVES **excusable** adj. **excusably** adv. **excusatory** adj.
– ORIGIN ME: from OFr. *escuser* (v.), from L. *excusare* 'to free from blame', from *ex-* 'out' + *causa* 'accusation, cause'.

**excuse-me** ● **n.** informal a social dance in which participants may interrupt other pairs to change partners.

**ex-directory** ● **adj.** Brit. (of a telephone number) not listed in a telephone directory at the wish of the subscriber.

**ex div.** ● **abbrev.** ex dividend.

**ex dividend** ● **adj. & adv.** (of stocks or shares) not including the next dividend.

**exeat** /'ɛksɪat/ ● **n.** Brit. a permission from a college or boarding school for temporary absence.
– ORIGIN C18: from L., lit. 'let him or her go out'.

**exec** /ɪg'zɛk, ɛg-/ ● **n.** informal an executive.

**execrable** /'ɛksɪkrəb(ə)l/ ● **adj.** extremely bad or unpleasant.
– DERIVATIVES **execrably** adv.
– ORIGIN ME: via OFr. from L. *execrabilis*, from *exsecrari* (see EXECRATE).

**execrate** /'ɛksɪkreɪt/ ● **v.** **1** feel or express great loathing for. **2** archaic curse; swear.
– DERIVATIVES **execration** n. **execrative** adj. **execratory** adj.
– ORIGIN C16 (earlier (ME) as *execration*): from L. *exsecrat-*, *exsecrari* 'curse'.

**executant** /ɪg'zɛkjʊt(ə)nt, ɛg-/ ● **n.** formal **1** a person who puts something into effect. **2** an artist or performer.

**execute** /'ɛksɪkju:t/ ● **v.** **1** carry out or put into effect (a plan, order, etc.). ➤perform (an activity or manoeuvre). ➤Law make (a legal instrument) valid by signing or sealing it. ➤Law carry out (a judicial sentence, the terms of a will, or other order). ➤Computing run (a file or program). **2** carry out a sentence of death on (a condemned person).
– DERIVATIVES **executable** adj. (Computing). **execution** n.
– ORIGIN ME: from OFr. *executer*, from med. L. *executare*, from L. *exsequi* 'follow up, carry out, punish'.

**executioner** ● **n.** an official who executes condemned criminals.

**executive** /ɪg'zɛkjʊtɪv, ɛg-/ ● **adj.** having the power to execute plans, actions, or laws. ● **n.** **1** a person with senior managerial responsibility in a business organization. ➤an executive committee within an organization. **2** (**the executive**) the branch of a government responsible for executing plans, actions, or laws.
– DERIVATIVES **executively** adv.
– ORIGIN ME (as adj.): from med. L. *executivus*, from *exsequi* (see EXECUTE).

**executive officer** ● **n.** an officer with executive power, in particular a naval officer who is second in command to the captain.

**executive session** ● **n.** US a meeting, especially a private one, of a legislative body for executive business.

**executor** /ɪɡˈzɛkjʊtə, ɛɡ-/ ● **n.** Law a person appointed by a testator to carry out the terms of their will.
– DERIVATIVES **executorial** /-ˈtɔːrɪəl/ adj. (rare). **executorship** n. **executory** adj.

**executrix** /ɪɡˈzɛkjuːtrɪks, ɛɡ-/ ● **n.** (pl. **executrices** /-trɪsiːz/ or **executrixes**) Law a female executor.

**exedra** /ˈɛksɪdrə, ɪkˈsiːdrə, ɛk-/ ● **n.** (pl. **exedrae** /-driː/) Architecture a room, portico, or arcade with a bench or seats where people may converse.
– ORIGIN L., from Gk *ex-* 'out of' + *hedra* 'seat'.

**exegesis** /ˌɛksɪˈdʒiːsɪs/ ● **n.** (pl. **exegeses** /-siːz/) critical explanation or interpretation of a text, especially of scripture.
– DERIVATIVES **exegetic** /-ˈdʒɛtɪk/ adj. **exegetical** adj.
– ORIGIN C17: from Gk *exēgēsis*, from *exēgeisthai* 'interpret'.

**exegete** /ˈɛksɪdʒiːt/ ● **n.** a person who interprets text, especially of scripture.
– ORIGIN C18: from Gk *exēgētēs*, from *exēgeisthai* 'interpret'.

**exemplar** /ɪɡˈzɛmplə, ɛɡ-/ ● **n.** a person or thing serving as a typical example or appropriate model.
– ORIGIN ME: from OFr. *exemplaire*, from late L. *exemplarium*, from L. *exemplum* (see **EXAMPLE**).

**exemplary** ● **adj.** **1** serving as a desirable model; very good. **2** (of a punishment) serving as a warning or deterrent. ➤ Law (of damages) exceeding the amount needed for simple compensation.
– DERIVATIVES **exemplarily** adv. **exemplariness** n. **exemplarity** n.

**exemplify** /ɪɡˈzɛmplɪfʌɪ, ɛɡ-/ ● **v.** (**-ies**, **-ied**) be or give a typical example of.
– DERIVATIVES **exemplification** /-fɪˈkeɪʃ(ə)n/ n.

**exemplum** /ɪɡˈzɛmpləm, ɛɡ-/ ● **n.** (pl. **exempla**) an example or model, especially a moralizing or illustrative story.
– ORIGIN from L.

**exempt** /ɪɡˈzɛm(p)t, ɛɡ-/ ● **adj.** free from an obligation or liability imposed on others. ● **v.** make exempt. ● **n.** a person who is exempt from something, especially the payment of tax.
– DERIVATIVES **exemption** n.
– ORIGIN ME: from L. *exempt-*, *eximere* 'take out, free'.

**exenteration** /ɪkˌsɛntəˈreɪʃ(ə)n, ɛk-/ ● **n.** Medicine complete surgical removal of the eyeball and other contents of the eye socket.
– ORIGIN C17 (orig. in the sense 'disembowelment'): from L. *exenterat-*, *exenterare* 'remove', based on Gk *enteron* 'intestine'.

**exequatur** /ˌɛksɪˈkweɪtə/ ● **n.** an official recognition by a government of a consul or other representative of a foreign state.
– ORIGIN L., lit. 'let him or her perform'.

**exequies** /ˈɛksɪkwi/ ● **pl. n.** (sing. **exequy**) formal funeral rites.
– ORIGIN ME: via OFr. from L. *exsequiae* 'funeral ceremonies', from *exsequi* 'follow after'.

**exercise** ● **n.** **1** activity requiring physical effort carried out for the sake of health and fitness. **2** a task set to practise or test a skill. **3** an activity carried out for a specific purpose: *an exercise in public relations.* ➤ (**exercises**) N. Amer. ceremonies. **4** a military drill or training manoeuvre. **5** the application of a faculty, right, or process: *the exercise of authority.* ● **v.** **1** use or apply (a faculty, right, or process). **2** take or subject to exercise. **3** worry or perplex.
– DERIVATIVES **exercisable** adj. **exerciser** n.
– ORIGIN ME: via OFr. from L. *exercitium*, from *exercere* 'keep busy, practise'.

**exercise bike** ● **n.** a stationary piece of exercise equipment resembling an ordinary bicycle.

**exercise book** ● **n.** Brit. a booklet with blank pages for students to write in.

**exercise price** ● **n.** Stock Exchange the price per share at which the owner of a traded option is entitled to buy or sell the underlying security.

**exercise yard** ● **n.** an enclosed area used for physical exercise in a prison.

**exergue** /ɪkˈsəːɡ, ɛkˈsəːɡ, ˈɛksəːɡ/ ● **n.** a small space or inscription below the principal emblem on a coin or medal, usually on the reverse side.
– ORIGIN C17: from Fr., from med. L. *exergum*, from *ex-* 'out' + Gk *ergon* 'work'.

**exert** /ɪɡˈzəːt, ɛɡ-/ ● **v.** **1** apply or bring to bear (a force, influence, or quality). **2** (**exert oneself**) make a physical or mental effort.
– DERIVATIVES **exertion** n.
– ORIGIN C17: from L. *exserere* 'put forth'.

**exeunt** /ˈɛksɪʌnt/ ● **v.** (as a stage direction) (actors) leave the stage.
– ORIGIN C15: L., lit. 'they go out'.

**exfiltrate** ● **v.** withdraw (troops or spies) surreptitiously.
– DERIVATIVES **exfiltration** n.

**exfoliant** ● **n.** a cosmetic for exfoliating the skin.

**exfoliate** /ɪksˈfəʊlɪeɪt, ɛks-/ ● **v.** **1** shed or be shed from a surface in scales or layers. **2** wash or rub (the skin) with a granular substance to remove dead cells.
– DERIVATIVES **exfoliation** n. **exfoliative** adj. **exfoliator** n.
– ORIGIN C17: from late L. *exfoliat-*, *exfoliare* 'strip of leaves', from *ex-* 'out, from' + *folium* 'leaf'.

**ex gratia** /ɛks ˈɡreɪʃə/ ● **adv. & adj.** (with reference to payment) done from a sense of moral obligation rather than because of any legal requirement.
– ORIGIN L., lit. 'from favour', from *ex* 'from' and *gratia* (see **GRACE**).

**exhale** /ɪksˈheɪl, ɛks-/ ● **v.** **1** breathe out. **2** give off (vapour or fumes).
– DERIVATIVES **exhalable** adj. **exhalation** n.
– ORIGIN ME: from OFr. *exhaler*, from L. *exhalare*, from *ex-* 'out' + *halare* 'breathe'.

**exhaust** /ɪɡˈzɔːst, ɛɡ-/ ● **v.** **1** [often as adj. **exhausted** or **exhausting**] tire out completely. **2** use up (resources or reserves) completely. ➤ explore (a subject) thoroughly. **3** expel (gas or steam) from an engine or other machine. ● **n.** waste gases or air expelled from an engine or other machine. ➤ the system through which such gases are expelled.
– DERIVATIVES **exhaustedly** adv. **exhauster** n. **exhaustibility** /-ˈbɪlɪti/ n. **exhaustible** adj. **exhaustingly** adv.
– ORIGIN C16: from L. *exhaust-*, *exhaurire* 'drain out'.

**exhaustion** ● **n.** **1** the action or state of exhausting something or of being exhausted. **2** Logic the process of establishing a conclusion by eliminating all the alternatives.

**exhaustive** ● **adj.** fully comprehensive.
– DERIVATIVES **exhaustively** adv. **exhaustiveness** n.

**exhibit** /ɪɡˈzɪbɪt, ɛɡ-/ ● **v.** **1** publicly display (an item) in an art gallery or museum. **2** manifest one's possession of (a quality). ➤ show as a sign or symptom. ● **n.** **1** an object or collection of objects on display in an art gallery or museum. **2** Law a document or other object produced in a court as evidence. **3** N. Amer. an exhibition.
– DERIVATIVES **exhibitor** n.
– ORIGIN ME: from L. *exhibit-*, *exhibere* 'hold out'.

**exhibition** ● **n.** **1** a public display of items in an art gallery or museum. **2** a display or demonstration of a particular skill or quality. **3** Brit. a scholarship awarded to a student at a school or university.
– PHRASES **make an exhibition of oneself** behave very foolishly in public.

**exhibitioner** ● **n.** Brit. a student who has been awarded an exhibition (scholarship).

**exhibitionism** ● **n.** **1** extravagant behaviour that is intended to attract attention to oneself. **2** Psychiatry a mental condition characterized by the compulsion to display one's genitals in public.
– DERIVATIVES **exhibitionist** n. **exhibitionistic** adj. **exhibitionistically** adv.

**exhilarate** /ɪɡˈzɪləreɪt, ɛɡ-/ ● **v.** [often as adj. **exhilarated** or **exhilarating**] cause to feel very happy or animated.

– DERIVATIVES **exhilaratingly** adv. **exhilaration** n.
– ORIGIN C16: from L. *exhilarat-*, *exhilarare* 'make cheerful', from *ex-* + *hilaris* 'cheerful'.

**exhort** /ɪɡ'zɔːt, ɛɡ-/ ● v. strongly encourage or urge (someone) to do something.
– DERIVATIVES **exhortation** n. **exhortative** adj. **exhortatory** /-tət(ə)ri/ adj. **exhorter** n.
– ORIGIN ME: from OFr. *exhorter* or L. *exhortari*, from *ex-* 'thoroughly' + *hortari* 'encourage'.

**exhume** /ɛks'(h)juːm, ɪɡ'zjuːm/ ● v. dig out (something buried, especially a corpse) from the ground.
– DERIVATIVES **exhumation** n.
– ORIGIN ME: from med. L. *exhumare*, from *ex-* 'out of' + *humus* 'ground'.

**ex hypothesi** /ˌɛks hʌɪ'pɒθəsʌɪ/ ● adv. according to the hypothesis proposed.
– ORIGIN from mod. L.

**exigency** /'ɛksɪdʒ(ə)nsi, 'ɛɡzɪ-, ɪɡ'zɪ-, ɛɡ'zɪ-/ (also **exigence**) ● n. (pl. **-ies**) urgent need or demand.
– ORIGIN C16: from late L. *exigentia*, from L. *exigere* (see EXACT).

**exigent** /'ɛksɪdʒ(ə)nt, 'ɛɡzɪ-/ ● adj. formal pressing; demanding.
– ORIGIN C17: from L. *exigent-*, *exigere* (see EXACT).

**exigible** /'ɛksɪdʒɪb(ə)l, 'ɛɡzɪ-/ ● adj. (of a tax or duty) able to be charged or levied.
– ORIGIN C17: from Fr., from *exiger*, from L. *exigere* (see EXACT).

**exiguous** /ɪɡ'zɪɡjʊəs, ɛɡ-/ ● adj. formal very small.
– DERIVATIVES **exiguity** /-'ɡjuːɪti/ n. **exiguously** adv. **exiguousness** n.
– ORIGIN C17: from L. *exiguus* 'scanty' (from *exigere* 'weigh exactly') + **-OUS**.

**exile** ● n. **1** the state of being barred from one's native country. **2** a person who lives in exile. ● v. expel and bar (someone) from their native country.
– ORIGIN ME: the noun is from OFr. *exil* 'banishment', *exile* 'banished person'; the verb is from OFr. *exiler*; all based on L. *exilium* 'banishment'.

**exilic** /ɪɡ'zɪlɪk, ɪk-, ɛɡ-, ɛk-/ ● adj. of or relating to a period of exile, especially that of the Jews in Babylon in the 6th century BC.

**exine** /'ɛksɪn, -ʌɪn/ ● n. Botany the decay-resistant outer coating of a pollen grain or spore.
– ORIGIN C19: perh. from EX-[2] + Gk *is*, *in-* 'fibre'.

**exist** ● v. **1** have objective reality or being. ➤be found: *two conflicting stereotypes exist.* **2** live, especially under adverse conditions.
– ORIGIN C17: prob. a back-form. from EXISTENCE.

**existence** ● n. **1** the fact or state of existing. ➤a way of living. **2** archaic a being or entity.
– ORIGIN ME: from OFr., or from late L. *existentia*, from L. *exsistere* 'come into being'.

**existent** ● adj. existing.

**existential** /ˌɛɡzɪ'stɛnʃ(ə)l/ ● adj. **1** of or relating to existence. ➤Logic (of a proposition) affirming or implying the existence of a thing. **2** Philosophy concerned with existentialism.
– DERIVATIVES **existentially** adv.

**existentialism** ● n. a philosophical theory which emphasizes the existence of the individual person as a free and responsible agent determining their own development through acts of the will.
– DERIVATIVES **existentialist** n. & adj.

**exit** ● n. **1** a way out of a building, room, or passenger vehicle. ➤a place for traffic to leave a major road or roundabout. **2** an act of leaving. ➤a departure of an actor from the stage. **3** poetic/literary a person's death. ● v. (**exited**, **exiting**) **1** go out of or leave a place. ➤(of an actor) leave the stage. ➤(**exit**) (as a stage direction) indicating that a character leaves the stage: *exit Pamela.* **2** poetic/literary die. **3** Computing terminate a process or program. **4** Bridge relinquish the lead.
– ORIGIN C16: from L. *exit* 'he or she goes out', third person sing. pres. tense of *exire*, from *ex-* 'out' + *ire* 'go'.

**exit poll** ● n. an opinion poll of people leaving a polling station, asking how they voted.

**ex libris** /ɛks 'lɪbrɪs, 'liːb-, 'lʌɪb-, 'liːbriːs/ ● adv. used as an inscription on a bookplate to show the name of the book's owner.
– ORIGIN L., lit. 'out of the books or library (of someone)'.

**Exmoor pony** ● n. a pony of a small hardy breed, originating on Exmoor in SW England.

**ex nihilo** /ɛks 'nʌɪhɪləʊ/ ● adv. formal out of nothing.
– ORIGIN from L.

**exo-** ● prefix external; from outside: *exoskeleton.*
– ORIGIN from Gk *exō* 'outside'.

**exobiology** ● n. the branch of science concerned with the possibility and likely nature of life on other planets or in space.
– DERIVATIVES **exobiological** adj. **exobiologist** n.

**exocarp** /'ɛksəʊkɑːp/ ● n. Botany the outer layer of the pericarp of a fruit.

**exocentric** /ˌɛksəʊ'sɛntrɪk/ ● adj. Linguistics denoting or being a construction which has no explicit head, for example *John slept.* Contrasted with ENDOCENTRIC.

**exocrine** /'ɛksə(ʊ)krʌɪn, -krɪn/ ● adj. Physiology relating to or denoting glands which secrete their products through ducts opening on to an epithelium rather than directly into the bloodstream.
– ORIGIN C20: from EXO- + Gk *krinein* 'sift'.

**exocytosis** /ˌɛksəʊsʌɪ'təʊsɪs/ ● n. Biology the release of the contents of a cell vacuole to the exterior.
– DERIVATIVES **exocytotic** adj.

**Exod.** ● abbrev. Exodus (in biblical references).

**exodus** /'ɛksədəs/ ● n. **1** a mass departure of people, especially emigrants. **2** (**Exodus**) the second book of the Bible, recounting the departure of the Israelites from Egypt.
– ORIGIN OE: via eccles. L. from Gk *exodos*, from *ex-* 'out of' + *hodos* 'way'.

**exoenzyme** ● n. Biochemistry an enzyme which acts outside the cell that produces it.

**ex officio** /ˌɛks ə'fɪʃɪəʊ/ ● adv. & adj. by virtue of one's position or status.
– ORIGIN L., from *ex* 'out of, from' + *officium* 'duty'.

**exogamy** /ɪk'sɒɡəmi, ɛk-/ ● n. **1** Anthropology the custom of marrying outside a community, clan, or tribe. Compare with ENDOGAMY. **2** Biology outbreeding or cross-pollination.
– DERIVATIVES **exogamous** adj.
– ORIGIN C19: from EXO- + Gk *gamos* 'marriage'.

**exogenic** /ˌɛksə(ʊ)'dʒɛnɪk/ ● adj. Geology formed or occurring on the surface of the earth. Often contrasted with ENDOGENIC.

**exogenous** /ɪk'sɒdʒɪnəs, ɛk-/ ● adj. of, relating to, or developing from external factors. Often contrasted with ENDOGENOUS.
– DERIVATIVES **exogenously** adv.

**exon**[1] /'ɛksən/ ● n. Biochemistry a segment of a DNA or RNA molecule containing information coding for a protein or peptide sequence. Compare with INTRON.
– ORIGIN C20: from *expressed* (see EXPRESS[1]) + **-ON**.

**exon**[2] /'ɛksɒn/ ● n. Brit. each of the four officers acting as commanders of the Yeomen of the Guard.
– ORIGIN C18: representing the pronunc. of Fr. *exempt* 'free from' (because they were exempt from normal duties).

**exonerate** /ɪɡ'zɒnəreɪt, ɛɡ-/ ● v. **1** officially absolve from blame. **2** (**exonerate someone from**) release someone from (a duty or obligation).
– DERIVATIVES **exoneration** n. **exonerative** adj.
– ORIGIN ME: from L. *exonerat-*, *exonerare* 'free from a burden' (based on *onus*, *oner-* 'a burden').

**exonuclease** /ˌɛksəʊ'njuːklɪeɪz/ ● n. Biochemistry an enzyme which removes successive nucleotides from the end of a polynucleotide molecule.

**exophthalmic goitre** ● n. another term for GRAVES' DISEASE.

**exophthalmos** /ˌɛksɒf'θalmɒs/ ● n. Medicine abnormal protrusion of the eyeball or eyeballs.
– DERIVATIVES **exophthalmic** adj.
– ORIGIN C17: from mod. L. *exophthalmus*, from Gk *exophthalmos* 'having prominent eyes'.

**exoplanet** ● n. a planet which orbits a star outside the solar system.

**exor** • abbrev. an executor (of a will).

**exorbitant** /ɪg'zɔːbɪt(ə)nt/ • adj. (of a price or amount charged) unreasonably high.
– DERIVATIVES **exorbitance** n. **exorbitantly** adv.
– ORIGIN ME: from late L. *exorbitant-*, *exorbitare* 'go off the track'.

**exorcize** /'ɛksɔːsʌɪz/ (also **-ise**) • v. drive out (a supposed evil spirit) from a person or place.
– DERIVATIVES **exorcism** n. **exorcist** n.
– ORIGIN ME (in sense 'conjure up (an evil spirit)'): from Fr. *exorciser* or eccles. L. *exorcizare*, from Gk *exorkizein*, from *ex-* 'out' + *horkos* 'oath'.

**exordium** /ɪg'zɔːdɪəm, ɛg-/ • n. (pl. **exordiums** or **exordia**) formal the beginning or introduction of a discourse or treatise.
– DERIVATIVES **exordial** adj.
– ORIGIN C16: from L., from *exordiri* 'begin'.

**exoskeleton** • n. Zoology a rigid external covering for the body in some invertebrate animals, especially arthropods. Compare with **ENDOSKELETON**.
– DERIVATIVES **exoskeletal** adj.

**exosphere** /'ɛksə(ʊ)sfɪə/ • n. Astronomy the outermost region of a planet's atmosphere.
– DERIVATIVES **exospheric** adj.

**exostosis** /ˌɛksɒs'təʊsɪs/ • n. (pl. **exostoses** /-siːz/) Medicine a benign outgrowth of cartilaginous tissue on a bone.
– ORIGIN C16: from Gk, from *ex-* 'out' + *osteon* 'bone'.

**exoteric** /ˌɛksə(ʊ)'tɛrɪk/ • adj. formal intended for or likely to be understood by the general public. The opposite of **ESOTERIC**.
– ORIGIN C17: via L. from Gk *exōterikos*, from *exōterō* 'outer'.

**exothermic** /ˌɛksə(ʊ)'θəːmɪk/ • adj. Chemistry (of a reaction) accompanied by the release of heat. The opposite of **ENDOTHERMIC**.
– DERIVATIVES **exothermically** adv.

**exotic** /ɪg'zɒtɪk, ɛg-/ • adj. **1** originating in or characteristic of a distant foreign country. **2** strikingly colourful or unusual. • n. an exotic plant or animal.
– DERIVATIVES **exotically** adv. **exoticism** n.
– ORIGIN C16: via L. from Gk *exōtikos* 'foreign', from *exō* 'outside'.

**exotica** /ɪg'zɒtɪkə, ɛg-/ • pl. n. objects considered exotic.
– ORIGIN C19: from L., neut. pl. of *exoticus* (see **EXOTIC**).

**exotic dancer** • n. a striptease dancer.

**exotoxin** • n. Microbiology a toxin released by a living bacterial cell into its surroundings. Compare with **ENDOTOXIN**.

**exp** • abbrev. **1** experience. **2** experimental. **3** expiry. **4** Mathematics the exponential function raising *e* to the power of the given quantity. **5** Photography exposures.

**expand** /ɪk'spand, ɛk-/ • v. **1** make or become larger or more extensive. **2** (often **expand on**) give a fuller version or account of. **3** become less reserved.
– DERIVATIVES **expandable** adj. **expander** n. **expansibility** n. **expansible** adj.
– ORIGIN ME: from L. *expans-*, *expandere* 'to spread out'.

**expanded** • adj. **1** denoting materials which have a light cellular structure. **2** denoting sheet metal slit and stretched into a mesh, used to reinforce concrete and other brittle materials. **3** relatively broad in shape.

**expanse** • n. **1** a wide continuous area of something, typically land or sea. **2** the distance to which something expands or can be expanded.

**expansile** • adj. Physics relating to or capable of expansion.

**expansion** • n. **1** the action or an instance of expanding. **2** the increase in the volume of fuel on combustion in the cylinder of an engine, or the piston stroke in which this occurs.
– DERIVATIVES **expansionary** adj.

**expansion bolt** • n. a bolt that expands when inserted, no thread being required in the surrounding material.

**expansionism** • n. the policy of territorial or economic expansion.
– DERIVATIVES **expansionist** n. & adj. **expansionistic** adj.

**expansion joint** • n. a joint that makes allowance for thermal expansion of the parts joined without distortion.

**expansive** • adj. **1** covering a wide area; extensive. **2** relaxed, genial, and communicative. **3** tending towards economic or territorial expansion.
– DERIVATIVES **expansively** adv. **expansiveness** n.

**expansivity** • n. Physics the amount a material expands or contracts per unit length due to a one-degree change in temperature.

**ex parte** /ɛks 'pɑːteɪ/ • adj. & adv. Law with respect to or in the interests of one side only.
– ORIGIN L., 'from a side'.

**expat** • n. & adj. informal short for **EXPATRIATE**.

**expatiate** /ɪk'speɪʃɪeɪt, ɛk-/ • v. speak or write at length or in detail.
– DERIVATIVES **expatiation** n.
– ORIGIN C16: from L. *exspatiari* 'move beyond one's usual bounds' (based on *spatium* 'space').

**expatriate** • n. /ɪks'patrɪət, -'peɪtrɪət, ɛks-/ a person who lives outside their native country. • adj. living outside one's native country. • v. /ɪks'patrɪeɪt, -'peɪtrɪeɪt, ɛks-/ settle abroad.
– DERIVATIVES **expatriation** n.
– ORIGIN C18 (as v.): from med. L. *expatriat-*, *expatriare*, from L. *ex-* 'out' + *patria* 'native country'.

**expect** • v. **1** regard as likely to happen, do, or be the case. ➤ suppose or assume: *I expect I'll be late.* **2** believe that (someone) will arrive soon. ➤ (**be expecting**) informal be pregnant. **3** require as appropriate or rightfully due.
– DERIVATIVES **expectable** adj.
– ORIGIN C16: from L. *exspectare* 'look out for'.

**expectancy** • n. (pl. **-ies**) **1** hope or anticipation that something, especially something pleasant, will happen. **2** a future prospect: *life expectancy.*

**expectant** • adj. **1** hoping or anticipating that something, especially something pleasant, is about to happen. **2** (of a woman) pregnant. • n. archaic a person who anticipates receiving something, especially high office.
– DERIVATIVES **expectantly** adv.

**expectation** • n. **1** belief that something will happen or be the case. **2** (**expectations**) archaic prospects of inheritance. **3** Mathematics another term for **EXPECTED VALUE**.

**expected value** • n. Mathematics a predicted value of a variable, calculated as the sum of all possible values each multiplied by the probability of its occurrence.

**expectorant** • n. a medicine which promotes the secretion of sputum by the air passages, used especially to treat coughs.

**expectorate** /ɪk'spɛktəreɪt, ɛk-/ • v. cough or spit out (phlegm) from the throat or lungs.
– DERIVATIVES **expectoration** n.
– ORIGIN C17: from L. *expectorat-*, *expectorare* 'expel from the chest', based on *pectus* 'breast'.

**expedient** /ɪk'spiːdɪənt, ɛk-/ • adj. **1** convenient and practical although possibly improper or immoral. **2** suitable or appropriate. • n. a means of attaining an end, especially one that is convenient but possibly improper.
– DERIVATIVES **expedience** n. **expediency** n. **expediently** adv.
– ORIGIN ME: from L. *expedient-*, *expedire* (see **EXPEDITE**).

**expedite** /'ɛkspɪdʌɪt/ • v. cause to happen sooner or be accomplished more quickly.
– DERIVATIVES **expediter** (also **expeditor**) n.
– ORIGIN C15: from L. *expedire* 'extricate (orig. by freeing the feet), put in order', from *ex-* 'out' + *pes, ped-* 'foot'.

**expedition** • n. **1** a journey undertaken by a group of people with a particular purpose. **2** formal promptness or speed in doing something.
– DERIVATIVES **expeditionary** adj.
– ORIGIN ME: via OFr. from L. *expeditio(n-)*, from *expedire* (see **EXPEDITE**).

**expeditious** /ˌɛkspɪ'dɪʃəs/ • adj. quick and efficient.
– DERIVATIVES **expeditiously** adv. **expeditiousness** n.

**expel** • v. (**expelled**, **expelling**) **1** force or drive out. **2** force (a pupil) to leave a school.
– DERIVATIVES **expellable** adj. **expellee** n. **expeller** n.
– ORIGIN ME: from L. *expellere*, from *ex-* 'out' + *pellere* 'to

drive'.

**expend** • **v.** spend or use up (a resource).
– ORIGIN ME: from L. *expendere*, from *ex-* 'out' + *pendere* 'weigh, pay'; cf. **SPEND**.

**expendable** • **adj.** not worth preserving after use; able to be sacrificed or abandoned.
– DERIVATIVES **expendability** n. **expendably** adv.

**expenditure** /ɪk'spɛndɪtʃə, ɛk-/ • **n.** the action of spending funds. ➤ the amount of money spent.

**expense** • **n. 1** cost incurred or required. ➤ **(expenses)** costs incurred in the performance of a job or task. **2** something on which money must be spent.
– PHRASES **at the expense of 1** paid for by. **2** to the detriment of.
– ORIGIN ME: from Anglo-Norman Fr., from late L. *expensa* (*pecunia*) '(money) spent', from L. *expendere* (see **EXPEND**).

**expense account** • **n.** an arrangement under which money spent in the course of business is later reimbursed by one's employer.

**expensive** • **adj.** costing a lot of money.
– DERIVATIVES **expensively** adv. **expensiveness** n.

**experience** • **n. 1** practical contact with and observation of facts or events. **2** knowledge or skill acquired over time. **3** an event or occurrence which leaves an impression on one. • **v.** encounter or undergo (an event or occurrence). ➤ feel (an emotion).
– DERIVATIVES **experienceable** adj. **experiencer** n. (Linguistics).
– ORIGIN ME: via OFr. from L. *experientia*, from *experiri* 'try'; cf. **EXPERIMENT** and **EXPERT**.

**experienced** • **adj.** having knowledge or skill in a particular field gained over time.

**experiential** /ɪkˌspɪərɪ'ɛntʃ(ə)l, ɛk-/ • **adj.** involving or based on experience and observation.
– DERIVATIVES **experientially** adv.

**experiment** • **n. 1** a scientific procedure undertaken to make a discovery, test a hypothesis, or demonstrate a known fact. **2** a course of action tentatively adopted without being sure of the eventual outcome. • **v. 1** perform a scientific experiment. **2** try out new things.
– DERIVATIVES **experimentation** n. **experimenter** n.
– ORIGIN ME: from OFr., or from L. *experimentum*, from *experiri* 'try'; cf. **EXPERIENCE** and **EXPERT**.

**experimental** • **adj. 1** based on untested ideas or techniques and not yet established or finalized. ➤ of or relating to scientific experiments. **2** (of art) radically new and innovative. **3** archaic based on experience as opposed to authority or conjecture.
– DERIVATIVES **experimentalism** n. **experimentalist** n. **experimentally** adv.

**experimental psychology** • **n.** the branch of psychology concerned with the scientific investigation of responses to stimuli in controlled situations.

**expert** • **n.** a person who is very knowledgeable about or skilful in a particular area. • **adj.** having or involving such knowledge or skill.
– DERIVATIVES **expertly** adv. **expertness** n.
– ORIGIN ME (as adj.): from Fr., from L. *expertus*, past part. of *experiri* 'try'; cf. **EXPERIENCE** and **EXPERIMENT**.

**expertise** /ˌɛkspəː'tiːz/ • **n.** great skill or knowledge in a particular field.

**expert system** • **n.** Computing a piece of software which uses databases of expert knowledge to offer advice or make decisions.

**expiate** /'ɛkspɪeɪt/ • **v.** atone for (guilt or sin).
– DERIVATIVES **expiable** adj. **expiation** n. **expiator** n. **expiatory** /'ɛkspɪət(ə)ri, ˌɛkspɪ'eɪt(ə)ri/ adj.
– ORIGIN C16 (earlier (ME) as *expiation*): from L. *expiat-*, *expiare* 'appease by sacrifice' (based on *pius* 'pious').

**expire** /ɪk'spʌɪə, ɛk-/ • **v. 1** (of a document or agreement) come to the end of the period of validity. ➤ (of a period of time) come to an end. **2** (of a person) die. **3** technical exhale (air) from the lung.
– DERIVATIVES **expiration** n. **expiratory** adj.
– ORIGIN ME: from OFr. *expirer*, from L. *exspirare* 'breathe out'.

**expiry** • **n. 1** the time when something expires. **2** archaic death.

**explain** • **v. 1** make (something) clear by describing it in more detail. **2** (**explain oneself**) excuse or justify one's motives or conduct. ➤ (**explain something away**) minimize the significance of something embarrassing by giving an excuse or justification. **3** give a reason or justification for.
– DERIVATIVES **explainable** adj. **explainer** n. **explanation** n.
– ORIGIN ME: from L. *explanare*, based on *planus* 'plain'.

**explanandum** /ˌɛksplə'nandəm/ • **n.** (pl. **explananda** /-'nandə/) Philosophy another term for **EXPLICANDUM**.
– ORIGIN C19: from L., 'something to be explained'.

**explanans** /ˌɛksplə'nanz/ • **n.** (pl. **explanantia** /-'nantɪə/) Philosophy another term for **EXPLICANS**.
– ORIGIN 1940s: L., 'explaining'.

**explanatory** /ɪk'splanəˌt(ə)ri, ɛk-/ • **adj.** serving to explain something.
– DERIVATIVES **explanatorily** adv.

**explant** Biology • **v.** /ɪks'plɑːnt, ɛks-/ transfer (living cells, tissues, or organs) from animals or plants to a nutrient medium. • **n.** /'ɛksplɑːnt/ an explanted cell, organ, or piece of tissue.
– DERIVATIVES **explantation** n.

**expletive** /ɪk'spliːtɪv, ɛk-/ • **n. 1** an oath or swear word. **2** Grammar a word or phrase used to fill out a sentence or a line of verse without adding to the sense. • **adj.** Grammar (of a word or phrase) serving to fill out a sentence or line of verse.
– ORIGIN ME (as adj.): from late L. *expletivus*, from *explere* 'fill out'.

**explicable** /ɪk'splɪkəb(ə)l, ɛk-, 'ɛksplɪˌkəb(ə)l/ • **adj.** able to be explained or accounted for.
– ORIGIN C16: from Fr., or from L. *explicabilis*, from *explicare* (see **EXPLICATE**).

**explicandum** /ˌɛksplɪ'kandəm/ • **n.** (pl. **explicanda** /-'kandə/) Philosophy something which is to be explained or explicated.
– ORIGIN C19: L., 'something to be explained'.

**explicans** /ˌɛksplɪ'kanz/ • **n.** (pl. **explicantia** /ˌɛksplɪ'kantɪə/) Philosophy the explanation or explication given for something.
– ORIGIN C19: L.

**explicate** /'ɛksplɪkeɪt/ • **v.** analyse and develop (an idea or principle) in detail. ➤ analyse (a literary work) in order to reveal its meaning.
– DERIVATIVES **explication** n. **explicative** /ɛk'splɪkətɪv, 'ɛksplɪkeɪtɪv/ adj. **explicator** n. **explicatory** /ɛk'splɪkət(ə)ri, 'ɛksplɪkeɪt(ə)ri/ adj.
– ORIGIN C16: from L. *explicat-*, *explicare* 'unfold'.

**explicit** /ɪk'splɪsɪt, ɛk-/ • **adj. 1** clear and detailed, with no room for confusion or doubt. **2** graphically describing or representing sexual activity.
– DERIVATIVES **explicitly** adv. **explicitness** n.
– ORIGIN C17: from Fr. *explicite* or L. *explicit-*, *explicare* (see **EXPLICATE**).

**explode** • **v. 1** burst or shatter violently, especially as a result of rapid combustion or excessive internal pressure. **2** suddenly give expression to violent emotion, especially anger. **3** show (a belief or theory) to be false or unfounded. **4** [as adj. **exploded**] (of a diagram) showing the components of a mechanism in the normal relative positions but slightly separated from each other. **5** increase suddenly in number or extent.
– DERIVATIVES **exploder** n.
– ORIGIN C16 (in the sense 'reject scornfully, discard'): from L. *explodere* 'drive out by clapping, hiss off the stage', from *ex-* 'out' + *plaudere* 'to clap'.

**exploit** • **v.** /ɪk'splɔɪt, ɛk-/ **1** make use of and derive benefit from (a resource). **2** make use of unfairly; benefit unjustly from the work or actions of. • **n.** /'ɛksplɔɪt/ a bold or daring feat.
– DERIVATIVES **exploitable** adj. **exploitation** n. **exploitative** adj. **exploiter** n. **exploitive** adj.
– ORIGIN ME (as n. in sense 'success, progress'): from OFr. *esploit*, based on L. *explicare* (see **EXPLICATE**); the verb is from mod. Fr. *exploiter*.

**explore** • **v. 1** travel through (an unfamiliar area) in

order to learn about it. **2** inquire into or discuss in detail. ➤evaluate (a new option or possibility). **3** examine by touch.
– DERIVATIVES **exploration** n. **explorational** adj. **explorative** adj. **exploratory** adj. **explorer** n.
– ORIGIN C16 (earlier (ME) as *exploratory*): from Fr. *explorer*, from L. *explorare* 'search out', from *ex-* 'out' + *plorare* 'utter a cry'.

**explosion** ● n. an act or instance of exploding.

**explosive** ● adj. **1** able or likely to explode. **2** likely to cause an eruption of anger or controversy. **3** (of an increase) sudden and dramatic. **4** Phonetics (of a vocal sound) produced with a sharp release of air. ● n. a substance which can be made to explode.
– DERIVATIVES **explosively** adv. **explosiveness** n.

**Expo** /ˈɛkspəʊ/ ● n. (pl. **-os**) a large international exhibition.
– ORIGIN 1960s: abbrev. of **EXPOSITION**.

**exponent** /ɪkˈspəʊnənt, ɛk-/ ● n. **1** a promoter of an idea or theory. **2** a person who does a particular thing skilfully. **3** Mathematics the power to which a given number or expression is raised (e.g. 3 in $2^3 = 2 \times 2 \times 2$). **4** Linguistics a linguistic unit that realizes another, more abstract unit.
– ORIGIN C16 (as adj. in the sense 'expounding'): from L. *exponent-*, *exponere* (see **EXPOUND**).

**exponential** /ˌɛkspəˈnɛnʃ(ə)l/ ● adj. **1** (of an increase) becoming more and more rapid. **2** Mathematics of or expressed by a mathematical exponent.
– DERIVATIVES **exponentially** adv.

**exponential function** ● n. Mathematics a function whose value is a constant raised to the power of the argument, especially the function where the constant is *e*.

**exponentiation** /ˌɛkspənɛnʃɪˈeɪʃ(ə)n/ ● n. Mathematics the operation of raising one quantity to the power of another.
– DERIVATIVES **exponentiate** v.

**export** ● v. /ɪkˈspɔːt, ɛk-, ˈɛk-/ **1** send (goods or services) to another country for sale. ➤spread or introduce (ideas or customs) to another country. **2** Computing transfer (data) in a format that can be used by other programs. ● n. /ˈɛkspɔːt/ **1** an exported commodity, article, or service. **2** the exporting of goods or services. ➤[as modifier] of a high standard suitable for export: *export ales*.
– DERIVATIVES **exportability** n. **exportable** adj. **exportation** n. **exporter** n.
– ORIGIN C15 (in the sense 'take away'): from L. *exportare*, from *ex-* 'out' + *portare* 'carry'.

**expose** ● v. **1** make (something) visible by uncovering it. ➤(**expose oneself**) publicly and indecently display one's genitals. **2** [as adj. **exposed**] unprotected from the weather. **3** (often **expose someone to**) cause (someone) to be vulnerable or at risk. **4** reveal the true, objectionable nature of. **5** subject (photographic film) to light. **6** leave (a child) in the open to die.
– DERIVATIVES **exposer** n.
– ORIGIN ME: from OFr. *exposer*, from L. *exponere* (see **EXPOUND**), but influenced by L. *expositus* 'put or set out' and OFr. *poser* 'to place'.

**exposé** /ɪkˈspəʊzeɪ, ɛk-/ ● n. a report in the media that reveals something discreditable.
– ORIGIN C19: from Fr., past part. of *exposer* (see **EXPOSE**).

**exposition** ● n. **1** a comprehensive description and explanation of a theory. **2** a large public exhibition of art or trade goods. **3** Music the part of a movement, especially in sonata form, in which the principal themes are first presented. **4** archaic the action of making public; exposure.
– DERIVATIVES **expositional** adj.
– ORIGIN ME: from L. *expositio(n-)*, from *exponere* (see **EXPOUND**).

**expositor** /ɪkˈspɒzɪtə, ɛk-/ ● n. a person or thing that explains complicated ideas or theories.
– DERIVATIVES **expository** adj.

**ex post** /ɛks ˈpəʊst/ ● adj. & adv. based on actual results rather than forecasts.
– ORIGIN mod. L., from *ex* 'from' and *post* 'after'.

**ex post facto** /ˌɛks pəʊst ˈfaktəʊ/ ● adj. & adv. with retrospective action or force.
– ORIGIN erroneous division of L. *ex postfacto* 'in the light of subsequent events'.

**expostulate** /ɪkˈspɒstjʊleɪt, ɛk-/ ● v. express strong disapproval or disagreement.
– DERIVATIVES **expostulation** n. **expostulatory** /-lət(ə)ri/ adj.
– ORIGIN C16: from L. *expostulat-*, *expostulare* 'demand'.

**exposure** ● n. **1** the state of being exposed to something harmful. ➤a physical condition resulting from being exposed to severe weather conditions. **2** the action of exposing a photographic film. ➤the quantity of light reaching a photographic film, as determined by shutter speed and lens aperture. **3** the revelation of something secret. ➤the publicizing of information or an event. **4** the direction in which a building faces.
– ORIGIN C17: from **EXPOSE**, on the pattern of words such as *enclosure*.

**exposure meter** ● n. Photography a device for measuring the strength of light, giving the correct exposure to use with a given film.

**expound** ● v. present and explain (a theory or idea) systematically.
– DERIVATIVES **expounder** n.
– ORIGIN ME *expoune*: from OFr. *espon-*, pres. tense stem of *espondre*, from L. *exponere* 'explain, publish', from *ex-* 'out' + *ponere* 'put'.

**express**[1] /ɪkˈsprɛs, ɛk-/ ● v. **1** convey (a thought or feeling) in words or by gestures and conduct. **2** squeeze out (liquid or air). **3** chiefly Mathematics represent by a figure, symbol, or formula. **4** (usu. **be expressed**) Genetics cause (an inherited characteristic or gene) to appear in a phenotype.
– DERIVATIVES **expresser** n. **expressible** adj.
– ORIGIN ME: from OFr. *expresser*, based on L. *ex-* 'out' + *pressare* 'to press'.

**express**[2] /ɪkˈsprɛs, ɛk-/ ● adj. operating at high speed. ➤denoting a service in which deliveries are made by a special messenger. ● adv. by express train or delivery service. ● n. **1** (also **express train**) a train that stops at few stations and so travels quickly. **2** a special delivery service. ● v. send by express messenger or delivery.
– ORIGIN C18: extension of **EXPRESS**[3]; the adjective is from *express train*, reflecting an earlier sense of *express* 'done or made for a special purpose', later interpreted in the sense 'rapid'.

**express**[3] /ɪkˈsprɛs, ɛk-, ˈɛksprɛs/ ● adj. stated explicitly. ➤specific.
– DERIVATIVES **expressly** adv.
– ORIGIN ME: from OFr. *expres*, from L. *expressus* 'distinctly presented', past part. of *exprimere* 'press out, express'.

**expression** ● n. **1** the action of expressing something. **2** the look on someone's face, seen as conveying a particular emotion. **3** a word or phrase expressing an idea. **4** Mathematics a collection of symbols that jointly express a quantity.
– DERIVATIVES **expressional** adj. **expressionless** adj. **expressionlessly** adv. **expressionlessness** n.

**expressionism** ● n. a style of painting, music, or drama in which the artist or writer seeks to express the inner world of emotion rather than external reality.
– DERIVATIVES **expressionist** n. & adj. **expressionistic** adj. **expressionistically** adv.

**expressive** ● adj. effectively conveying thought or feeling. ➤(**expressive of**) conveying (a specified quality or idea).
– DERIVATIVES **expressively** adv. **expressiveness** n. **expressivity** n.
– ORIGIN ME (in the sense 'tending to press out'): from Fr. *expressif*, *-ive* or med. L. *expressivus*, from *exprimere* (see **EXPRESS**[3]).

**expresso** /ɛkˈsprɛsəʊ/ ● n. variant spelling of **ESPRESSO**.

**express rifle** ● n. a rifle that discharges a bullet at high speed, used in big-game hunting.

**expressway** ● n. chiefly N. Amer. an urban motorway.

**expropriate** /ɪksˈprəʊprɪeɪt, ɛks-/ ● v. (of the state) take (property) from its owner for public use or benefit.
– DERIVATIVES **expropriation** n. **expropriator** n.

– ORIGIN C16 (earlier (ME) as *expropriation*): from med. L. *expropriat-*, *expropriare* 'take from the owner', from *ex-* 'out, from' + *proprium* 'property'.

**expulsion** ● n. the action of expelling.
– DERIVATIVES **expulsive** adj.
– ORIGIN ME: from L. *expulsio(n-)*, from *expellere* (see **EXPEL**).

**expunge** /ɪk'spʌn(d)ʒ, ɛk-/ ● v. obliterate or remove completely.
– DERIVATIVES **expunction** n. **expungement** n. **expunger** n.
– ORIGIN C17: from L. *expungere* 'mark for deletion by means of points', from *ex-* 'out' + *pungere* 'to prick'.

**expurgate** /'ɛkspəːgeɪt/ ● v. [often as adj. **expurgated**] remove matter regarded as obscene or unsuitable from (a text or account).
– DERIVATIVES **expurgation** n. **expurgator** n. **expurgatory** /ɛk'spəːgət(ə)ri/ adj.
– ORIGIN C17 (earlier (ME) as *expurgation* in the sense 'purging of excrement'): from L. *expurgat-*, *expurgare* 'cleanse thoroughly'.

**exquisite** /'ɛkskwɪzɪt, ɪk'skwɪzɪt, ɛk-/ ● adj. **1** of great beauty and delicacy. **2** acute: *the exquisite pain of love.* ➤highly sensitive: *exquisite taste.* ● n. dated a dandy.
– DERIVATIVES **exquisitely** adv. **exquisiteness** n.
– ORIGIN ME (in the sense 'precise'): from L. *exquisit-*, *exquirere* 'seek out'.

**exsanguination** /ɪk,saŋgwɪ'neɪʃ(ə)n, ɛk-/ ● n. Medicine the action of draining someone or something of blood.
– DERIVATIVES **exsanguinate** v.
– ORIGIN C20: from L. *exsanguinatus* 'drained of blood' (based on *sanguis* 'blood') + **-ION**.

**exsert** /ɪk'səːt, ɛk-/ ● v. Biology cause to protrude.
– ORIGIN C17: from L. *exsert-*, *exserere* (see **EXERT**).

**ex-service** ● adj. chiefly Brit. denoting or relating to former members of the armed forces.

**ex-serviceman** (or **ex-servicewoman**) ● n. (pl. **-men** or **-women**) chiefly Brit. a former member of the armed forces.

**ex silentio** /,ɛks sɪ'lɛnʃɪəʊ/ ● adj. & adv. (with reference to an argument or theory) based on lack of contrary evidence.
– ORIGIN L., 'from silence'.

**exsolve** /ɪk'sɒlv, ɛk-/ ● v. [usu. as adj. **exsolved**] Geology (with reference to minerals) separate out from solid solution in a rock.
– DERIVATIVES **exsolution** n.
– ORIGIN C20: orig. as *exsolution*, from **EX-**[1] + **SOLUTION**.

**ext.** ● abbrev. **1** extension (in a telephone number). **2** exterior. **3** external.

**extant** /ɪk'stant, ɛk-, 'ɛkst(ə)nt/ ● adj. still in existence.
– ORIGIN C16: from L. *exstant-*, *exstare* 'be visible or prominent, exist'.

**extemporaneous** /ɪk,stɛmpə'reɪnɪəs, ɛk-/ ● adj. another term for **EXTEMPORARY**.
– DERIVATIVES **extemporaneously** adv. **extemporaneousness** n.

**extemporary** /ɪk'stɛmp(ə)(rə)ri, ɛk-/ ● adj. spoken or done without preparation.
– DERIVATIVES **extemporarily** adv. **extemporariness** n.
– ORIGIN C16: from **EXTEMPORE**, on the pattern of *temporary*.

**extempore** /ɪk'stɛmp(ə)ri, ɛk-/ ● adj. & adv. spoken or done without preparation.
– ORIGIN C16: from L. *ex tempore* 'on the spur of the moment' (lit. 'out of the time').

**extemporize** /ɪk'stɛmpərʌɪz, ɛk-/ (also **-ise**) ● v. improvise.
– DERIVATIVES **extemporization** n.

**extend** ● v. **1** make larger or longer in space or time. ➤occupy a specified area or continue for a specified distance. **2** hold out towards someone. ➤offer. **3** (**extend to**) be applicable to.
– DERIVATIVES **extendability** n. **extendable** adj. **extendibility** n. **extendible** adj. **extensibility** n. **extensible** adj.
– ORIGIN ME: from L. *extens-*, *extendere* 'stretch out'.

**extended family** ● n. a family which extends beyond the nuclear family to include relatives, who live nearby or in the one household.

**extended-play** ● adj. denoting a record that plays for longer than most singles.

**extender** ● n. a person or thing that extends something. ➤a substance added to a product such as paint or glue to dilute its colour or increase its bulk.

**extensile** /ɪk'stɛnsʌɪl, ɛk-/ ● adj. capable of being extended.

**extension** ● n. **1** a part added to a structure or building to enlarge it. ➤the action or process of enlarging or extending something. ➤an additional period of time given to someone to hold office or fulfil an obligation. ➤chiefly Brit. permission granted to licensed premises for the sale of alcoholic drinks until later than usual. **2** (also **extension lead** or **cable**) a length of electric cable which permits the use of appliances at some distance from a fixed socket. **3** a subsidiary telephone, especially one with its own additional number on a line leading from a main switchboard. **4** [as modifier] denoting extramural instruction by a university or college. **5** the extending of a limb from a bent to a straight position. ➤Ballet the ability of a dancer to raise one leg above the waist, especially to the side. **6** Logic the range of a term or concept as measured by the objects which it denotes or contains. Often contrasted with **INTENSION**. **7** Physics & Philosophy the property of occupying space.
– DERIVATIVES **extensional** adj.
– ORIGIN ME: from late L. *extensio(n-)*, from *extendere* (see **EXTEND**).

**extensive** ● adj. **1** covering a large area. ➤large in amount or scale. **2** (of agriculture) obtaining a relatively small crop from a large area with a minimum of capital and labour. Often contrasted with **INTENSIVE**.
– DERIVATIVES **extensively** adv. **extensiveness** n.
– ORIGIN ME: from Fr. *extensif, -ive* or late L. *extensivus*, from *extens-*, *extendere* (see **EXTEND**).

**extensometer** /,ɛkstɛn'sɒmɪtə/ ● n. an instrument for measuring the deformation of a material under stress.

**extensor** /ɪk'stɛnsə, ɛk-/ ● n. Anatomy a muscle whose contraction extends a limb or other part of the body. Often contrasted with **FLEXOR**.

**extent** ● n. **1** the area covered by something. ➤the size or scale of something. **2** the particular degree to which something is the case: *everyone has to compromise to some extent.*
– ORIGIN ME (in the sense 'valuation of property'): from Anglo-Norman Fr. *extente*, from med. L. *extenta*, fem. past part. of L. *extendere* (see **EXTEND**).

**extenuate** /ɪk'stɛnjʊeɪt, ɛk-/ ● v. [usu. as adj. **extenuating**] lessen the seriousness of (guilt or an offence) by reference to a mitigating factor.
– DERIVATIVES **extenuation** n. **extenuatory** /-jʊət(ə)ri/ adj.
– ORIGIN ME (in the sense 'make thin'): from L. *extenuat-*, *extenuare* 'make thin', based on *tenuis* 'thin'.

**exterior** ● adj. forming, situated on, or relating to the outside. ➤(in filming) outdoor. ● n. the outer surface or structure of something. ➤a person's apparent behaviour or demeanour. ➤(in filming) an outdoor scene.
– DERIVATIVES **exteriority** n. **exteriorize** (also **-ise**) v. **exteriorly** adv.
– ORIGIN C16: from L., compar. of *exter* 'outer'.

**exterior angle** ● n. Geometry the angle between a side of a rectilinear figure and an adjacent side extended outward.

**exterminate** /ɪk'stəːmɪneɪt, ɛk-/ ● v. destroy completely; eradicate.
– DERIVATIVES **extermination** n. **exterminator** n. **exterminatory** /-nət(ə)ri/ adj.
– ORIGIN ME (in the sense 'drive out'): from L. *exterminat-*, *exterminare*, from *ex-* 'out' + *terminus* 'boundary'.

**extern** /ɪk'stəːn, ɛk-/ ● n. **1** N. Amer. a non-resident doctor or other worker in a hospital. **2** (in a strictly enclosed order of nuns) a sister who does not live exclusively within the enclosure and goes on outside errands.
– ORIGIN C16 (as an adj. in the sense 'external'): from Fr. *externe* or L. *externus*, from *exter* 'outer'.

**external** ● adj. **1** belonging to, situated on, or forming

the outside. **2** coming or derived from a source outside the subject affected. ➤coming from or relating to a country or institution other than the main subject. **3** for or concerning students registered with and taking the examinations of a university but not resident there. ● **n.** (**externals**) outward features.
– DERIVATIVES **externally** adv.
– ORIGIN ME: from med. L., from L. *exter* 'outer'.

**external ear** ● **n.** the parts of the ear outside the eardrum, especially the pinna.

**externalism** ● **n. 1** excessive regard for outward form in religion. **2** Philosophy the view that mental events and acts are essentially dependent on the world external to the mind.
– DERIVATIVES **externalist** n. & adj.

**externality** /ˌɛkstəːˈnalɪti/ ● **n.** (pl. **-ies**) Economics a consequence of an economic activity which affects other parties without this being reflected in market prices.

**externalize** (also **-ise**) ● **v.** give external existence or form to. ➤Psychology project (a mental image or process) on to a figure outside oneself.
– DERIVATIVES **externalization** n.

**exteroceptive** /ˌɛkstərə(ʊ)ˈsɛptɪv/ ● **adj.** Physiology of or denoting stimuli that are external to an organism. Compare with **INTEROCEPTIVE**.
– DERIVATIVES **exteroceptor** n.

**extinct** ● **adj. 1** (of a species or other large group) having no living members. ➤no longer in existence. ➤(of a volcano) not having erupted in recorded history. **2** (of a title of nobility) having no valid claimant.
– ORIGIN ME (in the sense 'no longer alight'): from L. *exstinct-*, *exstinguere* (see **EXTINGUISH**).

**extinction** ● **n. 1** the state or process of being or becoming extinct. **2** Physics reduction to zero of the intensity of light or other radiation passing through a medium, due to absorption, reflection, or scattering.

**extinguish** ● **v. 1** put out (a fire or light). **2** put an end to. **3** cancel (a debt) by full payment. ➤Law render (a right or obligation) void.
– DERIVATIVES **extinguishable** adj. **extinguisher** n. **extinguishment** n. (Law).
– ORIGIN C16: from L. *exstinguere*, from *ex-* 'out' + *stinguere* 'quench'.

**extirpate** /ˈɛkstəːpeɪt/ ● **v.** search out and destroy completely.
– DERIVATIVES **extirpation** n. **extirpator** n.
– ORIGIN ME: from L. *exstirpare*, from *ex-* 'out' + *stirps* 'a stem'.

**extol** /ɪkˈstəʊl, ɛk-/ ● **v.** (**extolled**, **extolling**) praise enthusiastically.
– DERIVATIVES **extoller** n. **extolment** n.
– ORIGIN ME: from L. *extollere*, from *ex-* 'out, upward' + *tollere* 'raise'.

**extort** /ɪkˈstɔːt, ɛk-/ ● **v.** obtain by force, threats, or other unfair means.
– DERIVATIVES **extorter** n. **extortion** n. **extortioner** n. **extortionist** n. **extortive** adj.
– ORIGIN C16 (earlier (ME) as *extortion*): from L. *extort-*, *extorquere* 'wrest', based on *torquere* 'twist'.

**extortionate** /ɪkˈstɔːʃ(ə)nət, ɛk-/ ● **adj. 1** (of a price) much too high. **2** using or given to extortion.
– DERIVATIVES **extortionately** adv.

**extra** ● **adj.** added to an existing or usual amount or number. ● **adv. 1** to a greater extent than usual. **2** in addition. ● **n. 1** an item for which an extra charge is made. **2** an extra item. **3** a person engaged temporarily to fill out a crowd scene in a film or play. **4** Cricket a run scored other than from a hit with the bat, credited to the batting side rather than to a batsman.
– ORIGIN C17 (as adj.): prob. a shortening of **EXTRAORDINARY**, suggested by similar forms in Fr. and Ger.

**extra-** ● **prefix** outside; beyond: *extracellular*. ➤beyond the scope of: *extra-curricular*.
– ORIGIN via med. L. from L. *extra* 'outside'.

**extracellular** ● **adj.** Biology situated or taking place outside a cell or cells.
– DERIVATIVES **extracellularly** adv.

**extracorporeal** /ˌɛkstrəkɔːˈpɔːrɪəl/ ● **adj.** situated or occurring outside the body.

**extra cover** ● **n.** Cricket a fielding position between cover point and mid-off but further from the wicket.

**extract** ● **v.** /ɪkˈstrakt, ɛk-/ **1** remove, especially by effort or force. ➤obtain (money, information, etc.) from someone unwilling to give it. ➤obtain (a substance or resource) from something by a special method. ➤select (a passage from a text, film, or piece of music) for quotation, performance, or reproduction. **2** Mathematics calculate (a root of a number). ● **n.** /ˈɛkstrakt/ **1** a short passage taken from a text, film, or piece of music. **2** a preparation containing the active ingredient of a substance in concentrated form: *vanilla extract*.
– DERIVATIVES **extractability** n. **extractable** adj. **extractive** adj.
– ORIGIN ME: from L. *extract-*, *extrahere* 'draw out'.

**extraction** ● **n. 1** the action of extracting. **2** the ethnic origin of someone's family: *he's of Polish extraction*.

**extractor** ● **n.** a machine or device used to extract something. ➤[as modifier] denoting a fan or other device for extracting odours and stale air.

**extra-curricular** ● **adj.** (of an activity at a school or college) pursued in addition to the normal curriculum.

**extradite** /ˈɛkstrədʌɪt/ ● **v.** hand over (a person accused or convicted of a crime) to the jurisdiction of the foreign state in which the crime was committed.
– DERIVATIVES **extraditable** adj. **extradition** n.
– ORIGIN C19 (as *extradition*): from Fr., from *ex-* 'out, from' + *tradition* 'delivery'.

**extrados** /ɪkˈstreɪdɒs, ɛk-/ ● **n.** Architecture the upper or outer curve of an arch. Often contrasted with **INTRADOS**.
– ORIGIN C18: from Fr., from L. *extra* 'outside' + Fr. *dos* 'back'.

**extragalactic** /ˌɛkstrəgəˈlaktɪk/ ● **adj.** Astronomy occurring or originating outside the Milky Way galaxy.

**extrajudicial** ● **adj.** Law (of a sentence) not legally authorized. ➤(of a settlement or statement) out-of-court.
– DERIVATIVES **extrajudicially** adv.

**extralimital** /ˌɛkstrəˈlɪmɪt(ə)l/ ● **adj.** chiefly Biology situated or occurring outside a particular area.

**extralinguistic** /ˌɛkstrəlɪŋˈgwɪstɪk/ ● **adj.** not involving or beyond the bounds of language.

**extramarital** /ˌɛkstrəˈmarɪt(ə)l/ ● **adj.** (especially of sexual relations) occurring outside marriage.
– DERIVATIVES **extramaritally** adv.

**extramural** /ˌɛkstrəˈmjʊər(ə)l/ ● **adj. 1** Brit. (of a course of study) arranged for people who are not full-time members of a university or other educational establishment. ➤additional to one's studies. **2** outside the walls or boundaries of a town or city.
– DERIVATIVES **extramurally** adv.
– ORIGIN C19: from L. *extra muros* 'outside the walls' + **-AL**.

**extraneous** /ɪkˈstreɪnɪəs, ɛk-/ ● **adj. 1** irrelevant or unrelated to the subject. **2** of external origin.
– DERIVATIVES **extraneously** adv. **extraneousness** n.
– ORIGIN C17: from L. *extraneus* + **-OUS**.

**extranet** ● **n.** an Intranet that can be partially accessed by authorized outside users, enabling businesses to exchange information over the Internet in a secure way.

**extraordinaire** /ɪkˌstrɔːdɪˈnɛː/ ● **adj.** [postpos.] outstanding in a particular capacity: *a gardener extraordinaire*.
– ORIGIN 1940s: Fr., 'extraordinary'.

**extraordinary** /ɪkˈstrɔːd(ə)n(ə)ri, ɛk-, ˌɛkstrəˈɔːdɪn(ə)ri/ ● **adj. 1** very unusual or remarkable. **2** (of a meeting) specially convened. ➤[postpos.] (of an official) specially employed: *Ambassador Extraordinary*.
– DERIVATIVES **extraordinarily** adv. **extraordinariness** n.
– ORIGIN ME: from L. *extraordinarius*, from *extra ordinem* 'outside the normal course of events'.

**extraordinary ray** ● **n.** Optics (in double refraction) the light ray that does not obey the ordinary laws of refraction.

**extrapolate** /ɪkˈstrapəleɪt, ɛk-/ ● **v. 1** extend (a graph) by inferring unknown values from trends in the known data. **2** extend the application of (a method, conclusion, etc.) to different or larger groups.

– DERIVATIVES **extrapolation** n. **extrapolative** adj. **extrapolator** n.
– ORIGIN C19: from **EXTRA-** + a shortened form of **INTERPOLATE**.

**extraposition** /ˌɛkstrəpəˈzɪʃ(ə)n/ ● **n.** Grammar the placing of a word or group of words outside or at the end of a clause, while retaining the sense (e.g. *it's no use crying over spilt milk*).

**extrapyramidal** /ˌɛkstrəpɪˈramɪd(ə)l/ ● **adj.** Anatomy & Medicine relating to motor nerves descending from the cortex to the spine but not part of the pyramidal system.

**extrasensory perception** /ɛkstrəˈsɛns(ə)ri/ ● **n.** the supposed faculty of perceiving things by means other than the known senses, e.g. by telepathy.

**extrasolar** ● **adj.** outside the solar system.

**extraterrestrial** /ˌɛkstrətəˈrɛstrɪəl/ ● **adj.** of or from outside the earth or its atmosphere. ● **n.** a hypothetical or fictional being from outer space.

**extraterritorial** /ˌɛkstrətɛrɪˈtɔːrɪəl/ ● **adj.** **1** situated or valid outside a country's territory. **2** denoting the freedom of embassy staff from the jurisdiction of the territory of residence.
– DERIVATIVES **extraterritoriality** n.

**extra time** ● **n.** chiefly Brit. a further period of play added on to a game if the scores are equal.

**extravagant** /ɪkˈstravəg(ə)nt, ɛk-/ ● **adj.** **1** lacking restraint in spending money or using resources. ➤ resulting from or showing this: *extravagant gifts.* **2** exceeding what is reasonable or appropriate: *extravagant claims.*
– DERIVATIVES **extravagance** n. **extravagancy** n. **extravagantly** adv.
– ORIGIN ME (in the sense 'unusual, unsuitable'): from med. L. *extravagant-*, *extravagari* 'diverge greatly', from L. *extra-* 'outside' + *vagari* 'wander'.

**extravaganza** /ɪkˌstravəˈganzə, ɛk-/ ● **n.** an elaborate and spectacular entertainment.
– ORIGIN C18 (in the sense 'extravagance in language or behaviour'): from Ital. *estravaganza* 'extravagance'.

**extravasate** /ɪkˈstravəseɪt, ɛk-/ ● **v.** [usu. as adj. **extravasated**] chiefly Medicine let or force out (a fluid, especially blood) from the vessel that naturally contains it.
– DERIVATIVES **extravasation** n.
– ORIGIN C17: from **EXTRA-** + L. *vas* 'vessel' + **-ATE**³.

**extravascular** /ˌɛkstrəˈvaskjʊlə/ ● **adj.** Medicine situated or occurring outside the vascular system.

**extravehicular** /ˌɛkstrəvɪˈhɪkjʊlə/ ● **adj.** of or relating to work performed in space outside a spacecraft.

**extravert** ● **n.** variant spelling of **EXTROVERT**.

**extra virgin** ● **adj.** denoting a particularly fine grade of olive oil made from the first pressing of the olives.

**extrema** plural form of **EXTREMUM**.

**extreme** ● **adj.** **1** very great. ➤ exceptional. ➤ very severe or serious. **2** far from moderate, especially politically. ➤ chiefly N. Amer. denoting or relating to a sport performed in a hazardous environment. **3** furthest from the centre or a given point. ● **n.** **1** either of two abstract things that are as different from each other as possible. ➤ the most extreme degree of something. **2** Logic the subject or predicate in a proposition, or the major or minor term in a syllogism.
– DERIVATIVES **extremely** adv. **extremeness** n.
– ORIGIN ME: via OFr. from L. *extremus* 'outermost, utmost', superlative of *exterus* 'outer'.

**extreme unction** ● **n.** (in the Roman Catholic Church) a former name for the sacrament of anointing of the sick, especially when administered to the dying.

**extremist** ● **n.** chiefly derogatory a person who holds extreme political or religious views.
– DERIVATIVES **extremism** n.

**extremity** /ɪkˈstrɛmɪti, ɛk-/ ● **n.** (pl. **-ies**) **1** the furthest point or limit. ➤ (**extremities**) the hands and feet. **2** severity or seriousness. ➤ extreme adversity.

**extremophile** /ɛksˈtrɛməfʌɪl/ ● **n.** Biology a microorganism that lives in extreme environmental conditions.

**extremum** /ɪkˈstriːməm, ɛk-/ ● **n.** (pl. **extremums** or **extrema**) Mathematics the maximum or minimum value of a function.
– ORIGIN C20: from L., neut. of *extremus* (see **EXTREME**).

**extricate** /ˈɛkstrɪkeɪt/ ● **v.** free from a constraint or difficulty.
– DERIVATIVES **extricable** adj. **extrication** n.
– ORIGIN C17 (in the sense 'unravel'): from L. *extricat-*, *extricare* 'unravel', from *ex-* 'out' + *tricae* 'perplexities'.

**extrinsic** /ɪkˈstrɪnsɪk, ɛk-/ ● **adj.** **1** not essential or inherent. **2** (of a muscle) having its origin some distance from the part which it moves.
– DERIVATIVES **extrinsically** adv.
– ORIGIN C16 (in the sense 'outward'): from late L. *extrinsecus* 'outward', based on *exter* 'outer'.

**extrorse** /ɛksˈtrɔːs/ ● **adj.** Botany & Zoology turned outwards. The opposite of **INTRORSE**.
– ORIGIN C19: from late L. *extrorsus* 'outwards' (adv.).

**extrovert** /ˈɛkstrəvəːt/ (also technical **extravert**) ● **n.** an outgoing, socially confident person. ➤ Psychology a person predominantly concerned with external things or objective considerations. Compare with **INTROVERT**. ● **adj.** of, denoting, or typical of an extrovert.
– DERIVATIVES **extroversion** n. **extroverted** adj.
– ORIGIN C20 (earlier (C17) as *extroversion*): from *extro-* (var. of **EXTRA-**) + L. *vertere* 'to turn'.

**extrude** /ɪkˈstruːd, ɛk-/ ● **v.** thrust or force out. ➤ shape (a material such as metal or plastic) by forcing it through a die.
– DERIVATIVES **extrudable** adj. **extrusile** adj. **extrusion** n.
– ORIGIN C16: from L. *extrudere*, from *ex-* 'out' + *trudere* 'to thrust'.

**extrusive** ● **adj.** Geology relating to or denoting rock that has been extruded at the earth's surface as lava or other volcanic deposits.

**exuberant** /ɪgˈzjuːb(ə)r(ə)nt, ɛg-/ ● **adj.** **1** lively and cheerful. **2** chiefly poetic/literary growing profusely.
– DERIVATIVES **exuberance** n. **exuberantly** adv.
– ORIGIN ME (in the sense 'overflowing'): from Fr. *exubérant*, from L. *exuberant-*, *exuberare* 'be abundantly fruitful' (based on *uber* 'fertile').

**exude** /ɪgˈzjuːd, ɛg-/ ● **v.** **1** (with reference to moisture or a smell) discharge or be discharged slowly and steadily. **2** display (an emotion or quality) strongly and openly.
– DERIVATIVES **exudate** n. **exudation** n. **exudative** /ɪgˈzjuːdətɪv, ɛg-/ adj.
– ORIGIN C16: from L. *exsudare*, from *ex-* 'out' + *sudare* 'to sweat'.

**exult** ● **v.** show or feel triumphant elation.
– DERIVATIVES **exultancy** n. **exultant** adj. **exultantly** adv. **exultation** n. **exulting** adj. **exultingly** adv.
– ORIGIN C16 (earlier (ME) as *exultation*): from L. *exsultare*, frequentative of *exsilire* 'leap up'.

**exurb** /ˈɛksəːb/ ● **n.** N. Amer. a prosperous area beyond a city's suburbs.
– DERIVATIVES **exurban** adj. **exurbanite** n. & adj.
– ORIGIN 1901 (as *exurban*): from L. *ex* 'out of' + **URBAN**, on the model of *suburban*.

**exurbia** /ɛkˈsəːbɪə/ ● **n.** the exurbs collectively.

**exuviae** /ɪgˈzjuːvɪiː, ɛg-/ ● **pl. n.** [also treated as sing.] Zoology the cast or sloughed skin of an animal, especially of an insect larva.
– DERIVATIVES **exuvial** adj.
– ORIGIN C17: from L., lit. 'animal skins'.

**exuviate** /ɪgˈzjuːvɪeɪt, ɛg-/ ● **v.** technical shed (a skin or shell).
– DERIVATIVES **exuviation** n.
– ORIGIN C19: from **EXUVIAE** + **-ATE**³.

**ex-voto** /ɛks ˈvəʊtəʊ/ ● **n.** (pl. **-os**) an offering given in order to fulfil a vow.
– ORIGIN C18: from L. *ex voto* 'from a vow'.

**ex-works** ● **adj. & adv.** Brit. direct from the factory or place of manufacture.

**-ey** ● **suffix** variant spelling of **-Y**² (as in *Charley*).

**eyas** /ˈʌɪəs/ ● **n.** (pl. **eyasses**) a young hawk, especially (in falconry) an unfledged nestling taken from the nest for training.
– ORIGIN C15 (orig. *nyas*): from Fr. *niais*, based on L. *nidus* 'nest'; the initial *n* was lost by wrong division of *a nyas*; cf. **ADDER**¹.

**eye** ● n. **1** the organ of sight in humans or other animals. ➤a person's attitude or feelings: *to European eyes, it may seem that the city is overcrowded.* **2** a rounded eye-like marking on an animal, such as those on the tail of a peacock. ➤a round, dark spot on a potato from which a new shoot can grow. **3** the small hole in a needle through which the thread is passed. ➤a small metal loop into which a hook is fitted as a fastener on a garment. ➤Nautical a loop at the end of a rope, especially one at the top end of a shroud or stay. **4** (**eyes**) Nautical the extreme forward part of a ship. ● v. (**eyeing** or **eying**) look at closely or with interest. ➤(**eye someone up**) informal look at someone in a way that reveals a sexual interest.
– PHRASES **be all eyes** be watching eagerly and attentively. **close** (or **shut**) **one's eyes to** refuse to acknowledge (something unpleasant). **an eye for an eye and a tooth for a tooth** retaliation in kind is the appropriate way to deal with an offence or crime. [with biblical allusion to Exod. 21: 24.] **the eye of the storm** the calm region at the centre of a storm. **the eye of the wind** the direction from which the wind is blowing. **eyes front** (or **left** or **right**) a military command to turn the head in the direction stated. **get one's eye in** Brit. improve one's judgement or skill through experience. **give someone the eye** informal look at someone with sexual interest. **half an eye** a partial degree of attention. **have an eye for** be able to recognize and make good judgements about. **have** (or **keep**) **one's eye on** keep under careful observation. ➤(**have one's eye on**) aim to acquire. **have** (or **with**) **an eye to** have (or having) as one's objective. (**only**) **have eyes for** be (exclusively) interested in. **have eyes in the back of one's head** know what is going on around one even when one cannot see it. **keep an eye on** keep under careful observation. **keep an eye out** (or **open**) look out for something. **keep one's eyes open** (or **peeled** or Brit. **skinned**) watch out for something. **make eyes at** look at in a way that indicates one's sexual interest. **one in the eye for** a disappointment or setback for. **open someone's eyes** cause someone to realize something. **see eye to eye** be in full agreement. **a twinkle** (or **gleam**) **in someone's eye** something that is as yet no more than an idea or dream. **up to the** (or **one's**) **eyes** (**in**) informal extremely busy. **with one's eyes open** fully aware of possible difficulties.
– DERIVATIVES **-eyed** adj. **eyeless** adj.
– ORIGIN OE *ēage*, of Gmc origin.

**eyeball** ● n. the round part of the eye of a vertebrate, within the eyelids and socket. ● v. informal, chiefly N. Amer. stare at closely.
– PHRASES **eyeball to eyeball** face to face with someone, especially in an aggressive way.

**eyebath** ● n. chiefly Brit. a small container used for applying cleansing solutions to the eye.

**eye bolt** ● n. a bolt or bar with an eye at the end for attaching a hook or ring to.

**eyebright** ● n. a small white-flowered plant, traditionally used as a remedy for eye problems. [*Euphrasia officinalis* and other species.]

**eyebrow** ● n. the strip of hair growing on the ridge above a person's eye socket.
– PHRASES **raise one's eyebrows** (or **an eyebrow**) show surprise or mild disapproval.

**eye candy** ● n. informal visual images that are superficially entertaining but intellectually undemanding.

**eye-catching** ● adj. immediately appealing or noticeable.
– DERIVATIVES **eye-catcher** n. **eye-catchingly** adv.

**eyecup** ● n. **1** a piece of an optical device such as a pair of binoculars which is contoured to provide a comfortable rest for the eye. **2** North American term for EYEBATH.

**eyeful** ● n. informal **1** a long steady look. **2** an eye-catching person or thing.

**eyeglass** ● n. **1** a single lens for correcting or assisting defective eyesight, especially a monocle. **2** (**eyeglasses**) chiefly N. Amer. another term for GLASSES. **3** another term for EYEPIECE.

**eyehole** ● n. a hole to look through.

**eyelash** ● n. each of the short hairs growing on the edges of the eyelids.

**eyelet** ● n. a small round hole in leather or cloth for threading a lace, string, or rope through. ➤a metal ring used to reinforce such a hole. ➤a small hole with stitching around its edge, used as a form of decoration in embroidery. ● v. (**eyeleted**, **eyeleting**) make eyelets in (fabric).
– ORIGIN ME *oilet*, from OFr. *oillet*, dimin. of *oil* 'eye', from L. *oculus*.

**eye level** ● n. the level of the eyes looking straight ahead.

**eyelid** ● n. each of the upper and lower folds of skin which cover the eye when closed.

**eyeliner** ● n. a cosmetic applied as a line round the eyes.

**eye-opener** ● n. informal **1** an unexpected revelation. **2** N. Amer. an alcoholic drink taken early in the day.
– DERIVATIVES **eye-opening** adj.

**eyepatch** ● n. a patch worn to protect an injured eye.

**eyepiece** ● n. the lens or group of lenses that is closest to the eye in a microscope or other optical instrument.

**eye-popping** ● adj. informal astonishingly large or blatant.

**eye rhyme** ● n. a similarity between words in spelling but not in pronunciation, for example *love* and *move*.

**eyeshade** ● n. a translucent visor used to protect the eyes from strong light.

**eyeshadow** ● n. a coloured cosmetic applied to the eyelids or to the skin around the eyes.

**eyeshot** ● n. the distance for which one can see.

**eyesight** ● n. a person's ability to see.

**eye socket** ● n. the cavity in the skull which encloses an eyeball with its surrounding muscles.

**eyesore** ● n. a thing that is very ugly, especially a building.

**eye splice** ● n. a splice made by turning the end of a rope back on itself and interlacing the strands, thereby forming a loop.

**eyespot** ● n. **1** Zoology a light-sensitive pigmented spot on a flatworm, starfish, or other organism. **2** a rounded eye-like marking, especially on a butterfly or moth. **3** a fungal disease of cereals and other grasses, characterized by yellowish oval spots.

**eyestripe** ● n. a stripe on a bird's head which encloses or appears to run through the eye.

**Eyetie** /ˈʌɪtʌɪ/ ● adj. & n. (pl. **Eyeties**) Brit. informal, offensive Italian or an Italian.
– ORIGIN 1920s: abbrev. of *Eyetalian*, representing a humorous pronunc. of *Italian*.

**eye tooth** ● n. a canine tooth, especially one in the upper jaw.
– PHRASES **give one's eye teeth for** (or **to be**) do anything in order to have or be.

**eyewash** ● n. **1** cleansing lotion for a person's eye. **2** informal nonsense.

**eyewitness** ● n. a person who has personally seen something happen and so can give a first-hand description of it.

**eye worm** ● n. **1** a filarial worm of equatorial Africa, affecting the eyes. [*Loa loa*.] **2** a nematode worm that occurs in the region of the eyelid and tear duct, found chiefly in hoofed mammals. [Genus *Thelazia*.]

**eyot** /ˈeɪət/ ● n. another term for AIT.

**eyra** /ˈeɪrə/ ● n. a reddish-brown form of the jaguarundi (cat).
– ORIGIN C17: from Sp., from Tupi *eirara*, *irara*.

**eyrie** /ˈɪəri, ˈʌɪri, ˈɛːri/ (US also **aerie**) ● n. a large nest of an eagle or other bird of prey, typically built high in a tree or on a cliff.
– ORIGIN C15: from med. L. *aeria*, *aerea*, *eyria*, prob. from OFr. *aire*, from L. *area* 'level piece of ground', in late L. 'nest of a bird of prey'.

**eyrir** /ˈeɪriːr/ ● n. (pl. **aurar** /ˈøɪrar/) a monetary unit of Iceland, equal to one hundredth of a krona.
– ORIGIN Icelandic, from ON, prob. from L. *aureus* 'golden, a gold coin'.

**Ezek.** ● abbrev. Ezekiel (in biblical references).

# F f

**F**[1] (also **f**) ● **n.** (pl. **Fs** or **F's**) **1** the sixth letter of the alphabet. **2** denoting the next after E in a set of items, categories, etc. **3** Music the fourth note of the diatonic scale of C major.

**F**[2] ● **abbrev. 1** Fahrenheit. **2** farad(s). **3** Chemistry faraday(s). **4** (in racing results) favourite. **5** female. **6** fighter (in designations of US aircraft types). **7** Biology filial generation. **8** Brit. fine (used in describing grades of pencil lead). **9** (in motor racing) formula. **10** Franc(s). **11** France (international vehicle registration). **12** (in tables of sports results) goals or points for. ● **symb. 1** the chemical element fluorine. **2** Physics force.

**f** ● **abbrev. 1** Grammar feminine. **2** femto- ($10^{-15}$). **3** (in textual references) folio. **4** Music forte. **5** (in racing results) furlong(s). **6** Chemistry denoting electrons and orbitals possessing three units of angular momentum. [*f* from *fundamental*, orig. applied to lines in atomic spectra.] ● **symb. 1** focal length. **2** Mathematics a function of a specified variable. **3** Electronics frequency.

**FA** ● **abbrev. 1** Fanny Adams. **2** (in the UK) Football Association.

**fa** ● **n.** variant spelling of **FAH**.

**FAA** ● **abbrev. 1** (in the US) Federal Aviation Administration. **2** (in the UK) Fleet Air Arm.

**fab**[1] ● **adj.** informal fabulous; wonderful.
– DERIVATIVES **fabbo** adj. **fabby** adj.

**fab**[2] ● **n.** Electronics a microchip fabrication plant or process.

**faba bean** /'fɑːbə/ ● **n.** variant spelling of **FAVA BEAN**.

**Fabian** /'feɪbɪən/ ● **n.** a member or supporter of the Fabian Society, an organization of socialists aiming to achieve socialism by non-revolutionary methods. ● **adj. 1** relating to or characteristic of the Fabians. **2** employing a cautiously persistent and dilatory strategy to wear out an enemy.
– DERIVATIVES **Fabianism** n. **Fabianist** n.
– ORIGIN C18: from the name of the Roman general Quintus *Fabius* Maximus Verrucosus, known for his delaying tactics.

**fable** /'feɪb(ə)l/ ● **n.** a short story, typically with animals as characters, conveying a moral. ➤ a supernatural story incorporating elements of myth and legend. ➤ myth and legend. ● **v.** archaic invent (an incident, person, or story).
– DERIVATIVES **fabler** n.
– ORIGIN ME: from OFr. *fable*, from L. *fabula* 'story', from *fari* 'speak'.

**fabled** ● **adj. 1** famous. **2** mythical or imaginary.

**fabless** ● **adj.** denoting or relating to a company which designs microchips but contracts out their production rather than owning its own fabrication plant.

**fabliau** /'fablɪəʊ/ ● **n.** (pl. **fabliaux** /-əʊz/) a metrical tale, typically a bawdy one, of a type found chiefly in early French poetry.
– ORIGIN from OFr. (Picard dial.) *fabliaux*, pl. of *fablel* 'short fable', dimin. of *fable*.

**Fablon** ● **n.** trademark flexible self-adhesive plastic sheeting used for covering table tops and working surfaces.

**fabric** ● **n. 1** material produced by weaving or knitting textile fibres; cloth. **2** a structure or framework, especially the walls, floor, and roof of a building. ➤ the essential structure of something abstract: *the fabric of society.*
– ORIGIN C15 (orig. denoting a building or machine, i.e. 'something made'): from Fr. *fabrique*, from L. *fabrica* 'something skilfully produced'.

**fabricate** ● **v. 1** invent, typically with deceitful intent. **2** construct or manufacture (an industrial product), especially from prepared components.
– DERIVATIVES **fabrication** n. **fabricator** n.
– ORIGIN ME: from L. *fabricat-*, *fabricare* 'manufacture', from *fabrica* (see **FABRIC**).

**fabulate** /'fabjʊleɪt/ ● **v.** tell invented stories.
– DERIVATIVES **fabulation** n.
– ORIGIN C17: from L. *fabulat-*, *fabulari* 'narrate as a fable'.

**fabulist** ● **n. 1** a person who composes fables. **2** a liar.

**fabulous** ● **adj. 1** extraordinary, especially extraordinarily large. ➤ informal wonderful. **2** mythical.
– DERIVATIVES **fabulosity** n. **fabulously** adv. **fabulousness** n.
– ORIGIN ME (in the sense 'known through fable'): from Fr. *fabuleux* or L. *fabulosus* 'celebrated in fable', from *fabula* (see **FABLE**).

**facade** /fə'sɑːd/ ● **n. 1** the face of a building, especially its principal front. **2** a deceptive outward appearance.
– ORIGIN C17: from Fr. *façade*, from *face* 'face', on the pattern of Ital. *facciata*.

**face** ● **n. 1** the front part of a person's head from the forehead to the chin, or the corresponding part in an animal. ➤ an aspect of something: *the unacceptable face of social drinking.* **2** an expression on someone's face. **3** the surface of a thing, especially one that is presented to the view or has a particular function. ➤ Geometry each of the surfaces of a solid. ➤ a vertical or sloping side of a mountain or cliff. ● **v. 1** be positioned with the face or front towards or in a specified direction. **2** confront and deal with. ➤ have (a difficult event or situation) in prospect. ➤ (**face off**) chiefly N. Amer. take up an attitude of confrontation, especially at the start of a fight or game. **3** (usu. **be faced with**) cover the surface of (something) with a layer of a different material.
– PHRASES **someone's face fits** Brit. someone has the necessary qualities for something. **face the music** be confronted with the unpleasant consequences of one's actions. **face to face** close together and looking directly at one another. **in face** (or **the face**) **of** when confronted with. ➤ despite. **lose** (or **save**) **face** incur (or avoid) humiliation. **on the face of it** apparently. **set one's face against** resist with determination. **to one's face** openly in one's presence.
– DERIVATIVES **-faced** adj.
– ORIGIN ME: from OFr., based on L. *facies* 'form, appearance, face'.

**faceache** ● **n.** informal an ugly or miserable-looking person.

**face card** ● **n.** chiefly N. Amer. another term for **COURT CARD**.

**facecloth** ● **n. 1** a small towelling cloth for washing one's face. **2** smooth-surfaced woollen cloth.

**face flannel** ● **n.** Brit. a facecloth.

**faceless** ● **adj.** remote and impersonal: *faceless bureaucrats.*
– DERIVATIVES **facelessness** n.

**facelift** ● **n.** a cosmetic surgical operation to remove unwanted wrinkles by tightening the skin of the face.

**face mask** ● **n. 1** a protective mask covering the nose and mouth or nose and eyes. **2** another term for **FACE PACK**.

**face-off** ● **n. 1** chiefly N. Amer. a direct confrontation. **2** Ice Hockey the start of play.

**face pack** ● **n.** chiefly Brit. a cosmetic preparation spread over the face to improve the skin.

**face paint** ● **n.** bold-coloured paint used to decorate the face.

– DERIVATIVES **face-painter** n. **face-painting** n.

**faceplate** • n. **1** an enlarged end or attachment on the end of the mandrel on a lathe, on which work can be mounted. **2** the transparent window of a diver's or astronaut's helmet. **3** the part of a cathode ray tube that carries the phosphor screen.

**facer** • n. informal, chiefly Brit. **1** a blow to the face. **2** a sudden difficulty.

**face-saving** • adj. preserving one's reputation or dignity.

– DERIVATIVES **face-saver** n.

**facet** /ˈfasɪt, -ɛt/ • n. **1** one side of something many-sided, especially of a cut gem. ➤ Zoology any of the individual units that make up the compound eye of an insect or crustacean. **2** a particular aspect of something.

– DERIVATIVES **-faceted** adj.

– ORIGIN C17: from Fr. *facette*, dimin. of *face* (see FACE).

**facetiae** /fəˈsiːʃiː/ • pl. n. dated pornographic literature.

– ORIGIN C16: from L., pl. of *facetia* 'jest'.

**facetious** /fəˈsiːʃəs/ • adj. trying but failing to be amusing, or using inappropriate humour.

– DERIVATIVES **facetiously** adv. **facetiousness** n.

– ORIGIN C16: from Fr. *facétieux*, from *facétie*, from L. *facetia* 'jest'.

**face value** • n. **1** the value printed or depicted on a coin, postage stamp, etc., especially when less than the actual value. **2** apparent worth or implication.

**faceworker** • n. a miner who works at the coalface.

**facia** • n. chiefly Brit. variant spelling of FASCIA.

**facial** /ˈfeɪʃ(ə)l/ • adj. of or affecting the face. • n. a beauty treatment for the face.

– DERIVATIVES **facially** adv.

**facial nerves** • pl. n. Anatomy the pair of cranial nerves supplying the facial muscles and the tongue.

**-facient** • comb. form producing a specified action or state: *abortifacient*.

– ORIGIN from L. *facient-* 'doing, making'.

**facies** /ˈfeɪʃiːz/ • n. (pl. same) **1** Medicine the facial expression of an individual that is typical of a particular disease or condition. **2** Geology the character of a rock expressed by its formation, composition, and fossil content.

– ORIGIN C17: from L., 'appearance, face'.

**facile** /ˈfasʌɪl, -sɪl/ • adj. **1** appearing comprehensive only by ignoring the complexities of an issue; superficial. **2** (of success, especially in sport) effortless.

– DERIVATIVES **facilely** adv. **facileness** n.

– ORIGIN C15: from Fr., or from L. *facilis* 'easy'.

**facilitate** /fəˈsɪlɪteɪt/ • v. make easy or easier.

– DERIVATIVES **facilitation** n. **facilitative** adj. **facilitator** n. **facilitatory** adj.

– ORIGIN C17: from Fr. *faciliter*.

**facility** • n. (pl. **-ies**) **1** a building, service, or piece of equipment provided for a particular purpose. ➤ an additional feature of a service or machine. **2** a natural aptitude. ➤ absence of difficulty or effort.

– ORIGIN C16: from Fr. *facilité* or L. *facilitas*.

**facing** • n. **1** a piece of material sewn on the inside of a garment, especially at the neck and armholes, to strengthen it. ➤ (**facings**) the cuffs, collar, and lapels of a military jacket, contrasting in colour with the rest of the garment. **2** an outer layer covering the surface of a wall. • adj. positioned so as to face.

**facsimile** /fakˈsɪmɪli/ • n. an exact copy, especially of written or printed material. • v. (**facsimiled**, **facsimileing**) make a copy of.

– ORIGIN C16 (orig. as *fac simile*): mod. L., from L. *fac!* (imper. of *facere* 'make') and *simile* (neut. of *similis* 'like').

**fact** • n. a thing that is indisputably the case. ➤ (**facts**) information used as evidence or as part of a report. ➤ chiefly Law the truth about events as opposed to interpretation.

– PHRASES **before** (or **after**) **the fact** Law before (or after) the committing of a crime. **a fact of life** something that must be accepted, even if unpalatable. **the facts of life** information about sexual matters, especially as given to children. **in** (**point of**) **fact** in reality.

– ORIGIN C15 (orig. meaning 'an act', later 'a crime', surviving in the phr. *before* (*or after*) *the fact*): from L. *factum*, neut. past part. of *facere* 'do'.

**facticity** /fakˈtɪsɪti/ • n. the quality or condition of being fact.

**faction**[1] • n. a small dissentient group within a larger one.

– DERIVATIVES **factional** adj. **factionalism** n. **factionally** adv.

– ORIGIN C15 (denoting the action of doing or making): via Fr. from L. *factio(n-)*, from *facere* 'do, make'.

**faction**[2] • n. a literary and cinematic genre in which real events are used as a basis for a fictional narrative or dramatization.

– ORIGIN 1960s: blend of FACT and FICTION.

**-faction** • comb. form in nouns of action derived from verbs ending in *-fy* (such as *torrefaction* from *torrefy*).

– ORIGIN from L. *factio(n)-*, from *facere* 'do, make'.

**factionalize** (also **-ise**) • v. (of an organized group) split into factions.

**factious** /ˈfakʃəs/ • adj. relating or inclined to dissension.

– DERIVATIVES **factiously** adv. **factiousness** n.

– ORIGIN C16: from Fr. *factieux* or L. *factiosus*, from *factio* (see FACTION[1]).

**factitious** /fakˈtɪʃəs/ • adj. artificial; contrived.

– DERIVATIVES **factitiously** adv. **factitiousness** n.

– ORIGIN C17 (in the sense 'made by human skill'): from L. *facticius* 'made by art'.

**factitive** /ˈfaktɪtɪv/ • adj. Linguistics denoting a verb having a sense of causing a result and taking a complement as well as an object, as in *he appointed me captain*.

– ORIGIN C19: from mod. L. *factitivus*, formed irregularly from L. *factitare*, frequentative of *facere* 'do, make'.

**factive** • adj. Linguistics denoting a verb that assigns the status of an established fact to its object (normally a clausal object), e.g. *know*. Contrasted with CONTRAFACTIVE, NON-FACTIVE.

**factoid** • n. **1** an item of unreliable information that is repeated so often that it becomes accepted as fact. **2** N. Amer. a brief or trivial item of information.

**factor** • n. **1** a circumstance, fact, or influence that contributes to a result. ➤ Biology a gene that determines a hereditary characteristic. **2** Mathematics a number or quantity that when multiplied with another produces a given number or expression. **3** Physiology any of a number of substances in the blood which are involved in coagulation. **4** a business agent. ➤ a company that buys a manufacturer's invoices at a discount and takes responsibility for collecting the payments due on them. ➤ chiefly Scottish a land agent or steward. • v. **1** Mathematics another term for FACTORIZE. **2** sell (one's receivable debts) to a factor. **3** (**factor something in/out**) include (or exclude) something as a relevant element when making a decision.

– DERIVATIVES **factorable** adj.

– ORIGIN ME (meaning 'doer', also in the Scots sense 'agent'): from Fr. *facteur* or L. *factor*, from *fact-*, *facere* 'do'.

**factor VIII** (also **factor eight**) • n. Physiology a blood protein involved in clotting, a deficiency of which causes one of the main forms of haemophilia.

**factorage** • n. the commission or charges payable to a factor.

**factor analysis** • n. Statistics a process in which the values of observed data are expressed as functions of a number of possible causes to determine which are most important.

**factorial** Mathematics • n. the product of an integer and all the integers below it; e.g. factorial four (*4!*) is equal to 24. (Symbol: **!**) ➤ the product of a series of factors in an arithmetical progression. • adj. relating to a factor or factorial.

– DERIVATIVES **factorially** adv.

**factorize** (also **-ise**) • v. Mathematics resolve or be resolvable into factors.

– DERIVATIVES **factorization** n.

**factory** • n. (pl. **-ies**) **1** a building or buildings where goods are manufactured or assembled chiefly by ma-

chine. **2** historical an establishment for traders carrying on business in a foreign country.
– ORIGIN C16: from late L. *factorium*, lit. 'oil press', and Port. *feitoria*.

**factory farming** ● n. a system of rearing poultry, pigs, or cattle indoors under strictly controlled conditions.
– DERIVATIVES **factory farm** n.

**factory floor** ● n. the workers in a company or industry, rather than the management.

**factory ship** ● n. a fishing or whaling ship with facilities for immediate processing of the catch.

**factory shop** (chiefly N. Amer. also **factory outlet**) ● n. a shop in which goods, especially surplus stock, are sold directly by the manufacturers at a discount.

**factotum** /fak'təʊtəm/ ● n. (pl. **factotums**) an employee who does all kinds of work.
– ORIGIN C16 (orig. in the phrs *dominum* (or *magister*) *factotum* 'master of everything' and *Johannes factotum* 'Jack of all trades'): from med. L., from L. *fac!* 'do!' (imper. of *facere*) + *totum* 'the whole thing' (neut. of *totus*).

**factual** /'faktʃʊəl, -tjʊəl/ ● adj. based on or concerned with fact or facts.
– DERIVATIVES **factuality** n. **factually** adv. **factualness** n.

**factum** /'faktəm/ ● n. (pl. **factums** or **facta**) Law a statement of the facts of a case.
– ORIGIN C18: from L., lit. 'something done or made'.

**facture** /'faktʃə/ ● n. an artist's characteristic handling of paint.
– ORIGIN ME (in the sense 'workmanship'): via OFr. from L. *factura* 'manufacture', from *facere* 'do, make'.

**facula** /'fakjʊlə/ ● n. (pl. **faculae** /-liː/) Astronomy a bright region on the surface of the sun, linked to the subsequent appearance of sunspots.
– DERIVATIVES **facular** adj.
– ORIGIN C18: from L., dimin. of *fax*, *fac-* 'torch'.

**facultative** /'fak(ə)l,tətɪv/ ● adj. **1** occurring optionally in response to circumstances rather than by nature. **2** Biology capable of but not restricted to a particular function or mode of life: *a facultative parasite*.
– DERIVATIVES **facultatively** adv.
– ORIGIN C19: from Fr. *facultatif*, *-ive*, from *faculté* (see FACULTY).

**faculty** ● n. (pl. **-ies**) **1** an inherent mental or physical power. ➤an aptitude or talent. **2** chiefly Brit. a group of university departments concerned with a major division of knowledge. ➤N. Amer. the teaching or research staff of a university or college. **3** an authorization, especially from a Church authority.
– ORIGIN ME: from OFr. *faculte*, from L. *facultas*, from *facilis* 'easy', from *facere* 'make, do'.

**FAD** ● abbrev. Biochemistry flavin adenine dinucleotide.

**fad** ● n. **1** a craze. **2** an idiosyncrasy or arbitrary like or dislike.
– DERIVATIVES **faddish** adj. **faddishly** adv. **faddishness** n. **faddism** n. **faddist** n.
– ORIGIN C19 (orig. dial.): prob. the second element of *fidfad*, contr. of FIDDLE-FADDLE.

**faddy** ● adj. (**-ier**, **-iest**) Brit. having many arbitrary likes and dislikes about food.
– DERIVATIVES **faddily** adv. **faddiness** n.

**fade** ● v. **1** gradually grow faint and disappear. ➤lose or cause to lose colour. ➤(of a vehicle brake) become temporarily less efficient as a result of frictional heating. **2** (with reference to film and television images) come or cause to come gradually into or out of view, or to merge into another shot. ➤(with reference to recorded sound) increase or decrease in volume or merge into another recording. **3** Golf (of the ball) deviate to the right (or, for a left-handed golfer, the left), typically as a result of spin. **4** N. Amer. informal (in craps) match the bet of (another player). ● n. **1** an act or instance of fading. **2** Golf a shot causing the ball to fade.
– DERIVATIVES **fadeless** adj.
– ORIGIN ME: from OFr. *fader*, from *fade* 'dull, insipid', prob. based on a blend of L. *fatuus* 'silly' and *vapidus* 'vapid'.

**fader** ● n. a device for varying the volume of sound, the intensity of light, or the gain on a video or audio signal.

**fadge** /fadʒ/ ● n. Austral./NZ a loose pack of wool containing less than a bale.
– ORIGIN C16 (orig. Engl. dial.): of unknown origin.

**fado** /'fɑːdəʊ/ ● n. (pl. **-os**) a type of popular Portuguese song, usually with a melancholy theme.
– ORIGIN Port., lit. 'fate'.

**faeces** /'fiːsiːz/ (US **feces**) ● pl. n. waste matter remaining after food has been digested, discharged from the bowels.
– DERIVATIVES **faecal** /'fiːk(ə)l/ adj.
– ORIGIN ME: from L., pl. of *faex* 'dregs'.

**faerie** /'feɪəri, 'fɛːri/ (also **faery**) ● n. archaic or poetic/literary fairyland.
– ORIGIN C16 (introduced by Spenser): pseudo-archaic var. of FAIRY.

**Faeroese** ● n. & adj. variant spelling of FAROESE.

**faff** Brit. informal ● v. bustle ineffectually. ● n. ineffectual activity.
– ORIGIN C18 (orig. dial. in the sense 'blow in puffs', describing the wind): imitative.

**fag**[1] ● n. informal, chiefly Brit. **1** a tiring or unwelcome task. **2** Brit. a junior pupil at a public school who does minor chores for a senior pupil. ● v. (**fagged**, **fagging**) **1** work hard. **2** Brit. (of a public-school pupil) act as a fag. **3** [as adj. **fagged out**] exhausted.
– ORIGIN C16 (in the sense 'grow weary'): of unknown origin; cf. FLAG[4].

**fag**[2] ● n. N. Amer. informal, derogatory a male homosexual.
– DERIVATIVES **faggy** adj.
– ORIGIN 1920s: short for FAGGOT (in sense 3).

**fag**[3] ● n. Brit. informal a cigarette.
– ORIGIN C19: elliptically from FAG END.

**fag end** ● n. informal, chiefly Brit. a cigarette end. ➤a useless remnant.
– ORIGIN C17: from C15 *fag* 'a flap', of unknown origin.

**faggot** /'fagət/ ● n. **1** Brit. a ball of seasoned chopped liver, baked or fried. **2** (US **fagot**) a bundle of sticks bound together as fuel. ➤a bundle of iron rods bound together for reheating, welding, and hammering into bars. **3** N. Amer. informal, derogatory a male homosexual. **4** Brit. informal, dated an unpleasant or contemptible woman. ● v. (**faggoted**, **faggoting**; US **fagoted**, **fagoting**) (in embroidery) join by faggoting.
– DERIVATIVES **faggoty** adj.
– ORIGIN ME: from OFr. *fagot*, from Ital. *fagotto*, based on Gk *phakelos* 'bundle'.

**faggoting** (US **fagoting**) ● n. embroidery in which threads are fastened together in bundles.

**fag hag** ● n. N. Amer. informal, derogatory a heterosexual woman who spends much of her time with homosexual men.

**fah** (also **fa**) ● n. Music (in tonic sol-fa) the fourth note of a major scale. ➤the note F in the fixed-doh system.
– ORIGIN ME: representing (as an arbitrary name for the note) the first syllable of *famuli*, taken from a Latin hymn.

**Fahr.** ● abbrev. Fahrenheit.

**Fahrenheit** /'far(ə)nhʌɪt, 'fɑː-/ (abbrev.: **F**) ● adj. [postpos. when used with a numeral] of or denoting a scale of temperature on which water freezes at 32° and boils at 212°. ● n. (also **Fahrenheit scale**) this scale of temperature.
– ORIGIN C18: named after the Ger. physicist Gabriel Daniel *Fahrenheit*.

**faience** /fʌɪ'ɒ̃s, feɪ-, -'ɑːns/ ● n. glazed ceramic ware, in particular decorated tin-glazed earthenware of the type which includes delftware.
– ORIGIN C17 (orig. denoting pottery made at Faenza): from Fr. *faïence*, from *Faïence*, the Fr. name for *Faenza*, a city in Italy.

**fail** ● v. **1** be unsuccessful in an undertaking. ➤be unable to meet the standards set by (a test). ➤judge (a candidate in an examination or test) not to have passed. **2** neglect to do something. ➤disappoint expectations: *commuter chaos has failed to materialize*. **3** stop working properly. ➤become weaker or less good. ➤go out of business. **4** desert or let down: *her nerve failed her*. ● n. a mark which is not high enough to pass an examination or test.

– PHRASES **without fail** whatever happens.
– ORIGIN ME: from OFr. *faillir* (v.), *faille* (n.), based on L. *fallere* 'deceive'.

**failing** ● **n.** a weakness, especially in someone's character. ● **prep.** if not.

**faille** /feɪl/ ● **n.** a soft, light-woven fabric with a ribbed texture.
– ORIGIN C16 (denoting a kind of hood or veil worn by women): from OFr.

**fail-safe** ● **adj. 1** causing a piece of machinery to revert to a safe condition in the event of a breakdown. **2** unlikely or unable to fail.

**failure** ● **n. 1** lack of success. ➤an unsuccessful person or thing. **2** the omission of expected or required action. **3** the action or state of not functioning. ➤a sudden cessation of power. ➤the collapse of a business.

**fain** archaic ● **adj. 1** pleased or willing under the circumstances. **2** obliged. ● **adv.** gladly.
– ORIGIN OE *fægen* 'happy', of Gmc origin; rel. to FAWN[2].

**fainéant** /'feɪneɪɒ̃/ ● **n.** archaic an idle or ineffective person.
– ORIGIN C17: from Fr., from *fait* 'does' + *néant* 'nothing'.

**faint** ● **adj. 1** (of a sight, smell, or sound) barely perceptible. ➤(of a hope, chance, or idea) slight. **2** close to losing consciousness. ● **v.** briefly lose consciousness because of a temporarily insufficient supply of oxygen to the brain. ● **n.** a sudden loss of consciousness.
– DERIVATIVES **faintly** adv. **faintness** n.
– ORIGIN ME: from OFr. *faint*, *feint*, past part. of *faindre*, *feindre* (see FEIGN).

**faint heart** ● **n.** a person who has a timid or reserved nature.
– DERIVATIVES **faint-hearted** adj. **faint-heartedly** adv. **faint-heartedness** n.

**fair**[1] ● **adj. 1** treating people equally. ➤just or appropriate in the circumstances. **2** (of hair or complexion) light; blonde. **3** considerable in size or amount. ➤moderately good. ➤Austral./NZ informal complete. **4** (of weather) fine and dry. **5** archaic beautiful. ● **adv. 1** in a fair manner. **2** dialect to a high degree. ● **n.** archaic a beautiful woman. ● **v.** dialect (of the weather) become fine.
– PHRASES **fair and square 1** with absolute accuracy. **2** honestly and straightforwardly. **fair dinkum** see DINKUM. **fair dos** Brit. informal a request for just treatment or an acceptance that it has been given. **fair enough** informal that is reasonable or acceptable. **the fair sex** (also **the fairer sex**) dated or humorous women. **fair's fair** informal a request for just treatment or an assertion that an arrangement is just. **for fair** US informal completely and finally. **in a fair way to** likely to. **it's a fair cop** informal an admission that the speaker has been caught doing wrong and deserves punishment.
– DERIVATIVES **fairish** adj. **fairness** n.
– ORIGIN OE *fæger* 'pleasing, attractive', of Gmc origin.

**fair**[2] ● **n. 1** a gathering of stalls and amusements for public entertainment. **2** a periodic gathering for the sale of goods. ➤an exhibition, especially to promote particular products.
– ORIGIN ME: from OFr. *feire*, from late L. *feria*, sing. of L. *feriae* 'holy days' (on which such fairs were often held).

**fair**[3] ● **v.** [usu. as adj. **faired**] streamline (a vehicle, boat, or aircraft) by adding fairings.
– ORIGIN OE in the senses 'beautify' and 'appear or become clean'.

**fair copy** ● **n.** written or printed matter transcribed or reproduced after final correction.

**fair game** ● **n.** a person or thing that is considered a reasonable target for criticism or exploitation.

**fairground** ● **n.** an outdoor area where a fair is held.

**fair-haired** ● **adj.** N. Amer. favourite; cherished.

**fairies' bonnets** ● **pl. n.** a small toadstool with a grooved yellowish-brown thimble-shaped cap. [*Coprinus disseminatus*.]

**fairing**[1] ● **n.** an external metal or plastic structure added to increase streamlining on a high-performance vehicle, boat, or aircraft.

**fairing**[2] ● **n.** Brit. archaic a small present bought at a fair.

**Fair Isle** ● **n.** a traditional multicoloured geometric design used in woollen knitwear.
– ORIGIN *Fair Isle* in the Shetlands, where the design was first devised.

**fairlead** /'fɛːliːd/ ● **n.** a ring mounted on a boat to keep a rope clear of obstructions and prevent chafing.

**fairly** ● **adv. 1** with justice. **2** moderately. **3** actually; positively: *he fairly snarled at her.*
– PHRASES **fairly and squarely** another term for ***fair and square*** (see FAIR[1]).

**fair-minded** ● **adj.** impartial; just.
– DERIVATIVES **fair-mindedly** adv. **fair-mindedness** n.

**fair play** ● **n.** respect for the rules or equal treatment of all concerned.
– PHRASES **fair play to** —— Irish an expression of approval when someone has done the right thing.

**fair trade** ● **n.** trade in which fair prices are paid to producers in developing countries.

**fairwater** ● **n.** a structure that improves the streamlining of a ship.

**fairway** ● **n. 1** the part of a golf course between a tee and the corresponding green, where the grass is kept short. **2** a navigable channel in a river or harbour. ➤a regular course followed by ships.

**fair-weather friend** ● **n.** a person who stops being a friend in times of difficulty.

**fairy** ● **n.** (pl. **-ies**) **1** a small imaginary being of human form that has magical powers. **2** a Central and South American hummingbird with a green back and long tail. [Genus *Heliothryx*: two species.] **3** informal, derogatory a male homosexual.
– DERIVATIVES **fairylike** adj.
– ORIGIN ME (denoting fairyland): from OFr. *faerie*, from *fae* 'a fairy', from L. *fata* 'the Fates', pl. of *fatum* (see FATE).

**fairy armadillo** ● **n.** a very small burrowing armadillo found in southern South America. [Genus *Clamyphorus*: two species.]

**fairy cake** ● **n.** Brit. a small individual sponge cake, usually with icing.

**fairy floss** ● **n.** Australian term for CANDYFLOSS.

**fairy godmother** ● **n.** a female character in some fairy stories who brings unexpected good fortune to the hero or heroine.

**fairyland** ● **n.** the imaginary home of fairies.

**fairy lights** ● **pl. n.** chiefly Brit. small coloured electric lights used for decoration, especially on a Christmas tree.

**fairy ring** ● **n.** a ring of grass that is darker in colour than the surrounding grass due to the growth of certain fungi, popularly believed to have been caused by fairies dancing.

**fairy shrimp** ● **n.** a small transparent crustacean which typically swims on its back, using its legs to filter food particles from the water. [Order Anostraca: many species.]

**fairy story** ● **n.** a children's tale about magical and imaginary beings and lands. ➤an untrue account.

**fairy tale** ● **n.** a fairy story. ➤[as modifier] denoting something regarded as resembling a fairy story in being magical or idealized: *a fairy-tale romance.*

**fait accompli** /ˌfeɪt ə'kɒmpli, French fɛt akɔ̃pli/ ● **n.** a thing that has been done or decided, leaving those affected with no option but to accept.
– ORIGIN C19: from Fr., lit. 'accomplished fact'.

**faith** ● **n. 1** complete trust or confidence. **2** strong belief in a religion, based on spiritual apprehension rather than proof. **3** a system of religious belief.
– ORIGIN ME: from OFr. *feid*, from L. *fides*.

**faithful** ● **adj. 1** remaining loyal and steadfast. ➤remaining sexually loyal to a lover or spouse. **2** true to the facts or the original. ● **n.** (**the faithful**) the believers in a particular religion, especially Islam.
– DERIVATIVES **faithfulness** n.

**faithfully** ● **adv.** in a faithful manner.
– PHRASES **yours faithfully** chiefly Brit. a formula for ending a formal letter in which the recipient is not addressed by name.

**faith healing** ● **n.** healing achieved by religious faith and prayer, rather than by medical treatment.
– DERIVATIVES **faith healer** n.

**faithless** ● **adj. 1** disloyal, especially to a spouse or lover. **2** without religious faith.
– DERIVATIVES **faithlessly** adv. **faithlessness** n.

**fajitas** /fəˈhiːtəz, fəˈdʒiːtəz/ ● **pl. n.** a dish of Mexican origin consisting of strips of spiced meat, chopped vegetables, and grated cheese, wrapped in a soft tortilla.
– ORIGIN Mex. Sp., lit. 'little strips'.

**fake[1]** ● **adj.** not genuine. ● **n.** a person or thing that is not genuine. ● **v.** forge or counterfeit. ➤ pretend to feel or suffer from (an emotion or illness).
– DERIVATIVES **faker** n. **fakery** n.
– ORIGIN C18 (orig. sl.): origin uncertain; perh. ult. rel. to Ger. *fegen* 'sweep, thrash'.

**fake[2]** ● **n. & v.** variant spelling of FLAKE[4].
– ORIGIN ME (as v.): of unknown origin.

**fakie** /ˈfeɪki/ ● **n.** (pl. **-ies**) (in skateboarding or snowboarding) a movement in which the board is ridden backwards.

**fakir** /ˈfeɪkɪə, ˈfa-/ ● **n.** a Muslim (or, loosely, a Hindu) religious ascetic who lives solely on alms.
– ORIGIN C17: via Fr. from Arab. *faḳīr* 'needy man'.

**falafel** /fəˈlaf(ə)l, -ˈlɑː-/ (also **felafel**) ● **n.** a Middle Eastern dish of spiced mashed chickpeas formed into balls and deep-fried.
– ORIGIN from colloq. Egyptian Arab. *falāfil*, pl. of Arab. *fulful, filfil* 'pepper'.

**Falangist** /fəˈlandʒɪst/ ● **n.** a member of the Falange, the Spanish Fascist movement founded in 1933 and later the ruling party under General Franco. ● **adj.** of or relating to the Falangists or Falangism.
– DERIVATIVES **Falangism** n.
– ORIGIN from Sp. *falange* (from L. *phalanx, phalang-*, see PHALANX) + -IST.

**Falasha** /fəˈlɑːʃə/ ● **n.** (pl. same or **Falashas**) a member of a group of people in Ethiopia who hold the Jewish faith.
– ORIGIN Amharic, lit. 'exile, immigrant'.

**falcate** /ˈfalkeɪt/ ● **adj.** Botany & Zoology curved like a sickle; hooked.
– ORIGIN C19: from L. *falcatus* from *falx, falc-* 'sickle'.

**falchion** /ˈfɔːl(t)ʃ(ə)n/ ● **n.** historical a broad, slightly curved sword with the cutting edge on the convex side.
– ORIGIN ME *fauchon*, from OFr., based on L. *falx, falc-* 'sickle'.

**falciform** /ˈfalsɪfɔːm/ ● **adj.** Anatomy & Zoology curved like a sickle; hooked.
– ORIGIN C18: from L. *falx, falc-* 'sickle' + -IFORM.

**falciparum** /falˈsɪpərəm/ (also **falciparum malaria**) ● **n.** the most severe form of malaria, caused by *Plasmodium falciparum*.
– ORIGIN 1930s: mod. L., from L. *falx, falc-* 'sickle' + *-parum* 'bearing'.

**falcon** /ˈfɔː(l)k(ə)n, ˈfɒlk(ə)n/ ● **n.** a fast-flying bird of prey with long pointed wings. [Genus *Falco*: many species.] ➤ Falconry the female of such a bird, especially a peregrine. Compare with TERCEL.
– ORIGIN ME *faucon*: from OFr., from late L. *falco*, from L. *falx, falc-* 'scythe', or of Gmc origin.

**falconer** ● **n.** a person who keeps, trains, or hunts with falcons or other birds of prey.

**falconet** /ˈfɔː(l)k(ə)nɪt/ ● **n. 1** historical a light cannon. **2** a very small South Asian (or South American) falcon, typically with bold black-and-white plumage. [Genus *Microhierax*.]
– ORIGIN C16: sense 1 from Ital. *falconetto*, dimin. of *falcone*, from L. *falco* (see FALCON): sense 2 from FALCON + -ET[1].

**falconry** ● **n.** the keeping and training of falcons or other birds of prey; the sport of hunting with such birds.

**falderal** /ˈfaldəral/ ● **n.** variant spelling of FOLDEROL.

**faldstool** /ˈfɔːldstuːl/ ● **n. 1** a folding chair used by a bishop when not occupying the throne or when officiating in a church other than his own. **2** a small movable folding desk or stool for kneeling at prayer.
– ORIGIN OE *fældestōl*, of Gmc origin, from the base of FOLD[1] and STOOL, influenced by med. L. *faldistolium*.

**fale** /ˈfɑːleɪ/ ● **n.** a Samoan house with open sides and a thatched roof.
– ORIGIN from Samoan.

**fall** ● **v.** (past **fell**; past part. **fallen**) **1** move from a higher to a lower level, typically rapidly and without control. ➤ (**fall off**) become detached and drop to the ground. ➤ hang down. ➤ slope downwards. ➤ (of someone's face) show dismay or disappointment by appearing to droop. **2** lose one's balance and collapse. ➤ be captured or defeated. ➤ Cricket (of a wicket) be taken by the bowling side. ➤ archaic yield to temptation. **3** decrease in number, amount, intensity, or quality. **4** pass into a specified state. ➤ (**fall to doing something**) begin to do something. ➤ (usu. **fall on**) occur. ➤ be classified in the way specified. ● **n. 1** an act of falling. ➤ Wrestling a move which pins the opponent's shoulders on the ground for a count of three. ➤ a downward difference in height between parts of a surface. ➤ a sudden onset or arrival. **2** a thing which falls or has fallen. ➤ a waterfall or cascade. **3** a decline. **4** a defeat or downfall. ➤ (**the Fall of Man**) the lapse of humankind into a state of sin, ascribed in Jewish and Christian theology to the disobedience of Adam and Eve. **5** N. Amer. autumn.
– PHRASES **fall foul** (or chiefly N. Amer. **afoul**) **of** come into conflict with. **fall in** (or **into**) **line** conform. [with ref. to military formation.] **fall into place** begin to make sense. **fall over oneself to do something** informal be excessively eager to do something. **fall short** (**of**) **1** (of a missile) fail to reach its target. **2** be deficient or inadequate. **take the fall** N. Amer. informal receive blame or punishment, typically in the place of another.
– PHRASAL VERBS **fall about** Brit. informal laugh uncontrollably. **fall apart** (or **to pieces**) informal lose one's capacity to cope. **fall back** retreat. **fall back on** have recourse to when in difficulty. **fall down** fail. **fall for** informal **1** fall in love with. **2** be deceived by. **fall in** take one's place in a military formation. **fall in with 1** meet by chance and become involved with. **2** agree to. **fall on** (or **upon**) **1** attack fiercely or unexpectedly. **2** (of someone's eyes or gaze) be directed towards. **3** (of a burden or duty) be borne or incurred by. **fall out 1** have an argument. **2** leave one's place in a military formation. **3** happen. **fall through** fail. **fall to** become the duty of. ➤ (of property) revert to the ownership of.
– ORIGIN OE *fallan, feallan*, of Gmc origin; the noun is partly from ON *fall* 'downfall, sin'.

**fallacy** /ˈfaləsi/ ● **n.** (pl. **-ies**) **1** a mistaken belief. **2** Logic a failure in reasoning which renders an argument invalid.
– DERIVATIVES **fallacious** adj. **fallaciously** adv. **fallaciousness** /fəˈleɪʃəsnɪs/ n.
– ORIGIN C15 (in the sense 'deception, guile'): from L. *fallacia*, from *fallax, fallac-* 'deceiving'.

**fallback** ● **n. 1** an alternative plan for use in an emergency. **2** a reduction.

**fallen** past participle of FALL. ● **adj. 1** dated (of a woman) regarded as having lost her honour through engaging in an extramarital sexual relationship. **2** killed in battle.
– DERIVATIVES **fallenness** n.

**fallen angel** ● **n.** (in Christian, Jewish, and Muslim tradition) an angel who rebelled against God and was cast out of heaven.

**faller** ● **n. 1** Brit. a person or thing that falls, especially a horse that falls during a race. **2** N. Amer. a person who fells trees for a living.

**fallfish** ● **n.** (pl. same or **-fishes**) a North American freshwater fish resembling the chub. [*Semotilus corporalis*.]

**fall guy** ● **n.** informal a scapegoat.

**fallible** /ˈfalɪb(ə)l/ ● **adj.** capable of making mistakes or being erroneous.
– DERIVATIVES **fallibility** n. **fallibly** adv.
– ORIGIN ME: from med. L. *fallibilis*, from L. *fallere* 'deceive'.

**falling-out** ● **n.** a quarrel.

**falling star** ● **n.** a meteor or shooting star.

**fall line** ● **n. 1** (**the fall line**) Skiing the route leading straight down any particular part of a slope. **2** a narrow zone marking the geological boundary between an upland region and a plain, distinguished by the occurrence of falls where rivers cross it.

**fall-off** • **n.** a decrease.

**Fallopian tube** /fəˈləʊpɪən/ • **n.** Anatomy (in a female mammal) either of a pair of tubes along which eggs travel from the ovaries to the uterus.
– ORIGIN C18: from *Fallopius*, Latinized form of the name of Gabriello *Fallopio*, the Ital. anatomist who first described them.

**fallout** • **n.** **1** radioactive particles carried into the atmosphere by a nuclear explosion and gradually falling to the ground over a wide area. **2** the adverse results of a situation.

**fallow**[1] • **adj.** **1** (of farmland) ploughed and harrowed but left for a period without being sown. **2** inactive: *a fallow period.* **3** (of a sow) not pregnant. • **n.** a piece of fallow land. • **v.** leave (land) fallow.
– DERIVATIVES **fallowness** n.
– ORIGIN OE *fealgian* 'to break up land for sowing', of Gmc origin.

**fallow**[2] • **n.** a pale brown or reddish yellow colour.
– ORIGIN OE *falu, fealu*, of Gmc origin.

**fallow deer** • **n.** a deer with branched palmate antlers, typically having a white-spotted reddish-brown coat in summer. [*Cervus dama.*]

**false** • **adj.** **1** not according with truth or fact. ➤ invalid or illegal: *false imprisonment.* **2** deliberately intended to deceive. ➤ artificial. **3** illusory. ➤ used in names of plants, animals, and gems that superficially resemble the thing properly so called, e.g. **false scorpion**. **4** disloyal.
– PHRASES **play someone false** deceive or cheat someone.
– DERIVATIVES **falsely** adv. **falseness** n. **falsity** n.
– ORIGIN OE *fals* 'fraud', from L. *falsum* 'fraud', neut. past part. of *fallere* 'deceive'; reinforced or re-formed in ME from OFr. *fals, faus* 'false'.

**false acacia** • **n.** a North American tree with compound leaves and dense hanging clusters of fragrant white flowers. [*Robinia pseudoacacia.*]

**false alarm** • **n.** a warning given about something that fails to happen.

**false card** • **n.** Bridge a card played to give one's opponents a misleading impression of one's strength in the suit led.

**false colour** • **n.** colour added during the processing of a photographic or computer image to aid interpretation of the subject.

**false dawn** • **n.** a transient light which precedes the rising of the sun by about an hour, commonly seen in Eastern countries.

**false economy** • **n.** an apparent financial saving that in fact leads to greater expenditure.

**false friend** • **n.** a word or expression having a similar form to one in a person's native language, but a different meaning (e.g. English *magazine* and French *magasin* 'shop').

**false fruit** • **n.** Botany a fruit (such as a fig) formed from the receptacle or other parts of the flower besides the ovary.

**falsehood** • **n.** the state of being untrue. ➤ a lie.

**false memory** • **n.** Psychology an apparent recollection of an event which did not actually occur, especially one of childhood sexual abuse arising from suggestion during psychoanalysis.

**false move** • **n.** an unwise action with potentially dangerous consequences.

**false pretences** • **pl. n.** behaviour intended to deceive.

**false rib** • **n.** another term for **FLOATING RIB**.

**false scorpion** • **n.** a minute arachnid with pincers but no long abdomen or sting. [Order Pseudoscorpiones.]

**false start** • **n.** an invalid start to a race.

**false step** • **n.** a slip or stumble. ➤ a mistake.

**false topaz** • **n.** another term for **CITRINE**.

**falsetto** /fɔːlˈsɛtəʊ, fɒl-/ • **n.** (pl. **-os**) Music a method of voice production used by male singers, especially tenors, to sing notes higher than their normal range.
– ORIGIN C18: from Ital., dimin. of *falso* 'false'.

**falsework** • **n.** temporary framework used to support a building during its construction.

**falsies** • **pl. n.** informal pads of material in women's clothing used to increase the apparent size of the breasts.

**falsify** /ˈfɔːlsɪfʌɪ, ˈfɒls-/ • **v.** (**-ies**, **-ied**) **1** alter (information or evidence) so as to mislead. **2** prove (a statement or theory) to be false.
– DERIVATIVES **falsifiability** n. **falsifiable** adj. **falsification** n.
– ORIGIN ME: from Fr. *falsifier* or med. L. *falsificare*, from L. *falsificus* 'making false', from *falsus* 'false'.

**Falstaffian** /fɔːlˈstɑːfɪən, fɒl-/ • **adj.** of or resembling Shakespeare's character Sir John Falstaff in being fat, jolly, and debauched.

**falter** /ˈfɔːltə, ˈfɒl-/ • **v.** lose strength or momentum. ➤ move or speak hesitantly.
– DERIVATIVES **falterer** n. **faltering** adj. **falteringly** adv.
– ORIGIN ME: perh. from **FOLD**[1] (which was occasionally used of the faltering of the legs or tongue) + *-ter* as in *totter.*

**fame** • **n.** the state of being famous.
– ORIGIN ME (also in the sense 'reputation', which survives in **HOUSE OF ILL FAME**): via OFr. from L. *fama.*

**famed** • **adj.** famous; well known.
– ORIGIN ME: past part. of archaic *fame* (v.), from OFr. *famer*, from L. *fama.*

**familiar** • **adj.** **1** well known. ➤ common; usual. **2** (**familiar with**) having a good knowledge of. **3** in close friendship. ➤ inappropriately intimate or informal. • **n.** **1** (also **familiar spirit**) a demon supposedly attending and obeying a witch. **2** (in the Roman Catholic Church) a person rendering certain services in a pope's or bishop's household. **3** a close friend or associate.
– DERIVATIVES **familiarity** n. (pl. **-ies**). **familiarly** adv.
– ORIGIN ME: from OFr. *familier*, from L. *familiaris*, from *familia* 'household servants, family'.

**familiarize** (also **-ise**) • **v.** (usu. **familiarize someone with**) make (someone) familiar with something.
– DERIVATIVES **familiarization** n.

**familist** /ˈfamɪlɪst/ • **adj.** of or relating to a social framework centred on family relationships.
– DERIVATIVES **familistic** adj.

**famille** /faˈmiː/ • **n.** Chinese enamelled porcelain of particular periods in the 17th and 18th centuries with a predominant colour, **famille jaune** /ʒəʊn/ (yellow), **famille noire** /nwɑː/ (black), **famille rose** /rəʊz/ (red), **famille verte** /vɛːt/ (green).
– ORIGIN Fr., lit. 'family'.

**family** • **n.** (pl. **-ies**) **1** [treated as sing. or pl.] a group consisting of two parents and their children living together as a unit. ➤ a group of people related by blood or marriage. ➤ the children of a person or couple. **2** all the descendants of a common ancestor. ➤ all the languages ultimately derived from a particular early language, regarded as a group. **3** a group united by a significant shared characteristic. ➤ Biology a principal taxonomic category ranking above genus and below order. • **adj.** designed to be suitable for children as well as adults.
– PHRASES **in the family way** informal pregnant.
– DERIVATIVES **familial** /fəˈmɪljəl/ adj.
– ORIGIN ME: from L. *familia* 'household servants, family', from *famulus* 'servant'.

**family credit** • **n.** (in the UK) a regular payment by the state to a family with an income below a certain level.

**family name** • **n.** a surname.

**family planning** • **n.** the practice of controlling the number of children in a family and the intervals between their births, particularly by means of contraception.

**family tree** • **n.** a diagram showing the relationship between people in several generations of a family.

**family values** • **pl. n.** values supposedly characteristic of a traditional family unit, typically those of high moral standards and discipline.

**famine** /ˈfamɪn/ • **n.** **1** extreme scarcity of food. ➤ a shortage. **2** archaic hunger.
– ORIGIN ME: from OFr., from *faim* 'hunger', from L.

*fames.*

**famish** ● v. archaic reduce or be reduced to extreme hunger.
– ORIGIN ME: from obs. *fame* 'starve, famish', from OFr. *afamer*, based on L. *fames* 'hunger'.

**famished** /ˈfamɪʃd/ ● adj. informal extremely hungry.

**famous** ● adj. **1** known about by many people. **2** informal magnificent.
– DERIVATIVES **famously** adv. **famousness** n.
– ORIGIN ME: from OFr. *fameus*, from L. *famosus* 'famed', from *fama* (see FAME).

**famulus** /ˈfamjʊləs/ ● n. (pl. **famuli** /-lʌɪ, -liː/) historical an assistant or servant, especially one working for a magician or scholar.
– ORIGIN C19: from L., 'servant'.

**Fan** /fan/ ● n. & adj. variant spelling of FANG.

**fan**[1] ● n. **1** an apparatus with rotating blades that creates a current of air for cooling or ventilation. **2** a hand-held device, typically folding and shaped like a segment of a circle when spread out, that is waved so as to cool the user. **3** a fan-shaped alluvial or talus deposit at the foot of a slope. ● v. (**fanned**, **fanning**) **1** cool by waving something to create a current of air. ➤ drive away with a waving movement. ➤ Baseball & Ice Hockey swing unsuccessfully at the ball or puck. ➤ Baseball strike out (a batter). **2** (of an air current) increase the strength of (a fire). ➤ cause (a belief or emotion) to become stronger. **3** (**fan out**) spread out from a central point to cover a wide area.
– DERIVATIVES **fan-like** adj. **fanner** n.
– ORIGIN OE *fann* (as a noun denoting a device for winnowing grain), *fannian* (v.), from L. *vannus* 'winnowing fan'.

**fan**[2] ● n. a person who has a strong interest in or admiration for a particular sport, art form, or famous person.
– DERIVATIVES **fandom** n.
– ORIGIN C19 (orig. US): abbrev. of FANATIC.

**Fanakalo** /ˌfanagaˈlɒ, ˈfanagalɒ/ (also **Fanagalo**) ● n. S. African a language developed as a lingua franca by the southern African mining companies, composed of elements of the Nguni languages, English, and Afrikaans.
– ORIGIN 1940s: from Nguni *fana ka lo*, from *fana* 'be like' + the possessive suffix *-ka* + *lo* 'this'.

**fanatic** /fəˈnatɪk/ ● n. a person filled with excessive zeal, especially for an extreme religious or political cause. ➤ informal a person with an obsessive enthusiasm for a pastime or hobby. ● adj. filled with or expressing excessive zeal.
– DERIVATIVES **fanatical** adj. **fanatically** adv. **fanaticism** n. **fanaticize** (also **-ise**) v.
– ORIGIN C16 (as an adjective describing behaviour or speech that might result from possession by a god or demon): from Fr. *fanatique* or L. *fanaticus* 'of a temple, inspired by a god', from *fanum* 'temple'.

**fan belt** ● n. (in a motor-vehicle engine) a belt that transmits motion from the driveshaft to the radiator fan and the dynamo or alternator.

**fancier** ● n. a person who has a special interest in or breeds a particular animal.

**fanciful** ● adj. **1** over-imaginative and unrealistic. ➤ existing only in the imagination. **2** highly ornamental or imaginative in design.
– DERIVATIVES **fancifully** adv. **fancifulness** n.

**fan club** ● n. an organized group of fans of a famous person or team.

**fancy** ● v. (**-ies**, **-ied**) **1** Brit. informal feel a desire for. ➤ find sexually attractive. **2** regard as a likely winner. **3** imagine. ➤ used to express surprise: *fancy that!* ● adj. (**-ier**, **-iest**) elaborate or highly decorated. ➤ chiefly N. Amer. (especially of foodstuffs) of high quality. ➤ (of flowers) of two or more colours. ➤ (of an animal) bred to develop particular points of appearance. ● n. (pl. **-ies**) **1** a superficial or transient feeling of liking or attraction. ➤ a favourite in a race or other sporting contest. **2** the faculty of imagination. ➤ an unfounded or tentative belief or idea. **3** (also **fancy cake**) a small iced cake or biscuit.
– PHRASES **take** (or **catch**) **someone's fancy** appeal to someone. **take a fancy to** become fond of, especially without an obvious reason.
– DERIVATIVES **fanciable** adj. (informal). **fancily** adv. **fanciness** n.
– ORIGIN ME: contr. of FANTASY.

**fancy dress** ● n. a costume worn to make someone look like a famous person, fictional character, or an animal.

**fancy-free** ● adj. without emotional commitments.

**fancy goods** ● pl. n. items for sale that are purely or chiefly ornamental.

**fancy man** ● n. informal, often derogatory a woman's lover.

**fancy woman** ● n. informal, often derogatory a married man's mistress.

**fancy-work** ● n. ornamental needlework, crochet, or knitting.

**fan dance** ● n. a dance in which the female performer is apparently nude and remains partly concealed throughout by large fans.

**fandangle** /fanˈdaŋg(ə)l/ ● n. archaic a useless or purely ornamental thing.
– ORIGIN C19: perh. from FANDANGO, influenced by *newfangle.*

**fandango** /fanˈdaŋgəʊ/ ● n. (pl. **-oes** or **-os**) **1** a lively Spanish dance for two people, typically accompanied by castanets or tambourine. **2** foolish nonsense. ➤ a useless or purely ornamental thing.
– ORIGIN C18: Sp., of unknown origin.

**fane** ● n. archaic a temple or shrine.
– ORIGIN ME: from L. *fanum.*

**fanfare** ● n. **1** a short ceremonial tune or flourish played on brass instruments, especially to introduce something. **2** an elaborate welcome or introduction.
– ORIGIN C18: from Fr., ult. of imitative origin.

**fanfaronade** /ˌfanfarəˈneɪd, -ˈnɑːd/ ● n. **1** arrogant or boastful talk. **2** a fanfare.
– ORIGIN C17: from Fr. *fanfaronnade*, from *fanfaron* 'braggart'.

**Fang** /faŋ/ (also **Fan**) ● n. (pl. same or **Fangs**) **1** a member of a people inhabiting parts of Cameroon, Equatorial Guinea, and Gabon. **2** the Bantu language of this people.
– ORIGIN Fr., prob. from Fang *Pangwe.*

**fang** ● n. a large sharp tooth, especially a canine tooth of a dog or wolf. ➤ a tooth with which a snake injects poison. ➤ the biting mouthpart of a spider.
– DERIVATIVES **fanged** adj. **fangless** adj.
– ORIGIN OE (denoting booty or spoils): from ON *fang* 'capture, grasp'; cf. VANG.

**fango** /ˈfaŋgəʊ/ ● n. mud from thermal springs in Italy, used in health treatments.
– ORIGIN C20: Ital., lit. 'mud'.

**fan jet** ● n. another term for TURBOFAN.

**fankle** /ˈfaŋk(ə)l/ ● v. Scottish entangle.
– ORIGIN ME: from Scots *fank* 'coil of rope' + -LE[4].

**fanlight** ● n. a small window, typically semicircular, over a door or another window. ➤ another term for SKYLIGHT.

**fanny** ● n. (pl. **-ies**) **1** Brit. vulgar slang a woman's genitals. **2** informal, chiefly N. Amer. a person's buttocks. ● v. (**fanny about/around**) Brit. informal mess around and waste time.
– ORIGIN C19: of unknown origin.

**Fanny Adams** (also **sweet Fanny Adams**) ● n. Brit. informal nothing at all.
– ORIGIN C19: orig. a naut. term for tinned meat or stew (darkly humorous ref. to the name of a murder victim *c.*1870), now often understood as a euphemism for *fuck all.*

**fanny pack** ● n. North American term for BUMBAG.

**fan palm** ● n. a palm with large lobed fan-shaped leaves. [*Chamaerops* and other genera: many species.]

**fantabulous** /fanˈtabjʊləs/ ● adj. informal excellent; wonderful.
– ORIGIN 1950s: blend of FANTASTIC and FABULOUS.

**fantail** ● n. **1** a fan-shaped tail or end. **2** chiefly N. Amer. the overhanging part of the stern of a warship. **3** a domestic pigeon of a broad-tailed variety. **4** (also **fantail flycatcher**) a SE Asian and Australasian flycatcher with a long tapering tail, often fanned out. [Genus *Rhipidura*: numerous species.]
– DERIVATIVES **fan-tailed** adj.

**fan-tan** /'fantan/ ● **n. 1** a Chinese gambling game in which players try to guess the remainder after the banker has divided a number of hidden objects into four groups. **2** a card game in which players build on sequences of sevens.
– ORIGIN C19: from Chin. *fān tān*, lit. 'repeated divisions'.

**fantasia** /fan'teɪzɪə, ˌfantə'ziːə/ ● **n.** a musical or other composition with a free form and often an improvisatory style.
– ORIGIN C18: from Ital., 'fantasy'.

**fantasize** (also **-ise**) ● **v.** indulge in daydreaming or speculation about something desired.
– DERIVATIVES **fantasist** n.

**fantast** /'fantast/ (also **phantast**) ● **n.** archaic or N. Amer. an impractical, impulsive person.
– ORIGIN C16: orig. via med. L. from Gk *phantastēs* 'boaster', from *phantazein* or *phantazesthai* (see **FANTASTIC**); in mod. use from Ger. *Phantast*.

**fantastic** ● **adj. 1** imaginative or fanciful; remote from reality. **2** informal extraordinarily good or attractive.
– DERIVATIVES **fantastical** adj. **fantasticality** n. **fantastically** adv.
– ORIGIN ME: from OFr. *fantastique*, via med. L. from Gk *phantastikos*, from *phantazein* 'make visible', *phantazesthai* 'have visions', from *phantos* 'visible'.

**fantasy** ● **n.** (pl. **-ies**) **1** the faculty or activity of imagining improbable or impossible things. ➤a fanciful mental image, especially one on which a person often dwells and which reflects their wishes. ➤an idea with no basis in reality. **2** a genre of imaginative fiction involving magic and adventure. **3** a fantasia. ● **v.** (**-ies**, **-ied**) poetic/literary fantasize about.
– ORIGIN ME: from OFr. *fantasie*, from L. *phantasia*, from Gk 'imagination, appearance', later 'phantom', from *phantazein* (see **FANTASTIC**).

**Fante** /'fanti/ (also **Fanti**) ● **n.** (pl. same or **Fantis**) **1** a member of a people of southern Ghana. **2** the dialect of Akan spoken by this people.
– ORIGIN the name in Akan.

**fantod** /'fantɒd/ ● **n.** N. Amer. informal a state of uneasiness or unreasonableness.
– ORIGIN C19: of unknown origin.

**fan worm** ● **n.** a tube-dwelling marine bristle worm which bears a fan-like crown of filaments for filtering the water for food. [Families Sabellidae and Serpulidae: many species.]

**fanzine** /'fanziːn/ ● **n.** a magazine for fans of a particular team, performer, or genre.
– ORIGIN 1940s: blend of **FAN**[2] and **MAGAZINE**.

**FAO** ● **abbrev. 1** Food and Agriculture Organization. **2** for the attention of.

**FAQ** ● **abbrev.** Computing frequently asked questions.

**far** ● **adv.** (**further**, **furthest** or **farther**, **farthest**) **1** at, to, or by a great distance. **2** a long way in space or time. **3** by a great deal. ● **adj. 1** situated at a great distance in space or time. ➤more distant than another object of the same kind. **2** distant from the centre; extreme.
– PHRASES **as far as 1** for as great a distance as. **2** to the extent that. **be a far cry from** be very different to. **by far** by a great amount. **far and away** by a very large amount. **far and wide** over a large area. **far be it from** (or **for**) **me to** used to express reluctance. **far from** very different from being; tending to the opposite of. **far gone 1** in a bad or worsening state. **2** advanced in time. **go far 1** achieve a great deal. **2** be worth or amount to much. **go so far as to do something** do something regarded as extreme. **go too far** exceed the limits of what is reasonable or acceptable. **so far 1** to a certain limited extent. **2** up to this time. (**in**) **so far as** (or **that**) to the extent that.
– ORIGIN OE *feorr*, of Gmc origin.

**farad** /'farad/ (abbrev.: **F**) ● **n.** the SI unit of electrical capacitance, equal to a capacitance in which one coulomb of charge causes a potential difference of one volt.
– ORIGIN C19: shortening of **FARADAY**.

**faradaic** /ˌfarə'deɪɪk/ ● **adj.** produced by or associated with electrical induction.

**faraday** /'farədeɪ/ (abbrev.: **F**) ● **n.** Chemistry a unit of electric charge equal to Faraday's constant.
– ORIGIN C20: from the name of the C19 Engl. physicist Michael *Faraday*.

**Faraday cage** ● **n.** Physics an earthed metal screen surrounding a piece of equipment in order to exclude electrostatic influences.

**Faraday effect** ● **n.** Physics the rotation of the plane of polarization of electromagnetic waves in certain substances in a magnetic field.

**Faraday's constant** ● **n.** Chemistry the quantity of electric charge carried by one mole of electrons (equal to roughly 96,490 coulombs).

**faradic** /fə'radɪk/ ● **adj.** another term for **FARADAIC**.

**farandole** /ˌfar(ə)n'dəʊl, 'far(ə)ndəʊl/ ● **n.** historical a lively Provençal dance in which the dancers join hands and wind in and out in a chain.
– ORIGIN C19: Fr., from mod. Provençal *farandoulo*.

**farang** /fa'raŋ/ ● **n.** (among Thais) a European or other foreigner.
– ORIGIN Thai, from **FRANK**[2].

**faraway** ● **adj. 1** distant in space or time. **2** seeming remote; dreamy: *a strange faraway look.*

**farce** ● **n. 1** a comic dramatic work or genre using buffoonery and horseplay and typically including ludicrously improbable situations. **2** an absurd event: *the debate turned into a drunken farce.*
– ORIGIN C16: from Fr., lit. 'stuffing' (used metaphorically for comic interludes 'stuffed' into religious plays), from *farcir* 'to stuff'.

**farceur** /fɑː'səː/ ● **n.** a writer of or performer in farces. ➤a joker or comedian.
– ORIGIN C17: Fr.

**farcical** ● **adj.** resembling farce; absurd or ridiculous.
– DERIVATIVES **farcicality** n. **farcically** adv.

**farcy** /'fɑːsi/ ● **n.** glanders in horses or cattle, in which nodules are formed by inflammation of lymph vessels.
– ORIGIN ME: from OFr. *farcin*, from late L. *farciminum*, from *farcire* 'to stuff' (because of the appearance of the swollen nodules).

**fardel** /'fɑːd(ə)l/ ● **n.** archaic a bundle.
– ORIGIN ME: from OFr.

**fare** ● **n. 1** the money a passenger on public transport has to pay. **2** a range of food: *traditional Scottish fare.* ● **v. 1** perform in a specified way in a particular situation or period: *the party fared badly in the elections.* ➤archaic happen; turn out. **2** archaic travel.
– ORIGIN OE *fær*, *faru* 'travelling, a journey or expedition', *faran* 'to travel', also 'get on (well or badly)', of Gmc origin; rel. to **FORD**.

**Far East** ● **n.** China, Japan, and other countries of east Asia.
– DERIVATIVES **Far Eastern** adj.

**fare-thee-well** (also **fare-you-well**) ● **n.** (in phr. **to a fare-thee-well**) US to perfection; thoroughly.

**farewell** ● **exclam.** used to express good wishes on parting. ● **n.** an act of parting or of marking someone's departure.
– ORIGIN ME: from the imper. of **FARE** + the adv. **WELL**[1].

**farfalle** /fɑː'faleɪ, -li/ ● **pl. n.** small pieces of pasta shaped like bows or butterflies' wings.
– ORIGIN Ital., pl. of *farfalla* 'butterfly'.

**far-fetched** ● **adj.** unconvincing; implausible.

**far-flung** ● **adj.** distant or remote. ➤widely distributed.

**farina** /fə'rʌɪnə, fə'riːnə/ ● **n. 1** flour or meal made of cereal grains, nuts, or starchy roots. **2** archaic a powdery substance.
– DERIVATIVES **farinaceous** /ˌfarɪ'neɪʃəs/ adj.
– ORIGIN ME: from L., from *far* 'corn'.

**farkleberry** /'fɑːk(ə)lˌb(ə)ri, -ˌbɛri/ ● **n.** a shrub with thick leathery leaves and inedible black berries, native to the south-eastern US. [*Vaccinium arboreum*.]
– ORIGIN C18: prob. an alt. of **WHORTLEBERRY**.

**farl** /fɑːl/ ● **n.** a thin Scottish cake of oatmeal or flour, typically triangular.
– ORIGIN C17: from obs. *fardel* 'quarter', contr. of *fourth deal* (i.e. **DEAL**[1] in the earlier sense 'portion, share').

**farm** ● **n.** an area of land and its buildings used for grow-

ing crops and rearing animals. ➤a farmhouse. ➤an establishment for breeding or growing something, or devoted to a particular thing: *a fish farm* | *a wind farm*. ● v. **1** make one's living by growing crops or keeping livestock. ➤use (land) for this purpose. ➤breed or grow (a type of livestock or crop) commercially. **2** (**farm someone/thing out**) send out or subcontract work to others. ➤arrange for a child to be looked after by someone. **3** historical allow someone to collect and keep the revenues from (a tax) on payment of a fee.
– DERIVATIVES **farmable** adj. **farming** n.
– ORIGIN ME, orig. denoting a fixed annual amount payable as rent or tax: from OFr. *ferme*, from med. L. *firma* 'fixed payment', from L. *firmare* 'fix, settle'; cf. FIRM².

**farman** ● n. variant of FIRMAN.

**farmer** ● n. **1** a person who owns or manages a farm. **2** historical a person who farms taxes.

**farmer's lung** ● n. informal term for ASPERGILLOSIS.

**farmhand** ● n. a worker on a farm.

**farmhouse** ● n. a house attached to a farm, especially the main house in which the farmer lives.

**farmland** ● n. (also **farmlands**) land used for farming.

**farmstead** ● n. a farm and its buildings.

**farmyard** ● n. a yard or enclosure attached to a farmhouse. ● adj. (of manners or language) coarse.

**faro** /ˈfɛːrəʊ/ ● n. a gambling card game in which players bet on the order in which the cards will appear.
– ORIGIN C18: from Fr. *pharaon* 'pharaoh', said to have been the name of the king of hearts.

**Faroese** /ˌfɛːrəʊˈiːz/ (also **Faeroese**) ● n. (pl. same) **1** a native or inhabitant of the Faroe Islands. **2** the language of the Faroe Islands, closely related to Icelandic.

**far-off** ● adj. remote in time or space.

**farouche** /fəˈruːʃ/ ● adj. sullen or shy in company.
– ORIGIN C18: from Fr., alt. of OFr. *forache*, based on L. *foras* 'out of doors'.

**far out** ● adj. **1** unconventional or avant-garde. **2** informal, dated excellent.

**farrago** /fəˈrɑːɡəʊ, fəˈreɪɡəʊ/ ● n. (pl. **-os** or US **-oes**) a confused mixture.
– DERIVATIVES **farraginous** /fəˈrɑːdʒɪnəs, -ˈreɪdʒ-/ adj.
– ORIGIN C17: from L., lit. 'mixed fodder', from *far* 'corn'.

**far-reaching** ● adj. having important and extensive effects or implications.

**farrier** /ˈfarɪə/ ● n. a smith who shoes horses.
– DERIVATIVES **farriery** n.
– ORIGIN C16: from OFr. *ferrier*, from L. *ferrarius*, from *ferrum* 'iron, horseshoe'.

**farrow** ● n. a litter of pigs. ● v. (of a sow) give birth to (piglets).
– ORIGIN OE *fearh*, *færh* 'young pig', of W. Gmc origin.

**farruca** /fəˈruːkə/ ● n. a type of flamenco dance.
– ORIGIN 1930s: Sp., fem. of *farruco* 'of or from Galicia or Asturias' (in Spain), from *Farruco*, familiar form of the given name *Francisco*.

**far-seeing** ● adj. having shrewd judgement and foresight.

**Farsi** /ˈfɑːsiː/ ● n. the modern form of the Persian language, spoken in Iran.
– ORIGIN from Arab. *fārsī*, from *Fārs*, from Pers. *Pārs* 'Persia'.

**far-sighted** ● adj. **1** far-seeing. **2** N. Amer. long-sighted.
– DERIVATIVES **far-sightedly** adv. **far-sightedness** n.

**fart** informal ● v. **1** emit wind from the anus. **2** (**fart about/around**) waste time on silly or trivial things. ● n. **1** an emission of wind from the anus. **2** a boring or contemptible person: *an old fart*.
– ORIGIN OE: of Gmc origin.

**farther** ● adv. & adj. variant form of FURTHER.

**farthermost** ● adj. variant form of FURTHERMOST.

**farthest** ● adj. & adv. variant form of FURTHEST.

**farthing** ● n. **1** a former monetary unit and coin of the UK, equal to a quarter of an old penny. **2** [usu. with neg.] the least possible amount.
– ORIGIN OE *fēorthing*, from *fēortha* 'fourth', perh. on the pattern of ON *fjórthungr* 'quarter'.

**farthingale** /ˈfɑːðɪŋɡeɪl/ ● n. historical a hooped petticoat or circular pad of fabric formerly worn under women's skirts to extend and shape them.
– ORIGIN C16: from Fr. *verdugale*, alt. of Sp. *verdugado*, from *verdugo* 'rod, stick'.

**fartlek** /ˈfɑːtlɛk/ ● n. Athletics a system of training for distance runners in which the terrain and pace are continually varied.
– ORIGIN 1940s: from Swed., from *fart* 'speed' + *lek* 'play'.

**FAS** ● abbrev. fetal alcohol syndrome, causing retarded fetal development and due to excessive consumption of alcohol by the pregnant mother.

**fasces** /ˈfasiːz/ ● pl. n. historical a bundle of rods with a projecting axe blade, carried by a lictor in ancient Rome as a symbol of a magistrate's power, and used as an emblem of authority in fascist Italy.
– ORIGIN L., pl. of *fascis* 'bundle'.

**fascia** (chiefly Brit. also **facia** except in sense 5) ● n. **1** /ˈfeɪʃɪə, -ʃə/ a board covering the ends of rafters or other fittings. **2** a signboard on a shopfront. **3** chiefly Brit. the dashboard of a motor vehicle. **4** (in classical architecture) a long flat surface between mouldings on an architrave. **5** /ˈfaʃə/ (pl. **fasciae** /-ʃɪiː/) Anatomy a thin sheath of fibrous tissue enclosing a muscle or other organ.
– DERIVATIVES **fascial** adj. (Anatomy).
– ORIGIN C16: from L., 'band, door frame', rel. to FASCES.

**fasciated** /ˈfaʃɪeɪtɪd, -ɪətɪd/ ● adj. Botany showing abnormal fusion of parts, resulting in a flattened ribbon-like structure.
– DERIVATIVES **fasciation** n.
– ORIGIN C18 (in the sense 'striped, banded'): from L. *fasciat-*, *fasciare* 'swathe' + -ED¹.

**fascicle** /ˈfasɪk(ə)l/ ● n. **1** (also **fascicule** /-kjuːl/) a separately published instalment of a book. **2** (also **fasciculus** /faˈsɪkjʊləs/) Anatomy & Biology a bundle of structures, such as nerves or muscle fibres.
– DERIVATIVES **fascicled** adj. **fascicular** adj. **fasciculate** /-ˈsɪkjʊlət/ adj.
– ORIGIN C15: from L. *fasciculus*, dimin. of *fascis* 'bundle'.

**fasciculation** /faˌsɪkjʊˈleɪʃ(ə)n/ ● n. **1** Medicine a brief spontaneous contraction affecting a small number of muscle fibres. **2** chiefly Biology arrangement in bundles.

**fasciitis** /ˌfasɪˈʌɪtɪs, ˌfaʃɪ-/ ● n. Medicine inflammation of the fascia of a muscle or organ.

**fascinate** ● v. **1** irresistibly attract the interest of. **2** archaic deprive (prey) of the ability to resist or escape by the power of a gaze.
– DERIVATIVES **fascinating** adj. **fascinatingly** adv. **fascination** n. **fascinator** n.
– ORIGIN C16: from L. *fascinat-*, *fascinare* 'bewitch', from *fascinum* 'spell, witchcraft'.

**fascine** /faˈsiːn/ ● n. a bundle of rods or pipes bound together, used as filling or strengthening material in civil and military engineering.
– ORIGIN C17: via Fr. from L. *fascina*, from *fascis* 'bundle'.

**fascism** /ˈfaʃɪz(ə)m, -sɪz(ə)m/ ● n. an authoritarian and nationalistic right-wing system of government.
– DERIVATIVES **fascist** n. & adj. **fascistic** adj.
– ORIGIN 1920s (with ref. to Mussolini's regime in Italy): from Ital. *fascismo*, from *fascio* 'bundle, political group', from L. *fascis* (see FASCES).

**fash** ● v. (**fash oneself**) Scottish feel upset or worried.
– ORIGIN C16: from early mod. Fr. *fascher*, based on L. *fastus* 'disdain, contempt'.

**fashion** ● n. **1** a popular trend, especially in dress. ➤the production and marketing of new styles of clothing and cosmetics. **2** a manner of doing something. ● v. make into a particular form or article.
– PHRASES **after a fashion** to a certain extent but not perfectly. **after** (or **in**) **the fashion of** in a manner similar to. **in** (or **out of**) **fashion** fashionable (or unfashionable).
– DERIVATIVES **fashioner** n.
– ORIGIN ME: from OFr. *façon*, from L. *factio(n-)*, from *facere* 'do, make'.

**fashionable** ● adj. characteristic of or influenced by a current popular trend or style.
– DERIVATIVES **fashionability** n. **fashionableness** n. **fashionably** adv.

**fashionista** /ˌfaʃənˈiːstə/ • **n.** informal **1** a designer of haute couture. **2** a devoted follower of fashion.
– ORIGIN from **FASHION** + the Sp. ending *-ista*, as in **SANDINISTA**.

**fashion victim** • **n.** informal a person who follows popular fashions slavishly.

**fast**[1] • **adj. 1** moving or capable of moving at high speed. ➤taking place or acting rapidly. **2** (of a clock or watch) showing a time ahead of the correct time. **3** firmly fixed or attached. ➤(of friends) close and loyal. ➤(of a dye) not fading in light or when washed. **4** Photography needing only a short exposure. **5** involving or engaging in exciting or shocking activities. • **adv. 1** at high speed. ➤within a short time. **2** so as to be hard to move; firmly or securely. **3** so as to be hard to wake: *fast asleep*.
– PHRASES **pull a fast one** informal try to gain an unfair advantage.
– ORIGIN OE *fæst* 'firmly fixed, steadfast' and *fæste* 'firmly, securely', of Gmc origin.

**fast**[2] • **v.** abstain from food or drink, especially as a religious observance. • **n.** an act or period of fasting.
– ORIGIN OE *fæstan* (v.), of Gmc origin.

**fastback** • **n.** a car with a rear that slopes continuously down to the bumper.

**fast breeder** • **n.** a breeder reactor in which the neutrons causing fission are not slowed by any moderator.

**fasten** • **v. 1** close or do up securely. ➤fix or hold in place. ➤(**fasten something off**) secure the end of a thread with stitches or a knot. **2** (**fasten on/upon**) single out (something) and concentrate on it obsessively.
– DERIVATIVES **fastener** n. **fastening** n.
– ORIGIN OE *fæstnian* 'make sure, confirm', also 'immobilize', of W. Gmc origin; rel. to **FAST**[1].

**fast food** • **n.** cooked food sold in snack bars and restaurants as a quick meal or to be taken away.

**fast forward** • **n.** a control on a tape or video player for advancing the tape rapidly. • **v.** (**fast-forward**) advance (a tape) rapidly with such a control.

**fastidious** /faˈstɪdɪəs/ • **adj. 1** very attentive to accuracy and detail. **2** very concerned about cleanliness.
– DERIVATIVES **fastidiously** adv. **fastidiousness** n.
– ORIGIN ME (in the sense 'distasteful', later 'disgusted'): from L. *fastidiosus*, from *fastidium* 'loathing'.

**fastigiate** /faˈstɪdʒɪət, -ieɪt/ • **adj.** Botany (of a tree) having the branches more or less parallel to the main stem.
– ORIGIN C17: from L. *fastigium* 'tapering point, gable' + **-ATE**[2].

**fastness** • **n. 1** a secure place well protected by natural features. **2** the ability of a dye to maintain its colour without fading or washing away.

**fast-talk** • **v.** informal, chiefly N. Amer. pressurize into doing something using rapid or misleading speech.

**fast track** • **n.** a rapid route or method. • **v.** (**fast-track**) accelerate the development or progress of.

**fat** • **n. 1** a natural oily substance in animal bodies, especially when deposited under the skin or around certain organs. ➤such a substance, or a similar one made from plants, used in cooking. **2** the presence of excess fat in a person or animal: *he was running to fat*. **3** Chemistry any of a group of natural esters of glycerol and various fatty acids, which are solid at room temperature and are the main constituents of animal and vegetable fat. Compare with **OIL**. • **adj.** (**fatter, fattest**) **1** (of a person or animal) having much excess fat; corpulent. **2** (of food) containing much fat. **3** informal substantial: *fat profits*. • **v.** (**fatted, fatting**) archaic make or become fat.
– PHRASES **kill the fatted calf** produce one's best food to celebrate, especially at a prodigal's return. [with biblical allusion to Luke 15.] **live off** (or **on**) **the fat of the land** have the best of everything.
– DERIVATIVES **fatless** adj. **fatly** adv. **fatness** n. **fattish** adj.
– ORIGIN OE *fǣtt*, of W. Gmc origin.

**fatal** /ˈfeɪt(ə)l/ • **adj.** causing death. ➤leading to failure or disaster.
– DERIVATIVES **fatally** adv.
– ORIGIN ME (in the senses 'destined by fate' and 'ominous'): from OFr., or from L. *fatalis*, from *fatum* (see **FATE**).

**fatalism** • **n.** the belief that all events are predetermined and therefore inevitable. ➤a submissive attitude to events.
– DERIVATIVES **fatalist** n. **fatalistic** adj. **fatalistically** adv.

**fatality** /fəˈtalɪti, feɪ-/ • **n.** (pl. **-ies**) **1** an occurrence of death by accident, in war, or from disease. **2** helplessness in the face of fate.

**Fata Morgana** /ˌfɑːtə mɔːˈɡɑːnə/ • **n.** a mirage.
– ORIGIN Ital., lit. 'fairy Morgan', with ref. to a mirage seen in the Straits of Messina, from the name of the legendary enchantress *Morgan le Fay*, sister of King Arthur.

**fatback** • **n. 1** N. Amer. fat from the upper part of a side of pork. **2** US informal term for **MENHADEN**.

**fat cat** • **n.** derogatory a wealthy and powerful businessman or politician.

**fat dormouse** • **n.** a squirrel-like burrowing dormouse found in Europe and Asia Minor, sometimes farmed or hunted for food. [*Glis glis*.]

**fate** • **n. 1** the development of events outside a person's control, regarded as predetermined by a supernatural power. **2** the outcome of a particular situation for someone or something, especially the end of a person's life. **3** (**the Fates**) Greek & Roman Mythology the three goddesses (Clotho, Lachesis, and Atropos) who preside over the birth and life of humans. • **v.** (**be fated**) be destined to happen, turn out, or act in a particular way.
– PHRASES **seal someone's fate** make it inevitable that something unpleasant will happen to someone.
– ORIGIN ME: from Ital. *fato* or (later) from its source, L. *fatum* 'that which has been spoken', from *fari* 'speak'.

**fateful** • **adj.** having far-reaching, especially disastrous consequences or implications.
– DERIVATIVES **fatefully** adv. **fatefulness** n.

**fat farm** • **n.** informal, chiefly N. Amer. a health farm for people who are overweight.

**fathead** • **n.** informal a stupid person.
– DERIVATIVES **fat-headed** adj. **fat-headedness** n.

**fat hen** • **n.** a herbaceous weed with mealy edible leaves. [*Chenopodium alba*.]
– ORIGIN C18: said to be so named because the seeds were eaten by poultry.

**father** • **n. 1** a man in relation to his natural child or children. ➤a male animal in relation to its offspring. ➤an important figure in the origin and early history of something. ➤a man who gives care and protection. ➤the oldest member or doyen of a society or other body. ➤(**the Father**) (in Christian belief) the first person of the Trinity; God. ➤(**Father**) used in proper names to suggest an old and venerable character: *Father Thames*. **2** (often as a title or form of address) a priest. **3** (**Fathers** or **Fathers of the Church**) early Christian theologians who are regarded as especially authoritative. • **v. 1** be the father of. ➤[usu. as noun **fathering**] treat with fatherly protective care. ➤be the source or originator of. **2** (**father someone/thing on**) assign paternity of a child or responsibility for something to.
– PHRASES **how's your father** Brit. informal used euphemistically to refer to sexual intercourse.
– DERIVATIVES **fatherhood** n. **fatherless** adj. **fatherlessness** n. **fatherlike** adj. & adv.
– ORIGIN OE *fæder*, of Gmc origin, from an Indo-Eur. root shared by L. *pater* and Gk *patēr*.

**Father Christmas** • **n.** an imaginary being said to bring presents for children on the night before Christmas Day.

**father-in-law** • **n.** (pl. **fathers-in-law**) the father of one's husband or wife.

**fatherland** • **n.** a person's native country. ➤(**the Fatherland**) Germany during the period of Hitler's control.

**fatherly** • **adj.** of, resembling, or characteristic of a father, especially in being protective and affectionate.
– DERIVATIVES **fatherliness** n.

**father of chapel** • **n.** Brit. the shop steward of a printers' trade union.

**Father of the House** • **n.** (in the UK) the member of the House of Commons with the longest continuous service.

**Father's Day** • **n.** a day of the year on which fathers are honoured with gifts and greetings cards (in the US and Britain usually the third Sunday in June).

**fathom** ● **n.** a unit of length equal to six feet (1.8 metres), chiefly used in reference to the depth of water. ● **v. 1** [usu. with neg.] understand (something) after much thought. **2** measure the depth of.
– DERIVATIVES **fathomable** adj. **fathomless** adj.
– ORIGIN OE *fæthm*, in the sense 'something which embraces', (pl.) 'the outstretched arms', of Gmc origin.

**fatigue** /fəˈtiːg/ ● **n. 1** extreme tiredness, especially resulting from mental or physical exertion or illness. **2** weakness in metal or other materials caused by repeated variations of stress. **3** (**fatigues**) menial non-military tasks performed by a soldier. ➤a group of soldiers ordered to do such a duty. ➤(**fatigues**) loose-fitting clothing of a sort worn by soldiers. ● **v.** (**fatigues**, **fatigued**, **fatiguing**) (often **be fatigued**) cause to suffer fatigue.
– DERIVATIVES **fatiguability** (also **fatigability**) n. **fatiguable** (also **fatigable**) adj.
– ORIGIN C17 (in the sense 'task or duty that causes weariness'): from Fr. *fatigue* (n.), *fatiguer* (v.), from L. *fatigare* 'tire out', from *ad fatim*, *affatim* 'to satiety or surfeit, to bursting'.

**Fatiha** /ˈfɑːtɪə, ˈfat-/ (also **Fatihah**) ● **n.** the short first sura of the Koran, used by Muslims as an essential element of ritual prayer.
– ORIGIN from Arab. *al-Fātiḥah*, from *fātiḥa* 'opening'.

**Fatimid** /ˈfatɪmɪd/ ● **n.** a member of a dynasty which ruled in parts of northern Africa, Egypt, and Syria from 909 to 1171.
– DERIVATIVES **Fatimite** n.
– ORIGIN named after *Fatima*, youngest daughter of Muhammad, from whom the dynasty is said to have descended.

**fatling** ● **n.** a young animal that has been fattened for slaughter.

**fatso** ● **n.** (pl. **-oes**) informal, derogatory a fat person.

**fatstock** ● **n.** Brit. livestock that has been fattened for slaughter.

**fatten** ● **v.** make or become fat or fatter.

**fattism** ● **n.** prejudice against people who are fat.
– DERIVATIVES **fattist** n. & adj.

**fatty** ● **adj.** (**-ier**, **-iest**) **1** containing a large amount of fat. **2** Medicine involving abnormal deposition of fat: *fatty degeneration.* ● **n.** (pl. **-ies**) informal a fat person.
– DERIVATIVES **fattiness** n.

**fatty acid** ● **n.** Chemistry an organic acid consisting of a hydrocarbon chain and a terminal carboxyl group.

**fatuous** /ˈfatjʊəs/ ● **adj.** silly and pointless.
– DERIVATIVES **fatuity** n. (pl. **-ies**). **fatuously** adv. **fatuousness** n.
– ORIGIN C17: from L. *fatuus* 'foolish' + **-ous**.

**fatwa** /ˈfatwɑː/ ● **n.** an authoritative ruling on a point of Islamic law.
– ORIGIN C17: from Arab. *fatwā*, from *ʼaftā* 'decide a point of law'.

**fauces** /ˈfɔːsiːz/ ● **pl. n.** Anatomy the arched opening at the back of the mouth leading to the pharynx.
– DERIVATIVES **faucial** /ˈfɔːʃ(ə)l/ adj.
– ORIGIN ME: from L., 'throat'.

**faucet** /ˈfɔːsɪt/ ● **n.** chiefly N. Amer. a tap.
– ORIGIN ME: from OFr. *fausset*, from Provençal *falset*, from *falsar* 'to bore'.

**faugh** /fɔː/ ● **exclam.** expressing disgust.

**fault** /fɔːlt, fɒlt/ ● **n. 1** an unattractive or unsatisfactory feature; a defect or mistake. ➤(in tennis and similar games) a service of the ball not in accordance with the rules. **2** responsibility for an accident or misfortune. **3** Geology an extended break in a rock formation, marked by the relative displacement and discontinuity of strata. ● **v. 1** criticize for inadequacy or mistakes. ➤archaic do wrong. **2** (**be faulted**) Geology be broken by a fault or faults.
– PHRASES **at fault 1** in the wrong. **2** mistaken or defective. **find fault** make an adverse criticism or objection, sometimes unfairly or destructively. —— **to a fault** displaying the specified commendable quality to an excessive extent.
– DERIVATIVES **faultless** adj. **faultlessly** adv. **faultlessness** n.
– ORIGIN ME *faut(e)* 'lack, failing', from OFr., based on L. *fallere* 'deceive'; *-l-* added to conform with L.

**faulty** ● **adj.** (**-ier**, **-iest**) having or displaying faults.
– DERIVATIVES **faultily** adv. **faultiness** n.

**faun** /fɔːn/ ● **n.** Roman Mythology a lustful rural god represented as a man with a goat's horns, ears, legs, and tail.
– ORIGIN ME: from the name of the pastoral god *Faunus*.

**fauna** /ˈfɔːnə/ ● **n.** the animals of a particular region, habitat, or geological period. Compare with **FLORA**.
– DERIVATIVES **faunal** adj. **faunistic** /-ˈnɪstɪk/ adj.
– ORIGIN C18: mod. L. *Fauna*, the name of a rural goddess, sister of *Faunus* (see **FAUN**).

**Fauntleroy** /ˈfɔːntlərɔɪ/ (also **Little Lord Fauntleroy**) ● **n.** an excessively well-mannered or elaborately dressed young boy.
– ORIGIN from the name of the boy hero of Frances Hodgson Burnett's novel *Little Lord Fauntleroy* (1886).

**Faustian** /ˈfaʊstɪən/ ● **adj.** relating to or characteristic of the 16th-century German astronomer and necromancer Johann Faust, reputed to have sold his soul to the Devil.

**faute de mieux** /fəʊt də ˈmjəː, French fot də mjø/ ● **adv.** for want of a better alternative.
– ORIGIN from Fr.

**fauteuil** /fəʊˈtəːi/ ● **n.** a wooden seat in the form of an armchair with open sides and upholstered arms.
– ORIGIN Fr., from OFr. *faudestuel*, from med. L. *faldistolium* (see **FALDSTOOL**).

**Fauve** /fəʊv, French fov/ ● **n.** a member of a group of early 20th-century French painters who favoured a vivid expressionistic and non-naturalistic use of colour.
– DERIVATIVES **fauvism** n. **fauvist** n. & adj.
– ORIGIN Fr., lit. 'wild beast', with ref. to a remark by the art critic Louis Vauxcelles.

**faux** /fəʊ/ ● **adj.** made in imitation; artificial.
– ORIGIN Fr., 'false'.

**faux naif** /ˌfəʊ nʌɪˈiːf, French fo naif/ ● **adj.** artificially or affectedly naive. ● **n.** a person who affects naivety.
– ORIGIN from Fr. *faux* 'false' + *naïf* 'naive'.

**faux pas** /fəʊ ˈpɑː, French fo pa/ ● **n.** (pl. same) a social blunder.
– ORIGIN Fr., lit. 'false step'.

**fava bean** /ˈfɑːvə/ (also **faba bean**) ● **n.** North American term for **BROAD BEAN**.
– ORIGIN Ital. *fava*, from L. *faba* 'bean'.

**fave** ● **n. & adj.** informal short for **FAVOURITE**.

**favela** /faˈvɛlə/ ● **n.** (in Brazil) a shack or shanty town.
– ORIGIN from Port.

**favour** (US **favor**) ● **n. 1** approval or liking. ➤overgenerous preferential treatment. **2** an act of kindness beyond what is due or usual. ➤(**one's favours**) dated a woman's consent to a man having sexual intercourse with her. **3** archaic a thing such as a badge that is given or worn as a mark of favour or support. ● **v. 1** regard or treat with favour. ➤work to the advantage of. **2** (**favour someone with**) give someone (something that they want). **3** informal resemble (a relative) in facial features.
– PHRASES **in** (or **out of**) **favour** meeting with (or having lost) approval. **in favour of 1** to be replaced by. **2** in support or to the advantage of.
– DERIVATIVES **favourer** n.
– ORIGIN ME: via OFr. from L. *favor*, from *favere* 'show kindness to'.

**favourable** (US **favorable**) ● **adj. 1** expressing approval or consent. **2** to the advantage of someone or something. ➤auspicious.
– DERIVATIVES **favourableness** n. **favourably** adv.

**favourite** (US **favorite**) ● **adj.** preferred to all others of the same kind. ● **n. 1** a favourite person or thing. **2** the competitor thought most likely to win.
– PHRASES **favourite son 1** a famous man who is particularly popular in his native area. **2** US a person supported as a presidential candidate by delegates from the candidate's home state.
– ORIGIN C16 (as n.): from obs. Fr. *favorit*, from Ital. *favorito*, past part. of *favorire* 'to favour'.

**favouritism** (US **favoritism**) ● **n.** the unfair favouring of one person or group at the expense of another.

**fawn**[1] ● **n. 1** a young deer in its first year. **2** a light brown colour. ● **v.** (of a deer) produce young.
– ORIGIN ME: from OFr. *faon*, based on L. *fetus* 'offspring'; cf. FETUS.

**fawn**[2] ● **v.** give a servile display of exaggerated flattery or affection. ➤(of an animal, especially a dog) show slavish devotion, especially by rubbing against someone.
– DERIVATIVES **fawning** adj. **fawningly** adv.
– ORIGIN OE *fagnian* 'make or be glad', of Gmc origin; rel. to FAIN.

**fax** ● **n.** an exact copy of a document made by electronic scanning and transmitted as data by telecommunications links. ➤the production or transmission of documents in this way. ➤(also **fax machine**) a machine for transmitting and receiving such documents. ● **v.** send (a document) by fax. ➤contact by fax.
– ORIGIN 1940s.: abbrev. of FACSIMILE.

**fay** ● **n.** poetic/literary a fairy.
– ORIGIN ME: from OFr. *fae, faie*, from L. *fata* 'the Fates', pl. of *fatum* (see FATE); cf. FAIRY.

**fayre** ● **n.** pseudo-archaic spelling of FAIR[2].

**faze** ● **v.** [usu. with neg.] (usu. **be fazed**) informal disturb or disconcert.
– ORIGIN C19 (orig. US): var. of dial. *feeze* 'drive off', from OE *fēsian*.

**fazenda** /fəˈzɛndə/ ● **n.** (in Portuguese-speaking countries) an estate or large farm.
– ORIGIN from Port.; cf. Sp. *hacienda*.

**FBA** ● **abbrev.** Fellow of the British Academy.

**FBI** ● **abbrev.** (in the US) Federal Bureau of Investigation.

**FC** ● **abbrev. 1** Football Club. **2** (in the UK) Forestry Commission.

**FCC** ● **abbrev.** (in the US) Federal Communications Commission.

**FCO** ● **abbrev.** (in the UK) Foreign and Commonwealth Office.

**FD** ● **abbrev.** Defender of the Faith.
– ORIGIN from L. *Fidei Defensor*.

**FDA** ● **abbrev.** (in the US) Food and Drug Administration.

**FDDI** ● **abbrev.** fibre distributed data interface, an industry standard for high-speed optical-fibre networks.

**FDIC** ● **abbrev.** Federal Deposit Insurance Corporation.

**FE** ● **abbrev.** (in the UK) further education.

**Fe** ● **symb.** the chemical element iron.
– ORIGIN from L. *ferrum*.

**fealty** /ˈfiːəlti/ ● **n.** historical a feudal tenant's or vassal's sworn loyalty to a lord.
– ORIGIN ME: from OFr. *feau(l)te, fealte*, from L. *fidelitas* (see FIDELITY).

**fear** ● **n. 1** an unpleasant emotion caused by the threat of danger, pain, or harm. ➤(**fear for**) a feeling of anxiety concerning the outcome of something or the safety of someone. ➤the likelihood of something unwelcome happening. **2** archaic a mixed feeling of dread and reverence. ● **v. 1** be afraid of. ➤(**fear for**) feel anxiety on behalf of. ➤used to express regret or apology. **2** archaic regard (God) with reverence and awe.
– PHRASES **for fear of** (or **that**) to avoid the risk of (or that). **never fear** used to reassure someone. **no fear** Brit. informal used as an emphatic expression of denial or refusal. **put the fear of God in** (or **into**) **someone** cause someone to be very frightened. **without fear or favour** impartially.
– DERIVATIVES **fearless** adj. **fearlessly** adv. **fearlessness** n.
– ORIGIN OE *fǣr* 'danger', *fǣran* 'frighten', also 'revere', of Gmc origin.

**fearful** ● **adj. 1** showing or causing fear. **2** informal very great.
– DERIVATIVES **fearfully** adv. **fearfulness** n.

**fearsome** ● **adj.** frightening, especially in appearance.
– DERIVATIVES **fearsomely** adv. **fearsomeness** n.

**feart** /ˈfɪət/ ● **adj.** Scottish afraid.

**feasible** /ˈfiːzɪb(ə)l/ ● **adj. 1** possible and practical to achieve easily or conveniently. **2** informal likely.
– DERIVATIVES **feasibility** n. **feasibly** adv.
– ORIGIN ME: from OFr. *faisible*, from *fais-*, stem of *faire* 'do, make', from L. *facere*.

**feast** ● **n. 1** a large meal, especially a celebratory one. ➤a plentiful supply of something enjoyable. **2** an annual religious celebration. ➤a day dedicated to a particular saint. ➤Brit. an annual village festival. ● **v.** eat and drink sumptuously. ➤give a sumptuous meal to.
– PHRASES **ghost** (or **skeleton**) **at the feast** a person or thing that brings gloom to an otherwise pleasant occasion. **feast one's eyes on** gaze at with pleasure.
– DERIVATIVES **feaster** n.
– ORIGIN ME: from OFr. *feste* (n.), *fester* (v.), from L. *festa*, neut. pl. of *festus* 'joyous'; cf. FÊTE and FIESTA.

**feast day** ● **n.** a day on which an annual Christian celebration is held.

**Feast of Dedication** ● **n.** another name for HANUKKAH.

**Feast of Tabernacles** ● **n.** another name for SUCCOTH.

**Feast of Weeks** ● **n.** another name for SHAVUOTH.

**feat** ● **n.** an achievement requiring great courage, skill, or strength.
– ORIGIN ME: from OFr. *fait*, from L. *factum* (see FACT).

**feather** ● **n. 1** any of the flat appendages growing from a bird's skin, consisting of a partly hollow horny shaft fringed with vanes of barbs. **2** (**feathers**) a fringe of long hair on the legs of a dog, horse, or other animal. ● **v. 1** rotate the blades of (a propeller) about their own axes in such a way as to lessen the air or water resistance. ➤Rowing turn (an oar) so that it passes through the air edgeways. **2** [as adj. **feathered**] covered or decorated with feathers. **3** float or move like a feather.
– PHRASES **a feather in one's cap** an achievement to be proud of. **feather one's (own) nest** make money illicitly and at someone else's expense.
– DERIVATIVES **featheriness** n. **featherless** adj. **feathery** adj.
– ORIGIN OE *fether*, of Gmc origin.

**feather bed** ● **n.** a bed with a mattress stuffed with feathers. ● **v.** (**feather-bed**) provide with excessively favourable economic or working conditions.

**feather-brain** ● **n.** a silly or absent-minded person.
– DERIVATIVES **feather-brained** adj.

**feather-cut** ● **v.** cut (hair) into wispy feather-like points. ● **n.** (**feathercut**) a hairstyle produced by such cutting.

**feather edge** ● **n.** a fine edge produced by tapering a board, plank, or other object.

**feathering** ● **n. 1** a bird's plumage. ➤the feathers of an arrow. ➤fringes of hairs on a dog. **2** feather-like markings or structure. ➤Architecture cusping in tracery.

**feather star** ● **n.** an echinoderm with a small disc-like body and long feathery arms. [Order Comatulida: many species.]

**feather stitch** ● **n.** ornamental zigzag sewing. ● **v.** (**feather-stitch**) [usu. as noun **feather-stitching**] sew with such a stitch.

**featherweight** ● **n. 1** a weight in boxing and other sports intermediate between bantamweight and lightweight. **2** a person or thing not worth serious consideration.

**feature** ● **n. 1** a distinctive attribute or aspect of something. ➤a part of the face, such as the mouth, making a significant contribution to its overall appearance. **2** a newspaper or magazine article or a broadcast programme devoted to a particular topic. ➤(also **feature film**) a full-length film intended as the main item in a cinema programme. ● **v.** have as a feature. ➤have as an important actor or participant. ➤be a feature of or take an important part in.
– DERIVATIVES **-featured** adj. **featureless** adj.
– ORIGIN ME: from OFr. *faiture* 'form', from L. *factura* (see FACTURE).

**Feb.** ● **abbrev.** February.

**febrifuge** /ˈfɛbrɪfjuːdʒ/ ● **n.** a medicine used to reduce fever.
– DERIVATIVES **febrifugal** /fɪˈbrɪfjʊg(ə)l, ˌfɛbrɪˈfjuːg(ə)l/ adj.

– ORIGIN C17: from Fr. *fébrifuge*, from L. *febris* 'fever' + *fugare* 'drive away'; cf. **FEVERFEW**.

**febrile** /ˈfiːbrʌɪl/ ● **adj.** **1** having or showing the symptoms of a fever. **2** having or showing a great deal of nervous excitement.
– DERIVATIVES **febrilely** adv. **febrility** n.
– ORIGIN C17: from Fr. *fébrile* or med. L. *febrilis*, from L. *febris* 'fever'.

**February** /ˈfɛbrʊəri, ˈfɛbjʊəri/ ● **n.** (pl. **-ies**) the second month of the year.
– ORIGIN ME *feverer*, from OFr. *feverier*, based on L. *februarius*, from *februa*, the name of a purification feast held in this month.

**feces** ● **n.** US spelling of **FAECES**.

**feckless** ● **adj.** **1** ineffectual; feeble. **2** unthinking and irresponsible.
– DERIVATIVES **fecklessly** adv. **fecklessness** n.
– ORIGIN C16: from Scots and north. Engl. dial. *feck* (from *effeck*, var. of **EFFECT**) + **-LESS**.

**feculent** /ˈfɛkjʊl(ə)nt/ ● **adj.** of or containing dirt, sediment, or waste matter.
– DERIVATIVES **feculence** n.
– ORIGIN C15: from Fr. *féculent* or L. *faeculentus*, from *faex*, *faec-* 'dregs'.

**fecund** /ˈfɛk(ə)nd, ˈfiːk-/ ● **adj.** highly fertile; able to produce offspring.
– DERIVATIVES **fecundity** /fɪˈkʌndɪti/ n.
– ORIGIN ME: from Fr. *fécond* or L. *fecundus*.

**fecundability** /fɪˌkʌndəˈbɪlɪti/ ● **n.** Medicine & Zoology the probability of a woman or female animal conceiving within a given period.

**fecundate** /ˈfɛk(ə)ndeɪt, ˈfiːk-/ ● **v.** archaic fertilize. ➤ poetic/literary make fruitful.
– DERIVATIVES **fecundation** n.
– ORIGIN C17: from L. *fecundat-*, *fecundare* 'make fruitful'.

**Fed** ● **n.** US informal **1** a member of the FBI or other federal agent or official. **2** (usu. **the Fed**) short for **FEDERAL RESERVE**.

**fed** past and past participle of **FEED**.

**fedayeen** /ˌfɛdəˈjiːn, fəˈdɑːjiːn/ ● **pl. n.** Arab guerrillas, especially those operating against Israel.
– ORIGIN 1950s: from colloq. Arab. *fidā'iyīn*, pl. of classical Arab. *fidā'ī* 'one who gives his life for another or for a cause'.

**federal** ● **adj.** **1** having or relating to a system of government in which several states form a unity but remain independent in internal affairs. **2** relating to or denoting the central government as distinguished from the separate units constituting a federation. ➤ (**Federal**) US historical of the Northern States in the Civil War.
– DERIVATIVES **federalism** n. **federalist** n. & adj. **federalization** (also **-isation**) n. **federalize** (also **-ise**) v. **federally** adv.
– ORIGIN C17: from L. *foedus*, *foeder-* 'league, covenant' + **-AL**.

**Federal Reserve** ● **n.** (in the US) the banking authority that performs the functions of a central bank.

**federate** ● **v.** /ˈfɛdəreɪt/ (of a number of states or organizations) organize or be organized on a federal basis. ● **adj.** /ˈfɛd(ə)rət/ of or relating to such an arrangement.
– DERIVATIVES **federative** adj.
– ORIGIN C18 (as adj.): from late L. *foederatus*, based on *foedus*, *foeder-* (see **FEDERAL**).

**federation** ● **n.** **1** a federal group of states. ➤ an organization within which smaller divisions have some degree of internal autonomy. **2** the action of federating.
– DERIVATIVES **federationist** n.

**fedora** /fɪˈdɔːrə/ ● **n.** a low, soft felt hat with a curled brim and the crown creased lengthways.
– ORIGIN C19 (orig. US): from *Fédora*, the title of a drama written by the Fr. dramatist Victorien Sardou.

**fed up** ● **adj.** (often **fed up with**) informal annoyed or bored.

**fee** ● **n.** **1** a payment made to a professional person or to a professional or public body in exchange for advice or services. ➤ a charge made for a privilege such as admission. **2** Law, historical an estate of land, especially one held on condition of feudal service. ● **v.** (**fees**, **fee'd** or **feed**, **feeing**) rare pay a fee to.
– PHRASES **hold something in fee** Law, historical hold an estate in return for feudal service to a superior.
– ORIGIN ME: from an Anglo-Norman Fr. var. of OFr. *feu*, *fief*, from med. L. *feodum*, *feudum*, ult. of Gmc origin; cf. **FEU** and **FIEF**.

**feeb** ● **n.** N. Amer. informal a feeble-minded person.

**feeble** ● **adj.** (**-er**, **-est**) lacking physical strength. ➤ lacking strength of character. ➤ failing to convince or impress: *a feeble excuse*.
– DERIVATIVES **feebleness** n. **feebly** adv.
– ORIGIN ME: from OFr. *fieble*, earlier *fleible*, from L. *flebilis* 'lamentable', from *flere* 'weep'.

**feeble-minded** ● **adj.** foolish; stupid. ➤ dated having less than average intelligence.
– DERIVATIVES **feeble-mindedly** adv. **feeble-mindedness** n.

**feed** ● **v.** (past and past part. **fed** /fɛd/) **1** give food to. ➤ provide an adequate supply of food for. **2** eat. ➤ (**feed on/off**) derive regular nourishment from (a particular substance). **3** supply with material, power, water, etc. ➤ prompt (an actor) with (a line). ➤ (in ball games) pass (the ball) to a player. **4** pass gradually through a confined space. **5** (**feed back**) (of an electrical or other system) produce feedback. ● **n.** **1** an act of feeding or of being fed. ➤ food for domestic animals. **2** a device or pipe for supplying material to a machine. ➤ the supply of raw material to a machine or device. **3** a prompt given to an actor on stage.
– ORIGIN OE *fēdan* (v.), of Gmc origin; rel. to **FOOD**.

**feedback** ● **n.** **1** information given in response to a product, a person's performance of a task, etc., used as a basis for improvement. **2** the modification or control of a process or system by its results or effects. **3** the return of a fraction of the output of an amplifier, microphone, or other device to the input, causing distortion or a whistling sound.

**feeder** ● **n.** **1** a person or animal that eats a particular food or in a particular manner. **2** a container filled with food for birds or mammals. ➤ Brit. a child's feeding bottle. **3** a thing that supplies something. ➤ a road or rail route linking outlying districts with a main system.

**feedforward** ● **n.** the modification or control of a process using its anticipated results or effects.

**feeding frenzy** ● **n.** **1** an aggressive and competitive group attack on prey by a number of sharks or piranhas. **2** an episode of frantic competition for something.

**feedstock** ● **n.** raw material to supply a machine or industrial process.

**feedstuff** ● **n.** fodder.

**feel** ● **v.** (past and past part. **felt**) **1** perceive, examine, or search by touch. ➤ be aware of (something happening) through physical sensation. ➤ give a sensation of a particular physical quality when touched: *the wool feels soft*. ➤ (**feel someone up**) informal fondle someone for one's own sexual stimulation. **2** experience (an emotion or sensation). ➤ consider oneself: *he doesn't feel obliged to visit*. ➤ (**feel up to**) have the strength and energy to. ➤ be emotionally affected by. ➤ have a specified reaction or attitude towards something. **3** have a belief or impression, especially without an identifiable reason. ● **n.** **1** an act of feeling. ➤ the sense of touch. **2** a sensation given by an object or material when touched. **3** the impression given by something.
– PHRASES **get a** (or **the**) **feel for** (or **of**) become accustomed to. **have a feel for** have a sensitive appreciation or understanding of. **make oneself** (or **one's presence**) **felt** have a noticeable effect.
– ORIGIN OE *fēlan*, of W. Gmc origin.

**feeler** ● **n.** **1** an animal organ such as an antenna that is used for testing things by touch or for searching for food. **2** a tentative proposal intended to ascertain someone's attitude or opinion.

**feeler gauge** ● **n.** a gauge consisting of a number of thin blades for measuring narrow gaps or clearances.

**feel-good** ● **adj.** informal causing a feeling of happiness and well-being: *a feel-good movie*.
– DERIVATIVES **feel-goodism** n.

**feeling** ● **n. 1** an emotional state or reaction. ➤ **(feelings)** emotional responses or tendencies to respond. ➤ strong emotion. **2** a belief or opinion. **3** the capacity to feel. ➤ the sensation of touching or being touched. **4** **(feeling for)** a sensitivity to or intuitive understanding of. ● **adj.** showing emotion or sensitivity.
– PHRASES **one's better feelings** one's conscience.
– DERIVATIVES **feelingless** adj. **feelingly** adv.

**fee simple** ● **n.** (pl. **fees simple**) Law a permanent and absolute tenure of an estate in land with freedom to dispose of it at will.

**feet** plural form of **FOOT**.

**fee tail** ● **n.** (pl. **fees tail**) Law a former type of tenure of an estate in land with restrictions or entailment regarding the line of heirs to whom it may be willed.
– ORIGIN ME: from Anglo-Norman Fr. *fee tailé* (see **FEE**, **TAIL**[2]).

**feign** ● **v. 1** pretend to be affected by (a feeling, state, or injury). **2** archaic invent (a story or excuse).
– ORIGIN ME: from OFr. *feign-*, stem of *feindre*, from L. *fingere* 'mould, contrive'; cf. **FICTION** and **FIGMENT**.

**feijoa** /feɪ'(d)ʒəʊə, fɛ-, fiː-, -'jəʊə/ ● **n. 1** an edible green fruit resembling a guava. **2** the small tree which bears this fruit, native to tropical South America. [Genus *Feijoa*.]
– ORIGIN C19: mod. L., named after the Brazilian naturalist J. da Silva *Feijó*.

**feijoada** /feɪ'(d)ʒwaðə, -də/ ● **n.** a Brazilian or Portuguese stew of black beans with pork or other meat and vegetables, served with rice.
– ORIGIN Port., from *feijão*, from L. *phaseolus* 'bean'.

**feint**[1] /feɪnt/ ● **n.** a deceptive or pretended blow, thrust, or other attacking movement, especially in boxing or fencing. ● **v.** make a feint.
– ORIGIN C17: from Fr. *feinte*, past part. (used as n.) of *feindre* 'feign'.

**feint**[2] /feɪnt/ ● **adj.** denoting paper printed with faint lines as a guide for handwriting.
– ORIGIN C19: var. of **FAINT**.

**feisty** /'fʌɪsti/ ● **adj.** (**-ier**, **-iest**) informal **1** spirited and exuberant. **2** touchy and aggressive.
– DERIVATIVES **feistily** adv. **feistiness** n.
– ORIGIN C19: from earlier *feist*, *fist* 'small dog', from *fisting cur* or *hound*, a derogatory term for a lapdog, from ME *fist* 'break wind'; cf. **FIZZLE**.

**felafel** /fə'laf(ə)l, -'lɑː-/ ● **n.** variant spelling of **FALAFEL**.

**Feldenkrais method** /'fɛld(ə)nkrʌɪs/ ● **n.** a system designed to promote bodily and mental well-being by analysis of neuromuscular activity via exercises which improve flexibility and coordination.
– ORIGIN 1930s: named after the Russian-born physicist and mechanical engineer Moshe *Feldenkrais*.

**feldspar** /'fɛldspɑː/ (also **felspar**) ● **n.** an abundant rock-forming aluminosilicate mineral, typically colourless or pale-coloured.
– DERIVATIVES **feldspathic** adj.
– ORIGIN C18: alt. of Ger. *Feldspat*, *Feldspath*, from *Feld* 'field' + *Spat*, *Spath* (see **SPAR**[3]); the form *felspar* is by mistaken assoc. with Ger. *Fels* 'rock'.

**felicitate** /fɪ'lɪsɪteɪt/ ● **v.** rare congratulate.
– ORIGIN C17: from late L. *felicitat-*, *felicitare* 'make happy'.

**felicitations** ● **pl. n.** congratulations.

**felicitous** /fɪ'lɪsɪtəs/ ● **adj.** well chosen or appropriate: *a felicitous phrase*. ➤ pleasing.
– DERIVATIVES **felicitously** adv. **felicitousness** n.

**felicity** ● **n.** (pl. **-ies**) **1** complete happiness. **2** the ability to express oneself appropriately. ➤ a felicitous feature of a work of literature or art.
– ORIGIN ME: from OFr. *felicite*, from L. *felicitas*, from *felix*, *felic-* 'happy'.

**felid** /'fiːlɪd/ ● **n.** Zoology a mammal of the cat family (Felidae).
– ORIGIN C19: from mod. L. *Felidae*, from L. *feles* 'cat'.

**feline** /'fiːlʌɪn/ ● **adj.** of, relating to, or resembling a cat. ● **n.** a cat or other animal of the cat family.
– DERIVATIVES **felinity** n.
– ORIGIN C17: from L. *felinus*, from *feles* 'cat'.

**felix culpa** /ˌfiːlɪks 'kʌlpə, ˌfeɪlɪks, 'kʊlpɑː/ ● **n.** Christian Theology the sin of Adam viewed as fortunate, because it brought about the blessedness of the Redemption.
– ORIGIN L., lit. 'happy fault'.

**fell**[1] past of **FALL**.

**fell**[2] ● **v. 1** cut down (a tree). ➤ knock down. **2** (also **flat-fell**) stitch down (the edge of a seam) to lie flat. ● **n.** an amount of wood cut.
– DERIVATIVES **feller** n.
– ORIGIN OE *fellan*, of Gmc origin; rel. to **FALL**.

**fell**[3] ● **n.** a hill or stretch of high moorland, especially in northern England.
– ORIGIN ME: from ON *fjall*, *fell* 'hill'.

**fell**[4] ● **adj.** poetic/literary of terrible evil or ferocity.
– PHRASES **in** (or **at**) **one fell swoop** all in one go. [from Shakespeare's *Macbeth* (IV. iii. 219).]
– ORIGIN ME: from OFr. *fel*, nominative of *felon* (see **FELON**[1]).

**fell**[5] ● **n.** archaic an animal's hide or skin with its hair.
– ORIGIN OE *fel*, *fell*, of Gmc origin.

**fellah** /'fɛlə/ ● **n.** (pl. **fellahin** /-'hiːn/) an Egyptian peasant.
– ORIGIN from Arab. *fallāḥ* 'tiller of the soil'.

**fellatio** /fɛ'leɪʃɪəʊ, -'lɑːt-/ ● **n.** oral stimulation of a man's penis.
– DERIVATIVES **fellate** v. **fellator** /fɛ'leɪtə/ n.
– ORIGIN C19: mod. L., from L. *fellare* 'to suck'.

**felloes** /'fɛləʊz/ (also **fellies** /'fɛliz/) ● **pl. n.** the outer rim of a wheel, to which the spokes are fixed.
– ORIGIN OE *felg* (sing.), of unknown origin.

**fellow** ● **n. 1** informal a man or boy. **2** a person in the same position or otherwise associated with another. ➤ a thing of the same kind as or otherwise associated with another. **3** a member of a learned society. ➤ Brit. an incorporated senior member of a college. ➤ (also **research fellow**) an elected graduate receiving a stipend for a period of research. ➤ a member of the governing body in some universities. ● **adj.** sharing a particular activity, quality, or condition: *a fellow sufferer*.
– ORIGIN OE *fēolaga* 'a colleague' (lit. 'one who lays down money in a joint enterprise'), from ON *félagi*, from *fé* 'property, money' + the Gmc base of **LAY**[1].

**fellow feeling** ● **n.** sympathy based on shared experiences.

**fellowship** ● **n. 1** friendliness and companionship based on shared interests. **2** a group of people meeting to pursue a shared interest or aim. ➤ a guild or corporation. **3** the status of a fellow of a college or society.

**fellow-traveller** ● **n.** a sympathizer with, but non-member of, the Communist Party.
– DERIVATIVES **fellow-travelling** adj.

**felo de se** /ˌfiːləʊ deɪ 'seɪ, ˌfɛ-/ ● **n.** (pl. **felos de se**) suicide.
– ORIGIN from Anglo-Latin, lit. 'felon of himself' (suicide was formerly a criminal act in the UK).

**felon**[1] /'fɛlən/ ● **n.** a person who has committed a felony. ● **adj.** archaic cruel; wicked.
– ORIGIN ME: from OFr., lit. 'wicked, a wicked person', from med. L. *fello*, *fellon-*, of unknown origin.

**felon**[2] /'fɛlən/ ● **n.** archaic term for **WHITLOW**.
– ORIGIN ME: perh. a specific use of **FELON**[1]; med. L. *fello*, *fellon-* had the same sense.

**felony** ● **n.** (pl. **-ies**) a crime, typically one involving violence, regarded in the US and other judicial systems (and formerly in the UK) as more serious than a misdemeanour.
– DERIVATIVES **felonious** adj. **feloniously** adv.

**felsic** /'fɛlsɪk/ ● **adj.** Geology relating to or denoting a group of light-coloured minerals including feldspar, quartz, and muscovite. Often contrasted with **MAFIC**.
– ORIGIN C20: from **FELDSPAR** + a contr. of **SILICA**.

**felspar** /'fɛlspɑː/ ● **n.** variant spelling of **FELDSPAR**.

**felt**[1] ● **n.** cloth made by rolling and pressing wool or another suitable textile accompanied by the application of moisture or heat, which causes the fibres to mat together. ● **v. 1** mat together or become matted. **2** cover with felt.
– DERIVATIVES **felty** adj.
– ORIGIN OE, of W. Gmc origin; rel. to **FILTER**.

**felt**[2] past and past participle of **FEEL**.

**felt-tip pen** (also **felt-tipped pen**) ● **n.** a pen with a writing point made of felt or tightly packed fibres.

**felucca** /fɛˈlʌkə/ ● **n.** a small boat propelled by oars or lateen sails or both, used on the Nile and formerly more widely in the Mediterranean region.
– ORIGIN C17: from Ital. *feluc(c)a*, ult. of Arab. origin.

**felwort** /ˈfɛlwəːt/ ● **n.** a gentian of dry grassland, which produces mauve flowers in the autumn. [*Gentianella amarella*.]
– ORIGIN OE *feldwyrt* (see **FIELD**, **WORT**).

**female** ● **adj. 1** of or denoting the sex that can bear offspring or produce eggs. ➤ relating to or characteristic of women or female animals. ➤ (of a plant or flower) having a pistil but no stamens. **2** (of a fitting) manufactured hollow so that a corresponding male part can be inserted. ● **n.** a female person, animal, or plant.
– DERIVATIVES **femaleness** n.
– ORIGIN ME: from OFr. *femelle*, from L. *femella*, dimin. of *femina* 'a woman'; the change in the ending was due to assoc. with **MALE**.

**female circumcision** ● **n.** (among some peoples) the action or traditional practice of cutting off the clitoris and sometimes the labia of girls or young women.

**female condom** ● **n.** a contraceptive device made of thin rubber, inserted into a woman's vagina before sexual intercourse.

**feme covert** /fiːm ˈkʌvət/ ● **n.** Law, historical a married woman.
– ORIGIN C16: from Anglo-Norman Fr., lit. 'a woman covered (i.e. protected by marriage)'.

**feme sole** /fiːm ˈsəʊl/ (also **femme sole**) ● **n.** Law, historical a woman without a husband, especially one that is divorced.
– ORIGIN C16: from Anglo-Norman Fr. *feme soule* 'a woman alone'.

**feminine** ● **adj. 1** having qualities traditionally associated with women, especially delicacy and prettiness. ➤ female. **2** Grammar of or denoting a gender of nouns and adjectives, conventionally regarded as female. ● **n.** (**the feminine**) the female sex or gender.
– DERIVATIVES **femineity** n. (archaic). **femininely** adv. **feminineness** n. **femininity** n.
– ORIGIN ME: from L. *femininus*, from *femina* 'woman'.

**feminine rhyme** ● **n.** Prosody a rhyme between stressed syllables followed by one or more unstressed syllables (e.g. *stocking/shocking*).

**feminism** ● **n.** the advocacy of women's rights on the grounds of sexual equality.
– DERIVATIVES **feminist** n. & adj.
– ORIGIN C19: from Fr. *féminisme*.

**feminize** (also **-ise**) ● **v.** make more feminine or female.
– DERIVATIVES **feminization** n.

**femme** /fɛm/ (also **fem**) ● **n.** informal a lesbian who takes a traditionally feminine sexual role.
– ORIGIN 1960s: Fr., 'woman'.

**femme fatale** /ˌfam fəˈtɑːl/ ● **n.** (pl. **femmes fatales** pronunc. same) an attractive and seductive woman.
– ORIGIN C20: Fr., lit. 'disastrous woman'.

**femto-** /ˈfɛmtəʊ/ ● **comb. form** denoting a factor of $10^{-15}$: *femtosecond*.
– ORIGIN from Dan. or Norw. *femten* 'fifteen'.

**femur** /ˈfiːmə/ ● **n.** (pl. **femurs** or **femora** /ˈfɛm(ə)rə/) **1** Anatomy the bone of the thigh or upper hindlimb. **2** Zoology the third segment of the leg in insects and some other arthropods.
– DERIVATIVES **femoral** /ˈfɛm(ə)r(ə)l/ adj.
– ORIGIN C15: from L. *femur*, *femor-* 'thigh'.

**fen**[1] ● **n.** a low and marshy or frequently flooded area of land. ➤ (**the Fens**) flat low-lying areas of Lincolnshire, Cambridgeshire, and Norfolk, formerly marshland but now largely drained. ➤ Ecology wetland with alkaline, neutral, or only slightly acid peaty soil. Compare with **BOG**.
– DERIVATIVES **fenny** adj.
– ORIGIN OE *fen(n)*, of Gmc origin.

**fen**[2] ● **n.** (pl. same) a monetary unit of China, equal to one hundredth of a yuan.
– ORIGIN from Chin. *fēn* 'a hundredth part'.

**fenberry** ● **n.** (pl. **-ies**) another term for **CRANBERRY**.

**fence** ● **n. 1** a barrier enclosing an area, typically consisting of posts connected by wire, wood, etc. ➤ a large upright obstacle in steeplechasing, showjumping, or cross-country. **2** a guard or guide on a plane or other tool. **3** informal a dealer in stolen goods. ● **v. 1** surround or protect with a fence. ➤ (**fence something in/off**) enclose or separate an area with a fence. **2** informal deal in (stolen goods). **3** practise the sport of fencing. ➤ conduct a discussion or argument in an evasive way.
– PHRASES **over the fence** Austral./NZ informal unreasonable or unacceptable. **sit on the fence** avoid making a decision.
– DERIVATIVES **fenceless** adj. **fencer** n.
– ORIGIN ME (in the sense 'defence'): shortening of **DEFENCE**; cf. **FENCIBLE** and **FEND**.

**fencerow** /ˈfɛnsrəʊ/ ● **n.** N. Amer. an uncultivated strip of land on each side of and below a fence.

**fencible** /ˈfɛnsɪb(ə)l/ ● **n.** historical a soldier belonging to a British militia which could be called up only for home service.
– ORIGIN ME (in the sense 'suitable for defence'): shortening of **DEFENSIBLE**; cf. **FENCE**, **FEND**.

**fencing** ● **n. 1** the sport of fighting with blunted swords according to a set of rules in order to score points. **2** a series of fences. ➤ material for making fences.

**fend** ● **v. 1** (**fend for oneself**) look after and provide for oneself. **2** (**fend someone/thing off**) defend oneself from an attack or attacker.
– ORIGIN ME: shortening of **DEFEND**; cf. **FENCE** and **FENCIBLE**.

**fender** ● **n. 1** a low frame bordering a fireplace to keep in falling coals. **2** a tyre or other cushioning device hung over a ship's side to protect it against impact. **3** N. Amer. the mudguard or area around the wheel well of a vehicle.

**fender bender** ● **n.** N. Amer. informal a minor collision between motor vehicles.

**fenestella** /ˌfɛnɪˈstɛlə/ ● **n.** Architecture a niche in a wall south of a church's altar, holding the piscina and often the credence.
– ORIGIN ME: from L., dimin. of *fenestra* 'window'.

**fenestra** /fɪˈnɛstrə/ ● **n.** (pl. **fenestrae** /-triː/) **1** Anatomy & Zoology a small hole or opening in a bone, especially either of two in the middle ear (**fenestra ovalis**, **fenestra rotunda**). **2** Medicine an artificial opening, especially one made by fenestration. **3** a perforation in a forceps blade.
– ORIGIN C19: from L., lit. 'window'.

**fenestrate** /ˈfɛnəstrət, fɪˈnɛstrət/ ● **adj.** Botany & Zoology having small window-like perforations or transparent areas.

**fenestrated** /ˈfɛnəˌstreɪtɪd, fɪˈnɛstreɪtɪd/ ● **adj. 1** provided with a window or windows. **2** chiefly Anatomy fenestrate; having fenestrae.

**fenestration** /ˌfɛnɪˈstreɪʃ(ə)n/ ● **n. 1** Architecture the arrangement of windows in a building. **2** Botany & Zoology the condition of being fenestrate. **3** Medicine a surgical operation in which a new opening is formed, especially in the labyrinth of the inner ear to improve hearing.

**feng shui** /ˌfɛŋ ˈʃuːi, ˌfʌŋ ˈʃweɪ/ ● **n.** (in Chinese thought) a system of laws considered to govern spatial arrangement and orientation in relation to the flow of energy, and whose effects are taken into account when siting and designing buildings.
– ORIGIN Chin., from *fēng* 'wind' and *shuǐ* 'water'.

**Fenian** /ˈfiːnɪən/ ● **n. 1** a member of the Irish Republican Brotherhood, a 19th-century revolutionary nationalist organization among the Irish in the US and Ireland. **2** informal, offensive (chiefly in Northern Ireland) a Protestant name for a Catholic.
– DERIVATIVES **Fenianism** n.
– ORIGIN from Old Ir. *féne*, the name of an ancient Ir. people, confused with *fiann*, *fianna* 'band of warriors', in particular the soldiers of the legendary king Finn Mac Cool.

**fenland** ● **n.** (also **fenlands**) land consisting of fens.

**fennec** /ˈfɛnɛk/ ● **n.** a small pale fox of North African and Arabian deserts, with large pointed ears. [*Vulpes zerda*.]
– ORIGIN C18: via Arab. from Pers. *fanak*, *fanaj*.

**fennel** /ˈfɛn(ə)l/ ● **n.** an aromatic yellow-flowered plant of the parsley family, with feathery leaves used as culinary herbs or eaten as a vegetable. [*Foeniculum vulgare, Ferula communis* (**giant fennel**), and other species.]
– ORIGIN OE *finule, fenol,* from L. *faeniculum,* dimin. of *faenum* 'hay'.

**fenugreek** /ˈfɛnjʊgriːk/ ● **n.** a white-flowered leguminous plant with aromatic seeds that are used as a spice. [*Trigonella foenum-graecum.*]
– ORIGIN OE *fenogrecum,* from L. *faenugraecum,* from *faenum graecum* 'Greek hay' (the Romans used the dried plant as fodder).

**feoffee** /fɛˈfiː, fiː-/ ● **n.** **1** a trustee invested with a freehold estate to hold in possession for a charitable purpose. **2** (in feudal law) a person to whom a feoffment is made.

**feoffment** /ˈfiːfm(ə)nt, ˈfɛf-/ ● **n.** (in feudal law) a grant of ownership of freehold property to someone.
– DERIVATIVES **feoffor** /ˈfɛfə/ n.
– ORIGIN ME: from an Anglo-Norman Fr. var. of OFr. *fieffer* 'put in legal possession', from *fief* (see **FEE** and **FIEF**).

**feral** /ˈfɛr(ə)l, ˈfɪə-/ ● **adj.** **1** (of an animal or plant) in a wild state, especially after having been domesticated or cultivated. **2** resembling a wild animal: *a feral snarl.*
– ORIGIN C17: from L. *fera* 'wild animal' + **-AL**.

**fer de lance** /ˌfɛː də ˈlɑːns/ ● **n.** (pl. **fers de lance** pronunc. same or **fer de lances**) a large and dangerous pit viper native to Central and South America. [*Bothrops atrox* and related species.]
– ORIGIN C19: from Fr., lit. 'iron (head) of a lance'.

**feria** /ˈfɛrɪə/ ● **n.** (in Spain and Spanish-speaking America) a fair.
– ORIGIN Sp., from L., lit. 'holiday'.

**ferial** /ˈfɪərɪəl, ˈfɛ-/ ● **adj.** Christian Church denoting an ordinary weekday, as opposed to one appointed for a festival or fast.
– ORIGIN ME: from med. L. *ferialis,* from L. *feria* 'holiday' (in late L. 'day of the week').

**feringhee** /fəˈrɪŋgi/ (also **feringhi**) ● **n.** **1** chiefly derogatory (in India and parts of the Middle and Far East) a foreigner, especially a white person. **2** archaic a person of Indian–Portuguese parentage.
– ORIGIN via Urdu from Pers. *firangī,* from the base of **FRANK**.

**fermata** /fəːˈmɑːtə/ ● **n.** Music a pause of unspecified length on a note or rest. ➤a sign indicating this.
– ORIGIN Ital., from *fermare* 'to stop'.

**Fermat's last theorem** ● **n.** Mathematics the theorem (proved in 1995) that if *n* is an integer greater than 2, the equation $x^n + y^n = z^n$ has no positive integral solutions.
– ORIGIN C19: named after the C17 Fr. mathematician Pierre de *Fermat.*

**ferment** ● **v.** /fəˈmɛnt/ **1** undergo or cause to undergo fermentation. **2** stir up (disorder). ● **n.** /ˈfəːmɛnt/ **1** agitation and social unrest. **2** dated a fermenting agent or enzyme.
– DERIVATIVES **fermentable** adj. **fermenter** (US also **fermentor**) n.
– ORIGIN ME: from OFr. *ferment* (n.), *fermenter* (v.), based on L. *fermentum* 'yeast', from *fervere* 'to boil'.

**fermentation** ● **n.** **1** the chemical breakdown of a substance by bacteria, yeasts, or other micro-organisms, especially that involved in the making of beers, wines, and spirits in which sugars are converted to ethyl alcohol. **2** archaic agitation and social unrest.
– DERIVATIVES **fermentative** adj.

**fermion** /ˈfəːmɪɒn/ ● **n.** Physics a subatomic particle, such as a nucleon, which has half-integral spin.
– ORIGIN 1940s: named after the Ital. physicist Enrico *Fermi* + **-ON**.

**fermium** /ˈfəːmɪəm/ ● **n.** the chemical element of atomic number 100, an artificially made radioactive metal of the actinide series. (Symbol: **Fm**)

**fern** ● **n.** (pl. same or **ferns**) a flowerless vascular plant which has feathery or leafy fronds and reproduces by spores released from the undersides of the fronds. [Class Filicopsida.]
– DERIVATIVES **fernery** n. (pl. **-ies**). **ferny** adj.
– ORIGIN OE *fearn,* of W. Gmc origin.

**ferocious** ● **adj.** **1** savagely fierce, cruel, or violent. **2** informal very great; extreme.
– DERIVATIVES **ferociously** adv. **ferociousness** n. **ferocity** n.
– ORIGIN C17 (earlier (C16) as *ferocity*): from L. *ferox, feroc-* 'fierce' + **-IOUS**.

**-ferous** (usu. **-iferous**) ● **comb. form** having, bearing, or containing (a specified thing): *Carboniferous.*
– DERIVATIVES **-ferously** comb. form. **-ferousness** comb. form.
– ORIGIN from Fr. *-fère* or L. *-fer* 'producing', from *ferre* 'to bear'.

**ferrate** /ˈfɛreɪt/ ● **n.** Chemistry a salt in which the anion contains both iron and oxygen: *sodium ferrate.*
– ORIGIN C19: from L. *ferrum* 'iron' + **-ATE**[1].

**ferrel** /ˈfɛr(ə)l/ ● **n.** variant spelling of **FERRULE**.

**ferret** /ˈfɛrɪt/ ● **n.** **1** a domesticated albino or brown polecat, used for catching rabbits. [*Mustela furo.*] **2** an assiduous search. ● **v.** (**ferreted**, **ferreting**) **1** hunt with ferrets. **2** search for something in a place or container. ➤(**ferret something out**) investigate something assiduously.
– DERIVATIVES **ferreter** n. **ferrety** adj.
– ORIGIN ME: from OFr. *fuiret,* alt. of *fuiron,* based on late L. *furo* 'thief, ferret', from L. *fur* 'thief'.

**ferri-** /ˈfɛri/ ● **comb. form** Chemistry of iron with a valency of three; ferric. Compare with **FERRO-**.
– ORIGIN from L. *ferrum* 'iron'.

**ferriage** /ˈfɛrɪɪdʒ/ ● **n.** archaic transportation by ferry.

**ferric** /ˈfɛrɪk/ ● **adj.** Chemistry of iron with a valency of three; of iron(III).
– ORIGIN C18: from L. *ferrum* 'iron' + **-IC**.

**ferrimagnetic** ● **adj.** Physics denoting or exhibiting a weak form of ferromagnetism associated with parallel but opposite alignment of adjacent electron spins.
– DERIVATIVES **ferrimagnetism** n.

**Ferris wheel** /ˈfɛrɪs/ ● **n.** a fairground ride consisting of a giant vertical revolving wheel with passenger cars suspended on its outer edge.
– ORIGIN C19: named after George W. G. *Ferris,* the Amer. engineer who invented it.

**ferrite** /ˈfɛrʌɪt/ ● **n.** **1** a ceramic ferrimagnetic oxide of iron and one or more other metals, used in high-frequency electrical components such as aerials. **2** Metallurgy a form of pure iron occurring in low-carbon steel.
– DERIVATIVES **ferritic** /fɛˈrɪtɪk/ adj.
– ORIGIN C19: from L. *ferrum* 'iron' + **-ITE**[1].

**ferro-** /ˈfɛrəʊ/ ● **comb. form** **1** containing iron: *ferroconcrete.* **2** Chemistry of iron with a valency of two; ferrous. Compare with **FERRI-**.
– ORIGIN from L. *ferrum* 'iron'.

**ferroconcrete** ● **n.** concrete reinforced with steel.

**ferroelectric** ● **adj.** Physics displaying or denoting permanent electric polarization which varies in strength with the applied electric field.
– DERIVATIVES **ferroelectricity** n.

**ferrofluid** ● **n.** a fluid containing a magnetic suspension.

**ferromagnetic** ● **adj.** Physics displaying or denoting the strong, persistent magnetism displayed by iron, associated with parallel magnetic alignment of neighbouring atoms.
– DERIVATIVES **ferromagnetism** n.

**ferrous** /ˈfɛrəs/ ● **adj.** **1** (chiefly of metals) containing or consisting of iron. **2** Chemistry of iron with a valency of two; of iron(II).
– ORIGIN C19: from L. *ferrum* 'iron' + **-OUS**.

**ferruginous** /fɛˈruːdʒɪnəs/ ● **adj.** **1** containing iron oxides or rust. **2** rust-coloured.
– ORIGIN C17: from L. *ferrugo, ferrugin-* 'rust, dark red' + **-OUS**.

**ferruginous duck** ● **n.** a diving duck related to the pochard, the male of which has mainly dark red-brown breeding plumage. [*Aythya nyroca.*]

**ferrule** /ˈfɛruːl, ˈfɛr(ə)l/ (also **ferrel**) ● **n.** a ring or cap which strengthens the end of a handle, stick, or tube. ➤a metal band strengthening or forming a joint.
– ORIGIN C17: alt. (prob. by assoc. with L. *ferrum* 'iron') of obs. *verrel,* from OFr. *virelle,* from L. *viriola,* dimin. of *viriae* 'bracelets'.

**ferry** • **n.** (pl. **-ies**) a boat or ship for conveying passengers and goods, especially as a regular service. • **v.** (**-ies, -ied**) convey by ferry or other transport, especially on short, regular trips.
– DERIVATIVES **ferryman** n. (pl. **-men**).
– ORIGIN ME: from ON *ferja* 'ferry boat', of Gmc origin and rel. to **FARE**.

**fertile** /ˈfəːtʌɪl/ • **adj.** **1** (of soil or land) producing or capable of producing abundant vegetation or crops. **2** (of a person, animal, or plant) able to conceive young or produce seed. ➤(of a seed or egg) capable of becoming a new individual. **3** productive in generating new ideas; inventive.
– DERIVATIVES **fertility** n.
– ORIGIN ME: via Fr. from L. *fertilis*, from *ferre* 'to bear'.

**fertility cult** • **n.** a religious system of some agricultural societies in which seasonal rites are performed to ensure good harvests and the well-being of the community.

**fertilize** (also **-ise**) • **v.** **1** cause (an egg, female animal, or plant) to develop a new individual by introducing male reproductive material. **2** make (soil or land) more fertile by adding fertilizer.
– DERIVATIVES **fertilizable** adj. **fertilization** n.

**fertilizer** (also **-iser**) • **n.** a chemical or natural substance added to soil to increase its fertility.

**ferule** /ˈfɛruːl/ • **n.** a flat ruler with a widened end, formerly used for beating children.
– ORIGIN ME: from L. *ferula* 'giant fennel, rod'.

**fervent** /ˈfəːv(ə)nt/ • **adj.** **1** intensely passionate. **2** archaic hot or glowing.
– DERIVATIVES **fervency** n. **fervently** adv.
– ORIGIN ME: via OFr. from L. *fervent-*, *fervere* 'boil'.

**fervid** /ˈfəːvɪd/ • **adj.** **1** intensely enthusiastic, especially to an excessive degree. **2** poetic/literary hot or glowing.
– DERIVATIVES **fervidly** adv.
– ORIGIN C16: from L. *fervidus*, from *fervere* 'to boil'.

**fervour** /ˈfəːvə/ (US **fervor**) • **n.** **1** intense and passionate feeling. **2** archaic intense heat.
– ORIGIN ME: via OFr. from L. *fervor*, from *fervere* 'to boil'.

**fescue** /ˈfɛskjuː/ • **n.** a narrow-leaved grass, some kinds of which are valuable for pasture and fodder. [Genera *Festuca* and *Vulpia*.]
– ORIGIN ME *festu*, *festue* 'straw, twig', from OFr. *festu*, based on L. *festuca* 'stalk, straw'.

**fess**[1] /fɛs/ (also **fesse**) • **n.** Heraldry an ordinary in the form of a broad horizontal stripe across the middle of the shield.
– PHRASES **in fess** across the middle third of the field.
– ORIGIN C15: from OFr. *fesse*, alt. of *faisse*, from L. *fascia* 'band'.

**fess**[2] /fɛs/ • **v.** (**fess up**) informal confess.

**fess point** • **n.** Heraldry a point at the centre of a shield.

**-fest** • **comb. form** informal in nouns denoting a festival or large gathering of a specified kind: *a media-fest.*
– ORIGIN from Ger. *Fest* 'festival'.

**festa** /ˈfɛstə/ • **n.** (in Italy) a religious or other festival.
– ORIGIN C19: from Ital., 'festival'.

**festal** • **adj.** relating to a festival; festive.
– DERIVATIVES **festally** adv.
– ORIGIN C15: via OFr. from late L. *festalis*, from L. *festum*, (pl.) *festa* 'feast'.

**fester** • **v.** [often as adj. **festering**] **1** (of a wound or sore) become septic. ➤(of food or rubbish) become rotten. **2** (of a negative feeling or a problem) intensify, especially through neglect. **3** deteriorate physically and mentally in isolated inactivity.
– ORIGIN ME: from *fester* 'fistula', later 'festering sore', or OFr. *festrir* (v.), both from OFr. *festre* (n.), from L. *fistula* 'reed, fistula'.

**festival** • **n.** **1** a day or period of celebration, typically for religious reasons. **2** an organized series of concerts, films, etc., typically one held annually in the same place.
– ORIGIN ME (as adj.): via OFr. from med. L. *festivalis*, from L. *festivus*, from *festum*, (pl.) *festa* 'feast'.

**festival of lights** • **n.** **1** another term for **HANUKKAH**. **2** another term for **DIWALI**.

**Festival of the Dead** • **n.** another term for **BON**.

**festive** • **adj.** **1** of or relating to a festival. **2** jovially celebratory.
– DERIVATIVES **festively** adv. **festiveness** n.
– ORIGIN C17: from L. *festivus* (see **FESTIVAL**).

**festivity** • **n.** (pl. **-ies**) joyful and exuberant celebration. ➤(**festivities**) celebratory activities or events.
– ORIGIN ME: from OFr. *festivite* or L. *festivitas*, from *festivus* (see **FESTIVAL**).

**festoon** /fɛˈstuːn/ • **n.** an ornamental chain or garland of flowers, leaves, or ribbons, hung in a curve. ➤a carved or moulded ornament representing this. • **v.** (often **be festooned with**) adorn with festoons or other decorations.
– ORIGIN C17: from Fr. *feston*, from Ital. *festone* 'festal ornament'.

**festoon blind** • **n.** a window blind consisting of vertical rows of horizontally gathered fabric.

**Festschrift** /ˈfɛstˌʃrɪft/ • **n.** (pl. **Festschriften** or **Festschrifts**) a collection of writings published in honour of a scholar.
– ORIGIN C19: from Ger., from *Fest* 'celebration' + *Schrift* 'writing'.

**FET** • **abbrev.** field-effect transistor.

**feta** /ˈfɛtə/ (also **feta cheese** or **fetta**) • **n.** a white salty Greek cheese made from the milk of ewes or goats.
– ORIGIN from mod. Gk *pheta*.

**fetal** /ˈfiːt(ə)l/ • **adj.** of or relating to a fetus. ➤denoting a posture characteristic of a fetus, with the back curved forwards and the limbs folded in front of the body.

**fetch**[1] • **v.** **1** go for and bring back. ➤cause to come to a place. **2** achieve (a particular price) when sold. **3** archaic bring forth (blood or tears). ➤take (a breath). **4** informal inflict (a blow) on (someone). **5** (**fetch up**) informal arrive or come to rest. • **n.** **1** the distance travelled by wind or waves across open water. ➤the distance a vessel must sail to reach open water. **2** an act of fetching. **3** archaic a stratagem or trick.
– PHRASES **fetch and carry** run backwards and forwards bringing things to someone in a servile fashion.
– DERIVATIVES **fetcher** n.
– ORIGIN OE *fecc(e)an*, var. of *fetian*, prob. rel. to *fatian* 'grasp', of Gmc origin.

**fetch**[2] • **n.** Brit., chiefly archaic the apparition or double of a living person, believed to be a warning of that person's impending death.
– ORIGIN C17: of unknown origin.

**fetching** • **adj.** attractive: *a fetching little garment.*
– DERIVATIVES **fetchingly** adv.

**fête** /feɪt/ • **n.** **1** Brit. an outdoor public function to raise funds for a charity or institution, typically involving entertainment and the sale of goods. **2** chiefly N. Amer. a celebration or festival. • **v.** (usu. **be fêted**) honour or entertain lavishly.
– ORIGIN ME (in the sense 'festival, fair'): from Fr., from OFr. *feste* (see **FEAST**).

**fête champêtre** /ˌfɛt ʃɒ̃ˈpɛtr(ə), French fɛt ʃɑ̃pɛtʀ/ • **n.** (pl. **fêtes champêtres** pronunc. same) an outdoor entertainment such as a garden party.
– ORIGIN Fr., lit. 'rural festival'.

**fête galante** /ˌfɛt gaˈlɒ̃t, French fɛt galɑ̃t/ • **n.** (pl. **fêtes galantes** pronunc. same) an outdoor entertainment or rural festival, especially as depicted in 18th-century French painting.
– ORIGIN Fr., lit. 'elegant festival'.

**feticide** /ˈfiːtɪsʌɪd/ • **n.** destruction or abortion of a fetus.

**fetid** /ˈfɛtɪd, ˈfiːt-/ (also **foetid**) • **adj.** smelling unpleasant.
– DERIVATIVES **fetidly** adv. **fetidness** n.
– ORIGIN ME: from L. *fetidus*, from *fetere* 'to stink'.

**fetish** /ˈfɛtɪʃ/ • **n.** **1** an inanimate object worshipped for its supposed magical powers or because it is considered to be inhabited by a spirit. **2** a form of sexual desire in which gratification is linked to an abnormal degree to a particular object, part of the body, or activity. **3** a course of action to which one has an excessive and irrational commitment.
– DERIVATIVES **fetishism** n. **fetishist** n. **fetishistic** adj.

**fetishization** (also **-isation**) n. **fetishize** (also **-ise**) v.
– ORIGIN C17: from Fr. *fétiche*, from Port. *feitiço* 'charm, sorcery'.

**fetlock** /ˈfɛtlɒk/ ● n. the joint of a horse's or other quadruped's leg between the cannon bone and the pastern.
– ORIGIN ME: ult. of Gmc origin; rel. to FOOT.

**feto-** ● comb. form representing FETUS.

**fetor** /ˈfiːtə/ ● n. a strong, foul smell.
– ORIGIN C15: from L., from *fetere* 'to stink'.

**fetta** ● n. variant spelling of FETA.

**fetter** ● n. a chain or shackle placed around a prisoner's ankles. ➤a restraint or check. ● v. restrain with fetters. ➤(often **be fettered**) restrict.
– ORIGIN OE *feter*, of Gmc origin.

**fetterlock** ● n. a D-shaped fetter for tethering a horse by the leg, now only as represented as a heraldic charge.

**fettle** ● n. condition: *the horse remains in fine fettle.* ● v. **1** trim or clean the rough edges of (a metal casting or a piece of pottery) before firing. **2** N. English make or repair.
– ORIGIN ME (in the general sense 'to prepare'): from dial. *fettle* 'strip of material', from OE *fetel*, of Gmc origin.

**fettler** ● n. **1** Brit. & Austral. a railway maintenance worker. **2** a person who fettles metal castings or pottery.

**fettuccine** /ˌfɛtʊˈtʃiːneɪ, -ni/ (also **fettucini**) ● pl. n. pasta made in ribbons.
– ORIGIN from Ital., pl. of *fettuccina*, dimin. of *fetta* 'ribbon'.

**fetus** /ˈfiːtəs/ (Brit. (in non-technical use) also **foetus**) ● n. (pl. **fetuses**) an unborn or unhatched offspring of a mammal, in particular an unborn human more than eight weeks after conception.
– ORIGIN ME: from L. *fetus* 'pregnancy, childbirth, offspring'.

**feu** /fjuː/ Scots Law ● n. a perpetual lease at a fixed rent. ➤a piece of land held by such a lease. ● v. (**feus, feued, feuing**) grant (land) on such a lease.
– ORIGIN C15: from OFr. (see FEE).

**feud** ● n. a prolonged and bitter quarrel or dispute. ➤a state of prolonged mutual hostility, typically between two families or communities. ● v. take part in a feud.
– ORIGIN ME *fede* 'hostility', from OFr. *feide*, from MDu., Mid. Low Ger. *vēde*, of Gmc origin; rel. to FOE.

**feudal** /ˈfjuːd(ə)l/ ● adj. according to, resembling, or denoting the system of feudalism.
– DERIVATIVES **feudalization** /-ˈzeɪʃ(ə)n/ (also **-isation**) n. **feudalize** (also **-ise**) v. **feudally** adv.
– ORIGIN C17: from med. L. *feudalis*, from *feudum* (see FEE).

**feudalism** ● n. the dominant social system in medieval Europe, in which the nobility held lands from the Crown in exchange for military service, and vassals were tenants of and protected by the nobles, giving their lords homage, labour, and a share of the produce.
– DERIVATIVES **feudalist** n. **feudalistic** adj.

**feudality** ● n. archaic the principles and practice of the feudal system.

**feudatory** /ˈfjuːdət(ə)ri/ historical ● adj. owing feudal allegiance to. ● n. (pl. **-ies**) a person who held land under the feudal system.
– ORIGIN C16: from med. L. *feudatorius*, from *feudare* 'enfeoff', from *feudum* (see FEE).

**feu de joie** /ˌfəː də ˈʒwɑː/ ● n. (pl. **feux de joie** pronunc. same) a rifle salute fired on a ceremonial occasion, each soldier firing in succession along the ranks.
– ORIGIN Fr., lit. 'fire of joy'.

**feudist** ● n. US a person taking part in a feud.

**feuilleton** /ˈfəːɪtɒ̃/ ● n. a part of a newspaper or magazine devoted to fiction, criticism, or light literature.
– ORIGIN C19: Fr., from *feuillet*, dimin. of *feuille* 'leaf'.

**fever** ● n. **1** an abnormally high body temperature, usually accompanied by shivering, headache, and in severe instances, delirium. **2** a state of nervous excitement or agitation. ● v. [as adj. **fevered**] **1** having or showing the symptoms of fever. **2** nervously excited or agitated.
– DERIVATIVES **feverish** adj. **feverishly** adv. **feverishness** n.
– ORIGIN OE *fēfor*, from L. *febris*; reinforced in ME by OFr. *fievre*, also from *febris*.

**feverfew** /ˈfiːvəfjuː/ ● n. a small bushy aromatic plant of the daisy family, with feathery leaves and daisy-like flowers, used as a herbal remedy for headaches. [*Tanacetum parthenium*.]
– ORIGIN OE *feferfuge*, from L. *febrifuga*, from *febris* 'fever' + *fugare* 'drive away'; cf. FEBRIFUGE.

**feverous** ● adj. archaic feverish.

**fever pitch** ● n. a state of extreme excitement.

**fever tree** ● n. **1** a North American tree used in the treatment of malaria during the Civil War. [*Pinckneya pubens*.] **2** a southern African tree formerly believed to cause malaria. [*Acacia xanthophloea*.]

**few** ● det., pron., & adj. **1** (**a few**) a small number of. **2** not many. ● n. [as pl. n. **the few**] a select minority. ➤(**the Few**) Brit. the RAF pilots who took part in the Battle of Britain.
– PHRASES **few and far between** scarce. **a good few** Brit. a fairly large number of. **no fewer than** a surprisingly large number of. **not a few** a considerable number. **quite a few** a fairly large number. **some few** some but not many.
– ORIGIN OE *fēawe*, *fēawa*, of Gmc origin.

**USAGE** few

Fewer, the comparative form of **few**, is correctly used with words denoting people or countable things, while **less** is used with mass nouns, denoting things which cannot be counted. In addition, **less** is normally used with numbers and expressions of measurement or time. The use of **less** with a count noun (*less people*) is incorrect in standard English.

**fey** /feɪ/ ● adj. **1** unworldly and vague. **2** having clairvoyant powers.
– DERIVATIVES **feyly** adv. **feyness** n.
– ORIGIN OE *fǣge*, of Gmc origin.

**Feynman diagram** ● n. Physics a diagram showing electromagnetic interactions between subatomic particles.
– ORIGIN named after the Amer. theoretical physicist Richard P. *Feynman*.

**fez** /fɛz/ ● n. (pl. **fezzes**) a flat-topped conical red hat with a black tassel on top, worn by men in some Muslim countries.
– DERIVATIVES **fezzed** adj.
– ORIGIN C19: from Turk. *fes*, named after *Fez*, a city in Morocco, once the chief place of manufacture.

**ff** ● abbrev. Music fortissimo.

**ff.** ● abbrev. **1** folios. **2** following pages.

**Fg Off** ● abbrev. (in the UK) Flying Officer.

**f-hole** ● n. either of a pair of soundholes resembling an ʃ and a reversed ʃ in shape, cut in the front of musical instruments of the violin family, and some other stringed instruments such as mandolins.

**FHSA** ● abbrev. (in the UK) Family Health Services Authority.

**fiacre** /fɪˈɑːkrə, -kə/ ● n. historical a small four-wheeled carriage for public hire.
– ORIGIN C17: from Fr., named after the Hôtel de St *Fiacre* in Paris, where such vehicles were first hired out.

**fiancé** /fɪˈɒnseɪ, -ˈɑːns-, -ˈɒ̃s-/ ● n. (fem. **fiancée** pronunc. same) a person to whom another is engaged to be married.
– ORIGIN C19: from Fr., past part. of *fiancer* 'betroth'.

**fianchetto** /ˌfɪənˈtʃɛtəʊ, -ˈkɛtəʊ/ Chess ● n. (pl. **-oes**) the development of a bishop by moving it one square to a long diagonal of the board. ● v. (**-oes, -oed**) develop (a bishop) in such a way.
– ORIGIN C19: from Ital., dimin. of *fianco* 'flank'.

**fiasco** /fɪˈaskəʊ/ ● n. (pl. **-os**) a ludicrous or humiliating failure.
– ORIGIN C19: from Ital., lit. 'bottle, flask', in the phr. *far fiasco*, lit. 'make a bottle', figuratively 'fail in a performance'.

**fiat** /ˈfʌɪat/ ● n. an official order or authorization.
– ORIGIN ME: from L., 'let it be done', from *fieri* 'be done or made'.

**fiat money** ● n. inconvertible paper money made legal tender by a government fiat.

**fib** ● **n.** a trivial lie. ● **v.** (**fibbed**, **fibbing**) tell a fib.
– DERIVATIVES **fibber** n.
– ORIGIN C16: perh. a shortening of obs. *fible-fable* 'nonsense', reduplication of **FABLE**.

**fiber** etc. ● **n.** US spelling of **FIBRE** etc.

**Fibonacci series** ● **n.** Mathematics a series of numbers in which each number (**Fibonacci number**) is the sum of the two preceding numbers (e.g. the series 1, 1, 2, 3, 5, 8, etc.).
– ORIGIN C19: named after the Ital. mathematician Leonardo *Fibonacci* (*c.*1170–*c.*1250), who discovered it.

**fibre** (US **fiber**) ● **n. 1** a thread or filament from which a plant or animal tissue, mineral substance, or textile is formed. **2** a substance formed of fibres. **3** dietary material containing substances such as cellulose, that are resistant to the action of digestive enzymes. **4** strength of character: *a weak person with no moral fibre.*
– DERIVATIVES **-fibred** adj. **fibreless** adj.
– ORIGIN ME (in the sense 'lobe of the liver', (pl.) 'entrails'): via Fr. from L. *fibra* 'fibre, entrails'.

**fibreboard** (US **fiberboard**) ● **n.** a building material made of wood or other plant fibres compressed into boards.

**fibrefill** ● **n.** synthetic material used for padding and insulation in garments and soft furnishings such as duvets.

**fibreglass** (US **fiberglass**) ● **n. 1** a reinforced plastic material composed of glass fibres embedded in a resin matrix. **2** a textile fabric made from woven glass filaments.

**fibre optics** ● **pl. n.** [treated as sing.] the use of thin flexible transparent fibres to transmit light signals, chiefly for telecommunications or for internal inspection of the body.
– DERIVATIVES **fibre-optic** adj.

**fibrescope** (US **fiberscope**) ● **n.** a fibre-optic device for viewing inaccessible internal structures, especially in the human body.

**fibril** /ˈfʌɪbrɪl/ ● **n.** technical a small or slender fibre.
– DERIVATIVES **fibrillar** adj. **fibrillary** adj.
– ORIGIN C17: from mod. L. *fibrilla*, dimin. of L. *fibra* (see **FIBRE**).

**fibrillate** /ˈfʌɪbrɪleɪt, ˈfɪb-/ ● **v. 1** (of a muscle, especially in the heart) make a quivering movement due to uncoordinated contraction of the individual fibrils. **2** (with reference to a fibre) split up or break into fibrils.
– DERIVATIVES **fibrillation** n.

**fibrin** /ˈfʌɪbrɪn, ˈfɪb-/ ● **n.** Biochemistry an insoluble protein formed as a fibrous mesh during the clotting of blood.
– DERIVATIVES **fibrinoid** adj. **fibrinous** adj.

**fibrinogen** /fʌɪˈbrɪnədʒ(ə)n, fɪ-/ ● **n.** Biochemistry a soluble protein present in blood plasma, from which fibrin is produced by the enzyme thrombin.

**fibrinolysis** /ˌfʌɪbrɪˈnɒlɪsɪs, ˌfɪb-/ ● **n.** Physiology the enzymatic breakdown of the fibrin in blood clots.
– DERIVATIVES **fibrinolytic** adj.

**fibro** /ˈfʌɪbrəʊ/ ● **n.** (pl. **-os**) Austral. a mixture of asbestos and cement, used in sheets for building.
– ORIGIN 1950s: abbrev. of *fibro-cement.*

**fibro-** /ˈfʌɪbrəʊ/ ● **comb. form** of, relating to, or characterized by fibres: *fibroblast.*
– ORIGIN from L. *fibra* 'fibre'.

**fibroblast** /ˈfʌɪbrə(ʊ)blast/ ● **n.** Physiology a cell in connective tissue which produces collagen and other fibres.

**fibroid** /ˈfʌɪbrɔɪd/ ● **adj.** of or characterized by fibres or fibrous tissue. ● **n.** Medicine a benign tumour of muscular and fibrous tissues, typically developing in the wall of the womb.

**fibroin** /ˈfʌɪbrəʊɪn/ ● **n.** a protein which is the chief constituent of silk.

**fibroma** /fʌɪˈbrəʊmə/ ● **n.** (pl. **fibromas** or **fibromata** /-mətə/) Medicine a benign fibrous tumour of connective tissue.
– ORIGIN C19: from L. *fibra* (see **FIBRE**) + **-OMA**.

**fibrosis** /fʌɪˈbrəʊsɪs/ ● **n.** Medicine the thickening and scarring of connective tissue, usually as a result of injury.
– DERIVATIVES **fibrotic** adj.

**fibrositis** /ˌfʌɪbrəˈsʌɪtɪs/ ● **n.** Medicine inflammation of fibrous connective tissue, typically affecting the back and causing stiffness and pain.
– DERIVATIVES **fibrositic** adj.

**fibrous** ● **adj.** consisting of or characterized by fibres.
– DERIVATIVES **fibrously** adv. **fibrousness** n.

**fibula** /ˈfɪbjʊlə/ ● **n.** (pl. **fibulae** /-liː/ or **fibulas**) **1** Anatomy the outer and usually smaller of the two bones between the knee and the ankle, parallel with the tibia. **2** Archaeology a brooch or clasp.
– DERIVATIVES **fibular** adj.
– ORIGIN C16: from L., 'brooch', perh. rel. to *figere* 'to fix'; the bone is so named because the shape it makes with the tibia resembles a clasp.

**-fic** (usu. as **-ific**) ● **suffix** (forming adjectives) producing; making: *prolific.*
– DERIVATIVES **-fically** suffix forming corresponding adverbs.
– ORIGIN from Fr. *-fique* or L. *-ficus*, from *facere* 'do, make'.

**-fication** (usu. as **-ification**) ● **suffix** forming nouns of action from verbs ending in *-fy* (such as *simplification* from *simplify*).
– ORIGIN from Fr., or from L. *-fication-* (from verbs ending in *-ficare*).

**fiche** ● **n.** short for **MICROFICHE**.

**fichu** /ˈfiːʃuː/ ● **n.** a small triangular shawl, worn round a woman's shoulders and neck.
– ORIGIN C18: from Fr., from *ficher* 'to fix, pin'.

**fickle** ● **adj.** changeable, especially as regards one's loyalties.
– DERIVATIVES **fickleness** n. **fickly** adv.
– ORIGIN OE *ficol* 'deceitful', of Gmc origin.

**fictile** /ˈfɪktʌɪl, -tɪl/ ● **adj.** made of clay by a potter. ➤ of or relating to pottery.
– ORIGIN C17: from L. *fictilis*, from *fict-*, *fingere* 'form'.

**fiction** ● **n. 1** prose literature, especially novels, describing imaginary events and people. **2** invention as opposed to fact. ➤ a false belief or statement, accepted as true because such acceptance is considered expedient.
– DERIVATIVES **fictional** adj. **fictionality** n. **fictionalization** (also **-isation**) n. **fictionalize** (also **-ise**) v. **fictionally** adv. **fictionist** n.
– ORIGIN ME: via OFr. from L. *fictio(n-)*, from *fingere* 'form, contrive'; cf. **FEIGN** and **FIGMENT**.

**fictitious** /fɪkˈtɪʃəs/ ● **adj. 1** not real or true, being imaginary or invented. **2** relating to or denoting the characters and events found in fiction.
– DERIVATIVES **fictitiously** adv. **fictitiousness** n.
– ORIGIN C17: from L. *ficticius* (from *fingere* 'contrive, form') + **-ous** (see also **-ITIOUS**[2]).

**fictive** ● **adj.** creating or created by imagination.
– DERIVATIVES **fictiveness** n.

**ficus** /ˈfiːkəs, ˈfʌɪkəs/ ● **n.** (pl. same) a tree, shrub, or climber of warm and tropical climates belonging to a large genus that includes the figs and the rubber plant. [Genus *Ficus*.]
– ORIGIN C19: from L., 'fig, fig tree'.

**fid** ● **n.** Nautical **1** a square wooden or iron bar which supports a topmast. **2** a conical pin or spike used in splicing rope.
– ORIGIN C17: of unknown origin.

**Fid. Def.** ● **abbrev.** Brit. Defender of the Faith.
– ORIGIN L. *Fidei Defensor.*

**fiddle** ● **n. 1** informal a violin. **2** informal, chiefly Brit. an act of fraud or cheating. **3** informal an unnecessarily intricate or awkward task. **4** Nautical a raised rim that prevents things from falling off a table in rough seas. ● **v.** informal **1** touch or fidget with something restlessly or nervously. **2** chiefly Brit. falsify (figures, data, or records).
– PHRASES **fiddle while Rome burns** be concerned with relatively trivial matters while ignoring the serious events going on around one. **(as) fit as a fiddle** in very good health. **on the fiddle** informal engaged in fraud or cheating. **play second fiddle to** take a subordinate role to.
– DERIVATIVES **fiddler** n. (informal).
– ORIGIN OE *fithele*, based on L. *vitulari* 'celebrate a festival'; cf. **VIOL**.

**fiddle-back** ● **n.** a thing shaped like the back of a violin, especially the back of a chair or the front of a chasuble.

**fiddle-de-dee** • **n.** dated nonsense.
– ORIGIN C18: from **FIDDLE** + a reduplication without meaning.

**fiddle-faddle** • **n.** trivial matters; nonsense. • **v.** fuss.
– ORIGIN C16: reduplication of **FIDDLE**.

**fiddlehead** • **n. 1** (also **fiddlehead greens**) N. Amer. the young, curled, edible frond of certain ferns. **2** a scroll-like carving at a ship's bows.

**fiddle pattern** • **n.** a style of spoons and forks, with handles shaped like the body of a violin.

**fiddler crab** • **n.** a small amphibious crab, the males of which have one greatly enlarged claw. [Genus *Uca*.]

**fiddlestick** informal • **exclam.** (**fiddlesticks**) nonsense. • **n.** a violin bow.

**fiddling** • **adj.** informal **1** annoyingly trivial. **2** involved in fraud.

**fiddly** • **adj.** (**-ier**, **-iest**) Brit. informal complicated and awkward to do or use.

**fideism** /ˈfʌɪdiːɪz(ə)m/ • **n.** the doctrine that knowledge depends on faith or revelation.
– DERIVATIVES **fideist** n. **fideistic** adj.
– ORIGIN C19: from L. *fides* 'faith' + **-ISM**.

**fidelity** /fɪˈdɛlɪti/ • **n. 1** continuing loyalty to a person, cause, or belief. **2** the degree of exactness with which something is copied or reproduced.
– ORIGIN ME: from OFr. *fidelite* or L. *fidelitas*, from *fidelis* 'faithful', from *fides* 'faith'; cf. **FEALTY**.

**fidelity insurance** • **n.** insurance taken out by an employer against losses incurred through dishonesty by employees.

**fidget** /ˈfɪdʒɪt/ • **v.** (**fidgeted**, **fidgeting**) make small movements through nervousness or impatience. • **n.** a person who fidgets. ➤ an act of fidgeting. ➤ (**fidgets**) mental or physical restlessness.
– DERIVATIVES **fidgeter** n. **fidgetiness** n. **fidgety** adj.
– ORIGIN C17: from obs. or dial. *fidge* 'to twitch'.

**fiducial** /fɪˈdjuːʃ(ə)l/ • **adj.** technical (of a point or line) assumed as a fixed basis of comparison.
– ORIGIN C16: from late L. *fiducialis*, from *fiducia* 'trust'.

**fiduciary** /fɪˈdjuːʃ(ə)ri/ • **adj. 1** Law involving trust, especially with regard to the relationship between a trustee and a beneficiary. **2** Finance (of a paper currency) depending for its value on securities or the reputation of the issuer. • **n.** (pl. **-ies**) a trustee.
– ORIGIN C16 (in the sense 'credentials'): from L. *fiduciarius*, from *fiducia* 'trust'.

**fidus Achates** /ˌfʌɪdəs əˈkeɪtiːz/ • **n.** a faithful friend or devoted follower.
– ORIGIN L., lit. 'faithful Achates' (a companion of Aeneas in Virgil's *Aeneid*).

**fie** /fʌɪ/ • **exclam.** archaic or humorous used to express disgust or outrage.
– ORIGIN ME: via OFr. from L. *fi*, an exclamation of disgust at a stench.

**fief** /fiːf/ • **n. 1** historical another term for **FEE** (in sense 2). **2** a person's sphere of operation or control.
– DERIVATIVES **fiefdom** n.
– ORIGIN C17: from Fr. (see **FEE**).

**field** • **n. 1** an area of open land, especially one planted with crops or pasture. ➤ a piece of land used for a sport or game. ➤ a large area of land or water completely covered in snow or ice. ➤ an area rich in a natural product, typically oil or gas. **2** a particular branch of study or sphere of activity. ➤ Computing a part of a record, representing an item of data. **3** a space or range within which objects are visible from a particular viewpoint or through a piece of apparatus. **4** (**the field**) all the participants in a contest or sport. ➤ Cricket fielders collectively. ➤ a fielder of specified ability. **5** Heraldry the surface of an escutcheon or of one of its divisions. **6** Physics the region in which a force such as gravity or magnetism is effective, regardless of the presence or absence of a material medium. **7** Mathematics a system subject to two binary operations analogous to those for the multiplication and addition of real numbers, and having similar commutative and distributive laws. • **v. 1** chiefly Cricket & Baseball attempt to catch or stop the ball and return it after it has been hit. ➤ catch or stop (the ball) and return it. **2** select for a particular game or to stand in an election. **3** deal with (a difficult question, telephone call, etc.). • **adj.** carried out or working in the natural environment, rather than in a laboratory or office. ➤ (of military equipment) light and mobile for use on campaign. ➤ used in names of animals or plants found in the open country, e.g. **field mouse**.
– PHRASES **hold the field** remain the most important. **in the field 1** engaged in combat or manoeuvres. **2** engaged in fieldwork. **play the field** informal indulge in a series of casual sexual relationships. **take the field 1** (of a team) go on to a field to begin a game. **2** start a military campaign.
– ORIGIN OE *feld*, of W. Gmc origin.

**field book** • **n.** a book in which a surveyor writes down technical notes taken in the field.

**fieldcraft** • **n.** the techniques involved in living or making military or scientific observations in the field.

**field day** • **n. 1** an opportunity for action or success, especially at the expense of others. **2** Military a review or an exercise, especially in manoeuvring. **3** chiefly N. Amer. a day devoted to athletics or other sporting events.

**field-effect transistor** • **n.** Electronics a transistor in which most current is carried along a channel whose effective resistance can be controlled by a transverse electric field.

**fielder** • **n.** chiefly Cricket & Baseball a player on the fielding team, especially one other than the bowler or pitcher.

**field events** • **pl. n.** athletic sports other than races, such as throwing and jumping events. Compare with **TRACK EVENTS**.

**fieldfare** • **n.** a large migratory thrush with a grey head, breeding in northern Eurasia. [*Turdus pilaris*.]
– ORIGIN OE *feldefare*, perh. from *feld* 'field' + the base of *faran* (see **FARE**).

**field glasses** • **pl. n.** binoculars for outdoor use.

**field goal** • **n. 1** American Football a goal scored by a place kick. **2** Basketball a goal scored while the clock is running and the ball is in play.

**field hockey** • **n.** hockey played on grass or a hard pitch, as opposed to ice hockey.

**field hospital** • **n.** a temporary hospital set up near a battlefield.

**field mark** • **n.** a visible mark used in identifying a bird or other animal in the field.

**field marshal** • **n.** the highest rank of officer in the British army.

**field mouse** • **n.** another term for **WOOD MOUSE**.

**field mushroom** • **n.** the common edible mushroom. [*Agaricus campestris*.]

**field mustard** • **n.** another term for **CHARLOCK**.

**field officer** • **n.** Military a major, lieutenant colonel, or colonel.

**field of honour** • **n.** the place where a duel or battle was fought, especially in the Middle Ages.

**field rank** • **n.** the rank attained by a military field officer.

**fieldsman** • **n.** (pl. **-men**) **1** Cricket a fielder. **2** an agent or salesman working for a company.

**field sports** • **pl. n.** outdoor sports, especially hunting, shooting, and fishing.

**fieldstone** • **n.** stone used in its natural form.

**field test** • **n.** a test carried out in the environment in which a product or device is to be used. • **v.** (**field-test**) test in such a way.

**field trial** • **n. 1** a field test. **2** a competition for gun dogs to test their levels of skill and training.

**fieldwork** • **n.** practical work conducted by a researcher in the field.
– DERIVATIVES **fieldworker** n.

**fiend** /fiːnd/ • **n. 1** an evil spirit or demon. ➤ a very wicked or cruel person. **2** informal an enthusiast or devotee: *a jazz fiend*.
– DERIVATIVES **fiendlike** adj.
– ORIGIN OE *fēond* 'an enemy, the devil', of Gmc origin.

**fiendish** • **adj. 1** extremely cruel or unpleasant. **2** extremely difficult.

– DERIVATIVES **fiendishly** adv. **fiendishness** n.

**fierce** • adj. violent or aggressive; ferocious. ➤ intense: *fierce opposition.* ➤ (of a mechanism) having a powerful abruptness of action.
– PHRASES **something fierce** informal, chiefly N. Amer. to a great extent.
– DERIVATIVES **fiercely** adv. **fierceness** n.
– ORIGIN ME: from OFr. *fiers* 'fierce, brave', from L. *ferus* 'untamed'.

**fieri facias** /ˌfʌɪərʌɪ ˈfeɪʃɪas/ • n. Law a writ to a sheriff for executing a judgement.
– ORIGIN L., 'cause to be made or done'.

**fiery** • adj. (**-ier**, **-iest**) **1** resembling or consisting of fire. **2** quick-tempered or passionate.
– DERIVATIVES **fierily** adv. **fieriness** n.

**fiery cross** • n. **1** a burning wooden cross carried as a symbol by the Ku Klux Klan. **2** historical a wooden cross, charred and dipped in blood, used among Scottish clans as a summons to battle.

**fiesta** /fɪˈɛstə/ • n. **1** (in Spanish-speaking countries) a religious festival. **2** a festive event.
– ORIGIN Sp., from L. *festum*, (pl.) *festa* (see **FEAST**).

**FIFA** /ˈfiːfə/ • abbrev. Fédération Internationale de Football Association, the international governing body of soccer.

**fi. fa.** • abbrev. fieri facias.

**fife** • n. a kind of small shrill flute used with the drum in military bands.
– DERIVATIVES **fifer** n.
– ORIGIN C16: from Ger. *Pfeife* 'pipe', or from Fr. *fifre* from Swiss Ger. *Pfifer* 'piper'.

**fife rail** • n. chiefly historical a rail round the mainmast of a sailing ship, holding belaying pins.
– ORIGIN C18: of unknown origin.

**FIFO** /ˈfʌɪfəʊ/ • abbrev. first in, first out (chiefly with reference to methods of stock valuation and data storage).

**fifteen** • cardinal number **1** equivalent to the product of three and five; one more than fourteen; 15. (Roman numeral: **xv** or **XV**.) **2** a team of fifteen players, especially in rugby. **3** (**15**) Brit. (of a film) classified as suitable for people of 15 years and over. **4** (**the Fifteen**) the Jacobite rebellion of 1715.
– DERIVATIVES **fifteenth** ordinal number.
– ORIGIN OE *fīftēne*, *fīftīene* (see **FIVE**, **-TEEN**).

**fifth** • ordinal number **1** constituting number five in a sequence; 5th. **2** (**a fifth/one fifth**) each of five equal parts into which something is or may be divided. **3** Music an interval spanning five consecutive notes in a diatonic scale, in particular (also **perfect fifth**) an interval of three tones and a semitone. ➤ the note which is higher by such an interval than the root of a diatonic scale. **4** US informal a fifth of a gallon, as a measure of alcoholic liquor.
– PHRASES **take the fifth** (in the US) exercise the right guaranteed by the Fifth Amendment to the Constitution of refusing to answer questions in order to avoid incriminating oneself.
– DERIVATIVES **fifthly** adv.

**fifth column** • n. a group within a country at war who are working for its enemies.
– DERIVATIVES **fifth columnist** n.
– ORIGIN from the Spanish Civil War, when General Mola, leading four columns of troops towards Madrid, declared that he had a fifth column inside the city.

**fifth-generation** • adj. denoting a proposed new class of computer or programming language employing artificial intelligence.

**Fifth-monarchy-man** • n. a member of a 17th-century sect expecting the immediate second coming of Christ and repudiating all other government.
– ORIGIN from *Fifth Monarchy*, denoting the last of the five great empires prophesied by Daniel (Dan. 2:44).

**fifth position** • n. **1** Ballet a posture in which the feet are placed turned outwards, one immediately in front of but touching the other so that the toe of the back foot just protrudes beyond the heel of the front foot. **2** Music a position of the left hand on the fingerboard of a stringed instrument nearer to the bridge than the fourth position.

**fifth wheel** • n. chiefly N. Amer. **1** a spare wheel for a four-wheeled vehicle. ➤ informal a superfluous person or thing. **2** a coupling between a vehicle used for towing and a trailer. **3** (also **fifth-wheel trailer**) a trailer with accommodation for camping out.

**fifty** • cardinal number (pl. **-ies**) the number equivalent to the product of five and ten; half of one hundred; 50. (Roman numeral: **l** or **L**.)
– DERIVATIVES **fiftieth** ordinal number. **fiftyfold** adj. & adv.
– ORIGIN OE *fīftig* (see **FIVE**, **-TY**[2]).

**fifty-fifty** • adj. & adv. with equal shares or chances.

**fig**[1] • n. **1** a soft pear-shaped fruit with sweet dark flesh and many small seeds. **2** (also **fig tree**) the deciduous tree or shrub bearing this fruit. [*Ficus carica*.] ➤ used in names of related plants, e.g. **strangling fig**.
– PHRASES **not give** (or **care**) **a fig** not care at all.
– ORIGIN ME: from OFr. *figue*, from Provençal *fig(u)a*, based on L. *ficus*.

**fig**[2] • n. (in phr. **full fig**) informal the complete set of clothes appropriate to a particular occasion or profession.
– ORIGIN C17 (as v.): var. of obs. *feague* 'liven up' (earlier 'whip'), perh. rel. to Ger. *fegen* 'sweep, thrash'; cf. **FAKE**[1].

**fig.** • abbrev. figure.

**fight** • v. (past and past part. **fought**) **1** take part in a violent struggle involving physical force or weapons. ➤ engage in (a war or contest). ➤ quarrel or argue. ➤ (**fight someone/thing off**) defend oneself against an attack by someone or something. **2** struggle to overcome, eliminate, or prevent. ➤ (**fight for**) try very hard to obtain or do. **3** (**fight one's way**) move forward with difficulty. • n. an act of fighting. ➤ the inclination or ability to fight or struggle.
– PHRASES **fight fire with fire** use the weapons or tactics of one's opponent, even if one finds them distasteful. **fight shy of** avoid through unwillingness. **fight or flight** the instinctive physiological response to a threatening situation, which readies one either to resist forcibly or to run away.
– ORIGIN OE *feohtan* (v.), *feoht(e)*, *gefeoht* (n.), of W. Gmc origin.

**fightback** • n. Brit. a rally or recovery.

**fighter** • n. **1** a person or animal that fights. **2** a fast military aircraft designed for attacking other aircraft.

**fighting chair** • n. N. Amer. a fixed chair on a boat used by a person trying to catch large fish.

**fighting chance** • n. a possibility of success if great effort is made.

**fighting fish** (also **Siamese fighting fish**) • n. a small labyrinth fish native to Thailand, the males of which fight vigorously. [*Betta splendens*.]

**fighting fit** • adj. in excellent health.

**fighting fund** • n. Brit. money raised to finance a campaign.

**fighting top** • n. historical a gun platform high on a warship's mast.

**fighting words** (also **fighting talk**) • pl. n. **1** informal words indicating a willingness to fight. **2** US insulting language, especially of an ethnic, racial, or sexist nature, considered unacceptable or illegal.

**fig leaf** • n. a leaf of a fig tree, often used for concealing the genitals in paintings and sculpture.
– ORIGIN C16: with ref. to the story of Adam and Eve (Gen. 3:7).

**figment** /ˈfɪgm(ə)nt/ • n. a thing believed to be real but existing only in the imagination.
– ORIGIN ME (denoting an invented statement): from L. *figmentum*, rel. to *fingere* 'form, contrive'; cf. **FEIGN** and **FICTION**.

**figura** /fɪˈgjʊərə/ • n. (pl. **figurae** /-riː/) (in literary theory) a person or thing representing or symbolizing a fact or ideal.
– ORIGIN L., lit. 'figure'.

**figural** /ˈfɪgjʊr(ə)l/ • adj. another term for **FIGURATIVE**.

**figurant** /ˈfɪgjʊr(ə)nt/ • n. (fem. **figurante** /ˌfɪgjʊˈrɒ̃t/) a supernumerary actor who has little or nothing to say.
– ORIGIN Fr., pres. part. of *figurer* 'to figure'.

**figuration** /ˌfɪgəˈreɪʃ(ə)n, -gjʊ-/ • n. **1** ornamentation by means of figures. ➤ Music use of florid counterpoint. **2** allegorical representation.

**figurative** ● adj. **1** departing from a literal use of words; metaphorical. **2** Art representing forms that are recognizably derived from life.
– DERIVATIVES **figuratively** adv. **figurativeness** n.

**figure** /ˈfɪɡə/ ● n. **1** a number or a numerical symbol. ➤ an amount of money. ➤ (**figures**) arithmetical calculations. **2** a person's bodily shape, especially that of a woman. ➤ a person seen indistinctly. ➤ a person of a particular kind: *a public figure.* ➤ an artistic representation of a human or animal form. **3** a shape defined by one or more lines in two dimensions, or one or more surfaces in three dimensions. ➤ a diagram or illustrative drawing. ➤ (in skating) a movement or series of movements following a prescribed pattern. ➤ a pattern formed by the movements of a group of people, for example in country dancing, as part of a longer dance or display. ➤ archaic external form or shape. **4** Music a short succession of notes producing a single impression. **5** Logic the form of a syllogism, classified according to the position of the middle term. ● v. **1** be a significant part of or contributor to something. **2** calculate arithmetically. **3** informal, chiefly N. Amer. think; consider. ➤ be perfectly understandable: *she supposed that figured.* ➤ (**figure someone/thing out**) informal reach an understanding of someone or something. **4** (**figure on**) N. Amer. informal count or rely on something happening or being the case. **5** represent in a diagram or picture. ➤ [usu. as adj. **figured**] embellish with a pattern.
– DERIVATIVES **figureless** adj.
– ORIGIN ME: from OFr. *figure* (n.), *figurer* (v.), from L. *figura* 'figure, form'; rel. to *fingere* 'form, contrive'.

**figured bass** ● n. Music a bass line with the intended harmonies indicated by figures rather than written out as chords, typical of continuo parts.

**figurehead** ● n. **1** a carved bust or full-length figure set at the prow of an old-fashioned sailing ship. **2** a nominal leader without real power.

**figure of eight** (N. Amer. **figure eight**) ● n. an object or movement having the shape of the number eight.

**figure of speech** ● n. a word or phrase used in a non-literal sense for rhetorical or vivid effect.

**figure skating** ● n. the sport of skating in prescribed patterns from a stationary position.
– DERIVATIVES **figure skater** n.

**figurine** /ˈfɪɡəriːn, -ɡjʊ-/ ● n. a small statue of a human form.
– ORIGIN C19: from Fr., from Ital. *figurina*, dimin. of *figura*, from L. *figura* (see **FIGURE**).

**figwort** ● n. a herbaceous plant with purplish-brown two-lobed flowers. [Genus *Scrophularia*: several species.]
– ORIGIN C16 (orig. denoting pilewort, used as a treatment for piles): from obs. *fig* 'piles' + **WORT**.

**Fijian** /fiːˈdʒiːən/ ● n. **1** a native or national of Fiji, or a person of Fijian descent. **2** the Austronesian language of the indigenous people of Fiji. ● adj. of or relating to Fiji, its people, or language.

**filagree** /ˈfɪləɡriː/ ● n. variant spelling of **FILIGREE**.

**filament** /ˈfɪləm(ə)nt/ ● n. **1** a slender thread-like object or fibre, especially one found in animal or plant structures. **2** a metal wire in an electric light bulb, made incandescent by an electric current. **3** Botany the slender part of a stamen that supports the anther.
– DERIVATIVES **filamentary** adj. **filamented** adj. **filamentous** adj.
– ORIGIN C16: from Fr., or from mod. L. *filamentum*, from late L. *filare* 'to spin'.

**filaria** /fɪˈlɛːrɪə/ ● n. (pl. **filariae** /-rɪiː/) a thread-like parasitic nematode worm which is transmitted by biting flies and mosquitoes in the tropics, causing disease. [Superfamily Filarioidea.]
– DERIVATIVES **filarial** adj. **filariasis** /fɪˌlɛːrɪˈeɪsɪs, ˌfɪləˈrʌɪəsɪs/ n.
– ORIGIN C19: from mod. L. *Filaria* (former genus name), from L. *filum* 'thread'.

**filature** /ˈfɪlətʃə, -tjə/ ● n. a place where silk thread is obtained from silkworm cocoons.
– ORIGIN C18: from Fr., from Ital. *filatura*, from *filare* 'to spin'.

**filbert** ● n. **1** a cultivated oval hazelnut. **2** the tree that bears these nuts. [*Corylus maxima* and other species.] **3** (also **filbert brush**) a brush with bristles forming a flattened oval head, used in oil painting.
– ORIGIN ME *fylberd*, from Anglo-Norman Fr. *philbert*, dial. Fr. *noix de filbert* (so named because it is ripe about 20 August, the feast day of St *Philibert*).

**filch** /fɪltʃ/ ● v. informal pilfer; steal.
– DERIVATIVES **filcher** n.
– ORIGIN ME: of unknown origin.

**file**[1] ● n. **1** a folder or box for keeping loose papers together and in order. **2** Computing a collection of data or programs stored under a single identifying name. ● v. **1** place (a document) in a file. ➤ submit (a legal document, application, or charge) to be officially placed on record. **2** (of a reporter) send (a story) to a newspaper or news organization.
– DERIVATIVES **filer** n. **filing** n.
– ORIGIN ME (as a verb meaning 'string documents on a thread or wire'): from Fr. *filer* 'to string', *fil* 'a thread', both from L. *filum* 'a thread'.

**file**[2] ● n. **1** a line of people or things one behind another. **2** Military a small detachment of men. **3** Chess each of the eight rows of eight squares on a chessboard running away from the player towards the opponent. Compare with **RANK**[1] (in sense 6). ● v. walk one behind the other.
– ORIGIN C16: from Fr. *file*, from *filer* 'to string'.

**file**[3] ● n. a tool with a roughened surface or surfaces, used for smoothing or shaping a hard material. ● v. smooth or shape with a file.
– DERIVATIVES **filer** n.
– ORIGIN OE *fīl*, of W. Gmc origin.

**filé** /ˈfiːleɪ/ ● n. N. Amer. pounded or powdered sassafras leaves used to flavour and thicken soup, especially gumbo.
– ORIGIN C19: from Fr., past part. of *filer* 'to twist'.

**filefish** ● n. (pl. same or **-fishes**) a fish with a dorsal spine and rough scales, occurring chiefly in tropical seas. [Family Balistidae: many species.]
– ORIGIN C18: from **FILE**[3] (because of its rough skin).

**filet** /ˈfiːleɪ, ˈfɪlɪt/ ● n. **1** French spelling of **FILLET**, used in the names of French or French-sounding dishes: *filet de boeuf.* **2** a kind of net or lace with a square mesh.
– ORIGIN C19: from Fr., 'net'.

**filet mignon** /ˌfiːleɪ ˈmiːnjɒ̃/ ● n. a small tender piece of beef from the end of the undercut.
– ORIGIN Fr., lit. 'dainty fillet'.

**filial** /ˈfɪlɪəl/ ● adj. **1** of, relating to, or due from a son or daughter. **2** Biology denoting the offspring of a cross.
– DERIVATIVES **filially** adv.
– ORIGIN ME: from OFr., or from eccles. L. *filialis*, from *filius* 'son', *filia* 'daughter'.

**filiation** /ˌfɪlɪˈeɪʃ(ə)n/ ● n. **1** the fact of being the child of a particular parent or parents. **2** the manner in which a thing is related to another from which it is derived or descended.
– ORIGIN ME: from Fr., from eccles. and med. L. *filiatio(n-)*, from L. *filius* 'son', *filia* 'daughter'.

**filibeg** /ˈfɪlɪbɛɡ/ (also **philibeg**) ● n. Scottish archaic a kilt.
– ORIGIN C18: from Sc. Gaelic *feileadh-beag* 'little kilt'.

**filibuster** /ˈfɪlɪbʌstə/ ● n. **1** prolonged speaking or other action which obstructs progress in a legislative assembly while not technically contravening the required procedures. **2** historical a person engaging in unauthorized warfare against a foreign state. ● v. [often as noun **filibustering**] obstruct legislation with a filibuster.
– ORIGIN C18: from Fr. *flibustier*, first applied to pirates who pillaged the Sp. colonies in the W. Indies, influenced by Sp. *filibustero*, denoting Amer. adventurers who incited revolution in Latin America; ult. from Du. *vrijbuiter* 'freebooter'.

**filicide** /ˈfɪlɪsʌɪd/ ● n. the killing of one's son or daughter. ➤ a person who does this.
– ORIGIN C17 from L. *filius* 'son', *filia* 'daughter' + **-CIDE**.

**filiform** /ˈfʌɪlɪfɔːm/ ● adj. Biology thread-like.
– ORIGIN C18: from L. *filum* 'thread' + **-IFORM**.

**filigree** /ˈfɪlɪɡriː/ (also **filagree**) ● n. delicate ornamental

work of fine gold, silver, or copper wire.
– DERIVATIVES **filigreed** adj.
– ORIGIN C17 (earlier as *filigreen*, *filigrane*): from Fr. *filigrane*, from Ital. *filigrana* (from L. *filum* 'thread' + *granum* 'seed').

**filing cabinet** • n. a large piece of office furniture with deep drawers for storing files.

**filings** • pl. n. small particles rubbed off by a file.

**Filipino** /ˌfɪlɪˈpiːnəʊ/ (also **Pilipino**) • n. (fem. **Filipina** /-nə/) (pl. **-os** or **-as**) **1** a native or national of the Philippines, or a person of Filipino descent. **2** the national language of the Philippines, a standardized form of Tagalog. • adj. of or relating to the Philippines, the Filipinos, or their language.
– ORIGIN Sp., from *las Islas Filipinas* 'the Philippine Islands'.

**fill** • v. **1** make or become full. ➤block up (a hole, gap, etc.). ➤pervade with an emotion or feeling. ➤(of a sail) curve out tautly from its supports as the wind blows into it. **2** appoint a person to hold (a vacant post). ➤hold and perform the duties of (a position or role). **3** occupy (a period of time). **4** chiefly N. Amer. be supplied with the items described in (a prescription or order). **5** Poker complete (a good hand) by drawing the necessary cards. • n. **1** (**one's fill**) as much as one wants or can bear. ➤enough to fill something: *a fill of tobacco.* **2** material which fills a space, especially in building or engineering work. **3** (in popular music) a short interjected instrumental phrase.
– PHRASES **fill someone's shoes** (or **boots**) informal take over someone's role and fulfil it satisfactorily.
– PHRASAL VERBS **fill in** act as a substitute. **fill someone in** inform someone more fully of a matter. **fill something in 1** Brit. add information to complete a form or document. **2** complete a drawing by adding colour or shade to the spaces within an outline. **fill out** put on weight. **fill something out** chiefly N. Amer. add information to complete a form or document. ➤give more details about something.
– ORIGIN OE *fyllan* (v.), *fyllu* (n.), of Gmc origin; rel. to **FULL**[1].

**fille de joie** /ˌfiː də ˈʒwɑː/ • n. euphemistic a prostitute.
– ORIGIN Fr., lit. 'girl of pleasure'.

**filler**[1] /ˈfɪlə/ • n. **1** something used to fill a gap or cavity, or to increase bulk. ➤an item serving only to fill space or time in a newspaper, broadcast, or recording. ➤a word or sound filling a pause in an utterance or conversation (e.g. *er*). **2** a person or thing that fills a space or container: *a shelf-filler.*

**filler**[2] /ˈfɪləː/ • n. (pl. same) a monetary unit of Hungary, equal to one hundredth of a forint.
– ORIGIN from Hungarian *fillér.*

**filler cap** • n. a cap closing the pipe leading to the petrol tank of a motor vehicle.

**fillet** • n. **1** a fleshy boneless piece of meat from near the loins or the ribs of an animal. ➤(also **fillet steak**) a beef steak cut from the lower part of a sirloin. ➤a boned side of a fish. **2** a band or ribbon binding the hair. **3** Architecture a narrow flat band separating two mouldings. ➤a small band between the flutes of a column. **4** a roughly triangular strip of material which rounds off an interior angle between two surfaces. **5** a plain line impressed on the cover of a book. • v. (**filleted**, **filleting**) remove the bones from (a fish). ➤cut (fish or meat) into fillets.
– DERIVATIVES **filleter** n.
– ORIGIN ME: from OFr. *filet* 'thread', based on L. *filum* 'thread'.

**filling** • n. **1** a quantity or piece of material that fills or is used to fill something. **2** N. Amer. another term for **WEFT**[1]. • adj. (of food) leaving one with a pleasantly satiated feeling.

**filling station** • n. a petrol station.

**fillip** /ˈfɪlɪp/ • n. **1** a stimulus or boost. **2** archaic a movement made by bending the last joint of the finger against the thumb and suddenly releasing it. • v. (**filliped**, **filliping**) archaic propel (a small object) with a flick of the fingers.
– ORIGIN ME: symbolic; cf. **FLICK**, **FLIP**[1].

**fillis** /ˈfɪlɪs/ • n. Brit. loosely twisted string, used especially for tying up plants.
– ORIGIN C20: from Fr. *filasse* 'tow'.

**filly** • n. (pl. **-ies**) **1** a young female horse, especially one less than four years old. **2** humorous a lively girl or young woman.
– ORIGIN ME: from ON *fylja*, of Gmc origin; rel. to **FOAL**.

**film** • n. **1** a thin flexible strip of plastic or other material coated with light-sensitive emulsion for exposure in a camera. **2** material in the form of a very thin flexible sheet. ➤a thin layer covering a surface. **3** a story or event recorded by a camera as a series of moving images and shown in a cinema or on television. • v. **1** make a film of; record on film. **2** become or appear to become covered with a thin film.
– ORIGIN OE *filmen* 'membrane', of W. Gmc origin; rel. to **FELL**[5].

**film badge** • n. a device containing photographic film which registers the wearer's exposure to radiation.

**filmic** • adj. of or relating to films or cinematography.

**film noir** /fɪlm ˈnwɑː, French film nwaʀ/ • n. a style or genre of cinematographic film marked by a mood of pessimism, fatalism, and menace.
– ORIGIN Fr., lit. 'black film'.

**filmography** • n. (pl. **-ies**) a list of films by one director or actor, or on one subject.
– ORIGIN 1960s: from **FILM** + **-GRAPHY**, on the pattern of *bibliography.*

**filmsetting** • n. Printing the setting of material to be printed by projecting it on to photographic film from which the printing surface is prepared.
– DERIVATIVES **filmset** v. **filmsetter** n.

**film star** • n. a well-known film actor or actress.

**filmstrip** • n. a series of transparencies in a strip for projection.

**filmy** • adj. (**-ier**, **-iest**) **1** (especially of fabric) thin and translucent. **2** covered with or as with a thin film.
– DERIVATIVES **filmily** adv. **filminess** n.

**filo** /ˈfiːləʊ/ (also **phyllo**) • n. a kind of flaky pastry stretched into very thin sheets, used especially in eastern Mediterranean cookery.
– ORIGIN 1950s: from mod. Gk *phullo* 'leaf'.

**Filofax** /ˈfʌɪlə(ʊ)faks/ • n. trademark a loose-leaf notebook for recording appointments, addresses, and notes.
– ORIGIN 1930s: representing a colloq. pronunc. of *file of facts.*

**filopodium** /ˌfʌɪlə(ʊ)ˈpəʊdɪəm/ • n. (pl. **filopodia**) Biology a long, slender, tapering pseudopodium.
– DERIVATIVES **filopodial** adj.
– ORIGIN C20: from L. *filium* 'thread' + **PODIUM**.

**filoselle** /ˈfɪlə(ʊ)sɛl/ • n. floss silk, or silk thread resembling this, used in embroidery.
– ORIGIN C16: from Fr., from Ital. *filosello.*

**filovirus** /ˈfiːləʊˌvʌɪrəs/ • n. a filamentous RNA virus of a group which causes severe haemorrhagic fevers.

**fils**[1] /fɪls/ • n. (pl. same) a monetary unit of Iraq, Bahrain, Jordan, Kuwait, and Yemen, equal to one hundredth of a riyal in Yemen and one thousandth of a dinar elsewhere.
– ORIGIN from a colloq. pronunc. of Arab. *fals*, denoting a small copper coin.

**fils**[2] /fiːs, French fis/ • n. used after a surname to distinguish a son from a father of the same name.
– ORIGIN Fr., 'son'.

**filter** • n. **1** a porous device for removing impurities or solid particles from a liquid or gas passed through it. ➤a screen, plate, or layer which absorbs some of the light passing through it. ➤a device for suppressing electrical or sound waves of frequencies not required. **2** Brit. an arrangement whereby vehicles may turn left (or right) while other traffic waiting to go straight ahead or turn right (or left) is stopped by a red light. **3** Computing a piece of software that processes text, e.g. by removing unwanted spaces. • v. **1** pass through a filter. **2** (often **filter in/out/through**) move gradually through something or in a specified direction. ➤(of information) gradually become known.
– DERIVATIVES **filterable** (also **filtrable**) adj.
– ORIGIN ME (denoting a piece of felt): from Fr. *filtre*, from med. L. *filtrum* 'felt used as a filter', of W. Gmc origin and

rel. to **FELT**[1].

**filter bed** ● **n.** a tank or pond containing a layer of sand or gravel, used for filtering large quantities of liquid.

**filter-feeding** ● **adj.** Zoology (of an aquatic animal) feeding by filtering out plankton or nutrients suspended in the water.
– DERIVATIVES **filter-feeder** n.

**filter press** ● **n.** a device consisting of a series of cloth filters fixed to frames, used for the large-scale filtration of liquid under pressure.

**filter tip** ● **n.** a filter attached to a cigarette for removing impurities from the inhaled smoke.
– DERIVATIVES **filter-tipped** adj.

**filth** ● **n. 1** disgusting dirt. ➤obscene and offensive language or printed material. ➤corrupt behaviour. **2** [as pl. n. **the filth**] Brit. informal, derogatory the police.
– ORIGIN OE *fȳlth* 'rotting matter', also 'corruption, obscenity', of Gmc origin; rel. to **FOUL**.

**filthy** ● **adj.** (**-ier**, **-iest**) disgustingly dirty. ➤obscene and offensive. ➤Brit. informal (of weather) very unpleasant. ➤informal (of a mood) very disagreeable. ● **adv.** informal extremely: *filthy rich.*
– DERIVATIVES **filthily** adv. **filthiness** n.

**filtrable** ● **adj.** variant spelling of **FILTERABLE**.

**filtrate** /ˈfɪltreɪt/ ● **n.** a liquid which has passed through a filter. ● **v.** rare filter.
– DERIVATIVES **filtration** n.
– ORIGIN C17: from mod. L. *filtrat-*, *filtrare* 'filter'.

**fimbria** /ˈfɪmbrɪə/ ● **n.** (pl. **fimbriae** /-ɪiː/) chiefly Anatomy a series of threads resembling a fringe. ➤a thread in such a structure, especially a finger-like projection at the end of a Fallopian tube.
– DERIVATIVES **fimbrial** adj.
– ORIGIN C18 (earlier (C15) as *fimbriated*): from late L., 'border, fringe'.

**fimbriated** /ˈfɪmbrɪeɪtɪd/ (also **fimbriate**) ● **adj. 1** Biology having a fringe of fimbriae. **2** Heraldry having a narrow border.

**fin** ● **n. 1** a flattened appendage on the body of a fish or other aquatic animal, used for propelling, steering, and balancing. ➤an underwater swimmer's flipper. **2** a small flattened projecting surface or attachment on an aircraft, rocket, or motor car, for providing aerodynamic stability. **3** a flattened projection for increasing heat transfer from an object. ● **v.** (**finned**, **finning**) swim under water by means of flippers.
– DERIVATIVES **finless** adj. **-finned** adj.
– ORIGIN OE *finn*, *fin*, of Gmc origin.

**finagle** /fɪˈneɪg(ə)l/ ● **v.** informal obtain or act dishonestly or deviously.
– DERIVATIVES **finagler** n.
– ORIGIN 1920s (orig. US): from dial. *fainaigue* 'cheat'.

**final** ● **adj. 1** coming at the end of a series. ➤reached as the outcome of a process: *the final cost will run into six figures.* **2** allowing no further doubt or dispute. ● **n. 1** the last game in a sports tournament or other competition, which will decide the overall winner. ➤(**finals**) a series of games constituting the final stage of a competition. **2** (**finals**) Brit. a series of examinations at the end of a degree course. ➤(**final**) N. Amer. an examination at the end of a term, school year, or particular class. **3** Music the principal note in a mode.
– DERIVATIVES **finality** n. **finally** adv.
– ORIGIN ME: from OFr., or from L. *finalis*, from *finis* 'end'.

**final cause** ● **n.** Philosophy the purpose of an action or the end towards which a thing naturally develops.

**final clause** ● **n.** Grammar a clause expressing purpose or intention (e.g. one introduced by *in order that*).

**final drive** ● **n.** the last part of the transmission system in a motor vehicle.

**finale** /fɪˈnɑːli, -leɪ/ ● **n.** the last part of a piece of music, an entertainment, or a public event.
– ORIGIN C18: from Ital.

**finalism** ● **n.** the doctrine that natural processes, for example evolution, are directed towards some goal.
– DERIVATIVES **finalistic** adj.

**finalist** ● **n. 1** a participant in the final or finals of a competition. **2** a student taking finals.

**finalize** (also **-ise**) ● **v. 1** complete (a transaction) after discussion of the terms. **2** produce or agree on a finished version of.
– DERIVATIVES **finalization** n.

**final solution** ● **n.** the Nazi policy (1941–5) of exterminating European Jews.
– ORIGIN translation of Ger. *Endlösung*.

**finance** /fʌɪˈnans, fɪ-, ˈfʌɪnans/ ● **n.** the management of large amounts of money, especially by governments or large companies. ➤monetary support for an enterprise. ➤(**finances**) the monetary resources and affairs of a state, organization, or person. ● **v.** provide funding for.
– ORIGIN ME (orig. in the sense 'payment of a debt, ransom, etc.'): from OFr., from *finer* 'settle a debt', from *fin* (see **FINE**[2]).

**finance company** (also **finance house**) ● **n.** a company concerned primarily with providing money, e.g. for hire-purchase transactions.

**financial** /fʌɪˈnanʃ(ə)l, fɪ-/ ● **adj. 1** of or relating to finance. **2** Austral./NZ informal possessing money.
– DERIVATIVES **financially** adv.

**financial year** ● **n.** Brit. a year as reckoned for taxing or accounting purposes (e.g. the British tax year, reckoned from 6 April).

**financier** /fʌɪˈnansɪə, fɪ-/ ● **n.** a person engaged in managing the finances of governments or other large organizations.
– ORIGIN C17: from Fr., from *finance* (see **FINANCE**).

**finback** ● **n.** another term for **FIN WHALE**.

**finca** /ˈfɪŋkə/ ● **n.** (in Spanish-speaking countries) a country estate or ranch.

**finch** ● **n.** a seed-eating songbird of a large group including the chaffinch, goldfinch, linnet, etc., typically with a stout bill and colourful plumage. [Many species, especially in family Fringillidae.]
– ORIGIN OE *finc*, of W. Gmc origin.

**find** ● **v.** (past and past part. **found**) **1** discover by chance or deliberately. ➤(**find something out** or **find out about something**) discover information or a fact. ➤succeed in obtaining: *she also found the time to raise a family.* ➤(of hunters or hounds) discover a fox or other game. ➤(**find someone out**) detect someone in a crime or lie. **2** recognize or discover to be present: *vitamin B12 is found in dairy products.* ➤discover or perceive to be the case. ➤ascertain by research or calculation. ➤Law (of a court) officially declare to be the case. ➤(**find against** or **for**) Law (of a court) make a decision against (or in favour of); judge to be guilty (or innocent). **3** reach or arrive at by a natural or normal process: *water finds its own level.* ➤(**find one's way**) reach one's destination without knowing or having been told in advance how to get there. ● **n.** a discovery of something valuable or interesting, typically an archaeological one. ➤a person who is found to be useful or interesting.
– PHRASES **all found** Brit. dated (of an employee's wages) with board and lodging provided free. **find one's feet** stand up and become able to walk. ➤establish oneself in a particular field. **find it in one's heart to do** [usu. with neg.] allow or force oneself to do.
– DERIVATIVES **findable** adj.
– ORIGIN OE *findan*, of Gmc origin.

**finder** ● **n. 1** a person that finds someone or something. **2** a small telescope attached to a large one to locate an object for observation. ➤a viewfinder.
– PHRASES **finders keepers (losers weepers)** informal whoever finds something is entitled to keep it.

**fin de siècle** /ˌfã də ˈsjɛkl(ə)/ ● **adj.** relating to or characteristic of the end of a century, especially the 19th century.
– ORIGIN Fr., 'end of century'.

**finding** ● **n. 1** a conclusion reached as a result of an inquiry, investigation, or trial. **2** (**findings**) N. Amer. small articles or tools used in making garments, shoes, or jewellery.

**fine**[1] /fʌɪn/ ● **adj. 1** of very high quality. ➤satisfactory. ➤in good health and feeling well. ➤(of speech or writing) sounding impressive but ultimately insincere: *fine words.*

➤(of gold or silver) containing a specified high proportion of pure metal. **2** (of the weather) bright and clear. **3** (of a thread, filament, or hair) thin. ➤consisting of small particles. ➤of delicate or intricate workmanship. ➤subtle and therefore perceptible with difficulty: *a fine distinction*. ➤(of feelings) refined; elevated. **4** Cricket behind the wicket and close to the line of flight of the bowling. ● **n.** (**fines**) very small particles found in mining or milling. ● **adv. 1** informal in a satisfactory or pleasing manner. **2** Cricket to a fine position. ● **v. 1** clarify (beer or wine) by causing the precipitation of sediment. **2** (usu. **fine something down** or **fine down**) make or become thinner. **3** (**fine up**) N. English & Austral./NZ informal (of the weather) become bright and clear.
– PHRASES **cut it** (or **things**) **fine** allow a very small margin of time. **one's finest hour** the time of one's greatest success. **not to put too fine a point on it** to speak bluntly. **one fine day** at some unspecified time.
– DERIVATIVES **finely** adv. **fineness** n.
– ORIGIN ME: from OFr. *fin*, based on L. *finire* (see **FINISH**).

**fine**[2] /fʌɪn/ ● **n.** a sum of money exacted as a penalty by a court of law or other authority. ● **v.** punish by a fine.
– DERIVATIVES **fineable** adj.
– ORIGIN ME: from OFr. *fin* 'end, payment', from L. *finis* 'end' (in med. L. denoting a sum paid on settling a lawsuit).

**fine**[3] /fiːn/ ● **n. 1** French brandy of high quality made from distilled wine. **2** short for **FINE CHAMPAGNE**.

**fine**[4] /ˈfiːneɪ/ ● **n.** Music the place where a piece of music finishes (when at the end of a repeated section rather than at the end of the score).
– ORIGIN Ital., from L. *finis* 'end'.

**fine art** ● **n.** (also **fine arts**) art intended to be appreciated primarily or solely for its aesthetic content.
– PHRASES **have** (or **get**) **something down to a fine art** achieve a high level of skill in something through experience.

**fine champagne** /ˌfiːn ʃɒ̃ˈpɑːnj(ə)/ ● **n.** brandy from the Champagne district of the Cognac region of which half or more of the content comes from the central Grande Champagne.
– ORIGIN Fr., 'fine (brandy from) Champagne'.

**fine chemicals** ● **pl. n.** highly pure chemicals prepared for use in research and industry.

**fine-draw** ● **v.** sew together so that the join is imperceptible.

**fine print** ● **n.** another term for **SMALL PRINT**.

**finery**[1] /ˈfʌɪn(ə)ri/ ● **n.** ostentatious clothes or decoration.
– ORIGIN C17: from **FINE**[1], on the pattern of *bravery*.

**finery**[2] /ˈfʌɪnəri/ ● **n.** (pl. **-ies**) historical a hearth where pig iron was converted into wrought iron.
– ORIGIN C16: from Fr. *finerie*, from OFr. *finer* 'refine'.

**fines herbes** /fiːnz ˈɛːb/ ● **pl. n.** mixed herbs used in cooking.
– ORIGIN Fr., lit. 'fine herbs'.

**fine-spun** ● **adj.** (especially of fabric) fine or delicate in texture.

**finesse** ● **n. 1** refinement and delicacy. ➤subtle skill in handling or manipulating people or situations. **2** (in bridge and whist) an attempt to win a trick with a card that is not a certain winner. ● **v. 1** do in a subtle and delicate manner. ➤slyly attempt to avoid blame when dealing with (a situation). **2** (in bridge and whist) play (a card) as a finesse.
– ORIGIN ME: from Fr., rel. to **FINE**[1].

**fine-tooth comb** (also **fine-toothed comb**) ● **n.** (in phr. **with a fine-tooth comb**) with a very thorough search or analysis.

**fine-tune** ● **v.** make small adjustments to in order to achieve the best performance.

**finfoot** ● **n.** (pl. **finfoots**) a grebe-like waterbird with a long bill, neck, and tail, and lobed feet. [Family Heliornithidae: three species.]

**finger** ● **n.** each of the four slender jointed parts attached to either hand (or five, if the thumb is included). ➤a measure of liquor in a glass, based on the breadth of a finger. ● **v. 1** touch or feel with the fingers. **2** (usu. **finger someone for**) informal, chiefly N. Amer. inform on to the police. ➤identify or choose (someone) for a particular purpose. **3** Music play (a passage) with a particular sequence of positions of the fingers. ➤mark (music) with signs indicating the fingering.
– PHRASES **be all fingers and thumbs** Brit. informal be clumsy. **pull one's finger out** Brit. informal cease prevaricating and start to act. **get one's fingers burned** (or **burnt**) (or **burn one's fingers**) suffer unpleasant consequences as a result of one's actions. **give someone the finger** N. Amer. informal make a gesture with the middle finger raised as an obscene sign of contempt. **have a finger in the pie** be involved in a matter. **have** (or **keep**) **one's finger on the pulse** be aware of the latest trends. **lay a finger on** touch (someone), especially with the intention of harming them. **put the finger on** informal inform on. **put one's finger on** identify (something) exactly. **snap** (or **click**) **one's fingers** make a sharp clicking sound by bending the last joint of the middle finger against the thumb and suddenly releasing it.
– DERIVATIVES **-fingered** adj. **fingerless** adj.
– ORIGIN OE, of Gmc origin.

**finger alphabet** ● **n.** a form of sign language using the fingers to spell out words.

**fingerboard** ● **n.** a flat strip on the neck of a stringed instrument, against which the strings are pressed to shorten the vibrating length and produce notes of higher pitches.

**finger bowl** ● **n.** a small bowl holding water for rinsing the fingers during or after a meal.

**finger-dry** ● **v.** dry and style (hair) by repeatedly running one's fingers through it.

**finger food** ● **n.** food served in a form that can conveniently be eaten with the fingers.

**fingering**[1] ● **n.** a manner or technique of using the fingers to play a musical instrument.

**fingering**[2] ● **n.** dated fine wool for hand knitting.
– ORIGIN C17 (as *fingram*): perh. from Fr. *fin grain* 'fine grain'; cf. **GROGRAM** and **GROSGRAIN**.

**fingerling** ● **n.** a salmon parr.
– ORIGIN C18: from **FINGER** (with ref. to its transverse dusky bars) + **-LING**.

**fingernail** ● **n.** the nail on the upper surface of the tip of each finger.

**finger-paint** ● **n.** thick paint designed to be applied with the fingers, used especially by young children.
– DERIVATIVES **finger-painting** n.

**fingerpick** ● **v.** play (a guitar or similar instrument) using the fingernails or plectrums worn on the fingertips. ● **n.** a plectrum worn on a fingertip.
– DERIVATIVES **fingerpicker** n.

**fingerplate** ● **n.** a piece of metal or porcelain fixed to a door above the handle to prevent fingermarks on the door itself.

**fingerpost** ● **n.** a post at a road junction from which signs project in the direction of the place indicated.

**fingerprint** ● **n.** a mark made on a surface by a person's fingertip, especially as consisting of a unique pattern used for purposes of identification. ● **v.** record the fingerprints of.

**fingerstall** ● **n.** a cover to protect a finger.

**fingertip** ● **adj.** using or operated by the fingers.
– PHRASES **at one's fingertips** (especially of information) readily available. **to one's fingertips** completely.

**finger wave** ● **n.** a wave set in wet hair using the fingers.

**fingle** ● **v.** W. Indian handle or finger.
– ORIGIN blend of obs. *fangle* 'to trifle' and **FINGER**.

**finial** /ˈfɪnɪəl, ˈfʌɪn-/ ● **n.** a distinctive section or ornament at the apex of a roof, pinnacle, or similar structure in a building. ➤an ornament at the top, end, or corner of an object.
– ORIGIN ME: from OFr. *fin* or L. *finis* 'end'.

**finical** /ˈfɪnɪk(ə)l/ ● **adj.** another term for **FINICKY**.
– DERIVATIVES **finicality** n. **finically** adv. **finicalness** n.
– ORIGIN C16: prob. from **FINE**[1] + **-ICAL**.

**finicking** ● adj. another term for **FINICKY**.
– ORIGIN C17: from **FINICAL** + **-ING**[2].

**finicky** ● adj. **1** fussy. **2** excessively detailed or elaborate.
– DERIVATIVES **finickiness** n.

**fining** ● n. a substance used for clarifying beer or wine.

**finis** /ˈfiːnɪs, ˈfɪnɪs, ˈfʌɪnɪs/ ● n. the end (printed at the end of a book or shown at the end of a film).
– ORIGIN ME: from L.

**finish** ● v. **1** bring or come to an end. ➤consume or get through the whole or the remainder of (food or drink). ➤(**finish with**) have nothing more to do with. ➤reach the end of a race or other sporting competition. ➤(**finish up**) chiefly Brit. end by doing something or being in a particular position. ➤(**finish someone off**) kill or comprehensively defeat someone. **2** complete the manufacture or decoration of (something) by giving it an attractive surface appearance. ➤complete the fattening of (livestock) before slaughter. **3** dated prepare (a girl) for entry into fashionable society. ● n. **1** an end or final stage. ➤the place at which a race or competition ends. **2** the manner in which a manufactured article is finished. ➤the surface appearance of a manufactured article. ➤the final taste impression of a wine or beer.
– PHRASES **a fight to the finish** a fight or contest which ends only with the complete defeat of one of the participants.
– ORIGIN ME: from OFr. *feniss-*, lengthened stem of *fenir*, from L. *finire*, from *finis* 'end'.

**finisher** ● n. **1** a person or thing that finishes something. **2** an animal that has been fattened for slaughter.

**finishing school** ● n. a private college where girls are prepared for entry into fashionable society.

**finishing touch** ● n. a final detail completing and enhancing a piece of work.

**finite** /ˈfʌɪnʌɪt/ ● adj. **1** limited in size or extent. **2** Grammar (of a verb form) having a specific tense, number, and person.
– DERIVATIVES **finitely** adv. **finiteness** n. **finitude** /ˈfɪnɪtjuːd/ n.
– ORIGIN ME: from L. *finitus*, *finire* (see **FINISH**).

**finitism** /ˈfʌɪnʌɪtɪz(ə)m/ ● n. Philosophy & Mathematics rejection of the belief that anything can be infinite.
– DERIVATIVES **finitist** n.

**finito** /fɪˈniːtəʊ/ ● adj. informal finished.
– ORIGIN from Ital.

**fink** N. Amer. informal ● n. **1** an unpleasant or contemptible person. **2** an informer. ● v. **1** (**fink on**) inform on. **2** (**fink out**) back out of a responsibility.
– ORIGIN C19: of unknown origin; perh. from Ger., lit. 'finch', but also a pejorative term.

**Finlandization** /ˌfɪnləndʌɪˈzeɪʃ(ə)n/ (also **-isation**) ● n. historical the process or result of being obliged for economic reasons to favour the interests of the former Soviet Union despite not being politically allied to it.
– DERIVATIVES **Finlandize** (also **-ise**) v.
– ORIGIN 1960s: translation of Ger. *Finnlandisierung*, referring to the case of Finland after 1944.

**Finn** ● n. a native or national of Finland or a person of Finnish descent.
– ORIGIN OE *Finnas* (pl.).

**finnan** /ˈfɪnən/ (also **finnan haddock**) ● n. haddock cured with the smoke of green wood, turf, or peat.
– ORIGIN C18: alt. of *Findon*, the name of a fishing village near Aberdeen, but sometimes confused with the Sc. river and village of *Findhorn*.

**finnesko** /ˈfɪnəskəʊ/ ● n. (pl. same) a boot of tanned reindeer skin with the hair on the outside.
– ORIGIN C19: from Norw. *finnsko*, from *Finn* (see **FINN**) + *sko* (see **SHOE**).

**Finnic** ● adj. **1** of or denoting a group of Finno-Ugric languages including Finnish and Estonian. **2** of or denoting the group of peoples which includes the Finns.

**Finnish** ● n. the Finno-Ugric language of the Finns. ● adj. of or relating to the Finns or their language.

**Finno-Ugric** /ˌfɪnəʊˈuːɡrɪk, -ˈjuːɡrɪk/ (also **Finno-Ugrian** /-ˈuːɡrɪən, -ˈjuːɡrɪən/) ● n. a major group of Uralic languages, including Finnish, Hungarian, and several north central Asian languages. ● adj. of or relating to this group of languages.

**finny** ● adj. poetic/literary or humorous of, relating to, or resembling a fish.

**fino** /ˈfiːnəʊ/ ● n. (pl. **-os**) a light-coloured dry sherry.
– ORIGIN Sp., lit. 'fine'.

**fin whale** ● n. a large rorqual with a small dorsal fin and white underparts. [*Balaenoptera physalus*.]

**fiord** ● n. variant spelling of **FJORD**.

**fioritura** /fɪˌɔːrɪˈt(j)ʊərə/ ● n. (pl. **fioriture** /fɪˌɔːrɪˈt(j)ʊəri, -reɪ/) Music an embellishment of a melody, especially as improvised by an operatic singer.
– ORIGIN Ital., lit. 'flowering'.

**fipple** /ˈfɪp(ə)l/ ● n. the mouthpiece of a recorder or similar wind instrument which is blown endwise, in which a thin channel cut through a block directs a stream of air against a sharp edge.
– ORIGIN C17: perh. rel. to Icelandic *flipi* 'horse's lip'.

**fipple flute** ● n. a flute, such as a recorder, played by blowing endwise.

**fir** ● n. an evergreen coniferous tree with upright cones and flat needle-shaped leaves. [Genus *Abies*: many species.]
– DERIVATIVES **firry** adj.
– ORIGIN ME: prob. from ON *fyri-*.

**fir cone** ● n. chiefly Brit. the dry fruit of a fir tree or other conifer.

**fire** ● n. **1** the state of burning, in which substances combine chemically with oxygen from the air and give out bright light, heat, and smoke. ➤a destructive burning. ➤one of the four elements in ancient and medieval philosophy and in astrology. **2** a collection of fuel burnt in a hearth or stove for heating or cooking. ➤Brit. (also **electric fire** or **gas fire**) a domestic heating appliance that uses electricity (or gas) as fuel. **3** a burning sensation. ➤passionate emotion or enthusiasm. **4** the firing of guns. ➤strong criticism. ● v. **1** propel (a bullet or projectile) from a gun or other weapon. ➤discharge (a gun or other weapon). ➤direct a rapid succession of (questions or statements) towards someone. **2** informal dismiss from a job. **3** supply (a furnace, power station, etc.) with fuel. ➤(of an internal-combustion engine) undergo ignition of its fuel. ➤set fire to. **4** stimulate (the imagination or an emotion). ➤fill with enthusiasm: *he was fired up for the Cup final.* **5** bake or dry (pottery, bricks, etc.) in a kiln.
– PHRASES **catch fire** begin to burn. **fire and brimstone** the supposed torments of hell. **fire away** informal go ahead. **firing on all (four) cylinders** functioning at a peak level. **go on fire** Scottish & Irish begin to burn. **go through fire (and water)** face any peril. **on fire 1** burning. **2** very excited. **set fire to** (or **set something on fire**) cause to burn. **set the world** (or Brit. **Thames**) **on fire** do something remarkable or sensational. **take fire** start to burn. **under fire 1** being shot at. **2** being rigorously criticized.
– DERIVATIVES **fireless** adj. **firer** n. **firing** n.
– ORIGIN OE *fȳr* (n.), *fȳrian* 'supply with material for a fire', of W. Gmc origin.

**fire alarm** ● n. a device making a loud noise that gives warning of a fire.

**fire ant** ● n. a tropical American ant with a painful sting. [*Solenopsis invicta* and other species.]

**firearm** ● n. a rifle, pistol, or other portable gun.

**fireback** ● n. **1** the back wall of a fireplace. **2** (also **fireback pheasant**) a SE Asian pheasant with a reddish rump. [Genus *Lophura*: three species.]

**fireball** ● n. **1** a ball of flame or fire. ➤a large bright meteor. **2** an energetic or hot-tempered person.

**fireballer** ● n. Baseball a pitcher known for throwing pitches at maximum speed.
– DERIVATIVES **fireballing** adj.

**fire blanket** ● n. a sheet of flexible material, typically woven fibreglass, used to smother a fire.

**fireblight** ● n. a serious bacterial disease of fruit trees and other plants, giving the leaves a scorched appearance.

**firebomb** ● n. a bomb designed to cause a fire. ● v. attack with a firebomb.

**firebox** • **n.** the chamber of a steam engine or boiler in which the fuel is burnt.

**firebrand** • **n.** a fervent supporter of a particular cause, especially one who incites unrest.

**firebrat** • **n.** a fast-moving brownish bristletail that frequents warm places indoors. [*Thermobia domestica*.]

**firebreak** • **n.** an obstacle to the spread of fire, e.g. a strip of open space in a forest.

**firebrick** • **n.** a brick capable of withstanding intense heat, used especially to line furnaces and fireplaces.

**fire brigade** • **n.** chiefly Brit. an organized body of people trained and employed to extinguish fires.

**firebug** • **n.** informal an arsonist.

**fireclay** • **n.** clay capable of withstanding high temperatures, chiefly used for making firebricks.

**fire company** • **n.** US term for **FIRE BRIGADE**.

**fire control** • **n.** the process of targeting and firing heavy weapons.

**fire coral** • **n.** a colonial coral-like hydrozoan which can inflict painful stings. [Genus *Millepora*.]

**firecracker** • **n.** chiefly N. Amer. a loud, explosive firework.

**firecrest** • **n.** a very small songbird with a red and orange crest, related to the goldcrest. [*Regulus ignicapillus*.]

**firedamp** • **n.** methane, especially as forming an explosive mixture with air in coal mines.

**fire department** • **n.** N. Amer. the department of a local or municipal authority in charge of preventing and fighting fires.

**firedog** • **n.** each of a pair of decorative metal supports for wood burning in a fireplace.

**fire door** • **n.** a fire-resistant door to prevent the spread of fire.

**firedrake** • **n.** Germanic Mythology a dragon.
– ORIGIN OE *fȳr-draca*, from *fȳr* (see **FIRE**) + *draca* 'dragon', from L. *draco*.

**fire drill** • **n.** a practice of the emergency procedures to be used in case of fire.

**fire-eater** • **n. 1** an entertainer who appears to eat fire. **2** dated an aggressive or quarrelsome person.

**fire engine** • **n.** a vehicle carrying firefighters and their equipment.

**fire escape** • **n.** a staircase or other apparatus used for escaping from a building on fire.

**fire extinguisher** • **n.** a portable device that discharges a jet of liquid, foam, or gas to extinguish a fire.

**firefight** • **n.** Military a battle using guns rather than bombs or other weapons.

**firefighter** • **n.** a person whose job is to extinguish fires.
– DERIVATIVES **firefighting** n.

**firefly** • **n.** (pl. **-flies**) a soft-bodied beetle related to the glow-worm, the winged male and flightless female of which both have luminescent organs. [*Luciola lusitanica* (Europe) and other species.]

**fireguard** • **n. 1** a protective screen or grid placed in front of an open fire. **2** N. Amer. a firebreak in a forest.

**firehouse** • **n.** N. Amer. a fire station.

**fire irons** • **pl. n.** tongs, a poker, and a shovel for tending a domestic fire.

**fireless cooker** • **n.** dated an insulated container capable of maintaining a temperature sufficient to cook food.

**firelight** • **n.** light from a fire in a fireplace.

**firelighter** • **n.** Brit. a piece of flammable material used to help start a fire.

**fire line** • **n.** N. Amer. a firebreak in a forest.

**firelock** • **n.** historical a musket in which the priming is ignited by sparks.

**fireman** • **n.** (pl. **-men**) **1** a male firefighter. **2** a person who tends a furnace or the fire of a steam engine or steamship.

**fire opal** • **n.** another term for **GIRASOL** (in sense 1).

**fireplace** • **n.** a partially enclosed space at the base of a chimney for a domestic fire.

**fireplug** • **n. 1** US a hydrant for a fire hose. **2** N. Amer. informal a short, stocky person, especially an athlete.

**firepower** • **n.** the destructive capacity of guns, missiles, or a military force.

**fire practice** • **n.** Brit. a fire drill.

**fireproof** • **adj.** able to withstand fire or great heat. • **v.** make fireproof.

**fire-raiser** • **n.** Brit. an arsonist.
– DERIVATIVES **fire-raising** n.

**fire salamander** • **n.** a short-tailed nocturnal salamander with black skin and bright red, orange, and yellow markings. [*Salamandra salamandra*.]

**fire sale** • **n.** a sale of goods remaining after a fire. ➤a sale of goods or assets at a very low price.

**fire screen** • **n.** a fireguard. ➤an ornamental screen placed in front of a fireplace when the fire is unlit.

**fireship** • **n.** historical a ship loaded with burning material and explosives and set adrift to burn an enemy's ships.

**fireside** • **n.** the area round a fireplace, especially as considered to be the focus of domestic life.

**fireside chat** • **n.** an informal and intimate conversation.

**fire starter** • **n.** North American term for **FIRELIGHTER**.

**fire station** • **n.** the headquarters of a fire brigade.

**fire step** • **n.** a step or ledge on which soldiers in a trench stand to fire.

**fire stone** • **n.** stone that can withstand fire and great heat, used especially for lining furnaces and ovens.

**firestorm** • **n.** a very intense and destructive fire (typically one caused by bombing) in which the blaze is fanned by strong currents of air drawn in from the surrounding area.

**firethorn** • **n.** another term for **PYRACANTHA**.

**fire trap** • **n.** a building without proper provision for escape in case of fire.

**fire-walking** • **n.** the practice of walking barefoot over hot stones or wood ashes, especially as a religious rite.
– DERIVATIVES **fire-walker** n.

**firewall** • **n. 1** a wall or partition designed to inhibit or prevent the spread of fire. **2** Computing a part of a computer system or network which is designed to block unauthorized access while permitting outward communication.

**fire warden** • **n.** N. Amer. a person employed to prevent or extinguish fires, especially in a town, camp, or forest.

**fire-watcher** • **n.** a person keeping watch for fires, especially forest fires or those caused by bombs.
– DERIVATIVES **fire-watching** n.

**firewater** • **n.** informal strong alcoholic liquor.

**fireweed** • **n.** a plant that springs up on burnt land, especially the rosebay willowherb.

**firewood** • **n.** wood that is burnt as fuel.

**firework** • **n. 1** a device containing gunpowder and other combustible chemicals which causes spectacular effects and explosions when ignited. **2** (**fireworks**) an outburst of anger or a display of brilliance.

**firing line** • **n. 1** the front line of troops in a battle. **2** a position where one is subject to criticism or blame.

**firing party** • **n. 1** a group of soldiers detailed to fire the salute at a military funeral. **2** another term for **FIRING SQUAD**.

**firing squad** • **n.** a group of soldiers detailed to shoot a condemned person.

**firing step** • **n.** another term for **FIRE STEP**.

**firkin** /ˈfəːkɪn/ • **n.** chiefly historical **1** a small cask used chiefly for liquids, butter, or fish. **2** a unit of liquid volume equal to half a kilderkin (usually 9 imperial gallons or about 41 litres).
– ORIGIN ME *ferdekyn*, prob. from the MDu. dimin. of *vierde* 'fourth' (a firkin orig. contained a quarter of a barrel).

**firm**[1] • **adj. 1** having an unyielding surface or structure. **2** solidly in place and stable. **3** having steady power or strength: *a firm grip*. ➤steadfast and enduring. **4** showing resolute determination. **5** (of a currency, a commodity, or shares) having a steady value or price which is

more likely to rise than fall. ● **v. 1** make stable or unyielding. **2** (of a price) rise to a level considered secure. **3** (often **firm something up**) make (an agreement or plan) explicit and definite. ● **adv.** in a resolute and determined manner: *she will stand firm.*
– PHRASES **be on firm ground** be sure of one's facts or secure in one's position. **a firm hand** strict discipline or control.
– DERIVATIVES **firmly** adv. **firmness** n.
– ORIGIN ME: from OFr. *ferme*, from L. *firmus*.

**firm²** ● **n. 1** a company or business partnership. **2** a group of hospital doctors working as a team.
– ORIGIN C16 (orig. denoting a signature, later the name under which the business of a firm was transacted): from Sp. and Ital. *firma*, based on L. *firmare* 'fix, settle' (in late L. 'confirm by signature'), from *firmus* 'firm'; cf. FARM.

**firmament** /'fəːməm(ə)nt/ ● **n.** poetic/literary the heavens; the sky.
– DERIVATIVES **firmamental** adj.
– ORIGIN ME: via OFr. from L. *firmamentum*, from *firmare* 'fix, settle'.

**firman** /'fəːmən, fəː'mɑːn/ (also **farman**) ● **n.** (pl. **-mans**) (in the Middle East) an official edict or permit.
– ORIGIN C17: from Pers. *firmān*, Sanskrit *pramāṇa* 'right measure, standard, authority'.

**firmware** ● **n.** Computing permanent software programmed into a read-only memory.

**first** ● **ordinal number 1** coming before all others in time or order; earliest; 1st. ➤ before doing something else specified or implied. ➤ for the first time. ➤ with a specified part or person in a leading position: *it plunged nose first into the river.* **2** foremost in position, rank, or importance. **3** informal something never previously achieved or occurring. **4** Brit. a place in the top grade in an examination for a degree. **5** Music performing the highest or chief of two or more parts for the same instrument or voice.
– PHRASES **at first** at the beginning. **first and foremost** most importantly; more than anything else. **first and last** fundamentally; on the whole. **first of all** before doing anything else; at the beginning. ➤ most importantly. **first off** informal, chiefly N. Amer. as a first point; first of all. **first past the post** winning a race by being the first to reach the finishing line. ➤ Brit. denoting an electoral system in which a candidate or party is selected by achievement of a simple majority. **first thing** early in the morning; before anything else. **first things first** important matters should be dealt with before other things. **first up** informal first of all. **in the first place** as the first consideration or point. ➤ at the beginning; to begin with. **of the first order** (or **magnitude**) excellent or considerable of its kind.
– ORIGIN OE *fyr(e)st*; of Gmc origin.

**first aid** ● **n.** help given to a sick or injured person until full medical treatment is available.
– DERIVATIVES **first-aider** n.

**firstborn** ● **adj.** denoting the first child to be born to someone. ● **n.** a firstborn child.

**First Cause** ● **n.** Philosophy a supposed ultimate cause of all events, which does not itself have a cause, identified with God.

**first class** ● **n. 1** a set of people or things grouped together as the best. **2** the best accommodation in an aircraft, train, or ship. **3** Brit. the highest division in the results of the examinations for a university degree. ● **adj. & adv.** (**first-class**) of or relating to the first class.

**first cost** ● **n.** another term for PRIME COST.

**first-day cover** ● **n.** an envelope bearing a stamp or set of stamps postmarked on their day of issue.

**first-degree** ● **adj. 1** Medicine denoting burns that affect only the surface of the skin and cause reddening. **2** Law, chiefly N. Amer. denoting the most serious category of a crime, especially murder.
– PHRASES **first-degree relative** a person's parent, sibling, or child.

**first down** ● **n.** American Football the score achieved by a team who have kept possession of the ball by advancing at least ten yards in a series of four downs.

**first finger** ● **n.** the index finger.

**first-foot** ● **v.** [usu. as noun **first-footing**] be the first person to cross someone's threshold in the New Year. ● **n.** the first person to cross a threshold in such a way.
– DERIVATIVES **first-footer** n.

**first fruits** ● **pl. n. 1** the first agricultural produce of a season. **2** the initial results of an enterprise or endeavour.

**first-hand** ● **adj. & adv.** (of information or experience) from the original source or personal experience; direct.
– PHRASES **at first hand** directly or from personal experience.

**first intention** ● **n.** Medicine the healing of a wound by natural contact of the parts involved.

**first lady** ● **n.** the wife of the President of the US or other head of state.

**first lieutenant** ● **n. 1** a naval officer with executive responsibility for a ship or other command. **2** a rank of officer in the US army or air force, above second lieutenant and below captain.

**firstling** ● **n.** (usu. **firstlings**) archaic the first agricultural produce or animal offspring of a season.

**firstly** ● **adv.** in the first place; first.

**first mate** ● **n.** the officer second in command to the master of a merchant ship.

**first name** ● **n.** a personal name given to someone at birth or baptism and used before a family name.
– PHRASES **on first-name terms** having a friendly and informal relationship.

**first night** ● **n.** the first public performance of a play or show.

**first offender** ● **n.** a person who is convicted of a criminal offence for the first time.

**first officer** ● **n. 1** the first mate on a merchant ship. **2** the second in command to the captain on an aircraft.

**first-order** ● **adj. 1** of the first order. **2** having an order of one, especially denoting mathematical equations involving only the first power of the independent variable or only the first derivative of a function.

**first person** ● **n.** see PERSON (sense 5).

**first position** ● **n. 1** Ballet a standing position in which the feet are turned outwards with the heels touching. **2** Music the position of the hand on the fingerboard of a stringed instrument furthest from the bridge.

**first post** ● **n.** (in the British armed forces) the first of two bugle calls giving notice of the hour of retiring at night.

**first principles** ● **pl. n.** the fundamental concepts or assumptions on which a theory, system, or method is based.

**first-rate** ● **adj.** of the best class, quality, or condition; excellent.

**first reading** ● **n.** the first presentation of a bill to a legislative assembly, to permit its introduction.

**first refusal** ● **n.** the privilege of deciding whether to accept or reject something before it is offered to others.

**first school** ● **n.** Brit. a school for children from five to nine years old.

**first sergeant** ● **n.** (in the US army) the highest-ranking non-commissioned officer in a unit.

**first strike** ● **n.** an opening attack with nuclear weapons.

**First World** ● **n.** the industrialized capitalist countries of western Europe, North America, Japan, Australia, and New Zealand.

**firth** ● **n.** a narrow inlet of the sea.
– ORIGIN ME (orig. Scots), from ON *fjǫrthr* (see FJORD).

**fisc** /fɪsk/ ● **n.** Roman History the public treasury of Rome or the emperor's privy purse.
– ORIGIN C16: from Fr., or from L. *fiscus* 'rush basket, purse, treasury'.

**fiscal** /'fɪsk(ə)l/ ● **adj. 1** of or relating to government revenue, especially taxes. **2** chiefly N. Amer. of or relating to financial matters. ➤ N. Amer. denoting a particular financial year: *the deficit for fiscal 1996.*
– DERIVATIVES **fiscally** adv.
– ORIGIN C16: from Fr., or from L. *fiscalis*, from *fiscus* (see FISC).

**fiscal year** • n. North American term for FINANCIAL YEAR.

**fish**[1] • n. (pl. same or **fishes**) **1** a limbless cold-blooded vertebrate animal with gills and fins, living wholly in water. ➤ the flesh of fish as food. **2** used in names of invertebrate animals living wholly in water, e.g. **shellfish**, **jellyfish**. **3** informal a person who is strange in a specified way: *he's a cold fish.* • v. **1** catch fish with a net or hook and line. ➤ fish in (a particular body of water). **2** (**fish something out**) pull or take something out of water or a receptacle. **3** grope or feel for something concealed. **4** try subtly or deviously to elicit a response or information.
– PHRASES **a big fish** an important person. **a big fish in a small pond** a person who is important only within a small community. **a fish out of water** a person who feels out of place in their surroundings. **have other** (or **bigger**) **fish to fry** have more important matters to attend to.
– DERIVATIVES **fishing** n.
– ORIGIN OE *fisc* (as a noun denoting any animal living exclusively in water), *fiscian* (v.), of Gmc origin.

**fish**[2] • n. **1** a flat plate fixed on a beam or across a joint to give additional strength. **2** a long curved piece of wood lashed to a ship's damaged mast or spar as a temporary repair. • v. **1** strengthen or mend with a fish. **2** join (rails) with a fishplate.
– ORIGIN C16: prob. from Fr. *fiche*, from *ficher* 'to fix', based on L. *figere*.

**fishbowl** • n. a round glass bowl for keeping pet fish in.

**fish cake** • n. a patty of shredded fish and mashed potato.

**fish eagle** • n. an eagle that preys largely on fish. [*Haliaeetus vocifer* (Africa) and other species.]

**fisher** • n. **1** a large brown marten found in North American woodland. [*Martes pennanti*.] **2** archaic a fisherman.

**fisherfolk** • pl. n. people who catch fish for a living.

**fisherman** • n. (pl. **-men**) a person who catches fish for a living or for sport.

**fisherman bat** • n. another term for BULLDOG BAT.

**fisherman's bend** • n. a knot tied by making a full turn round something, a half hitch through the turn, and a half hitch round the standing part of the rope.

**fisherman's knot** • n. a knot used to join two small ropes by tying an overhand knot in the end of each around the opposite standing part.

**fisherman's rib** (also **fisherman knit**) • n. a type of thick ribbed knitting.

**fishery** • n. (pl. **-ies**) **1** a place where fish are reared, or caught in numbers. **2** the occupation or industry of catching or rearing fish.

**fisheye** • n. **1** a very wide-angle lens with a field of vision covering up to 180°, the scale being reduced towards the edges. **2** US informal a suspicious or unfriendly look. **3** a defect in metal causing a spot to stand out brightly against its surroundings.

**fish finger** • n. Brit. a small oblong piece of flaked or minced fish coated in batter or breadcrumbs.

**fish hawk** • n. another term for OSPREY.

**fishing fly** • n. a natural or artificial flying insect used as bait in fishing.

**fishing line** • n. a long thread of silk or nylon attached to a baited hook, with a sinker or float, and used for catching fish.

**fishing pole** • n. N. Amer. a simple fishing rod with no reel.

**fishing rod** • n. a long, tapering rod to which a fishing line is attached.

**fish kettle** • n. an oval pan for boiling fish.

**fish knife** • n. a blunt knife with a broad blade used for eating or serving fish.

**fish louse** • n. a parasitic crustacean which attaches itself to the skin or gills of fish. [Many species in classes Branchiura and Copepoda.]

**fishmeal** • n. ground dried fish used as fertilizer or animal feed.

**fishmonger** • n. a person or shop that sells fish for food.

**fishnet** • n. a fabric with an open mesh resembling a fishing net.

**fishplate** • n. **1** a flat piece of metal used to connect adjacent rails in a railway track. **2** a flat piece of metal with ends like a fish's tail, used to position masonry.

**fish slice** • n. Brit. a kitchen utensil with a broad flat blade for lifting fish and fried foods.

**fishtail** • n. a thing resembling a fish's tail in shape or movement. • v. make or cause to make a fishtail movement.

**fishwife** • n. (pl. **-wives**) **1** a coarse-mannered woman who is prone to shouting. **2** archaic a woman who sells fish.

**fishy** • adj. (**-ier**, **-iest**) **1** of, relating to, or resembling fish or a fish. **2** informal arousing feelings of doubt or suspicion.
– DERIVATIVES **fishily** adv. **fishiness** n.

**fissile** /ˈfɪsʌɪl/ • adj. **1** (of an atom or element) able to undergo nuclear fission. **2** (chiefly of rock) easily split.
– DERIVATIVES **fissility** /-ˈsɪlɪti/ n.
– ORIGIN C17 (in the sense 'easily split'): from L. *fissilis*, from *fiss-*, *findere* 'split, crack'.

**fission** /ˈfɪʃ(ə)n/ • n. **1** the action of splitting or being split into two or more parts. **2** a reaction in which a heavy atomic nucleus splits in two, releasing much energy. **3** Biology reproduction by means of a cell or organism dividing into two or more new cells or organisms. • v. (chiefly of atoms) undergo fission.
– DERIVATIVES **fissionable** adj.
– ORIGIN C17: from L. *fissio(n-)*, from *findere* 'to split'.

**fission bomb** • n. another term for ATOM BOMB.

**fissiparous** /fɪˈsɪp(ə)rəs/ • adj. **1** inclined to cause or undergo fission. **2** Biology (of an organism) reproducing by fission.
– DERIVATIVES **fissiparity** n. **fissiparousness** n.
– ORIGIN C19: from L. *fissus*, past part. of *findere* 'split', on the pattern of *viviparous*.

**fissure** /ˈfɪʃə/ • n. **1** a long, narrow crack. **2** a state of division or disagreement. • v. [usu. as adj. **fissured**] split; crack.
– ORIGIN ME: from OFr., or from L. *fissura*, from *fiss-*, *findere* 'to split'.

**fist** • n. a person's hand when the fingers are bent in towards the palm and held there tightly. • v. **1** (of a goalkeeper) strike (a ball or shot) with the fist. **2** (also **fist-fuck**) vulgar slang penetrate (a person's anus or vagina) with one's fist.
– PHRASES **make a —— fist of** (or **at**) informal do something to the specified degree of success.
– DERIVATIVES **-fisted** adj. **fistful** n. (pl. **-fuls**).
– ORIGIN OE *fȳst*, of W. Gmc origin.

**fisticuffs** • pl. n. fighting with the fists.
– ORIGIN C17: prob. from obs. *fisty* 'relating to the fists or to fist fighting' + CUFF[2].

**fistula** /ˈfɪstjʊlə/ • n. (pl. **fistulas** or **fistulae** /-liː/) Medicine an abnormal or surgically made passage between a hollow or tubular organ and the body surface, or between two hollow or tubular organs.
– DERIVATIVES **fistular** adj. **fistulous** adj.
– ORIGIN ME: from L., 'pipe, flute, fistula'; cf. FESTER.

**fit**[1] • adj. (**fitter**, **fittest**) **1** of a suitable quality, standard, or type. ➤ socially acceptable: *a fit subject.* ➤ (**fit to do something**) informal having reached such an extreme condition as to be on the point of doing the thing specified: *they were fit to kill him.* **2** in good health, especially because of regular physical exercise. **3** Brit. informal sexually attractive. • v. (**fitted** (US also **fit**), **fitting**) **1** be of the right shape and size for. ➤ (usu. **be fitted for**) try clothing on (someone) in order to make or alter it to the correct size. **2** be or make able to occupy a particular position, place, or period of time. **3** fix into place. ➤ (often **be fitted with**) provide with a particular component or article. ➤ join or cause to join together to form a whole. **4** be or make suitable for. • n. **1** the particular way in which something fits. **2** Statistics the correspondence between observed data and the values expected by theory.
– PHRASES **fit to be tied** informal very angry. **fit to bust** with excessive energy. **see** (or **think**) **fit** consider it correct or

acceptable.
– PHRASAL VERBS **fit in 1** be compatible; be in harmony. **2** (also **fit into**) constitute part of a particular situation or larger structure. **fit someone/thing out** (or **up**) provide someone or something with necessary items. **fit someone up** Brit. informal incriminate someone by falsifying evidence against them.
– DERIVATIVES **fitly** adv. **fitter** n.
– ORIGIN ME: of unknown origin.

**fit**[2] ● n. **1** a sudden attack of convulsions. ➤a sudden attack of coughing, fainting, etc. **2** a sudden burst of intense feeling or activity.
– PHRASES **in** (or **by**) **fits and starts** with irregular bursts of activity.
– ORIGIN OE *fitt* 'conflict', in ME also 'position of danger' and 'short period'.

**fit**[3] (also **fytte**) ● n. archaic a section of a poem.
– ORIGIN OE *fitt*, perh. the same word as FIT[2], or rel. to Ger. *Fitze* 'skein of yarn'.

**fitch** ● n. old-fashioned term for POLECAT.
– ORIGIN ME: from MDu. *visse* 'polecat'.

**fitchew** /'fɪtʃu:/ ● n. archaic term for POLECAT.
– ORIGIN ME: from OFr. *ficheau*, *fissel*, dimin. rel. to MDu. *visse* (see FITCH).

**fitful** ● adj. active or occurring intermittently; not regular or steady.
– DERIVATIVES **fitfully** adv. **fitfulness** n.

**fitment** ● n. chiefly Brit. a fixed item of furniture or piece of equipment.

**fitness** ● n. **1** the state of being fit. **2** Biology an organism's ability to survive and reproduce in a particular environment.

**fitted** ● adj. **1** made to fill a space or to cover something closely. ➤chiefly Brit. (of a room) equipped with matching units of furniture. **2** attached to or provided with a particular component or article. **3** (**fitted for/to do**) being fit for or to do: *the type best fitted for the job.*

**fitting** ● n. **1** an attachment. **2** (**fittings**) items which are fixed in a building but can be removed when the owner moves. Compare with FIXTURE (in sense 1). **2** the action of fitting or being fitted. ● adj. **1** appropriate; right or proper. **2** [in combination] fitted in a specified way: *loose-fitting trousers.*
– DERIVATIVES **fittingly** adv. **fittingness** n.

**fitting room** ● n. a room in a shop in which one can try on clothes before purchase.

**fitting shop** ● n. a part of a factory where machine parts are put together.

**FitzGerald contraction** (also **FitzGerald–Lorentz contraction**) ● n. Physics the shortening of a moving body in the direction of its motion, especially at speeds close to that of light.
– ORIGIN named after George. F. *Fitzgerald*, Ir. physicist, and the Du. physicist H. A. *Lorentz*, who independently postulated the theory.

**five** ● cardinal number equivalent to the sum of two and three; one more than four, or half of ten; 5. (Roman numeral: **v** or **V**.)
– DERIVATIVES **fivefold** adj. & adv.
– ORIGIN OE *fīf*, of Gmc origin.

**five-alarm** ● adj. US informal **1** (of a fire) very large or serious. **2** (of food, such as chillies) extremely pungent.

**five-and-dime** (also **five-and-dime store** or **five-and-ten**) ● n. N. Amer. a shop selling a wide variety of inexpensive goods.

**five-a-side** ● n. a form of soccer with five players in each team.

**five-eighth** ● n. Rugby, chiefly Austral./NZ a player positioned between the scrum half and the three-quarters.

**five hundred** ● n. a form of euchre in which making 500 points wins a game.

**five o'clock shadow** ● n. a slight growth of beard visible on a man's chin several hours after he has shaved.

**fiver** ● n. **1** Brit. informal a five-pound note. **2** N. Amer. a five-dollar bill.

**fives** ● pl. n. [treated as sing.] a game in which a ball is hit with a gloved hand or a bat against a wall.
– ORIGIN C17: pl. of FIVE used as a sing. noun; the significance is unknown.

**five-spice** ● n. a blend of five powdered spices, typically fennel seeds, cinnamon, cloves, star anise, and peppercorns, used in Chinese cuisine.

**fivestones** ● n. Brit. a game of jacks played with five pieces of metal or stone and usually no ball.

**fix** ● v. **1** attach or position securely. ➤(**fix on**) direct or be directed unwaveringly toward: *her gaze fixed on Jess.* ➤discover the exact location of (something) by using radar, visual bearings, or astronomical observation. **2** decide or settle on. ➤(**be fixing to do something**) N. Amer. informal be intending or planning to do something. ➤assign or determine (a person's liability or responsibility) for legal purposes. **3** repair or restore. **4** make arrangements for. ➤informal, chiefly N. Amer. provide with food or drink. ➤(**fix someone up**) informal provide someone with something. **5** make unchanging or constant. ➤make (a dye, photographic image, or drawing) permanent. ➤Biology preserve or stabilize (a specimen) with a chemical substance. ➤(of a plant or micro-organism) assimilate (nitrogen or carbon dioxide) by forming a non-gaseous compound. **6** informal deviously influence the outcome of. **7** informal take an injection of a narcotic drug. **8** castrate or spay (an animal). ● n. **1** an act of fixing. **2** informal a difficult or awkward situation. **3** informal a dose of a narcotic drug to which one is addicted. **4** a position determined by visual or radio bearings or astronomical observations.
– PHRASES **get a fix on** determine the position of. ➤informal determine the nature or facts of.
– DERIVATIVES **fixable** adj. **fixed** adj. **fixedly** adv. **fixedness** n. **fixer** n.
– ORIGIN ME: partly from OFr. *fix* 'fixed', partly from med. L. *fixare* 'to fix', both from L. *fixus*, past part. of *figere* 'fix, fasten'.

**fixate** /fɪk'seɪt/ ● v. **1** (often **be fixated on**) cause to be obsessively interested in something or someone. ➤(in Freudian theory) arrest (a person or their libidinal energy) at an immature stage, causing an obsessive attachment. **2** direct one's eyes towards.
– ORIGIN C19: from L. *fixus*, past part. of *figere* (see FIX) + -ATE[3].

**fixation** ● n. **1** the action or condition of fixating or being fixated. **2** the action or process of fixing or being fixed, especially chemically or biologically.
– ORIGIN ME (orig. as an alchemical term denoting the process of reducing a volatile spirit or essence to a permanent bodily form): from med. L. *fixatio(n-)*, from *fixare* (see FIX).

**fixative** /'fɪksətɪv/ ● n. a substance used to fix, protect, or stabilize something. ● adj. (of a substance) used in such a way.

**fixed assets** ● pl. n. assets which are purchased for long-term use and are not likely to be converted quickly into cash, such as land, buildings, and equipment. Compare with CURRENT ASSETS.

**fixed capital** ● n. capital invested in fixed assets.

**fixed charge** ● n. a liability to a creditor which relates to specific assets of a company. Compare with FLOATING CHARGE.

**fixed costs** ● pl. n. business costs, such as rent, that are constant whatever the amount of goods produced.

**fixed-doh** ● adj. denoting a system of solmization in which C is called 'doh', D is called 'ray', etc., irrespective of the key in which they occur. Compare with MOVABLE-DOH.

**fixed income** ● n. an income from a pension or investment that is set at a particular figure and does not vary like a dividend or rise with the rate of inflation.

**fixed odds** ● pl. n. odds in betting (especially on soccer results) that are predetermined, as opposed to a pool system or a starting price.

**fixed oil** ● n. a non-volatile oil of animal or plant origin.

**fixed point** ● n. **1** Physics a well-defined reproducible temperature which can be used as a reference point, e.g. one defined by a change of phase. **2** [as modifier] Computing denoting a mode of representing a number by a single sequence of digits whose values depend on their location relative to a predetermined radix point.

**fixed star** ● n. Astronomy, historical a star, as distinguished from a planet by its fixed position.

**fixed-wing** ● adj. denoting aircraft of the conventional type as opposed to those with rotating wings, such as helicopters.

**fixing** ● n. **1** the action of fixing something. **2** (**fixings**) Brit. screws, bolts, etc. used to fix or assemble building material, furniture, or equipment. **3** (**fixings**) N. Amer. ingredients, apparatus, or equipment required for a meal or other purpose.

**fixity** ● n. the state of being unchanging or permanent.
– ORIGIN C17: partly from obs. *fix* 'fixed', partly from Fr. *fixité*.

**fixture** /'fɪkstʃə, -tjə/ ● n. **1** a piece of equipment or furniture which is fixed in position in a building or vehicle. ➤(**fixtures**) articles attached to a house or land and considered legally part of it so that they normally remain in place when an owner moves. Compare with **FITTING** (in sense 2). **2** informal a person or thing that has become established in a particular place. **3** Brit. a sporting event which takes place on a particular date.
– ORIGIN C16: alt. (first found in Shakespeare) of obs. *fixure* (from late L. *fixura*, from L. *figere* 'to fix'), with *t* inserted on the pattern of *mixture*.

**fizgig** /'fɪzgɪg/ ● n. **1** Austral. informal a police informer. **2** archaic a silly or flirtatious young woman.
– ORIGIN C16: prob. from **FIZZ** + obs. *gig* 'flighty girl'; cf. **GIG**[1] and **WHIRLIGIG**.

**fizz** ● v. **1** (of a liquid) produce bubbles of gas and make a hissing sound. **2** make a buzzing or crackling sound. ● n. **1** the action or sound of fizzing. **2** informal an effervescent drink, especially sparkling wine. **3** exuberance.
– ORIGIN C17: imitative; cf. **FIZZLE**.

**fizzer** ● n. informal **1** Brit. an outstandingly lively or excellent thing. **2** Austral./NZ a failure or fiasco.

**fizzle** ● v. **1** make a feeble hissing or spluttering sound. **2** (usu. **fizzle out**) end or fail in a weak or disappointing way. ● n. an instance of fizzling.
– ORIGIN ME (in the sense 'break wind quietly'): prob. imitative (cf. **FIZZ**), but perh. rel. to ME *fist* (see **FEISTY**).

**fizzog** ● n. variant of **PHIZ**.

**fizzy** ● adj. (**-ier**, **-iest**) **1** (of a drink) effervescent. **2** exuberant.
– DERIVATIVES **fizzily** adv. **fizziness** n.

**fjord** /fjɔːd, 'fiːɔːd/ (also **fiord**) ● n. a long, narrow, deep inlet of the sea between high cliffs, typically formed by submergence of a glaciated valley and found predominantly in Norway.
– ORIGIN C17: Norw., from ON *fjǫrthr*; cf. **FIRTH**.

**FL** ● abbrev. **1** Florida (in official postal use). **2** Liechtenstein (international vehicle registration). [from Ger. *Fürstentum Liechtenstein* 'Principality of Liechtenstein'.]

**fl.** ● abbrev. **1** floor. **2** floruit. **3** fluid.

**Fla** ● abbrev. Florida.

**flab** ● n. informal soft, loose flesh on a person's body; fat.
– ORIGIN 1950s: back-form. from **FLABBY**.

**flabbergast** /'flabəgɑːst/ ● v. [usu. as adj. **flabbergasted**] informal surprise greatly.
– ORIGIN C18: of unknown origin.

**flabby** ● adj. (**-ier**, **-iest**) **1** (of a part of a person's body) soft, loose, and fleshy. **2** not tightly controlled and therefore ineffective.
– DERIVATIVES **flabbily** adv. **flabbiness** n.
– ORIGIN C17: alt. of earlier *flappy*.

**flaccid** /'flasɪd, 'flaksɪd/ ● adj. soft and limp.
– DERIVATIVES **flaccidity** /flək'sɪdɪti, flə'sɪd-/ n. **flaccidly** adv.
– ORIGIN C17: from Fr. *flaccide* or L. *flaccidus*, from *flaccus* 'flabby'.

**flack**[1] N. Amer. informal ● n. a publicity agent. ● v. publicize or promote.
– DERIVATIVES **flackery** n.
– ORIGIN 1940s: of unknown origin.

**flack**[2] ● n. variant spelling of **FLAK**.

**flag**[1] ● n. **1** an oblong piece of cloth that is raised on a pole and used as an emblem, especially of nationality. **2** a ship's ensign. **3** a device or symbol resembling a flag, used as a marker. **4** a small paper badge given to people who donate to a charity appeal. ● v. (**flagged**, **flagging**) **1** mark for attention. **2** direct or alert by waving a flag or using hand signals. ➤(**flag someone down**) signal to a driver to stop. ➤(**flag someone off**) wave a flag at someone as a starting signal. **3** provide or decorate with a flag or flags.
– PHRASES **fly the flag** (of a ship) be registered in a particular country and sail under its flag. ➤(also **show** or **carry** or **wave the flag**) represent one's country or demonstrate one's affiliation with a party or organization. **put the flags** (or **flag**) **out** celebrate. **wrap oneself in the flag** chiefly N. Amer. make an excessive show of one's patriotism.
– DERIVATIVES **flagger** n.
– ORIGIN C16: perh. from obs. *flag* 'drooping', of unknown ultimate origin.

**flag**[2] ● n. a flat rectangular or square stone slab, used for paving.
– DERIVATIVES **flagged** adj.
– ORIGIN ME: prob. of Scand. origin and rel. to Icelandic *flag* 'spot from which a sod has been cut' and ON *flaga* 'slab of stone'.

**flag**[3] ● n. a waterside plant with long sword-shaped leaves. [*Iris pseudacorus* (**yellow flag**) and other species.]
– ORIGIN ME: of unknown ultimate origin.

**flag**[4] ● v. (**flagged**, **flagging**) become tired or less enthusiastic.
– ORIGIN C16: rel. to obs. *flag* 'hanging down'.

**flag boat** ● n. a boat serving as a mark in sailing matches.

**flag captain** ● n. the captain of a flagship.

**Flag Day** ● n. (in the US) 14 June, the anniversary of the adoption of the Stars and Stripes in 1777.

**flag day** ● n. Brit. a day on which money is collected in the street for a charity and contributors are given flags to wear.

**flagellant** /'fladʒ(ə)l(ə)nt, flə'dʒɛl(ə)nt/ ● n. a person who subjects themselves to flagellation.

**flagellate**[1] /'fladʒ(ə)leɪt/ ● v. flog, either as a religious discipline or for sexual gratification.
– DERIVATIVES **flagellation** n. **flagellator** n. **flagellatory** /-lət(ə)ri/ adj.
– ORIGIN C17 (earlier (C16) as *flagellant*): from L. *flagellat-*, *flagellare* 'whip'.

**flagellate**[2] /'fladʒ(ə)lət, -eɪt/ Zoology ● n. any of a large group of protozoans that have one or more flagella used for swimming. ● adj. bearing one or more flagella.
– ORIGIN C19: from **FLAGELLUM** + **-ATE**[2].

**flagellum** /flə'dʒɛləm/ ● n. (pl. **flagella**) Biology a slender thread-like structure, especially a microscopic whip-like appendage which enables many protozoans, bacteria, spermatozoa, etc. to swim.
– DERIVATIVES **flagellar** adj.
– ORIGIN C19 (denoting a whip or scourge): from L., dimin. of *flagrum* 'scourge'.

**flageolet**[1] /ˌfladʒə'lɛt, 'fladʒəlɪt, 'fla(d)ʒəleɪ/ (also **French flageolet**) ● n. **1** a very small flute-like instrument resembling a recorder but with four finger holes on top and two thumb holes below. **2** a tin whistle.
– ORIGIN C17: from Fr., dimin. of OFr. *flageol*, from Provençal *flaujol*, of unknown origin.

**flageolet**[2] /'fla(d)ʒəleɪ, ˌfladʒə'lɛt/ ● n. a French kidney bean of a small variety used in cooking.
– ORIGIN C19: from Fr., based on L. *phaseolus* 'bean'.

**flagitious** /flə'dʒɪʃəs/ ● adj. extremely and criminally wicked.
– DERIVATIVES **flagitiously** adv. **flagitiousness** n.
– ORIGIN ME: from L. *flagitiosus*, from *flagitium* 'importunity, shameful crime', from *flagitare* 'demand earnestly'.

**flag lieutenant** ● n. a lieutenant acting as an admiral's aide-de-camp.

**flagman** ● n. (pl. **-men**) a person who gives signals with a flag.

**flag of convenience** ● n. a flag of a country under which a ship is registered in order to avoid financial charges or restrictive regulations in the owner's country.

**flag officer** ● n. an admiral, vice admiral, or rear admiral, or the commodore of a yacht club.

**flag of truce** ● n. a white flag indicating a desire for a truce.

**flagon** /ˈflag(ə)n/ ● n. a large container for serving or consuming drinks. ➤a container used to hold the wine for the Eucharist. ➤a large bottle in which wine or cider is sold, typically holding 1.13 litres (about 2 pints).
– ORIGIN ME: from OFr. *flacon*, based on late L. *flasco*, *flascon-*, of unknown origin.

**flagpole** ● n. a pole used for flying a flag.

**flag rank** ● n. the rank attained by flag officers.

**flagrant** /ˈfleɪgr(ə)nt/ ● adj. conspicuous; blatant.
– DERIVATIVES **flagrancy** n. **flagrantly** adv.
– ORIGIN C15 (in the sense 'blazing, resplendent'): from Fr., or from L. *flagrant-*, *flagrare* 'blaze'.

**flagship** ● n. **1** the ship in a fleet which carries the commanding admiral. **2** the best or most important thing owned or produced by an organization.

**flagstaff** /ˈflagstɑːf/ ● n. a flagpole.

**flagstone** ● n. another term for FLAG[2].
– DERIVATIVES **flagstoned** adj.

**flail** /fleɪl/ ● n. a threshing tool consisting of a wooden staff with a short heavy stick swinging from it. ➤a similar device used as a weapon or for flogging. ➤a machine having a similar action. ● v. **1** swing or cause to swing wildly. **2** (**flail around/about**) flounder; struggle. **3** beat; flog.
– ORIGIN OE, of W. Gmc origin, based on L. *flagellum* (see FLAGELLUM).

**flair** ● n. **1** a natural ability or talent. **2** stylishness.
– ORIGIN C19: from Fr., from *flairer* 'to smell', based on L. *fragrare* 'smell sweet'.

**flak** (also **flack**) ● n. **1** anti-aircraft fire. **2** strong criticism.
– ORIGIN 1930s: from Ger., abbrev. of *Fliegerabwehrkanone*, lit. 'aviator-defence gun'.

**flake**[1] ● n. **1** a small, flat, very thin piece of something. **2** a snowflake. **3** Archaeology a piece of hard stone chipped off for use as a tool. **4** thin pieces of crushed dried food or bait for fish. **5** N. Amer. informal a crazy or eccentric person. ● v. **1** come away from a surface in flakes. **2** split or cause to split into flakes.
– DERIVATIVES **flaked** adj. **flakily** adv. **flakiness** n. **flaky** adj. (**-ier**, **-iest**).
– ORIGIN ME: the immediate source is unknown, the senses perh. deriving from different words; prob. of Gmc origin and rel. to FLAG[2] and FLAW[1].

**flake**[2] ● n. a rack for storing or drying food such as fish.
– ORIGIN ME (denoting a wicker hurdle): perh. of Scand. origin.

**flake**[3] ● v. (**flake out**) informal fall asleep; drop from exhaustion.
– ORIGIN C15 (in the senses 'become languid' and (of a garment) 'fall in folds'): var. of obs. *flack* and the verb FLAG[4].

**flake**[4] (also **fake**) Nautical ● n. a single turn of a coiled rope or hawser. ● v. lay (a rope) in loose coils in order to prevent it tangling. ➤lay (a sail) down in folds either side of the boom.
– ORIGIN C17: of unknown origin.

**flake white** ● n. a pure white pigment made from flakes of white lead.

**flak jacket** ● n. a sleeveless jacket made of heavy fabric reinforced with metal, worn as protection against bullets and shrapnel.

**flaky pastry** ● n. pastry consisting of a number of thin layers.

**flam** ● n. Music one of the basic patterns of drumming, consisting of a stroke preceded by a grace note.
– ORIGIN C18: prob. imitative.

**flambé** /ˈflɒmbeɪ/ ● adj. **1** [postpos.] (of food) covered with spirits and set alight briefly: *steak flambé*. **2** denoting or characterized by a lustrous red copper-based porcelain glaze with purple streaks. ● v. (**flambés**, **flambéed**, **flambéing**) cover (food) with spirits and set it alight briefly.
– ORIGIN C19: Fr., lit. 'singed', past part. of *flamber*, from *flambe* 'a flame'.

**flambeau** /ˈflambəʊ/ ● n. (pl. **flambeaus** or **flambeaux** /-əʊz/) **1** a flaming torch. **2** a branched candlestick.
– ORIGIN C17: from Fr., from *flambe* 'a flame'.

**flamboyant** /flamˈbɔɪənt/ ● adj. **1** conspicuously and confidently exuberant. **2** brightly coloured and showy. **3** Architecture of or denoting a style of French Gothic architecture marked by wavy flamelike tracery and ornate decoration. ● n. a Madagascan tree with bright red flowers, planted as a street tree in the tropics. [*Delonix regia*.]
– DERIVATIVES **flamboyance** n. **flamboyancy** n. **flamboyantly** adv.
– ORIGIN C19: from Fr., lit. 'flaming, blazing', pres. part. of *flamboyer*, from *flambe* 'a flame'.

**flame** ● n. **1** a hot glowing body of ignited gas that is generated by something on fire. **2** a thing compared to a flame's ability to burn fiercely or be extinguished: *the flame of hope*. **3** a brilliant orange-red colour. **4** Computing, informal a vitriolic or abusive message distributed electronically through a computer network. ● v. **1** give off flames. ➤apply a flame to; set alight. **2** (of an intense emotion) appear suddenly and fiercely. **3** (of a person's face) become red with embarrassment or anger. **4** Computing, informal send a flame. **5** (**flame out**) (of a jet engine) lose power through the extinction of the flame in the combustion chamber. **6** informal, chiefly N. Amer. fail conspicuously.
– PHRASES **old flame** informal a former lover.
– DERIVATIVES **flameless** adj. **flamer** n. (Computing, informal) **flamy** adj.
– ORIGIN ME: from OFr. *flame* (n.), *flamer* (v.), from L. *flamma* 'a flame'.

**flame gun** ● n. a device for producing a jet of flame.

**flamen** /ˈfleɪmɛn, ˈflɑː-/ ● n. (pl. **flamens** or **flamines**) Roman History a priest serving a particular deity.
– ORIGIN from L.

**flamenco** /fləˈmɛŋkəʊ/ ● n. a spirited style of Spanish guitar music accompanied by singing and dancing.
– ORIGIN C19: Sp., 'like a gypsy', lit. 'Fleming'.

**flameout** ● n. **1** an instance of the flame in the combustion chamber of a jet engine being extinguished, with a resultant loss of power. **2** informal, chiefly N. Amer. a conspicuous failure.

**flameproof** ● adj. **1** (of fabric) treated so as to be non-flammable. **2** (of cookware) able to be used either in an oven or on a hob. ● v. make flameproof.

**flame-thrower** ● n. a weapon that sprays out burning fuel.

**flame tree** ● n. a tree with brilliant red flowers. [*Brachychiton acerifolius* (Australia) and other species.]

**flaming** ● adj. **1** emitting flames. **2** very hot: *flaming June*. **3** of a flame colour. **4** (especially of an argument) passionate. **5** informal expressing annoyance: *that flaming dog*.

**flamingo** /fləˈmɪŋgəʊ/ ● n. (pl. **-os** or **-oes**) a tall wading bird with mainly pink or scarlet plumage, long legs and neck, and a crooked bill. [Family Phoenicopteridae: several species.]
– ORIGIN C16: from Sp. *flamengo*, earlier form of *flamenco* (see FLAMENCO); assoc., because of its colour, with L. *flamma* 'a flame'.

**flammable** /ˈflaməb(ə)l/ ● adj. easily set on fire.
– DERIVATIVES **flammability** n.
– ORIGIN C19: from L. *flammare*, from *flamma* 'a flame'.

**USAGE** flammable

The words **flammable** and **inflammable** have the same meaning: see INFLAMMABLE.

**flan** ● n. **1** a baked dish consisting of an open-topped pastry case with a savoury or sweet filling. **2** a disc of metal such as one from which a coin is made.
– ORIGIN C19: from Fr., from OFr. *flaon*, from med. L. *flado*,

*fladon-*, of W. Gmc origin.

**flâneur** /flɑˈnəː, French flanœʀ/ ● n. (pl. **flâneurs** pronunc. same) a saunterer.
– ORIGIN Fr., from *flâner* 'saunter, lounge'.

**flange** /flan(d)ʒ/ ● n. a projecting rim or piece.
– DERIVATIVES **flanged** adj. **flangeless** adj.
– ORIGIN C17: perh. based on OFr. *flanchir* 'to bend'.

**flanger** /ˈflan(d)ʒə/ ● n. an electronic device which alters a sound signal by introducing a cyclically varying phase shift into one of two identical copies of the signal and recombining them, used especially in popular music.

**flanging** /ˈflandʒɪŋ/ ● n. **1** the provision of a flange on an object. **2** the alteration of sound using a flanger.

**flank** ● n. **1** the side of a person's or animal's body between the ribs and the hip. **2** the side of something such as a building or mountain, or a gaming area. **3** the left or right side of a body of people. **4** (also **flank forward**) Rugby another term for WING (in sense 8). ● v. be situated on each or on one side of.
– PHRASES **in flank** Military at the side.
– ORIGIN OE, from OFr. *flanc*, of Gmc origin.

**flanker** ● n. **1** Rugby a wing forward. **2** American Football an offensive back who is positioned to the outside of an end. **3** Military a fortification to the side of a force or position.

**flannel** ● n. **1** a kind of soft-woven woollen or cotton fabric that is slightly milled and raised. **2** (**flannels**) men's trousers made of woollen flannel. **3** Brit. a small piece of towelling used for washing oneself. **4** Brit. informal bland, fluent talk used to gloss over a difficult subject. ● v. (**flannelled**, **flannelling**; US also **flanneled**, **flanneling**) informal, chiefly Brit. use such talk.
– ORIGIN ME: prob. from Welsh *gwlanen* 'woollen article', from *gwlân* 'wool'.

**flannelette** /ˌflanəˈlɛt/ ● n. a napped cotton fabric resembling flannel.

**flannelled** (US also **flanneled**) ● adj. wearing flannel trousers.

**flap** ● v. (**flapped**, **flapping**) **1** move or be moved up and down or from side to side. **2** (**flap at**) strike at loosely. **3** informal be agitated. ● n. **1** a piece of something that is attached on one side only. **2** a hinged or sliding section of an aircraft wing used to control lift. **3** a single flapping movement. **4** informal a state of agitation. **5** a large broad mushroom.
– DERIVATIVES **flappy** adj.
– ORIGIN ME: prob. imitative.

**flapdoodle** ● n. informal, chiefly N. Amer. **1** nonsense. **2** a fool.
– ORIGIN C19: an arbitrary formation.

**flapjack** ● n. **1** Brit. a soft, thick biscuit made from oats and butter. **2** N. Amer. a pancake.
– ORIGIN C17 (in the sense 'pancake'): from FLAP (in the dial. sense 'toss a pancake') + JACK[1].

**flapper** ● n. informal (in the 1920s) a young woman who wore fashionable clothing and flouted convention.

**flap valve** (also **flapper valve**) ● n. a valve opened and closed by a plate hinged at one side.

**flare** ● n. **1** a sudden brief burst of flame or light. **2** a device producing a very bright flame as a signal or marker. **3** a sudden burst of intense emotion. **4** Photography extraneous illumination on film caused by internal reflection in the camera. **5** a gradual widening towards the hem of a garment. ➤(**flares**) trousers of which the legs widen from the knees down. **6** an upward and outward curve of a ship's bows. ● v. **1** burn, shine, or be revealed with a sudden intensity. **2** (**flare up**) suddenly become intense, angry, or violent. **3** gradually become wider at one end. **4** (with reference to the nostrils) dilate or cause to dilate.
– DERIVATIVES **flared** adj.
– ORIGIN C16 (in the sense 'spread out (one's hair)'): of unknown origin.

**flarepath** ● n. an area illuminated to enable an aircraft to land or take off.

**flare star** ● n. Astronomy a dwarf star which displays spasmodic outbursts of radiation, believed to be due to extremely intense flares.

**flash**[1] ● v. **1** shine or cause to shine in a bright but brief, sudden, or intermittent way. **2** move, pass, or send very quickly in a particular direction. **3** display or be displayed briefly or repeatedly. ➤informal display conspicuously so as to impress: *they flash their money about.* ➤ informal (of a man) show one's genitals in public. **4** (**flash over**) make an electric circuit by sparking across a gap. ● n. **1** a sudden brief burst of bright light. **2** a camera attachment that produces a flash of light, for taking photographs in poor light. **3** a sudden or brief manifestation or occurrence. **4** a bright patch of colour. ➤Brit. a coloured patch of cloth worn on a uniform as a distinguishing emblem. **5** excess plastic or metal forced between facing surfaces as two halves of a mould close up, forming a thin projection on the finished object. **6** a rush of water, especially down a weir to take a boat over shallows. ● adj. **1** informal ostentatiously stylish or expensive. **2** archaic of or relating to the language of criminals or prostitutes.
– PHRASES **flash in the pan** a sudden but brief success. [with allusion to the priming of a firearm, the flash arising from an explosion of gunpowder within the lock.]
– DERIVATIVES **flasher** n.
– ORIGIN ME (in the sense 'splash water about'): prob. imitative; cf. FLUSH[1] and SPLASH.

**flash**[2] ● n. Brit. a water-filled hollow formed by subsidence.
– ORIGIN ME (in the sense 'a marshy place'): from OFr. *flache*, var. of Picard and Norman dial. *flaque*, from MDu. *vlacke*.

**flashback** ● n. **1** a scene in a film, novel, etc. set in a time earlier than the main story. **2** a sudden vivid memory of an event in the past. **3** a flame moving rapidly back through a combustible vapour.

**flashboard** ● n. a board used for sending more water from a mill dam into a mill race.

**flashbulb** ● n. a bulb for a flashgun.

**flash burn** ● n. a burn caused by brief exposure to intense radiant heat.

**flashcard** ● n. a card containing a clear display of a word or words, used in teaching reading.

**flash flood** ● n. a sudden case of local flooding resulting from extreme rainfall.

**flash-freeze** ● v. freeze (food or other material) very rapidly so as to prevent the formation of ice crystals.
– DERIVATIVES **flash-freezer** n.

**flashgun** ● n. a device which gives a brief flash of intense light, used for taking photographs in poor light.

**flashing** ● n. a strip of metal used to seal the junction of a roof with another surface.

**flash lamp** ● n. a flashgun.

**flashlight** ● n. **1** an electric torch with a strong beam. **2** a flashing light used for signals. **3** a flashgun.

**flash memory** ● n. Computing memory that retains data in the absence of a power supply.

**flashover** ● n. **1** a high-voltage electric short circuit made through the air between exposed conductors. **2** an instance of a fire spreading very rapidly through the air because of intense heat.

**flashpoint** ● n. **1** a point or place at which anger or violence flares up. **2** Chemistry the temperature at which a particular organic compound gives off sufficient vapour to ignite in air.

**flash suit** ● n. a set of heatproof protective clothing.

**flash tube** ● n. a gas-discharge tube used to provide a flash when a current is suddenly passed through it.

**flashy** ● adj. (**-ier**, **-iest**) ostentatiously stylish.
– DERIVATIVES **flashily** adv. **flashiness** n.

**flask** ● n. **1** a narrow-necked conical or spherical bottle. **2** Brit. a vacuum flask. **3** a hip flask. **4** (also **nuclear flask**) a lead-lined container for radioactive nuclear waste.
– ORIGIN ME (in the sense 'cask'): from med. L. *flasca*.

**flat**[1] ● adj. (**flatter**, **flattest**) **1** having a level surface; without raised areas or indentations. ➤not sloping. ➤having a broad level surface but little height or depth: *a flat box.* **2** (of shoes) without high heels. **3** dull; lifeless: *a flat voice.* ➤showing little or no activity: *sales were flat.* **4** (of a sparkling drink) having lost its effervescence.

**5** Brit. (of a battery) having exhausted its charge. **6** (of something kept inflated) having lost some or all of its air. **7** (of a photograph) lacking contrast. **8** (of a fee, charge, or price) unvarying; fixed. **9** (of a negative statement) definite and firm: *a flat denial.* **10** (of musical sound) below true or normal pitch. ➤ [postpos.] (of a key) having a flat or flats in the signature. ➤ [postpos.] (of a note) a semitone lower than a specified note. ● **adv. 1** in or to a horizontal position. ➤ lying in close juxtaposition to a surface. ➤ so as to become level and even. **2** informal completely; absolutely: *I'm turning you down flat.* **3** emphasizing the speed of an action or task: *in ten minutes flat.* **4** below the true or normal pitch of musical sound. ● **n. 1** the flat part of something. **2** an upright section of stage scenery. **3** informal a flat tyre. **4** N. Amer. a shallow container in which seedlings are grown. **5** (**flats**) chiefly N. Amer. shoes with a very low heel or no heel. **6** (**flats**) an area of low level ground, especially near water. **7** (**the Flat**) Brit. flat racing. **8** a musical note lowered a semitone below natural pitch. ➤ the sign (♭) indicating this. ● **v.** (**flatted**, **flatting**) **1** [usu. as adj. **flatted**] N. Amer. Music lower (a note) by a semitone. **2** archaic flatten.

– PHRASES **fall flat** fail to produce the intended effect. **flat out 1** as fast or as hard as possible. **2** informal, chiefly N. Amer. unequivocally. **3** lying down in a state of exhaustion. **on the flat 1** on level ground as opposed to uphill. **2** (**on the Flat**) (of a horse race) on a course without jumps.

– DERIVATIVES **flatly** adv. **flatness** n. **flattish** adj.

– ORIGIN ME: from ON *flatr.*

**flat²** ● **n.** chiefly Brit. a set of rooms comprising an individual place of residence within a larger building. ● **v.** (**flatted**, **flatting**) Austral./NZ live in or share a flat.

– PHRASES **go flatting** Austral./NZ leave one's family home to live in a flat.

– DERIVATIVES **flatlet** n.

– ORIGIN C19: alt. of obs. *flet* 'floor, dwelling', of Gmc origin and rel. to FLAT¹.

**flatbed** ● **n. 1** a long flat area or structure. **2** [as modifier] denoting a vehicle with a flat load-carrying area. **3** [as modifier] denoting a letterpress printing machine in which the forme is carried on a horizontal surface. **4** Computing a scanner, plotter, or other device which keeps paper flat during use.

**flatboat** ● **n.** a boat with a flat bottom for use in shallow water.

**flatbread** ● **n.** N. Amer. flat, thin, often unleavened bread.

**flatcar** ● **n.** chiefly N. Amer. a railway freight wagon without a roof or sides.

**flat-fell** ● **v.** see FELL² (sense 2).

**flat file** ● **n.** Computing a file having no internal hierarchy.

**flatfish** ● **n.** (pl. same or **-fishes**) a flounder, plaice, dab, sole, or other marine fish that swims on its side with both eyes on the upper side of its flattened body. [Order Pleuronectiformes.]

**flatfoot** ● **n.** (pl. **flatfoots** or **flatfeet**) informal, dated a police officer.

**flat foot** ● **n.** a foot with an arch that is lower than usual.

**flat-footed** ● **adj. 1** having flat feet. **2** informal clumsy.

– DERIVATIVES **flat-footedly** adv. **flat-footedness** n.

**flat-four** ● **adj.** (of an engine) having four horizontal cylinders, two on each side of the crankshaft. ● **n.** a flat-four engine.

**flathead** ● **n. 1** an edible tropical marine fish that has a pointed flattened head with the eyes on the top. [Family Platycephalidae: several species.] **2** (**Flathead**) a member of certain North American Indian peoples who practised or were believed to practise head-flattening, including the Chinook. **3** [as modifier] US denoting an engine having the valves and spark plugs in the cylinder block rather than the cylinder head. **4** [as modifier] N. Amer. denoting a countersunk screw.

**flat iron** ● **n.** historical an iron heated on a hotplate or fire.

**flatline** ● **v.** informal (of a person) die.

– DERIVATIVES **flatliner** n.

– ORIGIN 1980s: with ref. to the continuous straight line displayed on a heart monitor.

**flatmate** ● **n.** Brit. a person with whom one shares a flat.

**flat-pack** ● **n. 1** [as modifier] denoting furniture or other equipment that is sold in pieces and assembled by the buyer. **2** Electronics a package for an integrated circuit consisting of a rectangular sealed unit with a number of horizontal metal pins protruding from its sides.

– DERIVATIVES **flat-packed** adj.

**flat race** ● **n.** a horse race over a course with no jumps, as opposed to a steeplechase or hurdles.

– DERIVATIVES **flat racing** n.

**flatten** ● **v. 1** make or become flat or flatter. **2** press (oneself) against a surface. **3** raze to the ground. **4** informal strike (someone) so as to make them fall down. **5** Music lower (a note) in pitch by a semitone.

– DERIVATIVES **flattened** adj. **flattener** n.

**flatter** ● **v. 1** lavish compliments on, especially in order to further one's own interests. **2** (usu. **be flattered**) cause to feel honoured and pleased. **3** (**flatter oneself**) please, congratulate, or delude oneself. **4** (of clothing or a colour) enhance; make attractive. **5** give an unrealistically favourable impression of. **6** archaic please (the ear or eye).

– DERIVATIVES **flatterer** n. **flattering** adj. **flatteringly** adv. **flattery** n.

– ORIGIN ME (as *flattery*): from OFr. *flaterie*, from *flater* 'stroke, flatter', prob. of Gmc origin and rel. to FLAT¹.

**flattie** (also **flatty**) ● **n.** (pl. **-ies**) informal **1** a flat-heeled shoe. **2** a flatfish. **3** a flatboat. **4** informal, dated a police officer. [C19: abbrev. of FLATFOOT.]

**flat-top** ● **n. 1** US informal an aircraft carrier. **2** a man's hairstyle in which the hair is cropped short so that it bristles up into a flat surface. **3** an acoustic guitar that has a flat rather than a curved front.

**flatulent** /ˈflatjʊl(ə)nt/ ● **adj.** suffering from or marked by an accumulation of gas in the alimentary canal.

– DERIVATIVES **flatulence** n. **flatulency** n. **flatulently** adv.

– ORIGIN C16: via Fr. from mod. L. *flatulentus*, from L. *flatus* (see FLATUS).

**flatus** /ˈfleɪtəs/ ● **n.** formal gas in or from the stomach or intestines.

– ORIGIN C17: from L., lit. 'blowing', from *flare* 'to blow'.

**flatware** ● **n. 1** items of crockery such as plates and saucers. **2** N. Amer. domestic cutlery.

**flatworm** ● **n.** a worm of a phylum which includes the planarians, parasitic flukes, and tapeworms, distinguished by a simple flattened body lacking blood vessels. [Phylum Platyhelminthes.]

**flat-woven** ● **adj.** (of a carpet or rug) woven so as not to form a projecting pile.

– DERIVATIVES **flat-weave** n.

**flaunching** /ˈflɔːntʃɪŋ/ ● **n.** the sloping fillet of mortar embedding the base of a chimney pot.

– ORIGIN C18 (as *flaunch*, denoting a flange): perh. based on OFr. *flanchir* 'to bend'.

**flaunt** ● **v.** display ostentatiously.

– DERIVATIVES **flaunter** n. **flaunty** adj.

– ORIGIN C16: of unknown origin.

**USAGE** flaunt

It is a common error to use **flaunt** when **flout** is intended. **Flaunt** means 'display ostentatiously', while **flout** means 'openly disregard (a rule or convention)'. Around 20 per cent of the uses of **flaunt** in the British National Corpus are incorrect in this respect.

**flautist** /ˈflɔːtɪst/ ● **n.** a flute player.

– ORIGIN C19 (in Brit. use superseding C17 *flutist*): from Ital. *flautista*, from *flauto* 'flute'.

**flavescent** /fləˈvɛs(ə)nt/ ● **adj.** yellowish or turning yellow.

– ORIGIN C19: from L. *flavescent-*, *flavescere* 'turn yellow', from *flavus* 'yellow'.

**Flavian** /ˈfleɪvɪən/ ● **adj.** of or relating to a dynasty (AD 69–96) of Roman emperors. ● **n.** a member of this dynasty.

– ORIGIN from L. *Flavianus*, from *Flavius*, a given name used by this dynasty.

**flavin** /ˈfleɪvɪn/ ● **n.** Biochemistry any of a group of naturally occurring pigments including riboflavin, having a tricyclic aromatic molecular structure.

– ORIGIN C19: from L. *flavus* 'yellow' + -IN¹.

**flavone** /ˈfleɪvəʊn/ ● **n.** Chemistry a colourless crystalline organic compound which is the basis of a number of white or yellow plant pigments.
– DERIVATIVES **flavonoid** n.
– ORIGIN C19: from L. *flavus* 'yellow' + **-ONE**.

**flavoprotein** /ˌfleɪvə(ʊ)ˈprəʊtiːn/ ● **n.** Biochemistry any of a class of conjugated proteins that contain flavins and are involved in oxidation reactions in cells.
– ORIGIN 1930s: blend of **FLAVIN** and **PROTEIN**.

**flavour** (US **flavor**) ● **n. 1** the distinctive taste of a food or drink. **2** a quality reminiscent of something specified: *a European flavour.* **3** a sample of the distinctive quality of something: *a flavour of the content of the conversation.* **4** chiefly N. Amer. a flavouring. **5** Physics a quantized property of quarks with values designated up, down, charmed, strange, top, and bottom. ● **v.** give flavour to.
– PHRASES **flavour of the month** a person or thing that is currently popular.
– DERIVATIVES **flavoured** adj. **flavourful** adj. **flavourless** adj. **flavoursome** adj.
– ORIGIN ME (in the sense 'fragrance, aroma'): from OFr. *flaor*, perh. based on a blend of L. *flatus* 'blowing' and *foetor* 'stench'; the *-v-* appears to have been introduced in ME by assoc. with **SAVOUR**.

**flavouring** (US **flavoring**) ● **n.** a substance used to enhance the flavour of a food or drink.

**flaw**[1] ● **n. 1** a blemish; an imperfection. **2** a fundamental weakness. ● **v.** (usu. **be flawed**) mar or weaken.
– DERIVATIVES **flawed** adj. **flawless** adj. **flawlessly** adv. **flawlessness** n.
– ORIGIN ME (orig. in sense 'a flake of snow', later, 'a fragment or splinter'): perh. from ON *flaga* 'slab'.

**flaw**[2] ● **n.** poetic/literary a squall; a short storm.
– ORIGIN C16: prob. from MDu. *vlāghe*, Mid. Low Ger. *vlāge*.

**flax** ● **n. 1** a blue-flowered herbaceous plant that is cultivated for its seed (linseed) and for textile fibre made from its stalks. [*Linum usitatissimum*.] ➤ textile fibre obtained from this plant. **2** (also **New Zealand flax**) another term for **FLAX-LILY**.
– ORIGIN OE *flæx*, of W. Gmc origin.

**flaxen** ● **adj. 1** of flax. **2** poetic/literary (especially of hair) of the pale yellow colour of dressed flax.

**flax-lily** ● **n.** a New Zealand plant that yields fibre and is also grown as an ornamental. [*Phormium tenax*.]

**flaxseed** ● **n.** another term for **LINSEED**.

**flay** ● **v. 1** strip the skin from (a body or carcass). **2** whip or beat harshly. **3** criticize harshly.
– DERIVATIVES **flayer** n.
– ORIGIN OE *flēan*, of Gmc origin.

**F-layer** ● **n.** the highest and most strongly ionized region of the ionosphere.
– ORIGIN 1920s: arbitrary use of *F* + **LAYER**.

**flea** ● **n.** a small wingless jumping insect which feeds on the blood of mammals and birds. [*Pulex irritans* (**human flea**) and other species, order Siphonaptera.]
– PHRASES **(as) fit as a flea** in very good health. **a flea in one's ear** a sharp reproof.
– ORIGIN OE *flēa*, *flēah*, of Gmc origin.

**fleabag** ● **n.** N. Amer. informal a seedy hotel or other establishment.

**fleabane** ● **n.** a plant of the daisy family, reputed to drive away fleas. [*Pulicaria dysenterica* and other species.]

**flea beetle** ● **n.** a small jumping leaf beetle that can be a pest of plants such as crucifers. [*Phyllotreta* and other genera.]

**flea-bitten** ● **adj. 1** bitten by or infested with fleas. **2** dilapidated or disreputable.

**flea collar** ● **n.** a collar for a cat or dog that is impregnated with insecticide to kill or deter fleas.

**fleadh** /flɑː/ ● **n.** a festival of Irish or Celtic music, dancing, and culture.
– ORIGIN from Ir. *fleadh ceoil* 'music festival'.

**flea market** ● **n.** a street market selling second-hand goods.

**fleapit** ● **n.** chiefly Brit. a dingy, dirty place, especially a run-down cinema.

**fleawort** ● **n.** a plant related to ragwort, reputed to drive away fleas. [*Senecio integrifolius* and other species.]

**flèche** /fleɪʃ, flɛʃ/ ● **n.** a slender spire.
– ORIGIN C19: Fr., lit. 'arrow'.

**fleck** ● **n. 1** a very small patch of colour or light. **2** a speck. ● **v.** (usu. **be flecked**) mark or dot with flecks.
– ORIGIN ME: perh. from ON *flekkr* (n.), *flekka* (v.), or from Mid. Low Ger., MDu. *vlecke*.

**fled** past and past participle of **FLEE**.

**fledge** /flɛdʒ/ ● **v.** (with reference to a young bird) develop or allow to develop wing feathers that are large enough for flight.
– DERIVATIVES **fledged** adj.
– ORIGIN C16: from the obs. adj. *fledge* 'ready to fly', from OE, of Gmc origin; rel. to **FLY**[1].

**fledgling** (also **fledgeling**) ● **n. 1** a young bird that has just fledged. **2** [as modifier] denoting an inexperienced person or emergent system: *fledgling democracies.*
– ORIGIN C19: from the obs. adj. *fledge* (see **FLEDGE**), on the pattern of *nestling*.

**flee** ● **v.** (**flees**, **fleeing**; past and past part. **fled**) run away.
– ORIGIN OE *flēon*, of Gmc origin.

**fleece** ● **n. 1** the wool coat of a sheep. **2** a soft, warm fabric with a texture similar to sheep's wool, or a garment made from this. ● **v.** informal obtain an unfair amount of money from.
– DERIVATIVES **fleeced** adj. **fleecy** adj. **fleeciness** n.
– ORIGIN OE *flēos*, *flēs*, of W. Gmc origin.

**fleer** /flɪə/ ● **v.** poetic/literary laugh impudently or jeeringly. ● **n.** archaic an impudent or jeering look or speech.
– ORIGIN ME: prob. of Scand. origin and rel. to Norw. and Swed. dial. *flira* 'to grin'.

**fleet**[1] ● **n. 1** a group of ships sailing together. **2** (**the fleet**) a country's navy: *the US fleet.* **3** a number of vehicles or aircraft operating together.
– ORIGIN OE *flēot* 'ship, shipping', from *flēotan* (see **FLEET**[5]).

**fleet**[2] ● **adj.** fast and nimble: *fleet of foot.*
– DERIVATIVES **fleetly** adv. **fleetness** n.
– ORIGIN C16: prob. from ON *fljótr*, of Gmc origin and rel. to **FLEET**[5].

**fleet**[3] ● **n.** dialect a marshland creek, channel, or ditch.
– ORIGIN OE *flēot*, of Gmc origin; rel. to **FLEET**[5].

**fleet**[4] dialect ● **adj.** (of water) shallow. ● **adv.** at or to a small depth.
– ORIGIN C17: perh. based on an OE cognate of Du. *vloot* 'shallow' and rel. to **FLEET**[5].

**fleet**[5] ● **v.** poetic/literary move or pass quickly.
– ORIGIN OE *flēotan* 'float, swim', of Gmc origin; rel. to **FLIT** and **FLOAT**.

**Fleet Admiral** ● **n.** the highest rank of admiral in the US navy.

**fleeting** ● **adj.** lasting for a very short time.
– DERIVATIVES **fleetingly** adv.

**Fleming** /ˈflɛmɪŋ/ ● **n. 1** a native of Flanders. **2** a member of the Flemish-speaking people inhabiting northern and western Belgium. Compare with **WALLOON**.
– ORIGIN OE *Flæmingi*, from ON, reinforced by MDu. *Vlāming*, rel. to *Vlaanderen* 'Flanders'.

**Flemish** /ˈflɛmɪʃ/ ● **n. 1** (**the Flemish**) the people of Flanders, a region divided between Belgium, France, and the Netherlands. **2** the Dutch language as spoken in Flanders. ● **adj.** relating to the Flemish people or language.
– ORIGIN ME: from MDu. *Vlāmisch*, rel. to *Vlaanderen* 'Flanders'.

**Flemish bond** ● **n.** Building a pattern of bricks in a wall in which each course consists of alternate headers and stretchers.

**flense** /flɛns/ (also **flench** /flɛn(t)ʃ/, **flinch**) ● **v.** slice the skin or fat from (a carcass, especially that of a whale).
– DERIVATIVES **flenser** n.
– ORIGIN C19: from Dan. *flensa*.

**flesh** ● **n. 1** the soft substance in the body consisting of muscle tissue and fat. **2** the edible pulpy part of a fruit or vegetable. **3** the surface of the human body (with reference to its appearance or sensory properties). **4** (**the flesh**) the physicality of the human body as contrasted

with the mind or the soul. ● v. **1** (**flesh out**) make more substantial. **2** give (a hound or hawk) a piece of flesh in order to stimulate it to hunt. **3** remove the flesh from (a hide). **4** poetic/literary initiate in bloodshed or warfare.
– PHRASES **all flesh** all human and animal life. **in the flesh** in person or (of a thing) in its actual state. **make someone's flesh creep** (or **crawl**) cause someone to feel fear, horror, or disgust. **put flesh on** (**the bones of**) **something** flesh something out.
– DERIVATIVES **-fleshed** adj. **fleshless** adj.
– ORIGIN OE *flǣsc*, of Gmc origin.

**flesher** ● n. **1** chiefly Scottish a butcher. **2** N. Amer. a knife for fleshing hides.

**flesh fly** ● n. a fly that breeds in carrion. [Family Sarcophagidae: many species.]

**fleshly** ● adj. (**-ier**, **-iest**) **1** of or relating to the body; sensual. **2** having an actual physical presence.
– ORIGIN OE *flǣsclic* (see **FLESH**, **-LY**[1]).

**fleshpots** ● pl. n. places providing a hedonistic experience.
– ORIGIN C16: with biblical allusion to the *fleshpots of Egypt* (Exod. 16:3).

**flesh wound** ● n. a wound that breaks the skin but does not damage bones or vital organs.

**fleshy** ● adj. (**-ier**, **-iest**) **1** having a substantial amount of flesh; plump. **2** (of plant or fruit tissue) soft and thick. **3** resembling flesh.
– DERIVATIVES **fleshiness** n.

**fletch** /flɛtʃ/ ● v. provide (an arrow) with feathers.
– ORIGIN C17: alt. of **FLEDGE**, prob. influenced by *fletcher*.

**fletcher** ● n. chiefly historical a person who makes and sells arrows.
– ORIGIN ME: from OFr. *flechier*, from *fleche* 'arrow'.

**fletching** ● n. the feathers of an arrow.

**fleur-de-lis** /ˌfləːdəˈliː/ (also **fleur-de-lys**) ● n. (pl. **fleurs-de-lis** pronunc. same) **1** Art & Heraldry a stylized lily composed of three petals bound together near their bases. **2** a variety of iris.
– ORIGIN ME: from OFr. *flour de lys* 'flower of the lily'.

**fleuron** /ˈflʊərɒn, ˈfləː-/ ● n. a flower-shaped piece of ornamentation.
– ORIGIN ME: from OFr. *floron*, from *flour* 'flower'.

**fleury** /ˈflʊəri/ ● adj. variant spelling of **FLORY**.

**flew** past of **FLY**[1].

**flews** /fluːz/ ● pl. n. the thick hanging lips of a bloodhound or similar dog.
– ORIGIN C16: of unknown origin.

**flex**[1] ● v. **1** bend (a limb or joint). **2** contract or tense (a muscle). **3** warp or bend and then revert to shape. **4** [usu. as adj. **flexed**] Archaeology place (a corpse) with the legs drawn up under the chin.
– ORIGIN C16: from L. *flex-*, *flectere* 'bend'.

**flex**[2] ● n. chiefly Brit. a flexible insulated cable used for carrying electric current to an appliance.
– ORIGIN C20: abbrev. of **FLEXIBLE**.

**flexible** ● adj. **1** capable of bending easily without breaking. **2** readily adaptable.
– DERIVATIVES **flexibility** n. **flexibly** adv.
– ORIGIN ME: from OFr., or from L. *flexibilis*, from *flectere* 'to bend'.

**flexile** /ˈflɛksʌɪl/ ● adj. archaic pliant and flexible.
– DERIVATIVES **flexility** n.
– ORIGIN C17: from L. *flexilis*, from *flectere* 'to bend'.

**flexion** /ˈflɛkʃ(ə)n/ (also **flection**) ● n. the action of bending or the condition of being bent.
– ORIGIN C17: from L. *flexio(n-)*, from *flectere* 'to bend'.

**flexitime** (N. Amer. also **flextime**) ● n. a system allowing some flexibility in when workers put in their allotted hours.

**flexography** /flɛkˈsɒgrəfi/ ● n. a rotary relief printing method using rubber or plastic plates and fluid inks or dyes, for printing on impervious materials such as plastics, as well as on fabrics and paper.
– DERIVATIVES **flexographic** adj.

**flexor** /ˈflɛksə/ ● n. Anatomy a muscle whose contraction bends a limb or other part of the body.

**flexuous** /ˈflɛksjʊəs/ ● adj. full of bends and curves.
– DERIVATIVES **flexuosity** n. **flexuously** adv.

**flexure** /ˈflɛkʃə/ ● n. chiefly Anatomy & Geology **1** the action of bending or curving, or the condition of being bent or curved. **2** a bent or curved part.
– DERIVATIVES **flexural** adj.
– ORIGIN C16: from L. *flexura*, from *flectere* 'to bend'.

**flexwing** ● n. a flexible fabric wing, as used in hang-gliders.

**flibbertigibbet** /ˌflɪbətɪˈdʒɪbɪt/ ● n. a frivolous and restless person.
– ORIGIN ME: prob. imitative of idle chatter.

**flic** ● n. Computing a data file containing computer animations.
– ORIGIN C20: based on the cinematographic sense of **FLICK**.

**flick** ● n. **1** a sudden smart movement up and down or from side to side. **2** the sudden release of a finger or thumb held bent against another finger. **3** informal a cinema film. ➤(**the flicks**) the cinema. ● v. **1** make or cause to make a sudden sharp movement. **2** propel with a flick of the fingers. **3** (**flick through**) look quickly through (a volume or a collection of papers).
– PHRASES **give someone the flick** informal, chiefly Austral. reject in a casual or offhand way.
– ORIGIN ME: symbolic, *fl-* freq. beginning words denoting sudden movement.

**flicker**[1] ● v. **1** shine or burn unsteadily and fitfully. **2** (of a feeling) be briefly perceptible. **3** make small, quick movements. ● n. an instance of flickering.
– DERIVATIVES **flickering** adj. & n.
– ORIGIN OE *flicorian*, *flycerian* 'to flutter', prob. of Gmc origin.

**flicker**[2] ● n. an American woodpecker that often feeds on ants on the ground. [*Colaptes auratus* (**common** or **northern flicker**) and related species.]
– ORIGIN C19: imitative of its call.

**flick knife** ● n. Brit. a knife with a blade that springs out from the handle when a button is pressed.

**flick roll** ● n. another term for **SNAP ROLL**.

**flier** ● n. variant spelling of **FLYER**.

**flight** ● n. **1** the action or process of flying. ➤a journey made in an aircraft or in space. ➤the movement or trajectory of a projectile through the air. **2** a flock of birds or body of insects flying in the air. **3** a group of aircraft operating together, especially an RAF or USAF unit of about six aircraft. **4** the action of fleeing. **5** a series of steps between floors or levels. ➤a sequence of locks by which a canal ascends an incline. ➤a series of hurdles across a racetrack. **6** an uninhibited mental journey: *a flight of fancy*. **7** the tail of an arrow or dart. ● v. **1** Brit. (in soccer, cricket, etc.) deliver (a ball) with well-judged trajectory and pace. **2** provide (an arrow or dart) with a flight. **3** shoot (wildfowl) in flight.
– PHRASES **in full flight** having gained optimum momentum. **take flight 1** (of a bird) take off and fly. **2** flee.
– ORIGIN OE *flyht*, of Gmc origin; rel. to **FLY**[1].

**flight capital** ● n. capital which has been moved from an area in economic difficulties to a more stable region.

**flight control** ● n. **1** the activity of directing the movement of aircraft. **2** a control surface on an aircraft.

**flight deck** ● n. **1** the cockpit of a large aircraft. **2** the deck of an aircraft carrier, used for take-off and landing.

**flight envelope** ● n. the range of combinations of speed, altitude, angle of attack, etc., within which a flying object is aerodynamically stable.

**flight feather** ● n. any of the large primary or secondary feathers in a bird's wing, supporting it in flight.

**flightless** ● adj. (of a bird or insect) naturally unable to fly.
– DERIVATIVES **flightlessness** n.

**flight lieutenant** ● n. a rank of officer in the RAF, above flying officer and below squadron leader.

**flightline** ● n. the part of an airport around the hangars where aircraft can be parked and serviced.

**flight path** ● n. the course of an aircraft or spacecraft.

**flight recorder** ● n. a device in an aircraft to record

technical details during a flight, used in the event of an accident to discover its cause.

**flight sergeant** • n. a rank of non-commissioned officer in the RAF, above sergeant and below warrant officer.

**flight simulator** • n. a machine resembling a cockpit and simulating the conditions of an aircraft in flight, used for training pilots.

**flighty** • adj. (**-ier**, **-iest**) fickle; erratic; restlessly flirtatious.
– DERIVATIVES **flightily** adv. **flightiness** n.

**flimflam** informal • n. **1** insincere and unconvincing talk. **2** a confidence trick. • v. (**flimflammed**, **flimflamming**) swindle with a flimflam.
– DERIVATIVES **flimflammer** n. **flimflammery** n.
– ORIGIN C16: symbolic reduplication.

**flimsy** • adj. (**-ier**, **-iest**) **1** weak and insubstantial. **2** light and thin. **3** (of a pretext or account) weak; unconvincing. • n. (pl. **-ies**) Brit. **1** very thin paper. **2** a copy of a document, produced on very thin paper.
– DERIVATIVES **flimsily** adv. **flimsiness** n.
– ORIGIN C18: prob. from **FLIMFLAM**.

**flinch**[1] • v. **1** make a quick, nervous movement as an instinctive reaction to fear or pain. **2** (**flinch from**) avoid through fear or anxiety. • n. an act of flinching.
– DERIVATIVES **flincher** n. **flinching** adj. **flinchingly** adv.
– ORIGIN C16 (in the sense 'slink or sneak off'): from OFr. *flenchir* 'turn aside', of W. Gmc origin.

**flinch**[2] /flɪn(t)ʃ/ • v. variant spelling of **FLENSE**.

**flinders** • pl. n. small fragments or splinters.
– ORIGIN ME: prob. of Scand. origin.

**fling** • v. (past and past part. **flung**) **1** throw forcefully; hurl. **2** (**fling oneself into**) wholeheartedly engage in (an activity or enterprise). **3** move with speed: *he flung away to his study.* • n. **1** a short period of enjoyment or wild behaviour: *a final fling.* ➤a short sexual relationship. **2** short for **HIGHLAND FLING**.
– DERIVATIVES **flinger** n.
– ORIGIN ME: perh. rel. to ON *flengja* 'flog'.

**flint** • n. **1** a hard grey rock consisting of nearly pure silica (chert), occurring chiefly as nodules in chalk. **2** a piece of flint, especially one shaped to form a primitive tool or weapon. **3** a piece of flint used with steel to produce an igniting spark.
– ORIGIN OE; rel. to MDu. *vlint* and Old High Ger. *flins.*

**flint corn** • n. maize of a variety that has hard, slightly translucent grains.

**flint glass** • n. a pure lustrous kind of glass originally made with flint.

**flintlock** • n. an old-fashioned type of gun fired by a spark from a flint, or the lock producing the spark.

**flinty** • adj. (**-ier**, **-iest**) **1** of, containing, or reminiscent of flint. **2** (of a person or their expression) very hard and unyielding.
– DERIVATIVES **flintily** adv. **flintiness** n.

**flip**[1] • v. (**flipped**, **flipping**) **1** turn over or cause to turn over with a quick, smooth movement. **2** toss (something) into the air so that it turns over. **3** (**flip through**) flick through. **4** informal suddenly become deranged or very angry. • n. a flipping action or movement. • adj. flippant.
– PHRASES **flip one's lid** (or chiefly N. Amer. **one's wig**) informal suddenly become deranged or lose one's self-control.
– ORIGIN C16: prob. a contr. of **FILLIP**.

**flip**[2] • n. another term for **EGG-NOG**.
– ORIGIN C17: perh. from **FLIP**[1] in the sense 'whip up'.

**flip chart** • n. a very large pad of paper bound so that pages can be turned over at the top, used on a stand at presentations.

**flip-flop** • n. **1** a light sandal with a thong that passes between the big and second toes. **2** N. Amer. a backward somersault or handspring. **3** N. Amer. informal an abrupt reversal of policy. **4** Electronics a switching circuit which works by changing between two stable states. • v. **1** move with a flapping sound or motion. **2** N. Amer. informal make an abrupt reversal of policy.
– ORIGIN C17: imitative reduplication of **FLOP**.

**flippant** • adj. not showing a serious or respectful attitude.
– DERIVATIVES **flippancy** n. **flippantly** adv.
– ORIGIN C17 (early senses including 'nimble' and 'talkative', then 'playful'): from **FLIP**[1] + **-ANT**.

**flipper** • n. **1** a broad, flat limb without fingers, used for swimming by sea animals such as seals, whales, and turtles. **2** a flat rubber attachment worn on the foot for underwater swimming. **3** a pivoted arm in a pinball machine.

**flipping** • adj. informal, chiefly Brit. used for emphasis or to express mild annoyance.
– ORIGIN C20: from **FLIP**[1] + **-ING**[2].

**flip side** • n. informal **1** the less important side of a pop single; the B-side. **2** the reverse aspect or unwelcome concomitant of something.

**flip-top** • adj. denoting or having a lid that can be easily flipped open.

**flirt** • v. **1** behave playfully in a sexually enticing manner. **2** (**flirt with**) experiment casually with (an idea or activity). **3** (**flirt with**) deliberately risk (danger or death). **4** (of a bird) flap or wave (its wings or tail) with a quick flicking motion. • n. a person who habitually flirts.
– DERIVATIVES **flirtation** n. **flirtatious** adj. **flirtatiously** adv. **flirtatiousness** n. **flirty** adj. (**-ier**, **-iest**).
– ORIGIN C16 (orig. in sense 'give someone a sharp blow'; the earliest noun senses were 'joke, gibe' and 'flighty girl'): appar. symbolic, the elements *fl-* and *-irt* both suggesting sudden movement; cf. **FLICK**.

**flit** • v. (**flitted**, **flitting**) **1** move swiftly and lightly. **2** chiefly Scottish & N. English move house or leave one's home, especially in secrecy. • n. Brit. informal an act of leaving one's home in secrecy.
– ORIGIN ME: from ON *flytja*; rel. to **FLEET**[5].

**flitch** /flɪtʃ/ • n. **1** a slab of wood cut from a tree trunk. **2** (also **flitch plate**) the strengthening plate in a flitch beam. **3** chiefly dialect a side of bacon.
– ORIGIN OE *flicce*, orig. denoting the cured side of any meat, of Gmc origin.

**flitch beam** • n. a compound beam made of an iron plate between two slabs of wood.

**flitter** • v. move quickly in a random manner. • n. **1** a flittering movement. **2** (in science fiction) a small personal aircraft.
– ORIGIN ME: frequentative of **FLIT**.

**flittermouse** • n. (pl. **-mice**) old-fashioned term for **BAT**[2] (in sense 1).
– ORIGIN C16: on the pattern of Du. *vledermuis* or Ger. *Fledermaus.*

**flixweed** /ˈflɪkswiːd/ • n. a plant with small yellow flowers and finely divided leaves, formerly thought to cure dysentery. [*Descurainia sophia.*]
– ORIGIN C16: from obs. *flix* (var. of **FLUX**) + **WEED**.

**FLN** • abbrev. Front de Libération Nationale.

**float** • v. **1** rest or cause to rest on the surface of a liquid without sinking. **2** be suspended freely in a liquid or gas. **3** move slowly or hover in a liquid or the air. **4** (in sport) make (the ball) travel lightly and effortlessly through the air. **5** [usu. as adj. **floating**] remain unsettled in one's opinions, where one lives, etc. **6** put forward (an idea) as a suggestion or test of reactions. **7** offer the shares of (a company) for sale on the stock market for the first time. **8** (with reference to a currency) fluctuate or allow to fluctuate freely in value. • n. **1** any hollow or lightweight object or device used to achieve buoyancy in water. **2** a small floating object attached to a fishing line signalling the bite of a fish. **3** a floating device which forms part of a valve apparatus controlling a flow of water. **4** Brit. a small vehicle or cart powered by electricity. **5** a platform mounted on a truck and carrying a display in a procession. **6** Brit. a sum of money used for change at the beginning of a period of selling in a shop or stall. **7** a hand tool with a rectangular blade used for smoothing plaster. **8** a soft drink with a scoop of ice cream floating in it. **9** (in critical path analysis) the period of time by which the duration of an activity may be extended without affecting the overall time for the process.
– PHRASES **float someone's boat** informal appeal to or excite someone.
– DERIVATIVES **floatable** adj.

– ORIGIN OE *flotian*, of Gmc origin and rel. to **FLEET**[5].

**floatation** • n. variant spelling of **FLOTATION**.

**float chamber** • n. the cavity in a carburettor containing a device which floats on the surface of the fuel and seals off the flow as the level rises.

**floatel** /fləʊˈtɛl/ (also **flotel**) • n. a floating hotel or a vessel providing accommodation for oil-rig workers.

**floater** • n. 1 a person or thing that floats. ➤a loose particle within the eyeball which is apparent in one's field of vision. 2 Brit. informal, dated a mistake; a gaffe. 3 US an insurance policy covering loss of articles without specifying a location.

**float glass** • n. glass made by allowing it to solidify on molten metal.

**floating charge** • n. a liability to a creditor which relates to the company's assets as a whole. Compare with **FIXED CHARGE**.

**floating debt** • n. a debt which is repayable in the short term. Compare with **FUNDED DEBT**.

**floating-point** • n. [as modifier] Computing denoting a mode of representing numbers as two sequences of bits, one representing the digits in the number and the other an exponent which determines the position of the radix point.

**floating rib** • n. any of the lower ribs which are not attached directly to the breastbone.

**floating voter** • n. a person who has not decided which way to vote in an election, or one who does not consistently vote for the same party.

**floatplane** • n. a seaplane.

**float stone** • n. light, porous stone that floats, e.g. pumice.

**float valve** • n. a ball valve.

**floaty** • adj. chiefly Brit. (especially of a woman's garment or a fabric) light and flimsy.

**floc** /flɒk/ • n. technical a loosely clumped mass of fine particles.

– ORIGIN 1920s: abbrev. of **FLOCCULUS**.

**floccinaucinihilipilification** /ˌflɒksɪˌnɔːsɪˌnɪhɪlɪˌpɪlɪfɪˈkeɪʃ(ə)n/ • n. the action or habit of estimating something as worthless.

– ORIGIN C18: from L. *flocci, nauci, nihili, pili* (words meaning 'at little value') + **-FICATION**.

**floccose** /ˈflɒkəʊs/ • adj. chiefly Botany covered with or consisting of woolly tufts.

– ORIGIN C18: from late L. *floccosus*, from L. *floccus* 'flock'.

**flocculant** /ˈflɒkjʊl(ə)nt/ • n. a substance which promotes the clumping of particles, especially one used in treating waste water.

**flocculate** /ˈflɒkjʊleɪt/ • v. technical form or cause to form into small clumps or masses.

– DERIVATIVES **flocculation** n.

**floccule** /ˈflɒkjuːl/ • n. a small clump of material that resembles a tuft of wool.

– DERIVATIVES **flocculence** n. **flocculent** /ˈflɒkjʊl(ə)nt/ adj.

– ORIGIN C19: from mod. L. *flocculus*, dimin. of *floccus* 'flock'.

**flocculus** /ˈflɒkjʊləs/ • n. (pl. **flocculi** /-lʌɪ, -liː/) 1 Anatomy a small egg-shaped lobe on the underside of the cerebellum. 2 Astronomy a small cloudy wisp on the surface of the sun. 3 a floccule.

– ORIGIN C18: mod. L., dimin. of L. *floccus* (see **FLOCCUS**).

**floccus** /ˈflɒkəs/ • n. (pl. **flocci** /ˈflɒksʌɪ/) a tuft of wool or similar clump of fibres.

– ORIGIN C19: from L., 'lock or tuft of wool'; cf. **FLOCK**[2].

**flock**[1] • n. 1 a number of birds moving or resting together. ➤a number of domestic animals, especially sheep, goats, or geese, that are kept together. 2 (**a flock/flocks**) a large number or crowd. 3 a Christian congregation under the charge of a particular minister. • v. congregate or move in a flock.

– ORIGIN OE *flocc* (in the sense 'a band or body of people'), of unknown origin.

**flock**[2] • n. 1 a soft material for stuffing cushions and quilts, made of wool refuse or torn-up cloth. ➤powdered wool or cloth, used in making flock wallpaper. 2 a lock or tuft of wool or cotton.

– DERIVATIVES **flocky** adj.

– ORIGIN ME: from OFr. *floc*, from L. *floccus* (see **FLOCCUS**).

**flockmaster** • n. a sheep farmer.

**flock wallpaper** • n. wallpaper sized and sprinkled with powdered wool to make a raised pattern.

**floe** /fləʊ/ • n. a sheet of floating ice.

– ORIGIN C19: prob. from Norw. *flo*, from ON *fló* 'layer'.

**flog** • v. (**flogged**, **flogging**) 1 beat with a whip or stick as a punishment. 2 informal work at or promote repetitively or at excessive length. 3 Brit. informal sell or offer for sale. 4 Brit. informal make one's way with strenuous effort.

– PHRASES **flog a dead horse** waste energy on a lost cause or unalterable situation.

– DERIVATIVES **flogger** n.

– ORIGIN C17 (orig. sl.): perh. imitative, or from L. *flagellare* 'to whip'.

**flokati** /flɒˈkɑːti/ • n. (pl. **flokatis**) a Greek woven woollen rug with a thick loose pile.

– ORIGIN C20: from mod. Gk *phlokatē* 'peasant's blanket'.

**flood** • n. 1 an overflow of a large amount of water over dry land. ➤(**the Flood**) the biblical flood brought by God upon the earth because of the wickedness of the human race. 2 the inflow of the tide. ➤poetic/literary a river, stream, or sea. 3 an outpouring of tears or emotion. 4 an overwhelming quantity of things or people appearing at once. 5 short for **FLOODLIGHT**. • v. 1 cover or become covered with water in a flood. ➤(of a river) become swollen and overflow its banks. 2 arrive in or overwhelm with very large numbers. ➤fill or suffuse completely: *she flooded the room with light.* 3 overfill the carburettor of (an engine) with petrol. 4 (of a woman) experience a uterine haemorrhage.

– ORIGIN OE *flōd*, of Gmc origin; rel. to **FLOW**.

**floodgate** • n. 1 a gate that can be opened or closed to admit or exclude water, especially the lower gate of a lock. 2 (**the floodgates**) last restraints holding back a powerful outpouring.

**floodlight** • n. a large, powerful light used to illuminate a stage or sports ground. • v. (past and past part. **-lit**) [usu. as adj. **floodlit**] illuminate with floodlights.

**flood plain** • n. an area of low-lying ground adjacent to a river that is subject to flooding.

**flood tide** • n. an incoming tide.

**floor** • n. 1 the lower surface of a room, on which one may walk. ➤the bottom of the sea, a cave, etc.: *the ocean floor.* 2 a storey of a building. 3 (**the floor**) the part of a legislative assembly in which members sit and from which they speak. ➤the right to speak in an assembly. 4 a minimum level of prices or wages. • v. 1 provide with a floor. 2 informal knock or punch to the ground. ➤baffle or confound completely.

– DERIVATIVES **flooring** n.

– ORIGIN OE *flōr*, of Gmc origin.

**floorboard** • n. a long plank making up part of a wooden floor.

**floorcloth** • n. N. Amer. a thin canvas rug or similar light floor covering.

**floor lamp** • n. chiefly N. Amer. a standard lamp.

**floor leader** • n. US the leader of a party in a legislative assembly.

**floor manager** • n. 1 the stage manager of a television production. 2 a supervisor of shop assistants in a large store.

**floor show** • n. an entertainment presented on the floor of a nightclub or restaurant.

**floorwalker** • n. N. Amer. a shopwalker.

**floozy** (also **floozie**) • n. (pl. **-ies**) informal a disreputable or promiscuous girl or woman.

– ORIGIN C20: perh. rel. to **FLOSSY** or to dial. *floosy* 'fluffy'.

**flop** • v. (**flopped**, **flopping**) 1 fall, hang, or collapse in a heavy, loose, and ungainly way. 2 informal (of a performer or show) fail totally. 3 informal rest or sleep in an improvised place. • n. 1 a heavy, loose, and ungainly fall. 2 informal a total failure. 3 informal, chiefly US a cheap place to

sleep.
– ORIGIN C17: var. of **FLAP**.

**-flop** • **comb. form** Computing floating-point operations per second: *a gigaflop computer.*

**flophouse** • **n.** informal, chiefly N. Amer. a dosshouse.

**floppy** • **adj.** (**-ier**, **-iest**) tending to flop or hang loosely. • **n.** (pl. **-ies**) (also **floppy disk**) Computing a flexible removable magnetic disk used for storing data.
– DERIVATIVES **floppily** adv. **floppiness** n.

**floptical** /ˈflɒptɪk(ə)l/ • **adj.** Computing, trademark denoting a floppy-disk drive which uses a laser to position the read-write head.
– ORIGIN 1980s: blend of **FLOPPY** and **OPTICAL**.

**flor** • **n.** yeast allowed to develop in a whitish film on the surface of dry (fino) sherries during fermentation.
– ORIGIN C19: from Sp., lit. 'flower'.

**flor.** • **abbrev.** floruit.

**flora** • **n.** (pl. **floras** or **florae** /-riː/) **1** the plants of a particular region, habitat, or geological period. Compare with **FAUNA**. **2** [with modifier] the symbiotic bacteria occurring naturally in the intestines: *the gut flora.*
– ORIGIN C18: from L. *flos, flor-* 'flower'.

**floral** /ˈflɔːr(ə)l, ˈflɒ-/ • **adj.** **1** of or decorated with flowers. **2** Botany of flora or floras.
– DERIVATIVES **florally** adv.

**floreat** /ˈflɒrɪat/ • **exclam.** may (he, she, or it) flourish; long live!
– ORIGIN L., 'let flourish ...'.

**Florentine** /ˈflɒr(ə)ntʌɪn/ • **adj.** **1** of or relating to Florence in Italy. **2** (**florentine** /-tiːn/) [postpos.] (of a dish) served on a bed of spinach: *eggs florentine.* • **n.** **1** a native or citizen of Florence. **2** a biscuit consisting mainly of nuts and preserved fruit, coated on one side with chocolate.

**florescence** /flɔːˈrɛs(ə)ns, flə-/ • **n.** the process of flowering.
– ORIGIN C18: from mod. L. *florescentia*, from L. *florescent-*, *florescere* 'begin to flower', based on *flos, flor-* 'flower'.

**floret** /ˈflɒrɪt, ˈflɔː-/ • **n.** **1** Botany one of the small flowers making up a composite flower head. ➤ a small flower. **2** one of the flowering stems making up a head of cauliflower or broccoli.
– ORIGIN C17: from L. *flos, flor-* 'flower' + **-ET**[1].

**floriated** /ˈflɔːrɪeɪtɪd/ • **adj.** decorated with floral designs.

**floribunda** /ˌflɒrɪˈbʌndə, ˌflɔː-/ • **n.** a plant, especially a rose, which bears dense clusters of flowers.
– ORIGIN C19: mod. L., fem. (used as n.) of *floribundus* 'freely flowering'.

**florican** /ˈflɔːrɪkan/ • **n.** a small South Asian bustard, the male of which is mainly black with white wings. [*Houbaropsis begalensis* and *Sypheotides indica*.]
– ORIGIN C18: of unknown origin.

**floriculture** /ˈflɒrɪˌkʌltʃə, ˈflɔː-/ • **n.** the cultivation of flowers.
– DERIVATIVES **floricultural** adj. **floriculturist** n.

**florid** /ˈflɒrɪd/ • **adj.** **1** having a red or flushed complexion. **2** elaborately or excessively intricate or complicated. **3** Medicine (of a disease or its manifestations) occurring in a fully developed form.
– DERIVATIVES **floridity** n. **floridly** adv. **floridness** n.
– ORIGIN C17: from L. *floridus*, from *flos, flor-* 'flower'.

**Floridian** /flɒˈrɪdɪən/ • **n.** a native or inhabitant of Florida. • **adj.** of or relating to Florida.

**floriferous** /flɒˈrɪf(ə)rəs, flɔː-/ • **adj.** (of a plant) producing many flowers.

**florilegium** /ˌflɒrɪˈliːdʒɪəm, flɔː-/ • **n.** (pl. **florilegia** /-ˈliːdʒɪə/ or **florilegiums**) an anthology of literary extracts.
– ORIGIN C17: mod. L., lit. 'bouquet', translation of Gk *anthologion* (see **ANTHOLOGY**).

**florin** /ˈflɒrɪn/ • **n.** **1** a former British coin and monetary unit worth two shillings. **2** an English gold coin of the 14th century, worth six shillings and eight old pence. **3** a foreign coin of gold or silver, especially a Dutch guilder. **4** the basic monetary unit of Aruba, equal to 100 cents.
– ORIGIN via OFr. from Ital. *fiorino*, dimin. of *fiore* 'flower' (orig. referring to a Florentine coin bearing a fleur-de-lis).

**florist** • **n.** a person who sells and arranges cut flowers.
– DERIVATIVES **floristry** n.

**floristic** /flәˈrɪstɪk/ • **adj.** Botany relating to the study of the distribution of plants.
– DERIVATIVES **floristically** adv.

**floristics** • **pl. n.** [treated as sing.] Botany the branch of phytogeography concerned with the study of plant species present in an area.

**floruit** /ˈflɒrʊɪt, ˈflɔː-/ • **v.** used to indicate when a historical figure lived, worked, or was most active.
– ORIGIN L., lit. 'he or she flourished'.

**flory** /ˈflɔːri/ (also **fleury**) • **adj.** Heraldry **1** decorated with fleurs-de-lis. **2** (of a cross) having the end of each limb splayed out into three pointed lobes.
– ORIGIN ME: from OFr. *floure*, from *flour* 'flower'.

**floss** • **n.** **1** the rough silk enveloping a silkworm's cocoon. **2** untwisted silk fibres used in embroidery. **3** (also **dental floss**) a soft thread used to clean between the teeth. **4** the silky down in maize and other plants. • **v.** clean between (one's teeth) with dental floss.
– ORIGIN C18: from Fr. (*soie*) *floche*, from OFr. *flosche* 'down, nap of velvet'.

**flossy** • **adj.** (**-ier**, **-iest**) **1** of or like floss. **2** N. Amer. informal excessively showy.

**flotation** /fləʊˈteɪʃ(ə)n/ (also **floatation**) • **n.** **1** the action of floating or capacity to float. **2** the separation of small particles of a solid by their different capacities to float. **3** the process of offering a company's shares for sale on the stock market for the first time.

**flotation tank** • **n.** a lightproof, soundproof tank of salt water in which a person floats as a form of deep relaxation.

**flotel** • **n.** variant spelling of **FLOATEL**.

**flotilla** /fləˈtɪlə/ • **n.** a small fleet of ships or boats.
– ORIGIN C18: from Sp., dimin. of *flota* 'fleet'.

**flotsam** /ˈflɒts(ə)m/ • **n.** wreckage found floating on the sea. Compare with **JETSAM**.
– PHRASES **flotsam and jetsam** useless or discarded objects.
– ORIGIN C17: from Anglo-Norman Fr. *floteson*, from *floter* 'to float'.

**flounce**[1] • **v.** move in an exaggeratedly impatient or angry manner. • **n.** an exaggerated action expressing annoyance or impatience.
– ORIGIN C16: perh. of Scand. origin and rel. to Norw. *flunsa* 'hurry', or perh. symbolic, like *bounce* or *pounce.*

**flounce**[2] • **n.** a wide ornamental strip of material gathered and sewn to a skirt or dress; a frill.
– DERIVATIVES **flounced** adj. **flouncy** adj.
– ORIGIN C18: from an alt. of obs. *frounce* 'a fold or pleat', from OFr. *fronce.*

**flounder**[1] • **v.** **1** stagger clumsily in mud or water. **2** have trouble doing or understanding something.
– DERIVATIVES **flounderer** n.
– ORIGIN C16: perh. a blend of **FOUNDER**[3] and **BLUNDER**, or perh. symbolic.

**USAGE** flounder

On the confusion of **flounder** with **founder**, see **FOUNDER**[3].

**flounder**[2] • **n.** a small flatfish that typically occurs in shallow coastal water. [*Platichthys flesus* and other species.]
– ORIGIN ME: from OFr. *flondre*, prob. of Scand. origin.

**flour** • **n.** a powder obtained by grinding grain, used to make bread, cakes, and pastry. • **v.** **1** sprinkle with flour. **2** US grind (grain) into flour.
– DERIVATIVES **flouriness** n. **floury** adj.
– ORIGIN ME: a specific use of **FLOWER** in the sense 'the best part', used orig. to mean 'the finest quality of ground wheat'.

**flourish** • **v.** **1** grow or develop in a healthy or vigorous way. ➤ be working or at the height of one's career during a specified period. **2** wave (something) about dramatically. • **n.** **1** a bold or extravagant gesture or action. **2** an

ornamental flowing curve in handwriting or scrollwork. **3** Music an ornate musical passage. ➤a fanfare played by brass instruments.
– DERIVATIVES **flourisher** n.
– ORIGIN ME: from OFr. *floriss-*, lengthened stem of *florir*, based on L. *florere*, from *flos, flor-* 'a flower'.

**floury** ● adj. **1** covered with flour. ➤of or resembling flour. **2** (of a potato) having a soft, fluffy texture when cooked.
– DERIVATIVES **flouriness** n.

**flout** /flaʊt/ ● v. **1** openly disregard (a rule, law, or convention). **2** archaic mock; scoff.
– ORIGIN C16: perh. from Du. *fluiten* 'whistle, play the flute, hiss (in derision)'.

**USAGE** flout

On the confusion of **flout** with **flaunt**, see **FLAUNT**.

**flow** ● v. **1** move steadily and continuously in a current or stream. **2** (of the sea or a tidal river) move towards the land; rise. Compare with **EBB**. **3** move or issue forth steadily and freely. ➤[often as adj. **flowing**] hang loosely in a graceful manner: *a long flowing gown*. **4** (of a solid) undergo a permanent change of shape under stress, without melting. ● n. **1** the action or process of flowing. **2** the rise of a tide or a river. **3** a steady, continuous stream: *the flow of traffic*. **4** Scottish a watery swamp; a morass.
– PHRASES **go with the flow** informal be relaxed and accept a situation. **in full flow** talking or performing fluently and enthusiastically.
– DERIVATIVES **flowingly** adv.
– ORIGIN OE *flōwan*, of Gmc origin; rel. to **FLOOD**.

**flow chart** (also **flow diagram**) ● n. **1** a diagram of a sequence of movements or actions making up a complex system. **2** a graphical representation of a computer program in relation to its sequence of functions.

**flower** ● n. **1** the seed-bearing part of a plant, consisting of reproductive organs (stamens and carpels) typically surrounded by brightly coloured petals (the corolla) and green sepals (the calyx). **2** (often in phr. **in flower**) the state or period in which a plant's flowers have developed and opened. **3** (**the flower of**) the finest individuals out of a number of people or things. ● v. **1** [often as adj. **flowering**] (of a plant) produce flowers. **2** be in or reach an optimum stage of development.
– DERIVATIVES **flowerer** n. **flowerless** adj. **flower-like** adj.
– ORIGIN ME *flour*, from OFr. *flour, flor*, from L. *flos, flor-*; cf. **FLOUR**.

**flowered** ● adj. **1** having a floral design. **2** [in combination] bearing flowers: *yellow-flowered japonica*.

**floweret** /ˈflaʊərɪt/ ● n. a floret, especially of cauliflower or broccoli.

**flower head** ● n. a compact mass of flowers at the top of a stem, especially a capitulum.

**flowering plant** ● n. an angiosperm.

**flowerpecker** ● n. a very small songbird feeding chiefly on insects in flowers, native to Australasia and SE Asia. [Family Dicaeidae: many species.]

**flowerpot** ● n. a small earthenware container in which to grow a plant.

**flower power** ● n. the promotion by hippies of peace and love as means of changing the world.

**flowers of sulphur** ● pl. n. [treated as sing.] Chemistry a fine yellow powdered form of sulphur produced by sublimation.

**flowery** ● adj. **1** filled with or resembling flowers. **2** (of speech or writing) elaborate.
– DERIVATIVES **floweriness** n.

**flown** past participle of **FLY**[1].

**flowsheet** ● n. another term for **FLOW CHART**.

**flowstone** ● n. Geology rock deposited as a thin sheet by precipitation from flowing water.

**Flt Lt** ● abbrev. Flight Lieutenant.

**Flt Sgt** ● abbrev. Flight Sergeant.

**flu** ● n. influenza or any similar, milder infection.

**flub** N. Amer. informal ● v. (**flubbed**, **flubbing**) botch or bungle. ● n. something done badly or clumsily; a blunder.
– ORIGIN 1920s: of unknown origin.

**fluctuant** ● adj. poetic/literary fluctuating; unstable.

**fluctuate** /ˈflʌktʃʊeɪt, -tjʊ-/ ● v. rise and fall irregularly in number or amount.
– DERIVATIVES **fluctuation** n.
– ORIGIN C17 (earlier (ME) as *fluctuation*): from L. *fluctuat-*, *fluctuare* 'undulate', based on *fluere* 'to flow'.

**flue** /fluː/ ● n. a duct in a chimney for smoke and waste gases. ➤a channel for conveying heat.
– ORIGIN ME (denoting the mouthpiece of a hunting horn): of unknown origin.

**fluellen** /flʊˈɛlɪn/ ● n. a small creeping plant found in cornfields, with yellow and purple flowers. [Genus *Kickxia*: two species.]
– ORIGIN C16: alt. of Welsh *llysiau Llywelyn* 'Llewelyn's herbs'.

**fluence**[1] /ˈfluːəns/ ● n. Brit. informal magical or hypnotic power.
– ORIGIN C20: shortening of **INFLUENCE**.

**fluence**[2] /ˈfluːəns/ ● n. Physics the rate at which a stream of particles crosses a unit area.
– ORIGIN C17 (in the sense 'a flowing, a stream'): from Fr., from L. *fluentia*, from *fluere* 'to flow'.

**fluent** /ˈfluːənt/ ● adj. **1** speaking or writing easily and accurately, especially in a foreign language. ➤(of a language) used easily and accurately. **2** smoothly graceful and easy. **3** able to flow freely; fluid.
– DERIVATIVES **fluency** n. **fluently** adv.
– ORIGIN C16: from L. *fluent-*, *fluere* 'flow'.

**flue pipe** ● n. **1** a pipe acting as a flue. **2** an organ pipe into which the air enters directly without striking a reed.

**fluff** ● n. **1** soft fibres accumulated in small light clumps. ➤the fur or feathers of a young mammal or bird. **2** trivial or superficial entertainment or writing. **3** informal a mistake, especially in speech, sport, or music. ● v. **1** (usu. **fluff something up**) make something fuller and softer by shaking or patting it. **2** informal fail to accomplish (something) properly.
– ORIGIN C18: prob. a dial. alt. of C16 *flue* 'down, nap, fluff', appar. from Flemish *vluwe*.

**fluffy** ● adj. (**-ier**, **-iest**) **1** of, like, or covered with fluff. **2** (of food) light in texture. **3** informal frivolous, silly, or vague.
– DERIVATIVES **fluffily** adv. **fluffiness** n.

**flugelhorn** /ˈfluːg(ə)lhɔːn/ ● n. a valved brass musical instrument like a cornet but with a broader tone.
– ORIGIN C19: from Ger. *Flügelhorn*, from *Flügel* 'wing' + *Horn* 'horn'.

**fluid** ● n. a substance that has no fixed shape and yields easily to external pressure; a gas or (especially) a liquid. ● adj. **1** able to flow easily. **2** (of a clutch or coupling) using a liquid to transmit power. **3** not settled or stable. **4** smoothly elegant or graceful.
– DERIVATIVES **fluidity** n. **fluidly** adv.
– ORIGIN ME (as adj.): from Fr. *fluide* or L. *fluidus*, from *fluere* 'to flow'.

**fluidics** /fluːˈɪdɪks/ ● pl. n. [often treated as sing.] the technique of using small interacting fluid jets for functions usually performed by electronic devices.
– DERIVATIVES **fluidic** adj.

**fluidize** /ˈfluːɪdʌɪz/ (also **-ise**) ● v. technical cause (a finely divided solid) to acquire the characteristics of a fluid by passing a gas upwards through it.
– DERIVATIVES **fluidization** n.

**fluidized bed** ● n. a layer of a fluidized solid, used in chemical processes and in the efficient burning of coal for power generation.

**fluid mechanics** ● pl. n. [treated as sing.] the study of forces and flow within fluids.

**fluid ounce** ● n. **1** Brit. a unit of capacity equal to one twentieth of a pint (approximately 0.028 litre). **2** (also **fluidounce**) US a unit of capacity equal to one sixteenth of a US pint (approximately 0.03 litre).

**fluidram** /ˈfluːɪdram/ ● n. US a fluid drachm. See **DRACHM**.

**fluke**[1] ● n. an unlikely chance occurrence, especially a stroke of luck. ● v. achieve by luck rather than skill.
– DERIVATIVES **flukily** adv. **flukiness** n. **fluky** (also **flukey**) adj.

– ORIGIN C19 (orig. a term in games such as billiards denoting a lucky stroke): perh. a dial. word.

**fluke²** • **n.** **1** a parasitic flatworm which typically has suckers and hooks for attachment to the host. [Classes Trematoda and Monogenea.] **2** chiefly dialect or N. Amer. a flounder or other flatfish.
– ORIGIN OE *flōc* (in sense 2), of Gmc origin.

**fluke³** • **n.** **1** a broad triangular plate on the arm of an anchor. **2** either of the lobes of a whale's tail.
– ORIGIN C16: perh. from **FLUKE²** (because of the shape).

**flume** /fluːm/ • **n.** **1** an artificial channel conveying water, typically used for transporting logs. **2** a water slide or chute at a swimming pool or amusement park.
– ORIGIN ME (denoting a river or stream): from OFr. *flum*, from L. *flumen* 'river', from *fluere* 'to flow'.

**flummery** /ˈflʌm(ə)ri/ • **n.** (pl. **-ies**) **1** empty compliments; nonsense. **2** a sweet dish made with beaten eggs and sugar.
– ORIGIN C17: from Welsh *llymru*; perh. rel. to *llymrig* 'soft, slippery'.

**flummox** /ˈflʌməks/ • **v.** informal perplex; bewilder.
– ORIGIN C19: prob. of dial. origin.

**flump** • **v.** fall, sit, or throw down heavily. • **n.** the action or sound of a heavy fall.
– ORIGIN C17: imitative.

**flung** past and past participle of **FLING**.

**flunk** • **v.** informal, chiefly N. Amer. fail to reach the required standard in (an examination). ➤ **(flunk out)** be dismissed from school or college for failing examinations.
– ORIGIN C19: perh. rel. to **FUNK¹** or to US *flink* 'be a coward', perh. a var. of **FLINCH¹**.

**flunkey** (also **flunky**) • **n.** (pl. **-eys** or **-ies**) chiefly derogatory a liveried manservant or footman. ➤ a person who performs menial tasks.
– DERIVATIVES **flunkeyism** n.
– ORIGIN C18 (orig. Scots): perh. from **FLANK** in the sense 'a person who stands at one's flank'.

**fluoresce** /flʊəˈrɛs, flɔː-/ • **v.** shine or glow brightly due to fluorescence.

**fluorescein** /ˈflʊərəsiːn, -sɪn, ˈflɔː-/ • **n.** Chemistry an orange dye with a yellowish-green fluorescence, used as an indicator and tracer.

**fluorescence** /flʊəˈrɛs(ə)ns, flɔː-/ • **n.** light or other radiation emitted by a substance when it is exposed to incident radiation of a shorter wavelength such as X-rays or ultraviolet light. ➤ the property of emitting light in this way.
– ORIGIN C19: from **FLUORSPAR** (which fluoresces), on the pattern of *opalescence*.

**fluorescent** • **adj.** **1** having or showing fluorescence. ➤ denoting lighting based on fluorescence from a phosphor illuminated by ultraviolet light from mercury vapour inside a glass tube. **2** vividly colourful.

**fluorescent screen** • **n.** a transparent screen coated with fluorescent material to show images from X-rays.

**fluoridate** /ˈflʊərɪdeɪt, ˈflɔː-/ • **v.** add traces of fluorides to (something, especially a water supply).
– DERIVATIVES **fluoridation** n.

**fluoride** /ˈflʊərʌɪd, flɔː-/ • **n.** **1** Chemistry a compound of fluorine with another element or group: *calcium fluoride*. **2** sodium fluoride or another fluorine-containing salt added to water supplies or toothpaste in order to reduce tooth decay.

**fluorinate** /ˈflʊərɪneɪt, ˈflɔː-/ • **v.** **1** Chemistry introduce fluorine into (a compound). **2** another term for **FLUORIDATE**.
– DERIVATIVES **fluorination** n.

**fluorine** /ˈflʊəriːn, ˈflɔː-/ • **n.** the chemical element of atomic number 9, a poisonous pale yellow gas of the halogen series. (Symbol: **F**)
– ORIGIN C19: from *fluor* (see **FLUORSPAR**) + **-INE⁴**.

**fluorite** /ˈflʊərʌɪt, ˈflɔː-/ • **n.** a mineral consisting of calcium fluoride which typically occurs as cubic crystals, colourless when pure but often coloured by impurities.

**fluoro-** /ˈflʊərəʊ, ˈflɔː-/ • **comb. form** **1** representing **FLUORINE**. **2** representing **FLUORESCENCE**.

**fluorocarbon** • **n.** Chemistry a compound formed by replacing one or more of the hydrogen atoms in a hydrocarbon with fluorine atoms.

**fluorochrome** • **n.** a chemical that fluoresces, especially one used as a label in biological research.

**fluorography** /flʊəˈrɒgrəfi, flɔː-/ • **n.** photography in which the image is formed by fluorescence, used chiefly in biomedical research.
– DERIVATIVES **fluorograph** n.

**fluorometer** /flʊəˈrɒmɪtə, flɔː-/ (also **fluorimeter**) • **n.** an instrument for detecting and measuring fluorescence.
– DERIVATIVES **fluorometric** adj. **fluorometrically** adv. **fluorometry** n.

**fluoroscope** • **n.** an instrument with a fluorescent screen used for viewing X-ray images without taking and developing X-ray photographs.
– DERIVATIVES **fluoroscopic** adj. **fluoroscopy** n.

**fluorosis** /flʊəˈrəʊsɪs, flɔː-/ • **n.** Medicine a chronic condition caused by excessive intake of fluorine compounds, marked by mottling of the teeth and, if severe, calcification of the ligaments.

**fluorspar** /ˈflʊəspɑː, ˈflɔː-/ • **n.** another term for **FLUORITE**.
– ORIGIN C18: from *fluor* 'a flow, a mineral used as a flux, fluorspar' (based on L. *fluere* 'to flow') + **SPAR³**.

**fluoxetine** /fluːˈɒksətiːn/ • **n.** Medicine a synthetic compound which inhibits the uptake of serotonin in the brain and is taken to treat depression. Also called **PROZAC** (trademark).
– ORIGIN 1970s: from *fluo(rine)* + *ox(y)* + *-etine* (perh. from *e* + a blend of **TOLUENE** and **AMINE**).

**flurried** • **adj.** agitated, nervous, or anxious.

**flurry** • **n.** (pl. **-ies**) **1** a small swirling mass of snow, leaves, etc. moved by sudden gusts of wind. **2** a sudden short period of commotion or excitement. ➤ a number of things arriving suddenly and simultaneously. • **v.** (**-ies**, **-ied**) move in flurries; swirl.
– ORIGIN C17: from obs. *flurr* 'fly up, flutter, whirr' (imitative), prob. influenced by **HURRY**.

**flush¹** • **v.** **1** (of a person's skin or face) become red and hot, typically through illness or emotion. ➤ glow or cause to glow with warm colour or light. ➤ **(be flushed with)** be excited or elated by. **2** cleanse (something, especially a toilet) by passing large quantities of water through it. ➤ remove or dispose of in such a way. **3** drive (a bird or animal, especially a game bird) from cover. **4** (of a plant) send out fresh shoots. • **n.** **1** a reddening of the face or skin. ➤ an area of warm colour or light. **2** a sudden rush of intense emotion. ➤ a period of freshness and vigour: *the first flush of youth*. **3** an act of flushing. **4** a fresh growth of leaves, flowers, or fruit.
– DERIVATIVES **flusher** n.
– ORIGIN ME (in the sense 'move rapidly, spring or fly up'): symbolic; perh. influenced by **FLASH¹** and **BLUSH**.

**flush²** • **adj.** **1** completely level or even with another surface. **2** informal having plenty of money. • **v.** fill in (a joint) level with a surface.
– DERIVATIVES **flushness** n.
– ORIGIN C16 (in the sense 'perfect, lacking nothing'): prob. rel. to **FLUSH¹**.

**flush³** • **n.** (in poker or brag) a hand of cards all of the same suit.
– ORIGIN C16: from Fr. *flux* (formerly *flus*), from L. *fluxus* (see **FLUX**).

**flush⁴** • **n.** Ecology a piece of wet ground over which water flows without being confined to a definite channel.
– ORIGIN ME (in the sense 'marshy place'): var. of **FLASH²**.

**fluster** • **v.** [often as adj. **flustered**] make (someone) agitated or confused. • **n.** a flustered state.
– ORIGIN C17 (in the sense 'make slightly drunk'): perh. of Scand. origin and rel. to Icelandic *flaustra* 'hurry, bustle'.

**flute** • **n.** **1** a high-pitched wind instrument consisting of a tube with holes along it, usually held horizontally so that the breath can be directed against a fixed edge. **2** Architecture an ornamental vertical groove in a column. ➤ a trumpet-shaped frill on a garment. **3** a tall, narrow wine glass. • **v.** **1** speak in a melodious way. ➤ poetic/literary play a

flute or pipe. **2** [often as adj. **fluted**] make flutes or grooves in.
– DERIVATIVES **fluting** n. **fluty** (also **flutey**) adj.
– ORIGIN ME: from OFr. *flahute*, prob. from Provençal *flaüt*, perh. a blend of *flaujol* 'flageolet' + *laüt* 'lute'.

**flutist** ● n. US term for **FLAUTIST**.

**flutter** ● v. **1** fly unsteadily by flapping the wings quickly and lightly. **2** move or fall with a light irregular motion. **3** (of a pulse or heartbeat) beat feebly or irregularly. ● n. **1** an act or instance of fluttering. **2** a state or sensation of tremulous excitement. **3** Brit. informal a small bet. **4** Electronics rapid variation in the pitch or amplitude of a signal, especially of recorded sound. Compare with **wow²**. **5** Aeronautics undesired oscillation in a part of an aircraft under stress.
– DERIVATIVES **flutterer** n. **fluttering** adj. **flutteringly** adv. **fluttery** adj.
– ORIGIN OE *floterian*, *flotorian*, a frequentative form rel. to **FLEET⁵**.

**fluvial** /ˈfluːvɪəl/ ● adj. chiefly Geology of or found in a river.
– ORIGIN ME: from L. *fluvialis*, from *fluvius* 'river', from *fluere* 'to flow'.

**fluviatile** /ˈfluːvɪəˌtʌɪl/ ● adj. technical of, found in, or produced by a river.

**fluvio-** /ˈfluːvɪəʊ/ ● comb. form river; relating to rivers: *fluvioglacial*.
– ORIGIN from L. *fluvius* 'river'.

**fluvioglacial** ● adj. Geology relating to or denoting erosion or deposition caused by flowing meltwater from glaciers or ice sheets.

**fluvoxamine** /fluːˈvɒxəmiːn/ ● n. Medicine a synthetic antidepressant drug which acts by prolonging the effect of the neurotransmitter serotonin on the brain.

**flux** /flʌks/ ● n. **1** the action or process of flowing. **2** Medicine an abnormal discharge of blood or other matter from or within the body. ➤ archaic diarrhoea or dysentery. **3** continuous change. **4** Physics the amount of radiation, particles, etc. incident on or passing through an area in a given time. ➤ the total electric or magnetic field passing through a surface. **5** a substance mixed with a solid to lower the melting point, especially in soldering or smelting. ● v. treat (a metal object) with a flux to promote melting.
– ORIGIN ME: from L. *fluxus*, from *fluere* 'to flow'.

**fluxgate** ● n. a device consisting of one or more soft iron cores surrounded by coils, used for determining the characteristics of an external magnetic field.

**fluxion** /ˈflʌkʃ(ə)n/ ● n. Mathematics, dated a derivative.

**fluxional** ● adj. **1** subject to flux. **2** Mathematics, dated relating to fluxions.

**fly¹** ● v. (**flies**; past **flew**; past part. **flown**) **1** (of a winged creature or aircraft) move through the air under control. ➤ control the flight of (an aircraft). **2** move or be hurled quickly through the air. ➤ Baseball hit a ball high into the air. **3** go or move quickly. ➤ informal depart hastily. ➤ (of time) pass swiftly. ➤ [as adj. **flying**] hasty; brief: *a flying visit*. ➤ (**fly into**) suddenly go into (a rage or other strong emotion). ➤ (**fly at**) attack verbally or physically. **4** wave or flutter in the wind. ➤ (of a flag) be displayed on a flagpole. **5** archaic flee. ● n. (pl. **flies**) **1** (Brit. also **flies**) an opening at the crotch of a pair of trousers, closed with a zip or buttons. **2** a flap of material covering the opening of a tent. **3** (**the flies**) the space over the stage in a theatre. **4** (pl. usu. **flys**) Brit. historical a one-horse hackney carriage.
– PHRASES **fly in the face of** be openly at variance with (what is usual or expected). **fly a kite 1** informal try something out to test public opinion. **2** historical raise money by an accommodation bill. **fly off the handle** informal lose one's temper suddenly. **with flying colours** with distinction.
– DERIVATIVES **flyable** adj.
– ORIGIN OE *flēogan*, of Gmc origin; rel. to **FLY²**.

**fly²** ● n. (pl. **flies**) a flying insect of a large order characterized by a single pair of transparent wings and sucking or piercing mouthparts. [Order Diptera.] ➤ used in names of other flying insects, e.g. **dragonfly**, **firefly**. ➤ a fishing bait consisting of a mayfly or other natural or artificial flying insect.
– PHRASES **drop like flies** die or collapse in large numbers. **a fly in the ointment** a minor irritation that spoils the enjoyment of something. **fly on the wall** an unnoticed observer. **there are no flies on ——** the person specified is quick and astute.
– ORIGIN OE *flȳge*, *flēoge*, of W. Gmc origin; rel. to **FLY¹**.

**fly³** ● adj. (**flyer**, **flyest**) informal **1** Brit. knowing and clever; worldly-wise. **2** N. Amer. stylish and fashionable.
– DERIVATIVES **flyness** n.
– ORIGIN C19: of unknown origin.

**fly agaric** ● n. a poisonous toadstool which has a red cap with fluffy white spots. [*Amanita muscaria*.]

**fly ash** ● n. ash produced in small dark flecks and carried into the air.

**flyaway** ● adj. (of hair) fine and difficult to control.

**fly ball** ● n. Baseball a ball batted high into the air.

**flyblown** ● adj. contaminated by contact with flies and their eggs and larvae.

**fly boy** ● n. N. Amer. informal a pilot, especially one in the air force.

**flybridge** ● n. an open deck above the main bridge of a vessel, typically equipped with duplicate controls.

**fly-by-night** ● adj. unreliable or untrustworthy, especially in business or financial matters.

**fly-by-wire** ● n. a semi-automatic, usually computer-regulated system for controlling an aircraft or spacecraft.

**flycatcher** ● n. a perching bird that catches flying insects, especially in short flights from a perch. [Muscicapidae and other families: many species.]

**flyer** (also **flier**) ● n. **1** a person or thing that flies. ➤ informal a fast-moving person or thing. **2** a small handbill advertising an event or product. **3** a flying start. **4** informal, chiefly N. Amer. a speculative action or investment.

**fly-fishing** ● n. the sport of fishing using a rod and an artificial fly as bait.
– DERIVATIVES **fly-fish** v.

**fly half** ● n. Rugby another term for **STAND-OFF HALF**.

**flying boat** ● n. a large seaplane that lands with its fuselage in the water.

**flying bomb** ● n. a small pilotless aircraft with an explosive warhead.

**flying bridge** ● n. another term for **FLYBRIDGE**.

**flying buttress** ● n. Architecture a buttress slanting from a separate column, typically forming an arch with the wall it supports.

**flying doctor** ● n. (in Australia) a doctor who travels by aircraft to visit patients in remote areas of the country.

**flying fish** ● n. a fish of warm seas which leaps out of the water and uses its wing-like pectoral fins to glide for some distance. [*Exocoetus volitans* and other species.]

**flying fox** ● n. a large fruit bat with a foxlike face, found in Madagascar, SE Asia, and northern Australia. [*Pteropus* and two other genera: numerous species.]

**flying jacket** ● n. a short leather jacket with a warm lining or collar.

**flying lemur** ● n. a nocturnal lemur-like mammal with a membrane between the fore- and hindlimbs for gliding from tree to tree. [Genus *Cynocephalus*: two species.]

**flying lizard** (also **flying dragon**) ● n. an arboreal SE Asian lizard with expanding membranes along its body, used for gliding between trees. [Genus *Draco*: several species.]

**flying officer** ● n. a rank of commissioned officer in the RAF, above pilot officer and below flight lieutenant.

**flying phalanger** ● n. a small Australasian marsupial with a membrane between the fore- and hindlimbs for gliding. [Genera *Petaurus* and *Petauroides*: five species.]

**flying picket** ● n. Brit. a person who travels to picket a workplace where there is an industrial dispute.

**flying saucer** ● n. a disc-shaped flying craft supposedly piloted by aliens.

**flying squad** ● n. Brit. a division of a police force which is capable of reaching an incident quickly.

**flying squirrel** ● n. a squirrel that has skin joining the fore- and hindlimbs for gliding from tree to tree. [Many species, chiefly in subfamily Pteromyinae.]

**flying start** ● n. **1** a start of a race in which the starting point is passed at speed. **2** a good beginning, especially one giving an advantage over competitors.

**flying suit** ● n. a one-piece garment worn by the pilot and crew of a military or light aircraft.

**flying wing** ● n. an aircraft with little or no fuselage and no tailplane.

**flyleaf** ● n. (pl. **-leaves**) a blank page at the beginning or end of a book.

**flyover** ● n. chiefly Brit. a bridge carrying one road or railway line over another.

**flypaper** ● n. sticky, poison-treated strips of paper that are hung indoors to catch and kill flies.

**fly-past** ● n. Brit. a ceremonial flight of aircraft past a person or a place.

**fly-pitcher** ● n. Brit. informal a street trader.
– DERIVATIVES **fly-pitching** n.

**fly-post** ● v. Brit. put up (advertising posters) in unauthorized places.

**fly-poster** ● n. Brit. **1** an advertising poster put up in an unauthorized place. **2** a person who fly-posts.

**flysch** /flɪʃ/ ● n. Geology a sedimentary deposit consisting of thin beds of shale or marl alternating with coarser strata such as sandstone or conglomerate.
– ORIGIN C19: from Swiss Ger. dial.

**flysheet** ● n. **1** Brit. a fabric cover pitched over a tent to give extra protection against bad weather. **2** a tract or circular of two or four pages.

**flyspeck** ● n. **1** a tiny stain made by the excrement of an insect. **2** something contemptibly small or insignificant.
– DERIVATIVES **flyspecked** adj.

**fly strike** ● n. infestation of an animal with blowfly maggots.

**fly-tip** ● v. Brit. illegally dump waste.
– DERIVATIVES **fly-tipper** n.

**flyway** ● n. Ornithology a route regularly used by large numbers of migrating birds.

**flyweight** ● n. a weight in boxing and other sports intermediate between light flyweight and bantamweight.

**flywheel** ● n. a heavy revolving wheel in a machine which is used to increase momentum and thereby provide greater stability or a reserve of available power.

**FM** ● abbrev. **1** Field Marshal. **2** frequency modulation.

**Fm** ● symb. the chemical element fermium.

**fm** ● abbrev. fathom(s).

**FMV** ● abbrev. full-motion video.

**f-number** ● n. Photography the ratio of the focal length of a camera lens to the diameter of the aperture being used for a particular shot.

**FO** ● abbrev. **1** Flying Officer. **2** Foreign Office.

**fo.** ● abbrev. folio.

**FOAF** ● abbrev. friend of a friend, denoting a story or rumour which has no definite source and cannot be authenticated.

**foal** ● n. a young horse or related animal. ● v. (of a mare) give birth to a foal.
– ORIGIN OE *fola*, of Gmc origin; rel. to FILLY.

**foam** ● n. **1** a mass of small bubbles formed on or in liquid. ➤a liquid preparation containing many small bubbles. **2** a lightweight form of rubber or plastic made by solidifying foam. ● v. form or produce foam.
– DERIVATIVES **foamless** adj. **foamy** adj.
– ORIGIN OE *fām* (n.), *fǣman* (v.), of W. Gmc origin.

**fob**[1] ● n. a chain attached to a watch for carrying in a waistcoat or waistband pocket. ➤a small ornament attached to a watch chain. ➤(also **fob pocket**) a small pocket for carrying a watch. ➤a tab on a key ring.
– ORIGIN C17: origin uncertain; prob. rel. to Ger. dial. *Fuppe* 'pocket'.

**fob**[2] ● v. (**fobbed**, **fobbing**) (**fob someone off**) deceitfully attempt to satisfy someone by making excuses or giving them something inferior. ➤(**fob something off on**) give something inferior to.
– ORIGIN ME (in the sense 'cheat out of'): origin uncertain; perh. rel. to Ger. *foppen* 'deceive, banter', or to FOP.

**f.o.b.** ● abbrev. free on board.

**fob watch** ● n. a pocket watch.

**focaccia** /fə'katʃə/ ● n. a type of flat Italian bread made with olive oil and flavoured with herbs.
– ORIGIN from Ital.

**focal** /'fəʊk(ə)l/ ● adj. **1** of or relating to a focus, in particular the focus of a lens. **2** (of a disease or medical condition) occurring in one particular site in the body.
– DERIVATIVES **focalization** (also **-isation**) n. **focalize** (also **-ise**) v.

**focal length** ● n. the distance between the centre of a lens or curved mirror and its focus. ➤the equivalent distance in a compound lens or telescope.

**focal plane** ● n. the plane through the focus perpendicular to the axis of a mirror or lens.

**focal point** ● n. **1** the point at which rays or waves meet after reflection or refraction, or the point from which diverging rays or waves appear to proceed. **2** the centre of interest or activity.

**fo'c's'le** /'fəʊks(ə)l/ ● n. variant spelling of FORECASTLE.

**focus** ● n. (pl. **focuses** or **foci** /'fəʊsʌɪ/) **1** the centre of interest or activity. ➤an act of focusing on something. **2** Geology the point of origin of an earthquake. Compare with EPICENTRE. **3** Medicine the principal site of an infection or other disease. **4** the state or quality of having or producing clear visual definition. ➤another term for FOCAL POINT. ➤the point at which an object must be situated with respect to a lens or mirror for an image of it to be well defined. **5** Geometry one of the fixed points from which the distances to any point of an ellipse, parabola, or other curve are connected by a linear relation. **6** Linguistics another term for RHEME. ● v. (**focused**, **focusing** or **focussed**, **focussing**) **1** adapt to the prevailing level of light and become able to see clearly. ➤adjust the focus of (a telescope, camera, etc.). ➤(of rays or waves) meet at a single point. ➤(of light, radio waves, or other energy) become concentrated into a sharp beam of light or energy. **2** (**focus on**) pay particular attention to. **3** Linguistics place the focus on (a part of a sentence).
– DERIVATIVES **focuser** n.
– ORIGIN C17: from L., lit. 'domestic hearth'.

**focus group** ● n. a group of people assembled to assess a new product, political campaign, television series, etc.

**focus puller** ● n. a person responsible for keeping the lens of a video or film camera focused during filming.

**fodder** ● n. **1** food for cattle and other livestock. **2** a person or thing regarded only as material for a specific use: *young people ending up as factory fodder.* ● v. give fodder to (cattle or other livestock).
– ORIGIN OE *fōdor*, of Gmc origin; rel. to FOOD.

**fody** /'fəʊdi/ ● n. (pl. **-ies**) a songbird of the weaver family native to Madagascar and other islands in the Indian Ocean. [Genus *Foudia*: several species.]
– ORIGIN a local word.

**FoE** ● abbrev. Friends of the Earth.

**foe** ● n. formal or poetic/literary an enemy or opponent.
– ORIGIN OE *fāh* 'hostile' and *gefā* 'enemy', of W. Gmc origin; rel. to FEUD.

**foehn** ● n. variant spelling of FÖHN.

**foetid** ● adj. variant spelling of FETID.

**foetus** ● n. variant spelling of FETUS (chiefly in British non-technical use).
– DERIVATIVES **foetal** adj. **foeticide** n.

**fog**[1] ● n. **1** a thick cloud of tiny water droplets suspended in the atmosphere at or near the earth's surface which obscures or restricts visibility. ➤Photography cloudiness obscuring the image on a developed negative or print. **2** a state or cause of perplexity or confusion. ● v. (**fogged**, **fogging**) **1** cover or become covered with steam. ➤Photography make (a film, negative, or print) obscure or cloudy. **2** bewilder or puzzle. **3** treat with something, especially an insecticide, in the form of a spray.
– ORIGIN C16: perh. a back-form. from FOGGY.

**fog**[2] ● n. the grass which grows in a field after a crop of hay has been taken.
– ORIGIN ME: origin uncertain; perh. rel. to Norw. *fogg*.

**fog bank** ● n. a dense mass of fog, especially at sea.

**fogey** /ˈfəʊɡi/ (also **fogy**) ● n. (pl. **-eys** or **-ies**) a very old-fashioned or conservative person.
– DERIVATIVES **fogeydom** n. **fogeyish** adj. **fogeyism** n.
– ORIGIN C18: rel. to earlier *fogram*, of unknown origin.

**foggy** ● adj. (**-ier**, **-iest**) **1** full of or accompanied by fog. **2** confused.
– PHRASES **not have the foggiest (idea** or **notion)** informal, chiefly Brit. have no idea at all.
– DERIVATIVES **foggily** adv. **fogginess** n.
– ORIGIN C15: perh. from FOG².

**foghorn** ● n. a device making a loud, deep sound as a warning to ships in fog.

**fogou** /ˈfəʊɡuː, -ɡəʊ/ ● n. (pl. **fogous**) Archaeology a form of artificial underground passage or chamber found in Cornwall.
– ORIGIN from Cornish *fogo, fougo*.

**fog signal** ● n. a detonator placed on a railway line in fog to warn train drivers.

**fogy** ● n. variant spelling of FOGEY.

**föhn** /fəːn/ (also **foehn**) ● n. a hot southerly wind on the northern slopes of the Alps.
– ORIGIN C19: from Ger., based on L. (*ventus*) *Favonius* 'mild west wind', *Favonius* being the Roman personification of the west or west wind.

**foible** /ˈfɔɪb(ə)l/ ● n. **1** a minor weakness or eccentricity. **2** Fencing the part of a sword blade from the middle to the point. Compare with FORTE¹.
– ORIGIN C16 (as adj. in the sense 'feeble'): from obs. Fr., in OFr. *fieble* (see FEEBLE).

**foie gras** /fwɑː ˈɡrɑː/ ● n. short for PÂTÉ DE FOIE GRAS.

**foil¹** ● v. **1** prevent the success of. **2** Hunting (of a hunted animal) cross (a scent or track) in such a way as to confuse the hounds. ● n. **1** Hunting the track or scent of a hunted animal. **2** archaic a setback or defeat.
– ORIGIN ME (in the sense 'trample down'): perh. from OFr. *fouler* 'to full cloth, trample', based on L. *fullo* 'fuller'.

**foil²** ● n. **1** metal hammered or rolled into a thin flexible sheet. ➤a thin leaf of metal placed under a precious stone to increase its brilliance. **2** a person or thing that contrasts with and so enhances the qualities of another. **3** Architecture a leaf-shaped curve formed by the cusping of an arch or circle.
– ORIGIN ME: via OFr. from L. *folium* 'leaf'.

**foil³** ● n. a light, blunt-edged fencing sword with a button on its point.
– DERIVATIVES **foilist** n.
– ORIGIN C16: of unknown origin.

**foil⁴** ● n. each of the structures fitted to a hydrofoil's hull to lift it clear of the water at speed.

**foist** /fɔɪst/ ● v. (**foist someone/thing on**) impose an unwelcome or unnecessary person or thing on.
– ORIGIN C16 (in the sense 'dishonestly manipulate a dice'): from Du. dial. *vuisten* 'take in the hand', from *vuist* (see FIST).

**fol.** ● abbrev. folio.

**folacin** /ˈfəʊləsɪn/ ● n. another term for FOLIC ACID.

**fold¹** ● v. **1** bend (something) over on itself so that one part of it covers another. ➤[often as adj. **folding**] be able to be folded into a flatter shape. **2** use (a soft or flexible material) to cover or wrap something in. ➤affectionately clasp in one's arms. **3** informal (of a company) cease trading as a result of financial problems. ➤(of a sports player or team) suddenly stop performing well. **4** (**fold something in/into**) mix an ingredient gently with (another ingredient). **5** (in poker and other card games) drop out of a hand. **6** Geology cause (rock strata) to undergo bending or curvature. ● n. **1** a form produced by the gentle draping of a garment or piece of cloth. ➤an area of skin that sags or hangs loosely. **2** chiefly Brit. a slight hill or hollow. **3** Geology a bend or curvature of strata. **4** a line or crease produced by folding.
– PHRASES **fold one's arms** bring one's arms together and cross them over one's chest.
– DERIVATIVES **foldable** adj.
– ORIGIN OE *falden, fealden*, of Gmc origin.

**fold²** ● n. **1** a pen or enclosure for livestock, especially sheep. **2** (**the fold**) a group or community with shared aims and values. ● v. shut (livestock) in a fold.
– ORIGIN OE *fald*, of Gmc origin.

**-fold** ● suffix forming adjectives and adverbs from cardinal numbers: **1** in an amount multiplied by: *threefold*. **2** consisting of so many parts or facets: *twofold*.
– ORIGIN OE *-fald, -feald*; rel. to FOLD¹.

**foldaway** ● adj. designed to be folded up for ease of storage or transport.

**folder** ● n. **1** a folding cover or wallet for storing loose papers. **2** N. Amer. a leaflet or booklet made of folded sheets of paper. **3** Computing a directory containing related files or documents.

**folderol** /ˈfɒldərɒl/ (also **falderal**) ● n. **1** trivial or nonsensical fuss. **2** dated a showy but useless item.
– ORIGIN from a meaningless refrain in old songs.

**folding money** ● n. informal money in the form of notes.

**foley** /ˈfəʊli/ ● n. [as modifier] chiefly US relating to the addition of sound effects after the shooting of a film: *a foley artist*.
– ORIGIN named after the inventor of the editing process.

**folia** plural form of FOLIUM.

**foliaceous** /ˌfəʊlɪˈeɪʃəs/ ● adj. **1** of or resembling a leaf or leaves. **2** Geology consisting of thin sheets or laminae.
– ORIGIN C17: from L. *foliaceus* (from *folium* 'leaf') + **-OUS**.

**foliage** /ˈfəʊlɪɪdʒ/ ● n. plant leaves, collectively.
– ORIGIN ME *foilage*: from OFr. *feuillage*, from *feuille* 'leaf', from L. *folium*.

**foliar** /ˈfəʊlɪə/ ● adj. technical of or relating to leaves.

**foliar feed** ● n. nutrients supplied to plant leaves.
– DERIVATIVES **foliar feeding** n.

**foliate** ● adj. /ˈfəʊlɪət, -eɪt/ foliated. ● v. /ˈfəʊlɪeɪt/ **1** decorate with leaves or leaf-like motifs. **2** number the leaves of (a book) rather than the pages.

**foliated** ● adj. **1** decorated with leaves or leaf-like motifs. ➤Architecture decorated with foils. **2** chiefly Geology consisting of thin sheets or laminae.

**foliation** /ˌfəʊlɪˈeɪʃ(ə)n/ ● n. chiefly Geology the process of splitting into thin sheets or laminae.

**folic acid** /ˈfəʊlɪk, ˈfɒl-/ ● n. Biochemistry a vitamin of the B complex found especially in leafy green vegetables, liver, and kidney.
– DERIVATIVES **folate** n.
– ORIGIN 1940s: *folic* from L. *folium* 'leaf' + **-IC**.

**folie à deux** /ˌfɒlɪ a ˈdəː/ ● n. (pl. **folies à deux**) delusion or mental illness shared by two people in close association.
– ORIGIN Fr., lit. 'shared madness'.

**folie de grandeur** /ˌfɒlɪ də ɡrɒ̃ˈdəː/ ● n. delusions of grandeur.
– ORIGIN from Fr.

**folio** /ˈfəʊlɪəʊ/ ● n. (pl. **-os**) **1** a sheet of paper folded once to form two leaves (four pages) of a book. ➤a book made up of such sheets. **2** an individual leaf of paper or parchment numbered on the recto or front side only. ➤the page number in a printed book.
– ORIGIN ME: from L., ablative of *folium* 'leaf', in med. L. used to mean 'on leaf so-and-so'.

**foliose** /ˈfəʊlɪəʊs, -z/ ● adj. Botany (of a lichen) having a lobed, leaf-like shape.

**folium** /ˈfəʊlɪəm/ ● n. (pl. **folia**) technical a thin leaf-like structure, e.g. in some rocks or in the cerebellum.
– ORIGIN C18: from L., lit. 'leaf'.

**folivore** /ˈfəʊlɪvɔː/ ● n. Zoology an animal that feeds on leaves.
– DERIVATIVES **folivorous** adj. **folivory** n.

**folk** /fəʊk/ ● pl. n. **1** (also **folks**) informal people in general. ➤(**one's folks**) one's family, especially one's parents. **2** (also **folk music**) traditional music of unknown authorship, transmitted orally. **3** [as modifier] originating from the beliefs and customs of ordinary people: *folk wisdom*.
– ORIGIN OE *folc*, of Gmc origin.

**folk dance** ● n. a traditional dance associated with a particular people or area.
– DERIVATIVES **folk dancer** n. **folk dancing** n.

**folk devil** ● n. a person or thing held to be a bad influence on society.

**folk etymology** ● n. **1** a popular but mistaken account of the origin of a word or phrase. **2** the process by which the form of an unfamiliar or foreign word is adapted to a more familiar form through popular usage.

**folkie** • n. informal a singer, player, or fan of folk music.

**folkish** • adj. **1** characteristic of ordinary people or traditional culture. **2** resembling folk music.

**folklore** • n. the traditional beliefs and customs of a community, passed on by word of mouth.
– DERIVATIVES **folkloric** adj. **folklorist** n. **folkloristic** adj.

**folk memory** • n. a body of recollections or legends that persists among a people.

**folk rock** • n. popular music derived from folk music but having a stronger beat and using electric instruments.

**folksy** • adj. (**-ier**, **-iest**) traditional and unpretentious, especially in a contrived or artificial way.
– DERIVATIVES **folksiness** n.

**folk tale** • n. a traditional story originally transmitted orally.

**folkways** • pl. n. the traditional way of life of a particular community.

**folkweave** • n. Brit. a rough, loosely woven fabric.

**folky** • adj. (**-ier**, **-iest**) resembling or characteristic of folk music.
– DERIVATIVES **folkiness** n.

**follicle** /ˈfɒlɪk(ə)l/ • n. **1** the sheath of cells and connective tissue which surrounds the root of a hair. **2** short for **GRAAFIAN FOLLICLE**. **3** Botany a dry fruit derived from a single carpel and opening on one side only to release its seeds.
– DERIVATIVES **follicular** /fɒˈlɪkjʊlə/ adj. **folliculate** /-lət/ adj. **folliculated** adj.
– ORIGIN ME: from L. *folliculus* 'little bag', dimin. of *follis* 'bellows'.

**follicle-stimulating hormone** • n. Biochemistry a hormone secreted by the anterior pituitary gland which promotes the formation of ova or sperm.

**folliculitis** /fəˌlɪkjʊˈlʌɪtɪs/ • n. Medicine inflammation of the hair follicles.

**follis** /ˈfɒlɪs/ • n. (pl. **folles**) a bronze or copper coin used in late Roman and Byzantine times.
– ORIGIN from L.

**follow** • v. **1** move or travel behind. ➤go after (someone) in order to observe or monitor them. ➤go along (a route or path). **2** (**follow through**) (in sport) continue the movement of a stroke after the ball has been struck. ➤(**follow something through**) continue an action or task to its conclusion. ➤(**follow something up**) pursue or investigate something further. **3** come after in time or order. ➤(also **follow on from**) occur as a consequence or result of. **4** be a logical consequence: *it thus follows that the value must be negative.* **5** act according to (an instruction or precept). ➤act according to the lead or example of. **6** pay close attention to the movement, course, or progress of. ➤be a supporter or fan of. **7** understand the meaning of: *I still don't follow you.* **8** practise (a trade or profession). ➤undertake or carry out (a course of action or study). **9** archaic strive after; aim at: *I follow fame.*
– PHRASES **follow on** (of a cricket team) be required to bat again immediately after failing to reach a certain score in their first innings. **follow one's nose 1** trust to one's instincts. **2** go straight ahead. **follow suit 1** conform to another's actions. **2** (in bridge, whist, and other card games) play a card of the suit led.
– ORIGIN OE *folgian*, of Gmc origin.

**follower** • n. **1** a person who follows. **2** a supporter, fan, or disciple.

**following** • prep. coming after or as a result of. • n. a body of supporters or admirers. • adj. **1** next in time or order. ➤about to be mentioned: *the following information.* **2** (of a wind) blowing in the same direction as the course of a vessel.

**follow-the-leader** (also **follow-my-leader**) • n. a children's game in which the participants must copy the actions and words of a person acting as leader.

**follow-through** • n. the continuing of an action or task to its conclusion. ➤a continuation of a stroke after a ball has been struck.

**follow-up** • n. **1** a study carried out to monitor or further develop earlier work. **2** a work that follows or builds on an earlier work.

**folly** • n. (pl. **-ies**) **1** foolishness. **2** an ornamental building with no practical purpose, especially a tower or mock-Gothic ruin in a large garden or park. **3** (**Follies**) a theatrical revue with glamorous female performers.
– ORIGIN ME: from OFr. *folie* 'madness', from *fol* 'fool'.

**Folsom** /ˈfəʊlsəm/ • n. [as modifier] Archaeology denoting a Palaeo-Indian culture of Central and North America, dated to about 10,500–8,000 years ago.
– ORIGIN named after *Folsom* in New Mexico.

**foment** /fə(ʊ)ˈmɛnt/ • v. **1** instigate or stir up (revolution or strife). **2** archaic bathe (a part of the body) with warm or medicated lotions.
– DERIVATIVES **fomentation** n. **fomenter** n.
– ORIGIN ME: from Fr. *fomenter*, from late L. *fomentare*, from L. *fomentum* 'poultice, lotion'.

**fomites** /ˈfəʊmɪtiːz/ • pl. n. Medicine objects or materials which are likely to carry infection.
– ORIGIN C19: from L., pl. of *fomes*, lit. 'touchwood, tinder'.

**Fon** /fɒn/ • n. (pl. same or **Fons**) **1** a member of a people inhabiting the southern part of Benin. **2** the Kwa language of this people.
– ORIGIN the name in Fon.

**fond** • adj. **1** (**fond of**) having an affection or liking for. ➤affectionate; loving: *fond memories.* **2** (of a hope or belief) foolishly optimistic; naive.
– DERIVATIVES **fondly** adv. **fondness** n.
– ORIGIN ME (in the sense 'infatuated, foolish'): from obs. *fon* 'a fool, be foolish', of unknown origin; cf. **FUN**.

**fondant** /ˈfɒnd(ə)nt/ • n. a thick paste made of sugar and water, used in making sweets and icing cakes. ➤a sweet made of such a paste.
– ORIGIN C19: from Fr., lit. 'melting', pres. part. of *fondre*.

**fondle** • v. stroke or caress lovingly or erotically. • n. an act of fondling.
– DERIVATIVES **fondler** n.
– ORIGIN C17: back-form. from obs. *fondling* 'much-loved or petted person', from **FOND** + **-LING**.

**fondu** /fɒ̃ˈd(j)uː/ • adj. [postpos.] Ballet involving a lowering of the body by bending the knee of the supporting leg.
– ORIGIN Fr., lit. 'melted'.

**fondue** /ˈfɒnd(j)uː/ • n. a dish in which small pieces of food are dipped into a hot sauce or a hot cooking medium such as oil or broth.
– ORIGIN Fr., fem. past part. of *fondre* 'to melt'.

**fons et origo** /ˌfɒnz ɛt ˈɒrɪgəʊ, ɒˈrʌɪgəʊ/ • n. the source and origin of something.
– ORIGIN L., orig. as *fons et origo mali* 'the source and origin of evil'.

**font**[1] • n. **1** a receptacle in a church for the water used in baptism. **2** a reservoir for oil in an oil lamp.
– DERIVATIVES **fontal** adj.
– ORIGIN OE: from L. *fons*, *font-* 'spring, fountain'.

**font**[2] (Brit. also **fount**) • n. Printing a set of type of a particular face and size.
– ORIGIN C16 (denoting the action or process of casting or founding): from Fr. *fonte*, from *fondre* 'to melt'.

**fontanelle** /ˌfɒntəˈnɛl/ (US **fontanel**) • n. a soft area between the bones of the cranium in an infant or fetus, where the sutures are not yet fully formed.
– ORIGIN C16: from Fr., from mod. L. *fontanella*, from an OFr. dimin. of *fontaine* (see **FOUNTAIN**).

**fontina** /fɒnˈtiːnə/ • n. a pale yellow Italian cheese.
– ORIGIN from Ital.

**food** • n. any nutritious substance that people or animals eat or drink or that plants absorb in order to maintain life and growth.
– PHRASES **food for thought** something that warrants serious consideration.
– ORIGIN OE *fōda*, of Gmc origin; rel. to **FODDER**.

**food chain** • n. a series of organisms each dependent on the next as a source of food.

**foodie** (also **foody**) • n. (pl. **-ies**) informal a person with a particular interest in food; a gourmet.

**food poisoning** • n. illness caused by bacteria or other

toxins in food, typically with vomiting and diarrhoea.

**foodstuff** • n. a substance suitable for consumption as food.

**food value** • n. the nutritional value of a foodstuff.

**foo-foo** • n. variant spelling of **FUFU**.

**fool**[1] • n. **1** a person who acts unwisely. ➤ archaic a person who is duped or imposed on. **2** historical a jester or clown, especially one retained in a great household. • v. **1** trick, deceive, or dupe. **2** (usu. **fool about/around**) act in a joking or frivolous way. ➤ (**fool around**) N. Amer. engage in casual or extramarital sexual activity. • adj. N. Amer. informal foolish or silly.
– PHRASES **be no** (or **nobody's**) **fool** be shrewd or prudent. **make a fool of** trick or deceive (someone) so that they look foolish. ➤ (**make a fool of oneself**) appear foolish through incompetent or inappropriate behaviour. **more fool ——** the specified person is behaving unwisely.
– DERIVATIVES **foolery** n.
– ORIGIN ME: from OFr. *fol* 'fool, foolish', from L. *follis* 'bellows, windbag', by extension 'empty-headed person'.

**fool**[2] • n. chiefly Brit. a cold dessert made of puréed fruit mixed or served with cream or custard.
– ORIGIN C16: perh. from **FOOL**[1].

**foolhardy** • adj. (**-ier, -iest**) recklessly bold or rash.
– DERIVATIVES **foolhardily** adv. **foolhardiness** n.
– ORIGIN ME: from OFr. *folhardi*, from *fol* 'foolish' + *hardi* (see **HARDY**).

**foolish** • adj. lacking good sense or judgement; silly or unwise.
– DERIVATIVES **foolishly** adv. **foolishness** n.

**foolproof** • adj. incapable of going wrong or being misused.

**foolscap** /'fu:lzkap, 'fu:ls-/ • n. Brit. a size of paper, about 330 × 200 (or 400) mm.
– ORIGIN C17: said to be named from a former watermark representing a fool's cap.

**fool's errand** • n. a task or activity that has no hope of success.

**fool's gold** • n. a brassy yellow mineral that can be mistaken for gold, especially pyrite.

**fool's mate** • n. Chess checkmate forced by Black's queen on the second move of the game.

**fool's paradise** • n. a state of happiness based on not knowing about or ignoring potential trouble.

**fool's parsley** • n. a poisonous white-flowered plant of the parsley family, with fern-like leaves and an unpleasant smell. [*Aethusa cynapium*.]

**foot** • n. (pl. **feet** /fi:t/) **1** the lower extremity of the leg below the ankle, on which a person or animal stands or walks. **2** poetic/literary manner or speed of walking or running: *fleet of foot*. **3** [treated as pl.] Brit. infantry; foot soldiers. **4** the lower or lowest part of something vertical; the base or bottom. ➤ the end of a table furthest from the host. ➤ the end of a bed where the occupant's feet normally rest. **5** a unit of linear measure equal to 12 inches (30.48 cm). **6** Music a unit used in classifying sets of organ pipes or harpsichord strings by their pitch. **7** Prosody a group of syllables constituting a metrical unit. **8** a device on a sewing machine for holding the material steady as it is sewn. • v. **1** informal pay (a bill, especially a large or unreasonable one). **2** (**foot it**) cover a distance, especially a long one, on foot. ➤ archaic dance.
– PHRASES **feet of clay** a fundamental flaw or weakness in a person otherwise revered. **get** (or **start**) **off on the right** (or **wrong**) **foot** make a good (or bad) start at something. **have** (or **keep**) **one's feet on the ground** be (or remain) practical and sensible. **have** (or **get**) **a foot in the door** have (or gain) a first introduction to a profession or organization. **have one foot in the grave** humorous be very old or ill. **my foot!** informal said to express strong contradiction. **on** (or **by**) **foot** walking rather than travelling by car or using other transport. **put one's best foot forward** begin with as much effort and determination as possible. **put one's foot down** informal **1** adopt a firm policy when faced with opposition or disobedience. **2** Brit. accelerate a motor vehicle by pressing the accelerator pedal. **put one's foot in it** informal say or do something tactless or embarrassing. **put a foot wrong** [usu. with neg.] make a mistake. **set something on foot** archaic set an action or process in motion. **under one's feet** in one's way. **under foot** on the ground.
– DERIVATIVES **footless** adj.
– ORIGIN OE *fōt*, of Gmc origin.

**footage** • n. **1** a length of film made for cinema or television. **2** size or length measured in feet.

**foot-and-mouth disease** • n. a contagious viral disease of cattle and sheep, causing ulceration of the hoofs and around the mouth.

**football** • n. **1** any of a number of forms of team game involving kicking a ball, in particular (in the UK) soccer or (in the US) American football. **2** a large inflated ball used in such a game. **3** a topical issue that arouses controversy: *the use of education as a political football*.
– DERIVATIVES **footballer** n. **footballing** adj.

**footbed** • n. an insole in a boot or shoe.

**footbrake** • n. a foot-operated brake lever in a motor vehicle.

**footbridge** • n. a bridge for pedestrians.

**foot-candle** • n. a unit of illumination equal to that given by a source of one candela at a distance of one foot.

**-footed** • comb. form **1** for or involving a specified number of feet: *four-footed locomotion*. **2** using the foot specified: *right-footed*. **3** having feet of a specified kind.

**footer**[1] /'fʊtə/ • n. **1** [in combination] a person or thing of a specified number of feet in length or height: *a six-footer*. ➤ a kick of a football performed with a specified foot: *a low left-footer*. **2** variant of **FOOTY**. **3** a line or block of text appearing at the foot of each page of a book or document.

**footer**[2] /'fu:tə/ • v. Scottish fiddle about.
– ORIGIN C18: var. of obs. *foutre* 'valueless thing, contemptible person', from OFr.

**footfall** • n. **1** the sound of a footstep or footsteps. **2** the number of people entering a shop or shopping area in a given time.

**foot fault** • n. (in tennis, squash, etc.) an infringement of the rules made by overstepping the baseline when serving. • v. (**foot-fault**) make a foot fault.

**foothill** • n. a low hill at the base of a mountain or mountain range.

**foothold** • n. **1** a place where one can lodge a foot to give secure support while climbing. **2** a secure position from which further progress may be made: *a foothold in the Russian market*.

**footie** • n. variant spelling of **FOOTY**.

**footing** • n. **1** (**one's footing**) a secure grip with one's feet. **2** the basis on which something is established or operates. **3** the foundations of a wall, usually with a course of brickwork wider than the base of the wall.

**footle** /'fu:t(ə)l/ • v. chiefly Brit. engage in fruitless activity; mess about.
– ORIGIN C19: perh. from dial. *footer* 'idle, potter about', from C16 *foutre* 'worthless thing', from OFr., lit. 'have sexual intercourse with'.

**footlights** • pl. n. a row of spotlights along the front of a stage at the level of the actors' feet.

**footling** /'fu:tlɪŋ/ • adj. trivial and irritating.

**footlocker** • n. N. Amer. a small trunk or storage chest.

**footloose** • adj. free to go where one likes and do as one pleases.

**footman** • n. (pl. **-men**) **1** a liveried servant whose duties include admitting visitors and waiting at table. **2** historical a soldier in the infantry. **3** archaic a trivet to hang on the bars of a grate. **4** used in names of small moths of a subdued colour. [*Eilem lurideola* (**common footman**) and other species.]

**footmark** • n. a footprint.

**footnote** • n. an additional piece of information at the bottom of a page. • v. add a footnote or footnotes to.

**footpad** • n. historical a highwayman operating on foot rather than riding a horse.

**footpath** • n. a path for people to walk along, especially a right of way in the countryside.

**footplate** • n. chiefly Brit. the platform for the crew in the cab of a locomotive.

**foot-pound** ● **n.** a unit of energy equal to the amount required to raise 1 lb a distance of 1 foot.

**foot-pound-second system** ● **n.** a system of measurement with the foot, pound, and second as basic units.

**footprint** ● **n. 1** the impression left by a foot or shoe on the ground. **2** the area in which a broadcast signal can be received. **3** the area beneath an aircraft or a land vehicle which is affected by its noise or weight. **4** Computing the space taken up on a surface by a piece of hardware.

**footrest** ● **n.** a support for the feet, used when sitting.

**foot rot** ● **n. 1** a bacterial disease of the feet in sheep and other hoofed animals. **2** a fungal disease of plants in which the base of the stem rots.

**footsie** /ˈfʊtsi/ ● **n.** (usu. in phr. **play footsie**) informal the action of touching someone's feet lightly with one's own feet as a playful expression of romantic interest.
– ORIGIN 1940s: humorous dimin. of **FOOT**.

**footslog** ● **v.** (**-slogged**, **-slogging**) laboriously walk or march for a long distance. ● **n.** a long and exhausting walk or march.
– DERIVATIVES **footslogger** n.

**foot soldier** ● **n. 1** a soldier who fights on foot. **2** a low-ranking person who nevertheless does valuable work.

**footsore** ● **adj.** having sore feet from much walking.

**footstalk** ● **n.** the short supporting stalk of a leaf or flower.

**footstep** ● **n.** a step taken in walking, especially as heard by another person.
– PHRASES **follow** (or **tread**) **in someone's footsteps** do as another person did before.

**footstool** ● **n.** a low stool for resting the feet on when sitting.

**foot valve** ● **n.** a one-way valve at the inlet of a pipe or the base of a suction pump.

**footwall** ● **n.** Geology the block of rock which lies on the underside of an inclined fault or mineral vein.

**footwear** ● **n.** shoes, boots, and other coverings for the feet.

**footwell** ● **n.** a space for the feet in front of a seat in a vehicle.

**footwork** ● **n.** the manner in which one moves one's feet in dancing and sport.

**footy** (also **footie** or **footer**) ● **n.** Brit. informal term for **FOOTBALL** (in sense 1).

**foo yong** /fuː ˈjɒŋ/ ● **n.** a Chinese dish or sauce made with egg as a main ingredient.
– ORIGIN from Chin. *foō yung*, lit. 'hibiscus'.

**foozle** /ˈfuːz(ə)l/ informal ● **n.** a clumsy or botched attempt at something, especially a shot in golf. ● **v.** bungle.
– ORIGIN C19: from Ger. dial. *fuseln* 'work badly'.

**fop** ● **n.** a man who is excessively concerned with his clothes and appearance.
– DERIVATIVES **foppery** n. **foppish** adj. **foppishly** adv. **foppishness** n.
– ORIGIN ME (in the sense 'fool'): perh. rel. to **FOB**[2].

**for** ● **prep. 1** in favour of. **2** affecting or with regard to. **3** on behalf of or to the benefit of. **4** having as a purpose or function. **5** having as a reason or cause. **6** having as a destination. **7** representing. **8** in exchange for. ➤ charged as (a price). **9** in relation to the expected norm of. **10** indicating the extent of (a distance) or the length of (a period of time). **11** indicating an occasion in a series. ● **conj.** poetic/literary because; since.
– PHRASES **be for it** Brit. informal be about to be punished or get into trouble. **oh for** —— I long for ——.
– ORIGIN OE, prob. a reduction of a Gmc prep. meaning 'before' (in place or time); rel. to Ger. *für*, also to **FORE**.

**for-** ● **prefix 1** denoting prohibition: *forbid*. **2** denoting abstention, neglect, or renunciation: *forgive*. **3** used as an intensifier: *forlorn*.
– ORIGIN OE.

**f.o.r.** ● **abbrev.** free on rail. See ***free on board*** at **FREE**.

**fora** plural form of **FORUM** (in sense 3).

**forage** /ˈfɒrɪdʒ/ ● **v.** search widely for food or provisions. ➤ obtain (food) by searching. ➤ search (a place) so as to obtain food. ● **n. 1** food for horses and cattle. **2** an act of foraging.
– DERIVATIVES **forager** n.
– ORIGIN ME: from OFr. *fourrage* (n.), *fourrager* (v.), from *fuerre* 'straw', of Gmc origin and rel. to **FODDER**.

**forage cap** ● **n.** a soldier's peaked cap.

**forage fish** ● **n.** a species of fish which is the prey of more valuable game fish.

**foramen** /fəˈreɪmɛn/ ● **n.** (pl. **foramina** /-ˈramɪnə/) Anatomy an opening, hole, or passage, especially in a bone.
– ORIGIN C17: from L.

**foramen magnum** /ˈmagnəm/ ● **n.** Anatomy the hole in the base of the skull through which the spinal cord passes.
– ORIGIN L., 'large opening'.

**foraminifer** /ˌfɒrəˈmɪnɪfə/ ● **n.** (pl. **foraminifers** or **foraminifera** /ˌfɒrəmɪˈnɪf(ə)rə/) Zoology a single-celled planktonic animal with a perforated chalky shell through which slender protrusions of protoplasm extend. [Order Foraminiferida.]
– DERIVATIVES **foraminiferal** /ˌfɒrəmɪˈnɪf(ə)rəl/ adj. **foraminiferan** n. & adj. **foraminiferous** adj.
– ORIGIN C19: from L. *foramen, foramin-* (see **FORAMEN**) + *-fer* 'bearing'.

**forasmuch as** ● **conj.** archaic because; since.
– ORIGIN ME *for as much*, translating OFr. *por tant que* 'for so much as'.

**forastero** /ˌfɒrəˈstɛːrəʊ/ ● **n.** (pl. **-os**) a cacao tree of a variety providing the bulk of the world's cocoa beans.
– ORIGIN C19: from Sp., lit. 'foreign', because the tree was an import to Venezuela from the West Indies.

**foray** /ˈfɒreɪ/ ● **n. 1** a sudden attack or incursion into enemy territory. **2** a brief but spirited attempt to become involved in a new activity. ● **v.** make or go on a foray.
– DERIVATIVES **forayer** n.
– ORIGIN ME: back-form. from *forayer* 'a person who forays', from OFr. *forrier* 'forager', from *fuerre* (see **FORAGE**).

**forb** /fɔːb/ ● **n.** Botany a herbaceous flowering plant other than a grass.
– ORIGIN 1920s: from Gk *phorbē* 'fodder'.

**forbade** (also **forbad**) past of **FORBID**.

**forbear**[1] /fɔːˈbɛː/ ● **v.** (past **forbore**; past part. **forborne**) refrain from doing something.
– ORIGIN OE *forberan* (see **FOR-**, **BEAR**[1]).

**forbear**[2] /ˈfɔːbɛː/ ● **n.** variant spelling of **FOREBEAR**.

**forbearance** ● **n. 1** patient self-control. **2** Law abstention from enforcing the payment of a debt.

**forbearing** ● **adj.** patient and restrained.

**forbid** ● **v.** (**forbidding**; past **forbade** /-ˈbad, -ˈbeɪd/ or **forbad**; past part. **forbidden**) **1** refuse to allow. ➤ order not to do. **2** [as adj. **forbidden**] Physics (of a quantum transition) contrary to a selection rule.
– PHRASES **the forbidden degrees** the number of steps of descent from the same ancestor that bar two related people from marrying. **forbidden fruit** a thing that is desired all the more because it is not allowed. [with biblical allusion to Gen. 2:17.] **God** (or **Heaven**) **forbid** expressing a fervent wish that something does not happen.
– ORIGIN OE *forbēodan* (see **FOR-**, **BID**[2]).

**forbidding** ● **adj.** unfriendly or threatening.
– DERIVATIVES **forbiddingly** adv.

**forbore** past of **FORBEAR**[1].

**forborne** past participle of **FORBEAR**[1].

**forbye** /fəˈbʌɪ, fɔː-/ (also **forby**) ● **adv. & prep.** archaic or Scottish in addition; besides.

**force**[1] ● **n. 1** physical strength or energy as an attribute of action or movement. ➤ Physics an influence tending to change the motion of a body or produce motion or stress in a stationary body. **2** coercion backed by the use or threat of violence. **3** mental or moral power; influence. ➤ a person or thing exerting this. **4** an organized body of military personnel, police, or workers. ➤ (**forces**) troops and weaponry. ➤ (**the forces**) Brit. informal the army, navy, and air force. ● **v. 1** make a way through or into by force. ➤ push into a specified position using force. ➤ achieve by

effort. **2** artificially hasten the development or maturity of (a plant). **3** make (someone) do something against their will. ➤(**force something on/upon**) impose something on. **4** Baseball put out (a runner) by a force-out.
– PHRASES **by force of** by means of. **force the bidding** (at an auction) make bids to raise the price rapidly. **force someone's hand** make someone do something. **force the issue** compel the making of an immediate decision. **in force 1** in great strength or numbers. **2** (**in/into force**) in or into effect.
– DERIVATIVES **forceable** adj. **forcer** n.
– ORIGIN ME: from OFr. *force* (n.), *forcer* (v.), based on L. *fortis* 'strong'.

**force**[2] ● n. N. English a waterfall.
– ORIGIN ME: from ON *fors.*

**forced landing** ● n. an act of abruptly landing an aircraft in an emergency.
– DERIVATIVES **force-land** v.

**forced march** ● n. a fast march by soldiers, typically over a long distance.

**force-feed** ● v. force to eat food.

**force field** ● n. (chiefly in science fiction) an invisible barrier of force.

**forceful** ● adj. powerful, assertive, or vigorous.
– DERIVATIVES **forcefully** adv. **forcefulness** n.

**force majeure** /ˌfɔːs maˈʒəː/ ● n. **1** Law unforeseeable circumstances that prevent someone from fulfilling a contract. **2** superior strength.
– ORIGIN Fr., lit. 'superior strength'.

**forcemeat** ● n. a mixture of meat or vegetables chopped and seasoned for use as a stuffing or garnish.
– ORIGIN C17: from obs. *force* 'to stuff', alt. (influenced by the verb **FORCE**[1]) of *farce* (see **FARCE**).

**force-out** ● n. Baseball a play in which a runner is put out after being forced (by another runner) to advance to a base at which a fielder is holding the ball.

**forceps** /ˈfɔːsɛps, -sɪps/ (also **a pair of forceps**) ● pl. n. a pair of pincers used in surgery or in a laboratory. ➤a large instrument of such a type with broad blades, used to assist in the delivery of a baby.
– ORIGIN C16: from L., 'tongs, pincers'.

**force pump** ● n. a pump used to move liquid under greater than ambient pressure.

**force-ripe** ● adj. W. Indian (of a person) mature in certain respects without having developed fully in others.
– ORIGIN by assoc. with a fruit ripened by forcing.

**forcible** ● adj. done by force.
– DERIVATIVES **forcibly** adv.

**forcing** ● adj. Bridge (of a bid) requiring by convention a response from one's partner, no matter how weak their hand may be.

**ford** ● n. a shallow place in a river or stream that can be crossed on foot or in a vehicle. ● v. cross at a ford.
– DERIVATIVES **fordable** adj. **fordless** adj.
– ORIGIN OE, of W. Gmc origin; rel. to **FARE**.

**Fordism** ● n. the use in manufacturing industry of the mechanized mass-production methods pioneered by the American motor manufacturer Henry Ford (1863–1947).
– DERIVATIVES **Fordist** n. & adj.

**fore** ● adj. situated or placed in front. ● n. the front part of something, especially a ship. ● exclam. called out as a warning to people in the path of a golf ball.
– PHRASES **to the fore** in or to a conspicuous or leading position.
– ORIGIN OE: of Gmc origin.

**fore-** ● comb. form **1** (added to verbs) in front: *foreshorten.* ➤in advance: *forebode.* **2** (added to nouns) situated in front of: *forecourt.* ➤the front part of: *forebrain.* ➤preceding: *forefather.*
– ORIGIN OE (see **FORE**).

**fore and aft** ● adv. at the front and rear. ➤backwards and forwards. ● adj. **1** backwards and forwards. **2** (of a sail or rigging) set lengthwise, not on the yards.
– ORIGIN C17: perh. translating a phr. of Low Ger. origin.

**forearm**[1] /ˈfɔːrɑːm/ ● n. the part of a person's arm extending from the elbow to the wrist or the fingertips.

**forearm**[2] /fɔːrˈɑːm/ ● v. (usu. **be forearmed**) prepare in advance for danger or attack.

**forebear** (also **forbear**) ● n. an ancestor.
– ORIGIN C15: from **FORE** + *bear*, var. of obs. *beer* 'someone who exists'.

**forebode** ● v. archaic or poetic/literary act as an advance warning of (something bad).

**foreboding** ● n. fearful apprehension. ● adj. ominous.
– DERIVATIVES **forebodingly** adv.

**forebrain** ● n. Anatomy the anterior part of the brain, including the cerebral hemispheres, the thalamus, and the hypothalamus.

**forecast** ● v. (past and past part. **-cast** or **-casted**) predict or estimate (a future event or trend). ● n. a prediction or estimate, especially of the weather or a financial trend.
– DERIVATIVES **forecaster** n.

**forecastle** /ˈfəʊks(ə)l/ (also **fo'c's'le**) ● n. the forward part of a ship below the deck, traditionally used as the crew's living quarters.

**forecheck** ● v. Ice Hockey play an aggressive style of defence, checking opponents before they can attack.
– DERIVATIVES **forechecker** n.

**foreclose** ● v. **1** take possession of a mortgaged property as a result of defaults in mortgage payments. **2** rule out or prevent.
– DERIVATIVES **foreclosure** n.
– ORIGIN ME (orig. in the sense 'bar from escaping', 'shut out'): from OFr. *forclos, forclore*, from *for-* 'out' + *clore* 'to close'.

**forecourt** ● n. **1** an open area in front of a large building or petrol station. **2** Tennis the part of the court between the service line and the net.

**foredeck** ● n. the forward deck of a ship.

**foredoom** ● v. (usu. **be foredoomed**) condemn beforehand to certain failure.

**fore-edge** ● n. technical the outer vertical edge of the pages of a book.

**forefather** (or **foremother**) ● n. an ancestor.

**forefinger** ● n. the finger next to the thumb.

**forefoot** ● n. (pl. **forefeet**) **1** each of the front feet of a four-footed animal. **2** the foremost section of a shoe. **3** the foremost section of a ship's keel.

**forefront** ● n. the leading position or place.

**foregather** (also **forgather**) ● v. formal assemble.
– ORIGIN C15 (orig. Scots as *forgadder*): from Du. *vergaderen.*

**forego**[1] ● v. variant spelling of **FORGO**.

**forego**[2] ● v. (**-goes**; past **-went**; past part. **-gone**) archaic precede in place or time.
– DERIVATIVES **foregoer** n.

**foregoing** ● adj. previously mentioned.

**foregone** past participle of **FOREGO**[2]. ● adj. [often postpos.] archaic past.
– PHRASES **a foregone conclusion** an easily predictable result.

**foreground** ● n. **1** the part of a view or image nearest to the observer. **2** the most prominent or important position. ● v. place in the foreground.
– ORIGIN C17: from **FORE-** + **GROUND**[1], on the pattern of Du. *voorgrond.*

**foregut** ● n. Anatomy & Zoology the anterior part of the gut, towards the mouth.

**forehand** ● n. **1** (in tennis and other racket sports) a stroke played with the palm of the hand facing in the direction of the stroke. **2** the part of a horse in front of the saddle.

**forehanded** ● adv. (in tennis and other racket sports) with a forehand stroke. ● adj. US prudent or thrifty.

**forehead** /ˈfɒrɪd, ˈfɔːhɛd/ ● n. the part of the face above the eyebrows.
– ORIGIN OE *forhēafod* (see **FORE-**, **HEAD**).

**forehock** /ˈfɔːhɒk/ ● n. Brit. a foreleg cut of pork or bacon.

**foreign** /ˈfɒrɪn/ ● adj. **1** of, from, in, or characteristic of a country or language other than one's own. ➤dealing with or relating to other countries. **2** coming or introduced from outside. **3** (usu. **foreign to**) unfamiliar or

uncharacteristic.
– DERIVATIVES **foreignness** /'fɒr(ə)nnɪs/ n.
– ORIGIN ME *foren, forein,* from OFr. *forein, forain,* based on L. *foras, foris* 'outside', from *fores* 'door'.

**Foreign and Commonwealth Office** (also **Foreign Office**) • n. the British government department dealing with foreign affairs.

**foreign body** • n. an object or piece of extraneous matter that has entered the body by accident or design.

**foreigner** • n. a person born in or coming from a foreign country. ➤ informal a stranger or outsider.

**foreign exchange** • n. the currency of other countries.

**Foreign Legion** • n. a military formation of the French army composed chiefly of non-Frenchmen and originally founded to fight France's colonial wars.

**Foreign Secretary** • n. (in the UK) the government minister who heads the Foreign and Commonwealth Office.

**foreign service** • n. the government department concerned with the representation of a country abroad.

**foreknowledge** • n. awareness of something before it happens or exists.

**foreland** • n. **1** an area of land in front of a particular feature. **2** a cape or promontory.

**forelock** • n. a lock of hair growing just above the forehead.
– PHRASES **take time by the forelock** poetic/literary seize an opportunity. **touch** (or **tug**) **one's forelock** raise a hand to one's forehead in deference to a person of higher social rank.

**foreman** (or **forewoman**) • n. (pl. **-men** or **-women**) **1** a worker who supervises other workers. **2** (in a law court) a person who presides over a jury and speaks on its behalf.
– ORIGIN ME: perh. suggested by Du. *voorman.*

**foremast** • n. the mast of a ship nearest the bow.

**foremost** • adj. the most prominent in rank, importance, or position. • adv. in the first place.
– ORIGIN OE *formest, fyrmest,* from *forma* 'first' + **-EST**[1]; cf. **FIRST** and **FORMER**[1].

**forename** • n. another term for **FIRST NAME**.

**forenoon** • n. N. Amer. or Nautical the morning.

**forensic** /fə'rɛnsɪk/ • adj. **1** relating to or denoting the application of scientific methods and techniques to the investigation of crime. **2** of or relating to courts of law. • n. (**forensics**) forensic tests or techniques.
– DERIVATIVES **forensically** adv.
– ORIGIN C17: from L. *forensis* 'in open court, public', from *forum* (see **FORUM**).

**forensic medicine** • n. the application of medical knowledge to the investigation of crime, particularly in establishing the causes of injury or death.

**foreordain** /ˌfɔːrɔː'deɪn/ • v. (of God or fate) appoint or decree beforehand.
– DERIVATIVES **foreordination** n.

**forepeak** • n. the front end of the hold in the angle of the bows of a ship.

**foreplay** • n. sexual activity that precedes intercourse.

**forequarters** • pl. n. the front legs and adjoining parts of a quadruped.

**forerib** • n. a cut of beef for roasting, containing the rib from just in front of the sirloin.

**forerun** • v. (**-running**; past **-ran**; past part. **-run**) poetic/literary go before or indicate the coming of.

**forerunner** • n. **1** a precursor. **2** archaic an advance messenger.

**foresail** /'fɔːseɪl, -s(ə)l/ • n. the principal sail on a foremast.

**foresee** • v. (**-sees**, **-seeing**; past **-saw**; past part. **-seen**) be aware of beforehand; predict.
– DERIVATIVES **foreseeability** n. **foreseeable** adj. **foreseeably** adv. **foreseer** /-'siːə/ n.
– ORIGIN OE *foresēon* (see **FORE-**, **SEE**[1]).

**foreshadow** • v. be a warning or indication of.

**foresheet** • n. Nautical **1** a rope by which the lee corner of a foresail is kept in place. **2** (**foresheets**) the inner part of the bows.

**foreshock** • n. a mild tremor preceding a larger earthquake.

**foreshore** • n. the part of a shore between high- and low-water marks, or between the water and cultivated or developed land.

**foreshorten** • v. **1** represent as having less depth or distance than in reality, so as to convey an effect of perspective. **2** shorten or reduce in time or scale.

**foreshow** • v. (past part. **-shown**) archaic give warning or promise of.

**foresight** • n. **1** the ability to predict or action of predicting the future. **2** the front sight of a gun. **3** Surveying a sight taken forwards.
– DERIVATIVES **foresighted** adj. **foresightedly** adv. **foresightedness** n.
– ORIGIN ME: from **FORE-** + **SIGHT**, prob. suggested by ON *forsjá, forsjó.*

**foreskin** • n. the retractable roll of skin covering the end of the penis.

**forest** • n. **1** a large area covered chiefly with trees and undergrowth. ➤ historical an area, typically owned by the sovereign and partly wooded, kept for hunting and having its own laws. **2** a dense mass of vertical or tangled objects. • v. [usu. as adj. **forested**] plant with trees.
– DERIVATIVES **forestation** n.
– ORIGIN ME: via OFr. from late L. *forestis* (*silva*), lit. '(wood) outside', from L. *foris* (see **FOREIGN**).

**forestall** /fɔː'stɔːl/ • v. prevent or obstruct (something anticipated) by taking advance action. ➤ anticipate and prevent the action of. ➤ historical buy up (goods) before they come to market to profit from an enhanced price.
– DERIVATIVES **forestaller** n. **forestalment** n.
– ORIGIN OE *foresteall* 'an ambush' (see **FORE-** and **STALL**).

**forestay** /'fɔːsteɪ/ • n. a rope supporting a ship's foremast, running from its top to the deck at the bow.

**forester** • n. **1** a person in charge of a forest or skilled in forestry. **2** chiefly archaic a person or animal living in a forest. **3** a small day-flying moth with metallic green forewings. [Genus *Adscita.*] **4** (**Forester**) Brit. a member of the Ancient Order of Foresters, a friendly society.

**forestry** • n. **1** the science or practice of planting, managing, and caring for forests. **2** forests.

**foretaste** • n. a sample or suggestion of something that lies ahead.

**foretell** • v. (past and past part. **-told**) predict.
– DERIVATIVES **foreteller** n.

**forethought** • n. careful consideration of what will be necessary or may happen in the future.

**foretoken** • v. /fɔː'təʊk(ə)n/ poetic/literary be a sign of. • n. /'fɔːtəʊk(ə)n/ a sign of something to come.
– ORIGIN OE *foretācn* (noun: see **FORE-**, **TOKEN**).

**foretold** past and past participle of **FORETELL**.

**foretop** /'fɔːtɒp, -təp/ • n. a platform around the head of the lower section of a sailing ship's foremast.

**fore-topgallant-mast** • n. the third section of a sailing ship's foremast, above the foretopmast.

**fore-topgallant-sail** • n. the sail above a sailing ship's foretopsail.

**foretopmast** /fɔː'tɒpmɑːst, -məst/ • n. the second section of a sailing ship's foremast.

**foretopsail** /fɔː'tɒps(ə)l, -seɪl/ • n. the sail above a sailing ship's foresail.

**foretriangle** • n. the triangular space between the deck, foremast, and forestay of a sailing vessel.

**forever** • adv. **1** (also **for ever**) for all future time. ➤ a very long time (used hyperbolically). **2** continually.

**for evermore** (N. Amer. **forevermore**) • adv. Brit. forever.

**forewarn** • v. warn in advance.
– DERIVATIVES **forewarner** n.

**forewent** past of **FOREGO**[1], **FOREGO**[2].

**forewing** • n. either of the two front wings of a four-winged insect.

**foreword** • n. a short introduction to a book, typically by a person other than the author.
– ORIGIN C19: from **FORE-** + **WORD**, on the pattern of Ger. *Vorwort.*

**forex** ● abbrev. foreign exchange.

**foreyard** ● n. the lowest yard on a sailing ship's foremast.

**forfeit** /ˈfɔːfɪt/ ● v. (**forfeited**, **forfeiting**) lose or be deprived of (property or a right or privilege) as a penalty for wrongdoing. ➤ lose or give up as a necessary consequence: *she forfeited another hour in bed to muck out the horses.* ● n. a fine or penalty for wrongdoing. ➤ Law a forfeited item of property, right, or privilege. ➤ (**forfeits**) a game in which trivial penalties are exacted for minor misdemeanours. ● adj. lost or surrendered as a forfeit.
– DERIVATIVES **forfeitable** adj. **forfeiter** n. **forfeiture** n.
– ORIGIN ME (orig. denoting a crime or transgression): from OFr. *forfet*, *forfait*, *forfaire* 'transgress', from *for-* 'out' + *faire* 'do'.

**forfend** /fɔːˈfɛnd/ ● v. **1** archaic avert or prevent (something evil or unpleasant). **2** US protect by precautionary measures.
– PHRASES **God** (or **Heaven**) **forfend** archaic or humorous used to express dismay at the thought of something.

**forgather** ● v. variant spelling of **FOREGATHER**.

**forgave** past of **FORGIVE**.

**forge**[1] /fɔːdʒ/ ● v. **1** make or shape (a metal object) by heating it and beating or hammering it. **2** create: *the two women forged a close bond.* **3** produce a fraudulent copy or imitation of (a banknote, work of art, etc.). ● n. a blacksmith's workshop. ➤ a furnace or hearth for melting or refining metal.
– DERIVATIVES **forgeable** adj. **forger** n. **forgery** n.
– ORIGIN ME: from OFr. *forger*, from L. *fabricare* 'fabricate', from *fabrica* 'manufactured object, workshop'.

**forge**[2] /fɔːdʒ/ ● v. move forward gradually or steadily. ➤ (**forge ahead**) take the lead or make progress.
– ORIGIN C18: perh. an aberrant pronunc. of **FORCE**[1].

**forget** ● v. (**forgetting**; past **forgot**; past part. **forgotten** or chiefly US **forgot**) fail to remember. ➤ inadvertently neglect to do. ➤ cease to think of. ➤ (**forget oneself**) neglect to behave appropriately.
– DERIVATIVES **forgetful** adj. **forgetfully** adv. **forgetfulness** n. **forgettable** adj. **forgetter** n.
– ORIGIN OE *forgietan*, of W. Gmc origin; ult. rel. to **FOR-** and **GET**.

**forget-me-not** ● n. a low-growing plant of the borage family with bright blue flowers. [*Myosotis scorpioides* and other species.]
– ORIGIN C16: translating the OFr. name *ne m'oubliez mye*; said to ensure that the wearer of the flower would never be forgotten by a lover.

**forgive** ● v. (past **forgave**; past part. **forgiven**) stop feeling angry or resentful towards (someone) for an offence or mistake. ➤ excuse (an offence, flaw, or mistake).
– DERIVATIVES **forgivable** adj. **forgivably** adv. **forgiveness** n. **forgiver** n. **forgiving** adj. **forgivingly** adv.
– ORIGIN OE *forgiefan*, of Gmc origin, ult. rel. to **FOR-** and **GIVE**.

**forgo** (also **forego**) ● v. (**-goes**; past **-went**; past part. **-gone**) go without (something desirable).
– ORIGIN OE *forgān* (see **FOR-**, **GO**[1]).

**forgot** past of **FORGET**.

**forgotten** past participle of **FORGET**.

**forint** /ˈfɒrɪnt/ ● n. the basic monetary unit of Hungary, equal to 100 filler.
– ORIGIN Hungarian, from Ital. *fiorino* (see **FLORIN**).

**fork** ● n. **1** an implement with two or more prongs used for lifting or holding food. ➤ a farm or garden tool of larger but similar form used for digging or lifting. **2** each of a pair of supports in which a bicycle or motorcycle wheel revolves. **3** the point where something, especially a road or (N. Amer.) river, divides into two parts. ➤ either of two such parts. **4** Chess a simultaneous attack on two or more pieces by one. ● v. **1** divide into two parts. ➤ take one road or the other at a fork. **2** dig or lift with a fork. **3** (**fork out/up**) (or N. Amer. **fork over**) informal pay money for something, especially reluctantly. **4** Chess attack (two pieces) simultaneously with one.
– DERIVATIVES **forkful** n. (pl. **-fuls**).
– ORIGIN OE *forca*, *force*, based on L. *furca* 'pitchfork, forked stick'; reinforced in ME by Anglo-Norman Fr. *furke*.

**forkball** ● n. Baseball a pitch released from between the widely spread index finger and middle finger.

**forked** ● adj. having a divided or pronged end.

**forked lightning** ● n. lightning that is visible in the form of a zigzag or branching line across the sky.

**forklift truck** ● n. a vehicle with a pronged device in front for lifting and carrying heavy loads.

**forlorn** /fəˈlɔːn/ ● adj. **1** pitifully sad and lonely. **2** unlikely to succeed or be fulfilled.
– PHRASES **forlorn hope** a persistent or desperate hope that is unlikely to be fulfilled. [C16: from Du. *verloren hoop* 'lost troop', orig. denoting a band of soldiers picked to begin an attack, many of whom would not survive.]
– DERIVATIVES **forlornly** adv. **forlornness** n.
– ORIGIN OE *forloren* 'depraved', past part. of *forlēosan* 'lose', of Gmc origin; ult. rel. to **FOR-** and **LOSE**.

**form** ● n. **1** visible shape or configuration. ➤ style, design, and arrangement in an artistic work as distinct from its content. **2** a way in which a thing exists or appears. ➤ any of the ways in which a word may be spelled, pronounced, or inflected. ➤ Philosophy the essential nature of a species or thing, especially (in Plato's thought) regarded as an abstract ideal which real things imitate or participate in. **3** a type or variety of something. **4** the customary or correct method or procedure. ➤ a ritual or convention. **5** a printed document with blank spaces for information to be inserted. **6** chiefly Brit. a class or year in a school. **7** the state of a sports player with regard to their current standard of play. ➤ details of previous performances by a racehorse or greyhound. ➤ a person's mood and state of health. ➤ Brit. informal a criminal record. **8** Brit. a long bench without a back. **9** Printing, chiefly US variant spelling of **FORME**. **10** Brit. a hare's lair. **11** a temporary wooden structure used to hold concrete during setting. ● v. **1** bring together parts to create. ➤ go to make up. ➤ establish or develop. ➤ (**form people/things up** or **form up**) chiefly Military bring or be brought into a certain formation. ➤ articulate (a word or other linguistic unit). **2** (often **form something into** or **form into**) make or be made into a certain form.
– PHRASES **in** (or chiefly Brit. **on**) **form** playing or performing well. **off** (or chiefly Brit. **out of**) **form** not playing or performing well.
– DERIVATIVES **formability** n. **formable** adj. **formless** adj. **formlessly** adv. **formlessness** n.
– ORIGIN ME: from OFr. *forme* (n.), *fo(u)rmer* (v.), both based on L. *forma* 'a mould or form'.

**-form** (usu. as **-iform**) ● comb. form **1** having the form of: *cruciform.* **2** having a particular number of: *multiform.*
– ORIGIN from Fr. *-forme*, from L. *-formis*, from *forma* 'form'.

**forma** /ˈfɔːmə/ ● n. (pl. **formas** or **formae** /-miː/) Botany a taxonomic category that ranks below variety, representing e.g. a colour variant.
– ORIGIN C20: L., 'form'.

**formal** ● adj. **1** done in accordance with rules of convention or etiquette. ➤ having a conventionally recognized structure or set of rules: *he had little formal education.* ➤ of or denoting a style of writing or public speaking characterized by more elaborate grammatical structures and more conservative and technical vocabulary. ➤ (especially of a garden) arranged in a precise or symmetrical manner. **2** officially recognized: *a formal complaint.* **3** of or concerned with outward form rather than content. ➤ having the form without the spirit. ➤ of or relating to linguistic or logical form as opposed to function or meaning. ● n. N. Amer. an evening dress. ➤ an occasion on which evening dress is worn.
– DERIVATIVES **formally** adv.
– ORIGIN ME: from L. *formalis*, from *forma* (see **FORM**).

**formaldehyde** /fɔːˈmaldɪhʌɪd/ ● n. Chemistry a colourless pungent gas made by oxidizing methanol, and used in solution as a preservative for biological specimens.
– ORIGIN C19: blend of **FORMIC ACID** and **ALDEHYDE**.

**formalin** /ˈfɔːm(ə)lɪn/ ● n. a solution of formaldehyde in water.

**formalism** ● n. **1** excessive adherence to prescribed

forms. **2** concern or excessive concern with form rather than content in artistic creation. **3** a description in formal mathematical or logical terms.
– DERIVATIVES **formalist** n. **formalistic** adj.

**formality** • n. (pl. **-ies**) the rigid observance of rules or convention. ➤a thing that is done simply to comply with convention, regulations, or custom. ➤**(a formality)** something done or happening as a matter of course.

**formalize** (also **-ise**) • v. **1** give legal or formal status to. **2** give a definite form to.
– DERIVATIVES **formalization** n.

**formant** /ˈfɔːm(ə)nt/ • n. Phonetics any of the three characteristic pitch constituents of a vowel.
– ORIGIN C20: Ger., from L. *formant-*, *formare* 'form'.

**format** • n. the way in which something is arranged or presented. ➤Computing a defined structure for the processing, storage, or display of data. • v. **(formatted, formatting)** (especially in computing) arrange or put into a format. ➤prepare (a storage medium) to receive data.
– ORIGIN C19: via Fr. and Ger. from L. *formatus (liber)* 'shaped (book)'.

**formation** • n. **1** the action of forming or the process of being formed. **2** a structure or arrangement. ➤a formal arrangement of aircraft in flight or troops.
– DERIVATIVES **formational** adj.

**formation dancing** • n. a variety of competitive ballroom dancing in which a team of couples dance a prepared routine.

**formative** • adj. serving to form something, especially having a profound influence on a person's development. ➤Linguistics denoting or relating to any of the smallest meaningful units that are used to form words in a language, typically combining forms and inflections.
– DERIVATIVES **formatively** adv.
– ORIGIN C15: from OFr. *formatif, -ive* or med. L. *formativus*, from L. *formare* (see **FORM**).

**form class** • n. Linguistics a part of speech or subset of a part of speech.

**form criticism** • n. analysis of the Bible by tracing the history of its content by literary forms such as parables and psalms.

**form drag** • n. Aeronautics that part of the drag on an aerofoil which arises from its shape.

**forme** /fɔːm/ (also **form**) • n. Printing a body of type secured in a chase for printing. ➤a quantity of film arranged for making a plate.
– ORIGIN C15: var. of **FORM**.

**former**[1] • adj. **1** having been previously. ➤of or occurring in the past. **2** **(the former)** denoting the first or first-mentioned of two people or things.
– ORIGIN ME: from OE *forma* (see **FOREMOST**) + **-ER**[2].

**former**[2] • n. **1** a person or thing that forms something. **2** a transverse strengthening part in an aircraft wing or fuselage. **3** a frame or core around which an electrical coil can be wound. **4** [in combination] Brit. a person in a particular school year: *a fifth-former.*

**formerly** • adv. in the past.

**Formica** /fɔːˈmʌɪkə/ • n. trademark a hard durable plastic laminate used for worktops, cupboard doors, etc.
– ORIGIN 1920s (orig. US): of unknown origin.

**formic acid** /ˈfɔːmɪk/ • n. Chemistry an irritant volatile organic acid present in the fluid emitted by some ants. [HCOOH.]
– DERIVATIVES **formate** n.
– ORIGIN C18: *formic* from L. *formica* 'ant'.

**formication** /ˌfɔːmɪˈkeɪʃ(ə)n/ • n. a sensation like insects crawling over the skin.
– ORIGIN C18: from L. *formicatio(n-)*, from *formicare* 'crawl like an ant'.

**formidable** /ˈfɔːmɪdəb(ə)l, fɔːˈmɪd-/ • adj. inspiring fear or respect through being impressively large, powerful, or capable.
– DERIVATIVES **formidableness** n. **formidably** adv.
– ORIGIN ME: from Fr., or from L. *formidabilis*, from *formidare* 'to fear'.

**form letter** • n. a standardized letter to deal with frequently occurring matters.

**formol** /ˈfɔːmɒl/ • n. another term for **FORMALIN**.

**formula** /ˈfɔːmjʊlə/ • n. **1** (pl. **formulae** /-liː/) a mathematical relationship or rule expressed in symbols. ➤(also **chemical formula**) a set of chemical symbols showing the elements present in a compound and their relative proportions. **2** (pl. **formulas**) a fixed form of words, especially one used in particular contexts or as a conventional usage. ➤a rule or style unintelligently followed. **3** (pl. **formulas**) a method or procedure for achieving something. ➤a list of ingredients with which something is made. ➤an infant's liquid food preparation based on cow's milk or soya protein. **4** (usually followed by a numeral) a classification of racing car, especially by the engine capacity.
– DERIVATIVES **formulaic** adj. **formulaically** adv. **formularize** (also **-ise**) v.
– ORIGIN C17: from L., dimin. of *forma* 'shape, mould'.

**formulable** • adj. capable of being formulated.

**formulary** /ˈfɔːmjʊləri/ • n. (pl. **-ies**) **1** a collection of set forms, especially for use in religious ceremonies. **2** an official list giving details of prescribable medicines.
– ORIGIN C16: Fr. *formulaire* or med. L. *formularius (liber)* '(book) of formulae'.

**formulate** /ˈfɔːmjʊleɪt/ • v. create or prepare methodically. ➤express (an idea) in a concise or systematic way.
– DERIVATIVES **formulator** n.

**formulation** • n. **1** the action of formulating. **2** a material or mixture prepared according to a formula.

**formwork** • n. another term for **FORM** (in sense 11).

**formyl** /ˈfɔːmʌɪl, -mɪl/ • n. [as modifier] Chemistry of or denoting the acyl radical –CHO, derived from formic acid.

**fornent** /fɔːˈnɛnt, fə-/ (also **fornenst**) • prep. dialect, chiefly Scottish alongside, opposite, or close by.
– ORIGIN ME: blend of **FORE** and **ANENT**.

**fornicate** • v. formal or humorous have sexual intercourse with someone one is not married to.
– DERIVATIVES **fornication** n. **fornicator** n.
– ORIGIN C16 (earlier (ME) as *fornication*): from eccles. L. *fornicat-, fornicari* 'to arch', from L. *fornix, fornic-* 'vaulted chamber', later 'brothel'.

**forsake** • v. (past **forsook**; past part. **forsaken**) chiefly poetic/literary abandon. ➤renounce or give up.
– DERIVATIVES **forsakenness** n. **forsaker** n.
– ORIGIN OE *forsacan* 'renounce, refuse', of W. Gmc origin; ult. rel. to **FOR-** and **SAKE**[1].

**forsooth** /fəˈsuːθ/ • adv. archaic or humorous indeed: *a kind of wine bar for royals, forsooth.*
– ORIGIN OE *forsōth* (see **FOR**, **SOOTH**).

**forswear** • v. (past **forswore**; past part. **forsworn**) formal **1** agree to give up or do without. **2** **(forswear oneself/be forsworn)** commit perjury.
– ORIGIN OE *forswerian* (see **FOR-**, **SWEAR**).

**forsythia** /fɔːˈsʌɪθɪə, fə-/ • n. an ornamental shrub whose bright yellow flowers appear in early spring before its leaves. [Genus *Forsythia*: several species.]
– ORIGIN mod. L., named after the C18 Sc. botanist William *Forsyth*, said to have introduced the shrub into Britain from China.

**fort** • n. a fortified building or strategic position.
– ORIGIN ME: from OFr. *fort* or Ital. *forte*, from L. *fortis* 'strong'.

**forte**[1] /ˈfɔːteɪ, ˈfɔːti, fɔːt/ • n. **1** a thing at which someone excels. **2** Fencing the part of a sword blade from the hilt to the middle. Compare with **FOIBLE**.
– ORIGIN C17 (orig. as *fort*): from Fr. *fort* (masc.), *forte* (fem.) 'strong'.

**forte**[2] /ˈfɔːteɪ/ • adv. & adj. Music loud or loudly.
– ORIGIN Ital., lit. 'strong, loud'.

**Fortean** /ˈfɔːtɪən/ • adj. relating to or denoting paranormal phenomena.
– DERIVATIVES **Forteana** pl. n.
– ORIGIN 1970s: from the name of the Amer. student of paranormal phenomena Charles H. *Fort* (1874–1932).

**fortepiano** /ˌfɔːteɪˈpjɑːnəʊ, -ˈpjanəʊ/ • n. (pl. **-os**) Music a piano, especially of the kind made in the 18th and early 19th centuries.
– ORIGIN C18: from **FORTE**[2] + **PIANO**[2].

**forte piano** /ˌfɔːteɪ ˈpjɑːnəʊ/ • adv. & adj. Music loud or

loudly and then immediately soft.
– ORIGIN from Ital.

**forth** • **adv.** chiefly archaic **1** out from a starting point and forwards or into view. **2** onwards in time.
– PHRASES **and so forth** and so on.
– ORIGIN OE, of Gmc origin; rel. to **FORE-**.

**forthcoming** • **adj.** **1** about to happen or appear. **2** [often with neg.] ready or made available when required. **3** willing to divulge information.
– DERIVATIVES **forthcomingness** n.

**forthright** • **adj.** direct and outspoken.
– DERIVATIVES **forthrightly** adv. **forthrightness** n.
– ORIGIN OE *forthriht* 'straight forward, directly' (see **FORTH**, **RIGHT**).

**forthwith** /fɔːθ'wɪθ, -ð/ • **adv.** without delay.
– ORIGIN ME (in the sense 'at the same time'): partly from earlier *forthwithal*, partly representing *forth with* used alone without a following noun.

**fortify** /'fɔːtɪfʌɪ/ • **v.** (**-ies**, **-ied**) **1** provide with defensive works as protection against attack. **2** invigorate or encourage. **3** [often as adj. **fortified**] add spirits to (wine) to make port, sherry, etc. **4** increase the nutritive value of (food) by adding vitamins.
– DERIVATIVES **fortifiable** adj. **fortification** n. **fortifier** n.
– ORIGIN ME: from Fr. *fortifier*, from late L. *fortificare*, from L. *fortis* 'strong'.

**fortis** /'fɔːtɪs/ • **adj.** Phonetics (of a consonant) strongly articulated, especially more so than another consonant articulated in the same place. The opposite of **LENIS**.
– ORIGIN C20: from L., lit. 'strong'.

**fortissimo** /fɔː'tɪsɪməʊ/ • **adv. & adj.** Music very loud or loudly.
– ORIGIN Ital., from L. *fortissimus* 'very strong'.

**fortitude** /'fɔːtɪtjuːd/ • **n.** courage in adversity.
– ORIGIN ME: via Fr. from L. *fortitudo*, from *fortis* 'strong'.

**fortnight** • **n.** chiefly Brit. a period of two weeks. ➤ informal (preceded by a specified day) two weeks from that day.
– ORIGIN OE *fēowertīene niht* 'fourteen nights'.

**fortnightly** chiefly Brit. • **adj.** happening or produced every two weeks. • **adv.** every two weeks. • **n.** (pl. **-ies**) a magazine issued every two weeks.

**Fortran** /'fɔːtran/ • **n.** a high-level computer programming language used especially for scientific calculations.
– ORIGIN 1950s: contr. of *formula translation*.

**fortress** • **n.** a military stronghold, especially a strongly fortified town fit for a large garrison.
– ORIGIN ME: from OFr. *forteresse* 'strong place', based on L. *fortis* 'strong'.

**fortuitous** /fɔː'tjuːɪtəs/ • **adj.** happening by chance rather than design. ➤ informal happening by a lucky chance.
– DERIVATIVES **fortuitously** adv. **fortuitousness** n. **fortuity** n. (pl. **-ies**).
– ORIGIN C17: from L. *fortuitus*, from *forte* 'by chance'.

**fortunate** • **adj.** favoured by or involving good luck. ➤ auspicious or favourable.

**fortunately** • **adv.** it is fortunate that.

**fortune** • **n.** **1** chance as an arbitrary force affecting human affairs. ➤ luck, especially good luck. ➤ (**fortunes**) the success or failure of a person or enterprise. **2** a large amount of money or assets.
– PHRASES **a small fortune** informal a large amount of money. **tell someone's fortune** make predictions about a person's future by palmistry or similar divining methods.
– ORIGIN ME: via OFr. from L. *Fortuna*, the name of a goddess personifying luck or chance.

**Fortune 500** • **n.** (trademark in the US) an annual list of the five hundred most profitable US industrial corporations.

**fortune cookie** • **n.** N. Amer. a small biscuit containing a slip of paper bearing a prediction or motto, served in Chinese restaurants.

**fortune-hunter** • **n.** a person seeking wealth by marriage.
– DERIVATIVES **fortune-hunting** n.

**fortune-teller** • **n.** a person who tells people's fortunes.
– DERIVATIVES **fortune-telling** n.

**forty** • **cardinal number** (pl. **-ies**) **1** the number equivalent to the product of four and ten; ten less than fifty; 40. (Roman numeral: **xl** or **XL**.) **2** (**the Forties**) the central North Sea between Scotland and southern Norway, so called from its prevailing depth of forty fathoms or more.
– PHRASES **forty winks** informal a short daytime sleep.
– DERIVATIVES **fortieth** ordinal number. **fortyfold** adj. & adv.
– ORIGIN OE *fēowertig* (see **FOUR**, **-TY**[2]).

**forty-five** • **n.** a gramophone record played at 45 rpm.
– PHRASES **the Forty-five** an informal name for the Jacobite rebellion of 1745.

**forty-niner** • **n.** a seeker for gold in the California gold rush of 1849.

**forum** /'fɔːrəm/ • **n.** (pl. **forums**) **1** a meeting or medium for an exchange of views. **2** chiefly N. Amer. a court or tribunal. **3** (pl. **fora**) (in an ancient Roman city) a public square or marketplace used for judicial and other business.
– ORIGIN ME: from L., lit. 'what is out of doors'.

**forward** • **adv.** (also **forwards**) **1** in the direction that one is facing or travelling. ➤ in or near the front of a ship or aircraft. **2** onward so as to make progress. **3** in the normal order or sequence. **4** ahead in time. • **adj.** **1** towards the direction that one is facing or travelling. ➤ situated in or near the front of a ship or aircraft. **2** relating to the future. **3** bold or over-familiar in manner. **4** further advanced than expected or required. • **n.** **1** an attacking player in football, hockey, or other sports. **2** (**forwards**) agreements to trade specified assets at a specified price at a certain future date. Compare with **FUTURE** (in sense 4). • **v.** **1** send (a letter) on to a further destination. ➤ dispatch; send. **2** promote.
– DERIVATIVES **forwarder** n. **forwardly** adv. **forwardness** n.
– ORIGIN OE *forweard*, var. of *forthweard* (see **FORTH**, **-WARD**).

**forward-looking** • **adj.** progressive.

**forwent** past of **FORGO**.

**fossa**[1] /'fɒsə/ • **n.** (pl. **fossae** /-siː/) Anatomy a shallow depression or hollow.
– ORIGIN C17: from L., lit. 'ditch'.

**fossa**[2] /'fɒsə/ • **n.** a large nocturnal reddish-brown cat-like mammal of the civet family, found in Madagascar. [*Cryptoprocta ferox*.]
– ORIGIN C19: from Malagasy *fosa*.

**fosse** /fɒs/ • **n.** Archaeology a long narrow trench or ditch, especially in a fortification.
– ORIGIN OE, via OFr. from L. *fossa* (see **FOSSA**[1]).

**fossick** /'fɒsɪk/ • **v.** Austral./NZ informal rummage; search. ➤ search for gold in abandoned workings.
– DERIVATIVES **fossicker** n.
– ORIGIN C19: prob. from the Engl. dial. sense 'obtain by asking'.

**fossil** /'fɒs(ə)l, -sɪl/ • **n.** **1** the remains or impression of a prehistoric plant or animal embedded in rock and preserved in petrified form. **2** humorous an antiquated person or thing. **3** a word or phrase that has become obsolete except in set phrases or forms, e.g. *hue* in *hue and cry*.
– DERIVATIVES **fossiliferous** adj. **fossilization** (also **-isation**) n. **fossilize** (also **-ise**) v.
– ORIGIN C16: from Fr. *fossile*, from L. *fossilis* 'dug up'.

**fossil fuel** • **n.** a natural fuel such as coal or gas, formed in the geological past from the remains of living organisms.

**fossil ivory** • **n.** ivory from the tusks of a mammoth.

**fossorial** /fɒ'sɔːrɪəl/ • **adj.** Zoology (of an animal) burrowing. ➤ (of limbs) adapted for use in burrowing.
– ORIGIN C19: from med. L. *fossorius* (from L. *fossor* 'digger') + **-AL**.

**foster** • **v.** **1** promote the development of. **2** bring up (a child that is not one's own by birth). ➤ Brit. assign (a child) to be fostered.
– DERIVATIVES **fosterage** n. **fosterer** n.
– ORIGIN OE *fōstrian* 'feed, nourish', from *fōster* 'food, nourishment', of Gmc origin; rel. to **FOOD**.

**foster-** • **comb. form** denoting someone having a specified

family connection through fostering: *foster-parent.* ➤ concerned with fostering: *foster care.*
– ORIGIN OE.

**fosterling** ● n. chiefly archaic a foster-child.
– ORIGIN OE *fōstorling* (see **FOSTER**, **-LING**).

**fou** /fuː/ ● adj. Scottish drunk.
– ORIGIN C16: var. of **FULL**[1].

**fouetté** /ˈfwɛteɪ/ ● n. Ballet a pirouette performed with a circular whipping movement of the raised leg to the side. ➤ a quick shift of direction of the upper body, performed with one leg extended.
– ORIGIN Fr., past part. of *fouetter* 'to whip'.

**fought** past and past participle of **FIGHT**.

**foul** ● adj. **1** offensive to the senses. ➤ informal very disagreeable or unpleasant. ➤ (of the weather) wet and stormy. **2** morally offensive; wicked or obscene. ➤ done contrary to the rules of a sport. **3** polluted or contaminated. ➤ (**foul with**) clogged or choked with. ➤ Nautical (of a rope or anchor) entangled. ● n. (in sport) an unfair or invalid stroke or piece of play. ➤ a collision or entanglement in riding, rowing, or running. ● v. **1** make foul; pollute. ➤ (of an animal) dirty with excrement. **2** (in sport) commit a foul against. **3** (**foul something up** or **foul up**) make a mistake with or spoil something. **4** (of a ship) collide with or interfere with the passage of (another). ➤ cause (a cable, anchor, etc.) to become entangled or jammed.
– DERIVATIVES **foully** adv. **foulness** n.
– ORIGIN OE *fūl*, of Gmc origin.

**Foulah** /ˈfuːlə/ ● n. (pl. same or **Foulahs**) variant spelling of **FULA**.

**foulard** /ˈfuːlɑː(d)/ ● n. a thin, soft material of silk or silk and cotton.
– ORIGIN C19: from Fr.

**foul brood** ● n. a fatal bacterial disease of larval honeybees.

**foul line** ● n. Baseball either of the straight lines extending from home plate and marking the limit of the playing area within which a ball is deemed to be fair.

**foul mouth** ● n. a tendency to use bad language.
– DERIVATIVES **foul-mouthed** adj.

**foul play** ● n. **1** unfair play in a game or sport. **2** criminal or violent activity, especially murder.

**foumart** /ˈfuːmət, -mɑːt/ ● n. old-fashioned term for **POLECAT**.
– ORIGIN ME: from **FOUL** + OE *mearth* 'marten'; of Gmc origin and rel. to **MARTEN**.

**found**[1] past and past participle of **FIND**. ● adj. **1** (of an object or sound) collected in its natural state and presented in a new context as part of a work of art or piece of music. **2** (of a ship) equipped: *the ship was well found and seaworthy.*

**found**[2] ● v. **1** establish (an institution or organization). ➤ plan and begin the building of (a settlement). **2** (usu. **be founded on/upon**) base on a particular principle or concept. ➤ serve as a basis for.
– ORIGIN ME: from OFr. *fonder*, from L. *fundare*, from *fundus* 'bottom, base'.

**found**[3] ● v. melt and mould (metal). ➤ fuse (materials) to make glass. ➤ make by founding.
– ORIGIN C16: from Fr. *fondre*, from L. *fundere* 'melt, pour'.

**foundation** ● n. **1** the lowest load-bearing part of a building, typically below ground level. **2** an underlying basis or principle. ➤ [often with neg.] justification or reason. **3** the action of founding an institution or organization. ➤ an institution so established. **4** a cream or powder applied to the face as a base for other make-up.
– DERIVATIVES **foundational** adj.

**foundation course** ● n. Brit. a preparatory course taken at some colleges and universities, either in a wide range of subjects or in one subject at a basic level.

**foundation garment** ● n. a woman's supportive undergarment, such as a corset.

**foundation stone** ● n. a stone laid with ceremony to celebrate the founding of a building.

**founder**[1] ● n. a person who founds an institution or settlement.
– DERIVATIVES **foundress** n.

**founder**[2] ● n. the owner or operator of a foundry.
– ORIGIN ME: prob. from OFr. *fondeur*, from *fondre* (see **FOUND**[3]).

**founder**[3] ● v. **1** (of a ship) fill with water and sink. ➤ (of a plan or undertaking) fail. **2** (of a horse) stumble or fall. **3** chiefly N. Amer. (of a horse, pony, etc.) succumb to laminitis. ● n. chiefly N. Amer. laminitis in horses, ponies, etc.
– ORIGIN ME: from OFr. *fondrer*, *esfondrer* 'submerge, collapse', based on L. *fundus* 'bottom, base'.

**USAGE** founder

The words **founder** and **flounder** are often confused. **Founder** means, in its general and extended use, 'fail or come to nothing', while **flounder** means 'struggle; be in a state of confusion'.

**founding father** ● n. a founder. ➤ (**Founding Father**) a member of the convention that drew up the constitution of the US in 1787.

**foundling** ● n. an infant that has been abandoned by its parents and is discovered and cared for by others.
– ORIGIN ME: from **FOUND**[1] (past part.) + **-LING**.

**foundry** ● n. (pl. **-ies**) a workshop or factory for casting metal.

**fount**[1] ● n. **1** a source of a desirable quality. **2** poetic/literary a spring or fountain.
– ORIGIN C16: back-form. from **FOUNTAIN**, on the pattern of the pair *mountain, mount.*

**fount**[2] ● n. Brit. variant spelling of **FONT**[2].

**fountain** ● n. **1** an ornamental structure in a pool or lake from which one or more jets of water are pumped into the air. **2** poetic/literary or S. African a natural spring of water. **3** a source of a desirable quality. **4** Heraldry a circle with wavy horizontal stripes of blue and white. ● v. spurt or cascade like a fountain.
– ORIGIN ME: from OFr. *fontaine*, from late L. *fontana*, fem. of L. *fontanus*, from *fons, font-* 'a spring'.

**fountainhead** ● n. an original source.

**fountain pen** ● n. a pen with a reservoir or cartridge from which ink flows continuously to the nib.

**four** ● cardinal number **1** equivalent to the product of two and two; one more than three, or six less than ten; 4. (Roman numeral: **iv** or **IV**, archaic **iiii** or **IIII**.) **2** Cricket a hit that reaches the boundary after first striking the ground, scoring four runs. **3** a four-oared rowing boat or its crew.
– DERIVATIVES **fourfold** adj. & adv.
– ORIGIN OE *fēower*, of Gmc origin.

**fourchette** /fʊəˈʃɛt/ ● n. Anatomy a thin fold of skin at the back of the vulva.
– ORIGIN C18: from Fr., dimin. of *fourche* 'fork'.

**four-dimensional** ● adj. having four dimensions, typically the three dimensions of space (length, breadth, and depth) plus time.

**four-eyes** ● n. informal, derogatory a person who wears glasses.
– DERIVATIVES **four-eyed** adj.

**four-flush** N. Amer. ● n. a poker hand of little value, having four cards of the same suit and one of another. ● v. informal bluff.
– DERIVATIVES **four-flusher** n.

**four hundred** ● n. US the social elite of a community.
– ORIGIN C19: from Ward McAllister's remark 'There are only 400 people in New York that one really knows'.

**Fourierism** /ˈfʊrɪərɪz(ə)m/ ● n. a system for the reorganization of society into self-sufficient cooperatives, in accordance with the principles of the French socialist Charles Fourier (died 1837).
– DERIVATIVES **Fourierist** n. & adj.

**Fourier series** ● n. Mathematics an infinite series of trigonometric functions used to represent a given periodic function.
– ORIGIN named after the C19 Fr. mathematician Jean B. J. *Fourier.*

**Fourier transform** ● n. Mathematics a function derived from a given non-periodic function and representing it as a series of sinusoidal functions.

**four-in-hand** • **n. 1** a vehicle with four horses driven by one person. **2** N. Amer. a necktie tied in a loose knot with two hanging ends, popular in the late 19th and early 20th centuries.

**four-leaf clover** (also **four-leaved clover**) • **n.** a clover leaf with four lobes, thought to bring good luck.

**four-letter word** • **n.** any of several short words referring to sexual or excretory functions, regarded as coarse or offensive.

**four o'clock plant** • **n.** another term for **MARVEL OF PERU**.

**fourpenny one** • **n.** Brit. informal a blow.

**four-poster** (also **four-poster bed**) • **n.** a bed with a post at each corner supporting a canopy.

**fours** • **pl. n. 1** a race for four-oared rowing boats. **2** a competition for teams of four players, especially in bowls.

**fourscore** • **cardinal number** archaic eighty.

**foursome** • **n. 1** a group of four people. **2** a golf match between two pairs of players, with partners playing the same ball.

**four-square** • **adj. 1** (of a building) having a square shape and solid appearance. **2** firm and resolute. • **adv. 1** squarely and solidly. **2** firmly and resolutely.

**four-stroke** • **adj.** denoting an internal-combustion engine having a cycle of four strokes (intake, compression, combustion, and exhaust).

**fourteen** • **cardinal number** equivalent to the product of seven and two; one more than thirteen, or six less than twenty; 14. (Roman numeral: **xiv** or **XIV**.)
– DERIVATIVES **fourteenth** ordinal number.
– ORIGIN OE *fēowertīene* (see **FOUR**, **-TEEN**).

**fourth** • **ordinal number 1** constituting number four in a sequence; 4th. **2** (**a fourth/one fourth**) chiefly N. Amer. a quarter. **3** Music an interval spanning four consecutive notes in a diatonic scale, in particular (also **perfect fourth**) an interval of two tones and a semitone. ➤ Music the note which is higher by this interval than the tonic of a diatonic scale or root of a chord.
– PHRASES **the fourth estate** the press; journalism.
– DERIVATIVES **fourthly** adv.

**fourth dimension** • **n. 1** a postulated spatial dimension additional to those determining length, area, and volume. **2** time regarded as analogous to linear dimensions.

**fourth position** • **n. 1** Ballet a posture in which the feet are placed turned outwards one in front of the other, separated by the distance of one step. **2** Music a position of the left hand on the fingerboard of a stringed instrument nearer to the bridge than the third position.

**Fourth World** • **n.** those countries and communities considered to be the poorest and most underdeveloped of the Third World.

**4to** • **abbrev.** quarto.

**4WD** • **abbrev.** four-wheel drive.

**four-wheel drive** • **n.** a transmission system which provides power directly to all four wheels of a vehicle.

**fovea** /ˈfəʊvɪə/ • **n.** (pl. **foveae** /-vɪiː/) Anatomy a small depression in the retina of the eye where visual acuity is highest.
– DERIVATIVES **foveal** adj.
– ORIGIN C17: from L., lit. 'small pit'.

**fowl** • **n.** (pl. same or **fowls**) **1** (also **domestic fowl**) a domesticated bird derived from a junglefowl and kept for its eggs or flesh; a cock or hen. ➤ any domesticated bird, e.g. a turkey or duck. ➤ used in the names of birds that resemble the domestic fowl, e.g. **spurfowl**. **2** birds collectively, especially as the quarry of hunters.
– DERIVATIVES **fowler** n. **fowling** n.
– ORIGIN OE *fugol*, of Gmc origin; rel. to **FLY**[1].

**fowl pest** • **n.** Newcastle disease or fowl plague.

**fowl plague** • **n.** a serious infectious disease of poultry caused by an influenza virus.

**Fox** • **n.** (pl. same) **1** a member of an American Indian people formerly living in southern Wisconsin, and now mainly in Iowa, Nebraska, and Kansas. **2** the Algonquian language of this people.

**fox** • **n. 1** a carnivorous mammal of the dog family with a pointed muzzle, bushy tail, and typically a reddish coat. [*Vulpes vulpes* (**red fox**) and other species.] **2** informal a cunning or sly person. **3** N. Amer. informal a sexually attractive woman. • **v.** informal baffle or deceive.
– DERIVATIVES **foxlike** adj.
– ORIGIN OE, of Gmc origin; rel. to Ger. *Fuchs*.

**foxed** • **adj.** (of the paper of old books or prints) discoloured with brown spots.
– DERIVATIVES **foxing** n.

**foxfire** • **n.** N. Amer. the phosphorescent light emitted by certain fungi on decaying wood.

**foxglove** • **n.** a tall plant with erect spikes of typically pinkish-purple flowers shaped like the fingers of gloves. [*Digitalis purpurea* and related species.]

**foxhole** • **n.** a hole in the ground used by troops as a shelter against enemy fire or as a firing point.

**foxhound** • **n.** a dog of a smooth-haired breed with drooping ears, trained to hunt foxes in packs.

**fox-hunting** • **n.** the sport of hunting a fox across country with a pack of hounds by a group of people on foot and horseback.
– DERIVATIVES **fox-hunter** n.

**fox moth** • **n.** a reddish-brown moth with a velvety black and orange caterpillar. [*Macrothylacia rubi*.]

**foxtail** • **n.** a common meadow grass with soft brush-like flowering spikes. [*Alopecurus pratensis* and related species.]

**fox terrier** • **n.** a terrier of a short-haired or wire-haired breed originally used for unearthing foxes.

**foxtrot** • **n. 1** a ballroom dance having an uneven rhythm with alternation of slow and quick steps. ➤ music for the foxtrot. **2** a code word representing the letter F, used in radio communication. • **v.** (**-trotted**, **-trotting**) dance the foxtrot.

**foxy** • **adj.** (**-ier**, **-iest**) **1** resembling or likened to a fox. **2** informal cunning or sly. **3** N. Amer. informal (of a woman) sexually attractive. **4** (of wine) having a musky flavour. **5** (of paper or other material) foxed.
– DERIVATIVES **foxily** adv. **foxiness** n.

**foyer** /ˈfɔɪeɪ/ • **n.** an entrance hall or other open area in a public building, especially a hotel or theatre.
– ORIGIN C18 (denoting the centre of attention or activity): from Fr., 'hearth, home'.

**FP** • **abbrev.** former pupils (especially in the name of some rugby teams).

**fp** • **abbrev. 1** forte piano. **2** (**f.p.**) freezing point.

**FPA** • **abbrev.** (in the UK) Family Planning Association.

**FPS** • **abbrev.** Fellow of the Pharmaceutical Society of Great Britain.

**fps** (also **f.p.s.**) • **abbrev. 1** feet per second. **2** foot-pound-second. **3** frames per second.

**FPU** • **abbrev.** Computing floating-point unit.

**Fr** • **abbrev.** Father (as a courtesy title of priests). [from Fr. *frère*, lit. 'brother'.] • **symb.** the chemical element francium.

**fr.** • **abbrev.** franc(s).

**Fra** /frɑː/ • **n.** a prefixed title given to an Italian monk or friar.
– ORIGIN Ital., abbrev. of *frate* 'brother'.

**frabjous** /ˈfrabdʒəs/ • **adj.** humorous delightful; joyous.
– DERIVATIVES **frabjously** adv.
– ORIGIN 1871: coined by Lewis Carroll, appar. to suggest *fair* and *joyous*.

**fracas** /ˈfrakɑː/ • **n.** (pl. same /-kɑːz/ or US **fracases**) a noisy disturbance or quarrel.
– ORIGIN C18: Fr., from *fracasser*, from Ital. *fracassare* 'make an uproar'.

**fractal** /ˈfrakt(ə)l/ Mathematics • **n.** a curve or geometrical figure each part of which has the same statistical character as the whole. • **adj.** relating to or of the nature of a fractal or fractals.
– ORIGIN 1970s: from Fr., from L. *fract-*, *frangere* 'break'.

**fraction** /ˈfrakʃ(ə)n/ • **n. 1** a numerical quantity that is not a whole number (e.g. ½, 0.5). **2** a small or tiny part, amount, or proportion. ➤ a dissenting group within a larger one. **3** Chemistry each of the portions into which a

mixture may be separated according to a physical property such as boiling point or solubility. **4** (usu. **the Fraction**) (in the Christian Church) the breaking of the Eucharistic bread.
– ORIGIN ME: via OFr. from eccles. L. *fractio(n-)* 'breaking (bread)', from L. *frangere* 'to break'.

**fractional** • **adj.** **1** of, relating to, or expressed as a fraction. **2** small or tiny in amount. **3** Chemistry relating to or denoting the separation of a mixture into fractions.
– DERIVATIVES **fractionally** adv.

**fractionalize** (also **-ise**) • **v.** [usu. as adj. **fractionalized**] divide into separate groups or parts.
– DERIVATIVES **fractionalization** n.

**fractionate** /'frakʃ(ə)neɪt/ • **v.** chiefly Chemistry divide into fractions or components.
– DERIVATIVES **fractionation** n.

**fractious** /'frakʃəs/ • **adj.** **1** easily irritated. **2** difficult to control.
– DERIVATIVES **fractiously** adv. **fractiousness** n.
– ORIGIN C17: from **FRACTION**, prob. on the pattern of the pair *faction, factious.*

**fracture** • **n.** **1** the cracking or breaking of a hard object or material. ➤a crack or break, especially in a bone or a rock stratum. ➤the shape of the surface formed by a freshly broken rock or mineral. **2** Phonetics the replacement of a simple vowel by a diphthong owing to the influence of a following sound, typically a consonant. • **v.** break or cause to break. ➤(of a group or organization) break up or fragment.
– ORIGIN ME: from Fr., or from L. *fractura*, from *frangere* 'to break'.

**frae** /freɪ/ • **prep.** Scottish from.

**frag** N. Amer. military slang • **n.** a hand grenade. • **v.** (**fragged, fragging**) deliberately kill (an unpopular officer) with a hand grenade.
– ORIGIN C20: from *fragmentation grenade.*

**fragile** /'fradʒʌɪl/ • **adj.** **1** easily broken or damaged. **2** delicate and vulnerable.
– DERIVATIVES **fragilely** adv. **fragility** n.
– ORIGIN C15 (in the sense 'morally weak'): from L. *fragilis*, from *frangere* 'to break'.

**fragile X syndrome** • **n.** Medicine an inherited mental disability resulting from an X chromosome that is abnormally susceptible to damage.

**fragment** • **n.** /'fragm(ə)nt/ a small part broken off or detached. ➤an isolated or incomplete part. • **v.** /frag'mɛnt/ break or cause to break into fragments.
– DERIVATIVES **fragmental** adj. (chiefly Geology). **fragmentarily** adv. **fragmentary** adj. **fragmentation** n.
– ORIGIN ME: from Fr., or from L. *fragmentum*, from *frangere* 'to break'.

**fragmentation bomb** (or **fragmentation grenade**) • **n.** a bomb (or grenade) designed to break into small fragments as it explodes.

**fragrance** /'freɪgr(ə)ns/ • **n.** a pleasant, sweet smell. ➤a perfume or aftershave.
– DERIVATIVES **fragranced** adj. **fragrancy** n. (dated).

**fragrant** • **adj.** having a pleasant or sweet smell.
– DERIVATIVES **fragrantly** adv.
– ORIGIN ME: from Fr., or from L. *fragrant-, fragrare* 'smell sweet'.

**frail** • **adj.** **1** weak and delicate. **2** easily damaged or broken. • **n.** US informal, dated a woman.
– DERIVATIVES **frailly** adv. **frailness** n.
– ORIGIN ME: from OFr. *fraile*, from L. *fragilis* (see **FRAGILE**).

**frailty** • **n.** (pl. **-ies**) the condition of being frail. ➤weakness in character or morals.

**fraise** /frɛz, freɪz/ • **n.** (pl. pronounced same) **1** (in cookery) a strawberry. **2** a white brandy distilled from strawberries.
– ORIGIN from Fr.

**Fraktur** /'fraktʊə, German frak'tuːɐ/ • **n.** a German style of black-letter type.
– ORIGIN C19: Ger., from L. *fractura* 'fracture' (because of its angularity).

**framboesia** /fram'biːzɪə/ (US **frambesia**) • **n.** another term for **YAWS**.
– ORIGIN C19: mod. L., from Fr. *framboise* 'raspberry', so named because of the red swellings caused by the disease.

**framboise** /frɒm'bwɑːz/ • **n.** **1** (in cookery) a raspberry. **2** a white brandy distilled from raspberries.
– ORIGIN from Fr.

**frame** • **n.** **1** a rigid structure surrounding a picture, door, etc. ➤(**frames**) a metal or plastic structure holding the lenses of a pair of glasses. ➤the rigid supporting structure of a vehicle, aircraft, or other object. ➤a person's body with reference to its size or build. ➤a box-like structure of glass or plastic in which seeds or young plants are grown. **2** a basic underlying or supporting structure of a system, concept, or text. **3** Linguistics a structural environment within which a class of words or other linguistic units can be correctly used (e.g. *I —— him* is a frame for a large class of transitive verbs). **4** a single complete picture in a series forming a cinema, television, or video film. **5** the triangular structure for positioning the red balls in snooker. ➤a single game of snooker. • **v.** **1** place (a picture or photograph) in a frame. ➤surround so as to create a sharp or attractive image. **2** formulate. ➤archaic construct by fitting parts together or in accordance with a plan. **3** informal produce false incriminating evidence against (an innocent person).
– PHRASES **be in** (or **out of**) **the frame** be (or not be) eligible. ➤be wanted (or not wanted) by the police. **frame of mind** a particular mood.
– DERIVATIVES **framable** adj. **framed** adj. **frameless** adj. **framer** n. **framing** n.
– ORIGIN OE *framian* 'be useful', later 'prepare timber for building', 'make the wooden parts of a building': of Gmc origin and rel. to **FROM**.

**frame house** • **n.** chiefly N. Amer. a house constructed from a wooden skeleton covered with timber boards.

**frame of reference** • **n.** **1** a set of criteria in relation to which judgements can be made. **2** a system of geometrical axes in relation to which size, position, or motion can be defined.

**frame saw** • **n.** a saw with a thin blade kept rigid by being stretched in a frame.

**frameset** • **n.** the frame and front fork of a bicycle.

**frame tent** • **n.** chiefly Brit. a tent supported by a tall frame, giving it nearly perpendicular sides and standing headroom throughout.

**frame-up** • **n.** informal a conspiracy to incriminate someone falsely.

**framework** • **n.** an essential supporting or underlying structure.

**franc** /fraŋk/ • **n.** the basic monetary unit of France, Belgium, Switzerland, Luxembourg, and several other countries, equal to 100 centimes.
– ORIGIN from OFr., from L. *Francorum Rex* 'king of the Franks', the legend on gold coins struck in the 14th cent.

**franchise** /'fran(t)ʃʌɪz/ • **n.** **1** an authorization granted by a government or company to an individual or group enabling them to carry out specified commercial activities. ➤a business or service granted such authorization. ➤N. Amer. an authorization given by a professional league to own a sports team. ➤N. Amer. informal a team granted such authorization. **2** the right to vote in public elections, especially for members of parliament. • **v.** grant a franchise to. ➤grant a franchise for the sale of (goods) or the operation of (a service).
– DERIVATIVES **franchisee** n. **franchiser** (also **franchisor**) n.
– ORIGIN ME (denoting a grant of legal immunity): from OFr., based on *franc, franche* (see **FRANK**[1]).

**Franciscan** /fran'sɪsk(ə)n/ • **n.** a monk, nun, or lay member of a Christian religious order following the rule of St Francis of Assisi. • **adj.** of St Francis or the Franciscans.

**francium** /'fransɪəm/ • **n.** the chemical element of atomic number 87, an unstable radioactive member of the alkali metal group. (Symbol: **Fr**)
– ORIGIN 1940s: from the country *France* + **-IUM**.

**Franco-** (also **franco-**) • **comb. form** French; French and

...: *francophone.* ➤ relating to France: *Francophile.*
– ORIGIN from med. L. *Francus* 'Frank'.

**Francoist** ● **n.** a supporter of the Spanish dictator General Francisco Franco (1892–1975) or his policies. ● **adj.** of or relating to Franco's regime or policies.
– DERIVATIVES **Francoism** n.

**francolin** /'fraŋkə(ʊ)lɪn/ ● **n.** a large game bird resembling a partridge, found in Africa and South Asia. [Genus *Francolinus*: many species.]
– ORIGIN C17: from Fr., from Ital. *francolino.*

**Franconian** ● **n. 1** a native or inhabitant of Franconia, a medieval duchy of southern Germany. **2** a group of medieval West Germanic dialects, combining features of Low and High German. ➤ the group of modern German dialects of Franconia. ● **adj.** of or relating to Franconia or its inhabitants.

**Francophile** ● **n.** a person who is fond of or greatly admires France or the French.

**francophone** /'fraŋkə(ʊ)fəʊn/ ● **adj.** French-speaking. ● **n.** a French-speaking person.

**frangible** /'fran(d)ʒɪb(ə)l/ ● **adj.** formal fragile; brittle.
– ORIGIN ME: from OFr., or from med. L. *frangibilis*, from L. *frangere* 'to break'.

**frangipane** /'fran(d)ʒɪpeɪn/ ● **n.** an almond-flavoured cream or paste.
– ORIGIN C17 (orig. denoting the frangipani plant, the perfume of which was used to flavour frangipane): from Fr., named after the Marquis *Frangipani* (see **FRANGIPANI**).

**frangipani** /ˌfran(d)ʒɪ'pani, -'pɑːni/ ● **n.** (pl. **frangipanis**) a tropical American tree or shrub with clusters of fragrant white, pink, or yellow flowers. [*Plumeria rubra* and related species.] ➤ perfume obtained from this plant.
– ORIGIN C19: named after the Marquis Muzio *Frangipani*, a C16 Ital. nobleman who invented a perfume for scenting gloves.

**franglais** /'frɒ̃gleɪ/ ● **n.** a blend of French and English, either French that makes excessive use of English expressions, or unidiomatic French spoken by an English person.
– ORIGIN 1960s: coined in Fr., from a blend of *français* 'French' and *anglais* 'English'.

**Frank** ● **n.** a member of a Germanic people that conquered Gaul in the 6th century.
– DERIVATIVES **Frankish** adj. & n.
– ORIGIN OE *Franca*, of Gmc origin; perh. from the name of a weapon and rel. to OE *franca* 'javelin'; reinforced in ME by med. L. *Francus* and OFr. *Franc*, of the same origin and rel. to **FRENCH**.

**frank**[1] ● **adj. 1** candid and honest. ➤ sincere or undisguised. **2** Medicine unmistakable.
– DERIVATIVES **frankness** n.
– ORIGIN ME (in the sense 'free', also 'generous'): from OFr. *franc*, from med. L. *francus* 'free', from *Francus* (see **FRANK**: only Franks had full freedom in Frankish Gaul).

**frank**[2] ● **v.** stamp an official mark on (a letter or parcel) to indicate that postage has been paid or does not need to be paid. ➤ historical sign (a letter or parcel) to ensure delivery free of charge. ● **n.** a franking mark or signature on a letter or parcel.
– DERIVATIVES **franker** n. **franking** n.
– ORIGIN C18: from **FRANK**[1], an early sense being 'free of obligation'.

**franked investment income** ● **n.** (in the UK) income in the form of dividends paid to a company from earnings on which corporation tax has already been paid by the originating company.

**Frankenstein** /'fraŋk(ə)nstʌɪn/ (also **Frankenstein's monster**) ● **n.** a thing that becomes terrifying or destructive to its maker.
– ORIGIN Baron *Frankenstein*, a character in a novel (1818) by Mary Shelley, who creates a manlike monster which eventually destroys him.

**frankfurter** ● **n.** a seasoned smoked sausage made of beef and pork.
– ORIGIN from Ger. *Frankfurter Wurst* 'Frankfurt sausage'.

**frankincense** /'fraŋkɪnsɛns/ ● **n.** an aromatic gum resin obtained from an African tree (*Boswellia sacra*) and burnt as incense.
– ORIGIN ME: from OFr. *franc encens*, lit. 'high-quality incense', from *franc* (see **FRANK**[1]) in an obs. sense 'of high quality' + *encens* 'incense'.

**franklin** ● **n.** a landowner of free but not noble birth in the 14th and 15th centuries in England.
– ORIGIN ME: from Anglo-Latin *francalanus*, from *francalis* 'held without dues', from *francus* (see **FRANK**[1]).

**Franklin stove** ● **n.** N. Amer. a large cast-iron stove for heating a room, resembling an open fireplace in shape.
– ORIGIN C18: named after the Amer. statesman and inventor Benjamin *Franklin*.

**frankly** ● **adv.** in a frank manner. ➤ to be frank.

**frantic** ● **adj. 1** distraught with fear, anxiety, etc. **2** conducted in a hurried and chaotic way.
– DERIVATIVES **frantically** adv. **franticness** n.
– ORIGIN ME *frentik*, 'violently mad', from OFr. *frenetique* (see **FRENETIC**).

**frap** ● **v.** (**frapped, frapping**) Nautical bind tightly.
– ORIGIN ME (in the sense 'strike', now only dial.): from OFr. *fraper* 'to bind, strike'.

**frappé**[1] /'frapeɪ/ ● **adj.** [postpos.] (of a drink) iced or chilled. ● **n.** a drink served with ice or frozen to a slushy consistency.
– ORIGIN from Fr.

**frappé**[2] /'frapeɪ/ ● **adj.** [postpos.] Ballet (of a position) involving a beating action of the toe of one foot against the ankle of the supporting leg.
– ORIGIN Fr., lit. 'struck'.

**Frascati** /fra'skɑːti/ ● **n.** a wine, typically white, produced in the region of Frascati, Italy.

**frass** /fras/ ● **n. 1** powdery refuse produced by wood-boring insects. **2** the excrement of insect larvae.
– ORIGIN C19: from Ger. *Frass*, from *fressen* 'devour'.

**frat** ● **n.** N. Amer. informal a students' fraternity.

**fraternal** /frə'təːn(ə)l/ ● **adj. 1** of or like a brother or brothers. **2** of or denoting a fraternity. **3** (of twins) developed from separate ova and therefore not identical.
– DERIVATIVES **fraternalism** n. **fraternally** adv.
– ORIGIN ME: from med. L. *fraternalis*, from L. *fraternus*, from *frater* 'brother'.

**fraternity** /frə'təːnɪti/ ● **n.** (pl. **-ies**) **1** [treated as sing. or pl.] a group of people sharing a common profession or interests. ➤ N. Amer. a male students' society in a university or college. ➤ a religious or masonic society or guild. **2** friendship and mutual support within a group.
– ORIGIN ME: from OFr. *fraternite*, from L. *fraternitas*, from *fraternus* (see **FRATERNAL**).

**fraternize** /'fratənʌɪz/ (also **-ise**) ● **v.** (usu. **fraternize with**) be on friendly terms.
– DERIVATIVES **fraternization** n.
– ORIGIN C17: from Fr. *fraterniser*, from med. L. *fraternizare*, from L. *fraternus* (see **FRATERNAL**).

**fratricide** /'fratrɪsʌɪd/ ● **n. 1** the killing of one's brother or sister. ➤ a person who does this. **2** the accidental killing of one's own forces in war.
– DERIVATIVES **fratricidal** adj.
– ORIGIN C15: via Fr. from late L. *fratricidium*, from *frater* 'brother' + *-cidium* (see **-CIDE**).

**Frau** /fraʊ/ ● **n.** (pl. **Frauen** /'fraʊən/) a title or form of address for a married or widowed German-speaking woman.
– ORIGIN from Ger.

**fraud** /frɔːd/ ● **n. 1** wrongful or criminal deception intended to result in financial or personal gain. **2** a person or thing intended to deceive.
– DERIVATIVES **fraudster** n.
– ORIGIN ME: from OFr. *fraude*, from L. *fraus*, *fraud-* 'deceit, injury'.

**fraudulent** /'frɔːdjʊl(ə)nt/ ● **adj.** done by or involving fraud. ➤ deceitful or dishonest.
– DERIVATIVES **fraudulence** n. **fraudulently** adv.

**fraught** /frɔːt/ ● **adj. 1** (**fraught with**) filled with (something undesirable). **2** causing or affected by anxiety or stress.
– ORIGIN ME, past part. of obs. *fraught* 'load with cargo', from MDu. *vrachten*, from *vracht* 'ship's cargo'; cf.

**FREIGHT**.

**Fräulein** /'frɔɪlʌɪn, German 'frɔylaın/ ● **n.** a title or form of address for an unmarried German-speaking woman, especially a young woman.
– ORIGIN Ger., dimin. of **FRAU**.

**fraxinella** /ˌfraksɪ'nɛlə/ ● **n.** another term for **GAS PLANT**.
– ORIGIN C17: mod. L., dimin. of L. *fraxinus* 'ash tree' (because its leaves resemble those of the ash).

**fray**[1] ● **v. 1** (of a fabric, rope, or cord) unravel or become worn at the edge. **2** (of a person's nerves or temper) show the effects of strain.
– ORIGIN ME: from OFr. *freiier*, from L. *fricare* 'to rub'.

**fray**[2] ● **n.** (**the fray**) a situation of intense competitive activity. ➤a battle or fight.
– ORIGIN ME: from archaic *fray* 'to quarrel', from *affray* 'startle', from Anglo-Norman Fr. *afrayer* (see **AFFRAY**).

**frazil** /'freɪz(ə)l, frə'zɪl/ ● **n.** N. Amer. an accumulation of ice crystals in water that is too turbulent to freeze solid.
– ORIGIN C19: from Canad. Fr. *frasil*, from Fr. *fraisil* 'cinders'.

**frazzle** informal ● **v. 1** [usu. as adj. **frazzled**] cause to feel completely exhausted. **2** cause to shrivel up with burning. ● **n.** (**a frazzle**) **1** an exhausted state. **2** a charred or burnt state.
– ORIGIN C19 (orig. dial.): perh. a blend of **FRAY**[1] and obs. *fazle* 'ravel out', of Gmc origin.

**freak** ● **n. 1** (also **freak of nature**) a person, animal, or plant which is abnormal or deformed. **2** [often as modifier] a very unusual and unexpected event or situation: *a freak storm.* **3** informal a person who is obsessed with a particular activity or interest: *a fitness freak.* **4** archaic a whim. ● **v. 1** (usu. **freak out**) informal behave or cause to behave in a wild and irrational way. **2** archaic fleck or streak randomly.
– DERIVATIVES **freakish** adj. **freakishly** adv. **freakishness** n.
– ORIGIN C16: prob. from a dial. word.

**freaky** ● **adj.** (**-ier**, **-iest**) informal very odd or strange.
– DERIVATIVES **freakily** adv. **freakiness** n.

**freckle** ● **n.** a small light brown spot on the skin, often becoming more pronounced through exposure to the sun. ● **v.** cover or become covered with freckles.
– DERIVATIVES **freckly** adj.
– ORIGIN ME: alt. of dial. *frecken*, from ON *freknur* (pl.).

**free** ● **adj.** (**freer**, **freest**) **1** not under the control or in the power of another. ➤subject neither to foreign domination nor despotic government: *a free press.* ➤permitted to take a specified action. **2** not or no longer confined, obstructed, or fixed: *the researchers set the birds free.* ➤Physics (of power or energy) disengaged or available. ➤Physics & Chemistry not bound in an atom, molecule, or compound: *free oxygen.* **3** not subject to engagements or obligations. ➤not occupied or in use. **4** (**free of/from**) not subject to or affected by: *an area free from weeds.* **5** available without charge. **6** generous or lavish: *she was always free with her money.* ➤frank or unrestrained. **7** not subject to the normal conventions; improvised: *free jazz.* ➤(of a translation) conveying only the broad sense; not literal. **8** Sailing (of the wind) blowing from a favourable direction to the side or aft of a vessel. ● **adv. 1** without cost or payment. **2** Sailing with the sheets eased. ● **v.** (**frees**, **freed**, **freeing**) **1** make free; release. **2** make available.
– PHRASES **free and easy** informal and relaxed. **a free hand** freedom to act completely at one's own discretion. **free on board** (or **rail**) including delivery without charge to a ship or railway wagon. **a free ride** a situation in which someone benefits without having to make a fair contribution. **the free world** the non-communist countries of the world, as formerly opposed to the Soviet bloc. **make free with** treat without ceremony or proper respect.
– DERIVATIVES **freeness** n.
– ORIGIN OE *frēo* (adj.), *frēon* (v.), of Gmc origin; rel. to **FRIEND**.

**-free** ● **comb. form** free of or from: *tax-free.*

**free association** ● **n.** Psychology a psychoanalytic technique for investigation of the unconscious mind, in which words and thoughts are elicited from the subject as they occur, especially in response to key words or images put forward by the analyst.

**freebase** ● **n.** cocaine that has been purified by heating with ether, taken by inhaling the fumes or smoking the residue. ● **v.** take (cocaine) in such a way.

**freebie** ● **n.** informal a thing given free of charge.
– ORIGIN 1940s: an arbitrary form from **FREE**.

**freeboard** ● **n.** the height of a ship's side between the waterline and the deck.

**freebooter** ● **n.** a pirate or lawless adventurer.
– DERIVATIVES **freeboot** v.
– ORIGIN C16: from Du. *vrijbuiter*, from *vrij* 'free' + *buit* 'booty'.

**freeborn** ● **adj.** not born in slavery.

**Free Church** ● **n.** a Christian Church which has dissented or seceded from an established Church.

**free climbing** ● **n.** rock climbing without the use of devices such as pegs placed in the rock, but occasionally using ropes and belays. Compare with **AID CLIMBING**.
– DERIVATIVES **free climb** n. & v.

**freedman** ● **n.** (pl. **-men**) historical an emancipated slave.

**freedom** ● **n. 1** the power or right to act, speak, or think freely. **2** the state of being free. ➤unrestricted use of something. **3** (**freedom from**) exemption or immunity from. **4** the power of self-determination attributed to the will; the quality of being independent of fate or necessity. **5** a special privilege or right of access, especially that of full citizenship of a particular city given to a public figure as an honour: *he accepted the freedom of the City of Glasgow.* **6** archaic familiarity or openness in speech or behaviour.
– ORIGIN OE *frēodōm* (see **FREE**, **-DOM**).

**freedom fighter** ● **n.** a person who takes part in a revolutionary struggle.

**free energy** ● **n.** Physics a thermodynamic quantity equivalent to the capacity of a system to do work.

**free enterprise** ● **n.** an economic system in which private business operates in competition and largely free of state control.

**free fall** ● **n.** downward movement under the force of gravity only. ➤rapid descent or decline without means of stopping. ● **v.** (**free-fall**) move under the force of gravity only; fall rapidly.

**free flight** ● **n.** the flight of a spacecraft, rocket, or missile when the engine is not producing thrust.

**free-floating** ● **adj. 1** not attached to anything and able to move or act freely. **2** Psychiatry (of anxiety) chronic and generalized, without an obvious cause.
– DERIVATIVES **free-float** v. **free-floater** n.

**free-for-all** ● **n.** a disorganized or unrestricted situation or event in which everyone may take part, especially a fight or discussion.

**free-form** ● **adj.** not conforming to a regular or formal structure.

**freehand** ● **adj. & adv.** done manually without the aid of instruments such as rulers.

**free-handed** ● **adj.** generous, especially with money.
– DERIVATIVES **free-handedly** adv. **free-handedness** n.

**freehold** ● **n.** permanent and absolute tenure of land or property with freedom to dispose of it at will. ➤chiefly Brit. a piece of land or property held by such tenure.
– DERIVATIVES **freeholder** n.

**free house** ● **n.** Brit. a public house not controlled by a brewery and therefore not restricted to selling particular brands of beer or liquor.

**free kick** ● **n.** (in soccer and rugby) an unimpeded kick of the stationary ball awarded for a foul or infringement.

**freelance** /'fri:lɑ:ns/ ● **adj.** self-employed and hired to work for different companies on particular assignments. ● **adv.** earning one's living in such a way. ● **n. 1** a freelance worker. **2** historical a mercenary in medieval Europe. ● **v.** earn one's living as a freelance.
– DERIVATIVES **freelancer** n.
– ORIGIN C19 (orig. denoting a mercenary): from **FREE** + **LANCE**.

F

**free-living** ● adj. Biology living freely and independently, not as a parasite or attached to a substrate.

**freeloader** ● n. informal a person who takes advantage of others' generosity without giving anything in return.
– DERIVATIVES **freeload** v.

**free love** ● n. the idea or practice of having sexual relations without fidelity to one partner.

**freely** ● adv. **1** not under the control of another. **2** without restriction or interference. **3** in copious or generous amounts: *she drank freely.* **4** openly and honestly. ➤willingly and readily.

**freeman** ● n. (pl. **-men**) **1** a person who has been given the freedom of a city or borough. **2** historical a person who is not a slave or serf.

**free market** ● n. an economic system in which prices are determined by unrestricted competition between privately owned businesses.
– DERIVATIVES **free marketeer** n.

**freemartin** /ˈfriːmɑːtɪn/ ● n. a hermaphrodite or imperfect sterile female calf which is the twin of a male calf whose hormones affected its development.
– ORIGIN C17: of unknown origin.

**Freemason** ● n. a member of an international order established for mutual help and fellowship, which holds elaborate secret ceremonies.

**freemasonry** ● n. **1** the system and institutions of the Freemasons. **2** instinctive sympathy or fellow feeling between people with something in common.

**free pardon** ● n. an unconditional remission of the legal consequences of an offence or conviction.

**free port** ● n. **1** a port open to all traders. **2** a port area where goods in transit are exempt from customs duty.

**Freepost** ● n. Brit. a postal service whereby the cost of postage is paid by the business that receives the letter.

**free radical** ● n. Chemistry an uncharged molecule (typically highly reactive) having an unpaired valency electron.

**free-range** ● adj. (of livestock or their produce) kept or produced in natural conditions, where the animals have freedom of movement.

**freeride** ● n. a type of snowboard designed for all-round use on and off piste. ● v. ride such a snowboard.

**free safety** ● n. American Football a defensive back who is usually free from an assignment to cover a particular player on the opposing team.

**freesia** /ˈfriːzɪə/ ● n. a small plant with fragrant, colourful, tubular flowers, native to southern Africa. [Genus *Freesia*.]
– ORIGIN mod. L., named after the Ger. physician Friedrich H. T. *Freese* (died 1876).

**free skating** ● n. a type of figure skating performed to music, in which the skater has some choice of type and sequence of figures.

**free space** ● n. Physics space containing no electromagnetic or gravitational field, used as a standard or reference point.

**free-spoken** ● adj. archaic speaking candidly and openly.

**free-standing** ● adj. not attached to or supported by another structure.

**free state** ● n. historical a state of the US in which slavery did not exist.

**freestone** ● n. **1** a fine-grained stone which can be cut easily in any direction, in particular a type of sandstone or limestone. **2** a fruit in which the stone is easily separated from the flesh when the fruit is ripe. Contrasted with **CLINGSTONE**.

**freestyle** ● n. [often as modifier] a contest, race, or type of sport in which there are few restrictions on the style or technique that competitors employ: *freestyle wrestling.*
– DERIVATIVES **freestyler** n.

**free-tailed bat** ● n. a streamlined fast-flying insectivorous bat with a projecting tail. [Many species in family Molossidae.]

**freethinker** ● n. a person who rejects accepted opinions, especially those concerning religious belief.
– DERIVATIVES **freethinking** n. & adj.

**free throw** ● n. Basketball an unimpeded attempt at a goal awarded following a foul or other infringement.

**free trade** ● n. international trade left to its natural course without tariffs, quotas, or other restrictions.

**free vector** ● n. Mathematics a vector of which only the magnitude and direction are specified, not the position or line of action.

**free verse** ● n. poetry that does not rhyme or have a regular rhythm.

**free vote** ● n. chiefly Brit. a parliamentary division in which members vote according to their own beliefs rather than following a party policy.

**freeware** ● n. software that is available free of charge.

**freeway** ● n. N. Amer. **1** a dual-carriageway main road. **2** a toll-free highway.

**freewheel** ● n. a bicycle wheel which is able to revolve freely when no power is being applied to the pedals. ● v. **1** coast on a bicycle without using the pedals. **2** [as adj. **freewheeling**] cheerily unconcerned: *the freewheeling drug scene of the sixties.*
– DERIVATIVES **freewheeler** n.

**free will** ● n. the power of acting without the constraint of necessity or fate; the ability to act at one's own discretion. ● adj. voluntary: *free-will offerings.*

**freeze** ● v. (past **froze**; past part. **frozen**) **1** (with reference to a liquid) turn or be turned into ice or another solid as a result of extreme cold. ➤become or cause to become blocked or rigid with ice. **2** be or cause to be very cold. ➤store at a very low temperature as a means of preservation. **3** become suddenly motionless or paralysed with fear or shock. ➤(of a computer screen) suddenly become locked. **4** keep or stop at a fixed level or in a fixed state. ➤prevent (assets) from being used for a period of time. **5** (**freeze someone out**) informal behave in a hostile or obstructive way so as to exclude someone. ● n. **1** an act of freezing: *a pay freeze.* **2** informal a period of very cold weather: *the big freeze.*
– DERIVATIVES **freezable** adj.
– ORIGIN OE *frēosan*, of Gmc origin.

**freeze-dry** ● v. preserve by rapid freezing followed by subjection to a high vacuum which removes ice by sublimation.

**freeze-frame** ● n. **1** a single frame forming a motionless image from a film or videotape. **2** the facility or process of stopping a film or videotape to obtain such a frame.

**freezer** ● n. a refrigerated cabinet or room for preserving food at very low temperatures.

**freezing** ● adj. **1** below 0°C. ➤informal very cold. **2** (of fog or rain) consisting of droplets which freeze rapidly on contact with a surface. ● n. the freezing point of water (0°C).

**freezing point** ● n. the temperature at which a liquid turns into a solid when cooled.

**freight** /freɪt/ ● n. transport of goods in bulk, especially by truck, train, or ship. ➤goods transported by freight. ➤a charge for such transport. ● v. **1** transport by freight. **2** (**be freighted with**) be laden or burdened with: *each word was freighted with anger.*
– ORIGIN ME: from MDu., Mid. Low Ger. *vrecht*, var. of *vracht* 'ship's cargo'.

**freightage** ● n. the carrying of goods in bulk. ➤freight.

**freighter** ● n. **1** a large ship or aircraft designed to carry freight. **2** a person who loads, receives, or forwards goods for transport.

**French** ● adj. of or relating to France or its people or language. ● n. the language of France, also used in parts of Belgium, Switzerland, Canada, and certain other countries.
– PHRASES (**if you'll**) **excuse** (or **pardon**) **my French** informal used to apologize for swearing.
– DERIVATIVES **Frenchness** n.
– ORIGIN OE *Frencisc*, of Gmc origin, from the base of **FRANK**.

**French bean** ● n. Brit. a tropical American bean plant of which many varieties are commercially cultivated for food. [*Phaseolus vulgaris*.]

**French bread** ● n. white bread in a long, crisp loaf.

**French Canadian** • n. a Canadian whose native language is French. • adj. of or relating to French Canadians or their language.

**French chalk** • n. a kind of steatite used for marking cloth and removing grease and as a dry lubricant.

**French cricket** • n. an informal game resembling cricket but played with a soft ball which is bowled at the batter's legs.

**French cuff** • n. a shirt cuff that is folded back before fastening, creating a double-layered cuff.

**French door** • n. chiefly N. Amer. a French window.

**French dressing** • n. a salad dressing of vinegar, oil, and seasonings.

**French fries** • pl. n. chiefly N. Amer. potatoes deep-fried in thin strips; chips.

**French horn** • n. a brass instrument with a coiled tube, valves, and a wide bell, played with the right hand in the bell to soften the tone and increase the range of harmonics.

**Frenchie** • n. (pl. **-ies**) variant spelling of **FRENCHY**.

**Frenchify** • v. (**-ies**, **-ied**) often derogatory make French in form or character.

**French kiss** • n. a kiss with contact between tongues.
– DERIVATIVES **French kissing** n.

**French knickers** • pl. n. women's loose-fitting, wide-legged underpants.

**French leave** • n. informal, dated absence from work or duty without permission.
– ORIGIN C18: said to derive from the French custom of leaving a function without saying goodbye to the host or hostess.

**French letter** • n. Brit. informal, dated a condom.

**Frenchman** • n. (pl. **-men**) **1** a man who is French by birth or descent. **2** a knife with a right-angled bend in its blade, used in bricklaying.

**French mustard** • n. Brit. mild mustard mixed with vinegar.

**French plait** • n. a type of plait in which all the hair is gathered tightly and pulled back from the forehead and down the back of the head.

**French polish** • n. shellac polish that produces a high gloss on wood. • v. (**french-polish**) treat (wood) with French polish.

**French roll** • n. a hairstyle in which the hair is tucked into a vertical roll down the back of the head.

**French seam** • n. a seam with the raw edges enclosed.

**French stick** • n. a loaf of French bread.

**French tickler** • n. informal a ribbed condom.

**French toast** • n. **1** bread coated in egg and milk and fried. **2** Brit. bread buttered on one side and toasted on the other.

**French window** • n. each of a pair of glazed doors in an outside wall, opening on to a garden or balcony.

**Frenchwoman** • n. (pl. **-women**) a woman who is French by birth or descent.

**Frenchy** (also **Frenchie**) informal, chiefly derogatory • adj. French in character. • n. (pl. **-ies**) a French person.

**frenetic** /frəˈnɛtɪk/ • adj. fast and energetic in a rather wild and uncontrolled way.
– DERIVATIVES **frenetically** adv. **freneticism** n.
– ORIGIN ME (in the sense 'insane'): from OFr. *frenetique*, via L. from Gk *phrenitikos*, from *phrenitis* 'delirium'.

**frenulum** /ˈfriːnjʊləm/ • n. **1** Anatomy a small fold or ridge of tissue, in particular a fold of skin beneath the tongue or between the lip and the gum. **2** Entomology a bristle or row of bristles on an insect's hindwing which keeps it in contact with the forewing.
– ORIGIN C18: mod. L., dimin. of L. *frenum* 'bridle'.

**frenum** /ˈfriːnəm/ (also **fraenum**) • n. another term for **FRENULUM**.
– ORIGIN C18: from L., lit. 'bridle'.

**frenzy** • n. (pl. **-ies**) a state or period of uncontrolled excitement or wild behaviour.
– DERIVATIVES **frenzied** adj. **frenziedly** adv.
– ORIGIN ME: from OFr. *frenesie*, from med. L. *phrenesia*, from L. *phrenesis*, from Gk *phrēn* 'mind'.

**Freon** /ˈfriːɒn/ • n. trademark an aerosol propellant, refrigerant, or organic solvent consisting of one or more of a group of chlorofluorocarbons and related compounds.
– ORIGIN 1930s: of unknown origin.

**frequency** • n. (pl. **-ies**) **1** the rate at which something occurs over a particular period or in a given sample. **2** the fact or state of being frequent. **3** the rate per second of a vibration constituting a wave, e.g. sound, light, or radio waves. ➤the particular waveband at which radio signals are broadcast or transmitted.

**frequency distribution** • n. Statistics a mathematical function showing the number of instances in which a variable takes each of its possible values.

**frequency modulation** (abbrev.: **FM**) • n. the modulation of a radio or other wave by variation of its frequency, especially to carry an audio signal.

**frequency response** • n. Electronics the dependence on signal frequency of the output–input ratio of an amplifier or other device.

**frequent** • adj. /ˈfriːkw(ə)nt/ **1** occurring or done many times at short intervals. **2** habitual. • v. /frɪˈkwɛnt/ visit (a place) often or habitually.
– DERIVATIVES **frequentation** n. **frequenter** n. **frequently** adv.
– ORIGIN ME (in the sense 'profuse'): from Fr., or from L. *frequens*, *frequent-* 'crowded, frequent'.

**frequentative** /frɪˈkwɛntətɪv/ Grammar • adj. (of a verb or verbal form) expressing frequent repetition or intensity of action. • n. a frequentative form.

**fresco** /ˈfrɛskəʊ/ • n. (pl. **-oes** or **-os**) a type of painting done in watercolour on wet plaster on a wall or ceiling, in which the colours penetrate the plaster and become fixed as it dries.
– DERIVATIVES **frescoed** adj.
– ORIGIN C16: Ital., lit. 'cool, fresh'; first recorded in the phr. *in fresco*, representing Ital. *affresco*, *al fresco* 'on the fresh (plaster)'.

**fresh** • adj. **1** not previously known or used; new or different. **2** (of food) recently made or obtained; not tinned, frozen, or otherwise preserved. **3** full of energy and vigour. ➤(of a colour or a person's complexion) bright or healthy in appearance. **4** (of water) not salty. **5** (of the wind) cool and fairly strong. ➤pleasantly clean, invigorating, and cool: *fresh air.* **6** (**fresh from/out of**) newly come from; having just had (a particular experience): *we were fresh out of art school.* **7** informal presumptuous or impudent, especially sexually. **8** attractively youthful and inexperienced. • adv. newly; recently.
– PHRASES **be fresh out of** informal have just run out of.
– DERIVATIVES **freshly** adv. **freshness** n.
– ORIGIN OE *fersc* 'not salt, fit for drinking', superseded in ME by forms from OFr. *freis*, *fresche*; both ult. of Gmc origin.

**freshen** • v. **1** make or become fresh. ➤(**freshen up**) refresh oneself by washing oneself or changing one's clothes. **2** (of wind) become stronger and colder. **3** chiefly N. Amer. top up (a drink).

**fresher** • n. Brit. informal a first-year student at college or university.

**freshet** /ˈfrɛʃɪt/ • n. the flood of a river from heavy rain or melted snow. ➤a rush of fresh water flowing into the sea.
– ORIGIN C16: prob. from OFr. *freschete*, dimin. of *freis* 'fresh'.

**freshman** • n. (pl. **-men**) a first-year student at university or (N. Amer.) at high school.

**fresh-run** • adj. (of a migratory fish, especially a salmon) newly arrived in fresh water from the sea.

**freshwater** • adj. of or found in fresh water; not of the sea.

**fresnel lens** /freɪˈnɛl/ • n. Photography a flat lens made of a number of concentric rings, to reduce spherical aberration.
– ORIGIN C19: named after the Fr. physicist and civil engineer Augustin J. *Fresnel*.

**fret**[1] • v. (**fretted**, **fretting**) **1** be constantly or visibly anxious. **2** gradually wear away by rubbing or gnawing. **3** flow or move in small waves. • n. chiefly Brit. a state of

anxiety.
– ORIGIN OE *fretan* 'devour, consume', of Gmc origin.

**fret**[2] ● **n.** **1** Art & Architecture a repeating ornamental design of vertical and horizontal lines. **2** Heraldry a device of narrow diagonal bands interlaced through a diamond. ● **v.** (**fretted**, **fretting**) [usu. as adj. **fretted**] decorate with fretwork.
– ORIGIN ME: from OFr. *frete* 'trelliswork' and *freter* (v.), of unknown origin.

**fret**[3] ● **n.** each of a sequence of ridges on the fingerboard of some stringed instruments such as the guitar, used for fixing the positions of the fingers to produce the desired notes. ● **v.** (**fretted**, **fretting**) [often as adj. **fretted**] **1** provide with frets. **2** play (a note) while pressing against a fret.
– DERIVATIVES **fretless** adj.
– ORIGIN C16: of unknown origin.

**fret**[4] (also **sea fret**) ● **n.** N. English a sea mist or fog.
– ORIGIN C19: of unknown origin.

**fretboard** ● **n.** a fingerboard with frets.

**fretful** ● **adj.** anxious or irritated.
– DERIVATIVES **fretfully** adv. **fretfulness** n.

**fretsaw** ● **n.** a saw with a narrow blade stretched vertically on a frame, for cutting designs in thin wood or metal.

**fretwork** ● **n.** ornamental design, typically openwork, done with a fretsaw.

**Freudian** ● **adj.** relating to or influenced by Sigmund Freud (1856–1939) and his methods of psychoanalysis, especially with reference to the importance of sexuality in human behaviour. ➤ susceptible to analysis in terms of unconscious thoughts or desires: *a Freudian slip.* ● **n.** a follower of Freud or his methods.
– DERIVATIVES **Freudianism** n.

**Fri.** ● **abbrev.** Friday.

**friable** /ˈfrʌɪəb(ə)l/ ● **adj.** easily crumbled.
– DERIVATIVES **friability** n. **friableness** n.
– ORIGIN C16: from Fr., or from L. *friabilis*, from *friare* 'to crumble'.

**friar** ● **n.** a member of any of certain religious orders of men, especially the four mendicant orders (Augustinians, Carmelites, Dominicans, and Franciscans).
– ORIGIN ME: from OFr. *frere*, from L. *frater* 'brother'.

**friarbird** ● **n.** a large Australasian honeyeater with a dark, partly naked head and a long curved bill. [Genus *Philemon*: many species.]

**friar's balsam** ● **n.** a solution containing benzoin in alcohol, used chiefly as an inhalant.

**friary** ● **n.** (pl. **-ies**) a building occupied by friars.

**fribble** ● **n.** informal a foolish or inconsequential person or thing.
– ORIGIN C17: symbolic, from the earlier (now obs.) verb meaning 'stammer'.

**fricandeau** /ˈfrɪkandəʊ/ ● **n.** (pl. **fricandeaux** /-dəʊz/) a dish consisting of a veal fillet fried or stewed and served with a sauce.
– ORIGIN Fr., prob. rel. to *fricassée* (see **FRICASSÉE**).

**fricassée** /ˈfrɪkəsiː, ˌfrɪkəˈsiː/ ● **n.** a dish of stewed or fried pieces of meat served in a thick white sauce.
– DERIVATIVES **fricasséed** adj.
– ORIGIN Fr., fem. past part. of *fricasser* 'cut up and cook in a sauce'.

**fricative** /ˈfrɪkətɪv/ Phonetics ● **adj.** denoting a type of consonant (e.g. *f* and *th*) made by the friction of breath in a narrow opening. ● **n.** a fricative consonant.
– ORIGIN C19: from mod. L. *fricativus*, from L. *fricare* 'to rub'.

**friction** ● **n.** **1** the resistance that one surface or object encounters when moving over another. ➤ the action of one surface or object rubbing against another. **2** conflict or disagreement.
– DERIVATIVES **frictional** adj. **frictionless** adj.
– ORIGIN C16: via Fr. from L. *frictio(n-)*, from *fricare* 'to rub'.

**frictional unemployment** ● **n.** Economics unemployment due to people being in the process of moving between jobs.

**friction tape** ● **n.** another term for **INSULATING TAPE**.

**Friday** ● **n.** the day of the week before Saturday and following Thursday. ● **adv.** chiefly N. Amer. on Friday. ➤ (**Fridays**) on Fridays; each Friday.
– ORIGIN OE *Frīgedœg*, named after the Gmc goddess *Frigga*; translation of late L. *Veneris dies* 'day of the planet Venus'.

**fridge** ● **n.** short for **REFRIGERATOR**.

**fridge-freezer** ● **n.** chiefly Brit. an upright unit comprising a separate refrigerator and freezer.

**fried** past and past participle of **FRY**[1]. ● **adj.** **1** (of food) cooked in hot fat or oil. **2** N. Amer. informal exhausted.

**friend** ● **n.** **1** a person with whom one has a bond of mutual affection, typically one exclusive of sexual or family relations. ➤ used in polite address to an acquaintance or stranger. **2** a familiar or helpful thing. **3** a person who supports a particular cause or organization: *the Friends of the Welsh National Opera.* **4** (in battle) an ally. **5** (**Friend**) a member of the Religious Society of Friends; a Quaker. ● **v.** archaic befriend.
– PHRASES **be** (or **make**) **friends with** be (or become) on friendly terms with. **a friend at court** a person in a position to use their influence on one's behalf.
– DERIVATIVES **friendless** adj. **friendship** n.
– ORIGIN OE *frēond*, of Gmc origin; rel. to **FREE**.

**friendly** ● **adj.** (**-ier**, **-iest**) **1** kind and pleasant; of or like a friend. **2** Military of, belonging to, or allied with one's own forces. **3** favourable or serviceable. **4** [in combination] not harmful to a specified thing: *an environment-friendly policy.* ● **n.** (pl. **-ies**) Brit. a game or match not forming part of a serious competition.
– DERIVATIVES **friendlily** adv. **friendliness** n.

**friendly fire** ● **n.** Military weapon fire coming from one's own side that causes accidental injury or death to one's own forces.

**friendly society** ● **n.** (in the UK) a mutual association providing sickness benefits, life assurance, and pensions.

**friend of Dorothy** ● **n.** informal a homosexual man.
– ORIGIN from the name of *Dorothy*, a character played by the actress Judy Garland (a gay icon) in the film *The Wizard of Oz* (1939).

**frier** ● **n.** variant spelling of **FRYER**.

**Friesian** /ˈfriːʒ(ə)n/ ● **n.** Brit. an animal of a black-and-white breed of dairy cattle originally from Friesland in the Netherlands.

**frieze**[1] /friːz/ ● **n.** **1** a broad horizontal band of sculpted or painted decoration. **2** Architecture the part of an entablature between the architrave and the cornice.
– ORIGIN C16: from Fr. *frise*, from med. L. *frisium*, var. of *frigium*, from L. *Phrygium* (*opus*) '(work) of Phrygia'.

**frieze**[2] /friːz/ ● **n.** heavy, coarse woollen cloth with a nap, usually on one side only.
– ORIGIN ME: from Fr. *frise*, from med. L. *frisia*, 'Frisian wool'.

**frig** ● **v.** (**frigged**, **frigging**) vulgar slang have sexual intercourse with. ➤ masturbate.
– ORIGIN ME (orig. in sense 'move restlessly', later 'rub, chafe'): of unknown origin.

**frigate** /ˈfrɪgət/ ● **n.** a warship with a mixed armament, generally lighter than a destroyer. ➤ historical a sailing warship of a size and armament just below that of a ship of the line.
– ORIGIN C16: from Fr. *frégate*, from Ital. *fregata*, of unknown origin.

**frigate bird** ● **n.** a predatory tropical seabird with dark plumage, long narrow wings, a deeply forked tail, and a long hooked bill. [Genus *Fregata*: five species.]

**fright** ● **n.** a sudden intense feeling of fear. ➤ an experience causing fright; a shock. ● **v.** archaic frighten.
– PHRASES **look a fright** informal look ridiculous or grotesque. **take fright** suddenly become frightened.
– ORIGIN OE *fryhto*, *fyrhto* (n.), of Gmc origin.

**frighten** ● **v.** cause to be afraid. ➤ (**frighten someone off**) drive someone away by fear.
– DERIVATIVES **frightened** adj. **frightening** adj. **frighteningly** adv.

**frightener** ● **n.** a frightening person or thing. ➤ Brit. in-

formal a member of a criminal gang who intimidates its victims.
– PHRASES **put the frighteners on** Brit. informal threaten or intimidate (someone).

**frightful** ● adj. **1** very unpleasant, serious, or shocking. **2** informal terrible; awful: *her hair was a frightful mess.*
– DERIVATIVES **frightfully** adv. **frightfulness** n.

**fright wig** ● n. a wig with the hair arranged sticking out, as worn by a clown.

**frigid** /ˈfrɪdʒɪd/ ● adj. **1** very cold. **2** (of a woman) unable to be sexually responsive or aroused. **3** stiff or formal in behaviour or style.
– DERIVATIVES **frigidity** n. **frigidly** adv. **frigidness** n.
– ORIGIN ME: from L. *frigidus*, from *frigere* 'be cold'.

**frigidarium** /ˌfrɪdʒɪˈdɛːrɪəm/ ● n. (pl. **frigidaria** /-rɪə/) historical a cold room in an ancient Roman bath.
– ORIGIN from L.

**frigid zone** ● n. each of the two areas of the earth respectively north of the Arctic Circle and south of the Antarctic Circle.

**frill** ● n. **1** a strip of gathered or pleated material sewn by one side only on to a garment or piece of material as a decorative edging or ornament. **2** a frill-like fringe of feathers, hair, skin, etc. on a bird, reptile, or other animal. **3** (**frills**) unnecessary extra features or embellishments: *a comfortable flat with no frills.*
– DERIVATIVES **frilled** adj. **frillery** n. **frilliness** n. **frilly** adj.
– ORIGIN C16: from or rel. to Flemish *frul.*

**frilled lizard** (also **frill-necked lizard**) ● n. a large north Australian lizard with a membrane round the neck which can be erected to form a ruff for defensive display. [*Chlamydosaurus kingii.*]

**fringe** ● n. **1** a border of threads, tassels, or twists, used to edge clothing or material. **2** chiefly Brit. the front part of someone's hair, cut so as to hang over the forehead. ➤ a natural border of hair or fibres in an animal or plant. **3** the outer or marginal part of something. ➤ [as modifier] not part of the mainstream; unconventional: *fringe theatre.* **4** a band of contrasting brightness or darkness produced by diffraction or interference of light. ➤ a strip of false colour in an optical image. **5** N. Amer. short for **FRINGE BENEFIT**. ● v. provide with or form a fringe.
– DERIVATIVES **fringeless** adj. **fringing** n. **fringy** adj.
– ORIGIN ME: from OFr. *frenge*, based on late L. *fimbria*, earlier a pl. noun meaning 'fibres, shreds'.

**fringe benefit** ● n. an additional benefit, especially a benefit given to an employee, such as a company car or private health care.

**fringing reef** ● n. a coral reef that lies close to the shore.

**frippery** /ˈfrɪp(ə)ri/ ● n. (pl. **-ies**) showy or unnecessary ornament. ● adj. archaic frivolous and tawdry.
– ORIGIN C16 (denoting second-hand clothes): from Fr. *friperie*, from OFr. *freperie*, from *frepe* 'rag', of unknown ultimate origin.

**frisbee** /ˈfrɪzbi/ ● n. trademark a concave plastic disc designed for skimming through the air as an outdoor game.
– ORIGIN 1950s: said to be named after the pie tins of the *Frisbie* bakery (Bridgeport, Connecticut).

**frisée** /ˈfriːzeɪ/ ● n. a kind of endive with curled leaves.
– ORIGIN Fr., from *chicorée frisée* 'curly endive'.

**Frisian** /ˈfriːzɪən, ˈfriːʒ(ə)n, ˈfrɪ-/ ● n. **1** a native or inhabitant of Frisia or Friesland in the Netherlands. **2** the Germanic language spoken in northern parts of the Netherlands and adjacent islands. ● adj. of or relating to Frisia or Friesland, its people, or language.

**frisk** ● v. **1** (of a police officer or official) pass the hands over (someone) in a search for hidden weapons or drugs. **2** (of an animal or person) skip or move playfully; frolic. ● n. **1** a search by frisking. **2** a playful skip or leap.
– DERIVATIVES **frisker** n.
– ORIGIN C16: from obs. *frisk* 'lively', from OFr. *frisque* 'alert, lively'.

**frisket** /ˈfrɪskɪt/ ● n. N. Amer. (in painting or crafts) an adhesive substance or stencil used to cover areas of a surface on which paint is not wanted.
– ORIGIN C17: from Fr. *frisquette*, from Provençal *frisqueto*, from Sp. *frasqueta.*

**frisky** ● adj. (**-ier**, **-iest**) playful and full of energy.
– DERIVATIVES **friskily** adv. **friskiness** n.

**frisson** /ˈfriːsɔ̃, ˈfrɪsɒn/ ● n. a strong feeling of excitement or fear; a thrill.
– ORIGIN C18: Fr.

**frit** ● n. a mixture of silica and fluxes which is fused at high temperature to make glass. ➤ a similar calcined and pulverized mixture used to make soft-paste porcelain or ceramic glazes. ● v. (**fritted**, **fritting**) make into frit.
– ORIGIN C17: from Ital. *fritta*, fem. past part. of *friggere* 'to fry'.

**frit fly** ● n. a very small black fly whose larvae are a serious pest of cereal crops and maize. [*Oscinella frit.*]
– ORIGIN C19: from L. *frit* 'particle on an ear of corn'.

**fritillary** /frɪˈtɪləri/ ● n. **1** a plant of the lily family with hanging bell-like flowers. [*Fritillaria meleagris* (snake's head) and related species.] **2** a butterfly with orange-brown wings chequered with black. [*Argynnis* and other genera: numerous species.]
– ORIGIN C17: from mod. L. *fritillaria*, from L. *fritillus* 'dice-box' (prob. with ref. to the flower's chequered corolla).

**frittata** /frɪˈtɑːtə/ ● n. an Italian dish made with fried beaten eggs, resembling a Spanish omelette.
– ORIGIN Ital., from *fritto*, past part. of *friggere* 'to fry'.

**fritter**[1] ● v. **1** (often **fritter something away**) waste time, money, or energy on trifling matters. **2** archaic divide into small pieces.
– ORIGIN C18: based on obs. *fitter* 'break into fragments'.

**fritter**[2] ● n. a piece of fruit, vegetable, or meat that is coated in batter and deep-fried.
– ORIGIN ME: from OFr. *friture*, based on L. *frigere* (see **FRY**[1]).

**fritto misto** /ˌfrɪtəʊ ˈmɪstəʊ/ ● n. a dish of various foods, typically seafood, deep-fried in batter.
– ORIGIN Ital., 'mixed fry'.

**Fritz** ● n. Brit. informal, dated a German or the German people collectively, especially a soldier in the First World War.
– ORIGIN abbrev. of the Ger. given name *Friedrich.*

**fritz** ● n. (in phr. **go** (or **be**) **on the fritz**) N. Amer. informal (of a machine) stop working properly.
– ORIGIN C20: said to be with allusion to cheap Ger. imports into the US before the First World War.

**frivolous** ● adj. not having any serious purpose or value. ➤ (of a person) carefree and superficial.
– DERIVATIVES **frivolity** n. **frivolously** adv. **frivolousness** n.
– ORIGIN ME: from L. *frivolus* 'silly, trifling' + **-OUS**.

**frizz** /frɪz/ ● v. (of hair) form into a mass of small, tight curls. ● n. a mass of tightly curled hair.
– ORIGIN ME: from Fr. *friser.*

**frizzante** /frɪtˈzanteɪ, -ti/ ● adj. (of wine) semi-sparkling.
– ORIGIN from Ital.

**frizzle**[1] ● v. fry until crisp or burnt.
– ORIGIN C18: from **FRY**[1], prob. influenced by **SIZZLE**.

**frizzle**[2] ● v. form (hair) into tight curls. ● n. a tight curl in hair.
– DERIVATIVES **frizzly** adj.
– ORIGIN C16: from **FRIZZ** + **-LE**[4].

**frizzy** ● adj. (**-ier**, **-iest**) formed of a mass of small, tight, wiry curls.
– DERIVATIVES **frizziness** n.

**fro** ● adv. see **TO AND FRO**.
– ORIGIN ME: from ON *frá* (see **FROM**).

**frock** ● n. **1** chiefly Brit. a woman's or girl's dress. **2** a loose outer garment, in particular a long gown with flowing sleeves worn by monks, priests, or clergy. **3** archaic priestly office.
– DERIVATIVES **frocked** adj.
– ORIGIN ME: from OFr. *froc*, of Gmc origin.

**frock coat** ● n. a man's double-breasted, long-skirted coat, now worn chiefly on formal occasions.

**froe** /frəʊ/ ● n. a cleaving tool with a handle at right angles to the blade.
– ORIGIN C16: abbrev. of obs. *frower*, from **FROWARD** in the sense 'turned away'.

**frog**[1] ● n. **1** a tailless amphibian with a short squat body, moist smooth skin, and very long hind legs for leaping. [Many species, chiefly in family Ranidae.] **2** (**Frog**) derogatory a French person.
– PHRASES **have a frog in one's throat** informal lose one's voice or find it hard to speak because of hoarseness.
– DERIVATIVES **froggy** adj. **froglet** n.
– ORIGIN OE *frogga*, of Gmc origin; a general term of abuse in ME. Its application to the French (late 18th cent.) is partly alliterative, partly from the reputation of the French for eating frogs' legs.

**frog**[2] ● n. **1** a thing used to hold or fasten something. **2** an ornamental coat fastener consisting of a spindle-shaped button and a loop. **3** an attachment to a belt for holding a sword or bayonet. **4** a perforated or spiked device for holding the stems of flowers in an arrangement.
– DERIVATIVES **frogged** adj. **frogging** n.
– ORIGIN C18: perh. a use of **FROG**[1], influenced by Ital. *forchetta* or Fr. *fourchette* 'small fork', because of the shape.

**frog**[3] ● n. an elastic horny pad growing in the sole of a horse's hoof, helping to absorb the shock when the hoof hits the ground.
– ORIGIN C17: perh. from **FROG**[1]; perh. also influenced by Ital. *forchetta* or Fr. *fourchette* (see **FROG**[2]).

**frogbit** ● n. a floating freshwater plant with clusters of small rounded leaves. [*Hydrocharis morsus-ranae* (Eurasia) and *Hydromystria laevigatum* (N. America).]

**frogfish** ● n. (pl. same or **-fishes**) an anglerfish that typically lives on the seabed, where its warty skin provides camouflage. [*Antennaria hispidus* (Indo-Pacific) and other species.]

**froghopper** ● n. a jumping, plant-sucking bug, the larva of which produces cuckoo spit. [Family Cercopidae, many species.]

**frogman** ● n. (pl. **-men**) a diver equipped with a rubber suit, flippers, and breathing equipment for working under water.

**frogmarch** ● v. force (someone) to walk forward by holding and pinning their arms from behind.

**frogmouth** ● n. a nocturnal bird resembling a nightjar, occurring in SE Asia and Australasia. [*Podargus strigoides* (**tawny frogmouth**, Australia) and other species.]

**frog orchid** ● n. a small orchid with inconspicuous green flowers, growing chiefly on calcareous grassland in north temperate regions. [*Coeloglossum viride*.]

**frogspawn** ● n. a mass of frogs' eggs surrounded by transparent jelly.

**froideur** /frwʌˈdəː, French frwadœʀ/ ● n. coolness or reserve between people.
– ORIGIN Fr., from *froid* 'cold'.

**frolic** ● v. (**frolicked**, **frolicking**) play or move about in a cheerful and lively way. ● n. a playful action or movement. ● adj. archaic cheerful and playful.
– DERIVATIVES **frolicker** n.
– ORIGIN C16: from Du. *vrolijk* 'merry, cheerful'.

**frolicsome** ● adj. lively and playful.
– DERIVATIVES **frolicsomely** adv. **frolicsomeness** n.

**from** ● prep. **1** indicating the point in space or time at which a journey, process, or action starts. **2** indicating source or provenance. ➤indicating the raw material of manufacture. **3** indicating the starting point of a specified range. **4** indicating separation, removal, or prevention. **5** indicating a cause. **6** indicating a distinction.
– PHRASES **from day to day** (or **hour to hour** etc.) daily (or hourly etc.). **from time to time** occasionally.
– ORIGIN OE *fram*, *from*, of Gmc origin; rel. to ON *frá* (see **FRO**).

**fromage blanc** /ˌfrɒmɑːʒ ˈblɒ̃, French frɔmaʒ blɑ̃/ ● n. a type of soft French cheese having a creamy sour taste.
– ORIGIN Fr., lit. 'white cheese'.

**fromage frais** /ˌfrɒmɑːʒ ˈfreɪ, French frɔmaʒ frɛ/ ● n. a type of smooth soft fresh cheese.
– ORIGIN Fr., lit. 'fresh cheese'.

**frond** ● n. the leaf or leaf-like part of a palm, fern, or similar plant.
– DERIVATIVES **frondage** n. **fronded** adj. **frondose** adj.
– ORIGIN C18: from L. *frons, frond-* 'leaf'.

**frons** /frɒnz/ ● n. (pl. **frontes**) Zoology the forehead or equivalent part of an animal, especially the middle part of an insect's face between the eyes and above the clypeus.
– ORIGIN C19: from L., 'front, forehead'.

**front** ● n. **1** the side or part of an object that presents itself to view or that is normally seen or used first. ➤the position directly ahead. ➤the forward-facing part of a person's body. **2** the foremost line or part of an armed force; the furthest position that an army has reached. ➤[often in names] an organized political group: *the Patriotic Front*. **3** Meteorology the boundary of an advancing mass of air, in particular the leading edge (**warm front**) or trailing edge (**cold front**) of the warm sector of a low-pressure system. **4** a particular situation or sphere of operation: *good news on the jobs front*. **5** a deceptive appearance or mode of behaviour assumed by someone to conceal truth or genuine feelings. ➤a person or organization serving as a cover for subversive activities. **6** boldness and confidence of manner. ● adj. **1** of or at the front. **2** Phonetics (of a vowel sound) formed by raising the tongue towards the hard palate. ● v. **1** have the front facing towards. ➤place or be placed at the front of. **2** (usu. **be fronted**) provide with a front or facing. **3** lead or be at the forefront of. ➤present or host (a television or radio programme). **4** act as a front for. **5** Phonetics articulate (a vowel sound) with the tongue further forward. **6** archaic confront.
– PHRASES **front of house** the parts of a theatre in front of the proscenium arch. ➤the business of a theatre that concerns the audience, such as ticket sales. **in front 1** in a position just ahead or further forward. **2** on the front part or side. **3** (**in front of**) in the presence of. **out front** chiefly N. Amer. at or to the front; in front.
– DERIVATIVES **frontless** adj. **frontward** adj. & adv. **frontwards** adv.
– ORIGIN ME: from OFr. *front* (n.), *fronter* (v.), from L. *frons, front-* 'forehead, front'.

**frontage** ● n. **1** the facade of a building. **2** a strip or extent of land abutting on a street or waterway.

**frontager** /ˈfrɒntɪdʒə/ ● n. an owner of frontage.

**frontal** ● adj. **1** of or at the front. **2** of or relating to the forehead or front part of the skull: *the frontal sinuses*. ● n. a decorative cloth for covering the front of an altar.
– DERIVATIVES **frontally** adv.

**frontal bone** ● n. the bone which forms the front part of the skull and the upper part of the eye sockets.

**frontal lobe** ● n. each of the paired lobes of the brain lying immediately behind the forehead, including areas concerned with behaviour, learning, personality, and voluntary movement.

**front bench** ● n. (in the UK) the foremost seats in the House of Commons, occupied by the members of the cabinet and shadow cabinet.
– DERIVATIVES **frontbencher** n.

**front-end** ● adj. **1** of or relating to the front, especially of a vehicle. **2** informal (of money) paid or charged at the beginning of a transaction. **3** Computing (of a device or program) directly accessed by the user and allowing access to further devices or programs. ● n. Computing the front-end part of a computer or program.

**front-fanged** ● adj. denoting a snake (such as a cobra or viper) in which the front pair of teeth have grooves to conduct the venom. Compare with **BACK-FANGED**.

**frontier** /ˈfrʌntɪə, frʌnˈtɪə/ ● n. **1** a border separating two countries. **2** the extreme limit of settled land beyond which lies wilderness. **3** the extreme limit of understanding or achievement in a particular area.
– DERIVATIVES **frontierless** adj.
– ORIGIN ME: from OFr. *frontiere*, based on L. *frons, front-* 'front'.

**frontiersman** (or **frontierswoman**) ● n. (pl. **-men** or **-women**) a man (or woman) living in the region of a frontier, especially that between settled and unsettled country.

**frontispiece** /ˈfrʌntɪspiːs/ ● n. **1** an illustration facing the title page of a book. **2** Architecture the principal face of a

building. ➤a decorated entrance. ➤a pediment over a door or window.
– ORIGIN C16: from Fr. *frontispice* or late L. *frontispicium* 'facade', from L. *frons, front-* 'front' + *specere* 'to look'.

**frontlet** ● n. **1** an ornamental piece of cloth hanging over the upper part of an altar frontal. **2** another term for **PHYLACTERY**. **3** a piece of armour or harness for an animal's forehead.

**front line** ● n. the military line or part of an army that is closest to the enemy.

**frontman** ● n. (pl. **-men**) a person who acts as a front, in particular the leader of a band or the representative of an illegal organization.

**front office** ● n. chiefly N. Amer. the main administrative office of a business or other organization.

**fronton** /ˈfrʌnt(ə)n/ ● n. **1** a building where pelota or jai alai is played. **2** another term for **PEDIMENT** (in sense 1).
– ORIGIN C17: from Fr., from Ital. *frontone*, from *fronte* 'forehead', from L. *frons, front-* 'front, forehead'.

**front-runner** ● n. the contestant that is leading in a race or other competition. ➤an athlete or horse that runs best when in the front of the field.

**front-running** ● n. **1** Stock Exchange the practice by market-makers of dealing on advance information provided by their brokers and investment analysts, before their clients have been given the information. **2** US the practice of giving one's support to a competitor because they are in front.

**front-wheel drive** ● n. a transmission system that provides power to the front wheels of a motor vehicle.

**frost** ● n. **1** a deposit of small white ice crystals formed on the ground or other surfaces when the temperature falls below freezing. **2** a period of cold weather when frost forms. ● v. **1** cover or be covered with or as if with frost; freeze. **2** N. Amer. decorate with icing.
– PHRASES **degrees of frost** Brit. degrees below freezing point.
– DERIVATIVES **frostless** adj.
– ORIGIN OE *frost, forst*, of Gmc origin; rel. to **FREEZE**.

**frostbite** ● n. injury to body tissues, especially the nose, fingers, or toes, caused by exposure to extreme cold.

**frosted** ● adj. **1** covered with or as if with frost. **2** (of glass) having a translucent textured surface so that it is difficult to see through.

**frost heave** ● n. the uplift of soil or other surface deposits due to expansion of groundwater on freezing.
– DERIVATIVES **frost heaving** n.

**frosting** ● n. **1** N. Amer. icing. **2** a roughened matt finish on otherwise shiny material such as glass or steel.

**frosty** ● adj. (**-ier**, **-iest**) **1** (of the weather) very cold with frost forming on surfaces. **2** cold and unfriendly.
– DERIVATIVES **frostily** adv. **frostiness** n.

**froth** ● n. **1** a mass of small bubbles in liquid caused by agitation, fermentation, or salivating. ➤impure matter that rises to the surface of liquid. **2** worthless or insubstantial talk, ideas, or activities. ● v. form, produce, or contain froth.
– DERIVATIVES **frothily** adv. **frothy** adj.
– ORIGIN ME: from ON *frotha, frauth*.

**frottage** /ˈfrɒtɑːʒ/ ● n. **1** Art the technique or process of taking a rubbing from an uneven surface to form the basis of a work of art. **2** the practice of rubbing against the clothed body of another person in a crowd as a means of obtaining sexual gratification.
– DERIVATIVES **frotteur** n. (pl. same). **frotteurism** n.
– ORIGIN 1930s: Fr., 'rubbing, friction', from *frotter* 'to rub', of unknown origin.

**frottola** /ˈfrɒtələ/ ● n. (pl. **frottole** /-leɪ/) Music a form of Italian comic or amorous song, especially from the 15th and 16th centuries.
– ORIGIN Ital., lit. 'fib, tall story'.

**Froude number** /fraʊd/ ● n. a dimensionless number used in hydrodynamics to indicate how well a particular model works in relation to a real system.
– ORIGIN C19: named after the Engl. civil engineer William *Froude* (1810–79).

**frou-frou** /ˈfruːfruː/ ● n. **1** a rustling noise made by someone walking in a dress. **2** [often as modifier] frills or other ornamentation, particularly of women's clothes: *a little frou-frou skirt*.
– ORIGIN C19: from Fr., imitative.

**froward** /ˈfrəʊəd/ ● adj. archaic (of a person) difficult to deal with; contrary.
– DERIVATIVES **frowardly** adv. **frowardness** n.
– ORIGIN OE *frāward* 'leading away from, away', based on ON *frá* (see **FRO**, **FROM**).

**frown** ● v. furrow one's brows in an expression indicating disapproval, displeasure, or concentration. ➤(**frown on/upon**) disapprove of. ● n. an expression of this type.
– DERIVATIVES **frowner** n. **frowning** adj. **frowningly** adv.
– ORIGIN ME: from OFr. *froignier*, from *froigne* 'surly look', of Celtic origin.

**frowst** /fraʊst/ informal, chiefly Brit. ● n. a warm stuffy atmosphere in a room. ● v. lounge about in such an atmosphere.
– DERIVATIVES **frowster** n.

**frowsty** ● adj. (**-ier**, **-iest**) Brit. having a stale, warm, and stuffy atmosphere.
– DERIVATIVES **frowstiness** n.
– ORIGIN C19 (orig. dial.): var. of **FROWZY**.

**frowzy** /ˈfraʊzi/ (also **frowsy**) ● adj. (**-ier**, **-iest**) scruffy, dingy, and neglected in appearance.
– DERIVATIVES **frowziness** n.
– ORIGIN C17 (orig. dial.): of unknown origin.

**froze** past of **FREEZE**.

**frozen** past participle of **FREEZE**.

**frozen shoulder** ● n. Medicine chronic painful stiffness of the shoulder joint.

**FRS** ● abbrev. **1** (in the UK) Fellow of the Royal Society. **2** (in the UK) Financial Reporting Standard.

**fructification** /ˌfrʌktɪfɪˈkeɪʃ(ə)n/ ● n. **1** the process of fructifying. **2** Botany a spore-bearing or fruiting structure, especially in a fungus.

**fructify** /ˈfrʌktɪfʌɪ/ ● v. (**-ies**, **-ied**) **1** formal make or become fruitful. **2** bear fruit.
– ORIGIN ME: from OFr. *fructifier*, from L. *fructificare*, from *fructus* 'fruit'.

**fructose** /ˈfrʌktəʊz, -s/ ● n. Chemistry a sugar of the hexose class found especially in honey and fruit.
– ORIGIN C19: from L. *fructus* 'fruit' + **-OSE**².

**fructuous** /ˈfrʌktjʊəs/ ● adj. formal full of or producing a great deal of fruit.
– ORIGIN ME: from L. *fructuosus*, from *fructus* 'fruit'.

**frug** ● n. a vigorous dance to pop music, popular in the mid 1960s. ● v. (**frugged**, **frugging**) perform such a dance.
– ORIGIN of unknown origin.

**frugal** /ˈfruːg(ə)l/ ● adj. sparing or economical as regards money or food.
– DERIVATIVES **frugality** n. **frugally** adv. **frugalness** n.
– ORIGIN C16: from L. *frugalis*, from *frugi* 'economical, thrifty', from *frux, frug-* 'fruit'.

**frugivore** /ˈfruːdʒɪvɔː/ ● n. Zoology an animal that feeds on fruit.
– DERIVATIVES **frugivorous** adj.
– ORIGIN C20: from L. *frux, frug-* 'fruit' + *-vore* (see **-VOROUS**).

**fruit** ● n. **1** the sweet and fleshy product of a tree or other plant that contains seed and can be eaten as food. ➤Botany the seed-bearing structure of a plant, e.g. an acorn. ➤archaic or poetic/literary natural produce that can be used for food: *the fruits of the earth*. **2** the result or reward of work or activity. **3** archaic offspring. **4** informal, derogatory, chiefly N. Amer. a male homosexual. ● v. produce fruit.
– PHRASES **bear fruit** have good results. **in fruit** at the stage of producing fruit. **old fruit** informal, dated a friendly form of address used by one man to another.
– ORIGIN ME: from OFr., from L. *fructus* 'enjoyment of produce, harvest', from *frui* 'enjoy', rel. to *fruges* 'fruits of the earth', pl. of *frux, frug-* 'fruit'.

**fruitarian** ● n. a person who eats only fruit.
– DERIVATIVES **fruitarianism** n.

**fruit bat** ● n. a large bat which feeds chiefly on fruit or nectar, found mainly in the Old World tropics. [Family Pteropodidae: numerous species.]

**fruit body** ● n. another term for FRUITING BODY.

**fruitcake** ● n. **1** a cake containing dried fruit and nuts. **2** informal an eccentric or mad person.

**fruit cocktail** ● n. a finely chopped fruit salad, commercially produced in tins.

**fruit cup** ● n. **1** Brit. a drink consisting of a mixture of fruit juices. **2** N. Amer. a fruit salad.

**fruit drop** ● n. the shedding of unripe fruit from a tree.

**fruiterer** ● n. chiefly Brit. a retailer of fruit.
– ORIGIN ME: from *fruiter* + -ER¹; the reason for the addition of the suffix is unclear.

**fruit fly** ● n. a small fly which feeds on fruit in both its adult and larval stages. [Families Drosophilidae and Tephritidae: many species.]

**fruitful** ● adj. **1** producing much fruit; fertile. **2** producing good results; productive.
– DERIVATIVES **fruitfully** adv. **fruitfulness** n.

**fruiting body** ● n. Botany the spore-producing organ of a fungus, often seen as a toadstool.

**fruition** /frʊˈɪʃ(ə)n/ ● n. **1** the realization or fulfilment of a plan or project. **2** poetic/literary the state or action of producing fruit.
– ORIGIN ME (in the sense 'enjoyment'): via OFr. from late L. *fruitio(n-)*, from *frui* (see FRUIT).

**fruitless** ● adj. **1** failing to achieve the desired results; unproductive. **2** not producing fruit.
– DERIVATIVES **fruitlessly** adv. **fruitlessness** n.

**fruitlet** ● n. an immature or small fruit. ➤ Botany another term for DRUPEL.

**fruit machine** ● n. Brit. a coin-operated gambling machine that generates random combinations of symbols (typically representing fruit), certain combinations winning money for the player.

**fruit salad** ● n. a mixture of different types of chopped fruit served in syrup or juice.

**fruit sugar** ● n. another term for FRUCTOSE.

**fruity** ● adj. (-ier, -iest) **1** of, resembling, or containing fruit. **2** (of a voice) mellow, deep, and rich. ➤ Brit. informal sexually suggestive. **3** informal, chiefly US eccentric or crazy. **4** informal, derogatory, chiefly N. Amer. relating to or associated with homosexuals.
– DERIVATIVES **fruitily** adv. **fruitiness** n.

**frumenty** /ˈfruːm(ə)nti/ (also **furmety**) ● n. Brit. an old-fashioned dish consisting of hulled wheat boiled in milk and seasoned with cinnamon and sugar.
– ORIGIN ME: from OFr. *frumentee*, from *frument*, from L. *frumentum* 'corn'.

**frump** ● n. an unattractive woman who wears dowdy old-fashioned clothes.
– DERIVATIVES **frumpily** adv. **frumpiness** n. **frumpish** adj. **frumpishly** adv. **frumpy** adj.
– ORIGIN C16 (orig. in sense 'mocking speech', later 'bad-tempered woman'): prob. a contr. of ME *frumple* 'wrinkle', from MDu. *verrompelen*.

**frusemide** /ˈfruːsəmʌɪd/ (chiefly US also **furosemide**) ● n. Medicine a synthetic compound with a strong diuretic action, used especially in the treatment of oedema.
– ORIGIN 1960s: from *fru-* (alt. of *fur(yl)*, denoting a radical derived from furan) + *sem-* (of unknown origin) + -IDE.

**frustrate** ● v. **1** prevent (a plan or action) from progressing, succeeding, or being fulfilled. ➤ prevent (someone) from doing or achieving something. **2** cause to feel dissatisfied or unfulfilled. ● adj. archaic frustrated.
– DERIVATIVES **frustrated** adj. **frustratedly** adv. **frustrater** n. **frustrating** adj. **frustratingly** adv. **frustration** n.
– ORIGIN ME: from L. *frustrat-*, *frustrare* 'disappoint', from *frustra* 'in vain'.

**frustule** /ˈfrʌstjuːl/ ● n. Botany the silicified cell wall of a diatom, consisting of two valves or overlapping halves.
– ORIGIN C19: from L. *frustulum*, dimin. of *frustum* (see FRUSTUM).

**frustum** /ˈfrʌstəm/ ● n. (pl. **frusta** /-tə/ or **frustums**) Geometry the portion of a cone or pyramid which remains after its upper part has been cut off by a plane parallel to its base, or which is intercepted between two such planes.
– ORIGIN C17: from L., 'piece cut off'.

**fruticose** /ˈfruːtɪkəʊz, -s/ ● adj. Botany (of a lichen) having upright or pendulous branches.
– ORIGIN C17: from L. *fruticosus*, from *frutex*, *frutic-* 'bush, shrub'.

**fry¹** ● v. (-ies, -ied) **1** cook or be cooked in hot fat or oil. **2** informal (of a person) burn or overheat. ● n. (pl. -ies) **1** a fried dish or meal. ➤ (**fries**) N. Amer. short for FRENCH FRIES. **2** N. Amer. a social gathering where fried food is served.
– ORIGIN ME: from OFr. *frire*, from L. *frigere*.

**fry²** ● pl. n. young fish, especially when newly hatched. ➤ the young of other animals produced in large numbers, such as frogs.
– ORIGIN ME: from ON *frjó*.

**fryer** (also **frier**) ● n. **1** a large, deep container for frying food. **2** N. Amer. a small young chicken suitable for frying.

**frying pan** (N. Amer. also **frypan**) ● n. a shallow pan with a long handle, used for frying food.
– PHRASES **out of the frying pan into the fire** from a bad situation to one that is worse.

**fry-up** ● n. Brit. informal a dish or meal of fried food.

**FS** ● abbrev. (in the UK) Flight Sergeant.

**FSA** ● abbrev. (in the UK) Fellow of the Society of Antiquaries.

**FSH** ● abbrev. follicle-stimulating hormone.

**f-stop** ● n. Photography a camera setting corresponding to a particular f-number.

**FT** ● abbrev. (in the UK) Financial Times.

**Ft** ● abbrev. Fort.

**ft** ● abbrev. foot or feet.

**FTC** ● abbrev. (in the US) Federal Trade Commission.

**FTP** ● abbrev. Computing file transfer protocol, a standard for the exchange of program and data files across a network.

**FTSE index** (also **FT index**) ● n. a figure (published by the *Financial Times*) indicating the relative prices of shares on the London Stock Exchange.
– ORIGIN abbrev. of *Financial Times Stock Exchange*.

**fubsy** /ˈfʌbzi/ ● adj. (-ier, -iest) Brit. informal fat and squat.
– ORIGIN C18: from dial. *fubs* 'small fat person', perh. a blend of FAT and CHUB.

**fuchsia** /ˈfjuːʃə/ ● n. **1** an ornamental shrub native to America and New Zealand, with drooping tubular flowers that are typically of two contrasting colours. [Genus *Fuchsia*.] **2** a vivid purplish-red colour like that of a typical fuchsia flower.
– ORIGIN mod. L., named in honour of the C16 Ger. botanist Leonhard *Fuchs*.

**fuchsin** /ˈfuːksiːn/ (also **fuchsine**) ● n. a deep red synthetic dye used as a biological stain and disinfectant.
– ORIGIN C19: from Ger. *Fuchs* 'fox', translating Fr. *Renard* (the name of the chemical company which first produced fuchsin commercially) + -IN¹.

**fuck** vulgar slang ● v. **1** have sexual intercourse with. **2** damage or ruin. ● n. an act of sexual intercourse. ● exclam. a strong expression of annoyance, contempt, or impatience.
– PHRASES **fuck all** Brit. absolutely nothing.
– PHRASAL VERBS **fuck about** (or **around**) spend time doing unimportant or trivial things. **fuck someone around** (or **about**) waste someone's time. **fuck off** go away. **fuck someone up** damage or confuse someone emotionally. **fuck something up** (or **fuck up**) do something badly or ineptly.
– DERIVATIVES **fuckable** adj. **fucker** n.
– ORIGIN C16: of Gmc origin.

**fucoxanthin** /ˌfjuːkəˈzanθɪn/ ● n. Chemistry a brown carotenoid pigment occurring in and generally characteristic of the brown algae.
– ORIGIN C19: from FUCUS + *xanthin*, var. of XANTHINE.

**fucus** /ˈfjuːkəs/ ● n. (pl. **fuci** /ˈfjuːsʌɪ/) a seaweed of a large genus of brown algae having flat leathery fronds. [Genus *Fucus*.]
– DERIVATIVES **fucoid** adj. & n.
– ORIGIN C17 (denoting a cosmetic): from L., 'rock lichen, red dye, rouge', from Gk *phukos* 'seaweed', of Semitic

origin.

**fuddle** /ˈfʌd(ə)l/ ● **v.** [usu. as adj. **fuddled**] confuse or stupefy, especially with alcohol. ● **n.** a state of confusion or intoxication.
– ORIGIN C16 (in the sense 'go on a drinking bout'): of unknown origin.

**fuddy-duddy** ● **n.** (pl. **-ies**) informal a person who is very old-fashioned and pompous.
– ORIGIN C20 (orig. dial.): of unknown origin.

**fudge** ● **n. 1** a soft crumbly or chewy sweet made from sugar, butter, and milk or cream. **2** [as modifier] chiefly N. Amer. rich chocolate, used as a sauce or a filling for cakes. **3** an attempt to fudge an issue. ➤ archaic nonsense. **4** a piece of late news inserted in a newspaper page. ● **v.** present in a vague or inadequate way, especially to mislead. ➤ adjust or manipulate (facts or figures) so as to present a desired picture. ● **exclam.** dated used to express disbelief or annoyance.
– ORIGIN C17: prob. an alt. of obs. *fadge* 'to fit'; the sense in confectionery prob. arose from early verb usage 'merge together'.

**fuehrer** ● **n.** variant spelling of **FÜHRER**.

**fuel** ● **n. 1** material such as coal, gas, or oil that is burned to produce heat or power. ➤ food, drink, or drugs as a source of energy. **2** something that acts to sustain or inflame passion, argument, or other intense emotion. ● **v.** (**fuelled**, **fuelling**; US **fueled**, **fueling**) **1** supply or power with fuel. **2** sustain or inflame: *their anger is fuelled by bitterness over the regrading.*
– ORIGIN ME: from OFr. *fouaille*, based on L. *focus* 'hearth' (in late L. 'fire').

**fuel cell** ● **n.** a cell producing an electric current direct from a chemical reaction.

**fuel injection** ● **n.** the direct introduction of fuel under pressure into the combustion units of an internal-combustion engine.
– DERIVATIVES **fuel-injected** adj.

**fuel oil** ● **n.** oil used as fuel in an engine or furnace.

**fufu** /ˈfuːfuː/ (also **foo-foo**) ● **n.** dough made from boiled and ground plantain or cassava, used as a staple food in parts of West and central Africa.
– ORIGIN C18: from Twi *fufuu*.

**fug** ● **n.** Brit. informal a warm, stuffy atmosphere.
– DERIVATIVES **fuggy** adj.
– ORIGIN C19 (orig. dial. and schoolchildren's sl.): of unknown origin.

**fugacious** /fjʊˈgeɪʃəs/ ● **adj.** poetic/literary tending to disappear; fleeting.
– DERIVATIVES **fugaciously** adv. **fugaciousness** n. **fugacity** n.
– ORIGIN C17: from L. *fugax*, *fugac-* (from *fugere* 'flee') + **-IOUS**.

**fugal** /ˈfjuːg(ə)l/ ● **adj.** of or relating to a fugue.
– DERIVATIVES **fugally** adv.

**fugato** /fjuːˈgɑːtəʊ, fuː-/ ● **adj. & adv.** Music in the style of a fugue, but not in strict or complete fugal form.
– ORIGIN from Ital.

**-fuge** ● **comb. form** expelling or dispelling: *centrifuge.*
– ORIGIN from mod. L. *-fugus*, from L. *fugare* 'cause to flee'.

**fugitive** ● **n.** a person who has escaped from captivity or is in hiding. ● **adj.** quick to disappear; fleeting.
– ORIGIN ME: from OFr. *fugitif*, *-ive*, from L. *fugitivus*, from *fugere* 'flee'.

**fugleman** /ˈfjuːg(ə)lmən/ ● **n.** (pl. **-men**) **1** historical a soldier who stands in front of a regiment or company to act as a model in demonstrating drilling exercises. **2** a leader or spokesperson.
– ORIGIN C19: from Ger. *Flügelmann* 'leader of the file'.

**fugu** /ˈfuːguː/ ● **n.** a pufferfish that is eaten as a Japanese delicacy, after some highly poisonous parts have been removed.
– ORIGIN C20: from Japanese.

**fugue** /fjuːg/ ● **n. 1** Music a contrapuntal composition in which a short melody or phrase (the subject) is introduced by one part and successively taken up by others. **2** Psychiatry a state or period of loss of awareness of one's identity, often coupled with flight from one's usual environment, associated with certain forms of hysteria and epilepsy.
– ORIGIN C16: from Fr., or from Ital. *fuga*, from L. *fuga* 'flight'.

**führer** /ˈfjʊərə/ (also **fuehrer**) ● **n.** the title assumed by Hitler as leader of Germany.
– ORIGIN from Ger. *Führer* 'leader'.

**-ful** ● **suffix 1** (forming adjectives from nouns) full of; having the qualities of: *sorrowful.* **2** forming adjectives from adjectives or from Latin stems with little change of sense: *grateful.* **3** (forming adjectives from verbs) apt to; able to; accustomed to: *forgetful.* **4** (pl. **-fuls**) forming nouns denoting the amount needed to fill the specified container: *bucketful.*

**Fula** /ˈfuːlə/ (also **Foulah**) ● **n.** the language of the Fulani people, belonging to the Benue-Congo language family and widely used in West Africa as a lingua franca.
– ORIGIN from Fula *pulo* 'Fula person'.

**Fulani** /fuːˈlɑːni/ ● **n.** (pl. same) **1** a member of a mainly Muslim people living in regions of West Africa. **2** another term for **FULA**.
– ORIGIN the name in Hausa.

**fulcrum** /ˈfʊlkrəm, ˈfʌl-/ ● **n.** (pl. **fulcra** /-rə/ or **fulcrums**) the point against which a lever is placed to get a purchase, or on which it turns or is supported.
– ORIGIN C17: from L., lit. 'post of a couch', from *fulcire* 'to prop up'.

**fulfil** (US **fulfill**) ● **v.** (**fulfilled**, **fulfilling**) **1** achieve or realize (something desired, promised, or predicted). ➤ (**fulfil oneself**) gain happiness or satisfaction by fully achieving one's potential. **2** satisfy or meet (a requirement or condition).
– DERIVATIVES **fulfillable** adj. **fulfilled** adj. **fulfiller** n. **fulfilling** adj. **fulfilment** (US **fulfillment**) n.
– ORIGIN OE *fullfyllan* 'fill up, make full' (see **FULL[1]**, **FILL**).

**fulgent** /ˈfʌldʒ(ə)nt/ ● **adj.** poetic/literary shining brightly.
– ORIGIN ME: from L. *fulgent-*, *fulgere* 'to shine'.

**fulguration** /ˌfʌlgjʊˈreɪʃ(ə)n/ ● **n. 1** Medicine the destruction of small growths or areas of tissue using diathermy. **2** poetic/literary a flash like that of lightning.
– DERIVATIVES **fulgurant** adj. **fulgurate** v. **fulgurous** adj.
– ORIGIN C17: from L. *fulguratio(n-)* 'sheet lightning'.

**fulgurite** /ˈfʌlgjʊrʌɪt/ ● **n.** Geology vitreous material formed of sand or other sediment fused by lightning.
– ORIGIN C19: from L. *fulgur* 'lightning' + **-ITE[1]**.

**fuliginous** /fjuːˈlɪdʒɪnəs/ ● **adj.** poetic/literary sooty; dusky.
– ORIGIN C16 (orig. describing a vapour as 'thick and noxious'): from late L. *fuliginosus*, from *fuligo*, *fuligin-* 'soot'.

**full[1]** ● **adj. 1** containing or holding as much or as many as possible; having no empty space. ➤ (**full of**) having a large number or quantity of. **2** not lacking or omitting anything; complete. ➤ (of a covering material in bookbinding) used for the entire cover. **3** plump or rounded: *the fuller figure.* ➤ (of the hair) having body. ➤ (of a garment) made using much material. ➤ (of a sound or colour) strong and rich. **4** (**full of**) unable to stop talking or thinking about: *they had their photographs taken and he was full of it.* ➤ filled with intense emotion. **5** involving a lot of activities: *he lived a full life.* **6** informal, chiefly Austral./NZ & Scottish drunk. ● **adv. 1** straight; directly. **2** very: *he knew full well she was too polite to barge in.* ➤ archaic entirely. ● **n.** (**the full**) **1** archaic the period, point, or state of the greatest fullness or strength. **2** the state or time of full moon. ● **v. 1** black English make full; fill up. **2** gather or pleat so as to make a garment full. **3** dialect or US (of the moon or tide) become full.
– PHRASES **full and by** Sailing close-hauled but with sails filling. **full of oneself** very self-satisfied and with an exaggerated sense of self-worth. **full of years** archaic having lived to a considerable age. **full on 1** running at or providing maximum power or capacity. **2** so as to make a direct or significant impact. ➤ (**full-on**) informal not diluted in nature or effect; intense or uncompromising: *full-on boogie.* **full out 1** with maximum effort or power. **2** Printing flush with the margin. **full steam** (or **speed**) **ahead** proceeding with as much speed or energy as possible. **full up** filled to capacity. **in full 1** with nothing omitted. **2**

to the full amount due. **3** to the utmost; completely. **to the full** to the greatest possible extent.
– ORIGIN OE, of Gmc origin.
**full**[2] ● **v.** [often as noun **fulling**] clean, shrink, and felt (cloth) by heat, pressure, and moisture.
– ORIGIN ME: prob. a back-form. from *fuller*, influenced by OFr. *fouler* 'press hard upon' or med. L. *fullare*, based on L. *fullo* 'fuller', of unknown origin.
**fullback** ● **n.** a player in a defensive position near the goal in a ball game such as soccer, rugby, or field hockey.
**full beam** ● **n.** the brightest setting of a vehicle's headlights.
**full-blooded** ● **adj. 1** of unmixed ancestry. **2** vigorous and whole-hearted.
– DERIVATIVES **full-blood** n. **full-bloodedly** adv. **full-bloodedness** n.
**full-blown** ● **adj. 1** fully developed; complete. **2** (of a flower) in full bloom.
**full board** ● **n.** Brit. provision of accommodation and all meals at a hotel or guest house.
**full-bodied** ● **adj.** rich and satisfying in flavour or sound.
**full bore** chiefly N. Amer. ● **adv.** at full speed or maximum capacity. ● **adj. 1** denoting firearms of relatively large calibre. **2** complete; thoroughgoing: *a full-bore leftist*.
**full-court press** ● **n.** Basketball an aggressive tactic in which members of a team cover their opponents throughout the court and not just in the region near their own basket.
**full-cream** ● **adj.** Brit. (of milk) unskimmed.
**full dress** ● **n.** clothes worn on ceremonial or very formal occasions. ● **adj.** formal and serious: *a full-dress conference*.
**fuller**[1] ● **n.** a person whose occupation is fulling cloth.
**fuller**[2] ● **n.** a grooved or rounded tool on which iron is shaped. ● **v.** stamp (iron) using a fuller.
– ORIGIN C19: of unknown origin.
**fullerene** /'fʊləriːn/ ● **n.** Chemistry a form of carbon having a molecule consisting of a large spheroidal cage of atoms, produced chiefly by the action of arc discharges between carbon electrodes.
– ORIGIN C20: contr. of **BUCKMINSTERFULLERENE** (the first known example).
**fuller's earth** ● **n.** a type of clay used in fulling cloth and as an adsorbent.
**full face** ● **adv.** with all the face visible; facing directly at someone or something. ● **adj. 1** showing all of the face. **2** covering all of the face.
**full-fledged** ● **adj.** North American term for **FULLY FLEDGED**.
**full flood** ● **n.** the tide at its highest.
– PHRASES **in full flood** speaking enthusiastically and volubly.
**full forward** ● **n.** Australian Rules the centrally positioned player in front of the goal on the forward line of the attacking team.
**full-frontal** ● **adj.** with full exposure of the front of the body.
**full-grown** ● **adj.** having reached maturity.
**full-hearted** ● **adj.** with great enthusiasm and commitment; full of sincere feeling.
– DERIVATIVES **full-heartedly** adv. **full-heartedness** n.
**full house** ● **n. 1** a theatre or meeting that is filled to capacity. **2** a poker hand with three of a kind and a pair, which beats a flush and loses to four of a kind. **3** a winning card at bingo.
**full marks** ● **pl. n.** the maximum award in an examination or assessment.
**full moon** ● **n.** the phase of the moon in which its whole disc is illuminated.
**full-motion video** ● **n.** digital video data that is transmitted or stored on video discs for real-time reproduction at a rate of not less than 25 frames per second.
**full-mouthed** ● **adj. 1** (of cattle, sheep, etc.) having a full set of adult teeth. **2** spoken loudly or vigorously.
**full nelson** ● **n.** see **NELSON**.
**fullness** (also **fulness**) ● **n. 1** the state of being full. **2** richness or abundance.
– PHRASES **in the fullness of time** after a due length of time has elapsed; eventually.
**full point** ● **n.** another term for **FULL STOP** (as a punctuation mark).
**full professor** ● **n.** chiefly N. Amer. a professor of the highest grade in a university.
– DERIVATIVES **full professorship** n.
**full-rigged** ● **adj.** (of a sailing ship) having three or more masts that all carry square sails.
**full-scale** ● **adj. 1** (of a model or representation) of the same size as the thing represented. **2** unrestricted in extent or intensity: *a full-scale invasion*.
**full score** ● **n.** a score of a musical composition giving the parts for all performers on separate staves.
**full stop** ● **n.** a punctuation mark (.) used at the end of a sentence or an abbreviation.
**full-time** ● **adj.** occupying the whole of the time available. ● **adv.** on a full-time basis. ● **n.** (**full time**) the end of a sports match.
– DERIVATIVES **full-timer** n.
**full toss** Cricket ● **n.** a ball pitched right up to the batsman. ● **adv.** without the ball having touched the ground.
**fully** ● **adv. 1** completely or entirely; to the fullest extent. **2** no less or fewer than: *fully 65 per cent*.
**-fully** ● **suffix** forming adverbs corresponding to adjectives ending in *-ful* (such as *sorrowfully* corresponding to *sorrowful*).
**fully fashioned** ● **adj.** (of women's clothing) shaped and seamed to fit the body.
**fully fledged** ● **adj. 1** with fully developed wing feathers and able to fly. **2** Brit. completely developed or established; of full status.
**fulmar** /'fʊlmə/ ● **n.** a gull-sized grey and white northern seabird of the petrel family. [*Fulmarus glacialis*.]
– ORIGIN C17: from Hebridean Norn dial., from ON *fúll* 'stinking, foul' (because of its habit of regurgitating its stomach contents when disturbed) + *már* 'gull'.
**fulminant** /'fʊlmɪnənt, 'fʌl-/ ● **adj.** Medicine (of a disease or symptom) severe and sudden in onset.
– ORIGIN C17: from Fr., or from L. *fulminant-*, *fulminare* (see **FULMINATE**).
**fulminate** /'fʊlmɪneɪt, 'fʌl-/ ● **v. 1** express vehement protest. **2** poetic/literary explode violently or flash like lightning. **3** [usu. as adj. **fulminating**] Medicine (of a disease or symptom) develop suddenly and severely. ● **n.** Chemistry a salt or ester of fulminic acid.
– DERIVATIVES **fulminator** n.
– ORIGIN ME: from med. L. *fulminare*, from L. *fulminat-* 'struck by lightning', from *fulmen*, *fulmin-* 'lightning'.
**fulmination** ● **n. 1** an expression of vehement protest. **2** a violent explosion or a flash like lightning.
**fulminic acid** /fʌl'mɪnɪk, fʊl-/ ● **n.** Chemistry a very unstable acid isomeric with cyanic acid.
– ORIGIN C19: *fulminic* from L. *fulmen*, *fulmin-* 'lightning' + **-IC**.
**fulness** ● **n.** variant spelling of **FULLNESS**.
**fulsome** ● **adj. 1** flattering to an excessive degree. **2** of large size or quantity.
– DERIVATIVES **fulsomely** adv. **fulsomeness** n.
– ORIGIN ME: from **FULL**[1] + **-SOME**[1].
**fulvous** /'fʌlvəs, 'fʊl-/ ● **adj.** reddish yellow; tawny.
– ORIGIN C17: from L. *fulvus* + **-OUS**.
**fumaric acid** /fjuː'marɪk/ ● **n.** Chemistry a crystalline organic acid, isomeric with maleic acid, first obtained from the plant fumitory.
– DERIVATIVES **fumarate** n.
– ORIGIN C19: from mod. L. *Fumaria* 'fumitory' + **-IC**.
**fumarole** /'fjuːmərəʊl/ ● **n.** an opening in or near a volcano, through which hot sulphurous gases emerge.
– DERIVATIVES **fumarolic** adj.
– ORIGIN C19: from obs. Ital. *fumaruolo*, from late L. *fumariolum* 'vent, hole for smoke'.
**fumble** ● **v. 1** use the hands clumsily while doing or handling something. ➤ (of the hands) do or handle something clumsily. ➤ (**fumble about/around**) move about

clumsily using the hands to find one's way. ➤(in ball games) fail to catch or field (the ball) cleanly. **2** express oneself or deal with something clumsily or nervously. ● **n.** an act of fumbling. ➤ informal an act of fondling someone for sexual pleasure.
– DERIVATIVES **fumbler** n. **fumbling** adj. **fumblingly** adv.
– ORIGIN ME: from Low Ger. *fommeln* or Du. *fommelen*.

**fume** ● **n. 1** a gas or vapour that smells strongly or is dangerous to inhale. **2** poetic/literary a watery vapour rising from the earth or sea. ● **v. 1** emit fumes. **2** [usu. as adj. **fumed**] expose (something, especially wood) to ammonia fumes in order to produce dark tints. **3** feel great anger.
– DERIVATIVES **fuming** adj. **fumingly** adv. **fumy** adj.
– ORIGIN ME: from OFr. *fumer* (v.), from L. *fumare* 'to smoke'.

**fume cupboard** (US **fume hood**) ● **n.** a ventilated enclosure in a chemistry laboratory, in which harmful volatile chemicals can be used or kept.

**fumet** /fjuːˈmɛt/ ● **n.** a concentrated stock, especially of game or fish.
– ORIGIN C18 (in the sense 'game flavour'): from Fr., from *fumer* 'to smoke'.

**fumigate** ● **v.** disinfect or purify with the fumes of certain chemicals.
– DERIVATIVES **fumigant** n. **fumigation** n. **fumigator** n.
– ORIGIN C16 (in the sense 'to perfume'): from L. *fumigat-*, *fumigare*, from *fumus* 'smoke'.

**fumitory** /ˈfjuːmɪt(ə)ri/ ● **n.** a plant with spikes of small tubular pink or white flowers and finely divided greyish leaves. [Genus *Fumaria*.]
– ORIGIN ME: from OFr. *fumeterre*, from med. L. *fumus terrae* 'smoke of the earth' (because of its greyish leaves).

**fun** ● **n. 1** light-hearted pleasure or amusement. **2** a source of this. **3** playfulness or good humour: *she's full of fun.* ● **adj.** informal enjoyable. ● **v.** informal, chiefly N. Amer. joke or tease.
– PHRASES **in fun** not intended seriously. **make fun of** tease or laugh at in a mocking or unkind way.
– ORIGIN C17 (denoting a trick or hoax): from obs. *fun* 'to cheat or hoax', dial. var. of ME *fon* 'make a fool of, be a fool', rel. to *fon* 'a fool', of unknown origin; cf. **FOND**.

**funambulist** /fjuːˈnambjʊlɪst/ ● **n.** formal a tightrope walker.
– ORIGIN C18: from Fr. *funambule* or L. *funambulus* (from *funis* 'rope' + *ambulare* 'to walk') + **-IST**.

**funboard** ● **n.** a type of windsurfing board that is less stable but faster than a standard board.

**function** ● **n. 1** an activity that is natural to or the purpose of a person or thing. ➤a computer operation corresponding to a single instruction from the user. **2** a large or formal social event or ceremony. **3** Mathematics a relation or expression involving one or more variables. ➤a variable quantity regarded as depending on another variable; a consequence: *depreciation is a function of time.* **4** Chemistry a functional group. ● **v.** work or operate in a proper or particular way. ➤(**function as**) fulfil the purpose or task of (a specified thing).
– DERIVATIVES **functionless** adj.
– ORIGIN C16: from Fr. *fonction*, from L. *functio(n-)*, from *fungi* 'perform'.

**functional** ● **adj. 1** of, relating to, or having a function: *a functional role.* ➤relating to the way in which something functions: *there are functional differences between the left and right brain.* **2** designed to be practical and useful, rather than attractive. **3** working or operating. **4** (of a disease) affecting the operation rather than the structure of an organ. **5** (of a mental illness) having no discernible organic cause.
– DERIVATIVES **functionality** n. **functionally** adv.

**functional food** ● **n.** a food containing health-giving additives.

**functional group** ● **n.** Chemistry a group of atoms responsible for the characteristic reactions of a particular compound.

**functionalism** ● **n. 1** the theory that the design of an object should be determined by its function rather than by aesthetic considerations. **2** (in social sciences) the study or interpretation of phenomena in terms of the functions which they fulfil within an overall system.
– DERIVATIVES **functionalist** n. & adj.

**functionary** /ˈfʌŋ(k)ʃ(ə)n(ə)ri/ ● **n.** (pl. **-ies**) an official.

**function key** ● **n.** Computing a key on a computer keyboard to which software can assign a particular function.

**function word** ● **n.** Linguistics a word whose purpose is to contribute to the syntax rather than the meaning of a sentence, for example *do* in *we do not live here.*

**functor** /ˈfʌŋktə/ ● **n.** Logic & Mathematics a function; an operator.

**fund** ● **n. 1** a sum of money saved or made available for a particular purpose. **2** (**funds**) financial resources. **3** a large stock. ● **v.** provide with a fund.
– PHRASES **in funds** Brit. having money to spend.
– DERIVATIVES **funding** n.
– ORIGIN C17: from L. *fundus* 'bottom, piece of landed property'.

**fundal** /ˈfʌnd(ə)l/ ● **adj.** Medicine of or relating to a fundus.

**fundament** /ˈfʌndəm(ə)nt/ ● **n. 1** the foundation or basis of something. **2** humorous a person's buttocks or anus.
– ORIGIN ME: from OFr. *fondement*, from L. *fundamentum*, from *fundare* 'to found'.

**fundamental** /fʌndəˈmɛnt(ə)l/ ● **adj.** of or serving as a foundation or core; of central importance. ● **n. 1** a central or primary rule or principle. **2** Music a fundamental note, tone, or frequency.
– DERIVATIVES **fundamentality** n. **fundamentally** adv.

**fundamental frequency** ● **n. 1** Physics the lowest frequency produced by the oscillation of the whole of an object, as distinct from harmonics. **2** Music the principal frequency in a harmonic series.

**fundamentalism** ● **n. 1** a form of Protestant Christianity which upholds belief in the strict and literal interpretation of the Bible. **2** the strict maintenance of the ancient or fundamental doctrines of any religion or ideology.
– DERIVATIVES **fundamentalist** n. & adj.

**fundamental note** ● **n.** Music the lowest note of a chord in its original (uninverted) form.

**fundamental tone** ● **n.** Music the tone which represents the fundamental frequency of a vibrating object such as a string or bell.

**fundamental unit** ● **n.** each of a set of unrelated units of measurement from which other units are derived, for example (in the SI system) the metre, kilogram, and second.

**funded debt** ● **n.** debt in the form of securities with long-term or indefinite redemption. Compare with **FLOATING DEBT**.

**fundholding** ● **n.** (in the UK) a system of state funding in which a general practitioner is provided with and controls their own budget for the purchase of hospital services.
– DERIVATIVES **fundholder** n.

**fundi** plural form of **FUNDUS**.

**fundie** /ˈfʌndi/ (also **fundi**) ● **n.** (pl. **fundies** or **fundis**) informal a Christian fundamentalist.

**fund-raiser** ● **n. 1** a person engaged in seeking financial support for an organization or cause. **2** an event held to generate such financial support.
– DERIVATIVES **fund-raising** n.

**fundus** /ˈfʌndəs/ ● **n.** (pl. **fundi** /-dʌɪ/) Anatomy **1** the part of a hollow organ (such as the uterus or the gall bladder) that is furthest from the opening. **2** the part of the eyeball opposite the pupil.
– ORIGIN C18: from L., lit. 'bottom'.

**funeral** ● **n.** a ceremony in which a dead person is buried or cremated. ➤ archaic or poetic/literary a procession of mourners at a burial.
– PHRASES **it's one's funeral** informal it is one's own responsibility (used to imply that an undesirable outcome is possible).
– ORIGIN ME: from OFr. *funeraille*, from med. L. *funeralia*, neut. pl. of late L. *funeralis*, from L. *funus*, *funer-* 'funeral, death, corpse'.

**funeral director** • n. an undertaker.
**funeral parlour** (also **funeral home**, **funeral chapel**) • n. an establishment where the dead are prepared for burial or cremation.
**funeral pyre** (also **funeral pile**) • n. a pile of wood on which a corpse is burnt as part of a funeral ceremony.
**funeral urn** • n. an urn holding the ashes of a cremated body.
**funerary** /ˈfjuːn(ə)(rə)ri/ • adj. relating to a funeral or the commemoration of the dead.
**funereal** /fjuːˈnɪərɪəl/ • adj. having the sombre character appropriate to a funeral.
– DERIVATIVES **funereally** adv.
**funfair** • n. chiefly Brit. a fair consisting of rides, sideshows, and other amusements.
**fun fur** • n. an artificial fabric with a texture resembling fur.
**fungi** plural form of **FUNGUS**.
**fungible** /ˈfʌn(d)ʒɪb(ə)l/ • adj. Law (of goods contracted for without an individual specimen being specified) interchangeable with other identical items.
– DERIVATIVES **fungibility** n.
– ORIGIN C17: from med. L. *fungibilis*, from *fungi* 'perform, enjoy'.
**fungicide** /ˈfʌn(d)ʒɪsʌɪd, ˈfʌŋɡɪ-/ • n. a chemical that destroys fungus.
– DERIVATIVES **fungicidal** adj.
**fungistatic** /ˌfʌn(d)ʒɪˈstatɪk/ • adj. inhibiting the growth of fungi.
– DERIVATIVES **fungistatically** adv.
**fungivorous** /fʌŋˈdʒɪv(ə)rəs/ • adj. feeding on fungi or mushrooms.
**fungo** /ˈfʌŋɡəʊ/ • n. (pl. **-oes** or **-os**) **1** (also **fungo fly**) Baseball a fly ball hit for practice. **2** (also **fungo bat** or **stick**) a long lightweight bat for hitting fungoes.
– ORIGIN C19: of unknown origin.
**fungus** /ˈfʌŋɡəs/ • n. (pl. **fungi** /-ɡʌɪ, -(d)ʒʌɪ/ or **funguses**) any of a large group of spore-producing organisms which feed on organic matter and include moulds, yeast, mushrooms, and toadstools.
– DERIVATIVES **fungal** adj. **fungiform** adj. **fungoid** adj. **fungous** adj.
– ORIGIN ME: from L., perh. from Gk *spongos* (see **SPONGE**).
**funicle** /ˈfjuːnɪk(ə)l/ • n. **1** Botany a filamentous stalk attaching a seed or ovule to the placenta. **2** Entomology a filamentous section of an insect's antenna, supporting the club.
– ORIGIN C17: anglicized form of L. *funiculus* (see **FUNICULUS**).
**funicular** /fjʊˈnɪkjʊlə, fəˈnɪk-/ • adj. **1** (of a railway on a steep slope) operated by cable with ascending and descending cars counterbalanced. **2** of or relating to a rope or its tension. • n. a funicular railway.
– ORIGIN C17: from L. *funiculus* (see **FUNICULUS**) + **-AR**[1].
**funiculus** /fjʊˈnɪkjʊləs/ • n. (pl. **funiculi** /-lʌɪ, -liː/) **1** Anatomy a bundle of nerve fibres, especially forming one of the main tracts of white matter in the spinal cord. **2** another term for **FUNICLE**.
– ORIGIN C17: from L., dimin. of *funis* 'rope'.
**funk**[1] informal • n. (also **blue funk**) a state of panic or depression. • v. avoid out of fear.
– ORIGIN C18: perh. from **FUNK**[2] in the informal sense 'tobacco smoke', or from obs. Flemish *fonck* 'disturbance, agitation'.
**funk**[2] • n. **1** a style of popular dance music of US black origin, having a strong rhythm that typically accentuates the first beat in the bar. **2** N. Amer. informal, dated a strong musty smell of sweat or tobacco. • v. (**funk something up**) give music elements of funk.
– ORIGIN C17: perh. from Fr. dial. *funkier* 'blow smoke on'.
**funkia** /ˈfʌŋkɪə/ • n. another term for **HOSTA**.
– ORIGIN C19: mod. L. (former genus name), named after the Prussian botanist Heinrich Christian *Funck*.
**funkster** • n. informal a performer or fan of funk music.
**funky** • adj. (**-ier**, **-iest**) informal **1** (of music) having a strong dance rhythm. **2** unconventionally modern and stylish. **3** N. Amer. strongly musty.
– DERIVATIVES **funkily** adv. **funkiness** n.
**funnel** • n. **1** a utensil that is wide at the top and narrow at the bottom, used for guiding liquid or powder into a small opening. **2** a metal chimney on a ship or steam engine. • v. (**funnelled**, **funnelling**; US **funneled**, **funneling**) **1** guide or move through or as if through a funnel. **2** assume the shape of a funnel.
– ORIGIN ME: appar. via OFr. from Provençal *fonilh*, from late L. *fundibulum*, from L. *infundibulum*, from *infundere* 'pour into'.
**funnel cake** • n. US a cake made of batter that is poured through a funnel into hot fat or oil, deep-fried until crisp, and served sprinkled with sugar.
**funnel-web spider** • n. a dangerously venomous Australian spider that builds a funnel-shaped web. [Genera *Atrax* and *Hadronyche*.]
**funniosity** /ˌfʌnɪˈɒsɪti/ • n. (pl. **-ies**) Brit. humorous a comical person or thing.
**funny** • adj. (**-ier**, **-iest**) **1** causing laughter or amusement. **2** strange; peculiar. **3** arousing suspicion: *there was something funny going on.* **4** informal slightly unwell; out of sorts. **5** eccentric or slightly deranged. • n. (**funnies**) informal **1** amusing jokes. **2** N. Amer. the comic strips in newspapers.
– PHRASES **funny ha-ha** (or **funny peculiar**) funny in its sense 'amusing' rather than 'peculiar' (or vice versa). [coined by Ian Hay in his novel *Housemaster* (1936).]
– DERIVATIVES **funnily** adv. **funniness** n.
**funny bone** • n. informal the part of the elbow over which passes the ulnar nerve, which may cause numbness and pain along the forearm and hand if knocked.
**funny-face** • n. informal an affectionate form of address.
**funny farm** • n. informal a psychiatric hospital.
**funny man** • n. a professional clown or comedian.
**funny money** • n. informal currency that is forged or otherwise worthless.
**funny paper** • n. N. Amer. a section of a newspaper containing cartoons and humorous matter.
**fun run** • n. informal an uncompetitive run for sponsored runners, held in support of a charity.
**funster** • n. informal a joker.
**Fur** /fʊə, fəː/ • n. (pl. same) **1** a member of a Muslim people of the mountainous and desert regions of SW Sudan. **2** the Nilo-Saharan language of the Fur.
**fur** • n. **1** the short, fine, soft hair of certain animals. **2** the skin of an animal with fur on it, used in making or trimming garments. **3** a coat made from fur. **4** Heraldry any of several heraldic tinctures representing animal skins in stylized form (e.g. ermine, vair). **5** Brit. a coating formed by hard water on the inside surface of a pipe, kettle, etc. **6** a coating formed on the tongue as a symptom of sickness. • v. (**furred**, **furring**) **1** Brit. coat or clog with a deposit. **2** level (floor or wall timbers) by inserting strips of wood.
– PHRASES **fur and feather** game mammals and birds. **the fur will fly** informal there will be a dramatic argument.
– DERIVATIVES **furless** adj. **-furred** adj.
– ORIGIN ME: from OFr. *forrer* 'to line, sheathe', from *forre* 'sheath', of Gmc origin.
**fur.** • abbrev. furlong(s).
**furan** /ˈfjʊəran/ • n. Chemistry a volatile liquid organic compound with an unsaturated five-membered ring in its molecule.
– ORIGIN C19: from synonymous *furfuran*, from L. *furfur* 'bran' + **-AN**.
**furbelow** /ˈfəːbɪləʊ/ • n. **1** a flounce on a skirt or petticoat. **2** (**furbelows**) showy trimmings. • v. [usu. as adj. **furbelowed**] poetic/literary adorn with a furbelow or trimmings.
– ORIGIN C17: from Fr. *falbala* 'trimming, flounce'.
**furbish** /ˈfəːbɪʃ/ • v. **1** give a fresh look to; renovate. **2** archaic polish (a weapon).
– DERIVATIVES **furbisher** n.
– ORIGIN ME: from OFr. *forbiss-*, lengthened stem of *forbir*, of Gmc origin.
**furcate** • v. /ˈfəːkeɪt, fəːˈkeɪt/ divide into two or more

branches; fork. ● **adj.** /ˈfəːkeɪt, -kət/ furcated; forked.
– DERIVATIVES **furcation** n.
– ORIGIN C19 (earlier (C17) as *furcation*): from late L. *furcatus* 'cloven', from L. *furca* 'fork'.

**furcula** /ˈfəːkjʊlə/ ● **n.** (pl. **furculae** /-liː/) Zoology **1** the wishbone of a bird. **2** the forked appendage at the end of the abdomen in a springtail, by which the insect jumps.
– DERIVATIVES **furcular** adj.
– ORIGIN C19: from L., dimin. of *furca* 'fork'.

**furfuraceous** /ˌfəːf(j)əˈreɪʃəs/ ● **adj.** Botany & Medicine covered with or characterized by bran-like scales.
– ORIGIN C17: from late L. *furfuraceus* (from L. *furfur* 'bran') + **-ous**.

**furfural** /ˈfəːf(j)əral/ ● **n.** Chemistry a colourless liquid aldehyde derived from furan.

**furioso** /ˌfjʊərɪˈəʊzəʊ, -səʊ/ ● **adv. & adj.** Music furiously and wildly.
– ORIGIN from Ital.

**furious** ● **adj. 1** extremely angry. **2** full of energy or intensity.
– DERIVATIVES **furiously** adv. **furiousness** n.
– ORIGIN ME: from OFr. *furieus*, from L. *furiosus*, from *furia* 'fury'.

**furl** ● **v.** roll or fold up neatly and securely.
– DERIVATIVES **furlable** adj. **furled** adj.
– ORIGIN C16: from Fr. *ferler*.

**furling** ● **n.** equipment for furling sails around their yards or booms.

**furlong** ● **n.** an eighth of a mile, 220 yards.
– ORIGIN OE *furlang*, from *furh* 'furrow' + *lang* 'long' (orig. denoting the length of a furrow in a common field, also used as the equivalent of the Roman *stadium*, one eighth of a Roman mile).

**furlough** /ˈfəːləʊ/ ● **n.** leave of absence, especially from military duty. ● **v.** US grant furlough to.
– ORIGIN C17: from Du. *verlof*, of W. Gmc origin and rel. to **LEAVE**[2].

**furmety** /ˈfəːmɪti/ ● **n.** variant of **FRUMENTY**.

**furnace** ● **n. 1** an enclosed chamber in which material can be heated to very high temperatures. **2** chiefly N. Amer. a boiler serving a central heating system. **3** a very hot place.
– ORIGIN ME: from OFr. *fornais(e)*, from L. *fornax*, *fornac-*, from *fornus* 'oven'.

**furnish** ● **v. 1** provide (a room or building) with furniture and fittings. **2** supply with equipment or information. **3** be a source of; provide.
– DERIVATIVES **furnished** adj. **furnisher** n.
– ORIGIN ME: from OFr. *furniss-*, lengthened stem of *furnir*, ult. of W. Gmc origin.

**furnishing** ● **n. 1** (**furnishings**) furniture and fittings in a room or building. **2** [as modifier] denoting fabrics used for curtains or upholstery.

**furniture** ● **n. 1** the movable articles that are used to make a room or building suitable for living or working in, such as tables, chairs, or desks. **2** the small accessories or fittings that are required for a particular task or function.
– PHRASES **a part of the furniture** informal a person or thing that has become so familiar as to be unquestioned or unnoticed.
– ORIGIN C16: from Fr. *fourniture*, from *fournir* 'to furnish'.

**furniture beetle** ● **n.** a small brown beetle, the larva of which (the woodworm) bores holes in dead wood. [*Anobium punctatum*.]

**furore** /ˌfjʊ(ə)ˈrɔːri, ˌfjʊ(ə)ˈrɔː/ (US **furor** /ˈfjʊərɔː/) ● **n. 1** an outbreak of public anger or excitement. **2** archaic a craze.
– ORIGIN C18: from Ital.

**furosemide** /ˌfjʊəˈrɒsəmʌɪd/ ● **n.** variant spelling of **FRUSEMIDE**.

**furphy** /ˈfəːfi/ ● **n.** (pl. **-ies**) Austral. informal a far-fetched rumour.
– ORIGIN First World War: from the name painted on water and sanitary carts manufactured by the *Furphy* family of Shepparton, Victoria.

**furrier** /ˈfʌrɪə/ ● **n.** a person who prepares or deals in furs.
– DERIVATIVES **furriery** n.
– ORIGIN ME: from OFr. *forreor*, from *forrer* (see **FUR**).

**furring strip** ● **n.** a length of wood tapering to nothing, used in roofing and other construction work.

**furrow** ● **n. 1** a long, narrow trench made in the ground by a plough. **2** a rut or groove. **3** a deep wrinkle on a person's face. ● **v. 1** make a furrow in. **2** mark or be marked with furrows.
– DERIVATIVES **furrowy** adj.
– ORIGIN OE *furh*, of Gmc origin.

**furrow slice** ● **n.** a slice of earth turned up by the mouldboard of a plough.

**furry** ● **adj.** (**-ier**, **-iest**) covered with or resembling fur.
– DERIVATIVES **furriness** n.

**fur seal** ● **n.** a gregarious eared seal of the Pacific and southern oceans, whose thick underside fur is used commercially as sealskin. [*Callorhinus ursinus* and other species.]

**further** used as comparative of **FAR**. ● **adv.** (also **farther**) **1** at, to, or by a greater distance. **2** over a greater expanse of space or time. ➤ beyond the point already reached. **3** at or to a more advanced, successful, or desirable stage. **4** in addition; also. ● **adj. 1** (also **farther**) more distant in space. ➤ more remote from a central point. **2** additional: *a further ten minutes*. ● **v.** help the progress or development of.
– PHRASES **further to** formal following on from (used especially at the beginning of a letter). **until further notice** until another announcement is made.
– DERIVATIVES **furtherer** n.
– ORIGIN OE *furthor* (adv.), *furthra* (adj.), *fyrthrian* (v.), of Gmc origin; rel. to **FORTH**.

**furtherance** ● **n.** the advancement of a scheme or interest.

**further education** ● **n.** Brit. education below degree level for people above school age.

**furthermore** ● **adv.** in addition; besides.

**furthermost** (also **farthermost**) ● **adj.** at the greatest distance from a central point or implicit standpoint.

**furthest** (also **farthest**) used as superlative of **FAR**. ● **adj.** situated at the greatest distance. ➤ covering the greatest area or distance. ● **adv. 1** at or by the greatest distance. **2** over the greatest distance or area. ➤ indicating the most distant point reached in a specified direction: *it was the furthest north I had ever travelled*. **3** to the most extreme or advanced point.
– PHRASES **at the furthest** at most.
– ORIGIN ME: formed as a superlative of **FURTHER**.

**furtive** /ˈfəːtɪv/ ● **adj.** characterized by guilty or evasive secrecy; stealthy.
– DERIVATIVES **furtively** adv. **furtiveness** n.
– ORIGIN C17: from Fr. *furtif*, *-ive* or L. *furtivus*, from *furtum* 'theft'.

**furuncle** /ˈfjʊərʌŋk(ə)l/ ● **n.** technical term for **BOIL**[2].
– DERIVATIVES **furuncular** adj. **furunculous** adj.
– ORIGIN ME: from L. *furunculus*, lit. 'petty thief', also 'knob on a vine' (regarded as stealing the sap), from *fur* 'thief'.

**furunculosis** /fjʊˌrʌŋkjʊˈləʊsɪs/ ● **n. 1** Medicine the simultaneous or repeated occurrence of boils on the skin. **2** a bacterial disease of salmon and trout.

**fury** ● **n.** (pl. **-ies**) **1** extreme anger. **2** extreme strength or violence in an action or a natural phenomenon. **2** (**Fury**) Greek Mythology a spirit of punishment, often represented as one of three goddesses (identified at an early date with the Eumenides).
– PHRASES **like fury** informal with great energy or effort.
– ORIGIN ME: from OFr. *furie*, from L. *furia*, from *furiosus* 'furious', from *furere* 'be mad, rage'.

**furze** /fəːz/ ● **n.** another term for **GORSE**.
– DERIVATIVES **furzy** adj.
– ORIGIN OE *fyrs*, of unknown origin.

**fusarium** /fjʊˈzɛːrɪəm/ ● **n.** a mould that causes diseases of plants, especially wilting. [Genus *Fusarium*.]
– ORIGIN C20: mod. L., from L. *fusus* 'spindle'.

**fuscous** /ˈfʌskəs/ ● **adj.** technical or poetic/literary dark and sombre in colour.

– ORIGIN C17: from L. *fuscus* 'dusky' + **-OUS**.

**fuse**[1] • v. **1** join, blend, or coalesce to form a single entity. **2** melt (a material or object) with intense heat, so as to join it with something else. **3** Brit. (with reference to an electrical appliance) stop or cause to stop working when a fuse melts. **4** provide (a circuit or electrical appliance) with a fuse. • n. a safety device consisting of a strip of wire that melts and breaks an electric circuit if the current exceeds a safe level.
– ORIGIN C16: from L. *fus-*, *fundere* 'pour, melt'.

**fuse**[2] (US **fuze**) • n. a length of material along which a small flame moves to explode a bomb or firework. ➤a device in a bomb that controls the timing of the explosion. • v. fit a fuse to (a bomb).
– DERIVATIVES **fuseless** adj.
– ORIGIN C17: from Ital. *fuso*, from L. *fusus* 'spindle'.

**fuse box** (or **fuse board**) • n. a box or board housing the fuses for circuits in a building.

**fusee** /fjuːˈziː/ (US **fuzee**) • n. **1** a conical pulley or wheel in a watch or clock. **2** a large-headed match capable of staying alight in strong wind. **3** N. Amer. a railway signal flare.
– ORIGIN C16 (denoting a spindle-shaped figure): from Fr. *fusée* 'spindleful', based on L. *fusus* 'spindle'.

**fuselage** /ˈfjuːzəlɑːʒ, -lɪdʒ/ • n. the main body of an aircraft.
– ORIGIN C20: from Fr., from *fuseler* 'shape into a spindle'.

**fusel oil** /ˈfjuːz(ə)l/ • n. a mixture of several alcohols (chiefly amyl alcohol) produced as a by-product of alcoholic fermentation.
– ORIGIN C19: from Ger. *Fusel* 'bad liquor', prob. rel. to *fuseln* 'to bungle'.

**fuseway** • n. a fused connection point in a fuse box.

**fuse wire** • n. thin wire used in an electric fuse.

**fusible** /ˈfjuːzɪb(ə)l/ • adj. able to be fused or melted easily.
– DERIVATIVES **fusibility** n.

**fusiform** /ˈfjuːzɪfɔːm/ • adj. Botany & Zoology tapering at both ends; spindle-shaped.
– ORIGIN C18: from L. *fusus* 'spindle' + **-IFORM**.

**fusil**[1] /ˈfjuːzɪl/ • n. historical a light musket.
– ORIGIN C16 (denoting a flint in a tinderbox): from Fr., based on L. *focus* 'hearth, fire'.

**fusil**[2] /ˈfjuːzɪl/ • n. Heraldry an elongated lozenge.
– ORIGIN ME: from OFr. *fusel*, from a dimin. of L. *fusus* 'spindle'.

**fusilier** /ˌfjuːzɪˈlɪə/ (US also **fusileer**) • n. **1** (**Fusilier**) a member of any of several British regiments formerly armed with fusils. **2** historical a soldier armed with a fusil.

**fusillade** /ˌfjuːzɪˈleɪd, -ˈlɑːd/ • n. a series of shots fired at the same time or in rapid succession. • v. archaic fire a fusillade at.
– ORIGIN C19: from Fr.

**fusilli** /f(j)ʊˈziːli/ • pl. n. pasta pieces in the form of short spirals.
– ORIGIN Ital., lit. 'little spindles'.

**fusion** • n. **1** the process or result of fusing. **2** a reaction in which light atomic nuclei fuse to form a heavier nucleus, releasing much energy. **3** music that is a mixture of different styles, especially jazz and rock. **4** [as modifier] referring to food or cooking which incorporates elements of both eastern and western cuisine.
– DERIVATIVES **fusional** adj. **fusionism** n. **fusionist** n.
– ORIGIN C16: from L. *fusio(n-)*, from *fundere* 'pour, melt'.

**fusion bomb** • n. a bomb deriving its energy from nuclear fusion, especially a hydrogen bomb.

**fuss** • n. **1** a display of unnecessary or excessive excitement, activity, or interest. **2** a protest or complaint. • v. **1** show unnecessary or excessive concern about something. **2** Brit. disturb or bother. **3** treat with excessive attention or affection.
– PHRASES **not be fussed** Brit. informal not have strong feelings about something.
– DERIVATIVES **fusser** n.
– ORIGIN C18: perh. Anglo-Ir.

**fusspot** • n. informal a fussy person.

**fussy** • adj. (**-ier**, **-iest**) **1** fastidious about one's requirements and hard to please. **2** full of unnecessary detail or decoration.
– DERIVATIVES **fussily** adv. **fussiness** n.

**fustanella** /ˌfʌstəˈnɛlə/ • n. a stiff white kilt, worn by men in Albania and Greece.
– ORIGIN C19: from Ital.

**fustian** /ˈfʌstɪən/ • n. a thick, hard-wearing twilled cloth with a short nap.
– ORIGIN ME: from OFr. *fustaigne*, from med. L. *fustaneum*, from (*pannus*) *fustaneus* 'cloth from *Fostat*', a suburb of Cairo.

**fustic** /ˈfʌstɪk/ • n. **1** (also **old fustic**) a tropical American tree with heartwood that yields a yellow dye and other products. [*Maclura tinctoria*.] **2** (also **young fustic**) the smoke tree.
– ORIGIN ME: via Fr. from Sp. *fustoc*, from Arab. *fustuḳ*, from Gk *pistakē* 'pistachio tree'.

**fusty** • adj. (**-ier**, **-iest**) **1** smelling stale, damp, or stuffy. **2** old-fashioned.
– DERIVATIVES **fustily** adv. **fustiness** n.
– ORIGIN C15: from OFr. *fuste* 'smelling of the cask'.

**futhark** /ˈfuːθɑːk/ (also **futhorc** /ˈfuːθɔːk/, **futhork**) • n. the runic alphabet.
– ORIGIN C19: from its first six letters: *f*, *u*, *th*, *a* (or *o*), *r*, *k*.

**futile** • adj. producing no useful result; pointless.
– DERIVATIVES **futilely** adv. **futility** n.
– ORIGIN C16: from L. *futilis* 'leaky, futile', appar. from *fundere* 'pour'.

**futon** /ˈfuːtɒn/ • n. a padded unsprung mattress originating in Japan, that can be rolled up or folded in two.
– ORIGIN C19: Japanese.

**futtock** /ˈfʌtək/ • n. each of the middle timbers of a ship's frame, between the floor and the top timbers.
– ORIGIN ME: perh. from Mid. Low Ger., or from **FOOT** + **HOOK**.

**future** • n. **1** (**the future**) time that is still to come. ➤events or conditions occurring or existing in that time. **2** a prospect of success or happiness: *I might have a future as an artist.* **3** Grammar a tense of verbs expressing events that have not yet happened. **4** (**futures**) contracts for assets (especially commodities or shares) bought at agreed prices but delivered and paid for later. Compare with **FORWARD** (in sense 2). • adj. **1** existing or occurring in the future. ➤(of a person) planned or destined to hold a specified position: *his future wife.* **2** Grammar (of a tense) expressing an event yet to happen.
– PHRASES **in future** from now onwards.
– DERIVATIVES **futureless** adj.
– ORIGIN ME: via OFr. from L. *futurus*, future part. of *esse* 'be' (from the stem *fu-*, ult. from a base meaning 'grow, become').

**future history** • n. (in science fiction) a narration of imagined future events.

**future perfect** • n. Grammar a tense of verbs expressing expected completion in the future, in English exemplified by *will have done*.

**future-proof** • adj. (of a product) unlikely to become obsolete.
– DERIVATIVES **future-proofed** adj. **future-proofing** n.

**future shock** • n. a state of distress or disorientation due to rapid social or technological change.

**Futurism** • n. an artistic movement launched in Italy in 1909, which strongly rejected traditional forms and embraced the dynamism of modern technology.
– ORIGIN from Ital. *futurismo*.

**futurist** • n. **1** (**Futurist**) an adherent of Futurism. **2** a person who studies the future and makes predictions about it based on current trends. **3** Theology a person who believes that eschatological prophecies are still to be fulfilled. • adj. **1** (**Futurist**) of or relating to Futurism or the Futurists. **2** relating to a vision of the future.

**futuristic** • adj. **1** having or involving very modern technology or design. **2** (of a film or book) set in the future, typically in a world of highly advanced technology. **3** dated of or characteristic of Futurism.
– DERIVATIVES **futuristically** adv.

**futurity** /fjuːˈtjʊərɪti, -tʃ-/ ● **n.** (pl. **-ies**) **1** the future time. **2** a future event. **3** renewed or continuing existence. **4** US short for **FUTURITY RACE**.

**futurity race** (also **futurity stakes**) ● **n.** US a race for young horses for which entries may be made before the horses are born.

**futurology** /ˌfjuːtʃəˈrɒlədʒi/ ● **n.** systematic forecasting of the future based on present trends.
– DERIVATIVES **futurological** adj. **futurologist** n.

**futz** /fʌts/ ● **v.** (usu. **futz around**) N. Amer. informal idle or busy oneself aimlessly.
– ORIGIN 1930s: perh. an alt. of Yiddish *arumfartzen* 'fart about'.

**fuze** ● **n.** US spelling of **FUSE**[2].

**fuzee** ● **n.** US spelling of **FUSEE**.

**fuzz**[1] ● **n. 1** a frizzy mass of hair or fibre. **2** a blurred image. **3** a buzzing or distorted sound. ➤such a sound deliberately produced on an electric guitar. ● **v. 1** make or become fuzzy. **2** make a distorted buzzing sound with (a guitar).
– DERIVATIVES **fuzzed** adj.
– ORIGIN C16: prob. of Low Ger. or Du. origin.

**fuzz**[2] ● **n.** (**the fuzz**) informal the police.
– ORIGIN 1920s (orig. US): of unknown origin.

**fuzzbox** ● **n.** a device which adds fuzz to an electric guitar.

**fuzzy** ● **adj.** (**-ier**, **-iest**) **1** having a frizzy texture or appearance. **2** indistinct or vague. ➤(of an electric guitar) having a distorted, buzzing sound; fuzzed. **3** Computing & Logic of or relating to a form of set theory and logic in which predicates may have degrees of applicability, rather than simply being true or false.
– PHRASES **warm and fuzzy** N. Amer. informal sentimentally emotional.
– DERIVATIVES **fuzzily** adv. **fuzziness** n.

**fwd** ● **abbrev.** forward.

**f.w.d.** ● **abbrev. 1** four-wheel drive. **2** front-wheel drive.

**F-word** ● **n.** euphemistic the word 'fuck'.

**FX** ● **abbrev.** visual or sound effects.
– ORIGIN from the pronunc. of the two syllables of *effects*.

**FY** ● **abbrev. 1** Brit. financial year. **2** N. Amer. fiscal year.

**-fy** ● **suffix 1** (added to nouns) forming verbs denoting making or producing: *speechify*. ➤denoting transformation or the process of making into: *petrify*. **2** forming verbs denoting the making of a state defined by an adjective: *falsify*. **3** forming verbs expressing a causative sense: *horrify*.
– ORIGIN from Fr. *-fier*, from L. *-ficare*, *-facere*, from *facere* 'do, make'.

**FYI** ● **abbrev.** for your information.

**fyke** /fʌɪk/ ● **n.** chiefly US a bag net for catching fish.
– ORIGIN C19: from Du. *fuik* 'fish trap'.

**fyrd** /fəːd, fɪəd/ ● **n.** the English militia before 1066.
– ORIGIN OE, of Gmc origin; rel. to **FARE**.

**fytte** ● **n.** variant spelling of **FIT**[3].

# G g

**G**[1] (also **g**) ● **n.** (pl. **Gs** or **G's**) **1** the seventh letter of the alphabet. **2** denoting the next after F in a set of items, categories, etc. **3** Music the fifth note in the diatonic scale of C major.

**G**[2] ● **abbrev.** **1** Physics gauss. **2** giga- ($10^9$). **3** N. Amer. informal grand (a thousand dollars). **4** the force exerted by the earth's gravitational field. ● **symb.** **1** Chemistry Gibbs free energy. **2** Physics the gravitational constant ($6.67 \times 10^{-11}$ N $m^2$ $kg^{-2}$).

**g** ● **abbrev.** **1** Chemistry gas. **2** gelding. **3** gram(s). ● **symb.** Physics the acceleration due to gravity (9.81 m $s^{-2}$).

**G8** ● **abbrev.** Group of Eight, a group of eight leading industrial nations whose heads of government meet regularly.

**GA** ● **abbrev.** **1** general aviation. **2** Georgia (in official postal use).

**Ga** ● **symb.** the chemical element gallium.

**Ga.** ● **abbrev.** Georgia (US).

**gab** informal ● **v.** (**gabbed**, **gabbing**) talk at length. ● **n.** talk; chatter.
– PHRASES **the gift of the gab** the ability to speak with eloquence and fluency.
– DERIVATIVES **gabby** adj. (**-ier**, **-iest**).
– ORIGIN C18: var. of **GOB**[1].

**GABA** ● **abbrev.** gamma-aminobutyric acid.

**gabardine** ● **n.** variant spelling of **GABERDINE**.

**gabble** ● **v.** talk rapidly and unintelligibly. ● **n.** rapid, unintelligible talk.
– DERIVATIVES **gabbler** n.
– ORIGIN C16: from Du. *gabbelen*, of imitative origin.

**gabbro** /'gabrəʊ/ ● **n.** (pl. **-os**) Geology a dark, coarse-grained plutonic rock consisting mainly of pyroxene, plagioclase feldspar, and often olivine.
– DERIVATIVES **gabbroic** adj. **gabbroid** adj.
– ORIGIN C19: from Ital., from L. *glaber, glabr-* 'smooth'.

**gaberdine** /,gabə'di:n, 'gabədi:n/ ● **n.** **1** a smooth, durable twill-woven worsted or cotton cloth. **2** Brit. a raincoat made of gaberdine. **3** historical a loose, long upper garment worn particularly by Jews.
– ORIGIN C16: from OFr. *gauvardine*, earlier *gallevardine*, perh. from Mid. High Ger. *wallevart* 'pilgrimage' and orig. 'a garment worn by a pilgrim'.

**gabion** /'geɪbɪən/ ● **n.** a cylindrical basket or container filled with earth, stones, or other material and used as a component of civil engineering works.
– DERIVATIVES **gabionage** n.
– ORIGIN C16: via Fr. from Ital. *gabbione*, from *gabbia* 'cage'.

**gable** ● **n.** **1** the triangular upper part of a wall at the end of a ridged roof. **2** a gable-shaped canopy over a window or door.
– DERIVATIVES **gabled** adj.
– ORIGIN ME: via OFr. from ON *gafl*, of Gmc origin.

**Gabonese** /,gabə'ni:z/ ● **n.** (pl. same) a native or inhabitant of Gabon, a country in West Africa. ● **adj.** of or relating to Gabon or its people.

**gad**[1] ● **v.** (**gadded**, **gadding**) (**gad about/around**) informal go around from one place to another in the pursuit of pleasure.
– PHRASES **on the gad** archaic on the move.
– ORIGIN ME: back-form. from obs. *gadling* 'wanderer, vagabond', (earlier) 'companion', of Gmc origin.

**gad**[2] (also **by gad**) ● **exclam.** archaic expressing surprise or emphatic assertion.
– ORIGIN C15: euphemistic alt. of **GOD**.

**gadabout** ● **n.** informal a person who gads about.

**Gadarene** /'gadəri:n/ ● **adj.** involving or engaged in a headlong or disastrous rush.
– ORIGIN C19: from New Testament Gk *Gadarēnos* 'inhabitant of *Gadara*' (see Matt. 8:28–32).

**gadfly** ● **n.** (pl. **-flies**) **1** a fly that bites livestock, especially a horsefly, warble fly, or botfly. **2** an annoying and provocative person.
– ORIGIN C16: from **GAD**[1], or obs. *gad* 'goad, spike', from ON *gaddr*, of Gmc origin; rel. to **YARD**[1].

**gadget** ● **n.** a small mechanical device or tool.
– DERIVATIVES **gadgeteer** n. **gadgetry** n. **gadgety** adj.
– ORIGIN C19: prob. from Fr. *gâchette* 'lock mechanism' or from the Fr. dial. word *gagée* 'tool'.

**gadid** /'geɪdɪd/ ● **n.** Zoology a fish of the cod family (Gadidae).
– ORIGIN C19: from mod. L. *Gadidae*, from *gadus* 'cod'.

**gadoid** /'geɪdɔɪd, 'ga-/ ● **n.** Zoology a bony fish of an order (Gadiformes) that comprises cod, hake, and related fish.
– ORIGIN C19: from mod. L. *gadus* (from Gk *gados* 'cod') + **-OID**.

**gadolinite** /'gad(ə)lɪnʌɪt, gə'dəʊlɪnʌɪt/ ● **n.** a rare dark brown or black mineral, consisting of a silicate of iron, beryllium, and rare earths.
– ORIGIN C19: named after the Finnish mineralogist Johan *Gadolin*.

**gadolinium** /,gadə'lɪnɪəm/ ● **n.** the chemical element of atomic number 64, a soft silvery-white metal of the lanthanide series. (Symbol: **Gd**)
– ORIGIN C19: from **GADOLINITE**.

**gadroon** /gə'dru:n/ ● **n.** a decorative edging on silverware, wood, etc. formed by convex curves.
– DERIVATIVES **gadrooned** adj. **gadrooning** n.
– ORIGIN C17: from Fr. *godron*, prob. rel. to *goder* 'to pucker', also to **GODET**.

**gadwall** /'gadwɔ:l/ ● **n.** (pl. same or **gadwalls**) a brownish-grey freshwater duck. [*Anas strepera*.]
– ORIGIN C17: of unknown origin.

**gadzooks** /gad'zu:ks/ ● **exclam.** archaic expressing surprise or annoyance.
– ORIGIN C17: alt. of *God's hooks*, i.e. the nails by which Christ was fastened to the cross.

**Gael** /geɪl/ ● **n.** a Gaelic-speaking person.
– DERIVATIVES **Gaeldom** n.
– ORIGIN from Sc. Gaelic *Gaidheal*.

**Gaelic** /'geɪlɪk, 'galɪk/ ● **n.** **1** (also **Scottish Gaelic**) a Celtic language spoken in western Scotland, brought from Ireland in the 5th and 6th centuries AD. **2** (also **Irish Gaelic**) another term for **IRISH** (the language). ● **adj.** of or relating to the Goidelic group of Celtic languages, particularly Scottish Gaelic, and the speakers of these languages and their culture.

**Gaelic coffee** ● **n.** coffee served with cream and whisky.

**Gaelic football** ● **n.** a type of football played mainly in Ireland, with a goal resembling that used in rugby but having a net attached, the object being to kick or punch the ball into the net or over the crossbar.

**gaff**[1] ● **n.** **1** a stick with a hook or barbed spear, for landing large fish. **2** Sailing a spar to which the head of a fore-and-aft sail is bent. ● **v.** seize or impale with a gaff.
– ORIGIN ME: from Provençal *gaf* 'hook'; rel. to **GAFFE**.

**gaff**[2] ● **n.** (in phr. **blow the gaff**) Brit. informal reveal a plot or secret.
– ORIGIN C19: of unknown origin.

**gaff**[3] ● **n.** Brit. informal a person's house, flat, or shop.
– ORIGIN 1930s: of unknown origin.

**gaffe** /gaf/ (also **gaff**) ● **n.** an embarrassing blunder.
– ORIGIN C20: from Fr., lit. 'boathook', in colloq. use 'blunder'.

**gaffer** ● **n.** Brit. **1** informal an old man. **2** informal a boss. **3** the chief electrician in a film or television production unit.
– ORIGIN C16: prob. a contr. of **GODFATHER**; cf. **GAMMER**.

**gaffer tape** ● **n.** strong cloth-backed waterproof adhesive tape.

**gag**[1] ● **n.** **1** a piece of cloth put in or over a person's mouth to prevent them from speaking. **2** a device for keeping the patient's mouth open during a dental or surgical operation. **3** a restriction on free speech. ● **v.** (**gagged, gagging**) **1** put a gag on. **2** choke or retch.
– ORIGIN ME: perh. rel. to ON *gagháls* 'with the neck thrown back', or imitative of a person choking.

**gag**[2] ● **n.** a joke or funny story, especially one forming part of a comedian's act. ● **v.** tell jokes.
– ORIGIN C19 (orig. theatrical sl.): of unknown origin.

**gaga** /'gɑːgɑː, 'gagə/ ● **adj.** informal slightly mad, especially as a result of old age.
– ORIGIN C20: from Fr., 'senile, a senile person'.

**Gagauz** /gə'gaʊz/ ● **n.** (pl. same) **1** a member of a people living mainly in southern Moldova and speaking a Turkic language. **2** the language of this people, closely related to Turkish.

**gag bit** ● **n.** a powerful bit for use on difficult horses.

**gage**[1] /geɪdʒ/ archaic ● **n.** **1** a valued object deposited as a guarantee of good faith. **2** a pledge, especially a glove, thrown down as a challenge to fight. ● **v.** offer as a gage.
– ORIGIN ME: from OFr. *gage* (n.), *gager* (v.), of Gmc origin; rel. to **WAGE** and **WED**.

**gage**[2] ● **n. & v.** variant spelling of **GAUGE**.

**gage**[3] /geɪdʒ/ ● **n.** another term for **GREENGAGE**.
– ORIGIN C19: after the Engl. botanist Sir William *Gage*.

**gaggle** ● **n.** **1** a flock of geese. **2** informal a disorderly group of people.
– ORIGIN ME (as v.): imitative of the noise that a goose makes.

**gagster** ● **n.** a writer or performer of gags.

**Gaia** /'gʌɪə/ ● **n.** the earth viewed as a vast self-regulating organism.
– ORIGIN 1970s: coined by the Engl. scientist James Lovelock from the name of the Gk goddess *Gaia*.

**gaiety** (US also **gayety**) ● **n.** (pl. **-ies**) **1** the state or quality of being light-hearted and cheerful. **2** merrymaking; festivity.
– ORIGIN C17: from Fr. *gaieté*.

**gaijin** /gʌɪ'dʒɪn/ ● **n.** (pl. same) (in Japan) a foreigner.
– ORIGIN Japanese, contr. of *gaikoku-jin*, from *gaikoku* 'foreign country' + *jin* 'person'.

**gaillardia** /geɪ'lɑːdɪə/ ● **n.** an American plant of the daisy family, cultivated for its bright red and yellow flowers. [Genus *Gaillardia*.]
– ORIGIN mod. L., named in memory of *Gaillard* de Marentonneau, Fr. amateur botanist.

**gaily** ● **adv.** **1** in a light-hearted and cheerful manner. **2** without thinking of the consequences. **3** with a bright appearance.

**gain** ● **v.** **1** obtain or secure (something favourable). **2** reach or arrive at (a destination). **3** (**gain on**) come closer to (a person or thing pursued). **4** increase the amount or rate of (weight, speed, etc.). **5** increase in value. **6** (**gain in**) improve or advance in some respect: *canoeing is gaining in popularity.* **7** (of a clock or watch) become fast. ● **n.** **1** a thing that is gained. **2** an increase in wealth or resources: *personal gain.* **3** the factor by which power or voltage is increased in an amplifier or other electronic device, usually expressed as a logarithm.
– DERIVATIVES **gainable** adj. **gainer** n.
– ORIGIN C15 (orig. in the sense 'booty'): from OFr. *gaigne* (n.), *gaignier* (v.), of Gmc origin.

**gainful** ● **adj.** serving to increase wealth or resources.
– DERIVATIVES **gainfully** adv. **gainfulness** n.

**gainsay** /geɪn'seɪ/ ● **v.** (past and past part. **-said**) formal deny or contradict; speak against.
– DERIVATIVES **gainsayer** n.
– ORIGIN ME: from obs. *gain-* 'against' + **SAY**.

**'gainst** ● **prep.** poetic/literary short for **AGAINST**.

**gait** /geɪt/ ● **n.** **1** a person's manner of walking. **2** the paces of a horse or dog.
– ORIGIN ME (orig. Scots): var. of **GATE**[2].

**gaita** /'gʌɪtə/ ● **n.** a kind of bagpipe played in northern Spain and Portugal.
– ORIGIN from Sp. and Port.

**gaiter** ● **n.** **1** a covering of cloth or leather for the ankle and lower leg. **2** chiefly US a shoe or overshoe extending to the ankle or above. **3** a flexible covering for the base of a gear lever or other mechanical part.
– DERIVATIVES **gaitered** adj.
– ORIGIN C18: from Fr. *guêtre*, prob. of Gmc origin.

**Gal.** ● **abbrev.** Epistle to the Galatians (in biblical references).

**gal**[1] ● **n.** informal, chiefly N. Amer. a girl or young woman.
– ORIGIN C18: representing a pronunc.

**gal**[2] ● **n.** Physics a unit of gravitational acceleration equal to one centimetre per second per second.
– ORIGIN C20: named after *Galileo* (see **GALILEAN**[1]).

**gal.** ● **abbrev.** gallon(s).

**gala** /'gɑːlə, 'geɪlə/ ● **n.** **1** a festive entertainment or performance. **2** Brit. a special sports meeting, especially a swimming competition.
– ORIGIN C17 (in the sense 'showy dress'): via Ital. and Sp. from OFr. *gale* 'rejoicing'.

**galactagogue** /gə'laktəgɒg/ ● **n.** Medicine a food or drug that promotes the flow of a mother's milk.
– ORIGIN C19: from Gk *gala, galakt-* 'milk' + *agōgos* 'leading'.

**galactic** /gə'laktɪk/ ● **adj.** **1** of or relating to a galaxy or galaxies. **2** Astronomy measured relative to the galactic equator.
– ORIGIN C19: from Gk *galaktias* + **-IC**.

**galactic equator** ● **n.** Astronomy the great circle of the celestial sphere passing as closely as possible through the densest parts of the Milky Way.

**galactose** /gə'laktəʊz, -s/ ● **n.** Chemistry a sugar of the hexose class which is a constituent of lactose and many polysaccharides.
– ORIGIN C19: from Gk *gala, galaktos* 'milk' + **-OSE**[2].

**galago** /gə'leɪgəʊ/ ● **n.** (pl. **-os**) another term for **BUSHBABY**.
– ORIGIN mod. L. (genus name).

**galah** /gə'lɑː/ ● **n.** **1** a small Australian cockatoo with a grey back and rosy pink head and underparts, regarded as a pest. [*Eulophus roseicapillus*.] **2** Austral. informal a stupid person.
– ORIGIN C19: from Yuwaalaraay (an Aborig. lang.).

**Galahad** /'galəhad/ (also **Sir Galahad**) ● **n.** a person of great nobility and integrity.
– ORIGIN C19: the name of one of King Arthur's knights.

**galangal** /'gal(ə)ŋgal/ (also **galingale**) ● **n.** an Asian plant of the ginger family, the rhizome of which is used in cookery and herbal medicine. [Genera *Alpinia* and *Kaempferia*.]
– ORIGIN ME *galingale*, via OFr. from Arab. *ḵalanjān*, perh. from Chin. *gāoliángjiāng*, from *gāoliáng* (the name of a district in Guangdong Province, China) + *jiāng* 'ginger'.

**galant** /ga'lant, ga'lɒ̃/ ● **adj.** relating to or denoting a light and elegant style of 18th-century music.
– ORIGIN Fr. and Ger. (see **GALLANT**).

**galantine** /'gal(ə)ntiːn/ ● **n.** a dish of cooked meat or fish served cold in aspic.
– ORIGIN ME (in the sense 'sauce for fish'): from OFr., alt. of *galatine*, from med. L. *galatina*.

**Galatian** /gə'leɪʃ(ə)n/ ● **n.** an inhabitant of Galatia, an ancient region of Asia Minor. ● **adj.** of or relating to Galatia or its inhabitants.

**galaxy** ● **n.** (pl. **-ies**) **1** a system of millions or billions of stars, together with gas and dust, held together by gravitational attraction. ➤(**the Galaxy**) the galaxy of which the solar system is a part; the Milky Way. **2** a large and impressive group of people or things.
– ORIGIN ME (orig. referring to the Milky Way): via OFr. from med. L. *galaxia*, from Gk *galaxias* (*kuklos*) 'milky (vault)', from *gala, galakt-* 'milk'.

**galbanum** /ˈgalbənəm/ ● n. a bitter aromatic resin produced from a kind of fennel.
– ORIGIN ME: via L. from Gk *khalbanē*, prob. of Semitic origin.

**gale** ● n. **1** a very strong wind. **2** an outburst of laughter.
– ORIGIN C16: perh. rel. to ON *galinn* 'mad, frantic'.

**galea** /ˈgeɪlɪə/ ● n. (pl. **galeae** /-lɪiː/ or **galeas**) Botany & Zoology a structure shaped like a helmet.
– ORIGIN C19: from L., lit. 'helmet'.

**galena** /gəˈliːnə/ ● n. a metallic grey or black mineral consisting of lead sulphide.
– ORIGIN C17: from L., 'lead ore'.

**galenic** /gəˈlɛnɪk/ ● adj. Medicine **1** of or relating to the 2nd-century Greek physician Galen or his methods. **2** denoting a medicine made of natural rather than synthetic components.
– DERIVATIVES **galenical** adj.

**galette** /gəˈlɛt/ ● n. a savoury pancake made from grated potatoes or a buckwheat batter.
– ORIGIN from Fr.

**galia melon** /ˈgɑːlɪə/ ● n. a small rounded melon of a variety with rough skin and fragrant orange flesh.
– ORIGIN from the Heb. given name *Galia*.

**Galibi** /gəˈliːbi/ ● n. another term for **CARIB** (in sense 2).
– ORIGIN Carib, lit. 'strong man'.

**Galician** ● n. **1** a native or inhabitant of Galicia in NW Spain. **2** the language of Galicia in NW Spain, a Romance language closely related to Portuguese. **3** a native or inhabitant of Galicia in east central Europe. ● adj. **1** of or relating to Galicia in NW Spain, its people, or their language. **2** of or relating to Galicia in east central Europe.

**Galilean**[1] /ˌgalɪˈleɪən/ ● adj. of or relating to the Italian astronomer and physicist Galileo Galilei (1564–1642) or his methods.

**Galilean**[2] /ˌgalɪˈliːən/ ● n. **1** a native or inhabitant of Galilee. **2** archaic, derogatory a Christian. ● adj. **1** of or relating to Galilee or its people. **2** archaic, derogatory Christian.

**Galilean telescope** ● n. an astronomical telescope of the earliest type, with a biconvex objective and biconcave eyepiece.

**galilee** /ˈgalɪliː/ ● n. a chapel or porch at the entrance of a church.
– ORIGIN ME: from OFr., from med. L. *galilea* 'Galilee'; cf. **GALLERY**.

**galingale** /ˈgalɪŋˌgeɪl/ ● n. **1** (also **English** or **sweet galingale**) a Eurasian sedge with an aromatic rhizome, formerly used in perfumes. [*Cyperus longus*.] **2** variant spelling of **GALANGAL**.
– ORIGIN C16: var. of **GALANGAL**.

**galiot** ● n. variant spelling of **GALLIOT**.

**galipot** /ˈgalɪpɒt/ ● n. hardened resin deposits formed on the stem of the maritime pine.
– ORIGIN C18: from Fr.

**gall**[1] /gɔːl/ ● n. **1** bold and impudent behaviour. **2** archaic the contents of the gall bladder; bile. **3** an animal's gall bladder. **4** bitterness or cruelty: *life's gall*.
– ORIGIN OE *gealla* (denoting bile), of Gmc origin.

**gall**[2] /gɔːl/ ● n. **1** annoyance; humiliation. **2** a sore on the skin made by chafing. ● v. **1** annoy; humiliate. **2** make sore by chafing.
– DERIVATIVES **galling** adj. **gallingly** adv.
– ORIGIN OE *gealle* 'sore on a horse', perh. rel. to **GALL**[1].

**gall**[3] /gɔːl/ ● n. **1** an abnormal growth formed in response to the presence of insect larvae, mites, or fungi on plants and trees, especially oaks. **2** [as modifier] denoting insects or mites that produce galls.
– ORIGIN ME: via OFr. from L. *galla*.

**gall.** ● abbrev. gallon(s).

**Galla** /ˈgalə/ ● n. & adj. another term for **OROMO**.
– ORIGIN of unknown origin.

**gallant** /ˈgal(ə)nt/ ● adj. **1** brave; heroic. **2** /also gəˈlant/ (of a man) charming; chivalrous. **3** archaic of fine appearance; grand. ● n. /also gəˈlant/ **1** a man who is charmingly attentive to women. **2** archaic a dashing gentleman. ● v. /also gəˈlant/ archaic (of a man) be charmingly attentive to (a woman).
– DERIVATIVES **gallantly** adv.
– ORIGIN ME (in the sense 'finely dressed'): from OFr. *galant*, from *galer* 'have fun, make a show', from *gale* 'pleasure, rejoicing'.

**gallantry** ● n. (pl. **-ies**) **1** courageous behaviour, especially in battle. **2** polite attention or respect given by men to women. ➤ (**gallantries**) actions or words used when paying such attention. ➤ archaic sexual intrigue.

**gall bladder** ● n. a small sac-shaped organ beneath the liver, in which bile is stored.

**galleon** ● n. a large sailing ship in use from the 15th to the 18th centuries, typically square-rigged and with three or more decks and masts.
– ORIGIN C16: either via MDu. from Fr. *galion*, from *galie* 'galley', or from Sp. *galeón*.

**galleria** /ˌgaləˈriːə/ ● n. an arcade of small shops.
– ORIGIN Ital. (see **GALLERY**).

**gallery** ● n. (pl. **-ies**) **1** a room or building for the display or sale of works of art. **2** a balcony or upper floor projecting from a back or side wall inside a hall or church. **3** the highest balcony in a theatre, having the cheapest seats. **4** (**the gallery**) a group of spectators, especially those at a golf tournament. **5** a long room or passage forming a portico or colonnade. **6** a horizontal underground passage in a mine.
– PHRASES **play to the gallery** aim to attract popular attention.
– DERIVATIVES **galleried** adj.
– ORIGIN ME: via OFr. from Ital. *galleria* 'gallery', formerly also 'church porch', from med. L. *galeria*, perh. an alt. of *galilea* (see **GALILEE**).

**gallery forest** ● n. a forest restricted to the banks of a river or stream.

**gallery grave** ● n. Archaeology an underground megalithic burial chamber which may be divided into sections but has no separate entrance passage.

**galley** ● n. (pl. **-eys**) **1** historical a low, flat ship with one or more sails and up to three banks of oars, chiefly used for warfare or piracy and often manned by slaves or criminals. **2** a large, open rowing boat kept on a warship especially for use by the captain. **3** the kitchen in a ship or aircraft. **4** (also **galley proof**) a printer's proof in the form of long single-column strips.
– ORIGIN ME: via OFr. from med. L. *galea*, from med. Gk *galaia*, of unknown origin; sense 4 is from Fr. *galée* denoting an oblong tray for holding set-up type.

**galliambic** /ˌgalɪˈambɪk/ Prosody ● adj. relating to or written in a metre consisting of two catalectic iambic dimeters. ● n. galliambic verse.
– ORIGIN C19: from L. *galliambus*, a song of the *Galli* (name given to priests of Cybele) + **-IC**.

**Galliano** /ˌgalɪˈɑːnəʊ/ ● n. a golden-yellow Italian liqueur flavoured with herbs.
– ORIGIN named after Major Giuseppe *Galliáno*, a noted C19 military officer.

**galliard** /ˈgalɪɑːd, -ɪəd/ ● n. historical a lively dance in triple time for two people.
– ORIGIN ME (as adj. meaning 'valiant, sturdy' and 'lively, brisk'): from OFr. *gaillard* 'valiant', of Celtic origin.

**Gallic** /ˈgalɪk/ ● adj. **1** of or characteristic of France or the French. **2** of or relating to the Gauls.
– DERIVATIVES **Gallicize** (also **-ise**) v.
– ORIGIN C17: from L. *Gallicus*, from *Gallus* 'a Gaul'.

**gallic acid** ● n. Chemistry an organic acid extracted from oak galls and other plant products.
– DERIVATIVES **gallate** n.
– ORIGIN C18: from L. *galla* (see **GALL**[3]) + **-IC**.

**Gallican** /ˈgalɪk(ə)n/ ● adj. **1** of or relating to the ancient Church of Gaul or France. **2** of or holding a doctrine which asserted the freedom of the Roman Catholic Church in France and elsewhere from the ecclesiastical authority of the papacy. Compare with **ULTRAMONTANE**. ● n. an adherent of the Gallican doctrine.
– DERIVATIVES **Gallicanism** n.

**Gallicism** /ˈgalɪˌsɪz(ə)m/ ● n. a French word or idiom adopted in another language.

**galligaskins** /ˌgalɪˈgaskɪnz/ ● pl. n. Brit. historical breeches, trousers, or gaiters.

– ORIGIN C16: perh. an alt. (influenced by *galley* and *Gascon*) of obs. Fr. *gargesque*.

**gallimaufry** /ˌgalɪˈmɔːfri/ ● n. a jumble or medley of things.
– ORIGIN C16: from archaic Fr. *galimafrée* 'unappetizing dish'.

**gallimimus** /ˌgalɪˈmʌɪməs/ ● n. an ostrich dinosaur of the late Cretaceous period.
– ORIGIN mod. L., from L. *galli* 'of a cockerel' + *mimus* 'mime, pretence'.

**gallinaceous** /ˌgalɪˈneɪʃəs/ ● adj. of or relating to birds of an order (Galliformes) which includes domestic poultry and game birds.
– ORIGIN C18: from L. *gallinaceus*.

**gallinule** /ˈgalɪnjuːl/ ● n. **1** a marshbird of the rail family, with mainly black or dark plumage and a red bill. [*Porphyrula martinica* (**purple gallinule**, N. America) and other species.] **2** (**common gallinule**) North American term for MOORHEN.
– ORIGIN C18: from mod. L. *Gallinula* (genus term).

**galliot** /ˈgalɪət/ (also **galiot**) ● n. historical **1** a single-masted Dutch cargo boat or fishing vessel. **2** a small fast galley used in the Mediterranean.
– ORIGIN ME: from OFr. *galiote* or Du. *galjoot*, from a dimin. of med. L. *galea* 'galley'.

**gallipot** /ˈgalɪpɒt/ ● n. historical a small pot used to hold medicines or ointments.
– ORIGIN ME: prob. from GALLEY + POT[1] (because the pots were brought from the Mediterranean in galleys).

**gallium** /ˈgalɪəm/ ● n. the chemical element of atomic number 31, a soft, silvery-white metal which melts at about 30°C. (Symbol: **Ga**)
– ORIGIN C19: mod. L., from L. *Gallia* 'France' or *gallus* 'cock'; named by the Fr. chemist Paul-Émile *Lecoq de Boisbaudran*.

**gallivant** /ˈgalɪvant, ˌgalɪˈvant/ ● v. informal go from place to place in pursuit of pleasure.
– ORIGIN C19: perh. an alt. of GALLANT.

**galliwasp** /ˈgalɪwɒsp/ ● n. a marsh lizard found in the Caribbean and Central America. [*Diploglossus monotropis* and related species.]
– ORIGIN C17: of unknown origin.

**gall midge** ● n. a small fly which induces gall formation in plants. [Family Cecidomyiidae: many species.]

**Gallo-** /ˈgaləʊ/ ● comb. form French; French and ...: *Gallo-German*. ➤relating to France.
– ORIGIN from L. *Gallus* 'a Gaul'.

**gallon** /ˈgalən/ ● n. **1** a unit of volume for liquid measure equal to eight pints: in Britain (also **imperial gallon**), equivalent to 4.55 litres; in the US, equivalent to 3.79 litres. **2** (**gallons**) informal large quantities.
– DERIVATIVES **gallonage** n.
– ORIGIN ME: from Anglo-Norman Fr. *galon*, from the base of med. L. *galleta*, *galletum* 'pail, liquid measure', perh. of Celtic origin.

**galloon** /gəˈluːn/ ● n. a narrow ornamental strip of braid, lace, etc., used as a trim.
– ORIGIN C17: from Fr. *galon*.

**gallop** ● n. **1** the fastest pace of a horse or other quadruped, with all the feet off the ground together in each stride. **2** a ride on a horse at a gallop. **3** Brit. a track where horses are exercised at a gallop. ● v. (**galloped**, **galloping**) **1** go or cause to go at the pace of a gallop. **2** proceed at great speed: *he galloped through the service*.
– DERIVATIVES **galloper** n. **galloping** adj.
– ORIGIN C16: from OFr. *galop* (n.), *galoper* (v.), vars of ONorth. Fr. *walop*, *waloper* (see WALLOP).

**gallous** ● adj. variant spelling of GALLUS.

**galloway** /ˈgaləweɪ/ ● n. an animal of a black hornless breed of cattle which originated in Galloway in Scotland.

**gallows** ● pl. n. [usu. treated as sing.] a structure, typically consisting of two uprights and a crosspiece, used for hanging a person. ➤(**the gallows**) execution by hanging.
– ORIGIN OE *galga*, *gealga*, of Gmc origin.

**gallows humour** ● n. grim and ironical humour in a desperate or hopeless situation.

**gallows tree** ● n. another term for GALLOWS.

**gallstone** /ˈgɔːlstəʊn/ ● n. a small, hard crystalline mass formed abnormally in the gall bladder or bile ducts from bile pigments, cholesterol, and calcium salts.

**Gallup poll** /ˈgaləp/ ● n. trademark an assessment of public opinion by the questioning of a representative sample, used in forecasting voting results in an election.
– ORIGIN 1940s: named after the Amer. statistician George H. *Gallup*.

**gallus** /ˈgaləs/ (also **gallous**) ● adj. chiefly Scottish bold, cheeky, or flashy.
– ORIGIN ME (in the sense 'fit to be hanged'): var. of GALLOWS used attributively.

**galluses** /ˈgaləsɪz/ ● pl. n. Scottish & N. Amer. dated braces for a person's trousers.
– ORIGIN C19: pl. of *gallus*, var. of GALLOWS.

**galoot** /gəˈluːt/ ● n. N. Amer. & Scottish informal a clumsy or stupid person.
– ORIGIN C19 (orig. in naut. use meaning 'an inexperienced marine'): of unknown origin.

**galop** /ˈgaləp, gəˈlɒp/ ● n. a lively ballroom dance in duple time, popular in the late 18th century.
– ORIGIN C19: Fr., lit. 'gallop'.

**galore** ● adj. [postpos.] in abundance: *there were prizes galore*.
– ORIGIN C17: from Ir. *go leor*, lit. 'to sufficiency'.

**galosh** /gəˈlɒʃ/ ● n. a waterproof rubber overshoe.
– ORIGIN ME (denoting a type of clog): via OFr. from late L. *gallicula*, dimin. of L. *gallica* (*solea*) 'Gallic (shoe)'.

**galumph** /gəˈlʌmf/ ● v. informal move in a clumsy, ponderous, or noisy manner.
– DERIVATIVES **galumphing** adj.
– ORIGIN 1871 (in the sense 'prance in triumph'): coined by Lewis Carroll in *Through the Looking Glass*; perh. a blend of GALLOP and TRIUMPH.

**galvanic** /galˈvanɪk/ ● adj. **1** relating to or involving electric currents produced by chemical action. **2** sudden and dramatic.
– DERIVATIVES **galvanically** adv.
– ORIGIN C18: from Fr. *galvanique*, from the name of the Ital. physiologist Luigi *Galvani*, known for his discovery of the twitching of frogs' legs in an electric field.

**galvanic skin response** (also **galvanic skin reflex**) ● n. a change in the electrical resistance of the skin caused by emotional stress.

**galvanism** ● n. historical **1** electricity produced by chemical action. **2** the therapeutic use of electric currents.
– ORIGIN C18: from Fr. *galvanisme* (see GALVANIC).

**galvanize** /ˈgalvənʌɪz/ (also **-ise**) ● v. **1** shock or excite into action. **2** [often as adj. **galvanized**] coat (iron or steel) with a protective layer of zinc.
– DERIVATIVES **galvanization** n. **galvanizer** n.
– ORIGIN C19 (in the sense 'stimulate by electricity'): from Fr. *galvaniser* (see GALVANIC).

**galvanometer** /ˌgalvəˈnɒmɪtə/ ● n. an instrument for detecting and measuring small electric currents.
– DERIVATIVES **galvanometric** adj.

**gam** ● n. informal a leg.
– ORIGIN C18: prob. a var. of the heraldic term *gamb*, which denotes a charge representing an animal's leg.

**Gamay** /ˈgameɪ/ ● n. a variety of black wine grape native to the Beaujolais district of France. ➤a red wine made from this grape.
– ORIGIN from the name of a hamlet in Burgundy, eastern France.

**gamba** /ˈgambə/ ● n. short for VIOLA DA GAMBA.

**gambado**[1] /gamˈbeɪdəʊ/ ● n. (pl. **-os** or **-oes**) a gaiter attached to a saddle to protect the rider's leg.
– ORIGIN C17: from Ital. *gamba* 'leg' + -ADO.

**gambado**[2] /gamˈbeɪdəʊ, -ˈbɑːdəʊ/ (also **gambade** /-ˈbeɪd, -ˈbɑːd/) ● n. (pl. **-os** or **-oes**) a horse's leap.
– ORIGIN C19: from Sp. *gambada*, from *gamba* 'leg'.

**Gambian** /ˈgambɪən/ ● n. a native or inhabitant of Gambia, a country in West Africa. ● adj. of or relating to Gambia or its people.

**gambier** /ˈgambɪə/ ● n. an astringent extract of a tropical Asian plant, used in tanning.

– ORIGIN C19: from Malay *gambir*, the name of the plant.

**gambit** • n. **1** an action or remark that is calculated to gain an advantage. **2** (in chess) an opening move in which a player makes a sacrifice, typically of a pawn, for the sake of some compensating advantage.
– ORIGIN C17: orig. *gambett*, from Ital. *gambetto*, lit. 'tripping up'.

**gamble** • v. **1** play games of chance for money; bet. ➤ bet (a sum of money). **2** take risky action in the hope of a desired result. • n. **1** an act of gambling. **2** a risky undertaking or enterprise.
– DERIVATIVES **gambler** n.
– ORIGIN C18: from obs. *gamel* 'play games', or from the verb **GAME**[1].

**gamboge** /gam'bəʊʒ, -'buːʒ/ • n. a gum resin produced by certain East Asian trees, used as a yellow pigment and in medicine as a purgative.
– ORIGIN C18: from mod. L. *gambaugium*, from *Cambodia*.

**gambol** • v. (**gambolled**, **gambolling**; US **gamboled**, **gamboling**) run or jump about playfully. • n. an act of gambolling.
– ORIGIN C16: alt. of obs. *gambade*, via Fr. from Ital. *gambata* 'trip up'.

**gambrel** /'gambr(ə)l/ • n. **1** a roof having a shallower slope above a steeper one on each side. **2** Brit. a hipped roof with a small gable forming the upper part of each end.
– ORIGIN C16 (in the sense 'bent piece of wood or iron', later 'joint in the upper part of a horse's hind leg'): from ONorth. Fr. *gamberel*, from *gambier* 'forked stick'.

**game**[1] • n. **1** an activity engaged in for amusement. **2** a form of competitive activity or sport played according to rules. **3** a complete episode or period of play, ending in a final result. **4** a single portion of play, forming a scoring unit within a game. **5** (**games**) a meeting for sporting contests. **6** (**games**) Brit. athletics or sports as a period of activity and instruction in a school. **7** the equipment used in playing a board game, computer game, etc. **8** a type of activity or business regarded as a game. **9** a secret plan or trick: *I was on to his little game.* **10** wild mammals or birds hunted for sport or food. ➤ the flesh of these, as food. • adj. eager and willing to do something new or challenging: *they were game for anything.* • v.**1** [as noun **gaming**] playing at games of chance for money. **2** play video or computer games.
– PHRASES **ahead of the game** ahead of one's competitors or peers. **beat someone at their own game** use someone's own methods to outdo them. **the game is up** the deception or crime is revealed or foiled. **on the game** Brit. informal working as a prostitute. **play the game** behave in a fair or honourable way; abide by the rules.
– DERIVATIVES **gamely** adv. **gameness** n. **gamester** n.
– ORIGIN OE *gamen* 'amusement, fun', *gamenian* 'play, amuse oneself', of Gmc origin.

**game**[2] • adj. (of a person's leg) lame.
– ORIGIN C18: orig. dial., of unknown origin.

**game bird** • n. **1** a bird shot for sport or food. **2** a bird of a large group that includes pheasants, grouse, quails, guineafowl, etc. [Order Galliformes.]

**gamecock** (also **gamefowl**) • n. a cock bred and trained for cockfighting.

**game fish** • n. (pl. same) a fish caught by anglers for sport, especially (in fresh water) salmon and trout and (in the sea) billfishes, sharks, bass, and mackerel. Compare with **COARSE FISH**.

**gamekeeper** • n. a person employed to breed and protect game for a large estate.
– DERIVATIVES **gamekeeping** n.

**gamelan** /'gamәlan/ • n. a traditional instrumental ensemble in Java and Bali, including many bronze percussion instruments.
– ORIGIN C19: from Javanese.

**game plan** • n. a strategy worked out in advance, especially in sport, politics, or business.

**gameplay** • n. (in a computer game) the plot and the way the game is played, as distinct from the graphics and sound effects.

**game point** • n. (in tennis and other sports) a point which if won by a player or side will also win them the game.

**gamer** • n. **1** a person who plays a game or games, especially a participant in a computer or role-playing game. **2** N. Amer. (especially in sporting contexts) a person known for consistently making a strong effort.

**game show** • n. a programme on television in which people compete to win prizes.

**gamesmanship** • n. the art of winning games by using various ploys and tactics to gain a psychological advantage.
– DERIVATIVES **gamesman** n. (pl. **-men**).

**gamesome** • adj. playful and merry.
– DERIVATIVES **gamesomely** adv. **gamesomeness** n.

**gametangium** /,gamɪ'tan(d)ʒɪəm/ • n. (pl. **gametangia**) Botany a specialized organ in which gametes are formed in algae, ferns, and some other plants.
– ORIGIN C19: from mod. L. *gameta* (see **GAMETE**) + Gk *angeion* 'vessel' + **-IUM**.

**gamete** /'gamiːt/ • n. Biology a mature haploid male or female germ cell which is able to unite with another of the opposite sex in sexual reproduction to form a zygote.
– DERIVATIVES **gametic** /gə'mɛtɪk/ adj.
– ORIGIN C19: from mod. L. *gameta*, from Gk *gametē* 'wife', *gametēs* 'husband', from *gamos* 'marriage'.

**game theory** • n. the mathematical study of strategies for dealing with competitive situations where the outcome of a participant's choice of action depends critically on the actions of other participants. Compare with **DECISION THEORY**.

**gameto-** /gə'miːtəʊ/ • comb. form Biology representing **GAMETE**.

**gametocyte** /gə'miːtə(ʊ)sʌɪt/ • n. Biology a cell that divides (by meiosis) to form gametes.

**gametogenesis** /gə,miːtə(ʊ)'dʒɛnɪsɪs/ • n. Biology the process in which cells undergo meiosis to form gametes.
– DERIVATIVES **gametogenic** adj. **gametogeny** n.

**gametophyte** /gə'miːtə(ʊ)fʌɪt/ • n. Botany (in the life cycle of plants with alternating generations, e.g. ferns) the gamete-producing phase (typically haploid), which produces the zygote from which the sporophyte arises.
– DERIVATIVES **gametophytic** adj.

**gamey** • adj. variant spelling of **GAMY**.

**gamine** /ga'miːn/ • n. a girl with a mischievous, boyish charm. • adj. characteristic of a gamine.
– ORIGIN C19: Fr.

**gamma** /'gamə/ • n. **1** the third letter of the Greek alphabet (Γ, γ), transliterated as 'g'. ➤ [as modifier] denoting the third in a series of items or categories. ➤ Brit. a third-class mark given for a piece of work. **2** [as modifier] relating to gamma rays. **3** (pl. same) Physics a unit of magnetic field strength equal to $10^{-5}$ oersted.
– ORIGIN via L. from Gk.

**gamma-aminobutyric acid** /,gaməə,miːnəʊbjuː'tɪrɪk, -ə,mʌɪnəʊ-, -'amɪnəʊ-/ • n. Biochemistry an amino acid which acts to inhibit the transmission of nerve impulses.
– ORIGIN C20: *gamma* indicating the position of amino on the third carbon away from the acid group.

**gamma globulin** • n. Biochemistry a mixture of blood plasma proteins, mainly immunoglobulins, with relatively low mobility under electrophoresis.

**gamma-HCH** • n. another term for **LINDANE**.
– ORIGIN *HCH* from *hexachlorocyclohexane*.

**gamma rays** (also **gamma radiation**) • pl. n. penetrating electromagnetic radiation of shorter wavelength than X-rays.

**gammer** • n. archaic an old woman.
– ORIGIN C16: prob. a contr. of **GODMOTHER**; see also **GAFFER**.

**gammon**[1] • n. **1** ham which has been cured like bacon. **2** the bottom piece of a side of bacon, including a hind leg.
– ORIGIN C15: from ONorth. Fr. *gambon*, from *gambe* 'leg'.

**gammon**[2] • n. a victory in backgammon (carrying a

double score) in which the winner removes all his or her pieces before the loser has removed any. ● **v.** defeat with a gammon.
– ORIGIN C18: appar. from OE *gamen* or *gamenian* (see **GAME**[1]).

**gammon**[3] informal, dated, chiefly Brit. ● **n.** nonsense; rubbish. ● **v.** hoax or deceive.
– ORIGIN C18: origin uncertain; the term was first used as criminals' sl. in *give gammon to* 'give cover to (a pickpocket)' and *keep in gammon* 'distract (a victim) for a pickpocket'.

**gammy** ● **adj.** Brit. informal (especially of a leg) unable to function normally because of injury or chronic pain.
– ORIGIN C19 (in the sense 'bad, false'): dial. form of **GAME**[2].

**gamp** ● **n.** Brit. informal, dated a large umbrella.
– ORIGIN C19: named after Mrs *Gamp* in Charles Dickens's *Martin Chuzzlewit*, who carried one.

**gamut** /'gamət/ ● **n. 1** the complete range or scope of something. **2** Music a complete scale of musical notes; the compass or range of a voice or instrument. **3** a scale consisting of seven overlapping hexachords, containing all the recognized notes used in medieval music, covering almost three octaves from bass G to treble E. ➤ the lowest note in this scale.
– PHRASES **run the gamut** experience, display, or perform the complete range of something.
– ORIGIN ME: from med. L. *gamma ut* (in sense 3): the Greek letter Γ (gamma) was used for bass G, with *ut* indicating that it was the first note in the lowest of the hexachords or six-note scales.

**gamy** (also **gamey**) ● **adj.** (**-ier, -iest**) **1** (of meat) having the strong flavour or smell of game, especially when it is high. **2** chiefly N. Amer. racy or risqué.
– DERIVATIVES **gamily** adv. **gaminess** n.

**Gan** /gan/ ● **n.** a dialect of Chinese spoken mainly in Jiangxi province.

**ganache** /gə'naʃ/ ● **n.** a whipped filling of chocolate and cream, used in cakes and confectionery.
– ORIGIN from Fr.

**gander** /'gandə/ ● **n. 1** a male goose. **2** informal a look or glance.
– ORIGIN OE *gandra*, of Gmc origin, rel. to **GANNET**; sense 2 was orig. criminals' sl.

**gandy dancer** ● **n.** N. Amer. informal a track maintenance worker on a railway.
– ORIGIN C20: of unknown origin.

**gang**[1] ● **n. 1** an organized group of criminals or disorderly young people. ➤ informal a group of people who regularly associate together. ➤ an organized group of people doing manual work. **2** a set of switches, sockets, or other devices grouped together. ● **v. 1** (**gang together**) form a group or gang. ➤ (**gang up**) join together, typically in order to intimidate someone. **2** arrange (electrical devices or machines) together to work in coordination.
– ORIGIN OE, from ON *gangr, ganga* 'gait, course, going', of Gmc origin; rel. to **GANG**[2].

**gang**[2] ● **v.** Scottish go; proceed.
– PHRASAL VERBS **gang agley** (of a plan) go wrong.
– ORIGIN OE *gangan*, of Gmc origin; rel. to **GO**[1].

**gang bang** ● **n.** informal **1** a gang rape. ➤ a sexual orgy. **2** N. Amer. an instance of violence involving members of a criminal gang.
– DERIVATIVES **gang-bang** v. **gang banger** n.

**gangboard** ● **n.** another term for **GANGPLANK**.

**gangbuster** ● **n.** informal **1** a police officer engaged in breaking up criminal gangs. **2** [as modifier] N. Amer. very successful: *the restaurant did gangbuster business.*
– PHRASES **go** (or **like**) **gangbusters** N. Amer. with great vigour or success.

**ganger** ● **n.** Brit. the foreman of a gang of labourers.

**gangling** (also **gangly**) ● **adj.** tall, thin, and awkward.
– ORIGIN C19: from the verb **GANG**[2] + **-LE**[4] + **-ING**[2].

**ganglion** /'gaŋglɪən/ ● **n.** (pl. **ganglia** or **ganglions**) **1** Anatomy a structure containing a number of nerve cells, often forming a swelling on a nerve fibre. ➤ a well-defined mass of grey matter within the central nervous system. **2** Medicine an abnormal benign swelling on a tendon sheath.
– DERIVATIVES **ganglionic** adj.
– ORIGIN C17: from Gk *ganglion* 'tumour on or near sinews or tendons'.

**ganglioside** /'gaŋglɪə(ʊ)sʌɪd/ ● **n.** Biochemistry any of a group of complex lipids present in the grey matter of the human brain.
– ORIGIN 1940s: from **GANGLION** + *-oside* (see **-OSE**[2], **-IDE**).

**gangplank** ● **n.** a movable plank used to board or disembark from a ship or boat.

**gang rape** ● **n.** the rape of one person by a group of other people.
– DERIVATIVES **gang-rape** v.

**gangrene** /'gaŋgriːn/ ● **n.** Medicine localized death and decomposition of body tissue, resulting from either obstructed circulation or bacterial infection. ● **v.** become affected with gangrene.
– DERIVATIVES **gangrenous** /'gaŋgrɪnəs/ adj.
– ORIGIN C16: via Fr. from L. *gangraena*, from Gk *gangraina*.

**gangsta** ● **n. 1** N. Amer. black slang a gang member. **2** (also **gangsta rap**) a type of rap music featuring aggressive macho lyrics, often with reference to gang warfare.

**gangster** ● **n.** a member of an organized gang of violent criminals.
– DERIVATIVES **gangsterism** n.

**gangue** /gaŋ/ ● **n.** the commercially valueless material in which ore is found.
– ORIGIN C19: from Fr., from Ger. *Gang* 'course, lode'; rel. to **GANG**[1].

**gangway** ● **n. 1** a raised platform or walkway providing a passage. **2** a movable bridge linking a ship to the shore. ➤ an opening in the bulwarks by which a ship is entered or left. **3** Brit. a passage between rows of seats, especially in a theatre or aircraft. ● **exclam.** make way!

**ganister** /'ganɪstə/ ● **n.** a close-grained, hard siliceous rock used in northern England for furnace linings.
– ORIGIN C19: of unknown origin.

**ganja** /'gan(d)ʒə, 'gɑː-/ ● **n.** cannabis.
– ORIGIN C19: from Hindi *gāṁjā*.

**gannet** /'ganɪt/ ● **n. 1** a large seabird with mainly white plumage, catching fish by plunge-diving. [*Morus bassanus* and other species.] **2** Brit. informal a greedy person.
– ORIGIN OE *ganot*, of Gmc origin; rel. to **GANDER**.

**gannetry** ● **n.** (pl. **-ies**) a breeding colony of gannets, usually on an isolated rock.

**ganoid** /'ganɔɪd/ ● **adj.** Zoology (of fish scales) hard and bony with a shiny enamelled surface. Compare with **CTENOID** and **PLACOID**.
– ORIGIN C19: from Fr. *ganoïde*, from Gk *ganos* 'brightness'.

**gantlet** /'gantlɪt/ ● **n.** US spelling of **GAUNTLET**[2].

**gantline** /'gantlʌɪn/ ● **n.** Sailing a line passed through a block near the masthead and used to hoist sails or rigging.
– ORIGIN C18 (orig. *girtline*): of unknown origin.

**gantry** ● **n.** (pl. **-ies**) **1** a bridge-like overhead structure supporting equipment such as a crane or railway signals. ➤ a tall framework supporting a space rocket prior to launching. **2** a collection of inverted bottles with optics for serving measures in a bar.
– ORIGIN ME (denoting a wooden stand for barrels): prob. from dial. *gawn* (contr. of **GALLON**) + **TREE**.

**GAO** ● **abbrev.** General Accounting Office.

**gaol** ● **n.** Brit. variant spelling of **JAIL**.

**gap** ● **n. 1** a break or hole in an object or between two objects. **2** a space, interval, or break.
– DERIVATIVES **gapped** adj. **gappy** adj.
– ORIGIN ME: from ON, 'chasm'; rel. to **GAPE**.

**gape** ● **v. 1** be or become wide open. **2** stare with one's mouth open wide in amazement or wonder. ● **n. 1** a wide opening. ➤ an open-mouthed stare. ➤ a widely open mouth or beak. **2** (**the gapes**) a disease of birds with gaping of the mouth as a symptom, caused by infestation with gapeworm.
– DERIVATIVES **gaping** adj. **gapingly** adv.

– ORIGIN ME: from ON *gapa*; rel. to **GAP**.

**gaper** • n. **1** a burrowing bivalve mollusc, the shell valves of which have an opening at one or both ends. [Genus *Mya*.] **2** another term for **COMBER**[2]. **3** a deep-sea anglerfish that is able to inflate itself with water. [Genus *Chaunax*.] **4** a person who gapes.

**gapeworm** • n. a parasitic nematode worm that infests the trachea and bronchi of birds, causing the gapes.

**gapping** • n. Grammar the omission of a verb in the second of two coordinated clauses.

**gap year** • n. a period, typically an academic year, taken by a student as a break between school and university or college education.

**gar** • n. the freshwater garfish of North America.

**garage** /ˈgarɑː(d)ʒ, -ɪdʒ, gəˈrɑːʒ/ • n. **1** a building for housing a motor vehicle or vehicles. **2** an establishment which sells fuel or which repairs and sells motor vehicles. **3** a style of unpolished energetic rock music. [from the idea of amateur bands practising in garages.] **4** (also **UK garage**) a form of pop music incorporating elements of drum and bass, house music, and soul, characterized by a rhythm in which the 2nd and 4th beats of the bar are omitted. • v. put or keep (a motor vehicle) in a garage.

– ORIGIN C20: from Fr., from *garer* 'to shelter'.

**garage sale** • n. chiefly N. Amer. a sale of unwanted goods held in a garage or front garden.

**garam masala** /ˌgʌrəm məˈsɑːlə/ • n. a spice mixture used in Indian cookery.

– ORIGIN from Urdu *garam maṣālaḥ*, from *garam* 'hot, pungent' + *maṣālaḥ* 'spice'.

**garb**[1] • n. clothing or dress, especially of a distinctive or special kind. • v. dress in distinctive clothes.

– ORIGIN C16: via Fr. from Ital. *garbo* 'elegance', of Gmc origin; rel. to **GEAR**.

**garb**[2] • n. Heraldry a sheaf of wheat.

– ORIGIN C16: from ONorth. Fr. *garbe*; cf. Fr. *gerbe*.

**garbage** • n. chiefly N. Amer. **1** rubbish or waste, especially domestic refuse. **2** something worthless or meaningless.

– PHRASES **garbage in, garbage out** Computing, informal incorrect or poor-quality input will produce faulty output.

– ORIGIN ME (in the sense 'offal'): from Anglo-Norman Fr., of unknown ultimate origin.

**garbage collector** • n. **1** N. Amer. a dustman. **2** Computing a program that automatically removes unwanted data held temporarily in memory during processing.

**garbanzo** /gɑːˈbanzəʊ/ • n. (pl. **-os**) N. Amer. a chickpea.

– ORIGIN C18: from Sp.

**garble** • v. [often as adj. **garbled**] reproduce (a message or transmission) in a confused and distorted way. • n. a garbled account or transmission.

– DERIVATIVES **garbler** n.

– ORIGIN ME (in the sense 'sift out, cleanse'): from Anglo-Latin and Ital. *garbellare*, from Arab. *ġarbala* 'sift', perh. from late L. *cribellare* 'to sieve'.

**garboard** (also **garboard strake**) • n. the first range of planks or plates laid on a ship's bottom next to the keel.

– ORIGIN C17: from Du. *gaarboord*, perh. from *garen* 'gather' + *boord* 'board'.

**garbology** /gɑːˈbɒlədʒi/ • n. the study of a community or culture by analysing its refuse.

– DERIVATIVES **garbologist** n.

**garçon** /ˈgɑːsɒn, ˈgɑːsɔ̃, French garsɔ̃/ • n. a waiter in a French restaurant.

– ORIGIN Fr., lit. 'boy'.

**garçonnière** /ˌgɑːsɒnˈjɛː/ • n. a bachelor's flat or set of rooms.

– ORIGIN Fr., from *garçon* 'boy'.

**Garda** /ˈgɑːdə/ • n. [treated as sing. or pl.] the state police force of the Irish Republic. ➤ (pl. **Gardai** /-diː/) a member of the Irish police force.

– ORIGIN from Ir. *Garda Siochána* 'Civic Guard'.

**garden** • n. **1** chiefly Brit. a piece of ground adjoining a house, used for growing flowers, fruit, or vegetables. **2** (**gardens**) ornamental grounds laid out for public enjoyment. • v. cultivate or work in a garden.

– DERIVATIVES **gardener** n. **gardening** n.

– ORIGIN ME: from ONorth. Fr. *gardin*, var. of OFr. *jardin*, of Gmc origin; rel. to **YARD**[2].

**garden centre** • n. an establishment where plants and gardening equipment are sold.

**garden city** • n. a new town designed as a whole with much open space and greenery.

**garden cress** • n. a type of cress that is grown as a sprouting vegetable, often mixed with sprouting mustard, and used in salads. [*Lepidium sativum*.]

**gardenia** /gɑːˈdiːnɪə/ • n. a tree or shrub of warm climates, with large fragrant white or yellow flowers. [Genus *Gardenia*: several species, in particular the Cape jasmine.]

– ORIGIN mod. L., named in honour of the Sc. naturalist Dr Alexander *Garden* (1730–91).

**garden party** • n. a social event held on a lawn in a garden.

**garden pea** • n. a variety of pea grown for food.

**garden suburb** • n. Brit. a suburb set in rural surroundings or incorporating much landscaping.

**garden-variety** • adj. N. Amer. of the usual or ordinary type; commonplace.

**garden warbler** • n. a migratory songbird with drab plumage, frequenting woodland. [*Sylvia borin*.]

**garderobe** /ˈgɑːdrəʊb/ • n. **1** a toilet in a medieval building. **2** a wardrobe or storeroom in a medieval building.

– ORIGIN ME: Fr., from *garder* 'to keep' + *robe* 'robe, dress'; cf. **WARDROBE**.

**garfish** • n. (pl. same or **-fishes**) **1** a long, slender marine fish with beak-like jaws containing sharp teeth. [Family Belonidae: several species.] **2** N. Amer. a similar freshwater fish. [Genus *Lepisosteus*.]

– ORIGIN ME: appar. from OE *gār* 'spear' + **FISH**[1].

**garganey** /ˈgɑːg(ə)ni/ • n. (pl. same or **-eys**) a small duck, the male of which has a brown head with a white stripe from the eye to the neck. [*Anas querquedula*.]

– ORIGIN C17: from Ital. dial. *garganei*, of imitative origin.

**gargantuan** /gɑːˈgantjʊən/ • adj. enormous.

– ORIGIN C16: from *Gargantua*, the name of a voracious giant in Rabelais' book of the same name, + **-AN**.

**garget** /ˈgɑːgɪt/ • n. inflammation of a cow's or ewe's udder.

– ORIGIN C18: perh. a special use of OFr. *gargate* 'throat'; rel. to **GARGOYLE**.

**gargle** • v. wash one's mouth and throat with a liquid that is kept in motion by breathing through it with a gurgling sound. • n. **1** an act of gargling. ➤ a liquid used for gargling. **2** Brit. informal an alcoholic drink.

– ORIGIN C16: from Fr. *gargouiller* 'gurgle, bubble', from *gargouille* (see **GARGOYLE**).

**gargoyle** /ˈgɑːgɔɪl/ • n. a grotesque carved human or animal face or figure projecting from the gutter of a building, usually as a spout to carry water clear of a wall.

– ORIGIN ME: from OFr. *gargouille* 'throat', also 'gargoyle', rel. to Gk *gargarizein* 'to gargle' (of imitative origin).

**gargoylism** • n. another term for **HURLER'S SYNDROME**.

**garibaldi** /ˌgarɪˈbɔːldi, -ˈbaldi/ • n. (pl. **garibaldis**) **1** Brit. a thin biscuit containing a compressed layer of currants. **2** a small bright orange marine fish found off California. [*Hypsypops rubicundus*.]

– ORIGIN C19: named after the Ital. patriot G. *Garibaldi*.

**garish** /ˈgɛːrɪʃ/ • adj. obtrusively bright and showy.

– DERIVATIVES **garishly** adv. **garishness** n.

– ORIGIN C16: of unknown origin.

**garland** • n. **1** a wreath of flowers and leaves, worn on the head or hung as a decoration. **2** a prize or distinction. **3** archaic a literary anthology. • v. adorn with a garland.

– ORIGIN ME: from OFr. *garlande*, of unknown origin.

**garlic** • n. **1** a strong-smelling pungent-tasting bulb, used as a flavouring in cookery. **2** the central Asian plant, closely related to the onion, which produces this bulb. [*Allium sativum*.] ➤ used in names of plants with a similar smell or flavour, e.g. **wild garlic**.

– DERIVATIVES **garlicky** adj.

– ORIGIN OE *gārlēac*, from *gār* 'spear' (because the shape of a clove resembles the head of a spear) + *lēac* 'leek'.

**garment** ● n. an item of clothing.
– ORIGIN ME: from OFr. *garnement* 'equipment', from *garnir* (see **GARNISH**).

**garner** ● v. **1** gather or collect. **2** archaic store; deposit. ● n. archaic a storehouse for corn; a granary.
– ORIGIN ME: from OFr. *gernier*, from L. *granarium* 'granary'.

**garnet** /ˈɡɑːnɪt/ ● n. a vitreous silicate mineral, in particular a deep red form used as a gem.
– ORIGIN ME: prob. via MDu. from OFr. *grenat*, from med. L. *granatus*, perh. from *granatum* (see **POMEGRANATE**), because the garnet is similar in colour to the pulp of the fruit.

**garnish** ● v. **1** decorate or embellish (something, especially food). **2** Law serve notice on (a third party) for the purpose of legally seizing money belonging to a debtor or defendant. ➤seize (money, especially part of a person's salary) to settle a debt or claim. ● n. a decoration or embellishment, especially for food.
– DERIVATIVES **garnishment** n.
– ORIGIN ME (in the sense 'equip, arm'): from OFr. *garnir*, prob. of Gmc origin and rel. to **WARN**.

**garnishee** /ˌɡɑːnɪˈʃiː/ Law ● n. a third party who is garnished. ● v. (**garnishees**, **garnisheed**) another term for **GARNISH** (in sense 2).

**garniture** /ˈɡɑːnɪtʃə/ ● n. a set of decorative vases.
– ORIGIN C15: from Fr., from *garnir* 'to garnish'.

**garotte** ● v. & n. variant spelling of **GARROTTE**.

**garpike** ● n. another term for **GARFISH**.

**garret** ● n. a top-floor or attic room, especially a small dismal one.
– ORIGIN ME (in the sense 'watchtower'): from OFr. *garite*, from *garir* (see **GARRISON**).

**garrison** ● n. a body of troops stationed in a fortress or town to defend it. ● v. provide (a place) with a garrison.
– ORIGIN ME (in the sense 'safety, means of protection'): from OFr. *garison*, from *garir* 'defend, provide', of Gmc origin.

**garrison cap** ● n. US a peakless cap, especially one worn as part of a military uniform.

**garron** /ˈɡarən/ ● n. a small, sturdy workhorse of a breed originating in Ireland and Scotland.
– ORIGIN C16: from Sc. Gaelic *gearran*, Ir. *gearrán*.

**garrotte** /ɡəˈrɒt/ (also **garotte**; US **garrote**) ● v. kill by strangulation, especially with an iron collar or a length of wire or cord. ● n. a wire, cord, or apparatus used for garrotting.
– ORIGIN C17: via Fr. from Sp. *garrote* 'a cudgel, a garrotte', perh. of Celtic origin.

**garrulous** /ˈɡar(j)ʊləs/ ● adj. excessively talkative.
– DERIVATIVES **garrulity** /ɡəˈruːlɪti/ n. **garrulously** adv. **garrulousness** n.
– ORIGIN C17: from L. *garrulus* (from *garrire* 'to chatter, prattle') + **-OUS**.

**garryowen** /ˌɡarɪˈəʊɪn/ ● n. Rugby an up-and-under.
– ORIGIN 1960s: named after a rugby club in Limerick, Republic of Ireland.

**garter** ● n. a band worn around the leg to keep up a stocking or sock. ➤N. Amer. a suspender for a sock or stocking.
– DERIVATIVES **gartered** adj.
– ORIGIN ME: from OFr. *gartier*, from *garet* 'bend of the knee, calf of the leg', prob. of Celtic origin.

**garter belt** ● n. N. Amer. a suspender belt.

**garter snake** ● n. **1** a common, harmless North American snake with well-defined longitudinal stripes. [*Thamnophis sirtalis* and related species.] **2** a venomous burrowing African snake, typically dark with lighter bands. [Genus *Elapsoidea*.]

**garter stitch** ● n. knitting in which all of the rows are knitted in plain stitch, rather than alternating with purl rows.

**garth** ● n. **1** Brit. an open space surrounded by cloisters. **2** archaic a yard or garden.
– ORIGIN ME: from ON *garthr*; rel. to **YARD**[2].

**gas** ● n. (pl. **gases** or chiefly US **gasses**) **1** an air-like fluid substance which expands freely to fill any space available, irrespective of its quantity. ➤Physics a substance of this type that cannot be liquefied by pressure alone. Compare with **VAPOUR**. ➤a flammable substance of this type used as a fuel. **2** a gaseous anaesthetic such as nitrous oxide, used in dentistry. **3** chiefly N. Amer. flatulence. **4** Mining an explosive mixture of firedamp with air. **5** N. Amer. informal short for **GASOLINE**. **6** (**a gas**) informal an entertaining or amusing person or thing. ● v. (**gases**, **gassed**, **gassing**) **1** attack with, expose to, or kill with gas. ➤(of a storage battery or dry cell) give off gas. **2** N. Amer. informal fill the tank of (a motor vehicle) with petrol. **3** informal talk idly; chatter.
– DERIVATIVES **gasification** n. **gasify** v. **gasser** n.
– ORIGIN C17: invented by the Belgian chemist J. B. van Helmont to denote an occult principle which he believed to exist in all matter; suggested by Gk *khaos* 'chaos'.

**gasbag** ● n. informal a person who talks idly and excessively.

**gas chamber** ● n. an airtight room that can be filled with poisonous gas to kill people or animals.

**gas chromatography** ● n. chromatography employing a gas as the moving carrier medium.

**Gascon** /ˈɡask(ə)n/ ● n. **1** a native or inhabitant of Gascony, a region in SW France. **2** (**gascon**) archaic a boastful person.
– ORIGIN via OFr. from L. *Vasco*, *Vascon-*; rel. to **BASQUE**.

**gas constant** ● n. Chemistry the constant of proportionality in the gas equation, equal to 8.314 joule kelvin$^{-1}$ mole$^{-1}$.

**gaseous** /ˈɡasɪəs, ˈɡeɪsɪəs/ ● adj. relating to or having the characteristics of a gas.
– DERIVATIVES **gaseousness** n.

**gas equation** ● n. Chemistry the equation of state of an ideal gas, $PV = nRT$, where $P$ = pressure, $V$ = volume, $T$ = absolute temperature, $R$ = the gas constant, and $n$ = the number of moles of gas.

**gas gangrene** ● n. rapidly spreading gangrene affecting injured tissue infected by a soil bacterium and accompanied by the evolution of foul-smelling gas.

**gas guzzler** ● n. informal, chiefly N. Amer. a large motor car with a high fuel consumption.

**gash**[1] ● n. a long, deep slash, cut, or wound. ● v. make a gash in.
– ORIGIN ME *garse*, from OFr. *garcer* 'to chap, crack', perh. based on Gk *kharassein* 'sharpen, scratch, engrave'.

**gash**[2] ● n. Brit. informal rubbish or waste.
– ORIGIN C20 (orig. in naut. use): of unknown origin.

**gasket** /ˈɡaskɪt/ ● n. **1** a sheet or ring of rubber or other material sealing the junction between two surfaces in an engine or other device. **2** archaic a cord securing a furled sail to the yard of a sailing ship.
– ORIGIN C17: perh. from Fr. *garcette* 'thin rope' (orig. 'little girl').

**gaskin** /ˈɡaskɪn/ ● n. the muscular part of the hind leg of a horse between the stifle and the hock.
– ORIGIN C16: perh. from **GALLIGASKINS** (the orig. sense).

**gas laws** ● pl. n. Chemistry the physical laws that describe the properties of gases, including Boyle's and Charles's laws.

**gaslight** ● n. light from lamps in which an incandescent mantle is heated by a jet of burning gas.
– DERIVATIVES **gaslit** adj.

**gas–liquid chromatography** ● n. chromatography employing a gas as the moving carrier medium and a liquid as the stationary medium.

**gasman** ● n. (pl. **-men**) a man whose job is to install and service gas appliances, or to read gas meters.

**gas mask** ● n. a protective mask used to cover the face as a defence against poison gas.

**gasohol** /ˈɡasəhɒl/ ● n. a mixture of petrol and ethanol used as fuel in internal-combustion engines.

**gas oil** ● n. a type of fuel oil distilled from petroleum and heavier than paraffin oil.

**gasoline** (also **gasolene**) ● n. North American term for **PETROL**.

**gasometer** ● n. a large tank in which gas for use as fuel is stored before being distributed to consumers.

**gasp** ● v. **1** catch one's breath with an open mouth, owing to pain or astonishment. ➤(**gasp for**) strain to obtain (air) by gasping. **2** (**be gasping for**) informal be desperate to obtain or consume; crave: *I'm gasping for a drink!* ● n. a convulsive catching of breath.
– PHRASES **the last gasp** the point of exhaustion, death, or completion.
– ORIGIN ME: from ON *geispa* 'to yawn'.

**gasper** ● n. Brit. informal, dated a cigarette.

**gas-permeable** ● adj. (of a contact lens) allowing the diffusion of gases into and out of the cornea.

**gas plant** ● n. an aromatic plant of the rue family, with showy white flowers and fragrant leaves that emit a flammable vapour. [*Dictamnus albus*.]

**gassy** ● adj. (**-ier**, **-iest**) **1** resembling or full of gas. **2** informal verbose; idly chattering.
– DERIVATIVES **gassiness** n.

**Gastarbeiter** /'gast,ɑːbʌɪtə, German 'gast,arbaɪtɐ/ ● n. (pl. same or **Gastarbeiters**) a person with temporary permission to work in another country, especially in Germany.
– ORIGIN Ger., from *Gast* 'guest' + *Arbeiter* 'worker'.

**Gasthaus** /'gasthaʊs/ ● n. (pl. **Gasthäuser** /-,hɔɪzə/) a small inn or hotel in a German-speaking country.
– ORIGIN from Ger., from *Gast* 'guest' + *Haus* 'house'.

**Gasthof** /'gasthɒf, German 'gasthoːf/ ● n. (pl. **Gasthöfe** or **Gasthofs** /-,həːfə, German -,høːfə/) a hotel in a German-speaking country.
– ORIGIN from Ger., from *Gast* 'guest' + *Hof* 'hotel, large house'.

**gastr-** ● comb. form variant spelling of **GASTRO-** shortened before a vowel (as in *gastrectomy*).

**gastrectomy** /ga'strɛktəmi/ ● n. (pl. **-ies**) surgical removal of a part or the whole of the stomach.

**gastric** ● adj. of the stomach.
– ORIGIN C17: from mod. L. *gastricus*, from Gk *gastēr*, *gastr-* 'stomach'.

**gastric flu** ● n. a short-lived stomach disorder of unknown cause, popularly attributed to a virus.

**gastric juice** ● n. an acid fluid secreted by the stomach glands and active in promoting digestion.

**gastrin** ● n. Biochemistry a hormone which stimulates secretion of gastric juice, and is secreted into the bloodstream by the stomach wall in response to the presence of food.

**gastritis** /ga'strʌɪtɪs/ ● n. Medicine inflammation of the lining of the stomach.

**gastro-** /'gastrəʊ/ (also **gastr-** before a vowel) ● comb. form of or relating to the stomach: *gastro-enteritis*.
– ORIGIN from Gk *gastēr*, *gastr-* 'stomach'.

**gastrocnemius** /,gastrə(ʊ)'kniːmɪəs/ (also **gastrocnemius muscle**) ● n. (pl. **gastrocnemii** /-mɪʌɪ/) Anatomy the chief muscle of the calf of the leg, which flexes the knee and foot.
– ORIGIN C17: mod. L., from Gk *gastroknēmia* 'calf of the leg', from *gaster*, *gastr-* 'stomach' + *knēmē* 'leg' (from the bulging shape of the calf).

**gastro-enteritis** ● n. inflammation of the stomach and intestines, typically resulting from bacterial toxins or viral infection and causing vomiting and diarrhoea.

**gastroenterology** /,gastrəʊɛntə'rɒlədʒi/ ● n. the branch of medicine which deals with disorders of the stomach and intestines.
– DERIVATIVES **gastroenterological** adj. **gastroenterologist** n.

**gastrointestinal** /,gastrəʊɪn'tɛstɪn(ə)l, -ɪntɛs'tʌɪn(ə)l/ ● adj. of or relating to the stomach and the intestines.

**gastrolith** /'gastrə(ʊ)lɪθ/ ● n. **1** Zoology a small stone swallowed by a bird, reptile, or fish to aid digestion in the gizzard. **2** Medicine a hard concretion in the stomach.

**gastronome** /'gastrənəʊm/ ● n. a gourmet.

**gastronomy** /ga'strɒnəmi/ ● n. the practice or art of choosing, cooking, and eating good food.
– DERIVATIVES **gastronomic** adj. **gastronomical** adj. **gastronomically** adv.
– ORIGIN C19: from Fr. *gastronomie*, from Gk *gastronomia*, alt. of *gastrologia* (see **GASTRO-**, **-LOGY**).

**Gastropoda** /,gastrə'pəʊdə, gas'trɒpədə/ ● pl. n. Zoology a large class of molluscs which includes snails, slugs, and whelks.
– DERIVATIVES **gastropod** n.
– ORIGIN mod. L., from Gk *gastēr*, *gastr-* 'stomach' + *pous*, *pod-* 'foot'.

**gastroscope** ● n. an optical instrument used for inspecting the interior of the stomach.
– DERIVATIVES **gastroscopic** adj. **gastroscopy** n.

**Gastrotricha** /,gastrə'trʌɪkə/ ● pl. n. Zoology a small phylum of minute aquatic worm-like animals which bear bristles and cilia.
– DERIVATIVES **gastrotrich** /'gastrətrɪk/ n.
– ORIGIN mod. L., from Gk *gastēr*, *gastr-* 'stomach' + *thrix*, *trikh-* 'hair'.

**gastrula** /'gastrʊlə/ ● n. (pl. **gastrulae** /-liː/) Embryology an embryo at the stage following the blastula, when it is a hollow cup-shaped structure having three layers of cells.
– DERIVATIVES **gastrulation** n.
– ORIGIN C19: mod. L., from Gk *gastēr*, *gastr-* 'stomach' + the L. dimin. ending *-ula*.

**gas turbine** ● n. a turbine driven by expanding hot gases produced by burning fuel, as in a jet engine.

**gasworks** ● pl. n. [treated as sing.] a place where gas is manufactured and processed.

**gat**[1] ● n. informal a revolver or pistol.
– ORIGIN C20: abbrev. of **GATLING GUN**.

**gat**[2] archaic past of **GET**.

**gate**[1] ● n. **1** a hinged barrier used to close an opening in a wall, fence, or hedge. ➤an exit from an airport building to an aircraft. ➤a hinged or sliding barrier for controlling the flow of water: *a sluice gate*. **2** the number of people who pay to enter a sports ground for an event. **3** an arrangement of slots into which the gear lever of a motor vehicle moves to engage each gear. **4** an electric circuit with an output which depends on the combination of several inputs. **5** a device for holding each frame of a movie film in position behind the lens of a camera or projector. ● v. Brit. confine (a pupil or student) to school or college.
– PHRASES **get** (or **be given**) **the gate** N. Amer. informal be dismissed from a job.
– DERIVATIVES **gated** adj.
– ORIGIN OE *gæt*, *geat*, pl. *gatu*, of Gmc origin.

**gate**[2] ● n. Brit. (in place names) a street: *Kirkgate*.
– ORIGIN ME (also meaning 'way' in general): from ON *gata*.

**-gate** ● comb. form in nouns denoting a scandal, especially one involving a cover-up: *Irangate*.
– ORIGIN 1970s: suggested by the *Watergate* scandal in the US, 1972.

**gateau** /'gatəʊ/ ● n. (pl. **gateaus** or **gateaux** /-əʊz/) chiefly Brit. a rich cake, typically one containing layers of cream or fruit.
– ORIGIN C19: from Fr. *gâteau* 'cake'.

**gatecrash** ● v. enter (a party) without an invitation or ticket.
– DERIVATIVES **gatecrasher** n.

**gatefold** ● n. an oversized page in a book or magazine folded to the same size as the other pages but intended to be opened out for reading.

**gatehouse** ● n. **1** a house standing by a gateway, especially on a country estate. **2** historical a room over a city or palace gate, often used as a prison.

**gatekeeper** ● n. **1** an attendant at a gate. **2** an orange and brown butterfly with small eyespots on the wings. [*Pyronia tithonus*.]

**gateleg table** ● n. a table with hinged legs that may be swung out from the centre to support folding leaves.
– DERIVATIVES **gatelegged** adj.

**gatepost** ● n. a post on which a gate is hinged, or against which it shuts.

**gate valve** ● n. a valve with a sliding part that controls the extent of the aperture.

**gateway** ● n. **1** an opening that can be closed by a gate. ➤a frame or arch built around or over a gate. **2** Computing a device used to connect two different networks, especially a connection to the Internet.

**gather** ● v. **1** come or bring together; assemble or accumulate. ➤ harvest (a crop). ➤ collect plants, fruits, etc., for food: *hunting and gathering.* ➤ draw together or towards oneself. **2** summon up (a mental or physical attribute): *he gathered his thoughts together.* **3** develop a higher degree of: *the Green movement is gathering pace.* **4** infer; understand. **5** draw and hold together (fabric or a part of a garment) by running thread through it. ● n. (**gathers**) a part of a garment that is gathered or drawn in.
– PHRASES **gather way** (of a ship) begin to move.
– DERIVATIVES **gatherer** n.
– ORIGIN OE *gaderian*, of W. Gmc origin; rel. to **TOGETHER**.

**gathering** ● n. **1** an assembly or meeting, especially a social one. **2** a group of leaves taken together, one inside another, in binding a book.

**Gatling gun** ● n. an early type of machine gun, with clustered barrels.
– ORIGIN C19: named after the Amer. inventor Richard J. *Gatling*.

**gator** ● n. informal, chiefly N. Amer. an alligator.

**gauche** /gəʊʃ/ ● adj. unsophisticated and socially awkward.
– DERIVATIVES **gauchely** adv. **gaucheness** n.
– ORIGIN C18: Fr., lit. 'left'.

**gaucherie** /'gəʊʃ(ə)ri/ ● n. awkward or unsophisticated ways.

**Gaucher's disease** /'gəʊʃeɪz, gəʊ'ʃeɪz/ ● n. a hereditary abnormality of fat metabolism, with effects including bone fragility and enlargement of the liver and spleen.
– ORIGIN C20: named after the Fr. physician Phillippe C. E. *Gaucher*.

**gaucho** /'gaʊtʃəʊ, 'gɔː-/ ● n. (pl. **-os**) a cowboy from the South American pampas.
– ORIGIN Latin Amer. Sp., prob. from Araucanian *kauču* 'friend'.

**gaud** /gɔːd/ ● n. archaic a showy and purely ornamental thing.
– ORIGIN ME (denoting a trick or pretence): perh. via Anglo-Norman Fr. from OFr. *gaudir* 'rejoice', from L. *gaudere*.

**gaudy**[1] ● adj. (**-ier**, **-iest**) extravagantly or tastelessly bright or showy.
– DERIVATIVES **gaudily** adv. **gaudiness** n.
– ORIGIN C15: prob. from **GAUD** + **-Y**[1].

**gaudy**[2] ● n. (pl. **-ies**) Brit. a celebratory dinner or entertainment held by a college for old members.
– ORIGIN C16 (in the sense 'rejoicing, a celebration'): from L. *gaudium* 'joy', or from *gaude* 'rejoice!', imper. of *gaudere*.

**gauge** /geɪdʒ/ (chiefly US also **gage**) ● n. **1** an instrument that measures and gives a visual display of the amount, level, or contents of something. **2** the thickness, size, or capacity of a wire, sheet, tube, bullet, etc., especially as a standard measure. **3** the distance between the rails of a line of railway track. **4** Nautical, archaic the position of a sailing vessel to windward (**the weather gage**) or leeward (**the lee gage**) of another. ● v. **1** estimate or determine the amount or level of. ➤ judge or assess (a situation, mood, etc.). **2** measure the dimensions of with a gauge. ➤ [as adj. **gauged**] made in standard dimensions.
– DERIVATIVES **gaugeable** adj. **gauger** n.
– ORIGIN ME: from OFr. *gauge* (n.), *gauger* (v.), var. of ONorth. Fr. *jauge*, *jauger*, of unknown origin.

**gauge pressure** ● n. Engineering the amount by which the pressure measured in a fluid exceeds that of the atmosphere.

**gauge theory** ● n. Physics a quantum theory using mathematical functions to describe subatomic interactions in terms of particles that are not directly detectable.

**Gaul** /gɔːl/ ● n. a native or inhabitant of the ancient European region of Gaul.
– ORIGIN from L. *Gallus*, prob. of Celtic origin.

**Gauleiter** /'gaʊlʌɪtə, German 'gaʊlaɪtɐ/ ● n. **1** historical a political official governing a district under Nazi rule. **2** an overbearing official.
– ORIGIN 1930s: Ger., from *Gau* 'administrative district' + *Leiter* 'leader'.

**Gaulish** ● n. the Celtic language of the ancient Gauls. ● adj. relating to or denoting the ancient Gauls.

**Gaullism** /'gəʊlɪz(ə)m/ ● n. the principles and policies of the French statesman Charles de Gaulle (1890–1970), characterized by conservatism, nationalism, and advocacy of centralized government.
– DERIVATIVES **Gaullist** n. & adj.

**Gault clay** /gɔːlt/ ● n. Geology a series of Cretaceous clays and marls forming strata in southern England.
– ORIGIN C16: possibly rel. to Old Swed. *galt*, neut. of *galder* 'barren'.

**gaunt** ● adj. **1** lean and haggard, especially through suffering, hunger, or age. **2** (of a place) grim or desolate in appearance.
– DERIVATIVES **gauntly** adv. **gauntness** n.
– ORIGIN ME: of unknown origin.

**gauntlet**[1] ● n. a stout glove with a long loose wrist. ➤ historical an armoured glove.
– PHRASES **take up** (or **throw down**) **the gauntlet** accept (or issue) a challenge.
– ORIGIN ME: from OFr. *gantelet*, dimin. of *gant* 'glove', of Gmc origin.

**gauntlet**[2] (US also **gantlet**) ● n. (in phr. **run the gauntlet**) **1** go through an intimidating crowd or experience in order to reach a goal. **2** historical undergo the military punishment of receiving blows while running between two rows of men with sticks.
– ORIGIN C17: alt. of *gantlope* (from Swed. *gatlopp*, from *gata* 'lane' + *lopp* 'course'), assoc. with **GAUNTLET**[1].

**gaur** /'gaʊə/ ● n. a wild ox having a dark brown or black coat with white lower legs, native to India and Malaysia. [*Bos gaurus*.]
– ORIGIN C19: from Sanskrit *gaura*; rel. to **COW**[1].

**gauss** /gaʊs/ ● n. (pl. same or **gausses**) a unit of magnetic induction, equal to one ten-thousandth of a tesla.
– ORIGIN C19: named after the Ger. mathematician K. *Gauss*.

**Gaussian distribution** /'gaʊsɪən/ ● n. Statistics another term for **NORMAL DISTRIBUTION**.

**gauze** /gɔːz/ ● n. **1** a thin transparent fabric. ➤ Medicine thin, loosely woven cloth used for dressing and swabs. **2** (also **wire gauze**) a very fine wire mesh.
– DERIVATIVES **gauzily** adv. **gauziness** n. **gauzy** adj.
– ORIGIN C16: from Fr. *gaze*, perh. from *Gaza*, the name of a town in Palestine.

**gavage** /ga'vɑːʒ/ ● n. the administration of food or drugs by force, especially to an animal.
– ORIGIN C19: Fr., from *gaver* 'force-feed'.

**gave** past of **GIVE**.

**gavel** /'gav(ə)l/ ● n. a small hammer with which an auctioneer, judge, etc., hits a surface to call for attention or order. ● v. (**gavelled**, **gavelling**; US **gaveled**, **gaveling**) bring to order by use of a gavel.
– ORIGIN C19 (in the sense 'stonemason's mallet'): of unknown origin.

**gavelkind** /'gav(ə)lkʌɪnd/ ● n. historical a system of inheritance in which a deceased person's land is divided equally among all male heirs.
– ORIGIN ME: from obs. *gavel* 'payment, rent' + **KIND**[1].

**gavial** /'geɪvɪəl/ ● n. variant spelling of **GHARIAL**.

**gavotte** /gə'vɒt/ ● n. a medium-paced French dance, popular in the 18th century.
– ORIGIN Fr., from Provençal *gavoto* 'dance of the mountain people', from *Gavot* 'a native of the Alps'.

**gawk** ● v. stare openly and stupidly. ● n. an awkward or shy person.
– DERIVATIVES **gawker** n. **gawkish** adj.
– ORIGIN C17 (as n.): perh. rel. to obs. *gaw* 'to gaze', from ON *gá* 'heed'.

**gawky** ● adj. (**-ier**, **-iest**) nervously awkward and ungainly.
– DERIVATIVES **gawkily** adv. **gawkiness** n.

**gawp** ● v. Brit. informal stare openly in a stupid or rude manner.
– DERIVATIVES **gawper** n.
– ORIGIN C17: perh. an alt. of **GAPE**.

**gay** ● adj. (**-er**, **-est**) **1** (especially of a man) homosexual. ➤relating to or used by homosexuals. **2** dated light-hearted and carefree. **3** dated brightly coloured; showy. ● n. a homosexual person, especially a man.
– DERIVATIVES **gayness** n.
– ORIGIN ME: from OFr. *gai*, of unknown origin.

**gayal** /gʌɪ'jɑːl, -'jal/ ● n. a domesticated ox used in the Indian subcontinent. [*Bos frontalis*.]
– ORIGIN C18: from Bengali.

**gayety** ● n. US variant spelling of **GAIETY**.

**Gay-Lussac's law** /geɪ'luːsaks/ ● n. Chemistry a law stating that the volumes of gases undergoing a reaction at constant pressure and temperature are in a simple ratio to each other and to that of the product.
– ORIGIN C19: named after the Fr. scientist Joseph L. *Gay-Lussac*.

**gazania** /gə'zeɪnɪə/ ● n. a tropical herbaceous plant of the daisy family, with showy orange or yellow flowers. [Genus *Gazania*.]
– ORIGIN mod. L., named after the C15 Gk scholar Theodore of *Gaza*.

**gaze** ● v. look steadily and intently. ● n. a steady intent look.
– DERIVATIVES **gazer** n.
– ORIGIN ME: perh. rel. to obs. *gaw* (see **GAWK**).

**gazebo** /gə'ziːbəʊ/ ● n. (pl. **-os** or **-oes**) a small building, especially one in the garden of a house, that gives a wide view of the surrounding area.
– ORIGIN C18: perh. humorously from **GAZE**, in imitation of L. future tenses ending in *-ebo*: cf. **LAVABO**.

**gazelle** ● n. a small slender African or Asian antelope, typically having curved horns and fawn-coloured with white underparts. [*Gazella* and other genera: several species.]
– ORIGIN C17: from Fr., prob. via Sp. from Arab. *ghazāl*.

**gazette** ● n. **1** a journal or newspaper, especially the official one of an organization or institution. **2** historical a news-sheet. ● v. Brit. announce or publish in an official gazette. ➤publish the fact of the appointment of (someone) to a military or other official post.
– ORIGIN C17: via Fr. from Ital. *gazzetta*, orig. Venetian *gazeta de la novità* 'a halfpennyworth of news' (with ref. to a news-sheet sold for a *gazeta*, a Venetian coin of small value).

**gazetteer** /ˌgazə'tɪə/ ● n. a geographical index or dictionary.
– ORIGIN C17 (in the sense 'journalist'): via Fr. from Ital. *gazzettiere*, from *gazzetta* (see **GAZETTE**); current sense is from a gazetteer called *The Gazetteer's: or, Newsman's Interpreter*.

**gazillion** /gə'zɪljən/ (also **kazillion**) ● cardinal number N. Amer. informal a very large number or quantity.
– ORIGIN C20: fanciful formation on the pattern of *billion* and *million*.

**gazpacho** /gəs'patʃəʊ/ ● n. (pl. **-os**) a cold Spanish soup made from tomatoes, peppers, and other salad vegetables.
– ORIGIN from Sp.

**gazump** /gə'zʌmp/ ● v. Brit. informal make a higher offer for a house than (someone whose offer has already been accepted) and thus succeed in acquiring the property.
– DERIVATIVES **gazumper** n.
– ORIGIN 1920s (in sense 'swindle'): from Yiddish *gezumph* 'overcharge'.

**GB** ● abbrev. **1** Great Britain. **2** (also **Gb**) Computing gigabyte(s).

**GBA** ● abbrev. Alderney (international vehicle registration).

**GBE** ● abbrev. Knight or Dame Grand Cross of the Order of the British Empire.

**GBG** ● abbrev. Guernsey (international vehicle registration).

**GBH** ● abbrev. Brit. grievous bodily harm.

**GBJ** ● abbrev. Jersey (international vehicle registration)

**GBM** ● abbrev. Isle of Man (international vehicle registration).

**Gbyte** ● abbrev. gigabyte(s).

**GBZ** ● abbrev. Gibraltar (international vehicle registration).

**GC** ● abbrev. George Cross.

**GCA** ● abbrev. Guatemala (international vehicle registration).

**GCB** ● abbrev. Knight or Dame Grand Cross of the Order of the Bath.

**GCE** ● abbrev. General Certificate of Education.

**GCHQ** ● abbrev. Government Communications Headquarters.

**GCMG** ● abbrev. Knight or Dame Grand Cross of the Order of St Michael and St George.

**GCSE** ● abbrev. General Certificate of Secondary Education.

**GCVO** ● abbrev. Knight or Dame Grand Cross of the Royal Victorian Order.

**Gd** ● symb. the chemical element gadolinium.

**Gdns** ● abbrev. Gardens (as part of an address).

**GDP** ● abbrev. gross domestic product.

**GDR** ● abbrev. historical German Democratic Republic.

**Ge** ● symb. the chemical element germanium.

**gean** /giːn/ ● n. the wild or sweet cherry. [*Prunus avium*.]
– ORIGIN C16: from OFr. *guine*, of unknown origin.

**gear** ● n. **1** a toothed wheel that works with others to alter the relation between the speed of an engine and the speed of the driven parts (e.g. wheels). ➤a particular setting of engaged gears: *in fifth gear*. **2** informal apparatus or equipment. ➤clothing: *designer gear*. **3** informal illegal drugs. ● v. **1** design or adjust gears to give a specified speed or power output. **2** (often **gear something up**) make ready; prepare. ➤equip or adapt for a particular purpose. **3** (**gear down** or **up**) change to a lower (or higher) gear.
– PHRASES **in** (or **out of**) **gear** with a gear (or no gear) engaged.
– ORIGIN ME: of Scand. origin; cf. ON *gervi*.

**gearbox** ● n. a set of gears with its casing, especially in a motor vehicle; the transmission.

**geared** ● adj. **1** fitted with gears. **2** (of a company) having a specified ratio of loan capital (debt) to the value of its ordinary shares (equity).

**gearing** ● n. **1** the set or arrangement of gears in a machine. **2** the ratio of a company's loan capital (debt) to the value of its ordinary shares (equity).

**gear lever** (also **gearstick**) ● n. Brit. a lever used to engage or change gear in a motor vehicle.

**gear shift** ● n. chiefly N. Amer. a gear lever.

**gear train** ● n. a system of gears which transmits motion from one shaft to another.

**gearwheel** ● n. a toothed wheel in a set of gears. ➤(on a bicycle) a cogwheel driven directly by the chain.

**gecko** /'gɛkəʊ/ ● n. (pl. **-os** or **-oes**) a nocturnal lizard with adhesive pads on the feet, found in warm regions. [Gekkonidae and related families: many species.]
– ORIGIN C18: from Malay dial. *geko*, *gekok*, imitative of its cry.

**gee**[1] (also **gee whiz**) ● exclam. informal, chiefly N. Amer. a mild expression of surprise, enthusiasm, or sympathy.
– ORIGIN C19: perh. an abbrev. of **JESUS**.

**gee**[2] ● exclam. (**gee up**) a command to a horse to go faster. ● v. (**gees**, **geed**, **geeing**) (**gee someone/thing up**) command a horse to go faster. ➤encourage someone to work more quickly.
– ORIGIN C17: of unknown origin.

**geebung** /'dʒiːbʌŋ/ ● n. an Australian shrub or small tree with creamy-yellow flowers and small green fruit. [Genus *Persoonia*.]
– ORIGIN C19: from Dharuk.

**Geechee** /'giːtʃiː/ ● n. **1** an English creole spoken by blacks in parts of South Carolina and Georgia. Compare with **GULLAH**. **2** a speaker of this creole.
– ORIGIN from the name of the Ogeechee River, in Georgia.

**gee-gee** ● n. Brit. informal a child's word for a horse.
– ORIGIN C19: reduplication of **GEE**[2].

**geek** /giːk/ ● n. informal, chiefly N. Amer. an unfashionable or socially inept person. ➤a knowledgeable and obsessive

enthusiast: *a computer geek.*
– DERIVATIVES **geeky** adj.
– ORIGIN C19: from the rel. Engl. dial. word *geck* 'fool', of Gmc origin.

**geese** plural form of GOOSE.

**gee-string** • n. variant spelling of G-STRING.

**gee whiz** • exclam. another term for GEE[1].

**Geez** • exclam. variant spelling of JEEZ.

**Ge'ez** /'giːɛz/ • n. an ancient Semitic language of Ethiopia, which survives as the liturgical language of the Ethiopian Orthodox Church.
– ORIGIN of Ethiopic origin.

**geezer** /'giːzə/ • n. informal a man.
– ORIGIN C19: representing a dial. pronunc. of earlier *guiser* 'mummer'.

**gefilte fish** /gə'fɪltə/ • n. a dish of stewed or baked stuffed fish, or of fish cakes boiled in a fish or vegetable broth.
– ORIGIN Yiddish, 'stuffed fish', from *filn* 'to fill' + FISH[1].

**gegenschein** /'geɪgən,ʃʌɪn/ • n. Astronomy a patch of very faint reflected light sometimes seen in the night sky opposite the position of the sun.
– ORIGIN C19: Ger. *Gegenschein*, from *gegen* 'opposite' + *Schein* 'glow, shine'.

**Gehenna** /gə'hɛnə/ • n. a name for hell.
– ORIGIN via eccles. L. from Gk *geenna*, from Heb. *gē' hinnōm* 'hell', lit. 'valley of Hinnom', a place near Jerusalem where children were sacrificed to Baal.

**Geiger counter** • n. a device for measuring radioactivity by detecting and counting ionizing particles.
– ORIGIN C20: named after the Ger. physicist Hans *Geiger.*

**geisha** /'geɪʃə/ • n. (pl. same or **geishas**) a Japanese hostess trained to entertain men with conversation, dance, and song.
– ORIGIN Japanese, 'entertainer'.

**Geissler tube** /'gʌɪslə/ • n. a sealed tube of glass or quartz with a central constriction, filled with vapour for the production of a luminous electrical discharge.
– ORIGIN C19: named after its Ger. inventor Heinrich *Geissler.*

**Geist** /gʌɪst/ • n. the spirit of an individual or group.
– ORIGIN Ger.; rel. to GHOST.

**geitonogamy** /,gʌɪtə'nɒgəmi/ • n. Botany the fertilization of a flower by pollen from another flower on the same (or a genetically identical) plant. Compare with XENOGAMY.
– DERIVATIVES **geitonogamous** adj.
– ORIGIN C19: from Gk *geitōn, geitono-* 'neighbour' + *gamos* 'marriage'.

**gel[1]** /dʒɛl/ • n. a jelly-like substance containing a cosmetic, medicinal, or other preparation. ➤ Chemistry a semi-solid colloidal suspension of a solid dispersed in a liquid. • v. (**gelled, gelling**) **1** Chemistry form into a gel. **2** smooth (one's hair) with gel.
– ORIGIN C19: abbrev. of GELATIN.

**gel[2]** /dʒɛl/ • v. variant spelling of JELL.

**gelada** /dʒə'lɑːdə/ • n. (pl. same or **geladas**) a brownish baboon with a long mane and naked red rump, native to Ethiopia. [*Theropithecus gelada.*]
– ORIGIN C19: from Amharic *č'ällada.*

**gelati** plural form of GELATO.

**gelatin** /'dʒɛlətɪn/ (also **gelatine** /-tiːn/) • n. **1** a virtually colourless and tasteless water-soluble protein prepared from collagen and used in food preparation, in photographic processing, and for making glue. **2** a high explosive consisting chiefly of a gel of nitroglycerine with added cellulose nitrate.
– DERIVATIVES **gelatinization** (also **-isation**) n. **gelatinize** (also **-ise**) v.
– ORIGIN C19: from Fr. *gélatine*, from Ital. *gelatina*, from *gelata*, from L. (see JELLY).

**gelatinous** • adj. having a jelly-like consistency. ➤ of or like the protein gelatin.
– DERIVATIVES **gelatinously** adv.

**gelatin paper** • n. Brit. paper coated with sensitized gelatin for photographic use.

**gelation[1]** • n. technical solidification by freezing.
– ORIGIN C19: from L. *gelatio(n-)*, from *gelare* 'freeze'.

**gelation[2]** • n. Chemistry the process of forming a gel.

**gelato** /dʒə'lɑːtəʊ/ • n. (pl. **gelati** /dʒə'lɑːti/) an Italian or Italian-style ice cream.
– ORIGIN from Ital.

**gelcoat** /'dʒɛlkəʊt/ • n. the smooth, hard polyester resin surface coating of a fibreglass structure.

**geld** • v. castrate (a male animal).
– ORIGIN ME: from ON *gelda*, from *geldr* 'barren'.

**gelding** • n. a castrated animal, especially a male horse.

**gelid** /'dʒɛlɪd/ • adj. icy; extremely cold.
– ORIGIN C17: from L. *gelidus*, from *gelu* 'frost, intense cold'.

**gelignite** /'dʒɛlɪgnʌɪt/ • n. a high explosive made from a gel of nitroglycerine and nitrocellulose in a base of wood pulp and sodium or potassium nitrate, used particularly for blasting rock.
– ORIGIN C19: prob. from GELATIN + L. *(l)ignis* 'wood' + -ITE[1].

**gelsemium** /dʒɛl'siːmɪəm/ • n. a preparation of the rhizome of yellow jasmine, used in homeopathy to treat flu-like symptoms.
– ORIGIN C19: mod. L., from Ital. *gelsomino* 'jasmine'.

**gelt** /gɛlt/ • n. informal money.
– ORIGIN C16: from Ger. *Geld* 'money'.

**gem** • n. **1** a precious or semi-precious stone, especially when cut and polished or engraved. **2** an outstanding person or thing.
– DERIVATIVES **gem-like** adj. **gemmed** adj.
– ORIGIN OE *gim*, from L. *gemma* 'bud, jewel'; influenced in ME by OFr. *gemme.*

**Gemara** /gə'mɑːrə/ • n. (**the Gemara**) a rabbinical commentary on the Mishnah, forming the second part of the Talmud.
– ORIGIN from Aramaic *gĕmārā* 'completion'.

**gematria** /gɪ'meɪtrɪə/ • n. a Kabbalistic method of interpreting the Hebrew scriptures by computing the numerical value of words, based on those of their constituent letters.
– ORIGIN C17: from Aramaic *gīmaṭrēyā*, from Gk *gēometria* (see GEOMETRY).

**Gemeinschaft** /gə'mʌɪnʃaft/ • n. social relations based on close personal and family ties. Contrasted with GESELLSCHAFT.
– ORIGIN Ger., from *gemein* 'common' + *-schaft* (see -SHIP).

**geminal** /'dʒɛmɪn(ə)l/ • adj. Chemistry denoting substituent atoms or groups, especially protons, attached to the same atom in a molecule.
– DERIVATIVES **geminally** adv.
– ORIGIN C20: from L. *geminus* 'twin' + -AL.

**geminate** Phonetics • adj. /'dʒɛmɪneɪt, -nət/ consisting of identical adjacent speech sounds; doubled. • v. /'dʒɛmɪneɪt/ double or repeat (a speech sound).
– DERIVATIVES **gemination** n.
– ORIGIN ME: from L. *geminat-*, *geminare* 'double, pair with', from *geminus* 'twin'.

**Gemini** • n. **1** Astronomy a northern constellation (the Twins), said to represent the twins Castor and Pollux. **2** Astrology the third sign of the zodiac, which the sun enters about 21 May.
– DERIVATIVES **Geminian** /dʒɛmɪ'niːən/ n. & adj.
– ORIGIN L., pl. of *geminus* 'twin'.

**gemma** /'dʒɛmə/ • n. (pl. **gemmae** /-miː/) Biology **1** a small cellular body or bud that can separate to form a new organism. **2** another term for CHLAMYDOSPORE.
– ORIGIN C18: from L., lit. 'bud, jewel'.

**gemmation** /dʒɛ'meɪʃ(ə)n/ • n. Biology asexual reproduction by the production of gemmae; budding.
– ORIGIN C18: from Fr., from *gemmer* 'to bud', from *gemme* 'bud', from L. *gemma.*

**gemmiparous** /dʒɛ'mɪp(ə)rəs/ • adj. Biology reproducing by gemmation.

**gemmology** • n. the study of precious stones.
– DERIVATIVES **gemmological** adj. **gemmologist** n.

**gemmule** /'dʒɛmjuːl/ • n. Zoology a tough-coated dormant cluster of embryonic cells produced by a freshwater sponge for development in more favourable conditions.
– DERIVATIVES **gemmulation** n.

– ORIGIN C19: from Fr., from L. *gemmula*, dimin. of *gemma* 'bud, jewel'.

**gemsbok** /ˈxɛmzbɒk, ˈxɛms-/ ● **n.** a large antelope with distinctive black-and-white head markings and long straight horns, native to SW and East Africa. [*Oryx gazella*.]
– ORIGIN C18: via Afrik. from Du., lit. 'chamois'.

**gemstone** ● **n.** a precious or semi-precious stone, especially one cut, polished, and used in a piece of jewellery.

**gemütlich** /ɡəˈmuːtlɪx, German ɡəˈmyːtlɪç/ ● **adj.** pleasant and cheerful.
– ORIGIN from Ger.

**Gemütlichkeit** /ɡəˈmuːtlɪxkʌɪt, German ɡəˈmyːtlɪçkaɪt/ ● **n.** geniality; friendliness.
– ORIGIN from Ger.

**Gen.** ● **abbrev.** **1** General. **2** Genesis (in biblical references).

**gen** /dʒɛn/ Brit. informal ● **n.** information. ● **v.** (**genned**, **genning**) (**gen someone up**) provide someone with information. ➤(**gen up on**) find out about; learn about.
– ORIGIN Second World War (orig. in military use): perh. from *general information*.

**-gen** ● **comb. form** **1** Chemistry denoting a substance that produces something: *allergen*. **2** Botany denoting a substance or plant that is produced: *cultigen*.
– ORIGIN via Fr. *-gène* from Gk *genēs* '-born, of a specified kind', based on *gignomai* 'be born, become'.

**gendarme** /ˈʒɒndɑːm, French ʒɑ̃daʀm/ ● **n.** **1** a paramilitary police officer in French-speaking countries. **2** a rock pinnacle on a mountain, occupying and blocking an arête.
– ORIGIN C16 (denoting a mounted military officer): Fr., from *gens d'armes* 'men of arms'.

**gendarmerie** /ʒɒnˈdɑːməri, French ʒɑ̃daʀm(ə)ʀi/ ● **n.** a force of gendarmes. ➤the headquarters of such a force.

**gender** ● **n.** **1** Grammar a class (usually masculine, feminine, common, or neuter) into which nouns and pronouns are placed in some languages, distinguished by a particular inflection. ➤the property of belonging to such a class. **2** the state of being male or female (chiefly in cultural or social contexts). ➤the members of one or other sex: *differences between the genders*.
– DERIVATIVES **gendered** adj.
– ORIGIN ME: from OFr. *gendre* (mod. *genre*), based on L. *genus* 'birth, family, nation'.

**gender bender** ● **n.** informal a person who dresses and behaves in a way characteristic of the opposite sex.

**gender dysphoria** ● **n.** Medicine the condition of feeling one's emotional and psychological identity as male or female to be opposite to one's biological sex.

**gene** /dʒiːn/ ● **n.** Biology a unit of heredity which is transferred from a parent to offspring and is held to determine some characteristic of the offspring; in particular, a distinct sequence of DNA forming part of a chromosome.
– ORIGIN C20: from Ger. *Gen*, from *Pangen*, a supposed ultimate unit of heredity (from Gk *pan-* 'all' + *genos* 'race, kind, offspring').

**genealogical tree** ● **n.** a chart like an inverted branching tree showing the lines of descent of a family or of an animal species.

**genealogy** /dʒiːnɪˈalədʒi, dʒɛn-/ ● **n.** (pl. **-ies**) **1** a line of descent traced continuously from an ancestor. **2** the study of lines of descent.
– DERIVATIVES **genealogical** /ˌdʒiːnɪəˈlɒdʒɪk(ə)l, ˌdʒɛn-/ adj. **genealogically** adv. **genealogist** n. **genealogize** (also **-ise**) v.
– ORIGIN ME: via OFr. and late L. from Gk *genealogia*, from *genea* 'race, generation' + *-logia* (see **-LOGY**).

**gene pool** ● **n.** the stock of different genes in an interbreeding population.

**genera** plural form of **GENUS**.

**general** ● **adj.** **1** affecting or concerning all or most people or things; not specialized or limited. ➤normal or usual. **2** involving only the main features or elements and disregarding exceptions; overall. **3** chief or principal: *the general manager*. ● **n.** **1** a commander of an army, or an army officer ranking above lieutenant general. ➤short for **LIEUTENANT GENERAL** or **MAJOR GENERAL**. ➤the head of a religious order organized on quasi-military lines, e.g. the Jesuits or the Salvation Army. **2** (**the general**) archaic the general public.
– PHRASES **in general** **1** usually; mainly. **2** as a whole.
– DERIVATIVES **generalship** n.
– ORIGIN ME: via OFr. from L. *generalis*, from *genus*, *gener-* 'class, race, kind'.

**General American** ● **n.** the accent of English with which people speak in the greater part of the US, excluding New England, New York, and the South.

**general anaesthetic** ● **n.** an anaesthetic that affects the whole body and causes a loss of consciousness.

**general average** ● **n.** Law the apportionment of financial liability for the loss arising from the jettisoning of cargo among all those whose property has been preserved by the action.

**general delivery** ● **n.** North American term for **POSTE RESTANTE**.

**general election** ● **n.** the election of representatives to a legislature from constituencies throughout the country.

**general headquarters** ● **n.** [treated as sing. or pl.] the headquarters of a military commander.

**generalissimo** /ˌdʒɛn(ə)rəˈlɪsɪməʊ/ ● **n.** (pl. **-os**) the commander of a combined military force consisting of army, navy, and air force units.
– ORIGIN C17: Ital., 'having greatest authority', superlative of *generale* (see **GENERAL**).

**generalist** ● **n.** a person competent in several different fields or activities.

**generality** ● **n.** (pl. **-ies**) **1** a statement or principle having general rather than specific validity or force. ➤the quality or state of being general. **2** (**the generality**) the majority.

**generalize** (also **-ise**) ● **v.** **1** make a general or broad statement by inferring from specific cases. **2** make more common or more widely applicable. **3** [as adj. **generalized**] Medicine (of a disease) affecting much or all of the body; not localized.
– DERIVATIVES **generalizability** n. **generalizable** adj. **generalization** n. **generalizer** n.

**generally** ● **adv.** **1** in most cases. **2** without regard to particulars or exceptions. **3** widely.

**general meeting** ● **n.** a meeting open to all members of an organization.

**general of the air force** ● **n.** the highest rank of officer in the US air force, above general.

**general of the army** ● **n.** the highest rank of officer in the US army, above general.

**general paralysis of the insane** ● **n.** dementia, weakness, speech and hearing difficulty, and other symptoms, associated with the late stages of syphilis.

**general practitioner** ● **n.** a community doctor who treats patients with minor or chronic illnesses.
– DERIVATIVES **general practice** n.

**general-purpose** ● **adj.** having a range of potential uses or functions.

**general staff** ● **n.** [treated as sing. or pl.] the staff assisting a military commander.

**general strike** ● **n.** a strike of workers in all or most industries.

**generate** ● **v.** **1** cause to arise or come about. **2** produce (energy, especially electricity). **3** Mathematics & Linguistics produce (a set or sequence of items) by performing mathematical or logical operations on an initial set. **4** Mathematics form (a line, surface, or solid) by notionally moving a point, line, or surface.
– DERIVATIVES **generable** adj.
– ORIGIN C16 (earlier (ME) as *generation*), in the sense 'beget, procreate': from L. *generat-*, *generare*, 'create', from *genus*, *gener-* 'stock, race'.

**generation** ● **n.** **1** all of the people born and living at about the same time, regarded collectively. ➤the average period in which children grow up and have children of their own (usually reckoned as about thirty years). **2** a set of members of a family regarded as a single step or stage in descent. **3** the action of producing or generating.

➤ the propagation of living organisms; procreation.
– DERIVATIVES **generational** adj.

**generation gap** ● n. a difference in attitudes between people of different generations, leading to lack of understanding.

**Generation X** ● n. the generation born between the mid 1960s and the mid 1970s, perceived as being disaffected and directionless.
– DERIVATIVES **Generation Xer** n.

**generative** /ˈdʒɛn(ə)rətɪv/ ● adj. **1** relating to or capable of production or reproduction. **2** Linguistics relating to the application of a set of rules in order to produce all and only the well-formed items of a language.

**generative grammar** ● n. grammar which describes a language in terms of a set of logical rules whereby the infinite number of possible sentences of that language can be generated.

**generator** ● n. **1** a person or thing that generates. **2** a dynamo or similar machine for converting mechanical energy into electricity.

**generic** /dʒɪˈnɛrɪk/ ● adj. **1** referring to a class or group; not specific. **2** (of goods, especially medicinal drugs) having no brand name. **3** Biology relating to a genus.
– DERIVATIVES **generically** adv.
– ORIGIN C17: from Fr. *générique*, from L. *genus, gener-* 'stock, race'.

**generous** ● adj. **1** freely giving more of something than is necessary or expected. ➤ kind towards others. **2** larger or more plentiful than is usual.
– DERIVATIVES **generosity** n. **generously** adv. **generousness** n.
– ORIGIN C16 (ME as *generosity*), in sense 'of noble birth': via OFr. from L. *generosus* 'noble, magnanimous'.

**genesis** /ˈdʒɛnɪsɪs/ ● n. the origin or mode of formation of something. ➤ (**Genesis**) the first book of the Bible, which includes the story of the creation of the world.
– ORIGIN OE, via L. from Gk, 'generation, creation', from the base of *gignesthai* 'be born or produced'.

**genet** /ˈdʒɛnɪt/ ● n. a nocturnal catlike mammal with short legs and a long bushy ringed tail, found in Africa, SW Europe, and Arabia. [*Genetta genetta* and related species.]
– ORIGIN ME: from OFr. *genete*, prob. via Catalan, Port., or Sp. from Arab. *jarnaiṭ*.

**gene therapy** ● n. the introduction of normal genes into cells in place of missing or defective ones in order to correct genetic disorders.

**genetic** /dʒɪˈnɛtɪk/ ● adj. **1** of or relating to genes or heredity. ➤ of or relating to genetics. **2** of or relating to origin, or arising from a common origin.
– DERIVATIVES **genetical** adj. **genetically** adv.
– ORIGIN C19: from GENESIS.

**genetic code** ● n. the means by which DNA and RNA molecules carry genetic information in living cells.

**genetic engineering** ● n. the deliberate modification of the characteristics of an organism by manipulating its genetic material.

**genetic fingerprinting** (also **genetic profiling**) ● n. the analysis of DNA from samples of body tissues or fluids in order to identify individuals.

**genetic pollution** ● n. the spread of altered genes from genetically engineered organisms to other, non-engineered organisms, especially by cross-pollination.

**genetics** ● pl. n. **1** [treated as sing.] the study of heredity and the variation of inherited characteristics. **2** [treated as sing. or pl.] the genetic properties or features of an organism.
– DERIVATIVES **geneticist** n.

**Geneva bands** ● pl. n. two white cloth strips attached to the collar of some Protestants' clerical dress.
– ORIGIN *Geneva* in Switzerland, where orig. worn by Calvinists.

**genever** /dʒɪˈniːvə/ ● n. Dutch gin.
– ORIGIN C18: from Du., from OFr. *genevre*, from an alt. of L. *juniperus* (gin being flavoured with juniper berries).

**genial**[1] /ˈdʒiːnɪəl/ ● adj. **1** friendly and cheerful. **2** poetic/literary (of weather) pleasantly mild and warm.
– DERIVATIVES **geniality** n. **genially** adv.
– ORIGIN C16: from L. *genialis* 'nuptial, productive', from *genius* (see GENIUS).

**genial**[2] /dʒɪˈniːəl/ ● adj. Anatomy, rare relating to the chin.
– ORIGIN C19: from Gk *geneion* 'chin' + -AL.

**genic** /ˈdʒiːnɪk, ˈdʒɛn-/ ● adj. Biology of or relating to genes.

**-genic** ● comb. form **1** producing or produced by: *carcinogenic*. **2** well suited to: *mediagenic*. See word-formation panel.
– DERIVATIVES **-genically** suffix forming corresponding adverbs.
– ORIGIN from -GEN + -IC.

**geniculate** /dʒɪˈnɪkjʊlət/ ● adj. Anatomy bent at a sharp angle.
– ORIGIN C17: from L. *geniculatus*, from *geniculum* 'small knee, joint (of a plant)'.

**geniculate body** (also **geniculate nucleus**) ● n. Anatomy either of two protuberances on the thalamus which relay auditory or visual impulses to the cerebral cortex.

**genie** ● n. (pl. **genii** /ˈdʒiːnɪʌɪ/ or **genies**) (in Arabian folklore) a jinn or spirit, especially one imprisoned within a bottle or oil lamp and capable of granting wishes when summoned.
– ORIGIN C17 (denoting a guardian or protective spirit): from Fr. *génie*, from L. *genius* (see GENIUS), adopted in current sense because of its resemblance to Arab. *jinnī* 'jinn'.

**genii** plural form of GENIE, GENIUS.

**genip** /gɛˈnɪp/ (also **guinep**) ● n. the edible fruit of a tropical American tree.
– ORIGIN C18: from Amer. Sp. *quenepo, quenepa*.

**genipapo** /ˌdʒɛnɪˈpapəʊ/ (also **genipap** /ˈdʒɛnɪpap/) ● n. **1** a tropical American tree bearing a fruit with a jelly-like pulp which is used for flavouring drinks and to make a black dye. [*Genipa americana*.] **2** a drink, flavouring, or dye made from this fruit.
– ORIGIN C17: from Port. *jenipapo*, from Tupi.

**genital** ● adj. **1** of or relating to the human or animal reproductive organs. **2** Psychoanalysis relating to or denoting the final stage of psychosexual development reached in adulthood. ● n. (**genitals**) a person or animal's external organs of reproduction.
– ORIGIN ME: from OFr., or from L. *genitalis*, from *genit-*, *gignere* 'beget'.

**genitalia** /ˌdʒɛnɪˈteɪlɪə/ ● pl. n. formal or technical the genitals.

**genitive** /ˈdʒɛnɪtɪv/ Grammar ● adj. denoting a case indicating possession or close association. ● n. a word in the genitive case.
– DERIVATIVES **genitival** /-ˈtʌɪv(ə)l/ adj. **genitivally** adv.
– ORIGIN ME: from OFr. *genitif, -ive* or L. *genitivus* (*casus*) '(case) of production or origin', from *gignere* 'beget'.

**genitor** /ˈdʒɛnɪtə/ ● n. Anthropology a person's biological father. Often contrasted with PATER.
– ORIGIN ME: from OFr. *geniteur* or L. *genitor*, from the root of *gignere* 'beget'.

**genito-urinary** /ˌdʒɛnɪtəʊˈjʊərɪn(ə)ri/ ● adj. chiefly Medicine of or relating to the genital and urinary organs.

**geniture** /ˈdʒɛnɪtʃə/ ● n. archaic a person's birth or parentage.
– ORIGIN ME: from OFr. *geniture* or L. *genitura*, from the root of *gignere* 'beget'.

**genius** ● n. (pl. **geniuses**) **1** exceptional intellectual or creative power or other natural ability. **2** an exceptionally intelligent or able person. **3** (pl. **genii** /-nɪʌɪ/) (in some mythologies) a spirit associated with a person, place, or institution. **4** the prevalent character or spirit of a nation, period, etc.
– ORIGIN ME: from L., from the root of *gignere* 'beget'.

**genius loci** /ˈləʊsʌɪ, ˈlɒkiː/ ● n. the prevailing character or atmosphere of a place.
– ORIGIN L., lit. 'spirit of the place'.

**Genizah** /gɛˈniːzə/ ● n. a room attached to a synagogue and housing damaged, discarded, or heretical texts and relics.
– ORIGIN from Heb. *gĕnīzāh*, lit. 'hiding place'.

**genlock** /ˈdʒɛnlɒk/ ● n. a device for synchronizing two different video signals, or a video signal and a computer or audio signal, enabling video images and computer graphics to be mixed.

## Word *Formation*

**-genic** based on Greek *genēs* 'born'

➤ **1.** With the sense 'producing or produced by':

| | | |
|---|---|---|
| abiogenic | resulting from spontaneous generation | Gk *a-* 'without' + *bios* 'life' |
| allergenic | causing an allergic reaction | based on ALLERGY |
| allogenic | (in geology) transported from elsewhere | Gk *allos* 'other' |
| authigenic | (in geology) formed in the present position | Gk *authigenēs* 'born on the spot' |
| carcinogenic | having the potential to cause cancer | Gk *karkinos* 'crab' (see CANCER) |
| cryogenics | the production of very low temperatures (e.g. as a way of keeping a human being alive) | Gk *kruos* 'frost' |
| cryptogenic | (of a disease) of unknown origin | Gk *kruptos* 'hidden' |
| erotogenic | another term for EROGENOUS | Gk *erōs, erōt-* 'sexual love' |
| eugenics | the science of controlled breeding in a population | Gk *eu* 'well' |
| hypo-allergenic | not causing an allergic reaction | Gk *hupo* 'under' + ALLERGY |
| neurogenic | originating in the nervous system | Gk *neuron* 'nerve' |
| pathogenic | producing disease | Gk *pathos* 'disease' |
| pyrogenic | inducing fever | Gk *pur* 'fire' |

➤ Related words:

-gen forming nouns, as ***pathogen*** 'a bacterium, virus, etc. that can cause disease'

➤ **2.** With the sense 'well suited to':

The term ***photogenic*** is the earliest in this sense (first recorded in the 1920s): the others are formed by analogy with it, as ***telegenic*** 'well suited to television', ***mediagenic***, ***radiogenic***, etc.

– ORIGIN 1960s: from **GENERATOR** + **LOCK**[1].

**genoa** /ˈdʒɛnəʊə, dʒɛˈnəʊə/ (also **genoa jib**) ● **n.** Sailing a large jib or foresail whose foot extends aft of the mast, used especially on racing yachts.
– ORIGIN *Genoa*, a city in Italy.

**Genoa cake** ● **n.** a rich fruit cake with almonds on top.

**genocide** /ˈdʒɛnəsʌɪd/ ● **n.** the deliberate killing of a very large number of people from a particular ethnic group or nation.
– DERIVATIVES **genocidal** adj.
– ORIGIN 1940s: from Gk *genos* 'race' + **-CIDE**.

**genome** /ˈdʒiːnəʊm/ ● **n.** Biology **1** the haploid set of chromosomes of an organism. **2** the complete set of genetic material of an organism.
– DERIVATIVES **genomic** adj.
– ORIGIN 1930s: blend of **GENE** and **CHROMOSOME**.

**genomics** ● **pl. n.** [treated as sing.] the branch of molecular biology concerned with the structure, function, evolution, and mapping of genomes.

**genotype** /ˈdʒɛnətʌɪp, ˈdʒiːn-/ ● **n.** Biology the genetic constitution of an individual organism. Often contrasted with **PHENOTYPE**.
– DERIVATIVES **genotypic** /-ˈtɪpɪk/ adj.

**-genous** ● **comb. form 1** producing; inducing: *erogenous*. **2** originating in: *endogenous*.
– ORIGIN from **-GEN** + **-OUS**.

**genre** /ˈʒɒ̃rə, ˈ(d)ʒɒnrə/ ● **n. 1** a style or category of art or literature. **2** [as modifier] denoting a style of painting depicting scenes from ordinary life.
– ORIGIN C19: Fr., lit. 'a kind' (see **GENDER**).

**gens** /dʒɛnz/ ● **n.** (pl. **gentes** /-tiːz, -teɪz/) **1** a group of families in ancient Rome who shared a name and claimed a common origin. **2** Anthropology a group of people who are related through their male ancestors.
– ORIGIN L., from the root of *gignere* 'beget'.

**gent** ● **n.** informal a gentleman. ➤ **(the Gents)** Brit. a men's public toilet.

**genteel** ● **adj.** affectedly polite and refined.
– DERIVATIVES **genteelism** n. **genteelly** adv. **genteelness** n.
– ORIGIN C16 from Fr. *gentil* 'well-born'.

**gentian** /ˈdʒɛnʃ(ə)n/ ● **n.** a plant of temperate and mountainous regions with violet or blue trumpet-shaped flowers. [Genera *Gentiana* and *Gentianella*.]
– ORIGIN ME: from L. *gentiana*, allegedly named after *Gentius*, king of Illyria, who discovered the plant's medicinal properties.

**gentian violet** ● **n.** a synthetic violet dye derived from rosaniline, used as an antiseptic.

**gentile** /ˈdʒɛntʌɪl/ ● **adj. 1** (**Gentile**) not Jewish. **2** not belonging to one's own religious community, in particular (historical) non-Mormon. **3** chiefly Anthropology relating to or indicating a nation or clan, especially a gens. ● **n.** (**Gentile**) a person who is not Jewish.
– ORIGIN ME: from L. *gentilis* 'of a family or nation, of the same clan', from *gens, gent-* 'family, race'.

**gentility** /dʒɛnˈtɪlɪti/ ● **n.** socially superior or genteel character or behaviour.
– ORIGIN ME (in the sense 'honourable birth'): from OFr. *gentilite*, from *gentil* (see **GENTLE**[1]).

**gentle**[1] ● **adj.** (**-er, -est**) **1** mild and kind. **2** moderate: *a gentle breeze*. **3** archaic noble or courteous. ● **v.** make or become gentle. ➤ touch gently.
– DERIVATIVES **gentleness** n. **gently** adv.
– ORIGIN ME: from OFr. *gentil* 'high-born, noble', from L. *gentilis* (see **GENTILE**).

**gentle**[2] ● **n.** Fishing a maggot, especially the larva of a blowfly, used as bait.
– ORIGIN C16: prob. from an obs. sense of **GENTLE**[1], 'soft, pliant'.

**gentlefolk** ● **pl. n.** archaic people of noble birth or good social position.

**gentleman** ● **n.** (pl. **-men**) **1** a courteous or honourable

man. **2** a man of good social position, especially one of wealth and leisure. **3** (in polite or formal use) a man.
– DERIVATIVES **gentlemanliness** n. **gentlemanly** adj.

**gentleman-at-arms** • n. one of the bodyguards of the British monarch on ceremonial occasions.

**gentleman farmer** • n. (pl. **gentlemen farmers**) a country gentleman who has a farm as part of his estate.

**gentleman's agreement** • n. an arrangement or understanding which is based on trust rather than being legally binding.

**gentleman's gentleman** • n. a valet.

**gentlewoman** • n. (pl. **-women**) archaic a woman of noble birth or good social standing.

**gentoo** /dʒɛn'tuː/ • n. a tall penguin with a white triangular patch above the eye. [*Pygoscelis papua*.]
– ORIGIN C19: perh. from Anglo-Ind. *Gentoo* 'a Hindu', from Port. *gentio* 'gentile'.

**gentrify** • v. (**-ies**, **-ied**) renovate and improve (a house or district) so that it conforms to middle-class taste.
– DERIVATIVES **gentrification** n. **gentrifier** n.

**gentry** /'dʒɛntri/ • n. **1** (**the gentry**) people of good social position, specifically the class next below the nobility. **2** derogatory or humorous people of a specified kind: *devices beyond the comprehension of all but the bespectacled gentry who invented them.*
– ORIGIN ME (in the sense 'superiority of birth or rank'): from Anglo-Norman Fr. *genterie*, based on *gentil* (see GENTLE[1]).

**genuflect** /'dʒɛnjʊflɛkt/ • v. lower one's body briefly by bending one knee to the ground in worship or as a sign of respect.
– DERIVATIVES **genuflection** (also **genuflexion**) n. **genuflector** n.
– ORIGIN C17 (earlier (ME) as *genuflection*): from eccles. L. *genuflectere*, from L. *genu* 'knee' + *flectere* 'to bend'.

**genuine** • adj. **1** truly what it is said to be; authentic. **2** sincere; honest.
– DERIVATIVES **genuinely** adv. **genuineness** n.
– ORIGIN C16: from L. *genuinus*, from *genu* 'knee' (with ref. to the Roman custom of a father acknowledging paternity of a newborn child by placing it on his knee); later assoc. with *genus* 'birth, race, stock'.

**genus** /'dʒiːnəs, 'dʒɛnəs/ • n. (pl. **genera** /'dʒɛn(ə)rə/) **1** Biology a principal taxonomic category that ranks above species and below family, denoted by a capitalized Latin name, e.g. *Leo*. **2** a class of things which have common characteristics and which can be divided into subordinate kinds.
– ORIGIN C16: from L., 'birth, race, stock'.

**-geny** • comb. form denoting the mode by which something develops or is produced: *orogeny.*
– ORIGIN rel. to Fr. *-génie*; both forms derive from Gk *-geneia*, from *gen-* (root of *gignomai* 'be born, become' and *genos* 'a kind').

**Geo.** • abbrev. dated George.

**geo-** /'dʒiːəʊ/ • comb. form of or relating to the earth: *geocentric.*
– ORIGIN from Gk *gē* 'earth'.

**geobotany** • n. another term for PHYTOGEOGRAPHY.
– DERIVATIVES **geobotanical** adj. **geobotanist** n.

**geocentric** • adj. **1** having or representing the earth as the centre, as in former astronomical systems. Compare with HELIOCENTRIC. **2** Astronomy measured from or considered in relation to the centre of the earth.
– DERIVATIVES **geocentrically** adv. **geocentrism** n.

**geocentric latitude** • n. the latitude at which a planet would appear if viewed from the centre of the earth.

**geochemistry** • n. the study of the chemical composition of the earth and its rocks and minerals.
– DERIVATIVES **geochemical** adj. **geochemist** n.

**geochronology** • n. the branch of geology concerned with the dating of rock formations and geological events.
– DERIVATIVES **geochronological** adj. **geochronologist** n.

**geochronometric** /ˌdʒiːə(ʊ)ˌkrɒnə'mɛtrɪk/ • adj. of or relating to geochronological measurement.
– DERIVATIVES **geochronometry** n.

**geode** /'dʒiːəʊd/ • n. a small cavity in rock lined with crystals or other mineral matter. ➤a rock containing such a cavity.
– DERIVATIVES **geodic** /dʒiː'ɒdɪk/ adj.
– ORIGIN C17: via L. from Gk *geōdēs* 'earthy'.

**geodesic** /ˌdʒiːə(ʊ)'dɛsɪk, -'diːsɪk/ • adj. **1** relating to or denoting the shortest possible line between two points on a sphere or other curved surface. **2** (of a dome) constructed from struts which follow geodesic lines and form an open framework of triangles and polygons. **3** another term for GEODETIC.

**geodesy** /dʒɪ'ɒdɪsi/ • n. the branch of mathematics concerned with the shape and area of the earth or large portions of it.
– DERIVATIVES **geodesist** n.
– ORIGIN C16: from mod. L. *geodaesia*, from Gk *geōdaisia*, from *gē* 'earth' + *daiein* 'to divide'.

**geodetic** /ˌdʒiːə(ʊ)'dɛtɪk/ • adj. of or relating to geodesy, especially as applied to land surveying.

**geoduck** /'dʒiːəʊdʌk/ • n. a giant mud-burrowing bivalve mollusc found on the west coast of North America. [*Panopea generosa*.]
– ORIGIN C19: from Chinook Jargon.

**geographical** • adj. of or relating to geography.
– DERIVATIVES **geographic** adj. **geographically** adv.

**geographical latitude** • n. the angle made with the plane of the equator by a perpendicular to the earth's surface at any point.

**geographical mile** • n. a distance equal to one minute of longitude or latitude at the equator (about 1,850 metres).

**geography** • n. **1** the study of the physical features of the earth and of human activity as it relates to these. **2** the relative arrangement of places and physical features.
– DERIVATIVES **geographer** n.
– ORIGIN C15: from Fr. *géographie* or L. *geographia*, from Gk *geōgraphia*, from *gē* 'earth' + *-graphia* 'writing'.

**geoid** /'dʒiːɔɪd/ • n. (**the geoid**) the shape of the earth taken as mean sea level and its imagined extension under (or over) land areas.
– ORIGIN C19: from Gk *geoeidēs*, from *gē* 'earth' + *-oeidēs* (see **-OID**).

**geology** • n. **1** the science which deals with the physical structure and substance of the earth. **2** the geological features of a district.
– DERIVATIVES **geologic** adj. **geological** adj. **geologically** adv. **geologist** n. **geologize** (also **-ise**) v.
– ORIGIN C18: from mod. L. *geologia*, from Gk *gē* 'earth' + *-logia* (see **-LOGY**).

**geomagnetism** • n. the branch of geology concerned with the magnetic properties of the earth.
– DERIVATIVES **geomagnetic** adj. **geomagnetically** adv.

**geomancy** /'dʒiːə(ʊ)mansi/ • n. **1** the art of siting buildings auspiciously. **2** divination from the configuration of a handful of earth or random dots.
– DERIVATIVES **geomantic** adj.

**geometer** /dʒɪ'ɒmɪtə/ • n. **1** a person skilled in geometry. **2** Entomology a geometrid moth or its caterpillar.

**geometric** /ˌdʒɪə'mɛtrɪk/ • adj. **1** of or relating to geometry. **2** (of a design) characterized by or decorated with regular lines and shapes. ➤(**Geometric**) Archaeology of or denoting a period of Greek culture (*c.* 900–700 BC) characterized by geometrically decorated pottery. ➤(**Geometric**) Architecture relating to or denoting a style of early English Decorated tracery based on the geometry of circles.
– DERIVATIVES **geometrical** adj. **geometrically** adv.

**geometric mean** • n. the central number in a geometric progression (e.g. 9 in 3, 9, 27), also calculable as the nth root of a product of n numbers.

**geometric progression** (also **geometric series**) • n. a sequence of numbers with a constant ratio between each number and the one before (e.g. 1, 3, 9, 27, 81).

**geometrid** /dʒɪ'ɒmɪtrɪd/ • n. Entomology a moth of a large family (Geometridae), distinguished by having twig-like caterpillars that move by looping and straightening the

body.
– ORIGIN C19: from mod. L. *Geometridae*, from the genus name *Geometra*, from L. *geometres* 'geometer'.

**geometry** /dʒɪˈɒmɪtri/ ● **n.** (pl. **-ies**) **1** the branch of mathematics concerned with the properties and relations of points, lines, surfaces, solids, and higher dimensional analogues. **2** the shape and relative arrangement of the parts of something.
– DERIVATIVES **geometrician** /ˌdʒiːəmɪˈtrɪʃ(ə)n/ n.
– ORIGIN ME: via OFr. from L. *geometria*, from Gk, from *gē* 'earth' + *metria* (see **-METRY**).

**geomorphic** /ˌdʒiːə(ʊ)ˈmɔːfɪk/ ● **adj.** of or relating to the form of the landscape and other natural features of the earth's surface.

**geomorphology** /ˌdʒiːə(ʊ)mɔːˈfɒlədʒi/ ● **n.** the study of the physical features of the surface of the earth and their relation to its geological structures.
– DERIVATIVES **geomorphological** adj. **geomorphologist** n.

**geophagy** /dʒɪˈɒfədʒi/ ● **n.** the practice in some tribal societies of eating earth.
– ORIGIN C19: from **GEO-** + Gk *phagia* 'eating, feeding' (from *phagein* 'eat').

**geophysics** ● **pl. n.** [treated as sing.] the physics of the earth.
– DERIVATIVES **geophysical** adj. **geophysicist** n.

**geopolitics** ● **pl. n.** [treated as sing. or pl.] politics, especially international relations, as influenced by geographical factors.
– DERIVATIVES **geopolitical** adj. **geopolitically** adv. **geopolitician** n.

**Geordie** ● **n.** Brit. informal a person from Tyneside.
– ORIGIN C19: dimin. of the given name *George*.

**georgette** /dʒɔːˈdʒɛt/ ● **n.** a thin silk or crêpe dress material.
– ORIGIN C20: named after the Fr. dressmaker *Georgette* de la Plante.

**Georgian**[1] ● **adj. 1** of or characteristic of the reigns of the British Kings George I–IV (1714–1830). ➤ relating to British architecture of this period, characterized by restrained elegance and the use of neoclassical styles. **2** of or characteristic of the reigns of the British Kings George V and VI (1910–52). ➤ relating to a style of British pastoral poetry of 1910–20.

**Georgian**[2] ● **n. 1** a native or national of the country of Georgia. **2** the official language of Georgia, the main member of the small South Caucasian family. ● **adj.** of or relating to Georgia, its people, or their language.

**Georgian**[3] ● **n.** a native or inhabitant of the US state of Georgia. ● **adj.** of or relating to Georgia.

**georgic** /ˈdʒɔːdʒɪk/ ● **n.** a poem or book concerned with agriculture or rural topics. ● **adj.** poetic/literary rustic; pastoral.
– ORIGIN C16: via L. from Gk *geōrgikos*, from *geōrgos* 'farmer'.

**geoscience** ● **n.** (also **geosciences**) earth sciences, especially geology.
– DERIVATIVES **geoscientist** n.

**geostationary** ● **adj.** (of an artificial satellite) moving in a circular geosynchronous orbit so that it appears to be stationary above a fixed point on the surface.

**geostrophic** /ˌdʒiːə(ʊ)ˈstrɒfɪk, -ˈstrəʊf-/ ● **adj.** Meteorology & Oceanography denoting the component of a wind or current that arises from the balance between pressure gradients and coriolis forces.
– ORIGIN C20: from **GEO-** + Gk *strophē* 'a turn'.

**geosynchronous** /ˌdʒiːə(ʊ)ˈsɪŋkrənəs/ ● **adj.** another term for **SYNCHRONOUS** (in sense 2).

**geotechnics** ● **pl. n.** [treated as sing.] the branch of civil engineering concerned with the study and modification of soil and rocks.
– DERIVATIVES **geotechnic** adj. **geotechnical** adj.

**geothermal** ● **adj.** relating to or produced by the internal heat of the earth.

**geotropism** /ˌdʒiːə(ʊ)ˈtrəʊpɪz(ə)m/ ● **n.** Botany the growth of the parts of plants in response to the force of gravity.
– DERIVATIVES **geotropic** adj.
– ORIGIN C19: from **GEO-** + Gk *tropē* 'turning' + **-ISM**.

**geraniol** /dʒɪˈreɪnɪɒl/ ● **n.** Chemistry a fragrant liquid present in some floral oils and used in perfumery.
– ORIGIN C19: from Ger., from **GERANIUM** + **-OL**.

**geranium** /dʒɪˈreɪnɪəm/ ● **n.** a herbaceous plant or small shrub of a genus that comprises the cranesbills and their relatives. [Genus *Geranium*.] ➤ (in general use) a cultivated pelargonium.
– ORIGIN mod. L., from Gk *geranion*, from *geranos* 'crane'.

**gerbera** /ˈdʒəːb(ə)rə, ˈɡəː-/ ● **n.** a tropical plant of the daisy family, with large brightly coloured flowers. [Genus *Gerbera*: many species.]
– ORIGIN mod. L., named after the Ger. naturalist Traugott *Gerber* (died 1743).

**gerbil** /ˈdʒəːbɪl/ ● **n.** a burrowing mouse-like rodent found in arid regions of Africa and Asia. [*Gerbillus* and other genera: many species.]
– ORIGIN C19: from Fr. *gerbille*, from mod. L. *gerbillus*, dimin. of *gerboa* (see **JERBOA**).

**gerenuk** /ˈɡɛrənʊk/ ● **n.** a slender East African antelope with a long neck, often browsing on tall bushes by standing on its hind legs. [*Litocranius walleri*.]
– ORIGIN C19: from Somali.

**geriatric** /ˌdʒɛrɪˈatrɪk/ ● **adj. 1** of or relating to old people. **2** informal decrepit or out of date. ● **n.** an old person, especially one receiving special care.
– ORIGIN 1920s: from Gk *gēras* 'old age' + *iatros* 'doctor', on the pattern of *paediatric*.

**geriatrics** ● **pl. n.** [treated as sing. or pl.] the branch of medicine or social science concerned with the health and care of old people.
– DERIVATIVES **geriatrician** n.

**germ** ● **n. 1** a micro-organism, especially one which causes disease. **2** a portion of an organism capable of developing into a new one or part of one. ➤ the embryo in a cereal grain or other plant seed. **3** an initial stage from which something may develop: *the germ of a brilliant idea*.
– DERIVATIVES **germy** adj. (informal).
– ORIGIN ME: via OFr. from L. *germen* 'seed, sprout'.

**German** ● **n. 1** a native or national of Germany, or a person of German descent. **2** the West Germanic language of Germany, Austria, and parts of Switzerland. ● **adj.** of or relating to Germany, its people, or their language.
– DERIVATIVES **Germanist** n. **Germanization** (also **-isation**) n. **Germanize** (also **-ise**) v. **Germanizer** (also **-iser**) n.

**german** ● **adj.** archaic germane.
– ORIGIN ME: from OFr. *germain*, from L. *germanus* 'genuine, of the same parents'.

**germander** /dʒəˈmandə/ ● **n.** a plant of the mint family, some kinds of which are cultivated as ornamentals. [Genus *Teucrium*: many species.]
– ORIGIN ME: from med. L. *germandra*, based on Gk *khamaidrus*, lit. 'ground oak' (because the leaves of some species were thought to resemble those of the oak).

**germander speedwell** ● **n.** a speedwell with bright blue flowers and leaves resembling those of the germander. [*Veronica chamaedrys*.]

**germane** /dʒəːˈmeɪn/ ● **adj.** relevant to a subject under consideration.
– DERIVATIVES **germanely** adv. **germaneness** n.
– ORIGIN C17: var. of **GERMAN**.

**Germanic** ● **adj. 1** relating to or denoting the branch of the Indo-European language family that includes English, German, Dutch, Frisian, and the Scandinavian languages. ➤ relating to or denoting the peoples of ancient northern and western Europe speaking such languages. **2** characteristic of Germans or Germany. ● **n. 1** the Germanic languages collectively. **2** the unrecorded ancient language from which these developed.

**germanium** /dʒəːˈmeɪnɪəm/ ● **n.** the chemical element of atomic number 32, a shiny grey semimetal. (Symbol: **Ge**)
– ORIGIN C19: mod. L., from L. *Germanus* 'German'.

**German measles** ● **pl. n.** [usu. treated as sing.] another term for **RUBELLA**.

**Germano-** /dʒəːˈmanəʊ, ˈdʒəːmənəʊ/ ● **comb. form** German; German and ...: *Germanophile*. ➤ relating to Germany: *Germanocentric.*

**German shepherd** • **n.** a large dog of a breed often used as guard dogs or for police work; an Alsatian.

**German silver** • **n.** a white alloy of nickel, zinc, and copper.

**germ cell** • **n.** Biology a gamete, or an embryonic cell with the potential of developing into one.

**germicide** • **n.** a substance or other agent which destroys harmful micro-organisms.
– DERIVATIVES **germicidal** adj.

**germinal** • **adj. 1** relating to or of the nature of a germ cell or embryo. **2** in the earliest stage of development. ➤providing material for future development.
– DERIVATIVES **germinally** adv.
– ORIGIN C19: from L. *germen, germin-* 'sprout, seed' + **-AL**.

**germinate** /ˈdʒəːmɪneɪt/ • **v.** (of a seed or spore) begin to grow and put out shoots after a period of dormancy.
– DERIVATIVES **germination** n. **germinative** adj. **germinator** n.
– ORIGIN C16: from L. *germinat-, germinare* 'sprout forth, bud', from *germen, germin-* 'sprout, seed'.

**germ layer** • **n.** Embryology each of the three layers of cells (ectoderm, mesoderm, and endoderm) that are formed in the early embryo.

**germ line** • **n.** Biology a series of germ cells each descended or developed from earlier cells in the series, regarded as continuing through successive generations of an organism.

**germ plasm** • **n.** Biology germ cells collectively.

**germ warfare** • **n.** the use of disease-spreading micro-organisms as a military weapon.

**Geronimo** /dʒəˈrɒnɪməʊ/ • **exclam.** used to express exhilaration when leaping or moving quickly.
– ORIGIN Second World War: adopted as a slogan by Amer. paratroopers, by assoc. with the Apache chief *Geronimo.*

**gerontic** /dʒɛˈrɒntɪk/ • **adj.** technical of or relating to old age.
– ORIGIN C19: from Gk *gerōn, geront-* 'old man' + **-IC**.

**gerontocracy** /ˌdʒɛrənˈtɒkrəsi/ • **n.** a state, society, or group governed by old people. ➤government based on rule by old people.
– DERIVATIVES **gerontocrat** n. **gerontocratic** adj.

**gerontology** /ˌdʒɛrənˈtɒlədʒi/ • **n.** the scientific study of old age and old people.
– DERIVATIVES **gerontological** adj. **gerontologist** n.

**-gerous** • **comb. form** bearing (a specified thing): *armigerous.*
– ORIGIN from L. *-ger* 'bearing' (from the root of *gerere* 'to bear, carry') + **-OUS**.

**gerrymander** /ˈdʒɛrɪˌmandə/ (Brit. also **jerrymander**) • **v.** [often as noun **gerrymandering**] manipulate the boundaries of (an electoral constituency) so as to favour one party or class.
– DERIVATIVES **gerrymanderer** n.
– ORIGIN C19: from the name of Governor Elbridge *Gerry* of Massachusetts + **SALAMANDER**, from the supposed similarity between a salamander and the shape of a new voting district created when he was in office, which was felt to favour his party.

**gerund** /ˈdʒɛrʌnd/ • **n.** Grammar a verb form which functions as a noun, in Latin ending in *-ndum* (declinable), in English ending in *-ing* (e.g. *asking* in *do you mind my asking you?*).
– ORIGIN C16: from late L. *gerundium,* from *gerundum,* var. of *gerendum,* the gerund of L. *gerere* 'do'.

**gerundive** /dʒəˈrʌndɪv/ • **n.** Grammar a form of a Latin verb, ending in *-ndus* (declinable) and functioning as an adjective meaning 'that should or must be done'.
– ORIGIN ME (in the sense 'gerund'): from late L. *gerundivus* (*modus*) 'gerundive (mood)', from *gerundium* (see **GERUND**).

**Gesellschaft** /gəˈzɛlʃaft/ • **n.** social relations based on impersonal ties, as duty to a society or organization. Often contrasted with **GEMEINSCHAFT**.
– ORIGIN Ger., from *Gesell(e)* 'companion' + *-schaft* (see **-SHIP**).

**gesneriad** /gɛsˈnɪərɪad, dʒɛs-/ • **n.** a tropical plant of a family (Gesneriaceae) that includes African violets, gloxinias, and their relatives.
– ORIGIN C19: from mod. L. *Gesneria* (genus name), from the name of the Swiss naturalist Conrad von *Gesner* + **-AD**[1].

**gesso** /ˈdʒɛsəʊ/ • **n.** (pl. **-oes**) a hard compound of plaster of Paris or whiting in glue, used in sculpture or as a base for gilding or painting on wood.
– ORIGIN C16: Ital., from L. *gypsum* (see **GYPSUM**).

**gestalt** /gəˈʃtɑːlt, -ˈʃtalt/ • **n.** Psychology an organized whole that is perceived as more than the sum of its parts.
– DERIVATIVES **gestaltism** n. **gestaltist** n.
– ORIGIN 1920s: from Ger. *Gestalt,* lit. 'form, shape'.

**gestalt psychology** • **n.** a movement in psychology seeking to explain perceptions as gestalts rather than analysing their constituents.

**gestalt therapy** • **n.** a psychotherapeutic approach focusing on insight into gestalts in patients and often using role playing.

**Gestapo** /gəˈstɑːpəʊ/ • **n.** the German secret police under Nazi rule.
– ORIGIN Ger., from *Geheime Staatspolizei* 'secret state police'.

**gestation** • **n. 1** the process of carrying or being carried in the womb between conception and birth. **2** the development of a plan or idea over a period of time.
– DERIVATIVES **gestate** v.
– ORIGIN C16 (denoting exercise in the form of riding or travelling in a carriage): from L. *gestatio(n-),* from *gestare* 'carry, carry in the womb'.

**gesticulate** /dʒɛˈstɪkjʊleɪt/ • **v.** gesture dramatically in place of or to emphasize speech.
– DERIVATIVES **gesticulation** n. **gesticulative** adj. **gesticulator** n. **gesticulatory** adj.
– ORIGIN C17 (earlier (ME) as *gesticulation*): from L. *gesticulat-, gesticulari,* from *gesticulus,* dimin. of *gestus* 'action'.

**gesture** • **n. 1** a movement of part of the body, especially a hand or the head, to express an idea or meaning. **2** an action performed to convey one's feelings or intentions: *a kind gesture.* ➤an action performed for show in the knowledge that it will have no effect. • **v.** make a gesture.
– DERIVATIVES **gestural** adj.
– ORIGIN ME: from med. L. *gestura,* from L. *gerere* 'bear, wield, perform'.

**gesundheit** /gɛˈzʌndhʌɪt, German gɛˈzʊnthaɪt/ • **exclam.** used to wish good health to a person who has just sneezed.
– ORIGIN from Ger. *Gesundheit* 'health'.

**get** • **v.** (**getting**; past **got**; past part. **got**, N. Amer. or archaic **gotten**) **1** come to have or hold; receive. ➤experience, suffer, or be afflicted with (something bad). **2** succeed in attaining, achieving, or experiencing; obtain. **3** move in order to pick up, deal with, or bring. ➤tend to meet with or find. ➤travel by or catch (a form of transport). **4** bring or come into a specified state or condition. ➤used with past participle to form the passive mood: *the cat got drowned.* ➤begin to be or do something, especially gradually or by chance: *we got talking.* **5** come or go eventually or with some difficulty: *I got to the airport.* ➤move or come into a specified position or state: *she got into the car.* **6** (**have got**) see **HAVE**. **7** catch, apprehend, or thwart. ➤strike or wound with a blow or missile. ➤informal punish, injure, or kill, especially as retribution. ➤(**get one's**) informal be killed or suffer retribution. **8** informal understand (an argument or the person making it). **9** archaic acquire (knowledge) by study. • **n. 1** dated an animal's offspring. **2** Brit. informal or dialect an unpleasant or stupid person.
– PHRASES **get one's own back** informal have one's revenge. **getting on for** chiefly Brit. almost (a specified time, age, or amount). **get someone with child** archaic make a woman pregnant.
– PHRASAL VERBS **get something across** manage to communicate an idea clearly. **get ahead** become successful in one's life or career. **get along 1** chiefly N. Amer. another way of saying ***get on*** (in sense 2). **2** manage to live or

survive. **get at 1** reach or gain access to. ➤bribe or unfairly influence. **2** informal imply. **3** Brit. informal criticize subtly and repeatedly. **get away 1** escape. **2** informal said to express disbelief or scepticism. **get away with** escape blame or punishment for. **get back at** take revenge on. **get by** manage with difficulty to live or accomplish something. **get down** N. Amer. informal dance energetically. **get down to** begin to do or give serious attention to. **get off 1** informal escape a punishment; be acquitted. **2** go to sleep. **3** (usu. **get off with**) Brit. informal have a sexual encounter. **4** (often **get off on**) informal, chiefly N. Amer. be excited or aroused. **get on 1** manage or make progress with a task. ➤chiefly Brit. be successful in one's life or career. **2** chiefly Brit. have a harmonious or friendly relationship. **3** (**be getting on**) informal be old or comparatively old. **get out of** contrive to avoid or escape. **get over 1** recover from (an ailment or an unpleasant experience). **2** overcome (a difficulty). **get something over 1** manage to communicate an idea or theory. **2** promptly complete an unpleasant or tedious but necessary task. **get round** (or N. Amer. **around**) chiefly Brit. **1** coax or persuade (someone) to do or allow something. **2** deal successfully with (a problem). ➤evade (a regulation or restriction) without contravening it. **get round to** (or N. Amer. **around to**) chiefly Brit. deal with (a task) in due course. **get through 1** pass or endure (a difficult experience or period). **2** chiefly Brit. use up (a large amount or number of something). **3** make contact by telephone. ➤succeed in communicating with someone. **get to 1** informal annoy or upset by persistent action. **2** another way of saying ***get round to***. **get together** gather or assemble socially or to cooperate. **get up 1** rise from bed after sleeping. **2** (of wind or the sea) become strong or agitated. **get someone up** (usu. **be got up**) dress someone in a specified smart, elaborate, or unusual way. **get something up** prepare or organize a project or piece of work. **get up to** Brit. informal be involved in (something illicit or surprising).

– DERIVATIVES **gettable** adj.

– ORIGIN ME: from ON *geta* 'obtain, beget, guess'; rel. to OE *gietan*.

**get-at-able** ● adj. informal accessible.

**getaway** ● n. **1** an escape or quick departure, especially after committing a crime. **2** informal a short holiday.

**get-out** ● n. Brit. a means of avoiding something.

– PHRASES **as —— as all get-out** N. Amer. informal as —— as is possible.

**getter** ● n. **1** [in combination] a person or thing that gets a specified desirable thing: *an attention-getter.* **2** Electronics & Physics a substance used to remove residual gas from a vacuum tube, or impurities or defects from a semiconductor crystal.

**get-together** ● n. an informal gathering.

**get-up** ● n. informal a style or arrangement of dress, especially an elaborate or unusual one.

**geum** /'dʒiːəm/ ● n. a plant of a genus which comprises the avens. [Genus *Geum*.]

– ORIGIN mod. L., var. of L. *gaeum*.

**GeV** ● abbrev. gigaelectronvolt, equivalent to $10^9$ electronvolts.

**gewgaw** /'gjuːgɔː/ ● n. a showy thing, especially one that is useless or worthless.

– ORIGIN ME: of unknown origin.

**Gewürztraminer** /gə'vʊətstrəˌmiːnə, German gə'vyrts traˌmiːnɐ/ ● n. a variety of white grape grown mainly in Alsace, Austria, and the Rhine valley. ➤a wine made from this grape.

– ORIGIN Ger., from *Gewürz* 'spice' + **TRAMINER**.

**geyser** /'giːzə, 'gʌɪ-/ ● n. **1** a hot spring in which water intermittently boils, sending a tall column of water and steam into the air. **2** /'giːzə/ Brit. a gas-fired water heater through which water flows as it is rapidly heated.

– ORIGIN C18: from Icelandic *Geysir*, the name of a particular spring in Iceland; rel. to *geysa* 'to gush'.

**geyserite** ● n. a hard opaline siliceous deposit occurring around geysers and hot springs.

**GG** ● abbrev. Brit. Governor General.

**GH** ● abbrev. Ghana (international vehicle registration).

**Ghanaian** /gɑː'neɪən/ ● n. a native or inhabitant of Ghana. ● adj. of or relating to Ghana.

**gharana** /gʌ'rɑːnə/ ● n. a school or method of Indian classical music or dance.

– ORIGIN from Hindi *gharānā* 'family'.

**gharial** /'garɪɑːl, ˌgʌrɪ'ɑːl, 'gɛːrɪəl/ (also **gavial**) ● n. a large fish-eating crocodile with a long narrow snout that widens at the nostrils, native to the Indian subcontinent. [*Gavialis gangeticus*.]

– ORIGIN C19: from Hindi *ghaṛiyāl*.

**ghastly** ● adj. (**-ier**, **-iest**) **1** causing great horror or fear; macabre. **2** deathly white or pallid. **3** informal very objectionable or unpleasant.

– DERIVATIVES **ghastliness** n.

– ORIGIN ME: from obs. *gast* 'terrify', from OE *gǣstan*, of Gmc origin; rel. to (and influenced in spelling by) **GHOST**.

**ghat** /gɑːt/ ● n. **1** (in the Indian subcontinent) a flight of steps leading down to a river. ➤a level place on the edge of a river where Hindus cremate their dead. **2** (in the Indian subcontinent) a mountain pass.

– ORIGIN from Hindi *ghāṭ*.

**ghazal** /'gʌzʌl/ ● n. a Middle Eastern or Indian lyric poem with a fixed number of verses and a repeated rhyme.

– ORIGIN via Pers. from Arab. *ġazal*.

**Ghazi** /'gɑːzi/ ● n. (pl. **Ghazis**) a Muslim fighter against non-Muslims.

– ORIGIN from Arab. *al-ġāzī*, part. of *ġazā* 'invade, raid'.

**GHB** ● abbrev. (sodium) gamma-hydroxybutyrate, a designer drug with anaesthetic properties.

**ghee** /giː/ ● n. clarified butter used in Indian cooking.

– ORIGIN from Hindi *ghī*, from Sanskrit *ghṛtá* 'sprinkled'.

**Gheg** /gɛg/ ● n. (pl. same or **Ghegs**) **1** a member of one of the two main ethnic groups of Albania, living mainly in the north of the country. Compare with **TOSK**. **2** the dialect of Albanian spoken by this people.

– ORIGIN from Albanian *Geg*.

**gherao** /gɛ'raʊ/ ● n. (pl. **-os**) Indian a protest in which workers prevent employers leaving a place of work until demands are met.

– ORIGIN from Hindi *gherāo* 'surround, besiege'.

**gherkin** /'gəːkɪn/ ● n. a small variety of cucumber, or a young green cucumber, used for pickling.

– ORIGIN C17: from Du. *augurkje*, *gurkje*, dimin. of *augurk*, *gurk*, from Slavic, based on med. Gk *angourion* 'cucumber'.

**ghetto** /'gɛtəʊ/ ● n. (pl. **-os** or **-oes**) **1** a part of a city, especially a slum area, occupied by a minority group. **2** historical the Jewish quarter in a city.

– DERIVATIVES **ghettoization** (also **-isation**) n. **ghettoize** (also **-ise**) v.

– ORIGIN C17: perh. from Ital. *getto* 'foundry' (because the first ghetto was established on the site of a foundry in Venice), or from Ital. *borghetto*, dimin. of *borgo* 'borough'.

**ghetto blaster** ● n. informal a large portable radio and cassette or CD player.

**Ghibelline** /'gɪbɪlʌɪn/ ● n. a member of one of the two great political factions in Italian medieval politics, traditionally supporting the Holy Roman emperor against the Pope and his supporters, the Guelphs.

– ORIGIN from Ital. *Ghibellino*, perh. from Ger. *Waiblingen*, an estate belonging to Hohenstaufen emperors.

**ghibli** /'gɪbli/ ● n. a hot, dry southerly wind of North Africa.

– ORIGIN C19: from Arab. *ḳiblī* 'southern'.

**ghillie** ● n. variant spelling of **GILLIE**.

**ghost** ● n. **1** an apparition of a dead person which is believed to appear to the living, typically as a nebulous image. ➤archaic a spirit or soul. **2** a faint trace: *the ghost of a smile.* **3** a faint secondary image produced by a fault in an optical system or on a cathode ray screen. ● v. **1** act as ghost writer of. **2** glide smoothly and effortlessly.

– PHRASES **the ghost in the machine** Philosophy the mind viewed as distinct from the body. **give up the ghost** die or stop functioning.

– DERIVATIVES **ghostlike** adj.

– ORIGIN OE *gāst*, of Gmc origin.

**ghosting** ● **n.** the appearance of a secondary image on a television or other display screen.

**ghostly** ● **adj.** (**-ier**, **-iest**) of or like a ghost; eerie and unnatural.
– DERIVATIVES **ghostliness** n.

**ghost town** ● **n.** a town with few or no remaining inhabitants.

**ghost train** ● **n.** a miniature train at a funfair that travels through a dark tunnel in which there are eerie effects.

**ghost word** ● **n.** a word which is recorded in a dictionary but is not actually used.

**ghostwriter** ● **n.** a person employed to write material for another person, who is the named author.
– DERIVATIVES **ghostwrite** v.

**ghoul** /guːl/ ● **n. 1** an evil spirit or phantom, especially one supposed to rob graves and feed on dead bodies. **2** a person morbidly interested in death or disaster.
– DERIVATIVES **ghoulish** adj. **ghoulishly** adv. **ghoulishness** n.
– ORIGIN C18: from Arab. *ġūl*, a desert demon believed to rob graves and devour corpses.

**GHQ** ● **abbrev.** General Headquarters.

**ghyll** ● **n.** variant spelling of **GILL**[3].

**GI** ● **n.** (pl. **GIs**) a private soldier in the US army.
– ORIGIN 1930s (orig. denoting equipment supplied to US forces): abbrev. of *government* (or *general*) *issue*.

**gi** /giː/ ● **n.** the loose white jacket worn in judo.
– ORIGIN from Japanese.

**giant** ● **n. 1** an imaginary or mythical being of human form but superhuman size. **2** an abnormally tall or large person, animal, or plant. **3** Astronomy a star of relatively great size and luminosity. ● **adj.** of very great size or force; gigantic.
– DERIVATIVES **giantess** n. **giantlike** adj.
– ORIGIN ME *geant*, from OFr., via L. from Gk *gigas*, *gigant-*.

**giantism** ● **n.** a tendency towards abnormally large size; gigantism.

**giant-killer** ● **n.** a person or team that defeats a seemingly much more powerful opponent.
– DERIVATIVES **giant-killing** n.

**giant slalom** ● **n.** a long-distance slalom with fast, wide turns.

**giant squid** ● **n.** a deep-sea squid which is the largest known invertebrate, reaching a length of 18 m (59 ft) or more. [Genus *Architeuthis*.]

**giant toad** ● **n.** another term for **CANE TOAD**.

**giaour** /ˈdʒaʊə/ ● **n.** archaic, derogatory a non-Muslim, especially a Christian.
– ORIGIN from Turk. *gâvur*, from Pers. *gaur*, prob. from Arab. *kāfir* (see **KAFFIR**).

**giardiasis** /ˌdʒɪɑːˈdʌɪəsɪs/ ● **n.** infection of the intestine with a flagellate protozoan.
– ORIGIN C20: from mod. L. *Giardia* (from the name of the Fr. biologist Alfred M. *Giard*) + **-ASIS**.

**gibber**[1] /ˈdʒɪbə, ˈgɪbə/ ● **v.** speak rapidly and unintelligibly, typically through fear or shock.
– DERIVATIVES **gibbering** adj.
– ORIGIN C17: imitative.

**gibber**[2] /ˈgɪbə/ ● **n.** Austral. a stone or boulder.
– ORIGIN from Dharuk *giba* 'stone'.

**gibberellin** /ˌdʒɪbəˈrɛlɪn/ ● **n.** any of a group of plant hormones that stimulate stem elongation, germination, and flowering.
– ORIGIN 1930s: from mod. L. *Gibberella*, dimin. of the genus name *Gibbera*, from L. *gibber* 'hump', + **-IN**[1].

**gibberish** /ˈdʒɪb(ə)rɪʃ, ˈgɪb-/ ● **n.** unintelligible or meaningless speech or writing; nonsense.
– ORIGIN C16: perh. from **GIBBER**[1] (but recorded earlier) + **-ISH**[1].

**gibbet** historical ● **n. 1** a gallows. **2** an upright post with an arm on which the bodies of executed criminals were left hanging as a warning or deterrent to others. ● **v.** (**gibbeted**, **gibbeting**) hang up on a gibbet or execute by hanging.
– ORIGIN ME: from OFr. *gibet* 'staff, cudgel, gallows', dimin. of *gibe* 'club, staff', prob. of Gmc origin.

**gibbon** ● **n.** a small, slender tree-dwelling ape with long, powerful arms, native to the forests of SE Asia. [Genus *Hylobates*: several species.]
– ORIGIN C18: from Fr., from an Ind. dial. word.

**gibbous** /ˈgɪbəs/ ● **adj. 1** (of the moon) having the illuminated part greater than a semicircle and less than a circle. **2** convex or protuberant.
– DERIVATIVES **gibbosity** /-ˈbɒsɪti/ n. **gibbously** adv. **gibbousness** n.
– ORIGIN ME: from late L. *gibbosus*, from L. *gibbus* 'hump'.

**Gibbs free energy** ● **n.** Chemistry a thermodynamic quantity equal to enthalpy minus the product of the entropy and the absolute temperature.
– ORIGIN C20: named after the Amer. chemist J. W. *Gibbs*.

**gibe** /dʒʌɪb/ ● **n. & v.** variant spelling of **JIBE**[1].

**giblets** /ˈdʒɪblɪts/ ● **pl. n.** the liver, heart, gizzard, and neck of a chicken or other fowl, usually removed before the bird is cooked.
– ORIGIN ME (in the sense 'an inessential appendage', later 'garbage, offal'): from OFr. *gibelet* 'game bird stew', prob. from *gibier* 'birds or mammals hunted for sport'.

**Gibraltarian** /dʒɪbrɔːlˈtɛːrɪən/ ● **n.** a native or inhabitant of Gibraltar. ● **adj.** of or relating to Gibraltar.

**Gibson girl** ● **n.** a girl typifying the fashionable ideal of the late 19th and early 20th centuries.
– ORIGIN represented in the work of the Amer. artist and illustrator Charles D. *Gibson*.

**gibus** /ˈdʒʌɪbəs/ ● **n.** a kind of collapsible top hat.
– ORIGIN C19: named after the Fr. hatter *Gibus*.

**gid** /gɪd/ ● **n.** a fatal disease of sheep and goats, marked by loss of balance and caused by larvae of the dog tapeworm encysted in the brain.
– ORIGIN C17: back-form. from **GIDDY**.

**giddy** ● **adj.** (**-ier**, **-iest**) **1** having or causing a sensation of whirling and a tendency to fall or stagger; dizzy. **2** excitable and frivolous. ● **v.** (**-ies**, **-ied**) make (someone) feel excited to the point of disorientation.
– PHRASES **play the giddy goat** dated act irresponsibly; fool around.
– DERIVATIVES **giddily** adv. **giddiness** n.
– ORIGIN OE *gidig* 'insane', lit. 'possessed by a god', from the base of **GOD**.

**giddy-up** ● **exclam.** said to induce a horse to start moving or go faster.
– ORIGIN 1920s (orig. US as *giddap*): reproducing a pronunc. of *get up*.

**gidgee** /ˈgɪdʒiː/ ● **n.** Austral. an Australian acacia with unpleasant-smelling foliage. [*Acacia cambagei*.]
– ORIGIN C19: from Wiradhuri *gijir*.

**GIF** ● **n.** Computing a popular format for image files, with built-in data compression. ➤ (also **gif**) a file in this format.
– ORIGIN C20: acronym from *graphic interchange format*.

**GIFT** ● **n.** Medicine gamete intrafallopian transfer.

**gift** ● **n. 1** a thing given willingly to someone without payment; a present. ➤ informal a very easy task or unmissable opportunity. **2** a natural ability or talent. ● **v. 1** give as a gift, especially formally. ➤ informal inadvertently allow (an opponent) to have something. **2** (**gift someone with**) endow someone with (an ability or talent). ➤ [as adj. **gifted**] having exceptional talent or ability.
– PHRASES **in the gift of** (of a Church living or official appointment) in the power of (someone) to award.
– DERIVATIVES **giftedness** adj.
– ORIGIN ME: from ON *gipt*; rel. to **GIVE**.

**gift certificate** ● **n.** N. Amer. a gift token.

**gift token** (also **gift voucher**) ● **n.** Brit. a voucher given as a gift which is exchangeable for goods.

**giftware** ● **n.** goods sold as being suitable as gifts.

**gift wrap** ● **n.** decorative paper for wrapping gifts. ● **v.** (**gift-wrap**) [usu. as adj. **gift-wrapped**] wrap (a gift) in decorative paper.

**gig**[1] /gɪg/ ● **n. 1** chiefly historical a light two-wheeled carriage pulled by one horse. **2** a light, fast, narrow boat adapted for rowing or sailing.

– ORIGIN C18: appar. a transferred sense of obs. *gig* 'a flighty girl'.

**gig**[2] /gɪg/ informal • n. a live performance by a musician or other performer. • v. (**gigged**, **gigging**) perform a gig or gigs.

– ORIGIN 1920s: of unknown origin.

**gig**[3] /gɪg/ • n. a harpoon-like weapon used for catching fish. • v. (**gigged**, **gigging**) fish using such a weapon.

– ORIGIN C18: shortening of earlier *fizgig*, prob. from Sp. *fisga* 'harpoon'.

**gig**[4] /gɪg, dʒɪg/ • n. Computing, informal short for **GIGABYTE**.

**giga-** /'gɪgə, 'dʒɪgə/ • comb. form **1** denoting a factor of $10^9$: *gigahertz*. **2** Computing denoting a factor of $2^{30}$.

– ORIGIN from Gk *gigas* 'giant'.

**gigabyte** /'gɪgəbʌɪt, 'dʒ-/ • n. Computing a unit of information equal to one thousand million ($10^9$) or (strictly) $2^{30}$ bytes.

**gigaflop** /'gɪgəflɒp, 'dʒ-/ • n. Computing a unit of computing speed equal to one thousand million floating-point operations per second.

– ORIGIN 1970s: back-form. from *gigaflops* (see **GIGA-**, **-FLOP**).

**gigantic** • adj. of very great size or extent.

– DERIVATIVES **gigantically** adv.

– ORIGIN C17 (in the sense 'like or suited to a giant'): from L. *gigas*, *gigant-* (see **GIANT**) + **-IC**.

**gigantism** /'dʒʌɪgantɪz(ə)m, dʒʌɪ'gantɪz(ə)m/ • n. chiefly Biology unusual or abnormal largeness.

**gigantomachy** /ˌdʒʌɪgan'tɒməki/ • n. (in Greek mythology) the struggle between the gods and the giants.

– ORIGIN C16: from Gk *gigantomakhia*, from *gigas*, *gigant-* (see **GIANT**) + *-makhia* 'fighting'.

**giggle** • v. laugh lightly in a nervous, affected, or silly manner. • n. **1** a laugh of such a kind. **2** informal an amusing person or thing.

– DERIVATIVES **giggler** n. **giggly** adj. (**-ier**, **-iest**).

– ORIGIN C16: imitative.

**GIGO** /'gʌɪgəʊ/ • abbrev. chiefly Computing garbage in, garbage out.

**gigolo** /'(d)ʒɪgələʊ/ • n. (pl. **-os**) **1** a young man paid or financially supported by an older woman to be her escort or lover. **2** a professional male dancing partner.

– ORIGIN 1920s: from Fr., formed as the masc. of *gigole* 'dance hall woman', from colloq. *gigue* 'leg'.

**gigot** /'dʒɪgət/ • n. a leg of mutton or lamb.

– ORIGIN Fr., dimin. of colloq. *gigue* 'leg'.

**gigot sleeve** • n. a leg-of-mutton sleeve.

**gigue** /ʒiːg/ • n. Music a lively piece of music in the style of a dance, typically of the Renaissance or baroque period and in compound time.

– ORIGIN C17: Fr., lit. 'jig'.

**Gila monster** /'hiːlə/ • n. a large, slow-moving venomous lizard native to the south-western US and Mexico. [*Heloderma suspectum*.]

– ORIGIN C19: named after *Gila*, a river in New Mexico and Arizona.

**Gilbertese** • n. **1** a native or inhabitant of the Gilbert Islands in the SW Pacific. **2** the Micronesian language spoken there. • adj. of or relating to the Gilbert Islands.

**gild**[1] • v. **1** cover thinly with gold. **2** [as adj. **gilded**] wealthy and privileged: *gilded youth*.

– PHRASES **gild the lily** try to improve what is already beautiful or excellent.

– DERIVATIVES **gilder** n. **gilding** n.

– ORIGIN OE *gyldan*, of Gmc origin; rel. to **GOLD**.

**gild**[2] • n. archaic spelling of **GUILD**.

**gilded cage** • n. a luxurious but restrictive environment.

**gilet** /'ʒɪleɪ, 'ʒiːleɪ/ • n. (pl. **gilets** pronunc. same) a light sleeveless padded jacket.

– ORIGIN C19: Fr., 'waistcoat', from Sp. *jileco*, from Turk. *yelek*.

**gilgai** /'gɪlgʌɪ/ • n. Austral. a hollow where rainwater collects; a waterhole.

– ORIGIN from Wiradhuri and Kamilaroi *gilgaay*.

**gill**[1] /gɪl/ • n. **1** the paired respiratory organ of fishes and some amphibians, by which oxygen is extracted from water flowing over surfaces within or attached to the walls of the pharynx. **2** the vertical plates arranged radially on the underside of mushrooms and many toadstools. **3** (**gills**) the wattles or dewlap of a fowl. • v. **1** gut or clean (a fish). **2** catch (a fish) in a gill net.

– PHRASES **green about** (or **around**) **the gills** sickly-looking. **to the gills** until completely full.

– DERIVATIVES **-gilled** adj.

– ORIGIN ME: from ON.

**gill**[2] /dʒɪl/ • n. a unit of liquid measure, equal to a quarter of a pint.

– ORIGIN ME: from OFr. *gille* 'measure or container for wine', from late L. *gillo* 'water pot'.

**gill**[3] /gɪl/ (also **ghyll**) • n. chiefly N. English **1** a deep ravine, especially a wooded one. **2** a narrow mountain stream.

– ORIGIN ME: from ON *gil* 'deep glen'.

**gill**[4] /dʒɪl/ (also **jill**) • n. a female ferret. Compare with **HOB**[2].

– ORIGIN ME: abbrev. of the given name *Gillian*.

**gill cover** • n. a flap of skin protecting a fish's gills, typically stiffened by bony plates.

**gillie** /'gɪli/ (also **ghillie**) • n. **1** (in Scotland) an attendant on a hunting or fishing expedition. **2** historical a Highland chief's attendant. **3** a type of shoe with laces along the instep and no tongue, as used for Scottish country dancing.

– ORIGIN C16: from Sc. Gaelic *gille* 'lad, servant'.

**gill net** • n. a fishing net which is hung vertically so that fish get trapped in it by their gills.

– DERIVATIVES **gill-netter** n.

**gillyflower** /'dʒɪlɪˌflaʊə/ (also **gilliflower**) • n. any of a number of fragrant flowers, such as the wallflower or white stock.

– ORIGIN ME *gilofre* (in the sense 'clove'), from OFr. *gilofre*, *girofle*, via med. L. from Gk *karuophullon* (from *karuon* 'nut' + *phullon* 'leaf').

**gilt**[1] • adj. covered thinly with gold leaf or gold paint. • n. **1** gold leaf or gold paint applied in a thin layer to a surface. **2** (**gilts**) fixed-interest loan securities issued by the UK government.

– ORIGIN ME: archaic past part. of **GILD**[1].

**gilt**[2] • n. a young sow.

– ORIGIN ME: from ON *gyltr*.

**gilt-edged** • adj. relating to or denoting stocks or securities (such as gilts) that are regarded as extremely reliable investments.

**gimbal** /'dʒɪmb(ə)l, 'gɪm-/ (also **gimbals**) • n. a contrivance for keeping an instrument such as a compass or chronometer horizontal in a moving vessel or aircraft.

– DERIVATIVES **gimballed** adj.

– ORIGIN C16: var. of earlier *gimmal*, itself a var. of ME *gemel* 'twin, hinge', from OFr. *gemel* 'twin'.

**gimcrack** /'dʒɪmkrak/ • adj. showy but flimsy or poorly made. • n. a cheap and showy ornament.

– DERIVATIVES **gimcrackery** n.

– ORIGIN ME *gibecrake*, of unknown origin.

**gimlet** /'gɪmlɪt/ • n. **1** a small T-shaped tool with a screw-tip for boring holes. **2** a cocktail of gin or vodka and lime juice.

– ORIGIN ME: from OFr. *guimbelet*, dimin. of *guimble* 'drill', ult. of Gmc origin.

**gimlet eye** • n. an eye with a piercing stare.

– DERIVATIVES **gimlet-eyed** adj.

**gimme** informal • contr. give me. • n. chiefly N. Amer. something very easy to perform or obtain.

**gimmick** • n. a trick or device intended to attract attention rather than fulfil a useful purpose.

– DERIVATIVES **gimmickry** n. **gimmicky** adj.

– ORIGIN 1920s (in sense 'piece of magicians' apparatus'): perh. an approximate anagram of *magic*.

**gimp**[1] /gɪmp/ • n. **1** twisted, reinforced material used as upholstery trimming. **2** (in lacemaking) coarser thread forming the outline of the design. **3** fishing line made of silk bound with wire.

– ORIGIN C17: from Du.

**gimp**[2] /gɪmp/ N. Amer. informal, derogatory • n. **1** a physically handicapped or lame person. ➤ a limp. **2** a feeble or contemptible person. • v. limp; hobble.

– DERIVATIVES **gimpy** adj.
– ORIGIN 1920s: of unknown origin.

**gin**[1] ● **n.** **1** a clear alcoholic spirit distilled from grain or malt and flavoured with juniper berries. **2** (also **gin rummy**) a form of the card game rummy.
– ORIGIN C18: abbrev. of **GENEVER**.

**gin**[2] ● **n.** **1** a machine for separating cotton from its seeds. **2** a machine for raising and moving heavy weights. **3** a trap for catching small game. ● **v.** (**ginned**, **ginning**) treat (cotton) in a gin.
– DERIVATIVES **ginner** n. **ginnery** n.
– ORIGIN ME (in the sense 'a tool or device, a trick'): from OFr. *engin* (see **ENGINE**).

**gin**[3] ● **n.** Austral. offensive an Aboriginal woman.
– ORIGIN from Dharuk *diyin* 'woman, wife'.

**ginger** ● **n.** **1** a hot, fragrant spice made from the rhizome of a plant. **2** a SE Asian plant, resembling bamboo in appearance, from which ginger is taken. [*Zingiber officinale.*] See also **WILD GINGER**. **3** a light reddish-yellow colour. **4** spirit; mettle. ● **v.** **1** [usu. as adj. **gingered**] flavour with ginger. **2** (**ginger someone/thing up**) stimulate or enliven someone or something.
– DERIVATIVES **gingery** adj.
– ORIGIN OE *gingifer*, conflated in ME with OFr. *gingimbre*, from med. L. *gingiber*, from Gk *zingiberis*, from Pali *siṅgivera*, of Dravidian origin.

**ginger ale** (also **ginger beer**) ● **n.** an effervescent, sometimes alcoholic drink flavoured with ginger.

**gingerbread** ● **n.** **1** cake made with treacle or syrup and flavoured with ginger. **2** informal fancy decoration on a building.
– PHRASES **take the gilt off the gingerbread** make something no longer attractive or desirable.
– ORIGIN ME, from OFr. *gingembrat*, from med. L. *gingibratum*, from *gingiber* (see **GINGER**).

**ginger group** ● **n.** chiefly Brit. a highly active faction within a party or movement that presses for stronger action on a particular issue.

**gingerly** ● **adv.** in a careful or cautious manner. ● **adj.** showing great care or caution.
– DERIVATIVES **gingerliness** n.
– ORIGIN C16 (in the sense 'daintily, mincingly'): perh. from OFr. *gensor* 'delicate', compar. of *gent* 'graceful', from L. *genitus* '(well-) born'.

**ginger nut** ● **n.** a hard ginger-flavoured biscuit.

**gingham** /'gɪŋəm/ ● **n.** lightweight plain-woven cotton cloth, typically checked.
– ORIGIN C17: from Du. *gingang*, from Malay *genggang* (orig. an adj. meaning 'striped').

**gingili** /'dʒɪndʒɪli/ ● **n.** (in Indian cookery) sesame.
– ORIGIN from Hindi and Marathi *jiñjalī*, from Arab. *juljulān*.

**gingival** /dʒɪn'dʒʌɪv(ə)l/ ● **adj.** Medicine concerned with the gums.
– ORIGIN C17: from L. *gingiva* 'gum' + **-AL**.

**gingivitis** /ˌdʒɪndʒɪ'vʌɪtɪs/ ● **n.** Medicine inflammation of the gums.

**ginglymus** /'gɪŋglɪməs/ ● **n.** (pl. **ginglymi** /-mʌɪ/) Anatomy a hinge-like joint such as the elbow or knee.
– ORIGIN C16: mod. L., from Gk *ginglumos* 'hinge'.

**gink** /gɪŋk/ ● **n.** informal, chiefly N. Amer. a foolish or contemptible person.
– ORIGIN C20: of unknown origin.

**ginkgo** /'gɪŋkgəʊ, 'gɪŋkəʊ/ (also **gingko**) ● **n.** (pl. **-os** or **-oes**) a deciduous Chinese tree related to the conifers, with fan-shaped leaves and yellow flowers. [*Ginkgo biloba.*]
– ORIGIN C18: from Japanese *ginkyō*, from Chin. *yinxing*.

**gin mill** ● **n.** N. Amer. informal a seedy nightclub or bar.

**ginnel** /'gɪn(ə)l/ ● **n.** N. English a narrow passage between buildings; an alley.
– ORIGIN C17: perh. from Fr. *chenel* 'channel'.

**ginormous** ● **adj.** Brit. informal extremely large.
– ORIGIN 1940s (orig. military sl.): blend of **GIANT** and **ENORMOUS**.

**ginseng** /'dʒɪnsɛŋ/ ● **n.** **1** a plant tuber credited with various tonic and medicinal properties. **2** the plant from which this tuber is obtained, native to east Asia and North America. [Genus *Panax*: several species.]
– ORIGIN C17: from Chin. *rénshēn*, from *rén* 'man' + *shēn*, a kind of herb (because of the supposed resemblance of the forked root to a person).

**ginzo** /'gɪnzəʊ/ ● **n.** US informal, derogatory a person of Italian descent.
– ORIGIN C20: perh. from US sl. *Guinea*, denoting an Ital. or Sp. immigrant.

**gip** ● **n.** variant spelling of **GYP**[1].

**gippo** ● **n.** variant spelling of **GYPPO**.

**gippy tummy** /'dʒɪpi/ ● **n.** Brit. informal diarrhoea affecting visitors to hot countries.
– ORIGIN 1940s: *gippy*, abbrev. of **EGYPTIAN**.

**gipsy** ● **n.** variant spelling of **GYPSY**.

**giraffe** ● **n.** (pl. same or **giraffes**) a large African mammal with a very long neck and forelegs, the tallest living animal. [*Giraffa camelopardalis.*]
– ORIGIN C16: from Fr. *girafe*, Ital. *giraffa*, or Sp. and Port. *girafa*, based on Arab. *zarāfa*.

**girandole** /'dʒɪr(ə)ndəʊl/ ● **n.** a branched support for candles or other lights.
– ORIGIN C17: from Fr., from Ital. *girandola*, from *girare* 'gyrate, turn'.

**girasol** /'dʒɪrəsɒl, -səʊl/ (also **girasole** /-səʊl/) ● **n.** **1** a kind of opal reflecting a reddish glow. **2** North American term for **JERUSALEM ARTICHOKE**.
– ORIGIN C16 (in the sense 'sunflower'): from Fr., or from Ital. *girasole*, from *girare* 'to turn' + *sole* 'sun'.

**gird**[1] ● **v.** (past and past part. **girded** or **girt**) poetic/literary **1** encircle or secure with a belt or band. **2** (often in phr. **gird one's loins**) prepare and strengthen oneself for what is to come.
– ORIGIN OE *gyrdan*, of Gmc origin; rel. to **GIRDLE**[1] and **GIRTH**.

**gird**[2] archaic ● **v.** make cutting or critical remarks. ● **n.** a cutting or critical remark; a taunt.
– ORIGIN ME (in the sense 'strike, stab'): of unknown origin.

**girder** ● **n.** a large metal beam used in building bridges and large buildings.
– ORIGIN C17: from **GIRD**[1] in the archaic sense 'brace, strengthen'.

**girdle**[1] ● **n.** **1** a belt or cord worn round the waist. **2** a woman's elasticated corset extending from waist to thigh. **3** the part of a cut gem dividing the crown from the base and embraced by the setting. **4** a ring made around a tree by removing bark. ● **v.** **1** encircle with a girdle or belt. ➤ surround; encircle. **2** kill (a tree or branch) by cutting through the bark all the way round.
– DERIVATIVES **girdler** n.
– ORIGIN OE *gyrdel*, of Gmc origin; rel. to **GIRD**[1] and **GIRTH**.

**girdle**[2] ● **n.** Scottish and northern English term for **GRIDDLE** (in sense 1).

**girl** ● **n.** **1** a female child. **2** a young or relatively young woman. ➤ (**girls**) informal women who mix socially or belong to a group or team. ➤ a person's girlfriend. **3** dated a female servant.
– DERIVATIVES **girlhood** n. **girlish** adj. **girlishly** adv. **girlishness** n.
– ORIGIN ME (denoting a child or young person of either sex): perh. rel. to Low Ger. *gör* 'child'.

**girlfriend** ● **n.** a person's regular female companion in a romantic or sexual relationship. ➤ a woman's female friend.

**Girl Guide** ● **n.** a member of the Guides Association.

**girlie** ● **n.** (also **girly**) (pl. **-ies**) informal a girl or young woman. ● **adj.** **1** (usu. **girly**) often derogatory like or characteristic of a girl. **2** depicting nude or partially nude young women in erotic poses: *girlie magazines.*

**Girl Scout** ● **n.** a girl belonging to the Scout Association.

**girn** ● **v.** variant spelling of **GURN**.

**giro** /'dʒʌɪrəʊ/ ● **n.** (pl. **-os**) **1** a system of electronic credit transfer involving banks, post offices, and public utilities. **2** a cheque or payment by giro, especially a social

security payment.
– ORIGIN C19: via Ger. from Ital., 'circulation (of money)'.

**Girondist** /dʒɪ'rɒndɪst/ (also **Girondin** /dʒɪ'rɒndɪn, French ʒiʀɔ̃dɛ̃/) ● **n.** a member of the moderate republican party during the French Revolution.
– ORIGIN from archaic Fr. *Girondiste* (because the party leaders were the deputies from the department of the *Gironde*).

**girt**¹ past participle of **GIRD**¹.

**girt**² ● **n.** old-fashioned term for **GIRTH**.

**girth** ● **n.** **1** the measurement around the middle of something, especially a person's waist. **2** a band attached to a saddle and fastened around a horse's belly. ● **v.** archaic surround; encircle.
– ORIGIN ME: from ON *gjǫrth*.

**GIS** ● **abbrev.** geographic information system.

**gismo** ● **n.** variant spelling of **GIZMO**.

**gist** /dʒɪst/ ● **n.** **1** the substance or essence of a speech or text. **2** Law the real point of an action.
– ORIGIN C18: from OFr., third person sing. pres. tense of *gesir* 'to lie', in Anglo-Fr. legal phr. *cest action gist* 'this action lies', denoting that there were sufficient grounds to proceed.

**git** ● **n.** Brit. informal an unpleasant or contemptible person.
– ORIGIN 1940s: var. of the noun **GET**.

**gîte** /ʒiːt, French ʒit/ ● **n.** a small furnished holiday house in France.
– ORIGIN Fr., from OFr. *giste*; rel. to *gésir* 'to lie'.

**gittern** /'gɪtəːn/ ● **n.** a lute-like medieval stringed instrument, forerunner of the guitar.
– ORIGIN ME: from OFr. *guiterne*; perh. rel. to **CITTERN** and **GUITAR**.

**give** ● **v.** (past **gave**; past part. **given**) (usu. **give something to** or **give someone something**) **1** freely transfer the possession of; cause to receive or have. ➤communicate or impart (a message). ➤commit, consign, or entrust. ➤cause to experience or suffer: *you gave me a fright.* ➤allot (a score) to. **2** yield as a product or result. ➤(**give something off/out**) emit odour, vapour, etc. **3** carry out (an action). ➤produce (a sound). ➤provide (a party or meal) as host or hostess. **4** state or put forward (information or argument). ➤pledge or assign as a guarantee. ➤deliver (a judgement) authoritatively. **5** present (an appearance or impression): *he gave no sign of life.* **6** alter in shape under pressure rather than resist or break. ➤yield or give way to pressure. ➤N. Amer. informal concede defeat; surrender. **7** (of an umpire or referee) declare whether or not (a player) is out or offside. ➤adjudicate that (a goal) has been legitimately scored. **8** concede or yield (something) as valid or deserved in respect of (someone). ● **n.** capacity to bend or alter in shape under pressure.
– PHRASES **give oneself airs** act pretentiously or snobbishly. **give and take** mutual concessions and compromises. **give the game** (or **show**) **away** inadvertently reveal something secret or concealed. **give or take ——** informal **1** to within a specified amount. **2** apart from. **give rise to** cause or induce to happen. **give someone to understand** inform someone in a formal and rather indirect way. **give someone what for** informal, chiefly Brit. punish or scold someone severely. **not give a damn** (or **hoot** etc.) informal not care at all. **what gives?** informal what's the news?
– PHRASAL VERBS **give someone away 1** reveal incriminating or hidden information about someone. **2** hand over a bride ceremonially to her bridegroom. **give something away 1** reveal something secret or concealed. **2** (in sport) concede a goal or advantage to the opposition. **give in** cease fighting or arguing. **give on to** (or **into**) Brit. overlook or lead into. **give out** be completely used up. ➤stop functioning. **give over** Brit. informal stop doing something. **give up** cease making an effort; resign oneself to failure. **give someone up** deliver a wanted person to authority. **give something up 1** part with something that one would prefer to keep. **2** stop doing something. **give up on** stop having faith or belief in.
– DERIVATIVES **giver** n.
– ORIGIN OE *giefan*, *gefan*, of Gmc origin.

**giveaway** ● **n.** informal **1** something given free, especially for promotional purposes. **2** something that makes an inadvertent revelation.

**given** past participle of **GIVE**. ● **adj.** **1** specified or stated. **2** (**given to**) inclined or disposed to. **3** Law, archaic (of a document) signed and dated. ● **prep.** taking into account. ● **n.** a known or established fact or situation.

**given name** ● **n.** another term for **FIRST NAME**.

**gizmo** /'gɪzməʊ/ (also **gismo**) ● **n.** (pl. **-os**) informal a gadget, especially one whose name the speaker does not know or cannot recall.
– ORIGIN 1940s (orig. US): of unknown origin.

**gizzard** /'gɪzəd/ ● **n.** a muscular, thick-walled part of a bird's stomach for grinding food, typically with grit. ➤a muscular stomach of some fish, insects, molluscs, and other invertebrates.
– ORIGIN ME *giser*: from OFr., based on L. *gigeria* 'cooked entrails of fowl'.

**Gjetost** /'jɛtɒst/ ● **n.** a very sweet, firm, golden-brown Norwegian cheese, traditionally made with goat's milk.
– ORIGIN Norw., from *gjet, geit* 'goat' + *ost* 'cheese'.

**GLA** ● **abbrev.** gamma linolenic acid.

**glabella** /glə'bɛlə/ ● **n.** (pl. **glabellae** /-liː/) Anatomy the smooth part of the forehead above and between the eyebrows.
– DERIVATIVES **glabellar** adj.
– ORIGIN C19: mod. L., from L. *glabellus* (adj.), dimin. of *glaber* 'smooth'.

**glabrous** /'gleɪbrəs/ ● **adj.** technical free from hair or down; smooth.
– ORIGIN C17: from L. *glaber, glabr-* 'hairless, smooth' + **-OUS**.

**glacé** /'glaseɪ/ ● **adj.** **1** (of fruit) having a glossy surface due to preservation in sugar. **2** (of cloth or leather) smooth and highly polished.
– ORIGIN C19: Fr., lit. 'iced', past part. of *glacer*, from *glace* 'ice'.

**glacé icing** ● **n.** icing made with icing sugar and water.

**glacial** /'gleɪʃ(ə)l, -sɪəl/ ● **adj.** **1** relating to ice, especially in the form of glaciers or ice sheets. **2** extremely cold or unfriendly; icy. **3** Chemistry denoting pure organic acids (especially acetic acid) which form ice-like crystals on freezing. ● **n.** Geology a glacial period.
– DERIVATIVES **glacially** adv.
– ORIGIN C17: from Fr., or from L. *glacialis* 'icy'.

**glacial period** ● **n.** a period in the earth's history when ice sheets were unusually extensive; an ice age.

**glaciated** /'gleɪsɪeɪtɪd, 'glas-/ ● **adj.** covered or having been covered by glaciers or ice sheets.
– ORIGIN C19: past part. of obs. *glaciate*, from L. *glaciare* 'freeze'.

**glaciation** /ˌgleɪsɪ'eɪʃ(ə)n/ ● **n.** Geology **1** the condition or result of being glaciated. **2** a glacial period.

**glacier** /'glasɪə, 'gleɪs-/ ● **n.** a slowly moving mass of ice formed by the accumulation and compaction of snow on mountains or near the poles.
– ORIGIN C18: from Fr., from *glace* 'ice'.

**glaciology** /ˌgleɪsɪ'ɒlədʒi/ ● **n.** the study of glaciers.
– DERIVATIVES **glaciological** adj. **glaciologist** n.

**glacis** /'glasɪs, -si/ ● **n.** (pl. same /-sɪz, -siːz/) a bank sloping down from a fort which exposes attackers to the defenders' missiles.
– ORIGIN C17: from Fr., from OFr. *glacier* 'to slip'.

**glad** ● **adj.** (**gladder**, **gladdest**) **1** pleased; delighted. ➤causing happiness: *glad tidings.* **2** (often **glad of**) grateful. ● **v.** (**gladded**, **gladding**) poetic/literary make happy; please.
– PHRASES **give someone the glad eye** informal, dated look flirtatiously at someone.
– DERIVATIVES **gladly** adv. **gladness** n. **gladsome** adj. (poetic/literary).
– ORIGIN OE *glæd* (orig. in the sense 'bright, shining'), of Gmc origin; rel. to L. *glaber* 'smooth, hairless'.

**gladden** ● **v.** make glad.

**gladdon** /'glad(ə)n/ ● **n.** a purple-flowered iris which produces an unpleasant odour, especially when bruised. [*Iris foetidissima.*]

– ORIGIN OE *glædene*, based on L. *gladiolus* (see **GLADIOLUS**).

**glade** • **n.** an open space in a wood or forest.
– ORIGIN ME: of unknown origin; perh. rel. to **GLAD** or **GLEAM**, with ref. to the compar. brightness of a clearing.

**glad-hand** chiefly N. Amer. • **v.** (especially of a politician) greet or welcome warmly. • **n.** (**glad hand**) a warm and hearty greeting or welcome.
– DERIVATIVES **glad-hander** n.

**gladiator** /ˈɡladɪeɪtə/ • **n.** (in ancient Rome) a man trained to fight with weapons against other men or wild animals in an arena.
– DERIVATIVES **gladiatorial** adj.
– ORIGIN ME: from L., from *gladius* 'sword'.

**gladiolus** /ˌɡladɪˈəʊləs/ • **n.** (pl. **gladioli** /-lʌɪ/ or **gladioluses**) a plant of the iris family with sword-shaped leaves and spikes of brightly coloured flowers. [Genus *Gladiolus*.]
– ORIGIN OE (orig. denoting the gladdon), from L., dimin. of *gladius* 'sword'.

**glad rags** • **pl. n.** informal clothes for a party or special occasion.

**Gladstone bag** • **n.** a bag like a briefcase having two equal compartments joined by a hinge.
– ORIGIN C19: named after the Brit. Liberal statesman W. E. *Gladstone*.

**Glagolitic** /ˌɡlaɡəˈlɪtɪk/ • **adj.** denoting or relating to an alphabet based on Greek minuscules, formerly used in writing some Slavic languages.
– ORIGIN from mod. L. *glagoliticus*, from Serbo-Croat *glagòljica*, from Old Church Slavonic *glagolŭ* 'word'.

**glaikit** /ˈɡleɪkɪt/ • **adj.** Scottish & N. English stupid, foolish, or thoughtless.
– ORIGIN ME: rel. to Scots *glaiks* 'tricks, pranks'.

**glair** /ɡlɛː/ • **n.** a preparation made from egg white, used as an adhesive for bookbinding and gilding.
– DERIVATIVES **glairy** adj.
– ORIGIN ME: from OFr. *glaire*, based on L. *clara*, fem. of *clarus* 'clear'.

**glaive** /ɡleɪv/ • **n.** poetic/literary a sword.
– ORIGIN ME: from OFr., appar. from L. *gladius* 'sword'.

**Glam.** • **abbrev.** Glamorgan.

**glam** informal • **adj.** glamorous. • **n.** glamour. • **v.** (**glammed**, **glamming**) (**glam up**) make oneself look glamorous.

**glamorize** (also **glamourize** or **-ise**) • **v.** make (something) seem glamorous or desirable, especially spuriously so.
– DERIVATIVES **glamorization** n.

**glamour** (US also **glamor**) • **n.** **1** an attractive and exciting quality, especially sexual allure. **2** archaic enchantment; magic.
– DERIVATIVES **glamorous** adj. **glamorously** adv.
– ORIGIN C18: alt. of **GRAMMAR**, with ref. to the occult practices assoc. with learning in medieval times.

**glam rock** • **n.** a style of rock music characterized by male performers wearing exaggeratedly flamboyant clothes and make-up.

**glance**[1] • **v.** **1** take a brief or hurried look. **2** (often **glance off**) strike at an angle and bounce off obliquely. • **n.** **1** a brief or hurried look. **2** poetic/literary a flash or gleam of light. **3** Cricket a stroke with the bat's face turned slantwise to deflect the ball slightly.
– DERIVATIVES **glancing** adj. **glancingly** adv.
– ORIGIN ME: prob. a nasalized form of obs. *glace*, from OFr. *glacier* 'to slip', from *glace* 'ice'.

**glance**[2] • **n.** a shiny black or grey sulphide ore of lead, copper, or other metal.
– ORIGIN ME: from Ger. *Glanz* 'brightness, lustre'.

**gland**[1] • **n.** an organ of the body which secretes particular chemical substances. ➤ a lymph node.
– ORIGIN C17: from Fr. *glande*, alt. of OFr. *glandre*, from L. *glandulae* 'throat glands'.

**gland**[2] • **n.** a sleeve used to produce a seal round a piston rod or other shaft.
– ORIGIN C19: prob. a var. of Scots *glam* 'a vice or clamp'; rel. to **CLAMP**[1].

**glanders** /ˈɡlandəz/ • **pl. n.** [usu. treated as sing.] a rare contagious disease that mainly affects horses, characterized by swellings below the jaw and mucous discharge from the nostrils.
– ORIGIN C15: from OFr. *glandre* (see **GLAND**[1]).

**glandular** /ˈɡlandjʊlə, ˈɡlan(d)ʒʊlə/ • **adj.** relating to or affecting a gland or glands.

**glandular fever** • **n.** an infectious viral disease characterized by swelling of the lymph glands and prolonged lassitude.

**glans** /ɡlanz/ • **n.** (pl. **glandes** /ˈɡlandiːz/) Anatomy the rounded part forming the end of the penis or clitoris.
– ORIGIN C17: from L., lit. 'acorn'.

**glare** • **v.** **1** stare in an angry or fierce way. **2** shine with a strong or dazzling light. **3** [as adj. **glaring**] highly obvious or conspicuous. • **n.** **1** a fierce or angry stare. **2** strong and dazzling light.
– DERIVATIVES **glaringly** adv. **glary** adj.
– ORIGIN ME: from MDu. and Mid. Low Ger. *glaren* 'to gleam or glare': perh. rel. to **GLASS**.

**glare ice** • **n.** N. Amer. smooth, glassy ice.
– ORIGIN C19: prob. from obs. *glare* 'frost'; perh. rel. to **GLARE**.

**glasnost** /ˈɡlaznɒst, ˈɡlɑːs-/ • **n.** (in the former Soviet Union) the policy or practice of more open government and wider dissemination of information.
– ORIGIN from Russ. *glasnost'*, lit. 'the fact of being public, openness'.

**glass** • **n.** **1** a hard, brittle, usually transparent or translucent substance made by fusing sand with soda and lime. ➤ ornaments and other articles made from glass. ➤ greenhouses or cold frames considered collectively. **2** a drinking container made of glass. **3** a lens or optical instrument, in particular a monocle or a magnifying lens. **4** chiefly Brit. a mirror. • **v.** **1** cover or enclose with glass. **2** Brit. informal hit in the face with a beer glass. **3** scan (one's surroundings) with binoculars.
– DERIVATIVES **glassful** n. (pl. **-fuls**). **glassless** adj. **glasslike** adj. **glassware** n.
– ORIGIN OE *glæs*, of Gmc origin.

**glass-blowing** • **n.** the craft of making glassware by blowing semi-molten glass through a long tube.
– DERIVATIVES **glass-blower** n.

**glass ceiling** • **n.** an unacknowledged barrier to advancement in a profession, especially affecting women and members of minorities.

**glass cloth** • **n.** **1** Brit. a cloth covered with powdered glass or other abrasive, used for smoothing and polishing. **2** woven fabric of fine-spun glass thread.

**glass eel** • **n.** an elver at the time that it first enters brackish or fresh water, when it is translucent.

**glasses** • **pl. n.** a pair of lenses set in a frame that rests on the nose and ears, used to correct or assist defective eyesight.

**glass fibre** • **n.** chiefly Brit. a strong plastic, textile, or other material containing embedded glass filaments for reinforcement.

**glass harmonica** • **n.** a musical instrument consisting of a row of glass bowls, played by rubbing the rims with a finger or by keys.

**glasshouse** • **n.** **1** Brit. a greenhouse. **2** Brit. military slang a place of detention.

**glassine** /ˈɡlɑːsiːn/ • **n.** a glossy transparent paper.

**glass lizard** (also **glass snake**) • **n.** a legless burrowing lizard of snake-like appearance. [Genus *Ophisaurus*: several species.]

**glasspaper** • **n.** paper covered with powdered glass, used for smoothing and polishing.

**glass wool** • **n.** glass in the form of fine fibres used for packing and insulation.

**glasswort** • **n.** a salt-marsh plant with fleshy scale-like leaves, formerly burnt for use in glass-making. [Genus *Salicornia*: several species.]

**glassy** • **adj.** (**-ier**, **-iest**) **1** of or resembling glass. ➤ (of water) having a smooth surface. **2** (of a person's eyes or expression) showing no interest or animation.
– DERIVATIVES **glassily** adv. **glassiness** n.

**Glaswegian** /glazˈwiːdʒ(ə)n, glas-, glɑːz-, glɑːs-/ ● **n.** a native of Glasgow. ● **adj.** of or relating to Glasgow.

**Glauber's salt** /ˈglaʊbəz, ˈglɔː-/ ● **n.** a crystalline hydrated form of sodium sulphate, used chiefly as a laxative.
– ORIGIN C18: named after the Ger. chemist Johann R. *Glauber* (1604–1668).

**glaucoma** /glɔːˈkəʊmə/ ● **n.** Medicine a condition of increased pressure within the eyeball, causing gradual loss of sight.
– DERIVATIVES **glaucomatous** adj.
– ORIGIN C17: via L. from Gk *glaukōma*, based on *glaukos* 'bluish green or grey' (because of the grey-green haze in the pupil).

**glauconite** /ˈglɔːkənʌɪt/ ● **n.** a greenish clay mineral found chiefly in marine sands.
– ORIGIN C19: from Ger. *Glaukonit*, from Gk *glaukon* (neut. of *glaukos* 'bluish-green') + **-ITE**[1].

**glaucophane** /ˈglɔːkəfeɪn/ ● **n.** a bluish sodium-containing mineral found chiefly in schists and other metamorphic rocks.
– ORIGIN C19: from Ger. *Glaukophan*, from Gk *glaukos* 'bluish-green' + *-phanēs* 'shining'.

**glaucous** /ˈglɔːkəs/ ● **adj.** technical or poetic/literary **1** of a dull greyish-green or blue colour. **2** covered with a powdery bloom like that on grapes.
– ORIGIN C17: via L. from Gk *glaukos* + **-OUS**.

**glaucous gull** ● **n.** a large white and pale grey Arctic gull. [*Larus hyperboreus*.]

**glaze** ● **v. 1** fit panes of glass into (a window frame or similar structure). ➤ enclose or cover with glass. **2** cover with a glaze. **3** (often **glaze over**) lose brightness and animation. ● **n. 1** a vitreous substance fused on to the surface of pottery to form a hard, impervious decorative coating. **2** a thin topcoat of transparent paint used to modify the tone of an underlying colour. **3** a liquid such as milk or beaten egg, used to form a smooth shiny coating on food. **4** N. Amer. a thin, glassy coating of ice on the ground or water.
– DERIVATIVES **glazer** n. **glazing** n.
– ORIGIN ME *glase*, from **GLASS**.

**glazed frost** ● **n.** a glassy coating of ice, typically caused by rain freezing on impact.

**glazier** /ˈgleɪzɪə/ ● **n.** a person whose trade is fitting glass into windows and doors.

**GLC** ● **abbrev. 1** Chemistry gas–liquid chromatography. **2** Greater London Council.

**gleam** ● **v.** shine brightly, especially with reflected light. ● **n. 1** a faint or brief light. **2** a brief or faint show of a quality or emotion.
– PHRASES **a gleam in someone's eye** see **EYE**.
– DERIVATIVES **gleaming** adj. **gleamingly** adv. **gleamy** adj. (archaic).
– ORIGIN OE *glǣm* 'brilliant light', of Gmc origin.

**glean** /gliːn/ ● **v. 1** collect gradually from various sources. **2** historical gather (leftover grain) after a harvest.
– DERIVATIVES **gleaner** n.
– ORIGIN ME: from OFr. *glener*, from late L. *glennare*, prob. of Celtic origin.

**gleanings** ● **pl. n.** things gleaned from various sources rather than acquired as a whole.

**glebe** /gliːb/ ● **n. 1** historical a piece of land serving as part of a clergyman's benefice and providing income. **2** archaic land; fields.
– ORIGIN ME: from L. *gleba*, *glaeba* 'clod, land, soil'.

**glee** ● **n. 1** great delight. **2** a song for men's voices in three or more parts, usually unaccompanied.
– DERIVATIVES **gleesome** adj. (archaic).
– ORIGIN OE *glēo* 'entertainment, music, fun', of Gmc origin.

**glee club** ● **n.** a society for singing part songs.

**gleeful** ● **adj.** exuberantly or triumphantly joyful.
– DERIVATIVES **gleefully** adv. **gleefulness** n.

**gleeman** ● **n.** (pl. **-men**) historical a professional entertainer, especially a singer.

**gleet** /gliːt/ ● **n.** Medicine a watery discharge from the urethra caused by gonorrhoeal infection.
– DERIVATIVES **gleety** adj.
– ORIGIN ME: from OFr. *glette* 'slime, secretion', of unknown origin.

**Gleichschaltung** /ˈglʌɪxˌʃaltʊŋ, German ˈglaɪçˌʃaltʊŋ/ ● **n.** the standardization of political, economic, and social institutions as carried out in authoritarian states.
– ORIGIN Ger., from *gleich* 'same' + *schalten* 'force or bring into line'.

**glen** ● **n.** a narrow valley, especially in Scotland or Ireland.
– ORIGIN ME: from Sc. Gaelic and Ir. *gleann* (earlier *glenn*).

**glengarry** ● **n.** (pl. **-ies**) a brimless boat-shaped hat with a cleft down the centre, worn as part of Highland dress.
– ORIGIN C19: from *Glengarry*, the name of a valley in the Highlands of Scotland.

**glenoid cavity** /ˈgliːnɔɪd/ (also **glenoid fossa**) ● **n.** Anatomy a shallow depression on a bone into which another bone fits to form a joint, especially that on the scapula into which the head of the humerus fits.
– ORIGIN C18: *glenoid* from Fr. *glénoïde*, from Gk *glēnoeidēs*, from *glēnē* 'socket'.

**gley** /gleɪ/ ● **n.** Soil Science a sticky waterlogged soil lacking in oxygen, typically grey to blue in colour.
– ORIGIN 1920s: from Ukrainian, 'sticky blue clay'; rel. to **CLAY**.

**glia** /ˈglʌɪə, ˈgliːə/ ● **n.** Anatomy the connective tissue of the nervous system, consisting of several different types of cell associated with neurons.
– DERIVATIVES **glial** adj.
– ORIGIN C19: from Gk, lit. 'glue'.

**glib** ● **adj.** (**glibber**, **glibbest**) articulate and voluble but insincere and shallow.
– DERIVATIVES **glibly** adv. **glibness** n.
– ORIGIN C16: ult. of Gmc origin.

**glide** ● **v. 1** move with a smooth, quiet, continuous motion. **2** fly without power or in a glider. ● **n. 1** an instance of gliding. **2** Phonetics a sound produced as the vocal organs move towards or away from articulation of a vowel or consonant, for example /j/ in *duke* /djuːk/. **3** Cricket a glancing stroke which slightly deflects the ball, especially towards the leg side.
– DERIVATIVES **gliding** n.
– ORIGIN OE *glīdan*, of Gmc origin.

**glide path** ● **n.** an aircraft's line of descent to land, especially as indicated by ground radar.

**glider** ● **n. 1** a light aircraft designed to fly without using an engine. **2** a person or thing that glides. **3** another term for **FLYING PHALANGER**. **4** US a long swinging seat suspended from a frame in a porch.

**glimmer** ● **v.** shine faintly with a wavering light. ● **n. 1** a faint or wavering light. **2** a faint sign of a feeling or quality, especially a desirable one: *a glimmer of hope*.
– DERIVATIVES **glimmering** adj. & n. **glimmeringly** adv.
– ORIGIN ME: prob. of Scand. origin; rel. to Swed. *glimra* and Dan. *glimre*.

**glimpse** ● **n.** a momentary or partial view. ● **v.** see briefly or partially.
– ORIGIN ME (in the sense 'shine faintly'): prob. of Gmc origin; rel. to **GLIMMER**.

**glint** ● **v.** give out or reflect small flashes of light. ● **n.** a small flash of light, especially a reflected one.
– ORIGIN ME (in the sense 'move quickly or obliquely'): var. of dial. *glent*, prob. of Scand. origin and rel. to Swed. dial. *glänta*, *glinta* 'to slip, slide, gleam'.

**glioblastoma** /ˌglʌɪə(ʊ)blaˈstəʊmə/ ● **n.** (pl. **glioblastomas** or **glioblastomata** /-mətə/) Medicine a highly invasive glioma in the brain.

**glioma** /glʌɪˈəʊmə/ ● **n.** (pl. **gliomas** or **gliomata** /-mətə/) Medicine a malignant tumour of the glial tissue of the nervous system.
– ORIGIN C19: from Gk *glia* 'glue' + **-OMA**.

**glissade** /glɪˈsɑːd, -ˈseɪd/ ● **n. 1** a slide down a steep slope of snow or ice, typically on the feet with the support of an ice axe. **2** Ballet a movement in which one leg is brushed outwards from the body and then takes the weight while the second leg is brushed in to meet it. ● **v.** perform or move by means of a glissade.
– ORIGIN C19: Fr., from *glisser* 'to slip, slide'.

**glissando** /glɪˈsandəʊ/ ● n. (pl. **glissandi** /-di/ or **glissandos**) Music a continuous slide upwards or downwards between two notes.
– ORIGIN Ital., from Fr. *glisser* 'to slip, slide'.

**glissé** /gliːˈseɪ/ ● n. (pl. pronounced same) Ballet a movement in which one foot is slid outward from the body and briefly extended off the ground and the other is brought to meet it.
– ORIGIN Fr., lit. 'slipped, glided', past part. of *glisser.*

**glisten** ● v. (of something wet or greasy) shine or sparkle. ● n. a sparkling light reflected from something wet.
– ORIGIN OE *glisnian*, of Gmc origin.

**glister** /ˈglɪstə/ poetic/literary ● v. sparkle; glitter. ● n. a sparkle.
– ORIGIN ME: prob. from Mid. Low Ger. *glistern* or MDu. *glisteren.*

**glitch** ● n. informal **1** a sudden, usually temporary malfunction or irregularity of equipment. ➤ an unexpected setback in a plan. **2** Astronomy a brief irregularity in the rotation of a pulsar.
– DERIVATIVES **glitchy** adj.
– ORIGIN 1960s (orig. US): of unknown origin.

**glitter** ● v. **1** shine with a bright, shimmering reflected light. **2** [as adj. **glittering**] impressively successful or glamorous: *a glittering career.* ● n. **1** bright, shimmering reflected light. **2** tiny pieces of sparkling material used for decoration. **3** an attractive and exciting but superficial quality.
– DERIVATIVES **glitteringly** adv. **glittery** adj.
– ORIGIN ME: from ON *glitra.*

**glitterati** /ˌglɪtəˈrɑːti/ ● pl. n. informal fashionable people involved in show business or some other glamorous activity.
– ORIGIN 1950s (orig. US): blend of **GLITTER** and **LITERATI**.

**glitz** ● n. informal extravagant but superficial display.
– DERIVATIVES **glitzily** adv. **glitziness** n. **glitzy** adj.
– ORIGIN 1960s (as *glitzy*): from **GLITTER**, suggested by **RITZY** and perh. also by Ger. *glitzerig* 'glittering'.

**gloaming** ● n. (**the gloaming**) poetic/literary twilight; dusk.
– ORIGIN OE *glōmung*, from *glōm* 'twilight', of Gmc origin; rel. to **GLOW**.

**gloat** ● v. contemplate one's own success or another's misfortune with smugness or malignant pleasure. ● n. an act of gloating.
– DERIVATIVES **gloater** n. **gloating** adj. & n. **gloatingly** adv.
– ORIGIN C16 (in the sense 'give a sideways or furtive look'): of uncertain origin; perh. rel. to ON *glotta* 'to grin' and Mid. High Ger. *glotzen* 'to stare'.

**glob** ● n. informal a lump of a semi-liquid substance.
– ORIGIN C20: perh. a blend of **BLOB** and **GOB**².

**global** /ˈgləʊb(ə)l/ ● adj. **1** of or relating to the whole world; worldwide. **2** relating to or embracing the whole of something, or of a group of things. ➤ Computing operating or applying through the whole of a file or program.
– DERIVATIVES **globalist** n. **globalization** (also **-isation**) n. **globalize** (also **-ise**) v. **globally** adv.

**global village** ● n. the world considered as a single community linked by telecommunications.

**global warming** ● n. the gradual increase in the overall temperature of the earth's atmosphere due to the greenhouse effect caused by increased levels of carbon dioxide, CFCs, and other pollutants.

**globe** ● n. **1** a spherical or rounded object. ➤ a golden orb as an emblem of sovereignty. **2** a spherical representation of the earth with a map on the surface. **3** (**the globe**) the earth. ● v. poetic/literary form into a globe.
– DERIVATIVES **globe-like** adj. **globoid** adj. & n. **globose** adj.
– ORIGIN ME: from OFr., or from L. *globus.*

**globefish** ● n. (pl. same or **-fishes**) a pufferfish or a porcupine fish.

**globeflower** ● n. a plant of the buttercup family with globular yellow or orange flowers. [Genus *Trollius.*]

**globetrotter** ● n. informal a person who travels widely.
– DERIVATIVES **globetrot** v. **globetrotting** n. & adj.

**globigerina** /ˌgləʊbɪdʒəˈrʌɪnə/ ● n. (pl. **globigerinas** or **globigerinae** /-niː/) a planktonic marine protozoan with a calcareous shell. [Genus *Globigerina.*]
– ORIGIN mod. L., from L. *globus* 'spherical object, globe' (because of the globular chambers in its shell) + *-ger* 'carrying' + **-INA**.

**globular** /ˈglɒbjʊlə/ ● adj. **1** globe-shaped; spherical. **2** composed of globules.
– DERIVATIVES **globularity** n.

**globular cluster** ● n. Astronomy a large compact spherical star cluster, typically of old stars in the outer regions of a galaxy.

**globule** /ˈglɒbjuːl/ ● n. **1** a small round particle of a substance; a drop. **2** Astronomy a small dark cloud of gas and dust seen against a brighter background such as a luminous nebula.
– DERIVATIVES **globulous** adj.
– ORIGIN C17: from Fr., or from L. *globulus*, dimin. of *globus* 'spherical object, globe'.

**globulin** /ˈglɒbjʊlɪn/ ● n. Biochemistry any of a group of simple proteins soluble in salt solutions and forming a large fraction of blood serum protein.

**glochidium** /gləʊˈkɪdɪəm/ ● n. (pl. **glochidia**) Zoology a parasitic larva of certain freshwater bivalve molluscs, which attaches itself by hooks and suckers to the fins or gills of fish.
– ORIGIN C19: mod. L., based on Gk *glōkhis* 'arrowhead'.

**glockenspiel** /ˈglɒk(ə)nspiːl, -ʃpiːl/ ● n. a musical percussion instrument consisting of a set of tuned metal pieces mounted in a frame and struck with small hammers.
– ORIGIN C19: from Ger. *Glockenspiel*, lit. 'bell play'.

**glom** /glɒm/ ● v. (**glommed**, **glomming**) N. Amer. informal **1** steal. **2** (**glom on to**) become stuck or attached to.
– ORIGIN C20: var. of Scots *glaum*, of unknown origin.

**glomerulonephritis** /glɒˌmɛrjʊləʊnɪˈfrʌɪtɪs/ ● n. Medicine acute inflammation of the kidney, typically caused by an immune response.

**glomerulus** /glɒˈmɛr(j)ʊləs/ ● n. (pl. **glomeruli** /-lʌɪ, -liː/) Anatomy & Biology a cluster of nerve endings, spores, or small blood vessels, especially of capillaries around the end of a kidney tubule.
– DERIVATIVES **glomerular** adj.
– ORIGIN C19: mod. L., dimin. of L. *glomus, glomer-* 'ball of thread'.

**gloom** ● n. **1** partial or total darkness. **2** a state of depression or despondency. ● v. appear gloomy.
– ORIGIN ME (as v.): of unknown origin.

**gloomy** ● adj. (**-ier**, **-iest**) **1** poorly lit, especially so as to cause fear or depression. **2** causing or feeling depression or despondency.
– DERIVATIVES **gloomily** adv. **gloominess** n.

**gloop** ● n. informal sloppy or sticky semi-fluid matter.
– DERIVATIVES **gloopy** adj.
– ORIGIN C20: symbolic.

**glop** ● n. informal, chiefly N. Amer. sticky and amorphous matter. ➤ a soft, shapeless lump of something.
– DERIVATIVES **gloppy** adj. (**-ier**, **-iest**).
– ORIGIN 1940s: symbolic.

**Gloria** ● n. **1** a hymn beginning *Gloria in excelsis Deo* (Glory be to God in the highest), forming a set part of the Mass. **2** the doxology beginning *Gloria Patris* (Glory be to the Father), used after psalms and in formal prayer.

**glorify** ● v. (**-ies**, **-ied**) **1** praise and worship (God). ➤ reveal the glory of (God) through one's actions. **2** describe or represent as admirable, especially unjustifiably or undeservedly. **3** [as adj. **glorified**] represented as or appearing more elevated or special than is the case: *the word processor is not merely a glorified typewriter.*
– DERIVATIVES **glorification** n. **glorifier** n.

**glorious** ● adj. **1** having or bringing glory. **2** strikingly beautiful or impressive.
– DERIVATIVES **gloriously** adv. **gloriousness** n.

**glory** ● n. (pl. **-ies**) **1** high renown or honour won by notable achievements. **2** praise, worship, and thanksgiving offered to God. **3** magnificence; great beauty. ➤ the splendour and bliss of heaven. **4** a luminous ring or halo, especially as depicted around the head of Christ or a saint. ● v. (**glory in**) take great pride or pleasure in. ➤ exult in unpleasantly or boastfully.

– PHRASES **glory be!** expressing enthusiastic piety. **glory days** the most successful period of a person's past life. **go to glory** die. **in one's glory** informal in a state of extreme joy or exaltation.
– ORIGIN ME: from OFr. *glorie*, from L. *gloria*.

**glory box** • n. Austral./NZ a box for a woman's clothes and household items, stored in preparation for marriage.

**glory hole** • n. **1** informal an untidy room or cupboard used for storage. **2** N. Amer. an open quarry.

**glory-of-the-snow** • n. another term for **CHIONODOXA**.

**glory pea** • n. another term for **CLIANTHUS**.

**Glos.** • abbrev. Gloucestershire.

**gloss[1]** • n. **1** shine or lustre on a smooth surface. **2** a superficially attractive appearance or impression: *beneath the gloss of success.* • v. **1** give a glossy appearance to. **2** (**gloss something over**) try to conceal or pass over something embarrassing or unfavourable.
– DERIVATIVES **glosser** n.
– ORIGIN C16: of unknown origin.

**gloss[2]** • n. a translation or explanation of a word, phrase, or passage. • v. provide a gloss for (a text, word, etc.).
– ORIGIN C16: alt. of *gloze*, from OFr. *glose* (see **GLOZE**), suggested by med. L. *glossa* 'explanation of a difficult word'.

**glossal** /ˈglɒs(ə)l/ • adj. Anatomy, rare of the tongue; lingual.
– ORIGIN C19: from Gk *glōssa* 'tongue' + **-AL**.

**glossary** • n. (pl. **-ies**) an alphabetical list of words relating to a specific subject, text, or dialect, with explanations.
– DERIVATIVES **glossarial** adj. **glossarist** n.
– ORIGIN ME: from L. *glossarium*, from *glossa* (see **GLOSS[2]**).

**glossator** /glɒˈseɪtə/ • n. chiefly historical a person who wrote glosses, especially a scholarly commentator on legal texts.

**glossitis** /glɒˈsʌɪtɪs/ • n. Medicine inflammation of the tongue.

**glossolalia** /ˌglɒsəˈleɪlɪə/ • n. the phenomenon of apparently speaking in an unknown language during religious worship, regarded as a gift of the Holy Spirit.
– DERIVATIVES **glossolalic** adj.
– ORIGIN C19: from Gk *glōssa* 'language, tongue' + *lalia* 'speech'.

**glossopharyngeal nerves** /ˌglɒsə(ʊ)fəˈrɪn(d)ʒɪəl, -ˌfar(ə)nˈdʒiːəl/ • pl. n. Anatomy the pair of cranial nerves supplying the tongue and pharynx.

**glossy** • adj. (**-ier**, **-iest**) **1** shiny and smooth. **2** superficially attractive and stylish. • n. (pl. **-ies**) informal a magazine printed on glossy paper with many colour photographs.
– DERIVATIVES **glossily** adv. **glossiness** n.

**glost** • n. the second firing of ceramic ware, in which the glaze is fused.
– ORIGIN appar. a dial. alt. of **GLOSS[1]**.

**glottal** • adj. of or produced by the glottis.

**glottal stop** • n. a consonant formed by the audible release of the airstream after complete closure of the glottis.

**glottis** /ˈglɒtɪs/ • n. the part of the larynx consisting of the vocal cords and the slit-like opening between them.
– DERIVATIVES **glottic** adj.
– ORIGIN C16: mod. L., from Gk *glōttis*, from *glōtta*, var. of *glōssa* 'tongue'.

**Gloucester Old Spot** • n. a pig of a white breed with black spots.

**glove** • n. a covering for the hand having separate parts for each finger and the thumb. ➤ a padded protective covering for the hand used in boxing and other sports.
– PHRASES **fit like a glove** (of clothes) fit exactly.
– DERIVATIVES **gloved** adj. **gloveless** adj.
– ORIGIN OE *glōf*, of Gmc origin.

**glovebox** • n. **1** a glove compartment. **2** a closed chamber with sealed-in gloves for handling radioactive or other hazardous material.

**glove compartment** • n. a recess with a flap in the dashboard of a motor vehicle, used for storing small items.

**glove puppet** • n. chiefly Brit. a cloth puppet fitted on the hand and worked by the fingers.

**glover** • n. a maker of gloves.

**glow** • v. **1** give out steady light without flame. ➤ have an intense colour and a slight shine. **2** convey deep pleasure through one's expression and bearing. ➤ [as adj. **glowing**] expressing great praise. • n. **1** a steady radiance of light or heat. ➤ a feeling or appearance of warmth. **2** a strong feeling of pleasure or well-being: *a glow of pride.*
– DERIVATIVES **glowingly** adv.
– ORIGIN OE *glōwan*, of Gmc origin.

**glow discharge** • n. a luminous sparkless electrical discharge from a pointed conductor in a gas at low pressure.

**glower** /ˈglaʊə/ • v. have an angry or sullen look on one's face; scowl. • n. an angry or sullen look.
– DERIVATIVES **glowering** adj. **gloweringly** adv.
– ORIGIN C15: perh. a Scots var. of dial. *glore*, or from obs. *glow* 'to stare', both possibly of Scand. origin.

**glow-worm** • n. a soft-bodied beetle whose larvalike wingless female emits light to attract males. [*Lampyris noctiluca* (Europe), *Zarhipis integripennis* (N. America), and other species.]

**gloxinia** /glɒkˈsɪnɪə/ • n. a tropical American plant with large, velvety, bell-shaped flowers. [Genera *Gloxinia* and *Sinningia*: several species.]
– ORIGIN mod. L., named after the C18 Ger. botanist Benjamin P. *Gloxin*.

**gloze** /gləʊz/ • v. archaic **1** make excuses for. **2** use ingratiating or fawning language. **3** make a comment or comments.
– ORIGIN ME: from OFr. *gloser*, from *glose* 'a gloss, comment', based on L. *glossa* (see **GLOSS[2]**).

**glucagon** /ˈgluːkəg(ə)n, -gɒn/ • n. Biochemistry a hormone formed in the pancreas which promotes the breakdown of glycogen to glucose in the liver.
– ORIGIN 1920s: from Gk *glukus* 'sweet' + *agōn* 'leading, bringing'.

**glucocorticoid** /ˌgluːkə(ʊ)ˈkɔːtɪkɔɪd/ • n. Biochemistry any of a group of corticosteroids (e.g. hydrocortisone) which are involved in the metabolism of carbohydrates, proteins, and fats and have anti-inflammatory activity.

**glucose** /ˈgluːkəʊs, -z/ • n. a simple sugar which is an important energy source in living organisms and is a component of many carbohydrates. ➤ a syrup containing glucose and other sugars, made by hydrolysis of starch and used in the food industry.
– ORIGIN C19: from Fr., from Gk *gleukos* 'sweet wine'.

**glucoside** /ˈgluːkəsʌɪd/ • n. Biochemistry a glycoside derived from glucose.
– DERIVATIVES **glucosidic** adj.

**glue** • n. an adhesive substance used for sticking objects or materials together. • v. (**glues**, **glued**, **gluing** or **glueing**) **1** fasten or join with glue. **2** (**be glued to**) informal be paying very close attention to.
– DERIVATIVES **glue-like** adj. **gluey** adj.
– ORIGIN ME: from OFr. *glu* (n.), *gluer* (v.), from late L. *glus*, *glut-*, from L. *gluten*.

**glue ear** • n. blocking of the Eustachian tube by mucus occurring especially in children, and causing impaired hearing.

**glue pot** • n. a pot with an outer container holding water, used to heat glue that sets when it cools.

**glue-sniffing** • n. the practice of inhaling intoxicating fumes from the solvents in adhesives.
– DERIVATIVES **glue-sniffer** n.

**glug** informal • v. (**glugged**, **glugging**) pour or drink (liquid) with a hollow gurgling sound. • n. a hollow gurgling sound as of liquid being poured from a bottle.
– DERIVATIVES **gluggable** adj.
– ORIGIN C17: imitative.

**Glühwein** /ˈgluːvʌɪn, German ˈglyːvaɪn/ ● **n.** mulled wine.
– ORIGIN Ger., from *glühen* 'to mull' + *Wein* 'wine'.

**glum** ● **adj.** (**glummer**, **glummest**) dejected; morose.
– DERIVATIVES **glumly** adv. **glumness** n.
– ORIGIN C16: rel. to dial. *glum* 'to frown', var. of **GLOOM**.

**glume** /gluːm/ ● **n.** Botany each of two membranous bracts surrounding the spikelet of a grass (forming the husk of a cereal grain) or one surrounding the florets of a sedge.
– ORIGIN C18: from L. *gluma* 'husk'.

**gluon** /ˈgluːɒn/ ● **n.** Physics a hypothetical massless subatomic particle believed to transmit the force binding quarks together in hadrons.
– ORIGIN 1970s: from **GLUE** + **-ON**.

**glut** ● **n.** an excessively abundant supply of something. ● **v.** (**glutted**, **glutting**) supply or fill to excess. ➤archaic satisfy fully.
– ORIGIN ME: prob. via OFr. from L. *gluttire* 'to swallow'; rel. to **GLUTTON**.

**glutamate** /ˈgluːtəmeɪt/ ● **n.** Biochemistry a salt or ester of glutamic acid. ➤short for **MONOSODIUM GLUTAMATE**.

**glutamic acid** /gluːˈtamɪk/ ● **n.** Biochemistry an acidic amino acid which is a constituent of many proteins.
– ORIGIN C19: from **GLUTEN** + **AMINE** + **-IC**.

**glutamine** /ˈgluːtəmiːn/ ● **n.** Biochemistry a hydrophilic amino acid which is a constituent of most proteins.
– ORIGIN C19: blend of **GLUTAMIC ACID** and **AMINE**.

**glutathione** /ˌgluːtəˈθʌɪəʊn/ ● **n.** Biochemistry a compound involved as a coenzyme in oxidation-reduction reactions in cells.

**glute** ● **n.** informal short for **GLUTEUS**.

**gluten** /ˈgluːt(ə)n/ ● **n.** a substance present in cereal grains, especially wheat, which is responsible for the elastic texture of dough.
– ORIGIN C16 (orig. denoting protein from animal tissue): via Fr. from L., lit. 'glue'.

**gluteus** /ˈgluːtɪəs, gluːˈtiːəs/ ● **n.** (pl. **glutei** /-tɪʌɪ, -ˈtiːʌɪ/) any of three muscles in each buttock which move the thigh, the largest of which is the **gluteus maximus**.
– DERIVATIVES **gluteal** adj.
– ORIGIN C17: mod. L., from Gk *gloutos* 'buttock'.

**glutinous** /ˈgluːtɪnəs/ ● **adj.** like glue in texture; sticky.
– DERIVATIVES **glutinously** adv. **glutinousness** n.
– ORIGIN ME: from OFr. *glutineux* or L. *glutinosus*, from *gluten* 'glue'.

**glutton** ● **n.** **1** an excessively greedy eater. ➤a person who is very fond of something: *he is a glutton for poetry.* **2** old-fashioned term for **WOLVERINE**.
– PHRASES **a glutton for punishment** a person who is always eager to undertake hard or unpleasant tasks.
– DERIVATIVES **gluttonize** (also **-ise**) v. **gluttonous** adj. **gluttonously** adv.
– ORIGIN ME: from OFr. *gluton*, from L. *glutto(n-)*, rel. to *gluttire* 'to swallow', *gluttus* 'greedy', and *gula* 'throat'.

**gluttony** ● **n.** habitual greed or excess in eating.

**glyceride** /ˈglɪs(ə)rʌɪd/ ● **n.** a fatty acid ester of glycerol.

**glycerine** /ˈglɪs(ə)riːn, -ɪn/ (US **glycerin**) ● **n.** another term for **GLYCEROL**.
– ORIGIN C19: from Fr. *glycerin*, from Gk *glukeros* 'sweet'.

**glycerol** /ˈglɪs(ə)rɒl/ ● **n.** a colourless, sweet, viscous liquid formed as a by-product in soap manufacture, used as an emollient and laxative and for making explosives and antifreeze.

**glyceryl** /ˈglɪs(ə)rʌɪl, -rɪl/ ● **n.** [as modifier] Chemistry denoting a radical derived from glycerol by replacement of one or more hydrogen atoms.

**glycine** /ˈglʌɪsiːn/ ● **n.** Biochemistry the simplest naturally occurring amino acid, a constituent of most proteins.
– ORIGIN C19: from Gk *glukus* 'sweet' + **-INE**[4].

**glyco-** ● **comb. form** of, relating to, or producing sugar: *glycoside*.
– ORIGIN from Gk *glukus* 'sweet'.

**glycogen** /ˈglʌɪkədʒ(ə)n/ ● **n.** Biochemistry a polysaccharide deposited in bodily tissues as a store of carbohydrates.
– DERIVATIVES **glycogenic** /-ˈdʒɛnɪk/ adj.

**glycogenesis** /ˌglʌɪkə(ʊ)ˈdʒɛnɪsɪs/ ● **n.** Biochemistry the formation of glycogen from sugar.

**glycol** /ˈglʌɪkɒl/ ● **n.** **1** short for **ETHYLENE GLYCOL**. **2** another term for **DIOL**.
– ORIGIN C19: from **GLYCERINE** + **-OL**.

**glycolysis** /glʌɪˈkɒlɪsɪs/ ● **n.** Biochemistry the breakdown of glucose by enzymes, releasing energy and pyruvic acid.
– DERIVATIVES **glycolytic** /ˌglʌɪkəˈlɪtɪk/ adj.

**glycoprotein** /ˌglʌɪkə(ʊ)ˈprəʊtiːn/ ● **n.** Biochemistry any of a class of proteins which have carbohydrate groups attached to the polypeptide chain.

**glycosaminoglycan** /ˌglʌɪkəʊsˌəmiːnə(ʊ)ˈglʌɪkan/ ● **n.** Biochemistry another term for **MUCOPOLYSACCHARIDE**.

**glycoside** /ˈglʌɪkə(ʊ)sʌɪd/ ● **n.** Biochemistry a compound formed from a simple sugar and another compound by replacement of a hydroxyl group in the sugar molecule.
– DERIVATIVES **glycosidic** adj.
– ORIGIN C19: from **GLYCO-**, on the pattern of *glucoside*.

**glycosuria** /ˌglʌɪkə(ʊ)ˈsjʊərɪə/ ● **n.** Medicine a condition characterized by an excess of sugar in the urine, typically associated with diabetes or kidney disease.
– DERIVATIVES **glycosuric** adj.
– ORIGIN C19: from Fr. *glycosurie*, from *glucos* 'glucose'.

**glyph** /glɪf/ ● **n.** **1** a hieroglyphic character; a pictograph or sculptured symbol. **2** Architecture an ornamental carved groove or channel, as on a Greek frieze. **3** Computing a small graphic symbol.
– DERIVATIVES **glyphic** adj.
– ORIGIN C18: from Fr. *glyphe*, from Gk *gluphē* 'carving'.

**glyphosate** /ˈglʌɪfə(ʊ)seɪt/ ● **n.** a synthetic compound which is a non-selective systemic herbicide.
– ORIGIN 1970s: from **GLYCINE** + **PHOSPHO-** + **-ATE**[1].

**glyptic** /ˈglɪptɪk/ ● **adj.** of or concerning carving or engraving.
– ORIGIN C19: from Fr. *glyptique* or Gk *gluptikos*, from *gluptēs* 'carver', from *gluphein* 'carve'.

**glyptodont** /ˈglɪptə(ʊ)dɒnt/ ● **n.** a fossil South American edentate mammal of the Cenozoic era, related to armadillos but much larger.
– ORIGIN C19: from Gk *gluptos* 'carved' + *odous, odont-* 'tooth'.

**glyptography** /glɪpˈtɒgrəfi/ ● **n.** the art or scientific study of gem engraving.
– ORIGIN C18: from Gk *gluptos* 'carved' + **-GRAPHY**.

**GM** ● **abbrev.** **1** general manager. **2** General Motors. **3** genetically modified. **4** George Medal. **5** Chess grandmaster. **6** (of a school) grant-maintained.

**gm** ● **abbrev.** gram(s).

**G-man** ● **n.** informal **1** US an FBI agent. **2** Irish a political detective.
– ORIGIN C20: prob. an abbrev. of *Government man*.

**GMS** ● **abbrev.** (with reference to schools) grant maintained status.

**GMT** ● **abbrev.** Greenwich Mean Time.

**GMWU** ● **abbrev.** General and Municipal Workers' Union.

**gn** ● **abbrev.** guinea(s).

**gnamma** /ˈnamə/ ● **n.** Austral. a natural hole in a rock in which rainwater collects.
– ORIGIN from Nyungar.

**gnarl** /nɑːl/ ● **n.** a rough, knotty protuberance, especially on a tree.
– ORIGIN C19: back-form. from **GNARLED**.

**gnarled** ● **adj.** knobbly, rough, and twisted, especially with age.
– ORIGIN C17: var. of *knarled*, from **KNAR**.

**gnarly** ● **adj.** (**-ier**, **-iest**) **1** gnarled. **2** N. Amer. informal difficult, dangerous, or challenging. ➤unpleasant or unattractive.

**gnash** /naʃ/ ● **v.** grind (one's teeth) together, especially as a sign of anger.
– ORIGIN ME: perh. rel. to ON *gnastan* 'a gnashing of teeth'.

**gnashers** ● pl. n. Brit. informal teeth.

**gnat** /nat/ ● n. a small two-winged fly resembling a mosquito, typically forming large swarms. [*Culex pipiens* and many other species, especially in the family Culicidae.]
– ORIGIN OE *gnætt*, of Gmc origin.

**gnatcatcher** ● n. a tiny grey-backed New World songbird with a long tail. [Genus *Polioptila*.]

**gnathic** /ˈnaθɪk, ˈneɪ-/ ● adj. rare of or relating to the jaws.
– ORIGIN C19: from Gk *gnathos* 'jaw' + **-IC**.

**gnaw** /nɔː/ ● v. **1** bite at or nibble persistently. **2** [often as adj. **gnawing**] cause persistent anxiety or distress.
– DERIVATIVES **gnawingly** adv.
– ORIGIN OE *gnagen*, of Gmc origin; ult. imitative.

**gneiss** /nʌɪs/ ● n. a typically coarse-grained metamorphic rock with a banded or foliated structure.
– DERIVATIVES **gneissic** adj. **gneissose** adj.
– ORIGIN C18: from Ger., from Old High Ger. *gneisto* 'spark' (because of the rock's sheen).

**gnocchi** /ˈn(j)ɒki, ˈgnɒki/ ● pl. n. (in Italian cooking) small dumplings made from potato, semolina, or flour.
– ORIGIN Ital., pl. of *gnocco*, alt. of *nocchio* 'knot in wood'.

**gnome**[1] /nəʊm/ ● n. **1** a legendary dwarfish creature supposed to guard the earth's treasures underground. **2** a small garden ornament in the form of a bearded man with a pointed hat. **3** informal a person having secret or sinister influence, especially in financial matters: *the gnomes of Zurich*.
– DERIVATIVES **gnomish** adj.
– ORIGIN C17: from Fr., from mod. L. *gnomus*, a word used by the C16 Swiss physician Paracelsus as a synonym of *Pygmaeus* (see **PYGMY**).

**gnome**[2] /nəʊm, ˈnəʊmi/ ● n. a short statement encapsulating a general truth; a maxim.
– ORIGIN C16: from Gk *gnōmē* 'thought, opinion'.

**gnomic** /ˈnəʊmɪk/ ● adj. **1** in the form of short, pithy maxims or aphorisms. **2** enigmatic; ambiguous.
– DERIVATIVES **gnomically** adv.

**gnomon** /ˈnəʊmɒn/ ● n. **1** the projecting piece on a sundial that shows the time by its shadow. **2** Geometry the part of a parallelogram left when a similar parallelogram has been taken from its corner. **3** Astronomy a structure used in observing the sun's meridian altitude.
– DERIVATIVES **gnomonic** /-ˈmɒnɪk/ adj.
– ORIGIN C16: via L. from Gk *gnōmōn* 'indicator, carpenter's square'.

**gnosis** /ˈnəʊsɪs/ ● n. knowledge of spiritual mysteries.
– ORIGIN C16: from Gk *gnōsis* 'knowledge'.

**gnostic** /ˈnɒstɪk/ ● adj. **1** of or relating to knowledge, especially esoteric mystical knowledge. **2** (**Gnostic**) of or relating to Gnosticism. ● n. (**Gnostic**) an adherent of Gnosticism.
– ORIGIN C16: via eccles. L. from Gk *gnōstikos*, from *gnōstos* 'known'.

**Gnosticism** /ˈnɒstɪˌsɪz(ə)m/ ● n. a heretical movement of the 2nd-century Christian Church, teaching that esoteric knowledge (gnosis) of the supreme divine being enabled the redemption of the human spirit.

**gnotobiotic** /ˌnəʊtə(ʊ)bʌɪˈɒtɪk/ ● adj. Biology denoting or relating to an environment in which all micro-organisms are either known or excluded.
– ORIGIN 1940s: from Gk *gnōtos* 'known' + **BIOTIC**.

**GNP** ● abbrev. gross national product.

**Gnr** ● abbrev. Gunner.

**gns** ● abbrev. guineas.

**gnu** /(g)nuː, (g)njuː/ ● n. a large African antelope with a long head, a beard and mane, and a sloping back. [Genus *Connochaetes*: two species.]
– ORIGIN C18: from Khoikhoi and San, perh. imitative of the sound made by the animal when alarmed.

**GNVQ** ● abbrev. General National Vocational Qualification.

**go**[1] ● v. (**goes**, **going**; past **went**; past part. **gone**) **1** move from one place to another; travel. ➤ engage in a specified activity: *she used to go hunting*. ➤ (**go to**) attend or visit for a particular purpose. ➤ pass time in a particular way: *they went for two months without talking*. ➤ lie or extend in a certain direction. **2** leave; depart. ➤ (of time) pass or elapse. ➤ come to an end; cease to exist. ➤ disappear or be used up. **3** (**be going to be/do something**) used to express a future tense: *I'm going to be late*. **4** pass into or be in a specified state, especially an undesirable one: *her mind went blank*. ➤ (**go to/into**) enter into a specified state or course of action: *she went back to sleep*. ➤ make a sound of a specified kind. ➤ (**go by/under**) be known or called by (a specified name). **5** turn out in a specified way. ➤ be acceptable or permitted: *anything goes*. **6** be harmonious, complementary, or matching. **7** (of a machine or device) function. ➤ continue in operation or existence. **8** fit into or be regularly kept in a particular place. **9** informal use a toilet; urinate or defecate. **10** informal say. ● n. (pl. **goes**) informal **1** an attempt or trial. ➤ chiefly Brit. a state of affairs. ➤ chiefly Brit. an attack of illness. **2** a person's turn to do or use something. **3** spirit, animation, or energy. ➤ Brit. vigorous activity: *it's all go*.
– PHRASES **all the go** Brit. informal, dated in fashion. **from the word go** informal from the very beginning. **go figure!** N. Amer. informal said to express the belief that something is amazing or incredible. **go halves** (or **shares**) share something equally. **going!, gone!** an auctioneer's announcement that bidding is closing or closed. **going on** —— (Brit. also **going on for** ——) approaching a specified time, age, or amount. **go to show** (or **prove**) serve as evidence or proof. **have a go at** chiefly Brit. attack or criticize. **have —— going for one** informal be in one's favour or to one's advantage. **make a go of** informal be successful in. **no go** informal impossible, hopeless, or forbidden. **on the go** informal very active or busy. **to be going on with** Brit. to start with; for the time being. **to go** chiefly N. Amer. (of food or drink from a restaurant or cafe) to be eaten or drunk off the premises. **who goes there?** said by a sentry as a challenge.
– PHRASAL VERBS **go about 1** begin or carry on work at: *you went about it in the wrong way*. **2** Sailing change to an opposite tack. **go against** oppose or resist. ➤ be contrary to or unfavourable for. **go ahead** proceed or be carried out. **go along with** consent or agree to. **go at** energetically attack or tackle. **go back on** fail to keep (a promise). **go down 1** be defeated in a contest. **2** be recorded or remembered in a particular way. **3** elicit a specified reaction. **4** N. Amer. informal happen. **5** Brit. informal be sent to prison. **go for 1** decide on; choose. **2** attempt to gain or attain. **3** launch oneself at; attack. **4** end up having a specified value or effect. **5** apply to; have relevance for. **go in for 1** enter (a contest) as a competitor. **2** like or habitually take part in. **go into 1** investigate or enquire into. **2** (of a whole number) be capable of dividing another, typically without a remainder. **go off 1** (of a gun or bomb) explode or fire. ➤ (of an alarm) begin to sound. **2** chiefly Brit. (of food) begin to decompose. **3** informal, chiefly Brit. begin to dislike. **4** go to sleep. **go on 1** continue or persevere. ➤ talk at great or excessive length. ➤ continue speaking or doing something after a short pause. ➤ informal said when encouraging someone or expressing disbelief. **2** happen; take place. **3** proceed to do. **4** [usu. with neg.] informal have a specified amount of care or liking for. **go out 1** (of a fire or light) be extinguished. **2** (of the tide) ebb; recede to low tide. **3** leave home to go to an entertainment or social event. ➤ carry on a regular romantic relationship with someone. **4** (in some card games) be the first to dispose of one's cards. **go over 1** examine or check the details of. **2** change one's allegiance or religion. **3** be received in a specified way. **go round** chiefly Brit. (chiefly US also **go around**) **1** spin; revolve. **2** be sufficient to supply everybody present. **go through 1** undergo (a difficult or painful period or experience). **2** search through or examine carefully. **3** be officially approved or completed. **4** informal use up or spend. **go to!** archaic said to express disbelief, impatience, or admonition. **go under** (of a business) become bankrupt. **go up** explode or suddenly burst into flames. **go with 1** give one's consent or agreement to. **2** have a romantic or sexual relationship with. **go without** suffer lack or deprivation.
– ORIGIN OE *gān*, of Gmc origin; the form *went* was orig. the past tense of **WEND**.

**go²** • **n.** a Japanese board game of territorial possession and capture.
– ORIGIN C19: Japanese.

**goad** /gəʊd/ • **n.** **1** a spiked stick used for driving cattle. **2** a thing that stimulates someone into action. • **v.** **1** provoke to action or reaction. **2** urge on with a goad.
– ORIGIN OE *gād*, of Gmc origin.

**go-ahead** informal • **n.** (usu. **the go-ahead**) permission to proceed. • **adj.** **1** enthusiastic about new projects; enterprising. **2** N. Amer. denoting the run or score which gives a team the lead in a game.

**goal** • **n.** **1** (in soccer, rugby, etc.) a pair of posts linked by a crossbar and forming a space into or over which the ball has to be sent in order to score. **2** an instance of sending the ball into or over a goal. **3** an aim or desired result. ➤ the destination of a journey.
– PHRASES **in goal** in the position of goalkeeper.
– DERIVATIVES **goalless** adj.
– ORIGIN ME (in the sense 'limit, boundary'): of unknown origin.

**goal area** • **n.** Soccer a rectangular area in front of the goal from within which goal kicks must be taken.

**goal average** • **n.** Soccer the ratio of the numbers of goals scored for and against a team in a series of matches.

**goalball** • **n.** a game for visually handicapped players, played with a large ball containing bells.

**goal difference** • **n.** Soccer the difference between the number of goals scored for and against a team in a series of matches.

**goalie** • **n.** informal a goalkeeper or goaltender.

**goalkeeper** • **n.** a player in soccer or field hockey whose special role is to stop the ball from entering the goal.
– DERIVATIVES **goalkeeping** n.

**goal kick** • **n.** **1** Soccer a free kick taken by the defending side from within their goal area after attackers send the ball over the byline. **2** Rugby an attempt to kick a goal.
– DERIVATIVES **goal-kicker** n. (Rugby). **goal-kicking** n. (Rugby).

**goal line** • **n.** a line across a football or hockey field on which the goal is placed or which acts as the boundary beyond which a try or touchdown is scored.

**goalmouth** • **n.** the area just in front of a goal in soccer or hockey.

**goalpost** • **n.** either of the two upright posts of a goal.
– PHRASES **move the goalposts** unfairly alter the conditions or rules of a procedure during its course.

**goaltender** • **n.** chiefly N. Amer. a goalkeeper, especially in ice hockey.
– DERIVATIVES **goaltending** n.

**Goan** /ˈgəʊən/ (also **Goanese** /ˌgəʊəˈniːz/) • **n.** a native or inhabitant of the Indian state of Goa. • **adj.** of or relating to Goa.

**goanna** /gəʊˈanə/ • **n.** Austral. a monitor lizard.
– ORIGIN C19: alt. of IGUANA.

**go-around** (also **go-round**) • **n.** **1** a flight path taken by an aircraft after an aborted approach to landing. **2** US informal a confrontation or argument.

**goat** • **n.** **1** a hardy domesticated ruminant mammal that has backward-curving horns and (in the male) a beard. [*Capra hircus*.] ➤ a wild mammal related to this, such as the ibex, markhor, and tur. **2** informal a lecherous man. **3** Brit. informal a stupid person; a fool. **4** US informal a scapegoat.
– PHRASES **get someone's goat** informal irritate someone.
– DERIVATIVES **goatish** adj. **goaty** adj.
– ORIGIN OE *gāt* 'nanny goat', of Gmc origin; rel. to L. *haedus* 'kid'.

**goat-antelope** • **n.** a ruminant mammal of a group including the chamois and musk ox, with characteristics of both goats and antelopes. [Subfamily Caprinae.]

**goatee** /gəʊˈtiː/ • **n.** a small pointed beard like that of a goat.
– DERIVATIVES **goateed** adj.

**goatfish** • **n.** (pl. same or **-fishes**) North American term for RED MULLET.

**goatherd** • **n.** a person who tends goats.
– ORIGIN OE, from GOAT + obs. *herd* 'herdsman'.

**goat moth** • **n.** a large greyish moth, the caterpillar of which bores into wood and has a goat-like smell. [*Cossus cossus*.]

**goat's beard** • **n.** **1** a plant resembling a dandelion, with slender grass-like leaves. [*Tragopogon pratensis*.] **2** a plant with long plumes of white flowers. [*Aruncus dioicus*.]

**goatskin** • **n.** leather made from the skin of a goat.

**goatsucker** • **n.** another term for NIGHTJAR.

**go-away bird** • **n.** a mainly grey, crested, long-tailed African bird with a call that resembles the words 'go away'. [*Corythaixoides concolor* and other species.]

**gob¹** • **n.** informal, chiefly Brit. a person's mouth.
– ORIGIN C16: perh. from Sc. Gaelic *gob* 'beak, mouth'.

**gob²** informal • **n.** **1** Brit. a lump or clot of a slimy or viscous substance. ➤ N. Amer. a small lump. **2** (**gobs of**) N. Amer. a lot of. • **v.** (**gobbed**, **gobbing**) Brit. spit.
– ORIGIN ME: from OFr. *gobe* 'mouthful, lump', from *gober* 'to swallow, gulp', perh. of Celtic origin.

**gob³** • **n.** informal, dated an American sailor.
– ORIGIN C20: of unknown origin.

**gobbet** /ˈgɒbɪt/ • **n.** **1** a piece or lump of flesh, food, or other matter. **2** an extract from a text set for translation or comment in an examination.
– ORIGIN ME: from OFr. *gobet*, dimin. of *gobe* (see GOB²).

**gobble¹** • **v.** (often **gobble something up**) eat hurriedly and noisily. ➤ use a large amount of very quickly.
– DERIVATIVES **gobbler** n.
– ORIGIN C17: prob. from GOB².

**gobble²** • **v.** (of a turkeycock) make a characteristic swallowing sound in the throat.
– DERIVATIVES **gobbler** n.
– ORIGIN C17: imitative, perh. influenced by GOBBLE¹.

**gobbledegook** /ˈgɒb(ə)ldɪˌguːk, -ˌgʊk/ (also **gobbledygook**) • **n.** informal meaningless or unintelligible language, especially when over-technical or pompous.
– ORIGIN 1940s (orig. US): prob. imitating a turkey's gobble.

**go-between** • **n.** an intermediary or negotiator.

**gobi** /ˈgəʊbi/ • **n.** Indian term for CAULIFLOWER or CABBAGE.
– ORIGIN from Punjabi.

**goblet** • **n.** **1** a drinking glass with a foot and a stem. ➤ archaic a bowl-shaped metal or glass drinking cup. **2** Brit. a receptacle forming part of a liquidizer.
– ORIGIN ME: from OFr. *gobelet*, dimin. of *gobel* 'cup', of unknown origin.

**goblet cell** • **n.** Anatomy a column-shaped cell found in the respiratory and intestinal tracts, which secretes the main component of mucus.

**goblin** • **n.** a mischievous, ugly, dwarf-like creature of folklore.
– ORIGIN ME: from OFr. *gobelin*, possibly rel. to Ger. *Kobold* (see KOBOLD) or to Gk *kobalos* 'mischievous goblin'.

**gobo¹** /ˈgəʊbəʊ/ • **n.** (pl. **-os**) **1** a screen used to shield a lens from light or a microphone from noise. **2** Theatre a partial screen used in front of a spotlight to project a shape.
– ORIGIN 1930s: of unknown origin, perh. from *go between*.

**gobo²** /ˈgəʊbəʊ/ • **n.** a vegetable root used in oriental cookery.
– ORIGIN from Japanese.

**gobony** /gɒˈbəʊni/ • **adj.** Heraldry another term for COMPONY.

**gobshite** /ˈgɒbʃʌɪt/ • **n.** vulgar slang, chiefly Irish a stupid or incompetent person.

**gobsmacked** • **adj.** Brit. informal utterly astonished.
– DERIVATIVES **gobsmacking** adj.

**gobstopper** • **n.** chiefly Brit. a large, hard spherical sweet.

**goby** /ˈgəʊbi/ • **n.** (pl. **-ies**) a small marine fish, typically with a sucker on the underside. [Family Gobiidae: many species.]
– ORIGIN C18: from L. *gobius*, from Gk *kōbios*.

**go-by** • **n.** informal, dated (in phr. **give someone the go-by**) avoid or snub. ➤ end a romantic relationship with.

**GOC** • **abbrev.** Brit. General Officer Commanding.

**go-cart** ● n. **1** variant spelling of **GO-KART**. **2** a handcart. **3** a pushchair. **4** archaic a baby walker.

**God** ● n. **1** (in Christianity and other monotheistic religions) the creator and ruler of the universe; the supreme being. **2** (**god**) a superhuman being or spirit worshipped as having power over nature or human fortunes; a deity. ➤ an image of a god; an idol. **3** (**god**) a greatly admired or influential person. **4** (**the gods**) informal the gallery in a theatre. ● exclam. used to express surprise, anger, distress, etc. or for emphasis.
– PHRASES **God's acre** archaic a churchyard. **God the Father** (in Christian doctrine) the first person of the Trinity, God as creator and supreme authority. **God the Son** (in Christian doctrine) Christ regarded as the second person of the Trinity; God as incarnate and resurrected saviour. **play God** behave as if all-powerful or supremely important. **with God** dead and in heaven.
– DERIVATIVES **godhood** n. **godlike** adj. **godship** n. **godward** adj. & adv. **godwards** adv.
– ORIGIN OE, of Gmc origin.

**God-awful** ● adj. informal extremely bad or unpleasant.

**godchild** ● n. (pl. **-children**) a person in relation to a godparent.

**goddam** (also **goddamn, goddamned**) ● adj. & adv. informal, chiefly N. Amer. used for emphasis, especially to express anger or frustration.

**god-daughter** ● n. a female godchild.

**goddess** ● n. **1** a female deity. **2** a woman who is adored, especially for her beauty.

**godet** /gəʊ'dɛt, 'gəʊdeɪ/ ● n. a triangular piece of material inserted in a garment to make it flared or for ornamentation.
– ORIGIN C19: from Fr.

**godetia** /gə(ʊ)'di:ʃə/ ● n. a North American plant with showy lilac to red flowers. [Genus *Clarkia* (or *Godetia*).]
– ORIGIN mod. L., named after the Swiss botanist Charles H. *Godet*.

**go-devil** ● n. N. Amer., chiefly historical **1** a crude sled used for dragging logs. **2** a jointed apparatus for cleaning pipelines.

**godfather** ● n. **1** a male godparent. **2** a man who is influential or pioneering in a movement or organization. **3** a person directing an illegal organization, especially a leader of the American Mafia.

**God-fearing** ● adj. earnestly religious.

**godforsaken** ● adj. lacking any merit or attraction.

**godhead** ● n. **1** (usu. **the Godhead**) God. ➤ divine nature. **2** informal an adored, admired, or influential person.

**godless** ● adj. lacking or not recognizing God. ➤ profane; wicked.
– DERIVATIVES **godlessness** n.

**godly** ● adj. (**-ier, -iest**) devoutly religious; pious.
– DERIVATIVES **godliness** n.

**godmother** ● n. a female godparent.

**godown** /'gəʊdaʊn, gəʊ'daʊn/ ● n. (in east Asia, especially India) a warehouse.
– ORIGIN C16: from Port. *gudão*, from Tamil *kiṭaṅku*, Malayalam *kiṭaṅṅu*, or Kannada *gadaṅgu*.

**godparent** ● n. a person nominated to present a child at baptism and promising to take responsibility for their religious education.

**God Save the Queen** (or **King**) ● n. the British national anthem.

**godsend** ● n. something very helpful or opportune.

**God's gift** ● n. chiefly ironic the ideal or best possible person or thing.

**godson** ● n. a male godchild.

**Godspeed** ● exclam. dated an expression of good wishes to a person starting a journey.

**God's truth** ● n. the absolute truth.

**godwit** ● n. a large, long-legged wader with a long straight or slightly upcurved bill. [Genus *Limosa*: four species.]
– ORIGIN C16: of unknown origin.

**Godwottery** /gɒd'wɒt(ə)ri/ ● n. Brit. humorous affectedly archaic or elaborate speech or writing.
– ORIGIN 1930s: from the line 'A garden is a lovesome thing, God wot!', in T. E. Brown's poem *My Garden* (1876).

**goer** ● n. **1** a person who attends a specified place or event: *a theatre-goer.* **2** informal a person or thing that goes. **3** informal a sexually unrestrained woman.

**goes** third person singular present of **GO**[1].

**goest** /'gəʊɪst/ archaic second person singular present of **GO**[1].

**goeth** /'gəʊɪθ/ archaic third person singular present of **GO**[1].

**Goethean** /'gə:tɪən/ (also **Goethian**) ● adj. of or relating to the German poet and dramatist Johann Wolfgang von Goethe (1749–1832).

**goethite** /'gə:tʌɪt/ ● n. a dark or yellowish-brown mineral consisting of hydrated iron oxide.
– ORIGIN C19: from *Goethe* (see **GOETHEAN**).

**gofer** /'gəʊfə/ (also **gopher**) ● n. informal, chiefly N. Amer. a person who runs errands, especially on a film set or in an office; a dogsbody.
– ORIGIN 1960s: from *go for* (i.e. go and fetch).

**goffer** /'gɒfə/ ● v. [usu. as adj. **goffered**] **1** crimp or flute (a lace edge or frill) with heated irons. **2** [as adj. **goffered**] (of the gilt edges of a book) embossed with a repeating design. ● n. an iron used to crimp or flute lace.
– ORIGIN C16: from Fr. *gaufrer*, from *gaufre* 'honeycomb', from Mid. Low Ger. *wāfel* (see **WAFFLE**[2]).

**go-getter** ● n. informal an aggressively enterprising person.
– DERIVATIVES **go-getting** adj.

**goggle** ● v. look with wide open eyes, typically in amazement or wonder. ➤ (of the eyes) protrude or open wide. ● adj. (of the eyes) protuberant or rolling. ● n. (**goggles**) **1** close-fitting protective glasses with side shields. **2** the staggers (a disease of sheep).
– DERIVATIVES **goggled** adj.
– ORIGIN ME (in the sense 'look to one side, squint'): prob. from a base symbolic of oscillating movement.

**goggle-box** ● n. Brit. informal a television set.

**goggle-eye** ● n. an edible fish with large eyes, occurring on tropical and subtropical reefs. [*Priacanthus hamrur* and *Selar crumenophthalmus* (**goggle-eye jack**).]

**goggle-eyed** ● adj. having goggle eyes, especially through astonishment.

**go-go** ● adj. **1** denoting an unrestrained and erotic style of dancing to popular music. **2** assertively dynamic. ● n. a style of popular music with an incessant funk beat.
– ORIGIN 1960s: reduplication of **GO**[1], perh. influenced by **A GOGO**.

**Goidelic** /gɔɪ'dɛlɪk/ ● n. the northern group of Celtic languages, including Irish, Scottish Gaelic, and Manx. Compare with **BRYTHONIC**. ● adj. relating to or denoting these languages.

**going** ● n. **1** the condition of the ground viewed in terms of suitability for horse racing or travel. **2** conditions for, or progress in, an endeavour: *when the going gets tough, the tough get going.* ● adj. **1** chiefly Brit. existing or available; to be had. **2** (of a price) fair or correct; current: *the going rate.*

**going concern** ● n. a business that is operating and making a profit.

**going-over** ● n. informal **1** a thorough cleaning or inspection. **2** a beating.

**goings-on** ● pl. n. events or behaviour, especially of an unusual or suspect nature.

**goitre** /'gɔɪtə/ (US **goiter**) ● n. a swelling of the neck resulting from enlargement of the thyroid gland.
– DERIVATIVES **goitred** adj. **goitrous** adj.
– ORIGIN C17: from Fr., a back-form. from *goitreux* 'having a goitre', or from OFr. *goitron* 'gullet', both based on L. *guttur* 'throat'.

**go-kart** (also **go-cart**) ● n. a small racing car with a lightweight or skeleton body.
– DERIVATIVES **go-karting** n.

**Golconda** /gɒl'kɒndə/ ● n. a source of wealth, advantages, or happiness.
– ORIGIN C19: from the name of a city near Hyderabad, India, famous for its diamonds.

**gold** • n. **1** a yellow precious metal, the chemical element of atomic number 79, used in jewellery and decoration and as a monetary medium. (Symbol: **Au**) **2** a deep lustrous yellow or yellow-brown colour. **3** coins or articles made of gold. ➤money in large sums; wealth. **4** the bullseye of an archery target.
– PHRASES **pot** (or **crock**) **of gold** a large but distant or imaginary reward. [with allusion to the story of a crock of gold supposedly to be found at the end of a rainbow.]
– ORIGIN OE, of Gmc origin.

**gold-beater's skin** • n. a membrane used to separate leaves of gold during beating.

**gold brick** US informal • n. (also **gold-bricker**) a swindler or shirker. • v. (**gold-brick**) **1** invent excuses to avoid a task; shirk. **2** swindle or cheat.

**goldbug** • n. informal, chiefly US a person favouring gold as an investment.

**goldcrest** • n. a very small warbler with a black-bordered yellow or orange crest. [*Regulus regulus*.]

**gold-digger** • n. informal a woman who forms relationships with men purely to extract money from them.
– DERIVATIVES **gold-digging** adj.

**gold disc** • n. a framed golden disc awarded to a recording artist or group for sales exceeding a specified figure.

**gold dust** • n. **1** fine particles of gold. **2** something very valuable. **3** a cultivated evergreen alyssum, with grey-green leaves and numerous small yellow flowers. [*Alyssum saxatile*.]

**golden** • adj. **1** made of, coloured like, or shining like gold. **2** (of a period) very happy and prosperous. **3** (of an opportunity) very favourable.
– DERIVATIVES **goldenly** adv.

**golden age** • n. **1** an idyllic, often imaginary past time of peace, prosperity, and happiness. **2** the period when a specified art or activity is at its peak.

**golden ager** • n. N. Amer. euphemistic an old person.

**golden boy** (or **golden girl**) • n. informal a very popular or successful young man or woman.

**golden chain** • n. the common laburnum.

**Golden Delicious** • n. a widely grown dessert apple of a greenish-yellow, soft-fleshed variety.

**golden eagle** • n. a large eagle with yellow-tipped head feathers in the mature adult. [*Aquila chrysaetos*.]

**goldeneye** • n. (pl. same or **goldeneyes**) a migratory northern diving duck, the male of which has a dark head with a white cheek patch and yellow eyes. [Genus *Bucephala*: two species.]

**golden goal** • n. (in some soccer competitions) the first goal scored during extra time, which ends the match and gives victory to the scoring side.

**golden goose** • n. a continuing source of wealth or profit that may be exhausted if it is misused. See also ***kill the goose that lays the golden eggs*** at EGG[1].

**golden handcuffs** • pl. n. informal benefits provided by an employer to discourage an employee from taking employment elsewhere.

**golden handshake** • n. informal a payment given to someone who is made redundant or retires early.

**golden jubilee** • n. the fiftieth anniversary of a significant event.

**golden mean** • n. **1** the ideal moderate position between two extremes. **2** another term for GOLDEN SECTION.

**golden number** • n. the number showing a year's place in the Metonic lunar cycle, used to fix the date of Easter for that year.

**golden oldie** • n. informal **1** an old song of enduring popularity. **2** a person who is no longer young but is still successful.

**golden orfe** • n. an orfe (fish) of an ornamental yellow variety, widely kept in aquaria and ponds.

**golden parachute** • n. informal a payment guaranteed to a company executive should they be dismissed as a result of a merger or takeover.

**golden perch** • n. another term for CALLOP.

**golden plover** • n. a northern plover with a gold-speckled back and black face and underparts. [*Pluvialis apricaria* and related species.]

**golden retriever** • n. a retriever of a breed with a thick golden-coloured coat.

**goldenrod** • n. a plant of the daisy family, with tall spikes of small bright yellow flowers. [Genus *Solidago*.]

**golden rule** • n. a basic principle which should always be followed.

**golden section** • n. the division of a line so that the whole is to the greater part as that part is to the smaller part (i.e. in a ratio of 1 to ½ ($\sqrt{5}$ + 1)), a proportion which is considered to be particularly pleasing to the eye.

**golden share** • n. Brit. a share in a company that gives control of at least 51 per cent of the voting rights, especially when held by the government.

**golden syrup** • n. Brit. a pale treacle.

**golden wedding** • n. the fiftieth anniversary of a wedding.

**goldfield** • n. a district in which gold is found as a mineral.

**goldfinch** • n. a brightly coloured finch with yellow feathers in the plumage. [*Carduelis carduelis* (Eurasia), *C. tristis* (**American goldfinch**), and related species.]

**goldfish** • n. (pl. same or **-fishes**) a small reddish-golden carp popular in ponds and aquaria. [*Carassius auratus*.]

**goldfish bowl** • n. chiefly Brit. **1** a spherical glass container for goldfish. **2** a place or situation lacking privacy.

**goldilocks** • n. **1** informal a person with golden hair. **2** a woodland buttercup. [*Ranunculus auricomus*.] **3** a yellow-flowered plant resembling the Michaelmas daisy. [*Aster linosyris*.]

**gold leaf** • n. gold that has been beaten into a very thin sheet, used in gilding.

**gold medal** • n. a medal made of or coloured gold, customarily awarded for first place in a race or competition.

**gold mine** • n. **1** a place where gold is mined. **2** a source of great wealth or valuable resources.
– DERIVATIVES **gold miner** n.

**gold of pleasure** • n. a yellow-flowered Mediterranean plant of the cabbage family, which yields fibre, oilseed, and seed for cage birds. [*Camelina sativa*.]

**gold plate** • n. **1** a thin layer of gold applied as a coating to another metal. **2** plates, dishes, etc. made of or plated with gold. • v. (**gold-plate**) cover with gold plate.

**gold reserve** • n. a quantity of gold held by a central bank.

**gold rush** • n. a rapid movement of people to a newly discovered goldfield.

**goldsmith** • n. a person who makes gold articles.

**gold standard** • n. historical the system by which the value of a currency was defined in terms of gold, for which the currency could be exchanged.

**Gold Stick** • n. (in the UK) a ceremonial officer in the Sovereign's household, entitled to carry a gilt rod on state occasions.

**golem** /ˈɡəʊləm, ˈɡɔɪl-/ • n. **1** (in Jewish legend) a clay figure brought to life by magic. **2** an automaton or robot.
– ORIGIN C19: from Yiddish *goylem*, from Heb. *gōlem* 'shapeless mass'.

**golf** • n. **1** a game played on a large open-air course, the aim of which is to strike a small, hard ball with a club into a series of small holes with the fewest possible strokes. **2** a code word representing the letter G, used in radio communication. • v. [often as noun **golfing**] play golf.
– DERIVATIVES **golfer** n.
– ORIGIN ME (orig. Scots): perh. rel. to Du. *kolf* 'club, bat'.

**golf ball** • n. **1** a small, hard ball used in the game of golf. **2** (**golfball**) a small metal globe used in some electric typewriters to carry the type.

**golf club** • n. see CLUB[2] (sense 2).

**golf course** • n. a course on which golf is played.

**Golgi body** /ˈɡɒldʒi, -ɡi/ (also **Golgi apparatus**) • n. Biology a complex of vesicles and folded membranes within

## Word *Formation*

**-gon** 'a plane figure with a specified number of straight sides', from Greek *-gōnos* '-angled'

| | | |
|---|---|---|
| decagon | ten sides | Gk *deka* 'ten' |
| dodecagon | twelve sides | Gk *dōdeka* 'twelve' |
| hendecagon | eleven sides | Gk *hendeka* 'eleven' |
| heptagon | seven sides | Gk *hepta* 'seven' |
| hexagon | six sides | Gk *hex* 'six' |
| nonagon | nine sides | L. *nonus* 'ninth' |
| octagon | eight sides | Gk *oktō* 'eight' |
| pentagon | five sides | Gk *pente* 'five' |
| polygon | many sides | Gk *polloi* 'many' |
| trigon | (archaic) a triangle; also denoting a type of harp | Gk *treis* 'three' |
| undecagon | another term for ***hendecagon*** | L. *undecim* 'eleven' |

the cytoplasm of a cell, involved in secretion and intracellular transport.
– ORIGIN named after the Ital. scientist Camillo *Golgi*.

**goliath beetle** ● **n.** a very large tropical beetle, the male of which has a forked horn on the head. [*Goliathus giganteus* (Africa, the largest known beetle) and related species.]
– ORIGIN after the Philistine giant *Goliath* in the Bible.

**goliath frog** ● **n.** a giant frog of West Central Africa. [*Rana goliath*.]

**golliwog** ● **n.** a soft doll with a black face and fuzzy hair.
– ORIGIN C19: from *Golliwogg*, the name of a doll character in books by Bertha Upton; perh. suggested by **GOLLY**[1] and **POLLIWOG**.

**gollop** /ˈgɒləp/ Brit. informal ● **v.** (**golloped**, **golloping**) swallow (food) hastily or greedily. ● **n.** a hasty gulp.
– ORIGIN C19: perh. from **GULP**, influenced by **GOBBLE**[1].

**golly**[1] ● **exclam.** informal used to express surprise or delight.
– ORIGIN C18: euphemism for **GOD**.

**golly**[2] ● **n.** (pl. **-ies**) Brit. informal short for **GOLLIWOG**.

**gombeen** /gɒmˈbiːn/ ● **n.** [as modifier] Irish involved in the practice of usury: *a gombeen man*.
– ORIGIN C19: from Ir. *gaimbín*, perh. from the same Celtic source as med. L. *cambire* 'to change'.

**-gon** ● **comb. form** in nouns denoting plane figures with a specified number of angles and sides: *hexagon*. See word-formation panel.
– ORIGIN from Gk *-gōnos* '-angled'.

**gonad** /ˈgəʊnad/ ● **n.** Physiology & Zoology an organ that produces gametes; a testis or ovary.
– DERIVATIVES **gonadal** /gə(ʊ)ˈneɪd(ə)l/ adj.
– ORIGIN C19: from mod. L. *gonades*, pl. of *gonas*, from Gk *gonē* 'generation, seed'.

**gonadotrophin** /ˌgəʊnadə(ʊ)ˈtrəʊfɪn/ (also **gonadotropin** /-ˈtrəʊpɪn, -ˈtrɒpɪn/) ● **n.** Biochemistry any of a group of hormones secreted by the pituitary which stimulate the activity of the gonads.
– DERIVATIVES **gonadotrophic** adj.

**Gond** /gɒnd, gəʊnd/ (also **Gondi** /ˈgɒndi/) ● **n.** (pl. same) **1** a member of an indigenous people living in the hill forests of central India. **2** the Dravidian language of this people.
– ORIGIN from Sanskrit *goṇḍa*.

**gondola** /ˈgɒndələ/ ● **n. 1** a light flat-bottomed boat used on Venetian canals, having a high point at each end and worked by one oar at the stern. **2** a cabin on a ski lift, or suspended from an airship or balloon. **3** (also **gondola car**) N. Amer. an open railway freight wagon. **4** Brit. a free-standing block of shelves used to display goods in a supermarket.
– ORIGIN C16: from Venetian Ital., from Rhaeto-Romance *gondolà* 'to rock, roll'.

**gondolier** /ˌgɒndəˈlɪə/ ● **n.** a person who propels and steers a gondola.

**gone** past participle of **GO**[1]. ● **adj. 1** no longer present; departed. ➤no longer in existence; dead or extinct. **2** informal in a trance or stupor, especially through exhaustion, drink, or drugs. **3** informal, chiefly N. Amer. lost; hopeless. **4** informal having reached a specified time in a pregnancy. **5** US informal, dated excellent; inspired. ● **prep.** Brit. **1** (of time) past: *it's gone half past eleven*. **2** (of age) older than.
– PHRASES **be gone on** informal be infatuated with. **gone away!** a huntsman's cry, indicating that a fox has been started.

**goner** /ˈgɒnə/ ● **n.** informal a person or thing that is doomed or cannot be saved.

**gonfalon** /ˈgɒnf(ə)lən/ ● **n.** a banner or pennant hung from a crossbar.
– DERIVATIVES **gonfalonier** /ˌgɒnfələˈnɪə/ n.
– ORIGIN C16: from Ital. *gonfalone*, from a Gmc compound whose second element is rel. to **VANE**.

**gong** ● **n. 1** a metal disc with a turned rim, giving a resonant note when struck. **2** Brit. informal a medal or decoration. ● **v.** sound a gong or make a sound like that of a gong.
– ORIGIN C17: from Malay *gong*, *gung*, of imitative origin.

**gongoozler** /gɒŋˈguːzlə/ ● **n.** informal an idle spectator.
– ORIGIN C20: perh. from Lincolnshire dial. *gawn* and *gooze* 'stare, gape'.

**goniatite** /ˈgəʊnɪətʌɪt/ ● **n.** Palaeontology an ammonoid fossil of an early type with simple angular suture lines.
– ORIGIN C19: from mod. L. *Goniatites*, from Gk *gōnia* 'angle'.

**gonif** /ˈgɒnɪf/ (also **goniff**) ● **n.** N. Amer. informal a disreputable or dishonest person.
– ORIGIN C19: from Yiddish *ganev*, from Heb. *gannāḇ* 'thief'.

**goniometer** /ˌgəʊnɪˈɒmɪtə/ ● **n.** an instrument for the precise measurement of angles, especially the angles between the faces of crystals.
– DERIVATIVES **goniometric** adj. **goniometrical** adj. **goniometry** n.
– ORIGIN C18: from Fr. *goniomètre*, from Gk *gōnia* 'angle' + Fr. *-mètre* '(instrument) measuring'.

**gonna** ● **contr.** informal going to.

**gonococcus** /ˌgɒnəˈkɒkəs/ ● **n.** (pl. **gonococci** /-k(s)ʌɪ, -k(s)iː/) a bacterium which causes gonorrhoea. [*Neisseria gonorrhoeae*.]
– DERIVATIVES **gonococcal** adj.

**gonorrhoea** /ˌgɒnəˈrɪə/ (US **gonorrhea**) ● **n.** a venereal disease involving inflammatory discharge from the urethra or vagina.
– DERIVATIVES **gonorrhoeal** adj.
– ORIGIN C16: via late L. from Gk *gonorrhoia*, from *gonos* 'semen' + *rhoia* 'flux'.

**gonzo** ● **adj.** informal, chiefly N. Amer. **1** of or denoting journalism of an exaggerated, subjective, and fictionalized style. **2** bizarre or crazy.
– ORIGIN 1970s: perh. from Ital. *gonzo* 'foolish' or Sp. *ganso* 'goose, fool'.

**goo** ● **n.** informal **1** a sticky or slimy substance. **2** sickly sentiment.
– ORIGIN C20: perh. from *burgoo*, a naut. sl. term for porridge, based on Pers. *bulġūr* 'bruised grain'.

**good** ● **adj.** (**better**, **best**) **1** to be desired or approved of;

welcome; pleasant. ➤(**good for**) beneficial to. ➤expressing good wishes on meeting: *good morning.* **2** having the required qualities; of a high standard. ➤appropriate. ➤(of language) with correct grammar and pronunciation. ➤strictly adhering to the principles of a religion or cause: *a good Catholic girl.* **3** morally right; virtuous. ➤(of a child) obedient; well behaved. **4** enjoyable or satisfying: *a good time.* ➤(of clothes) smart and formal. **5** thorough: *a good look around.* ➤at least; no less than: *a good twenty years.* **6** chiefly N. Amer. (of a ticket) valid. ● **n. 1** that which is morally right; righteousness. **2** benefit or advantage. **3** (**goods**) merchandise or possessions. ➤[often as modifier] Brit. freight: *a goods train.*

– PHRASES **as good as** —— very nearly or inevitably ——. **be any** (or **no** or **much**) **good** have some (or none or a lot of) merit. **be to the good** have a net profit or advantage. **come up with** (or **deliver**) **the goods** informal do what is expected or required. **do good 1** act virtuously, especially by helping others. **2** make a helpful contribution. **do someone good** be beneficial, especially to health. **for good** forever. (**as**) **good as gold** (of a child) extremely well behaved. **the Good Book** the Bible. **good for** (or **on**) **you!** well done! **the Good Shepherd** a name for Jesus. **a good word** words in recommendation or defence of a person. **in good time 1** with no risk of being late. **2** (also **all in good time**) in due course but without haste. **make good** be successful. **make something good 1** compensate for loss, damage, or expense. **2** fulfil a promise or claim. **take something in good part** not be offended. **up to no good** doing something wrong.

– ORIGIN OE *gōd*, of Gmc origin.

**goodbye** (US also **goodby**) ● **exclam.** used to express good wishes when parting or ending a conversation. ● **n.** (pl. **goodbyes**; US also **goodbys**) an instance of saying 'goodbye'; a parting.

– ORIGIN C16: contr. of *God be with you!*

**good faith** ● **n.** honesty or sincerity of intention.

**goodfella** ● **n.** US informal a gangster, especially a member of a Mafia family.

**good form** ● **n.** behaviour complying with social conventions.

**good-for-nothing** ● **adj.** (of a person) worthless. ● **n.** a worthless person.

**Good Friday** ● **n.** the Friday before Easter Sunday, on which the Crucifixion of Christ is commemorated in the Christian Church.

**good-hearted** ● **adj.** kind and well meaning.

– DERIVATIVES **good-heartedness** n.

**good-humoured** ● **adj.** genial; cheerful.

– DERIVATIVES **good-humouredly** adv.

**goodie** ● **n.** variant spelling of **GOODY**[1].

**goodish** ● **adj.** fairly good. ➤fairly large.

**Good King Henry** ● **n.** an edible plant with large dark green leaves and insignificant clusters of flowers. [*Chenopodium bonus-henricus.*]

**good-looking** ● **adj.** (of a person) attractive.

– DERIVATIVES **good-looker** n.

**goodly** ● **adj.** (**-ier**, **-iest**) **1** considerable in size or quantity. **2** archaic attractive, excellent, or virtuous.

– DERIVATIVES **goodliness** n.

**goodman** ● **n.** (pl. **-men**) archaic, chiefly Scottish the male head of a household.

**good nature** ● **n.** a kind and unselfish disposition.

– DERIVATIVES **good-natured** adj. **good-naturedly** adv.

**goodness** ● **n. 1** the quality of being good. **2** the beneficial or nourishing element of food. ● **exclam.** (as a substitution for 'God') expressing surprise, anger, etc.

– PHRASES **goodness of fit** Statistics the extent to which observed data match the values expected by theory.

**goodnight** ● **exclam.** expressing good wishes on parting at night or before going to bed.

**good-oh** /ˈgʊdəʊ, gʊdˈəʊ/ ● **exclam.** dated used to express pleasure or approval.

**goods and chattels** ● **pl. n.** chiefly Law all kinds of personal possessions.

**good-tempered** ● **adj.** not easily irritated or made angry.

– DERIVATIVES **good-temperedly** adv.

**good-time** ● **adj.** (of a person) recklessly pursuing pleasure. ➤(of music) intended purely to entertain.

– DERIVATIVES **good-timer** n.

**goodwife** ● **n.** (pl. **-wives**) archaic, chiefly Scottish the female head of a household.

**goodwill** ● **n. 1** friendly or helpful feelings or attitude. **2** the established reputation of a business regarded as a quantifiable asset.

**good works** ● **pl. n.** charitable acts.

**goody**[1] ● **n.** (also **goodie**) (pl. **-ies**) informal **1** Brit. a good or favoured person, especially a hero in a story or film. **2** (usu. **goodies**) something tasty to eat. ● **exclam.** expressing childish delight.

**goody**[2] ● **n.** (pl. **-ies**) archaic (with a name) an elderly woman of humble position: *Goody Blake.*

– ORIGIN C16: familiar form of **GOODWIFE**; cf. **HUSSY**.

**goody-goody** informal ● **n.** a smug or obtrusively virtuous person. ● **adj.** smug or obtrusively virtuous.

**gooey** ● **adj.** (**-ier**, **-iest**) informal **1** soft and sticky. **2** mawkishly sentimental.

– DERIVATIVES **gooeyness** n.

**goof** informal, chiefly N. Amer. ● **n. 1** a mistake. **2** a foolish or stupid person. ● **v. 1** fool around. ➤(**goof off**) evade a duty; idle or shirk. **2** make a mistake; blunder.

– ORIGIN C20: of unknown origin; cf. **GOOP**[1].

**goofball** ● **n.** informal, chiefly N. Amer. **1** a naive or stupid person. **2** a narcotic drug in pill form, especially a barbiturate.

**goofus** /ˈguːfəs/ ● **n.** US informal a foolish or stupid person.

– ORIGIN 1920s: based on **GOOF**.

**goofy** ● **adj.** (**-ier**, **-iest**) informal **1** chiefly N. Amer. foolish; harmlessly eccentric. **2** having protruding or crooked front teeth.

– DERIVATIVES **goofily** adv. **goofiness** n.

**goog** ● **n.** Austral./NZ informal an egg.

– PHRASES (**as**) **full as a goog** very drunk.

– ORIGIN C20: abbrev. of *googie*, from Sc. dial. *goggie*, child's word for an egg.

**googly** ● **n.** (pl. **-ies**) Cricket an off break bowled with an apparent leg-break action.

– ORIGIN C20: of unknown origin.

**googol** /ˈguːgɒl/ ● **cardinal number** equivalent to ten raised to the power of a hundred ($10^{100}$).

– ORIGIN 1940s: said to have been coined by the young nephew of the Amer. mathematician E. Kasner.

**googolplex** /ˈguːg(ə)lplɛks/ ● **cardinal number** equivalent to ten raised to the power of a googol.

**goo-goo** ● **adj.** informal **1** amorously adoring: *making goo-goo eyes.* **2** (of speech or vocal sounds) childish or meaningless.

– ORIGIN C20: possibly rel. to **GOGGLE**.

**gook**[1] /guːk, gʊk/ ● **n.** offensive, chiefly N. Amer. a foreigner, especially a person of SE Asian descent.

– ORIGIN 1930s: of unknown origin.

**gook**[2] /guːk, gʊk/ ● **n.** informal a sloppy wet or viscous substance.

– ORIGIN 1970s: var. of **GUCK**.

**goolie** /ˈguːli/ (also **gooly**) ● **n.** (pl. **-ies**) **1** Brit. informal a testicle. **2** Austral./NZ informal a stone, boulder, or pebble.

– ORIGIN 1930s: appar. of Ind. origin; cf. Hindi *golī* 'bullet, ball, pill'.

**goombah** /guːmˈbɑː/ ● **n.** N. Amer. informal an associate or accomplice, especially a senior member of a criminal gang.

– ORIGIN 1960s: prob. a dial. alt. of Ital. *compàre* 'godfather, friend, accomplice'.

**goombay** /ˈguːmbeɪ/ ● **n.** W. Indian **1** a goatskin drum played with the hands. **2** (chiefly in the Bahamas) a festival of music and dance.

– ORIGIN perh. from Kikongo *ngoma*, denoting a type of drum.

**goon** ● **n.** informal **1** a foolish or eccentric person. **2** chiefly N. Amer. a bully or thug, especially a member of an armed force. **3** Brit. a guard in a German prisoner-of-war camp during the Second World War.

– ORIGIN C19: perh. from dial. *gooney* 'booby'; later influenced by the Amer. cartoon character 'Alice the *Goon*'.

**goonda** /'gu:ndə/ ● **n.** Indian a hired thug or bully.
– ORIGIN from Hindi *gundā* 'rascal'.

**gooney bird** ● **n.** informal, chiefly US an albatross.
– ORIGIN C19: of unknown origin.

**goop**[1] ● **n.** informal a stupid person.
– DERIVATIVES **goopiness** n. **goopy** adj.
– ORIGIN C20 (orig. US): of unknown origin; cf. **GOOF**.

**goop**[2] ● **n.** informal, chiefly N. Amer. another term for **GLOOP**.
– DERIVATIVES **goopiness** n. **goopy** adj.

**goosander** /gu:'sandə/ ● **n.** (pl. same or **goosanders**) a large merganser (diving duck), the male of which has a dark green head and whitish underparts. [*Mergus merganser*.]
– ORIGIN C17: prob. from **GOOSE** + *-ander* as in dial. *bergander* 'shelduck'.

**goose** /gu:s/ ● **n.** (pl. **geese** /gi:s/) **1** a large waterbird with a long neck, short legs, webbed feet, and a short, broad bill. [Several genera in the family Anatidae.] ➤ the female of such a bird. **2** informal a foolish person. **3** (pl. **gooses**) a tailor's smoothing iron. ● **v.** informal **1** poke (someone) in the bottom. **2** N. Amer. give a boost to; invigorate.
– ORIGIN OE *gōs*, of Gmc origin.

**goose barnacle** ● **n.** a stalked barnacle which hangs from floating objects, catching passing prey with its feathery legs. [Genus *Lepas*.]

**gooseberry** ● **n.** (pl. **-ies**) **1** a round edible yellowish-green or reddish berry with a thin translucent hairy skin. **2** the thorny European shrub which bears this fruit. [*Ribes grossularia*.] **3** Brit. informal a third person in the company of two people, especially lovers, who would prefer to be alone.
– ORIGIN C16: the first element perh. from **GOOSE**, or perh. based on OFr. *groseille*.

**goosebumps** ● **pl. n.** chiefly N. Amer. another term for **GOOSE PIMPLES**.

**goose egg** ● **n.** N. Amer. informal a zero score in a game.

**goosefish** ● **n.** (pl. same or **-fishes**) N. Amer. a bottom-dwelling anglerfish. [*Lophius americanus* and other species.]

**gooseflesh** ● **n.** a pimply state of the skin with the hairs erect, produced by cold or fright.

**goosefoot** ● **n.** (pl. **goosefoots**) a plant with divided leaves which are said to resemble the foot of a goose. [Genus *Chenopodium*.]

**goosegog** /'gʊzgɒg, 'gu:sgɒg/ ● **n.** Brit. informal a gooseberry.

**goosegrass** ● **n.** a widely distributed scrambling plant related to bedstraws, with hooked bristles on the stem, leaves, and seeds. [*Galium aparine*.]

**gooseneck** ● **n.** a support or pipe curved like a goose's neck.

**goose pimples** ● **pl. n.** the pimples that form gooseflesh.

**gooseskin** ● **n.** another term for **GOOSEFLESH**.

**goose step** ● **n.** a military marching step in which the legs are not bent at the knee. ● **v.** (**goose-step**) march with such a step.

**goosey** (also **goosy**) ● **adj.** (**-ier**, **-iest**) informal **1** exhibiting gooseflesh. **2** US sensitive to being tickled.

**GOP** ● **abbrev.** informal Grand Old Party (a name for the US Republican Party).

**gopak** /'gəʊpak/ (also **hopak**) ● **n.** an energetic Ukrainian dance traditionally performed by men.
– ORIGIN 1920s: via Russ., from Ukrainian *hopak*.

**gopher** /'gəʊfə/ ● **n. 1** (also **pocket gopher**) a burrowing American rodent with fur-lined pouches on its cheeks. [Family Geomyidae: many species.] ➤ informal North American term for **GROUND SQUIRREL**. ➤ [as modifier] in names of various burrowing reptiles: *gopher tortoise*. **2** Computing an Internet system which searches for documents on topics of interest. **3** variant spelling of **GOFER**.
– ORIGIN C18: perh. from Canad. Fr. *gaufre* 'honeycomb' (because the gopher 'honeycombs' the ground with its burrows).

**gopher wood** ● **n.** (in biblical use) the timber from which Noah's ark was made.
– ORIGIN C17: *gopher* from Heb. *gōper*.

**gopik** /'gəʊpɪk/ ● **n.** (pl. same or **gopiks**) a monetary unit of Azerbaijan, equal to one hundredth of a manat.

**goral** /'gɔ:r(ə)l/ ● **n.** a long-haired goat-antelope with backward-curving horns, found in mountainous regions of east Asia. [Genus *Nemorhaedus*.]
– ORIGIN C19: a local word in the Himalayas.

**gorblimey** Brit. informal ● **exclam.** an expression of surprise or indignation. ● **n.** [as modifier] dated denoting various kinds of unusual clothing.
– ORIGIN C19: alt. of *God blind me*.

**gorcock** /'gɔ:kɒk/ ● **n.** Scottish & N. English the male of the red grouse.
– ORIGIN C17: from *gor-* (of unknown origin) + **COCK**[1].

**Gordian knot** /'gɔ:dɪən/ ● **n.** (in phr. **cut the Gordian knot**) solve a difficult problem in a direct or forceful way.
– ORIGIN C16: from the legendary knot tied by *Gordius*, king of Gordium, and cut through by Alexander the Great in response to the prophecy that whoever untied it would rule Asia.

**Gordon Bennett** ● **exclam.** expressing surprise, incredulity, or exasperation.
– ORIGIN 1890s: prob. an alt. of **GORBLIMEY**, after the Amer. publisher James *Gordon Bennett*.

**Gordon setter** ● **n.** a setter of a black-and-tan breed, used as a gun dog.
– ORIGIN C19: named after the 4th Duke of *Gordon*.

**gore**[1] ● **n.** blood that has been shed, especially as a result of violence.
– ORIGIN OE *gor* 'dung, dirt', of Gmc origin.

**gore**[2] ● **v.** (of an animal such as a bull) pierce or stab with a horn or tusk.
– ORIGIN ME: of unknown origin.

**gore**[3] ● **n. 1** a triangular or tapering piece of material used in making a garment, sail, or umbrella. **2** archaic a triangular piece of land. ● **v.** shape with a gore or gores.
– ORIGIN OE *gāra*, of Gmc origin; prob. rel. to OE *gār* 'spear'.

**Gore-tex** /'gɔ:tɛks/ ● **n.** trademark a breathable waterproof fabric used in outdoor clothing.

**gorge** ● **n. 1** a steep, narrow valley or ravine. **2** (usu. in phr. **one's gorge rises**) the contents of the stomach. **3** archaic the throat. **4** Architecture the narrow rear entrance to a fortification. ● **v.** eat a large amount greedily.
– DERIVATIVES **gorger** n.
– ORIGIN ME: from OFr. *gorger*, from *gorge* 'throat', based on L. *gurges* 'whirlpool'.

**gorged** ● **adj.** [postpos.] Heraldry having the neck encircled by a coronet or collar.

**gorgeous** ● **adj. 1** beautiful; very attractive. **2** informal very pleasant.
– DERIVATIVES **gorgeously** adv. **gorgeousness** n.
– ORIGIN C15: from OFr. *gorgias* 'fine, elegant', of unknown origin.

**gorget** /'gɔ:dʒɪt/ ● **n. 1** historical an article of clothing or piece of armour covering the throat. ➤ a wimple. **2** a patch of colour on the throat of a bird or other animal.
– ORIGIN ME: from OFr. *gorgete*, from *gorge* (see **GORGE**).

**gorgio** /'gɔ:dʒɪəʊ/ ● **n.** (pl. **-os**) the gypsy name for a non-gypsy.
– ORIGIN from Romany *gorjo*.

**gorgon** /'gɔ:g(ə)n/ ● **n. 1** Greek Mythology each of three sisters with snakes for hair, who had the power to turn anyone who looked at them to stone. **2** a fierce, frightening, or repulsive woman.
– ORIGIN via L. from Gk *Gorgō*, from *gorgos* 'terrible'.

**gorgonian** /gɔ:'gəʊnɪən/ ● **n.** Zoology a colonial coral of an order (Gorgonacea) having a horny tree-like skeleton, including the sea fans and precious red coral.
– ORIGIN C19: from mod. L. *Gorgonia*, from L. *Gorgo* (see **GORGON**) + **-AN**.

**Gorgonzola** /ˌgɔ:g(ə)n'zəʊlə/ ● **n.** a rich, strong-flavoured Italian cheese with bluish-green veins.
– ORIGIN named after *Gorgonzola*, a village in northern Italy.

**gorilla** ● **n.** **1** a powerfully built great ape of central Africa, the largest living primate. [*Gorilla gorilla.*] **2** informal a heavily built aggressive-looking man.
– ORIGIN C19: from Gk, representing an alleged Afr. word for a wild or hairy person.

**Gorkhali** /gɔːˈkɑːli/ ● **n.** variant spelling of **GURKHALI**.

**gormandize** /ˈgɔːm(ə)ndʌɪz/ (also **-ise**) ● **v.** variant spelling of **GOURMANDIZE**.
– DERIVATIVES **gormandizer** n.

**gormless** ● **adj.** informal, chiefly Brit. lacking sense or initiative; foolish.
– DERIVATIVES **gormlessly** adv. **gormlessness** n.
– ORIGIN C18 (orig. as *gaumless*): from dial. *gaum* 'understanding' (from ON *gaumr* 'care, heed') + **-LESS**.

**gorp** ● **n.** N. Amer. informal another term for **TRAIL MIX**.
– ORIGIN C20: origin uncertain, perh. an acronym from *good ol' raisins and peanuts.*

**gorse** ● **n.** a yellow-flowered shrub of the pea family, the leaves of which have the form of spines. [*Ulex europaeus* and related species.]
– DERIVATIVES **gorsy** adj.
– ORIGIN OE *gors, gorst*, from an Indo-Eur. root meaning 'rough, prickly'.

**Gorsedd** /ˈgɔːsɛð/ ● **n.** a council of Welsh or other Celtic bards and Druids.
– ORIGIN Welsh, 'mound, throne, assembly'.

**gory** ● **adj.** (**-ier**, **-iest**) **1** involving or showing violence and bloodshed. **2** covered in blood.
– PHRASES **the gory details** humorous the explicit details of something.
– DERIVATIVES **gorily** adv. **goriness** n.

**gosh** ● **exclam.** informal used to express surprise or give emphasis.
– ORIGIN C18: euphemism for **GOD**.

**goshawk** /ˈgɒshɔːk/ ● **n.** a short-winged hawk resembling a large sparrowhawk. [*Accipiter gentilis* and other species.]
– ORIGIN OE *gōshafoc*, from *gōs* 'goose' + *hafoc* 'hawk'.

**gosht** /gəʊʃt/ ● **n.** Indian red meat (beef, lamb, or mutton).
– ORIGIN from Hindi *gośt.*

**gosling** /ˈgɒzlɪŋ/ ● **n.** a young goose.
– ORIGIN ME (orig. *gesling*): from ON *gǿslingr*, from *gás* 'goose' + **-LING**.

**go-slow** ● **n.** chiefly Brit. a form of industrial action in which work is delayed or slowed down.

**gospel** ● **n.** **1** the teaching or revelation of Christ. **2** (**Gospel**) the record of Christ's life and teaching in the first four books of the New Testament. ➤each of these books. **3** (also **gospel truth**) something absolutely true. **4** (also **gospel music**) a fervent style of black American evangelical religious singing.
– DERIVATIVES **gospelize** (also **-ise**) v.
– ORIGIN OE *gōdspel*, from *gōd* 'good' + *spel* 'news, a story', translating eccles. L. *bona annuntiatio* or *bonus nuntius*, used to gloss eccles. L. *evangelium*, from Gk *euangelion* 'good news'.

**gospeller** (US **gospeler**) ● **n.** **1** a zealous preacher. **2** the reader of the Gospel in a Communion service.

**Gospel side** ● **n.** (in a church) the north side of the altar, at which the Gospel is read.

**goss** ● **n.** Brit. informal gossip.

**gossamer** ● **n.** a fine, filmy substance consisting of cobwebs spun by small spiders, seen especially in autumn. ● **adj.** very fine and insubstantial: *gossamer wings.*
– DERIVATIVES **gossamery** adj.
– ORIGIN ME: appar. from **GOOSE** + **SUMMER**[1], perh. from the time of year around St Martin's day (11 November) when geese were eaten.

**gossan** /ˈgɒz(ə)n/ ● **n.** Geology & Mining an iron-containing secondary deposit of oxides, typically yellowish or reddish, occurring above an ore deposit.
– ORIGIN C18: prob. of Cornish origin.

**gossip** ● **n.** **1** casual conversation or unsubstantiated reports about other people. **2** chiefly derogatory a person who likes talking about other people's private lives. ● **v.** (**gossiped**, **gossiping**) engage in gossip.
– DERIVATIVES **gossiper** n. **gossipy** adj.
– ORIGIN OE *godsibb* 'godfather or godmother', later 'a close friend, a person with whom one gossips' (see **SIB**).

**gossip column** ● **n.** a section of a newspaper devoted to gossip about well-known people.
– DERIVATIVES **gossip columnist** n.

**gossoon** /gɒˈsuːn/ ● **n.** Irish a lad.
– ORIGIN C17: from Fr. *garçon* 'boy'.

**gossypol** /ˈgɒsɪpɒl/ ● **n.** Chemistry a toxic crystalline compound present in cotton-seed oil.
– ORIGIN C19: from mod. L. *Gossypium* (genus name), from L. *gossypinum, -pion* 'cotton plant' + **-OL**.

**got** past and past participle of **GET**.

**gotcha** (also **gotcher**) ● **exclam.** informal I have got you.

**Goth** /gɒθ/ ● **n.** **1** a member of a Germanic people that invaded the Roman Empire between the 3rd and 5th centuries. **2** (**goth**) a style of rock music typically having apocalyptic or mystical lyrics. ➤a member of a subculture favouring black clothing and goth music.
– ORIGIN OE *Gota*, superseded in ME by the adoption of late L. *Gothi*, from Gk *Gothoi*, from Gothic *Gutthiuda* 'the Gothic people'.

**Gothic** ● **adj.** **1** of or relating to the ancient Goths or their East Germanic language. **2** of or in the style of architecture prevalent in western Europe in the 12th–16th centuries (and revived in the 18th and 19th centuries), characterized by pointed arches. **3** (also pseudo-archaic **Gothick**) portentously gloomy or horrifying. **4** (of lettering) derived from the angular style of handwriting with broad vertical downstrokes used in medieval western Europe. **5** (**gothic**) of or relating to goths or their rock music. ● **n.** **1** the language of the Goths. **2** the Gothic style of architecture. **3** Gothic type.
– DERIVATIVES **Gothically** adv. **Gothicism** n.

**gothic novel** ● **n.** an English genre of fiction popular in the 18th to early 19th centuries, characterized by an atmosphere of mystery and horror.

**gotta** ● **contr.** informal **1** have got a. **2** have got to.

**gotten** N. Amer. past participle of **GET**.

**USAGE gotten**

The form **gotten** is very common in North American English, though even there it is often regarded as non-standard.

**gouache** /guˈɑːʃ, gwɑːʃ/ ● **n.** a method of painting using opaque pigments ground in water and thickened with a glue-like substance. ➤paint of this kind; opaque watercolour.
– ORIGIN C19: Fr., from Ital. *guazzo.*

**Gouda** /ˈgaʊdə/ ● **n.** a flat round Dutch cheese with a yellow rind.
– ORIGIN orig. made in *Gouda* in the Netherlands.

**gouge** /gaʊdʒ, guːdʒ/ ● **v.** **1** make (a rough hole or indentation) in a surface. **2** (**gouge something out**) cut or force something out roughly or brutally. **3** N. Amer. informal overcharge; swindle. ● **n.** **1** a chisel with a concave blade. **2** an indentation or groove made by gouging.
– DERIVATIVES **gouger** n.
– ORIGIN ME: from OFr., from late L. *gubia, gulbia*, perh. of Celtic origin; cf. Old Ir. *gulba* 'beak' and Welsh *gylf* 'beak, pointed instrument'.

**goujons** /ˈguː(d)ʒənz/ ● **pl. n.** Brit. deep-fried strips of chicken or fish.
– ORIGIN from Fr. *goujon* 'gudgeon'.

**goulash** /ˈguːlaʃ/ ● **n.** **1** a highly seasoned Hungarian soup or stew of meat and vegetables, flavoured with paprika. **2** (in informal bridge) a redealing of the cards, unshuffled and several at a time, after no player has bid.
– ORIGIN from Hungarian *gulyás-hús*, from *gulyás* 'herdsman' + *hús* 'meat'.

**gourami** /gʊ(ə)ˈrɑːmi, ˈgʊərəmi/ ● **n.** (pl. same or **gouramis**) an Asian labyrinth fish of a large group including many kinds popular in aquaria. [Osphronemidae (the **giant gouramis**), Belontiidae, and other families.]
– ORIGIN C19: from Malay *gurami.*

**gourd** /gʊəd, gɔːd/ ● **n.** **1** a large fleshy fruit with a hard skin. ➤a drinking vessel or water container made from the hollowed and dried skin of a gourd. **2** a climbing or trailing plant which bears this fruit. [*Cucurbita* and

other genera.]
– PHRASES **out of one's gourd** N. Amer. informal **1** out of one's mind; crazy. **2** under the influence of alcohol or drugs.
– DERIVATIVES **gourdful** n. (pl. **-fuls**).
– ORIGIN ME: from OFr. *gourde*, based on L. *cucurbita*.

**gourde** /gʊəd/ • n. the basic monetary unit of Haiti, equal to 100 centimes.
– ORIGIN the Franco-Amer. name for a dollar.

**gourmand** /ˈgʊəmənd, ˈgɔː-/ • n. **1** a person who enjoys eating, sometimes to excess. **2** a gourmet.
– DERIVATIVES **gourmandism** n.
– ORIGIN ME: from OFr., of unknown origin.

**gourmandize** /ˌgʊəm(ə)nˈdiːz, ˈgɔː-/ (also **-ise**, **gormandize**) • v. indulge in good eating; eat greedily. • n. appreciation or consumption of good food.

**gourmet** /ˈgʊəmeɪ, ˈgɔː-/ • n. a connoisseur of good food. ➤[as modifier] suitable for a gourmet: *a gourmet meal*.
– ORIGIN C19: Fr., orig. 'wine taster', influenced by **GOURMAND**.

**gout** /gaʊt/ • n. **1** a disease in which defective metabolism of uric acid causes arthritis, especially in the smaller bones of the feet. **2** poetic/literary a drop or spot.
– DERIVATIVES **goutiness** n. **gouty** adj.
– ORIGIN ME: from OFr. *goute*, from med. L. *gutta*, lit. 'drop' (because gout was believed to be caused by the dropping of diseased matter from the blood into the joints).

**goutweed** • n. ground elder (formerly used to treat gout).

**gov.** • abbrev. **1** government. **2** governor.

**govern** /ˈgʌv(ə)n/ • v. **1** conduct the policy and affairs of (a state, organization, or people). ➤control or influence. **2** constitute a rule, standard, or principle for. ➤serve to decide (a legal case). **3** Grammar (of a word) require that (another word or group of words) be in a particular case.
– DERIVATIVES **governability** n. **governable** adj.
– ORIGIN ME: from OFr. *governer*, from L. *gubernare* 'to steer, rule', from Gk *kubernan* 'to steer'.

**governance** • n. the action or manner of governing. ➤archaic control.

**governess** • n. a woman employed to teach children in a private household.
– DERIVATIVES **governessy** adj.
– ORIGIN ME: from OFr. *governeresse*, fem. of *governeour* (see **GOVERNOR**).

**governing body** • n. a group of people who govern an institution in partnership with the managers.

**government** /ˈgʌv(ə)nˌm(ə)nt, ˈgʌvəm(ə)nt/ • n. **1** [treated as sing. or pl.] the governing body of a state. ➤the system by which a state or community is governed. ➤the action or manner of governing a state, organization, or people. **2** Grammar the relation between a governed and a governing word.
– DERIVATIVES **governmental** adj. **governmentally** adv.

**Government House** • n. Brit. the official residence of a governor.

**government paper** • n. bonds or other promissory certificates issued by the government.

**government securities** • pl. n. another term for **GOVERNMENT PAPER**.

**government surplus** • n. unused equipment sold by the government.

**governor** • n. **1** an official appointed to govern a town or region. ➤the elected executive head of a state of the US. ➤the representative of the British Crown in a colony or in a Commonwealth state that regards the monarch as head of state. **2** the head of a public institution. ➤a member of a governing body. **3** Brit. informal the person in authority. **4** a device automatically regulating the supply of fuel, steam, or water to a machine.
– DERIVATIVES **governorate** n. **governorship** n.
– ORIGIN ME: from OFr. *governeour*, from L. *gubernator*, from *gubernare* (see **GOVERN**).

**Governor General** • n. (pl. **Governors General**) the chief representative of the Crown in a Commonwealth country of which the British monarch is head of state.

**govt** • abbrev. government.

**gowan** /ˈgaʊən/ • n. Scottish & N. English a wild white or yellow flower, especially a daisy.
– ORIGIN C16: prob. a var. of dial. *gollan*, denoting various yellow-flowered plants.

**gowk** /gaʊk/ • n. dialect **1** an awkward or foolish person. **2** a cuckoo.
– ORIGIN ME: from ON *gaukr*.

**gown** • n. a long dress worn on formal occasions. ➤a protective garment worn in hospital by surgical staff or patients. ➤a loose cloak indicating one's profession or status, worn by a lawyer, teacher, academic, or university student. ➤the members of a university as distinct from the residents of a town. Often contrasted with **TOWN**. • v. (**be gowned**) be dressed in a gown.
– ORIGIN ME: from OFr. *goune*, from late L. *gunna* 'fur garment'.

**goy** /gɔɪ/ • n. (pl. **goyim** /ˈgɔɪɪm/ or **goys**) informal, offensive a Jewish name for a non-Jew.
– DERIVATIVES **goyish** adj.
– ORIGIN from Heb. *gōy* 'people, nation'.

**GP** • abbrev. **1** general practitioner. **2** Grand Prix.

**Gp Capt** • abbrev. Group Captain.

**gph** • abbrev. gallons per hour.

**GPI** • abbrev. general paralysis of the insane.

**gpm** • abbrev. gallons per minute.

**GPO** • abbrev. **1** historical (in the UK) General Post Office. **2** (in the US) Government Printing Office.

**GPRS** • abbrev. general packet radio services, a technology for radio transmission of small packets of data, especially between mobile phones and the Internet.

**GPS** • abbrev. Global Positioning System (a satellite navigational system).

**GR** • abbrev. **1** Greece (international vehicle registration). **2** King George. [from L. *Georgius Rex*.]

**gr.** • abbrev. **1** grain(s). **2** gram(s). **3** grey. **4** gross.

**Graafian follicle** /ˈgrɑːfɪən/ • n. Physiology a fluid-filled structure in the ovary within which an ovum develops prior to ovulation.
– ORIGIN C19: named after the C17 Du. anatomist R. de *Graaf*.

**grab** • v. (**grabbed**, **grabbing**) **1** seize suddenly and roughly. ➤informal obtain quickly or opportunistically. ➤(of a brake on a vehicle) grip the wheel harshly or jerkily. **2** [usu. with neg. or in questions] informal impress: *how does that grab you?* • n. **1** a quick sudden clutch or attempt to seize. ➤[as modifier] denoting a bar or strap to hold on to for support or in a moving vehicle. **2** a mechanical device for clutching, lifting, and moving loads.
– PHRASES **up for grabs** informal available.
– DERIVATIVES **grabber** n.
– ORIGIN C16: from Mid. Low Ger. and MDu. *grabben*; perh. rel. to **GRIP**, **GRIPE**, and **GROPE**.

**grab bag** • n. N. Amer. a lucky dip in which wrapped items are chosen blindly from a bag. ➤an assortment of items in a sealed bag which one buys or is given without knowing what the contents are.

**grabble** • v. archaic feel or search with the hands.
– ORIGIN C16: prob. from Du. *grabbelen* 'scramble for a thing', from MDu. *grabben* (see **GRAB**).

**grabby** • adj. informal, chiefly N. Amer. **1** greedy. **2** attracting attention.

**graben** /ˈgrɑːb(ə)n/ • n. (pl. same or **grabens**) Geology an elongated block of the earth's crust lying between two faults and displaced downwards, as in a rift valley.
– ORIGIN C19: from Ger. *Graben* 'a ditch'.

**grace** • n. **1** elegance of movement. **2** courteous good will. ➤(**graces**) an attractively polite manner of behaving. **3** (in Christian belief) the free and unearned favour of God. ➤a divinely given talent or blessing. ➤a person's favour. **4** a period officially allowed for fulfilment of an obligation. **5** a short prayer of thanks said before or after a meal. **6** (**His**, **Her**, or **Your Grace**) used as forms of description or address for a duke, duchess, or archbishop. • v. lend honour to by one's presence. ➤be an attractive presence in or on.
– PHRASES **be in someone's good** (or **bad**) **graces** be regarded by someone with favour (or disfavour). **the (Three) Graces** Greek Mythology three beautiful goddesses,

daughters of Zeus, believed to personify and bestow charm, grace, and beauty. **with good** (or **bad**) **grace** in a willing (or reluctant) manner.
– DERIVATIVES **graceless** adj. **gracelessly** adv. **gracelessness** n.
– ORIGIN ME: via OFr. from L. *gratia*, from *gratus* 'pleasing, thankful'; rel. to **GRATEFUL**.

**grace and favour** • **adj.** Brit. denoting accommodation occupied by permission of a sovereign or government.

**graceful** • **adj.** having or showing grace or elegance.
– DERIVATIVES **gracefully** adv. **gracefulness** n.

**grace note** • **n.** Music an extra note added as an embellishment and not essential to the harmony or melody.

**gracile** /ˈɡrasɪl, ˈɡrasʌɪl/ • **adj.** Anthropology (of a hominid species) of slender build.
– ORIGIN C17: from L. *gracilis* 'slender'.

**gracility** /ɡrəˈsɪlɪti/ • **n.** archaic the state of being gracefully slender.

**gracious** • **adj.** **1** courteous, kind, and pleasant. **2** showing the elegance and comfort brought by wealth. **3** (in Christian belief) showing divine grace. **4** Brit. a polite epithet used of royalty or their acts. • **exclam.** expressing polite surprise.
– DERIVATIVES **graciously** adv. **graciousness** n.
– ORIGIN ME: via OFr. from L. *gratiosus*, from *gratia* (see **GRACE**).

**grackle** • **n.** **1** a songbird of the American blackbird family, the male of which is shiny black with a blue-green sheen. [*Quiscalus quiscula* and other species.] **2** an Asian mynah or starling with mainly black plumage. [*Gracula* and other genera.]
– ORIGIN C18: from mod. L. *Gracula*, from L. *graculus* 'jackdaw'.

**grad**[1] • **n.** informal term for **GRADUATE**.

**grad**[2] • **abbrev.** gradient.

**gradable** • **adj.** Grammar denoting an adjective that can be used in the comparative and superlative and take a submodifier.
– DERIVATIVES **gradability** n.

**gradation** • **n.** **1** a scale of successive changes, stages, or degrees. **2** a stage in a such a scale. **3** a minute change from one shade, tone, or colour to another. **4** Linguistics another term for **ABLAUT**.
– DERIVATIVES **gradate** v. **gradational** adj. **gradationally** adv.
– ORIGIN C16: from L. *gradatio(n-)*, based on *gradus* 'step'.

**grade** • **n.** **1** a particular level of rank, quality, proficiency, or value. **2** a mark indicating the quality of a student's work. **3** N. Amer. (with specifying ordinal number) those pupils in a school who are grouped by age or ability for teaching at a particular level for a year. **4** Linguistics a relative position in a series of forms involving ablaut. **5** chiefly N. Amer. a gradient or slope. **6** a variety of cattle produced by crossing with a superior breed. • **v.** **1** arrange in or allocate to grades. **2** chiefly N. Amer. give a mark to. **3** pass gradually from one level to another. **4** reduce (a road) to an easy gradient. **5** cross (livestock) with a superior breed.
– PHRASES **at grade** N. Amer. on the same level. **make the grade** informal succeed.
– ORIGIN C16: from Fr., or from L. *gradus* 'step'.

**grade crossing** • **n.** North American term for **LEVEL CROSSING**.

**gradely** • **adj.** N. English fine or respectable.
– ORIGIN ME: from ON *greithligr*, from *greithr* 'ready'.

**grader** • **n.** **1** a person or thing that grades. **2** a wheeled machine for levelling the ground, especially in making roads. **3** [in combination] N. Amer. a pupil of a specified grade in a school.

**grade school** • **n.** N. Amer. elementary school.
– DERIVATIVES **grade schooler** n.

**gradient** /ˈɡreɪdɪənt/ • **n.** **1** a sloping part of a road or railway. **2** the degree of such a slope, expressed as change of height divided by distance travelled. ➤ Mathematics the degree of steepness of a graph. **3** Physics a change in the magnitude of a property (e.g. temperature) observed in passing from one point or moment to another.
– ORIGIN C19: from **GRADE**, on the pattern of *salient*.

**gradine** /ɡrəˈdiːn/ (also **gradin** /ˈɡreɪdɪn/) • **n.** archaic a low step or ledge, especially one at the back of an altar.
– ORIGIN C19: from Ital. *gradino*, dimin. of *grado* 'step'.

**gradiometer** /ˌɡreɪdɪˈɒmɪtə/ • **n.** **1** a surveying instrument for setting out or measuring a gradient. **2** Physics an instrument for measuring the gradient of a gravitational, magnetic, or other field.

**gradual** /ˈɡradʒʊəl/ • **adj.** **1** taking place in stages over an extended period. **2** (of a slope) not steep or abrupt. • **n.** (in the Western Christian Church) a response sung or recited between the Epistle and Gospel in the Mass.
– DERIVATIVES **gradually** adv. **gradualness** n.
– ORIGIN ME: from med. L. *gradualis*, from L. *gradus* 'step'.

**gradualism** • **n.** a policy or theory of gradual rather than sudden change.
– DERIVATIVES **gradualist** n. **gradualistic** adj.

**graduand** /ˈɡradʒʊand, -dj-, -ənd/ • **n.** Brit. a person who is about to receive an academic degree.
– ORIGIN C19: from med. L. *graduandus*, gerundive of *graduare* (see **GRADUATE**).

**graduate** • **n.** /ˈɡradʒʊət, -djʊət/ a person who has been awarded a first academic degree, or (N. Amer.) a high-school diploma. • **v.** /ˈɡradʒʊeɪt, -djʊeɪt/ **1** successfully complete a degree, course, or (N. Amer.) high school. ➤ N. Amer. confer a degree or other academic qualification on. **2** (**graduate to**) move up to (something more advanced). **3** arrange or mark out in gradations. **4** change gradually.
– DERIVATIVES **graduation** n.
– ORIGIN ME: from med. L. *graduat-* 'graduated', from *graduare* 'take a degree', from L. *gradus* 'degree, step'.

**graduate school** • **n.** N. Amer. a department of a university for advanced work by graduates.

**Graecism** /ˈɡriːsɪz(ə)m, ˈɡrʌɪ-/ (also **Grecism**) • **n.** **1** a Greek idiom, especially as adopted by speakers of another language. **2** the qualities typical of Greece and the Greeks, especially as imitated in a work of art.
– ORIGIN C16: from Fr. *grécisme* or med. L. *Graecismus*, from *Graecus* (see **GREEK**).

**Graeco-** /ˈɡriːkəʊ, ˈɡrʌɪ-/ (also **Greco-**) • **comb. form** Greek; Greek and ...: *Graecophile*.
– ORIGIN from L. *Graecus* (see **GREEK**).

**Graeco-Roman** • **adj.** **1** of or relating to the ancient Greeks and Romans. **2** denoting a style of wrestling in which holds below the waist are prohibited.

**graffiti** /ɡrəˈfiːti/ • **pl. n.** (sing. **graffito** /-təʊ/) [treated as sing. or pl.] unauthorized writing or drawings on a surface in a public place. • **v.** write or draw graffiti on.
– DERIVATIVES **graffitist** n.
– ORIGIN C19: from Ital., from *graffio* 'a scratch'.

**USAGE** graffiti

In Italian the word **graffiti** is a plural noun and its singular form is **graffito**. In modern English, **graffiti** is used as a plural in some specialist fields such as archaeology but in normal general use it is treated as if it were a mass noun (with a singular verb), similar to a word like **writing**. This use is now widely accepted as standard.

**graft**[1] • **n.** **1** Horticulture a scion inserted into a slit of stock, from which it receives sap. **2** Medicine a piece of living tissue that is transplanted surgically. ➤ an operation in which tissue is transplanted. • **v.** **1** insert or transplant as a graft. **2** integrate in or attach to something else, especially inappropriately.
– ORIGIN ME *graff*, from OFr. *grafe*, via L. from Gk *graphion* 'writing implement' (with ref. to the tapered tip of the scion), from *graphein* 'write'.

**graft**[2] Brit. informal • **n.** hard work. • **v.** work hard.
– DERIVATIVES **grafter** n.
– ORIGIN C19: perh. rel. to the phr. *spade's graft* 'the amount of earth that one stroke of a spade will move'.

**graft**[3] • **n.** informal bribery and other corrupt measures pursued for gain in politics or business. • **v.** make money by graft.
– DERIVATIVES **grafter** n.
– ORIGIN C19: of unknown origin.

**graham** ● adj. N. Amer. denoting wholewheat flour, or biscuits or bread made from this.
– ORIGIN C19: named after the Amer. advocate of dietary reform Sylvester *Graham.*

**Graham's law** ● n. Chemistry a law stating that the rates of diffusion and effusion of a gas are inversely proportional to the square root of its density.
– ORIGIN C19: named after the Sc. chemist Thomas *Graham.*

**Grail** (also **Holy Grail**) ● n. (in medieval legend) the cup or platter used by Christ at the Last Supper and in which Joseph of Arimathea received Christ's blood, especially as the object of quests by knights.
– ORIGIN from OFr. *graal*, from med. L. *gradalis* 'dish'.

**grain** ● n. **1** wheat or other cultivated cereal used as food. ➤ a single seed or fruit of a cereal. **2** a small, hard particle of a substance such as sand. ➤ a discrete particle or crystal in a metal, igneous rock, etc. **3** the smallest unit of weight in the troy and avoirdupois systems, equal to 1/5760 of a pound troy and 1/7000 of a pound avoirdupois (approximately 0.0648 grams). ➤ the smallest possible amount: *there wasn't a grain of truth in what he said.* **4** the longitudinal arrangement of fibres in wood, paper, etc. ➤ the texture of wood, stone, etc. **5** the rough or wrinkled outer surface of leather. **6** Photography a grainy appearance of a photograph or negative. **7** historical kermes or cochineal, or dye made from either of these. ● v. **1** give a rough surface or texture to. **2** form into grains. **3** [usu. as noun **graining**] paint in imitation of the grain of wood or marble. **4** remove hair from (a hide).
– PHRASES **against the grain** contrary to one's nature or instinct.
– DERIVATIVES **-grained** adj. **grainer** n. **grainless** adj.
– ORIGIN ME: from OFr. *grain*, from L. *granum*; sense 3 arose because the weight was orig. equivalent to that of a grain of wheat.

**grains of Paradise** ● pl. n. the seeds of a West African plant (*Aframomum melegueta*), used as a spice and in herbal medicine.

**grain whisky** ● n. whisky made mainly from unmalted wheat or maize.

**grainy** ● adj. (**-ier**, **-iest**) **1** granular. ➤ (of a photograph) showing visible grains of emulsion. **2** (of wood) having prominent grain.
– DERIVATIVES **graininess** n.

**gralloch** /ˈgralək/ ● n. the entrails of a dead deer. ● v. disembowel (a deer that has been shot).
– ORIGIN C19: from Sc. Gaelic *grealach*.

**gram**[1] (Brit. also **gramme**) (abbrev.: **g**) ● n. a metric unit of mass equal to one thousandth of a kilogram.
– ORIGIN C18: from Fr. *gramme*, from late L. *gramma* 'a small weight'.

**gram**[2] ● n. chickpeas or other pulses used as food.
– ORIGIN C18: from Port. *grão*, from L. *granum* 'grain'.

**-gram**[1] ● comb. form forming nouns denoting something written or recorded: *cryptogram.*
– DERIVATIVES **-grammatic** comb. form in corresponding adjectives.
– ORIGIN from Gk *gramma* 'thing written, letter of the alphabet'.

**-gram**[2] ● comb. form forming nouns denoting a person paid to deliver a novelty greeting or message: *kissogram.*
– ORIGIN on the pattern of *telegram*.

**gramicidin** /ˌgramɪˈsʌɪdɪn/ ● n. Medicine a widely used bacterial antibiotic.
– ORIGIN 1940s: from *Gram* (see **GRAM STAIN**) + **-I-** + **-CIDE** + **-IN**[1].

**graminaceous** /ˌgramɪˈneɪʃəs/ ● adj. Botany relating to or denoting plants of the grass family (Gramineae).
– ORIGIN C19: from L. *gramen, gramin-* 'grass' + **-ACEOUS**.

**graminivorous** /ˌgramɪˈnɪv(ə)rəs/ ● adj. Zoology (of an animal) feeding on grass.
– ORIGIN C18: from L. *gramen, gramin-* 'grass' + **-VOROUS**.

**gramma** ● n. N. Amer. informal one's grandmother.

**grammalogue** /ˈgraməlɒg/ ● n. (in shorthand) a word represented by a single sign or symbol.
– ORIGIN C19: formed irregularly from Gk *gramma* 'thing written' + *logos* 'word'.

**grammar** ● n. **1** the whole system and structure of a language or of languages in general, usually taken as consisting of syntax and morphology. ➤ a particular analysis of this. **2** a book on grammar. **3** a set of prescriptive notions about correct use of a language. **4** the basic elements of an area of knowledge or skill.
– ORIGIN ME: from OFr. *gramaire*, via L. from Gk *grammatikē* (*tekhnē*) '(art) of letters', from *gramma, grammat-* 'letter of the alphabet'.

**grammarian** /grəˈmɛːrɪən/ ● n. a person who studies and writes about grammar.

**grammar school** ● n. **1** (in the UK, especially formerly) a state secondary school to which pupils are admitted on the basis of ability. ➤ historical a school founded in or before the 16th century for teaching Latin, later becoming a secondary school teaching academic subjects. **2** US another term for **ELEMENTARY SCHOOL**.

**grammatical** /grəˈmatɪk(ə)l/ ● adj. **1** of or relating to grammar. **2** in accordance with the rules of grammar.
– DERIVATIVES **grammaticality** n. **grammatically** adv. **grammaticalness** n.
– ORIGIN C16: from late L. *grammaticalis*, via L. from Gk *grammatikos*, from *gramma, grammatos* 'letter of the alphabet'.

**grammaticalize** (also **-ise**) ● v. Linguistics change (an element with lexical meaning) into one having a largely grammatical function.
– DERIVATIVES **grammaticalization** n.

**gramme** ● n. variant spelling of **GRAM**[1].

**Grammy** ● n. (pl. **Grammys** or **Grammies**) each of a number of annual awards given by the American National Academy of Recording Arts and Sciences for achievement in the record industry.
– ORIGIN 1950s: blend of **GRAMOPHONE** and **EMMY**.

**Gram-negative** ● adj. see **GRAM STAIN**.

**gramophone** ● n. chiefly Brit. old-fashioned term for **RECORD PLAYER**.
– DERIVATIVES **gramophonic** adj.
– ORIGIN C19: formed by inversion of elements of *phonogram* 'sound recording'.

**gramophone record** ● n. fuller form of **RECORD** (in sense 4).

**gramp** (also **gramps**, **grampy**) ● n. dialect or informal one's grandfather.

**Gram-positive** ● adj. see **GRAM STAIN**.

**grampus** /ˈgrampəs/ ● n. (pl. **grampuses**) **1** a killer whale or other cetacean of the dolphin family. **2** Brit. dated someone or something breathing loudly and heavily.
– ORIGIN C16: alt. (by assoc. with **GRAND**) of OFr. *grapois*, from med. L. *craspiscis*, from L. *crassus piscis* 'fat fish'.

**Gram stain** ● n. Medicine a staining technique for the preliminary distinction of bacteria between two categories (**Gram-positive** and **Gram-negative**).
– ORIGIN C19: named after the Dan. physician Hans C. J. *Gram.*

**gran** ● n. informal, chiefly Brit. one's grandmother.

**granadilla** /gran-/ (also **grenadilla**) ● n. a passion fruit.
– ORIGIN C16: Sp., dimin. of *granada* 'pomegranate'.

**granary** ● n. (pl. **-ies**) **1** a storehouse for threshed grain. **2** a region supplying large quantities of corn: *Egypt was the granary of Rome.*
– ORIGIN C16: from L. *granarium*.

**granary bread** ● n. Brit. trademark a type of brown bread containing whole grains of wheat.

**grand** ● adj. **1** magnificent and imposing. ➤ large, ambitious, or impressive in scope or scale. ➤ dignified, noble, or proud. **2** of chief importance. ➤ of the highest rank (used especially in official titles). ➤ Law (of a crime) serious. Compare with **PETTY** (in sense 3). **3** informal excellent. **4** [in combination] (in names of family relationships) denoting one generation removed in ascent or descent. ● n. **1** (pl. same) informal a thousand dollars or pounds. **2** a grand piano.
– DERIVATIVES **grandly** adv. **grandness** n.
– ORIGIN ME: from OFr. *grant, grand*, from L. *grandis* 'full-grown, great'.

**grandad** (also **granddad**) • **n. 1** informal one's grandfather. **2** [as modifier] denoting a style of shirt or neckline with a collar in the form of a narrow upright band fastened with buttons.

**grandam** /ˈgrandam/ (also **grandame**) • **n.** archaic term for **GRANDMOTHER**.
– ORIGIN ME: from Anglo-Norman Fr. *graund dame* (see **GRAND, DAME**).

**grandchild** • **n.** (pl. **-children**) a child of one's son or daughter.

**grand cru** /grɒ̃ ˈkruː, French grɑ̃ kry/ • **n.** (pl. **grands crus** pronunc. same) (chiefly in France) a wine of the most superior grade. Compare with **PREMIER CRU**.
– ORIGIN Fr., lit. 'great growth'.

**granddad** • **n.** variant spelling of **GRANDAD**.

**granddaughter** • **n.** a daughter of one's son or daughter.

**grand duchess** • **n. 1** the wife or widow of a grand duke. **2** a woman holding the rank of grand duke in her own right.

**grand duke** • **n. 1** a prince or nobleman ruling over a territory in certain European countries. **2** historical a son (or son's son) of a Russian tsar.
– DERIVATIVES **grand duchy** n.

**grande dame** /grɒ̃d ˈdam/ • **n.** an influential woman within a particular sphere.
– ORIGIN Fr., lit. 'grand lady'.

**grandee** /granˈdiː/ • **n.** a Spanish or Portuguese nobleman of the highest rank. ➤ a man of high rank or eminence.
– ORIGIN C16: from Sp. and Port. *grande* 'grand', used as n.; the change of ending was due to assoc. with **-EE**.

**grandeur** /ˈgrandjə, -(d)ʒə/ • **n.** splendour and impressiveness. ➤ high rank or social importance.
– ORIGIN C16 (denoting tall stature): from Fr., from *grand* (see **GRAND**).

**grandfather** • **n. 1** the father of one's father or mother. **2** a founder or originator. • **v.** N. Amer. informal make exempt by a grandfather clause.
– DERIVATIVES **grandfatherly** adj.

**grandfather clause** • **n.** N. Amer. informal a clause exempting certain pre-existing classes of people or things from the requirements of a piece of legislation.
– ORIGIN from a clause in the constitutions of some Southern states, exempting from voting restrictions the descendants of men who voted before the Civil War.

**grandfather clock** • **n.** a clock in a tall free-standing wooden case, driven by weights.

**Grand Guignol** /ˌgrɒ̃ giːˈnjɒl, French grɑ̃ giɲɔl/ • **n.** a dramatic entertainment of a sensational or horrific nature, originally as performed at the Grand Guignol theatre in Paris.
– ORIGIN Fr., lit. 'Great Punch'.

**grandiflora** /ˌgrandɪˈflɔːrə/ • **adj.** denoting cultivated plant varieties with large flowers.
– ORIGIN C20: mod. L., from L. *grandis* 'great' + *flos, flor-* 'flower'.

**grandiloquent** /granˈdɪləkwənt/ • **adj.** pompous or extravagant in language, style, or manner.
– DERIVATIVES **grandiloquence** n. **grandiloquently** adv.
– ORIGIN C16: from L. *grandiloquus* lit. 'grand-speaking'; the ending was alt. in Engl. by assoc. with **ELOQUENT**.

**Grand Inquisitor** • **n.** historical the director of the court of Inquisition, especially in Spain and Portugal.

**grandiose** /ˈgrandɪəʊs/ • **adj. 1** impressive or magnificent, especially pretentiously so. **2** conceived on a very ambitious scale.
– DERIVATIVES **grandiosely** adv. **grandiosity** n.
– ORIGIN C19: from Fr., from Ital. *grandioso*, from *grande* 'grand'.

**grand jeté** /grɒ̃ ˈʒɛteɪ, ʒəˈteɪ/ • **n.** Ballet a jump in which a dancer springs from one foot to land on the other with one leg forward of their body and the other stretched backwards while in the air.

**grand jury** • **n.** US Law a jury selected to examine the validity of an accusation prior to trial.

**grand larceny** • **n.** Law (in many US states and formerly in Britain) theft of personal property having a value above a legally specified amount.

**grandma** • **n.** informal one's grandmother.

**grand mal** /grɒ̃ ˈmal/ • **n.** a serious form of epilepsy with muscle spasms and prolonged loss of consciousness. Compare with **PETIT MAL**.
– ORIGIN C19: from Fr., lit. 'great sickness'.

**grandmama** (also **grandmamma**) • **n.** archaic form of **GRANDMA**.

**Grand Marnier** /grɒ̃ ˈmɑːnɪeɪ/ • **n.** trademark an orange-flavoured cognac-based liqueur.
– ORIGIN from Fr.

**grand master** • **n. 1** (usu. **grandmaster**) a chess player of the highest class, especially one who has won an international tournament. **2** (**Grand Master**) the head of an order of chivalry or of Freemasons.

**grandmother** • **n.** the mother of one's father or mother.
– PHRASES **teach one's grandmother to suck eggs** presume to advise a more experienced person.
– DERIVATIVES **grandmotherly** adj.

**grandmother clock** • **n.** a clock similar to a grandfather clock but about two thirds the size.

**Grand National** • **n.** an annual steeplechase held at Aintree, Liverpool.

**grand opera** • **n.** an opera on a serious theme in which the entire libretto (including dialogue) is sung.

**grandpa** • **n.** informal one's grandfather.

**grandpapa** • **n.** old-fashioned term for **GRANDFATHER**.

**grandpappy** • **n.** (pl. **-ies**) North American term for **GRANDFATHER**.

**grandparent** • **n.** a grandmother or grandfather.
– DERIVATIVES **grandparental** adj. **grandparenthood** n.

**Grand Penitentiary** • **n.** (in the Roman Catholic Church) a cardinal presiding over the penitentiary.

**grand piano** • **n.** a large, full-toned piano which has the body, strings, and soundboard arranged horizontally and in line with the keys and is supported by three legs.

**Grand Prix** /grɒ̃ ˈpriː/ • **n.** (pl. **Grands Prix** pronunc. same) any of a world championship series of international motor-racing or motorcycling contests.
– ORIGIN C19: Fr., lit. 'great or chief prize'.

**grand seigneur** /ˌgrɒ̃ seɪˈnjəː/ • **n.** a man whose rank or position allows him to command others.
– ORIGIN Fr., lit. 'great lord'.

**grand siècle** /ˌgrɒ̃ sɪˈɛkl(ə), French grɑ̃ sjɛkl/ • **n.** the reign of Louis XIV, seen as France's period of political and cultural pre-eminence.
– ORIGIN Fr., lit. 'great century or age'.

**grandsire** • **n. 1** archaic term for **GRANDFATHER**. **2** Bell-ringing a method of change-ringing involving an odd number of bells.

**grand slam** • **n. 1** the winning of each of a group of major championships or matches in a particular sport in the same year. **2** Bridge the bidding and winning of all thirteen tricks. **3** Baseball a home run hit when each of the three bases is occupied by a runner.

**grandson** • **n.** the son of one's son or daughter.

**grandstand** • **n.** the main stand commanding the best view for spectators at racecourses or sports grounds. • **v.** [usu. as noun **grandstanding**] derogatory seek to attract favourable public or media attention.

**grandstand finish** • **n.** a close or exciting finish to a race or competition.

**grand total** • **n.** the final amount after everything is added up.

**grand tour** • **n.** historical a cultural tour of Europe conventionally undertaken by a young man of the upper classes.

**grand unified theory** • **n.** Physics a theory attempting to give a single explanation of the strong, weak, and electromagnetic interactions between subatomic particles.

**grange** • **n.** Brit. **1** a country house with farm buildings attached. **2** archaic a barn.
– ORIGIN ME: from OFr., from med. L. *granica* (*villa*) 'grain house or farm', based on L. *granum* 'grain'.

**graniferous** /graˈnɪf(ə)rəs/ • **adj.** Botany (of a plant) producing grain or a grain-like seed.
– ORIGIN C17: from L. *granum* 'grain' + **-FEROUS**.

**granita** /graˈniːtə/ • **n.** (pl. **granite** /-ˈniːteɪ/) a coarse Italian-style water ice.
– ORIGIN from Ital.

**granite** /ˈgranɪt/ • **n.** a very hard, granular, crystalline igneous rock consisting mainly of quartz, mica, and feldspar.
– DERIVATIVES **granitic** adj. **granitoid** adj. & n.
– ORIGIN C17: from Ital. *granito*, lit. 'grained'.

**graniteware** • **n. 1** a speckled form of earthenware imitating the appearance of granite. **2** a kind of enamelled ironware.

**granivorous** /graˈnɪv(ə)rəs/ • **adj.** Zoology (of an animal) feeding on grain.
– DERIVATIVES **granivore** n.
– ORIGIN C17: from L. *granum* 'grain' + **-VOROUS**.

**granny** (also **grannie**) • **n.** (pl. **-ies**) informal one's grandmother.
– ORIGIN C17: from *grannam* (representing a colloq. pronunc. of **GRANDAM**) + **-Y**².

**granny bond** • **n.** Brit. informal a form of index-linked National Savings certificate, originally available only to pensioners.

**granny flat** • **n.** informal a part of a house made into self-contained accommodation suitable for an elderly relative.

**granny glasses** • **pl. n.** informal round metal-rimmed glasses.

**granny knot** • **n.** a reef knot with the ends crossed the wrong way and therefore liable to slip.

**Granny Smith** • **n.** a dessert apple of a bright green variety with crisp sharp-flavoured flesh, originating in Australia.
– ORIGIN C19: named after Maria Ann (*Granny*) *Smith*.

**granodiorite** /ˌgranə(ʊ)ˈdʌɪərʌɪt/ • **n.** Geology a coarse-grained plutonic rock between granite and diorite in composition.

**granola** /graˈnəʊlə/ • **n.** N. Amer. **1** a kind of breakfast cereal resembling muesli. **2** [as modifier] informal, chiefly derogatory denoting people with liberal or Green political views, typified as eating health foods.
– ORIGIN C19: from *gran-* (representing **GRANULAR** or **GRAIN**) + *-ola* (suffix chiefly in US usage).

**granolithic** /ˌgranə(ʊ)ˈlɪθɪk/ • **adj.** (of concrete) containing fine granite chippings or crushed granite, used to render floors and surfaces.
– ORIGIN C19: from *grano-* (irregular combining form from L. *granum* 'grain') + Gk *lithos* 'stone' + **-IC**.

**granophyre** /ˈgranə(ʊ)ˌfʌɪə/ • **n.** Geology a granitic rock containing intergrown feldspar and quartz crystals.
– ORIGIN C19: from Ger. *Granophyr*, from *Granit* 'granite'+ *Porphyr* (see **PORPHYRY**).

**grant** • **v. 1** agree to give or allow (something requested) to. ➤ give (a right, property, etc.) formally or legally to. **2** agree or admit to (someone) that (something) is true. • **n. 1** a sum of money given by a government or public body for a particular purpose. **2** formal the action of granting something. **3** Law a legal conveyance or formal conferment.
– PHRASES **take for granted 1** fail to appreciate through over-familiarity. **2** (**take something for granted**) assume that something is true.
– DERIVATIVES **grantable** adj. **grantee** n. (chiefly Law). **granter** n. **grantor** n. (chiefly Law).
– ORIGIN ME: from OFr. *granter* 'consent to support', var. of *creanter* 'to guarantee', based on L. *credere* 'entrust'.

**grant aid** Brit. • **n.** financial assistance granted by central government to local government or an institution. • **v.** (**grant-aid**) give such financial assistance to.

**granted** • **adv.** admittedly; it is true. • **conj.** (**granted that**) even assuming that.

**grant-in-aid** • **n.** (pl. **grants-in-aid**) a grant given to local government, an institution, or a particular scholar.

**grant-maintained** • **adj.** Brit. (of a school) funded by central rather than local government, and self-governing.

**gran turismo** /ˌgran tʊˈrɪzməʊ/ • **n.** (pl. **-os**) a high-performance model of motor car.
– ORIGIN C20: Ital., lit. 'great touring'.

**granular** • **adj. 1** resembling or consisting of granules. **2** having a roughened surface or structure.
– DERIVATIVES **granularity** n.

**granulate** • **v. 1** [usu. as adj. **granulated**] form into or take the form of granules. **2** [often as adj. **granulating**] Medicine (of a wound or lesion) form multiple small prominences as part of the healing process. **3** [as adj. **granulated**] chiefly Biology having a roughened surface.
– DERIVATIVES **granulation** n. **granulator** n.

**granule** /ˈgranjuːl/ • **n.** a small compact particle.
– ORIGIN C17: from late L. *granulum*, dimin. of L. *granum* 'grain'.

**granulite** • **n.** Geology a fine-grained granular metamorphic rock consisting mainly of feldspars and quartz.
– DERIVATIVES **granulitic** adj.

**granulocyte** /ˈgranjʊlə(ʊ)ˌsʌɪt/ • **n.** Physiology a white blood cell with secretory granules in its cytoplasm.
– DERIVATIVES **granulocytic** adj.

**granuloma** /ˌgranjʊˈləʊmə/ • **n.** (pl. **granulomas** or **granulomata** /-mətə/) Medicine a mass of granulated connective tissue, typically produced in response to infection, inflammation, or a foreign substance.
– DERIVATIVES **granulomatous** adj.

**granulometric** /ˌgranjʊlə(ʊ)ˈmɛtrɪk/ • **adj.** relating to the distribution or measurement of grain sizes in sand, rock, or other deposits.

**grape** • **n. 1** a green, purple, or black berry growing in clusters on a vine, eaten as fruit and used in making wine. ➤ (**the grape**) informal wine. **2** short for **GRAPESHOT**.
– DERIVATIVES **grapey** (also **grapy**) adj.
– ORIGIN ME: from Old Fr., 'bunch of grapes', prob. from *graper* 'gather (grapes)', from *grap* 'hook' (used in harvesting grapes), of Gmc origin.

**grapefruit** • **n.** (pl. same) **1** a large round yellow citrus fruit with an acid juicy pulp. **2** the tree bearing this fruit. [*Citrus paradisi*.]
– ORIGIN C19: from **GRAPE** + **FRUIT** (prob. because the fruits grow in clusters).

**grape hyacinth** • **n.** a small plant of the lily family, with clusters of small globular blue flowers, cultivated as an ornamental or for use in perfume. [Genus *Muscari*.]

**grape ivy** • **n.** an evergreen climbing vine, grown as a house plant. [*Cissus rhombifolia* and other species.]

**grapeseed oil** • **n.** oil extracted from the residue of grapes which have been juiced.

**grapeshot** • **n.** historical ammunition consisting of a number of small iron balls fired together from a cannon.

**grape sugar** • **n.** dextrose present in or derived from grapes.

**grapevine** • **n. 1** a vine bearing grapes. [*Vitis vinifera* and related species.] **2** (**the grapevine**) informal the circulation of rumours and unofficial information.

**graph**¹ /grɑːf, graf/ • **n. 1** a diagram showing the relation between variable quantities, typically of two variables measured along a pair of axes at right angles. **2** Mathematics a collection of points whose coordinates satisfy a given relation. • **v.** plot or trace on a graph.
– ORIGIN C19: abbrev. of *graphic formula*.

**graph**² /grɑːf, graf/ • **n.** Linguistics a visual symbol representing a unit of sound or other feature of speech.
– ORIGIN 1930s: from Gk *graphē* 'writing'.

**-graph** • **comb. form 1** in nouns denoting something written or drawn in a specified way: *autograph*. **2** in nouns denoting an instrument that records: *seismograph*.
– ORIGIN from Fr. *-graphe*, based on Gk *graphos* 'written, writing'.

**grapheme** /ˈgrafiːm/ • **n.** Linguistics the smallest meaningful contrastive unit in a writing system.
– DERIVATIVES **graphemic** adj. **graphemically** adv. **graphemics** pl. n.

**-grapher** • **comb. form** indicating a person concerned with a subject denoted by a noun ending in *-graphy*.

– ORIGIN from Gk *-graphos* 'writer' + **-ER**[1].

**graphic** ● adj. **1** of or relating to visual art, especially involving drawing, engraving, or lettering. **2** giving vividly explicit detail. **3** Computing relating to or denoting a visual image. **4** of or in the form of a graph. **5** Geology of or denoting rocks having a surface texture resembling cuneiform writing. ● n. Computing a graphical item displayed on a screen or stored as data.
– DERIVATIVES **graphically** adv. **graphicness** n.
– ORIGIN C17: via L. from Gk *graphikos*, from *graphē* 'writing, drawing'.

**-graphic** ● comb. form in adjectives corresponding to nouns ending in *-graphy*.
– DERIVATIVES **-graphically** comb. form in corresponding adverbs.
– ORIGIN suggested by Gk *-graphikos*, from *graphē* 'writing, drawing'; partly from **-GRAPHY** or **-GRAPH** + **-IC**.

**graphicacy** /ˈgrafɪkəsi/ ● n. the ability to understand maps or graphs.
– ORIGIN 1960s: from **GRAPHIC**, on the pattern of *literacy* and *numeracy*.

**graphical** ● adj. **1** of or in the form of a graph. **2** of or relating to visual art or computer graphics.
– DERIVATIVES **graphically** adv.

**-graphical** ● comb. form equivalent to **-GRAPHIC**.

**graphical user interface** ● n. Computing a visual way of interacting with a computer using items such as windows and icons.

**graphic arts** ● pl. n. the visual arts based on the use of line and tone rather than three-dimensional work or the use of colour.
– DERIVATIVES **graphic artist** n.

**graphic design** ● n. the art or skill of combining text and pictures in advertisements, magazines, or books.
– DERIVATIVES **graphic designer** n.

**graphic equalizer** ● n. an electronic device or computer program which allows the separate control of the strength and quality of selected frequency bands.

**graphic novel** ● n. a novel in comic-strip format.

**graphics** ● pl. n. [usu. treated as sing.] **1** the products of the graphic arts, especially commercial design or illustration. **2** the use of diagrams in calculation and design. **3** [treated as pl.] visual images produced or manipulated by computer processing. ➤[treated as sing.] the use of computers to generate and manipulate visual images.

**graphics tablet** ● n. Computing an input device which the user draws on or points at with a special stylus, to guide a pointer displayed on the screen.

**graphite** ● n. a grey, crystalline, electrically conducting form of carbon which is used as a solid lubricant, as pencil lead, and as a moderator in nuclear reactors.
– DERIVATIVES **graphitic** adj. **graphitization** (also **-isation**) n. **graphitize** (also **-ise**) v.
– ORIGIN C18: from Ger. *Graphit*, from Gk *graphein* 'write' (because of its use in pencils).

**graphology** ● n. **1** the study of handwriting, especially as used to infer a person's character. **2** Linguistics the study of written and printed symbols and of writing systems.
– DERIVATIVES **graphological** adj. **graphologist** n.
– ORIGIN C19: from Gk *graphē* 'writing' + **-LOGY**.

**graph paper** ● n. paper printed with a network of small squares to assist the drawing of graphs etc.

**-graphy** ● comb. form in nouns denoting: **1** a descriptive science: *geography*. **2** a technique of producing images: *radiography*. **3** a style or method of writing or drawing: *calligraphy*. **4** writing about (a specified subject): *hagiography*. **5** a written or printed list: *filmography*. See word-formation panel.
– ORIGIN from or suggested by Gk *-graphia* 'writing'.

**grapnel** /ˈgrapn(ə)l/ ● n. **1** a grappling hook. **2** a small anchor with several flukes.
– ORIGIN ME: from an Anglo-Norman Fr. dimin. of OFr. *grapon*, of Gmc origin.

**grappa** /ˈgrapə/ ● n. a brandy distilled from the fermented residue of grapes after they have been pressed in winemaking.
– ORIGIN Ital., lit. 'grape stalk'.

**grapple** ● v. **1** engage in a close fight or struggle without weapons. ➤(**grapple with**) struggle to deal with. **2** archaic seize with a grapnel. ● n. **1** an act of grappling. **2** a grapnel.
– DERIVATIVES **grappler** n.
– ORIGIN ME: from OFr. *grapil*, from Provençal, dimin. of *grapa* 'hook', of Gmc origin; rel. to **GRAPE**.

**grappling hook** (also **grappling iron**) ● n. a device with iron claws, attached to a rope and used for dragging or grasping.

**graptolite** /ˈgraptəlʌɪt/ ● n. a fossil planktonic invertebrate animal, believed to be related to the pterobranchs.
– ORIGIN C19: from Gk *graptos* 'marked with letters' + **-LITE**: so named because impressions left on hard shales resemble slate pencil marks.

**grasp** /grɑːsp/ ● v. **1** seize and hold firmly. **2** comprehend fully. ● n. **1** a firm grip. ➤a person's capacity to attain something. **2** a person's understanding.
– DERIVATIVES **graspable** adj. **grasper** n.
– ORIGIN ME: perh. rel. to **GROPE**.

**grasping** ● adj. greedy.
– DERIVATIVES **graspingly** adv. **graspingness** n.

**grass** ● n. **1** vegetation consisting of short plants with long narrow leaves, growing wild or cultivated on lawns and pasture. ➤ground covered with this. **2** a plant with jointed stems and spikes of small wind-pollinated flowers, predominant in such vegetation. [Family Gramineae: many species.] **3** informal cannabis. **4** Brit. informal a police informer. ● v. **1** cover with grass. **2** (often **grass on**) Brit. informal inform the police of criminal activity or plans. **3** land (a fish). **4** chiefly Rugby & Australian Rules knock down.
– PHRASES **at grass** grazing. **not let the grass grow under one's feet** not delay in taking action. **put out to grass** put (an animal) out to graze. ➤(**put someone out to grass**) informal force someone to retire.
– DERIVATIVES **grassless** adj. **grass-like** adj.
– ORIGIN OE *græs*, of Gmc origin; ult. rel. to **GREEN** and **GROW**. The sense 'police informer' is perh. rel. to C19 rhyming sl. *grasshopper* 'copper'.

**grassbird** ● n. a brown streaked warbler frequenting long grass and reed beds. [Genus *Megalurus* (Australasia and Asia) and *Sphenoeacus afer* (southern Africa).]

**grassbox** ● n. a receptacle on a lawnmower for collecting the cut grass.

**grass carp** ● n. a large Chinese freshwater fish, farmed for food in SE Asia. [*Ctenopharyngodon idella*.]

**grasscloth** ● n. a fine, light cloth resembling linen, woven from the fibres of the ramie plant.

**grasshopper** ● n. a plant-eating insect with long hind legs which are used for jumping and for producing a chirping sound. [Family Acrididae: many species.]

**grasshopper warbler** ● n. a secretive warbler whose song is a prolonged mechanical-sounding trill. [*Locustella naevia* and other species.]

**grassland** ● n. (also **grasslands**) a large area of grass-covered land, especially one used for grazing.

**grass of Parnassus** ● n. a northern plant of damp meadows, with a solitary white flower. [*Parnassia palustris*.]

**grass parakeet** ● n. Austral. a small parrot frequenting grassy country. [*Psephotus*, *Neophema*, and other genera.]

**grass pea** ● n. a leguminous plant cultivated as food for animals and humans. [*Lathyrus sativus*.]

**grassquit** /ˈgrɑːskwɪt/ ● n. a small Caribbean and tropical American songbird related to the buntings. [*Tiaris* and other genera.]

**grass roots** ● pl. n. the most basic level of an activity or organization. ➤ordinary people regarded as the main body of an organization's membership.

**grass sickness** ● n. a disease of horses which affects the bowel and is usually fatal.

**grass ski** ● n. each of a pair of devices resembling caterpillar tracks, worn on the feet for going down grass-covered slopes as if on skis.
– DERIVATIVES **grass skiing** n.

**grass skirt** ● n. a skirt made of long grass and leaves

## Word *Formation*

### **-graphy** from Greek *-graphia* 'writing'

➤ A number of **-graphy** words in English relate directly to writing, both the techniques used and the subject matter addressed:

| | | |
|---|---|---|
| autobiography | an account of one's own life | Gk *autos* 'self' + *bios* 'life' |
| biography | an account of a person's life | Gk *bios* 'life' |
| calligraphy | decorative handwriting | Gk *kallos* 'beauty' |
| chirography | handwriting, esp. as distinct from printed matter | Gk *kheir* 'hand' |
| epigraphy | the interpretation of ancient inscriptions | Gk *epigraphein* 'write on' |
| hagiography | a biography idealizing its subject | Gk *hagios* 'holy' |
| haplography | the inadvertent omission of a letter or letters in writing | Gk *haploos* 'single' (i.e. the letter is written only once, not twice) |
| orthography | spelling, esp. correct spelling | Gk *orthos* 'correct' |
| palaeography | the study of ancient writing | Gk *palaios* 'ancient' |
| stenography | writing and transcribing shorthand | Gk *stenos* 'narrow' |
| typography | the process of setting type; the style of printed matter | Gk *tupos* 'impression, force' |

➤ Other **-graphy** words relate to the production of images, graphs, or diagrams:

| | | |
|---|---|---|
| cartography | the science of drawing maps | OFr. *carte*, from L. *carta, charta*, from Gk *khartēs* 'papyrus leaf' |
| encephalography | a technique for recording electrical activity in the brain | Gk *enkephalos* 'brain' |
| holography | the production of three-dimensional images (holograms) | Gk *holos* 'whole' |
| lithography | a printing process | Gk *lithos* 'stone' |
| mammography | the use of X-rays to locate breast abnormalities | L. *mamma* 'breast' |
| photography | the taking of photographs | Gk *phōs, phōt-*, 'light' |
| pornography | writing and images designed to stimulate sexual excitement | Gk *pornographos* 'writing about prostitutes' |
| radiography | the production of images by X-rays, gamma rays, etc. | based on RADIO- |
| tomography | a technique for producing an image showing a cross-section through the body | Gk *tomos* 'slice' |
| topography | the arrangement of physical features of an area | Gk *topos* 'place' |

➤ One of the most productive uses in English forms words with the meaning 'a descriptive science or study' (many of the words listed above also have this meaning):

| | | |
|---|---|---|
| cosmography | the science of the universe | Gk *kosmos* 'order, world' |
| crystallography | the science of crystals | Gk *krustallos* 'crystal' |
| ethnography | the study of different peoples | Gk *ethnos* 'nation' |
| geography | the study of the physical features of the earth and their relation to human populations | Gk *gē* 'earth' |
| oceanography | the science of the sea | based on OCEAN |
| petrography | the study of rocks | Gk *petros* 'stone' |

fastened to a waistband, associated especially with female dancers from some Pacific islands.

**grass snake** ● **n. 1** a common harmless snake, typically grey-green with a yellowish band around the neck. [*Natrix natrix*.] **2** North American term for **GREEN SNAKE**.

**grass tree** ● **n.** another term for **BLACKBOY**.

**grass widow** ● **n.** a woman whose husband is away often or for a prolonged period.
– ORIGIN C16 (denoting an unmarried woman with a child): from **GRASS** + **WIDOW**, perh. from the idea of a couple having lain on the grass instead of in bed.

**grassy** ● **adj.** (**-ier, -iest**) **1** of or covered with grass. **2** characteristic of or resembling grass.
– DERIVATIVES **grassiness** n.

**grate**[1] ● **v. 1** reduce (food) to small shreds by rubbing it on a grater. **2** make an unpleasant rasping sound. **3** have an irritating effect.
– ORIGIN ME: from OFr. *grater*, of Gmc origin.

**grate**[2] ● **n.** the recess of a fireplace or furnace. ➤ a metal frame confining fuel in a fireplace or furnace.
– ORIGIN ME (meaning 'a grating'): from OFr., based on L. *cratis* 'hurdle'.

**grateful** ● **adj. 1** feeling or showing gratitude. **2** archaic received with gratitude.
– DERIVATIVES **gratefully** adv. **gratefulness** n.
– ORIGIN C16: from obs. *grate* 'pleasing, thankful' (from L. *gratus*) + **-FUL**.

**grater** ● **n.** a device having a surface covered with sharp-edged holes, used for grating food.

**graticule** /ˈgratɪkjuːl/ ● **n. 1** a network of lines representing meridians and parallels, on which a map or plan can be represented. **2** a series of fine lines in an eyepiece or oscilloscope screen, used as a measuring scale or an aid in locating objects.
– ORIGIN C19: from Fr., from med. L. *graticula* 'a little grating'.

**gratify** ● **v.** (**-ies, -ied**) **1** give pleasure or satisfaction. **2** indulge or satisfy (a desire).
– DERIVATIVES **gratification** n. **gratifier** n. **gratifying** adj. **gratifyingly** adv.

– ORIGIN ME: from Fr. *gratifier* or L. *gratificari* 'give or do as a favour', from *gratus* 'pleasing, thankful'.

**gratin** /'gratã, 'gratan/ • **n.** a dish cooked au gratin.
– ORIGIN Fr., from *gratter*, earlier *grater* 'to grate'.

**gratiné** /,gratɪ'neɪ/ (also **gratinée**) • **adj.** [postpos.] another term for **AU GRATIN**.
– DERIVATIVES **gratinéed** adj.
– ORIGIN Fr., past part. of *gratiner* 'cook au gratin'.

**grating**[1] • **adj.** **1** sounding harsh and unpleasant. **2** irritating.
– DERIVATIVES **gratingly** adv.

**grating**[2] • **n.** **1** a framework of parallel or crossed bars, typically preventing access through an opening. **2** (also **diffraction grating**) Optics a set of equally spaced parallel wires or ruled lines, used to produce spectra by diffraction.

**gratis** /'gratɪs, 'grɑː-, 'greɪ-/ • **adv. & adj.** free of charge.
– ORIGIN ME: from L., contr. of *gratiis* 'as a kindness', from *gratia* 'grace, kindness'.

**gratitude** • **n.** thankfulness; appreciation of kindness.
– ORIGIN ME: from OFr., or from med. L. *gratitudo*, from L. *gratus* 'pleasing, thankful'.

**gratuitous** /grə'tjuːɪtəs/ • **adj.** **1** uncalled for. **2** free of charge.
– DERIVATIVES **gratuitously** adv. **gratuitousness** n.
– ORIGIN C17: from L. *gratuitus* 'given freely, spontaneous' + **-OUS**.

**gratuity** /grə'tjuːɪti/ • **n.** (pl. **-ies**) **1** formal a tip given to a waiter, porter, etc. **2** Brit. a sum of money paid to an employee at the end of a period of employment.
– ORIGIN C15 (denoting graciousness): from OFr. *gratuité* or med. L. *gratuitas* 'gift'.

**graunch** /grɔːn(t)ʃ/ • **v.** Brit. informal make a crunching or grinding noise.
– ORIGIN C19 (orig. dial.): imitative.

**gravadlax** /'gravəd,laks/ • **n.** variant spelling of **GRAVLAX**.

**gravamen** /grə'veɪmɛn/ • **n.** (pl. **gravamina** /-mɪnə/) chiefly Law the essence or most serious part of a complaint or accusation.
– ORIGIN C17: from late L., lit. 'physical inconvenience'.

**grave**[1] • **n.** a hole dug in the ground to receive a coffin or corpse. ➤ (**the grave**) death.
– PHRASES **dig one's own grave** do something foolish which causes one's downfall. **turn** (N. Amer. also **turn over**) **in one's grave** (of a dead person) be thought of as angry or distressed about something had they been alive.
– ORIGIN OE *græf*, of Gmc origin.

**grave**[2] • **adj.** **1** giving cause for alarm. **2** solemn.
– DERIVATIVES **gravely** adv. **graveness** n.
– ORIGIN C15: from OFr. *grave* or L. *gravis* 'heavy, serious'.

**grave**[3] • **v.** (past part. **graven** or **graved**) **1** archaic engrave (an inscription or image) on a surface. **2** poetic/literary fix indelibly in the mind.
– ORIGIN OE *grafan* 'dig', of Gmc origin; rel. to **GRAVE**[1] and **GROOVE**.

**grave**[4] • **v.** historical clean (a ship's bottom) by burning off the accretions and then tarring it.
– ORIGIN ME: perh. from Fr. dial. *grave*, var. of OFr. *greve* 'shore'.

**grave accent** /grɑːv/ • **n.** a mark (`) placed over a vowel in some languages to indicate a feature such as altered sound quality.
– ORIGIN C17: Fr. *grave* (see **GRAVE**[2]).

**gravel** • **n.** **1** a loose aggregation of small stones and coarse sand, often used for paths and roads. **2** Medicine aggregations of crystals formed in the urinary tract. • **v.** (**gravelled**, **gravelling**; US **graveled**, **graveling**) **1** cover with gravel. **2** US informal anger or annoy.
– ORIGIN ME: from OFr., dimin. of *grave* (see **GRAVE**[4]).

**gravelly** • **adj.** **1** resembling, containing, or consisting of gravel. **2** (of a voice) deep and rough-sounding.

**graven** past participle of **GRAVE**[3].

**graven image** • **n.** a carved figure of a god used as an idol.
– ORIGIN with biblical allusion to Exod. 20:4.

**Gravenstein** /'grɑːv(ə)n,stʌɪn/ • **n.** a cooking and dessert apple of a variety with yellow, red-streaked skin.
– ORIGIN C19: the Ger. form of *Graasten*, a village in Denmark.

**graver** • **n.** **1** a burin or other engraving tool. **2** archaic an engraver.

**Graves** /grɑːv, French gʀav/ • **n.** a red or white wine from Graves, a district of SW France.

**Graves' disease** • **n.** a swelling of the neck and protrusion of the eyes resulting from an overactive thyroid gland.
– ORIGIN C19: named after the Ir. physician Robert J. *Graves*.

**gravestone** • **n.** an inscribed headstone marking a grave.

**Gravettian** /grə'vɛtɪən/ • **adj.** Archaeology relating to or denoting an Upper Palaeolithic culture in Europe following the Aurignacian, dated to about 28,000–19,000 years ago.
– ORIGIN 1930s: from *la Gravette* in SW France, where objects from this culture were found.

**graveyard** • **n.** a burial ground beside a church.

**graveyard shift** • **n.** chiefly N. Amer. a work shift that runs from midnight to 8 a.m.

**gravid** /'gravɪd/ • **adj.** **1** technical pregnant. **2** poetic/literary full of meaning or a specified quality.
– ORIGIN C16: from L. *gravidus* 'laden, pregnant'.

**gravimeter** /grə'vɪmɪtə/ • **n.** an instrument for measuring the force of gravity at different places.
– ORIGIN C18: from Fr. *gravimètre*, from *grave* 'heavy' + *-mètre* '(instrument) measuring'.

**gravimetric** /gravɪ'mɛtrɪk/ • **adj.** **1** of or relating to the measurement of weight. **2** of or relating to the measurement of gravity.
– DERIVATIVES **gravimetry** /grə'vɪmɪtri/ n.

**graving dock** • **n.** another term for **DRY DOCK**.
– ORIGIN C19: *graving* from **GRAVE**[4].

**gravitas** /'gravɪtas, -tɑːs/ • **n.** dignity or solemnity of manner.
– ORIGIN L., from *gravis* 'serious'.

**gravitate** /'gravɪteɪt/ • **v.** **1** be drawn towards a place, person, or thing. **2** Physics move, or tend to move, towards a centre of gravity.
– ORIGIN C17: from mod. L. *gravitat-*, *gravitare*, from L. *gravitas* 'weight'.

**gravitation** • **n.** **1** movement, or a tendency to move, towards a centre of gravity. **2** Physics the force responsible for this; gravity.
– DERIVATIVES **gravitational** adj. **gravitationally** adv.

**gravitational constant** (abbrev.: **G**) • **n.** Physics the constant in Newton's law of gravitation relating gravity to the masses and separation of particles, equal to $6.67 \times 10^{-11}$ N $m^2$ $kg^{-2}$.

**gravitational lens** • **n.** Astronomy a massive object whose gravitational field distorts light passing through it, producing a multiple image of a more remote object.

**graviton** /'gravɪtɒn/ • **n.** Physics a hypothetical particle representing a quantum of gravitational energy.

**gravity** • **n.** **1** Physics the force that attracts a body towards the centre of the earth, or towards any other physical body having mass. ➤ the degree of intensity of this, measured by acceleration. **2** extreme importance; seriousness. ➤ solemnity of manner.
– ORIGIN C15: from OFr., or from L. *gravitas* 'weight, seriousness'.

**gravity feed** • **n.** a supply system making use of gravity to maintain the flow of material.
– DERIVATIVES **gravity-fed** adj.

**gravity wave** • **n.** Physics **1** a hypothetical wave carrying gravitational energy. **2** a wave propagated on a liquid surface or in a fluid through the effects of gravity.

**gravlax** /'gravlaks/ (also **gravadlax**) • **n.** a Scandinavian dish of dry-cured salmon marinated in herbs.
– ORIGIN Swed., from *grav* 'trench' + *lax* 'salmon' (from the former practice of burying the salmon in salt in a hole in the ground).

**gravure** /grə'vjʊə/ • **n.** short for **PHOTOGRAVURE**.

**gravy** ● n. (pl. **-ies**) **1** the fat and juices exuding from meat during cooking. ➤a sauce made from these juices together with stock and other ingredients. **2** informal unearned or unexpected money.
– ORIGIN ME: perh. from a misreading (as *gravé*) of OFr. *grané*, prob. from *grain* 'spice', from L. *granum* 'grain'.

**gravy boat** ● n. a long narrow jug used for serving gravy.

**gravy train** ● n. informal a situation in which someone can easily make a lot of money.

**gray**[1] (abbrev.: **Gy**) ● n. Physics the SI unit of the absorbed dose of ionizing radiation, corresponding to one joule per kilogram.
– ORIGIN 1970s: named after the Engl. radiobiologist Louis H. *Gray*.

**gray**[2] ● adj. US spelling of **GREY**.

**graybeard** etc. ● n. US spelling of **GREYBEARD** etc.

**grayling** ● n. **1** an edible silvery-grey freshwater fish with horizontal violet stripes and a long high dorsal fin. [Genus *Thymallus*: several species.] **2** a mainly brown butterfly having wings with bright eyespots and greyish undersides. [*Hipparchia semele*.]
– ORIGIN ME: from *gray* (var. of **GREY**) + **-LING**.

**grayscale** ● n. US spelling of **GREYSCALE**.

**graywacke** ● n. US spelling of **GREYWACKE**.

**graze**[1] ● v. **1** (of cattle, sheep, etc.) eat grass in a field. ➤feed on (grass or grassland). **2** informal eat frequent snacks at irregular intervals. **3** informal, chiefly N. Amer. casually sample something.
– DERIVATIVES **grazer** n.
– ORIGIN OE *grasian*, from *græs* 'grass'.

**graze**[2] ● v. **1** scrape and break the skin on (part of the body). **2** touch or scrape lightly in passing. ● n. a superficial injury caused by grazing the skin.
– ORIGIN C16: perh. a specific use of **GRAZE**[1].

**grazier** /ˈɡreɪzɪə/ ● n. a person who rears or fattens cattle or sheep for market.
– ORIGIN ME: from **GRASS** + **-IER**.

**grazing** ● n. grassland suitable for pasturage.

**grease** ● n. **1** a thick oily substance, especially as used as a lubricant. **2** animal fat used or produced in cooking. ● v. smear or lubricate with grease.
– PHRASES **grease the palm of** informal bribe. [*grease* expressing the sense 'cause to run smoothly' and *palm*, by assoc. with the taking of money.] **grease the wheels** (N. Amer. also **the skids**) informal help matters run smoothly. **like greased lightning** informal extremely rapidly.
– DERIVATIVES **greaseless** adj.
– ORIGIN ME: from OFr. *graisse*, based on L. *crassus* 'thick, fat'.

**grease gun** ● n. a device for pumping grease under pressure to a particular point.

**grease monkey** ● n. informal a mechanic.

**greasepaint** ● n. a waxy substance used as make-up by actors.

**greaseproof** ● adj. (especially of paper used in cooking) impermeable to grease.

**greaser** ● n. **1** a motor mechanic or unskilled engineer on a ship. **2** informal a young man with long hair belonging to a motorcycle gang. **3** US informal, offensive a Hispanic American, especially a Mexican.

**greasewood** ● n. a resinous dwarf shrub with hard yellow wood, growing in dry areas of the western US. [*Sarcobatus vermiculatus*.]

**greasy** ● adj. (**-ier**, **-iest**) **1** covered with or resembling grease. ➤producing more body oils than average. ➤containing or cooked with too much oil or fat. **2** effusively polite in a repellently insincere way.
– DERIVATIVES **greasily** adv. **greasiness** n.

**greasy pole** ● n. informal a pole covered with grease, especially as climbed or walked along for entertainment. ➤the difficult route to the top of a profession.

**greasy spoon** ● n. informal a cheap, run-down cafe or restaurant serving fried foods.

**great** ● adj. **1** of an extent, amount, or intensity considerably above average. ➤(**Greater**) (of a city) including adjacent urban areas. **2** of ability, quality, or eminence considerably above average. ➤(**the Great**) a title denoting the most important person of the name. ➤informal excellent. **3** denoting the most important element of something. ➤particularly deserving a specified description: *I was a great fan of Hank's.* **4** [in combination] (in names of family relationships) denoting one degree further removed upwards or downwards. ● n. **1** a distinguished person. **2** (**Greats**) another term for **LITERAE HUMANIORES**. ● adv. informal very well.
– PHRASES **the great and the good** often ironic distinguished and worthy people collectively. **great and small** of all sizes, classes, or types. **Great Scott!** expressing surprise or amazement. [arbitrary euphemism for *Great God!*]
– DERIVATIVES **greatness** n.
– ORIGIN OE *grēat* 'big', of W. Gmc origin.

**great ape** ● n. a large ape of a family closely related to humans, including the gorilla and chimpanzees. [Family Pongidae.]

**great auk** ● n. a large flightless auk of the North Atlantic, exterminated in the 19th century. [*Alca impennis*.]

**great-aunt** ● n. an aunt of one's father or mother.

**great circle** ● n. a circle on the surface of a sphere which lies in a plane passing through the sphere's centre, especially as representing the shortest path between two given points on the sphere.

**greatcoat** ● n. a long heavy overcoat.

**Great Dane** ● n. a dog of a very large, powerful, short-haired breed.

**great divide** ● n. **1** the boundary between two contrasting groups, cultures, etc., that is very difficult to overcome. **2** the boundary between life and death.

**great-hearted** ● adj. dated having a noble and generous spirit.
– DERIVATIVES **great-heartedness** n.

**greatly** ● adv. very much.

**great-nephew** ● n. a son of one's nephew or niece.

**great-niece** ● n. a daughter of one's nephew or niece.

**great organ** ● n. the chief keyboard in a large organ and its related pipes and mechanism.

**Great Russian** ● adj. & n. former term for **RUSSIAN** (language and people), as distinguished from other peoples and languages of the old Russian Empire.

**Great Seal** ● n. a seal used for the authentication of state documents of the highest importance.

**great tit** ● n. a common titmouse with a black and white head, grey back, and yellow breast. [*Parus major*.]

**great-uncle** ● n. an uncle of one's mother or father.

**great white shark** ● n. a very large predatory shark with a brownish or grey back and white underparts. [*Carcharodon carcharias*.]

**greave** ● n. historical a piece of armour for the shin.
– ORIGIN ME: from OFr. *greve* 'shin, greave'.

**grebe** /ɡriːb/ ● n. a diving waterbird with a long neck, lobed toes, and a very short tail. [Family Podicipedidae: several species.]
– ORIGIN C18: from Fr. *grèbe*.

**grebo** /ˈɡriːbəʊ/ ● n. (pl. **-os**) informal a youth favouring heavy metal or punk rock music and long hair.
– ORIGIN 1980s: perh. from **GREASER**, on the pattern of words such as *dumbo*.

**Grecian** ● adj. of or relating to ancient Greece, especially its architecture.
– ORIGIN ME: from OFr. *grecien*, from L. *Graecia* 'Greece'.

**Grecian nose** ● n. a straight nose that continues the line of the forehead without a dip.

**Grecism** ● n. variant spelling of **GRAECISM**.

**Greco-** ● comb. form variant spelling of **GRAECO-**.

**greed** ● n. intense and selfish desire for wealth, power, or food.
– ORIGIN C16: back-form. from **GREEDY**.

**greedy** ● adj. (**-ier**, **-iest**) having or showing greed.
– DERIVATIVES **greedily** adv. **greediness** n.
– ORIGIN OE *grǣdig*, of Gmc origin.

**greegree** ● n. variant spelling of **GRIS-GRIS**.

**Greek** ● n. **1** a native or national of Greece, or a person of Greek descent. ➤a Greek-speaking native of one of the

ancient city states of Greece and the eastern Mediterranean. **2** the ancient or modern Indo-European language of Greece. ● **adj.** of or relating to Greece, its people, or their language.
– PHRASES **it's (all) Greek to me** informal I can't understand it at all.
– DERIVATIVES **Greekness** n.
– ORIGIN OE *Grēcas* 'the Greeks', from L. *Graeci*, from Gk *Graikoi*, which according to Aristotle was the prehistoric name of the Hellenes.

**Greek coffee** ● **n.** very strong black coffee served with the fine grounds in it.

**Greek cross** ● **n.** a cross of which all four arms are of equal length.

**Greek fire** ● **n.** historical a combustible composition first used by the Greeks besieged in Constantinople (673–8), used to set fire to enemy ships.

**Greek key** ● **n.** a pattern of interlocking right-angled spirals.

**Greek Orthodox Church** (also **Greek Church**) ● **n.** the Eastern Orthodox Church which uses the Byzantine rite in Greek, in particular the national Church of Greece.

**green** ● **adj. 1** of the colour between blue and yellow in the spectrum; coloured like grass. **2** covered with grass or other vegetation. **3** (of a plant or fruit) young or unripe. ➤(of food, wood, pottery, or leather) in its untreated or original state; not cured, seasoned, fired, etc. **4** inexperienced or naive. **5** pale and sickly-looking. **6** (usu. **Green**) concerned with or supporting protection of the environment as a political principle. **7** (of a ski run) of the lowest level of difficulty. ● **n. 1** green colour, pigment, or material. ➤green foliage or growing plants. **2** a piece of common grassy land, especially in the centre of a village. ➤an area of smooth, very short grass immediately surrounding a hole on a golf course. **3** (**greens**) green vegetables. **4** (usu. **Green**) a member or supporter of an environmentalist group or party. ● **v. 1** make or become green. **2** make less harmful to the environment.
– DERIVATIVES **greenish** adj. **greenly** adv. **greenness** n. **greeny** adj.
– ORIGIN OE *grēne* (adj.), *grēnian* (v.), of Gmc origin; rel. to GRASS and GROW.

**green algae** ● **pl. n.** algae which contain chlorophyll and store starch in discrete chloroplasts. [Division Chlorophyta.]

**greenback** ● **n.** US informal a dollar.

**green belt** ● **n. 1** an area of open land around a city, on which building is restricted. **2** a green belt marking a level of proficiency below that of a brown belt in judo, karate, or other martial arts.

**Green Beret** ● **n.** informal a British commando or a member of the US Army Special Forces.

**greenbottle** ● **n.** a metallic green fly which sometimes lays eggs in wounds on sheep or other animals. [*Lucilia caesar* and related species.]

**green card** ● **n. 1** (in the UK) an international insurance document for motorists. **2** (in the US) a permit allowing a foreign national to live and work permanently in the US.

**Green Cloth** (in full **Board of Green Cloth**) ● **n.** (in the UK) the Lord Steward's department of the royal household.

**green crop** ● **n.** Brit. a crop used in a green or unripe state as fodder.

**green earth** ● **n.** another term for TERRE VERTE.

**greenery** ● **n.** green foliage or vegetation.

**green-eyed monster** ● **n.** (**the green-eyed monster**) informal, humorous jealousy personified.
– ORIGIN from Shakespeare's *Othello* (III. 3. 166).

**green fat** ● **n.** the green gelatinous part of a turtle, highly regarded by gourmets.

**greenfeed** ● **n.** Austral./NZ forage grown to be fed fresh to livestock.

**greenfield** ● **adj.** relating to or denoting previously undeveloped sites for commercial development.

**greenfinch** ● **n.** a large finch with green and yellow plumage. [*Carduelis chloris*.]

**green fingers** ● **pl. n.** Brit. informal natural ability in growing plants.
– DERIVATIVES **green-fingered** adj.

**greenfly** ● **n.** (pl. same or **-flies**) chiefly Brit. a green aphid.

**greengage** ● **n. 1** a sweet greenish fruit resembling a small plum. **2** the tree bearing this fruit. [*Prunus domestica*.]
– ORIGIN C18: named after the Engl. botanist Sir William *Gage*.

**greengrocer** ● **n.** Brit. a retailer of fruit and vegetables.
– DERIVATIVES **greengrocery** n.

**greenhead** ● **n. 1** (also **greenhead fly**) chiefly US a biting horsefly with green eyes. [Genus *Chrysops*.] **2** Austral. a stinging ant with a green head. [*Rhytidoponera metallica*.]

**greenheart** ● **n.** a South American evergreen tree yielding hard greenish wood used for marine work. [*Ocotea rodiaei*.]

**greenhorn** ● **n.** informal, chiefly N. Amer. an inexperienced or naive person.

**greenhouse** ● **n.** a glass building in which plants that need protection from cold weather are grown.

**greenhouse effect** ● **n.** the trapping of the sun's warmth in a planet's lower atmosphere, due to the greater transparency of the atmosphere to visible radiation from the sun than to infrared radiation emitted from the planet's surface.

**greenhouse gas** ● **n.** a gas, such as carbon dioxide, that contributes to the greenhouse effect by absorbing infrared.

**greenie** ● **n.** informal, often derogatory a campaigner for Green issues.

**greening** ● **n.** an apple of a variety that is green when ripe.
– ORIGIN C17: prob. from MDu. *groeninc*, a kind of apple.

**green jersey** ● **n.** (in a cycling race involving stages) a green jersey worn each day by the rider accumulating the highest number of points, and presented at the end of the race to the rider with the highest overall points total.

**Greenlander** ● **n.** an inhabitant of Greenland.

**Greenlandic** /griːn'landɪk/ ● **n.** an Inuit dialect which is one of the official languages of Greenland.

**green leek** ● **n.** Austral. a green-faced or mainly green parrot.

**greenlet** /'griːnlɪt/ ● **n.** a small vireo with drab plumage, found in Central and South America. [Genus *Hylophilus*: several species.]

**green light** ● **n.** a green traffic light giving permission to proceed. ➤permission to go ahead with a project. ● **v.** (**green-light**) chiefly N. Amer. give permission to go ahead with.

**greenling** ● **n.** a spiny-finned edible fish of the North Pacific. [Family Hexagrammidae: several species.]

**greenmail** ● **n.** Stock Exchange the practice of buying enough shares in a company to threaten a takeover, forcing the owners to buy them back at a higher price in order to retain control.
– DERIVATIVES **greenmailer** n.
– ORIGIN 1980s: blend of GREEN and BLACKMAIL.

**green man** ● **n.** historical a man dressed up in greenery to represent a wild man of the woods or seasonal fertility.

**green manure** ● **n.** growing plants ploughed back into the soil as fertilizer.

**Green Paper** ● **n.** (in the UK) a preliminary report of government proposals published to stimulate discussion.

**green pepper** ● **n.** the mild-flavoured unripe fruit of a sweet pepper.

**green plover** ● **n.** Brit. the lapwing.

**green pound** ● **n.** the exchange rate for the pound applied to payments for agricultural produce in the EU.

**green revolution** ● **n.** a large increase in crop production in developing countries achieved by the use of artificial fertilizers, pesticides, and high-yield crop varieties.

**green room** • n. a room in a theatre or studio in which performers can relax when they are not performing.

**greensand** • n. Geology a greenish kind of sandstone, often loosely consolidated.

**greenshank** • n. a large grey and white sandpiper with long greenish legs. [*Tringa nebularia*.]

**green snake** • n. a harmless American snake with a green back and white or yellowish underparts. [Genus *Opheodrys*: two species.]

**greenstick fracture** • n. a fracture of the bone, occurring typically in children, in which one side of the bone is broken and the other only bent.

**greenstone** • n. **1** Geology a greenish igneous rock containing feldspar and hornblende. **2** chiefly NZ a variety of jade.

**greensward** /ˈgriːnˌswɔːd/ • n. archaic or poetic/literary grass-covered ground.

**green tea** • n. tea made from unfermented leaves, produced mainly in China and Japan.

**green thumb** • n. North American term for **GREEN FINGERS**.

**green vitriol** • n. archaic crystalline ferrous sulphate.

**greenwash** • n. disinformation disseminated by an organization so as to present an environmentally responsible public image.
– DERIVATIVES **greenwashing** n.
– ORIGIN from **GREEN**, on the pattern of *whitewash*.

**greenway** • n. N. Amer. a strip of undeveloped land near an urban area, set aside for recreational use or environmental protection.

**Greenwich Mean Time** • n. the mean solar time at the Greenwich meridian, adopted as the standard time in a zone that includes the British Isles.
– ORIGIN *Greenwich* in London, former site of the Royal Observatory.

**Greenwich meridian** • n. the meridian of zero longitude, passing through Greenwich.

**greenwood** • n. archaic a wood or forest in leaf, especially as a refuge for outlaws.

**green woodpecker** • n. a large green and yellow woodpecker with a red crown and a laughing call. [*Picus viridis*.]

**greet**[1] • v. **1** give a word or sign of welcome when meeting (someone). **2** receive or acknowledge in a specified way: *the idea was warmly greeted.* **3** (of a sight or sound) become apparent to (a person arriving somewhere).
– DERIVATIVES **greeter** n.
– ORIGIN OE *grētan* 'approach, attack, or salute', of W. Gmc origin.

**greet**[2] • v. Scottish weep; cry.
– ORIGIN OE, partly from *grētan* 'cry out, rage', partly from *grēotan* 'lament', both of Gmc origin.

**greeting** • n. **1** a word or sign of welcome or recognition. ➤ the action of greeting. **2** (usu. **greetings**) a formal expression of goodwill.

**greetings card** (N. Amer. **greeting card**) • n. a decorative card sent to convey good wishes.

**gregarious** /grɪˈgɛːrɪəs/ • adj. **1** fond of company; sociable. **2** (of animals) living in flocks or colonies. **3** (of plants) growing in clusters.
– DERIVATIVES **gregariously** adv. **gregariousness** n.
– ORIGIN C17: from L. *gregarius* (from *grex, greg-* 'a flock') + **-OUS**.

**Gregorian calendar** /grɪˈgɔːrɪən/ • n. the modified form of the Julian calendar introduced in 1582 by Pope Gregory XIII, and still used today.

**Gregorian chant** • n. medieval church plainsong.
– ORIGIN C18: named after St *Gregory* the Great (*c.*540–604).

**Gregorian telescope** • n. an early reflecting telescope in which light reflected from a concave elliptical secondary mirror passes through a hole in the primary mirror.
– ORIGIN C18: named after the C17 Sc. mathematician James *Gregory*.

**greisen** /ˈgrʌɪz(ə)n/ • n. Geology a light-coloured rock resulting from the alteration of granite by hot vapour from magma.
– ORIGIN C19: from Ger., prob. a dial. word, from *greis* 'grey with age'.

**gremlin** • n. a mischievous sprite regarded as responsible for unexplained mechanical or electrical faults.
– ORIGIN 1940s: perh. suggested by **GOBLIN**.

**Grenache** /grəˈnaʃ/ • n. a variety of black wine grape native to the Languedoc-Roussillon region of France. ➤ a sweet red dessert wine made from this grape.
– ORIGIN from Fr.

**grenade** /grəˈneɪd/ • n. **1** a small bomb thrown by hand or launched mechanically. **2** a glass receptacle containing chemicals which are released on impact, used for testing drains and extinguishing fires.
– ORIGIN C16 (in the sense 'pomegranate', which the bomb supposedly resembled in shape): from Fr., alt. of OFr. *(pome) grenate* (see **POMEGRANATE**), on the pattern of Sp. *granada*.

**Grenadian** /grɪˈneɪdɪən/ • n. a native or inhabitant of the Caribbean country of Grenada. • adj. of or relating to Grenada.

**grenadier** /ˌgrɛnəˈdɪə/ • n. **1** historical a soldier armed with grenades. ➤ (**Grenadiers** or **Grenadier Guards**) the first regiment of the royal household infantry. **2** a common bottom-dwelling fish with a large head, a long tapering tail, and typically a luminous gland on the belly. [Family Macrouridae: numerous species.] **3** a reddish-brown African waxbill with a red bill and a bright blue rump. [Genus *Uraeginthus*: two species.]

**grenadilla** /ˌgrɛnəˈdɪlə/ • n. variant spelling of **GRANADILLA**.

**grenadine**[1] /ˈgrɛnədiːn/ • n. a sweet cordial made in France from pomegranates.
– ORIGIN Fr., from *grenade* (see **GRENADE**).

**grenadine**[2] /ˈgrɛnədiːn/ • n. dress fabric of loosely woven silk or silk and wool.
– ORIGIN C19: from Fr. (earlier *grenade*), 'grained silk'.

**Gresham's law** • n. Economics the tendency for money of lower intrinsic value to circulate more freely than money of higher intrinsic and equal nominal value (often expressed as 'Bad money drives out good').
– ORIGIN from the name of the C16 Engl. financier Sir Thomas *Gresham*.

**grew** past of **GROW**.

**grey** (US **gray**) • adj. **1** of a colour intermediate between black and white, as of ashes or lead. **2** (of hair) turning grey or white with age. ➤ informal, chiefly N. Amer. relating to old people as a group: *grey power.* **3** (of the weather) cloudy and dull; without sun. **4** dull and nondescript: *grey, faceless men.* **5** (of financial or trading activity) not accounted for in official statistics: *the grey economy.* • n. grey colour or pigment. • v. (especially of hair) become grey with age.
– DERIVATIVES **greyish** adj. **greyly** adv. **greyness** n.
– ORIGIN OE *grǣg*, of Gmc origin.

**grey area** • n. an ill-defined area of activity not readily conforming to an existing category or set of rules.

**greybeard** (US **graybeard**) • n. **1** humorous or derogatory an old man. **2** archaic a large stoneware jug for spirits.

**grey eminence** • n. another term for **ÉMINENCE GRISE**.

**Grey Friar** • n. a friar of the Franciscan order (who wear grey habits).

**greyhen** • n. the female of the black grouse.

**greyhound** • n. a dog of a swift, slender, keen-sighted breed, used in racing and coursing.
– ORIGIN OE *grīghund*; the first element, rel. to ON *grey* 'bitch', is of unknown origin.

**greylag** • n. a large goose with mainly grey plumage, the ancestor of the domestic goose. [*Anser anser*.]
– ORIGIN C18: prob. from **GREY** + dial. *lag* 'goose', of unknown origin.

**grey matter** • n. **1** the darker tissue of the brain and spinal cord, consisting mainly of nerve cell bodies and branching dendrites. **2** informal intelligence.

**grey mullet** • n. a thick-bodied, blunt-headed food fish of inshore or estuarine waters. [Family Mugilidae: several species.]

**greyscale** (US **grayscale**) ● **n.** Computing a range of grey shades from white to black, as used in a monochrome display or printout.

**grey seal** ● **n.** a large North Atlantic seal with a spotted greyish coat. [*Halichoerus grypus.*]

**grey squirrel** ● **n.** a tree squirrel with mainly grey fur, native to eastern North America and introduced to Britain and elsewhere. [*Sciurus carolinensis.*]

**greywacke** /ˈgreɪwakə/ (US **graywacke**) ● **n.** Geology a dark coarse-grained sandstone containing more than 15 per cent clay.
– ORIGIN C18 (as *grauwacke*): from Ger. *Grauwacke*, from *grau* 'grey' + **WACKE**.

**grey water** ● **n.** technical the relatively clean waste water from baths, sinks, and washing machines. Compare with **BLACK WATER**.

**gribble** ● **n.** a small marine isopod crustacean that bores into submerged wooden structures. [*Limnoria lignorum.*]
– ORIGIN C18: perh. rel. to **GRUB**.

**gricer** /ˈgrʌɪsə/ ● **n.** Brit. informal a trainspotter.
– DERIVATIVES **gricing** n.
– ORIGIN 1960s: origin uncertain; perh. a humorous representation of an upper-class pronunc. of *grouser* 'grouse-shooter'.

**grid** ● **n. 1** a framework of spaced bars that are parallel to or cross each other. **2** a network of lines that cross each other to form a series of squares or rectangles. ➤a numbered grid on a map that enables a place to be precisely located. **3** a network of cables or pipes for distributing power, especially high-voltage electricity. **4** a pattern of lines marking the starting places on a motor-racing track. **5** Electronics an electrode placed between the cathode and anode of a thermionic valve or cathode ray tube, serving to control or modulate the flow of electrons. ● **v.** [usu. as adj. **gridded**] put into or set out as a grid.
– ORIGIN C19: back-form. from **GRIDIRON**.

**grid bias** ● **n.** Electronics a fixed voltage applied between the cathode and the control grid of a thermionic valve which determines its operating conditions.

**gridder** ● **n.** US an American football player.

**griddle** ● **n. 1** a circular iron plate that is heated and used for cooking food. **2** historical a miner's wire-bottomed sieve. ● **v. 1** cook on a griddle. **2** historical screen (ore) with a griddle.
– ORIGIN ME (denoting a gridiron): from OFr. *gredil*, from L. *craticula*, dimin. of *cratis* 'hurdle'; rel. to **CRATE**, **GRATE**[2], and **GRILL**[1].

**gridiron** /ˈgrɪdʌɪən/ ● **n. 1** a frame of parallel metal bars used for grilling meat or fish over an open fire. **2** a frame of parallel beams for supporting a ship in dock. **3** a field for American football, marked with regularly spaced parallel lines. ➤N. Amer. the game of American football. **4** a grid pattern, especially of streets.
– ORIGIN ME *gredire*, alt. of *gredile* 'griddle' by assoc. with **IRON**.

**gridlock** ● **n.** a traffic jam affecting a whole network of intersecting streets.
– DERIVATIVES **gridlocked** adj.

**grief** ● **n. 1** intense sorrow, especially caused by someone's death. **2** informal trouble or annoyance.
– PHRASES **come to grief** have an accident; meet with disaster. **good grief!** an exclamation of surprise or alarm.
– ORIGIN ME: from OFr. *grief*, from *grever* (see **GRIEVE**[1]).

**grievance** ● **n.** a real or imagined cause for complaint.
– ORIGIN ME: from OFr. *grevance*, from *grever* (see **GRIEVE**[1]).

**grieve**[1] ● **v. 1** suffer grief. **2** cause great distress to.
– DERIVATIVES **griever** n.
– ORIGIN ME: from OFr. *grever* 'burden, encumber', based on L. *gravare*, from *gravis* (see **GRAVE**[2]).

**grieve**[2] ● **n.** Scottish an overseer, manager, or bailiff on a farm.
– ORIGIN C15: rel. to **REEVE**[1].

**grievous** ● **adj.** formal (of something bad) very severe or serious.
– DERIVATIVES **grievously** adv. **grievousness** n.
– ORIGIN ME: from OFr. *greveus*, from *grever* (see **GRIEVE**[1]).

**grievous bodily harm** ● **n.** Law serious physical injury inflicted on a person by the deliberate action of another, considered more serious than actual bodily harm.

**griffin** (also **gryphon** or **griffon**) ● **n.** a mythical creature with the head and wings of an eagle and the body of a lion.
– ORIGIN ME: from OFr. *grifoun*, based on late L. *gryphus*, via L. from Gk *grups*, *grup-*.

**griffon** /ˈgrɪf(ə)n/ ● **n. 1** a dog of a small terrier-like breed. **2** (also **griffon vulture**) a large Old World vulture with predominantly pale brown plumage. [*Gyps fulvus* and related species.] **3** variant spelling of **GRIFFIN**.
– ORIGIN ME: var. of **GRIFFIN**.

**grift** N. Amer. informal ● **v.** engage in petty swindling. ● **n.** a petty swindle.
– DERIVATIVES **grifter** n.
– ORIGIN C20: alt. of **GRAFT**[2].

**grig** ● **n.** dialect **1** a small eel. **2** a grasshopper or cricket.
– PHRASES **(as) merry** (or **lively**) **as a grig** full of fun; extravagantly lively.
– ORIGIN ME (in the sense 'dwarf'): of unknown origin.

**gri-gri** ● **n.** variant spelling of **GRIS-GRIS**.

**grike** /grʌɪk/ (also **gryke**) ● **n.** a fissure separating blocks or clints in a limestone pavement.
– ORIGIN C18 (orig. north. Engl. dial.): of unknown origin.

**grill**[1] ● **n.** Brit. **1** a device on a cooker that radiates heat downwards for cooking food. **2** a gridiron used for cooking food on an open fire. **3** a dish of food, especially meat, cooked using a grill. **4** a restaurant serving grilled food. ● **v. 1** cook with a grill. **2** informal subject to intense questioning or interrogation.
– DERIVATIVES **griller** n.
– ORIGIN C17: from Fr. *gril* (n.), *griller* (v.), from OFr. *graille* 'grille'.

**grill**[2] ● **n.** variant spelling of **GRILLE**.

**grillade** /grɪˈleɪd, -ˈjɑːd, ˈgriːɑːd/ ● **n.** a kind of French or Cajun meat stew.
– ORIGIN from Fr.

**grillage** /ˈgrɪlɪdʒ/ ● **n.** a heavy framework of cross-timbering or metal beams forming a foundation for building on difficult ground.

**grille** (also **grill**) ● **n.** a grating or screen of metal bars or wires.
– ORIGIN C17: from Fr., from med. L., *craticula*, dimin. of *cratis* 'hurdle'; rel. to **CRATE**, **GRATE**[2], and **GRIDDLE**.

**grilse** /grɪls/ ● **n.** a salmon that has returned to fresh water after a single winter at sea.
– ORIGIN ME: of unknown origin.

**grim** ● **adj.** (**grimmer**, **grimmest**) **1** very serious or gloomy; forbidding. ➤(of humour) black or ironic. **2** unappealing, unattractive, or depressing.
– PHRASES **like** (or **for**) **grim death** with great determination.
– DERIVATIVES **grimly** adv. **grimness** n.
– ORIGIN OE, of Gmc origin.

**grimace** /grɪˈmeɪs, ˈgrɪməs/ ● **n.** an ugly, twisted expression on a person's face, typically expressing disgust, pain, or wry amusement. ● **v.** make a grimace.
– DERIVATIVES **grimacer** n.
– ORIGIN C17: from Fr., from Sp. *grimazo* 'caricature', from *grima* 'fright'.

**grimalkin** /grɪˈmalkɪn, -ˈmɔːl-/ ● **n.** archaic **1** a cat. **2** a spiteful old woman.
– ORIGIN C16: from **GREY** + *Malkin* (familiar form of the given name *Matilda*).

**grime** ● **n.** dirt ingrained on a surface. ● **v.** blacken or make dirty with grime.
– DERIVATIVES **grimily** adv. **griminess** n. **grimy** adj. (**-ier**, **-iest**).
– ORIGIN ME: from Mid. Low Ger. and MDu.

**Grimm's law** ● **n.** Linguistics the observation that certain consonants undergo regular changes in the Germanic languages which are not seen in others such as Greek or Latin.
– ORIGIN from the name of the Ger. philologist and folklorist Jacob *Grimm*.

**grimoire** /grɪm'wɑː/ ● n. a book of magic spells and invocations.
– ORIGIN C19: Fr., alt. of *grammaire* 'grammar'.

**grin** ● v. (**grinned**, **grinning**) **1** smile broadly. **2** grimace grotesquely in a way that reveals the teeth. ● n. a smile or grimace produced by grinning.
– PHRASES **grin and bear it** suffer pain or misfortune in a stoical manner.
– DERIVATIVES **grinner** n. **grinning** adj. **grinningly** adv.
– ORIGIN OE *grennian* 'bare the teeth in pain or anger', of Gmc origin; prob. rel. to **GROAN**.

**grind** ● v. (past and past part. **ground**) **1** reduce to small particles or powder by crushing. **2** sharpen, smooth, or produce by crushing or friction. ➤operate (a mill or machine) by turning the handle. **3** (**grind someone down**) wear someone down with harsh treatment. ➤(**grind something out**) produce something slowly and laboriously. ➤[as adj. **grinding**] oppressive and seemingly endless: *grinding poverty*. **4** rub together gratingly. ➤move noisily and laboriously. **5** (often **grind away**) work or study hard. **6** informal (of a dancer) rotate the hips. ➤Brit. vulgar slang, dated have sexual intercourse. ● n. **1** an act or process of grinding. **2** hard dull work: *the daily grind*.
– PHRASES **grind to a halt** (or **come to a grinding halt**) stop laboriously and noisily.
– DERIVATIVES **grinder** n. **grindingly** adv.
– ORIGIN OE *grindan*, prob. of Gmc origin.

**grindstone** ● n. **1** a thick revolving disc of abrasive material used for sharpening or polishing metal objects. **2** a millstone.
– PHRASES **keep one's nose to the grindstone** work hard and continuously.

**gringo** /'grɪŋgəʊ/ ● n. (pl. **-os**) informal (in Latin America) a white English-speaking person.
– ORIGIN Sp., lit. 'foreign, foreigner, or gibberish'.

**griot** /'griːəʊ/ ● n. a West African travelling poet, musician, and storyteller.
– ORIGIN Fr., earlier *guiriot*, perh. from Port. *criado*.

**grip** ● v. (**gripped**, **gripping**) **1** take and keep a firm hold of; grasp tightly. **2** deeply affect or afflict. ➤[often as adj. **gripping**] compel the attention or interest of. ● n. **1** a firm hold; a tight grasp or clasp. ➤effective control. ➤intellectual understanding. **2** a part or attachment by which something is held in the hand. ➤a hairgrip. **3** a travelling bag. **4** a stage hand in a theatre. ➤a member of a camera crew responsible for moving and setting up equipment.
– PHRASES **come** (or **get**) **to grips with 1** engage in combat with. **2** begin to deal with or understand. **get** (or **take**) **a grip on** take control of. **lose one's grip** become unable to understand or control one's situation.
– DERIVATIVES **gripper** n. **grippingly** adv. **grippy** adj.
– ORIGIN OE *grippa* (v.), *gripe* 'grasp, clutch' (n.), *gripa* 'handful, sheath'; rel. to **GRIPE**.

**gripe** ● v. **1** informal express a trivial complaint; grumble. **2** affect with gastric or intestinal pain. **3** archaic grasp tightly; clutch. **4** Nautical secure with gripes. **5** Sailing (of a ship) turn to face the wind in spite of the helm. ● n. **1** informal a trivial complaint. **2** gastric or intestinal pain; colic. **3** archaic an act of grasping tightly. **4** (**gripes**) Nautical lashings securing a boat in its place on deck or in davits.
– DERIVATIVES **griper** n.
– ORIGIN OE *grīpan* 'grasp, clutch', of Gmc origin; rel. to **GRIP** and **GROPE**.

**gripe water** ● n. Brit. trademark a solution given to babies for the relief of colic, wind, and indigestion.

**grippe** /grɪp/ ● n. dated influenza.
– ORIGIN C18: Fr., from *gripper* 'seize'.

**Griqua** /'griːkwə/ ● n. (pl. same or **Griquas**) a member of a South African people of mixed European and Khoikhoi origin.
– ORIGIN the name in Nama.

**grisaille** /grɪ'zeɪl, -li/ ● n. a method of painting in grey monochrome, typically to imitate sculpture.
– ORIGIN C19: Fr., from *gris* 'grey'.

**griseofulvin** /ˌgrɪzɪə(ʊ)'fʊlvɪn/ ● n. Medicine an antibiotic used against fungal infections of the hair and skin.
– ORIGIN 1930s: from mod. L. (*Penicillium*) *griseofulvum* (the source bacterium), from med. L. *griseus* 'greyish' + L. *fulvus* 'reddish yellow'.

**grisette** /grɪ'zɛt/ ● n. **1** an edible woodland mushroom with a brown or grey cap. [*Amanita vaginata* and *A. fulva*.] **2** dated a young working-class Frenchwoman.
– ORIGIN Fr., from *gris* 'grey' + the dimin. suffix *-ette* (in sense 2 with ref. to a characteristic grey dress material).

**gris-gris** /'griːgriː/ (also **gri-gri**, **greegree**) ● n. (pl. same) **1** an African or Caribbean charm or amulet. **2** the use of such charms, especially in voodoo.
– ORIGIN C17: from Fr. *grisgris*, of W. Afr. origin.

**griskin** /'grɪskɪn/ ● n. Brit. the lean part of a loin of pork.
– ORIGIN C17: perh. from archaic *grice* 'pig' + **-KIN**.

**grisly** /'grɪzli/ ● adj. (**-ier**, **-iest**) causing horror or revulsion.
– DERIVATIVES **grisliness** n.
– ORIGIN OE *grislic* 'terrifying', of Gmc origin.

**grison** /'grɪz(ə)n, 'grʌɪs(ə)n/ ● n. a weasel-like mammal with dark fur and a white stripe across the forehead, found in Central and South America. [Genus *Galictis*: two species.]
– ORIGIN C18: from Fr., from *gris* 'grey'.

**grissini** /grɪ'siːni/ ● pl. n. thin, crisp Italian breadsticks.
– ORIGIN from Ital.

**grist** ● n. **1** corn that is ground to make flour. **2** malt crushed to make mash for brewing.
– PHRASES **grist to the mill** useful experience or knowledge.
– ORIGIN OE 'grinding', of Gmc origin; rel. to **GRIND**.

**gristle** /'grɪs(ə)l/ ● n. cartilage, especially when found as tough inedible tissue in meat.
– DERIVATIVES **gristly** adj.
– ORIGIN OE, of unknown origin.

**grit** ● n. **1** small loose particles of stone or sand. **2** (also **gritstone**) a coarse sandstone. **3** courage and resolve. ● v. (**gritted**, **gritting**) **1** clench (the teeth), especially in order to keep one's resolve. **2** spread grit on (an icy road). **3** move with or make a grating sound.
– DERIVATIVES **gritter** n.
– ORIGIN OE *grēot*, of Gmc origin; rel. to **GROATS**.

**grits** ● pl. n. US coarsely ground maize kernels, served boiled with water or milk.
– ORIGIN OE *grytt*, *grytte* 'bran, mill dust', of Gmc origin: rel. to **GROATS**.

**gritty** ● adj. (**-ier**, **-iest**) **1** containing or covered with grit. **2** showing courage and resolve. ➤tough and uncompromising: *a gritty look at urban life*.
– DERIVATIVES **grittily** adv. **grittiness** n.

**grivet monkey** /'grɪvɪt/ ● n. another term for **VERVET MONKEY**.
– ORIGIN C19: from Fr., of unknown origin.

**grizzle**[1] ● v. informal, chiefly Brit. (of a child) cry or whimper fretfully.
– DERIVATIVES **grizzler** n.
– ORIGIN C18 (in the sense 'show the teeth, grin'): of unknown origin.

**grizzle**[2] ● n. a mixture of dark and white hairs.
– ORIGIN ME: from OFr. *grisel*, from *gris* 'grey'.

**grizzled** ● adj. having grey or grey-streaked hair.

**grizzly bear** ● n. a brown bear of a large race often with white-tipped fur, native to western North America.
– ORIGIN C19: *grizzly* from **GRIZZLE**[2].

**groan** ● v. **1** make a deep inarticulate sound in response to pain or despair. **2** make a low creaking sound when pressure or weight is applied. **3** (**groan beneath/under**) be oppressed by. ● n. a groaning sound.
– DERIVATIVES **groaner** n. **groaning** adj. **groaningly** adv.
– ORIGIN OE *grānian*, of Gmc origin; prob. rel. to **GRIN**.

**groat** ● n. historical an English silver coin worth four old pence.
– ORIGIN from MDu. *groot* or Mid. Low Ger. *grōte* 'great, thick', hence 'thick penny'; cf. **GROSCHEN**.

**groats** ● pl. n. hulled or crushed grain, especially oats.
– ORIGIN OE *grotan* (pl.): rel. to **GRIT** and **GRITS**.

**Gro-bag** • n. trademark for **GROWBAG**.

**grocer** • n. a person who sells food and small household goods.
– ORIGIN ME (orig. 'a person who sold things by the gross'): from OFr. *grossier*, from med. L. *grossarius*, from late L. *grossus* 'gross'.

**grocery** • n. (pl. **-ies**) **1** a grocer's shop or business. **2** (**groceries**) items of food sold in a grocer's shop or supermarket.

**grockle** • n. Brit. informal, derogatory a holidaymaker, especially one in the West Country.
– ORIGIN an invented word, orig. a fantastic creature in a children's comic, popularized by the film *The System* (1962).

**grog** • n. spirits (originally rum) mixed with water. ➤ informal alcoholic drink.
– ORIGIN C18: said to be from *Old Grog*, the reputed nickname (because of his grogram cloak) of Admiral Vernon, who ordered diluted (instead of neat) rum to be served out to sailors.

**groggy** • adj. (**-ier**, **-iest**) dazed and unsteady after intoxication, sleep, etc.
– DERIVATIVES **groggily** adv. **grogginess** n.

**grogram** /ˈgrɒgrəm/ • n. a coarse fabric made of silk, often combined with mohair or wool and stiffened with gum.
– ORIGIN C16: from Fr. *gros grain* 'coarse grain' (see also **GROSGRAIN**).

**groin**[1] • n. **1** the area between the abdomen and the thigh on either side of the body. ➤ informal the region of the genitals. **2** Architecture a curved edge formed by two intersecting vaults.
– DERIVATIVES **groined** adj. (Architecture).
– ORIGIN ME *grynde*, perh. from OE *grynde* 'depression, abyss'.

**groin**[2] • n. US spelling of **GROYNE**.

**grok** • v. (**grokked**, **grokking**) US informal understand intuitively.
– ORIGIN C20: invented word.

**grommet** /ˈgrɒmɪt/ • n. **1** a protective eyelet in a hole that a rope or cable passes through. **2** Medicine a tube surgically implanted in the eardrum to drain fluid from the middle ear.
– ORIGIN C17 (in sense 'a circle of rope used as a fastening'): from obs. Fr. *grommette*, from *gourmer* 'to curb', of unknown ultimate origin.

**gromwell** • n. a plant of the borage family with white or blue flowers. [*Lithospermum officinale* and other species.]
– ORIGIN ME: from OFr. *gromil*, prob. from a med. L. phr. meaning 'crane's millet'.

**groom** • v. **1** brush and clean the coat of (a horse or dog). ➤ give a neat and tidy appearance to. **2** prepare or train for a particular purpose or activity. • n. **1** a person employed to take care of horses. **2** a bridegroom. **3** Brit. any of various officials of the royal household.
– ORIGIN ME (in the sense 'boy', later 'man, male servant'): of unknown origin.

**groomsman** • n. (pl. **-men**) a male friend officially attending the bridegroom at a wedding.

**groove** • n. **1** a long, narrow cut or depression in a hard material. ➤ a spiral track cut in a gramophone record, into which the stylus fits. **2** an established routine or habit. **3** informal a rhythmic pattern in popular or jazz music. • v. **1** make a groove or grooves in. **2** informal dance to or play popular or jazz music. ➤ enjoy oneself.
– PHRASES **in** (or **into**) **the groove** informal **1** performing confidently. **2** enjoying oneself, especially by dancing.
– DERIVATIVES **grooved** adj.
– ORIGIN ME (denoting a mine or shaft): from Du. *groeve* 'furrow, pit'; rel. to **GRAVE**[1].

**groovy** • adj. (**-ier**, **-iest**) informal, dated or humorous fashionable and exciting.
– DERIVATIVES **groovily** adv. **grooviness** n.

**grope** • v. **1** feel about or search blindly or uncertainly with the hands. **2** informal feel or fondle (someone) for sexual pleasure, especially against their will. • n. informal an act of groping someone.
– DERIVATIVES **groping** adj. **gropingly** adv.
– ORIGIN OE *grāpian*, of W. Gmc origin; rel. to **GRIPE**.

**groper**[1] • n. a person who gropes.

**groper**[2] • n. **1** chiefly Austral./NZ variant spelling of **GROUPER**. **2** (also **blue groper**) a large Australian wrasse which is a popular sporting fish. [*Achoerodus gouldii*.]

**grosbeak** /ˈgrəʊsbiːk/ • n. a finch or related songbird with a stout conical bill and brightly coloured plumage. [Several species in the families Fringillidae and Emberizidae.]
– ORIGIN C17 (denoting the hawfinch): from Fr. *grosbec*, from *gros* 'big, fat' + *bec* 'beak'.

**groschen** /ˈgrəʊʃ(ə)n, ˈgrɒʃ(ə)n/ • n. (pl. same) **1** a monetary unit of Austria, equal to one hundredth of a schilling. **2** historical a small German silver coin.
– ORIGIN Ger., from Mid. High Ger. *grosse*, from med. L. (*denarius*) *grossus* 'thick (penny)'; cf. **GROAT**.

**grosgrain** /ˈgrəʊgreɪn/ • n. a heavy ribbed fabric, typically of silk or rayon.
– ORIGIN C19: Fr., 'coarse grain' (see also **GROGRAM**).

**gros point** /grəʊ ˈpwã/ • n. a type of needlepoint embroidery consisting of stitches crossing two or more threads of the canvas in each direction.
– ORIGIN C19: Fr., lit. 'large stitch', from *gros point de Venise*, a type of lace orig. from Venice.

**gross** • adj. **1** unattractively large or bloated. **2** vulgar; unrefined. ➤ informal very unpleasant; repulsive. **3** complete; blatant: *a gross exaggeration.* **4** (of income, profit, or interest) without deduction of tax or other contributions; total. Often contrasted with **NET**[2]. ➤ (of weight) including contents or other variable items; overall. • adv. without tax or other contributions having been deducted. • v. **1** produce or earn (an amount of money) as gross profit or income. ➤ (**gross something up**) add deductions such as tax to a net amount. **2** (**gross someone out**) informal, chiefly N. Amer. disgust someone with repulsive behaviour or appearance. • n. **1** (pl. same) an amount equal to twelve dozen; 144. **2** (pl. **grosses**) a gross profit or income.
– DERIVATIVES **grossly** adv. **grossness** n.
– ORIGIN ME (in the sense 'thick, massive, bulky'): from OFr. *gros*, *grosse* 'large', from late L. *grossus*; sense 1 of the noun is from Fr. *grosse douzaine*, lit. 'large dozen'.

**gross domestic product** • n. the total value of goods produced and services provided within a country during one year.

**gross national product** • n. the total value of goods produced and services provided by a country during one year, equal to the gross domestic product plus the net income from foreign investments.

**grossular** /ˈgrɒsjʊlə/ • n. a mineral of the garnet group.
– ORIGIN C19: from mod. L. *grossularia* 'gooseberry' (from the yellow-green colour of one variety).

**grosz** /grɔːʃ/ • n. (pl. **groszy** or **grosze**) a monetary unit of Poland, equal to one hundredth of a zloty.
– ORIGIN Polish; cf. **GROSCHEN**.

**grot**[1] • n. Brit. informal something unpleasant, dirty, or of poor quality; rubbish.
– ORIGIN 1960s: back-form. from **GROTTY**.

**grot**[2] • n. poetic/literary a grotto.
– ORIGIN C16: from Fr. *grotte*, from Ital. *grotta*, via L. from Gk *kruptē* 'vault, crypt'.

**grotesque** /grə(ʊ)ˈtɛsk/ • adj. **1** comically or repulsively ugly or distorted. **2** shockingly incongruous or inappropriate. • n. **1** a grotesque figure or image. **2** a style of decorative painting or sculpture consisting of the interweaving of human and animal forms with flowers and foliage. **3** Printing a family of 19th-century sans serif typefaces.
– DERIVATIVES **grotesquely** adv. **grotesqueness** n.
– ORIGIN C16 (as n.): from Fr. *crotesque*, from Ital. *grottesca*, from *opera* or *pittura grottesca* 'work or painting resembling that found in a grotto'.

**grotesquerie** /grəʊˈtɛskəri/ • n. (pl. **-ies**) grotesque quality or things.

**grotto** • n. (pl. **-oes** or **-os**) a small picturesque cave, especially an artificial one in a park or garden.

– DERIVATIVES **grottoed** adj.
– ORIGIN C17: from Ital. *grotta*, via L. from Gk *kruptē* (see **CRYPT**).

**grotty** • adj. (-ier, -iest) Brit. informal **1** unpleasant and of poor quality. **2** unwell.
– DERIVATIVES **grottiness** n.
– ORIGIN 1960s: from **GROTESQUE** + **-Y**[1].

**grouch** /graʊtʃ/ informal • n. **1** a habitually grumpy person. **2** a complaint or grumble. • v. complain ill-temperedly; grumble.
– ORIGIN C19: var. of obs. *grutch*, from OFr. *grouchier* 'to grumble, murmur', of unknown origin; cf. **GRUDGE**.

**grouchy** • adj. (-ier, -iest) irritable and bad-tempered; grumpy.
– DERIVATIVES **grouchily** adv. **grouchiness** n.

**ground**[1] • n. **1** the solid surface of the earth. ➤ land of a specified kind: *marshy ground*. ➤ an area of land or sea with a specified use: *fishing grounds*. ➤ (**grounds**) an area of enclosed land surrounding a large house. ➤ Brit. the floor of a room. **2** (**grounds**) factors forming a basis for action or the justification for a belief. **3** a prepared surface to which paint or other decoration is applied. ➤ a substance used to prepare a surface for painting. ➤ a piece of wood fixed to a wall as a base for boards, plaster, or joinery. **4** (**grounds**) solid particles, especially of coffee, which form a residue. **5** N. Amer. electrical connection to the earth. • v. **1** prohibit or prevent (a pilot or aircraft) from flying. ➤ informal, chiefly N. Amer. (of a parent) refuse to allow (a child) to go out socially, as a punishment. **2** run (a ship) aground. **3** (usu. **be grounded in**) give a firm theoretical or practical basis to. ➤ [as adj. **grounded**] well balanced and sensible. **4** place on the ground or touch the ground with. **5** N. Amer. connect (an electrical device) with the ground.
– PHRASES **be thick** (or **thin**) **on the ground** exist in large (or small) numbers or amounts. **break new ground** be innovative. **gain ground 1** become more popular or accepted. **2** (usu. **gain ground on**) get closer to someone being pursued. **get off the ground** start happening or functioning successfully. **give** (or **lose**) **ground** retreat or lose one's advantage. **go to ground** (of a fox or other animal) enter its earth or burrow. **hold** (or **stand**) **one's ground** not retreat or lose one's advantage. **on the ground** in a place where real, practical work is done. **on one's own ground** in one's own territory or area of knowledge. **work** (or **run**) **oneself into the ground** exhaust oneself by working or running very hard.
– ORIGIN OE *grund*, of Gmc origin.

**ground**[2] past and past participle of **GRIND**.

**groundbait** • n. Brit. bait thrown into the water while fishing.
– DERIVATIVES **groundbaiting** n.

**ground ball** • n. Baseball a ball hit along the ground.

**ground bass** • n. Music a short bass theme which is constantly repeated as the other parts of the music vary.

**ground-breaking** • adj. innovative; pioneering.
– DERIVATIVES **ground-breaker** n.

**ground control** • n. [treated as sing. or pl.] the personnel and equipment that monitor and direct the flight and landing of aircraft or spacecraft.
– DERIVATIVES **ground controller** n.

**ground cover** • n. low-growing, spreading plants that help to stop weeds growing.

**ground effect** • n. the aerodynamic buoyancy produced by a cushion of air below a vehicle moving close to the ground.

**ground elder** • n. a common weed of the parsley family, with leaves that resemble those of the elder and spreading underground stems. [*Aegopodium podagraria*.]

**grounder** • n. Baseball a ground ball.

**ground floor** • n. Brit. the floor of a building at ground level.

**ground frost** • n. Brit. frost formed on the surface of the ground or in the top layer of soil.

**ground glass** • n. **1** glass with a smooth ground surface that renders it non-transparent. **2** glass ground into an abrasive powder.

**groundhog** • n. North American term for **WOODCHUCK**.

**groundhopper** • n. a small predominantly brown insect that resembles a grasshopper and has well-developed wings. [*Tetrix undulata* and other species.]

**grounding** • n. basic training or instruction in a subject.

**ground ivy** • n. a creeping plant of the mint family, with bluish-purple flowers. [*Glechoma hederacea*.]

**groundless** • adj. not based on any good reason.
– DERIVATIVES **groundlessly** adv. **groundlessness** n.

**groundling** /ˈgraʊn(d)lɪŋ/ • n. **1** a spectator or reader of inferior taste. **2** a person on the ground as opposed to one in a spacecraft or aircraft. **3** a fish that lives at the bottom of lakes and streams, especially a gudgeon or loach. **4** a creeping or dwarf plant.

**groundmass** • n. Geology the compact, finer-grained material in which the crystals are embedded in a porphyritic rock.

**groundnut** • n. **1** another term for **PEANUT**. **2** a North American plant of the pea family with a sweet edible tuber. [*Apios tuberosa*.]

**ground pine** • n. **1** a small yellow-flowered plant of the mint family, resembling a pine seedling. [*Ajuga chamaepitys*.] **2** a North American clubmoss with small shiny leaves. [*Lycopodium obscurum* and related species.]

**ground rent** • n. Brit. rent paid under the terms of a lease by the owner of a building to the owner of the land on which it is built.

**ground rule** • n. a basic principle established to regulate action or facilitate cooperation.

**groundsel** /ˈgraʊn(d)s(ə)l/ • n. a plant of the daisy family with small yellow rayless flowers. [*Senecio vulgaris* (a common weed) and related species.]
– ORIGIN OE *gundæswelgiæ* (later *grundeswylige*), prob. from *gund* 'pus' + *swelgan* 'to swallow' (with ref. to its use in poultices).

**groundsheet** • n. a waterproof sheet spread on the ground inside a tent.

**groundskeeper** • n. North American term for **GROUNDSMAN**.

**ground sloth** • n. a very large extinct terrestrial edentate mammal of the Cenozoic era in America.

**groundsman** • n. (pl. **-men**) Brit. a person who maintains a sports ground or the grounds of a large building.

**ground speed** • n. an aircraft's speed relative to the ground.

**ground squirrel** • n. a burrowing northern squirrel of a large group including the sousliks and chipmunks. [*Spermophilus* and other genera.]

**ground state** • n. Physics the lowest energy state of an atom or other particle.

**groundstroke** • n. Tennis a stroke played after the ball has bounced, as opposed to a volley.

**groundswell** /ˈgraʊn(d),swɛl/ • n. **1** a build-up of opinion in a large section of the population. **2** a large or extensive swell in the sea.

**ground tackle** • n. the equipment used to anchor or moor a boat or ship.

**groundwater** • n. water held underground in the soil or in pores and crevices in rock.

**ground wave** • n. a radio wave which reaches a receiver from a transmitter directly, without reflection from the ionosphere.

**groundwork** • n. preliminary or basic work.

**ground zero** • n. the point on the earth's surface directly above or below an exploding nuclear bomb.

**group** • n. [treated as sing. or pl.] **1** a number of people or things located, gathered, or classed together. **2** a number of musicians who play popular music together. **3** Chemistry a set of elements occupying a column in the periodic table and having broadly similar properties. **4** Chemistry a combination of atoms having a recognizable identity in a number of compounds. **5** Mathematics a set of elements, together with an associative binary operation, which contains an inverse for each element and an identity element. **6** a division of an air force, usually consisting of two or more stations. • v. place in or form a group or

groups.
– DERIVATIVES **grouping** n.
– ORIGIN C17: from Fr. *groupe*, from Ital. *gruppo*, of Gmc origin; rel. to **CROP**.

**group captain** • n. a rank of officer in the RAF, above wing commander and below air commodore.

**group dynamics** • pl. n. Psychology the processes involved when people in a group interact with each other.

**grouper** (chiefly Austral./NZ also **groper**) • n. a large heavy-bodied fish of the sea bass family, found in warm seas. [*Epinephelus*, *Mycteroperca*, and other genera: many species.]
– ORIGIN C17: from Port. *garoupa*, prob. from a local term in South America.

**groupie** • n. informal a young woman who devotedly follows a pop group or celebrity, especially in the hope of a sexual relationship with them.

**groupset** • n. the brakes and gears for a bicycle.

**group therapy** • n. a form of psychiatric therapy in which patients meet to discuss their problems.

**groupthink** • n. chiefly N. Amer. unchallenged, poor-quality decision-making by a group.

**groupuscule** /ˈgruːpəˌskjuːl/ • n. a political or religious splinter group.
– ORIGIN C20: from Fr., dimin. of *groupe* 'group'.

**group velocity** • n. Physics the speed at which the energy of a wave travels.

**groupware** • n. Computing software designed to facilitate collective working by a number of different users.

**grouse**[1] • n. (pl. same) a medium-sized game bird with a plump body and feathered legs. [*Lagopus lagopus* (**red** or **willow grouse**) and other species.]
– ORIGIN C16: perh. rel. to med. L. *gruta* or to OFr. *grue* 'crane'.

**grouse**[2] • v. complain pettily; grumble. • n. a grumble or complaint.
– DERIVATIVES **grouser** n.
– ORIGIN C19: of unknown origin; cf. **GROUCH**.

**grout** /graʊt/ • n. a mortar or paste for filling crevices, especially the gaps between wall or floor tiles. • v. fill in with grout.
– DERIVATIVES **grouter** n. **grouting** n.
– ORIGIN C17: perh. from obs. *grout* (see **GROUTS**) or rel. to Fr. dial. *grouter* 'grout a wall'.

**grouts** /graʊt/ • pl. n. archaic sediment; dregs; grounds.
– ORIGIN OE *grūt*, of Gmc origin; rel. to **GRITS** and **GROATS**.

**grove** • n. a small wood, orchard, or group of trees.
– DERIVATIVES **grovy** adj.
– ORIGIN OE *grāf*, of Gmc origin.

**grovel** • v. (**grovelled**, **grovelling**; US **groveled**, **groveling**) **1** crouch or crawl abjectly on the ground. **2** act obsequiously to obtain forgiveness or favour.
– DERIVATIVES **groveller** n. **grovelling** adj. **grovellingly** adv.
– ORIGIN ME: back-form. from the obs. adv. *grovelling*, from obs. *groof*, *grufe* 'the face or front' (from ON *á grúfu* 'face downwards') + the suffix *-ling*.

**grow** /grəʊ/ • v. (past **grew** /gruː/; past part. **grown** /grəʊn/) **1** (of a living thing) undergo natural development by increasing in size and changing physically. ➤(**grow up**) advance to maturity; become an adult. ➤(**grow out of** or **into**) become too large (or large enough) to wear. **2** (of a plant) germinate and develop. ➤produce by cultivation. **3** become larger or greater over a period of time; increase. **4** become gradually or increasingly: *we grew braver.* **5** (**grow on**) become gradually more appealing to.
– DERIVATIVES **growable** adj. **grower** n.
– ORIGIN OE *grōwan*, of Gmc origin; rel. to **GRASS** and **GREEN**.

**growbag** (also trademark **Gro-bag**) • n. Brit. a bag containing potting compost, in which plants such as tomatoes can be grown.

**growing pains** • pl. n. **1** neuralgic pains occurring in the limbs of young children. **2** difficulties experienced in the early stages of an enterprise.

**growl** • v. **1** (especially of a dog) make a low guttural sound of hostility in the throat. **2** say something in a low grating voice. **3** make a low or harsh rumbling sound. • n. a growling sound.
– DERIVATIVES **growling** n. & adj. **growlingly** adv.
– ORIGIN C17: prob. imitative.

**growler** • n. **1** a person or thing that growls. **2** a small iceberg. **3** archaic a four-wheeled hansom cab.

**grown** past participle of **GROW**.

**grown-up** • adj. adult. • n. informal an adult.

**growth** • n. **1** the process of growing. **2** something that has grown or is growing. ➤Medicine & Biology a tumour or other abnormal formation. **3** a vineyard or crop of grapes of a specified classification of quality.

**growth factor** • n. Biology a substance, such as a vitamin or hormone, which is required for the stimulation of growth in living cells.

**growth hormone** • n. a hormone which stimulates growth in animal or plant cells.

**growth industry** • n. an industry that is developing particularly rapidly.

**growth ring** • n. a concentric layer of wood, shell, or bone developed during an annual or other regular period of growth.

**growth stock** • n. a company stock that tends to increase in capital value rather than yield high income.

**groyne** (US **groin**) • n. a low wall or barrier built out into the sea from a beach to check erosion and drifting.
– ORIGIN C16: from dial. *groin* 'snout', from OFr. *groign*, from late L. *grunium* 'pig's snout'.

**grozing iron** /ˈgrəʊzɪŋ/ • n. chiefly historical a pair of pliers for clipping the edges of pieces of glass.
– ORIGIN ME: *grozing* from MDu., from the stem of *gruizen* 'crush, trim glass', from *gruis* 'fragments'.

**GRP** • abbrev. glass-reinforced plastic.

**grt** • abbrev. gross registered tonnage.

**grub** • n. **1** the larva of an insect, especially a beetle. ➤a maggot or small caterpillar. **2** informal food. • v. (**grubbed**, **grubbing**) **1** dig shallowly in soil. ➤(**grub something up**) dig something up. **2** search clumsily and unmethodically; rummage. **3** do demeaning or humiliating work in order to achieve something.
– ORIGIN ME: perh. rel. to Du. *grobbelen*, also to **GRAVE**[1].

**grubber** • n. **1** a person who is determined to amass something, especially in an unscrupulous manner: *a money-grubber.* **2** an implement for digging up plants. **3** (in ball games) a ball that runs closely along the ground.

**grubby** • adj. (**-ier**, **-iest**) **1** dirty; grimy. **2** disreputable; sordid.
– DERIVATIVES **grubbily** adv. **grubbiness** n.

**grub screw** • n. Brit. a small headless screw, used typically to attach a handle to a spindle.

**grubstake** N. Amer. informal • n. an amount of material or money supplied to an enterprise in return for a share in the resulting profits. • v. provide with a grubstake.

**Grub Street** • n. the world or class of impoverished journalists and writers.
– ORIGIN the name of a street (later Milton Street) in London inhabited by such authors in the 17th cent.

**grudge** • n. a persistent feeling of ill will or resentment resulting from a past insult or injury. • v. **1** be resentfully unwilling to grant or allow (something). **2** feel resentful that (someone) has achieved (something).
– DERIVATIVES **grudger** n. **grudging** adj. **grudgingly** adv. **grudgingness** n.
– ORIGIN ME: var. of obs. *grutch* 'complain, murmur, grumble', from OFr. *grouchier*, of unknown origin; cf. **GROUCH**.

**gruel** • n. a thin liquid food of oatmeal or other meal boiled in milk or water.
– ORIGIN ME: from OFr., of Gmc origin.

**gruelling** (US **grueling**) • adj. extremely tiring and demanding.
– DERIVATIVES **gruellingly** adv.
– ORIGIN C19: from *gruel* 'exhaust, punish', from an old phr. *get one's gruel* 'receive one's punishment'.

**gruesome** ● **adj.** causing repulsion or horror; grisly. ➤ informal extremely unpleasant.
– DERIVATIVES **gruesomely** adv. **gruesomeness** n.
– ORIGIN C16: from Sc. *grue* 'to feel horror, shudder' (of Scand. origin) + **-SOME**[1].

**gruff** ● **adj.** **1** (of a voice) rough and low in pitch. **2** abrupt or taciturn in manner.
– DERIVATIVES **gruffly** adv. **gruffness** n.
– ORIGIN C15 (in the sense 'coarse-grained'): from Flemish and Du. *grof* 'coarse, rude', of W. Gmc origin.

**grumble** ● **v.** **1** complain or protest in a bad-tempered but muted way. **2** make a low rumbling sound. **3** [as adj. **grumbling**] (of an internal organ) giving intermittent discomfort. ● **n.** an instance of grumbling; a complaint.
– DERIVATIVES **grumbler** n. **grumblingly** adv. **grumbly** adj.
– ORIGIN C16: from obs. *grumme* (prob. of Gmc origin) + **-LE**[4].

**grump** informal ● **n.** **1** a grumpy person. **2** a fit of sulking. ● **v.** act in a sulky, grumbling manner.
– DERIVATIVES **grumpish** adj. **grumpishly** adv.
– ORIGIN C18: imitating sounds expressing displeasure.

**grumpy** ● **adj.** (**-ier**, **-iest**) bad-tempered and sulky.
– DERIVATIVES **grumpily** adv. **grumpiness** n.

**grunge** ● **n.** **1** chiefly N. Amer. grime; dirt. **2** a style of rock music characterized by a raucous guitar sound and lazy vocal delivery. **3** a casual style of fashion including loose, layered clothing and ripped jeans.
– DERIVATIVES **grunginess** n. **grungy** adj.
– ORIGIN 1970s: back-form. from *grungy*, perh. suggested by **GRUBBY** and **DINGY**.

**grunion** /ˈgrʌnjən/ ● **n.** a small, slender Californian fish that swarms on to beaches to spawn. [*Leuresthes tenuis*.]
– ORIGIN C20: prob. from Sp. *gruñón* 'grunter'.

**grunt** ● **v.** **1** (of an animal, especially a pig) make a low, short guttural sound. **2** make a low inarticulate sound to express effort or indicate assent. ● **n.** **1** a grunting sound. **2** informal, chiefly N. Amer. a low-ranking soldier or worker. **3** informal power, especially in a motor vehicle. **4** an edible fish of tropical coasts and reefs, able to make a loud noise. [Family Pomadasyidae: many species.]
– DERIVATIVES **grunter** n.
– ORIGIN OE *grunnettan*, of Gmc origin; prob. orig. imitative.

**gruntled** ● **adj.** humorous pleased; satisfied.
– ORIGIN 1930s: back-form. from **DISGRUNTLED**.

**Gruyère** /ˈgruːjɛː/ ● **n.** a firm, tangy Swiss cheese.
– ORIGIN named after *Gruyère*, a district in Switzerland.

**gryke** ● **n.** variant spelling of **GRIKE**.

**gryphon** ● **n.** variant spelling of **GRIFFIN**.

**grysbok** /ˈgrʌɪsbɒk, ˈxreɪs-/ ● **n.** a small mainly nocturnal antelope with small vertical horns, found in SW Africa. [Genus *Raphicerus*: two species.]
– ORIGIN C18: from Afrik., from Du. *grijs* 'grey' + *bok* 'buck'.

**gs** ● **abbrev.** historical guineas.

**GSM** ● **abbrev.** Global System (or Standard) for Mobile.

**gsm** ● **abbrev.** grams per square metre.

**GSOH** ● **abbrev.** good sense of humour.

**G-spot** ● **n.** a sensitive area of the anterior wall of the vagina believed by some to be highly erogenous.
– ORIGIN 1944 (as *Gräfenberg spot*): *G* from *Gräfenberg* and Dickinson, who first described it.

**GSR** ● **abbrev.** galvanic skin response.

**G-string** (also **gee-string**) ● **n.** a skimpy undergarment covering the genitals, consisting of a narrow strip of cloth attached to a waistband.

**G-suit** ● **n.** a garment with inflatable pressurized pouches, worn by fighter pilots and astronauts to enable them to withstand high gravitational forces.
– ORIGIN 1940s: from *g* (symbol of *gravity*) + **SUIT**.

**GT** ● **n.** a high-performance car.
– ORIGIN 1960s: abbrev. of Ital. **GRAN TURISMO**.

**Gt** ● **abbrev.** Great.

**GTi** ● **n.** a GT car with a fuel-injected engine.

**guacamole** /ˌgwɑːkəˈməʊleɪ, -li/ ● **n.** a dish of mashed avocado mixed with chilli peppers, tomatoes, etc.
– ORIGIN Latin Amer. Sp., from Nahuatl *ahuacamolli*, from *ahuacatl* 'avocado' + *molli* 'sauce'.

**guacharo** /ˈgwɑːtʃərəʊ/ ● **n.** (pl. **-os**) North American term for **OILBIRD**.
– ORIGIN C19: from Sp. *guácharo*, of South Amer. origin.

**Guadeloupian** /ˌgwɑːdəˈluːpɪən/ ● **n.** a native or inhabitant of Guadeloupe, a group of islands in the Lesser Antilles. ● **adj.** of or relating to Guadeloupe.

**guaiac** /ˈgwʌɪak/ ● **n.** brown resin obtained from guaiacum trees, used as a flavouring and in varnishes.

**guaiacol** /ˈgwʌɪəkɒl/ ● **n.** Chemistry an oily yellow liquid with a penetrating odour, obtained by distilling wood tar or guaiac, used as a flavouring and an expectorant.

**guaiacum** /ˈgwʌɪəkəm/ ● **n.** an evergreen tree of the Caribbean and tropical America, formerly important for its hard, heavy, oily wood. [*Guaiacum officinale* and *G. sanctum*.] ➤ another term for **GUAIAC**.
– ORIGIN C16: mod. L., via Sp. from Taino *guayacan*.

**Guamanian** /gwɑːˈmeɪnɪən/ ● **n.** a native or inhabitant of Guam, in the Mariana Islands. ● **adj.** of or relating to Guam.

**guan** /gwɑːn/ ● **n.** a large pheasant-like tree-dwelling bird of tropical American rainforests. [*Penelope* and other genera: several species.]
– ORIGIN C17: via Amer. Sp. from Miskito *kwamu*.

**guanaco** /gwəˈnɑːkəʊ/ ● **n.** (pl. **-os**) a wild Andean mammal similar to the domestic llama, with a valuable pale brown pelt. [*Lama guanicoe*.]
– ORIGIN C17: via Sp. from Quechua *huanacu*.

**guanidine** /ˈgwɑːnɪdiːn/ ● **n.** Chemistry a strongly basic crystalline compound derived from urea.
– ORIGIN C19: from **GUANO** + **-IDE** + **-INE**[4].

**guanine** /ˈgwɑːniːn/ ● **n.** Biochemistry a compound that occurs in guano and fish scales, and is one of the four constituent bases of nucleic acids.

**guano** /ˈgwɑːnəʊ/ ● **n.** (pl. **-os**) **1** the excrement of seabirds. **2** an artificial fertilizer resembling natural guano, especially one made from fish.
– ORIGIN C17: from Sp., or from Latin Amer. Sp. *huano*, from Quechua *huanu* 'dung'.

**guanosine** /ˈgwɑːnəsiːn/ ● **n.** Biochemistry a nucleoside consisting of guanine combined with ribose.

**guar** /gwɑː/ ● **n.** a drought-resistant African and Asian plant grown as a vegetable and for gum used in the food and paper industries. [*Cyamopsis tetragonoloba*.]
– ORIGIN C19: from Hindi *guār*.

**guarana** /gwəˈrɑːnə/ ● **n.** **1** a Brazilian shrub. [*Paullinia cupana*.] **2** a substance prepared from the seeds of this shrub, used as a tonic or stimulant.
– ORIGIN from Tupi.

**Guarani** /ˌgwɑːrəˈniː/ ● **n.** (pl. same) **1** a member of an American Indian people of Paraguay and adjacent regions. **2** the Tupi-Guarani language of this people. **3** (**guarani**) the basic monetary unit of Paraguay, equal to 100 centimos.
– ORIGIN from Sp.

**guarantee** ● **n.** **1** a formal assurance that certain conditions will be fulfilled, especially that restitution will be made if a product is not of a specified quality. **2** something that gives a certainty of outcome. **3** variant spelling of **GUARANTY**. **4** less common term for **GUARANTOR**. ● **v.** (**guarantees**, **guaranteed**, **guaranteeing**) **1** provide a guarantee: *the company guarantees to refund your money.* ➤ provide a guarantee for (a product). ➤ provide financial security for; underwrite. **2** promise with certainty.
– ORIGIN C17: perh. from Sp. *garante*, corresp. to Fr. *garant* (see **WARRANT**), influenced by Fr. *garantie* 'guaranty'.

**guarantee fund** ● **n.** a sum of money pledged as a contingent indemnity for loss.

**guarantor** /ˌgar(ə)nˈtɔː/ ● **n.** a person or organization that gives or acts as a guarantee.

**guaranty** /ˈgar(ə)nti/ (also **guarantee**) ● **n.** (pl. **-ies**) an undertaking to answer for the payment of a debt or for the performance of an obligation by another person liable in the first instance. ➤ a thing serving as security for such an undertaking.
– ORIGIN C16: from OFr. *garantie*, from *garantir*; rel. to **WARRANT**.

**guard** ● **v.** **1** watch over in order to keep safe; protect.

➤watch over in order to control or restrict. **2** (**guard against**) take precautions against. **3** Basketball stay close to (an opponent) to prevent them getting or passing the ball. ● **n. 1** a person, especially a soldier, who guards or keeps watch. ➤N. Amer. a prison warder. **2** [treated as sing. or pl.] a body of soldiers serving to protect a place or person. ➤(**Guards**) the household troops of the British army. **3** a device worn or fitted to prevent injury or damage. **4** (often in phr. **on** (or **off**) **guard**) a defensive posture adopted in a fight. ➤a state of vigilance against adverse circumstances: *he let his guard slip.* **5** Brit. an official who rides on and is in general charge of a train. **6** Basketball each of two players chiefly responsible for marking opposing players. **7** American Football each of two players either side of the centre.
– PHRASES **guard of honour** a group of soldiers ceremonially welcoming an important visitor. **take guard** Cricket (of a batsman) stand in position ready to receive the ball.
– ORIGIN ME (in the sense 'care, custody'): from OFr. *garde* (n.), *garder* (v.), of W. Gmc origin; cf. **WARD**.

**guardant** /ˈgɑːd(ə)nt/ ● **adj.** Heraldry (of an animal) depicted with the body sideways and the face towards the viewer.

**guard cell** ● **n.** Botany each of a pair of curved cells that surround a stoma.

**guarded** ● **adj.** cautious and having possible reservations: *he gave a guarded welcome to the idea.*
– DERIVATIVES **guardedly** adv. **guardedness** n.

**guardee** ● **n.** Brit. informal a guardsman.

**guard hair** ● **n.** long, coarse hair forming an animal's outer fur.

**guardhouse** ● **n.** a building used to accommodate a military guard or to detain military prisoners.

**guardian** ● **n. 1** a defender, protector, or keeper. **2** a person legally responsible for someone unable to manage their own affairs, especially a child whose parents have died. **3** the superior of a Franciscan convent.
– DERIVATIVES **guardianship** n.
– ORIGIN ME: from OFr. *garden*, of Gmc origin; cf. **WARD** and **WARDEN**.

**guardian angel** ● **n.** a spirit that is thought to watch over and protect a person or place.

**guard rail** ● **n.** a rail that prevents people from falling off or being hit by something.

**guard ring** ● **n.** a ring-shaped electrode used to limit the extent of an electric field, especially in a capacitor.

**guardroom** ● **n.** a room in a military base used to accommodate a guard or detain prisoners.

**guardsman** ● **n.** (pl. **-men**) **1** (in the UK) a soldier of a regiment of Guards. **2** (in the US) a member of the National Guard.

**guard's van** ● **n.** Brit. a carriage or wagon occupied by the guard on a train.

**Guatemalan** /ˌgwɑːtəˈmɑːlən/ ● **n.** a native or inhabitant of Guatemala in Central America. ● **adj.** of or relating to Guatemala.

**guava** /ˈgwɑːvə/ ● **n. 1** a tropical American fruit with pink juicy flesh and a strong, sweet aroma. **2** the small tree which bears this fruit. [*Psidium guajava* and related species.]
– ORIGIN C16: from Sp. *guayaba*, prob. from Taino.

**guayule** /gwʌɪˈuːli/ ● **n. 1** a silver-leaved Mexican shrub which yields large amounts of latex. [*Parthenium argentatum.*] **2** a rubber substitute made from this latex.
– ORIGIN C20: via Latin Amer. Sp. from Nahuatl *cuauhuli.*

**gubbins** ● **pl. n.** Brit. informal **1** [treated as sing. or pl.] miscellaneous items; paraphernalia; rubbish. **2** [treated as sing.] a gadget.
– ORIGIN C16 (in the sense 'fragments'): from obs. *gobbon* 'piece, slice, gob', from OFr.; prob. rel. to **GOBBET**.

**gubernatorial** /ˌg(j)uːbənəˈtɔːrɪəl/ ● **adj.** of or relating to a governor, particularly that of a state in the US.
– ORIGIN C18: from L. *gubernator* 'governor' + **-IAL**.

**guck** ● **n.** N. Amer. informal a slimy, dirty, or otherwise unpleasant substance.
– ORIGIN possibly a blend of **GOO** and **MUCK**.

**guddle** Scottish ● **v.** fish with the hands by groping under the stones or banks of a stream. ● **n.** a muddle; a mess.
– DERIVATIVES **guddler** n.
– ORIGIN C17: of unknown origin.

**gudgeon**[1] /ˈgʌdʒ(ə)n/ ● **n. 1** a small freshwater fish often used as bait by anglers. [*Gobio gobio.*] **2** archaic a credulous or easily fooled person.
– ORIGIN ME: from OFr. *goujon*, from L. *gobio(n-)*, from *gobius* 'goby'.

**gudgeon**[2] /ˈgʌdʒ(ə)n/ ● **n. 1** a pivot or spindle on which a bell or other object swings or rotates. **2** the tubular part of a hinge into which the pin fits. **3** a socket at the stern of a boat, into which the rudder is fitted. **4** a pin holding two blocks of stone together.
– ORIGIN ME: from OFr. *goujon*, dimin. of *gouge* (see **GOUGE**).

**gudgeon pin** ● **n.** a pin holding a piston rod and a connecting rod together.

**guelder rose** /ˈgɛldə/ ● **n.** a deciduous shrub with flattened heads of fragrant creamy-white flowers, followed by translucent red berries. [*Viburnum opulus.*]
– ORIGIN C16: from Du. *geldersche roos* 'rose of *Gelderland*' (a province of the Netherlands).

**Guelph** /gwɛlf/ ● **n. 1** a member of one of two great factions in Italian medieval politics, traditionally supporting the Pope against the Holy Roman emperor and his supporters, the Ghibellines. **2** a member of a German princely family from which the British royal house is descended.
– DERIVATIVES **Guelphic** adj.
– ORIGIN from Ital. *Guelfo*, from Mid. High Ger. *Welf*, the name of the founder of the Guelph faction.

**guenon** /gəˈnɒn/ ● **n.** a long-tailed African monkey of a group including the vervet and patas monkeys. [Genus *Cercopithecus*: several species.]
– ORIGIN C19: from Fr., of unknown origin.

**guerdon** /ˈgəːd(ə)n/ archaic ● **n.** a reward or recompense. ● **v.** give a reward to.
– ORIGIN ME: from OFr., from med. L. *widerdonum*, alt. (by assoc. with L. *donum* 'gift') of a W. Gmc compound represented by Old High Ger. *widarlōn* 'repayment'.

**Guernsey** /ˈgəːnzi/ ● **n.** (pl. **-eys**) **1** an animal of a breed of dairy cattle from Guernsey, noted for producing rich, creamy milk. **2** (**guernsey**) a thick sweater made with oiled wool, originally worn by fishermen. ➤Austral. a football jumper.

**Guernsey lily** ● **n.** a nerine with large heads of pink lily-like flowers. [*Nerine sarniensis.*]

**guerrilla** /gəˈrɪlə/ (also **guerilla**) ● **n.** a member of a small independent group taking part in irregular warfare, typically against larger regular forces.
– ORIGIN C19: from Sp., dimin. of *guerra* 'war'.

**guess** ● **v. 1** estimate or suppose (something) without sufficient information to be sure of being correct. **2** correctly conjecture or perceive. **3** (**I guess**) informal, chiefly N. Amer. I suppose. ● **n.** an estimate or conjecture.
– PHRASES **be anybody's** (or **anyone's**) **guess** be very difficult or impossible to determine.
– DERIVATIVES **guessable** adj. **guesser** n.
– ORIGIN ME: origin uncertain; perh. from Du. *gissen*, and prob. rel. to **GET**.

**guesstimate** (also **guestimate**) informal ● **n.** /ˈgɛstɪmət/ an estimate based on a mixture of guesswork and calculation. ● **v.** /ˈgɛstɪmeɪt/ form such an estimate of.

**guesswork** ● **n.** the process or results of guessing.

**guest** ● **n. 1** a person who is invited to visit someone's home or take part in a function. ➤a visiting performer invited to take part in an entertainment. **2** a person lodging at a hotel or boarding house. ● **v.** informal appear as a guest.
– PHRASES **be my guest** informal please do! **guest of honour** the most important guest at an occasion.
– ORIGIN ME: from ON *gestr*, of Gmc origin.

**guest beer** ● **n.** Brit. a draught beer offered only temporarily or in addition to those produced by the parent brewery.

**guest house** • n. a private house offering accommodation to paying guests.

**guestimate** • n. & v. variant spelling of **GUESSTIMATE**.

**guest rope** • n. **1** a second rope fastened to a boat in tow to keep it steady. **2** a rope slung outside a ship to give a hold for boats coming alongside.

**guest worker** • n. English term for **GASTARBEITER**.

**guff** • n. **1** informal trivial or worthless talk or ideas. **2** Scottish an unpleasant smell.
– ORIGIN C19 (in the sense 'puff, whiff of a bad smell'): imitative.

**guffaw** /gəˈfɔː/ • n. a loud and boisterous laugh. • v. laugh in such a way.
– ORIGIN C18 (orig. Scots): imitative.

**GUI** • abbrev. Computing graphical user interface.

**guidance** • n. **1** advice or information aimed at resolving a problem or difficulty. **2** the directing of the motion or position of something.

**guide** • n. **1** a person who advises or shows the way to others. ➤a professional mountain climber in charge of a group. **2** a directing principle or standard. ➤a book providing information on a subject. **3** a structure or marking which directs the motion or positioning of something. **4** (**Guide**) chiefly Brit. a member of the Guides Association, a girls' organization corresponding to the Scouts. • v. **1** show or indicate the way to. **2** direct the motion, positioning, or course of. ➤[as adj. **guided**] directed by remote control or internal equipment: *a guided missile*.
– DERIVATIVES **guidable** adj. **guider** n.
– ORIGIN ME: from OFr. *guide* (n.), *guider* (v.), of Gmc origin; rel. to **WIT**².

**guidebook** • n. a book of information about a place for visitors or tourists.

**guide dog** • n. a dog that has been trained to lead a blind person.

**guideline** • n. a general rule, principle, or piece of advice.

**guidepost** • n. archaic term for **SIGNPOST**.

**Guider** • n. Brit. an adult leader in the Guides Association.

**guideway** • n. a groove or track along which something moves.

**guidon** /ˈgʌɪd(ə)n/ • n. a pennant that narrows to a point or fork, especially one used as the standard of a light cavalry regiment.
– ORIGIN C16: from Fr., from Ital. *guidone*, from *guida* 'a guide'.

**guild** • n. **1** a medieval association of craftsmen or merchants. **2** an association of people for mutual aid or the pursuit of a common goal. **3** Ecology a group of species with similar roles within a community.
– ORIGIN OE: prob. from Mid. Low Ger. and MDu. *gilde*, of Gmc origin; rel. to **YIELD**.

**guilder** /ˈgɪldə/ • n. (pl. same or **guilders**) **1** the basic monetary unit of the Netherlands, equal to 100 cents. **2** historical a gold or silver coin formerly used in the Netherlands, Germany, and Austria.
– ORIGIN alt. of Du. *gulden* (see **GULDEN**).

**guildhall** • n. a building used as the meeting place of a guild or corporation. ➤Brit. a town hall. ➤(**the Guildhall**) the hall of the Corporation of the City of London.

**guile** /gʌɪl/ • n. sly or cunning intelligence.
– DERIVATIVES **guileful** adj. **guilefully** adv. **guileless** adj. **guilelessly** adv. **guilelessness** n.
– ORIGIN ME: from OFr., prob. from ON; cf. **WILE**.

**Guillain–Barré syndrome** /ˌgɪjãˈbareɪ/ • n. Medicine an acute disorder of the peripheral nerves causing weakness and often paralysis of the limbs.
– ORIGIN 1916: named after the Fr. physicians Georges *Guillain* and Jean *Barré*, who described the syndrome.

**guillemot** /ˈgɪlɪmɒt/ • n. an auk with a narrow pointed bill, typically nesting on cliff ledges. [*Uria aalge* and other species.]
– ORIGIN C17: from Fr., dimin. of *Guillaume* 'William'.

**guilloche** /gɪˈləʊʃ, -ˈlɒʃ/ • n. ornamentation resembling braided or interlaced ribbons.
– ORIGIN C19: from Fr. *guillochis*, denoting the ornamentation, or *guilloche*, a carving tool.

**guillotine** /ˈgɪlətiːn, ˌgɪləˈtiːn/ • n. **1** a machine with a heavy blade sliding vertically in grooves, used for beheading people. **2** a device with a descending or sliding blade used for cutting paper or sheet metal. **3** a surgical instrument with a sliding blade used typically for the removal of the tonsils. **4** Brit. (in parliament) a procedure used to limit discussion of a legislative bill by fixing times at which various parts of it must be voted on. • v. **1** execute by guillotine. **2** Brit. (in parliament) apply a guillotine to (a bill or debate).
– ORIGIN C18: from Fr., named after the Fr. physician Joseph-Ignace *Guillotin*.

**guilt** • n. **1** the fact of having committed an offence or crime. **2** a feeling of having committed wrong or failed in an obligation.
– DERIVATIVES **guiltless** adj. **guiltlessly** adv. **guiltlessness** n.
– ORIGIN OE *gylt*, of unknown origin.

**guilt trip** informal • n. a feeling of guilt, especially when self-indulgent or unjustified. • v. (**guilt-trip**) make (someone) feel guilty, especially in order to induce them to do something.

**guilty** • adj. (**-ier, -iest**) **1** (often **guilty of**) culpable of a specified wrongdoing. ➤justly chargeable with a particular fault or error. **2** having or showing a feeling of guilt: *a guilty conscience*.
– DERIVATIVES **guiltily** adv. **guiltiness** n.

**guimpe** /gɪmp/ (also **guimp**) • n. historical a high-necked blouse or undergarment worn showing beneath a low-necked dress.
– ORIGIN C19: from Fr.; rel. to **WIMPLE**.

**guinea** /ˈgɪni/ • n. Brit. **1** the sum of £1.05 (21 shillings in pre-decimal currency), used mainly for determining professional fees and auction prices. **2** a former British gold coin with a value of 21 shillings.
– ORIGIN named after *Guinea* in West Africa (the source of the gold from which the first guineas were minted).

**guineafowl** • n. (pl. same) a large African game bird with slate-coloured, white-spotted plumage. [*Numida meleagris* (**helmeted guineafowl**) and other species.]

**Guinean** /ˈgɪniən/ • n. a native or inhabitant of Guinea, a country on the west coast of Africa. • adj. of or relating to Guinea.

**guinea pig** • n. **1** a tailless South American cavy, now completely domesticated as a pet or laboratory animal. [*Cavia porcellus*.] **2** a person or thing used as a subject for experiment.

**Guinea worm** • n. a very long parasitic nematode worm which lives under the skin of infected humans and other mammals in rural Africa and Asia. [*Dracunculus medinensis*.]

**guinep** /gɪˈnɛp/ • n. variant spelling of **GENIP**.

**guipure** /gɪˈpjʊə/ • n. heavy lace consisting of embroidered motifs held together by large connecting stitches.
– ORIGIN C19: from Fr., from *guiper* 'cover with silk'.

**guiro** /ˈgwɪərəʊ/ • n. (pl. **-os**) a musical instrument with a serrated surface which gives a rasping sound when scraped with a stick.
– ORIGIN Sp., 'gourd'.

**guise** /gʌɪz/ • n. an external form, appearance, or manner of presentation.
– ORIGIN ME: from OFr., of Gmc origin; rel. to **WISE**².

**guiser** /ˈgʌɪzə/ • n. archaic a mummer in a folk play.
– ORIGIN C15: from the archaic verb *guise* 'dress fantastically', from the noun **GUISE**.

**guitar** • n. a stringed musical instrument with a fretted fingerboard and six or twelve strings, played by plucking or strumming with the fingers or a plectrum.
– DERIVATIVES **guitarist** n.
– ORIGIN C17: from Sp. *guitarra* (partly via Fr.), from Gk *kithara*, denoting an instrument similar to the lyre.

**guitarfish** • n. (pl. same or **-fishes**) a fish related to the rays, with a guitar-like body shape. [*Rhinobatus rhinobatus* and other species.]

**guiver** • n. variant spelling of **GUYVER**.

**Gujarati** /ˌguːdʒəˈrɑːti, ˌgʊ-/ (also **Gujerati**) • n. (pl. **Guja-**

**ratis**) **1** a native or inhabitant of the Indian state of Gujarat. **2** the Indic language of the Gujaratis. ● **adj.** of or relating to the Gujaratis or their language.

**gulab jamun** /gʊˌlɑːb ˈjɑːmʌn/ ● **n.** an Indian sweet consisting of a ball of deep-fried paneer boiled in a sugar syrup.
– ORIGIN from Hindi *gulāb* 'rose water' and *jāmun* 'fruit'.

**Gulag** /ˈguːlag/ ● **n.** (**the Gulag**) a system of harsh labour camps maintained in the Soviet Union 1930–1955.
– ORIGIN Russ., from *G(lavnoe) u(pravlenie ispravitel'no-trudovykh) lag(ereĭ)* 'Chief Administration for Corrective Labour Camps'.

**gular** /ˈgjuːlə/ ● **adj.** Zoology of or relating to the throat, especially of a reptile, fish, or bird.
– ORIGIN C19: from L. *gula* 'throat' + **-AR**[1].

**gulch** /gʌltʃ/ ● **n.** N. Amer. a narrow, steep-sided ravine marking the course of a fast stream.
– ORIGIN C19: perh. from dial. *gulch* 'to swallow'.

**gulden** /ˈgʊld(ə)n/ ● **n.** (pl. same or **guldens**) another term for **GUILDER**.
– ORIGIN Du. and Ger., lit. 'golden'.

**gules** /gjuːlz/ ● **n.** red, as a heraldic tincture.
– ORIGIN ME: from OFr. *goles* (pl. of *gole* 'throat', from L. *gula*), used to denote pieces of red-dyed fur used as a neck ornament.

**gulf** ● **n.** **1** a deep inlet of the sea almost surrounded by land, with a narrow mouth. **2** a deep ravine, chasm, or abyss. **3** a substantial difference between two people, concepts, or situations.
– ORIGIN ME: from OFr. *golfe*, from Ital. *golfo*, based on Gk *kolpos* 'bosom, gulf'.

**Gulf War syndrome** ● **n.** an unexplained medical condition affecting some veterans of the 1991 Gulf War, causing fatigue, chronic headaches, and skin and respiratory disorders.

**gulfweed** ● **n.** another term for **SARGASSUM**.

**gull**[1] ● **n.** a long-winged, web-footed seabird typically having white plumage with a grey or black mantle. [Family Laridae: many species.]
– ORIGIN ME: of Celtic origin; rel. to Welsh *gwylan* and Breton *gwelan*.

**gull**[2] ● **v.** fool or deceive (someone). ● **n.** a person who is fooled or deceived.
– ORIGIN C16: of unknown origin.

**Gullah** /ˈgʌlə/ ● **n.** **1** a member of a black people living on the coast of South Carolina and nearby islands. **2** the Creole language of this people, having an English base with West African elements.
– ORIGIN perh. a shortening of *Angola*, or from *Gola*, the name of a people of Liberia and Sierra Leone.

**gullery** ● **n.** (pl. **-ies**) a breeding colony or roost of gulls.

**gullet** ● **n.** the passage by which food passes from the mouth to the stomach; the oesophagus.
– ORIGIN ME: from OFr. *goulet*, dimin. of *goule* 'throat', from L. *gula*.

**gulley** ● **n.** (pl. **-eys**) variant spelling of **GULLY**.

**gullible** ● **adj.** easily persuaded to believe something; credulous.
– DERIVATIVES **gullibility** n. **gullibly** adv.
– ORIGIN C19: from **GULL**[2] + **-IBLE**.

**gull-wing** ● **n.** [as modifier] (of a door on a car or aircraft) opening upwards.

**gully** ● **n.** (pl. **-ies**) **1** (also **gulley**) a water-worn ravine. ➤ a gutter or drain. **2** Cricket a fielding position on the off side between point and the slips. ● **v.** (also **gulley**) [usu. as adj. **gullied**] erode gullies into (land) by water action.
– ORIGIN C16 (in the sense 'gullet'): from Fr. *goulet* (see **GULLET**).

**gulp** ● **v.** **1** swallow (drink or food) quickly or in large mouthfuls, often audibly. **2** make an effortful swallowing motion, typically in response to strong emotion. ● **n.** **1** an act of gulping food or drink. ➤ a large mouthful of liquid hastily drunk. **2** an effortful swallowing motion.
– DERIVATIVES **gulpy** adj.
– ORIGIN ME: prob. from MDu. *gulpen*, of imitative origin.

**gulpera** ● **n.** a deep-sea eel with very large jaws that open to give an enormous gape. [Order Saccopharyngiformes: many species.]

**GUM** ● **abbrev.** genito-urinary medicine.

**gum**[1] ● **n.** **1** a viscous secretion of some trees and shrubs that hardens on drying but is soluble in water. ➤ a sticky secretion collecting in the corner of the eye. **2** glue used for sticking paper or other light materials together. **3** chewing gum or bubble gum. **4** a firm, jelly-like sweet made with gelatin or gum arabic. **5** a gum tree, especially a eucalyptus. **6** North American term for **GUMBOOT**. ● **v.** (**gummed**, **gumming**) cover or fasten with gum or glue. ➤ (**gum something up**) clog up a mechanism and prevent it from working properly.
– ORIGIN ME: from OFr. *gomme*, based on L. *gummi*, from Gk *kommi*, from Egyptian *kemai*.

**gum**[2] ● **n.** the firm area of flesh around the roots of the teeth in the upper or lower jaw.
– ORIGIN OE *gōma* 'inside of the mouth or throat', of Gmc origin.

**gum**[3] ● **n.** (in phr. **by gum!**) chiefly N. English an exclamation used for emphasis.
– ORIGIN C19: euphemistic alt. of *God*.

**gum arabic** ● **n.** a gum exuded by some kinds of acacia and used as glue and in incense.

**gum benjamin** ● **n.** gum benzoin (see **BENZOIN**).

**gumbo** ● **n.** (pl. **-os**) N. Amer. **1** okra, especially the gelatinous pods used in cooking. ➤ (in Cajun cooking) a spicy chicken or seafood soup thickened with okra or rice. **2** (**Gumbo**) a French-based patois spoken by some blacks and Creoles in Louisiana. **3** a fine clayey soil that becomes sticky and impervious when wet. **4** a type of Cajun music consisting of a lively blend of styles and sounds.
– ORIGIN C19: from the Angolan word *kingombo* 'okra'.

**gumboil** ● **n.** a small swelling formed on the gum over an abscess at the root of a tooth.

**gumboot** ● **n.** dated, chiefly Brit. a long rubber boot; a wellington.

**gumdrop** ● **n.** a firm, jelly-like sweet made with gelatin or gum arabic.

**gumma** /ˈgʌmə/ ● **n.** (pl. **gummas** or **gummata** /-mətə/) Medicine a small soft swelling which is characteristic of the late stages of syphilis and occurs in the connective tissue of the liver, brain, testes, and heart.
– DERIVATIVES **gummatous** adj.
– ORIGIN C18: mod. L., from L. *gummi* (see **GUM**[1]).

**gummosis** /gəˈməʊsɪs/ ● **n.** the copious production and exudation of gum by a diseased or damaged tree.

**gummy**[1] ● **adj.** (**-ier**, **-iest**) viscous; sticky.
– DERIVATIVES **gumminess** n.

**gummy**[2] ● **adj.** (**-ier**, **-iest**) toothless: *a gummy grin.*
– DERIVATIVES **gummily** adv.

**gummy shark** ● **n.** a small edible shark of Australasian coasts, with rounded teeth that it uses to crush hard-shelled prey. [*Mustelus antarcticus*.]

**gum olibanum** ● **n.** another term for **FRANKINCENSE**.

**gumption** /ˈgʌm(p)ʃ(ə)n/ ● **n.** informal shrewd or spirited initiative and resourcefulness.
– ORIGIN C18 (orig. Scots): of unknown origin.

**gum resin** ● **n.** a plant secretion consisting of resin mixed with gum.

**gumshield** ● **n.** a pad or plate held in the mouth by a sports player to protect the teeth and gums.

**gumshoe** ● **n.** N. Amer. informal a detective.
– ORIGIN C20: from *gumshoes* in the sense 'sneakers', suggesting stealth.

**gum tree** ● **n.** a tree that exudes gum, especially a eucalyptus.
– PHRASES **up a gum tree** Brit. informal in or into a predicament.

**gun** ● **n.** **1** a weapon incorporating a metal tube from which bullets or shells are propelled by explosive force. ➤ N. Amer. a gunman: *a hired gun.* **2** a device for discharging something (e.g. grease) in a required direction. ● **v.** (**gunned**, **gunning**) **1** (**gun someone down**) shoot someone with a gun. **2** (**gun for**) aggressively pursue or act against. ➤ strive for determinedly. **3** informal cause (an engine) to race. ➤ accelerate (a vehicle).
– PHRASES **go great guns** informal proceed forcefully, vigor-

ously, or successfully. **jump the gun** informal act before the proper or appropriate time. **stick to one's guns** informal refuse to compromise or change, despite criticism. **top gun** a (or the) most important person. **under the gun** N. Amer. informal under great pressure.
– DERIVATIVES **gunless** adj. **-gunned** adj.
– ORIGIN ME *gunne, gonne,* perh. from a familiar form of the Scand. name *Gunnhildr,* from *gunnr* + *hildr,* both meaning 'war'.

**gunboat** • n. a small ship mounting guns, for use in shallow coastal waters and rivers.

**gunboat diplomacy** • n. foreign policy supported by the use or threat of military force.

**gun carriage** • n. a wheeled support for a piece of artillery.

**guncotton** • n. a highly nitrated form of nitrocellulose, used as an explosive.

**gun deck** • n. a deck on a ship on which guns are placed. ➤ historical the lowest such deck on a ship of the line.

**gundi** /'gʌndi/ • n. (pl. **gundis**) a small desert-dwelling rodent of North and East Africa. [Family Ctenodactylidae: several species.]
– ORIGIN C18: from N. Afr. Arab.

**gun dog** • n. a dog trained to retrieve game for a gamekeeper or the members of a shoot.

**gunfight** • n. a fight involving an exchange of fire with guns.
– DERIVATIVES **gunfighter** n.

**gunfire** • n. the repeated firing of a gun or guns.

**gunge** Brit. informal • n. a sticky, viscous, and unpleasantly messy material. • v. (**gunged**, **gungeing**) (**gunge something up**) clog or obstruct something with gunge.
– DERIVATIVES **gungy** adj.
– ORIGIN 1960s: perh. suggested by **GOO** and **GUNK**.

**gung-ho** /gʌŋ'həʊ/ • adj. unthinkingly enthusiastic and eager, especially about taking part in fighting or warfare.
– ORIGIN Second World War: from Chin. *gōnghé,* taken to mean 'work together' and adopted as a slogan by US Marines.

**gunk** • n. informal unpleasantly sticky or messy matter.
– ORIGIN 1930s (orig. US): the proprietary name of a detergent.

**gunlock** • n. a mechanism by which the charge of a gun is exploded.

**gunman** • n. (pl. **-men**) a man who uses a gun to commit a crime or terrorist act.

**gunmetal** • n. **1** a grey corrosion-resistant form of bronze containing zinc. **2** a dull bluish-grey colour.

**gun microphone** • n. a microphone with an elongated barrel which can be directed from a distance at a localized sound source.

**gunnel**[1] /'gʌn(ə)l/ • n. an elongated, laterally compressed marine fish with a dorsal fin running along most of the back. [Family Pholidae: several species.]
– ORIGIN C17: of unknown origin.

**gunnel**[2] • n. variant spelling of **GUNWALE**.

**gunner** • n. **1** a person who operates a gun. ➤ a British artillery soldier (an official term for a private). **2** historical a naval warrant officer in charge of a ship's guns and ordnance stores.

**gunnera** /'gʌn(ə)rə, gʌ'nɪərə/ • n. a South American plant with extremely large leaves, grown as a waterside ornamental. [Genus *Gunnera*.]
– ORIGIN mod. L., named after the C18 Norw. botanist Johann E. *Gunnerus.*

**gunnery** • n. the design, manufacture, or firing of heavy guns.

**gunnery sergeant** • n. a rank of non-commissioned officer in the US marines, above staff sergeant and below master sergeant.

**gunny** /'gʌni/ • n. chiefly N. Amer. coarse sacking, typically made of jute fibre.
– ORIGIN C18: from Marathi *gōnī,* from Sanskrit *goṇī* 'sack'.

**gunplay** • n. chiefly N. Amer. the use of guns.

**gunpoint** • n. (in phr. **at gunpoint**) while threatening someone or being threatened with a gun.

**gunpowder** • n. **1** an explosive consisting of a powdered mixture of saltpetre, sulphur, and charcoal. **2** a fine green China tea of granular appearance.

**gunroom** • n. **1** a room for storing guns. **2** Brit. dated a set of quarters for midshipmen or other junior officers in a warship.

**gunrunner** • n. a person engaged in the illegal sale or importing of firearms.
– DERIVATIVES **gunrunning** n.

**gunsel** /'gʌns(ə)l/ • n. US informal **1** a criminal carrying a gun. **2** dated a homosexual youth.
– ORIGIN C20: from Yiddish *gendzel* 'little goose', influenced by **GUN**.

**gunship** • n. a heavily armed helicopter.

**gunshot** • n. a shot fired from a gun.

**gun-shy** • adj. (especially of a hunting dog) alarmed at the sound of a gun.

**gunsight** • n. a device on a gun enabling it to be aimed accurately.

**gunslinger** • n. informal a man who carries a gun.
– DERIVATIVES **gunslinging** adj.

**gunsmith** • n. a person who makes and sells small firearms.

**gunstock** • n. the wooden support to which the barrel of a gun is attached.

**gunter** • n. Sailing **1** a fore-and-aft sail which is nearly triangular. **2** historical a type of rig in which the topmast slid up and down the lower mast on rings.
– ORIGIN C18: named after the C17 Engl. mathematician Edmund *Gunter.*

**gunwale** /'gʌn(ə)l/ (also **gunnel**) • n. the upper edge or planking of the side of a boat.
– ORIGIN ME: from **GUN** + **WALE** (because it was formerly used to support guns).

**gunyah** /'gʌnjə/ • n. Austral. an Aboriginal bush hut, typically made of bark and branches.
– ORIGIN from Dharuk *ganya* 'house, hut'.

**guppy** /'gʌpi/ • n. (pl. **-ies**) a small live-bearing freshwater fish, native to tropical America and widely kept in aquaria. [*Poecilia reticulata.*]
– ORIGIN 1920s: named after the Trinidadian clergyman R. J. Lechmere *Guppy,* who sent the first specimen to the British Museum.

**Gur** /gəː/ • n. a branch of the Niger–Congo family of languages, spoken in parts of West Africa.

**gur** /gʊr/ • n. (in the Indian subcontinent) unrefined, solid brown sugar made by boiling sugar cane juice until dry.
– ORIGIN from Hindi *guṛ* and Marathi *gūḷ,* from Sanskrit *guḍa.*

**gurdwara** /gʊə'dwɑːrə, gəː'dwɑːrə/ • n. a Sikh place of worship.
– ORIGIN from Punjabi *gurduārā,* from Sanskrit *guru* 'teacher' + *dvāra* 'door'.

**gurgle** • v. make a hollow bubbling sound. • n. a gurgling sound.
– ORIGIN ME: imitative, or directly from Du. *gorgelen,* Ger. *gurgeln,* or med. L. *gurgulare,* all from L. *gurgulio* 'gullet'.

**Gurkha** /'gəːkə, 'gʊəkə/ • n. **1** a member of any of several Nepalese peoples noted for their military prowess. **2** a member of a regiment in the British army established for Nepalese recruits.
– ORIGIN name of a locality, from Sanskrit *gorakṣa* 'cowherd' (from *go* 'cow' + *rakṣ-* 'protect'), used as an epithet of their patron deity.

**Gurkhali** /gəː'kɑːli/ (also **Gorkhali**) • n. another term for **NEPALI** (the language).

**Gurmukhi** /'gʊəmʊki/ • n. the script used by Sikhs for writing Punjabi.
– ORIGIN Punjabi, from Sanskrit *guru* (see **GURU**) + *mukha* 'mouth'.

**gurn** /gəːn/ (also **girn**) • v. Brit. pull a grotesque face.
– DERIVATIVES **gurner** n.
– ORIGIN C20: dial. var. of **GRIN**.

**gurnard** /'gəːnəd/ • n. a small coastal fish with three finger-like pectoral rays with which it searches for food

and walks on the seabed. [*Eutrigla gurnardus* and other species, family Triglidae.]
– ORIGIN ME: from OFr. *gornart*, from *grondir* 'to grunt', from L. *grundire*, *grunnire*.

**gurney** /'gəːni/ ● **n.** (pl. **-eys**) chiefly N. Amer. a wheeled stretcher for transporting hospital patients.
– ORIGIN C19: appar. named after the patentee of a new cab design, J. T. *Gurney*.

**gurry** /'gʌri/ ● **n.** chiefly N. Amer. fish or whale offal.
– ORIGIN C18: of unknown origin.

**guru** /'gʊruː, 'guːruː/ ● **n. 1** a Hindu spiritual teacher. **2** each of the ten first leaders of the Sikh religion. **3** an influential teacher: *a management guru*.
– ORIGIN from Hindi and Punjabi, from Sanskrit *guru* 'weighty, grave' (cf. L. *gravis*), hence 'elder, teacher'.

**gush** ● **v. 1** send out or flow in a rapid and plentiful stream. **2** speak or write effusively. ● **n. 1** a rapid and plentiful stream. **2** effusiveness.
– DERIVATIVES **gushing** adj. **gushingly** adv.
– ORIGIN ME: prob. imitative.

**gusher** ● **n. 1** an oil well from which oil flows profusely without being pumped. **2** an effusive person.

**gushy** ● **adj.** (**-ier**, **-iest**) excessively effusive.
– DERIVATIVES **gushily** adv. **gushiness** n.

**gusset** /'gʌsɪt/ ● **n. 1** a piece of material sewn into a garment to strengthen or enlarge a part of it, e.g. the crotch of an undergarment. **2** a bracket strengthening an angle of a structure.
– DERIVATIVES **gusseted** adj.
– ORIGIN ME: from OFr. *gousset*, dimin. of *gousse* 'pod, shell', of unknown origin.

**gussy** ● **v.** (**-ies**, **-ied**) (**gussy someone/thing up**) informal, chiefly N. Amer. make someone or something more attractive, especially in a showy way.
– ORIGIN 1940s: perh. from *Gussie*, familiar form of the given name *Augustus*.

**gust** ● **n. 1** a brief, strong rush of wind. **2** a burst of rain, sound, emotion, etc. ● **v.** blow in gusts.
– ORIGIN C16: from ON *gustr*, rel. to *gjósa* 'to gush'.

**gustation** ● **n.** formal the action or faculty of tasting.
– DERIVATIVES **gustative** adj. **gustatory** /gʌ'steɪt(ə)ri, 'gʌstət(ə)ri/ adj.
– ORIGIN C16: from L. *gustatio(n-)*, from *gustare* 'to taste', from *gustus* 'taste'.

**gusto** ● **n.** (pl. **-os** or **-oes**) **1** enjoyment or vigour. **2** archaic a relish or liking. **3** archaic style of artistic execution.
– ORIGIN C17: from Ital., from L. *gustus* 'taste'.

**gusty** ● **adj.** (**-ier**, **-iest**) **1** characterized by or blowing in gusts. **2** showing gusto.
– DERIVATIVES **gustily** adv. **gustiness** n.

**gut** ● **n. 1** the stomach or belly. ➤ Medicine & Biology the intestine. ➤ (**guts**) entrails that have been removed or exposed. **2** (**guts**) the internal parts or essence of something. **3** (**guts**) used in names attributing negative characteristics: *greedy guts*. **4** (**guts**) informal personal courage and determination. **5** [as modifier] informal (of a feeling or reaction) instinctive. **6** fibre from the intestines of animals, used especially for violin or racket strings. **7** a narrow passage or strait. ● **v.** (**gutted**, **gutting**) **1** take out the internal organs of (a fish or other animal) before cooking. **2** remove or destroy the internal parts of.
– PHRASES **bust a gut** informal make a strenuous effort. **hate someone's guts** informal dislike someone intensely. **have someone's guts for garters** informal, humorous used as a threat of punishment. **sweat** (or **work**) **one's guts out** informal work extremely hard.
– ORIGIN OE *guttas* (pl.), prob. rel. to *gēotan* 'pour'.

**gutbucket** ● **n.** informal **1** Brit. a glutton. **2** [as modifier] chiefly N. Amer. (of jazz or blues) raw and spirited in style.

**Guthrie test** ● **n.** Medicine a routine blood test for phenylketonuria, carried out on newborn babies.
– ORIGIN named after the Amer. microbiologist Robert *Guthrie*.

**gutless** ● **adj.** informal lacking courage or determination.
– DERIVATIVES **gutlessly** adv. **gutlessness** n.

**gut rot** ● **n.** Brit. informal **1** another term for ROTGUT. **2** a stomach upset.

**gutsy** ● **adj.** (**-ier**, **-iest**) informal **1** showing courage and determination. **2** strongly flavoursome. **3** greedy.
– DERIVATIVES **gutsily** adv. **gutsiness** n.

**gutta-percha** /ˌgʌtə'pəːtʃə/ ● **n.** the hard tough coagulated latex of certain Malaysian trees, resembling rubber.
– ORIGIN C19: from Malay *getah perca*, from *getah* 'gum' + *perca* 'strips of cloth' (which it resembles), alt. by assoc. with obs. *gutta* 'gum', from L. *gutta* 'a drop'.

**guttate** /'gʌteɪt/ ● **adj.** chiefly Biology having drops or droplike markings.
– ORIGIN C19: from L. *guttatus* 'speckled', from *gutta* 'a drop'.

**guttation** /gʌ'teɪʃ(ə)n/ ● **n.** the secretion of droplets of water from the pores of plants.
– ORIGIN C19: from L. *gutta* 'drop' + -ATION.

**gutted** ● **adj.** Brit. informal bitterly disappointed or upset.

**gutter** ● **n. 1** a shallow trough beneath the edge of a roof, or a channel at the side of a street, for carrying off rainwater. ➤ technical a groove or channel for flowing liquid. **2** (**the gutter**) a poor or squalid environment. **3** the blank space between facing pages of a book or between adjacent columns of type or stamps in a sheet. ● **v. 1** (of a flame) flicker and burn unsteadily. **2** archaic channel or furrow with streams, tears, etc.
– ORIGIN ME: from OFr. *gotiere*, from L. *gutta* 'a drop'.

**guttering** ● **n.** chiefly Brit. the gutters of a building.

**gutter press** ● **n.** chiefly Brit. newspapers engaging in sensational journalism.

**guttersnipe** ● **n.** a street urchin.

**guttural** /'gʌt(ə)r(ə)l/ ● **adj. 1** (of a speech sound) produced in the throat. **2** (of speech) characterized by guttural sounds. ● **n.** a guttural consonant (e.g. *k*, *g*).
– DERIVATIVES **gutturally** adv.
– ORIGIN C16: from Fr., or from med. L. *gutturalis*, from L. *guttur* 'throat'.

**gutty**[1] ● **n.** Irish & Scottish informal a plimsoll.

**gutty**[2] ● **adj.** (**-ier**, **-iest**) N. Amer. informal determined and spirited.

**guv** ● **n.** Brit. informal (as a form of address) sir.

**GUY** ● **abbrev.** Guyana (international vehicle registration).

**guy**[1] ● **n. 1** informal a man. ➤ (**guys**) chiefly N. Amer. people of either sex. **2** Brit. a figure representing the Catholic conspirator Guy Fawkes, burnt on a bonfire on 5 November to commemorate a plot to blow up Parliament in 1605. ● **v.** ridicule.

**guy**[2] ● **n.** a rope or line fixed to the ground to secure a tent. ● **v.** secure with a guy or guys.
– ORIGIN ME: prob. of Low Ger. origin; rel. to Du. *gei* 'brail' and Ger. *Geitaue* 'brails'.

**Guyanese** /ˌgʌɪə'niːz/ ● **n.** (pl. same) a native or inhabitant of Guyana, a country on the NE coast of South America. ● **adj.** of or relating to Guyana.

**Guy Fawkes Night** ● **n.** another term for BONFIRE NIGHT.

**guyot** /'giːəʊ/ ● **n.** Geology a seamount with a flat top.
– ORIGIN 1940s: named after the C19 Swiss geographer Arnold H. *Guyot*.

**guyver** /'gʌɪvə/ (also **guiver**, **gyver**) ● **n.** Austral./NZ informal ingratiating or affected speech or behaviour.
– ORIGIN C19: of unknown origin.

**guzzle** ● **v.** eat or drink greedily.
– DERIVATIVES **guzzler** n.
– ORIGIN C16: perh. from OFr. *gosillier* 'chatter, vomit', from *gosier* 'throat', from late L. *geusiae* 'cheeks'.

**Gy** ● **abbrev.** Physics gray(s).

**gybe** /dʒʌɪb/ (US **jibe**) Sailing ● **v.** change course by swinging the sail across a following wind. ➤ (of a sail or boom) swing across the wind. ● **n.** an act of gybing.
– ORIGIN C17: from obs. Du. *gijben*.

**gym** ● **n.** informal **1** a gymnasium. **2** gymnastics.

**gymkhana** /dʒɪm'kɑːnə/ ● **n. 1** an event comprising competitions on horseback, typically for children. **2** Indian a public place with facilities for athletics.
– ORIGIN C19: from Urdu *gendḵānah* 'racket court', from Hindi *gem̐d* 'ball' + Pers. *ḵānah* 'house', alt. by assoc. with GYMNASTICS.

**gymnasium** /dʒɪm'neɪzɪəm/ ● **n.** (pl. **gymnasiums** or **gymnasia** /-zɪə/) **1** a hall or building equipped for gymnastics and other physical exercise. **2** /also gɪm'nɑːzɪəm/ a school in Germany, Scandinavia, or central Europe that prepares pupils for university.
– DERIVATIVES **gymnasial** adj.
– ORIGIN C16: via L. from Gk *gumnasion*, from *gumnazein* 'exercise naked', from *gumnos* 'naked'.

**gymnast** ● **n.** a person trained in gymnastics.
– ORIGIN C16: from Fr. *gymnaste* or Gk *gumnastēs* 'trainer of athletes', from *gumnazein* (see **GYMNASIUM**).

**gymnastics** ● **pl. n.** [also treated as sing.] **1** exercises involving physical agility, flexibility, and coordination, especially tumbling and acrobatic feats. **2** physical or mental agility of a specified kind: *vocal gymnastics.*
– DERIVATIVES **gymnastic** adj. **gymnastically** adv.

**gymno-** /'dʒɪmnəʊ/ ● **comb. form** bare; naked: *gymnosophist* | *gymnosperm.*
– ORIGIN from Gk *gumnos* 'naked'.

**gymnosophist** /dʒɪm'nɒsəfɪst/ ● **n.** a member of an ancient Hindu sect who wore very little clothing and were given to asceticism and contemplation.
– DERIVATIVES **gymnosophy** n.
– ORIGIN ME: from Fr. *gymnosophiste*, via L. from Gk *gumnosophistai* (pl.), from *gumnos* 'naked' + *sophistēs* (see **SOPHIST**).

**gymnosperm** /'dʒɪmnə(ʊ)spəːm/ ● **n.** Botany a plant of a group (subdivision Gymnospermae) that comprises those that have seeds unprotected by an ovary or fruit, including conifers and cycads. Compare with **ANGIOSPERM**.
– DERIVATIVES **gymnospermous** /-'spəːməs/ adj.

**gymslip** ● **n.** Brit. dated a sleeveless belted tunic reaching from the shoulder to the knee, formerly worn by schoolgirls.

**gynaeceum** /dʒʌɪ'niːsɪəm, g-/ ● **n.** (pl. **gynaecea**) a part of an ancient Greek or Roman house set apart for women.
– ORIGIN L., from Gk.

**gynaeco-** /'gʌɪnɪkɒ, gʌɪ'niːkəʊ, dʒ-/ (US **gyneco-**) ● **comb. form** relating to women; female: *gynaecocracy.*
– ORIGIN from Gk *gunē, gunaik-* 'woman, female'.

**gynaecocracy** /,gʌɪnɪ'kɒkrəsi, dʒ-/ ● **n.** another term for **GYNARCHY**.

**gynaecology** /,gʌɪnɪ'kɒlədʒi, dʒ-/ (US **gynecology**) ● **n.** the branch of physiology and medicine concerned with the functions and diseases specific to women and girls, especially those affecting the reproductive system.
– DERIVATIVES **gynaecologic** adj. **gynaecological** adj. **gynaecologically** adv. **gynaecologist** n.

**gynaecomastia** /,gʌɪnɪkə(ʊ)'mastɪə, gʌɪ'niːkə(ʊ)-, dʒ-/ (US **gynecomastia**) ● **n.** Medicine enlargement of a man's breasts, due to hormone imbalance or hormone therapy.

**gynaecophobia** /,gʌɪnɪkə(ʊ)'fəʊbɪə, gʌɪ'niːkə(ʊ)-, dʒ-/ (US **gynecophobia**) ● **n.** another term for **GYNOPHOBIA**.

**gynandromorph** /dʒɪ'nandrəmɔːf, gʌɪ-/ ● **n.** Zoology & Medicine an abnormal individual, especially an insect, having male and female characteristics.
– DERIVATIVES **gynandromorphic** adj. **gynandromorphy** n.
– ORIGIN C19: from Gk *gunandros* (see **GYNANDROUS**) + *morphē* 'form'.

**gynandrous** /dʒɪ'nandrəs, gʌɪ-/ ● **adj.** Botany **1** (of a flower) having stamens and pistil united in one column, as in orchids. **2** (of a person or animal) hermaphrodite.
– ORIGIN C19: from Gk *gunandros* 'of doubtful sex' (from *gunē* 'woman' + *anēr, andr-* 'man, male') + **-OUS**.

**gynarchy** /'gʌɪnɑːki, 'dʒʌɪ-/ ● **n.** (pl. **-ies**) rule by women or a woman.

**gyneco-** ● **comb. form** US spelling of **GYNAECO-**.

**gynocentric** /,gʌɪnə(ʊ)'sɛntrɪk, ,dʒʌɪ-/ ● **adj.** concerned exclusively with women; taking a female (or feminist) point of view.

**gynoecium** /gʌɪ'niːsɪəm, dʒ-/ ● **n.** (pl. **gynoecia** /-sɪə/) Botany the female part of a flower, consisting of one or more carpels.
– ORIGIN C19: mod. L., from Gk *gunaikeion* 'women's apartments', from *gunē, gunaik-* 'woman, female' + *oikos* 'house'.

**gynophobia** /,gʌɪnə(ʊ)'fəʊbɪə, ,dʒʌɪ-/ ● **n.** extreme or irrational fear of women.
– DERIVATIVES **gynophobic** adj.

**-gynous** ● **comb. form** Botany having female organs or pistils of a specified kind or number: *epigynous.*
– ORIGIN based on mod. L. *-gynus* (from Gk *-gunos*, from *gunē* 'woman') + **-OUS**.

**gyp**[1] /dʒɪp/ (also **gip**) ● **n.** Brit. informal pain or discomfort.
– ORIGIN C19: perh. from *gee-up* (see **GEE**[2]).

**gyp**[2] /dʒɪp/ ● **n.** Brit. a college servant at the Universities of Cambridge and Durham.
– ORIGIN C18: perh. from obs. *gippo* 'menial kitchen servant', orig. denoting a man's short tunic, from obs. Fr. *jupeau.*

**gyp**[3] /dʒɪp/ informal ● **v.** (**gypped**, **gypping**) cheat or swindle (someone). ● **n.** a swindle.
– ORIGIN C19: of unknown origin.

**gyppo** /'dʒɪpəʊ/ (also **gippo**) ● **n.** (pl. **-os**) informal, derogatory a gypsy.

**gypsophila** /dʒɪp'sɒfɪlə/ ● **n.** a plant of a genus which includes baby's breath. [Genus *Gypsophila.*]
– ORIGIN mod. L., from Gk *gupsos* 'chalk, gypsum' + *philos* 'loving'.

**gypsum** /'dʒɪpsəm/ ● **n.** a soft white or grey mineral consisting of hydrated calcium sulphate, used to make plaster of Paris and in the building industry.
– DERIVATIVES **gypsiferous** /-'sɪf(ə)rəs/ adj.
– ORIGIN ME: from L., from Gk *gupsos.*

**gypsy** (also **gipsy**) ● **n.** (pl. **-ies**) a member of a travelling people with dark skin and hair, speaking a language (Romany) related to Hindi, and traditionally living by itinerant trade and fortune telling.
– DERIVATIVES **gypsyish** adj.
– ORIGIN C16: orig. *gipcyan*, short for **EGYPTIAN** (because gypsies were believed to have come from Egypt).

**gypsy moth** ● **n.** a tussock moth having a brown male and larger white flightless female. [*Lymantria dispar.*]

**gypsywort** ● **n.** a white-flowered plant of the mint family, growing in damp habitats. [*Lycopus europaeus.*]
– ORIGIN C18: so named because it was reputed to have been used by gypsies to stain the skin brown.

**gyral** /'dʒʌɪr(ə)l/ ● **adj.** chiefly Anatomy of or relating to a gyrus or gyri.

**gyrate** ● **v.** move or cause to move in a circle or spiral.
– DERIVATIVES **gyration** n. **gyrator** n.
– ORIGIN C19 (earlier (C17) as *gyration*): from L. *gyrat-*, *gyrare* 'revolve', from Gk *guros* 'a ring'.

**gyratory** /dʒʌɪ'reɪt(ə)ri, 'dʒʌɪrət-/ ● **adj.** of or involving circular or spiral motion. ● **n.** (pl. **-ies**) a traffic system requiring the circular movement of traffic.

**gyre** /'dʒʌɪə, 'gʌɪə/ ● **v.** poetic/literary whirl; gyrate. ● **n.** **1** a spiral; a vortex. **2** Geography a circular pattern of currents in an ocean basin.
– ORIGIN ME: from late L. *gyrare*, from L. *gyrus* 'a ring', from Gk *guros.*

**gyrfalcon** /'dʒəː,fɔː(l)k(ə)n, -,fɒlk(ə)n/ ● **n.** a large arctic falcon, occurring in several colour forms including a mainly white one. [*Falco rusticolus.*]
– ORIGIN ME: from OFr. *gerfaucon*, of Gmc origin, prob. rel. to Old High Ger. *gēr* 'spear'.

**gyri** plural form of **GYRUS**.

**gyro**[1] /'dʒʌɪrəʊ/ ● **n.** (pl. **-os**) short for **GYROSCOPE** or **GYROCOMPASS**.

**gyro**[2] /'dʒʌɪrəʊ/ ● **n.** (pl. **-os**) N. Amer. a sandwich of spiced meat cooked on a spit, served in pitta bread.
– ORIGIN 1970s: from mod. Gk *guros* 'turning'.

**gyro-** /'dʒʌɪrəʊ/ ● **comb. form** **1** relating to rotation: *gyromagnetic.* **2** gyroscopic: *gyrostabilizer.*
– ORIGIN from Gk *guros* 'a ring'.

**gyrocompass** ● **n.** a compass in which the direction of true north is maintained by a gyroscope rather than magnetism.

**gyrocopter** ● **n.** a small single-seater autogiro.

**gyromagnetic** ● **adj.** **1** Physics relating to or denoting the magnetic and mechanical properties of a rotating charged particle. **2** combining a gyroscope and a magnetic compass.

**gyron** /ˈdʒʌɪr(ə)n/ ● **n.** Heraldry a triangular ordinary formed by two lines from the edge of the shield meeting at the fess point at 45 degrees.
– ORIGIN C16: from OFr. *giron* 'gusset'.

**gyronny** /dʒʌɪˈrɒni/ ● **adj.** Heraldry (of a shield) divided into eight gyrons.
– ORIGIN ME: from Fr. *gironné*, from *giron* (see **GYRON**).

**gyropilot** ● **n.** a gyrocompass providing automatic steering for a ship or aircraft.

**gyroplane** ● **n.** an autogiro or similar aircraft.

**gyroscope** ● **n.** a device, used to provide stability or maintain a fixed orientation, consisting of a wheel or disc spinning rapidly about an axis which is itself free to alter in direction.
– DERIVATIVES **gyroscopic** adj. **gyroscopically** adv.
– ORIGIN C19: from Fr., from Gk *guros* 'a ring' + mod. L. *scopium* (see **-SCOPE**).

**gyrostabilizer** ● **n.** a gyroscopic device for maintaining the equilibrium of a ship, aircraft, platform etc.

**gyrus** /ˈdʒʌɪrəs/ ● **n.** (pl. **gyri** /-rʌɪ/) Anatomy a ridge or fold on the cerebral surface in the brain.
– ORIGIN C19: from L., from Gk *guros* 'a ring'.

**Gy Sgt** ● **abbrev.** Gunnery Sergeant.

**gyttja** /ˈjɪtʃə/ ● **n.** Geology sediment rich in organic matter at the bottom of a eutrophic lake.
– ORIGIN C19: Swed., lit. 'mud, ooze'.

**gyve** /dʒʌɪv, gʌɪv/ ● **n.** archaic a fetter or shackle.
– DERIVATIVES **gyved** adj.
– ORIGIN ME: of unknown origin.

**gyver** ● **n.** variant spelling of **GUYVER**.

**H¹** (also **h**) ● **n.** (pl. **Hs** or **H's**) **1** the eighth letter of the alphabet. **2** denoting the next after G in a set of items, categories, etc. **3** (**H**) Music (in the German system) the note B natural.

**H²** ● **abbrev. 1** (of a pencil lead) hard. **2** height. **3** Physics henry(s). **4** informal heroin. **5** Hungary (international vehicle registration). **6** Brit. (on street signs) hydrant. ● **symb. 1** Chemistry enthalpy. **2** the chemical element hydrogen. **3** Physics magnetic field strength.

**h** ● **abbrev. 1** (in measuring the height of horses) hand(s). **2** hecto-. **3** Brit. (with reference to sporting fixtures) home. **4** horse. **5** hot. **6** hour(s). ● **symb.** Physics Planck's constant.

**ha¹** (also **hah**) ● **exclam.** expressing surprise, suspicion, triumph, etc.
– ORIGIN natural utterance: first recorded in ME.

**ha²** ● **abbrev.** hectare(s).

**haaf** /hɑːf, haf/ ● **n.** (in Orkney and Shetland) the area of sea used for deep-sea fishing.
– ORIGIN C18: from ON *haf* 'high sea, ocean'.

**haar** /hɑː/ ● **n.** a cold sea fog on the east coast of England or Scotland.
– ORIGIN C17: perh. from ON *hárr* 'hoar, hoary'.

**Hab.** ● **abbrev.** Habakkuk (in biblical references).

**habanera** /ˌhabəˈnɛːrə, ˌɑːbə-/ ● **n.** a Cuban dance in slow duple time.
– ORIGIN C19: Sp., short for *danza habanera* 'dance of Havana'.

**Habanero** /ˌabəˈnɛːrəʊ/ ● **n.** North American term for **SCOTCH BONNET**.
– ORIGIN Sp., lit. 'of Havana'.

**habdabs** ● **pl. n.** variant spelling of **ABDABS**.

**Habdalah** /havˈdɑːlə/ (also **Havdalah**) ● **n.** a Jewish ceremony or prayer marking the end of the Sabbath.
– ORIGIN from Heb. *haḇdālāh* 'separation, division'.

**habeas corpus** /ˌheɪbɪəs ˈkɔːpəs/ ● **n.** Law a writ requiring a person to be brought before a judge or into court, especially to investigate the lawfulness of their detention.
– ORIGIN ME: L., lit. 'thou shalt have the body (in court)'.

**habendum** /həˈbɛndəm/ ● **n.** Law the part of a deed or conveyance which states the estate or quantity of interest to be granted.
– ORIGIN L., lit. 'that is to be had', gerundive of *habere* 'have'.

**haberdasher** /ˈhabəˌdaʃə/ ● **n. 1** Brit. a dealer in dressmaking and sewing goods. **2** N. Amer. a dealer in men's clothing.
– DERIVATIVES **haberdashery** n. (pl. **-ies**).
– ORIGIN ME: prob. based on Anglo-Norman Fr. *hapertas*, perh. the name of a fabric, of unknown origin.

**habergeon** /ˈhabədʒ(ə)n, həˈbəːdʒ(ə)n/ ● **n.** historical a sleeveless coat of mail or scale armour.
– ORIGIN ME: from OFr. *haubergeon*, from *hauberc* (see **HAUBERK**).

**habiliment** /həˈbɪlɪm(ə)nt/ ● **n.** archaic clothing.
– ORIGIN ME: from OFr. *habillement*, from *habiller* 'fit out', from L. *habilis* (see **ABLE**).

**habilitate** /həˈbɪlɪteɪt/ ● **v.** qualify for office, especially as a teacher in a German university.
– DERIVATIVES **habilitation** n.
– ORIGIN C17: from med. L. *habilitat-*, *habilitare* 'make able', from *habilitas* (see **ABILITY**).

**habit** ● **n. 1** a settled or regular tendency or practice. **2** general shape or mode of growth, especially of a plant or a mineral. **3** a long, loose garment worn by a member of a religious order. ➤ archaic dress; attire. **4** archaic a person's health or constitution. ● **v.** (usu. **be habited**) archaic dress.
– PHRASES **break** (or informal **kick**) **the habit** stop engaging in a habitual practice.
– ORIGIN ME: from OFr. *abit, habit*, from L. *habitus* 'condition, appearance', from *habere* 'have, consist of'.

**habitable** ● **adj.** suitable to live in.
– DERIVATIVES **habitability** n.
– ORIGIN ME: via OFr. from L. *habitabilis*, from *habitare* 'possess, inhabit'.

**habitant** ● **n. 1** /abiːˈtɒ̃/ an early French settler in Canada (especially Quebec) or Louisiana. **2** /ˈhabɪt(ə)nt/ archaic an inhabitant.
– ORIGIN ME: from OFr., from *habiter*, from L. *habitare* 'inhabit'.

**habitat** ● **n.** the natural home or environment of an organism.
– ORIGIN C18: from L., lit. 'it dwells', from *habitare* (see **HABITABLE**).

**habitation** ● **n. 1** the state or process of inhabiting. **2** formal a house or home.
– ORIGIN ME: via OFr. from L. *habitatio(n-)*, from *habitare* 'inhabit'.

**habit-forming** ● **adj.** addictive.

**habitual** /həˈbɪtʃʊəl, -tjʊəl/ ● **adj. 1** done constantly or as a habit. **2** regular; usual: *his habitual dress.*
– DERIVATIVES **habitually** adv.
– ORIGIN ME (in the sense 'part of one's character'): from med. L. *habitualis*, from *habitus* (see **HABIT**).

**habituate** ● **v.** chiefly Zoology make or become accustomed to something.
– DERIVATIVES **habituation** n.
– ORIGIN C15 (earlier (ME) as *habituation*): from late L. *habituat-*, *habituare* 'accustom', from *habitus* (see **HABIT**).

**habitude** ● **n.** rare a habitual tendency.
– ORIGIN ME: via OFr. from L. *habitudo*, from *habere* 'have' (cf. **HABIT**).

**habitué** /(h)əˈbɪtjʊeɪ/ ● **n.** a resident of or frequent visitor to a place.
– ORIGIN C19: Fr., lit. 'accustomed', past part. of *habituer*.

**habitus** /ˈhabɪtəs/ ● **n.** chiefly Medicine & Psychology general constitution, especially bodily build.
– ORIGIN C19: from L.

**haboob** /həˈbuːb/ ● **n.** (especially in Sudan) a violent and oppressive summer wind bringing sand from the desert.
– ORIGIN C19: from Arab. *habūb* 'blowing furiously'.

**háček** /ˈhɑːtʃɛk, ˈha-/ ● **n.** a diacritic mark (ˇ) placed over a letter to modify the sound in Slavic and other languages.
– ORIGIN Czech, dimin. of *hák* 'hook'.

**hachures** /haˈʃjʊəz/ ● **pl. n.** parallel lines used in hill-shading on maps, their closeness indicating steepness of gradient.
– DERIVATIVES **hachured** adj.
– ORIGIN C19: from Fr., from *hacher* (see **HATCH³**).

**hacienda** /ˌhasɪˈɛndə, Spanish aˈθjenda, aˈsjenda/ ● **n.** (in Spanish-speaking countries) a large estate with a house.
– ORIGIN Sp., from L. *facienda* 'things to be done', from *facere* 'make, do'.

**hack¹** ● **v. 1** cut with rough or heavy blows. **2** kick wildly or roughly. **3** use a computer to gain unauthorized access to data. **4** [usu. with neg.] (**hack it**) informal manage; cope. **5** (**hack someone off**) informal annoy someone. **6** (**hack around**) N. Amer. pass one's time idly. ● **n. 1** a rough cut or

blow. ➤ archaic a gash or wound. **2** a tool for rough striking or cutting. **3** informal an instance of computer hacking.
– PHRASES **hacking cough** a dry, frequent cough.
– DERIVATIVES **hacker** n.
– ORIGIN OE *haccian* 'cut in pieces', of W. Gmc origin.

**hack**[2] ● n. **1** a writer producing dull, unoriginal work. ➤ a person who does dull routine work. **2** a horse for ordinary riding. ➤ an inferior or worn-out horse. ➤ a horse let out for hire. ➤ a ride on a horse. **3** N. Amer. a taxi. ● v. [usu. as noun **hacking**] ride a horse.
– DERIVATIVES **hackery** n.
– ORIGIN ME: abbrev. of **HACKNEY**.

**hack**[3] ● n. **1** Falconry a board on which a hawk's meat is laid. **2** a wooden frame for drying bricks, cheeses, etc.
– PHRASES **at hack** (of a young hawk) not yet allowed to hunt for itself.
– ORIGIN ME (denoting the lower half of a divided door): var. of **HATCH**[1].

**hackamore** /'hakəmɔː/ ● n. a bitless bridle which exerts pressure on the horse's nose.
– ORIGIN C19: perh. from Sp. *jaquima*, earlier *xaquima* 'halter'.

**hackberry** ● n. (pl. **-ies**) **1** a tree with leaves that resemble those of nettles. [*Celtis occidentalis* (N. America) and other species.] **2** the purple berry of this tree.
– ORIGIN C18: var. of north. Engl. dial. *hagberry*, of Scand. origin.

**hacking jacket** ● n. a riding jacket with slits at the side or back.

**hackle** ● n. **1** (**hackles**) erectile hairs along an animal's back, which rise when it is angry or alarmed. **2** a long, narrow feather on the neck or saddle of a domestic cock or other bird. **3** Fishing a feather wound around a fishing fly so that its filaments are splayed out. **4** a bunch of feathers in a military headdress. **5** a steel comb for dressing flax. ● v. dress or comb with a hackle.
– PHRASES **make someone's hackles rise** make someone angry or indignant.
– ORIGIN ME: var. of obs. *hatchel*, of W. Gmc origin.

**hackmatack** /'hakmətak/ ● n. N. Amer. a tamarack or similar coniferous tree.
– ORIGIN C18: perh. from W. Abnaki.

**hackney** ● n. (pl. **-eys**) chiefly historical **1** a light horse with a high-stepping trot, used in harness. **2** a horse-drawn vehicle kept for hire.
– ORIGIN ME: prob. from *Hackney* in East London, where horses were pastured.

**hackney carriage** ● n. Brit. the official term for a taxi.

**hackneyed** ● adj. (of a phrase or idea) unoriginal and trite.
– ORIGIN from the obs. v. *hackney* 'use (a horse) for general purposes', later 'make commonplace by overuse'.

**hacksaw** ● n. a saw with a narrow blade set in a frame, used for cutting metal. ● v. (past part. **-sawn** or **-sawed**) cut with a hacksaw.

**had** past and past participle of **HAVE**.

**haddock** ● n. (pl. same) a silvery-grey bottom-dwelling fish of North Atlantic coastal waters, popular as a food fish. [*Melanogrammus aeglefinus*.]
– ORIGIN ME: from Anglo-Norman Fr. *hadoc*, from OFr. *hadot*, of unknown origin.

**hade** /heɪd/ Geology ● n. the inclination of a mineral vein or fault from the vertical. ● v. incline from the vertical.
– ORIGIN C17: perh. a dial. form of **HEAD** (v.).

**Hades** /'heɪdiːz/ ● n. **1** Greek Mythology the underworld; the abode of the spirits of the dead. **2** informal hell.
– ORIGIN from Gk *Haidēs* (a name of Pluto, the god of the dead), of unknown origin.

**Hadith** /ha'diːθ/ ● n. (pl. same or **Hadiths**) a collection of Islamic traditions containing sayings of the prophet Muhammad.
– ORIGIN from Arab. *ḥadīṯ* 'tradition'.

**Hadley cell** ● n. Meteorology a large-scale atmospheric convection cell in which air rises at the equator and sinks at medium latitudes.
– ORIGIN 1950s: named after the C18 Engl. scientific writer George *Hadley*.

**hadn't** ● contr. had not.

**hadron** /'hadrɒn/ ● n. Physics a subatomic particle that can take part in the strong interaction, such as a baryon or meson.
– DERIVATIVES **hadronic** adj.
– ORIGIN 1960s: from Gk *hadros* 'bulky' + **-ON**.

**hadrosaur** /'hadrəsɔː/ ● n. a large herbivorous mainly bipedal dinosaur with jaws flattened like the bill of a duck.
– ORIGIN C19: from mod. L. *Hadrosaurus* (genus name), from Gk *hadros* 'thick, stout' + *sauros* 'lizard'.

**hadst** archaic second person singular past of **HAVE**.

**haecceity** /hɛk'siːɪti, hiːk-/ ● n. Philosophy **1** the quality of a thing that makes it unique or describable as 'this (one)'. **2** individuality.
– ORIGIN C17: from med. L. *haecceitas*, from L. *haec*, fem. of *hic* 'this'.

**haem** /hiːm/ (US **heme**) ● n. Biochemistry an iron-containing compound of the porphyrin class which forms the non-protein part of haemoglobin.
– ORIGIN 1920s: back-form. from **HAEMOGLOBIN**.

**haemal** /'hiːm(ə)l/ (US **hemal**) ● adj. **1** Physiology of or concerning the blood. **2** Zoology situated on the same side of the body as the heart and major blood vessels (i.e. in chordates, ventral).
– ORIGIN C19: from Gk *haima* 'blood' + **-AL**.

**haematin** /'hiːmətɪn/ (US **hematin**) ● n. Biochemistry a bluish-black compound derived from haemoglobin by removal of the protein part and oxidation of the iron atom.
– ORIGIN C19: from Gk *haima, haimat-* 'blood' + **-IN**[1].

**haematite** /'hiːmətʌɪt/ (US **hematite**) ● n. a reddish-black mineral consisting of ferric oxide.
– ORIGIN ME: via L. from Gk *haimatitēs* (*lithos*) 'blood-like (stone)', from *haima, haimat-* 'blood'.

**haemato-** (US **hemato-**) ● comb. form of or relating to the blood: *haematoma*.
– ORIGIN from Gk *haima, haimat-* 'blood'.

**haematocele** /'hiːmətə(ʊ)siːl/ (US **hematocele**) ● n. Medicine a swelling caused by blood collecting in a body cavity.

**haematocrit** /'hiːmətə(ʊ)krɪt/ (US **hematocrit**) ● n. Physiology the ratio of the volume of red blood cells to the total volume of blood.
– ORIGIN C19: from **HAEMATO-** + Gk *kritēs* 'judge'.

**haematogenous** /ˌhiːmə'tɒdʒɪnəs/ (US **hematogenous**) ● adj. Medicine originating in or carried by the blood.

**haematology** /ˌhiːmə'tɒlədʒi/ (US **hematology**) ● n. the study of the physiology of the blood.
– DERIVATIVES **haematologic** adj. **haematological** adj. **haematologist** n.

**haematoma** /ˌhiːmə'təʊmə/ (US **hematoma**) ● n. (pl. **haematomas** or **haematomata** /-mətə/) Medicine a solid swelling of clotted blood within the tissues.

**haematophagous** /ˌhiːmə'tɒfəgəs/ (US **hematophagous**) ● adj. Zoology feeding on blood.

**haematopoiesis** /ˌhiːmatə(ʊ)pɔɪ'iːsɪs/ (US **hematopoiesis**) ● n. another term for **HAEMOPOIESIS**.
– DERIVATIVES **haematopoietic** adj.

**haematoxylin** /ˌhiːmə'tɒksɪlɪn/ (US **hematoxylin**) ● n. Chemistry a colourless compound present in logwood, which is easily converted into dyes and is used as a biological stain.
– ORIGIN C19: from mod. L. *Haematoxylum* (genus name), from **HAEMATO-** + Gk *xulon* 'wood'.

**haematuria** /ˌhiːmə'tjʊərɪə/ (US **hematuria**) ● n. Medicine the presence of blood in the urine.

**-haemia** ● comb. form variant spelling of **-AEMIA**.

**haemo-** (US **hemo-**) ● comb. form equivalent to **HAEMATO-**.
– ORIGIN from Gk *haima* 'blood'.

**haemochromatosis** /ˌhiːmə(ʊ)ˌkrəʊmə'təʊsɪs/ (US **hemochromatosis**) ● n. Medicine a hereditary liver disorder in which iron salts are deposited in the tissues.

**haemocoel** /'hiːməsiːl/ (US **hemocoel**) ● n. Zoology the primary body cavity of most invertebrates, containing circulatory fluid.

– ORIGIN C19: from **HAEMO-** + Gk *koilos* 'hollow, cavity'.

**haemocyanin** /ˌhiːmə(ʊ)ˈsʌɪənɪn/ (US **hemocyanin**) • **n.** Biochemistry a protein containing copper, responsible for transporting oxygen in the blood plasma of arthropods and molluscs.

– ORIGIN C19: from **HAEMO-** + **CYAN** + **-IN**[1].

**haemodialysis** /ˌhiːmə(ʊ)dʌɪˈalɪsɪs/ (US **hemodialysis**) • **n.** (pl. **haemodialyses** /-siːz/) Medicine kidney dialysis.

**haemodynamic** (US **hemodynamic**) • **adj.** Physiology of or relating to the flow of blood within the body.

– DERIVATIVES **haemodynamically** adv. **haemodynamics** pl. n.

**haemoglobin** /ˌhiːməˈgləʊbɪn/ (US **hemoglobin**) • **n.** Biochemistry a red protein containing iron, responsible for transporting oxygen in the blood of vertebrates.

– ORIGIN C19: a contracted form of *haematoglobulin*, in the same sense.

**haemolymph** /ˈhiːmə(ʊ)lɪmf/ (US **hemolymph**) • **n.** a fluid equivalent to blood in most invertebrates.

**haemolysis** /hiːˈmɒlɪsɪs/ (US **hemolysis**) • **n.** the rupture or destruction of red blood cells.

– DERIVATIVES **haemolytic** /ˌhiːməˈlɪtɪk/ adj.

**haemolytic disease of the newborn** • **n.** Medicine a severe form of anaemia caused in a fetus or newborn infant by incompatibility with the mother's blood type.

**haemophilia** /ˌhiːməˈfɪlɪə/ (US **hemophilia**) • **n.** a medical condition in which the ability of the blood to clot is severely reduced, causing severe bleeding from even a slight injury.

– DERIVATIVES **haemophiliac** n. **haemophilic** adj.

**haemopoiesis** /ˌhiːmə(ʊ)pɔɪˈiːsɪs/ (US **hemopoiesis**) • **n.** the production of blood cells and platelets in the bone marrow.

– DERIVATIVES **haemopoietic** adj.

– ORIGIN C20: from **HAEMO-** + Gk *poiēsis* 'making'.

**haemoptysis** /hiːˈmɒptɪsɪs/ (US **hemoptysis**) • **n.** the coughing up of blood.

– ORIGIN C17: from **HAEMO-** + Gk *ptusis* 'spitting'.

**haemorrhage** /ˈhɛmərɪdʒ/ (US **hemorrhage**) • **n. 1** an escape of blood from a ruptured blood vessel. **2** a damaging loss of something valuable: *a haemorrhage of highly qualified teachers.* • **v. 1** suffer a haemorrhage. **2** expend in large amounts, seemingly uncontrollably.

– DERIVATIVES **haemorrhagic** /ˌhɛməˈradʒɪk/ adj.

– ORIGIN C17: alt. of obs. *haemorrhagy*, via L. from Gk *haimorrhagia*, from *haima* 'blood' + the stem of *rhēgnunai* 'burst'.

**haemorrhoid** /ˈhɛmərɔɪd/ (US **hemorrhoid**) • **n.** (usu. **haemorrhoids**) a swollen vein or group of veins (piles) in the region of the anus.

– DERIVATIVES **haemorrhoidal** adj.

– ORIGIN ME: via OFr. and L. from Gk *haimorrhoides (phlebes)* 'bleeding (veins)', from *haima* 'blood' + an element rel. to *rhein* 'to flow'.

**haemostasis** /ˌhiːmə(ʊ)ˈsteɪsɪs/ (US **hemostasis**) • **n.** Medicine the stopping of a flow of blood.

– DERIVATIVES **haemostatic** adj.

**haemostat** /ˈhiːməstat/ (US **hemostat**) • **n.** Medicine an instrument for preventing blood flow by compression of a blood vessel.

– DERIVATIVES **haemostatic** adj.

**haere mai** /ˌhʌɪrə ˈmʌɪ/ • **exclam.** used as a Maori greeting.

– ORIGIN Maori, lit. 'come hither'.

**hafiz** /ˈhɑːfɪz/ • **n.** a Muslim who knows the Koran by heart.

– ORIGIN Pers., from Arab. *ḥāfiẓ* 'guardian', from *ḥafiẓa* 'guard, know by heart'.

**hafnium** /ˈhafnɪəm/ • **n.** the chemical element of atomic number 72, a hard silver-grey metal resembling zirconium. (Symbol: **Hf**)

– ORIGIN 1920s: from *Hafnia*, Latinized form of Dan. *Havn*, former name of Copenhagen.

**haft** /hɑːft/ • **n.** the handle of a knife, axe, or spear. • **v.** [often as adj. **hafted**] provide with a haft.

– ORIGIN OE *hæft*, of Gmc origin: rel. to **HEAVE**.

**Haftorah** /hɑːfˈtəʊrɑː/ (also **Haphtarah**, **Haphtorah**) • **n.** (pl. **Haftoroth** /-rəʊt/) Judaism a short reading from the Prophets following the reading from the Law in a synagogue.

– ORIGIN from Heb. *hapṭārāh* 'dismissal'.

**Hag.** • **abbrev.** Haggai (in biblical references).

**hag**[1] • **n.** a witch. ➤ an ugly old woman.

– DERIVATIVES **haggish** adj.

– ORIGIN ME: perh. from OE *hægtesse*, *hegtes*, of unknown ultimate origin.

**hag**[2] • **n.** Scottish & N. English a soft place on a moor or a firm place in a bog.

– ORIGIN ME: from ON *hǫgg* 'gap', from *hǫggva* 'hack, hew'.

**hagfish** • **n.** (pl. same or **-fishes**) a primitive jawless marine fish with a slimy eel-like body, a slit-like mouth, and a rasping tongue used for feeding on dead or dying fish. [*Myxine* and other genera, family Myxinidae.]

**Haggadah** /həˈgɑːdə, hagaˈdɑː/ • **n.** (pl. **Haggadoth** or **Haggadot** /-dəʊt/) Judaism **1** the text recited at the Seder on the first two nights of the Passover. **2** a legend or anecdote used to illustrate a point of the Law in the Talmud. ➤ this (non-legal) element of the Talmud.

– DERIVATIVES **Haggadic** /-ˈgadɪk, -ˈgɑːdɪk/ adj. **Haggadist** n.

– ORIGIN from Heb. *Haggāḏāh*, 'tale, parable', from *higgīḏ* 'tell, expound'.

**haggard** • **adj. 1** looking exhausted and unwell. **2** (of a hawk) caught and trained as an adult. • **n.** a haggard hawk.

– DERIVATIVES **haggardly** adv. **haggardness** n.

– ORIGIN C16: from Fr. *hagard*; perh. rel. to **HEDGE**.

**haggis** • **n.** (pl. same) a Scottish dish consisting of seasoned sheep's or calf's offal mixed with suet and oatmeal, boiled in a bag traditionally made from the animal's stomach.

– ORIGIN ME: prob. from earlier *hag* 'hack, hew', from ON *hǫggva*.

**haggle** • **v.** dispute or bargain persistently, especially over a price. • **n.** a period of haggling.

– DERIVATIVES **haggler** n.

– ORIGIN C16 (in the sense 'hack, mangle'): from ON *hǫggva* 'hew'.

**hagio-** • **comb. form** relating to saints or holiness: *hagiographer.*

– ORIGIN from Gk *hagios* 'holy'.

**Hagiographa** /ˌhagɪˈɒgrəfə/ • **pl. n.** the twelve books of the bible comprising the last of the three major divisions of the Hebrew scriptures, other than the Law and the Prophets.

– ORIGIN via late L. from Gk.

**hagiographer** /ˌhagɪˈɒgrəfə/ • **n. 1** a writer of the lives of the saints. **2** Theology a writer of any of the Hagiographa.

**hagiography** /ˌhagɪˈɒgrəfi/ • **n. 1** the writing of the lives of saints. **2** a biography idealizing its subject.

– DERIVATIVES **hagiographic** adj. **hagiographical** adj.

**hagiolatry** /ˌhagɪˈɒlətri/ • **n.** the worship of saints.

**hagiology** /ˌhagɪˈɒlədʒi/ • **n.** literature concerned with the lives and legends of saints.

– DERIVATIVES **hagiological** adj. **hagiologist** n.

**hag-ridden** • **adj.** afflicted by nightmares or anxieties.

**hah** • **exclam.** variant spelling of **HA**[1].

**ha-ha** • **n.** a ditch with a wall on its inner side below ground level, forming a boundary to a park or garden without interrupting the view.

– ORIGIN C18: from Fr., said to be from the cry of surprise on encountering such an obstacle.

**ha ha** • **exclam.** used to represent laughter.

– ORIGIN natural utterance: first recorded in OE.

**haham** /ˈhɑːhəm/ (also **chacham**) • **n.** a spiritual leader among Sephardic Jews, or a person learned in Jewish law.

– ORIGIN from Heb. *ḥāḵām* 'wise'.

**Haida** /ˈhʌɪdə/ • **n.** (pl. same or **Haidas**) **1** a member of an American Indian people living on the Pacific coast of Canada. **2** the language of this people.

– ORIGIN the name in Haida, lit. 'people'.

**haik** /heɪk, ˈhɑːɪk/ (also **haick**) • **n.** a large outer wrap

worn by people from North Africa.
– ORIGIN C18: from Arab. *ḥā'ik*.

**haiku** /'hʌɪkuː/ ● **n.** (pl. same or **haikus**) a Japanese poem of seventeen syllables, in three lines of five, seven, and five.
– ORIGIN Japanese, contr. of *haikai no ku* 'light verse'.

**hail**[1] ● **n.** **1** pellets of frozen rain falling in showers from cumulonimbus clouds. **2** a large number of things hurled forcefully through the air. ● **v.** (**it hails, it is hailing**, etc.) hail falls.
– ORIGIN OE *hagol, hægl* (n.), *hagalian* (v.), of Gmc origin.

**hail**[2] ● **v.** **1** call out to (someone) to attract attention. ➤ signal for (a taxi). **2** acclaim enthusiastically as something: *he has been hailed as the new James Dean.* **3** (**hail from**) have one's home or origins in. ● **exclam.** archaic expressing greeting or acclaim. ● **n.** a call to attract attention.
– PHRASES **within hail** within earshot.
– DERIVATIVES **hailer** n.
– ORIGIN ME: from the obs. adj. *hail* 'healthy' (used in greetings and toasts), from ON *heill*, rel. to **HALE**[1] and **WHOLE**.

**hail-fellow-well-met** ● **adj.** showing excessive familiarity.

**Hail Mary** ● **n.** (pl. **Hail Marys**) a prayer to the Virgin Mary used chiefly by Roman Catholics.

**hailstone** ● **n.** a pellet of hail.

**hair** ● **n.** **1** any of the fine thread-like strands growing from the skin of mammals and other animals, or from the epidermis of a plant. ➤ such strands collectively, especially those on a person's head. **2** a very small quantity or extent.
– PHRASES **hair of the dog** informal an alcoholic drink taken to cure a hangover. [from *hair of the dog that bit you*, formerly recommended as an efficacious remedy for the bite of a mad dog.] **a hair's breadth** a very small margin. **in** (or **out of**) **someone's hair** informal burdening (or ceasing to burden) someone. **keep your hair on!** Brit. informal stay calm. **let one's hair down** informal behave wildly or uninhibitedly. **make someone's hair stand on end** alarm someone. **not turn a hair** remain apparently unmoved. **split hairs** make overfine distinctions.
– DERIVATIVES **-haired** adj. **hairless** adj.
– ORIGIN OE *hǣr*, of Gmc origin.

**hairball** ● **n.** a ball of hair which collects in the stomach of a cat or similar animal as a result of the animal licking its coat.

**hairband** ● **n.** a band for securing or tying back one's hair.

**hairbrush** ● **n.** a brush for smoothing one's hair.

**haircloth** ● **n.** stiff cloth with a cotton or linen warp and horsehair weft.

**haircut** ● **n.** **1** the style in which someone's hair is cut. **2** an act of cutting someone's hair.

**hairdo** ● **n.** (pl. **-os**) informal the style of a woman's hair.

**hairdresser** ● **n.** a person who cuts and styles hair.
– DERIVATIVES **hairdressing** n.

**hairdryer** (also **hairdrier**) ● **n.** an electrical device for drying the hair with warm air.

**hair grass** ● **n.** a slender-stemmed grass of temperate and cool regions. [*Deschampsia*, *Aira*, and other genera.]

**hairgrip** ● **n.** Brit. a flat hairpin with the ends close together.

**hairline** ● **n.** **1** the edge of a person's hair. **2** [as modifier] very thin or fine: *a hairline fracture.*

**hairnet** ● **n.** a fine mesh for confining the hair.

**hairpiece** ● **n.** a patch or bunch of false hair used to augment a person's natural hair.

**hairpin** ● **n.** a U-shaped pin for fastening the hair.

**hairpin bend** ● **n.** Brit. a sharp U-shaped bend in a road.

**hair-raising** ● **adj.** terrifying.

**hair shirt** ● **n.** a shirt of haircloth, formerly worn by penitents and ascetics.
– DERIVATIVES **hair-shirted** adj.

**hairslide** ● **n.** Brit. a clip for keeping a woman's hair in position.

**hair-splitting** ● **n.** the action of making overfine distinctions.
– DERIVATIVES **hair-splitter** n.

**hairspray** ● **n.** a solution sprayed on to hair to keep it in place.

**hairspring** ● **n.** a slender flat coiled spring regulating the movement of the balance wheel in a watch.

**hairstreak** ● **n.** a butterfly with a narrow streak or row of dots on the underside of the hindwing. [*Callophrys rubi* (**green hairstreak**) and other species.]

**hairstyle** ● **n.** a way in which someone's hair is cut or arranged.
– DERIVATIVES **hairstyling** n. **hairstylist** n.

**hair trigger** ● **n.** a trigger of a firearm set for release at the slightest pressure.

**hair worm** ● **n.** a long slender worm related to the nematodes, the larvae being parasites of arthropods. [Phylum Nematomorpha.]

**hairy** ● **adj.** (**-ier, -iest**) **1** covered with hair. ➤ having the feel of hair. **2** informal alarming and difficult.
– DERIVATIVES **hairily** adv. **hairiness** n.

**Haitian** /'heɪʃɪən, -ʃ(ə)n/ ● **n.** **1** a native or inhabitant of Haiti. **2** (also **Haitian Creole**) the French-based Creole language spoken in Haiti. ● **adj.** of or relating to Haiti, its inhabitants, or their language.

**haji** /'hadʒiː/ (also **hajji**) ● **n.** (pl. **hajis**) a Muslim who has been to Mecca as a pilgrim.
– ORIGIN from Pers. and Turk. *ḥājjī, ḥājī*, from Arab. *ḥajj* (see **HAJJ**).

**hajj** /hadʒ/ (also **haj**) ● **n.** the pilgrimage to Mecca which all Muslims are expected to make at least once.
– ORIGIN from Arab. (*al-*) *ḥajj* '(the Great) Pilgrimage'.

**haka** /'hɑːkə/ ● **n.** a Maori ceremonial war dance involving chanting.
– ORIGIN from Maori.

**hake** ● **n.** a large-headed elongated food fish with long jaws and strong teeth. [*Merluccius merluccius* and other species.]
– ORIGIN ME: perh. from OE *haca* 'hook'.

**Hakenkreuz** /'hɑːk(ə)nˌkrɔɪts, German 'hɑːkənˌkrɔyts/ ● **n.** a swastika, especially as a Nazi symbol.
– ORIGIN Ger., from *Haken* 'hook' + *Kreuz* 'cross'.

**hakim** /ha'kiːm/ ● **n.** **1** a physician using traditional remedies in India and Muslim countries. **2** a judge or ruler in India and Muslim countries.
– ORIGIN from Arab. *ḥakīm* 'wise man, physician, ruler'.

**Hakka** /'hakə/ ● **n.** **1** a member of a people of SE China who migrated from the north during the 12th century. **2** the dialect of Chinese spoken by this people.
– ORIGIN from Chin. (Cantonese dial.) *haàk ka* 'stranger'.

**Halacha** /ˌhalɑː'xɑː, hə'lɑːkə/ (also **Halakah**) ● **n.** Jewish law and jurisprudence, based on the Talmud.
– DERIVATIVES **Halachic** adj.
– ORIGIN from Heb. *hălāḵāh* 'law'.

**halal** /hə'lɑːl/ ● **adj.** denoting or relating to meat prepared as prescribed by Muslim law. ● **n.** halal meat.
– ORIGIN C19: from Arab. *ḥalāl* 'according to religious law'.

**halala** /hə'lɑːlə/ ● **n.** (pl. same or **halalas**) a monetary unit of Saudi Arabia, equal to one hundredth of a rial.
– ORIGIN from Arab.

**halation** /hə'leɪʃ(ə)n/ ● **n.** the spreading of light to form a fog round the edges of a bright image in a photograph or on a television screen.
– ORIGIN C19: formed irregularly from **HALO** + **-ATION**.

**halberd** /'halbəːd/ (also **halbert**) ● **n.** historical a combined spear and battleaxe.
– ORIGIN C15: from Fr. *hallebarde*, from Ital. *alabarda*, from Mid. High Ger. *helmbarde* (from *helm* 'handle' + *barde* 'hatchet').

**halberdier** /ˌhalbə'dɪə/ ● **n.** historical a man armed with a halberd.

**halcyon** /'halsɪən, -ʃ(ə)n/ ● **adj.** denoting a past time that was idyllically happy and peaceful. ● **n.** **1** a tropical Asian and African kingfisher with brightly coloured plumage. [Genus *Halcyon*: many species.] **2** a mythical bird said to breed in a nest floating at sea, charming the wind and waves into calm.

– ORIGIN ME: via L. from Gk *alkuōn* 'kingfisher' (also *halkuōn*, by assoc. with *hals* 'sea' and *kuōn* 'conceiving').

**haldi** /ˈhʌldi/ • **n.** Indian term for **TURMERIC**.
– ORIGIN via Hindi from Sanskrit *haridrā*.

**hale**[1] • **adj.** (of an old person) strong and healthy.
– ORIGIN OE, northern var. of *hāl* 'whole'.

**hale**[2] • **v.** archaic haul.
– ORIGIN ME: from OFr. *haler*, from ON *hala*.

**haler** /ˈhɑːlə/ • **n.** (pl. same or **haleru** /ˈhɑːləruː/) a monetary unit of the Czech Republic and Slovakia, equal to one hundredth of a koruna.
– ORIGIN from Czech *haléř*, from Mid. High Ger. *haller*, from *Schwäbisch Hall*, a Ger. town where coins were minted.

**half** • **n.** (pl. **halves**) **1** either of two equal or corresponding parts into which something is or can be divided. ➤ either of two equal periods into which a sports game or performance is divided. **2** Brit. informal half a pint of beer. **3** informal a half-price fare or ticket. **4** Golf a score for a hole that is the same as one's opponent's. **5** a halfback. • **predet. & pron.** an amount equal to a half. • **adj.** forming a half. • **adv.** to the extent of half. ➤ partly: *half-cooked*.
– PHRASES **half a chance** informal the slightest opportunity. **the half of it** [usu. with neg.] informal the most important part or aspect. **half one** (**two**, etc.) informal way of saying ***half past one (two***, etc.). **half past one** (**two**, etc.) thirty minutes after one (two, etc.) o'clock. **not do things by halves** do things thoroughly or extravagantly. **not half 1** not nearly: *he is not half such a fool as they thought*. **2** informal not at all: *the players are not half bad*. **3** Brit. informal to an extreme degree: *she didn't half flare up!* **too —— by half** excessively ——: *too superstitious by half*.
– ORIGIN OE *half*, *healf*, of Gmc origin.

**half a crown** • **n.** another term for **HALF-CROWN**.

**half a dozen** • **n.** another term for **HALF-DOZEN**.

**half-and-half** • **adv. & adj.** in equal parts. • **n.** N. Amer. a mixture of milk and cream.

**half-arsed** • **adj.** vulgar slang incompetent; inadequate.

**halfback** • **n.** a player in a ball game whose position is between the forwards and fullbacks.

**half-baked** • **adj.** incompetently planned or considered.

**halfbeak** • **n.** a slender coastal fish related to the flying fishes, with the lower jaw lengthened into a beak. [*Euleptorhamphus viridis* and other species.]

**half binding** • **n.** a type of bookbinding in which the spine and corners are bound in a different material to the rest of the cover.
– DERIVATIVES **half-bound** adj.

**half blood** • **n. 1** the relationship between people having one parent in common. ➤ a person related to another in this way. **2** offensive another term for **HALF-BREED**.
– DERIVATIVES **half-blooded** adj.

**half board** • **n.** Brit. provision of bed, breakfast, and a main meal at a hotel or guest house.

**half-boot** • **n.** a boot reaching up to the calf.

**half-breed** • **n.** offensive a person of mixed race.

**half-brother** (or **half-sister**) • **n.** a brother (or sister) with whom one has only one parent in common.

**half-caste** • **n.** offensive a person of mixed race.

**half-century** • **n. 1** a period of fifty years. **2** a score of fifty in a sporting event, especially cricket.

**half-cock** • **n.** the partly raised position of the cock of a gun.
– PHRASES **at half-cock 1** (of a gun) with the cock partly raised. **2** when only partly ready.
– DERIVATIVES **half-cocked** adj.

**half-crown** (also **half a crown**) • **n.** a former British coin and monetary unit equal to two shillings and sixpence (12½p).

**half-cut** • **adj.** Brit. informal drunk.

**half-dozen** (also **half a dozen**) • **n.** a group of six.

**half-duplex** • **adj.** (of a communications system or computer circuit) allowing the transmission of signals in both directions but not simultaneously.

**half-hardy** • **adj.** (of a plant) able to grow outdoors except in severe frost.

**half-hearted** • **adj.** without enthusiasm or energy.
– DERIVATIVES **half-heartedly** adv. **half-heartedness** n.

**half hitch** • **n.** a knot formed by passing the end of a rope round its standing part and then through the loop.

**half holiday** • **n.** a half day taken as a holiday, especially at school.

**half-hose** • **n.** archaic socks.

**half-hour** • **n. 1** (also **half an hour**) a period of thirty minutes. **2** a point in time thirty minutes after a full hour of the clock.
– DERIVATIVES **half-hourly** adj. & adv.

**half-hunter** • **n.** a pocket watch with a small opening in the cover allowing one to read the approximate time.

**half-inch** • **n.** a unit of length half as large as an inch. • **v.** Brit. informal steal. [1920s: rhyming sl. for 'pinch'.]

**half landing** • **n.** Brit. a landing where a flight of stairs turns through 180 degrees.

**half-lap** • **n.** another term for **LAP JOINT**.

**half-length** • **n.** a painting or sculpture of a person down to their waist.

**half-life** • **n. 1** the time taken for the radioactivity of an isotope to fall to half its original value. **2** the time required for any specified property to decrease by half.

**half-light** • **n.** dim light, as at dusk.

**half mast** • **n. 1** a position of a flag halfway down its mast, as a mark of respect for a person who has died. **2** humorous a position lower than normal, especially for clothes.

**half measure** • **n.** an inadequate action or policy.

**half-moon** • **n. 1** the moon when only half its surface is visible from the earth. **2** a semicircular or crescent-shaped object.

**half nelson** • **n.** see **NELSON**.

**half note** • **n.** Music, chiefly N. Amer. a minim.

**halfpenny** /ˈheɪpni/ (also **ha'penny**) • **n.** (pl. **-pennies** (for separate coins); **-pence** (for a sum of money) /ˈheɪp(ə)ns/) a former British coin equal to half an old or new penny.

**halfpennyworth** /ˈheɪpəθ, ˈheɪpnɪˌwəθ/ (also **ha'p'orth**) • **n.** Brit. **1** as much as could be bought for a halfpenny. **2** [usu. with neg.] (**ha'p'orth**) informal a negligible amount.

**half-pie** • **adj.** NZ informal imperfect; mediocre.
– ORIGIN *pie* perh. from Maori *pai* 'good'.

**half plate** • **n.** Brit. a photographic plate measuring 4¾ × 6½ inches (*c*.16.5 × 10.8 cm).

**half relief** • **n.** a method of moulding, carving, or stamping a design in which figures project to half their true proportions.

**half seas over** • **adj.** Brit. informal, dated fairly drunk.

**half-sovereign** • **n.** a former British gold coin worth ten shillings (50p).

**half step** • **n.** Music a semitone.

**half-term** • **n.** Brit. a short holiday halfway through a school term.

**half-tester** • **n.** historical a canopy extending over half the length of a bed.

**half-timbered** • **adj.** having walls with a timber frame and a brick or plaster filling.
– DERIVATIVES **half-timbering** n.

**half-time** • **n.** a short interval between two halves of a game.

**half-title** • **n.** the title of a book, printed on the right-hand page before the title page. ➤ the title of a section of a book printed on the right-hand page before it.

**half-tone** • **n. 1** a reproduction of an image in which the tones of grey or colour are produced by variously sized dots. **2** Music, chiefly N. Amer. a semitone.

**half-track** • **n.** a vehicle with wheels at the front and caterpillar tracks at the rear.

**half-truth** • **n.** a statement conveying only part of the truth.

**half-volley** • **n.** (chiefly in tennis and soccer) a strike or kick of the ball immediately after it bounces.

**halfway** • **adv. & adj. 1** at or to a point equidistant between two others. **2** [as adv.] to some extent: *halfway decent*.

**halfway house** • n. **1** the halfway point in a progression. **2** a compromise. **3** a centre for rehabilitating former prisoners or psychiatric patients. **4** historical an inn midway between two towns.

**halfwit** • n. informal a stupid person.
– DERIVATIVES **half-witted** adj. **half-wittedly** adv. **half-wittedness** n.

**half-yearly** • adj. & adv. at intervals of six months.

**halibut** /ˈhalɪbət/ • n. (pl. same) a large marine flatfish, used as food. [*Hippoglossus hippoglossus* (N. Atlantic), *H. stenolepis* (N. Pacific), and other species.]
– ORIGIN ME: from *haly* 'holy' + obs. *butt* 'flatfish' (because it was often eaten on holy days).

**halide** /ˈheɪlʌɪd/ • n. Chemistry a binary compound of a halogen with another element or group.

**halite** /ˈhalʌɪt/ • n. sodium chloride as a mineral; rock salt.
– ORIGIN C19: from Gk *hals* 'salt' + **-ITE**[1].

**halitosis** /ˌhalɪˈtəʊsɪs/ • n. unpleasant-smelling breath.
– ORIGIN C19: from L. *halitus* 'breath' + **-OSIS**.

**hall** • n. **1** the room or space just inside the front entrance of a house. ➤N. Amer. a passage in a building. **2** a large room for meetings, concerts, etc. ➤the dining room of a college, university, or school. ➤the principal living room of a medieval house. **3** (also **hall of residence**) chiefly Brit. a university building in which students live. **4** Brit. a large country house. **5** the building of a guild.
– ORIGIN OE *hall*, *heall*; of Gmc origin.

**Hall effect** • n. Physics the production of a potential difference across an electrical conductor when a magnetic field is applied perpendicular to the current direction.
– ORIGIN C20: named after the Amer. physicist E. H. *Hall*.

**hallelujah** /ˌhalɪˈluːjə/ (also **alleluia**) • exclam. God be praised. • n. an utterance of the word 'hallelujah'. ➤a piece of music or church liturgy containing this.
– ORIGIN OE, via eccles. L. *alleluia* from Gk *allēlouia*, or directly from Heb. *hallĕlūyāh* 'praise ye the Lord'.

**hallmark** • n. **1** a mark stamped on articles of gold, silver, or platinum by the British assay offices, certifying purity. **2** a distinctive feature, especially of excellence. • v. **1** stamp with a hallmark. **2** designate as distinctive.
– ORIGIN C18: from *Goldsmiths' Hall* in London, where articles were tested and stamped.

**hallo** • exclam. variant spelling of **HELLO**.

**Hall of Fame** • n. chiefly N. Amer. the group of people who have excelled in a particular sphere.

**halloo** • exclam. used to incite dogs to the chase during a hunt. ➤used to attract someone's attention. • n. a cry of 'halloo'. • v. (**halloos**, **hallooed**) cry or shout 'halloo'.
– ORIGIN C16: prob. from the rare v. *hallow* 'pursue or urge on with shouts', from imitative OFr. *haloer*.

**halloumi** /həˈluːmi/ • n. a firm white Cypriot cheese made from goats' or ewes' milk, used especially in cooked dishes.
– ORIGIN Egyptian Arab. *ḥalūm*, prob. from Arab. *ḥaluma* 'to be mild'.

**hallow** /ˈhaləʊ/ • v. **1** make holy; consecrate. **2** honour as holy. ➤[as adj. **hallowed**] greatly revered. • n. archaic a saint or holy person.
– ORIGIN OE *hālgian* (v.), *hālga* (n.), of Gmc origin; rel. to **HOLY**.

**Halloween** (also **Hallowe'en**) • n. the night of 31 October, the eve of All Saints' Day.
– ORIGIN C18: contr. of *All Hallow Even* (see **HALLOW**, **EVEN**[2]).

**hall porter** • n. Brit. a concierge or person who carries guests' luggage in a hotel.

**hallstand** (US **hall tree**) • n. a coat stand in the hall of a house.

**halluces** plural form of **HALLUX**.

**hallucinate** /həˈluːsɪneɪt/ • v. experience a seemingly real perception of something not actually present.
– DERIVATIVES **hallucinant** adj. & n. **hallucination** n. **hallucinator** n. **hallucinatory** adj.
– ORIGIN C17: from L. *hallucinat-*, *hallucinari* 'go astray in thought', from Gk *alussein* 'be uneasy or distraught'.

**hallucinogen** /həˈluːsɪnədʒ(ə)n/ • n. a drug causing hallucinations.
– DERIVATIVES **hallucinogenic** adj.

**hallux** /ˈhaləks/ • n. (pl. **halluces** /-jʊsiːz, -ləsiːz/) **1** Anatomy the big toe. **2** Zoology the innermost digit of the hind foot of vertebrates.
– ORIGIN C19: mod. L. alt. of med. L. *allex*, L. *hallus*.

**hallway** • n. another term for **HALL** (in sense 1).

**halma** /ˈhalmə/ • n. a game played by two or four people using a board of 256 squares, with pieces advancing by being moved over other pieces into vacant squares.
– ORIGIN C19: from Gk, lit. 'leap'.

**halo** /ˈheɪləʊ/ • n. (pl. **-oes** or **-os**) **1** (in a painting) a circle of light surrounding the head of a holy person. **2** a circle of light round the sun or moon caused by refraction through ice crystals in the atmosphere. • v. (**-oes**, **-oed**) surround with or as if with a halo.
– ORIGIN C16: from med. L., from L. *halos*, from Gk *halōs* 'disc of the sun or moon'.

**halo-** /ˈheɪləʊ/ • comb. form **1** relating to salinity: *halophile*. [from Gk *hals*, *halo-* 'salt'.] **2** representing **HALOGEN**.

**halocarbon** • n. Chemistry a compound in which the hydrogen of a hydrocarbon is replaced by halogens.

**halo effect** • n. the tendency for an impression created in one area to influence opinion in another area.

**halogen** /ˈhalədʒ(ə)n, ˈheɪl-/ • n. **1** Chemistry any of the group of reactive, non-metallic elements fluorine, chlorine, bromine, iodine, and astatine. **2** [as modifier] denoting lamps and radiant heat sources using a filament surrounded by halogen vapour.
– DERIVATIVES **halogenic** adj.
– ORIGIN C19: from Gk *hals*, *halo-* 'salt' + **-GEN**.

**halogenate** /həˈlɒdʒɪneɪt/ • v. [usu. as adj. **halogenated**] Chemistry introduce one or more halogen atoms into (a compound or molecule).
– DERIVATIVES **halogenation** n.

**halon** /ˈheɪlɒn/ • n. any of a number of unreactive gaseous compounds of carbon with halogens, used in fire extinguishers.
– ORIGIN 1960s: from **HALOGEN** + **-ON**.

**haloperidol** /ˌhalə(ʊ)ˈpɛrɪdɒl, ˌheɪlə(ʊ)-/ • n. Medicine a synthetic antidepressant used chiefly in the treatment of psychotic conditions.
– ORIGIN 1960s: blend of **HALOGEN** and **PIPERIDINE** + **-OL**.

**halophile** /ˈhalə(ʊ)fʌɪl, ˈheɪl-/ • n. Ecology an organism that grows in or can tolerate saline conditions.
– DERIVATIVES **halophilic** adj.

**halophyte** /ˈhaləfʌɪt, ˈheɪlə-/ • n. Botany a plant adapted to growing in saline conditions.

**halothane** /ˈhalə(ʊ)θeɪn/ • n. Medicine a volatile synthetic organic compound used as a general anaesthetic.
– ORIGIN 1950s: blend of **HALOGEN** and **ETHANE**.

**halt**[1] • v. bring or come to an abrupt stop. • n. **1** a suspension of movement or activity. **2** Brit. a minor stopping place on a local railway line.
– PHRASES **call a halt** order a stop.
– ORIGIN C16: orig. in the phr. *make halt*, from Ger. *haltmachen*, from *halten* 'to hold'.

**halt**[2] archaic • adj. lame. • v. walk with a limp.
– ORIGIN OE *healtian* (v.), *halt*, *healt* (adj.), of Gmc origin.

**halter** • n. **1** a rope or strap placed around the head of an animal and used to lead or tether it. **2** archaic a noose for hanging a person. **3** a strap passing behind the neck by which the bodice of a sleeveless dress or top is held in place. • v. put a halter on (an animal). ➤archaic hang (someone).
– ORIGIN OE *hælftre*, of Gmc origin, meaning 'something to hold things by'; rel. to **HELVE**.

**halter-break** • v. accustom (a horse) to wearing a halter.

**halteres** /halˈtɪəz/ • pl. n. Entomology a pair of knobbed filaments that replace the hindwings of a two-winged fly and act as balancing organs during flight.
– ORIGIN C16 (orig. denoting weights held to give impetus when jumping): from Gk *haltēres*, from *hallesthai* 'to leap'.

**halter neck** • n. a style of neckline incorporating a halter.

**halting** • adj. slow and hesitant.
– DERIVATIVES **haltingly** adv.

**halva** /ˈhalvɑː, -və/ (also **halvah**) • n. a Middle Eastern sweet made of sesame flour and honey.
– ORIGIN Yiddish, or from Turk. *helva*, from Arab. and Pers. *ḥalwā* 'sweetmeat'.

**halve** • v. **1** divide into two parts of equal size. ➤share (something) equally with another person. **2** reduce or be reduced by half. **3** Golf use the same number of strokes as an opponent and thus draw (a hole or match). **4** [usu. as noun **halving**] fit (crossing timbers) together by cutting out half the thickness of each.
– ORIGIN ME: from **HALF**.

**halvers** /ˈhɑːvəz/ • pl. n. (in phr. **go halvers**) informal, chiefly Scottish, N. English, & N. Amer. go halves.

**halves** plural form of **HALF**.

**halwa** /ˈhalwɑː/ (also **halwah**) • n. a sweet Indian dish with carrots or semolina, almonds, and cardamom.
– ORIGIN from Arab., lit. 'sweetmeat'.

**halyard** /ˈhaljəd/ • n. a rope used for raising and lowering a sail, yard, or flag on a ship.
– ORIGIN ME *halier*, from **HALE**[2] + **-IER**; the change in the ending was due to assoc. with **YARD**[1].

**ham**[1] • n. **1** meat from the upper part of a pig's leg salted and dried or smoked. **2** (**hams**) the back of the thigh or the thighs and buttocks.
– ORIGIN OE *ham*, *hom* (denoting the back of the knee), from a Gmc base meaning 'be crooked'.

**ham**[2] • n. **1** an inexpert or unsubtle actor or piece of acting. **2** (also **radio ham**) informal an amateur radio operator. • v. (**hammed**, **hamming**) (usu. **ham it up**) informal overact.
– ORIGIN C19: perh. from the first syllable of **AMATEUR**; cf. the US sl. term *hamfatter* 'inexpert performer'.

**hamadryad** /ˌhaməˈdrʌɪəd, -ad/ • n. **1** Greek & Roman Mythology a nymph who lives in a tree and dies when it dies. **2** another term for **KING COBRA**.
– ORIGIN via L. from Gk *Hamadruas*, from *hama* 'together' + *drus* 'tree'.

**hamadryas** /ˌhaməˈdrʌɪəs, -as/ • n. a large Arabian and NE African baboon, the male of which has a silvery-grey cape of hair and a naked red face and rump. [*Papio hamadryas*.]
– ORIGIN 1930s: mod. L. (see **HAMADRYAD**).

**hamamelis** /ˌhaməˈmiːlɪs/ • n. the witch hazel.
– ORIGIN C18: mod. L. (genus name), from Gk *hamamēlis* 'medlar'.

**hamartia** /həˈmɑːtɪə/ • n. a fatal flaw leading to the downfall of a tragic hero or heroine.
– ORIGIN C18: Gk, 'fault, failure, guilt'.

**hamate bone** /ˈheɪmət/ • n. Anatomy a hook-shaped carpal bone to which muscles of the little finger are attached.
– ORIGIN C18: from L. *hamatus* 'hooked'.

**hamba** /ˈhambə/ • v. S. African go away.
– ORIGIN from Xhosa and Zulu.

**hambone** /ˈhambəʊn/ • n. N. Amer. informal an inferior actor or performer.

**hamburger** • n. a round patty of minced beef, fried or grilled and typically served in a bread roll.
– ORIGIN C19: from Ger., from *Hamburg*, a city in northern Germany.

**hamerkop** • n. variant spelling of **HAMMERKOP**.

**hames** /heɪmz/ • pl. n. two curved bars forming the collar of a draught horse, to which the traces are attached.
– ORIGIN ME: from MDu.

**ham-fisted** • adj. informal clumsy; awkward.
– DERIVATIVES **ham-fistedly** adv. **ham-fistedness** n.

**ham-handed** • adj. another term for **HAM-FISTED**.
– DERIVATIVES **ham-handedly** adv. **ham-handedness** n.

**Hamite** /ˈhamʌɪt/ • n. a member of a group of North African peoples, including the ancient Egyptians and Berbers, supposedly descended from Ham, son of Noah.

**Hamitic** /həˈmɪtɪk/ • adj. of or denoting a hypothetical language family including Berber and ancient Egyptian.

**Hamito-Semitic** /ˌhamɪtəʊsɪˈmɪtɪk/ • adj. former term for **AFRO-ASIATIC**.

**hamlet** • n. a small village, especially (in Britain) one without a church.
– ORIGIN ME: from OFr. *hamelet*, dimin. of *hamel* 'little village'; rel. to **HOME**.

**hammer** • n. **1** a tool consisting of a heavy metal head mounted at the end of a handle, used for breaking things and driving in nails. ➤an auctioneer's mallet, tapped to indicate a sale. **2** a part of a mechanism that hits another, e.g. one exploding the charge in a gun or striking piano strings. **3** a heavy metal ball attached to a wire for throwing in an athletic contest. **4** another term for **MALLEUS**. • v. **1** hit or beat repeatedly with or as with a hammer. **2** (**hammer away**) work hard and persistently. **3** (**hammer something in/into**) inculcate something forcefully or repeatedly. **4** (**hammer something out**) laboriously work out the details of a plan or agreement. **5** (**hammer something out**) play a tune loudly and unskilfully, especially on the piano. **6** informal utterly defeat. **7** Stock Exchange declare (someone) a defaulter. ➤informal beat down the price of (a stock).
– PHRASES **come** (or **go**) **under the hammer** be sold at an auction. **hammer and tongs** informal enthusiastically or vehemently: *they fought hammer and tongs.*
– DERIVATIVES **hammering** n. **hammerless** adj.
– ORIGIN OE *hamor*, *hamer*, of Gmc origin.

**hammer and sickle** • n. the symbols of the industrial worker and the peasant used as the emblem of the former USSR and of international communism.

**hammer beam** • n. a short wooden beam projecting from a wall to support a principal rafter or one end of an arch.

**hammer drill** • n. a power drill that delivers a rapid succession of blows.

**hammerhead** • n. **1** a shark with flattened blade-like extensions on either side of the head. [Genus *Sphyrna*: several species.] **2** another term for **HAMMERKOP**.

**hammerkop** /ˈhaməkɒp/ (also **hamerkop**) • n. a brown African marshbird related to the storks, with a crest that looks like a backward projection of the head. [*Scopus umbretta*.]
– ORIGIN C19: from Afrik. *hamerkop*, from *hamer* 'hammer' + *kop* 'head'.

**hammerlock** • n. an armlock in which a person's arm is bent up behind their back.

**hammer toe** • n. a toe that is bent permanently downwards, typically as a result of pressure from footwear.

**hammock** • n. a wide strip of canvas or rope mesh suspended by two ends, used as a bed.
– ORIGIN C16 (in the Sp. form *hamaca*): via Sp. from Taino *hamaka*.

**Hammond organ** • n. trademark a type of electronic organ.
– ORIGIN 1930s: named after the Amer. mechanical engineer Laurens *Hammond*.

**hammy** • adj. (**-ier**, **-iest**) **1** informal (of acting or an actor) exaggerated or over-theatrical. **2** (of a hand or thigh) thick and solid.
– DERIVATIVES **hammily** adv. **hamminess** n.

**hamper**[1] • n. a basket with a carrying handle and a hinged lid, used for food, cutlery, etc. on a picnic. ➤Brit. a box containing food and drink for a special occasion.
– ORIGIN ME: from Anglo-Norman Fr. *hanaper* 'case for a goblet', from OFr. *hanap* 'goblet', of Gmc origin.

**hamper**[2] • v. hinder or impede the movement or progress of. • n. Nautical necessary but cumbersome equipment on a ship.
– ORIGIN ME: perh. rel. to Ger. *hemmen* 'restrain'.

**hamster** • n. a burrowing rodent with a short tail and large cheek pouches, native to Europe and North Asia. [*Mesocricetus auratus* (**golden hamster**, often kept as a pet), *Cricetus cricetus* (**common hamster**), and other species.]
– ORIGIN C17: from Ger., from Old High Ger. *hamustro* 'corn-weevil'.

**hamstring** • n. any of five tendons at the back of a person's knee. ➤the great tendon at the back of a quadruped's hock. • v. (past and past part. **hamstrung**) **1** cripple by

cutting the hamstrings. **2** severely restrict; thwart.
– ORIGIN C16: from **HAM**[1] + **STRING**.

**hamulus** /ˈhamjʊləs/ ● n. (pl. **hamuli** /-lʌɪ, -liː/) Anatomy & Zoology a small hook or hook-like projection, especially one of a number linking the fore- and hindwings of a bee or wasp.
– ORIGIN C18: from L., dimin. of *hamus* 'hook'.

**hamza** /ˈhamzə/ ● n. (in Arabic script) a symbol representing a glottal stop.
– ORIGIN Arab., lit. 'compression'.

**Han** /han/ ● n. **1** the Chinese dynasty that ruled almost continuously from 206 BC until AD 220. **2** the dominant ethnic group in China.

**hand** ● n. **1** the end part of the arm beyond the wrist, including the palm, fingers, and thumb. ➤W. Indian a person's arm, including the hand. ➤[as modifier] operated by or held in the hand. ➤[as modifier or in combination] done or made manually. **2** a pointer on a clock or watch indicating the passing of units of time. **3** (**hands**) with reference to someone's power or control: *taking the law into their own hands*. ➤(usu. **a hand**) an active role. ➤(usu. **a hand**) help in doing something. **4** a person engaging in manual labour, especially in a factory, on a farm, or on board a ship. **5** informal a round of applause. **6** the set of cards dealt to a player in a card game. ➤a round or short spell of play in a card game. **7** a person's handwriting. **8** a unit of measurement of a horse's height, equal to 4 inches (10.16 cm). [denoting the breadth of a hand.] **9** a pledge of marriage by a woman. ● v. **1** pick (something) up and give it to (someone). **2** hold the hand of, in order to guide or assist. **3** Sailing take in or furl (a sail).
– PHRASES **all hands on deck** a cry or signal used on board ship to indicate that all crew members are to go on deck. **at hand 1** close by; readily accessible. **2** close in time; about to happen. **at** (or **by**) **the hands** (or **hand**) **of** through the agency of. **by hand** by a person and not a machine. **get** (or **keep**) **one's hand in** become (or remain) practised in something. **give** (or **lend**) **a hand** assist. **hand in glove** in close association. **hand in hand** closely associated; together. **(from) hand to mouth** satisfying only one's immediate needs because of lack of money. **hands down** easily and decisively. **hands-off** not involving or requiring direct intervention. **hands-on** involving or offering active participation. **a hand's turn** [usu. with neg.] informal a stroke of work. **have one's hands tied** informal be unable to act freely. **have to hand it to someone** informal used to acknowledge the merit or achievement of someone. **in hand 1** in progress; requiring immediate attention. **2** ready for use if required. **3** under one's control. ➤(of land) farmed directly by its owner and not let to tenants. **in safe hands** protected by someone trustworthy from harm or damage. **make** (or **lose** or **spend**) **money hand over fist** informal make (or lose or spend) money very rapidly. **off someone's hands** not having to be dealt with by the person specified. **on every hand** all around. **on hand 1** present and available. **2** needing to be dealt with. **on someone's hands 1** under the responsibility of the person specified. **2** at someone's disposal. **on the one** (or **the other**) **hand** used to present factors for (and against). **out of hand 1** not under control. **2** without taking time to think: *they rejected negotiations out of hand*. **a safe pair of hands** denoting someone who is capable or reliable. **set** (or **put**) **one's hand to** start work on. **stay someone's hand** restrain someone from acting. **take a hand** become influential; intervene: *fate was about to take a hand*. **to hand** within easy reach. **turn one's hand to** undertake (an activity different from one's usual occupation). **wait on someone hand and foot** attend to all someone's needs or requests, especially when unreasonable.
– PHRASAL VERBS **hand something down 1** pass something on to a successor. **2** announce something formally or publicly. **hand someone off** Rugby push away a tackling opponent with one's hand. **hand something on** pass something to the next person. **hand something out 1** distribute something among a group of people. **2** impose a penalty or misfortune on someone. **hand over** pass to someone else. **hand something round** (or **around**) offer something to each of a number of people in turn.
– DERIVATIVES **handless** adj.
– ORIGIN OE *hand*, *hond*, of Gmc origin.

**handbag** ● n. Brit. a small bag used by a woman to carry everyday personal items.

**handball** ● n. **1** a game similar to fives, in which the ball is hit with the hand in a walled court. **2** Soccer touching of the ball with the hand or arm, constituting a foul.

**handbasin** ● n. Brit. a washbasin.

**handbell** ● n. a small bell, especially one of a set tuned to a range of notes and played by a group of people.

**handbill** ● n. a small printed advertisement or other notice distributed by hand.

**handbook** ● n. a book giving brief information such as basic facts on a particular subject or instructions for operating a machine.

**handbrake** ● n. a brake operated by hand, used to hold an already stationary vehicle.

**h & c** ● abbrev. Brit. hot and cold (water).

**handcar** ● n. N. Amer. a light railway vehicle propelled by cranks or levers, used by workers inspecting the track.

**handcart** ● n. a small cart pushed or drawn by hand.

**handclap** ● n. a clapping of the hands.

**handcraft** ● v. [usu. as adj. **handcrafted**] make skilfully by hand. ● n. another term for **HANDICRAFT**.

**handcuff** ● n. (**handcuffs**) a pair of lockable linked metal rings for securing a prisoner's wrists. ● v. put handcuffs on.

**-handed** ● comb. form **1** for or involving a specified number of hands: *a two-handed back-hand*. **2** using the hand specified: *right-handed*. **3** having hands as specified: *empty-handed*.
– DERIVATIVES **-handedly** adv. **-handedness** n.

**handful** ● n. (pl. **-fuls**) **1** a quantity that fills the hand. ➤a small number or amount. **2** informal a person who is difficult to deal with or control.

**hand grenade** ● n. a hand-thrown grenade.

**handgrip** ● n. **1** a handle for holding something by. **2** a soft bag with handles.

**handgun** ● n. a gun designed for use by one hand, chiefly either a pistol or a revolver.

**handhold** ● n. something for a hand to grip on.

**handicap** ● n. **1** a condition that markedly restricts a person's ability to function physically, mentally, or socially. **2** a disadvantage imposed on a superior competitor in sports such as golf and horse racing in order to make the chances more equal. ➤the extra weight given as a handicap to a racehorse or other competitor. ➤the number of strokes by which a golfer normally exceeds par for a course. ● v. (**handicapped**, **handicapping**) act as a handicap to; place at a disadvantage.
– PHRASES **out of the handicap** Horse Racing having a handicap rating that would merit carrying a weight below the minimum specified for a race.
– ORIGIN C17: from the phr. *hand in cap*, a game in which players showed acceptance or rejection of a disputed object's valuation by bringing their hands either full or empty out of a cap in which forfeit money had been deposited. In the 18th cent. a similar practice was used to signify agreement or disagreement with an allocation of additional weight to be carried in horse races.

**handicapped** ● adj. having a handicap.

**handicapper** ● n. **1** a person appointed to assess a competitor's handicap. **2** a person or horse having a specified handicap.

**handicraft** ● n. (often **handicrafts**) **1** a particular skill of making decorative domestic or other objects by hand. **2** an object made using a skill of this kind.
– ORIGIN ME: alt. of **HANDCRAFT**, on the pattern of *handiwork*.

**handiwork** ● n. **1** (**one's handiwork**) something that one has made or done. **2** the making of things by hand.
– ORIGIN OE *handgeweorc*, from **HAND** + *geweorc* 'something made', interpreted as *handy* + *work*.

**handjob** ● n. vulgar slang an act of male masturbation.

**handkerchief** /'haŋkətʃɪf/ • **n.** (pl. **handkerchiefs** or **handkerchieves** /-tʃiːvz/) a square of cotton or other material for wiping one's nose.

**handle** • **v. 1** feel or manipulate with the hands. ➤(of a vehicle) respond or behave in a specified way when being driven: *the new model does not handle well.* **2** manage or cope with (a situation, person, or problem). ➤control or manage commercially. **3** deal with. ➤receive or deal in (stolen goods). **4** (**handle oneself**) conduct oneself. • **n. 1** the part by which a thing is held, carried, or controlled. **2** a means of understanding, controlling, or approaching a person or situation: *it'll give people some kind of handle on these issues.* **3** informal the name of a person or place: *that's some handle for a baby.* **4** the feel of goods, especially textiles, when handled. **5** US informal the total amount of money bet over a particular time or at a particular event.
– DERIVATIVES **handleability** /-'bɪlɪti/ n. **handleable** adj. **-handled** adj. **handleless** adj. **handling** n.
– ORIGIN OE *handle* (n.), *handlian* (v.), from **HAND**.

**handlebar** (also **handlebars**) • **n.** the steering bar of a bicycle, motorbike, or other similar vehicle.

**handlebar moustache** • **n.** a wide, thick moustache with the ends curving slightly upwards.

**handler** • **n. 1** a person who handles a particular type of article or commodity. **2** a person who trains or has charge of an animal, in particular a police officer in charge of a dog. **3** a person who trains or manages another person. ➤a person who trains and acts as second to a boxer. ➤a publicity agent.

**handlist** • **n.** a short list of something such as essential reading or the items in a collection.

**handmade** • **adj.** made by hand rather than machine.

**handmaid** • **n. 1** archaic a female servant. **2** a subservient partner or element.

**handmaiden** • **n.** another term for **HANDMAID**.

**hand-me-down** • **n.** a garment or other item that has been passed on from another person.

**handoff** • **n.** American Football an exchange made by handing the ball to a teammate.

**handout** • **n. 1** an amount of money or other aid given to a needy person or organization. **2** a piece of printed information provided free of charge, especially to accompany a lecture or advertise something.

**handover** • **n.** chiefly Brit. an act or instance of handing something over.

**hand-pick** • **v.** [usu. as adj. **hand-picked**] select carefully.

**handprint** • **n.** the mark left by the impression of a hand.

**handpump** • **n.** a pump operated by hand.

**handrail** • **n.** a rail fixed to posts or a wall for people to hold on to for support.

**handsel** • **n. & v.** variant spelling of **HANSEL**.

**handset** • **n. 1** the part of a telephone that is held up to speak into and listen to. **2** a hand-held control device for a piece of electronic equipment.

**hands-free** • **adj.** (especially of a telephone) designed to be operated without the use of the hands.

**handshake** • **n.** an act of shaking a person's hand.
– DERIVATIVES **handshaking** n.

**handsome** • **adj.** (**-er**, **-est**) **1** (of a man) good-looking. ➤(of a woman) striking and imposing rather than conventionally pretty. **2** (of a thing) well made, imposing, and of obvious quality. **3** (of an amount) substantial.
– DERIVATIVES **handsomely** adv. **handsomeness** n.
– ORIGIN ME: from **HAND** + **-SOME**[1]; the original sense was 'easy to handle or use', hence 'apt, clever'.

**handspike** • **n.** historical a wooden rod with an iron tip, used as a lever on board ship and by artillery soldiers.

**handspring** • **n.** a jump through the air on to one's hands followed by another on to one's feet.

**handstand** • **n.** an act of balancing upside down on one's hands.

**handstroke** • **n.** Bell-ringing a pull of the sally of the rope so as to swing the bell through a full circle. Compare with **BACKSTROKE**.

**hand-to-hand** • **adj.** (of fighting) at close quarters.

**handwriting** • **n.** writing with a pen or pencil rather than by typing or printing. ➤a person's particular style of writing.

**handwritten** • **adj.** written with a pen, pencil, or other hand-held implement.

**handy** • **adj.** (**-ier**, **-iest**) **1** convenient to handle or use; useful. **2** ready to hand. ➤placed or occurring conveniently. **3** skilful.
– PHRASES **come in handy** informal turn out to be useful.
– DERIVATIVES **handily** adv. **handiness** n.

**handyman** • **n.** (pl. **-men**) a person employed to do general decorating or domestic repairs.

**hang** • **v.** (past and past part. **hung** except in sense 2) **1** suspend or be suspended from above with the lower part not attached. ➤attach or be attached so as to allow free movement about the point of attachment: *hanging a door.* ➤(of fabric or a garment) fall or drape in a specified way. ➤paste (wallpaper) to a wall. **2** (past and past part. **hanged**) kill or be killed by tying a rope attached from above around the neck and removing the support from beneath the feet (used as a form of capital punishment). **3** attach (meat or game) to a hook and leave it until dry, tender, or high. **4** remain static in the air. ➤be present or imminent, especially oppressively or threateningly. **5** Computing come unexpectedly to a state in which no further operations can be carried out. **6** Baseball deliver (a pitch) which does not change direction and is easily hit by a batter. • **n.** a downward droop or bend. ➤the way in which something hangs or is hung. • **exclam.** dated used in expressions as a mild oath: *well, hang it all!*
– PHRASES **get the hang of** informal learn how to operate or do. **hang fire** delay or be delayed in taking action. **hang one's hat** N. Amer. informal be resident. **hang a left** (or **right**) informal, chiefly N. Amer. make a left (or right) turn. **hang someone out to dry** informal, chiefly N. Amer. leave someone in a difficult or vulnerable situation. **hang ten** ride a surfboard with all ten toes curled over the board's front edge. **hang tough** N. Amer. be or remain inflexible or firmly resolved. **let it all hang out** informal be very relaxed or uninhibited. **not care** (or **give**) **a hang** informal not care at all.
– PHRASAL VERBS **hang around** (or **round** or Brit. **about**) **1** loiter; wait around. **2** (**hang around with**) associate with. **hang back** remain behind. ➤show reluctance to act or move. **hang in** informal, chiefly N. Amer. remain persistent and determined in difficult circumstances. **hang on 1** hold tightly. ➤informal remain firm or resolved. **2** informal wait for a short time. **3** be contingent or dependent on. **4** listen closely to. **hang out** informal spend time relaxing or enjoying oneself. **hang together 1** make sense; be consistent. **2** (of people) help or support one another. **hang up** end a telephone conversation by cutting the connection.
– ORIGIN OE *hangian* (v.), of W. Gmc origin, reinforced by the ON verb *hanga*.

**hangar** /'haŋə/ • **n.** a large building with extensive floor area, typically for housing aircraft.
– DERIVATIVES **hangarage** n.
– ORIGIN C17 (in the sense 'shelter'): from Fr.; prob. from Gmc bases meaning 'hamlet' and 'enclosure'.

**hangdog** • **adj.** having a dejected or guilty appearance; shamefaced.

**hanger**[1] • **n. 1** a person who hangs something. **2** (also **coat hanger**) a shaped piece of wood, plastic, or metal with a hook at the top, for hanging clothes from a rail.

**hanger**[2] • **n.** Brit. a wood on the side of a steep hill.
– ORIGIN OE *hangra*, from *hangian* 'hang'.

**hanger-on** • **n.** (pl. **hangers-on**) a person who associates sycophantically with another person.

**hang-glider** • **n.** an unpowered flying apparatus for a single person, consisting of a frame with a fabric aerofoil stretched over it from which the operator is suspended in a harness, controlling flight by body movement.
– DERIVATIVES **hang-glide** v. **hang-gliding** n.

**hangi** /'haŋi, 'hɑːŋi/ • **n.** NZ a pit in which food is cooked on heated stones. ➤the food or meal cooked in such a pit.
– ORIGIN from Maori.

**hanging** ● n. **1** the practice of hanging condemned people as a form of capital punishment. **2** a decorative piece of fabric hung on the wall of a room or around a bed. ● adj. **1** suspended in the air. **2** situated or designed so as to appear to hang down.

**hanging paragraph** ● n. a paragraph in which all lines except the first are indented.

**hanging valley** ● n. a valley which is cut across by a deeper valley or a cliff.

**hangman** ● n. (pl. **-men**) an executioner who hangs condemned people.

**hangnail** ● n. a piece of torn skin at the root of a fingernail.
– ORIGIN C17: alt. of *agnail* 'painful swelling around a nail', influenced by **HANG**.

**hang-out** ● n. informal a place one lives in or frequently visits.

**hangover** ● n. **1** a severe headache or other after-effects caused by drinking an excess of alcohol. **2** a thing that has survived from the past.

**hang-up** ● n. informal an emotional problem or inhibition.

**hank** ● n. **1** a coil or skein of wool, hair, or other material. **2** a measurement of the length per unit mass of cloth or yarn (equal to 840 yards for cotton yarn and 560 yards for worsted). **3** Sailing a ring for securing a staysail to the stay.
– ORIGIN ME: from ON *hǫnk*; cf. Swed. *hank* 'string' and Dan. *hank* 'handle'.

**hanker** ● v. (**hanker after/for/to do something**) feel a strong desire for or to do something.
– DERIVATIVES **hankerer** n.
– ORIGIN C17: prob. rel. to **HANG**.

**hanky** (also **hankie**) ● n. (pl. **-ies**) informal a handkerchief.

**hanky-panky** ● n. informal, humorous behaviour considered improper but not seriously so.
– ORIGIN C19: perh. an alt. of **HOKEY-POKEY**.

**Hanoverian** /ˌhanə(ʊ)ˈvɪərɪən/ ● adj. of or relating to the royal house of Hanover, who ruled as monarchs in Britain from 1714 (accession of George I) to 1901 (death of Queen Victoria). ● n. **1** (usu. **the Hanoverians**) any of the British sovereigns from George I to Victoria. **2** a medium-built horse of a German breed, developed for use both as a riding horse and in harness.

**Hansard** /ˈhansɑːd, -səd/ ● n. the official verbatim record of debates in the British, Canadian, Australian, or New Zealand parliament.
– ORIGIN C19: named after the Engl. printer Thomas C. *Hansard*.

**Hanse** /ˈhansə/ ● n. a medieval guild of merchants. ➤(**the Hanse**) the Hanseatic League, a powerful medieval association of north German cities.
– DERIVATIVES **Hanseatic** adj.
– ORIGIN ME: from OFr. *hanse* 'guild, company', from Old High Ger. *hansa* 'company, troop'.

**hansel** /ˈhans(ə)l/ (also **handsel**) archaic or US ● n. a gift given at the beginning of the year or the start of an enterprise, supposedly to bring good luck. ● v. (**hanselled, hanselling**; US **hanseled, hanseling**) give a hansel to. ➤inaugurate.
– ORIGIN ME (denoting luck): appar. rel. to OE *handselen* 'giving into a person's hands', and ON *handsal* 'giving of the hand to seal a promise', from **HAND** + an element rel. to **SELL**.

**Hansen's disease** /ˈhans(ə)nz/ ● n. another term for **LEPROSY**.
– ORIGIN 1930s: named after the Norw. physician Gerhard H. A. *Hansen* (1841–1912).

**hansom** /ˈhans(ə)m/ (also **hansom cab**) ● n. historical a two-wheeled horse-drawn cab with space for two inside, with the driver seated behind.
– ORIGIN C19: named after the Engl. architect Joseph A. *Hansom*, who patented it.

**hantavirus** /ˈhantəˌvʌɪrəs/ ● n. a virus of a genus carried by rodents and causing various febrile haemorrhagic diseases, often with kidney damage or failure.
– ORIGIN 1980s: from *Hantaan* (a river in Korea where the virus was first isolated).

**Hants** ● abbrev. Hampshire.

**Hanukkah** /ˈhanʊkə, x-/ (also **Chanukkah**) ● n. an eight-day Jewish festival of lights held in December, commemorating the rededication of the Jewish Temple in Jerusalem in 165 BC after its desecration.
– ORIGIN from Heb. *ḥănukkāh* 'consecration'.

**hanuman** /ˌhʌnʊˈmɑːn/ (also **hanuman langur**) ● n. a pale-coloured langur monkey of the Indian subcontinent, venerated by Hindus. [*Presbytis entellus*, family Cercopithecidae.]

**hap** archaic ● n. luck; fortune. ● v. (**happed, happing**) come about by chance; happen.
– ORIGIN ME: from ON *happ*.

**hapax legomenon** /ˌhapaks lɪˈɡɒmɪnɒn/ ● n. (pl. **hapax legomena** /-mɪnə/) a term of which only one instance of use is recorded.
– ORIGIN C17: Gk, 'a thing said once', from *hapax* 'once' and the passive part. of *legein* 'to say'.

**ha'penny** ● n. variant spelling of **HALFPENNY**.

**haphazard** /hapˈhazəd/ ● adj. lacking order or organization.
– DERIVATIVES **haphazardly** adv. **haphazardness** n.
– ORIGIN C16: from **HAP** + **HAZARD**.

**Haphtarah** /ˌhɑːftɑːˈrɑː/ (also **Haphtorah**) ● n. (pl. **Haphtaroth**, **Haphtoroth** /-rəʊt/) variant spelling of **HAFTORAH**.

**hapless** ● adj. unlucky; unfortunate.
– DERIVATIVES **haplessly** adv. **haplessness** n.
– ORIGIN ME: from **HAP** + **-LESS**.

**haplo-** ● comb. form single; simple: *haploid*.
– ORIGIN from Gk *haploos* 'single'.

**haplodiploid** /ˌhaplə(ʊ)ˈdɪplɔɪd/ ● adj. Biology denoting or possessing a genetic system in which females develop from fertilized (diploid) eggs and males from unfertilized (haploid) ones.

**haplography** /hapˈlɒɡrəfi/ ● n. the inadvertent omission of a repeated letter or letters in writing (e.g. writing *philogy* for *philology*).

**haploid** /ˈhaplɔɪd/ ● adj. Genetics (of a cell or nucleus) having a single set of unpaired chromosomes. Compare with **DIPLOID**.
– DERIVATIVES **haploidy** n.

**haplology** /hapˈlɒlədʒi/ ● n. the omission of one occurrence of a sound or syllable which is repeated within a word (e.g. in *February* pronounced as /ˈfɛbri/).

**ha'p'orth** ● n. variant spelling of **HALFPENNYWORTH**.

**happen** ● v. **1** take place; occur. **2** come about by chance. ➤chance to do something or come about. ➤(**happen on**) come across by chance. ➤used as a polite formula in questions: *do you happen to know who her doctor is?* **3** (**happen to**) be experienced by; befall. ➤become of. ● adv. N. English perhaps; maybe.
– PHRASES **as it happens** actually; as a matter of fact.
– ORIGIN ME (superseding the verb *hap*): from the noun **HAP** + **-EN**[1].

**happening** ● n. **1** an event or occurrence. **2** a partly improvised or spontaneous performance, typically involving audience participation. ● adj. informal fashionable; trendy.

**happenstance** /ˈhap(ə)nˌstans/ ● n. chiefly N. Amer. coincidence.
– ORIGIN C19: blend of **HAPPEN** and **CIRCUMSTANCE**.

**happi** /ˈhapi/ ● n. (pl. **happis**) a loose informal Japanese coat.
– ORIGIN C19: Japanese.

**happy** ● adj. (**-ier, -iest**) **1** feeling or showing pleasure or contentment. ➤willing to do something. **2** fortunate and convenient: *a happy coincidence*. **3** [in combination] informal inclined to use a specified thing excessively or at random: *trigger-happy*.
– DERIVATIVES **happily** adv. **happiness** n.
– ORIGIN ME: from the noun **HAP** + **-Y**[1].

**happy-go-lucky** ● adj. cheerfully unconcerned about the future.

**happy hour** ● n. a period of the day when drinks are sold at reduced prices in a bar or other establishment.

**happy hunting ground** ● n. a place where success or enjoyment is obtained.

– ORIGIN orig. referring to the optimistic hope of Amer. Indians for good hunting grounds in the afterlife.

**hapten** /ˈhaptən/ ● n. Physiology a small molecule which, when combined with a protein, can elicit the production of antibodies.
– ORIGIN C20: from Gk *haptein* 'fasten'.

**haptic** /ˈhaptɪk/ ● adj. technical of or relating to the sense of touch.
– ORIGIN C19: from Gk *haptikos* 'able to touch or grasp', from *haptein* 'fasten'.

**haptoglobin** /ˌhaptə(ʊ)ˈgləʊbɪn/ ● n. Biochemistry a protein present in blood serum which binds to and removes free haemoglobin from the bloodstream.
– ORIGIN 1940s: from Gk *haptein* 'fasten' + (*haemo*)*globin*.

**hara-kiri** /ˌharəˈkɪri/ ● n. ritual suicide by disembowelment with a sword, formerly practised in Japan by samurai as an honourable alternative to disgrace or execution.
– ORIGIN C19: colloq. Japanese, from *hara* 'belly' + *kiri* 'cutting'.

**haram** /hɑːˈrɑːm/ ● adj. forbidden or proscribed by Islamic law.
– ORIGIN from Arab. *ḥarām* 'forbidden'.

**harangue** /həˈraŋ/ ● v. criticize at length in an aggressive and hectoring manner. ● n. a forceful and aggressive speech.
– DERIVATIVES **haranguer** n.
– ORIGIN ME: from OFr. *arenge*, from med. L. *harenga*, perh. of Gmc origin; altered to conform with Fr. *harangue* (n.), *haranguer* (v.).

**harass** /ˈharəs, həˈras/ ● v. torment by subjecting to constant interference or intimidation.
– DERIVATIVES **harassed** adj. **harasser** n. **harassing** adj. **harassingly** adv. **harassment** n.
– ORIGIN C17: from Fr. *harasser*, from *harer* 'set a dog on', from Gmc *hare*, a cry urging a dog to attack.

**USAGE** harass

The word **harass** is pronounced either with the stress on the **har-** or with the stress on the **-rass**. The former pronunciation is the older and is regarded by some as the only correct one.

**harbinger** /ˈhɑːbɪn(d)ʒə/ ● n. a person or thing that announces or signals the approach of something.
– ORIGIN ME (orig. 'a person who provides or goes ahead to find lodging', later 'a herald'): from OFr. *herbergere*, from *herbergier* 'provide lodging for', from *herberge* 'lodging', from Old Saxon *heriberga* 'shelter for an army, lodging'.

**harbour** (US **harbor**) ● n. a place on the coast where ships may moor in shelter, either naturally formed or artificially created. ● v. **1** keep (a thought or feeling) secretly in one's mind. **2** give a refuge or shelter to. ➤ carry the germs of (a disease). **3** archaic moor in a harbour.
– DERIVATIVES **harbourless** adj.
– ORIGIN OE *herebeorg* 'shelter', *herebeorgian* 'occupy shelter', of Gmc origin.

**harbourage** (US **harborage**) ● n. a harbour or other place of shelter.

**harbour master** (US **harbormaster**) ● n. an official in charge of a harbour.

**hard** ● adj. **1** solid, firm, and rigid; not easily broken, bent, or pierced. ➤ (of a person) not showing any signs of weakness; tough. ➤ (of prices of shares, commodities, etc.) high and stable; firm. **2** requiring or demonstrating a great deal of endurance or effort; difficult. ➤ strict and demanding: *a hard taskmaster.* **3** (of information or a subject of study) concerned with precise and verifiable facts: *hard science.* **4** harsh or unpleasant to the senses. ➤ (of a season or the weather) severe. ➤ (of wine) harsh or sharp to the taste, especially because of tannin. **5** done with a great deal of force or strength: *a hard whack.* **6** very potent, strong, or intense. ➤ (of liquor) strongly alcoholic; spirit rather than beer or wine. ➤ (of a drug) potent and addictive. ➤ (of radiation) highly penetrating. ➤ (of pornography) highly obscene and explicit. **7** denoting an extreme or dogmatic faction within a political party: *the hard left.* **8** (of water) containing mineral salts. **9** (of a consonant) pronounced as a velar plosive (as *c* in *cat*, *g* in *go*). ● adv. **1** with a great deal of effort. ➤ with a great deal of force; violently. **2** so as to be solid or firm. **3** to the fullest extent possible: *put the wheel hard over to starboard.* ● n. Brit. a road leading down across a foreshore.
– PHRASES **be hard put (to it)** find it very difficult. **go hard with** dated turn out to (someone's) disadvantage. **hard and fast** [usu. with neg.] (of a rule or distinction) fixed and definitive. **hard at it** informal busily working. **hard by** close to. **hard done by** Brit. harshly or unfairly treated. **hard feelings** [usu. with neg.] feelings of resentment. **hard going** difficult to understand or enjoy. **hard luck** (or **lines**) Brit. informal used to express sympathy or commiserations. **hard of hearing** not able to hear well. **hard on** (or **upon**) close to; following soon after. **hard up** informal short of money. **play hard to get** informal deliberately adopt an aloof or uninterested attitude. **put the hard word on** Austral./NZ informal ask a favour of.
– DERIVATIVES **hardish** adj. **hardness** n.
– ORIGIN OE *hard, heard*, of Gmc origin.

**hardback** ● n. a book bound in stiff covers.

**hardball** ● n. N. Amer. baseball, especially as contrasted with softball.

**hardbitten** ● adj. tough and cynical.

**hardboard** ● n. stiff board made of compressed and treated wood pulp.

**hard-boiled** ● adj. **1** (of an egg) boiled until solid. **2** (of a person) tough and cynical. ➤ denoting a tough, realistic style of detective fiction.

**hard cash** ● n. negotiable coins and banknotes as opposed to other forms of payment.

**hard coal** ● n. another term for **ANTHRACITE**.

**hard-code** ● v. Computing fix (data or parameters) in a program in such a way that they cannot easily be altered.

**hard copy** ● n. a printed version on paper of data held in a computer.

**hard core** ● n. **1** the most active, committed, or doctrinaire members of a group. **2** popular music that is experimental in nature and typically characterized by high volume and aggressive presentation. **3** pornography of a very explicit kind. **4** Brit. broken bricks and rubble used as a filling or foundation in building.

**hardcover** ● adj. & n. chiefly N. Amer. another term for **HARDBACK**.

**hard disk** (also **hard drive**) ● n. Computing a rigid non-removable magnetic disk with a large data storage capacity.

**harden** ● v. **1** make or become hard or harder. **2** (of prices of shares, commodities, etc.) rise and remain steady at a higher level. **3** (**harden something off**) inure a plant to cold by gradually increasing its exposure to the outside.
– DERIVATIVES **hardened** adj. **hardener** n.

**hard fern** ● n. a heathland fern with long, narrow leathery fronds consisting of a row of thin lobes on each side of the stem. [*Blechnum spicant*.]

**hard hat** ● n. a rigid protective helmet, as worn by factory and building workers.

**hardhead** ● n. **1** (**hardheads**) Brit. knapweed. **2** an Australasian diving duck with mainly dark brown plumage. [*Aythya australis*.] **3** a North American Atlantic catfish, the male of which incubates the eggs inside its mouth. [*Arius felis*.]

**hard-headed** ● adj. tough and realistic.
– DERIVATIVES **hard-headedly** adv. **hard-headedness** n.

**hard-hearted** ● adj. unfeeling.
– DERIVATIVES **hard-heartedly** adv. **hard-heartedness** n.

**hardihood** ● n. dated boldness; daring.

**hard labour** ● n. heavy manual work as a punishment.

**hard line** ● n. an uncompromising adherence to a firm policy.
– DERIVATIVES **hardliner** n.

**hardly** ● adv. **1** scarcely; barely. ➤ only with great difficulty. ➤ no or not (suggesting surprise at or disagreement with a statement). **2** archaic harshly.

**hard-nosed** ● adj. informal realistic and tough-minded.

**hard-on** ● n. vulgar slang an erection of the penis.

**hard pad** ● n. hardening of the pads of the feet, a symptom of distemper in dogs and other animals.

**hard palate** • n. the bony front part of the palate.

**hardpan** • n. a hardened impervious layer, typically of clay, occurring in or below the soil.

**hard-paste** • adj. denoting true porcelain made of fusible and infusible materials (usually kaolin and china stone) fired at a high temperature.

**hard-pressed** • adj. **1** closely pursued. **2** in difficulties.

**hard rock** • n. highly amplified rock music with a heavy beat.

**hard sauce** • n. a sauce of butter and sugar, typically with brandy, rum, or vanilla added.

**hard sell** • n. a policy or technique of aggressive selling or advertising.

**hard-shell** • adj. **1** having a hard shell. **2** chiefly N. Amer. rigid or uncompromising.

**hardship** • n. severe suffering or privation.

**hard shoulder** • n. Brit. a hardened strip alongside a motorway for use in an emergency.

**hardstanding** • n. Brit. ground surfaced with a hard material for parking vehicles on.

**hardstone** • n. precious or semi-precious stone used for intaglio, mosaic work, etc.

**hard tack** • n. archaic hard dry bread or biscuit, especially as rations for sailors or soldiers.

**hardtop** • n. a motor vehicle with a rigid roof which in some cases is detachable.

**hardware** • n. **1** heavy military equipment such as tanks and missiles. **2** the machines, wiring, and other physical components of a computer. Compare with SOFTWARE. **3** tools, implements, and other items used in the home and in activities such as gardening.

**hard-wired** • adj. Electronics involving or achieved by permanently connected circuits rather than software.
– DERIVATIVES **hard-wire** v. & adj.

**hardwood** • n. **1** the wood from a broadleaved tree as distinguished from that of conifers. **2** (in gardening) mature growth on shrubs from which cuttings may be taken.

**hardy** • adj. (**-ier**, **-iest**) capable of enduring difficult conditions; robust. ➤ (of a plant) able to survive outside during winter.
– DERIVATIVES **hardily** adv. **hardiness** n.
– ORIGIN ME: from OFr. *hardi*, past part. of *hardir* 'become bold', of Gmc origin; rel. to HARD.

**hare** • n. a fast-running, long-eared mammal resembling a large rabbit, with very long hind legs. [*Lepus europaeus* (**brown hare**) and other species.] • v. run with great speed.
– PHRASES **run with the hare and hunt with the hounds** Brit. try to remain on good terms with both sides in a conflict. **start a hare** Brit. dated raise a topic of conversation.
– ORIGIN OE *hara*, of Gmc origin.

**harebell** • n. a bellflower with slender stems and pale blue flowers in late summer. [*Campanula rotundifolia*.]

**hare-brained** • adj. rash; ill-judged.

**Haredi** /ha'rɛdi/ • n. (pl. **Haredim** /-dɪm/) a member of any of various Orthodox Jewish sects characterized by strict adherence to traditional Jewish law.
– ORIGIN Heb., lit. 'one who trembles (in awe at the word of God)'.

**Hare Krishna** /ˌharɪ 'krɪʃnə, ˌhɑːreɪ/ • n. a member of the International Society for Krishna Consciousness, a religious sect based on the worship of the Hindu god Krishna.
– ORIGIN 1960s: Sanskrit, lit. 'O Vishnu Krishna'.

**harelip** • n. another term for CLEFT LIP.
– DERIVATIVES **harelipped** adj.
– ORIGIN C16: from a perceived resemblance to the mouth of a hare.

**harem** /'hɑːriːm, hɑː'riːm, 'hɛːrəm/ • n. **1** the separate part of a Muslim household reserved for wives, concubines, and female servants. **2** the wives (or concubines) of a polygamous man. ➤ a group of female animals sharing a single mate.
– ORIGIN C17: from Arab. *ḥaram*, *ḥarīm*, lit. 'prohibited place', from *ḥarama* 'be prohibited'.

**hare's-foot** • n. a slender clover which has soft hairs around the flowers. [*Trifolium arvense*.]

**hare's-tail** • n. a Mediterranean grass with white silky flowering heads and woolly grey-green leaves. [*Lagurus ovatus*.]

**harewood** • n. stained sycamore wood used for making furniture.
– ORIGIN C17: from Ger. dial. *Ehre* (from L. *acer* 'maple') + WOOD.

**haricot** /'harɪkəʊ/ • n. a French bean of a variety with small white seeds, which can be dried and used as a vegetable.
– ORIGIN C17: Fr., perh. from Aztec *ayacotli*.

**Harijan** /'hʌrɪdʒ(ə)n, 'harɪdʒan/ • n. a member of a hereditary Hindu group of the lowest social and ritual status. See UNTOUCHABLE.
– ORIGIN from Sanskrit *harijana*, lit. 'a person dedicated to Vishnu', from *Hari* 'Vishnu' + *jana* 'person'.

**harissa** /'arɪsə/ • n. a hot sauce or paste used in North African cuisine, made from chilli peppers, paprika, and olive oil.
– ORIGIN from Arab.

**hark** • v. **1** poetic/literary listen. **2** (**hark at**) informal used to draw attention to an ill-advised or foolish remark or action: *just hark at you!* **3** (**hark back**) recall an earlier period.
– ORIGIN ME: of Gmc origin.

**harken** • v. variant spelling of HEARKEN.

**harlequin** /'hɑːlɪkwɪn/ • n. **1** (**Harlequin**) a mute character in traditional pantomime, typically masked and dressed in a diamond-patterned costume. ➤ historical a stock comic character in Italian commedia dell'arte. **2** a small duck of fast-flowing streams around the Arctic and North Pacific, the male having mainly grey-blue plumage with bold white markings. [*Histrionicus histrionicus*.] • adj. in varied colours; variegated.
– ORIGIN C16: from obs. Fr., from earlier *Herlequin*, the leader of a legendary troop of demon horsemen.

**harlequinade** /ˌhɑːlɪkwɪ'neɪd/ • n. **1** historical the section of a traditional pantomime in which Harlequin played a leading role. **2** dated a piece of buffoonery.

**harlequin fish** • n. a small brightly coloured freshwater fish of SE Asia. [*Rasbora heteromorpha*.]

**harlot** /'hɑːlət/ • n. archaic a prostitute or promiscuous woman.
– DERIVATIVES **harlotry** n.
– ORIGIN ME (denoting a vagabond or beggar, later a lecherous man or woman): from OFr. *harlot*, *herlot* 'young man, knave'.

**harm** • n. physical injury, especially that which is deliberately inflicted. ➤ material damage. ➤ actual or potential ill effect. • v. physically injure. ➤ have an adverse effect on.
– PHRASES **out of harm's way** in a safe place.
– ORIGIN OE *hearm* (n.), *hearmian* (v.), of Gmc origin.

**harmattan** /hɑː'mat(ə)n/ • n. a very dry, dusty easterly or north-easterly wind on the West African coast, occurring from December to February.
– ORIGIN C17: from Twi *haramata*.

**harmful** • adj. causing or likely to cause harm.
– DERIVATIVES **harmfully** adv. **harmfulness** n.

**harmless** • adj. not able or likely to cause harm.
– DERIVATIVES **harmlessly** adv. **harmlessness** n.

**harmonic** /hɑː'mɒnɪk/ • adj. **1** of, relating to, or characterized by harmony. **2** Music relating to or denoting a harmonic or harmonics. **3** Mathematics of or relating to a harmonic progression. ➤ Physics of or denoting components of a complex oscillation or wave whose frequencies are exact multiples of the basic frequency. **4** Astrology of or relating to a division of the zodiacal circle by a whole number. • n. **1** Music an overtone accompanying a fundamental tone at a fixed interval, produced by vibration of a string, column of air, etc. in an exact fraction of its length. ➤ a note produced on a musical instrument as an overtone, e.g. by lightly touching a string while sounding

it. **2** Physics a harmonic component of a complex oscillation or wave.
– DERIVATIVES **harmonically** adv.

**harmonica** /hɑːˈmɒnɪkə/ ● n. a small rectangular wind instrument with a row of metal reeds along its length, held against the lips and moved from side to side to produce different notes by blowing or sucking.
– ORIGIN C18: from L., fem. sing. or neut. pl. of *harmonicus*, from Gk *harmonikos*, from *harmonia* (see **HARMONY**).

**harmonic minor** ● n. Music a scale containing a minor third, minor sixth, and major seventh, forming the basis of conventional harmony in minor keys.

**harmonic progression** ● n. **1** Music a series of chord changes forming the underlying harmony of a piece of music. **2** Mathematics a sequence of quantities whose reciprocals are in arithmetical progression (e.g. 1, ⅓, ⅕, ⅐, etc.).

**harmonic series** ● n. **1** Music a set of frequencies consisting of a fundamental and the harmonics related to it by an exact fraction. **2** Mathematics a harmonic progression.

**harmonious** ● adj. **1** tuneful; not discordant. **2** free from conflict.
– DERIVATIVES **harmoniously** adv. **harmoniousness** n.

**harmonist** ● n. a person skilled in musical harmony.

**harmonium** /hɑːˈməʊnɪəm/ ● n. a keyboard instrument in which the notes are produced by air driven through metal reeds by foot-operated bellows.
– ORIGIN C19: from Fr., from L. *harmonia* (see **HARMONY**) or Gk *harmonios* 'harmonious'.

**harmonize** (also **-ise**) ● v. **1** Music provide harmony for. **2** make or be harmonious. **3** make consistent: *plans to harmonize the railways of Europe.*
– DERIVATIVES **harmonization** n.

**harmony** ● n. (pl. **-ies**) **1** the combination of simultaneously sounded musical notes to produce chords and chord progressions having a pleasing effect. **2** agreement or concord. **3** an arrangement of the four Gospels which presents a single continuous narrative text.
– PHRASES **harmony of the spheres** see **SPHERE**.
– ORIGIN ME: via OFr. from L. *harmonia* 'joining, concord', from Gk, from *harmos* 'joint'.

**harness** ● n. **1** a set of straps and fittings by which a horse or other draught animal is fastened to a cart, plough, etc. and is controlled by its driver. **2** a similar arrangement of straps, as for fastening a parachute to a person's body or for restraining a young child. ● v. **1** fit with a harness. **2** control and make use of (resources).
– PHRASES **in harness 1** (of an animal) used for draught work. **2** in the routine of daily work: *an ordinary man who died in harness.* **3** in close partnership.
– DERIVATIVES **harnesser** n.
– ORIGIN ME: from OFr. *harneis* 'military equipment', from ON, from *herr* 'army' + *nest* 'provisions'.

**harness racing** ● n. another term for **TROTTING**.

**harp** ● n. a musical instrument, roughly triangular in shape, consisting of a frame supporting a graduated series of parallel strings, played by plucking with the fingers. ● v. **1** (**harp on**) talk or write persistently and tediously on a particular topic. **2** archaic play on a harp.
– DERIVATIVES **harper** n. **harpist** n.
– ORIGIN OE *hearpe*, of Gmc origin.

**harpoon** ● n. a barbed spear-like missile attached to a long rope and thrown by hand or fired from a gun, used for catching whales and other large sea creatures. ● v. spear with a harpoon.
– DERIVATIVES **harpooner** n.
– ORIGIN C17: from Fr. *harpon*, from *harpe* 'dog's claw, clamp'.

**harp seal** ● n. a slender North Atlantic seal that typically has a dark harp-shaped mark on its grey back. [*Phoca groenlandica*.]

**harp shell** ● n. a marine mollusc with a large vertically ribbed shell, found chiefly in the Indo-Pacific. [Family Harpidae: many species.]

**harpsichord** /ˈhɑːpsɪkɔːd/ ● n. a keyboard instrument similar in shape to a grand piano, with horizontal strings plucked by points operated by depressing the keys.
– DERIVATIVES **harpsichordist** n.
– ORIGIN C17: from obs. Fr. *harpechorde*, from late L. *harpa* 'harp' + *chorda* 'string'.

**harpy** ● n. (pl. **-ies**) Greek & Roman Mythology a rapacious monster usually depicted with a woman's head and body and a bird's wings and claws.
– ORIGIN ME: from L. *harpyia*, from Gk *harpuiai* 'snatchers'.

**harpy eagle** ● n. a very large crested eagle of tropical rainforests. [*Harpia harpyja* (S. America) and *Harpyopsis novaeguineae* (New Guinea).]

**harquebus** /ˈhɑːkwɪbəs/ (also **arquebus**) ● n. historical an early type of portable gun supported on a tripod or a forked rest.
– ORIGIN C16: from Fr. *harquebuse*, based on Mid. Low Ger. *hakebusse*, from *hake* 'hook' + *busse* 'gun'.

**harridan** /ˈharɪd(ə)n/ ● n. a strict, bossy, or belligerent old woman.
– ORIGIN C17 (orig. sl.): perh. from Fr. *haridelle* 'old horse'.

**harrier**[1] ● n. a person who harries others.

**harrier**[2] ● n. a hound of a breed used for hunting hares.
– ORIGIN ME *hayrer*, from **HARE** + **-ER**[1].

**harrier**[3] ● n. a long-winged, slender-bodied bird of prey with low quartering flight. [Genus *Circus*: several species.]
– ORIGIN C16 (as *harrower*): from *harrow* 'harry, rob' (var. of **HARRY**); spelling influenced by **HARRIER**[1].

**Harris tweed** ● n. trademark handwoven tweed made traditionally on the island of Lewis and Harris in Scotland.

**Harrovian** /həˈrəʊvɪən/ ● n. a past or present member of Harrow School, a boys' public school in NW London.
– ORIGIN C19: from mod. L. *Harrovia* 'Harrow' + **-AN**.

**harrow** ● n. an implement consisting of a heavy frame set with teeth or tines which is dragged over ploughed land to break up or spread the soil. ● v. **1** draw a harrow over. **2** [usu. as adj. **harrowing**] cause distress to: *a harrowing film about racism.*
– DERIVATIVES **harrower** n. **harrowingly** adv.
– ORIGIN ME: from ON *herfi*.

**harrumph** /həˈrʌmf/ ● v. **1** clear the throat noisily. **2** grumpily express dissatisfaction: *sceptics tend to harrumph at case histories like this.*
– ORIGIN 1930s: imitative.

**harry** ● v. (**-ies**, **-ied**) **1** persistently carry out attacks on (an enemy). **2** persistently harass.
– ORIGIN OE *herian*, *hergian*, of Gmc origin.

**harsh** ● adj. **1** unpleasantly rough or jarring to the senses. **2** cruel or severe. ➤ (of reality or a fact) grim and unpalatable.
– DERIVATIVES **harshen** v. **harshly** adv. **harshness** n.
– ORIGIN ME: from Mid. Low Ger. *harsch* 'rough', lit. 'hairy', from *haer* 'hair'.

**hart** ● n. an adult male deer, especially a red deer over five years old.
– ORIGIN OE *heorot*, *heort*, of Gmc origin.

**hartal** /ˈhɑːtɑːl, ˈhəːtɑːl/ ● n. (in the Indian subcontinent) a closure of shops and offices as a protest or a mark of sorrow.
– ORIGIN from Hindi *haṛtāl*, *haṭṭāl*, lit. 'locking of shops'.

**hartebeest** /ˈhɑːtɪbiːst/ ● n. a large African antelope with a long head and sloping back. [*Alcelaphus buselaphus* (**red hartebeest**) and other species.]
– ORIGIN C18: from S. Afr. Du., from Du. *hert* 'hart' + *beest* 'beast'.

**hartshorn** /ˈhɑːtsˌhɔːn/ ● n. archaic aqueous ammonia solution used as smelling salts, formerly prepared from the horns of deer.

**hart's tongue** ● n. a fern whose long, narrow undivided fronds are said to resemble the tongues of deer. [*Phyllitis scolopendrium*.]

**harum-scarum** /ˌhɛːrəmˈskɛːrəm/ ● adj. reckless; impetuous.
– ORIGIN C17: reduplication based on **HARE** and **SCARE**.

**haruspex** /həˈrʌspɛks/ ● n. (pl. **haruspices** /-spɪsiːz/) (in ancient Rome) a religious official who interpreted omens

by inspecting the entrails of sacrificial animals.
– DERIVATIVES **haruspicy** /həˈrʌspɪsi/ n.
– ORIGIN L., from an unrecorded element meaning 'entrails' + *-spex* (from *specere* 'look at').

**harvest** • n. the process or period of gathering in crops. ➤the season's yield or crop. • v. **1** gather as a harvest. **2** remove (cells or tissue) from a person or animal for experimental or transplantation purposes.
– DERIVATIVES **harvestable** adj. **harvester** n.
– ORIGIN OE *hærfest* 'autumn', of Gmc origin.

**harvest home** • n. the gathering in of the final part of the year's harvest. ➤a festival marking the end of the harvest period.

**harvestman** • n. (pl. **-men**) an arachnid with a globular body and very long thin legs. [Order Opiliones: many species.]

**harvest mite** • n. a minute mite whose parasitic larvae live on or under the skin of animals where they cause dermatitis and can transmit scrub typhus. [Genus *Trombicula*.]

**harvest moon** • n. the full moon that is seen closest to the time of the autumn equinox.

**harvest mouse** • n. **1** a small North Eurasian mouse with a prehensile tail, nesting among the stalks of growing cereals. [*Micromys minutus*.] **2** a nocturnal mouse found in North and Central America. [Genus *Reithrodontomys*: several species.]

**Harvey Wallbanger** • n. a cocktail made from vodka or gin, orange juice, and Galliano.

**has** third person singular present of **HAVE**.

**has-been** • n. informal a person or thing that is outmoded or no longer of any significance.

**hash**[1] • n. **1** a dish of diced cooked meat reheated with potatoes. ➤N. Amer. a finely chopped mixture. **2** a jumble; a mess. • v. **1** make or chop into a hash. **2** (**hash something out**) come to agreement after lengthy and vigorous discussion.
– PHRASES **make a hash of** informal make a mess of. **settle someone's hash** informal deal with and subdue someone in no uncertain manner.
– ORIGIN C16: from Fr. *hacher*, from *hache* (see **HATCHET**).

**hash**[2] • n. informal short for **HASHISH**.

**hash**[3] • n. the symbol #.
– ORIGIN 1980s: prob. from **HATCH**[3], alt. by folk etymology.

**hash browns** (also **hashed browns**) • pl. n. chiefly N. Amer. a dish of chopped and fried cooked potatoes.

**Hashemite** /ˈhaʃɪmʌɪt/ • n. a member of an Arab princely family claiming descent from Hashim, great-grandfather of Muhammad.

**Hashimoto's disease** /ˌhaʃɪˈməʊtəʊz/ • n. an autoimmune disease causing chronic inflammation and consequential failure of the thyroid gland.
– ORIGIN 1930s: named after the Japanese surgeon Hakaru *Hashimoto*.

**hashish** /ˈhaʃiːʃ, -ʃɪʃ, haˈʃiːʃ/ • n. cannabis.
– ORIGIN C16: from Arab. *ḥašīš* 'dry herb, powdered hemp leaves'.

**Hasid** /ˈhasɪd/ (also **Chasid**, **Chassid**, or **Hassid**) • n. (pl. **Hasidim**) an adherent of Hasidism.
– DERIVATIVES **Hasidic** /-ˈsɪdɪk/ adj.
– ORIGIN from Heb. *ḥāsīḏ* 'pious'.

**Hasidism** /ˈhasɪˌdɪz(ə)m/ (also **Chasidism**, **Chassidism**, or **Hassidism**) • n. a mystical Jewish movement founded in Poland in the 18th century, represented today by fundamentalist communities in Israel and New York.

**haslet** /ˈhazlɪt, ˈheɪzlɪt/ • n. chiefly Brit. a cold meat consisting of chopped and compressed pork offal.
– ORIGIN ME: from OFr. *hastelet*, dimin. of *haste* 'roast meat, spit', prob. of Gmc origin.

**hasn't** • contr. has not.

**hasp** /hɑːsp/ • n. a slotted hinged metal plate that forms part of a fastening for a door or lid and is fitted over a metal loop and secured by a pin or padlock.
– ORIGIN OE *hæpse*, *hæsp*, of Gmc origin.

**Hassid** • n. variant spelling of **HASID**.

**Hassidism** • n. variant spelling of **HASIDISM**.

**hassium** /ˈhasɪəm/ • n. the chemical element of atomic number 108, a very unstable element made by high-energy atomic collisions. (Symbol: **Hs**)
– ORIGIN 1990s: mod. L., from L. *Hassias* 'Hesse', the Ger. state where it was discovered.

**hassle** informal • n. irritating inconvenience. ➤deliberate harassment. • v. harass; pester.
– ORIGIN C19 (orig. dial. in the sense 'hack or saw at'): of unknown origin.

**hassock** /ˈhasək/ • n. **1** chiefly Brit. a cushion for kneeling on in church. ➤N. Amer. a footstool. **2** a firm clump of grass or vegetation in marshy ground.
– ORIGIN OE *hassuc*, of unknown origin.

**hast** archaic second person singular present of **HAVE**.

**hastate** /ˈhasteɪt/ • adj. Botany (of a leaf) having a narrow triangular shape like that of a spearhead.
– ORIGIN C18: from L. *hastatus*, from *hasta* 'spear'.

**haste** • n. excessive speed or urgency of action. • v. archaic term for **HASTEN**: *haste ye back!*
– ORIGIN ME: from OFr. *haste* (n.), *haster* (v.), of Gmc origin.

**hasten** • v. **1** be quick to do something; move quickly. **2** cause to happen sooner than anticipated.

**hasty** • adj. (**-ier**, **-iest**) **1** done or acting with haste; hurried. **2** archaic quick-tempered.
– DERIVATIVES **hastily** adv. **hastiness** n.

**hasty pudding** • n. a pudding containing wheat or maize flour stirred to a thick batter in boiling milk or water.

**hat** • n. a shaped covering for the head, typically with a brim and a crown.
– PHRASES **hat in hand** see ***cap in hand*** at **CAP**. **keep something under one's hat** keep something a secret. **pass the hat round** (or N. Amer. **pass the hat**) collect contributions of money. **pick something out of a hat** select something at random. **take one's hat off to** used to express admiration or praise for. **talk through one's hat** informal talk foolishly or ignorantly. **throw one's hat into the ring** express willingness to take up a challenge.
– DERIVATIVES **hatful** n. (pl. **-fuls**). **hatless** adj. **hatted** adj.
– ORIGIN OE *hætt*, of Gmc origin; rel. to **HOOD**[1].

**hatband** • n. a decorative ribbon encircling a hat, held in position above the brim.

**hatbox** • n. a large cylindrical box used to store hats.

**hatch**[1] • n. **1** a small opening in a floor, wall, or roof allowing access from one area to another, in particular that in the deck of a boat leading to the cabin or lower level. ➤a door in an aircraft, spacecraft, or submarine. **2** short for **HATCHBACK**.
– PHRASES **down the hatch** informal used as a toast. **under (the) hatches** below deck in a ship.
– ORIGIN OE *hæcc* (denoting the lower half of a divided door), of Gmc origin.

**hatch**[2] • v. **1** (of a young bird, fish, or reptile) emerge from its egg. ➤(of an egg) open and produce a young animal. ➤cause (a young animal) to emerge from its egg. **2** conspire to devise (a plot or plan). • n. a newly hatched brood.
– ORIGIN ME *hacche*, rel. to Swed. *häcka* and Dan. *hække*.

**hatch**[3] • v. (in technical drawing) shade with closely drawn parallel lines.
– DERIVATIVES **hatching** n.
– ORIGIN C15 (in the sense 'inlay with strips of metal'): from OFr. *hacher*, from *hache* (see **HATCHET**).

**hatchback** • n. a car with a door across the full width at the back end that opens upwards to provide easy access for loading.

**hatchery** • n. (pl. **-ies**) an establishment where fish or poultry eggs are hatched.

**hatchet** • n. a small axe with a short handle for use in one hand.
– PHRASES **bury the hatchet** end a quarrel or conflict. [in allusion to an American Indian custom.]
– ORIGIN ME: from OFr. *hachette*, dimin. of *hache* 'axe'.

**hatchet-faced** • adj. informal sharp-featured and grim-looking.

**hatchetfish** • n. (pl. same or **-fishes**) a deep-bodied laterally compressed tropical freshwater fish of the New

World, able to fly short distances in the air by beating its broad pectoral fins. [Family Gasteropelecidae: several species.]

**hatchet job** ● n. informal a fierce verbal or written attack.

**hatchet man** ● n. informal **1** a person employed to carry out controversial or disagreeable tasks. **2** a harsh critic.

**hatchling** ● n. a newly hatched young animal.

**hatchment** ● n. a large diamond-shaped tablet bearing the coat of arms of someone who has died, displayed in their honour.
– ORIGIN C16: prob. from obs. Fr. *hachement*, from OFr. *acesmement* 'adornment'.

**hatchway** ● n. an opening or hatch, especially in a ship's deck.

**hate** ● v. feel intense dislike for or a strong aversion towards. ● n. **1** intense dislike; strong aversion. **2** informal a disliked person or thing: *Richard's pet hate is filling in tax forms.*
– DERIVATIVES **hatable** (also **hateable**) adj. **hater** n.
– ORIGIN OE *hatian* (v.), *hete* (n.), of Gmc origin.

**hateful** ● adj. arousing or deserving of hatred.
– DERIVATIVES **hatefully** adv. **hatefulness** n.

**hath** archaic third person singular present of **HAVE**.

**hatha yoga** /'hʌtə, 'haθə/ ● n. a system of physical exercises and breathing control used in yoga.
– ORIGIN from Sanskrit *haṭha* 'force'.

**hatpin** ● n. a long pin used to hold a woman's hat in position.

**hatred** ● n. intense dislike.
– ORIGIN ME: from **HATE** + *-red* (from OE *rǣden* 'condition').

**hatstand** ● n. a tall free-standing post fitted with large hooks for hanging hats on.

**hatter** ● n. a person who makes and sells hats.
– PHRASES **(as) mad as a hatter** informal completely crazy. [with allusion to the effects of mercury poisoning from the use of mercurous nitrate in the manufacture of felt hats.]

**hat-trick** ● n. three successes of the same kind, especially (in soccer) the scoring of three goals in a game by one player or (in cricket) the taking of three wickets by the same bowler with successive balls.
– ORIGIN C19: orig. referring to the club presentation of a new hat to a bowler taking three wickets successively.

**hauberk** /'hɔːbəːk/ ● n. historical a full-length coat of mail.
– ORIGIN ME: from OFr. *hauberc, hausberc*, of Gmc origin.

**haugh** /hɔː, hɑːx/ ● n. Scottish & N. English a piece of flat alluvial land by the side of a river.
– ORIGIN ME: prob. from OE *healh* 'corner, nook'.

**haughty** ● adj. (**-ier**, **-iest**) arrogantly superior and disdainful.
– DERIVATIVES **haughtily** adv. **haughtiness** n.
– ORIGIN C16: from obs. *haught*, earlier *haut*, from OFr., from L. *altus* 'high'.

**haul** ● v. **1** pull or drag with effort or force. **2** transport in a truck or cart. **3** (especially of a sailing ship) make an abrupt change of course. ● n. **1** a quantity of something obtained, especially illegally. **2** a number of fish caught at one time. **3** a distance to be travelled.
– PHRASES **haul off** N. Amer. informal leave; withdraw. **haul someone over the coals** see **COAL**.
– DERIVATIVES **hauler** n.
– ORIGIN C16 (orig. in the naut. sense 'trim sails for sailing closer to the wind'): var. of **HALE**[2].

**haulage** ● n. the commercial transport of goods.

**haulier** /'hɔːlɪə/ ● n. **1** Brit. a person or company employed in the commercial transport of goods by road. **2** a miner who is responsible for transporting coal within a mine.

**haulm** /hɔːm/ ● n. a stalk or stem. ➤ the stalks or stems of peas, beans, or potatoes collectively, as used for bedding.
– ORIGIN OE *healm, halm*, of Gmc origin.

**haunch** ● n. **1** the buttock and thigh considered together, in a human or animal. ➤ the leg and loin of an animal, as food. **2** Architecture the side of an arch, between the crown and the pier.
– ORIGIN ME: from OFr. *hanche*, of Gmc origin.

**haunt** ● v. **1** (of a ghost) manifest itself regularly at (a place). ➤ (of a person) frequent (a place). **2** be persistently and disturbingly present in the mind: *cities haunted by the shadow of cholera.* ● n. a place frequented by a specified person: *a favourite haunt of pickpockets.*
– DERIVATIVES **haunter** n.
– ORIGIN ME: from OFr. *hanter*, of Gmc origin; distantly rel. to **HOME**.

**haunted** ● adj. **1** (of a place) frequented by a ghost. **2** having or showing signs of mental anguish.

**haunting** ● adj. poignant; evocative.
– DERIVATIVES **hauntingly** adv.

**haurient** /'hɔːrɪənt/ ● adj. [postpos.] Heraldry (of a fish or marine creature) depicted swimming vertically.
– ORIGIN C16: from L. *haurient-* 'drawing in (air, water, etc.)', from *haurire*.

**Hausa** /'haʊsə/ ● n. (pl. same or **Hausas**) **1** a member of a people of northern Nigeria and adjacent regions. **2** the Chadic language of this people, used as a lingua franca in parts of West Africa.
– ORIGIN the name in Hausa.

**hausfrau** /'haʊsfraʊ/ ● n. a German housewife, especially with reference to orderliness and efficiency.
– ORIGIN C18: from Ger., from *Haus* 'house' + *Frau* 'woman, wife'.

**haustellum** /hɔː'stɛləm/ ● n. (pl. **haustella**) Zoology the sucking organ or proboscis of an insect or crustacean.
– DERIVATIVES **haustellate** /'hɔːstələt, -leɪt/ adj.
– ORIGIN C19: mod. L. dimin. of *haustrum* 'scoop', from *haust-, haurire* 'draw in'.

**haustorium** /hɔː'stɔːrɪəm/ ● n. (pl. **haustoria** /-rɪə/) Botany a slender projection from the root of a parasitic plant or from the hyphae of a parasitic fungus, enabling the parasite to penetrate the tissues of its host.
– DERIVATIVES **haustorial** adj.
– ORIGIN C19: mod. L., from L. *haustor* 'thing that draws in', from *haurire*.

**hautboy** /'(h)əʊbɔɪ/ ● n. archaic form of **OBOE**.
– ORIGIN C16: from Fr. *hautbois*, from *haut* 'high' + *bois* 'wood'.

**haute couture** /ˌəʊt kʊ'tjʊə/ ● n. the designing and making of high-quality fashionable clothes by leading fashion houses.
– ORIGIN Fr., lit. 'high dressmaking'.

**haute cuisine** /ˌəʊt kwɪ'ziːn/ ● n. high-quality cooking following the style of traditional French cuisine.
– ORIGIN Fr., lit. 'high cookery'.

**haute école** /ˌəʊt eɪ'kɒl/ ● n. the art or practice of advanced classical dressage.
– ORIGIN Fr., lit. 'high school'.

**hauteur** /əʊ'təː, French 'otœʀ/ ● n. proud haughtiness of manner.
– ORIGIN Fr., from *haut* 'high'.

**haut monde** /əʊ 'mɒ̃d/ ● n. fashionable society.
– ORIGIN Fr., lit. 'high world'.

**Havana** /hə'vanə/ ● n. a cigar made in Cuba or from Cuban tobacco.
– ORIGIN named after *Havana*, the capital of Cuba.

**Havdalah** ● n. variant spelling of **HABDALAH**.

**have** ● v. (**has**; past and past part. **had**) **1** (also **have got**) possess, own, or hold. ➤ be made up of; comprise. ➤ be able to make use of. ➤ know (a language or subject): *I had only a little French.* **2** experience; undergo. ➤ (also **have got**) suffer from (an illness or disability). ➤ cause to be in a particular state. ➤ cause to be done for one by someone else. **3** (**have to** or **have got to**) be obliged to; must. ➤ be strongly recommended to. **4** perform the action indicated by the noun specified: *he had a look round.* ➤ eat or drink. ➤ give birth to or be due to give birth to. **5** (also **have got**) demonstrate (a personal attribute): *he had little patience.* ➤ [with neg.] refuse to tolerate. **6** (also **have got**) place, hold, or keep in a particular position. **7** be the recipient or host of. **8** (usu. **be had**) informal cheat or deceive: *I realized I'd been had.* **9** vulgar slang engage in sexual intercourse with. **10** (also **have got**) informal have put (someone) at a disadvantage in an argument: *you've got me there.* ● aux. v. used with a past participle to form the

perfect, pluperfect, and future perfect tenses, and the conditional mood. ● **n. 1** (usu. in phr. **the haves and the have-nots**) informal people with plenty of money. **2** Brit. informal, dated a swindle.
– PHRASES **have had it** informal **1** be beyond repair or revival: *the car has had it.* **2** be unable to tolerate any longer. **have it away** (or **off**) Brit. vulgar slang have sexual intercourse. **have (got) it in for** informal behave in a hostile way towards. **have (got) it in one (to do something)** informal have the capacity or potential (to do something). **have it out** informal attempt to resolve a contentious matter by open confrontation. **have (got) nothing on** informal be not nearly as good as. **have nothing** (or **something**) **on someone** informal know nothing (or something) discreditable or incriminating about someone.
– PHRASAL VERBS **have someone on** Brit. informal try to make someone believe something that is untrue, especially as a joke. **have something out** undergo an operation to extract a part of one's body. **have someone up** (usu. **be had up**) Brit. informal bring someone before a court of justice to answer for an alleged offence.
– ORIGIN OE *habban*, of Gmc origin; prob. rel. to **HEAVE**.

**have-a-go** ● **adj.** Brit. informal (of a member of the public) intervening to stop a criminal during the course of a crime: *he was a classic have-a-go hero.*

**haveli** /ˌhʌvəˈliː/ ● **n.** (pl. **havelis**) Indian a mansion.
– ORIGIN via Hindi from Arab. *havelī.*

**haven** ● **n. 1** a place of safety or refuge. **2** a harbour or small port.
– ORIGIN OE *hæfen*, from ON *hǫfn.*

**have-nots** ● **pl. n.** informal economically disadvantaged people.

**haven't** ● **contr.** have not.

**haver** /ˈheɪvə/ ● **v. 1** Scottish talk foolishly; babble. **2** Brit. act in an indecisive manner.
– ORIGIN C18: of unknown origin.

**haversack** /ˈhavəsak/ ● **n.** a small, stout bag carried on the back or over the shoulder, used especially by soldiers and walkers.
– ORIGIN C18: from Fr. *havresac*, from obs. Ger. *Habersack*, denoting a bag used to carry oats as horse feed, from dial. *Haber* 'oats' + *Sack* 'sack, bag'.

**Haversian canal** /həˈvəːsɪən/ ● **n.** Anatomy any of the minute tubes which form a network in bone and contain blood vessels.
– ORIGIN C19: named after the C17 Engl. anatomist Clopton *Havers.*

**haversine** /ˈhavəsʌɪn/ (also **haversin**) ● **n.** Mathematics half of a versed sine.
– ORIGIN C19: contr. of *half versed sine.*

**havildar** /ˈhavɪldɑː/ ● **n.** (in the Indian subcontinent) a soldier or police officer corresponding to a sergeant.
– ORIGIN from Urdu *hawildār*, from Pers. *ḥawāldār* 'trust-holder'.

**havoc** ● **n. 1** widespread destruction. **2** great confusion or disorder. ● **v.** (**havocked, havocking**) archaic lay waste to.
– PHRASES **play havoc with** completely disrupt.
– ORIGIN ME: from Anglo-Norman Fr. *havok*, alt. of OFr. *havot*, of unknown origin; the word was orig. used in the phr. *cry havoc* 'to give an army the order *havoc*', which was the signal for plundering.

**haw**[1] ● **n.** the red fruit of the hawthorn.
– ORIGIN OE *haga*, of Gmc origin.

**haw**[2] ● **n.** the third eyelid or nictitating membrane in certain mammals, especially dogs and cats.
– ORIGIN ME (denoting a discharge from the eye): of unknown origin.

**haw**[3] ● **v.** see ***hum and haw*** at **HUM**[1].

**Hawaiian** ● **n. 1** a native or inhabitant of Hawaii. **2** the Austronesian language of Hawaii. ● **adj.** of or relating to Hawaii or its people or language.

**Hawaiian guitar** ● **n.** a steel-stringed guitar in which a characteristic glissando effect is produced by sliding a metal bar along the strings as they are plucked.

**hawfinch** ● **n.** a large finch with a massive bill for cracking open cherry stones and other hard seeds. [Genus *Coccothraustes*: three species.]
– ORIGIN C17: from **HAW**[1] + **FINCH**.

**hawk**[1] ● **n. 1** a fast-flying bird of prey with broad rounded wings and a long tail, such as a sparrowhawk. [*Accipiter* and other genera: many species.] ➤ N. Amer. a buzzard or similar large bird of prey. ➤ any bird used in falconry. **2** a person who advocates an aggressive or warlike foreign policy. **3** used in names of hawkmoths, e.g. **eyed hawk**. ● **v. 1** hunt game with a trained hawk. **2** (of a bird or dragonfly) hunt on the wing for food.
– DERIVATIVES **hawkish** adj. **hawkishly** adv. **hawkishness** n.
– ORIGIN OE *hafoc, heafoc*, of Gmc origin.

**hawk**[2] ● **v.** carry about and offer (goods) for sale in the street.
– ORIGIN C15: prob. a back-form. from **HAWKER**[1].

**hawk**[3] ● **v.** clear the throat noisily. ➤ bring (phlegm) up from the throat.
– ORIGIN C16: prob. imitative.

**hawk**[4] ● **n.** a plasterer's square board with a handle underneath for carrying plaster or mortar.
– ORIGIN ME: of unknown origin.

**hawkbit** ● **n.** a plant which resembles a dandelion, with a rosette of leaves and yellow flowers. [Genus *Leontodon.*]
– ORIGIN C18: blend of **HAWKWEED** and **DEVIL'S BIT**.

**hawk eagle** ● **n.** a small tropical eagle with broad wings and a long tail. [Genera *Spizaetus* and *Spizastur*: several species.]

**hawker**[1] ● **n.** a person who travels about selling goods.
– ORIGIN C16: prob. from Low Ger. or Du. and rel. to **HUCKSTER**.

**hawker**[2] ● **n. 1** a falconer. **2** a slender-bodied dragonfly that remains airborne for long periods. [Aeshnidae and other families: many species.]
– ORIGIN OE *hafocere*, from *hafoc* 'hawk'.

**hawkmoth** ● **n.** a large swift-flying moth with a stout body and narrow forewings, typically feeding on nectar while hovering. [Family Sphingidae: many species.]

**hawk-nosed** ● **adj.** (of a person) having a nose which is curved like a hawk's beak.

**hawk owl** ● **n.** a long-tailed day-flying owl of northern coniferous forests. [*Surnia ulula.*]

**hawksbeard** ● **n.** a plant of the daisy family which resembles a dandelion but has a branched stem with several flowers. [Genus *Crepis.*]

**hawksbill turtle** ● **n.** a small tropical sea turtle with hooked jaws and overlapping horny plates on the shell, hunted as the traditional source of tortoiseshell. [*Eretmochelys imbricata.*]

**hawkweed** ● **n.** a plant of the daisy family, with yellow dandelion-like flower heads. [Genus *Hieracium.*]
– ORIGIN OE, rendering L. *hieracium*, based on Gk *hierax* 'hawk'.

**hawse** /hɔːz/ ● **n.** the part of a ship's bows through which the anchor cables pass. ➤ the space between the head of an anchored vessel and the anchors.
– PHRASES **a foul hawse** a situation in which an anchored ship's port and starboard cables are crossed.
– ORIGIN ME *halse*, prob. from ON *háls* 'neck, ship's bow'.

**hawse hole** ● **n.** a hole in the deck of a ship through which an anchor cable passes.

**hawsepipe** ● **n.** a pipe housing the shank of the anchor when the anchor is raised.

**hawser** /ˈhɔːzə/ ● **n.** a thick rope or cable for mooring or towing a ship.
– ORIGIN ME: from Anglo-Norman Fr. *haucer*, from OFr. *haucier* 'to hoist', based on L. *altus* 'high'.

**hawser-laid** ● **adj.** another term for **CABLE-LAID**.

**hawthorn** ● **n.** a thorny shrub or tree with white, pink, or red blossom and small dark red fruits (haws). [*Crataegus monogyna* and related species.]
– ORIGIN OE *hagathorn*, prob. lit. 'hedge thorn' (see **HAW**[1], **THORN**).

**hay** ● **n.** grass that has been mown and dried for use as fodder.
– PHRASES **hit the hay** informal go to bed. **make hay (while the sun shines)** make good use of an opportunity while

it lasts.
– DERIVATIVES **haying** n.
– ORIGIN OE *hēg, hīeg, hīg*, of Gmc origin; rel. to **HEW**.
**haybox** ● n. historical a box stuffed with hay in which heated food was left to continue cooking.
**haycock** ● n. a conical heap of hay left in the field to dry.
**hay fever** ● n. an allergy caused by pollen or dust in which the mucous membranes of the eyes and nose are inflamed, causing sneezing and watery eyes.
**haylage** /'heɪlɪdʒ/ ● n. silage made from grass which has been partially dried.
– ORIGIN 1960s: blend of **HAY[1]** and **SILAGE**.
**hayloft** ● n. a loft over a stable used for storing hay or straw.
**haymaker** ● n. **1** a person who is involved in making hay. **2** an apparatus for shaking and drying hay. **3** informal a forceful blow.
– DERIVATIVES **haymaking** n.
**haymow** /'heɪməʊ/ ● n. a stack of hay or part of a barn in which hay is stored.
**hayrick** ● n. another term for **HAYSTACK**.
**hayride** ● n. chiefly N. Amer. a ride taken for pleasure in a wagon carrying hay.
**hayseed** ● n. **1** grass seed obtained from hay. **2** informal, chiefly N. Amer. a simple, unsophisticated country person.
**haystack** ● n. a large packed pile of hay.
**haywire** ● adj. informal erratic; out of control.
– ORIGIN C20: from **HAY** + **WIRE**, from the use of hay-baling wire in makeshift repairs.
**hazard** /'hazəd/ ● n. **1** a danger or risk. **2** a permanent feature of a golf course which presents an obstruction to playing a shot. **3** poetic/literary chance; probability. **4** a gambling game using two dice. **5** (in real tennis) each of the winning openings in the court. **6** Billiards a stroke with which a ball is pocketed. ➤(**losing hazard**) the pocketing of the cue ball off another ball. ➤(**winning hazard**) the pocketing of the object ball. ● v. **1** venture to say: *he hazarded a guess.* **2** risk the loss of.
– ORIGIN ME: from OFr. *hasard*, from Sp. *azar*, from Arab. *az-zahr* 'chance', from Pers. *zār* or Turk. *zar* 'dice'.
**hazard lights** ● pl. n. flashing right and left indicator lights on a vehicle, used to warn that the vehicle is stationary or unexpectedly slow.
**hazardous** ● adj. risky; dangerous.
– DERIVATIVES **hazardously** adv. **hazardousness** n.
**hazard pay** ● n. US term for **DANGER MONEY**.
**haze[1]** ● n. **1** a slight obscuration of the lower atmosphere, typically caused by fine suspended particles. **2** a state of obscurity or confusion: *through an alcoholic haze.*
– ORIGIN C18: prob. a back-form. from **HAZY**.
**haze[2]** ● v. N. Amer. **1** torment or harass (a new student or recruit) by subjection to strenuous, humiliating, or dangerous tasks. **2** drive (cattle) while on horseback.
– ORIGIN C17 (orig. Scots and dial. in the sense 'frighten, scold, or beat'): perh. rel. to obs. Fr. *haser* 'tease or insult'.
**hazel** ● n. **1** a shrub or small tree bearing prominent catkins in spring and edible nuts in autumn. [*Corylus avellana* and related species.] **2** a rich reddish-brown colour.
– ORIGIN OE *hæsel*, of Gmc origin.
**hazel grouse** ● n. a small woodland grouse with mainly greyish plumage. [*Bonasa bonasia*.]
**hazelnut** ● n. the round brown edible hard-shelled nut of the hazel.
**hazy** ● adj. (**-ier**, **-iest**) **1** covered by a haze. **2** vague, indistinct, or ill-defined.
– DERIVATIVES **hazily** adv. **haziness** n.
– ORIGIN C17: of unknown origin.
**HB** ● abbrev. **1** half board. **2** (also **hb**) hardback. **3** hard black (as a medium grade of pencil lead).
**Hb** ● symb. haemoglobin.
**HBM** ● abbrev. Her or His Britannic Majesty (or Majesty's).
**H-bomb** ● n. short for **HYDROGEN BOMB**.
**HC** ● abbrev. **1** Holy Communion. **2** (in the UK) House of Commons. **3** hydrocarbon.
**HCF** ● abbrev. Mathematics highest common factor.
**HCFC** ● n. Chemistry hydrochlorofluorocarbon, any of a class of inert compounds of carbon, hydrogen, hydrocarbons, chlorine, and fluorine.
**HDD** ● abbrev. Computing hard disk drive.
**HDTV** ● abbrev. high-definition television.
**HE** ● abbrev. **1** high explosive. **2** His Eminence. **3** His or Her Excellency.
**He** ● symb. the chemical element helium.
**he** ● pron. [third person sing.] **1** used to refer to a man, boy, or male animal previously mentioned or easily identified. **2** used to refer to a person or animal of unspecified sex (in modern use, now largely replaced by 'he or she' or 'they'). **3** any person (in modern use, now largely replaced by 'anyone' or 'the person'). ● n. a male; a man.
– ORIGIN OE *he, hē*, of Gmc origin.
**head** ● n. **1** the upper part of the human body, or the front or upper part of the body of an animal, typically separated from the rest of the body by a neck, and containing the brain, mouth, and sense organs. **2** the front, forward, or upper part or end of something. ➤the source of a river or stream. ➤the end of a lake or inlet at which a river enters. ➤[usu. in place names] a promontory: *Beachy Head.* ➤the top of a ship's mast. ➤the bows of a ship. ➤the foam on top of a glass of beer, or the cream on the top of milk. **3** the cutting or operational end of a tool or mechanism. ➤the flattened or knobbed end of a nail, pin, screw, or match. **4** a compact mass of leaves or flowers at the top of a stem, especially a capitulum. ➤the edible leafy part at the top of the stem of vegetables such as cabbage and lettuce. ➤one saleable unit of certain vegetables such as cabbage or celery. **5** a person in charge; a director or leader. **6** a person considered as a numerical unit: *they paid fifty pounds a head.* ➤[treated as pl.] a number of cattle or game as specified: *seventy head of dairy cattle.* **7** a component in an audio, video, or information system by which information is transferred from an electrical signal to the recording medium, or vice versa. ➤the part of a record player that holds the playing cartridge and stylus. **8** a body of water kept at a particular height in order to provide a supply at sufficient pressure: *an 8 m head of water in the shafts.* ➤the pressure exerted by such water. **9** Nautical slang a toilet, especially on a ship. **10** Geology a superficial deposit of rock fragments, formed at the edge of an ice sheet by repeated freezing and thawing and then moved downhill. **11** (**heads**) the side of a coin bearing the image of a head (used when tossing a coin to determine a winner). **12** the antlers of a deer. **13** Grammar the word that governs all the other words in a phrase in which it is used. ● adj. chief; principal. ● v. **1** be or act as the head of. **2** give a title or heading to. **3** move in a specified direction: *he was heading for the exit.* **4** (**head someone/thing off**) intercept and turn aside someone or something; forestall something. **5** Soccer shoot or pass (the ball) with the head. **6** lop off the upper part or branches of (a plant or tree). **7** (of a lettuce or cabbage) form a head. **8** (**head up**) Sailing steer towards the wind.
– PHRASES **be banging one's head against a brick wall** be doggedly attempting the impossible. **bang** (or **knock**) **people's heads together** reprimand people in an attempt to stop them arguing. **be hanging over someone's head** threaten to affect someone at any moment. **be on someone's** (**own**) **head** be someone's sole responsibility. **by the head** Nautical (of a boat or ship) deeper in the water forward than astern. **come to a head** reach a crisis. **do someone's head in** Brit. informal cause someone to feel annoyed, confused, or frustrated. **get one's head down** Brit. informal **1** sleep. **2** concentrate on the task in hand. **get one's head round** (or **around**) informal understand or come to terms with. **give someone his** (or **her**) **head** allow someone complete freedom of action. **give someone head** vulgar slang perform oral sex on someone. **go to someone's head 1** (of alcohol) make someone slightly drunk. **2** (of success) make someone conceited. **a head for** an aptitude for or tolerance of: *a head for heights.* —— **one's head off** informal talk, laugh, shout, etc. unrestrainedly: *he was laughing his head off.* **head over heels 1** turning over completely in forward

motion, as in a somersault. **2** madly in love. **a head start** an advantage granted or gained at the beginning. **heads will roll** people will be dismissed or forced to resign. **in one's head** by mental process without use of physical aids. **keep one's head** remain calm. **keep one's head above water** avoid succumbing to difficulties. **knock something on the head** dismiss an idea or rumour once and for all. **lose one's head** lose self-control; panic. **make head or tail of** [usu. with neg.] understand at all. **off** (or **out of**) **one's head** informal crazy. **off the top of one's head** without careful thought or investigation. **over someone's head 1** (also **above someone's head**) beyond someone's ability to understand. **2** without consultation or involvement. **put their** (or **our** or **your**) **heads together** consult and work together. **stand** (or **turn**) **something on its head** completely reverse an idea or argument. **turn someone's head** make someone conceited. **turn heads** attract a great deal of attention.

– DERIVATIVES **-headed** adj. **headless** adj. **headward** adj. & adv. **headwards** adv.

– ORIGIN OE *hēafod*, of Gmc origin.

**-head¹** ● **suffix** equivalent to **-HOOD**.

– ORIGIN ME *-hed*, *-hede*.

**-head²** ● **comb. form 1** denoting the head or end of a specified thing: *spearhead*. **2** in nouns used informally to express disparagement of a person: *airhead*. **3** in nouns used informally to denote an addict of a specified drug: *crackhead*.

**headache** ● **n. 1** a continuous pain in the head. **2** informal something that causes worry or trouble.

– DERIVATIVES **headachy** adj.

**headage** ● **n.** the number of animals held as stock on a farm.

**headband** ● **n. 1** a band of fabric worn around the head as a decoration or to keep the hair off the face. **2** an ornamental strip of coloured silk fastened to the top of the spine of a book.

**headbanger** ● **n.** informal **1** a fan or performer of heavy metal music. **2** a mad or eccentric person.

**headbanging** ● **n.** violent rhythmic shaking of the head by fans of heavy metal music.

**headboard** ● **n. 1** an upright panel at the head of a bed. **2** a board or sign, especially on the front of a train. **3** Sailing a reinforcement at the top of a triangular sail such as a mainsail.

**headbutt** ● **v.** attack (someone) using a forceful and aggressive thrust with the head. ● **n.** an act of headbutting.

**head case** ● **n.** informal a mentally ill or unstable person.

**headcheese** ● **n.** North American term for **BRAWN** (in sense 2).

**headcount** ● **n.** a count of the number of people present or available.

**headdress** ● **n.** an ornamental covering for the head, especially one worn on ceremonial occasions.

**header** ● **n. 1** Soccer a shot or pass made with the head. **2** informal a headlong fall or dive. **3** a brick or stone laid at right angles to the face of a wall. Compare with **STRETCHER** (in sense 5). **4** (also **header tank**) a raised tank of water maintaining pressure in a plumbing system. **5** a line or block of text appearing at the top of each page of a book or document.

**head first** ● **adj. & adv. 1** with the head in front of the rest of the body. **2** without sufficient forethought.

**head gasket** ● **n.** the gasket which fits between the cylinder head and the cylinders or cylinder block in an internal-combustion engine.

**headgear** ● **n.** hats, helmets, and other items worn on the head.

**headhunt** ● **v. 1** [as noun **headhunting**] the practice among some peoples of collecting the heads of dead enemies as trophies. **2** identify and approach (someone employed elsewhere) to fill a business position.

– DERIVATIVES **headhunter** n.

**heading** ● **n. 1** a title at the head of a page or section of a book. **2** a direction or bearing. **3** the top of a curtain extending above the hooks or wire by which it is suspended. **4** a horizontal passage made in preparation for building a tunnel. ➤ Mining another term for **DRIFT**.

**headland** ● **n. 1** a narrow piece of land projecting into the sea. **2** a strip of land left unploughed at the end of a field.

**headlight** (also **headlamp**) ● **n.** a powerful light at the front of a motor vehicle or railway engine.

**headline** ● **n.** a heading at the top of an article or page in a newspaper or magazine. ➤ **(the headlines)** a summary of the most important items of news. ● **v. 1** provide with a headline. **2** appear as the star performer at (a concert).

**headliner** ● **n.** the performer or act promoted as the star attraction on a bill.

**headlock** ● **n.** a method of restraining someone by holding an arm firmly around their head.

**headlong** ● **adv. & adj. 1** with the head foremost. **2** in a rush; with reckless haste.

– ORIGIN ME *headling*, from **HEAD** + the adverbial suffix *-ling*.

**head louse** ● **n.** a louse which infests the hair of the human head. [*Pediculus humanus capitis*.]

**headman** ● **n.** (pl. **-men**) the chief or leader of a tribe.

**headmaster** ● **n.** chiefly Brit. a male head teacher.

– DERIVATIVES **headmasterly** adj.

**headmistress** ● **n.** chiefly Brit. a female head teacher.

– DERIVATIVES **headmistressy** adj.

**headmost** ● **adj.** archaic (chiefly of a ship) holding a position in advance of others; foremost.

**headnote** ● **n. 1** a note at the head of an article or document. **2** Law a summary of a decided case prefixed to the case report.

**head of state** ● **n.** the chief public representative of a country, who may also be the head of government.

**head-on** ● **adj. & adv. 1** with or involving the front of a vehicle. **2** with or involving direct confrontation.

**headphones** ● **pl. n.** a pair of earphones joined by a band placed over the head.

**headpiece** ● **n. 1** a device worn on the head. **2** an illustration or ornamental motif at the head of a chapter in a book. **3** the part of a halter or bridle that fits over the top of a horse's head behind the ears.

**headquarter** ● **v.** (**be headquartered**) have headquarters at a specified place.

**headquarters** ● **n.** [treated as sing. or pl.] the managerial and administrative centre of an organization. ➤ the premises of a military commander and their staff.

**headrest** ● **n.** a padded support for the head on the back of a seat or chair.

**headroom** ● **n.** the space between the top of a person's head and the ceiling or other structure above.

**headsail** /ˈhɛdseɪl, -s(ə)l/ ● **n.** a sail on a ship's foremast or bowsprit.

**headscarf** ● **n.** (pl. **-scarves**) a square of fabric worn as a covering for the head, often folded into a triangle and knotted under the chin.

**head sea** ● **n.** a mass of waves approaching the front of a ship.

**headset** ● **n. 1** a set of headphones with a microphone attached. **2** the bearing assembly which links the front fork of a bicycle to its frame.

**headship** ● **n.** the position of leader or chief. ➤ chiefly Brit. the position of head teacher in a school.

**headshrinker** ● **n.** informal, chiefly N. Amer. a psychiatrist.

**headsman** ● **n.** (pl. **-men**) historical **1** an executioner who beheaded prisoners. **2** a person in command of a whaling boat.

**headspring** ● **n.** a spring that is the main source of a stream.

**headsquare** ● **n.** another term for **HEADSCARF**.

**headstall** /ˈhɛdstɔːl/ ● **n.** chiefly N. Amer. **1** a halter. **2** another term for **HEADPIECE** (in sense 3).

**headstander** ● **n.** a small freshwater fish of the Amazon region, popular in aquaria, that swims at an oblique angle with the head down. [Genus *Abramites*: two species.]

**headstay** • n. another term for **FORESTAY**.

**headstock** • n. **1** a set of bearings in a machine, supporting a revolving part. **2** the piece at the end of a guitar neck to which the tuning pegs are fixed.

**headstone** • n. an inscribed stone slab set up at the head of a grave.

**headstream** • n. a headwater stream.

**headstrong** • adj. energetically wilful and determined.

**heads-up** N. Amer. informal • n. an advance warning of something. • adj. showing alertness or perceptiveness.

**head teacher** • n. the teacher in charge of a school.

**head-to-head** • adj. & adv. involving two parties confronting each other. • n. a conversation or confrontation between two parties.

**head-turning** • adj. extremely noticeable or attractive.
– DERIVATIVES **head-turner** n.

**head-up display** (N. Amer. also **heads-up display**) • n. a display of instrument readings in an aircraft or vehicle that can be seen without lowering the eyes, typically through being projected on to the windscreen or visor.

**head voice** • n. one of the high registers of the voice in speaking or singing, above chest voice.

**headwater** • n. a tributary stream of a river close to or forming part of its source.

**headway** • n. **1** forward movement or progress. **2** the average interval between trains or buses on a regular service.

**headwind** • n. a wind blowing from directly in front.

**headword** • n. a word which begins a separate entry in a reference work.

**headwork** • n. **1** activities taxing the mind; mental work. **2** (**headworks**) apparatus for controlling the flow of water in a river or canal.

**heady** • adj. (**-ier**, **-iest**) **1** (of liquor) potent; intoxicating. **2** having a strong or exhilarating effect.
– DERIVATIVES **headily** adv. **headiness** n.

**heal** • v. **1** make or become sound or healthy again. **2** correct or put right (an undesirable situation).
– DERIVATIVES **healable** adj. **healer** n.
– ORIGIN OE *hǣlan*, of Gmc origin; rel. to **WHOLE**.

**heal-all** • n. **1** a universal remedy; a panacea. **2** any of a number of medicinal plants, especially roseroot and selfheal.

**heald** /hiːld/ • n. another term for **HEDDLE**.
– ORIGIN OE *hefel*, *hefeld* 'the warp and weft', of Gmc origin, from a base meaning 'raise'.

**health** • n. the state of being free from illness or injury. ➤a person's mental or physical condition.
– ORIGIN OE *hǣlth*, of Gmc origin; rel. to **WHOLE**.

**health centre** • n. an establishment housing local medical services or the practice of a group of doctors.

**health farm** • n. a residential establishment where people seek improved health by a regimen of dieting, exercise, and treatment.

**health food** • n. natural food that is thought to have health-giving qualities.

**healthful** • adj. having or conducive to good health.
– DERIVATIVES **healthfully** adv. **healthfulness** n.

**health physics** • pl. n. [treated as sing.] the branch of radiology concerned with the health of people working with radioactive materials.

**health service** • n. a public service providing medical care.

**health visitor** • n. Brit. a nurse who visits the homes of the chronically ill or parents with very young children.

**healthy** • adj. (**-ier**, **-iest**) **1** in good health; not unwell or diseased. ➤promoting good health: *a healthy diet.* **2** normal, natural, or desirable: *a healthy attitude.* ➤of a very satisfactory size or amount: *a healthy profit.*
– DERIVATIVES **healthily** adv. **healthiness** n.

**heap** • n. **1** a mound or pile of a substance. ➤an untidy collection of objects piled up haphazardly. **2** informal a large amount or number: *we have heaps of room.* **3** informal an untidy or dilapidated place or vehicle. • v. put in or form a heap. ➤load copiously with. ➤[as adj. **heaped**] Brit. (of a spoon) with the contents piled above the brim or edge.
– ORIGIN OE *hēap* (n.), *hēapian* (v.), of Gmc origin.

**hear** • v. (past and past part. **heard**) **1** perceive (a sound) with the ear. **2** be told or informed of. ➤(**have heard of**) be aware of the existence of. ➤(**hear from**) receive a letter or phone call from. ➤(**hear someone out**) listen to all that someone has to say. **3** Law listen to and judge (a case or plaintiff). **4** listen to and grant (a prayer).
– PHRASES **hear! hear!** used to express wholehearted agreement with something said in a speech. **will** (or **would**) **not hear of** will (or would) not allow or agree to.
– DERIVATIVES **hearable** adj. **hearer** n.
– ORIGIN OE *hīeran*, *hēran*, of Gmc origin.

**hearing** • n. **1** the faculty of perceiving sounds. ➤the range within which sounds may be heard; earshot. **2** an opportunity to state one's case. **3** Law an act of listening to evidence, especially a trial before a judge without a jury.

**hearing aid** • n. a small amplifying device worn on the ear by a partially deaf person.

**hearken** /ˈhɑːk(ə)n/ (also **harken**) • v. (usu. **hearken to**) archaic listen.
– ORIGIN OE *heorcnian*; prob. rel. to **HARK**.

**hearsay** • n. information which cannot be adequately substantiated; rumour.

**hearsay evidence** • n. Law evidence given by a witness based on information received from others rather than personal knowledge.

**hearse** /həːs/ • n. a vehicle for conveying the coffin at a funeral.
– ORIGIN ME (denoting a latticework canopy placed over the coffin of a distinguished person in church): from Anglo-Norman Fr. *herce* 'harrow, frame', from L. *hirpex* 'rake'.

**heart** • n. **1** a hollow muscular organ that pumps the blood through the circulatory system by rhythmic contraction and dilation. **2** the central, innermost, or vital part of something. **3** a conventional representation of a heart with two equal curves meeting at a point at the bottom and a cusp at the top. **4** (**hearts**) one of the four suits in a conventional pack of playing cards, denoted by a red figure of such a shape. ➤a card of this suit. **5** a person's feeling of or capacity for love or compassion. ➤mood or feeling: *they had a change of heart.* ➤courage or enthusiasm: *they may lose heart as the work mounts up.* **6** the close compact head of a cabbage or lettuce. **7** the condition of agricultural land as regards fertility.
– PHRASES **after one's own heart** sharing one's tastes. **at heart** in one's real nature, in contrast to how one may appear. **break someone's heart** overwhelm someone with sadness. **by heart** from memory. **close** (or **dear**) **to one's heart** of deep interest and concern to one. **from the** (or **the bottom of one's**) **heart** with sincere feeling. **have a heart** be merciful; show pity. **have a heart of gold** have a generous or compassionate nature. **have one's heart in one's mouth** be greatly alarmed or apprehensive. **have one's heart in the right place** be sincere or well intentioned. **one's heart's desire** something that one greatly wishes for. **one's heartstrings** used in reference to one's deepest feelings of love or compassion. **in one's heart of hearts** in one's innermost feelings. **take something to heart** take criticism seriously and be affected by it. **wear one's heart on one's sleeve** make one's feelings apparent.
– DERIVATIVES **-hearted** adj.
– ORIGIN OE *heorte*, of Gmc origin.

**heartache** • n. emotional anguish or grief.

**heart attack** • n. a sudden occurrence of coronary thrombosis, typically resulting in the death of part of a heart muscle.

**heartbeat** • n. **1** a pulsation of the heart. **2** an animating force or influence.
– PHRASES **a heartbeat away** very close.

**heartbreak** • n. overwhelming distress.
– DERIVATIVES **heartbreaker** n.

**heartbreaking** • adj. causing overwhelming distress.

– DERIVATIVES **heartbreakingly** adv.

**heartbroken** • **adj.** suffering from overwhelming distress; very upset.

**heartburn** • **n.** a form of indigestion felt as a burning sensation in the chest, caused by acid regurgitation into the oesophagus.

**hearten** • **v.** make more cheerful or confident.
– DERIVATIVES **heartening** adj. **hearteningly** adv.

**heart failure** • **n.** severe failure of the heart to function properly, especially as a cause of death.

**heartfelt** • **adj.** sincere; deeply and strongly felt.

**hearth** /hɑːθ/ • **n.** **1** the floor or surround of a fireplace (often used as a symbol of home). **2** the base or lower part of a furnace, where molten metal collects.
– ORIGIN OE *heorth*, of W. Gmc origin.

**hearthrug** • **n.** a rug laid in front of a fireplace.

**hearthstone** • **n.** a flat stone forming a hearth.

**heartily** • **adv.** **1** in a hearty manner. **2** very; to a great degree: *they were heartily sick of the subject.*

**heartland** • **n.** the central or most important part of a country or area.

**heartless** • **adj.** completely lacking in feeling or consideration.
– DERIVATIVES **heartlessly** adv. **heartlessness** n.

**heart-lung machine** • **n.** a machine that temporarily takes over the functions of the heart and lungs, especially during heart surgery.

**heart of palm** • **n.** the edible bud of a palm tree.

**heart-rending** • **adj.** causing great sadness or distress.
– DERIVATIVES **heart-rendingly** adv.

**heart-searching** • **n.** thorough examination of one's feelings and motives.

**heartsease** /ˈhɑːtsiːz/ • **n.** a wild pansy with purple and yellow flowers, source of most garden varieties. [*Viola tricolor.*]

**heartsick** (also **heartsore**) • **adj.** chiefly poetic/literary despondent from grief or loss of love.
– DERIVATIVES **heartsickness** n.

**heartsink patient** • **n.** Brit. informal (among doctors) a patient who makes frequent visits to a surgery, complaining of persistent but unidentifiable ailments.

**heart-stopping** • **adj.** thrilling; full of suspense.
– DERIVATIVES **heart-stopper** n. **heart-stoppingly** adv.

**heart-throb** • **n.** informal a man whose good looks excite romantic feelings in women.

**heart-to-heart** • **adj.** (of a conversation) intimate and personal. • **n.** an intimate and personal conversation.

**heart-warming** • **adj.** emotionally rewarding or uplifting.

**heartwood** • **n.** the dense inner part of a tree trunk, yielding the hardest wood.

**heartworm** • **n.** a parasitic nematode worm which infests the hearts of dogs and other animals. [*Dirofilaria immitis.*]

**hearty** • **adj.** (**-ier**, **-iest**) **1** loudly vigorous and cheerful. ➤(of a feeling or opinion) heartfelt. **2** strong and healthy. **3** (of a person's appetite) robust and healthy. ➤(of food) wholesome and substantial. • **n.** Brit. informal **1** a vigorously cheerful and sporty person. **2** (**me hearties**) a form of address ascribed to sailors.
– DERIVATIVES **heartiness** n.

**heat** • **n.** **1** the quality of being hot; high temperature. ➤Physics heat seen as a form of energy arising from the random motion of the molecules of bodies. ➤technical the amount of heat needed for or evolved in a specific process. ➤a source or level of heat for cooking. **2** intensity of feeling, especially of anger or excitement. ➤(**the heat**) informal intensive and unwelcome pressure. **3** a preliminary round in a race or contest. • **v.** **1** make or become hot or warm. **2** (**heat up**) become more intense and exciting. ➤[as adj. **heated**] inflamed with passion or conviction: *a heated argument.* ➤archaic inflame; excite.
– PHRASES **in the heat of the moment** while temporarily angry or excited and without stopping for thought. **on** (or N. Amer. **in**) **heat** (of a female mammal) in the receptive period of the sexual cycle; in oestrus.
– DERIVATIVES **heatedly** adv.
– ORIGIN OE *hǣtu* (n.), *hǣtan* (v.), of Gmc origin; rel. to HOT.

**heat barrier** • **n.** the limitation of the speed of an aircraft or other flying object by heat resulting from air friction.

**heat capacity** • **n.** another term for THERMAL CAPACITY.

**heat death** • **n.** Physics a state of uniform distribution of energy, especially viewed as a possible fate of the universe.

**heat engine** • **n.** a device for producing motive power from heat.

**heater** • **n.** **1** a device for heating something, especially a room. **2** Baseball a fast ball. **3** N. Amer. informal, dated a gun.

**heat-exchanger** • **n.** a device for transferring heat from one medium to another.

**heath** • **n.** **1** chiefly Brit. an area of open uncultivated land, typically on acid sandy soil and covered with heather, gorse, and coarse grasses. **2** a dwarf shrub with small leathery leaves and small pink or purple flowers, characteristic of heathland and moorland. [*Erica tetralix* (**cross-leaved heath**) and other species.] **3** used in names of heathland butterflies and moths, e.g. **small heath**.
– DERIVATIVES **heathy** adj.
– ORIGIN OE *hǣth*, of Gmc origin.

**heathen** /ˈhiːð(ə)n/ • **n.** derogatory **1** a person who does not belong to a widely held religion (especially Christianity, Judaism, or Islam) as regarded by those who do. **2** informal a person lacking culture or moral principles. • **adj.** of or relating to heathens.
– DERIVATIVES **heathendom** n. **heathenish** adj. **heathenism** n.
– ORIGIN OE *hǣthen*, prob. from a Gmc adj. meaning 'inhabiting open country, savage', from the base of HEATH.

**heather** • **n.** a purple-flowered heath typical of moorland and heathland. [*Calluna vulgaris.*] ➤informal any plant of this family (Ericaceae); a heath.
– DERIVATIVES **heathery** adj.
– ORIGIN OE *hadre, hedre*, of unknown origin.

**Heath Robinson** • **adj.** Brit. ingeniously or ridiculously over-complicated in design or construction.
– ORIGIN C20: named after the Engl. cartoonist William *Heath Robinson.*

**heating** • **n.** equipment or devices used to provide heat, especially to a building.

**heatproof** • **adj.** able to resist great heat.

**heat pump** • **n.** a device that transfers heat from a colder area to a hotter area by using mechanical energy, as in a refrigerator.

**heat-seeking** • **adj.** (of a missile) able to detect and home in on infrared radiation emitted by a target, such as the exhaust vent of a jet aircraft.

**heat shield** • **n.** a device or coating for protection from excessive heat, in particular an outer covering on a spacecraft to protect it from the heat generated during re-entry into the earth's atmosphere.

**heat sink** • **n.** a device or substance for absorbing excessive or unwanted heat.

**heatstroke** • **n.** a feverish condition caused by failure of the body's temperature-regulating mechanism when exposed to excessively high temperatures.

**heat treatment** • **n.** the use of heat for therapeutic purposes in medicine or to modify the properties of a material, especially in metallurgy.
– DERIVATIVES **heat-treat** v.

**heatwave** • **n.** a prolonged period of abnormally hot weather.

**heave** /hiːv/ • **v.** (past and past part. **heaved** or chiefly Nautical **hove**) **1** lift or haul (a heavy thing) with great effort. ➤informal throw (something heavy). **2** produce (a sigh). **3** rise and fall rhythmically or spasmodically. **4** make an effort to vomit; retch. **5** (**heave to**) Nautical come to a stop, especially by turning across the wind leaving the headsail backed. ➤(**heave in sight** or **into view**) come into view. • **n.** **1** an act of heaving. **2** (**heaves**) another term for **COPD** in horses. **3** Geology a sideways displacement in a fault.

– DERIVATIVES **heaver** n.
– ORIGIN OE *hebban*, of Gmc origin.

**heave-ho** • exclam. a cry emitted with an action that requires physical effort. • n. (**the heave-ho**) informal dismissal.

**heaven** • n. **1** a place regarded in various religions as the abode of God or the gods and of the good after death, often depicted as being above the sky. **2** (**the heavens**) poetic/literary the sky. **3** informal a place or state of supreme bliss. **4** (also **heavens**) used in exclamations as a substitute for 'God': *heaven knows!*
– PHRASES **the heavens open** it suddenly starts to rain very heavily. **in seventh heaven** in a state of ecstasy. **move heaven and earth to do something** make extraordinary efforts to do a thing. **stink** (or **smell**) **to high heaven** informal smell very bad.
– DERIVATIVES **heavenward** adj. & adv. **heavenwards** adv.
– ORIGIN OE *heofon*, of Gmc origin.

**heavenly** • adj. **1** of heaven; divine. **2** of or relating to the sky. **3** informal very pleasing; wonderful.
– DERIVATIVES **heavenliness** n.

**heavenly body** • n. a planet, star, or other celestial body.

**heavenly host** • n. a literary or biblical term for the angels.

**heaven-sent** • adj. (of an event or opportunity) occurring at a very favourable time.

**heaving** • adj. Brit. informal (of a place) extremely crowded.

**Heaviside layer** (also **Heaviside–Kennelly layer**) • n. another name for **E-LAYER**.
– ORIGIN C20: named after the Engl. physicist Oliver *Heaviside* and the Amer. engineer Arthur E. *Kennelly*.

**heavy** • adj. (**-ier**, **-iest**) **1** of great weight; difficult to lift or move. **2** of great density; thick or substantial. ➤(of food) hard to digest; too filling. ➤(of ground) muddy or full of clay. ➤not delicate or graceful; coarse or slow-moving. ➤(of a smell) overpowering. **3** of more than the usual size, amount, or force: *a heavy cold.* ➤(**heavy on**) using a lot of. ➤doing something to excess: *a heavy smoker.* **4** striking or falling with force. **5** needing much physical effort. ➤mentally oppressive; hard to endure. ➤very important or serious. **6** (of music, especially rock) having a strong bass component and a forceful rhythm. **7** informal strict, harsh, or difficult to deal with. **8** Physics containing atoms of an isotope of greater than the usual mass: *heavy water.* • n. (pl. **-ies**) **1** something large or heavy of its kind. ➤informal a large, strong man, especially one hired for protection. ➤informal an important person. **2** chiefly Scottish strong beer, especially bitter.
– PHRASES **heavy going** a person or situation that is difficult or boring to deal with.
– DERIVATIVES **heavily** adv. **heaviness** n. **heavyish** adj.
– ORIGIN OE *hefig*, of Gmc origin; rel. to **HEAVE**.

**heavy breathing** • n. breathing that is audible through being deep or laboured.

**heavy chemicals** • pl. n. bulk chemicals used in industry and agriculture.

**heavy cream** • n. North American term for **DOUBLE CREAM**.

**heavy-duty** • adj. **1** designed to withstand the stresses of demanding use. **2** informal intense, important, or abundant.

**heavy-handed** • adj. clumsy, insensitive, or overly forceful.
– DERIVATIVES **heavy-handedly** adv. **heavy-handedness** n.

**heavy-hearted** • adj. feeling depressed or melancholy.

**heavy horse** • n. a large, strong, heavily built horse of a type used for draught work.

**heavy hydrogen** • n. another term for **DEUTERIUM**.

**heavy industry** • n. the manufacture of large, heavy articles and materials in bulk.

**heavy metal** • n. **1** a metal of relatively high density, or of high relative atomic weight. **2** a type of highly amplified harsh-sounding rock music with a strong beat.

**heavy oil** • n. any of the relatively dense hydrocarbons (denser than water) derived from petroleum, coal tar, and similar materials.

**heavy petting** • n. erotic contact between two people involving stimulation of the genitals but stopping short of intercourse.

**heavy water** • n. water in which the hydrogen in the molecules is partly or wholly replaced by the isotope deuterium, used especially as a moderator in nuclear reactors.

**heavyweight** • n. **1** a weight in boxing and other sports, typically the heaviest category. **2** informal a person of influence or importance. • adj. **1** of above-average weight. **2** informal serious, important, or influential.

**Heb.** • abbrev. **1** Epistle to the Hebrews. **2** Hebrew.

**hebdomadal** /hɛbˈdɒməd(ə)l/ • adj. formal weekly.
– ORIGIN C17: from late L. *hebdomadalis*, from Gk *hebdomas, hebdomad-* 'the number seven, seven days', from *hepta* 'seven'.

**Hebe** /ˈhiːb/ • n. US informal, offensive a Jewish person.
– ORIGIN C20: abbrev. of **HEBREW**.

**hebe** /ˈhiːbi/ • n. an evergreen flowering shrub with spikes of mauve, pink, or white flowers, native to New Zealand. [Genus *Hebe*.]
– ORIGIN mod. L., named after the Gk goddess *Hebe*.

**hebephrenia** /ˌhiːbɪˈfriːnɪə/ • n. a form of chronic schizophrenia involving disordered thought, hallucinations, and bizarre behaviour.
– DERIVATIVES **hebephrenic** /-ˈfrɛnɪk/ adj. & n.
– ORIGIN C19 (orig. assoc. with behaviour in puberty): from the Gk goddess of youth *Hebe* + Gk *phrēn* 'mind' + **-IA**[1].

**hebetude** /ˈhɛbɪtjuːd/ • n. poetic/literary the state of being dull or lethargic.
– ORIGIN C17: from late L. *hebetudo*, from *hebes, hebet-* 'blunt'.

**Hebraic** /hɪˈbreɪɪk/ • adj. of Hebrew or the Hebrews.
– DERIVATIVES **Hebraically** adv.

**Hebraism** /ˈhiːbreɪɪz(ə)m/ • n. **1** a Hebrew idiom or expression. **2** the Jewish religion, culture, or character.
– DERIVATIVES **Hebraistic** adj. **Hebraize** (also **-ise**) v.

**Hebraist** /ˈhiːbreɪɪst/ • n. a scholar of the Hebrew language.

**Hebrew** /ˈhiːbruː/ • n. **1** a member of an ancient people living in what is now Israel and Palestine, who established the kingdoms of Israel and Judah. **2** old-fashioned and sometimes offensive term for **JEW**. **3** the Semitic language of the Hebrews, in its ancient or modern form.
– ORIGIN from OFr. *Ebreu*, via L. from late Gk *Hebraios*, from Aramaic *ʿibray*, based on Heb. *ʿiḇrî* understood to mean 'one from the other side (of the river)'.

**Hebrew Bible** • n. the sacred writings of Judaism, called by Christians the Old Testament.

**Hebridean** /ˈhɛbrɪdiːən/ • n. a native or inhabitant of the Hebrides off the NW coast of Scotland. • adj. of or relating to the Hebrides.

**hecatomb** /ˈhɛkətuːm/ • n. (in ancient Greece or Rome) a great public sacrifice, originally of a hundred oxen.
– ORIGIN C16: via L. from Gk *hekatombē* (from *hekaton* 'hundred' + *bous* 'ox').

**heck** • exclam. expressing surprise, frustration, or dismay. ➤(**the heck** or **a heck of a** ——) used for emphasis.
– ORIGIN C19 (orig. north. Engl. dial.): euphemistic alt. of **HELL**.

**heckelphone** /ˈhɛk(ə)lfəʊn/ • n. a woodwind instrument resembling a large oboe, with a range about an octave lower.
– ORIGIN C20: named after the Ger. instrument-maker Wilhelm *Heckel*, on the pattern of *saxophone*.

**heckle** • v. **1** interrupt (a public speaker) with derisive comments or abuse. **2** dress (flax or hemp) to split and straighten the fibres for spinning. • n. a heckling comment.
– DERIVATIVES **heckler** n.
– ORIGIN ME: from *heckle* 'flax comb', a dial. form of **HACKLE**; for the development in sense, cf. **TEASE**.

**hectare** /ˈhɛktɛː, -ɑː/ (abbrev.: **ha**) • n. a metric unit of square measure, equal to 10,000 square metres (2.471 acres).

## Word *Formation*

**-hedron** from Greek *hedra* 'base'

➤ Most **-hedron** words are used with the sense 'a solid figure having a specified number of plane faces':

| | | |
|---|---|---|
| decahedron | ten faces | Gk *deka* 'ten' |
| dodecahedron | twelve faces | Gk *dōdeka* 'twelve' |
| heptahedron | seven faces | Gk *hepta* 'seven' |
| hexahedron | six faces | Gk *hex* 'six' |
| icosahedron | twenty faces | Gk *eikosi* 'twenty' |
| octahedron | eight faces | Gk *oktō* 'eight' |
| pentahedron | five faces | Gk *pente* 'five' |
| polyhedron | many faces | Gk *polloi* 'many' |
| tetrahedron | four faces (a triangular pyramid) | Gk *tettares* 'four' |
| trihedron | three faces (in addition to the ends) | Gk *treis* 'three' |

– DERIVATIVES **hectarage** n.
– ORIGIN C19: from Fr., from Gk *hekaton* 'hundred' + **ARE**[2].

**hectic** ● adj. **1** full of incessant or frantic activity. **2** Medicine, archaic affected by or denoting a recurrent fever typically accompanying tuberculosis, with flushed cheeks and hot, dry skin. ● n. Medicine, archaic a hectic fever or flush.
– DERIVATIVES **hectically** adv.
– ORIGIN ME *etik*, via OFr. from late L. *hecticus*, from Gk *hektikos* 'habitual'.

**hecto-** ● comb. form a hundred: *hectometre.*
– ORIGIN from Fr., formed irregularly by contr. of Gk *hekaton* 'hundred'.

**hectocotylus** /ˌhɛktə(ʊ)ˈkɒtɪləs/ ● n. (pl. **hectocotyli** /-lʌɪ, -liː/) Zoology a modified arm used by male octopuses and some other cephalopods to transfer sperm to the female.
– ORIGIN C19: mod. L., from **HECTO-** + Gk *kotulē* 'hollow thing'.

**hectogram** (also **hectogramme**) (abbrev.: **hg**) ● n. a metric unit of mass equal to one hundred grams.

**hectolitre** /ˈhɛktə(ʊ)ˌliːtə/ (US **hectoliter**) (abbrev.: **hl**) ● n. a metric unit of capacity equal to one hundred litres.

**hectometre** /ˈhɛktə(ʊ)ˌmiːtə/ (US **hectometer**) (abbrev.: **hm**) ● n. a metric unit of length equal to one hundred metres.

**hector** /ˈhɛktə/ ● v. talk to (someone) in a bullying way.
– DERIVATIVES **hectoring** adj. **hectoringly** adv.
– ORIGIN ME (orig. denoting a hero, later a braggart or bully): from the Trojan warrior *Hector* in Homer's *Iliad.*

**he'd** ● contr. **1** he had. **2** he would.

**heddle** /ˈhɛd(ə)l/ ● n. a looped wire or cord with an eye in the centre through which a warp yarn is passed in a loom before going through the reed.
– ORIGIN C16: appar. from an alt. of OE *hefeld* (see **HEALD**).

**heder** /ˈhɛdə, ˈxɛdə/ ● n. (pl. **hedarim** /hɛˈdɑːrɪm, xɛ-/ or **heders**) variant spelling of **CHEDER**.

**hedge** ● n. **1** a fence or boundary formed by closely growing bushes or shrubs. **2** a contract entered into or asset held as a protection against possible financial loss. **3** a word or phrase used to allow for additional possibilities or to avoid over-precise commitment, for example *etc.* or *usually.* ● v. **1** surround or bound with a hedge. **2** limit or qualify by conditions or exceptions. ➤avoid making a definite statement or commitment. **3** protect (one's investment or an investor) against loss by making balancing or compensating contracts or transactions.
– PHRASES **hedge one's bets** avoid committing oneself when faced with a difficult choice.
– DERIVATIVES **hedger** n. **hedging** n.
– ORIGIN OE *hegg*, of Gmc origin.

**hedge brown** ● n. another term for **GATEKEEPER** (in sense 2).

**hedge garlic** ● n. another term for **JACK-BY-THE-HEDGE**.

**hedgehog** ● n. **1** a nocturnal insectivorous mammal with a spiny coat and short legs, able to roll itself into a ball for defence. [*Erinaceus europaeus* and other species, family Erinaceidae.] **2** [as modifier] used in names of plants or fruits having spines, e.g. **hedgehog cactus**.

**hedge-hop** ● v. fly an aircraft at a very low altitude.
– DERIVATIVES **hedge-hopper** n.

**hedgerow** ● n. a hedge of wild shrubs and occasional trees bordering a field.
– ORIGIN OE: from **HEDGE** + obs. *rew* 'hedgerow'.

**hedge sparrow** ● n. another term for **DUNNOCK**.

**hedonic** /hiːˈdɒnɪk, hɛ-/ ● adj. Psychology & Philosophy relating to or considered in terms of pleasant (or unpleasant) sensations.
– ORIGIN C17: from Gk *hēdonikos*, from *hēdonē* 'pleasure'.

**hedonism** /ˈhiːd(ə)nɪz(ə)m, ˈhɛ-/ ● n. **1** the pursuit of pleasure; sensual self-indulgence. **2** Philosophy the ethical theory that pleasure (in the sense of the satisfaction of desires) is the highest good and proper aim of human life.
– DERIVATIVES **hedonist** n. **hedonistic** adj. **hedonistically** adv.
– ORIGIN C19: from Gk *hēdonē* 'pleasure' + **-ISM**.

**-hedron** ● comb. form (pl. **-hedra** or **-hedrons**) in nouns denoting geometrical solids having a specified number of plane faces: *decahedron.* ➤denoting geometrical solids having faces of a specified shape: *rhombohedron.* See word-formation panel.
– DERIVATIVES **-hedral** comb. form in corresponding adjectives.
– ORIGIN from Gk *hedra* 'seat, base'.

**heebie-jeebies** ● pl. n. (**the heebie-jeebies**) informal a state of nervous fear or anxiety.
– ORIGIN 1920s (orig. US): of unknown origin.

**heed** ● v. pay attention to; take notice of. ● n. (usu. in phr. **pay** (or **take**) **heed**) careful attention.
– DERIVATIVES **heedful** adj. **heedfully** adv. **heedfulness** n.
– ORIGIN OE *hēdan*, of W. Gmc origin.

**heedless** ● adj. showing a reckless lack of care or attention.
– DERIVATIVES **heedlessly** adv. **heedlessness** n.

**hee-haw** ● n. the loud, harsh cry of a donkey or mule. ● v. make such a cry.

**heel**[1] ● n. **1** the back part of the foot below the ankle. ➤the part of the palm of the hand next to the wrist. **2** the part of a shoe or boot supporting the heel. **3** informal, dated an inconsiderate or untrustworthy person. **4** the end of a violin bow at which it is held. **5** the part of the head of a golf club nearest the shaft. **6** a crusty end of a loaf of bread. **7** a piece of the main stem of a plant left attached to the base of a cutting. ● exclam. a command to a dog to walk close behind its owner. ● v. **1** fit or renew a heel on (a shoe or boot). **2** Rugby push or kick (the ball) out of the back of the scrum with one's heel. **3** Golf strike (the ball) with the heel of the club. **4** touch the ground with the heel when dancing.
– PHRASES **at** (or **on**) **the heels of** following closely after. **bring someone to heel** bring someone under control.

**cool** (or Brit. **kick**) **one's heels** be kept waiting. **kick up one's heels** chiefly N. Amer. have a lively, enjoyable time. **take to one's heels** run away. **turn** (**on one's**) **heel** turn sharply.
– DERIVATIVES **-heeled** adj. **heelless** adj.
– ORIGIN OE *hēla*, *hǣla*, of Gmc origin; rel. to **HOUGH**.

**heel**[2] ● **v.** (of a ship) lean over owing to the pressure of wind or an uneven load. ● **n.** an instance of heeling, or the amount that a ship heels.
– ORIGIN C16: from obs. *heeld*, *hield* 'incline', of Gmc origin.

**heel**[3] ● **v.** (**heel something in**) set a plant in the ground and cover its roots; plant something temporarily.
– ORIGIN OE *helian* 'cover, hide', of Gmc origin.

**heelball** ● **n.** a mixture of hard wax and lampblack used by shoemakers for polishing or in brass rubbing.

**heel bar** ● **n.** a small shop or stall where shoes are repaired.

**heel bone** ● **n.** the calcaneus.

**heeltap** ● **n. 1** a layer of leather or other material of which a shoe heel is made. **2** dated an amount of liquor left at the bottom of a glass after drinking.

**heft** ● **v. 1** lift or carry (something heavy). **2** lift or hold (something) to test its weight. ● **n.** chiefly N. Amer. **1** weight. **2** ability or influence.
– ORIGIN ME: prob. from **HEAVE**, on the pattern of words such as *cleft* and *weft*.

**hefty** ● **adj.** (**-ier**, **-iest**) large, heavy, and powerful.
– DERIVATIVES **heftily** adv. **heftiness** n.

**Hegelian** /heɪˈgiːlɪən, hɪ-, -ˈgeɪl-/ ● **adj.** of or relating to the German philosopher Georg Hegel (1770–1831) or his philosophy of objective idealism. ● **n.** a follower of Hegel.
– DERIVATIVES **Hegelianism** n.

**hegemony** /hɪˈdʒɛməni, -ˈgɛ-/ ● **n.** leadership or dominance, especially by one state or social group over others.
– DERIVATIVES **hegemonic** adj.
– ORIGIN C16: from Gk *hēgemonia*, from *hēgemōn* 'leader', from *hēgeisthai* 'to lead'.

**Hegira** /ˈhɛdʒɪrə/ (also **Hejira** or **Hijra**) ● **n. 1** Muhammad's departure from Mecca to Medina in AD 622, marking the consolidation of the first Muslim community. ➤ the Muslim era reckoned from this date. See also **AH**. **2** (**hegira**) an exodus or migration.
– ORIGIN via med. L. from Arab. *hijra* 'departure'.

**heifer** /ˈhɛfə/ ● **n.** a cow that has not borne a calf, or has borne only one calf. Compare with **cow**[1].
– ORIGIN OE *heahfore*, of unknown origin.

**heigh** ● **exclam.** archaic expressing encouragement or enquiry.

**heigh-ho** /heɪˈhəʊ/ ● **exclam.** informal expressing boredom, resignation, or jollity.

**height** ● **n. 1** the measurement of someone or something from head to foot or from base to top. ➤ the quality of being tall or high. **2** elevation above ground or a recognized level (typically sea level). ➤ a high place or area. **3** the most intense part or period of something. ➤ an extreme instance or example of something: *the height of bad manners*.
– ORIGIN OE *hēhthu*, of Gmc origin; rel. to **HIGH**.

**heighten** ● **v. 1** make higher. **2** make or become more intense.

**height of land** ● **n.** N. Amer. a watershed.

**Heimlich procedure** /ˈhʌɪmlɪç/ (also **Heimlich manoeuvre**) ● **n.** a first-aid procedure for dislodging an obstruction from a person's windpipe, in which a sudden strong pressure is applied on the abdomen between the navel and the ribcage.
– ORIGIN 1970s: named after the Amer. physician Henry J. *Heimlich*.

**heinie** /ˈhʌɪni/ ● **n.** US informal a person's buttocks.
– ORIGIN 1960s: alt. of **HINDER**[2], var. of **HIND**[1].

**heinous** /ˈheɪnəs, ˈhiːnəs/ ● **adj.** utterly odious or wicked: *a heinous crime*.
– DERIVATIVES **heinously** adv. **heinousness** n.
– ORIGIN ME: from OFr. *haineus*, from *hair* 'to hate', of Gmc origin.

**heir** /ɛː/ ● **n. 1** a person legally entitled to the property or rank of another on that person's death. **2** a person who continues the work of a predecessor.
– DERIVATIVES **heirdom** n. **heirless** adj. **heirship** n.
– ORIGIN ME: via OFr. from L. *heres*.

**heir apparent** ● **n.** (pl. **heirs apparent**) **1** an heir whose claim cannot be set aside by the birth of another heir. Compare with **HEIR PRESUMPTIVE**. **2** a person who is most likely to succeed to the place of another.

**heir-at-law** ● **n.** (pl. **heirs-at-law**) an heir by right of blood, especially to the real property of an intestate.

**heiress** ● **n.** a female heir, especially to vast wealth.

**heirloom** ● **n.** a valuable object that has belonged to a family for several generations.
– ORIGIN ME: from **HEIR** + **LOOM**[1] (which formerly had the senses 'tool, heirloom').

**heir presumptive** ● **n.** (pl. **heirs presumptive**) an heir whose claim may be set aside by the birth of another heir. Compare with **HEIR APPARENT**.

**heist** /hʌɪst/ informal, chiefly N. Amer. ● **n.** a robbery. ● **v.** steal.
– ORIGIN C19: representing a local pronunc. of **HOIST**.

**Hejira** ● **n.** variant spelling of **HEGIRA**.

**HeLa cells** /ˈhiːlə/ ● **pl. n.** human epithelial cells of a strain maintained in tissue culture since 1951 and used in research, especially in virology.
– ORIGIN 1950s: from the name of *He*nrietta *La*cks, whose cervical carcinoma provided the original cells.

**held** past and past participle of **HOLD**[1].

**Heldentenor** /ˈhɛld(ə)nˌtɛnɔː/ ● **n.** a powerful tenor voice suitable for heroic roles in opera.
– ORIGIN 1920s: Ger., lit. 'hero tenor'.

**helenium** /hɛˈliːnɪəm/ ● **n.** an American plant of the daisy family, with red to yellow flowers, each having a prominent central disc. [Genus *Helenium*.]
– ORIGIN mod. L., from Gk *helenion*, orig. denoting the herb *elecampane*, possibly in commemoration of Helen of Troy (said to have planted elecampane).

**heli-** ● **comb. form** relating to helicopters: *helipad*.

**heliacal** /hɪˈlʌɪək(ə)l/ ● **adj.** Astronomy denoting the first rising (or last setting) of a star or planet which occurs at the same time as the rising of the sun.
– ORIGIN C17: via late L. from Gk *hēliakos* (from *hēlios* 'sun') + **-AL**.

**helianthemum** /ˌhiːlɪˈanθɪməm/ ● **n.** a low evergreen shrub with saucer-shaped flowers, grown as an ornamental. [Genus *Helianthemum*.]
– ORIGIN mod. L., from Gk *hēlios* 'sun' + *anthemon* 'flower'.

**helical** /ˈhɛlɪk(ə)l, ˈhiː-/ ● **adj.** having the shape or form of a helix; spiral.
– DERIVATIVES **helically** adv.

**helices** plural form of **HELIX**.

**helichrysum** /ˌhɛlɪˈkrʌɪsəm/ ● **n.** a plant of the daisy family, with flowers retaining their shape and colour when dried. [Genus *Helichrysum*.]
– ORIGIN L., from Gk *helikhrusos*, from *helix* 'spiral' + *khrusos* 'gold'.

**helicity** /hiːˈlɪsɪti/ ● **n. 1** chiefly Biochemistry helical character, especially of DNA. **2** Physics a combination of the spin and the linear motion of a subatomic particle.

**helicoid** /ˈhiːlɪkɔɪd/ ● **adj.** of the form of a helix. ● **n.** a helicoid object or surface.
– DERIVATIVES **helicoidal** adj.

**helicon** /ˈhɛlɪk(ə)n/ ● **n.** a large spiral bass tuba played encircling the player's head and resting on the shoulder.
– ORIGIN C19: from L., assoc. with **HELIX**.

**helicopter** ● **n.** a type of aircraft deriving both lift and propulsion from one or two sets of horizontally revolving rotors and capable of moving vertically and horizontally. ● **v.** transport or fly by helicopter.
– ORIGIN C19: from Fr. *hélicoptère*, from Gk *helix* 'spiral' + *pteron* 'wing'.

**helio-** /ˈhiːlɪəʊ/ ● **comb. form** of or relating to the sun: *heliostat*.

– ORIGIN from Gk *hēlios* 'sun'.

**heliocentric** ● **adj. 1** having or representing the sun as the centre, as in the accepted astronomical model of the solar system. Compare with **GEOCENTRIC**. **2** Astronomy measured from or considered in relation to the centre of the sun.
– DERIVATIVES **heliocentrically** adv.

**heliogram** ● **n.** a message sent by reflecting sunlight in flashes from a movable mirror.

**heliograph** ● **n. 1** a signalling device by which sunlight is reflected in flashes from a movable mirror. ➤a message sent in such a way; a heliogram. **2** a telescopic apparatus for photographing the sun. **3** historical a type of early photographic engraving made using a sensitized silver plate and an asphalt or bitumen varnish. ● **v. 1** send (a message) by heliograph. **2** take a heliographic photograph of.
– DERIVATIVES **heliographic** adj. **heliography** n.

**heliogravure** /ˌhiːlɪəʊgraˈvjʊə/ ● **n.** another term for **PHOTOGRAVURE**.

**heliometer** /ˌhiːlɪˈɒmɪtə/ ● **n.** Astronomy a refracting telescope with a split objective lens, used for finding the angular distance between two stars.

**heliopause** ● **n.** Astronomy the boundary of the heliosphere.

**heliosphere** ● **n.** Astronomy the region of space, encompassing the solar system, in which the solar wind has a significant influence.
– DERIVATIVES **heliospheric** adj.

**heliostat** /ˈhiːlɪə(ʊ)stat/ ● **n.** an apparatus containing a movable mirror, used to reflect sunlight in a fixed direction.

**heliotherapy** ● **n.** the therapeutic use of sunlight.

**heliotrope** /ˈhiːlɪətrəʊp, ˈhɛl-/ ● **n.** a plant of the borage family, cultivated for its fragrant purple or blue flowers. [Genus *Heliotropium*.]
– ORIGIN OE *eliotropus* (orig. applied to various plants whose flowers turn towards the sun), via L. from Gk *hēliotropion*, from *hēlios* 'sun' + *trepein* 'to turn'.

**heliotropism** /ˌhiːlɪə(ʊ)ˈtrəʊpɪz(ə)m/ ● **n.** Biology growth or movement of a plant or other organism in response to sunlight.
– DERIVATIVES **heliotropic** adj.

**helipad** ● **n.** a landing and take-off area for helicopters.

**heliport** ● **n.** an airport or landing place for helicopters.

**heli-skiing** ● **n.** skiing in which the skier is taken up the mountain by helicopter.
– DERIVATIVES **heli-ski** v. **heli-skier** n.

**helium** /ˈhiːlɪəm/ ● **n.** the chemical element of atomic number 2, an inert gas which is the lightest member of the noble gas series. (Symbol: **He**)
– ORIGIN C19: mod. L., from Gk *hēlios* 'sun', because its existence was inferred from an emission line in the sun's spectrum.

**helix** /ˈhiːlɪks/ ● **n.** (pl. **helices** /ˈhiːlɪsiːz, ˈhɛl-/) **1** an object having a three-dimensional shape like that of a wire wound uniformly in a single layer around a cylinder or cone, as in a corkscrew or spiral staircase. ➤ Biochemistry an extended spiral chain of atoms in a protein, nucleic acid, or other polymeric molecule. **2** Architecture a spiral ornament. **3** Anatomy the rim of the external ear.
– ORIGIN C16: via L. from Gk.

**hell** ● **n. 1** a place regarded in various religions as a spiritual realm of evil and suffering, often depicted as a place of perpetual fire beneath the earth to which the wicked are consigned after death. **2** a state or place of great suffering. ● **exclam.** used to express annoyance or surprise or for emphasis.
– PHRASES **all hell breaks** (or **is let**) **loose** informal suddenly there is pandemonium. **come hell or high water** whatever difficulties may occur. **for the hell of it** informal just for fun. **get hell** informal be severely reprimanded. **give someone hell** informal severely reprimand or make things very unpleasant for someone. **go to hell in a handbasket** (or **handcart**) N. Amer. informal deteriorate rapidly. **hell for leather** as fast as possible. **hell's bells** informal an exclamation of annoyance or anger. **hell's half acre** N. Amer. a great distance. **like hell** informal **1** very fast, much, hard, etc. **2** used in ironic expressions of scorn or disagreement. **not a hope in hell** informal no chance at all. **play hell** (or **merry hell**) informal create havoc or cause damage. **there will be hell to pay** informal serious trouble will result. **until hell freezes over** forever.
– DERIVATIVES **hellward** adv. & adj.
– ORIGIN OE *hel*, *hell*, of Gmc origin.

**he'll** ● **contr.** he shall or he will.

**hellacious** /hɛˈleɪʃəs/ ● **adj.** N. Amer. informal very great, bad, or overwhelming.
– DERIVATIVES **hellaciously** adv.
– ORIGIN 1930s: from **HELL** + **-ACIOUS**, perh. suggested by *bodacious*.

**Helladic** /hɛˈladɪk/ ● **adj.** Archaeology relating to or denoting the Bronze Age cultures of mainland Greece (*c.*3000–1050 BC).
– ORIGIN C19: from Gk *Helladikos*, from *Hellas*, *Hellad-* 'Greece'.

**hellbender** ● **n.** an aquatic giant salamander with greyish skin and a flattened head, native to North America. [*Cryptobranchus alleganiensis*.]

**hell-bent** ● **adj.** determined to achieve something at all costs.

**hellcat** ● **n.** a spiteful, violent woman.

**hellebore** /ˈhɛlɪbɔː/ ● **n.** a poisonous winter-flowering plant with coarse divided leaves and large white, green, or purplish flowers. [Genus *Helleborus*: several species.]
– ORIGIN OE, from OFr. *ellebre*, *elebore* or med. L. *eleborus*, via L. from Gk *helleboros*.

**helleborine** /ˈhɛlɪbəˌriːn, -ˌrʌɪn/ ● **n.** an orchid with greenish, white, or pink flowers, occurring chiefly in woodland. [Genera *Epipactis* and *Cephalanthera*.]
– ORIGIN C16: Fr. or L., from Gk *helleborinē*, a plant like hellebore, from *helleboros* 'hellebore'.

**Hellene** /ˈhɛliːn/ ● **n.** a Greek.
– ORIGIN from Gk *Hellēn* 'a Greek'.

**Hellenic** /hɛˈlɛnɪk, -ˈliːnɪk/ ● **adj. 1** Greek. **2** Archaeology relating to or denoting Iron Age and Classical Greek culture (between Helladic and Hellenistic). ● **n.** the branch of the Indo-European language family comprising classical and modern Greek. ➤ the Greek language.
– DERIVATIVES **Hellenism** n. **Hellenist** n. **Hellenization** (also **-isation**) n. **Hellenize** (also **-ise**) v. **Hellenizer** n.

**Hellenistic** ● **adj.** of or relating to Greek culture in the Mediterranean and Near East from the death of Alexander the Great (323 BC) to the defeat of Cleopatra and Mark Antony by Octavian in 31 BC.

**hellfire** ● **n.** the fire regarded as existing in hell.

**hellgrammite** /ˈhɛlgrəmʌɪt/ ● **n.** N. Amer. the aquatic larva of a dobsonfly, often used as fishing bait.
– ORIGIN C19: of unknown origin.

**hellhole** ● **n.** an oppressive or unbearable place.

**hellhound** ● **n.** a demon in the form of a dog.

**hellion** /ˈhɛljən/ ● **n.** N. Amer. informal a rowdy or mischievous person, especially a child.
– ORIGIN C19: perh. from dial. *hallion* 'a worthless fellow', changed by assoc. with **HELL**.

**hellish** ● **adj. 1** of or like hell. **2** informal extremely difficult or unpleasant. ● **adv.** Brit. informal very; extremely.
– DERIVATIVES **hellishly** adv. **hellishness** n.

**hello** (also **hallo** or **hullo**) ● **exclam. 1** used as a greeting or to begin a telephone conversation. **2** Brit. used to express surprise or as a cry to attract someone's attention.
– ORIGIN C19: var. of earlier *hollo*; rel. to **HOLLA**.

**hellraiser** ● **n.** a person who causes trouble by violent, drunken, or outrageous behaviour.
– DERIVATIVES **hellraising** adj. & n.

**Hell's Angel** ● **n.** a member of a gang of male motorcycle enthusiasts notorious for lawless behaviour.

**helluva** ● **contr.** a hell of a (representing a non-standard pronunciation).

**helm**[1] ● **n. 1** a tiller or wheel for steering a ship or boat. **2** (**the helm**) a position of leadership. ● **v. 1** steer (a boat or ship). **2** manage the running of.
– ORIGIN OE *helma*; prob. rel. to **HELVE**.

**helm**[2] ● **n.** archaic a helmet.

– DERIVATIVES **helmed** adj.
– ORIGIN OE, of Gmc origin; rel. to **HELMET**.

**helmet** ● n. **1** a hard or padded protective hat. **2** Botany the arched upper part (galea) of the corolla in some flowers. **3** (also **helmet shell**) a predatory mollusc with a squat heavy shell, living in tropical and temperate seas. [Family Cassidae.]
– DERIVATIVES **helmeted** adj.
– ORIGIN ME: from OFr., dimin. of *helme*, of Gmc origin; rel. to **HELM**[2].

**helminth** /'hɛlmɪnθ/ ● n. a parasitic worm; a fluke, tapeworm, or nematode.
– DERIVATIVES **helminthic** adj. **helminthological** adj. **helminthologist** n. **helminthology** n.
– ORIGIN C19: from Gk *helmins*, *helminth-* 'intestinal worm'.

**helminthiasis** /ˌhɛlmɪn'θʌɪəsɪs/ ● n. Medicine infestation with parasitic worms.

**helmsman** ● n. (pl. **-men**) a person who steers a boat.

**helot** /'hɛlət/ ● n. **1** a member of a class of serfs in ancient Sparta, intermediate in status between slaves and citizens. **2** a serf or slave.
– DERIVATIVES **helotage** n. **helotism** n. **helotry** n.
– ORIGIN via L. from Gk *Heilōtes* (pl.), traditionally taken as referring to *Helos*, a Laconian town whose inhabitants were enslaved.

**help** ● v. **1** make it easier for (someone) to do something. ➤ improve (a situation or problem); be of benefit to. ➤ assist (someone) to move in a specified direction. **2** (**help someone to**) serve someone with (food or drink). ➤ (**help oneself**) take something without permission. **3** (**can/could not help**) cannot or could not avoid. ➤ (**can/could not help oneself**) cannot or could not stop oneself from acting in a certain way. ● n. **1** assistance or a source of assistance. **2** [as modifier] Computing giving assistance to a user in the form of displayed instructions: *a help menu*. **3** a domestic servant or employee. ● exclam. used as an appeal for urgent assistance.
– PHRASES **so help me (God)** used to emphasize that one means what one is saying. **there is no help for it** there is no way of avoiding or remedying a situation.
– DERIVATIVES **helper** n.
– ORIGIN OE *helpan* (v.), *help* (n.), of Gmc origin.

**helper cell** ● n. Physiology a T-lymphocyte that influences or controls the differentiation or activity of other cells of the immune system.

**helpful** ● adj. **1** giving or ready to give help. **2** useful.
– DERIVATIVES **helpfully** adv. **helpfulness** n.

**helping** ● n. a portion of food served to one person at one time.

**helpless** ● adj. **1** unable to defend oneself or to act without help. **2** uncontrollable: *helpless laughter*.
– DERIVATIVES **helplessly** adv. **helplessness** n.

**helpline** ● n. a telephone service providing help with problems.

**helpmate** (also **helpmeet**) ● n. a helpful companion or partner.
– ORIGIN C17 (as *helpmeet*): from an erroneous reading of Gen. 2:18, 20, where Adam's future wife is described as 'an help meet for him' (i.e. a suitable helper for him).

**helter-skelter** ● adj. & adv. in disorderly haste or confusion. ● n. Brit. a tall spiral slide winding around a tower at a fair.
– ORIGIN C16: a rhyming jingle of unknown origin, perh. symbolic of running feet or from ME *skelte* 'hasten'.

**helve** /hɛlv/ ● n. the handle of a weapon or tool.
– ORIGIN OE *helfe*, of Gmc origin; rel. to **HALTER**.

**Helvetian** (also **Helvetic**) ● adj. Swiss. ● n. a native of Switzerland.
– ORIGIN from L. *Helvetia* 'Switzerland' + **-AN**.

**hem**[1] ● n. the edge of a piece of cloth or clothing which has been turned under and sewn. ● v. (**hemmed**, **hemming**) **1** turn under and sew the edge of (a piece of cloth). **2** (**hem someone/thing in**) surround and restrict the space or movement of someone or something.
– ORIGIN OE 'the border of a piece of cloth', of W. Gmc origin.

**hem**[2] ● exclam. expressing the sound made when coughing or clearing the throat to attract someone's attention or show hesitation. ● v. (**hemmed**, **hemming**) archaic make such a sound.
– PHRASES **hem and haw** another way of saying ***hum and haw*** (see **HUM**[1]).
– ORIGIN C15: imitative.

**hemal** etc. ● adj. US spelling of **HAEMAL** etc.

**he-man** ● n. informal a very well-built, masculine man.

**hemato-** ● comb. form US spelling of **HAEMATO-**.

**heme** ● n. US spelling of **HAEM**.

**hemerocallis** /ˌhɛm(ə)rə(ʊ)'kalɪs/ ● n. (pl. same) a plant of a genus that comprises the day lilies. [Genus *Hemerocallis*.]
– ORIGIN mod. L., from Gk *hēmerokallis* 'a lily that flowers for a day'.

**hemi-** ● prefix half.
– ORIGIN from Gk *hēmi-*; rel. to L. *semi-*.

**-hemia** ● comb. form US spelling of **-AEMIA**.

**hemianopia** /ˌhɛmɪə'nəʊpɪə/ (also **hemianopsia** /-'nɒpsɪə/) ● n. blindness over half the field of vision.

**hemicellulose** ● n. Biochemistry a constituent of the cell walls of plants, consisting of polysaccharides of simpler structure than cellulose.

**Hemichordata** /ˌhɛmɪkɔː'deɪtə/ ● pl. n. Zoology a small phylum of marine invertebrates that comprises the acorn worms.
– DERIVATIVES **hemichordate** n. & adj.

**hemicycle** ● n. a semicircular shape or structure.

**hemicylindrical** ● adj. having the shape of half a cylinder (divided lengthways).

**hemidemisemiquaver** /ˌhɛmɪdɛmɪ'sɛmɪkweɪvə/ ● n. Music, chiefly Brit. a note with the time value of half a demisemiquaver, represented by a large dot with a four-hooked stem.

**hemihydrate** /ˌhɛmɪ'hʌɪdreɪt/ ● n. Chemistry a crystalline hydrate containing one molecule of water for every two molecules of the compound in question.

**hemimetabolous** /ˌhɛmɪmɛ'tabələs/ ● adj. Entomology (of an insect) having no pupal stage in the transition from larva to adult.
– DERIVATIVES **hemimetabolic** adj.

**hemimorphite** /ˌhɛmɪ'mɔːfʌɪt/ ● n. a mineral consisting of hydrated zinc silicate, typically occurring as flat white prisms.

**hemiola** /ˌhɛmɪ'əʊlə/ ● n. Music a musical figure in which two groups of three beats are replaced by three groups of two beats, giving the effect of a shift between triple and duple metre.
– ORIGIN ME: via med. L. from Gk *hēmiolia* 'in the ratio of one and a half to one'.

**hemiparasite** ● n. Botany a plant which obtains part of its food by parasitism but also photosynthesizes, e.g. mistletoe.

**hemiparesis** /ˌhɛmɪpə'riːsɪs/ ● n. another term for **HEMIPLEGIA**.

**hemipenis** /'hɛmɪpiːnɪs/ ● n. (pl. **hemipenes**) Zoology each of the paired male reproductive organs in snakes and lizards.

**hemiplegia** /ˌhɛmɪ'pliːdʒə/ ● n. Medicine paralysis of one side of the body.
– DERIVATIVES **hemiplegic** n. & adj.

**hemipode** /'hɛmɪpəʊd/ ● n. another term for **BUTTON-QUAIL**.
– ORIGIN C19: from mod. L. *Hemipodius*, from Gk *hemi-* 'half' + *pous*, *pod-* 'foot'.

**Hemiptera** /hɛ'mɪpt(ə)rə/ ● pl. n. Entomology a large order of insects comprising the bugs, which include aphids, cicadas, and leafhoppers.
– DERIVATIVES **hemipteran** n. & adj. **hemipterous** adj.
– ORIGIN mod. L., from Gk *hemi-* 'half' + *pteron* 'wing' (because of the forewing structure, partly hardened at the base and partly membranous).

**hemisphere** ● n. **1** a half of a sphere. **2** a half of the earth, usually as divided into northern and southern halves by the equator, or into western and eastern halves by an imaginary line passing through the poles. ➤ a half of the celestial sphere. **3** (also **cerebral hemisphere**)

each of the two parts of the cerebrum (left and right) in the brain of a vertebrate.
– DERIVATIVES **hemispheric** adj. **hemispherical** adj. **hemispherically** adv.
– ORIGIN ME: from OFr. *emisphere*, via L. from Gk *hēmisphairion*, from *hēmi-* 'half' + *sphaira* 'sphere'.

**hemistich** /ˈhɛmɪstɪk/ ● n. (chiefly in Old English verse) a half of a line of verse.
– ORIGIN C16: via late L. from Gk *hēmistikhion*, from *hemi-* 'half' + *stikhos* 'row, line of verse'.

**hemline** ● n. the level of the lower edge of a garment such as a skirt, dress, or coat.

**hemlock** ● n. **1** a highly poisonous plant of the parsley family, with fern-like leaves, small white flowers, and an unpleasant smell. [*Conium maculatum*.] ➤a sedative or poisonous potion obtained from this plant. **2** (also **hemlock fir** or **spruce**) a North American conifer with dark green foliage which is said to smell like hemlock when crushed. [Genus *Tsuga*: several species.]
– ORIGIN OE *hymlice, hemlic*, of unknown origin.

**hemo-** ● comb. form US spelling of **HAEMO-**.

**hemp** ● n. **1** (also **Indian hemp**) the cannabis plant. ➤the fibre of this plant, extracted from the stem and used to make rope, stout fabrics, fibreboard, and paper. ➤used in names of other plants that yield fibre, e.g. **Manila hemp**. **2** the drug cannabis.
– DERIVATIVES **hempen** adj. (archaic).
– ORIGIN OE *henep, hænep*, of Gmc origin; rel. to Gk *kannabis*.

**hemp agrimony** ● n. a plant of the daisy family resembling a valerian, with clusters of pale purple flowers and hairy stems. [*Eupatorium cannabinum*.]

**hemp-nettle** ● n. a nettle-like plant of the mint family. [Genus *Galeopsis*.]

**hemstitch** ● n. a decorative stitch used especially alongside a hem, in which several adjacent threads are pulled out and the crossing threads are tied into bunches, making a row of small openings. ● v. incorporate such a decoration in the hem of.

**hen** ● n. **1** a female bird, especially of a domestic fowl. ➤(**hens**) domestic fowls of either sex. ➤used in names of various rails and other birds, e.g. **native hen**. ➤a female lobster, crab, or salmon. **2** Scottish used as an affectionate term of address to a girl or woman.
– PHRASES **as rare** (or **scarce**) **as hen's teeth** extremely rare.
– ORIGIN OE *henn*, of Gmc origin.

**hen and chickens** ● n. a houseleek or other plant producing additional small flower heads or offshoots. [*Jovibarba sobilifera* and other species.]

**henbane** /ˈhɛnbeɪn/ ● n. a poisonous plant of the nightshade family, with sticky hairy leaves and an unpleasant smell. [*Hyoscyamus niger*.]

**henbit** /ˈhɛnbɪt/ ● n. a dead-nettle with purple flowers and partly prostrate stems. [*Lamium amplexicaule*.]
– ORIGIN C16: appar. a translation of Low Ger. or Du. *hoenderbeet* 'hen's bed'.

**hence** ● adv. **1** as a consequence; for this reason. **2** from now; in the future. **3** (also **from hence**) archaic from here.
– ORIGIN ME *hennes*: from earlier *henne* (from OE *heonan*, of Gmc origin, rel. to **HE**) + **-S**³.

**henceforth** (also **henceforward**) ● adv. from this or that time on.

**henchman** ● n. (pl. **-men**) **1** chiefly derogatory a faithful follower or political supporter, especially one prepared to engage in crime or dishonest practices. **2** historical a squire or page of honour to a person of rank. ➤(in Scotland) the principal attendant of a Highland chief.
– ORIGIN ME, from OE *hengest* 'male horse' + **MAN**, the original sense being prob. 'groom'.

**hendeca-** /ˈhɛndɛkə, hɛnˈdɛkə/ ● comb. form eleven; having eleven: *hendecasyllable*.
– ORIGIN from Gk *hendeka* 'eleven'.

**hendecagon** /hɛnˈdɛkəg(ə)n/ ● n. a plane figure with eleven straight sides and angles.
– DERIVATIVES **hendecagonal** /ˌhɛndɪˈkag(ə)n(ə)l/ adj.

**hendecasyllable** /ˌhɛndɛkəˈsɪləbəl/ ● n. Prosody a line of verse containing eleven syllables.
– DERIVATIVES **hendecasyllabic** adj.

**hendiadys** /hɛnˈdʌɪədɪs/ ● n. the expression of a single idea by two words connected with 'and', e.g. *nice and warm*, when one could be used to modify the other, as in *nicely warm*.
– ORIGIN C16: via med. L. from Gk *hen dia duoin* 'one thing by two'.

**henequen** /ˈhɛnɪkɛn/ ● n. **1** a fibre resembling sisal, used for binder twine and paper pulp. **2** a Central American agave from which such fibre is obtained. [*Agave fourcroydes*.]
– ORIGIN C17: from Sp. *jeniquen*, from a local word.

**henge** /hɛn(d)ʒ/ ● n. a prehistoric monument consisting of a circle of stone or wooden uprights.
– ORIGIN C18: back-form. from the megalithic monument *Stonehenge* in Wiltshire, from OE *stān* 'stone' + an element rel. to *hengan* 'to hang'.

**hen harrier** ● n. a harrier of open country, the male of which is mainly pale grey and the female brown. [*Circus cyaneus*.]

**Henle's loop** ● n. another term for **LOOP OF HENLE**.

**henna** ● n. **1** the powdered leaves of a tropical shrub, used as a reddish-brown dye to colour the hair and decorate the body. **2** the shrub which produces these leaves, with small pink, red, or white flowers. [*Lawsonia inermis*] ● v. (**hennas**, **hennaed**, **hennaing**) dye with henna.
– ORIGIN C17: from Arab. *ḥinnā'*.

**hen night** ● n. Brit. informal a celebration held for a woman who is about to get married, attended only by women.

**henotheism** /ˈhɛnəʊˌθiːɪz(ə)m/ ● n. adherence to one particular god out of several.
– ORIGIN C19: from Gk *heis, henos* 'one' + *theos* 'god' + **-ISM**.

**hen party** ● n. informal a social gathering of women.

**henpeck** ● v. [usu. as adj. **henpecked**] (of a woman) continually criticize and order about (her husband).

**henry** (abbrev.: **H**) ● n. (pl. **henries** or **henrys**) Physics the SI unit of inductance, equal to an electromotive force of one volt in a closed circuit with a uniform rate of change of current of one ampere per second.
– ORIGIN C19: named after the Amer. physicist Joseph Henry.

**Henry's law** ● n. Chemistry a law stating that the mass of a dissolved gas in a given volume of solvent at equilibrium is proportional to the partial pressure of the gas.
– ORIGIN C19: named after the Engl. chemist William Henry.

**hep**¹ ● adj. old-fashioned term for **HIP**³.

**hep**² ● n. archaic or dialect term for **HIP**².

**heparin** /ˈhɛpərɪn/ ● n. Biochemistry a compound occurring in the liver and other tissues which inhibits blood coagulation, used as an anticoagulant in the treatment of thrombosis.
– DERIVATIVES **heparinization** (also **-isation**) n. **heparinize** (also **-ise**) v.
– ORIGIN C20: via late L. from Gk *hēpar* 'liver' + **-IN**¹.

**hepatic** /hɪˈpatɪk/ ● adj. of or relating to the liver. ● n. Botany less common term for **LIVERWORT**.
– ORIGIN ME: via L. from Gk *hēpatikos*, from *hēpar, hēpat-* 'liver'.

**hepatica** /hɪˈpatɪkə/ ● n. a plant of the buttercup family, with anemone-like flowers, native to north temperate regions. [Genus *Hepatica*.]
– ORIGIN from med. L. *hepatica* (*herba*) 'plant having liver-shaped parts, or one used to treat liver diseases'.

**Hepaticae** /hɛˈpatɪkiː/ ● pl. n. Botany a class of lower plants that comprises the liverworts.

**hepatitis** /ˌhɛpəˈtʌɪtɪs/ ● n. a disease characterized by inflammation of the liver.
– ORIGIN C18: mod. L., from Gk *hēpar, hēpat-* 'liver' + **-ITIS**.

**hepatitis A** ● n. a form of viral hepatitis transmitted in food, causing fever and jaundice.

**hepatitis B** ● n. a severe form of viral hepatitis transmitted in infected blood, causing fever, debility, and jaundice.

**hepatitis C** ● **n.** a form of viral hepatitis transmitted in infected blood, causing chronic liver disease.

**hepato-** /ˈhɛpətəʊ, hɛˈpatə(ʊ)-/ ● **comb. form** of or relating to the liver.
– ORIGIN from Gk *hēpar, hēpat-* 'liver'.

**hepatocyte** /ˈhɛpətəʊsʌɪt, hɛˈpatə(ʊ)-/ ● **n.** Physiology a liver cell.

**hepatoma** /ˌhɛpəˈtəʊmə/ ● **n.** (pl. **hepatomas** or **hepatomata** /-mətə/) Medicine a cancer of the cells of the liver.

**hepatomegaly** /ˌhɛpətəʊˈmɛɡəli, hɛˌpatəʊ-/ ● **n.** Medicine abnormal enlargement of the liver.

**hepatotoxic** /ˌhɛpətəʊˈtɒksɪk, hɛˌpatəʊ-/ ● **adj.** damaging or destructive to liver cells.
– DERIVATIVES **hepatotoxicity** n. **hepatotoxin** n.

**hepcat** ● **n.** informal, dated a stylish or fashionable person.

**hepta-** ● **comb. form** seven; having seven: *heptathlon.*
– ORIGIN from Gk *hepta* 'seven'.

**heptachlor** /ˈhɛptəklɔː/ ● **n.** a chlorinated hydrocarbon used as an insecticide.

**heptad** /ˈhɛptad/ ● **n.** technical a group or set of seven.
– ORIGIN C17: from Gk *heptas, heptad-*, from *hepta* 'seven'.

**heptagon** /ˈhɛptəɡ(ə)n/ ● **n.** a plane figure with seven straight sides and angles.
– DERIVATIVES **heptagonal** adj.
– ORIGIN C16: from Gk *heptagonon*, neut. (used as n.) of *heptagonos* 'seven-angled'.

**heptahedron** /ˌhɛptəˈhiːdrən, -ˈhɛd-/ ● **n.** (pl. **heptahedra** or **heptahedrons**) a solid figure with seven plane faces.
– DERIVATIVES **heptahedral** adj.

**heptamerous** /hɛpˈtamərəs/ ● **adj.** Botany & Zoology having parts arranged in groups of seven. ➤ consisting of seven joints or parts.

**heptameter** /hɛpˈtamɪtə/ ● **n.** Prosody a line of verse consisting of seven metrical feet.

**heptane** /ˈhɛpteɪn/ ● **n.** Chemistry a colourless liquid hydrocarbon of the alkane series, present in petroleum spirit.
– ORIGIN C19: from **HEPTA-** 'seven' (denoting seven carbon atoms) + **-ANE**[2].

**heptarchy** /ˈhɛptɑːki/ ● **n.** (pl. **-ies**) a state or region consisting of seven autonomous regions. ➤ government by seven rulers.
– DERIVATIVES **heptarchic** /-ˈtɑːkɪk/ adj. **heptarchical** /-ˈtɑːkɪk(ə)l/ adj.
– ORIGIN C16: from **HEPTA-** + Gk *arkhia* 'rule', on the pattern of *tetrarchy.*

**Heptateuch** /ˈhɛptəˌtjuːk/ ● **n.** the first seven books of the Bible (Genesis to Judges) collectively.
– ORIGIN C17: via late L. from Gk *heptateukhos*, from *hepta* 'seven' + *teukhos* 'book, volume'.

**heptathlon** /hɛpˈtaθlɒn, -lən/ ● **n.** an athletic contest for women that consists of seven separate events.
– DERIVATIVES **heptathlete** n.
– ORIGIN 1970s: from **HEPTA-** + Gk *athlon* 'contest', on the pattern of words such as *decathlon.*

**heptavalent** /ˌhɛptəˈveɪl(ə)nt/ ● **adj.** Chemistry having a valency of seven.

**heptyl** /ˈhɛptʌɪl, -tɪl/ ● **n.** [as modifier] Chemistry of or denoting an alkyl radical $-C_7H_{15}$, derived from heptane.

**her** ● **pron.** [third person sing.] **1** used as the object of a verb or preposition to refer to a female person or animal previously mentioned. ➤ referring to a ship, country, or other inanimate thing regarded as female. **2** archaic or N. Amer. dialect herself. ● **possess. det. 1** belonging to or associated with a female person or animal previously mentioned. **2** (**Her**) used in titles.
– PHRASES **her indoors** Brit. informal, humorous one's wife.
– ORIGIN OE *hire*, genitive and dative of *hīo, hēo* 'she'.

**herald** ● **n. 1** historical a person who carried official messages, made proclamations, and oversaw tournaments. **2** a person or thing viewed as a sign that something is about to happen: *primroses are the herald of spring.* **3** an official employed to oversee state ceremonial, precedence, and the use of armorial bearings. ➤ (in the UK) an official of the College of Arms ranking above a pursuivant. **4** a brown moth with dull orange markings. [*Scoliopteryx libatrix.*] ● **v. 1** signal the imminence of. **2** acclaim.
– ORIGIN ME: from OFr. *herault* (n.), *herauder* (v.), of Gmc origin.

**heraldic** /hɛˈraldɪk/ ● **adj.** of or relating to heraldry.
– DERIVATIVES **heraldically** adv.

**heraldry** ● **n.** the system by which coats of arms and other armorial bearings are devised, described, and regulated. ➤ armorial bearings or other heraldic symbols.
– DERIVATIVES **heraldist** n.

**herb** ● **n. 1** any plant with leaves, seeds, or flowers used for flavouring, food, medicine, or perfume. **2** Botany any seed-bearing plant which does not have a woody stem and dies down to the ground after flowering.
– DERIVATIVES **herby** adj. (**-ier, -iest**).
– ORIGIN ME: via OFr. from L. *herba* 'grass, green crops, herb'.

**herbaceous** /həːˈbeɪʃəs/ ● **adj.** denoting or relating to herbs (in the botanical sense).

**herbaceous border** ● **n.** a garden border containing flowering plants, typically herbaceous perennials.

**herbaceous perennial** ● **n.** a plant whose growth dies down annually but whose roots or other underground parts survive.

**herbage** ● **n. 1** herbaceous vegetation. ➤ the succulent part of this vegetation, used as pasture. **2** historical the right of pasture on another person's land.

**herbal** ● **adj.** relating to or made from herbs, especially those used in cooking and medicine. ● **n.** a book that describes herbs and their culinary and medicinal properties.

**herbalism** ● **n.** the study or practice of the medicinal and therapeutic use of plants.

**herbalist** ● **n. 1** a practitioner of herbalism or dealer in herbs. **2** an early botanical writer.

**herbarium** /həːˈbɛːrɪəm/ ● **n.** (pl. **herbaria** /-rɪə/) a systematically arranged collection of dried plants.

**herbary** ● **n.** (pl. **-ies**) archaic a herb garden.

**herb bennet** ● **n.** another term for **WOOD AVENS**.
– ORIGIN ME: from OFr. *herbe beneite*, from med. L. *herba benedicta* 'blessed herb' (appar. first applied to a plant thought to ward off the Devil).

**herb Christopher** ● **n.** the common baneberry.
– ORIGIN C16: translation of med. L. *herba Christophori* 'herb of St *Christopher*'.

**herbed** ● **adj.** (of food) cooked or flavoured with herbs.

**herb Gerard** /ˈdʒɛrɑːd/ ● **n.** ground elder, which was formerly used to treat gout.
– ORIGIN named after the C10 St *Gerard* of Toul.

**herbicide** /ˈhəːbɪsʌɪd/ ● **n.** a toxic substance used to destroy unwanted vegetation.

**herbivore** /ˈhəːbɪvɔː/ ● **n.** an animal that feeds on plants.
– DERIVATIVES **herbivorous** /-ˈbɪv(ə)rəs/ adj.
– ORIGIN C19: from L. *herba* 'herb' + *-vore* (see **-VOROUS**).

**herb Paris** ● **n.** a woodland plant of the lily family, which has a single unbranched stem bearing a green and purple flower above four unstalked leaves. [*Paris quadrifolia.*]
– ORIGIN translating med. L. *herba paris*, prob. lit. 'herb of a pair', referring to the resemblance of the four leaves to a true-love knot.

**herb Robert** ● **n.** a common cranesbill with pungent-smelling red-stemmed leaves and pink flowers. [*Geranium robertianum.*]
– ORIGIN translating med. L. *herba Roberti*, variously supposed to refer to *Robert* Duke of Normandy, St *Robert*, or St Rupert.

**Herculean** /ˌhəːkjʊˈliːən, həːˈkjuːlɪən/ ● **adj.** requiring or having great strength or effort: *a Herculean task.*
– ORIGIN C16: from the name of the Gk mythological hero *Hercules* (famed for his strength) + **-AN**.

**Hercules beetle** ● **n.** a very large tropical American rhinoceros beetle, the male of which has two long curved horns extending from the head and one from the thorax. [*Dynastes hercules.*]

**Hercynian** /həːˈsɪnɪən/ ● **adj.** Geology denoting a major mountain-forming period in western Europe, eastern North America, and the Andes, in the Upper Palaeozoic era.
– ORIGIN C16: from L. *Hercynia silva*, the ancient name of an area of forested mountains in central Germany.

**herd** ● **n.** **1** a large group of animals, especially hoofed mammals, that live or are kept together. **2** derogatory a large group or class of people. ● **v.** **1** move in a large group. **2** keep or look after (livestock).
– DERIVATIVES **herder** n.
– ORIGIN OE *heord*, of Gmc origin.

**herd book** ● **n.** Brit. a book recording the pedigrees of cattle, goats, or other livestock.

**herd instinct** ● **n.** an inclination in people or animals to behave or think like the majority.

**herdsman** ● **n.** (pl. **-men**) the owner or keeper of a herd of domesticated animals.

**Herdwick** /ˈhəːdwɪk/ ● **n.** a sheep of a hardy mountain breed from the north of England.
– ORIGIN C19: from obs. *herdwick* 'pasture ground'.

**here** ● **adv.** **1** in, at, or to this place or position. **2** (usu. **here is/are**) used when introducing or handing over something or someone. **3** used when indicating a time, point, or situation that has arrived or is happening. ● **exclam.** used to attract someone's attention.
– PHRASES **here and now** at the present time. **here and there** in various places. **here goes** said to indicate that one is about to start something difficult or exciting. **here's to** used to wish health or success before drinking. **here we go again** said to indicate that the same events, typically undesirable ones, are recurring. **neither here nor there** of no importance or relevance.
– ORIGIN OE *hēr*, of Gmc origin; rel. to **HE**.

**hereabouts** (also **hereabout**) ● **adv.** near this place.

**hereafter** ● **adv.** formal from now on or at some time in the future. ➤after death. ● **n.** (**the hereafter**) life after death.

**hereat** ● **adv.** archaic as a result of this.

**hereby** ● **adv.** formal as a result of this document or utterance.

**hereditable** /hɪˈrɛdɪtəb(ə)l/ ● **adj.** less common term for **HERITABLE**.

**hereditament** /ˌhɛrɪˈdɪtəm(ə)nt, hɪˈrɛdɪt-/ ● **n.** Law, dated any item of property that can be inherited. ➤an item of inheritance.
– ORIGIN ME: from med. L. *hereditamentum*, from eccles. L. *hereditare* 'inherit'.

**hereditarian** /hɪˌrɛdɪˈtɛːrɪən/ ● **adj.** relating to or denoting the theory that heredity is the primary influence on human characteristics. ● **n.** an advocate of such a view.
– DERIVATIVES **hereditarianism** n.

**hereditary** /hɪˈrɛdɪt(ə)ri/ ● **adj.** **1** conferred by, based on, or relating to inheritance. ➤(of a characteristic or disease) able to be passed on from parents to their offspring or descendants. **2** Mathematics (of a set) defined such that every element which has a given relation to a member of the set is also a member of the set.
– DERIVATIVES **hereditarily** adv. **hereditariness** n.
– ORIGIN ME: from L. *hereditarius*, from *hereditas* (see **HEREDITY**).

**heredity** /hɪˈrɛdɪti/ ● **n.** **1** the passing on of physical or mental characteristics genetically from one generation to another. ➤a person's ancestry. **2** inheritance of title, office, or right.
– ORIGIN C18: from Fr. *hérédité*, from L. *hereditas* 'heirship', from *heres, hered-* 'heir'.

**Hereford** /ˈhɛrɪfəd/ ● **n.** an animal of a breed of red and white beef cattle.
– ORIGIN from *Hereford* in west central England.

**herein** ● **adv.** formal in this document, book, or matter.

**hereinafter** ● **adv.** formal further on in this document.

**hereinbefore** ● **adv.** formal before this point in this document.

**hereof** ● **adv.** formal of this document.

**Herero** /həˈrɛːrəʊ, -ˈrɪərəʊ/ ● **n.** (pl. same or **-os**) **1** a member of a people living in Namibia, Angola, and Botswana. **2** the Bantu language of this people.
– ORIGIN Herero, from *Otshi-Herero*, the Herero word for the lang.

**heresiarch** /hɛˈriːzɪɑːk/ ● **n.** the founder of a heresy or the leader of a heretical sect.
– ORIGIN C16: via eccles. L. from eccles. Gk *hairesiarkhēs*, from *hairesis* 'heretical sect, heresy' + *arkhēs* 'ruler'.

**heresy** /ˈhɛrɪsi/ ● **n.** (pl. **-ies**) **1** belief or opinion contrary to orthodox religious (especially Christian) doctrine. **2** opinion profoundly at odds with what is generally accepted.
– ORIGIN ME: from OFr. *heresie*, based on L. *haeresis*, from Gk *hairesis* 'choice' (in eccles. Gk 'heretical sect').

**heretic** /ˈhɛrɪtɪk/ ● **n.** a person believing in or practising heresy.
– DERIVATIVES **heretical** /hɪˈrɛtɪk(ə)l/ adj. **heretically** adv.

**hereto** ● **adv.** formal to this matter or document.

**heretofore** ● **adv.** formal before now.

**hereunder** ● **adv.** formal as provided for under the terms of this document. ➤further on in this document.

**hereunto** ● **adv.** archaic or formal to this document.

**hereupon** ● **adv.** archaic after or as a result of this.

**herewith** ● **adv.** formal with this letter.

**heriot** /ˈhɛrɪət/ ● **n.** Brit. historical a tribute paid to a lord on the death of a tenant, originally the return of borrowed military equipment.
– ORIGIN OE *heregeatwa*, from *here* 'army' + *geatwa* 'trappings'.

**heritable** ● **adj.** able to be inherited.
– DERIVATIVES **heritability** n. **heritably** adv.

**heritage** ● **n.** **1** property that is or may be inherited; an inheritance. **2** valued things such as historic buildings that have been passed down from previous generations. ➤[as modifier] of special value and worthy of preservation. **3** archaic a special or individual possession; an allotted portion. ➤God's chosen people (the people of Israel, or the Christian Church).

**heritor** /ˈhɛrɪtə/ ● **n.** **1** Scots Law a proprietor of a heritable object. **2** a person who inherits.

**herl** /həːl/ ● **n.** a barb or filament of a feather used in dressing a fishing fly.
– ORIGIN ME: appar. of Gmc origin.

**herm** /həːm/ ● **n.** a squared stone pillar with a carved head on top (typically of the god Hermes), used in ancient Greece as a boundary marker or a signpost.

**hermaphrodite** /həːˈmafrədʌɪt/ ● **n.** **1** a person or animal having both male and female sex organs or other sexual characteristics. **2** Botany a plant having stamens and pistils in the same flower. **3** archaic a person or thing combining opposite qualities or characteristics. ● **adj.** of or denoting a person, animal, or plant of this kind.
– DERIVATIVES **hermaphroditic** adj. **hermaphroditical** adj. **hermaphroditism** n.
– ORIGIN ME: via L. from Gk *hermaphroditos*, orig. the name of the son of Hermes and Aphrodite who became joined in one body with the nymph Salmacis.

**hermaphrodite brig** ● **n.** a two-masted sailing ship with a square-rigged foremast and, on the mainmast, a square topsail above a fore-and-aft gaff mainsail.

**hermeneutic** /ˌhəːmɪˈnjuːtɪk/ ● **adj.** concerning interpretation, especially of the Bible or literary texts.
– DERIVATIVES **hermeneutical** adj. **hermeneutically** adv. **hermeneutics** pl. n.
– ORIGIN C17: from Gk *hermēneutikos*, from *hermēneuein* 'interpret'.

**hermetic** /həːˈmɛtɪk/ ● **adj.** **1** (of a seal or closure) complete and airtight. **2** insulated or protected from outside influences. **3** (also **Hermetic**) of or denoting an ancient occult tradition encompassing alchemy, astrology, and theosophy. ➤esoteric; cryptic.
– DERIVATIVES **hermetically** adv. **hermeticism** n.
– ORIGIN C17: from mod. L. *hermeticus*, from *Hermes Trismegistus*, the legendary founder of alchemy and astrology identified with the Gk god Hermes.

**hermit** ● **n.** a person living in solitude as a religious discipline. ➤a reclusive or solitary person.
– DERIVATIVES **hermitage** n. **hermitic** adj.

– ORIGIN ME: from OFr. *hermite*, from late L. *eremita*, from Gk *erēmitēs*, from *erēmos* 'solitary'.

**hermit crab** ● n. a crab with a soft abdomen, which lives in a cast-off mollusc shell for protection. [Superfamily Paguroidea: many species.]

**hermit thrush** ● n. a small migratory North American thrush, noted for its melodious song. [*Catharus guttatus*.]

**hernia** /ˈhəːnɪə/ ● n. (pl. **hernias** or **herniae** /-nɪiː/) a condition in which part of an organ (most commonly, the intestine) is displaced and protrudes through the wall of the cavity containing it.

– DERIVATIVES **hernial** adj. **herniated** adj. **herniation** n.

– ORIGIN ME: from L.

**hero** ● n. (pl. **-oes**) **1** a person, typically a man, who is admired for their courage or outstanding achievements. ➤ (in mythology and folklore) a person of superhuman qualities, in particular one of those whose exploits were the subject of ancient Greek legends. **2** the chief male character in a book, play, or film. **3** (also **hero sandwich**) chiefly N. Amer. another term for **HOAGIE**.

– DERIVATIVES **heroism** n. **heroize** (also **-ise**) v.

– ORIGIN ME: via L. from Gk *hērōs*.

**heroic** ● adj. **1** having the characteristics of a hero or heroine; very brave. ➤ of or representing heroes or heroines. **2** (of language or a work of art) grand or grandiose in scale or intention. ➤ Sculpture (of a statue) larger than life size but less than colossal. ● n. (**heroics**) **1** behaviour or talk that is bold or dramatic. **2** short for **HEROIC VERSE**.

– DERIVATIVES **heroically** adv.

**heroic age** ● n. the period in Greek history and legend before the Trojan War and its aftermath, in which the legends of the heroes were set.

**heroic couplet** ● n. (in verse) a pair of rhyming iambic pentameters.

**heroic verse** ● n. a type of verse used for epic or heroic subjects, such as the iambic pentameter.

**heroin** ● n. a highly addictive analgesic drug derived from morphine, often used illicitly as a narcotic.

– ORIGIN C19: from Ger. *Heroin*, from L. *heros* 'hero' (because of its effects on the user's self-esteem).

**heroine** ● n. **1** a woman admired for her courage or outstanding achievements. ➤ (in mythology and folklore) a woman of superhuman qualities, in particular one whose dealings with the gods were the subject of ancient Greek legends. **2** the chief female character in a book, play, or film.

**heron** ● n. a large fish-eating wading bird with long legs, a long S-shaped neck, and a long pointed bill. [*Ardea cinerea* (**grey heron**) and other species, family Ardeidae.]

– ORIGIN ME: from OFr., of Gmc origin.

**heronry** ● n. (pl. **-ies**) a breeding colony of herons, typically in a group of trees.

**hero worship** ● n. excessive admiration for someone. ● v. (**hero-worship**) admire excessively.

– DERIVATIVES **hero-worshipper** n.

**herpes** /ˈhəːpiːz/ ● n. a disease caused by a herpesvirus, affecting the skin (often with blisters) or the nervous system.

– DERIVATIVES **herpetic** adj.

– ORIGIN ME: via L. from Gk *herpēs* 'shingles', lit. 'creeping', from *herpein* 'to creep'.

**herpes simplex** ● n. a form of herpes which can produce cold sores, genital inflammation, or conjunctivitis.

**herpesvirus** /ˈhəːpiːzˌvʌɪrəs/ ● n. Medicine any of a group of DNA viruses causing herpes and other diseases.

**herpes zoster** /ˈzɒstə/ ● n. medical name for **SHINGLES**.

– ORIGIN ME: from **HERPES** and L. *zoster*, from Gk *zōstēr* 'girdle, shingles'.

**herpetology** /ˌhəːpɪˈtɒlədʒi/ ● n. the branch of zoology concerned with reptiles and amphibians.

– DERIVATIVES **herpetological** adj. **herpetologist** n.

– ORIGIN C19: from Gk *herpeton* 'creeping thing' (from *herpein* 'to creep') + **-LOGY**.

**herptile** /ˈhəːptʌɪl/ ● n. a reptile or amphibian.

– ORIGIN blend of **HERPETOLOGY** and **REPTILE**.

**Herr** /hɛː, German hɛr/ ● n. (pl. **Herren** /ˈhɛr(ə)n/) a title or form of address used of or to a German-speaking man, corresponding to *Mr* and also used before a rank or occupation.

– ORIGIN Ger., from Old High Ger. *hērro*, compar. of *hēr* 'exalted'.

**Herrenvolk** /ˈhɛr(ə)nˌfɒlk/ ● n. the German nation as considered by the Nazis to be innately superior to others.

– ORIGIN Ger., 'master race'.

**herring** ● n. a silvery fish which is most abundant in coastal waters and is an important food fish. [*Clupea harengus* (N. Atlantic) and other species, family Clupeidae.]

– ORIGIN OE *hǣring*, *hēring*, of W. Gmc origin.

**herringbone** ● n. **1** a pattern consisting of columns of short parallel lines, with all the lines in one column sloping one way and all the lines in the next column sloping the other way. ➤ a cross stitch with a pattern resembling this. **2** Skiing a method of ascending a slope by walking with the skis pointing outwards. ● v. **1** mark with a herringbone pattern. ➤ work with a herringbone stitch. **2** Skiing ascend a slope using the herringbone technique.

**herring gull** ● n. a common northern gull with grey black-tipped wings. [*Larus argentatus*.]

**Herrnhuter** /ˈhɛːnhuːtə, ˈhɛːr(ə)n-/ ● n. a member of a Moravian Church.

– ORIGIN C18: Ger., from *Herrnhut* (lit. 'the Lord's keeping'), the name of the first Ger. settlement of the Moravian Church.

**hers** ● possess. pron. used to refer to a thing or things belonging to or associated with a female person or animal previously mentioned.

**herself** ● pron. [third person sing.] **1** [reflexive] used as the object of a verb or preposition to refer to a female person or animal previously mentioned as the subject of the clause. **2** [emphatic] she or her personally.

**Herts.** /hɑːts/ ● abbrev. Hertfordshire.

**hertz** /həːts/ (abbrev.: **Hz**) ● n. (pl. same) the SI unit of frequency, equal to one cycle per second.

– ORIGIN C19: named after the Ger. physicist H. R. *Hertz*.

**Herzegovinian** /ˌhɛːtsəˈɡɒvɪnɪən/ ● n. a native or inhabitant of the Balkan region of Herzegovina. ● adj. of or relating to Herzegovina.

**he's** ● contr. **1** he is. **2** he has.

**Heshvan** /ˈhɛʃv(ə)n/ ● n. variant spelling of **HESVAN**.

**hesitant** ● adj. slow to act or speak through indecision or reluctance.

– DERIVATIVES **hesitance** n. **hesitancy** n. **hesitantly** adv.

– ORIGIN ME: from L. *haesitant-*, *haesitare* (see **HESITATE**).

**hesitate** ● v. pause in indecision. ➤ be reluctant to do something.

– DERIVATIVES **hesitater** n. **hesitating** adj. **hesitatingly** adv. **hesitation** n.

– ORIGIN C17: from L. *haesitat-*, *haesitare* 'stick fast, leave undecided'.

**Hesperian** /hɛˈspɪərɪən/ ● adj. **1** Greek Mythology of or concerning the Hesperides, a group of nymphs who guarded the garden of golden apples at the western extremity of the earth. **2** poetic/literary western.

– ORIGIN C15: from L. *hesperius* (from Gk *hesperios*, from *Hesperia* 'land of the west', from *hesperos* (see **HESPERUS**)) + **-AN**.

**hesperidium** /ˌhɛspəˈrɪdɪəm/ ● n. (pl. **hesperidia** /-dɪə/) Botany a fruit with sectioned pulp inside a separable rind, e.g. an orange.

– ORIGIN C19: based on mod. L *Hesperideae* (former order name), named after the golden apples of the Hesperides (see **HESPERIAN**) + **-IUM**.

**Hesperus** /ˈhɛspərəs/ ● n. poetic/literary the planet Venus.

– ORIGIN L., from Gk *hesperos* 'western', (as n.) 'the evening star'.

**hessian** ● n. a strong, coarse fabric made from hemp or jute, used especially for sacks and in upholstery.

– ORIGIN C19: from *Hesse*, a state of western Germany, + **-IAN**.

**Hessian boot** • n. a high tasselled leather boot, originally worn by troops from Hesse in Germany.

**Hessian fly** • n. a gall midge whose larvae are a pest of cereal crops. [*Mayetiola destructor.*]
– ORIGIN C18: so named because it was supposed (erroneously) to have been carried to America by troops from Hesse in Germany during the War of Independence.

**hest** • n. archaic form of **BEHEST**.
– ORIGIN OE *hǣs*, of Gmc origin; rel. to **HIGHT**.

**Hesvan** /ˈhɛsv(ə)n/ (also **Heshvan**) • n. (in the Jewish calendar) the second month of the civil and eighth of the religious year, usually coinciding with parts of October and November.
– ORIGIN from Heb. *ḥešwān*.

**hetaera** /hɪˈtɪərə/ (also **hetaira** /-ˈtʌɪrə/) • n. (pl. **hetaeras** or **hetaerae** /-ˈtɪəriː/ or **hetairas** or **hetairai** /-ˈtʌɪrʌɪ/) a courtesan or mistress, especially an educated one in ancient Greece.
– ORIGIN from Gk *hetaira*, fem. of *hetairos* 'companion'.

**hetero-** • comb. form other; different: *heterosexual.*
– ORIGIN from Gk *heteros* 'other'.

**heterocercal** /ˌhɛtərəʊˈsəːkəl/ • adj. Zoology (of a fish's tail) having unequal upper and lower lobes, usually with the vertebral column passing into the upper.
– ORIGIN C19: from **HETERO-** + Gk *kerkos* 'tail'.

**heterochromatic** /ˌhɛt(ə)rəʊkrəˈmatɪk/ • adj. of several different colours or (in physics) wavelengths.

**heteroclite** /ˈhɛt(ə)rə(ʊ)klʌɪt/ formal • adj. abnormal. • n. **1** an abnormal thing or person. **2** an irregularly declined word, especially a Greek or Latin noun.
– DERIVATIVES **heteroclitic** adj.
– ORIGIN C15: via late L. from Gk *heteroklitos*, from *heteros* 'other' + *-klitos* 'inflected'.

**heterocyclic** /ˌhɛt(ə)rə(ʊ)ˈsʌɪklɪk, -ˈsɪklɪk/ • adj. Chemistry denoting a compound whose molecule contains a ring of atoms of at least two elements (one of which is generally carbon).

**heterodox** /ˈhɛt(ə)rə(ʊ)dɒks/ • adj. not conforming with orthodox standards or beliefs.
– DERIVATIVES **heterodoxy** n.
– ORIGIN C17: via late L. from Gk *heterodoxos*, from *heteros* 'other' + *doxa* 'opinion'.

**heterodyne** /ˈhɛt(ə)rə(ʊ)dʌɪn/ • adj. Electronics relating to or denoting the production of a lower frequency from the combination of two almost equal high frequencies, as used in radio transmission.
– DERIVATIVES **heterodyning** n.
– ORIGIN C20: from **HETERO-** + *-dyne*, suffix formed irregularly from Gk *dunamis* 'power'.

**heterogametic** /ˌhɛt(ə)rə(ʊ)gəˈmɛtɪk/ • adj. Biology denoting the sex which has sex chromosomes that differ in morphology, e.g. (in mammals) the male and (in birds) the female.

**heterogamy** /ˌhɛtəˈrɒgəmi/ • n. **1** chiefly Zoology alternation of generations, especially between sexual and parthenogenetic generations. **2** Botany a state in which the flowers of a plant are of two or more types. **3** marriage between people from different backgrounds.
– DERIVATIVES **heterogamous** adj.
– ORIGIN C19: from **HETERO-** + Gk *gamos* 'marriage'.

**heterogeneous** /ˌhɛt(ə)rə(ʊ)ˈdʒiːnɪəs, -ˈdʒɛn-/ • adj. **1** diverse in character or content. **2** Chemistry denoting a process involving substances in different phases (solid, liquid, or gaseous): *heterogeneous catalysis.*
– DERIVATIVES **heterogeneity** /-dʒɪˈniːɪti, -ˈneɪɪti/ n. **heterogeneously** adv. **heterogeneousness** n.
– ORIGIN C17: from med. L. *heterogeneus*, from Gk *heterogenēs*, from *heteros* 'other' + *genos* 'a kind'.

**heteroglossia** /ˌhɛtərəʊˈglɒsɪə/ • n. the presence of two or more voices in a text or other artistic work.

**heterograft** • n. another term for **XENOGRAFT**.

**heterologous** /ˌhɛtəˈrɒləgəs/ • adj. chiefly Medicine & Biology not homologous.
– DERIVATIVES **heterology** n.

**heteromerous** /ˌhɛtəˈrɒm(ə)rəs/ • adj. Biology having or composed of parts that differ in number or position.

**heteromorphic** /ˌhɛt(ə)rə(ʊ)ˈmɔːfɪk/ • adj. Biology occurring in two or more different forms, especially at different stages in the life cycle.
– DERIVATIVES **heteromorph** n. **heteromorphism** n. **heteromorphy** n.

**heteronomous** /ˌhɛtəˈrɒnəməs/ • adj. **1** subject to a law or standard external to itself. **2** Biology subject to different laws of growth and development.
– DERIVATIVES **heteronomy** n.

**heteronym** /ˈhɛtərə(ʊ)nɪm/ • n. Linguistics **1** each of two or more words which are spelled identically but have different sounds and meanings (e.g. **TEAR**[1] and **TEAR**[2]). **2** each of two or more words which are used to refer to the identical thing in different geographical areas of a speech community, e.g. *nappy* and *diaper.*
– DERIVATIVES **heteronymic** adj. **heteronymous** adj.

**heteropolar** /ˌhɛtərəʊˈpəʊlə/ • adj. chiefly Physics characterized by opposite or alternating polarity.

**Heteroptera** /ˌhɛtəˈrɒpt(ə)rə/ • pl. n. Entomology a group of bugs comprising those, such as the predatory and water bugs, in which the forewings are non-uniform, having a thickened base and membranous tip. Compare with **HOMOPTERA**.
– DERIVATIVES **heteropteran** n. & adj. **heteropterous** adj.
– ORIGIN mod. L., from Gk *heteros* 'other' + *pteron* 'wing'.

**heterosexism** • n. discrimination or prejudice against homosexuals on the assumption that heterosexuality is the norm.
– DERIVATIVES **heterosexist** adj.

**heterosexual** • adj. sexually attracted to the opposite sex. ➤ involving or characterized by such sexual attraction. • n. a heterosexual person.
– DERIVATIVES **heterosexuality** n. **heterosexually** adv.

**heterosis** /ˌhɛtəˈrəʊsɪs/ • n. technical term for **HYBRID VIGOUR**.
– DERIVATIVES **heterotic** adj.
– ORIGIN C20: from Gk *heterōsis* 'alteration'.

**heterostyly** /ˈhɛtərə(ʊ)ˌstʌɪli/ • n. Botany the condition (e.g. in primroses) of having styles of different lengths relative to the stamens in the flowers of different individual plants, to reduce self-fertilization.
– DERIVATIVES **heterostylous** adj.
– ORIGIN C19: from **HETERO-** + Gk *stulos* 'column' + **-Y**[3].

**heterotransplant** • n. another term for **XENOGRAFT**.

**heterotroph** /ˈhɛt(ə)rə(ʊ)trəʊf, -trɒf/ • n. Biology an organism that derives nutrients from complex organic substances. Compare with **AUTOTROPH**.
– DERIVATIVES **heterotrophic** adj. **heterotrophy** n.

**heterozygote** /ˌhɛt(ə)rə(ʊ)ˈzʌɪgəʊt/ • n. Genetics an individual having two different alleles of a particular gene or genes, and so giving rise to varying offspring. Compare with **HOMOZYGOTE**.
– DERIVATIVES **heterozygosity** n. **heterozygous** adj.

**hetman** /ˈhɛtmən/ • n. (pl. **-men**) a Polish or Cossack military commander.
– ORIGIN Polish, prob. from Ger. *Hauptmann* 'captain'.

**het up** • adj. informal angry and agitated.
– ORIGIN C19: from dial. *het* 'heated, hot'.

**heuchera** /ˈhɔɪkərə, ˈhjuːk-/ • n. a North American plant with dark green round or heart-shaped leaves and slender stems of tiny flowers. [Genus *Heuchera*: many species.]
– ORIGIN mod. L., named after the C18 Ger. botanist Johann H. von *Heucher.*

**heuriger** /ˈhɔɪrɪgə/ (also **heurige**) • n. (pl. **heurigen** /-g(ə)n/) (in Austria) wine from the latest harvest. ➤ an establishment where this is served.
– ORIGIN Austrian Ger., lit. 'this year's (wine)'.

**heuristic** /ˌhjʊ(ə)ˈrɪstɪk/ • adj. **1** enabling a person to discover or learn something for themselves. **2** Computing proceeding to a solution by trial and error or by rules that are only loosely defined. • n. a heuristic process or method. ➤ (**heuristics**) [usu. treated as sing.] the study and use of heuristic techniques.
– DERIVATIVES **heuristically** adv.
– ORIGIN C19: formed irregularly from Gk *heuriskein* 'find'.

**HEW** • abbrev. (the US Department of) Health, Education, and Welfare.

**hew** /hjuː/ • v. (past part. **hewn** or **hewed**) **1** chop or cut

(wood, coal, etc.) with an axe, pick, or other tool. ➤(usu. **be hewn**) make or shape by cutting or chopping a hard material. **2** (**hew to**) N. Amer. conform to.
– ORIGIN OE *hēawan*, of Gmc origin.

**hewer** ● n. dated a person who hews something, especially a miner who cuts coal from a seam.
– PHRASES **hewers of wood and drawers of water** menial drudges. [with biblical allusion to Josh. 9:21.]

**hex**[1] chiefly N. Amer. ● v. cast a spell on. ● n. **1** a magic spell. **2** a witch.
– ORIGIN C19 (as v.): from Pennsylvanian Ger. *hexe* (v.), *Hex* (n.), from Ger. *hexen* (v.), *Hexe* (n.).

**hex**[2] ● adj. & n. short for **HEXADECIMAL**.

**hexa-** (also **hex-** before a vowel) ● comb. form six; having six.
– ORIGIN from Gk *hex* 'six'.

**hexachord** /'hɛksəkɔːd/ ● n. a musical scale of six notes with a semitone between the third and fourth.

**hexad** /'hɛksad/ ● n. technical a group or set of six.
– ORIGIN C17: from Gk *hexas, hexad-*, from *hex* 'six'.

**hexadecimal** /ˌhɛksə'dɛsɪm(ə)l/ ● adj. Computing relating to or using a system of numerical notation that has 16 rather than 10 as its base.
– DERIVATIVES **hexadecimally** adv.

**hexagon** /'hɛksəg(ə)n/ ● n. a plane figure with six straight sides and angles.
– DERIVATIVES **hexagonal** adj.
– ORIGIN C16: via late L. from Gk *hexagōnon*, neut. of *hexagōnos* 'six-angled'.

**hexagram** ● n. **1** a star-shaped figure formed by two intersecting equilateral triangles. **2** any of a set of sixty-four figures made up of six parallel whole or broken lines, occurring in the ancient Chinese I Ching.
– ORIGIN C19: from **HEXA-** + Gk *gramma* 'line'.

**hexahedron** /ˌhɛksə'hiːdrən, -'hɛd-/ ● n. (pl. **hexahedra** or **hexahedrons**) a solid figure with six plane faces.
– DERIVATIVES **hexahedral** adj.
– ORIGIN C16: from Gk *hexaedron*, neut. of *hexaedros* 'six-faced'.

**hexamerous** /hɛk'sam(ə)rəs/ ● n. Botany & Zoology having parts arranged in groups of six.

**hexameter** /hɛk'samɪtə/ ● n. Prosody a line of verse consisting of six metrical feet.

**hexane** /'hɛkseɪn/ ● n. Chemistry a colourless liquid hydrocarbon of the alkane series, present in petroleum spirit. [$C_6H_{14}$.]
– ORIGIN C19: from **HEXA-** 'six' (denoting six carbon atoms) + **-ANE**[2].

**hexapla** /'hɛksəplə/ ● n. a sixfold text in parallel columns, especially of the Old Testament.
– ORIGIN C17: from Gk, neut. pl. of *hexaploos* 'sixfold'.

**hexaploid** /'hɛksəplɔɪd/ ● adj. Genetics having or denoting cells or nuclei containing six homologous sets of chromosomes.
– DERIVATIVES **hexaploidy** n.

**Hexapoda** /ˌhɛksə'pəʊdə/ ● pl. n. Entomology a class of six-legged arthropods that comprises the insects (especially when distinguished from the primitive apterygotes).
– DERIVATIVES **hexapod** n.
– ORIGIN mod. L., from Gk *hexapous, hexapod-*, from **HEXA-** + *pous* 'foot'.

**hexastyle** /'hɛksəstʌɪl/ ● adj. Architecture (of a portico) having six columns.
– ORIGIN C18: from Gk *hexastulos*, from *hex* 'six' + *stulos* 'column'.

**Hexateuch** /'hɛksətjuːk/ ● n. the first six books of the Bible collectively.
– ORIGIN C19: from **HEXA-** + Gk *teukhos* 'book'.

**hexavalent** /ˌhɛksə'veɪl(ə)nt/ ● adj. Chemistry having a valency of six.

**hexose** /'hɛksəʊz, -s/ ● n. Chemistry any of the class of simple sugars whose molecules contain six carbon atoms (e.g. glucose).

**hexyl** /'hɛksʌɪl, -sɪl/ ● n. [as modifier] Chemistry of or denoting an alkyl radical $-C_6H_{13}$, derived from hexane.

**hey** ● exclam. used to attract attention or to express surprise, interest, etc.

**heyday** ● n. (**one's heyday**) the period of one's greatest success, activity, or vigour.
– ORIGIN C16 (denoting good spirits or passion): from archaic *heyday!*, an exclam. of joy or surprise.

**hey presto** ● exclam. see **PRESTO**.

**HF** ● abbrev. Physics high frequency.

**Hf** ● symb. the chemical element hafnium.

**hf** ● abbrev. half.

**HFC** ● abbrev. hydrofluorocarbon.

**HG** ● abbrev. Brit. **1** Her or His Grace. **2** historical Home Guard.

**Hg** ● symb. the chemical element mercury.
– ORIGIN abbrev. of mod. L. *hydrargyrum*.

**hg** ● abbrev. hectogram(s).

**HGH** ● abbrev. human growth hormone.

**HGV** ● abbrev. Brit. heavy goods vehicle.

**HH** ● abbrev. **1** Brit. Her or His Highness. **2** His Holiness. **3** extra hard (as a grade of pencil lead).

**hh.** ● abbrev. hands (as a unit of measurement of a horse's height).

**hhd** ● abbrev. hogshead(s).

**H-hour** ● n. the time of day at which an attack or other military operation is scheduled to begin.
– ORIGIN First World War: from *H* (for *hour*) + **HOUR**.

**HI** ● abbrev. Hawaii (in official postal use).

**hi** ● exclam. informal used as a friendly greeting.

**hiatus** /hʌɪ'eɪtəs/ ● n. (pl. **hiatuses**) a pause or gap in continuity. ➤ Prosody & Grammar a break between two vowels coming together but not in the same syllable, as in *the ear*.
– DERIVATIVES **hiatal** adj.
– ORIGIN C16: from L., lit. 'gaping'.

**hiatus hernia** (also **hiatal hernia**) ● n. Medicine the protrusion of an organ (usually the stomach) through the oesophageal opening in the diaphragm.

**Hib** ● n. a bacterium that causes infant meningitis.
– ORIGIN C20: acronym from *Haemophilus influenzae type B*.

**hibachi** /hɪ'batʃi, 'hɪbətʃi/ ● n. (pl. **hibachis**) a portable cooking apparatus similar to a small barbecue. ➤(in Japan) a large earthenware pan or brazier in which charcoal is burnt to provide indoor heating.
– ORIGIN C19: Japanese *hibachi, hi-hachi*, from *hi* 'fire' + *hachi* 'bowl, pot'.

**hibernate** ● v. (of an animal or plant) spend the winter in a dormant state.
– DERIVATIVES **hibernation** n. **hibernator** n.
– ORIGIN C19 (earlier (C17) as *hibernation*): from L. *hibernare*, from *hiberna* 'winter quarters'.

**Hibernian** /hʌɪ'bəːnɪən/ ● adj. of or concerning Ireland (now chiefly used in names). ● n. a native of Ireland (now chiefly used in names).
– ORIGIN from L. *Hibernia* (alt. of *Iverna*), from Gk *I(w)ernē*, of Celtic origin.

**Hibernianism** (also **Hibernicism**) ● n. an Irish idiom or expression.

**Hiberno-** /hʌɪ'bəːnəʊ/ ● comb. form Irish; Irish and ...: *Hiberno-English*.
– ORIGIN from med. L. *Hibernus* 'Irish'; see also **HIBERNIAN**.

**hibiscus** /hɪ'bɪskəs/ ● n. a plant of the mallow family with large brightly coloured flowers. [Genus *Hibiscus*: many species.]
– ORIGIN L., from Gk *hibiskos* 'marsh mallow'.

**hic** ● exclam. used in writing to express the sound of a hiccup.
– ORIGIN C19: imitative.

**hiccup** (also **hiccough** (pronunc. same)) ● n. **1** an involuntary spasm of the diaphragm and respiratory organs, with a sudden closure of the glottis and a characteristic gulping sound. **2** a minor difficulty or setback. ● v. (**hiccuped, hiccuping**) make the sound of a hiccup or series of hiccups.
– DERIVATIVES **hiccupy** adj.
– ORIGIN C16: imitative; the form *hiccough* arose by assoc. with **COUGH**.

**hic jacet** /hɪk 'dʒeɪsɛt, 'jakɛt/ ● n. poetic/literary an

epitaph.
– ORIGIN L., 'here lies', the first words of a Latin epitaph.

**hick** • **n.** informal, chiefly N. Amer. a country-dweller, regarded as unintelligent or parochial.
– ORIGIN C16: familiar form of the given name *Richard.*

**hickey** • **n.** (pl. **-eys**) **1** N. Amer. informal a gadget. **2** a blemish in printing, especially an uninked area in a solid. **3** N. Amer. informal a love bite.
– ORIGIN C20: of unknown origin.

**hickory** • **n. 1** a chiefly North American tree which yields tough, heavy wood and bears edible nuts. [Genus *Carya*: several species.] **2** a stick made of hickory wood.
– ORIGIN C17: abbrev. of *pohickery*, the local Virginian name, from Algonquian *pawcohiccora*.

**hid** past of HIDE[1].

**hidalgo** /hɪˈdalɡəʊ/ • **n.** (pl. **-os**) a gentleman in a Spanish-speaking country.
– ORIGIN C16: Sp., from *hijo de algo*, lit. 'son of something'.

**Hidatsa** /hɪˈdatsə/ • **n.** (pl. same or **Hidatsas**) **1** a member of an American Indian people living on the upper Missouri River. **2** the Siouan language of this people.
– ORIGIN from Hidatsa *hiratsa* 'willow wood lodge'.

**hidden** past participle of HIDE[1].
– DERIVATIVES **hiddenness** n.

**hidden agenda** • **n.** a secret or ulterior motive.

**hidden reserves** • **pl. n.** a company's funds that are not declared on its balance sheet.

**hide[1]** • **v.** (past **hid**; past part. **hidden**) put or keep out of sight. ➤keep secret. ➤conceal oneself. • **n.** Brit. a camouflaged shelter used to observe wildlife at close quarters.
– PHRASES **hide one's light under a bushel** keep quiet about one's talents or accomplishments. [with biblical allusion to Matt. 15.]
– DERIVATIVES **hider** n.
– ORIGIN OE *hȳdan*, of W. Gmc origin.

**hide[2]** • **n.** the skin of an animal, especially when tanned or dressed.
– PHRASES **hide or hair of** [with neg.] the slightest trace of. **save one's hide** escape from difficulty. **tan** (or **whip**) **someone's hide** beat or flog someone.
– DERIVATIVES **hided** adj.
– ORIGIN OE *hȳd*, of Gmc origin.

**hide[3]** • **n.** a former measure of land used in England, typically equal to between 60 and 120 acres, being the amount that would support a family.
– ORIGIN OE *hīd, hīgid*, from the base of *hīgan, hīwan* 'household members', of Gmc origin.

**hide-and-seek** • **n.** a children's game in which one or more players hide and the other or others have to look for them.

**hideaway** • **n.** a hiding place, especially as a retreat from others.

**hidebound** • **adj.** constrained by tradition or convention; narrow-minded.
– ORIGIN C16 (orig. referring to malnourished cattle, later extended to emaciated human beings, hence the sense 'narrow in outlook'): from HIDE[2] + BOUND[4].

**hideous** • **adj.** extremely ugly. ➤extremely unpleasant.
– DERIVATIVES **hideously** adv. **hideousness** n.
– ORIGIN ME: from OFr. *hidos, hideus*, from *hide, hisde* 'fear'.

**hideout** • **n.** a hiding place, especially one used by someone who has broken the law.

**hidey-hole** (also **hidy-hole**) • **n.** informal a hiding place.

**hiding[1]** • **n. 1** a physical beating. **2** informal a severe defeat.
– PHRASES **be on a hiding to nothing** Brit. be unlikely to succeed.
– ORIGIN C19: from HIDE[2] + -ING[1].

**hiding[2]** • **n.** the action of hiding or the state of being hidden.
– ORIGIN ME: from HIDE[1] + -ING[1].

**hie** /hʌɪ/ • **v.** (**hies**, **hied**, **hieing** or **hying**) archaic go quickly.
– ORIGIN ME: from OE *hīgian* 'strive, pant'.

**hierarch** /ˈhʌɪərɑːk/ • **n.** a chief priest, archbishop, or other leader.
– ORIGIN ME: via med. L. from Gk *hierarkhēs*, from *hieros* 'sacred' + *arkhēs* 'ruler'.

**hierarchy** /ˈhʌɪərɑːki/ • **n.** (pl. **-ies**) **1** a ranking system ordered according to status or authority. ➤(**the hierarchy**) the upper echelons of a hierarchical system. ➤an arrangement according to relative importance or inclusiveness. **2** (**the hierarchy**) the clergy of the Catholic Church or of an episcopal Church. **3** Theology the traditional system of orders of angels and other heavenly beings.
– DERIVATIVES **hierarchic** adj. **hierarchical** adj. **hierarchically** adv. **hierarchization** (also **-isation**) n. **hierarchize** (also **-ise**) v.
– ORIGIN ME: via OFr. and med. L. from Gk *hierarkhia*, from *hierarkhēs* (see HIERARCH).

**hieratic** /ˌhʌɪəˈratɪk/ • **adj. 1** of or concerning priests. **2** of or in the ancient Egyptian writing of abridged hieroglyphics used by priests. Compare with DEMOTIC. **3** of or concerning Egyptian or Greek styles of art adhering to early methods as laid down by religious tradition.
– DERIVATIVES **hieratically** adv.
– ORIGIN C17 (orig. as *hieratical*): via L. from Gk *hieratikos*, from *hierasthai* 'be a priest'.

**hiero-** /ˈhʌɪrəʊ/ • **comb. form** sacred; holy.
– ORIGIN from Gk *hieros* 'sacred'.

**hierocracy** /hʌɪˈrɒkrəsi/ • **n.** (pl. **-ies**) rule by priests. ➤a ruling body of priests.
– DERIVATIVES **hierocratic** adj.

**hieroglyph** /ˈhʌɪrəɡlɪf/ • **n.** a stylized picture of an object representing a word, syllable, or sound, as found in ancient Egyptian and certain other writing systems.
– ORIGIN C16: back-form. from HIEROGLYPHIC.

**hieroglyphic** • **n.** (**hieroglyphics**) writing consisting of hieroglyphs. • **adj.** of or written in hieroglyphs.
– DERIVATIVES **hieroglyphical** adj. **hieroglyphically** adv.
– ORIGIN C16: from Fr. *hiéroglyphique*, from Gk *hieroglyphikos*, from *hieros* 'sacred' + *gluphē* 'carving'.

**hierogram** /ˈhʌɪrə(ʊ)ɡram/ • **n.** a sacred inscription or symbol.

**hierology** /hʌɪˈrɒlədʒi/ • **n.** sacred literature or lore.

**hierophant** /ˈhʌɪrə(ʊ)fant/ • **n.** a person, especially a priest, who interprets sacred or esoteric mysteries.
– DERIVATIVES **hierophantic** adj.
– ORIGIN C17: via late L. from Gk *hierophantēs*, from *hieros* 'sacred' + *phainein* 'show'.

**hi-fi** informal • **adj.** of or relating to the reproduction of high fidelity sound. • **n.** (pl. **hi-fis**) a set of equipment for high-fidelity sound reproduction.

**higgle** • **v.** archaic spelling of HAGGLE.

**higgledy-piggledy** • **adv. & adj.** in confusion or disorder.
– ORIGIN C16: rhyming jingle, prob. with ref. to the irregular herding together of pigs.

**higgler** • **n.** W. Indian a pedlar.

**Higgs boson** (also **Higgs particle**) • **n.** Physics a subatomic particle postulated to exist by the theory which unified the weak and electromagnetic interactions.
– ORIGIN 1970s: named after the Engl. physicist Peter W. Higgs.

**high** • **adj. 1** of great vertical extent. ➤of a specified height. ➤far above ground or sea level. ➤extending above the normal level. ➤(of latitude) near the North or South Pole. **2** great in amount, value, size, or intensity. ➤(of a period or movement) at its peak. **3** great in rank or status. ➤morally or culturally superior. **4** (of a sound or note) having a frequency at the upper end of the auditory range. **5** informal euphoric, especially from the effects of drugs or alcohol. **6** (of food) strong-smelling because beginning to go bad. ➤(of game) slightly decomposed and so ready to cook. **7** Phonetics (of a vowel) produced with the tongue relatively near the palate. • **n. 1** a high point, level, or figure. **2** an anticyclone. **3** informal a state of euphoria. **4** informal, chiefly N. Amer. high school. • **adv. 1** at or to a considerable or specified height. **2** highly. ➤at a high price. **3** (of a sound) at or to a high pitch.
– PHRASES **ace** (or **king** or **queen** etc.) **high** (in card games) having the ace (or another specified card) as the

highest-ranking. **from on high** from remote high authority or heaven. **high and dry 1** stranded by the sea as it retreats. **2** without resources. **high and low** in many different places. **high and mighty** informal arrogant. **the high ground** a position of superiority. **a high old time** informal a most enjoyable time. **high, wide, and handsome** informal expansive and impressive. [from *Arizona Nights* by the Amer. author Stewart E. White (1873–1946).] **it is high time that ——** it is past the time when something should have happened or been done. **on one's high horse** informal behaving arrogantly or pompously. **run high 1** (of a river) be full and close to overflowing, with a strong current. **2** (of feelings) be intense.
– ORIGIN OE *hēah*, of Gmc origin.

**high altar** • **n.** the chief altar of a church.

**highball** N. Amer. • **n. 1** a long drink consisting of a spirit and a mixer such as soda, served with ice. **2** informal a railway signal to proceed. • **v.** informal travel fast.

**highbinder** /ˈhʌɪbʌɪndə/ • **n.** US informal a corrupt and unscrupulous person.
– ORIGIN C19: first recorded as *Highbinders*, the name of a New York gang.

**highboy** • **n.** N. Amer. a tall chest of drawers on legs.

**highbrow** • **adj.** often derogatory intellectual or rarefied in taste.

**high chair** • **n.** a small chair with long legs for a baby or small child, fitted with a tray and used at mealtimes.

**High Church** • **n.** a tradition within the Anglican Church emphasizing ritual, priestly authority, sacraments, and historical continuity with Catholic Christianity.
– DERIVATIVES **High Churchman** n. (pl. **-men**).

**high colour** • **n.** a flushed complexion.

**high command** • **n.** the commander-in-chief and associated senior staff of an army, navy, or air force.

**high commission** • **n.** an embassy of one Commonwealth country in another.
– DERIVATIVES **high commissioner** n.

**high court** • **n.** a supreme court of justice. ➤(in full **High Court of Justice**) (in England and Wales) the court of unlimited civil jurisdiction forming part of the Supreme Court. ➤(in full **High Court of Justiciary**) the supreme criminal court of Scotland.

**high day** • **n.** Brit. the day of a religious festival.
– PHRASES **high days and holidays** informal special occasions.

**high-dependency** • **adj.** Brit. of or relating to hospital patients requiring a high level of medical treatment and supervision.

**high enema** • **n.** an enema delivered into the colon.

**Higher** • **n.** (in Scotland) the more advanced of the two main levels of the Scottish Certificate of Education. Compare with **ORDINARY GRADE**.

**higher animals** • **pl. n.** mammals and other vertebrates, regarded as having relatively advanced characteristics.

**higher court** • **n.** Law a court that can overrule the decision of another.

**higher criticism** • **n.** the study of the literary methods and sources discernible in biblical texts.

**higher education** • **n.** education at universities or similar educational establishments, especially to degree level.

**higher mathematics** • **pl. n.** [usu. treated as sing.] the more advanced aspects of mathematics, such as number theory and topology.

**higher plants** • **pl. n.** vascular plants, regarded as having relatively advanced characteristics.

**highest common factor** • **n.** the highest number that can be divided exactly into each of two or more numbers.

**high explosive** • **n.** a powerful chemical explosive of the kind used in shells and bombs.

**highfalutin** /ˌhʌɪfəˈluːtɪn/ (also **highfaluting** /-tɪŋ/) • **adj.** informal pompous or pretentious.
– ORIGIN C19 (orig. US): perh. from **HIGH** + *fluting* (pres. part. of **FLUTE**).

**high fashion** • **n.** another term for **HAUTE COUTURE**.

**high fidelity** • **n.** the reproduction of sound with little distortion.

**high finance** • **n.** financial transactions involving large sums.

**high five** • **n.** informal, chiefly N. Amer. a gesture of celebration or greeting in which two people slap each other's palms with their arms raised.

**high-flown** • **adj.** (especially of language) extravagant or grandiose.

**high-flyer** (also **high-flier**) • **n.** a person who is or has the potential to be very successful.
– DERIVATIVES **high-flying** adj.

**high frequency** • **n.** (in radio) a frequency of 3–30 megahertz.

**high gear** • **n.** a gear that causes a wheeled vehicle to move fast.

**High German** • **n.** the standard literary and spoken form of German, originally used in the highlands in the south of Germany.

**high-handed** • **adj.** domineering or inconsiderate.
– DERIVATIVES **high-handedly** adv. **high-handedness** n.

**high hat** • **n. 1** a top hat. **2** N. Amer. informal a snobbish or supercilious person. **3** (**high-hat**) variant form of **HI-HAT**. • **adj.** (**high-hat**) N. Amer. informal snobbish. • **v.** (**high-hat**) (**-hatted**, **-hatting**) N. Amer. informal treat superciliously.

**High Holidays** (also **High Holy Days**) • **pl. n.** the Jewish festivals of Yom Kippur and Rosh Hashana.

**high-impact** • **adj. 1** (of plastic or a similar substance) able to withstand great impact without breaking. **2** denoting extremely strenuous aerobic exercises.

**high jinks** • **pl. n.** boisterous fun.
– ORIGIN C17: see **JINK**.

**high jump** • **n.** (**the high jump**) an athletic event in which competitors jump as high as possible over a bar of adjustable height.
– PHRASES **be for the high jump** Brit. informal be about to be severely reprimanded.
– DERIVATIVES **high jumper** n.

**high-key** (also **high-keyed**) • **adj.** Art & Photography having a predominance of light or bright tones.

**highland** • **n.** (also **highlands**) an area of high or mountainous land. ➤(**the Highlands**) the mountainous northern part of Scotland.
– DERIVATIVES **highlander** n. **highlandman** n. (pl. **-men**).
– ORIGIN OE *hēahlond* 'a high promontory' (see **HIGH**, **LAND**).

**Highland cattle** • **pl. n.** animals of a shaggy-haired breed of cattle with long, curved widely spaced horns.

**Highland dress** • **n.** the kilt and other clothing in the traditional style of the Scottish Highlands, now worn chiefly on formal occasions.

**Highland fling** • **n.** a vigorous solo Scottish dance consisting of a series of complex steps.

**Highland Games** • **pl. n.** a meeting for athletic events, playing of the bagpipes, and dancing, held in the Scottish Highlands or by Scots elsewhere.

**high-level** • **adj. 1** of relatively high importance. **2** Computing denoting a programming language (e.g. BASIC) that has instructions resembling an existing language such as English.

**high life** • **n. 1** (also **high living**) an extravagant social life as enjoyed by the wealthy. **2** (usu. **highlife**) a style of dance music of West African origin, influenced by rock and jazz.

**highlight** • **n. 1** an outstanding part of an event or period of time. **2** a bright or reflective area in a painting, picture, or design. ➤(usu. **highlights**) a bright tint in the hair, produced by bleaching or dyeing. • **v. 1** draw attention to. ➤mark with a highlighter. **2** create highlights in (hair).

**highlighter** • **n. 1** a broad marker pen used to overlay transparent fluorescent colour on text or a part of an illustration. **2** a cosmetic that is lighter than the wearer's foundation or skin, used to emphasize the cheekbones or other features.

**high-low** • **n.** a lace-up ankle boot with a low heel, worn by the military in the 18th and early 19th centuries.

**highly** • adv. **1** to a high degree or level. **2** favourably.

**highly strung** • adj. Brit. very nervous and easily upset.

**High Mass** • n. a Roman Catholic or Anglo-Catholic mass with full ceremonial, including music and incense.

**high-minded** • adj. having strong moral principles.
– DERIVATIVES **high-mindedly** adv. **high-mindedness** n.

**high muck-a-muck** (also **high muckety-muck**) • n. N. Amer. informal a self-important or conceited person.
– ORIGIN C19: perh. from Chinook *hiyu* 'plenty' + *muckamuck* 'food', with *high* substituted for *hiyu*.

**highness** • n. **1** (**His/Your** etc. **Highness**) a title given to a person of royal rank, or used in addressing them. **2** the state of being high.

**high-octane** • adj. **1** denoting petrol having a high octane number and thus good anti-knock properties. **2** powerful or dynamic.

**high polymer** • n. a polymer having a high molecular weight, such as those used in plastics and resins.

**high-powered** • adj. (of a person) dynamic and forceful.

**high priest** • n. a chief priest of a non-Christian religion, especially of historic Judaism. ➤(or **high priestess**) the leader of a cult or movement.

**high relief** • n. see RELIEF (sense 6).

**high-rise** • adj. (of a building) having many storeys.

**high road** • n. **1** a main road. **2** N. Amer. a morally superior approach.

**high roller** • n. informal, chiefly N. Amer. a person who gambles or spends large sums of money.
– DERIVATIVES **high-rolling** adj.
– ORIGIN with ref. to rolling dice.

**high school** • n. **1** N. Amer. a secondary school. **2** (in the UK except Scotland) used chiefly in names of grammar schools or independent fee-paying secondary schools.
– DERIVATIVES **high schooler** n.

**high seas** • pl. n. (**the high seas**) the open ocean, especially that not within any country's jurisdiction.

**high season** • n. Brit. the most popular time of year for a holiday, when prices are highest.

**high sheriff** • n. see SHERIFF.

**high sign** • n. N. Amer. informal a surreptitious gesture indicating a warning or that all is well.

**high spirits** • pl. n. lively and cheerful behaviour or mood.
– DERIVATIVES **high-spirited** adj. **high-spiritedness** n.

**high spot** • n. the most enjoyable or significant part of an experience or period of time.
– PHRASES **hit the high spots** informal visit the most exciting places in town.

**high-stick** • v. [often as noun **high-sticking**] Ice Hockey strike (an opponent) on or above the shoulders with one's stick, for which a penalty may be assessed.

**high street** • n. Brit. the main street and often the principal shopping area of a town. ➤[as modifier] (of retail goods) catering to the needs of the ordinary public.

**hight** /hʌɪt/ • adj. archaic or poetic/literary named.
– ORIGIN ME, from OE *heht*, past tense of *hātan* 'call or name', of Gmc origin.

**high table** • n. Brit. a table in a dining hall at which high-ranking people, such as the fellows of a college, sit.

**hightail** • v. informal, chiefly N. Amer. move or travel fast.

**high tea** • n. Brit. a late-afternoon or early-evening meal, typically consisting of a cooked dish and tea.

**high-tech** (also **hi-tech**) • adj. **1** employing, requiring, or involved in high technology. **2** (of architecture and interior design) employing a functional style and industrial materials, such as steel and plastic. • n. (**high tech**) short for HIGH TECHNOLOGY.

**high technology** • n. advanced technological development, especially in electronics.

**high-tensile** • adj. (of metal) very strong under tension.

**high-test** • adj. US (of petrol) high-octane.

**high-ticket** • adj. another term for BIG-TICKET.

**high tide** • n. the state of the tide when at its highest level.

**high-top** • adj. denoting a soft-soled sports shoe with a laced upper that extends above the ankle. • n. (**high-tops**) a pair of such shoes.

**high treason** • n. see TREASON.

**high water** • n. another term for HIGH TIDE.

**high-water mark** • n. the level reached by the sea at high tide, or by a lake or river in time of flood. ➤a maximum recorded level or value.

**highway** • n. chiefly N. Amer. a main road. ➤(chiefly in official use) a public road.

**highwayman** • n. (pl. **-men**) historical a man, typically on horseback, who held up and robbed travellers.

**high wire** • n. a high tightrope.

**high yellow** • n. US offensive a light-skinned person with one black and one white parent.

**HIH** • abbrev. Brit. Her or His Imperial Highness.

**hi-hat** (also **high-hat**) • n. a pair of foot-operated cymbals forming part of a drum kit.

**hijab** /ˈhidʒab/ • n. a head covering worn in public by some Muslim women. ➤the religious code which governs the wearing of such clothing.
– ORIGIN Pers., from Arab. *ḥajaba* 'to veil'.

**hijack** • v. illegally seize control of (an aircraft, ship, or vehicle) while in transit. • n. an instance of hijacking.
– DERIVATIVES **hijacker** n.
– ORIGIN 1920s (orig. US): of unknown origin.

**Hijra** /ˈhɪdʒrə/ • n. variant spelling of HEGIRA.

**hijra** /ˈhɪdʒrə/ • n. Indian a transvestite or eunuch.
– ORIGIN from Hindi.

**hike** • n. **1** a long walk or walking tour. **2** a sharp increase, especially in price. • v. **1** go on a hike. **2** pull or lift up (clothing). **3** increase (a price) sharply.
– PHRASES **take a hike** informal, chiefly N. Amer. go away.
– DERIVATIVES **hiker** n.
– ORIGIN C19 (orig. dial.): of unknown origin.

**hila** plural form of HILUM.

**hilar** /ˈhʌɪlə/ • adj. Anatomy & Botany of or relating to a hilus or hilum.

**hilarious** /hɪˈlɛːrɪəs/ • adj. extremely funny or merry.
– DERIVATIVES **hilariously** adv. **hilarity** n.
– ORIGIN C19 (ME as *hilarity*): from L. *hilaris* (from Gk *hilaros* 'cheerful') + **-ous**.

**Hilary term** • n. Brit. (in some universities) the university term beginning in January.
– ORIGIN ME: named after the 4th-cent. Fr. bishop St *Hilary*.

**Hilbert space** • n. Mathematics an infinite-dimensional analogue of Euclidean space.
– ORIGIN C20: named after the Ger. mathematician David *Hilbert*.

**hill** • n. a naturally raised area of land, not as high or craggy as a mountain. ➤a heap or mound. • v. form into a heap. ➤bank up (a plant) with soil.
– PHRASES **a hill of beans** [with neg.] N. Amer. informal a small amount. **over the hill** informal old; past one's best.
– ORIGIN OE *hyll*, of Gmc origin.

**hillbilly** • n. (pl. **-ies**) N. Amer. informal an unsophisticated country person, originally one from the Appalachians.
– ORIGIN C20: from HILL + *Billy* (familiar form of the given name *William*).

**hill climb** • n. a race for vehicles up a steep hill.
– DERIVATIVES **hill-climber** n. **hill-climbing** n.

**hill figure** • n. an outline of a horse, human, or other design cut into the turf of a hill, especially in the chalk downs of southern England.

**hill fort** • n. a fort built on a hill, in particular an Iron Age system of defensive banks and ditches.

**hillock** • n. a small hill or mound.
– DERIVATIVES **hillocky** adj.

**hillside** • n. the sloping side of a hill.

**hill station** • n. a town in the low mountains of the Indian subcontinent, popular as a holiday resort during the hot season.

**hilltop** • n. the summit of a hill.

**hillwalking** • n. the pastime of walking in hilly country.

– DERIVATIVES **hillwalker** n.

**hilly** ● adj. (**-ier**, **-iest**) having many hills.
– DERIVATIVES **hilliness** n.

**hilt** ● n. the handle of a sword, dagger, or knife.
– PHRASES **(up) to the hilt** completely.
– DERIVATIVES **hilted** adj.
– ORIGIN OE *hilt*, *hilte*, of Gmc origin.

**hilum** /ˈhʌɪləm/ ● n. (pl. **hila** /-lə/) **1** Botany the scar on a seed marking the point of attachment to its seed vessel. **2** Anatomy another term for **HILUS**.
– ORIGIN C17: from L., lit. 'little thing, trifle', once thought to mean 'that which sticks to a bean'.

**hilus** /ˈhʌɪləs/ ● n. (pl. **hili** /ˈhʌɪlʌɪ/) Anatomy an indentation in the surface of a kidney or other organ, where blood vessels, nerve fibres, etc. enter or leave it.
– ORIGIN C19: mod. L., alt. of **HILUM**.

**HIM** ● abbrev. Brit. Her or His Imperial Majesty.

**him** ● pron. [third person sing.] **1** used as the object of a verb or preposition to refer to a male person or animal previously mentioned. **2** referring to a person or animal of unspecified sex (now largely replaced by 'him or her' or 'they'). **3** archaic or N. Amer. dialect himself.
– ORIGIN OE, dative sing. form of *he*, *hē* 'he' and *hit* 'it'.

**Himalayan** ● adj. of or relating to the Himalayas.

**himation** /hɪˈmatɪɒn/ ● n. an outer garment worn by the ancient Greeks over the left shoulder and under the right.
– ORIGIN from Gk.

**himself** ● pron. [third person sing.] **1** [reflexive] used as the object of a verb or preposition to refer to a male person or animal previously mentioned as the subject of the clause. **2** [emphatic] he or him personally. ➤ chiefly Irish an important male third party, especially the master of the house.

**hin** ● n. a Hebrew unit of liquid capacity equal to approximately 5 litres (about one gallon).
– ORIGIN ME: from biblical Heb. *hīn*.

**Hinayana** /ˌhiːnəˈjɑːnə/ (also **Hinayana Buddhism**) ● n. a name given by the followers of Mahayana Buddhism to the more orthodox schools of early Buddhism, which survived in Sri Lanka as the Theravada school.
– ORIGIN from Sanskrit *hīna* 'lesser' + *yāna* 'vehicle'.

**hind**[1] ● adj. situated at the back.
– ORIGIN ME: perh. shortened from OE *behindan* (see **BEHIND**).

**hind**[2] ● n. a female deer, especially a red deer or sika in and after the third year.
– ORIGIN OE, of Gmc origin.

**hind**[3] ● n. archaic, chiefly Scottish a skilled farm worker, typically married and with a tied cottage. ➤ a peasant.
– ORIGIN OE *hīne* 'household servants', appar. from *hīgna*, *hīna*, genitive pl. of *hīgan*, *hīwan* 'family members'.

**hind-** ● comb. form (added to nouns) posterior: *hindquarters*.

**hindbrain** ● n. the lower part of the brainstem, comprising the cerebellum, pons, and medulla oblongata.

**hinder**[1] /ˈhɪndə/ ● v. delay or impede.
– ORIGIN OE *hindrian* 'damage', of Gmc origin; rel. to **BEHIND**.

**hinder**[2] /ˈhʌɪndə/ ● adj. (especially of a bodily part) hind.
– ORIGIN ME: perh. from OE *hinderweard* 'backward', rel. to **BEHIND**.

**Hindi** /ˈhɪndi/ ● n. an Indic language of northern India derived from Sanskrit, an official language of India. ● adj. of or relating to Hindi.
– ORIGIN from Urdu *hindī*, from *Hind* 'India'.

**hindmost** ● adj. furthest back.

**hindquarters** ● pl. n. the hind legs and adjoining parts of a quadruped.

**hindrance** /ˈhɪndr(ə)ns/ ● n. a thing that hinders.

**hindsight** ● n. understanding of a situation or event only after it has happened.

**Hindu** /ˈhɪnduː, hɪnˈduː/ ● n. (pl. **Hindus**) a follower of Hinduism. ● adj. of or relating to Hindus or Hinduism.
– ORIGIN Urdu, from Pers. *hindū*, from *Hind* 'India'.

**Hinduism** ● n. a major religious and cultural tradition of the Indian subcontinent, including belief in reincarnation and the worship of a large pantheon of deities.
– DERIVATIVES **Hinduize** (also **-ise**) v.

**Hindustani** /ˌhɪndʊˈstɑːni/ ● n. a group of mutually intelligible languages and dialects spoken in NW India, principally Hindi and Urdu. ➤ the Delhi dialect of Hindi, widely used throughout India as a lingua franca. ● adj. of or relating to the culture of NW India.

**Hindutva** /hɪnˈdʊtvə/ ● n. Indian a very strong sense of Hindu identity, seeking the creation of a Hindu state.
– ORIGIN from Hindi.

**hinge** ● n. a movable joint or mechanism by which a door, gate, or lid opens and closes or which connects linked objects. ● v. (**hingeing** or **hinging**) **1** attach or join with or as if with a hinge. **2** (**hinge on**) depend entirely on.
– DERIVATIVES **hingeless** adj.
– ORIGIN ME *henge*; rel. to **HANG**.

**hinky** ● adj. (**-ier**, **-iest**) US informal dishonest or suspect.
– ORIGIN 1950s: of obscure origin.

**hinny**[1] ● n. (pl. **-ies**) the offspring of a female donkey and a male horse. Compare with **MULE**[1].
– ORIGIN C17: via L. from Gk *hinnos*.

**hinny**[2] (also **hinnie**) ● n. (pl. **-ies**) Scottish & N. English used as a term of endearment.
– ORIGIN C19: var. of **HONEY**.

**hinoki** /hɪˈnəʊki/ ● n. a tall slow-growing Japanese cypress with bright green leaves that yields a valuable wood. [*Chamaecyparis obtusa*.]
– ORIGIN C18: from Japanese.

**hint** ● n. **1** a slight or indirect indication. ➤ a very small trace. **2** a small piece of practical information. ● v. indicate indirectly. ➤ (**hint at**) be a slight indication of.
– ORIGIN C17 (in the sense 'occasion, opportunity'): appar. from obs. *hent* 'grasp', from OE *hentan*, of Gmc origin; rel. to **HUNT**.

**hinterland** /ˈhɪntəland/ ● n. **1** the remote areas of a country away from the coast or the banks of major rivers. ➤ the area around or beyond a major town or port. **2** an area lying beyond what is visible or known.
– ORIGIN C19: from Ger., from *hinter* 'behind' + *Land* 'land'.

**hip**[1] ● n. **1** a projection of the pelvis and upper thigh bone on each side of the body. ➤ (**hips**) the circumference of the body at the buttocks. **2** the edge formed where two sloping sides of a roof meet.
– ORIGIN OE *hype*, of Gmc origin; rel. to **HOP**[1].

**hip**[2] (also **rose hip**) ● n. the fruit of a rose, especially a wild kind.
– ORIGIN OE *hēope*, *hīope*, of W. Gmc origin.

**hip**[3] ● adj. (**hipper**, **hippest**) informal **1** fashionable. **2** (**hip to**) aware of or informed about.
– DERIVATIVES **hipness** n.
– ORIGIN C20 (orig. US): of unknown origin.

**hip**[4] ● exclam. introducing a communal cheer.
– ORIGIN C18: of unknown origin.

**hip bath** ● n. a portable bath large enough to sit rather than lie down in.

**hip bone** ● n. a large bone forming the main part of the pelvis on each side of the body and consisting of the fused ilium, ischium, and pubis.

**hip flask** ● n. a small flask for spirits, of a kind intended to be carried in a hip pocket.

**hip hop** ● n. a style of popular music of US black and Hispanic origin, featuring rap with an electronic backing.
– ORIGIN 1980s: reduplication prob. based on **HIP**[3].

**hipped**[1] ● adj. **1** [in combination] having hips of a specified kind. **2** (of a roof) having a hip or hips.

**hipped**[2] ● adj. (**hipped on**) informal, chiefly N. Amer. obsessed or infatuated with.
– ORIGIN 1920s.: from **HIP**[3], or as the past part. of *hip* 'make someone hip (i.e. aware)'.

**hippie** ● n. & adj. variant spelling of **HIPPY**[1].

**hippo** ● n. (pl. same or **-os**) informal term for **HIPPOPOTAMUS**.

**hippocampus** /ˌhɪpə(ʊ)ˈkampəs/ ● n. (pl. **hippocampi** /-pi, -pʌɪ/) Anatomy the system of elongated ridges on the floor of the lateral ventricles of the brain, thought to be

the centre of emotion, memory, and the autonomic nervous system.
– ORIGIN C16: via L. from Gk *hippokampos*, from *hippos* 'horse' + *kampos* 'sea monster'.

**hippocras** /ˈhɪpəkras/ ● **n.** historical wine flavoured with spices.
– ORIGIN ME: from OFr. *ipocras* 'Hippocrates' (see **HIPPOCRATIC OATH**), translating med. L. *vinum Hippocraticum* 'Hippocratic wine' (because it was strained through a filter called a *Hippocrates' sleeve*).

**Hippocratic oath** /ˌhɪpəˈkratɪk/ ● **n.** a former oath taken by those beginning medical practice, affirming their obligations and proper conduct, parts of which are still used in some medical schools.
– ORIGIN C18: *Hippocratic* from med. L. *Hippocraticus* 'relating to *Hippocrates*', a Gk physician of the 5th cent. BC.

**Hippocrene** /ˈhɪpəkriːn/ ● **n.** poetic/literary poetic or literary inspiration.
– ORIGIN C17: via L. from Gk *Hippokrēnē, Hippou krēnē*, lit. 'fountain of the horse', the name of a fountain on Mount Helicon sacred to the Muses, which according to legend was produced by a stroke of Pegasus' hoof.

**hippodrome** /ˈhɪpədrəʊm/ ● **n. 1** [in names] a theatre or concert hall. **2** (in ancient Greece or Rome) a course for chariot or horse races.
– ORIGIN C16: from Fr., via L. from Gk *hippodromos*, from *hippos* 'horse' + *dromos* 'race, course'.

**hippogriff** /ˈhɪpə(ʊ)ɡrɪf/ (also **hippogryph**) ● **n.** a mythical creature with the body of a horse and a griffin's wings and head.
– ORIGIN C17: from Fr. *hippogriffe*, from Ital. *ippogrifo*, from Gk *hippos* 'horse' + Ital. *grifo* 'griffin'.

**hippopotamus** /ˌhɪpəˈpɒtəməs/ ● **n.** (pl. **hippopotamuses** or **hippopotami** /-mʌɪ/) a large thick-skinned semiaquatic African mammal, with massive jaws. [*Hippopotamus amphibius* and *Choeropsis liberiensis* (**pygmy hippopotamus**).]
– ORIGIN ME: via L. from Gk *hippopotamos*, earlier *hippos ho potamios*, 'river horse'.

**hippuric acid** /hɪˈpjʊərɪk/ ● **n.** Biochemistry an organic acid present in the urine of herbivores and other mammals.
– DERIVATIVES **hippurate** n.
– ORIGIN C19: from Gk *hippos* 'horse' + *ouron* 'urine' + **-IC**.

**hippy**[1] (also **hippie**) ● **n.** (pl. **-ies**) (especially in the 1960s) a young person associated with a subculture which rejected traditional social values, advocated peace and free love, and adopted an unconventional appearance.
– DERIVATIVES **hippiedom** n. **hippiness** n. **hippyish** adj.
– ORIGIN 1950s: from **HIP**[3] + **-Y**[1].

**hippy**[2] ● **adj.** (of a woman) having large hips.

**hippy-dippy** ● **adj.** informal adopting hippy values in a way perceived to be unconsidered or foolishly idealistic.

**hipshot** ● **adv.** N. Amer. in a posture with one hip lower than the other.

**hipster**[1] Brit. ● **adj.** (of a garment) having the waistline at the hips rather than the waist. ● **n.** (**hipsters**) trousers with such a waistline.

**hipster**[2] ● **n.** informal a person who follows the latest trends and fashions.
– DERIVATIVES **hipsterism** n.
– ORIGIN 1940s: from **HIP**[3] + **-STER**.

**hiragana** /ˌhɪrəˈɡɑːnə, ˌhɪərə-/ ● **n.** the more cursive form of syllabic writing used in Japanese, primarily used for function words and inflections.
– ORIGIN Japanese, 'plain kana'.

**hircine** /ˈhəːsʌɪn/ ● **adj.** archaic of or resembling a goat.
– ORIGIN C17: from L. *hircinus*, from *hircus* 'he-goat'.

**hire** ● **v. 1** chiefly Brit. obtain the temporary use of in return for payment. ➤(**hire something out**) grant the temporary use of something in return for payment. **2** employ for wages. ➤obtain the services of (someone) to do a particular job. ● **n. 1** the action of hiring. **2** N. Amer. a recently recruited employee.
– PHRASES **for** (or **on**) **hire** available to be hired.
– DERIVATIVES **hireable** (US also **hirable**) adj. **hirer** n.
– ORIGIN OE *hȳrian* 'employ for wages', *hȳr* 'payment under contract for the use of something', of W. Gmc origin.

**hired girl** (or **hired man**) ● **n.** N. Amer. a domestic servant, especially on a farm.

**hired gun** ● **n.** N. Amer. informal **1** an expert brought in to resolve complex legal or financial problems, disputes, etc. ➤a lobbyist or similar person able to attain power or influence for others quickly and efficiently. **2** a bodyguard, mercenary, or other person hired to protect or fight for another. ➤a hired assassin.

**hireling** ● **n.** chiefly derogatory a person who is hired, especially for morally dubious or illegal work.

**hire purchase** ● **n.** Brit. a system by which someone pays for a thing in regular instalments while having the use of it.

**hirple** /ˈhəːp(ə)l/ ● **v.** chiefly Scottish & N. English hobble.
– ORIGIN C15: of unknown origin.

**hirsute** /ˈhəːsjuːt/ ● **adj.** formal, often humorous hairy: *their hirsute chests.*
– DERIVATIVES **hirsuteness** n.
– ORIGIN C17: from L. *hirsutus*.

**hirsutism** /ˈhəːsjuːtɪz(ə)m/ ● **n.** Medicine abnormal growth of hair on a woman's face and body.

**hirundine** /ˈhɪrʌndʌɪn, hɪˈrʌndʌɪn/ ● **n.** Ornithology a bird of the swallow family (Hirundinidae).
– ORIGIN C19: from L. *hirundo* 'swallow' + **-INE**[1].

**his** ● **possess. det. 1** belonging to or associated with a male person or animal previously mentioned. ➤belonging to or associated with a person or animal of unspecified sex (in modern use chiefly replaced by 'his or her' or 'their'). **2** (**His**) used in titles. ● **possess. pron.** used to refer to a thing or things belonging to or associated with a male person or animal previously mentioned.
– ORIGIN OE, genitive sing. form of *he*, *hē* 'he' and *hit* 'it'.

**Hispanic** /hɪˈspanɪk/ ● **adj.** of or relating to Spain or to Spanish-speaking countries, especially those of Central and South America. ➤of or relating to Spanish-speaking people or their culture, especially in the US. ● **n.** a Spanish-speaking person, especially one of Latin American descent, living in the US.
– DERIVATIVES **Hispanicize** (also **-ise**) v.
– ORIGIN from L. *Hispanicus*, from *Hispania* 'Spain'.

**Hispanist** /ˈhɪspənɪst/ (also **Hispanicist** /hɪˈspanɪsɪst/) ● **n.** an expert in or student of Hispanic language and culture.

**Hispano-** /hɪˈspanəʊ/ ● **comb. form** Spanish; Spanish and ...: *Hispano-Argentine.*
– ORIGIN from L. *Hispanus* 'Spanish'.

**hispid** /ˈhɪspɪd/ ● **adj.** Botany & Zoology covered with stiff hair or bristles.
– ORIGIN C17: from L. *hispidus*.

**hiss** ● **v.** make a sharp sibilant sound as of the letter *s*, often as a sign of disapproval or derision. ➤whisper something in an urgent or angry way. ● **n.** a hissing sound. ➤electrical interference at audio frequencies.
– ORIGIN ME: imitative.

**hissy fit** ● **n.** N. Amer. informal an angry outburst; a temper tantrum.
– ORIGIN 1930s (as *hissy*): perh. from *hysterics* (see **HYSTERIC**).

**hist** ● **exclam.** archaic used to attract attention or call for silence.
– ORIGIN C16: natural exclam.

**hist-** ● **comb. form** variant spelling of **HISTO-** shortened before a vowel (as in *histidine*).

**histamine** /ˈhɪstəmiːn/ ● **n.** Biochemistry a compound which is released by cells in response to injury and in allergic and inflammatory reactions, causing muscle contraction and capillary dilation.
– DERIVATIVES **histaminic** adj.
– ORIGIN C20: blend of **HISTIDINE** and **AMINE**.

**histidine** /ˈhɪstɪdiːn/ ● **n.** Biochemistry an amino acid which is a constituent of most proteins and is essential in the human diet.
– ORIGIN C19: from Gk *histos* 'web, tissue' + **-IDE** + **-INE**[4].

**histiocyte** /ˈhɪstɪə(ʊ)sʌɪt/ ● **n.** Physiology a stationary

phagocytic cell present in connective tissue.
– ORIGIN C20: from Gk *histion* (dimin. of *histos* 'tissue, web') + **-CYTE**.

**histo-** /ˈhɪstəʊ/ (also **hist-** before a vowel) ● **comb. form** Biology relating to organic tissue: *histochemistry*.
– ORIGIN from Gk *histos* 'web, tissue'.

**histochemistry** ● **n.** the branch of science concerned with the chemical constituents of tissues and their study using stains, indicators, and microscopy.
– DERIVATIVES **histochemical** adj.

**histocompatibility** ● **n.** Medicine compatibility between the tissues of different individuals.

**histogram** ● **n.** Statistics a diagram consisting of rectangles whose positions and dimensions represent the values of a variable quantity.
– ORIGIN C19: from Gk *histos* 'mast, web' + **-GRAM**[1].

**histology** /hɪˈstɒlədʒi/ ● **n.** the branch of biology concerned with the microscopic structure of tissues.
– DERIVATIVES **histological** adj. **histologist** n.

**histolysis** /hɪˈstɒlɪsɪs/ ● **n.** Biology the breaking down of tissues (e.g. during animal metamorphosis).
– DERIVATIVES **histolytic** adj.

**histone** /ˈhɪstəʊn/ ● **n.** Biochemistry any of a group of basic proteins found in chromatin.
– ORIGIN C19: Ger. *Histon*, perh. from Gk *histanai* 'arrest' or from *histos* 'web, tissue'.

**histopathology** ● **n.** the branch of medicine concerned with the changes in tissues caused by disease.
– DERIVATIVES **histopathological** adj. **histopathologist** n.

**histoplasmosis** /ˌhɪstəʊplazˈməʊsɪs/ ● **n.** Medicine infection by a fungus found in the droppings of birds and bats in humid areas.
– ORIGIN C20: from mod. L. *Histoplasma* (genus name of the fungus) + **-OSIS**.

**historian** ● **n.** an expert in or student of history.

**historiated** /hɪˈstɔːrɪeɪtɪd/ ● **adj.** (of an initial letter in an illuminated manuscript) decorated with designs representing scenes from the text.
– ORIGIN C19: from Fr. *historié*, past part. of *historier* in an obs. sense 'illustrate', from med. L. *historiare*, from *historia* (see **HISTORY**).

**historic** ● **adj.** **1** famous or important in history, or potentially so. ➤ archaic of the past. **2** Grammar (of a tense) used in the narration of past events, especially Latin and Greek imperfect and pluperfect.

**historical** ● **adj.** of or concerning history. ➤ belonging to or set in the past. ➤ (of the study of a subject) based on an analysis of its development over a period.
– DERIVATIVES **historically** adv.

**historical materialism** ● **n.** another term for **DIALECTICAL MATERIALISM**.

**historicism** ● **n.** **1** the theory that social and cultural phenomena are determined by history. ➤ the belief that historical events are governed by natural laws. **2** the tendency to regard historical development as the most basic aspect of human existence. **3** (in art and architecture) excessive regard for past styles.
– DERIVATIVES **historicist** n. **historicization** (also **-isation**) n. **historicize** (also **-ise**) v.

**historicity** /ˌhɪstəˈrɪsɪti/ ● **n.** historical authenticity.

**historic present** ● **n.** Grammar the present tense used instead of the past in vivid narrative.

**historiography** /hɪˌstɔːrɪˈɒgrəfi, -ˌstɒrɪ-/ ● **n.** the study of the writing of history and of written histories. ➤ the writing of history.
– DERIVATIVES **historiographer** n. **historiographic** adj. **historiographical** adj.
– ORIGIN C16: via med. L. from Gk *historiographia*, from *historia* 'history' + *-graphia* 'writing'.

**history** ● **n.** (pl. **-ies**) **1** the study of past events. **2** the past considered as a whole. ➤ the whole series of past events connected with someone or something. ➤ an eventful past. **3** a continuous, typically chronological, record of past events or trends.
– PHRASES **be history** informal used to indicate imminent departure, dismissal, or death. **the rest is history** the events succeeding those already related are so well known that they need not be recounted again.
– ORIGIN ME: via L. from Gk *historia* 'narrative, history', from *histōr* 'learned, wise man'.

**histosol** /ˈhɪstəsɒl/ ● **n.** Soil Science a peaty soil with a deep surface layer of purely organic material.

**histrionic** /ˌhɪstrɪˈɒnɪk/ ● **adj.** **1** overly theatrical or melodramatic. **2** formal of or concerning actors or acting. ● **n.** (**histrionics**) exaggerated dramatic behaviour designed to attract attention.
– DERIVATIVES **histrionically** adv.
– ORIGIN C17: from late L. *histrionicus*, from L. *histrio(n-)* 'actor'.

**hit** ● **v.** (**hitting**; past and past part. **hit**) **1** direct a blow at with one's hand or a tool or weapon. ➤ accidentally strike (part of one's body) against something. ➤ (of a moving object or body) come into contact with (someone or something stationary) quickly and forcefully. **2** strike (a target). **3** cause harm or distress to. ➤ (**hit out**) make a strongly worded criticism or attack. ➤ informal, chiefly N. Amer. attack and rob or kill. **4** informal reach or arrive at. ➤ take effect. ➤ be suddenly and vividly realized by: *it hit her that I wanted to settle down here.* ➤ (**hit on**) discover or think of, especially by chance. ➤ (**hit on**) N. Amer. informal make sexual advances towards. **5** propel (a ball) with a bat, racket, etc. ➤ score (runs or points) in this way. ● **n.** **1** an instance of hitting or being hit. **2** informal, chiefly N. Amer. a murder carried out by a criminal organization. **3** Baseball short for **BASE HIT**. **4** Computing an instance of identifying an item of data which matches the requirements of a search. **5** a successful and popular film, pop record, person, etc. **6** informal a dose of a narcotic drug.
– PHRASES **hit-and-miss** done or occurring at random. **hit-and-run** **1** denoting a road accident from which the perpetrator escapes before being discovered and without lending assistance. **2** denoting an attack or aggressive enterprise from which the aggressor withdraws rapidly on achieving their goal. **hit someone below the belt** **1** Boxing give one's opponent an illegal low blow. **2** behave unfairly towards someone. **hit someone for six** Brit. affect someone very severely. [with allusion to a forceful hit that scores six runs in cricket.] **hit the ground running** informal proceed at a fast pace with enthusiasm. **hit it off** informal be naturally friendly or well suited. **hit the nail on the head** find exactly the right answer. **hit-or-miss** as likely to be unsuccessful as successful. **hit the road** (or N. Amer. **trail**) informal set out on a journey. **hit wicket** Cricket the action of a batsman stepping on or knocking over their own wicket, resulting in their dismissal.
– DERIVATIVES **hitter** n.
– ORIGIN OE *hittan*, from ON *hitta* 'come upon, meet with'.

**hitch** ● **v.** **1** move (something) into a different position with a jerk. **2** informal travel or obtain (a lift) by hitch-hiking. **3** fasten or tether with a rope. ➤ harness (a draught animal or team). ● **n.** **1** a temporary difficulty. **2** a knot of a kind used to fasten one thing temporarily to another: *an overhand hitch*. ➤ N. Amer. a device for attaching one thing to another. **3** informal an act of hitch-hiking. **4** N. Amer. informal a period of service.
– PHRASES **get hitched** informal marry. **hitch one's wagon to a star** try to succeed by forming a relationship with a successful person.
– ORIGIN ME: of unknown origin.

**hitcher** ● **n.** a hitch-hiker.

**hitch-hike** ● **v.** travel by getting free lifts in passing vehicles. ● **n.** a journey made by hitch-hiking.
– DERIVATIVES **hitch-hiker** n.

**hither** ● **adv.** archaic or poetic/literary to or towards this place. ● **adj.** archaic situated on this side.
– ORIGIN OE *hider*, of Gmc origin; rel. to **HE** and **HERE**.

**hither and thither** (also **hither and yon**) ● **adv.** to and fro.

**hitherto** ● **adv.** until the point in time under discussion.

**hitherward** ● **adv.** archaic to or towards this place.

**Hitler** ● **n.** **1** an authoritarian or tyrannical person. **2** [as modifier] used with reference to Hitler's rule or personal characteristics: *a Hitler moustache*.
– DERIVATIVES **Hitlerian** adj. **Hitlerism** n. **Hitlerite**

n. & adj.
– ORIGIN from Adolf *Hitler* (1889–1945), Austrian-born Nazi leader, Chancellor of Germany 1933–45.

**hit list** ● n. a list of people to be killed for criminal or political reasons.

**hit man** ● n. informal a hired assassin.

**hit-out** ● n. Austral. **1** Australian Rules an instance of hitting the ball towards a teammate after it has been bounced by the umpire or at a boundary throw-in. **2** informal a brisk run.

**hit parade** ● n. dated a weekly listing of the current best-selling pop records.

**Hittite** /ˈhɪtʌɪt/ ● n. **1** a member of an ancient people who established an empire in Asia Minor and Syria *c.*1700–1200 BC. ➤a member of a Canaanite or Syrian people mentioned in the Bible (11th to 8th century BC). **2** the language of the Hittites, the oldest attested Indo-European language. ● adj. of or relating to the Hittites, their empire, or their language.
– ORIGIN from Heb. *Ḥittīm*, ult. from Hittite *Ḫatti*.

**HIV** ● abbrev. human immunodeficiency virus, a retrovirus which causes Aids.

**hive** ● n. **1** a beehive. **2** a busy swarming place. ● v. place (bees) in a hive.
– PHRASAL VERBS **hive something off** chiefly Brit. separate something from a larger group or organization.
– ORIGIN OE *hȳf*, of Gmc origin.

**hives** ● pl. n. [treated as sing. or pl.] another term for URTICARIA.
– ORIGIN C16 (orig. Scots): of unknown origin.

**HIV-positive** ● adj. having had a positive result in a blood test for HIV.

**hiya** ● exclam. an informal greeting.
– ORIGIN 1940s: alt. of *how are you?*

**HK** ● abbrev. Hong Kong.

**HKJ** ● abbrev. Jordan (international vehicle registration).
– ORIGIN from *Hashemite Kingdom of Jordan*.

**HL** ● abbrev. (in the UK) House of Lords.

**hl** ● abbrev. hectolitre(s).

**HM** ● abbrev. **1** headmaster or headmistress. **2** Brit. heavy metal (music). **3** (in the UK) Her (or His) Majesty('s).

**hm** ● abbrev. hectometre(s).

**HMG** ● abbrev. (in the UK) Her or His Majesty's Government.

**HMI** ● abbrev. historical (in the UK) Her or His Majesty's Inspector (of Schools).

**hmm** ● exclam. & n. variant spelling of HEM², HUM².

**Hmong** /hmɒŋ/ ● n. (pl. same) **1** a member of a people living in the mountains of SE Asia. **2** the language of this people. ● adj. relating to or denoting this people or their language.

**HMS** ● abbrev. Her or His Majesty's Ship.

**HMSO** ● abbrev. (in the UK) Her or His Majesty's Stationery Office, which publishes government documents and legislation.

**HNC** ● abbrev. (in the UK) Higher National Certificate.

**HND** ● abbrev. (in the UK) Higher National Diploma.

**Ho** ● symb. the chemical element holmium.

**ho¹** ● exclam. **1** an expression of surprise, triumph, or derision. **2** used to call for attention. ➤Nautical used to draw attention to something: *land ho!*
– ORIGIN ME: natural exclam.

**ho²** (also **hoe**) ● n. (pl. **-os** or **-oes**) black slang a prostitute.
– ORIGIN 1960s: dial. pronunc. of WHORE.

**ho.** ● abbrev. house.

**hoagie** /ˈhəʊgi/ ● n. (pl. **-ies**) chiefly N. Amer. a sandwich made of a long roll filled with meat, cheese, and salad.
– ORIGIN of unknown origin.

**hoar** /hɔː/ archaic or poetic/literary ● adj. grey or grey-haired with age. ● n. hoar frost.
– ORIGIN OE *hār*, of Gmc origin.

**hoard** ● n. a store of money or valued objects. ➤an amassed store of useful information. ● v. amass and hide or store away.
– DERIVATIVES **hoarder** n.
– ORIGIN OE *hord* (n.), *hordian* (v.), of Gmc origin.

**hoarding** ● n. Brit. **1** a large board used to display advertisements. **2** a temporary board fence around a building site.
– ORIGIN C19: from obs. *hoard* in the same sense.

**hoar frost** ● n. frozen water vapour deposited in clear still weather on vegetation, fences, etc.

**hoarhound** ● n. variant spelling of HOREHOUND.

**hoarse** ● adj. (of a voice) rough and harsh.
– DERIVATIVES **hoarsely** adv. **hoarsen** v. **hoarseness** n.
– ORIGIN OE *hās*, of Gmc origin.

**hoarstone** ● n. Brit. an ancient boundary stone.

**hoary** ● adj. (**-ier**, **-iest**) **1** greyish-white. ➤having grey hair; aged. **2** old and trite.
– DERIVATIVES **hoarily** adv. **hoariness** n.

**hoatzin** /həʊˈatsɪn/ ● n. a large tree-dwelling tropical American bird with weak flight. [*Opisthocomus hoazin*.]
– ORIGIN C17: from Amer. Sp., from Nahuatl *uatzin*, prob. imitative of its call.

**hoax** ● n. a humorous or malicious deception. ● v. deceive with a hoax.
– DERIVATIVES **hoaxer** n.
– ORIGIN C18: prob. a contr. of HOCUS.

**hob¹** ● n. **1** Brit. a cooking appliance, or the flat top part of a cooker, with hotplates or burners. ➤a flat metal shelf at the side of a fireplace, used for heating pans. **2** a machine tool for cutting gears or screw threads. **3** a peg or pin used as a mark in throwing games.
– ORIGIN C16 (in sense 3): alt. of HUB.

**hob²** ● n. **1** a male ferret. Compare with GILL⁴. **2** archaic or dialect a hobgoblin.
– PHRASES **play** (or **raise**) **hob** N. Amer. cause mischief.
– ORIGIN ME (in the sense 'country fellow'): familiar form of *Rob*, short for *Robin* or *Robert*.

**Hobbesian** /ˈhɒbzɪən/ ● adj. of or relating to the English political philosopher Thomas Hobbes (1588–1679) or his philosophy.

**hobbit** ● n. a member of an imaginary race similar to humans, of small size and with hairy feet, in stories by J. R. R. Tolkien.
– ORIGIN 1937: invented by Tolkien in his book *The Hobbit*, and said by him to mean 'hole-dweller'.

**hobble** ● v. **1** walk awkwardly, typically because of pain. **2** strap together the legs of (a horse) to prevent straying. ➤cause to limp. **3** be or cause a problem for. ● n. **1** an awkward way of walking. **2** a rope or strap for hobbling a horse.
– DERIVATIVES **hobbler** n.
– ORIGIN ME: prob. of Du. or Low Ger. origin and rel. to Du. *hobbelen* 'rock from side to side'.

**hobblebush** ● n. a North American viburnum bearing clusters of white or pink flowers and purple-black berries. [*Viburnum alnifolium*.]

**hobbledehoy** /ˈhɒb(ə)ldɪˌhɔɪ/ ● n. informal, dated a clumsy or awkward youth.
– ORIGIN C16: of unknown origin.

**hobble skirt** ● n. a skirt so narrow at the hem as to impede walking, popular in the 1910s.

**hobby¹** ● n. (pl. **-ies**) **1** an activity done regularly for pleasure. **2** archaic a small horse or pony. **3** historical an early type of velocipede.
– ORIGIN ME (in sense 'small horse', later 'toy horse or hobby horse') *hobyn*, *hoby*, from familiar forms of the given name *Robin*.

**hobby²** ● n. (pl. **-ies**) a small migratory falcon which hunts birds and insects on the wing. [*Falco subbuteo*.]
– ORIGIN ME: from OFr. *hobet*, dimin. of *hobe* 'falcon'.

**hobby horse** ● n. **1** a child's toy consisting of a stick with a model of a horse's head at one end. ➤a rocking horse. ➤a model of a horse used in morris dancing. **2** a favourite topic.

**hobbyist** ● n. a person with a particular hobby.

**hobday** ● v. Brit. operate on (a horse) to improve its breathing.
– ORIGIN 1930s: named after the Brit. veterinary surgeon Sir Frederick T. G. *Hobday*.

**hobgoblin** ● n. a mischievous imp; a bogey.
– ORIGIN C16: from HOB² + GOBLIN.

**hobnail** • n. **1** a short heavy-headed nail used to reinforce the soles of boots. **2** a blunt projection, especially in cut or moulded glassware.
– DERIVATIVES **hobnailed** adj.
– ORIGIN C16: from **HOB**[1] + **NAIL**.

**hobnail liver** (also **hobnailed liver**) • n. a liver with small knobbly projections due to cirrhosis.

**hobnob** • v. (**hobnobbed**, **hobnobbing**) informal mix socially, especially with those of higher social status.
– ORIGIN C19 (in the sense 'drink together, drink each other's health'): from archaic *hob or nob, hob and nob*, prob. meaning 'give and take'.

**hobo** • n. (pl. **-oes** or **-os**) N. Amer. a vagrant.
– ORIGIN C19: of unknown origin.

**Hobson's choice** • n. a choice of taking what is offered or nothing at all.
– ORIGIN C17: named after Thomas *Hobson*, who hired out horses, making the customer take the one nearest the door or none at all.

**hock**[1] • n. **1** the joint in a quadruped's hind leg between the knee and the fetlock. **2** a knuckle of meat, especially pork or ham.
– ORIGIN ME: var. of **HOUGH**.

**hock**[2] • n. Brit. a dry white wine from the German Rhineland.
– ORIGIN abbrev. of obs. *hockamore*, alt. of Ger. *Hochheimer (Wein)* '(wine) from Hochheim'.

**hock**[3] • v. informal pawn (an object).
– PHRASES **in hock** having been pawned. ➤ in debt.
– ORIGIN C19: from Du. *hok* 'hutch, prison, debt'.

**hocket** • n. Music a spasmodic or interrupted effect, produced by dividing a melody between two parts, notes in one part coinciding with rests in the other.
– DERIVATIVES **hocketing** n.
– ORIGIN C18: from Fr. *hoquet* 'hiccup'.

**hockey**[1] /'hɒki/ • n. a game played between two teams of eleven players each, using hooked sticks to drive a small hard ball towards a goal.
– ORIGIN C16: of unknown origin.

**hockey**[2] /'ɒki, 'hɒki/ • n. variant spelling of **OCHE**.

**Hocktide** • n. (in England) a festival formerly kept on the second Monday and Tuesday after Easter, originally to raise money for the Church and parish.
– ORIGIN of unknown origin.

**hocus** /'həʊkəs/ • v. (**hocussed**, **hocussing** or **hocused**, **hocusing**) archaic **1** deceive (someone). **2** stupefy with drugs. ➤ drug (liquor).
– ORIGIN C17: from obs. *hocus* 'trickery', from **HOCUS-POCUS**.

**hocus-pocus** • n. **1** meaningless talk used for trickery. **2** a form of words used by a conjuror.
– ORIGIN C17: from *hax pax max Deus adimax*, a pseudo-Latin phr. used as a magic formula by conjurors.

**hod** • n. **1** a builder's V-shaped open trough on a pole, used for carrying bricks. **2** a coal scuttle.
– ORIGIN C16: var. of north. Engl. dial. *hot* 'a basket for carrying earth', from OFr. *hotte* 'pannier'.

**hodden** /'hɒd(ə)n/ • n. chiefly Scottish & N. English coarse woollen cloth.
– ORIGIN C16: of unknown origin.

**Hodge** • n. Brit. archaic a typical English agricultural labourer.
– ORIGIN ME: familiar form of the given name *Roger*.

**hodgepodge** • n. N. Amer. variant of **HOTCHPOTCH**.
– ORIGIN ME: changed by assoc. with **HODGE**.

**Hodgkin's disease** • n. a malignant disease of lymphatic tissues typically causing enlargement of the lymph nodes, liver, and spleen.
– ORIGIN C19: named after the Engl. physician Thomas *Hodgkin*.

**hodiernal** /ˌhɒdɪ'əːn(ə)l, ˌhəʊdɪ-/ • adj. rare of or relating to the present day.
– ORIGIN C17: from L. *hodiernus* (from *hodie* 'today') + **-AL**.

**hodman** • n. (pl. **-men**) Brit. a labourer carrying a hod.

**hodograph** /'hɒdəgrɑːf/ • n. Mathematics a curve the radius vector of which represents in magnitude and direction the velocity of a moving object.
– ORIGIN C19: from Gk *hodos* 'way' + **-GRAPH**.

**hodoscope** /'hɒdəskəʊp/ • n. Physics an instrument for observing the paths of cosmic rays or other particles.
– ORIGIN C20: from Gk *hodos* 'way' + **-SCOPE**.

**hoe**[1] • n. a long-handled gardening tool with a thin metal blade, used mainly for weeding. • v. (**-oes**, **-oed**, **-oeing**) **1** use a hoe to dig up (earth or plants). **2** (**hoe in**) Austral./NZ informal eat eagerly. ➤ (**hoe into**) attack or criticize.
– DERIVATIVES **hoer** n.
– ORIGIN ME: from OFr. *houe*, of Gmc origin; rel. to **HEW**.

**hoe**[2] • n. variant spelling of **HO**[2].

**hoecake** • n. US a coarse cake of maize flour, originally baked on the blade of a hoe.

**hoedown** • n. N. Amer. a lively folk dance.

**hog** • n. **1** a pig, especially a castrated male reared for slaughter. **2** informal a greedy person. **3** (also **hogg**) dialect a young sheep before the first shearing. • v. (**hogged**, **hogging**) **1** informal take or hoard selfishly. **2** distort (a ship) by supporting the centre and allowing the bow and stern to droop.
– PHRASES **go the whole hog** informal do something completely or thoroughly. **live high on** (or **off**) **the hog** N. Amer. informal have a luxurious lifestyle.
– DERIVATIVES **hogger** n. **hoggery** n. **hoggish** adj. **hoggishly** adv. **hog-like** adj.
– ORIGIN OE *hogg*, *hocg*, perh. of Celtic origin.

**hogan** /'həʊg(ə)n/ • n. a traditional Navajo Indian hut of logs and earth.
– ORIGIN from Navajo.

**hogback** (also **hog's back**) • n. a long steep hill or mountain ridge.

**hog badger** • n. a badger with a long mobile snout, found in the forests of east Asia. [*Arctonyx collaris*.]

**hogfish** • n. (pl. same or **-fishes**) a large colourful wrasse found chiefly in the western Atlantic. [*Lachnolaimus maximus* and other species.]

**hogg** • n. variant spelling of **HOG** (in sense 3).

**hogget** /'hɒgɪt/ • n. Brit. a yearling sheep. ➤ NZ a lamb between weaning and first shearing.
– ORIGIN ME: from **HOG** + **-ET**[1].

**hoggin** • n. a mixture of sand and gravel, used especially in road-building.
– ORIGIN C19: of unknown origin.

**hog line** • n. Curling a line marked across either end of a curling rink, over which a stone must cross to count.

**Hogmanay** /'hɒgməneɪ, ˌhɒgmə'neɪ/ • n. (in Scotland) New Year's Eve.
– ORIGIN C17: perh. from *hoguinané*, Norman Fr. form of OFr. *aguillanneuf* 'last day of the year, new year's gift'.

**hog-nosed bat** • n. a tiny insectivorous bat with a pig-like nose and no tail, native to Thailand. [*Craseonycteris thonglongyai*.]

**hognose snake** • n. a harmless burrowing American snake that has an upturned snout and inflates itself when alarmed. [Genus *Heterodon*: several species.]

**hognut** • n. another term for **EARTHNUT**.

**hog plum** • n. **1** a Caribbean tree with yellow fruit. [*Spondias mombin*.] **2** an American tree with bitter fruit whose wood is used as a sandalwood substitute. [*Ximenia americana*.]
– ORIGIN C17: so named because the fruit is common food for hogs.

**hog's back** • n. variant of **HOGBACK**.

**hogshead** • n. **1** a large cask. **2** a measure of liquid volume equal to 52.5 imperial gallons (63 US gallons, 238.7 litres) for wine or 54 imperial gallons (64 US gallons, 245.5 litres) for beer.
– ORIGIN ME: from **HOG** + **HEAD**; the reason for the term is unknown.

**hog-tie** • v. N. Amer. **1** secure (a person or animal) by fastening the hands and feet or all four feet together. **2** impede.

**hogwash** • n. informal nonsense.
– ORIGIN C15 (meaning 'kitchen swill for pigs'): from **HOG** + **WASH**.

**hogweed** • n. a large white-flowered weed of the parsley family, formerly used as forage for pigs. [Genus

*Heracleum*: several species.]

**hog-wild** • adj. N. Amer. informal overenthusiastic.

**ho ho** • exclam. **1** used to represent deep laughter. **2** used to express triumph.

**ho-hum** • exclam. used to express boredom or resignation.
– ORIGIN 1920s: imitative of a yawn.

**hoick** Brit. informal • v. lift or pull with a jerk. • n. a jerky pull.
– ORIGIN C19: perh. a var. of HIKE.

**hoicks** /hɔɪks/ • exclam. variant of YOICKS.

**hoi polloi** /ˌhɔɪ pɒˈlɔɪ/ • pl. n. derogatory the common people.
– ORIGIN C17: Gk, lit. 'the many'.

USAGE **hoi polloi**

Hoi polloi is sometimes used incorrectly to mean 'upper class', i.e. the exact opposite of its normal meaning. The confusion probably arose by association with the similar-sounding but otherwise unrelated word **hoity-toity**.

**hoisin sauce** /ˈhɔɪzɪn/ • n. a sweet, spicy dark red sauce made from soya beans, used in Chinese cooking.
– ORIGIN Cantonese *hoisin* 'seafood', from *hoi* 'sea' + *sin* 'fresh'.

**hoist** • v. raise by means of ropes and pulleys. ➤haul up. • n. **1** an act of hoisting. **2** an apparatus for hoisting something. **3** the part of a flag nearest the staff. **4** a group of flags raised as a signal.
– PHRASES **hoist one's flag** (of an admiral) take up command. **hoist the flag** stake one's claim to territory by displaying a flag.
– DERIVATIVES **hoister** n.
– ORIGIN C15: alt. of dial. *hoise*, prob. from Du. *hijsen* or Low Ger. *hiesen*.

**hoity-toity** • adj. **1** haughty. **2** archaic frolicsome.
– ORIGIN C17: from obs. *hoit* 'indulge in riotous mirth', of unknown origin.

**Hokan** /ˈhəʊkan/ • n. a group of American Indian languages of California and western Mexico. • adj. relating to this hypothetical language family.
– ORIGIN from Hokan *hok* 'about two' + -AN.

**hoke** /həʊk/ • v. (usu. **hoke something up**) informal, chiefly N. Amer. (of an actor) overact (a part).
– ORIGIN C20: back-form. from HOKUM.

**hokey** • adj. (**-ier**, **-iest**) N. Amer. informal excessively sentimental or contrived.
– DERIVATIVES **hokeyness** (also **hokiness**) n.
– ORIGIN 1940s: from HOKUM + -Y[1].

**hokey-cokey** • n. a communal song and dance performed in a circle with synchronized shaking of the limbs in turn.
– ORIGIN 1940s: perh. from HOCUS-POCUS.

**hokey-pokey** • n. informal **1** dated ice cream sold by Italian street vendors. **2** US term for HOKEY-COKEY.
– ORIGIN C19: of unknown origin.

**hoki** /ˈhəʊki/ • n. an edible marine fish related to the hakes, found off the southern coasts of New Zealand. [*Macruronus novaezeelandiae*.]
– ORIGIN C19: from Maori.

**hokku** /ˈhɒkuː/ • n. (pl. same) another term for HAIKU.
– ORIGIN Japanese, lit. 'opening verse'.

**hokonui** /ˈhɒkənʊi/ • n. NZ illicitly distilled spirits, especially whisky.
– ORIGIN from a Maori place name.

**hokum** /ˈhəʊkəm/ • n. informal **1** nonsense. **2** sentimental or unrealistic situations and dialogue in a film or other work.
– ORIGIN C20: of unknown origin.

**Holarctic** /hə(ʊ)ˈlɑːktɪk/ • adj. Zoology relating to or denoting a zoogeographical region comprising the Nearctic and Palaearctic regions combined.
– ORIGIN C19: from HOLO- + ARCTIC.

**hold**[1] • v. (past and past part. **held**) **1** grasp, carry, or support. **2** keep or detain. ➤keep possession of. ➤keep in a specified position. ➤continue to follow (a course). ➤stay or cause to stay at a certain value or level. ➤(in sport) manage to achieve a draw against. **3** remain secure or intact. ➤be or remain valid or available. ➤(**hold to**) refuse to abandon or change (a principle). ➤(**hold someone to**) cause someone to adhere to (a commitment). **4** contain or be capable of containing. ➤be able to drink (a reasonable amount of alcohol) without suffering ill effects. **5** have in one's possession. ➤have or occupy (a job or position). ➤have in store: *I don't know what the future holds.* ➤have (a belief or opinion). ➤consider to be responsible for a situation. ➤(**hold someone/thing in**) regard someone or something with (a specified feeling): *the speed limit is held in contempt.* ➤(of a judge or court) rule. **6** reserve. ➤maintain (a telephone connection). **7** N. Amer. informal refrain from adding or using. ➤(**hold it**) informal wait or stop doing something. **8** arrange and take part in (a meeting or conversation). • n. **1** a grip. **2** a handhold. **3** a degree of power or control.
– PHRASES **be left holding the baby** (or N. Amer. **bag**) informal be left with an unwelcome responsibility. **get hold of** grasp. ➤informal find or contact. **hold court** be the centre of attention. **hold something dear** value something greatly. **hold fast** remain tightly secured. ➤continue to adhere to a principle. **hold the fort** take responsibility for something temporarily. **hold good** (or **true**) remain true or valid. **hold hard** Brit. stop or wait. **hold someone/thing harmless** Law indemnify someone or something. **hold one's horses** informal wait a moment. **hold the line** not yield to pressure. **hold someone to bail** Law bind someone by bail. **hold one's tongue** informal remain silent. **hold water** (of a theory) appear sound. **no holds barred 1** (in wrestling) with no restrictions on the kinds of holds that are used. **2** without rules or restrictions. **on hold 1** waiting to be connected by telephone. **2** pending. **take hold** start to have an effect.
– PHRASAL VERBS **hold something against** allow past events to have a negative influence on one's present attitude towards. **hold back** hesitate. **hold something down** informal succeed in keeping a job. **hold forth** talk at length or tediously. **hold off** (of bad weather) fail to occur. **hold someone/thing off** resist an attacker or challenge. ➤postpone an action or decision. **hold on 1** wait; stop. **2** keep going in difficult circumstances. **hold out 1** resist difficult circumstances. **2** continue to be sufficient. **hold out for** continue to demand. **hold out on** informal refuse to give something to. **hold something over 1** postpone something. **2** use information to threaten. **hold up** remain strong or vigorous. **hold someone/thing up 1** delay the progress of someone or something. **2** rob someone using the threat of violence. **3** present someone or something as an example. **hold with** [with neg.] informal approve of.
– DERIVATIVES **holdable** adj. **holder** n.
– ORIGIN OE *haldan*, *healdan*, of Gmc origin.

**hold**[2] • n. a storage space in the lower part of a ship or aircraft.
– ORIGIN C16: from obs. *holl*, from OE *hol* (see HOLE); the *-d* was added by assoc. with HOLD[1].

**holdall** • n. Brit. a large bag with handles and a shoulder strap.

**holdfast** • n. **1** a staple or clamp securing an object. **2** Biology a stalked organ by which a simple aquatic organism attaches itself to a substrate.

**holding** • n. **1** an area of land held by lease. **2** (**holdings**) financial assets.

**holding company** • n. a company created to buy shares in other companies, which it then controls.

**holding pattern** • n. the flight path maintained by an aircraft awaiting permission to land.

**hold-up** • n. **1** a cause of delay. **2** a robbery conducted with the threat of violence. **3** a stocking held up by an elasticated top.

**hole** • n. **1** an empty space in a solid body or surface. ➤an aperture. ➤a cavity on a golf course into which the ball must be hit. **2** Physics a position from which an electron is absent, regarded as a mobile carrier of positive charge in a semiconductor. **3** informal a small or unpleasant place. ➤an awkward situation. • v. **1** make a hole or holes in. **2** Golf hit (the ball) into a hole. **3** (**hole out**) Cricket (of a batsman) hit the ball to a fielder and be caught. **4** (**hole up**) informal hide oneself.

– PHRASES **blow a hole in** ruin the effectiveness of. **in the hole** N. Amer. informal in debt. **in holes** worn so much that holes have formed. **make a hole in** use a large amount of.
– DERIVATIVES **holey** adj.
– ORIGIN OE *hol* (n.), *holian* (v.), of Gmc origin.

**hole-and-corner** • adj. secret.

**hole card** • n. **1** (in stud poker) a card which has been dealt face down. **2** informal, chiefly N. Amer. a secret advantage.

**hole-in-one** • n. (pl. **holes-in-one**) Golf a shot that enters the hole from the tee.

**hole in the heart** • n. Medicine a congenital defect in the heart septum, resulting in inadequate circulation of oxygenated blood.

**hole in the wall** • n. informal **1** Brit. an automatic cash dispenser installed in an outside wall. **2** a small dingy place.

**hole saw** • n. a tool for making circular holes, consisting of a metal cylinder with a toothed edge.

**Holi** /ˈhəʊliː/ • n. a Hindu spring festival celebrated in honour of Krishna.
– ORIGIN via Hindi from Sanskrit *holī*.

**holiday** chiefly Brit. • n. **1** an extended period of recreation, especially away from home. **2** a day of festivity or recreation when no work is done. **3** [with modifier] a short period during which the payment of instalments, tax, etc. may be suspended. • v. spend a holiday.
– ORIGIN OE *hāligdæg* 'holy day'.

**holiday camp** • n. Brit. a site for holidaymakers with accommodation and entertainments.

**holidaymaker** • n. Brit. a tourist.

**holier-than-thou** • adj. self-righteous.

**holiness** • n. **1** the state of being holy. **2** (**His/Your Holiness**) the title of the Pope, Orthodox patriarchs, and the Dalai Lama.

**holism** /ˈhəʊlɪz(ə)m, ˈhɒl-/ • n. **1** chiefly Philosophy the theory that certain wholes are greater than the sum of their parts. The opposite of **ATOMISM**. **2** Medicine the treating of the whole person, rather than just the symptoms of a disease.
– DERIVATIVES **holist** adj. & n. **holistic** adj. **holistically** adv.
– ORIGIN 1920s: from **HOLO-** + **-ISM**.

**holla** /ˈhɒlə/ • exclam. archaic used to call attention to something.
– ORIGIN C16: from Fr. *holà*, from *ho* 'ho!' + *là* 'there'.

**holland** • n. a kind of smooth, hard-wearing linen, used for soft furnishings.
– ORIGIN ME: from *Holland*, where the cloth was made.

**hollandaise sauce** /ˌhɒlənˈdeɪz, ˈhɒlənˌdeɪz/ • n. a creamy sauce for fish, made of butter, egg yolks, and vinegar.
– ORIGIN Fr. *hollandaise*, fem. of *hollandais* 'Dutch'.

**Hollander** • n. dated a native of the Netherlands.

**Hollands** • n. archaic Dutch gin.
– ORIGIN from archaic Du. *hollandsch genever* 'Dutch gin'.

**holler** informal • v. give a loud shout. • n. a loud shout. ➤(also **field holler**) chiefly US a melodic cry used originally by black slaves at work in the fields.
– ORIGIN C17: var. of the rare verb *hollo*; rel. to **HALLOO**.

**hollow** • adj. **1** having a hole or empty space inside. ➤concave. **2** (of a sound) echoing. **3** insincere. • n. **1** a hole or depression. **2** a small valley. • v. (usu. **hollow something out**) make hollow. ➤form by hollowing.
– PHRASES **beat someone hollow** defeat someone thoroughly.
– DERIVATIVES **hollowly** adv. **hollowness** n.
– ORIGIN OE *holh* 'cave'; obscurely rel. to **HOLE**.

**hollowware** • n. hollow cookware or crockery, such as pots or jugs.

**holly** • n. an evergreen shrub, with prickly dark green leaves, small white flowers, and red berries. [*Ilex aquifolium* and other species.]
– ORIGIN ME *holi*, shortened form of OE *holegn*, *holen*, of Gmc origin.

**hollyhock** • n. a tall plant of the mallow family, with large showy flowers. [*Alcea rosea*.]
– ORIGIN ME: from **HOLY** + obs. *hock* 'mallow', of unknown origin.

**holly oak** • n. the holm oak or the kermes oak.

**holm** /həʊm/ (also **holme**) • n. Brit. **1** an islet. **2** a flood plain.
– ORIGIN OE, from ON *holmr*.

**holmium** /ˈhəʊlmɪəm/ • n. the chemical element of atomic number 67, a soft silvery-white metal of the lanthanide series. (Symbol: **Ho**)
– ORIGIN C19: mod. L., from *Holmia*, Latinized form of *Stockholm*, the capital of Sweden (because holmium and related minerals are found there).

**holm oak** • n. an evergreen oak with dark green glossy leaves. [*Quercus ilex*.]
– ORIGIN ME: alt. of dial. *hollin*, from OE *holen* 'holly'.

**holo-** • comb. form whole; complete: *holocaust* | *holophytic*.
– ORIGIN from Gk *holos* 'whole'.

**holocaust** /ˈhɒləkɔːst/ • n. **1** destruction or slaughter on a mass scale. ➤(**the Holocaust**) the mass murder of Jews under the German Nazi regime in World War II. **2** historical a Jewish sacrificial offering burnt on an altar.
– ORIGIN ME: from OFr. *holocauste*, via late L. from Gk *holokauston*, from *holos* 'whole' + *kaustos* 'burnt'.

**Holocene** /ˈhɒləsiːn/ • adj. Geology relating to or denoting the present epoch (from about 10,000 years ago, following the Pleistocene).
– ORIGIN C19: coined in Fr. from **HOLO-** + Gk *kainos* 'new'.

**holoenzyme** /ˌhɒləʊˈɛnzʌɪm/ • n. Biochemistry a biochemically active compound of an enzyme combined with a coenzyme.

**hologram** /ˈhɒləgram/ • n. **1** a three-dimensional image formed by the interference of light beams from a laser or other coherent light source. **2** a photograph of an interference pattern which, when suitably illuminated, produces a three-dimensional image.
– DERIVATIVES **holographic** adj. **holographically** adv. **holography** n.

**holograph** /ˈhɒləgrɑːf/ • n. a manuscript handwritten by its author.

**holophytic** /ˌhɒlə(ʊ)ˈfɪtɪk/ • adj. Biology able to photosynthesize.

**holothurian** /ˌhɒlə(ʊ)ˈθjʊərɪən/ • n. Zoology a sea cucumber.
– ORIGIN C19: from the mod. L. genus name *Holothuria* (from Gk *holothourion*, denoting a kind of zoophyte) + **-AN**.

**Holothuroidea** /ˌhɒlə(ʊ)θjʊəˈrɔɪdɪə/ • pl. n. Zoology a class of echinoderms that comprises the sea cucumbers.
– DERIVATIVES **holothuroid** /ˈhɒlə(ʊ)θjʊərɔɪd/ n. & adj.
– ORIGIN mod. L., based on Gk *holothourion* (see **HOLOTHURIAN**).

**holotype** /ˈhɒlətʌɪp/ • n. Botany & Zoology a single type specimen upon which the description and name of a new species is based.

**hols** • pl. n. Brit. informal holidays.

**Holstein** /ˈhɒlstʌɪn, -iːn/ • n. an animal of a typically black-and-white breed of large dairy cattle.
– ORIGIN from *Holstein* in NW Germany.

**holster** /ˈhəʊlstə, ˈhɒl-/ • n. a holder for carrying a handgun, typically worn on a belt or under the arm. • v. put (a gun) into its holster.
– ORIGIN C17: rel. to Du. *holster*, of unknown origin.

**holt**[1] /həʊlt/ • n. **1** the den of an otter. **2** dialect, chiefly N. Amer. a grip or hold.
– ORIGIN ME: var. of **HOLD**[1].

**holt**[2] /həʊlt/ • n. archaic or dialect a wood or wooded hill.
– ORIGIN OE, of Gmc origin.

**holus-bolus** /ˌhəʊləsˈbəʊləs/ • adv. Canadian or archaic all at once.
– ORIGIN C19 (orig. dial.): perh. pseudo-Latin for 'whole bolus, whole lump'.

**holy** • adj. (**-ier, -iest**) **1** dedicated to God or a religious purpose. **2** morally and spiritually excellent and to be revered.
– ORIGIN OE *hālig*, of Gmc origin; rel. to **WHOLE**.

**Holy City** • n. **1** a city held sacred by the adherents of a religion, especially Jerusalem. **2** heaven.

**Holy Cross Day** • **n.** the day of the feast of the Exaltation of the Cross, 14 September.

**holy day** • **n.** a religious festival.

**Holy Family** • **n.** Christ as a child with Mary and Joseph (and often John the Baptist or St Anne), as a subject for a painting.

**Holy Father** • **n.** the Pope.

**Holy Ghost** • **n.** another term for **Holy Spirit**.

**Holy Joe** • **n.** informal a pious man. ➤a clergyman.
– ORIGIN C19: orig. naut. sl.

**Holy Name** • **n.** the name of Jesus as an object of devotion.

**Holy Office** • **n.** the Inquisition.

**holy of holies** • **n. 1** historical the inner chamber of the sanctuary in the Jewish Temple in Jerusalem. **2** a place regarded as most sacred or special.

**holy orders** • **pl. n.** the sacrament or rite of ordination as a member of the clergy.

**holy place** • **n.** historical the outer chamber of the sanctuary in the Jewish Temple in Jerusalem.

**holy roller** • **n.** informal, derogatory a member of an evangelical Christian group expressing religious fervour by frenzied excitement.

**Holy Roman Empire** • **n.** the western part of the Roman empire, as revived by Charlemagne in 800.

**Holy Rood Day** • **n. 1** the day of the feast of the Invention of the Cross, 3 May. **2** another term for **Holy Cross Day**.

**Holy Saturday** • **n.** the Saturday preceding Easter Sunday.

**Holy Scripture** • **n.** the Bible.

**Holy See** • **n.** the papacy or the papal court.

**Holy Spirit** • **n.** (in Christianity) the third person of the Trinity; God as spiritually active in the world.

**holystone** /ˈhəʊlɪstəʊn/ chiefly historical • **n.** a piece of soft sandstone for scouring a ship's deck. • **v.** scour (a deck) with a holystone.
– ORIGIN C19: prob. from **holy** + **stone**; perh. because the stones were used while kneeling.

**Holy Thursday** • **n. 1** (in the Roman Catholic Church) Maundy Thursday. **2** dated (in the Anglican Church) Ascension Day.

**holy war** • **n.** a war waged in support of a religious cause.

**holy water** • **n.** water blessed by a priest and used in religious ceremonies.

**Holy Week** • **n.** the week before Easter.

**Holy Writ** • **n.** sacred writings collectively, especially the Bible.

**Holy Year** • **n.** (in the Roman Catholic Church) a period of remission from the penal consequences of sin, granted under certain conditions for a year.

**hom** /həʊm/ (also **homa** /ˈhəʊmə/) • **n.** the soma plant, the juice of which was a sacred drink of the Parsees.
– ORIGIN C19: from Pers. *hūm* or Avestan *haoma*.

**homage** /ˈhɒmɪdʒ/ • **n. 1** honour or respect shown publicly. **2** formal public acknowledgement of feudal allegiance.
– ORIGIN ME: OFr., from med. L. *hominaticum*, from L. *homo, homin-* 'man'.

**hombre** /ˈɒmbreɪ/ • **n.** informal, chiefly N. Amer. a man.
– ORIGIN C19: Sp., 'man'.

**homburg** /ˈhɒmbəːg/ • **n.** a man's felt hat having a narrow curled brim and a lengthwise indentation in the crown.
– ORIGIN C19: named after *Homburg*, a town in western Germany, where such hats were first worn.

**home** • **n. 1** the place where one lives permanently. ➤a house or flat. **2** an institution for people needing professional care. **3** a place where something flourishes or from which it originated. **4** the finishing point in a race. **5** (in games) the place where a player is free from attack. **6** (in lacrosse) each of the three players nearest their opponents' goal. • **adj. 1** of or relating to one's home. ➤made, done, or intended for use in the home. **2** relating to one's own country. **3** (of a team or player) belonging to the place in which a sporting event occurs. ➤played on a team's own ground. • **adv. 1** to or at one's home. **2** to the end or conclusion of something. **3** to the intended or correct position. • **v. 1** (of an animal) return by instinct to its territory. **2** (**home in on**) move or be aimed towards. **3** provide (a pet) with a home.
– PHRASES **at home 1** comfortable and at ease. **2** ready to receive visitors. **bring something home to** make (someone) realize the significance of something. **close** (or **near**) **to home** (of a remark) accurate to the point that one feels uncomfortable. **come home** Golf play the last nine holes in a round of eighteen. **drive** (or **hammer**) **something home** stress a point forcefully. **hit** (or **strike**) **home** (of words) have the intended effect. ➤(of the significance of a situation) be fully realized. **home and dry** (N. Amer. **home free**, Austral./NZ **home and hosed**) chiefly Brit. having achieved one's objective.
– DERIVATIVES **homeless** adj. **homelessness** n. **homelike** adj.
– ORIGIN OE *hām*, of Gmc origin.

**home bird** • **n.** Brit. informal a person who likes to stay at home.

**homebody** • **n.** (pl. **-ies**) informal, chiefly N. Amer. another term for **home bird**.

**homeboy** (or **homegirl**) • **n.** US & S. African informal a person from one's own town or neighbourhood.

**home brew** • **n.** beer or other alcoholic drink brewed at home.
– DERIVATIVES **home-brewed** adj.

**homecoming** • **n. 1** an instance of returning home. **2** N. Amer. a reunion of former students of a college or high school.

**home economics** • **pl. n.** [often treated as sing.] the study of cookery and household management.

**home farm** • **n.** Brit. & S. African a farm on an estate that provides produce for the estate owner.

**home fries** • **pl. n.** N. Amer. fried sliced potatoes.

**home-grown** • **adj.** grown or produced in one's own garden or country.

**Home Guard** • **n.** the British citizen army organized in 1940 to defend the UK against invasion.

**home help** • **n.** Brit. a person employed to help in another's home.

**home key** • **n. 1** Music the basic key in which a work is written. **2** a key on a keyboard acting as the base position for one's fingers in touch-typing.

**homeland** • **n. 1** a person's native land. **2** an autonomous state occupied by a particular people. ➤historical any of ten partially self-governing areas in South Africa designated for indigenous African peoples.

**homely** • **adj.** (**-ier**, **-iest**) **1** Brit. simple but comfortable. ➤unsophisticated. **2** N. Amer. unattractive.
– DERIVATIVES **homeliness** n.

**home-made** • **adj.** made at home.

**homemaker** • **n.** a person who manages a home.
– DERIVATIVES **homemaking** n.

**home movie** • **n.** a film made at home or without professional equipment.

**homeobox** /ˌhɒmɪə(ʊ)ˈbɒks, ˌhəʊm-/ (also **homoeobox**) • **n.** Genetics any of a group of closely similar gene sequences which are involved in regulating embryonic development in a wide range of species.
– ORIGIN 1980s: from *homeotic* (see **homeosis**) + **box**[1].

**Home Office** • **n.** the British government department dealing with law and order, immigration, etc. in England and Wales.

**homeomorphism** /ˌhɒmɪə(ʊ)ˈmɔːfɪz(ə)m, ˌhəʊm-/ • **n.** Mathematics an instance of topological equivalence.
– DERIVATIVES **homeomorphic** adj.
– ORIGIN from Gk *homoios* 'like' + *morphē* 'form' + **-ism**.

**homeopath** /ˈhəʊmɪəpaθ, ˈhɒm-/ (also **homoeopath**) • **n.** a person who practises homeopathy.

**homeopathy** /ˌhəʊmɪˈɒpəθi, hɒm-/ (also **homoeopathy**) • **n.** a system of complementary medicine in which disease is treated by minute doses of natural substances

that in a healthy person would produce symptoms of disease. Often contrasted with **ALLOPATHY**.
– DERIVATIVES **homeopathic** adj. **homeopathically** adv. **homeopathist** n.
– ORIGIN C19: coined in Ger. from Gk *homoios* 'like' + *patheia* (see **-PATHY**).

**homeosis** /ˌhɒmɪˈəʊsɪs/ (also **homoeosis**) ● **n.** (pl. **homeoses** /-siːz/) Biology the replacement of part of one segment of an insect or other segmented animal by a structure characteristic of a different segment, especially through mutation.
– DERIVATIVES **homeotic** adj.
– ORIGIN C19: from Gk *homoiōsis* 'becoming like'.

**homeostasis** /ˌhɒmɪə(ʊ)ˈsteɪsɪs, ˌhəʊm-/ (also **homoeostasis**) ● **n.** (pl. **homeostases** /-siːz/) the maintenance of a stable equilibrium, especially through physiological processes.
– DERIVATIVES **homeostatic** adj.
– ORIGIN 1920s: mod. L., from Gk *homoios* 'like' + **-STASIS**.

**homeotherm** /ˈhɒmɪə(ʊ)ˌθəːm/ (also **homoiotherm**) ● **n.** Zoology an organism that maintains its body temperature at a constant level by its metabolic activity. Often contrasted with **POIKILOTHERM**.
– DERIVATIVES **homeothermal** adj. **homeothermic** adj. **homeothermy** n.
– ORIGIN C19: mod. L., from Gk *homoios* 'like' + *thermē* 'heat'.

**homeowner** ● **n.** a person who owns their own home.

**home page** ● **n.** Computing a person's or organization's introductory document on the World Wide Web.

**home plate** ● **n.** Baseball the five-sided flat white rubber base which must be touched in scoring a run.

**homer** ● **n. 1** Baseball a home run. **2** a homing pigeon.

**Homeric** /həʊˈmɛrɪk/ ● **adj. 1** of, or in the style of, the ancient Greek poet Homer (8th century BC) or the epic poems ascribed to him. **2** of Bronze Age Greece as described in these poems.

**homeroom** ● **n.** N. Amer. a classroom in which a group of students assembles daily with the same teacher before dispersing to other classes.

**home rule** ● **n.** the government of a place by its own citizens.

**home run** ● **n.** Baseball a hit that allows the batter to make a complete circuit of the bases.

**Home Secretary** ● **n.** (in the UK) the Secretary of State in charge of the Home Office.

**homesick** ● **adj.** upset due to absence from one's home.
– DERIVATIVES **homesickness** n.

**home signal** ● **n.** Brit. a railway signal controlling entry to the immediate section of the line.

**homespun** ● **adj. 1** simple and unsophisticated. **2** (of cloth or yarn) made or spun at home. ● **n.** cloth of this type.

**homestead** ● **n. 1** a house, especially a farmhouse, and outbuildings. **2** N. Amer. historical an area of land (usually 160 acres) granted to a settler as a home. **3** (in South Africa) a hut or cluster of huts occupied by one family or clan.
– DERIVATIVES **homesteader** n. **homesteading** n.
– ORIGIN OE *hāmstede* 'a settlement' (see **HOME**, **STEAD**).

**home straight** (also **home stretch**) ● **n.** the concluding stretch of a racecourse.

**homestyle** ● **adj.** N. Amer. simple and unpretentious.

**home truth** ● **n.** an unpleasant fact about oneself.

**home unit** ● **n.** Austral./NZ a flat occupied by the owner, that is one of several in a building.

**homeward** ● **adv.** (also **homewards**) towards home. ● **adj.** going or leading towards home.

**homework** ● **n. 1** school work that a pupil is required to do at home. **2** preparation. **3** paid work done in one's own home, especially piecework.

**homeworker** ● **n.** a person who works from home.

**homey** (also **homy**) ● **adj.** (**-ier**, **-iest**) **1** comfortable and cosy. **2** unsophisticated. ● **n.** US informal a homeboy.
– DERIVATIVES **homeyness** (also **hominess**) n.

**homicide** ● **n.** murder. ➤ dated a murderer.
– DERIVATIVES **homicidal** adj.
– ORIGIN ME: from OFr., from L. *homicidium*, from *homo*, *homin-* 'man' + *caedere* 'to kill'.

**homie** (also **homey**) ● **n.** (pl. **-ies**) informal, chiefly US a homeboy or homegirl.

**homiletic** /ˌhɒmɪˈlɛtɪk/ ● **adj.** of or like a homily. ● **n.** (**homiletics**) the art of preaching or writing sermons.
– ORIGIN C17: via late L. from Gk *homilētikos*, based on *homilia* (see **HOMILY**).

**homiliary** /hɒˈmɪlɪəri/ ● **n.** (pl. **-ies**) historical a book of homilies.
– ORIGIN C19: from med. L. *homiliarius*, from eccles. L. *homilia* (see **HOMILY**).

**homily** /ˈhɒmɪli/ ● **n.** (pl. **-ies**) **1** a religious discourse intended for spiritual edification rather than instruction. **2** a tedious moralizing discourse.
– DERIVATIVES **homilist** n.
– ORIGIN ME: via OFr. from eccles. L. *homilia*, from Gk, 'discourse' (in eccles. use, 'sermon'), from *homilos* 'crowd'.

**homing** ● **adj. 1** (of a pigeon or other animal) able to return home from a great distance. **2** (of a weapon) able to find and hit a target electronically.

**hominid** /ˈhɒmɪnɪd/ ● **n.** Zoology a primate of a family (Hominidae) which includes humans and their fossil ancestors.
– ORIGIN C19: from mod. L. *Hominidae* (pl.), from L. *homo*, *homin-* 'man'.

**hominoid** /ˈhɒmɪnɔɪd/ ● **n.** Zoology a primate of a group (superfamily Hominoidea) that includes humans, their fossil ancestors, and the great apes.

**hominy** /ˈhɒmɪni/ ● **n.** US coarsely ground corn (maize) used to make grits.
– ORIGIN shortened from Virginia Algonquian *uskatahomen*.

**Homo** /ˈhəʊməʊ, ˈhɒməʊ/ ● **n.** the genus of primates of which modern humans (*Homo sapiens*) are the present-day representatives.
– ORIGIN L., 'man'.

**homo** /ˈhəʊməʊ/ informal, chiefly derogatory ● **n.** (pl. **-os**) a homosexual man. ● **adj.** homosexual.

**homo-** ● **comb. form 1** same: *homogametic*. **2** relating to homosexual love: *homoerotic*.
– ORIGIN from Gk *homos* 'same'.

**homocentric**[1] ● **adj.** having the same centre.

**homocentric**[2] ● **adj.** another term for **ANTHROPOCENTRIC**.

**homocercal** /ˌhɒmə(ʊ)ˈsəːk(ə)l, ˌhəʊm-/ ● **adj.** Zoology (of a fish's tail) symmetrical in appearance but with the vertebral column passing into the upper lobe.
– ORIGIN C19: from **HOMO-** + Gk *kerkos* 'tail' + **-AL**.

**homocysteine** /ˌhɒmə(ʊ)ˈsɪstiːn, ˌhəʊm-, -tɪɪn, -teɪn, -tiːn/ ● **n.** Biochemistry an amino acid produced as an intermediate in the metabolism of methionine and cysteine.

**homoeobox** ● **n.** variant spelling of **HOMEOBOX**.

**homoeopath** ● **n.** variant spelling of **HOMEOPATH**.

**homoeopathy** ● **n.** variant spelling of **HOMEOPATHY**.

**homoeosis** ● **n.** variant spelling of **HOMEOSIS**.

**homoeostasis** ● **n.** variant spelling of **HOMEOSTASIS**.

**homoerotic** /ˌhəʊməʊɪˈrɒtɪk, ˌhɒməʊ-/ ● **adj.** concerning or arousing sexual desire centred on a person of the same sex.
– DERIVATIVES **homoeroticism** n.

**homogametic** /ˌhɒmə(ʊ)gəˈmɛtɪk, -ˈmiːtɪk, ˌhəʊm-/ ● **adj.** Biology denoting the sex which has sex chromosomes that do not differ in morphology, e.g. (in mammals) the female and (in birds) the male.

**homogamy** /hɒˈmɒgəmi/ ● **n. 1** Biology inbreeding. **2** marriage between people from similar backgrounds. **3** Botany a state in which the flowers of a plant are all of one type. **4** Botany the simultaneous ripening of the stamens and pistils of a flower, ensuring self-pollination. Compare with **DICHOGAMY**.
– DERIVATIVES **homogamous** adj.
– ORIGIN C19: from **HOMO-** + Gk *gamos* 'marriage'.

**homogenate** /həˈmɒdʒɪneɪt/ ● **n.** Biology a suspension of cell fragments and constituents obtained when tissue is homogenized.

**homogeneous** /ˌhɒmə(ʊ)ˈdʒiːnɪəs, -ˈdʒɛn-, ˌhəʊm-/ ● **adj.**

**1** of the same kind. ➤ consisting of parts all of the same kind. **2** Chemistry denoting a process involving substances in the same phase (solid, liquid, or gaseous): *homogeneous catalysis.*
– DERIVATIVES **homogeneity** /-dʒɪ'niːɪti, -dʒɪ'neɪɪti/ n. **homogeneously** adv. **homogeneousness** n.
– ORIGIN C17 (as *homogeneity*): from med. L. *homogeneus*, from Gk *homogenēs*, from *homos* 'same' + *genos* 'race, kind'.

**homogenize** (also **-ise**) ● v. **1** make homogeneous. **2** [often as adj. **homogenized**] subject (milk) to a process in which the fat droplets are emulsified and the cream does not separate.
– DERIVATIVES **homogenization** /-'zeɪʃ(ə)n/ n. **homogenizer** n.

**homogenous** /hə'mɒdʒɪnəs/ ● adj. Biology old-fashioned term for **HOMOLOGOUS**.
– ORIGIN C19: from **HOMO-** + Gk *genos* 'race, kind' + **-OUS**.

**homograft** /'hɒməgrɑːft, 'həʊm-/ ● n. a tissue graft from a donor of the same species.

**homograph** ● n. each of two or more words spelled the same but having different meanings and origins.
– DERIVATIVES **homographic** adj.

**homoiotherm** /'hɒmɔɪə(ʊ),θəːm/ ● n. variant spelling of **HOMEOTHERM**.

**homoiousian** /,hɒmɔɪ'uːsɪən, -'aʊ-, -z-/ ● n. historical a person who held that God the Father and God the Son are of like but not identical substance. Compare with **HOMOOUSIAN**.
– ORIGIN C17: via eccles. L. from Gk *homoiousios*, from *homoios* 'like' + *ousia* 'essence, substance'.

**homolog** ● n. US variant spelling of **HOMOLOGUE**.

**homologate** /hə'mɒləgeɪt/ ● v. **1** formal agree with or approve of. **2** approve (a vehicle or engine) for sale or for a class of racing.
– DERIVATIVES **homologation** n.
– ORIGIN C16: from med. L. *homologat-*, *homologare* 'agree', from Gk *homologein* 'confess'.

**homologous** /hɒ'mɒləgəs/ ● adj. **1** having the same relation, relative position, or structure. **2** Biology (of organs) similar in position, structure, and evolutionary origin. Often contrasted with **ANALOGOUS**. **3** Biology (of chromosomes) pairing at meiosis and having the same structure and pattern of genes. **4** Chemistry (of a series of chemical compounds) similar in properties but differing in composition by a fixed group of atoms.
– DERIVATIVES **homologize** (also **-ise**) v. **homology** /hɒ'mɒlədʒi/ n.
– ORIGIN C17: via med. L. from Gk *homologos* 'agreeing, consistent', from *homos* 'same' + *logos* 'ratio, proportion'.

**homologue** /'hɒməlɒg/ (US **homolog**) ● n. technical a homologous thing.

**homomorphic** ● adj. technical of the same or similar form.
– DERIVATIVES **homomorphically** adv.

**homonym** /'hɒmənɪm/ ● n. **1** each of two or more words having the same spelling or pronunciation but different meanings and origins (e.g. **POLE**[1] and **POLE**[2]). **2** Biology a Latin name which is identical to that of a different organism, the newer name being invalid.
– DERIVATIVES **homonymic** adj. **homonymous** adj. **homonymy** /hə'mɒnɪmi/ n.
– ORIGIN C17: via L. from Gk *homōnumon*, neut. of *homōnumos* 'having the same name', from *homos* 'same' + *onoma* 'name'.

**homoousian** /,hɒməʊ'uːsɪən, -'aʊ-, -z-, ,həʊməʊ-/ (also **homousian**) ● n. historical a person who held that God the Father and God the Son are of the same substance. Compare with **HOMOIOUSIAN**.
– ORIGIN C16: via eccles. L. *homousianus*, from Gk *homoousios*, from *homos* 'same' + *ousia* 'essence, substance'.

**homophobia** /,hɒmə'fəʊbɪə, ,həʊmə-/ ● n. an extreme and irrational aversion to homosexuality and homosexuals.
– DERIVATIVES **homophobe** n. **homophobic** adj.

**homophone** /'hɒməfəʊn, 'həʊm-/ ● n. **1** each of two or more words having the same pronunciation but different meanings, origins, or spelling (e.g. *new* and *knew*). **2** a symbol denoting the same sound as another.

**homophonic** ● adj. **1** Music characterized by the movement of accompanying parts in the same rhythm as the melody. **2** another term for **HOMOPHONOUS**.
– DERIVATIVES **homophonically** adv.

**homophonous** /hə'mɒf(ə)nəs/ ● adj. **1** (of music) homophonic. **2** (of a word or words) having the same pronunciation as another but different meaning, origin, or spelling.
– DERIVATIVES **homophony** n.

**homopolar** ● adj. having equal or unchanging polarity.

**Homoptera** /hɒ'mɒpt(ə)rə/ ● pl. n. Entomology a group of bugs comprising those with uniform forewings, such as the plant bugs, aphids, and cicadas. Compare with **HETEROPTERA**.
– DERIVATIVES **homopteran** n. & adj. **homopterous** adj.
– ORIGIN mod. L., from **HOMO-** + Gk *pteron* 'wing'.

**homorganic** /,hɒmɔː'ganɪk/ ● adj. denoting sets of speech sounds produced using the same vocal organs, e.g. *p*, *b*, and *m*.

**Homo sapiens** /,həʊməʊ 'sapɪɛnz, ,hɒməʊ/ ● n. the primate species to which modern humans belong.
– ORIGIN L., lit. 'wise man'.

**homosexual** /,hɒmə(ʊ)'sɛksjʊəl, ,həʊm-, -ʃʊəl/ ● adj. feeling or involving sexual attraction to people of one's own sex. ● n. a homosexual person.
– DERIVATIVES **homosexuality** n. **homosexually** adv.
– ORIGIN C19: from **HOMO-** + **SEXUAL**.

**homosocial** ● adj. of or relating to social interaction between members of the same sex.

**homotransplant** ● n. another term for **ALLOGRAFT**.

**homousian** ● n. variant spelling of **HOMOOUSIAN**.

**homozygote** /,hɒmə(ʊ)'zʌɪgəʊt, ,həʊm-/ ● n. Genetics an individual having two identical alleles of a particular gene or genes and so breeding true for the corresponding characteristic. Compare with **HETEROZYGOTE**.
– DERIVATIVES **homozygosity** n. **homozygous** adj.

**homunculus** /hɒ'mʌŋkjʊləs/ (also **homuncule** /-kjuːl/) ● n. (pl. **homunculi** /-lʌɪ/ or **homuncules**) a very small human or humanoid creature.
– ORIGIN C17: from L., dimin. of *homo*, *homin-* 'man'.

**homy** ● adj. variant spelling of **HOMEY**.

**Hon** ● abbrev. **1** (in official job titles) Honorary. **2** (in titles of the British nobility, members of parliament, and (in the US) judges) Honourable.

**hon** ● n. informal short for **HONEY** (as a form of address).

**honcho** /'hɒn(t)ʃəʊ/ informal ● n. (pl. **-os**) a leader. ● v. (**-oes**, **-oed**) N. Amer. be in charge of.
– ORIGIN 1940s: from Japanese *hanchō* 'group leader'.

**Honduran** /hɒn'djʊər(ə)n/ ● n. a native or inhabitant of Honduras, a country in Central America. ● adj. of or relating to Honduras.

**hone** ● v. sharpen with a whetstone. ➤ (usu. **be honed**) make sharper or more focused or efficient. ● n. a whetstone, especially one used to sharpen razors.
– ORIGIN ME: from OE *hān* 'stone', of Gmc origin.

**honest** ● adj. **1** free of deceit; truthful and sincere. **2** fairly earned: *an honest living.* **3** (of an action) well intentioned even if misguided. **4** simple and unpretentious: *good honest food with no gimmicks.* ● adv. informal genuinely; really.
– PHRASES **earn** (or **turn**) **an honest penny** earn money fairly. **make an honest woman of** dated or humorous marry a woman, especially to avoid scandal if she is pregnant.
– ORIGIN ME: via OFr. from L. *honestus*, from *honos* (see **HONOUR**).

**honest broker** ● n. an impartial mediator.

**honestly** ● adv. **1** in an honest way. **2** really: *honestly, that man is the limit!*

**honest-to-God** informal ● adj. genuine; real. ● adv. genuinely; really.

**honest-to-goodness** ● adj. genuine and straightforward.

**honesty** ● n. **1** the quality of being honest. **2** a plant with purple or white flowers and round, flat, translucent seed

pods. [Genus *Lunaria*.]
– ORIGIN ME: from OFr. *honeste*, from L. *honestas*, from *honestus* (see **HONEST**); the plant is so named from its seed pods, translucency symbolizing lack of deceit.

**honewort** /ˈhəʊnwəːt/ ● **n.** a wild plant of the parsley family. [*Cryptotaenia canadensis* (N. America and eastern Asia) and *Trinia glauca* (Europe).]
– ORIGIN C17: from obs. *hone* 'swelling' (for which the plant was believed to be a remedy) + **WORT**.

**honey** ● **n.** (pl. **-eys**) **1** a sweet, sticky yellowish-brown fluid made by bees and other insects from flower nectar. **2** informal an excellent example of something. **3** chiefly N. Amer. darling; sweetheart.
– ORIGIN OE *hunig*, of Gmc origin.

**honey ant** ● **n.** an ant that stores honeydew and nectar in its elastic abdomen, regurgitating it to feed nest mates. [*Myrmecocystus* and other genera.]

**honey badger** ● **n.** another term for **RATEL**.

**honeybee** ● **n.** see **BEE** (sense 1).

**honeybird** ● **n.** a small, drab African bird of the honeyguide family. [Genus *Prodotiscus*: three species.]

**honey bucket** ● **n.** N. Amer. informal a toilet without water, which has to be emptied manually.

**honeybun** (also **honeybunch**) ● **n.** N. Amer. informal darling.

**honey buzzard** ● **n.** a large broad-winged bird of prey feeding chiefly on bees and wasps and their nests. [*Pernis apivorus* and related species.]

**honeycomb** ● **n. 1** a structure of hexagonal cells of wax, made by bees to store honey and eggs. **2** a structure of linked cavities. **3** a raised hexagonal or cellular pattern on fabric. **4** tripe from the second stomach of a ruminant. ● **v.** fill with cavities or tunnels.

**honeycreeper** ● **n. 1** a tropical American tanager with a long curved bill, feeding on nectar and insects. [Genera *Cyanerpes* and *Chlorophanes*.] **2** a Hawaiian songbird, several kinds of which are endangered. [Family Drepanididae: several species.]

**honeydew** ● **n. 1** a sweet, sticky substance excreted by aphids. **2** poetic/literary an ideally sweet substance. **3** (also **honeydew melon**) a melon of a variety with smooth pale skin and sweet green flesh.

**honeyeater** ● **n.** an Australasian songbird with a long brush-like tongue for feeding on nectar. [Family Meliphagidae: numerous species.]

**honeyed** (also **honied**) ● **adj. 1** containing or coated with honey. **2** having a warm yellow colour. **3** (of words or a tone of voice) soothing and soft.

**honey fungus** (also **honey mushroom**) ● **n.** a parasitic fungus producing honey-coloured toadstools at the base of trees. [*Armillaria mellea*.]

**honeyguide** ● **n. 1** a small, drab tropical songbird, feeding chiefly on beeswax and bee grubs. [Family Indicatoridae: several species.] **2** Botany a marking on a flower petal thought to guide insects to nectar.

**honey locust** ● **n.** a spiny leguminous tree, grown for its fern-like foliage. [*Gleditsia triacanthos* (N. America) and related species.]

**honeymoon** ● **n. 1** a holiday taken by a newly married couple. **2** an initial period of enthusiasm or goodwill. ● **v.** spend a honeymoon.
– DERIVATIVES **honeymooner** n.
– ORIGIN C16: from **HONEY** + **MOON** (orig. referring to affection waning like the moon, later denoting the first month after marriage).

**honey parrot** ● **n.** Australian term for **LORIKEET**.

**honey possum** ● **n.** a tiny shrew-like marsupial of SW Australia, having a long snout and a prehensile tail and feeding on nectar and pollen. [*Tarsipes rostratus*.]

**honeypot** ● **n. 1** a container for honey. **2** a place to which many people are attracted.

**honeysuckle** ● **n.** a climbing shrub with fragrant tubular flowers, typically yellow and pink. [Genus *Lonicera*: many species.]
– ORIGIN ME *honysoukil*, extension of *honysouke*, from OE *hunigsūce* (see **HONEY**, **SUCK**).

**honeytrap** ● **n.** a stratagem in which an attractive person entices another person into revealing information.

**honeywort** ● **n.** a Mediterranean plant with greyish-green leaves and tubular yellow or purple flowers that are a favoured source of nectar for bees. [*Cerinthe major* and other species.]

**hongi** /ˈhɒŋi/ ● **n.** NZ the traditional Maori greeting in which people press their noses together.
– ORIGIN from Maori.

**honied** ● **adj.** variant spelling of **HONEYED**.

**Honiton lace** /ˈhɒnɪt(ə)n, ˈhʌn-/ ● **n.** a type of lace with a pattern of floral sprigs.
– ORIGIN C19: from *Honiton*, a town in Devon.

**honk** ● **n. 1** the cry of a goose. **2** the sound of a car horn. ● **v. 1** emit or cause to emit a honk. **2** Brit. informal vomit.
– DERIVATIVES **honker** n.
– ORIGIN C19: imitative.

**honky** ● **n.** (pl. **-ies**) N. Amer. informal, derogatory a white person or white people collectively.
– ORIGIN 1960s: of unknown origin.

**honky-tonk** ● **n.** informal **1** chiefly N. Amer. a cheap or disreputable bar or club. **2** ragtime piano music.
– ORIGIN C19: of unknown origin.

**honnête homme** /ˌɒnɛt ˈɒm/ ● **n.** a gentleman.
– ORIGIN Fr., lit. 'honest man'.

**honor** ● **n. & v.** US spelling of **HONOUR**.

**honorable** ● **adj.** US spelling of **HONOURABLE**.

**honorand** /ˈɒnərand/ ● **n.** a person to be honoured, especially with an honorary degree.
– ORIGIN 1950s: from L. *honorandus* 'to be honoured', gerundive of *honorare* 'to honour'.

**honorarium** /ˌɒnəˈrɛːrɪəm/ ● **n.** (pl. **honorariums** or **honoraria** /-rɪə/) a payment for professional services that are rendered nominally without charge.
– ORIGIN C17: from L., denoting a gift made on being admitted to public office, from *honorarius* (see **HONORARY**).

**honorary** ● **adj. 1** (of a title or position) conferred as an honour. ➤ holding such a title or position. **2** Brit. (of an office or its holder) unpaid.
– ORIGIN C17: from L. *honorarius*, from *honor* 'honour'.

**honorific** ● **adj.** given as a mark of respect. ● **n.** a title or word expressing respect.
– DERIVATIVES **honorifically** adv.
– ORIGIN C17: from L. *honorificus*, from *honor* 'honour'.

**honoris causa** /ɒˌnɔːrɪs ˈkaʊzə/ ● **adv.** (especially of a degree awarded without examination) as a mark of esteem.
– ORIGIN L., lit. 'for the sake of honour'.

**honour** (US **honor**) ● **n. 1** high respect. ➤ a feeling of pride and pleasure from being shown such respect. ➤ a person or thing that brings credit. **2** a clear sense of what is morally right. **3** a thing conferred as a distinction. ➤ (**honours**) a special distinction for proficiency in an examination. ➤ (**honours**) a course of degree studies more specialized than for an ordinary pass. **4** (**His**, **Your**, etc. **Honour**) a title of respect for a circuit judge, a US mayor, and (in Irish or rustic speech) any person of rank. **5** Golf the right of driving off first, having won the previous hole. **6** dated a woman's chastity. **7** Bridge an ace, king, queen, jack, or ten. ➤ (**honours**) possession of at least four of these cards in the trump suit, or of all four aces in no trumps, for which a bonus is scored. ➤ (in whist) an ace, king, queen, or jack of trumps. ● **v. 1** regard with great respect. ➤ pay public respect to. **2** grace; privilege: *the Princess honoured the ball with her presence.* **3** fulfil (an obligation) or keep (an agreement). ➤ accept (a bill) or pay (a cheque) when due.
– PHRASES **do the honours** informal perform a social duty for others, especially serve food or drink. **honour bright** Brit. dated on my honour. **honours are even** Brit. there is equality in the contest. **in honour of** as an expression of respect for. **on one's honour** under a moral obligation. **on** (or **upon**) **my honour** used to express sincerity.
– ORIGIN ME: from OFr. *onor* (n.), *onorer* (v.), from L. *honor*.

**honourable** (US **honorable**) ● **adj. 1** bringing or worthy of honour. ➤ formal or humorous (of the intentions of a man courting a woman) directed towards marriage. **2** (**Honourable**) a title given to certain high officials, the children of some ranks of the nobility, and MPs.

– DERIVATIVES **honourableness** n. **honourably** adv.

**honourable mention** ● n. a commendation for a candidate in an examination or competition not awarded a prize.

**honour point** ● n. Heraldry the point halfway between the top of a shield and the fess point.

**honours list** ● n. a list of people to be awarded honours.

**honours of war** ● pl. n. privileges granted to a capitulating force, e.g. that of marching out with colours flying.

**honour system** ● n. a system of payment or examinations relying on the honesty of those concerned.

**Hon. Sec.** ● abbrev. honorary secretary.

**hooch** /huːtʃ/ (also **hootch**) ● n. informal alcoholic liquor, especially inferior or illicit whisky.
– ORIGIN C19: abbrev. of *Hoochinoo*, an Alaskan Indian people who made liquor.

**hood**[1] ● n. **1** a covering for the head and neck with an opening for the face, typically part of a coat or cloak. ➤a similar garment worn over a university gown or surplice to indicate the wearer's degree. ➤Falconry a leather covering for a hawk's head. **2** Brit. a folding waterproof cover of a vehicle or pram. **3** N. Amer. the bonnet of a vehicle. **4** a canopy to protect users of machinery or to remove fumes from it. **5** a hood-like structure or marking on the head or neck of an animal. **6** the upper part of a flower such as a dead-nettle. ● v. put a hood on or over.
– DERIVATIVES **hoodless** adj. **hood-like** adj.
– ORIGIN OE *hōd*, of W. Gmc origin; rel. to **HAT**.

**hood**[2] ● n. informal, chiefly N. Amer. a gangster or violent criminal.
– ORIGIN 1930s: abbrev. of **HOODLUM**.

**hood**[3] ● n. informal, chiefly US a neighbourhood.

**-hood** ● suffix forming nouns: **1** denoting a condition or quality: *womanhood*. **2** denoting a collection or group: *brotherhood*.
– ORIGIN OE *-hād*, orig. an independent noun meaning 'person, condition, quality'.

**hooded** ● adj. **1** having or wearing a hood. **2** (of eyes) having drooping upper eyelids.

**hooded crow** ● n. a bird of the North and East European race of the carrion crow, having a grey body with a black head, wings, and tail. [*Corvus corone cornix*.]

**hooded seal** ● n. a North Atlantic seal with a grey and white blotched coat, the male having a nasal sac that inflates into a hood during display. [*Cystophora cristata*.]

**hoodie** ● n. Scottish term for **HOODED CROW**.

**hoodlum** /ˈhuːdləm/ ● n. a hooligan or gangster.
– ORIGIN C19 (orig. US): of unknown origin.

**hood mould** (also **hood moulding**) ● n. Architecture a dripstone.

**hoodoo** ● n. **1** voodoo. **2** bad luck. ➤a cause of bad luck. **3** chiefly N. Amer. a column or pinnacle of weathered rock. ● v. (**hoodoos, hoodooed**) bewitch.
– ORIGIN C19 (orig. US, denoting a person practising voodoo): appar. an alt. of **VOODOO**; sense 3 is appar. due to the strange forms of the columns.

**hoodwink** ● v. deceive or trick.
– ORIGIN C16 (orig. meaning 'to blindfold'): from **HOOD**[1] + an obs. sense of **WINK** 'close the eyes'.

**hooey** ● n. informal nonsense.
– ORIGIN 1920s (orig. US): of unknown origin.

**hoof** ● n. (pl. **hoofs** or **hooves**) the horny part of the foot of an ungulate, especially a horse. ● v. informal **1** kick (a ball) powerfully. **2** (**hoof it**) go on foot. ➤dance.
– PHRASES **on the hoof 1** (of livestock) not yet slaughtered. **2** informal without great thought or preparation.
– DERIVATIVES **hoofed** adj.
– ORIGIN OE *hōf*, of Gmc origin.

**hoofer** ● n. informal a professional dancer.

**hoo-ha** ● n. informal a commotion.
– ORIGIN 1930s: of unknown origin.

**hook** ● n. **1** a piece of curved metal or other material for catching hold of things or hanging things on. ➤(also **fish hook**) a bent piece of metal, typically barbed and baited, for catching fish. **2** a thing designed to catch people's attention. ➤a catchy chorus or repeated passage in a pop or rock song. **3** a curved cutting instrument. **4** a short swinging punch made with the elbow bent and rigid. **5** a hooking stroke in sport. **6** Music an added stroke transverse to the stem in the symbol for a quaver or other note. **7** a curved promontory or sand spit. ● v. **1** be or become attached or fastened with a hook. **2** (**hook up**) link or be linked to electronic equipment. **3** bend or be bent into the shape of a hook. **4** Rugby secure (the ball) and pass it backward with the foot in the scrum. **5** catch with a hook. ➤archaic, informal steal. **6** (**be hooked**) informal be captivated or addicted. **7** Cricket hit (the ball) round to the on side with a slightly upward swing of the bat at shoulder height. ➤(in sport) strike (the ball) so that it deviates in the direction of the follow-through. **8** Boxing punch one's opponent with the elbow bent and rigid. **9** (**hook it**) Brit. informal, dated run away.
– PHRASES **by hook or by crook** by any possible means. **get one's hooks into** informal get hold of. **get** (or **give someone**) **the hook** N. Amer. informal be dismissed (or dismiss someone) from a job. **hook, line, and sinker** entirely: *he fell hook, line, and sinker for the joke*. **off the hook 1** informal no longer in difficulty or trouble. **2** (of a telephone receiver) not on its rest. **on the hook for** N. Amer. informal (in a financial context) responsible for. **on one's own hook** informal, dated, chiefly US by oneself. **sling one's hook** Brit. informal leave.
– DERIVATIVES **hookless** adj. **hooklet** n. **hook-like** adj.
– ORIGIN OE *hōc*, of Gmc origin.

**hookah** /ˈhʊkə/ ● n. an oriental tobacco pipe with a long, flexible tube which draws the smoke through water in a bowl.
– ORIGIN C18: from Urdu, from Arab. *ḥuḳḳa* 'casket, jar'.

**hook and eye** ● n. a small metal hook and loop used to fasten a garment.

**hooked** ● adj. **1** having or resembling a hook or hooks. **2** (of a rug) made by pulling woollen yarn through canvas with a hook.

**hooker**[1] ● n. **1** Rugby the player in the middle of the front row of the scrum, who tries to hook the ball. **2** informal, chiefly N. Amer. a prostitute.

**hooker**[2] ● n. **1** a one-masted sailing boat, especially as used in Ireland for fishing. **2** Nautical, informal an old boat.
– ORIGIN C17: from Du. *hoeker*, from *hoek* 'hook' (earlier *hoekboot*, denoting a two-masted fishing vessel).

**hooker**[3] ● n. N. Amer. informal a drink of undiluted brandy, whisky, or other spirit.
– ORIGIN C19: of unknown origin.

**Hooke's law** ● n. Physics a law stating that the strain in a solid is proportional to the applied stress, within the elastic limit of that solid.
– ORIGIN C19: named after the C17 Engl. scientist Robert *Hooke*.

**hookey** (also **hooky**) ● n. (in phr. **play hookey**) N. Amer. informal play truant.
– ORIGIN C19: of unknown origin.

**hook nose** ● n. an aquiline nose.
– DERIVATIVES **hook-nosed** adj.

**hooktip** ● n. a slender moth with hooked tips to the forewings. [*Drepana* and other genera.]

**hook-up** ● n. a connection, especially to mains electricity or a communications system.

**hookworm** ● n. a parasitic nematode worm inhabiting the intestines and feeding by attaching itself to the wall of the gut with hook-like mouthparts. [*Ancylostoma*, *Uncinaria*, *Necator*, and other genera.]

**hooky**[1] ● adj. (of a tune) catchy.

**hooky**[2] ● n. variant spelling of **HOOKEY**.

**hooley** ● n. (pl. **-eys**) informal, chiefly Irish a wild or noisy party.
– ORIGIN C19: of unknown origin.

**hooligan** ● n. a violent young troublemaker.
– DERIVATIVES **hooliganism** n.
– ORIGIN C19: perh. from *Hooligan*, the surname of a fictional rowdy Irish family in a music-hall song.

**hoon** Austral./NZ informal ● n. a lout. ● v. behave like a lout.
– ORIGIN 1930s: of unknown origin.

**hoop** ● n. **1** a rigid circular band, especially one used for

binding the staves of barrels or forming a framework. ➤ a large ring used as a toy or for circus performers to jump through. ➤ historical a circle of flexible material used to expand a woman's petticoat. **2** chiefly Brit. a metal arch through which the balls are hit in croquet. **3** a contrasting horizontal band on a sports shirt or cap. ➤ Austral. informal a jockey. ● **v.** bind or encircle with or as with hoops.
– PHRASES **put someone** (or **go**) **through the hoops** make someone undergo (or be made to undergo) a gruelling test.
– DERIVATIVES **hooped** adj.
– ORIGIN OE *hōp*, of W. Gmc origin.

**hooper** ● **n.** old-fashioned term for **COOPER**.

**hoopla** /'hu:plɑ:/ ● **n. 1** Brit. a game in which rings are thrown in an attempt to encircle a prize. **2** informal unnecessary fuss.
– ORIGIN 1909: from **HOOP** + *la!*, used to direct attention or as an exclamation of surprise.

**hoopoe** /'hu:pu:, -pəʊ/ ● **n.** a salmon-pink bird with a long downcurved bill, a large crest, and black-and-white wings and tail. [*Upupa epops*.]
– ORIGIN C17: alt. of obs. *hoop*, from OFr. *huppe*, from L. *upupa*, imitative of the bird's call.

**hooray** ● **exclam. 1** hurrah. **2** Austral./NZ goodbye.

**Hooray Henry** ● **n.** (pl. **Hooray Henrys** or **Hooray Henries**) Brit. informal a lively but ineffectual young upper-class man.

**hoosegow** /'hu:sgaʊ/ ● **n.** informal, chiefly N. Amer. a prison.
– ORIGIN C20: via Latin Amer. Sp. from Sp. *juzgado* 'tribunal'.

**Hoosier** /'hu:ʒɪə/ ● **n.** a native or inhabitant of the US state of Indiana.
– ORIGIN C19: of unknown origin.

**hoot** ● **n. 1** a low musical sound made by many kinds of owl. ➤ a similar sound made by a horn, siren, etc. **2** a shout expressing scorn or disapproval. **3** an outburst of laughter. ➤ **(a hoot)** informal an amusing person or thing. ● **v. 1** make or cause to make a hoot. **2** (**hoot something down**) express loud scornful disapproval of something.
– PHRASES **not care** (or **give**) **a hoot** (or **two hoots**) informal not care at all.
– ORIGIN ME: perh. imitative.

**hootch** ● **n.** variant spelling of **HOOCH**.

**hootenanny** /'hu:t(ə),nani/ ● **n.** (pl. **-ies**) informal, chiefly US an informal gathering with folk music.
– ORIGIN 1920s (orig. US, denoting a 'thingummy'): of unknown origin.

**hooter** ● **n. 1** Brit. a siren, steam whistle, or horn. **2** informal a nose. **3** (**hooters**) N. Amer. vulgar slang a woman's breasts.

**hoots** ● **exclam.** Scottish & N. English archaic or humorous expressing dissatisfaction or impatience.
– ORIGIN C16: natural exclam.

**Hoover** Brit. ● **n.** trademark a vacuum cleaner. ● **v.** (**hoover**) clean with a vacuum cleaner.
– ORIGIN 1920s: named after the Amer. industrialist William H. *Hoover*.

**hooves** plural form of **HOOF**.

**hop**[1] ● **v.** (**hopped**, **hopping**) **1** move by jumping on one foot. ➤ (of a bird or animal) move by jumping with two or all feet at once. ➤ jump over. ➤ informal jump on to (a vehicle). **2** informal move or go quickly. ➤ (**hop it**) Brit. go away. ➤ [usu. as noun **hopping**] pass quickly from one place to another: *island-hopping*. ● **n. 1** a hopping movement. **2** a short journey or distance. **3** an informal dance.
– PHRASES **hop, skip** (or **step**), **and jump 1** old-fashioned term for **TRIPLE JUMP**. **2** informal a short distance. **hop the twig** (or **stick**) Brit. informal depart suddenly or die. **on the hop** Brit. informal **1** unprepared. **2** busy.
– ORIGIN OE *hoppian*, of Gmc origin.

**hop**[2] ● **n. 1** (**hops**) the dried cone-like flowers of a twining climbing plant, used in brewing to give a bitter flavour and as a mild sterilant. ➤ Austral./NZ informal beer. **2** the plant from which hops are obtained. [*Humulus lupulus*.] **3** US informal, dated opium or another narcotic. ● **v.** (**hopped, hopping**) **1** flavour with hops. **2** (**be hopped up**) informal be intoxicated by or as if by a narcotic drug.
– DERIVATIVES **hoppy** adj.
– ORIGIN ME *hoppe*, from Mid. Low Ger. or MDu.

**hopak** ● **n.** variant spelling of **GOPAK**.

**hop bine** ● **n.** the climbing stem of the hop.

**hope** ● **n. 1** a feeling of expectation and desire. ➤ a person or thing that gives cause for hope. ➤ grounds for hoping. **2** archaic a feeling of trust. ● **v.** expect and desire. ➤ intend if possible to do something.
– PHRASES **hope against hope** cling to a mere possibility. **not a** (or **some**) **hope** informal no chance at all.
– DERIVATIVES **hoper** n.
– ORIGIN OE *hopa* (n.), *hopian* (v.), of Gmc origin.

**hope chest** ● **n.** N. Amer. a chest in which household linen is stored by a woman in preparation for marriage.

**hopeful** ● **adj.** feeling or inspiring hope. ● **n.** a person likely or hoping to succeed.
– DERIVATIVES **hopefulness** n.

**hopefully** ● **adv. 1** in a hopeful manner. **2** it is to be hoped that: *hopefully it should be finished by next year.*

**USAGE hopefully**

The traditional sense of **hopefully**, 'in a hopeful manner', has been used since the 17th century. In the 20th century a new use arose, with the meaning 'it is to be hoped that'. This sense is regarded by some traditionalists as incorrect, despite the fact that it is now the dominant use, accounting for more than 90 per cent of citations for **hopefully** in the British National Corpus.

**hopeless** ● **adj. 1** feeling or causing despair. **2** inadequate; incompetent.
– DERIVATIVES **hopelessly** adv. **hopelessness** n.

**hophead** ● **n.** informal **1** US a drug addict. **2** Austral./NZ a heavy drinker.

**Hopi** /'həʊpi/ ● **n.** (pl. same or **Hopis**) **1** a member of a Pueblo Indian people living chiefly in NE Arizona. **2** the Uto-Aztecan language of this people.
– ORIGIN the name in Hopi.

**hoplite** /'hɒplʌɪt/ ● **n.** a heavily armed foot soldier of ancient Greece.
– ORIGIN from Gk *hoplitēs*, from *hoplon* 'weapon'.

**hopper**[1] ● **n. 1** a container for grain, rock, or rubbish, typically one that tapers downward and discharges its contents at the bottom. ➤ a tapering container, working with a hopping motion, through which grain passes into a mill. **2** a railway wagon able to discharge bulk material through its floor. **3** a barge for carrying away and discharging mud from a dredging-machine. **4** a person or thing that hops. ➤ a hopping insect, especially a young locust.

**hopper**[2] ● **n.** a person who picks hops.

**hopping** ● **adj.** informal, chiefly N. Amer. very active or lively.
– PHRASES **hopping mad** informal extremely angry.

**hopple** ● **v. & n.** Riding another term for **HOBBLE** (in sense 2).
– ORIGIN C16: prob. of Low Ger. origin.

**hopsack** ● **n. 1** a coarse clothing fabric of a loose weave. **2** a coarse hemp sack for hops.

**hopscotch** ● **n.** a children's game of hopping into and over squares marked on the ground to retrieve a marker.
– ORIGIN C19: from **HOP**[1] + **SCOTCH**[1].

**hop tree** ● **n.** a North American shrub with bitter fruit that was formerly used in brewing as a substitute for hops. [*Ptelea trifoliata*.]

**hora** /'hɔ:rə/ (also **horah**) ● **n.** a Romanian and Israeli dance performed by a ring of dancers.
– ORIGIN C19: from Romanian *horă*, Heb. *hōrāh*.

**horary** /'hɔ:rəri/ ● **adj.** archaic of or relating to hours. ➤ occurring every hour.
– ORIGIN C17: from med. L. *horarius*, from L. *hora* 'hour'.

**Horatian** /hə'reɪʃ(ə)n, -ʃɪən/ ● **adj. 1** of or relating to the Roman poet Horace (65–8 BC) or his work. **2** (of an ode) of several stanzas each of the same metrical pattern.

**horde** ● **n. 1** chiefly derogatory a large group of people. **2** an army or tribe of nomadic warriors. **3** Anthropology a loosely knit small social group typically consisting of about five families.
– ORIGIN C16: from Polish *horda*, from Turk. *ordu* '(royal)

camp'.

**horehound** /ˈhɔːhaʊnd/ (also **hoarhound**) ● **n.** a strong-smelling hairy plant of the mint family, traditionally used as a medicinal herb. [*Marrubium vulgare* (**white horehound**) and *Ballota nigra* (**black horehound**).]
– ORIGIN OE *hāre hūne*, from *hār* (see **HOAR**) + *hūne*, the name of the white horehound.

**horizon** ● **n. 1** the line at which the earth's surface and the sky appear to meet. ➤(also **apparent horizon**) this line represented as a circle, ignoring irregularities and obstructions. ➤(also **true horizon**) Astronomy a great circle of the celestial sphere, the plane of which passes through the centre of the earth and is parallel to that of the apparent horizon. **2** the limit of a person's mental perception, experience, or interest. **3** Geology & Archaeology a layer or level with particular characteristics or representing a particular period.
– PHRASES **on the horizon** imminent.
– ORIGIN ME: via OFr. from late L. *horizon*, from Gk *horizōn* (*kuklos*) 'limiting (circle)'.

**horizontal** ● **adj. 1** parallel to the plane of the horizon. **2** uniform; based on uniformity. ➤combining firms engaged in the same stage or type of production: *a horizontal merger.* **3** of or at the horizon. ● **n. 1** a horizontal line or plane. **2** a horizontal structure.
– DERIVATIVES **horizontality** n. **horizontally** adv.

**hormone** ● **n.** Physiology a regulatory substance produced by a living organism and transported in tissue fluids to stimulate specific cells or tissues into action.
– DERIVATIVES **hormonal** adj.
– ORIGIN C20: from Gk *hormōn*, pres. part. of *horman* 'set in motion'.

**hormone replacement therapy** ● **n.** treatment with oestrogens to alleviate menopausal symptoms or osteoporosis.

**horn** ● **n. 1** a hard permanent outgrowth of bone encased in hardened skin, often curved and pointed, found in pairs on the heads of cattle, sheep, and other animals. ➤a projection of similar appearance on the head of another animal, e.g. a snail's tentacle. ➤(**horns**) archaic a pair of horns as an emblem of a cuckold. **2** the substance of which horns are composed. ➤a receptacle or instrument made of horn, such as a drinking container. **3** a sharp promontory or mountain peak. ➤(**the Horn**) Cape Horn. ➤an arm or branch of a river or bay. ➤the extremity of the moon or other crescent. **4** a wind instrument, conical in shape or wound into a spiral, originally made of horn (now typically brass). **5** an instrument sounding a warning or other signal. **6** Brit. vulgar slang an erect penis. ● **v. 1** butt or gore with the horns. **2** (**horn in**) informal interfere.
– PHRASES **blow** (or **toot**) **one's own horn** N. Amer. informal boast about oneself or one's achievements. **draw** (or **pull**) **in one's horns** become less assertive or ambitious. **on the horn** N. Amer. informal on the telephone. **on the horns of a dilemma** faced with a decision involving equally unfavourable alternatives.
– DERIVATIVES **horned** adj. **hornist** n. **hornless** adj. **horn-like** adj.
– ORIGIN OE, of Gmc origin.

**hornbeam** ● **n.** a deciduous tree with oval serrated leaves, tough winged nuts, and hard pale wood. [Genus *Carpinus*: several species.]
– ORIGIN ME: so named because of the tree's hard wood.

**hornbill** ● **n.** a medium to large tropical bird with a very large curved bill that typically has a large horny or bony casque. [Family Bucerotidae: numerous species.]

**hornblende** /ˈhɔːnblɛnd/ ● **n.** a dark brown, black, or green mineral consisting of a silicate of calcium, magnesium, and iron and present in many rocks.
– ORIGIN C18: from Ger., from *Horn* 'horn' + *blende* (see **BLENDE**).

**hornbook** ● **n.** historical a teaching aid consisting of a leaf of paper showing the alphabet, and often the Lord's Prayer, mounted on a wooden tablet and protected by a thin plate of horn.

**horned lizard** ● **n.** another term for **HORNED TOAD** (in sense 1).

**horned owl** (also **great horned owl**) ● **n.** a large owl found throughout North and South America, with horn-like ear tufts. [*Bubo virginianus*.]

**horned poppy** ● **n.** a poppy with greyish-green lobed leaves, large flowers, and a long curved seed capsule. [*Glaucium flavum* (**yellow horned poppy**) and related species.]

**horned toad** ● **n. 1** an American lizard with spiny skin and large spines on the head. [*Phrynosoma cornutum* and other species.] **2** a large toad with horn-shaped projections of skin over the eyes. [*Megophrys* (SE Asia), *Ceratophrys* (S. America), and other genera.]

**hornero** /hɔːˈnɛːrəʊ/ ● **n.** (pl. **-os**) a tropical American ovenbird, often building its mud nest on the top of a fence post. [Genus *Furnarius*: several species.]
– ORIGIN C19: from Sp., lit. 'baker'.

**hornet** ● **n.** a large wasp which is typically red and yellow or red and black and usually nests in hollow trees. [*Vespa crabro* (Europe) and other species.]
– PHRASES **stir up a hornets' nest** provoke opposition or difficulties.
– ORIGIN OE *hyrnet*, of Gmc origin.

**hornfels** /ˈhɔːnfɛlz/ ● **n.** a dark, fine-grained metamorphic rock consisting largely of quartz, mica, and feldspars.
– ORIGIN C19: from Ger., lit. 'horn rock'.

**horn of plenty** ● **n. 1** a cornucopia. **2** an edible woodland mushroom with a funnel-shaped cap that bears spores on its outer surface. [*Craterellus cornucopioides*.]

**hornpipe** ● **n.** a lively solo dance traditionally performed by sailors. ➤a piece of music for such a dance.
– ORIGIN ME (denoting a wind instrument made of horn, played to accompany dancing): from **HORN** + **PIPE**.

**horn-rimmed** ● **adj.** (of glasses) having rims made of horn or a similar substance.

**hornswoggle** /ˈhɔːnswɒg(ə)l/ ● **v.** informal, chiefly N. Amer. outwit by cheating or deception.
– ORIGIN C19 (orig. US): of unknown origin.

**hornworm** ● **n.** N. Amer. a hawkmoth caterpillar with a spike on its tail, some kinds of which are pests of tobacco and other crops.

**hornwort** ● **n.** a submerged aquatic plant with narrow forked leaves that become translucent and horny as they age. [*Cratophyllum demersum* and related species.]

**horny** ● **adj.** (**-ier**, **-iest**) **1** of or resembling horn. ➤hard and rough. **2** informal sexually aroused or arousing.
– DERIVATIVES **horniness** n.

**horologe** /ˈhɒrəlɒdʒ/ ● **n.** archaic a timepiece.
– ORIGIN ME: from OFr., via L. from Gk *hōrologion*, from *hōra* 'time' + *-logos* '-telling'.

**horology** /hɒˈrɒlədʒi/ ● **n. 1** the study and measurement of time. **2** the art of making clocks and watches.
– DERIVATIVES **horologer** n. **horologic** adj. **horological** adj. **horologist** n.
– ORIGIN C19: from Gk *hōra* 'time' + **-LOGY**.

**horoscope** ● **n.** a forecast of a person's future based on the relative positions of the stars and planets at the time of their birth.
– DERIVATIVES **horoscopic** /-ˈskɒpɪk/ adj. **horoscopy** /hɒˈrɒskəpi/ n.
– ORIGIN OE: via L. from Gk *hōroskopos*, from *hōra* 'time' + *skopos* 'observer'.

**horrendous** /hɒˈrɛndəs/ ● **adj.** extremely unpleasant or horrifying.
– DERIVATIVES **horrendously** adv.
– ORIGIN C17: from L. *horrendus* (gerundive of *horrere* (see **HORRID**)) + **-OUS**.

**horrent** /ˈhɒr(ə)nt/ ● **adj.** poetic/literary **1** (of a person's hair) standing on end. **2** feeling or expressing horror.
– ORIGIN C17: from L. *horrent-*, *horrere* (see **HORRID**).

**horrible** ● **adj. 1** causing or likely to cause horror. **2** informal very unpleasant.
– DERIVATIVES **horribleness** n. **horribly** adv.
– ORIGIN ME: via OFr. from L. *horribilis*, from *horrere* (see **HORRID**).

**horrid** ● **adj. 1** causing horror. **2** informal very unpleasant. **3** poetic/literary rough; bristling.
– DERIVATIVES **horridly** adv. **horridness** n.

– ORIGIN C16: from L. *horridus*, from *horrere* 'shudder, (of hair) stand on end'.

**horrific** ● **adj.** causing horror.
– DERIVATIVES **horrifically** adv.
– ORIGIN C17: from L. *horrificus*, from *horrere* (see **HORRID**).

**horrify** ● **v.** (**-ies**, **-ied**) fill with horror.
– DERIVATIVES **horrification** n. **horrified** adj. **horrifiedly** adv. **horrifying** adj. **horrifyingly** adv.
– ORIGIN C18: from L. *horrificare*, from *horrificus* (see **HORRIFIC**).

**horripilation** /hɒˌrɪpɪˈleɪʃ(ə)n/ ● **n.** poetic/literary the erection of hairs on the skin due to cold, fear, or excitement.
– DERIVATIVES **horripilate** v.
– ORIGIN C17: from late L. *horripilatio(n-)*, from L. *horrere* (see **HORRID**) + *pilus* 'hair'.

**horror** ● **n. 1** an intense feeling of fear, shock, or disgust. ➤ a thing causing such a feeling. ➤ intense dismay. **2** informal a bad or mischievous person, especially a child.
– ORIGIN ME: via OFr. from L. *horror*, from *horrere* (see **HORRID**).

**horror vacui** /ˌhɒrə ˈvakjuːʌɪ/ ● **n.** a fear or dislike of leaving empty spaces, especially in an artistic composition.
– ORIGIN mod. L., 'horror of a vacuum'.

**hors concours** /ˌɔː kɒ̃ˈkʊə/ ● **adj. 1** poetic/literary unrivalled. **2** formal (of an exhibit or exhibitor) not competing for a prize.
– ORIGIN Fr., lit. 'out of the competition'.

**hors de combat** /ˌɔː də ˈkɒ̃bɑː/ ● **adj.** out of action due to injury or damage.
– ORIGIN Fr., lit. 'out of the fight'.

**hors d'oeuvre** /ɔː ˈdəːv, ˈdəːvr(ə)/ ● **n.** (pl. same or **hors d'oeuvres** pronunc. same or /ˈdəːvz/) a savoury appetizer.
– ORIGIN Fr., lit. 'outside the work'.

**horse** ● **n. 1** a solid-hoofed plant-eating quadruped with a flowing mane and tail, domesticated for riding and as a draught animal. [*Equus caballus* and other species, family Equidae.] ➤ an adult male horse, as opposed to a mare or colt. ➤ [treated as sing. or pl.] cavalry. **2** a frame or structure on which something is mounted or supported, especially a sawhorse. ➤ Nautical a horizontal bar, rail, or rope in the rigging of a sailing ship for supporting something. **3** informal a unit of horsepower. **4** informal heroin. **5** Mining an obstruction in a vein. ● **v. 1** provide with a horse or horses. **2** (**horse around/about**) informal fool about.
– PHRASES **from the horse's mouth** (of information) from an authoritative source. **to horse** (as a command) mount your horses!
– DERIVATIVES **horseless** adj. **horse-like** adj.
– ORIGIN OE *hors*, of Gmc origin.

**horse-and-buggy** ● **adj.** N. Amer. informal old-fashioned.

**horseback** ● **adj. & adv.** mounted on a horse.

**horsebean** ● **n.** a field bean of a variety with relatively large seeds, used as fodder.

**horsebox** ● **n.** Brit. a motorized vehicle or a trailer for transporting one or more horses.

**horse chestnut** ● **n. 1** a deciduous tree with large leaves of five leaflets, upright conical clusters of white, pink, or red flowers, and nuts enclosed in a spiny case. [*Aesculus hippocastanum* and related species.] **2** the nut of this tree; a conker.
– ORIGIN C16: translating (now obs.) botanical L. *Castanea equina*; its fruit is said to have been an Eastern remedy for chest diseases in horses.

**horse-coper** ● **n.** Brit. archaic a person who deals in horses.
– ORIGIN *coper* (C17) from obs. *cope* 'exchange or bargain', from MDu., Mid. Low Ger. *kōpen*.

**horseflesh** ● **n.** horses considered collectively.

**horsefly** ● **n.** (pl. **-flies**) a stoutly built fly, the female of which is a bloodsucker and inflicts painful bites on horses and other large mammals. [*Haematopota pluvialis* and other species, family Tabanidae.]

**Horse Guards** ● **pl. n.** (in the UK) the mounted squadrons provided from the Household Cavalry for ceremonial duties.

**horsehair** ● **n.** hair from the mane or tail of a horse, used in furniture for padding.

**horse latitudes** ● **pl. n.** a belt of calm air and sea occurring in both the northern and southern hemispheres between the trade winds and the westerlies.
– ORIGIN C18: of uncertain origin.

**horse laugh** ● **n.** a loud, coarse laugh.

**horseleech** ● **n.** a large predatory leech of freshwater and terrestrial habitats which feeds on carrion and small invertebrates. [Genus *Haemopis*.]

**horseless carriage** ● **n.** archaic or humorous a motor car.

**horse mackerel** ● **n.** a shoaling edible fish of the eastern Atlantic. [*Trachurus trachurus*.]

**horseman** (or **horsewoman**) ● **n.** (pl. **-men** or **-women**) a rider on horseback, especially a skilled one.
– DERIVATIVES **horsemanship** n.

**horse mushroom** ● **n.** a large edible mushroom with a creamy-white cap. [*Agaricus arvensis*.]

**horse mussel** ● **n.** a large marine mussel. [Genus *Modiolus*.]

**horse opera** ● **n.** N. Amer. informal a western film.

**horse pistol** ● **n.** historical a large pistol carried at the pommel of the saddle by a rider.

**horseplay** ● **n.** rough, boisterous play.

**horseplayer** ● **n.** N. Amer. a person who regularly bets on horse races.

**horsepower** (abbrev.: **h.p.**) ● **n.** (pl. same) an imperial unit of power equal to 550 foot-pounds per second (about 750 watts). ➤ engine power measured in terms of this.

**horse racing** ● **n.** a sport in which horses and their riders take part in races, either on a flat course or over hurdles or fences.

**horseradish** ● **n.** a plant of the cabbage family with long dock-like leaves, grown for its pungent root which is often made into a sauce. [*Armoracia rusticana*.]

**horse sense** ● **n.** informal common sense.

**horseshoe** ● **n.** a shoe for a horse formed of a narrow band of iron in the form of an extended circular arc. ➤ (**horseshoes**) [treated as sing.] chiefly N. Amer. a game resembling quoits in which horseshoes are thrown at a peg.

**horseshoe bat** ● **n.** an insectivorous bat with a horseshoe-shaped ridge on the nose. [Genus *Rhinolophus*: many species.]

**horseshoe crab** ● **n.** a large marine arthropod with a domed horseshoe-shaped shell and a long tail spine. [*Limulus polyphemus* (N. America) and other species.]

**horse's neck** ● **n.** informal a drink consisting of ginger ale, a twist of lemon peel, and brandy or other spirits.

**horsetail** ● **n.** a flowerless spore-producing plant with a hollow jointed stem bearing whorls of narrow leaves. [Genus *Equisetum*, class Sphenopsida.]

**horse-trading** ● **n.** informal hard and shrewd bargaining.
– DERIVATIVES **horse-trade** v. **horse-trader** n.

**horsewhip** ● **n.** a long whip used for driving and controlling horses. ● **v.** (**-whipped**, **-whipping**) beat with such a whip.

**horsey** (also **horsy**) ● **adj.** (**-ier**, **-iest**) **1** of or resembling a horse. **2** concerned with or devoted to horses or horse racing.
– DERIVATIVES **horsily** adv. **horsiness** n.

**horst** /hɔːst/ ● **n.** Geology a raised elongated block of the earth's crust lying between two faults.
– ORIGIN C19: from Ger. *Horst* 'heap'.

**hortatory** /ˈhɔːtət(ə)ri/ ● **adj.** formal tending or aiming to exhort.
– DERIVATIVES **hortation** n. **hortative** adj.
– ORIGIN C16: from L. *hortatorius*, from *hortari* 'exhort'.

**horticulture** /ˈhɔːtɪˌkʌltʃə/ ● **n.** the art or practice of garden cultivation and management.
– DERIVATIVES **horticultural** adj. **horticulturalist** n. **horticulturist** n.
– ORIGIN C17: from L. *hortus* 'garden' + **CULTURE**.

**hortus siccus** /ˌhɔːtəs ˈsɪkəs/ ● **n.** (pl. **horti sicci** /ˌhɔːtʌɪ ˈsɪkʌɪ, -tiː, -kiː/) a herbarium.
– ORIGIN L., lit. 'dry garden'.

**Hos.** ● **abbrev.** Hosea (in biblical references).

**hosanna** (also **hosannah**) ● **n. & exclam.** (especially in biblical use) a cry of praise or joy.
– ORIGIN OE, via late L. from Gk *hōsanna*, from Rabbinical Heb. *hōšaʿnā*, abbrev. of biblical *hōšīʿā-nnā* 'save, we pray' (Ps. 118:25).

**hose** ● **n. 1** a flexible tube conveying water, used chiefly for watering plants and in firefighting. **2** [treated as pl.] stockings, socks, and tights. ➤historical breeches. ● **v.** water or spray with a hose.
– ORIGIN OE *hosa*, of Gmc origin.

**hosel** /ˈhəʊz(ə)l/ ● **n.** the socket of a golf club head which the shaft fits into.
– ORIGIN C16: dimin. of **HOSE**, in the dial. sense 'sheathing'.

**hosepipe** ● **n.** British term for **HOSE** (in sense 1).

**hosier** /ˈhəʊzɪə/ ● **n.** a manufacturer or seller of hosiery.

**hosiery** ● **n.** stockings, socks, and tights collectively.

**hospice** ● **n. 1** a home providing care for the sick or terminally ill. **2** archaic a lodging for travellers, especially one run by a religious order.
– ORIGIN C19: from Fr., from L. *hospitium*, from *hospes, hospit-* (see **HOST**[1]).

**hospitable** /hɒˈspɪtəb(ə)l, ˈhɒspɪt-/ ● **adj. 1** showing or inclined to show hospitality. **2** (of an environment) pleasant and favourable for living in.
– DERIVATIVES **hospitably** adv.
– ORIGIN C16: from Fr., from obs. *hospiter* 'receive a guest', based on L. *hospes, hospit-* (see **HOST**[1]).

**hospital** ● **n. 1** an institution providing medical and surgical treatment and nursing care for sick or injured people. **2** historical a hospice, especially one run by the Knights Hospitallers.
– DERIVATIVES **hospitalization** (also **-isation**) n. **hospitalize** (also **-ise**) v.
– ORIGIN ME: via OFr. from med. L. *hospitale*, neut. of L. *hospitalis* 'hospitable', from *hospes, hospit-* (see **HOST**[1]).

**hospital corners** ● **pl. n.** overlapping folds used to tuck sheets neatly and securely under the mattress at the corners, in a manner used in hospitals.

**hospital fever** ● **n.** historical louse-borne typhus acquired in overcrowded, insanitary conditions in an old-fashioned hospital.

**hospitalism** ● **n.** the adverse effects of a prolonged stay in hospital.

**hospitality** ● **n.** the friendly and generous reception and entertainment of guests or strangers.
– ORIGIN ME: from OFr. *hospitalite*, based on L. *hospitalitas*, from *hospitalis* (see **HOSPITAL**).

**hospitaller** /ˈhɒspɪt(ə)lə/ (US **hospitaler**) ● **n.** a member of a charitable religious order.
– ORIGIN ME: from OFr. *hospitalier*, from med. L. *hospitalarius*, from *hospitale* (see **HOSPITAL**).

**hospital ship** ● **n.** a ship which functions as a hospital, especially to receive or take home sick or wounded military personnel.

**hospital trust** ● **n.** (in the UK) a National Health Service hospital which has opted to withdraw from local authority control and be managed by a trust instead.

**host**[1] ● **n. 1** a person who receives or entertains other people as guests. ➤the presenter of a television or radio programme. **2** Biology an animal or plant on or in which a parasite or commensal organism lives. **3** the recipient of transplanted tissue or a transplanted organ. **4** a computer which mediates multiple access to databases or provides other services to a network. ● **v.** act as host at (an event) or for (a television or radio programme).
– ORIGIN ME: from OFr. *hoste*, from L. *hospes, hospit-* 'host, guest'.

**host**[2] ● **n. 1** (**a host/hosts of**) a large number of. **2** archaic an army.
– ORIGIN ME: from OFr. *ost, hoost*, from L. *hostis* 'stranger, enemy' (in med. L. 'army').

**host**[3] ● **n.** (**the Host**) the bread consecrated in the Eucharist.
– ORIGIN ME: from OFr. *hoiste*, from L. *hostia* 'victim'.

**hosta** /ˈhɒstə/ ● **n.** an East Asian plant cultivated in the West chiefly for its shade-tolerant ornamental foliage. [Genus *Hosta*.]
– ORIGIN mod. L., named after the Austrian physician Nicolaus T. *Host*.

**hostage** ● **n.** a person seized or held as security for the fulfilment of a condition.
– PHRASES **a hostage to fortune** an act or remark regarded as unwise because it invites trouble.
– ORIGIN ME: from OFr., based on late L. *obsidatus* 'the state of being a hostage', from L. *obses, obsid-* 'hostage'.

**hostel** ● **n. 1** an establishment which provides cheap food and lodging for a specific group of people. **2** archaic an inn providing accommodation.
– ORIGIN ME: from OFr., from med. L. *hospitale* (see **HOSPITAL**).

**hostelling** (US **hosteling**) ● **n.** the practice of staying in youth hostels when travelling.
– DERIVATIVES **hosteller** n.

**hostelry** ● **n.** (pl. **-ies**) archaic or humorous an inn or pub.
– ORIGIN ME: from OFr. *hostelerie* from *hostelier* 'innkeeper', from *hostel* (see **HOSTEL**).

**hostess** ● **n.** a female host. ➤a woman employed to welcome and entertain customers at a nightclub or bar. ➤a stewardess on an aircraft, train, etc.

**hostile** ● **adj.** antagonistic; opposed. ➤of or belonging to a military enemy. ➤(of a takeover bid) opposed by the company to be bought.
– DERIVATIVES **hostilely** adv. **hostility** n. (pl. **-ies**).
– ORIGIN ME (as *hostility*): from Fr., or from L. *hostilis*, from *hostis* 'stranger, enemy'.

**hostile witness** ● **n.** Law a witness who is antagonistic to the party calling them.

**hostler** ● **n.** variant spelling of **OSTLER**.

**hot** ● **adj.** (**hotter, hottest**) **1** having a high temperature. ➤feeling or producing an uncomfortable sensation of heat. ➤causing a burning sensation in the mouth. ➤informal at a high voltage; live. ➤informal radioactive. **2** feeling or showing intense excitement, anger, lust, or other emotion. **3** currently popular, fashionable, or interesting. ➤Hunting (of the scent) fresh and strong. ➤(in children's games) very close to finding or guessing something. ➤informal (of goods) stolen and difficult to dispose of because easily identifiable. **4** (often **hot on**) informal very knowledgeable or skilful. ➤[usu. with neg.] good; promising. **5** (**hot on**) informal strict about. ● **v.** (**hotted, hotting**) **1** (**hot up** or **hot something up**) Brit. informal become or make more intense or exciting. **2** W. Indian make or become hot.
– PHRASES **go hot and cold** experience a sudden feeling of fear or shock. **have the hots for** informal be sexually attracted to. **hot and heavy** N. Amer. informal intense; with intensity. **hot under the collar** informal angry or resentful. **in hot water** informal in trouble or disgrace. **make it** (or **things**) **hot for** informal stir up trouble for (someone).
– DERIVATIVES **hotly** adv. **hotness** n. **hottish** adj.
– ORIGIN OE *hāt*, of Gmc origin.

**hot air** ● **n.** informal empty or boastful talk.

**hotbed** ● **n. 1** a bed of earth heated by fermenting manure, for raising or forcing plants. **2** an environment promoting the growth of an activity or trend.

**hot-blooded** ● **adj.** lustful; passionate.

**hot button** ● **n.** N. Amer. informal an issue that is highly charged emotionally or politically.

**hotchpot** ● **n.** Law the reunion and blending together of properties so as to distribute them equally.
– ORIGIN ME: from Anglo-Norman Fr. and OFr. *hochepot*, from *hocher* 'to shake' + *pot* 'pot'.

**hotchpotch** (N. Amer. **hodgepodge**) ● **n. 1** a confused mixture. **2** archaic a mutton stew with mixed vegetables.
– ORIGIN ME: var. of **HOTCHPOT**.

**hot cross bun** ● **n.** a bun marked with a cross and containing dried fruit, traditionally eaten on Good Friday.

**hot-desking** ● **n.** the allocation of desks to office workers when they are required or on a rota system.

**hot dog** ● **n. 1** a hot sausage served in a long, soft roll. **2** N. Amer. informal a person, especially a skier or surfer, who performs stunts. ● **exclam.** N. Amer. informal used to express enthusiastic approval. ● **v.** (**hotdog**) N. Amer. informal perform stunts.
– DERIVATIVES **hotdogger** n.

**hotel** ● **n. 1** an establishment providing accommodation

and meals for travellers and tourists. ➤ chiefly Austral./NZ a public house. **2** a code word representing the letter H, used in radio communication.
– ORIGIN C18: from Fr. *hôtel*, from OFr. *hostel* (see **HOSTEL**).

**hotelier** • **n.** a person who owns or manages a hotel.
– ORIGIN C20: from Fr. *hôtelier*.

**hot flash** • **n.** chiefly N. Amer. another term for **HOT FLUSH**.

**hot flush** • **n.** a sudden feeling of feverish heat, typically as a symptom of the menopause.

**hotfoot** • **adv.** in eager haste. • **v.** (**hotfoot it**) hurry eagerly.

**hot gospel** • **n.** informal zealous evangelism.
– DERIVATIVES **hot gospeller** n.

**hothead** • **n.** an impetuous or quick-tempered person.
– DERIVATIVES **hot-headed** adj. **hot-headedly** adv. **hot-headedness** n.

**hothouse** • **n. 1** a heated greenhouse. **2** an environment that encourages rapid growth or development. • **v.** educate (a child) to a higher level than is usual for their age.

**hot key** • **n.** Computing a key or combination of keys providing quick access to a function within a program.

**hotline** • **n.** a direct telephone line set up for a specific purpose, especially for use in emergencies or for communication between heads of government.

**hot metal** • **n.** a typesetting technique in which type is newly made each time from molten metal.

**hot money** • **n.** capital which is frequently transferred between financial institutions in an attempt to maximize interest or capital gain.

**hot pants** • **pl. n.** women's very tight, brief shorts.

**hotplate** • **n.** a flat heated metal or ceramic surface on an electric cooker.

**hotpot** • **n.** Brit. a casserole of meat and vegetables with a covering layer of sliced potato.

**hot potato** • **n.** informal a controversial and awkward issue or situation.

**hot press** • **n.** a press of glazed boards and hot metal plates for smoothing paper or cloth or making plywood. • **v.** (**hot-press**) press with such a device.

**hot rod** • **n.** a motor vehicle that has been specially modified to give it extra power and speed. • **v.** (**hot-rod**) **1** modify (a vehicle or other device) to make it faster or more powerful. **2** drive a hot rod.
– DERIVATIVES **hot-rodder** n.

**hot seat** • **n.** (**the hot seat**) informal **1** the position of a person who carries full responsibility for something. **2** chiefly N. Amer. the electric chair.

**hot shoe** • **n.** a socket on a camera with direct electrical contacts for an attached flashgun or other accessory.

**hot-short** • **adj.** (of a metal) brittle when hot.
– ORIGIN C18: from **HOT** + *short* suggested by the earlier *red-short*, from Swed. *rödskör* (from *röd* 'red' + *skör* 'brittle').

**hotshot** • **n.** informal an important or exceptionally able person. ➤ a sports player with a good aim.

**hot spot** • **n. 1** a small area with a relatively high temperature. **2** a place of significant activity or danger.

**hot spring** • **n.** a spring of naturally hot water, typically heated by subterranean volcanic activity.

**hotspur** /ˈhɒtspəː, -spə/ • **n.** archaic a rash person.
– ORIGIN ME: lit. 'a person whose spur is hot from rash or constant riding'.

**hot stuff** • **n.** informal a person or thing of outstanding talent or interest. ➤ a sexually exciting person, book, etc.

**hot-swap** • **v.** informal fit or replace (a computer part) with the power still connected.
– DERIVATIVES **hot-swappable** adj.

**hotsy-totsy** • **adj.** US term for **HOITY-TOITY**.
– ORIGIN C20: fanciful reduplication of **HOT**.

**hot-tempered** • **adj.** easily angered.

**Hottentot** /ˈhɒt(ə)ntɒt/ • **n. & adj.** used to refer to Khoikhoi peoples.
– ORIGIN Du., perh. a repetitive formula in a Nama dancing song, transferred by Du. sailors to the people themselves, or from Ger. *hotteren-totteren* 'stutter' (with ref. to their click language).

**USAGE** Hottentot

The word **Hottentot** is now regarded as offensive with reference to people (where **Khoikhoi** is the standard term) but is still standard when used in the names of some animals and plants.

**Hottentot fig** • **n.** a succulent mat-forming plant with bright yellow or lilac daisy-like flowers and edible fruit, native to South Africa and naturalized elsewhere. [*Carpobrotus edulis*.]

**hot ticket** • **n.** informal a person or thing that is much in demand.

**hottie** (also **hotty**) • **n.** (pl. **-ies**) informal **1** Brit. a hot-water bottle. **2** US a sexually attractive young woman.

**hotting** • **n.** Brit. informal joyriding in stolen high-performance cars.
– DERIVATIVES **hotter** n.

**hot tub** • **n.** a large tub filled with hot aerated water used for recreation or physical therapy.

**hot war** • **n.** a war with active military hostilities.

**hot-water bottle** (US also **hot-water bag**) • **n.** a flat, oblong rubber container that is filled with hot water and used for warming a bed or part of the body.

**hot-wire** • **v.** informal start the engine of (a vehicle) by bypassing the ignition switch.

**houbara bustard** /huːˈbɑːrə/ • **n.** a bustard of arid open country, found from the Canary Islands to central Asia. [*Chlamydotis undulata*.]
– ORIGIN C19: from mod. L. (former genus name), from Arab. *ḥubārā*.

**Houdini** /huːˈdiːni/ • **n.** a person skilled at escaping.
– ORIGIN C20: from the name of Harry *Houdini* (Erik Weisz), Amer. magician and escape artist.

**hough** /hɒk/ • **n.** Brit. variant spelling of **HOCK**[1] (in sense 1). ➤ a joint of meat consisting of the part extending from the hock some way up the leg.
– ORIGIN OE *hōh* 'heel', of Gmc origin; rel. to **HEEL**[1].

**hoummos** • **n.** variant spelling of **HUMMUS**.

**hound** • **n. 1** a dog of a breed used for hunting, especially one able to track by scent. **2** a person keen in pursuit of something: *a publicity hound*. **3** used in names of dogfishes, e.g. **nurse hound**. • **v.** harass or pursue relentlessly.
– ORIGIN OE *hund*, of Gmc origin.

**hound's tongue** • **n.** a tall plant with small purplish flowers, tongue-shaped leaves, and a mousy smell. [*Cynoglossum officinale*.]

**houndstooth** • **n.** a large dog-tooth pattern.

**houngan** /ˈhuːŋg(ə)n/ • **n.** a voodoo priest.
– ORIGIN C20: from Fon, from *hun*, a deity represented by a fetish, + *ga* 'chief'.

**hour** • **n. 1** a period of time equal to a twenty-fourth part of a day and night and divided into 60 minutes. **2** a time of day specified as an exact number of hours from midnight or midday. ➤ (**hours**) [with preceding numeral] a time so specified on the 24-hour clock. **3** a period set aside for a particular purpose or marked by a specific activity: *leisure hours*. ➤ a point in time: *the shop is half-full even at this hour*. **4** (**hours**) (in the Western (Latin) Church) a short service of psalms and prayers to be said at a particular time of day. **5** Astronomy 15° of longitude or right ascension (one twenty-fourth part of a circle).
– PHRASES **on the hour 1** at an exact hour, or on each hour, of the day or night. **2** after a period of one hour.
– ORIGIN ME: from Anglo-Norman Fr. *ure*, via L. from Gk *hōra* 'season, hour'.

**hourglass** • **n.** an invertible device with two connected glass bulbs containing sand that takes an hour to pass from the upper to the lower bulb.

**houri** /ˈhʊəri/ • **n.** (pl. **houris**) **1** a beautiful young woman. **2** one of the virgin companions of the faithful in the Muslim Paradise.
– ORIGIN C18: from Fr., from Pers. *ḥūrī*, from Arab. *ḥūr*, pl. of *ʼaḥwar* 'having eyes with a marked contrast of black and white'.

**hourly** ● adj. **1** done or occurring every hour. **2** reckoned hour by hour. ● adv. **1** every hour. **2** by the hour.

**house** ● n. /haʊs/ **1** a building for human habitation. ➤ chiefly Scottish a dwelling that is one of several in a building. ➤ a building in which animals live or in which things are kept. **2** a building in which people meet for a particular activity. ➤ a firm or institution: *a fashion house.* ➤ (**the House**) Brit. informal the Stock Exchange. ➤ a restaurant or inn. **3** a religious community that occupies a particular building. ➤ chiefly Brit. a body of pupils living in the same building at a boarding school. ➤ Brit. formal a college of a university. **4** a legislative or deliberative assembly. ➤ (**the House**) (in the UK) the House of Commons or Lords; (in the US) the House of Representatives. **5** a dynasty. **6** (also **house music**) a style of fast popular dance music typically using drum machines and synthesized bass lines. **7** Astrology a twelfth division of the celestial sphere. ● adj. **1** (of an animal or plant) kept in, frequenting, or infesting buildings. **2** of or relating to medical staff resident at a hospital. **3** of or relating to a firm, institution, or society. ● v. /haʊz/ **1** provide with shelter or accommodation. **2** provide space for. ➤ enclose or encase.
– PHRASES **get on** (or **along**) **like a house on fire** informal have a very good and friendly relationship. **go** (**all**) **round the houses** take a circuitous route. **keep** (or **make**) **a House** Brit. secure the presence of enough members for a quorum in the House of Commons. **keep house** run a household. **on the house** (of a drink or meal in a bar or restaurant) at the management's expense. **put** (or **set** or **get**) **one's house in order** make necessary reforms.
– DERIVATIVES **houseful** n. (pl. **-fuls**). **houseless** adj.
– ORIGIN OE *hūs* (n.), *hūsian* (v.), of Gmc origin.

**house arrest** ● n. the state of being kept as a prisoner in one's own house.

**houseboat** ● n. a boat which is fitted for use as a dwelling.

**housebound** ● adj. unable to leave one's house, typically due to illness or old age.

**houseboy** ● n. a boy or man employed to undertake domestic duties.

**housebreak** ● v. chiefly N. Amer. another term for **HOUSE-TRAIN**.

**housebreaking** ● n. the action of breaking into a building, especially in daytime, to commit a crime (replaced as a statutory crime in English law by burglary).
– DERIVATIVES **housebreaker** n.

**housecarl** /ˈhaʊskɑːl/ (also **housecarle**) ● n. historical a member of the bodyguard of a Danish or English king or noble.
– ORIGIN OE *hūscarl*, from ON *húskarl* 'manservant'.

**house church** ● n. **1** a charismatic Church independent of traditional denominations. **2** a group meeting for Christian worship in a private house.

**housecoat** ● n. a woman's long, loose, lightweight robe for informal wear around the house.

**house cricket** ● n. a cricket with a birdlike warble, native to North Africa and SW Asia and found in warm buildings elsewhere. [*Acheta domesticus*.]

**housefather** (or **housemother**) ● n. a person in charge of and living in a boarding school house or children's home.

**house finch** ● n. a common red-breasted brown finch, native to western North America. [*Carpodacus mexicanus*.]

**housefly** ● n. (pl. **-flies**) a common small fly occurring in and around human habitation and laying its eggs in decaying material. [*Musca domestica*.]

**household** ● n. a house and its occupants regarded as a unit.

**Household Cavalry** ● n. (in the British army) the two cavalry regiments with responsibility for guarding the monarch.

**householder** ● n. a person who owns or rents a house.

**household gods** ● pl. n. gods presiding over a household, especially (in ancient Rome) the lares and penates.

**household name** (also **household word**) ● n. a famous person or thing.

**household troops** ● pl. n. (in the UK) troops nominally employed to guard the sovereign.

**house-hunting** ● n. the process of seeking a house to buy or rent.
– DERIVATIVES **house-hunter** n.

**house husband** ● n. a man who lives with a partner and carries out the household duties traditionally done by a housewife.

**housekeeper** ● n. a person, typically a woman, employed to manage a household.
– DERIVATIVES **housekeep** v. (dated).

**housekeeping** ● n. **1** the management of household affairs. ➤ money set aside for this. **2** non-productive but necessary routine operations such as record-keeping or administration in a computer or other system.

**houseleek** /ˈhaʊsliːk/ ● n. a succulent plant with rosettes of fleshy leaves and small pink flowers, growing on walls and roofs. [*Sempervivum tectorum* and other species.]

**house lights** ● pl. n. the lights in the auditorium of a theatre.

**housemaid** ● n. a female domestic employee who cleans rooms.

**housemaid's knee** ● n. inflammation of the fluid-filled cavity covering the kneecap, often due to excessive kneeling.

**houseman** ● n. (pl. **-men**) **1** Brit. another term for **HOUSE OFFICER**. **2** N. Amer. another term for **HOUSEBOY**.

**house martin** ● n. a black-and-white bird of the swallow family which builds mud nests on the walls of buildings. [*Delichon urbica*.]

**housemaster** (or **housemistress**) ● n. a teacher in charge of a house at a boarding school.

**house mouse** ● n. a greyish-brown mouse found abundantly as a scavenger in human dwellings. [*Mus musculus*.]

**House of Commons** ● n. (in the UK) the elected chamber of Parliament.

**house of correction** ● n. historical an institution where vagrants and minor offenders were confined and set to work.

**house officer** ● n. Brit. a recent medical graduate receiving supervised training in a hospital and acting as an assistant physician or surgeon.

**house of God** ● n. a place of religious worship, especially a church.

**house of ill fame** (also **house of ill repute**) ● n. archaic or humorous a brothel.

**House of Keys** ● n. (in the Isle of Man) the elected chamber of Tynwald.

**House of Lords** ● n. (in the UK) the chamber of Parliament composed of peers and bishops. ➤ a committee of specially qualified members of this, appointed as the ultimate judicial appeal court of England and Wales.

**House of Representatives** ● n. the lower house of the US Congress and other legislatures.

**house plant** ● n. a plant which is grown indoors.

**house-proud** ● adj. attentive to, or preoccupied with, the care and appearance of one's home.

**houseroom** ● n. space or accommodation in one's house.
– PHRASES **not give something houseroom** Brit. be unwilling to have or consider something.

**house-sit** ● v. live in and look after a house while its owner is away.
– DERIVATIVES **house-sitter** n.

**Houses of Parliament** ● pl. n. (in the UK) the Houses of Lords and Commons regarded together.

**house sparrow** ● n. a common brown and grey sparrow that nests in the eaves and roofs of houses. [*Passer domesticus*.]

**house-to-house** ● adj. & adv. performed at or taken to each house in turn.

**house-train** ● v. chiefly Brit. train (a pet) to excrete outside the house.

**house-warming** ● n. a party celebrating a move to a new home.

**housewife** ● n. (pl. **-wives**) **1** a married woman whose main occupation is caring for her family and running the household. **2** /ˈhʌzɪf/ a small case for needles, thread, and other small sewing items.
– DERIVATIVES **housewifely** adj. **housewifery** n.

**housework** ● n. regular work done in housekeeping, such as cleaning and cooking.

**housey-housey** (also **housie-housie**) ● n. Brit. old-fashioned term for **BINGO**.

**housing**[1] ● n. **1** houses and flats considered collectively. ➤ the provision of accommodation. **2** a rigid casing that houses a piece of moving or delicate equipment. **3** a recess or groove cut in a piece of wood to allow another piece to be attached to it.

**housing**[2] ● n. archaic a cloth covering put on a horse for protection or ornament.
– ORIGIN ME: from OFr. *houce*, from med. L. *hultia*, of Gmc origin.

**housing estate** ● n. Brit. a residential area planned and built as a unit.

**houting** /ˈhaʊtɪŋ/ ● n. a whitefish with a pointed snout, found mainly in the Baltic and adjacent rivers. [*Coregonus oxyrhinchus*.]
– ORIGIN C19: from Du., from MDu. *houtic*.

**hove** chiefly Nautical past of **HEAVE**.

**hovel** ● n. **1** a small squalid or poorly constructed dwelling. **2** historical a conical building enclosing a kiln.
– ORIGIN ME: of unknown origin.

**hover** ● v. remain in one place in the air. ➤ linger close at hand in an uncertain manner. ➤ remain at or near a particular level. ● n. an act of hovering.
– DERIVATIVES **hoverer** n.
– ORIGIN ME: from archaic *hove* 'hover, linger'.

**hovercraft** ● n. (pl. same) a vehicle or craft that travels over land or water on a cushion of air provided by a downward blast.

**hoverfly** ● n. (pl. **-flies**) a fly, typically black and yellow, which frequently hovers in the air and feeds on the nectar of flowers. [Family Syrphidae: many species.]

**hoverport** ● n. a terminal for hovercraft.

**how**[1] ● adv. **1** in what way or by what means. **2** in what condition or health. **3** to what extent or degree. **4** that. ➤ however.
– PHRASES **and how!** informal very much so. **how about?** would you like? **the how and why** the methods and reasons for doing something. **how do you do?** a formal greeting. **how many** what number. **how much** what amount or price. **how now?** archaic what is the meaning of this? **how's that?** Cricket is the batsman out or not? (said to an umpire).
– ORIGIN OE *hū*, of W. Gmc origin; rel. to **WHO** and **WHAT**.

**how**[2] ● exclam. a greeting attributed to North American Indians.
– ORIGIN C19: perh. from Sioux *háo* or Omaha *hou*.

**howbeit** ● adv. archaic nevertheless.

**howdah** /ˈhaʊdə/ ● n. (in the Indian subcontinent) a seat for riding on the back of an elephant, usually having a canopy.
– ORIGIN from Urdu *haudah*, from Arab. *hawdaj* 'litter'.

**how-do-you-do** (also **how-de-do** or **how-d'ye-do**) ● n. informal an awkward or annoying situation.

**howdy** ● exclam. N. Amer. an informal friendly greeting.
– ORIGIN C19: alt. of *how d'ye*.

**howe** ● n. N. English a tumulus or barrow.
– ORIGIN ME: from ON *haugr* 'mound', from a Gmc base meaning 'high'.

**however** ● adv. **1** used to introduce a statement contrasting with a previous one. **2** in whatever way. ➤ to whatever extent.

**howff** /haʊf/ ● n. Scottish a favourite haunt, especially a pub.
– ORIGIN C16 (as the name of the main burial ground in Dundee): of unknown origin.

**howitzer** /ˈhaʊɪtsə/ ● n. a short gun for firing shells on high trajectories at low velocities.
– ORIGIN C17: from Du. *houwitser*, from Ger. *Haubitze*, from Czech *houfnice* 'catapult'.

**howk** /haʊk/ ● v. chiefly Scottish dig out or up.
– ORIGIN ME *holk*: rel. to **HOLE**.

**howl** ● n. a long doleful cry uttered by an animal such as a dog. ➤ a loud cry of pain, amusement, etc. ➤ Electronics a wailing noise in a loudspeaker due to feedback. ● v. make a howling sound.
– ORIGIN ME *houle* (v.), prob. imitative.

**howler** ● n. **1** informal a ludicrous mistake. **2** (also **howler monkey**) a fruit-eating monkey with a loud howling call, native to the forests of tropical America. [Genus *Alouatta*: several species.]

**howling** ● adj. informal great: *a howling success.*

**howsoever** formal or archaic ● adv. to whatever extent. ● conj. in whatever way.

**howzat** ● exclam. Cricket shortened form of ***how's that*** (see **HOW**[1]).

**hoy**[1] ● exclam. used to attract someone's attention. ● n. Austral. a game resembling bingo, using playing cards.
– ORIGIN ME: natural exclam.

**hoy**[2] ● n. historical a small coastal sailing vessel, typically single-masted.
– ORIGIN ME: from MDu. *hoei*, of unknown origin.

**hoy**[3] ● v. Austral. & N. English informal throw.
– ORIGIN C19: of unknown origin.

**hoya** /ˈhɔɪə/ ● n. a evergreen climbing shrub with ornamental foliage and waxy flowers, native to SE Asia and the Pacific. [Genus *Hoya*.]
– ORIGIN C19: mod. L., named after the Engl. gardener Thomas *Hoy*.

**hoyden** /ˈhɔɪd(ə)n/ ● n. dated a boisterous girl.
– DERIVATIVES **hoydenish** adj.
– ORIGIN C16 (denoting a rude man): prob. from MDu. *heiden* (see **HEATHEN**).

**Hoyle** ● n. (in phr. **according to Hoyle**) according to plan or the rules.
– ORIGIN C20: from the name of Edmond *Hoyle* (1672–1769), Engl. writer on card games.

**h.p.** (also **HP**) ● abbrev. **1** high pressure. **2** Brit. hire purchase. **3** horsepower.

**HPV** ● abbrev. human papilloma virus.

**HQ** ● abbrev. headquarters.

**HR** ● abbrev. (in the US) House of Representatives.

**hr** ● abbrev. hour.

**HRH** ● abbrev. Brit. Her or His Royal Highness (as a title).

**hrs** ● abbrev. hours.

**HRT** ● abbrev. hormone replacement therapy.

**Hs** ● symb. the chemical element hassium.

**HSH** ● abbrev. Her or His Serene Highness (as a title).

**Hsiang** ● n. variant of **XIANG**.

**HST** ● abbrev. (in the UK) high-speed train.

**HT** ● abbrev. (electrical) high tension.

**HTML** ● n. Computing Hypertext Mark-up Language.

**HTTP** ● abbrev. Computing Hypertext Transport (or Transfer) Protocol.

**huarache** /waˈrɑːtʃi/ ● n. a leather-thonged sandal, originally worn by Mexican Indians.
– ORIGIN C19: Mex. Sp.

**hub** ● n. **1** the central part of a wheel, rotating on or with the axle, and from which the spokes radiate. **2** the centre of an activity, region, or network.
– ORIGIN C16 (denoting a shelf at the side of a fireplace used for heating pans): of unknown origin (cf. **HOB**[1]).

**hubba hubba** ● exclam. N. Amer. informal an expression of approval, excitement, or enthusiasm.
– ORIGIN 1940s: of unknown origin.

**hubble-bubble** ● n. a hookah.
– ORIGIN C17: imitative repetition of **BUBBLE**.

**Hubble's law** ● n. Astronomy a law stating that the speed of recession of a galaxy (due to the expansion of the universe) is related to its distance by a constant factor (**Hubble's constant**).
– ORIGIN 1930s: named after the Amer. astronomer Edwin P. *Hubble*.

**hubbub** ● n. a chaotic din caused by a crowd. ➤a busy, noisy situation.
– ORIGIN C16: perh. of Ir. origin; cf. the Ir. exclamations *ababú, abú*, used in battle cries.

**hubby** ● n. (pl. **-ies**) informal a husband.

**hubcap** ● n. a cover for the hub of a motor vehicle's wheel.

**hubris** /ˈhjuːbrɪs/ ● n. excessive pride or self-confidence. ➤(in Greek tragedy) excessive pride or presumption towards the gods, leading to nemesis.
– DERIVATIVES **hubristic** adj.
– ORIGIN from Gk.

**huckaback** ● n. a strong linen or cotton fabric with a rough surface, used for towelling and glass cloths.
– ORIGIN C17: of unknown origin.

**huckleberry** ● n. **1** a soft edible blue-black fruit resembling a currant. **2** the low-growing North American plant of the heath family which bears this fruit. [Genus *Gaylussacia*.]
– ORIGIN C16: prob. orig. a dial. name for the bilberry, from dial. *huckle* 'hip, haunch' (because of the plant's jointed stems).

**huckster** ● n. **1** a person who sells small items, either door-to-door or from a stall. **2** N. Amer. a person who uses aggressive selling techniques. ● v. chiefly N. Amer. **1** promote or sell aggressively. **2** bargain.
– DERIVATIVES **hucksterism** n.
– ORIGIN ME: prob. of Low Ger. origin.

**huddle** ● v. crowd together. ➤curl one's body into a small space. ● n. a number of people or things crowded together. ➤a brief gathering of players during a game to receive instructions, especially in American football.
– ORIGIN C16 (in the sense 'conceal'): perh. of Low Ger. origin.

**Hudson's Bay blanket** ● n. Canadian a durable woollen blanket, typically with a coloured border.
– ORIGIN C19: orig. sold by the *Hudson's Bay* Company.

**hue** ● n. **1** a colour or shade. ➤technical the attribute of a colour, dependent on its dominant wavelength, by virtue of which it is discernible as red, green, etc. **2** aspect.
– DERIVATIVES **-hued** adj. **hueless** adj.
– ORIGIN OE *hīw, hēow*, of Gmc origin.

**hue and cry** ● n. **1** a loud clamour or public outcry. **2** historical a loud cry calling for the pursuit and capture of a criminal.
– ORIGIN ME: from the Anglo-Norman Fr. legal phr. *hu e cri*, lit. 'outcry and cry'.

**huff** ● v. **1** (often **huff and puff**) blow out noisily. ➤show (one's annoyance) in an obvious way. **2** (in draughts) remove (an opponent's piece that could have made a capture) from the board as a forfeit. [from the former practice of blowing on the piece.] ● n. a fit of petty annoyance.
– DERIVATIVES **huffish** adj.
– ORIGIN C16: imitative of the sound of blowing.

**huffy** ● adj. (**-ier, -iest**) easily offended.
– DERIVATIVES **huffily** adv. **huffiness** n.

**hug** ● v. (**hugged, hugging**) **1** squeeze or hold tightly in one's arms. **2** keep close to: *a few craft hugged the shore.* ● n. an act of hugging. ➤a squeezing grip in wrestling.
– DERIVATIVES **huggable** adj.
– ORIGIN C16: prob. of Scand. origin.

**huge** ● adj. (**huger, hugest**) extremely large.
– DERIVATIVES **hugeness** n.
– ORIGIN ME: shortening of OFr. *ahuge*, of unknown origin.

**hugely** ● adv. very much; to a very great extent.

**hugger-mugger** ● adj. **1** confused. **2** secret. ● n. **1** confusion. **2** secrecy.
– ORIGIN C16: prob. rel. to **HUDDLE** and to dial. *mucker* 'hoard money, conceal'.

**Hughie** ● n. Austral./NZ informal an imaginary being held to be responsible for controlling the weather and waves.
– ORIGIN C20: dimin. of the given name *Hugh*.

**Huguenot** /ˈhjuːgənəʊ, -nɒt/ ● n. a French Protestant of the 16th–17th centuries.
– ORIGIN Fr., alt. (by assoc. with the name of a Geneva burgomaster, Besançon *Hugues*) of *eiguenot*, from Du. *eedgenot*, from Swiss Ger. *Eidgenoss* 'confederate'.

**huh** ● exclam. used to express scorn or surprise, or in questions to invite agreement.

**hula** /ˈhuːlə/ (also **hula-hula**) ● n. a dance performed by Hawaiian women, characterized by six basic steps, undulating hips, and symbolic gestures.
– ORIGIN C19: Hawaiian.

**hula hoop** (also US trademark **Hula-Hoop**) ● n. a large hoop spun round the body by gyrating the hips.

**hula skirt** ● n. a long grass skirt as worn by a hula dancer.

**hulk** ● n. **1** an old ship stripped of fittings and permanently moored, especially for use as storage or (formerly) as a prison. **2** a large or clumsy boat, object, or person.
– ORIGIN OE *hulc* 'fast ship'; prob. of Mediterranean origin and rel. to Gk *holkas* 'cargo ship'.

**hulking** ● adj. informal very large or clumsy.

**hull**[1] ● n. the main body of a ship or other vessel, including the bottom, sides, and deck but not the superstructure, engines, and other fittings. ● v. hit and pierce the hull of.
– DERIVATIVES **-hulled** adj.
– ORIGIN ME: perh. the same word as **HULL**[2], or rel. to **HOLD**[2].

**hull**[2] ● n. **1** the outer covering of a fruit or seed. **2** the green calyx of a strawberry or raspberry. ● v. [usu. as adj. **hulled**] remove the hulls from.
– ORIGIN OE *hulu*, of Gmc origin; rel. to **HEEL**[3].

**hullabaloo** ● n. informal a commotion or uproar.
– ORIGIN C18: reduplication of *hallo, hullo*, etc.

**hullo** ● exclam. variant spelling of **HELLO**.

**hum**[1] ● v. (**hummed, humming**) **1** make a low, steady continuous sound like that of a bee. ➤sing with closed lips. **2** informal be in a state of great activity. **3** Brit. informal smell unpleasant. ● n. a low, steady continuous sound. ➤an unwanted low-frequency noise in an amplifier.
– PHRASES **hum and haw** (or **ha**) Brit. be indecisive.
– DERIVATIVES **hummable** adj. **hummer** n.
– ORIGIN ME: imitative.

**hum**[2] ● exclam. used to express hesitation or dissent.
– ORIGIN C16: imitative; rel. to **HUM**[1].

**human** ● adj. of, relating to, or characteristic of humankind. ➤of or characteristic of people as opposed to God or animals or machines: *human error.* ➤showing the better qualities of humankind, such as sensitivity. ● n. a human being.
– DERIVATIVES **humanness** n.
– ORIGIN ME *humaine*, from OFr. *humain(e)*, from L. *humanus*, from *homo* 'man, human being'.

**human being** ● n. a man, woman, or child of the species *Homo sapiens*.

**human chain** ● n. a line of people formed for passing things quickly from one site to another.

**humane** /hjʊˈmeɪn/ ● adj. **1** compassionate or benevolent. ➤inflicting the minimum of pain. **2** formal (of a branch of learning) intended to have a civilizing effect.
– DERIVATIVES **humanely** adv. **humaneness** n.
– ORIGIN ME: the earlier form of **HUMAN**, restricted to the senses above in the 18th cent.

**human geography** ● n. the branch of geography concerned with how human activity affects or is influenced by the earth's surface.

**human interest** ● n. the aspect of a news story concerned with the experiences or emotions of individuals.

**humanism** ● n. **1** a rationalistic outlook or system of thought attaching prime importance to human rather than divine or supernatural matters. **2** a Renaissance cultural movement which turned away from medieval scholasticism and revived interest in ancient Greek and Roman thought.
– DERIVATIVES **humanist** n. & adj. **humanistic** adj. **humanistically** adv.

**humanitarian** /hjʊˌmanɪˈtɛːrɪən/ ● adj. concerned with or seeking to promote human welfare. ● n. a humanitarian person.
– DERIVATIVES **humanitarianism** n.

**humanity** ● n. (pl. **-ies**) **1** the human race. ➤human nature. **2** compassion or benevolence. **3** (**humanities**) learning or literature concerned with human culture, especially literature, history, art, music, and philosophy.

**humanize** (also **-ise**) ● **v. 1** make more humane. **2** give a human character to.
– DERIVATIVES **humanization** n.

**humankind** ● **n.** human beings considered collectively.

**humanly** ● **adv.** from a human point of view; in a human manner. ➤ within human ability.

**human nature** ● **n.** the general psychological characteristics, feelings, and behavioural traits of humankind.

**humanoid** /ˈhjuːmənɔɪd/ ● **adj.** having an appearance or character resembling that of a human. ● **n.** (especially in science fiction) a humanoid being.

**human right** ● **n.** (usu. **human rights**) a right which is believed to belong justifiably to every person.

**humble** ● **adj.** (**-er**, **-est**) **1** having or showing a modest or low estimate of one's own importance. **2** of low rank. **3** of modest pretensions or dimensions. ● **v.** lower in dignity or importance. ➤ decisively defeat (a sporting opponent previously thought to be superior).
– PHRASES **eat humble pie** make a humble apology and accept humiliation. [*humble pie* is from a pun based on **UMBLES** 'offal', considered inferior food.]
– DERIVATIVES **humbleness** n. **humbly** adv.
– ORIGIN ME: from OFr., from L. *humilis* 'low, lowly', from *humus* 'ground'.

**humble-bee** ● **n.** another term for **BUMBLEBEE**.
– ORIGIN ME: prob. from Mid. Low Ger. *hummelbē*, from *hummel* 'to buzz' + *bē* 'bee'.

**humbug** ● **n. 1** deceptive or false talk or behaviour. ➤ a hypocrite. **2** Brit. a boiled peppermint sweet. ● **v.** (**humbugged**, **humbugging**) deceive; trick.
– DERIVATIVES **humbuggery** n.
– ORIGIN C18: of unknown origin.

**humdinger** /hʌmˈdɪŋə/ ● **n.** informal a remarkable or outstanding person or thing of its kind.
– ORIGIN C20 (orig. US): of unknown origin.

**humdrum** ● **adj.** dull or monotonous. ● **n.** monotonous routine.
– ORIGIN C16: prob. a reduplication of **HUM**[1].

**humectant** /hjʊˈmɛkt(ə)nt/ ● **adj.** retaining or preserving moisture. ● **n.** a substance, especially a skin lotion or a food additive, used to reduce the loss of moisture.
– ORIGIN C19: from L. *humectant-*, *humectare* 'moisten'.

**humeral** /ˈhjuːm(ə)r(ə)l/ ● **adj. 1** of or relating to the humerus. **2** (in Catholic use) denoting a plain vestment worn around the shoulders when administering the sacrament.

**humerus** /ˈhjuːm(ə)rəs/ ● **n.** (pl. **humeri** /-rʌɪ/) **1** Anatomy the bone of the upper arm or forelimb, between the shoulder and the elbow. **2** Entomology the structure forming the front basal corner of an insect's wing or wing case.
– ORIGIN ME: from L., 'shoulder'.

**humic** /ˈhjuːmɪk/ ● **adj.** relating to or consisting of humus.

**humid** /ˈhjuːmɪd/ ● **adj.** marked by a relatively high level of water vapour in the atmosphere.
– DERIVATIVES **humidly** adv.
– ORIGIN ME: from Fr. *humide* or L. *humidus*, from *humere* 'be moist'.

**humidify** ● **v.** (**-ies**, **-ied**) [often as adj. **humidified**] increase the level of moisture in (air).
– DERIVATIVES **humidification** n. **humidifier** n.

**humidity** ● **n.** (pl. **-ies**) the state or quality of being humid. ➤ a quantity representing the amount of water vapour in the atmosphere or a gas.

**humidor** /ˈhjuːmɪdɔː/ ● **n.** an airtight container for keeping cigars or tobacco moist.
– ORIGIN C20: from **HUMID**, on the pattern of *cuspidor*.

**humify** /ˈhjuːmɪfʌɪ/ ● **v.** (**-ies**, **-ied**) convert (plant remains) into humus.
– DERIVATIVES **humification** n.

**humiliate** ● **v.** injure the dignity and self-respect of.
– DERIVATIVES **humiliating** adj. **humiliatingly** adv. **humiliation** n. **humiliator** n.
– ORIGIN C16 (earlier (ME) as *humiliation*): from late L. *humiliat-*, *humiliare* 'make humble' from *humilis* (see **HUMBLE**).

**humility** ● **n.** a humble view of one's own importance.
– ORIGIN ME: from OFr. *humilite*, from L. *humilitas*, from *humilis* (see **HUMBLE**).

**Humint** /ˈh(j)uːmɪnt/ ● **n.** covert intelligence-gathering.
– ORIGIN C20: from *human intelligence*.

**hummingbird** ● **n.** a small long-billed nectar-feeding American bird, typically with colourful iridescent plumage, that is able to hover by beating its wings extremely fast. [Family Trochilidae: many species.]

**hummingbird hawkmoth** ● **n.** a day-flying hawkmoth that hovers in front of flowers to feed on nectar. [*Macroglossum stellatarum*.]

**hummock** ● **n.** a hillock or knoll. ➤ a hump or ridge in an ice field. ➤ N. Amer. a piece of forested ground rising above a marsh.
– DERIVATIVES **hummocky** adj.
– ORIGIN C16: of unknown origin.

**hummus** /ˈhʊməs/ (also **hoummos** or **humous**) ● **n.** a thick dip of Middle Eastern origin, made from ground chickpeas and sesame seeds, olive oil, lemon, and garlic.
– ORIGIN from Arab. *ḥummuṣ*.

**humongous** /hjuːˈmʌŋgəs/ (also **humungous**) ● **adj.** informal enormous.
– ORIGIN 1970s (orig. US): perh. based on **HUGE** and **MONSTROUS**, influenced by the stress pattern of *stupendous*.

**humor** ● **n.** US spelling of **HUMOUR**.

**humoral** /ˈhjuːm(ə)r(ə)l/ ● **adj. 1** Medicine of or relating to the body fluids, in particular (of immunity) involving the action of circulating antibodies. Often contrasted with **CELL-MEDIATED**. **2** historical of or relating to the four bodily humours.
– ORIGIN ME: from OFr., or from med. L. *humoralis*, from L. *humor* (see **HUMOUR**).

**humoresque** /ˌhjuːməˈrɛsk/ ● **n.** a short, lively piece of music.
– ORIGIN C19: from Ger. *Humoreske*, from *Humor* 'humour'.

**humorist** ● **n.** a humorous writer, performer, or artist.

**humorous** ● **adj.** causing amusement. ➤ having or showing a sense of humour.
– DERIVATIVES **humorously** adv. **humorousness** n.

**humour** (US **humor**) ● **n. 1** the quality of being amusing or comic, especially as expressed in literature or speech. ➤ the ability to appreciate or express humour. **2** a state of mind: *her good humour vanished*. ➤ archaic an inclination or whim. **3** (also **cardinal humour**) historical each of four fluids of the body (blood, phlegm, yellow bile or choler, and black bile or melancholy), formerly held to determine a person's physical and mental qualities. ● **v.** comply with the wishes or whims of.
– PHRASES **out of humour** in a bad mood.
– DERIVATIVES **humourless** adj. **humourlessly** adv. **humourlessness** n.
– ORIGIN ME (orig. in the sense 'bodily fluid', surviving in *aqueous humour* and *vitreous humour*): via OFr. from L. *humor* 'moisture', from *humere* (see **HUMID**).

**hump** ● **n. 1** a rounded protuberance found on the back of a camel or other animal or as an abnormality on a person's back. **2** a rounded raised mass of earth or land. ● **v. 1** informal lift or carry (a heavy object) with difficulty. **2** make hump-shaped. **3** vulgar slang have sexual intercourse with.
– PHRASES **get** (or **have**) **the hump** Brit. informal become or be annoyed or sulky. **over the hump** informal past the most difficult part of something.
– DERIVATIVES **humped** adj. **humpless** adj. **humpy** adj. (**-ier**, **-iest**).
– ORIGIN C18: prob. rel. to Low Ger. *humpe* 'hump'.

**humpback** ● **n.** another term for **HUNCHBACK**.
– DERIVATIVES **humpbacked** adj.

**humpback bridge** ● **n.** Brit. a small road bridge with a steep ascent and descent.

**humpback whale** ● **n.** a baleen whale which has a hump (instead of a dorsal fin) and long white flippers. [*Megaptera novaeangliae*.]

**humph** ● **exclam.** used to express doubt or dissatisfaction.

**humpty-dumpty** ● **n.** (pl. **-ies**) informal **1** a short fat person. **2** a person or thing that once overthrown cannot be restored.
– ORIGIN C18: from the egg-like nursery-rhyme character *Humpty-Dumpty*, who fell off a wall and could not be put together again.

**humungous** ● **adj.** variant spelling of **HUMONGOUS**.

**humus** /ˈhjuːməs/ ● **n.** the organic component of soil, formed by the decomposition of leaves and other plant material by soil micro-organisms.
– ORIGIN C18: from L., 'soil'.

**Humvee** /ˈhʌmviː/ ● **n.** trademark, chiefly N. Amer. a modern military jeep.
– ORIGIN C20: alt. from the initials of *high-mobility multi-purpose vehicle*.

**Hun** ● **n. 1** a member of a warlike Asiatic nomadic people who invaded and ravaged Europe in the 4th–5th centuries. **2** informal, derogatory a German (especially in military contexts during the First and Second World Wars).
– DERIVATIVES **Hunnish** adj.
– ORIGIN OE *Hūne, Hūnas* (pl.), from late L. *Hunni*, from Gk *Hounnoi*, of Middle Iranian origin.

**hunch** ● **v.** raise (one's shoulders) and bend the top of one's body forward. ➤sit or stand in such a position. ● **n. 1** a feeling or guess based on intuition. **2** chiefly dialect a thick piece.
– ORIGIN C15 (orig. in the sense 'push, shove' (n. and v.)): of unknown origin.

**hunchback** ● **n.** a back deformed by a sharp forward angle, forming a hump, typically caused by collapse of a vertebra. ➤often offensive a person with such a deformity.
– DERIVATIVES **hunchbacked** adj.

**hundred** ● **cardinal number** (pl. **hundreds** or (with numeral or quantifying word) **hundred**) **1** (**a/one hundred**) the number equivalent to the product of ten and ten; ten more than ninety; 100. (Roman numeral: **c** or **C**.) **2** (**hundreds**) informal an unspecified large number. **3** used to express whole hours in the twenty-four-hour system. ● **n.** Brit. historical a subdivision of a county or shire, having its own court.
– PHRASES **a** (or **one**) **hundred per cent** entirely. ➤[usu. with neg.] informal completely fit and healthy. ➤informal maximum effort and commitment.
– DERIVATIVES **hundredfold** adj. & adv. **hundredth** ordinal number.
– ORIGIN OE, from *hund* 'hundred' + a second element meaning 'number', of Gmc origin; the noun was perh. orig. equivalent to a hundred hides of land (see **HIDE**[3]).

**hundreds and thousands** ● **pl. n.** Brit. tiny sugar beads of varying colours used for decorating cakes and desserts.

**hundredweight** (abbrev.: **cwt.**) ● **n.** (pl. same or **-weights**) **1** (also **long hundredweight**) Brit. a unit of weight equal to 112 lb avoirdupois (about 50.8 kg). **2** (also **short hundredweight**) US a unit of weight equal to 100 lb (about 45.4 kg). **3** (also **metric hundredweight**) a unit of weight equal to 50 kg.

**hung** past and past participle of **HANG**. ● **adj. 1** (of an elected body) having no political party with an overall majority. ➤(of a jury) unable to agree on a verdict. **2** (**hung up**) informal emotionally confused or disturbed.

**Hungarian** /hʌŋˈɡɛːrɪən/ ● **n. 1** a native or national of Hungary, or a person of Hungarian descent. **2** the official Finno-Ugric language of Hungary. ● **adj.** of or relating to Hungary, its people, or their language.

**hunger** ● **n. 1** a feeling of discomfort or weakness caused by lack of food, coupled with the desire to eat. **2** a strong desire. ● **v. 1** (**hunger after/for**) have a strong desire for. **2** archaic feel or suffer hunger.
– ORIGIN OE *hungor* (n.), *hyngran* (v.), of Gmc origin.

**hunger march** ● **n.** a protest march against unemployment or poverty, especially one undertaken by unemployed workers in Britain during the 1920s and 1930s.
– DERIVATIVES **hunger marcher** n.

**hunger strike** ● **n.** a prolonged refusal to eat, carried out as a protest by a prisoner.
– DERIVATIVES **hunger striker** n.

**hung-over** ● **adj.** suffering from a hangover.

**hungry** ● **adj.** (**-ier, -iest**) **1** feeling, showing, or causing hunger. **2** (often **hungry for**) having a strong desire.
– DERIVATIVES **hungrily** adv. **hungriness** n.
– ORIGIN OE *hungrig*, of W. Gmc origin; rel. to **HUNGER**.

**hunk** ● **n. 1** a large piece cut or broken from something larger. **2** informal a large, strong, sexually attractive man.
– DERIVATIVES **hunky** adj. (**-ier, -iest**).
– ORIGIN C19: prob. of Du. or Low Ger. origin.

**hunker** ● **v. 1** squat or crouch down low. **2** (**hunker down**) apply oneself seriously to a task.
– ORIGIN C18: prob. rel. to Ger. *hocken*.

**hunkers** ● **pl. n.** informal haunches.
– ORIGIN C18 (orig. Scots): from **HUNKER**.

**hunky-dory** ● **adj.** informal excellent.
– ORIGIN C19 (orig. US): *hunky* from Du. *honk* 'home' (in games); the origin of *dory* is unknown.

**hunt** ● **v. 1** pursue and kill (a wild animal) for sport or food. ➤(of an animal) chase and kill (its prey). ➤(of the police) pursue (a criminal). ➤(**hunt someone down**) pursue and capture someone. ➤[as adj. **hunted**] appearing alarmed or harassed as if being hunted. **2** search diligently for. **3** (of a device or system) oscillate about a desired speed, position, or state. **4** (**hunt down/up**) (in change-ringing) move the place of a bell in a simple progression. ● **n.** an act or the process of hunting. ➤an association of people who meet regularly to hunt, especially with hounds. ➤an area where hunting takes place.
– ORIGIN OE *huntian*, of Gmc origin.

**hunt-and-peck** ● **adj.** denoting or using an inexpert form of typing with only one or two fingers.

**huntaway** ● **n.** NZ a dog trained to drive sheep forward.

**hunter** ● **n. 1** a person or animal that hunts. ➤a horse of a breed developed for stamina in fox-hunting. **2** a watch with a hinged cover protecting the glass.
– DERIVATIVES **huntress** n.

**hunter-gatherer** ● **n.** a member of a nomadic people who live chiefly by hunting and fishing, and harvesting wild food.

**hunter-killer** ● **adj.** (of a naval vessel, especially a submarine) equipped to locate and destroy enemy vessels.

**hunter's moon** ● **n.** the first full moon after a harvest moon.

**hunting** ● **n. 1** the activity of hunting wild animals or game, especially for food or sport. **2** (also **plain hunting**) Bell-ringing a simple system of changes in which bells move through the order in a regular progression.

**hunting crop** (also **hunting whip**) ● **n.** a short rigid riding whip with a handle at right angles to the stock and a long leather thong, used chiefly in hunting.

**hunting dog** (also **Cape hunting dog**) ● **n.** an African wild dog that has a dark coat with pale markings and a white-tipped tail, living and hunting in packs. [*Lycaon pictus*.]

**hunting ground** ● **n.** a place likely to be a fruitful source of something desired or sought.

**hunting horn** ● **n.** a straight horn blown to give signals during hunting.

**Huntington's disease** ● **n.** a hereditary disease marked by degeneration of brain cells, causing chorea and progressive dementia.
– ORIGIN C19: named after the Amer. neurologist George *Huntington*.

**hunt saboteur** ● **n.** a person who attempts to disrupt a hunt.

**huntsman** ● **n.** (pl. **-men**) a person who hunts. ➤a hunt official in charge of hounds.

**Huon pine** /ˈhjuːɒn/ ● **n.** a tall Tasmanian conifer with yew-like berries and fragrant red wood. [*Dacrydium franklinii*.]
– ORIGIN C19: from *Huon*, the name of a river in the south of Tasmania.

**hurdle** ● **n. 1** one of a series of upright frames which athletes in a race must jump over. ➤(**hurdles**) a hurdle race. **2** an obstacle or difficulty. **3** a portable rectangular frame

strengthened with withies or wooden bars, used as a temporary fence. ➤a horse race over a series of such frames. ➤Brit. historical a frame on which traitors were dragged to execution. ● v. **1** [often as noun **hurdling**] run in a hurdle race. ➤jump over (a hurdle or other obstacle) while running. **2** enclose or fence off with hurdles.
– DERIVATIVES **hurdler** n.
– ORIGIN OE *hyrdel* 'temporary fence', of Gmc origin.

**hurdy-gurdy** /ˈhəːdɪˌɡəːdi/ ● n. (pl. **-ies**) a musical instrument with a droning sound played by turning a handle, which is typically attached to a rosined wheel sounding a series of drone strings, with keys worked by the left hand. ➤informal a barrel organ.
– ORIGIN C18: prob. imitative of the instrument's sound.

**hurl** ● v. throw or impel with great force. ➤utter (abuse) vehemently. ● n. Scottish informal a ride in a vehicle.
– ORIGIN ME: prob. imitative, but corresp. in form and partly in sense with Low Ger. *hurreln*.

**hurler** ● n. **1** N. Amer. informal a baseball pitcher. **2** a player of hurling.

**Hurler's syndrome** /ˈhəːləz/ ● n. Medicine a defect in metabolism arising from congenital absence of an enzyme, resulting in mental retardation, a protruding abdomen, and an abnormally large head.
– ORIGIN 1930s: named after the Austrian paediatrician Gertrud *Hurler*.

**hurley** ● n. **1** a stick used in the game of hurling. **2** another term for **HURLING**.
– ORIGIN C19: from **HURL**.

**hurling** ● n. an Irish game resembling hockey, played with a shorter stick with a broader oval blade.

**hurly-burly** ● n. busy, boisterous activity.
– ORIGIN ME: reduplication based on **HURL**.

**Huron** /ˈhjʊərɒn/ ● n. (pl. same or **Hurons**) a member of a confederation of native North American peoples formerly living in the region east of Lake Huron.
– ORIGIN Fr., lit. 'having hair standing in bristles on the head', from OFr. *hure* 'head of a wild boar'.

**hurrah** (also **hooray**, **hurray**) ● exclam. used to express joy or approval.
– ORIGIN C17: alt. of **HUZZA**; perh. orig. a sailors' cry when hauling.

**Hurrian** /ˈhʌrɪən/ ● n. **1** a member of an ancient people who settled in Syria and northern Mesopotamia during the 3rd–2nd millennia BC. **2** the language of the Hurrians, written in cuneiform. ● adj. of or relating to this people or their language.
– ORIGIN Hittite and Assyrian *Ḫarri*, *Ḫurri*.

**hurricane** /ˈhʌrɪk(ə)n, -keɪn/ ● n. a storm with a violent wind, in particular a tropical cyclone in the Caribbean.
– ORIGIN C16: from Sp. *huracán*, prob. from Taino *hurakán* 'god of the storm'.

**hurricane deck** ● n. a covered deck at or near the top of a ship's superstructure.

**hurricane lamp** ● n. an oil lamp with a glass chimney, designed to protect the flame even in high winds.

**hurricane tape** ● n. US strong adhesive tape used on windows to keep the glass in place in strong winds.

**hurry** ● v. (**-ies**, **-ied**) move or act quickly or more quickly. ➤do or finish (something) quickly. ● n. great haste. ➤[with neg. and in questions] a need for haste; urgency.
– PHRASES **in a hurry 1** rushed; in a rushed manner. **2** [usu. with neg.] informal easily; readily.
– DERIVATIVES **hurried** adj. **hurriedly** adv. **hurriedness** n.
– ORIGIN C16: imitative.

**hurry-up** ● adj. US informal showing or involving haste or urgency: *a hurry-up visit*.

**hurst** ● n. archaic (except in place names) **1** a hillock or wooded rise. **2** a sandbank.
– ORIGIN OE *hyrst*, of Gmc origin.

**hurt** ● v. (past and past part. **hurt**) **1** cause physical pain or injury to. ➤(of a part of the body) suffer pain. **2** cause mental pain or distress to. ➤feel mental pain or distress: *he was hurting badly*. **3** (**hurt for**) N. Amer. informal have a pressing need for. ● n. injury or pain; harm.
– ORIGIN ME (orig. in the senses 'to strike' and 'a blow'): from OFr. *hurter* (v.), *hurt* (n.), perh. ult. of Gmc origin.

**hurtful** ● adj. causing mental pain or distress.
– DERIVATIVES **hurtfully** adv. **hurtfulness** n.

**hurtle** ● v. move or cause to move at great speed, typically in a wildly uncontrolled manner.
– ORIGIN ME (in the sense 'collide with'): frequentative of **HURT**.

**husband** ● n. a married man considered in relation to his wife. ● v. use (resources) economically.
– DERIVATIVES **husbander** n. (rare). **husbandhood** n. **husbandless** adj. **husbandly** adj.
– ORIGIN OE (in the senses 'male head of a household' and 'steward'), from ON *húsbóndi* 'master of a house', from *hús* 'house' + *bóndi* 'occupier and tiller of the soil'.

**husbandman** ● n. (pl. **-men**) archaic a farmer.
– ORIGIN ME: from **HUSBAND** in the obs. sense 'farmer' + **MAN**.

**husbandry** ● n. **1** the care, cultivation, and breeding of crops and animals. **2** management and conservation of resources.
– ORIGIN ME: from **HUSBAND** in the obs. sense 'farmer' + **-RY**.

**hush** ● v. **1** make or become quiet. **2** (**hush something up**) suppress public mention of something. ● n. a silence.
– ORIGIN C16: back-form. from obs. *husht* 'silent', from an interjection *husht* 'quiet!'

**hushaby** (also **hushabye**) ● exclam. archaic used to lull a child.
– ORIGIN C18: from **HUSH** + *-by* as in **BYE-BYE**.

**hush-hush** ● adj. informal highly secret or confidential.

**hush money** ● n. informal money paid to someone to prevent them from disclosing embarrassing or discreditable information.

**hush puppy** ● n. US maize bread which has been quickly deep-fried.

**husk**[1] ● n. **1** the dry outer covering of some fruits or seeds. **2** a dry or rough discarded outer layer. ● v. remove the husk from.
– ORIGIN ME: prob. from Low Ger. *hūske* 'sheath', lit. 'little house'.

**husk**[2] ● n. **1** bronchitis in cattle, sheep, or pigs caused by parasitic infestation, typically marked by a husky cough. **2** huskiness.
– ORIGIN C18: partly from **HUSKY**[1], partly from the earlier verb *husk* 'cough'.

**husky**[1] ● adj. (**-ier**, **-iest**) **1** (of a voice) sounding low-pitched and slightly hoarse. **2** strong; hefty. **3** like or consisting of husks.
– DERIVATIVES **huskily** adv. **huskiness** n.

**husky**[2] ● n. (pl. **-ies**) a powerful dog of a breed with a thick double coat, used in the Arctic for pulling sledges.
– ORIGIN C19 (orig. denoting the Eskimo lang. or an Eskimo): abbrev. of obs. *Ehuskemay* or Newfoundland dial. *Huskemaw* 'Eskimo'.

**huss** /hʌs/ ● n. Brit. a dogfish, especially the nurse hound. [Genus *Scyliorhinus*.]
– ORIGIN ME *husk*, of unknown origin.

**hussar** /hʊˈzɑː/ ● n. historical (except in titles) **1** a soldier in a light cavalry regiment which adopted a dress uniform modelled on that of the Hungarian hussars. **2** a Hungarian light horseman of the 15th century.
– ORIGIN from Hungarian *huszár*, from Old Serbian *husar*, from Ital. *corsaro* (see **CORSAIR**).

**Hussite** /ˈhʌsʌɪt/ ● n. a member or follower of the religious movement begun by John Huss, a 15th-century Bohemian reformer and supporter of John Wyclif. ● adj. of or relating to the Hussites.
– DERIVATIVES **Hussitism** n.

**hussy** ● n. (pl. **-ies**) dated or humorous a promiscuous or immoral girl or woman.
– ORIGIN ME: contr. of **HOUSEWIFE**.

**hustings** ● n. [treated as pl. or sing.] a meeting at which candidates in an election address potential voters.
– ORIGIN OE *husting* 'deliberative assembly, council', from ON *hústhing* 'household assembly held by a leader', from *hús* 'house' + *thing* 'assembly, parliament'.

**hustle** ● v. **1** push roughly; jostle. ➤force to move hurriedly or unceremoniously: *I was hustled away*. **2** informal, chiefly N. Amer. obtain illicitly or by forceful action or per-

suasion. ➤(**hustle someone into**) coerce or pressure someone into doing something. ➤sell aggressively. **3** N. Amer. informal engage in prostitution. ● **n. 1** busy movement and activity. **2** N. Amer. informal a fraud or swindle.
– ORIGIN C17: from MDu. *hutselen*.

**hustler** ● **n.** informal, chiefly N. Amer. **1** a person adept at aggressive selling or illicit dealing. **2** a prostitute.

**hut** ● **n.** a small single-storey building of simple or crude construction. ● **v.** (**hutted**, **hutting**) provide with huts.
– ORIGIN C16 (in the sense 'wooden shelter for troops'): from Fr. *hutte*, from Mid. High Ger. *hütte*.

**hutch** ● **n. 1** a box or cage for keeping rabbits or other small domesticated animals. **2** N. Amer. a storage chest. ➤a cupboard or dresser.
– ORIGIN ME (in the sense 'storage chest'): from OFr. *huche*, from med. L. *hutica*, of unknown origin.

**hutia** /hʌ'tiːə/ ● **n.** a Caribbean rodent resembling a cavy, with short legs and tail. [Family Capromyidae: several species.]
– ORIGIN C16: from Sp., from Taino *huti*, *cuti*.

**hutment** ● **n.** Military an encampment of huts.

**Hutterite** /'hʌtərʌɪt/ ● **n. 1** a member of an Anabaptist Christian sect established in Moravia in the 16th century. **2** a member of a North American community holding similar beliefs. ● **adj.** of or relating to Hutterites.
– ORIGIN from the name of the C16 Moravian Anabaptist Jacob *Hutter*.

**Hutu** /'huːtuː/ ● **n.** (pl. same or **Hutus** or **Bahutu** /bə'huːtuː/) a member of a Bantu-speaking people forming the majority population in Rwanda and Burundi.
– ORIGIN a local name.

**huzza** /hʊ'zɑː/ (also **huzzah**) ● **exclam.** archaic used to express approval or delight.
– ORIGIN C16: perh. used orig. as a sailor's cry when hauling.

**HWM** ● **abbrev.** high-water mark.

**hwyl** /'huːɪl/ ● **n.** (in Welsh use) a stirring, emotional feeling.
– ORIGIN from Welsh.

**hyacinth** /'hʌɪəsɪnθ/ ● **n. 1** a bulbous plant of the lily family with a spike of bell-shaped fragrant flowers. [Genus *Hyacinthus*: several species. See also WILD HYACINTH.] **2** another term for JACINTH.
– DERIVATIVES **hyacinthine** /-'sɪnθiːn, -θʌɪn/ adj.
– ORIGIN C16 (denoting a gem): from Fr. *hyacinthe*, via L. from Gk *huakinthos*, with ref. to the Gk mythological story of Hyacinthus, a youth loved by Apollo but accidentally killed by him, from whose blood Apollo caused a flower to grow.

**hyaena** ● **n.** variant spelling of HYENA.

**hyalin** /'hʌɪəlɪn/ ● **n.** Physiology a clear substance produced especially by the degeneration of epithelial or connective tissues.
– ORIGIN C19: via L. from Gk *hualinos*, from *hualos* 'glass'.

**hyaline** /'hʌɪəlɪn, -iːn, -ʌɪn/ ● **adj.** Anatomy & Zoology **1** (chiefly of cartilage) glassy and translucent in appearance. **2** relating to or consisting of hyalin.

**hyalite** /'hʌɪəlʌɪt/ ● **n.** a translucent, colourless variety of opal.
– ORIGIN C18: from Gk *hualos* 'glass' + -ITE[1].

**hyaloid** /'hʌɪəlɔɪd/ ● **adj.** Anatomy glassy; transparent.
– ORIGIN C19: from Fr. *hyaloïde*, or via late L. from Gk *hualoeidēs* 'like glass', from *hualos* 'glass'.

**hyaloid membrane** ● **n.** a thin transparent membrane enveloping the vitreous humour of the eye.

**hyaluronic acid** /ˌhʌɪəljʊə'rɒnɪk/ ● **n.** Biochemistry a viscous fluid carbohydrate present in connective tissue, synovial fluid, and the humours of the eye.
– DERIVATIVES **hyaluronate** n.
– ORIGIN 1930s: from a blend of HYALOID and *uronic acid* (an oxidized sugar, from URO-[1] 'urine').

**hybrid** /'hʌɪbrɪd/ ● **n. 1** Biology the offspring of two plants or animals of different species or varieties, such as a mule. **2** a thing made by combining two different elements. ➤a word formed from elements taken from different languages.
– DERIVATIVES **hybridism** n. **hybridity** n.
– ORIGIN C17: from L. *hybrida* 'offspring of a tame sow and wild boar, child of a freeman and slave, etc.'

**hybridize** (also **-ise**) ● **v.** cross-breed to produce hybrids.
– DERIVATIVES **hybridizable** adj. **hybridization** n.

**hybrid vigour** ● **n.** Genetics the tendency of a cross-bred individual to show qualities superior to those of both parents.

**hydantoin** /hʌɪ'dantəʊɪn/ ● **n.** Chemistry a crystalline compound present in sugar beet and used in the manufacture of some anticonvulsant drugs.
– ORIGIN C19: from Gk *hudōr* 'water' + *allantoic* (see ALLANTOIS) + -IN[1].

**hydathode** /'hʌɪdəθəʊd/ ● **n.** Botany a modified pore, especially on a leaf, which exudes drops of water.
– ORIGIN C19: from Gk *hudōr*, *hudat-* 'water' + *hodos* 'way'.

**hydatid** /'hʌɪdətɪd/ ● **n.** Medicine a cyst containing watery fluid, in particular one formed by and containing a tapeworm larva.
– ORIGIN C17: from mod. L. *hydatis*, from Gk *hudatis*, *hudatid-* 'watery vesicle', from *hudōr*, *hudat-* 'water'.

**hydatidiform mole** /ˌhʌɪdə'tɪdɪfɔːm/ ● **n.** Medicine a cluster of fluid-filled sacs formed in the womb by the degeneration of chorionic tissue around an aborting embryo.

**hydr-** ● **comb. form** variant spelling of HYDRO- shortened before a vowel (as in *hydraulic*).

**hydra** ● **n.** a minute freshwater coelenterate with a stalk-like tubular body and a ring of tentacles around the mouth. [Genus *Hydra*.]
– ORIGIN named after the *Hydra* of Gk mythology, a many-headed snake whose heads regrew as they were cut off: so named because, if cut into pieces, each section can grow into a whole animal.

**hydrangea** /hʌɪ'dreɪn(d)ʒə/ ● **n.** a shrub with flowering heads of white, blue, or pink florets, native to Asia and America. [*Hydrangea macrophylla* and related species.]
– ORIGIN mod. L., from Gk *hudro-* 'water' + *angeion* 'vessel' (from the cup shape of its seed capsule).

**hydrant** /'hʌɪdr(ə)nt/ ● **n.** a water pipe with a nozzle to which a fire hose can be attached.
– ORIGIN C19: formed from HYDRO- + -ANT.

**hydrate** ● **n.** /'hʌɪdreɪt/ Chemistry a compound in which water molecules are chemically bound to another compound or an element. ● **v.** /hʌɪ'dreɪt/ cause to absorb or combine with water.
– DERIVATIVES **hydratable** adj. **hydration** n. **hydrator** n.
– ORIGIN C19: coined in Fr. from Gk *hudōr* 'water'.

**hydraulic** /hʌɪ'drɔːlɪk, hʌɪ'drɒlɪk/ ● **adj. 1** denoting or relating to a liquid moving in a confined space under pressure. **2** of or relating to the science of hydraulics. **3** (of cement) hardening under water.
– DERIVATIVES **hydraulically** adv.
– ORIGIN C17: via L. from Gk *hudraulikos*, from *hudro-* 'water' + *aulos* 'pipe'.

**hydraulic ram** ● **n.** an automatic pump in which a large volume of water flows through a valve which it periodically forces shut, the sudden pressure change being used to raise a smaller volume of water to a higher level.

**hydraulics** ● **pl. n.** [usu. treated as sing.] the branch of science and technology concerned with the conveyance of liquids through pipes and channels.

**hydrazine** /'hʌɪdrəziːn/ ● **n.** Chemistry a volatile alkaline liquid with powerful reducing properties, used in some rocket fuels. [$N_2H_4$.]
– ORIGIN C19: from HYDROGEN + AZO- + -INE[4].

**hydria** /'hʌɪdrɪə/ ● **n.** (pl. **hydriae** or **hydriai**) Archaeology an ancient Greek pitcher with three handles.
– ORIGIN via L. from Gk *hudria*.

**hydric** /'hʌɪdrɪk/ ● **adj.** Ecology containing plenty of moisture; very wet. Compare with MESIC[1] and XERIC.
– ORIGIN C20: from HYDRO- + -IC.

**hydride** /'hʌɪdrʌɪd/ ● **n.** Chemistry a binary compound of hydrogen with a metal.

**hydriodic acid** /ˌhʌɪdrɪ'ɒdɪk, -ʌɪ'ɒdɪk/ ● **n.** Chemistry a strongly acidic solution of the gas hydrogen iodide. [HI.]

**hydro** ● **n.** (pl. **-os**) **1** Brit. a hotel or clinic originally providing hydropathic treatment. **2** a hydroelectric power plant. ➤ hydroelectricity. ➤ Canadian electricity.

**hydro-** (also **hydr-**) ● **comb. form 1** water; relating to water: *hydraulic.* ➤ Medicine affected with an accumulation of serous fluid: *hydrocephalus.* **2** Chemistry combined with hydrogen: *hydrocarbon.*
– ORIGIN from Gk *hudōr* 'water'.

**hydrobromic acid** /ˌhʌɪdrə(ʊ)ˈbrəʊmɪk/ ● **n.** Chemistry a strongly acidic solution of the gas hydrogen bromide. [HBr.]

**hydrocarbon** ● **n.** Chemistry a compound of hydrogen and carbon, such as any of those which are the chief components of petroleum and natural gas.

**hydrocele** /ˈhʌɪdrə(ʊ)siːl/ ● **n.** Medicine abnormal accumulation of serous fluid in a sac in the body.

**hydrocephalus** /ˌhʌɪdrəˈsɛf(ə)ləs, -ˈkɛf-/ ● **n.** Medicine a condition in which fluid accumulates in the brain.
– DERIVATIVES **hydrocephalic** adj. **hydrocephaly** n.
– ORIGIN C17: mod. L., from Gk *hudrokephalon,* from *hudro-* 'water' + *kephalē* 'head'.

**hydrochloric acid** ● **n.** Chemistry a strongly acidic solution of the gas hydrogen chloride. [HCl.]

**hydrochloride** ● **n.** Chemistry a compound of an organic base with hydrochloric acid.

**hydrocolloid** /ˌhʌɪdrə(ʊ)ˈkɒlɔɪd/ ● **n.** a substance which forms a gel in the presence of water.

**hydrocortisone** ● **n.** Biochemistry a steroid hormone produced by the adrenal cortex, used medicinally to treat inflammation and rheumatism.

**hydrocyanic acid** /ˌhʌɪdrə(ʊ)sʌɪˈanɪk/ ● **n.** Chemistry a highly poisonous acidic solution of hydrogen cyanide.

**hydrodynamics** ● **pl. n.** [treated as sing.] the branch of science concerned with forces acting on or exerted by fluids (especially liquids).
– DERIVATIVES **hydrodynamic** adj. **hydrodynamical** adj. **hydrodynamicist** n.

**hydroelectric** ● **adj.** relating to or denoting the generation of electricity using flowing water to drive a turbine which powers a generator.
– DERIVATIVES **hydroelectricity** n.

**hydrofluoric acid** /ˌhʌɪdrə(ʊ)ˈflʊərɪk/ ● **n.** Chemistry an acidic, extremely corrosive solution of the liquid hydrogen fluoride. [HF.]

**hydrofoil** ● **n.** a boat fitted underneath with shaped vanes (foils) which lift the hull clear of the water at speed. ➤ each of the foils of such a craft.
– ORIGIN 1920s: from **HYDRO-**, on the pattern of *aerofoil.*

**hydrogel** ● **n.** a gel in which the liquid component is water.

**hydrogen** /ˈhʌɪdrədʒ(ə)n/ ● **n.** a colourless, odourless, highly flammable gas, the chemical element of atomic number 1. (Symbol: **H**)
– DERIVATIVES **hydrogenous** /-ˈdrɒdʒɪnəs/ adj.
– ORIGIN C18: coined in Fr. from Gk *hudro-* 'water' + *-genēs* (see **-GEN**).

**hydrogenase** /hʌɪˈdrɒdʒəneɪz/ ● **n.** Biochemistry an enzyme which promotes the reduction of a particular substance by hydrogen.

**hydrogenate** /hʌɪˈdrɒdʒəneɪt, ˈhʌɪdrədʒəneɪt/ ● **v.** [often as adj. **hydrogenated**] charge with or cause to combine with hydrogen.
– DERIVATIVES **hydrogenation** n.

**hydrogen bomb** ● **n.** a nuclear bomb whose destructive power comes from the fusion of isotopes of hydrogen (deuterium and tritium).

**hydrogen bond** ● **n.** Chemistry a weak chemical bond resulting from electrostatic attraction between a proton in one molecule and an electronegative atom in another.

**hydrogen cyanide** ● **n.** Chemistry a highly poisonous gas or volatile liquid with an odour of bitter almonds, made by the action of acids on cyanides. [HCN.]

**hydrogen peroxide** ● **n.** Chemistry a colourless viscous liquid with strong oxidizing properties, used in some disinfectants and bleaches. [$H_2O_2$.]

**hydrogen sulphide** ● **n.** Chemistry a colourless poisonous gas with a smell of bad eggs, made by the action of acids on sulphides. [$H_2S$.]

**hydrogeology** ● **n.** the branch of geology concerned with underground or surface water.
– DERIVATIVES **hydrogeological** adj. **hydrogeologist** n.

**hydrography** /hʌɪˈdrɒɡrəfi/ ● **n.** the science of surveying and charting bodies of water.
– DERIVATIVES **hydrographer** n. **hydrographic** adj. **hydrographical** adj. **hydrographically** adv.

**hydroid** /ˈhʌɪdrɔɪd/ ● **n.** Zoology a coelenterate of an order (Hydroida) which includes the hydras.

**hydrolase** /ˈhʌɪdrəleɪz/ ● **n.** Biochemistry an enzyme that promotes the hydrolysis of a particular substrate.

**hydrology** ● **n.** the branch of science concerned with the properties and distribution of water on the earth's surface.
– DERIVATIVES **hydrologic** adj. **hydrological** adj. **hydrologically** adv. **hydrologist** n.

**hydrolyse** /ˈhʌɪdrəlʌɪz/ (also **hydrolyze**) ● **v.** Chemistry break down (a compound) by chemical reaction with water.

**hydrolysis** /hʌɪˈdrɒlɪsɪs/ ● **n.** Chemistry the chemical breakdown of a compound due to reaction with water.
– DERIVATIVES **hydrolytic** adj.

**hydromagnetics** ● **pl. n.** another term for **MAGNETOHYDRODYNAMICS**.
– DERIVATIVES **hydromagnetic** adj.

**hydromassage** ● **n.** massage using jets of water.

**hydromechanics** ● **pl. n.** [treated as sing.] the mechanics of liquids; hydrodynamics.
– DERIVATIVES **hydromechanical** adj.

**hydrometer** /hʌɪˈdrɒmɪtə/ ● **n.** an instrument for measuring the density of liquids.
– DERIVATIVES **hydrometric** adj. **hydrometry** n.

**hydronic** /hʌɪˈdrɒnɪk/ ● **adj.** denoting cooling or heating systems using circulating water.

**hydronium ion** /hʌɪˈdrəʊnɪəm/ ● **n.** Chemistry another term for **HYDROXONIUM ION**.

**hydropathy** /hʌɪˈdrɒpəθi/ ● **n.** the treatment of illness through the use of water, either internally or externally.
– DERIVATIVES **hydropathic** adj. **hydropathist** n.

**hydrophilic** /ˌhʌɪdrə(ʊ)ˈfɪlɪk/ ● **adj.** having a tendency to mix with, dissolve in, or be wetted by water.
– DERIVATIVES **hydrophilicity** n.

**hydrophobia** /ˌhʌɪdrə(ʊ)ˈfəʊbɪə/ ● **n.** **1** extreme or irrational fear of water, especially as a symptom of rabies. **2** rabies.

**hydrophobic** ● **adj.** **1** tending to repel or fail to mix with water. **2** of or suffering from hydrophobia.
– DERIVATIVES **hydrophobicity** n.

**hydrophone** ● **n.** a microphone which detects sound waves under water.

**hydrophyte** ● **n.** Botany a plant which grows only in or on water.
– DERIVATIVES **hydrophytic** adj.

**hydroplane** ● **n.** **1** a light, fast motor boat. **2** a fin-like attachment which enables a moving submarine to rise or fall in the water. **3** US a seaplane. ● **v.** chiefly N. Amer. another term for **AQUAPLANE**.

**hydroponics** /ˌhʌɪdrə(ʊ)ˈpɒnɪks/ ● **pl. n.** [treated as sing.] the process of growing plants in sand, gravel, or liquid, with added nutrients but without soil.
– DERIVATIVES **hydroponic** adj. **hydroponically** adv.
– ORIGIN 1930s: from **HYDRO-** + Gk *ponos* 'labour' + **-ICS**.

**hydropower** ● **n.** hydroelectric power.

**hydroquinone** /ˌhʌɪdrəˈkwɪnəʊn/ ● **n.** Chemistry a crystalline compound made by the reduction of benzoquinone.

**hydrospeed** (also **hydrospeeding**) ● **n.** a sport that involves jumping into fast-flowing white water and being carried along at high speed while buoyed up by a float.

**hydrosphere** ● **n.** the seas, lakes, and other waters of the earth's surface, considered collectively.

**hydrostatic** ● **adj.** relating to or denoting the equilibrium of liquids and the pressure exerted by liquid at rest.
– DERIVATIVES **hydrostatical** adj. **hydrostatically** adv. **hydrostatics** pl. n.
– ORIGIN C17: prob. from Gk *hudrostatēs* 'hydrostatic bal-

ance', from *hudro-* 'water' + *statikos* (see **STATIC**).

**hydrotherapy** ● n. **1** the therapeutic use of exercises in a pool. **2** another term for **HYDROPATHY**.
– DERIVATIVES **hydrotherapist** n.

**hydrothermal** ● adj. relating to or denoting the action of heated water in the earth's crust.
– DERIVATIVES **hydrothermally** adv.

**hydrothermal vent** ● n. an opening in the sea floor out of which heated mineral-rich water flows.

**hydrothorax** ● n. Medicine the condition of having fluid in the pleural cavity.

**hydrotropism** /hʌɪ'drɒtrəpɪz(ə)m/ ● n. Botany the growth or turning of plant roots towards moisture.

**hydrous** ● adj. chiefly Chemistry & Geology containing water as a constituent.
– ORIGIN C19: from Gk *hudro-* 'water' + **-OUS**.

**hydroxide** ● n. Chemistry a compound containing the hydroxide ion $OH^-$ or the group –OH.

**hydroxonium ion** /ˌhʌɪdrɒk'səʊnɪəm/ ● n. Chemistry the ion $H_3O^+$, present in all aqueous acids.
– ORIGIN 1920s: from **HYDRO-** (relating to hydrogen) + **OXY-**[2] + the suffix *-onium* (from **AMMONIUM**).

**hydroxy-** ● comb. form Chemistry representing **HYDROXYL** or **HYDROXIDE**.

**hydroxyl** /hʌɪ'drɒksʌɪl, -sɪl/ ● n. [as modifier] Chemistry of or denoting the radical –OH, present in alcohols and many other organic compounds.

**Hydrozoa** /ˌhʌɪdrə(ʊ)'zəʊə/ ● pl. n. Zoology a class of coelenterates which includes hydras and Portuguese men-of-war.
– DERIVATIVES **hydrozoan** n. & adj.
– ORIGIN mod. L., from **HYDRO-** + Gk *zōion* 'animal'.

**hyena** (also **hyaena**) ● n. a doglike carnivorous African mammal with long forelimbs and an erect mane. [Family Hyaenidae: three species.]
– ORIGIN ME: via L. from Gk *huaina*, fem. of *hus* 'pig' (prob. because of the resemblance of the mane to a hog's bristles).

**hygiene** ● n. conditions or practices conducive to maintaining health and preventing disease, especially cleanliness.
– ORIGIN C16: via Fr. from mod. L. *hygieina*, from Gk *hugieinē (tekhnē)* '(art) of health', from *hugiēs* 'healthy'.

**hygienic** ● adj. promoting or conducive to hygiene; sanitary.
– DERIVATIVES **hygienically** adv.

**hygienist** ● n. a specialist in the promotion of hygiene.

**hygro-** ● comb. form relating to moisture: *hygrometer.*
– ORIGIN from Gk *hugros* 'wet'.

**hygrometer** /hʌɪ'grɒmɪtə/ ● n. an instrument for measuring humidity.
– DERIVATIVES **hygrometric** adj. **hygrometry** n.

**hygrophilous** /hʌɪ'grɒfɪləs/ ● adj. Botany (of a plant) growing in damp conditions.

**hygrophyte** /'hʌɪgrəfʌɪt/ ● n. Botany a plant which grows in wet conditions.

**hygroscope** /'hʌɪgrə(ʊ)skəʊp/ ● n. an instrument which gives an indication (though not necessarily a measurement) of the humidity of the air.

**hygroscopic** ● adj. (of a substance) tending to absorb moisture from the air.
– DERIVATIVES **hygroscopically** adv.

**hying** present participle of **HIE**.

**Hyksos** /'hɪksɒs/ ● pl. n. a people of mixed Semitic and Asian descent who invaded Egypt *c.*1640 BC.
– ORIGIN from Gk *Huksōs*, from Egyptian *heqa khoswe* 'foreign rulers'.

**hyla** /'hʌɪlə/ ● n. a tree frog, typically bright green in colour. [Genus *Hyla*: many species.]
– ORIGIN mod. L., from Gk *hulē* 'timber'.

**hylo-** ● comb. form of or relating to matter: *hylozoism.*
– ORIGIN from Gk *hulē* 'matter'.

**hylomorphism** /ˌhʌɪlə(ʊ)'mɔːfɪz(ə)m/ ● n. Philosophy the doctrine that matter is the first cause of the universe and that physical objects result from the combination of matter and form.
– DERIVATIVES **hylomorphic** adj.
– ORIGIN C19: from **HYLO-** + Gk *morphē* 'form'.

**hylozoism** /ˌhʌɪlə(ʊ)'zəʊɪz(ə)m/ ● n. Philosophy the doctrine that all matter has life.
– ORIGIN C17: from **HYLO-** + Gk *zōē* 'life'.

**hymen** /'hʌɪmən/ ● n. a membrane which partially closes the opening of the vagina and whose presence is traditionally taken to be a mark of virginity.
– DERIVATIVES **hymenal** adj.
– ORIGIN C16: via late L. from Gk *humēn* 'membrane'.

**hymeneal** /ˌhʌɪmɪ'niːəl/ ● adj. poetic/literary of or concerning marriage.
– ORIGIN C17: from L. *hymenaeus*, from *Hymen* (from Gk *Humēn*), the name of the god of marriage.

**hymenium** /hʌɪ'miːnɪəm/ ● n. (pl. **hymenia** /-nɪə/) Botany (in higher fungi) a surface consisting mainly of spore-bearing structures.
– DERIVATIVES **hymenial** adj.
– ORIGIN C19: from Gk *humenion*, dimin. of *humēn* 'membrane'.

**Hymenoptera** /ˌhʌɪmə'nɒpt(ə)rə/ ● pl. n. Entomology a large order of insects including the bees, wasps, ants, and sawflies, having four transparent wings.
– DERIVATIVES **hymenopteran** n. & adj. **hymenopterous** adj.
– ORIGIN mod. L., from Gk *humenopteros* 'membrane-winged'.

**hymn** ● n. a religious song of praise, typically a Christian song in praise of God. ● v. praise or celebrate with or as if with a hymn.
– DERIVATIVES **hymnic** /'hɪmnɪk/ adj.
– ORIGIN OE, via L. from Gk *humnos* 'ode or song in praise'.

**hymnal** /'hɪmn(ə)l/ ● n. a book of hymns. ● adj. of or relating to hymns.

**hymnary** /'hɪmnəri/ ● n. (pl. **-ies**) another term for **HYMNAL**.

**hymnody** /'hɪmnədi/ ● n. the singing or composition of hymns.
– DERIVATIVES **hymnodist** n.
– ORIGIN C18: via med. L. from Gk *humnōidia*, from *humnos* 'hymn'.

**hymnographer** /hɪm'nɒgrəfə/ ● n. a writer of hymns.
– DERIVATIVES **hymnography** n.

**hymnology** /hɪm'nɒlədʒi/ ● n. the study or composition of hymns.
– DERIVATIVES **hymnological** adj. **hymnologist** n.

**hyoid** /'hʌɪɔɪd/ Anatomy & Zoology ● n. a U-shaped bone in the neck which supports the tongue. ● adj. relating to or denoting this bone.
– ORIGIN C19: via Fr. from mod. L. *hyoïdes*, from Gk *huoeidēs* 'shaped like the letter upsilon (υ)'.

**hyoscine** /'hʌɪəsiːn/ ● n. Chemistry a poisonous plant alkaloid used as an anti-emetic in motion sickness and as a preoperative medication for examination of the eye.
– ORIGIN C19: from mod. L. *hyoscyamus* (see **HYOSCYAMINE**).

**hyoscyamine** /ˌhʌɪə(ʊ)'sʌɪəmiːn, -ɪn/ ● n. Chemistry a poisonous compound present in henbane, with similar properties to hyoscine.
– ORIGIN C19: from mod. L. *hyoscyamus* (from Gk *huoskuamos* 'henbane') + **-INE**[4].

**hyp-** ● comb. form variant spelling of **HYPO-** shortened before a vowel or *h* (as in *hypaesthesia*).

**hypaesthesia** /ˌhʌɪpiːs'θiːzɪə, -pɛs-/ (US **hypesthesia**) ● n. Medicine a diminished capacity for physical sensation.
– DERIVATIVES **hypaesthetic** adj.
– ORIGIN C19: from **HYPO-** + Gk *aisthēsis* 'sensation'.

**hypaethral** /hʌɪ'piːθr(ə)l, hɪ-/ (also **hypethral**) ● adj. (of a classical building) having no roof.
– ORIGIN C18: via L. from Gk *hupaithros* (from *hupo* 'under' + *aithēr* 'air') + **-AL**.

**hypallage** /hʌɪ'palədʒiː, hɪ-/ ● n. Rhetoric a transposition of the natural relations of two elements in a proposition, e.g. in the sentence '*Melissa shook her doubtful curls*'.
– ORIGIN C16: via late L. from Gk *hupallagē*, from *hupo* 'under' + *allassein* 'to exchange'.

**hypalon** /ˈhʌɪpəlɒn/ ● **n.** trademark a kind of synthetic rubber made of chlorinated and sulphonated polyethylene.
– ORIGIN C20: of unknown origin.

**hype**[1] informal ● **n.** extravagant or intensive publicity or promotion. ➤a deception or hoax. ● **v.** promote or publicize intensively or extravagantly.
– ORIGIN 1920s (orig. US in the sense 'short-change, cheat'): of unknown origin.

**hype**[2] informal ● **n.** a hypodermic needle or injection. ➤a drug addict. ● **v.** (usu. **be hyped up**) stimulate or excite.
– ORIGIN 1920s: abbrev. of **HYPODERMIC**.

**hyper** ● **adj.** informal hyperactive or unusually energetic.

**hyper-** ● **prefix 1** over; beyond; above: *hypersonic*. ➤excessively; above normal: *hyperthyroidism*. **2** relating to hypertext: *hyperlink*.
– ORIGIN from Gk *huper* 'over, beyond'.

**hyperactive** ● **adj.** abnormally or extremely active.
– DERIVATIVES **hyperactivity** n.

**hyperaemia** /ˌhʌɪpərˈiːmɪə/ (US **hyperemia**) ● **n.** Medicine an excess of blood in an organ or other part of the body.
– DERIVATIVES **hyperaemic** adj.

**hyperaesthesia** /ˌhʌɪpəriːsˈθiːzɪə, -ɛsˈθiː-/ (US **hyperesthesia**) ● **n.** Medicine excessive physical sensitivity.
– DERIVATIVES **hyperaesthetic** adj.
– ORIGIN C19: from **HYPER-** + Gk *aisthēsis* 'sensation'.

**hyperalgesia** /ˌhʌɪpəralˈdʒiːzɪə/ ● **n.** Medicine abnormally heightened sensitivity to pain.
– DERIVATIVES **hyperalgesic** adj.
– ORIGIN from Gk *huperalgein* 'to be in great pain', based on *algos* 'pain'.

**hyperalimentation** ● **n.** Medicine artificial supply of nutrients, typically intravenously.

**hyperbaric** /ˌhʌɪpəˈbarɪk/ ● **adj.** relating to or denoting a gas at a pressure greater than normal.
– ORIGIN 1960s: from **HYPER-** + Gk *baros* 'heavy'.

**hyperbaton** /hʌɪˈpəːbətɒn/ ● **n.** Rhetoric an inversion of the normal order of words, especially for emphasis, as in '*this I must see*'.
– ORIGIN C16: via L. from Gk *huperbaton* 'overstepping'.

**hyperbola** /hʌɪˈpəːbələ/ ● **n.** (pl. **hyperbolas** or **hyperbolae** /-liː/) Mathematics a symmetrical open curve (or pair of curves) formed by the intersection of a cone (or pair of oppositely directed cones) with a plane at a smaller angle with its axis than the side of the cone.
– ORIGIN C17: mod. L., from Gk *huperbolē* 'excess' (from *huper* 'above' + *ballein* 'to throw').

**hyperbole** /hʌɪˈpəːbəli/ ● **n.** deliberate exaggeration, not meant to be taken literally.
– DERIVATIVES **hyperbolical** adj. **hyperbolically** adv. **hyperbolism** n.
– ORIGIN ME: via L. from Gk *huperbolē* (see **HYPERBOLA**).

**hyperbolic** /ˌhʌɪpəˈbɒlɪk/ ● **adj. 1** of or relating to a hyperbola. ➤Mathematics denoting trigonometrical functions defined with reference to a hyperbola rather than a circle. **2** (of language) deliberately exaggerated.

**hyperboloid** /hʌɪˈpəːbəlɔɪd/ ● **n.** a solid or surface having plane sections that are hyperbolas, ellipses, or circles.
– DERIVATIVES **hyperboloidal** adj.

**hyperborean** /ˌhʌɪpəbɔːˈriːən, -ˈbɔːrɪən/ poetic/literary ● **n. 1** an inhabitant of the extreme north. **2** (**Hyperborean**) Greek Mythology a member of a race worshipping Apollo and living in a land of sunshine beyond the north wind. ● **adj.** of or relating to the extreme north.
– ORIGIN ME: from late L. *hyperboreanus*, from Gk *huperboreos*, from *huper* 'beyond' + *boreas* 'north wind'.

**hypercholesterolaemia** /ˌhʌɪpəkəˌlɛstərɒˈliːmɪə/ (US **hypercholesterolemia**) ● **n.** Medicine an excess of cholesterol in the bloodstream.

**hypercorrection** ● **n.** the use of an erroneous word form or pronunciation based on a false analogy with a correct or prestigious form, such as the use of *I* in *he invited my husband and I to lunch*.
– DERIVATIVES **hypercorrect** adj.

**hypercritical** ● **adj.** excessively critical.
– DERIVATIVES **hypercritically** adv.

**hypercube** ● **n.** a geometrical figure in four or more dimensions which is analogous to a cube in three dimensions.

**hyperdrive** ● **n.** (in science fiction) a supposed propulsion system for travel in hyperspace.

**hyperemia** ● **n.** US spelling of **HYPERAEMIA**.

**hyperesthesia** ● **n.** US spelling of **HYPERAESTHESIA**.

**hyperextend** ● **v.** forcefully extend a limb or joint beyond its normal limits.
– DERIVATIVES **hyperextension** n.

**hyperfocal distance** ● **n.** the distance between a camera lens and the closest object which is in focus when the lens is focused at infinity.

**hypergamy** /hʌɪˈpəːgəmi/ ● **n.** marriage to a person of a superior class.
– ORIGIN C19: from **HYPER-** + Gk *gamos* 'marriage'.

**hyperglycaemia** /ˌhʌɪpəglʌɪˈsiːmɪə/ (US **hyperglycemia**) ● **n.** Medicine an excess of glucose in the bloodstream, often associated with diabetes mellitus.
– DERIVATIVES **hyperglycaemic** adj.
– ORIGIN C19: from **HYPER-** + **GLYCO-** + **-AEMIA**.

**hypergolic** /ˌhʌɪpəˈgɒlɪk/ ● **adj.** (of a rocket propellant) igniting spontaneously on mixing with another substance.
– ORIGIN 1940s: from Ger. *Hypergol*, prob. from **HYPER-** + Gk *ergon* 'work' + **-OL**.

**hypericin** /hʌɪˈpɛrɪsɪn/ ● **n.** a substance found in St John's wort, credited with chemical and pharmacological properties similar to those of antidepressants.
– ORIGIN from **HYPERICUM**.

**hypericum** /hʌɪˈpɛrɪkəm/ ● **n.** a yellow-flowered plant of a genus that includes the St John's worts, tutsan, and rose of Sharon. [Genus *Hypericum*.]
– ORIGIN L., from Gk *hupereikon*, from *huper* 'over' + *ereikē* 'heath'.

**hyperimmune** ● **adj.** Medicine having a high concentration of antibodies produced in reaction to repeated injections of an antigen.
– DERIVATIVES **hyperimmunized** adj.

**hyperinflation** ● **n.** monetary inflation occurring at a very high rate.

**hyperkeratosis** /ˌhʌɪpəkɛrəˈtəʊsɪs/ ● **n.** Medicine abnormal thickening of the outer layer of the skin.

**hyperkinesis** /ˌhʌɪpəkɪˈniːsɪs, -kʌɪ-/ (also **hyperkinesia**) ● **n. 1** Medicine muscle spasm. **2** Psychiatry a disorder of children marked by hyperactivity and inability to concentrate.
– DERIVATIVES **hyperkinetic** adj.
– ORIGIN C19: from **HYPER-** + Gk *kinēsis* 'motion'.

**hyperlink** ● **n.** Computing a link from a hypertext document to another location, activated by clicking on a highlighted word or image.

**hyperlipaemia** /ˌhʌɪpəlɪˈpiːmɪə/ (US **hyperlipemia**) ● **n.** Medicine an abnormally high concentration of fats or lipids in the blood.
– DERIVATIVES **hyperlipaemic** adj.

**hyperlipidaemia** /ˌhʌɪpəˌlɪpɪˈdiːmɪə/ (US **hyperlipidemia**) ● **n.** another term for **HYPERLIPAEMIA**.
– DERIVATIVES **hyperlipidaemic** adj.

**hypermarket** ● **n.** chiefly Brit. a very large supermarket.
– ORIGIN 1970s: translation of Fr. *hypermarché*, from **HYPER-** + *marché* 'market'.

**hypermedia** ● **n.** Computing an extension to hypertext providing multimedia facilities, such as sound and video.

**hypermetropia** /ˌhʌɪpəmɪˈtrəʊpɪə/ ● **n.** long-sightedness.
– DERIVATIVES **hypermetropic** adj.
– ORIGIN C19: from Gk *hupermetros* 'beyond measure' + *ōps* 'eye'.

**hypermnesia** /ˌhʌɪpəmˈniːzɪə/ ● **n.** unusual power of memory, typically under abnormal conditions such as trauma or narcosis.
– ORIGIN C19: from **HYPER-** + Gk *mnēsia* 'memory'.

**hypermutable** ● **adj.** Genetics relating to or denoting a state in which mutation is abnormally frequent.
– DERIVATIVES **hypermutation** n.

**hyperon** /ˈhʌɪp(ə)rɒn/ ● **n.** Physics an unstable subatomic particle of the baryon class which is heavier than a neu-

tron or proton.
– ORIGIN 1950s: from **HYPER-** + **-ON**.

**hyperopia** /ˌhʌɪpərˈəʊpɪə/ ● n. another term for **HYPERMETROPIA**.
– DERIVATIVES **hyperopic** adj.
– ORIGIN C19: from **HYPER-** + Gk *ōps* 'eye'.

**hyperparasite** ● n. Biology a parasite whose host is itself a parasite.
– DERIVATIVES **hyperparasitic** adj. **hyperparasitism** n.

**hyperparathyroidism** /ˌhʌɪpəˌparəˈθʌɪrɔɪdɪz(ə)m/ ● n. Medicine an abnormally high concentration of parathyroid hormone in the blood, resulting in weakening of the bones through loss of calcium.
– DERIVATIVES **hyperparathyroid** adj.

**hyperplasia** /ˌhʌɪpəˈpleɪzɪə/ ● n. Medicine & Biology the enlargement of an organ or tissue caused by an increase in the reproduction rate of its cells, often as an initial stage in the development of cancer.
– ORIGIN C19: from **HYPER-** + Gk *plasis* 'formation'.

**hyperreal** ● adj. **1** exaggerated in comparison to reality. **2** (of art) extremely realistic in detail.
– DERIVATIVES **hyperrealism** n. **hyperrealist** adj. **hyperrealistic** adj. **hyperreality** n.

**hypersensitive** ● adj. abnormally or excessively sensitive, either emotionally or in physical response.
– DERIVATIVES **hypersensitiveness** n. **hypersensitivity** n.

**hypersonic** ● adj. **1** relating to speeds of more than five times the speed of sound (Mach 5). **2** relating to sound frequencies above about a thousand million hertz.
– DERIVATIVES **hypersonically** adv.

**hyperspace** ● n. **1** space of more than three dimensions. **2** (in science fiction) a notional space-time continuum in which it is possible to travel faster than light.
– DERIVATIVES **hyperspatial** adj.

**hypersthene** /ˈhʌɪpəsθiːn/ ● n. a greenish rock-forming mineral consisting of a magnesium iron silicate.
– ORIGIN C19: coined in Fr., from **HYPER-** + Gk *sthenos* 'strength' (because it is harder than hornblende).

**hypertension** ● n. Medicine abnormally high blood pressure.

**hypertensive** Medicine ● adj. exhibiting hypertension. ● n. a person with high blood pressure.

**hypertext** ● n. Computing a system allowing extensive cross-referencing between related sections of text.

**hyperthermia** /ˌhʌɪpəˈθəːmɪə/ ● n. Medicine the condition of having a body temperature greatly above normal.
– DERIVATIVES **hyperthermic** adj.
– ORIGIN C19: from **HYPER-** + Gk *thermē* 'heat'.

**hyperthyroidism** /ˌhʌɪpəˈθʌɪrɔɪdɪz(ə)m/ ● n. Medicine overactivity of the thyroid gland, resulting in a rapid heartbeat and an increased rate of metabolism.
– DERIVATIVES **hyperthyroid** adj. **hyperthyroidic** adj.

**hypertonic** /ˌhʌɪpəˈtɒnɪk/ ● adj. **1** Biology having a higher osmotic pressure than a particular fluid. **2** Physiology of or in a state of abnormally high muscle tone.
– DERIVATIVES **hypertonia** n. **hypertonicity** n.

**hypertrophy** /hʌɪˈpəːtrəfi/ ● n. Physiology enlargement of an organ or tissue resulting from an increase in size of its cells.
– DERIVATIVES **hypertrophic** adj. **hypertrophied** adj.
– ORIGIN C19: from **HYPER-** + Gk *-trophia* 'nourishment'.

**hyperventilate** ● v. **1** breathe at an abnormally rapid rate, increasing the rate of loss of carbon dioxide. **2** be or become overexcited.
– DERIVATIVES **hyperventilation** n.

**hypesthesia** ● n. US spelling of **HYPAESTHESIA**.

**hypethral** ● adj. variant spelling of **HYPAETHRAL**.

**hypha** /ˈhʌɪfə/ ● n. (pl. **hyphae** /-fiː/) Botany each of the filaments that make up the mycelium of a fungus.
– DERIVATIVES **hyphal** adj.
– ORIGIN C19: mod. L., from Gk *huphē* 'web'.

**hyphen** /ˈhʌɪf(ə)n/ ● n. the sign (-) used to join words to indicate that they have a combined meaning or that they are grammatically linked, or to indicate word division at the end of a line.
– ORIGIN C17: via late L. from Gk *huphen* 'together'.

**hyphenate** ● v. write or separate with a hyphen.
– DERIVATIVES **hyphenation** n.

**hypnagogic** /ˌhɪpnəˈgɒdʒɪk/ (also **hypnogogic**) ● adj. Psychology of or relating to the state immediately before falling asleep.
– ORIGIN C19: from Fr. *hypnagogique*, from Gk *hupnos* 'sleep' + *agōgos* 'leading'.

**hypno-** ● comb. form **1** relating to sleep: *hypnopaedia*. **2** relating to hypnosis: *hypnotherapy*.
– ORIGIN from Gk *hupnos* 'sleep'.

**hypnopaedia** /ˌhɪpnəʊˈpiːdɪə/ (US **hypnopedia**) ● n. learning by hearing while asleep or under hypnosis.
– ORIGIN C20: from **HYPNO-** + Gk *paideia* 'learning'.

**hypnopompic** /ˌhɪpnə(ʊ)ˈpɒmpɪk/ ● adj. Psychology of or relating to the state immediately preceding waking up.
– ORIGIN C20: from Gk *hupnos* 'sleep' + *pompē* 'sending away' + **-IC**.

**hypnosis** ● n. the induction of a state of consciousness in which a person loses the power of voluntary action and is highly responsive to suggestion or direction.
– ORIGIN C19: from Gk *hupnos* 'sleep' + **-OSIS**.

**hypnotherapy** ● n. the use of hypnosis as a therapeutic technique.
– DERIVATIVES **hypnotherapist** n.

**hypnotic** ● adj. **1** of, producing, or relating to hypnosis. **2** having a compelling or soporific effect. **3** Medicine (of a drug) sleep-inducing. ● n. **1** Medicine a sleep-inducing drug. **2** a person under or open to hypnosis.
– DERIVATIVES **hypnotically** adv.
– ORIGIN C17: from Fr. *hypnotique*, via late L. from Gk *hupnōtikos* 'causing sleep', from *hupnoun* 'put to sleep'.

**hypnotism** ● n. the study or practice of hypnosis.
– DERIVATIVES **hypnotist** n.

**hypnotize** (also **-ise**) ● v. produce a state of hypnosis in.
– DERIVATIVES **hypnotizable** adj.

**hypo**[1] ● n. the chemical sodium thiosulphate (formerly called hyposulphite) used as a photographic fixer.

**hypo**[2] ● n. (pl. **-os**) informal term for **HYPODERMIC**.

**hypo**[3] ● n. (pl. **-os**) informal an attack of hypoglycaemia.

**hypo-** (also **hyp-**) ● prefix **1** under: *hypodermic*. ➤below normal: *hypoglycaemia*. **2** slightly: *hypomanic*. **3** Chemistry containing an element with an unusually low valency: *hypochlorous*.
– ORIGIN from Gk *hupo* 'under'.

**hypo-allergenic** ● adj. (especially of cosmetics and textiles) unlikely to cause an allergic reaction.

**hypoblast** /ˈhʌɪpə(ʊ)blast/ ● n. Biology former term for **ENDODERM**.

**hypocalcaemia** /ˌhʌɪpəʊkalˈsiːmɪə/ (US **hypocalcemia**) ● n. Medicine deficiency of calcium in the bloodstream.

**hypocaust** /ˈhʌɪpə(ʊ)kɔːst/ ● n. an ancient Roman heating system, comprising a hollow space under the floor into which hot air was directed.
– ORIGIN from L. *hypocaustum*, from Gk *hupokauston* 'place heated from below'.

**hypochlorous acid** /ˌhʌɪpə(ʊ)ˈklɔːrəs/ ● n. Chemistry a weak acid with oxidizing and bleaching properties, formed when chlorine dissolves in cold water. [HOCl.]
– DERIVATIVES **hypochlorite** n.
– ORIGIN C19: from **HYPO-** + **CHLORINE** + **-OUS**.

**hypochondria** /ˌhʌɪpəˈkɒndrɪə/ ● n. abnormal chronic anxiety about one's health.
– ORIGIN ME: via late L. from Gk *hupokhondria*, denoting the soft body area below the ribs, orig. thought to be the seat of melancholy.

**hypochondriac** ● n. a person who is abnormally anxious about their health. ● adj. (also **hypochondriacal**) related to or affected by hypochondria.

**hypochondriasis** /ˌhʌɪpə(ʊ)kɒnˈdrʌɪəsɪs/ ● n. technical term for **HYPOCHONDRIA**.

**hypocoristic** /ˌhʌɪpə(ʊ)kəˈrɪstɪk/ ● adj. of or denoting a pet name or diminutive form of a name. ● n. a hypocoristic name or form.
– DERIVATIVES **hypocorism** n.

– ORIGIN C19: from Gk *hupokorisma*, from *hupokorizesthai* 'play the child'.

**hypocotyl** /ˌhʌɪpə(ʊ)ˈkɒtɪl/ ● **n.** Botany the part of the stem of an embryo plant between the stalks of the cotyledons and the root.
– ORIGIN C19: from **HYPO-** + **COTYLEDON**.

**hypocrisy** ● **n.** (pl. **-ies**) the practice of claiming to have higher standards or beliefs than is the case.
– ORIGIN ME: from OFr. *ypocrisie*, via eccles. L. from Gk *hupokrisis* 'acting of a theatrical part', from *hupokrinesthai* 'play a part, pretend'.

**hypocrite** ● **n.** a person who indulges in hypocrisy.
– DERIVATIVES **hypocritical** adj. **hypocritically** adv.

**hypocycloid** /ˌhʌɪpə(ʊ)ˈsʌɪklɔɪd/ ● **n.** Mathematics the curve traced by a point on the circumference of a circle which is rolling on the interior of another circle.
– DERIVATIVES **hypocycloidal** adj.

**hypodermic** ● **adj. 1** Medicine of or relating to the region immediately beneath the skin. **2** (of a needle or syringe) used to inject beneath the skin. ➤ (of a drug) injected beneath the skin. ● **n.** a hypodermic syringe or injection.
– DERIVATIVES **hypodermically** adv.
– ORIGIN C19: from **HYPO-** + Gk *derma* 'skin' + **-IC**.

**hypogastrium** /ˌhʌɪpə(ʊ)ˈgastrɪəm/ ● **n.** (pl. **hypogastria** /-rɪə/) Anatomy the front central region of the abdomen.
– DERIVATIVES **hypogastric** adj.
– ORIGIN C17: mod. L., from Gk *hupogastrion*, from *hupo* 'under' + *gastēr* 'belly'.

**hypogeal** /ˌhʌɪpə(ʊ)ˈdʒiːəl/ (also **hypogean**) ● **adj.** Botany remaining or occurring underground. Compare with **EPIGEAL**.
– ORIGIN C17: via late L. from Gk *hupogeios* (from *hupo* 'under' + *gē* 'earth') + **-AL**.

**hypogene** /ˈhʌɪpə(ʊ)dʒiːn/ ● **adj.** Geology produced or occurring under the surface of the earth.
– DERIVATIVES **hypogenic** adj.
– ORIGIN C19: from **HYPO-** + Gk *genēs* '-born'.

**hypogeum** /ˌhʌɪpə(ʊ)ˈdʒiːəm/ ● **n.** (pl. **hypogea**) an underground chamber.
– ORIGIN C17: from L., from Gk *hupogeion*, neut. of *hupogeios* 'underground'.

**hypoglossal nerves** /ˌhʌɪpə(ʊ)ˈglɒs(ə)l/ ● **pl. n.** Anatomy the pair of cranial nerves supplying the muscles of the tongue.
– ORIGIN C19: *hypoglossal* from **HYPO-** + Gk *glōssa* 'tongue'.

**hypoglycaemia** /ˌhʌɪpəʊglʌɪˈsiːmɪə/ (US **hypoglycemia**) ● **n.** Medicine deficiency of glucose in the bloodstream.
– DERIVATIVES **hypoglycaemic** adj.
– ORIGIN C19: from **HYPO-** + **GLYCO-** + **-AEMIA**.

**hypogonadism** /ˌhʌɪpə(ʊ)ˈgəʊnadɪz(ə)m/ ● **n.** Medicine reduction or absence of hormone secretion or other physiological activity of the gonads (testes or ovaries).
– DERIVATIVES **hypogonadal** adj. **hypogonadic** n. & adj.

**hypogynous** /hʌɪˈpɒdʒɪnəs/ ● **adj.** Botany (of a plant or flower) having the stamens situated below the carpels (or gynoecium). Compare with **EPIGYNOUS** and **PERIGYNOUS**.
– DERIVATIVES **hypogyny** n.

**hypoid** /ˈhʌɪpɔɪd/ (also **hypoid gear**) ● **n.** a bevel wheel with teeth engaging with a spiral pinion mounted at right angles to the wheel's axis, used to connect non-intersecting shafts in vehicle transmissions.
– ORIGIN 1920s: perh. a contr. of **HYPERBOLOID**.

**hypokalaemia** /ˌhʌɪpəʊkəˈliːmɪə/ (US **hypokalemia**) ● **n.** Medicine deficiency of potassium in the bloodstream.
– DERIVATIVES **hypokalaemic** adj.
– ORIGIN 1940s: from **HYPO-** + mod. L. *kalium* 'potassium'.

**hypolimnion** /ˌhʌɪpə(ʊ)ˈlɪmnɪən/ ● **n.** (pl. **hypolimnia** /-nɪə/) the lower layer of water in a stratified lake. Compare with **EPILIMNION**.
– ORIGIN C20: from **HYPO-** + Gk *limnion* (dimin. of *limnē* 'lake').

**hypomagnesaemia** /ˌhʌɪpə(ʊ)ˌmagnɪˈziːmɪə/ (US **hypomagnesemia**) ● **n.** Medicine deficiency of magnesium in the blood.
– DERIVATIVES **hypomagnesaemic** adj.

**hypomania** ● **n.** Psychiatry a mild form of mania, marked by elation and hyperactivity.
– DERIVATIVES **hypomanic** adj.

**hypoparathyroidism** /ˌhʌɪpəʊˌparəˈθʌɪrɔɪdɪz(ə)m/ ● **n.** Medicine diminished concentration of parathyroid hormone in the blood, causing deficiencies of calcium and phosphorus compounds.
– DERIVATIVES **hypoparathyroid** adj.

**hypophysis** /hʌɪˈpɒfɪsɪs/ ● **n.** (pl. **hypophyses** /-siːz/) Anatomy technical term for **PITUITARY**.
– DERIVATIVES **hypophyseal** /ˌhʌɪpə(ʊ)ˈfɪzɪəl/ (also **hypophysial**) adj.
– ORIGIN C17: mod. L., from Gk *hupophusis* 'offshoot'.

**hypopituitarism** /ˌhʌɪpəʊpɪˈtjuːɪt(ə)rɪz(ə)m/ ● **n.** Medicine diminished hormone secretion by the pituitary gland, causing dwarfism and premature ageing.
– DERIVATIVES **hypopituitary** adj.

**hypospadias** /ˌhʌɪpəʊˈspeɪdɪəs/ ● **n.** Medicine a congenital condition in males in which the opening of the urethra is on the underside of the penis.
– ORIGIN C19: from Gk *hupospadias* 'person having hypospadias'.

**hypostasis** /hʌɪˈpɒstəsɪs/ ● **n.** (pl. **hypostases** /-siːz/) **1** Medicine the accumulation of fluid or blood in parts of the body or organs, as occurs in cases of poor circulation or after death. **2** Philosophy an underlying reality or substance. **3** Theology each of the three persons of the Trinity. ➤ the single person of Christ, as contrasted with his dual human and divine nature.
– ORIGIN C16: via eccles. L. from Gk *hupostasis* 'essence'.

**hypostasize** (also **-ise**) ● **v.** formal treat or represent as concrete reality.

**hypostatic** /ˌhʌɪpə(ʊ)ˈstatɪk/ ● **adj.** Theology relating to the persons of the Trinity.
– DERIVATIVES **hypostatical** adj.

**hypostatize** ● **v.** North American term for **HYPOSTASIZE**.

**hypostyle** /ˈhʌɪpə(ʊ)stʌɪl/ ● **adj.** Architecture having a roof supported by pillars. ● **n.** a building having such a roof.
– ORIGIN C19: from Gk *hupostulos*, from *hupo* 'under' + *stulos* 'column'.

**hypotension** ● **n.** Medicine abnormally low blood pressure.
– DERIVATIVES **hypotensive** adj.

**hypotenuse** /hʌɪˈpɒtənjuːz, -s/ ● **n.** the longest side of a right-angled triangle, opposite the right angle.
– ORIGIN C16: via L. *hypotenusa* from Gk *hupoteinousa* (*grammē*) 'subtending (line)', from *hupo* 'under' + *teinein* 'stretch'.

**hypothalamus** /ˌhʌɪpə(ʊ)ˈθaləməs/ ● **n.** (pl. **hypothalami** /-mʌɪ/) Anatomy a region of the forebrain below the thalamus, controlling body temperature, thirst, and hunger, and involved in sleep and emotional activity.
– DERIVATIVES **hypothalamic** adj.

**hypothecate** /hʌɪˈpɒθɪkeɪt/ ● **v.** pledge (money) by law to a specific purpose.
– DERIVATIVES **hypothecation** n.
– ORIGIN C17: from med. L. *hypothecat-*, *hypothecare* 'give as a pledge', based on Gk *hupothēkē* 'deposit'.

**hypothermia** /ˌhʌɪpə(ʊ)ˈθəːmɪə/ ● **n.** Medicine the condition of having an abnormally (typically dangerously) low body temperature.
– ORIGIN C19: from **HYPO-** + Gk *thermē* 'heat'.

**hypothesis** /hʌɪˈpɒθɪsɪs/ ● **n.** (pl. **hypotheses** /-siːz/) a supposition or proposed explanation made on the basis of limited evidence as a starting point for further investigation. ➤ Philosophy a proposition made as a basis for reasoning.
– DERIVATIVES **hypothesize** (also **-ise**) v.
– ORIGIN C16: via late L. from Gk *hupothesis* 'foundation'.

**hypothetical** /ˌhʌɪpəˈθɛtɪk(ə)l/ ● **adj. 1** of, based on, or serving as a hypothesis. ➤ supposed but not necessarily real or true. **2** Logic denoting or containing a proposition of the logical form *if p then q*. ● **n.** a hypothetical proposition or statement.
– DERIVATIVES **hypothetically** adv.

**hypothyroidism** /ˌhʌɪpəʊˈθʌɪrɔɪdɪz(ə)m/ ● **n.** Medicine ab-

normally low activity of the thyroid gland, resulting in retardation of growth and mental development.
– DERIVATIVES **hypothyroid** n. & adj.

**hypotonic** /ˌhʌɪpə(ʊ)ˈtɒnɪk/ • **adj.** **1** Biology having a lower osmotic pressure than a particular fluid. **2** Physiology of or in a state of abnormally low muscle tone.
– DERIVATIVES **hypotonia** n. **hypotonicity** n.

**hypoventilation** • **n.** Medicine breathing at an abnormally slow rate, resulting in an increased amount of carbon dioxide in the blood.

**hypovolaemia** /ˌhʌɪpə(ʊ)vəˈliːmɪə/ (US **hypovolemia**) • **n.** Medicine a decreased volume of circulating blood in the body.
– DERIVATIVES **hypovolaemic** adj.
– ORIGIN C20: from **HYPO-** + **VOLUME** + Gk *haima* 'blood'.

**hypoxaemia** /ˌhʌɪpɒkˈsiːmɪə/ (US **hypoxemia**) • **n.** Medicine an abnormally low concentration of oxygen in the blood.
– ORIGIN C19: from **HYPO-** + **OXYGEN** + **-AEMIA**.

**hypoxia** /hʌɪˈpɒksɪə/ • **n.** Medicine deficiency in the amount of oxygen reaching the tissues.
– DERIVATIVES **hypoxic** adj.
– ORIGIN 1940s: from **HYPO-** + **OXYGEN** + **-IA**[1].

**hypsilophodont** /ˌhɪpsɪˈlɒfədɒnt/ • **n.** a small bipedal dinosaur, adapted for swift running.
– ORIGIN C19: from mod. L. *Hypsilophodontidae* (family name), from Gk *hupsilophos* 'high-crested' + *odous, odont-* 'tooth'.

**hypso-** • **comb. form** relating to height: *hypsometer.*
– ORIGIN from Gk *hupsos* 'height'.

**hypsography** /hɪpˈsɒgrəfi/ • **n.** the study and mapping of the relative altitudes of different areas of the earth's surface.
– DERIVATIVES **hypsographic** adj. **hypsographical** adj.

**hypsometer** /hɪpˈsɒmɪtə/ • **n.** a device for measuring the boiling point of water, especially in order to determine height above sea level.
– DERIVATIVES **hypsometric** adj.

**hyracotherium** /ˌhʌɪrəkə(ʊ)ˈθɪərɪəm/ • **n.** the earliest fossil ancestor of the horse, a small forest animal of the Eocene epoch with four toes on the front feet and three on the back.
– ORIGIN mod. L.: from *hyraco-* (combining form from **HYRAX**) + Gk *thērion* 'wild animal'.

**hyrax** /ˈhʌɪraks/ • **n.** a small short-tailed herbivorous mammal, found in Africa and Arabia. [Family Procaviidae: several species.]
– ORIGIN C19: mod. L., from Gk *hurax* 'shrew-mouse'.

**hyssop** /ˈhɪsəp/ • **n.** **1** a small bushy aromatic plant of the mint family, the leaves of which are used in cookery and herbal medicine. [*Hyssopus officinalis.*] **2** (in biblical use) a wild shrub whose twigs were used for sprinkling in ancient Jewish rites of purification.
– ORIGIN OE *hysope*, via L. from Gk *hyssōpos*, of Semitic origin.

**hysterectomy** /ˌhɪstəˈrɛktəmi/ • **n.** (pl. **-ies**) a surgical operation to remove all or part of the womb.
– ORIGIN C19: from Gk *hustera* 'womb' + **-ECTOMY**.

**hysteresis** /ˌhɪstəˈriːsɪs/ • **n.** Physics the phenomenon in which the value of a physical property lags behind changes in the effect causing it, especially that involving magnetic induction and a magnetizing force.
– ORIGIN C19: from Gk *husterēsis* 'shortcoming'.

**hysteria** • **n.** **1** Psychiatry a psychological disorder whose symptoms include selective amnesia, volatile emotions, and attention-seeking behaviour. **2** exaggerated or uncontrollable emotion or excitement.
– ORIGIN C19: from L. *hystericus* (see **HYSTERIC**).

**hysteric** • **n.** **1** (**hysterics**) informal wildly emotional behaviour. ➤ uncontrollable laughter. **2** a person suffering from hysteria. • **adj.** another term for **HYSTERICAL**.
– ORIGIN C17: via L. from Gk *husterikos* 'of the womb', from *hustera* 'womb' (hysteria being thought to be assoc. with the womb).

**hysterical** • **adj.** **1** Psychiatry associated with or suffering from hysteria. **2** wildly uncontrolled: *the band were mobbed by hysterical fans.* ➤ informal extremely funny.
– DERIVATIVES **hysterically** adv.

**hysteron proteron** /ˌhɪstərɒn ˈprɒtərɒn/ • **n.** Rhetoric a figure of speech in which the natural order of elements is reversed.
– ORIGIN C16: late L., from Gk *husteron proteron* 'the latter (put in place of) the former'.

**Hystricomorpha** /ˌhɪstrɪkə(ʊ)ˈmɔːfə/ • **pl. n.** Zoology a major division of the rodents, occurring chiefly in South America, which includes the guinea pigs, coypu, and porcupines.
– DERIVATIVES **hystricomorph** n. & adj.
– ORIGIN mod. L., from L. *hystrix, hystric-* 'porcupine' + Gk *morphē* 'form'.

**Hz** • **abbrev.** hertz.

**I**[1] (also **i**) ● **n.** (pl. **Is** or **I's**) **1** the ninth letter of the alphabet. **2** denoting the next after H in a set of items, categories, etc. **3** the Roman numeral for one.

**I**[2] ● **pron.** [first person sing.] used by a speaker to refer to himself or herself.
– ORIGIN OE, of Gmc origin.

**I**[3] ● **abbrev. 1** (**I.**) Island(s) or Isle(s) (chiefly on maps). **2** Italy (international vehicle registration). ● **symb. 1** electric current. **2** the chemical element iodine.

**i** ● **symb.** (*i*) Mathematics the imaginary quantity equal to the square root of minus one. Compare with **J**.

**-i**[1] ● **suffix** forming the plural: **1** of nouns adopted from Latin ending in *-us*: *foci*. **2** of nouns adopted from Italian ending in *-e* or *-o*: *dilettanti*.

**-i**[2] ● **suffix** forming adjectives from place names in the Near or Middle East: *Azerbaijani*.
– ORIGIN from Semitic and Indo-Iranian adj. endings.

**-i-** ● **suffix** a connecting vowel chiefly forming words ending in *-ana*, *-ferous*, *-fic*, *-form*, *-fy*, *-gerous*, *-vorous*.

**IA** ● **abbrev.** Iowa (in official postal use).

**-ia**[1] ● **suffix 1** forming nouns adopted from Latin or Greek (such as *mania*), and modern Latin terms (such as *utopia*). **2** forming names of: ➤ Medicine states and disorders: *anaemia*. ➤ Botany & Zoology genera and higher groups: *dahlia*. **3** forming place names: *India*.
– ORIGIN representing L. or Gk endings.

**-ia**[2] ● **suffix** forming noun plurals: **1** from Greek neuter nouns ending in *-ion* or from those in Latin ending in *-ium* or *-e*: *paraphernalia*. **2** Zoology in the names of classes: *Reptilia*.

**IAA** ● **abbrev.** Biochemistry indoleacetic acid.

**IAEA** ● **abbrev.** International Atomic Energy Agency.

**-ial** ● **suffix** forming adjectives such as *celestial*.
– ORIGIN from Fr. *-iel* or L. *-ialis*.

**iamb** /ˈʌɪam(b)/ ● **n.** Prosody another term for **IAMBUS**.

**iambic** /ʌɪˈambɪk/ ● **adj.** Prosody of or using iambuses. ● **n.** (**iambics**) verse using iambuses.

**iambus** /ʌɪˈambəs/ ● **n.** (pl. **iambuses** or **iambi** /-bʌɪ/) Prosody a metrical foot consisting of one short (or unstressed) syllable followed by one long (or stressed) syllable.
– ORIGIN C16: L., from Gk *iambos* 'iambus, lampoon', from *iaptein* 'attack verbally' (because the iambic trimeter was first used by Greek satirists).

**-ian** ● **suffix** forming adjectives and nouns such as *antediluvian* and *Bostonian*.
– ORIGIN from Fr. *-ien* or L. *-ianus*.

**-iasis** ● **suffix** a common form of **-ASIS**.

**IATA** /ʌɪˈɑːtə/ ● **abbrev.** International Air Transport Association.

**iatro-** /ʌɪˈatrəʊ/ ● **comb. form** relating to medical treatment: *iatrogenic*.
– ORIGIN from Gk *iatros* 'physician', from *iasthai* 'heal'.

**iatrogenic** /ʌɪˌatrə(ʊ)ˈdʒɛnɪk/ ● **adj.** of or relating to illness caused by medical treatment.
– DERIVATIVES **iatrogenesis** n.

**IB** ● **abbrev.** International Baccalaureate.

**IBA** ● **abbrev.** Independent Broadcasting Authority.

**Iban** /ˈiːban/ ● **n.** (pl. same) **1** a member of an indigenous people of Kalimantan and Sarawak; a Sea Dayak. **2** the Austronesian language of this people.
– ORIGIN the name in Iban.

**I-beam** ● **n.** a girder which has the shape of a capital I when viewed in section.

**Iberian** ● **n. 1** a native of Iberia (the Iberian peninsula), especially in ancient times. **2** the extinct Romance language spoken in the Iberian peninsula in late classical times. **3** the extinct Celtic language spoken in the Iberian peninsula in ancient times. ● **adj.** relating to or denoting Iberia.

**iberis** /ʌɪˈbɪərɪs/ ● **n.** (pl. same) a plant of a genus that comprises the candytufts. [Genus *Iberis*.]
– ORIGIN mod. L., prob. from Gk *ibēris* 'pepperwort'.

**ibex** /ˈʌɪbɛks/ ● **n.** (pl. **ibexes**) a wild mountain goat with long, thick ridged horns and a beard. [*Capra ibex* (Eurasia and NE Africa), and *C. pyrenaica* (Pyrenees).]
– ORIGIN C17: from L.

**IBF** ● **abbrev.** International Boxing Federation.

**Ibibio** /ˌɪbɪˈbiːəʊ/ ● **n.** (pl. same or **-os**) **1** a member of a people of southern Nigeria. **2** the Benue-Congo language of this people.
– ORIGIN the name in Ibibio.

**ibid.** /ˈɪbɪd/ ● **adv.** in the same source (referring to a previously cited work).
– ORIGIN abbrev. of L. *ibidem* 'in the same place'.

**-ibility** ● **suffix** forming nouns corresponding to adjectives ending in *-ible* (such as *accessibility* corresponding to *accessible*).
– ORIGIN from Fr. *-ibilité* or L. *-ibilitas*.

**I.Biol.** ● **abbrev.** Institute of Biology.

**ibis** /ˈʌɪbɪs/ ● **n.** (pl. **ibises**) a large wading bird with a long downcurved bill, long neck, and long legs. [*Threskiornis*, *Plegadis*, and other genera: numerous species.]
– ORIGIN ME: via L. from Gk.

**Ibizan** /ɪˈbiːθən/ ● **n.** a native or inhabitant of Ibiza, the westernmost of the Balearic Islands. ● **adj.** of or relating to Ibiza.

**Ibizan hound** ● **n.** a dog of a breed of hound from Ibiza, characterized by large pointed ears.

**-ible** ● **suffix** forming adjectives: **1** able to be: *defensible*. **2** suitable for being: *edible*. **3** causing: *horrible*.
– ORIGIN from Fr. *-ible* or L. *-ibilis*.

**-ibly** ● **suffix** forming adverbs corresponding to adjectives ending in *-ible* (such as *audibly* corresponding to *audible*).

**IBM** ● **abbrev.** International Business Machines.

**Ibo** /ˈiːbəʊ/ ● **n. & adj.** variant form of **IGBO**.

**ibogaine** /ɪˈbəʊgəˌiːn/ ● **n.** a hallucinogenic compound from the roots of a West African shrub, sometimes used to treat heroin or cocaine addiction.
– ORIGIN C20: from a blend of *iboga* (local name for the compound) and **COCAINE**.

**IBRD** ● **abbrev.** International Bank for Reconstruction and Development.

**IBS** ● **abbrev.** irritable bowel syndrome.

**ibuprofen** /ˌʌɪbjuːˈprəʊf(ə)n/ ● **n.** a synthetic compound used as an analgesic and anti-inflammatory drug.
– ORIGIN 1960s: from elements of the chemical name *2-(4-isobutylphenyl) propionic acid*.

**IC** ● **abbrev. 1** integrated circuit. **2** internal-combustion.

**i/c** ● **abbrev. 1** in charge of. **2** in command.

**-ic** ● **suffix 1** forming adjectives such as *Islamic*, *terrific*. **2** forming nouns such as *lyric*, *mechanic*. **3** Chemistry denoting an element in a higher valency: *ferric*. Compare with **-OUS**.
– ORIGIN from Fr. *-ique*, L. *-icus*, or Gk *-ikos*.

**-ical** ● **suffix** forming adjectives: **1** corresponding to nouns or adjectives usually ending in *-ic* (such as *comical* corresponding to *comic*). **2** corresponding to nouns ending

in *-y* (such as *pathological* corresponding to *pathology*).
– DERIVATIVES **-ically** suffix forming corresponding adverbs.

**ICAO** • abbrev. International Civil Aviation Organization.

**ICBM** • abbrev. intercontinental ballistic missile.

**ICC** • abbrev. **1** International Chamber of Commerce. **2** International Cricket Council. **3** Interstate Commerce Commission.

**ICE** • abbrev. **1** Institution of Civil Engineers. **2** internal-combustion engine.

**ice** • n. **1** frozen water, a brittle transparent crystalline solid. ➤ chiefly Brit. an ice cream or water ice. **2** informal diamonds. • v. **1** decorate with icing. **2** (usu. **ice up/over**) become covered or blocked with ice. **3** N. Amer. informal clinch (a victory or deal). **4** N. Amer. informal kill.
– PHRASES **break the ice** relieve tension or get conversation going at the start of a party or between strangers. **on ice 1** (of wine or food) kept chilled using ice. **2** suspended; on hold. **on thin ice** in a precarious or risky situation.
– DERIVATIVES **iced** adj.
– ORIGIN OE *īs*, of Gmc origin.

**-ice** • suffix forming nouns such as *service, police*, and abstract nouns such as *justice*.
– ORIGIN from OFr. *-ice*, from L. *-itia, -itius, -itium*.

**ice age** • n. a period or series of periods when ice sheets were unusually extensive across the earth's surface, in particular during the Pleistocene period.

**ice axe** • n. a small axe used by climbers for cutting footholds in ice.

**ice beer** • n. a type of strong lager matured at a low temperature after the main fermentation is complete.

**iceberg** • n. a large mass of ice floating in the sea.
– PHRASES **the tip of an** (or **the**) **iceberg** the small perceptible part of a much larger situation or problem.
– ORIGIN C18: from Du. *ijsberg*, from *ijs* 'ice' + *berg* 'hill'.

**iceberg lettuce** • n. a lettuce of a variety having a dense round head of crisp pale leaves.

**iceblink** • n. a bright appearance of the sky caused by reflection from a distant ice sheet.

**iceboat** • n. **1** a light, wind-driven vehicle with sails and runners, used for travelling on ice. **2** a boat used for breaking ice.

**icebox** • n. a chilled container for keeping food cold. ➤ Brit. a compartment in a refrigerator for making and storing ice. ➤ US dated a refrigerator.

**ice-breaker** • n. a ship designed for breaking a channel through ice.

**ice cap** • n. a permanent covering of ice over a large area, especially on the polar region of a planet.

**ice cream** • n. a semi-soft frozen dessert made with sweetened and flavoured milk fat.

**ice cube** • n. a small block of ice made in a freezer, used for adding to drinks.

**ice dancing** • n. a form of ice skating incorporating choreographed dance moves based on ballroom dances.
– DERIVATIVES **ice dance** n. & v. **ice dancer** n.

**iced tea** (also **ice tea**) • n. a chilled drink of sweetened black tea.

**icefall** • n. **1** a steep part of a glacier like a frozen waterfall. **2** an avalanche of ice.

**ice field** • n. a large permanent expanse of ice, especially in polar regions.

**icefish** • n. (pl. same or **-fishes**) **1** another term for CAPELIN. **2** a scaleless Antarctic fish of pallid appearance with spiny gill covers and a snout shaped like a duck's bill. [*Chaenocephalus aceratus*.] • v. (**ice-fish**) fish through holes in the ice on a lake or river.
– DERIVATIVES **ice-fishing** n.

**ice hockey** • n. a fast contact sport developed from field hockey, played on an ice rink between two teams of six skaters, who attempt to drive a small rubber disc or puck into the opposing goal with hooked sticks.

**ice house** • n. a building for storing ice.

**Icelander** • n. a native or inhabitant of Iceland.

**Icelandic** /ʌɪsˈlandɪk/ • n. the language of Iceland. • adj. of or relating to Iceland, its people, or its language.

**Iceland moss** (also **Iceland lichen**) • n. a brown branching lichen with stiff spines along the margins of the fronds, which can be boiled to produce an edible jelly. [*Cetraria islandica*.]

**Iceland poppy** • n. a tall poppy with colourful flowers, native to arctic and north temperate regions. [*Papaver nudicaule*.]

**Iceland spar** • n. a transparent variety of calcite, showing strong double refraction.

**ice lolly** (also **iced lolly**) • n. Brit. a piece of flavoured water ice or ice cream on a stick.

**iceman** • n. (pl. **-men**) chiefly N. Amer. a man who sells or delivers ice.

**ice milk** • n. N. Amer. a frozen dessert similar to ice cream but containing less butterfat.

**Iceni** /ʌɪˈsiːni, -nʌɪ/ • pl. n. a tribe of ancient Britons inhabiting an area of SE England in present-day East Anglia, whose queen was Boudicca (Boadicea).
– ORIGIN from L.

**ice pack** • n. **1** a bag or piece of cloth filled with ice and applied to the body to reduce swelling or lower temperature. **2** an expanse of large pieces of floating ice forming a nearly continuous mass, as occurs in polar seas.

**ice pick** • n. a small pick as used by climbers or for breaking ice.

**ice plant** • n. **1** a South African succulent which has leaves covered with glistening fluid-filled hairs that resemble ice crystals. [Genera *Mesembryanthemum* and *Dorotheanthus*.] **2** an Asian stonecrop which bears domed heads of tiny pink flowers. [*Sedum spectabile*.]

**ice shelf** • n. a floating sheet of ice permanently attached to a land mass.

**ice skate** • n. a boot with a blade attached to the sole, used for skating on ice. • v. (**ice-skate**) skate on ice as a sport or pastime.
– DERIVATIVES **ice skater** n. **ice skating** n.

**ice tea** • n. another term for ICED TEA.

**I.Chem.E.** • abbrev. Institution of Chemical Engineers.

**I Ching** /iː ˈtʃɪŋ/ • n. an ancient Chinese manual of divination based on eight symbolic trigrams and sixty-four hexagrams, interpreted in terms of the principles of yin and yang.
– ORIGIN from Chin. *yijing* 'book of changes'.

**ichneumon** /ɪkˈnjuːmən/ • n. **1** (also **ichneumon wasp** or **ichneumon fly**) a slender parasitic wasp with long antennae, which deposits its eggs in or on the larvae of other insects. [Family Ichneumonidae: many species.] **2** the Egyptian mongoose. [*Herpestes ichneumon*.]
– ORIGIN C15: via L. from Gk *ikhneumōn* 'tracker', from *ikhneuein* 'to track'.

**ichnography** /ɪkˈnɒɡrəfi/ • n. (pl. **-ies**) a ground plan of a building or map of a region.
– ORIGIN C16: from Fr. *ichnographie*, or via L. from Gk, from *ikhnos* 'track' + *-graphia* (see -GRAPHY).

**ichor** /ˈʌɪkɔː/ • n. **1** Greek Mythology the fluid said to flow like blood in the veins of the gods. **2** archaic a watery fetid discharge from a wound.
– DERIVATIVES **ichorous** /ˈʌɪk(ə)rəs/ adj.
– ORIGIN C17: from Gk *ikhōr*.

**ichthyo-** /ˈɪkθɪəʊ/ • comb. form relating to fish; fishlike: *ichthyosaur*.
– ORIGIN from Gk *ikhthus* 'fish'.

**ichthyology** /ˌɪkθɪˈɒlədʒi/ • n. the branch of zoology concerned with fishes.
– DERIVATIVES **ichthyological** adj. **ichthyologist** n.

**ichthyosaur** /ˈɪkθɪəsɔː/ (also **ichthyosaurus** /ˌɪkθɪəˈsɔːrəs/) • n. a fossil marine reptile of the Mesozoic era, resembling a dolphin with a long pointed head, four flippers, and a vertical tail.

**ichthyosis** /ˌɪkθɪˈəʊsɪs/ • n. Medicine a congenital skin condition which causes the epidermis to become dry and horny like fish scales.
– DERIVATIVES **ichthyotic** adj.

**ICI** • abbrev. Imperial Chemical Industries.

**-ician** • suffix (forming nouns) denoting a person involved in a particular subject: *statistician*.

– ORIGIN from Fr. *-icien*.

**icicle** • **n.** a hanging, tapering piece of ice formed by the freezing of dripping water.

– ORIGIN ME: from **ICE** + dial. *ickle* 'icicle' (from OE *gicel*).

**icing** • **n. 1** a mixture of sugar with liquid or fat, used as a coating for cakes or biscuits. **2** the formation of ice on a vehicle or in an engine.

– PHRASES **the icing on the cake** an attractive but inessential addition or enhancement.

**icing sugar** • **n.** chiefly Brit. finely powdered sugar used to make icing.

**-icity** • **suffix** forming abstract nouns especially from adjectives ending in *-ic* (such as *authenticity* from *authentic*).

**ick** informal, chiefly N. Amer. • **n.** a sticky or congealed substance. • **exclam.** an expression of disgust.

– DERIVATIVES **ickiness** n. **icky** adj.

– ORIGIN 1940s: prob. imitative.

**-icle** • **suffix** forming nouns which were originally diminutives: *particle*.

– ORIGIN see **-CULE**.

**icon** /ˈʌɪkɒn, -k(ə)n/ • **n. 1** (also **ikon**) a devotional painting of Christ or another holy figure, typically on wood, venerated in the Byzantine and other Eastern Churches. **2** a person or thing regarded as a representative symbol or as worthy of veneration. **3** Computing a symbol or graphic representation on a VDU screen of a program, option, or window. **4** Linguistics a sign which has a characteristic in common with the thing it signifies, for example the word *snarl* pronounced in a snarling way.

– ORIGIN C16 (in the sense 'simile'): via L. from Gk *eikōn* 'image'.

**iconic** • **adj.** of, relating to, or of the nature of an icon. ➤(of a classical Greek statue) depicting a victorious athlete in a conventional style.

– DERIVATIVES **iconically** adv. **iconicity** n. (chiefly Linguistics).

**iconify** • **v.** (**-ies**, **-ied**) Computing reduce (a window on a VDU screen) to an icon.

**icono-** • **comb. form 1** of an image or likeness: *iconology*. **2** relating to icons.

– ORIGIN from Gk *eikōn* 'likeness'.

**iconoclast** /ʌɪˈkɒnəklast/ • **n. 1** a person who attacks cherished beliefs or institutions. **2** a person who destroys images used in religious worship, especially one belonging to a movement opposing such images in the Byzantine Church during the 8th and 9th century.

– DERIVATIVES **iconoclasm** n. **iconoclastic** adj. **iconoclastically** adv.

– ORIGIN C17: via med. L. from eccles. Gk *eikonoklastēs*, from *eikōn* 'likeness' + *klan* 'to break'.

**iconography** /ˌʌɪkəˈnɒgrəfi/ • **n.** (pl. **-ies**) **1** the use or study of images or symbols in visual arts. ➤the visual images, symbols, or modes of representation collectively associated with a person or movement. **2** the illustration of a subject by drawings or figures.

– DERIVATIVES **iconographer** n. **iconographic** adj. **iconographical** adj. **iconographically** adv.

**iconolatry** /ˌʌɪkəˈnɒlətri/ • **n.** chiefly derogatory the worship of icons.

– ORIGIN C17: from eccles. Gk *eikonolatreia*, from *eikōn* 'likeness' + *-latria* 'worship'.

**iconology** /ˌʌɪkəˈnɒlədʒi/ • **n.** the study of visual imagery and its symbolism. ➤symbolism.

– DERIVATIVES **iconological** adj.

**iconostasis** /ˌʌɪkəˈnɒstəsɪs/ • **n.** (pl. **iconostases** /-siːz/) a screen bearing icons, separating the sanctuary of many Eastern churches from the nave.

– ORIGIN C19: from mod. Gk *eikonostasis*, from *eikōn* 'likeness' + *stasis* 'standing'.

**icosahedron** /ˌʌɪkɒsəˈhiːdrən, -ˈhɛd-/ • **n.** (pl. **icosahedra** or **icosahedrons**) a three-dimensional shape having twenty plane faces, in particular a regular solid figure with twenty equal triangular faces.

– DERIVATIVES **icosahedral** adj.

– ORIGIN C16: via late L. from Gk *eikosaedron*, neut. (used as n.) of *eikosaedros* 'twenty-faced'.

**-ics** • **suffix** (forming nouns) denoting a subject of study or branch of knowledge, or a field of activity: *politics*.

– ORIGIN from Fr. *-iques*, L. *-ica*, or Gk *-ika*, pl. forms.

**icterine warbler** /ˈɪkt(ə)rʌɪn/ • **n.** a warbler with bright yellow underparts. [*Hippolais icterina*.]

– ORIGIN C19: *icterine* from **ICTERUS** + **-INE**[1].

**icterus** /ˈɪkt(ə)rəs/ • **n.** Medicine technical term for **JAUNDICE**.

– DERIVATIVES **icteric** /ɪkˈtɛrɪk/ adj.

– ORIGIN C18: via L. from Gk *ikteros*.

**ictus** /ˈɪktəs/ • **n.** (pl. same or **ictuses**) **1** Prosody a rhythmical or metrical stress. **2** Medicine a stroke or seizure.

– DERIVATIVES **ictal** adj. (Medicine).

– ORIGIN C18 (denoting the beat of the pulse): from L., lit. 'a blow'.

**icy** • **adj.** (**-ier**, **-iest**) **1** covered with or consisting of ice. ➤very cold. **2** very unfriendly or hostile.

– DERIVATIVES **icily** adv. **iciness** n.

**ID** • **abbrev. 1** Idaho (in official postal use). **2** identification or identity.

**Id** • **n.** variant spelling of **EID**.

**I'd** • **contr. 1** I had. **2** I should or I would.

**id** /ɪd/ • **n.** Psychoanalysis the part of the mind in which innate instinctive impulses and primary processes are manifest. Compare with **EGO** and **SUPEREGO**.

– ORIGIN 1920s: from L., lit. 'that', translating Ger. *es*.

**id.** • **abbrev.** idem.

**-id**[1] • **suffix** forming adjectives such as *putrid*.

– ORIGIN from Fr. *-ide* from L. *-idus*.

**-id**[2] • **suffix 1** forming nouns such as *pyramid*. **2** Biology forming names of structural constituents: *plastid*. **3** Botany forming names of plants belonging to a family with a name ending in *-idaceae*: *orchid*.

– ORIGIN from or suggested by Fr. *-ide*, via L. *-idis* from Gk *-is*, *-id-*.

**-id**[3] • **suffix** forming nouns: **1** Zoology denoting an animal belonging to a family with a name ending in *-idae* or to a class with a name ending in *-ida*: *arachnid*. **2** denoting a member of a specified dynasty or family. **3** Astronomy denoting a meteor in a shower radiating from a specified constellation: *Geminids*.

– ORIGIN from or suggested by L. *-ides* (pl. *-idae*, *-ida*), from Gk.

**IDA** • **abbrev.** International Development Association.

**Idahoan** /ˈʌɪdəhəʊən/ • **n.** a native or inhabitant of the US state of Idaho. • **adj.** of or relating to Idaho.

**IDE** • **abbrev.** Computing Integrated Drive Electronics.

**ide** /ʌɪd/ • **n.** another term for **ORFE**.

– ORIGIN C19: from mod. L. *idus*, from Swed. *id*.

**-ide** • **suffix** Chemistry forming nouns: ➤denoting binary compounds of a non-metallic element or group: *chloride*. ➤denoting other compounds: *peptide*. ➤denoting elements of a series in the periodic table: *lanthanide*.

– ORIGIN orig. used in *oxide*.

**idea** • **n. 1** a thought or suggestion as to a possible course of action. ➤a mental impression. ➤a belief. **2** (**the idea**) the aim. **3** Philosophy (in Platonic thought) an eternally existing pattern of which individual things in any class are imperfect copies. ➤(in Kantian thought) a concept of pure reason, not empirically based in experience.

– PHRASES **get** (or **give someone**) **ideas** informal become (or make someone) ambitious, conceited, or tempted to do something. **have no idea** informal not know at all. **that's the idea** informal that's right. **the very idea!** informal an exclamation of disapproval or disagreement.

– ORIGIN ME: via L. from Gk *idea* 'form, pattern', from the base of *idein* 'to see'.

**ideal** • **adj. 1** most suitable; perfect. **2** desirable or perfect but existing only in the imagination: *in an ideal world*. ➤representing an abstract or hypothetical optimum. • **n.** a perfect type. ➤a standard of perfection.

– DERIVATIVES **ideally** adv.

– ORIGIN ME (as a term in Platonic philosophy, in the sense 'existing as an archetype'): from late L. *idealis*, from L. *idea* (see **IDEA**).

**ideal gas** • **n.** Chemistry a hypothetical gas whose molecules occupy negligible space and have no interactions, and which consequently obeys the gas laws exactly.

**idealism** • **n.** **1** the practice of forming or pursuing ideals, especially unrealistically. **2** (in art or literature) the representation of things in ideal form. **3** Philosophy any of various systems of thought in which the objects of knowledge are held to be in some way dependent on the activity of mind.
– DERIVATIVES **idealist** n. **idealistic** adj. **idealistically** adv.

**ideality** /ˌʌɪdɪˈalɪti/ • **n.** (pl. **-ies**) formal the state or quality of being ideal.

**idealize** (also **-ise**) • **v.** [often as adj. **idealized**] regard or represent as perfect or better than in reality.
– DERIVATIVES **idealization** n. **idealizer** n.

**ideate** /ˈʌɪdɪeɪt/ • **v.** [often as adj. **ideated**] chiefly Psychology imagine. ➤form ideas.
– DERIVATIVES **ideation** n. **ideational** adj. **ideationally** adv.
– ORIGIN C17: from med. L. *ideat-*, *ideare* 'form an idea', from L. *idea* (see **IDEA**).

**idée fixe** /ˌiːdeɪ ˈfiːks/ • **n.** (pl. **idées fixes** pronunc. same) an obsession.
– ORIGIN Fr., lit. 'fixed idea'.

**idée reçue** /ˌiːdeɪ rəˈs(j)uː/ • **n.** (pl. **idées reçues** pronunc. same) a generally accepted concept.
– ORIGIN Fr., lit. 'received idea'.

**idem** /ˈʌɪdɛm, ˈɪdɛm/ • **adv.** used in citations to indicate an author or word that has just been mentioned.
– ORIGIN L., 'the same'.

**idempotent** /ˌʌɪdɛmˈpəʊt(ə)nt, ʌɪˈdɛmpət(ə)nt/ • **n.** Mathematics an element of a set which is unchanged in value when operated on by itself.
– ORIGIN C19: from L. *idem* 'same' + **POTENT**[1].

**identical** • **adj.** **1** exactly alike. ➤(of twins) developed from a single fertilized ovum, and therefore of the same sex and usually very similar in appearance. Compare with **FRATERNAL** (in sense 3). **2** Logic & Mathematics expressing an identity.
– DERIVATIVES **identically** adv.
– ORIGIN C16: from med. L. *identicus*, from late L. *identitas* (see **IDENTITY**).

**identification** • **n.** the action or process of identifying or the fact of being identified. ➤an official document or other proof of a person's identity.

**identify** • **v.** (**-ies**, **-ied**) **1** establish the identity of. **2** recognize or select by analysis. **3** (**identify someone/thing with**) associate someone or something closely with. ➤(**identify with**) regard oneself as sharing the same characteristics or thinking as (someone else).
– DERIVATIVES **identifiable** adj. **identifiably** adv. **identifier** n.
– ORIGIN C17: from med. L. *identificare*, from late L. *identitas* (see **IDENTITY**) + L. *-ficare* (from *facere* 'make').

**identikit** /ʌɪˈdɛntɪkɪt/ • **n.** trademark a picture of a person sought by the police, reconstructed from typical facial features according to witnesses' descriptions. • **adj.** often derogatory having typical features and few unique ones; formulaic.

**identity** • **n.** (pl. **-ies**) **1** the fact of being who or what a person or thing is. ➤the characteristics determining this. ➤[as modifier] serving to establish the identity of the owner: *an identity card.* **2** a close similarity or affinity. **3** Mathematics (also **identity operation**) a transformation that leaves an object unchanged. ➤(also **identity element**) an element of a set which, if combined with another element, leaves that element unchanged. **4** Mathematics an equation expressing the equality of two expressions for all values of the variables, e.g. $(x + 1)^2 = x^2 + 2x + 1$.
– ORIGIN C16: from late L. *identitas*, from L. *idem* 'same'.

**identity parade** • **n.** Brit. a group of people assembled for the purpose of having an eyewitness identify a suspect for a crime from among them.

**ideogram** /ˈɪdɪə(ʊ)gram, ˈʌɪd-/ • **n.** a character symbolizing the idea of a thing without indicating the sounds used to say it (e.g. a numeral).
– ORIGIN C19: from Gk *idea* 'form' + **-GRAM**[1].

**ideograph** /ˈɪdɪə(ʊ)grɑːf, ˈʌɪd-/ • **n.** another term for **IDEOGRAM**.
– DERIVATIVES **ideographic** adj. **ideography** n.

**ideologue** /ˈʌɪdɪəlɒg, ˈɪd-/ • **n.** a dogmatic or uncompromising adherent of an ideology.

**ideology** /ˌʌɪdɪˈɒlədʒi, ɪd-/ • **n.** **1** (pl. **-ies**) a system of ideas and ideals forming the basis of an economic or political theory. ➤the set of beliefs characteristic of a social group or individual. **2** archaic the study of the origin and nature of ideas.
– DERIVATIVES **ideological** adj. **ideologically** adv. **ideologist** n.
– ORIGIN C18: from Fr. *idéologie*, from Gk *idea* 'form' + *-logos* (denoting discourse or compilation).

**ides** /ʌɪdz/ • **pl. n.** (in the ancient Roman calendar) a day falling roughly in the middle of each month (the 15th day of March, May, July, and October, and the 13th of other months) from which other dates were calculated.
– ORIGIN OE: from OFr., from L. *idus* (pl.).

**idio-** /ˈɪdɪəʊ/ • **comb. form** personal; own: *idiotype.*
– ORIGIN from Gk *idios* 'own, distinct'.

**idiocy** • **n.** (pl. **-ies**) extremely stupid behaviour.
– ORIGIN C16: from **IDIOT**.

**idiolect** /ˈɪdɪəlɛkt/ • **n.** the speech habits peculiar to a particular person.
– ORIGIN 1940s: from **IDIO-** + *-lect* as in *dialect*.

**idiom** • **n.** **1** a group of words established by usage as having a meaning not deducible from those of the individual words (e.g. *over the moon*). ➤a form of expression natural to a language, person, or group. **2** a characteristic mode of expression in music or art.
– DERIVATIVES **idiomatic** adj. **idiomatically** adv.
– ORIGIN C16: from Fr. *idiome*, or via late L. from Gk *idiōma* 'private property'.

**idiopathy** /ˌɪdɪˈɒpəθi/ • **n.** (pl. **-ies**) Medicine a disease or condition which arises spontaneously or for which the cause is unknown.
– DERIVATIVES **idiopathic** adj.
– ORIGIN C17: from mod. L. *idiopathia*, from Gk *idiopatheia*, from *idios* 'own' + *-patheia* 'suffering'.

**idiosyncrasy** /ˌɪdɪə(ʊ)ˈsɪŋkrəsi/ • **n.** (pl. **-ies**) **1** a mode of behaviour or way of thought peculiar to an individual. ➤a distinctive characteristic of a thing. **2** Medicine an abnormal physical reaction by an individual to a food or drug.
– DERIVATIVES **idiosyncratic** adj. **idiosyncratically** adv.
– ORIGIN C17: from Gk *idiosunkrasia*, from *idios* 'own' + *sun* 'with' + *krasis* 'mixture'.

**idiot** • **n.** **1** informal a stupid person. **2** Medicine, archaic a mentally handicapped person.
– DERIVATIVES **idiotic** adj. **idiotically** adv.
– ORIGIN ME: via OFr. from L. *idiota* 'ignorant person', from Gk *idiōtēs* 'layman, ignorant person', from *idios* 'own'.

**idiot board** • **n.** informal a board displaying a television script to a speaker as an aid to memory.

**idiot box** • **n.** N. Amer. informal a television set.

**idiot light** • **n.** N. Amer. informal a warning light indicating a fault in a device.

**idiot savant** /ˌiːdjəʊ saˈvɒ̃, ˌɪdɪəʊ/ • **n.** (pl. **idiot savants** or **idiots savants** pronunc. same) a person considered to be mentally handicapped but who displays brilliance in a specific area, especially one involving memory.
– ORIGIN Fr., lit. 'knowledgeable idiot'.

**idiotype** /ˈɪdɪə(ʊ)tʌɪp/ • **n.** **1** Biology the set of genetic determinants of an individual. **2** Physiology a set of antigen-binding sites which characterizes the antibodies produced by a clone of cells.

**idle** • **adj.** (**idler**, **idlest**) **1** avoiding work; lazy. ➤not working or in use. ➤(of money) held in cash or in accounts paying no interest. **2** having no purpose or basis: *idle threats.* • **v.** **1** spend time doing nothing. ➤move aimlessly. ➤N. Amer. take out of use or employment. **2** (of an engine) run slowly while disconnected from a load or out of gear.
– DERIVATIVES **idleness** n. **idly** adv.
– ORIGIN OE *īdel* 'empty, useless', of W. Gmc origin.

**idler** • **n.** **1** a person who idles. **2** a pulley that transmits no power but guides or tensions a belt or rope. **3** an idle wheel.

**idle wheel** • **n.** an intermediate wheel between two

geared wheels, to allow them to rotate in the same direction.

**idli** /ˈɪdliː/ ● **n.** (pl. same or **idlis**) a south Indian steamed cake of rice.
– ORIGIN from Malayalam and Kannada *iḍḍali*.

**Ido** /ˈiːdəʊ/ ● **n.** an artificial universal language developed from Esperanto.
– ORIGIN C19: Ido, lit. 'offspring'.

**idol** ● **n.** **1** an image or representation of a god used as an object of worship. **2** an object of adulation: *a soccer idol.*
– ORIGIN ME: from OFr. *idole*, from L. *idolum* 'image', from Gk *eidōlon*, from *eidos* 'form'.

**idolatry** ● **n.** **1** worship of idols. **2** adulation.
– DERIVATIVES **idolater** n. **idolatrous** adj.
– ORIGIN ME: from OFr. *idolatrie*, based on Gk *eidōlolatreia*, from *eidōlon* (see **IDOL**) + *-latreia* 'worship'.

**idolize** (also **-ise**) ● **v.** revere or love greatly or excessively.
– DERIVATIVES **idolization** n. **idolizer** n.

**idyll** /ˈɪdɪl/ (also **idyl**) ● **n.** **1** a blissful or peaceful period or situation. **2** a short description in verse or prose of a picturesque pastoral scene or incident.
– DERIVATIVES **idyllic** adj. **idyllically** adv.
– ORIGIN C16: from L. *idyllium*, from Gk *eidullion*, dimin. of *eidos* 'form'.

**i.e.** ● **abbrev.** that is to say.
– ORIGIN from L. *id est* 'that is'.

**-ie** ● **suffix** **1** variant spelling of **-Y**[2] (as in *auntie*). **2** archaic variant spelling of **-Y**[1], **-Y**[3].
– ORIGIN earlier form of *-y*.

**IEE** ● **abbrev.** Institution of Electrical Engineers.

**IEEE** ● **abbrev.** Institute of Electrical and Electronics Engineers.

**-ier** ● **suffix** forming personal nouns denoting an occupation or interest: **1** pronounced with stress on the preceding element: *grazier.* **2** pronounced with stress on the final element: *brigadier.*
– ORIGIN sense 1 from ME: var. of **-ER**[1]; sense 2 from Fr. *-ier*, from L. *-arius*.

**IF** ● **abbrev.** intermediate frequency.

**if** ● **conj.** **1** introducing a conditional clause: ➤on the condition or supposition that. ➤(with past tense) introducing a hypothetical situation. ➤every time. **2** despite the possibility that. ➤despite being. **3** whether. **4** expressing a polite request or tentative opinion. **5** expressing surprise or regret. ● **n.** a condition or supposition.
– PHRASES **if and only if** used to introduce a condition which is necessary as well as sufficient. **if anything** used to suggest tentatively that something may be the case. **if not** perhaps even (used to introduce a more extreme term than one first mentioned). **if only** even if for no other reason than. **if so** if that is the case.
– ORIGIN OE *gif*, of Gmc origin.

**IFC** ● **abbrev.** International Finance Corporation.

**-iferous** ● **comb. form** common form of **-FEROUS**.

**iff** ● **conj.** Logic & Mathematics if and only if.
– ORIGIN 1950s: arbitrary extension of *if.*

**iffy** ● **adj.** (**-ier**, **-iest**) informal doubtful. ➤of doubtful quality or legality.

**-ific** ● **suffix** common form of **-FIC**.

**-ification** ● **suffix** common form of **-FICATION**.

**-iform** ● **comb. form** common form of **-FORM**.

**IFR** ● **abbrev.** instrument flight rules.

**Ig** ● **abbrev.** Biochemistry immunoglobulin.

**Igbo** /ˈiːbəʊ/ (also **Ibo**) ● **n.** (pl. same or **-os**) **1** a member of a people of SE Nigeria. **2** the language of this people, belonging to the Kwa group.
– ORIGIN a local name.

**igloo** ● **n.** a dome-shaped Eskimo house, typically built from blocks of solid snow.
– ORIGIN C19: from Inuit *iglu* 'house'.

**igneous** /ˈɪɡnɪəs/ ● **adj.** Geology **1** (of rock) having solidified from lava or magma. **2** relating to or involving volcanic or plutonic processes.
– ORIGIN C17: from L. *igneus* (from *ignis* 'fire') + **-OUS**.

**ignimbrite** /ˈɪɡnɪmbrʌɪt/ ● **n.** Geology a volcanic rock formed by the consolidation of material deposited by pyroclastic flows.
– ORIGIN 1930s: from L. *ignis* 'fire' + *imber, imbr-* 'shower of rain, storm cloud' + **-ITE**[1].

**ignis fatuus** /ˌɪɡnɪs ˈfatjʊəs/ ● **n.** (pl. **ignes fatui** /ˌɪɡniːz ˈfatjʊʌɪ, ˌɪɡneɪz, ˈfatjʊiː/) a will-o'-the-wisp.
– ORIGIN C16: mod. L., lit. 'foolish fire' (because of its erratic movement).

**ignite** /ɪɡˈnʌɪt/ ● **v.** **1** catch fire or cause to catch fire. **2** provoke or inflame (an emotion or situation).
– DERIVATIVES **ignitability** n. **ignitable** adj.
– ORIGIN C17: from L. *ignire* 'set on fire', from *ignis* 'fire'.

**igniter** ● **n.** **1** a device for igniting a fuel mixture in an engine. **2** a device for causing an electric arc.

**ignition** ● **n.** **1** the action of igniting or the state of being ignited. **2** the process of starting the combustion of fuel in the cylinders of an internal-combustion engine.

**ignitron** /ɪɡˈnʌɪtrɒn/ ● **n.** a kind of rectifier with a mercury cathode, able to carry large electric currents.
– ORIGIN 1930s: from **IGNITE** or **IGNITION** + **-TRON**.

**ignoble** ● **adj.** (**-er**, **-est**) **1** not honourable; base. **2** of humble origin or social status.
– DERIVATIVES **ignobility** n. **ignobly** adv.
– ORIGIN ME: from Fr., or from L. *ignobilis*, from *in-* 'not' + *gnobilis*, older form of *nobilis* 'noble'.

**ignominious** /ˌɪɡnəˈmɪnɪəs/ ● **adj.** deserving or causing public disgrace or shame.
– DERIVATIVES **ignominiously** adv. **ignominiousness** n. **ignominy** n.
– ORIGIN ME: from Fr. *ignominieux*, or L. *ignominiosus*, from *ignominia*, from *in-* 'not' + a var. of *nomen* 'name'.

**ignoramus** /ˌɪɡnəˈreɪməs/ ● **n.** (pl. **ignoramuses**) an ignorant or stupid person.
– ORIGIN C16 (as the endorsement made by a grand jury on an indictment considered to be backed by insufficient evidence to bring before a petty jury): L., lit. 'we do not know' (in legal use 'we take no notice of it').

**ignorant** ● **adj.** **1** lacking knowledge or awareness in general. ➤(often **ignorant of**) uninformed about or unaware of a specific subject or fact. **2** informal discourteous. **3** black English easily angered.
– DERIVATIVES **ignorance** n. **ignorantly** adv.
– ORIGIN ME: via OFr. from L. *ignorant-*, *ignorare* (see **IGNORE**).

**ignoratio elenchi** /ˌɪɡnəˈreɪʃɪəʊ ɪˈlɛŋkʌɪ/ ● **n.** (pl. **ignorationes elenchi** /-ˈəʊniːz/) Philosophy a logical fallacy which consists in apparently refuting an opponent while actually disproving something not asserted.
– ORIGIN L., lit. 'ignorance of the elenchus'.

**ignore** ● **v.** disregard intentionally. ➤fail to consider (something significant).
– DERIVATIVES **ignorable** adj. **ignorer** n.
– ORIGIN C15 (in the sense 'be ignorant of'): from Fr. *ignorer* or L. *ignorare* 'not know'.

**iguana** /ɪˈɡwɑːnə/ ● **n.** a large lizard with a spiny crest along the back. [*Iguana iguana* (**green iguana**, tropical America) and other species, family Iguanidae.]
– DERIVATIVES **iguanid** n.
– ORIGIN C16: from Sp., from Arawak *iwana*.

**iguanodon** /ɪˈɡwɑːnədɒn/ ● **n.** a large partly bipedal herbivorous dinosaur of the early to mid Cretaceous period, with a broad stiff tail and the thumb developed into a spike.
– ORIGIN mod. L., from **IGUANA** + Gk *odous, odont-* 'tooth' (because its teeth resemble those of the iguana).

**i.h.p.** ● **abbrev.** indicated horsepower.

**IHS** ● **abbrev.** Jesus.
– ORIGIN ME: from late L., representing Gk ΙΗΣ as an abbrev. of *Iēsous* 'Jesus', but later often taken as an abbrev. of various L. phrs.

**ikat** /ˈiːkat, ɪˈkat/ ● **n.** fabric made using an Indonesian decorative technique in which warp or weft threads, or both, are tie-dyed before weaving.
– ORIGIN 1930s: Malay, lit. 'fasten, tie'.

**ikebana** /ˌɪkɪˈbɑːnə/ ● **n.** the art of Japanese flower arrangement, with formal display according to strict rules.
– ORIGIN Japanese, lit. 'living flowers'.

**ikon** ● n. variant spelling of ICON (in sense 1).

**IL** ● abbrev. **1** Illinois (in official postal use). **2** Israel (international vehicle registration).

**il-** ● prefix variant spelling of IN-¹, IN-² assimilated before *l* (as in *illustrate*).

**-il** ● suffix forming adjectives and nouns such as *civil*.
– ORIGIN from OFr., from L. *-ilis*.

**-ile** ● suffix **1** forming adjectives and nouns such as *agile*. **2** Statistics forming nouns denoting a value of a variate which divides a population into the indicated number of equal-sized groups, or one of the groups itself: *percentile*.
– ORIGIN var. of -IL especially in adoptions from Fr.

**ileitis** /ˌɪlɪˈʌɪtɪs/ ● n. Medicine inflammation of the ileum.

**ileostomy** /ˌɪlɪˈɒstəmi/ ● n. (pl. **-ies**) a surgical operation in which a damaged part is removed from the ileum and the end diverted to an artificial opening.
– ORIGIN C19: from ILEUM + Gk *stoma* 'mouth'.

**ileum** /ˈɪlɪəm/ ● n. (pl. **ilea**) Anatomy the third portion of the small intestine, between the jejunum and the caecum.
– DERIVATIVES **ileac** adj. **ileal** adj.
– ORIGIN C17: from med. L., var. of ILIUM.

**ileus** /ˈɪlɪəs/ ● n. Medicine a painful obstruction of the ileum or other part of the intestine.
– ORIGIN C17: from L., from Gk *eileos, ilios* 'colic'.

**ilex** /ˈʌɪlɛks/ ● n. **1** the holm oak. **2** a tree or shrub of a genus that includes holly. [Genus *Ilex*.]
– ORIGIN ME: from L.

**iliac** /ˈɪlɪak/ ● adj. of or relating to the ilium or the nearby regions of the lower body.
– ORIGIN C16: from late L. *iliacus*, from *ilia* 'entrails'.

**ilium** /ˈɪlɪəm/ ● n. (pl. **ilia**) the large broad bone forming the upper part of each half of the pelvis.
– ORIGIN ME (orig. denoting the ileum): from L., sing. of *ilia* 'flanks, entrails'.

**ilk** ● n. **1** a type: *fascists, racists, and others of that ilk*. **2** (**of that ilk**) Scottish, chiefly archaic of the place or estate of the same name.
– ORIGIN OE *ilca* 'same', of Gmc origin; rel. to ALIKE.

**Ill.** ● abbrev. Illinois.

**I'll** ● contr. I shall; I will.

**ill** ● adj. **1** not in full health; unwell. **2** poor in quality. ➤harmful or hostile. ➤unfavourable. ● adv. **1** badly, wrongly, or imperfectly: *ill-chosen*. ➤unfavourably. **2** only with difficulty. ● n. a problem or misfortune. ➤evil or harm.
– PHRASES **ill at ease** uncomfortable or embarrassed. **speak** (or **think**) **ill of** say (or think) something critical about.
– ORIGIN ME: from ON *illr* 'evil, difficult'.

**ill-advised** ● adj. unwise. ➤badly thought out.
– DERIVATIVES **ill-advisedly** adv.

**ill-assorted** ● adj. not well matched.

**illation** /ɪˈleɪʃ(ə)n/ ● n. old-fashioned term for INFERENCE.
– ORIGIN C16: from L. *illatio(n-)*, from *illat-*, *inferre* (see INFER).

**illative** /ɪˈleɪtɪv/ ● adj. **1** of the nature of or stating an inference. ➤proceeding by inference. **2** Grammar relating to or denoting a case of nouns in some languages used to express motion into something.
– DERIVATIVES **illatively** adv.
– ORIGIN C16: from L. *illativus*, from *illat-* (see ILLATION).

**ill-bred** ● adj. badly brought up or rude.
– DERIVATIVES **ill breeding** n.

**ill-disposed** ● adj. unfriendly or unsympathetic.

**illegal** ● adj. contrary to or forbidden by law. ● n. chiefly N. Amer. an illegal immigrant.
– DERIVATIVES **illegality** n. (pl. **-ies**). **illegally** adv.

**illegible** /ɪˈlɛdʒɪb(ə)l/ ● adj. not clear enough to be read.
– DERIVATIVES **illegibility** n. **illegibly** adv.

**illegitimate** /ˌɪlɪˈdʒɪtɪmət/ ● adj. **1** not in accordance with the law or accepted standards. **2** (of a child) born of parents not lawfully married to each other.
– DERIVATIVES **illegitimacy** n. **illegitimately** adv.

**ill fame** ● n. dated disrepute.

**ill-fated** ● adj. destined to fail or have bad luck.

**ill-favoured** (US **ill-favored**) ● adj. unattractive or offensive.

**ill-gotten** ● adj. acquired by illegal or unfair means.

**ill humour** ● n. irritability or bad temper.
– DERIVATIVES **ill-humoured** adj.

**illiberal** ● adj. **1** opposed to liberal principles. **2** archaic ill-bred or unrefined.
– DERIVATIVES **illiberality** n. **illiberally** adv.

**illicit** ● adj. forbidden by law, rules, or custom.
– DERIVATIVES **illicitly** adv. **illicitness** n.
– ORIGIN C16: from Fr., or from L. *illicitus*, from *in-* 'not' + *licitus* (see LICIT).

**illimitable** ● adj. limitless.
– DERIVATIVES **illimitability** n. **illimitably** adv.

**Illinoisan** /ˌɪlɪˈnɔɪən/ ● n. a native or inhabitant of the US state of Illinois. ● adj. of or relating to Illinois.

**illiquid** /ɪˈlɪkwɪd/ ● adj. **1** (of assets) not easily converted into cash. **2** (of a market) with a low volume of activity.
– DERIVATIVES **illiquidity** n.

**illiterate** /ɪˈlɪt(ə)rət/ ● adj. **1** unable to read or write. **2** ignorant in a particular subject or activity: *politically illiterate*. ● n. a person who is unable to read or write.
– PHRASES **functionally illiterate** lacking the literacy necessary for coping with most jobs and daily situations.
– DERIVATIVES **illiteracy** n. **illiterately** adv. **illiterateness** n.

**ill-natured** ● adj. bad-tempered and churlish.
– DERIVATIVES **ill-naturedly** adv.

**illness** ● n. a disease or period of sickness.

**illocution** /ˌɪləˈkjuːʃ(ə)n/ ● n. an action performed by saying or writing something, e.g. ordering or promising.
– DERIVATIVES **illocutionary** adj.

**illogical** ● adj. lacking sense or sound reasoning.
– DERIVATIVES **illogic** n. **illogicality** n. (pl. **-ies**). **illogically** adv.

**ill-omened** ● adj. attended by bad omens.

**ill-starred** ● adj. unlucky.

**ill-tempered** ● adj. irritable or morose.

**ill-treat** ● v. act cruelly towards.
– DERIVATIVES **ill-treatment** n.

**illude** /ɪˈl(j)uːd/ ● v. poetic/literary trick; delude.
– ORIGIN ME: from L. *illudere* 'to mock'.

**illume** /ɪˈl(j)uːm/ ● v. poetic/literary illuminate.
– ORIGIN ME: abbrev. of ILLUMINE.

**illuminance** /ɪˈl(j)uːmɪnəns/ ● n. Physics the amount of luminous flux per unit area.

**illuminant** ● n. technical a means of lighting or source of light. ● adj. giving off light.

**illuminate** /ɪˈl(j)uːmɪneɪt/ ● v. **1** light up. **2** [usu. as adj. **illuminating**] help to clarify or explain. **3** [often as adj. **illuminated**] decorate (a page or initial letter in a manuscript) with gold, silver, or coloured designs.
– DERIVATIVES **illuminatingly** adv. **illuminative** adj. **illuminator** n.
– ORIGIN ME: from L. *illuminat-*, *illuminare* 'illuminate', from *in-* 'upon' + *lumen, lumin-* 'light'.

**illuminati** /ɪˌl(j)uːmɪˈnɑːti/ ● pl. n. people claiming to possess special enlightenment or knowledge.
– DERIVATIVES **illuminism** n. **illuminist** n.
– ORIGIN C16: pl. of Ital. *illuminato* or L. *illuminatus* 'enlightened', past part. of *illuminare* (see ILLUMINATE).

**illumination** ● n. **1** lighting or light. ➤(**illuminations**) lights used in decorating a building or other structure. **2** the action or process of illuminating.

**illumine** ● v. poetic/literary light up; illuminate.
– ORIGIN ME: from OFr. *illuminer*, from L. *illuminare* (see ILLUMINATE).

**ill-use** ● v. ill-treat. ● n. (**ill use**) ill-treatment.

**illusion** /ɪˈl(j)uːʒ(ə)n/ ● n. a false or unreal perception. ➤a deceptive appearance or impression. ➤a false idea or belief.
– PHRASES **be under the illusion that** believe mistakenly that.
– DERIVATIVES **illusional** adj.
– ORIGIN ME: via OFr. from L. *illusio(n-)*, from *illudere* 'to mock'.

**illusionism** • n. the use of perspective in art to give an appearance of three-dimensionality.
– DERIVATIVES **illusionistic** adj.

**illusionist** • n. a person who performs tricks that deceive the eye; a magician.

**illusive** /ɪˈl(j)uːsɪv/ • adj. chiefly poetic/literary deceptive; illusory.
– ORIGIN C17: from med. L. *illusivus*, from L. *illus-*, *illudere* (see **ILLUSION**).

**illusory** /ɪˈl(j)uːs(ə)ri/ • adj. based on illusion; not real.
– DERIVATIVES **illusorily** adv. **illusoriness** n.

**illustrate** • v. **1** provide (a book or periodical) with pictures. **2** elucidate by using examples, charts, etc. ➤ serve as an example of.
– DERIVATIVES **illustrator** n.
– ORIGIN C16 (earlier (ME) as *illustration*): from L. *illustrat-*, *illustrare* 'light up'.

**illustration** • n. **1** a picture illustrating a book or periodical. **2** the action or fact of illustrating. ➤ an illustrative example.
– DERIVATIVES **illustrational** adj.

**illustrative** • adj. serving as an example or explanation.
– DERIVATIVES **illustratively** adv.

**illustrious** /ɪˈlʌstrɪəs/ • adj. well known and admired for past achievements.
– DERIVATIVES **illustriously** adv. **illustriousness** n.
– ORIGIN C16: from L. *illustris* 'clear, bright' + **-OUS**.

**ill will** • n. animosity.

**Illyrian** • n. **1** a native or inhabitant of Illyria, an ancient region on the east coast of the Adriatic. **2** the branch of the Indo-European family of languages represented by modern Albanian. • adj. **1** of or relating to ancient Illyria. **2** of or denoting the branch of Indo-European languages represented by modern Albanian.

**illywhacker** /ˈɪlɪˌwakə/ • n. Austral. informal a small-time confidence trickster.
– ORIGIN 1940s: of unknown origin.

**ilmenite** /ˈɪlmənʌɪt/ • n. a black mineral consisting of oxides of iron and titanium.
– ORIGIN C19: named after the *Ilmen* mountains in the Urals + **-ITE**[1].

**ILO** • abbrev. International Labour Organization.

**ILP** • abbrev. Independent Labour Party.

**ILR** • abbrev. Independent Local Radio.

**ILS** • abbrev. instrument landing system.

**-ily** • suffix forming adverbs corresponding to adjectives ending in *-y* (such as *happily* corresponding to *happy*).
– ORIGIN see **-Y**[1], **-LY**[2].

**I'm** • contr. I am.

**im-** • prefix variant spelling of **IN-**[1], **IN-**[2] assimilated before *b*, *m*, *p* (as in *imbibe*, *impart*).

**image** • n. **1** a representation of the external form of a person or thing in art. ➤ a visible impression obtained by a camera, telescope, or other device, or displayed on a video screen. ➤ an optical appearance produced by light from an object reflected in a mirror or refracted through a lens. ➤ a mental representation. **2** the general impression that a person, organization, or product presents to the public. **3** a simile or metaphor. **4** a person or thing closely resembling another. ➤ likeness. ➤ (in biblical use) an idol. **5** Mathematics a point or set formed by mapping from another point or set. • v. make or form an image of.
– DERIVATIVES **imageless** adj.
– ORIGIN ME: from OFr., from L. *imago*; rel. to **IMITATE**.

**image intensifier** • n. a device used to make a brighter version of an image on a photoelectric screen.

**imager** • n. an electronic or other device which records images.

**imagery** • n. **1** figurative language, especially in a literary work. ➤ visual symbolism. **2** visual images collectively.

**imagesetter** • n. Computing a very high-quality type of colour printer.

**imaginable** • adj. possible to be thought of or believed.
– DERIVATIVES **imaginably** adv.

**imaginal** /ɪˈmadʒɪn(ə)l/ • adj. **1** of or relating to an image. **2** Entomology of or relating to an adult insect or imago.
– ORIGIN C19: from L. *imago*, *imagin-* 'image' + **-AL**.

**imaginary** • adj. **1** existing only in the imagination. **2** Mathematics (of a number or quantity) expressed in terms of the square root of −1 (represented by *i* or *j*).
– DERIVATIVES **imaginarily** adv.
– ORIGIN ME: from L. *imaginarius*, from *imago*, *imagin-* 'image'.

**imagination** • n. the faculty or action of forming ideas or mental images. ➤ the ability of the mind to be creative or resourceful.
– ORIGIN ME: via OFr. from L. *imaginatio(n-)*, from *imaginari* 'picture to oneself', from *imago*, *imagin-* 'image'.

**imaginative** • adj. having or showing creativity or inventiveness.
– DERIVATIVES **imaginatively** adv. **imaginativeness** n.

**imagine** • v. **1** form a mental image or concept of. ➤ [often as adj. **imagined**] believe (something unreal) to exist. **2** suppose or assume.
– DERIVATIVES **imaginer** n.
– ORIGIN ME: from OFr. *imaginer*, from L. *imaginare* 'form an image of' and *imaginari* 'picture to oneself', both from *imago*, *imagin-* 'image'.

**imagineer** /ɪˌmadʒɪˈnɪə/ • n. a person who devises a highly imaginative concept or technology, especially the attractions in Walt Disney theme parks.
– DERIVATIVES **imagineering** n.
– ORIGIN 1940s: from **IMAGINE**, on the pattern of *engineer*.

**imagines** plural form of **IMAGO**.

**imaginings** • pl. n. thoughts or fantasies.

**imagism** /ˈɪmɪdʒɪz(ə)m/ • n. a movement in early 20th-century English and American poetry which sought clarity of expression through the use of precise images.
– DERIVATIVES **imagist** n. **imagistic** adj.

**imago** /ɪˈmeɪgəʊ/ • n. (pl. **imagos** or **imagines** /ɪˈmeɪdʒɪniːz/) **1** Entomology the final and fully developed adult stage of an insect. **2** Psychoanalysis an unconscious idealized mental image of someone, which influences a person's behaviour.
– ORIGIN C18: mod. L. use of L. *imago* 'image'.

**imam** /ɪˈmɑːm/ • n. **1** the person who leads prayers in a mosque. **2** (**Imam**) a title of various Muslim leaders, especially of one succeeding Muhammad as leader of Shiite Islam.
– DERIVATIVES **imamate** n.
– ORIGIN from Arab. *'imām* 'leader'.

**Imam Bayildi** /ɪˌmɑːm ˈbɑːjɪldi/ • n. a Turkish dish consisting of aubergines stuffed with an onion and tomato mixture and baked.
– ORIGIN Turk., lit. 'the imam fainted' (from enjoyment or the cost of the dish).

**Imari** /ɪˈmɑːri/ • n. a type of richly decorated Japanese porcelain.
– ORIGIN C19: from the name of a port in NW Kyushu, Japan, from which it was shipped.

**IMAX** /ˈʌɪmaks/ • n. trademark a cinematographic technique which produces an image approximately ten times larger than that from standard 35 mm film.
– ORIGIN 1960s: from *i-* (prob. representing a pronunc. of **EYE**) + *max* (short for **MAXIMUM**).

**imbalance** • n. a lack of proportion or balance.

**imbecile** /ˈɪmbɪsiːl/ • n. informal a stupid person. • adj. stupid.
– DERIVATIVES **imbecilic** adj. **imbecility** n. (pl. **-ies**).
– ORIGIN C16 (as adj. in the sense 'physically weak'): via Fr. from L. *imbecillus*, lit. 'without a supporting staff'.

**imbed** • v. variant spelling of **EMBED**.

**imbibe** /ɪmˈbʌɪb/ • v. formal or humorous drink (alcohol). ➤ absorb (ideas or knowledge). ➤ chiefly Botany absorb (water) into ultramicroscopic spaces or pores.
– DERIVATIVES **imbiber** n. **imbibition** /ɪmbɪˈbɪʃ(ə)n/ n. (chiefly Botany).
– ORIGIN ME: from L. *imbibere*, from *in-* 'in' + *bibere* 'to drink'.

**imbricate** chiefly Zoology & Botany • v. /ˈɪmbrɪkeɪt/ [usu. as adj.

**imbricated**] arrange in an overlapping manner like roof tiles. ● **adj.** /ˈɪmbrɪkət/ (of scales, sepals, etc.) having adjacent edges overlapping. Compare with **VALVATE**.
– DERIVATIVES **imbrication** n.
– ORIGIN C17 (in the sense 'shaped like a pantile'): from L. *imbricat-*, *imbricare* 'cover with roof tiles'.

**imbroglio** /ɪmˈbrəʊlɪəʊ/ ● **n.** (pl. **-os**) **1** an extremely confused or complicated situation. **2** archaic a confused heap.
– ORIGIN C18: Ital., from *imbrogliare* 'confuse'.

**imbrue** /ɪmˈbruː/ ● **v.** (**imbrues**, **imbrued**, **imbruing**) archaic or poetic/literary stain, especially with blood.
– ORIGIN ME: from OFr. *embruer* 'bedaub', ult. of Gmc origin and rel. to **BROTH**.

**imbue** /ɪmˈbjuː/ ● **v.** (**imbues**, **imbued**, **imbuing**) (often **be imbued with**) fill with a feeling or quality.
– ORIGIN ME (in the sense 'saturate'): from Fr. *imbu* 'moistened', from L. *imbut-*, *imbuere* 'moisten'.

**I.Mech.E.** ● **abbrev.** Institution of Mechanical Engineers.

**IMF** ● **abbrev.** International Monetary Fund.

**IMHO** ● **abbrev.** in my humble opinion.

**imidazole** /ˌɪmɪˈdeɪzəʊl, ɪˈmɪdəzəʊl/ ● **n.** Chemistry a crystalline heterocyclic compound with mildly basic properties.
– ORIGIN C19: from **IMIDE** + **AZO-** + **-OLE**.

**imide** /ˈɪmʌɪd/ ● **n.** Chemistry an organic compound containing the group –CONHCO–.
– ORIGIN C19: from Fr., arbitrary alt. of **AMIDE**.

**I.Min.E.** ● **abbrev.** Institution of Mining Engineers.

**imine** /ˈɪmiːn/ ● **n.** Chemistry an organic compound containing the group –C=NH or –C=NR (where R is an alkyl group).
– ORIGIN C19: from **AMINE**, on the pattern of the pair *amide*, *imide*.

**imipramine** /ɪˈmɪprəmiːn/ ● **n.** Medicine a synthetic compound used to treat depression.
– ORIGIN 1950s: from *imi(ne)* + *pr(opyl)* + **AMINE**.

**imitate** ● **v.** follow as a model. ➤ copy (a person's speech or mannerisms), especially for comic effect. ➤ copy or simulate.
– DERIVATIVES **imitable** adj. **imitator** n.
– ORIGIN C16 (earlier (ME) as *imitation*): from L. *imitat-*, *imitari* 'copy'; rel. to *imago* 'image'.

**imitation** ● **n.** **1** the action of imitating. ➤ a copy. **2** Music the repetition of a phrase or melody in another part or voice, usually at a different pitch.

**imitative** /ˈɪmɪtətɪv/ ● **adj.** **1** following a model. **2** (of a word) reproducing a natural sound (e.g. *fizz*) or pronounced in a way thought to correspond to the appearance or character of the object or action described (e.g. *blob*).
– DERIVATIVES **imitatively** adv. **imitativeness** n.

**imli** /ˈɪmliː/ ● **n.** Indian term for **TAMARIND**.
– ORIGIN via Hindi from Sanskrit *amlikā*.

**immaculate** ● **adj.** **1** perfectly clean, neat, or tidy. **2** free from flaws or mistakes. ➤ Catholic Theology free from sin. **3** Botany & Zoology uniformly coloured without spots or other marks.
– DERIVATIVES **immaculacy** n. **immaculately** adv. **immaculateness** n.
– ORIGIN ME: from L. *immaculatus*, from *in-* 'not' + *maculatus* 'stained'.

**Immaculate Conception** ● **n.** the Roman Catholic doctrine that God preserved the Virgin Mary from the taint of original sin from the moment she was conceived. ➤ the feast commemorating the Immaculate Conception on December 8th.

**immanent** /ˈɪmənənt/ ● **adj.** existing or operating within. ➤ (of God) permanently pervading the universe. Often contrasted with **TRANSCENDENT**.
– DERIVATIVES **immanence** n. **immanency** n. **immanentism** n. **immanentist** n.
– ORIGIN C16: from late L. *immanent-*, *immanere* 'remain within'.

**immaterial** ● **adj.** **1** irrelevant. **2** Philosophy spiritual rather than physical.
– DERIVATIVES **immateriality** n. **immaterially** adv.

**immaterialism** ● **n.** the belief that matter has no objective existence.
– DERIVATIVES **immaterialist** n.

**immature** ● **adj.** not fully developed. ➤ having or showing emotional or intellectual development appropriate to someone younger.
– DERIVATIVES **immaturely** adv. **immaturity** n.

**immeasurable** ● **adj.** too large, extensive, or extreme to measure.
– DERIVATIVES **immeasurability** n. **immeasurably** adv.

**immediate** ● **adj.** **1** occurring or done at once. ➤ most urgent; current. **2** nearest in time, space, or relationship. ➤ (of a relation or action) direct. **3** Philosophy (of knowledge or reaction) intuitive.
– DERIVATIVES **immediacy** n. **immediateness** n.
– ORIGIN ME: from OFr. *immediat*, or from late L. *immediatus*, from *in-* 'not' + *mediatus* 'intervening', past part. of *mediare* (see **MEDIATE**).

**immediately** ● **adv.** **1** at once. **2** very close or adjacent in time or space. ➤ in direct or very close relation. ● **conj.** chiefly Brit. as soon as.

**Immelmann** /ˈɪm(ə)lmən/ (also **Immelmann turn**) ● **n.** an aerobatic manoeuvre consisting of a half loop followed by a half roll.
– ORIGIN C20: named after the Ger. fighter pilot Max *Immelmann*.

**immemorial** ● **adj.** very old or long past: *from time immemorial.*
– DERIVATIVES **immemorially** adv.
– ORIGIN C17: from med. L. *immemorialis*, from *in-* 'not' + *memorialis* 'relating to the memory'.

**immense** ● **adj.** extremely large or great.
– DERIVATIVES **immensity** n.
– ORIGIN ME: via Fr. from L. *immensus* 'immeasurable', from *in-* 'not' + *mensus* 'measured'.

**immensely** ● **adv.** to a great extent; extremely.

**immerse** ● **v.** **1** dip or submerge in a liquid. **2** (**immerse oneself** or **be immersed**) involve oneself deeply in a particular activity or interest.
– ORIGIN C17 (earlier (C15) as *immersion*): from L. *immers-*, *immergere* 'dip into'.

**immersion** ● **n.** **1** the action of immersing or the state of being immersed. **2** chiefly N. Amer. a method of teaching a foreign language by the exclusive use of that language. **3** Astronomy the disappearance of a celestial body in the shadow of or behind another.

**immersion heater** ● **n.** an electric heating element that is positioned in the liquid to be heated, typically in a domestic hot-water tank.

**immersive** ● **adj.** (of a computer display) generating a three-dimensional image which appears to surround the user.

**immigrant** ● **n.** a person who comes to live permanently in a foreign country.

**immigrate** ● **v.** come to live permanently in a foreign country.
– DERIVATIVES **immigration** n.
– ORIGIN C17: from L. *immigrat-*, *immigrare* 'immigrate', from *in-* 'into' + *migrare* 'migrate'.

**imminent** ● **adj.** **1** about to happen. **2** archaic overhanging.
– DERIVATIVES **imminence** n. **imminently** adv.
– ORIGIN ME: from L. *imminent-*, *imminere* 'overhang, impend', from *in-* 'upon, towards' + *minere* 'to project'.

**immiscible** /ɪˈmɪsɪb(ə)l/ ● **adj.** (of liquids) not forming a homogeneous mixture when added together.
– DERIVATIVES **immiscibility** n. **immiscibly** adv.

**immiseration** /ɪˌmɪzəˈreɪʃ(ə)n/ ● **n.** economic impoverishment.
– DERIVATIVES **immiserate** v.
– ORIGIN 1940s: translating Ger. *Verelendung*.

**immittance** /ɪˈmɪt(ə)ns/ ● **n.** Physics admittance and impedance (as a combined concept).

**immobile** ● **adj.** not moving. ➤ incapable of moving or being moved.
– DERIVATIVES **immobility** n.

**immobilize** (also **-ise**) ● **v.** prevent from moving or operating as normal. ➤ restrict the movements of (a limb or

patient) to allow healing.
– DERIVATIVES **immobilization** n. **immobilizer** n.

**immoderate** • **adj.** lacking moderation; excessive.
– DERIVATIVES **immoderately** adv. **immoderation** n.

**immodest** • **adj.** not humble, decent, or decorous.
– DERIVATIVES **immodestly** adv. **immodesty** n.

**immolate** /ˈɪməleɪt/ • **v.** kill or offer as a sacrifice, especially by burning.
– DERIVATIVES **immolation** n. **immolator** n.
– ORIGIN C16 (earlier (ME) as *immolation*): from L. *immolat-*, *immolare* 'sprinkle with sacrificial meal', based on *mola* 'meal'.

**immoral** • **adj.** not conforming to accepted standards of morality.
– DERIVATIVES **immorality** n. (pl. **-ies**). **immorally** adv.

**immoral earnings** • **pl. n.** earnings from prostitution.

**immoralism** • **n.** a system of thought or behaviour that does not accept moral principles.
– DERIVATIVES **immoralist** n.

**immortal** /ɪˈmɔːt(ə)l/ • **adj.** living forever. ➤deserving to be remembered forever. • **n.** an immortal being, especially a god of ancient Greece or Rome. ➤a person of enduring fame. ➤(**Immortal**) a member of the French Academy.
– DERIVATIVES **immortality** /ɪmɔːˈtalɪti/ n. **immortalization** (also **-isation**) n. **immortalize** (also **-ise**) v. **immortally** adv.

**immortelle** /ˌɪmɔːˈtɛl/ • **n.** **1** another term for **EVERLASTING**. **2** W. Indian a Caribbean tree with a spiny trunk and red, orange, or pinkish flowers. [Genus *Erythrina*.]
– ORIGIN Fr. (fem. adj.), lit. 'everlasting'.

**immovable** (also **immoveable**) • **adj.** not able to be moved or changed. ➤Law (of property) consisting of land, buildings, or other permanent items. • **n.** (**immovables**) Law immovable property.
– DERIVATIVES **immovability** n. **immovably** adv.

**immune** • **adj.** **1** resistant to a particular infection owing to the presence of specific antibodies or sensitized white blood cells. ➤Biology of or relating to such resistance: *the immune system*. **2** exempt from an obligation or penalty. **3** (often **immune to**) not susceptible.
– DERIVATIVES **immunity** n. (pl. **-ies**).
– ORIGIN ME: from L. *immunis* 'exempt from public service or charge', from *in-* 'not' + *munis* 'ready for service'.

**immune response** • **n.** the reaction of the cells and fluids of the body to the presence of an antigen.

**immunize** (also **-ise**) • **v.** make immune to infection, typically by inoculation.
– DERIVATIVES **immunization** n. **immunizer** n.

**immuno-** /ˈɪmjʊnəʊ, ɪˈmjuːnəʊ/ • **comb. form** Medicine representing **IMMUNE**, **IMMUNITY**, or **IMMUNOLOGY**.

**immunoassay** /ˌɪmjʊnəʊˈaseɪ, ɪˌmjuːnəʊ-/ • **n.** Biochemistry a procedure for detecting or measuring substances through their properties as antigens or antibodies.

**immunoblotting** • **n.** a technique for analysing or identifying proteins in a mixture, involving separation by electrophoresis followed by staining with antibodies.

**immunochemistry** • **n.** the branch of biochemistry concerned with immune responses and systems.

**immunocompetent** /ˌɪmjʊnəʊˈkɒmpɪtənt, ɪˌmjuːnəʊ-/ • **adj.** Medicine having a normal immune response.
– DERIVATIVES **immunocompetence** n.

**immunocompromised** • **adj.** Medicine having an impaired immune system.

**immunodeficiency** • **n.** Medicine reduced ability of the immune system to protect the body from infection.

**immunogenic** /ˌɪmjʊnəʊˈdʒɛnɪk, ɪˌmjuːnəʊ-/ • **adj.** (of a substance) able to produce an immune response.
– DERIVATIVES **immunogenicity** n.

**immunoglobulin** /ˌɪmjʊnəʊˈglɒbjʊlɪn, ɪˌmjuːnəʊ-/ • **n.** Biochemistry any of a class of blood proteins which function as antibodies.

**immunology** • **n.** the branch of medicine and biology concerned with immunity.
– DERIVATIVES **immunologic** adj. **immunological** adj. **immunologically** adv. **immunologist** n.

**immunosorbent** • **adj.** Biochemistry denoting techniques making use of the absorption of antibodies by insoluble preparations of antigens.

**immunosuppression** • **n.** Medicine suppression of an immune response, especially as induced to help the survival of an organ after a transplant operation.
– DERIVATIVES **immunosuppressant** n. **immunosuppressed** adj.

**immunosuppressive** • **adj.** Medicine (chiefly of drugs) partially or completely suppressing the immune response of an individual. • **n.** a drug of this kind.

**immunotherapy** • **n.** Medicine the prevention or treatment of disease with substances that stimulate the immune response.

**immure** /ɪˈmjʊə/ • **v.** confine or imprison.
– DERIVATIVES **immurement** n.
– ORIGIN C16: from Fr. *emmurer* or med. L. *immurare*, from *in-* 'in' + *murus* 'wall'.

**immutable** /ɪˈmjuːtəb(ə)l/ • **adj.** unchanging or unchangeable.
– DERIVATIVES **immutability** n. **immutably** adv.

**IMO** • **abbrev.** International Maritime Organization.

**i-Mode** • **n.** a technology that allows data to be transferred to and from Internet sites via mobile phone.
– ORIGIN from **I**[2] (referring to the user's ability to interact directly with the Internet) + **MODE**.

**IMP** • **abbrev.** Bridge International Match Point.

**imp** • **n.** a mischievous child. ➤a small, mischievous devil or sprite. • **v.** repair a damaged feather in (the wing of a trained hawk) by attaching part of a new feather.
– ORIGIN OE (in ME denoting a descendant of the devil or an evil person): *impa*, *impe* 'young shoot, scion', from *impian* 'to graft', based on Gk *emphuein* 'to implant'.

**impact** • **n.** /ˈɪmpakt/ **1** the action of one object coming forcibly into contact with another. **2** a marked effect or influence. • **v.** /ɪmˈpakt/ **1** come into forcible contact with another object. ➤chiefly N. Amer. come into forcible contact with. **2** (often **impact on**) have a strong effect. **3** press firmly.
– DERIVATIVES **impactive** adj. **impactor** n.
– ORIGIN C17: from L. *impact-*, *impingere* (see **IMPINGE**).

**impacted** • **adj.** **1** (of a tooth) wedged between another tooth and the jaw. **2** (of a fractured bone) having the parts crushed together. **3** (of faeces) lodged in the intestine.
– DERIVATIVES **impaction** n.

**impair** • **v.** weaken or damage.
– DERIVATIVES **impairment** n.
– ORIGIN ME *enpeire*, from OFr. *empeirier*, based on late L. *pejorare* (from L. *pejor* 'worse').

**impaired** • **adj.** [often in combination] having a disability of a specified kind: *hearing-impaired*.

**impala** /ɪmˈpɑːlə, -ˈpalə/ • **n.** (pl. same) a graceful antelope of southern and East Africa, with lyre-shaped horns. [*Aepyceros melampus*.]
– ORIGIN C19: from Zulu *i-mpala*.

**impale** • **v.** **1** transfix or pierce with a sharp instrument. **2** Heraldry display (a coat of arms) side by side with another on the same shield, separated by a vertical line.
– DERIVATIVES **impalement** n. **impaler** n.
– ORIGIN C16: from Fr. *empaler* or med. L. *impalare*, from L. *in-* 'in' + *palus* 'a stake'.

**impalpable** • **adj.** **1** unable to be felt by touch. **2** not easily comprehended.
– DERIVATIVES **impalpability** n. **impalpably** adv.

**impanel** (also **empanel**) • **v.** (**impanelled**, **impanelling**; US **impaneled**, **impaneling**) enrol (a jury) or enrol (someone) on to a jury.
– DERIVATIVES **impanelment** n.
– ORIGIN ME: from Anglo-Norman Fr. *empaneller*, from *em-* 'in' + OFr. *panel* 'panel'.

**impark** • **v.** historical enclose (animals) in a park. ➤enclose (land) to make it into a park.
– ORIGIN ME: from OFr. *emparquer*, from *em-* 'within' + *parc* 'park'.

**impart** • **v.** communicate (information). ➤bestow (a quality).
– DERIVATIVES **impartation** n.
– ORIGIN ME (in the sense 'give a share of'): from OFr. *impartir*, from L. *impartire*, from *in-* 'in' + *pars*, *part-*

'part'.

**impartial** • **adj.** treating all rivals or disputants equally.
– DERIVATIVES **impartiality** n. **impartially** adv.

**impassable** • **adj.** impossible to travel along or over.
– DERIVATIVES **impassability** n. **impassableness** n. **impassably** adv.

**impasse** /am'pɑːs, 'ampɑːs/ • **n.** a deadlock.
– ORIGIN C19: from Fr., from *im-* (expressing negation) + the stem of *passer* 'to pass'.

**impassion** • **v.** make passionate.
– ORIGIN C16: from Ital. *impassionnare*, from *im-* (expressing intensive force) + *passione* 'passion'.

**impassioned** • **adj.** filled with or showing great emotion.

**impassive** • **adj.** not feeling or showing emotion.
– DERIVATIVES **impassively** adv. **impassiveness** n. **impassivity** n.

**impasto** /ɪm'pastəʊ/ • **n.** Art the process or technique of laying on paint or pigment thickly so that it stands out from a surface.
– ORIGIN C18: from Ital., from *impastare*, from *im-* 'upon' + *pasta* 'a paste'.

**impatiens** /ɪm'patɪɛnz/ • **n.** a plant of a genus that includes busy Lizzie and its many hybrids. [Genus *Impatiens*.]
– ORIGIN mod. L. , from L., lit. 'impatient' (because the capsules of the plant readily burst open when touched).

**impatient** • **adj. 1** having or showing a lack of patience or tolerance. **2** restlessly eager.
– DERIVATIVES **impatience** n. **impatiently** adv.

**impeach** • **v. 1** call into question the integrity or validity of (a practice). **2** Brit. charge with treason or another crime against the state. ➤ chiefly US charge (the holder of a public office) with misconduct.
– DERIVATIVES **impeachable** adj. **impeachment** n.
– ORIGIN ME: from OFr. *empecher* 'impede', from late L. *impedicare* 'entangle' (based on L. *pes, ped-* 'foot').

**impeccable** /ɪm'pɛkəb(ə)l/ • **adj.** in accordance with the highest standards. ➤ Theology, rare not liable to sin.
– DERIVATIVES **impeccability** n. **impeccably** adv.
– ORIGIN C16: from L. *impeccabilis*, from *in-* 'not' + *peccare* 'to sin'.

**impecunious** /ˌɪmpɪ'kjuːnɪəs/ • **adj.** having little or no money.
– DERIVATIVES **impecuniosity** n. **impecuniousness** n.
– ORIGIN C16: from **IN-**[1] + obs. *pecunious* 'wealthy' (from L. *pecuniosus*, from *pecunia* 'money').

**impedance** /ɪm'piːd(ə)ns/ • **n.** the effective resistance to an alternating electric current arising from the combined effects of ohmic resistance and reactance. See also **ACOUSTIC IMPEDANCE.**

**impede** /ɪm'piːd/ • **v.** delay or block the progress or action of.
– ORIGIN C16 (earlier (ME) as *impediment*): from L. *impedire* 'shackle the feet of', based on *pes, ped-* 'foot'.

**impediment** /ɪm'pɛdɪm(ə)nt/ • **n. 1** a hindrance or obstruction. **2** (also **speech impediment**) a defect in a person's speech, such as a lisp or stammer.
– DERIVATIVES **impedimental** adj.

**impedimenta** /ɪmˌpɛdɪ'mɛntə/ • **pl. n.** equipment for an activity or expedition, especially when an encumbrance.
– ORIGIN C17: from L., pl. of *impedimentum* 'impediment', from *impedire* (see **IMPEDE**).

**impel** /ɪm'pɛl/ • **v.** (**impelled**, **impelling**) drive, force, or urge to do something. ➤ drive forward.
– ORIGIN ME: from L. *impellere*, from *in-* 'towards' + *pellere* 'to drive'.

**impeller** (also **impellor**) • **n.** the rotating part of a centrifugal pump, compressor, etc. designed to move a fluid. ➤ a similar device used to measure speed or distance travelled through water.

**impend** /ɪm'pɛnd/ • **v.** [usu. as adj. **impending**] be about to happen. ➤ (of something bad) loom.
– ORIGIN C16: from L. *impendere*, from *in-* 'towards, upon' + *pendere* 'hang'.

**impenetrable** /ɪm'pɛnɪtrəb(ə)l/ • **adj. 1** impossible to pass through or enter. ➤ impervious to new ideas or influences. **2** impossible to understand. **3** Physics (of matter) incapable of occupying the same space as other matter at the same time.
– DERIVATIVES **impenetrability** n. **impenetrably** adv.
– ORIGIN ME: via Fr. from L. *impenetrabilis*, from *in-* 'not' + *penetrabilis* 'able to be pierced', from *penetrare* (see **PENETRATE**).

**impenitent** • **adj.** not feeling shame or regret.
– DERIVATIVES **impenitence** n. **impenitency** n. **impenitently** adv.

**imperative** • **adj. 1** of vital importance. **2** giving an authoritative command. ➤ Grammar denoting the mood of a verb that expresses a command or exhortation, as in *come here!* • **n.** an essential or urgent thing. ➤ a factor or influence making something necessary.
– DERIVATIVES **imperatival** /ɪmˌpɛrə'tʌɪv(ə)l/ adj. **imperatively** adv. **imperativeness** n.
– ORIGIN ME: from late L. *imperativus* (lit. 'specially ordered'), from *imperare* 'to command', from *in-* 'towards' + *parare* 'make ready'.

**imperator** /ˌɪmpə'rɑːtɔː/ • **n.** Roman History commander (a title conferred under the Republic on a victorious general and under the Empire on the emperor).
– DERIVATIVES **imperatorial** /ˌɪmpɛrə'tɔːrɪəl, ɪmˌpɛrə-/ adj.
– ORIGIN L., from *imperare* 'to command'.

**imperceptible** • **adj.** so slight, gradual, or subtle as not to be perceived.
– DERIVATIVES **imperceptibility** n. **imperceptibly** adv.

**imperceptive** • **adj.** lacking in perception or insight.

**impercipient** • **adj.** failing to perceive something.
– DERIVATIVES **impercipience** n.

**imperfect** • **adj. 1** faulty or incomplete. **2** Grammar (of a tense) denoting a past action in progress but not completed at the time in question. **3** Music (of a cadence) ending on the dominant chord. **4** Law (of a gift, title, etc.) transferred without all the necessary conditions or requirements being met.
– DERIVATIVES **imperfection** n. **imperfectly** adv.

**imperfective** • **adj.** Grammar relating to or denoting an aspect of verbs in Slavic languages that expresses action without reference to its completion. The opposite of **PERFECTIVE.**

**imperfect rhyme** • **n.** a rhyme that only partly satisfies the usual criteria (e.g. *love* and *move*).

**imperforate** /ɪm'pəːf(ə)rət/ • **adj. 1** (of a postage stamp or a block or sheet of stamps) lacking perforations. **2** Anatomy & Zoology lacking the normal opening.

**imperial** • **adj. 1** of or relating to an empire or an emperor. ➤ characteristic of an emperor; majestic or magnificent. **2** relating to or denoting the system of non-metric weights and measures formerly used for all measures in the UK, and still used for some. **3** chiefly historical (of a size of paper) measuring (in the UK) 762 × 559 mm (30 × 22 inches). • **n.** a small pointed beard growing below the lower lip (associated with Napoleon III of France).
– DERIVATIVES **imperially** adv.
– ORIGIN ME: via OFr. from L. *imperialis*, from *imperium* 'command, empire'; rel. to *imperare* 'to command'.

**imperial gallon** • **n.** see **GALLON** (sense 1).

**imperialism** • **n. 1** a policy of extending a country's power and influence through colonization, use of military force, or other means. **2** chiefly historical rule by an emperor.
– DERIVATIVES **imperialist** n. & adj. **imperialistic** adj. **imperialistically** adv. **imperialize** (also **-ise**) v.

**imperil** • **v.** (**imperilled**, **imperilling**; US **imperiled**, **imperiling**) put into danger.
– ORIGIN ME: from **PERIL**, prob. on the pattern of *endanger*.

**imperious** /ɪm'pɪərɪəs/ • **adj.** arrogant and domineering.
– DERIVATIVES **imperiously** adv. **imperiousness** n.
– ORIGIN C16: from L. *imperiosus*, from *imperium* (see **IMPERIUM**).

**imperishable** ● **adj.** enduring forever.
– DERIVATIVES **imperishability** /-ˈbɪlɪti/ n. **imperishableness** n. **imperishably** adv.

**imperium** /ɪmˈpɪərɪəm/ ● **n.** absolute power.
– ORIGIN C17: from L., 'command, empire'; rel. to *imperare* 'to command'.

**impermanent** ● **adj.** not permanent.
– DERIVATIVES **impermanence** n. **impermanency** n. **impermanently** adv.

**impermeable** /ɪmˈpəːmɪəb(ə)l/ ● **adj.** not allowing fluid to pass through.
– DERIVATIVES **impermeability** n.

**impersonal** ● **adj. 1** not influenced by or involving personal feelings. ➤featureless and anonymous. **2** not existing as a person: *an impersonal God.* **3** Grammar (of a verb) used only with a formal subject (in English usually *it*) and expressing an action not attributable to a definite subject (as in *it is snowing*).
– DERIVATIVES **impersonality** n. **impersonally** adv.

**impersonal pronoun** ● **n.** the pronoun *it* when used without definite reference or antecedent, as in *it was snowing*.

**impersonate** ● **v.** pretend to be (another person) for entertainment or fraud.
– DERIVATIVES **impersonation** n. **impersonator** n.
– ORIGIN C17 (in the sense 'personify'): from **IN-**[2] + L. *persona* 'person', on the pattern of *incorporate*.

**impertinent** ● **adj. 1** not showing proper respect. **2** formal not pertinent.
– DERIVATIVES **impertinence** n. **impertinently** adv.
– ORIGIN ME: from OFr., or from late L. *impertinent-* 'not having reference to', from L. *in-* 'not' + *pertinere* 'pertain'.

**imperturbable** /ˌɪmpəˈtəːbəb(ə)l/ ● **adj.** unable to be upset or excited.
– DERIVATIVES **imperturbability** n. **imperturbably** adv.
– ORIGIN ME: from late L. *imperturbabilis*, from *in-* 'not' + *perturbare* (see **PERTURB**).

**impervious** /ɪmˈpəːvɪəs/ ● **adj. 1** not allowing fluid to pass through. **2** (**impervious to**) unable to be affected by.
– DERIVATIVES **imperviously** adv. **imperviousness** n.

**impetigo** /ˌɪmpɪˈtʌɪgəʊ/ ● **n.** a contagious bacterial skin infection forming pustules and yellow crusty sores.
– ORIGIN ME: from L., from *impetere* 'to attack'.

**impetuous** ● **adj. 1** acting or done quickly and rashly. **2** moving forcefully or rapidly.
– DERIVATIVES **impetuosity** n. **impetuously** adv. **impetuousness** n.
– ORIGIN ME: from OFr. *impetueux*, from late L. *impetuosus*, from *impetere* 'to attack'.

**impetus** ● **n.** the force or energy with which a body moves. ➤a driving force.
– ORIGIN C17: from L., 'assault, force'.

**impi** /ˈɪmpi/ ● **n.** (pl. **impis**) a body of Zulu warriors. ➤an armed band of Zulus involved in urban or rural conflict.
– ORIGIN Zulu, 'regiment, armed band'.

**impiety** /ɪmˈpʌɪɪti/ ● **n.** (pl. **-ies**) lack of piety or reverence.

**impinge** ● **v.** (**impinging**) (usu. **impinge on**) have an effect. ➤come into contact; encroach.
– DERIVATIVES **impingement** n. **impinger** n.
– ORIGIN C16 (orig. in the sense 'thrust at forcibly', then 'come into forcible contact'): from L. *impingere* 'drive something in or at'.

**impious** /ˈɪmpɪəs, ɪmˈpʌɪəs/ ● **adj.** not showing respect or reverence. ➤wicked.
– DERIVATIVES **impiously** adv. **impiousness** n.

**impish** ● **adj.** mischievous.
– DERIVATIVES **impishly** adv. **impishness** n.

**implacable** ● **adj.** unable to be appeased. ➤relentless.
– DERIVATIVES **implacability** n. **implacably** adv.

**implant** ● **v.** /ɪmˈplɑːnt/ **1** insert or fix (tissue or an artificial object) into the body. ➤(of a fertilized egg) become attached to the wall of the uterus. **2** establish (an idea) in the mind. ● **n.** /ˈɪmplɑːnt/ a thing implanted.
– DERIVATIVES **implantation** n.
– ORIGIN ME: from late L. *implantare* 'engraft'.

**implausible** ● **adj.** not seeming reasonable or probable.
– DERIVATIVES **implausibility** n. **implausibly** adv.

**implement** ● **n.** /ˈɪmplɪm(ə)nt/ **1** a tool, utensil, or other piece of equipment, used for a particular purpose. **2** Scots Law performance of an obligation. ● **v.** /ˈɪmplɪmɛnt/ put into effect.
– DERIVATIVES **implementation** n. **implementer** n.
– ORIGIN ME: partly from med. L. *implementa* (pl.), partly from late L. *implementum* 'filling up', both from L. *implere* 'fill up' (later 'employ').

**implicate** ● **v.** /ˈɪmplɪkeɪt/ **1** show to be involved in a crime. ➤(**be implicated in**) bear some of the responsibility for (an action or process). **2** convey (a meaning or intention) indirectly; imply. ● **n.** /ˈɪmplɪkət/ chiefly Logic a thing implied.
– DERIVATIVES **implicative** /ɪmˈplɪkətɪv/ adj. **implicatively** adv.
– ORIGIN ME (orig. in the sense 'entwine'; cf. **EMPLOY** and **IMPLY**): from L. *implicatus* 'folded in', past part. of *implicare* (see **IMPLY**).

**implication** ● **n. 1** the implicit conclusion that can be drawn from something. ➤a likely consequence. **2** the action of implicating or the state of being implicated.
– DERIVATIVES **implicational** adj.

**implicature** /ˈɪmplɪˌkətʃə, -ˌkeɪtʃə/ ● **n.** the action of implying a meaning beyond the literal sense of what is explicitly stated, for example saying *the frame is nice* and implying *I don't like the picture in it.*

**implicit** /ɪmˈplɪsɪt/ ● **adj. 1** implied though not directly expressed. **2** (**implicit in**) always to be found in. **3** with no qualification or question: *an implicit faith in God.* **4** Mathematics (of a function) not expressed directly in terms of independent variables.
– DERIVATIVES **implicitly** adv. **implicitness** n.
– ORIGIN C16: from Fr. *implicite* or L. *implicitus*, later form of *implicatus* 'entwined', past part. of *implicare* (see **IMPLY**).

**implode** /ɪmˈpləʊd/ ● **v.** collapse or cause to collapse violently inwards.
– DERIVATIVES **implosion** n. **implosive** adj.
– ORIGIN C19: from **IN-**[2] + L. *plodere*, *plaudere* 'to clap', on the pattern of *explode*.

**implore** ● **v.** beg earnestly or desperately. ➤archaic beg earnestly for.
– DERIVATIVES **imploring** adj. **imploringly** adv.
– ORIGIN C16: from Fr. *implorer* or L. *implorare* 'invoke with tears'.

**imply** ● **v.** (**-ies**, **-ied**) indicate by suggestion rather than explicit reference. ➤(of a fact or occurrence) suggest as a logical consequence.
– DERIVATIVES **implied** adj. **impliedly** adv.
– ORIGIN ME (orig. in the sense 'entangle'): from OFr. *emplier*, from L. *implicare*, from *in-* 'in' + *plicare* 'to fold'; cf. **EMPLOY** and **IMPLICATE**.

**impolite** ● **adj.** not having or showing good manners.
– DERIVATIVES **impolitely** adv. **impoliteness** n.

**impolitic** /ɪmˈpɒlɪtɪk/ ● **adj.** failing to possess or display prudence.
– DERIVATIVES **impoliticly** adv.

**imponderable** ● **adj. 1** difficult or impossible to estimate or assess. **2** archaic or poetic/literary very light. ● **n.** an imponderable factor.
– DERIVATIVES **imponderability** /-ˈbɪlɪti/ n. **imponderably** adv.

**import** ● **v. 1** bring (goods or services) into a country from abroad. **2** Computing transfer (data) into a file or document. **3** archaic indicate or signify. ● **n. 1** an imported commodity, article, or service. ➤the action or process of importing. **2** the implied meaning of something. ➤importance.
– DERIVATIVES **importable** adj. **importation** n. **importer** n.
– ORIGIN ME: from L. *importare* 'bring in' (in med. L. 'imply, be of consequence').

**important** ● **adj. 1** of great significance or value. **2** having high rank or status.
– DERIVATIVES **importance** n. **importantly** adv.

– ORIGIN ME: from med. L. *important-*, *importare* (see **IMPORT**).

**importunate** /ɪmˈpɔːtjʊnət/ • **adj.** persistent or pressing.
– DERIVATIVES **importunately** adv. **importunity** n. (pl. **-ies**).
– ORIGIN C16: from L. *importunus* 'inconvenient', based on *Portunus*, the name of the god who protected harbours; cf. **OPPORTUNE**.

**importune** /ˌɪmpɔːˈtjuːn/ • **v. 1** harass with persistent requests. **2** [usu. as noun **importuning**] approach to offer one's services as a prostitute.
– ORIGIN C16: from Fr. *importuner* or med. L. *importunari*, from L. *importunus* (see **IMPORTUNATE**).

**impose** • **v. 1** force to be accepted, undertaken, or complied with. **2** (often **impose on**) take advantage of someone. **3** Printing arrange (pages of type) so as to be in the correct order after printing and folding.
– DERIVATIVES **imposition** n.
– ORIGIN C15 (earlier (ME) as *imposition*): from Fr. *imposer*, from L. *imponere* 'inflict, deceive', but influenced by *impositus* 'inflicted' and OFr. *poser* 'to place'.

**imposing** • **adj.** grand and impressive.
– DERIVATIVES **imposingly** adv.

**impossible** • **adj.** not able to occur, exist, or be done. ➤very difficult to deal with.
– DERIVATIVES **impossibility** n. (pl. **-ies**). **impossibly** adv.

**impost**[1] /ˈɪmpəʊst/ • **n. 1** a tax or similar compulsory payment. **2** Horse Racing the weight carried by a horse as a handicap.
– ORIGIN C16: from Fr., from med. L. *impostus*, from L. *impositus*, past part. of *imponere* (see **IMPOSE**).

**impost**[2] /ˈɪmpəʊst/ • **n.** Architecture the top course of a pillar that supports an arch.
– ORIGIN C15: from Ital. *imposta*, fem. past part. of *imporre*, from L. *imponere* (see **IMPOSE**).

**impostor** (also **imposter**) • **n.** a person who assumes a false identity in order to deceive or defraud.
– ORIGIN C16: from Fr. *imposteur*, from late L. *impostor*, contr. of *impositor*, from L. *imponere* (see **IMPOSE**).

**imposture** • **n.** an instance of assuming a false identity.

**impotent** /ˈɪmpət(ə)nt/ • **adj. 1** helpless or powerless. **2** (of a man) abnormally unable to achieve an erection or orgasm.
– DERIVATIVES **impotence** n. **impotency** n. **impotently** adv.

**impound** • **v. 1** seize and take legal custody of. **2** shut up (domestic animals) in a pound. **3** (of a dam) hold back or confine (water).
– DERIVATIVES **impoundable** adj. **impounder** n. **impoundment** n.

**impoverish** • **v. 1** make poor. **2** exhaust the strength or natural fertility of.
– DERIVATIVES **impoverishment** n.
– ORIGIN ME: from OFr. *empoveriss-*, lengthened stem of *empoverir*, based on *povre* 'poor'.

**impracticable** • **adj.** impossible in practice to do or carry out.
– DERIVATIVES **impracticability** n. **impracticably** adv.

**impractical** • **adj. 1** not adapted for use or action; not sensible. **2** chiefly N. Amer. impracticable.
– DERIVATIVES **impracticality** n. **impractically** adv.

**imprecation** • **n.** formal a spoken curse.
– DERIVATIVES **imprecatory** adj.
– ORIGIN ME: from L. *imprecatio(n-)*, from *imprecari* 'invoke (evil)', from *in-* 'towards' + *precari* 'pray'.

**imprecise** • **adj.** lacking exactness.
– DERIVATIVES **imprecisely** adv. **impreciseness** n. **imprecision** n.

**impregnable** • **adj.** unable to be captured or broken into. ➤unable to be overcome.
– DERIVATIVES **impregnability** n. **impregnably** adv.

**impregnate** /ˈɪmprɛgneɪt/ • **v. 1** (usu. **be impregnated with**) soak or saturate with a substance. ➤fill with a feeling or quality. **2** make pregnant; fertilize.
– DERIVATIVES **impregnation** n.
– ORIGIN C17 (earlier (ME) as *impregnation*): from late L. *impregnat-*, *impregnare* 'make pregnant'.

**impresario** /ˌɪmprɪˈsɑːrɪəʊ/ • **n.** (pl. **-os**) a person who organizes and often finances theatrical or musical productions. ➤chiefly historical the manager of a musical, theatrical, or operatic company.
– ORIGIN C18: from Ital., from *impresa* 'undertaking'.

**imprescriptible** /ˌɪmprɪˈskrɪptɪb(ə)l/ • **adj.** Law (of rights) unable to be taken away by prescription or by lapse of time.
– ORIGIN C16: from med. L. *imprescriptibilis*.

**impress**[1] • **v. 1** make (someone) feel admiration and respect. **2** make a mark or design on using a stamp or seal. **3** (**impress something on**) emphasize an idea in the mind of. **4** apply (an electric current or potential) from an external source. • **n. 1** an act of making an impression. ➤a mark made by a seal or stamp. **2** a person's characteristic mark or quality.
– DERIVATIVES **impressible** adj.
– ORIGIN ME: from OFr. *empresser*, from *em-* 'in' + *presser* 'to press', influenced by L. *imprimere* (see **IMPRINT**).

**impress**[2] • **v.** historical force to serve in an army or navy. ➤commandeer (goods or equipment) for public service.
– DERIVATIVES **impressment** n.
– ORIGIN C16: from **IN-**[2] + **PRESS**[2].

**impression** • **n. 1** an idea, feeling, or opinion. ➤an effect produced on someone: *her quick wit made a good impression.* **2** an imitation of a person or thing, done to entertain. **3** a mark impressed on a surface. ➤Dentistry a negative copy of the teeth or mouth made by pressing them into a soft substance. **4** the printing of a number of copies of a publication for issue at one time. ➤chiefly Brit. a particular printed version of a book, especially one reprinted with no or only minor alteration. ➤a print taken from an engraving.
– DERIVATIVES **impressional** adj.

**impressionable** • **adj.** easily influenced.
– DERIVATIVES **impressionability** n. **impressionably** adv.

**Impressionism** • **n. 1** a style or movement in painting characterized by a concern with depicting the visual impression of the moment, especially in terms of the shifting effect of light. **2** a literary or artistic style that seeks to capture a feeling or experience rather than to achieve accurate depiction. **3** Music a style of composition in which clarity of structure and theme is subordinate to harmonic effects.
– DERIVATIVES **Impressionist** n. & adj.
– ORIGIN from Fr. *impressionnisme*, from *impressionniste*, orig. applied unfavourably with ref. to Monet's painting *Impression: soleil levant* (1872).

**impressionist** • **n.** an entertainer who impersonates famous people.

**impressionistic** • **adj. 1** based on subjective impressions presented unsystematically. **2** (**Impressionistic**) in the style of Impressionism.
– DERIVATIVES **impressionistically** adv.

**impressive** • **adj.** evoking admiration through size, quality, or skill.
– DERIVATIVES **impressively** adv. **impressiveness** n.

**imprest** • **n.** a fund used by a business for small items of expenditure and restored to a fixed amount periodically. ➤a sum of money advanced to a person for a particular purpose.
– ORIGIN C16: from the earlier phr. *in prest* 'as a loan', influenced by Ital. or med. L. *imprestare* 'lend'.

**imprimatur** /ˌɪmprɪˈmeɪtə, -ˈmɑːtə, -ˈmɑːtʊə/ • **n.** an official licence issued by the Roman Catholic Church to print an ecclesiastical or religious book. ➤authority or approval.
– ORIGIN C17: from L., 'let it be printed'.

**imprint** • **v. 1** (usu. **be imprinted**) impress or stamp (a mark or outline) on a surface or body. **2** make an impression or mark on. ➤fix (an idea) firmly in someone's mind. **3** (**imprint on**) Zoology (of a young animal) come to recognize (another animal, person, or thing) as a parent or object of habitual trust. • **n. 1** an impressed mark or outline. **2** a printer's or publisher's name and other details in a book or other publication. ➤a brand name under which books are published, typically the name of a former publishing house now part of a larger group.

– ORIGIN ME: from OFr. *empreinter*, based on L. *imprimere*, from *in-* 'into' + *premere* 'to press'.

**imprison** ● v. put or keep in prison.
– DERIVATIVES **imprisonment** n.
– ORIGIN ME *emprison*, from OFr. *emprisoner*.

**impro** ● n. (pl. **-os**) informal improvisation, especially as a theatrical technique.

**improbable** ● adj. not likely to be true or to happen. ➤unexpected and apparently inauthentic.
– DERIVATIVES **improbability** n. (pl. **-ies**). **improbably** adv.

**improbity** /ɪm'prəʊbɪti, -'prɒb-/ ● n. formal wickedness or dishonesty.

**impromptu** /ɪm'prɒm(p)tjuː/ ● adj. & adv. unplanned or unrehearsed. ● n. (pl. **impromptus**) a short piece of instrumental music, especially a solo, reminiscent of an improvisation.
– ORIGIN C17 (as adv.): from Fr., from L. *in promptu* 'in readiness', from *promptus* (see PROMPT).

**improper** ● adj. not in accordance with accepted standards of behaviour. ➤unseemly or indecent.
– DERIVATIVES **improperly** adv.

**improper fraction** ● n. a fraction in which the numerator is greater than the denominator, such as 5/4.

**impropriate** /ɪm'prəʊprɪeɪt/ ● v. [usu. as adj. **impropriated**] grant (an ecclesiastical benefice) to a corporation or person as their property. ➤place (tithes or ecclesiastical property) in lay hands.
– DERIVATIVES **impropriation** n.
– ORIGIN C16: from Anglo-Latin *impropriat-*, *impropriare* 'appropriate', based on L. *proprius* 'one's own'.

**impropriator** ● n. a person to whom a benefice is granted as their property.

**impropriety** /ˌɪmprə'prʌɪəti/ ● n. (pl. **-ies**) improper behaviour or character.

**improv** ● n. another term for IMPRO.

**improve** ● v. **1** make or become better. ➤(**improve on/upon**) achieve or produce something better than. **2** [as adj. **improving**] giving moral or intellectual benefit.
– DERIVATIVES **improvability** n. **improvable** adj. **improvement** n. **improver** n.
– ORIGIN C16 (as *emprowe* or *improwe*): from Anglo-Norman Fr. *emprower*, based on OFr. *prou* 'profit'.

**improvident** ● adj. lacking foresight; thoughtless.
– DERIVATIVES **improvidence** n. **improvidently** adv.

**improvise** ● v. **1** create and perform (music, drama, or verse) spontaneously or without preparation. **2** produce or make (something) from whatever is available.
– DERIVATIVES **improvisation** n. **improvisational** adj. **improvisatorial** adj. **improvisatory** adj. **improviser** n.
– ORIGIN C19 (earlier (C18) as *improvisation*): from Fr. *improviser* or Ital. *improvvisare*, from *improvviso* 'extempore'.

**imprudent** ● adj. not showing care for the consequences of an action; rash.
– DERIVATIVES **imprudence** n. **imprudently** adv.

**impudent** /'ɪmpjʊd(ə)nt/ ● adj. not showing due respect for another person; impertinent.
– DERIVATIVES **impudence** n. **impudently** adv.
– ORIGIN ME (in the sense 'immodest, indelicate'): from L. *impudent-*, from *in-* 'not' + *pudent-* 'ashamed, modest'.

**impudicity** /ˌɪmpjʊ'dɪsɪti/ ● n. formal lack of modesty.

**impugn** /ɪm'pjuːn/ ● v. dispute the truth, validity, or honesty of (a statement or motive).
– DERIVATIVES **impugnable** adj. **impugnment** n.
– ORIGIN ME: from L. *impugnare* 'assail'.

**impuissant** /ɪm'pjuːɪs(ə)nt, -'pwiː-, -'pwɪs-/ ● adj. poetic/literary unable to take effective action; powerless.
– DERIVATIVES **impuissance** n.

**impulse** ● n. **1** a sudden strong and unreflective urge or desire to act. **2** a driving or motivating force; an impetus. **3** a pulse of electrical energy; a brief current. **4** Physics a force acting briefly on a body and producing a change of momentum.
– ORIGIN C17 (earlier (ME) as *impulsion*), as a verb in the sense 'give an impulse to', from L. *impuls-*, *impellere* (see IMPEL).

**impulsion** ● n. **1** a strong urge to do something. **2** the force or motive behind an action or process.

**impulsive** ● adj. **1** acting or done without forethought. **2** Physics acting as an impulse.
– DERIVATIVES **impulsively** adv. **impulsiveness** n. **impulsivity** n.

**impunity** /ɪm'pjuːnɪti/ ● n. (usu. in phr. **with impunity**) exemption from punishment or freedom from the injurious consequences of an action.
– ORIGIN C16: from L. *impunitas*, from *impunis* 'unpunished'.

**impure** ● adj. **1** mixed with foreign matter; adulterated or tainted. **2** morally wrong, especially in sexual matters. ➤defiled or contaminated according to ritual prescriptions.
– DERIVATIVES **impurely** adv. **impureness** n.

**impurity** ● n. (pl. **-ies**) **1** the quality or condition of being impure. **2** a constituent which impairs the purity of something. **3** Electronics a trace element deliberately added to a semiconductor; a dopant.

**impute** /ɪm'pjuːt/ ● v. **1** (usu. **impute something to**) attribute (something, especially something bad) to someone. **2** Theology ascribe (righteousness, guilt, etc.) to some-one by virtue of a similar quality in another. **3** Finance assign (a value) to something by inference from the value of the products or processes to which it contributes.
– DERIVATIVES **imputable** adj. **imputation** n.
– ORIGIN ME: from OFr. *imputer*, from L. *imputare* 'enter in the account'.

**imshi** /'ɪmʃiː/ ● exclam. military slang go away; be off.
– ORIGIN from colloq. Arab. *'mšī* 'go!'

**I.Mun.E.** ● abbrev. Institution of Municipal Engineers.

**IN** ● abbrev. Indiana (in official postal use).

**In** ● symb. the chemical element indium.

**in** ● prep. **1** expressing the situation of being enclosed or surrounded by something. **2** expressing motion that results in being within or surrounded by something. **3** expressing a period of time during which an event takes place or a situation remains the case. **4** expressing the length of time before a future event is expected to take place. **5** expressing a state, condition, or quality. **6** expressing inclusion or involvement. **7** indicating someone's occupation or profession. **8** indicating the language or medium used. **9** expressing a value as a proportion of (a whole). ● adv. **1** expressing movement that results in being enclosed or surrounded by something. **2** expressing the situation of being enclosed or surrounded by something. ➤present at one's home or office. ➤Cricket batting. **3** expressing arrival at a destination. **4** (of the tide) rising or at its highest level. ● adj. informal fashionable.
– PHRASES **be in for** have good reason to expect (something, typically something unpleasant). **be in for it** have good reason to expect trouble or retribution. **in on** privy to (a secret). **in that** for the reason that. **in with** informal enjoying friendly relations with. **the ins and outs** informal all the details of something.
– ORIGIN OE *in* (prep.), *inn*, *inne* (adv.), of Gmc origin.

**in.** ● abbrev. inch(es).

**in-**[1] (also **il-** before *l*; **im-** before *b*, *m*, *p*; **ir-** before *r*) ● prefix **1** (added to adjectives) not: *infertile*. **2** (added to nouns) without; a lack of: *inappreciation*.
– ORIGIN from L.

**in-**[2] (also **il-** before *l*; **im-** before *b*, *m*, *p*; **ir-** before *r*) ● prefix in; into; towards; within: *influx*.
– ORIGIN representing IN or the L. prep. *in*.

**-in**[1] ● suffix Chemistry forming names of organic compounds, pharmaceutical products, proteins, etc: *insulin*.
– ORIGIN alt. of -INE[4].

**-in**[2] ● comb. form denoting a gathering of people for a common purpose, typically as a form of protest: *sit-in*.

**-ina** ● suffix **1** denoting feminine names and titles: *tsarina*. **2** denoting names of musical instruments: *concertina*. **3** denoting names of plant and animal groups: *globigerina*.
– ORIGIN from Ital., Sp., or L.

**inability** ● n. the state of being unable to do something.

**in absentia** /ˌɪn ab'sɛntɪə/ ● adv. while not present.
– ORIGIN L., 'in absence'.

**inaccessible** • adj. **1** unable to be reached. ➤ unable to be seen or used. **2** difficult to understand or appreciate. **3** not open to advances or influence; unapproachable.
– DERIVATIVES **inaccessibility** n. **inaccessibly** adv.

**inaccurate** • adj. not accurate.
– DERIVATIVES **inaccuracy** n. **inaccurately** adv.

**inaction** • n. lack of action where some is expected or appropriate.

**inactivate** • v. make inactive or inoperative.
– DERIVATIVES **inactivation** n. **inactivator** n.

**inactive** • adj. not active, working, or energetic.
– DERIVATIVES **inactively** adv. **inactivity** n.

**inadequate** • adj. **1** lacking the quality or quantity required; insufficient for a purpose. **2** (of a person) unable to deal with a situation or with life.
– DERIVATIVES **inadequacy** n. (pl. **-ies**). **inadequately** adv.

**inadmissible** • adj. **1** (especially of evidence in court) not accepted as valid. **2** not to be allowed or tolerated.
– DERIVATIVES **inadmissibility** n. **inadmissibly** adv.

**inadvertent** • adj. not resulting from or achieved through deliberate planning.
– DERIVATIVES **inadvertence** n. **inadvertency** n. **inadvertently** adv.
– ORIGIN C17: from IN-[1] + L. *advertent-*, *advertere* 'turn the mind to'.

**inadvisable** • adj. likely to have unfortunate consequences; unwise.
– DERIVATIVES **inadvisability** n.

**inalienable** • adj. unable to be taken away from or given away by the possessor.
– DERIVATIVES **inalienability** n. **inalienably** adv.

**inalterable** • adj. unable to be changed.
– DERIVATIVES **inalterability** n. **inalterably** adv.

**inamorato** /ɪˌnaməˈrɑːtəʊ/ • n. (fem. **inamorata**) (pl. **-os** or **-as**) a person's lover.
– ORIGIN C16: Ital., lit. 'enamoured', past part. of *inamorare*, based on L. *amor* 'love'.

**inane** • adj. lacking sense or meaning; silly.
– DERIVATIVES **inanely** adv. **inaneness** n. **inanity** n. (pl. **-ies**).
– ORIGIN C16: from L. *inanis* 'empty, vain'.

**inanimate** • adj. **1** not alive, especially not in the manner of animals and humans. **2** showing no sign of life; lifeless.
– DERIVATIVES **inanimately** adv.

**inanition** /ˌɪnəˈnɪʃ(ə)n/ • n. **1** exhaustion caused by lack of nourishment. **2** lack of vigour and enthusiasm.
– ORIGIN ME: from late L. *inanitio(n-)*, from L. *inanire* 'make empty', from *inanis* 'empty, vain'.

**inapparent** • adj. Medicine causing no noticeable signs or symptoms.

**inappetence** • n. chiefly Veterinary Medicine lack of appetite.
– DERIVATIVES **inappetent** adj.

**inapplicable** • adj. not relevant or appropriate.
– DERIVATIVES **inapplicability** n. **inapplicably** adv.

**inapposite** /ɪnˈapəzɪt/ • adj. out of place; inappropriate.
– DERIVATIVES **inappositely** adv. **inappositeness** n.

**inappreciable** • adj. **1** too small or insignificant to be valued or perceived. **2** archaic too valuable to be properly estimated.
– DERIVATIVES **inappreciably** adv.

**inappreciative** • adj. another term for UNAPPRECIATIVE.
– DERIVATIVES **inappreciation** n.

**inappropriate** • adj. not suitable or appropriate.
– DERIVATIVES **inappropriately** adv. **inappropriateness** n.

**inapt** • adj. not suitable or appropriate.
– DERIVATIVES **inaptitude** n. **inaptly** adv.

**inarch** • v. Horticulture graft (a plant) by connecting a growing branch without separating it from its parent stock.

**inarguable** • adj. another term for UNARGUABLE.
– DERIVATIVES **inarguably** adv.

**inarticulate** /ˌɪnɑːˈtɪkjʊlət/ • adj. **1** unable to speak distinctly or express oneself clearly. ➤ unspoken or not expressed in words. **2** without joints or articulations.
– DERIVATIVES **inarticulacy** n. **inarticulately** adv. **inarticulateness** n.

**inartistic** • adj. having or showing a lack of skill or talent in art.
– DERIVATIVES **inartistically** adv.

**inasmuch** • adv. (in phr. **inasmuch as**) **1** to the extent that; in so far as. **2** considering that; since.

**inattentive** • adj. not paying attention. ➤ failing to attend to the comfort or wishes of others.
– DERIVATIVES **inattention** n. **inattentively** adv. **inattentiveness** n.

**inaudible** • adj. unable to be heard.
– DERIVATIVES **inaudibility** n. **inaudibly** adv.

**inaugurate** /ɪˈnɔːgjʊreɪt/ • v. **1** begin or introduce (a system, period, project, etc.). **2** admit formally to office.
– DERIVATIVES **inaugural** adj. **inauguration** n. **inaugurator** n. **inauguratory** adj.
– ORIGIN C16: from L. *inaugurat-* 'interpreted as omens (from the flight of birds)', based on *augurare* 'to augur'.

**inauspicious** • adj. not conducive to success; unpromising.
– DERIVATIVES **inauspiciously** adv. **inauspiciousness** n.

**inauthentic** • n. not authentic, genuine, or sincere.
– DERIVATIVES **inauthentically** adv. **inauthenticity** n.

**in-between** • adj. informal situated somewhere between two extremes; intermediate.
– DERIVATIVES **in-betweener** n.

**inboard** • adv. & adj. within or towards the centre of a ship, aircraft, or vehicle.

**inborn** • adj. existing from birth. ➤ natural to a person or animal.

**inbound** • adj. & adv. travelling towards a particular place, especially when returning to the original point of departure.

**inbred** • adj. **1** produced by inbreeding. **2** existing in a person or animal from birth; congenital.

**inbreed** • v. (past and past part. **inbred**) [often as noun **inbreeding**] breed from closely related people or animals, especially over many generations.

**inbuilt** • adj. existing as an original or essential part.

**Inc.** • abbrev. N. Amer. Incorporated.

**Inca** • n. **1** a member of a South American Indian people living in the central Andes before the Spanish conquest. **2** the supreme ruler of this people.
– DERIVATIVES **Incaic** /ɪŋˈkeɪɪk/ adj. **Incan** adj.
– ORIGIN the name in Quechua, lit. 'lord, royal person'.

**inca** • n. a South American hummingbird with mainly blackish or bronze-coloured plumage. [Genus *Coeligena*: four species.]

**incalculable** • adj. **1** too great to be calculated or estimated. **2** not able to be calculated, estimated, or predicted.
– DERIVATIVES **incalculability** n. **incalculably** adv.

**in camera** • adv. see CAMERA[2].

**incandesce** /ˌɪnkanˈdɛs/ • v. glow with heat.

**incandescent** • adj. **1** emitting light as a result of being heated. ➤ (of an electric light) containing a filament which glows white-hot when heated by a current passed through it. **2** informal extremely angry.
– DERIVATIVES **incandescence** n. **incandescently** adv.
– ORIGIN C18: from Fr., from L. *incandescent-*, *incandescere* 'glow'.

**incant** /ɪnˈkant/ • v. chant or intone.

**incantation** • n. a series of words said as a magic spell or charm.
– DERIVATIVES **incantatory** adj.
– ORIGIN ME: via OFr. from late L. *incantatio(n-)*, from L. *incantare* 'chant, bewitch', based on *cantare* 'sing'.

**incapable** • adj. **1** (**incapable of**) unable to do or achieve. ➤ not able to be treated in a certain way. **2** unable to behave rationally or manage one's own affairs.
– DERIVATIVES **incapability** n. **incapably** adv.

**incapacitant** • n. a substance capable of temporarily incapacitating a person without wounding or killing them.

**incapacitate** /ˌɪnkəˈpasɪteɪt/ • v. **1** prevent from functioning in a normal way. **2** Law deprive (someone) of their legal capacity.

– DERIVATIVES **incapacitation** n.

**incapacity** • n. (pl. **-ies**) **1** physical or mental inability to do something or to manage one's affairs. **2** legal disqualification.

**incarcerate** /ɪnˈkɑːsəreɪt/ • v. imprison or confine.

– DERIVATIVES **incarceration** n. **incarcerator** n.

– ORIGIN C16 (earlier (ME) as *incarceration*): from med. L. *incarcerat-*, *incarcerare*, based on L. *carcer* 'prison'.

**incarnadine** /ɪnˈkɑːnədʌɪn/ poetic/literary • v. colour (something) a bright crimson or pinkish-red. • n. a bright crimson or pinkish-red colour.

– ORIGIN C16: from Fr. *incarnadin(e)*, from Ital. *incarnadino*, var. of *incarnatino* 'flesh colour', based on L. *incarnare* (see **INCARNATE**).

**incarnate** • adj. /ɪnˈkɑːnət/ [often postpos.] **1** (of a deity or spirit) embodied in flesh; in human form. **2** represented in the ultimate or most extreme form: *capitalism incarnate*. • v. /ˈɪnkɑːneɪt, -ˈkɑːneɪt/ **1** embody or represent (a deity or spirit) in human form. **2** be the living embodiment of (a quality).

– ORIGIN ME: from eccles. L. *incarnat-*, *incarnare* 'make flesh', from L. *in-* 'into' + *caro*, *carn-* 'flesh'.

**incarnation** • n. **1** a living embodiment of a deity, spirit, or abstract quality. **2** (**the Incarnation**) (in Christian theology) the embodiment of God the Son in human flesh as Jesus Christ. **3** (with reference to reincarnation) each of a series of earthly lifetimes or forms.

**incase** • v. variant spelling of **ENCASE**.

**incautious** • adj. heedless of potential problems or risks.

– DERIVATIVES **incaution** n. **incautiously** adv. **incautiousness** n.

**incendiary** /ɪnˈsɛndɪəri/ • adj. **1** (of a device or attack) designed to cause fires. **2** tending to stir up conflict or excitement. • n. (pl. **-ies**) an incendiary bomb or device.

– DERIVATIVES **incendiarism** n.

– ORIGIN ME: from L. *incendiarius*, from *incendium* 'conflagration', from *incendere* 'set fire to'.

**incense**[1] /ˈɪnsɛns/ • n. a gum, spice, or other substance that is burned for the sweet smell it produces. • v. perfume with incense or a similar fragrance.

– DERIVATIVES **incensation** n.

– ORIGIN ME: from OFr. *encens* (n.), *encenser* (v.), from eccles. L. *incensum* 'something burnt, incense', neut. past part. of *incendere* 'set fire to'.

**incense**[2] /ɪnˈsɛns/ • v. make very angry.

– ORIGIN ME (in the sense 'inflame or excite with a strong feeling'): from OFr. *incenser*, from L. *incendere* 'set fire to'.

**incensory** /ˈɪnsɛns(ə)ri/ • n. (pl. **-ies**) another term for **CENSER**.

**incentive** • n. a thing that motivates or encourages someone to do something. ➤ a payment or concession to stimulate greater output or investment.

– DERIVATIVES **incentivize** (also **-ise**) v.

– ORIGIN ME: from L. *incentivum* 'something that sets the tune or incites', from *incantare* 'to chant or charm'.

**incentre** (US **incenter**) • n. Geometry the centre of the incircle of a triangle or other figure.

**incept** /ɪnˈsɛpt/ • v. Brit. historical graduate from a university with an academic degree.

– DERIVATIVES **inceptor** n.

**inception** • n. the establishment or starting point of an institution or activity.

– ORIGIN ME: from L. *inceptio(n-)*, from *incipere* 'begin'.

**inceptisol** /ɪnˈsɛptɪsɒl/ • n. Soil Science a freely draining soil in which the formation of distinct horizons is not far advanced.

– ORIGIN 1960s: from L. *inceptum* 'beginning' + **-SOL**.

**inceptive** • adj. **1** relating to or marking the beginning of something; initial. **2** Grammar (of a verb) expressing the beginning of an action. • n. Grammar an inceptive verb.

**incertitude** • n. a state of uncertainty or hesitation.

**incessant** • adj. (especially of something unpleasant) continuing without pause or interruption.

– DERIVATIVES **incessancy** n. **incessantly** adv. **incessantness** n.

– ORIGIN ME: via OFr. from late L. *incessant-*, from L. *in-* 'not' + *cessant-*, *cessare* 'cease'.

**incest** • n. sexual relations between people classed as being too closely related to marry each other.

– ORIGIN ME: from L. *incestus*, *incestum* 'unchastity, incest', from *in-* 'not' + *castus* 'chaste'.

**incestuous** /ɪnˈsɛstjʊəs/ • adj. **1** involving or guilty of incest. **2** (of human relations) excessively close and resistant to outside influence.

– DERIVATIVES **incestuously** adv. **incestuousness** n.

**inch**[1] • n. **1** a unit of linear measure equal to one twelfth of a foot (2.54 cm). ➤ (**inches**) informal a person's height or waist measurement. ➤ a very small amount or distance. **2** a quantity of rainfall that would cover a horizontal surface to a depth of one inch. **3** (also **inch of mercury**) a unit of atmospheric pressure able to support a column of mercury one-inch high in a barometer. • v. move along slowly and carefully.

– PHRASES **every inch 1** the whole surface, distance, or area. **2** entirely; very much so. (**to**) **within an inch of one's life** almost to the point of death.

– ORIGIN OE *ynce*, from L. *uncia* 'twelfth part', from *unus* 'one' (prob. denoting a unit): cf. **OUNCE**[1].

**inch**[2] • n. chiefly Scottish (in place names) a small island or a small area of high land.

– ORIGIN ME: from Sc. Gaelic *innis*.

**-in-chief** • comb. form supreme: *commander-in-chief*.

**inchmeal** • adv. by inches; little by little.

– ORIGIN C16: from **INCH**[1] + *-meal* from OE *mǣlum*, in the sense 'measure, quantity taken at one time'.

**inchoate** • adj. /ɪnˈkəʊeɪt, ˈɪnk-, -ət/ **1** not fully formed or developed; rudimentary. ➤ confused or incoherent. **2** Law (of an offence, such as incitement or conspiracy) anticipating a further criminal act.

– DERIVATIVES **inchoately** adv. **inchoateness** n.

– ORIGIN C16: from L. *inchoat-*, *inchoare*, var. of *incohare* 'begin'.

**inchoative** /ɪnˈkəʊətɪv/ • adj. Grammar denoting an aspect of a verb expressing the beginning of an action, typically one occurring of its own accord. Compare with **ERGATIVE**. • n. an inchoative verb.

**inchworm** • n. North American term for **LOOPER**.

**incidence** • n. **1** the occurrence, rate, or frequency of a disease, crime, or other undesirable thing. **2** Physics the intersection of a line, or something moving in a straight line, such as a beam of light, with a surface. **3** the way in which the burden of a tax falls upon the population.

– ORIGIN ME: from OFr., or from med. L. *incidentia*, from L. *incidere* (see **INCIDENT**).

**incident** • n. **1** an event or occurrence; an instance of something happening. ➤ a violent event, such as an assault or skirmish. **2** Law a privilege, burden, or right attaching to an office, estate, or other holding. • adj. **1** (**incident to**) liable to happen because of; resulting from. **2** (especially of light or other radiation) falling on or striking something. ➤ of or relating to incidence. **3** (**incident to**) Law attaching to.

– ORIGIN ME: via OFr. from L. *incident-*, *incidere* 'to fall upon, happen to'.

**incidental** • adj. **1** occurring as a minor accompaniment. ➤ occurring by chance in connection with something else. **2** (**incidental to**) liable to happen as a consequence of. • n. an incidental detail, expense, event, etc.

**incidentally** • adv. **1** as an incidental comment; by the way. **2** in an incidental manner.

**incidental music** • n. music used in a film or play as a background.

**incinerate** /ɪnˈsɪnəreɪt/ • v. destroy (something, especially waste material) by burning.

– DERIVATIVES **incineration** n.

– ORIGIN C15: from med. L. *incinerat-*, *incinerare* 'burn to ashes'.

**incinerator** • n. an apparatus for incinerating waste material, especially industrial waste.

**incipient** /ɪnˈsɪpɪənt/ • adj. in an initial stage; beginning to happen or develop.

– DERIVATIVES **incipience** n. **incipiency** n. **incipiently** adv.

– ORIGIN C16 (as n. denoting a beginner): from L. *incipient-*, *incipere*, 'undertake, begin'.

**incipit** /ˈɪnsɪpɪt/ ● **n.** the opening of a manuscript, early printed book, or chanted liturgical text.
– ORIGIN L., lit. '(here) begins'.

**incircle** ● **n.** Geometry a circle inscribed in a triangle or other figure so as to touch (but not cross) each side.

**incise** ● **v.** make a cut or cuts in (a surface). ➤ cut (a mark or decoration) into a surface.
– ORIGIN C16 (earlier (ME) as *incision*): from Fr. *inciser*, from L. *incis-*, *incidere* 'cut into'.

**incision** ● **n. 1** a surgical cut made in skin or flesh. **2** the action or process of cutting into something.
– DERIVATIVES **incisional** adj.

**incisive** ● **adj. 1** intelligently analytical and concise. **2** (of an action) quick and direct.
– DERIVATIVES **incisively** adv. **incisiveness** n.

**incisor** ● **n.** a narrow-edged tooth at the front of the mouth, adapted for cutting.

**incisure** /ɪnˈsɪʒə/ (also **incisura** /ˌɪnsɪˈʒʊərə/) ● **n.** (pl. **incisures** or **incisurae** /-riː/) Anatomy a deep indentation or notch in an edge or surface.

**incite** ● **v.** encourage or stir up (violent or unlawful behaviour). ➤ urge or persuade to act in a violent or unlawful way.
– DERIVATIVES **incitation** n. **inciteful** adj. **incitement** n. **inciter** n.
– ORIGIN C15 (earlier (ME) as *incitation*): from Fr. *inciter*, from L. *incitare*, from *in-* 'towards' + *citare* 'rouse'.

**incivility** ● **n.** (pl. **-ies**) rude or unsociable speech or behaviour.

**incl.** ● **abbrev.** including.

**inclement** /ɪnˈklɛm(ə)nt/ ● **adj.** (of the weather) unpleasantly cold or wet.
– DERIVATIVES **inclemency** n. (pl. **-ies**).

**inclination** ● **n. 1** a natural tendency or urge to act or feel in a particular way. ➤ (**inclination for/to/towards**) an interest in or liking for. **2** a slope or slant. ➤ a dip of a magnetic needle. **3** the angle at which a straight line or plane is inclined to another.

**incline** ● **v. 1** (usu. **be inclined to/towards/to do something**) be favourably disposed towards or willing to do. **2** (usu. **be inclined to/to do something**) have a specified tendency, disposition, or talent. **3** lean or turn away from a given plane or direction, especially the vertical or horizontal. ➤ bend (one's head) forwards and downwards. ● **n.** an inclined surface, slope, or plane.
– DERIVATIVES **inclinable** adj. **incliner** n.
– ORIGIN ME: from OFr. *encliner*, from L. *inclinare* 'to bend towards'.

**inclined plane** ● **n.** a plane inclined at an angle to the horizontal.

**inclinometer** /ˌɪnklɪˈnɒmɪtə/ ● **n.** a device for measuring the angle of inclination of something, especially from the horizontal.

**inclose** ● **v.** variant spelling of **ENCLOSE**.

**inclosure** ● **n.** variant spelling of **ENCLOSURE**.

**include** ● **v. 1** comprise or contain as part of a whole. **2** make part of a whole or set. ➤ allow (someone) to share in an activity or privilege. ➤ (**include someone out**) informal specifically exclude someone.
– ORIGIN ME: from L. *includere*, from *in-* 'into' + *claudere* 'to shut'.

**including** ● **prep.** containing as part of the whole being considered.

**inclusion** ● **n. 1** the action or state of including or of being included. ➤ a person or thing that is included. **2** chiefly Geology a body or particle of distinct composition embedded in a rock or other material.

**inclusive** ● **adj. 1** (**inclusive of**) containing (a specified element) as part of a whole. ➤ including all the expected or required services or items. ➤ [postpos.] between the extreme limits stated: *the ages of 55 to 59 inclusive.* **2** not excluding any section of society or any party. ➤ (of language) deliberately non-sexist, especially avoiding the use of masculine pronouns to cover both men and women.
– DERIVATIVES **inclusively** adv. **inclusiveness** n. **inclusivism** n. **inclusivist** n. & adj.

**inclusive fitness** ● **n.** Genetics the ability of an individual organism to pass on its genes to the next generation, taking into account the shared genes passed on by the organism's close relatives.

**incognito** /ˌɪnkɒgˈniːtəʊ, ɪnˈkɒgnɪtəʊ/ ● **adj. & adv.** having one's true identity concealed. ● **n.** (pl. **-os**) an assumed or false identity.
– ORIGIN C17: from Ital., lit. 'unknown'.

**incognizant** (also **incognisant**) ● **adj.** formal lacking knowledge or awareness.
– DERIVATIVES **incognizance** n.

**incoherent** ● **adj. 1** incomprehensible or confusing in speech or writing. ➤ internally inconsistent; illogical. **2** Physics (of waves) having no definite or stable phase relationship.
– DERIVATIVES **incoherence** n. **incoherency** n. (pl. **-ies**). **incoherently** adv.

**incohesion** ● **n.** lack of social cohesion.

**incombustible** ● **adj.** (especially of a building material) not inflammable.
– DERIVATIVES **incombustibility** n.

**income** ● **n.** money received, especially on a regular basis, for work or through investments.
– ORIGIN ME (in the sense 'entrance, arrival'): in early use from ON *innkoma*, later from **IN** + **COME**.

**incomer** ● **n.** chiefly Brit. a person who has come to live in an area in which they have not grown up.

**income support** ● **n.** (in the UK and Canada) payment made by the state to people on a low income.

**income tax** ● **n.** tax levied directly on personal income.

**incoming** ● **adj.** in the process of coming in. ➤ (of a message) being received rather than sent. ➤ (of an official or administration) having just been elected or appointed to succeed another. ● **n.** (**incomings**) revenue; income.

**incommensurable** /ˌɪnkəˈmɛnʃ(ə)rəb(ə)l, -sjə-/ ● **adj. 1** not able to be judged or measured by the same standards; having no common standard. **2** Mathematics (of numbers) in a ratio that cannot be expressed as a ratio of integers. ● **n.** an incommensurable quantity.
– DERIVATIVES **incommensurability** n. **incommensurably** adv.

**incommensurate** /ˌɪnkəˈmɛnʃ(ə)rət, -sjə-/ ● **adj. 1** (**incommensurate with**) out of keeping or proportion with. **2** another term for **INCOMMENSURABLE** (in sense 1).
– DERIVATIVES **incommensurately** adv. **incommensurateness** n.

**incommode** ● **v.** formal cause inconvenience to.
– ORIGIN C16: from Fr. *incommoder* or L. *incommodare*, from *in-* 'not' + *commodus* 'convenient'.

**incommodious** ● **adj.** formal or dated causing inconvenience or discomfort.
– DERIVATIVES **incommodiously** adv. **incommodiousness** n.

**incommunicable** ● **adj.** not able to be communicated to others.
– DERIVATIVES **incommunicability** n. **incommunicableness** n. **incommunicably** adv.

**incommunicado** /ˌɪnkəmjuːnɪˈkɑːdəʊ/ ● **adj. & adv.** not able to communicate with other people.
– ORIGIN C19: from Sp. *incomunicado*, past part. of *incomunicar* 'deprive of communication'.

**incommunicative** ● **adj.** another term for **UNCOMMUNICATIVE**.
– DERIVATIVES **incommunicatively** adv. **incommunicativeness** n.

**incommutable** ● **adj.** not capable of being changed or exchanged.
– DERIVATIVES **incommutably** adv.

**incomparable** /ɪnˈkɒmp(ə)rəb(ə)l/ ● **adj. 1** without an equal in quality or extent; matchless. **2** unable to be compared; totally different.
– DERIVATIVES **incomparability** n. **incomparably** adv.

**incompatible** ● **adj.** (of two things) not able to exist or

be used together. ➤ (of two people) unable to live together harmoniously.
– DERIVATIVES **incompatibility** n. **incompatibly** adv.

**incompetent** • **adj. 1** not sufficiently skilful to do something successfully. **2** Law not qualified to act in a particular capacity. • **n.** an incompetent person.
– DERIVATIVES **incompetence** n. **incompetency** n. **incompetently** adv.

**incomplete** • **adj.** not complete.
– DERIVATIVES **incompletability** n. **incompletable** adj. **incompletely** adv. **incompleteness** n. **incompletion** n.

**incompleteness theorem** • **n.** Logic the theorem, proposed by Kurt Gödel, that in any sufficiently powerful, logically consistent formulation of logic or mathematics there must be true formulas which are neither provable nor disprovable.

**incomprehensible** • **adj.** not able to be understood.
– DERIVATIVES **incomprehensibility** n. **incomprehensibleness** n. **incomprehensibly** adv. **incomprehension** n.

**incompressible** • **adj.** not able to be compressed.
– DERIVATIVES **incompressibility** n.

**incomputable** • **adj.** rare unable to be calculated or estimated.

**inconceivable** • **adj.** not capable of being imagined or grasped mentally; unbelievable.
– DERIVATIVES **inconceivability** n. **inconceivableness** n. **inconceivably** adv.

**inconclusive** • **adj.** not conclusive.
– DERIVATIVES **inconclusively** adv. **inconclusiveness** n.

**incongruent** /ɪnˈkɒŋɡrʊənt/ • **adj. 1** incongruous. **2** Chemistry affecting the components of an alloy or other substance differently: *incongruent melting.*
– DERIVATIVES **incongruence** n. **incongruently** adv.

**incongruous** /ɪnˈkɒŋɡrʊəs/ • **adj.** not in keeping with the surroundings or other elements; out of place.
– DERIVATIVES **incongruity** n. (pl. **-ies**). **incongruously** adv.

**inconnu** /ˈãkɒnuː, ˌãkɒˈn(j)uː/ • **n. 1** an unknown person or thing. **2** (pl. same) an edible predatory freshwater whitefish related to the salmon. [*Stenodus leucichthys.*]
– ORIGIN C19: Fr., lit. ‘unknown’.

**inconsecutive** • **adj.** not in order or following continuously.
– DERIVATIVES **inconsecutively** adv.

**inconsequent** • **adj. 1** not connected or following logically; irrelevant. **2** inconsequential.
– DERIVATIVES **inconsequence** n. **inconsequently** adv.

**inconsequential** • **adj.** not important or significant.
– DERIVATIVES **inconsequentiality** n. (pl. **-ies**). **inconsequentially** adv. **inconsequentialness** n.

**inconsiderable** • **adj.** [usu. with neg.] of small size, amount, or extent. ➤ unimportant or insignificant.

**inconsiderate** • **adj.** thoughtlessly causing hurt or inconvenience to others.
– DERIVATIVES **inconsiderately** adv. **inconsiderateness** n. **inconsideration** n.

**inconsistent** • **adj.** not consistent.
– DERIVATIVES **inconsistency** n. **inconsistently** adv.

**inconsolable** • **adj.** not able to be comforted or consoled.
– DERIVATIVES **inconsolability** n. **inconsolably** adv.

**inconsonant** • **adj.** rare not in agreement or harmony; not compatible.
– DERIVATIVES **inconsonance** n. **inconsonantly** adv.

**inconspicuous** • **adj.** not clearly visible or attracting attention.
– DERIVATIVES **inconspicuously** adv. **inconspicuousness** n.

**inconstant** • **adj.** frequently changing; variable or irregular.
– DERIVATIVES **inconstancy** n. (pl. **-ies**). **inconstantly** adv.

**incontestable** • **adj.** not able to be disputed.
– DERIVATIVES **incontestability** n. **incontestably** adv.

**incontinent** • **adj. 1** lacking voluntary control over urination or defecation. **2** lacking self-restraint; uncontrolled.
– DERIVATIVES **incontinence** n. **incontinently** adv.

**incontrovertible** • **adj.** not able to be denied or disputed.
– DERIVATIVES **incontrovertibility** n. **incontrovertibly** adv.

**inconvenience** • **n.** the state or fact of being slightly troublesome or difficult. • **v.** cause inconvenience to.
– DERIVATIVES **inconvenient** adj. **inconveniently** adv.

**inconvertible** • **adj.** not able to be converted.
– DERIVATIVES **inconvertibility** n. **inconvertibly** adv.

**incoordination** • **n.** chiefly technical lack of coordination.

**incorporate** • **v. 1** take in or include as part of a whole. **2** constitute (a company, city, or other organization) as a legal corporation. • **adj. 1** constituted as a legal corporation; incorporated. **2** poetic/literary having a bodily form; embodied.
– DERIVATIVES **incorporation** n. **incorporative** adj. **incorporator** n.
– ORIGIN ME: from late L. *incorporat-*, *incorporare* ‘embody’, based on L. *corpus, corpor-* ‘body’.

**incorporeal** /ˌɪnkɔːˈpɔːrɪəl/ • **adj. 1** not composed of matter; having no material existence. **2** Law having no physical existence.
– DERIVATIVES **incorporeality** n. **incorporeally** adv. **incorporeity** n.

**incorrect** • **adj.** not in accordance with fact or particular standards; wrong.
– DERIVATIVES **incorrectly** adv. **incorrectness** n.

**incorrigible** • **adj.** not able to be corrected or reformed: *she's an incorrigible flirt.*
– DERIVATIVES **incorrigibility** n. **incorrigibly** adv.

**incorruptible** • **adj. 1** not susceptible to corruption, especially by bribery. **2** not subject to death or decay; everlasting.
– DERIVATIVES **incorruptibility** n. **incorruptibly** adv.

**increase** • **v.** make or become greater in size, amount, or degree. • **n.** an instance of increasing.
– DERIVATIVES **increasable** adj. **increasing** adj. **increasingly** adv.
– ORIGIN ME: from OFr. *encreistre*, from L. *increscere*, from *in-* ‘into’ + *crescere* ‘grow’.

**incredible** • **adj. 1** impossible to believe. **2** difficult to believe; extraordinary. ➤ informal amazingly good.
– DERIVATIVES **incredibility** n. **incredibly** adv.

**incredulous** • **adj.** unwilling or unable to believe something.
– DERIVATIVES **incredulity** n. **incredulously** adv. **incredulousness** n.

**increment** /ˈɪŋkrɪm(ə)nt/ • **n. 1** an increase or addition, especially one of a series on a fixed scale. ➤ a regular increase in salary on such a scale. **2** Mathematics a small positive or negative change in a variable quantity or function.
– DERIVATIVES **incremental** adj. **incrementally** adv.
– ORIGIN ME: from L. *incrementum*, from the stem of *increscere* (see **INCREASE**).

**incrementalism** • **n.** belief in or advocacy of change by degrees.
– DERIVATIVES **incrementalist** n. & adj.

**incriminate** /ɪnˈkrɪmɪneɪt/ • **v.** make (someone) appear guilty of a crime or wrongdoing.
– DERIVATIVES **incrimination** n. **incriminatory** adj.
– ORIGIN C18 (earlier (C17) as *incrimination*): from late L. *incriminat-*, *incriminare* ‘accuse’, based on L. *crimen* ‘crime’.

**in-crowd** • **n.** (**the in-crowd**) informal a small group of people that are particularly fashionable or popular.

**incrust** • **v.** variant spelling of **ENCRUST**.

**incubate** /ˈɪŋkjʊbeɪt/ • **v. 1** (of a bird) sit on (eggs) in order to keep them warm and bring them to hatching. **2** develop (something, especially an infectious disease) slowly without outward or perceptible signs.
– DERIVATIVES **incubation** n. **incubative** adj. **incubatory** /ˈɪŋkjʊbeɪt(ə)ri/ adj.
– ORIGIN C17: from L. *incubat-*, *incubare* ‘lie on’.

**incubator** • **n. 1** an apparatus used to hatch eggs or grow micro-organisms under controlled conditions. **2** an enclosed apparatus providing a controlled and protective environment for the care of premature babies.

**incubus** /ˈɪŋkjʊbəs/ ● **n.** (pl. **incubi** /-bʌɪ/) **1** a male demon believed to have sexual intercourse with sleeping women. **2** archaic a nightmare.
– ORIGIN ME: late L. form of L. *incubo* 'nightmare', from *incubare* (see **INCUBATE**).

**incudes** plural form of **INCUS**.

**inculcate** /ˈɪnkʌlkeɪt/ ● **v.** instil (an idea or habit) by persistent instruction.
– DERIVATIVES **inculcation** n. **inculcator** n.
– ORIGIN C16: from L. *inculcat-*, *inculcare* 'press in'.

**inculpate** /ˈɪnkʌlpeɪt/ ● **v.** archaic accuse, blame, or incriminate.
– DERIVATIVES **inculpation** n. **inculpatory** adj.
– ORIGIN C18: from late L. *inculpat-*, *inculpare* 'make culpable'.

**inculturation** /ɪnˌkʌltʃəˈreɪʃ(ə)n/ ● **n.** variant spelling of **ENCULTURATION**.

**incumbency** ● **n.** (pl. **-ies**) the period during which an office is held.

**incumbent** /ɪnˈkʌmb(ə)nt/ ● **adj.** **1** (**incumbent on/upon**) necessary for (someone) as a duty or responsibility. **2** (of an official or regime) currently holding office. ● **n.** the holder of an office or post.
– ORIGIN ME (as n.): from Anglo-Latin *incumbens*, from L. *incumbere* 'lie or lean on'.

**incunabulum** /ˌɪnkjʊˈnabjʊləm/ (also **incunable** /ɪnˈkjuːnəb(ə)l/) ● **n.** (pl. **incunabula**) an early printed book, especially one printed before 1501.
– ORIGIN C19: from L. *incunabula* (neut. pl.) 'swaddling clothes, cradle'.

**incur** ● **v.** (**incurred**, **incurring**) become subject to (something unwelcome or unpleasant) as a result of one's actions.
– DERIVATIVES **incurrence** n.
– ORIGIN ME: from L. *incurrere*, from *in-* 'towards' + *currere* 'run'.

**incurable** ● **adj.** not able to be cured. ● **n.** an incurable person.
– DERIVATIVES **incurability** n. **incurably** adv.

**incurious** ● **adj.** not eager to know something; lacking curiosity.
– DERIVATIVES **incuriosity** n. **incuriously** adv. **incuriousness** n.

**incurrent** ● **adj.** chiefly Zoology (of a vessel or opening) conveying fluid inwards. The opposite of **EXCURRENT**.
– ORIGIN C16 (in the sense 'falling within (a period)'): from L. *incurrent-*, *incurrere* (see **INCUR**).

**incursion** /ɪnˈkəːʃ(ə)n/ ● **n.** an invasion or attack, especially a sudden or brief one.
– DERIVATIVES **incursive** adj.
– ORIGIN ME: from L. *incursio(n-)*, from *incurrere* (see **INCUR**).

**incurvate** ● **v.** /ˈɪnkəːveɪt/ [usu. as adj. **incurvated**] curve inwards. ● **adj.** /ɪnˈkəːvət/ curved inwards.
– DERIVATIVES **incurvation** n.
– ORIGIN ME: from L. *incurvat-*, *incurvare* 'bend into a curve'.

**incurve** ● **v.** [usu. as adj. **incurved**] curve inwards.

**incus** /ˈɪŋkəs/ ● **n.** (pl. **incudes** /ˈɪŋkjʊdiːz, ɪnˈkjuːdiːz/) Anatomy a small anvil-shaped bone in the middle ear, transmitting vibrations between the malleus and stapes.
– ORIGIN C17: from L., lit. 'anvil'.

**incuse** /ɪnˈkjuːz/ ● **n.** an impression hammered or stamped on a coin. ● **v.** mark (a coin) by impressing it with a stamp.
– ORIGIN C19: from L. *incus-*, *incudere* 'forge with a hammer'.

**IND** ● **abbrev.** India (international vehicle registration).

**Ind.** ● **abbrev.** **1** Independent. **2** India. **3** Indian. **4** Indiana.

**indebted** ● **adj.** owing money or gratitude.
– DERIVATIVES **indebtedness** n.
– ORIGIN ME *endetted*, from OFr. *endetter* 'involve in debt', assoc. with med. L. *indebitare*.

**indecent** ● **adj.** not conforming with generally accepted standards of behaviour or propriety.
– DERIVATIVES **indecency** n. **indecently** adv.

**indecent assault** ● **n.** sexual assault that does not involve rape.

**indecent exposure** ● **n.** the crime of intentionally showing one's sexual organs in public.

**indecipherable** /ˌɪndɪˈsʌɪf(ə)rəb(ə)l/ ● **adj.** not able to be read or understood.

**indecisive** ● **adj.** **1** not able to make decisions quickly and effectively. **2** not settling an issue.
– DERIVATIVES **indecision** n. **indecisively** adv. **indecisiveness** n.

**indeclinable** /ˌɪndɪˈklʌɪnəb(ə)l/ ● **adj.** Grammar (of a noun, pronoun, or adjective) having no inflections.

**indecorous** ● **adj.** not in keeping with good taste and propriety; improper.
– DERIVATIVES **indecorously** adv. **indecorousness** n.

**indecorum** /ˌɪndɪˈkɔːrəm/ ● **n.** failure to conform to good taste, propriety, or etiquette.

**indeed** ● **adv.** **1** used to emphasize a statement, description, or response. **2** used to introduce a further and stronger or more surprising point. **3** used in a response to express interest, incredulity, or contempt.
– ORIGIN ME: orig. as *in deed*.

**indefatigable** /ˌɪndɪˈfatɪgəb(ə)l/ ● **adj.** persisting tirelessly; unflagging.
– DERIVATIVES **indefatigability** n. **indefatigably** adv.
– ORIGIN C17: from Fr., or from L. *indefatigabilis*, from *in-* 'not' + *de-* 'away, completely' + *fatigare* 'wear out'.

**indefeasible** /ˌɪndɪˈfiːzɪb(ə)l/ ● **adj.** chiefly Law & Philosophy not able to be lost, annulled, or overturned.
– DERIVATIVES **indefeasibility** n. **indefeasibly** adv.

**indefectible** /ˌɪndɪˈfɛktɪb(ə)l/ ● **adj.** rare **1** not liable to fail, end, or decay. **2** perfect; faultless.

**indefensible** ● **adj.** **1** not justifiable by argument. **2** not able to be protected against attack.
– DERIVATIVES **indefensibility** n. **indefensibly** adv.

**indefinable** ● **adj.** not able to be defined or described exactly.
– DERIVATIVES **indefinably** adv.

**indefinite** ● **adj.** **1** not clearly expressed or defined; vague. ➤lasting for an unknown or unstated length of time. **2** Grammar (of a word, inflection, or phrase) not determining the person or thing referred to.
– DERIVATIVES **indefinitely** adv. **indefiniteness** n.

**indefinite article** ● **n.** Grammar a determiner (*a* and *an* in English) that introduces a noun phrase and implies that the thing referred to is non-specific.

**indefinite integral** ● **n.** Mathematics an integral expressed without limits, and so containing an arbitrary constant.

**indefinite pronoun** ● **n.** Grammar a pronoun that does not refer to any person or thing in particular, e.g. *anything*, *something*, *anyone*, *everyone*.

**indehiscent** /ˌɪndɪˈhɪs(ə)nt/ ● **adj.** Botany (of a pod or fruit) not splitting open to release the seeds when ripe.
– DERIVATIVES **indehiscence** n.

**indelible** /ɪnˈdɛlɪb(ə)l/ ● **adj.** **1** (of ink or a mark) unable to be removed. **2** unable to be forgotten.
– DERIVATIVES **indelibility** n. **indelibly** adv.
– ORIGIN C15 (as *indeleble*): from Fr., or from L. *indelebilis*, from *in-* 'not' + *delebilis* (from *delere* 'efface, delete').

**indelicate** ● **adj.** **1** lacking sensitive understanding or tact. **2** slightly indecent.
– DERIVATIVES **indelicacy** n. (pl. **-ies**). **indelicately** adv.

**indemnify** /ɪnˈdɛmnɪfʌɪ/ ● **v.** (**-ies**, **-ied**) **1** compensate in respect of harm or loss. **2** secure (someone) against legal responsibility for their actions.
– DERIVATIVES **indemnification** n. **indemnifier** n.

**indemnity** /ɪnˈdɛmnɪti/ ● **n.** (pl. **-ies**) **1** security or protection against a loss or other financial burden. ➤security against or exemption from legal responsibility for one's actions. **2** a sum of money paid as compensation, especially by a country defeated in war.
– ORIGIN ME: from Fr. *indemnite*, from late L. *indemnitas*, from L. *indemnis* 'unhurt, free from loss', based on *damnum* 'loss, damage'.

**indemonstrable** /ˌɪndɪˈmɒnstrəb(ə)l, ɪnˈdɛmən-/ ● **adj.**

not able to be proved or demonstrated. ➤ Philosophy (of a truth) axiomatic and hence not provable.

**indene** /ˈɪndiːn/ ● **n.** Chemistry a colourless liquid hydrocarbon, obtained from coal tar and used in making synthetic resins.
– ORIGIN C19: from **INDOLE** + **-ENE**.

**indent¹** ● **v.** /ɪnˈdɛnt/ **1** form deep recesses or notches in. **2** position or begin (a line or block of text) further from the margin than the main part of the text. **3** make a requisition or written order for something. **4** historical divide (a document drawn up in duplicate) into its two copies with a zigzag line, thus ensuring identification. ➤ draw up (a legal document) in exact duplicate. **5** [as adj. **indented**] Heraldry divided or edged with a zigzag line. ● **n.** /ˈɪndɛnt/ **1** Brit. an official order or requisition for goods or stores. **2** a space left by indenting text. **3** a deep recess or notch. **4** an indenture.
– DERIVATIVES **indentation** n. **indenter** n. **indention** n. (archaic). **indentor** n.
– ORIGIN ME: from Anglo-Norman Fr. *endenter* or med. L. *indentare*, from *en-*, *in-* 'into' + L. *dens*, *dent-* 'tooth'.

**indent²** /ɪnˈdɛnt/ ● **v.** make a dent or depression in.

**indenture** /ɪnˈdɛntʃə/ ● **n. 1** a formal agreement, contract, or list, formerly one of which copies with indented edges were made for the contracting parties. **2** an agreement binding an apprentice to a master. **3** historical a contract by which a person agreed to work for a set period for a colonial landowner in exchange for passage to the colony. ● **v.** chiefly historical bind by an indenture.
– DERIVATIVES **indentureship** n.

**independent** ● **adj. 1** free from outside control; not subject to another's authority. ➤ (of a country) self-governing. **2** not depending on another for livelihood or subsistence. **3** not connected with another; separate. **4** (**Independent**) historical Congregational. ● **n.** an independent person or body.
– DERIVATIVES **independence** n. **independency** n. **independently** adv.

**independent variable** ● **n.** Mathematics a variable (often denoted by *x*) whose variation does not depend on that of another.

**in-depth** ● **adj.** comprehensive and thorough.

**indescribable** ● **adj.** too unusual, extreme, or indefinite to be adequately described.
– DERIVATIVES **indescribability** n. **indescribably** adv.

**indestructible** ● **adj.** not able to be destroyed.
– DERIVATIVES **indestructibility** n. **indestructibly** adv.

**indeterminable** ● **adj. 1** not able to be determined. **2** Law (of a dispute or difficulty) not able to be resolved.
– DERIVATIVES **indeterminably** adv.

**indeterminacy principle** ● **n.** another term for **UNCERTAINTY PRINCIPLE**.

**indeterminate** /ˌɪndɪˈtəːmɪnət/ ● **adj. 1** not exactly known, established, or defined. ➤ Mathematics (of a quantity) having no definite or definable value. ➤ Medicine (of a condition) from which a diagnosis of the underlying cause cannot be made. **2** Botany (of a shoot) not having all the axes terminating in flower buds and so potentially of indefinite length.
– DERIVATIVES **indeterminacy** n. **indeterminately** adv. **indeterminateness** n.

**indeterminate vowel** ● **n.** Phonetics another term for **SCHWA**.

**indetermination** ● **n.** the state of being uncertain or undecided.

**indeterminism** ● **n. 1** Philosophy the doctrine that not all events are wholly determined by antecedent causes. **2** the state of being uncertain or undecided.
– DERIVATIVES **indeterminist** n. **indeterministic** adj.

**index** /ˈɪndɛks/ ● **n.** (pl. **indexes** or especially in technical use **indices** /ˈɪndɪsiːz/) **1** an alphabetical list of names, subjects, etc., with references to the places in a book where they occur. ➤ an alphabetical list or catalogue of books or documents. **2** an indicator, sign, or measure of something. ➤ a number representing the relative value or magnitude of something in terms of a standard: *a price index*. **3** Mathematics an exponent or other superscript or subscript number appended to a quantity. **4** Printing a symbol shaped like a pointing hand used to draw attention to a note. ● **v. 1** record in or provide with an index. **2** link the value of (prices, wages, etc.) automatically to the value of a price index. **3** [often as noun **indexing**] (of a machine or part) move from one predetermined position to another to carry out a sequence of operations.
– DERIVATIVES **indexable** adj. **indexation** n. **indexer** n. **indexible** adj.
– ORIGIN ME: from L. *index*, *indic-* 'forefinger, informer, sign', from *in-* 'towards' + a second element rel. to *dicere* 'say' or *dicare* 'make known'; cf. **INDICATE**.

**index finger** ● **n.** the forefinger.

**index futures** ● **pl. n.** contracts to buy a range of shares at an agreed price but delivered and paid for later.

**indexical** /ɪnˈdɛksɪk(ə)l/ ● **adj.** Linguistics another term for **DEICTIC**.

**index-linked** ● **adj.** Brit. adjusted according to the value of a retail price index.
– DERIVATIVES **index-linking** n.

**India ink** ● **n.** North American term for **INDIAN INK**.

**Indiaman** ● **n.** (pl. **-men**) historical a ship engaged in trade with India or the East or West Indies, especially an East Indiaman.

**Indian** ● **n. 1** a native or national of India, or a person of Indian descent. **2** an American Indian. ● **adj. 1** of or relating to India. **2** of or relating to the indigenous peoples of America.
– DERIVATIVES **Indianism** n. **Indianization** (also **-isation**) n. **Indianize** (also **-ise**) v. **Indianness** n.
– ORIGIN American native peoples were called 'Indian' as a result of Christopher Columbus and others believing that, when they reached the east coast of America, they had reached part of India by a new route.

**USAGE** **Indian**

The terms **Indian** and **Red Indian** are today regarded as old-fashioned, recalling, as they do, the stereotypical portraits of the Wild West. The term **American Indian**, however, is well established.

**Indianan** /ˌɪndɪˈan(ə)n/ ● **n.** a native or inhabitant of the US state of Indiana. ● **adj.** of or relating to Indiana.

**Indian club** ● **n.** each of a pair of bottle-shaped clubs swung to exercise the arms in gymnastics.

**Indian corn** ● **n.** another term for **MAIZE**.

**Indian file** ● **n.** another term for **SINGLE FILE**.

**Indian ink** (also N. Amer. **India ink**) ● **n.** deep black ink containing dispersed carbon particles, used especially in drawing and technical graphics.
– ORIGIN C17: orig. applied to Chinese and Japanese pigments prepared in solid blocks and imported to Europe via India.

**Indian meal** ● **n.** N. Amer. meal ground from maize.

**Indian red** ● **n.** a red ferric oxide pigment made typically by roasting ferrous salts.

**Indian rope-trick** ● **n.** the supposed feat of climbing an upright, unsupported length of rope.

**Indian runner** ● **n.** a domestic duck of a slender upright breed, typically with white or fawn plumage.

**Indian sign** ● **n.** dated a magic spell or curse.

**Indian summer** ● **n.** a period of dry, warm weather occurring in late autumn.

**India paper** ● **n. 1** soft, absorbent paper used for proofs of engravings. **2** very thin, tough, opaque printing paper, used especially for Bibles.

**India rubber** ● **n.** natural rubber.

**India rubber tree** ● **n.** another term for **RUBBER TREE**.

**Indic** /ˈɪndɪk/ ● **n.** the group of Indo-European languages comprising Sanskrit and the modern Indian languages which are its descendants. ● **adj.** relating to or denoting this language group.

**indicate** ● **v. 1** point out; show. ➤ be a sign or symptom of; strongly imply. ➤ state briefly or indirectly. ➤ (of a gauge or meter) register a reading of. **2** suggest as a desirable or necessary course of action: *treatment for shock may be indicated*. **3** chiefly Brit. (of a driver) use an indicator to signal an intention to change lanes or turn.

– DERIVATIVES **indicant** n. **indication** n.
– ORIGIN C17 (earlier (ME) as *indication*): from L. *indicat-*, *indicare* 'point out'.

**indicative** /ɪn'dɪkətɪv/ • **adj. 1** serving as a sign or indication. **2** Grammar denoting a mood of verbs expressing simple statement of a fact. Compare with **SUBJUNCTIVE**. • **n.** Grammar a verb in the indicative mood.
– DERIVATIVES **indicatively** adv.

**indicator** • **n. 1** a thing that indicates a state or level. **2** a gauge or meter of a specified kind. **3** a flashing light on a vehicle to show that it is about to change lanes or turn. **4** Brit. an information board or screen in a railway station, airport, etc. **5** Chemistry a compound which changes colour at a specific pH value or in the presence of a particular substance, and can be used to monitor a chemical change.

**indicator diagram** • **n.** a diagram of the variation of pressure and volume within a cylinder of a reciprocating engine.

**indicatory** /ɪn'dɪkət(ə)ri, ˌɪndɪ'keɪt(ə)ri/ • **adj.** rare term for **INDICATIVE**.

**indices** plural form of **INDEX**.

**indicia** /ɪn'dɪʃɪə, -sɪə/ • **pl. n.** formal signs, indications, or distinguishing marks.
– ORIGIN C17: pl. of L. *indicium*, from *index*, *indic-* 'informer, sign'.

**indict** /ɪn'dʌɪt/ • **v.** formally accuse or charge with a serious crime.
– DERIVATIVES **indictee** n. **indicter** n.
– ORIGIN ME *endite*, *indite*, from Anglo-Norman Fr. *enditer*, based on L. *indicere* 'proclaim, appoint'.

**indictable** • **adj.** (of an offence) rendering a person who commits it liable to be charged with a serious crime that warrants a trial by jury.

**indiction** /ɪn'dɪkʃ(ə)n/ • **n.** historical a fiscal period of fifteen years used as a means of dating events and transactions in the Roman Empire and in the papal and some royal courts.

**indictment** /ɪn'dʌɪtm(ə)nt/ • **n. 1** Law a formal charge or accusation of a serious crime. **2** an indication that a system or situation is bad and deserves to be condemned.

**indie** informal • **adj.** (of a pop group or record label) not belonging or affiliated to a major record company. • **n. 1** a pop group or record label of this type. **2** an independent film company.

**indifferent** • **adj. 1** having no particular interest or sympathy; unconcerned. **2** neither good nor bad; mediocre. ➤ not especially good; fairly bad.
– DERIVATIVES **indifference** n. **indifferently** adv.
– ORIGIN ME: via OFr. from L. *indifferent-* 'making no difference', from *in-* 'not' + *different-*, *differre* (see **DIFFER**).

**indifferentism** • **n.** the belief that differences of religious belief are of no importance.
– DERIVATIVES **indifferentist** n.

**indigene** /'ɪndɪdʒiːn/ • **n.** an indigenous person.
– ORIGIN C16: from Fr. *indigène*, from L. *indigena*, from *indi-* (strengthened form of *in-* 'into') + an element rel. to *gignere* 'beget'.

**indigenize** /ɪn'dɪdʒɪnʌɪz/ (also **-ise**) • **v.** bring under the control of native people.
– DERIVATIVES **indigenization** n.

**indigenous** • **adj.** originating or occurring naturally in a particular place; native.
– DERIVATIVES **indigenously** adv. **indigenousness** n.

**indigent** /'ɪndɪdʒ(ə)nt/ • **adj.** poor; needy. • **n.** a needy person.
– DERIVATIVES **indigence** n.
– ORIGIN ME: via OFr. from late L. *indigent-*, *indigere* 'to lack'.

**indigested** • **adj.** archaic term for **UNDIGESTED**.

**indigestible** • **adj. 1** (of food) difficult or impossible to digest. **2** difficult to read or understand.
– DERIVATIVES **indigestibility** n. **indigestibly** adv.

**indigestion** • **n.** pain or discomfort in the stomach associated with difficulty in digesting food.
– DERIVATIVES **indigestive** adj.

**indignation** • **n.** annoyance provoked by what is perceived as unfair treatment.
– DERIVATIVES **indignant** adj. **indignantly** adv.
– ORIGIN ME: from L. *indignatio(n-)*, from *indignari* 'regard as unworthy'.

**indignity** • **n.** (pl. **-ies**) treatment or circumstances that cause one to feel shame or to lose one's dignity.

**indigo** /'ɪndɪgəʊ/ • **n.** (pl. **-os** or **-oes**) **1** a tropical plant formerly widely cultivated as a source of dark blue dye. [*Indigofera tinctoria* and related species.] **2** the dark blue dye obtained from this plant. ➤ a colour between blue and violet in the spectrum.
– ORIGIN C16: from Port. *índigo*, via L. from Gk *indikon*, from *indikos* 'Indian (dye)'.

**indigo snake** • **n.** a large harmless American snake, typically bluish-black. [*Drymarchon corais.*]

**Indio** /'ɪndɪəʊ/ • **n.** (pl. **-os**) a member of any of the indigenous peoples of America or east Asia in areas formerly subject to Spain or Portugal.
– ORIGIN C19: from Sp. and Port., lit. 'Indian'.

**indirect** • **adj. 1** not direct. ➤ Soccer denoting a free kick from which a goal may not be scored directly. **2** (of costs) deriving from overhead charges or subsidiary work. **3** (of taxation) levied on goods and services rather than income or profits.
– DERIVATIVES **indirection** n. **indirectly** adv. **indirectness** n.

**indirect object** • **n.** Grammar a noun phrase referring to a person or thing that is affected by the action of a transitive verb but is not the primary object (e.g. *him* in *give him the book*).

**indirect question** • **n.** Grammar a question in reported speech (e.g. *they asked who I was*).

**indirect speech** • **n.** another term for **REPORTED SPEECH**.

**indiscernible** /ˌɪndɪ'səːnɪb(ə)l/ • **adj.** impossible to see or clearly distinguish.
– DERIVATIVES **indiscernibility** n. **indiscernibly** adv.

**indiscipline** • **n.** lack of discipline.

**indiscreet** • **adj.** too ready to reveal things that should remain secret or private.
– DERIVATIVES **indiscreetly** adv. **indiscretion** n.

**indiscrete** • **adj.** rare not divided into distinct parts.

**indiscriminate** /ˌɪndɪ'skrɪmɪnət/ • **adj.** done or acting at random or without careful judgement.
– DERIVATIVES **indiscriminately** adv. **indiscriminateness** n. **indiscrimination** n.
– ORIGIN C16: from **IN-**[1] + L. *discriminat-*, *discriminare* (see **DISCRIMINATE**).

**indiscriminating** • **adj.** making no distinctions; indiscriminate.

**indispensable** • **adj.** absolutely necessary.
– DERIVATIVES **indispensability** n. **indispensableness** n. **indispensably** adv.

**indispose** • **v.** archaic make unfit for or averse to something.

**indisposed** • **adj. 1** slightly unwell. **2** averse; unwilling.
– DERIVATIVES **indisposition** n.

**indisputable** • **adj.** unable to be challenged or denied.
– DERIVATIVES **indisputability** n. **indisputably** adv.

**indissociable** • **adj.** unable to be dissociated.

**indissoluble** /ˌɪndɪ'sɒljʊb(ə)l/ • **adj.** unable to be destroyed; lasting.
– DERIVATIVES **indissolubility** n. **indissolubly** adv.

**indistinct** • **adj.** not clear or sharply defined.
– DERIVATIVES **indistinctly** adv. **indistinctness** n.

**indistinguishable** • **adj.** not able to be identified as different or distinct.
– DERIVATIVES **indistinguishably** adv.

**indite** /ɪn'dʌɪt/ • **v.** archaic write; compose.
– ORIGIN ME *endite*, from OFr. *enditier*, based on L. *indicere* (see **INDICT**).

**indium** /'ɪndɪəm/ • **n.** the chemical element of atomic number 49, a soft, silvery-white metal occurring naturally in association with zinc and some other metals. (Symbol: **In**)
– ORIGIN C19: from **INDIGO** (because there are two charac-

teristic indigo lines in its spectrum) + **-IUM**.

**individual** ● **adj.** **1** single; separate. **2** of or for a particular person. ➤designed for use by one person. **3** striking or unusual; original. ● **n.** **1** a single human being or item as distinct from a group. ➤informal a person of a specified kind: *a most selfish, egotistical individual.* **2** a distinctive or original person.
– DERIVATIVES **individualization** (also **-isation**) n. **individualize** (also **-ise**) v. **individually** adv.
– ORIGIN ME (in the sense 'indivisible'): from med. L. *individualis*, from L. *individuus*, based on *dividere* 'to divide'.

**individualism** ● **n.** **1** independence and self-reliance. ➤self-centred feeling or conduct; egoism. **2** a social theory favouring freedom of action for individuals over collective or state control.
– DERIVATIVES **individualist** n. & adj. **individualistic** adj. **individualistically** adv.

**individuality** ● **n.** **1** distinctive quality or character. **2** separate existence.

**individuate** ● **v.** distinguish from others of the same kind; single out.
– DERIVATIVES **individuation** n.

**indivisible** ● **adj.** unable to be divided or separated. ➤(of a number) unable to be divided by another number exactly without leaving a remainder.
– DERIVATIVES **indivisibility** n. **indivisibly** adv.

**Indo-** /ˈɪndəʊ/ ● **comb. form** (especially in linguistic and ethnological terms) Indian; Indian and ...: *Indo-Iranian.* ➤relating to India.

**Indo-Aryan** ● **adj.** **1** relating to or denoting an Indo-European people who invaded NW India in the 2nd millennium BC. **2** another term for **INDIC**.

**Indo-Chinese** ● **adj.** of or relating to the peninsula of Indo-China, which contains Burma (Myanmar), Thailand, Malaya, Laos, Cambodia, and Vietnam.

**indocile** ● **adj.** difficult to teach or discipline; not submissive.
– DERIVATIVES **indocility** n.

**indoctrinate** /ɪnˈdɒktrɪneɪt/ ● **v.** **1** cause to accept a set of beliefs uncritically through repeated instruction. **2** archaic teach or instruct.
– DERIVATIVES **indoctrination** n. **indoctrinator** n. **indoctrinatory** adj.
– ORIGIN C17: from **IN-**[2] + **DOCTRINE** + **-ATE**[3], or from obs. *indoctrine* (v.), from Fr. *endoctriner.*

**Indo-European** ● **n.** **1** the ancestral Proto-Indo-European language. **2** the family of languages spoken over the greater part of Europe and Asia as far as northern India. **3** a speaker of an Indo-European language, especially Proto-Indo-European. ● **adj.** relating to or denoting Indo-European.

**Indo-Germanic** ● **n.** & **adj.** former term for **INDO-EUROPEAN**.

**Indo-Iranian** ● **n.** a subfamily of Indo-European languages spoken in northern India and Iran. ● **adj.** relating to or denoting Indo-Iranian.

**indole** /ˈɪndəʊl/ ● **n.** Chemistry a crystalline organic compound with an unpleasant odour, present in coal tar and in faeces.
– ORIGIN C19: blend of **INDIGO** (because obtained artificially from indigo blue) and L. *oleum* 'oil'.

**indoleacetic acid** /ˌɪndəʊləˈsiːtɪk, -ˈsɛtɪk/ ● **n.** Biochemistry a compound which is an acetic acid derivative of indole, especially one found as a natural growth hormone (auxin) in plants.

**indolent** /ˈɪnd(ə)l(ə)nt/ ● **adj.** **1** wanting to avoid activity or exertion; lazy. **2** Medicine (of an ulcer or other disease condition) slow to develop or heal.
– DERIVATIVES **indolence** n. **indolently** adv.
– ORIGIN C17: from late L. *indolent-*, from *in-* 'not' + *dolere* 'suffer or give pain'.

**Indology** /ɪnˈdɒlədʒi/ ● **n.** the study of Indian history, literature, philosophy, and culture.
– DERIVATIVES **Indologist** n.

**indomitable** /ɪnˈdɒmɪtəb(ə)l/ ● **adj.** impossible to subdue or defeat.
– DERIVATIVES **indomitability** n. **indomitableness** n. **indomitably** adv.
– ORIGIN C17 (in the sense 'untameable'): from late L. *indomitabilis*, from *in-* 'not' + L. *domitare* 'to tame'.

**Indonesian** ● **n.** **1** a native or national of Indonesia, or a person of Indonesian descent. **2** the group of Austronesian languages spoken in Indonesia. ● **adj.** of or relating to Indonesia, Indonesians, or their languages.

**indoor** ● **adj.** situated, conducted, or used within a building or under cover.

**indoors** ● **adv.** into or within a building. ● **n.** the area or space inside a building.

**Indo-Pacific** ● **adj.** **1** of or relating to the Indian Ocean and the adjacent parts of the Pacific. **2** another term for **AUSTRONESIAN**.

**indorse** ● **v.** US spelling of **ENDORSE**.

**indorsement** ● **n.** chiefly US variant spelling of **ENDORSEMENT**.

**indraught** /ˈɪndrɑːft/ (US **indraft**) ● **n.** the drawing in of something. ➤an inward flow or current, especially of air.

**indrawn** ● **adj.** **1** (of breath) taken in. **2** (of a person) shy and introspective.

**indri** /ˈɪndri/ ● **n.** (pl. **indris**) a large, short-tailed Madagascan lemur. [*Indri indri.*]
– ORIGIN C19: from Malagasy *indry!* 'behold!' or *indry izy!* 'there he is!', mistaken for its name.

**indubitable** /ɪnˈdjuːbɪtəb(ə)l/ ● **adj.** impossible to doubt; unquestionable.
– DERIVATIVES **indubitably** adv.
– ORIGIN ME: from L. *indubitabilis*, from *in-* 'not' + *dubitabilis* (see **DUBITABLE**).

**induce** /ɪnˈdjuːs/ ● **v.** **1** succeed in persuading or leading (someone) to do something. **2** bring about or give rise to. ➤produce (an electric charge or current or a magnetic state) by induction. **3** Medicine bring on (childbirth or abortion) artificially, typically by the use of drugs. **4** Logic derive by inductive reasoning.
– DERIVATIVES **inducer** n. **inducible** adj.
– ORIGIN ME: from L. *induct-*, *inducere* 'lead in', or from Fr. *enduire.*

**inducement** ● **n.** a thing that persuades or leads someone to do something. ➤a bribe.

**induct** /ɪnˈdʌkt/ ● **v.** **1** admit formally to a post or organization. ➤formally introduce (a member of the clergy) into possession of a benefice. ➤US enlist (someone) for military service. **2** archaic install in a seat or room.
– DERIVATIVES **inductee** n.
– ORIGIN ME: from L. *induct-*, *inducere* (see **INDUCE**).

**inductance** ● **n.** Physics the property of an electric conductor or circuit that causes an electromotive force to be generated by a change in the current flowing.

**induction** ● **n.** **1** the action or process of inducting someone to a post, organization, etc. **2** the action or process of inducing something. **3** Logic the inference of a general law from particular instances. Often contrasted with **DEDUCTION**. ➤the production of facts to prove a general statement. **4** Mathematics the proof of a theorem by showing that if it is true of any particular case it is true of the next case in a series, and then showing that it is indeed true in one particular case. **5** the production of an electric or magnetic state by the proximity (without contact) of an electrified or magnetized body. ➤the production of an electric current in a conductor by varying an applied magnetic field. **6** the drawing of the fuel mixture into the cylinders of an internal-combustion engine.

**induction coil** ● **n.** a coil for generating intermittent high voltage from a direct current.

**induction hardening** ● **n.** Metallurgy a process for hardening steel surfaces by induction heating followed by quenching.

**induction heating** ● **n.** heating of a material by inducing an electric current within it.

**induction loop** ● **n.** a sound system in which a loop of wire around an area in a building produces an electromagnetic signal received directly by hearing aids.

**inductive** ● **adj.** **1** Logic characterized by the inference of general laws from particular instances. **2** of or relating to

electric or magnetic induction. ➤ possessing inductance.
– DERIVATIVES **inductively** adv. **inductiveness** n. **inductivism** n. **inductivist** n. & adj.

**inductor** ● n. **1** a component in an electric or electronic circuit which possesses inductance. **2** a substance that promotes an equilibrium reaction by reacting with one of the substances produced.

**indue** ● v. variant spelling of **ENDUE**.

**indulge** ● v. **1** (**indulge in**) allow oneself to enjoy the pleasure of. ➤ become involved in (an activity that is undesirable or disapproved of). **2** satisfy or yield freely to (a desire or interest). ➤ allow (someone) to enjoy a desired pleasure.
– DERIVATIVES **indulger** n.
– ORIGIN C17 (earlier (ME) as *indulgence*), in the sense 'treat with excessive kindness': from L. *indulgere* 'give free rein to'.

**indulgence** ● n. **1** the action or fact of indulging. ➤ a thing that is indulged in; a luxury. **2** the state or attitude of being indulgent or tolerant. **3** an extension of the time in which a bill or debt has to be paid. **4** chiefly historical (in the Roman Catholic Church) a grant by the Pope of remission of the temporal punishment in purgatory still due for sins after absolution.

**indulgent** ● adj. **1** readily indulging someone or overlooking their faults; tolerant or lenient. **2** self-indulgent.
– DERIVATIVES **indulgently** adv.

**induline** /ˈɪndjʊliːn, lɪn/ ● n. any of a group of insoluble blue azine dyes.
– ORIGIN C19: from *indo-* (denoting indigo) + **-ULE** + **-INE**[4].

**indult** /ɪnˈdʌlt/ ● n. (in the Roman Catholic Church) a licence granted by the Pope authorizing an act that the common law of the Church does not sanction.
– ORIGIN C15: from Fr., from late L. *indultum* 'grant, concession', neut. past part. of L. *indulgere* 'indulge'.

**indumentum** /ˌɪndjʊˈmɛntəm/ ● n. (pl. **indumenta**) Botany & Zoology a covering of hairs (or feathers) on an animal or plant.
– ORIGIN C19: from L., lit. 'garment'.

**induna** /ɪnˈduːnə/ ● n. S. African **1** a tribal councillor or headman. **2** an African foreman.
– ORIGIN Xhosa and Zulu, from the nominal prefix *in-* + *duna* 'captain, councillor'.

**indurate** /ˈɪndjʊreɪt/ ● v. [usu. as adj. **indurated**] harden.
– DERIVATIVES **induration** n. **indurative** adj.
– ORIGIN C16 (earlier (ME) as *induration*): from L. *indurat-*, *indurare* 'make hard'.

**indusium** /ɪnˈdjuːzɪəm/ ● n. (pl. **indusia**) chiefly Botany a thin membranous covering, especially a shield covering a sorus on a fern frond.
– ORIGIN C18: from L., lit. 'tunic'.

**industrial** ● adj. **1** of, used in, or characterized by industry. **2** relating to or denoting a type of harsh, uncompromising rock music incorporating sounds resembling those produced by industrial machinery. ● n. (**industrials**) shares in industrial companies.
– DERIVATIVES **industrially** adv.

**industrial action** ● n. Brit. action taken by employees of a company as a protest, especially striking or working to rule.

**industrial archaeology** ● n. the study of equipment and buildings formerly used in industry.

**industrial diamond** ● n. a small diamond, not of gem quality, used in abrasives and in cutting and drilling tools.

**industrial estate** ● n. chiefly Brit. an area of land developed as a site for factories and other industrial use.

**industrialism** ● n. a social or economic system in which manufacturing industries are prevalent.

**industrialist** ● n. a person involved in the ownership and management of industry.

**industrialize** (also **-ise**) ● v. [often as adj. **industrialized**] develop industries in (a country or region) on a wide scale.
– DERIVATIVES **industrialization** n.

**industrial park** ● n. North American term for **INDUSTRIAL ESTATE**.

**industrial relations** ● pl. n. the relations between management and workers in industry.

**industrial-strength** ● adj. very strong or powerful.

**industrious** ● adj. diligent and hard-working.
– DERIVATIVES **industriously** adv. **industriousness** n.

**industry** ● n. (pl. **-ies**) **1** economic activity concerned with the processing of raw materials and manufacture of goods in factories. ➤ a particular branch of economic or commercial activity: *the tourist industry.* **2** hard work: *the kitchen became a hive of industry.*
– ORIGIN ME: from Fr. *industrie* or L. *industria* 'diligence'.

**indwell** ● v. (past and past part. **indwelt**) **1** be permanently present or living in. **2** [as adj. **indwelling**] Medicine (of a catheter, needle, etc.) fixed in a person's body for a long period of time.
– DERIVATIVES **indweller** n.
– ORIGIN ME: orig. translating L. *inhabitare*.

**Indy** ● n. a form of motor racing in which cars are driven round a banked, regular oval circuit.
– ORIGIN 1950s: named after the US city of *Indianapolis*, where the principal race is held.

**-ine**[1] /ʌɪn, ɪn, iːn/ ● suffix **1** (forming adjectives) belonging to; resembling: *canine.* **2** forming adjectives from the names of genera or subfamilies (such as *bovine* from the genus *Bos*). See word-formation panel.
– ORIGIN from Fr. *-in*, *-ine*, or from L. *-inus*.

**-ine**[2] /ʌɪn/ ● suffix forming adjectives from the names of minerals, plants, etc.: *crystalline.*
– ORIGIN from L. *-inus*, from Gk *-inos*.

**-ine**[3] /ɪn, iːn/ ● suffix forming feminine nouns such as *heroine.*
– ORIGIN from Fr., via L. *-ina* from Gk *-inē*, or from Ger. *-in*.

**-ine**[4] /iːn, ɪn/ ● suffix **1** forming chiefly abstract nouns and diminutives such as *doctrine, medicine.* **2** Chemistry forming names of alkaloids, halogens, amino acids, and other substances: *cocaine.*
– ORIGIN from Fr., from the L. fem. form *-ina*.

**inebriate** ● v. /ɪˈniːbrɪeɪt/ [usu. as adj. **inebriated**] make drunk; intoxicate. ● adj. /ɪˈniːbrɪət/ drunk; intoxicated.
– DERIVATIVES **inebriation** n. **inebriety** n.
– ORIGIN ME: from L. *inebriatus*, past part. of *inebriare* 'intoxicate'.

**inedible** ● adj. not fit for eating.
– DERIVATIVES **inedibility** n.

**ineducable** /ɪnˈɛdjʊkəb(ə)l/ ● adj. considered incapable of being educated.
– DERIVATIVES **ineducability** n.

**ineffable** /ɪnˈɛfəb(ə)l/ ● adj. **1** too great or extreme to be expressed in words: *the ineffable natural beauty of the Everglades.* **2** too sacred to be uttered.
– DERIVATIVES **ineffability** n. **ineffably** adv.

**ineffaceable** /ɪnɪˈfeɪsəb(ə)l/ ● adj. unable to be erased or forgotten.
– DERIVATIVES **ineffaceability** n. **ineffaceably** adv.

**ineffective** ● adj. not producing any or the desired effect.
– DERIVATIVES **ineffectively** adv. **ineffectiveness** n.

**ineffectual** ● adj. not producing any or the desired effect. ➤ lacking ability to cope with a role or situation: *she was ineffectual as a parent.*
– DERIVATIVES **ineffectuality** n. **ineffectually** adv. **ineffectualness** n.

**inefficacious** /ˌɪnɛfɪˈkeɪʃəs/ ● adj. not producing the desired effect.
– DERIVATIVES **inefficacy** n.

**inefficient** ● adj. not achieving maximum productivity; failing to make the best use of time or resources.
– DERIVATIVES **inefficiency** n. **inefficiently** adv.

**inegalitarian** /ˌɪnɪgalɪˈtɛːrɪən/ ● adj. characterized by or promoting inequality.

**inelastic** ● adj. **1** (of a material) not elastic. **2** Economics (of demand or supply) insensitive to changes in price or income. **3** Physics (of a collision) involving an overall loss of translational kinetic energy.

## Word *Formation*

**-ine** forming adjectives relating to animals

➤ Some **-ine** words in this group are used in general vocabulary, while others relate to a specific group (sometimes a subfamily ending in *-inae*) and are found only in technical contexts:

**1.** Mammals

| | | |
|---|---|---|
| bovine | relating to cattle | L. *bos, bov-* 'ox' |
| canine | relating to dogs | L. *canis* 'dog' |
| caprine | relating to goats | L. *caper, capr-* 'goat' |
| equine | relating to horses | L. *equus* 'horse' |
| feline | relating to cats | L. *feles* 'cat' |
| hircine | (archaic) relating to goats | L. *hircus* 'billy goat' |
| leonine | relating to lions | L. *leo, leon-* 'lion' |
| leporine | relating to hares | L. *lepus, lepor-* 'hare' |
| lupine | relating to wolves | L. *lupus* 'wolf' |
| murine | relating to mice or other rodents | L. *mus, mur-* 'mouse' |
| ovine | relating to sheep | L. *ovis* 'sheep' |
| phocine | relating to the true seals (family Phocidae) | Gk *phōkē* 'seal' |
| porcine | relating to pigs | L. *porcus* 'pig' |
| taurine | relating to bulls | L. *taurus* 'bull' |
| ursine | relating to bears | L. *ursus* 'bear' |
| vulpine | relating to foxes | L. *vulpes* 'fox' |

**2.** Birds

| | | |
|---|---|---|
| anserine | relating to geese | L. *anser* 'goose' |
| aquiline | relating to eagles | L. *aquila* 'eagle' |
| corvine | relating to crows or ravens | L. *corvus* 'raven' |
| hirundine | a bird of the swallow family | L. *hirundo* 'swallow' |
| passerine | denoting perching birds | L. *passer* 'sparrow' |
| pavonine | relating to peacocks | L. *pavo, pavon-* 'peacock' |

– DERIVATIVES **inelastically** adv. **inelasticity** n.

**inelegant** • adj. lacking elegance or refinement.
– DERIVATIVES **inelegance** n. **inelegantly** adv.

**ineligible** • adj. not eligible.
– DERIVATIVES **ineligibility** n. **ineligibly** adv.

**ineluctable** /ˌɪnɪˈlʌktəb(ə)l/ • adj. unable to be resisted or avoided; inescapable.
– DERIVATIVES **ineluctability** /-ˈbɪlɪti/ n. **ineluctably** adv.
– ORIGIN C17: from L. *ineluctabilis*, from *in-* 'not' + *eluctari* 'struggle out'.

**inept** • adj. incompetent; awkward or clumsy.
– DERIVATIVES **ineptitude** n. **ineptly** adv. **ineptness** n.
– ORIGIN C16 (in the sense 'unsuitable'): from L. *ineptus*, from *in-* 'not' + *aptus* (see **APT**).

**inequality** • n. (pl. **-ies**) **1** lack of equality. **2** Mathematics a symbolic expression of the fact that two quantities are not equal, employing a sign such as ≠ 'not equal to', > 'greater than', or < 'less than'. **3** archaic lack of smoothness or regularity in a surface.

**inequitable** • adj. unfair; unjust.
– DERIVATIVES **inequitably** adv.

**inequity** • n. (pl. **-ies**) lack of fairness or justice.

**ineradicable** /ˌɪnɪˈradɪkəb(ə)l/ • adj. unable to be destroyed or removed.
– DERIVATIVES **ineradicably** adv.

**inerrant** • adj. incapable of being wrong.
– DERIVATIVES **inerrancy** n. **inerrantist** n.

**inert** • adj. **1** lacking the ability or strength to move. ➤lacking vigour. **2** chemically inactive.
– DERIVATIVES **inertly** adv. **inertness** n.
– ORIGIN C17: from L. *iners, inert-* 'unskilled, inactive', from *in-* + *ars, art-* 'skill, art'.

**inert gas** • n. another term for **NOBLE GAS**.

**inertia** /ɪˈnəːʃə/ • n. **1** a tendency to do nothing or to remain unchanged. **2** Physics a property of matter by which it continues in its existing state of rest or uniform motion in a straight line, unless changed by an external force. ➤resistance to change in some other physical property: *the thermal inertia of the oceans.*
– ORIGIN C18: from L., from *iners, inert-* (see **INERT**).

**inertial** • adj. **1** chiefly Physics of, relating to, or arising from inertia. **2** (of navigation) depending on internal instruments which measure a craft's acceleration and compare the calculated position with stored data.

**inertia reel** • n. a reel device which allows a vehicle seat belt to unwind freely but which locks under force of impact or rapid deceleration.

**inertia selling** • n. Brit. the sending of unsolicited goods to potential customers in the hope of making a sale.

**inescapable** • adj. unable to be avoided or denied.
– DERIVATIVES **inescapability** n. **inescapably** adv.

**inescutcheon** /ˌɪnɪˈskʌtʃ(ə)n, ˌɪnɛ-/ • n. Heraldry a small shield placed within a larger one.

**in esse** /ɪn ˈɛsi, ˈɛseɪ/ • adv. in actual existence.
– ORIGIN from L.

**inessential** • adj. not absolutely necessary. • n. an inessential thing.

**inestimable** • adj. not able to be measured; very great.
– DERIVATIVES **inestimably** adv.

**inevitable** • adj. certain to happen; unavoidable. • n. (**the inevitable**) a situation that is unavoidable.
– DERIVATIVES **inevitability** n. **inevitably** adv.
– ORIGIN ME: from L. *inevitabilis*, from *in-* 'not' + *evitabilis* 'avoidable'.

**inexact** • adj. not quite accurate.
– DERIVATIVES **inexactitude** n. **inexactly** adv. **inexactness** n.

**inexcusable** • adj. too bad to be justified or tolerated.
– DERIVATIVES **inexcusably** adv.

**inexhaustible** • adj. **1** (of a supply) never ending; incapable of being used up. **2** tireless.
– DERIVATIVES **inexhaustibility** n. **inexhaustibly** adv.

**inexorable** /ɪnˈɛks(ə)rəb(ə)l/ • adj. **1** impossible to stop or prevent: *the inexorable march of new technology.* **2** impossible to persuade by request or entreaty.
– DERIVATIVES **inexorability** n. **inexorably** adv.

– ORIGIN C16: from Fr., or from L. *inexorabilis*, from *in-* 'not' + *exorabilis* (from *exorare* 'entreat').

**inexpedient** • adj. not practical, suitable, or advisable.
– DERIVATIVES **inexpediency** n.

**inexpensive** • adj. not costing a great deal; cheap.
– DERIVATIVES **inexpensively** adv. **inexpensiveness** n.

**inexperience** • n. lack of experience.
– DERIVATIVES **inexperienced** adj.

**inexpert** • adj. lacking skill or knowledge.
– DERIVATIVES **inexpertly** adv.

**inexpertise** • n. lack of expertise.

**inexpiable** /ɪnˈɛkspɪəb(ə)l/ • adj. (of an offence) not able to be expiated.
– DERIVATIVES **inexpiably** adv.

**inexplicable** /ˌɪnɪkˈsplɪkəb(ə)l, ˌɪnɛk-, ɪnˈɛksplɪ-/ • adj. unable to be explained or accounted for.
– DERIVATIVES **inexplicability** n. **inexplicably** adv.

**inexplicit** • adj. not clearly expressed or explained.

**inexpressible** • adj. not able to be expressed.
– DERIVATIVES **inexpressibly** adv.

**inexpressive** • adj. showing no expression.
– DERIVATIVES **inexpressively** adv. **inexpressiveness** n.

**inextensible** /ˌɪnɪkˈstɛnsɪb(ə)l, ˌɪnɛk-/ • adj. unable to be extended or stretched out.

**in extenso** /ˌɪn ɛkˈstɛnsəʊ/ • adv. in full.
– ORIGIN L., from *in* 'in' + *extensus*, past part. of *extendere* 'stretch out'.

**inextinguishable** • adj. unable to be extinguished.

**in extremis** /ˌɪn ɛkˈstriːmɪs/ • adv. **1** in an extremely difficult situation. **2** at the point of death.
– ORIGIN L., from *in* 'in' + *extremis*, ablative pl. of *extremus* 'outermost'.

**inextricable** /ɪnˈɛkstrɪkəb(ə)l, ˌɪnɪkˈstrɪk-, ˌɪnɛk-/ • adj. **1** impossible to disentangle or separate. **2** impossible to escape from.
– DERIVATIVES **inextricability** n. **inextricably** adv.

**INF** • abbrev. intermediate-range nuclear force(s).

**infallibility** • n. **1** the quality of being infallible. **2** (**papal infallibility**) (in the Roman Catholic Church) the doctrine that in specified circumstances the Pope is incapable of error in pronouncing dogma.

**infallible** /ɪnˈfalɪb(ə)l/ • adj. **1** incapable of making mistakes or being wrong. **2** never failing; always effective: *infallible cures.*
– DERIVATIVES **infallibly** adv.

**infamous** /ˈɪnfəməs/ • adj. **1** well known for some bad quality or deed: *an infamous war criminal.* **2** morally bad; shocking: *infamous misconduct.*
– DERIVATIVES **infamously** adv. **infamy** /ˈɪnfəmi/ n. (pl. **-ies**).

**infancy** • n. **1** the state or period of early childhood or babyhood. **2** the early stage in the development or growth of something. **3** Law the condition of being a minor.

**infant** • n. **1** a very young child or baby. **2** Brit. a schoolchild between the ages of five and seven. **3** [as modifier] denoting something in an early stage of development: *the infant universe.* **4** Law a person who has not attained legal majority.
– ORIGIN ME: from OFr. *enfant*, from L. *infant-* 'unable to speak', from *in-* 'not' + *fant-*, *fari* 'speak'.

**infanta** /ɪnˈfantə/ • n. historical a daughter of the ruling monarch of Spain or Portugal, especially the eldest daughter who was not heir to the throne.
– ORIGIN C16: Sp. and Port., fem. of **INFANTE**.

**infante** /ɪnˈfanteɪ/ • n. historical a son of the ruling monarch of Spain or Portugal other than the heir to the throne, specifically the second son.
– ORIGIN C16: Sp. and Port., from L. *infans, infant-* (see **INFANT**).

**infanteer** /ˌɪnf(ə)nˈtɪə/ • n. military slang an infantryman.

**infanticide** /ɪnˈfantɪsʌɪd/ • n. the killing of an infant. ➤ the practice in some societies of killing unwanted children soon after birth.
– DERIVATIVES **infanticidal** adj.

**infantile** /ˈɪnf(ə)ntʌɪl/ • adj. **1** of or occurring among infants. **2** derogatory childish.
– DERIVATIVES **infantility** n. (pl. **-ies**).

**infantile paralysis** • n. dated poliomyelitis.

**infantilism** /ɪnˈfantɪlɪz(ə)m/ • n. **1** childish behaviour. **2** Psychology the persistence of infantile characteristics or behaviour in adult life.

**infantilize** /ɪnˈfantɪlʌɪz/ (also **-ise**) • v. treat as a child.
– DERIVATIVES **infantilization** n.

**infantine** /ˈɪnf(ə)ntʌɪn/ • adj. archaic term for **INFANTILE**.

**infant mortality** • n. the death of children under the age of one year.

**infantry** • n. foot soldiers collectively.
– DERIVATIVES **infantryman** n.
– ORIGIN C16: from Fr. *infanterie*, from Ital. *infanteria*, from *infante* 'youth, infantryman', from L. *infant-* (see **INFANT**).

**infarct** /ˈɪnfɑːkt, ɪnˈfɑːkt/ • n. Medicine a small localized area of dead tissue resulting from failure of blood supply.
– ORIGIN C19: from mod. L. *infarctus*, from *infarcire* 'stuff into or with'.

**infarction** /ɪnˈfɑːkʃ(ə)n/ • n. the obstruction of the blood supply, typically by a thrombus or embolus, causing local death of the tissue.

**infatuate** • v. (**be infatuated with**) be inspired with an intense but short-lived passion for.
– DERIVATIVES **infatuation** n.
– ORIGIN C16: from L. *infatuat-*, *infatuare* 'make foolish'.

**infauna** /ˈɪnfɔːnə/ • n. Ecology animals living in the sediments of the ocean floor or river or lake beds. Compare with **EPIFAUNA**.
– DERIVATIVES **infaunal** adj.

**infeasible** • adj. inconvenient or impracticable.
– DERIVATIVES **infeasibility** n.

**infect** • v. **1** affect (a person, organism, cell, etc.) with a disease-causing organism. **2** Computing affect with a virus. **3** contaminate; affect adversely.
– DERIVATIVES **infector** n.
– ORIGIN ME: from L. *infect-*, *inficere* 'taint', from *in-* 'into' + *facere* 'put, do'.

**infection** • n. **1** the process of infecting or the state of being infected. **2** an infectious disease.

**infectious** • adj. **1** (of a disease or disease-causing organism) liable to be transmitted through the environment. ➤ liable to spread infection. **2** likely to spread to or influence others: *her enthusiasm is infectious.*
– DERIVATIVES **infectiously** adv. **infectiousness** n.

**infective** • adj. capable of causing infection.
– DERIVATIVES **infectiveness** n.

**infeed** • n. the action or process of supplying material to a machine.

**infelicitous** • adj. unfortunate; inappropriate.
– DERIVATIVES **infelicitously** adv.

**infelicity** • n. (pl. **-ies**) **1** an act or thing that is inapt or inappropriate, especially a remark or expression. **2** archaic unhappiness; misfortune.

**infer** • v. (**inferred**, **inferring**) deduce from evidence and reasoning rather than from explicit statements.
– DERIVATIVES **inferable** (also **inferrable**) adj.
– ORIGIN C15 (in the sense 'bring about, inflict'): from L. *inferre* 'bring in, bring about'.

**inference** /ˈɪnf(ə)r(ə)ns/ • n. **1** a conclusion reached on the basis of evidence and reasoning. **2** the process of reaching a conclusion by inferring.
– DERIVATIVES **inferential** adj. **inferentially** adv.

**inferior** • adj. **1** lower in rank, status, or quality. ➤ of low standard or quality. **2** Law (of a court or tribunal) able to have its decisions overturned by a higher court. **3** Economics denoting goods or services which are in greater demand during a recession. **4** chiefly Anatomy low or lower in position. ➤ Botany (of the ovary of a flower) situated below the sepals. **5** (of a letter or symbol) written or printed below the line. • n. **1** a person lower than another in rank, status, or ability. **2** Printing an inferior letter, figure, or symbol.
– DERIVATIVES **inferiority** n. **inferiorly** adv. (Anatomy).
– ORIGIN ME: from L., compar. of *inferus* 'low'.

**inferiority complex** • n. a feeling of general inadequacy caused by actual or supposed inferiority, marked by aggressive behaviour or withdrawal.

**inferior planet** • n. Astronomy either of the two planets Mercury and Venus, whose orbits are closer to the sun than the earth's.

**infernal** • adj. **1** of or relating to hell or the underworld. **2** informal terrible; awful: *you're an infernal nuisance.*
– DERIVATIVES **infernally** adv.
– ORIGIN ME: from OFr., from Christian L. *infernalis*, from L. *infernus* 'below, underground', used in Christianity to mean 'hell'.

**inferno** • n. (pl. **-os**) **1** a large fire that is dangerously out of control. **2** (**Inferno**) hell (with reference to Dante's *Divine Comedy*).
– ORIGIN C19: from Ital., from Christian L. *infernus* (see **INFERNAL**).

**infertile** • adj. **1** unable to reproduce. **2** (of land) unable to sustain crops or vegetation.
– DERIVATIVES **infertility** n.

**infest** • v. (of insects or organisms) be present in large numbers, typically so as to cause damage or disease.
– DERIVATIVES **infestation** n.
– ORIGIN ME (in the sense 'torment, harass'): from Fr. *infester* or L. *infestare* 'assail', from *infestus* 'hostile'.

**infeudation** /ˌɪnfjuːˈdeɪʃ(ə)n/ • n. historical (under the feudal system) the action of putting someone in possession of a fee or fief.
– ORIGIN C15: from med. L. *infeudatio(n-)*, from *infeudare* 'enfeoff' (based on *feudum* 'fee').

**infibulation** • n. the practice in some societies of removing the clitoris and labia of a girl or woman and stitching together the edges of the vulva to prevent sexual intercourse.
– DERIVATIVES **infibulate** v.
– ORIGIN C17: from L. *infibulat-*, *infibulare* 'fasten with a clasp'.

**infidel** /ˈɪnfɪd(ə)l/ • n. chiefly archaic a person who has no religion or whose religion is not that of the majority.
– ORIGIN C15: from Fr. *infidèle* or L. *infidelis*, from *in-* 'not' + *fidelis* 'faithful'.

**infidelity** • n. (pl. **-ies**) **1** the action or state of being sexually unfaithful. **2** lack of religious faith.

**infield** • n. **1** Cricket the part of the field closer to the wicket. **2** Baseball the area within and near the four bases. **3** the land around or near a farmstead. • adv. into or towards the infield.
– DERIVATIVES **infielder** n.

**infighting** • n. **1** hidden conflict within a group or organization. **2** boxing closer to an opponent than at arm's length.
– DERIVATIVES **infighter** n.

**infill** • n. (also **infilling**) material or buildings used to fill a space or hole. • v. fill or block up (a space or hole).

**infiltrate** /ˈɪnfɪltreɪt/ • v. **1** surreptitiously and gradually enter or gain access to (an organization, place, etc.). **2** permeate or cause to permeate by filtration. • n. Medicine an infiltrating substance or group of cells.
– DERIVATIVES **infiltration** n. **infiltrator** n.

**infimum** /ɪnˈfʌɪməm/ • n. Mathematics the largest quantity that is less than or equal to each of a given set or subset of quantities. The opposite of **SUPREMUM**.
– ORIGIN 1940s: from L., lit. 'lowest part'.

**in fine** /ɪn ˈfʌɪni, ˈfiːneɪ/ • adv. finally; to sum up.
– ORIGIN from L.

**infinite** /ˈɪnfɪnɪt/ • adj. **1** limitless in space, extent, or size. ➤very great in amount or degree. **2** Mathematics greater than any assignable quantity or countable number.
– DERIVATIVES **infinitely** adv. **infiniteness** n. **infinitude** /ɪnˈfɪnɪtjuːd/ n.
– ORIGIN ME: from L. *infinitus*, from *in-* 'not' + *finitus* 'finished, finite'.

**infinitesimal** /ˌɪnfɪnɪˈtɛsɪm(ə)l/ • adj. extremely small. • n. Mathematics an indefinitely small quantity; a value approaching zero.
– DERIVATIVES **infinitesimally** adv.
– ORIGIN C17: from mod. L. *infinitesimus*, from L. *infinitus* (see **INFINITE**), on the pattern of *centesimal.*

**infinitesimal calculus** • n. see **CALCULUS**.

**infinitive** /ɪnˈfɪnɪtɪv/ • n. the basic form of a verb, without an inflection binding it to a particular subject or tense (normally occurring in English with the word *to*, as in *to see, to ask*).
– DERIVATIVES **infinitival** /-ˈtʌɪv(ə)l/ adj. **infinitivally** adv.
– ORIGIN ME (as an adj.): from L. *infinitivus*, from *infinitus* (see **INFINITE**).

**infinity** • n. (pl. **-ies**) **1** the state or quality of being infinite. ➤a very great number or amount. **2** Mathematics a number greater than any assignable quantity or countable number (symbol ∞). **3** a point in space or time that is or seems infinitely distant: *the lawns stretched into infinity.*

**infirm** • adj. **1** not physically strong, especially through age. **2** archaic irresolute; weak.
– DERIVATIVES **infirmly** adv.
– ORIGIN ME: from L. *infirmus*, from *in-* 'not' + *firmus* 'firm'.

**infirmarer** /ɪnˈfəːm(ə)rə/ • n. historical a person in charge of the infirmary in a medieval monastery.
– ORIGIN ME: from OFr. *enfermerier*, from *enfermerie* 'infirmary', based on L. *infirmus* (see **INFIRM**).

**infirmary** • n. (pl. **-ies**) a place for the care of those who are ill or injured; a hospital.

**infirmity** • n. (pl. **-ies**) physical or mental weakness.

**infix** • v. /ɪnˈfɪks/ **1** implant or insert firmly in something. **2** Grammar insert (a formative element) into the body of a word. • n. /ˈɪnfɪks/ Grammar a formative element inserted in a word.
– DERIVATIVES **infixation** n.

**in flagrante delicto** /ɪn fləˌgranteɪ dɪˈlɪktəʊ, fləˌgranti/ • adv. in the very act of wrongdoing, especially in an act of sexual misconduct.
– ORIGIN L., 'in the heat of the crime' (lit. 'in blazing crime').

**inflame** • v. **1** intensify or aggravate: *high fines further inflamed public feelings.* ➤provoke (someone) to strong feelings. **2** (usu. **be inflamed**) cause inflammation in. **3** poetic/literary light up with or as if with flames.
– DERIVATIVES **inflamer** n.

**inflammable** • adj. easily set on fire. • n. a substance which is easily set on fire.
– DERIVATIVES **inflammability** n. **inflammableness** n. **inflammably** adv.

**USAGE** inflammable

The words **inflammable** and **flammable** both mean 'easily set on fire'. **Inflammable** is formed using the Latin prefix **in-** which has the meaning 'into' (rather than the more common use of **in-** to indicate negation), and here has the effect of intensifying the meaning of the word in English.

**inflammation** • n. a localized physical condition in which part of the body becomes reddened, swollen, hot, and often painful, especially as a reaction to injury or infection.

**inflammatory** • adj. **1** relating to or causing inflammation. **2** arousing or intended to arouse angry or violent feelings: *inflammatory language.*

**inflatable** • adj. capable of being inflated. • n. a plastic or rubber object that must be inflated before use.

**inflate** • v. **1** to expand or cause to expand by filling with air or gas. **2** [usu. as adj. **inflated**] increase by a large or excessive amount. ➤exaggerate. **3** bring about inflation of (a currency) or in (an economy).
– DERIVATIVES **inflatedly** adv. **inflater** (also **inflator**) n.
– ORIGIN ME: from L. *inflat-*, *inflare* 'blow into', from *in-* 'into' + *flare* 'to blow'.

**inflation** • n. **1** the action of inflating or the condition of being inflated. **2** Economics a general increase in prices and fall in the purchasing value of money. **3** Astronomy (in some theories of cosmology) a very brief exponential expansion of the early universe, interrupting the standard linear expansion.
– DERIVATIVES **inflationary** adj. **inflationism** n. **inflationist** n. & adj.

**inflect** • v. **1** Grammar change or be changed by inflection. **2** vary the intonation or pitch of (the voice), especially to

express mood or feeling. **3** technical bend or deflect from a straight course, especially inwards.
– DERIVATIVES **inflective** adj.
– ORIGIN ME: from L. *inflectere*, from *in-* 'into' + *flectere* 'to bend'.

**inflection** (chiefly Brit. also **inflexion**) ● **n.** **1** Grammar a change in the form of a word (typically the ending) to express a grammatical function or attribute such as tense, mood, person, number, case, and gender. **2** the modulation of intonation or pitch. **3** chiefly Mathematics a change of curvature from convex to concave.
– DERIVATIVES **inflectional** adj. **inflectionally** adv. **inflectionless** adj.

**inflexed** ● **adj.** technical bent or curved inwards.

**inflexible** ● **adj.** **1** unwilling to change; not able to be changed or adapted. **2** not able to be bent; stiff.
– DERIVATIVES **inflexibility** n. **inflexibly** adv.

**inflict** ● **v.** cause (something unpleasant or painful) to be suffered by someone else.
– DERIVATIVES **inflictable** adj. **inflicter** n. **infliction** n.
– ORIGIN C16 (in the sense 'afflict, trouble'): from L. *inflict-*, *infligere* 'strike against'.

**in-flight** ● **adj.** occurring or provided during an aircraft flight.

**inflorescence** /ˌɪnflɔːˈrɛs(ə)ns, -flə-/ ● **n.** Botany **1** the complete flower head of a plant including stems, stalks, bracts, and flowers. **2** the process of flowering.
– ORIGIN C18: from mod. L. *inflorescentia*, from late L. *inflorescere* 'come into flower'.

**inflow** ● **n.** **1** the action of flowing or moving in. **2** something, such as water or money, that flows or moves in.
– DERIVATIVES **inflowing** n. & adj.

**influence** ● **n.** **1** the capacity to have an effect on the character or behaviour of someone or something, or the effect itself. **2** the power arising out of status, contacts, or wealth. **3** a person or thing with such a capacity or power. **4** Physics, archaic electrical or magnetic induction. ● **v.** have an influence on.
– PHRASES **under the influence** informal affected by alcoholic drink.
– DERIVATIVES **influenceable** adj. **influencer** n.
– ORIGIN ME (orig. in the sense 'influx'): from OFr., or from med. L. *influentia* 'inflow', from L. *influere*, from *in-* 'into' + *fluere* 'to flow'.

**influent** /ˈɪnflʊənt/ ● **adj.** flowing in. ● **n.** a stream flowing into another stream or lake.
– ORIGIN ME: from L. *influent-*, *influere* 'flow in'.

**influential** ● **adj.** having great influence.
– DERIVATIVES **influentially** adv.

**influenza** ● **n.** a highly contagious viral infection of the respiratory passages causing fever, severe aching, and catarrh.
– DERIVATIVES **influenzal** adj.
– ORIGIN C18: from Ital., lit. 'influence', from med. L. *influentia* (see INFLUENCE); the Ital. word was applied to an influenza epidemic which began in Italy in 1743, later adopted in Engl. as the name of the disease.

**influx** /ˈɪnflʌks/ ● **n.** **1** the arrival or entry of large numbers of people or things. **2** an inflow of water into a river, lake, or the sea.
– ORIGIN C16: from late L. *influxus*, from *influere* (see INFLUENCE).

**info** ● **n.** informal short for INFORMATION.

**infomediary** ● **n.** an Internet company that gathers and links information on particular subjects on behalf of commercial organizations and their potential customers.

**infomercial** /ˌɪnfə(ʊ)ˈməːʃ(ə)l/ ● **n.** chiefly N. Amer. an advertising film which promotes a product in an informative and supposedly objective style.
– ORIGIN 1980s: blend of INFORMATION and COMMERCIAL.

**inform** ● **v.** **1** give facts or information to. **2** (**inform on**) give incriminating information about (someone) to the police or other authority. **3** give an essential or formative principle or quality to.
– ORIGIN ME *enforme*, *informe* 'give form or shape to', from OFr. *enfourmer*, from L. *informare* 'shape, describe'.

**informal** ● **adj.** **1** relaxed and unofficial; not formal. **2** of or denoting the grammatical structures, vocabulary, and idiom suitable to everyday language and conversation rather than to official or formal contexts.
– DERIVATIVES **informality** n. **informally** adv.

**informal vote** ● **n.** Austral./NZ an invalid vote or voting paper.

**informant** ● **n.** **1** a person who gives information to another. **2** another term for INFORMER.

**informatics** /ˌɪnfəˈmatɪks/ ● **pl. n.** [treated as sing.] Computing the science of processing data for storage and retrieval.

**information** ● **n.** **1** facts or knowledge provided or learned as a result of research or study. **2** what is conveyed or represented by a particular sequence of symbols, impulses, etc.: *genetically transmitted information.* **3** Law a charge lodged with a magistrates' court.
– DERIVATIVES **informational** adj. **informationally** adv.

**information retrieval** ● **n.** Computing the tracing and recovery of information from stored data.

**information science** ● **n.** Computing the study of processes for storing and retrieving information.

**information superhighway** ● **n.** an extensive electronic network such as the Internet, used for the rapid transfer of information in digital form.

**information technology** ● **n.** the study or use of systems (especially computers and telecommunications) for storing, retrieving, and sending information.

**information theory** ● **n.** the mathematical study of the coding of information in the form of sequences of symbols, impulses, etc. and of how rapidly such information can be transmitted.

**informative** ● **adj.** providing useful information.
– DERIVATIVES **informatively** adv. **informativeness** n.

**informatory** /ɪnˈfɔːmət(ə)ri/ ● **adj.** informative.

**informed** ● **adj.** having or showing knowledge. ➤(of a judgement) based on a sound understanding of the facts.
– DERIVATIVES **informedly** /ɪnˈfɔːmɪdli/ adv. **informedness** /ɪnˈfɔːmɪdnɪs/ n.

**informer** ● **n.** a person who informs on another person to the police or other authority.

**infotainment** ● **n.** broadcast material which is intended both to entertain and to inform.
– ORIGIN 1980s (orig. US): blend of INFORMATION and ***entertainment*** (see ENTERTAIN).

**infotech** ● **n.** short for INFORMATION TECHNOLOGY.

**infra-** /ˈɪnfrə/ ● **prefix** below: *infrasonic.*
– ORIGIN from L. *infra* 'below'.

**infraclass** ● **n.** Biology a taxonomic category that ranks below a subclass.

**infraction** ● **n.** chiefly Law a violation or infringement of a law or agreement.
– DERIVATIVES **infractor** n.
– ORIGIN ME: from L. *infractio(n-)*, from *infringere* (see INFRINGE).

**infradian** /ɪnˈfreɪdɪən/ ● **adj.** Physiology recurring less than once a day. Compare with ULTRADIAN.
– ORIGIN C20: from INFRA- 'below', on the pattern of *circadian.*

**infra dig** /ˌɪnfrə ˈdɪɡ/ ● **adj.** informal beneath one; demeaning.
– ORIGIN C19: abbrev. of L. *infra dignitatem* 'beneath (one's) dignity'.

**infrangible** /ɪnˈfran(d)ʒɪb(ə)l/ ● **adj.** formal unbreakable; inviolable.
– DERIVATIVES **infrangibility** n. **infrangibly** adv.

**infraorder** ● **n.** Biology a taxonomic category that ranks below a suborder.

**infrared** ● **n.** electromagnetic radiation having a wavelength just greater than that of red light but less than that of microwaves, emitted particularly by heated objects. ● **adj.** of or denoting such radiation.

**infrasonic** ● **adj.** referring to sound waves with a frequency below the lower limit of human audibility.

**infrasound** ● **n.** infrasonic sound waves.

**infrastructure** ● **n.** the basic physical and organizational structures (e.g. buildings, roads, power supplies) needed for the operation of a society or enterprise.

– DERIVATIVES **infrastructural** adj.

**infrequent** ● **adj.** not occurring often; rare.
– DERIVATIVES **infrequency** n. **infrequently** adv.

**infringe** ● **v. 1** violate (a law, agreement, etc.). **2** encroach on (a right or privilege).
– DERIVATIVES **infringement** n. **infringer** n.
– ORIGIN C16: from L. *infringere*, from *in-* 'into' + *frangere* 'to break'.

**infundibulum** /ˌɪnfʌnˈdɪbjʊləm/ ● **n.** (pl. **infundibula** /-ˈdɪbjʊlə/) Anatomy & Zoology a funnel-shaped cavity or structure.
– DERIVATIVES **infundibular** adj.
– ORIGIN C16: from L., 'funnel'.

**infuriate** ● **v.** /ɪnˈfjʊərɪeɪt/ make irritated or angry.
– DERIVATIVES **infuriating** adj. **infuriatingly** adv.
– ORIGIN C17: from med. L. *infuriat-*, *infuriare* 'make angry'.

**infuse** ● **v. 1** pervade; fill. **2** instil (a quality) in someone or something. ➤ Medicine allow (a liquid) to flow into a patient, vein, etc. **3** soak (tea, herbs, etc.) to extract the flavour or healing properties.
– DERIVATIVES **infuser** n.
– ORIGIN ME: from L. *infus-*, *infundere* 'pour in'.

**infusible** ● **adj.** not able to be melted or fused.
– DERIVATIVES **infusibility** n.

**infusion** ● **n. 1** a drink, remedy, or extract prepared by infusing. **2** the action or process of infusing.

**-ing[1]** ● **suffix 1** denoting a verbal action, activity, or result: *building*. **2** denoting material used for or associated with a process: *piping*. **3** forming the gerund of verbs (such as *painting* as in *I love painting*).
– ORIGIN OE *-ung*, *-ing*, of Gmc origin.

**-ing[2]** ● **suffix 1** forming the present participle of verbs: *calling*. **2** forming adjectives from nouns: *hulking*.
– ORIGIN ME: alt. of earlier *-ende*, later *-inde*.

**-ing[3]** ● **suffix** a thing belonging to or having the quality of: *farthing*.
– ORIGIN OE, of Gmc origin.

**ingenious** /ɪnˈdʒiːnɪəs/ ● **adj.** clever, original, and inventive.
– DERIVATIVES **ingeniously** adv. **ingeniousness** n.
– ORIGIN ME: from Fr. *ingénieux* or L. *ingeniosus*, from *ingenium* 'mind, intellect'; cf. ENGINE.

**ingénue** /ˈãʒən(j)uː/ ● **n.** an innocent or unsophisticated young woman.
– ORIGIN Fr., fem. of *ingénu* 'ingenuous'.

**ingenuity** /ˌɪndʒɪˈnjuːɪti/ ● **n.** the quality of being ingenious.
– ORIGIN C16: from L. *ingenuitas* 'ingenuousness', from *ingenuus* 'inborn'; the current meaning arose by confusion of *ingenuous* with *ingenious*.

**ingenuous** /ɪnˈdʒɛnjʊəs/ ● **adj.** innocent, artless, and unsuspecting.
– DERIVATIVES **ingenuously** adv. **ingenuousness** n.
– ORIGIN C16 (orig. in sense 'noble, generous'): from L. *ingenuus* lit. 'native, inborn'.

**ingest** ● **v.** take (food or drink) into the body by swallowing or absorbing it.
– DERIVATIVES **ingestion** n. **ingestive** adj.
– ORIGIN C17: from L. *ingest-*, *ingerere* 'bring in'.

**ingle** ● **n.** chiefly dialect a domestic fire or fireplace.
– ORIGIN C16 (orig. Scots): perh. from Sc. Gaelic *aingeal* 'light, fire', Ir. *aingeal* 'live ember'.

**inglenook** ● **n.** a space on either side of a large fireplace.

**inglorious** ● **adj. 1** not worthy of honour. **2** not famous or renowned.
– DERIVATIVES **ingloriously** adv. **ingloriousness** n.

**ingoing** ● **adj.** going towards or into.

**ingot** /ˈɪŋgət/ ● **n.** a rectangular block of steel, gold, or other metal.
– ORIGIN ME (denoting a mould): perh. from IN + OE *goten*, past part. of *geotan* 'pour, cast'.

**ingraft** ● **v.** variant spelling of ENGRAFT.

**ingrain** ● **v.** (also **engrain**) firmly fix or establish (a habit, belief, or attitude) in a person. ● **adj.** (of a textile) composed of fibres which have been dyed different colours before being woven.
– ORIGIN ME: from EN-[1], IN-[2] + GRAIN; the adjective is from *in grain* 'fast-dyed', from the old use of *grain* meaning 'kermes, cochineal'.

**ingrained** ● **adj.** (also **engrained**) **1** (of a habit or attitude) firmly established. **2** (of dirt) deeply embedded.

**ingrate** /ˈɪngreɪt, ɪnˈgreɪt/ formal or poetic/literary ● **n.** an ungrateful person. ● **adj.** ungrateful.
– ORIGIN ME: from L. *ingratus*, from *in-* 'not' + *gratus* 'grateful'.

**ingratiate** /ɪnˈgreɪʃɪeɪt/ ● **v.** (**ingratiate oneself**) bring oneself into favour with someone by flattering or trying to please them.
– DERIVATIVES **ingratiating** adj. **ingratiatingly** adv. **ingratiation** n.
– ORIGIN C17: from L. *in gratiam* 'into favour'.

**ingratitude** ● **n.** a discreditable lack of gratitude.

**ingredient** ● **n. 1** any of the foods or substances that are combined to make a particular dish. **2** a component part or element.
– ORIGIN ME: from L. *ingredient-*, *ingredi* 'enter', from *in-* 'into' + *gradi* 'walk'.

**ingress** /ˈɪngrɛs/ ● **n. 1** the action or fact of entering or coming in: *the sides are sealed against the ingress of water.* **2** a place or means of access. **3** Astronomy & Astrology the arrival of the sun, moon, or a planet in a specified constellation or part of the sky.
– DERIVATIVES **ingression** n.
– ORIGIN ME: from L. *ingressus*, from *ingredi* 'enter'.

**in-group** ● **n.** an exclusive group of people with a shared interest or identity.

**ingrown** ● **adj. 1** growing or having grown within; innate: *ingrown habit.* **2** inward-looking. **3** (of a toenail) having grown into the flesh.
– DERIVATIVES **ingrowing** adj. **ingrowth** n.

**inguinal** /ˈɪŋgwɪn(ə)l/ ● **adj.** Anatomy of the groin.
– DERIVATIVES **inguinally** adv.
– ORIGIN ME: from L. *inguinalis*, from *inguen*, *inguin-* 'groin'.

**ingulf** ● **v.** archaic spelling of ENGULF.

**ingurgitate** /ɪnˈgəːdʒɪteɪt/ ● **v.** poetic/literary swallow greedily.
– DERIVATIVES **ingurgitation** n.
– ORIGIN C16: from L. *ingurgitat-*, *ingurgitare* 'pour in', from *in-* 'into' + *gurges*, *gurgit-* 'whirlpool, gulf'.

**Ingush** /ˈɪŋgʊʃ/ ● **n.** (pl. same or **Ingushes**) **1** a member of a people living mainly in the Ingush republic in the central Caucasus region. **2** the North Caucasian language of this people.
– ORIGIN from Russ.

**inhabit** ● **v.** (**inhabited**, **inhabiting**) live in or occupy.
– DERIVATIVES **inhabitability** /-təˈbɪlɪti/ n. **inhabitable** adj. **inhabitation** n.
– ORIGIN ME, from OFr. *enhabiter* or L. *inhabitare*, from *in-* 'in' + *habitare* 'dwell'.

**inhabitant** ● **n.** a person or animal that lives in or occupies a place.

**inhalant** ● **n.** a medicinal preparation for inhaling. ➤ a solvent or other material producing vapour that is inhaled by drug abusers. ● **adj.** chiefly Zoology serving for inhalation.
– DERIVATIVES **inhalator** n.

**inhale** /ɪnˈheɪl/ ● **v.** breathe in (air, gas, smoke, etc.).
– DERIVATIVES **inhalation** n.
– ORIGIN C18 (earlier (C17) as *inhalation*): from L. *inhalare* 'breathe in'.

**inhaler** ● **n.** a portable device for administering a drug which is to be inhaled.

**inhaul** ● **n.** Sailing a rope used to haul in the clew of a sail.

**inhere** /ɪnˈhɪə/ ● **v.** (**inhere in/within**) **1** formal exist essentially or permanently in. **2** Law (of rights, powers, etc.) be vested in (a person or group) or attached to the ownership of (a property).
– ORIGIN C16: from L. *inhaerere* 'stick to'.

**inherent** /ɪnˈhɪər(ə)nt, -ˈhɛr(ə)nt/ ● **adj. 1** existing in something as a permanent or essential attribute. **2** Law

vested in someone as a right or privilege.
– DERIVATIVES **inherence** n. **inherently** adv.

**inherit** • v. (**inherited**, **inheriting**) **1** receive (money, property, or a title) as an heir at the death of the previous holder. **2** derive (a quality or characteristic) from one's parents or ancestors. ➤receive or be left with (a situation, object, etc.) from a predecessor or former owner.
– DERIVATIVES **inheritability** n. **inheritable** adj. **inheritor** n.
– ORIGIN ME *enherite* 'receive as a right', from OFr. *enheriter*, from late L. *inhereditare* 'appoint as heir'.

**inheritance** • n. **1** a thing that is inherited. **2** the action of inheriting.

**inheritance tax** • n. (in the UK) tax levied on property and money acquired by gift or inheritance (introduced in 1986).

**inhibit** • v. (**inhibited**, **inhibiting**) **1** hinder, restrain, or prevent (an action or process). **2** make (someone) unable to act in a relaxed and natural way.
– DERIVATIVES **inhibited** adj. **inhibitive** adj.
– ORIGIN ME: from L. *inhibere* 'hinder', from *in-* 'in' + *habere* 'hold'.

**inhibition** • n. **1** the action or process of inhibiting or being inhibited. **2** a feeling that makes one unable to act in a relaxed and natural way. ➤Psychology a restraint on the direct expression of an instinct. **3** Law, Brit. an order or writ of prohibition.

**inhibitor** • n. **1** a substance which slows down or prevents a particular chemical reaction or other process. **2** Genetics a gene whose presence prevents the expression of some other gene at a different locus. **3** Scots Law a person who takes out an inhibition.
– DERIVATIVES **inhibitory** adj.

**in-home** • adj. provided or taking place within a person's home.

**inhomogeneous** /ˌɪnhɒmə(ʊ)'dʒiːnɪəs, ˌɪnhəʊm-, -'dʒɛn-/ • adj. not homogeneous.
– DERIVATIVES **inhomogeneity** n.

**inhospitable** /ˌɪnhɒ'spɪtəb(ə)l, ɪn'hɒspɪt-/ • adj. not hospitable.
– DERIVATIVES **inhospitableness** n. **inhospitably** adv. **inhospitality** n.

**in-house** • adj. & adv. within an organization.

**inhuman** • adj. **1** lacking positive human qualities; cruel and barbaric. **2** not human in nature or character.
– DERIVATIVES **inhumanly** adv.

**inhumane** • adj. without compassion for misery or suffering; cruel.
– DERIVATIVES **inhumanely** adv.

**inhumanity** • n. (pl. **-ies**) cruel and brutal behaviour.

**inhumation** /ˌɪnhjʊ'meɪʃ(ə)n/ • n. chiefly Archaeology **1** the action or practice of burying the dead. **2** a burial or buried corpse.

**inhume** /ɪn'hjuːm/ • v. poetic/literary bury.
– ORIGIN C17: from L. *inhumare*, from *in-* 'into' + *humus* 'ground'.

**inimical** /ɪ'nɪmɪk(ə)l/ • adj. tending to obstruct or harm; hostile.
– DERIVATIVES **inimically** adv.
– ORIGIN C16: from late L. *inimicalis*, from L. *inimicus* (see **ENEMY**).

**inimitable** /ɪ'nɪmɪtəb(ə)l/ • adj. impossible to imitate; unique.
– DERIVATIVES **inimitability** n. **inimitably** adv.

**iniquity** /ɪ'nɪkwɪti/ • n. (pl. **-ies**) injustice or immoral behaviour.
– DERIVATIVES **iniquitous** adj. **iniquitously** adv. **iniquitousness** n.
– ORIGIN ME: from OFr. *iniquite*, from L. *iniquitas*, from *iniquus*, from *in-* 'not' + *aequus* 'equal, just'.

**initial** • adj. existing or occurring at the beginning. • n. the first letter of a name or word, especially that of a person's given name. • v. (**initialled**, **initialling**; N. Amer. **initialed**, **initialing**) mark or sign with one's initials as a sign of approval or endorsement.
– DERIVATIVES **initially** adv.
– ORIGIN C16: from L. *initialis*, from *initium* 'beginning'.

**initialism** • n. an abbreviation consisting of initial letters pronounced separately (e.g. *BBC*).

**initialize** (also **-ise**) • v. Computing set to the appropriate starting value or condition.
– DERIVATIVES **initialization** n.

**initiate** • v. /ɪ'nɪʃɪeɪt/ **1** cause (a process or action) to begin. **2** admit formally into a society or group, typically with a ritual. **3** (**initiate someone into**) introduce someone to (a new activity or skill). • n. /ɪ'nɪʃɪət/ a person who has been initiated.
– DERIVATIVES **initiation** n. **initiatory** adj.
– ORIGIN C16: from L. *initiat-*, *initiare* 'begin'.

**initiative** • n. **1** the ability to initiate. ➤the power or opportunity to act before others do: *we have lost the initiative.* **2** a fresh approach.
– PHRASES **on one's own initiative** without being prompted by others.

**initiator** • n. **1** a person or thing that initiates. **2** Chemistry a substance which starts a chain reaction. **3** an explosive or device used to detonate the main charge.

**inject** • v. **1** introduce (a liquid, especially a drug or vaccine) into the body with a syringe. ➤administer a drug or medicine to (a person or animal) in this way. **2** introduce or feed (something) under pressure into another substance. **3** introduce (a new or different element): *she tried to inject scorn into her tone.*
– DERIVATIVES **injectable** adj. & n. **injector** n.
– ORIGIN C16: from L. *inject-*, *inicere* 'throw in'.

**injection** • n. **1** an act of injecting or being injected. **2** a substance that is injected. **3** short for **FUEL INJECTION**.

**injection moulding** • n. the shaping of rubber or plastic articles by injecting heated material into a mould.
– DERIVATIVES **injection-moulded** adj.

**in-joke** • n. a joke that is shared exclusively by a small group.

**injudicious** • adj. showing poor judgement; unwise.
– DERIVATIVES **injudiciously** adv. **injudiciousness** n.

**injunct** /ɪn'dʒʌŋ(k)t/ • v. issue a legal injunction against.
– ORIGIN C19: from L. *injunct-*, *injungere* (see **ENJOIN**).

**injunction** • n. **1** Law a judicial order restraining a person from an action, or compelling a person to carry out a certain act. **2** an authoritative warning.
– DERIVATIVES **injunctive** adj.

**injure** • v. **1** do or undergo physical harm to; wound. **2** archaic do injustice or wrong to.
– DERIVATIVES **injurer** n.
– ORIGIN ME: back-form. from **INJURY**.

**injured** • adj. **1** physically harmed or wounded. **2** offended; wronged: *the injured party.*

**injurious** /ɪn'dʒʊərɪəs/ • adj. **1** causing or likely to cause injury. **2** (of language) maliciously insulting; libellous.
– DERIVATIVES **injuriously** adv. **injuriousness** n.

**injury** • n. (pl. **-ies**) **1** an instance of being injured. **2** the fact of being injured; harm or damage.
– ORIGIN ME: from Anglo-Norman Fr. *injurie*, from L. *injuria* 'a wrong'.

**injury time** • n. Brit. (in soccer and other sports) extra playing time allowed to compensate for time lost as a result of injuries.

**injustice** • n. **1** lack of justice. **2** an unjust act or occurrence.

**ink** • n. **1** a coloured fluid used for writing, drawing, or printing. **2** Zoology a black liquid ejected by a cuttlefish, octopus, or squid to confuse a predator. • v. **1** write or mark with ink. ➤cover (type or a stamp) with ink before printing. **2** informal, chiefly N. Amer. sign and secure (a contract).
– DERIVATIVES **inker** n.
– ORIGIN ME *enke*, *inke*, from OFr. *enque*, via late L. from Gk *enkauston*, denoting the purple ink used by Roman emperors for signatures, from *enkaiein* 'burn in'.

**ink-blot test** • n. another term for **RORSCHACH TEST**.

**ink cap** • n. a mushroom with a tall, narrow cap and slender white stem, turning into a black liquid after the spores are shed. [*Coprinus atramentarius* and related species.]

**inkhorn** ● **n.** historical a small portable container for ink, originally made from a horn.

**ink-jet printer** ● **n.** a printer in which the characters are formed by minute jets of ink.

**inkling** ● **n.** a slight suspicion; a hint.
– ORIGIN ME: from *inkle* 'utter in an undertone', of unknown origin.

**inkstand** ● **n.** a stand for ink bottles, pens, and other stationery items.

**inkwell** ● **n.** a container for ink, normally housed in a hole in a desk.

**inky** ● **adj.** (**-ier, -iest**) **1** as dark as ink. **2** stained with ink.
– DERIVATIVES **inkiness** n.

**INLA** ● **abbrev.** Irish National Liberation Army.

**inlaid** past and past participle of **INLAY**.

**inland** ● **adj. & adv. 1** in or into the interior of a country. **2** [as adj.] chiefly Brit. carried on within the limits of a country; domestic. ● **n.** the interior of a country or region.
– DERIVATIVES **inlander** n.

**inland revenue** ● **n.** Brit. public revenue consisting of income tax and some other direct taxes.

**inland sea** ● **n.** an entirely landlocked large body of salt or fresh water.

**in-law** ● **n.** a relative by marriage. ● **comb. form** related by marriage: *father-in-law.*

**inlay** ● **v.** (past and past part. **inlaid**) ornament by embedding pieces of a different material in a surface. ● **n. 1** an inlaid design or piece of material. ➤a material or substance used for inlaying. ➤inlaid work or decoration. **2** a filling shaped to fit a tooth cavity. **3** a printed insert supplied with a CD, video, etc.
– DERIVATIVES **inlayer** n.

**inlet** ● **n. 1** a small arm of the sea, a lake, or a river. **2** a place or means of entry: *an air inlet.* **3** (in tailoring and dressmaking) an inserted piece of material.

**inlier** /ˈɪnlʌɪə/ ● **n.** Geology an older rock formation isolated among newer rocks.

**in-line** ● **adj. 1** having parts arranged in a line. **2** constituting an integral part of a continuous sequence of operations or machines.

**in-liner** ● **n.** an in-line skater. ➤an in-line skate.

**in-line skate** ● **n.** a type of roller skate in which the wheels are fixed in a single line along the sole.
– DERIVATIVES **in-line skater** n. **in-line skating** n.

**in loco parentis** /ɪn ˌləʊkəʊ pəˈrɛntɪs/ ● **adv. & adj.** (of a teacher or other adult) in the place of a parent.
– ORIGIN from L.

**inly** /ˈɪnli/ ● **adv.** poetic/literary inwardly.

**inlying** /ˈɪnlʌɪɪŋ/ ● **adj.** within or near a centre.

**inmate** ● **n.** a person living in an institution such as a prison or hospital.
– ORIGIN C16 (denoting a lodger or subtenant): prob. orig. from **INN** + **MATE**[1], later assoc. with **IN**.

**in medias res** /ɪn ˌmiːdɪas ˈreɪz/ ● **adv.** in or into the midst or middle; without preamble.
– ORIGIN from L.

**in memoriam** /ˌɪn mɪˈmɔːrɪam/ ● **prep.** in memory of (a dead person).
– ORIGIN from L.

**inmost** ● **adj.** innermost.

**inn** ● **n.** a public house, traditionally an establishment also providing food and lodging.
– ORIGIN OE: of Gmc origin; rel. to **IN**.

**innards** ● **pl. n.** informal **1** internal organs; entrails. **2** the internal workings of a device or machine.
– ORIGIN C19: representing a dial. pronunc. of **INWARDS**.

**innate** /ɪˈneɪt, ˈɪneɪt/ ● **adj. 1** inborn; natural. **2** Philosophy originating in the mind.
– DERIVATIVES **innately** adv. **innateness** n.
– ORIGIN ME: from L. *innatus*, past part. of *innasci*, from *in-* 'into' + *nasci* 'be born'.

**inner** ● **adj. 1** situated inside; close to the centre. **2** mental or spiritual; not visible: *inner strength.* ➤private; not expressed. ● **n. 1** an inner part. **2** (in archery and shooting) a division of the target next to the bullseye.
– DERIVATIVES **innerly** adv. (poetic/literary). **innerness** n. (poetic/literary).

**inner bar** ● **n.** (in the UK) Queen's or King's Counsel collectively.

**inner city** ● **n.** the area near the centre of a city, especially when associated with social and economic problems.

**inner ear** ● **n.** the part of the ear embedded in the temporal bone, consisting of the semicircular canals and cochlea.

**innermost** ● **adj. 1** furthest in; closest to the centre. **2** (of thoughts) most private and deeply felt.

**inner space** ● **n. 1** the region between the earth and outer space, or below the surface of the sea. **2** the part of the mind not normally accessible to consciousness.

**inner tube** ● **n.** a separate inflatable tube inside a pneumatic tyre casing.

**innervate** /ˈɪnəveɪt, ɪˈnəːveɪt/ ● **v.** Anatomy & Zoology supply (an organ or other body part) with nerves.
– DERIVATIVES **innervation** n.
– ORIGIN C19: from **IN-**[2] + **NERVE** + **-ATE**[3].

**inning** ● **n.** Baseball each division of a game during which both sides have a turn at batting.
– ORIGIN OE *innung* 'a putting or getting in', rel. to **IN**.

**innings** ● **n.** (pl. same) [treated as sing.] Cricket each of the divisions of a game during which one side has a turn at batting. ➤a player's turn at batting.
– PHRASES **have had a good innings** Brit. informal have had a long and fulfilling life or career.

**innkeeper** ● **n.** chiefly archaic a person who runs an inn.

**innocent** ● **adj. 1** not guilty of a crime or offence. ➤not responsible or directly involved: *an innocent bystander.* **2** free from moral wrong; not corrupted. **3** not intended to cause offence; harmless. **4** (**innocent of**) without experience or knowledge of: *a man innocent of war's cruelties.* ➤without; lacking. ● **n.** an innocent person.
– DERIVATIVES **innocence** n. **innocency** n. (archaic). **innocently** adv.
– ORIGIN ME: from OFr., or from L. *innocent-* 'not harming', from *in-* 'not' + *nocere* 'to hurt'.

**innocuous** /ɪˈnɒkjʊəs/ ● **adj.** not harmful or offensive.
– DERIVATIVES **innocuously** adv. **innocuousness** n.
– ORIGIN C16: from L. *innocuus*, from *in-* 'not' + *nocuus* (see **NOCUOUS**).

**Inn of Court** ● **n.** (in the UK) each of the four legal societies having the exclusive right of admitting people to the English bar.

**innominate** /ɪˈnɒmɪnət/ ● **adj.** not named or classified.
– ORIGIN C17: from late L. *innominatus*, from *in-* 'not' + *nominatus* 'named'.

**innominate artery** ● **n.** Anatomy a large artery which branches from the aortic arch and divides into the right carotid subclavian arteries.

**innominate bone** ● **n.** Anatomy the hip bone.

**innominate vein** ● **n.** Anatomy either of two large veins of the neck.

**innovate** /ˈɪnəveɪt/ ● **v.** make changes in something already existing, as by introducing new methods, ideas, or products.
– DERIVATIVES **innovation** n. **innovational** adj. **innovative** adj. **innovator** n. **innovatory** adj.
– ORIGIN C16 (earlier (ME) as *innovation*): from L. *innovat-*, *innovare* 'renew, alter', from *in-* 'into' + *novare* 'make new'.

**innuendo** /ˌɪnjʊˈɛndəʊ/ ● **n.** (pl. **-oes** or **-os**) an allusive or oblique remark, typically a suggestive or disparaging one.
– ORIGIN C16 (as an adv. in legal documents, meaning 'that is to say'): L., 'by nodding at, by pointing to', ablative gerund of *innuere*, from *in-* 'towards' + *nuere* 'to nod'.

**innumerable** ● **adj.** too many to be counted.
– DERIVATIVES **innumerability** n. **innumerably** adv.

**innumerate** ● **adj.** without a basic knowledge of mathematics and arithmetic. ● **n.** an innumerate person.
– DERIVATIVES **innumeracy** n.

**innutritious** ● **adj.** not nourishing.

**inoculant** ● **n.** a substance used for inoculation.

**inoculate** /ɪˈnɒkjʊleɪt/ ● **v. 1** another term for **VACCIN-**

**ATE.** ➤ introduce (an infective agent) into an organism. **2** introduce (cells or organisms) into a culture medium.
– DERIVATIVES **inoculable** adj. **inoculation** n. **inoculator** n.
– ORIGIN ME (in the sense 'graft a bud or shoot'): from L. *inoculat-*, *inoculare* 'engraft', from *in-* 'into' + *oculus* 'eye, bud'.

**inoculum** /ɪˈnɒkjʊləm/ ● **n.** (pl. **inocula**) Medicine a substance used for inoculation.
– ORIGIN C20: mod. L., from L. *inoculare* (see **INOCULATE**).

**inodorous** ● **adj.** having no smell; odourless.

**in-off** ● **n.** Billiards & Snooker the pocketing of the cue ball (a scoring stroke in billiards, a foul in snooker) by bouncing it off another ball.

**inoffensive** ● **adj.** not objectionable or harmful.
– DERIVATIVES **inoffensively** adv. **inoffensiveness** n.

**inoperable** ● **adj. 1** Medicine not able to be suitably operated on. **2** not able to be used or operated. **3** impractical; unworkable.
– DERIVATIVES **inoperability** n. **inoperably** adv.

**inoperative** ● **adj.** not working or taking effect.

**inopportune** ● **adj.** occurring at an inconvenient time.
– DERIVATIVES **inopportunely** adv. **inopportuneness** n.

**inordinate** /ɪˈnɔːdɪnət/ ● **adj. 1** unusually large; excessive. **2** archaic unrestrained in feelings or behaviour; disorderly.
– DERIVATIVES **inordinately** adv.
– ORIGIN ME: from L. *inordinatus*, from *in-* 'not' + *ordinatus* 'set in order'.

**inorganic** ● **adj. 1** not arising from natural growth. **2** Chemistry relating to or denoting compounds which are not organic (broadly, compounds not containing carbon). Compare with **ORGANIC**. **3** without organized physical structure.
– DERIVATIVES **inorganically** adv.

**inosculate** /ɪˈnɒskjʊleɪt/ ● **v.** formal join by intertwining or fitting closely together.
– DERIVATIVES **inosculation** n.
– ORIGIN C17: from **IN-**[2] + L. *osculare* 'provide with a mouth or outlet'.

**inosine** /ˈɪnə(ʊ)siːn/ ● **n.** Biochemistry a compound which is formed in the metabolism of purine and is a nucleoside containing ribose.
– ORIGIN C20: from Gk *is*, *in-* 'fibre, muscle' + **-OSE**[2] + **-INE**[4].

**inositol** /ʌɪˈnəʊsɪtɒl/ ● **n.** Biochemistry a simple carbohydrate which occurs in animal and plant tissue and is a vitamin of the B group.
– ORIGIN C19: from the earlier name *inosite* + **-OL**.

**inpatient** ● **n.** a patient who lives in hospital while under treatment.

**in personam** /ˌɪn pəˈsəʊnam/ ● **adj. & adv.** Law made against or affecting a specific person only. Compare with **IN REM**.
– ORIGIN L., 'against a person'.

**in-phase** ● **adj.** of or relating to electrical signals that are in phase.

**in propria persona** /ɪn ˌprəʊprɪə pəːˈsəʊnə/ ● **adv.** in his or her own person.
– ORIGIN from L.

**input** ● **n. 1** what is put in, taken in, or operated on by any process or system. ➤ a person's contribution: *her input on issues was appreciated.* **2** the action or process of putting or feeding something in. **3** energy supplied to a device or system; an electrical signal. **4** Electronics a place or device from which energy or information enters a system. ● **v.** (**inputting**; past and past part. **input** or **inputted**) put (data) into a computer.
– DERIVATIVES **inputter** n.

**input-output** ● **adj.** Electronics of, relating to, or for both input and output.

**inquest** ● **n.** Law a judicial inquiry to ascertain the facts relating to an incident. ➤ Brit. an inquiry by a coroner's court into the cause of a death. ➤ Brit. a coroner's jury.
– ORIGIN ME from OFr. *enqueste*, based on L. *inquirere* (see **ENQUIRE**).

**inquietude** /ɪnˈkwʌɪətjuːd/ ● **n.** physical or mental unease.

**inquiline** /ˈɪnkwɪlʌɪn, -liːn/ ● **n.** Zoology an animal exploiting the living space of another, e.g. an insect that lays its eggs in a gall.
– ORIGIN C17: from L. *inquilinus* 'lodger', from *in-* + *colere* 'dwell'.

**inquire** ● **v.** another term for **ENQUIRE**.
– DERIVATIVES **inquirer** n.

**inquiry** ● **n.** (pl. **-ies**) another term for **ENQUIRY**.

**inquisition** ● **n. 1** a period of prolonged and intensive questioning or investigation. ➤ the verdict of a coroner's jury. **2** (**the Inquisition**) an ecclesiastical tribunal established *c.*1232 for the suppression of heresy, notorious for its use of torture.
– DERIVATIVES **inquisitional** adj.
– ORIGIN ME: via OFr. from L. *inquisitio(n-)* 'examination', from *inquirere* (see **ENQUIRE**).

**inquisitive** ● **adj.** curious or enquiring. ➤ unduly curious; prying.
– DERIVATIVES **inquisitively** adv. **inquisitiveness** n.

**inquisitor** /ɪnˈkwɪzɪtə/ ● **n.** a person making an inquiry or conducting an inquisition, especially when regarded as harsh or very searching.

**inquisitorial** ● **adj. 1** of or like an inquisitor. **2** Law (of a trial) in which the judge has an examining role. Compare with **ACCUSATORIAL**, **ADVERSARIAL**.
– DERIVATIVES **inquisitorially** adv.

**inquorate** /ɪnˈkwɔːrət, -eɪt/ ● **adj.** Brit. (of an assembly) not having a quorum.

**in re** /ɪn ˈriː, ˈreɪ/ ● **prep.** in the legal case of; with regard to.
– ORIGIN L., 'in the matter of'.

**in rem** /ɪn ˈrɛm/ ● **adj.** Law made against or affecting a thing, and therefore other people generally. Compare with **IN PERSONAM**.
– ORIGIN L., 'against a thing'.

**INRI** ● **abbrev.** Jesus of Nazareth, King of the Jews (the inscription over Christ's head at the Crucifixion).
– ORIGIN from the initials of L. *Iesus Nazarenus Rex Iudaeorum*.

**inro** /ˈɪnrəʊ/ ● **n.** (pl. same or **-os**) an ornamental box with compartments for seals or medicines, worn suspended from a girdle as part of traditional Japanese dress.
– ORIGIN C17: from Japanese *inrō*, from *in* 'seal' + *rō* 'basket'.

**inroad** ● **n. 1** an instance of something being encroached or intruded upon. **2** a hostile attack.

**inrush** ● **n.** a sudden inward rush or flow.
– DERIVATIVES **inrushing** adj. & n.

**INS** ● **abbrev.** Immigration and Naturalization Service.

**insalubrious** /ˌɪnsəˈluːbrɪəs/ ● **adj.** seedy; unwholesome.
– DERIVATIVES **insalubrity** n.

**insane** ● **adj. 1** in or relating to an unsound state of mind; seriously mentally ill. **2** extremely foolish; irrational.
– DERIVATIVES **insanely** adv. **insanity** n.
– ORIGIN C16: from L. *insanus*, from *in-* 'not' + *sanus* 'healthy'.

**insanitary** ● **adj.** so dirty or germ-ridden as to be a danger to health.

**insatiable** /ɪnˈseɪʃəb(ə)l/ ● **adj.** impossible to satisfy.
– DERIVATIVES **insatiability** n. **insatiably** adv.

**inscribe** ● **v.** (usu. **be inscribed**) **1** write or carve (words or symbols) on a surface, especially as a formal or permanent record. **2** write a dedication to someone in (a book). **3** Geometry draw (a figure) within another so that their boundaries touch but do not intersect. Compare with **CIRCUMSCRIBE**. **4** archaic enter the name of (someone) on a list; enrol.
– DERIVATIVES **inscribable** adj. **inscriber** n.
– ORIGIN ME: from L. *inscribere*, from *in-* 'into' + *scribere* 'write'.

**inscription** ● **n. 1** a thing inscribed, as on a monument or in a book. **2** the action of inscribing.
– DERIVATIVES **inscriptional** adj. **inscriptive** adj.
– ORIGIN ME: from L. *inscriptio(n-)*, from *inscribere* (see **INSCRIBE**).

**inscrutable** /ɪnˈskru:təb(ə)l/ ● **adj.** impossible to understand or interpret.
– DERIVATIVES **inscrutability** n. **inscrutably** adv.
– ORIGIN ME: from eccles. L. *inscrutabilis*, from *in-* 'not' + *scrutari* (see **SCRUTINY**).

**inseam** ● **n.** N. Amer. another term for **INSIDE LEG**.

**insect** ● **n.** an arthropod animal of a large class (Insecta) having a head, thorax, and abdomen, six legs, two antennae, and one or two pairs of wings. ➤ informal any small invertebrate animal such as a spider or tick.
– ORIGIN C17: from L. (*animal*) *insectum* 'segmented (animal)' (translating Gk *zōion entomon*), from *insecare* 'cut up or into'.

**insectarium** /ˌɪnsɛkˈtɛ:rɪəm/ (also **insectary** /ɪnˈsɛktəri/) ● **n.** (pl. **insectariums** or **insectaries**) a place where insects are kept, exhibited, and studied.

**insecticide** ● **n.** a substance used for killing insects.
– DERIVATIVES **insecticidal** adj.

**insectile** ● **adj.** resembling an insect.

**Insectivora** /ˌɪnsɛkˈtɪvərə/ ● **pl. n.** Zoology an order of small mammals that includes the shrews, moles, hedgehogs, and tenrecs.

**insectivore** /ɪnˈsɛktɪvɔ:/ ● **n. 1** an animal that feeds on insects and other invertebrates. **2** Zoology a mammal of the order Insectivora.
– DERIVATIVES **insectivorous** adj.

**insecure** ● **adj. 1** not confident or assured. **2** (of a thing) not firm or firmly fixed. ➤ not permanent: *insecure employment.* **3** easily broken into; not protected.
– DERIVATIVES **insecurely** adv. **insecurity** n.

**inselberg** /ˈɪns(ə)lbə:g, -z-/ ● **n.** Geology an isolated hill rising abruptly from a plain.
– ORIGIN C20: from Ger., from *Insel* 'island' + *Berg* 'mountain'.

**inseminate** /ɪnˈsɛmɪneɪt/ ● **v.** introduce semen into (a woman or a female animal).
– DERIVATIVES **insemination** n. **inseminator** n.
– ORIGIN C17: from L. *inseminat-*, *inseminare* 'sow', from *in-* 'into' + *seminare* 'sow'.

**insensate** ● **adj. 1** lacking physical sensation. **2** lacking sympathy; unfeeling. **3** completely lacking sense or reason.
– DERIVATIVES **insensately** adv.

**insensible** ● **adj. 1** without one's mental faculties; unconscious. ➤ numb; without feeling. **2** (**insensible of/to**) unaware of; indifferent to. **3** too small or gradual to be perceived: *varying by insensible degrees.*
– DERIVATIVES **insensibly** adv. **insensibility** n.

**insensitive** ● **adj. 1** showing or feeling no concern for others' feelings. **2** not sensitive to physical sensation. **3** not appreciative of or able to respond to something.
– DERIVATIVES **insensitively** adv. **insensitiveness** n. **insensitivity** n.

**insentient** ● **adj.** incapable of feeling; inanimate.
– DERIVATIVES **insentience** n.

**inseparable** ● **adj.** unable to be separated or treated separately.
– DERIVATIVES **inseparability** n. **inseparably** adv.

**insert** ● **v.** /ɪnˈsə:t/ **1** place, fit, or incorporate (something) in something else. ➤ include (text) in a piece of writing. **2** (**be inserted**) Anatomy & Zoology (of a muscle or other organ) be attached to a part, especially that which is moved. ● **n.** /ˈɪnsə:t/ **1** a loose page or section in a magazine, typically one carrying an advertisement. **2** an ornamental section of cloth inserted into a garment. **3** a shot inserted in a film or video.
– DERIVATIVES **insertable** adj. **inserter** n.
– ORIGIN C15: from L. *insert-*, *inserere* 'put in', from *in-* 'into' + *serere* 'to join'.

**insertion** ● **n. 1** the action of inserting. **2** an amendment or addition inserted in a text. ➤ each appearance of an advertisement in a newspaper or periodical. **3** an insert in a garment. **4** Anatomy & Zoology the manner or place of attachment of an organ or muscle.

**in-service** ● **adj.** (of training) intended to take place during the course of employment.

**inset** ● **n.** /ˈɪnsɛt/ a thing inserted; an insert. ➤ a small picture or map inserted within the border of a larger one. ● **v.** /ɪnˈsɛt/ (**insetting**; past and past part. **inset** or **insetted**) **1** put in as an inset. **2** decorate with an inset.
– DERIVATIVES **insetter** n.

**inshallah** /ɪnˈʃalə/ ● **exclam.** if Allah wills it.
– ORIGIN from Arab. *in šā' Allāh.*

**inshore** ● **adj.** at sea but close to the shore; operating near the coast: *an inshore lifeboat.* ● **adv.** towards or closer to the shore.

**inside** ● **n.** /ɪnˈsʌɪd/ **1** the inner side or surface of a thing. ➤ the part of a road furthest from the centre. ➤ the side of a bend where the edge is shorter. **2** the inner part; the interior. ➤ (**insides**) informal the stomach and bowels. **3** (**the inside**) informal a position affording private information: *will you be my spy on the inside?* ● **adj.** /ˈɪnsʌɪd/ **1** situated on or in, or derived from, the inside. **2** (in hockey, soccer, and other sports) denoting positions nearer to the centre of the field. ● **prep. & adv.** /ɪnˈsʌɪd/ **1** situated or moving within. ➤ within (the body or mind of a person). **2** informal in prison. **3** (in soccer, rugby, and other sports) closer to the centre of the field than. **4** in less than (the period of time specified).
– PHRASES **inside of** N. Amer. informal **1** within. **2** in less than (the period of time specified).

**inside job** ● **n.** informal a crime committed by or with the assistance of a person associated with the premises where it occurred.

**inside leg** ● **n.** the length of a person's leg or trouser leg from crotch to ankle.

**inside out** ● **adv.** with the inner surface turned outwards.
– PHRASES **know something inside out** know something very thoroughly.

**insider** ● **n.** a person within an organization, especially someone privy to information unavailable to others.

**insider dealing** (also **insider trading**) ● **n.** the illegal practice of trading on the stock exchange to one's own advantage through having access to confidential information.

**insidious** /ɪnˈsɪdɪəs/ ● **adj.** proceeding in a gradual, subtle way, but with harmful effects.
– DERIVATIVES **insidiously** adv. **insidiousness** n.
– ORIGIN C16: from L. *insidiosus* 'cunning'.

**insight** ● **n. 1** the capacity to gain an accurate and deep intuitive understanding of something. ➤ an understanding of this kind. **2** Psychiatry awareness by a mentally ill person that their mental experiences are not based in external reality.
– DERIVATIVES **insightful** adj. **insightfully** adv.
– ORIGIN ME: prob. of Scand. and Low Ger. origin.

**insignia** /ɪnˈsɪgnɪə/ ● **n.** (pl. same) **1** a badge or distinguishing mark of military rank, office, or membership. **2** chiefly poetic/literary a token of something.
– ORIGIN C17: from L., pl. of *insigne* 'sign, badge', neut. of *insignis* 'distinguished'.

**insignificant** ● **adj.** too small or unimportant to be worth consideration.
– DERIVATIVES **insignificance** n. **insignificancy** n. **insignificantly** adv.

**insincere** ● **adj.** not expressing genuine feelings.
– DERIVATIVES **insincerely** adv. **insincerity** n. (pl. **-ies**).

**insinuate** /ɪnˈsɪnjʊeɪt/ ● **v. 1** suggest or hint (something bad) in an indirect and unpleasant way. **2** (**insinuate oneself into**) manoeuvre oneself gradually into (a favourable position).
– DERIVATIVES **insinuating** adj. **insinuatingly** adv. **insinuator** n.
– ORIGIN C16 (in the sense 'enter (a document) on the official register'): from L. *insinuat-*, *insinuare* 'introduce tortuously', from *in-* 'in' + *sinuare* 'to curve'.

**insinuation** ● **n.** an unpleasant hint or suggestion.

**insipid** /ɪnˈsɪpɪd/ ● **adj. 1** lacking flavour. **2** lacking vigour or interest.
– DERIVATIVES **insipidity** n. **insipidly** adv. **insipidness** n.
– ORIGIN C17: from Fr. *insipide* or late L. *insipidus*, from *in-* 'not' + *sapidus* (see **SAPID**).

**insist** ● **v.** demand or state forcefully, without accepting refusal or contradiction. ➤ (**insist on**) persist in (doing).

– ORIGIN C16: from L. *insistere* 'persist', from *in-* 'upon' + *sistere* 'stand'.

**insistent** ● adj. **1** insisting or very demanding. **2** repeated and demanding attention: *a telephone started ringing, loud and insistent.*
– DERIVATIVES **insistence** n. **insistency** n. **insistently** adv.

**in situ** /ɪn ˈsɪtjuː/ ● adv. & adj. in the original or appropriate position.
– ORIGIN from L.

**insobriety** ● n. drunkenness.

**insofar** ● adv. variant spelling of *in so far* (see **FAR**).

**insolation** /ˌɪnsəˈleɪʃ(ə)n/ ● n. technical exposure to the sun's rays. ➤the amount of solar radiation reaching a given area.
– ORIGIN C17: from L. *insolatio(n-)*, from *insolare*, from *in-* 'towards' + *sol* 'sun'.

**insole** ● n. a removable sole worn in a shoe for warmth or to improve the fit. ➤the fixed inner sole of a boot or shoe.

**insolent** ● adj. rude and disrespectful.
– DERIVATIVES **insolence** n. **insolently** adv.
– ORIGIN ME: from L. *insolent-* 'immoderate, arrogant'.

**insoluble** ● adj. **1** impossible to solve. **2** (of a substance) incapable of being dissolved.
– DERIVATIVES **insolubility** n. **insolubilize** (also **-ise**) v. **insolubly** adv.

**insolvent** ● adj. **1** unable to pay debts owed. **2** of or relating to bankruptcy. ● n. an insolvent person.
– DERIVATIVES **insolvency** n.

**insomnia** ● n. habitual sleeplessness.
– DERIVATIVES **insomniac** n. & adj.
– ORIGIN C17: from L., from *insomnis* 'sleepless'.

**insomuch** ● adv. (**insomuch that/as**) to the extent that.

**insouciant** /ɪnˈsuːsɪənt/ ● adj. casually unconcerned.
– DERIVATIVES **insouciance** n. **insouciantly** adv.
– ORIGIN C18: Fr., from *insouciant*, from *in-* 'not' + *souciant* 'worrying' (pres. part. of *soucier*).

**inspan** /ɪnˈspan/ ● v. (**inspanned**, **inspanning**) S. African **1** yoke (draught animals) to a vehicle. **2** use for a particular purpose.
– ORIGIN C19: from Du. *inspannen* 'to stretch'.

**inspect** ● v. look at closely. ➤examine officially.
– DERIVATIVES **inspection** n.
– ORIGIN C17 (earlier (ME) as *inspection*): from L. *inspect-*, *inspicere* 'look into, examine', or from its frequentative, *inspectare*.

**inspector** ● n. **1** an official who ensures that regulations are obeyed. ➤Brit. an official who examines bus or train tickets for validity. **2** a police officer ranking below a chief inspector.
– DERIVATIVES **inspectorate** n. **inspectorial** adj. **inspectorship** n.

**inspector general** ● n. **1** the head of a body of inspectors. **2** Military a staff officer who conducts inspections and investigations.

**inspector of taxes** (also **tax inspector**) ● n. (in the UK) an official of the Inland Revenue responsible for collecting taxes.

**inspiration** ● n. **1** the process or quality of being inspired. ➤a person or thing that inspires. ➤a sudden brilliant or timely idea. ➤the divine influence supposed to have led to the writing of the Bible. **2** inhalation.
– DERIVATIVES **inspirational** adj.

**inspiratory** /ɪnˈspʌɪrət(ə)ri/ ● adj. Physiology relating to inhalation.

**inspire** ● v. **1** fill with the urge or ability to do or feel something. ➤create (a feeling) in a person. ➤(**inspire someone with**) animate someone with (a feeling). **2** give rise to. **3** inhale.
– DERIVATIVES **inspirer** n. **inspiring** adj. **inspiringly** adv.
– ORIGIN ME *enspire*, from OFr. *inspirer*, from L. *inspirare* 'breathe or blow into'.

**inspired** ● adj. **1** showing or characterized by inspiration: *an inspired contribution to the debate.* **2** (of air or another substance) having been inhaled.
– DERIVATIVES **inspiredly** adv.

**inspirit** ● v. (**inspirited**, **inspiriting**) [usu. as adj. **inspiriting**] encourage and enliven.
– DERIVATIVES **inspiritingly** adv.

**inspissate** /ɪnˈspɪseɪt/ ● v. [usu. as adj. **inspissated**] thicken or congeal.
– DERIVATIVES **inspissation** n.
– ORIGIN C17: from late L. *inspissat-*, *inspissare* 'thicken'.

**inspissator** /ˈɪnspɪˌseɪtə/ ● n. a heating device for thickening a liquid.

**inst.** ● abbrev. **1** dated (in business letters) instant. **2** institute; institution.

**instability** ● n. (pl. **-ies**) lack of stability.

**install** (also **instal**) ● v. (**installed**, **installing**) **1** place or fix (equipment) in position ready for use. **2** establish in a new place, condition, or role.
– DERIVATIVES **installer** n.
– ORIGIN ME: from med. L. *installare*, from *in-* 'into' + *stallum* 'place, stall'.

**installation** ● n. **1** the action or process of installing or being installed. **2** a large piece of equipment installed for use. **3** a military or industrial establishment. **4** an art exhibit constructed within a gallery.

**instalment** (US also **installment**) ● n. **1** a sum of money due as one of several equal payments for something, spread over an agreed period of time. **2** one of several parts of something which are published or broadcast in sequence at intervals.
– ORIGIN C18: alt. of obs. *estalment* (prob. by assoc. with **INSTALLATION**), from Anglo-Norman Fr. *estalement*, from OFr. *estaler* 'to fix'.

**instance** ● n. an example or single occurrence of something. ➤a particular case. ● v. cite as an example.
– PHRASES **at first instance** Law at the first court hearing concerning a case. **at the instance of** formal at the request or instigation of. **for instance** as an example. **in the first** (or **second** etc.) **instance** in the first (or second etc.) place or stage of a proceeding.
– ORIGIN ME (orig. 'urgent entreaty', later 'example to the contrary'): via OFr. from L. *instantia* 'presence, urgency', from *instare* 'be present, press upon', from *in-* 'upon' + *stare* 'to stand'.

**instancy** ● n. archaic urgency.

**instant** ● adj. **1** immediate. ➤(of food) processed to allow quick preparation. **2** urgent; pressing. **3** [postpos.] dated (in business letters) of the current month: *your letter of the 6th instant.* **4** archaic of the present. ● n. **1** a precise moment of time. **2** a very short time.
– DERIVATIVES **instantly** adv.
– ORIGIN ME: via OFr. from L. *instant-*, *instare* 'be at hand', from *in-* 'in, at' + *stare* 'to stand'.

**instantaneous** /ˌɪnst(ə)nˈteɪnɪəs/ ● adj. **1** occurring or done instantly. **2** Physics existing or measured at a particular instant.
– DERIVATIVES **instantaneity** n. **instantaneously** adv. **instantaneousness** n.
– ORIGIN C17: from med. L. *instantaneus*, from L. *instant-* (from *instare* 'be at hand').

**instanter** /ɪnˈstantə/ ● adv. archaic or humorous immediately.
– ORIGIN from L.

**instantiate** /ɪnˈstanʃɪeɪt/ ● v. represent as or by an instance. ➤(**be instantiated**) Philosophy (of a universal or abstract concept) be represented by an actual example.
– DERIVATIVES **instantiation** n.
– ORIGIN 1940s: from L. *instantia* (see **INSTANCE**) + **-ATE**³.

**instar** /ˈɪnstɑː/ ● n. Zoology a phase between two periods of moulting in the development of an insect larva or other invertebrate.
– ORIGIN C19: from L., lit. 'form, likeness'.

**instate** ● v. install or establish.
– ORIGIN C17: from **IN-**² + **STATE**; cf. earlier **REINSTATE**.

**in statu pupillari** /ɪn ˌstatjuː ˌpjuːpɪˈlɑːri/ ● adj. **1** under guardianship as a pupil. **2** in a junior position at university; not having a master's degree.
– ORIGIN from L.

**instauration** /ˌɪnstɔːˈreɪʃ(ə)n/ ● n. formal restoration or renewal.
– DERIVATIVES **instaurator** /ˈɪnstɔːreɪtə/ n.

– ORIGIN C17: from L. *instauratio(n-)*, from *instaurare* 'renew'.

**instead** ● **adv.** as an alternative or substitute. ➤(**instead of**) in place of.

– ORIGIN ME: from **IN** + **STEAD**.

**instep** ● **n.** the part of a person's foot between the ball and the ankle. ➤the part of a shoe which fits over or under this.

– ORIGIN ME: of unknown origin; cf. W. Frisian *ynstap* 'opening in a shoe for insertion of the foot'.

**instigate** /ˈɪnstɪɡeɪt/ ● **v.** bring about or initiate. ➤(**instigate someone to/to do something**) incite someone to do something.

– DERIVATIVES **instigation** n. **instigator** n.

– ORIGIN C16 (earlier (ME) as *instigation*): from L. *instigat-*, *instigare* 'urge, incite'.

**instil** /ɪnˈstɪl/ (also **instill**) ● **v.** (**instilled**, **instilling**) **1** gradually but firmly establish in someone's mind. **2** put (a liquid) into something in drops.

– DERIVATIVES **instillation** n. **instilment** n.

– ORIGIN ME: from L. *instillare*, from *in-* 'into' + *stillare* 'to drop'.

**instinct** ● **n. 1** an innate pattern of behaviour in animals in response to certain stimuli. ➤a natural or intuitive way of acting or thinking. **2** a natural propensity or skill. ● **adj.** (**instinct with**) formal imbued or filled with (a quality).

– DERIVATIVES **instinctual** adj. **instinctually** adv.

– ORIGIN ME: from L. *instinctus* 'impulse', from *instinguere*, from *in-* 'towards' + *stinguere* 'to prick'.

**instinctive** ● **adj.** relating to or prompted by instinct. ➤apparently natural or automatic.

– DERIVATIVES **instinctively** adv.

**institute** ● **n. 1** an organization for the promotion of science, education, etc. **2** archaic a treatise or summary of principles, especially of law. ● **v. 1** set in motion or establish. ➤begin (legal proceedings). **2** appoint to a position, especially as a cleric.

– ORIGIN ME: from L. *institut-*, *instituere* 'establish'.

**institution** ● **n. 1** an organization founded for a religious, educational, or social purpose. ➤an organization providing residential care for people with special needs. ➤an official organization with an important role in a country. **2** an established law or custom. ➤informal a well-established and familiar person or thing: *he became a national institution.* **3** the action of instituting.

**institutional** ● **adj. 1** of, in, or like an institution. ➤regimented or unimaginative. ➤expressed or organized through institutions: *institutional religion.* **2** (of advertising) intended to create prestige.

– DERIVATIVES **institutionalism** n. **institutionally** adv.

**institutionalize** (also **-ise**) ● **v. 1** establish as a convention in an organization or culture. **2** place in a residential institution. ➤(**be/become institutionalized**) suffer the deleterious effects of long-term residence in an institution.

– DERIVATIVES **institutionalization** n.

**Inst.P.** ● **abbrev.** Institute of Physics.

**instruct** ● **v. 1** direct or command. **2** teach. **3** chiefly Brit. authorize (a solicitor or barrister) to act on one's behalf. ➤(of a solicitor) inform (a barrister) about a case. **4** inform of a fact or situation.

– ORIGIN ME: from L. *instruct-*, *instruere* 'construct, equip, teach', from *in-* 'upon, towards' + *struere* 'pile up'.

**instruction** ● **n. 1** a direction or order. ➤(**instructions**) Law directions to a solicitor, counsel, or jury. **2** Computing a code in a program which defines and carries out an operation. **3** education.

– DERIVATIVES **instructional** adj.

**instruction set** ● **n.** Computing the complete set of instructions in machine code that can be recognized by a central processing unit.

**instructive** ● **adj.** useful and informative.

– DERIVATIVES **instructively** adv. **instructiveness** n.

**instructor** (or **instructress**) ● **n.** a teacher. ➤N. Amer. a university teacher ranking below assistant professor.

– DERIVATIVES **instructorship** n.

**instrument** ● **n. 1** a tool or implement, especially for precision work. **2** a measuring device, especially in a vehicle or aircraft. **3** (also **musical instrument**) a device for producing musical sounds. **4** a means of pursuing an aim. **5** a person who is made use of. **6** a formal or legal document. ● **v.** equip with measuring instruments.

– ORIGIN ME: from OFr., or from L. *instrumentum* 'equipment, implement', from *instruere* 'construct, equip'.

**instrumental** ● **adj. 1** serving as a means of pursuing an aim. **2** (of music) performed on instruments. **3** of or relating to an implement or measuring device. **4** Grammar denoting or relating to a case of nouns and pronouns indicating a means or instrument. ● **n.** a piece of music performed by instruments, with no vocals.

– DERIVATIVES **instrumentality** n. **instrumentally** adv.

**instrumentalism** ● **n. 1** a pragmatic philosophical approach which regards an activity (e.g. science, law, or education) chiefly as an instrument for some practical purpose. **2** Music, rare instrumental technique.

**instrumentalist** ● **n. 1** a player of a musical instrument. **2** an adherent of instrumentalism. ● **adj.** of or in terms of instrumentalism.

**instrumentation** ● **n. 1** the instruments used in a piece of music. ➤the arrangement of a piece of music for particular instruments. **2** measuring instruments collectively. ➤the design or use of such instruments.

**insubordinate** ● **adj.** disobedient.

– DERIVATIVES **insubordinately** adv. **insubordination** n.

**insubstantial** ● **adj.** lacking strength and solidity. ➤imaginary.

– DERIVATIVES **insubstantiality** n. **insubstantially** adv.

**insufferable** ● **adj.** intolerable. ➤unbearably arrogant or conceited.

– DERIVATIVES **insufferableness** n. **insufferably** adv.

– ORIGIN ME: perh. via Fr. (now dial.) *insouffrable*, based on L. *sufferre* (see **SUFFER**).

**insufficiency** ● **n.** the condition of being insufficient. ➤Medicine the inability of an organ to perform normally.

**insufficient** ● **adj.** not enough.

– DERIVATIVES **insufficiently** adv.

**insufflate** /ˈɪnsəfleɪt/ ● **v. 1** Medicine blow or breathe (vapour, a powdered medicine, etc.) into or through a body cavity. **2** Theology breathe on to symbolize spiritual influence.

– DERIVATIVES **insufflation** n.

– ORIGIN C17: from late L. *insufflat-*, *insufflare* 'blow into'.

**insufflator** ● **n. 1** a device for blowing powder on to a surface to reveal fingerprints. **2** an instrument for medical insufflation.

**insula** /ˈɪnsjʊlə/ ● **n.** (pl. **insulae** /-liː/) **1** (in ancient Rome) a tenement in a city. **2** Anatomy a region of the cerebral cortex.

– ORIGIN L., lit. 'island'.

**insulant** ● **n.** an insulating material.

**insular** ● **adj. 1** lacking contact with other people. ➤narrow-minded. **2** of, relating to, or from an island. **3** of or relating to the art of Britain and Ireland in the early Middle Ages. **4** (of climate) equable because of the influence of the sea. **5** Anatomy of or relating to the insula of the brain.

– DERIVATIVES **insularity** n. **insularly** adv.

– ORIGIN C16 (as n. denoting an islander): from late L. *insularis*, from *insula* 'island'.

**insulate** ● **v. 1** protect by interposing material to prevent loss of heat or intrusion of sound. ➤cover with non-conducting material to prevent the passage of electricity. **2** protect from something unpleasant. **3** archaic make (land) into an island.

– ORIGIN C16: from L. *insula* 'island' + **-ATE**[3].

**insulating tape** ● **n.** adhesive tape used to cover exposed electric wires.

**insulation** ● **n. 1** the action of insulating or state of being insulated. **2** material used to insulate something.

**insulator** ● **n.** a substance which does not readily allow the passage of heat, sound, or electricity. ➤a block of glass, ceramic, or other insulating material enclosing an electric wire where it crosses a support.

**insulin** ● **n.** Biochemistry a pancreatic hormone which regulates glucose levels in the blood, a lack of which causes

diabetes.
– ORIGIN C20: from L. *insula* 'island' (with ref. to the islets of Langerhans in the pancreas) + **-IN**[1].

**insulin shock** • **n.** Medicine an acute condition resulting from excess insulin in the blood, involving weakness, convulsions, and potentially coma.

**insult** • **v.** /ɪn'sʌlt/ speak to or treat with disrespect or abuse. • **n.** /'ɪnsʌlt/ **1** an insulting remark or action. ➤a thing so worthless or contemptible as to be offensive: *the pay offer is an absolute insult.* **2** Medicine an event which causes damage to a tissue or organ.
– DERIVATIVES **insulter** n. **insulting** adj. **insultingly** adv.
– ORIGIN C16: from L. *insultare* 'jump or trample on'; the noun is from Fr. *insulte* or eccles. L. *insultus*.

**insuperable** /ɪn's(j)uːp(ə)rəb(ə)l/ • **adj.** impossible to overcome.
– DERIVATIVES **insuperability** n. **insuperably** adv.
– ORIGIN ME: from OFr., or from L. *insuperabilis*, from *in-* 'not' + *superabilis* (from *superare* 'overcome').

**insupportable** • **adj. 1** unable to be supported or justified. **2** intolerable.
– DERIVATIVES **insupportably** adv.

**insurance** • **n. 1** the action of insuring someone or something. ➤the business of providing insurance policies. ➤money paid for this, or as compensation under an insurance policy. **2** a thing providing protection against a possible eventuality.

**insurance broker** • **n.** an agent selling insurance.

**insurance carrier** • **n.** N. Amer. an insurance company.

**insurance policy** • **n.** a contract of insurance.

**insurance stamp** • **n.** Brit. a stamp certifying that a weekly payment has been made towards National Insurance.

**insure** /ɪn'ʃʊə/ • **v. 1** arrange for compensation in the event of damage to or loss of (property, life, or a person), in exchange for regular payments to a company. ➤secure the payment of (a sum) in this way. ➤(**insure someone against**) protect someone against (a possible contingency). **2** another term for **ENSURE**.
– DERIVATIVES **insurability** n. **insurable** adj. **insurer** n.
– ORIGIN ME: alt. of **ENSURE**.

**insured** • **adj.** covered by insurance. • **n.** (**the insured**) (pl. same) a person covered by insurance.

**insurgent** /ɪn'səːdʒ(ə)nt/ • **adj.** rising in active revolt. • **n.** a rebel or revolutionary.
– DERIVATIVES **insurgence** n. **insurgency** n. (pl. **-ies**).
– ORIGIN C18: via Fr. from L. *insurgent-*, *insurgere* 'arise'.

**insurmountable** /ˌɪnsə'maʊntəb(ə)l/ • **adj.** too great to be overcome.
– DERIVATIVES **insurmountably** adv.

**insurrection** /ˌɪnsə'rɛkʃ(ə)n/ • **n.** a violent uprising against authority.
– DERIVATIVES **insurrectionary** adj. **insurrectionist** n. & adj.
– ORIGIN ME: via OFr. from late L. *insurrectio(n-)*, from *insurgere* 'rise up'.

**insusceptible** • **adj.** not susceptible.
– DERIVATIVES **insusceptibility** n.

**inswinger** • **n.** Cricket a ball bowled with a swing from the off to the leg side.

**int.** • **abbrev. 1** interior. **2** internal. **3** international.

**intact** • **adj.** not damaged or impaired.
– DERIVATIVES **intactness** n.
– ORIGIN ME: from L. *intactus*, from *in-* 'not' + *tactus* (past part. of *tangere* 'touch').

**intagliated** /ɪn'talɪeɪtɪd/ • **adj.** archaic carved or engraved.
– ORIGIN C18: from Ital. *intagliato* 'engraved', past part. of *intagliare* (see **INTAGLIO**).

**intaglio** /ɪn'talɪəʊ, -'tɑːl-/ • **n.** (pl. **-os**) an incised or engraved design. ➤a gem with an incised design. ➤a printing process in which the type or design is engraved. • **v.** (**-oes, -oed**) [usu. as adj. **intaglioed**] engrave.
– ORIGIN C17: Ital., from *intagliare* 'engrave'.

**intake** • **n. 1** an amount or quantity taken in. ➤an act of taking someone or something in. **2** a location or structure through which something is taken in. **3** N. English land reclaimed from a moor or common.

**intangible** • **adj.** unable to be touched; not solid or real. ➤vague and abstract. • **n.** an intangible thing.
– DERIVATIVES **intangibility** n. **intangibly** adv.

**intarsia** /ɪn'tɑːsɪə/ • **n. 1** a method of knitting, in which a separate length or ball of yarn is used for each area of colour. **2** elaborate marquetry or inlaid work, especially as practised in 15th-century Italy.
– ORIGIN from Ital. *intarsio*; superseding earlier *tarsia* (from Ital., 'marquetry').

**integer** /'ɪntɪdʒə/ • **n. 1** a whole number. **2** a thing complete in itself.
– ORIGIN C16: from L., 'intact, whole', from *in-* (expressing negation) + the root of *tangere* 'to touch'; cf. **ENTIRE**.

**integral** • **adj.** /'ɪntɪgr(ə)l, ɪn'tɛgr(ə)l/ **1** necessary to make a whole complete; fundamental. ➤included as part of a whole. ➤having all the parts necessary to be complete. **2** Mathematics of or denoted by an integer or integers. • **n.** /'ɪntɪgr(ə)l/ Mathematics a function of which a given function is the derivative, and which may express the area under the curve of a graph of the function.
– DERIVATIVES **integrality** n. **integrally** adv.
– ORIGIN C16: from late L. *integralis*, from *integer* (see **INTEGER**).

**USAGE** integral

There are two possible pronunciations for the adjective **integral**: one with the stress on the **in-** and the other with the stress on the **-teg-**. In British English, the second pronunciation is sometimes frowned on, but both are broadly accepted as standard.

**integral calculus** • **n.** Mathematics the part of calculus concerned with the integrals of functions.

**integrand** /'ɪntɪgrand/ • **n.** Mathematics a function that is to be integrated.
– ORIGIN C19: from L. *integrandus*, gerundive of *integrare* (see **INTEGRATE**).

**integrant** /'ɪntɪgr(ə)nt/ • **adj.** (of parts) constituent.
– ORIGIN C17: from Fr. *intégrant*, from *intégrer*, from L. *integrare* (see **INTEGRATE**).

**integrate** • **v.** /'ɪntɪgreɪt/ **1** combine or be combined to form a whole. **2** bring or come into equal participation in an institution or body. **3** Mathematics find the integral of. ➤[usu. as adj. **integrated**] find the mean value or total sum of (a variable quantity or property).
– DERIVATIVES **integrability** /ˌɪntɪgrə'bɪlɪti/ n. **integrable** /'ɪntɪgrəb(ə)l/ adj. **integrative** /'ɪntɪgrətɪv/ adj. **integrator** n.
– ORIGIN C17: from L. *integrat-*, *integrare* 'make whole', from *integer* (see **INTEGER**).

**integrated circuit** • **n.** an electronic circuit on a small piece of semiconducting material, performing the same function as a larger circuit of discrete components.

**integrated services digital network** (abbrev.: **ISDN**) • **n.** a telecommunications network through which sound, images, and data can be transmitted as digitized signals.

**integration** • **n. 1** the action or process of integrating. **2** Mathematics the finding of an integral or integrals. **3** Psychology the coordination of processes in the nervous system. **4** Psychoanalysis the process by which a well-balanced psyche becomes whole as the developing ego organizes the id.
– DERIVATIVES **integrationist** n.

**integrity** /ɪn'tɛgrɪti/ • **n. 1** the quality of having strong moral principles. **2** the state of being whole. ➤the condition of being unified or sound in construction. ➤internal consistency or lack of corruption in electronic data.
– ORIGIN ME: from Fr. *intégrité* or L. *integritas*, from *integer* (see **INTEGER**).

**integument** /ɪn'tɛgjʊm(ə)nt/ • **n.** a tough outer protective layer, especially of an animal or plant.
– DERIVATIVES **integumental** adj. **integumentary** adj.
– ORIGIN C17: from L. *integumentum*, from *integere*, from *in-* 'in' + *tegere* 'to cover'.

**intellect** • n. **1** the faculty of reasoning and understanding objectively. ➤one's mental powers. **2** a clever person.
– ORIGIN ME: from L. *intellectus* 'understanding', from *intellegere* (see **INTELLIGENCE**).

**intellection** • n. the action or process of understanding.
– DERIVATIVES **intellective** adj.

**intellectual** /ˌɪntəˈlɛktʃʊəl, -tjʊəl/ • adj. of, relating to, or appealing to the intellect. ➤having a highly developed intellect. • n. a person with a highly developed intellect.
– DERIVATIVES **intellectuality** n. **intellectually** adv.

**intellectualism** • n. **1** the exercise of the intellect at the expense of the emotions. **2** Philosophy rationalism.
– DERIVATIVES **intellectualist** n.

**intellectualize** (also **-ise**) • v. **1** give an intellectual character to. **2** talk or write intellectually.

**intellectual property** • n. Law intangible property that is the result of creativity, e.g. patents or copyrights.

**intelligence** • n. **1** the ability to acquire and apply knowledge and skills. **2** a person with this ability. **3** the gathering of information of military or political value. ➤information gathered in this way. **4** archaic news.
– DERIVATIVES **intelligential** adj. (archaic).
– ORIGIN ME: via OFr. from L. *intelligentia*, from *intelligere* 'understand', var. of *intellegere* 'understand', from *inter* 'between' + *legere* 'choose'.

**intelligence quotient** (abbrev.: **IQ**) • n. a number representing a person's reasoning ability, compared to the statistical norm, 100 being average.

**intelligencer** • n. archaic a person who gathers intelligence.

**intelligent** • adj. **1** having intelligence, especially of a high level. **2** (of a device) able to vary its state or action in response to varying situations and past experience. ➤(of a computer terminal) having its own processing capability.
– DERIVATIVES **intelligently** adv.

**intelligentsia** /ɪnˌtɛlɪˈdʒɛntsɪə/ • n. [treated as sing. or pl.] intellectuals or highly educated people, regarded as possessing culture and political influence.
– ORIGIN C20: from Russ. *intelligentsiya*, from Polish *inteligencja*, from L. *intelligentia* (see **INTELLIGENCE**).

**intelligible** /ɪnˈtɛlɪdʒɪb(ə)l/ • adj. able to be understood. ➤Philosophy able to be understood only by the intellect.
– DERIVATIVES **intelligibility** n. **intelligibly** adv.
– ORIGIN ME: from L. *intelligibilis*, from *intelligere* (see **INTELLIGENCE**).

**intemperate** • adj. showing a lack of self-control. ➤characterized by excessive indulgence, especially in alcohol.
– DERIVATIVES **intemperance** n. **intemperately** adv. **intemperateness** n.

**intend** • v. **1** have as one's aim or plan. ➤(**intend something as/to do something**) plan that something should be or act as something. ➤plan that speech should have (a particular meaning). **2** (**intend for/to do something**) design or destine for a particular purpose. ➤(**be intended for**) be meant for the use of.
– DERIVATIVES **intender** n.
– ORIGIN ME *entend* ('direct the attention to'), from OFr. *entendre*, from L. *intendere* 'intend, extend, direct'.

**intendant** • n. **1** the administrator of an opera house or theatre. **2** chiefly historical a title of a high-ranking official, especially in France, Spain, or Portugal.
– DERIVATIVES **intendancy** n.

**intended** • adj. planned or meant. • n. (**one's intended**) informal one's fiancé(e).
– DERIVATIVES **intendedly** adv.

**intendment** • n. Law the sense in which the law understands something.

**intense** • adj. (**-er**, **-est**) **1** of extreme force, degree, or strength: *intense concentration*. **2** extremely earnest or serious: *an intense young woman*.
– DERIVATIVES **intensely** adv. **intenseness** n.
– ORIGIN ME: from OFr., or from L. *intensus* 'stretched tightly, strained', past part. of *intendere* (see **INTEND**).

**intensifier** • n. **1** Photography a chemical used to intensify a negative. **2** Grammar an adverb used to give force or emphasis.

**intensify** • v. (**-ies**, **-ied**) **1** make or become more intense. **2** Photography increase the opacity of (a negative) using a chemical.
– DERIVATIVES **intensification** n.
– ORIGIN C19: coined by Coleridge.

**intension** • n. **1** Logic the internal content of a concept. Often contrasted with **EXTENSION**. **2** archaic determination.
– DERIVATIVES **intensional** adj. **intensionally** adv.
– ORIGIN C17: from L. *intensio(n-)*, from *intendere* (see **INTEND**).

**intensity** • n. (pl. **-ies**) **1** the quality of being intense. **2** chiefly Physics the measurable amount of a property.

**intensive** • adj. **1** very thorough or vigorous. **2** (of agriculture) aiming to achieve maximum production within a limited area. Often contrasted with **EXTENSIVE**. **3** [in combination] concentrating on or making much use of something: *computer-intensive methods*. **4** Grammar giving force or emphasis. **5** denoting a property measured in terms of intensity rather than extent. • n. Grammar an intensifier.
– DERIVATIVES **intensively** adv. **intensiveness** n.
– ORIGIN ME: from Fr. *intensif*, *-ive* or med. L. *intensivus*, from *intendere* (see **INTEND**).

**intensive care** • n. special medical treatment of a dangerously ill patient.

**intent** • n. intention or purpose. • adj. **1** (**intent on/upon**) resolved or determined to do. ➤attentively occupied with. **2** showing earnest and eager attention.
– PHRASES **to all intents and purposes** in all important respects. **with intent** Law with the intention of committing a crime.
– DERIVATIVES **intently** adv. **intentness** n.
– ORIGIN ME: from OFr. *entent*, *entente*, based on L. *intendere* (see **INTEND**).

**intention** • n. **1** an aim or plan. ➤the action or fact of intending. ➤(**one's intentions**) a person's, especially a man's, designs in respect to marriage. **2** Medicine the healing process of a wound. **3** (**intentions**) Logic conceptions formed by directing the mind towards an object.
– DERIVATIVES **-intentioned** adj.

**intentional** • adj. deliberate.
– DERIVATIVES **intentionality** n. **intentionally** adv.

**intention tremor** • n. a trembling of a body part when attempting a precise movement.

**inter** /ɪnˈtəː/ • v. (**interred**, **interring**) (usu. **be interred**) place (a corpse) in a grave or tomb.
– ORIGIN ME: from OFr. *enterrer*, based on L. *in-* 'into' + *terra* 'earth'.

**inter.** • abbrev. intermediate.

**inter-** • prefix **1** between; among: *interbreed*. **2** mutually; reciprocally: *interatomic*.
– ORIGIN from OFr. *entre-* or L. *inter* 'between, among'.

**interact** • v. act in such a way as to have an effect on another.
– DERIVATIVES **interactant** adj. & n.

**interaction** • n. reciprocal action or influence.
– DERIVATIVES **interactional** adj.

**interactionism** • n. **1** Philosophy the theory that there are two entities, mind and body, each affecting the other. **2** (also **symbolic interactionism**) Sociology a view of social behaviour that emphasizes the role of linguistic communication and its subjective understanding.
– DERIVATIVES **interactionist** n. & adj.

**interactive** • adj. **1** (of two people or things) influencing each other. **2** (of a computer or other electronic device) allowing a two-way flow of information between it and a user, responding to the user's input.
– DERIVATIVES **interactively** adv. **interactivity** n.

**inter alia** /ˌɪntər ˈeɪlɪə, ˈalɪə/ • adv. among other things.
– ORIGIN from L.

**inter alios** /ˌɪntər ˈeɪlɪəʊs, ˈalɪəʊs/ • adv. among other people.
– ORIGIN from L.

**inter-allied** • adj. of or relating to two or more states cooperating for military purposes.

**interarticular** /ˌɪntərɑːˈtɪkjʊlə/ ● **adj.** Anatomy existing or acting between the adjacent surfaces of a joint.

**interatomic** ● **adj.** Physics existing or acting between atoms.

**interbed** ● **v.** (**-bedded**, **-bedding**) (**be interbedded**) Geology (of a stratum) be embedded between others.

**interbreed** ● **v.** (past and past part. **-bred**) breed or cause to breed with an animal of a different race or species.

**intercalary** /ɪnˈtəːkəl(ə)ri, ˌɪntəˈkal(ə)ri/ ● **adj. 1** (of a day or month) inserted in the calendar to harmonize it with the solar year, e.g. 29 February. **2** (of an academic period) additional to the standard course and taken at a different institution. **3** Botany denoting meristem tissue located between its daughter cells.
– ORIGIN C17: from L. *intercalarius*, from *intercalare* (see **INTERCALATE**).

**intercalate** /ɪnˈtəːkəleɪt/ ● **v. 1** insert (an intercalary period) in a calendar. **2** (usu. **be intercalated**) insert between layers in a crystal lattice or other structure.
– DERIVATIVES **intercalation** n.
– ORIGIN C17: from L. *intercalat-*, *intercalare* 'proclaim as inserted in the calendar'.

**intercede** /ˌɪntəˈsiːd/ ● **v.** intervene on behalf of another.
– DERIVATIVES **interceder** n.
– ORIGIN C16: from Fr. *intercéder* or L. *intercedere* 'intervene', from *inter-* 'between' + *cedere* 'go'.

**intercellular** ● **adj.** Biology located or occurring between cells.

**intercensal** /ˌɪntəˈsɛns(ə)l/ ● **adj.** of or relating to the interval between two censuses.

**intercept** ● **v.** /ˌɪntəˈsɛpt/ **1** obstruct and prevent from continuing to a destination. **2** Mathematics mark or cut off (part of a space, line, or surface). ● **n.** /ˈɪntəsɛpt/ **1** an act of intercepting. **2** Mathematics the point at which a given line cuts a coordinate axis.
– DERIVATIVES **interception** n. **interceptive** adj.
– ORIGIN ME: from L. *intercept-*, *intercipere* 'catch between'.

**interceptor** ● **n. 1** a person or thing that intercepts another. **2** a fast aircraft for stopping or repelling hostile aircraft.

**intercession** /ˌɪntəˈsɛʃ(ə)n/ ● **n.** the action of intervening on behalf of another. ➤the action of saying a prayer on behalf of another person.
– DERIVATIVES **intercessor** n. **intercessory** adj.
– ORIGIN ME: from L. *intercessio(n-)*, from *intercedere* (see **INTERCEDE**).

**interchange** ● **v.** /ɪntəˈtʃeɪn(d)ʒ/ (of two people) exchange (things) with each other. ➤put each of (two things) in the other's place. ● **n.** /ˈɪntətʃeɪn(d)ʒ/ **1** the action of interchanging. ➤an exchange of words. **2** alternation: *the interchange of woods and meadows.* **3** a road junction on several levels so that traffic streams do not intersect. **4** a station where passengers may change from one railway line or bus service to another.
– DERIVATIVES **interchangeability** n. **interchangeable** adj. **interchangeableness** n. **interchangeably** adv.

**intercity** ● **adj.** existing or travelling between cities.

**intercollegiate** ● **adj.** existing or conducted between colleges or universities.

**intercolonial** ● **adj.** existing or conducted between colonies.

**intercolumniation** /ˌɪntəkəlʌmnɪˈeɪʃ(ə)n/ ● **n.** Architecture the distance between adjacent columns.
– DERIVATIVES **intercolumnar** adj.

**intercom** ● **n.** an electrical device allowing one-way or two-way communication.
– ORIGIN Second World War: abbrev. of ***intercommunication*** (see **INTERCOMMUNICATE**).

**intercommunicate** ● **v. 1** engage in two-way communication. **2** (of rooms) have a common connecting door.
– DERIVATIVES **intercommunication** n.

**intercommunion** ● **n.** participation in Holy Communion by members of different denominations.

**interconnect** ● **v.** connect with each other.
– DERIVATIVES **interconnection** n.

**intercontinental** ● **adj.** relating to or travelling between continents.
– DERIVATIVES **intercontinentally** adv.

**interconvert** ● **v.** (usu. **be interconverted**) cause to be converted into each other.
– DERIVATIVES **interconversion** n. **interconvertible** adj.

**intercooler** ● **n.** an apparatus for cooling gas between successive compressions, especially in a supercharged engine.
– DERIVATIVES **intercool** v.

**intercorrelation** /ˌɪntəkɒrəˈleɪʃ(ə)n/ ● **n.** a mutual connection between two or more things.
– DERIVATIVES **intercorrelate** v.

**intercostal** /ˌɪntəˈkɒst(ə)l/ Anatomy ● **adj.** situated between the ribs. ● **n.** an intercostal muscle.
– DERIVATIVES **intercostally** adv.

**intercourse** ● **n. 1** communication or dealings between people. **2** short for **SEXUAL INTERCOURSE**.
– ORIGIN ME: from OFr. *entrecours* 'exchange, commerce', from L. *intercursus*, from *intercurrere* 'intervene', from *inter-* 'between' + *currere* 'run'.

**intercrop** ● **v.** (**-cropped**, **-cropping**) [often as noun **intercropping**] grow (a crop) among plants of a different kind.

**intercross** ● **v.** interbreed or cause to interbreed. ● **n.** an instance of interbreeding. ➤a hybrid.

**intercrural** /ˌɪntəˈkrʊər(ə)l/ ● **adj.** between the legs.

**intercurrent** ● **adj. 1** Medicine (of a disease) occurring during the progress of another. **2** rare intervening.
– ORIGIN C17: from L. *intercurrent-*, *intercurrere* 'intervene'.

**intercut** ● **v.** (**-cutting**; past and past part. **-cut**) alternate (scenes) with contrasting scenes in a film.

**interdenominational** /ˌɪntədɪnɒmɪˈneɪʃ(ə)n(ə)l/ ● **adj.** of or relating to more than one religious denomination.
– DERIVATIVES **interdenominationally** adv.

**interdepartmental** ● **adj.** of or relating to more than one department.
– DERIVATIVES **interdepartmentally** adv.

**interdependent** ● **adj.** dependent on each other.
– DERIVATIVES **interdepend** v. **interdependence** n. **interdependency** n.

**interdict** ● **n.** /ˈɪntədɪkt/ **1** Law, chiefly Scottish a court order forbidding an act. **2** (in the Roman Catholic Church) a sentence debarring a person or place from ecclesiastical functions and privileges. ● **v.** /ˌɪntəˈdɪkt/ chiefly N. Amer. **1** prohibit or forbid. **2** intercept (a prohibited commodity). **3** Military impede (an enemy force), especially by bombing lines of communication or supply.
– DERIVATIVES **interdiction** n.
– ORIGIN ME *entredite*, from OFr. *entredit*, from L. *interdictum*, past part. of *interdicere* 'interpose, forbid by decree'.

**interdigital** ● **adj.** between the fingers or toes.

**interdigitate** /ˌɪntəˈdɪdʒɪteɪt/ ● **v.** interlock like the fingers of clasped hands.
– ORIGIN C19: from **INTER-** + **DIGIT** + **-ATE**[3].

**interdisciplinary** ● **adj.** of or relating to more than one branch of knowledge.

**interest** ● **n. 1** the state of wanting to know about something or someone. ➤a quality exciting curiosity or holding the attention: *a tale full of interest.* ➤a subject in which one is concerned. **2** money paid for the use of money lent, or for delaying the repayment of a debt. **3** the advantage or benefit of someone. ➤archaic self-interest. **4** a share or involvement in an undertaking. ➤a legal concern, title, or right in property. **5** a group having a common concern, especially in politics or business. ● **v. 1** excite the curiosity or attention of. ➤(**interest someone in**) persuade someone to undertake or acquire. **2** [as adj. **interested**] having an interest or involvement; not impartial: *seeking views from interested parties.*
– PHRASES **at interest** (of money borrowed) on the condition that interest is payable. **declare an** (or **one's**) **interest** make known one's financial interests in an undertaking before it is discussed. **in the interests** (or **interest**) **of something** for the benefit of.
– DERIVATIVES **interestedly** adv. **interestedness** n.

– ORIGIN ME (orig. as *interess* 'the possession of a share in or a right to something'): from Anglo-Norman Fr. *interesse*, from L. *interesse* 'differ, be important', from *inter-* 'between' + *esse* 'be'; the *-t* was added by assoc. with OFr. *interest* 'damage, loss'.

**interest-free** ● adj. & adv. with no interest charged.

**interesting** ● adj. arousing curiosity or interest.
– PHRASES **in an interesting condition** archaic, euphemistic pregnant.
– DERIVATIVES **interestingly** adv. **interestingness** n.

**interface** ● n. **1** a point where two things meet and interact. ➤chiefly Physics a surface forming a boundary between two portions of matter or space. **2** Computing a device or program enabling a user to communicate with a computer, or for connecting two items of hardware or software. ● v. (**interface with**) **1** interact with. **2** Computing connect with (something) by an interface.

**interfacial** ● adj. **1** included between two faces of a crystal or other solid. **2** relating to or denoting an interface.

**interfacing** ● n. an extra layer of material or an adhesive stiffener, applied to the facing of a garment to add support.

**interfaith** ● adj. of, relating to, or between different religions.

**interfere** ● v. **1** (**interfere with**) prevent from continuing or being carried out properly. ➤get in the way of. ➤handle or adjust without permission. ➤Law attempt to bribe or intimidate (a witness). **2** intervene without invitation or necessity. **3** (**interfere with**) Brit. euphemistic sexually molest. **4** Physics interact to produce interference. **5** (of a horse) knock one foot against the fetlock of another leg.
– DERIVATIVES **interferer** n. **interfering** adj. **interferingly** adv.
– ORIGIN ME: from OFr. *s'entreferir* 'strike each other', from *entre-* 'between' + *ferir* (from L. *ferire* 'to strike').

**interference** ● n. **1** the action of interfering or process of being interfered with. **2** Physics the combination of two or more waveforms to form a resultant wave in which the displacement is either reinforced or cancelled. ➤disturbance to radio signals caused by unwanted signals from other sources.
– DERIVATIVES **interferential** adj.

**interference fit** ● n. a fit in which the external dimension of one part exceeds the internal dimension of the part into which it has to fit.

**interferogram** /ˌɪntəˈfɪərə(ʊ)gram/ ● n. Physics a photograph or other record of a pattern formed by wave interference.

**interferometer** /ˌɪntəfəˈrɒmɪtə/ ● n. Physics an instrument in which wave interference is employed to make precise measurements in terms of the wavelength.
– DERIVATIVES **interferometric** adj. **interferometrically** adv. **interferometry** n.

**interferon** /ˌɪntəˈfɪərɒn/ ● n. Biochemistry a protein released by animal cells which inhibits virus replication.
– ORIGIN 1950s: from INTERFERE + -ON.

**interfile** ● v. file together or into an existing sequence.

**interfluve** /ˈɪntəfluːv/ ● n. Geology a region between the valleys of adjacent watercourses.
– DERIVATIVES **interfluvial** adj.
– ORIGIN C19 (as *interfluvial*).

**interfuse** ● v. poetic/literary join or mix together.
– DERIVATIVES **interfusion** n.

**intergalactic** ● adj. of, relating to, or situated between galaxies.
– DERIVATIVES **intergalactically** adv.

**intergeneric** /ˌɪntədʒɪˈnɛrɪk/ ● adj. Biology existing between or obtained from different genera.

**interglacial** Geology ● adj. relating to or denoting a period of milder climate between two glacial periods. ● n. an interglacial period.

**intergovernmental** ● adj. of, relating to, or conducted between governments.
– DERIVATIVES **intergovernmentally** adv.

**intergrade** ● v. Biology pass into another form by a series of intervening forms.
– DERIVATIVES **intergradation** n.

**intergrow** ● v. (past **-grew**; past part. **-grown**) [usu. as adj. **intergrown**] grow into each other.
– DERIVATIVES **intergrowth** n.

**interim** /ˈɪnt(ə)rɪm/ ● n. the intervening time. ● adj. **1** provisional. **2** chiefly Brit. relating to less than a full year's business activity: *interim profits*. ● adv. archaic meanwhile.
– ORIGIN C16: from L., 'meanwhile'.

**interior** ● adj. **1** situated within or inside; inner. ➤(**interior to**) chiefly technical situated further in or within. **2** inland. **3** relating to a country's internal or domestic affairs. ● n. **1** the interior part of something. **2** the internal affairs of a country.
– DERIVATIVES **interiorize** (also **-ise**) v. **interiorly** adv.
– ORIGIN C15: from L., 'inner', compar. adj. from *inter* 'within'.

**interior angle** ● n. the angle between adjacent sides of a rectilinear figure.

**interior decoration** ● n. the decoration of the interior of a building or room, especially with regard for colour combination and artistic effect.
– DERIVATIVES **interior decorator** n.

**interior design** ● n. the design or decoration of the interior of a room or building.
– DERIVATIVES **interior designer** n.

**interiority** ● n. the quality of being interior or inward.

**interior monologue** ● n. a piece of writing expressing a character's thoughts.

**interject** /ˌɪntəˈdʒɛkt/ ● v. say abruptly, especially as an interruption.
– DERIVATIVES **interjectory** adj.
– ORIGIN C16 (earlier (ME) as *interjection*): from L. *interject-*, *interjicere* 'interpose', from *inter-* 'between' + *jacere* 'to throw'.

**interjection** ● n. an exclamation, especially as a part of speech (e.g. *ah!*, *dear me!*).
– DERIVATIVES **interjectional** adj.

**interlace** ● v. **1** interweave. ➤(**interlace something with**) mingle or intersperse something with. **2** Electronics scan (a video image) in such a way that alternate lines form one sequence which is followed by the other lines in a second sequence.
– DERIVATIVES **interlacement** n.

**interlanguage** ● n. a language or form of language having features of two others, e.g. a pidgin.

**interlard** ● v. (**interlard something with**) intersperse or embellish something with (different material).
– ORIGIN ME (in the sense 'mix with alternate layers of fat'): from Fr. *entrelarder*, from *entre-* 'between' + *larder* 'to lard'.

**interlay** ● v. (past and past part. **-laid**) interpose. ● n. an inserted layer.

**interleaf** ● n. (pl. **-leaves**) an extra page, typically a blank one, between the leaves of a book.

**interleave** ● v. **1** insert interleaves between the pages of (a book). ➤place something between the layers of. **2** Telecommunications mix (digital signals) by alternating between them. **3** Computing divide (memory or processing power) between a number of tasks by allocating successive segments of it to each task in turn.

**interleukin** /ˌɪntəˈluːkɪn/ ● n. Biochemistry any of a class of glycoproteins produced by leucocytes for regulating immune responses.
– ORIGIN 1970s: from INTER- + *leukocyte* (var. of LEUCOCYTE) + -IN[1].

**interline**[1] ● v. insert words between the lines of (a document).

**interline**[2] ● v. put an extra lining in (a garment, curtain, etc.).

**interlinear** ● adj. written between the lines of a text.

**interlingua** /ˌɪntəˈlɪŋgwə/ ● n. an artificial language devised for machine translation. ➤(**Interlingua**) an artificial international language formed of elements common to the Romance languages.
– ORIGIN C20: from INTER- + L. *lingua* 'tongue'.

**interlingual** ● adj. **1** between or relating to two languages. **2** of or relating to an interlingua.

**interlining** ● n. material used to interline a garment, curtain, etc.

**interlink** ● v. join or connect together.
– DERIVATIVES **interlinkage** n.

**interlobular** /ˌɪntəˈlɒbjʊlə/ ● adj. Anatomy situated between lobes.

**interlock** ● v. (of two or more things) engage with each other by overlapping or fitting together. ● n. **1** a device or mechanism for connecting or coordinating the function of components. **2** (also **interlock fabric**) a fabric with closely interlocking stitches allowing it to stretch.
– DERIVATIVES **interlocker** n.

**interlocutor** /ˌɪntəˈlɒkjʊtə/ ● n. formal a person who takes part in a dialogue.
– DERIVATIVES **interlocution** n.
– ORIGIN C16: mod. L., from L. *interlocut-*, *interloqui* 'interrupt (with speech)', from *inter-* 'between' + *loqui* 'speak'.

**interlocutory** /ˌɪntəˈlɒkjʊt(ə)ri/ ● adj. **1** Law (of a decree or judgement) given provisionally during the course of a legal action. **2** rare of or relating to dialogue.

**interloper** /ˈɪntələʊpə/ ● n. a person who interferes in another's affairs; an intruder.
– DERIVATIVES **interlope** v.
– ORIGIN C16: from **INTER-** + *-loper* as in archaic *landloper* 'vagabond' (from MDu. *landlooper*).

**interlude** ● n. **1** an intervening period of time. ➤a pause between the acts of a play. **2** a thing occurring or done during an interval. ➤a piece of music played between other pieces or between the verses of a hymn. **3** a temporary amusement or diversion: *a romantic interlude.*
– ORIGIN ME: from med. L. *interludium*, from *inter-* 'between' + *ludus* 'play'.

**intermarriage** ● n. **1** marriage between people of different races, castes, or religions. **2** marriage between close relations.
– DERIVATIVES **intermarry** v.

**intermediary** /ˌɪntəˈmiːdɪəri/ ● n. (pl. **-ies**) a mediator. ● adj. intermediate.
– ORIGIN C18: from Fr. *intermédiaire*, from Ital. *intermediario*, from L. *intermedius* (see **INTERMEDIATE**).

**intermediate** /ˌɪntəˈmiːdɪət/ ● adj. **1** coming between two things in time, place, character, etc. **2** having more than basic knowledge or skills but not yet advanced. ● n. **1** an intermediate person or thing. **2** a chemical compound formed by one reaction and then taking part in another. ● v. /ˌɪntəˈmiːdɪeɪt/ mediate.
– DERIVATIVES **intermediacy** n. **intermediately** adv. **intermediateness** n. **intermediation** n. **intermediator** n.
– ORIGIN ME: from med. L. *intermediatus*, from L. *intermedius*, from *inter-* 'between' + *medius* 'middle'.

**intermediate technology** ● n. technology suitable for developing countries, typically using local resources.

**interment** /ɪnˈtəːm(ə)nt/ ● n. the burial of a corpse in a grave or tomb.

**intermesh** ● v. mesh together.

**intermezzo** /ˌɪntəˈmɛtsəʊ/ ● n. (pl. **intermezzi** /-ˈmɛtsi/ or **intermezzos**) **1** a short connecting instrumental movement in an opera or other musical work. ➤a short piece for a solo instrument. **2** a light dramatic or other performance between the acts of a play.
– ORIGIN C18: from Ital., from L. *intermedium* 'interval'.

**interminable** ● adj. endless.
– DERIVATIVES **interminableness** n. **interminably** adv.
– ORIGIN ME: from OFr., or from late L. *interminabilis*, from *in-* 'not' + *terminare* (see **TERMINATE**).

**intermingle** ● v. mix or mingle together.

**intermission** ● n. a pause or break. ➤an interval between parts of a play or film.
– ORIGIN ME: from L. *intermissio(n-)*, from *intermittere* (see **INTERMIT**).

**intermit** /ˌɪntəˈmɪt/ ● v. (**intermitted**, **intermitting**) suspend or discontinue for a time. ➤(especially of a fever or pulse) stop for a time.
– ORIGIN C16: from L. *intermittere*, from *inter-* 'between' + *mittere* 'let go'.

**intermittent** ● adj. occurring at irregular intervals.
– DERIVATIVES **intermittence** n. **intermittency** n. **intermittently** adv.

**intermix** ● v. mix together.
– DERIVATIVES **intermixable** adj. **intermixture** n.

**intermodal** ● adj. involving two or more different modes of transport.

**intermolecular** ● adj. existing or occurring between molecules.

**intern** ● n. /ˈɪntəːn/ (also **interne**) chiefly N. Amer. a recent medical graduate receiving supervised training in a hospital and acting as an assistant physician or surgeon. ➤a student or trainee who does a job to gain work experience or for a qualification. ● v. **1** /ɪnˈtəːn/ confine as a prisoner. **2** /ˈɪntəːn/ chiefly N. Amer. serve as an intern.
– DERIVATIVES **internment** n. **internship** n.
– ORIGIN C16 (as an adj. in the sense 'internal'): from Fr. *interne* (adj.), *interner* (v.), from L. *internus* 'inward, internal'.

**internal** ● adj. **1** of or situated on the inside. ➤inside the body. ➤existing within an organization. ➤relating to affairs and activities within a country. **2** experienced in one's mind. **3** intrinsic. **4** Brit. (of a student) attending a university as well as taking its examinations. ● n. (**internals**) inner parts or features.
– DERIVATIVES **internality** n. **internally** adv.
– ORIGIN C16: from mod. L. *internalis*, from L. *internus* 'inward, internal'.

**internal-combustion engine** ● n. an engine in which petrol or other fuel is burned with air and the hot gases produced are used to do work such as driving a piston.

**internal evidence** ● n. evidence derived from the contents of the thing discussed.

**internal exile** ● n. penal banishment from a part of one's own country.

**internalize** (also **-ise**) ● v. **1** Psychology make (attitudes or behaviour) part of one's nature by learning or unconscious assimilation. ➤acquire knowledge of (the rules of a language). **2** Economics incorporate (costs) as part of a pricing structure.
– DERIVATIVES **internalization** n.

**internal market** ● n. **1** another term for **SINGLE MARKET**. **2** a system in the National Health Service whereby hospital departments purchase each other's services contractually.

**internal rhyme** ● n. a rhyme involving a word in the middle of a line and another at the end of the line or in the middle of the next.

**international** ● adj. existing or occurring between nations. ➤agreed on by all or many nations. ➤used by people of many nations. ● n. **1** Brit. a game or contest between teams representing different countries. ➤a player who has taken part in such a contest. **2** (**International**) any of four associations founded (1864–1936) to promote socialist or communist action.
– DERIVATIVES **internationality** n. **internationally** adv.

**International Baccalaureate** ● n. a set of examinations qualifying candidates for higher education in any of several countries.

**international candle** ● n. see **CANDLE**.

**International Date Line** ● n. see **DATE LINE**.

**Internationale** /ˌɪntənaʃəˈnɑːl/ ● n. **1** (**the Internationale**) a revolutionary song composed in France and adopted by socialists. **2** variant spelling of **INTERNATIONAL** (in sense 2).
– ORIGIN Fr., fem. of *international* 'international'.

**internationalism** ● n. **1** the advocacy of cooperation and understanding between nations. **2** the state or process of being international. **3** (**Internationalism**) the principles of any of the four Internationals.
– DERIVATIVES **internationalist** n.

**internationalize** (also **-ise**) ● v. **1** make international. **2** bring under the protection or control of two or more nations.
– DERIVATIVES **internationalization** n.

**international law** ● n. a body of rules established by custom or treaty and recognized by nations as binding in their relations with one another.

**International Phonetic Alphabet** • **n.** an internationally recognized set of phonetic symbols.

**international style** • **n.** a functional style of 20th-century architecture characterized by the use of steel and reinforced concrete, wide windows, uninterrupted interior spaces, simple lines, and strict geometric forms.

**international system of units** • **n.** the SI system of units.

**international unit** • **n.** a unit of activity for a particular vitamin, hormone, etc. in terms of the activity of a standard quantity.

**interne** • **n.** variant spelling of **INTERN**.

**internecine** /ɪntəˈniːsʌɪn/ • **adj.** destructive to both sides in a conflict. ➤of or relating to conflict within a group.
– ORIGIN C17: from L. *internecinus*, based on *inter-* 'among' + *necare* 'to kill'.

**internee** /ˌɪntəːˈniː/ • **n.** a prisoner.

**internegative** • **n.** Photography a second negative of an image made from the original negative.

**Internet** • **n.** an international information network linking computers, accessible to the public via modem links.
– ORIGIN C20: from **INTER-** + **NETWORK**.

**interneuron** /ˌɪntəˈnjʊərɒn/ (also **interneurone** /-rəʊn/) • **n.** Physiology an internuncial neuron.
– DERIVATIVES **interneuronal** adj.

**internist** • **n.** Medicine, chiefly N. Amer. a specialist in internal diseases.

**internode** /ˈɪntənəʊd/ • **n. 1** Botany a part of a plant stem between nodes. **2** Anatomy a stretch of a nerve, sheathed with myelin, between two nodes of Ranvier.

**internuclear** • **adj.** between nuclei.

**internuncial** /ˌɪntəˈnʌnʃ(ə)l/ • **adj.** Physiology (of neurons) forming connections between other neurons.
– ORIGIN C19: from L. *internuntius* (from *inter-* 'between' + *nuntius* 'messenger') + **-AL**.

**interoceanic** • **adj.** between or connecting two oceans.

**interoceptive** /ˌɪntərəʊˈsɛptɪv/ • **adj.** Physiology of or denoting stimuli that are produced within an organism. Compare with **EXTEROCEPTIVE**.
– DERIVATIVES **interoceptor** n.

**interoperable** • **adj.** (of computer systems or software) able to operate in conjunction.
– DERIVATIVES **interoperability** n.

**interosseous** /ˌɪntərˈɒsɪəs/ • **adj.** Anatomy situated between bones.

**interpellate** /ɪnˈtəːpɪleɪt/ • **v.** (in a parliament) interrupt the order of the day by demanding an explanation from (the minister concerned).
– DERIVATIVES **interpellation** n. **interpellator** n.
– ORIGIN C16: from L. *interpellat-*, *interpellare* 'interrupt (with speech)', from *inter-* 'between' + *pellere* 'to drive'.

**interpenetrate** • **v.** mix or merge together.
– DERIVATIVES **interpenetration** n. **interpenetrative** adj.

**interpersonal** • **adj.** of or relating to relationships or communication between people.
– DERIVATIVES **interpersonally** adv.

**interphase** • **n.** Biology the resting phase between successive mitotic divisions of a cell, or between the first and second divisions of meiosis.

**interplanetary** • **adj.** situated or travelling between planets.

**interplant** • **v.** plant (a crop or plant) together with another. ➤plant with a mixture of crops.

**interplay** • **n.** the way in which two or more things affect each other.

**interpleader** • **n.** Law a suit pleaded between two parties to determine a matter of right to property held by a third party.

**Interpol** /ˈɪntəpɒl/ • **n.** an organization based in France that coordinates investigations made by the police forces of member countries into international crimes.
– ORIGIN from *Inter(national) pol(ice)*.

**interpolate** /ɪnˈtəːpəleɪt/ • **v. 1** insert (words) in a book, especially to give a false impression as to its date. ➤make such insertions in (a book). **2** interject (a remark) in a conversation. **3** Mathematics insert (an intermediate term) into a series by estimating or calculating it from surrounding known values.
– DERIVATIVES **interpolation** n. **interpolative** adj. **interpolator** n.
– ORIGIN C17: from L. *interpolat-*, *interpolare* 'refurbish, alter', from *inter-* 'between' + *-polare* (rel. to *polire* 'to polish').

**interpose** • **v. 1** insert between one thing and another. **2** intervene between parties. **3** say as an interruption. **4** exercise or advance (a veto or objection).
– DERIVATIVES **interposition** n.
– ORIGIN C16: from Fr. *interposer*, from L. *interponere* 'put in' (from *inter-* 'between' + *ponere* 'put'), but influenced by *interpositus* 'inserted' and OFr. *poser* 'to place'.

**interpret** • **v.** (**interpreted**, **interpreting**) **1** explain the meaning of (words, actions, etc.). ➤translate orally the words of a person speaking a different language. **2** perform (a creative work) in a way that conveys one's understanding of the creator's ideas. ➤understand as having a particular meaning or significance.
– DERIVATIVES **interpretability** n. **interpretable** adj. **interpretation** n. **interpretational** adj. **interpretative** adj. **interpretatively** adv. **interpretive** adj. **interpretively** adv.
– ORIGIN ME: from OFr. *interpreter* or L. *interpretari* 'explain, translate', from *interpres*, *interpret-* 'agent, translator, interpreter'.

**interpreter** • **n. 1** a person who interprets foreign speech orally. **2** Computing a program that can analyse and execute a program line by line.

**interprovincial** • **adj.** existing or carried on between provinces of the same country.

**interracial** • **adj.** existing between or involving different races.
– DERIVATIVES **interracially** adv.

**interregnum** /ˌɪntəˈrɛgnəm/ • **n.** (pl. **interregnums** or **interregna** /-nə/) a period when normal government is suspended, especially between successive reigns or regimes.
– ORIGIN C16: from L., from *inter-* 'between' + *regnum* 'reign'.

**interrelate** • **v.** relate or connect to one other.
– DERIVATIVES **interrelatedness** n. **interrelation** n. **interrelationship** n.

**interrogate** • **v. 1** ask questions of (someone) closely, aggressively, or formally. **2** obtain data or information automatically from (a device, database, etc.).
– DERIVATIVES **interrogation** n. **interrogational** adj. **interrogator** n.
– ORIGIN C15 (earlier (ME) as *interrogation*): from L. *interrogat-*, *interrogare* 'question', from *inter-* 'between' + *rogare* 'ask'.

**interrogation point** (also **interrogation mark**) • **n.** another term for **QUESTION MARK**.

**interrogative** /ˌɪntəˈrɒgətɪv/ • **adj.** having the force of a question. ➤Grammar used in questions. Contrasted with **AFFIRMATIVE** and **NEGATIVE**. • **n.** an interrogative word, e.g. *how* or *what*.
– DERIVATIVES **interrogatively** adv.

**interrogatory** /ˌɪntəˈrɒgət(ə)ri/ • **adj.** questioning. • **n.** (pl. **-ies**) Law a written question which is formally put to one party in a case by another party and which must be answered.

**interrupt** • **v. 1** stop the continuous progress of. ➤stop (a person who is speaking) by saying or doing something. **2** break the continuity of (a line, surface, or view): *a sunken fence which doesn't interrupt the view across the fields.*
– DERIVATIVES **interruptible** adj. **interruption** n. **interruptive** adj.
– ORIGIN ME: from L. *interrupt-*, *interrumpere* 'break, interrupt', from *inter-* 'between' + *rumpere* 'to break'.

**interrupter** (also **interruptor**) • **n. 1** a person or thing that interrupts. **2** a device that automatically breaks an electric circuit if a fault develops.

**inter se** /ˌɪntə ˈseɪ/ • **adv.** between or among themselves.

– ORIGIN from L.

**intersect** ● v. divide (something) by passing or lying across it. ➤ (of lines, roads, etc.) cross or cut each other.
– ORIGIN C17 (earlier (C16) as *intersection*): from L. *intersect-*, *intersecare* 'cut, intersect'.

**intersection** ● n. a point or line common to lines or surfaces that intersect. ➤ a point at which two or more things, especially roads, intersect.
– DERIVATIVES **intersectional** adj.

**interseptal** /ɪntəˈsɛpt(ə)l/ ● adj. Anatomy & Zoology situated between septa or partitions.

**intersex** ● n. hermaphroditism. ➤ a hermaphrodite.

**intersexual** ● adj. **1** existing or occurring between the sexes. **2** relating to or having the condition of hermaphroditism.
– DERIVATIVES **intersexuality** n.

**interspace** ● n. a space between objects. ● v. (usu. **be interspaced**) put or occupy a space between.

**interspecific** /ˌɪntəspəˈsɪfɪk/ ● adj. Biology existing or occurring between different species.
– DERIVATIVES **interspecifically** adv.

**intersperse** ● v. (usu. **be interspersed**) scatter among or between other things. ➤ diversify with other things at intervals.
– DERIVATIVES **interspersion** n.
– ORIGIN C16: from L. *interspers-*, *interspergere* 'scatter between'.

**interstadial** /ˌɪntəˈsteɪdɪəl/ Geology ● adj. relating to or denoting a minor period of less cold climate during a glacial period. ● n. an interstadial period.
– ORIGIN C20: from **INTER-** + *stadial* from L. *stadialis*, from *stadium* 'stage'.

**interstate** ● adj. existing or carried on between states, especially of the US. ● n. one of a system of motorways running between US states. ● adv. Austral. from one state to another.

**interstellar** /ˌɪntəˈstɛlə/ ● adj. occurring or situated between stars.

**interstice** /ɪnˈtəːstɪs/ ● n. a small intervening space.
– ORIGIN ME: from L. *interstitium*, from *intersistere* 'stand between'.

**interstitial** /ˌɪntəˈstɪʃ(ə)l/ ● adj. of, forming, or occupying interstices.
– DERIVATIVES **interstitially** adv.

**intersubjective** ● adj. Philosophy existing between conscious minds.
– DERIVATIVES **intersubjectively** adv. **intersubjectivity** n.

**intertextuality** /ˌɪntətɛkstjʊˈalɪti/ ● n. the relationship between texts.
– DERIVATIVES **intertextual** adj. **intertextually** adv.

**intertidal** ● adj. Ecology of or denoting the area of a seashore which is covered at high tide and uncovered at low tide.

**intertribal** ● adj. existing or occurring between different tribes.

**intertrigo** /ˌɪntəˈtrʌɪgəʊ/ ● n. Medicine inflammation caused by the rubbing of one area of skin on another.
– ORIGIN C18: from L., from *interterere* 'rub against each other'.

**intertwine** ● v. twist or twine together.
– DERIVATIVES **intertwinement** n.

**interval** ● n. **1** an intervening time or space. **2** a pause or break. ➤ Brit. a period of time separating parts of a theatrical or musical performance or a sports match. **3** a gap. **4** the difference in pitch between two sounds.
– PHRASES **at intervals** with time or spaces between, not continuously.
– DERIVATIVES **intervallic** adj.
– ORIGIN ME: from OFr. *entrevalle*, based on L. *intervallum* 'space between ramparts, interval'.

**intervalometer** /ˌɪntəvəˈlɒmɪtə/ ● n. Photography a device on a camera that operates the shutter regularly at set intervals over a period.

**intervene** ● v. **1** come between so as to prevent or alter something. ➤ occur as a delay or obstacle to something being done. ➤ interrupt verbally. ➤ Law interpose in a lawsuit as a third party. **2** [usu. as adj. **intervening**] occur in time between events. ➤ be situated between things.
– DERIVATIVES **intervener** (also **intervenor**) n. **intervenient** adj.
– ORIGIN C16 (earlier (ME) as *intervention*): from L. *intervenire*, from *inter-* 'between' + *venire* 'come'.

**intervention** ● n. **1** the action or process of intervening. ➤ interference by a state in another's affairs. **2** action taken to improve a medical disorder.
– DERIVATIVES **interventional** adj. .

**interventionist** ● adj. favouring intervention, especially by a government in its domestic economy or by one state in the affairs of another. ● n. an interventionist person.
– DERIVATIVES **interventionism** n.

**intervertebral** /ˌɪntəˈvəːtɪbr(ə)l/ ● adj. situated between vertebrae.

**interview** ● n. **1** a conversation between a journalist or broadcaster and a person of public interest. **2** an oral examination of an applicant for a job or college place. ➤ a session of formal questioning of a person by the police. ● v. hold an interview with.
– DERIVATIVES **interviewee** n. **interviewer** n.
– ORIGIN C16 (formerly also as *enterview*): from Fr. *entrevue*, from *s'entrevoir* 'see each other', from *voir* 'to see', on the pattern of *vue* 'a view'.

**inter vivos** /ˌɪntə ˈviːvəʊs/ ● adv. & adj. (especially of a gift as opposed to a legacy) between living people.
– ORIGIN from L.

**interwar** ● adj. existing in the period between two wars, especially the two world wars.

**interweave** ● v. (past **-wove**; past part. **-woven**) weave or become woven together.

**interwind** /ˌɪntəˈwʌɪnd/ ● v. (past and past part. **-wound**) wind together.

**interwork** ● v. Computing (of items of hardware or software) be able to connect, communicate, or exchange data.

**intestate** /ɪnˈtɛsteɪt/ ● adj. not having made a will before one dies. ● n. a person who has died intestate.
– DERIVATIVES **intestacy** /-təsi/ n.
– ORIGIN ME: from L. *intestatus*, from *in-* 'not' + *testatus* (see **TESTATE**).

**intestine** (also **intestines**) ● n. the lower part of the alimentary canal from the end of the stomach to the anus. ➤ (in invertebrates) the whole alimentary canal.
– DERIVATIVES **intestinal** adj.
– ORIGIN ME: from L. *intestinum*, neut. of *intestinus*, from *intus* 'within'.

**intifada** /ˌɪntɪˈfɑːdə/ ● n. the Palestinian uprising against Israeli occupation of the West Bank and Gaza Strip, beginning in 1987.
– ORIGIN from Arab. *intifāda* 'an uprising', from *intifaḍa* 'be shaken, shake oneself'.

**intima** /ˈɪntɪmə/ ● n. (pl. **intimae** /-miː/) Anatomy & Zoology the innermost membrane of a vein, artery, or other part.
– DERIVATIVES **intimal** adj.
– ORIGIN C19: shortening of mod. L. *tunica intima* 'innermost sheath'.

**intimacy** ● n. (pl. **-ies**) **1** close familiarity or friendship. **2** an intimate act, especially sexual intercourse. ➤ an intimate remark.

**intimate**[1] /ˈɪntɪmət/ ● adj. **1** closely acquainted; familiar. ➤ having an informal friendly atmosphere. **2** private and personal. ➤ euphemistic having a sexual relationship. **3** involving very close connection. **4** (of knowledge) detailed. ● n. a very close friend.
– DERIVATIVES **intimately** adv.
– ORIGIN C17 (as n.): from late L. *intimatus*, past part. of L. *intimare* 'impress, make familiar', from *intimus* 'inmost'.

**intimate**[2] /ˈɪntɪmeɪt/ ● v. state or make known. ➤ imply or hint.
– DERIVATIVES **intimation** n.
– ORIGIN C16 (earlier (ME) as *intimation*): from late L. *intimat-*, *intimare* (see **INTIMATE**[1]).

**intimidate** ● v. frighten or overawe.

– DERIVATIVES **intimidating** adj. **intimidatingly** adv. **intimidation** n. **intimidator** n. **intimidatory** adj.
– ORIGIN C17: from med. L. *intimidat-*, *intimidare* 'make timid' (based on *timidus* 'timid').

**intinction** /ɪn'tɪŋ(k)ʃ(ə)n/ ● **n.** the action of dipping the bread in the wine at a Eucharist so that a communicant receives both together.
– ORIGIN C16: from late L. *intinctio(n-)*, from L. *intingere*, from *in-* 'into' + *tingere* 'dip'.

**intitule** /ɪn'tɪtjuːl/ ● **v.** Brit. give a title to (an Act of Parliament).
– ORIGIN C15 (formerly also as *entitule*): from OFr. *entituler*, *intituler* (see **ENTITLE**).

**into** ● **prep. 1** expressing motion or direction to a point on or within. **2** indicating a route to a destination. **3** indicating the direction towards which someone or something is turned. **4** indicating an object of interest. **5** expressing a change of state. **6** expressing the result of an action. **7** expressing division. **8** informal taking a lively and active interest in.
– ORIGIN OE *intō* (see **IN**, **TO**).

**intolerable** ● **adj.** unable to be endured.
– DERIVATIVES **intolerably** adv.

**intolerant** ● **adj.** not tolerant.
– DERIVATIVES **intolerance** n. **intolerantly** adv.

**intonation** ● **n. 1** the rise and fall of the voice in speaking. ➤ the action of intoning. **2** accuracy of pitch. **3** the opening phrase of a plainsong melody.
– DERIVATIVES **intonational** adj.

**intone** /ɪn'təʊn/ ● **v.** say or recite with little rise and fall of the pitch of the voice.
– DERIVATIVES **intoner** n.
– ORIGIN C15 (orig. as *entone*): from OFr. *entoner* or med. L. *intonare*, from *in-* 'into' + L. *tonus* 'tone'.

**in toto** /ɪn 'təʊtəʊ/ ● **adv.** as a whole.
– ORIGIN from L.

**intoxicant** ● **n.** an intoxicating substance.

**intoxicate** ● **v.** [usu. as adj. **intoxicated**] **1** (of alcoholic drink or a drug) cause (someone) to lose control of their faculties. **2** poison. **3** excite or exhilarate.
– DERIVATIVES **intoxicating** adj. **intoxicatingly** adv. **intoxication** n.
– ORIGIN ME: from med. L. *intoxicare*, from *in-* 'into' + *toxicare* 'to poison', from L. *toxicum* (see **TOXIC**).

**intoximeter** /ɪn'tɒksɪmiːtə/ ● **n.** a non-portable instrument for measuring the alcohol content of a person's breath.

**intra-** /'ɪntrə/ ● **prefix** (added to adjectives) on the inside; within: *intramural*.
– ORIGIN from L. *intra* 'inside'.

**intracellular** ● **adj.** Biology located or occurring within a cell or cells.
– DERIVATIVES **intracellularly** adv.

**intracranial** ● **adj.** within the skull.
– DERIVATIVES **intracranially** adv.

**intractable** /ɪn'traktəb(ə)l/ ● **adj.** hard to control or deal with. ➤ stubborn.
– DERIVATIVES **intractability** n. **intractableness** n. **intractably** adv.

**intrados** /ɪn'treɪdɒs/ ● **n.** Architecture the lower or inner curve of an arch. Often contrasted with **EXTRADOS**.
– ORIGIN C18: from Fr., from *intra-* 'on the inside' + *dos* 'the back' (from L. *dorsum*).

**intramolecular** ● **adj.** existing or occurring within a molecule.
– DERIVATIVES **intramolecularly** adv.

**intramural** /ˌɪntrə'mjʊər(ə)l/ ● **adj. 1** situated or done within a building. ➤ chiefly N. Amer. within a single educational institution. ➤ forming part of normal university or college studies. **2** Medicine & Biology situated within a hollow organ or a cell. **3** situated or done within a community.
– DERIVATIVES **intramurally** adv.
– ORIGIN C19: from **INTRA-** + L. *murus* 'wall' + **-AL**.

**intramuscular** ● **adj.** situated or taking place within, or administered into, a muscle.
– DERIVATIVES **intramuscularly** adv.

**Intranet** /'ɪntrənɛt/ ● **n.** Computing a private communications network created using Internet technology, accessible only to members of a particular company.

**intransigent** /ɪn'transɪdʒ(ə)nt, -'trɑː-, -nz-/ ● **adj.** unwilling to change one's views or to agree. ● **n.** an intransigent person.
– DERIVATIVES **intransigence** n. **intransigency** n. **intransigently** adv.
– ORIGIN C19: from Fr. *intransigeant*, from Sp. *los intransigentes* (a name adopted by the extreme republicans in the Cortes); based on L. *in-* 'not' + *transigere* 'come to an understanding'.

**intransitive** /ɪn'transɪtɪv, -'trɑː-, -nz-/ ● **adj.** (of a verb or a sense or use of a verb) not taking a direct object, e.g. *look* in *look at the sky*. The opposite of **TRANSITIVE**.
– DERIVATIVES **intransitively** adv. **intransitivity** n.

**intrapreneur** /ˌɪntrəprə'nəː/ ● **n.** a manager within a company who promotes innovative product development and marketing.
– ORIGIN 1970s (orig. US): from **INTRA-** + a shortened form of **ENTREPRENEUR**.

**intraspecific** ● **adj.** Biology occurring or existing within a species.

**intrathecal** /ˌɪntrə'θiːk(ə)l/ ● **adj.** Medicine occurring within or administered into the spinal theca.
– DERIVATIVES **intrathecally** adv.

**intrauterine** /ˌɪntrə'juːtərʌɪn, -rɪn/ ● **adj.** within the uterus.

**intrauterine device** (abbrev.: **IUD**) ● **n.** a contraceptive device fitted inside the uterus and physically preventing the implantation of fertilized ova.

**intravascular** /ˌɪntrə'vaskjʊlə/ ● **adj.** Medicine & Biology situated or occurring within the vascular system.
– DERIVATIVES **intravascularly** adv.

**intravenous** /ˌɪntrə'viːnəs/ (abbrev.: **IV**) ● **adj.** within or into a vein or veins.
– DERIVATIVES **intravenously** adv.

**in tray** ● **n.** chiefly Brit. a tray on a desk for letters and documents that have to be dealt with.

**intrench** ● **v.** variant spelling of **ENTRENCH**.

**intrepid** ● **adj.** fearless; adventurous.
– DERIVATIVES **intrepidity** n. **intrepidly** adv.
– ORIGIN C17: from Fr. *intrépide* or L. *intrepidus*, from *in-* 'not' + *trepidus* 'alarmed'.

**intricacy** /'ɪntrɪkəsi/ ● **n.** (pl. **-ies**) **1** the quality of being intricate. **2** (**intricacies**) details.

**intricate** ● **adj.** very complicated or detailed.
– DERIVATIVES **intricately** adv.
– ORIGIN ME: from L. *intricat-*, *intricare* 'entangle', from *in-* 'into' + *tricae* 'tricks, perplexities'.

**intrigant** /'ɪntrɪg(ə)nt/ ● **n.** a person who plots something illicit or harmful.
– ORIGIN C18: var. of Fr. *intriguant*, from *intriguer* 'to intrigue'.

**intrigue** ● **v.** /ɪn'triːg/ (**intrigues**, **intrigued**, **intriguing**) **1** arouse the curiosity or interest of. **2** plot something illicit or harmful. ● **n.** /ɪn'triːg, 'ɪn-/ **1** the plotting of something illicit or harmful. ➤ a secret love affair. **2** a mysterious or fascinating quality.
– DERIVATIVES **intriguer** n. **intriguing** adj. **intriguingly** adv.
– ORIGIN C17: from Fr. *intrigue* 'plot', *intriguer* 'to tangle, to plot', via Ital. from L. *intricare* (see **INTRICATE**).

**intrinsic** /ɪn'trɪnsɪk/ ● **adj.** belonging naturally; essential.
– DERIVATIVES **intrinsically** adv.
– ORIGIN C15 (in the sense 'interior, inner'): from Fr. *intrinsèque*, from late L. *intrinsecus*, from the earlier adv. *intrinsecus* 'inwardly, inwards'.

**intro** ● **n.** (pl. **-os**) informal an introduction.

**intro-** ● **prefix** into; inwards: *introvert*.
– ORIGIN from L. *intro* 'to the inside'.

**introduce** ● **v. 1** bring into use or operation for the first time. ➤ bring (a plant, animal, or disease) to a place for the first time. ➤ (**introduce something to**) bring a subject to the attention of (someone) for the first time. ➤ present (new legislation) for debate in a legislative assembly. **2** present (someone) by name to another. **3** insert or bring into something. **4** occur at

the start of. ➤provide an opening announcement for.
– DERIVATIVES **introducer** n.
– ORIGIN ME: from L. *introducere*, from *intro-* 'to the inside' + *ducere* 'to lead'.

**introduction** ● **n. 1** the action of introducing or being introduced. ➤a thing, such as a product, plant, etc., newly brought in. **2** a formal presentation of one person to another, in which each is told the other's name. **3** a preliminary thing, such as an explanatory section at the beginning of a book, report, etc. ➤a preliminary section in a piece of music, often thematically different from the main section. **4** a book or course of study intended to introduce a subject to a person. ➤a person's first experience of a subject or thing.

**introductory** ● **adj.** serving as an introduction; basic or preliminary.

**introgression** /ˌɪntrə(ʊ)ˈɡrɛʃ(ə)n/ ● **n.** Biology the transfer of genetic information from one species to another through hybridization and repeated backcrossing.
– ORIGIN C17: from L. *intro-* 'to the inside' on the pattern of *egression*, *ingression*.

**introit** /ˈɪntrɔɪt, ɪnˈtrəʊɪt/ ● **n.** a psalm or antiphon sung or said while the priest approaches the altar for the Eucharist.
– ORIGIN ME: via OFr. from L. *introitus*, from *introire* 'enter', from *intro-* 'to the inside' + *ire* 'go'.

**introjection** /ˌɪntrə(ʊ)ˈdʒɛkʃ(ə)n/ ● **n.** Psychoanalysis the unconscious adoption of the ideas or attitudes of others.
– DERIVATIVES **introject** v.
– ORIGIN C19: from **INTRO-**, on the pattern of *projection*.

**intromission** ● **n.** the inserting of the penis into the vagina in sexual intercourse.

**intromittent organ** /ˌɪntrə(ʊ)ˈmɪt(ə)nt/ ● **n.** Zoology the male copulatory organ of an animal, especially a hermaphrodite.
– ORIGIN C19: from L. *intromittent-*, *intromittere* 'introduce', from *intro-* 'to the inside' + *mittere* 'send'.

**intron** /ˈɪntrɒn/ ● **n.** Biochemistry a segment of a DNA or RNA molecule which does not code for proteins and interrupts the sequence of genes. Compare with **EXON**[1].
– DERIVATIVES **intronic** adj.
– ORIGIN 1970s: from **INTRA-** + **-ON**.

**introrse** /ɪnˈtrɔːs/ ● **adj.** Botany & Zoology turned inwards. The opposite of **EXTRORSE**.
– ORIGIN C19: from L. *introrsus*, from *introversus* 'turned inwards'.

**introspect** /ˌɪntrə(ʊ)ˈspɛkt/ ● **v.** examine one's own thoughts or feelings.
– ORIGIN C17: from L. *introspect-*, *introspicere* 'look into', or from *introspectare* 'keep looking into'.

**introspection** ● **n.** the examination of one's own thoughts or feelings.
– DERIVATIVES **introspective** adj. **introspectively** adv. **introspectiveness** n.

**introvert** ● **n.** a shy, reticent person. ➤Psychology a person predominantly concerned with their own thoughts and feelings rather than with external things. Compare with **EXTROVERT**. ● **adj.** of, denoting, or typical of an introvert.
– DERIVATIVES **introversion** n. **introversive** /-ˈvəːsɪv/ adj.
– ORIGIN C17: from mod. L. *introvertere*, from *intro-* 'to the inside' + *vertere* 'to turn'.

**introverted** ● **adj. 1** of, denoting, or typical of an introvert. **2** Anatomy & Zoology (of an organ etc.) turned or pushed inward on itself.

**intrude** ● **v. 1** come into a place or situation where one is unwelcome or uninvited. ➤introduce into or enter with adverse effect. **2** Geology (of igneous rock) be forced or thrust into (a pre-existing formation).
– ORIGIN C16 (orig. as *entrude*): from L. *intrudere*, from *in-* 'into' + *trudere* 'to thrust'.

**intruder** ● **n.** a person who intrudes, especially into a building with criminal intent.

**intrusion** ● **n.** the action of intruding. ➤a thing that intrudes.
– ORIGIN ME: from med. L. *intrusio(n-)*, from L. *intrudere* (see **INTRUDE**).

**intrusive** ● **adj. 1** intruding or tending to intrude. **2** Phonetics (of a sound) added between words or syllables to facilitate pronunciation, e.g. an *r* in *saw a film*. **3** Geology relating to or formed by the intrusion of igneous rock.
– DERIVATIVES **intrusively** adv. **intrusiveness** n.

**intrust** ● **v.** archaic spelling of **ENTRUST**.

**intubate** /ˈɪntjʊbeɪt/ ● **v.** Medicine insert a tube into.
– DERIVATIVES **intubation** n.
– ORIGIN C19: from **IN-**[2] + L. *tuba* 'tube' + **-ATE**[3].

**intuit** /ɪnˈtjuːɪt/ ● **v.** understand or work out by instinct.
– DERIVATIVES **intuitable** adj.
– ORIGIN C18 (earlier (ME) as *intuition*): from L. *intuit-*, *intueri* 'contemplate', from *in-* 'upon' + *tueri* 'to look'.

**intuition** ● **n.** the ability to understand something immediately, without the need for conscious reasoning.
– DERIVATIVES **intuitional** adj.

**intuitionism** ● **n.** Philosophy the theory that primary truths and principles are known by intuition.
– DERIVATIVES **intuitionist** n. & adj.

**intuitive** ● **adj. 1** instinctive. **2** (chiefly of computer software) easy to use and understand.
– DERIVATIVES **intuitively** adv. **intuitiveness** n.

**intumesce** /ˌɪntjʊˈmɛs/ ● **v.** rare swell up.
– DERIVATIVES **intumescence** n. **intumescent** adj.
– ORIGIN C18: from L. *intumescere*, from *in-* 'into' + *tumescere* 'begin to swell' (from *tumere* 'swell').

**intussusception** /ˌɪntəsəˈsɛpʃ(ə)n/ ● **n. 1** Medicine the inversion of one portion of the intestine within another. **2** Botany the growth of a cell wall by the deposition of cellulose.
– ORIGIN C18: from mod. L. *intussusceptio(n-)*, from L. *intus* 'within' + *susceptio(n-)* (from *suscipere* 'take up').

**intwine** ● **v.** archaic spelling of **ENTWINE**.

**Inuit** /ˈɪnjʊɪt, ˈɪnʊɪt/ ● **n. 1** the members of an indigenous people of northern Canada and parts of Greenland and Alaska. **2** the Eskimo-Aleut language of this people.
– ORIGIN Inuit, pl. of *inuk* 'person'.

**USAGE Inuit**

The term **Inuit** has official status in Canada, and is also used elsewhere as a synonym for **Eskimo** in general. However, this latter use, in including people from Siberia who are not Inupiaq-speakers, is, strictly speaking, not accurate. See also **ESKIMO**.

**Inuk** /ˈɪnʊk/ ● **n.** (pl. **Inuit**) a member of the Inuit people.
– ORIGIN Inuit, lit. 'person'.

**Inuktitut** /ɪˈnʊktɪtʊt/ (also **Inuktituk** /-tʊk/) ● **n.** the Inuit language.
– ORIGIN Inuit, lit. 'the Inuk way', used as the title of a periodical.

**inulin** /ˈɪnjʊlɪn/ ● **n.** Biochemistry a substance derived from fructose, present in the roots of various plants.
– ORIGIN C19: from L. *inula* 'elecampane' + **-IN**[1].

**inunction** /ɪˈnʌŋ(k)ʃ(ə)n/ ● **n.** chiefly Medicine the rubbing of ointment or oil into the skin.
– ORIGIN C15: from L. *inunctio(n-)*, from *inunguere* 'smear on'.

**inundate** /ˈɪnʌndeɪt/ ● **v.** (usu. **be inundated**) **1** flood. **2** overwhelm with things to be dealt with.
– DERIVATIVES **inundation** n.
– ORIGIN C16 (earlier (ME) as *inundation*): from L. *inundat-*, *inundare* 'flood', from *in-* 'into, upon' + *undare* 'to flow' (from *unda* 'a wave').

**Inupiaq** /ɪˈnuːpɪak/ (also **Inupiat** /-pɪat/, **Inupik** /-pɪk/) ● **n.** (pl. same) **1** a member of a group of Inuit people inhabiting northern Alaska. **2** the Inuit language. ● **adj.** of or relating to this people or their language.
– ORIGIN Inuit, from *inuk* 'person' + *piaq* 'genuine'.

**inure** /ɪˈnjʊə/ ● **v. 1** (usu. **be inured to**) accustom to something, especially something unpleasant. **2** Law variant spelling of **ENURE**.
– DERIVATIVES **inurement** n.
– ORIGIN ME *inure*, *enure*, from an Anglo-Norman Fr. phr. meaning 'in use or practice', from *en* 'in' + OFr. *euvre* 'work' (from L. *opera*).

**in utero** /ɪn ˈjuːtərəʊ/ ● **adv. & adj.** in a woman's uterus; before birth.
– ORIGIN from L.

**in vacuo** /ɪn 'vakjʊəʊ/ ● **adv.** in a vacuum.
– ORIGIN from L.

**invade** ● **v. 1** enter (a country) as or with an army so as to subjugate or occupy it. ➤enter in large numbers, especially intrusively. ➤(of a parasite or disease) attack and spread into (an organism or bodily part). **2** intrude on: *he felt his privacy was being invaded.*
– DERIVATIVES **invader** n.
– ORIGIN ME: from L. *invadere*, from *in-* 'into' + *vadere* 'go'.

**invagination** ● **n.** chiefly Anatomy & Biology the action or process of being turned inside out or folded back on itself to form a cavity or pouch. ➤a cavity or pouch so formed.
– DERIVATIVES **invaginate** v.
– ORIGIN C17: from mod. L. *invaginatio(n-)*, based on **IN-**[2] + L. *vagina* 'sheath'.

**invalid**[1] /'ɪnvəliːd, -lɪd/ ● **n.** a person made weak or disabled by illness or injury. ● **v.** (**invalided**, **invaliding**) (usu. **be invalided**) remove from active service in the armed forces because of injury or illness. ➤disable by injury or illness.
– DERIVATIVES **invalidism** n.
– ORIGIN C17 (as adj. in the sense 'infirm or disabled'): a special sense of **INVALID**[2], with a change of pronunc.

**invalid**[2] /ɪn'valɪd/ ● **adj. 1** not legally recognized because contravening a regulation or law. **2** not true because based on erroneous information or unsound reasoning.
– DERIVATIVES **invalidate** v. **invalidation** n. **invalidly** adv.
– ORIGIN C16 (earlier than *valid*): from L. *invalidus*, from *in-* 'not' + *validus* (see **VALID**).

**invalidity** ● **n. 1** Brit. the condition of being an invalid. **2** the fact of being invalid.

**invaluable** ● **adj.** extremely useful.
– DERIVATIVES **invaluably** adv.

**Invar** /'ɪnvɑː/ ● **n.** trademark an alloy of iron and nickel with a negligible coefficient of expansion.
– ORIGIN C20: abbrev. of **INVARIABLE**.

**invariable** ● **adj.** never changing. ➤(of a noun in an inflected language) having the same form in both the singular and the plural. ➤Mathematics (of a quantity) constant.
– DERIVATIVES **invariability** n. **invariableness** n.

**invariably** ● **adv.** always.

**invariant** ● **adj.** never changing. ● **n.** Mathematics a function which remains unchanged when a specified transformation is applied.
– DERIVATIVES **invariance** n.

**invasion** ● **n.** an instance of invading. ➤the action or process of being invaded.

**invasive** ● **adj.** tending to invade or intrude. ➤(of medical procedures) involving the introduction of instruments or other objects into the body or body cavities.
– ORIGIN ME: from obs. Fr. *invasif, -ive* or med. L. *invasivus*, from L. *invadere* (see **INVADE**).

**invected** ● **adj.** Heraldry having convex semicircular projections along the edge. Compare with **ENGRAILED**.
– ORIGIN C17: from L. *invehect-, invehere* 'carry in' + **-ED**[2].

**invective** ● **n.** strongly abusive or critical language.
– ORIGIN ME (orig. as adj. meaning 'abusive'): from OFr. *invectif, -ive*, from late L. *invectivus* 'attacking', from *invehere* (see **INVEIGH**).

**inveigh** /ɪn'veɪ/ ● **v.** (**inveigh against**) speak or write about with great hostility.
– ORIGIN C15 (in the sense 'carry in'): from L. *invehere* 'carry in', *invehi* 'be carried into, assail'.

**inveigle** /ɪn'viːg(ə)l, ɪn'veɪg(ə)l/ ● **v.** (usu. **inveigle someone into**) persuade by deception or flattery.
– DERIVATIVES **inveiglement** n.
– ORIGIN C15: from Anglo-Norman Fr. *envegler*, alt. of OFr. *aveugler* 'to blind'.

**invent** ● **v.** create or design (a new device, process, etc.). ➤make up (a name, story, etc.), especially so as to deceive.
– DERIVATIVES **inventor** n. **inventress** n.
– ORIGIN C15 (earlier (ME) as *invention* in the sense 'discovery'): from L. *invent-, invenire* 'contrive, discover'.

**invention** ● **n. 1** the action of inventing. ➤something invented. ➤a fabricated story. **2** creative ability.

**Invention of the Cross** ● **n.** a festival, held on 3 May, commemorating the reputed finding of the Cross of Christ by Helena, mother of the emperor Constantine, in AD 326.

**inventive** ● **adj.** having or showing creativity or original thought.
– DERIVATIVES **inventively** adv. **inventiveness** n.

**inventory** /'ɪnv(ə)nt(ə)ri/ ● **n.** (pl. **-ies**) a complete list of items such as goods in stock or the contents of a building. ➤a quantity of goods in stock. ➤(in accounting) the entire stock of a business, including materials and finished product. ● **v.** (**-ies**, **-ied**) make an inventory of.
– ORIGIN ME: from med. L. *inventorium*, alt. of late L. *inventarium*, lit. 'a list of what is found', from L. *invenire* 'come upon'.

**inverse** /'ɪnvəːs, ɪn'vəːs/ ● **adj.** opposite in position, direction, order, or effect. ● **n. 1** a thing that is the opposite or reverse of another. **2** Mathematics a reciprocal quantity.
– DERIVATIVES **inversely** adv.
– ORIGIN ME: from L. *inversus*, past part. of *invertere* (see **INVERT**[1]).

**inverse proportion** (also **inverse ratio**) ● **n.** a relation between two quantities such that one increases in proportion as the other decreases.

**inverse square law** ● **n.** Physics a law stating that the intensity of an effect changes in inverse proportion to the square of the distance from the source.

**inversion** ● **n. 1** the action of inverting or the state of being inverted. ➤reversal of the normal order of words, typically for rhetorical effect. ➤Music an inverted interval, chord, or phrase. **2** (also **temperature** or **thermal inversion**) a reversal of the normal decrease of air temperature with altitude, or of water temperature with depth. **3** Mathematics the process of finding an inverse or reciprocal quantity from a given one. **4** Chemistry a reaction causing a change from one optically active configuration to the opposite configuration. **5** (also **sexual inversion**) Psychology, dated homosexuality.
– DERIVATIVES **inversive** adj.

**invert**[1] ● **v.** /ɪn'vəːt/ **1** put upside down or in the opposite position, order, or arrangement. **2** Music modify (a phrase) by reversing the direction of pitch changes. ➤alter (an interval or chord) by changing the relative position of the notes in it. **3** chiefly Mathematics subject to inversion. ● **n.** /'ɪnvəːt/ **1** an inverted arch, as at the lower surface of a sewer. **2** Psychology, dated a homosexual. **3** Philately a postage stamp printed with an error such that all or part of its design is upside down.
– DERIVATIVES **invertibility** n. **invertible** adj.
– ORIGIN C16: from L. *invertere*, lit. 'turn inside out'.

**invert**[2] /'ɪnvəːt/ ● **n.** informal short for **INVERTEBRATE**.

**invertase** /'ɪnvəːteɪz, ɪn'vəːt-/ ● **n.** Biochemistry an enzyme produced by yeast which promotes the hydrolysis of sucrose, forming invert sugar.

**invertebrate** /ɪn'vəːtɪbrət/ ● **n.** an animal lacking a backbone, such as an arthropod, mollusc, annelid, etc. Compare with **VERTEBRATE**. ● **adj.** of or relating to this division of animals.
– ORIGIN C19: from mod. L. *invertebrata* (pl.) (former taxonomic group), from Fr. *invertébrés*, from *in-* 'without' + L. *vertebra* (see **VERTEBRA**).

**inverted comma** ● **n.** chiefly Brit. another term for **QUOTATION MARK**.

**inverted snobbery** ● **n.** derogatory the attitude of disdaining anything associated with wealth or high social status, while elevating those things associated with lack of wealth and social position.
– DERIVATIVES **inverted snob** n.

**inverter** ● **n. 1** an apparatus which converts direct current into alternating current. **2** Electronics a device that converts either of the two binary digits or signals into the other.

**invert sugar** ● **n.** a mixture of glucose and fructose obtained by the hydrolysis of sucrose.
– ORIGIN C19: from *inverted* with ref. to inversion of optical activity.

**invest** ● **v. 1** put money into financial schemes, shares, or property with the expectation of achieving a profit. ➤devote (one's time or energy) to an undertaking with the

expectation of a worthwhile result. ➤(**invest in**) informal buy (something) whose usefulness will repay the cost. **2** (**invest someone/thing with**) endow someone or something with (a particular quality or attribute). ➤endow someone with (a rank or office). ➤(**invest something in**) establish a right or power in. **3** archaic clothe or cover with a garment. **4** archaic surround (a place) in order to besiege or blockade it.
– DERIVATIVES **investable** adj. **investible** adj. **investor** n.
– ORIGIN C16: from Fr. *investir* or L. *investire*, from *in-* 'into, upon' + *vestire* 'clothe'; sense 1 is influenced by Ital. *investire*.

**investigate** ● v. carry out a systematic or formal inquiry into (an incident or allegation) so as to establish the truth. ➤carry out research into (a subject). ➤make a search or systematic inquiry.
– DERIVATIVES **investigable** adj. **investigation** n. **investigator** n. **investigatory** adj.
– ORIGIN C16 (earlier (ME) as *investigation*): from L. *investigat-*, *investigare* 'trace out'.

**investigative** /ɪnˈvɛstɪɡətɪv, -ɡeɪtɪv/ ● adj. of or concerned with investigating. ➤(of journalism or a journalist) investigating and seeking to expose malpractice or the miscarriage of justice.

**investiture** /ɪnˈvɛstɪtjə, -tʃə/ ● n. the action of formally investing a person with honours or rank. ➤a ceremony at which this takes place.
– ORIGIN ME: from med. L. *investitura*, from *investire* (see INVEST).

**investment** ● n. the action or process of investing. ➤a thing worth buying because it may be profitable or useful in the future.

**investment bank** ● n. (in the US) a bank that purchases large holdings of newly issued shares and resells them to investors.

**investment bond** ● n. (in the UK) a single-premium life insurance policy linked to a unit trust for long-term investment.

**investment casting** ● n. a technique for making small, accurate castings in metal using a mould formed around a pattern of wax which is removed by melting.

**investment trust** ● n. a limited company which buys and sells shares in selected companies to make a profit for its members.

**inveterate** /ɪnˈvɛt(ə)rət/ ● adj. having a long-standing and firmly established habit or activity. ➤(of a feeling or habit) firmly established.
– DERIVATIVES **inveteracy** n. **inveterately** adv.
– ORIGIN ME (referring to disease, in the sense 'chronic'): from L. *inveteratus* 'made old', past part. of *inveterare*.

**invidious** /ɪnˈvɪdɪəs/ ● adj. unacceptable, unfair, and likely to arouse resentment or anger in others.
– DERIVATIVES **invidiously** adv. **invidiousness** n.
– ORIGIN C17: from L. *invidiosus*, from *invidia* (see ENVY).

**invigilate** /ɪnˈvɪdʒɪleɪt/ ● v. Brit. supervise candidates during an examination.
– DERIVATIVES **invigilation** n. **invigilator** n.
– ORIGIN C16 (in the general sense 'watch over'): from L. *invigilat-*, *invigilare* 'watch over'.

**invigorate** /ɪnˈvɪɡəreɪt/ ● v. give strength or energy to.
– DERIVATIVES **invigorating** adj. **invigoratingly** adv. **invigoration** n. **invigorator** n.
– ORIGIN C17: from med. L. *invigorat-*, *invigorare* 'make strong'.

**invincible** /ɪnˈvɪnsɪb(ə)l/ ● adj. too powerful to be defeated or overcome.
– DERIVATIVES **invincibility** n. **invincibly** adv.
– ORIGIN ME (earlier than *vincible*): via OFr. from L. *invincibilis*, from *in-* 'not' + *vincibilis* (see VINCIBLE).

**in vino veritas** /ɪn ˌviːnəʊ ˈvɛrɪtɑːs/ ● exclam. under the influence of alcohol, a person tells the truth.
– ORIGIN L., lit. 'truth in wine'.

**inviolable** /ɪnˈvʌɪələb(ə)l/ ● adj. never to be infringed or dishonoured.
– DERIVATIVES **inviolability** n. **inviolably** adv.

**inviolate** /ɪnˈvʌɪələt/ ● adj. free from injury or violation.
– DERIVATIVES **inviolacy** n. **inviolately** adv.
– ORIGIN ME: from L. *inviolatus*, from *in-* 'not' + *violare* 'violate'.

**inviscid** /ɪnˈvɪsɪd/ ● adj. Physics having no or negligible viscosity.

**invisible** ● adj. **1** unable to be seen, either by nature or because concealed. ➤treated as if unable to be seen; ignored. **2** Economics relating to or denoting earnings which a country makes from the sale of services or other items not constituting tangible commodities. ● n. (**invisibles**) invisible exports and imports.
– DERIVATIVES **invisibility** n. **invisibly** adv.

**invisible ink** ● n. a type of ink used to produce writing that cannot be seen until the paper is heated or otherwise treated.

**invitation** ● n. **1** a written or verbal request inviting someone to go somewhere or to do something. ➤the action of inviting. **2** a situation or action inviting a particular outcome or response.

**invitational** ● adj. N. Amer. (especially of a competition) open only to those invited.

**invite** ● v. **1** ask in a friendly or formal way to go somewhere or to do something. **2** request (something) formally or politely from someone. **3** (of an action or situation) tend to elicit (a particular outcome or response). ● n. informal an invitation.
– DERIVATIVES **invitee** n. **inviter** n.
– ORIGIN C16 (earlier (ME) as *invitation*): from OFr. *inviter*, or from L. *invitare*.

**inviting** ● adj. tempting or attractive.
– DERIVATIVES **invitingly** adv.

**in vitro** /ɪn ˈviːtrəʊ/ ● adj. & adv. Biology (of processes) taking place in a test tube, culture dish, or elsewhere outside a living organism.
– ORIGIN L., lit. 'in glass'.

**in vivo** /ɪn ˈviːvəʊ/ ● adv. & adj. Biology (of processes) taking place in a living organism.
– ORIGIN L., 'in a living thing'.

**invocation** ● n. the action of invoking. ➤an incantation used to invoke a deity or the supernatural. ➤(in the Christian Church) a form of words introducing a prayer, sermon, etc.
– DERIVATIVES **invocatory** /ɪnˈvɒkət(ə)ri/ adj.

**invoice** ● n. a list of goods sent or services provided, with a statement of the sum due. ● v. send an invoice to. ➤send an invoice for (goods or services provided).
– ORIGIN C16: orig. the pl. of obs. *invoy*, from obs. Fr. *envoy*, from *envoyer* (see ENVOY[1]).

**invoke** /ɪnˈvəʊk/ ● v. **1** appeal to as an authority or in support of an argument. ➤call on (a deity or spirit) in prayer or as a witness. ➤call earnestly for. ➤summon (a spirit) by charms or incantation. **2** Computing cause (a procedure) to be carried out.
– DERIVATIVES **invoker** n.
– ORIGIN C15 (earlier (ME) as *invocation*): from Fr. *invoquer*, from L. *invocare*.

**involucre** /ˈɪnvəl(j)uːkə/ ● n. **1** Anatomy a membranous envelope. **2** Botany a whorl of bracts surrounding an inflorescence or at the base of an umbel.
– ORIGIN C16: from Fr., or from L. *involucrum*, from *involvere* (see INVOLVE).

**involuntary** ● adj. **1** done without conscious control. ➤(especially of muscles or nerves) concerned in bodily processes that are not under the control of the will. **2** done against someone's will.
– DERIVATIVES **involuntarily** adv. **involuntariness** n.

**involute** /ˈɪnvəl(j)uːt/ ● adj. **1** formal complicated. **2** technical curled spirally. ➤Zoology (of a shell) having the whorls wound closely round the axis. ➤Botany rolled inwards at the edges. ● n. Geometry the locus of a point considered as the end of a taut string being unwound from a given curve in the plane of that curve. Compare with EVOLUTE.
– ORIGIN C17: from L. *involutus*, past part. of *involvere* (see INVOLVE).

**involuted** ● adj. complicated; abstruse.

**involution** ● n. **1** Physiology the shrinkage of an organ in old age or when inactive. **2** Mathematics a function, transformation, or operator that is equal to its inverse. **3** formal

the process or state of complication.
– DERIVATIVES **involutional** adj.
– ORIGIN ME (in the sense '(part) curling inwards'): from L. *involutio(n-)*, from *involvere* (see INVOLVE).

**involve** • v. **1** (of a situation or event) include as a necessary part or result. ➤cause to experience or participate in an activity or situation. **2** [as adj. **involved**] connected, typically on an emotional or personal level. **3** [as adj. **involved**] complicated.
– DERIVATIVES **involvement** n.
– ORIGIN ME (in the senses 'enfold' and 'entangle'): from L. *involvere*, from *in-* 'into' + *volvere* 'to roll'.

**invulnerable** • adj. impossible to harm or damage.
– DERIVATIVES **invulnerability** n. **invulnerably** adv.
– ORIGIN C16 (earlier than *vulnerable*): from L. *invulnerabilis*, from *in-* 'not' + *vulnerabilis* (see VULNERABLE).

**-in-waiting** • comb. form **1** denoting a position as attendant to a royal personage: *lady-in-waiting.* **2** awaiting a turn or about to happen: *a political administration-in-waiting.*

**inwale** /'ɪnweɪl/ • n. an internal gunwale.

**inward** • adj. directed or proceeding towards the inside. ➤mental or spiritual. • adv. variant of INWARDS.
– DERIVATIVES **inwardly** adv. **inwardness** n.

**inward investment** • n. investment made within a country from outside.

**inward-looking** • adj. self-absorbed or insular.

**inwards** (also **inward**) • adv. towards the inside. ➤into or towards the mind, spirit, or soul.

**inwrought** /ɪn'rɔːt, 'ɪnrɔːt/ • adj. poetic/literary (of a fabric or garment) intricately embroidered.

**in-your-face** • adj. informal blatantly aggressive or provocative.
– ORIGIN 1970s: from *in your face*, used as a derisive insult.

**I/O** • abbrev. Electronics input-output.

**IOC** • abbrev. International Olympic Committee.

**iod-** • comb. form variant spelling of IODO- shortened before a vowel (as in *iodic*).

**iodic acid** /ʌɪ'ɒdɪk/ • n. Chemistry a crystalline acid with strong oxidizing properties, made by oxidation of iodine. [$HIO_3$.]
– DERIVATIVES **iodate** n.

**iodide** /'ʌɪədʌɪd/ • n. Chemistry a compound of iodine with another element or group: *sodium iodide.*

**iodine** /'ʌɪədiːn, -ʌɪn, -ɪn/ • n. the chemical element of atomic number 53, a halogen forming black crystals and a violet vapour. (Symbol: **I**) ➤an antiseptic solution of this in alcohol.
– DERIVATIVES **iodinate** v. **iodination** n.
– ORIGIN C19: from Fr. *iode* (from Gk *iōdēs* 'violet-coloured') + -INE[4].

**iodism** /'ʌɪədɪz(ə)m/ • n. Medicine iodine poisoning.

**iodo-** (usu. **iod-** before a vowel) • comb. form Chemistry representing IODINE.

**iodoform** /ʌɪ'əʊdə(ʊ)fɔːm, 'ʌɪədə(ʊ)-, ʌɪ'ɒdə(ʊ)-/ • n. a volatile pale yellow sweet-smelling crystalline compound with antiseptic properties. [$CHI_3$.]
– ORIGIN C19: from IODINE, on the pattern of *chloroform.*

**iodophor** /ʌɪ'əʊdə(ʊ)fɔː, 'ʌɪəd-/ • n. a disinfectant containing iodine in combination with a surfactant.

**IOM** • abbrev. Isle of Man.

**ion** /'ʌɪən/ • n. an atom or molecule with a net electric charge through loss or gain of electrons, either positive (a **cation**) or negative (an **anion**).
– ORIGIN C19: from Gk, neut. pres. part. of *ienai* 'go'.

**-ion** • suffix **1** forming nouns denoting verbal action or an instance of this: *communion.* **2** denoting a resulting state or product: *oblivion.*
– ORIGIN via Fr. from L. *-ion-*.

**ion exchange** • n. the exchange of ions of the same charge between an insoluble solid and a solution in contact with it, used in purification and separation processes.
– DERIVATIVES **ion exchanger** n.

**Ionian** • n. **1** a member of an ancient Hellenic people inhabiting Attica, parts of western Asia Minor, and the Aegean islands in pre-classical times. **2** a native or inhabitant of the Ionian Islands, a chain of islands off the western coast of mainland Greece. • adj. of or relating to the Ionians, Ionia, or the Ionian Islands.
– ORIGIN C16: via L. from Gk *Iōnios*, from *Iōnia* 'Ionia', an ancient region on the west coast of Asia Minor.

**Ionian mode** • n. Music the mode represented by the natural diatonic scale C–C (the major scale).

**Ionic** /ʌɪ'ɒnɪk/ • adj. **1** relating to or denoting a classical order of architecture characterized by a column with scroll shapes on either side of the capital. **2** another term for IONIAN. • n. **1** the Ionic order of architecture. **2** the ancient Greek dialect used in Ionia.

**ionic** /ʌɪ'ɒnɪk/ • adj. relating to ions. ➤(of a chemical bond) formed by the electrostatic attraction of oppositely charged ions. Often contrasted with COVALENT.
– DERIVATIVES **ionically** adv.

**ionize** /'ʌɪənʌɪz/ (also **-ise**) • v. convert (an atom, molecule, or substance) into an ion or ions, typically by removing one or more electrons.
– DERIVATIVES **ionizable** adj. **ionization** n.

**ionizer** • n. a device which produces ions, especially one used to improve the quality of the air in a room.

**ionizing radiation** • n. radiation consisting of particles, X-rays, or gamma rays which produce ions in the medium through which it passes.

**ionophore** /ʌɪ'ɒnə(ʊ)fɔː/ • n. Biochemistry a substance which is able to transport particular ions through a lipid membrane in a cell.

**ionosphere** /ʌɪ'ɒnəsfɪə/ • n. the layer of the atmosphere above the mesosphere, which contains a high concentration of ions and electrons and is able to reflect radio waves.
– DERIVATIVES **ionospheric** adj.

**iontophoresis** /ʌɪˌɒntə(ʊ)fə'riːsɪs/ • n. Medicine a technique of introducing ionic medicinal compounds through the skin by applying a local electric current.
– ORIGIN C20: from ION, on the pattern of *electrophoresis.*

**-ior** • suffix forming adjectives of comparison: *senior.*
– ORIGIN from L.

**iota** /ʌɪ'əʊtə/ • n. **1** the ninth letter of the Greek alphabet (**Ι, ι**), transliterated as 'i'. **2** [usu. with neg.] an extremely small amount.
– ORIGIN from Gk *iōta*; sense 2 derives from *iota* being the smallest letter of the Greek alphabet (cf. JOT).

**IOU** • n. a signed document acknowledging a debt.
– ORIGIN C18: representing the pronunc. of *I owe you.*

**-ious** • suffix (forming adjectives) characterized by; full of: *cautious.*
– ORIGIN from Fr. *-ieux*, from L. *-iosus.*

**IOW** • abbrev. Isle of Wight.

**Iowan** /'ʌɪəw(ə)n/ • n. a native or inhabitant of the US state of Iowa. • adj. of or relating to Iowa.

**IP** • abbrev. Computing Internet Protocol.

**IPA** • abbrev. International Phonetic Alphabet.

**ipecacuanha** /ˌɪpɪkakjʊ'anə/ • n. the dried rhizome of a South American shrub, used as an emetic and expectorant drug.
– ORIGIN C17: from Port., from Tupi-Guarani *ipekaaguéne* 'emetic creeper'.

**IPMS** • abbrev. Institution of Professionals, Managers, and Specialists.

**IPO** • abbrev. initial public offering, the first issue of a company's shares to the public, used as a means of raising start-up or expansion capital.

**ippon** /'ɪpɒn/ • n. a full point scored in judo, karate, and other martial sports.
– ORIGIN from Japanese.

**IPR** • abbrev. intellectual property rights.

**ipse dixit** /ˌɪpseɪ 'dɪksɪt, ˌɪpsiː/ • n. a dogmatic and unproven statement.
– ORIGIN L., lit. 'he himself said it', translating Gk *autos epha*, a phr. used of Pythagoras by his followers.

**ipsilateral** /ˌɪpsɪ'lat(ə)r(ə)l/ • adj. belonging to or occurring on the same side of the body.
– ORIGIN C20: formed irregularly from L. *ipse* 'self' + LATERAL.

**ipsissima verba** /ɪpˌsɪsɪmə ˈvəːbə/ ● **pl. n.** the precise words.
– ORIGIN from L.

**ipso facto** /ˌɪpsəʊ ˈfaktəʊ/ ● **adv.** by that very fact or act.
– ORIGIN from L.

**IQ** ● **abbrev.** intelligence quotient.

**-ique** ● **suffix** archaic spelling of **-IC**.

**IR** ● **abbrev.** **1** infrared. **2** Iran (international vehicle registration).

**Ir** ● **symb.** the chemical element iridium.

**ir-** ● **prefix** variant spelling of **IN-**[1], **IN-**[2] assimilated before *r* (as in *irradiate*).

**IRA** ● **abbrev.** Irish Republican Army.

**Iranian** ● **n.** a native or national of Iran, or a person of Iranian descent. ● **adj.** **1** relating to Iran or its people. **2** relating to or denoting the group of Indo-European languages that includes Persian (Farsi), Pashto, Avestan, and Kurdish.

**Iraqi** ● **n.** (pl. **Iraqis**) **1** a native or national of Iraq, or a person of Iraqi descent. **2** the form of Arabic spoken in Iraq. ● **adj.** relating to Iraq or its people.

**irascible** /ɪˈrasɪb(ə)l/ ● **adj.** hot-tempered; irritable.
– DERIVATIVES **irascibility** n. **irascibly** adv.
– ORIGIN ME: via Fr. from late L. *irascibilis*, from L. *irasci* 'grow angry', from *ira* 'anger'.

**irate** /ʌɪˈreɪt/ ● **adj.** extremely angry.
– DERIVATIVES **irately** adv. **irateness** n.
– ORIGIN C19: from L. *iratus*, from *ira* 'anger'.

**IRBM** ● **abbrev.** intermediate-range ballistic missile.

**IRC** ● **abbrev.** Internet Relay Chat, a system that provides software allowing Internet users to join groups for online chatting.

**ire** /ˈʌɪə/ ● **n.** chiefly poetic/literary anger.
– DERIVATIVES **ireful** adj.
– ORIGIN ME: via OFr. from L. *ira*.

**irenic** ● **adj.** variant spelling of **EIRENIC**.

**iridaceous** /ˌʌɪrɪˈdeɪʃəs, ˌɪrɪ-/ ● **adj.** Botany relating to or denoting plants of the iris family (Iridaceae).
– ORIGIN C19: from mod. L. *Iridaceae*, based on Gk *iris, irid-* 'rainbow', + **-OUS**.

**iridescent** /ˌɪrɪˈdɛs(ə)nt/ ● **adj.** showing luminous colours that seem to change when seen from different angles.
– DERIVATIVES **iridescence** n. **iridescently** adv.
– ORIGIN C18: from L. *iris, irid-* 'rainbow' + **-ESCENT**.

**iridium** /ɪˈrɪdɪəm, ʌɪ-/ ● **n.** the chemical element of atomic number 77, a hard, dense silvery-white metal. (Symbol: **Ir**)
– ORIGIN C19: mod. L., from L. *iris, irid-* 'rainbow' (so named because it forms compounds of various colours).

**iridology** /ˌʌɪrɪˈdɒlədʒi, ˌɪrɪ-/ ● **n.** (in alternative medicine) diagnosis by examination of the iris of the eye.
– DERIVATIVES **iridologist** n.
– ORIGIN C20: from Gk *iris, irid-* 'iris' + **-LOGY**.

**irie** /ˈʌɪriː/ black English ● **adj.** nice, good, or pleasing. ● **exclam.** used by Rastafarians as a friendly greeting.
– ORIGIN perh. representing a pronunc. of *all right*.

**iris** ● **n.** **1** a flat, coloured, ring-shaped membrane behind the cornea of the eye, with an adjustable circular opening (pupil) in the centre. **2** a plant with showy flowers, typically purple or yellow, and sword-shaped leaves. [Genus *Iris*: many species.] **3** (also **iris diaphragm**) an adjustable diaphragm of thin overlapping plates for regulating the size of a central aperture. ● **v.** open or close in the manner of an iris.
– ORIGIN mod. L., via L. from Gk *iris* 'rainbow, iris'.

**Irish** ● **n.** (also **Irish Gaelic**) the Celtic language of Ireland. ● **adj.** **1** of or relating to Ireland, its people, or the Celtic language traditionally and historically spoken there. **2** offensive illogical or apparently so.
– DERIVATIVES **Irishman** n. (pl. **-men**). **Irishness** n. **Irishwoman** n. (pl. **-women**).
– ORIGIN ME: from OE *Īr-* (stem of *Īras* 'the Irish' and *Īrland* 'Ireland', obscurely rel. to **HIBERNIAN**) + **-ISH**[1].

**Irish coffee** ● **n.** coffee mixed with a dash of Irish whiskey and served with cream on top.

**Irish moss** ● **n.** another term for **CARRAGEEN**.

**Irish setter** ● **n.** a dog of a breed of setter with a long, silky dark red coat and a long feathered tail.

**Irish stew** ● **n.** a stew made with mutton, potatoes, and onions.

**Irish terrier** ● **n.** a terrier of a rough-haired light reddish-brown breed.

**Irish wolfhound** ● **n.** a large, typically greyish hound of a rough-coated breed.

**iritis** /ʌɪˈrʌɪtɪs/ ● **n.** inflammation of the iris of the eye.

**irk** /əːk/ ● **v.** irritate; annoy.
– DERIVATIVES **irksome** adj. **irksomely** adv.
– ORIGIN ME: perh. from ON *yrkja* 'to work'.

**IRL** ● **abbrev.** the Republic of Ireland (international vehicle registration).

**IRO** ● **abbrev.** **1** Inland Revenue Office. **2** International Refugee Organization.

**iroko** /ɪˈrəʊkəʊ, iː-/ ● **n.** (pl. **-os**) a tropical African hardwood tree producing pale wood. [*Chlorophora excelsa* and related species.]
– ORIGIN C19: from Yoruba.

**iron** ● **n.** **1** a strong, hard magnetic silvery-grey metal, the chemical element of atomic number 26, used in construction and manufacturing (especially as steel). (Symbol: **Fe**) **2** a tool or implement made of iron. ➤(**irons**) fetters or handcuffs. **3** a hand-held implement with a heated flat steel base, used to smooth clothes and linen. **4** a golf club with an angled metal head used for lofting the ball. ● **v.** **1** smooth (clothes) with an iron. **2** (**iron something out**) settle a difficulty or problem.
– PHRASES **have many** (or **other**) **irons in the fire** have a range of options or interests. **in irons** **1** having the feet or hands fettered. **2** Sailing stalled head to wind and unable to come about or tack either way. **an iron hand** (or **fist**) **in a velvet glove** firmness or ruthlessness cloaked in outward gentleness.
– DERIVATIVES **ironer** n. **ironware** n.
– ORIGIN OE *īren, īsen, īsern*, of Gmc origin.

**Iron Age** ● **n.** a prehistoric period that followed the Bronze Age, when weapons and tools came to be made of iron.

**ironbark** ● **n.** an Australian eucalyptus with thick, solid bark and hard, dense wood. [*Eucalyptus paniculata* (**grey ironbark**) and other species.]

**ironclad** ● **adj.** **1** covered or protected with iron. **2** impossible to weaken or change. ● **n.** a 19th-century warship with armour plating.

**Iron Curtain** ● **n.** (**the Iron Curtain**) a notional barrier separating the former Soviet bloc and the West prior to the decline of communism in eastern Europe in 1989.

**iron horse** ● **n.** archaic a steam railway locomotive.

**ironic** /ʌɪˈrɒnɪk/ ● **adj.** using or characterized by irony. ➤happening in the opposite way to what is expected.
– DERIVATIVES **ironical** adj. **ironically** adv.
– ORIGIN C17: from Fr. *ironique* or late L. *ironicus*, from Gk *eirōnikos* 'dissembling', from *eirōneia* (see **IRONY**[1]).

**ironing** ● **n.** clothes and linen that need to be or have just been ironed.

**ironing board** ● **n.** a long, narrow board having folding legs, on which clothes are ironed.

**ironist** /ˈʌɪr(ə)nɪst/ ● **n.** a person who uses irony.
– DERIVATIVES **ironize** (also **-ise**) v.

**iron lung** ● **n.** a rigid case fitted over a patient's body, used for administering prolonged artificial respiration by means of mechanical pumps.

**iron maiden** ● **n.** a former instrument of torture consisting of a coffin-shaped box lined with iron spikes.

**iron man** ● **n.** an exceptionally strong or robust man, especially a sportsman. ➤a multi-event sporting contest demanding stamina, in particular a consecutive triathlon of swimming, cycling, and running.

**ironmaster** ● **n.** a manufacturer of iron, especially (in former times) the proprietor of an ironworks.

**ironmonger** ● **n.** Brit. a retailer of tools and other hardware.
– DERIVATIVES **ironmongery** n. (pl. **-ies**).

**iron mould** (US **iron mold**) ● **n.** a spot caused by rust or an ink stain, especially on fabric.

**iron rations** ● **pl. n.** a small emergency supply of food.

**ironstone** ● **n. 1** sedimentary rock containing a substantial proportion of iron compounds. **2** a kind of dense, opaque stoneware.

**ironwood** ● **n.** a tree that produces very hard wood. [*Ostrya virginiana* (N. America) and other species.]

**ironwork** ● **n.** things made of iron.

**ironworks** ● **n.** [treated as sing. or pl.] a place where iron is smelted or iron goods are made.

**irony**[1] /ˈʌɪrəni/ ● **n.** (pl. **-ies**) the expression of meaning through the use of language signifying the opposite, typically for humorous effect. ➤a state of affairs that appears perversely contrary to what one expects. ➤(also **dramatic** or **tragic irony**) a literary technique, originally used in Greek tragedy, by which the significance of a character's words or actions are clear to the audience or reader although unknown to the character.
– ORIGIN C16: via L. from Gk *eirōneia* 'simulated ignorance', from *eirōn* 'dissembler'.

**irony**[2] /ˈʌɪəni/ ● **adj.** of or like iron.

**Iroquoian** ● **n.** a language family of eastern North America, including Cherokee and Mohawk. ● **adj.** of or relating to the Iroquois people or the Iroquoian language family.

**Iroquois** /ˈɪrəkwɔɪ, -kɔɪ/ ● **n.** (pl. same) **1** a member of a former confederacy of six American Indian peoples (Mohawk, Oneida, Seneca, Onondaga, Cayuga, and Tuscarora) who lived mainly in southern Ontario and Quebec and northern New York State. **2** any of the Iroquoian languages of these peoples.
– ORIGIN Fr., from an Algonquian lang.

**IRQ** ● **abbrev.** Iraq (international vehicle registration).

**irradiance** ● **n. 1** Physics the flux of radiant energy per unit area. **2** poetic/literary the fact of shining brightly.

**irradiant** ● **adj.** poetic/literary shining brightly.

**irradiate** ● **v. 1** expose to radiation. **2** shine light on.
– ORIGIN C16: from L. *irradiat-*, *irradiare* 'shine upon'.

**irradiation** ● **n. 1** the process or fact of irradiating or being irradiated. **2** Optics the apparent extension of the edges of an illuminated object seen against a dark background.

**irrational** ● **adj. 1** not logical or reasonable. **2** Mathematics (of a number or quantity) not expressible as a ratio of two integers (e.g. $\pi$).
– DERIVATIVES **irrationality** n. **irrationalize** (also **-ise**) v. **irrationally** adv.

**irrationalism** ● **n.** a system of belief or action that disregards rational principles.
– DERIVATIVES **irrationalist** n. & adj.

**irrebuttable** /ˌɪrɪˈbʌtəb(ə)l/ ● **adj.** unable to be rebutted.

**irreclaimable** ● **adj.** not able to be reclaimed.
– DERIVATIVES **irreclaimably** adv.

**irreconcilable** ● **adj. 1** (of ideas, facts, etc.) incompatible. **2** mutually and implacably hostile. ● **n.** any of two or more irreconcilable ideas, facts, etc.
– DERIVATIVES **irreconcilability** n. **irreconcilably** adv.

**irrecoverable** ● **adj.** not able to be recovered or remedied.
– DERIVATIVES **irrecoverably** adv.

**irrecusable** /ˌɪrɪˈkjuːzəb(ə)l/ ● **adj.** rare (of evidence or a statement) not able to be challenged or rejected.
– ORIGIN C18: via Fr. from late L. *irrecusabilis*, from *in-* 'not' + *recusabilis* 'that should be refused'.

**irredeemable** ● **adj. 1** not able to be saved, improved, or corrected. **2** (of securities) on which no date is given for repayment of the capital sum.
– DERIVATIVES **irredeemability** /-ˈbɪlɪti/ n. **irredeemably** adv.

**irredentist** /ˌɪrɪˈdɛntɪst/ ● **n.** (especially in 19th-century Italian politics) a person advocating the restoration to their country of any territory formerly belonging to it.
– DERIVATIVES **irredentism** n.
– ORIGIN from Ital. *irredentista*, from (*Italia*) *irredenta* 'unredeemed (Italy)'.

**irreducible** ● **adj.** not able to be reduced or simplified.
– DERIVATIVES **irreducibility** n. **irreducibly** adv.

**irrefragable** /ɪˈrɛfrəgəb(ə)l/ ● **adj.** indisputable.
– DERIVATIVES **irrefragably** adv.
– ORIGIN C16: from late L. *irrefragabilis*, from *in-* 'not' + *refragari* 'oppose'.

**irrefutable** /ɪˈrɛfjʊtəb(ə)l, ˌɪrɪˈfjuː-/ ● **adj.** impossible to deny or disprove.
– DERIVATIVES **irrefutability** n. **irrefutably** adv.

**irregardless** ● **adj. & adv.** informal regardless.
– ORIGIN C20: prob. a blend of **IRRESPECTIVE** and **REGARDLESS**.

**irregular** ● **adj. 1** not regular in shape, arrangement, or occurrence. **2** contrary to a rule, standard, or convention. ➤not belonging to regular army units. **3** Grammar (of a word) having inflections that do not conform to the usual rules. ● **n. 1** a member of an irregular military force. **2** chiefly N. Amer. an imperfect item of merchandise sold at a reduced price.
– DERIVATIVES **irregularity** n. (pl. **-ies**). **irregularly** adv.

**irrelative** ● **adj.** rare unconnected; unrelated.
– DERIVATIVES **irrelatively** adv.

**irrelevant** ● **adj.** not relevant.
– DERIVATIVES **irrelevance** n. **irrelevancy** n. (pl. **-ies**). **irrelevantly** adv.

**irreligious** ● **adj.** indifferent or hostile to religion.
– DERIVATIVES **irreligion** n. **irreligiously** adv. **irreligiousness** n.

**irremediable** /ˌɪrɪˈmiːdɪəb(ə)l/ ● **adj.** impossible to remedy.
– DERIVATIVES **irremediably** adv.

**irremissible** ● **adj.** rare **1** (of a crime) unpardonable. **2** (of an obligation or duty) binding.
– ORIGIN ME: from OFr., or from eccles. L. *irremissibilis*.

**irremovable** ● **adj.** incapable of being removed.
– DERIVATIVES **irremovability** n. **irremovably** adv.

**irreparable** /ɪˈrɛp(ə)rəb(ə)l/ ● **adj.** impossible to rectify or repair.
– DERIVATIVES **irreparability** /-ˈbɪlɪti/ n. **irreparably** adv.

**irreplaceable** ● **adj.** impossible to replace if lost or damaged.
– DERIVATIVES **irreplaceably** adv.

**irrepressible** ● **adj.** not able to be restrained.
– DERIVATIVES **irrepressibility** n. **irrepressibly** adv.

**irreproachable** ● **adj.** beyond criticism.
– DERIVATIVES **irreproachability** n. **irreproachably** adv.

**irresistible** ● **adj.** too tempting or powerful to be resisted.
– DERIVATIVES **irresistibility** n. **irresistibly** adv.

**irresolute** ● **adj.** uncertain.
– DERIVATIVES **irresolutely** adv. **irresoluteness** n. **irresolution** n.

**irresolvable** ● **adj.** (of a problem) impossible to solve.

**irrespective** ● **adj.** (**irrespective of**) regardless of.
– DERIVATIVES **irrespectively** adv.

**irresponsible** ● **adj.** not showing a proper sense of responsibility.
– DERIVATIVES **irresponsibility** n. **irresponsibly** adv.

**irresponsive** ● **adj.** not responsive.
– DERIVATIVES **irresponsiveness** n.

**irretrievable** ● **adj.** not able to be retrieved.
– DERIVATIVES **irretrievability** n. **irretrievably** adv.

**irreverent** /ɪˈrɛv(ə)r(ə)nt/ ● **adj.** disrespectful.
– DERIVATIVES **irreverence** n. **irreverential** adj. **irreverently** adv.

**irreversible** ● **adj.** impossible to be reversed or altered.
– DERIVATIVES **irreversibility** n. **irreversibly** adv.

**irrevocable** /ɪˈrɛvəkəb(ə)l/ ● **adj.** not able to be changed, reversed, or recovered.
– DERIVATIVES **irrevocability** n. **irrevocably** adv.
– ORIGIN ME: from OFr., or from L. *irrevocabilis*.

**irrigate** /ˈɪrɪgeɪt/ ● **v. 1** supply water to (land or crops) by means of channels. ➤(of a river or stream) supply (land) with water. **2** Medicine apply a flow of water or medication to (an organ or wound).
– DERIVATIVES **irrigable** adj. **irrigation** n. **irrigator** n.
– ORIGIN C17: from L. *irrigat-*, *irrigare* 'moisten'.

**irritable** ● **adj. 1** easily annoyed or angered. **2** Medicine

characterized by abnormal sensitivity. **3** Biology able to respond actively to physical stimuli.
– DERIVATIVES **irritability** n. **irritableness** n. **irritably** adv.

**irritable bowel syndrome** ● **n.** a condition involving recurrent abdominal pain and diarrhoea or constipation, often associated with stress or previous infection.

**irritant** ● **n.** a substance that irritates part of the body. ➤a source of continual annoyance. ● **adj.** causing irritation to the body.
– DERIVATIVES **irritancy** n.

**irritate** ● **v. 1** make annoyed or angry. **2** cause inflammation in (a part of the body). **3** Biology stimulate (an organism, cell, etc.) to produce an active response.
– DERIVATIVES **irritated** adj. **irritatedly** adv. **irritating** adj. **irritatingly** adv. **irritation** n. **irritative** adj. **irritator** n.
– ORIGIN C16 (earlier (ME) as *irritation*), in sense 'excite, provoke': from L. *irritat-*, *irritare* 'irritate'.

**irrupt** /ɪ'rʌpt/ ● **v. 1** enter forcibly or suddenly. **2** (chiefly of a bird) migrate into an area in abnormally large numbers.
– DERIVATIVES **irruption** n. **irruptive** adj.
– ORIGIN C19 (earlier (C16) as *irruption*): from L. *irrupt-*, *irrumpere* 'break into'.

**IRS** ● **abbrev.** Internal Revenue Service.

**IS** ● **abbrev.** Iceland (international vehicle registration).
– ORIGIN from Icelandic *Ísland*.

**Is.** ● **abbrev. 1** (also **Isa.**) Isaiah (in biblical references). **2** Island(s). **3** Isle(s).

**is** third person singular present of **BE**.

**ISA** ● **abbrev. 1** individual savings account. **2** Computing industry standard architecture.

**isagogics** /ˌʌɪsə'gɒdʒɪks/ ● **pl. n.** [treated as sing.] introductory study, especially of the literary and external history of the Bible prior to exegesis.
– DERIVATIVES **isagogic** adj.
– ORIGIN C19: pl. of *isagogic*, via L. from Gk *eisagōgikos*, from *eisagōgē* 'introduction'.

**isatin** /'ʌɪsətɪn/ ● **n.** Chemistry a red crystalline compound used in dye manufacture.
– ORIGIN C19: from L. *isatis* 'woad' + **-IN**[1].

**ISBN** ● **abbrev.** international standard book number.

**ischaemia** /ɪ'skiːmɪə/ (US **ischemia**) ● **n.** Medicine an inadequate blood supply to a part of the body, especially the heart muscles.
– DERIVATIVES **ischaemic** adj.
– ORIGIN C19 (denoting the staunching of bleeding): mod. L., from Gk *iskhaimos* 'stopping blood'.

**ischium** /'ɪskɪəm/ ● **n.** (pl. **ischia** /-kɪə/) the curved bone forming the base of each half of the pelvis.
– DERIVATIVES **ischial** adj.
– ORIGIN C17: from L., from Gk *iskhion* 'hip joint', later 'ischium'.

**ISDN** ● **abbrev.** integrated services digital network.

**-ise**[1] ● **suffix** variant spelling of **-IZE**.

**USAGE -ise**

There are some verbs which must be spelled **-ise** and are not variants of the **-ize** ending. Most reflect a French influence; they include **advertise, televise, compromise,** and **improvise**. See also **-IZE**.

**-ise**[2] ● **suffix** forming nouns of quality, state, or function: *expertise*.
– ORIGIN from OFr. *-ise*, from L. *-itia*, *-itium*.

**isentropic** /ˌʌɪsɛn'trɒpɪk/ ● **adj.** Physics having equal entropy.
– ORIGIN from **ISO-** + **ENTROPIC**.

**-ish**[1] ● **suffix** forming adjectives: **1** (from nouns) having the qualities or characteristics of: *girlish*. ➤of the nationality of: *Swedish*. **2** (from adjectives) somewhat: *yellowish*. ➤informal denoting an approximate age or time of day: *sixish*.
– ORIGIN OE *-isc*, of Gmc origin.

**-ish**[2] ● **suffix** forming verbs such as *abolish*.
– ORIGIN from Fr. *-iss-* (from stems of verbs ending in *-ir*), from L. *-isc-* (suffix forming inceptive verbs).

**Ishmaelite** /'ɪʃməˌlʌɪt/ ● **n.** a descendant of Ishmael, a son of Abraham and Hagar (Gen. 16:12), and in Islamic belief the traditional ancestor of Muhammad and of the Arab peoples.

**isinglass** /'ʌɪzɪŋˌglɑːs/ ● **n. 1** a kind of gelatin obtained from fish, especially sturgeon. **2** chiefly US mica or a similar material in thin transparent sheets.
– ORIGIN C16: alt. (by assoc. with **GLASS**) of obs. Du. *huysenblas* 'sturgeon's bladder'.

**Islam** /'ɪzlɑːm, ɪz'lɑːm, -lam/ ● **n.** the religion of the Muslims, a monotheistic faith regarded as revealed through Muhammad as the Prophet of Allah. ➤the Muslim world.
– DERIVATIVES **Islamism** n. **Islamist** n. **Islamization** (also **-isation**) n. **Islamize** (also **-ise**) v.
– ORIGIN from Arab. *'islām* 'submission', from *'aslama* 'submit (to God)'.

**Islamic** /ɪz'lamɪk, ɪz'lɑːmɪk/ ● **adj.** of or relating to Islam.
– DERIVATIVES **Islamicization** (also **isation**) n. **Islamicize** (also **-ise**) v.

**island** ● **n. 1** a piece of land surrounded by water. **2** a thing that is isolated, detached, or surrounded. ➤Anatomy a detached portion of tissue or group of cells. Compare with **ISLET**.
– DERIVATIVES **islander** n.
– ORIGIN OE *īegland*, from *īeg* 'island' (from a base meaning 'watery') + **LAND**; spelling influenced by **ISLE**.

**isle** ● **n.** poetic/literary (except in place names) an island.
– ORIGIN ME *ile*, from OFr., from L. *insula*.

**islet** /'ʌɪlɪt/ ● **n. 1** a small island. **2** Anatomy a portion of tissue structurally distinct from its surroundings. Compare with **ISLAND**.
– ORIGIN C16: from OFr., dimin. of *isle* (see **ISLE**).

**islets of Langerhans** /'laŋəhanz/ ● **pl. n.** groups of pancreatic cells secreting insulin and glucagon.
– ORIGIN C19: named after the Ger. anatomist Paul *Langerhans*.

**ism** /'ɪz(ə)m/ ● **n.** informal, chiefly derogatory an unspecified system, philosophy, or ideological movement.
– ORIGIN C17: independent usage of **-ISM**.

**-ism** ● **suffix** forming nouns: **1** denoting an action or its result: *baptism*. ➤denoting a state or quality: *barbarism*. **2** denoting a system, principle, or ideological movement: *Anglicanism*. ➤denoting a basis for prejudice or discrimination: *racism*. **3** denoting a peculiarity in language: *colloquialism*. **4** denoting a pathological condition: *alcoholism*.
– ORIGIN from Fr. *-isme*, via L. from Gk *-ismos*, *-isma*.

**Ismaili** /ˌɪsmʌɪ'iːli, ˌɪsmɑː-/ ● **n.** (pl. **Ismailis**) a member of a Shiite Muslim sect believing that Ismail, the son of the sixth Shiite imam, should have become the seventh imam.

**Isnik** ● **adj.** variant spelling of **IZNIK**.

**isn't** ● **contr.** is not.

**ISO** ● **abbrev. 1** historical Imperial Service Order. **2** International Organization for Standardization. [from Gk *isos* 'equal'; the term is technically not an abbrev.]

**iso-** ● **comb. form 1** equal: *isosceles*. **2** Chemistry (chiefly of hydrocarbons) isomeric: *isooctane*.
– ORIGIN from Gk *isos* 'equal'.

**isobar** /'ʌɪsə(ʊ)bɑː/ ● **n. 1** Meteorology a line on a map connecting points having the same atmospheric pressure. **2** Physics each of two or more isotopes of different elements, with the same atomic weight.
– DERIVATIVES **isobaric** adj.
– ORIGIN C19: from Gk *isobaros* 'of equal weight'.

**isobutylene** ● **n.** Chemistry an easily liquefied hydrocarbon gas used in the making of butyl rubber. [$C_4H_8$.]

**isocheim** /'ʌɪsə(ʊ)kʌɪm/ ● **n.** Meteorology a line on a map connecting points having the same average temperature in winter.
– ORIGIN C19: from **ISO-** + Gk *kheima* 'winter weather'.

**isochromatic** /ˌʌɪsə(ʊ)krə'matɪk/ ● **adj.** of a single colour.

**isochron** /'ʌɪsə(ʊ)krɒn/ ● **n.** chiefly Geology a line on a diagram or map connecting points relating to the same time or equal times.

**isochronous** /ʌɪˈsɒkrənəs/ ● **adj.** **1** occurring at the same time. **2** occupying equal time.
– DERIVATIVES **isochronously** adv.
– ORIGIN C18: from mod. L. *isochronus* (from Gk *isokhronos*, from *isos* 'equal' + *khronos* 'time') + **-OUS**.

**isoclinal** /ˌʌɪsə(ʊ)ˈklʌɪn(ə)l/ ● **adj.** Geology denoting a fold in which the two limbs are parallel.
– ORIGIN C19: from **ISO-** + Gk *klinein* 'to lean' + **-AL**.

**isoclinic** /ʌɪsə(ʊ)ˈklɪnɪk/ ● **adj.** Geography denoting a line on a map connecting points where the dip of the earth's magnetic field is the same.

**isocyanide** ● **n.** Chemistry an organic compound containing the group –NC.

**isodynamic** ● **adj.** Geography denoting a line on a map connecting points where the intensity of the magnetic force is the same.

**isoelectric** ● **adj.** having or involving no net electric charge or potential difference.

**isoelectric focusing** ● **n.** Biochemistry a technique of electrophoresis in which the resolution is improved by maintaining a pH gradient between the electrodes.

**isoelectronic** ● **adj.** Chemistry having the same numbers of electrons or the same electronic structure.

**isoenzyme** ● **n.** Biochemistry each of two or more enzymes with identical function but different structure.

**isogamy** /ʌɪˈsɒgəmi/ ● **n.** Biology sexual reproduction by the fusion of similar gametes. Compare with **ANISOGAMY**.
– DERIVATIVES **isogamete** n. **isogamous** adj.
– ORIGIN C19: from **ISO-** + Gk *gamos* 'marriage'.

**isogeotherm** /ˌʌɪsə(ʊ)ˈdʒiːə(ʊ)θəːm/ ● **n.** Geography a line or surface on a diagram of the earth's interior connecting points having the same temperature.
– DERIVATIVES **isogeothermal** adj.
– ORIGIN C19: from **ISO-** + **GEO-** + Gk *thermē* 'heat'.

**isogloss** /ˈʌɪsə(ʊ)glɒs/ ● **n.** Linguistics a line on a map marking an area having a distinct linguistic feature.
– ORIGIN C20: from **ISO-** + Gk *glōssa* 'tongue, word'.

**isogonic** /ˌʌɪsə(ʊ)ˈgɒnɪk/ ● **adj.** Geography denoting a line on a map connecting points at which the magnetic declination is the same.
– ORIGIN C19: from Gk *isogōnios* 'equiangular' + **-IC**.

**isohel** /ˈʌɪsə(ʊ)hɛl/ ● **n.** Meteorology a line on a map connecting points having the same duration of sunshine.
– ORIGIN C20: from **ISO-** + Gk *hēlios* 'sun'.

**isohyet** /ˌʌɪsə(ʊ)ˈhʌɪɪt/ ● **n.** Meteorology a line on a map connecting points having the same amount of rainfall.
– ORIGIN C19: from **ISO-** + Gk *huetos* 'rain'.

**isokinetic** /ˌʌɪsə(ʊ)kɪˈnɛtɪk/ ● **adj.** characterized by or producing a constant speed or rate.

**isolate** ● **v.** **1** place apart or alone; cut off. ➤place in quarantine. **2** Chemistry & Biology obtain or extract (a compound, micro-organism, etc.) in a pure form. **3** cut off the electrical or other connection to (a part of a network). ● **n.** a person or thing that has become isolated.
– DERIVATIVES **isolable** adj. **isolatable** adj. **isolator** n.
– ORIGIN C19: back-form. from **ISOLATED**.

**isolated** ● **adj.** **1** remote; lonely. **2** single; exceptional.
– ORIGIN C18: from Fr. *isolé*, from Ital. *isolato*, from late L. *insulatus* 'made into an island', based on L. *insula* 'island'.

**isolating** ● **adj.** (of a language) tending to have each element as an independent word without inflections.

**isolation** ● **n.** the process or fact of isolating or being isolated.
– PHRASES **in isolation** without relation to others; separately.

**isolationism** ● **n.** a policy of remaining apart from the political affairs of other countries.
– DERIVATIVES **isolationist** n.

**isoleucine** /ˌʌɪsə(ʊ)ˈluːsiːn/ ● **n.** Biochemistry a hydrophobic amino acid that is a constituent of most proteins and is an essential nutrient in the diet.

**isomer** /ˈʌɪsəmə/ ● **n.** **1** Chemistry each of two or more compounds with the same formula but a different arrangement of atoms in the molecule and different properties. **2** Physics each of two or more atomic nuclei with the same atomic number and mass number but different energy states.
– DERIVATIVES **isomeric** adj. **isomerism** n. **isomerize** (also **-ise**) v.
– ORIGIN C19: from Gk *isomerēs* 'sharing equally', from *isos* 'equal' + *meros* 'a share'.

**isomerase** /ʌɪˈsɒməreɪz/ ● **n.** Biochemistry an enzyme which promotes the conversion of a specified compound to an isomer.

**isomerous** /ʌɪˈsɒm(ə)rəs/ ● **adj.** Biology having parts that are similar in number or position.

**isometric** ● **adj.** **1** of or having equal dimensions. **2** Physiology (of muscular action) in which tension is developed without contraction. **3** denoting a method of perspective drawing in which the three principal dimensions are represented by three axes 120° apart. **4** Mathematics (of a transformation) without change of shape or size.
– DERIVATIVES **isometrically** adv. **isometry** n.
– ORIGIN C19: from Gk *isometria* 'equality of measure' (from *isos* 'equal' + *-metria* 'measuring') + **-IC**.

**isometrics** ● **pl. n.** a system of physical exercises in which muscles are caused to act against each other or against a fixed object.

**isomorphic** /ˌʌɪsə(ʊ)ˈmɔːfɪk/ ● **adj.** corresponding or similar in form and relations.
– DERIVATIVES **isomorphism** n. **isomorphous** adj.

**-ison** ● **suffix** (forming nouns) equivalent to **-ATION** (as in *comparison*).
– ORIGIN from OFr. *-aison*, *-eison*, etc., from L. *-atio(n)-*.

**isoniazid** /ˌʌɪsə(ʊ)ˈnʌɪəzɪd/ ● **n.** Medicine a synthetic compound used as a bacteriostatic drug, chiefly to treat tuberculosis.
– ORIGIN 1950s: from **ISO-** + *ni(cotinic acid)* + *(hydr)azine* + **-IDE**.

**isooctane** /ˌʌɪsəʊˈɒkteɪn/ ● **n.** Chemistry a liquid hydrocarbon present in petroleum, used as a standard in the system of octane numbers.

**isophote** /ˈʌɪsə(ʊ)fəʊt/ ● **n.** a line on a diagram connecting points where the intensity of light is the same.
– ORIGIN C20: from **ISO-** + Gk *phōs, phōt-* 'light'.

**isopleth** /ˈʌɪsə(ʊ)plɛθ/ ● **n.** Meteorology a line on a map connecting points having equal incidence of a specified feature.
– ORIGIN C20: from Gk *isoplēthēs* 'equal in quantity', from Gk *isos* 'equal' + *plēthos* 'multitude, quantity'.

**Isopoda** /ˌʌɪsəˈpəʊdə/ ● **pl. n.** Zoology an order of crustaceans that includes the woodlice and many aquatic forms.
– DERIVATIVES **isopod** n.
– ORIGIN mod. L., from Gk *isos* 'equal' + *pous, pod-* 'foot'.

**isoprene** /ˈʌɪsə(ʊ)priːn/ ● **n.** Chemistry a volatile liquid hydrocarbon whose molecule forms the basic structural unit of rubber.
– ORIGIN C19: appar. from **ISO-** + *pr(opyl)ene*.

**isopropanol** /ˌʌɪsə(ʊ)ˈprəʊpənɒl/ ● **n.** Chemistry an alcohol used as a solvent and in the industrial production of acetone.

**isopropyl** /ˌʌɪsəʊˈprəʊpʌɪl, -pɪl/ ● **n.** [as modifier] Chemistry of or denoting the alkyl radical $-CH(CH_3)_2$, derived from propane.

**isopropyl alcohol** ● **n.** Chemistry another term for **ISOPROPANOL**.

**isoproterenol** /ˌʌɪsə(ʊ)prəʊtəˈriːnɒl/ ● **n.** Medicine a synthetic derivative of adrenalin, used for the relief of bronchial asthma and pulmonary emphysema.
– ORIGIN 1950s: from elements of the semi-systematic name *N-isopropylarterenol*.

**isosceles** /ʌɪˈsɒsɪliːz/ ● **adj.** (of a triangle) having two sides of equal length.
– ORIGIN C16: via late L. from Gk *isoskelēs*, from *isos* 'equal' + *skelos* 'leg'.

**isoseismal** /ˌʌɪsə(ʊ)ˈsʌɪzm(ə)l/ ● **adj.** Geology denoting a line on a map connecting places where an earthquake was experienced with equal strength.
– DERIVATIVES **isoseismic** adj.

**isospin** /ˈʌɪsə(ʊ)spɪn/ ● **n.** Physics a quantum number assigned to subatomic particles, such that similar particles differing only in charge-related properties (independent

of the strong interaction) can be treated as different states of a single particle.
– ORIGIN 1960s: contr. of *isotopic spin, isobaric spin.*

**isostasy** /ʌɪ'sɒstəsi/ • **n.** Geology the equilibrium that exists between parts of the earth's crust, which rise if material (such as an ice cap) is removed and sink if material is deposited.
– DERIVATIVES **isostatic** adj.
– ORIGIN C19: from **ISO-** + Gk *stasis* 'station'.

**isothere** /'ʌɪsə(ʊ)θɪə/ • **n.** Meteorology a line on a map connecting points having the same average temperature in summer.
– ORIGIN C19: from Fr. *isothère*, from Gk *isos* 'equal' + *theros* 'summer'.

**isotherm** /'ʌɪsə(ʊ)θə:m/ • **n.** a line on a map or diagram connecting points having the same temperature.
– DERIVATIVES **isothermal** adj. & n. **isothermally** adv.
– ORIGIN C19: from Fr. *isotherme*, from Gk *isos* 'equal' + *thermē* 'heat'.

**isotonic** /ˌʌɪsə(ʊ)'tɒnɪk/ • **adj.** **1** Physiology (of muscle action) taking place with normal contraction. **2** Physiology having the same osmotic pressure. **3** (of a drink) containing essential salts and minerals in the same concentration as in the body.
– DERIVATIVES **isotonically** adv. **isotonicity** n.
– ORIGIN C19: from Gk *isotonos*, from *isos* 'equal' + *tonos* 'tone'.

**isotope** /'ʌɪsətəʊp/ • **n.** Chemistry each of two or more forms of the same element that contain equal numbers of protons but different numbers of neutrons in their nuclei.
– DERIVATIVES **isotopic** adj. **isotopically** adv. **isotopy** n.
– ORIGIN 1913: from **ISO-** + Gk *topos* 'place' (because the isotopes occupy the same place in the periodic table).

**isotropic** /ˌʌɪsə(ʊ)'trɒpɪk/ • **adj.** Physics having the same magnitude or properties when measured in different directions.
– DERIVATIVES **isotropically** adv. **isotropy** /ʌɪ'sɒtrəpi/ n.
– ORIGIN C19: from **ISO-** + Gk *tropos* 'a turn' + **-IC**.

**isozyme** /'ʌɪsə(ʊ)zʌɪm/ • **n.** Biochemistry another term for **ISOENZYME**.

**ISP** • **abbrev.** Internet service provider.

**ispaghul** /'ɪspəgu:l/ (also **ispaghula** /ˌɪspə'gu:lə/) • **n.** the dried seeds of an Asian plantain, used medicinally in the treatment of dysentery.
– ORIGIN C19: from Pers. and Urdu *ispağol*, from *asp* 'horse' + *ğol* 'ear' (because of the shape of the leaves).

**Israeli** /ɪz'reɪli/ • **n.** (pl. **Israelis**) a native or national of Israel, or a person of Israeli descent. • **adj.** of or relating to the modern country of Israel.

**Israelite** /'ɪzrəlʌɪt/ • **n.** a member of the ancient Hebrew nation. ➤ old-fashioned and sometimes offensive term for **JEW**. • **adj.** of or relating to the Israelites.

**Issa** /'i:sɑ:/ • **n.** (pl. same or **Issas**) a member of a Somali people living in the Republic of Djibouti.
– ORIGIN the name in Somali.

**issei** /'i:seɪ/ • **n.** (pl. same) N. Amer. a Japanese immigrant to North America. Compare with **NISEI** and **SANSEI**.
– ORIGIN Japanese, lit. 'generation'.

**ISSN** • **abbrev.** international standard serial number.

**issuant** /'ɪʃ(j)ʊənt, 'ɪsjʊ-/ • **adj.** Heraldry (of the upper part of an animal) shown rising up or out from another bearing.

**issue** /'ɪʃ(j)u:, 'ɪsju:/ • **n.** **1** an important topic for debate or resolution. **2** the action of issuing. **3** each of a regular series of publications. ➤ a number or set of items issued at one time. **4** formal or Law children of one's own. **5** dated a result or outcome. • **v.** (**issues, issued, issuing**) **1** supply or distribute for use or sale. ➤ (**issue someone with**) supply someone with. ➤ formally send out or make known. **2** (**issue from**) come, go, or flow out from.
– PHRASES **at issue** under discussion. **make an issue of** treat too seriously or as a problem. **take issue with** challenge.
– DERIVATIVES **issuable** adj. **issuance** n. **issueless** adj. **issuer** n.
– ORIGIN ME (in the sense 'outflowing'): from OFr., based on L. *exit-*, *exire* 'go out'.

**issue of fact** • **n.** Law a dispute in court in which the significance of a fact or facts is denied.

**issue of law** • **n.** Law a dispute in court in which the application of the law is contested.

**-ist** • **suffix** forming personal nouns and some related adjectives: **1** denoting an adherent of a system of beliefs expressed by nouns ending in *-ism*: *hedonist.* ➤ denoting a person who subscribes to a prejudice or practises discrimination: *sexist.* **2** denoting a member of a profession or business activity: *dentist.* ➤ denoting a person who uses something: *flautist.* ➤ denoting a person who does something expressed by a verb ending in *-ize*: *plagiarist.*
– ORIGIN from OFr. *-iste*, L. *-ista*, from Gk *-istēs*.

**isthmian** /'ɪsθmɪən, 'ɪstm-, 'ɪsm-/ • **adj.** of or relating to an isthmus.

**isthmus** /'ɪsθməs, 'ɪstməs, 'ɪsməs/ • **n.** **1** (pl. **isthmuses**) a narrow strip of land with sea on either side, linking two larger areas of land. **2** (pl. **isthmi**) Anatomy a narrow organ or other part connecting two larger parts.
– ORIGIN C16: via L. from Gk *isthmos*.

**ISV** • **abbrev.** independent software vendor.

**IT** • **abbrev.** information technology.

**it**[1] • **pron.** [third person sing.] **1** used to refer to a thing previously mentioned or easily identified. ➤ referring to an animal or child of unspecified sex. **2** used to identify a person. **3** used in the normal subject position in statements about time, distance, or weather. **4** used in the normal subject or object position when a more specific subject or object is given later in the sentence. **5** used to emphasize a following part of a sentence. **6** the situation or circumstances. **7** exactly what is needed or desired. **8** informal sexual intercourse or sex appeal. **9** (in children's games) the player who has to catch the others.
– PHRASES **that's it 1** that is the main point or difficulty. **2** that is enough. **this is it** the expected event is about to happen.
– ORIGIN OE *hit*, neut. of **HE**, of Gmc origin.

**it**[2] • **n.** Brit. informal, dated Italian vermouth.

**ITA** • **abbrev.** initial teaching alphabet.

**ital** /'ɪtal/ • **n.** (in Rastafarian culture) organically grown vegetarian food, cooked without salt.
– ORIGIN from *I* (used by Rastafarians to signify value) + **VITAL** or **VITTLE**.

**ital.** • **abbrev.** italic.

**Italian** • **n.** **1** a native or national of Italy, or a person of Italian descent. **2** the Romance language of Italy, descended from Latin. • **adj.** of or relating to Italy, its people, or their language.
– DERIVATIVES **Italianize** (also **-ise**) v.

**Italianate** • **adj.** Italian in character or appearance.
– ORIGIN C16: from Ital. *italianato*.

**Italianism** • **n.** **1** an Italian characteristic, expression, or custom. **2** attachment to Italy or Italian ideas or practices.

**Italian vermouth** • **n.** a type of bitter-sweet vermouth made in Italy.

**Italic** /ɪ'talɪk/ • **n.** the branch of Indo-European languages that includes Latin and the Romance languages. • **adj.** relating to or denoting the Italic group of languages.
– ORIGIN C19: via L. from Gk *Italikos* (see **ITALIC**).

**italic** /ɪ'talɪk/ • **adj.** Printing of the sloping kind of typeface used especially for emphasis and in foreign words. ➤ (of handwriting) cursive and sloping and with elliptical or pointed letters, in the style of 16th-century Italian handwriting. • **n.** (also **italics**) an italic typeface or letter.
– DERIVATIVES **italicization** (also **-isation**) n. **italicize** (also **-ise**) v.
– ORIGIN ME (in the general sense 'Italian'): via L. from Gk *Italikos*, from *Italia* 'Italy'.

**Italiot** /ɪ'talɪət/ • **n.** an inhabitant of any of the Greek colonies in ancient Italy. • **adj.** of or relating to these people.
– ORIGIN from Gk *Italiōtēs*, from *Italia* 'Italy'.

**Italo-** /'ɪtələʊ, ɪ'taləʊ/ • **comb. form** Italian; Italian and ...: *Italophile.*

**ITC** • **abbrev.** Independent Television Commission.

## Word *Formation*

**-itis** denoting an inflammatory disease

In Greek, **-itis** is the feminine form of adjectives ending in *itēs*, and was already used in Greek forms with the noun *nosos* 'disease' understood, even though not expressed.

➤ There are many common words in English formed with **-itis**:

| | | |
|---|---|---|
| appendicitis | inflammation of the appendix | based on APPENDIX |
| arthritis | disease causing inflammation of joints | Gk *arthron* 'joint' |
| bronchitis | inflammation of the bronchial tubes | Gk *bronkhos* 'windpipe' |
| bursitis | inflammation of a bursa | based on BURSA |
| cystitis | inflammation of the urinary bladder | Gk *kustis* 'bladder' |
| encephalomyelitis | inflammation of the brain and spinal cord | Gk *enkephalos* 'brain' + *muelos* 'marrow' |
| gastro-enteritis | inflammation of the stomach and intestine | Gk *gaster*, *gastr-* 'stomach' + *enteron* 'intestine' |
| hepatitis | disease causing inflammation of the liver | Gk *hēpar*, *hēpat-*, 'liver' |
| laryngitis | inflammation of the larynx | based on LARYNX |
| meningitis | disease causing inflammation of the meninges | MENINGES: Gk *mēninx*, *mēning-* 'membrane' |

The form **-itis** is also used in the humorous coinage of words with the sense 'a particular state of mind or tendency seen as a disease' e.g. ***electionitis*** (used in 1945 by Winston Churchill); ***media-itis***; ***phone-itis***.

**itch** ● **n.** **1** an uncomfortable sensation or condition that causes a desire to scratch the skin. **2** informal an impatient desire. ● **v.** **1** be the site of or experience an itch. **2** informal feel an impatient desire to do something.
– PHRASES **an itching palm** an avaricious nature.
– ORIGIN OE *gycce* (n.), *gyccan* (v.), of W. Gmc origin.

**itching powder** ● **n.** a powder used to make someone's skin itch, typically as a practical joke.

**itch mite** ● **n.** a parasitic mite which burrows under the skin, causing scabies or (in animals) sarcoptic mange. [*Sarcoptes scabiei*.]

**itchy** ● **adj.** (**-ier**, **-iest**) having or causing an itch.
– PHRASES **get** (or **have**) **itchy feet** informal have or develop a strong urge to travel.
– DERIVATIVES **itchiness** n.

**it'd** ● **contr.** **1** it had. **2** it would.

**-ite**[1] ● **suffix** **1** forming names denoting natives of a country: *Israelite*. ➤ often derogatory denoting followers of a movement: *Luddite*. **2** used in scientific and technical terms: ➤ forming names of minerals or fossil organisms: *ammonite*. ➤ forming names of constituent parts of a body or organ: *somite*. ➤ forming names of explosives and other commercial products: *dynamite*. ➤ Chemistry forming names of salts or esters of acids ending in *-ous*: *sulphite*.
– ORIGIN from Fr. *-ite*, via L. *-ita* from Gk *-ītes*.

**-ite**[2] ● **suffix** **1** forming adjectives such as *composite*. **2** forming nouns such as *appetite*. **3** forming verbs such as *unite*.
– ORIGIN from L. *-itus*, past part. of verbs ending in *-ere* and *-ire*.

**item** ● **n.** an individual article or unit. ➤ a piece of news or information. ➤ an entry in an account. ● **adv.** archaic (used to introduce each item in a list) also.
– PHRASES **be an item** informal (of a couple) be in a romantic or sexual relationship.
– ORIGIN ME (as adv.): from L., 'in like manner, also'.

**itemize** (also **-ise**) ● **v.** present as a list of individual items or parts.
– DERIVATIVES **itemization** /-ˈzeɪʃ(ə)n/ n. **itemizer** n.

**iterate** /ˈɪtəreɪt/ ● **v.** **1** perform or utter repeatedly. **2** make repeated use of a mathematical or computational procedure, applying it each time to the result of the previous application.
– DERIVATIVES **iteration** n.
– ORIGIN C16 (ME as *iteration*): from L. *iterat-*, *iterare* 'repeat'.

**iterative** ● **adj.** **1** relating to or involving iteration, especially of a mathematical or computational process. **2** Grammar another term for **FREQUENTATIVE**.
– DERIVATIVES **iteratively** adv.

**ithyphallic** /ˌɪθɪˈfalɪk/ ● **adj.** (especially of a statue) having an erect penis.
– ORIGIN C17 (as a noun denoting a sexually explicit poem): via late L. from Gk *ithuphallikos*, from *ithus* 'straight' + *phallos* 'phallus'.

**Iti** ● **n.** (pl. **Ities**) & **adj.** variant spelling of **EYETIE**.

**-itic** ● **suffix** forming adjectives and nouns corresponding to nouns ending in *-ite* (such as *Semitic* corresponding to *Semite*). ➤ corresponding to nouns ending in *-itis* (such as *arthritic* corresponding to *arthritis*). ➤ from other bases: *syphilitic*.
– ORIGIN from Fr. *-itique*, via L. *-iticus* from Gk *-itikos*.

**itinerant** /ɪˈtɪn(ə)r(ə)nt, ʌɪ-/ ● **adj.** travelling from place to place. ● **n.** an itinerant person.
– DERIVATIVES **itineracy** n. **itinerancy** n.
– ORIGIN C16: from late L. *itinerant-*, *itinerari* 'travel'.

**itinerary** /ʌɪˈtɪn(ə)(rə)ri, ɪ-/ ● **n.** (pl. **-ies**) a planned route or journey. ➤ a travel document recording this.
– ORIGIN ME: from late L. *itinerarium*, neut. of *itinerarius* 'of a journey or roads', from L. *iter*, *itiner-* 'journey, road'.

**itinerate** /ɪˈtɪnəreɪt, ʌɪ-/ ● **v.** (especially of a Church minister or a magistrate) travel from place to place to perform one's professional duty.
– DERIVATIVES **itineration** n.
– ORIGIN C17: from late L. *itinerat-*, *itinerari* 'travel'.

**-ition** ● **suffix** (forming nouns) equivalent to **-ATION** (as in *audition*).
– ORIGIN from Fr., or from L. *-itio(n)-*.

**-itious**[1] ● **suffix** forming adjectives corresponding to nouns ending in *-ition* (such as *ambitious* corresponding to *ambition*).
– ORIGIN from L. *-itiosus*.

**-itious**[2] ● **suffix** (forming adjectives) related to; having the nature of: *fictitious*.
– ORIGIN from late L. *-itius*, alt. of L. *-icius*.

**-itis** ● **suffix** forming names of inflammatory diseases: *cystitis*. See word-formation panel.
– ORIGIN from Gk fem. form of adjectives ending in *-itēs* (combined with *nosos* 'disease' implied).

**-itive** ● **suffix** (forming adjectives) equivalent to **-ATIVE** (as in *positive*).

– ORIGIN from Fr. *-itif, -itive* or L. *-itivus* (from past participial stems ending in *-it*).

**it'll** • **contr.** **1** it shall. **2** it will.

**-itous** • **suffix** forming adjectives corresponding to nouns ending in *-ity* (such as *calamitous* corresponding to *calamity*).

– ORIGIN from Fr. *-iteux*, from L. *-itosus*.

**its** • **possess. det.** belonging to or associated with a thing previously mentioned or easily identified. ➤ belonging to or associated with a child or animal of unspecified sex.

**it's** • **contr.** **1** it is. **2** it has.

**itself** • **pron.** [third person sing.] **1** [reflexive] used as the object of a verb or preposition to refer to a thing or animal previously mentioned as the subject of the clause. **2** [emphatic] used to emphasize a particular thing or animal mentioned. ➤ used to emphasize what a perfect example of a particular quality someone or something is.

– PHRASES **in itself** viewed in its essential qualities.

**itsy-bitsy** (also **itty-bitty**) • **adj.** informal very small.

– ORIGIN 1930s: from a child's form of **LITTLE** + *bitsy* (from **BIT**[1] + **-SY**).

**ITU** • **abbrev.** International Telecommunication Union.

**ITV** • **abbrev.** Independent Television.

**-ity** • **suffix** forming nouns denoting quality or condition: *humility.* ➤ denoting an instance or degree of this: *a profanity.*

– ORIGIN from Fr. *-ité*, from L. *-itas, -itatis*.

**IU** • **abbrev.** international unit.

**IUD** • **abbrev.** **1** intrauterine death (of the fetus before birth). **2** intrauterine device.

**-ium** • **suffix** **1** forming nouns adopted unchanged from Latin (such as *alluvium*) or based on Latin or Greek words (such as *euphonium*). **2** (also **-um**) forming names of metallic elements: *cadmium.* **3** denoting a region of the body: *pericardium.* **4** denoting a biological structure: *mycelium.*

– ORIGIN mod. L. in senses 2, 3, and 4, via L. from Gk *-ion*.

**IUPAC** • **abbrev.** International Union of Pure and Applied Chemistry.

**IV** • **abbrev.** intravenous or intravenously.

**I've** • **contr.** I have.

**-ive** • **suffix** (forming adjectives, also nouns derived from them) tending to; having the nature of: *palliative.*

– DERIVATIVES **-ively** suffix forming corresponding adverbs. **-iveness** suffix forming corresponding nouns.

– ORIGIN from Fr. *-if, -ive*, from L. *-ivus*.

**ivermectin** /ˌʌɪvəˈmɛktɪn/ • **n.** a compound of the avermectin group, used as an anthelmintic in veterinary medicine and as a treatment for river blindness.

– ORIGIN 1980s: from *i* + **AVERMECTIN**.

**IVF** • **abbrev.** in vitro fertilization.

**ivied** • **adj.** **1** covered in ivy. **2** US of or relating to the academic institutions of the Ivy League.

**Ivorian** /ʌɪˈvɔːrɪən/ • **n.** a person from the Ivory Coast, a country in West Africa. • **adj.** relating to the Ivory Coast.

**ivory** • **n.** (pl. **-ies**) **1** a hard creamy-white substance composing the main part of the tusks of an elephant, walrus, or narwhal. **2** the creamy-white colour of ivory. **3** (**the ivories**) informal the keys of a piano. **4** (**ivories**) informal a person's teeth.

– DERIVATIVES **ivoried** adj.

– ORIGIN ME: from Anglo-Norman Fr. *ivurie*, based on L. *ebur*.

**ivory black** • **n.** a black carbon pigment made from charred ivory or bone, used in drawing and painting.

**ivory nut** • **n.** the seed of a tropical American palm (*Phytelephas macrocarpa*), which, when hardened, is a source of vegetable ivory.

**ivory tower** • **n.** a state of privileged seclusion or separation from the facts and practicalities of the real world.

– ORIGIN C20: translating Fr. *tour d'ivoire*, used by the C19 French writer Charles Augustin Sainte-Beuve.

**ivy** • **n.** a woody evergreen climbing plant, typically with shiny five-pointed leaves. [*Hedera helix* and related species.] ➤ used in names of other climbing plants, e.g. **poison ivy**.

– ORIGIN OE *īfig*, of Gmc origin.

**Ivy League** • **n.** a group of long-established and prestigious universities in the eastern US.

– ORIGIN with ref. to the ivy traditionally growing over their walls.

**IWC** • **abbrev.** International Whaling Commission.

**iwi** /ˈiːwi/ • **n.** (pl. same) NZ a community or people.

– ORIGIN from Maori.

**IWW** • **abbrev.** Industrial Workers of the World.

**ixia** /ˈɪksɪə/ • **n.** a South African plant of the iris family, bearing showy six-petalled starlike flowers. [Genus *Ixia*: many cultivars.]

– ORIGIN mod. L., from L., denoting a kind of thistle.

**Iyyar** /ˈiːjɑː/ • **n.** (in the Jewish calendar) the eighth month of the civil and second of the religious year, usually coinciding with parts of April and May.

– ORIGIN from Heb. *'iyyār*.

**izard** /ˈɪzəd/ • **n.** (in the Pyrenees) a chamois.

– ORIGIN C18: from Fr. *isard* or Gascon *isart*.

**-ize** (also **-ise**) • **suffix** forming verbs meaning: **1** make or become: *privatize.* ➤ cause to resemble: *Americanize.* **2** treat in a specified way: *pasteurize.* ➤ treat or cause to combine with a specified substance: *carbonize.* **3** follow a specified practice: *agonize.* ➤ subject to a practice: *hospitalize.*

– DERIVATIVES **-ization** suffix forming corresponding nouns. **-izer** suffix forming agent nouns.

– ORIGIN from Fr. *-iser*, via late L. *-izare* from Gk verbs ending in *-izein*.

**USAGE** -ize

The forms **-ize** and **-ise** are, in many cases, straightforward spelling variants. However, the **-ise** spelling is obligatory in certain cases: first, where it forms part of a larger word element, such as *-mise* in **compromise**; and second, in verbs corresponding to nouns with **-s-** in the stem, such as **advertise** and **televise**.

**Iznik** /ˈɪznɪk/ (also **Isnik**) • **adj.** denoting ceramics produced during the 16th and 17th centuries in Iznik (ancient Nicaea), a town in NW Turkey.

# Jj

**J**[1] (also **j**) ● **n.** (pl. **Js** or **J's**) **1** the tenth letter of the alphabet. **2** denoting the next after I in a set of items, categories, etc. **3** archaic (as a Roman numeral) used instead of an I when in a final position.

**J**[2] ● **abbrev. 1** jack. **2** Japan (international vehicle registration). **3** Physics joule(s). **4** (in titles) Journal (of).

**j** ● **symb.** (*j*) (in electrical engineering and electronics) the imaginary quantity equal to the square root of minus one. Compare with **I**.

**jab** ● **v.** (**jabbed**, **jabbing**) poke roughly or quickly with something sharp or pointed. ● **n. 1** a quick, sharp poke or blow. **2** Brit. informal a hypodermic injection, especially a vaccination.
– ORIGIN C19 (orig. Scots): var. of **JOB**[2].

**jabber** ● **v.** talk rapidly and excitedly but with little sense. ● **n.** such talk.
– ORIGIN C15: imitative.

**jabberwocky** /ˈdʒabə,wɒki/ ● **n.** (pl. **-ies**) invented or meaningless language.
– ORIGIN C20: from the title of a nonsense poem in Lewis Carroll's *Through the Looking Glass* (1871).

**jabiru** /ˈdʒabɪruː/ ● **n.** a large black-necked stork with an upturned bill. [*Ephippiorhynchus mycteria* (Central and S. America) and related species.]
– ORIGIN C18: from Tupi-Guarani *jabirú*.

**jab jab** ● **n.** W. Indian a devil, in particular as represented in a carnival masquerade.
– ORIGIN Fr. Creole, from Fr. *diable diable* 'devil devil'.

**jaborandi** /,dʒabəˈrandi/ ● **n. 1** a drug made from the dried leaves of certain South American plants, which contain the alkaloid pilocarpine and promote salivation when chewed. **2** a plant that yields this drug. [*Pilocarpus jaborandi* and other species.]
– ORIGIN C17: from Tupi-Guarani *jaburandi*, lit. 'a person who spits'.

**jabot** /ˈʒabəʊ/ ● **n.** an ornamental ruffle on the front of a shirt or blouse.
– ORIGIN C19: Fr., orig. 'crop of a bird'.

**jacal** /həˈkɑːl/ ● **n.** (pl. **jacales** /həˈkɑːleɪz/) (in Mexico and the south-western US) a thatched wattle-and-daub hut.
– ORIGIN Mex. Sp., from Nahuatl *xacalli*, contr. of *xamitl calli* 'adobe house'.

**jacamar** /ˈdʒakəmɑː/ ● **n.** an insectivorous bird of tropical American forests, with a long pointed bill, a long tail, and iridescent plumage. [Family Galbulidae: several species.]
– ORIGIN C19: from Fr., appar. from Tupi.

**jacana** /ˈdʒakənə/ (also **jaçana** /,dʒasəˈnɑː/) ● **n.** a small tropical wading bird with greatly elongated toes and claws that enable it to walk on floating vegetation. [Family Jacanidae: several species.]
– ORIGIN C18: from Port. *jaçanã*, from Tupi-Guarani *jasanã*.

**jacaranda** /,dʒakəˈrandə/ ● **n.** a tropical American tree which has blue trumpet-shaped flowers, fern-like leaves, and fragrant wood. [Genus *Jacaranda*.]
– ORIGIN C18: from Port., from Tupi-Guarani *jakara'nda*.

**jacinth** /ˈdʒasɪnθ, ˈdʒeɪ-/ ● **n.** a reddish-orange gem variety of zircon.
– ORIGIN ME: from OFr. *iacinte* or med. L. *iacintus*, alt. of L. *hyacinthus* (see **HYACINTH**).

**jack**[1] ● **n. 1** a device for lifting heavy objects, especially one for raising the axle of a motor vehicle. **2** a playing card bearing a representation of a soldier, page, or knave, normally ranking next below a queen. **3** (also **jack socket**) a socket designed to receive a jack plug. **4** (in bowls) a small white ball at which the players aim. **5** (also **jackstone**) a small round pebble or star-shaped piece of metal or plastic used in tossing and catching games. ➤ (**jacks**) a game played by tossing and catching jacks. **6** a small version of a national flag flown at the bow of a vessel in harbour. **7** US informal money. **8** a device for turning a spit. **9** a part of the mechanism in a spinet or harpsichord that connects a key to its corresponding string. **10** a perch-like marine fish, typically with a row of large spiky scales along each side. [Family Carangidae: numerous species.] **11** the male of various animals, especially a merlin or (N. Amer.) an ass. **12** used in names of animals and plants that are smaller than similar kinds, e.g. **jack pine**. ● **v. 1** (**jack something up**) raise something with a jack. **2** (**jack something up**) informal increase something by a considerable amount. **3** (**jack in/into**) log into or connect up (a computer or electronic device).
– PHRASES **every man jack** informal every single person. **jack of all trades** (**and master of none**) a person who can do many different types of work (but has special skill in none.).
– PHRASAL VERBS **jack someone around** N. Amer. informal cause someone inconvenience or problems. **jack something in** Brit. informal cease doing something. **jack off** vulgar slang masturbate. **jack up 1** informal inject oneself with a narcotic drug. **2** Austral. give up or refuse to participate.
– ORIGIN ME: from *Jack*, familiar form of the given name *John*, used orig. to denote an ordinary man, hence the 'knave' in cards and 'male animal', also denoting various devices saving human labour.

**jack**[2] ● **n.** historical **1** another term for **BLACKJACK** (in sense 5). **2** a sleeveless padded tunic worn by foot soldiers. [ME: from OFr. *jaque*; origin uncertain, perh. based on Arab.]

**jack**[3] ● **adj.** Austral./NZ tired of or bored with someone or something.
– ORIGIN C19: from *jack up* 'give up'.

**jackal** /ˈdʒakəl, -kɔːl/ ● **n.** a slender, long-legged wild dog that often hunts or scavenges in packs, found in Africa and southern Asia. [Genus *Canis*: four species.]
– ORIGIN C17: from Turk. *çakal*.

**jackanapes** /ˈdʒakəneɪps/ ● **n. 1** dated an impertinent person. **2** archaic a tame monkey.
– ORIGIN C16 (orig. as *Jack Napes*): perh. from a playful name for a tame ape, the initial *n-* by elision of *an ape*.

**Jack and Jill party** ● **n.** N. Amer. a party held for a couple soon to be married, to which both men and women are invited.

**jackaroo** /,dʒakəˈruː/ Austral. informal ● **n.** a young, inexperienced worker on a sheep or cattle station. ● **v.** work as a jackaroo.
– ORIGIN C19: alt. of Aborig. term *dhugai-iu* 'wandering white man'.

**jackass** ● **n. 1** a stupid person. **2** a male ass or donkey. **3** Austral. short for **LAUGHING JACKASS**.

**jackboot** ● **n.** a large leather military boot reaching to the knee.
– DERIVATIVES **jackbooted** adj.

**Jack-by-the-hedge** ● **n.** a white-flowered plant of the cabbage family, which typically grows in hedgerows and has leaves that smell of garlic when crushed. [*Alliaria petiolata*, family Cruciferae.]

**jackdaw** ● **n.** a small grey-headed crow, noted for its inquisitiveness. [Genus *Corvus*: two species, in particular the Eurasian *C. monedula*.]
– ORIGIN from **JACK**[1] + earlier *daw* (of Gmc origin).

**jackeen** /dʒa'ki:n/ ● **n.** Irish, chiefly derogatory a city-dweller, especially a Dubliner.
– ORIGIN C19: dimin. of the pet name *Jack* (see **JACK**[1], **-EEN**).

**jacket** ● **n.** **1** an outer garment extending to the waist or hips, with sleeves and a fastening down the front. **2** an outer covering placed around something for protection or insulation. **3** the skin of a potato. **4** a steel frame fixed to the seabed to support an oil production platform. ● **v.** (**jacketed**, **jacketing**) cover with a jacket.
– DERIVATIVES **-jacketed** adj.
– ORIGIN ME: from OFr. *jaquet*, dimin. of *jaque* (see **JACK**[2]).

**jacket potato** ● **n.** Brit. a baked potato served with the skin on.

**jackfish** ● **n.** (pl. same or **-fishes**) chiefly N. Amer. a pike or sauger, especially the northern pike.

**Jack Frost** ● **n.** a personification of frost.

**jackfruit** ● **n.** the very large edible fruit of a fast-growing tropical Asian tree (*Artocarpus heterophyllus*), resembling a breadfruit.
– ORIGIN C16: from Port. *jaca* (from Malayalam *chakka*) + **FRUIT**.

**jackhammer** chiefly N. Amer. ● **n.** a portable pneumatic hammer or drill. ● **v.** beat or hammer heavily or loudly and repeatedly.

**jack-in-the-box** ● **n.** a toy consisting of a box containing a figure on a spring which pops up when the lid is opened.

**Jack-in-the-pulpit** ● **n.** **1** another term for **CUCKOO PINT**. **2** a North American arum with a green or purple-brown spathe. [*Arisaema triphyllum.*]
– ORIGIN C19: so named because the erect spadix over-arched by the spathe resembles a person in a pulpit.

**jackknife** ● **n.** (pl. **-knives**) **1** a large knife with a folding blade. **2** a dive in which the body is bent at the waist and then straightened. ● **v.** (**-knifed**, **-knifing**) **1** move (one's body) into a bent or doubled-up position. **2** (of an articulated vehicle) bend into a V-shape in an uncontrolled skidding movement. **3** (of a diver) perform a jackknife.

**jackknife clam** ● **n.** North American term for **RAZOR SHELL**.

**jackknife fish** ● **n.** a strikingly marked fish with a long upright dorsal fin, which lives in the warm waters of the western Atlantic. [*Equetus lanceolatus.*]

**jackleg** ● **n.** US informal an incompetent, unskilful, or dishonest person.

**jack mackerel** ● **n.** a game fish of the jack family, found in the eastern Pacific. [*Trachurus symmetricus.*]

**jack-o'-lantern** ● **n.** **1** a lantern made from a hollowed-out pumpkin or turnip in which holes are cut to represent facial features. **2** archaic a will-o'-the wisp.

**jack pine** ● **n.** a small, hardy North American pine with short needles. [*Pinus banksiana.*]

**jack plane** ● **n.** a medium-sized plane for use in rough joinery.

**jack plug** ● **n.** a plug consisting of a single shaft used to make a connection which transmits a signal, typically used in sound equipment.

**jackpot** ● **n.** a large cash prize or accumulated stake in a game or lottery.
– PHRASES **hit the jackpot** informal **1** win a jackpot. **2** have great or unexpected success.
– ORIGIN C19 (orig. used in a form of poker): from **JACK**[1] + **POT**[1].

**jackrabbit** ● **n.** a hare found on the prairies and steppes of North America. [Genus *Lepus*: several species.]
– ORIGIN C19: abbrev. of *jackass-rabbit*, because of its long ears.

**Jack Russell** (also **Jack Russell terrier**) ● **n.** a terrier of a small working breed with short legs.
– ORIGIN C20: named after the Engl. clergyman Revd John (*Jack*) *Russell*, a breeder of such terriers.

**jack screw** ● **n.** **1** a screw which can be turned to adjust the position of an object into which it fits. **2** another term for **SCREW JACK**.

**jacksie** (also **jacksy**) ● **n.** Brit. informal a person's bottom.
– ORIGIN C19: dimin. of **JACK**[1].

**jackstaff** ● **n.** a short staff at a ship's bow, on which a jack is hoisted.

**jackstone** ● **n.** see **JACK**[1] (sense 5).

**jackstraw** ● **n.** another term for **SPILLIKIN**.

**jacksy** ● **n.** (pl. **-ies**) variant spelling of **JACKSIE**.

**Jack tar** ● **n.** Brit. informal, dated a sailor.

**Jack the Lad** ● **n.** informal a brash, cocky young man.
– ORIGIN nickname of *Jack* Sheppard, C18 thief.

**Jacobean** /ˌdʒakə'bi:ən/ ● **adj.** of or relating to the reign of James I of England (1603–25). ➤denoting the architectural style prevalent at this time, consisting of a blend of Gothic and classical features. ➤(of furniture) made in the style prevalent at this time, characterized by the use of dark oak. ● **n.** a person who lived in the Jacobean period.
– ORIGIN C19: from mod. L. *Jacobaeus* (from eccles. L. *Jacobus* 'James') + **-AN**.

**Jacobin** /'dʒakəbɪn/ ● **n.** **1** historical a member of a radical democratic club established in Paris in 1789, in the wake of the French Revolution. **2** an extreme political radical. **3** chiefly historical a Dominican friar. **4** (**jacobin**) a pigeon of a breed with reversed feathers on the back of its neck like a cowl.
– DERIVATIVES **Jacobinic** adj. **Jacobinical** adj. **Jacobinism** n.
– ORIGIN ME (denoting the Dominican friars): from OFr., via med. L. from eccles. L. *Jacobus* 'James', after the church in Paris, St Jacques, near which the friars built their first convent; the latter eventually became the headquarters of the French revolutionary group.

**Jacobite**[1] /'dʒakəbʌɪt/ ● **n.** a supporter of the deposed James II and his descendants in their claim to the British throne after the Revolution of 1688.
– DERIVATIVES **Jacobitical** adj. **Jacobitism** n.
– ORIGIN from L. *Jacobus* 'James' + **-ITE**[1].

**Jacobite**[2] /'dʒakəbʌɪt/ ● **n.** a member of the Syrian Orthodox Church (Monophysite).
– ORIGIN C15: from med. L. *Jacobita*, from the name of *Jacobus* Baradaeus, a C6 Syrian monk.

**Jacob's ladder** ● **n.** **1** a herbaceous plant with blue or white flowers and slender pointed leaves formed in ladder-like rows. [*Polemonium caeruleum.*] **2** a rope ladder with wooden rungs.
– ORIGIN C18: with biblical allusion to Jacob's dream of a ladder reaching to heaven (Gen. 28:12).

**Jacobson's organ** ● **n.** Zoology a scent organ situated in the mouth of snakes, lizards, and some other vertebrates.
– ORIGIN C19: named after the Du. anatomist Ludwig L. *Jacobson*.

**Jacob's staff** ● **n.** a rod with a sliding cursor formerly used for measuring distances and heights.
– ORIGIN C16 (denoting a pilgrim's staff): alluding to St James (*Jacobus* in eccles. L.), whose symbols are a pilgrim's staff and a scallop shell.

**jaconet** /'dʒakənɪt/ ● **n.** a lightweight cotton cloth with a smooth and slightly stiff finish.
– ORIGIN C18: from Hindi *Jagannāth(purī)* (now *Puri*) in India, its place of origin.

**jacquard** /'dʒakɑ:d, -kəd/ ● **n.** **1** an apparatus consisting of perforated cards, fitted to a loom to facilitate the weaving of figured and brocaded fabrics. ➤[as modifier] denoting a loom fitted with a jacquard. **2** a fabric made on a jacquard loom.
– ORIGIN C19: named after the Fr. weaver Joseph M. *Jacquard*.

**jacquerie** /'dʒeɪk(ə)ri/ ● **n.** a communal uprising or revolt.
– ORIGIN C16: from OFr., lit. 'villeins', from *Jacques*, a given name used in the sense 'peasant'.

**jactitation** /ˌdʒaktɪ'teɪʃ(ə)n/ ● **n.** Medicine restless tossing or twitching of the body.
– ORIGIN C17: expressive extension of earlier *jactation*, from L. *jactare* 'to throw'.

**jacuzzi** /dʒə'ku:zi/ ● **n.** (pl. **jacuzzis**) trademark a large bath incorporating jets of water to massage the body.
– ORIGIN 1960s: named after the Italian-born Amer. in-

ventor Candido *Jacuzzi*.

**jade**[1] ● **n. 1** a hard, typically green, stone consisting of the minerals jadeite or nephrite, used for ornaments and jewellery. **2** the light bluish green colour of jade.
– ORIGIN C16: from Fr. *le jade* (earlier *l'ejade*), from Sp. *piedra de ijada* 'stone of the flank' (i.e. stone for colic, which it was believed to cure).

**jade**[2] ● **n.** archaic **1** a bad-tempered or disreputable woman. **2** an inferior or worn-out horse.
– ORIGIN ME: of unknown origin.

**jaded** ● **adj.** tired or lacking enthusiasm after having had a surfeit of something.
– DERIVATIVES **jadedly** adv. **jadedness** n.
– ORIGIN C16 (in the sense 'disreputable'): from **JADE**[2].

**jadeite** /ˈdʒeɪdʌɪt/ ● **n.** a green, blue, or white silicate mineral which is one of the forms of jade.

**j'adoube** /ʒɑːˈduːb/ ● **exclam.** Chess a declaration by a player intending to adjust the placing of a chessman without making a move with it.
– ORIGIN Fr., lit. 'I adjust'.

**jaeger** /ˈdʒeɪɡə/ ● **n.** N. Amer. a skua. [*Stercorarius parasiticus* (**parasitic jaeger**, Arctic skua) and other species.]
– ORIGIN C19: from Ger. *Jäger* 'hunter'.

**Jaffa** /ˈdʒafə/ ● **n.** Brit. a large oval orange of a thick-skinned variety.
– ORIGIN from the city of *Jaffa* in Israel.

**jag**[1] ● **v.** (**jagged**, **jagging**) stab, pierce, or prick. ● **n. 1** a sharp projection. **2** chiefly Scottish a prick or injection.
– DERIVATIVES **jagger** n.
– ORIGIN ME: perh. symbolic of sudden movement or unevenness (cf. **JAM**[1] and **RAG**[1]).

**jag**[2] ● **n.** informal, chiefly N. Amer. **1** a bout of unrestrained activity or emotion: *a crying jag*. **2** dialect a bundle.
– ORIGIN C16 (in sense 'a load of hay or wood', later 'as much alcohol as one can hold'): of unknown origin.

**jagged** /ˈdʒaɡɪd/ ● **adj.** with rough, sharp points protruding.
– DERIVATIVES **jaggedly** adv. **jaggedness** n.
– ORIGIN ME: from **JAG**[1].

**jaggery** /ˈdʒaɡ(ə)ri/ ● **n.** a coarse brown sugar made in India from the sap of palm trees.
– ORIGIN C16: from Port. *xagara*, *jag(a)ra*, from Malayalam *cakkarā*, from Sanskrit *śarkarā* 'sugar'.

**jaggy** ● **adj.** (**-ier**, **-iest**) **1** jagged. **2** (also **jaggie**) Scottish prickly.

**jaguar** /ˈdʒaɡjʊə/ ● **n.** a large, heavily built cat that has a yellowish-brown coat with black spots, found mainly in the dense forests of Central and South America. [*Panthera onca*.]
– ORIGIN C17: from Port., from Tupi-Guarani *yaguára*.

**jaguarundi** /ˌdʒaɡwəˈrʌndi/ ● **n.** (pl. **jaguarundis**) a small American wild cat with a uniform red or grey coat, slender body, and short legs, found from Arizona to Argentina. [*Felis yagouaroundi*.]
– ORIGIN C19: from Port., from Tupi-Guarani, from *yaguára* 'jaguar' + *undi* 'dark'.

**Jah** /dʒɑː, jɑː/ ● **n.** the Rastafarian name of God.
– ORIGIN representing Heb. *Yāh*, abbrev. of **YAHWEH**.

**jai alai** /ˌhʌɪ əˈlʌɪ/ ● **n.** a game like pelota played with large curved wicker baskets.
– ORIGIN Sp., from Basque *jai* 'festival' + *alai* 'merry'.

**jail** (Brit. also **gaol**) ● **n.** a place for the confinement of people accused or convicted of a crime. ● **v.** put (someone) in jail.
– DERIVATIVES **jailer** (also **gaoler**) n.
– ORIGIN ME: based on L. *cavea* (see **CAGE**); the word came into Engl. in two forms, *jaiole* from OFr. and *gayole* from Anglo-Norman Fr. *gaole* (surviving in the spelling *gaol*).

**jailbait** ● **n.** [treated as sing. or pl.] informal a young woman, or young women collectively, considered in sexual terms but under the age of consent.

**jailbird** ● **n.** informal a person who is or has repeatedly been in prison.

**jailbreak** ● **n.** an escape from jail.

**jailhouse** ● **n.** chiefly N. Amer. a prison.

**Jain** /dʒeɪn/ ● **n.** an adherent of Jainism. ● **adj.** of or relating to Jainism.
– ORIGIN via Hindi from Sanskrit *jaina* 'of or concerning a *Jina*' (see **JINA**).

**Jainism** ● **n.** a non-theistic religion founded in India in the 6th century BC, in opposition to Brahmanism.
– DERIVATIVES **Jainist** n.

**jake** /dʒeɪk/ ● **adj.** N. Amer. & Austral./NZ informal all right; satisfactory.
– ORIGIN C20: of unknown origin.

**jakes** /dʒeɪks/ ● **n.** archaic an outdoor toilet.
– ORIGIN C16: perh. from the given name *Jacques*, or as the genitive of the pet name *Jack* (see **JACK**[1]).

**jalap** /ˈdʒaləp, ˈdʒɒləp/ ● **n.** a purgative drug obtained chiefly from the tuberous roots of a Mexican climbing plant (*Ipomoea purga*).
– ORIGIN C17: from Fr., from Sp. (*purga de*) *Jalapa*, from the name of the Mexican city *Jalapa*.

**jalapeño** /ˌhaləˈpeɪnjəʊ, -ˈpiːnəʊ/ ● **n.** (pl. **-os**) a very hot green chilli pepper.
– ORIGIN 1940s (orig. US): from Mex. Sp. (*chile*) *jalapeño* (see **JALAP**).

**jalebi** /dʒəˈleɪbi/ ● **n.** (pl. **jalebis**) an Indian sweet made of a coil of batter fried and steeped in syrup.
– ORIGIN from Hindi *jalebī*.

**jalfrezi** /dʒalˈfreɪzi/ ● **n.** a medium-hot Indian dish consisting of chicken or lamb with fresh chillies, tomatoes, and onions.
– ORIGIN from Bengali *jalfrezi*, from *jal* 'hot'.

**jalopy** /dʒəˈlɒpi/ ● **n.** (pl. **-ies**) informal an old car in a dilapidated condition.
– ORIGIN 1920s (orig. US): of unknown origin.

**jalousie** /ˈʒalʊziː/ ● **n.** a blind or shutter made of a row of angled slats.
– ORIGIN C18: Fr., lit. 'jealousy', from Ital. *geloso* 'jealous', also (by extension) 'screen', assoc. with the screening of women from view in the Middle East.

**Jam.** ● **abbrev. 1** Jamaica. **2** James (in biblical references).

**jam**[1] ● **v.** (**jammed**, **jamming**) **1** squeeze or pack tightly into a space. ➤ push roughly and forcibly into a position. ➤ crowd so as to block (a road, telephone line, etc.). **2** become or make unable to move or work due to a part becoming stuck. **3** (**jam something on**) apply something forcibly: *he jammed on the brakes*. **4** make (a radio transmission) unintelligible by causing interference. **5** informal (in jazz or blues) improvise with other musicians. ● **n. 1** an instance of jamming. **2** informal an awkward situation or predicament: *I'm in a jam*. **3** Climbing a handhold obtained by jamming a part of the body into a crack in the rock. **4** informal (in jazz or blues) an improvised performance by a group of musicians.
– DERIVATIVES **jammer** n.
– ORIGIN C18: prob. symbolic; cf. **JAG**[1] and **CRAM**.

**jam**[2] ● **n. 1** chiefly Brit. a conserve and spread made from fruit and sugar. **2** Brit. something easy or pleasant. ● **v.** (**jammed**, **jamming**) make (fruit) into jam.
– PHRASES **jam tomorrow** a desirable thing that is promised but rarely materializes. [phr. from Lewis Carroll's *Through the Looking Glass* (1871).]
– ORIGIN C18: perh. from **JAM**[1].

**Jamaican** /dʒəˈmeɪkən/ ● **n.** a native or inhabitant of Jamaica. ● **adj.** of or relating to Jamaica or its people.

**Jamaica pepper** ● **n.** another term for **ALLSPICE** (in senses 1 and 2).

**jamb** /dʒam/ ● **n.** a side post of a doorway, window, or fireplace.
– ORIGIN ME: from OFr. *jambe* 'leg, vertical support', based on Gk *kampē* 'joint'.

**jambalaya** /ˌdʒambəˈlʌɪə/ ● **n.** a Cajun dish of rice with shrimps, chicken, and vegetables.
– ORIGIN Louisiana Fr., from Provençal *jambalaia*.

**jamboree** /ˌdʒambəˈriː/ ● **n. 1** a lavish or boisterous celebration or party. **2** a large rally of Scouts or Guides.
– ORIGIN C19 (orig. US sl.): of unknown origin.

**jammy** ● **adj.** (**-ier**, **-iest**) **1** covered, filled with, or resembling jam. **2** Brit. informal lucky.

**jam-packed** ● **adj.** informal extremely crowded or full to capacity.

**Jan.** • **abbrev.** January.

**jane** • **n.** informal, chiefly US a woman.
– PHRASES **plain Jane** an unattractive girl or woman.
– ORIGIN C20: from the given name *Jane*.

**jangle** • **v.** **1** make or cause to make a ringing metallic sound. **2** (of one's nerves) be set on edge. • **n.** an instance of jangling.
– DERIVATIVES **jangly** adj.
– ORIGIN ME (in the sense 'talk excessively or noisily, squabble'): from OFr. *jangler*, of unknown origin.

**janissary** /'dʒanɪs(ə)ri/ (also **janizary** /-z(ə)ri/) • **n.** (pl. **-ies**) historical a Turkish infantryman in the Sultan's guard.
– ORIGIN C16: from Fr. *janissaire*, based on Turk. *yeniçeri*, from *yeni* 'new' + *çeri* 'troops'.

**janitor** /'dʒanɪtə/ • **n.** chiefly N. Amer. a caretaker of a building.
– DERIVATIVES **janitorial** adj.
– ORIGIN C16: from L., from *janua* 'door'.

**jankers** /'dʒaŋkəz/ • **n.** Brit. military slang punishment for committing a military offence.
– ORIGIN C20: of unknown origin.

**Jansenism** • **n.** a rigorous Christian movement of the 17th and 18th centuries, based on the writings of the Catholic theologian Cornelius Jansen (1585–1638).
– DERIVATIVES **Jansenist** n.

**January** /'dʒanjʊ(ə)ri/ • **n.** (pl. **-ies**) the first month of the year.
– ORIGIN OE, from L. *Januarius* (*mensis*) '(month) of *Janus*' (the Roman god who presided over doors and beginnings).

**Jap** • **n. & adj.** informal, offensive short for **JAPANESE**.

**japan** • **n.** a black glossy varnish of a type originating in Japan. • **v.** (**japanned**, **japanning**) cover with japan.
– DERIVATIVES **japanned** adj. **japanning** n.

**Japanese** • **n.** (pl. same) **1** a native or national of Japan, or a person of Japanese descent. **2** the language of Japan. • **adj.** of or relating to Japan, its people, or their language.

**Japanese beetle** • **n.** a metallic green and copper chafer which is a pest of fruit and foliage as an adult and of grass roots as a larva. [*Popillia japonica*.]

**Japanese cedar** • **n.** another term for **CRYPTOMERIA**.

**Japanese lantern** • **n.** another term for **CHINESE LANTERN** (in sense 1).

**Japanimation** /dʒə,panɪ'meɪʃ(ə)n/ • **n.** another term for **ANIME**.

**jape** • **n.** a practical joke. • **v.** say or do something in jest or mockery.
– DERIVATIVES **japery** n.
– ORIGIN ME: appar. combining the form of OFr. *japer* 'to yelp, yap' with the sense of OFr. *gaber* 'to mock'.

**Japlish** /'dʒaplɪʃ/ • **n.** informal a blend of Japanese and English spoken in Japan.

**japonica** /dʒə'pɒnɪkə/ • **n.** an Asian shrub of the rose family, with bright red flowers followed by edible fruits. [*Chaenomeles speciosa* (Japanese quince) and related species.]
– ORIGIN C19: mod. L., fem. of *japonicus* 'Japanese'.

**jar**[1] • **n.** **1** a wide-mouthed cylindrical container made of glass or pottery. **2** Brit. informal a glass of beer.
– ORIGIN C16: from Fr. *jarre*, from Arab. *jarra*.

**jar**[2] • **v.** (**jarred**, **jarring**) **1** send a painful or uncomfortable shock through (a part of the body). ➤ strike against something with an unpleasant vibration or jolt. **2** have a disturbing or incongruous effect. • **n.** an instance of jarring.
– DERIVATIVES **jarring** adj. **jarringly** adv.
– ORIGIN C15 (as a noun in the sense 'disagreement, dispute'): prob. imitative.

**jar**[3] • **n.** (in phr. **on the jar**) informal or dialect ajar.
– ORIGIN C17: later form of obs. *char* 'turn' (see also **AJAR**[1] and **CHARWOMAN**).

**jardinière** /,ʒɑːdɪn'jɛː/ • **n.** **1** an ornamental pot or stand for displaying plants. **2** a garnish of mixed vegetables.
– ORIGIN C19: Fr., lit. 'female gardener'.

**jargon**[1] /'dʒɑːg(ə)n/ • **n.** words or expressions used by a particular profession or group that are difficult for others to understand.
– DERIVATIVES **jargonistic** adj. **jargonize** (also **-ise**) v.
– ORIGIN ME (orig. in the sense 'twittering, chattering', later 'gibberish'): from OFr. *jargoun*, of unknown origin.

**jargon**[2] /'dʒɑːg(ə)n/ (also **jargoon** /dʒɑː'guːn/) • **n.** a translucent, colourless, or smoky gem variety of zircon.
– ORIGIN C18: from Fr.; prob. ult. rel. to **ZIRCON**.

**Jargonelle** /,dʒɑːgə'nɛl/ • **n.** Brit. a pear of an early ripening variety.
– ORIGIN C17: from Fr., dimin. of **JARGON**[2] (with ref. to the colour).

**jarl** /jɑːl/ • **n.** historical a Norse or Danish chief.
– ORIGIN ON, lit. 'man of noble birth'; rel. to **EARL**.

**Jarlsberg** /'jɑːlzbəːg/ • **n.** a firm, mild Norwegian cheese.
– ORIGIN named after the town of *Jarlsberg*, Norway.

**jarrah** /'dʒarə/ • **n.** a eucalyptus tree native to western Australia. [*Eucalyptus marginata*.]
– ORIGIN C19: from Nyungar *djarryl*, *jerrhyl*.

**Jas.** • **abbrev.** James (especially in biblical references).

**jasmine** /'dʒazmɪn, 'dʒas-/ (also **jessamine**) • **n.** a shrub or climbing plant with fragrant flowers, often yellow. [*Jasminum nudiflorum* (**winter jasmine**, China), *Gelsemium sempervirens* (**yellow jasmine**, US) and other species.]
– ORIGIN C16: from Fr. *jasmin* and obs. Fr. *jessemin*.

**jasmine tea** • **n.** a tea perfumed with dried jasmine flowers.

**jaspé** /'dʒaspeɪ/ • **adj.** randomly mottled like jasper.
– ORIGIN C19: Fr., past part. of *jasper* 'to marble', from *jaspe* (see **JASPER**).

**jasper** • **n.** an opaque reddish-brown variety of chalcedony.
– ORIGIN ME: from OFr. *jasp(r)e*, from L. *iaspis*, from Gk, of oriental origin.

**Jat** /dʒɑːt/ • **n.** a member of a people distributed throughout the north-west of the Indian subcontinent.
– ORIGIN from Hindi *Jāṭ*.

**Jataka** /'dʒʌtəkə/ • **n.** any of the various stories of the former lives of the Buddha found in Buddhist literature.
– ORIGIN from Sanskrit *jātaka* 'born under'.

**jati** /'dʒɑːti/ • **n.** (pl. same or **jatis**) Indian a caste or subcaste.
– ORIGIN via Hindi from Sanskrit *jāti* 'birth'.

**JATO** /'dʒeɪtəʊ/ • **abbrev.** Aeronautics jet-assisted take-off.

**jaundice** /'dʒɔːndɪs/ • **n.** **1** Medicine yellowing of the skin due to an excess of bile pigments in the blood. **2** bitterness or resentment.
– DERIVATIVES **jaundiced** adj.
– ORIGIN ME *jaunes*, from OFr. *jaunice* 'yellowness', from *jaune* 'yellow'.

**jaunt** • **n.** a short excursion for pleasure. • **v.** go on a jaunt.
– ORIGIN C16: of unknown origin.

**jaunty** • **adj.** (**-ier**, **-iest**) having a lively and self-confident manner.
– DERIVATIVES **jauntily** adv. **jauntiness** n.
– ORIGIN C17 (in the sense 'well-bred, genteel'): from Fr. *gentil* (see **GENTLE**[1], **GENTEEL**).

**Java** /'dʒɑːvə/ • **n.** trademark a computer programming language designed to work across different computer systems.

**java** /'dʒɑːvə/ • **n.** N. Amer. informal coffee.

**Javan** /'dʒɑːvən/ • **n.** a native or inhabitant of the Indonesian island of Java. • **adj.** of or relating to Java.

**Javanese** • **n.** (pl. same) **1** a native or inhabitant of Java, or a person of Javanese descent. **2** the Indonesian language of central Java. • **adj.** of or relating to Java.

**Java sparrow** • **n.** a waxbill with a large red bill and black-and-white head, native to Java and Bali and popular as a cage bird. [*Padda oryzivora*.]

**javelin** /'dʒav(ə)lɪn/ • **n.** a long, light spear thrown in a competitive sport or as a weapon.
– ORIGIN ME: from OFr. *javeline*, of Celtic origin.

**javelina** /ˌhavəˈliːnə/ • **n.** North American term for **PECCARY**.
– ORIGIN C19: from Sp. *jabalina*, from the fem. form of *jabalí* 'wild boar'.

**jaw** • **n.** **1** each of the upper and lower bony structures in vertebrates forming the framework of the mouth and containing the teeth. ➤(**jaws**) the grasping, biting, or crushing mouthparts of an invertebrate. **2** (**jaws**) the gripping parts of a wrench, vice, etc. **3** (**jaws**) the grasping or destructive power of something: *the jaws of death*. **4** informal tedious talk. • **v.** informal talk at length.
– DERIVATIVES **-jawed** adj. **jawless** adj.
– ORIGIN ME: from OFr. *joe* 'cheek, jaw', of unknown origin.

**jawbone** • **n.** a bone of the jaw, especially that of the lower jaw (the mandible).

**jawbreaker** • **n.** **1** informal a word that is very long or hard to pronounce. **2** chiefly N. Amer. a large gobstopper.

**jaw-dropping** • **adj.** informal amazing.
– DERIVATIVES **jaw-droppingly** adv.

**jaw-jaw** informal • **n.** lengthy or pointless talk. • **v.** talk pointlessly or at length.
– ORIGIN C19: reduplication of **JAW**.

**jawline** • **n.** the contour of the lower edge of a person's jaw.

**Jaws of Life** • **n.** N. Amer. trademark a hydraulic apparatus used to pry apart the wreckage of crashed vehicles in order to free people trapped inside.

**jay** • **n.** **1** a bird of the crow family with boldly patterned plumage, typically with blue feathers in the wings or tail and a harsh chattering call. [*Garrulus glandarius* (Eurasia) and other species.] **2** informal, dated a prattler.
– ORIGIN C15: via OFr. from late L. *gaius*, *gaia*, perh. from the L. given name *Gaius*.

**Jaycee** /dʒeɪˈsiː/ • **n.** N. Amer. informal a member of a Junior Chamber of Commerce.
– ORIGIN 1940s: representing the initials of *Junior Chamber*.

**jaywalk** • **v.** chiefly N. Amer. walk in or across a road without regard for approaching traffic.
– DERIVATIVES **jaywalker** n.
– ORIGIN C20: from **JAY** in the colloq. sense 'silly person' + **WALK**.

**jazz** • **n.** a type of music of black American origin characterized by improvisation, syncopation, and a regular rhythm, and typically played on brass and woodwind instruments. • **v.** **1** dated play or dance to jazz. **2** (**jazz something up**) make something more lively.
– PHRASES **and all that jazz** informal and such similar things.
– DERIVATIVES **jazzer** n.
– ORIGIN C20: of unknown origin.

**jazz age** • **n.** the 1920s in the US, characterized as a period of hedonism, freedom, and exuberance.

**jazzbo** • **n.** (pl. **-os**) informal a jazz musician or enthusiast.
– ORIGIN C20: of unknown origin.

**jazzy** • **adj.** (**-ier**, **-iest**) **1** of or in the style of jazz. **2** bright, colourful, and showy.
– DERIVATIVES **jazzily** adv. **jazziness** n.

**JCB** • **n.** Brit. trademark a type of mechanical excavator with a shovel at the front and a digging arm at the rear.
– ORIGIN 1960s: the initials of *J. C. B*amford, the makers.

**JCL** • **abbrev.** Computing job control language.

**J-cloth** • **n.** trademark (in the UK) a type of cloth used for household cleaning.
– ORIGIN C20: *J* from *J*ohnson and Johnson, the original makers.

**JCR** • **abbrev.** Brit. Junior Common (or Combination) Room.

**JCS** • **abbrev.** Joint Chiefs of Staff.

**jealous** • **adj.** **1** envious of someone else's possessions, achievements, or advantages. ➤suspicious or resentful of a perceived sexual rival. **2** fiercely protective or vigilant of one's rights or possessions. **3** (of God) demanding faithfulness and exclusive worship.
– DERIVATIVES **jealously** adv. **jealousy** n.
– ORIGIN ME: from OFr. *gelos*, from med. L. *zelosus* (see **ZEALOUS**).

**jean** • **n.** **1** heavy twilled cotton cloth, especially denim. **2** (in commercial use) a pair of jeans: *a button-fly jean*.
– ORIGIN C15 (as adj.): from OFr. *Janne* (now *Gênes*), from med. L. *Janua* 'Genoa', the place of original production.

**jeans** • **pl. n.** hard-wearing trousers made of denim or other cotton fabric.
– ORIGIN C19: pl. of **JEAN**.

**jebel** /ˈdʒɛbɛl/ • **n.** (in the Middle East and North Africa) a mountain or hill, or a range of hills.
– ORIGIN colloq. Arab. form of *jabal* 'mountain'.

**jeep** • **n.** trademark a small, sturdy motor vehicle with four-wheel drive, especially one used by the army.
– ORIGIN Second World War (orig. US): from the initials *GP*, standing for *general purpose*, influenced by 'Eugene the Jeep', a creature in the *Popeye* comic strip.

**jeepers** (also **jeepers creepers**) • **exclam.** informal, chiefly N. Amer. expressing surprise or alarm.
– ORIGIN 1920s: alt. of **JESUS**.

**jeer** • **v.** make rude and mocking remarks at someone. • **n.** a rude and mocking remark.
– DERIVATIVES **jeering** adj. & n. **jeeringly** adv.
– ORIGIN C16: of unknown origin.

**jeera** /ˈdʒiːrə/ (also **zeera** /ˈʒiːrə/) • **n.** Indian term for **CUMIN**.
– ORIGIN from Hindi *jīrā*.

**jeet kune do** /ˈdʒiːt kuːn duː/ • **n.** a modern martial art incorporating elements of kung fu, fencing, and boxing, devised by the American actor Bruce Lee (1941–73).
– ORIGIN from Cantonese, lit. 'the way of the intercepting fist'.

**Jeez** (also **Jeeze** or **Geez**) • **exclam.** informal expressing surprise or annoyance.
– ORIGIN 1920s: abbrev. of **JESUS**.

**jehad** • **n.** variant spelling of **JIHAD**.

**Jehovah** /dʒɪˈhəʊvə/ • **n.** a form of the Hebrew name of God used in some translations of the Bible.
– ORIGIN from med. L. *Iehouah*, *Iehoua*, from Heb. *YHWH* or *JHVH*, the consonants of the name of God, with the inclusion of vowels taken from *'ăḏōnāy* 'my lord'; cf. **YAHWEH**.

**Jehovah's Witness** • **n.** a member of a fundamentalist Christian sect that denies many traditional Christian doctrines (including the divinity of Christ) and preaches the Second Coming.

**jejune** /dʒɪˈdʒuːn/ • **adj.** **1** naive and simplistic. **2** (of ideas or writings) dull.
– DERIVATIVES **jejunely** adv. **jejuneness** n.
– ORIGIN C17: from L. *jejunus* 'fasting, barren'.

**jejunum** /dʒɪˈdʒuːnəm/ • **n.** Anatomy the part of the small intestine between the duodenum and ileum.
– DERIVATIVES **jejunal** adj.
– ORIGIN C16: from med. L., neut. of *jejunus* 'fasting' (because it is usu. found to be empty after death).

**Jekyll** /ˈdʒɛk(ə)l/ • **n.** (in phr. **a Jekyll and Hyde**) a person displaying alternately good and evil personalities.
– ORIGIN after the central character in Robert Louis Stevenson's story *The Strange Case of Dr Jekyll and Mr Hyde* (1886).

**jell** (also **gel**) • **v.** (**jelled**, **jelling**) **1** (of jelly or a similar substance) set or become firmer. **2** take definite form or begin to work well.

**jellaba** • **n.** variant spelling of **DJELLABA**.

**jello** (also trademark **Jell-O**) • **n.** N. Amer. a fruit-flavoured gelatin dessert made up from a powder.

**jelly** • **n.** (pl. **-ies**) **1** chiefly Brit. a dessert consisting of a sweet, fruit-flavoured liquid set with gelatin to form a semi-solid mass. ➤a small sweet made with gelatin. **2** a similar preparation made with fruit or other ingredients as a condiment. ➤a savoury preparation made from gelatin and meat stock. **3** any substance of a similar semi-solid consistency. **4** Brit. informal a tablet of the drug Temazepam. **5** Brit. informal term for **GELIGNITE**. • **v.** (**-ies**, **-ied**) [usu. as adj. **jellied**] set (food) as or in a jelly.
– DERIVATIVES **jellification** n. **jellify** v.
– ORIGIN ME: from OFr. *gelee* 'frost, jelly', from L. *gelata* 'frozen'.

**jelly baby** ● **n.** Brit. a jelly sweet in the stylized shape of a baby.

**jelly bag** ● **n.** a fine mesh bag used for straining the juice from cooked fruit in the preparation of a jelly.

**jelly bean** ● **n.** a jelly sweet in the shape of a bean.

**jellyfish** ● **n.** (pl. same or **-fishes**) a free-swimming marine coelenterate with a jelly-like bell- or saucer-shaped body that has stinging tentacles around the edge. [Classes Scyphozoa and Cubozoa.]

**jelly roll** ● **n.** N. Amer. a Swiss roll.

**jelly shoe** (also **jelly sandal**) ● **n.** a sandal made from translucent moulded plastic.

**jelutong** /dʒɛˈluːtɒŋ/ ● **n.** a Malaysian tree with pale lightweight wood. [Genus *Dyera*: several species.]
– ORIGIN C19: from Malay.

**jemmy** (N. Amer. **jimmy**) ● **n.** (pl. **-ies**) a short crowbar. ● **v.** (**-ies**, **-ied**) informal force open with a jemmy.
– ORIGIN C19: familiar form of the given name *James*.

**je ne sais quoi** /ˌʒə nə seɪ ˈkwɑː, French ʒən sɛ kwa/ ● **n.** a quality that cannot be easily identified.
– ORIGIN Fr., lit. 'I do not know what'.

**jenny** ● **n.** (pl. **-ies**) **1** a female donkey or ass. **2** short for **SPINNING JENNY**.
– ORIGIN C17 (denoting a female mammal or bird): familiar form of the given name *Janet*, used as a feminine prefix and in names of machines (cf. **JACK**[1]).

**jenny wren** ● **n.** Brit. informal a wren.

**jeon** /dʒʌn/ ● **n.** (pl. same) a monetary unit of South Korea, equal to one hundredth of a won.
– ORIGIN from Korean.

**jeopardize** /ˈdʒɛpədʌɪz/ (also **-ise**) ● **v.** put into a situation in which there is a danger of loss, harm, or failure.

**jeopardy** /ˈdʒɛpədi/ ● **n.** **1** danger of loss, harm, or failure. **2** Law danger arising from being on trial for a criminal offence.
– ORIGIN ME *iuparti*, from OFr. *ieu parti* '(evenly) divided game', orig. used in chess to denote a position in which the chances of winning or losing were evenly balanced.

**Jer.** ● **abbrev.** Jeremiah (in biblical references).

**jerboa** /dʒəːˈbəʊə, ˈdʒəːbəʊə/ ● **n.** a desert-dwelling rodent with very long hind legs that enable it to perform long jumps, found from North Africa to central Asia. [Family Dipodidae: several species.]
– ORIGIN C17: mod. L., from Arab. *yarbūʻ*.

**jeremiad** /ˌdʒɛrɪˈmʌɪad/ ● **n.** a long, mournful complaint or lamentation; a list of woes.
– ORIGIN C18: from Fr. *jérémiade*, with ref. to the Lamentations of Jeremiah in the Old Testament.

**Jeremiah** /ˌdʒɛrɪˈmʌɪə/ ● **n.** a person who complains continually or foretells disaster.
– ORIGIN C18: from *Jeremiah* (see **JEREMIAD**).

**jerk**[1] ● **n.** **1** a quick, sharp, sudden movement. **2** Weightlifting the raising of a barbell above the head from shoulder level by an abrupt straightening of the arms and legs. **3** informal, chiefly N. Amer. a contemptibly foolish person. ● **v.** **1** move or cause to move with a jerk. **2** Weightlifting raise (a barbell) with a jerk. **3** (**jerk someone around**) N. Amer. informal deal with someone dishonestly or unfairly. **4** (**jerk off**) vulgar slang, chiefly N. Amer. masturbate.
– DERIVATIVES **jerker** n.
– ORIGIN C16 (denoting a stroke with a whip): prob. imitative.

**jerk**[2] ● **v.** [usu. as adj. **jerked**] **1** cure (meat) by cutting it into strips and drying it (originally in the sun). **2** prepare (pork or chicken) by marinating it in spices and barbecuing it over a wood fire. ● **n.** jerked meat.
– ORIGIN C18: from Latin Amer. Sp. *charquear*, from *charqui*, from Quechua *echarqui* 'dried flesh'.

**jerkin** ● **n.** **1** a sleeveless jacket. **2** historical a man's close-fitting skirted jacket, typically of leather.
– ORIGIN C16: of unknown origin.

**jerkin head** ● **n.** Architecture the end of a roof that is hipped for only part of its height, leaving a truncated gable.
– ORIGIN C19: perh. from an alt. of *jerking* (from **JERK**[1]) + **HEAD**.

**jerkwater** ● **adj.** N. Amer. informal of or associated with remote and insignificant rural settlements.
– ORIGIN C19: from **JERK**[1] + **WATER**, from the need for early railway engines to be supplied with water in remote areas, by dipping a bucket into a stream and 'jerking' it out by rope.

**jerky**[1] ● **adj.** (**-ier**, **-iest**) characterized by abrupt stops and starts.
– DERIVATIVES **jerkily** adv. **jerkiness** n.

**jerky**[2] ● **n.** strips of meat that has been cured by drying; jerked meat.

**jeroboam** /ˌdʒɛrəˈbəʊəm/ ● **n.** a wine bottle with a capacity four times larger than that of an ordinary bottle.
– ORIGIN C19: named after *Jeroboam*, a king of Israel.

**Jerry** ● **n.** (pl. **-ies**) Brit. informal, dated a German or Germans collectively (especially in military contexts).
– ORIGIN First World War: prob. an alt. of **GERMAN**.

**jerry** ● **n.** (pl. **-ies**) Brit. informal, dated a chamber pot.
– ORIGIN C19: prob. a dimin. of **JEROBOAM**.

**jerry-built** ● **adj.** badly or hastily built.
– DERIVATIVES **jerry-builder** n. **jerry-building** n.
– ORIGIN C19: origin unknown; sometimes said to be from the name of a firm of builders in Liverpool, or to allude to the walls of Jericho, which fell down at the sound of Joshua's trumpets (Josh. 6:20).

**jerrycan** (also **jerrican**) ● **n.** a large flat-sided metal container for storing or transporting liquids.
– ORIGIN Second World War: from **JERRY** + **CAN**[2], because such containers were first used in Germany.

**jerrymander** ● **v.** Brit. variant spelling of **GERRYMANDER**.

**jersey** ● **n.** (pl. **-eys**) **1** a knitted garment with long sleeves, worn over the upper body. **2** a distinctive shirt worn by a player or competitor in certain sports. **3** a soft knitted fabric. **4** (**Jersey**) an animal of a breed of light brown dairy cattle from Jersey.
– ORIGIN C16 (denoting woollen worsted fabric): from *Jersey*, where the fabric was made.

**Jerusalem artichoke** ● **n.** **1** a knobbly tuber with white flesh, eaten as a vegetable. **2** the tall North American plant, closely related to the sunflower, which produces this tuber. [*Helianthus tuberosus*.]
– ORIGIN C17: *Jerusalem*, alt. of Ital. *girasole* 'sunflower'.

**jess** Falconry ● **n.** a short leather strap that is fastened round each leg of a hawk, to which a leash may be attached. ● **v.** put a jess or jesses on (a hawk).
– ORIGIN ME: from OFr. *ges*, based on L. *jactus* 'a throw'.

**jessamine** /ˈdʒɛsəmɪn/ ● **n.** variant spelling of **JASMINE**.

**jessie** (also **jessy**) ● **n.** (pl. **-ies**) Brit. informal, derogatory an effeminate, weak, or over-sensitive man.
– ORIGIN 1920s: from the female given name *Jessie*.

**jest** ● **n.** a joke. ● **v.** speak or act in a joking manner.
– ORIGIN ME (orig. 'exploit, heroic deed', later 'a narrative of such deeds'): from earlier *gest*, from OFr. *geste*, from L. *gesta* 'actions, exploits'.

**jester** ● **n.** historical a professional joker or 'fool' at a medieval court.

**Jesuit** /ˈdʒɛz(j)ʊɪt/ ● **n.** a member of a Roman Catholic order of priests founded by St Ignatius Loyola and others in 1534.
– ORIGIN from Fr. *jésuite* or mod. L. *Jesuita*, from Christian L. *Iesus* 'Jesus'.

**Jesuitical** ● **adj.** **1** of or concerning the Jesuits. **2** dissembling or equivocating, in a manner once associated with Jesuits.
– DERIVATIVES **Jesuitically** adv.

**Jesus** (also **Jesus Christ**) ● **n.** the central figure of the Christian religion, considered by Christians to be the Christ or Messiah and the Son of God. ● **exclam.** informal expressing irritation, dismay, or surprise.

**Jesus freak** ● **n.** informal, derogatory a fervent evangelical Christian.

**JET** ● **abbrev.** Joint European Torus.

**jet**[1] ● **n.** **1** a rapid stream of liquid or gas forced out of a small opening. **2** a jet engine. ➤ an aircraft powered by jet engines. ● **v.** (**jetted**, **jetting**) **1** spurt out in a jet. **2** travel by jet aircraft.

– ORIGIN C16: from Fr. *jeter* 'to throw', based on L. *jactare*, frequentative of *jacere* 'to throw'.

**jet**[2] ● **n. 1** a hard black semi-precious variety of lignite. **2** a glossy black colour.
– ORIGIN ME: from OFr. *jaiet*, from L. *Gagates*, from Gk *gagatēs* 'from *Gagai*', a town in Asia Minor.

**jeté** /ˈʒɛteɪ, ʒəˈteɪ/ ● **n.** Ballet a spring from one foot to the other, with the following leg extended backwards while in the air.
– ORIGIN Fr., past part. of *jeter* 'to throw'.

**jet engine** ● **n.** an engine using jet propulsion for forward thrust.

**jet lag** ● **n.** extreme tiredness and other effects felt by a person after a long flight across different time zones.
– DERIVATIVES **jet-lagged** adj.

**jetliner** ● **n.** a large jet aircraft carrying passengers.

**jetsam** /ˈdʒɛts(ə)m/ ● **n.** unwanted material or goods that have been thrown overboard from a ship and washed ashore. Compare with **FLOTSAM**.
– ORIGIN C16 (as *jetson*): contr. of **JETTISON**.

**jet set** ● **n.** (**the jet set**) informal wealthy people who travel widely and frequently for pleasure.
– DERIVATIVES **jet-setter** n. **jet-setting** adj.

**jet ski** ● **n.** trademark a small jet-propelled vehicle which skims across the surface of water and is ridden in a similar way to a motorcycle. ● **v.** (**jet-ski**) ride on a jet ski.
– DERIVATIVES **jet-skier** n. **jet-skiing** n.

**jet stream** ● **n. 1** any of several narrow variable bands of very strong predominantly westerly air currents encircling the globe several miles above the earth. **2** a flow of exhaust gases from a jet engine.

**jettison** /ˈdʒɛtɪs(ə)n, -z(ə)n/ ● **v. 1** throw or drop from an aircraft or ship. **2** abandon or discard. ● **n.** the action of jettisoning.
– ORIGIN ME: from OFr. *getaison*, from L. *jactatio(n-)*, from *jactare* (see **JET**[1]).

**jetton** /ˈdʒɛt(ə)n/ ● **n.** a counter or token used as a gambling chip or to operate slot machines.
– ORIGIN C18: from Fr. *jeton*, from *jeter* 'throw, add up accounts' (see **JET**[1]); so named because the term was formerly used in accounting.

**jetty** ● **n.** (pl. **-ies**) **1** a landing stage or small pier. **2** a bridge or staircase used by passengers boarding an aircraft. **3** a construction built out into the water to protect a harbour, stretch of coast, or riverbank.
– ORIGIN ME: from OFr. *jetee*, past part. of *jeter* (see **JET**[1]).

**jetway** ● **n.** (trademark in the UK) another term for **AIR BRIDGE**.

**jeu d'esprit** /ʒəː dɛˈspriː, French ʒø dɛspʀi/ ● **n.** (pl. **jeux d'esprit** pronunc. same) a light-hearted display of wit.
– ORIGIN Fr., lit. 'game of the mind'.

**jeunesse dorée** /ʒəːˌnɛs ˈdɔːreɪ, French ʒœnɛs dɔʀe/ ● **n.** young people of wealth, fashion, and flair.
– ORIGIN C19: Fr., lit. 'gilded youth'.

**Jew** ● **n.** a member of the people whose traditional religion is Judaism and who trace their origins to the ancient Hebrew people of Israel.
– ORIGIN ME: from OFr. *juiu*, via L. from Gk *Ioudaios*, via Aramaic from Heb. *yĕhūḏī*, from *yĕhūḏāh* 'Judah'.

**jewel** ● **n. 1** a precious stone, especially a single crystal or a cut and polished piece of a lustrous or translucent mineral. ➤ (**jewels**) pieces of jewellery. ➤ a hard precious stone used as a bearing in a watch, compass, etc. **2** a highly valued person or thing.
– DERIVATIVES **jewelled** (US **jeweled**) adj.
– PHRASES **the jewel in the** (or **one's**) **crown** the most valuable or successful part of something.
– ORIGIN ME: from OFr. *joel*, from *jeu* 'game, play', from L. *jocus* 'jest'.

**jewel beetle** ● **n.** a chiefly tropical beetle that has bold metallic colours and patterns, the larvae of which are mainly wood-borers and may be serious pests of wood. [Family Buprestidae.]

**jewel box** ● **n. 1** a box for the storage of jewellery. **2** a bivalve mollusc which has a robust shell with a rough or spiny surface. [Family Chamidae: *Chama* and other genera.] **3** (also **jewel case**) a storage box for a compact disc.

**jewelfish** ● **n.** (pl. same or **-fishes**) a scarlet and green tropical freshwater cichlid. [*Hemichromis bimaculatus*.]

**jeweller** (US **jeweler**) ● **n.** a person or company that makes or sells jewels or jewellery.

**jeweller's rouge** ● **n.** finely ground ferric oxide, used as a polish for metal and optical glass.

**jewellery** (US also **jewelry**) ● **n.** personal ornaments, such as necklaces, rings, or bracelets, that are made from or contain jewels and precious metal.

**Jewess** ● **n.** a Jewish woman or girl.

**jewfish** ● **n.** (pl. same or **-fishes**) a large sporting or food fish of warm coastal waters. [*Epinephelus itajara* (N. America) and other species elsewhere.]

**Jewish** ● **adj.** relating to, associated with, or denoting Jews or Judaism.
– DERIVATIVES **Jewishly** adv. **Jewishness** n.

**Jewish New Year** ● **n.** another term for **ROSH HASHANA**.

**Jewry** /ˈdʒʊəri/ ● **n.** (pl. **-ies**) **1** Jews collectively. **2** historical a Jewish quarter in a town or city.

**Jew's ear** ● **n.** a common fungus with a brown rubbery cup-shaped fruiting body, growing on dead or dying trees. [*Auricularia auricula-judae*.]
– ORIGIN C16: a mistranslation of med. L. *auricula Judae* 'Judas's ear', from its shape, and because it grows on the elder, which was said to be the tree from which Judas Iscariot hanged himself.

**Jew's harp** ● **n.** a small lyre-shaped musical instrument held between the teeth and struck with a finger.

**Jezebel** /ˈdʒɛzəbɛl/ ● **n.** a shameless or immoral woman.
– ORIGIN C16: *Jezebel*, wife of Ahab in the Bible.

**-ji** /dʒi/ ● **comb. form** Indian used with names and titles to show respect: *guruji.*
– ORIGIN via Hindi from Sanskrit *jaya* 'conquering'.

**jiao** /dʒaʊ/ ● **n.** (pl. same) a monetary unit of China, equal to one tenth of a yuan.
– ORIGIN from Chin. *jiǎo*.

**jib**[1] ● **n. 1** Sailing a triangular staysail set forward of the mast. **2** the projecting arm of a crane.
– ORIGIN C17: of unknown origin.

**jib**[2] ● **v.** (**jibbed**, **jibbing**) **1** (usu. **jib at**) (of a person) be unwilling to do or accept something. **2** (of a horse) stop and refuse to go on.
– DERIVATIVES **jibber** n.
– ORIGIN C19: perh. rel. to Fr. *regimber* (earlier *regiber*) 'to buck, rear'; cf. **JIBE**[1].

**jibba** /ˈdʒɪbə/ (also **djibba**) ● **n.** a long coat worn by Muslim men.
– ORIGIN C19: Egyptian var. of Arab. *jubba*.

**jib boom** ● **n.** Sailing a spar run out forward as an extension of the bowsprit.

**jibe**[1] (also **gibe**) ● **n.** an insulting or mocking remark. ● **v.** make jibes.
– ORIGIN C16: perh. from OFr. *giber* 'handle roughly' (in mod. dial. 'kick'); cf. **JIB**[2].

**jibe**[2] ● **v. & n.** US variant of **GYBE**.

**jibe**[3] ● **v.** N. Amer. informal be in accordance; agree.
– ORIGIN C19: of unknown origin.

**jib sheet** ● **n.** Sailing a rope by which a jib is trimmed.

**jicama** /ˈhiːkəmə/ ● **n.** the crisp white-fleshed edible tuber of the yam bean, used in Mexican cookery.
– ORIGIN C17: from Mex. Sp. *jícama*.

**jiffy** (also **jiff**) ● **n.** informal a moment.
– ORIGIN C18: of unknown origin.

**Jiffy bag** ● **n.** trademark a padded envelope for protecting fragile items in the post.

**jig** ● **n. 1** a lively dance with leaping movements. ➤ a piece of music for a jig, typically in compound time. **2** a device that guides tools and holds materials or parts securely. **3** Fishing a type of artificial bait that is jerked up and down through the water. ● **v.** (**jigged**, **jigging**) **1** dance a jig. **2** move up and down with a quick jerky motion. **3** equip (a workshop) with a jig or jigs. **4** fish with a jig.
– PHRASES **in jig time** N. Amer. informal extremely quickly. **the jig is up** N. Amer. informal the game is up.
– ORIGIN C16: of unknown origin.

**jigaboo** /ˈdʒɪɡəbuː/ ● **n.** N. Amer. offensive a black person.
– ORIGIN C20: rel. to sl. *jig* (in the same sense); cf. the pair *bug, bugaboo.*

**jigger**[1] ● **n. 1** a machine or vehicle with a part that rocks or moves to and fro. **2** a person who dances a jig. **3** a small sail set at the stern of a ship. **4** a small tackle consisting of a double and single block with a rope. **5** a measure or small glass of spirits or wine. **6** informal a rest for a billiard cue. **7** Golf, dated a metal golf club with a narrow face. ● **v.** informal rearrange or tamper with.

**jigger**[2] ● **n.** variant spelling of **CHIGGER**.

**jiggered** ● **adj.** Brit. informal damaged, broken, or exhausted.
– PHRASES **I'll be jiggered** expressing astonishment.
– ORIGIN C19: from **JIGGER**[1]; prob. euphemism for *buggered.*

**jiggery-pokery** ● **n.** informal, chiefly Brit. deceitful or dishonest behaviour.
– ORIGIN C19: prob. a var. of Scots *joukery-pawkery,* from *jouk* 'dodge, skulk', of unknown origin.

**jiggle** ● **v.** move or cause to move lightly and quickly from side to side or up and down. ● **n.** an instance of jiggling.
– DERIVATIVES **jiggly** adj.
– ORIGIN C19: partly an alt. of **JOGGLE**[1], reinforced by **JIG**.

**jigsaw** ● **n. 1** a puzzle consisting of a picture printed on cardboard or wood and cut into numerous interlocking shapes that have to be fitted together. **2** a machine saw with a fine blade enabling it to cut curved lines in a sheet of wood, metal, etc.

**jihad** /dʒɪˈhɑːd, -ˈhad/ (also **jehad**) ● **n.** a holy war undertaken by Muslims against unbelievers.
– ORIGIN from Arab. *jihād,* lit. 'effort'.

**jill** ● **n.** variant spelling of **GILL**[4].

**jillion** /ˈdʒɪljən/ ● **cardinal number** informal, chiefly N. Amer. an extremely large number.
– ORIGIN 1940s: fanciful formation on the pattern of *billion* and *million.*

**jilt** ● **v.** abruptly break a relationship with (a lover). ● **n.** archaic a person, especially a woman, who capriciously rejects a lover.
– ORIGIN C17: (in the sense 'deceive, trick'): of unknown origin.

**Jim Crow** ● **n.** US **1** the former practice of segregating black people in the US. **2** offensive a black person. **3** an implement for straightening iron bars or bending rails by screw pressure.
– DERIVATIVES **Jim Crowism** n.
– ORIGIN C19: the name of a black character in a plantation song.

**jim-dandy** N. Amer. informal ● **adj.** very pleasing; excellent. ● **n.** an excellent person or thing.
– ORIGIN C19: from the given name *Jim* (familiar form of *James*) + **DANDY**.

**jim-jams**[1] ● **pl. n.** informal a fit of depression or nervousness.
– ORIGIN C16 (orig. denoting a small article or knick-knack): fanciful reduplication.

**jim-jams**[2] ● **pl. n.** Brit. informal pyjamas.
– ORIGIN C20: abbrev. of *pie-jim-jams,* alt. of **PYJAMAS**.

**Jimmy** ● **n.** Brit. informal **1** an act of urination. [1930s: from *Jimmy Riddle,* rhyming sl. for 'piddle'.] **2** chiefly Scottish used as a term of address to a male stranger.

**jimmy** ● **n. & v.** US spelling of **JEMMY**.

**jimson weed** /ˈdʒɪms(ə)n/ (also **jimpson weed**) ● **n.** North American term for **THORN APPLE**.
– ORIGIN C17 (orig. as *Jamestown weed*): named after *Jamestown* in Virginia.

**Jina** /ˈdʒɪnə/ ● **n.** (in Jainism) a great teacher who has attained liberation from karma.
– ORIGIN from Sanskrit, lit. 'victor'.

**jingle** ● **n. 1** a light, loose ringing sound such as that made by metal objects being shaken together. **2** a short easily remembered slogan, verse, or tune. ● **v. 1** make or cause to make a jingle. **2** (of writing) be full of alliteration or rhymes.
– DERIVATIVES **jingler** n. **jingly** adj.
– ORIGIN ME: imitative.

**jingle shell** ● **n.** a bivalve mollusc with a fragile, slightly translucent shell. [Family Anomidae.]

**jingo** /ˈdʒɪŋɡəʊ/ ● **n.** (pl. **-oes**) dated, chiefly derogatory a vociferous supporter of a patriotic war policy.
– PHRASES **by jingo!** an exclamation of surprise.
– ORIGIN C17 (orig. a conjuror's word): from a popular song adopted by those supporting the sending of a Brit. fleet into Turk. waters to resist Russia in 1878.

**jingoism** ● **n.** chiefly derogatory extreme patriotism, especially in the form of aggressive foreign policy.
– DERIVATIVES **jingoist** n. **jingoistic** adj.

**jings** /dʒɪŋz/ ● **exclam.** (also **by jings**) chiefly Scottish used to express surprise.
– ORIGIN C18: alt. of **JINGO**.

**jink** /dʒɪŋk/ ● **v.** change direction suddenly and nimbly. ● **n.** a sudden quick change of direction.
– ORIGIN C17 (orig. Scots as *high jinks,* denoting antics at drinking parties): prob. symbolic of nimble motion.

**jinker** /ˈdʒɪŋkə/ Austral./NZ ● **n.** a wheeled conveyance for moving heavy logs. ● **v.** convey in a jinker.
– ORIGIN C19: var. of Scots *janker,* a long pole on wheels for carrying logs.

**jinn** /dʒɪn/ (also **djinn**) ● **n.** (pl. same or **jinns**) (in Arabian and Muslim mythology) an intelligent spirit able to appear in human and animal form.
– ORIGIN from Arab. *jinnī,* pl. *jinn.*

**jinx** ● **n.** a person or thing that brings bad luck. ● **v.** (usu. **be jinxed**) bring bad luck to.
– ORIGIN C20 (orig. US): prob. a var. of *jynx* 'wryneck' (because the bird was used in witchcraft).

**jird** /dʒəːd/ ● **n.** a long-tailed burrowing rodent related to the gerbils, found in deserts and steppes from North Africa to China. [Genus *Meriones*: several species.]
– ORIGIN from Berber *(a)gherda.*

**jism** /ˈdʒɪz(ə)m/ (also **jissom** /ˈdʒɪsəm/ or **jizz**) ● **n.** vulgar slang semen.
– ORIGIN C19: of unknown origin.

**JIT** ● **abbrev.** (of manufacturing systems) just-in-time.

**jit** /dʒɪt/ (also **jit jive**) ● **n.** a style of dance music popular in Zimbabwe.
– ORIGIN Shona, from *jit* 'to dance'.

**jitney** /ˈdʒɪtni/ ● **n.** (pl. **-eys**) N. Amer. informal a small bus carrying passengers for a low fare.
– ORIGIN C20 (orig. denoting a five-cent piece): of unknown origin.

**jitter** informal ● **n. 1** (**the jitters**) a feeling of extreme nervousness. **2** slight, irregular movement, variation, or unsteadiness in an electrical signal or electronic device. ● **v. 1** act nervously. **2** (of a signal or device) suffer from jitter.
– DERIVATIVES **jitteriness** n. **jittery** adj.
– ORIGIN 1920s: of unknown origin.

**jitterbug** ● **n.** a fast dance performed to swing music, popular in the 1940s. ● **v.** (**-bugged, -bugging**) dance the jitterbug.

**jiu-jitsu** ● **n.** variant spelling of **JU-JITSU**.

**Jivaro** /ˈhiːvərəʊ/ ● **n.** (pl. same or **-os**) **1** a member of an indigenous people living widely scattered throughout the Amazon region. **2** any of the group of languages spoken by this people.
– DERIVATIVES **Jivaroan** adj. & n.
– ORIGIN from Sp. *jíbaro,* prob. from the local name *Shuara, Shiwora.*

**jive** ● **n. 1** a style of lively dance popular in the 1940s and 1950s, performed to swing music or rock and roll. **2** a style of dance music popular in South Africa. **3** (also **jive talk**) a form of slang associated with black American jazz musicians. **4** informal, chiefly N. Amer. deceptive or worthless talk. ● **v. 1** dance the jive. **2** N. Amer. informal taunt or sneer at. **3** informal, chiefly N. Amer. talk nonsense. ● **adj.** N. Amer. informal deceitful or worthless.
– DERIVATIVES **jiver** n. **jivey** adj.
– ORIGIN 1920s (orig. US, denoting meaningless or misleading speech): of unknown origin; the later musical sense 'jazz' gave rise to 'dance performed to jazz' (1940s).

**jizz**[1] ● **n.** informal (among birdwatchers and naturalists) the characteristic impression given by a particular species of animal or plant.

– ORIGIN 1920s: of unknown origin.

**jizz**[2] ● n. vulgar slang variant of **JISM**.

**Jn** ● abbrev. **1** (with preceding numeral) an Epistle of John (in biblical references). **2** the Gospel of John.

**Jnr** ● abbrev. Junior (in names).

**jo** ● n. (pl. **-oes**) Scottish archaic a sweetheart.
– ORIGIN C16: var. of **JOY**.

**joanna** ● n. Brit. rhyming slang a piano.

**job**[1] ● n. **1** a paid position of regular employment. **2** a task or piece of work. ➤a responsibility or duty. ➤informal a crime, especially a robbery. ➤Computing an operation or group of operations treated as a distinct unit. **3** informal a procedure to improve the appearance of something: *a nose job*. **4** informal a thing of a specified nature: *the car was a fast job*. ● v. (**jobbed, jobbing**) **1** [usu. as adj. **jobbing**] do casual or occasional work. **2** buy and sell (stocks) as a broker-dealer, especially on a small scale. **3** N. Amer. informal cheat; betray. **4** archaic turn a public office or a position of trust to private advantage.
– PHRASES **be** (or **have**) **a job** be or have a difficult task. **a good job** informal, chiefly Brit. a fortunate fact or circumstance. **jobs for the boys** Brit. the practice of giving paid employment to one's friends, supporters, or relations. **just the job** Brit. informal exactly what is needed. **on the job 1** while working; at work. **2** Brit. informal engaged in sexual intercourse.
– DERIVATIVES **jobless** adj. **joblessness** n.
– ORIGIN C16: of unknown origin.

**job**[2] archaic ● v. (**jobbed, jobbing**) prod or stab. ● n. an act of prodding or stabbing.
– ORIGIN ME: appar. symbolic of a brief forceful action (cf. **JAB**).

**jobber** ● n. **1** (in the UK) a principal or wholesaler dealing only on the Stock Exchange with brokers, not directly with the public (term officially replaced by **broker-dealer** in 1986). **2** N. Amer. a wholesaler. **3** a person who does casual or occasional work.

**jobbery** ● n. the practice of using a public office or position of trust for one's own gain or advantage.

**jobbie** ● n. informal **1** an object or product of a specified kind: *these computer jobbies*. **2** a piece of excrement.

**jobcentre** ● n. (in the UK) a government office in a local area, giving information about available jobs and administering benefits to unemployed people.

**job club** ● n. (in the UK) an organization providing support and practical help for the long-term unemployed in seeking work.

**job control language** ● n. Computing a language enabling the user to define the tasks to be undertaken by the operating system.

**job lot** ● n. a batch of articles sold or bought at one time, especially at a discount.

**Job's comforter** /dʒəʊbz/ ● n. a person who aggravates distress under the guise of giving comfort.
– ORIGIN C18: alluding to the biblical story (Job 16:2) of the patriarch *Job*.

**job-share** ● v. (of two part-time employees) jointly do a full-time job. ● n. an arrangement of such a kind.
– DERIVATIVES **job-sharer** n.

**Job's tears** /dʒəʊbz/ ● pl. n. a SE Asian grass which bears its seeds inside shiny pear-shaped receptacles, which are sometimes used as beads. [*Coix lacryma-jobi*.]
– ORIGIN C16: named after the biblical patriarch *Job*.

**jobsworth** ● n. Brit. informal an official who mindlessly upholds petty rules.
– ORIGIN 1970s: from 'it's more than my *job's worth* (not) to...'.

**Jock** ● n. informal, often offensive a Scotsman.
– ORIGIN C16: Scots form of the given name *Jack* (see **JACK**[1]).

**jock**[1] ● n. informal **1** a disc jockey. **2** N. Amer. an enthusiast or participant in a specified activity: *a computer jock*.
– ORIGIN C18 (denoting a jockey): abbrev.

**jock**[2] ● n. N. Amer. informal **1** another term for **JOCKSTRAP**. **2** an enthusiastic male athlete or sports fan.
– DERIVATIVES **jockish** adj.

**jock**[3] ● n. US informal a pilot or astronaut.
– ORIGIN C20: prob. an abbrev. of **JOCKEY**, from its informal use in combinations such as *jet jockey*.

**jockey** ● n. (pl. **-eys**) a professional rider in horse races. ● v. (**-eys, -eyed**) **1** struggle to gain or achieve something. **2** handle or manipulate in a skilful manner.
– DERIVATIVES **jockeyship** n.
– ORIGIN C16: dimin. of **JOCK**, orig. denoting an ordinary man, later 'mounted courier' and 'horse dealer'.

**jockey cap** ● n. a strengthened cap with a long peak of a kind worn by jockeys.

**jock itch** ● n. N. Amer. informal a fungal infection of the groin area.
– ORIGIN 1970s: *jock* from **JOCKSTRAP**.

**jockstrap** ● n. a support or protection for the male genitals, worn especially by sportsmen.
– ORIGIN C19: from sl. *jock* 'genitals' (of unknown origin) + **STRAP**.

**jocose** /dʒə'kəʊs/ ● adj. formal playful or humorous.
– DERIVATIVES **jocosely** adv. **jocoseness** n. **jocosity** /-'kɒsɪti/ n. (pl. **-ies**).
– ORIGIN C17: from L. *jocosus*, from *jocus* (see **JOKE**).

**jocular** /'dʒɒkjʊlə/ ● adj. fond of or characterized by joking; humorous.
– DERIVATIVES **jocularity** n. **jocularly** adv.
– ORIGIN C17: from L. *jocularis*, from *joculus*, dimin. of *jocus* (see **JOKE**).

**jocund** /'dʒɒk(ə)nd, 'dʒəʊk-/ ● adj. formal cheerful and light-hearted.
– DERIVATIVES **jocundity** n. (pl. **-ies**). **jocundly** adv.
– ORIGIN ME: via OFr. from L. *jocundus*, var. (influenced by *jocus* 'joke') of *jucundus* 'pleasant, agreeable'.

**jodhpurs** /'dʒɒdpəz/ ● pl. n. trousers worn for horse riding that are close-fitting below the knee and have reinforced patches on the inside of the leg.
– ORIGIN C19: named after the Indian city of *Jodhpur*.

**joe** ● n. **1** an ordinary man. [C19: familiar form of the given name *Joseph*.] **2** N. Amer. informal coffee. [1940s: of unknown origin.]

**Joe Bloggs** (N. Amer. **Joe Blow**) ● n. Brit. informal a name used to represent the average person.

**Joe Public** ● n. Brit. informal a name used to represent the general public.

**joe-pye weed** ● n. a tall North American plant of the daisy family, with small purple flowers. [*Eupatorium purpureum* and *E. maculatum*.]
– ORIGIN C19: of unknown origin.

**Joe Sixpack** ● n. informal, chiefly US a name used to represent the ordinary working man.

**joey** ● n. (pl. **-eys**) Austral. **1** a young kangaroo, wallaby, or possum. **2** informal a baby or young child.
– ORIGIN from Aborig. *joè*.

**jog** ● v. (**jogged, jogging**) **1** run at a steady, gentle pace, especially as a form of exercise. ➤(of a horse) move at a slow trot. ➤(**jog along/on**) continue in a steady, uneventful way. **2** nudge or knock slightly. ➤trigger; stimulate. ● n. **1** a spell of jogging. **2** a gentle running pace. **3** a slight push or nudge.
– ORIGIN ME (in the sense 'stab, pierce'): var. of **JAG**[1].

**jogger** ● n. **1** a person who jogs. **2** (**joggers**) tracksuit trousers worn for jogging.

**joggle**[1] ● v. move or cause to move with repeated small bobs or jerks. ● n. a joggling movement.
– ORIGIN C16: frequentative of **JOG**.

**joggle**[2] ● n. a joint between two pieces of stone, concrete, or timber, consisting of a projection in one of the pieces fitting into a notch in the other, or a small piece let in between the two. ● v. join with a joggle.
– ORIGIN C18: perh. rel. to **JAG**[1].

**jog-shuttle** ● n. a facility on some video recorders which allows the speed at which the tape is played to be varied.

**jogtrot** ● n. a slow trot.

**john** ● n. informal **1** chiefly N. Amer. a toilet. **2** a prostitute's client.
– ORIGIN C20: from the given name *John*.

**John Barleycorn** ● n. a personification of barley, or of malt liquor.

**johnboat** • n. N. Amer. a small flat-bottomed boat with square ends, used chiefly on inland waterways.

**John Bull** • n. a personification of England or the typical Englishman.
– ORIGIN C18: from the name of a character in John Arbuthnot's satire *Law is a Bottomless Pit; or, the History of John Bull* (1712).

**John Doe** • n. **1** Law, chiefly N. Amer. an anonymous party in a legal action. **2** N. Amer. informal a hypothetical average man.
– ORIGIN C18: orig. in legal use as a name of a fictitious plaintiff, corresp. to *Richard Roe*, a fictitious defendant.

**John Dory** • n. (pl. **-ies**) an edible dory (fish) of the eastern Atlantic and Mediterranean, with a black oval mark on each side. [*Zeus faber.*]

**Johne's disease** /ˈjəʊnəz/ • n. a form of chronic enteritis in cattle and sheep, caused by a mycobacterium.
– ORIGIN C20: named after the Ger. veterinary surgeon Heinrich A. *Johne.*

**johnny** • n. (pl. **-ies**) Brit. informal **1** a man. **2** a condom.
– ORIGIN C17: familiar form of the given name *John.*

**johnnycake** • n. **1** N. Amer. maize flour bread baked or fried on a griddle. **2** Austral./NZ a small unleavened wheat loaf baked in wood ashes.
– ORIGIN C18: also as *journey cake*, perh. the original form.

**johnny-come-lately** • n. informal a newcomer or late starter.

**John Q. Public** • n. North American term for **JOE PUBLIC**.

**joie de vivre** /ˌʒwɑː də ˈviːvr(ə), French ʒwad vivʀ/ • n. exuberant enjoyment of life.
– ORIGIN Fr., lit. 'joy of living'.

**join** • v. **1** link or become linked or connected to. ➤ unite. **2** become a member or employee of. ➤ take part in. ➤ (**join up**) become a member of the armed forces. ➤ come into the company of. ➤ support in an activity. • n. a place where two or more things are joined.
– PHRASES **join battle** formal begin fighting. **join forces** combine efforts.
– DERIVATIVES **joinable** adj.
– ORIGIN ME: from OFr. *joindre*, from L. *jungere* 'to join'.

**joinder** /ˈdʒɔɪndə/ • n. Law the action of bringing together.
– ORIGIN ME: from Anglo-Norman Fr., from OFr. *joindre* 'to join'.

**joiner** • n. **1** a person who constructs the wooden components of a building. **2** informal a person who readily joins groups.

**joinery** • n. the wooden components of a building collectively.

**joint** • n. **1** a point at which parts are joined. ➤ Geology a break or fracture in a mass of rock. ➤ a piece of flexible material forming the hinge of a book cover. **2** a structure in a body by which two bones are fitted together. ➤ a section of a body or limb between connecting places. ➤ Brit. a large piece of meat. ➤ the part of a plant stem from which a leaf or branch grows. ➤ a section of a plant stem between such parts. **3** informal an establishment of a specified kind: *a burger joint.* ➤ (**the joint**) N. Amer. prison. **4** informal a cannabis cigarette. • adj. shared, held, or made by two or more people. ➤ sharing in an achievement or activity. ➤ Law applied or regarded together. Contrasted with **SEVERAL**. • v. **1** provide or fasten with joints. ➤ prepare (a board) to be joined to another by planing its edge. **2** point (masonry or brickwork). **3** cut (the body of an animal) into joints.
– PHRASES **out of joint** (of a joint of the body) dislocated. ➤ in a state of disorder or disorientation.
– DERIVATIVES **jointless** adj. **jointly** adv.
– ORIGIN ME: from OFr., past part. of *joindre* (see **JOIN**).

**joint and several** • adj. (of a legal obligation) undertaken by two or more people, each having liability for the whole.

**jointer** • n. **1** a plane for preparing a wooden edge for joining to another. **2** a tool for pointing masonry and brickwork. **3** a person who joints pipes or wires.

**jointress** • n. Law, dated a widow holding a jointure.
– ORIGIN C17: fem. of obs. *jointer* 'joint owner'.

**joint-stock company** • n. Finance a company whose stock is owned jointly by the shareholders.

**jointure** /ˈdʒɔɪntʃə/ • n. Law an estate settled on a wife for the period during which she survives her husband.
– ORIGIN ME (orig. denoting the joint holding of property): from OFr., from L. *junctura* (see **JUNCTURE**).

**joist** /dʒɔɪst/ • n. a length of timber or steel supporting part of the structure of a building.
– DERIVATIVES **joisted** adj.
– ORIGIN ME *giste*, from OFr., 'beam supporting a bridge', based on L. *jacere* 'lie down'.

**jojoba** /həˈhəʊbə, həʊ-/ • n. **1** (also **jojoba oil**) an oil extracted from the seeds of a North American shrub, widely used in cosmetics. **2** the leathery-leaved evergreen shrub that produces these seeds. [*Simmondsia chinensis.*]
– ORIGIN C20: from Mex. Sp.

**joke** • n. **1** a thing said to cause amusement. ➤ a trick played for fun. **2** informal a ridiculously inadequate person or thing. • v. make jokes. ➤ archaic poke fun at.
– PHRASES **be no joke** informal be a serious or difficult matter. **be beyond a joke** informal be serious or worrying.
– DERIVATIVES **jokey** (also **joky**) adj. **jokily** adv. **jokiness** n. **joking** adj. **jokingly** adv.
– ORIGIN C17: perh. from L. *jocus* 'jest, wordplay'.

**joker** • n. **1** a person who is fond of joking. ➤ informal a foolish or inept person. **2** a playing card with the figure of a jester, used as a wild card. **3** US a clause in a bill or document affecting its operation in a way not immediately apparent.
– PHRASES **the joker in the pack** an unpredictable person or factor.

**jolie laide** /ˌʒɒlɪ ˈlɛd/ • n. (pl. **jolies laides** pronunc. same) a woman who is attractive despite having ugly features.
– ORIGIN Fr., from *jolie* 'pretty' and *laide* 'ugly'.

**jollification** • n. merrymaking.

**jollity** • n. (pl. **-ies**) lively and cheerful activity. ➤ the quality of being jolly.

**jolly**[1] • adj. (**-ier**, **-iest**) happy and cheerful. ➤ informal, dated lively and entertaining. • v. (**-ies**, **-ied**) informal encourage in a friendly way. ➤ (**jolly someone/thing up**) make someone or something more jolly. • adv. Brit. informal very. • n. (pl. **-ies**) Brit. informal a party or celebration.
– PHRASES **get one's jollies** informal have fun. **jolly well** Brit. informal used for emphasis: *I should jolly well hope so!*
– DERIVATIVES **jollily** adv. **jolliness** n.
– ORIGIN ME: from OFr. *jolif*, an earlier form of *joli* 'pretty', perh. from ON *jól* (see **YULE**).

**jolly**[2] (also **jolly boat**) • n. (pl. **-ies**) a clinker-built ship's boat that is smaller than a cutter.
– ORIGIN C18: perh. rel. to **YAWL**.

**Jolly Roger** • n. a pirate's flag with a white skull and crossbones on a black background.
– ORIGIN C18: of unknown origin.

**jolt** /dʒəʊlt, dʒɒlt/ • v. **1** push or shake abruptly and roughly. **2** shock (someone) in order to make them act or change. • n. **1** an act of jolting. **2** a surprise or shock.
– DERIVATIVES **jolty** adj.
– ORIGIN C16: of unknown origin.

**Jon.** • abbrev. **1** Jonah (in biblical references). **2** Jonathan.

**jones** US, chiefly black slang • n. an addiction. • v. (**jones on/for**) be addicted to.
– ORIGIN 1960s: said to come from *Jones* Alley, in Manhattan, assoc. with drug addicts.

**Joneses** • n. (in phr. **keep up with the Joneses**) strive not be outdone by one's neighbours.
– ORIGIN C19: from the surname *Jones.*

**jong** /jɒŋ/ • n. S. African, chiefly historical a young black male servant. ➤ offensive a black man.
– ORIGIN Afrik., from earlier S. Afr. Du. *jongen* 'lad'.

**jongleur** /dʒɔ̃ˈgləː/ • n. historical an itinerant minstrel.
– ORIGIN Fr., var. of *jougleur* 'juggler', earlier *jogleor* 'pleasant, smiling', from L. *joculator* 'joker'.

**jonquil** /ˈdʒʌŋkwɪl, ˈdʒɒn-/ • n. a narcissus with small fragrant yellow flowers and cylindrical leaves. [*Narcissus jonquilla.*]

– ORIGIN C17: from mod. L. *jonquilla* or Fr. *jonquille*, from Sp. *junquillo*, dimin. of *junco*, from L. *juncus* 'rush, reed'.

**Jordanian** ● **n.** a native or inhabitant of Jordan. ● **adj.** of or relating to Jordan or the River Jordan in the Middle East.

**jorum** /'dʒɔːrəm/ ● **n.** historical a large bowl or jug for serving drinks.
– ORIGIN C18: perh. from *Joram* (2 Sam. 8:10), who 'brought with him vessels of silver, and vessels of gold' to King David.

**Jos.** ● **abbrev.** **1** Joseph. **2** Joshua (in biblical references).

**Josephson junction** ● **n.** Physics an electrical device in which two superconducting metals are separated by a thin layer of insulator, across which an electric current may flow in the absence of a potential difference.
– ORIGIN 1960s: named after the Brit. physicist Brian D. *Josephson*.

**Josh.** ● **abbrev.** Joshua (in biblical references).

**josh** informal ● **v.** tease playfully; banter. ● **n.** N. Amer. good-natured banter.
– DERIVATIVES **josher** n.
– ORIGIN C19: of unknown origin.

**Joshua tree** ● **n.** a tall branching yucca of SW North America, with clusters of spiky leaves. [*Yucca brevifolia*.]
– ORIGIN C19: appar. from *Joshua* (Josh. 8:18), the plant being likened to a man with a spear.

**joss**[1] ● **n.** a Chinese idol.
– ORIGIN C18: from Javanese *dejos*, from obs. Port. *deos*, from L. *deus* 'god'.

**joss**[2] ● **n.** informal, chiefly Austral. an important person.
– ORIGIN C19: from dial. *joss* 'foreman', of unknown origin.

**josser** ● **n.** informal **1** Brit. a man, typically one regarded with contempt: *an old josser.* **2** Austral. a clergyman.
– ORIGIN C19: from **JOSS**[1] + **-ER**[1].

**joss house** ● **n.** a Chinese temple.

**joss stick** ● **n.** a thin stick of a fragrant substance, burnt as incense.

**jostle** ● **v.** push or bump against roughly. ➤**(jostle for)** struggle or compete forcefully for. ● **n.** the action of jostling.
– ORIGIN ME *justle*, from *just*, an earlier form of **JOUST**.

**jot** ● **v.** **(jotted, jotting)** write quickly. ● **n.** [usu. with neg.] a very small amount.
– ORIGIN C15: via L. from Gk *iōta*, the smallest letter of the Gk alphabet (see **IOTA**).

**jota** /'xəʊtə/ ● **n.** a Spanish folk dance for couples, in fast triple time.
– ORIGIN from Sp.

**jotter** ● **n.** Brit. a small notebook.

**jotting** ● **n.** a brief note.

**joual** /ʒwal, ʒuː'ɑːl/ ● **n.** a non-standard form of Canadian French, influenced by English.
– ORIGIN Canad. Fr. dial., from Fr. *cheval* 'horse', appar. from the way *cheval* is pronounced in rural Quebec.

**jougs** /dʒuːgz/ ● **pl. n.** a hinged iron collar chained to a wall or post, used in medieval Scotland as a punishment.
– ORIGIN C16: from Fr. *joug* or L. *jugum* 'yoke'.

**jouissance** /'ʒwiːsɒ̃s, French ʒwisɑ̃s/ ● **n.** formal pleasure.
– ORIGIN Fr., from *jouir* 'enjoy'.

**jouk** /dʒuːk/ ● **v.** Scottish & N. English turn or bend quickly to avoid something.
– ORIGIN C16: perh. rel. to **DUCK**[2].

**joule** /dʒuːl/ (abbrev.: **J**) ● **n.** the SI unit of work or energy, equal to the work done by a force of one newton when its point of application moves one metre in the direction of action of the force.
– ORIGIN C19: named after the Engl. physicist James P. *Joule*.

**Joule's law** ● **n.** Physics a law stating that the heat produced by an electric current $i$ flowing through a resistance $R$ for a time $t$ is proportional to $i^2Rt$.

**Joule–Thomson effect** ● **n.** Physics an increase or decrease in the temperature of a gas when it is allowed to expand without doing any external work.

**jounce** /dʒaʊns/ ● **v.** jolt or bounce.
– ORIGIN ME: prob. symbolic; cf. **BOUNCE**.

**journal** /'dʒəːn(ə)l/ ● **n.** **1** a newspaper or magazine dealing with a particular subject. **2** a diary. ➤Nautical a logbook. ➤**(the Journals)** a record of the daily proceedings in the Houses of Parliament. ➤(in bookkeeping) a daily record of business transactions. **3** the part of a shaft or axle that rests on bearings.
– ORIGIN ME: from OFr. *jurnal*, from late L. *diurnalis* (see **DIURNAL**).

**journalese** ● **n.** informal a hackneyed writing style supposedly characteristic of journalists.

**journalism** ● **n.** the activity or profession of being a journalist.

**journalist** ● **n.** a person who writes for newspapers or magazines or prepares news to be broadcast on radio or television.
– DERIVATIVES **journalistic** adj. **journalistically** adv.

**journalize** (also **-ise**) ● **v.** dated enter (information) in a journal.

**journey** ● **n.** (pl. **-eys**) an act of travelling from one place to another. ● **v.** **(-eys, -eyed)** travel.
– DERIVATIVES **journeyer** n.
– ORIGIN ME: from OFr. *jornee* 'day, a day's travel, a day's work', based on L. *diurnum* 'daily portion', from *diurnus* (see **DIURNAL**).

**journeyman** ● **n.** (pl. **-men**) **1** a skilled worker who is employed by another. **2** a worker who is reliable but not outstanding.
– ORIGIN ME: from **JOURNEY** (in the obs. sense 'day's work') + **MAN**; so named because the journeyman was paid by the day.

**journo** ● **n.** (pl. **-os**) informal a journalist.

**joust** /dʒaʊst/ ● **v.** **1** [often as noun **jousting**] (of a medieval knight) engage in a contest in which two opponents on horseback fight with lances. **2** compete for superiority. ● **n.** a jousting contest.
– DERIVATIVES **jouster** n.
– ORIGIN ME: from OFr. *jouster* 'bring together', based on L. *juxta* 'near'.

**J'Ouvert** /dʒuː'veɪ/ ● **n.** (in the Caribbean) the official start of carnival, at dawn on the Monday preceding Lent.
– ORIGIN Fr. Creole, from Fr. *jour ouvert* 'day opened'.

**Jove** /'dʒəʊv/ ● **n.** (in phr. **by Jove**) dated used for emphasis or to indicate surprise.
– ORIGIN from *Jove*, the chief of the Roman gods, equivalent to Jupiter.

**jovial** /'dʒəʊvɪəl, -vj(ə)l/ ● **adj.** cheerful and friendly.
– DERIVATIVES **joviality** n. **jovially** adv.
– ORIGIN C16: from Fr., from late L. *jovialis* 'of Jupiter', with ref. to the supposed influence of the planet Jupiter on those born under it.

**Jovian** /'dʒəʊvɪən/ ● **adj.** **1** (in Roman mythology) of or like the god Jove (or Jupiter). **2** of, relating to, or resembling the planet Jupiter.

**jowar** /dʒaʊ'ɑː/ ● **n.** another term for **DURRA**.
– ORIGIN from Hindi *jawār*.

**jowl** ● **n.** the lower part of a cheek, especially when fleshy or drooping. ➤N. Amer. the cheek of a pig as meat. ➤the dewlap of cattle or wattle of birds.
– DERIVATIVES **-jowled** adj. **jowly** adj.
– ORIGIN OE *ceole*, partly merged with OE *ceafl* 'jaw'.

**joy** ● **n.** **1** a feeling of great pleasure and happiness. ➤a cause of joy. **2** [usu. with neg.] Brit. informal success or satisfaction. ● **v.** poetic/literary rejoice.
– PHRASES **be full of the joys of spring** be lively and cheerful. **wish someone joy** Brit., chiefly ironic congratulate someone.
– DERIVATIVES **joyless** adj. **joylessly** adv.
– ORIGIN ME: from OFr. *joie*, based on L. *gaudium*, from *gaudere* 'rejoice'.

**joyful** ● **adj.** feeling or causing joy.
– DERIVATIVES **joyfully** adv. **joyfulness** n.

**joyous** ● **adj.** chiefly poetic/literary full of happiness and joy.
– DERIVATIVES **joyously** adv. **joyousness** n.

**joypad** • n. a device for a computer games console which uses buttons to control an image on the screen.
– ORIGIN C20: blend of JOYSTICK and KEYPAD.

**joyride** • n. informal **1** a fast ride in a stolen vehicle. **2** a ride for enjoyment.
– DERIVATIVES **joyrider** n. **joyriding** n.

**joystick** • n. informal **1** the control column of an aircraft. **2** a lever for controlling the movement of an image on a computer screen.

**JP** • abbrev. Justice of the Peace.

**JPEG** /ˈdʒeɪpɛg/ • n. Computing a format for compressing images.
– ORIGIN 1990s: abbrev. of *Joint Photographic Experts Group*.

**Jr** • abbrev. (in names) junior.

**jube** • n. Austral./NZ a jujube lozenge.

**jubilant** • adj. happy and triumphant.
– DERIVATIVES **jubilance** n. **jubilantly** adv.
– ORIGIN C17: from L. *jubilant-*, *jubilare* (see JUBILATION).

**Jubilate** /ˌdʒuːbɪˈlɑːteɪ/ • n. Psalm 100, beginning *Jubilate deo*, especially as used as a canticle.
– ORIGIN L., 'shout for joy!', imper. of *jubilare* (see JUBILATION).

**jubilation** /ˌdʒuːbɪˈleɪʃ(ə)n/ • n. a feeling of great happiness and triumph.
– DERIVATIVES **jubilate** v.
– ORIGIN ME: from L. *jubilat-*, *jubilare* 'shout for joy'.

**jubilee** • n. **1** a special anniversary, especially one celebrating twenty-five or fifty years of something. **2** Jewish History a year of emancipation and restoration, kept every fifty years. **3** a period of remission from the penal consequences of sin, granted by the Roman Catholic Church under certain conditions for a year, at intervals of twenty-five years.
– ORIGIN ME: from OFr. *jubile*, from late L. *jubilaeus (annus)* '(year) of jubilee', based on Heb. *yōḇēl*, orig. 'ram's-horn trumpet', with which the jubilee was proclaimed.

**Jubilee clip** • n. trademark an adjustable steel band secured with a screw.

**Jud.** • abbrev. **1** Judges (in biblical references). **2** Judith (Apocrypha) (in biblical references).

**Judaean** /dʒuːˈdiːən/ • n. a native or inhabitant of Judaea, the southern part of ancient Palestine. • adj. of or relating to Judaea.

**Judaeo-** /dʒuːˈdiːəʊ/ (US **Judeo-**) • comb. form **1** Jewish; Jewish and ...: *Judaeo-Christian*. **2** relating to Judaea.
– ORIGIN from L. *Judaeus* 'Jewish'.

**Judaic** /dʒuːˈdeɪɪk/ • adj. of or relating to Judaism or the ancient Jews.

**Judaism** /ˈdʒuːdeɪɪz(ə)m/ • n. **1** the monotheistic religion of the Jews, based on the Old Testament and the Talmud. **2** Jews collectively.
– DERIVATIVES **Judaist** n.
– ORIGIN ME: from late L. *Judaismus*, from Gk *Ioudaïsmos*, from *Ioudaios* (see JEW).

**Judaize** /ˈdʒuːdeɪʌɪz/ (also **-ise**) • v. **1** make Jewish. **2** follow Jewish customs or religious rites.
– DERIVATIVES **Judaization** n.

**Judas** /ˈdʒuːdəs/ • n. a person who betrays a friend.
– ORIGIN from the name of *Judas* Iscariot, the disciple who betrayed Christ.

**judas** (also **judas hole**) • n. a peephole in a door.
– ORIGIN C19: from *Judas* Iscariot (see JUDAS), because of his assoc. with betrayal.

**Judas tree** • n. a Mediterranean tree of the pea family, with purple flowers that appear before the rounded leaves. [*Cercis siliquastrum*.]

**judder** • v. chiefly Brit. shake and vibrate rapidly and forcefully. • n. an instance of juddering.
– DERIVATIVES **juddery** adj.
– ORIGIN 1930s: imitative; cf. SHUDDER.

**judenrein** /ˈjuːd(ə)nrʌɪn/ • adj. (in Nazi Germany) denoting a place from which Jews were excluded.
– ORIGIN Ger., 'free of Jews'.

**Judeo-** • comb. form US spelling of JUDAEO-.

**Judg.** • abbrev. Judges (in biblical references).

**judge** • n. **1** a public officer appointed to decide cases in a law court. ➤ a person who decides the results of a competition. ➤ a person able or qualified to give an opinion: *a good judge of character*. **2** a leader having temporary authority in ancient Israel in the period between Joshua and the kings. • v. form an opinion about. ➤ give a verdict on in a law court. ➤ decide the results of.
– DERIVATIVES **judgeship** n.
– ORIGIN ME: from OFr. *juge* (n.), *juger* (v.), from L. *judex*, *judic-*, from *jus* 'law' + *dicere* 'to say'.

**judge advocate** • n. Law a barrister who advises a court martial on points of law and sums up the case.

**Judge Advocate General** • n. an officer in supreme control of the courts martial, excluding (in the UK) that of the navy.

**judgement** (also **judgment**) • n. **1** the ability to make considered decisions or form sensible opinions. ➤ an opinion or conclusion. ➤ a decision of a law court or judge. **2** formal or humorous a misfortune viewed as a divine punishment.
– PHRASES **against one's better judgement** contrary to what one feels to be wise.

**judgemental** (also **judgmental**) • adj. **1** of or concerning the use of judgement. **2** having an excessively critical point of view.
– DERIVATIVES **judgementally** adv.

**Judgement Day** • n. the time of the Last Judgement.

**judgement in default** • n. Law judgement awarded to the plaintiff on the defendant's failure to plead.

**Judges' Rules** • pl. n. English Law rules regarding the admissibility of an accused's statements as evidence.

**judicature** /ˈdʒuːdɪkəˌtʃə, dʒʊˈdɪk-/ • n. **1** the administration of justice. **2** (**the judicature**) the judiciary.
– DERIVATIVES **judicatory** adj.
– ORIGIN C16: from med. L. *judicatura*, from L. *judicare* 'to judge'.

**judicial** /dʒuːˈdɪʃ(ə)l/ • adj. of, by, or appropriate to a law court or judge.
– DERIVATIVES **judicially** adv.
– ORIGIN ME: from L. *judicialis*, from *judicium* 'judgement', from *judex* (see JUDGE).

**judicial factor** • n. Scots Law an agent appointed to administer a person's estate.

**judicial review** • n. **1** (in the UK) a procedure by which a court can pronounce on an administrative action by a public body. **2** (in the US) review by the Supreme Court of the constitutional validity of a legislative act.

**judicial separation** • n. another term for LEGAL SEPARATION (in sense 1).

**judiciary** /dʒʊˈdɪʃ(ə)ri/ • n. (pl. **-ies**) (usu. **the judiciary**) the judicial authorities of a country.

**judicious** /dʒʊˈdɪʃəs/ • adj. having or done with good judgement.
– DERIVATIVES **judiciously** adv. **judiciousness** n.
– ORIGIN C16: from Fr. *judicieux*, from L. *judicium* (see JUDICIAL).

**judo** • n. a sport of unarmed combat derived from ju-jitsu, using holds and leverage to unbalance the opponent.
– DERIVATIVES **judoist** n.
– ORIGIN C19: Japanese, from *jū* 'gentle' + *dō* 'way'.

**judoka** /ˈdʒuːdəʊˌkə/ • n. a person who practises judo.
– ORIGIN Japanese, from JUDO + *-ka* 'person, profession'.

**Judy** • n. (pl. **-ies**) **1** the wife of Punch (see PUNCH[4]). **2** Brit. informal, dated a woman.

**jug** • n. **1** Brit. a cylindrical container with a handle and a lip, for holding and pouring liquids. ➤ N. Amer. a large container for liquids, with a narrow mouth. **2** (**the jug**) informal prison. **3** (**jugs**) vulgar slang a woman's breasts. • v. (**jugged**, **jugging**) **1** [usu. as adj. **jugged**] stew or boil (a hare or rabbit) in a covered container. **2** informal, chiefly N. Amer. prosecute and imprison.
– DERIVATIVES **jugful** n. (pl. **-fuls**).
– ORIGIN C16: perh. from *Jug*, familiar form of the given names *Joan*, *Joanna*, and *Jenny*.

**jug band** • n. a group of jazz, blues, or folk musicians using simple or improvised instruments such as jugs and washboards.

**Jugendstil** /'ju:gənd,ʃti:l, German 'ju:gnt,ʃtil/ ● **n.** German name for **ART NOUVEAU.**
– ORIGIN Ger., from *Jugend* 'youth' + *Stil* 'style'.

**juggernaut** /'dʒʌgənɔ:t/ ● **n. 1** Brit. a large heavy vehicle, especially an articulated truck. **2** a huge and overwhelming force.
– ORIGIN C19: via Hindi from Sanskrit *Jagannātha* 'Lord of the world', the name of an image of the Hindu god Krishna carried in procession on a heavy chariot.

**juggins** ● **n.** Brit. informal, dated a simpleton.
– ORIGIN C19: perh. from the surname *Juggins*; cf. **MUGGINS.**

**juggle** ● **v. 1** continuously toss into the air and catch a number of objects so as to keep at least one in the air at any time. **2** cope with by adroitly balancing (several activities). **3** misrepresent (facts). ● **n.** an act of juggling.
– DERIVATIVES **juggler** n. **jugglery** n.
– ORIGIN ME: back-form. from *juggler*, or from OFr. *jogler*, from L. *joculari* 'to jest', from *joculus*, dimin. of *jocus* 'jest'.

**Jugoslav** ● **n. & adj.** old-fashioned spelling of **YUGOSLAV.**

**jugular** /'dʒʌgjʊlə/ ● **adj. 1** of the neck or throat. **2** Zoology (of fish's pelvic fins) located in front of the pectoral fins. ● **n.** short for **JUGULAR VEIN.**
– ORIGIN C16: from late L. *jugularis*, from L. *jugulum* 'collarbone, throat', dimin. of *jugum* 'yoke'.

**jugular vein** ● **n.** any of several large veins in the neck, carrying blood from the head.

**jugulate** /'dʒʌgjʊleɪt/ ● **v.** archaic kill by cutting the throat.

**jugum** /'dʒu:gəm/ ● **n.** (pl. **juga**) chiefly Zoology a connecting ridge or projection, especially on a bone.
– DERIVATIVES **jugal** adj.
– ORIGIN C19: from L., lit. 'yoke'.

**juice** ● **n. 1** the liquid present in fruit or vegetables. ➤a drink made from this. **2** (**juices**) fluid secreted by the body, especially in the stomach. **3** (**juices**) liquid coming from meat or other food in cooking. **4** informal electrical energy. ➤petrol. **5** (**juices**) one's vitality or creative faculties. **6** N. Amer. informal alcoholic drink. ● **v. 1** extract the juice from. **2** (**juice something up**) informal, chiefly N. Amer. liven something up. **3** [as adj. **juiced**] N. Amer. informal drunk.
– DERIVATIVES **juiceless** adj.
– ORIGIN ME: via OFr. from L. *jus* 'broth, vegetable juice'.

**juicer** ● **n.** an appliance for extracting juice from fruit and vegetables.

**juicy** ● **adj.** (**-ier, -iest**) **1** full of juice. **2** informal interestingly scandalous. **3** informal profitable.
– DERIVATIVES **juicily** adv. **juiciness** n.

**ju-jitsu** /dʒu:'dʒɪtsu:/ (also **jiu-jitsu** or **ju-jutsu** /-'jʌtsu:/) ● **n.** a Japanese system of unarmed combat and physical training.
– ORIGIN Japanese *jūjutsu*, from *jū* 'gentle' + *jutsu* 'skill'.

**juju**[1] /'dʒu:dʒu:/ ● **n.** a style of Nigerian music characterized by the use of guitars and variable-pitch drums.
– ORIGIN perh. from Yoruba *jo jo* 'dance'.

**juju**[2] /'dʒu:dʒu:/ ● **n.** a charm or fetish, especially as used by some West African peoples. ➤supernatural power.
– ORIGIN C17: of W. Afr. origin, perh. from Fr. *joujou* 'toy'.

**jujube** /'dʒu:dʒu:b/ ● **n. 1** the edible berry-like fruit of the jujube bush, formerly taken as a cough cure. ➤chiefly N. Amer. a jujube-flavoured lozenge or sweet. **2** (also **jujube bush**) the shrub that produces this fruit. [*Ziziphus jujuba*.]
– ORIGIN ME: from Fr., or from med. L. *jujuba*, based on Gk *zizuphos*.

**juke** N. Amer. informal ● **n.** (also **juke joint**) a roadhouse, nightclub, or bar, especially one providing food, drinks, and music for dancing. ● **v. 1** dance, especially to the music of a jukebox. **2** (in sport) make a sham move to confuse or mislead an opponent. ➤move in a zigzag fashion: *I juked down an alley.*
– ORIGIN 1930s: from Gullah *juke* 'disorderly'.

**jukebox** ● **n.** a machine that automatically plays a selected musical recording when a coin is inserted.

**juku** /'dʒʊku:/ ● **n.** (pl. same) (in Japan) a private school attended in addition to an ordinary educational institution.
– ORIGIN from Japanese.

**Jul.** ● **abbrev.** July.

**julep** /'dʒu:lɛp/ ● **n.** a sweet drink made from sugar syrup, sometimes containing alcohol or medicine.
– ORIGIN ME: from OFr., from med. L. *julapium*, via Arab. from Pers. *gulāb*, from *gul* 'rose' + *āb* 'water'.

**Julian** /'dʒu:lɪən/ ● **adj.** of or associated with the Roman general and statesman Julius Caesar (100–44 BC).

**Julian calendar** ● **n.** a calendar introduced by Julius Caesar, in which the year consisted of 365 days, every fourth year having 366, replaced by the Gregorian calendar.

**julienne** /,dʒu:lɪ'ɛn/ ● **n.** a portion of food cut into short, thin strips.
– ORIGIN C18: Fr., from the male given names *Jules* or *Julien*, of obscure development.

**Juliet** /'dʒu:lɪɛt/ ● **n.** a code word representing the letter J, used in radio communication.

**Juliet cap** ● **n.** a small ornamental cap of lace or net, typically worn by brides.
– ORIGIN C20: so named because it is part of the usual costume of Juliet in Shakespeare's *Romeo and Juliet.*

**July** ● **n.** (pl. **Julys**) the seventh month of the year.
– ORIGIN ME: from L. *Julius* (*mensis*) '(month) of July', named after the Roman general Julius Caesar.

**jumar** /'dʒu:mə/ Climbing ● **n.** a clamp attached to a fixed rope that tightens when weight is applied and relaxes when it is removed. ● **v.** (**jumared, jumaring**) climb using a jumar.
– ORIGIN 1960s: orig. in Swiss use, of unknown origin.

**jumbie** /'dʒʌmbi/ ● **n.** W. Indian an evil spirit of a dead person.
– ORIGIN from Kikongo *zumbi* 'fetish'.

**jumble** ● **n. 1** an untidy collection of things. **2** Brit. articles collected for a jumble sale. ● **v.** mix up in a confused way.
– ORIGIN C16: prob. symbolic.

**jumble sale** ● **n.** Brit. a sale of miscellaneous second-hand goods, typically for charity.

**jumbo** informal ● **n.** (pl. **-os**) a very large person or thing. ➤(also **jumbo jet**) a very large airliner (specifically a Boeing 747). ● **adj.** very large.
– ORIGIN C19: prob. the second element of **MUMBO-JUMBO.**

**jumbuck** /'dʒʌmbʌk/ ● **n.** Austral. informal a sheep.
– ORIGIN C19: perh. Austral. pidgin for *jump up.*

**jump** ● **v. 1** push oneself off the ground using the muscles in one's legs and feet. ➤pass over by jumping. ➤get on or off (a vehicle) quickly. **2** move suddenly and quickly. ➤make a sudden involuntary movement in surprise. ➤informal attack suddenly and unexpectedly. ➤(**jump on**) informal attack or criticize suddenly. ➤pass abruptly from one subject or state to another. ➤rise or increase suddenly. **3** informal fail to stop at (a red traffic light). **4** informal (of a place) be very lively. **5** (**jump at/on**) accept eagerly. **6** vulgar slang, chiefly N. Amer. have sexual intercourse with. **7** Bridge make a bid that is higher than necessary, in order to signal a strong hand. **8** N. Amer. take summary possession of (land) after alleged abandonment or forfeiture by the former occupant. ● **n. 1** an act of jumping. ➤a sudden dramatic increase. ➤a large or sudden change. **2** a sudden startled movement. ➤(**the jumps**) informal extreme nervousness. **3** an obstacle to be jumped, especially by a horse in a competition. **4** vulgar slang, chiefly N. Amer. an act of sexual intercourse. **5** Bridge a bid that is higher than necessary.
– PHRASES **get** (or **have**) **the jump on** informal, chiefly N. Amer. get (or have) an advantage over (someone) due to prompt action. **jump down someone's throat** informal respond in a sudden and angry way. **jump out of one's skin** informal be startled. **jump the queue** (or N. Amer. **jump in line**) push into a queue of people. ➤take unfair precedence over others. **jump the rails** (or **track**) (of a train) become dislodged from the track. **jump rope** N. Amer. skip with a rope. **jump ship** (of a sailor) leave a ship without permission. **jump through hoops** be made to go through a complicated procedure. **jump** (or **leap**) **to**

**conclusions** (or **the conclusion**) form an opinion hastily without considering all the facts. **jump to it!** informal act promptly. **one jump ahead** one stage ahead of a rival.
– DERIVATIVES **jumpable** adj.
– ORIGIN C16: prob. imitative of the sound of feet landing on the ground.

**jump ball** • n. Basketball a ball put in play by the referee, who throws it up between two opposing players.

**jumped-up** • adj. informal considering oneself to be more important than one really is.

**jumper**[1] • n. **1** Brit. a pullover or sweater. **2** historical a loose outer jacket for sailors. **3** N. Amer. a pinafore dress.
– ORIGIN C19: prob. from dial. *jump* 'short coat', perh. from Scots *jupe* 'loose jacket or tunic', via OFr. from Arab. *jubba*.

**jumper**[2] • n. **1** a person or animal that jumps. **2** (also **jumper wire**) a short wire used to shorten or close an electric circuit. **3** Nautical a rope made fast to keep a yard or mast from jumping. **4** a heavy chisel-ended iron bar for drilling blast holes.

**jumper cable** • n. North American term for **JUMP LEAD**.

**jumping bean** • n. a plant seed, chiefly Mexican, that jumps due to the movement of a moth larva developing inside it.

**jumping jack** • n. **1** Brit. dated a small firework producing repeated explosions. **2** a toy figure of a man, with movable limbs. **3** a jump done from a standing position with the arms and legs pointing outwards.

**jumping-off place** (also **jumping-off point**) • n. a starting place.

**jump jet** • n. a jet aircraft that can take off and land vertically.

**jump lead** • n. Brit. each of a pair of cables for recharging a battery in a motor vehicle by connecting it to a battery in another.

**jump-off** • n. a deciding round in a showjumping competition.

**jump rope** • n. N. Amer. a skipping rope.

**jump seat** • n. chiefly N. Amer. an extra seat in a car that folds back when not in use.

**jump-start** • v. start (a car with a flat battery) with jump leads or by a sudden release of the clutch while it is being pushed. • n. an act of jump-starting a car.

**jumpsuit** • n. a garment incorporating trousers and a sleeved top in one piece.
– ORIGIN 1940s: so named because it was first used to denote a parachutist's garment.

**jump-up** • n. **1** a Caribbean dance or celebration. **2** Austral. informal an escarpment.

**jumpy** • adj. (**-ier**, **-iest**) informal **1** anxious and uneasy. **2** stopping and starting abruptly.
– DERIVATIVES **jumpily** adv. **jumpiness** n.

**Jun.** • abbrev. **1** June. **2** (in names) junior.

**jun** /dʒʌn/ • n. (pl. same) a monetary unit of North Korea, equal to one hundredth of a won.
– ORIGIN from Korean.

**junco** /ˈdʒʌŋkəʊ/ • n. (pl. **-os** or **-oes**) a North American songbird related to the buntings, with largely grey and brown plumage. [Genus *Junco*: several species.]
– ORIGIN C18 (orig. 'reed bunting'): from Sp., from L. *juncus* 'rush, reed'.

**junction** • n. **1** a point where two or more things, especially roads or railway lines, meet or are joined. **2** Electronics a region of transition in a semiconductor between a part where conduction is mainly by electrons and a part where it is mainly by holes. **3** the action of joining or being joined.
– ORIGIN C18: from L. *junctio(n-)*, from *jungere* 'to join'.

**junction box** • n. a box containing a junction of electric wires or cables.

**juncture** /ˈdʒʌŋ(k)tʃə/ • n. **1** a particular point in time. **2** a place where things join. **3** Phonetics the features in speech that enable a hearer to detect a word boundary (e.g. distinguishing *I scream* from *ice cream*).
– ORIGIN ME: from L. *junctura* 'joint', from *jungere* 'to join'.

**June** • n. the sixth month of the year.
– ORIGIN ME: from OFr. *juin*, from L. *Junius* (*mensis*) '(month) of June', var. of *Junonius* 'sacred to the goddess Juno'.

**juneberry** • n. (pl. **-ies**) **1** a North American shrub of the rose family. [Genus *Amelanchier*: many species.] **2** the edible berry of this plant.

**June bug** • n. chiefly N. Amer. a chafer or similar beetle which often flies in June.

**Jungian** /ˈjʊŋɪən/ • adj. of or relating to the Swiss psychologist Carl Jung (1875–1961) or his system of analytical psychology. • n. a follower of Jung or his system.

**jungle** • n. **1** an area of land with dense forest and tangled vegetation, typically in the tropics. ➤a tangled mass, especially of vegetation. **2** a very bewildering or competitive place. **3** (also **jungle music**) a style of dance music with very fast electronic drum tracks and slower synthesized bass lines.
– PHRASES **the law of the jungle** the principle that those who are strongest and most selfish will be most successful.
– DERIVATIVES **jungled** adj. **junglist** n. & adj. **jungly** adj.
– ORIGIN C18: via Hindi from Sanskrit *jāṅgala* 'rough and arid (terrain)'.

**jungle fever** • n. a severe form of malaria.

**junglefowl** • n. (pl. same) a southern Asian game bird related to the domestic fowl. [*Gallus gallus* and other species.]

**jungle gym** • n. N. Amer. an extensive apparatus in a park or playground for children to climb on.

**jungle juice** • n. informal powerful or roughly prepared alcoholic liquor.

**junior** • adj. **1** of, for, or denoting young or younger people. ➤ Brit. of, for, or denoting schoolchildren aged 7–11. ➤ N. Amer. of or for students in the third year of a four-year course at college or high school. **2** [postpos.] denoting the younger of two with the same name in a family. **3** low or lower in rank or status. • n. **1** a person who is a specified amount younger than someone else: *he's five years her junior*. **2** Brit. a child at a junior school. ➤ N. Amer. a student in the third year at college or high school. ➤(in sport) a young competitor, typically under 16 or 18. **3** N. Amer. informal a nickname for one's son. **4** a person with low rank or status.
– DERIVATIVES **juniority** /-ˈɒrɪti/ n.
– ORIGIN ME: from L., compar. of *juvenis* 'young'.

**junior college** • n. (in the US) a college offering courses for two years beyond high school.

**junior common room** • n. Brit. a room used for social purposes by the undergraduates of a college.

**junior high school** • n. (in the US and Canada) a school intermediate between an elementary school and a high school.

**junior lightweight** • n. a weight in boxing of 57.1–59 kilograms.

**junior middleweight** • n. a weight in boxing of 66.7–69.8 kilograms.

**junior school** • n. a school for young children, especially (in England and Wales) for those aged 7–11.

**junior technician** • n. a rank in the RAF, above senior aircraftman or aircraftwoman and below corporal.

**junior welterweight** • n. a weight in boxing of 61.2–63.5 kilograms.

**juniper** /ˈdʒuːnɪpə/ • n. an evergreen shrub or small tree bearing berry-like cones, many kinds having aromatic cones or foliage. [*Juniperus communis* and related species.]
– ORIGIN ME: from L. *juniperus*.

**junk**[1] • n. **1** informal useless or worthless articles. ➤nonsense. **2** Finance junk bonds. **3** informal heroin. **4** the lump of oily fibrous tissue in a sperm whale's head, containing spermaceti. • v. informal discard unceremoniously.
– ORIGIN ME (denoting an old or inferior rope): of unknown origin.

**junk**[2] • n. a flat-bottomed sailing vessel with a prominent stem, used in China and the East Indies.

– ORIGIN C16: from obs. Fr. *juncque* or Port. *junco*, from Malay *jong*, reinforced by Du. *jonk*.

**junk bond** ● n. a high-yielding high-risk security, typically issued to finance a takeover.

**Junker** /ˈjʊŋkə/ ● n. historical a German nobleman or aristocrat, especially one of the Prussian aristocracy.
– DERIVATIVES **junkerdom** n.
– ORIGIN Ger., earlier *Junkher*, from Mid. High Ger. *junc* 'young' + *herre* 'lord'.

**junket** /ˈdʒʌŋkɪt/ ● n. **1** a dish of sweetened and flavoured curds of milk, often served with fruit. **2** informal an extravagant trip, especially one by an official at public expense. ● v. (**junketed**, **junketing**) [often as noun **junketing**] informal go on such a trip.
– ORIGIN ME (denoting cream cheese, formerly made in a rush basket): from OFr. *jonquette* 'rush basket', from *jonc* 'rush', from L. *juncus*.

**junk food** ● n. food with little nutritional value.

**junkie** (also **junky**) ● n. informal a drug addict.
– ORIGIN 1920s (orig. US): from **JUNK**[1].

**junk mail** ● n. informal unsolicited advertising material sent by post.

**junk shop** ● n. informal a shop selling second-hand goods or inexpensive antiques.

**junky** informal ● adj. regarded as junk. ● n. (pl. **-ies**) variant spelling of **JUNKIE**.

**junkyard** ● n. N. Amer. a scrapyard.

**Junoesque** /ˌdʒuːnəʊˈɛsk/ ● adj. (of a woman) tall and shapely.
– ORIGIN C19: from the name of *Juno*, goddess of ancient Rome and wife of Jupiter, + **-ESQUE**.

**Junr** ● abbrev. (in names) Junior.

**junta** /ˈdʒʌntə, ˈhʊ-/ ● n. **1** a military or political group ruling a country after taking power by force. **2** historical a deliberative or administrative council in Spain or Portugal.
– ORIGIN C17: from Sp. and Port., from L. *juncta*, fem. past part. of *jungere* 'to join'.

**Jupiter** ● n. the largest planet in the solar system, fifth in order from the sun and one of the brightest objects in the night sky.

**jural** /ˈdʒʊər(ə)l/ ● adj. **1** formal of or relating to the law. **2** Philosophy of or relating to rights and obligations.
– ORIGIN C17: from L. *jus*, *jur-* 'law, right' + **-AL**.

**Jurassic** /dʒʊˈrasɪk/ ● adj. Geology relating to or denoting the second period of the Mesozoic era (between the Triassic and Cretaceous periods, about 208 to 146 million years ago), a time when large reptiles were dominant and the first birds appeared.
– ORIGIN C19: from Fr. *jurassique*; named after the *Jura* Mountains on the border of France and Switzerland.

**jurat** /ˈdʒʊərat/ ● n. Law **1** (in the Channel Islands) a magistrate or other public official. **2** a statement on an affidavit of when, where, and before whom it was sworn.
– ORIGIN ME: based on L. *juratus* 'sworn', past part. of L. *jurare*.

**juridical** /dʒʊˈrɪdɪk(ə)l/ ● adj. Law of or relating to judicial proceedings and the law.
– DERIVATIVES **juridically** adv.
– ORIGIN C16: from L. *juridicus* (from *jus*, *jur-* 'law' + *dicere* 'say') + **-AL**.

**jurisconsult** /ˌdʒʊərɪskənˈsʌlt/ ● n. Law, chiefly historical an expert on law.
– ORIGIN C17: from L. *jurisconsultus*, from *jus*, *jur-* 'law' + *consultus* 'skilled' (from *consulere* 'take counsel').

**jurisdiction** /ˌdʒʊərɪsˈdɪkʃ(ə)n/ ● n. **1** the official power to make legal decisions and judgements. ➤the territory or sphere over which the legal authority of a court or other institution extends. **2** a system of law courts.
– DERIVATIVES **jurisdictional** adj.
– ORIGIN ME: from OFr. *jurediction*, from L. *jurisdictio(n-)*, from *jus*, *jur-* 'law' + *dictio* 'saying' (from *dicere* 'say').

**jurisprudence** /ˌdʒʊərɪsˈpruːd(ə)ns/ ● n. **1** the theory or philosophy of law. **2** a legal system.
– DERIVATIVES **jurisprudent** adj. & n. **jurisprudential** adj.
– ORIGIN C17: from late L. *jurisprudentia*, from L. *jus*, *jur-* 'law' + *prudentia* 'knowledge'.

**jurist** /ˈdʒʊərɪst/ ● n. **1** an expert in law. **2** N. Amer. a lawyer or a judge.
– DERIVATIVES **juristic** adj.
– ORIGIN C15: from Fr. *juriste*, med. L. *jurista*, from *jus*, *jur-* 'law'.

**juror** ● n. **1** a member of a jury. **2** historical a person taking an oath.
– ORIGIN ME: from OFr. *jureor*, from L. *jurator*, from *jurare* 'swear', from *jus*, *jur-* 'law'.

**jury**[1] ● n. (pl. **-ies**) a body of people (typically twelve) sworn to give a verdict on the basis of evidence submitted in court. ➤a body of people judging a competition. ● v. (**-ies**, **-ied**) chiefly N. Amer. judge (an art or craft exhibit).
– PHRASES **the jury is out** a decision has not yet been reached.
– ORIGIN ME: from OFr. *juree* 'oath, inquiry', from L. *jurata*, fem. past part. of *jurare* (see **JUROR**).

**jury**[2] ● adj. Nautical denoting improvised or temporary fittings: *a jury rudder.*
– ORIGIN C17: perh. based on OFr. *ajurie* 'aid'.

**jury box** ● n. a segregated area for the jury in a court of law.

**jury-rigged** ● adj. **1** (of a ship) having makeshift rigging. **2** chiefly N. Amer. makeshift; improvised.

**jus** /ʒuː, French ʒy/ ● n. (especially in French cuisine) a sauce.
– ORIGIN from Fr.

**jussive** /ˈdʒʌsɪv/ ● adj. Grammar (of a verb form) expressing a command.
– ORIGIN C19: from L. *juss-*, *jubere* 'command' + **-IVE**.

**just** ● adj. morally right and fair. ➤appropriate or deserved. ➤(of an opinion or appraisal) well founded. ● adv. **1** exactly. ➤exactly or nearly at this or that moment. **2** very recently. **3** barely; by a little. **4** simply; only. ➤really: *they're just great.* **5** expressing agreement.
– PHRASES **just in case** as a precaution. **just so 1** arranged or done very carefully. **2** expressing agreement.
– DERIVATIVES **justly** adv. **justness** n.
– ORIGIN ME: via OFr. from L. *justus*, from *jus* 'law, right'.

**juste milieu** /ˌʒuːst mɪˈljəː, French ʒystə miljø/ ● n. the happy medium.
– ORIGIN Fr., lit. 'correct mean'.

**justice** ● n. **1** just behaviour or treatment. ➤the quality of being just. **2** the administration of the law or authority in maintaining this. **3** a judge or magistrate.
– PHRASES **bring someone to justice** arrest and try someone in court for a crime. **do oneself justice** perform as well as one is able. **do someone/thing justice** treat or represent with due fairness. **Mr** (or **Mrs**) **Justice** Brit. a form of address to a judge of the supreme court.
– DERIVATIVES **justiceship** n.
– ORIGIN OE *iustise* 'administration of the law', via OFr. from L. *justitia*, from *justus* (see **JUST**).

**Justice of the Peace** ● n. (in the UK) a lay magistrate appointed to hear minor cases, grant licences, etc., in a town or county.

**justiciable** /dʒʌˈstɪʃəb(ə)l/ ● adj. Law subject to trial in a court of law.
– ORIGIN ME: from OFr., from *justicier* 'bring to trial', based on L. *justitia* 'equity', from *justus* (see **JUST**).

**justiciar** /dʒʌˈstɪʃə/ ● n. historical **1** a regent and deputy presiding over the court of a Norman or early Plantagenet king of England. **2** either of two supreme judges in medieval Scotland.
– ORIGIN C15: from med. L. *justitiarius*, from L. *justitia*, from *justus* (see **JUST**).

**justiciary** /dʒʌˈstɪʃ(ə)ri/ ● n. (pl. **-ies**) chiefly Scottish **1** an administrator of justice. **2** the administration of justice.

**justifiable** ● adj. able to be justified.
– DERIVATIVES **justifiability** n. **justifiableness** n. **justifiably** adv.

**justify** /ˈdʒʌstɪfʌɪ/ ● v. (**-ies**, **-ied**) **1** prove to be right or reasonable. ➤be a good reason for. **2** Theology declare or make righteous in the sight of God. **3** Printing [often as adj. **justified**] adjust (text or a line of type) so that the print

fills a space evenly or forms a straight edge.
– DERIVATIVES **justification** n. **justificatory** adj. **justifier** n.
– ORIGIN ME: from OFr. *justifier*, from Christian L. *justificare* 'do justice to', from L. *justus* (see **JUST**).

**just-in-time** ● **adj.** denoting a manufacturing system in which materials are delivered immediately before use in order to minimize storage costs.

**jut** ● **v.** (**jutted**, **jutting**) extend out, over, or beyond the main body or line of something. ● **n.** a point that sticks out.
– ORIGIN C16: var. of **JET**[1].

**Jute** /dʒuːt/ ● **n.** a member of a Germanic people, possibly from Jutland, that settled in southern Britain in the 5th century.
– DERIVATIVES **Jutish** adj.
– ORIGIN OE *Eotas, Iotas*, influenced by med. L. *Jutae, Juti*.

**jute** /dʒuːt/ ● **n. 1** rough fibre made from the stems of a tropical plant, used for making rope or woven into sacking. **2** the plant cultivated for this fibre, with edible young shoots. [*Corchorus capsularis* (China) and *C. olitorius* (India).]
– ORIGIN C18: from Bengali *jhūṭo*, from Prakrit *juṭṭi*.

**juvenescence** /ˌdʒuːvəˈnɛs(ə)ns/ ● **n.** formal youth.
– DERIVATIVES **juvenescent** adj.
– ORIGIN C19: from L. *juvenescent-*, *juvenescere* 'reach the age of youth', from *juvenis* 'young'.

**juvenile** /ˈdʒuːvənʌɪl/ ● **adj.** of, for, or relating to young people, birds, or animals. ➤ childish. ● **n.** a young person, bird, or animal. ➤ Law a person below the age at which ordinary criminal prosecution is possible (18 in most countries).
– DERIVATIVES **juvenility** /-ˈnɪlɪti/ n. **juvenilize** (also **-ise**) v.
– ORIGIN C17: from L. *juvenilis*, from *juvenis* 'young, a young person'.

**juvenile court** ● **n.** a court for the trial or legal supervision of juveniles.

**juvenile delinquency** ● **n.** the habitual committing of criminal acts by a juvenile.
– DERIVATIVES **juvenile deliquent** n.

**juvenile hormone** ● **n.** Entomology a hormone regulating larval development in insects.

**juvenilia** /ˌdʒuːvəˈnɪlɪə/ ● **pl. n.** works produced by an author or artist when young.
– ORIGIN C17: from L., neut. pl. of *juvenilis* (see **JUVENILE**).

**juxtapose** /ˌdʒʌkstəˈpəʊz/ ● **v.** place close together.
– DERIVATIVES **juxtaposition** n. **juxtapositional** adj.
– ORIGIN C19 (earlier (ME) as *juxtaposition*): from Fr. *juxtaposer*, from L. *juxta* 'next' + Fr. *poser* 'to place'.

**K**[1] (also **k**) ● **n.** (pl. **Ks** or **K's**) **1** the eleventh letter of the alphabet. **2** denoting the next after J in a set of items, categories, etc.

**K**[2] ● **abbrev. 1** Cambodia (international vehicle registration). [from *Kampuchea*.] **2** kelvin(s). **3** Computing kilobyte(s). **4** kilometre(s). **5** king (used in describing play in card games and chess). **6** Köchel (catalogue of Mozart's works). **7** informal thousand. [from **KILO-**.] ● **symb.** the chemical element potassium. [from mod. L. *kalium*.]

**k** ● **abbrev.** kilo-. ● **symb. 1** a constant in a formula or equation. **2** Chemistry Boltzmann's constant.

**ka** /kɑː/ ● **n.** (in ancient Egypt) the supposed spiritual part of an individual, which survived after death.
– ORIGIN from Egyptian.

**Kaaba** /ˈkɑːəbə/ (also **Caaba**) ● **n.** a square building in Mecca, the site most holy to Muslims, containing a sacred black stone.
– ORIGIN from Arab. *(al-)kaʻba*, lit. '(the) square house'.

**kabaddi** /ˈkʌbədi/ ● **n.** a sport of Indian origin in which players attempt to tag or capture opponents.
– ORIGIN from Tamil, of uncertain origin: players must repeat the word 'kabaddi' to show that they are holding their breath.

**Kabardian** /kəˈbɑːdɪən/ ● **n. 1** a member of an indigenous people of the NW Caucasus. **2** the North Caucasian language of this people.
– ORIGIN from Russ. *Kabarda*, a district in SW Russia.

**Kabbalah** /kəˈbɑːlə, ˈkabələ/ (also **Kabbala**, **Cabbala**, **Cabala**, or **Qabalah**) ● **n.** the ancient Jewish tradition of mystical interpretation of the Bible.
– DERIVATIVES **Kabbalism** n. **Kabbalist** n. **Kabbalistic** adj.
– ORIGIN from med. L. *cabala*, *cabbala*, from Rabbinical Heb. *qabbālāh* 'tradition', from *qibbēl* 'receive, accept'.

**Kabinett** /ˌkabɪˈnɛt/ ● **n.** a wine of German origin or style of superior quality.
– ORIGIN from Ger. *Kabinettwein*, lit. 'chamber wine'.

**kabob** /kəˈbɑːb/ ● **n.** US spelling of **KEBAB**.

**kabuki** /kəˈbuːki/ ● **n.** a form of traditional Japanese drama performed by men, with highly stylized song, mime, and dance.
– ORIGIN Japanese, orig. as a verb meaning 'act dissolutely', later interpreted as if from *ka* 'song' + *bu* 'dance' + *ki* 'art'.

**Kabyle** /kəˈbʌɪl/ ● **n. 1** a member of a Berber people of northern Algeria. **2** the Berber dialect of this people.
– ORIGIN prob. from Arab. *ḳabā'il*, pl. of *ḳabīla* 'tribe'.

**Kachin** /ˈkatʃɪn/ ● **n. 1** a member of a people living in northern Burma (Myanmar) and adjacent parts of China and India. **2** the Tibeto-Burman language of this people.
– ORIGIN from Burmese.

**kachina** /kəˈtʃiːnə/ (also **katsina**) ● **n.** (pl. **kachinas**) a deified ancestral spirit in the mythology of Pueblo Indians. ➤(also **kachina dancer**) a dancer representing such a spirit.
– ORIGIN from Hopi *kacina* 'supernatural'.

**Kaddish** /ˈkadɪʃ/ ● **n.** an ancient Jewish prayer sequence recited in the synagogue service. ➤a form of this recited for the dead.
– ORIGIN from Aramaic *qaddīš* 'holy'.

**kadi** ● **n.** (pl. **kadis**) variant spelling of **CADI**.

**Kaffir** /ˈkafə/ ● **n.** offensive, chiefly S. African a black African.
– ORIGIN from Arab. *kāfir* 'infidel', from *kafara* 'not believe'.

**USAGE** Kaffir

The word **Kaffir** was originally simply a descriptive term for a particular ethnic group. Now it is a racially abusive and offensive term, and in South Africa its use is actionable.

**Kaffir lily** ● **n. 1** a South African plant with strap-like leaves and star-shaped flowers. [*Schizostylis coccinea*.] **2** another term for **CLIVIA**.

**kaffiyeh** ● **n.** variant spelling of **KEFFIYEH**.

**Kafir** /ˈkafə/ ● **n.** a member of a people of the Hindu Kush mountains of NE Afghanistan.
– DERIVATIVES **Kafiri** adj. & n.
– ORIGIN from Arab. *kāfir* (see **KAFFIR**).

**kafir** /ˈkafɪə/ ● **n.** (among Muslims) a person who is not a Muslim.
– ORIGIN from Arab. *kāfir* 'infidel, unbeliever'; cf. **KAFFIR**.

**Kafkaesque** /ˌkafkəˈɛsk/ ● **adj.** of or relating to the Czech novelist Franz Kafka (1883–1924) or his nightmarish fictional world.

**kaftan** /ˈkaftan/ (also **caftan**) ● **n.** a man's long belted tunic, worn in the Near East. ➤a woman's long loose dress. ➤a loose shirt or top.
– ORIGIN C16: from Turk., from Pers. *ḵaftān*, partly influenced by Fr. *cafetan*.

**kagoul** ● **n.** variant spelling of **CAGOULE**.

**kagu** /ˈkɑːguː/ ● **n.** a crested, almost flightless bluish-grey bird found only on the Pacific island of New Caledonia. [*Rhynochetos jubatus*.]
– ORIGIN C19: from Melanesian.

**kahuna** /kəˈhuːnə/ ● **n. 1** (in Hawaii) a wise man or shaman. **2** N. Amer. informal an important person.
– ORIGIN from Hawaiian.

**kainite** /ˈkʌɪnʌɪt, ˈkeɪnʌɪt/ ● **n.** a white mineral consisting of a double salt of hydrated magnesium sulphate and potassium chloride.
– ORIGIN C19: from Ger. *Kainit*, from Gk *kainos* 'new, recent', because of the mineral's recent formation.

**kairos** /ˈkʌɪrɒs/ ● **n.** chiefly Theology a propitious moment.
– ORIGIN C20: Gk, lit. 'opportunity'.

**kaiser** /ˈkʌɪzə/ ● **n. 1** historical the German Emperor, the Emperor of Austria, or the head of the Holy Roman Empire. **2** (also **kaiser roll**) N. Amer. a crisp bread roll in the shape of a pinwheel.
– DERIVATIVES **kaisership** n.
– ORIGIN ME *cayser*, from ON *keisari*, based on L. *Caesar* (see **CAESAR**).

**kaizen** /kʌɪˈzɛn/ ● **n.** a Japanese business philosophy of continuous improvement.
– ORIGIN Japanese, lit. 'improvement'.

**kaka** /ˈkɑːkɑː/ ● **n.** a large New Zealand parrot with olive-brown and dull green upper parts and reddish underparts. [*Nestor meridionalis*.]
– ORIGIN C18: from Maori.

**kakapo** /ˈkɑːkəpəʊ/ ● **n.** (pl. **-os**) an endangered nocturnal flightless New Zealand parrot, with greenish plumage. [*Strigops habroptilus*.]
– ORIGIN C19: from Maori, lit. 'night kaka'.

**kakemono** /ˌkɑːkɪˈməʊnəʊ, ˌkakɪ-/ ● **n.** (pl. **-os**) a Japanese painting on paper or silk, displayed as a wall hanging.
– ORIGIN C19: Japanese, from *kake-* 'hang, suspend' + *mono* 'thing'.

**kala-azar** /ˌkɑːlə,əˈzɑː/ ● **n.** a form of the disease leishmaniasis affecting the internal organs, with emaciation, anaemia, and fever.

– ORIGIN C19: from Assamese, from *kālā* 'black' + *āzār* 'disease' (because of the bronzing of the skin often assoc. with it).

**kalanchoe** /ˌkalən'kəʊi/ ● **n.** a tropical succulent plant with clusters of tubular flowers, sometimes producing miniature plants along the edges of the leaves. [Genus *Kalanchoe*.]
– ORIGIN C19: mod. L., from Fr., based on Chin. *gāláncài*.

**Kalashnikov** /kə'laʃnɪkɒf, -'lɑːʃ-/ ● **n.** a type of rifle or sub-machine gun made in Russia.
– ORIGIN 1970s: named after the Russ. designer Mikhail T. *Kalashnikov*.

**kale** /keɪl/ ● **n.** a hardy cabbage of a variety which produces erect stems with large leaves and no compact head.
– ORIGIN ME: north. Engl. form of **COLE**.

**kaleidoscope** /kə'lʌɪdəskəʊp/ ● **n. 1** a toy consisting of a tube containing mirrors and pieces of coloured glass or paper, whose reflections produce changing patterns when the tube is rotated. **2** a constantly changing pattern or sequence.
– DERIVATIVES **kaleidoscopic** adj. **kaleidoscopically** adv.
– ORIGIN C19: from Gk *kalos* 'beautiful' + *eidos* 'form' + **-SCOPE**.

**kalends** ● **pl. n.** variant spelling of **CALENDS**.

**kalimba** /kə'lɪmbə/ ● **n.** a type of African thumb piano.
– ORIGIN 1950s: a local word; rel. to **MARIMBA**.

**kalmia** /'kalmɪə/ ● **n.** an evergreen leathery-leaved shrub of the heather family with clusters of pink or red flowers, native to North America and Cuba. [Genus *Kalmia*.]
– ORIGIN mod. L., named after the C18 Swed. botanist Pehr *Kalm*.

**Kalmyk** /'kalmʌk/ (also **Kalmuck**) ● **n.** (pl. same or **Kalmyks** or **Kalmucks**) **1** a member of a Buddhist Mongolian people living chiefly in Kalmykia, a republic in SW Russia. **2** the Altaic language of this people.
– ORIGIN from Russ. *kalmyk*.

**kalong** /'kɑːlɒŋ/ ● **n.** a flying fox found in SE Asia and Indonesia. [*Pteropus vampyrus* and other species.]
– ORIGIN C19: from Javanese.

**kalpa** /'kalpə/ ● **n.** (in Hindu and Buddhist tradition) the period between the creation and end of the world, reckoned as 4,320 million human years, and considered as the day of Brahma.
– ORIGIN from Sanskrit.

**Kama Sutra** /ˌkɑːmə 'suːtrə/ ● **n.** an ancient Sanskrit treatise on the art of love and sexual technique.
– ORIGIN Sanskrit, from *kāma* 'love' + *sūtra* 'thread'.

**Kamba** /'kambə/ ● **n.** (pl. same, **Kambas**, or **Wakamba**) **1** a member of a people of central Kenya. **2** the Bantu language of this people.
– ORIGIN the name in Kamba.

**kame** /keɪm/ ● **n.** Geology a steep mound of sand and gravel deposited by a melting ice sheet.
– ORIGIN C18: Scots form of **COMB**.

**kameez** /kə'miːz/ ● **n.** (pl. same or **kameezes**) a long tunic worn by people from the Indian subcontinent.
– ORIGIN from Arab. *ḳamīṣ*, perh. from late L. *camisia* (see **CHEMISE**).

**kami** /'kɑːmi/ ● **n.** (pl. same) a divine being in the Shinto religion.
– ORIGIN from Japanese.

**kamikaze** /ˌkamɪ'kɑːzi/ ● **n.** (in the Second World War) a Japanese aircraft loaded with explosives and making a deliberate suicidal crash on an enemy target. ● **adj.** reckless or potentially self-destructive.
– ORIGIN Japanese, from *kami* 'divinity' + *kaze* 'wind'.

**Kamilaroi** /kə'mɪlərɔɪ/ ● **n.** (pl. same) **1** a member of a group of Australian Aboriginal peoples of New South Wales. **2** the extinct language of these peoples.
– ORIGIN the name in Kamilaroi.

**kampong** /kam'pɒŋ, 'kampɒŋ/ ● **n.** a Malaysian enclosure or village.
– ORIGIN Malay; cf. **COMPOUND**[2].

**Kampuchean** /ˌkampʊ'tʃiːən/ ● **n. & adj.** another term for **CAMBODIAN**.

**Kan.** ● **abbrev.** Kansas.

**kana** /'kɑːnə/ ● **n.** the system of syllabic writing used for Japanese.
– ORIGIN from Japanese.

**kanaka** /kə'nakə, -'nɑːkə/ ● **n.** historical a Pacific Islander employed as an indentured labourer in Australia.
– ORIGIN Hawaiian, lit. 'man'.

**Kanarese** /ˌkanə'riːz/ (also **Canarese**) ● **n.** (pl. same) **1** a member of a people living mainly in Kanara, a district in SW India. **2** another term for **KANNADA**. ● **adj.** of or relating to Kanara, its people, or their language.

**kanban** /'kanban/ ● **n.** a Japanese manufacturing system in which the supply of components is regulated by way of an instruction card sent along the production line.
– ORIGIN C20: Japanese, lit. 'billboard, sign'.

**kangaroo** ● **n.** a large plant-eating marsupial with a long powerful tail and strongly developed hindlimbs that enable it to travel by leaping, found only in Australia and New Guinea. [Genus *Macropus*: several species.]
– ORIGIN C18: the name of a specific kind of kangaroo in an extinct Aborig. lang.

**kangaroo court** ● **n.** an unofficial court formed by a group of people to settle disputes among themselves.

**kangaroo mouse** ● **n.** a small hopping rodent with large cheek pouches and long hind legs, found in North America. [Genus *Microdipodops*: two species.]

**kangaroo paw** ● **n.** an Australian plant with strap-like leaves and tubular flowers with woolly outer surfaces. [Genera *Anigozanthos* and *Macropidia*: several species.]

**kangaroo rat** ● **n.** a seed-eating hopping rodent with large cheek pouches and long hind legs, found from Canada to Mexico. [Genus *Dipodomys*: several species.]

**kangaroo vine** ● **n.** an Australian evergreen vine, grown as a house plant. [*Cissus antarctica*.]

**kangha** /'kʌŋhə/ ● **n.** a comb worn in the hair as one of the five distinguishing signs of the Sikh Khalsa.
– ORIGIN from Punjabi *kanghā*.

**kanji** /'kandʒi, 'kɑːn-/ ● **n.** a system of Japanese writing using Chinese characters.
– ORIGIN Japanese, from *kan* 'Chinese' + *ji* 'character'.

**Kannada** /'kanədə/ ● **n.** a Dravidian language spoken in SW India, related to Telugu and using a similar script.
– ORIGIN the name in Kannada.

**Kans.** ● **abbrev.** Kansas.

**Kansan** /'kanzən/ ● **n.** a native or inhabitant of the US state of Kansas. ● **adj.** of or relating to Kansas.

**Kantian** /'kantɪən/ ● **adj.** of or relating to the German philosopher Immanuel Kant (1724–1804) or his philosophy. ● **n.** an adherent of Kant's philosophy.
– DERIVATIVES **Kantianism** n.

**KANU** /'kɑːnuː/ ● **abbrev.** Kenya African National Union.

**kaolin** /'keɪəlɪn/ ● **n.** a fine soft white clay, used for making porcelain and china and in medicinal absorbents.
– DERIVATIVES **kaolinize** (also **-ise**) v.
– ORIGIN C18: from Fr., from Chin. *gāolǐng*, lit. 'high hill', the name of a mountain in Jiangxi province where the clay is found.

**kaolinite** /'keɪəlɪnʌɪt/ ● **n.** a clay mineral which is the chief constituent of kaolin.

**kaon** /'keɪɒn/ ● **n.** Physics a meson with a mass several times that of a pion.
– ORIGIN 1950s: from *ka* representing the letter *K* (as a symbol for the particle) + **-ON**.

**kapellmeister** /kə'pɛlˌmʌɪstə/ ● **n.** (in German-speaking countries) the leader or conductor of an orchestra or choir.
– ORIGIN C19: Ger., from *Kapelle* 'court orchestra' + *Meister* 'master'.

**kapok** /'keɪpɒk/ ● **n.** a fine fibrous substance which grows around the seeds of a ceiba or silk-cotton tree, used as stuffing for cushions.
– ORIGIN C18: from Malay *kapuk*.

**Kaposi's sarcoma** /kə'pəʊsɪz/ ● **n.** Medicine a form of cancer involving multiple tumours of the lymph nodes or skin, occurring chiefly as a result of Aids.
– ORIGIN C19: named after the Hungarian dermatologist Moritz K. *Kaposi*.

**kappa** /ˈkapə/ ● **n.** the tenth letter of the Greek alphabet (Κ, κ), transliterated as 'k'.
– ORIGIN from Gk.

**kapu** /ˈkapuː/ ● **n.** (in Hawaiian culture and religion) a set of rules and prohibitions for everyday life.
– ORIGIN from Hawaiian.

**kapur** /ˈkapə/ ● **n.** a large tropical tree which yields light brown wood, edible fruit, and camphor. [Genus *Dryobalanops*.]
– ORIGIN C20: from Malay.

**kaput** /kəˈpʊt/ ● **adj.** informal broken and useless.
– ORIGIN C19: from Ger. *kaputt*, from Fr. (*être*) *capot* '(be) without tricks in a card game'; cf. **CAPOT**.

**kara** /ˈkɑːrə/ ● **n.** a steel bangle worn on the right wrist as one of the five distinguishing signs of the Sikh Khalsa.
– ORIGIN from Punjabi *karā*.

**karabiner** /ˌkarəˈbiːnə/ (also **carabiner**) ● **n.** a coupling link with a safety closure, used by rock climbers.
– ORIGIN 1930s: from Ger. *Karabiner-haken* 'spring hook'.

**karahi** /kʌˈrʌɪ/ ● **n.** (pl. **karahis**) a small bowl-shaped Indian frying pan with two handles, used for balti dishes.
– ORIGIN from Hindi *karāhī*.

**Karaite** /ˈkɛːrəʌɪt/ ● **n.** a member of a Jewish sect which rejects rabbinical interpretation in favour of a literal interpretation of the scriptures.
– ORIGIN C18: from Heb. *Qārāʾīm* 'those who adhere closely to the scriptures' (from *qārā'* 'read') + **-ITE**[1].

**karakul** /ˈkarəkʊl/ (also **caracul**) ● **n. 1** a sheep of an Asian breed with a dark curled fleece when young. **2** cloth or fur made from or resembling this fleece.
– ORIGIN C19: from Russ.

**karaoke** /ˌkarəˈəʊki, ˌkarɪ-/ ● **n.** a form of entertainment in which people sing popular songs over pre-recorded backing tracks.
– ORIGIN 1970s: from Japanese, lit. 'empty orchestra'.

**karat** ● **n.** US spelling of **CARAT** (in sense 2).

**karate** /kəˈrɑːti/ ● **n.** an oriental system of unarmed combat using the hands and feet to deliver and block blows.
– ORIGIN Japanese, from *kara* 'empty' + *te* 'hand'.

**karateka** /kəˈrɑːtɪkɑː/ ● **n.** (pl. same or **karatekas**) a practitioner of karate.
– ORIGIN from Japanese.

**Karelian** /kəˈriːlɪən/ ● **n.** a native or inhabitant of Karelia, a region on the border between Russia and Finland. ● **adj.** of or relating to Karelia.

**Karen** /kəˈrɛn/ ● **n.** (pl. same or **Karens**) **1** a member of a people of eastern Burma (Myanmar) and western Thailand. **2** the Sino-Tibetan language of this people.
– ORIGIN from Burmese *ka-reng* 'wild unclean man'.

**karma** /ˈkɑːmə, ˈkəːmə/ ● **n.** (in Hinduism and Buddhism) the sum of a person's actions in this and previous states of existence, viewed as affecting their future fate. ➤ informal the sum of good or bad luck, viewed as resulting from one's actions.
– DERIVATIVES **karmic** adj. **karmically** adv.
– ORIGIN from Sanskrit *karman* 'action, effect, fate'.

**karoshi** /kaˈrəʊʃi/ ● **n.** (in Japan) death caused by overwork.
– ORIGIN Japanese, from *ka* 'excess' + *rō* 'labour' + *shi* 'death'.

**karri** /ˈkari/ ● **n.** (pl. **karris**) a tall Australian eucalyptus with hard red wood. [*Eucalyptus diversicolor*.]
– ORIGIN C19: from Nyungar.

**karst** /kɑːst/ ● **n.** Geology landscape underlain by limestone which has been eroded by dissolution, producing towers, fissures, sinkholes, etc.
– DERIVATIVES **karstic** adj. **karstification** n. **karstify** v. (**-ies, ied**).
– ORIGIN C19: from Ger. *Karst*, the name of a limestone region in Slovenia.

**kart** ● **n.** a small unsprung motor-racing vehicle with a tubular frame and a rear-mounted engine.
– DERIVATIVES **karting** n.
– ORIGIN C20: shortening of **GO-KART**.

**karyo-** ● **comb. form** Biology denoting the nucleus of a cell: *karyotype*.
– ORIGIN from Gk *karuon* 'kernel'.

**karyokinesis** /ˌkarɪəʊkɪˈniːsɪs, -kʌɪ-/ ● **n.** Biology division of a cell nucleus during mitosis.

**karyotype** /ˈkarɪə(ʊ)tʌɪp/ ● **n.** Biology & Medicine the number and visual appearance of the chromosomes in the cell nuclei of an organism.
– DERIVATIVES **karyotypic** adj.

**kasbah** /ˈkazbɑː/ (also **casbah**) ● **n.** a North African citadel. ➤ the area surrounding a citadel.
– ORIGIN C18: from Fr. *casbah*, from Arab. *ḳaṣaba* 'citadel'.

**kasha** /ˈkaʃə/ ● **n.** (in Russia and Poland) porridge made from cooked buckwheat or similar grain.
– ORIGIN from Russ.

**Kashmir goat** ● **n.** a goat of a Himalayan breed yielding fine, soft wool, which is used to make cashmere.

**Kashmiri** /kaʃˈmɪəri/ ● **n. 1** a native or inhabitant of Kashmir, a region on the border of India and Pakistan. **2** the Indic language of Kashmir. ● **adj.** of or relating to Kashmir, its people, or their language.

**kashrut** /kaʃˈruːt/ (also **kashruth**) ● **n.** the body of Jewish religious laws concerning the suitability of food, the use of ritual objects, etc.
– ORIGIN Heb., lit. 'legitimacy (in religion)'.

**kata** /ˈkɑːtɑː/ ● **n.** a system of individual training exercises in karate and other martial arts.
– ORIGIN from Japanese.

**katabatic** /ˌkatəˈbatɪk/ ● **adj.** Meteorology (of a wind) caused by local downward motion of cool air.
– ORIGIN C19: from Gk *katabatikos*, from *katabainein* 'go down'.

**katabolism** ● **n.** variant spelling of **CATABOLISM**.

**katakana** /ˌkatəˈkɑːnə/ ● **n.** an angular form of Japanese kana, used especially for words of foreign origin.
– ORIGIN C18: Japanese, lit. 'side kana'.

**katana** /kəˈtɑːnə/ ● **n.** a long, single-edged sword used by Japanese samurai.
– ORIGIN C17: Japanese.

**Kathak** /ˈkʌtək/ ● **n. 1** a type of northern Indian classical dance with passages of mime. **2** (pl. same or **Kathaks**) a member of an Indian caste of storytellers and musicians.
– ORIGIN from Sanskrit *kathaka* 'professional storyteller', from *kathā* 'story'.

**Kathakali** /ˌkɑːtəˈkɑːli, ˌkʌtəˈkʌli/ ● **n.** a type of dramatic dance from southern India, based on Hindu literature.
– ORIGIN from Malayalam, from Sanskrit *kathā* 'story' + Malayalam *kaḷi* 'play'.

**katharevousa** /ˌkaθəˈrɛvuːsə/ ● **n.** a heavily archaized form of modern Greek used in traditional literary writing. Compare with **DEMOTIC**.
– ORIGIN C20: mod. Gk, lit. 'purified'.

**katsina** ● **n.** (pl. **katsinam**) variant of **KACHINA**.

**katsura** /katˈsʊərə/ ● **n. 1** an ornamental East Asian tree which has leaves resembling those of the Judas tree. [*Cercidiphyllum japonicum*.] **2** a type of Japanese wig worn mainly by women.
– ORIGIN C20: from Japanese.

**katydid** /ˈkeɪtɪdɪd/ ● **n.** a large bush cricket native to North America, the male of which makes a characteristic sound which resembles the name. [*Microcentrum* and other genera.]

**kauri** /ˈkaʊri/ ● **n.** (pl. **kauris**) (also **kauri pine**) a tall coniferous forest tree native to New Zealand, which produces valuable wood and resin. [*Agathis australis*.]
– ORIGIN C19: from Maori.

**kava** /ˈkɑːvə/ ● **n. 1** a narcotic drink made in Polynesia from the crushed roots of a plant of the pepper family. **2** the Polynesian shrub from which this root is obtained. [*Piper methysticum*.]
– ORIGIN C18: from Tongan.

**kawa-kawa** /ˈkɑːwəˌkɑːwə/ ● **n.** a New Zealand shrub of the pepper family with aromatic leaves, cultivated as an ornamental. [*Macropiper excelsum*.]
– ORIGIN C19: from Maori.

**Kawasaki disease** ● **n.** a disease in young children with an unknown cause, giving rise to a rash, glandular swelling, and sometimes damage to the heart.

– ORIGIN 1960s: named after the Japanese physician Tomisaku *Kawasaki*.

**kayak** /'kʌɪak/ ● **n.** a canoe of a type used originally by the Inuit, made of a light frame with a watertight covering having a small opening for the seat. ● **v.** (**kayaked, kayaking**) [usu. as noun **kayaking**] travel in a kayak.
– ORIGIN C18: from Inuit *qayaq*.

**kayo** /keɪ'əʊ/ Boxing, informal ● **n.** (pl. **-os**) a knockout. ● **v.** (**-oes, -oed**) knock (someone) out.
– ORIGIN 1920s: representing the pronunc. of *KO*.

**Kazakh** /kə'zak, 'kazak/ ● **n. 1** a member of a people living chiefly in Kazakhstan. **2** the Turkic language of this people.
– ORIGIN Russ., from Turkic (see **COSSACK**).

**kazillion** /kə'zɪljən/ ● **cardinal number** another term for **GAZILLION**.

**kazoo** /kə'zuː/ ● **n.** a simple musical instrument consisting of a pipe with a hole in it, over which is a membrane that vibrates and adds a buzzing sound when the player hums into the pipe.
– ORIGIN C19: appar. imitative of the sound produced.

**KB** ● **abbrev. 1** (also **Kb**) kilobyte(s). **2** (in the UK) King's Bench.

**kb** ● **abbrev.** Biochemistry kilobase(s).

**KBE** ● **abbrev.** (in the UK) Knight Commander of the Order of the British Empire.

**Kbps** ● **abbrev.** kilobits per second.

**kbyte** ● **abbrev.** kilobyte(s).

**KC** ● **abbrev.** King's Counsel.

**kc** ● **abbrev.** kilocycle(s).

**kcal** ● **abbrev.** kilocalorie(s).

**KCB** ● **abbrev.** (in the UK) Knight Commander of the Order of the Bath.

**KCMG** ● **abbrev.** (in the UK) Knight Commander of the Order of St Michael and St George.

**kc/s** ● **abbrev.** kilocycles per second.

**KCVO** ● **abbrev.** (in the UK) Knight Commander of the Royal Victorian Order.

**KE** ● **abbrev.** kinetic energy.

**kea** /'kiːə/ ● **n.** a New Zealand mountain parrot with a long, narrow bill and mainly olive-green plumage, sometimes feeding on carrion. [*Nestor notabilis.*]
– ORIGIN C19: from Maori, imitative of its call.

**kebab** /kɪ'bab, kə'bɑːb/ (N. Amer. also **kabob**) ● **n.** a dish of pieces of meat, fish, or vegetables roasted or grilled on a skewer or spit.
– ORIGIN C17: from Arab. *kabāb*, partly via Urdu, Pers., and Turk.

**kecks** ● **pl. n.** Brit. informal trousers or underpants.
– ORIGIN 1960s: phonetic respelling of obs. *kicks* 'trousers'.

**ked** (also **sheep ked**) ● **n.** a wingless louse fly that parasitizes sheep. [*Melophagus ovinus.*]
– ORIGIN C16: of unknown origin.

**kedge** /kɛdʒ/ ● **v.** move (a boat) by hauling in a hawser attached at a distance to an anchor. ● **n.** (also **kedge anchor**) a small anchor used for such a purpose.
– ORIGIN C15: perh. a specific use of dial. *cadge* 'bind, tie'.

**kedgeree** /'kɛdʒəriː/ ● **n. 1** an Indian dish consisting chiefly of rice, split pulses, onions, and eggs. **2** a European dish consisting chiefly of smoked fish, rice, and hard-boiled eggs.
– ORIGIN from Hindi *khichṛī*, from Sanskrit *khiccā*.

**keech** /kiːx/ ● **n.** Scottish informal excrement.
– ORIGIN from *cach*, Scots var. of **CACK**.

**keek** Scottish ● **v.** peep surreptitiously. ● **n.** a surreptitious peep.
– ORIGIN ME: perh. rel. to Du. *kijken* 'have a look'.

**keel**[1] ● **n. 1** a lengthwise structure along the base of a ship, in some vessels extended downwards as a ridge to increase stability. **2** Zoology a ridge along the breastbone of many birds to which the flight muscles are attached; the carina. **3** Botany a prow-shaped pair of petals present in flowers of the pea family. ● **v.** (**keel over**) **1** (of a boat or ship) turn over on its side; capsize. **2** informal fall over.
– DERIVATIVES **keeled** adj. **keelless** adj.
– ORIGIN ME: from ON *kjǫlr*, of Gmc origin.

**keel**[2] ● **n.** Brit. a flat-bottomed boat of a kind formerly used on the Rivers Tyne and Wear for loading colliers.
– ORIGIN ME: from Mid. Low Ger. *kēl*, MDu. *kiel* 'ship, boat'.

**keelback** ● **n.** a harmless Australian snake which lives close to water. [*Amphiesma mairii.*]
– ORIGIN so named because each scale on the back has a keel.

**keelboat** ● **n. 1** a yacht built with a permanent keel rather than a centreboard. **2** a large, flat freight boat used on American rivers.

**keelhaul** ● **v. 1** historical punish (someone) by dragging them through the water from one side of a boat to the other, under the keel. **2** humorous punish or reprimand severely.

**keelie** /'kiːli/ ● **n.** (pl. **-ies**) Scottish & N. English a disreputable inhabitant of a town or city, especially Glasgow.
– ORIGIN C19: perh. rel. to **GILLIE**.

**keelson** /'kiːls(ə)n/ (also **kelson**) ● **n.** a structure running the length of a ship, that fastens the timbers or plates of the floor to the keel.
– ORIGIN ME *kelswayn*, from *kiel* 'keel of a ship' + *swīn* 'swine' (used as the name of a timber).

**keen**[1] ● **adj. 1** eager; enthusiastic. ➤(**keen on**) interested in or attracted by. **2** (of the edge or point of a blade) sharp. ➤(of a sense or mental faculty) acute or quick. ➤(of the air or wind) cold and biting. **3** Brit. (of prices) very low; competitive.
– DERIVATIVES **keenly** adv. **keenness** n.
– ORIGIN OE *cēne* 'wise, clever', also 'brave, daring', of Gmc origin.

**keen**[2] ● **v.** wail in grief for a dead person. ➤make an eerie wailing sound. ● **n.** an Irish funeral song accompanied with wailing in lamentation for the dead.
– DERIVATIVES **keener** n.
– ORIGIN C19: from Ir. *caoinim* 'I wail'.

**keep** ● **v.** (past and past part. **kept** /kɛpt/) **1** have or retain possession of. ➤retain or reserve for use in the future. ➤put or store in a regular place. ➤(of a perishable commodity) remain in good condition. **2** continue or cause to continue in a specified condition, position, or activity: *she kept quiet about it.* ➤(**keep something from**) cause something to stay out of. ➤(**keep something from**) cause something to remain a secret from. ➤(**keep from**) avoid doing something. ➤(**keep someone from**) guard or protect someone from. **3** provide for the sustenance of. ➤own and look after (an animal). ➤[as adj. **kept**] supported financially in return for sexual favours. **4** delay or detain; cause to be late. **5** honour or fulfil (a commitment or undertaking). ➤observe or pay due regard to (a law, custom, or religious occasion). **6** record or regularly maintain (a note or diary). ● **n. 1** food, clothes, and other essentials for living. **2** archaic charge; control. **3** the strongest or central tower of a castle.
– PHRASES **for keeps** informal permanently; indefinitely.
– PHRASAL VERBS **keep something in** restrain oneself from expressing a feeling. **keep off** (of bad weather) fail to occur. **keep on** continue to do something. **keep on about** speak about (something) repeatedly. **keep on at** harass with constant requests. **keep someone/thing on** continue to use or employ someone or something. **keep to 1** avoid leaving (a path, road, or place). **2** adhere to (a schedule). **3** observe (a promise). **4** confine or restrict oneself to. **keep up** move or progress at the same rate as someone or something else. **keep up with 1** learn about or be aware of (current events or developments). **2** continue to be in contact with (someone). **3** meet a regular commitment to pay or do (something). **keep someone up** prevent someone from going to bed or to sleep. **keep something up** continue a course of action.
– DERIVATIVES **keepable** adj.
– ORIGIN OE *cēpan* 'seize, take in', also 'care for, attend to', of unknown origin.

**keeper** ● **n. 1** a person who manages or looks after something or someone. **2** short for **GOALKEEPER** or **WICKETKEEPER**. **3** an object which protects or secures another. **4** a bar of soft iron placed across the poles of a horseshoe magnet to maintain its strength. **5** American Football a play in which the quarterback receives the ball from the centre and runs with it.

– DERIVATIVES **keepership** n.

**keep-fit** • **n.** chiefly Brit. regular exercises to improve personal fitness and health.

**keeping** • **n.** the action of keeping something.
– PHRASES **in someone's keeping** in someone's care or custody. **in** (or **out of**) **keeping with** in (or out of) harmony or conformity with.

**keepnet** • **n.** Fishing a net secured in the water and keeping alive the fish that have been caught.

**keepsake** • **n.** a small item kept in memory of the person who gave it or originally owned it.

**keeshond** /'keɪshɒnd/ • **n.** a dog of a Dutch breed with long thick grey hair, resembling a large Pomeranian.
– ORIGIN 1920s: Du., from *Kees* (familiar form of the given name *Cornelius*) + *hond* 'dog'.

**keester** /'ki:stə/ • **n.** variant spelling of **KEISTER**.

**kef** /kɛf/ • **n. & adj.** variant spelling of **KIF**.

**keffiyeh** /kə'fi:(j)ə/ (also **kaffiyeh**) • **n.** a Bedouin Arab's kerchief worn as a headdress.
– ORIGIN C19: from Arab. *keffiyya, kūfiyya*.

**keftedes** /kɛf'tɛði:z/ • **pl. n.** (in Greek cookery) small meatballs made with herbs and onions.
– ORIGIN from Gk *kephtedes*, pl. of *kephtes*, via Turk. from Pers. *koftah* (see **KOFTA**).

**keg** • **n. 1** a small barrel, especially one of less than 10 gallons or (in the US) 30 gallons. **2** short for **KEG BEER**.
– ORIGIN C17: var. of Scots and US dial. *cag*, from ON *kaggi*.

**keg beer** • **n.** Brit. beer supplied in a keg, to which carbon dioxide has been added.

**keiretsu** /keɪ'rɛtsu:/ • **n.** (pl. same) (in Japan) a conglomeration of businesses linked together by cross-shareholdings to form a robust corporate structure.
– ORIGIN Japanese, from *kei* 'systems' + *retsu* 'tier'.

**keister** /'ki:stə/ (also **keester**) • **n.** N. Amer. informal **1** a person's buttocks. **2** dated a suitcase, bag, or box for carrying possessions or merchandise.
– ORIGIN C19 (in sense 2): of unknown origin.

**Kejia** /keɪ'dʒjɑ:/ • **n.** another term for **HAKKA**.

**kelim** • **n.** variant spelling of **KILIM**.

**keloid** /'ki:lɔɪd/ • **n.** Medicine an area of irregular fibrous tissue formed at the site of a scar or injury.
– ORIGIN C19: via Fr. from Gk *khēlē* 'crab's claw' + **-OID**.

**kelp** • **n. 1** a very large brown seaweed that typically has a long, tough stalk with a broad frond divided into strips. [*Laminaria* and other genera, family Laminariaceae.] **2** the calcined ashes of seaweed, used as a source of various salts.
– ORIGIN ME: of unknown origin.

**kelpie** /'kɛlpi/ • **n. 1** a water spirit of Scottish folklore, typically taking the form of a horse. **2** a sheepdog of an Australian breed with a smooth coat, originally bred from a Scottish collie.
– ORIGIN C17: perh. from Sc. Gaelic *cailpeach, colpach* 'bullock, colt'.

**kelson** /'kɛls(ə)n/ • **n.** variant spelling of **KEELSON**.

**kelt** • **n.** a salmon or sea trout after spawning and before returning to the sea.
– ORIGIN ME: of unknown origin.

**kelvin** (abbrev.: **K**) • **n.** the SI base unit of thermodynamic temperature, equal in magnitude to the degree Celsius.
– ORIGIN C19: named after the Brit. physicist William T. *Kelvin*.

**Kelvin scale** • **n.** a scale of temperature with absolute zero as zero, and the triple point of water as exactly 273.16 degrees.

**kemp** • **n.** a coarse hair or fibre in wool.
– DERIVATIVES **kempy** adj.
– ORIGIN ME: from ON *kampr* 'beard, whisker'.

**kempt** • **adj.** maintained in a neat and clean condition.
– ORIGIN OE *cemd-*, past part. of *cemban* 'to comb', of Gmc origin; rel. to **COMB**.

**ken** • **n.** (**one's ken**) one's range of knowledge or sight. • **v.** (**kenning**; past and past part. **kenned** or **kent**) Scottish & N. English **1** know. **2** recognize; identify.
– ORIGIN OE *cennan* 'tell, make known', of Gmc origin.

**kenaf** /kə'naf/ • **n.** a brown plant fibre similar to jute, used to make ropes and coarse cloth.
– ORIGIN C19: from Pers., var. of *kanab* 'hemp'.

**Kendal Green** /'kɛnd(ə)l/ • **n. 1** a kind of rough green woollen cloth. **2** the green colour of this cloth.
– ORIGIN from the name of *Kendal* in Cumbria.

**Kendal mint cake** • **n.** a hard peppermint-flavoured sweet produced in flat rectangular blocks.

**kendo** /'kɛndəʊ/ • **n.** a Japanese form of fencing with two-handed bamboo swords.
– DERIVATIVES **kendoist** n.
– ORIGIN Japanese, from *ken* 'sword' + *dō* 'way'.

**kennel** • **n. 1** a small shelter for a dog. **2** (**kennels**) [treated as sing. or pl.] a boarding or breeding establishment for dogs. • **v.** (**kennelled**, **kennelling**; US **kenneled**, **kenneling**) put or keep (a dog) in a kennel or kennels.
– ORIGIN ME: from an ONorth. Fr. var. of OFr. *chenil*, from L. *canis* 'dog'.

**Kennelly layer** (also **Kennelly–Heaviside layer**) • **n.** another name for **E-LAYER**.

**kennelmaid** • **n.** a woman who works in a kennels.

**kennelman** • **n.** (pl. **-men**) a man who works in a kennels, especially for a hunt.

**kenning** • **n.** a compound expression in Old English and Old Norse poetry with metaphorical meaning, e.g. *oar-steed* = ship.
– ORIGIN C19: from ON, from *kenna* 'know, perceive'; rel. to **KEN**.

**keno** /'ki:nəʊ/ • **n.** a game of chance similar to bingo, based on the drawing of numbers and covering of corresponding numbers on cards.
– ORIGIN C19: from Fr. *kine*, denoting a set of five winning lottery numbers.

**kenosis** /kɪ'nəʊsɪs/ • **n.** (in Christian theology) the full or partial renunciation of his divine nature by Christ in the Incarnation.
– DERIVATIVES **kenotic** adj.
– ORIGIN C19: from Gk *kenōsis* 'an emptying', from *kenoein* 'to empty', with biblical allusion (Phil. 2:7) to Gk *heauton ekenōse*, lit. 'emptied himself'.

**kenspeckle** /'kɛn,spɛk(ə)l/ • **adj.** Scottish easily recognizable; conspicuous.
– ORIGIN C16: of Scand. origin, prob. based on ON *kenna* 'know, perceive' and *spak-, spek-* 'wise or wisdom'.

**kent** past and past participle of **KEN**.

**kente** /'kɛntə/ • **n.** a brightly coloured material consisting of separate strips sewn together, made in Ghana.
– ORIGIN C20: from Twi, 'cloth'.

**kentia palm** /'kɛntɪə/ • **n.** an Australasian palm tree popular as a house plant. [*Howeia* (formerly *Kentia*) *forsteriana*.]
– ORIGIN C19: mod. L., named after the botanical collector William *Kent*.

**Kentish** • **adj.** of or relating to the English county of Kent.

**Kentish glory** • **n.** a large moth with orange-brown and white markings. [*Endromis versicolora*.]

**Kentuckian** /kɛn'tʌkiən/ • **n.** a native or inhabitant of the US state of Kentucky. • **adj.** of or relating to Kentucky.

**Kenyan** /'kɛnjən/ • **n.** a native or inhabitant of Kenya. • **adj.** of or relating to Kenya.

**kepi** /'kɛpi, 'keɪpi/ • **n.** (pl. **kepis**) a French military cap with a horizontal peak.
– ORIGIN C19: from Fr. *képi*, from Swiss Ger. *Käppi*, dimin. of *Kappe* 'cap'.

**kept** past and past participle of **KEEP**.

**Keralite** /'kɛrəlʌɪt, kə'rɑ:lʌɪt/ • **n.** a native or inhabitant of the Indian state of Kerala. • **adj.** of or relating to Kerala.

**kerat-** • **comb. form** variant spelling of **KERATO-** shortened before a vowel (as in *keratectomy*).

**keratectomy** /,kɛrə'tɛktəmi/ • **n.** surgical removal of a section or layer of the cornea, usually performed using a laser to correct myopia.

**keratin** /'kɛrətɪn/ • **n.** a fibrous protein forming the main structural constituent of hair, feathers, hoofs, claws, and horns.

– DERIVATIVES **keratinous** adj.
– ORIGIN C19: from Gk *keras, kerat-* 'horn' + **-IN**[1].

**keratinize** /'kɛrətɪnʌɪz, kə'rat-/ (also **-ise**) • **v.** Biology change or become changed into a form containing keratin.
– DERIVATIVES **keratinization** n.

**keratinocyte** /ˌkɛrə'tɪnə(ʊ)sʌɪt/ • **n.** Biology an epidermal cell which produces keratin.

**keratitis** /ˌkɛrə'tʌɪtɪs/ • **n.** Medicine inflammation of the cornea of the eye.

**kerato-** (also **kerat-**) • **comb. form 1** relating to keratin or horny tissue. **2** relating to the cornea.
– ORIGIN from Gk *keras, kerat-* 'horn'.

**keratoplasty** /'kɛrətə(ʊ),plasti/ • **n.** Medicine surgery carried out on the cornea, especially corneal transplantation.

**keratosis** /ˌkɛrə'təʊsɪs/ • **n.** (pl. **keratoses**) Medicine a horny growth, especially on the skin.

**keratotomy** /ˌkɛrə'tɒtəmi/ • **n.** a surgical operation involving cutting into the cornea of the eye, especially (**radial keratotomy**) performed to correct myopia.

**kerb** (US **curb**) • **n.** a stone edging to a pavement or raised path.
– ORIGIN C17 (denoting a raised border or frame): var. of **CURB**.

**kerb-crawling** • **n.** Brit. the action of driving slowly along the edge of the road in search of a prostitute or in an attempt to entice a passer-by.
– DERIVATIVES **kerb-crawler** n.

**kerb drill** • **n.** Brit. a set of precautions taken before crossing the road, as taught to children.

**kerbing** • **n. 1** the stones collectively forming a kerb. **2** the action of hitting a kerb with a car tyre.

**kerbstone** (US **curbstone**) • **n.** a long, narrow stone or concrete block, laid end to end with others to form a kerb.

**kerb weight** • **n.** the weight of a motor car without occupants or baggage.

**kerchief** /'kəːtʃɪf/ • **n. 1** a piece of fabric used to cover the head. **2** a handkerchief.
– DERIVATIVES **kerchiefed** adj.
– ORIGIN ME *kerchef*, from OFr. *cuevrechief*, from *couvrir* 'to cover' + *chief* 'head'.

**Keres** /'kɛrɛs/ • **n.** (pl. same) **1** a member of a Pueblo Indian people inhabiting parts of New Mexico. **2** the language of this people, of unknown affinity.
– ORIGIN from Amer. Sp. *Queres*, from Amer. Ind.

**kerf** /kəːf/ • **n. 1** a slit made by cutting with a saw. **2** the cut end of a felled tree.
– DERIVATIVES **kerfed** adj.
– ORIGIN OE *cyrf* 'cutting, a cut', of W. Gmc origin; rel. to **CARVE**.

**kerfuffle** /kə'fʌf(ə)l/ • **n.** informal, chiefly Brit. a commotion or fuss.
– ORIGIN C19: perh. from Scots *curfuffle* (prob. from Sc. Gaelic *car* 'twist, bend' + imitative Scots *fuffle* 'to disorder'), or rel. to Ir. *cior thual* 'confusion, disorder'.

**kermes** /'kəːmɪz/ • **n.** a red dye obtained from the dried bodies of a scale insect (*Kermes illicis*) which makes berry-like galls on the kermes oak.
– ORIGIN C16 (denoting the kermes oak): from Fr. *kermès*, from Arab. *ḳirmiz*; rel. to **CRIMSON**.

**kermes oak** • **n.** a very small evergreen Mediterranean oak with prickly, holly-like leaves, formerly prized as a host plant for kermes insects. [*Quercus coccifera*.]

**kermis** /'kəːmɪs/ • **n. 1** a summer fair held in towns and villages in the Netherlands. **2** US a fair or carnival, especially one held to raise money for a charity.
– ORIGIN C16: Du., orig. denoting a mass on the anniversary of the dedication of a church, when a fair was held, from *kerk* 'church' + *mis* 'Mass'.

**kern**[1] Printing • **n.** a part of a metal type projecting beyond the body or shank, or a part of a printed character that overlaps its neighbours. • **v. 1** provide (metal type or a printed character) with a kern. **2** [usu. as noun **kerning**] adjust the spacing between (characters).
– ORIGIN C17: perh. from Fr. *carne* 'corner', from L. *cardo, cardin-* 'hinge'.

**kern**[2] (also **kerne**) • **n. 1** historical a light-armed Irish foot soldier. **2** archaic a peasant; a rustic.
– ORIGIN ME: from Ir. *ceithearn*, from Old Ir. *ceithern* 'band of foot soldiers'.

**kernel** /'kəːn(ə)l/ • **n. 1** a softer part of a nut, seed, or fruit stone contained within its hard shell. ➤the seed and hard husk of a cereal, especially wheat. **2** the central or most important part of something. ➤Computing the most basic level or core of an operating system.
– ORIGIN OE *cyrnel*, dimin. of **CORN**[1].

**kerosene** /'kɛrəsiːn/ (also **kerosine**) • **n.** a light fuel oil obtained by distilling petroleum; paraffin oil.
– ORIGIN C19: from Gk *kēros* 'wax' + **-ENE**.

**kerria** /'kɛrɪə/ • **n.** an East Asian shrub of the rose family, cultivated for its yellow flowers. [*Kerria japonica*.]
– ORIGIN C19: mod. L., named after the Engl. botanical collector William *Ker(r)*.

**Kerry** • **n.** (pl. **-ies**) an animal of a breed of small black dairy cattle.
– ORIGIN from *Kerry* in Ireland.

**Kerry blue** • **n.** a terrier of a breed with a silky blue-grey coat.
– ORIGIN from *Kerry* in Ireland.

**Kerry Hill** • **n.** a sheep of a breed having a thick fleece and black markings near the muzzle and feet.
– ORIGIN C20: from *Kerry*, a town and neighbouring hill range in Powys, Wales.

**kersey** /'kəːzi/ • **n.** a kind of coarse, ribbed cloth with a short nap, woven from short-stapled wool.
– ORIGIN ME: prob. from *Kersey*, a town in Suffolk where woollen cloth was made.

**kerseymere** /'kəːzɪmɪə/ • **n.** a fine twilled woollen cloth.
– ORIGIN C18: alt. of *cassimere*, var. of **CASHMERE**, changed by assoc. with **KERSEY**.

**keskidee** /ˌkɛskɪ'diː/ • **n.** variant spelling of **KISKADEE**.

**kestrel** • **n.** a small falcon that hunts by hovering with rapidly beating wings. [*Falco tinnunculus* (Eurasia and Africa), *F. sparverius* (N. America), and other species.]
– ORIGIN ME *castrel*, perh. from *casserelle*, dial. var. of OFr. *crecerelle*, perh. imitative of its call.

**ketamine** /'kiːtəmiːn/ • **n.** a synthetic compound used as an anaesthetic and analgesic drug and also illicitly as a hallucinogen.
– ORIGIN C20: blend of **KETONE** and **AMINE**.

**ketch** • **n.** a two-masted, fore-and-aft rigged sailing boat with a mizzenmast stepped forward of the rudder and smaller than its foremast.
– ORIGIN C17: later form of obs. *catch*, prob. from **CATCH**.

**ketchup** /'kɛtʃəp, -ʌp/ (also **catchup**, US also **catsup**) • **n.** a spicy sauce made chiefly from tomatoes and vinegar, used as a relish.
– ORIGIN C17: perh. from Chin. (Cantonese dial.) *k'ē chap* 'tomato juice'.

**keto-** /'kiːtəʊ/ • **comb. form** Chemistry denoting ketones or the carbonyl group characteristic of them.

**ketonaemia** /ˌkiːtə(ʊ)'niːmɪə/ (US **ketonemia**) • **n.** Medicine the presence of an abnormally high concentration of ketone bodies in the blood.

**ketone** /'kiːtəʊn/ • **n.** Chemistry an organic compound containing a carbonyl group =C=O bonded to two alkyl groups, e.g. acetone.
– DERIVATIVES **ketonic** /kɪ'tɒnɪk/ adj.
– ORIGIN C19: from Ger. *Keton*, alt. of *Aketon* 'acetone'.

**ketone bodies** • **pl. n.** Biochemistry three related compounds (one of which is acetone) produced during the metabolism of fats.

**ketonuria** /ˌkiːtə(ʊ)'njʊərɪə/ • **n.** Medicine the excretion of abnormally large amounts of ketone bodies in the urine, characteristic of diabetes mellitus, starvation, or other medical conditions.

**ketosis** /kɪ'təʊsɪs/ • **n.** Medicine a condition characterized by raised levels of ketone bodies in the body, associated with abnormal fat metabolism and diabetes mellitus.
– DERIVATIVES **ketotic** adj.

**kettle** • **n.** a metal or plastic container with a lid, spout,

and handle, used for boiling water.
– PHRASES **a different kettle of fish** informal a person or matter that is altogether different from the one just mentioned. **the pot calling the kettle black** the criticisms a person is aiming at someone else could equally well apply to themselves. **a pretty** (or **fine**) **kettle of fish** informal an awkward state of affairs.
– ORIGIN OE *cetel*, *cietel*, of Gmc origin, based on L. *catillus*, dimin. of *catinus* 'deep container for cooking or serving food'.

**kettledrum** • n. a large drum shaped like a bowl, with a membrane adjustable for tension (and so pitch) stretched across.
– DERIVATIVES **kettledrummer** n.

**kettle hole** • n. Geology a hollow, typically filled by a lake, resulting from the melting of a mass of ice trapped in glacial deposits.

**Keuper** /ˈkɔɪpə/ • n. Geology a European series of sedimentary rocks of Upper Triassic age, represented in England chiefly by marls and sandstones.
– ORIGIN C19 (orig. a miners' term): Ger.

**keV** • abbrev. kilo-electronvolt(s).

**kevel** /ˈkɛv(ə)l/ • n. a large cleat fitted to the gunwale of a ship and used in belaying ropes.
– ORIGIN ME: of unknown origin.

**Kevlar** /ˈkɛvlɑː/ • n. trademark a synthetic fibre of high tensile strength used especially as a reinforcing agent in the manufacture of tyres and other rubber products.
– ORIGIN 1970s: an arbitrary formation.

**kewpie** /ˈkjuːpi/ (also **kewpie doll**) • n. (trademark in the US) a type of doll characterized by a large head, big eyes, chubby cheeks, and a curl or topknot on top of its head.
– ORIGIN C20 (orig. US): from *Cupid*, the name of the Roman god of love (represented as a naked winged boy).

**key**[1] • n. (pl. **-eys**) **1** a small piece of shaped metal with incisions cut to fit the wards of a particular lock, which is inserted into the lock and rotated to open or close it or to operate a switch. ➤an instrument for grasping and turning a screw, peg, or nut. ➤a pin, bolt, or wedge inserted into a hole or between parts so as to lock the parts together. **2** a lever depressed by the finger in playing an instrument such as the organ, piano, flute, or concertina. **3** each of several buttons on a panel for operating a typewriter, word processor, or computer terminal. **4** a lever operating a mechanical device for making or breaking an electric circuit. **5** a thing that provides access to or understanding of something: *a key to success*. ➤an explanatory list of symbols used in a map or table. ➤a set of answers to exercises or problems. ➤a word or system for solving a cipher or code. ➤the first move in the solution of a chess problem. **6** Music a group of notes based on a particular note and comprising a scale, regarded as forming the tonal basis of a passage of music. ➤the tone or pitch of someone's voice. **7** the dry winged fruit of an ash, maple, or sycamore; a samara. **8** roughness on a surface, provided to assist adhesion of plaster or other material. **9** Basketball the keyhole-shaped area marked on the court near each basket. • adj. of crucial importance: *a key figure*. • v. (**-eys**, **-eyed**) **1** enter or operate on (data) by means of a computer keyboard. **2** fasten into position with a pin, wedge, or bolt. **3** (**key to**) link with. ➤(**key into/in with**) be connected or in harmony with. **4** (**be keyed up**) be nervous, tense, or excited. **5** roughen (a surface) to provide a key.
– PHRASES **in** (or **out of**) **key** in (or out of) harmony.
– DERIVATIVES **keyed** adj. **keyer** n. **keyless** adj.
– ORIGIN OE *cǣg*, *cǣge*, of unknown origin.

**key**[2] • n. a low-lying island or reef (especially in the Caribbean).
– ORIGIN C17: from Sp. *cayo* 'reef', influenced by QUAY.

**keyboard** • n. **1** a panel of keys for use with a computer or typewriter. **2** a set of keys on a piano or similar musical instrument. **3** an electronic musical instrument with keys arranged as on a piano. • v. enter (data) by means of a keyboard.
– DERIVATIVES **keyboarder** n. **keyboardist** n.

**key card** • n. a small plastic card bearing magnetically encoded data that can be read by an electronic device, used instead of a door key.

**key grip** • n. the person in a film crew who is in charge of the camera equipment.

**keyholder** • n. a person who is entrusted with keeping a key to commercial or industrial premises.

**keyhole** • n. a hole in a lock into which the key is inserted.

**keyhole saw** • n. a saw with a long, narrow blade for cutting small holes such as keyholes.

**keyhole surgery** • n. minimally invasive surgery carried out through a very small incision, with special instruments and techniques including fibre optics.

**key industry** • n. an industry that is essential to the functioning of others, such as the manufacture of machine tools.

**key light** • n. the main source of light in a photograph or film.

**Key lime** • n. a small yellowish lime with a sharp flavour.
– ORIGIN named after the Florida *Keys*.

**key map** • n. a map in bare outline, to simplify the use of a full map.

**key money** • n. a payment required from a new tenant in exchange for the provision of a key to the premises.

**Keynesian** /ˈkeɪnzɪən/ • adj. of or relating to the theories of the English economist John Maynard Keynes (1883–1946). • n. an adherent of Keynesian theories.
– DERIVATIVES **Keynesianism** n.

**keynote** • n. **1** a prevailing tone or central theme. ➤[as modifier] (of a speech) setting out the central theme of a conference. **2** Music the note on which a key is based.
– DERIVATIVES **keynoter** n.

**keypad** • n. a miniature keyboard or set of buttons for operating a portable electronic device, telephone, or other equipment.

**keypunch** • n. a device for transferring data by means of punched holes or notches on a series of cards or paper tape. • v. transfer (data) to a keypunch.
– DERIVATIVES **keypuncher** n.

**key ring** • n. a metal ring for holding keys together in a bunch.

**key signature** • n. Music any of several combinations of sharps or flats after the clef at the beginning of each stave, indicating the key of a composition.

**Key Stage** • n. (in the UK) any of the four fixed stages into which the national curriculum is divided, at the end of which pupils are required to complete standard assessment tasks.

**keystone** • n. **1** a central stone at the summit of an arch, locking the whole together. **2** the central principle or part of a policy or system.

**keystroke** • n. a single depression of a key on a keyboard.

**keyway** • n. a slot cut in a part of a machine or an electrical connector, to ensure correct orientation with another part which is fitted with a key.

**keyword** • n. **1** a word which acts as the key to a cipher or code. **2** a word or concept of great significance. ➤a word used in an information retrieval system to indicate the content of a document. ➤a significant word mentioned in an index.

**KG** • abbrev. (in the UK) Knight of the Order of the Garter.

**kg** • abbrev. kilogram(s).

**Kgs** • abbrev. Kings (in biblical references).

**khadi** /ˈkɑdə/ (also **khaddar**) • n. an Indian homespun cotton cloth.
– ORIGIN from Punjabi, from Hindi *khādī*.

**khaki** /ˈkɑːki/ • n. (pl. **khakis**) **1** a cotton or wool fabric of a dull brownish-yellow colour, used especially in military clothing. ➤(**khakis**) clothing made of khaki. **2** a dull brownish-yellow colour.
– ORIGIN C19: from Urdu *ḵākī* 'dust-coloured', from *ḵāk* 'dust', from Pers.

**Khalkha** /ˈkɑːlkə/ • n. (pl. same or **Khalkas**) **1** a member of a section of the Mongolian people, constituting the bulk of the population of Mongolia. **2** the language of the

Khalka, a demotic form of Mongolian adopted as the official language of Mongolia.
– ORIGIN of unknown origin.

**Khalsa** /ˈkʌlsə/ ● **n.** the company of fully initiated Sikhs to which devout orthodox Sikhs are ritually admitted at puberty.
– ORIGIN via Urdu from Pers., from the fem. form of Arab. *ḵāliṣ* 'pure, belonging to'.

**khamsin** /ˈkamsɪn/ ● **n.** an oppressive, hot southerly or south-easterly wind blowing in Egypt in spring.
– ORIGIN C17: from Arab. *ḵamsīn*, from *ḵamsūn* 'fifty' (being the approximate duration in days).

**khan**[1] /kɑːn, kan/ ● **n. 1** a title given to rulers and officials in central Asia, Afghanistan, and certain other Muslim countries. **2** any of the successors of Genghis Khan, supreme rulers of the Turkish, Tartar, and Mongol peoples and emperors of China in the Middle Ages.
– DERIVATIVES **khanate** n.
– ORIGIN ME: from OFr. *chan*, med. L. *canus*, *caanus*, from Turkic *ḵān* 'lord, prince'.

**khan**[2] /kɑːn, kan/ ● **n.** (in the Middle East) an inn for travellers, built around a central courtyard.
– ORIGIN from Pers. *ḵān*.

**khat** /kɑːt/ ● **n. 1** the leaves of an Arabian shrub, which are chewed (or drunk as an infusion) as a stimulant. **2** the shrub that produces these leaves. [*Catha edulis*.]
– ORIGIN C19: from Arab. *ḵāt*.

**Khazar** /kəˈzɑː/ ● **n.** a member of a Turkic people who occupied a large part of southern Russia from the 6th to the 11th centuries.
– ORIGIN of unknown origin.

**khazi** /ˈkɑːzi/ ● **n.** (pl. **khazies**) Brit. informal a toilet.
– ORIGIN 1960s: from Ital. *casa* 'house'.

**Khedive** /kɪˈdiːv/ ● **n.** the title of the viceroy of Egypt under Turkish rule 1867–1914.
– DERIVATIVES **Khedival** adj. **Khedivial** adj.
– ORIGIN via Fr. from Ottoman Turk. *ḵediv*, from Pers. *ḵadiw* 'prince'.

**Khmer** /kmɛː/ ● **n. 1** a native or inhabitant of the ancient kingdom of Khmer in SE Asia. **2** a native or inhabitant of Cambodia. **3** the language of the Khmers, the official language of Cambodia.
– ORIGIN the name in Khmer.

**Khoikhoi** /ˈkɔɪkɔɪ/ (also **Khoi-khoin** /-kɔɪn/, **Khoi**) ● **n.** (pl. same) a member of a group of indigenous peoples of South Africa and Namibia, including the Nama.
– ORIGIN Nama, lit. 'men of men'.

**Khoisan** /ˈkɔɪsɑːn/ ● **n. 1** [usu. treated as pl.] a collective term for the Khoikhoi and San peoples of southern Africa. **2** a language family of southern Africa, including the languages of the Khoikhoi and San, notable for the use of clicks as additional consonants.
– ORIGIN blend of **KHOIKHOI** and **SAN**.

**Khoja** /ˈkəʊdʒə/ ● **n.** a member of a Muslim sect found mainly in western India.
– ORIGIN C17 (in the sense 'Muslim scribe or teacher'): from Turk. *hoca*.

**khoum** /kuːm/ ● **n.** a monetary unit of Mauritania, equal to one fifth of an ouguiya.
– ORIGIN from Arab. *ḵums* 'one fifth'.

**khus-khus** /ˈkʌskʌs/ ● **n.** another term for **VETIVER**.
– ORIGIN C19: from Urdu and Pers. *ḵasḵas*.

**kHz** ● **abbrev.** kilohertz.

**ki** ● **n.** variant spelling of **CHI**[2].

**kiang** /kɪˈaŋ/ ● **n.** a wild ass of a Tibetan race with a thick furry coat.
– ORIGIN C19: from Tibetan *kyang*.

**kia ora** /ˌkɪə ˈɔːrə/ ● **exclam.** (in New Zealand) a greeting wishing good health.
– ORIGIN from Maori.

**kibble**[1] /ˈkɪb(ə)l/ ● **v.** [usu. as adj. **kibbled**] grind or chop (beans, grain, etc.) coarsely. ● **n.** N. Amer. ground meal shaped into pellets, especially for pet food.
– ORIGIN C18: of unknown origin.

**kibble**[2] /ˈkɪb(ə)l/ ● **n.** Brit. an iron hoisting bucket used in mines.
– ORIGIN ME: from Mid. High Ger. *kübel*, from med. L. *cupellus* 'corn measure', dimin. of *cuppa* 'cup'.

**kibbutz** /kɪˈbʊts/ ● **n.** (pl. **kibbutzim** /-ˈtsiːm/) a communal farming settlement in Israel.
– ORIGIN 1930s: from mod. Heb. *qibbūṣ* 'gathering'.

**kibbutznik** /kɪˈbʊtsnɪk/ ● **n.** a member of a kibbutz.

**kibe** /kʌɪb/ ● **n.** archaic an ulcerated chilblain.
– ORIGIN ME: of unknown origin.

**kibitka** /kɪˈbɪtkə/ ● **n. 1** a type of Russian hooded sledge. **2** a circular tent, covered with felt, formerly used by Tartars.
– ORIGIN C18: Russ., from Tartar and Kyrgyz *kibit* (from Arab. *qubbat* 'dome') + the Russ. suffix *-ka*.

**kibitz** /ˈkɪbɪts/ ● **v.** informal, chiefly N. Amer. **1** look on and offer unwelcome advice, especially at a card game. **2** speak informally; chat.
– DERIVATIVES **kibitzer** n.
– ORIGIN 1920s: Yiddish, from colloq. Ger., from Ger. *Kiebitz* 'interfering onlooker'.

**kiblah** /ˈkɪblə/ (also **qibla**) ● **n.** the direction of the Kaaba in Mecca, to which Muslims turn when at prayer.
– ORIGIN C17: from Arab. *ḵibla* 'that which is opposite'.

**kibosh** /ˈkʌɪbɒʃ/ (also **kybosh**) ● **n.** (in phr. **put the kibosh on**) informal put a decisive end to.
– ORIGIN C19: of unknown origin.

**kick**[1] ● **v. 1** strike or propel forcibly with the foot. ➤strike out with the foot or feet. ➤(chiefly in rugby) score (a goal) by a kick. ➤(**kick oneself**) be annoyed with oneself. ➤(**kick against**) express disagreement or frustration with. ➤(**kick someone/thing out**) informal expel or dismiss someone or something. **2** informal succeed in giving up (a habit or addiction). **3** (of a gun) recoil when fired. ● **n. 1** an instance of kicking. **2** Brit. (chiefly in rugby) a player of specified kicking ability. **3** informal a sharp stimulant effect. ➤a thrill of pleasurable excitement. **4** Billiards & Snooker an irregular movement of the ball caused by dust.
– PHRASES **kick the bucket** informal die. **a kick in the teeth** informal a grave setback or disappointment. **kick someone upstairs** informal remove someone from an influential position in a business by giving them an ostensible promotion.
– PHRASAL VERBS **kick around** (or **about**) (of a thing) lie unwanted or unexploited. ➤(of a person) drift idly from place to place. **kick someone around** (or **about**) treat someone roughly or without respect. **kick something around** (or **about**) discuss an idea casually or experimentally. **kick back** N. Amer. informal be at leisure; relax. **kick in** become activated; come into effect. **kick something in** N. Amer. informal contribute something, especially money. **kick off** (of a football match) be started or resumed by a player kicking the ball from the centre spot.
– DERIVATIVES **kickable** adj.
– ORIGIN ME: of unknown origin.

**kick**[2] ● **n.** archaic an indentation in the bottom of a glass bottle, diminishing the internal capacity.
– ORIGIN C19: of unknown origin.

**Kickapoo** /ˈkɪkəpuː/ ● **n.** (pl. same or **Kickapoos**) **1** a member of an American Indian people formerly living in Wisconsin, and now in Kansas, Oklahoma, and northern Mexico. **2** the Algonquian language of this people.
– ORIGIN from Kickapoo *kiikaapoa*.

**kick-ass** ● **adj.** informal, chiefly N. Amer. forceful, vigorous, and aggressive.

**kickback** ● **n. 1** a sudden forceful recoil. **2** informal a payment made to someone who has facilitated a transaction or appointment, especially illicitly.

**kickball** ● **n.** N. Amer. an informal game combining elements of baseball and soccer.

**kick-boxing** ● **n.** a form of martial art which combines boxing with elements of karate, in particular kicking with bare feet.
– DERIVATIVES **kick-boxer** n.

**kick-down** ● **n.** Brit. a device for changing gear in a motor vehicle with automatic transmission by full depression of the accelerator.

**kick drum** ● **n.** informal a bass drum played using a pedal.

**kicker** ● **n. 1** a person or animal that kicks. **2** a player in a team who scores or gains positional advantage by kicking. **3** N. Amer. informal an unwelcome discovery or turn of events. **4** an extra clause in a contract. **5** informal a small outboard motor. **6** (in poker) a high third card retained in the hand with a pair at the draw.

**kicking** ● **adj.** informal (especially of music) lively and exciting.

**kicking strap** ● **n.** **1** a strap used to prevent a horse from kicking. **2** Sailing a rope lanyard fixed to a boom to prevent it from rising.

**kick-off** ● **n.** the start or resumption of a football match, in which a player kicks the ball from the centre spot.

**kick plate** ● **n.** a metal plate at the base of a door or panel to protect it from damage or wear.

**kick-pleat** ● **n.** an inverted pleat in a narrow skirt to allow freedom of movement.

**kickshaw** ● **n.** **1** archaic a fancy but insubstantial cooked dish. **2** chiefly N. Amer. an elegant but insubstantial trinket.
– ORIGIN C16: from Fr. *quelque chose* 'something'.

**kicksorter** ● **n.** informal a device for analysing electrical pulses according to amplitude.

**kickstand** ● **n.** a metal rod attached to a bicycle or motorcycle that may be kicked into a vertical position to support the vehicle when it is stationary.

**kick-start** ● **v.** **1** start (an engine on a motorcycle) with a downward thrust of a pedal. **2** provide an impetus to start or restart (a process). ● **n.** **1** an act or instance of kick-starting. **2** a device to kick-start an engine.

**kick-turn** ● **n.** **1** (in skiing) a turn carried out while stationary by lifting first one and then the other ski through 180°. **2** (in skateboarding) a turn performed with the front wheels lifted off the ground.

**kicky** ● **adj.** N. Amer. informal exciting or fashionable.

**kid**[1] ● **n.** **1** a young goat. ➤leather made from a young goat's skin. **2** informal a child or young person. ● **v.** (**kidded, kidding**) (of a goat) give birth.
– PHRASES **handle** (or **treat**) **someone/thing with kid gloves** deal with someone or something very carefully. **kids' stuff** informal something that is easy or simple to do.
– ORIGIN ME: from ON *kith*, of Gmc origin.

**kid**[2] ● **v.** (**kidded, kidding**) informal **1** deceive playfully; tease. **2** fool into believing something.
– DERIVATIVES **kidder** n. **kidding** adj. **kiddingly** adv.
– ORIGIN C19: perh. from KID[1], expressing the notion 'make a child or goat of'.

**kid**[3] ● **n.** archaic a small wooden tub, especially a sailor's mess tub for grog or rations.
– ORIGIN C18: perh. a var. of KIT[1].

**kid brother** ● **n.** informal a younger brother.

**Kidderminster carpet** ● **n.** a reversible carpet made of two cloths of different colours woven together.
– ORIGIN C17: named after *Kidderminster* in Worcestershire, a centre of carpet-making.

**kiddie** (also **kiddy**) ● **n.** (pl. **-ies**) informal a young child.

**kiddiewink** ● **n.** Brit. humorous a small child.
– ORIGIN 1950s: a familiar extension of KIDDIE.

**kiddle** /ˈkɪd(ə)l/ ● **n.** **1** a dam or barrier in a river, with an opening fitted with nets to catch fish. **2** an arrangement of fishing nets hung on stakes along the seashore.
– ORIGIN ME: from OFr. *quidel*.

**kiddush** /ˈkɪdʊʃ/ ● **n.** a Jewish ceremony of prayer and blessing over wine, performed at a meal preceding the Sabbath or a holy day.
– ORIGIN C18: from Heb. *qiddūš* 'sanctification'.

**kidnap** ● **v.** (**kidnapped, kidnapping**; US also **kidnaped, kidnaping**) abduct and hold captive, typically to obtain a ransom. ● **n.** an instance of kidnapping.
– DERIVATIVES **kidnapper** n.
– ORIGIN C17: back-form. from *kidnapper*, from KID[1] + sl. *nap* 'nab, seize'.

**kidney** ● **n.** (pl. **-eys**) **1** each of a pair of organs in the abdominal cavity, with one concave and one convex side, that excrete urine. ➤the kidney of a sheep, ox, or pig as food. **2** nature or temperament: *of similar kidney.*
– ORIGIN ME: of obscure origin.

**kidney bean** ● **n.** a kidney-shaped bean, especially a dark red one from a dwarf French bean plant.

**kidney dish** ● **n.** (in medicine) a kidney-shaped receptacle.

**kidney machine** ● **n.** an artificial kidney or dialysis machine.

**kidney stone** ● **n.** a hard mass formed in the kidneys, typically consisting of insoluble calcium compounds; a renal calculus.

**kidney vetch** ● **n.** a yellow- or orange-flowered leguminous grassland plant, sometimes grown as a fodder crop. [*Anthyllis vulneraria*.]

**kidology** /kɪˈdɒlədʒi/ ● **n.** informal, chiefly Brit. the art or practice of deliberately deceiving or teasing people.

**kid sister** ● **n.** informal a younger sister.

**kidstakes** /ˈkɪdsteɪkz/ ● **pl. n.** Austral./NZ informal nonsense; pretence.
– ORIGIN C20: prob. a humorous formation based on sl. *kid* 'humbug'.

**kiekie** /ˈkiːkiː/ ● **n.** a New Zealand climbing plant with edible bracts, and leaves which are used for basket-making and weaving. [*Freycinetia banksii*.]
– ORIGIN C19: from Maori.

**kielbasa** /kiːlˈbasə/ ● **n.** a type of highly seasoned Polish sausage.
– ORIGIN Polish, lit. 'sausage'.

**Kierkegaardian** /ˈkɪəkəˌgɑːdɪən/ ● **adj.** of or relating to the work of the Danish philosopher Søren Kierkegaard (1813–55).

**kieselguhr** /ˈkiːz(ə)lˌgʊə/ ● **n.** a form of diatomaceous earth used in various manufacturing and laboratory processes, chiefly as a filter, filler, or insulator.
– ORIGIN C19: from Ger., from *Kiesel* 'gravel' + dial. *Guhr* (lit. 'yeast').

**kif** /kɪf/ (also **kef**) ● **n.** a substance, especially cannabis, smoked to produce a drowsy state.
– ORIGIN C19: from Arab. *kayf* 'enjoyment, well-being'.

**kike** /kʌɪk/ ● **n.** N. Amer. offensive a Jew.
– ORIGIN C20: of unknown origin.

**kikoi** /kɪˈkɔɪ/ ● **n.** (pl. **kikois**) a distinctive East African striped cloth with an end fringe.
– ORIGIN C20: from Kiswahili.

**Kikongo** /kɪˈkɒŋgəʊ/ ● **n.** either of two similar Bantu languages spoken in the Congo, the Democratic Republic of Congo (Zaire), and adjacent areas.
– ORIGIN the name in Kikongo.

**Kikuyu** /kɪˈkuːjuː/ ● **n.** (pl. same or **Kikuyus**) **1** a member of a people forming the largest ethnic group in Kenya. **2** the Bantu language of this people. **3** (**kikuyu, kikuyu grass**) a creeping perennial grass which is native to Kenya and cultivated elsewhere as a lawn and fodder grass. [*Pennisetum clandestinum*.]
– ORIGIN the name in Kikuyu.

**kilderkin** /ˈkɪldəkɪn/ ● **n.** a cask for liquids or other substances, holding 16 or 18 gallons.
– ORIGIN ME: from MDu. *kinderkin*, var. of *kinerkijn*, dimin. of *kintal* (see QUINTAL).

**kilim** /kɪˈliːm, ˈkiːlɪm/ (also **kelim**) ● **n.** a flat-woven carpet or rug made in Turkey, Kurdistan, and neighbouring areas.
– ORIGIN C19: via Turk. from Pers. *gelīm*.

**kill** ● **v.** **1** cause the death of. ➤put an end to. ➤stop (a computing process). ➤(**kill oneself**) overexert oneself. ➤(**kill out**) (of an animal) yield a specified amount of meat when slaughtered. **2** informal overwhelm with an emotion: *the suspense is killing me.* ➤cause pain or anguish to. **3** pass (time). **4** (in soccer and other ball games) make (the ball) stop. ➤Tennis hit (the ball) so that it cannot be returned. ● **n.** **1** an act of killing, especially of one animal by another: *a lion has made a kill.* ➤an animal or animals killed by a hunter or another animal. **2** informal an act of destroying or disabling an enemy aircraft, submarine, etc.
– PHRASES **be in at the kill** be present at or benefit from the successful conclusion of an enterprise. **go for the kill** take ruthless or decisive action to secure an advantage. **kill someone with kindness** spoil someone with overindulgence.
– ORIGIN ME (in the sense 'strike, beat', also 'put to death'):

prob. of Gmc origin and rel. to **QUELL**.

**killdeer** /'kɪldɪə/ ● **n.** a widespread American plover with a plaintive call that resembles its name. [*Charadrius vociferus*.]

**killer** ● **n. 1** a person or thing that kills. **2** informal a formidable person or thing. **3** informal a hilarious joke.

**killer bee** ● **n.** informal, chiefly US an Africanized honeybee.

**killer cell** ● **n.** Physiology a white blood cell (a type of lymphocyte) which destroys infected or cancerous cells.

**killer instinct** ● **n.** a ruthless determination to succeed or win.

**killer whale** ● **n.** a large, toothed whale with distinctive black-and-white markings and a prominent dorsal fin, living in groups that hunt fish, seals, and penguins cooperatively. [*Orcinus orca*.]

**killick** /'kɪlɪk/ ● **n. 1** a heavy stone used as an anchor. ➤ a small anchor. **2** Brit. nautical slang a leading seaman. [so named because the leading seaman's badge bore the symbol of an anchor.]
– ORIGIN C17: of unknown origin.

**killifish** /'kɪlɪfɪʃ/ ● **n.** (pl. same or **-fishes**) a small, typically brightly coloured fish of fresh or brackish water, mainly native to America. [Families Cyprinodontidae and Poeciliidae: many species.]
– ORIGIN C19: appar. from **KILL** and **FISH**[1].

**killing** ● **n.** an act of causing death. ● **adj. 1** [in combination] causing the death of a specified thing: *weed-killing*. **2** informal overwhelming or unbearable.
– PHRASES **make a killing** have a great financial success.
– DERIVATIVES **killingly** adv.

**killing bottle** ● **n.** a bottle containing poisonous vapour to kill insects collected as specimens.

**killing field** ● **n.** (usu. **killing fields**) a place where many people have been massacred or killed.

**killing zone** (also **kill zone**) ● **n. 1** the area of a military engagement with a high concentration of deaths. **2** an area of the body where entry of a bullet, arrow, etc. would kill.

**killjoy** ● **n.** a person who deliberately spoils the enjoyment of others through resentful or overly sober behaviour.

**kiln** ● **n.** a furnace or oven for burning, baking, or drying, especially one for calcining lime or firing pottery.
– ORIGIN OE *cylene*, from L. *culina* 'kitchen, cooking stove'.

**kiln-dry** ● **v.** [usu. as adj. **kiln-dried**] dry in a kiln.

**Kilner jar** /'kɪlnə/ ● **n.** trademark a glass jar with a lid which forms an airtight seal, used to bottle fruit and vegetables.
– ORIGIN C20: from the name of the manufacturing company.

**kilo** ● **n.** (pl. **-os**) **1** a kilogram. **2** a code word representing the letter K, used in radio communication.
– ORIGIN C19: from Fr., abbrev. of *kilogramme*.

**kilo-** /'kɪləʊ, 'kiːləʊ/ ● **comb. form** denoting a factor of 1,000: *kilolitre*.
– ORIGIN via Fr. from Gk *khilioi* 'thousand'.

**kilobase** (abbrev.: **kb**) ● **n.** Biochemistry (in expressing the lengths of nucleic acid molecules) one thousand bases.

**kilobit** ● **n.** Computing a unit of memory or data equal to 1,024 bits.

**kilobyte** (abbrev.: **Kb** or **KB**) ● **n.** Computing a unit of memory or data equal to 1,024 bytes.

**kilocalorie** ● **n.** a unit of energy of one thousand calories (equal to one large calorie).

**kilocycle** (abbrev.: **kc**) ● **n.** a former measure of frequency, equivalent to 1 kilohertz.

**kilogram** (also **kilogramme**) (abbrev.: **kg**) ● **n.** the SI unit of mass, equal to 1,000 grams (approximately 2.205 lb) and equivalent to the international standard kept at Sèvres near Paris.
– ORIGIN C18: from Fr. *kilogramme* (see **KILO-**, **GRAM**[1]).

**kilohertz** (abbrev.: **kHz**) ● **n.** a measure of frequency equivalent to 1,000 cycles per second.

**kilojoule** (abbrev.: **kJ**) ● **n.** 1,000 joules, especially as a measure of the energy value of foods.

**kilolitre** (US **kiloliter**) (abbrev.: **kl**) ● **n.** 1,000 litres (equivalent to 220 imperial gallons).

**kilometre** /'kɪlə,miːtə, kɪ'lɒmɪtə/ (US **kilometer**) (abbrev.: **km**) ● **n.** a metric unit of measurement equal to 1,000 metres (approximately 0.62 miles).
– DERIVATIVES **kilometric** adj.
– ORIGIN C18: from Fr. *kilomètre* (see **KILO-**, **METRE**[1]).

**USAGE** kilometre

There are two possible pronunciations for **kilometre**: one with the stress on the **ki-** and the other with the stress on the **-lo-**. The first is traditionally considered the correct one, while the second is still regarded as incorrect by some people, especially in British English.

**kiloton** (also **kilotonne**) ● **n.** a unit of explosive power equivalent to 1,000 tons of TNT.

**kilovolt** (abbrev.: **kV**) ● **n.** 1,000 volts.

**kilowatt** (abbrev.: **kW**) ● **n.** 1,000 watts.

**kilowatt-hour** (abbrev.: **kWh**) ● **n.** a measure of electrical energy equivalent to a power consumption of one thousand watts for one hour.

**kilt** ● **n.** a knee-length skirt of pleated tartan cloth, traditionally worn by men as part of Scottish Highland dress and also worn by women and girls. ● **v. 1** arrange (a garment or material) in vertical pleats. **2** (**kilt something up**) hoist or tuck up one's skirt or coat.
– DERIVATIVES **kilted** adj.
– ORIGIN ME (as v. in the sense 'tuck up around the body'): of Scand. origin.

**kilter** ● **n.** (in phr. **out of kilter**) out of harmony or balance.
– ORIGIN C17: of unknown origin.

**kiltie** /'kɪlti/ (also **kilty**) ● **n.** informal a Scot.

**kimberlite** /'kɪmbəlʌɪt/ ● **n.** Geology a rare, blue-tinged, coarse-grained intrusive igneous rock sometimes containing diamonds, found in South Africa and Siberia.
– ORIGIN C19: from *Kimberley*, a S. Afr. city and diamond-mining centre, + **-ITE**[1].

**kimchi** /'kɪmtʃi/ ● **n.** spicy pickled cabbage, the national dish of Korea.
– ORIGIN from Korean.

**kimono** /kɪ'məʊnəʊ/ ● **n.** (pl. **-os**) a long, loose robe having wide sleeves and tied with a sash, originally worn as a formal garment in Japan.
– DERIVATIVES **kimonoed** adj.
– ORIGIN C17: Japanese, from *ki* 'wearing' + *mono* 'thing'.

**kin** ● **n.** [treated as pl.] one's family and relations. ● **adj.** (of a person) related.
– DERIVATIVES **kinless** adj.
– ORIGIN OE *cynn*, of Gmc origin.

**-kin** ● **suffix** forming diminutive nouns such as *catkin*.
– ORIGIN from MDu. *-kijn*, *-ken*, Mid. Low Ger. *-kīn*.

**kina**[1] /'kiːnə/ ● **n.** (pl. same) the basic monetary unit of Papua New Guinea, equal to 100 toea.
– ORIGIN from Papuan.

**kina**[2] /'kiːnə/ ● **n.** (pl. same) an edible sea urchin occurring on New Zealand coasts. [*Evechinus chloroticus*.]
– ORIGIN C20: from Maori.

**kinaesthesia** /,kɪnɪs'θiːzɪə, ,kʌɪn-/ (US **kinesthesia**) ● **n.** awareness of the position and movement of the parts of the body by means of sensory organs (proprioceptors) in the muscles and joints.
– DERIVATIVES **kinaesthetic** adj.
– ORIGIN C19: from Gk *kinein* 'to move' + *aisthēsis* 'sensation'.

**kinase** /'kʌɪneɪz/ ● **n.** Biochemistry an enzyme that promotes the transfer of a phosphate group from ATP to a specified molecule.
– ORIGIN C20: from Gk *kinein* 'to move' + **-ASE**.

**kincob** /'kɪŋkɒb/ ● **n.** a rich Indian fabric brocaded with gold or silver.
– ORIGIN C18: from Urdu and Pers. *kamḵāb*, alt. of *kamḵā* 'damask silk'.

**kind**[1] ● **n. 1** a class or type of people or things having similar characteristics. **2** character; nature: *the trials were different in kind from any that preceded them.* **3** each of the elements (bread and wine) of the Eucharist.
– PHRASES **in kind 1** in the same way. **2** (of payment) in

goods or services as opposed to money. **kind of** informal rather. **nothing of the kind** not at all like the thing in question. ➤expressing emphatic denial: *he did nothing of the kind.* **of its kind** within the limitations of its class. **of a kind** hardly or only partly deserving the name: *there is tribute, of a kind, in such popularity.* **one of a kind** unique. **two** (or **three, four**, etc.) **of a kind 1** the same or very similar. **2** (of cards) having the same face value but of a different suit.
– ORIGIN OE *cynd(e), gecynd(e)*, of Gmc origin; rel. to **KIN**.

**kind**[2] ● **adj. 1** considerate and generous. **2** (**kind to**) (of a product) not harmful to. **3** archaic affectionate; loving.
– ORIGIN OE *gecynde* 'natural, native', in ME 'well-born or well-bred', whence 'courteous, gentle'.

**kinda** ● **contr.** informal kind of.

**kindergarten** /'kɪndə,gɑːt(ə)n/ ● **n.** a nursery school.
– DERIVATIVES **kindergartener** n.
– ORIGIN C19: from Ger., lit. 'children's garden'.

**kind-hearted** ● **adj.** kind and sympathetic.
– DERIVATIVES **kind-heartedly** adv. **kind-heartedness** n.

**kindle**[1] /'kɪnd(ə)l/ ● **v. 1** light (a flame); set on fire. **2** (with reference to an emotion) arouse or be aroused.
– DERIVATIVES **kindler** n.
– ORIGIN ME: based on ON *kynda*, influenced by ON *kindill* 'candle, torch'.

**kindle**[2] /'kɪnd(ə)l/ ● **v.** (of a hare or rabbit) give birth.
– ORIGIN ME: appar. a frequentative of **KIND**[1].

**kindling** ● **n. 1** small sticks or twigs used for lighting fires. **2** (in neurology) a process by which an event in the brain is initiated and its recurrence made more likely.

**kindly**[1] ● **adv. 1** in a kind manner. **2** please (used in a polite request): *will you kindly sign this letter.*
– PHRASES **look kindly on** regard sympathetically. **not take kindly to** not welcome or be pleased by. **take something kindly** like or be pleased by something. **thank someone kindly** thank someone very much.
– ORIGIN OE *gecyndelīce* 'naturally, characteristically' (see **KIND**[2], **-LY**[2]).

**kindly**[2] ● **adj.** (**-ier, -iest**) **1** kind; warm-hearted. **2** archaic native-born.
– DERIVATIVES **kindliness** n.

**kindness** ● **n. 1** the quality of being kind. **2** a kind act.

**kindred** /'kɪndrɪd/ ● **n. 1** [treated as pl.] one's family and relations. **2** relationship by blood. ● **adj.** similar in kind; related.
– ORIGIN ME: from **KIN** + *-red* (from OE *rǣden* 'condition'), with insertion of *-d-* in the mod. spelling through phonetic development (as in *thunder*).

**kindred spirit** ● **n.** a person whose interests or attitudes are similar to one's own.

**kine** /kʌɪn/ ● **pl. n.** archaic cows collectively.

**kinematics** /,kɪnɪ'matɪks, ,kʌɪn-/ ● **pl. n.** [treated as sing.] the branch of mechanics concerned with the motion of objects without reference to the forces which cause the motion. Compare with **DYNAMICS**.
– DERIVATIVES **kinematic** adj. **kinematically** adv.
– ORIGIN C19: from Gk *kinēma, kinēmat-* 'motion'.

**kinematic viscosity** ● **n.** Mechanics a quantity representing the dynamic viscosity of a fluid per unit density.

**kinematograph** /,kɪnɪ'matəgrɑːf/ ● **n.** variant spelling of **CINEMATOGRAPH**.

**kinesics** /kɪ'niːsɪks, kʌɪ-/ ● **pl. n.** [treated as sing.] the study of the way in which certain gestures and movements of the body serve for non-verbal communication.
– ORIGIN 1950s: from Gk *kinēsis* 'motion' + **-ICS**.

**kinesiology** /kɪ,niːsɪ'ɒlədʒi, kʌɪ-/ ● **n.** the study of the mechanics of body movements.
– DERIVATIVES **kinesiological** adj. **kinesiologist** n.
– ORIGIN C19: from Gk *kinēsis* 'movement' + **-LOGY**.

**kinesis** /kɪ'niːsɪs, kʌɪ-/ ● **n.** (pl. **kineses**) **1** movement; motion. **2** Biology an undirected movement of a cell, organism, or part in response to an external stimulus. Compare with **TAXIS**. **3** Zoology mobility of the bones of the skull, as in some birds and reptiles.
– ORIGIN C17: from Gk *kinēsis* 'movement'.

**kinesthesia** ● **n.** US spelling of **KINAESTHESIA**.

**kinetic** /kɪ'nɛtɪk, kʌɪ-/ ● **adj. 1** of, relating to, or resulting from motion. **2** (of a work of art) depending on movement for its effect.
– DERIVATIVES **kinetically** adv.
– ORIGIN C19: from Gk *kinētikos*, from *kinein* 'to move'.

**kinetic energy** ● **n.** Physics energy which a body possesses by virtue of being in motion. Compare with **POTENTIAL ENERGY**.

**kinetics** /kɪ'nɛtɪks, kʌɪ-/ ● **pl. n.** [treated as sing.] **1** the branch of chemistry concerned with the rates of chemical reactions. **2** Physics another term for **DYNAMICS** (in sense 1).

**kinetic theory** ● **n.** the body of theory which explains the physical properties of matter in terms of the motions of its constituent particles.

**kinetin** /'kʌɪnɪtɪn/ ● **n.** a synthetic compound similar to kinin, used to stimulate cell division in plants.
– ORIGIN 1950s: from Gk *kinetos* 'movable' + **-IN**[1].

**kineto-** ● **comb. form** relating to movement: *kinetoscope.*
– ORIGIN from Gk *kinētos* 'movable'.

**kinetochore** /kɪ'niːtəʊkɔː, kʌɪ-/ ● **n.** another term for **CENTROMERE**.
– ORIGIN C20: from **KINETO-** + Gk *khōros* 'place'.

**kinetoscope** /kɪ'niːtəʊskəʊp, kʌɪ-/ ● **n.** an early motion-picture device in which the images were viewed through a peephole.

**kinfolk** ● **pl. n.** another term for **KINSFOLK**.

**king** ● **n. 1** the male ruler of an independent state, especially one who inherits the position by right of birth. **2** a person or thing regarded as the finest or most important in its sphere or group. **3** used in names of animals and plants that are particularly large, e.g. **king cobra**. **4** the most important chess piece, which the opponent has to checkmate in order to win. **5** a piece in draughts with extra capacity for moving, made by crowning an ordinary piece that has reached the opponent's baseline. **6** a playing card bearing a representation of a king, ranking next below an ace. ● **v. 1** archaic make (someone) king. **2** (**king it**) act in an unpleasantly superior manner.
– DERIVATIVES **kinghood** n. **kingless** adj. **kingliness** n. **kingly** adj. **kingship** n.
– ORIGIN OE *cyning, cyng*, of Gmc origin; rel. to **KIN**.

**kingbird** ● **n.** a large American tyrant flycatcher, typically with a grey head and back and yellowish or white underparts. [Genus *Tyrannus*: several species.]

**kingbolt** ● **n.** a kingpin.

**King Charles spaniel** ● **n.** a spaniel of a small breed, typically with a white, black, and tan coat.

**king cobra** ● **n.** a brownish cobra native to the Indian subcontinent, the largest of all venomous snakes. [*Ophiophagus hannah*.]

**king crab** ● **n. 1** another term for **HORSESHOE CRAB**. **2** N. Amer. an edible crab of the North Pacific, resembling a spider crab. [Genus *Paralithodes*.]

**kingcraft** ● **n.** archaic the art of ruling as a king, especially the use of clever diplomacy in dealing with subjects.

**kingcup** ● **n.** British term for **MARSH MARIGOLD**.

**kingdom** ● **n. 1** a country, state, or territory ruled by a king or queen. **2** a realm associated with a particular person or thing. **3** the spiritual reign or authority of God. ➤heaven as the abode of God and of the faithful after death. **4** each of the three divisions (animal, vegetable, and mineral) in which natural objects have conventionally been classified. ➤Biology the highest category in taxonomic classification.
– PHRASES **come into** (or **to**) **one's kingdom** achieve recognition or supremacy. **till** (or **until**) **kingdom come** informal forever. **to kingdom come** informal into the next world: *the truck was blown to kingdom come.*
– ORIGIN OE *cyningdōm* 'kingship' (see **KING**, **-DOM**).

**King Edward** ● **n.** an oval potato of a variety with a white skin mottled with red.
– ORIGIN 1920s: named after *King Edward* VII.

**kingfish** ● **n.** (pl. same or **-fishes**) a large sea fish, generally valued for food or sport. [*Scomberomorus cavalla* (mackerel family, W. Atlantic) and other species.]

**kingfisher** ● **n.** a colourful bird with a large head and long sharp beak which dives to catch fish in streams, ponds, etc. [*Alcedo atthis* and other species, family Alcedinidae.]

**kingfisher blue** • n. a brilliant turquoise-blue colour.

**King in Council** • n. (in the UK) the Privy Council as issuing Orders in Council or receiving petitions when the reigning monarch is a king.

**King James Bible** (also **King James Version**) • n. another name for **AUTHORIZED VERSION**.

**kingklip** /ˈkɪŋklɪp/ • n. a cusk-eel of South African waters, important as a food fish. [*Genypterus capensis*.]
– ORIGIN C19: abbrev. of *kingklipfish*, partly translating Afrik. *koningklipvis* 'king rock fish'.

**kinglet** • n. **1** chiefly derogatory a minor king. **2** chiefly N. Amer. a very small warbler of a group that includes the goldcrest. [Genus *Regulus*.]

**kingmaker** • n. a person who brings leaders to power through the exercise of political influence.
– ORIGIN used orig. with ref. to the Earl of Warwick (1428–71), known as Warwick the *Kingmaker*.

**King of Arms** • n. Heraldry (in the UK) a chief herald.

**king of beasts** • n. chiefly poetic/literary the lion.

**king of birds** • n. chiefly poetic/literary the eagle.

**King of Kings** • n. (in the Christian Church) God.

**King of the Castle** • n. Brit. a children's game in which the object is to beat one's rivals to an elevated position at the top of a mound or other high place.

**kingpin** • n. **1** a main or large bolt in a central position. ➤a vertical bolt used as a pivot. **2** a person or thing that is essential to the success of an organization or operation.

**king post** • n. an upright post extending from the tie beam to the apex of a roof truss.

**king prawn** • n. a large edible prawn. [Genus *Penaeus*.]

**kin group** • n. another term for **KINSHIP GROUP**.

**King's Bench** • n. in the reign of a king, the term for **QUEEN'S BENCH**.

**king's bishop** • n. Chess each player's bishop on the kingside at the start of a game.

**King's bounty** • n. historical (in the UK) a sum of money given from royal funds to a mother who had had a multiple birth of three or more.

**King's Champion** • n. another term for **CHAMPION OF ENGLAND**.

**King's Counsel** • n. in the reign of a king, the term for **QUEEN'S COUNSEL**.

**King's English** • n. in the reign of a king, the term for **QUEEN'S ENGLISH**.

**King's evidence** • n. in the reign of a king, the term for **QUEEN'S EVIDENCE**.

**king's evil** • n. (usu. **the king's evil**) historical scrofula, formerly held to be curable by the royal touch.

**kingside** • n. Chess the half of the board on which each king stands at the start of a game.

**king-sized** (also **king-size**) • adj. of a larger size than the standard; very large.

**king's knight** • n. Chess each player's knight on the kingside at the start of a game.

**king's pawn** • n. Chess the pawn immediately in front of each player's king at the start of a game.

**king's rook** • n. Chess each player's rook on the kingside at the start of a game.

**King's speech** • n. in the reign of a king, the term for **QUEEN'S SPEECH**.

**kinin** /ˈkʌɪnɪn/ • n. **1** Biochemistry a substance, such as bradykinin, produced in response to injury and causing vasodilation and smooth muscle contraction. **2** Botany a compound that promotes cell division and inhibits ageing in plants.
– ORIGIN 1950s: from Gk *kinein* 'to move' + **-IN**[1].

**kink** • n. **1** a sharp twist or curve in something linear. **2** a flaw or obstacle in a plan or operation. **3** a quirk of character or behaviour. • v. form or cause to form a kink.
– ORIGIN C17: from Mid. Low Ger. *kinke*, prob. from Du. *kinken* 'to kink'.

**kinkajou** /ˈkɪŋkəˌdʒuː/ • n. a fruit-eating mammal with a prehensile tail, found in the tropical forests of Central and South America. [*Potos flavus*.]
– ORIGIN C18: from Fr. *quincajou*, alt. of **CARCAJOU**.

**kinky** • adj. (**-ier**, **-iest**) **1** having kinks or twists. **2** informal involving or given to unusual sexual behaviour. ➤(of clothing) sexually provocative.
– DERIVATIVES **kinkily** adv. **kinkiness** n.
– ORIGIN C19: from **KINK** + **-Y**[1].

**kinnikinnick** /ˌkɪnɪkɪˈnɪk/ (also **-nic** or **-nik**) • n. **1** a mixture used by North American Indians as a substitute for tobacco, typically consisting of dried sumac leaves and willow or dogwood bark. **2** N. Amer. the bearberry, also sometimes used in this mixture.
– ORIGIN C18: from a Delaware word meaning 'admixture'.

**kino** /ˈkiːnəʊ/ • n. a gum obtained from certain tropical trees, used as an astringent and in tanning.
– ORIGIN C18: appar. from a W. Afr. lang.

**-kins** • suffix equivalent to **-KIN**, typically expressing endearment.

**kin selection** • n. Zoology natural selection in favour of behaviour by individuals which may decrease their own chance of survival but increases that of their kin.

**kinsfolk** (also **kinfolk**) • pl. n. **1** (in anthropological or formal use) a person's blood relations, regarded collectively. **2** a group of people related by blood.

**kinship** • n. **1** blood relationship. **2** a sharing of characteristics or origins: *they felt a kinship with architects.*

**kinship group** • n. Anthropology a family, clan, or other group based on blood relationship.

**kinsman** (also **kinswoman**) • n. (pl. **-men** or **-women**) (in anthropological or formal use) one of a person's blood relations.

**kiosk** /ˈkiːɒsk/ • n. **1** a small open-fronted hut or cubicle from which newspapers, refreshments, tickets, etc. are sold. **2** (usu. **telephone kiosk**) Brit. a public telephone booth. **3** (in Turkey and Iran) a light open pavilion or summer house.
– ORIGIN C17: from Fr. *kiosque*, from Turk. *köşk* 'pavilion'.

**kip**[1] informal • n. **1** Brit. a sleep; a nap. **2** chiefly Scottish a bed. **3** Irish a dirty or sordid place. • v. (**kipped**, **kipping**) Brit. sleep.
– ORIGIN C18 (in the sense 'brothel'): perh. rel. to Dan. *kippe* 'hovel, tavern'.

**kip**[2] • n. (in leather-making) the hide of a young or small animal. ➤a set or bundle of such hides.
– ORIGIN ME: perh. rel. to MDu. *kip*, *kijp* 'bundle (of hides)'.

**kip**[3] • n. (pl. same or **kips**) the basic monetary unit of Laos, equal to 100 ats.
– ORIGIN from Thai.

**kip**[4] • n. (in Australia) a small piece of wood from which coins are spun in the game of two-up.
– ORIGIN C19: perh. rel. to Ir. *cipin* 'small stick, dibble'.

**Kiplingesque** /kɪplɪŋˈɛsk/ • adj. reminiscent of the work of the British writer Rudyard Kipling (1865–1936).

**kipper**[1] • n. **1** a herring that has been split open, salted, and dried or smoked. **2** a male salmon in the spawning season. • v. [usu. as adj. **kippered**] cure (a herring) in such a way.
– ORIGIN OE *cypera*, of Gmc origin; perh. rel. to **COPPER**[1].

**kipper**[2] • n. Austral. an Aboriginal male who has been initiated into manhood.
– ORIGIN from Dharuk *gibara*, from *giba* 'a stone' (because of its use in the ceremonial extraction of teeth).

**kipper tie** • n. a brightly coloured and very wide tie.

**kipsie** /ˈkɪpsi/ (also **kipsy**) • n. (pl. **-ies**) Austral. informal an improvised dwelling or shelter.
– ORIGIN C20: perh. from **KIP**[1].

**Kir** /kɪə/ • n. trademark a drink made from dry white wine and crème de cassis.
– ORIGIN 1960s: named after Canon Félix *Kir*, a mayor of Dijon, said to have invented the recipe.

**kirby grip** /ˈkəːbi/ (also trademark **Kirbigrip**) • n. Brit. a hairgrip consisting of a thin folded and sprung metal strip.
– ORIGIN 1920s: named after *Kirby*, Beard & Co. Ltd, the

original manufacturers.

**Kirghiz** ● n. variant spelling of **KYRGYZ**.

**kirk** /kəːk/ ● n. Scottish & N. English **1** a church. **2** (**the Kirk** or **the Kirk of Scotland**) the Church of Scotland.
– ORIGIN ME: from ON *kirkja*, from OE *cirice* (see **CHURCH**).

**kirkman** /'kəːkmən/ ● n. (pl. **-men**) Scottish a clergyman or member of the Church of Scotland.

**Kirk session** ● n. the lowest court in the Church of Scotland, composed of the minister and elders of the parish.

**Kirlian photography** /'kəːlɪən/ ● n. a technique for recording images of corona discharges and hence, supposedly, the auras of living creatures.
– ORIGIN C20: from the name of the Russ. electricians Semyon D. and Valentina K. *Kirlian*.

**kirpan** /kəː'pɑːn/ ● n. a short curved sword, worn as one of the five distinguishing signs of the Sikh Khalsa.
– ORIGIN from Punjabi and Hindi *kirpān*, from Sanskrit *kṛpāṇa* 'sword'.

**kirsch** /kɪəʃ/ (also **kirschwasser** /'kɪəʃvasə/) ● n. brandy distilled from the fermented juice of cherries.
– ORIGIN Ger., abbrev. of *Kirschenwasser*, from *Kirsche* 'cherry' + *Wasser* 'water'.

**kirtan** /'kɪətʌn/ ● n. Hinduism a devotional song in which a group repeats lines sung by a leader.
– ORIGIN from Sanskrit *kīrtana*.

**kirtle** /'kəːt(ə)l/ ● n. archaic **1** a woman's gown or outer petticoat. **2** a man's tunic or coat.
– ORIGIN OE *cyrtel*, of Gmc origin, prob. based on L. *curtus* 'short'.

**kish** /kɪʃ/ ● n. graphite scum formed on iron during smelting.
– ORIGIN C19: perh. rel. to Fr. dial. *quiasse*.

**kishke** /'kɪʃkə/ ● n. **1** a beef intestine stuffed with a savoury filling. **2** (**kishkes**) US informal a person's guts.
– ORIGIN C20: Yiddish, from Polish *kiszka* or Ukrainian *kishka*.

**kiskadee** /ˌkɪskə'diː/ (also **keskidee**) ● n. a large tropical American tyrant flycatcher with a black-and-white-striped head and bright yellow breast. [*Pitangus sulphuratus* and *Philohydor lictor*.]
– ORIGIN C19: imitative of its call.

**Kislev** /'kɪslɛf/ (also **Kislew**) ● n. (in the Jewish calendar) the third month of the civil and ninth of the religious year, usually coinciding with parts of November and December.
– ORIGIN from Heb. *kislēw*.

**kismet** /'kɪzmɛt, -mɪt, -s-/ ● n. destiny; fate.
– ORIGIN C19: from Turk., from Arab. *ḳismat* 'division, portion, lot', from *ḳasama* 'to divide'.

**kiss** ● v. **1** touch or caress with the lips as a sign of love, affection, or greeting. **2** Billiards & Snooker (of a ball) lightly touch (another ball). **3** (**kiss someone/thing off**) N. Amer. informal dismiss someone rudely; end a relationship abruptly. **4** (**kiss up to**) N. Amer. informal behave obsequiously towards. ● n. **1** a touch or caress with the lips. **2** Billiards & Snooker a slight touch of a ball against another ball. **3** N. Amer. a small cake, biscuit, or sweet.
– PHRASES **kiss and tell** chiefly derogatory recount one's sexual exploits concerning a famous person. **kiss someone's arse** (or N. Amer. **ass**) vulgar slang behave obsequiously towards someone. **kiss of death** an action that ensures failure, especially when apparently benign. **kiss of life 1** mouth-to-mouth resuscitation. **2** something that revives a failing enterprise. **kiss of peace** a ceremonial kiss signifying unity, especially during the Eucharist. **kiss the rod** accept punishment submissively.
– DERIVATIVES **kissable** adj.
– ORIGIN OE *cyssan* (v.), of Gmc origin.

**kiss curl** ● n. a small curl of hair on the forehead, at the nape of the neck, or in front of the ear.

**kissel** /'kɪs(ə)l/ ● n. a dessert of fruit juice or purée thickened with cornflour.
– ORIGIN from Russ. *kisel'*, from a base shared by *kislyĭ* 'sour'.

**kisser** ● n. **1** a person who kisses someone. **2** informal a person's mouth.

**kissing bug** ● n. a bloodsucking North American bug which inflicts a painful bite, often on the face. [*Melanolestes picipes*.]

**kissing cousin** ● n. a relative known well enough to greet with a kiss.

**kissing gate** ● n. Brit. a small gate hung in a U- or V-shaped enclosure, letting one person through at a time.

**kiss-off** ● n. informal, chiefly N. Amer. a rude or abrupt dismissal.

**kissogram** ● n. a novelty greeting delivered by a man or woman who accompanies it with a kiss.

**kissy** ● adj. informal characterized by or given to kissing.

**kist** ● n. **1** variant spelling of **CIST**[1]. **2** S. African a storage chest. [S. Afr. Du., from Du.]

**Kiswahili** /ˌkiːswə'hiːli, ˌkɪswɑː-/ ● n. another term for **SWAHILI** (the language).
– ORIGIN from the Bantu prefix *ki-* (used in names of langs) + **SWAHILI**.

**kit**[1] ● n. **1** a set of articles or equipment for a specific purpose. **2** Brit. the clothing and other items needed for an activity. **3** a set of all the parts needed to assemble something. **4** Brit. a large basket or box, especially for fish. ● v. (**kit someone/thing out/up**) chiefly Brit. provide someone or something with appropriate clothing or equipment.
– PHRASES **get one's kit off** Brit. informal take off one's clothes.
– ORIGIN ME: from MDu. *kitte* 'wooden vessel', of unknown origin.

**kit**[2] ● n. the young of certain animals, e.g. the beaver, ferret, and mink. ➤ informal a kitten.

**kit**[3] ● n. historical a small violin, especially one used by a dancing master.
– ORIGIN C16: perh. from L. *cithara* (see **CITTERN**).

**kitbag** ● n. a long, cylindrical canvas bag for carrying a soldier's possessions.

**kit-cat** ● n. a canvas of a standard size (typically 36 × 28 in., 91.5 × 71 cm), especially as used for a portrait showing the sitter's head, shoulders, and hands.
– ORIGIN C18: named after portraits of members of the *Kit-Cat* Club, an association of Whigs and literary figures.

**kitchen** ● n. **1** a room where food is prepared and cooked. **2** informal the percussion section of an orchestra. **3** [as modifier] (of a language) in an uneducated or domestic form.
– ORIGIN OE *cycene*, of W. Gmc origin, based on L. *coquere* 'to cook'.

**kitchen cabinet** ● n. informal a group of unofficial advisers considered to be unduly influential.

**kitchener** ● n. historical a kitchen range.

**kitchenette** ● n. a small kitchen or part of a room equipped as a kitchen.

**kitchen garden** ● n. a garden where vegetables, fruit, etc. are grown for domestic use.

**kitchen midden** ● n. a prehistoric refuse heap marking an ancient settlement.

**kitchen paper** ● n. absorbent paper used for drying and cleaning in a kitchen.

**kitchen roll** ● n. Brit. kitchen paper.

**kitchen-sink** ● adj. (chiefly of drama) realistic in the depiction of drab or sordid subjects.

**kitchen tea** ● n. Austral./NZ a party before a wedding to which female guests bring kitchen equipment for the bride-to-be.

**kitchenware** ● n. kitchen utensils.

**kite** ● n. **1** a toy consisting of a light frame with thin material stretched over it, flown in the wind at the end of a long string. **2** Brit. informal, dated an aircraft. **3** Sailing, informal a spinnaker. **4** a long-winged bird of prey with a forked tail, frequently soaring. [*Milvus milvus* (**red kite**) and other species.] **5** informal a fraudulent cheque, bill, or receipt. ➤ an illicit or surreptitious letter. ➤ archaic a dishonest person. **6** Geometry a quadrilateral figure having two pairs of equal adjacent sides, symmetrical only about one diagonal. ● v. **1** [usu. as noun **kiting**] fly a kite. ➤ fly; move quickly. **2** informal, chiefly N. Amer. write or use (a fraudulent cheque, bill, or receipt).
– PHRASES (**as**) **high as a kite** informal intoxicated with drugs or alcohol.

– ORIGIN OE *cȳta* (in sense 4); prob. of imitative origin.

**kite-flying** ● **n.** **1** the action of trying something out to test public opinion. **2** informal the using of a fraudulent cheque, bill, or receipt.

**Kitemark** ● **n.** trademark (in the UK) an official kite-shaped mark on goods approved by the British Standards Institution.

**kit fox** ● **n.** a small nocturnal fox found in the southwestern US. [*Vulpes macrotis.*]
– ORIGIN C19: prob. from **KIT**[2] (because of its small size).

**kith** /kɪθ/ ● **n.** (in phr. **kith and kin**) one's relations.
– ORIGIN OE *cȳthth* 'knowledge', 'one's native land', and 'friends and neighbours', of Gmc origin; rel. to **COUTH**.

**kitsch** /kɪtʃ/ ● **n.** garish, tasteless, or sentimental art, objects, or design.
– DERIVATIVES **kitschiness** n. **kitschy** adj.
– ORIGIN 1920s: Ger.

**kitten** ● **n.** **1** a young cat. ➤the young of certain other animals, such as the rabbit and beaver. **2** used in names of a group of furry grey and white moths. [Genus *Furcula.*] ● **v.** give birth to kittens.
– PHRASES **have kittens** Brit. informal be extremely nervous or upset.
– ORIGIN ME *kitoun, ketoun*, from an Anglo-Norman Fr. var. of OFr. *chitoun*, dimin. of *chat* 'cat'.

**kitten heel** ● **n.** a type of low stiletto heel.

**kittenish** ● **adj.** playful, lively, or flirtatious.
– DERIVATIVES **kittenishly** adv. **kittenishness** n.

**kittiwake** /ˈkɪtɪweɪk/ ● **n.** a small gull that nests in colonies on sea cliffs and has a loud call that resembles its name. [*Rissa tridactyla.*]

**kittle** /ˈkɪt(ə)l/ (also **kittle-cattle**) ● **adj.** archaic difficult to deal with.
– ORIGIN C16: from *kittle* 'to tickle' (now Scots and dial.), prob. from ON *kitla*.

**kitty**[1] ● **n.** (pl. **-ies**) **1** a fund of money for communal use. **2** a pool of money in some card games. **3** (in bowls) the jack.
– ORIGIN C19 (denoting a jail): of unknown origin.

**kitty**[2] ● **n.** (pl. **-ies**) a pet name for a cat.

**kitty-corner** ● **adj. & adv.** N. Amer. another term for **CATER-CORNERED**.

**kiva** /ˈkiːvə/ ● **n.** a chamber, typically underground, used by male Pueblo Indians for religious rites.
– ORIGIN C19: from Hopi *kíva*.

**Kiwanis Club** /kɪˈwɑːnɪs/ ● **n.** a North American society of business and professional people.
– DERIVATIVES **Kiwanian** n. & adj.
– ORIGIN C20: of unknown origin.

**kiwi** ● **n.** (pl. **kiwis**) **1** a flightless, tailless New Zealand bird with hair-like feathers and a long downcurved bill. [Genus *Apteryx*: three species.] **2** (**Kiwi**) informal a New Zealander.
– ORIGIN C19: from Maori.

**kiwi fruit** ● **n.** (pl. same) the fruit of an East Asian climbing plant (*Actinidia chinensis*), with a thin hairy skin, green flesh, and black seeds.

**kJ** ● **abbrev.** kilojoule(s).

**KKK** ● **abbrev.** Ku Klux Klan.

**KL** ● **abbrev.** informal Kuala Lumpur.

**kl** ● **abbrev.** kilolitre(s).

**Klamath** /ˈklaməθ/ ● **n.** (pl. same or **Klamaths**) **1** a member of an American Indian people of the Oregon–California border. **2** the Penutian language of this people.
– ORIGIN from Chinook.

**Klansman** (or **Klanswoman**) ● **n.** (pl. **-men** or **-women**) a member of the Ku Klux Klan.

**klatch** /klatʃ/ ● **n.** N. Amer. a social gathering.
– ORIGIN C20: from Ger. *Klatsch* 'gossip'.

**klaxon** /ˈklaks(ə)n/ ● **n.** trademark a vehicle horn or warning hooter.
– ORIGIN 1910: name of the manufacturers.

**klebsiella** /ˌklɛbzɪˈɛlə/ ● **n.** a bacterium of a genus causing respiratory, urinary, and wound infections. [Genus *Klebsiella.*]
– ORIGIN mod. L., from the name of the C19 Ger. bacteriologist Theodore *Klebs*.

**Kleenex** ● **n.** (pl. same or **Kleenexes**) trademark a paper tissue.

**Klein bottle** ● **n.** Mathematics a closed surface with only one side, formed by passing one end of a tube through the side of the tube and joining it to the other end.
– ORIGIN 1940s.: named after the Ger. mathematician Felix *Klein*.

**klepht** /klɛft/ ● **n.** **1** a Greek independence fighter, especially one who fought the Turks in the 15th century. **2** a brigand.
– ORIGIN from mod. Gk *klephtēs*, from Gk *kleptēs* 'thief' (because the original klephts were mountain outlaws).

**kleptocrat** ● **n.** a ruler who uses their power to steal their country's resources.
– DERIVATIVES **kleptocracy** n. **kleptocratic** adj.

**kleptomania** /ˌklɛptə(ʊ)ˈmeɪnɪə/ ● **n.** a recurrent urge to steal.
– DERIVATIVES **kleptomaniac** n. & adj.
– ORIGIN C19: from Gk *kleptēs* 'thief' + **-MANIA**.

**kleptoparasite** ● **n.** Zoology a bird, insect, or other animal which habitually robs another species of food.
– DERIVATIVES **kleptoparasitic** adj. **kleptoparasitism** n.

**klezmer** /ˈklɛzmə/ ● **n.** (pl. **klezmorim** /-rɪm/) **1** traditional eastern European Jewish music. **2** a musician who plays this.
– ORIGIN C20: Yiddish, contr. of Heb. *kĕlē zemer* 'musical instruments'.

**klick** ● **n.** informal a kilometre.
– ORIGIN C20 (orig. used in the Vietnam War): of unknown origin.

**klieg light** /kliːg/ ● **n.** a powerful electric lamp used in filming.
– ORIGIN 1920s: named after the Amer. brothers, Anton T. *Kliegl* and John H. *Kliegl*, who invented it.

**Klinefelter's syndrome** /ˈklʌɪnˌfɛltəz/ ● **n.** Medicine a syndrome affecting males in which the cells have an extra X chromosome, characterized by a tall thin physique, small infertile testes, and enlarged breasts.
– ORIGIN C20: named after the Amer. physician Harry F. *Klinefelter*.

**klipspringer** /ˈklɪpˌsprɪŋə/ ● **n.** a small rock-dwelling antelope with a yellowish-grey coat, native to southern Africa. [*Oreotragus oreotragus.*]
– ORIGIN C18: from Afrik., from Du. *klip* 'rock' + *springer* 'jumper'.

**Klondike** /ˈklɒndʌɪk/ ● **n.** a source of valuable material.
– ORIGIN from *Klondike* in Yukon, Canada, where gold was found in 1896.

**klong** /klɒŋ/ ● **n.** (in Thailand) a canal.
– ORIGIN from Thai.

**kloof** /kluːf/ ● **n.** S. African a wooded ravine or valley.
– ORIGIN Afrik., from MDu. *clove* 'cleft'.

**kludge** /klʌdʒ, kluːdʒ/ ● **n.** informal something hastily or badly put together, especially a computer program.
– ORIGIN 1960s: invented word, perh. influenced by **BODGE** and **FUDGE**.

**klutz** /klʌts/ ● **n.** informal, chiefly N. Amer. a clumsy, awkward, or foolish person.
– DERIVATIVES **klutzy** adj.
– ORIGIN 1960s: from Yiddish *klots* 'wooden block'.

**klystron** /ˈklʌɪstrɒn/ ● **n.** an electron tube that generates or amplifies microwaves by velocity modulation.
– ORIGIN 1930s: from Gk *kluzein*, 'wash over' + **-TRON**.

**km** ● **abbrev.** kilometre(s).

**K-meson** ● **n.** another term for **KAON**.
– ORIGIN 1950s: from *K* (for **KAON**) + **MESON**.

**kn.** ● **abbrev.** knot(s).

**knack** ● **n.** an acquired or natural skill at performing a task. ➤a tendency to do something.
– ORIGIN ME: prob. rel. to obs. *knack* 'sharp blow or sound', of imitative origin.

**knacker** Brit. ● **n.** **1** a person who disposes of dead or unwanted animals. **2** (**knackers**) vulgar slang testicles. ● **v.** [often as adj. **knackered**] informal exhaust; wear out.
– ORIGIN C16 (orig. denoting a harness-maker): possibly from obs. *knack* 'trinket'; sense 2 may be from dial.

*knacker* 'castanet'.

**knacker's yard** • n. Brit. a place where old or injured animals are slaughtered.

**knackwurst** /ˈnakwəːst/ (also **knockwurst**) • n. a type of short, fat, highly seasoned German sausage.
– ORIGIN C20: from Ger. *Knackwurst*, from *knacken* 'make a cracking noise' + *Wurst* 'sausage'.

**knag** /nag/ • n. **1** a short dead branch. **2** a knot in wood.
– ORIGIN ME: from Low Ger. *knagge*.

**knap**[1] /nap/ • n. archaic the crest of a hill.
– ORIGIN OE *cnæpp, cnæp*.

**knap**[2] /nap/ • v. (**knapped**, **knapping**) **1** Architecture & Archaeology shape (a stone) by striking it, so as to make a tool or a flat stone for building walls. **2** archaic knock.
– DERIVATIVES **knapper** n.
– ORIGIN ME: imitative.

**knapsack** • n. a soldier's or hiker's bag with shoulder straps, carried on the back.
– ORIGIN C17: from Mid. Low Ger., from Du. *knapzack*, prob. from Ger. *knappen* 'to bite' + *zak* 'sack'.

**knapweed** • n. a tough-stemmed plant with purple thistle-like flower heads. [*Centaurea nigra* and related species.]
– ORIGIN ME (orig. as *knopweed*): from **KNOP** (because of its rounded flower heads) + **WEED**.

**knar** /nɑː/ • n. archaic a knot or protuberance on a tree trunk or root.
– ORIGIN ME *knarre* (denoting a rugged rock or stone).

**knave** • n. **1** archaic a scoundrel. **2** (in cards) a jack.
– DERIVATIVES **knavery** n. (pl. **-ies**). **knavish** adj. **knavishly** adv. **knavishness** n.
– ORIGIN OE *cnafa* 'boy, servant', of W. Gmc origin.

**knawel** /ˈnɔːɪl/ • n. a low-growing inconspicuous plant of the pink family. [Genus *Scleranthus*.]
– ORIGIN C16: from Ger. *Knauel, Knäuel* 'knotgrass'.

**knead** • v. **1** work (dough or clay) with the hands. **2** massage as if kneading.
– DERIVATIVES **kneadable** adj. **kneader** n.
– ORIGIN OE *cnedan*, of Gmc origin.

**knee** • n. **1** the joint between the thigh and the lower leg. ➤a person's lap. **2** an angled piece of wood or metal supporting the beams of a wooden ship. **3** an abrupt obtuse or right-angled bend in a graph. • v. (**knees**, **kneed**, **kneeing**) hit with the knee.
– PHRASES **at one's mother's** (or **father's**) **knee** at an early age. **bend** (or **bow**) **the** (or **one's**) **knee** (**to**) submit. **bring someone** (or **something**) **to their** (or **its**) **knees** reduce someone or something to a state of weakness or submission. **on bended knee(s)** kneeling.
– ORIGIN OE *cnēow, cnēo*, of Gmc origin.

**kneeboard** • n. a short board for surfing or waterskiing in a kneeling position.
– DERIVATIVES **kneeboarder** n. **kneeboarding** n.

**knee breeches** • pl. n. archaic short trousers fastened at or just below the knee.

**kneecap** • n. the convex bone in front of the knee joint; the patella. • v. (**-capped**, **-capping**) shoot in the knee or leg as a punishment.

**knee-deep** • adj. **1** immersed up to the knees. ➤deeply involved in something. **2** so deep as to reach the knees.

**knee-high** • adj. & adv. so high as to reach the knees. • n. a stocking with an elasticated top reaching to the knee.
– PHRASES **knee-high to a grasshopper** informal very small or young.

**kneehole** • n. a space for the knees, especially under a desk.

**knee-jerk** • n. an involuntary reflex kick caused by a blow on the tendon just below the knee. • adj. automatic and unthinking.

**kneel** • v. (past and past part. **knelt** or chiefly N. Amer. also **kneeled**) fall or rest on a knee or the knees.
– ORIGIN OE *cnēowlian*, from *cnēow* (see **KNEE**).

**knee-length** • adj. reaching up or down to the knees.

**kneeler** • n. **1** a person who kneels. **2** a cushion or bench for kneeling on.

**knee-pan** • n. dated a kneecap.

**knees-up** • n. Brit. informal a lively party.

**knee-trembler** • n. informal an act of sexual intercourse between people in a standing position.

**knell** /nɛl/ poetic/literary • n. the sound of a bell, especially when rung solemnly for a death or funeral. ➤something regarded as a warning of disaster. • v. (of a bell) ring solemnly. ➤proclaim by or as if by a knell.
– ORIGIN OE *cnyll* (n.), *cnyllan* (v.), of W. Gmc origin; the spelling is perh. influenced by **BELL**[1].

**knelt** past and past participle of **KNEEL**.

**Knesset** /ˈknɛsɛt/ • n. the parliament of modern Israel.
– ORIGIN Heb., lit. 'gathering'.

**knew** past of **KNOW**.

**knickerbocker** • n. **1** (**knickerbockers**) loose-fitting breeches gathered at the knee or calf. **2** (**Knickerbocker**) informal a New Yorker.
– DERIVATIVES **knickerbockered** adj.
– ORIGIN C19: named after Diedrich *Knickerbocker*, pretended author of W. Irving's *History of New York* (1809); sense 1 is said to be from the knee breeches worn by Du. settlers in Irving's book.

**Knickerbocker Glory** • n. Brit. a dessert consisting of ice cream, fruit, and cream in a tall glass.

**knickers** • pl. n. Brit. **1** a woman's or girl's undergarment, covering the body from the waist or hips to the top of the thighs and having two holes for the legs. **2** N. Amer. knickerbockers.
– PHRASES **get one's knickers in a twist** Brit. informal become upset or angry.
– DERIVATIVES **knickered** adj. **knickerless** adj.
– ORIGIN C19: abbrev. of *knickerbockers* (see **KNICKERBOCKER**).

**knick-knack** (also **nick-nack**) • n. a small worthless object, especially an ornament.
– DERIVATIVES **knick-knackery** n.
– ORIGIN C16 (in the sense 'a petty trick'): reduplication of **KNACK**.

**knick point** /ˈnɪk/ • n. Geology an abrupt change of gradient in the profile of a stream or river.
– ORIGIN C20: partial translation of Ger. *Knickpunkt*, from *Knick* 'bend'.

**knife** • n. (pl. **knives**) **1** a cutting instrument consisting of a blade fixed into a handle. **2** a cutting blade on a machine. • v. **1** stab with a knife. **2** cut like a knife.
– PHRASES **before you can say knife** informal very quickly. **that one could cut with a knife** (of an accent or atmosphere) very obvious. **get** (or **stick**) **the knife into** (or **in**) informal treat in a hostile or aggressive manner. **go** (or **be**) **under the knife** informal have surgery.
– DERIVATIVES **knife-like** adj. **knifer** n.
– ORIGIN OE *cnīf*, from ON *knífr*, of Gmc origin.

**knife block** • n. a block of wood with long hollow grooves into which kitchen knives can be inserted.

**knife-edge** • n. **1** the cutting edge of a knife. **2** a very tense or dangerous situation. **3** [as modifier] (of creases or pleats) very fine. **4** a steel wedge on which a pendulum or other device oscillates or is balanced. **5** an arête.

**knifeman** • n. (pl. **-men**) a man who uses a knife as a weapon.

**knife pleat** • n. a sharp, narrow pleat on a skirt.

**knifepoint** • n. the pointed end of a knife.
– PHRASES **at knifepoint** under threat of injury from a knife.

**knight** • n. **1** (in the Middle Ages) a man raised to honourable military rank after service as a page and squire. ➤(also **knight of the shire**) historical a gentleman representing a shire or county in Parliament. ➤poetic/literary a man devoted to a cause or the service of a woman. **2** (in the UK) a man awarded a non-hereditary title by the sovereign and entitled to use the honorific 'Sir' in front of his name. **3** a chess piece, typically shaped like a horse's head, that moves by jumping to the opposite corner of a rectangle two squares by three. **4** (in ancient Rome) a member of the class of equites. **5** (in ancient Greece) a citizen of the second class in Athens, called *hippeus* in Greek. • v. invest with the title of knight.
– PHRASES **knight in shining armour** (or **knight on a white charger**) an idealized chivalrous man. **knight of**

**the road** informal a man who frequents the roads, e.g. a salesman, tramp, or (formerly) a highwayman.
– DERIVATIVES **knighthood** n. **knightliness** n. **knightly** adj. & (poetic/literary) adv.
– ORIGIN OE *cniht* 'boy, youth, servant', of W. Gmc origin.

**knight bachelor** ● n. (pl. **knights bachelor**) a knight not belonging to any particular order.

**knight commander** ● n. a very high class in some orders of knighthood.

**knight errant** ● n. a medieval knight wandering in search of chivalrous adventures.
– DERIVATIVES **knight-errantry** n.

**knight marshal** ● n. historical an officer of the royal household with judicial functions.

**knight service** ● n. (in the Middle Ages) the tenure of land by a knight on condition of performing military service.

**kniphofia** /nɪˈfəʊfɪə, nʌɪ-, nɪpˈhəʊfɪə/ ● n. a plant of a genus comprising the red-hot pokers. [Genus *Kniphofia*.]
– ORIGIN mod. L.; named after the C18 Ger. botanist Johann H. *Kniphof*.

**knish** /knɪʃ/ ● n. a baked or fried dumpling of flaky dough with a savoury filling.
– ORIGIN Yiddish, from Russ. *knish, knysh*, denoting a bun or dumpling.

**knit** ● v. (**knitting**; past and past part. **knitted** or (especially in sense 2) **knit**) **1** make by interlocking loops of yarn with knitting needles or on a machine. ➤make (a plain stitch) in knitting. **2** unite or cause to unite. ➤(of parts of a broken bone) become joined. **3** tighten (one's eyebrows) in a frown. ● n. (**knits**) knitted garments.
– DERIVATIVES **knitter** n.
– ORIGIN OE *cnyttan*, of W. Gmc origin; rel. to KNOT[1].

**knitbone** ● n. another term for COMFREY.

**knitting** ● n. the craft or action of knitting.

**knitting needle** ● n. a long, thin, pointed rod used as part of a pair for hand knitting.

**knitwear** ● n. knitted garments.

**knives** plural form of KNIFE.

**knob** ● n. **1** a rounded lump or ball, especially at the end or on the surface of something. **2** a ball-shaped handle on a door or drawer. **3** a round button on a machine. **4** a small lump of something. **5** chiefly N. Amer. a prominent round hill. **6** vulgar slang a man's penis. ● v. (**knobbed, knobbing**) Brit. vulgar slang (of a man) have sexual intercourse with.
– PHRASES **with (brass) knobs on** Brit. informal and something more, used especially for returning an insult.
– DERIVATIVES **knobbed** adj. **knobby** adj. **knob-like** adj.
– ORIGIN ME: from Mid. Low Ger. *knobbe* 'knot, knob, bud'.

**knobble** ● n. Brit. a small lump on something.
– DERIVATIVES **knobbly** adj. (**-ier, -iest**).
– ORIGIN ME: dimin. of KNOB.

**knobkerrie** /ˈnɒbˌkɛri/ (also **knobkierie**) ● n. a short stick with a knobbed head, used as a weapon by South African tribesmen.
– ORIGIN C19: from KNOB + *-kerrie* (from Nama *kieri* 'knobkerrie'), suggested by Afrik. *knopkierie*.

**knobstick** ● n. **1** another term for KNOBKERRIE. **2** archaic term for BLACKLEG (in sense 1).

**knock** ● v. **1** strike a surface noisily to attract attention. ➤strike or thump together or against something. ➤(of a motor) make a thumping or rattling noise. **2** collide forcefully with. ➤force to move or fall with a blow or collision. ➤damage by striking. **3** make (a hole, dent, etc.) in something by striking it. ➤bring into a specified condition by blows or rough treatment: *two rooms had been knocked into one.* **4** informal criticize. ● n. **1** a sudden short sound caused by a blow. ➤a continual thumping or rattling made by an engine. **2** a blow or collision. **3** a setback. ➤informal a critical comment. **4** Cricket, informal an innings.
– PHRASES **knock it off** informal stop doing something. **knock someone on the head** euphemistic kill someone. **knock something on the head** Brit. informal put an end to an idea, plan, etc. **knock spots off** Brit. informal easily outdo. **the school of hard knocks** painful or difficult but useful life experiences.
– PHRASAL VERBS **knock about** (or **around**) informal **1** spend time or travel without a specific purpose. **2** happen to be present. **knock something back** informal consume a drink quickly. **knock something down 1** (at an auction) confirm a sale by a knock with a hammer. ➤informal reduce the price of an article. **2** US informal earn a specified sum as a wage. **3** Austral./NZ informal spend a pay cheque freely. **knock off** informal stop work. **knock someone off 1** informal kill someone. **2** Brit. vulgar slang have sexual intercourse with a woman. **knock something off 1** informal produce a piece of work quickly and easily. **2** informal deduct an amount from a total. **3** Brit. informal steal something. ➤N. Amer. informal rob a shop. ➤N. Amer. informal make an illegal copy of something. **knock on 1** informal grow old. **2** (also **knock the ball on**) Rugby illegally drive the ball with the hand or arm towards the opponents' goal line. **knock someone out 1** make someone unconscious. ➤knock down (a boxer) for a count of ten. ➤informal astonish or greatly impress someone. **2** eliminate a competitor from a knockout competition. **knock something out 1** destroy or disable equipment. **2** informal produce work at a steady fast rate. **3** Austral./NZ informal earn a specified sum of money. **knock something over** N. Amer. informal rob a shop. **knock someone sideways** informal astonish someone. **knock something together** assemble something roughly and hastily. **knock up** Brit. informal (in a racket game) practise before play begins. **knock someone up 1** Brit. awaken someone by knocking at their door. **2** informal, chiefly N. Amer. make a woman pregnant. **knock something up 1** Brit. make something hurriedly. **2** Cricket score runs rapidly.
– ORIGIN OE *cnocian*, of imitative origin.

**knockabout** ● adj. **1** denoting rough, slapstick comedy. **2** (of clothes) suitable for rough use. ● n. **1** US & Austral. a tramp. **2** Austral./NZ a farm or station handyman. **3** N. Amer. a small yacht or dinghy.

**knock-back** ● n. informal a refusal or setback.

**knock-down** ● adj. **1** informal (of a price) very low. **2** capable of knocking someone or something down. ➤(of furniture) easily dismantled. ● n. **1** Boxing an act of knocking an opponent down. **2** Austral./NZ informal an introduction.

**knocker** ● n. **1** an object hinged to a door and rapped by visitors to attract attention. **2** informal a person who buys or sells from door to door. **3** informal a person who continually finds fault. **4** (**knockers**) informal a woman's breasts.
– PHRASES **on the knocker** informal **1** Brit. going from door to door. **2** Austral./NZ (of payment) immediately.

**knocker-up** ● n. (pl. **knockers-up**) Brit. historical a person who woke workers by knocking at their doors or windows.

**knock-for-knock agreement** ● n. Brit. an agreement between insurance companies by which each pays its own policyholders regardless of liability.

**knocking shop** ● n. Brit. informal a brothel.

**knock knees** ● pl. n. a condition in which the legs curve inwards at the knee.
– DERIVATIVES **knock-kneed** adj.

**knock-off** ● n. informal a copy or imitation.

**knock-on** ● n. **1** chiefly Brit. a secondary, indirect, or cumulative effect. **2** Rugby an act of knocking on.

**knockout** ● n. **1** an act of knocking someone out. **2** Brit. a tournament in which the loser in each round is eliminated. **3** informal an extremely attractive or impressive person or thing.

**knockout drops** ● pl. n. a liquid drug added to a drink to cause unconsciousness.

**knock-up** ● n. Brit. (in racket sports) a period of practice play before a game.

**knockwurst** /ˈnɒkwəːst/ ● n. variant spelling of KNACKWURST.

**knoll**[1] /nəʊl/ ● n. a small hill or mound.
– ORIGIN OE *cnoll*, of Gmc origin.

**knoll**[2] /nəʊl/ ● v. & n. archaic form of KNELL.
– ORIGIN ME: prob. an imitative alt. of KNELL.

**knop** /nɒp/ ● n. **1** an ornamental knob. **2** an ornamental loop or tuft in yarn.

– ORIGIN ME: from Mid. Low Ger. and MDu. *knoppe*.

**knot**[1] ● n. **1** a fastening made by looping a piece of string, rope, etc. on itself and tightening it. ➤a tangled mass in hair, wool, etc. ➤an ornamental ribbon. **2** a protuberance or node in a stem, branch, or root. ➤a hard mass in wood at the intersection of a trunk with a branch. ➤a hard lump of bodily tissue. **3** a small group of people. **4** a unit of speed equivalent to one nautical mile per hour, used of ships, aircraft, or winds. ➤chiefly historical a length marked by knots on a log line, as a measure of speed. ● v. (**knotted, knotting**) **1** fasten with a knot. ➤make (a carpet) with knots. ➤tangle. **2** cause (a muscle) to become tense and hard. ➤(of the stomach) tighten as a result of tension.
– PHRASES **at a rate of knots** Brit. informal very fast. **get knotted** Brit. informal go away. **tie someone (up) in knots** informal confuse someone completely. **tie the knot** informal get married.
– DERIVATIVES **knotless** adj. **knotter** n.
– ORIGIN OE *cnotta*, of W. Gmc origin.

**knot**[2] ● n. (pl. same or **knots**) a short-billed northern sandpiper. [*Calidris canutus*.]
– ORIGIN ME: of unknown origin.

**knot garden** ● n. an intricately designed formal garden.

**knotgrass** ● n. a common plant of the dock family, with jointed creeping stems and small pink flowers. [*Polygonum aviculare* and related species.]

**knothole** ● n. a hole in a piece of wood where a knot has fallen out.

**knotting** ● n. the action or craft of tying knots in yarn to make carpets or other decorative items. ➤the knots in such an item.

**knotty** ● adj. (**-ier, -iest**) **1** full of knots. **2** extremely difficult or intricate.
– DERIVATIVES **knottily** adv. **knottiness** n.

**knotweed** ● n. knotgrass or a related plant.

**knotwork** ● n. ornamental work consisting of or representing intertwined cords.

**knout** /naʊt/ ● n. (in imperial Russia) a whip used for punishment. ● v. flog with such a whip.
– ORIGIN C17: via Fr. from Russ. *knut*, from ON *knútr*; rel. to KNOT[1].

**know** ● v. (past **knew**; past part. **known**) **1** be aware of through observation, inquiry, or information. ➤have knowledge or information concerning. ➤be absolutely sure of something. **2** be familiar or friendly with. ➤have a good command of (a subject or language). ➤have personal experience of. ➤(usu. **be known as**) regard as having a specified characteristic or title. **3** archaic have sexual intercourse with.
– PHRASES **be in the know** be aware of something known only to a few people. **God** (or **goodness** or **heaven**) **knows** I have no idea. **I know (what)** I have a new idea. **know better than** be wise enough to avoid doing something. **know someone by sight** recognize someone without knowing their name or being well acquainted with them. **know no bounds** have no limits. **know one's own mind** be decisive and certain. **know the ropes** have experience of the appropriate procedures. **know what's what** informal be experienced and competent in a particular area. **not want to know** informal refuse to react or take notice. **what do you know (about that)?** N. Amer. informal used as an expression of surprise. **you know** informal implying something generally known or known by the listener. ➤used as a gap-filler in conversation.
– DERIVATIVES **knowable** adj. **knower** n.
– ORIGIN OE *cnāwan* (earlier *gecnāwan*) 'recognize, identify', of Gmc origin; rel. to CAN[1] and KEN.

**know-all** (also **know-it-all**) ● n. informal a person who behaves as if they know everything.

**knowbot** /ˈnəʊbɒt/ ● n. Computing an Internet search program which operates independently and has reasoning and decision-making capabilities.
– ORIGIN C20: from *knowledgeable robot*.

**know-how** ● n. expertise.

**knowing** ● adj. **1** suggesting that one has secret knowledge. **2** chiefly derogatory experienced or shrewd, especially excessively or prematurely so. ● n. the state of being aware or informed.
– PHRASES **there is no knowing** no one can tell.
– DERIVATIVES **knowingly** adv. **knowingness** n.

**knowledge** ● n. **1** information and skills acquired through experience or education. ➤the sum of what is known. ➤Philosophy true, justified belief, as opposed to opinion. **2** awareness or familiarity gained by experience.
– PHRASES **come to one's knowledge** become known to one. **to (the best of) my knowledge 1** so far as I know. **2** as I know for certain.
– ORIGIN ME (orig. as v. in the sense 'acknowledge, recognize'): from an OE compound based on *cnāwan* (see KNOW).

**knowledgeable** (also **knowledgable**) ● adj. intelligent and well informed.
– DERIVATIVES **knowledgeability** n. **knowledgeably** adv.

**knowledge worker** ● n. a person whose job involves handling or using information.

**known** past participle of KNOW. ● adj. **1** recognized, familiar, or within the scope of knowledge. **2** publicly acknowledged to be. **3** Mathematics (of a quantity or variable) having a value that can be stated.

**know-nothing** ● n. **1** an ignorant person. **2** (**Know-Nothing**) a member of a 19th century US political party which was antagonistic towards immigrants, and whose members denied its existence.
– DERIVATIVES **know-nothingism** n.

**Knt** ● abbrev. Knight.

**knuckle** ● n. **1** a part of a finger at a joint where the bone is near the surface. **2** a projection of the carpal or tarsal joint of a quadruped. ➤a joint of meat consisting of such a projection together with the adjoining parts. ● v. rub or press with the knuckles.
– PHRASES **go the knuckle** Austral. informal fight with fists. **near the knuckle** Brit. informal verging on the indecent or offensive. **rap someone on** (or **over**) **the knuckles** rebuke or criticize someone.
– PHRASAL VERBS **knuckle down 1** apply oneself seriously to a task. **2** (also **knuckle under**) submit.
– DERIVATIVES **knuckly** adj.
– ORIGIN ME *knokel*, from Mid. Low Ger., MDu. *knökel*, dimin. of *knoke* 'bone'; the verb *knuckle (down)* expressed setting the knuckles down to start a game of marbles.

**knuckleball** ● n. Baseball a slow pitch made by releasing the ball from the knuckles of the index and middle finger.
– DERIVATIVES **knuckleballer** n.

**knuckle bone** ● n. **1** a bone forming or corresponding to a knuckle. ➤a knuckle of meat. **2** (**knuckle bones**) animal knuckle bones used in the game of jacks.

**knuckleduster** ● n. a metal guard worn over the knuckles in fighting to increase the effect of blows.

**knucklehead** ● n. informal a stupid person.

**knuckle joint** ● n. a hinged joint in which a projection in one part fits into a recess in the other.

**knuckle sandwich** ● n. informal a punch in the mouth.

**knurl** /nəːl/ ● n. a small projecting knob or ridge.
– DERIVATIVES **knurled** adj.
– ORIGIN C17: appar. a derivative of ME *knur*, var. of *knarre* (see KNAR).

**KO**[1] ● abbrev. kick-off.

**KO**[2] Boxing ● n. a knockout in a boxing match. ● v. (**KO's, KO'd, KO'ing**) knock out in a boxing match.
– ORIGIN 1920s: abbrev.

**koa** /ˈkəʊə/ ● n. a large Hawaiian forest tree yielding dark red wood. [*Acacia koa*.]
– ORIGIN C19: from Hawaiian.

**koala** /kəʊˈɑːlə/ ● n. a bear-like arboreal Australian marsupial that has thick grey fur and feeds on eucalyptus leaves. [*Phascolarctos cinereus*.]
– ORIGIN C19: from Dharuk.

**koan** /ˈkəʊɑːn, ˈkəʊan/ ● n. a paradoxical anecdote or riddle, used in Zen Buddhism to show the inadequacy of logical reasoning and provoke enlightenment.
– ORIGIN Japanese, lit. 'matter for public thought', from

Chin. *gōngàn* 'official business'.

**kob** ● **n.** (pl. same) a southern African antelope with a reddish coat and lyre-shaped horns. [*Kobus kob.*]
– ORIGIN C18: from Wolof *kooba.*

**kobo** /ˈkəʊbəʊ/ ● **n.** (pl. same) a monetary unit of Nigeria, equal to one hundredth of a naira.
– ORIGIN corruption of **COPPER**[1].

**kobold** /ˈkəʊbəld/ ● **n.** (in Germanic mythology) a spirit who haunts houses or lives underground.
– ORIGIN from Ger. *Kobold.*

**Kodiak bear** /ˈkəʊdɪak/ ● **n.** a large brown bear of a race found on Kodiak and other Alaskan islands.

**koel** /ˈkəʊəl/ ● **n.** an all-black or dark Asian and Australasian cuckoo. [*Eudynamys scolopacea.*]
– ORIGIN C19: from Hindi *koël*, from Sanskrit *kokila.*

**kofta** /ˈkɒftə, ˈkəʊftə/ ● **n.** (pl. same or **koftas**) (in Middle Eastern and Indian cookery) a savoury ball of minced meat, paneer, or vegetables.
– ORIGIN from Urdu and Pers. *koftah* 'pounded meat'.

**kohen** /ˈkɒhɛn, kɔɪn/ (also **cohen**) ● **n.** (pl. **kohanim** /-nɪm/or **cohens**) Judaism a member of the priestly caste.
– ORIGIN from Heb., lit. 'priest'.

**kohl** /kəʊl/ ● **n.** a black powder, usually antimony sulphide or lead sulphide, used as eye make-up.
– ORIGIN C18: from Arab. *kuḥl.*

**kohlrabi** /kəʊlˈrɑːbi/ ● **n.** (pl. **kohlrabies**) a cabbage of a variety with an edible turnip-like swollen stem.
– ORIGIN C19: via Ger. from Ital. *cavoli rape*, pl. of *cavola rapa*, from med. L. *caulorapa*, from L. *caulis* (see **COLE**) + *rapum, rapa* 'turnip'.

**koi** /kɔɪ/ ● **n.** (pl. same) a large common carp of a Japanese ornamental variety.
– ORIGIN C18: from Japanese, 'carp'.

**koine** /ˈkɔɪniː/ ● **n. 1** the common language of the Greeks from the close of the classical period to the Byzantine era. **2** a lingua franca.
– ORIGIN C19: from Gk *koinē* (*dialektos*) 'common (language)'.

**koinonia** /kɔɪˈnəʊnɪə/ ● **n.** Theology Christian fellowship.
– ORIGIN C20: from Gk *koinōnia* 'fellowship'.

**kokanee** /ˈkəʊkani/ ● **n.** (pl. same or **kokanees**) a dwarf sockeye salmon which lives in landlocked lakes in western North America.
– ORIGIN C19: from Salish.

**kola** ● **n.** variant spelling of **COLA** (in sense 2).

**kolinsky** /kəˈlɪnski/ ● **n.** (pl. **-ies**) a dark brown bushy-tailed weasel, found from Siberia to Japan. [*Mustela sibirica.*]
– ORIGIN C19: from *Kola*, a port in NW Russia, + the pseudo-Russ. ending *-insky.*

**kolkhoz** /ˈkɒlkɒz, kʌlkˈhɔːz/ ● **n.** (pl. same or **kolkhozes** or **kolkhozy**) a collective farm in the former USSR.
– ORIGIN 1920s: Russ., from *kol(lektivnoe) khoz(yaĭstvo)* 'collective farm'.

**Kol Nidre** /kɒl ˈniːdreɪ/ ● **n.** an Aramaic prayer annulling vows made before God, sung by Jews on the eve of Yom Kippur.
– ORIGIN from Aramaic *kol niḏrē* 'all the vows' (the opening words of the prayer).

**komatiite** /kəˈmatɪʌɪt/ ● **n.** Geology a magnesium-rich extrusive rock, often with a characteristic texture of criss-crossing olivine crystals.
– ORIGIN C20: from *Komati* (a river in southern Africa) + **-ITE**[1].

**komatik** /ˈkɒmətɪk/ ● **n.** a dog sled used by the people of Labrador.
– ORIGIN C19: from Inuit *qamutik.*

**Komodo dragon** ● **n.** a very large monitor lizard native to Komodo and neighbouring Indonesian islands. [*Varanus komodoensis.*]

**Komsomol** /ˈkɒmsəmɒl/ ● **n.** an organization for communist youth in the former Soviet Union.
– ORIGIN Russ., from *Kommunisticheskiĭ Soyuz Molodëzhi* 'Communist League of Youth'.

**Kongo** /ˈkɒŋgəʊ/ ● **n.** (pl. same or **-os**) **1** a member of an indigenous people inhabiting the region of the River Congo in west central Africa. **2** Kikongo, the Bantu language of this people.
– ORIGIN the name in Kikongo.

**Konkani** /ˈkəʊŋkəni/ ● **n.** an Indic language spoken in Goa and parts of Maharashtra in western India.
– ORIGIN from Marathi and Hindi *koṅkaṇī*, from Sanskrit *koṅkaṇa* 'Konkan' (a coastal region of western India).

**kook** ● **n.** N. Amer. informal a mad or eccentric person.
– ORIGIN 1960s: prob. from **CUCKOO.**

**kookaburra** /ˈkʊkəˌbʌrə/ ● **n.** a very large Australasian kingfisher that feeds on reptiles and birds and has a loud cackling call. [*Dacelo novaeguineae.*]
– ORIGIN C19: from Wiradhuri *gugubarra.*

**kooky** ● **adj.** (**-ier**, **-iest**) informal strange or eccentric.
– DERIVATIVES **kookily** adv. **kookiness** n.

**koori** /ˈkʊəri/ ● **n.** (pl. **koories**) Austral. an Aboriginal.
– ORIGIN from Awabakal (an Aborig. lang.), lit. 'man'.

**kop** ● **n.** Brit. a high bank of terracing at a soccer ground.
– ORIGIN Afrik., from Du., 'head'; the term entered Engl. from *Spion Kop* in S. Africa, site of a Boer War battle.

**kopek** /ˈkəʊpɛk, ˈkɒpɛk/ (also **copeck** or **kopeck**) ● **n.** a monetary unit of Russia and some other countries of the former USSR, equal to one hundredth of a rouble.
– ORIGIN from Russ. *kopeĭka*, dimin. of *kop'ë* 'lance' (from the figure on the coin (1535) of Tsar Ivan IV, bearing a lance).

**koppie** /ˈkɒpi/ (also **kopje**) ● **n.** S. African a small hill.
– ORIGIN Afrik., from Du. *kopje*, dimin. of *kop* 'head'.

**kora** /ˈkɔːrə/ ● **n.** a West African musical instrument shaped like a lute and played like a harp.
– ORIGIN C18: a local word.

**Koran** /kɔːˈrɑːn, kə-/ (also **Quran** or **Qur'an** /kʊ-/) ● **n.** the Islamic sacred book, believed to be the word of God as dictated to Muhammad and written down in Arabic.
– DERIVATIVES **Koranic** /-ˈranɪk, -ˈrɑːnɪk/ adj.
– ORIGIN from Arab. *ḳur'ān* 'recitation', from *ḳara'a* 'read, recite'.

**Korean** ● **adj.** of or relating to North or South Korea or its people or language. ● **n. 1** a native or national of North or South Korea, or a person of Korean descent. **2** the language of Korea, distantly related to Japanese.

**korfball** /ˈkɔːfbɔːl/ ● **n.** a game similar to basketball, played by teams each consisting of six men and six women.
– ORIGIN C20: from Du. *korfbal*, from *korf* 'basket' + *bal* 'ball'.

**korma** /ˈkɔːmə/ ● **n.** a mild Indian curry of meat or fish marinaded in yogurt or curds.
– ORIGIN from Urdu *ḳormā*, from Turk. *kavurma.*

**Korsakoff's syndrome** /ˈkɔːsəkɒfs/ ● **n.** Psychiatry a serious mental illness with loss of recent memory, typically the result of chronic alcoholism.
– ORIGIN C20: named after the C19 Russ. psychiatrist Sergei S. *Korsakoff.*

**koruna** /ˈkɒrʊnə, kəˈruːnə/ ● **n.** the basic monetary unit of Bohemia, Moravia, and Slovakia, equal to 100 haleru.
– ORIGIN Czech, lit. 'crown'.

**Koryak** /ˈkɒrjak/ ● **n.** (pl. same or **Koryaks**) **1** a member of an indigenous people of the northern Kamchatka peninsula. **2** the language of this people, related to Chukchi.
– ORIGIN from Russ. *koryaki* (pl.).

**kosher** /ˈkəʊʃə/ ● **adj. 1** satisfying the requirements of Jewish law with regards to the preparation of food. **2** informal genuine and legitimate. ● **v.** prepare (food) according to Jewish law.
– ORIGIN C19: from Heb. *kāšēr* 'proper'.

**Kosovar** /ˈkɒsəvɑː/ ● **n.** a native or inhabitant of Kosovo, a province of Serbia whose population is largely of Albanian descent.
– DERIVATIVES **Kosovan** n. & adj.

**koto** /ˈkəʊtəʊ/ ● **n.** (pl. **-os**) a Japanese zither about six feet long, with thirteen strings.
– ORIGIN C18: Japanese.

**koulibiac** ● **n.** variant spelling of **COULIBIAC.**

**koumiss** /ˈkuːmɪs/ ● **n.** a fermented liquor prepared from mare's milk, used as a drink and medicine by Asian nomads.

– ORIGIN C16: based on Tartar *kumiz.*

**kouprey** /ˈkuːpreɪ/ ● **n.** a very rare grey ox found in the forests of SE Asia. [*Bos sauveli.*]
– ORIGIN 1940s: from Khmer.

**kowhai** /ˈkəʊwʌɪ, ˈkɔːfʌɪ/ ● **n.** a tree native to New Zealand and Chile, with hanging clusters of yellow flowers. [*Sophora tetraptera.*]
– ORIGIN C19: from Maori.

**kowtow** /kaʊˈtaʊ/ ● **v. 1** historical kneel and touch the ground with the forehead in submission as part of Chinese custom. **2** be excessively subservient towards someone. ● **n.** historical an act of kowtowing.
– DERIVATIVES **kowtower** n.
– ORIGIN C19: from Chin. *kētóu*, from *kē* 'knock' + *tóu* 'head'.

**kph** ● **abbrev.** kilometres per hour.

**Kr** ● **symb.** the chemical element krypton.

**kraal** /krɑːl/ S. African ● **n. 1** a traditional African village of huts, typically enclosed by a fence. **2** an animal enclosure. ● **v.** drive (animals) into a kraal.
– ORIGIN Du., from Port. *curral* (see **CORRAL**).

**kraft** /krɑːft/ (also **kraft paper**) ● **n.** a kind of strong, smooth brown wrapping paper.
– ORIGIN C20: from Swed., lit. 'strength'.

**krait** /krʌɪt/ ● **n.** a highly venomous Asian cobra. [Genus *Bungarus*: several species.]
– ORIGIN C19: from Hindi *karait.*

**kraken** /ˈkrɑːk(ə)n/ ● **n.** a mythical sea monster said to appear off the coast of Norway.
– ORIGIN from Norw.

**krantz** /krɑːns/ (also **krans**) ● **n.** S. African a precipitous or overhanging wall of rocks.
– ORIGIN S. Afr. Du., from Du. *krans* 'coronet'.

**Kraut** /kraʊt/ ● **n.** informal, offensive a German.
– ORIGIN First World War: shortening of **SAUERKRAUT**.

**Krebs cycle** /krɛbz/ ● **n.** Biochemistry the sequence of reactions by which living cells generate energy during aerobic respiration.
– ORIGIN 1940s: named after the German-born Brit. biochemist Sir Hans *Krebs.*

**kremlin** /ˈkrɛmlɪn/ ● **n.** a citadel within a Russian town. ➤ (**the Kremlin**) the citadel in Moscow, housing the Russian government.
– ORIGIN C17: via Fr. from Russ. *kreml'* 'citadel'.

**kreplach** /ˈkrɛplɑːx/ ● **pl. n.** (in Jewish cookery) triangular noodles filled with chopped meat or cheese and served with soup.
– ORIGIN from Yiddish *kreplekh*, pl. of *krepel*, from Ger. dial. *Kräppel* 'fritter'.

**kriegspiel** /ˈkriːgspiːl/ ● **n. 1** a war game in which blocks representing armies are moved about on maps. **2** a form of chess with an umpire, in which each player has only limited information about the opponent's moves.
– ORIGIN C19: from Ger., from *Krieg* 'war' + *Spiel* 'game'.

**krill** ● **pl. n.** small shrimp-like planktonic crustaceans which are the principal food of baleen whales. [*Meganyctiphanes norvegica* and other species, order Euphausiacea.]
– ORIGIN C20: from Norw. *kril* 'small fish fry'.

**krimmer** /ˈkrɪmə/ ● **n.** tightly curled grey or black fur made from the wool of Crimean lambs.
– ORIGIN C19: from Ger., from *Krim* 'Crimea'.

**Krio** /ˈkriːəʊ/ ● **n.** an English-based creole language of Sierra Leone.
– ORIGIN prob. an alt. of **CREOLE**.

**kris** /kriːs/ (also archaic **creese**) ● **n.** a Malay or Indonesian dagger with a wavy-edged blade.
– ORIGIN C16: based on Malay *keris.*

**Krishnaism** /ˈkrɪʃnəɪz(ə)m/ ● **n.** Hinduism the worship of Krishna as an incarnation of the supreme deity Vishnu.

**krona** /ˈkrəʊnə/ ● **n. 1** (pl. **kronor** pronunc. same) the basic monetary unit of Sweden, equal to 100 öre. **2** (pl. **kronur** pronunc. same) the basic monetary unit of Iceland, equal to 100 aurar.
– ORIGIN Swed. and Icelandic, lit. 'crown'.

**krone** /ˈkrəʊnə/ ● **n.** (pl. **kroner** pronunc. same) the basic monetary unit of Denmark and Norway, equal to 100 øre.
– ORIGIN Dan. and Norw., lit. 'crown'.

**kroon** /kruːn/ ● **n.** (pl. **kroons** or **krooni**) the basic monetary unit of Estonia, equal to 100 sents.
– ORIGIN Estonian, lit. 'crown'.

**Kru** /kruː/ ● **n.** (pl. same) **1** a member of a seafaring people of the coast of Liberia and Ivory Coast. **2** the Niger-Congo language of this people.
– ORIGIN from a W. Afr. lang.

**krugerrand** /ˈkruːgərand/ (also **Kruger**) ● **n.** a South African gold coin with a portrait of President Kruger on the obverse.
– ORIGIN 1967: from the name of Paul *Kruger*, President of Transvaal 1883–99, + **RAND**[1].

**krummholz** /ˈkrʌmhɒlts/ ● **n.** stunted wind-blown trees growing near the tree line on mountains.
– ORIGIN C20: from Ger., lit. 'crooked wood'.

**krummhorn** /ˈkrʌmhɔːn, ˈkrʊm-/ (also **crumhorn**) ● **n.** a medieval wind instrument with an enclosed double reed and an upward-curving end.
– ORIGIN from Ger., from *krumm* 'crooked' + *Horn* 'horn'.

**krypton** /ˈkrɪptɒn/ ● **n.** the chemical element of atomic number 36, a member of the noble gas group. (Symbol: **Kr**)
– ORIGIN C19: from Gk *krupton*, neut. of *kruptos* 'hidden'.

**KS** ● **abbrev. 1** Kansas (in official postal use). **2** Kaposi's sarcoma. **3** (in the UK) King's Scholar.

**Kshatriya** /ˈkʃatrɪə/ ● **n.** a member of the second-highest Hindu caste, that of the military.
– ORIGIN C18: from Sanskrit *kṣatriya*, from *kṣhatra* 'rule, authority'.

**KStJ** ● **abbrev.** Knight of the Order of St John.

**KT** ● **abbrev. 1** (in the UK) Knight of the Order of the Thistle. **2** Knight Templar.

**Kt** ● **abbrev.** Knight.

**kt** ● **abbrev.** knot(s).

**K/T boundary** ● **n.** Geology the boundary between the Cretaceous and Tertiary periods, about 65 million years ago, marked by the extinction of dinosaurs and many other groups of animals.
– ORIGIN from symbols for *Cretaceous* and *Tertiary.*

**kuccha** /ˈkʌtʃtʃʌ/ ● **pl. n.** short trousers worn as one of the five distinguishing signs of the Sikh Khalsa.
– ORIGIN from Punjabi.

**kudos** /ˈkjuːdɒs/ ● **n.** praise and honour.
– ORIGIN C18: Gk.

**kudu** /ˈkuːduː, ˈkʊdʊ/ ● **n.** (pl. same or **kudus**) a striped African antelope, the male of which has long spirally curved horns. [*Tragelaphus strepsiceros* and *T. imberbis.*]
– ORIGIN C18: from Afrik. *koedoe*, from Xhosa *i-qudu.*

**kudzu** /ˈkʊdzuː/ ● **n.** a quick-growing East Asian climbing plant with reddish-purple flowers. [*Pueraria lobata.*]
– ORIGIN C19: from Japanese *kuzu.*

**Kufic** /ˈkjuːfɪk/ (also **Cufic**) ● **n.** an early angular form of the Arabic alphabet found chiefly in decorative inscriptions. ● **adj.** of or in this type of script.
– ORIGIN C18: from the name *Kufa*, a city south of Baghdad, Iraq (because it was attributed to the city's scholars), + **-IC**.

**kugel** /ˈkuːg(ə)l/ ● **n.** (in Jewish cookery) a kind of savoury pudding of potatoes or other vegetables.
– ORIGIN Yiddish, lit. 'ball'.

**Ku Klux Klan** /ˌkuː klʌks ˈklan/ ● **n.** an extreme white supremacist secret society in the US.
– DERIVATIVES **Ku Kluxer** n.
– ORIGIN perh. from Gk *kuklos* 'circle' and **CLAN**.

**kukri** /ˈkʊkri/ ● **n.** (pl. **kukris**) a curved knife broadening towards the point, used by Gurkhas.
– ORIGIN C19: from Nepalese *khukuri.*

**kulak** /ˈkuːlak/ ● **n.** historical a peasant in Russia wealthy enough to own a farm and hire labour.
– ORIGIN Russ., lit. 'fist, tight-fisted person', from Turkic *kol* 'hand'.

**kulan** /ˈkuːlən/ ● **n.** a wild ass of a race native to the central Asian steppes.
– ORIGIN C18: from Turkic.

**kulcha** /ˈkʊltʃə/ ● **n.** a small, round Indian flatbread, typically stuffed with meat or vegetables.
– ORIGIN from Pers. *kulīca.*

**kulfi** /ˈkʊlfi/ ● **n.** a type of Indian ice cream, typically served in the shape of a cone.
– ORIGIN from Hindi *kulfī.*

**Kulturkampf** /kʊlˈtʊəkampf, German kʊlˈtuːɐkampf/ ● **n.** the late 19th-century conflict between the German government and the Catholic Church, especially regarding education.
– ORIGIN Ger., from *Kultur* 'culture' + *Kampf* 'struggle'.

**kumara** /ˈkuːmərə/ ● **n.** (pl. same) NZ a sweet potato.
– ORIGIN C18: from Maori.

**Kumbh Mela** /kʊm ˈmeɪlɑː/ ● **n.** a Hindu festival, held once every twelve years, at which pilgrims bathe in the Ganges and Jumna Rivers.
– ORIGIN from Sanskrit, lit. 'pitcher festival', from *kumbh* 'pitcher' + *melā* 'assembly'.

**kumkum** /ˈkʊmkʊm/ ● **n.** a red pigment used by Hindu women to make a mark on the forehead.
– ORIGIN C20: from Sanskrit *kuṅkuma* 'saffron'.

**kümmel** /ˈkʊm(ə)l/ ● **n.** a sweet liqueur flavoured with caraway and cumin seeds.
– ORIGIN from Ger., from Old High Ger. *kumil,* var. of *kumîn* 'cumin'.

**kumquat** /ˈkʌmkwɒt/ (also **cumquat**) ● **n. 1** an East Asian citrus-like fruit with an edible sweet rind and acid pulp. **2** the tree which yields this fruit. [Genus *Fortunella.*]
– ORIGIN C17: from Chin. (Cantonese dial.) *kam kwat* 'little orange'.

**Kuna** /ˈkuːnə/ (also **Cuna**) ● **n.** (pl. same or **Kunas**) **1** a member of an American Indian people of the isthmus of Panama. **2** the Chibchan language of this people.
– ORIGIN the name in Kuna.

**kuna** /ˈkuːnə/ ● **n.** (pl. **kune**) the basic monetary unit of Croatia, equal to 100 lipa.
– ORIGIN from Serbo-Croat, lit. 'marten' (the fur of the marten was formerly a medium of exchange).

**kundalini** /ˈkʊndəˌlɪni/ ● **n.** (in yoga) latent female energy believed to lie coiled at the base of the spine.
– ORIGIN Sanskrit, lit. 'snake'.

**Kung** /kʊŋ/ ● **n. 1** (pl. same) a member of a San (Bushman) people of the Kalahari Desert in southern Africa. **2** the Khoisan language of this people.
– ORIGIN Khoikhoi *!Kung,* lit. 'people'.

**kung fu** /kʊŋ ˈfuː, kʌŋ/ ● **n.** a Chinese martial art resembling karate.
– ORIGIN from Chin. *gongfu,* from *gong* 'merit' + *fu* 'master'.

**kunzite** /ˈkʌntsʌɪt, ˈkʌnzʌɪt/ ● **n.** a lilac-coloured gem variety of spodumene.
– ORIGIN C20: from the name of the Amer. gemmologist George F. *Kunz,* + **-ITE**[1].

**Kupffer cell** /ˈkʊpfə/ ● **n.** Anatomy a phagocytic liver cell, involved in the breakdown of red blood cells.
– ORIGIN C20: named after the Bavarian anatomist Karl Wilhelm von *Kupffer.*

**kurbash** /ˈkʊəbaʃ/ ● **n.** a whip used for punishment in Turkey and Egypt.
– ORIGIN C19: from Arab. *kurbāj,* from Turk. *kırbaç* 'whip'.

**Kurd** /kəːd/ ● **n.** a member of a mainly pastoral Islamic people living in Kurdistan.
– ORIGIN the name in Kurdish.

**kurdaitcha** /kəˈdʌɪtʃə/ ● **n.** Austral. the use among Aboriginals of a bone in spells intended to cause sickness or death.
– ORIGIN prob. from Aranda.

**Kurdish** /ˈkəːdɪʃ/ ● **n.** the Iranian language of the Kurds. ● **adj.** of or relating to the Kurds or their language.

**kurgan** /kʊəˈɡɑːn/ ● **n.** Archaeology **1** a prehistoric burial mound of a type found in southern Russia and the Ukraine. **2** (**Kurgan**) a member of the ancient people who built such mounds.
– ORIGIN Russ., of Turkic origin.

**kurrajong** /ˈkʌrədʒɒŋ/ ● **n.** an Australian plant which produces useful tough fibre. [*Brachychiton populneus* and other species.]
– ORIGIN C19: from Dharuk *garrajung* 'fibre fishing line'.

**kursaal** /ˈkʊəsɑːl, -z-/ ● **n.** a building for the entertainment of visitors at a German spa.
– ORIGIN C19: from Ger., from *Kur* 'cure' + *Saal* 'room'.

**kurta** /ˈkəːtə/ ● **n.** a loose collarless shirt worn by people from the Indian subcontinent.
– ORIGIN from Urdu and Pers. *kurtah.*

**kurtosis** /kəːˈtəʊsɪs/ ● **n.** Statistics the sharpness of the peak of a frequency-distribution curve.
– ORIGIN C20: from Gk *kurtōsis* 'a bulging', from *kurtos* 'bulging, convex'.

**kuru** /ˈkʊruː/ ● **n.** Medicine a fatal brain disease occurring in New Guinea, spread by cannibalism and believed to be caused by a prion.
– ORIGIN 1950s: a local word.

**kurus** /kəˈruːʃ/ ● **n.** (pl. same) a monetary unit of Turkey, equal to one hundredth of a lira.
– ORIGIN from Turk. *kuruş.*

**Kushan** /ˈkʊʃɑːn/ ● **n.** (pl. same or **Kushans**) a member of an Iranian dynasty which established a powerful empire in the Indian subcontinent in the 1st–3rd centuries AD.
– ORIGIN from Prakrit *kuṣāṇa* (adj.), from Iranian.

**kusti** /ˈkʊstiː/ ● **n.** (pl. **kustis**) a cord of seventy-two threads worn round the waist by Parsees, representing the chapters of a portion of the Zend-Avesta.
– ORIGIN C19: Pers. and Gujarati.

**Kuwaiti** /kʊˈweɪti/ ● **n.** a native or inhabitant of Kuwait. ● **adj.** of or relating to Kuwait.

**kV** ● **abbrev.** kilovolt(s).

**kvass** /kvɑːs/ ● **n.** a Russian fermented drink made from rye flour or bread with malt.
– ORIGIN from Russ. *kvas.*

**kvell** /kvɛl/ ● **v.** N. Amer. informal feel happy and proud.
– ORIGIN 1960s: from Yiddish *kveln,* from Mid. High Ger., lit. 'well up'.

**kvetch** /kvɛtʃ/ N. Amer. informal ● **n. 1** a person who complains a great deal. **2** a complaint. ● **v.** complain.
– ORIGIN 1960s: from Yiddish *kvetsh* (n.), *kvetshn* (v.), from Mid. High Ger. *quetschen,* lit. 'crush'.

**kW** ● **abbrev.** kilowatt(s).

**Kwa** /kwɑː/ ● **n.** a major branch of the Niger–Congo family of languages, spoken from the Ivory Coast to Nigeria.
– ORIGIN the name in Kwa.

**kwacha** /ˈkwɑːtʃə/ ● **n.** the basic monetary unit of Zambia and Malawi, equal to 100 ngwee in Zambia and 100 tambala in Malawi.
– ORIGIN from a Bantu word meaning 'dawn', used as a Zambian nationalist slogan calling for a new 'dawn' of freedom.

**Kwakiutl** /ˈkwɑːˌkjʊt(ə)l/ ● **n.** (pl. same or **Kwakiutls**) **1** a member of an American Indian people of the NW Pacific coast. **2** the Wakashan language of this people.
– ORIGIN the name in Kwakiutl.

**kwanza** /ˈkwanzə/ ● **n.** (pl. same or **kwanzas**) the basic monetary unit of Angola, equal to 100 lwei.
– ORIGIN perh. from a Kiswahili word meaning 'first'.

**Kwanzaa** /ˈkwanzɑː/ ● **n.** N. Amer. a secular festival observed by many African Americans from 26 December to 1 January as a celebration of their cultural heritage.
– ORIGIN from Kiswahili *matunda ya kwanza,* lit. 'first fruits (of the harvest)', from *kwanza* 'first'.

**kwashiorkor** /ˌkwɒʃɪˈɔːkɔː, ˌkwa-/ ● **n.** malnutrition caused by protein deficiency.
– ORIGIN 1930s: a local word in Ghana.

**kwela** /ˈkweɪlə/ ● **n.** a style of rhythmical popular African music resembling jazz.
– ORIGIN C20: Afrik., perh. from Zulu *khwela* 'mount, climb'.

**kWh** ● **abbrev.** kilowatt-hour(s).

**KWIC** ● **abbrev.** Computing keyword in context.

**KWT** ● **abbrev.** Kuwait (international vehicle registration).

**KY** ● **abbrev.** Kentucky (in official postal use).

**Ky** ● **abbrev.** Kentucky.

**kyanite** /ˈkʌɪənʌɪt/ ● **n.** a blue or green mineral consisting of aluminium silicate, used in heat-resistant ceramics.
– ORIGIN C18: from Gk *kuanos*, *kuaneos* 'dark blue' + **-ITE**[1].

**kyanize** /ˈkʌɪənʌɪz/ (also **-ise**) ● **v.** treat (wood) with a solution of mercuric chloride to prevent decay.
– ORIGIN C19: named after the Ir. inventor John H. *Kyan*.

**kyat** /kiːˈɑːt/ ● **n.** (pl. same or **kyats**) the basic monetary unit of Burma (Myanmar), equal to 100 pyas.
– ORIGIN from Burmese.

**kybosh** ● **n.** variant spelling of **KIBOSH**.

**kyle** /kʌɪl/ ● **n.** Scottish a narrow sea channel.
– ORIGIN C16: from Sc. Gaelic *caol* 'strait', (as adj.) 'narrow'.

**kylie** /ˈkʌɪli/ ● **n.** Austral. a boomerang.
– ORIGIN from Nyungar (and other Aborig. langs) *garli*.

**kylin** /ˈkiːlɪn/ ● **n.** a mythical composite animal figured on Chinese and Japanese ceramics.
– ORIGIN C19: from Chin. *qilin*, from *qi* 'male' + *lin* 'female'.

**kylix** /ˈkʌɪlɪks, ˈkɪl-/ ● **n.** (pl. **kylikes** or **kylixes**) an ancient Greek cup with a shallow bowl and a tall stem.
– ORIGIN from Gk *kulix*.

**kyloe** /ˈkʌɪləʊ/ ● **n.** Scottish an animal of the breed of Highland cattle.
– ORIGIN C19: from Sc. Gaelic *gaidhealach* 'Gaelic, Highland'.

**kymograph** /ˈkʌɪmə(ʊ)grɑːf/ ● **n.** an instrument for recording variations in pressure, e.g. in sound waves or in circulating blood.
– DERIVATIVES **kymographic** adj.
– ORIGIN C19: from Gk *kuma* 'wave' + **-GRAPH**.

**kype** /kʌɪp/ ● **n.** a hook formed on the lower jaw of adult male salmon and trout during the breeding season.
– ORIGIN C20: var. of Scots *kip*, perh. influenced by **PIKE**[1].

**kyphosis** /kʌɪˈfəʊsɪs/ ● **n.** Medicine excessive forward curvature of the spine, causing a hunched back. Compare with **LORDOSIS**.
– DERIVATIVES **kyphotic** adj.
– ORIGIN C19: from Gk *kuphōsis*, from *kuphos* 'bent, hunchbacked'.

**Kyrgyz** /kɪəˈgiːz, ˈkəːgɪz/ (also **Kirghiz**) ● **n.** (pl. same) **1** a member of a people of central Asia, living chiefly in Kyrgyzstan. **2** the Turkic language of this people.
– ORIGIN the name in Kyrgyz.

**Kyrie** /ˈkɪrɪeɪ/ (also **Kyrie eleison** /ɪˈleɪɪzɒn, -sɒn, ɛˈleɪ-/) ● **n.** a short repeated invocation (in Greek or in translation) used in many Christian liturgies.
– ORIGIN from Gk *Kuriē eleēson* 'Lord, have mercy'.

**kyte** /kʌɪt/ ● **n.** Scottish a person's belly or stomach.
– ORIGIN C16: of unknown origin.

**kyu** /kjuː/ ● **n.** a grade of the less advanced level of proficiency in martial arts.
– ORIGIN from Japanese *kyū* 'class'.

# Ll

**L**[1] (also **l**) ● **n.** (pl. **Ls** or **L's**) **1** the twelfth letter of the alphabet. **2** denoting the next after K in a set of items, categories, etc. **3** the Roman numeral for 50.

**L**[2] ● **abbrev. 1** Chemistry laevorotatory. **2** (**L.**) Lake, Loch, or Lough. **3** large (as a clothes size). **4** Brit. learner driver. **5** (**L.**) Linnaeus (as the source of names of animal and plant species). **6** lire. **7** (in tables of sports results) lost. **8** Luxembourg (international vehicle registration).

**l** ● **abbrev. 1** left. **2** (in horse racing) length(s). **3** (**l.**) line. **4** Chemistry liquid. **5** litre(s). **6** (**l.**) archaic pound(s). ● **symb.** (in mathematical formulae) length.

**£** ● **abbrev.** pound(s) (of money).
– ORIGIN the initial letter of L. *libra* 'pound, balance'.

**LA** ● **abbrev. 1** Library Association. **2** Los Angeles. **3** Louisiana (in official postal use).

**La** ● **abbrev.** (**La.**) Louisiana. ● **symb.** the chemical element lanthanum.

**la** ● **n.** Music variant spelling of **LAH**.

**laager** /'lɑːɡə/ S. African ● **n. 1** historical an encampment formed by a circle of wagons. **2** an entrenched position or viewpoint. ● **v.** historical form or enclose with a laager.
– ORIGIN S. Afr. Du., from Du. *leger, lager* 'camp'; cf. **LAGER**, **LAIR**[1], and **LEAGUER**[2].

**Lab** ● **abbrev. 1** Brit. Labour. **2** Labrador.

**lab** ● **n.** informal a laboratory.

**labarum** /'labərəm/ ● **n. 1** a symbolic banner. **2** Constantine the Great's imperial standard, with Christian symbols added to Roman military symbols.
– ORIGIN C17: from late L., of unknown origin.

**labdanum** /'labdənəm/ ● **n.** variant spelling of **LADANUM**.

**labefaction** /ˌlabɪ'fakʃ(ə)n/ ● **n.** archaic deterioration or downfall.
– ORIGIN C17: from L. *labefactio(n-)*, from *labefacere* 'weaken', from *labi* 'to fall' + *facere* 'make'.

**label** ● **n. 1** a small piece of paper, fabric, etc. attached to an object and giving information about it. ➤ a piece of fabric sewn inside a garment and bearing the brand name, size, or care instructions. **2** the name or trademark of a fashion company. ➤ a company that produces recorded music. **3** a classifying name applied to a person or thing, especially inaccurately. ➤ (in a dictionary entry) a word or words used to specify the subject area, register, or geographical origin of the word being defined. ➤ Computing a string of characters used to refer to a particular instruction in a program. **4** Biology & Chemistry a radioactive isotope, fluorescent dye, or enzyme used to make something identifiable. **5** Heraldry a narrow horizontal strip superimposed on a coat of arms by an eldest son during the life of his father. **6** Architecture another term for **DRIPSTONE**. ● **v.** (**labelled**, **labelling**; US **labeled**, **labeling**) **1** attach a label to. **2** assign to a category, especially inaccurately. **3** Biology & Chemistry make (a substance, cell, etc.) identifiable using a label.
– DERIVATIVES **labeller** n.
– ORIGIN ME: from OFr., 'ribbon', prob. of Gmc origin and rel. to **LAP**[1].

**labellum** /lə'bɛləm/ ● **n.** (pl. **labella**) **1** Entomology a lobe at the tip of the proboscis in some insects. **2** Botany a larger central petal at the base of an orchid flower.
– ORIGIN C19: from L., dimin. of *labrum* 'lip'.

**labia** plural form of **LABIUM**.

**labial** /'leɪbɪəl/ ● **adj. 1** chiefly Anatomy & Biology of or relating to the lips or a labium. **2** Phonetics (of a consonant) requiring partial or complete closure of the lips (e.g. *p* or *w*), or (of a vowel) requiring rounded lips (e.g. *oo*).
– DERIVATIVES **labialize** (also **-ise**) v. **labially** adv.
– ORIGIN C16: from med. L. *labialis*, from L. *labium* 'lip'.

**labia majora** /mə'dʒɔːrə/ ● **pl. n.** Anatomy the larger outer folds of the vulva.

**labia minora** /mɪ'nɔːrə/ ● **pl. n.** Anatomy the smaller inner folds of the vulva.

**labiate** /'leɪbɪət/ ● **adj. 1** Botany of or relating to the mint family (Labiatae), plants of which have distinctive two-lobed flowers. **2** Botany & Zoology resembling or possessing a lip or labium.
– ORIGIN C18: from mod. L. *labiatus*, from *labium* 'lip'.

**labile** /'leɪbɪl, -ʌɪl/ ● **adj. 1** technical liable to change; easily altered. **2** Chemistry easily broken down or displaced.
– DERIVATIVES **lability** /lə'bɪlɪti/ n.
– ORIGIN ME (in the sense 'liable to err or sin'): from late L. *labilis*, from *labi* 'to fall'.

**labio-** /'leɪbɪəʊ/ ● **comb. form** of or relating to the lips: *labiodental*.
– ORIGIN from L. *labium* 'lip'.

**labiodental** ● **adj.** Phonetics (of a sound) made with the lips and teeth, e.g. *f* and *v*.

**labiovelar** ● **adj.** Phonetics (of a sound) made with the lips and soft palate, e.g. *w*.

**labium** /'leɪbɪəm/ ● **n.** (pl. **labia** /-bɪə/) **1** Entomology a fused mouthpart forming the floor of the mouth of an insect. **2** Botany the lower lip of the flower of a labiate plant. **3** (**labia**) Anatomy the labia majora or minora.
– ORIGIN C16: from L., 'lip'; rel. to **LABRUM**.

**lablab** /'lablab/ ● **n.** a tropical Asian plant of the pea family, grown for its edible seeds and pods. [*Lablab purpureus*.]
– ORIGIN C19: from Arab. *lablāb*.

**labor** etc. ● **n.** US and Australian spelling of **LABOUR** etc.

**laboratory** /lə'bɒrəˌt(ə)ri, 'lab(ə)rəˌt(ə)ri/ ● **n.** (pl. **-ies**) a room or building for scientific experiments, research, or teaching, or for the manufacture of drugs or chemicals.
– ORIGIN C17: from med. L. *laboratorium*, from L. *laborare* 'to labour'.

**labored** ● **adj.** US spelling of **LABOURED**.

**laborer** ● **n.** US spelling of **LABOURER**.

**laborious** /lə'bɔːrɪəs/ ● **adj.** requiring considerable time and effort. ➤ (especially of speech or writing) showing obvious signs of effort.
– DERIVATIVES **laboriously** adv. **laboriousness** n.
– ORIGIN ME: from OFr. *laborieux*, from L. *laboriosus*, from *labor* 'labour'.

**laborism** ● **n.** US spelling of **LABOURISM**.

**Laborite** ● **n.** US spelling of **LABOURITE**.

**labour** (US & Austral. **labor**) ● **n. 1** work, especially hard physical work. **2** workers, especially manual workers, collectively. **3** (**Labour**) [treated as sing. or pl.] the Labour Party. **4** the process of childbirth from the start of uterine contractions to delivery. ● **v. 1** work hard. ➤ work at an unskilled manual job. ➤ archaic till (the ground). **2** have difficulty despite working hard. ➤ (of an engine) work noisily and with difficulty. ➤ move with difficulty. ➤ (of a ship) roll or pitch heavily. **3** (**labour under**) be misled by (a mistaken belief).
– PHRASES **a labour of love** a task done for pleasure, not reward. **labour the point** explain or discuss something at excessive length.
– ORIGIN ME: from OFr. *labour* (n.), *labourer* (v.), both from L. *labor* 'toil, trouble'.

**labour camp** ● **n.** a prison camp with a regime of hard labour.

**Labour Day** ● n. a public holiday held in honour of working people in some countries on 1 May, or (in the US and Canada) on the first Monday in September.

**laboured** (US **labored**) ● adj. **1** done with great difficulty. **2** not spontaneous or fluent.

**labourer** (US **laborer**) ● n. a person doing unskilled manual work.

**labour exchange** ● n. former term for **JOBCENTRE**.

**labour force** ● n. the members of a population who are able to work.

**labour-intensive** ● adj. needing a large workforce or a large amount of work in relation to output.

**labourism** (US **laborism**) ● n. the principles of a Labour Party or the labour movement.
– DERIVATIVES **labourist** n. & adj.

**Labourite** (US **Laborite**) ● n. a member or supporter of a Labour Party.

**labour-saving** ● adj. (of an appliance) designed to reduce or eliminate work.

**labour theory of value** ● n. the Marxist theory that the value of a commodity should be determined by the amount of human labour used in its production.

**labour union** ● n. chiefly N. Amer. a trade union.

**labra** plural form of **LABRUM**.

**Labrador** /ˈlabrədɔː/ (also **Labrador retriever**) ● n. a retriever of a breed typically having a black or yellow coat, widely used as a gun dog or guide dog.
– ORIGIN C20: named after the *Labrador* Peninsula of eastern Canada, where the breed was developed.

**labradorite** /ˌlabrəˈdɔːrʌɪt/ ● n. a mineral of the plagioclase feldspar group, found in many igneous rocks.

**Labrador tea** ● n. a low-growing northern shrub with fragrant leathery evergreen leaves, sometimes used in Canada to make tea. [Genus *Ledum*.]

**labret** /ˈleɪbrɪt/ ● n. a small piece of shell, bone, etc. inserted into the lip as an ornament in some cultures.
– ORIGIN C19: dimin. of **LABRUM**.

**labrum** /ˈleɪbrəm/ ● n. (pl. **labra** /-brə/) Zoology a structure corresponding to a lip, especially the upper border of the mouthparts of a crustacean or insect.
– DERIVATIVES **labral** adj.
– ORIGIN C18: from L., lit. 'lip'; rel. to **LABIUM**.

**Labrusca** /ləˈbrʊskə/ ● n. a variety of grape obtained from a wild vine (*Vitis labrusca*) native to the eastern US. ➤a wine made from this grape.
– ORIGIN from L. *labrusca*, denoting a wild vine.

**laburnum** /ləˈbəːnəm/ ● n. a small hardwood tree with hanging clusters of yellow flowers followed by pods of poisonous seeds. [Genus *Laburnum*.]
– ORIGIN mod. L., from L.

**labyrinth** /ˈlab(ə)rɪnθ/ ● n. **1** a complicated irregular network of passages or paths. ➤an intricate and confusing arrangement. **2** Anatomy a complex fluid-filled bony structure in the inner ear which contains the organs of hearing and balance.
– DERIVATIVES **labyrinthian** adj.
– ORIGIN ME (referring to the maze constructed by Daedalus in Gk mythology to house the Minotaur): from Fr. *labyrinthe* or L. *labyrinthus*, from Gk *laburinthos*.

**labyrinth fish** ● n. a freshwater fish of a large group including gouramis, with poorly developed gills and a labyrinthine accessory breathing organ. [Suborder Anabantoidei.]

**labyrinthine** /ˌlabəˈrɪnθʌɪn/ ● adj. like a labyrinth, especially in being complicated or twisted.

**labyrinthodont** /ˌlabəˈrɪnθədɒnt/ Zoology & Palaeontology ● adj. (of teeth) having the enamel deeply folded to form a labyrinthine structure. ● n. a fossil amphibian of a large group having such teeth.
– ORIGIN C19: from mod. L. *Labyrinthodontia* (pl. n.), from Gk *laburinthos* 'labyrinth' + *odous, odont-* 'tooth'.

**LAC** ● abbrev. Leading Aircraftman.

**lac**[1] ● n. a resinous substance secreted as a protective covering by the lac insect, used to make varnish, shellac, etc.
– ORIGIN ME: from med. L. *lac, lac(c)a*, from Port. *laca*, based on Hindi *lākh* or Pers. *lāk*.

**lac**[2] ● n. variant spelling of **LAKH**.

**Lacanian** /laˈkeɪnɪən/ ● adj. of or relating to the French psychoanalyst and writer Jacques Lacan (1901–81). ● n. a follower of Lacan.
– DERIVATIVES **Lacanianism** n.

**laccolith** /ˈlakəlɪθ/ ● n. Geology a lens-shaped mass of igneous rock intruded between rock strata, causing doming.
– ORIGIN C19: from Gk *lakkos* 'reservoir' + **-LITH**.

**lace** ● n. **1** a fine open fabric of cotton or silk made by looping, twisting, or knitting thread in patterns, used especially as a trimming. ➤braid used for trimming, especially on military dress uniforms. **2** a cord or leather strip passed through eyelets or hooks to fasten a shoe or garment. ● v. **1** fasten or be fastened with a lace or laces. ➤tighten a laced corset around the waist of. ➤[as adj. **laced**] trimmed or fitted with a lace or laces. **2** entwine. **3** (often **be laced with**) add an ingredient, especially alcohol, to (a drink or dish) to enhance its flavour or strength. **4** (**lace into**) informal assail or tackle.
– ORIGIN ME: from OFr. *laz, las* (n.), *lacier* (v.), based on L. *laqueus* 'noose'; cf. **LASSO**.

**lace bug** ● n. a small plant-eating bug with a patterned upper surface. [Family Tingidae.]

**Lacedaemonian** /ˌlasɪdɪˈməʊnɪən/ ● n. a native or inhabitant of Lacedaemon, an area of ancient Greece comprising the city of Sparta and its surroundings. ● adj. of Lacedaemon or its inhabitants; Spartan.

**lace pillow** ● n. a cushion placed on the lap to provide support in lacemaking.

**lacerate** /ˈlasəreɪt/ ● v. tear or deeply cut (the flesh or skin).
– DERIVATIVES **laceration** n.
– ORIGIN ME: from L. *lacerat-*, *lacerare* 'mangle', from *lacer* 'torn'.

**Lacertilia** /ˌlasəˈtɪlɪə/ ● pl. n. Zoology a suborder of reptiles that comprises the lizards.
– DERIVATIVES **lacertilian** n. & adj.
– ORIGIN mod. L., from L. *lacerta* 'lizard'.

**lacewing** ● n. a slender delicate insect with large clear membranous wings, predatory on aphids. [Chrysopidae (**green lacewings**) and other families.]

**lacewood** ● n. the wood of the plane tree.

**laches** /ˈlatʃɪz, ˈleɪ-/ ● n. Law unreasonable delay in making an assertion or claim, which may result in refusal.
– ORIGIN ME (in the sense 'negligence'): from OFr. *laschesse*, from *lasche* 'lax', based on L. *laxus*.

**lachrymal** /ˈlakrɪm(ə)l/ (also **lacrimal** or **lacrymal**) ● adj. **1** formal or poetic/literary connected with weeping or tears. **2** (**lacrimal**) Physiology & Anatomy concerned with the secretion of tears. ● n. (**lacrimal** or **lacrimal bone**) Anatomy a small bone forming part of the eye socket.
– ORIGIN ME: from med. L. *lachrymalis*, from L. *lacrima* 'tear'.

**lachrymal vase** ● n. historical a phial holding the tears of mourners at a funeral.

**lachrymation** /ˌlakrɪˈmeɪʃ(ə)n/ (also **lacrimation** or **lacrymation**) ● n. poetic/literary or Medicine the flow of tears.
– ORIGIN C16: from L. *lacrimatio(n-)*, from *lacrimare* 'weep'.

**lachrymator** /ˈlakrɪˌmeɪtə/ (also **lacrimator**) ● n. chiefly Medicine a substance that irritates the eyes and causes tears to flow.

**lachrymatory** /ˈlakrɪməˌt(ə)ri/ (also **lacrimatory**) ● adj. technical or poetic/literary relating to, causing, or containing tears. ● n. (pl. **-ies**) a phial of a kind found in ancient Roman tombs and thought to be a lachrymal vase.
– ORIGIN C17: from L. *lacrima* 'tear'.

**lachrymose** /ˈlakrɪməʊs, -z/ ● adj. formal or poetic/literary **1** tearful. **2** inducing tears; sad.
– DERIVATIVES **lachrymosely** adv. **lachrymosity** n.
– ORIGIN C17 (in the sense 'like tears'): from L. *lacrimosus*, from *lacrima* 'tear'.

**lacing** ● n. **1** a laced fastening of a shoe or garment. **2** a dash of spirits added to a drink.

**lacing course** ● n. a strengthening course of bricks built into an arch or wall.

**laciniate** /ləˈsɪnɪət/ (also **laciniated** /-eɪtɪd/) ● adj. Botany

& Zoology divided into deep narrow irregular segments.
– ORIGIN C18: from L. *lacinia* 'fringe or flap of a garment' + **-ATE**[2].

**lac insect** • **n.** an Asian scale insect which lives on croton trees and produces lac. [*Laccifer lacca*.]

**lack** • **n.** absence or deficiency of something. • **v.** (also **lack for**) be without or deficient in.
– ORIGIN ME: corresp. to, and perh. partly from, MDu. and Mid. Low Ger. *lak* 'deficiency', MDu. *laken* 'lack'.

**lackadaisical** /ˌlakəˈdeɪzɪk(ə)l/ • **adj.** lacking enthusiasm and thoroughness.
– DERIVATIVES **lackadaisically** adv.
– ORIGIN C18: from the archaic interjection *lackaday, lackadaisy* (see **ALACK**) + **-ICAL**.

**lackey** • **n.** (pl. **-eys**) **1** a servant, especially a liveried footman or manservant. **2** a servile or obsequious person. **3** a brownish moth whose caterpillars live in groups in a silken shelter. [*Malacosoma neustria*.] • **v.** (**-eys, -eyed**) archaic behave servilely towards.
– ORIGIN C16: from Fr. *laquais*, perh. from Catalan *alacay*, from Arab. *al-ḳā'id* 'the chief'. Sense 3 derives from the resemblance of the coloured stripes of the caterpillars to a footman's livery.

**lacking** • **adj.** absent or deficient.

**lacklustre** (US **lackluster**) • **adj.** **1** lacking in vitality, force, or conviction. **2** not shining; dull.

**Laconian** /ləˈkəʊnɪən/ • **n.** a native or inhabitant of Laconia, a region of Greece. • **adj.** of or relating to Laconia.

**laconic** /ləˈkɒnɪk/ • **adj.** using very few words; terse.
– DERIVATIVES **laconically** adv. **laconicism** n. **laconism** n.
– ORIGIN C16 (in the sense 'Laconian'): via L. from Gk *Lakōnikos*, from *Lakōn* 'Laconia, Sparta', the Spartans being known for their terse speech.

**lacquer** /ˈlakə/ • **n.** **1** a liquid made of shellac dissolved in alcohol, or of synthetic substances, that dries to form a hard protective coating for wood, metal, etc. **2** the sap of the lacquer tree used to varnish wood or other materials. **3** decorative wooden ware coated with lacquer. **4** Brit. a chemical substance sprayed on hair to keep it in place. • **v.** [often as adj. **lacquered**] coat with lacquer.
– DERIVATIVES **lacquerer** n.
– ORIGIN C16: from obs. Fr. *lacre* 'sealing wax', from Port. *laca* (see **LAC**[1]).

**lacquer tree** • **n.** an East Asian tree with a sap used as a hard-wearing varnish. [*Rhus verniciflua*.]

**lacrimal** • **adj.** & **n.** variant spelling of **LACHRYMAL**.

**lacrimation** • **n.** variant spelling of **LACHRYMATION**.

**lacrimator** • **n.** variant spelling of **LACHRYMATOR**.

**lacrimatory** • **adj.** variant spelling of **LACHRYMATORY**.

**lacrosse** /ləˈkrɒs/ • **n.** a team game in which a ball is thrown, carried, and caught with a long-handled stick having a curved L-shaped or triangular frame at one end with a piece of netting in the angle.
– ORIGIN C19: from Fr. (*le jeu de*) *la crosse* '(the game of) the hooked stick'; cf. **CROSSE**.

**lacrymal** • **adj.** & **n.** variant spelling of **LACHRYMAL**.

**lacrymation** • **n.** variant spelling of **LACHRYMATION**.

**lactam** /ˈlaktam/ • **n.** Chemistry an organic compound containing an amide group –NHCO– as part of a ring.
– ORIGIN C19: blend of **LACTONE** and **AMIDE**.

**lactase** /ˈlakteɪz/ • **n.** Biochemistry an enzyme which converts lactose to glucose and galactose.
– ORIGIN C19: from **LACTOSE** + **-ASE**.

**lactate**[1] /lakˈteɪt/ • **v.** (of a female mammal) secrete milk.
– ORIGIN C19: back-form. from **LACTATION**.

**lactate**[2] /ˈlakteɪt/ • **n.** Chemistry a salt or ester of lactic acid.

**lactation** • **n.** **1** the secretion of milk by the mammary glands. **2** the suckling of young.
– DERIVATIVES **lactational** adj.
– ORIGIN C17: from L. *lactatio(n-)*, from *lactare* 'suckle'.

**lacteal** /ˈlaktɪəl/ • **adj.** **1** of milk. **2** Anatomy conveying chyle or other milky fluid. • **n.** (**lacteals**) Anatomy the lymphatic vessels of the small intestine which absorb digested fats.
– ORIGIN C17: from L. *lacteus* (from *lac, lact-* 'milk') + **-AL**.

**lactescent** /lakˈtɛs(ə)nt/ • **adj.** technical milky in appearance.
– DERIVATIVES **lactescence** n.

**lactic** /ˈlaktɪk/ • **adj.** of, relating to, or obtained from milk.
– ORIGIN C18: from L. *lac, lact-* 'milk' + **-IC**.

**lactic acid** • **n.** Biochemistry a syrupy organic acid present in sour milk, and produced in the muscles during strenuous exercise.

**lactiferous** /lakˈtɪf(ə)rəs/ • **adj.** chiefly Anatomy forming or conveying milk or milky fluid.
– ORIGIN C17: from L. *lac, lact-* 'milk' + **-FEROUS**.

**lacto-** • **comb. form** **1** of or relating to milk: *lactometer.* **2** of or relating to lactic acid or lactose: *lactobacillus.*
– ORIGIN from L. *lac, lact-* 'milk'.

**lactobacillus** /ˌlaktəʊbəˈsɪləs/ • **n.** (pl. **lactobacilli** /-lʌɪ/) Biology a rod-shaped bacterium which produces lactic acid from the fermentation of carbohydrates. [Genus *Lactobacillus*.]

**lactometer** /lakˈtɒmɪtə/ • **n.** an instrument for measuring the density of milk.

**lactone** /ˈlaktəʊn/ • **n.** Chemistry an organic compound containing an ester group –OCO– as part of a ring.

**lactoprotein** • **n.** the protein component of milk.

**lactose** /ˈlaktəʊz, -s/ • **n.** Chemistry a compound sugar present in milk, containing glucose and galactose units.

**lacto-vegetarian** • **n.** a person who eats only dairy products and vegetables.

**lacuna** /ləˈkjuːnə/ • **n.** (pl. **lacunae** /-niː/ or **lacunas**) **1** a gap or missing portion. **2** Anatomy a cavity or depression, especially in bone.
– DERIVATIVES **lacunal** adj. **lacunar** adj. **lacunary** adj. **lacunate** adj. **lacunose** adj.
– ORIGIN C17: from L., 'pool'.

**lacustrine** /ləˈkʌstrʌɪn, -trɪn/ • **adj.** technical or poetic/literary of or relating to lakes.
– ORIGIN C19: from L. *lacus* 'lake' (the stem *lacustr-* influenced by L. *palustris* 'marshy') + **-INE**[1].

**LACW** • **abbrev.** Leading Aircraftwoman.

**lacy** • **adj.** (**-ier, -iest**) made of, resembling, or trimmed with lace.
– DERIVATIVES **lacily** adv. **laciness** n.

**lad** • **n.** **1** informal a boy or young man. ➤(**lads**) chiefly Brit. a group of men sharing recreational or working interests. ➤Brit. a boisterously macho or high-spirited man. **2** Brit. a stable worker (regardless of age or sex).
– DERIVATIVES **laddish** adj. **laddishness** n.
– ORIGIN ME: of unknown origin.

**Ladakhi** /ləˈdɑːki/ • **n.** (pl. **Ladakhis**) **1** a native or inhabitant of Ladakh, a region of NW India, Pakistan, and China. **2** the language of Ladakh, a dialect of Tibetan. • **adj.** of or relating to Ladakh, the Ladakhis, or their language.
– ORIGIN the name in Ladakhi.

**ladanum** /ˈlad(ə)nəm/ (also **labdanum**) • **n.** a gum resin obtained from a rock rose, used in perfumery and for fumigation.
– ORIGIN C16: via L. from Gk *ladanon, lēdanon*, from *lēdon* 'mastic'.

**ladder** • **n.** **1** a structure consisting of a series of bars or steps between two upright lengths of wood, metal, or rope, used for climbing up or down. **2** a hierarchical structure, especially as providing a means of advancement. **3** Brit. a vertical strip of unravelled fabric in tights or stockings. • **v.** Brit. (with reference to tights or stockings) develop or cause to develop a ladder.
– ORIGIN OE *hlǣd(d)er*, of W. Gmc origin.

**ladder-back** • **n.** an upright chair with a back resembling a ladder.

**ladder stitch** • **n.** a stitch in embroidery consisting of transverse bars.

**laddie** • **n.** informal, chiefly Scottish a boy or young man.

**laddu** /ˈlʌduː/ (also **laddoo** or **ladoo**) • **n.** (pl. **laddus**) an Indian sweet made from flour, sugar, and shortening,

which is fried and then shaped into a ball.
– ORIGIN from Hindi *laḍḍū*.

**lade** /leɪd/ ● v. (past part. **laden**) archaic put cargo on board (a ship). ➤ship (goods) as cargo.
– DERIVATIVES **lading** n.
– ORIGIN OE *hladan*, of W. Gmc origin; rel. to **LADLE**.

**laden** ● adj. heavily loaded or weighed down.
– ORIGIN C16: past part. of **LADE**.

**ladette** ● n. Brit. informal a young woman who behaves in a boisterously assertive or crude manner and engages in heavy drinking sessions.

**la-di-da** (also **lah-di-dah**) ● adj. informal pretentious or snobbish.
– ORIGIN C19: imitative of an affected manner of speech.

**ladies** plural form of **LADY**.

**ladies' chain** ● n. a figure in a quadrille or other dance.

**ladies' fingers** ● pl. n. Brit. another term for **OKRA**.

**ladies' man** (also **lady's man**) ● n. informal a man who enjoys spending time and flirting with women.

**ladies' night** ● n. a function at a men's institution or club to which women are invited.

**ladies' room** ● n. chiefly N. Amer. a toilet for women in a public or institutional building.

**Ladin** /ləˈdiːn/ ● n. the Rhaeto-Romance dialect of the Engadine in Switzerland.
– ORIGIN C19: from L. *Latinus* (see **LATIN**).

**Ladino** /ləˈdiːnəʊ/ ● n. (pl. **-os**) **1** the language of some Sephardic Jews, especially formerly in Mediterranean countries, based on medieval Spanish with some Hebrew, Greek, and Turkish words. **2** a mestizo or Spanish-speaking white person in Central America.
– ORIGIN Sp., from L. *Latinus* (see **LATIN**).

**ladino** /ləˈdiːnəʊ/ ● n. (pl. **-os**) a white clover of a large variety native to Italy and cultivated for fodder in North America.
– ORIGIN 1920s: from Ital.

**ladle** ● n. **1** a large long-handled spoon with a cup-shaped bowl, used for serving soup or sauce. **2** a container for transporting molten metal in a foundry. ● v. **1** serve or transfer with a ladle. **2** (**ladle something out**) distribute something in large amounts.
– DERIVATIVES **ladleful** n. (pl. **-fuls**). **ladler** n.
– ORIGIN OE *hlædel*, from *hladan* (see **LADE**).

**ladoo** ● n. variant spelling of **LADDU**.

**lad's love** ● n. another term for **SOUTHERNWOOD**.

**lady** ● n. (pl. **-ies**) **1** (in polite or formal use) a woman. **2** a woman of superior social position. ➤(**Lady**) a title used by peeresses, female relatives of peers, the wives and widows of knights, etc. ➤a courteous or genteel woman. **3** (**one's lady**) dated a man's wife. ➤historical a woman to whom a knight is chivalrously devoted. **4** (**the Ladies**) Brit. a women's public toilet.
– PHRASES **find the lady** another term for **THREE-CARD TRICK**. **it isn't over till the fat lady sings** there is still time for a situation to change. [by assoc. with the final aria in tragic opera.] **My Lady** a polite form of address to female judges and certain noblewomen.
– DERIVATIVES **ladyhood** n.
– ORIGIN OE *hlǣfdīge*, from *hlāf* 'loaf' + a Gmc base meaning 'knead', rel. to **DOUGH**; cf. **LORD**.

**ladybird** ● n. a small beetle with a domed back, typically red or yellow with black spots. [Family Coccinellidae: many species.]

**ladybug** ● n. North American term for **LADYBIRD**.

**Lady chapel** ● n. a chapel dedicated to the Virgin Mary in a church or cathedral.

**Lady Day** ● n. the feast of the Annunciation, 25 March.

**lady fern** ● n. a tall, graceful fern of moist, shady habitats. [*Athyrium filix-femina* and other species.]

**ladyfinger** ● n. North American term for **LADY'S FINGER** (in sense 2).

**ladyfy** ● v. (**-ies**, **-ied**) **1** [as adj. **ladyfied**] having the manner of a socially superior woman. **2** archaic give (a woman) the title of Lady.

**lady-in-waiting** ● n. (pl. **ladies-in-waiting**) a woman who attends a queen or princess.

**ladykiller** ● n. informal a charming man who habitually seduces women.

**ladylike** ● adj. appropriate for or typical of a well-mannered, decorous woman or girl.
– DERIVATIVES **ladylikeness** n.

**Lady Mayoress** ● n. the title of the wife of a Lord Mayor.

**lady of the bedchamber** ● n. (in the UK) a female attendant to the queen or queen mother, ranking in the royal household above woman of the bedchamber.

**lady of the night** ● n. euphemistic a prostitute.

**lady's bedstraw** ● n. a yellow-flowered bedstraw which smells of hay when dried and was formerly used to make mattresses. [*Galium verum*.]

**lady's companion** ● n. Brit. a small case or bag containing needlework items.

**lady's finger** ● n. Brit. **1** another term for **KIDNEY VETCH**. **2** a finger-shaped sponge cake with a sugar topping.

**ladyship** ● n. (**Her/Your Ladyship**) a respectful form of reference or address to a Lady.

**lady's maid** ● n. chiefly historical a maid who attended to the personal needs of her mistress.

**lady's man** ● n. variant spelling of **LADIES' MAN**.

**lady's mantle** ● n. a plant with inconspicuous greenish flowers, formerly valued in herbal medicine. [*Alchemilla vulgaris*.]

**lady's slipper** ● n. an orchid whose flower has a pouch- or slipper-shaped lip. [Genus *Cypripedium*.]

**lady's smock** ● n. another term for **CUCKOOFLOWER**.

**lady's tresses** ● pl. n. [usu. treated as sing.] a short orchid with small white flowers. [Genus *Spiranthes*.]

**Lady Superior** ● n. the head of a convent or nunnery in certain orders.

**laevo-** /ˈliːvəʊ/ (also **levo-**) ● comb. form on or to the left: *laevorotatory*.
– ORIGIN from L. *laevus* 'left'.

**laevorotatory** /ˌliːvəʊˈrəʊtət(ə)ri/ (US **levorotatory**) ● adj. Chemistry (of a compound) having the property of rotating the plane of a polarized light ray to the left, i.e. anticlockwise facing the oncoming radiation. The opposite of **DEXTROROTATORY**.
– DERIVATIVES **laevorotation** n.

**laevulose** /ˈliːvjʊləʊz, -s/ (US **levulose**) ● n. Chemistry another term for **FRUCTOSE**.

**Laffer curve** /ˈlafə/ ● n. Economics a supposed relationship between economic activity and the rate of taxation which suggests that there is an optimum tax rate which maximizes revenue.
– ORIGIN 1970s: named after the Amer. economist Arthur Laffer.

**lag**[1] ● v. (**lagged**, **lagging**) **1** fall behind; follow after a delay. **2** N. Amer. another term for **STRING** (in sense 6). ● n. (also **time lag**) a period of time between two events; a delay.
– DERIVATIVES **lagger** n.
– ORIGIN C16 (as n. in the sense 'hindmost person'): rel. to the dial. adj. *lag* (perh. from a fanciful distortion of **LAST**[1], or of Scand. origin).

**lag**[2] ● v. (**lagged**, **lagging**) enclose or cover (a boiler, pipes, etc.) with insulating material.
– DERIVATIVES **lagger** n.
– ORIGIN C19: from earlier *lag* 'piece of insulating cover'.

**lag**[3] ● n. Brit. informal a habitual convict.
– ORIGIN C16: of unknown origin.

**lagan** /ˈlag(ə)n/ ● n. archaic (in legal contexts) goods or wreckage lying on the bed of the sea.
– ORIGIN C16: from OFr.

**lager** ● n. an effervescent beer, light in colour and body.
– ORIGIN C19: from Ger. *Lagerbier* 'beer brewed for keeping', from *Lager* 'storehouse'; cf. **LAAGER** and **LAIR**[1].

**lager lout** ● n. Brit. informal a young man who behaves offensively as a result of excessive drinking.

**laggard** /ˈlagəd/ ● n. a person who falls behind others. ● adj. slower than desired or expected.
– DERIVATIVES **laggardly** adj. & adv. **laggardness** n.
– ORIGIN C18 (as adj.): from **LAG**[1].

**lagging** ● n. material providing heat insulation for a

boiler, pipes, etc.
– ORIGIN C19: from **LAG²**.

**lagniappe** /la'njap/ ● **n.** N. Amer. something given as a bonus or gratuity.
– ORIGIN Louisiana Fr., from Sp. *la ñapa*.

**Lagomorpha** /'lagə,mɔːfə/ ● **pl. n.** Zoology an order of mammals that comprises the hares, rabbits, and pikas, distinguished by the possession of double incisor teeth.
– DERIVATIVES **lagomorph** n. & adj.
– ORIGIN mod. L., from Gk *lagōs* 'hare' + *morphē* 'form'.

**lagoon** ● **n. 1** a stretch of salt water separated from the sea by a low sandbank or coral reef. **2** N. Amer. & Austral./NZ a small freshwater lake near a larger lake or river. **3** an artificial pool for the treatment of effluent or to accommodate an overspill from surface drains.
– DERIVATIVES **lagoonal** adj.
– ORIGIN C17: from Ital. and Sp. *laguna*, from L. *lacuna* (see **LACUNA**).

**Lagrangian point** /lə'grɒ̃ʒɪən/ ● **n.** Astronomy each of five points in the plane of orbit of one body around another at which a small third body can remain stationary with respect to the others.
– ORIGIN C19: named after the Italian-born Fr. mathematician Joseph Louis *Lagrange*.

**lah** (also **la**) ● **n.** Music (in tonic sol-fa) the sixth note of a major scale. ➤ the note A in the fixed-doh system.
– ORIGIN ME: representing (as an arbitrary name for the note) the first syllable of L. *labii*, taken from a Latin hymn.

**lahar** /'lɑːhɑː/ ● **n.** Geology a destructive flow of mud on the slopes of a volcano.
– ORIGIN 1920s: from Javanese.

**lah-di-dah** ● **n.** variant spelling of **LA-DI-DA**.

**Lahnda** /'lɑːndə/ ● **n.** an Indic language of the western Punjab and adjacent areas of Pakistan.
– ORIGIN C20: from Punjabi *lahandā*, lit. 'western'.

**Lahu** /lɑː'huː/ ● **n.** (pl. same or **Lahus**) **1** a member of an indigenous people of SW China and Laos. **2** the Tibeto-Burman language of this people.
– ORIGIN the name in Lahu.

**laic** /'leɪɪk/ ● **adj.** formal of the laity; secular.
– DERIVATIVES **laical** adj. **laically** adv. **laicity** n.
– ORIGIN C16: from late L. *laicus* (see **LAY²**).

**laicize** /'leɪɪsʌɪz/ (also **-ise**) ● **v.** formal withdraw clerical character, control, or status from.
– DERIVATIVES **laicism** n. **laicization** n.

**laid** past and past participle of **LAY¹**.

**laid-back** ● **adj.** informal relaxed and easy-going.

**laid paper** ● **n.** paper that has a finely ribbed appearance. Compare with **WOVE PAPER**.

**lain** past participle of **LIE¹**.

**lair¹** ● **n. 1** a wild animal's resting place. **2** a person's hiding place or den.
– ORIGIN OE *leger* 'resting place, bed', of Gmc origin; rel. to **LIE¹**; cf. **LAAGER** and **LAGER**.

**lair²** Austral./NZ informal ● **n.** a flashily dressed man who enjoys showing off. ● **v.** dress or behave in a flashy manner.
– DERIVATIVES **lairy** adj.
– ORIGIN 1930s: back-form. from *lairy* (earlier as Cockney sl. in the sense 'knowing, conceited'), alt. of **LEERY**.

**lairage** /'lɛːrɪdʒ/ ● **n.** a place where cattle or sheep may be rested on the way to market or slaughter.

**laird** /lɛːd/ ● **n.** (in Scotland) a person who owns a large estate.
– DERIVATIVES **lairdship** n.
– ORIGIN ME: Scots form of **LORD**.

**laissez-aller** /,lɛseɪ'aleɪ, French leseale/ ● **n.** absence of restraint.
– ORIGIN Fr., lit. 'allow to go'.

**laissez-faire** /,lɛseɪ'fɛː, French lɛsefɛʀ/ ● **n.** a policy of non-interference, especially abstention by governments from interfering in the workings of the free market.
– DERIVATIVES **laisser-faireism** n.
– ORIGIN Fr., lit. 'allow to do'.

**laissez-passer** /,lɛseɪ'pɑːseɪ, French lɛsepase/ ● **n.** a permit allowing the holder to go somewhere.
– ORIGIN Fr., lit. 'allow to pass'.

**laissez vibrer** /,lɛse 'viːbreɪ, French lɛse vibʀe/ ● **v.** a musical instruction used to indicate that a note made by striking or plucking should be allowed to fade away without damping.
– ORIGIN Fr., lit. 'allow to vibrate'.

**laity** /'leɪɪti/ ● **n.** (**the laity**) [usu. treated as pl.] lay people.
– ORIGIN ME: from **LAY²** + **-ITY**.

**lake¹** ● **n.** a large area of water surrounded by land. ➤ (**the Lakes**) another name for the **LAKE DISTRICT**.
– DERIVATIVES **lakelet** n.
– ORIGIN OE, from OFr. *lac*, from L. *lacus* 'pool, lake'.

**lake²** ● **n. 1** an insoluble pigment made by combining a soluble organic dye and an insoluble mordant. **2** a purplish-red pigment of this kind, originally one made with lac.
– ORIGIN C17: var. of **LAC¹**.

**Lake District** ● **n.** a region of lakes and mountains in Cumbria.

**lake dwelling** ● **n.** a prehistoric hut built on piles driven into the bed or shore of a lake.
– DERIVATIVES **lake-dweller** n.

**Lakeland terrier** ● **n.** a terrier of a small stocky breed originating in the Lake District.

**laker** ● **n.** N. Amer. informal **1** a lake trout. **2** a ship constructed for sailing on the Great Lakes.

**lake trout** ● **n.** a large charr living in the Great Lakes of North America. [*Salvelinus namaycush*.]

**lakh** /lak, lɑːk/ (also **lac**) ● **n.** Indian a hundred thousand.
– ORIGIN via Hindi from Sanskrit *lakṣa*.

**Lakota** /lə'kəʊtə/ ● **n.** (pl. same or **Lakotas**) **1** a member of an American Indian people of western South Dakota. **2** the Siouan language of this people.
– ORIGIN the name in Lakota, rel. to the word **DAKOTA**.

**laksa** /'lɑːksə/ ● **n.** a Malaysian dish of Chinese origin, consisting of rice noodles served in a curry sauce or hot soup.
– ORIGIN from Malay.

**la-la land** ● **n.** N. Amer. informal **1** Los Angeles or Hollywood, especially with regard to the film and television industry. **2** a dreamworld.
– ORIGIN *la-la*, reduplication of LA (i.e. Los Angeles).

**lalapalooza** ● **n.** variant spelling of **LOLLAPALOOZA**.

**laldy** /'laldi/ ● **n.** Scottish informal a beating.
– PHRASES **give it laldy** do something vigorously or enthusiastically.
– ORIGIN C19: perh. imitative, or from OE *læl* 'whip, weal'.

**Lallans** /'lalənz/ ● **n.** a distinctive Scottish literary form of English, based on standard older Scots.
– ORIGIN C18: Scots var. of *Lowlands*, with ref. to a central Lowlands dial.

**lallation** /la'leɪʃ(ə)n/ ● **n.** imperfect speech, especially the pronunciation of *r* as *l*.
– ORIGIN C17: from L. *lallatio(n-)*, from *lallare* 'sing a lullaby'.

**lallygag** /'lalɪgag/ ● **v.** variant spelling of **LOLLYGAG**.

**Lam.** ● **abbrev.** Lamentations (in biblical references).

**lam¹** ● **v.** (**lammed**, **lamming**) (often **lam into**) informal hit hard or repeatedly.
– ORIGIN C16: perh. of Scand. origin.

**lam²** N. Amer. informal ● **n.** (in phr. **on the lam**) in flight, especially from the police. ● **v.** (**lammed**, **lamming**) flee.
– ORIGIN C19: from **LAM¹**.

**lama** /'lɑːmə/ ● **n. 1** an honorific title applied to a spiritual leader in Tibetan Buddhism. **2** a Tibetan or Mongolian Buddhist monk.
– DERIVATIVES **Lamaism** n. **Lamaist** n. & adj.
– ORIGIN C17: from Tibetan *bla-ma* (with silent *b*), lit. 'superior one'.

**Lamarckism** /la'mɑːkɪz(ə)m/ ● **n.** the theory of evolution based on the supposed inheritance of acquired characteristics, devised by the French naturalist Jean Baptiste de Lamarck (1744–1829).
– DERIVATIVES **Lamarckian** n. & adj.

**lamasery** /ˈlɑːməs(ə)ri, ləˈmɑːs(ə)ri/ ● n. (pl. **-ies**) a monastery of lamas.

**lamb** ● n. **1** a young sheep. **2** a mild-mannered, gentle, or innocent person. ● v. (of a ewe) give birth to lambs. ➤ tend (ewes) at lambing time.
– PHRASES **in lamb** (of a ewe) pregnant.
– DERIVATIVES **lamber** n. **lambing** n. **lambkin** n. **lamblike** adj.
– ORIGIN OE, of Gmc origin.

**lambada** /lamˈbɑːdə/ ● n. a fast erotic Brazilian dance which couples perform in close physical contact.
– ORIGIN 1980s: Port., lit. 'a beating'.

**lambaste** /lamˈbeɪst/ (also **lambast** /-ˈbast/) ● v. criticize harshly.
– DERIVATIVES **lambasting** n.
– ORIGIN C17 (in the sense 'beat'): from LAM¹ + BASTE³.

**lambda** /ˈlamdə/ ● n. **1** the eleventh letter of the Greek alphabet (Λ, λ), transliterated as 'l'. **2** Anatomy the point at the back of the skull where the parietal bones and the occipital bone meet. ● symb. (λ) **1** wavelength. **2** Astronomy celestial longitude.
– ORIGIN from Gk.

**lambent** /ˈlamb(ə)nt/ ● adj. poetic/literary glowing or flickering with a soft radiance.
– DERIVATIVES **lambency** n. **lambently** adv.
– ORIGIN C17: from L. *lambent-*, *lambere* 'to lick'.

**lambert** /ˈlambət/ ● n. a former unit of luminance, equal to the emission or reflection of one lumen per square centimetre.
– ORIGIN C20: named after the C18 Ger. physicist Johann H. *Lambert*.

**Lamb of God** ● n. a title of Jesus Christ (see John 1:29).

**lambrequin** /ˈlambrɪkɪn/ ● n. **1** N. Amer. a short piece of drapery hung over the top of a door or window or draped from a mantelpiece. **2** a cloth covering the back of a medieval knight's helmet, represented in heraldry as the mantling.
– ORIGIN C18: from Fr., from Du. dimin. of *lamper* 'veil'.

**Lambrusco** /lamˈbrʊskəʊ/ ● n. a variety of wine grape grown in the Emilia-Romagna region of North Italy. ➤ a sparkling red or white wine made from this grape.
– ORIGIN Ital., lit. 'grape of the wild vine'.

**lamb's ears** ● pl. n. [usu. treated as sing.] a SW Asian ornamental plant of the mint family, with grey-green woolly leaves. [*Stachys byzantina*.]

**lamb's fry** ● n. Brit. lamb's testicles or other offal as food.

**lamb's lettuce** ● n. a small blue-flowered herbaceous plant, used in salad. [*Valerianella locusta*.]

**lamb's quarter** (also **lamb's quarters**) ● n. North American term for FAT HEN.

**lamb's-tails** ● pl. n. Brit. catkins from the hazel tree.

**lamb's tongue** ● n. another term for LAMB'S EARS.

**lambswool** ● n. soft, fine wool from lambs, used to make knitted garments.

**lame** ● adj. **1** disabled in the leg or foot. **2** (of an explanation or excuse) unconvincingly feeble. ● v. make lame.
– DERIVATIVES **lamely** adv. **lameness** n.
– ORIGIN OE *lama*, of Gmc origin.

**lamé** /ˈlɑːmeɪ/ ● n. fabric with interwoven gold or silver threads.
– ORIGIN 1920s: Fr., from L. *lamina* (see LAMINA).

**lamebrain** ● n. informal a stupid person.
– DERIVATIVES **lamebrained** adj.

**lame duck** ● n. **1** an ineffectual or unsuccessful person or thing. **2** N. Amer. a President or administration in the final period of office, after the election of a successor.

**lamella** /ləˈmɛlə/ ● n. (pl. **lamellae** /-liː/) **1** a thin layer, membrane, or plate of tissue, especially in bone. **2** Botany a membranous fold in a chloroplast.
– DERIVATIVES **lamellar** adj. **lamellate** adj. **lamelliform** adj. **lamellose** adj.
– ORIGIN C17: from L., dimin. of *lamina* 'thin plate'.

**lamellibranch** /ləˈmɛlɪbraŋk/ ● n. another term for BIVALVE.
– ORIGIN C19: from mod. L. *Lamellibranchia* (former class name), from L. LAMELLA + Gk *brankhia* 'gills'.

**lament** ● n. **1** a passionate expression of grief. **2** a song, piece of music, or poem expressing grief or regret. ● v. **1** mourn (a person's death). ➤ [as adj. **lamented**] (usu. **late lamented**) a conventional way of referring to a dead person. **2** express regret or disappointment about.
– DERIVATIVES **lamentation** n. **lamenter** n.
– ORIGIN ME (as v.): from Fr. *lamenter* or L. *lamentari*, from *lamenta* (pl.) 'weeping'.

**lamentable** /ˈlaməntəb(ə)l/ ● adj. **1** deplorable or regrettable. **2** archaic sorrowful.
– DERIVATIVES **lamentably** adv.

**lamia** /ˈleɪmɪə/ ● n. (pl. **lamias** or **lamiae** /-ɪiː/) a mythical monster with the body of a woman, supposed to prey on human beings and suck the blood of children.
– ORIGIN via L. from Gk, denoting a carnivorous fish or mythical monster.

**lamina** /ˈlamɪnə/ ● n. (pl. **laminae** /-niː/) technical a thin layer, plate, or scale of sedimentary rock, organic tissue, or other material.
– DERIVATIVES **laminose** adj.
– ORIGIN C17: from L.

**laminar** /ˈlamɪnə/ ● adj. **1** consisting of laminae. **2** Physics denoting flow that takes place along constant streamlines, without turbulence.

**laminate** ● v. /ˈlamɪneɪt/ [often as adj. **laminated**] **1** overlay (a flat surface) with a layer of protective material. **2** manufacture by placing layer on layer. **3** split into layers or leaves. **4** beat or roll (metal) into thin plates. ● n. /ˈlamɪnət/ a laminated structure or material. ● adj. in the form of a lamina or laminae.
– DERIVATIVES **laminable** adj. **lamination** n. **laminator** n.
– ORIGIN C17: from LAMINA + -ATE².

**laminectomy** /ˌlamɪˈnɛktəmi/ ● n. (pl. **-ies**) a surgical operation to remove the back of one or more vertebrae.

**lamington** /ˈlamɪŋtən/ ● n. Austral./NZ a square of sponge cake dipped in melted chocolate and grated coconut.
– ORIGIN appar. from the name of Lord *Lamington*, Governor of Queensland (1895–1901).

**laminitis** /ˌlamɪˈnʌɪtɪs/ ● n. inflammation of layers of tissue inside the hoof in horses and other animals.

**Lammas** /ˈlaməs/ (also **Lammas Day**) ● n. the first day of August, formerly observed as harvest festival.
– ORIGIN OE *hlāfmæsse* (see LOAF¹, MASS), later interpreted as if from LAMB + MASS.

**lammergeier** /ˈlaməˌɡʌɪə/ (also **lammergeyer**) ● n. a long-winged, long-tailed Old World vulture, noted for dropping bones to break them and get at the marrow. [*Gypaetus barbatus*.]
– ORIGIN C19: from Ger. *Lämmergeier*, from *Lämmer* 'lambs' + *Geier* 'vulture'.

**lamp** ● n. **1** an electric, oil, or gas device for giving light. **2** an electrical device producing ultraviolet or other radiation. ● v. **1** supply with lamps; illuminate. **2** [usu. as noun **lamping**] hunt at night for rabbits using lamps.
– DERIVATIVES **lamper** n. **lampless** adj.
– ORIGIN ME: via OFr. from late L. *lampada*, from L. *lampas*, *lampad-* 'torch', from Gk.

**lampas** /ˈlampəs/ ● n. swelling of the fleshy lining of the roof of a horse's mouth.
– ORIGIN C16: from Fr.

**lampblack** ● n. a black pigment made from soot.

**lamp chimney** ● n. a glass cylinder encircling the wick of an oil lamp and providing a draught for the flame.

**lampern** /ˈlampən/ ● n. a lamprey of rivers and coastal waters in NW Europe. [*Lampetra fluviatilis*.]
– ORIGIN ME: from OFr. *lampreion*, dimin. of *lampreie* 'lamprey'.

**lamplight** ● n. the light cast by a lamp.
– DERIVATIVES **lamplit** adj.

**lamplighter** ● n. historical a person employed to light street gaslights by hand.

**lampoon** /lamˈpuːn/ ● v. publicly satirize or ridicule. ● n. a satirical attack.
– DERIVATIVES **lampooner** n. **lampoonist** n.
– ORIGIN C17: from Fr. *lampon*, said to be from *lampons* 'let us drink'.

**lamprey** /ˈlampri/ ● n. (pl. **-eys**) an eel-like jawless fish,

often parasitic, that has a sucker mouth with horny teeth and a rasping tongue. [Family Petromyzonidae: several species.]
– ORIGIN ME: from OFr. *lampreie*, from med. L. *lampreda*, prob. from L. *lambere* 'to lick' + *petra* 'stone' (because the lamprey attaches itself to stones by its mouth).

**lamprophyre** /ˈlamprəˌfʌɪə/ ● **n.** Geology an igneous rock containing biotite crystals in a fine-grained feldspathic groundmass.
– ORIGIN C19: from Gk *lampros* 'bright' + *porphureos* 'purple'.

**lampshade** ● **n.** a cover for a lamp, used to soften or direct its light.

**lamp shell** ● **n.** a marine invertebrate resembling a bivalve mollusc, with arms of ciliated tentacles used for filter-feeding. [Phylum Brachiopoda.]
– ORIGIN C19: from its resemblance to an ancient oil lamp.

**LAN** ● **abbrev.** local area network.

**lanai** /ləˈnʌɪ/ ● **n.** (pl. **lanais**) a porch or veranda.
– ORIGIN from Hawaiian.

**Lancashire** /ˈlaŋkəʃə/ ● **n.** a mild crumbly white cheese, originally made in Lancashire.

**Lancashire hotpot** ● **n.** a stew of meat and vegetables, covered with a layer of sliced potato.

**Lancastrian** /laŋˈkastrɪən/ ● **n. 1** a native of Lancashire or Lancaster. **2** a follower of the House of Lancaster in the Wars of the Roses. ● **adj.** of or relating to Lancashire or Lancaster, or the House of Lancaster.

**lance** ● **n. 1** a long weapon with a wooden shaft and a pointed steel head, formerly used by a horseman in charging. **2** a similar weapon used in hunting fish or whales. **3** a metal pipe supplying a jet of oxygen to a furnace or to make a very hot flame for cutting. ● **v. 1** Medicine prick or cut open with a sharp instrument. **2** pierce with or as if with a lance. **3** move suddenly and quickly.
– ORIGIN ME: from OFr. *lance* (n.), *lancier* (v.), from L. *lancea* (n.).

**lance bombardier** ● **n.** a rank of non-commissioned officer in an artillery regiment of the British army, corresponding to that of a lance corporal in the infantry.

**lance corporal** ● **n.** a rank of non-commissioned officer in the British army, above private and below corporal.
– ORIGIN C18: on the analogy of obs. *lancepesade*, the lowest grade of non-commissioned officer, based on Ital. *lancia spezzata* 'broken lance'.

**lancelet** /ˈlɑːnslɪt/ ● **n.** a jawless fish-like marine animal that possesses a notochord and typically burrows in sand, e.g. amphioxus. [Family Branchiostomidae.]

**lanceolate** /ˈlɑːnsɪələt/ ● **adj.** technical of a narrow oval shape tapering to a point at each end.
– ORIGIN C18: from late L. *lanceolatus*, from L. *lanceola*, dimin. of *lancea* 'a lance'.

**lancer** ● **n. 1** a cavalry soldier armed with a lance. ➤ (**Lancer**) a soldier of a regiment originally armed with lances. **2** (**lancers**) [treated as sing.] a quadrille for eight or sixteen pairs.

**lance sergeant** ● **n.** a rank in the Foot Guards equivalent to corporal.

**lancet** /ˈlɑːnsɪt/ ● **n.** a small, broad two-edged surgical knife or blade with a sharp point.
– DERIVATIVES **lanceted** adj.
– ORIGIN ME (also denoting a small lance): from OFr. *lancette*, dimin. of *lance* 'a lance'.

**lancet arch** ● **n.** an arch with an acutely pointed head.

**lancet window** ● **n.** a narrow window with an acutely pointed head.

**lancewood** ● **n.** a tree with tough elastic wood. [*Oxandra lanceolata* (Caribbean) and *Pseudopanax crassifolius* (New Zealand).]

**Lancs.** ● **abbrev.** Lancashire.

**Land** /land, German lant/ ● **n.** (pl. **Länder** /ˈlɛndə, German ˈlɛndɐ/) a province of Germany or Austria.
– ORIGIN Ger., lit. 'land'.

**land** ● **n. 1** the part of the earth's surface that is not covered by water. ➤ an area of ground, especially in terms of its ownership or use. ➤ S. African a field. **2** a country or state. **3** the space between the rifling-grooves in a gun. ● **v. 1** put or go ashore. ➤ unload (goods) from a ship. ➤ bring (a fish) to land with a net or rod. ➤ informal succeed in obtaining or achieving (something desirable). **2** (with reference to aircraft, birds, etc.) come or bring down to the ground. ➤ come to rest after falling or being thrown. **3** (**land up**) reach a place or destination. ➤ (**land up with**) end up with (an unwelcome situation). **4** (**land someone in**) informal cause someone to be in (a difficult situation). ➤ (**land someone with**) inflict (an unwelcome task or a difficult situation) on someone. **5** informal inflict (a blow) on someone.
– PHRASES **how the land lies** what the state of affairs is. **in the land of the living** humorous alive or awake. **the land of Nod** humorous a state of sleep. [punningly, with biblical allusion to the place name *Nod* (Gen. 4:16).] **land** (or **fall**) **on one's feet** have good luck or success.
– DERIVATIVES **landless** adj. **landlessness** n.
– ORIGIN OE, of Gmc origin.

**land agent** ● **n.** Brit. **1** a person employed to manage an estate on behalf of its owners. **2** a person who deals with the sale of land.
– DERIVATIVES **land agency** n.

**landau** /ˈlandɔː, -aʊ/ ● **n.** a four-wheeled enclosed horse-drawn carriage with a removable front cover and a back cover that can be raised and lowered.
– ORIGIN C18: named after *Landau* in Germany.

**landaulet** /ˌlandɔːˈlɛt, -də-/ ● **n. 1** a small landau. **2** chiefly historical a car with a folding hood over the rear seats.

**land bank** ● **n. 1** a large body of land held in trust for future development or disposal. **2** a bank providing loans for land purchase.

**land breeze** ● **n.** a breeze blowing towards the sea from the land.

**land bridge** ● **n.** an area of land formerly connecting two land masses which are now separate.

**land crab** ● **n.** a crab that lives in burrows on land and migrates to the sea to breed. [Family Gecarcinidae.]

**land drain** ● **n.** a drain made of porous or perforated piping and placed in a gravel-filled trench, used for subsoil drainage.

**landed** ● **adj.** owning much land, especially through inheritance. ➤ consisting of or relating to such land.

**Länder** plural form of **LAND**.

**lander** ● **n.** a spacecraft designed to land on the surface of a planet or moon.

**landfall** ● **n. 1** an arrival at land on a sea or air journey. **2** a collapse of a mass of land.

**landfill** ● **n. 1** the disposal of waste material by burying it, especially as a method of filling in and reclaiming excavated pits. **2** waste material used in this way.

**landform** ● **n.** a natural feature of the earth's surface.

**land girl** ● **n.** (in the UK) a woman doing farm work during the Second World War.

**landgrave** /ˈlan(d)greɪv/ ● **n.** historical **1** a count having jurisdiction over a territory. **2** the title of certain German princes.
– ORIGIN ME: from Mid. Low Ger., from *land* 'land' + *grave* 'count'.

**landholder** ● **n.** a landowner, especially one who either makes their living from it or rents it out.
– DERIVATIVES **landholding** n.

**landing** ● **n. 1** the process of coming to or bringing something to land. **2** a place where people and goods can be landed from a boat. **3** a level area at the top of a staircase or between flights of stairs.

**landing craft** ● **n.** a boat specially designed for putting troops and military equipment ashore on a beach.

**landing gear** ● **n.** the undercarriage of an aircraft.

**landing stage** ● **n.** a platform on to which passengers or cargo can be landed from a boat.

**landlady** ● **n.** (pl. **-ies**) **1** a woman who leases land or property. **2** a woman who keeps lodgings, a boarding house, or (Brit.) a public house.

**ländler** /ˈlɛndlə/ ● **n.** an Austrian folk dance in triple time, a precursor of the waltz.
– ORIGIN C19: Ger., from *Landl* 'Upper Austria'.

**landline** • n. a conventional telecommunications connection by cable laid across land.

**landlocked** • adj. almost or entirely surrounded by land.

**landlord** • n. **1** a man (in legal use also a woman) who leases land or property. **2** a man who keeps lodgings, a boarding house, or (Brit.) a public house.

**landlordism** • n. the system whereby land (or property) is owned by landlords to whom tenants pay a fixed rent.

**landlubber** • n. informal a person unfamiliar with the sea or sailing.

**landmark** • n. **1** an object or feature of a landscape or town that is easily seen and recognized from a distance. ➤ historical the boundary of an area of land, or an object marking this. **2** an event, discovery, or change marking an important stage or turning point.

**land mass** • n. a continent or other large body of land.

**landmine** • n. an explosive mine laid on or just under the surface of the ground.

**land office** • n. chiefly N. Amer. a government office recording dealings in public land.
– PHRASES **do a land-office business** N. Amer. informal do a lot of successful trading.

**landowner** • n. a person who owns land.
– DERIVATIVES **landownership** n. **landowning** adj. & n.

**landrace** • n. a pig of a large white breed, originally developed in Denmark.
– ORIGIN 1930s: from Dan.

**landrail** • n. another term for **CORNCRAKE**.

**landscape** • n. **1** all the visible features of an area of land. **2** a picture representing an area of countryside. **3** the distinctive features of a sphere of intellectual activity. **4** [as modifier] denoting a format of printed matter which is wider than it is high. Compare with **PORTRAIT**. • v. improve the aesthetic appearance of (a piece of land) by changing its contours, planting trees and shrubs, etc.
– DERIVATIVES **landscaper** n. **landscapist** n.
– ORIGIN C16: from MDu. *lantscap*, from *land* 'land' + *scap* (equivalent of **-SHIP**).

**landscape architecture** • n. the art and practice of designing the outdoor environment, especially designing parks or gardens to harmonize with buildings or roads.
– DERIVATIVES **landscape architect** n.

**landscape gardening** • n. the art and practice of laying out grounds in a way which is ornamental or which imitates natural scenery.
– DERIVATIVES **landscape gardener** n.

**landside** • n. the side of an airport terminal to which the general public has unrestricted access.

**landsknecht** /ˈlan(d)sknɛkt/ • n. a member of a class of mercenary soldiers in the German and other continental armies in the 16th and 17th centuries.
– ORIGIN from Ger. *Landsknecht*, lit. 'soldier of the land'.

**landslide** • n. **1** (chiefly Brit. also **landslip**) the sliding down of a mass of earth or rock from a mountain or cliff. **2** an overwhelming majority of votes for one party in an election.

**Landsmål** /ˈlantsmɔːl/ • n. another term for **NYNORSK**.
– ORIGIN Norw., lit. 'language of the land'.

**landsman** • n. (pl. **-men**) a person unfamiliar with the sea or sailing.

**land tax** • n. tax levied on landed property.

**landtie** • n. a beam or piece of masonry supporting a wall or other vertical structure by connecting it with the ground.

**landward** • adv. (also **landwards**) towards land. • adj. facing towards land as opposed to sea.

**land yacht** • n. a wind-powered wheeled vehicle with sails, used for recreation and sport.

**lane** • n. **1** a narrow road, especially in a rural area. ➤ [in place names] an urban street. **2** a division of a road intended to separate single lines of traffic according to speed or direction. **3** each of a number of parallel strips of track or water for runners, rowers, or swimmers in a race. **4** a path or course prescribed for or regularly followed by ships or aircraft.
– ORIGIN OE: of unknown ultimate origin.

**langlauf** /ˈlaŋlaʊf/ • n. cross-country skiing.
– ORIGIN 1920s: from Ger., lit. 'long run'.

**langouste** /ˈlɒŋguːst/ • n. a spiny lobster, especially when prepared and cooked.
– ORIGIN Fr., from Old Provençal *lagosta*, based on L. *locusta* 'locust, crustacean'.

**langoustine** /ˈlɒŋgʊstiːn/ • n. a Norway lobster.
– ORIGIN Fr., from *langouste* (see **LANGOUSTE**).

**lang syne** /laŋ ˈsʌɪn/ Scottish archaic • adv. long ago. • n. times gone by.
– ORIGIN C16: from *lang*, Scots var. of **LONG**[1] + **SYNE**.

**language** • n. **1** the method of human communication, either spoken or written, consisting of the use of words in a structured and conventional way. ➤ any method of expression or communication: *body language*. **2** the system of communication used by a particular community or country. ➤ the phraseology and vocabulary of a particular group. ➤ Computing a system of symbols and rules for writing programs or algorithms. **3** the manner or style of a piece of writing or speech. ➤ (usu. **bad/foul/strong language**) coarse or offensive language.
– PHRASES **speak the same language** understand one another as a result of shared opinions or values.
– ORIGIN ME: from OFr. *langage*, based on L. *lingua* 'tongue'.

**language engineering** • n. the use of computers to process language for purposes such as speech recognition, speech synthesis, and machine translation.

**language laboratory** • n. a room equipped with audio and visual equipment for learning a foreign language.

**language of flowers** • n. a set of symbolic meanings attached to different flowers.

**langue** /lɒ̃g/ • n. (pl. pronounced same) Linguistics a language viewed as an abstract system used by a speech community. Contrasted with **PAROLE**.
– ORIGIN 1920s: Fr.

**langued** /ˈlaŋgd/ • adj. Heraldry having the tongue of a specified tincture.
– ORIGIN ME: from Fr. *langué* 'tongued' + **-ED**[2].

**langue de chat** /ˌlɒ̃(g) də ˈʃɑː/ • n. a very thin finger-shaped crisp biscuit or piece of chocolate.
– ORIGIN Fr., lit. 'cat's tongue'.

**langue d'oc** /lɒ̃(g) ˈdɒk, French lɑ̃g dɔk/ • n. the form of medieval French spoken south of the Loire, generally characterized by the use of *oc* to mean 'yes', and forming the basis of modern Provençal.
– ORIGIN OFr., lit. 'language of *oc*' (see above).

**langue d'oïl** /lɒ̃(g) ˈdɔɪl, French lɑ̃g dɔjl/ • n. the form of medieval French spoken north of the Loire, generally characterized by the use of *oïl* to mean 'yes', and forming the basis of modern French.
– ORIGIN OFr., lit. 'language of *oïl*' (see above).

**languid** • adj. **1** having or showing a disinclination for physical exertion. **2** weak or faint from illness or fatigue.
– DERIVATIVES **languidly** adv. **languidness** n.
– ORIGIN C16: from Fr. *languide* or L. *languidus*, from *languere* (see **LANGUISH**).

**languish** • v. **1** grow weak or feeble. ➤ archaic pine with love or grief. **2** be kept in an unpleasant place or situation: *he was languishing in jail.*
– DERIVATIVES **languisher** n. **languishment** n. (archaic).
– ORIGIN ME: from OFr. *languiss-*, lengthened stem of *languir*, from a var. of L. *languere*, rel. to *laxus* 'lax'.

**languor** /ˈlaŋgə/ • n. **1** tiredness or inactivity, especially when pleasurable. **2** an oppressive stillness of the air.
– DERIVATIVES **languorous** adj. **languorously** adv.
– ORIGIN ME (orig. in the sense 'illness, distress', later 'faintness, lassitude'): via OFr. from L., from *languere* (see **LANGUISH**).

**langur** /ˈlaŋgə, lanˈgʊə/ • n. a long-tailed Asian monkey with a characteristic loud call. [*Presbytis* and other genera: several species.]
– ORIGIN C19: via Hindi from Sanskrit *lāṅgūla*.

**laniard** • n. variant spelling of **LANYARD**.

**lank**[1] • adj. **1** (of hair) long, limp, and straight. **2** lanky.
– DERIVATIVES **lankly** adv. **lankness** n.
– ORIGIN OE *hlanc* 'thin', of Gmc origin.

**lank**[2] ● **adj.** S. African informal **1** very numerous or plentiful. **2** very good.
– ORIGIN sense 1 is perh. from Afrik. *geld lank* 'money galore'; sense 2 is perh. rel. to Afrik. *lank nie sleg nie* 'not at all bad'.

**lanky** ● **adj.** (**-ier**, **-iest**) ungracefully thin and tall.
– DERIVATIVES **lankily** adv. **lankiness** n.

**lanner** /'lanə/ ● **n.** a falcon with a dark brown back and buff cap, found in SE Europe, the Middle East, and Africa. [*Falco biarmicus*.] ➤ Falconry the female of this bird.
– ORIGIN ME: from OFr. *lanier*.

**lanneret** /'lanərɪt/ ● **n.** Falconry a male lanner, which is smaller than the female.

**lanolin** ● **n.** a fatty substance found naturally on sheep's wool and used as a base for ointments.
– ORIGIN C19: coined in Ger. from L. *lana* 'wool' + *oleum* 'oil' + **-IN**[1].

**lansquenet** /'lɑːnskə,nɛt, 'lans-/ ● **n. 1** historical a gambling game of German origin involving betting on cards turned up by the dealer. **2** archaic variant of **LANDSKNECHT**.
– ORIGIN C17: via Fr. from Ger. *Landsknecht* (see **LANDSKNECHT**).

**lantana** /lan'tɑːnə, -'teɪnə/ ● **n.** a tropical evergreen flowering shrub, several kinds of which are cultivated as ornamentals. [*Lantana camara* (S. America) and related species.]
– ORIGIN mod. L., from the name of the wayfaring tree *Viburnum lantana*, which it resembles superficially.

**lantern** ● **n. 1** a lamp with a transparent case protecting the flame or electric bulb. ➤ the light chamber at the top of a lighthouse. **2** a square, curved, or polygonal structure on the top of a dome or a room, with glazed or open sides.
– ORIGIN ME: from OFr. *lanterne*, from L. *lanterna*, from Gk *lamptēr* 'lamp', from *lampein* 'to shine'.

**Lantern Festival** ● **n.** another name for **BON**.

**lanternfish** ● **n.** (pl. same or **-fishes**) a deep-sea fish with light-emitting organs on its body. [Family Myctophidae.]

**lantern fly** ● **n.** a brightly coloured tropical bug which typically has a bizarrely shaped head and was formerly thought to be luminescent. [Family Fulgoridae.]

**lantern jaw** ● **n.** a long, thin jaw and prominent chin.
– DERIVATIVES **lantern-jawed** adj.

**lantern slide** ● **n.** historical a mounted photographic transparency for projection by a magic lantern.

**lantern wheel** ● **n.** a cylindrical gearwheel.

**lanthanide** /'lanθənʌɪd/ ● **n.** Chemistry any of the series of fifteen metallic elements from lanthanum (atomic number 57) to lutetium (atomic number 71) in the periodic table. See also **RARE EARTH**.

**lanthanum** /'lanθənəm/ ● **n.** the chemical element of atomic number 57, a silvery-white rare-earth metal. (Symbol: **La**)
– ORIGIN C19: from Gk *lanthanein* 'escape notice' (because it was long undetected in cerium oxide) + **-UM**.

**lanugo** /lə'njuːgəʊ/ ● **n.** fine, soft hair, especially that which covers the body and limbs of a human fetus.
– ORIGIN C17: from L., 'down', from *lana* 'wool'.

**lanyard** /'lanjəd/ (also **laniard**) ● **n. 1** a rope used to secure or raise and lower something such as a ship's sails. **2** a cord passed round the neck, shoulder, or wrist for holding a whistle or similar object.
– ORIGIN ME *lanyer*, from OFr. *laniere*, alt. by assoc. with **YARD**[1].

**LAO** ● **abbrev.** Laos (international vehicle registration).

**Lao** /laʊ/ ● **n.** (pl. same or **Laos**) **1** a member of an indigenous people of Laos and NE Thailand. **2** the language of this people.
– ORIGIN the name in Lao.

**Laodicean** /,leɪə(ʊ)dɪ'siːən/ archaic ● **adj.** half-hearted or indifferent, especially with respect to religion or politics. ● **n.** a person with such an attitude.
– ORIGIN C17: from L. *Laodicea* in Asia Minor, with ref. to the early Christians there (Rev. 3:16), + **-AN**.

**laogai** /laʊ'gʌɪ/ ● **n.** (**the laogai**) (in China) a system of labour camps, many of whose inmates are political dissidents.
– ORIGIN Chin., 'reform through labour'.

**Laotian** /laʊʃ(ə)n/ ● **n.** a native or inhabitant of the country of Laos in SE Asia. ● **adj.** of or relating to Laos.

**lap**[1] ● **n. 1** the flat area between the waist and knees of a seated person. **2** archaic a hanging flap on a garment or a saddle.
– PHRASES **fall** (or **drop**) **into someone's lap** be acquired by or happen to someone without any effort. **in someone's lap** as someone's responsibility. **in the lap of the gods** open to chance. **in the lap of luxury** in conditions of great comfort and wealth.
– DERIVATIVES **lapful** n. (pl. **-fuls**).
– ORIGIN OE *læppa* (orig. in the sense 'fold, flap', later meaning the front of a skirt when held up to carry something), of Gmc origin.

**lap**[2] ● **n. 1** one circuit of a track or racetrack. **2** a part of a journey. **3** an overlapping or projecting part. ➤ the amount by which one thing overlaps or covers a part of another. **4** a single turn of rope, thread, or cable round a drum or reel. ➤ a layer or sheet of cotton or wool, wound on a roller during manufacture. **5** a rotating abrasive disc for polishing gems, metal, and optical glass. ● **v.** (**lapped**, **lapping**) **1** overtake (a competitor in a race) to become one or more laps ahead. **2** (**lap someone/thing in**) poetic/literary enfold someone or something protectively in. **3** project beyond or overlap. **4** polish with a lap.
– ORIGIN ME: from **LAP**[1].

**lap**[3] ● **v.** (**lapped**, **lapping**) **1** (of an animal) take up (liquid) with the tongue. **2** (**lap something up**) accept something with obvious pleasure. **3** (of water) wash against with a gentle rippling sound. ● **n.** the action of water lapping.
– ORIGIN OE *lapian*, of Gmc origin.

**laparoscopy** /,lapə'rɒskəpi/ ● **n.** (pl. **-ies**) a surgical procedure in which a fibre-optic instrument is inserted through the abdominal wall to view the organs in the abdomen or permit small-scale surgery.
– DERIVATIVES **laparoscope** n. **laparoscopic** adj. **laparoscopically** adv.
– ORIGIN C19: from Gk *lapara* 'flank' + **-SCOPY**.

**laparotomy** /,lapə'rɒtəmi/ ● **n.** (pl. **-ies**) a surgical incision into the abdominal cavity, for diagnosis or in preparation for major surgery.

**lap dance** ● **n.** chiefly N. Amer. an erotic dance or striptease performed near to or on the lap of a person watching.
– DERIVATIVES **lap dancer** n. **lap dancing** n.

**lapdog** ● **n. 1** a small pampered pet dog. **2** a person who is completely under the influence of another.

**lapel** ● **n.** the part on each side of a coat or jacket immediately below the collar which is folded back against the front opening.
– DERIVATIVES **-lapelled** adj.
– ORIGIN C17: dimin. of **LAP**[1].

**lapidary** /'lapɪd(ə)ri/ ● **adj. 1** of or relating to the engraving, cutting, or polishing of stones and gems. **2** (of language) elegant and concise, suitable for engraving on stone. ● **n.** (pl. **-ies**) a person who cuts, polishes, or engraves stones and gems.
– ORIGIN ME (as n.): from L. *lapidarius* (in late L. 'stonecutter'), from *lapis, lapid-* 'stone'.

**lapilli** /lə'pɪlʌɪ/ ● **pl. n.** Geology rock fragments ejected from a volcano.
– ORIGIN C18: via Ital. from L., pl. of *lapillus*, dimin. of *lapis* 'stone'.

**lapis lazuli** /,lapɪs 'lazjʊlʌɪ, -li/ (also **lapis**) ● **n. 1** a bright blue metamorphic rock consisting largely of lazurite, used in jewellery. **2** ultramarine, originally made by crushing this rock.
– ORIGIN ME: from L. *lapis* 'stone' and med. L. *lazuli*, genitive of *lazulum*, from Pers. *lāžward* 'lapis lazuli'; cf. **AZURE**.

**lap joint** ● **n.** a joint made by halving the thickness of each member at the joint and fitting them together.

**Laplander** /'laplandə/ ● **n.** a native or inhabitant of Lapland in northern Europe.

**lap of honour** ● **n.** Brit. a celebratory circuit of a sports field, track, etc. by the victorious person or team.

**Lapp** • n. **1** a member of an indigenous people of the extreme north of Scandinavia. **2** the Finno-Ugric language of this people.
– ORIGIN Swed., perh. orig. a term of contempt and rel. to Mid. High Ger. *lappe* 'simpleton'.

USAGE **Lapp**

Although the term **Lapp** is still widely used and is the most familiar term to many people, the people themselves prefer to be called **Sami**.

**lappet** /ˈlapɪt/ • n. **1** a fold or hanging piece of flesh in some animals. **2** a loose or overlapping part of a garment. **3** (also **lappet moth**) a brownish moth, the caterpillars of which have fleshy lappets along each side of the body. [*Gastropacha quercifilia* and other species.]
– DERIVATIVES **lappeted** adj.
– ORIGIN ME (denoting a lobe of the ear, liver, etc.): dimin. of LAP[1].

**Lappish** • n. the Lapp language. • adj. of or relating to the Lapps (Sami) or their language.

**lap robe** • n. N. Amer. a travelling rug.

**lapsang souchong** /ˈlapsaŋ/ • n. a variety of souchong tea with a smoky flavour.
– ORIGIN C19: from an invented first element + SOUCHONG.

**lapse** • n. **1** a brief failure of concentration, memory, or judgement. ➤a decline from previously high standards. **2** an interval of time. **3** Law the termination of a right or privilege through disuse or failure to follow appropriate procedures. • v. **1** (of a right, privilege, or agreement) become invalid because it is not used, claimed, or renewed. **2** cease to follow the rules and practices of a religion or doctrine. **3** (**lapse into**) pass gradually into (a different, often worse, state or condition).
– ORIGIN ME: from L. *lapsus*, from *labi* 'to slip or fall'.

**lapse rate** • n. the rate at which air temperature falls with increasing altitude.

**lapstrake** chiefly N. Amer. • n. a clinker-built boat. • adj. (also **lapstraked**) clinker-built.

**lapsus calami** /ˌlapsəs ˈkaləmʌɪ/ • n. (pl. same) formal a slip of the pen.
– ORIGIN from L.

**lapsus linguae** /ˌlapsəs ˈlɪŋgwʌɪ/ • n. (pl. same) formal a slip of the tongue.
– ORIGIN from L.

**laptop** • n. a portable microcomputer suitable for use while travelling.

**lapwing** • n. a large crested plover with a dark green back, black-and-white head and underparts, and a loud call. [*Vanellus vanellus*.]
– ORIGIN OE *hlēapewince*, from *hlēapan* 'to leap' and a base meaning 'move from side to side' (because of the way it flies); the spelling was changed by assoc. with LAP[2] and WING.

**LAR** • abbrev. Libya (international vehicle registration).
– ORIGIN from *Libyan Arab Republic*.

**larboard** /ˈlɑːbɔːd, -bəd/ • n. Nautical archaic term for PORT[3].
– ORIGIN ME *ladebord* (see LADE, BOARD), referring to the side on which cargo was loaded; the change to *lar-* was due to assoc. with STARBOARD.

**larceny** /ˈlɑːs(ə)ni/ • n. (pl. **-ies**) theft of personal property (in English law replaced as a statutory crime by theft in 1968).
– DERIVATIVES **larcener** n. (archaic). **larcenist** n. **larcenous** adj.
– ORIGIN C15: from OFr. *larcin*, from L. *latrocinium*, from *latro(n-)* 'robber'.

**larch** • n. a northern coniferous tree with bunches of deciduous bright green needles and tough wood. [*Larix decidua* and related species.]
– ORIGIN C16: from Mid. High Ger. *larche*, based on L. *larix*.

**lard** • n. fat from the abdomen of a pig, rendered and clarified for use in cooking. • v. **1** insert strips of fat or bacon in (meat) before cooking. **2** (usu. **be larded with**) embellish (talk or writing) excessively with esoteric or technical expressions.
– DERIVATIVES **lardy** adj.
– ORIGIN ME: from OFr. 'bacon', from L. *lardum, laridum*, rel. to Gk *larinos* 'fat'.

**lardass** /ˈlɑːdɑːs, ˈlɑːdas/ • n. N. Amer. informal, derogatory a fat person.

**larder** • n. a room or large cupboard for storing food.
– ORIGIN ME (denoting a store of meat): from OFr. *lardier*, from med. L. *lardarium*, from *laridum* (see LARD).

**lardon** /ˈlɑːdən/ (also **lardoon** /-ˈduːn/) • n. a chunk or strip of bacon used to lard meat.
– ORIGIN ME: from Fr., from *lard* (see LARD).

**lardy cake** • n. Brit. a cake made with bread dough, lard, and currants.

**lares** /ˈlɑːriːz/ • pl. n. protective gods of the household, worshipped in ancient Rome along with the penates.
– ORIGIN from L.

**large** • adj. **1** of considerable or relatively great size, extent, or capacity. **2** pursuing an occupation or activity on a significant scale. **3** of wide range or scope. • v. (**large it**) Brit. informal go out and have a good time.
– PHRASES **at large 1** escaped or not yet captured. **2** as a whole: *society at large*. **in large measure** (or **part**) to a great extent.
– DERIVATIVES **largeness** n. **largish** adj.
– ORIGIN ME (in the sense 'lavish, ample'): via OFr. from L. *larga*, fem. of *largus* 'copious'.

**large-hearted** • adj. sympathetic and generous.

**large intestine** • n. Anatomy the caecum, colon, and rectum collectively.

**largely** • adv. on the whole; mostly.

**large-scale** • adj. extensive.

**largesse** /lɑːˈ(d)ʒɛs/ (also **largess**) • n. **1** generosity. **2** money or gifts given generously.
– ORIGIN ME: from OFr., from L. *largus* 'copious'.

**larghetto** /lɑːˈgɛtəʊ/ • adv. & adj. Music in a fairly slow tempo.
– ORIGIN Ital., dimin. of *largo* 'broad'.

**largo** /ˈlɑːgəʊ/ • adv. & adj. Music in a slow tempo and dignified in style.
– ORIGIN Ital., from L. *largus* 'copious'.

**lari** /ˈlɑːriː/ • n. (pl. same or **laris**) a monetary unit of the Maldives, equal to one hundredth of a rufiyaa.
– ORIGIN from Pers.

**lariat** /ˈlarɪət/ • n. a rope used as a lasso or for tethering.
– ORIGIN C19: from Sp. *la reata*, from *la* 'the' and *reatar* 'tie again'.

**lark[1]** • n. a songbird with brown streaky plumage, elongated hind claws, and a song that is delivered on the wing. [*Alauda arvensis* (**skylark**) and other species, family Alaudidae.] ➤used in names of similar birds of other families, e.g. **meadowlark**.
– PHRASES **be up with the lark** get out of bed very early in the morning.
– ORIGIN OE *lāferce, lǣwerce*; of unknown ultimate origin.

**lark[2]** informal • n. **1** an amusing adventure or escapade. **2** Brit. an activity regarded as foolish or a waste of time: *he's serious about this music lark*. • v. behave in a playful and mischievous way.
– DERIVATIVES **larkiness** n. **larky** adj.
– ORIGIN C19: perh. from dial. *lake* 'play', but cf. SKYLARK in the same sense, which is recorded earlier.

**larkspur** • n. a Mediterranean plant resembling a delphinium, with spikes of spurred flowers. [Genus *Consolida*.]

**larn** • v. dialect form of LEARN.

**larrikin** /ˈlarɪkɪn/ • n. Austral./NZ **1** a boisterous, often loutish, young man. **2** a person who disregards convention.
– ORIGIN C19: from Engl. dial., perh. from the given name *Larry* + -KIN, or from a pronunc. of *larking*.

**larrup** /ˈlarəp/ • v. (**larruped, larruping**) informal thrash or whip.
– ORIGIN C19 (orig. dial.): perh. rel. to LATHER or LEATHER.

**larva** /ˈlɑːvə/ • n. (pl. **larvae** /-viː/) an active immature form of an insect or other animal that undergoes metamorphosis, e.g. a caterpillar or tadpole.

– DERIVATIVES **larval** adj. **larvicide** n.
– ORIGIN C17 (denoting a disembodied spirit or ghost): from L., lit. 'ghost, mask'.

**laryngeal** /lə'rɪn(d)ʒɪəl/ • **adj. 1** of or relating to the larynx. **2** Phonetics (of a speech sound) made in the larynx with the vocal cords partly closed and partly vibrating.

**laryngitis** /ˌlarɪn'dʒʌɪtɪs/ • **n.** inflammation of the larynx.
– DERIVATIVES **laryngitic** /-'dʒɪtɪk/ adj.

**laryngology** /ˌlarɪŋ'gɒlədʒi/ • **n.** the branch of medicine concerned with the larynx and its diseases.
– DERIVATIVES **laryngologist** n.

**laryngoscope** /lə'rɪŋgəskəʊp/ • **n.** an instrument for examining the larynx, or for inserting a tube through it.
– DERIVATIVES **laryngoscopy** n.

**laryngotomy** /ˌlarɪŋ'gɒtəmi/ • **n.** surgical incision into the larynx, typically to provide an air passage when breathing is obstructed.

**larynx** /'larɪŋks/ • **n.** (pl. **larynges** /lə'rɪn(d)ʒiːz/) Anatomy the hollow muscular organ forming an air passage to the lungs and containing the vocal cords.
– ORIGIN C16: mod. L., from Gk *larunx*.

**lasagne** /lə'zanjə, -'san-, -'sɑːn-, -'zɑːn-/ • **n. 1** pasta in the form of sheets or wide strips. **2** an Italian dish consisting of this baked with meat or vegetables and a cheese sauce.
– ORIGIN Ital., pl. of *lasagna*, based on L. *lasanum* 'chamber pot', perh. also 'cooking pot'.

**Lascar** /'laskə/ • **n.** dated a sailor from India or SE Asia.
– ORIGIN C17: from Port. *lascari*, from Urdu and Pers. *laškarī* 'soldier'.

**lascivious** /lə'sɪvɪəs/ • **adj.** feeling or revealing an overt or offensive sexual desire.
– DERIVATIVES **lasciviously** adv. **lasciviousness** n.
– ORIGIN ME: from late L. *lasciviosus*, from L. *lascivia* 'lustfulness'.

**lase** /leɪz/ • **v.** function as or in a laser.

**laser** • **n.** a device that generates an intense narrow beam of coherent monochromatic light by stimulating the emission of photons from excited atoms or molecules.
– ORIGIN 1960s: acronym from *light amplification by stimulated emission of radiation*, based on the earlier **MASER**.

**laserdisc** • **n.** a disc that resembles a compact disc but is the size of a long-playing record, used for high-quality video and for interactive multimedia.

**laser printer** • **n.** a computer printer in which a laser is used to form a pattern of electrostatically charged dots on a light-sensitive drum, which attracts toner.

**lash** • **v. 1** strike or beat with a whip or stick. ➤beat forcefully against: *waves lashed the coast.* ➤(**lash out**) hit or kick out. ➤(**lash out**) launch a verbal attack. **2** (of an animal) move (a part of the body, especially the tail) quickly and violently. **3** fasten securely with a cord or rope. **4** (**lash out**) Brit. spend money extravagantly. • **n. 1** a sharp blow or stroke with a whip or stick. **2** the flexible leather part of a whip. **3** an eyelash.
– DERIVATIVES **-lashed** adj. **lasher** n. **lashless** adj.
– ORIGIN ME (in the sense 'make a sudden movement'): prob. imitative.

**lashing** • **n. 1** a whipping or beating. **2** a cord used to fasten something securely.

**lashings** • **pl. n.** Brit. informal a copious amount of something, especially food or drink.

**lash-up** • **n.** informal, chiefly Brit. a makeshift, improvised structure or arrangement.

**lass** (also **lassie**) • **n.** chiefly Scottish & N. English a girl or young woman.
– ORIGIN ME: based on ON *laskura* 'unmarried'.

**Lassa fever** /'lasə/ • **n.** an acute and often fatal viral disease occurring chiefly in West Africa.
– ORIGIN 1970s: named after the village of *Lassa*, in NW Nigeria, where it was first reported.

**lassi** /'lasi/ • **n.** a sweet or savoury Indian drink made from a yogurt or buttermilk base with water.
– ORIGIN from Hindi *lassī*.

**lassitude** /'lasɪtjuːd/ • **n.** physical or mental weariness; lack of energy.
– ORIGIN ME: from Fr., from L. *lassitudo*, from *lassus* 'tired'.

**lasso** /lə'suː, 'lasəʊ/ • **n.** (pl. **-os** or **-oes**) a rope with a noose at one end, used especially in North America for catching cattle. • **v.** (**-oes**, **-oed**) catch with a lasso.
– DERIVATIVES **lassoer** n.
– ORIGIN C18: representing an Amer. Sp. pronunc. of Sp. *lazo*, based on L. *laqueus* 'noose'.

**last**[1] • **adj. 1** coming after all others in time or order; final. ➤lowest in importance or rank. ➤(**the last**) the least likely or suitable. **2** most recent in time; latest. **3** immediately preceding in order; previous in a sequence or enumeration. **4** only remaining. • **adv. 1** on the last occasion before the present; previously. **2** [in combination] after all others in order or sequence: *the last-named film.* **3** (in enumerating points) lastly. • **n.** (pl. same) the last person or thing. ➤(**the last of**) the only remaining part. ➤(**the last**) the end or last moment, especially death.
– PHRASES **at last** (or **at long last**) in the end; after much delay. **last thing** late in the evening, especially immediately before going to bed.
– ORIGIN OE *latost*, of Gmc origin; rel. to **LATE**.

**last**[2] • **v. 1** continue for a specified period of time. **2** remain operating or usable for a considerable or specified length of time. **3** (of provisions or resources) be adequate or sufficient for a specified length of time.
– ORIGIN OE *lǣstan*, of Gmc origin, rel. to **LAST**[3].

**last**[3] • **n.** a shoemaker's model for shaping or repairing a shoe or boot.
– ORIGIN OE *lǣste*, of Gmc origin, from a base meaning 'follow'.

**last-ditch** • **adj.** denoting a final desperate attempt to achieve something.

**last-gasp** • **adj.** informal at the last possible moment.

**last hurrah** • **n.** chiefly N. Amer. a final act, performance, or effort.

**lasting** • **adj.** enduring or able to endure over a long period of time.
– DERIVATIVES **lastingly** adv. **lastingness** n.

**Last Judgement** • **n.** the judgement of humankind expected in some religious traditions to take place at the end of the world.

**lastly** • **adv.** in the last place; last.

**last minute** (also **last moment**) • **n.** the latest possible time before an event.

**last name** • **n.** one's surname.

**last offices** • **pl. n.** the preparation of a corpse for burial; laying out.

**last post** • **n.** (in the British armed forces) the second of two bugle calls giving notice of the hour of retiring at night, played also at military funerals and acts of remembrance.

**last rites** • **pl. n.** (in the Christian Church) rites administered to a person who is about to die.

**Last Supper** • **n.** the supper eaten by Jesus and his disciples on the night before the Crucifixion.

**last trump** • **n.** the trumpet blast that in some religious beliefs is thought will wake the dead on Judgement Day.

**last word** • **n. 1** a final or definitive pronouncement on a subject. **2** the most modern or advanced example of something.

**lat**[1] /lat/ • **n.** (pl. **lati** /'lati/ or **lats**) the basic monetary unit of Latvia, equal to 100 santims.
– ORIGIN from the first syllable of *Latvija* 'Latvia'.

**lat**[2] /lat/ • **n.** informal (in bodybuilding) a latissimus muscle.

**lat.** • **abbrev.** latitude.

**latch** • **n. 1** a bar with a catch and lever used for fastening a door or gate. **2** a spring lock for an outer door, which catches when the door is closed and can only be opened from the outside with a key. **3** Electronics a circuit which retains whatever output state results from a momentary input signal until reset by another signal. • **v. 1** fasten with a latch. **2** Electronics (of a device) become fixed

in a particular state. **3** (**latch on**) understand the meaning of something. **4** (usu. **latch on to something**) become attached. ➤associate oneself enthusiastically with something.
– PHRASES **on the latch** (of a door or gate) closed but not locked.
– ORIGIN OE *læccan* 'take hold of, grasp', of Gmc origin.

**latchet** /ˈlatʃɪt/ ● **n.** archaic a narrow thong or lace for fastening a shoe or sandal.
– ORIGIN ME: from OFr. *lachet*, var. of *lacet*, from *laz* 'lace'.

**latchkey** ● **n.** (pl. **-eys**) a key of an outer door of a house.

**latchkey child** ● **n.** a child who is alone at home after school until a parent returns from work.

**late** ● **adj.** **1** acting, arriving, or happening after the expected or usual time. **2** belonging or taking place far on in a particular time or period. **3** far on in the day or night. **4** (**the/one's late**) (of a specified person) no longer alive. ➤no longer having the specified status; former. **5** (**latest**) of most recent date or origin. ● **adv.** **1** after the expected or usual time. **2** towards the end of a period. **3** far on in the day or night. **4** (**later**) at a time in the near future; afterwards. **5** (**late of**) formerly but not now living or working in a specified place or institution. ● **n.** (**the latest**) the most recent news or fashion.
– PHRASES **at the latest** no later than the time specified. **late in the day** (or N. Amer. **game**) at a late stage in proceedings. **of late** recently.
– DERIVATIVES **lateness** n.
– ORIGIN OE *læt* (adj.), *late* (adv.), of Gmc origin.

**latecomer** ● **n.** a person who arrives late.

**lateen sail** /ləˈtiːn/ ● **n.** a triangular sail on a long yard at an angle of 45° to the mast.
– ORIGIN C16: from Fr. (*voile*) *Latine* 'Latin (sail)', so named because it was common in the Mediterranean.

**late Latin** ● **n.** Latin of about AD 200–600.

**lately** ● **adv.** recently; not long ago.

**latent** ● **adj.** existing but not yet developed, manifest, or active: *her latent talent.*
– DERIVATIVES **latency** n. **latently** adv.
– ORIGIN ME: from L. *latent-*, *latere* 'be hidden'.

**latent heat** ● **n.** Physics the heat required to convert a solid into a liquid or vapour, or a liquid into a vapour, without change of temperature.

**latent image** ● **n.** Photography an image on film that has not yet been made visible by developing.

**latent period** ● **n.** Medicine the period between infection and the onset of symptoms.

**-later** ● **comb. form** denoting a person who worships a specified thing: *idolater.*
– ORIGIN from Gk *-latrēs* 'worshipper'.

**lateral** ● **adj.** **1** of, at, towards, or from the side or sides. **2** Phonetics (of a consonant, especially the English clear *l*) pronounced with partial closure of the air passage by the tongue, which allows the breath to flow on one or both sides of the point of contact. ● **n.** **1** a side part of something, especially a shoot or branch growing out from the side of a stem. **2** Phonetics a lateral consonant. **3** American Football a pass thrown sideways or back.
– DERIVATIVES **laterally** adv.
– ORIGIN ME: from L. *lateralis*, from *latus, later-* 'side'.

**laterality** ● **n.** dominance of one side of the brain in controlling particular activities or functions, or of one of a pair of organs such as the eyes or hands.

**lateralize** ● **v.** (**be lateralized**) Physiology & Medicine be localized to one or other side of the brain.
– DERIVATIVES **lateralization** n.

**lateral line** ● **n.** Zoology a visible line along the side of a fish, consisting of a series of sense organs which detect pressure and vibration.

**lateral thinking** ● **n.** chiefly Brit. the solving of problems by an indirect and creative approach.

**lateral ventricle** ● **n.** Anatomy each of the first and second ventricles in the centre of each cerebral hemisphere of the brain.

**laterite** /ˈlatərʌɪt/ ● **n.** a reddish clayey material, hard when dry, forming a topsoil in some tropical regions and sometimes used for building.
– DERIVATIVES **lateritic** adj.
– ORIGIN C19: from L. *later* 'brick' + **-ITE**[1].

**latex** /ˈleɪtɛks/ ● **n.** (pl. **latexes** or **latices** /-tɪsiːz/) **1** a milky fluid found in many plants, notably the rubber tree, which coagulates on exposure to the air. **2** a synthetic product resembling this, used to make paints, coatings, etc.
– ORIGIN C17 (denoting various bodily fluids): from L., lit. 'liquid, fluid'.

**lath** /lɑːθ, laθ/ ● **n.** (pl. **laths** /lɑːθs, lɑːðz, laθs/) a thin, flat strip of wood, especially one of a series forming a foundation for the plaster of a wall. ● **v.** cover with laths.
– ORIGIN OE *lætt*, of Gmc origin; rel. to **LATTICE**.

**lathe** /leɪð/ ● **n.** a machine for shaping wood or metal by means of a rotating drive which turns the piece being worked on against changeable cutting tools.
– ORIGIN ME: prob. from Old Dan. *lad* 'structure, frame', perh. from ON *hlath* 'pile, heap', rel. to **LADE**.

**lather** /ˈlɑːðə, ˈlaðə/ ● **n.** **1** a frothy white mass of bubbles produced by soap when mixed with water. **2** heavy sweat visible on a horse's coat as a white foam. **3** (**a lather**) informal a state of agitation or nervous excitement. ● **v.** **1** form or cause to form a lather. ➤rub with soap until a lather is produced. **2** cover or spread liberally with (a substance). **3** informal thrash (someone).
– DERIVATIVES **lathery** adj.
– ORIGIN OE *læthor*, *lēthran* (v.), of Gmc origin.

**lathi** /ˈlɑːtiː/ ● **n.** (pl. **lathis**) (in the Indian subcontinent) a long metal-bound bamboo stick used as a weapon, especially by police.
– ORIGIN from Hindi *lāṭhī*.

**latices** plural form of **LATEX**.

**latifundium** /ˌlɑːtɪˈfʌndɪəm, ˌlatɪ-/ ● **n.** (pl. **latifundia**) a large landed estate or ranch worked by peasants or slaves, especially in Spain or Latin America.
– ORIGIN C17: from L., from *latus* 'broad' + *fundus* 'landed estate'.

**Latin** ● **n.** **1** the language of ancient Rome and its empire. **2** a native or inhabitant of a country whose language developed from Latin, e.g. a Latin American. ● **adj.** **1** of or relating to the Latin language. **2** relating to or denoting countries using languages that developed from Latin, especially Latin America. **3** relating to or denoting the Western or Roman Catholic Church. **4** historical of or relating to ancient Latium in Italy.
– DERIVATIVES **Latinism** n. **Latinist** n. **Latinity** n.
– ORIGIN from L. *Latinus* 'of Latium'.

**Latina** /ləˈtiːnə/ ● **n.** fem. of **LATINO**.

**Latin American** ● **adj.** of or relating to the parts of the American continent where Spanish or Portuguese is the main national language. ● **n.** a native or inhabitant of this region.

**Latinate** /ˈlatɪneɪt/ ● **adj.** (of language) having the character of Latin.

**Latin Church** ● **n.** the Roman Catholic Church as distinguished from Orthodox and Uniate Churches.

**Latin cross** ● **n.** a plain cross in which the vertical part below the horizontal is longer than the other three parts.

**Latinize** (also **-ise**) ● **v.** **1** give a Latin or Latinate form to (a word). ➤archaic translate into Latin. **2** cause to conform to the ideas and customs of the ancient Romans or the Latin Church.
– DERIVATIVES **Latinization** n. **Latinizer** n.

**Latino** /ləˈtiːnəʊ/ ● **n.** (fem. **Latina**) (pl. **-os** or **-as**) chiefly N. Amer. a Latin American inhabitant of the United States.
– ORIGIN from Latin Amer. Sp.

**Latin square** ● **n.** an arrangement of letters in a square array of $n^2$ compartments, each letter appearing $n$ times but never twice in the same row or column.

**latissimus** /lɑːˈtɪsɪməs/ (also **latissimus dorsi** /ˈdɔːsʌɪ, -siː/) ● **n.** (pl. **latissimi** /lɑːˈtɪsɪmʌɪ, -miː/) Anatomy either of a pair of large, roughly triangular muscles covering the lower part of the back.
– ORIGIN C17: mod. L., from *musculus latissimus dorsi*, lit. 'broadest muscle of the back'.

## Word *Formation*

**-latry** from Greek *latreia* 'worship'

In modern English, most **-latry** words are relatively uncommon or obscure, the only well established one being ***idolatry***. Most are used in a derogatory sense.

| | | |
|---|---|---|
| anthropolatry | worship of humans as if gods | Gk *anthrōpos* 'human being' |
| bardolatry | worship of Shakespeare | 'the Bard' |
| bibliolatry | excessive reverence for books | Gk *biblion* 'book' |
| demonolatry | demon worship | based on DEMON |
| gyneolatry | adoration of women | Gk *gunē, gunaik-* 'woman' |
| hagiolatry | worship of saints | Gk *hagios* 'holy' |
| Mariolatry | idolatrous worship of the Virgin Mary | L. *Maria* 'Mary' |
| zoolatry | worship of animals | Gk *zōion* 'animal' |

**latitude** /ˈlatɪtjuːd/ ● **n.** **1** the angular distance of a place north or south of the equator. **2** (**latitudes**) regions with reference to their temperature and distance from the equator: *northern latitudes.* **3** scope for freedom of action or thought.
– DERIVATIVES **latitudinal** adj. **latitudinally** adv.
– ORIGIN ME: from L. *latitudo* 'breadth', from *latus* 'broad'.

**latitudinarian** /ˌlatɪtjuːdɪˈnɛːrɪən/ ● **adj.** liberal, especially in religious views. ● **n.** a person with a latitudinarian attitude.
– DERIVATIVES **latitudinarianism** n.

**latke** /ˈlʌtkə/ ● **n.** (in Jewish cookery) a pancake, especially one made with grated potato.
– ORIGIN from Yiddish.

**latria** /ləˈtrʌɪə, ˈlatrɪə/ ● **n.** (in Roman Catholic theology) supreme worship allowed to God alone. Compare with **DULIA**.
– ORIGIN C16: from late L., from Gk *latreia* 'worship'.

**latrine** /ləˈtriːn/ ● **n.** a toilet, especially a communal one in a camp or barracks.
– ORIGIN ME: via Fr. from L. *latrina*, contr. of *lavatrina*, from *lavare* 'to wash'.

**-latry** ● **comb. form** denoting worship of a specified thing: *idolatry.* See word-formation panel.
– ORIGIN from Gk *-latria* 'worship'.

**latte** /ˈlɑːteɪ, ˈlateɪ/ ● **n.** short for **CAFFÈ LATTE**.

**latten** /ˈlat(ə)n/ ● **n.** historical an alloy of copper and zinc resembling brass, hammered into thin sheets and used to make monumental brasses and church ornaments.
– ORIGIN ME: from OFr. *laton*, of unknown origin.

**latter** ● **adj.** **1** nearer to the end of something than to the beginning. ➤belonging to the final stages of something, especially of a person's life. ➤recent: *in latter years.* **2** (**the latter**) denoting the second or second-mentioned of two people or things.
– ORIGIN OE *lætra* 'slower', compar. of *læt* (see **LATE**).

**latter-day** ● **adj.** modern or contemporary, especially when mirroring some person or thing of the past: *a latter-day Noah.*

**Latter-Day Saints** ● **pl. n.** the Mormons' name for themselves.

**latterly** ● **adv.** **1** recently. **2** in the later stages of a period of time.

**lattice** ● **n.** **1** a structure or pattern consisting of strips crossing each other with square or diamond-shaped spaces left between. **2** Physics a regular repeated three-dimensional arrangement of atoms, ions, or molecules in a metal or other crystalline solid.
– DERIVATIVES **latticed** adj. **latticework** n.
– ORIGIN ME: from OFr. *lattis*, from *latte* 'lath', of Gmc origin.

**lattice frame** (also **lattice girder**) ● **n.** an iron or steel structure consisting of two horizontal beams connected by diagonal struts.

**lattice window** ● **n.** a window with small panes set in diagonally crossing strips of lead.

**Latvian** ● **n.** **1** a native or citizen of Latvia, or a person of Latvian descent. **2** the Baltic language of Latvia. ● **adj.** of or relating to Latvia, its people, or their language.

**laud** /lɔːd/ ● **v.** formal praise highly, especially in a public context. ● **n.** archaic praise.
– DERIVATIVES **laudation** n.
– ORIGIN ME: the noun from OFr. *laude*, the verb from L. *laudare*, both from L. *laus, laud-* 'praise'.

**laudable** ● **adj.** deserving praise and commendation.
– DERIVATIVES **laudability** n. **laudably** adv.

**laudanum** /ˈlɔːd(ə)nəm, ˈlɒ-/ ● **n.** an alcoholic solution containing morphine, prepared from opium and formerly used as a narcotic painkiller.
– ORIGIN C16: mod. L., perh. a var. of L. *ladanum* (see **LADANUM**).

**laudatory** /ˈlɔːdət(ə)ri/ ● **adj.** expressing praise and commendation.

**lauds** /lɔːdz/ ● **n.** a service of morning prayer in the Divine Office of the Western Christian Church, traditionally said or chanted at daybreak.
– ORIGIN ME: from the frequent use, in Psalms 148–150, of the L. imper. *laudate!* 'praise ye!'.

**laugh** ● **v.** **1** make the sounds and movements that express lively amusement and sometimes also derision. ➤(**laugh at**) ridicule; scorn. **2** (**laugh something off**) dismiss something by treating it in a light-hearted way. **3** (**be laughing**) informal be in a fortunate or successful position. ● **n.** **1** an act of laughing. **2** (**a laugh**) informal a person or thing that causes laughter.
– PHRASES **have the last laugh** be finally vindicated. **a laugh a minute** very funny. **laugh on the other side of one's face** (or N. Amer. **out of the other side of one's mouth**) be discomfited after feeling confident or triumphant. **laugh out of court** dismiss with contempt as being obviously ridiculous. **laugh up one's sleeve** be secretly or inwardly amused. **no laughing matter** something serious that should not be joked about.
– DERIVATIVES **laugher** n. **laughing** adj. **laughingly** adv.
– ORIGIN OE *hlæhhan, hliehhan*, of Gmc origin.

**laughable** ● **adj.** so ludicrous as to be amusing.
– DERIVATIVES **laughably** adv.

**laughing gas** ● **n.** non-technical term for **NITROUS OXIDE**.

**laughing hyena** ● **n.** a southern African hyena with a loud laughing call. [*Crocuta crocuta*.]

**laughing jackass** ● **n.** Austral. the kookaburra.

**laughing stock** ● **n.** a person subjected to general mockery or ridicule.

**laughter** ● **n.** the action or sound of laughing.
– ORIGIN OE *hleahtor*, of Gmc origin.

**launch**[1] ● **v.** **1** set (a boat or ship) afloat, especially by sliding it into the water. **2** send out or hurl forcefully (a rocket or other missile). **3** begin (an enterprise) or introduce (a new product). ➤(**launch into**) begin (something) energetically and enthusiastically. ● **n.** an act or instance of launching something.
– ORIGIN ME: from Anglo-Norman Fr. *launcher*, var. of OFr. *lancier* (see **LANCE**).

**launch**[2] ● **n.** **1** a large motor boat. **2** historical the largest

boat carried on a man-of-war.
– ORIGIN C17: from Sp. *lancha* 'pinnace', perh. from Malay *lancharan*, from *lanchar* 'swift, nimble'.

**launcher** • n. a structure that holds a rocket or missile during launching.

**launch pad** (also **launching pad**) • n. the area on which a rocket stands for launching.

**launder** • v. **1** wash and iron (clothes or linen). **2** informal transfer (illegally obtained money) to conceal its origins. • n. **1** a trough for holding or conveying water, especially (in mining) one used for washing ore. **2** a channel for conveying molten metal to a ladle or mould.
– DERIVATIVES **launderer** n.
– ORIGIN ME (as n. denoting a person who washes linen): contr. of *lavender*, from OFr. *lavandier*, based on L. *lavanda* 'things to be washed', from *lavare* 'to wash'.

**launderette** (also **laundrette**) • n. an establishment with coin-operated washing machines and dryers for public use.

**laundress** • n. a woman employed to launder clothes and linen.

**laundromat** • n. chiefly N. Amer. (trademark in the US) a launderette.

**laundry** • n. (pl. **-ies**) **1** clothes and linen that need to be washed or that have been newly washed. **2** a room or building where clothes and linen are washed and ironed.
– ORIGIN C16: contr. of ME *lavendry*, from OFr. *lavanderie*, from *lavandier* (see **LAUNDER**).

**laureate** /ˈlɒrɪət, ˈlɔː-/ • n. **1** a person given an award for outstanding creative or intellectual achievement: *a Nobel laureate*. **2** short for **POET LAUREATE**. • adj. poetic/literary wreathed with laurel as a mark of honour.
– DERIVATIVES **laureateship** n.
– ORIGIN ME (as adj.): from L. *laureatus*, from *laurea* 'laurel wreath'.

**laurel** • n. **1** an aromatic evergreen shrub or small tree with dark green glossy leaves. [*Laurus* and other genera, family Lauraceae.] **2** (**laurels**) a crown woven from the foliage of the bay tree and awarded as an emblem of victory or mark of honour in classical times. ➤ honour or praise. • v. (**laurelled**, **laurelling**; US **laureled**, **laureling**) adorn with or as if with a laurel.
– PHRASES **look to one's laurels** be careful not to lose one's superior position to a rival. **rest on one's laurels** be so satisfied with what one has already achieved that one makes no further effort.
– ORIGIN ME *lorer*, from OFr. *lorier*, from Provençal *laurier*, from earlier *laur*, from L. *laurus*.

**laurustinus** /ˌlɒrəˈstʌɪnəs, ˌlɔː-/ • n. an evergreen winter-flowering viburnum with dense glossy green leaves and white or pink flowers. [*Viburnum tinus*.]
– ORIGIN C17: mod. L., from L. *laurus* 'laurel' + *tinus* 'wild laurel'.

**lav** • n. informal a lavatory.

**lava** • n. hot molten or semi-fluid rock erupted from a volcano or fissure, or solid rock resulting from cooling of this.
– ORIGIN C18: from Ital. (orig. denoting a stream caused by sudden rain), from *lavare* 'to wash', from L.

**lavabo** /ləˈveɪbəʊ, ləˈvɑː-/ • n. (pl. **-os**) **1** a towel or basin used for the ritual washing of the celebrant's hands at the offertory of the Catholic Mass. ➤ ritual washing of this type. **2** /ˈlavəbəʊ/ a washing trough in a monastery. **3** archaic a washbasin.
– ORIGIN C18: from L., lit. 'I will wash', in *Lavabo inter innocentes manus meas* 'I will wash my hands in innocence' (Ps. 26:6).

**lavage** /ˈlavɪdʒ, laˈvɑːʒ/ • n. Medicine washing out of a body cavity, such as the colon or stomach, with water or a medicated solution.
– ORIGIN C18 (in the general sense 'washing, a wash'): from Fr., from *laver* 'to wash'.

**lava lamp** • n. a transparent electric lamp containing a viscous liquid in which a suspended waxy substance rises and falls in constantly changing shapes.

**lavatorial** • adj. **1** of, relating to, or resembling lavatories. **2** (of conversation or humour) characterized by undue reference to lavatories and their use.

**lavatory** • n. (pl. **-ies**) a toilet.
– ORIGIN ME: from late L. *lavatorium* 'place for washing', from L. *lavare* 'to wash'.

**lave** /leɪv/ • v. poetic/literary wash or wash over.
– DERIVATIVES **lavation** n.
– ORIGIN OE *lafian*, from L. *lavare* 'to wash'; reinforced in ME by OFr. *laver*.

**lavender** • n. **1** a small aromatic evergreen shrub of the mint family, with narrow leaves and bluish-purple flowers. [Genus *Lavandula*.] ➤ (also **lavender oil**) a scented oil distilled from lavender flowers. ➤ used in names of similar plants, e.g. **sea lavender**. **2** a pale blue colour with a trace of mauve. • v. perfume with lavender.
– ORIGIN ME: from Anglo-Norman Fr. *lavendre*, based on med. L. *lavandula*.

**lavender cotton** • n. another term for **COTTON LAVENDER**.

**lavender water** • n. a perfume made from distilled lavender, alcohol, and ambergris.

**laver**[1] /ˈlɑːvə, ˈleɪvə/ (also **purple laver**) • n. an edible seaweed with thin reddish-purple and green sheet-like fronds. [*Porphyra umbilicaulis*.]
– ORIGIN OE, from L.

**laver**[2] /ˈleɪvə/ • n. **1** archaic or poetic/literary a basin or similar container used for washing oneself. **2** (in biblical use) a large brass bowl for Jewish priests' ritual ablutions.
– ORIGIN ME: from OFr. *laveoir*, from late L. *lavatorium* (see **LAVATORY**).

**laver bread** • n. a Welsh dish of laver which is boiled, dipped in oatmeal, and fried.

**lavish** • adj. **1** sumptuously rich, elaborate, or luxurious. **2** giving or given in profusion. • v. (usu. **lavish something on**) bestow or cover in generous or extravagant quantities.
– DERIVATIVES **lavishly** adv. **lavishness** n.
– ORIGIN ME (as n. denoting profusion): from OFr. *lavasse* 'deluge of rain', from *laver* 'to wash', from L. *lavare*.

**law** • n. **1** a rule or system of rules recognized by a country or community as regulating the actions of its members and enforced by the imposition of penalties. ➤ such rules as a subject of study or as the basis of the legal profession. ➤ statute law and the common law. ➤ something regarded as having binding force or effect: *his word was law*. ➤ (**the law**) informal the police. **2** a statement of fact, deduced from observation, to the effect that a particular natural or scientific phenomenon always occurs if certain conditions are present. **3** a rule defining correct procedure or behaviour in a sport. **4** the body of divine commandments as expressed in the Bible or other religious texts. ➤ (**the Law**) the Pentateuch. ➤ (also **the Law of Moses**) the precepts of the Pentateuch.
– PHRASES **be a law unto oneself** behave in an unconventional or unpredictable manner. **lay down the law** issue instructions in an authoritative or dogmatic way. **take the law into one's own hands** illegally or violently punish someone according to one's own ideas of justice.
– ORIGIN OE *lagu*, from ON *lag* 'something laid down or fixed', of Gmc origin and rel. to **LAY**[1].

**law-abiding** • adj. obedient to the laws of society.
– DERIVATIVES **law-abidingness** n.

**law agent** • n. (in Scotland) a solicitor.

**lawbreaker** • n. a person who breaks the law.
– DERIVATIVES **lawbreaking** n. & adj.

**law centre** • n. (in the UK) an independent publicly funded advisory service on legal matters.

**law court** • n. a court of law.

**lawful** • adj. conforming to, permitted by, or recognized by law or rules. ➤ dated (of a child) born within a lawful marriage.
– DERIVATIVES **lawfully** adv. **lawfulness** n.

**lawgiver** • n. a person who draws up and enacts laws.

**lawks** • exclam. dated (in cockney speech) expressing surprise, awe, or consternation.
– ORIGIN C18: alt. of **LORD**.

**lawless** • adj. not governed by or obedient to laws.
– DERIVATIVES **lawlessly** adv. **lawlessness** n.

**law lord** ● n. (in the UK) a member of the House of Lords qualified to perform its legal work.

**lawmaker** ● n. a legislator.
– DERIVATIVES **law-making** adj. & n.

**lawman** ● n. (pl. **-men**) (in the US) a law-enforcement officer, especially a sheriff.

**lawn**[1] ● n. an area of mown grass in a garden or park.
– DERIVATIVES **lawned** adj.
– ORIGIN C16: alt. of dial. *laund* 'glade, pasture', from OFr. *launde* 'wooded district, heath', of Celtic origin.

**lawn**[2] ● n. a fine linen or cotton fabric used for making clothes.
– DERIVATIVES **lawny** adj.
– ORIGIN ME: prob. from *Laon*, the name of a city in France important for linen manufacture.

**lawn bowling** ● n. North American term for **BOWLS**.

**lawnmower** ● n. a machine for cutting the grass on a lawn.

**lawn tennis** ● n. dated or formal tennis.

**law of averages** ● n. the supposed principle that future events are likely to turn out so that they balance any past deviation from a presumed average.

**law office** ● n. N. Amer. a lawyer's office.

**law of mass action** ● n. Chemistry the principle that the rate of a chemical reaction is proportional to the concentrations of the reacting substances.

**law of nations** ● n. Law international law.

**law of nature** ● n. **1** another term for **NATURAL LAW**. **2** informal a regularly occurring phenomenon observable in human society.

**law of succession** ● n. the law regulating the inheritance of property.

**lawrencium** /lɒˈrɛnsɪəm/ ● n. the chemical element of atomic number 103, an artificially made radioactive metal. (Symbol: **Lr**)
– ORIGIN 1960s: named after the Amer. physicist Ernest O. *Lawrence*.

**lawsuit** ● n. a claim or dispute brought to a law court for adjudication.

**lawyer** ● n. a person who practises or studies law, especially (in the UK) a solicitor or a barrister or (in the US) an attorney.
– DERIVATIVES **lawyering** n. **lawyerly** adj.

**lax** ● adj. **1** not sufficiently strict, severe, or careful. **2** (of the limbs or muscles) relaxed. **3** Phonetics (of a speech sound, especially a vowel) pronounced with the vocal muscles relaxed. The opposite of **TENSE**[1].
– DERIVATIVES **laxity** n. **laxly** adv. **laxness** n.
– ORIGIN ME: from L. *laxus*.

**laxative** ● adj. tending to stimulate or facilitate evacuation of the bowels. ● n. a laxative drug or medicine.
– ORIGIN ME: via OFr. *laxatif, -ive* or late L. *laxativus*, from L. *laxare* 'loosen'.

**lay**[1] ● v. (past and past part. **laid**) **1** put down, especially gently or carefully. **2** put down and set in position for use. ➤set cutlery on (a table) in preparation for a meal. ➤put the material for (a fire) in place. ➤make ready (a trap). ➤(**lay something before**) present material for consideration and action to (someone). **3** (with an abstract noun) put or place: *lay the blame*. **4** (of a female bird, reptile, etc.) produce (an egg) from inside the body. **5** stake (an amount of money) in a wager. **6** cause (a ghost) to stop appearing; exorcize. **7** vulgar slang have sexual intercourse with. **8** trim (a hedge) by cutting the branches half through, bending them down, and interweaving them. **9** Nautical follow (a specified course). ● n. **1** the general appearance of an area of land. ➤the position or direction in which something lies: *roll the carpet against the lay of the nap*. **2** vulgar slang a sexual partner or act of sexual intercourse. **3** the laying of eggs or the period during which they are laid.
– PHRASES **lay claim to** assert one's right to or possession of. **lay hands on** find and take possession of or acquire. **lay hold of** (or **on**) catch at or gain possession of. **lay someone low** reduce someone to inactivity, illness, or lowly position. **lay something on thick** (or **with a trowel**) informal grossly exaggerate or overemphasize something. **lay someone open to** expose someone to the risk of. **lay someone/thing to rest 1** bury a body in a grave. **2** soothe and dispel fear, anxiety, etc.
– PHRASAL VERBS **lay about** beat or attack violently. ➤(**lay about one**) strike out wildly on all sides. **lay something down 1** formulate and enact a rule or principle. **2** begin to construct a ship or railway. **3** build up a deposit of a substance. **4** store wine in a cellar. **5** pay or wager money. **6** informal record a piece of music. **lay something in/up** build up a stock of something in case of need. **lay into** informal attack violently. **lay off** informal give up. **lay someone off** discharge a worker temporarily or permanently because of a shortage of work. **lay something off 1** chiefly Soccer pass the ball to a teammate. **2** (of a bookmaker) insure against a loss resulting from a large bet by placing a similar bet with another bookmaker. **lay something on** chiefly Brit. provide a service or amenity. **lay someone out 1** prepare someone for burial after death. **2** informal knock someone unconscious. **lay something out 1** spread something out to its full extent. **2** construct or arrange buildings or gardens according to a plan. ➤arrange and present material for printing and publication. **3** informal spend a sum of money. **lay someone up** put someone out of action through illness or injury. **lay something up 1** see ***lay something in***. **2** take a ship or other vehicle out of service.
– ORIGIN OE *lecgan*, of Gmc origin; rel. to **LIE**[1].

**lay**[2] ● adj. **1** not ordained into or belonging to the clergy. **2** not having professional qualifications or expert knowledge.
– ORIGIN ME: from OFr. *lai*, via late L. from Gk *laïkos*, from *laos* 'people'.

**lay**[3] ● n. **1** a short lyric or narrative poem meant to be sung. **2** poetic/literary a song.
– ORIGIN ME: from OFr. *lai*, corresp. to Provençal *lais*, of unknown origin.

**lay**[4] past of **LIE**[1].

**layabout** ● n. derogatory a person who habitually does little or no work.

**layaway** ● n. N. Amer. a system of paying a deposit to secure an article for later purchase.

**lay brother** (or **lay sister**) ● n. a person who has taken the vows of a religious order but is not ordained and is employed in ancillary or manual work.

**lay-by** ● n. (pl. **lay-bys**) **1** Brit. an area at the side of a road where vehicles may pull off the road and stop. **2** Austral./NZ & S. African a system of paying a deposit to secure an article for later purchase.

**layer** ● n. **1** a sheet or thickness of material, typically one of several, covering a surface or body. **2** a person or thing that lays something. **3** a shoot fastened down to take root while attached to the parent plant. ● v. [often as adj. **layered**] **1** arrange or cut in a layer or layers. **2** propagate (a plant) as a layer.
– ORIGIN ME (denoting a mason): from **LAY**[1] + **-ER**[1].

**layer cake** ● n. chiefly N. Amer. a cake of two or more layers with jam, cream, or icing between.

**layer-out** ● n. (pl. **layers-out**) dated a person who prepares a corpse for burial.

**layette** ● n. a set of clothing and bedclothes for a newborn child.
– ORIGIN C19: from Fr., dimin. of OFr. *laie* 'drawer'.

**lay figure** ● n. a dummy or jointed manikin of a human body used by artists.
– ORIGIN C18: from obs. *layman*, from Du. *leeman*, from obs. *led*, earlier form of *lid* 'joint'.

**layman** (or **layperson**) ● n. (pl. **-men**) **1** a non-ordained member of a Church. **2** a person without professional or specialized knowledge.

**layoff** ● n. **1** a temporary or permanent discharge of a worker or workers. **2** a period during which someone is unable to take part in a sport or other activity due to injury or illness.

**layout** ● n. **1** the way in which something, especially a page, is laid out. **2** a thing set out in a particular way: *a model railway layout*.

**layover** ● n. chiefly N. Amer. a period of rest or waiting before a further stage in a journey.

**lay reader** ● n. (in the Anglican Church) a layperson licensed to preach and to conduct some services but not to celebrate the Eucharist.

**layshaft** ● n. Brit. a second or intermediate transmission shaft in a machine.

**laywoman** ● n. (pl. **-women**) a non-ordained female member of a Church.

**lazar** /ˈleɪzə, ˈlazə/ ● n. archaic a poor and diseased person, especially a leper.
– ORIGIN ME: from med. L. *lazarus*, with biblical allusion to *Lazarus*, a beggar covered in sores (Luke 16:20).

**lazarette** /ˌlazəˈrɛt/ (also **lazaret**) ● n. **1** the after part of a ship's hold, used for stores. **2** a lazaretto.
– ORIGIN C17: from Fr. *lazaret*, from Ital. *lazaretto* (see **LAZARETTO**).

**lazaretto** /ˌlazəˈrɛtəʊ/ ● n. (pl. **-os**) chiefly historical an isolation hospital for people with infectious diseases, especially leprosy or plague.
– ORIGIN C16: from Ital., dimin. of *lazzaro* 'beggar', from med. L. *lazarus* (see **LAZAR**).

**laze** ● v. spend time in a relaxed, lazy manner. ● n. a spell of lazing.

**lazurite** /ˈlazjʊrʌɪt/ ● n. a bright blue mineral which is the chief constituent of lapis lazuli and consists chiefly of a silicate and sulphate of sodium and aluminium.

**lazy** ● adj. (**-ier**, **-iest**) **1** unwilling to work or use energy. **2** showing a lack of effort or care. **3** (of a river) slow-moving.
– DERIVATIVES **lazily** adv. **laziness** n.
– ORIGIN C16: perh. rel. to Low Ger. *lasich* 'languid, idle'.

**lazybones** ● n. (pl. same) informal a lazy person.

**lazy eye** ● n. an eye with poor vision due to underuse, especially the unused eye in a squint.

**lazy Susan** ● n. a revolving stand or tray on a table, used especially for holding condiments.

**LB** ● abbrev. Liberia (international vehicle registration).

**lb** ● abbrev. **1** pound(s) (in weight). [from L. *libra*.] **2** Cricket leg bye(s).

**LBDR** ● abbrev. Lance Bombardier.

**LBO** ● abbrev. leveraged buyout.

**lbw** ● abbrev. Cricket leg before wicket.

**l.c.** ● abbrev. **1** in the passage cited. [from L. *loco citato*.] **2** letter of credit. **3** lower case.

**LCC** ● abbrev. historical London County Council.

**LCD** ● abbrev. **1** Electronics & Computing liquid crystal display. **2** Mathematics lowest (or least) common denominator.

**LCM** ● abbrev. Mathematics lowest (or least) common multiple.

**LCPL** ● abbrev. Lance Corporal.

**LD** ● abbrev. lethal dose (of a toxic compound, drug, or pathogen).

**Ld** ● abbrev. Lord.

**LDC** ● abbrev. less-developed country.

**Ldg** ● abbrev. Leading (in navy ranks).

**LDL** ● abbrev. Biochemistry low-density lipoprotein.

**l-dopa** ● n. Biochemistry see **DOPA**.

**L-driver** ● n. Brit. a learner driver.

**LDS** ● abbrev. **1** Latter-Day Saints. **2** Licentiate in Dental Surgery.

**LE** ● abbrev. language engineering.

**-le**[1] ● suffix **1** forming names of appliances or instruments: *bridle*. **2** forming names of animals and plants: *beetle*.
– ORIGIN OE, of Gmc origin.

**-le**[2] (also **-el**) ● suffix forming nouns having or originally having a diminutive sense: *mantle*.
– ORIGIN ME *-el*, *-elle*, partly from OE and partly from OFr. (based on L. forms).

**-le**[3] ● suffix (forming adjectives from an original verb) apt to; liable to: *brittle*.
– ORIGIN ME: from earlier *-el*, of Gmc origin.

**-le**[4] ● suffix forming verbs, chiefly expressing repeated action or movement (as in *babble*, *dazzle*), or having diminutive sense (as in *nestle*).
– ORIGIN OE *-lian*, of Gmc origin.

**LEA** ● abbrev. Local Education Authority.

**lea** ● n. poetic/literary an open area of grassy or arable land.
– ORIGIN OE *lēa(h)*, of Gmc origin.

**leach** ● v. remove (a soluble substance) from soil or other material by the action of percolating liquid, especially rainwater.
– ORIGIN OE *leccan* 'to water', of W. Gmc origin.

**leachate** ● n. technical water that has percolated through a solid and leached out some of the constituents.

**lead**[1] /liːd/ ● v. (past and past part. **led** /lɛd/) **1** cause (a person or animal) to go with one by drawing them along. ➤show (someone) the way to a destination by preceding or accompanying them. ➤(**lead someone on**) deceive someone into believing that one is attracted to them. **2** (usu. **lead to**) be a route or means of access to a particular place. ➤culminate or result in. ➤(**lead someone to/to do something**) be someone's reason or motive for. ➤(**lead up to**) precede or provide an introduction to. ➤(often **lead (off) with**) begin a report or text with a particular item. **3** be in charge or command of. **4** have the advantage in a race or game. ➤be superior to (a competitor). **5** have or experience (a particular way of life). **6** (**lead with**) Boxing make an attack with (a particular punch or fist). **7** (in card games) play (the first card) in a trick or round of play. ● n. **1** the initiative in an action: *Britain should be taking the environmental lead.* **2** a clue to be followed in the resolution of a problem. **3** (**the lead**) a position of advantage in a contest; first place. ➤an amount by which a competitor is ahead of the others. **4** the chief part in a play or film. ➤[as modifier] playing the chief part in a musical group: *the lead singer.* ➤[as modifier] denoting the principal item in a report or text: *the lead article.* **5** Brit. a strap or cord for restraining and guiding a dog. **6** a wire conveying electric current from a source to an appliance, or connecting two points of a circuit together. **7** the distance advanced by a screw in one turn. **8** (in card games) an act or right of playing first in a trick or round of play. **9** an artificial watercourse leading to a mill. ➤a channel of water in an ice field.
– PHRASES **lead someone astray** cause someone to act or think foolishly or wrongly. **lead someone up** (or N. Amer. **down**) **the garden path** informal give someone misleading clues or signals. **lead with one's chin** informal **1** (of a boxer) leave one's chin unprotected. **2** behave or speak incautiously.
– ORIGIN OE *lǣdan*, of Gmc origin; rel. to **LOAD** and **LODE**.

**lead**[2] /lɛd/ ● n. **1** a heavy bluish-grey soft ductile metal, the chemical element of atomic number 82. (Symbol: **Pb**) **2** graphite used as the part of a pencil that makes a mark. **3** Printing a blank space between lines of print (originally created by a metal strip). **4** Nautical a lump of lead suspended on a line to determine the depth of water. **5** (**leads**) Brit. sheets or strips of lead covering a roof. **6** (**leads**) lead frames holding the glass of a lattice or stained-glass window.
– PHRASES **go down** (or N. Amer. **over**) **like a lead balloon** (of a speech, proposal, or joke) be poorly received.
– ORIGIN OE *lēad*, of W. Gmc origin.

**lead crystal** ● n. another term for **LEAD GLASS**.

**leaded** ● adj. **1** framed, covered, or weighted with lead. **2** (of petrol) containing tetraethyl lead. **3** (of type) having the lines separated by leads.

**leaden** ● adj. **1** dull, heavy, or slow. **2** of the colour of lead; dull grey. **3** archaic made of lead.
– DERIVATIVES **leadenly** adv. **leadenness** n.

**leaden seal** ● n. chiefly historical a seal made of lead, used especially for papal documents.

**leader** ● n. **1** the person who leads, commands, or precedes a group, organization, or country. ➤(also **Leader of the House**) Brit. a member of the government officially responsible for initiating business in Parliament. **2** the principal player in a music group. **3** Brit. a leading article in a newspaper. **4** a short strip of non-functioning material at each end of a reel of film or recording tape for connection to the spool. **5** a length of filament attached to the end of a fishing line to carry the hook or fly. **6** a shoot of a plant at the apex of a stem or main branch. **7** (**leaders**) Printing a series of dots or dashes across the page to guide the eye, especially in tabulated material.
– DERIVATIVES **leaderless** adj. **leadership** n.

**leader board** ● **n.** a scoreboard showing the names and current scores of the leading competitors, especially in a golf match.

**lead-footed** ● **adj.** N. Amer. informal **1** slow; clumsy. **2** tending to drive too quickly.

**lead-free** ● **adj.** (of petrol) without added tetraethyl lead.

**lead glass** ● **n.** glass containing a substantial proportion of lead oxide, making it more refractive.

**lead-in** ● **n.** **1** an introduction or preamble. **2** a wire leading in from outside, especially from an aerial to a receiver or transmitter.

**leading**[1] /'li:dɪŋ/ ● **adj.** most important or in first place.

**leading**[2] /'lɛdɪŋ/ ● **n.** the amount of blank space between lines of print.

**leading aircraftman** (or **leading aircraftwoman**) ● **n.** a rank in the RAF above aircraftman (or aircraftwoman) and below senior aircraftman (or senior aircraftwoman).

**leading article** ● **n.** Brit. a newspaper article giving the editorial opinion.

**leading counsel** ● **n.** the senior barrister of the team which represents either party in a legal case.

**leading edge** ● **n.** **1** Aeronautics the foremost edge of an aerofoil, especially a wing or propeller blade. **2** the forefront or vanguard, especially of technological development. **3** Electronics the part of a pulse in which the amplitude increases.

**leading light** ● **n.** a person who is prominent or influential in a particular field or organization.

**leading man** (or **leading lady**) ● **n.** the actor playing the principal part in a play, film, or television show.

**leading note** ● **n.** Music another term for **SUBTONIC**.

**leading question** ● **n.** a question that prompts or encourages the answer wanted.

**leading rein** ● **n.** a rein used to lead a horse along.

**leading seaman** ● **n.** a rank in the Royal Navy, above able seaman and below petty officer.

**leading tone** ● **n.** Music North American term for **SUBTONIC**.

**lead tetraethyl** ● **n.** Chemistry another term for **TETRAETHYL LEAD**.

**lead time** ● **n.** the time between the initiation and completion of a production process.

**lead-up** ● **n.** an event or sequence that leads up to something else.

**leadwort** /'lɛdwəːt/ ● **n.** another term for **PLUMBAGO** (in sense 2).

**leaf** ● **n.** (pl. **leaves**) **1** a flattened structure of a plant, typically green and blade-like, in which photosynthesis and transpiration mainly take place. ➤(often in phr. **in/into leaf**) the state of having leaves. **2** a single thickness of paper, especially in a book. **3** gold, silver, or other metal in the form of very thin foil. **4** the part of a door, shutter, or table that is hinged or may be inserted. ● **v.** **1** (of a plant) put out new leaves. **2** (**leaf through**) turn over (pages or papers), reading them quickly or casually.
– PHRASES **turn over a new leaf** start to act or behave in a better way.
– DERIVATIVES **leafage** n. **-leafed** adj. **leafless** adj. **leaflike** adj.
– ORIGIN OE *lēaf*, of Gmc origin.

**leaf beetle** ● **n.** a small beetle of a large group that are typically metallic in appearance and include some serious crop pests. [Family Chrysomelidae.]

**leafcutter ant** ● **n.** a tropical ant which cuts pieces from leaves and uses them to cultivate fungi for food. [Genus *Atta*.]

**leafcutter bee** ● **n.** a solitary bee which cuts pieces from leaves and uses them to construct cells in its nest. [Genus *Megachile*.]

**leaf fat** ● **n.** dense fat occurring in layers around the kidneys of some animals, especially pigs.

**leaf green** ● **n.** a bright, deep green colour.

**leafhopper** ● **n.** a small plant bug which leaps when disturbed. [Family Cicadellidae.]

**leaf insect** ● **n.** a large slow-moving tropical insect with a flattened leaf-like body. [Family Phylliidae.]

**leaflet** ● **n.** **1** a printed sheet of paper containing information or advertising and usually distributed free. **2** a small leaf, especially a component of a compound leaf. ● **v.** (**leafleted**, **leafleting**) distribute leaflets to.

**leaf miner** ● **n.** a small fly, moth, or sawfly whose larvae burrow between the two surfaces of a leaf.

**leaf monkey** ● **n.** a leaf-eating Asian monkey related to the langurs. [Genus *Presbytis*: several species.]

**leaf mould** ● **n.** **1** soil consisting chiefly of decayed leaves. **2** a fungal disease of tomatoes in which mould develops on the leaves.

**leaf roll** ● **n.** a virus disease of potatoes marked by upward curling of the leaves.

**leaf roller** ● **n.** a moth or other insect whose larvae roll up the leaves of plants which they feed upon.

**leaf spot** ● **n.** a fungal, bacterial, or viral plant disease which causes leaves to develop discoloured spots.

**leaf spring** ● **n.** a spring made of a number of strips of metal curved slightly upwards and clamped together one above the other.

**leaf warbler** ● **n.** a slender, typically greenish warbler of a group including the willow warbler and chiffchaff. [Genus *Phylloscopus*.]

**leafy** ● **adj.** (**-ier**, **-iest**) having many leaves or much foliage.
– DERIVATIVES **leafiness** n.

**league**[1] ● **n.** **1** a collection of people, countries, or groups that combine for mutual protection or cooperation. **2** a group of sports clubs which play each other over a period for a championship. **3** a class or category of quality or excellence: *the two men were not in the same league.* ● **v.** (**leagues**, **leagued**, **leaguing**) join in a league or alliance.
– PHRASES **in league** conspiring with another or others.
– ORIGIN ME: via Fr. from Ital. *lega*, from *legare* 'to bind', from L. *ligare*.

**league**[2] ● **n.** a former measure of distance by land, usually about three miles.
– ORIGIN ME: from late L. *leuga*, *leuca*, late Gk *leugē*, or from Provençal *lega* (mod. Fr. *lieue*).

**leaguer**[1] ● **n.** chiefly N. Amer. a member of a particular league, especially a sports player.

**leaguer**[2] ● **n.** & **v.** variant of **LAAGER**.

**league table** ● **n.** Brit. a list of the competitors in a league ranked according to performance. ➤a comparison of achievement or merit in a competitive area.

**leak** ● **v.** **1** (of a container or covering) accidentally lose or admit contents through a hole or crack. ➤(of liquid, gas, etc.) pass in or out through a hole or crack in such a way. **2** (of secret information) become known. ➤intentionally disclose (secret information). ● **n.** **1** a hole in a container or covering through which contents leak. ➤an instance of leaking in such a way. **2** an intentional disclosure of secret information.
– PHRASES **have** (or **take**) **a leak** informal urinate.
– DERIVATIVES **leakage** n. **leaker** n. **leakiness** n. **leaky** adj.
– ORIGIN ME: prob. of Low Ger. or Du. origin and rel. to **LACK**.

**leal** /li:l/ ● **adj.** Scottish archaic loyal and honest.
– ORIGIN ME: from OFr. *leel*, earlier form of *loial* (see **LOYAL**).

**lean**[1] ● **v.** (past and past part. **leaned** or chiefly Brit. **leant**) **1** be in or move into a sloping position. ➤(**lean against/on**) incline from the perpendicular and rest against. **2** (**lean on**) rely on or derive support from. **3** (**lean on**) informal put pressure on (someone) to act in a certain way. **4** (**lean to/towards**) incline or be partial to (a view or position). ➤[as noun **leaning**] a tendency or partiality. ● **n.** a deviation from the perpendicular; an inclination.
– ORIGIN OE *hleonian*, *hlinian*, of Gmc origin.

**lean**[2] ● **adj.** **1** (of a person) thin, especially healthily so. ➤(of meat) containing little fat. ➤informal (of an industry or company) efficient and with no wastage. **2** offering little reward, substance, or nourishment: *the lean years.* **3** (of a vaporized fuel mixture) having a high proportion of air. ● **n.** the lean part of meat.

– DERIVATIVES **leanly** adv. **leanness** n.
– ORIGIN OE *hlǣne*, of Gmc origin.

**lean-burn** • adj. (of an internal-combustion engine) designed to run on a lean mixture to reduce pollution.

**lean-to** • n. (pl. **-os**) a building sharing a wall with a larger building and having a roof that leans against that wall.

**leap** • v. (past or past part. **leaped** or **leapt**) **1** jump or spring a long way. ➤jump across. **2** move quickly and suddenly. ➤(**leap at**) accept (an opportunity) eagerly. ➤(**leap out**) (especially of writing) be conspicuous; stand out. **3** (of a price or figure) increase dramatically. • n. **1** an instance of leaping; a forceful jump or quick movement. **2** a sudden abrupt change or transition.
– PHRASES **a leap in the dark** a daring step or enterprise with unpredictable consequences. **by** (or **in**) **leaps and bounds** with startlingly rapid progress. **leap to the eye** (especially of writing) be immediately apparent.
– DERIVATIVES **leaper** n.
– ORIGIN OE *hlēapan* (v.), *hlȳp* (n.), of Gmc origin; rel. to LOPE.

**leap day** • n. the intercalary day in a leap year; 29 February.

**leapfrog** • n. a game in which players in turn vault with parted legs over others who are bending down. • v. (**-frogged**, **-frogging**) **1** perform such a vault. **2** surpass or overtake a competitor or obstacle to move into a leading position.

**leap second** • n. a second which is occasionally inserted into the atomic scale of reckoning time in order to bring it into line with solar time.

**leap year** • n. a year, occurring once every four years, which has 366 days including 29 February as an intercalary day.
– ORIGIN ME: prob. from the fact that feast days after February in such a year fell two days later than in the previous year, rather than one day later as in other years, and could be said to have 'leaped' a day.

**learn** • v. (past and past part. **learned** or chiefly Brit. **learnt**) **1** acquire knowledge of or skill in (something) through study or experience or by being taught. ➤commit to memory. ➤become aware of by information or from observation. **2** archaic or dialect teach.
– DERIVATIVES **learnability** n. **learnable** adj. **learner** n.
– ORIGIN OE *leornian*, of W. Gmc origin; rel. to LORE[1].

**learned** /ˈləːnɪd/ • adj. having or characterized by much knowledge acquired by study.
– DERIVATIVES **learnedly** adv. **learnedness** n.

**learned helplessness** • n. Psychiatry a condition characterized by a sense of powerlessness, arising from a traumatic event or persistent failure to succeed.

**learning** • n. knowledge or skills acquired through experience or study or by being taught.

**learning curve** • n. the rate of a person's progress in gaining experience or new skills.

**learning difficulties** • pl. n. difficulties in acquiring knowledge and skills to the normal level expected of those of the same age, especially because of mental handicap or cognitive disorder.

**learning disability** • n. a condition giving rise to learning difficulties, especially when not associated with physical handicap.

**lease** • n. a contract by which one party conveys land, property, services, etc. to another for a specified time. • v. **1** grant (property) on lease; let. **2** take (property) on lease; rent.
– PHRASES **a new lease of** (or N. Amer. **on**) **life** a substantially improved prospect of life or use after rejuvenation or repair.
– DERIVATIVES **leasable** adj.
– ORIGIN ME: from OFr. *lais*, *leis*, from *lesser*, *laissier* 'let, leave', from L. *laxare* 'make loose', from *laxus* 'loose, lax'.

**leaseback** • n. the leasing of a property back to the vendor.

**leasehold** • n. the holding of property by lease. ➤a piece of land or property held by lease.
– DERIVATIVES **leaseholder** n.

**leash** • n. **1** a dog's lead. **2** Falconry a thong or string attached to the jesses of a hawk, used for tying it to a perch or creance. • v. put a leash on (a dog).
– ORIGIN ME: from OFr. *lesse*, *laisse*, from *laissier* in the specific sense 'let run on a slack lead' (see LEASE).

**least** • det. & pron. (usu. **the least**) smallest in amount, extent, or significance. • adj. used in names of very small animals and plants: *least shrew*. • adv. to the smallest extent or degree.
– PHRASES **at least 1** not less than; at the minimum. **2** if nothing else. **3** anyway. **at the least** (or **very least**) **1** not less than; at the minimum. **2** taking the most pessimistic or unfavourable view. **not in the least** not in the smallest degree; not at all. **not least** in particular; notably. **to say the least** using moderate terms; to put it mildly.
– ORIGIN OE *lǣst*, *lǣsest*, of Gmc origin; rel. to LESS.

**least common denominator** • n. another term for LOWEST COMMON DENOMINATOR.

**least common multiple** • n. another term for LOWEST COMMON MULTIPLE.

**least significant bit** • n. Computing the bit in a binary number which is of the lowest numerical value.

**least squares** • n. a method of estimating a quantity or fitting a graph to data so as to minimize the sum of the squares of the differences between the observed values and the estimated values.

**leastways** (also **leastwise**) • adv. dialect or informal at least.

**leat** /liːt/ • n. Brit. an open watercourse conducting water to a mill.
– ORIGIN C16: from OE *-gelǣt* in *wætergelǣt* 'water channel', rel. to *lǣtan* 'to let'.

**leather** • n. **1** a material made from the skin of an animal by tanning or a similar process. **2** a piece of leather as a polishing cloth. **3** (**leathers**) leather clothes worn by a motorcyclist. • v. **1** [usu. as adj. **leathered**] cover with leather. **2** informal beat or thrash.
– ORIGIN OE *lether*, of Gmc origin.

**leatherback turtle** • n. a very large black turtle with a thick leathery shell, living chiefly in tropical seas. [*Dermochelys coriacea*.]

**leathercloth** • n. strong, coated fabric embossed to resemble leather.

**leatherette** • n. imitation leather.

**leatherjacket** • n. **1** Brit. the tough-skinned larva of a large crane fly, living in the soil. **2** a slender fish of American coastal waters, with a greenish back and a bright yellow tail. [*Oligoplites saurus*.] ➤a filefish or triggerfish.

**leathern** • adj. archaic made of leather.

**leatherneck** • n. US informal a marine.
– ORIGIN C19: with allusion to the leather lining inside the collar of a marine's uniform.

**leathery** • adj. having a tough, hard texture like leather.
– DERIVATIVES **leatheriness** n.

**leave[1]** • v. (past and past part. **left**) **1** go away from. ➤depart from permanently: *he left home at 16*. ➤cease attending or working for (an organization, school, etc.). ➤abandon (a spouse or partner). **2** allow or cause to remain. ➤deposit (something) to be collected or attended to. ➤have as (a surviving relative) after one's death. ➤(**leave off**) discontinue (an activity). ➤(**leave something off**) omit to add or put on something. ➤(**leave someone/thing out**) fail to include someone or something. **3** (**be left**) remain to be used or dealt with. **4** cause to be in a particular state or position. ➤let (someone) do or deal with something without offering help or assistance. ➤(**leave something to**) entrust a decision, choice, or action to. **5** bequeath. • n. (in snooker, croquet, and other games) the position in which a player leaves the balls for the next player.
– PHRASES **be left for dead** be abandoned as being almost dead or certain to die. **be left to oneself** be left alone or allowed to do what one wants. **leave someone be** informal refrain from disturbing or interfering with someone. **leave go** informal remove one's hold or grip. **leave hold of**

cease holding. **leave much** (or **a lot**) **to be desired** be highly unsatisfactory.
– DERIVATIVES **leaver** n.
– ORIGIN OE *lǣfan*, of Gmc origin.

**leave**[2] • n. **1** (also **leave of absence**) time when one has permission to be absent from work or duty. **2** (often in phr. **by your leave**) formal permission.
– PHRASES **take one's leave** formal say goodbye. **take leave to do something** formal venture or presume to do something.
– ORIGIN OE *lēaf* 'permission', of W. Gmc origin; rel. to LIEF and LOVE.

**leaved** • adj. having a leaf or leaves of a particular kind or number.

**leaven** /ˈlɛv(ə)n/ • n. **1** a substance, typically yeast, added to dough to make it ferment and rise. ➤dough reserved from an earlier batch in order to start a later one fermenting. **2** a pervasive influence that modifies something or transforms it for the better. • v. **1** [usu. as adj. **leavened**] cause (dough or bread) to ferment and rise by adding leaven. **2** permeate and modify or transform for the better.
– ORIGIN ME: from OFr. *levain*, based on L. *levamen* 'relief' (lit. 'means of raising'), from *levare* 'to lift'.

**leaves** plural form of LEAF.

**leave-taking** • n. an act of saying goodbye.

**leavings** • pl. n. things that have been left as worthless.

**Lebanese** /ˈlɛbəniːz/ • n. (pl. same) a native or inhabitant of Lebanon. • adj. of or relating to Lebanon.

**Lebensraum** /ˈleɪb(ə)nzˌraʊm, German ˈleːbnsˌraʊm/ • n. territory which a state or nation believes is needed for its natural development.
– ORIGIN Ger., lit. 'living space'.

**leccy** /ˈlɛki/ • n. Brit. informal electricity.

**lech** /lɛtʃ/ informal, derogatory • n. **1** a lecher. **2** a lecherous urge or desire. • v. act in a lecherous or lustful manner.

**Le Chatelier's principle** /ˌlə ʃaˈtɛljeɪz/ • n. Chemistry a principle stating that if a constraint is applied to a system in equilibrium, the equilibrium will shift so as to tend to counteract the effect of the constraint.
– ORIGIN C20: named after the Fr. chemist Henry *le Chatelier*.

**lecher** /ˈlɛtʃə/ • n. a lecherous man.
– DERIVATIVES **lechery** n.

**lecherous** • adj. having or showing excessive or offensive sexual desire.
– DERIVATIVES **lecherously** adv. **lecherousness** n.
– ORIGIN ME: from OFr. *lecheros*, from *lecheor*, from *lechier* 'live in debauchery or gluttony', ult. of W. Gmc origin and rel. to LICK.

**lechwe** /ˈlɛːtʃwi/ • n. (pl. same) an antelope with long horns, found in southern Africa and the Sudan. [Genus *Kobus*: two species.]
– ORIGIN C19: from Setswana.

**lecithin** /ˈlɛsɪθɪn/ • n. Biochemistry a substance found in egg yolk and other animal and plant tissues, consisting of phospholipids linked to choline.
– ORIGIN C19: from Gk *lekithos* 'egg yolk' + -IN[1].

**lectern** /ˈlɛkt(ə)n, -təːn/ • n. a tall stand with a sloping top from which a speaker can read while standing up.
– ORIGIN ME: from OFr. *letrun*, from med. L. *lectrum*, from *legere* 'to read'.

**lectin** • n. Biochemistry a protein which binds specifically to a sugar and causes agglutination of particular cell types.
– ORIGIN 1950s: from L. *lect-*, *legere* 'choose' + -IN[1].

**lection** /ˈlɛkʃ(ə)n/ • n. archaic a reading of a text found in a particular copy or edition.
– ORIGIN ME (in the sense 'election'): from L. *lectio(n-)*, from *legere* 'read or choose'.

**lectionary** /ˈlɛkʃ(ə)n(ə)ri/ • n. (pl. **-ies**) a list or book of portions of the Bible appointed to be read at divine service.

**lector** /ˈlɛktɔː/ • n. **1** a reader, especially someone who reads lessons in a church service. **2** (fem. **lectrice** /lɛkˈtriːs/) a person employed in a foreign university to teach in their native language.
– ORIGIN ME: from L., from *lect-*, *legere* 'read, choose'.

**lecture** • n. **1** an educational talk to an audience, especially one of students in a university. **2** a long serious speech, especially one given as a scolding or reprimand. • v. **1** deliver an educational lecture or lectures. **2** talk seriously or reprovingly to.
– ORIGIN ME (in the sense 'reading, a text to read'): from OFr., or from med. L. *lectura*, from L. *lect-*, *legere* 'read, choose'.

**lecturer** • n. a person who gives lectures, especially as a teacher in higher education.

**lectureship** • n. a post as a lecturer.

**lecythus** /ˈlɛsɪθəs/ • n. (pl. **lecythi** /-θʌɪ/) a thin narrow-necked vase or flask from ancient Greece.
– ORIGIN via late L. from Gk *lēkuthos*.

**LED** • abbrev. light-emitting diode, a semiconductor diode which glows when a voltage is applied.

**led** past and past participle of LEAD[1].

**lederhosen** /ˈleɪdəˌhəʊz(ə)n/ • pl. n. leather shorts with H-shaped braces, traditionally worn by men in Alpine regions such as Bavaria.
– ORIGIN from Ger., from *Leder* 'leather' + *Hosen* 'trousers'.

**ledge** • n. **1** a narrow horizontal surface projecting from a wall, cliff, etc. **2** an underwater ridge, especially one of rocks near the seashore. **3** Mining a stratum of metal-bearing rock.
– DERIVATIVES **ledged** adj. **ledgy** adj.
– ORIGIN ME (denoting a strip of wood or other material fixed across a door or gate): perh. from an early form of LAY[1].

**ledger** • n. **1** a book or other collection of financial accounts. **2** a flat stone slab covering a grave. **3** a horizontal scaffolding pole, parallel to the face of the building. **4** a weight used on a fishing line to anchor the bait in a particular place. • v. fish using a ledger.
– ORIGIN ME *legger*, *ligger* (denoting a large bible or breviary), prob. from vars of LAY[1] and LIE[1], influenced by Du. *legger* and *ligger*.

**ledger line** • n. Music variant spelling of LEGER LINE.

**lee** • n. **1** shelter from wind or weather given by an object. **2** (also **lee side**) the sheltered side; the side away from the wind. Contrasted with WEATHER.
– PHRASES **lee ho** Sailing a helmsman's command or warning indicating the moment of going about.
– ORIGIN OE *hlēo*, *hlēow* 'shelter', of Gmc origin; prob. rel. to *luke-* in LUKEWARM.

**leeboard** • n. a plank frame fixed to the side of a flat-bottomed boat and let down into the water to reduce drifting to the leeward side.

**leech**[1] • n. **1** a parasitic or predatory annelid worm with suckers at both ends, examples of which were formerly used in medicine for bloodletting. [*Hirudo medicinalis* (**medicinal leech**) and other species, class Hirudinea.] **2** a person who extorts profit from or lives off others. • v. (**leech on/off**) habitually exploit or rely on.
– PHRASES **like a leech** persistently or clingingly.
– ORIGIN OE *lǣce*, *lȳce*.

**leech**[2] • n. archaic a doctor or healer.
– DERIVATIVES **leechcraft** n.
– ORIGIN OE *lǣce*, of Gmc origin.

**leech**[3] • n. Sailing the after or leeward edge of a fore-and-aft sail, the leeward edge of a spinnaker, or a vertical edge of a square sail.
– ORIGIN C15: prob. of Scand. origin and rel. to Swed. *lik* and Dan. *lig*.

**lee helm** • n. Sailing the tendency of a ship to turn its bow to the leeward side.

**leek** • n. a plant related to the onion, with flat overlapping leaves forming an elongated cylindrical bulb which together with the leaf bases is eaten as a vegetable. [*Allium porrum*.]
– ORIGIN OE *lēac*, of Gmc origin.

**leer** • v. look or gaze in a lascivious or unpleasant way. • n. a lascivious or unpleasant look.
– DERIVATIVES **leering** adj. **leeringly** adv.
– ORIGIN C16 (in the general sense 'look sideways or askance'): perh. from obs. *leer* 'cheek', from OE *hlēor*.

**leery** ● **adj.** (**-ier**, **-iest**) cautious or wary due to realistic suspicions.
– DERIVATIVES **leeriness** n.
– ORIGIN C17: from obs. *leer* 'looking askance', from **LEER** + **-Y**[1].

**lees** ● **pl. n.** the sediment of wine in the barrel; dregs.
– ORIGIN ME: pl. of obs. *lee* in the same sense, from OFr. *lie*, from med. L. *liae* (pl.), of Gaulish origin.

**lee shore** ● **n.** a shore lying on the leeward side of a ship (and on to which the ship could be blown).

**leet**[1] (also **court leet**) ● **n.** historical **1** a yearly or half-yearly court of record held by the lords of certain manors. **2** the jurisdiction of such a court.
– ORIGIN ME: from Anglo-Norman Fr. *lete* or Anglo-Latin *leta*, of unknown origin.

**leet**[2] ● **n.** Scottish a list of candidates selected for a post.
– ORIGIN ME: prob. from OFr. *lit(t)e*, var. of *liste* 'list'.

**leeward** /'li:wəd, 'lu:əd/ ● **adj. & adv.** on or towards the side sheltered from the wind or towards which the wind is blowing; downwind. Contrasted with **WINDWARD**. ● **n.** the leeward side.

**lee wave** ● **n.** a standing wave generated on the sheltered side of a mountain by an air current.

**leeway** ● **n.** **1** the amount of freedom to move or act that is available. ➤margin of safety. **2** the sideways drift of a ship to leeward of the desired course.
– PHRASES **make up (the) leeway** Brit. struggle out of a bad position, especially by recovering lost time.

**left**[1] ● **adj.** **1** on, towards, or relating to the side of a human body or of a thing which is to the west when the person or thing is facing north. **2** of or relating to a left-wing person or group. ● **adv.** on or to the left side. ● **n.** **1** (**the left**) the left-hand part, side, or direction. ➤a left turn. ➤a person's left fist, or a blow given with it. **2** (often **the Left**) [treated as sing. or pl.] a group or party favouring radical, reforming, or socialist views.
– PHRASES **have two left feet** be clumsy or awkward. **left, right, and centre** (also **left and right** or **right and left**) on all sides.
– DERIVATIVES **leftish** adj. **leftmost** adj. **leftward** adj. & adv. **leftwards** adv.
– ORIGIN OE *lyft*, *left* 'weak', of W. Gmc origin.

**left**[2] past and past participle of **LEAVE**[1].

**left back** ● **n.** a defender in soccer or field hockey who plays primarily on the left of the field.

**left bank** ● **n.** the bank of a river on the left as one faces downstream.

**left brain** ● **n.** the left-hand side of the human brain, which is believed to be associated with linear and analytical thought.

**left field** ● **n.** Baseball the part of the outfield to the left of the batter when facing the pitcher. ● **adj.** (**left-field**) unconventional or unusual.
– DERIVATIVES **left fielder** n.

**left hand** ● **n.** **1** the hand of a person's left side. **2** the region or direction on the left side. ● **adj.** **1** on or towards the left side. **2** done with or using the left hand.

**left-hand drive** ● **n.** a motor-vehicle steering system with the steering wheel and other controls fitted on the left side, for use in countries where vehicles drive on the right-hand side of the road.

**left-handed** ● **adj.** **1** using or done with the left hand. **2** turning to the left; towards the left. ➤(of a screw) advanced by turning anticlockwise. ➤Zoology sinistral. **3** perverse or ambiguous.
– DERIVATIVES **left-handedly** adv. **left-handedness** n.

**left-hander** ● **n.** **1** a left-handed person. **2** a blow struck with a person's left hand.

**leftie** ● **n.** variant spelling of **LEFTY**.

**leftism** ● **n.** the political views or policies of the left.
– DERIVATIVES **leftist** n. & adj.

**left luggage** ● **n.** Brit. travellers' luggage left in temporary storage at a railway station, bus station, or airport.

**leftover** ● **n.** something, especially food, remaining after the rest has been used. ● **adj.** remaining; surplus.

**left wing** ● **n.** **1** the radical, reforming, or socialist section of a political party or system. [with ref. to the National Assembly in France (1789–91), where the nobles sat to the president's right and the commons to the left.] **2** the left side of a sports team on the field or of an army.
– DERIVATIVES **left-winger** n.

**lefty** (also **leftie**) ● **n.** (pl. **-ies**) informal **1** a left-wing person. **2** a left-handed person.

**leg** ● **n.** **1** each of the limbs on which a person or animal walks and stands. ➤a leg of an animal or bird as food. ➤a part of a garment covering a leg or part of a leg. ➤(**legs**) informal sustained momentum or success. **2** a long, thin support or prop, especially of a chair or table. **3** a section or stage of a journey or process. ➤(in sport) each of two or more games or stages constituting a round or match. ➤Sailing a run made on a single tack. **4** a branch of a forked object. **5** (also **leg side**) Cricket the half of the field away from which the batsman's feet are pointed when standing to receive the ball. The opposite of **OFF**. **6** archaic an obeisance made by drawing back one leg and bending it while keeping the front leg straight. ● **v.** (**legged**, **legging**) **1** (**leg it**) informal travel by foot; walk. ➤run away. **2** chiefly historical propel (a boat) through a canal tunnel by pushing with one's legs against the tunnel roof or sides.
– PHRASES **feel** (or **find**) **one's legs** become able to stand or walk. **get one's leg over** vulgar slang (of a man) have sexual intercourse. **have the legs of** Brit. be able to go faster or further than (a rival). **not have a leg to stand on** have no sound justification for one's arguments or actions. **on one's last legs** near the end of life, usefulness, or existence.
– DERIVATIVES **-legged** adj. **-legger** n.
– ORIGIN ME: from ON *leggr*, of Gmc origin.

**legacy** ● **n.** (pl. **-ies**) **1** an amount of money or property left to someone in a will. **2** something handed down by a predecessor. ● **adj.** Computing denoting software or hardware that has been superseded but is difficult to replace because of its wide use.
– ORIGIN ME (also denoting the function or office of a legate): from OFr. *legacie*, from med. L. *legatia* 'legateship', from *legatus* (see **LEGATE**).

**legal** ● **adj.** **1** of, based on, or required by the law. **2** permitted by law.
– DERIVATIVES **legally** adv.
– ORIGIN ME: from Fr., or from L. *legalis*, from *lex*, *leg-* 'law'.

**legal aid** ● **n.** payment from public funds allowed, in cases of need, to help pay for legal advice or proceedings.

**legal clinic** ● **n.** N. Amer. a place where one can obtain legal advice and assistance, paid for by legal aid.

**legal eagle** (also **legal beagle**) ● **n.** informal a lawyer.

**legalese** /ˌli:gə'li:z/ ● **n.** informal the formal and technical language of legal documents.

**legal fiction** ● **n.** an assumption of the truth of something, though unproven or unfounded, for legal purposes.

**legal holiday** ● **n.** N. Amer. a public holiday established by law.

**legalism** ● **n.** **1** excessive adherence to the details of law. **2** Theology adherence to moral law rather than personal religious faith.
– DERIVATIVES **legalist** n. & adj. **legalistic** adj. **legalistically** adv.

**legality** ● **n.** (pl. **-ies**) **1** the quality or state of being legal. **2** (**legalities**) obligations imposed by law.

**legalize** (also **-ise**) ● **v.** make legal.
– DERIVATIVES **legalization** n.

**legal person** ● **n.** Law an individual, company, or other entity which has legal rights and is subject to obligations.

**legal separation** ● **n.** **1** an arrangement by which a husband or wife remain married but live apart, following a court order. **2** an arrangement by which a child lives apart from a natural parent and with another natural or foster-parent of their choice, following a court decree.

**legal tender** ● **n.** coins or banknotes that must be accepted if offered in payment of a debt.

**legate** /'lɛgət/ ● **n.** **1** a member of the clergy who represents the Pope. **2** a general or governor of an ancient Roman province, or their deputy. **3** archaic an ambassador

or messenger.
– DERIVATIVES **legateship** n. **legatine** /-tɪn/ adj.
– ORIGIN OE, from OFr. *legat*, from L. *legatus*, *legare* 'depute, delegate, bequeath'.

**legate a latere** /ˌlɛgət ɑː ˈlatəreɪ, -ri/ • **n.** a papal legate of the highest class, with full powers.
– ORIGIN C16: from **LEGATE** + L. *a latere* 'by a third party'.

**legatee** /ˌlɛgəˈtiː/ • **n.** a person who receives a legacy.
– ORIGIN C17: from *legate* 'bequeath' (from L. *legare* 'delegate, bequeath') + **-EE**.

**legation** • **n. 1** a diplomatic mission. **2** the official residence of a diplomat. **3** archaic the sending of a papal legate on a mission. ➤ a legateship.
– ORIGIN ME: from L. *legatio(n-)*, from *legare* 'depute, delegate, bequeath'.

**legato** /lɪˈgɑːtəʊ/ • **adv. & adj.** Music in a smooth, flowing manner.
– ORIGIN Ital., lit. 'bound'.

**legator** /lɪˈgeɪtə/ • **n.** a person leaving a legacy.

**leg before wicket** (also **leg before**) • **adv. & adj.** Cricket (of a batsman) adjudged to be out through obstructing the ball with the leg (or other part of the body) when the ball would otherwise have hit the wicket.

**leg break** • **n.** Cricket a ball which spins from the leg side towards the off side after pitching.

**leg bye** • **n.** Cricket a run scored from a ball that has touched the batsman's body without touching the bat, the batsman having made an attempt to hit it.

**leg-cutter** • **n.** Cricket a fast leg break.

**legend** • **n. 1** a traditional story popularly regarded as historical but which is not authenticated. **2** an extremely famous or notorious person: *a screen legend*. **3** an inscription, caption, or key. **4** historical the written account of a saint's life. • **adj.** very well known.
– ORIGIN ME: from OFr. *legende*, from med. L. *legenda* 'things to be read', from L. *legere* 'read'.

**legendary** • **adj. 1** of, described in, or based on legends. **2** remarkable enough to be famous; very well known.
– DERIVATIVES **legendarily** adv.
– ORIGIN C16 (as n. denoting a collection of lives of saints): from med. L. *legendarius*, from *legenda* (see **LEGEND**).

**legerdemain** /ˌlɛdʒədɪˈmeɪn/ • **n. 1** skilful use of one's hands when performing conjuring tricks. **2** deception; trickery.
– ORIGIN ME: from Fr. *léger de main* 'dexterous', lit. 'light of hand'.

**leger line** /ˈlɛdʒə/ (also **ledger line**) • **n.** Music a short line added for notes above or below the range of a stave.
– ORIGIN C19: *leger*, var. of **LEDGER**.

**leggings** • **pl. n. 1** a woman's tight-fitting stretchy garment covering the legs, hips, and bottom. **2** stout protective overgarments for the legs.

**leggy** • **adj.** (**-ier, -iest**) **1** long-legged. ➤ (of a woman) having attractively long legs. **2** (of a plant) having a long and straggly stem or stems.
– DERIVATIVES **legginess** n.

**leghorn** /lɛˈgɔːn, ˈlɛghɔːn/ • **n. 1** fine plaited straw. ➤ a hat made of this. **2** (**Leghorn**) a chicken of a small hardy breed.
– ORIGIN C18: anglicized from the Ital. name *Leghorno* (now *Livorno*), from where the straw and fowls were imported.

**legible** • **adj.** (of handwriting or print) clear enough to read.
– DERIVATIVES **legibility** n. **legibly** adv.
– ORIGIN ME: from late L. *legibilis*, from *legere* 'to read'.

**legion** • **n. 1** a division of 3,000–6,000 men in the ancient Roman army. **2** (**the Legion**) the Foreign Legion. **3** a national association of former servicemen and servicewomen, such as the Royal British Legion. **2** (**a legion/legions of**) a vast number of people or things. • **adj.** great in number: *her fans are legion*.
– DERIVATIVES **legionary** adj. & n. **legioned** adj.
– ORIGIN ME: via OFr. from L. *legio(n-)*, from *legere* 'choose, levy'.

**legionella** /ˌliːdʒəˈnɛlə/ • **n.** (pl. **legionellae** /-liː/) the bacterium responsible for legionnaires' disease. [*Legionella pneumophila*.]
– ORIGIN C20: mod. L., from **LEGION** + the dimin. suffix *-ella*.

**legionnaire** /ˌliːdʒəˈnɛː/ • **n.** a member of a legion.

**legionnaires' disease** • **n.** a form of bacterial pneumonia spread chiefly in water droplets through air conditioning and similar systems.
– ORIGIN 1976 (identified after an outbreak at an American Legion meeting).

**leg iron** • **n.** a metal band or chain placed around a prisoner's ankle as a restraint.

**legislate** /ˈlɛdʒɪsleɪt/ • **v. 1** make or enact laws. **2** effect by making or enacting laws.
– ORIGIN C18: back-form. from **LEGISLATION**.

**legislation** • **n.** laws, considered collectively.
– ORIGIN C17: from late L. *legis latio(n-)*, lit. 'proposing of a law'.

**legislative** /ˈlɛdʒɪslətɪv/ • **adj. 1** of or having the power to make laws. **2** of or relating to laws or a legislature.
– DERIVATIVES **legislatively** adv.

**legislator** • **n.** a person who makes laws; a member of a legislative body.
– ORIGIN C15: from L. *legis lator*, lit. 'proposer of a law', from *lex* 'law' and *lator* 'proposer, mover'.

**legislature** /ˈlɛdʒɪslətʃə/ • **n.** the legislative body of a state.

**legit** /lɪˈdʒɪt/ • **adj.** informal legitimate.

**legitimate** • **adj.** /lɪˈdʒɪtɪmət/ **1** conforming to the law or to rules. **2** able to be defended with logic or justification. **3** (of a child) born of parents lawfully married to each other. **4** (of a sovereign) having a title based on strict hereditary right. • **v.** /lɪˈdʒɪtɪmeɪt/ make legitimate.
– DERIVATIVES **legitimacy** n. **legitimately** adv. **legitimation** n. **legitimatization** (also **-isation**) n. **legitimatize** (also **-ise**) v.
– ORIGIN ME: from med. L. *legitimatus*, *legitimare* 'make legal'.

**legitimism** • **n.** support for the authority of a legitimate sovereign.
– DERIVATIVES **legitimist** n. & adj.

**legitimize** (also **-ise**) • **v.** make legitimate.
– DERIVATIVES **legitimization** n.

**legless** • **adj. 1** having no legs. **2** Brit. informal extremely drunk.

**legman** • **n.** (pl. **-men**) N. Amer. a reporter whose job it is to gather information at source.

**Lego** • **n.** trademark a toy consisting of interlocking plastic building blocks.
– ORIGIN 1950s: from Dan. *leg godt* 'play well'.

**leg-of-mutton sleeve** • **n.** a sleeve which is full on the upper arm but close-fitting on the forearm and wrist.

**legroom** • **n.** space in which a seated person can put their legs.

**leg rope** • **n.** Austral./NZ a noosed rope used to secure an animal by one hind leg.

**leg slip** • **n.** Cricket a fielding position just behind the batsman on the leg side.

**leg spin** • **n.** Cricket bowling of leg breaks.
– DERIVATIVES **leg-spinner** n.

**legume** /ˈlɛgjuːm/ • **n. 1** a leguminous plant grown as a crop. **2** a seed, pod, or other edible part of a leguminous plant, used as food. **3** Botany the long seed pod of a leguminous plant.
– ORIGIN C17: from Fr. *légume*, from L. *legumen*, *legere* 'to pick'.

**leguminous** /lɪˈgjuːmɪnəs/ • **adj.** Botany relating to or denoting plants of the pea family (Leguminosae), typically having seeds in pods, distinctive flowers, and root nodules containing nitrogen-fixing bacteria.
– ORIGIN ME: from med. L. *leguminosus*, from *legumen* (see **LEGUME**).

**leg-up** • **n. 1** an act of helping someone to mount a horse or high object. **2** a boost to improve one's position.

**leg warmers** • **pl. n.** a pair of tubular knitted garments covering the legs from ankle to knee or thigh.

**legwork** • **n.** work that involves tiring or tedious movement from place to place.

**lei**[1] /leɪ, ˈleɪi/ • **n.** a Polynesian garland of flowers.

– ORIGIN from Hawaiian.

**lei**[2] plural form of LEU.

**Leibnizian** /lʌɪbˈnɪtsɪən/ ● **adj.** of or relating to the work of the German philosopher and mathematician Gottfried Leibniz (1646–1716). ● **n.** a follower of Leibniz.

**Leicester** /ˈlɛstə/ ● **n. 1** (also **Red Leicester**) a kind of mild, firm orange-coloured cheese originally made in Leicestershire. **2** (also **Border Leicester**) a sheep of a breed often crossed with other breeds to produce lambs for the meat industry.

**Leics.** ● **abbrev.** Leicestershire.

**leishmania** /liːˈʃmeɪnɪə/ ● **n.** (pl. same or **leishmanias** or **leishmaniae** /-ˈmeɪnɪʌɪ/) a single-celled parasitic protozoan which is transmitted to vertebrates by the bite of sandflies. [Genus *Leishmania*.]
– ORIGIN mod. L., from William B. *Leishman*, Brit. pathologist.

**leishmaniasis** /ˌliːʃməˈnʌɪəsɪs/ ● **n.** a tropical and subtropical disease caused by leishmania and transmitted by the bite of sandflies.

**leister** /ˈliːstə/ ● **n.** a pronged spear used for catching salmon. ● **v.** spear with a leister.
– ORIGIN C16: from ON *ljóstr*, from *ljósta* 'to strike'.

**leisure** /ˈlɛʒə/ ● **n.** time spent in or free for relaxation or enjoyment.
– PHRASES **at leisure 1** not occupied; free. **2** in an unhurried manner. **at one's leisure** at one's convenience. **lady** (or **man** or **gentleman**) **of leisure** a person who does not need to earn money.
– DERIVATIVES **leisured** adj.
– ORIGIN ME: from OFr. *leisir*, based on L. *licere* 'be allowed'.

**leisure centre** (or **complex**) ● **n.** a public building or complex offering facilities for sport and recreation.

**leisurely** ● **adj.** relaxed and unhurried. ● **adv.** without hurry.
– DERIVATIVES **leisureliness** n.

**leisurewear** ● **n.** casual clothes worn for leisure activities.

**leitmotif** /ˈlʌɪtməʊˌtiːf/ (also **leitmotiv**) ● **n.** a recurring theme in a musical or literary composition.
– ORIGIN C19: from Ger. *Leitmotiv*, from *leit-* 'leading' + *Motiv* 'motive'.

**lek**[1] /lɛk/ ● **n.** the basic monetary unit of Albania, equal to 100 qintars.
– ORIGIN from Albanian.

**lek**[2] /lɛk/ ● **n.** a patch of ground used for communal display in the breeding season by the males of certain birds and mammals, especially black grouse.
– DERIVATIVES **lekking** n.
– ORIGIN C19: perh. from Swed. *leka* 'to play'.

**lekker** /ˈlɛkə, ˈlʌkə/ S. African informal ● **adj.** good; pleasant. ● **adv. 1** well. **2** extremely.
– ORIGIN Afrik., from Du., lit. 'delicious'.

**leman** /ˈlɛmən, ˈliː-/ ● **n.** (pl. **lemans**) archaic a lover or sweetheart.
– ORIGIN ME *lēofman*, from *lēof* (see LIEF) + MAN.

**lemma**[1] /ˈlɛmə/ ● **n.** (pl. **lemmas** or **lemmata** /-mətə/) **1** a subsidiary or intermediate theorem in an argument or proof. **2** a heading indicating the subject of a literary composition, annotation, or dictionary entry.
– ORIGIN C16: via L. from Gk *lēmma* 'something assumed'.

**lemma**[2] /ˈlɛmə/ ● **n.** (pl. **lemmas** or **lemmata** /-mətə/) Botany the lower bract of the floret of a grass. Compare with PALEA.
– ORIGIN C18 (denoting the husk or shell of a fruit): from Gk, from *lepein* 'to peel'.

**lemme** ● **contr.** informal let me.

**lemming** ● **n. 1** a short-tailed, thickset Arctic rodent, noted for fluctuating populations and periodic mass migrations. [*Lemmus lemmus* and other species.] **2** a person who unthinkingly joins a mass movement, especially a headlong rush to destruction.
– ORIGIN C18: from Norw. and Dan.; rel. to ON *lómundr*.

**lemon** ● **n. 1** a pale yellow oval citrus fruit with thick skin and fragrant, acidic juice. ➤a drink made from or flavoured with lemon juice. **2** the evergreen citrus tree which produces this fruit. [*Citrus limon*.] **3** a pale yellow colour. **4** informal a feeble or unsatisfactory person or thing.
– DERIVATIVES **lemony** adj.
– ORIGIN ME: via OFr. *limon* from Arab. *līmūn*; cf. LIME[2].

**lemonade** ● **n.** a sweetened drink made from lemon juice or lemon flavouring and still or carbonated water.
– ORIGIN C17: from Fr. *limonade*, from *limon* 'lemon'.

**lemon balm** ● **n.** a bushy lemon-scented herb of the mint family. [*Melissa officinalis*.]

**lemon curd** (Brit. also **lemon cheese**) ● **n.** a conserve made from lemons, butter, eggs, and sugar.

**lemon grass** ● **n.** a fragrant tropical grass which yields an oil that smells of lemon, used in Asian cooking and in perfumery and medicine. [*Cymbopogon citratus*.]

**lemon sole** ● **n.** a common flatfish of the plaice family. [*Microstomus kitt*.]
– ORIGIN C19: *lemon* from Fr. *limande*.

**lemon thyme** ● **n.** thyme of a hybrid variety with lemon-scented leaves. [*Thymus* × *citriodorus*.]

**lemon verbena** ● **n.** a South American shrub with lemon-scented leaves used as flavouring and to make a sedative tea. [*Aloysia triphylla*.]

**lempira** /lɛmˈpɪərə/ ● **n.** the basic monetary unit of Honduras, equal to 100 centavos.
– ORIGIN named after *Lempira*, a C16 Ind. chieftain who opposed the Sp. conquest of Honduras.

**lemur** /ˈliːmə/ ● **n.** an arboreal primate with a pointed snout and typically a long tail, found only in Madagascar. [Lemuridae and other families: several species.]
– ORIGIN C18: mod. L., from L. *lemures* 'spirits of the dead' (from their spectre-like faces).

**lend** ● **v.** (past and past part. **lent**) **1** grant to (someone) the use of (something) on the understanding that it shall be returned. **2** allow (a person) the use of (a sum of money) under an agreement to pay it back later, typically with interest. **3** contribute or add (a quality) to. **4** (**lend oneself to**) accommodate or adapt oneself to. ➤(**lend itself to**) (of a thing) be suitable for.
– DERIVATIVES **lendable** adj. **lender** n.
– ORIGIN OE *lǣnan*, of Gmc origin; rel. to LOAN[1].

**lending library** ● **n.** a public library from which books may be borrowed and taken away for a limited time.

**length** /lɛŋθ, lɛŋkθ/ ● **n. 1** the measurement or extent of something from end to end; the greater or greatest of two or more dimensions of a body. ➤the length of a horse, boat, etc., as a measure of the lead in a race. **2** the amount of time occupied by something. **3** the quality of being long. **4** the full distance that a thing extends for: *the muscles running the length of my spine*. **5** the extent of a garment in a vertical direction when worn. **6** Prosody & Phonetics the metrical quantity or duration of a vowel or syllable. **7** (in bridge or whist) the number of cards of a suit held in one's hand. **8** a stretch or piece of something. **9** a degree or extreme to which a course of action is taken. **10** Cricket the distance from the batsman at which a well-bowled ball pitches.
– PHRASES **at length 1** in detail; fully. **2** after a long time. **the length and breadth of** the whole extent of.
– ORIGIN OE *lengthu*, of Gmc origin; rel. to LONG[1].

**-length** ● **comb. form 1** reaching up or down to the place specified: *knee-length*. **2** of the size, duration, or extent specified: *full-length*.

**lengthen** ● **v.** make or become longer.

**lengthman** ● **n.** (pl. **-men**) Brit. archaic a person employed to maintain a section of road or railway.

**lengthways** ● **adv.** in a direction parallel with a thing's length.

**lengthwise** ● **adv.** lengthways. ● **adj.** lying or moving lengthways.

**lengthy** ● **adj.** (**-ier**, **-iest**) of considerable or unusual duration.
– DERIVATIVES **lengthily** adv. **lengthiness** n.

**lenient** /ˈliːnɪənt/ ● **adj. 1** merciful or tolerant. **2** archaic emollient.
– DERIVATIVES **lenience** n. **leniency** n. **leniently** adv.
– ORIGIN C17: from L. *lenient-*, *lenire* 'soothe', from *lenis* 'mild, gentle'.

**Leninism** • n. Marxism as interpreted and applied by the Soviet premier Lenin (1870–1924).
– DERIVATIVES **Leninist** n. & adj. **Leninite** n. & adj.

**lenis** /ˈlɛnɪs, ˈleɪnɪs, ˈliːnɪs/ • adj. Phonetics (of a consonant) weakly articulated, especially the less or least strongly articulated of two or more similar consonants. The opposite of **FORTIS**.
– ORIGIN C20: from L., lit. 'mild, gentle'.

**lenition** /lɪˈnɪʃ(ə)n/ • n. (in Celtic languages) the process or result of palatalizing a consonant.
– ORIGIN C20: from L. *lenis* 'soft' + **-ITION**, suggested by Ger. *Lenierung*.

**lenitive** /ˈlɛnɪtɪv/ Medicine, archaic • adj. (of a medicine) laxative. • n. a medicine of this type.
– ORIGIN ME: from med. L. *lenitivus*, from *lenit-*, *lenire* 'soften'.

**lenity** /ˈlɛnɪti/ • n. poetic/literary kindness; gentleness.
– ORIGIN ME: from OFr. *lenite*, or from L. *lenitas*, from *lenis* 'gentle'.

**leno** /ˈliːnəʊ/ • n. (pl. **-os**) an openwork fabric with the warp threads twisted in pairs before weaving.
– ORIGIN C18: from Fr. *linon*, from *lin* 'flax'; cf. **LINEN**.

**lens** • n. **1** a piece of glass or other transparent material with one or both sides curved for concentrating or dispersing light rays. ➤ Anatomy the transparent elastic structure behind the iris by which light is focused on to the retina of the eye. ➤ short for **CONTACT LENS**. **2** the light-gathering device of a camera, containing a group of compound lenses. **3** Physics an object or device which focuses or otherwise modifies a beam of radiation, sound, electrons, etc.
– DERIVATIVES **lensed** adj. **lensless** adj.
– ORIGIN C17: from L., 'lentil' (because of the similarity in shape).

**lensman** • n. (pl. **-men**) a professional photographer or cameraman.

**Lent** • n. (in the Christian Church) the period preceding Easter (in the Western Church from Ash Wednesday to Holy Saturday), which is devoted to fasting, abstinence, and penitence in commemoration of Christ's fasting in the wilderness.
– ORIGIN ME: abbrev. of **LENTEN**.

**lent** past and past participle of **LEND**.

**-lent** • suffix forming adjectives such as *pestilent*.
– ORIGIN from L. *-lentus*.

**Lenten** • adj. of, in, or appropriate to Lent.
– ORIGIN OE *lencten* 'spring, Lent', of Gmc origin, rel. to **LONG**[1] (perh. with ref. to the lengthening of the day in spring); now interpreted as being from **LENT** + **-EN**[2].

**Lenten rose** • n. a hellebore that is cultivated for its flowers, which appear in late winter or early spring. [*Helleborus orientalis*.]

**lentic** /ˈlɛntɪk/ • adj. Ecology inhabiting or situated in still fresh water. Compare with **LOTIC**.
– ORIGIN C20: from L. *lentus* 'calm, slow' + **-IC**.

**lenticel** /ˈlɛntɪsɛl/ • n. Botany one of many raised pores in the stem of a woody plant allowing gas exchange between the atmosphere and the internal tissues.
– ORIGIN C19: from mod. L. *lenticella*, dimin. of L. *lens*, *lent-* 'lentil'.

**lenticular** /lɛnˈtɪkjʊlə/ • adj. **1** shaped like a lentil; biconvex. **2** of or relating to the lens of the eye.
– ORIGIN ME: from L. *lenticularis*, from *lenticula*, dimin. of *lens*, *lent-* 'lentil'.

**lentiform nucleus** • n. Anatomy the lower of the two grey nuclei of the corpus striatum.
– ORIGIN C18: *lentiform* from L. *lens*, *lent-* 'lentil' + **-IFORM**.

**lentigo** /lɛnˈtʌɪɡəʊ/ • n. (pl. **lentigines** /-ˈtɪdʒɪniːz/) a condition marked by small brown patches on the skin.
– ORIGIN ME: from L., from *lens*, *lent-* 'lentil'.

**lentil** • n. **1** a high-protein pulse which is dried and then soaked and cooked prior to eating. **2** the plant which yields this pulse, native to the Mediterranean and Africa. [*Lens culinaris*.]
– ORIGIN ME: from OFr. *lentille*, from L. *lenticula*, dimin. of *lens*, *lent-* 'lentil'.

**lentisc** /lɛnˈtɪsk/ • n. the mastic tree.
– ORIGIN ME: from L. *lentiscus*.

**lentivirus** /ˈlɛntɪˌvʌɪrəs/ • n. Medicine any of a group of retroviruses producing illnesses characterized by a delay in the onset of symptoms after infection.
– ORIGIN 1970s: from L. *lentus* 'slow' + **VIRUS**.

**lent lily** • n. Brit. the European wild daffodil, which typically has pale creamy-white outer petals. [*Narcissus pseudonarcissus*.]

**lento** /ˈlɛntəʊ/ • adv. & adj. Music slow or slowly.
– ORIGIN from Ital.

**lentoid** /ˈlɛntɔɪd/ • adj. another term for **LENTICULAR** (in sense 1).
– ORIGIN C19: from L. *lens*, *lent-* 'lentil' + **-OID**.

**Leo** • n. **1** Astronomy a large constellation (the Lion), said to represent the lion slain by Hercules. **2** Astrology the fifth sign of the zodiac, which the sun enters about 23 July.
– DERIVATIVES **Leonian** n. & adj.
– ORIGIN from L.

**Leonberg** /ˈliːənbəːɡ/ (also **Leonberger**) • n. a large dog of a breed produced by crossing a St Bernard and a Newfoundland.
– ORIGIN C20: named after a town in SW Germany.

**leone** /liːˈəʊn/ • n. the basic monetary unit of Sierra Leone, equal to 100 cents.

**Leonine** /ˈliːənʌɪn/ • adj. **1** of or relating to one of the popes named Leo, especially the part of Rome fortified by Leo IV. **2** Prosody (of medieval Latin verse) in hexameter or elegiac metre with internal rhyme. ➤ (of English verse) with internal rhyme. • n. (**Leonines**) Prosody Leonine verse.
– ORIGIN ME: from the name *Leo*, from L. *leo* 'lion'.

**leonine** /ˈliːənʌɪn/ • adj. of or resembling a lion or lions.
– ORIGIN ME: from OFr., or from L. *leoninus*, from *leo*, *leon-* 'lion'.

**leopard** • n. (fem. **leopardess**) a large solitary cat that has a fawn or brown coat with black spots, found in the forests of Africa and southern Asia. [*Panthera pardus*.] ➤ Heraldry the spotted leopard as a heraldic device; also, a lion passant guardant as in the arms of England. ➤ [as modifier] spotted like a leopard.
– ORIGIN ME: via OFr. from late L. *leopardus*, from late Gk *leopardos*, from *leōn* 'lion' + *pardos* (see **PARD**).

**leopard cat** • n. a small East Asian wild cat that has a yellowish-brown coat with black spots and often lives near water. [*Felis bengalensis*.]

**leopard frog** • n. a common greenish-brown North American frog which has dark leopard-like spots with a pale border. [*Rana pipiens*.]

**leopard moth** • n. a large white moth with black spots, the larvae of which tunnel into trees and can cause damage. [*Zeuzera pyrina*.]

**leopard's bane** • n. a herbaceous plant of the daisy family, with large yellow flowers. [Genus *Doronicum*.]

**leopard seal** • n. a large grey Antarctic seal which has leopard-like spots and preys on penguins and other seals. [*Hydrurga leptonyx*.]

**leotard** /ˈliːətɑːd/ • n. a close-fitting, stretchy one-piece garment covering the body to the top of the thighs, worn for dance, gymnastics, and exercise.
– ORIGIN C20: named after the Fr. trapeze artist Jules *Léotard*.

**Lepcha** /ˈlɛptʃə/ • n. **1** a member of a people living mainly in mountain valleys in Sikkim, western Bhutan, and parts of Nepal and West Bengal. **2** the Tibeto-Burman language of this people.
– ORIGIN from Nepali *lāpche*.

**leper** • n. **1** a person suffering from leprosy. **2** a person who is shunned by others.
– ORIGIN ME: prob. from an attributive use of *leper* 'leprosy', from OFr. *lepre*, via L. from Gk *lepra*, fem. of *lepros* 'scaly'.

**lepidolite** /ˈlɛpɪdəlʌɪt, lɪˈpɪdəlʌɪt/ • n. a mineral of the mica group containing lithium, typically grey or lilac in colour.
– ORIGIN C18: from Gk *lepis*, *lepid-* 'scale' + **-LITE**.

**Lepidoptera** /ˌlɛpɪˈdɒpt(ə)rə/ • pl. n. Entomology an order

of insects comprising the butterflies and moths.
– DERIVATIVES **lepidopteran** adj. & n. **lepidopterist** n. **lepidopterous** adj.
– ORIGIN mod. L., from Gk *lepis, lepid-* 'scale' + *pteron* 'wing'.

**leporine** /ˈlɛpərʌɪn/ ● adj. of or resembling a hare or hares.
– ORIGIN C17: from L. *leporinus*, from *lepus, lepor-* 'hare'.

**leprechaun** /ˈlɛprəkɔːn/ ● n. (in Irish folklore) a small, mischievous sprite.
– ORIGIN C17: from Ir. *leipreachán*, based on Old Ir. *luchorpán*, from *lu* 'small' + *corp* 'body'.

**lepromatous** /lɛˈprəʊmətəs/ ● adj. Medicine relating to or denoting the more severe of the two principal forms of leprosy. Compare with **TUBERCULOID**.

**leprosarium** /ˌlɛprəˈsɛːrɪəm/ ● n. a hospital for people with leprosy.

**leprosy** ● n. a contagious bacterial disease that affects the skin, mucous membranes, and nerves, causing discoloration and lumps on the skin and, in severe cases, disfigurement and deformities.
– ORIGIN C16 (superseding ME *lepry*): from **LEPROUS** + **-Y**[3].

**leprous** ● adj. relating to, resembling, or suffering from leprosy.
– ORIGIN ME: via OFr. from late L. *leprosus*, from L. *lepra* (see **LEPER**).

**lepta** plural form of **LEPTON**[1].

**leptin** ● n. Biochemistry a protein produced by fatty tissue which is believed to regulate fat storage in the body.
– ORIGIN 1990s: from Gk *leptos* 'fine, thin' + **-IN**[1].

**lepto-** ● comb. form small; narrow: *leptocephalic*.
– ORIGIN from Gk *leptos* 'fine, thin, delicate'.

**leptocephalic** /ˌlɛptə(ʊ)sɪˈfalɪk, -kɛˈfalɪk-/ (also **leptocephalous** /-ˈsɛf(ə)ləs, -ˈkɛf-/) ● adj. narrow-skulled.

**leptomeninges** /ˌlɛptəʊmɪˈnɪndʒiːz/ ● pl. n. Anatomy the inner two meninges, the arachnoid and the pia mater, between which circulates the cerebrospinal fluid.
– DERIVATIVES **leptomeningeal** adj.

**lepton**[1] /ˈlɛptɒn/ ● n. (pl. **lepta**) a monetary unit of Greece used only in calculations, worth one hundredth of a drachma.
– ORIGIN from Gk *lepton*, neut. of *leptos* 'small'.

**lepton**[2] /ˈlɛptɒn/ ● n. Physics a subatomic particle that does not take part in the strong interaction, such as an electron, muon, or neutrino.
– DERIVATIVES **leptonic** adj.
– ORIGIN 1940s: from Gk *leptos* 'small' + **-ON**.

**lepton number** ● n. Physics a quantum number assigned to subatomic particles that is ±1 for leptons and 0 for other particles and is conserved in all known interactions.

**leptospirosis** /ˌlɛptə(ʊ)spʌɪˈrəʊsɪs/ ● n. an infectious bacterial disease of rodents, dogs, and other mammals, transmissible to humans.
– ORIGIN 1920s: from mod. L. *Leptospira*, genus name of the bacteria (from **LEPTO-** + Gk *speira* 'coil') + **-OSIS**.

**leptotene** /ˈlɛptə(ʊ)tiːn/ ● n. Biology the first stage of the prophase of meiosis, during which each chromosome becomes visible as two fine threads (chromatids).
– ORIGIN C20: from **LEPTO-** + Gk *tainia* 'band, ribbon'.

**Lesbian** ● adj. of or relating to the Greek island of Lesbos.

**lesbian** ● n. a homosexual woman. ● adj. of or relating to lesbians or lesbianism.
– DERIVATIVES **lesbianism** n.
– ORIGIN C19: via L. from Gk *Lesbios*, from *Lesbos*, Gk island and home of Sappho, who expressed affection for women in her poetry, + **-IAN**.

**lese-majesty** /liːzˈmadʒɪsti/ ● n. the insulting of a sovereign; treason.
– ORIGIN ME: from Fr. *lèse-majesté*, from L. *laesa majestas* 'injured sovereignty'.

**lesion** /ˈliːʒ(ə)n/ ● n. chiefly Medicine a region in an organ or tissue which has suffered damage through injury or disease.
– ORIGIN ME: via OFr. from L. *laesio(n-)*, from *laedere* 'injure'.

**less** ● det. & pron. **1** a smaller amount of; not as much. **2** fewer in number. ● adj. archaic of lower rank or importance: *James the Less*. ● adv. to a smaller extent; not so much. ● prep. minus.
– ORIGIN OE *lǣssa*, of Gmc origin.

**USAGE** less
On the difference in use between **less** and **fewer**, see **FEW**.

**-less** ● suffix forming adjectives and adverbs: **1** (from nouns) not having; without; free from: *flavourless*. **2** (from verbs) not affected by or not carrying out the action of the verb: *tireless*.
– DERIVATIVES **-lessly** suffix forming corresponding adverbs. **-lessness** suffix forming corresponding nouns.
– ORIGIN OE *-lēas*, from *lēas* 'devoid of'.

**lessee** /lɛˈsiː/ ● n. a person who holds the lease of a property.
– DERIVATIVES **lesseeship** n.
– ORIGIN C15: from OFr. *lesse*, past part. of *lesser* 'to let, leave', + **-EE**.

**lessen** ● v. make or become less.

**lesser** ● adj. not so great or important as the other or the rest.
– ORIGIN ME: from **LESS** + **-ER**[2].

**lesson** ● n. **1** a period of learning or teaching. ➤ a thing learned. ➤ a thing that serves as a warning or encouragement. **2** a passage from the Bible read aloud during a church service. ● v. archaic instruct or rebuke (someone).
– ORIGIN ME: from OFr. *leçon*, from L. *lectio* (see **LECTION**).

**lessor** /lɛˈsɔː, ˈlɛsɔː/ ● n. a person who leases or lets a property to another.
– ORIGIN ME: from Anglo-Norman Fr., from OFr. *lesser* 'let, leave'.

**lest** ● conj. formal **1** with the intention of preventing; to avoid the risk of. **2** because of the possibility of.
– ORIGIN OE *thȳ lǣs the* 'whereby less that', later *the lǣste*.

**let**[1] ● v. (**letting**; past and past part. **let**) **1** not prevent or forbid; allow. **2** used in the imperative to express an intention, proposal, or instruction: *let's have a drink*. **3** used to express an assumption upon which a theory or calculation is to be based: *let A and B stand for X and Y*. **4** allow someone to have the use of (a room or property) in return for payment. **5** award (a contract for a project) to an applicant. ● n. Brit. a period during which a room or property is rented: *a short let*.
– PHRASES **let alone** not to mention. **let someone/thing be** stop interfering with someone or something. **let fall** Geometry draw (a perpendicular) from an outside point to a line. **let fly** attack physically or verbally. **let oneself go 1** act in an uninhibited way. **2** become careless or untidy in one's habits or appearance. **let someone/thing go 1** allow someone or something to go free. **2** dismiss an employee. **3** (also **let go** or **let go of**) relinquish one's grip on someone or something. **let someone have it** informal attack someone. **to let** available for rent.
– PHRASAL VERBS **let down** (of an aircraft) descend prior to making a landing. **let someone down** fail to support or help someone. ➤ (**let someone/thing down**) have a detrimental effect on someone or something. **let oneself in for** informal involve oneself in (something difficult or unpleasant). **let someone in on/into** allow someone to know or share (something secret). **let something into** set something back into (a surface). **let someone off 1** refrain from punishing someone. **2** excuse someone from a task or obligation. **let something off** cause a gun, firework, or bomb to fire or explode. **let on** informal **1** divulge information. **2** pretend. **let someone out** release someone from obligation or suspicion. **let something out 1** utter a sound or cry. **2** make a garment looser or larger. **3** reveal a piece of information. **let up** informal become less intense. ➤ relax one's efforts.
– DERIVATIVES **letting** n.
– ORIGIN OE *lǣtan* 'leave behind, leave out', of Gmc origin; rel. to **LATE**.

**let**[2] ● n. (in racket sports) a circumstance under which a

service is nullified and has to be retaken, especially (in tennis) when the ball clips the top of the net and falls within bounds. ● v. (**letting**; past and past part. **letted** or **let**) archaic hinder.
– PHRASES **let or hindrance** formal obstruction or impediment. **play a let** (in racket sports) play a point again because the ball or one of the players has been obstructed.
– ORIGIN OE *lettan* 'hinder', of Gmc origin; rel. to **LATE**.

**-let** ● suffix **1** (forming nouns) denoting a smaller or lesser kind: *booklet.* **2** denoting articles of ornament or dress: *anklet.*
– ORIGIN orig. corresp. to Fr. *-ette* added to nouns ending in *-el.*

**let-down** ● n. **1** a disappointment. **2** the release of milk in a nursing mother or lactating animal as a reflex response to suckling or massage.

**lethal** ● adj. **1** sufficient to cause death. **2** very harmful or destructive.
– DERIVATIVES **lethality** n. **lethally** adv.
– ORIGIN C16: from L. *lethalis*, from *lethum*, a var. (influenced by Gk *lēthē* 'forgetfulness'), of *letum* 'death'.

**lethargy** /ˈlɛθədʒi/ ● n. **1** a lack of energy and enthusiasm. **2** Medicine a pathological state of sleepiness or deep unresponsiveness.
– DERIVATIVES **lethargic** adj. **lethargically** adv.
– ORIGIN ME: via OFr. from late L. *lethargia*, from Gk *lēthargia*, from *lēthargos* 'forgetful'.

**Lethean** /liːˈθiən/ ● adj. poetic/literary causing forgetfulness and oblivion.
– ORIGIN from the name of the *Lethe*, a river of the underworld in Gk mythology whose water when drunk made the souls of the dead forget their life on earth.

**let-off** ● n. informal an instance of unexpectedly escaping or avoiding something.

**let-out** ● n. Brit. informal an opportunity to escape from or avoid a difficult situation.

**let-out clause** ● n. informal a clause specifying a circumstance in which the terms of an agreement shall not apply.

**let's** ● contr. let us.

**Lett** ● n. old-fashioned term for **LATVIAN**.
– DERIVATIVES **Lettish** adj.
– ORIGIN from Ger. *Lette*, from Latvian *Latvi.*

**letter** ● n. **1** a character representing one or more of the sounds used in speech; any of the symbols of an alphabet. ➤ US a school or college initial as a mark of proficiency, especially in sport. **2** a written, typed, or printed communication, sent by post or messenger. **3** the precise terms of a statement or requirement: *adherence to the letter of the law.* **4** (**letters**) literature: *the world of letters.* **5** (**letters**) archaic erudition: *a man of letters.* **6** Printing a style of typeface. ● v. **1** inscribe or provide with letters. **2** US informal be awarded a letter as a mark of proficiency in sport.
– PHRASES **to the letter** with adherence to every detail.
– DERIVATIVES **lettering** n.
– ORIGIN ME: from OFr. *lettre*, from L. *litera, littera* 'letter of the alphabet', (pl.) 'epistle, literature, culture'.

**letter bomb** ● n. an explosive device hidden in a small package and detonated when the package is opened.

**letter box** ● n. **1** chiefly Brit. a slot in a door through which mail is delivered. **2** (**letterbox**) a format for presenting widescreen films on a standard television screen, in which the image fills the width but not the height of the screen. ● v. (**letterbox**) record on to video in letterbox format.

**letter-carrier** ● n. N. Amer. a postman or postwoman.

**lettered** ● adj. dated formally educated.

**letterhead** ● n. a printed heading on stationery, stating the sender's name and address.

**letter missive** (also **letters missive**) ● n. a letter from the monarch to a dean and chapter nominating a person to be elected bishop.

**letter of comfort** ● n. an assurance about a debt, short of a legal guarantee, given to a bank by a third party.

**letter of credence** ● n. a letter of introduction, especially of an ambassador.

**letter of credit** ● n. a letter issued by one bank to another to serve as a guarantee for payments made to a specified person.

**letter of marque** ● n. historical a licence to fit out an armed vessel and use it in the capture of enemy merchant shipping and to commit acts which would otherwise have constituted piracy.
– ORIGIN ME: Law Fr. *marque*, from OFr. *marque* 'right of reprisal'.

**letterpress** ● n. **1** printing from a hard, raised image under pressure, using viscous ink. **2** Brit. printed text as opposed to illustrations.

**letterset** ● n. a method of printing in which ink is transferred from a raised surface to a cylinder and from that to the paper.
– ORIGIN 1960s: blend of **LETTERPRESS** and **OFFSET**.

**letters of administration** ● pl. n. Law authority to administer the estate of someone who has died without making a will.

**letters patent** ● pl. n. an open document issued by a monarch or government conferring a patent or other right.
– ORIGIN ME: from med. L. *litterae patentes*, lit. 'letters lying open'.

**letters rogatory** /ˈrəʊgət(ə)ri/ ● pl. n. Law documents making a request through a foreign court for the obtaining of information or evidence from a specified person within the jurisdiction of that court.
– ORIGIN C19: *rogatory* from med. L. *rogatorius* 'interrogatory'.

**lettuce** ● n. **1** a cultivated plant of the daisy family, with edible leaves that are eaten in salads. [*Lactuca sativa.*] **2** used in names of other plants with edible green leaves, e.g. **lamb's lettuce**.
– ORIGIN ME: from OFr. *letues, laitues*, pl. of *laitue*, from L. *lactuca*, from *lac, lact-* 'milk' (because of its milky juice).

**let-up** ● n. informal a pause or reduction in the intensity of something dangerous, difficult, or tiring.

**Letzeburgesch** /ˌlɛts(ə)bəːˈgɛʃ, ˈlɛts(ə)ˌbəːgɪʃ/ (also **Letzebuergesch**) ● n. another term for **LUXEMBURGISH**.
– ORIGIN from a local name for *Luxembourg* + *-esch* (equivalent of **-ISH**[1]).

**leu** /ˈleɪuː/ ● n. (pl. **lei** /leɪ/) the basic monetary unit of Romania, equal to 100 bani.
– ORIGIN Romanian, lit. 'lion'.

**leucine** /ˈluːsiːn/ ● n. Biochemistry a hydrophobic amino acid which is an essential nutrient in the diet of vertebrates.
– ORIGIN C19: coined in Fr. from Gk *leukos* 'white' + **-INE**[4].

**leucistic** /luːˈsɪstɪk/ ● adj. Zoology having whitish fur, plumage, or skin due to a lack of pigment.
– ORIGIN from **LEUCO-** + the adjectival suffix *-istic.*

**leuco-** (also **leuko-**) ● comb. form **1** white: *leucoma.* **2** representing **LEUCOCYTE**.
– ORIGIN from Gk *leukos* 'white'.

**leucocyte** /ˈluːkə(ʊ)sʌɪt/ (also **leukocyte**) ● n. Physiology a colourless cell which circulates in the blood and body fluids and is involved in counteracting foreign substances and disease; a white (blood) cell.
– DERIVATIVES **leucocytic** adj.

**leucocytosis** /ˌluːkə(ʊ)sʌɪˈtəʊsɪs/ (also **leukocytosis**) ● n. Medicine an increase in the number of white cells in the blood, especially during an infection.
– DERIVATIVES **leucocytotic** adj.

**leucoderma** /ˌluːkə(ʊ)ˈdəːmə/ ● n. another term for **VITILIGO**.

**leucoma** /luːˈkəʊmə/ ● n. Medicine a white opacity in the cornea of the eye.
– ORIGIN C18: mod. L., from Gk *leukōma.*

**leucopenia** /ˌluːkə(ʊ)ˈpiːnɪə/ (also **leukopenia**) ● n. Medicine a reduction in the number of white cells in the blood.
– DERIVATIVES **leucopenic** adj.
– ORIGIN C19: from Gk *leukos* 'white' + *penia* 'poverty'.

**leucoplast** /ˈluːkə(ʊ)plast, -plɑːst/ ● n. Botany a colourless organelle found in plant cells, used for the storage of starch or oil.

**leucorrhoea** /ˌluːkəˈriːə/ (US **leucorrhea, leukorrhea**) ● **n.** a whitish or yellowish discharge of mucus from the vagina.

**leucosis** /luːˈkəʊsɪs/ (also **leukosis**) ● **n.** a leukaemic disease of animals, especially one of a group of malignant viral diseases of poultry or cattle.
– DERIVATIVES **leucotic** adj.

**leucotomy** /luːˈkɒtəmi/ ● **n.** (pl. **-ies**) the surgical cutting of white nerve fibres within the brain, especially prefrontal lobotomy, formerly used to treat mental illness.

**leukaemia** /luːˈkiːmɪə/ (US **leukemia**) ● **n.** a malignant progressive disease in which the bone marrow and other blood-forming organs produce increased numbers of immature or abnormal leucocytes, suppressing the production of normal blood cells.
– DERIVATIVES **leukaemic** adj.
– ORIGIN C19: coined in Ger. from Gk *leukos* 'white' + *haima* 'blood'.

**leukaemogenic** /luːˌkiːmə(ʊ)ˈdʒɛnɪk/ (US **leukemogenic**) ● **adj.** Medicine relating to or promoting the development of leukaemia.
– DERIVATIVES **leukaemogen** /luːˈkiːmədzən/ n. **leukaemogenesis** n.

**leuko-** ● **comb. form** variant spelling of LEUCO-.

**leukotriene** /ˌluːkə(ʊ)ˈtrʌɪiːn/ ● **n.** Biochemistry any of a group of biologically active compounds produced in the body from arachidonic acid.
– ORIGIN from LEUKO- (because they were orig. isolated from leucocytes) + TRIENE.

**Lev.** ● **abbrev.** Leviticus (in biblical references).

**lev** /lɛv, lɛf/ (also **leva** /ˈlɛvə/) ● **n.** (pl. **leva** or **levas** or **levs**) the basic monetary unit of Bulgaria, equal to 100 stotinki.
– ORIGIN Bulgarian, var. of *lǎv* 'lion'.

**Levant** /lɪˈvant/ ● **n.** (**the Levant**) archaic the eastern part of the Mediterranean.
– DERIVATIVES **Levantine** n. & adj.
– ORIGIN C15: from Fr., lit. 'rising', pres. part. of *lever* 'to lift' used as a noun in the sense 'point of sunrise, east'.

**levant** /lɪˈvant/ ● **v.** Brit. archaic abscond leaving unpaid debts.
– ORIGIN C17: perh. from LEVANT: cf. Fr. *faire voile en Levant* 'be stolen or spirited away', lit. 'set sail for the Levant'.

**levanter** /lɪˈvantə/ ● **n.** a strong easterly wind in the Mediterranean region.

**levator** /lɪˈveɪtə/ ● **n.** Anatomy a muscle whose contraction causes the raising of a part of the body.
– ORIGIN C17: from L., lit. 'a person who lifts', from *levare* 'raise, lift'.

**levee¹** /ˈlɛvi, ˈlɛveɪ/ ● **n.** a reception or assembly of people.
– ORIGIN C17: from Fr. *levé*, var. of *lever* 'rising', from the verb *lever*.

**levee²** /ˈlɛvi, lɪˈviː/ ● **n. 1** an embankment built to prevent the overflow of a river. ➤a ridge of sediment deposited naturally alongside a river. **2** chiefly N. Amer. a landing place; a quay.
– ORIGIN C18 (orig. US): from Fr. *levée*, fem. past part. of *lever* 'to lift'.

**level** ● **n. 1** a horizontal plane or line with respect to the distance above or below a given point. **2** a height or distance from the ground or another base. ➤a floor within a multi-storey building. **3** a position or stage on a scale of quantity, extent, rank, or quality. **4** a flat tract of land. **5** an instrument giving a line parallel to the plane of the horizon for testing whether things are horizontal. ➤Surveying an instrument for giving a horizontal line of sight. ● **adj. 1** having a flat, horizontal surface. ➤(of a quantity of a dry substance) with the contents not rising above the brim of the measure: *a level teaspoon.* **2** at the same height as someone or something else. **3** having the same relative position; not in front or behind. **4** calm and steady: *a level voice.* ● **v.** (**levelled, levelling**; US **leveled, leveling**) **1** make or become level. ➤demolish (a building or town). **2** aim or direct (a weapon, criticism, or accusation). **3** (**level with**) informal be frank or honest with. **4** Surveying ascertain differences in the height of (land).
– PHRASES **do one's level best** make all possible efforts. **level of attainment** Brit. a rating of the ability of a school pupil, on a scale of 1 to 10. **be level pegging** Brit. be equal in score or achievement during a contest. **a level playing field** a situation in which everyone has an equal chance of succeeding. **on the level** informal honest; truthful.
– DERIVATIVES **levelly** adv. **levelness** n.
– ORIGIN ME: from OFr. *livel*, based on L. *libella*, dimin. of *libra* 'scales, balance'.

**level crossing** ● **n.** Brit. a place where a railway and a road cross at the same level.

**level-headed** ● **adj.** calm and sensible.
– DERIVATIVES **level-headedly** adv. **level-headedness** n.

**leveller** (US **leveler**) ● **n. 1** a person or thing that levels something. **2** (**Leveller**) a member of a group of radical dissenters in the English Civil War (1642–9).

**lever** /ˈliːvə/ ● **n.** a rigid bar resting on a pivot, used to move a load with one end when pressure is applied to the other. ➤a projecting arm or handle that is moved to operate a mechanism. ● **v. 1** lift or move with a lever. **2** cause to move with a concerted physical effort: *she levered herself up.*
– ORIGIN ME: from OFr. *levier, leveor*, from *lever* 'to lift'.

**leverage** ● **n. 1** the exertion of force by means of a lever. **2** the power to influence: *political leverage.* **3** Finance another term for GEARING (in sense 2). ● **v.** [usu. as adj. **leveraged**] use borrowed capital for (an investment), expecting the profits made to be greater than the interest payable.

**leveraged buyout** ● **n.** the purchase of a controlling share in a company by its management using outside capital.

**lever escapement** ● **n.** a mechanism in a watch connecting the escape wheel and the balance wheel using two levers.

**leveret** /ˈlɛv(ə)rɪt/ ● **n.** a young hare in its first year.
– ORIGIN ME: from Anglo-Norman Fr., dimin. of *levre*, from L. *lepus, lepor-* 'hare'.

**lever watch** ● **n.** a watch with a lever escapement.

**leviathan** /lɪˈvʌɪəθ(ə)n/ ● **n. 1** (in biblical use) a sea monster. ➤a very large aquatic creature, especially a whale. ➤something very large or powerful. **2** an autocratic monarch or state. [with allusion to Hobbes' *Leviathan* (1651).]
– ORIGIN via late L. from Heb. *liwyāṯān*.

**levigate** /ˈlɛvɪgeɪt/ ● **v.** archaic reduce to a fine powder or smooth paste.
– DERIVATIVES **levigation** n.
– ORIGIN C16 (earlier (C15) as *levigation*): from L. *levigat-*, *levigare* 'to make smooth, polish', from *levis* 'smooth'.

**levin** /ˈlɛvɪn/ ● **n.** archaic lightning; thunderbolts.
– ORIGIN ME: prob. of Scand. origin.

**levirate** /ˈliːvɪrət, ˈlɛv-/ ● **n.** (usu. **the levirate**) a custom of the ancient Hebrews and some other peoples by which a man may be obliged to marry his brother's widow.
– ORIGIN C18: from L. *levir* 'brother-in-law' + -ATE¹.

**levitate** /ˈlɛvɪteɪt/ ● **v.** rise or cause to rise and hover in the air.
– DERIVATIVES **levitation** n. **levitator** n.
– ORIGIN C17: from L. *levis* 'light', on the pattern of *gravitate*.

**Levite** /ˈliːvʌɪt/ ● **n.** a member of the Hebrew tribe of Levi, in particular an assistant to the priests in the Jewish temple.
– ORIGIN ME: from late L. *levita*, from Gk *leuitēs*, from Heb. *Lēwī* 'Levi'.

**Levitical** /lɪˈvɪtɪk(ə)l/ ● **adj. 1** of or relating to the Levites or the tribe of Levi. **2** Judaism (of a rule of conduct, temple ritual, etc.) derived from the biblical Book of Leviticus.

**levity** /ˈlɛvɪti/ ● **n.** the treatment of a serious matter with humour or lack of respect.
– ORIGIN C16: from L. *levitas*, from *levis* 'light'.

**levo-** ● **comb. form** US spelling of LAEVO-.

**levodopa** /ˌliːvə(ʊ)ˈdəʊpə/ ● **n.** another term for L-DOPA.

**levonorgestrel** /ˌliːvəʊnɔːˈdʒɛstr(ə)l/ ● **n.** Biochemistry a

synthetic steroid hormone which has a similar effect to progesterone and is used in some contraceptive pills.
– ORIGIN 1970s: from **LEVO-** (it being a laevorotatory isomer) + *norgestrel*, a synthetic steroid hormone.

**levulose** • **n.** US spelling of **LAEVULOSE**.

**levy** /ˈlɛvi/ • **n. 1** the imposition of a tax, fee, fine, or subscription. ➤ a sum of money raised by such a levy. **2** an item or set of items of property seized to satisfy a legal judgement. **3** archaic a body of enlisted troops. • **v.** (**-ies, -ied**) **1** impose or seize as a levy. **2** archaic enlist for miltary service. **3** archaic begin to wage (war).
– DERIVATIVES **leviable** adj.
– ORIGIN ME: from OFr. *levee*, fem. past part. of *lever* 'raise', from L. *levare*, from *levis* 'light'.

**lewd** • **adj.** crude and offensive in a sexual way.
– DERIVATIVES **lewdly** adv. **lewdness** n.
– ORIGIN OE *lǣwede* (orig. in sense 'belonging to the laity', later 'belonging to the common people, vulgar'): of unknown origin.

**lewis** • **n.** a steel device for lifting heavy blocks of stone or concrete, consisting of three pieces arranged to form a dovetail.
– ORIGIN ME: prob. from OFr. *lous*, pl. of *lou(p)* 'wolf', the name of a kind of siege engine.

**Lewis acid** • **n.** Chemistry a compound or ionic species which can accept an electron pair from a donor compound.
– ORIGIN 1940s: named after the Amer. chemist Gilbert N. *Lewis*.

**Lewis base** • **n.** Chemistry a compound or ionic species which can donate an electron pair to an acceptor compound.
– ORIGIN 1960s: see **LEWIS ACID**.

**Lewis gun** • **n.** chiefly historical a light air-cooled machine gun with a magazine operated by gas from its own firing, used mainly in the First World War.
– ORIGIN C20: named after the Amer. colonel Isaac N. *Lewis*.

**Lewisian** /luːˈɪsɪən/ • **adj.** Geology of or denoting the earlier stage of the Proterozoic aeon in NW Scotland, when the oldest rocks in Britain were deposited.
– ORIGIN C19: from the island of *Lewis* in the Outer Hebrides (where the chief outcrops of these rocks are found) + **-IAN**.

**lewisite** /ˈluːɪsʌɪt/ • **n.** a dark oily liquid producing an irritant gas that causes blisters, developed for use in chemical warfare.
– ORIGIN 1920s: named after the Amer. chemist Winford L. *Lewis*.

**lexeme** /ˈlɛksiːm/ • **n.** Linguistics a basic lexical unit of a language consisting of one or several words, the elements of which do not separately convey the meaning of the whole.
– ORIGIN 1940s: from **LEXICON** + **-EME**.

**lex fori** /lɛks ˈfɔːrʌɪ/ • **n.** Law the law of the country in which an action is brought.
– ORIGIN L., 'law of the court'.

**lexical** /ˈlɛksɪk(ə)l/ • **adj. 1** of or relating to the words or vocabulary of a language. **2** relating to or of the nature of a lexicon or dictionary.
– DERIVATIVES **lexically** adv.
– ORIGIN C19: from Gk *lexikos* 'of words' + **-AL**.

**lexicography** /ˌlɛksɪˈkɒgrəfi/ • **n.** the practice of compiling dictionaries.
– DERIVATIVES **lexicographer** n. **lexicographic** adj. **lexicographical** /-kəˈgrafɪk(ə)l/ adj. **lexicographically** adv.

**lexicology** • **n.** the study of the form, meaning, and behaviour of words.
– DERIVATIVES **lexicological** adj. **lexicologically** adv.

**lexicon** /ˈlɛksɪk(ə)n/ • **n. 1** the vocabulary of a person, language, or branch of knowledge. **2** a dictionary.
– ORIGIN C17: mod. L., from Gk *lexikon* (*biblion*) '(book) of words', from *lexis* 'word'.

**lexigram** /ˈlɛksɪgram/ • **n.** a symbol representing a word, especially one used in learning a language.

**lexis** /ˈlɛksɪs/ • **n.** the total stock of words in a language.
– ORIGIN 1950s: from Gk, lit. 'word'.

**lex loci** /lɛks ˈləʊsʌɪ/ • **n.** Law the law of the country in which a transaction is performed, a tort is committed, or a property is situated.
– ORIGIN L., 'law of the place'.

**lex talionis** /lɛks ˌtalɪˈəʊnɪs/ • **n.** the law of retaliation, whereby a punishment resembles the offence committed in kind and degree.
– ORIGIN L., from *lex* 'law' and *talio(n-)* 'retaliation' (from *talis* 'such').

**ley**[1] /leɪ/ • **n.** a piece of land temporarily put down to grass, clover, etc., in contrast to permanent pasture.
– ORIGIN OE *lǣge* 'fallow' (recorded in *lǣghrycg* 'ridge left at the edge of a ploughed field)'; rel. to **LAY**[1] and **LIE**[1].

**ley**[2] /leɪ, liː/ (also **ley line**) • **n.** a supposed straight line connecting three or more ancient sites, sometimes regarded as the line of a former track and associated by some with lines of energy and other paranormal phenomena.
– ORIGIN 1920s: var. of **LEA**.

**Leyden jar** /ˈlʌɪd(ə)n/ • **n.** an early form of capacitor consisting of a glass jar with layers of metal foil on the outside and inside.
– ORIGIN C18: named after *Leyden* (or *Leiden*), the city in the Netherlands where it was invented (1745).

**ley farming** • **n.** chiefly Brit. the alternate growing of crops and grass.

**Leyland cypress** /ˈleɪlənd/ • **n.** a fast-growing hybrid conifer, widely grown as a screening plant or for shelter. [× *Cupressocyparis leylandii*.]
– ORIGIN 1930s: named after the Brit. horticulturalist Christopher J. *Leyland*.

**leylandii** /leɪˈlandɪʌɪ/ • **n.** (pl. same) a Leyland cypress.
– ORIGIN from the mod. L. taxonomic name.

**LF** • **abbrev.** low frequency.

**LGV** • **abbrev.** Brit. large goods vehicle.

**LH** • **abbrev.** Biochemistry luteinizing hormone.

**l.h.** • **abbrev.** left hand.

**Lhasa apso** /ˈapsəʊ/ • **n.** (pl. **-os**) a dog of a small long-coated breed, typically gold or grey and white.
– ORIGIN C20: from *Lhasa* in Tibet + Tibetan *a-sob*.

**LHD** • **abbrev.** left-hand drive.

**LI** • **abbrev. 1** Light Infantry. **2** (in the US) Long Island.

**Li** • **symb.** the chemical element lithium.

**li** /liː/ • **n.** (pl. same) a Chinese unit of distance, equal to about 0.6 km (0.4 mile).
– ORIGIN from Chin. *lǐ*.

**liability** • **n.** (pl. **-ies**) **1** the state of being liable. **2** a thing for which someone is liable, especially a financial obligation. **3** a person or thing likely to cause one embarrassment or put one at a disadvantage.

**liable** • **adj. 1** responsible by law; legally answerable. ➤ (**liable to**) subject by law to. **2** (**liable to do something**) likely to do something. **3** (**liable to**) likely to experience (something undesirable): *areas liable to flooding*.
– ORIGIN ME: perh. from Anglo-Norman Fr., from Fr. *lier* 'to bind', from L. *ligare*.

**liaise** /lɪˈeɪz/ • **v. 1** cooperate on a matter of mutual concern. **2** (**liaise between**) act as a link to assist communication between.
– ORIGIN 1920s (orig. military sl.): back-form. from **LIAISON**.

**liaison** • **n. 1** communication or cooperation between people or organizations. **2** a sexual relationship, especially one that is secret. **3** the binding or thickening agent of a sauce. **4** Phonetics the sounding of a consonant that is normally silent at the end of a word, because the next word begins with a vowel.
– ORIGIN C17 (as a cookery term): from Fr., from *lier* 'to bind'.

**liana** /lɪˈɑːnə/ (also **liane** /-ˈɑːn/) • **n.** a woody climbing plant that hangs from trees, especially in tropical rainforests. ➤ the free-hanging stem of such a plant.
– ORIGIN C18: from Fr. *liane* 'clematis, liana'.

**liar** • **n.** a person who tells lies.
– ORIGIN OE *lēogere* (see **LIE**[2], **-AR**[4]).

**liar dice** • **n.** a gambling game resembling poker dice, in which the thrower conceals the dice thrown and sometimes declares a false score.

**lias** /ˈlʌɪəs/ ● **n.** **1** (**Lias**) Geology the earliest epoch of the Jurassic period, from about 208 to 178 million years ago. **2** (also **blue lias**) a blue-grey clayey limestone of this epoch, found chiefly in SW England.
– DERIVATIVES **liassic** adj.
– ORIGIN ME: from OFr. *liais* 'hard limestone', prob. from *lie* (see **LEES**).

**liatris** /lʌɪˈatrɪs/ ● **n.** (pl. same) a plant of a genus which includes the blazing stars of the daisy family. [Genus *Liatris*.]
– ORIGIN mod. L., of unknown origin.

**Lib.** ● **abbrev.** Liberal.

**lib** ● **n.** informal (in the names of political movements) the liberation of a specified group: *women's lib.*
– DERIVATIVES **libber** n.

**libation** /lʌɪˈbeɪʃ(ə)n/ ● **n.** **1** the pouring out of a drink as an offering to a deity. ➤such a drink. **2** humorous an alcoholic drink.
– ORIGIN ME: from L. *libatio(n-)*, from *libare* 'pour as an offering'.

**Lib Dem** ● **n.** informal (in the UK) Liberal Democrat.

**libel** ● **n.** **1** Law the publication of a false statement that is damaging to a person's reputation. Compare with **SLANDER**. ➤such a statement; a written defamation. **2** (in admiralty and ecclesiastical law) a plaintiff's written declaration. ● **v.** (**libelled**, **libelling**; US **libeled**, **libeling**) **1** Law defame by publishing a libel. **2** (in admiralty and ecclesiastical law) bring a suit against.
– DERIVATIVES **libeller** n. **libellous** (US also **libelous**) adj. **libellously** (US also **libelously**) adv.
– ORIGIN ME (in the general sense 'a document, a written statement'): via OFr. from L. *libellus*, dimin. of *liber* 'book'.

**liberal** ● **adj.** **1** respectful and accepting of behaviour or opinions different from one's own; open to new ideas. ➤(of a society, law, etc.) favourable to individual rights and freedoms. ➤Theology regarding many traditional beliefs as dispensable, invalidated by modern thought, or liable to change. **2** (in a political context) favouring individual liberty, free trade, and moderate political and social reform. ➤(**Liberal**) (in the UK) of or relating to the Liberal Democrat party. **3** (of education) concerned with broadening general knowledge and experience. **4** (especially of an interpretation of a law) broadly construed; not strictly literal. **5** given, used, or giving in generous amounts. ● **n.** **1** a person of liberal views. **2** (**Liberal**) (in the UK) a Liberal Democrat.
– DERIVATIVES **liberalism** n. **liberalist** n. **liberalistic** adj. **liberality** n. **liberally** adv. **liberalness** n.
– ORIGIN ME (orig. in sense 'suitable for a free man' hence 'suitable for a gentleman'): via OFr. from L. *liberalis*, from *liber* 'free (man)'.

**liberal arts** ● **pl. n.** **1** chiefly N. Amer. arts subjects such as literature and history, as distinct from science and technology. **2** historical the medieval trivium and quadrivium.

**Liberal Democrat** ● **n.** (in the UK) a member of a party formed from the Liberal Party and members of the Social Democratic Party.

**liberalize** (also **-ise**) ● **v.** remove or loosen restrictions on (something, typically an economic or political system).
– DERIVATIVES **liberalization** n. **liberalizer** n.

**liberal studies** ● **pl. n.** [usu. treated as sing.] Brit. an additional course in arts subjects taken by students studying for a qualification in science, technology, or the humanities.

**liberate** ● **v.** **1** set free, especially from imprisonment or oppression. ➤[as adj. **liberated**] free from social conventions, especially with regard to sexual roles. **2** Chemistry & Physics release (gas, energy, etc.) as a result of chemical reaction or physical decomposition.
– DERIVATIVES **liberated** adj. **liberating** adj. **liberation** n. **liberationist** n. **liberator** n.
– ORIGIN C16 (earlier (ME) as *liberation*): from L. *liberat-*, *liberare* 'to free', from *liber* 'free'.

**liberation theology** ● **n.** a movement in Christian theology which attempts to address the problems of poverty and social injustice as well as spiritual matters.

**Liberian** /lʌɪˈbɪərɪən/ ● **n.** a native or inhabitant of Liberia, a country in West Africa. ● **adj.** of or relating to Liberia or Liberians.

**libero** /ˈliːbərəʊ/ ● **n.** (pl. **-os**) Soccer another term for **SWEEPER** (in sense 2).
– ORIGIN 1960s: from Ital., abbrev. of *battitore libero* 'free defender', lit. 'free beater'.

**libertarian** /ˌlɪbəˈtɛːrɪən/ ● **n.** **1** an adherent of libertarianism. **2** a person who advocates civil liberty. **3** a person who believes in free will.
– ORIGIN C18: from **LIBERTY**, on the pattern of words such as *unitarian*.

**libertarianism** ● **n.** an extreme laissez-faire political philosophy advocating only minimal state intervention in the lives of citizens.

**libertine** /ˈlɪbətiːn, -tɪn, -tʌɪn/ ● **n.** **1** a person who is freely indulgent in sensual pleasures. **2** a freethinker in matters of religion. ● **adj.** **1** characterized by free indulgence in sensual pleasures. **2** freethinking.
– DERIVATIVES **libertinage** n. **libertinism** n.
– ORIGIN ME (denoting a freed slave or the son of one): from L. *libertinus* 'freedman', from *liber* 'free', influenced by Fr. *libertin*.

**liberty** ● **n.** (pl. **-ies**) **1** the state of being free from oppression or imprisonment. **2** a right or privilege, especially a statutory one. **3** the power or scope to act as one pleases. **4** informal a presumptuous remark or action. **5** Nautical shore leave granted to a sailor.
– PHRASES **at liberty** **1** not imprisoned. **2** allowed or entitled to do something. **take liberties** **1** behave in an unduly familiar manner towards a person. **2** treat something freely, without strict faithfulness to the facts or to an original. **take the liberty** venture to do something without first asking permission.
– ORIGIN ME: from OFr. *liberte*, from L. *libertas*, from *liber* 'free'.

**liberty boat** ● **n.** Brit. a boat carrying sailors who have leave to go on shore.

**liberty bodice** ● **n.** Brit. trademark a girl's or woman's bodice made from thick or quilted cotton, formerly worn as an undergarment.

**liberty cap** ● **n.** **1** a small toadstool which has a greyish-brown cap with a distinct boss and a long thin stem, containing the hallucinogen psilocybin. [*Psilocybe semilanceata*.] **2** another term for **CAP OF LIBERTY**.

**Liberty Hall** ● **n.** a place where one may do as one likes.

**liberty horse** ● **n.** a horse that performs in a circus without a rider.

**liberty man** ● **n.** Brit. a sailor with leave to go ashore.

**Liberty ship** ● **n.** a prefabricated US-built freighter of the Second World War.

**libidinous** /lɪˈbɪdɪnəs/ ● **adj.** having or showing excessive sexual drive.
– DERIVATIVES **libidinously** adv. **libidinousness** n.
– ORIGIN ME: from L. *libidinosus*, from *libido* 'desire, lust'.

**libido** /lɪˈbiːdəʊ, lɪˈbʌɪdəʊ/ ● **n.** (pl. **-os**) **1** sexual desire. **2** Psychoanalysis the energy of the sexual drive as a component of the life instinct.
– DERIVATIVES **libidinal** adj. **libidinally** adv.
– ORIGIN C20: from L., lit. 'desire, lust'.

**LIBOR** /ˈlʌɪbɔː/ ● **abbrev.** London interbank offered rate.

**Libra** /ˈliːbrə, ˈlɪb-, ˈlʌɪb-/ ● **n.** **1** Astronomy a small constellation (the Scales or Balance), said to represent a pair of scales symbolizing justice. **2** Astrology the seventh sign of the zodiac, which the sun enters at the northern autumnal equinox (about 23 September).
– DERIVATIVES **Libran** n. & adj.
– ORIGIN from L.

**libra** /ˈlʌɪbrə/ ● **n.** (pl. **librae** /ˈlʌɪbriː/) (in ancient Rome) a unit of weight equivalent to 12 ounces (0.34 kg), the forerunner of the pound.
– ORIGIN L., 'pound, balance'.

**librarian** ● **n.** a person in charge of or assisting in a library.

– DERIVATIVES **librarianship** n.
– ORIGIN C17 (denoting a scribe or copyist): from L. *librarius* 'relating to books' + **-AN**.

**library** • n. (pl. **-ies**) **1** a building or room containing a collection of books and periodicals for use by the public or the members of an institution. **2** a private collection of books. ➤a series of books or recordings issued by a company as a set. ➤(also **software library**) Computing a collection of programs and software packages made generally available.
– ORIGIN ME: via OFr. from L. *libraria* 'bookshop', from *liber, libr-* 'book'.

**libration** /lʌɪˈbreɪʃ(ə)n/ • n. Astronomy an apparent or real oscillation of the moon, by which parts near the edge of the disc that are often not visible from the earth sometimes come into view.
– DERIVATIVES **librate** v.
– ORIGIN C17: from L. *libratio(n-)*, from *librare* 'weigh', from *libra* 'a balance'.

**libretto** /lɪˈbrɛtəʊ/ • n. (pl. **libretti** /-ti/ or **librettos**) the text of an opera or other long vocal work.
– DERIVATIVES **librettist** n.
– ORIGIN C18: from Ital., dimin. of *libro* 'book'.

**Librium** /ˈlɪbrɪəm/ • n. trademark for **CHLORDIAZEPOXIDE**.
– ORIGIN 1960s: of unknown origin.

**Libyan** /ˈlɪbɪən/ • n. a native or inhabitant of Libya. • adj. of or relating to Libya or Libyans.

**lice** plural form of **LOUSE**.

**licence** (US **license**) • n. **1** a permit from an authority to own or use something, do a particular thing, or carry on a trade (especially in alcoholic liquor). ➤formal or official permission. **2** a writer's or artist's conventional freedom to deviate from facts or accepted rules. **3** freedom to behave without restraint.
– ORIGIN ME: via OFr. from L. *licentia* 'freedom, licentiousness' (in med. L. 'authority, permission'), from *licere* 'be lawful or permitted'.

**license** (also **licence**) • v. **1** grant a licence to. **2** authorize.
– DERIVATIVES **licensable** adj. **licensed** adj. **licenser** n. **licensing** adj. **licensor** n.
– ORIGIN ME: from **LICENCE**; the spelling *-se* arose by analogy with pairs such as *practice, practise*.

**licensee** • n. the holder of a licence, especially to sell alcoholic drinks.

**license plate** • n. North American term for **NUMBER PLATE**.

**licentiate** /lʌɪˈsɛnʃɪət/ • n. **1** the holder of a certificate of competence to practise a particular profession. **2** (in some foreign universities) a degree between that of bachelor and master or doctor. **3** a licensed preacher not yet having an appointment, especially in a Presbyterian Church.
– DERIVATIVES **licentiateship** n.
– ORIGIN C15: from med. L., noun use of *licentiatus* 'having freedom', based on *licentia* 'freedom'.

**licentious** /lʌɪˈsɛnʃəs/ • adj. **1** promiscuous and unprincipled in sexual matters. **2** archaic disregarding accepted rules or conventions, especially in grammar or literary style.
– DERIVATIVES **licentiously** adv. **licentiousness** n.
– ORIGIN ME: from L. *licentiosus*, from *licentia* 'freedom'.

**lichen** /ˈlʌɪk(ə)n, ˈlɪtʃ(ə)n/ • n. **1** a simple composite plant consisting of a fungus in association with an alga, typically growing on rocks, walls, and trees. **2** a skin disease in which small, round, hard lesions occur close together.
– DERIVATIVES **lichened** adj. **lichenology** n. **lichenous** adj.
– ORIGIN C17: via L. from Gk *leikhēn*.

**licit** /ˈlɪsɪt/ • adj. not forbidden; lawful.
– DERIVATIVES **licitly** adv.
– ORIGIN C15: from L. *licitus*, *licere* 'allow'.

**lick** • v. **1** pass the tongue over (something), typically in order to taste, moisten, or clean it. **2** move lightly and quickly like a tongue. **3** informal defeat comprehensively. • n. **1** an act of licking. ➤a place where animals come to lick salt. **2** informal a small amount or quick application of something. **3** informal a short phrase or solo in jazz or popular music. **4** informal a smart blow.
– PHRASES **at a lick** informal at a fast pace. **a lick and a promise** informal a hasty wash. **lick someone's boots** (or vulgar slang **arse**) be excessively obsequious towards someone.
– DERIVATIVES **-licker** n. **licking** n.
– ORIGIN OE *liccian*, of W. Gmc origin.

**lickerish** /ˈlɪkərɪʃ/ • adj. **1** lecherous. **2** W. Indian or archaic fond of eating; greedy.
– DERIVATIVES **lickerishly** adv.
– ORIGIN C15: alt. of obs. *lickerous*, from an Anglo-Norman Fr. var. of OFr. *lecheros* (see **LECHEROUS**).

**lickety-split** • adv. N. Amer. informal at full speed.
– ORIGIN C19 (in the phr. *as fast as lickety* 'at full speed'): from a fanciful extension of **LICK** + **SPLIT**.

**lickspittle** • n. a person who behaves obsequiously to those in power.

**licorice** • n. US spelling of **LIQUORICE**.

**lictor** /ˈlɪktə/ • n. (in ancient Rome) an officer attending a consul or magistrate.
– ORIGIN L., perh. rel. to *ligare* 'to bind'.

**lid** • n. **1** a removable or hinged cover for the top of a container. **2** an eyelid. **3** the top crust of a pie. **4** Botany the operculum of a moss capsule.
– DERIVATIVES **lidded** adj. **lidless** adj.
– ORIGIN OE *hlid*, of Gmc origin, from a base meaning 'cover'.

**lidar** /ˈlʌɪdɑː/ • n. a detection system which works on the principle of radar, but uses light from a laser.
– ORIGIN 1960s: blend of **LIGHT**[1] and **RADAR**.

**lido** /ˈliːdəʊ, ˈlʌɪ-/ • n. (pl. **-os**) a public open-air swimming pool or bathing beach.
– ORIGIN C17: from Ital. *Lido*, the name of a bathing beach near Venice, from *lido* 'shore'.

**lidocaine** /ˈlɪdə(ʊ)keɪn/ • n. chiefly N. Amer. another term for **LIGNOCAINE**.
– ORIGIN 1940s: from *(acetani)lid(e)* + *-caine* (from **COCAINE**).

**lie**[1] • v. (**lying**; past **lay**; past part. **lain**) **1** be in or assume a horizontal or resting position on a supporting surface. ➤be buried in a particular place. **2** be or remain in a specified state. **3** reside or be found: *the solution lies in a return to traditional values.* ➤be situated in a specified position or direction. **4** Law (of an action, charge, or claim) be admissible or sustainable. • n. **1** the way, direction, or position in which something lies or comes to rest. **2** the place of cover of an animal or a bird.
– PHRASES **let something lie** take no action regarding a sensitive matter. **lie low** keep out of sight; avoid attention. **the lie** (N. Amer. **lay**) **of the land 1** the features or characteristics of an area. **2** the current situation or state of affairs. **take something lying down** accept an insult, setback, or rebuke without protest.
– PHRASAL VERBS **lie behind** be the real reason for. **lie in 1** Brit. remain in bed after the normal time for getting up. **2** archaic (of a pregnant woman) go to bed to give birth. **lie off** Nautical (of a ship) stand some distance from shore or from another ship. **lie over** US break one's journey. **lie to** Nautical (of a ship) come almost to a stop with its head towards the wind. **lie up** (of a ship) go into dock or be out of commission. ➤(**lie something up**) put a boat in dock or out of commission. **lie with** archaic have sexual intercourse with.
– ORIGIN OE *licgan*, of Gmc origin.

**lie**[2] • n. an intentionally false statement. ➤a situation involving deception or founded on a mistaken impression: *she had been living a lie.* • v. (**lies, lied, lying**) tell a lie or lies. ➤(of a thing) present a false impression.
– PHRASES **give the lie to** serve to show that (something assumed to be true) is not true. **lie through one's teeth** informal tell an outright lie.
– ORIGIN OE *lyge* (n.), *lēogan* (v.), of Gmc origin.

**Liebfraumilch** /ˈliːbfraʊˌmɪlʃ, German ˈliːpfraʊˌmɪlç/ • n. a light white wine from the Rhine region.
– ORIGIN Ger., from *lieb* 'dear' + *Frau* 'lady' (referring to the Virgin Mary, patroness of the convent where it was

first made) + *Milch* 'milk'.

**Liechtensteiner** /'lɪktən,stʌɪnə, German 'lɪçtn,ʃtaɪnɐ/ ● n. a native or inhabitant of Liechtenstein.

**lied** /liːd, -t/ ● n. (pl. **lieder** /'liːdə/) a type of German song, especially of the Romantic period, typically for solo voice with piano accompaniment.
– ORIGIN from Ger. *Lied*.

**lie detector** ● n. an instrument for determining whether a person is telling the truth by testing for physiological changes considered to be associated with lying.

**lie-down** ● n. chiefly Brit. a short rest on a bed or sofa.

**lief** /liːf/ ● adv. (**as lief**) archaic as happily; as gladly.
– ORIGIN OE *lēof* 'dear, pleasant', of Gmc origin: rel. to LEAVE² and LOVE.

**liege** /liːdʒ/ historical ● adj. concerned with or relating to the relationship between a feudal superior and a vassal. ● n. **1** (also **liege lord**) a feudal superior or sovereign. **2** a vassal or subject.
– ORIGIN ME: via OFr. *lige, liege* from med. L. *laeticus*, prob. of Gmc origin.

**liegeman** ● n. (pl. **-men**) historical a vassal who owes feudal service or allegiance to a nobleman.

**lie-in** ● n. chiefly Brit. a prolonged stay in bed in the morning.

**lien** /liːn, 'liːən, 'lʌɪən/ ● n. Law a right to keep possession of property belonging to another person until a debt owed by that person is discharged.
– ORIGIN C16: from Fr., via OFr. *loien* from L. *ligamen* 'bond'.

**lierne** /lɪ'əːn/ ● n. Architecture (in vaulting) a short rib connecting the bosses and intersections of the principal ribs.
– ORIGIN ME: from Fr., perh. a transferred use of dial. *lierne* (standard Fr. *liane*) 'clematis'.

**lieu** /ljuː, luː/ ● n. (in phr. **in lieu (of)**) instead (of).
– ORIGIN ME: via Fr. from L. *locus* 'place'.

**Lieut.** ● abbrev. Lieutenant.

**lieutenant** /lɛf'tɛnənt/ ● n. **1** a deputy or substitute acting for a superior. **2** a rank of officer in the British army, above second lieutenant and below captain. **3** a rank of officer in the navy, above sub lieutenant and below lieutenant commander. **4** (in the US) a police officer next in rank below captain.
– DERIVATIVES **lieutenancy** n. (pl. **-ies**).
– ORIGIN ME: from OFr. (see LIEU, TENANT).

**lieutenant colonel** ● n. a rank of officer in the army and the US air force, above major and below colonel.

**lieutenant commander** ● n. a rank of officer in the navy, above lieutenant and below commander.

**lieutenant general** ● n. a high rank of officer in the army, above major general and below general.

**lieutenant governor** ● n. the acting or deputy governor of a state or province.

**life** ● n. (pl. **lives**) **1** the condition that distinguishes animals and plants from inorganic matter, including the capacity for growth, functional activity, and continual change preceding death. ➤living things and their activity. ➤a particular type or aspect of people's existence: *school life*. **2** the existence of an individual human being or animal. ➤a biography. ➤(in various games) each of a specified number of chances each player has before being put out. **3** informal a sentence of imprisonment for life. **4** vitality, vigour, or energy. **5** [as modifier] (in art) based on a living rather than an imagined form: *a life drawing*.
– PHRASES **come** (or **bring**) **to life 1** regain or cause to regain consciousness. **2** become or cause to become active, lively, or interesting. **for dear** (or **one's**) **life** as if or in order to escape death. **for the life of me** informal however hard I try. **as large as** (or **larger than**) **life** informal conspicuously present. **the life and soul of the party** a vivacious and sociable person. **a matter of life and death** a matter of vital importance. **not on your life** informal emphatically not. **see life** gain a wide experience of the world. **take one's life in one's hands** risk being killed.
– ORIGIN OE *līf*, of Gmc origin; rel. to LIVE¹.

**life assurance** ● n. chiefly Brit. another term for LIFE INSURANCE.

**lifebelt** ● n. chiefly Brit. a ring of buoyant or inflatable material used to help a person who has fallen into water to stay afloat.

**lifeblood** ● n. **1** poetic/literary blood, as being necessary to life. **2** an indispensable factor or force giving something its strength and vitality.

**lifeboat** ● n. **1** a specially constructed boat launched from land to rescue people in distress at sea. **2** a small boat kept on a ship for use in an emergency.
– DERIVATIVES **lifeboatman** n. (pl. **-men**).

**lifebuoy** ● n. chiefly Brit. a buoyant support such as a lifebelt for keeping a person afloat in water.

**life cycle** ● n. the series of changes in the life of an organism including reproduction.

**life expectancy** ● n. the period that a person may expect to live.

**life force** ● n. the force that gives something its life, vitality, or strength.

**life form** ● n. any living thing.

**lifeguard** ● n. a person employed to rescue bathers who get into difficulty at a beach or swimming pool.

**Life Guards** ● pl. n. (in the UK) a regiment of the Household Cavalry.

**life imprisonment** ● n. a long term of imprisonment (rarely the whole of a person's life), which (in the UK) is now the only sentence for murder and the maximum for any crime.

**life insurance** ● n. insurance that pays out a sum of money either on the death of the insured person or after a set period.

**life jacket** ● n. a sleeveless buoyant or inflatable jacket for keeping a person afloat in water.

**lifeless** ● adj. **1** dead or apparently dead. ➤devoid of living things. **2** lacking vigour, vitality, or excitement.
– DERIVATIVES **lifelessly** adv. **lifelessness** n.

**lifelike** ● adj. accurate in its representation of a living person or thing.

**lifeline** ● n. **1** a rope or line used for life-saving, typically one thrown to rescue someone in difficulties in water or one used by sailors to secure themselves to a boat. ➤a line used by a diver for sending signals to the surface. **2** a thing which is essential for the continued existence of someone or something or which provides a means of escape from a difficult situation. **3** (in palmistry) a line on the palm of a person's hand, regarded as indicating how long they will live.

**lifelong** ● adj. lasting or remaining in a particular state throughout a person's life.

**life member** ● n. a person who has lifelong membership of a society.
– DERIVATIVES **life membership** n.

**life office** ● n. an office or company dealing in life insurance.

**life peer** (or **peeress**) ● n. (in the UK) a peer (or peeress) whose title cannot be inherited.
– DERIVATIVES **life peerage** n.

**life preserver** ● n. **1** a life jacket or lifebelt. **2** Brit. a short truncheon with a heavily loaded end.

**lifer** ● n. **1** informal a person serving a life sentence. **2** N. Amer. a person who spends their life in a particular career, especially in the armed forces.

**life raft** ● n. an inflatable raft for use in an emergency at sea.

**lifesaver** ● n. **1** informal a thing that saves one from serious difficulty. **2** Austral./NZ a lifeguard on a beach.

**life sciences** ● pl. n. the sciences concerned with the study of living organisms, including biology, botany, zoology, and related subjects.
– DERIVATIVES **life scientist** n.

**life sentence** ● n. a punishment of life imprisonment.

**life-size** (also **life-sized**) ● adj. of the same size as the person or thing represented.

**lifespan** ● n. the length of time for which a person or animal lives or a thing functions.

**lifestyle** ● n. the way in which one lives.

**lifestyle drug** • n. a pharmaceutical product characterized as improving the quality of life rather than alleviating or curing disease.

**life support** • n. Medicine maintenance of vital functions following disablement or in an adverse environment.

**life table** • n. a table of statistics relating to life expectancy and mortality.

**life-threatening** • adj. potentially fatal.

**lifetime** • n. **1** the duration of a person's life. ➤ the duration of a thing or its usefulness. **2** informal a very long time.

**LIFO** /ˈlʌɪfəʊ/ • abbrev. last in, first out (chiefly with reference to methods of stock valuation and data storage).

**lift** • v. **1** raise or be raised to a higher position or level. ➤ raise (someone's spirits or confidence). ➤ dig up. **2** pick up and move to a different position. ➤ transport by air. ➤ (**lift off**) (of an aircraft, spacecraft, etc.) take off, especially vertically. **3** formally remove or end (a legal restriction, decision, etc.). **4** carry off or win (a prize or event). ➤ informal steal. **5** informal arrest. • n. **1** Brit. a platform or compartment housed in a shaft for raising and lowering people or things. ➤ a device for carrying people up or down a mountain. **2** a built-up heel or device in a boot or shoe. **3** an act or instance of lifting. ➤ upward force exerted by the air on an aerofoil or other structure, counteracting gravity. ➤ the maximum weight that an aircraft can raise. **4** a free ride in another person's vehicle. **5** a feeling of increased cheerfulness.
– PHRASES **lift a finger** (or **hand**) [usu. with neg.] make the slightest effort.
– DERIVATIVES **liftable** adj. **lifter** n.
– ORIGIN ME: from ON *lypta*, of Gmc origin; rel. to **LOFT**.

**lift-off** • n. the vertical take-off of a spacecraft, rocket, etc.

**lig** Brit. informal • v. (**ligged**, **ligging**) take advantage of free parties, shows, or travel offered by companies for publicity purposes. • n. a free party or show of this type.
– DERIVATIVES **ligger** n.
– ORIGIN 1960s: from a dial. var. of **LIE**[1], lit. 'lie about, loaf', whence 'freeload'.

**ligament** /ˈlɪɡəm(ə)nt/ • n. Anatomy a short band of tough, flexible, fibrous connective tissue which connects two bones or cartilages or holds together a joint. ➤ a membranous fold that supports an organ and keeps it in position.
– DERIVATIVES **ligamental** adj. **ligamentary** adj. **ligamentous** adj.
– ORIGIN ME: from L. *ligamentum* 'bond', from *ligare* 'to bind'.

**ligand** /ˈlɪɡ(ə)nd/ • n. **1** Chemistry an ion or molecule attached to a metal atom by coordinate bonding. **2** Biochemistry a molecule that binds to another.
– ORIGIN 1950s: from L. *ligandus* 'that can be tied'.

**ligase** /ˈlɪɡeɪz/ • n. Biochemistry an enzyme which brings about ligation.
– ORIGIN 1960s: from L. *ligare* 'to bind' + **-ASE**.

**ligate** /lɪˈɡeɪt/ • v. Surgery tie up (an artery or vessel).
– ORIGIN C16 (earlier (ME) as *ligation*): from L. *ligat-*, *ligare* 'to tie'.

**ligation** • n. **1** the surgical procedure of tying a ligature tightly around a blood vessel or other duct or tube in the body. **2** Biochemistry the joining of two DNA strands or other molecules by a phosphate ester linkage.

**ligature** /ˈlɪɡətʃə/ • n. **1** a thing used for tying something tightly. ➤ a cord used in surgery, especially to tie up a bleeding artery. **2** Music a slur or tie. **3** Printing a character consisting of two or more joined letters, e.g. *æ*. • v. bind or connect with a ligature.
– ORIGIN ME: via late L. *ligatura* from L. *ligat-*, *ligare* 'to tie'.

**liger** /ˈlʌɪɡə/ • n. the hybrid offspring of a male lion and a tigress.

**light**[1] • n. **1** the natural agent that stimulates sight and makes things visible; electromagnetic radiation from about 390 to 740 nm in wavelength. ➤ a source of illumination. ➤ (**lights**) traffic lights. ➤ Law the light falling on windows, the obstruction of which by a neighbour is illegal. **2** an expression in someone's eyes. ➤ enlightenment: *light dawned in her eyes.* ➤ (**lights**) a person's opinions, standards, and abilities. **3** an area that is brighter or paler than its surroundings. **4** a device producing a flame or spark. **5** a window or opening to let light in. ➤ a perpendicular division of a mullioned window. ➤ a pane of glass in a greenhouse or cold frame. **6** a person eminent in a particular sphere. • v. (past **lit**; past part. **lit** or **lighted**) **1** provide with light. ➤ (**light up**) become illuminated. ➤ (**light up**) (of the face or eyes) suddenly become animated with liveliness or joy. **2** ignite or be ignited. ➤ (**light up**) ignite a cigarette, cigar, or pipe and begin to smoke it. • adj. **1** having a considerable or sufficient amount of light. **2** (of a colour or object) reflecting a lot of light; pale.
– PHRASES **bring** (or **come**) **to light** make (or become) widely known or evident. **go out like a light** informal fall asleep or lose consciousness suddenly. **in a —— light** in the way specified: *the audit portrayed them in a favourable light.* **in (the) light of** taking (something) into consideration. **light at the end of the tunnel** an indication that a period of difficulty is ending. **the light of day** general public attention. **the light of someone's life** a much loved person. **lit up** informal, dated drunk. **punch someone's lights out** beat someone up. **see the light** understand or realize something. ➤ undergo religious conversion. **see the light of day** be born. ➤ come into existence. **throw** (or **cast** or **shed**) **light on** help to explain by providing further information.
– DERIVATIVES **lightish** adj. **lightless** adj. **lightness** n.
– ORIGIN OE *lēoht*, *līht* (n. and adj.), *līhtan* (v.), of Gmc origin.

**light**[2] • adj. **1** of little weight. ➤ deficient in weight. ➤ carrying or suitable for small loads. ➤ carrying only light armaments. ➤ (of a vehicle, ship, etc.) unladen or with less than a full load. ➤ (of food or a meal) small in quantity and easy to digest. ➤ low in fat, cholesterol, sugar, or alcohol. ➤ (of soil) friable, porous, and workable. **2** not strongly or heavily built. **3** relatively low in density, amount, or intensity. ➤ (**light on**) rather short of. ➤ (of sleep or a sleeper) easily disturbed. ➤ easily borne or done: *some light housework.* **4** gentle or delicate. ➤ (of type) having thin strokes. **5** not profound or serious. ➤ free from worry: *I left with a light heart.* **6** Physics containing atoms of an isotope of relatively low mass. **7** archaic (of a woman) promiscuous.
– PHRASES **make light of** treat as unimportant. **make light work of** accomplish quickly and easily. **travel light** travel with a minimum load or little luggage.
– DERIVATIVES **lightish** adj. **lightly** adv. **lightness** n.
– ORIGIN OE *lēocht*, *līht* (n.), *lēohte* (adv.), of Gmc origin.

**light**[3] • v. (past and past part. **lit** or **lighted**) **1** (**light on/upon**) come upon or discover by chance. **2** archaic descend. ➤ (**light on**) fall or land on. **3** (**light into**) N. Amer. informal attack. **4** (**light out**) N. Amer. informal depart hurriedly.
– ORIGIN OE *līhtan*, from **LIGHT**[2]; cf. **ALIGHT**[1].

**light box** • n. a box with a translucent top and containing an electric light, providing an evenly lighted flat surface for viewing transparencies.

**light bulb** • n. a glass bulb containing inert gas, fitted into a lamp or ceiling socket, which provides light when an electric current is passed through it.

**light-emitting diode** • n. see **LED**.

**lighten**[1] • v. **1** make or become lighter in weight. **2** make or become less serious.

**lighten**[2] • v. **1** make or become brighter. **2** archaic enlighten spiritually. **3** (**it lightens**, **it is lightening**, etc.) rare flash with lightning.

**light engine** • n. a railway locomotive with no vehicles attached.

**lightening** • n. a drop in the level of the womb during the last weeks of pregnancy as the head of the fetus engages in the pelvis.

**lighter**[1] • n. a device producing a small flame, used to light cigarettes.

**lighter**[2] • n. a flat-bottomed barge used to transfer goods to and from ships in harbour.
– DERIVATIVES **lighterman** n. (pl. **-men**).

– ORIGIN ME: from **LIGHT**[2] (in the sense 'unload'), or from Mid. Low Ger. *luchter.*

**lighterage** • n. the transference of cargo using a lighter.

**lightfast** • adj. (of a pigment) not prone to discolour when exposed to light.
– DERIVATIVES **lightfastness** n.

**light-fingered** • adj. prone to steal.

**light flyweight** • n. the lowest weight in amateur boxing.

**light-footed** • adj. fast, nimble, or stealthy on one's feet.
– DERIVATIVES **light-footedly** adv.

**light gun** • n. Computing a hand-held gunlike photosensitive device, used for passing information to a computer.

**light-headed** • adj. dizzy and slightly faint.
– DERIVATIVES **light-headedly** adv. **light-headedness** n.

**light-hearted** • adj. amusing and entertaining.
– DERIVATIVES **light-heartedly** adv. **light-heartedness** n.

**light heavyweight** • n. a weight in boxing and other sports intermediate between middleweight and heavyweight.

**lighthouse** • n. a tower or other structure containing a beacon light to warn ships at sea.

**light industry** • n. the manufacture of small or light articles.

**lighting** • n. equipment for producing light. ➤the arrangement or effect of lights.

**lighting-up time** • n. Brit. the time at which motorists are required by law to switch their vehicles' lights on.

**light meter** • n. an instrument measuring the intensity of light, used when taking photographs.

**light middleweight** • n. a weight in amateur boxing intermediate between welterweight and middleweight.

**lightning** • n. **1** the occurrence of a brief natural high-voltage electrical discharge between a cloud and the ground or within a cloud, accompanied by a bright flash and often thunder. **2** [as modifier] very quick: *lightning speed.*
– ORIGIN ME: special use of *lightening* (verbal noun from **LIGHTEN**[2]).

**lightning bug** • n. North American term for **FIREFLY**.

**lightning conductor** (also chiefly N. Amer. **lightning rod**) • n. Brit. a metal rod or wire fixed in a high and exposed place to divert lightning into the ground.

**lightning strike** • n. Brit. a strike by workers at short notice, especially without union backing.

**light pen** • n. **1** Computing a hand-held pen-like photosensitive device held to a computer display screen for passing information to the computer. **2** a hand-held device for reading bar codes.

**light pollution** • n. excessive brightening of the night sky by street lights and other man-made sources.

**lightproof** • adj. able to block out light completely.

**light railway** • n. a railway for light traffic.

**light reaction** • n. Biochemistry (in photosynthesis) the reaction in which light is absorbed and converted to chemical energy in the form of ATP.

**lights** • pl. n. the lungs of sheep, pigs, or bullocks as food for pets.
– ORIGIN ME: use of **LIGHT**[2] as a noun (so named because of their lightness); cf. **LUNG**.

**lightship** (also **light vessel**) • n. an anchored boat with a beacon light to warn ships at sea.

**lightsome** • adj. chiefly poetic/literary **1** carefree. **2** gracefully nimble.
– DERIVATIVES **lightsomely** adv. **lightsomeness** n.

**light water** • n. **1** water containing the normal proportion (or less) of deuterium oxide. **2** firefighting foam which floats on flammable liquids lighter than water.

**lightweight** • n. **1** a weight in boxing and other sports intermediate between featherweight and welterweight. **2** informal a person of little importance or influence. • adj. **1** of thin material or build. **2** informal having little importance or influence.

**light well** • n. an open area or vertical shaft in the centre of a building, typically roofed with glass.

**light welterweight** • n. a weight in amateur boxing intermediate between lightweight and welterweight.

**light year** • n. Astronomy a unit of distance equivalent to the distance that light travels in one year, $9.4607 \times 10^{12}$ km (nearly 6 million million miles).

**ligneous** /ˈlɪɡnɪəs/ • adj. made, consisting of, or resembling wood.
– ORIGIN C17: from L. *ligneus* 'relating to wood' + **-OUS**.

**ligni-** • comb. form relating to wood: *lignify.*
– ORIGIN from L. *lignum* 'wood'.

**lignify** /ˈlɪɡnɪfʌɪ/ • v. (**-ies**, **-ied**) [usu. as adj. **lignified**] Botany make rigid and woody by the deposition of lignin in cell walls.
– DERIVATIVES **lignification** n.

**lignin** /ˈlɪɡnɪn/ • n. Botany a complex organic polymer deposited in the cell walls of many plants, making them rigid and woody.
– ORIGIN C19: from **LIGNI-** + **-IN**[1].

**lignite** /ˈlɪɡnʌɪt/ • n. soft brownish coal, intermediate between bituminous coal and peat.
– DERIVATIVES **lignitic** adj.
– ORIGIN C19: coined in Fr. from L. *lignum* 'wood' + **-ITE**[1].

**ligno-** • comb. form **1** relating to wood: *lignotuber.* **2** representing **LIGNIN**: *lignocellulose.*
– ORIGIN from L. *lignum* 'wood'.

**lignocaine** /ˈlɪɡnə(ʊ)keɪn/ • n. Medicine a synthetic compound used as a local anaesthetic, e.g. for dental surgery, and in treating abnormal heart rhythms.
– ORIGIN 1950s: from **LIGNO-** (L. equivalent of **XYLO-**, used in the earlier name *xylocaine* and reflecting chemical similarity to **XYLENE**) + *-caine* (from **COCAINE**).

**lignocellulose** /ˌlɪɡnə(ʊ)ˈsɛljʊləʊz, -s/ • n. Botany a complex of lignin and cellulose present in the cell walls of woody plants.

**lignotuber** /ˈlɪɡnəʊˌtjuːbə/ • n. Botany a rounded woody growth at or below ground level on some shrubs and trees that grow in areas subject to fire or drought, containing a mass of buds and food reserves.

**lignum vitae** /ˌlɪɡnəm ˈvʌɪtiː, ˈviːtʌɪ/ • n. another term for **GUAIACUM**.
– ORIGIN L., 'wood of life'.

**ligroin** /ˈlɪɡrəʊɪn/ • n. Chemistry a volatile hydrocarbon mixture obtained from petroleum, used as a solvent.
– ORIGIN C19: of unknown origin.

**ligula** /ˈlɪɡjʊlə/ • n. (pl. **ligulae** /-liː/) Entomology the strap-shaped end of an insect's labium.
– DERIVATIVES **ligular** adj.
– ORIGIN C18: from L. 'strap'.

**ligule** /ˈlɪɡjuːl/ • n. Botany a narrow strap-shaped part of a plant, especially a membranous scale on the inner side of the leaf sheath in grasses.
– DERIVATIVES **ligulate** adj.
– ORIGIN C19: from L. *ligula* 'strap'.

**Ligurian** /lɪˈɡ(j)ʊərɪən/ • n. a native or inhabitant of Liguria, a region of NW Italy. • adj. of or relating to Liguria.

**ligustrum** /lɪˈɡʌstrəm/ • n. a plant of a genus that comprises the privets. [Genus *Ligustrum.*]
– ORIGIN C17: from L.

**likable** • adj. variant spelling of **LIKEABLE**.

**like**[1] • prep. **1** similar to. ➤in the manner of. ➤in a way appropriate to. ➤characteristic of. ➤used to ask about someone's or something's characteristics. **2** in this manner. **3** such as. • conj. informal **1** in the same way that. **2** as though. • n. a similar person or thing. ➤(**the like**) things of the same kind. • adj. having similar characteristics to another. • adv. **1** informal used in speech as a meaningless filler. **2** (**like as/to**) archaic in the manner of.
– PHRASES **and the like** et cetera. **like anything** informal to a great degree. (**as**) **like as not** probably. **like so** informal in this manner. **the likes of** informal a person such as.
– ORIGIN ME: from ON *líkr*; rel. to **ALIKE**.

**like**[2] • v. **1** find agreeable, enjoyable, or satisfactory. **2** wish for; want. ➤prefer. ➤(in questions) feel about or regard. • n. (**likes**) the things one likes.
– ORIGIN OE *līcian* 'be pleasing', of Gmc origin.

**-like** ● comb. form (added to nouns) similar to; characteristic of: *crust-like*.

**likeable** (also **likable**) ● adj. pleasant; easy to like.
– DERIVATIVES **likeability** n. **likeableness** n. **likeably** adv.

**likelihood** ● n. the state or fact of being likely.

**likely** ● adj. (**-ier, -iest**) **1** such as well might happen or be true. **2** promising. ● adv. probably.
– PHRASES **a likely story!** used to express disbelief. **as likely as not** probably. **not likely!** informal certainly not.
– DERIVATIVES **likeliness** n.
– ORIGIN ME: from ON *líkligr*, from *líkr* (see LIKE[1]).

**like-minded** ● adj. having similar tastes or opinions.
– DERIVATIVES **like-mindedness** n.

**liken** ● v. (**liken someone/thing to**) point out the resemblance of someone or something to.

**likeness** ● n. resemblance. ➤ the semblance or outward appearance of. ➤ a portrait or representation.
– ORIGIN OE *gelīknes* (see ALIKE, -NESS).

**likewise** ● adv. **1** also; moreover. **2** similarly.
– ORIGIN ME: from the phr. *in like wise*.

**liking** ● n. **1** a regard or fondness for something. **2** one's taste.

**likuta** /lɪˈkuːtə/ ● n. (pl. **makuta** /məˈkuːtə/) a monetary unit of Zaire (Democratic Republic of Congo), equal to one hundredth of a zaire.
– ORIGIN from Kikongo.

**lilac** ● n. **1** a shrub or small tree with fragrant violet, pink, or white blossom. [Genus *Syringa*; several species.] **2** a pale pinkish-violet colour.
– ORIGIN C17: from obs. Fr., via Sp. and Arab. from Pers. *līlak*, var. of *nīlak* 'bluish', from *nīl* 'blue'.

**lilangeni** /ˌliːlaŋˈgeɪni/ ● n. (pl. **emalangeni** /ɪˌmalaŋˈgeɪni/) the basic monetary unit of Swaziland, equal to 100 cents.
– ORIGIN from the Bantu prefix *li-* (used to denote a sing.) + *-langeni* 'member of a royal family'.

**liliaceous** /ˌlɪlɪˈeɪʃəs/ ● adj. Botany relating to or denoting plants of the lily family (Liliaceae).

**Lilliputian** /ˌlɪlɪˈpjuːʃ(ə)n/ ● adj. trivial or very small. ● n. a Lilliputian person or thing.
– ORIGIN C18: from the imaginary country of *Lilliput* in Jonathan Swift's *Gulliver's Travels* (1726), inhabited by 6-inch high people, + -IAN.

**lilo** /ˈlʌɪləʊ/ (also trademark **Li-lo**) ● n. (pl. **-os**) an inflatable mattress used as a bed or for floating on water.
– ORIGIN 1930s: alt. of *lie low*.

**lilt** ● n. a pleasant gentle accent. ➤ a gentle rhythm in a tune. ➤ archaic, chiefly Scottish a cheerful tune. ● v. [often as adj. **lilting**] speak, sing, or sound with a lilt.
– ORIGIN ME *lulte* (in the senses 'sound (an alarm)' or 'lift up (the voice)'), of unknown origin.

**lily** ● n. **1** a bulbous plant with large trumpet-shaped, typically fragrant, flowers on a tall, slender stem. [Genus *Lilium*: many species.] ➤ used in names of other similar plants, e.g. **arum lily**. **2** a heraldic fleur-de-lis.
– DERIVATIVES **lilied** adj.
– ORIGIN OE *lilie*, from L. *lilium*, from Gk *leirion*.

**lily-livered** ● adj. cowardly.

**lily of the valley** ● n. a plant of the lily family, with broad leaves and fragrant white bell-shaped flowers. [Genus *Convallaria*.]

**lily pad** ● n. a leaf of a water lily.

**lily-trotter** ● n. (especially in Africa) a jacana.

**lily-white** ● adj. **1** pure white. **2** totally innocent or immaculate.

**lima bean** /ˈliːmə/ ● n. **1** an edible flat whitish bean. **2** the tropical American plant which yields this bean. [*Phaseolus lunatus*.]
– ORIGIN C18: from the name of the Peruvian capital *Lima*.

**limb**[1] ● n. **1** an arm, leg, or wing. **2** a large branch of a tree. ➤ a branch of a cross. **3** a projecting landform such as a spur of a mountain range. ➤ a projecting section of a building.
– PHRASES **life and limb** life and bodily faculties. **out on a limb 1** isolated. **2** in a position not supported by anyone else. **tear someone limb from limb** violently dismember someone.
– DERIVATIVES **-limbed** adj. **limbless** adj.
– ORIGIN OE *lim*, of Gmc origin.

**limb**[2] ● n. **1** Astronomy a specified edge of the disc of the sun, moon, or other celestial object. **2** Botany the blade or broad part of a leaf or petal. ➤ the spreading upper part of a tube-shaped flower. **3** the graduated arc of a quadrant or other scientific instrument.
– ORIGIN ME: from Fr. *limbe* or L. *limbus* 'hem, border'.

**Limba** /ˈlɪmbə/ ● n. (pl. same or **Limbas**) **1** a member of a West African people of Sierra Leone and Guinea. **2** the Niger–Congo language of this people.
– ORIGIN the name in Limba.

**limber**[1] /ˈlɪmbə/ ● adj. supple; flexible. ● v. (often **limber up**) warm up in preparation for exercise or activity.
– DERIVATIVES **limberness** n.
– ORIGIN C16: perh. from LIMBER[2] in the dial. sense 'cart shaft', with allusion to the to-and-fro motion.

**limber**[2] /ˈlɪmbə/ ● n. the detachable front part of a gun carriage. ● v. attach a limber to (a gun).
– ORIGIN ME *lymour*, appar. rel. to med. L. *limonarius* from *limo, limon-* 'shaft'.

**limberneck** ● n. a kind of botulism affecting poultry.

**limber pine** ● n. a small pine tree with tough pliant branches, native to the Rocky Mountains of North America. [*Pinus flexilis*.]

**limbic system** /ˈlɪmbɪk/ ● n. a complex system of nerves and networks in the brain, controlling the basic emotions and drives.
– ORIGIN C19: *limbic* from Fr. *limbique*, from L. LIMBUS.

**limbo**[1] ● n. **1** (in some Christian beliefs) the supposed abode of the souls of unbaptized infants, and of the just who died before Christ. **2** an uncertain period of awaiting a decision or resolution: *he was left in limbo*.
– ORIGIN ME: from the med. L. phr. *in limbo*, from *limbus* 'hem, border, limbo'.

**limbo**[2] ● n. (pl. **-os**) a West Indian dance in which the dancer bends backwards to pass under a horizontal bar which is progressively lowered toward the ground. ● v. dance the limbo.
– ORIGIN 1950s: from LIMBER[1].

**Limburger** ● n. a soft white cheese with a strong smell, originally made in the Belgian province of Limburg.

**limbus** /ˈlɪmbəs/ ● n. (pl. **limbi** /-bʌɪ/) Anatomy the border of a structure, especially the junction of the cornea and sclera in the eye.
– ORIGIN ME: from L., 'edge, border'.

**lime**[1] ● n. **1** quicklime, slaked lime, or any salt or alkali containing calcium. **2** archaic birdlime. ● v. **1** treat with lime. **2** archaic catch (a bird) with birdlime.
– DERIVATIVES **limy** adj. (**-ier, -iest**).
– ORIGIN OE *līm*, of Gmc origin; rel. to LOAM.

**lime**[2] ● n. **1** a rounded green citrus fruit similar to a lemon. ➤ a drink made from lime juice. **2** (also **lime tree**) the evergreen citrus tree which produces this fruit. [*Citrus aurantifolia*.] **3** a bright light green colour.
– ORIGIN C17: from Fr., from mod. Provençal *limo*, Sp. *lima*, from Arab. *līma*; cf. LEMON.

**lime**[3] (also **lime tree**) ● n. a deciduous tree with heart-shaped leaves and fragrant yellowish blossom. [Genus *Tilia*: many species.]
– ORIGIN C17: alt. of obs. *line*, from OE *lind* (see LINDEN).

**limeade** ● n. a drink made from lime juice sweetened with sugar.

**limekiln** ● n. a kiln in which quicklime is produced.

**limelight** ● n. **1** (**the limelight**) the focus of public attention. **2** an intense white light produced by heating lime in an oxyhydrogen flame, formerly used in theatres.

**limen** /ˈlʌɪmɛn, ˈliː-/ ● n. (pl. **limens** or **limina** /ˈlʌɪmɪnə, ˈliː-/) Psychology a threshold below which a stimulus is not perceived or distinguished from another.
– ORIGIN C17: from L., 'threshold'.

**limepit** ● n. historical a pit of lime in which hides were placed to remove hair and fur.

**limerick** /ˈlɪm(ə)rɪk/ ● n. a humorous five-line poem with a rhyme scheme *aabba*.
– ORIGIN C19: said to be from the chorus 'will you come up

to Limerick?', sung between improvised verses at a gathering.

**limestone** ● n. a hard sedimentary rock composed mainly of calcium carbonate, used as building material and in cement.

**lime sulphur** ● n. an insecticide and fungicide containing calcium polysulphides.

**limewash** ● n. a mixture of lime and water for coating walls. ● v. apply limewash to.

**lime water** ● n. Chemistry an alkaline solution of calcium hydroxide in water.

**Limey** ● n. (pl. **-eys**) N. Amer. & Austral., chiefly derogatory a British person.
– ORIGIN C19: from **LIME**[2] + **-Y**[1], because of the former enforced consumption of lime juice in the Brit. navy.

**liminal** /ˈlɪmɪn(ə)l/ ● adj. technical **1** of or relating to a transitional or initial stage. **2** at a boundary or threshold.
– DERIVATIVES **liminality** n.
– ORIGIN C19: from L. *limen, limin-* 'threshold' + **-AL**.

**limit** ● n. **1** a point beyond which something does not or may not pass. ➤a terminal point or boundary. ➤the furthest extent of one's endurance. **2** a restriction on the size or amount of something: *an age limit*. **3** Mathematics a value which a sequence, function, or sum can be made to approach progressively. ● v. (**limited**, **limiting**) set or serve as a limit to.
– PHRASES **be the limit** informal be intolerable. **off limits** out of bounds. **within limits** up to a point.
– DERIVATIVES **limitary** adj. (rare). **limitative** adj. **limiter** n. **limitless** adj. **limitlessly** adv. **limitlessness** n.
– ORIGIN ME: from L. *limes, limit-* 'boundary, frontier'; the verb is from L. *limitare*, from *limes*.

**limitation** ● n. **1** a restriction. ➤a defect or failing. **2** (also **limitation period**) Law a legally specified period beyond which an action may be defeated or a property right is not to continue.

**limited** ● adj. **1** restricted in size, amount, or extent. ➤not great in ability. **2** (of a monarchy or government) exercised under limitations of power prescribed by a constitution. **3** (**Limited**) Brit. denoting a limited company.
– DERIVATIVES **limitedness** n.

**limited company** (also **limited liability company**) ● n. Brit. a private company whose owners are legally responsible for its debts only to the extent of the amount of capital they invested.

**limited liability** ● n. Brit. the condition of being legally responsible for the debts of a company only to the extent of the nominal value of one's shares.

**limn** /lɪm/ ● v. poetic/literary depict or describe in painting or words. ➤suffuse or highlight with bright colour or light.
– DERIVATIVES **limner** n.
– ORIGIN ME (in the sense 'illuminate a manuscript'): alt. of obs. *lumine* 'illuminate', via OFr. *luminer* from L. *luminare* 'make light'.

**limnology** /lɪmˈnɒlədʒi/ ● n. the study of lakes and other bodies of fresh water.
– DERIVATIVES **limnological** adj. **limnologist** n.
– ORIGIN C19: from Gk *limnē* 'lake' + **-LOGY**.

**limo** ● n. (pl. **-os**) informal a limousine.

**limonene** /ˈlɪməniːn/ ● n. Chemistry a colourless liquid hydrocarbon with a lemon-like scent, present in lemon oil, orange oil, etc.
– ORIGIN C20: from Ger. *Limonen*, from *Limone* 'lemon', + **-ENE**.

**limonite** /ˈlʌɪmənʌɪt/ ● n. a form of iron ore consisting of a brownish mixture of hydrous ferric oxides.
– ORIGIN C19: from Ger. *Limonit*, prob. from Gk *leimōn* 'meadow'.

**Limousin** /ˈlɪmʊzã, French limuzɛ̃/ ● n. **1** a native or inhabitant of Limousin, a region of central France. **2** an animal of a French breed of beef cattle.

**limousine** /ˈlɪməziːn, ˌlɪməˈziːn/ ● n. a large, luxurious car, typically with a partition behind the driver. ➤chiefly N. Amer. a passenger vehicle carrying people to and from an airport.
– ORIGIN C20: from Fr., fem. adj. orig. denoting a caped cloak worn in the region of *Limousin*.

**limp**[1] ● v. walk with difficulty because of an injured leg or foot. ➤(of a damaged ship or aircraft) proceed with difficulty. ● n. a limping gait.
– ORIGIN ME: rel. to obs. *limphalt* 'lame', and prob. of Gmc origin.

**limp**[2] ● adj. **1** not stiff or firm. ➤(of a book cover) not stiffened with board. **2** without energy or will.
– DERIVATIVES **limply** adv. **limpness** n.
– ORIGIN C18: of unknown origin; perh. rel. to **LIMP**[1].

**limpet** ● n. a marine mollusc with a shallow conical shell and a broad muscular foot for clinging tightly to rocks. [*Patella vulgata* and other species.]
– ORIGIN OE *lempedu*, from med. L. *lampreda* 'limpet, lamprey'.

**limpet mine** ● n. a mine that attaches magnetically to a ship's hull and explodes after a certain time.

**limpid** ● adj. (of a liquid or the eyes) clear. ➤(especially of writing or music) clear and accessible or melodious.
– DERIVATIVES **limpidity** n. **limpidly** adv.
– ORIGIN ME: from L. *limpidus*; perh. rel. to **LYMPH**.

**limpkin** ● n. a wading marshbird with long legs and a long bill, found in the south-eastern US and tropical America. [*Aramus guarauna*.]
– ORIGIN C19: from **LIMP**[1] (with ref. to the bird's limping gait) + **-KIN**.

**limp-wristed** ● adj. informal effeminate.

**linac** /ˈlɪnak/ ● n. short for **LINEAR ACCELERATOR**.

**linage** /ˈlʌɪnɪdʒ/ ● n. the number of lines in printed or written matter.

**linchpin** (also **lynchpin**) ● n. **1** a pin through the end of an axle keeping a wheel in position. **2** an indispensable person or thing.
– ORIGIN ME: from OE *lynis* (in the sense 'linchpin') + **PIN**.

**Lincoln green** ● n. bright green woollen cloth formerly made at Lincoln in eastern England.

**Lincoln red** ● n. an animal of a breed of red shorthorn cattle.

**Lincs.** ● abbrev. Lincolnshire.

**linctus** /ˈlɪŋktəs/ ● n. Brit. thick liquid medicine, especially cough mixture.
– ORIGIN C17: from L., from *lingere* 'to lick'.

**lindane** /ˈlɪndeɪn/ ● n. a synthetic insecticide, now restricted in use owing to its persistence in the environment.
– ORIGIN 1940s: named after the Du. chemist Teunis van der *Linden*.

**linden** ● n. another name for the lime tree (**LIME**[3]).
– ORIGIN OE: from *lind* 'lime tree' (cf. **LIME**[3]) + **-EN**[3].

**line**[1] ● n. **1** a long, narrow mark or band. ➤Mathematics a straight or curved continuous extent of length without breadth. ➤a wrinkle in the skin. ➤a contour or outline as a feature of design. ➤a curve connecting all points having a common property on a map or graph. ➤the starting or finishing point in a race. ➤(**the Line**) the equator. ➤a notional limit or boundary. ➤Physics a narrow range of the spectrum that is noticeably brighter or darker than the adjacent parts. ➤[as modifier] Printing & Computing denoting an image consisting of lines and solid areas, with no gradation of tone. ➤each of (usually five) horizontal lines forming a stave in musical notation. ➤a sequence of notes or tones forming a melody. **2** a length of cord, wire, etc. serving a purpose. ➤a telephone connection. ➤a railway track or route. ➤a company providing a form of passenger transport on particular routes: *a shipping line*. **3** a row of written or printed words. ➤(**lines**) the words of an actor's part. ➤(**lines**) a number of repetitions of a sentence written out as a school punishment. **4** a row or connected series of people or things. ➤N. Amer. a queue. ➤a range of commercial goods. **5** a sphere of activity. ➤a direction, course, or channel. ➤(**lines**) a way of doing something: *thinking along the same lines*. ➤a policy. ➤informal a false or exaggerated story. **6** a connected series of military defences facing an enemy force. ➤a line of battle. ➤(**the line**) regular army regiments. ● v. **1** stand or be positioned at intervals along. **2** (**line someone/thing up**) arrange people or things in a row. **3** (**line someone/thing up**) have someone or something prepared. **4** [usu. as adj. **lined**] mark or cover with lines. **5** (**line out**) Baseball be caught out after hitting a line drive.

– PHRASES **above** (or **below**) **the line** Finance denoting or relating to money spent on items of current (or capital) expenditure. **come** (or **bring**) **into line** conform (or cause to conform). **the end of the line** the point at which one can go no further. **get a line on** informal learn something about. **in line** under control. **in line for** likely to receive. **in the line of duty** while one is working or serving in a military force. **in** (or **out of**) **line with** in (or not in) alignment or accordance with. **lay** (or **put**) **it on the line** speak frankly. **line of credit** an amount of credit extended to a borrower. **line of fire** the expected path of gunfire or a missile. **line of force** an imaginary line representing the strength and direction of a magnetic, gravitational, or electric field at any point. **line of march** the route taken in marching. **line of scrimmage** American Football the imaginary line separating the teams at the beginning of a play. **line of sight** a straight line along which an observer has unobstructed vision. **line of vision** the straight line along which an observer looks. **on the line 1** at serious risk. **2** (of a picture) hung with its centre about level with the spectator's eye. **out of line** informal behaving inappropriately or incorrectly.

– ORIGIN OE *līne* 'rope, series', prob. of Gmc origin, from L. *linea* (*fibra*) 'flax (fibre)', from L. *linum* 'flax', reinforced in ME by OFr. *ligne*, based on L. *linea*.

**line**[2] • v. cover the inner surface of (something) with a layer of different material. ➤cover as if with a lining. ➤informal fill (one's stomach).

– ORIGIN ME: from obs. *line* 'flax', with ref. to the use of linen for linings.

**lineage** /ˈlɪnɪdʒ/ • n. **1** ancestry or pedigree. **2** Biology a sequence of species each of which is considered to have evolved from its predecessor.

– ORIGIN ME: from OFr. *lignage*, from L. *linea* (see LINE[1]).

**lineal** /ˈlɪnɪəl/ • adj. **1** in a direct line of descent or ancestry. **2** linear.

– DERIVATIVES **lineally** adv.

– ORIGIN ME: via OFr. from late L. *linealis*, from *linea* (see LINE[1]).

**lineament** /ˈlɪnɪəm(ə)nt/ • n. **1** poetic/literary a distinctive feature, especially of the face. **2** Geology a linear feature on the earth's surface.

– ORIGIN ME: from L. *lineamentum*, from *lineare* 'make straight', from *linea* (see LINE[1]).

**linear** /ˈlɪnɪə/ • adj. **1** arranged in or extending along a straight line. ➤consisting of lines or outlines. ➤involving one dimension only. **2** sequential. **3** Mathematics able to be represented by a straight line on a graph. ➤involving directly proportional change in two related quantities.

– DERIVATIVES **linearity** n. **linearization** (also **-isation**) n. **linearize** (also **-ise**) v. **linearizer** n. **linearly** adv.

– ORIGIN C17: from L. *linearis*, from *linea* (see LINE[1]).

**linear accelerator** • n. Physics an accelerator in which particles travel in straight lines, not in closed orbits.

**linear equation** • n. an equation between two variables that gives a straight line when plotted on a graph.

**linear motor** • n. an electric induction motor producing straight-line motion by means of a linear stator and rotor placed in parallel.

**linear programming** • n. a mathematical technique for maximizing or minimizing a linear function of several variables.

**lineation** /ˌlɪnɪˈeɪʃ(ə)n/ • n. the action of drawing lines or marking with lines. ➤a line or linear marking.

**linebacker** • n. American Football a defensive player positioned just behind the line of scrimmage.

**line dancing** • n. a type of country and western dancing in which a line of dancers follow a choreographed pattern of steps.

– DERIVATIVES **line-dance** v. **line dancer** n.

**line drawing** • n. a drawing consisting only of lines.

**line drive** • n. Baseball a powerfully struck shot that travels along or close to the ground.

**linefeed** • n. the advancing of paper in a printing machine by the space of one line. ➤Computing the analogous movement of text on a VDU screen.

**lineman** • n. (pl. **-men**) **1** a person who lays and maintains railway tracks. ➤North American term for LINESMAN (in sense 2). **2** American Football a player on the line of scrimmage.

**line manager** • n. chiefly Brit. a manager to whom an employee is directly responsible.

– DERIVATIVES **line management** n.

**linen** • n. cloth woven from flax. ➤articles such as sheets or clothes made, or originally made, of linen.

– ORIGIN OE *līnen* (as adj. in the sense 'made of flax'), of W. Gmc origin; rel. to obs. *line* 'flax'.

**linen basket** • n. chiefly Brit. a basket for soiled clothing.

**linenfold** • n. carved or moulded ornaments representing folds or scrolls of linen.

**line of battle** • n. a disposition of troops for action in battle.

**line-out** • n. Rugby Union a formation of parallel lines of opposing forwards at right angles to the touchline when the ball is thrown in.

**line printer** • n. a machine that prints computer output a line at a time rather than character by character.

**liner**[1] • n. **1** a large passenger ship of a type formerly used on a regular line. **2** a fine paintbrush. ➤a cosmetic for outlining or accentuating a facial feature. **3** a boat engaged in sea fishing with lines.

**liner**[2] • n. a lining of a garment, container, etc.

**-liner** • comb. form informal denoting a text of a specified number of lines: *two-liner*.

**liner note** • n. text printed on the paper insert of a compact disc or on the sleeve of a gramophone record.

**linesman** • n. (pl. **-men**) **1** (in games played on a field or court) an official who assists the referee or umpire, especially in deciding whether the ball is out of play. **2** Brit. a person who repairs and maintains telephone or electricity power lines.

**line-up** • n. **1** a group of people or things assembled for a particular purpose. **2** an identity parade.

**ling**[1] • n. a long-bodied edible marine fish of the cod family. [*Molva molva* (E. Atlantic) and other species.]

– ORIGIN ME *lenge*, prob. from MDu.; rel. to LONG[1].

**ling**[2] • n. the common heather. [*Calluna vulgaris*.]

– ORIGIN ME: from ON *lyng*, of unknown origin.

**-ling** • suffix **1** forming nouns from nouns (e.g. *hireling*, *sapling*). **2** forming nouns from adjectives and adverbs (e.g. *darling*, *underling*). **3** forming diminutive nouns: *gosling*. ➤with depreciatory reference: *princeling*.

– ORIGIN OE; sense 3 from ON.

**Lingala** /lɪŋˈɡɑːlə/ • n. a Bantu language used as a lingua franca in Congo and Zaire (Democratic Republic of Congo).

– ORIGIN the name in Lingala.

**lingam** /ˈlɪŋɡam/ (also **linga** /ˈlɪŋɡə/) • n. Hinduism a phallus or phallic object as a symbol of Shiva.

– ORIGIN from Sanskrit *liṅga*, lit. 'mark, (sexual) characteristic'.

**lingcod** /ˈlɪŋkɒd/ • n. (pl. same) a large slender greenish-brown fish with golden spots, of the Pacific coast of North America. [*Ophiodon elongatus*.]

**linger** • v. be slow or reluctant to leave. ➤(**linger over**) spend a long time over. ➤be slow to disappear or die.

– DERIVATIVES **lingerer** n. **lingering** adj. **lingeringly** adv.

– ORIGIN ME: frequentative of obs. *leng* 'prolong', of Gmc origin; rel. to LONG[1].

**lingerie** /ˈlãʒ(ə)ri/ • n. women's underwear and nightclothes.

– ORIGIN C19: from Fr., from *linge* 'linen'.

**lingo** • n. (pl. **-os** or **-oes**) informal, often humorous a foreign language. ➤the jargon of a particular subject or group.

– ORIGIN C17: prob. via Port. *lingoa* from L. *lingua* 'tongue'.

**lingonberry** /ˈlɪŋ(ə)nˌb(ə)ri, -ˌbɛri/ • n. (pl. **-ies**) another term for COWBERRY.

– ORIGIN 1950s: from Swed. *lingon* 'cowberry' + BERRY.

**lingua franca** /ˌlɪŋɡwə ˈfraŋkə/ • n. (pl. **lingua francas**) **1** a language used as a common language between speakers whose native languages are different. **2** historical

a mixture of Italian with French, Greek, Arabic, and Spanish, formerly used in the eastern Mediterranean.
– ORIGIN C17: from Ital., lit. 'Frankish tongue'.

**lingual** /ˈlɪŋɡw(ə)l/ • **adj.** technical **1** of, relating to, or near the tongue. ➤(of a sound) formed by the tongue. **2** of or relating to speech or language.
– DERIVATIVES **lingually** adv.
– ORIGIN C17: from med. L. *lingualis*, from L. *lingua* 'tongue, language'.

**linguine** /lɪŋˈɡwiːneɪ, -ni/ • **pl. n.** small ribbons of pasta.
– ORIGIN Ital., pl. of *linguina*, dimin. of *lingua* 'tongue'.

**linguist** • **n. 1** a person skilled in foreign languages. **2** a person who studies linguistics.
– ORIGIN C16: from L. *lingua* 'language' + **-IST**.

**linguistic** • **adj.** of or relating to language or linguistics.
– DERIVATIVES **linguistically** adv.

**linguistics** /lɪŋˈɡwɪstɪks/ • **pl. n.** [treated as sing.] the scientific study of language and its structure.
– DERIVATIVES **linguistician** /-ˈstɪʃ(ə)n/ n.

**lingulate** /ˈlɪŋɡjʊleɪt/ • **adj. 1** Botany & Zoology tongue-shaped. **2** Zoology denoting a burrowing brachiopod with an inarticulate shell and a long pedicle.
– ORIGIN C19: from L. *lingulatus*, based on *lingua* 'tongue'.

**liniment** /ˈlɪnɪm(ə)nt/ • **n.** an embrocation, especially one made with oil.
– ORIGIN ME: from late L. *linimentum*, from L. *linire* 'to smear'.

**lining** • **n.** a layer of different material covering or attached to the inside of something.

**link**[1] • **n. 1** a relationship or connection between people or things. ➤something that enables communication between people. ➤a means of contact or transport between two places. ➤Computing a code or instruction connecting one part of a program or an element in a list to another. **2** a loop in a chain. ➤a unit of measurement of length equal to one hundredth of a surveying chain (7.92 inches). • **v.** make, form, or suggest a link with or between. ➤join physically. ➤clasp; intertwine.
– DERIVATIVES **linker** n.
– ORIGIN ME: from ON *hlekkr*, of Gmc origin.

**link**[2] • **n.** historical a torch of pitch and tow for lighting the way in dark streets.
– ORIGIN C16: perh. from med. L. *li(n)chinus* 'wick'.

**linkage** • **n. 1** the action of linking or the state of being linked. ➤a system of links. **2** Genetics the tendency of groups of genes on the same chromosome to be inherited together.

**linking** • **adj.** connecting or joining two things. ➤Phonetics denoting a consonant that is sounded at a boundary where two vowels would otherwise be adjacent, as in *law(r) and order*.

**linkman** • **n.** (pl. **-men**) Brit. **1** a person serving as a connection between others. **2** a person providing continuity between items on radio or television.

**links** • **pl. n. 1** (also **golf links**) [treated as sing. or pl.] a golf course, especially on linksland. **2** another term for **LINKSLAND**.
– ORIGIN OE *hlinc* 'rising ground', perh. rel. to **LEAN**[1].

**linksland** • **n.** Scottish sandy ground near the sea, covered by coarse grass.

**link-up** • **n.** an instance of two or more people or things linking. ➤a connection enabling people or machines to communicate with each other.

**linn** • **n.** Scottish archaic a waterfall. ➤the pool below a waterfall. ➤a steep precipice.
– ORIGIN C16, from Sc. Gaelic *linne*, Ir. *linn*, rel. to Welsh *llyn* 'lake'.

**Linnaean** /lɪˈniːən/ (also **Linnean**) • **adj.** of or relating to the Swedish botanist Linnaeus (Latinized name of Carl von Linné) (1707–78) or his system of binomial nomenclature in the classification of animals and plants. • **n.** a follower of Linnaeus.

**linnet** • **n.** a mainly brown and grey finch with a reddish breast and forehead. [Genus *Acanthis*: three species.]
– ORIGIN C16: from OFr. *linette*, from *lin* 'flax' (because the bird feeds on flaxseeds).

**lino** • **n.** (pl. **-os**) informal, chiefly Brit. linoleum.

**linocut** • **n.** a design carved in relief on a block of linoleum, used for printing.
– DERIVATIVES **linocutting** n.

**linoleic acid** /ˌlɪnə(ʊ)ˈliːɪk, -ˈleɪɪk/ • **n.** Chemistry a polyunsaturated fatty acid present in linseed oil and other oils and essential in the human diet.
– DERIVATIVES **linoleate** n.
– ORIGIN C19: from L. *linum* 'flax' + **OLEIC ACID**.

**linolenic acid** /ˌlɪnə(ʊ)ˈlɛnɪk, -ˈliːnɪk/ • **n.** Chemistry a polyunsaturated fatty acid of similar properties and occurrence to linoleic acid.
– DERIVATIVES **linolenate** n.
– ORIGIN C19: from Ger. *Linolensaüre*, from *Linolsaüre* 'linoleic acid', with the insertion of *-en-* (from **-ENE**).

**linoleum** /lɪˈnəʊlɪəm/ • **n.** a material consisting of a canvas backing thickly coated with a preparation of linseed oil and powdered cork, used as a floor covering.
– DERIVATIVES **linoleumed** adj.
– ORIGIN C19: from L. *linum* 'flax' + *oleum* 'oil'.

**Linotype** /ˈlʌɪnə(ʊ)tʌɪp/ • **n.** Printing, trademark a composing machine producing lines of words as single strips of metal.
– ORIGIN C19: alt. of the phr. *line o' type*.

**linsang** /ˈlɪnsaŋ/ • **n.** a small civet found in SE Asia and West Africa. [Genera *Prionodon* and *Poiana*: three species.]
– ORIGIN C19: via Javanese from Malay.

**linseed** • **n.** the seeds of the flax plant.
– ORIGIN OE *līnsǣd*, from *līn* 'flax' + *sǣd* 'seed'.

**linseed cake** • **n.** pressed linseed used as cattle food.

**linseed oil** • **n.** oil extracted from linseed, used especially in paint and varnish.

**linsey-woolsey** /ˌlɪnzɪˈwʊlzi/ • **n.** a strong, coarse fabric with a linen or cotton warp and a woollen weft.
– ORIGIN C15: from *linsey*, orig. denoting a coarse linen fabric (prob. from *Lindsey*, a village in Suffolk) + **WOOL** + *-sey* as a rhyming suffix.

**linstock** • **n.** a long pole used to hold a match for firing a cannon.
– ORIGIN C16: from earlier *lintstock*, from Du. *lontstok*, from *lont* 'match' + *stok* 'stick'.

**lint** • **n. 1** short, fine fibres which separate from cloth or yarn during processing. ➤Scottish flax fibres prepared for spinning. ➤the fibrous material of a cotton boll. **2** Brit. a fabric with a raised nap on one side, used for dressing wounds.
– DERIVATIVES **linty** adj.
– ORIGIN ME *lynnet* 'flax prepared for spinning', perh. from OFr. *linette* 'linseed', from *lin* 'flax'.

**lintel** • **n.** a horizontal support across the top of a door or window.
– DERIVATIVES **lintelled** (US **linteled**) adj.
– ORIGIN ME: from OFr., based on late L. *liminare*, from L. *limen* 'threshold'.

**linter** • **n.** a machine for removing the short fibres from cotton seeds after ginning. ➤(**linters**) fibres of this kind.

**liny** • **adj.** (**-ier**, **-iest**) informal marked with lines.

**lion** • **n. 1** a large tawny-coloured cat of Africa and NW India, of which the male has a shaggy mane. [*Panthera leo*.] **2** a brave, strong, or fierce person. ➤dated a celebrity. **3** (**Lion**) a member of a touring international rugby union team representing the British Isles.
– PHRASES **the lion's den** an intimidating or unpleasant place. **the lion's share** the largest part of something.
– DERIVATIVES **lioness** n. **lion-like** adj.
– ORIGIN ME: from Anglo-Norman Fr. *liun*, from L. *leo*, *leon-*, from Gk *leōn*, *leont-*.

**lion-hearted** • **adj.** brave and determined.

**lionize** /ˈlʌɪənʌɪz/ (also **-ise**) • **v.** treat as a celebrity.
– DERIVATIVES **lionization** n. **lionizer** n.

**lion's paw** • **n.** a large Caribbean bivalve mollusc with a thick reddish fan-shaped shell. [*Chlamys nodosus*.]

**lion tamarin** • **n.** a tamarin with a golden or black and golden coat and an erect mane, found only in Brazil. [*Leontopithecus rosalia* and three other species.]

**lip** ● n. **1** either of the two fleshy parts forming the edges of the mouth opening. ➤another term for LABIUM (in senses 1 and 2). **2** the edge of a hollow container or an opening. **3** informal impudent talk. ● v. (**lipped**, **lipping**) **1** (of water) lap against. **2** Golf (of the ball) hit the rim of (a hole) but fail to go in.
– PHRASES **bite one's lip** stifle laughter or a retort. **curl one's lip** sneer. **pass one's lips** be eaten, drunk, or spoken. **pay lip service to** express approval or support for insincerely.
– DERIVATIVES **lipless** adj. **lip-like** adj. **-lipped** adj.
– ORIGIN OE *lippa*, of Gmc origin.

**lipa** /ˈliːpə/ ● n. (pl. same or **lipas**) a monetary unit of Croatia, equal to one hundredth of a kuna.
– ORIGIN from Serbo-Croat, lit. 'lime tree'.

**lipaemia** /lɪˈpiːmɪə/ (US **lipemia**) ● n. Medicine the presence in the blood of an abnormally high concentration of emulsified fat.
– ORIGIN C19: from Gk *lipos* 'fat' + -AEMIA.

**lipase** /ˈlɪpeɪz, ˈlʌɪp-/ ● n. Biochemistry a pancreatic enzyme that promotes the breakdown of fats.
– ORIGIN C19: from Gk *lipos* 'fat' + -ASE.

**lipgloss** ● n. a glossy cosmetic applied to the lips.

**lipid** ● n. Chemistry any of a class of fatty acids or their derivatives that are insoluble in water and include many natural oils, waxes, and steroids.
– ORIGIN C20: from Fr. *lipide*, based on Gk *lipos* 'fat'.

**lipidosis** /ˌlɪpɪˈdəʊsɪs/ (also **lipoidosis**) ● n. (pl. **lipidoses** /-siːz/) Medicine a disorder of lipid metabolism in the tissues.

**Lipizzaner** /ˌlɪpɪˈtsɑːnə, ˌlɪpɪˈzeɪnə/ ● n. a horse of a white breed used especially in dressage.
– ORIGIN C20: from Ger., from *Lippiza*, site of the former Austrian Imperial stud near Trieste.

**lipline** ● n. the outline of the lips.

**lipliner** ● n. a cosmetic applied to the outline of the lips.

**lipo-** /ˈlɪpəʊ, ˈlʌɪpəʊ/ ● comb. form relating to fat or other lipids: *liposuction*.
– ORIGIN from Gk *lipos* 'fat'.

**lipogenesis** /ˌlɪpə(ʊ)ˈdʒɛnɪsɪs, ˌlʌɪ-/ ● n. Physiology the metabolic formation of fat.
– DERIVATIVES **lipogenic** adj.

**lipogram** ● n. a composition from which the writer omits a certain letter or letters.
– DERIVATIVES **lipogrammatic** adj.
– ORIGIN C18: back-form. from Gk *lipogrammatos* 'lacking a letter', from *lip-* *leipein* 'leave (out)' + *gramma* 'letter'.

**lipoidosis** /ˌlɪpɔɪˈdəʊsɪs/ ● n. variant spelling of LIPIDOSIS.

**lipolysis** /lɪˈpɒlɪsɪs/ ● n. Physiology the breakdown of lipids by hydrolysis.
– DERIVATIVES **lipolytic** adj.

**lipoma** /lɪˈpəʊmə/ ● n. (pl. **lipomas** or **lipomata** /-mətə/) Medicine a benign tumour of fatty tissue.

**lipoprotein** ● n. Biochemistry a soluble protein that combines with and transports lipids in the blood.

**liposome** /ˈlɪpəsəʊm, ˈlʌɪ-/ ● n. Biochemistry a minute artificial spherical sac of phospholipid molecules enclosing a water droplet, used to carry drugs or other substances into the tissues.

**liposuction** /ˈlɪpə(ʊ)ˌsʌkʃ(ə)n, ˈlʌɪ-/ ● n. a technique in cosmetic surgery for removing excess fat from under the skin by suction.

**lippy** informal ● adj. (**-ier**, **-iest**) impertinent. ● n. (also **lippie**) lipstick.

**lip-read** ● v. understand speech from observing a speaker's lip movements.
– DERIVATIVES **lip-reader** n.

**lipsalve** ● n. Brit. a preparation to prevent or relieve sore lips.

**lipstick** ● n. coloured cosmetic applied to the lips from a small solid stick.

**lip-sync** (also **-synch**) ● n. the movement of a performer's lips in synchronization with a pre-recorded soundtrack. ● v. perform (a song or speech) in this way.
– DERIVATIVES **lip-syncer** n.

**liquate** /lɪˈkweɪt/ ● v. Metallurgy separate or purify (a metal) by melting it.
– DERIVATIVES **liquation** n.
– ORIGIN C19: from L. *liquat-*, *liquare* 'make liquid'.

**liquefy** /ˈlɪkwɪfʌɪ/ (also **liquify**) ● v. (**-ies**, **-ied**) make or become liquid.
– DERIVATIVES **liquefaction** n. **liquefactive** adj. **liquefiable** adj. **liquefier** n.
– ORIGIN ME: from Fr. *liquéfier* from L. *liquefacere* 'make liquid', from *liquere* 'be liquid'.

**liquescent** /lɪˈkwɛs(ə)nt/ ● adj. poetic/literary becoming or apt to become liquid.

**liqueur** /lɪˈkjʊə/ ● n. a strong, sweet flavoured alcoholic spirit.
– ORIGIN C18: from Fr., 'liquor'.

**liquid** ● adj. **1** having a consistency like that of water or oil, i.e. flowing freely but of constant volume. ➤having the translucence of water. ➤denoting a gas that has been liquefied. **2** not fixed or stable. **3** (of a sound) clear and flowing. **4** (of assets) held in or easily converted into cash. ➤having ready cash or liquid assets. ● n. a liquid substance.
– DERIVATIVES **liquidly** adv. **liquidness** n.
– ORIGIN ME: from L. *liquidus*, from *liquere* 'be liquid'.

**liquidambar** /ˌlɪkwɪdˈambə/ ● n. **1** a North American or Asian tree with maple-like leaves. [Genus *Liquidambar*: several species.] **2** liquid balsam obtained from such a tree, used medicinally and in perfume.
– ORIGIN C16: mod. L., appar. formed irregularly from L. *liquidus* 'liquid' + med. L. *ambar* 'amber'.

**liquidate** ● v. **1** wind up the affairs of (a company) by ascertaining liabilities and apportioning assets. ➤convert (assets) into cash. ➤pay off (a debt). **2** informal eliminate; kill.
– DERIVATIVES **liquidation** n. **liquidator** n.
– ORIGIN C16 (in the sense 'set out (accounts) clearly)': from med. L. *liquidat-*, *liquidare* 'make clear', from L. *liquidus* (see LIQUID).

**liquid crystal** ● n. a liquid with some degree of ordering in the arrangement of its molecules.

**liquid crystal display** ● n. an electronic visual display in which the application of an electric current to a liquid crystal layer makes it opaque.

**liquidity** /lɪˈkwɪdɪti/ ● n. Finance the availability of liquid assets to a market or company. ➤liquid assets.

**liquidize** (also **-ise**) ● v. Brit. convert (solid food) into a liquid or purée.

**liquidizer** (also **-iser**) ● n. Brit. a machine for liquidizing.

**liquid measure** ● n. a unit for measuring the volume of liquids.

**liquid paraffin** ● n. chiefly Brit. a colourless, odourless oily liquid obtained from petroleum, used as a laxative.

**liquify** ● v. variant spelling of LIQUEFY.

**liquor** /ˈlɪkə/ ● n. **1** alcoholic drink, especially spirits. **2** water used in brewing. **3** liquid that has been produced in or used for cooking. **4** the liquid from which a substance has been crystallized or extracted. ● v. **1** dress (leather) with grease or oil. **2** steep in water.
– ORIGIN ME: from OFr. *lic(o)ur*, from L. *liquor*; rel. to *liquare* 'liquefy', *liquere* 'be fluid'.

**liquorice** /ˈlɪk(ə)rɪs, -rɪʃ/ (US **licorice**) ● n. **1** a sweet, chewy, aromatic black substance made from the juice of a root and used as a sweet and in medicine. **2** a leguminous plant from which liquorice is obtained. [Genus *Glycyrrhiza*; many species.]
– ORIGIN ME: from OFr. *licoresse*, from late L. *liquiritia*, from Gk *glukurrhiza*, from *glukus* 'sweet' + *rhiza* 'root'.

**liquorish** /ˈlɪkərɪʃ/ ● adj. **1** archaic form of LICKERISH. **2** fond of liquor.
– DERIVATIVES **liquorishness** n.

**lira** /ˈlɪərə/ ● n. (pl. **lire** /ˈlɪərə, ˈlɪəreɪ, ˈlɪəri/) **1** the basic monetary unit of Italy, notionally equal to 100 centesimos. **2** the basic monetary unit of Turkey, equal to 100 kurus.
– ORIGIN Ital., from Provençal *liura*, from L. *libra* 'pound'.

**lis** /lɪs/ ● n. Law a lawsuit.
– ORIGIN C18: from L. *lis* 'dispute'.

**lisente** plural form of SENTE.

**lisle** /lʌɪl/ ● n. a fine, smooth cotton thread used for stockings.
– ORIGIN C16: from *Lisle*, former spelling of *Lille*, a city in northern France where lisle was originally made.

**Lisp** ● n. a high-level computer programming language devised for list processing.
– ORIGIN 1950s: from *lis(t) p(rocessor)*.

**lisp** ● n. a speech defect in which *s* is pronounced like *th* in *thick* and *z* is pronounced like *th* in *this*. ● v. speak with a lisp.
– DERIVATIVES **lisper** n. **lisping** n. & adj. **lispingly** adv.
– ORIGIN OE *wlispian*, from *wlisp* (adj.) 'lisping', of imitative origin.

**Lissajous figure** /'lɪsaʒuː/ ● n. Mathematics a looped or curved figure traced out by a point undergoing two independent simple harmonic motions at right angles with frequencies in a simple ratio.
– ORIGIN C19: named after the Fr. physicist Jules A. *Lissajous*.

**lissom** (also **lissome**) ● adj. slim, supple, and graceful.
– DERIVATIVES **lissomness** n.
– ORIGIN C18: contr., from LITHE + -SOME[1].

**list**[1] ● n. **1** a number of connected items or names written consecutively. **2** (**lists**) historical palisades enclosing an area for a tournament. ➤ the scene of a contest. **3** a selvedge of a piece of fabric. ● v. **1** make a list of. ➤ include in a list. **2** archaic enlist for military service.
– PHRASES **enter the lists** issue or accept a challenge.
– DERIVATIVES **listable** adj.
– ORIGIN OE *līste* (in sense 'a border or edging'), of Gmc origin; sense 2 from OFr. *lisse*.

**list**[2] ● v. (of a ship) lean over to one side. ● n. an instance of listing.
– ORIGIN C17: of unknown origin.

**list**[3] archaic ● v. want; like. ● n. desire; inclination.
– ORIGIN OE *lystan* (v.), of Gmc origin, from a base meaning 'pleasure'.

**listed** ● adj. **1** (of a building in the UK) officially designated as being of historical importance and so protected. **2** denoting companies whose shares are quoted on the main market of the London Stock Exchange.

**listen** ● v. give one's attention to a sound. ➤ respond to advice or a request. ➤ make an effort to hear something. ➤ (**listen in**) listen to a private conversation. ➤ (**listen in**) listen to a radio broadcast. ● n. an act of listening.
– DERIVATIVES **listener** n.
– ORIGIN OE *hlysnan* 'pay attention to', of Gmc origin.

**listenable** ● adj. easy or pleasant to listen to.
– DERIVATIVES **listenability** n.

**listening post** ● n. a station for intercepting electronic communications. ➤ a point near enemy lines for detecting movements by sound.

**lister** ● n. US a plough with a double mouldboard.
– ORIGIN C19: from LIST[1] in the C18 US sense 'prepare land for a crop' + -ER[1].

**listeria** /lɪ'stɪərɪə/ ● n. a type of bacterium which infects humans and other animals through contaminated food.
– ORIGIN 1940s: mod. L., named after the Engl. surgeon Joseph *Lister*.

**listeriosis** /lɪˌstɪərɪ'əʊsɪs/ ● n. disease caused by infection with listeria, which can resemble influenza or meningitis and may cause miscarriage.

**listing** ● n. **1** a list or catalogue. ➤ an entry in a list. **2** a selvedge of a piece of fabric.

**listless** ● adj. lacking energy or enthusiasm.
– DERIVATIVES **listlessly** adv. **listlessness** n.
– ORIGIN ME: from LIST[3] + -LESS.

**list price** ● n. the price of an article as listed by the manufacturer.

**LISTSERV** ● n. trademark an electronic mailing list of people who wish to receive specified information from the Internet.

**list system** ● n. a system of voting in which votes are cast for a list of candidates to allow a degree of proportional representation.

**lit** past and past participle of LIGHT[1], LIGHT[3].

**litany** /'lɪt(ə)ni/ ● n. (pl. **-ies**) **1** a series of petitions used in church services, usually recited by the clergy and responded to by the people. ➤ (**the Litany**) such petitions in the Book of Common Prayer. **2** a tedious recital.
– ORIGIN ME: from OFr. *letanie*, via eccles. L. from Gk *litaneia* 'prayer', from *litē* 'supplication'.

**litas** /'liːtas/ ● n. (pl. same) the basic monetary unit of Lithuania, equal to 100 centas.
– ORIGIN from Lithuanian.

**litchi** ● n. variant spelling of LYCHEE.

**lite** ● adj. **1** of or relating to low-fat or low-sugar versions of food or drink products. **2** N. Amer. informal lacking substance.
– ORIGIN 1950s: a deliberate respelling of LIGHT[2].

**-lite** ● suffix forming names of rocks, minerals, and fossils: *rhyolite*.
– ORIGIN from Fr., from Gk *lithos* 'stone'.

**liter** ● n. US spelling of LITRE.

**literacy** ● n. the ability to read and write.
– ORIGIN C19: from LITERATE, on the pattern of *illiteracy*.

**literae humaniores** /ˌlɪtərʌɪ hjuːˌmanɪ'ɔːriːz/ ● pl. n. [treated as sing.] the honours course in classics, philosophy, and ancient history at Oxford University.
– ORIGIN L., lit. 'the more humane studies'.

**literal** ● adj. **1** taking words in their usual or most basic sense without metaphor or allegory. ➤ free from distortion. ➤ informal absolute. **2** (of a translation) representing the exact words of the original text. **3** lacking imagination. **4** of, in, or expressed by a letter of the alphabet. ● n. Brit. Printing a misprint of a letter.
– DERIVATIVES **literality** n. **literalize** (also **-ise**) v. **literalness** n.
– ORIGIN ME: from OFr., or from late L. *litteralis*, from L. *littera* (see LETTER).

**literalism** ● n. the literal interpretation of words.
– DERIVATIVES **literalist** n. **literalistic** adj.

**literally** ● adv. in a literal manner or sense. ➤ informal used for emphasis while not being literally true: *we were literally killing ourselves laughing.*

**literary** ● adj. **1** concerning the writing, study, or content of literature, especially of the kind valued for quality of form. ➤ concerned with literature as a profession. **2** associated with literary works or formal writing.
– DERIVATIVES **literarily** adv. **literariness** n.
– ORIGIN C17 (in the sense 'relating to the letters of the alphabet'): from L. *litterarius*, from *littera* (see LETTER).

**literary criticism** ● n. the art or practice of judging the qualities and character of literary works.
– DERIVATIVES **literary critic** n.

**literary executor** ● n. a person entrusted with a dead writer's papers and works.

**literary history** ● n. the history of the treatment of a subject in literature.
– DERIVATIVES **literary historian** n.

**literate** ● adj. able to read and write. ➤ educated or knowledgeable: *politically literate*. ● n. a literate person.
– DERIVATIVES **literately** adv.
– ORIGIN ME: from L. *litteratus*, from *littera* (see LETTER).

**literati** /ˌlɪtə'rɑːti/ ● pl. n. educated people who are interested in literature.
– ORIGIN C17: from L., pl. of *literatus* 'acquainted with letters', from *littera* (see LETTER).

**literatim** /ˌlɪtə'rɑːtɪm, -'reɪtɪm/ ● adv. formal letter by letter.
– ORIGIN from med. L.

**literature** ● n. written works, especially those regarded as having artistic merit. ➤ books and writings on a particular subject. ➤ leaflets and other material used in advertising or to give advice.
– ORIGIN ME (in the sense 'knowledge of books'): via Fr. from L. *litteratura*, from *littera* (see LETTER).

**-lith** ● suffix denoting types of stone: *monolith*.
– ORIGIN from Gk *lithos* 'stone'.

**litharge** /'lɪθɑːdʒ/ ● n. lead monoxide, especially a red form used as a pigment in glass and ceramics.
– ORIGIN ME: from OFr. *litarge*, via L. from Gk *litharguros*, from *lithos* 'stone' + *arguros* 'silver'.

**lithe** ● adj. slim, supple, and graceful.

– DERIVATIVES **lithely** adv. **litheness** n.
– ORIGIN OE *līthe* 'gentle, meek', also 'mellow', of Gmc origin.

**lithesome** ● **adj.** poetic/literary lithe.

**lithia** /ˈlɪθɪə/ ● **n.** Chemistry lithium oxide, a white alkaline solid.
– ORIGIN C19: mod. L., alt. of earlier *lithion*, from Gk, neut. of *litheios*, from *lithos* 'stone'.

**lithiasis** /lɪˈθʌɪəsɪs/ ● **n.** Medicine the formation of stones in an internal organ such as the kidney or gall bladder.
– ORIGIN C17: from med. L., based on Gk *lithos* 'stone'.

**lithic** /ˈlɪθɪk/ ● **adj.** **1** chiefly Archaeology & Geology of, like, or relating to stone. **2** Medicine, dated relating to calculi.
– ORIGIN C18: from Gk *lithikos*, from *lithos* 'stone'.

**lithify** /ˈlɪθɪfʌɪ/ ● **v.** (**-ies**, **-ied**) chiefly Geology transform into stone.
– DERIVATIVES **lithification** n.
– ORIGIN C19: from Gk *lithos* 'stone' + **-FY**.

**lithium** /ˈlɪθɪəm/ ● **n.** **1** the chemical element of atomic number 3, the lightest of the alkali metals. (Symbol: **Li**) **2** a lithium salt used as a mood-stabilizing drug.
– ORIGIN C19: from **LITHIA** + **-IUM**.

**litho** /ˈlʌɪθəʊ, ˈlɪθ-/ ● **n.** (pl. **-os**) short for **LITHOGRAPHY** or **LITHOGRAPH**.

**litho-** ● **comb. form** **1** of or relating to stone: *lithosol*. **2** relating to a calculus: *lithotomy*.
– ORIGIN from Gk *lithos* 'stone'.

**lithograph** /ˈlɪθəgrɑːf, ˈlʌɪ-/ ● **n.** a print made by lithography. ● **v.** print by lithography.
– DERIVATIVES **lithographic** adj. **lithographically** adv.

**lithography** /lɪˈθɒgrəfi/ ● **n.** **1** the process of printing from a flat metal (formerly stone) surface treated so as to repel the ink except where it is required for printing. **2** Electronics an analogous method for making printed circuits.
– DERIVATIVES **lithographer** n.

**lithology** /lɪˈθɒlədʒi/ ● **n.** the study of the physical characteristics of rocks.
– DERIVATIVES **lithological** adj.

**lithophyte** /ˈlɪθə(ʊ)fʌɪt, ˈlʌɪ-/ ● **n.** Botany a plant that grows on bare rock or stone.

**lithopone** /ˈlɪθəpəʊn/ ● **n.** a white pigment made from zinc sulphide and barium sulphate.
– ORIGIN C19: from **LITHO-** + Gk *ponos* '(thing) produced by work'.

**lithosphere** /ˈlɪθəsfɪə/ ● **n.** Geology the rigid outer part of the earth, consisting of the crust and upper mantle.
– DERIVATIVES **lithospheric** adj.

**lithotomy** /lɪˈθɒtəmi/ ● **n.** surgical removal of a calculus (stone) from the bladder, kidney, or urinary tract.
– DERIVATIVES **lithotomist** n.
– ORIGIN C17: via late L. from Gk *lithotomia* (see **LITHO-**, **-TOMY**).

**lithotripsy** /ˈlɪθəˌtrɪpsi/ ● **n.** Surgery a treatment using ultrasound to shatter a urinary calculus so that it can be passed out by the body.
– DERIVATIVES **lithotripter** (also **lithotriptor**) n. **lithotriptic** adj.
– ORIGIN C19: from **LITHO-** + Gk *tripsis* 'rubbing'.

**Lithuanian** ● **n.** **1** a native or citizen of Lithuania, or a person of Lithuanian descent. **2** the Baltic language of Lithuania. ● **adj.** of or relating to Lithuania, its people, or its language.

**litigant** ● **n.** a person involved in litigation. ● **adj.** [postpos.] archaic involved in litigation.

**litigate** /ˈlɪtɪgeɪt/ ● **v.** go to law; be a party to a lawsuit. ➤ take (a dispute) to a law court.
– DERIVATIVES **litigation** n. **litigator** n.
– ORIGIN C17 (earlier (C16) as *litigation*): from L. *litigat-*, *litigare* 'to dispute in a lawsuit', from *lis*, *lit-* 'lawsuit'.

**litigious** /lɪˈtɪdʒəs/ ● **adj.** tending to go to law to settle disputes. ➤ concerned with or disputable by litigation.
– DERIVATIVES **litigiously** adv. **litigiousness** n.
– ORIGIN ME: from OFr. *litigieux* or L. *litigiosus* from *litigium* 'litigation', from *lis*, *lit-* 'lawsuit'.

**litmus** /ˈlɪtməs/ ● **n.** a dye obtained from certain lichens that is red under acid conditions and blue under alkaline conditions.
– ORIGIN ME: from ON *lit-mosi*, from *litr* 'dye' + *mosi* 'moss'.

**litmus paper** ● **n.** paper stained with litmus, used as a test for acids or alkalis.

**litmus test** ● **n.** **1** Chemistry a test using litmus. **2** a decisively indicative test.

**litotes** /lʌɪˈtəʊtiːz/ ● **n.** ironical understatement in which an affirmative is expressed by the negative of its contrary (e.g. *I shan't be sorry* for *I shall be glad*).
– ORIGIN C16: via late L. from Gk *litotēs*, from *litos* 'plain, meagre'.

**litre** (US **liter**) (abbrev.: **l**) ● **n.** a metric unit of capacity, formerly the volume of one kilogram of water under standard conditions, now equal to 1,000 cubic centimetres (about 1.75 pints).
– DERIVATIVES **litreage** /ˈliːt(ə)rɪdʒ/ n.
– ORIGIN C18: from Fr., alt. of *litron* (an obs. measure of capacity), via med. L. from Gk *litra*, a Sicilian monetary unit.

**LittD** ● **abbrev.** Doctor of Letters.
– ORIGIN from L. *Litterarum Doctor*.

**litter** ● **n.** **1** rubbish left in an open or public place. ➤ an untidy collection of things. **2** a number of young born to an animal at one time. **3** (also **cat litter**) granular absorbent material lining a tray for a cat to urinate and defecate in indoors. **4** straw or other plant matter used as animal bedding. **5** (also **leaf litter**) decomposing leaves and other matter forming a layer on top of soil. **6** historical a vehicle containing a bed or seat enclosed by curtains and carried by men or animals. ➤ a framework with a couch for transporting the sick. ● **v.** **1** make untidy with discarded articles. ➤ (usu. **be littered with**) leave (rubbish or objects) lying about untidily. **2** archaic provide (an animal) with litter as bedding.
– ORIGIN ME (in sense 6 of the noun): from OFr. *litiere*, from med. L. *lectaria*, from L. *lectus* 'bed'.

**littérateur** /ˌlɪtərɑːˈtəː/ ● **n.** a literary person.
– ORIGIN C19: Fr.

**litterbug** (Brit. also **litter lout**) ● **n.** informal a person who carelessly drops litter.

**little** ● **adj.** small in size, amount, or degree. ➤ (of a person) young or younger: *my little brother*. ➤ denoting something that is the smaller or smallest of those so named. ➤ of short distance or duration. ➤ trivial, unimportant, or humble. ● **det. & pron.** **1** (**a little**) a small amount of. ➤ a short time or distance. **2** not much. ● **adv.** (**less**, **least**) **1** (**a little**) to a small extent. **2** hardly or not at all.
– PHRASES **little by little** gradually. **little or nothing** hardly anything. **no little** considerable. **not a little** a great deal (of). ➤ very.
– DERIVATIVES **littleness** n.
– ORIGIN OE *lȳtel*, of Gmc origin.

**little auk** ● **n.** a small, stubby short-billed auk breeding in the Arctic. [*Alle alle*.]

**little end** ● **n.** Mechanics the smaller end of a connecting rod, attached to the piston.

**Little Englander** ● **n.** informal a person opposed to an international role or policy for Britain.

**little finger** ● **n.** the smallest finger, at the outer side of the hand.
– PHRASES **twist** (or **wind** or **wrap**) **someone around one's little finger** be able to make someone do whatever one wants.

**little grebe** ● **n.** a small grebe with a short neck and bill and a trilling call. [*Tachybaptus ruficollis*.]

**little green man** ● **n.** informal an imaginary being from outer space.

**little hours** ● **pl. n.** (in the Western Church) the offices of prime, terce, sext, and none.

**Little League** ● **n.** N. Amer. organized baseball for children aged 8–12.

**little ones** ● **pl. n.** young children.

**little owl** ● **n.** a small owl with speckled plumage, native to Eurasia and Africa. [*Athene noctua*.]

**little people** ● **pl. n.** **1** the ordinary people of a country or organization. **2** fairies or leprechauns.

**Little Russian** ● **n. & adj.** former term for **Ukrainian**.

**little toe** ● **n.** the smallest toe, on the outer side of the foot.

**littoral** /ˈlɪt(ə)r(ə)l/ ● **adj.** of, relating to, or on the shore of the sea or a lake. ● **n.** a littoral region.
– ORIGIN C17: from L. *littoralis*, from *litus, litor-* 'shore'.

**liturgical** /lɪˈtəːdʒɪk(ə)l/ ● **adj.** of or related to liturgy or public worship.
– DERIVATIVES **liturgically** adv. **liturgist** /ˈlɪtədʒɪst/ n.

**liturgics** /lɪˈtəːdʒɪks/ ● **pl. n.** [treated as sing.] the study of liturgies.

**liturgy** /ˈlɪtədʒi/ ● **n.** (pl. **-ies**) **1** a form or formulary according to which public religious worship, especially Christian worship, is conducted. ➤ (**the Liturgy**) the Communion office of the Orthodox Church. **2** (in ancient Athens) a public office or duty performed voluntarily by a rich citizen.
– ORIGIN C16: via Fr. or late L. from Gk *leitourgia* 'public service, worship of the gods'.

**Litvak** /ˈlɪtvak/ ● **n.** a Jew from the region of Lithuania.
– ORIGIN C19: Yiddish, from Polish *Litwak* 'Lithuanian'.

**livable** ● **adj.** variant spelling of **liveable**.

**live**[1] /lɪv/ ● **v. 1** remain alive. ➤ be alive at a specified time. ➤ spend one's life in a particular way. ➤ supply oneself with the means of subsistence. **2** make one's home in a particular place or with a particular person. **3** survive in someone's mind: *her name lived on.*
– PHRASES **live and breathe something** be devoted to a subject or activity. **live in the past** have outdated ideas and attitudes. **live it up** informal lead a life of extravagance and exciting social activity. **live rough** live outdoors as a result of being homeless. **live with oneself** be able to retain one's self-respect as a consequence of one's actions. **long live ——!** said to express loyalty or support for a specified person or thing. **where one lives** N. Amer. informal at, to, or in the right or most vulnerable spot.
– PHRASAL VERBS **live something down** [usu. with neg.] succeed in making others forget something embarrassing. **live for** regard as the most important aspect of one's life. **live in** (or **out**) (of an employee or student) reside at (or away from) the place where one works or studies. **live off** (or **on**) depend on as a source of income or support. ➤ have (a particular amount of money) with which to buy food and other necessities. **live something out 1** do in reality that which one has imagined. **2** spend the rest of one's life in a particular place or particular circumstances. **live through** survive (an unpleasant experience or period). **live together** (of a couple not married to each other) share a home and have a sexual relationship. **live up to** fulfil. **live with 1** share a home and have a sexual relationship with (someone to whom one is not married). **2** accept or tolerate (something unpleasant).
– ORIGIN OE *libban, lifian*, of Gmc origin; rel. to **life** and **leave**[1].

**live**[2] /lʌɪv/ ● **adj. 1** living. ➤ (of yogurt) containing the living micro-organisms by which it is formed. **2** (of a musical performance) given in concert. ➤ (of a broadcast) transmitted at the time of occurrence. **3** (of a wire or device) connected to a source of electric current. ➤ of, containing, or using undetonated explosive. ➤ (of coals) burning. ➤ (of a wheel or axle in machinery) moving or imparting motion. **4** of current or continuing interest and importance. ● **adv.** as or at an actual event or performance.
– PHRASES **go live** Computing (of a system) become operational.
– ORIGIN C16: shortening of **alive**.

**liveable** (US also **livable**) ● **adj.** worth living. ➤ fit to live in. ➤ (**liveable with**) informal easy to live with.
– DERIVATIVES **liveability** n.

**live action** ● **n.** action in films involving real people or animals, as contrasted with animation or computer-generated effects.

**live bait** ● **n.** small living fish or worms used as bait.

**live-bearing** ● **adj.** bearing live young rather than laying eggs.
– DERIVATIVES **livebearer** n.

**lived-in** ● **adj. 1** (of a room or building) showing comforting signs of wear and habitation. **2** informal (of a person's face) marked by experience.

**live-in** ● **adj.** (of a domestic employee) resident in an employer's house. ➤ (of a person) living with another in a sexual relationship. ➤ residential. ● **n.** informal a live-in sexual partner or employee.

**livelihood** ● **n.** a means of securing the necessities of life.
– ORIGIN OE *līflād* 'way of life', from *līf* 'life' + *lād* 'course' (see **lode**), assoc. with **lively** and **-hood**.

**live load** ● **n.** the weight of people or goods in a structure or vehicle.

**livelong**[1] /ˈlɪvlɒŋ/ ● **adj.** poetic/literary (of a period of time) entire: *all this livelong day.*
– ORIGIN ME *leve longe* 'dear long' (see **lief, long**[1]), assoc. with **live**[1].

**livelong**[2] /ˈlɪvlɒŋ/ ● **n.** a stonecrop, especially orpine.

**lively** ● **adj.** (**-ier, -iest**) full of life, energy, or activity. ➤ intellectually stimulating or perceptive. ➤ ironic, chiefly Brit. difficult. ➤ (of a boat) rising lightly to the waves.
– PHRASES **look lively** informal move more quickly and energetically.
– DERIVATIVES **livelily** adv. **liveliness** n.
– ORIGIN OE *līflic* 'living' (see **life, -ly**[1]).

**liven** ● **v.** (usu. **liven something up**) make or become more lively or interesting.

**live oak** ● **n.** a large, spreading, evergreen North American oak. [*Quercus virginiana*.]

**liver**[1] ● **n. 1** a large lobed glandular organ in the abdomen, involved in processing digestive products, neutralizing toxins, secreting bile, and other metabolic processes. ➤ the flesh of an animal's liver as food. **2** (also **liver colour**) a dark reddish brown.
– ORIGIN OE *lifer*, of Gmc origin.

**liver**[2] ● **n.** a person who lives in a specified way: *a clean liver.*

**liver chestnut** ● **n.** a horse of a dark chestnut colour.

**liver fluke** ● **n.** a fluke of which the adult lives in the liver of a vertebrate and the larva in a secondary host such as a snail or fish. [*Fasciola hepatica* and other species.]

**liverish** ● **adj.** slightly ill, as though having a disordered liver. ➤ unhappy and bad-tempered.
– DERIVATIVES **liverishly** adv. **liverishness** n.

**Liverpudlian** /ˌlɪvəˈpʌdlɪən/ ● **n. 1** a native or inhabitant of Liverpool. **2** the dialect or accent of people from Liverpool. ● **adj.** of or relating to Liverpool.
– ORIGIN C19: humorous formation from *Liverpool* + **puddle**.

**liver rot** ● **n.** disease of the liver, especially that caused in sheep by the liver fluke.

**liver salts** ● **pl. n.** Brit. salts taken in water to relieve indigestion or nausea.

**liver sausage** ● **n.** chiefly Brit. a savoury meat paste in the form of a sausage containing cooked liver, or a mixture of liver and pork.

**liver spot** ● **n.** a small brown spot on the skin, especially as caused by a skin condition such as lentigo.
– DERIVATIVES **liver-spotted** adj.

**liverwort** /ˈlɪvəwəːt/ ● **n.** a small flowerless green plant with leaf-like stems or lobed leaves, lacking true roots and reproducing by spores. [Class Hepaticae.]
– ORIGIN OE, from **liver**[1] + **wort**, translating med. L. *hepatica.*

**livery**[1] ● **n.** (pl. **-ies**) **1** a special uniform worn by a servant, an official, or a member of a City Company. ➤ a distinctive design and colour scheme used on the vehicles, aircraft, or products of a company. **2** (in the UK) the members of a City livery company collectively. **3** historical a provision of food or clothing for servants. **4** (in full **livery of seisin**) Brit. historical the ceremonial procedure at common law of conveying freehold land to a grantee.
– PHRASES **at livery** (of a horse) kept for the owner and fed and cared for at a fixed charge.
– DERIVATIVES **liveried** adj.
– ORIGIN ME (in the sense 'the dispensing of food, provi-

sions, or clothing to servants', also 'allowance of provender for horses', surviving in the phr. *at livery* and in **LIVERY STABLE**): from OFr. *livree* 'delivered', fem. past part. of *livrer*, from L. *liberare* 'liberate'.

**livery**[2] • **adj. 1** resembling liver in colour or consistency. ➤ informal liverish. **2** dialect (of soil) heavy.

**livery company** • **n.** (in the UK) any of a number of Companies of the City of London descended from the medieval trade guilds.

**liveryman** • **n.** (pl. **-men**) (in the UK) a member of a livery company.

**livery stable** (also **livery yard**) • **n.** a stable where horses are kept at livery or let out for hire.

**lives** plural form of **LIFE**.

**livestock** • **n.** farm animals regarded as an asset.

**live wire** • **n.** informal an energetic and lively person.

**livid** • **adj. 1** informal furiously angry. **2** (of a colour or the skin) having a dark inflamed appearance.
– DERIVATIVES **lividity** n. **lividly** adv. **lividness** n.
– ORIGIN ME: from Fr. *livide* or L. *lividus*, from *livere* 'be bluish'.

**living** • **n.** an income sufficient to live on, or the means of earning it. ➤ Brit. (in church use) a position as a vicar or rector with an income or property. • **adj.** alive. ➤ (of a language) still spoken and used. ➤ poetic/literary (of water) perennially flowing.
– PHRASES **in** (or **within**) **living memory** within or during a time that is remembered by people still alive. **the living image of** an exact copy or likeness of.

**living death** • **n.** a state of existence characterized by total emptiness or misery.

**living rock** • **n.** rock that is not detached but still forms part of the earth.

**living room** • **n.** a room in a house for general everyday use.

**living stone** • **n.** a small succulent southern African flowering plant resembling a pebble in appearance. [Genus *Lithops*.]

**living wage** • **n.** a wage which is high enough to maintain a normal standard of living.

**living will** • **n.** a written statement detailing a person's desires regarding their medical treatment in circumstances in which they are no longer able to express informed consent.

**Livonian** /lɪˈvəʊnɪən/ • **n.** a native or inhabitant of Livonia, a region on the east coast of the Baltic Sea. • **adj.** of or relating to Livonia.

**lixiviate** /lɪkˈsɪvɪeɪt/ • **v.** Chemistry, archaic separate (a substance) into soluble and insoluble constituents by percolation.
– DERIVATIVES **lixiviation** n.
– ORIGIN C17: from mod. L. *lixiviat-*, *lixiviare* 'impregnate with lye'.

**lizard** • **n.** a reptile that typically has a long body and tail, four legs, movable eyelids, and a rough, scaly, or spiny skin. [Suborder Lacertilia: many species.]
– ORIGIN ME: from OFr. *lesard(e)*, from L. *lacertus* 'lizard, sea fish', also 'muscle'.

**lizard orchid** • **n.** a tall orchid with greenish flowers that have a very long twisted lip and a goat-like smell. [*Himantoglossum hircinum*.]

**LJ** • **abbrev.** (pl. **L JJ**) (in the UK) Lord Justice.

**Lk.** • **abbrev.** the Gospel of Luke (in biblical references).

**ll.** • **abbrev.** (in textual references) lines.

**'ll** • **contr.** shall; will.

**llama** /ˈlɑːmə/ • **n.** a domesticated pack animal of the camel family found in the Andes, valued for its soft woolly fleece. [*Lama glama*.] ➤ the wool of the llama.
– ORIGIN C17: from Sp., prob. from Quechua.

**llanero** /laˈnɛːrəʊ, lj-/ • **n.** (pl. **-os**) (in South America) an inhabitant of a llano, in particular one who works as a cowboy.
– ORIGIN from Sp.

**llano** /ˈlɑːnəʊ, ˈljɑː-/ • **n.** (pl. **-os**) (in South America) a treeless grassy plain.
– ORIGIN Sp., from L. *planum* 'plain'.

**LLB** • **abbrev.** Bachelor of Laws.
– ORIGIN from L. *legum baccalaureus*.

**LLD** • **abbrev.** Doctor of Laws.
– ORIGIN from L. *legum doctor*.

**LLM** • **abbrev.** Master of Laws.
– ORIGIN from L. *legum magister*.

**Lloyd's** • **n. 1** an incorporated society of insurance underwriters in London, made up of private syndicates. **2** short for **LLOYD'S REGISTER**.
– ORIGIN named after the coffee house of Edward *Lloyd* (*fl.* 1688–1726), in which underwriters and merchants congregated and where *Lloyd's List* was started.

**Lloyd's Register** (in full **Lloyd's Register of Shipping**) • **n.** a classified list of merchant ships over a certain tonnage, published annually in London. ➤ the corporation that produces this list and lays down the specifications for ships on which it is based.

**LM** /lɛm/ • **abbrev.** long metre.

**lm** • **abbrev.** lumen(s).

**LMS** • **abbrev.** (in the UK) local management of schools.

**LMT** • **abbrev.** Local Mean Time.

**ln** • **abbrev.** Mathematics natural logarithm.
– ORIGIN from mod. L. *logarithmus naturalis*.

**LNB** • **abbrev.** low noise blocker.

**LNG** • **abbrev.** liquefied natural gas.

**lo** • **exclam.** archaic used to draw attention to an interesting event.
– PHRASES **lo and behold** used to present a new scene or situation.
– ORIGIN natural exclam.: first recorded as *lā* in OE; reinforced in ME by a shortened form of *loke* 'look!'

**loa** /ˈləʊə/ • **n.** (pl. same or **loas**) a god in the voodoo cult of Haiti.
– ORIGIN from Haitian Creole.

**loach** /ləʊtʃ/ • **n.** a small, elongated freshwater fish with several barbels near the mouth. [Families Cobitidae and Homalopteridae: numerous species.]
– ORIGIN ME: from OFr. *loche*, of unknown origin.

**load** • **n. 1** a heavy or bulky thing that is being carried or is about to be carried. ➤ [in combination] the total number or amount that can be carried in a vehicle or container: *a carload of people*. **2** a weight or source of pressure. ➤ the amount of work to be done by a person or machine. ➤ a burden of responsibility, worry, or grief. **3** (**a load of**) informal a lot of. ➤ (**a load/loads**) plenty. **4** the amount of power supplied by a source. ➤ the resistance of moving parts to be overcome by a motor. ➤ Electronics an impedance or circuit that receives or develops the output of a transistor or other device. • **v. 1** put a load on or in (a vehicle, ship, etc.). ➤ (of a ship or vehicle) take on a load. **2** make (someone or something) carry or hold a large amount of heavy things. ➤ (**load someone/thing with**) supply someone or something in overwhelming abundance or to excess with. **3** insert (something) into a device so that it will operate. ➤ charge (a firearm) with ammunition. **4** bias towards a particular outcome.
– PHRASES **get a load of** informal used to draw attention to someone or something. **get** (or **have**) **a load on** N. Amer. informal become drunk. **load the bases** Baseball have base runners on all three bases. **load the dice against** (or **in favour of**) put at a disadvantage (or advantage).
– ORIGIN OE *lād* 'journey, conveyance', of Gmc origin: rel. to **LEAD**[1]; cf. **LODE**.

**loaded** • **adj. 1** carrying or bearing a load. ➤ informal wealthy. ➤ N. Amer. informal drunk. ➤ N. Amer. informal (of a car) equipped with many optional extras. **2** weighted or biased towards a particular outcome. ➤ charged with an underlying meaning.

**loader** • **n. 1** a machine or person that loads something. **2** [in combination] a gun, machine, or truck which is loaded in a specified way: *a front-loader*.

**load factor** • **n.** the ratio of the average or actual amount of some quantity and the maximum possible or permissible.

**loading** • **n. 1** the application of a load to something. ➤ the amount of this. **2** an increase in an insurance premium due to a factor increasing the risk involved. **3** Austral. an increment added to a basic wage for special skills or qualifications.

**loading gauge** • n. the maximum permitted height and width for rolling stock on a railway.

**load line** • n. another term for **PLIMSOLL LINE**.

**loadmaster** • n. the member of an aircraft's crew responsible for the cargo.

**load-shedding** • n. action to reduce the load on something, especially the interruption of an electricity supply to avoid excessive load on the generating plant.

**loadstone** • n. variant spelling of **LODESTONE**.

**loaf**[1] • n. (pl. **loaves**) a quantity of bread that is shaped and baked in one piece.
– PHRASES **use one's loaf** Brit. informal use one's common sense. [prob. from *loaf of bread*, rhyming sl. for 'head'.]
– ORIGIN OE *hlāf*, of Gmc origin.

**loaf**[2] • v. idle one's time away in aimless loitering.
– ORIGIN C19: prob. a back-form. from **LOAFER**.

**loafer** • n. **1** a person who idles their time away. **2** trademark a leather shoe shaped like a moccasin, with a flat heel.
– ORIGIN C19: perh. from Ger. *Landläufer* 'tramp'.

**loam** • n. **1** a fertile soil of clay and sand containing humus. **2** a paste of clay and water with sand and chopped straw, used in making bricks and plastering walls.
– DERIVATIVES **loaminess** n. **loamy** adj.
– ORIGIN OE *lām* 'clay', of W. Gmc origin: rel. to **LIME**[1].

**loan**[1] • n. a thing that is borrowed, especially a sum of money that is expected to be paid back with interest. ➤ the action of lending. ➤ short for **LOANWORD**. • v. give as a loan.
– PHRASES **on loan** being borrowed.
– DERIVATIVES **loanable** adj. **loanee** n. **loaner** n.
– ORIGIN ME: from ON *lán*, of Gmc origin; rel. to **LEND**.

**loan**[2] (also **loaning**) • n. [usu. in place names] Scottish **1** a lane. **2** an open piece of land where cows are milked.
– ORIGIN ME: var. of **LANE**.

**loanholder** • n. a person or organization holding the securities for a loan; a mortgagee.

**loan shark** • n. informal a moneylender who charges exorbitant rates of interest, typically illicitly.

**loan translation** • n. an expression adopted by one language from another in a more or less literally translated form.

**loanword** • n. a word adopted from a foreign language with little or no modification.

**loath** /ləʊθ/ (also **loth**) • adj. reluctant; unwilling: *I was loath to leave.*
– ORIGIN OE *lāth* 'hostile', of Gmc origin.

**loathe** /ləʊð/ • v. feel hatred or disgust for.
– DERIVATIVES **loather** n.
– ORIGIN OE *lāthian*, of Gmc origin; rel. to **LOATH**.

**loathsome** • adj. causing hatred or disgust.
– DERIVATIVES **loathsomely** adv. **loathsomeness** n.
– ORIGIN ME: from archaic *loath* 'disgust' + **-SOME**[1].

**loaves** plural form of **LOAF**[1].

**lob** • v. (**lobbed**, **lobbing**) throw or hit (a ball or missile) in a high arc. ➤ (in soccer or tennis) kick or hit the ball over (an opponent) in such a way. • n. a ball lobbed over an opponent or a stroke producing this result. ➤ Cricket a ball bowled with a slow underarm action.
– ORIGIN C16 (in the senses 'cause or allow to hang heavily' and 'behave like a lout'): from the archaic noun *lob* 'lout', 'pendulous object', prob. from Low Ger. or Du.

**lobar** /ˈləʊbə/ • adj. chiefly Anatomy & Medicine of or relating to a lobe, especially a lobe of a lung.

**lobate** /ˈləʊbeɪt/ • adj. Biology having a lobe or lobes.
– DERIVATIVES **lobation** n.

**lobby** • n. (pl. **-ies**) **1** a room out of which one or more other rooms or corridors lead, typically one near the entrance of a public building. **2** (in the UK) any of several large halls in the Houses of Parliament in which MPs may meet members of the public. ➤ (also **division lobby**) each of two corridors in the Houses of Parliament to which MPs retire to vote. **3** a group of people seeking to influence legislators on a particular issue. ➤ an organized attempt by members of the public to influence legislators. • v. (**-ies**, **-ied**) seek to influence (a legislator).
– DERIVATIVES **lobbyist** n.
– ORIGIN C16 (in the sense 'monastic cloister'): from med. L. *lobia*, *lobium* 'covered walk'.

**lobby correspondent** • n. (in the UK) a senior political journalist of a group receiving direct but unattributable briefings from the government.

**lobe** • n. a roundish and flattish projecting or hanging part of something, often one of two or more such parts divided by a fissure.
– DERIVATIVES **lobed** adj. **lobeless** adj.
– ORIGIN ME: via late L. from Gk *lobos* 'lobe, pod'.

**lobectomy** • n. (pl. **-ies**) surgical removal of a lobe of an organ such as the lung or brain.

**lobelia** /ləˈbiːlɪə/ • n. a plant of the bellflower family, typically with blue or scarlet flowers. [Genus *Lobelia*: many species.]
– ORIGIN mod. L., named after the Flemish botanist Matthias de *Lobel* (1538–1616).

**loblolly pine** /ˈlɒblɒli/ • n. a pine tree with very long slender needles, native to the south-eastern US. [*Pinus taeda*.]
– ORIGIN from obs. *loblolly* 'thick gruel', US dial. 'mudhole'.

**lobo** /ˈləʊbəʊ/ • n. (pl. **-os**) N. Amer. (in the south-western US and Mexico) a timber wolf.
– ORIGIN C19: from Sp.

**lobola** /ləˈbəʊlə/ (also **lobolo** /ləˈbəʊləʊ/) • n. (among southern African peoples) a bride price, especially one paid with cattle.
– ORIGIN from Zulu and Xhosa.

**lobopod** /ˈləʊbə(ʊ)pɒd/ • n. Zoology the lobopodium of an onychophoran. ➤ an onychophoran.

**lobopodium** /ˌləʊbə(ʊ)ˈpəʊdɪəm/ • n. (pl. **lobopodia** /-ɪə/) Zoology **1** the primitive leg of an onychophoran. **2** a lobe-like pseudopodium in an amoeba.
– DERIVATIVES **lobopodial** adj.
– ORIGIN C20: from mod. L. *lobosus* 'having many lobes' + **PODIUM**.

**lobotomize** (also **-ise**) • v. Surgery perform a lobotomy on. ➤ informal reduce the mental ability to function of.
– DERIVATIVES **lobotomization** n.

**lobotomy** /ləˈbɒtəmi/ • n. (pl. **-ies**) a surgical operation involving incision into the prefrontal lobe of the brain, formerly used to treat mental illness.

**lobscouse** /ˈlɒbskaʊs/ • n. a stew formerly eaten by sailors, consisting of meat, vegetables, and ship's biscuit.
– ORIGIN C18: of unknown origin; cf. Du. *lapskous* and Ger. *Lapskaus*.

**lobster** • n. a large marine crustacean with a cylindrical body, stalked eyes, and the first of its five pairs of limbs modified as pincers. [*Homarus* and other genera.] ➤ the flesh of this animal as food. • v. catch lobsters.
– ORIGIN OE *lopustre*, alt. of L. *locusta* 'crustacean, locust'.

**lobster moth** • n. a brown moth with a long-legged caterpillar having an upturned tail reminiscent of a lobster. [*Stauropus fagi*.]

**lobster Newburg** /ˈnjuːbəːɡ/ • n. a dish of lobster cooked in a thick cream sauce containing sherry or brandy.
– ORIGIN prob. named after *Newburgh*, New York.

**lobster pot** • n. a basket-like trap in which lobsters are caught.

**lobster thermidor** /ˈθəːmɪdɔː/ • n. a dish of lobster cooked in a cream sauce, returned to its shell, sprinkled with cheese, and browned under the grill.
– ORIGIN *thermidor* from *Thermidor*, the eleventh month of the French Republican calendar.

**lobule** /ˈlɒbjuːl/ • n. chiefly Anatomy a small lobe.
– DERIVATIVES **lobular** adj. **lobulate** /-lət/ adj. **lobulated** adj.

**lobworm** • n. a large earthworm used as fishing bait.
– ORIGIN C17: from **LOB** in the obs. sense 'pendulous object'.

**local** • adj. relating or restricted to a particular area or one's neighbourhood. ➤ (in technical use) relating to a particular region or part, or to each of any number of these: *a local infection.* ➤ Computing only available for use

in one part of a program. ● n. a local person or thing. ➤ Brit. informal a pub convenient to a person's home. ➤ N. Amer. a local branch of a trade union. ➤ Stock Exchange slang a floor trader who trades on their own account, rather than on behalf of other investors.
– DERIVATIVES **locally** adv. **localness** n.
– ORIGIN ME: from late L. *localis*, from L. *locus* 'place'.

**local anaesthetic** ● n. an anaesthetic that affects a restricted area of the body.

**local area network** ● n. a computer network that links devices within a building or group of adjacent buildings.

**local authority** ● n. Brit. an administrative body in local government.

**local colour** ● n. **1** the characteristic customs or other aspects of a place or period. **2** Art the actual colour of a thing in ordinary daylight, without the influence of other colours in proximity.

**local derby** ● n. see **DERBY**[1].

**locale** /ləʊˈkɑːl/ ● n. a place associated with particular events.
– ORIGIN C18: from Fr. *local* (n.), respelled to indicate stress on the final syllable; cf. **MORALE**.

**local government** ● n. the administration of a particular county or district, with representatives elected by those who live there.

**localism** ● n. **1** preference for one's own locality, particularly when this results in a limitation of outlook. **2** a characteristic of a particular locality, such as an idiom.
– DERIVATIVES **localist** n. & adj.

**locality** ● n. (pl. **-ies**) the position or site of something. ➤ an area or neighbourhood.
– ORIGIN C17: from Fr. *localité* or late L. *localitas*, from *localis* (see **LOCAL**).

**localize** (also **-ise**) ● v. **1** [often as adj. **localized**] restrict or assign to a particular place. **2** make local in character.
– DERIVATIVES **localizable** adj. **localization** n.

**local option** ● n. a choice available to a local administration to accept or reject national legislation.

**local preacher** ● n. a Methodist layperson authorized to conduct services in a particular circuit.

**local time** ● n. time as reckoned in a particular region or time zone.

**locate** /lə(ʊ)ˈkeɪt/ ● v. **1** discover the exact place or position of. **2** (**be located**) be situated in a particular place. ➤ N. Amer. establish oneself or one's business in a specified place.
– DERIVATIVES **locatable** adj. **locator** n.
– ORIGIN C16 (orig. as a legal term meaning 'let out on hire'): from L. *locat-*, *locare* 'to place'.

**location** ● n. **1** a particular place or position. ➤ the action or process of locating. **2** an actual place in which a film or broadcast is made, as distinct from a simulation in a studio. **3** S. African former term for **TOWNSHIP** (sense 1).
– DERIVATIVES **locational** adj.

**locative** /ˈlɒkətɪv/ ● adj. Grammar relating to or denoting a case in some languages of nouns, pronouns, and adjectives, expressing location.

**loc. cit.** ● abbrev. in the passage already cited.
– ORIGIN from L. *loco citato*.

**loch** /lɒk, lɒx/ ● n. Scottish a lake. ➤ (also **sea loch**) an arm of the sea, especially when narrow or partially landlocked.
– ORIGIN ME: from Sc. Gaelic.

**lochan** /ˈlɒk(ə)n, ˈlɒx(ə)n/ ● n. Scottish a small loch.
– ORIGIN C17: from Sc. Gaelic, dimin. of *loch*.

**lochia** /ˈlɒkɪə, ˈləʊ-/ ● n. Medicine the normal discharge from the uterus after childbirth.
– DERIVATIVES **lochial** adj.
– ORIGIN C17: mod. L., from Gk *lokhia*, neut. pl. (used as n.) of *lokhios* 'of childbirth'.

**loci** plural form of **LOCUS**.

**loci classici** plural form of **LOCUS CLASSICUS**.

**lock**[1] ● n. **1** a mechanism for keeping a door, lid, or container fastened, typically operated by a key. ➤ a similar device used to prevent the operation of a vehicle or other machine. **2** a short section of a canal or river with gates and sluices at each end which can be opened or closed to change the water level, used for raising and lowering boats. **3** the turning of the front wheels of a vehicle to change its direction of motion. **4** (in wrestling and martial arts) a hold that prevents an opponent from moving a limb. **5** (also **lock forward**) Rugby a player in the second row of a scrum. **6** (**a lock**) N. Amer. informal a certainty. **7** archaic a mechanism for exploding the charge of a gun. ● v. **1** fasten or be fastened with a lock. ➤ enclose or secure by locking a door. ➤ (**lock someone up/away**) imprison someone. ➤ (**lock someone out of**) exclude someone from. **2** make or become rigidly fixed or immovable. ➤ (**lock someone/thing in**) engage or entangle someone or something in (an embrace or struggle). ➤ (**lock on to**) locate (a target) by radar or similar means and then track. **3** go through a lock on a canal.
– PHRASES **have a lock on** N. Amer. informal have an unbreakable hold on. **lock horns** engage in conflict. **lock, stock, and barrel** including everything. [referring to the complete mechanism of a firearm.]
– DERIVATIVES **lockable** adj. **lockless** adj.
– ORIGIN OE *loc*, of Gmc origin.

**lock**[2] ● n. **1** a piece of a person's hair that coils or hangs together. ➤ (**locks**) chiefly poetic/literary a person's hair. **2** a tuft of wool or cotton.
– DERIVATIVES **-locked** adj.
– ORIGIN OE *locc*, of Gmc origin.

**lockage** ● n. the construction or use of locks on waterways. ➤ the amount of rise and fall of water levels resulting from the use of locks.

**lockdown** ● n. N. Amer. the confining of prisoners to their cells, typically in order to regain control during a riot.

**locker** ● n. **1** a small lockable cupboard or compartment, typically as one of a number placed together for public use. ➤ a chest or compartment on a ship or boat for clothes, stores, or ammunition. **2** a device that locks something.

**locker room** ● n. a room containing lockers, especially a sports changing room. ➤ [as modifier] characteristic of a men's locker room, especially in being coarse or ribald.

**locket** ● n. **1** a small ornamental case worn round a person's neck on a chain and used to hold things of sentimental value. **2** a metal plate or band on a scabbard.
– ORIGIN ME: from OFr. *locquet*, dimin. of *loc* 'latch, lock', of Gmc origin; rel. to **LOCK**[1].

**lockfast** ● adj. Scottish secured with a lock.

**lock forward** ● n. another term for **LOCK**[1] (in sense 5).

**lock-in** ● n. **1** an arrangement according to which a person or company is obliged to negotiate or trade only with a specific company. **2** a period during which customers are locked into a bar or pub after closing time to continue drinking privately.

**lockjaw** ● n. non-technical term for **TRISMUS**.

**lock-knit** ● adj. (of a fabric) knitted with an interlocking stitch.

**locknut** ● n. **1** a nut screwed down on another to keep it tight. **2** a nut designed so that, once tightened, it cannot be accidentally loosened.

**lockout** ● n. the exclusion of employees by their employer from their place of work until certain terms are agreed to.

**locksmith** ● n. a person who makes and repairs locks.

**lockstep** ● n. a way of marching with each person as close as possible to the one in front.

**lock stitch** ● n. a stitch made by a sewing machine by firmly linking together two threads or stitches.

**lock-up** ● n. **1** a jail, especially a temporary one. **2** Brit. non-residential premises that can be locked up, typically a garage. **3** an investment in assets which cannot readily be realized or sold on in the short term.

**loco**[1] ● n. (pl. **-os**) informal a locomotive.

**loco**[2] ● adj. informal crazy.
– ORIGIN C19: from Sp., 'insane'.

**locomotion** ● n. movement or the ability to move from one place to another.
– DERIVATIVES **locomotory** adj.

– ORIGIN C17: from L. *loco*, ablative of *locus* 'place' + *motio* (see **MOTION**).

**locomotive** • n. a powered railway vehicle used for pulling trains. • adj. of or relating to locomotion. ➤archaic (of a machine, vehicle, or animal) having the power of progressive motion.

– ORIGIN C17 (as adj.): from mod. L. *locomotivus*, from L. *loco* (ablative of *locus* 'place') + late L. *motivus* 'motive'.

**locomotor** • adj. chiefly Biology of or relating to locomotion.

**locoweed** • n. N. Amer. a plant which can cause a brain disorder if eaten by livestock. [Genera *Astragalus* and *Oxytropis*.]

**locule** /'lɒkjuːl/ • n. another term for **LOCULUS**.

**loculus** /'lɒkjʊləs/ • n. (pl. **loculi** /-lʌɪ, -liː/) chiefly Botany each of a number of small separate cavities, especially in an ovary.

– DERIVATIVES **locular** adj.

– ORIGIN C19: from L., 'compartment'.

**locum** /'ləʊkəm/ • n. informal short for **LOCUM TENENS**.

**locum tenens** /ˌləʊkəm 'tiːnɛnz, 'tɛn-/ • n. (pl. **locum tenentes** /tɪ'nɛntiːz, tɛ-/) a temporary deputy, especially one acting for a cleric or doctor.

– DERIVATIVES **locum tenency** n.

– ORIGIN C17: from med. L., lit. 'one holding a place' (see **LOCUS**, **TENANT**).

**locus** /'ləʊkəs/ • n. (pl. **loci** /-sʌɪ, -kʌɪ, -kiː/) **1** technical a particular position, point, or place. **2** Mathematics a curve or other figure formed by all the points satisfying a particular condition.

– ORIGIN C18: from L., 'place'.

**locus classicus** /ˌləʊkəs 'klasɪkəs, ˌlɒkəs/ • n. (pl. **loci classici** /ˌləʊsʌɪ 'klasɪsʌɪ, ˌlɒkiː 'klasɪkiː/) the best known or most authoritative passage on a subject.

– ORIGIN L., lit. 'classical place'.

**locus standi** /ˌləʊkəs 'standʌɪ, ˌlɒkəs/ • n. (pl. **loci standi** /ˌləʊsʌɪ 'standʌɪ, ˌlɒkiː 'standiː/) Law the right or capacity to bring an action or to appear in a court.

– ORIGIN L., lit. 'place of standing'.

**locust** • n. **1** a large, mainly tropical grasshopper which migrates in vast swarms and is very destructive to vegetation. [*Locusta migratoria* and other species.] **2** (also **locust tree**) a carob tree, false acacia, or similar pod-bearing tree.

– ORIGIN ME: via OFr. *locuste* from L. *locusta* 'locust, crustacean'.

**locution** /lə'kjuːʃ(ə)n/ • n. **1** a word or phrase, especially with regard to style or idiom. ➤a person's style of speech. **2** an utterance regarded in terms of its intrinsic meaning or reference, as distinct from its function or purpose in context.

– DERIVATIVES **locutionary** adj.

– ORIGIN ME: from OFr., or from L. *locutio(n-)*, from *loqui* 'speak'.

**lode** /ləʊd/ • n. a vein of metal ore in the earth.

– ORIGIN OE *lād* 'way, course', var. of **LOAD**.

**loden** /'ləʊd(ə)n/ • n. **1** a thick waterproof woollen cloth. **2** the dark green colour in which such cloth is often made.

– ORIGIN C20: from Ger. *Loden*.

**lodestar** • n. a star that is used to guide the course of a ship, especially the pole star.

– ORIGIN ME: from **LODE** in the obs. sense 'way, course' + **STAR**.

**lodestone** (also **loadstone**) • n. a piece of magnetite or other naturally magnetized mineral, able to be used as a magnet.

**lodge** • n. **1** a small house at the gates of a park or in the grounds of a large house, occupied by a gatekeeper or other employee. ➤a small country house occupied in season for sports such as hunting and shooting. ➤[in names] a large house or hotel. ➤a porter's quarters at the main entrance of a college or other large building. **2** an American Indian tent or other dwelling. **3** a beaver's den. **4** a branch or meeting place of an organization such as the Freemasons. • v. **1** present (a complaint, appeal, etc.) formally to the proper authorities. **2** make or become firmly fixed in a place. **3** rent accommodation in another person's house. ➤provide with such accommodation. **4** (**lodge something in/with**) leave money or a valuable item in (a place) or with (someone) for safe keeping. **5** (of wind or rain) flatten (a standing crop).

– ORIGIN ME *loge*, via OFr. *loge* 'arbour, hut' from med. L. *laubia*, *lobia* (see **LOBBY**), of Gmc origin.

**lodgement** • n. **1** chiefly poetic/literary a place in which a person or thing is lodged. **2** the depositing of money in a particular bank or account.

**lodgepole pine** • n. a straight-trunked pine tree of the mountains of western North America. [*Pinus contorta* var. *latifolia*.]

– ORIGIN so called because its wood was used by American Indians to construct lodges.

**lodger** • n. a person who pays rent to live in a property with the owner.

**lodging** • n. a temporary place of residence. ➤(**lodgings**) a rented room or rooms, usually in the same residence as the owner.

**lodging house** • n. a private house providing rented accommodation.

**lodicule** /'lɒdɪkjuːl/ • n. Botany a small green or white scale below the ovary of a grass flower.

– ORIGIN C19: from L. *lodicula*, dimin. of *lodix* 'coverlet'.

**loess** /'ləʊɪs, lɜːs/ • n. Geology a loosely compacted yellowish-grey deposit of wind-blown sediment.

– DERIVATIVES **loessial** adj. **loessic** adj.

– ORIGIN C19: from Ger. *Löss*, from Swiss Ger. *lösch* 'loose'.

**lo-fi** (also **low-fi**) • adj. of or employing sound reproduction of a lower quality than hi-fi.

– ORIGIN 1950s: from an alt. of **LOW**[1] + *-fi* on the pattern of *hi-fi*.

**loft** • n. **1** a room or storage space directly under the roof of a house or other building. ➤a gallery in a church or hall. ➤a large, open area in a shop, warehouse, or other large building that has been converted into living space. ➤a pigeon house. **2** Golf upward inclination given to the ball in a stroke. ➤backward slope of the head of a club, designed to give such inclination. **3** the thickness of insulating matter in an object such as a sleeping bag. • v. **1** kick, hit, or throw (a ball or missile) high up. **2** [usu. as adj. **lofted**] give loft to the head of (a golf club).

– ORIGIN OE, from ON *lopt* 'air, upper room', of Gmc origin.

**lofty** • adj. (**-ier**, **-iest**) **1** of imposing height. **2** noble; elevated. ➤haughty and aloof. **3** (of wool and other textiles) thick and resilient.

– DERIVATIVES **loftily** adv. **loftiness** n.

– ORIGIN ME: from **LOFT**, influenced by **ALOFT**.

**log**[1] • n. **1** a part of the trunk or a large branch of a tree that has fallen or been cut off. **2** (also **logbook**) an official record of events during the voyage of a ship or aircraft. **3** an apparatus for determining the speed of a ship, originally one consisting of a float attached to a knotted line. • v. (**logged**, **logging**) **1** enter in a log. ➤achieve (a certain distance, speed, or time). **2** (**log in/on** or **off/out**) go through the procedures to begin (or conclude) use of a computer system. **3** cut down (an area of forest) to exploit the wood commercially.

– DERIVATIVES **logger** n. **logging** n.

– ORIGIN ME: of unknown origin.

**log**[2] • n. short for **LOGARITHM**.

**$\log_e$** • symb. natural logarithm.

**-log** • comb. form US spelling of **-LOGUE**.

**loganberry** /'ləʊg(ə)n,b(ə)ri, -ˌbɛri/ • n. **1** an edible dull-red soft fruit, considered to be a hybrid of a raspberry and an American dewberry. **2** the plant bearing this fruit. [*Rubus loganobaccus*.]

– ORIGIN C19: from the name of John H. *Logan*, Amer. horticulturalist, + **BERRY**.

**logan stone** /'lɒg(ə)n, 'ləʊg(ə)n/ • n. another term for **ROCKING STONE**.

– ORIGIN C18: from *logging* (from dial. *log* 'to rock').

**logarithm** /'lɒgərɪð(ə)m, -rɪθ-/ • n. a quantity representing the power to which a fixed number (the base) must be raised to produce a given number.

– DERIVATIVES **logarithmic** adj. **logarithmically** adv.

– ORIGIN C17: from mod. L. *logarithmus*, from Gk *logos* 'reckoning, ratio' + *arithmos* 'number'.

**logbook** • **n.** **1** another term for **LOG**[1] (in sense 2). **2** Brit. another term for **REGISTRATION DOCUMENT**.

**loge** /ləʊʒ/ • **n.** a private box or enclosure in a theatre.
– ORIGIN C18: from Fr.

**-loger** • **comb. form** equivalent to **-LOGIST**.
– ORIGIN on the pattern of words such as *(astro)loger*.

**loggerhead** • **n.** **1** (also **loggerhead turtle**) a large-headed reddish-brown turtle of warm seas. [*Caretta caretta*.] **2** archaic a foolish person.
– PHRASES **at loggerheads** in violent dispute or disagreement. [perh. a use of *loggerhead* in the C17 sense 'long-handled iron instrument for heating liquids' (when wielded as a weapon).]
– ORIGIN C16: from dial. *logger* 'block of wood for hobbling a horse' + **HEAD**.

**loggia** /ˈləʊdʒə, ˈlɒ-, -dʒɪə/ • **n.** a gallery or room with one or more open sides, especially one having one side open to a garden.
– ORIGIN C18: from Ital., 'lodge'.

**logia** plural form of **LOGION**.

**logic** • **n.** **1** reasoning conducted or assessed according to strict principles of validity. ➤a particular system or codification of this. ➤the ability to reason correctly. ➤(**the logic of**) the course of action following as a necessary consequence of. **2** a system or set of principles underlying the arrangements of elements in a computer or electronic device so as to perform a specified task.
– DERIVATIVES **logician** n.
– ORIGIN ME: via OFr. *logique* and late L. *logica* from Gk *logikē* (*tekhnē*) '(art) of reason'.

**-logic** • **comb. form** equivalent to **-LOGICAL** (as in *pharmacologic*).
– ORIGIN from Gk *-logikos*.

**logical** • **adj.** of or according to the rules of logic. ➤capable of or showing rational thought. ➤expected or reasonable under the circumstances.
– DERIVATIVES **logicality** /-ˈkalɪti/ n. **logically** adv.

**-logical** • **comb. form** in adjectives corresponding chiefly to nouns ending in *-logy* (such as *pharmacological* corresponding to *pharmacology*).

**logical atomism** • **n.** Philosophy the theory that all propositions can be analysed into simple independent elements of meaning corresponding to elements making up facts about the world.

**logical necessity** • **n.** that state of things which obliges something to be as it is because no alternative is logically possible.

**logical positivism** (also **logical empiricism**) • **n.** a form of positivism which considers that the only meaningful philosophical problems are those which can be solved by logical analysis.

**logic bomb** • **n.** Computing a set of instructions secretly incorporated into a program so that if a particular condition is satisfied they will be carried out, usually with harmful effects.

**logion** /ˈlɒgɪɒn, ˈləʊ-/ • **n.** (pl. **logia** /-gɪə/) a saying attributed to Christ, especially one not recorded in the canonical Gospels.
– ORIGIN C19: from Gk, 'oracle'.

**-logist** • **comb. form** indicating a person skilled or involved in a branch of study denoted by a noun ending in *-logy* (such as *biologist* corresponding to *biology*).

**logistic** • **adj.** of or relating to logistics.
– DERIVATIVES **logistical** adj. **logistically** adv.

**logistics** /ləˈdʒɪstɪks/ • **pl. n.** [treated as sing. or pl.] the detailed coordination of a large and complex operation.
– ORIGIN C19 (meaning 'movement and supply of troops and equipment'): from Fr. *logistique*, from *loger* 'lodge'.

**logjam** • **n.** **1** a crowded mass of logs blocking a river. **2** a deadlock. **3** a backlog.

**log line** • **n.** a line to which a ship's log is attached.

**log-normal** • **adj.** Statistics of or denoting a set of data in which the logarithm of the variate follows a normal distribution.
– DERIVATIVES **log-normality** n. **log-normally** adv.

**logo** /ˈlɒgəʊ, ˈləʊgəʊ/ • **n.** (pl. **-os**) an emblematic design adopted by an organization to identify its products.
– ORIGIN 1930s: abbrev. of **LOGOGRAM** or **LOGOTYPE**.

**logocentric** • **adj.** regarding words and language as a fundamental expression of an external reality.
– DERIVATIVES **logocentrism** n.
– ORIGIN 1930s: from Gk *logos* 'word, reason' + **-CENTRIC**.

**logogram** • **n.** a sign or character representing a word or phrase, as used in shorthand and some ancient writing systems.
– ORIGIN C19: from Gk *logos* 'word' + **-GRAM**[1].

**logograph** • **n.** another term for **LOGOGRAM**.
– DERIVATIVES **logographic** adj.

**logomachy** /ləˈgɒməki/ • **n.** (pl. **-ies**) rare an argument about words.
– ORIGIN C16: from Gk *logomakhia*, from *logos* 'word' + *-makhia* 'fighting'.

**logophile** /ˈlɒgə(ʊ)fʌɪl/ • **n.** a lover of words.
– ORIGIN C20: from Gk *logos* 'word' + **-PHILE**.

**logorrhoea** /ˌlɒgəˈrɪə/ (US **logorrhea**) • **n.** a tendency to extreme loquacity.
– DERIVATIVES **logorrhoeic** adj.
– ORIGIN C20: from Gk *logos* 'word' + *rhoia* 'flow'.

**Logos** /ˈlɒgɒs/ • **n.** **1** Theology the Word of God, or principle of divine reason and creative order, identified with the second person of the Trinity incarnate in Jesus Christ. **2** (in Jungian psychology) the principle of reason and judgement, associated with the animus. Often contrasted with **EROS**.
– ORIGIN Gk, 'word, reason'.

**logotype** • **n.** Printing a single piece of type that prints a word, a group of separate letters, or a logo.
– ORIGIN C19: from Gk *logos* 'word' + **TYPE**.

**logrolling** • **n.** N. Amer. **1** informal the exchange of favours between politicians by reciprocal voting for each other's proposed legislation. [from the phr. *you roll my log and I'll roll yours*.] **2** a sport in which two contestants stand on a floating log and spin it with their feet to try to dislodge their opponent.
– DERIVATIVES **logroller** n.

**logrunner** • **n.** a ground-dwelling Australasian songbird with a spine-tipped tail. [Genus *Orthonyx*: two species.]

**-logue** (US also **-log**) • **comb. form** **1** denoting discourse of a specified type: *dialogue*. **2** denoting compilation: *catalogue*. **3** equivalent to **-LOGIST**. See word-formation panel.
– ORIGIN from Fr. *-logue*, from Gk *-logos*, *-logon*.

**logwood** • **n.** a spiny Caribbean tree, the dark heartwood of which yields haematoxylin and other dyes. [*Haematoxylon campechianum*.]

**logy** /ˈləʊgi/ • **adj.** (**-ier**, **-iest**) N. Amer. sluggish.
– ORIGIN C19: of uncertain origin; cf. Du. *log* 'heavy, dull'.

**-logy** • **comb. form** **1** (usu. as **-ology**) denoting a subject of study or interest: *psychology*. **2** denoting a characteristic of speech or language: *eulogy*. ➤denoting a type of discourse: *trilogy*. See word-formation panel.
– ORIGIN from Fr. *-logie* or med. L. *-logia*, from Gk.

**loin** • **n.** **1** the part of the body on both sides of the spine between the lowest ribs and the hip bones. ➤a joint of meat that includes the vertebrae of the loins. **2** (**loins**) poetic/literary the region of the sexual organs, regarded as the source of erotic or procreative power.
– ORIGIN ME: from OFr. *loigne*, based on L. *lumbus*.

**loincloth** • **n.** a single piece of cloth wrapped round the hips, typically worn by men in some hot countries as their only garment.

**loiter** • **v.** stand around or move without apparent purpose.
– PHRASES **loiter with intent** English Law, dated stand around with the intention of committing an offence.
– DERIVATIVES **loiterer** n.
– ORIGIN ME: perh. from MDu. *loteren* 'wag about'.

**Lolita** /lə(ʊ)ˈliːtə/ • **n.** a sexually precocious young girl.
– ORIGIN from the eponymous character in the novel *Lolita* (1958) by Vladimir Nabokov.

**loll** • **v.** **1** sit, lie, or stand in a lazy, relaxed way. **2** hang loosely.

## Word *Formation*

**-logue** from Greek *logos* 'word, speech, telling'

➤ Some of the most common **-logue** words (full entries and definitions to be found in this dictionary), typically relating to a particular type of speech or text:

| | | |
|---|---|---|
| catalogue | a list of items systematically ordered | Gk *katalegein* 'pick out' (from *kata* 'down') |
| dialogue | a conversation | Gk *dia* 'through' |
| duologue | a play for two actors | DUO- 'two' |
| eclogue | a pastoral poem | Gk *eklogē* 'selection (of poems)' |
| epilogue | a section serving as a comment at the end of a text | Gk *epi* 'in addition' |
| ideologue | a dogmatic supporter of an ideology | based on IDEA |
| monologue | a long speech by a single actor | Gk *monos* 'alone' |
| prologue | a separate introductory section to a work | Gk *pro* 'before' |
| travelogue | a film or text about travel experiences | based on TRAVEL |

Many **-logue** words are spelled **-log** in US English, as ***catalog***, ***dialog***, and ***epilog***.

The word ***analogue*** relates to *logos* meaning 'ratio, proportion', and means literally 'up to proportion'.

– ORIGIN ME: prob. symbolic of dangling.

**lollapalooza** /ˌlɒləpəˈluːzə/ (also **lalapalooza**) ● n. N. Amer. informal a particularly impressive or attractive person or thing.
– ORIGIN C19: of fanciful formation.

**Lollard** /ˈlɒləd/ ● n. a follower of the English religious reformer John Wyclif (*c.*1330–84).
– DERIVATIVES **Lollardism** n. **Lollardy** n.
– ORIGIN orig. a derogatory term, derived from a Du. word meaning 'mumbler', based on *lollen* 'to mumble'.

**lollipop** ● n. **1** a large, flat, rounded boiled sweet on the end of a stick. ➤ British term for ICE LOLLY. **2** informal a short, entertaining, but undemanding piece of classical music.
– ORIGIN C18: perh. from dial. *lolly* 'tongue' + POP[1].

**lollipop lady** (or **lollipop man**) ● n. Brit. informal a person employed to help children cross the road safely near a school by holding up a circular sign on a pole to stop the traffic.

**lollop** ● v. (**lolloped**, **lolloping**) move in an ungainly way in a series of clumsy bounds.
– ORIGIN C18: prob. from LOLL, assoc. with TROLLOP.

**lollo rosso** /ˌlɒləʊ ˈrɒsəʊ/ ● n. lettuce of a variety with deeply divided red-edged leaves.
– ORIGIN Ital., from *lolla* 'husk, chaff' + *rosso* 'red'.

**lolly** ● n. (pl. **-ies**) informal **1** chiefly Brit. a lollipop. ➤ Austral./NZ a boiled sweet. **2** Brit. money.

**lollygag** (also **lallygag**) ● v. (**lollygagged**, **lollygagging**) N. Amer. informal spend time or move aimlessly.
– ORIGIN C19: of unknown origin.

**Lombard** /ˈlɒmbəd, -bɑːd/ ● n. **1** a member of a Germanic people who invaded Italy in the 6th century. **2** a native of Lombardy in northern Italy. **3** the Italian dialect of Lombardy.
– DERIVATIVES **Lombardic** adj.
– ORIGIN from Ital. *lombardo*, representing late L. *Langobardus*, of Gmc origin, from the base of LONG[1] + the ethnic name *Bardi*.

**Lombardy poplar** ● n. a black poplar of an Italian variety with a distinctive tall, slender columnar form. [*Populus nigra* var. *italica*.]

**loment** /ˈləʊmɛnt/ (also **lomentum** /lə(ʊ)ˈmɛntəm/) ● n. Botany the pod of some leguminous plants, breaking up when mature into one-seeded joints.
– ORIGIN C19: from L., lit. 'bean meal' (orig. used as a cosmetic).

**London clay** ● n. clay forming an extensive layer in SE England, dating from the lower Eocene period.

**Londoner** ● n. a native or inhabitant of London.

**London plane** ● n. a hybrid plane tree which is resistant to pollution and widely planted in towns. [*Platanus* × *hispanica*.]

**London pride** ● n. a saxifrage with rosettes of fleshy leaves and stems of pink starlike flowers. [*Saxifraga* × *urbium*.]

**lone** ● adj. having no companions; solitary. ➤ lacking the support of others. ➤ poetic/literary unfrequented and remote.
– ORIGIN ME: shortening of ALONE.

**lone hand** ● n. (in euchre or quadrille) a hand played against the rest.
– PHRASES **play a lone hand** act on one's own without help.

**lonely** ● adj. (**-ier**, **-iest**) sad because one has no friends or company. ➤ solitary. ➤ unfrequented and remote.
– DERIVATIVES **loneliness** n.

**lonely hearts** ● pl. n. people looking for a lover or friend by advertising in a newspaper.

**loner** ● n. a person who prefers not to associate with others.

**lonesome** ● adj. chiefly N. Amer. lonely.
– PHRASES **by** (or Brit. **on**) **one's lonesome** informal all alone.
– DERIVATIVES **lonesomeness** n.

**lone wolf** ● n. a person who prefers to act alone.

**long**[1] ● adj. (**-er**, **-est**) **1** of a great distance or duration. ➤ of a specified distance or duration. ➤ (of a ball in sport) travelling a great distance, or further than expected. **2** relatively great in extent. ➤ having a specified extent. **3** Phonetics (of a vowel) categorized as long with regard to quality and length (e.g. in standard British English the vowel /uː/ in *food*). ➤ Prosody (of a vowel or syllable) having the greater of the two recognized durations. **4** (of odds or a chance) reflecting or representing a low level of probability. **5** Finance (of shares or other assets) bought in advance, with the expectation of a rise in price. ➤ (of a security) maturing at a distant date. **6** (of a drink) large and refreshing, and in which alcohol, if present, is not concentrated. **7** (**long on**) informal well supplied with. ● n. **1** a long time. **2** a long sound, vowel, or syllable. **3** (**longs**) Finance long securities or assets. ● adv. (**longer**; **longest**) **1** for a long time. ➤ at a distant time: *long ago.* ➤ throughout a specified period of time: *all day long.* **2** (with reference to the ball in sport) at, to, or over a great distance.
– PHRASES **as** (or **so**) **long as 1** during the whole time that. **2** provided that. **be long** take a long time. **in the long run** (or **term**) eventually. **the long and the short of it** all that can or need be said. **long in the tooth** rather old. [orig. said of horses, from the recession of the gums with age.]
– DERIVATIVES **longish** adj.

## Word *Formation*

**-logy** from Greek *logos* 'word, discourse, account, etc.'

➤ The chief sense in English **-logy** words is 'a subject of study or interest', and there are many hundreds of such words, represented here by some of the most widely used:

| | | |
|---|---|---|
| anthropology | the study of humankind | Gk *anthrōpos* 'human being' |
| archaeology | the study of human history and prehistory through excavations etc. | Gk *arkhaios* 'ancient' |
| astrology | the study of the stars and planets as having an influence on human affairs | Gk *astron* 'star' |
| biology | the study of living organisms | Gk *bios* 'life' |
| ecology | the study of organisms in relation to their environment | Gk *oikos* 'house' |
| entomology | the study of insects | Gk *entomon* 'insect' |
| epidemiology | the study of diseases | Gk *epidēmia* 'prevalence of disease' (from *epi-* 'on, above' + *dēmos* 'people') |
| geology | the science of the physical structure of the earth | Gk *gē* 'earth' |
| gynaecology | the branch of medicine relating to women | Gk *gunē, gunaik-* 'woman' |
| meteorology | the science of the atmosphere | Gk *meteōron*, from *meteōros* 'lofty' |
| oncology | the branch of medicine relating to tumours | Gk *onkos* 'mass' |
| philology | the study of the development of languages | Gk *philologos* 'fond of words' |
| sociology | the study of human society | L. *socius* 'companion' |

➤ The **-logy** suffix is also used with the senses relating more generally to types of language or discourse:

| | | |
|---|---|---|
| anthology | a published collection of works | Gk *anthos* 'flower' (i.e. 'the flowers of verse') |
| antilogy | (archaic) a contradiction in ideas | Gk *anti-* 'against' |
| apology | expression of acknowledgement of fault | Gk *apologia* 'speech in one's defence' (from *apo* 'away') |
| etymology | the study of word origins | Gk *etumon*, from *etumos* 'true' |
| eulogy | a song or speech of praise | Gk *eulogia* 'praise' (from *eu* 'well') |
| ideology | a system of (political) ideas on which a theory is based | Gk *idea* 'form' |
| methodology | a system of methods | Gk *methodos* 'pursuit of knowledge' |
| tautology | unnecessary repetition within a statement using different words | Gk *tauto-* 'same' |
| trilogy | three related works | Gk *treis* 'three' |

➤ Some of the oldest **-logy** words:

| | | |
|---|---|---|
| genealogy | 14th century: line of continuous descent from an ancestor | Gk *genea* 'race, generation' |
| mythology | 15th century: a set of myths relating to a particular tradition | Gk *muthos* 'myth' |
| theology | 14th century: the study of religion and the nature of God | Gk *theos* 'God' |

Some important **-logy** words are of relatively recent origin: ***biology***, ***ecology***, and ***sociology***, for example, date from the 19th century.

– ORIGIN OE *lang, long* (adj.), *lange, longe* (adv.), of Gmc origin.

**long**[2] ● v. (**long for/to do**) have a strong wish for or to do.

– ORIGIN OE *langian* 'grow long', also 'yearn', of Gmc origin.

**long.** ● abbrev. longitude.

**-long** ● comb. form (added to nouns) for the duration of: *lifelong*.

**longan** /ˈlɒŋg(ə)n/ ● n. an edible juicy fruit from a SE Asian plant (*Dimocarpus longan*) related to the lychee.

– ORIGIN C18: from Chin. *lóngyǎn*, lit. 'dragon's eye'.

**long-and-short work** ● n. Architecture alternating tall quoins and horizontal slabs forming a corner of a medieval church or other building.

**longboard** ● n. a type of long surfboard.

**longboat** ● n. a large boat which may be launched from a sailing ship. ➤another term for LONGSHIP.

**longbow** ● n. a large bow drawn by hand and shooting a long feathered arrow.

**long-case clock** ● n. another term for GRANDFATHER CLOCK.

**long-dated** ● adj. (of securities) not due for early payment or redemption.

**long-day** ● adj. (of a plant) needing a long daily period of light to initiate flowering.

**long distance** ● adj. **1** travelling or operating between distant places. **2** Athletics denoting or relating to a race distance of 6 miles or 10,000 metres (6 miles 376 yds), or longer. ● adv. between distant places.

**long division** ● n. division of numbers with details of intermediate calculations written down.

**long-drawn** (also **long-drawn-out**) ● adj. prolonged, especially unduly.

**longe** ● n. variant of LUNGE[2].

**longeron** /ˈlɒn(d)ʒərɒn/ ● n. a longitudinal structural

component of an aircraft's fuselage.
– ORIGIN C20: from Fr., lit. 'girder'.

**longevity** /lɒnˈdʒɛvɪti/ • n. long life.
– ORIGIN C17: from late L. *longaevitas*, from L. *longus* 'long' + *aevum* 'age'.

**long face** • n. an unhappy or disappointed expression.
– DERIVATIVES **long-faced** adj.

**longhair** • n. **1** a person with long hair or characteristics associated with it, such as a hippy. **2** a cat of a long-haired breed.

**longhand** • n. ordinary handwriting (as opposed to shorthand, typing, or printing).

**long haul** • n. **1** a long distance (with reference to the transport of goods or passengers). **2** a lengthy and difficult task.
– PHRASES **over the long haul** chiefly N. Amer. over an extended period of time.

**long-headed** • adj. dated having or showing foresight and good judgement.
– DERIVATIVES **long-headedness** n.

**long hop** • n. Cricket a short-pitched, easily hit ball.

**longhorn** • n. an animal of a breed of cattle with long horns.

**longhorn beetle** • n. an elongated beetle with long antennae, the larva of which typically bores in wood. [Family Cerambycidae.]

**longhouse** • n. (among the Iroquois and other North American Indians) a traditional dwelling shared by several nuclear families. ➤a large communal village house in parts of Malaysia and Indonesia.

**longicorn** /ˈlɒn(d)ʒɪkɔːn/ • n. former term for **LONGHORN BEETLE**.
– ORIGIN C19: from mod. L. *longicornis*, from L. *longus* 'long' + *cornu* 'horn'.

**longing** • n. a yearning desire. • adj. having or showing such desire.
– DERIVATIVES **longingly** adv.

**longitude** /ˈlɒn(d)ʒɪtjuːd, ˈlɒŋgɪ-/ • n. the angular distance of a place east or west of a standard meridian, especially the Greenwich meridian.
– ORIGIN ME: from L. *longitudo*, from *longus* 'long'.

**longitudinal** /ˌlɒndʒɪˈtjuːdɪn(ə)l, ˌlɒŋgɪ-/ • adj. **1** running lengthwise. **2** of or relating to longitude. **3** involving information about an individual or group gathered over a prolonged period.
– DERIVATIVES **longitudinally** adv.

**longitudinal wave** • n. Physics a wave vibrating in the direction of propagation.

**long johns** • pl. n. informal underpants with closely fitted legs extending to the wearer's ankles.

**long jump** • n. (**the long jump**) an athletic event in which competitors jump as far as possible along the ground in one leap.
– DERIVATIVES **long jumper** n.

**long leg** • n. Cricket a fielding position far behind the batsman on the leg side.

**long-life** • adj. (of perishable goods) treated so as to stay fresh for longer than usual.

**longline** • n. a deep-sea fishing line with a large number of hooks attached to it.

**longliner** • n. chiefly N. Amer. a fishing vessel which uses longlines.

**long measure** • n. archaic a measure of length; a linear measure.

**long metre** • n. **1** a metrical pattern for hymns in which the stanzas have four lines with eight syllables each. **2** Prosody a quatrain of iambic tetrameters with alternate lines rhyming.

**long off** • n. Cricket a fielding position far behind the bowler and towards the off side.

**long on** • n. Cricket a fielding position far behind the bowler and towards the on side.

**long pig** • n. a translation of a term formerly used in some Pacific Islands for human flesh as food.

**long-playing** • adj. (of a gramophone record) about 30 cm in diameter and designed to rotate at 33⅓ revolutions per minute.
– DERIVATIVES **long-player** n.

**long-range** • adj. **1** able to be used or be effective over long distances. **2** relating to a period of time far into the future.

**long s** • n. an obsolete form of lower-case s, written or printed as ſ.

**longship** • n. a long, narrow warship, with oars and a sail, used by the Vikings and other ancient northern European peoples.

**longshore** • adj. of, relating to, or moving along the seashore.
– ORIGIN C19: from *along shore*.

**longshore drift** • n. the movement of material along a coast by waves which approach at an angle to the shore but recede directly away from it.

**longshoreman** • n. (pl. **-men**) N. Amer. a docker.

**long shot** • n. a venture or guess that has only the slightest chance of succeeding or being accurate.
– PHRASES **(not) by a long shot** informal (not) by far or at all.

**long sight** • n. the abnormal inability to see things clearly if they are relatively close to the eyes.

**long-sighted** • adj. having long sight.
– DERIVATIVES **long-sightedly** adv. **long-sightedness** n.

**longspur** • n. a North American bunting with brownish plumage and a boldly marked head in the male. [Genus *Calcarius*.]

**long-standing** • adj. having existed for a long time.

**longstop** • n. Cricket a fielding position (not normally used in the modern game) directly behind the wicket-keeper.

**long-suffering** • adj. bearing problems or provocation with patience.
– DERIVATIVES **long-sufferingly** adv.

**long suit** • n. **1** (in bridge or whist) a holding of several cards of one suit in a hand, typically 5 or more out of the 13. **2** [usu. with neg.] an outstanding personal quality or achievement.

**long-tailed tit** • n. a small songbird with largely black, pink, and white plumage and a long slender tail. [*Aegithalos caudatus* and other species, family Aegithalidae.]

**longueur** /lɒ̃(ŋ)ˈgəː/ • n. a tedious passage or period.
– ORIGIN Fr., lit. 'length'.

**long vacation** • n. Brit. the summer break of three months taken by universities and (formerly) law courts.

**long waist** • n. a low waist on a dress or a person's body.
– DERIVATIVES **long-waisted** adj.

**longwall** • adj. Mining of or involving a single long face worked (usually mechanically) along its whole length.

**long wave** • n. a radio wave of a wavelength above one kilometre (and a frequency below 300 kHz). ➤broadcasting using radio waves of 1 to 10 km wavelength.

**longways** (also **longwise**) • adv. lengthways.

**long-winded** • adj. **1** tediously lengthy. **2** archaic capable of doing something for a long time without becoming breathless.
– DERIVATIVES **long-windedly** adv. **long-windedness** n.

**lonicera** /lɒˈnɪs(ə)rə/ • n. a plant of a genus which comprises the honeysuckles. [Genus *Lonicera*.]
– ORIGIN mod. L., named after the C16 Ger. botanist Adam *Lonitzer*.

**lonning** • n. another term for **LOAN**[2].

**Lonsdale belt** • n. Boxing an ornate belt awarded to a professional boxer winning a British title fight.
– ORIGIN C20: named after the fifth Earl of *Lonsdale*.

**loo**[1] • n. Brit. informal a toilet.
– ORIGIN 1940s: many theories have been put forward about the word's origin: one suggests the source is *Waterloo*, a trade name for iron cisterns in the early 20th cent.

**loo**[2] • n. a gambling card game in which a player who fails to win a trick must pay a sum to a pool.
– ORIGIN C17: abbrev. of obs. *lanterloo* from Fr. *lanturlu*, a meaningless song refrain.

**loofah** /ˈluːfə/ • n. **1** the fibrous matter of the fluid-transport system of a marrow-like fruit, which is used

dried as a bath sponge. **2** the tropical climbing plant of the gourd family which produces these fruits, which are also edible. [*Luffa cylindrica.*]
– ORIGIN C19: from Egyptian Arab. *lūfa*, denoting the plant.

**look** • v. **1** direct one's gaze in a specified direction. ➤have an outlook in a specified direction. ➤(**look through**) ignore by pretending not to see. ➤(**look something over**) inspect something with a view to establishing its merits. ➤(**look at/on**) regard in a specified way. ➤(**look at**) examine (a matter) and consider what action to take. ➤(**look into**) investigate. ➤(**look for**) attempt to find. **2** have the appearance or give the impression of being. ➤(**look like**) informal show a likelihood of. **3** (**look to**) rely on (someone) to do something. ➤hope or expect to do. ➤archaic make sure. • n. **1** an act of looking. ➤an expression of a feeling or thought by such an act. **2** appearance, especially as expressing a particular quality. ➤(**looks**) a person's facial appearance considered aesthetically. ➤a style or fashion. • exclam. (also **look here!**) used to call attention to what one is going to say.
– PHRASES **look down one's nose at** another way of saying *look down on*. **look someone in the eye** (or **face**) look directly at someone without showing embarrassment, fear, or shame. **look lively** informal be quick; get moving. **look sharp** be quick.
– PHRASAL VERBS **look after** take care of. **look back** [with neg.] suffer a setback or interrupted progress. **look down on** regard with a feeling of superiority. **look in** make a short visit or call. **look on** watch without getting involved. **look out** be vigilant and take notice. **look something out** Brit. search for and produce something. **look up** improve. **look someone up** informal make social contact with someone. **look something up** search for and find a piece of information in a reference book or in a database. **look up to** have a great deal of respect for.
– ORIGIN OE *lōcian* (v.), of W. Gmc origin.

**lookalike** • n. a person or thing that closely resembles another.

**look-and-say** • n. [as modifier] denoting a method of teaching reading based on the visual recognition of words rather than the association of sounds and letters.

**looker** • n. a person with a specified appearance: *she's not a bad looker.* ➤informal a very attractive person.

**look-in** • n. informal a chance of participation or success.

**looking glass** • n. a mirror. ➤[as modifier] opposite to what is normal or expected.

**lookism** • n. prejudice or discrimination on the grounds of appearance.
– DERIVATIVES **lookist** n. & adj.

**lookout** • n. **1** a place from which to keep watch or view landscape. ➤a person stationed to keep watch. **2** informal, chiefly Brit. a good or bad prospect or outcome. **3** (**one's lookout**) Brit. informal one's own concern.
– PHRASES **be on the lookout** (or **keep a lookout**) **for** be alert to. ➤keep searching for.

**look-see** • n. informal a brief look or inspection.
– ORIGIN C19: from, or in imitation of, pidgin Engl.

**lookup** • n. [usu. as modifier] the action of systematic electronic information retrieval. ➤a facility for this.

**loom**[1] • n. an apparatus for making fabric by weaving yarn or thread.
– ORIGIN OE *gelōma* 'tool', shortened to *lome* in ME.

**loom**[2] • v. appear as a vague form, especially one that is threatening. ➤(of an event regarded as threatening) seem about to happen. • n. a vague first appearance of an object seen in darkness or fog, especially at sea.
– ORIGIN C16: prob. from Low Ger. or Du.

**loon**[1] • n. informal a silly or foolish person.
– ORIGIN C19: from LOON[2] (referring to the bird's actions when escaping from danger), perh. influenced by LOONY.

**loon**[2] • n. North American term for DIVER (in sense 2).
– ORIGIN C17: prob. by alt. of Shetland dial. *loom*, denoting especially a guillemot or a diver.

**loon**[3] • v. Brit. informal act in a foolish or desultory way.
– ORIGIN 1960s: of unknown origin.

**loonie** • n. (pl. **-ies**) Canadian informal a Canadian one-dollar coin.
– ORIGIN from LOON[2] (after the image on the coin) + -IE.

**loons** (also **loon pants**) • pl. n. Brit. dated close-fitting casual trousers widely flared from the knees downwards.
– ORIGIN 1970s: from LOON[3].

**loony** informal • n. (pl. **-ies**) a mad or silly person. • adj. (**-ier**, **-iest**) mad or silly.
– DERIVATIVES **looniness** n.
– ORIGIN C19: abbrev. of LUNATIC.

**loony bin** • n. informal, derogatory an institution for people with mental illnesses.

**loop** • n. **1** a shape produced by a curve that bends round and crosses itself. ➤a length of thread or similar material forming such a shape, used as a fastening or handle. ➤(also **loop line**) a length of railway track which is connected at either end to the main line and on to which trains can be diverted. ➤(also **loop-the-loop**) a manoeuvre in which an aircraft describes a vertical circle in the air. ➤Skating a manoeuvre describing a loop, made on a single edge. **2** a structure, series, or process the end of which is connected to the beginning. ➤an endless strip of tape or film allowing continuous repetition. ➤a complete circuit for an electric current. ➤Computing a programmed sequence of instructions that is repeated until or while a particular condition is satisfied. • v. form into a loop or loops; encircle. ➤follow a course that forms a loop or loops. ➤put into or execute a loop of tape, film, or computing instructions. ➤(also **loop the loop**) circle an aircraft vertically in the air.
– PHRASES **in** (or **out of**) **the loop** informal, chiefly N. Amer. aware (or unaware) of information known to only a privileged few. **throw** (or **knock**) **someone for a loop** N. Amer. informal surprise or astonish someone.
– ORIGIN ME: of unknown origin; cf. Sc. Gaelic *lùb* 'loop'.

**loop diuretic** • n. a powerful diuretic which inhibits resorption of water and sodium from the loop of Henle.

**looper** • n. **1** a caterpillar of a geometrid moth, which moves forward by arching itself into loops. **2** a device for making loops.

**loophole** • n. **1** an ambiguity or inadequacy in the law or a set of rules. **2** an arrow slit in a wall.
– DERIVATIVES **loopholed** adj.
– ORIGIN C16: from obs. *loop* 'embrasure' + HOLE.

**loop of Henle** /ˈhɛnli/ • n. the part of a kidney tubule from which water and salts are resorbed into the blood.
– ORIGIN C19: named after the Ger. anatomist F. G. J. *Henle*.

**loop stitch** • n. a method of sewing or knitting in which each stitch incorporates a free loop of thread, for ornament or to give a thick pile.
– DERIVATIVES **loop-stitched** adj. **loop stitching** n.

**loopy** • adj. (**-ier**, **-iest**) **1** informal mad or silly. **2** having many loops.
– DERIVATIVES **loopiness** n.

**loose** /luːs/ • adj. **1** not firmly or tightly fixed in place. ➤not held, tied or packaged together. ➤not bound or tethered. ➤(of the ball in a game) in play but not in any player's possession. **2** not fitting tightly or closely. **3** relaxed; physically slack. ➤not strict or exact. ➤careless and indiscreet: *loose talk.* ➤dated promiscuous; immoral. **4** not dense or compact. ➤(of play, especially in rugby) with the players far apart. • n. (**the loose**) Rugby loose play. • v. **1** set free. ➤untie; unfasten. ➤relax (one's grip). **2** (usu. **loose something off**) discharge; fire.
– PHRASES **hang loose** informal, chiefly N. Amer. be relaxed. **on the loose** having escaped from confinement.
– DERIVATIVES **loosely** adv. **looseness** n.
– ORIGIN ME *loos* 'free from bonds', from ON *lauss*, of Gmc origin.

**loose box** • n. Brit. a stable or stall in which a horse is kept without a tether.

**loose cannon** • n. an unpredictable person who is liable to cause unintentional damage.

**loose cover** • n. Brit. a removable fitted cloth cover for a chair or sofa.

**loose end** • n. a detail that is not yet settled or explained.
– PHRASES **be at a loose end** (or N. Amer. **at loose ends**) have nothing specific to do.

**loose-footed** • adj. (of a boat's sail) having no boom or not secured to a boom at the foot.

**loose forward** • n. Rugby a forward who plays at the back of the scrum.

**loose head** • n. Rugby the forward in the front row of a scrummage who is nearest to the scrum half as the ball is put in.

**loose-leaf** • adj. (of a notebook or folder) having each sheet of paper separate and removable.

**loosen** • v. make or become loose. ➤make more lax. ➤(**loosen up**) warm up in preparation for an activity.
– PHRASES **loosen someone's tongue** make someone talk freely.
– DERIVATIVES **loosener** n.

**loose scrum** • n. Rugby a scrum formed by the players round the ball during play, not ordered by the referee.

**loosestrife** /ˈluːsˌstrʌɪf/ • n. a waterside plant with a tall upright spike of flowers. [*Lythrum salicaria* (**purple loosestrife**), *Lysimachia vulgaris* (**yellow loosestrife**), and related plants.]
– ORIGIN C16: from LOOSE + STRIFE, taking the Gk name *lusimakheion* (actually from *Lusimakhos*, the name of its discoverer) to be directly from *luein* 'undo' + *makhē* 'battle'.

**loot** • n. **1** private property taken from an enemy in war or stolen by thieves. **2** informal money. • v. steal goods from, especially during a war or riot. ➤steal (goods).
– DERIVATIVES **looter** n.
– ORIGIN C19 (as v.): from Hindi *lūṭ*, from Sanskrit *luṇṭh-* 'rob'.

**lop**[1] • v. (**lopped**, **lopping**) cut off (a branch or limb) from a tree or body. ➤informal remove (something regarded as unnecessary or burdensome): *the new rail link lops an hour off journey times.* • n. (also **lop and top**) branches and twigs lopped off trees.
– DERIVATIVES **lopper** n.
– ORIGIN ME (as n.): of unknown origin.

**lop**[2] • v. (**lopped**, **lopping**) N. Amer. or archaic **1** hang loosely or limply. **2** lope.
– ORIGIN C16: prob. symbolic of limpness; cf. LOB.

**lope** • v. run with a long bounding stride. • n. a long bounding stride.
– ORIGIN ME: var. of Scots *loup*, from ON *hlaupa* 'leap'.

**lop-eared** • adj. (of an animal) having drooping ears.
– DERIVATIVES **lop ears** pl. n.

**loperamide** /ləʊˈpɛrəmʌɪd/ • n. Medicine a synthetic drug of the opiate class used to treat diarrhoea.
– ORIGIN 1970s: prob. from (*ch*)*lo*(*ro-*) + (*pi*)*per*(*idine*) + AMIDE.

**lopho-** • comb. form Zoology crested: *lophophore.*
– ORIGIN from Gk *lophos* 'crest'.

**lophophore** /ˈləʊfəˌfɔː, ˈlɒf-/ • n. Zoology a horseshoe-shaped structure around the mouth in bryozoans, brachiopods, and some other aquatic invertebrates, bearing ciliated tentacles.
– DERIVATIVES **lophophorate** adj. & n.

**lopolith** /ˈlɒpə(ʊ)lɪθ/ • n. Geology a large saucer-shaped intrusion of igneous rock.
– ORIGIN C20: from Gk *lopas* 'basin' + -LITH.

**lopsided** • adj. with one side lower or smaller than the other.
– DERIVATIVES **lopsidedly** adv. **lopsidedness** n.
– ORIGIN C18: from LOP[2] + SIDE + -ED[1].

**loquacious** /lɒˈkweɪʃəs/ • adj. talkative.
– DERIVATIVES **loquaciously** adv. **loquaciousness** n. **loquacity** n.
– ORIGIN C17 (earlier (ME) as *loquacity*): from L. *loquax*, *loquac-* (from *loqui* 'talk') + -IOUS.

**loquat** /ˈləʊkwɒt/ • n. a small yellow egg-shaped acidic fruit from an East Asian tree (*Eriobotrya japonica*).
– ORIGIN C19: from Chin. dial. *luh kwat* 'rush orange'.

**loquitur** /ˈlɒkwɪtə/ (abbrev.: **loq.**) • v. (he or she) speaks (as a stage direction).
– ORIGIN L., from *loqui* 'talk, speak'.

**lor** • exclam. Brit. informal used to indicate surprise or dismay.
– ORIGIN C19: abbrev. of LORD.

**Loran** /ˈlɔːran, ˈlɒ-/ • n. a system of long-distance navigation in which position is determined from the intervals between signal pulses received from widely spaced radio transmitters.
– ORIGIN 1940s: from *lo*(*ng-*)*ra*(*nge*) *n*(*avigation*).

**lord** • n. a man of noble rank or high office. ➤(**Lord**) a title given formally to a baron, and less formally to a marquess, earl, or viscount (prefixed to a family or territorial name). ➤(**the Lords**) the House of Lords, or its members collectively. ➤(**Lord**) a courtesy title given to a younger son of a duke or marquess (prefixed to a Christian name). ➤a feudal superior, especially the owner of a manor house. ➤(**Lord**) a name for God or Christ. • exclam. (**Lord**) used in exclamations expressing surprise or worry, or for emphasis. • v. (**lord it over**) act in a superior and domineering manner towards.
– PHRASES **Lord** (**God**) **of hosts** God as Lord over earthly or heavenly armies. **the Lord's Day** Sunday. **the Lord's Prayer** the prayer taught by Christ to his disciples, beginning 'Our Father.' **the Lord's Supper** the Eucharist (especially in Protestant use). **My Lord** a polite form of address to judges, bishops, and certain noblemen.
– DERIVATIVES **lordless** adj. **lord-like** adj.
– ORIGIN OE *hlāford*, from *hlāfweard* 'bread-keeper', from a Gmc base (see LOAF[1], WARD); cf. LADY.

**Lord Advocate** • n. the principal Law Officer of the Crown in Scotland.

**Lord Bishop** • n. the formal title of a bishop, in particular that of a diocesan bishop.

**Lord Chamberlain** (also **Lord Chamberlain of the Household**) • n. (in the UK) the official in charge of the royal household, formerly the licenser of plays.

**Lord Chancellor** • n. (in the UK) the highest officer of the Crown, presiding in the House of Lords, the Chancery Division, or the Court of Appeal.

**Lord Chief Justice** • n. (in the UK) the officer presiding over the Queen's Bench Division and the Court of Appeal.

**Lord Commissioner** • n. **1** the representative of the Crown at the General Assembly of the Church of Scotland. **2** (**Lords Commissioners**) (in the UK) the members of a board performing the duties of a high state office put in commission.

**Lord Great Chamberlain of England** • n. the hereditary holder of a ceremonial office who attends the monarch at a coronation.

**Lord High Chancellor** • n. another term for LORD CHANCELLOR.

**Lord High Commissioner** • n. another term for LORD COMMISSIONER.

**Lord High Treasurer** • n. see TREASURER.

**Lord Justice** (also **Lord Justice of Appeal**) • n. (pl. **Lords Justices**) (in the UK) a judge in the Court of Appeal.

**Lord Lieutenant** • n. (in the UK) the chief executive authority and head of magistrates in each county. ➤historical the viceroy of Ireland.

**lordling** • n. archaic, chiefly derogatory a minor lord.

**lordly** • adj. (**-ier**, **-iest**) of, characteristic of, or suitable for a lord.
– DERIVATIVES **lordliness** n.

**Lord Mayor** • n. the title of the mayor in London and some other large cities.

**Lord of Appeal** (in full **Lord of Appeal in Ordinary**) • n. formal term for LAW LORD.

**Lord Ordinary** • n. (in Scotland) any of the judges of the Outer House of the Court of Session.

**lordosis** /lɔːˈdəʊsɪs/ • n. Medicine excessive backward curvature of the spine, causing concavity of the back. Compare with KYPHOSIS.
– DERIVATIVES **lordotic** adj.
– ORIGIN C18: mod. L., from Gk *lordōsis*, from *lordos* 'bent backwards'.

**Lord President of the Council** • n. (in the UK) the cabinet minister presiding at the Privy Council.

**Lord Privy Seal** • n. (in the UK) a senior cabinet minister without specified official duties.

**Lord Protector of the Commonwealth** • n. see PROTECTOR (sense 2).

**Lord Provost** • n. the head of a municipal corporation or borough in certain Scottish cities.

**lords and ladies** • n. another term for CUCKOO PINT.

**lordship** • n. **1** supreme power or rule. **2** archaic the authority or state of being a lord. ➤ historical a piece of land belonging to a lord. **3** (**His/Your** etc. **Lordship**) a form of address to a judge, bishop, or titled man.

**Lords of Session** • pl. n. (in Scotland) the judges of the Court of Session.

**Lords spiritual** • pl. n. the bishops in the House of Lords.

**Lords temporal** • pl. n. the members of the House of Lords other than the bishops.

**Lord Treasurer** • n. see TREASURER.

**Lordy** • exclam. informal used to express surprise or dismay.

**lore**[1] • n. a body of traditions and knowledge on a subject: *farming lore*.
– ORIGIN OE *lār* 'instruction', of Gmc origin: rel. to LEARN.

**lore**[2] • n. Zoology the surface on each side of a bird's head between the eye and the upper base of the beak, or between the eye and nostril in snakes.
– ORIGIN C19: from L. *lorum* 'strap'.

**Lorentz force** • n. Physics the force exerted by a magnetic field on a moving electric charge.
– ORIGIN 1930s: named after the Du. theoretical physicist Hendrik Antoon *Lorentz*.

**lorgnette** /lɔːˈnjɛt/ (also **lorgnettes**) • n. a pair of glasses or opera glasses held by a long handle at one side.
– ORIGIN C19: from Fr., from *lorgner* 'to squint'.

**lorica** /ləˈrʌɪkə/ • n. (pl. **loricae** /-kiː/ or **loricas**) Zoology the rigid case or shell of some rotifers and protozoans.
– DERIVATIVES **loricate** adj.
– ORIGIN L., lit. 'breastplate'.

**lorikeet** /ˈlɒrɪkiːt/ • n. a small bird of the lory family, found chiefly in New Guinea. [*Charmosyna* and other genera: several species.]
– ORIGIN C18: dimin. of LORY, on the pattern of *parakeet*.

**loris** /ˈlɔːrɪs/ • n. (pl. **lorises**) a small, slow-moving nocturnal primate living in dense vegetation in South Asia. [*Loris tardigradus* (**slender loris**) and genus *Nycticebus* (**slow loris**).]
– ORIGIN C18: from Fr., perh. from obs. Du. *loeris* 'clown'.

**lorn** • adj. poetic/literary forlorn.
– ORIGIN ME: past part. of obs. *lese* from OE *lēosan* 'lose'.

**lorry** /ˈlɒri/ • n. (pl. **-ies**) Brit. a large, heavy motor vehicle for transporting goods or troops.
– PHRASES **fall off of the back a lorry** informal (of goods) be acquired in dubious circumstances.
– ORIGIN C19: perh. from the given name *Laurie*.

**lory** /ˈlɔːri/ • n. (pl. **-ies**) a small Australasian or SE Asian parrot with a brush-tipped tongue. [Family Loridae: many species.]
– ORIGIN C17: from Malay *lūrī*.

**Los Angeleno** • n. variant of ANGELENO.

**lose** /luːz/ • v. (past and past part. **lost**) **1** be deprived of or cease to have or retain. ➤ be deprived of (a relative or friend) through their death. ➤ (of a pregnant woman) miscarry (a baby). ➤ (**be lost**) be destroyed or killed. ➤ decrease in (body weight). ➤ (of a clock) become slow by (a specified amount of time). ➤ (**lose it**) informal lose control of one's temper or emotions. **2** become unable to find. ➤ evade or shake off (a pursuer). ➤ N. Amer. informal get rid of. ➤ (**lose oneself in/be lost in**) be or become deeply absorbed in. **3** fail to win. **4** earn less (money) than one is spending. **5** waste or fail to take advantage of: *he may have lost his chance*. **6** (**lose out**) be disadvantaged.
– PHRASES **lose face** lose one's credibility. **lose heart** become discouraged. **lose one's mind** (or **marbles**) informal go insane. **lose one's** (or **the**) **way** become lost.
– ORIGIN OE *losian* 'perish, destroy', also 'become unable to find', from *los* 'loss'.

**loser** • n. a person or thing that loses or has lost. ➤ informal a person who fails frequently.
– PHRASES **be on** (or **on to**) **a loser** informal be involved in something that is bound to fail.

**losing battle** • n. a struggle in which failure seems certain.

**loss** • n. the fact or process of losing something or someone. ➤ a defeat in sport. ➤ the feeling of grief after losing a valued person or thing. ➤ a person or thing that is badly missed when lost.
– PHRASES **at a loss 1** uncertain or puzzled. **2** making less money than is spent in operation or production.
– ORIGIN OE *los* 'destruction', of Gmc origin; rel. to LOOSE; later prob. a back-form. from *lost*, past part. of LOSE.

**loss adjuster** • n. an insurance agent who assesses the amount of compensation that should be paid to a claimant.

**loss-leader** • n. a product sold at a loss to attract customers.

**lossless** • adj. **1** without dissipation of electrical or electromagnetic energy. **2** Computing (of data compression) without loss of information.

**lossy** • adj. **1** having or involving dissipation of electrical or electromagnetic energy. **2** Computing (of data compression) in which unnecessary information is discarded.

**lost** past and past participle of LOSE.
– PHRASES **be lost for words** be so surprised or upset that one cannot think what to say. **be lost on** fail to be noticed or appreciated by. **get lost!** informal go away!

**lost cause** • n. a person or thing that can no longer hope to succeed or be changed for the better.

**lost generation** • n. **1** a generation with many of its men killed in war, especially the First World War. **2** an unfulfilled generation maturing during a period of instability.

**lost labour** • n. archaic fruitless effort.

**lot** • pron. (**a lot** or **lots**) informal a large number or amount; a great deal. ➤ (**the lot** or **the whole lot**) chiefly Brit. the whole number or quantity. • adv. (**a lot** or **lots**) informal a great deal. • n. **1** [treated as sing. or pl.] informal a particular group or set of people or things. **2** an item or set of items for sale at an auction. **3** a method of deciding something by random selection, especially of one from a number of pieces of paper. ➤ the choice resulting from such a process. **4** a person's destiny, luck, or condition in life. **5** chiefly N. Amer. a plot of land. ➤ (also **parking lot**) a car park. • v. (**lotted**, **lotting**) divide into lots for sale at an auction.
– PHRASES **draw** (or **cast**) **lots** decide by lot. **fall to someone's lot** become someone's task or responsibility. **throw in one's lot with** decide to share the fate of.
– ORIGIN OE *hlot* (n.) (orig. in sense 3 and 4), of Gmc origin.

**loth** • adj. variant spelling of LOATH.

**Lothario** /ləˈθɛːrɪəʊ, -ˈθɑː-/ • n. (pl. **-os**) a womanizer.
– ORIGIN from a character in Nicholas Rowe's tragedy *The Fair Penitent* (1703).

**loti** /ˈləʊti, ˈluːti/ • n. (pl. **maloti** /məˈləʊti, -ˈluːti/) the basic monetary unit of Lesotho, equal to 100 lisente.
– ORIGIN from Sesotho.

**lotic** /ˈləʊtɪk/ • adj. Ecology inhabiting or situated in rapidly moving fresh water. Compare with LENTIC.
– ORIGIN C20: from L. *lotus* 'washing' + **-IC**.

**lotion** • n. a thick liquid preparation applied to the skin as a medicine or cosmetic.
– ORIGIN ME: from OFr., or from L. *lotio(n-)*, from *lot-*, *lavare* 'wash'.

**lottery** • n. (pl. **-ies**) a means of raising money by selling numbered tickets and giving prizes to the holders of numbers drawn at random. ➤ something whose success is governed by chance.
– ORIGIN C16: prob. from Du. *loterij*, from *lot* 'lot'.

**lotto** • n. **1** a children's game similar to bingo, using illustrated counters or cards. **2** chiefly N. Amer. a lottery.
– ORIGIN C18: from Ital.

**lotus** • n. **1** a large water lily, now or formerly regarded as sacred. [*Nymphaea lotus* and *N. caerulea* (Egypt) and *Nelumbo nucifera* (**sacred lotus**, Asia).] **2** (in Greek

mythology) a legendary plant whose fruit induces a dreamy forgetfulness and an unwillingness to leave.
– ORIGIN C15: via L. from Gk *lōtos*, of Semitic origin.

**lotus-eater** • n. a person given to indulgence in pleasure and luxury.
– DERIVATIVES **lotus-eating** adj.

**lotus position** • n. a cross-legged position for meditation, with the feet resting on the thighs.

**louche** /luːʃ/ • adj. disreputable; dubious.
– ORIGIN C19: from Fr., lit. 'squinting'.

**loud** • adj. **1** producing or capable of producing much noise. **2** strong in expression: *loud protests.* ➤ obtrusive; gaudy. • adv. with a great deal of volume.
– PHRASES **out loud** audibly.
– DERIVATIVES **louden** v. **loudly** adv. **loudness** n.
– ORIGIN OE *hlūd*, of W. Gmc origin; from an Indo-Eur. root meaning 'hear'.

**loudhailer** • n. chiefly Brit. a megaphone.

**loudmouth** • n. informal a person who talks too much, especially tactlessly.
– DERIVATIVES **loud-mouthed** adj.

**loudspeaker** • n. an apparatus converting electrical impulses into sound, typically as part of a public address system.

**Lou Gehrig's disease** • n. another term for **AMYOTROPHIC LATERAL SCLEROSIS**.
– ORIGIN 1940s: named after the Amer. baseball star Henry *Louis Gehrig*, who died from the disease.

**lough** /lɒk, lɒx/ • n. Anglo-Irish spelling of **LOCH**.
– ORIGIN ME: from Ir. *loch*.

**louis** /ˈluːi/ (also **louis d'or** /-ˈdɔː/) • n. (pl. same /ˈluːɪz/) **1** a French gold coin issued between 1640 and 1793. **2** another term for **NAPOLEON** (in sense 1).
– ORIGIN from *Louis*, the name of many kings of France.

**Louisianan** /luːˌiːzɪˈan(ə)n/ (also **Louisianian** /luːˌiːzɪˈanɪ(ə)n/) • n. a native or inhabitant of the US state of Louisiana. • adj. of or relating to Louisiana.

**lounge** • v. recline or stand in a relaxed or lazy way. • n. **1** Brit. a sitting room. ➤ a public sitting room in a hotel or theatre. ➤ a seating area in an airport for waiting passengers. **2** Brit. a spell of lounging.
– ORIGIN C16 (in the sense 'move indolently'): perh. symbolic of slow movement.

**lounge bar** • n. Brit. a more comfortable bar in a pub or hotel.

**lounge lizard** • n. informal an idle, pleasure-seeking man who spends his time in fashionable society.

**lounger** • n. **1** a comfortable chair, especially an outdoor chair that reclines. **2** a person spending their time lazily or in a relaxed way.

**lounge suit** • n. Brit. a man's suit for ordinary day wear.

**loupe** /luːp/ • n. a small magnifying glass used by jewellers and watchmakers.
– ORIGIN C19: from Fr.

**louping-ill** /ˈlaʊpɪŋɪl/ • n. a tick-borne viral disease of animals, especially sheep, causing staggering and jumping.
– ORIGIN ME: from *loup* (dial. var. of **LEAP**) + the noun **ILL**.

**lour** /ˈlaʊə/ (also **lower**) • v. **1** scowl. **2** (of the sky) look dark and threatening. • n. **1** a scowl. **2** a louring appearance of the sky.
– DERIVATIVES **louring** adj. **louringly** adv. **loury** adj.
– ORIGIN ME: of unknown origin.

**louse** • n. **1** (pl. **lice**) a small wingless parasitic insect which infests human skin and hair. [*Pediculus humanus* (see **BODY LOUSE, HEAD LOUSE**).] ➤ a related insect which lives on the skin of mammals or birds. [Orders Anoplura (**sucking lice**) and Mallophaga (**biting lice**).] ➤ used in names of small invertebrates that parasitize aquatic animals or infest plants, e.g. **fish louse**. **2** (pl. **louses**) informal a contemptible person. • v. **1** (**louse something up**) informal spoil something. **2** archaic remove lice from.
– ORIGIN OE *lūs*, (pl.) *lȳs*, of Gmc origin.

**louse fly** • n. a flattened bloodsucking fly which typically spends much of its life on an individual host. [Family Hippoboscidae: many species.]

**louser** • n. informal, chiefly Irish a contemptible person.

**lousewort** • n. a partially parasitic herbaceous plant, typically favouring damp habitats and formerly reputed to harbour lice. [Genus *Pedicularis*: several species.]

**lousy** • adj. (**-ier, -iest**) **1** informal very poor or bad. **2** infested with lice. ➤ (**lousy with**) informal teeming with (something undesirable).
– DERIVATIVES **lousily** adv. **lousiness** n.

**lout** • n. an uncouth or aggressive man.
– DERIVATIVES **loutish** adj. **loutishly** adv. **loutishness** n.
– ORIGIN C16: perh. from archaic *lout* 'to bow down', of Gmc origin.

**louvar** /ˈluːvɑː/ • n. a large brightly coloured fish with a high forehead, living in warm open seas and feeding on jellyfish. [*Luvarus imperialis*.]

**louvre** /ˈluːvə/ (US also **louver**) • n. **1** each of a set of angled slats fixed at regular intervals in a door, shutter, or cover to allow air or light through. **2** a domed structure on a roof, with side openings for ventilation.
– DERIVATIVES **louvred** adj.
– ORIGIN ME: from OFr. *lover, lovier* 'skylight', prob. of Gmc origin and rel. to **LODGE**.

**lovable** (also **loveable**) • adj. inspiring love or affection.
– DERIVATIVES **lovability** n. **lovableness** n. **lovably** adv.

**lovage** /ˈlʌvɪdʒ/ • n. a large edible white-flowered plant of the parsley family. [*Levisticum officinale* (Mediterranean) and other species.]
– ORIGIN ME *loveache*, alt. (as if from **LOVE** + obs. *ache* 'parsley') of OFr. *luvesche, levesche*, via late L. *levisticum* from L. *ligusticum*, neut. of *ligusticus* 'Ligurian'.

**lovat** /ˈlʌvət/ (also **lovat green**) • n. a muted green used especially in tweed and woollen garments.
– ORIGIN C20: from *Lovat*, a place in Highland Scotland.

**love** • n. **1** an intense feeling of deep affection. ➤ a deep romantic or sexual attachment to someone. ➤ a great interest and pleasure in something. ➤ affectionate greetings. **2** (**Love**) love personified, often as the Roman god Cupid. **3** a person or thing that one loves. ➤ Brit. informal a friendly form of address. **4** (in tennis, squash, etc.) a score of zero. [appar. from the phr. *play for love* (i.e. the love of the game, not for money).] • v. feel a deep romantic or sexual attachment to. ➤ like very much. ➤ [as adj. **loving**] showing love or great care.
– PHRASES **for love** for pleasure not profit. **for the love of God** used with an urgent request or to express annoyance. **make love 1** have sexual intercourse. **2** (**make love to**) dated pay amorous attention to. **not for love or money** informal not in any circumstances. **there's no love lost between** there is mutual dislike between.
– DERIVATIVES **loveless** adj. **lovelessly** adv. **lovelessness** n. **loveworthy** adj. **lovingly** adv. **lovingness** n.
– ORIGIN OE *lufu*, of Gmc origin; rel. to **LEAVE**[2] and **LIEF**.

**loveable** • adj. variant spelling of **LOVABLE**.

**love affair** • n. **1** a romantic or sexual relationship, especially outside marriage. **2** an intense enthusiasm for something.

**love apple** • n. archaic a tomato.

**lovebird** • n. **1** a very small mainly green African or Madagascan parrot, noted for the affectionate behaviour of mated birds. [Genus *Agapornis*: several species.] **2** (**lovebirds**) informal an affectionate couple.

**love bite** • n. a temporary red mark on the skin caused by biting or sucking during sexual play.

**love child** • n. a child born to parents who are not married to each other.

**love feast** • n. a feast in token of fellowship among early Christians.

**love game** • n. (in tennis, squash, etc.) a game in which the loser does not score.

**love handles** • pl. n. informal deposits of excess fat at the waistline.

**love-in** • n. informal (especially among hippies in the 1960s) a gathering at which people are encouraged to express friendship and physical attraction.

**love-in-a-mist** • n. a plant of the buttercup family whose blue flowers are surrounded by thread-like green bracts, giving them a hazy appearance. [*Nigella damascena*.]

**love interest** ● n. an actor whose main role in a story or film is that of a lover of the central character.

**love-lies-bleeding** ● n. a South American plant with long drooping tassels of crimson flowers. [*Amaranthus caudatus*.]

**love life** ● n. the part of one's life concerning relationships with lovers.

**lovelock** ● n. archaic a curl of hair at the temple or forehead.

**lovelorn** ● adj. unhappy because of unrequited love.

**lovely** ● adj. (**-ier**, **-iest**) exquisitely beautiful. ➤informal very pleasant. ● n. (pl. **-ies**) informal a beautiful woman or girl.
– DERIVATIVES **lovelily** adv. **loveliness** n.
– ORIGIN OE *luflic* (see LOVE, -LY[1]).

**love match** ● n. a marriage based on love.

**love nest** ● n. informal a secluded place where two lovers spend time together.

**lover** ● n. **1** a person having a sexual or romantic relationship with another. **2** a person who enjoys a specified thing: *a music lover.*
– DERIVATIVES **loverless** adj.

**love seat** ● n. a sofa designed in an S-shape so that two people can face each other.

**lovesick** ● adj. pining or feeling weak due to being in love.
– DERIVATIVES **lovesickness** n.

**lovesome** ● adj. poetic/literary lovely or lovable.

**lovey** ● n. (pl. **-eys**) Brit. informal used as an affectionate form of address.

**lovey-dovey** ● adj. informal very affectionate or romantic.

**loving cup** ● n. a two-handled cup passed round at banquets.

**loving kindness** ● n. tenderness and consideration.

**low[1]** ● adj. **1** of less than average height. ➤situated not far above the ground, horizon, etc. ➤(of latitude) near the equator. ➤(of women's clothing) cut so as to reveal the upper part of the breasts. **2** (of a sound) deep. **3** below average in amount, extent, or intensity: *a low income.* ➤(of a sound) not loud. **4** lacking importance, prestige, or quality; inferior: *training was given low priority.* ➤unscrupulous or dishonest. ➤unfavourable: *a low opinion.* **5** depressed or lacking energy. **6** Phonetics (of a vowel) open. ● n. **1** a low point, level or figure. **2** an area of low barometric pressure. ● adv. **1** in or into a low position or state. **2** quietly. ➤at or to a low pitch.
– DERIVATIVES **lowish** adj. **lowness** n.
– ORIGIN ME: from ON *lágr*, of Gmc origin; rel. to LIE[1].

**low[2]** ● v. (of a cow) moo. ● n. a moo.
– ORIGIN OE *hlōwan*, of Gmc origin.

**lowball** ● n. Baseball a ball pitched so as to pass over the plate below knee-level. ➤[as modifier] N. Amer. informal (of an estimate) unrealistically low.
– DERIVATIVES **lowballing** n.

**lowboy** ● n. N. Amer. a low chest or table with drawers.

**lowbrow** ● adj. informal, chiefly derogatory not highly intellectual or cultured.

**Low Church** ● n. a tradition within the Anglican Church giving relatively little emphasis to ritual and sacraments.
– DERIVATIVES **Low Churchman** n. (pl. **-men**).

**low comedy** ● n. comedy bordering on farce.

**low-density lipoprotein** ● n. the form of lipoprotein by which cholesterol is transported in the blood.

**low-down** informal ● adj. mean and unfair. ● n. (**the low-down**) the relevant information.

**lower[1]** ● adj. comparative of LOW[1]. **1** less high. ➤denoting the first of two numbered forms through which pupils pass in successive years. ➤(often **Lower**) Geology & Archaeology denoting an older (and hence typically deeper) part of a stratigraphic or archaeological division: *the Lower Cretaceous.* **2** [in place names] situated to the south. ● adv. in or into a lower position.
– DERIVATIVES **lowermost** adj.

**lower[2]** ● v. **1** cause to move downward. ➤reduce the height, pitch, or elevation of. **2** make or become less in amount, extent, or value. ➤(**lower oneself**) demean oneself.

**lower[3]** ● v. & n. variant spelling of LOUR.

**lower animals** ● pl. n. invertebrate animals, regarded as having relatively primitive characteristics.

**lower case** ● n. small letters.

**lower chamber** ● n. another term for LOWER HOUSE.

**lower class** ● n. [treated as sing. or pl.] the working class. ● adj. of or relating to the lower class.

**lower court** ● n. Law a court whose decisions may be overruled by another.

**lower criticism** ● n. dated another term for TEXTUAL CRITICISM.

**lower deck** ● n. **1** the deck of a ship immediately above the hold. **2** the petty officers and crew of a ship.

**lower house** ● n. the larger, typically elected, body of a bicameral parliament. ➤(**the Lower House**) (in the UK) the House of Commons.

**lower plants** ● pl. n. plants without vascular systems, e.g. algae, mosses, and liverworts, regarded as having relatively primitive characteristics.

**lower regions** ● pl. n. archaic hell.

**lowest common denominator** ● n. **1** Mathematics the lowest common multiple of the denominators of several vulgar fractions. **2** the least desirable common feature of members of a group.

**lowest common multiple** ● n. Mathematics the lowest quantity that is a multiple of two or more given quantities.

**low-fi** ● adj. variant spelling of LO-FI.

**low frequency** ● n. (in radio) 30–300 kilohertz.

**low gear** ● n. a gear that causes a wheeled vehicle to move slowly.

**Low German** ● n. a German dialect spoken in much of northern Germany.

**low-impact** ● adj. **1** denoting exercises, especially aerobics, putting little stress on the body. **2** affecting or altering the environment as little as possible.

**low-key** ● adj. modest or restrained.

**lowland** /ˈləʊlənd/ ● n. (also **lowlands**) low-lying country. ➤(**the Lowlands**) the part of Scotland lying south and east of the Highlands.
– DERIVATIVES **lowlander** n.

**Low Latin** ● n. medieval and later forms of Latin.

**low-level** ● adj. **1** of relatively little importance. **2** Computing denoting a programming language that is close to machine code in form.

**low life** ● n. disreputable or criminal people or activities. ➤(**lowlife**) informal a person of this type.
– DERIVATIVES **low-lifer** n.

**lowlight** ● n. **1** (**lowlights**) darker dyed streaks in the hair. **2** informal a disappointing or dull event or feature.
– ORIGIN C20: from LOW[1], suggested by HIGHLIGHT.

**low-loader** ● n. Brit. a truck with a low floor and no sides, for heavy loads.

**lowly** ● adj. (**-ier**, **-iest**) **1** low in status or importance. **2** (of an organism) primitive or simple. ● adv. to a low degree: *lowly paid workers.*
– DERIVATIVES **lowlily** adv. **lowliness** n.

**low-lying** ● adj. at low altitude above sea level.

**Low Mass** ● n. (in the Catholic Church) Mass with no music and a minimum of ceremony.

**low-minded** ● adj. vulgar or sordid.
– DERIVATIVES **low-mindedness** n.

**low relief** ● n. see RELIEF (sense 6).

**low-rider** ● n. US a customized vehicle with a chassis that can be lowered nearly to the road.

**low-rise** ● adj. (of a building) having few storeys.

**low season** ● n. Brit. the least popular time of year for a holiday, when prices are lowest.

**low spirits** ● pl. n. sadness and despondency.
– DERIVATIVES **low-spirited** adj. **low-spiritedness** n.

**Low Sunday** ● n. the Sunday after Easter.
– ORIGIN perh. in contrast to the high days of Holy Week

and Easter.

**low-tech** • **adj.** involved in or employing low technology.

**low technology** • **n.** less advanced technological development or equipment.

**low tide** • **n.** the state of the tide when at its lowest level.

**low water** • **n.** low tide.

**low-water mark** • **n. 1** the level reached by the sea at low tide. **2** a minimum recorded level or value.

**Low Week** • **n.** the week beginning with Low Sunday.

**lox**[1] /lɒks/ • **n.** liquid oxygen.
– ORIGIN C20: acronym from *liquid oxygen explosive*, later interpreted as being from *liquid oxygen*.

**lox**[2] /lɒks/ • **n.** N. Amer. smoked salmon.
– ORIGIN 1940s: from Yiddish *laks*.

**loxodrome** /ˈlɒksədrəʊm/ • **n.** another term for **RHUMB** (in sense 1).
– DERIVATIVES **loxodromic** adj.
– ORIGIN C17 (as *loxodromic*): from Fr. *loxodromique*, from Gk *loxos* oblique + *dromos* course.

**loyal** • **adj.** showing firm and constant support or allegiance to a person or institution.
– DERIVATIVES **loyally** adv.
– ORIGIN C16: from Fr., via OFr. *loial* from L. *legalis* (see **LEGAL**).

**loyalist** • **n.** a person who remains loyal to the established ruler or government, especially in the face of a revolt. ➤(**Loyalist**) a supporter of union between Great Britain and Northern Ireland.
– DERIVATIVES **loyalism** n.

**loyal toast** • **n.** a toast to one's sovereign.

**loyalty** • **n.** (pl. **-ies**) the state of being loyal. ➤ a strong feeling of support or allegiance.

**loyalty card** • **n.** Brit. a card issued by a retailer to its customers, on which credits are accumulated for future discounts every time a transaction is recorded.

**lozenge** /ˈlɒzɪn(d)ʒ/ • **n. 1** a rhombus or diamond shape. ➤Heraldry a charge in the shape of a solid diamond. **2** a small medicinal tablet, originally of this shape, for dissolving in the mouth.
– ORIGIN ME: from OFr. *losenge*, prob. derived from the base of Sp. *losa*, Port. *lousa* 'slab', late L. *lausiae* (*lapides*) 'stone slabs'.

**LP** • **abbrev. 1** long-playing (gramophone record). **2** low pressure.

**l.p.** • **abbrev.** low pressure.

**LPG** • **abbrev.** liquefied petroleum gas.

**L-plate** • **n.** Brit. a sign bearing the letter L, attached to a vehicle to indicate that the driver is a learner.

**LPO** • **abbrev.** London Philharmonic Orchestra.

**Lr** • **symb.** the chemical element lawrencium.

**LS** • **abbrev.** Lesotho (international vehicle registration).

**LSB** • **abbrev.** Computing least significant bit.

**LSD** • **n.** a synthetic crystalline compound, lysergic acid diethylamide, which is a powerful hallucinogenic drug.
– ORIGIN 1950s: abbrev.

**LSE** • **abbrev.** London School of Economics.

**LSO** • **abbrev.** London Symphony Orchestra.

**Lt** • **abbrev. 1** Lieutenant. **2** (also **lt**) Military light.

**LTA** • **abbrev.** Lawn Tennis Association.

**Ltd** • **abbrev.** Brit. (after a company name) Limited.

**LTP** • **abbrev.** Physiology long-term potentiation.

**Lu** • **symb.** the chemical element lutetium.

**luau** /ˈluːaʊ/ • **n.** (pl. same or **luaus**) a Hawaiian party or feast.
– ORIGIN from Hawaiian *lu'au*.

**lubber** • **n.** archaic or dialect a big, clumsy person.
– DERIVATIVES **lubberlike** adj. **lubberly** adj. & adv.
– ORIGIN ME: perh. via OFr. *lobeor* 'swindler, parasite' from *lober* 'deceive'.

**lubber line** • **n.** a line on a compass, showing the direction straight ahead.

**lube** /luːb/ informal, chiefly N. Amer. & Austral./NZ • **n.** a lubricant. • **v.** lubricate.

**lubricant** • **n.** a substance, e.g. oil or grease, for lubricating an engine or component. • **adj.** lubricating.

**lubricate** /ˈluːbrɪkeɪt/ • **v. 1** apply oil or grease to (an engine or component) to minimize friction. **2** informal make convivial with alcohol.
– DERIVATIVES **lubrication** n. **lubricator** n.
– ORIGIN C17: from L. *lubricat-*, *lubricare* 'make slippery', from *lubricus* 'slippery'.

**lubricious** /luːˈbrɪʃəs/ (also **lubricous** /ˈluːbrɪkəs/) • **adj. 1** lewd. **2** smooth and slippery with oil or grease.
– DERIVATIVES **lubriciously** adv. **lubricity** n.
– ORIGIN C16 (earlier (C15) as *lubricity*): from L. *lubricus* 'slippery' + **-IOUS**.

**Lucan** /ˈluːk(ə)n/ • **adj.** of or relating to St Luke.
– ORIGIN via eccles. L. from Gk *Loukas* 'Luke' + **-AN**.

**luce** /luːs/ • **n.** (pl. same) a pike (fish), especially when full-grown.
– ORIGIN ME: via OFr. *lus*, *luis* from late L. *lucius*.

**lucent** /ˈluːs(ə)nt/ • **adj.** poetic/literary shining.
– DERIVATIVES **lucency** n.
– ORIGIN ME: from L. *lucent-*, *lucere* (see **LUCID**).

**lucerne** /luːˈsəːn/ • **n.** another term for **ALFALFA**.
– ORIGIN C17: from Fr. *luzerne*, from mod. Provençal *luzerno* 'glow-worm' (with ref. to its shiny seeds).

**lucid** /ˈluːsɪd/ • **adj. 1** clear; easy to understand. ➤showing an ability to think clearly. ➤Psychology denoting a dream in which the sleeper is aware of dreaming. **2** poetic/literary bright or luminous.
– DERIVATIVES **lucidity** n. **lucidly** adv.
– ORIGIN C16 (in sense 2): from L. *lucidus* (perh. via Fr. *lucide* or Ital. *lucido*) from *lucere* 'shine', from *lux*, *luc-* 'light'.

**Lucifer** /ˈluːsɪfə/ • **n. 1** the Devil. **2** poetic/literary the planet Venus in the morning. **3** (**lucifer**) archaic a match.
– ORIGIN OE, from L., 'light-bringing, morning star', from *lux*, *luc-* 'light' + *-fer* 'bearing'.

**lucite** /ˈluːsʌɪt/ • **n.** trademark, chiefly N. Amer. a tough transparent plastic made of an acrylic resin, used as a substitute for glass.
– ORIGIN 1930s: from L. *lux*, *luc-* 'light' + **-ITE**[1].

**luck** • **n.** success or failure apparently brought by chance. ➤chance considered as a force causing success or failure. • **v.** informal **1** (**luck into/upon**) chance to find or acquire. **2** (**luck out**) N. Amer. succeed due to good luck.
– PHRASES **one's luck is in** one is fortunate. **no such luck** informal unfortunately not. **try one's luck** attempt something risky. **worse luck** informal unfortunately.
– ORIGIN ME (as v.): perh. from Mid. Low Ger. or MDu. *lucken*; the noun is from Mid. Low Ger. *lucke*, of W. Gmc origin, possibly rel. to **LOCK**[1].

**luckily** • **adv.** it is fortunate that.

**luckless** • **adj.** unfortunate.
– DERIVATIVES **lucklessly** adv. **lucklessness** n.

**lucky** • **adj.** (**-ier**, **-iest**) having, bringing, or resulting from good luck.
– DERIVATIVES **luckiness** n.

**lucky bag** • **n.** Brit. another term for **GRAB BAG**.

**lucky bean** • **n.** a plant of the pea family producing poisonous shiny scarlet beans with a black eye, sometimes used as amulets. [*Abrus precatorius* and other species.] ➤a bean of this plant.

**lucky dip** • **n.** Brit. a game in which small prizes are concealed in a container and chosen at random by participants.

**lucrative** /ˈluːkrətɪv/ • **adj.** profitable.
– DERIVATIVES **lucratively** adv. **lucrativeness** n.
– ORIGIN ME: from L. *lucrativus*, from *lucrat-*, *lucrari* 'to gain', from *lucrum* (see **LUCRE**).

**lucre** /ˈluːkə/ • **n.** poetic/literary money, especially when gained dishonourably.
– ORIGIN ME: from Fr. *lucre* or L. *lucrum*; the phr. *filthy lucre* is with biblical allusion to Tit. 1:11.

**lucubrate** /ˈluːkjʊbreɪt/ • **v.** archaic discourse learnedly in writing.
– DERIVATIVES **lucubrator** n.
– ORIGIN C17 (earlier (C16) as *lucubration*): from L. *lucubrat-*, *lucubrare* 'work by lamplight'.

**lucubration** • **n.** formal study; meditation. ➤ a piece of writing, typically a pedantic or over-elaborate one.

**luculent** /ˈluːkjʊl(ə)nt/ ● **adj.** rare **1** clearly expressed. **2** shining brightly.
– DERIVATIVES **luculently** adv.
– ORIGIN ME: from L. *luculentus*, from *lux*, *luc-* 'light'.

**Lucullan** /luːˈkʌlən, lʊ-/ ● **adj.** (especially of food) luxurious.
– ORIGIN C19: from the name of Licinius *Lucullus*, a Roman general famous for his lavish banquets, + **-AN**.

**lud** ● **n.** (**m'lud** or **my lud**) Brit. used to address a judge in court.
– ORIGIN C18: alt. of **LORD**.

**Luddite** /ˈlʌdʌɪt/ ● **n. 1** a member of any of the bands of English workers who opposed mechanization and destroyed machinery in the early 19th century. **2** a person opposed to industrialization or new technology.
– DERIVATIVES **Luddism** n. **Udditism** n.
– ORIGIN perh. named after Ned *Lud*, a participant in the destruction of machinery, + **-ITE**[1].

**ludic** /ˈluːdɪk/ ● **adj.** formal spontaneous; playful.
– ORIGIN 1940s: from Fr. *ludique*, from L. *ludere* 'to play'.

**ludicrous** ● **adj.** absurd; ridiculous.
– DERIVATIVES **ludicrously** adv. **ludicrousness** n.
– ORIGIN C17 (in the sense 'intended as a jest'): from L. *ludicrus* (prob. from *ludicrum* 'stage play') + **-OUS**.

**ludo** ● **n.** Brit. a board game in which players move counters according to throws of a dice.
– ORIGIN C19: from L., 'I play'.

**lues** /ˈl(j)uːiːz/ (also **lues venerea** /vɪˈnɪərɪə/) ● **n.** dated syphilis.
– DERIVATIVES **luetic** /l(j)uːˈɛtɪk/ adj.
– ORIGIN C17: from L., lit. 'plague'; *venerea* from L. *venereus* (see **VENEREAL**).

**luff** chiefly Sailing ● **n.** the edge of a fore-and-aft sail next to the mast or stay. ● **v. 1** steer (a yacht) nearer the wind. ➤obstruct (an opponent in yacht racing) by sailing closer to the wind. **2** raise or lower (the jib of a crane).
– ORIGIN ME: from OFr. *lof*, prob. from Low Ger.

**Luftwaffe** /ˈlʊftwafə, German ˈlʊftvafə/ ● **n.** the German air force until the end of the Second World War.
– ORIGIN Ger., from *Luft* 'air' + *Waffe* 'weapon'.

**lug**[1] ● **v.** (**lugged**, **lugging**) carry or drag with great effort. ● **n.** a box for transporting fruit.
– ORIGIN ME: prob. of Scand. origin.

**lug**[2] ● **n. 1** Scottish & N. English or informal an ear. **2** a projection on an object by which it may be carried or fixed in place. **3** informal, chiefly N. Amer. a lout.
– ORIGIN C15 (denoting the ear flap of a hat): prob. of Scand. origin.

**lug**[3] ● **n.** short for **LUGWORM**.

**Luganda** /luːˈgandə/ ● **n.** the Bantu language of the Baganda people.

**luge** /luːʒ/ ● **n.** a light toboggan ridden in a sitting or supine position. ● **v.** ride on a luge.
– ORIGIN C19 (as v.): from Swiss Fr.

**Luger** /ˈluːgə/ ● **n.** (trademark in the US) a type of German automatic pistol.
– ORIGIN C20: named after the Ger. firearms expert George *Luger*.

**luggage** ● **n.** suitcases or other bags for a traveller's belongings.
– ORIGIN C16 (denoting inconveniently heavy baggage): from **LUG**[1] + **-AGE**.

**lugger** ● **n.** a small ship with two or three masts and a lugsail on each.
– ORIGIN C18: from **LUGSAIL** + **-ER**[1].

**lughole** ● **n.** Brit. informal an ear.

**lugsail** /ˈlʌgseɪl, -s(ə)l/ ● **n.** an asymmetrical four-sided sail, bent on and hoisted from a steeply inclined yard.
– ORIGIN C17: prob. from **LUG**[2] + **SAIL**.

**lugubrious** /lʊˈguːbrɪəs/ ● **adj.** mournful; sad and dismal.
– DERIVATIVES **lugubriously** adv. **lugubriousness** n.
– ORIGIN C17: from L. *lugubris* (from *lugere* 'mourn') + **-OUS**.

**lugworm** ● **n.** a bristle worm living in muddy sand and leaving characteristic worm casts, widely used as fishing bait. [*Arenicola marina*.]
– ORIGIN C19: from earlier *lug* (of unknown origin) + **WORM**.

**lukewarm** ● **adj. 1** only moderately warm. **2** unenthusiastic.
– DERIVATIVES **lukewarmly** adv. **lukewarmness** n.
– ORIGIN ME: from dial. *luke* (prob. from dial. *lew* 'lukewarm' and rel. to **LEE**) + **WARM**.

**lull** ● **v.** calm or send to sleep with soothing sounds or movements. ➤cause to feel deceptively secure. ➤allay (doubts, fears, etc.), typically by deception. ➤(of noise or a storm) abate. ● **n.** a temporary period of quiet or inactivity.
– ORIGIN ME: imitative of sounds used to quieten a child.

**lullaby** ● **n.** (pl. **-ies**) a soothing song sung to send a child to sleep. ● **v.** (**-ies**, **-ied**) rare sing to sleep.
– ORIGIN C16: from **LULL** + *bye-bye*, a sound used as a refrain in lullabies.

**lulu** ● **n.** informal an outstanding person or thing.
– ORIGIN C19: perh. from *Lulu*, familiar form of the given name *Louise*.

**lum** /lʌm/ ● **n.** Scottish & N. English a chimney.
– ORIGIN C16: perh. from OFr. *lum* 'light', from L. *lumen*.

**luma** /ˈluːma/ ● **n.** (pl. same or **lumas**) a monetary unit of Armenia, equal to one hundredth of a dram.
– ORIGIN from Armenian.

**lumbago** /lʌmˈbeɪgəʊ/ ● **n.** pain in the lower back.
– ORIGIN C17: from L., from *lumbus* 'loin'.

**lumbar** /ˈlʌmbə/ ● **adj.** relating to the lower back.
– ORIGIN C17: from med. L. *lumbaris*, from L. *lumbus* 'loin'.

**lumbar puncture** ● **n.** Medicine the withdrawal of spinal fluid from the lower back through a hollow needle, typically for diagnostic purposes.

**lumber**[1] ● **v.** move in a slow, heavy, awkward way.
– ORIGIN ME *lomere*, perh. symbolic of clumsy movement.

**lumber**[2] ● **n. 1** chiefly Brit. disused articles of furniture that inconveniently take up space. **2** chiefly N. Amer. partly prepared timber. ● **v. 1** (usu. **be lumbered with**) Brit. informal burden with an unwanted responsibility. **2** [usu. as noun **lumbering**] chiefly N. Amer. cut and prepare forest timber for transport and sale.
– ORIGIN C16: perh. from **LUMBER**[1]; later assoc. with obs. *lumber* 'pawnbroker's shop'.

**lumber**[3] Scottish informal ● **v.** casually strike up a relationship with (a prospective sexual partner). ● **n.** a prospective sexual partner.
– ORIGIN 1960s: of unknown origin.

**lumberer** ● **n.** chiefly N. Amer. a person working in the lumber trade.

**lumberjack** (also **lumberman**) ● **n.** a person who fells trees, cuts them into logs, or transports them.

**lumberjacket** ● **n.** a thick jacket, typically with a bright check pattern, of the kind worn by lumberjacks.

**lumber room** ● **n.** Brit. a room for storing disused or bulky things.

**lumbersome** ● **adj.** unwieldy; awkward.

**lumen**[1] /ˈluːmɛn/ (abbrev.: **lm**) ● **n.** Physics the SI unit of luminous flux, equal to the amount of light emitted per second in a unit solid angle of one steradian from a uniform source of one candela.
– ORIGIN C19: from L., lit. 'light'.

**lumen**[2] /ˈluːmən/ ● **n.** (pl. **lumina** /-mɪnə/) Anatomy the central cavity of a hollow structure in an organism or cell.
– DERIVATIVES **luminal** /ˈluːmɪn(ə)l/ adj.
– ORIGIN C19: from L., lit. 'opening'.

**luminaire** /ˈluːmɪnɛː, ˌluːmɪˈnɛː/ ● **n.** a complete electric light unit.
– ORIGIN C20: from Fr.

**luminance** /ˈluːmɪn(ə)ns/ ● **n. 1** Physics the intensity of light emitted from a surface per unit area in a given direction. **2** the component of a television signal which carries information on the brightness of the image.
– ORIGIN C19: from L. *luminant-* *luminare* 'illuminate' + **-ANCE**.

**luminary** /ˈluːmɪn(ə)ri/ ● **n.** (pl. **-ies**) **1** a person who inspires or influences others. **2** poetic/literary a natural light-

giving body, especially the sun or moon.
– ORIGIN ME: from OFr. *luminarie* or late L. *luminarium*, from L. *lumen, lumin-* 'light'.

**luminesce** /ˌluːmɪˈnɛs/ • **v.** emit light by luminescence.

**luminescence** /ˌluːmɪˈnɛs(ə)ns/ • **n.** the emission of light by a substance that has not been heated, as in fluorescence and phosphorescence.
– DERIVATIVES **luminescent** adj.
– ORIGIN C19: from L. *lumen, lumin-* 'light' + *-escence* (denoting a state).

**luminiferous** /ˌluːmɪˈnɪf(ə)rəs/ • **adj.** chiefly archaic producing light.

**luminosity** • **n.** (pl. **-ies**) luminous quality. ➤Astronomy the intrinsic brightness of an object (as distinct from its apparent brightness).

**luminous** /ˈluːmɪnəs/ • **adj. 1** bright or shining, especially in the dark. **2** Physics of or relating to visible light.
– DERIVATIVES **luminously** adv. **luminousness** n.
– ORIGIN ME: from OFr. *lumineux* or L. *luminosus*, from *lumen, lumin-* 'light'.

**lumme** /ˈlʌmi/ • **exclam.** Brit. informal, dated an expression of surprise.
– ORIGIN C19: from *(Lord) love me.*

**lummox** /ˈlʌməks/ • **n.** informal, chiefly N. Amer. a clumsy, stupid person.
– ORIGIN C19: of unknown origin.

**lump**[1] • **n. 1** a compact mass, especially one without a definite or regular shape. ➤a swelling under the skin. **2** informal a heavy, ungainly, or slow-witted person. **3** (**the lump**) Brit. informal casual employment in the building trade. • **v. 1** (often **lump things together**) put in an indiscriminate mass or group. **2** Brit. carry (a heavy load) somewhere with difficulty.
– PHRASES **a lump in the throat** a feeling of tightness in the throat caused by strong emotion. **take** (or **get**) **one's lumps** informal, chiefly N. Amer. be attacked, punished, or defeated.
– DERIVATIVES **lumper** n.
– ORIGIN ME: perh. from a Gmc base meaning 'shapeless piece'.

**lump**[2] • **v.** (**lump it**) informal accept or tolerate something whether one likes it or not.
– ORIGIN C16 (in the sense 'look sulky'): symbolic of displeasure; cf. words such as *dump* and *grump.*

**lumpectomy** • **n.** (pl. **-ies**) a surgical operation in which a lump, typically a tumour, is removed from the breast.

**lumpen** • **adj. 1** (in Marxist contexts) uninterested in revolutionary advancement. ➤boorish and stupid. **2** lumpy and misshapen.
– ORIGIN C20: back-form. from **LUMPENPROLETARIAT**; the sense 'misshapen' by assoc. with **LUMPISH**.

**lumpenproletariat** /ˌlʌmpənprəʊlɪˈtɛːrɪət/ • **n.** [treated as sing. or pl.] (especially in Marxist terminology) the apolitical lower orders of society uninterested in revolutionary advancement.
– ORIGIN C20: from Ger. (orig. used by Karl Marx), from *Lumpen* 'rag, rogue' + **PROLETARIAT**.

**lumpfish** • **n.** (pl. same or **-fishes**) a North Atlantic lumpsucker with edible roe. [*Cyclopterus lumpus.*]
– ORIGIN C17: from Mid. Low Ger. *lumpen*, MDu. *lompe* + **FISH**[1].

**lumpish** • **adj. 1** roughly or clumsily formed. **2** stupid and lethargic.
– DERIVATIVES **lumpishly** adv. **lumpishness** n.

**lumpsucker** • **n.** a globular northern coastal fish with a ventral sucker and spiny fins. [Family Cyclopteridae: several species.]

**lump sum** • **n.** a single payment made at one time, as opposed to many instalments.

**lumpy** • **adj.** (**-ier, -iest**) **1** full of or covered with lumps. **2** Nautical (of water) formed by the wind into small waves.
– DERIVATIVES **lumpily** adv. **lumpiness** n.

**lunacy** • **n.** (pl. **-ies**) insanity (not in technical use). ➤extreme folly.
– ORIGIN C16 from **LUNATIC** + **-ACY**.

**luna moth** • **n.** a large North American moth having pale green wings with long tails and transparent eyespots bearing crescent-shaped markings. [*Actias luna.*]
– ORIGIN C19: from L. *luna* 'moon' (from its markings).

**lunar** /ˈluːnə/ • **adj.** of, determined by, or resembling the moon.
– ORIGIN ME: from L. *lunaris*, from *luna* 'moon'.

**lunar cycle** • **n.** another term for **METONIC CYCLE**.

**lunar day** • **n.** the interval between two successive crossings of the meridian by the moon (roughly 24 hours and 50 minutes).

**lunar distance** • **n.** the angular distance of the moon from the sun, a planet, or a star, used in finding longitude at sea.

**lunar eclipse** • **n.** an eclipse in which the moon passes into the earth's shadow.

**lunar month** • **n.** a month measured between successive new moons (roughly 29½ days). ➤(in general use) four weeks.

**lunar node** • **n.** Astronomy each of the two points at which the moon's orbit cuts the ecliptic.

**lunar observation** • **n.** the measurement of longitude by lunar distance.

**lunar year** • **n.** a period of twelve lunar months (approximately 354 days).

**lunate** /ˈluːneɪt/ • **adj.** crescent-shaped. • **n. 1** Archaeology a crescent-shaped stone implement. **2** (also **lunate bone**) Anatomy a crescent-shaped carpal bone in the centre of the wrist.
– ORIGIN C18: from L. *lunatus*, from *luna* 'moon'.

**lunatic** • **n.** a person who is mentally ill (not in technical use). ➤an extremely foolish person.
– ORIGIN ME: from OFr. *lunatique*, from late L. *lunaticus*, from L. *luna* 'moon' (from the belief that changes of the moon caused intermittent insanity).

**lunatic asylum** • **n.** dated an institution for the mentally ill.

**lunatic fringe** • **n.** an extreme or eccentric minority.

**lunation** /luːˈneɪʃ(ə)n/ • **n.** Astronomy another term for **LUNAR MONTH**.
– ORIGIN ME: from med. L. *lunatio(n-)*, from L. *luna* 'moon'.

**lunch** • **n.** a meal eaten in the middle of the day. • **v.** eat lunch. ➤take (someone) out for lunch.
– PHRASES **do lunch** informal, chiefly N. Amer. meet for lunch. **out to lunch** informal unbalanced or stupid.
– DERIVATIVES **luncher** n.
– ORIGIN C19: abbrev. of **LUNCHEON**.

**lunch box** • **n. 1** a container for a packed meal. **2** humorous a man's genitals.

**luncheon** • **n.** formal lunch.
– ORIGIN C16 (in the sense 'thick piece, hunk'): possibly an extension of obs. *lunch* 'thick piece, hunk', from Sp. *lonja* 'slice'.

**luncheonette** • **n.** N. Amer. a small restaurant serving light lunches.

**luncheon meat** • **n.** finely minced cooked pork mixed with cereal, sold in a tin.

**luncheon voucher** • **n.** Brit. a voucher given to employees and exchangeable for food at restaurants and shops.

**lunch hour** • **n.** a break from work when lunch is eaten.

**lunchtime** • **n.** the time when lunch is eaten.

**lune** /luːn/ • **n.** a crescent-shaped figure formed on a sphere or plane by two arcs intersecting at two points.
– ORIGIN C18: from Fr., from L. *luna* 'moon'.

**lunette** /luːˈnɛt/ • **n. 1** an arched aperture or window in a domed ceiling. **2** a crescent-shaped or semicircular alcove containing a painting or statue. **3** a fortification with two faces forming a projecting angle, and two flanks. **4** Christian Church a holder for the consecrated host in a monstrance. **5** a ring on a vehicle, by which it can be towed.
– ORIGIN C16 (denoting a semicircular horseshoe): from Fr., dimin. of *lune* 'moon', from L. *luna*.

**lung** • **n.** each of the pair of organs within the ribcage into which air is drawn in breathing, so that oxygen can pass into the blood and carbon dioxide be removed.
– DERIVATIVES **-lunged** adj. **lungful** n. (pl. **-fuls**). **lungless** adj.

– ORIGIN OE *lungen*, of Gmc origin; rel. to **LIGHT**[2] and **LIGHTS**.

**lunge**[1] ● **n.** a sudden forward movement of the body. ➤a thrust in fencing, in which the leading leg is bent while the back leg remains straightened. ● **v.** (**lunging** or **lungeing**) make a lunge. ➤make a sudden forward thrust with.
– ORIGIN C18: from earlier *allonge*, from Fr. *allonger* 'lengthen'.

**lunge**[2] (also **longe**) ● **n.** a long rein on which a horse is made to move in a circle round its trainer. ● **v.** (**lungeing**) exercise (a horse or rider) on a lunge.
– ORIGIN C18: from Fr. *longe*, from *allonge* 'lengthening out'.

**lunge**[3] ● **n.** N. Amer. short for **MUSKELLUNGE**.

**lungfish** ● **n.** (pl. same or **-fishes**) an elongated freshwater fish with one or two sacs which function as lungs, enabling it to breathe air and aestivate in mud to survive drought. [Subclass Dipnoi: several species.]

**lungi** /'lʊŋgiː/ ● **n.** (pl. **lungis**) a length of cotton cloth worn as a loincloth in India or as a skirt in Burma (Myanmar).
– ORIGIN from Urdu.

**lungworm** ● **n.** a parasitic nematode worm found in the lungs of mammals. [*Dictyocaulus* and other genera.]

**lungwort** ● **n. 1** a bristly pink-flowered plant with white-spotted leaves said to resemble a diseased lung. [*Pulmonaria officinalis* and related species.] **2** (also **tree lungwort**) a large lichen which grows on trees, formerly used to treat lung disease. [*Lobaria pulmonaria*.]

**lunisolar** /ˌluːnɪ'səʊlə/ ● **adj.** of or concerning the sun and moon.
– ORIGIN C17: from L. *luna* 'moon' + **SOLAR**[1].

**lunk** ● **n.** short for **LUNKHEAD**.

**lunker** ● **n.** N. Amer. informal a very large animal, especially a fish.
– ORIGIN C20: of unknown origin.

**lunkhead** ● **n.** informal a slow-witted person.
– ORIGIN C19: prob. from an alt. of **LUMP**[1] + **HEAD**.

**lunula** /'luːnjʊlə/ ● **n.** (pl. **lunulae** /-liː/) **1** the white area at the base of a fingernail. **2** a crescent-shaped Bronze Age ornament.
– DERIVATIVES **lunular** adj. **lunulate** adj.
– ORIGIN C16: from L., dimin. of *luna* 'moon'.

**lunule** /'luːnjuːl/ ● **n.** another term for **LUNULA**.

**Luo** /'luːəʊ/ ● **n.** (pl. same or **-os**) **1** a member of an East African people of Kenya and the upper Nile valley. **2** the Nilotic language of this people.
– ORIGIN the name in Luo.

**lupara** /lʊ'pɑːrə/ ● **n.** a sawn-off shotgun.
– ORIGIN Ital., sl. term from *lupa* 'she-wolf'.

**lupin** /'luːpɪn/ (also **lupine** /-pɪn/) ● **n.** a plant of the pea family, with deeply divided leaves and tall colourful tapering spikes of flowers. [Genus *Lupinus*: several species.]
– ORIGIN ME: from L. *lupinus*.

**lupine** /'luːpʌɪn/ ● **adj.** of or like a wolf or wolves.
– ORIGIN C17: from L. *lupinus*, from *lupus* 'wolf'.

**lupus** /'luːpəs/ ● **n.** Medicine an ulcerous skin condition, especially one due to direct infection with tuberculosis.
– DERIVATIVES **lupoid** adj. **lupous** adj.
– ORIGIN C16: from L., lit. 'wolf'.

**lupus erythematosus** /ˌɛrɪθiːmə'təʊsəs/ ● **n.** an inflammatory disease causing scaly red patches on the skin.
– ORIGIN from **LUPUS** + mod. L. *erythematosus*, from Gk *eruthēma* 'reddening'.

**lur** /lʊə/ (also **lure**) ● **n.** a Scandinavian S-shaped bronze trumpet dating from the Bronze Age.
– ORIGIN from Dan. and Norw.

**lurch**[1] ● **n.** a sudden unsteady movement. ● **v.** make such a movement; stagger.
– ORIGIN C17: of unknown origin.

**lurch**[2] ● **n.** (in phr. **leave someone in the lurch**) leave someone in a difficult situation without assistance or support.
– ORIGIN C16: from Fr. *lourche*, the name of a game resembling backgammon, used in the phr. *demeurer lourche* 'be discomfited'.

**lurcher** ● **n. 1** Brit. a cross-bred dog, typically a retriever, collie, or sheepdog crossed with a greyhound, originally used for hunting and by poachers. **2** archaic a prowler, swindler, or petty thief.
– ORIGIN C16: from obs. *lurch*, var. of **LURK**.

**lure**[1] /l(j)ʊə/ ● **v.** tempt to do something or to go somewhere. ● **n. 1** a thing that lures a person or animal to do something. ➤a type of bait used in fishing or hunting. ➤Falconry a bunch of feathers with a piece of meat attached to a long string, swung around the head of a falconer to recall a hawk. **2** the attractive qualities of a person or thing.
– ORIGIN ME: from OFr. *luere*, of Gmc origin.

**lure**[2] /lʊə/ ● **n.** variant spelling of **LUR**.

**lurex** /'l(j)ʊərɛks/ ● **n.** trademark yarn or fabric incorporating a glittering metallic thread.
– ORIGIN 1940s: of unknown origin.

**lurgy** /'ləːgi/ ● **n.** (pl. **-ies**) Brit. humorous an unspecified illness.
– ORIGIN C20: of unknown origin; freq. used in the Brit. radio series *The Goon Show*, of the 1950s and 1960s.

**lurid** /'l(j)ʊərɪd/ ● **adj. 1** unpleasantly vivid in colour. **2** (of a description) shocking or sensational.
– DERIVATIVES **luridly** adv. **luridness** n.
– ORIGIN C17 (in the sense 'pale and dismal'): from L. *luridus*; rel. to *luror* 'wan or yellow colour'.

**lurk** ● **v. 1** be or remain hidden so as to wait in ambush. **2** be present in a latent or barely discernible state. ● **n.** Austral./NZ informal a dodge or scheme.
– DERIVATIVES **lurker** n.
– ORIGIN ME: perh. from **LOUR** + the frequentative suffix *-k* (as in *talk*).

**luscious** ● **adj. 1** having a pleasingly rich, sweet taste. **2** richly verdant or opulent. **3** (of a woman) sexually attractive.
– DERIVATIVES **lusciously** adv. **lusciousness** n.
– ORIGIN ME: perh. an alt. of obs. *licious*, shortened form of **DELICIOUS**.

**lush**[1] ● **adj. 1** (of vegetation) luxuriant. ➤luxurious. ➤(of colour or music) rich. **2** informal sexually attractive.
– DERIVATIVES **lushly** adv. **lushness** n.
– ORIGIN ME: perh. an alt. of obs. *lash* 'soft, lax', from OFr. *lasche* 'lax', by assoc. with **LUSCIOUS**.

**lush**[2] informal, chiefly N. Amer. ● **n.** a drunkard. ● **v.** dated make (someone) drunk.
– ORIGIN C18: perh. a humorous use of **LUSH**[1].

**lusophone** /'luːsəfəʊn/ ● **adj.** Portuguese-speaking.
– ORIGIN 1970s: from *luso-* (representing *Lusitania*, an ancient Roman province corresp. to mod. Portugal) + **-PHONE**.

**lust** ● **n.** strong sexual desire. ➤a passionate desire for something. ➤chiefly Theology a sensuous appetite regarded as sinful. ● **v.** (usu. **lust for/after**) feel lust for someone or something.
– DERIVATIVES **lustful** adj. **lustfully** adv. **lustfulness** n.
– ORIGIN OE, of Gmc origin.

**luster** ● **n.** US spelling of **LUSTRE**[1], **LUSTRE**[2].

**lusterware** ● **n.** US spelling of **LUSTREWARE**.

**lustra** plural form of **LUSTRUM**.

**lustral** /'lʌstr(ə)l/ ● **adj.** relating to or used in ceremonial purification.
– ORIGIN C16: from L. *lustralis*, from *lustrum* (see **LUSTRUM**).

**lustrate** /'lʌstreɪt/ ● **v.** rare purify by expiatory sacrifice, ceremonial washing, or other ritual action.
– DERIVATIVES **lustration** n.
– ORIGIN C17: from L. *lustrat-*, *lustrare* 'purify by lustral rites', from *lustrum* (see **LUSTRUM**).

**lustre**[1] (US **luster**) ● **n. 1** a gentle sheen or soft glow. ➤the manner in which the surface of a mineral reflects light. **2** a thin metallic coating giving an iridescent glaze to ceramics. ➤lustreware. **3** glory or distinction. **4** a fabric or yarn with a sheen. ➤Brit. a thin dress material of cotton and wool, with a glossy surface. **5** a prismatic glass pendant on a chandelier. ➤a cut-glass chandelier or candelabra.

– DERIVATIVES **lustred** adj. **lustreless** adj. **lustrous** adj. **lustrously** adv. **lustrousness** n.
– ORIGIN C16: from Fr., from Ital. *lustro*, from *lustrare*, from L. *lustrare* 'illuminate'.

**lustre**[2] (US **luster**) • n. another term for LUSTRUM.

**lustreware** (US **lusterware**) • n. ceramic articles with an iridescent metallic glaze.

**lustring** • n. historical a glossy silk or satin fabric.
– ORIGIN C17: from Fr. *lustrine* or from Ital. *lustrino*, from *lustro* 'lustre'.

**lustrum** /ˈlʌstrəm/ • n. (pl. **lustra** /-trə/ or **lustrums**) chiefly poetic/literary or historical a period of five years.
– ORIGIN C16: from L., orig. denoting a purificatory sacrifice after a quinquennial census.

**lusty** • adj. (**-ier**, **-iest**) healthy and strong; vigorous.
– DERIVATIVES **lustily** adv. **lustiness** n.
– ORIGIN ME: from LUST (in the early sense 'vigour') + **-Y**[1].

**lusus naturae** /ˌluːsəs nəˈtjʊəriː, -rʌɪ/ • n. (pl. same /-suːs/ or **lususes**) rare a freak of nature.
– ORIGIN L., lit. 'a sport of nature'.

**lutanist** • n. variant spelling of LUTENIST.

**lute**[1] • n. a stringed instrument with a long neck and a rounded body with a flat front, played by plucking.
– ORIGIN ME: from OFr. *lut*, *leut*, prob. via Provençal from Arab. *al-ʿūd*.

**lute**[2] • n. (also **luting**) liquid clay or cement used to seal a joint, coat a crucible, or protect a graft. ➤a rubber seal for a jar. • v. seal, join, or coat with lute.
– ORIGIN ME: from OFr. *lut* or med. L. *lutum*, a special use of L. *lutum* 'potter's clay'.

**luteal** /luːˈtɪəl/ • adj. Physiology of or relating to the corpus luteum.

**lutein** /ˈluːtɪɪn/ • n. Biochemistry a deep yellow pigment found in plant leaves, egg yolk, and the corpus luteum.
– ORIGIN C19: from L. *luteum* 'egg yolk' (neut. of *luteus* 'yellow') + **-IN**[1].

**luteinizing hormone** /ˈluːtənʌɪzɪŋ/ (also **-ising**) • n. Biochemistry a pituitary hormone that stimulates ovulation in females and the synthesis of androgen in males.

**lutenist** /ˈluːt(ə)nɪst/ (also **lutanist**) • n. a lute player.
– ORIGIN C17: from med. L. *lutanista*, from *lutana* 'lute'.

**luteo-** /ˈluːtɪəʊ/ • comb. form **1** orange-coloured: *luteofulvous*. **2** relating to the corpus luteum: *luteotrophic*.
– ORIGIN from L. *luteus* (or neut. *luteum*) 'yellow'.

**luteofulvous** /ˌluːtɪəʊˈfʌlvəs/ • adj. of an orange-tawny colour.

**luteotrophic hormone** /ˌluːtɪə(ʊ)ˈtrəʊfɪk, -ˈtrɒfɪk/ • n. another term for PROLACTIN.

**luteous** /ˈluːtɪəs, ˈljuː-/ • adj. Biology of a deep orange-yellow or greenish yellow colour.
– ORIGIN C17: from L. *luteus* 'yellow' + **-OUS**.

**lutetium** /luːˈtiːʃɪəm, -sɪəm/ • n. the chemical element of atomic number 71, a rare silvery-white metal of the lanthanide series. (Symbol: **Lu**)
– ORIGIN C20: from Fr. *lutécium*, from L. *Lutetia*, the ancient name of Paris.

**Lutheran** • n. a follower of the German protestant theologian Martin Luther (1483–1546). ➤a member of the Lutheran Church. • adj. of or characterized by the theology of Martin Luther. ➤of or relating to the Lutheran Church.
– DERIVATIVES **Lutheranism** n. **Lutheranize** (also **-ise**) v.

**Lutheran Church** • n. the Protestant Church founded on the doctrines of Martin Luther, with justification by faith alone as a cardinal doctrine.

**luthier** /ˈluːtɪə/ • n. a maker of stringed instruments.
– ORIGIN C19: from Fr., from *luth* 'lute'.

**luting** • n. see LUTE[2].

**lutino** /luːˈtiːnəʊ/ • n. (pl. **-os**) a cage bird with more yellow in the plumage than usual for the species.
– ORIGIN C20: from L. *luteus* 'yellow', on the pattern of *albino*.

**lutist** • n. **1** a lute player. **2** a lute maker.

**lutz** /lʊts/ • n. a jump in skating from the backward outside edge of one skate to the backward outside edge of the other, with a full turn in the air.
– ORIGIN 1930s: named after the Austrian skater Alois *Lutz* (1899–1918).

**luvvy** (also **luvvie**) • n. (pl. **-ies**) Brit. informal **1** an effusive or affected actor or actress. **2** variant spelling of LOVEY.
– DERIVATIVES **luvviedom** n.

**lux** /lʌks/ (abbrev.: **lx**) • n. (pl. same) the SI unit of illuminance, equal to one lumen per square metre.
– ORIGIN C19: from L., lit. 'light'.

**luxate** /ˈlʌkseɪt/ • v. Medicine dislocate.
– DERIVATIVES **luxation** n.
– ORIGIN C17: from L. *luxat-*, *luxare* 'dislocate', from *luxus* 'out of joint'.

**luxe** /lʌks, lʊks/ • n. luxury.
– ORIGIN C16: from Fr., from L. *luxus* 'abundance'.

**Luxembourger** /ˈlʌksəmbəːgə/ • n. a native or inhabitant of Luxembourg.

**Luxemburgish** /ˈlʌksəmˌbəːgɪʃ/ • n. a form of German spoken in Luxembourg.

**luxuriant** /lʌgˈʒʊərɪənt, lʌgˈzjʊə-, lʌkˈsjʊə-/ • adj. **1** (of vegetation) rich and profuse in growth. **2** (of hair) thick and healthy.
– DERIVATIVES **luxuriance** n. **luxuriantly** adv.
– ORIGIN C16: from L. *luxuriant-*, *luxuriare* 'grow rankly', from *luxuria* 'luxury, rankness'.

**luxuriate** /lʌgˈʒʊərɪeɪt, lʌgˈzjʊə-, lʌkˈsjʊə-/ • v. (**luxuriate in/over**) enjoy as a luxury.
– ORIGIN C17: from L. *luxuriat-*, *luxuriare* 'grow in abundance'.

**luxurious** • adj. characterized by luxury. ➤giving self-indulgent pleasure.
– DERIVATIVES **luxuriously** adv. **luxuriousness** n.
– ORIGIN ME: from OFr. *luxurios*, from L. *luxuriosus*, from *luxuria* 'luxury'.

**luxury** • n. (pl. **-ies**) **1** the state of great comfort and extravagant living. **2** an inessential but desirable item. • adj. of the nature of a luxury.
– ORIGIN ME (denoting lechery): from OFr. *luxurie*, *luxure*, from L. *luxuria*, from *luxus* 'excess'.

**LVO** • abbrev. Lieutenant of the Royal Victorian Order.

**lwei** /ləˈweɪ/ • n. (pl. same) a monetary unit of Angola, equal to one hundredth of a kwanza.
– ORIGIN a local word.

**LWM** • abbrev. low-water mark.

**lx** • abbrev. Physics lux.

**LXX** • symb. Septuagint.
– ORIGIN special use of the Roman numeral for 70.

**-ly**[1] • suffix forming adjectives meaning: **1** having the qualities of: *brotherly*. **2** recurring at intervals of: *hourly*.
– ORIGIN OE *-lic*, of Gmc origin; rel. to LIKE[1].

**-ly**[2] • suffix forming adverbs from adjectives: *greatly*.
– ORIGIN OE *-līce*, of Gmc origin.

**lycanthrope** /ˈlʌɪk(ə)nˌθrəʊp/ • n. a werewolf.
– ORIGIN C17: from mod. L. *lycanthropus*, from Gk *lukanthrōpos* (see LYCANTHROPY).

**lycanthropy** /lʌɪˈkanθrəpi/ • n. the mythical transformation of a person into a wolf. ➤archaic a form of madness involving the delusion of being an animal, usually a wolf.
– DERIVATIVES **lycanthropic** adj.
– ORIGIN C16: from mod. L. *lycanthropia*, from Gk *lukanthrōpia*, from *lukos* 'wolf' + *anthrōpos* 'man'.

**lycée** /ˈliːseɪ, French lise/ • n. (pl. pronounced same) a French secondary school funded by the state.
– ORIGIN Fr., from L. *lyceum* (see LYCEUM).

**Lyceum** /lʌɪˈsiːəm/ • n. **1** the garden at Athens in which Aristotle taught philosophy. ➤Aristotelian philosophy and its followers. **2** (**lyceum**) US archaic a literary institution, lecture hall, or teaching place.
– ORIGIN via L. from Gk *Lukeion*, neut. of *Lukeios*, epithet of Apollo (from whose neighbouring temple the Lyceum was named).

**lychee** /ˈlʌɪtʃiː, ˈlɪ-/ (also **litchi**) • n. **1** a small rounded fruit with sweet white scented flesh, a large stone, and thin rough skin. **2** the Chinese tree which bears this fruit. [*Nephelium litchi*.]
– ORIGIN C16: from Chin. *lìzhī*.

**lychgate** /ˈlɪtʃgeɪt/ • n. a roofed gateway to a church-

yard, formerly used at burials for sheltering a coffin until the clergyman's arrival.
– ORIGIN C15: from OE *līc* 'body' + **GATE**[1].

**lychnis** /ˈlɪknɪs/ ● **n.** a plant of a genus which includes the campions and ragged robin. [Genus *Lychnis*.]
– ORIGIN mod. L., via L. from Gk *lukhnis*, denoting a red flower, from *lukhnos* 'lamp'.

**lycopene** /ˈlʌɪkə(ʊ)piːn/ ● **n.** Biochemistry a red carotenoid pigment present in tomatoes and many berries and fruits.
– ORIGIN 1930s: from the var. *lycopin* (from mod. L. *Lycopersicon*, a genus name including the tomato) + **-ENE**.

**lycopodium** /ˌlʌɪkə(ʊ)ˈpəʊdɪəm/ ● **n. 1** a plant of a genus that includes the common clubmosses. [Genus *Lycopodium*.] **2** a fine flammable powder consisting of clubmoss spores, formerly used as an absorbent in surgery and in making fireworks.
– DERIVATIVES **lycopod** n.
– ORIGIN mod. L., from Gk *lukos* 'wolf' + *pous, pod-* 'foot' (because of the claw-like shape of the root).

**Lycra** /ˈlʌɪkrə/ ● **n.** trademark an elastic polyurethane fibre or fabric used especially for close-fitting sports clothing.
– ORIGIN C20: of unknown origin.

**lyddite** /ˈlɪdʌɪt/ ● **n.** a high explosive containing picric acid, used by the British during the First World War.
– ORIGIN C19: named after *Lydd*, a town in Kent where the explosive was first tested, + **-ITE**[1].

**Lydian** ● **n. 1** a native or inhabitant of the ancient region of Lydia in western Asia Minor. **2** the extinct language of the Lydians. ● **adj.** of or relating to the Lydians or their language.

**Lydian mode** ● **n.** Music the mode represented by the natural diatonic scale F–F (containing an augmented 4th).

**lye** ● **n.** a strongly alkaline solution, especially of potassium hydroxide, used for washing or cleansing.
– ORIGIN OE *lēag*, of Gmc origin: rel. to **LATHER**.

**lying**[1] present participle of **LIE**[1].

**lying**[2] present participle of **LIE**[2]. ● **adj.** not telling the truth.
– DERIVATIVES **lyingly** adv.

**lying-in** ● **n.** archaic seclusion before and after childbirth.

**lying-in-state** ● **n.** the display of the corpse of a public figure for public tribute before it is buried or cremated.

**lyke wake** /lʌɪk/ ● **n.** Brit. a night spent watching over a dead body.
– ORIGIN ME: from *lyke* (from OE *līc* 'body': cf. **LYCHGATE**) + **WAKE**[1].

**Lyme disease** /lʌɪm/ ● **n.** a form of arthritis caused by bacteria that are transmitted by ticks.
– ORIGIN 1970s: named after *Lyme*, a town in Connecticut, US, where an outbreak occurred.

**lymph** /lɪmf/ ● **n. 1** Physiology a colourless fluid containing white blood cells, which bathes the tissues and drains through the lymphatic system into the bloodstream. ➤fluid exuding from a sore or inflamed tissue. **2** poetic/literary pure water.
– DERIVATIVES **lymphous** adj.
– ORIGIN C16: from Fr. *lymphe* or L. *lympha*, *limpa* 'water'.

**lymph-** ● **comb. form** variant spelling of **LYMPHO-** shortened before a vowel, as in *lymphangitis*.

**lymphadenitis** /ˌlɪmfadɪˈnʌɪtɪs/ ● **n.** Medicine inflammation of the lymph nodes.
– ORIGIN C19: from **LYMPH-** + Gk *adēn* 'gland' + **-ITIS**.

**lymphadenopathy** /ˌlɪmfadɪˈnɒpəθi/ ● **n.** Medicine a disease affecting the lymph nodes.

**lymphangitis** /ˌlɪmfanˈdʒʌɪtɪs/ ● **n.** Medicine inflammation of the walls of the lymphatic vessels.

**lymphatic** ● **adj. 1** Physiology of or relating to lymph or its secretion. **2** archaic (of a person) pale, flabby, or sluggish. ● **n.** Anatomy a vein-like vessel conveying lymph in the body.
– ORIGIN C17 (in the sense 'frenzied, mad'): from L. *lymphaticus* 'mad', from Gk *nympholēptos* 'seized by nymphs'; now assoc. with **LYMPH**.

**lymphatic system** ● **n.** the network of vessels through which lymph drains from the tissues into the blood.

**lymph gland** ● **n.** less technical term for **LYMPH NODE**.

**lymph node** ● **n.** Physiology each of a number of small swellings in the lymphatic system where lymph is filtered and lymphocytes are formed.

**lympho-** (also **lymph-** before a vowel) ● **comb. form** representing **LYMPH**: *lymphocyte*.

**lymphoblast** /ˈlɪmfə(ʊ)blast/ ● **n.** Medicine an abnormal cell resembling a large lymphocyte, produced in large numbers in a form of leukaemia.
– DERIVATIVES **lymphoblastic** adj.

**lymphocyte** /ˈlɪmfə(ʊ)sʌɪt/ ● **n.** Physiology a form of small leucocyte (white blood cell) with a single round nucleus, occurring especially in the lymphatic system.
– DERIVATIVES **lymphocytic** adj.

**lymphoid** /ˈlɪmfɔɪd/ ● **adj.** Anatomy relating to or denoting tissue responsible for producing lymphocytes and antibodies.

**lymphokine** /ˈlɪmfə(ʊ)kʌɪn/ ● **n.** Physiology a substance of a type produced by lymphocytes and having an effect on other cells of the immune system.
– ORIGIN 1960s: from **LYMPHO-** + Gk *kinein* 'to move'.

**lymphoma** /lɪmˈfəʊmə/ ● **n.** (pl. **lymphomas** or **lymphomata** /-mətə/) Medicine cancer of the lymph nodes.

**lymphoreticular** /ˌlɪmfə(ʊ)rɪˈtɪkjʊlə/ ● **adj.** another term for **RETICULOENDOTHELIAL**.

**lynch** ● **v.** (of a group) kill (someone) for an alleged offence without a legal trial, especially by hanging.
– DERIVATIVES **lyncher** n.
– ORIGIN C19: from *Lynch's law*, named after Capt. William *Lynch*, head of a self-constituted judicial tribunal in Virginia *c.*1780.

**lynchet** /ˈlɪn(t)ʃɪt/ ● **n.** a ridge or ledge formed along the downhill side of a plot by ploughing in ancient times.
– ORIGIN C17: prob. from dial. *linch* 'rising ground'; cf. **LINKS**.

**lynchpin** ● **n.** variant spelling of **LINCHPIN**.

**lynx** ● **n.** a wild cat with a short tail and tufted ears. [*Lynx lynx* (northern Eurasia) and other species.]
– ORIGIN ME: via L. from Gk *lunx*.

**lynx-eyed** ● **adj.** keen-sighted.

**lyonnaise** /ˌliːəˈneɪz/ ● **adj.** (of sliced potatoes) cooked with onions or with a white wine and onion sauce.
– ORIGIN Fr., 'characteristic of the city of Lyons'.

**lyophilic** /ˌlʌɪə(ʊ)ˈfɪlɪk/ ● **adj.** Chemistry (of a colloid) readily dispersed by a solvent and not easily precipitated.
– ORIGIN C20: from Gk *luein* 'loosen, dissolve' + *philos* 'loving'.

**lyophilize** /lʌɪˈɒfɪlʌɪz/ (also **-ise**) ● **v.** technical freeze-dry.
– DERIVATIVES **lyophilization** n.

**lyophobic** /ˌlʌɪəˈfəʊbɪk/ ● **adj.** Chemistry (of a colloid) not lyophilic.

**lyrate** /ˈlʌɪreɪt/ ● **adj.** Biology lyre-shaped.

**lyre** ● **n.** a stringed instrument like a small U-shaped harp with strings fixed to a crossbar, used especially in ancient Greece.
– ORIGIN ME: via OFr. *lire* and L. *lyra* from Gk *lura*.

**lyrebird** ● **n.** a large Australian songbird, the male of which has a long lyre-shaped tail. [Genus *Menura*: *Menura novaehollandiae* (**superb lyrebird**) and *M. alberti*.]

**lyric** ● **n. 1** (also **lyrics**) the words of a song. **2** a lyric poem or verse. ● **adj. 1** (of poetry) expressing the writer's emotions, usually briefly and in stanzas or recognized forms. **2** (of a singing voice) using a light register.
– ORIGIN C16: from Fr. *lyrique* or L. *lyricus*, from Gk *lurikos*, from *lura* 'lyre'.

**lyrical** ● **adj. 1** (of literature, art, or music) expressing the writer's emotions in an imaginative and beautiful way. ➤(of poetry) lyric. **2** of or relating to the words of a popular song.
– PHRASES **wax lyrical** talk in a highly enthusiastic and effusive way.
– DERIVATIVES **lyrically** adv.

## Word *Formation*

**-lysis** 'decomposition', from Greek *lusis* 'loosening'

➤ Most **-lysis** words are used in technical fields, in which the first element indicates either the agent of decomposition or the substance affected by decomposition:

| | | |
|---|---|---|
| catalysis | using a catalyst to accelerate a chemical reaction | Gk *kataluein* 'dissolve' (*kata* 'down' + *luein* 'loosen') |
| electrolysis | chemical decomposition using an electric current | ELECTRO- |
| fibrinolysis | breakdown by enzymes of the fibrin in blood clots | based on FIBRIN |
| glycolysis | breakdown by enzymes of glucose | Gk *glukus* 'sugar, sweet' |
| histolysis | breakdown of tissue | Gk *histos* 'web, tissue' |
| hydrolysis | chemical breakdown due to reaction with water | Gk *hudōr* 'water' |

➤ A number of words containing the same element are of earlier origin and tend to have less technical meanings:

| | | |
|---|---|---|
| analysis | detailed examination | Gk *analuein* 'unloosen' |
| paralysis | loss of the ability to move | Gk *paraluein* (*para* 'beside, beyond') |

**lyricism** ● n. an artist's expression of emotion in an imaginative and beautiful way; lyrical quality.

**lyricist** ● n. a person who writes the words to popular songs.

**lyrist** ● n. **1** /ˈlʌɪərɪst/ a person who plays the lyre. **2** /ˈlɪrɪst/ a lyric poet.

**lysate** /ˈlʌɪzeɪt/ ● n. Biology a preparation containing the products of lysis of cells.

**lyse** /lʌɪz/ ● v. Biology undergo or cause to undergo lysis.

**lysergic acid** /lʌɪˈsəːdʒɪk/ ● n. Chemistry a crystalline compound prepared from natural ergot alkaloids or synthetically, from which the drug LSD (**lysergic acid diethylamide**) can be made.
– ORIGIN 1930s: *lysergic* from (*hydro*)*lys*(*is*) + *erg*(*ot*) + **-IC**.

**lysin** /ˈlʌɪsɪn/ ● n. Biology an antibody or other substance able to cause lysis of cells (especially bacteria).

**lysine** /ˈlʌɪsiːn/ ● n. Biochemistry a basic amino acid which is a constituent of most proteins, an essential nutrient in the diet of vertebrates.

**lysis** /ˈlʌɪsɪs/ ● n. Biology the disintegration of a cell by rupture of the cell wall or membrane.
– ORIGIN C19: from L., from Gk *lusis* 'loosening', from *luein* 'loosen'.

**-lysis** ● comb. form forming nouns denoting disintegration or decomposition: *hydrolysis* | *haemolysis*. See word-formation panel.
– ORIGIN via L. from Gk *lusis* 'loosening'.

**Lysol** /ˈlʌɪsɒl/ ● n. trademark a disinfectant consisting of a mixture of cresols and soft soap.
– ORIGIN C19: from **-LYSIS** + **-OL**.

**lysosome** /ˈlʌɪsəsəʊm/ ● n. Biology an organelle in the cytoplasm of eukaryotic cells containing degradative enzymes enclosed in a membrane.
– DERIVATIVES **lysosomal** adj.

**lysozyme** /ˈlʌɪsəzʌɪm/ ● n. Biochemistry an enzyme which catalyses the destruction of the cell walls of certain bacteria, found notably in tears and egg white.

**lytic** /ˈlɪtɪk/ ● adj. Biology of, relating to, or causing lysis.
– DERIVATIVES **lytically** adv.

**-lytic** ● comb. form in adjectives corresponding to nouns ending in *-lysis* (such as *hydrolytic* corresponding to *hydrolysis*).

**M**[1] (also **m**) ● **n.** (pl. **Ms** or **M's**) **1** the thirteenth letter of the alphabet. **2** denoting the next after L in a set of items, categories, etc. **3** the Roman numeral for 1,000. [from L. *mille.*]

**M**[2] ● **abbrev. 1** Cricket (on scorecards) maiden over(s). **2** male. **3** Malta (international vehicle registration). **4** medium (as a clothes size). **5** mega-. **6** Astronomy Messier (catalogue of nebulae). **7** Chemistry (with reference to solutions) molar. **8** used with following numeral in measures of money supply. **9** Monsieur. **10** (in UK road designations) motorway. ● **symb.** Physics mutual inductance.

**m** ● **abbrev. 1** metre(s). **2** mile(s). **3** masculine. **4** (***m-***) Chemistry meta-. **5** milli-: *100 mA.* **6** million(s). **7** married. **8** minute(s). **9** mare. ● **symb.** Physics mass.

**m'** ● **possess. det.** Brit. short for **MY** (representing the pronunciation used by lawyers in court to refer to or address the judge or a fellow barrister on the same side).

**'m**[1] ● **abbrev.** informal am.

**'m**[2] ● **n.** informal madam.

**MA** ● **abbrev. 1** Massachusetts (in official postal use). **2** Master of Arts. **3** Morocco (international vehicle registration). [from Fr. *Maroc.*]

**ma** ● **n.** informal one's mother.

**ma'am** ● **n.** a respectful form of address for a woman, in particular for female royalty or (N. Amer. or archaic) any woman.

**maar** /mɑː/ ● **n.** Geology a broad, shallow crater formed by a volcanic explosion with little lava.
– ORIGIN C19: from Ger. dial.

**Maasai** ● **n. & adj.** variant spelling of **MASAI**.

**Mac** ● **n.** informal, chiefly N. Amer. a form of address for a man whose name is unknown to the speaker.
– ORIGIN C17 (orig. a form of address to a Scotsman): from *Mac-*, a patronymic prefix in many Scots and Ir. surnames.

**mac** (also **mack**) ● **n.** Brit. informal a mackintosh.

**macabre** /mə'kɑːbr(ə)/ ● **adj.** disturbing and horrifying because concerned with death and injury.
– ORIGIN C19: from Fr. *macabre*, from *Danse Macabre* 'dance of death', from OFr., perh. from *Macabé* 'a Maccabee', with ref. to a miracle play depicting the slaughter of the Maccabees.

**macadam** /mə'kadəm/ ● **n.** broken stone used in compacted layers for surfacing roads and paths, typically bound with tar or bitumen.
– DERIVATIVES **macadamed** adj. **macadamize** (also **-ise**) v.
– ORIGIN C19: named after the Brit. surveyor John L. *McAdam.*

**macadamia** /ˌmakə'deɪmɪə/ ● **n.** an Australian rainforest tree with slender, glossy evergreen leaves. [Genus *Macadamia*: several species.] ➤ the globular edible nut of this tree.
– ORIGIN mod. L., named after the C19 Austral. chemist John *Macadam.*

**Macanese** /ˌmakə'niːz/ ● **n.** (pl. same) **1** a native or inhabitant of Macao on the SE coast of China. **2** a Portuguese creole formerly used in Macao. ● **adj.** of or relating to Macao.

**macaque** /mə'kɑːk, -'kak/ ● **n.** a medium-sized monkey with a long face and cheek pouches for holding food. [Genus *Macaca*: several species.]
– ORIGIN C17: via Fr. and Port.; based on Bantu *ma-* (denoting a pl.) + *kaku* 'monkey'.

**macaroni** /ˌmakə'rəʊni/ ● **n.** (pl. **-ies**) **1** a variety of pasta formed in narrow tubes. **2** an 18th-century British dandy affecting Continental fashions.
– ORIGIN C16: from Ital. *maccaroni*, pl. of *maccarone*, from late Gk *makaria* 'food made from barley'.

**macaronic** /ˌmakə'rɒnɪk/ ● **adj.** denoting language, especially burlesque verse, containing words or inflections from one language introduced into the context of another. ● **n.** (**macaronics**) macaronic verse.
– ORIGIN C17 (in sense 'characteristic of a jumble'): from mod. L. *macaronicus*, from obs. Ital. *macaronico*, a humorous formation from *macaroni* (see **MACARONI**).

**macaroni cheese** ● **n.** a savoury dish of macaroni in a cheese sauce.

**macaroni penguin** ● **n.** a penguin with an orange crest, breeding on islands in the Antarctic. [*Eudyptes chrysolophus.*]
– ORIGIN C19: so named because the orange crest was thought to resemble the hairstyle of the *macaronies* (see **MACARONI** in sense 2).

**macaroon** /ˌmakə'ruːn/ ● **n.** a light biscuit made with egg white, sugar, and ground almonds or coconut.
– ORIGIN C16: from Fr. *macaron*, from Ital. *maccarone* (see **MACARONI**).

**Macassar** /mə'kasə/ (also **Macassar oil**) ● **n.** a kind of oil formerly used by men to make their hair shine and lie flat.
– ORIGIN C17: from *Makassar* (now Ujung Pandang) in Indonesia.

**Macassarese** ● **n. & adj.** archaic spelling of **MAKASARESE**.

**macaw** /mə'kɔː/ ● **n.** a large long-tailed parrot with brightly coloured plumage, native to Central and South America. [*Ara* and related genera: several species.]
– ORIGIN C17: from Port. *macau*, of unknown origin.

**Macc.** ● **abbrev.** Maccabees (Apocrypha) (in biblical references).

**Maccabees** /'makəbiːz/ ● **pl. n.** the followers or family of the 2nd-century Jewish leader Judas Maccabaeus.
– DERIVATIVES **Maccabean** /ˌmakə'biːən/ adj.

**McCarthyism** ● **n.** a campaign against alleged communists in the US government and other institutions carried out under Senator Joseph McCarthy from 1950–4.
– DERIVATIVES **McCarthyist** adj. & n. **McCarthyite** adj. & n.

**macchiato** /ˌmakɪ'ɑːtəʊ/ ● **n.** espresso coffee with a dash of frothy steamed milk.
– ORIGIN Ital., lit. 'stained, marked'.

**McCoy** ● **n.** (in phr. **the real McCoy**) informal the real thing; the genuine article.
– ORIGIN C19: origin uncertain: perh. from *the real Mackay*, an advertising slogan used by the whisky distillers G. Mackay and Co.; the form *McCoy* may come from the name of the Amer. inventor Elijah *McCoy.*

**Mace** ● **n.** trademark an irritant chemical used in an aerosol to disable attackers.

**mace**[1] ● **n. 1** historical a heavy club with a metal head and spikes. **2** a staff of office, especially that which lies on the table in the House of Commons when the Speaker is in the chair.
– ORIGIN ME: from OFr. *masse* 'large hammer'.

**mace**[2] ● **n.** the reddish fleshy outer covering of the nutmeg, dried as a spice.
– ORIGIN ME *macis* (taken as pl.), via OFr. from L. *macir.*

**macédoine** /'masɪdwɑːn/ ● **n.** a mixture of vegetables or fruit cut into small pieces or in jelly.
– ORIGIN Fr., lit. 'Macedonia', with ref. to the mixture of peoples in the Macedonian Empire of Alexander the

Great.

**Macedonian** ● n. **1** a native or inhabitant of the republic of Macedonia, of ancient Macedonia, or of the modern Greek region of Macedonia. **2** the Southern Slavic language of the republic of Macedonia and adjacent parts of Bulgaria. ● adj. of or relating to Macedonia or Macedonian.

**macer** /ˈmeɪsə/ ● n. (in Scotland) an official who keeps order in a law court.
– ORIGIN ME: from OFr. *massier*, from *masse* (see MACE[1]).

**macerate** /ˈmasəreɪt/ ● v. **1** soften or break up (food) by soaking in a liquid. **2** archaic cause to grow thinner or waste away.
– DERIVATIVES **maceration** n. **macerator** n.
– ORIGIN C16: from L. *macerat-*, *macerare* 'make soft, soak'.

**macfarlane** /məkˈfɑːlən/ ● n. dated a type of overcoat with a shoulder cape and slits for access to pockets in clothing worn underneath.
– ORIGIN 1920s: prob. from the name of the designer or original manufacturer of the coat.

**McGuffin** ● n. an object or device in a film or a book which serves merely as a trigger for the plot.
– ORIGIN C20: a Scottish surname, said to have been borrowed by the Engl. film director Alfred Hitchcock.

**Mach** /mɑːk, mak/ (also **Mach number**) ● n. the ratio of the speed of a body to the speed of sound in the surrounding medium, used with a numeral (as **Mach 1**, **Mach 2**, etc.) to indicate the speed of sound, twice the speed of sound, etc.
– ORIGIN 1930s: named after the Austrian physicist Ernst *Mach*.

**machair** /ˈmakə, ˈmaxə/ ● n. (in Scotland) low-lying land formed near the coast from sand and shell fragments deposited by the wind.
– ORIGIN C17: from Sc. Gaelic.

**mache** /mɑːʃ/ ● n. another term for LAMB'S LETTUCE.
– ORIGIN C17: from Fr. *mâche*.

**macher** /ˈmaxə/ ● n. US informal, chiefly derogatory an important or overbearing person.
– ORIGIN 1930s: from Yiddish *makher*, from Mid. High Ger. *Macher* 'doer, active person'.

**machete** /məˈtʃɛti, -ˈʃɛti/ ● n. a broad, heavy knife used as an implement or weapon.
– ORIGIN C16: from Sp., from *macho* 'hammer'.

**Machiavellian** /ˌmakɪəˈvɛlɪən/ ● adj. cunning, scheming, and unscrupulous, especially in politics or business. ● n. (also **Machiavelli**) a Machiavellian person.
– DERIVATIVES **Machiavellianism** n.
– ORIGIN from the name of the Ital. statesman and writer Niccolò *Machiavelli*, whose work *The Prince* (1532) advises that the acquisition and use of power may necessitate unethical methods.

**machicolate** /məˈtʃɪkəleɪt/ ● v. [usu. as adj. **machicolated**] provide with machicolations.
– ORIGIN C18: from Anglo-Latin *machicollare*, based on Provençal *machacol*, from *macar* 'to crush' + *col* 'neck'.

**machicolation** ● n. (in medieval fortifications) an opening between the supporting corbels of a projecting structure, through which stones or burning objects could be dropped on attackers. ➤a projecting structure containing machicolations.

**machinable** /məˈʃiːnəb(ə)l/ ● adj. (of a material) able to be worked by a machine tool.
– DERIVATIVES **machinability** n.

**machinate** /ˈmakɪneɪt, ˈmaʃ-/ ● v. engage in plots and intrigues; scheme.
– DERIVATIVES **machination** n. **machinator** n.
– ORIGIN C16 (earlier (ME) as *machination*): from L. *machinat-*, *machinari* 'contrive', from *machina* (see MACHINE).

**machine** ● n. **1** an apparatus using or applying mechanical power and having several parts, each with a definite function and together performing a particular task. ➤technical any device that transmits a force or directs its application. **2** an efficient and well-organized group of powerful people: *the party machine.* **3** a person who acts with the mechanical efficiency of a machine. ● v. make or operate on with a machine. ➤Brit. sew or make with a sewing machine.
– ORIGIN C16: from Fr., via L. from Doric Gk *makhana* (Gk *mēkhanē*, from *mēkhos* 'contrivance').

**machine code** (also **machine language**) ● n. a computer programming language consisting of binary or hexadecimal instructions which a computer can respond to directly.

**machine gun** ● n. an automatic gun that fires bullets in rapid succession for as long as the trigger is pressed. ● v. (**machine-gun**) shoot with a machine gun.
– DERIVATIVES **machine-gunner** n.

**machine head** ● n. each of the small pegs on the head of a guitar, used for tightening the strings.

**machine-readable** ● adj. (of data or text) in a form that a computer can process.

**machinery** ● n. **1** machines collectively, or the components of a machine. **2** the organization or structure of something: *the machinery of the state.*

**machine screw** ● n. a fastening device similar to a bolt but having a socket in its head which allows it to be turned with a screwdriver.

**machine tool** ● n. a non-portable powered tool for cutting or shaping metal, wood, etc.
– DERIVATIVES **machine-tooled** adj.

**machine translation** ● n. translation carried out by a computer.

**machinist** ● n. **1** a person who operates a machine, especially a machine tool or (Brit.) a sewing machine. **2** a person who makes machinery.

**machismo** /məˈtʃɪzməʊ, -ˈkɪz-/ ● n. strong or aggressive masculine pride.
– ORIGIN 1940s: from Mex. Sp., from *macho* 'male'.

**Machmeter** /ˈmɑːkmiːtə, ˈmak-/ ● n. an instrument in an aircraft indicating airspeed as a Mach number.

**macho** /ˈmatʃəʊ/ ● adj. showing aggressive pride in one's masculinity. ● n. machismo.
– ORIGIN 1920s: from Mex. Sp., 'masculine or vigorous'.

**Mach's principle** ● n. Physics the hypothesis that a body's inertial mass results from its interaction with the rest of the matter in the universe.

**Machtpolitik** /ˈmɑːxtpɒlɪˌtiːk/ ● n. power politics.
– ORIGIN from Ger.

**macintosh** ● n. variant spelling of MACKINTOSH.

**McIntosh** (also **McIntosh red**) ● n. a dessert apple of a Canadian variety with deep red skin.
– ORIGIN C19: named after the Canad. farmer John *McIntosh* on whose farm the apple was discovered.

**McJob** /məkˈdʒɒb/ ● n. a low-paid job with few prospects, typically one taken by an overqualified person.

**mack** ● n. variant spelling of MAC.

**mackerel** ● n. (pl. same or **mackerels**) a surface-dwelling marine fish with a greenish-blue back, commercially important as a food fish. [*Scomber scombrus* (N. Atlantic) and other species.]
– ORIGIN ME: from OFr. *maquerel*, of unknown origin.

**mackerel shark** ● n. another term for PORBEAGLE.

**mackerel sky** ● n. a sky dappled with rows of small white fleecy (typically cirrocumulus) clouds, like the pattern on a mackerel's back.

**mackinaw** /ˈmakɪnɔː/ (also **mackinaw coat** or **jacket**) ● n. chiefly N. Amer. a short coat or jacket made of a thick, heavy woollen cloth.
– ORIGIN C19: named after *Mackinaw* City, Michigan.

**mackintosh** (also **macintosh**) ● n. Brit. a full-length waterproof coat.
– ORIGIN C19: named after the Sc. inventor Charles *Macintosh*.

**mackle** /ˈmak(ə)l/ ● n. a blurred impression in printing.
– ORIGIN C16: from Fr. *macule*, from L. *macula* 'stain'.

**macle** /ˈmak(ə)l/ ● n. **1** a diamond or other crystal that is twinned. **2** another term for CHIASTOLITE.
– ORIGIN C19: from Fr., from Anglo-Latin *mascula* 'mesh'.

**macramé** /məˈkrɑːmi/ ● n. the craft of knotting cord or string in patterns to make decorative articles.
– ORIGIN C19: Fr., from Turk. *makrama* 'tablecloth or towel', from Arab. *miḳrama* 'bedspread'.

**macro** ● n. (pl. **-os**) **1** (also **macro instruction**) Computing a single instruction that expands automatically into a set of instructions to perform a particular task. **2** Photography a macro lens. ● adj. large-scale; overall.

**macro-** ● comb. form **1** long; over a long period: *macroevolution*. **2** large or large-scale: *macromolecule*.
– ORIGIN from Gk *makros* 'long, large'.

**macrobiotic** /ˌmakrə(ʊ)bʌɪˈɒtɪk/ ● adj. relating to or denoting a diet of whole pure prepared foods which is based on Buddhist principles of the balance of yin and yang. ● n. (**macrobiotics**) [treated as sing.] the use or theory of such a diet.

**macrocarpa** /ˌmakrə(ʊ)ˈkɑːpə/ ● n. a Californian cypress tree with a large spreading crown of horizontal branches and leaves that smell of lemon when crushed. [*Cupressus macrocarpa*.]
– ORIGIN C20: mod. L., from **MACRO-** + Gk *karpos* 'fruit'.

**macrocephalic** /ˌmakrə(ʊ)sɪˈfalɪk, -kɛˈfalɪk-/ (also **macrocephalous**) ● adj. Anatomy having an unusually large head.
– DERIVATIVES **macrocephaly** n.

**macrocosm** /ˈmakrə(ʊ)kɒz(ə)m/ ● n. **1** the universe; the cosmos. **2** the whole of a complex structure, especially as represented or epitomized in a small part of itself (a microcosm).
– DERIVATIVES **macrocosmic** adj. **macrocosmically** adv.

**macrocyclic** /ˌmakrə(ʊ)ˈsʌɪklɪk, -ˈsɪk-/ ● adj. Chemistry relating to or denoting a ring composed of a relatively large number of atoms.
– DERIVATIVES **macrocycle** n.

**macroeconomics** ● pl. n. [treated as sing.] the part of economics concerned with large-scale or general economic factors, such as interest rates and national productivity.
– DERIVATIVES **macroeconomic** adj.

**macroeconomy** ● n. a large-scale economic system.

**macroevolution** ● n. Biology major evolutionary change, in particular the evolution of whole taxonomic groups over long periods of time.
– DERIVATIVES **macroevolutionary** adj.

**macro lens** ● n. Photography a lens suitable for taking photographs unusually close to the subject.

**macrolepidoptera** /ˌmakrəʊlɛpɪˈdɒpt(ə)rə/ ● pl. n. Entomology the butterflies and larger moths, comprising those of interest to the general collector.

**macromolecule** ● n. Chemistry a molecule containing a very large number of atoms, such as a protein, nucleic acid, or synthetic polymer.
– DERIVATIVES **macromolecular** adj.

**macron** /ˈmakrɒn/ ● n. a written or printed mark (¯) used to indicate a long vowel in some languages and phonetic transcription systems, or a stressed vowel in verse.
– ORIGIN C19: from Gk *makron*, neut. of *makros* 'long'.

**macronutrient** ● n. Biology a substance required in relatively large amounts by living organisms.

**macrophage** /ˈmakrə(ʊ)feɪdʒ/ ● n. Physiology a large phagocytic cell found in stationary form in the tissues or as a mobile white blood cell, especially at sites of infection.

**macrophotography** ● n. the photography of small items larger than life size.

**macrophyte** /ˈmakrə(ʊ)fʌɪt/ ● n. Botany a plant, especially an aquatic plant, large enough to be seen by the naked eye.

**macropod** /ˈmakrə(ʊ)pɒd/ ● n. Zoology a plant-eating marsupial mammal of an Australasian family (Macropodidae) that comprises the kangaroos and wallabies.
– ORIGIN C19: from mod. L. *Macropodidae*, from **MACRO-** + Gk *pous, pod-* 'foot'.

**macroscopic** /ˌmakrə(ʊ)ˈskɒpɪk/ ● adj. **1** visible to the naked eye; not microscopic. **2** of or relating to large-scale or general analysis.
– DERIVATIVES **macroscopically** adv.

**macrostructure** ● n. the large-scale or overall structure of something, e.g. an organism, a mechanical construction, or a written text.
– DERIVATIVES **macrostructural** adj.

**macula** /ˈmakjʊlə/ ● n. (pl. **maculae** /-liː/) **1** another term for **MACULE**. **2** (also **macula lutea**) /ˈluːtɪə/ (pl. **maculae luteae**) /-tɪiː/ Anatomy an oval yellowish area surrounding the fovea near the centre of the retina in the eye, which is the region of greatest visual acuity.
– DERIVATIVES **macular** adj.
– ORIGIN ME: from L., 'spot'.

**maculate** /ˈmakjʊleɪt/ poetic/literary ● adj. spotted or stained. ● v. mark with a spot or spots; stain.
– DERIVATIVES **maculation** n.
– ORIGIN ME: from L. *maculat-*, *maculare* 'to stain', from *macula* 'spot'.

**macule** /ˈmakjuːl/ ● n. a distinct spot, such as a discoloured spot on the skin.
– ORIGIN C15: from Fr., or from L. *macula* 'spot'.

**macumba** /məˈkʊmbə/ ● n. a religious cult practised by black people in Brazil, using sorcery, ritual dance, and fetishes.
– ORIGIN from Port.

**macushla** /məˈkʊʃlə/ ● n. a fond Irish form of address.
– ORIGIN from Ir. *mo* 'my' + *cuisle* 'pulse' (see also **ACUSHLA**).

**mad** ● adj. (**madder**, **maddest**) **1** mentally ill; insane. ➤extremely foolish or ill-advised. ➤(of a dog) rabid. **2** informal frenzied. ➤very enthusiastic about something: *he's football-mad*. **3** informal very angry. ● v. (**madded**, **madding**) archaic make mad or insane.
– PHRASES **like mad** informal with great intensity, energy, or enthusiasm. **mad keen** informal extremely enthusiastic.
– DERIVATIVES **madly** adv. **madness** n.
– ORIGIN OE *gemǣd(e)d* 'maddened', participial form rel. to *gemād* 'mad', of Gmc origin.

**Madagascan** /ˌmadəˈgaskən/ ● n. a native or inhabitant of Madagascar. ● adj. of or relating to Madagascar.

**madam** ● n. **1** a polite form of address for a woman. **2** Brit. informal a conceited or precocious girl. **3** a female brothel-keeper.
– ORIGIN ME: from OFr. *ma dame* 'my lady'.

**Madame** /məˈdɑːm, ˈmadəm, French madam/ ● n. (pl. **Mesdames**) a title or form of address for a French-speaking woman.
– ORIGIN Fr.; cf. **MADAM**.

**madarosis** /ˌmadəˈrəʊsɪs/ ● n. Medicine absence or loss of the eyelashes (and sometimes the eyebrows) as a congenital condition or through an infection.
– ORIGIN C17: mod. L., from Gk, 'baldness'.

**madcap** ● adj. amusingly eccentric. ➤crazy or reckless. ● n. an eccentric person.

**mad cow disease** ● n. informal term for **BSE**.

**madden** ● v. **1** drive (someone) insane. **2** [often as adj. **maddening**] irritate or annoy greatly.
– DERIVATIVES **maddeningly** adv.

**madder** ● n. a plant related to the bedstraws, with roots that yield a red dye. [*Rubia tinctorum* and other species.] ➤a red dye or pigment obtained from this plant.
– ORIGIN OE *mædere*, of Gmc origin.

**madding** ● adj. poetic/literary **1** acting madly; frenzied. **2** maddening.

**made** past and past participle of **MAKE**.

**Madeira** /məˈdɪərə/ ● n. a fortified white wine from the island of Madeira.

**Madeira cake** ● n. Brit. a close-textured, rich kind of sponge cake.

**Madeiran** /məˈdɪərən/ ● n. a native or inhabitant of Madeira. ● adj. of or relating to Madeira.

**madeleine** /ˈmadleɪn, ˈmad(ə)lɛn/ ● n. a small rich sponge cake, often decorated with coconut and jam.
– ORIGIN Fr., prob. named after *Madeleine* Paulmier, C19 Fr. pastry cook.

**made man** ● n. N. Amer. a man whose success in life is assured.

**Mademoiselle** /ˌmadəmwəˈzɛl, French madmwazɛl/ ● n. (pl. **Mesdemoiselles**) **1** a title or form of address for an unmarried French-speaking woman. **2** (**mademoiselle**) a young Frenchwoman. ➤dated a French governess.
– ORIGIN Fr., from *ma* 'my' + *demoiselle* 'damsel'.

**made road** ● n. Brit. a road surfaced with a material such as tarmac or concrete.

**made to measure** ● **adj.** chiefly Brit. (of clothes) specially made to fit a particular person.

**made to order** ● **adj.** specially made according to a customer's specifications.

**made-up** ● **adj. 1** wearing make-up. **2** invented; untrue.

**madhouse** ● **n. 1** historical a mental institution. ➤ informal a psychiatric hospital. **2** informal a scene of extreme confusion or uproar.

**Madison** /'madɪs(ə)n/ ● **n.** an energetic group dance popular in the 1960s.
– ORIGIN of unknown origin.

**madman** (or **madwoman**) ● **n.** (pl. **-men** or **-women**) a person who is mentally ill. ➤ a foolish or reckless person.

**Madonna** ● **n.** (**the Madonna**) the Virgin Mary.
– ORIGIN C16 (as a respectful form of address for an Ital. woman): Ital., from *ma* (old form of *mia* 'my') + *donna* 'lady' (from L. *domina*).

**madonna lily** ● **n.** a tall white-flowered lily with golden pollen, often depicted in paintings of the Madonna. [*Lilium candidum*.]

**madras** /mə'drɑːs, -'dras/ ● **n. 1** a strong cotton fabric, typically patterned with colourful stripes or checks. **2** a hot spiced curry dish.
– ORIGIN C19: by assoc. with the Indian city of *Madras*.

**madrasa** /mə'drasə/ (also **madrasah** or **medrese**) ● **n.** a college for Islamic instruction.
– ORIGIN Arab., from *darasa* 'to study'.

**Madreporaria** /ˌmadrɛpə'rɛːrɪə/ ● **pl. n.** Zoology another term for **Scleractinia**.
– DERIVATIVES **madreporarian** n. & adj. **madrepore** n. (dated).
– ORIGIN mod. L., from *Madrepora* (genus name), from Ital., prob. from *madre* 'mother', with ref. to the prolific growth of the coral.

**madrigal** /'madrɪg(ə)l/ ● **n.** a 16th- or 17th-century part song for several voices, typically unaccompanied and arranged in elaborate counterpoint.
– DERIVATIVES **madrigalian** /-'geɪlɪən/ adj. **madrigalist** n.
– ORIGIN from Ital. *madrigale*, from med. L. *carmen matricale* 'simple song'.

**madrilene** /ˌmadrɪ'liːn, -'lɛn/ ● **n.** a clear soup, usually served cold.
– ORIGIN from Fr. (*consommé à la*) *madrilène*, lit. 'soup in the Madrid style'.

**Madrileño** /ˌmadrɪ'lɛnjəʊ/ ● **n.** (pl. **-os**) a native or inhabitant of Madrid.
– DERIVATIVES **Madrilenian** /ˌmadrɪ'leɪnɪən/ n. & adj.

**madroño** /mə'drəʊnjəʊ/ (also **madroña** /-njə/) ● **n.** (pl. **-os**) an evergreen tree related to the strawberry tree, with white flowers, red berries, and glossy leaves. [*Arbutus menziesii*.]
– ORIGIN C19: from Sp.

**Madurese** /ˌmadjʊ'riːz/ ● **n.** (pl. same) **1** a native or inhabitant of the island of Madura in Indonesia. **2** the Indonesian language of Madura and nearby parts of Java. ● **adj.** of or relating to the inhabitants of Madura or their language.

**Maecenas** /mʌɪ'siːnəs/ ● **n.** a generous patron of literature or art.
– ORIGIN C16: from the name of Gaius *Maecenas* (*c.*70–8 BC), Roman statesman and patron of poets.

**maelstrom** /'meɪlstrəm/ ● **n. 1** a powerful whirlpool. **2** a scene of confused movement or upheaval.
– ORIGIN C17: from early mod. Du., from *maalen* 'grind, whirl' + *stroom* 'stream'.

**maenad** /'miːnad/ ● **n.** (in ancient Greece) a female follower of Bacchus, traditionally associated with divine possession and frenzied rites.
– DERIVATIVES **maenadic** adj.
– ORIGIN C16: via L. from Gk *Mainas*, *Mainad-*, from *mainesthai* 'to rave'.

**maestoso** /mʌɪ'stəʊzəʊ, -səʊ/ ● **adv. & adj.** Music in a majestic manner.
– ORIGIN from Ital.

**maestro** /'mʌɪstrəʊ/ ● **n.** (pl. **maestri** /-stri/ or **maestros**) **1** a distinguished conductor or performer of classical music. **2** a distinguished figure in any sphere.
– ORIGIN C18: Ital., 'master', from L. *magister*.

**Mae West** ● **n.** informal, dated an inflatable life jacket, originally as issued to RAF personnel during the Second World War.
– ORIGIN 1940s: from the name of the Amer. film actress *Mae West*, noted for her large bust.

**MAFF** ● **abbrev.** (in the UK) Ministry of Agriculture, Fisheries, and Food.

**Mafia** /'mafɪə/ ● **n.** [treated as sing. or pl.] **1** (**the Mafia**) an organized international body of criminals originating in Sicily and having a complex and ruthless behavioural code. **2** (usu. **mafia**) a group exerting a hidden sinister influence: *the British literary mafia.*
– ORIGIN Ital. (Sicilian dial.), orig. in the sense 'bragging'.

**mafic** /'mafɪk/ ● **adj.** Geology relating to or denoting a group of dark-coloured, mainly ferromagnesian minerals such as pyroxene and olivine. Often contrasted with **felsic**.
– ORIGIN C20: blend of **magnesium** and **ferric**.

**Mafioso** /ˌmafɪ'əʊzəʊ, -səʊ/ ● **n.** (pl. **Mafiosi** /-zi, -si/) a member of the Mafia.

**mag**[1] ● **n.** informal **1** a magazine. **2** magnesium or magnesium alloy. **3** a magneto. **4** magnitude (of stars or other celestial objects).

**mag**[2] Austral./NZ informal ● **v.** chatter incessantly. ● **n.** a gossip or chat.
– ORIGIN C19: orig. Engl. dial.; rel. to **magpie**.

**Magahi** /'mʌgəhi/ ● **n.** a Bihari language spoken in central Bihar and West Bengal.
– ORIGIN from Hindi *Magadhī* 'of Magadha'.

**magazine** ● **n. 1** a periodical publication containing articles and illustrations. ➤ a regular television or radio programme comprising a variety of items. **2** a chamber for holding a supply of cartridges to be fed automatically to the breech of a gun. **3** a store for arms, ammunition, and explosives.
– ORIGIN C16: from Fr. *magasin*, from Ital. *magazzino*, from Arab. *makzin*, *makzan* 'storehouse'.

**magdalen** /'magdəlɪn/ ● **n. 1** (**the Magdalen** or **the Magdalene**) St Mary Magdalene, to whom Jesus appeared after his resurrection. **2** archaic a reformed prostitute.

**Magdalenian** /ˌmagdə'liːnɪən/ ● **adj.** Archaeology relating to or denoting the final Palaeolithic culture in Europe, following the Solutrean and dated to about 17,000–11,500 years ago.
– ORIGIN C19: from Fr. *Magdalénien* 'from La Madeleine', a site in the Dordogne, France, where objects from this culture were found.

**Magdeburg hemispheres** ● **pl. n.** a pair of copper or brass hemispheres joined to form a hollow globe from which the air can be extracted to demonstrate the pressure of the atmosphere, which then prevents them from being pulled apart.
– ORIGIN C19: named after the German city of *Magdeburg*, where they were invented.

**mage** /meɪdʒ/ ● **n.** archaic or poetic/literary a magician or learned person.
– ORIGIN ME: anglicized form of L. *magus* (see **magus**).

**Magen David** /mɑːˌgɛn dɑː'viːd/ ● **n.** a hexagram used as a symbol of Judaism.
– ORIGIN C20: Heb., lit. 'shield of David', with ref. to David, King of Israel.

**magenta** /mə'dʒɛntə/ ● **n. 1** a light mauvish-crimson which is one of the primary subtractive colours, complementary to green. **2** the dye fuchsin.
– ORIGIN C19: named after *Magenta* in northern Italy, site of a battle (1859) fought shortly before the dye (of bloodlike colour) was discovered.

**Maggid** /'mɑːgɪd/ ● **n.** (pl. **Maggidim** /-ɪm/) an itinerant Jewish preacher.
– ORIGIN C19: from Heb. *maggīd* 'narrator'.

**maggot** ● **n. 1** a soft-bodied legless larva, especially that of a fly or other insect and found in decaying matter. **2** archaic a whimsical fancy.
– DERIVATIVES **maggoty** adj.

– ORIGIN ME: perh. an alt. of dial. *maddock*, from ON *mathkr*, of Gmc origin.

**magi** plural form of **MAGUS**. ● **pl. n.** (**the Magi**) the three wise men from the East who brought gifts to the infant Jesus (Matt. 2:1).
– DERIVATIVES **Magian** adj. & n.

**magic** ● **n. 1** the power of apparently influencing the course of events by using mysterious or supernatural forces. ➤mysterious tricks performed as entertainment. **2** a mysterious and enchanting quality. ➤informal exceptional skill or talent. ● **adj. 1** having or apparently having supernatural powers. **2** informal very exciting or good. ● **v.** (**magicked**, **magicking**) move, change, or create by or as if by magic.
– DERIVATIVES **magical** adj. **magically** adv.
– ORIGIN ME: from OFr. *magique*, from L. *magicus* (adj.), late L. *magica* (n.), from Gk *magikē* (*tekhnē*) '(art of) a magus'.

**magical realism** ● **n.** another term for **MAGIC REALISM**.

**magic bullet** ● **n.** informal a medicine or other remedy, especially a hypothetical one, with advanced and highly specific properties.

**magic carpet** ● **n.** a mythical carpet that is able to transport people through the air.

**magic circle** ● **n.** a small group of people privileged to receive confidential information or make important decisions.

**magic eye** ● **n. 1** informal a photoelectric cell or similar electrical device used for identification, detection, or measurement. **2** a small cathode ray tube in some radio receivers that displays a pattern which enables the radio to be accurately tuned.

**magician** ● **n.** a person with magical powers. ➤a conjuror.

**magick** ● **n.** archaic spelling of **MAGIC**.
– DERIVATIVES **magickal** adj.

**magic lantern** ● **n.** historical a simple form of image projector used for showing photographic slides.

**Magic Marker** ● **n.** trademark an indelible marker pen.

**magic mushroom** ● **n.** informal a toadstool with hallucinogenic properties, especially the liberty cap and its relatives.

**magic realism** (also **magical realism**) ● **n.** a literary or artistic genre in which realistic narrative and naturalistic technique are combined with surreal elements of dream or fantasy.
– DERIVATIVES **magic realist** n. & adj.

**magic square** ● **n.** a square divided into smaller squares each containing a number, such that the figures in each vertical, horizontal, and diagonal row add up to the same value.

**magilp** ● **n.** variant spelling of **MEGILP**.

**magister** /ˈmadʒɪstə, məˈdʒɪstə/ ● **n.** archaic a title or form of address for a scholar, especially one teaching in a medieval university.
– ORIGIN ME: from L., 'master'.

**magisterial** /ˌmadʒɪˈstɪərɪəl/ ● **adj. 1** having or showing great authority. ➤domineering; dictatorial. **2** relating to or conducted by a magistrate.
– DERIVATIVES **magisterially** adv.

**magisterium** /ˌmadʒɪˈstɪərɪəm/ ● **n.** the teaching or authority of the Roman Catholic Church, especially as exercised by bishops or the Pope.
– ORIGIN C19: L., 'the office of master', from *magister* (see **MAGISTER**).

**magistracy** /ˈmadʒɪstrəsi/ ● **n.** (pl. **-ies**) the office or authority of a magistrate. ➤(**the magistracy**) magistrates collectively.

**magistral** /ˈmadʒɪstr(ə)l, məˈdʒɪstr(ə)l/ ● **adj.** formal or archaic relating to a master or masters.

**magistrand** /ˈmadʒɪstrand/ ● **n.** Scottish a final-year undergraduate (now only at the University of St Andrews).
– ORIGIN C17: from med. L. *magistrandus* 'someone who is suitable to become a Master of Arts'.

**magistrate** /ˈmadʒɪstrət, -streɪt/ ● **n.** a civil officer or lay judge who administers the law, especially one who conducts a court concerned with minor offences and holds preliminary hearings for more serious ones.
– DERIVATIVES **magistrature** /-trətʃə/ n.
– ORIGIN ME: from L. *magistratus* 'administrator', from *magister* 'master'.

**Maglemosian** /ˌmagləˈməʊsɪən, -z-/ ● **adj.** Archaeology relating to or denoting a northern European Mesolithic culture, dated to about 9,500–7,700 years ago.
– ORIGIN C20: from *Maglemose*, the name of a town in Denmark where objects from this culture were found, + **-IAN**.

**maglev** /ˈmaglɛv/ ● **n.** a transport system in which trains glide above a track, supported by magnetic repulsion and propelled by a linear motor.
– ORIGIN C20: from *mag(netic) lev(itation)*.

**magma** /ˈmagmə/ ● **n. 1** hot fluid or semi-fluid material within the earth's crust from which lava and other igneous rock is formed by cooling. **2** dated, chiefly US a fluid medicinal suspension of a solid.
– DERIVATIVES **magmatic** adj.
– ORIGIN ME (in the sense 'residue left after evaporation or pressing of a semi-liquid substance'): via L. from Gk *magma* (from *massein* 'knead').

**magmatism** ● **n.** Geology the motion or activity of magma.

**magna cum laude** /ˌmagnə kʌm ˈlɔːdi, ˌmagnɑː kʊm ˈlaʊdeɪ/ ● **adv. & adj.** chiefly N. Amer. with great distinction (with reference to university degrees and diplomas).
– ORIGIN L., lit. 'with great praise'.

**magnanimous** /magˈnanɪməs/ ● **adj.** very generous or forgiving, especially towards a rival or less powerful person.
– DERIVATIVES **magnanimity** /ˌmagnəˈnɪmɪti/ n. **magnanimously** adv.
– ORIGIN C16: from L. *magnanimus* (from *magnus* 'great' + *animus* 'soul') + **-OUS**.

**magnate** /ˈmagneɪt/ ● **n.** a wealthy and influential person, especially in business.
– ORIGIN ME: from late L. *magnas*, *magnat-* 'great man', from L. *magnus* 'great'.

**magnesia** /magˈniːʒə, -zɪə, -ʃə/ ● **n.** Chemistry magnesium oxide. [MgO.] ➤hydrated magnesium carbonate used as an antacid and laxative.
– DERIVATIVES **magnesian** adj.
– ORIGIN ME: via med. L. from Gk *Magnēsia*, denoting a mineral from Magnesia in Asia Minor.

**magnesite** /ˈmagnɪsʌɪt/ ● **n.** a whitish mineral consisting of magnesium carbonate, used as a refractory lining in furnaces.

**magnesium** /magˈniːzɪəm/ ● **n.** the chemical element of atomic number 12, a silver-white metal of the alkaline earth series. (Symbol: **Mg**)

**magnesium flare** (also **magnesium light**) ● **n.** a brilliant white flare containing metallic magnesium wire or ribbon.

**magnet** ● **n. 1** a piece of iron or other material, typically in the form of a bar or horseshoe, that has the property of attracting similar objects or aligning itself in an external magnetic field. **2** a person or thing that has a powerful attraction.
– ORIGIN ME: from L. *magnes*, *magnet-*, from Gk *magnēs lithos* 'lodestone', prob. influenced by Anglo-Norman Fr. *magnete*.

**magnetic** ● **adj. 1** exhibiting magnetism. **2** (of a bearing in navigation) measured relative to magnetic north. **3** very attractive or alluring.
– DERIVATIVES **magnetically** adv.

**magnetic equator** ● **n.** the irregular imaginary line, passing round the earth near the equator, on which a magnetic needle has no dip.

**magnetic field** ● **n.** a region around a magnetic material or a moving electric charge within which the force of magnetism acts.

**magnetic inclination** ● **n.** another term for **DIP** (in sense 4).

**magnetic induction** • n. **1** magnetic flux or flux density. **2** the process by which an object or material is magnetized by an external magnetic field.

**magnetic mine** • n. a mine detonated by the proximity of a magnetized body such as a ship or tank.

**magnetic moment** • n. Physics the property of a magnet that interacts with an applied field to give a mechanical moment.

**magnetic needle** • n. a piece of magnetized steel used as an indicator on the dial of a compass and in magnetic and electrical apparatus.

**magnetic north** • n. the direction in which the north end of a compass needle or other freely suspended magnet will point in response to the earth's magnetic field.

**magnetic pole** • n. **1** each of the points near the extremities of the axis of rotation of the earth where a magnetic needle dips vertically. **2** each of the two points or regions of a magnet to and from which the lines of magnetic force are directed.

**magnetic resonance imaging** • n. a technique for producing images of bodily organs by measuring the response of atomic nuclei to radio waves when placed in a strong magnetic field.

**magnetic storm** • n. a disturbance of the magnetic field of the earth.

**magnetic tape** • n. tape used in recording sound, pictures, or computer data.

**magnetism** • n. **1** a physical phenomenon produced by the motion of electric charge, which results in attractive and repulsive forces between objects. **2** the ability to attract and charm people.

**magnetite** /ˈmagnɪtʌɪt/ • n. a grey-black magnetic mineral which consists of an oxide of iron and is an important form of iron ore.

**magnetize** (also **-ise**) • v. make magnetic.
– DERIVATIVES **magnetizable** adj. **magnetization** n. **magnetizer** n.

**magneto** • n. (pl. **-os**) a small electric generator containing a permanent magnet and used to provided high-voltage pulses, especially (formerly) in the ignition systems of internal-combustion engines.

**magneto-** /magˈniːtəʊ/ • comb. form relating to a magnet or magnetism: *magneto-electric*.

**magneto-electric** • adj. of or relating to electric currents generated in a material by its motion in a magnetic field.
– DERIVATIVES **magneto-electricity** n.

**magnetograph** • n. an instrument for recording measurements of magnetic forces.

**magnetohydrodynamics** /mag,niːtəʊ,hʌɪdrə(ʊ)dʌɪˈnamɪks/ • pl. n. [treated as sing.] the branch of physics concerned with the behaviour of an electrically conducting fluid (such as a plasma or molten metal) acted on by a magnetic field.
– DERIVATIVES **magnetohydrodynamic** adj.

**magnetometer** /ˌmagnɪˈtɒmɪtə/ • n. an instrument used for measuring magnetic forces, especially the earth's magnetism.
– DERIVATIVES **magnetometry** n.

**magnetomotive force** /mag,niːtə(ʊ)ˈməʊtɪv/ • n. Physics a quantity representing the sum of the magnetizing forces along a circuit.

**magneton** /ˈmagnɪtɒn/ • n. a unit of magnetic moment in atomic and nuclear physics.

**magnetopause** • n. the outer limit of a magnetosphere.

**magnetoresistance** • n. Physics the dependence of the electrical resistance of a body on an external magnetic field.
– DERIVATIVES **magnetoresistive** adj.

**magnetosphere** • n. the region surrounding the earth or another astronomical body in which its magnetic field is the predominant effective magnetic field.
– DERIVATIVES **magnetospheric** adj.

**magnetotail** • n. Astronomy the broad elongated extension of the earth's magnetosphere on the side away from the sun.

**magnetron** /ˈmagnɪtrɒn/ • n. an electron tube for amplifying or generating microwaves, with the flow of electrons controlled by an external magnetic field.

**Magnificat** /magˈnɪfɪkat/ • n. the hymn of the Virgin Mary (Luke 1:46–55) used as a canticle, especially at vespers and evensong.
– ORIGIN ME: L., lit. 'magnifies', from the opening words, which translate as 'my soul magnifies the Lord'.

**magnificence** • n. **1** the quality of being magnificent. **2** (**His/Your** etc. **Magnificence**) a title or form of address for a monarch or other distinguished person.

**magnificent** • adj. **1** impressively beautiful, elaborate, or extravagant. **2** very good; excellent.
– DERIVATIVES **magnificently** adv.
– ORIGIN ME: via OFr. from L. *magnificent-* 'making great, serving to magnify', based on *magnus* 'great'.

**magnifico** /magˈnɪfɪkəʊ/ informal • n. (pl. **-oes**) an eminent, powerful, or illustrious person. • adj. magnificent.
– ORIGIN C16: Ital., 'magnificent', orig. used to denote a Venetian magnate.

**magnify** • v. (**-ies**, **-ied**) **1** make (something) appear larger than it is, especially with a lens or microscope. ➤ intensify or exaggerate. **2** archaic extol; glorify.
– DERIVATIVES **magnification** n. **magnifier** n.
– ORIGIN ME: from OFr. *magnifier* or L. *magnificare*, based on L. *magnus* 'great'.

**magnifying glass** • n. a lens that produces an enlarged image, used to examine small or finely detailed things.

**magniloquent** /magˈnɪləkwənt/ • adj. using high-flown or bombastic language.
– DERIVATIVES **magniloquence** n. **magniloquently** adv.

**magnitude** /ˈmagnɪtjuːd/ • n. **1** great size, extent, or importance. **2** size. **3** Astronomy the brightness of a star, as represented by a number on a logarithmic scale.
– ORIGIN ME: from L. *magnitudo*, from *magnus* 'great'.

**magnolia** /magˈnəʊlɪə/ • n. **1** a tree or shrub with large, typically creamy-pink, waxy flowers. [Genus *Magnolia*.] **2** a pale creamy-white colour like that of magnolia blossom.
– ORIGIN mod. L., named after the C17 Fr. botanist Pierre *Magnol*.

**magnox** /ˈmagnɒks/ • n. a magnesium-based alloy used to enclose uranium fuel elements in some nuclear reactors.
– ORIGIN 1950s: from the phr. *mag(nesium) n(o) ox(idation)*.

**magnum** /ˈmagnəm/ • n. (pl. **magnums**) **1** a wine bottle of twice the standard size, normally 1½ litres. **2** (trademark in the US) a gun designed to fire cartridges that are more powerful than its calibre would suggest.
– ORIGIN C18: from L., neut. (used as n.) of *magnus* 'great'.

**magnum opus** /ˌmagnəm ˈəʊpəs, ˈɒpəs/ • n. (pl. **magnum opuses** or **magna opera** /ˌmagnə ˈəʊpərə, ˈɒpərə/) a large and important work of art, music, or literature, especially the most important work of an artist, writer, etc.
– ORIGIN C18: from L., 'great work'.

**magpie** • n. **1** a long-tailed bird of the crow family, typically with pied plumage and a raucous voice. [*Pica pica* and other species.] ➤ a black-and-white Australian butcher-bird with musical calls. [*Gymnorhina tibicen*.] **2** a person who obsessively collects things or who chatters idly. **3** the division of a circular target next to the outer one, or a shot which strikes this.
– ORIGIN C16: prob. shortening of dial. *Magot* (ME familiar form of the given name *Marguerite*) + PIE[2].

**magpie moth** • n. a white moth with black and yellow spots whose caterpillars can be pests of fruit bushes. [*Abraxas grossulariata* and related species.]

**maguey** /ˈmagweɪ/ • n. an agave plant, especially one yielding pulque.
– ORIGIN C16: via Sp. from Taino.

**magus** /ˈmeɪgəs/ • n. (pl. **magi** /ˈmeɪdʒʌɪ/) **1** a member of a priestly caste of ancient Persia. **2** a sorcerer.
– ORIGIN ME: via L. and Gk from Old Pers. *maguš*.

**mag wheel** • n. N. Amer. a motor-vehicle wheel made from lightweight magnesium steel, typically having a pattern of holes or spokes around the hub.

**Magyar** /ˈmagjɑː/ ● **n.** **1** a member of a people predominating in Hungary. **2** the Uralic language of this people; Hungarian.
– ORIGIN the name in Hungarian.

**mahant** /məˈhʌnt/ ● **n.** Hinduism a chief priest of a temple or the head of a monastery.
– ORIGIN from Hindi.

**maharaja** /ˌmɑː(h)əˈrɑːdʒə, ˌməhɑː-/ (also **maharajah**) ● **n.** historical an Indian prince.
– ORIGIN from Hindi *mahārājā*, from Sanskrit *mahā* 'great' + *rājan* 'raja'.

**maharani** /ˌmɑː(h)əˈrɑːni, ˌməhɑː-/ (also **maharanee**) ● **n.** a maharaja's wife or widow.
– ORIGIN from Hindi *mahārānī*, from Sanskrit *mahā* 'great' + *rājñī* 'ranee'.

**Maharashtrian** /ˌmɑːhəˈraʃtrɪən, -ˈrɑːʃtrɪən/ ● **n.** a native or inhabitant of the Indian state of Maharashtra. ● **adj.** of or relating to Maharashtra.

**Maharishi** /ˌmɑː(h)əˈrɪʃi/ ● **n.** a great Hindu sage or spiritual leader.
– ORIGIN alt. of Sanskrit *maharṣi*, from *mahā* 'great' + *ṛṣi* 'rishi'.

**mahatma** /məˈhatmə, məˈhɑː-/ ● **n.** **1** (in the Indian subcontinent) a holy person or sage. **2** (in some forms of theosophy) a person in India or Tibet said to have preternatural powers.
– ORIGIN from Sanskrit *mahātman*, from *mahā* 'great' + *ātman* 'soul'.

**Mahayana** /ˌmɑː(h)əˈjɑːnə, ˌməhɑː-/ (also **Mahayana Buddhism**) ● **n.** one of the two major traditions of Buddhism (the other being Theravada), practised especially in China, Tibet, Japan, and Korea.
– ORIGIN from Sanskrit, from *mahā* 'great' + *yāna* 'vehicle'.

**Mahdi** /ˈmɑːdi/ ● **n.** (pl. **Mahdis**) **1** (in popular Muslim belief) a spiritual and temporal leader who will rule before the end of the world and restore religion and justice. ➤ a person claiming to be this leader, notably Muhammad Ahmad of Dongola in Sudan (1843–85). **2** (in Shiite belief) the twelfth imam, who is expected to return and triumph over injustice.
– DERIVATIVES **Mahdism** n. **Mahdist** n. & adj.
– ORIGIN from Arab. *(al-)mahdī* 'he who is guided in the right way'.

**Mahican** /ˈmahɪk(ə)n/ (also **Mohican**) ● **n.** **1** a member of an American Indian people formerly inhabiting the Upper Hudson Valley. Compare with **MOHEGAN**. **2** the extinct Algonquian language of this people. ● **adj.** of or relating to the Mahicans or their language.
– ORIGIN the name in Mahican, said to mean 'wolf'.

**mahimahi** /ˈmɑːhɪˌmɑːhi/ ● **n.** Hawaiian term for **DORADO** (in sense 1).

**mah-jong** /mɑːˈdʒɒŋ/ (also **mah-jongg**) ● **n.** a Chinese game played, usually by four people, with 136 or 144 rectangular tiles.
– ORIGIN C20: from Chin. dial. *ma-tsiang*, lit. 'sparrows'.

**mahlstick** /ˈmɔːlstɪk/ ● **n.** US spelling of **MAULSTICK**.

**mahogany** /məˈhɒgəni/ ● **n.** **1** hard reddish-brown wood from a tropical tree, used for furniture. **2** the tree which produces this wood. [*Swietenia mahagoni* (tropical America) and other species.] **3** a rich reddish-brown colour.
– ORIGIN C17: of unknown origin.

**mahonia** /məˈhəʊnɪə/ ● **n.** an evergreen shrub of the barberry family, which produces clusters of small fragrant yellow flowers followed by purple or black berries. [Genus *Mahonia*.]
– ORIGIN mod. L., named after the Amer. botanist Bernard Mc*Mahon* (c.1775–1816).

**mahout** /məˈhaʊt/ ● **n.** (in the Indian subcontinent and SE Asia) a person who works with and rides an elephant.
– ORIGIN from Hindi *mahāvat*.

**Mahratta** ● **n.** variant spelling of **MARATHA**.

**Mahratti** ● **n.** variant spelling of **MARATHI**.

**mahseer** /ˈmɑːsɪə/ ● **n.** a large edible carp of northern India and the Himalayan region. [Genus *Tor*: several species.]
– ORIGIN via Hindi from Sanskrit *mahā* 'great' + *śaphara* 'carp'.

**mahua** /ˈmʌhʊə/ (also **mahwa** /ˈməʊwə/) ● **n.** **1** an Indian tree which has fleshy edible flowers and yields oil-rich seeds. [*Madhuca latifolia*.] **2** an alcoholic drink produced from the nectar-rich flowers of this tree.
– ORIGIN C17: via Hindi from Sanskrit *madhūka*, from *madhu* 'sweet'.

**maid** ● **n.** **1** a female domestic servant. **2** archaic or poetic/literary a girl or young woman. ➤ a virgin.
– ORIGIN ME: abbrev. of **MAIDEN**.

**maidan** /mʌɪˈdɑːn/ ● **n.** (in the Indian subcontinent) an open space in or near a town.
– ORIGIN from Urdu and Pers. *maidān*, from Arab. *maydān*.

**maiden** ● **n.** **1** archaic or poetic/literary a girl or young woman. ➤ a virgin. **2** (also **maiden over**) Cricket an over in which no runs are scored. ● **adj.** **1** (of a woman, especially an older one) unmarried. ➤ (of a female animal) unmated. **2** being or involving the first attempt or act of its kind: *the Titanic's maiden voyage*. **3** denoting a horse that has never won a race, or a race intended for such horses.
– DERIVATIVES **maidenhood** n. **maidenish** adj. **maidenlike** adj. **maidenly** adj.
– ORIGIN OE *mægden*, from a Gmc dimin. meaning 'maid, virgin'.

**maidenhair** (also **maidenhair fern**) ● **n.** a fern having slender-stalked fronds with small round or wedge-shaped divided lobes. [*Adiantum capillus-veneris* and related species.]

**maidenhair tree** ● **n.** the ginkgo, whose leaves resemble those of the maidenhair fern.

**maidenhead** ● **n.** archaic virginity. ➤ the hymen.

**maiden name** ● **n.** the surname that a married woman used before she was married.

**maid of honour** ● **n.** **1** an unmarried noblewoman attending a queen or princess. **2** N. Amer. a principal bridesmaid. **3** Brit. a small tart filled with flavoured milk curds.

**maidservant** ● **n.** dated a female domestic servant.

**maieutic** /meɪˈjuːtɪk/ ● **adj.** of or denoting the Socratic mode of enquiry, which aims to bring a person's latent ideas into clear consciousness. ● **n.** (**maieutics**) [treated as sing.] the maieutic method.
– ORIGIN C17: from Gk *maieutikos*, from *maieuesthai* 'act as a midwife', from *maia* 'midwife'.

**maigre** /ˈmeɪgə/ ● **adj.** (in the Roman Catholic Church) denoting a day on which abstinence from meat is ordered.
– ORIGIN C17: from Fr., lit. 'lean'.

**mail**[1] ● **n.** letters and parcels sent by post. ➤ (N. Amer. & W. Indian also **the mails**) the postal system. ➤ Computing email. ● **v.** send (a letter or parcel) by post. ➤ Computing send (someone) email.
– DERIVATIVES **mailable** adj.
– ORIGIN ME (in the sense 'travelling bag'): from OFr. *male* 'wallet', of W. Gmc origin.

**mail**[2] ● **n.** **1** historical armour made of metal rings or plates joined together flexibly. **2** the protective shell or scales of certain animals. ● **v.** [often as adj. **mailed**] clothe or cover with mail.
– ORIGIN ME: from OFr. *maille*, from L. *macula* 'spot or mesh'.

**mailbag** ● **n.** **1** a large sack or bag for carrying mail. **2** the letters received by a person, especially a public figure.

**mail bomb** ● **n.** **1** US a letter bomb. **2** an overwhelming quantity of email messages sent to one address.

**mailbox** ● **n.** chiefly N. Amer. **1** a box into which mail is delivered, especially one mounted on a post at the entrance to a person's property. ➤ N. Amer. a post box. **2** a computer file in which email messages are stored.

**mail drop** ● **n.** **1** N. Amer. a receptacle for mail, especially one in which mail is kept until collected. **2** Brit. a delivery of mail.

**mailer** • **n. 1** chiefly N. Amer. the sender of a letter or package by post. **2** a piece of advertising material sent out by post. **3** a container used for conveying items by post. **4** Computing a program that sends email messages.

**mailing** • **n.** something sent by mail, especially a piece of mass advertising.

**mailing list** • **n.** a list of the names and addresses of people to whom advertising matter or information may be mailed regularly.

**maillot** /mʌɪˈjəʊ/ • **n.** (pl. pronounced same) **1** a pair of tights worn for dancing or gymnastics. **2** chiefly N. Amer. a woman's tight-fitting one-piece swimsuit. **3** a jersey or top, especially one worn in sports such as cycling.
– ORIGIN from Fr.

**mailman** • **n.** (pl. **-men**) N. Amer. a postman.

**mail merge** • **n.** Computing the automatic addition of names and addresses from a database to letters and envelopes in order to facilitate sending mail to many addresses.

**mail order** • **n.** the ordering of goods by post.

**mailshot** • **n.** Brit. an item, especially a piece of advertising material, sent to a large number of addresses.

**maim** • **v.** wound or injure (someone) so that part of the body is permanently damaged.
– ORIGIN ME: from OFr. *mahaignier*, of unknown origin.

**main**[1] • **adj.** chief in size or importance. • **n. 1** a principal pipe carrying water or gas or a cable carrying electricity. ➤ **(the mains)** Brit. the source of public water, gas, or electricity supply through pipes or cables. **2** **(the main)** archaic or poetic/literary the open ocean. **3** Nautical short for **MAINSAIL** or **MAINMAST**.
– PHRASES **by main force** through sheer strength. **in the main** on the whole.
– ORIGIN ME: from OE *mægen* 'physical force', reinforced by ON *meginn*, *megn* 'strong, powerful', both from a Gmc base meaning 'have power'.

**main**[2] • **n. 1** (in the game of hazard) a number (5, 6, 7, 8, or 9) called by a player before dice are thrown. **2** historical a match between fighting cocks.
– ORIGIN C16: prob. from the phr. *main chance*.

**main brace** • **n.** the brace attached to the main yard of a sailing ship.

**main clause** • **n.** Grammar a clause that can form a complete sentence standing alone, having a subject and a predicate.

**main course** • **n. 1** the most substantial course of a meal. **2** the mainsail of a square-rigged sailing ship.

**maincrop** • **adj.** Brit. denoting a vegetable produced as a principal crop of the season.

**main drag** • **n.** informal, chiefly N. Amer. the main street of a town.

**Maine Coon** • **n.** a large, powerful cat of a long-haired breed, originally from America.
– ORIGIN 1970s: so named because of a resemblance to the raccoon.

**Mainer** • **n.** a native or inhabitant of the US state of Maine.

**mainframe** • **n. 1** a large high-speed computer, especially one supporting numerous workstations or peripherals. **2** the central processing unit and primary memory of a computer.

**mainland** • **n.** a large continuous extent of land that includes the greater part of a country or territory, as opposed to offshore islands and detached territories.
– DERIVATIVES **mainlander** n.

**main line** • **n. 1** a chief railway line. **2** N. Amer. a chief road or street. **3** informal a principal vein as a site for a drug injection. • **v.** **(mainline)** informal inject (a drug) intravenously.
– DERIVATIVES **mainliner** n.

**mainly** • **adv.** more than anything else. ➤ for the most part.

**main man** • **n. 1** informal, chiefly N. Amer. a close and trusted friend. **2** a principal figure in an organization, team, etc.

**mainmast** • **n.** the principal mast of a ship.

**mainplane** • **n.** the principal wing or other supporting surface of an aircraft, as opposed to a tailplane.

**mainsail** /ˈmeɪnseɪl, -s(ə)l/ • **n.** the principal sail of a ship. ➤ the sail set on the after part of the mainmast in a fore-and-aft rigged vessel.

**main sequence** • **n.** Astronomy a series of types to which most stars other than giants, supergiants, and white dwarfs belong.
– ORIGIN 1920s: so named because they occupy a broad band on a graph of magnitude against spectral type.

**mainsheet** • **n.** a sheet used for controlling and trimming the mainsail of a sailing boat.

**mainspring** • **n. 1** the principal spring in a watch, clock, etc. **2** a prime source of motivation or support.

**mainstay** • **n. 1** a stay which extends from the maintop to the foot of the foremast of a sailing ship. **2** the chief support or main part.

**mainstream** • **n.** **(the mainstream)** normal or conventional ideas, attitudes, or activities. • **adj.** belonging to or characteristic of the mainstream.

**maintain** • **v. 1** cause or enable (a condition or state of affairs) to continue. ➤ keep at the same level or rate. **2** keep (a building, machine, etc.) in good condition by checking or repairing it regularly. **3** provide with necessities for life or existence. ➤ archaic give one's support to; uphold. **4** assert something to be the case.
– DERIVATIVES **maintainability** n. **maintainable** adj.
– ORIGIN ME: from OFr. *maintenir*, from L. *manu tenere* 'hold in the hand'.

**maintained school** • **n.** Brit. a school financed with public money.

**maintainer** • **n. 1** a person or thing that maintains. **2** (also **maintainor**) Law, historical a person guilty of aiding a party in a legal action without lawful cause.

**maintenance** • **n. 1** the process or state of maintaining or being maintained. **2** a husband's or wife's provision for a spouse after separation or divorce. **3** Law, historical the former offence of aiding a party in a legal action without lawful cause.

**maintop** • **n.** a platform around the head of the lower section of a sailing ship's mainmast.

**maintopmast** /meɪnˈtɒpməst/ • **n.** the second section of a sailing ship's mainmast.

**maiolica** /məˈjɒlɪkə, mʌɪˈɒlɪkə/ • **n.** fine earthenware with coloured decoration on an opaque white tin glaze, originating in Italy during the Renaissance.
– ORIGIN C16: Ital., from *Maiolica* 'Majorca'.

**maisonette** /ˌmeɪzəˈnɛt/ • **n.** a set of rooms for living in, typically on two storeys of a larger building and having a separate entrance.
– ORIGIN C18: from Fr. *maisonnette*, dimin. of *maison* 'house'.

**mai tai** /ˈmʌɪ tʌɪ/ • **n.** chiefly US a cocktail based on light rum, curaçao, and fruit juices.
– ORIGIN from Polynesian.

**Maithili** /ˈmʌɪtɪli/ • **n.** a Bihari language spoken especially in northern Bihar.
– ORIGIN Sanskrit, from *Mithilā*, a place in northern Bihar.

**maître d'hôtel** /ˌmeɪtrə dəʊˈtɛl, French mɛtʀ dotɛl/ (also **maître d'** /ˌmeɪtrə ˈdiː/) • **n.** (pl. **maîtres d'hôtel** pronunc. same or **maître d's**) **1** the head waiter of a restaurant. **2** the manager of a hotel.
– ORIGIN C16: Fr., lit. 'master of (the) house'.

**maize** • **n.** chiefly Brit. a cereal plant originating in Central America and yielding large grains (corn or sweetcorn) set in rows on a cob. [*Zea mays*.]
– ORIGIN C16: from Sp. *maíz*, from Taino *mahiz*.

**Maj.** • **abbrev.** Major.

**majestic** • **adj.** having or showing impressive beauty or

dignity.
– DERIVATIVES **majestically** adv.

**majesty** ● n. (pl. **-ies**) **1** impressive stateliness, dignity, or beauty. **2** royal power. ➤(**His**, **Your**, etc. **Majesty**) a title given to a sovereign or a sovereign's wife or widow.
– ORIGIN ME: from OFr. *majeste*, from L. *majestas*, from a var. of *majus*, *major-* (see **MAJOR**).

**majlis** /'madʒlɪs, madʒ'lɪs/ ● n. the parliament of various North African and Middle Eastern countries, especially Iran.
– ORIGIN Arab., lit. 'assembly'.

**majolica** /mə'jɒlɪkə, -'dʒɒl-/ ● n. a kind of earthenware made in imitation of Italian maiolica, especially in England during the 19th century.
– ORIGIN var. of **MAIOLICA**.

**major** ● adj. **1** important, serious, or significant. ➤greater or more important; main. **2** Music (of a scale) having intervals of a semitone between the third and fourth, and seventh and eighth degrees. Contrasted with **MINOR**. ➤(of an interval) equivalent to that between the tonic and another note of a major scale, and greater by a semitone than the corresponding minor interval. ➤[postpos.] (of a key) based on a major scale: *Prelude in G Major.* **3** Brit. dated (appended to a surname in public schools) indicating the elder of two brothers. **4** Logic (of a term) occurring as the predicate in the conclusion of a categorical syllogism. ➤(of a premise) containing the major term in a categorical syllogism. ● n. **1** a rank of officer in the army and the US air force, above captain and below lieutenant colonel. ➤an officer in charge of a section of band instruments: *a trumpet major.* **2** Music a major key, interval, or scale. **3** a major organization, company, or competition. **4** N. Amer. a student's principal subject or course. ➤a student specializing in a specified subject: *a math major.* **5** Logic a major term or premise. **6** Bell-ringing a system of change-ringing using eight bells. ● v. (**major in**) N. Amer. & Austral./NZ specialize in (a particular subject) at college or university.
– ORIGIN ME: from L., compar. of *magnus* 'great'; perh. influenced by Fr. *majeur.*

**major axis** ● n. Geometry the longer axis of an ellipse, passing through its foci.

**Majorcan** /mə'jɔːkən/ ● n. a native or inhabitant of Majorca. ● adj. of or relating to Majorca.

**major-domo** /ˌmeɪdʒə'dəʊməʊ/ ● n. (pl. **-os**) the chief steward of a large household.
– ORIGIN C16: via Sp. and Ital. from med. L. *major domus* 'highest official of the household'.

**major general** ● n. a rank of officer in the army and the US air force, above brigadier or brigadier general and below lieutenant general.

**majoritarian** /məˌdʒɒrɪ'tɛːrɪən/ ● adj. governed by or believing in decision by a majority. ● n. a majoritarian person.
– DERIVATIVES **majoritarianism** n.

**majority** ● n. (pl. **-ies**) **1** the greater number. **2** Brit. the number by which the votes cast for one party or candidate exceed those for the next. ➤US the number by which votes for one candidate are more than those for all other candidates together. **3** the age when a person is legally considered a full adult, usually 18 or 21. **4** the rank or office of a major.
– ORIGIN C16 (denoting superiority): from Fr. *majorité*, from med. L. *majoritas*, from L. *major* (see **MAJOR**).

**majority rule** ● n. the principle that the greater number should exercise greater power.

**majority verdict** ● n. English Law a verdict agreed by all but one or two of the members of a jury.

**major league** ● n. N. Amer. the highest-ranking league in a particular professional sport, especially baseball.
– DERIVATIVES **major-leaguer** n.

**majorly** ● adv. informal very; extremely.

**major piece** ● n. Chess a rook or queen.

**major planet** ● n. any of the nine principal planets of the solar system, as distinct from an asteroid or moon.

**major prophet** ● n. any of the prophets after whom the longer prophetic books of the Bible are named; Isaiah, Jeremiah, or Ezekiel.

**major suit** ● n. Bridge spades or hearts.

**majuscule** /'madʒəskjuːl/ ● n. a large letter, either capital or uncial.
– DERIVATIVES **majuscular** /mə'dʒʌskjʊlə/ adj.
– ORIGIN C18: from Fr., from L. *majuscula* (*littera*) 'somewhat greater (letter)'.

**Makasarese** /məˌkasə'riːz/ (also archaic **Makassarese**) ● n. (pl. same) **1** a native or inhabitant of Makassar (now Ujung Pandang) in Indonesia. **2** the Indonesian language of this people. ● adj. of or relating to this people or their language.

**make** ● v. (past and past part. **made**) **1** form by putting parts together or combining substances. ➤(**make something into**) alter something so that it forms (something else). ➤arrange bedclothes tidily on (a bed) ready for use. ➤arrange and light materials for (a fire). ➤Electronics complete or close (a circuit). **2** cause to exist or come about; bring about or perform. ➤cause to be, become, or seem. ➤appoint to a position. ➤chiefly archaic enter into a contract of (marriage). **3** compel (someone) to do something. **4** constitute, amount to, or serve as. ➤consider to be; estimate as. ➤agree or decide on (a specified arrangement). **5** gain or earn (money or profit). ➤Cricket score (a specified number of runs). ➤(in sport) enable a teammate to score (a goal) by one's play. **6** manage to arrive at (a place) or catch (a train or other transport). ➤(**make it**) become successful. ➤achieve a place in. ➤chiefly N. Amer. achieve the rank of. **7** prepare to go in a particular direction or do a particular thing. **8** informal, chiefly N. Amer. induce (someone) to have sexual intercourse with one. **9** (in bridge, whist, etc.) win (a trick). ➤win the number of tricks that fulfils (a contract). ➤shuffle (a pack of cards) for dealing. **10** (of the tide) begin to flow or ebb. ● n. **1** the manufacturer or trade name of a product. ➤the structure or composition of something. **2** the making of electrical contact.
– PHRASES **be made of money** [usu. with neg.] informal be very rich. **have (got) it made** informal be in a position where success is certain. **make a day of it** devote a whole day to an activity. **make someone's day** make an otherwise ordinary day pleasingly memorable for someone. **make a House** Brit. secure the presence of enough members for a quorum or support in the House of Commons. **make do** manage with the limited or inadequate means available. **make like** N. Amer. informal pretend to be. **make or break** be the factor which decides whether (something) will succeed or fail. **make sail** Sailing spread a sail or sails. ➤start a voyage. **make time 1** find an occasion when time is available to do something. **2** N. Amer. informal make sexual advances to someone. **make up one's mind** make a decision. **make way 1** allow room for someone or something else. **2** chiefly Nautical make progress; travel. **on the make** informal intent on gain. ➤looking for a sexual partner. **put the make on** N. Amer. informal make sexual advances to.
– PHRASAL VERBS **make after** pursue. **make away with** another way of saying ***make off with***. ➤kill (someone) furtively and illicitly. **make for 1** move or head towards. ➤approach (someone) to attack them. **2** tend to result in or be received as. **3** (**be made for**) be eminently suited for (a particular function or partnership). **make something of** give or ascribe a specified amount of attention or importance to. ➤understand or derive advantage from. **make off** leave hurriedly. **make off with** carry away illicitly. **make out** informal **1** make progress; fare. **2** N. Amer. engage in sexual activity. **make someone/thing out 1** manage with some difficulty to see, hear, or understand. **2** represent as or pretend. **3** draw up or write out a list or document. **make something over** transfer the possession of. **make someone over** give someone a new image with cosmetics, hairstyling, etc. **make up** be reconciled after a quarrel. **make someone up** apply cosmetics to. **make something up 1** (also **make up for**) compensate for something lost, missed, or deficient. ➤(**make it up to**) compensate (someone) for negligent or unfair treatment. **2** (**make up**) (of parts) compose or constitute (a whole). **3** put together or prepare something

from parts or ingredients. ➤ Printing arrange type and illustrations into a page or pages. **4** concoct or invent a story. **make up to** informal attempt to win the favour of. **make with** US informal proceed to use or supply.
– DERIVATIVES **makable** (also **makeable**) adj.
– ORIGIN OE *macian*, of W. Gmc origin; rel. to **MATCH**[1].

**make-believe** • **n.** the action of pretending or imagining. • **adj.** imitating something real. • **v.** (**make believe**) pretend; imagine.

**makeover** • **n.** a complete transformation of a person's appearance with cosmetics, hairstyling, etc.

**maker** • **n. 1** a person or thing that makes or produces something. **2** (**our**, **the**, etc. **Maker**) God.
– PHRASES **meet one's Maker** chiefly humorous die.

**makeshift** • **adj.** interim and temporary. • **n.** a temporary substitute or device.

**make-up** • **n. 1** cosmetics such as lipstick or powder applied to the face. **2** the composition or constitution of something. **3** Printing the arrangement of type, illustrations, etc. on a printed page.

**makeweight** • **n. 1** something put on a scale to make up the required weight. **2** an extra person or thing needed to complete something.

**make-work** chiefly N. Amer. • **adj.** denoting an activity that serves to keep someone busy but is of little value in itself. • **n.** work or activity of this kind.

**making** • **n. 1** the process of making or producing something. **2** (**makings**) informal earnings or profit. **3** (**makings**) the necessary qualities: *she had the makings of a great teacher.* **4** (**makings**) N. Amer. & Austral./NZ informal paper and tobacco for rolling a cigarette.
– PHRASES **be the making of someone** bring about someone's success or favourable development. **in the making** in the process of developing or being made. **of one's (own) making** (of a difficulty) caused by oneself.

**mako**[1] /ˈmɑːkəʊ, ˈmeɪkəʊ/ • **n.** (pl. **-os**) a large, fast-moving oceanic shark with a deep blue back and white underparts. [Genus *Isurus*: two species.]
– ORIGIN C19: from Maori.

**mako**[2] /ˈmɑːkəʊ, ˈmakəʊ/ • **n.** (pl. **-os**) a small New Zealand tree which bears large clusters of pink flowers followed by dark red berries. [*Aristotelia racemosa*.]
– ORIGIN C19: from Maori.

**Makonde** /məˈkɒndeɪ/ • **n.** (pl. same or **Makondes**) **1** a member of a people inhabiting southern Tanzania and NE Mozambique. **2** the Bantu language of this people.
– ORIGIN the name in Makonde.

**Makua** /ˈmakuːə/ • **n.** (pl. same or **Makuas**) **1** a member of a people inhabiting the border regions of Mozambique, Malawi, and Tanzania. **2** the Bantu language of this people.
– ORIGIN the name in Makua.

**makuta** plural form of **LIKUTA**.

**MAL** • **abbrev.** Malaysia (international vehicle registration).

**Mal.** • **abbrev.** Malachi (in biblical references).

**mal-** • **comb. form 1** in an unpleasant degree: *malodorous.* **2** in a faulty manner: *malfunction.* ➤ in an improper manner: *malpractice.* ➤ in an inadequate manner: *malnourishment.* **3** not: *maladroit.*
– ORIGIN from Fr. *mal*, from L. *male* 'badly'.

**malacca** /məˈlakə/ • **n.** brown cane (obtained from a Malaysian climbing palm *Calamus scipionum*) that is widely used for walking sticks and umbrella handles. ➤ a walking stick of malacca cane.
– ORIGIN C19: from the name *Malacca* (or Melaka), a state of Malaysia.

**malachite** /ˈmaləkʌɪt/ • **n.** a bright green mineral consisting of hydrated basic copper carbonate.
– ORIGIN ME: from OFr. *melochite*, via L. from Gk *molokhitis*, from *molokhē*, var. of *malakhē* 'mallow'.

**malaco-** /ˈmaləkəʊ/ • **comb. form** soft: *malacostracan.*
– ORIGIN from Gk *malakos* 'soft'.

**malacology** /ˌmaləˈkɒlədʒi/ • **n.** the branch of zoology concerned with molluscs. Compare with **CONCHOLOGY**.
– DERIVATIVES **malacological** adj. **malacologist** n.

**Malacostraca** /ˌmaləˈkɒstrəkə/ • **pl. n.** Zoology a large class of crustaceans including crabs, shrimps, lobsters, isopods, and amphipods, having compound eyes that are typically on stalks.
– DERIVATIVES **malacostracan** adj. & n.
– ORIGIN mod. L., from **MALACO-** + Gk *ostrakon* 'shell'.

**maladaptive** • **adj.** not providing adequate or appropriate adjustment to the environment or situation.
– DERIVATIVES **maladaptation** n. **maladapted** adj.

**maladjusted** • **adj.** failing to cope with the demands of a normal social environment.
– DERIVATIVES **maladjustment** n.

**maladminister** • **v.** formal manage or administer badly or dishonestly.
– DERIVATIVES **maladministration** n.

**maladroit** /ˌmaləˈdrɔɪt/ • **adj.** inefficient or ineffective; clumsy.
– DERIVATIVES **maladroitly** adv. **maladroitness** n.
– ORIGIN C17: Fr.

**malady** • **n.** (pl. **-ies**) a disease or ailment.
– ORIGIN ME: from OFr. *maladie*, from *malade* 'sick', based on L. *male* 'ill' + *habitus* 'having (as a condition)'.

**mala fides** /ˌmeɪlə ˈfʌɪdiːz, ˌmalə ˈfiːdeɪz/ chiefly Law • **n.** bad faith; intent to deceive. • **adj. & adv.** (**mala fide**) in bad faith; with intent to deceive.
– ORIGIN from L.

**Malaga** /ˈmaləgə/ • **n.** a sweet fortified wine from Malaga in Spain.

**Malagasy** /ˌmaləˈgasi/ • **n.** (pl. same or **-ies**) **1** a native or national of Madagascar. **2** the Austronesian language of Madagascar.

**malagueña** /ˌmaləˈgeɪnjə/ • **n.** a Spanish dance similar to the fandango.
– ORIGIN C19: Sp., lit. 'of Málaga' (a port in southern Spain).

**malaguetta** /ˌmaləˈgɛtə/ (also **malagueta**) • **n.** another term for **GRAINS OF PARADISE**.
– ORIGIN C16: prob. from Fr. *malaguette*, perh. based on a dimin. of Ital. *melica* 'millet'.

**malaise** /maˈleɪz/ • **n.** a general feeling of discomfort, illness, or unease.
– ORIGIN C18: from Fr., from OFr. *mal* 'bad' (from L. *malus*) + *aise* 'ease'.

**malamute** /ˈmaləmjuːt/ (also **malemute**) • **n.** a powerful dog of a breed with a thick, grey coat, bred by the Inuit and typically used to pull sledges.
– ORIGIN C19: from Inuit *malimiut*, the name of a people of Kotzebue Sound, Alaska, who developed the breed.

**malanga** /məˈlaŋgə/ • **n.** another term for **TANNIA**.
– ORIGIN C20: from Amer. Sp.

**malapert** /ˈmaləpəːt/ archaic • **adj.** presumptuous and impudent. • **n.** a malapert person.
– ORIGIN ME: from **MAL-** + archaic *apert* 'insolent'.

**malapropism** /ˈmaləprɒˌpɪz(ə)m/ (US also **malaprop**) • **n.** the mistaken use of a word in place of a similar-sounding one (e.g. 'dance a *flamingo*' instead of *flamenco*).
– ORIGIN C19: from the name of the character Mrs *Malaprop* in Sheridan's play *The Rivals* (1775) + **-ISM**.

**malapropos** /ˌmalaprəˈpəʊ/ formal • **adv.** inopportunely; inappropriately. • **adj.** inopportune; inappropriate. • **n.** (pl. same) something inappropriately said or done.
– ORIGIN C17: from Fr. *mal à propos*, from *mal* 'ill' + *à* 'to' + *propos* 'purpose'.

**malar** /ˈmeɪlə/ • **adj.** Anatomy & Medicine of or relating to the cheek. • **n.** (also **malar bone**) another term for **ZYGOMATIC BONE**.
– ORIGIN C18: from mod. L. *malaris*, from L. *mala* 'jaw'.

**malaria** • **n.** a mosquito-borne intermittent and remittent fever endemic to warmer regions and caused by a protozoan parasite (genus *Plasmodium*).
– DERIVATIVES **malarial** adj. **malarian** adj. **malarious** adj.
– ORIGIN C18: from Ital., from *mal'aria*, contracted form of *mala aria* 'bad air' (orig. denoting the unwholesome exhalations of marshes, to which the disease was formerly attributed).

**malariology** /məˌlɛːrɪˈɒlədʒi/ • **n.** the scientific study of malaria.
– DERIVATIVES **malariological** adj. **malariologist** n.

**malarkey** /mə'lɑːki/ ● **n.** informal nonsense.
– ORIGIN 1920s: of unknown origin.

**malathion** /ˌmalə'θʌɪən/ ● **n.** a synthetic organophosphorus compound which is used as an insecticide and is relatively harmless to plants and other animals.
– ORIGIN 1950s: from *(diethyl) mal(eate)* (see **MALEIC ACID**) + **THIO-** + **-ON**.

**Malawian** /mə'lɑːwiən/ ● **n.** a native or inhabitant of Malawi. ● **adj.** of or relating to Malawi or Malawians.

**Malay** /mə'leɪ/ ● **n. 1** a member of a people inhabiting Malaysia and Indonesia. ➤a person of Malay descent. **2** the Austronesian language of the Malays.

**Malayalam** /ˌmalə'jɑːləm/ ● **n.** the Dravidian language of the Indian state of Kerala, closely related to Tamil. ● **adj.** of or relating to this language or its speakers.
– ORIGIN C19: from Malayalam, from *mala* 'mountain' + *āḷ* 'man'.

**Malayan** ● **n.** another term for **MALAY**. ● **adj.** of or relating to Malays, the Malay language, or Malaya (now part of Malaysia).

**Malayo-** ● **comb. form** Malay; Malay and ...: *Malayo-Polynesian.*

**Malayo-Polynesian** ● **n.** another term for **AUSTRONESIAN**.

**Malaysian** /mə'leɪzɪən, -'leɪʒən/ ● **n.** a native or inhabitant of Malaysia. ● **adj.** of or relating to Malaysia or Malaysians.

**malcontent** /'malkəntɛnt/ ● **n.** a discontented person. ● **adj.** discontented; complaining.
– DERIVATIVES **malcontented** adj.
– ORIGIN C16: from Fr., from *mal* 'badly, ill' + *content* 'pleased'.

**mal de mer** /ˌmal də 'mɛː, French mal də mɛʀ/ ● **n.** seasickness.
– ORIGIN from Fr.

**Maldivian** /mɔːl'dɪvɪən/ ● **n. 1** a native or inhabitant of the Maldives. **2** the Indic language spoken in the Maldives. ● **adj.** of or relating to the Maldives, the Maldivians, or their language.

**male** ● **adj. 1** of or denoting the sex that can fertilize or inseminate the female to engender offspring. ➤relating to or characteristic of men or male animals. ➤(of a plant or flower) bearing stamens but lacking functional pistils. **2** (of a fitting) manufactured to fit inside a corresponding female part. ● **n.** a male person, animal, or plant.
– DERIVATIVES **maleness** n.
– ORIGIN ME: from OFr. *masle*, from L. *masculus*, from *mas* 'a male'.

**malediction** /ˌmalɪ'dɪkʃ(ə)n/ ● **n.** a curse.
– DERIVATIVES **maledictive** adj. **maledictory** adj.
– ORIGIN ME: from L. *maledictio(n-)*, from *maledicere* 'speak evil of'.

**malefactor** /'malɪˌfaktə/ ● **n.** formal a person who commits a crime or some other wrong.
– DERIVATIVES **malefaction** n.
– ORIGIN ME: from L., from *malefact-*, *malefacere* 'do wrong'.

**male fern** ● **n.** a fern with brown scales on the stalks of the fronds. [*Dryopteris filix-mas* and related species.]

**malefic** /mə'lɛfɪk/ ● **adj. 1** poetic/literary causing harm. **2** Astrology relating to the planets Saturn and Mars, traditionally considered to have an unfavourable influence.
– DERIVATIVES **maleficence** n. **maleficent** adj.
– ORIGIN C17: from L. *maleficus*, from *male* 'ill' + *-ficus* 'doing'.

**maleic acid** /mə'leɪɪk/ ● **n.** Chemistry a crystalline acid made by distilling malic acid, used in making synthetic resins.
– DERIVATIVES **maleate** n.
– ORIGIN C19: *maleic* from Fr. *maléique*, alt. of *malique* (see **MALIC ACID**).

**male menopause** ● **n.** a stage in a middle-aged man's life supposedly corresponding to the menopause of a woman, associated with loss of vigour and a crisis of identity (not in technical use).

**malemute** ● **n.** variant spelling of **MALAMUTE**.

**malevolent** /mə'lɛv(ə)l(ə)nt/ ● **adj.** wishing evil to others.
– DERIVATIVES **malevolence** n. **malevolently** adv.
– ORIGIN C16: from L. *malevolent-* 'wishing evil', from *male* 'ill' + *volent-*, *velle* 'to wish'.

**malfeasance** /mal'fiːz(ə)ns/ ● **n.** Law wrongdoing, especially (US) by a public official.
– DERIVATIVES **malfeasant** n. & adj.
– ORIGIN C17: from Anglo-Norman Fr. *malfaisance*, from *mal-* 'evil' + OFr. *faisance* 'activity'.

**malformation** ● **n.** abnormality of shape or form in a part of the body.
– DERIVATIVES **malformed** adj.

**malfunction** ● **v.** (of a piece of equipment or machinery) fail to function normally. ● **n.** a failure of this type.

**Malian** /'mɑːliən/ ● **n.** a native or inhabitant of Mali, a country in West Africa. ● **adj.** of or relating to Mali or Malians.

**Malibu** /'malɪbuː/ (also **Malibu board**) ● **n.** (pl. **Malibus**) a lightweight surfboard.
– ORIGIN 1960s: named after *Malibu* beach in southern California.

**malic acid** /'malɪk/ ● **n.** Chemistry a crystalline acid present in unripe apples and other fruits.
– DERIVATIVES **malate** n.
– ORIGIN C18: *malic* from Fr. *malique*, from L. *malum* 'apple'.

**malice** ● **n. 1** the desire to do harm to someone; ill will. **2** Law wrongful intention, especially as increasing the guilt of certain offences.
– ORIGIN ME: via OFr. from L. *malitia*, from *malus* 'bad'.

**malice aforethought** ● **n.** Law the intention to kill or harm, held to distinguish unlawful killing from murder.

**malicious** ● **adj.** characterized by malice; intending or intended to do harm.
– DERIVATIVES **maliciously** adv. **maliciousness** n.

**malign** /mə'lʌɪn/ ● **adj.** harmful or evil in nature or effect. ● **v.** speak ill of.
– DERIVATIVES **maligner** n. **malignity** /mə'lɪgnɪti/ n. **malignly** adv.
– ORIGIN ME: via OFr. *maligne* (adj.), *malignier* (v.), based on L. *malignus* 'tending to evil', from *malus* 'bad'.

**malignancy** /mə'lɪgnənsi/ ● **n.** (pl. **-ies**) **1** the state or presence of a malignant tumour; cancer. ➤a cancerous growth. ➤a form of cancer. **2** the quality of being malign or malevolent.

**malignant** ● **adj. 1** harmful; malevolent. **2** (of a tumour) tending to invade normal tissue or to recur after removal; cancerous. Contrasted with **BENIGN**.
– DERIVATIVES **malignantly** adv.
– ORIGIN C16: from late L. *malignant-*, *malignare* 'contrive maliciously'.

**malignant pustule** ● **n.** a form of anthrax causing severe skin ulceration.

**malik** /'mɑːlɪk/ ● **n.** (in parts of the Indian subcontinent and the Middle East) the chief of a village or community.
– ORIGIN from Arab., active part. of *malaka* 'possess or rule'.

**malimbe** /mə'lɪmbi/ ● **n.** a weaver bird found mainly in west and central Africa, having black plumage with red on the head or throat. [Genus *Malimbus*.]
– ORIGIN C20: named after the town of *Malimbe* in Angola.

**malinger** /mə'lɪŋgə/ ● **v.** exaggerate or feign illness in order to escape duty or work.
– DERIVATIVES **malingerer** n.
– ORIGIN C19: back-form. from *malingerer*, appar. from Fr. *malingre*, perh. formed as *mal-* 'wrongly, improperly' + *haingre* 'weak', prob. of Gmc origin.

**Malinke** /mə'lɪŋkeɪ/ ● **n.** (pl. same or **Malinkes**) **1** a member of a West African people living mainly in Senegal, Mali, and the Ivory Coast. **2** the Mande language of this people.
– ORIGIN the name in Malinke.

**malison** /'malɪz(ə)n, -s-/ ● **n.** archaic a curse.
– ORIGIN ME: from OFr., from L. *maledictio(n-)* (see **MALEDICTION**).

**mall** /mal, mɔːl, mɒl/ ● **n. 1** a large enclosed shopping

area from which traffic is excluded. **2** a sheltered walk or promenade. **3** historical another term for the game **PALL-MALL**. ➤an alley used for this.
– ORIGIN C17: prob. a shortening of **PALL-MALL**; from *The Mall* in St James's Park, London, former site of a pall-mall alley.

**mallam** /'maləm/ ● **n.** (in parts of Africa) a learned man or scribe.
– ORIGIN from Hausa *mālam(i)*.

**mallard** ● **n.** (pl. same or **mallards**) the commonest duck of the northern hemisphere, the male having a dark green head and white collar. [*Anas platyrhynchos*.]
– ORIGIN ME: from OFr. 'wild drake', from *masle* 'male'.

**malleable** /'malɪəb(ə)l/ ● **adj. 1** (of a metal or other material) able to be hammered or pressed into shape without breaking or cracking. **2** easily influenced; pliable.
– DERIVATIVES **malleability** n. **malleably** adv.
– ORIGIN ME: via OFr. from med. L. *malleabilis*, from L. *malleus* 'a hammer'.

**mallee** /'mali/ ● **n.** a low-growing bushy Australian eucalyptus. [*Eucalyptus dumosa* and other species.]
– ORIGIN C19: from Wuywurung (an Aborig. lang.).

**malleolus** /mə'li:ələs/ ● **n.** (pl. **malleoli** /-lʌɪ/) Anatomy a bony projection with a shape likened to a hammer head, especially each of those on either side of the ankle.
– ORIGIN C17: from L., dimin. of *malleus* 'hammer'.

**mallet** ● **n. 1** a hammer with a large wooden head. **2** a long-handled wooden stick with a head like a hammer, used for hitting a croquet or polo ball.
– ORIGIN ME: from OFr. *maillet*, from *mail* 'hammer', from L. *malleus*.

**malleus** /'malɪəs/ ● **n.** (pl. **mallei** /'malɪʌɪ/) Anatomy a small bone in the middle ear which transmits vibrations of the eardrum to the incus.
– ORIGIN C17: from L., lit. 'hammer'.

**malling** /'mɔ:lɪŋ/ ● **n.** N. Amer. **1** the development of shopping malls. **2** the action of passing time in a shopping mall.

**Mallophaga** /mə'lɒfəgə/ ● **pl. n.** Entomology an order of insects that comprises the biting lice.
– DERIVATIVES **mallophagan** n. & adj.
– ORIGIN mod. L., from Gk *mallos* 'lock of wool' + *-phagos* 'eating'.

**mallow** ● **n.** a herbaceous plant with hairy stems, pink or purple flowers, and disc-shaped fruit. [Genus *Malva*, family Malvaceae: many species.]
– ORIGIN OE *meal(u)we*, from L. *malva*; cf. **MAUVE**.

**malm** /mɑ:m/ ● **n. 1** a soft, crumbly chalky rock, or the fertile loamy soil produced as it weathers. **2** a fine-quality brick made originally from malm, marl, or a similar chalky clay.
– ORIGIN OE *mealm-*, of Gmc origin; rel. to **MEAL**[2].

**malmsey** /'mɑ:mzi/ ● **n. 1** a fortified Madeira wine of the sweetest type. **2** historical a strong, sweet white wine imported from Greece and the eastern Mediterranean islands.
– ORIGIN ME: from MDu. *malemeseye*, via OFr. from *Monemvasia*, the name of a port in SE Greece; cf. **MALVOISIE**.

**malnourished** ● **adj.** suffering from malnutrition.
– DERIVATIVES **malnourishment** n.

**malnutrition** ● **n.** lack of proper nutrition, caused by not having enough to eat, not eating enough of the right things, or being unable to use the food eaten.

**malocclusion** ● **n.** Dentistry imperfect positioning of the teeth when the jaws are closed.

**malodorous** ● **adj.** smelling very unpleasant.

**malodour** ● **n.** a very unpleasant smell.

**malolactic** /ˌmalə(ʊ)'laktɪk/ ● **adj.** of or denoting bacterial fermentation which converts malic acid to lactic acid, especially as a secondary process used to reduce the acidity of some wines. ● **n.** fermentation of this kind.

**malope** /'maləpi/ ● **n.** a plant of the mallow family, with wide, trumpet-shaped flowers. [Genus *Malope*.]

**maloti** plural form of **LOTI**.

**Malpighian layer** /mal'pɪgɪən/ ● **n.** Zoology & Anatomy a layer in the epidermis in which skin cells are continually formed by division.
– ORIGIN C19: named after the C17 Ital. microscopist Marcello *Malpighi*.

**Malpighian tubule** ● **n.** Zoology a tubular excretory organ, numbers of which open into the gut in insects and some other arthropods.

**malpractice** ● **n.** improper, illegal, or negligent professional activity or treatment.

**malpresentation** ● **n.** Medicine abnormal positioning of a fetus at the time of delivery.

**malt** /mɔ:lt, mɒlt/ ● **n. 1** barley or other grain that has been steeped, germinated, and dried, used especially for brewing or distilling and vinegar-making. **2** chiefly Brit. short for **MALT WHISKY**. **3** N. Amer. short for **MALTED MILK**. ● **v. 1** convert (grain) into malt. **2** (of a seed) become malt when germination is checked by drought.
– DERIVATIVES **maltiness** n. **malty** adj.
– ORIGIN OE *m(e)alt*, of Gmc origin; rel. to **MELT**.

**Malta fever** ● **n.** another term for **UNDULANT FEVER**.
– ORIGIN C19: named after *Malta*, where it was once prevalent.

**maltase** /'mɒlteɪz, 'mɔ:l-/ ● **n.** Biochemistry an enzyme, present in saliva and pancreatic juice, which catalyses the breakdown of maltose and similar sugars to form glucose.

**malted** ● **adj.** mixed with malt or a malt extract.

**malted milk** ● **n.** a hot drink made from dried milk and a malt preparation.

**Maltese** /mɔ:l'ti:z, mɒl-/ ● **n.** (pl. same) **1** a native or national of Malta or a person of Maltese descent. **2** the national language of Malta. ● **adj.** of or relating to Malta, its people, or their language.

**Maltese cross** ● **n.** a cross with arms of equal length which broaden from the centre and have their ends indented in a shallow V-shape.
– ORIGIN so named because the cross was formerly worn by the Knights of Malta, a religious order.

**Maltese dog** (also **Maltese terrier**) ● **n.** a dog of a very small long-haired breed, typically with white hair.

**malthouse** ● **n.** a building in which malt is prepared and stored.

**Malthusian** /mal'θju:zɪən/ ● **adj.** of or relating to the theory of the English economist Thomas Malthus (1766–1834), that without the practice of 'moral restraint' the population tends to increase at a greater rate than its means of subsistence, resulting in the population checks of war, famine, and epidemic. ● **n.** an adherent of Malthus.
– DERIVATIVES **Malthusianism** n.

**maltings** ● **n.** Brit. a malthouse.

**malt liquor** ● **n.** alcoholic liquor made from malt by fermentation rather than distillation, for example beer.

**maltodextrin** ● **n.** dextrin containing maltose, used as a food additive.

**maltose** /'mɔ:ltəʊz, -s, mɒlt-/ ● **n.** Chemistry a sugar produced by the breakdown of starch, e.g. by enzymes found in malt and saliva.
– ORIGIN C19: from **MALT** + **-OSE**[2].

**maltreat** ● **v.** treat cruelly or with violence.
– DERIVATIVES **maltreater** n. **maltreatment** n.
– ORIGIN C18: from Fr. *maltraiter*.

**maltster** ● **n.** chiefly Brit. a person who makes malt.

**malt whisky** ● **n.** whisky made only from malted barley and not blended with grain whisky.

**malvaceous** /mal'veɪʃəs/ ● **adj.** Botany relating to or denoting plants of the mallow family (Malvaceae).
– ORIGIN C17: from mod. L. *Malvaceae*, based on L. *malva* 'mallow', + **-OUS**.

**Malvasia** /ˌmalvə'si:ə, -'zi:ə/ ● **n.** a variety of grape used to make white and red wines, especially in Italy.
– ORIGIN Ital. form of the place name *Monemvasia*, in the Peloponnese (see **MALMSEY**).

**malversation** /ˌmalvə'seɪʃ(ə)n/ ● **n.** formal corrupt behaviour by a person in public office or a position of trust.
– ORIGIN C16: from Fr., from *malverser*, from L. *male* 'badly' + *versari* 'behave'.

**malvoisie** /'malvɔɪzi, ˌmalvɔɪ'zi:, French malvwazi/ ● **n.**

(in French-speaking countries) any of several grape varieties used to make full-flavoured white wines.
– ORIGIN from OFr. *malvesie*, from the Fr. form of *Monemvasia* (see **MALMSEY**).

**mam** ● n. informal **1** chiefly Brit. one's mother. **2** chiefly US a term of respectful address used for any woman.
– ORIGIN sense 1 (C16) is perh. imitative of a child's first syllables; sense 2 is a var. of **MA'AM**.

**mama** /ˈmamə, məˈmɑː/ (also **mamma**) ● n. **1** dated or N. Amer. one's mother. **2** US informal a mature woman: *the ultimate tough blues mama*.
– ORIGIN C16: imitative of a child's first syllables *ma, ma*.

**mamaguy** /ˈmaməgʌɪ/ ● v. W. Indian try to deceive (someone), especially with flattery or untruths.
– ORIGIN from Sp. *mamar gallo* 'make a monkey of'.

**mamba** /ˈmambə/ ● n. a large, agile, highly venomous African snake. [*Dendroaspis polylepis* (**black mamba**) and related species.]
– ORIGIN C19: from Zulu *imamba*.

**mambo** /ˈmambəʊ/ ● n. (pl. **-os**) **1** a Latin American dance similar in rhythm to the rumba. **2** a voodoo priestess. ● v. (**-oes**, **-oed**) dance the mambo.
– ORIGIN 1940s: from Amer. Sp.

**mamee** ● n. variant spelling of **MAMMEE**.

**mamelon** /ˈmamɪlən/ ● n. Biology a small rounded structure.
– ORIGIN C19: from Fr. 'nipple'.

**Mameluke** /ˈmaməluːk/ ● n. a member of a regime descended from slaves, that formerly ruled parts of the Middle East.
– ORIGIN from Fr. *mameluk*, from Arab. *mamlūk* (passive part. used as a noun meaning 'slave'), from *malaka* 'possess'.

**mamey** ● n. variant spelling of **MAMMEE**.

**mamilla** /maˈmɪlə/ (also **mammilla**) ● n. (pl. **mamillae** /-liː/) Anatomy a nipple.
– ORIGIN C17: from L., dimin. of *mamma* (see **MAMMA²**).

**mamillary** /ˈmamɪləri/ (also **mammillary**) ● adj. **1** (of minerals) having several smoothly rounded convex surfaces. **2** Anatomy denoting two rounded bodies in the floor of the hypothalamus in the brain.
– ORIGIN C17: from mod. L. *mamillaris*, from *mamilla* (see **MAMILLA**).

**mamillated** /ˈmamɪleɪtɪd/ (also **mammillated**) ● adj. **1** covered with rounded mounds or lumps. **2** (of minerals) mamillary.
– DERIVATIVES **mamillate** adj.
– ORIGIN C18: from **MAMILLA** + the adjectival suffix *-ated*.

**mamma¹** /ˈmamə, məˈmɑː/ ● n. variant spelling of **MAMA**.

**mamma²** /ˈmamə/ ● n. (pl. **mammae** /-miː/) a milk-secreting organ of female mammals (in humans, the breast).
– DERIVATIVES **mammiform** adj.
– ORIGIN OE, from L., 'breast'.

**mammal** ● n. a warm-blooded vertebrate animal of a class (Mammalia) that is distinguished by the possession of hair or fur, the secretion of milk, and (typically) the birth of live young.
– DERIVATIVES **mammalian** adj.
– ORIGIN C19: anglicized form of mod. L. *mammalia*, neut. pl. of L. *mammalis* (adj.), from *mamma* (see **MAMMA²**).

**mammaliferous** /ˌmaməˈlɪf(ə)rəs/ ● adj. Geology containing mammalian fossil remains.

**mammalogy** /maˈmalədʒi/ ● n. the branch of zoology concerned with mammals.
– DERIVATIVES **mammalogist** n.

**mammary** /ˈmaməri/ ● adj. denoting or relating to the human female breasts or the milk-secreting organs of other mammals. ● n. (pl. **-ies**) informal a breast.
– ORIGIN C17: from **MAMMA²** + **-ARY¹**.

**mammary gland** ● n. the milk-producing gland of women or other female mammals.

**mammee** /maˈmiː/ (also **mamee**, **mamey**) ● n. **1** (also **mammee apple**) a tropical American tree having large edible red fruit with sweet yellow flesh. [*Mammea americana*.] **2** (also **mammee sapote**) a Central American tree having edible russet fruit with spicy red flesh. [*Pouteria sapota*.]
– ORIGIN C16: from Sp. *mamei*, from Taino; *sapote* in sense 2 from Sp. *zapote* 'sapodilla'.

**mammilla** ● n. variant spelling of **MAMILLA**.

**mammogram** /ˈmaməgram/ ● n. an image obtained by mammography.

**mammography** /maˈmɒgrəfi/ ● n. Medicine a technique using X-rays to diagnose and locate tumours of the breasts.
– ORIGIN 1930s: from **MAMMA²** + **-GRAPHY**.

**Mammon** /ˈmamən/ ● n. wealth regarded as an evil influence or false object of worship (taken by medieval writers as the name of the devil of covetousness).
– DERIVATIVES **Mammonism** n. **Mammonist** n.
– ORIGIN ME: via late L. from New Testament Gk *mamōnas* (see Matt. 6:24, Luke 16:9–13), from Aramaic *māmōn* 'riches'.

**mammoth** ● n. a large extinct elephant of the Pleistocene epoch, typically hairy and with long curved tusks. [*Mammuthus primigenius* (**woolly mammoth**) and related species.] ● adj. huge.
– ORIGIN C18: from Russ. *mamo(n)t*, prob. of Siberian origin.

**mammy** ● n. (pl. **-ies**) informal **1** a child's name for their mother. **2** offensive (formerly in the southern United States) a black nursemaid or nanny in charge of white children.
– ORIGIN C16: from **MAM** + **-Y²**.

**Man.** ● abbrev. Manitoba.

**man** ● n. (pl. **men**) **1** an adult human male. **2** a male member of a workforce, team, etc. **3** a husband or lover: *man and wife*. **4** a person. ➤human beings in general; the human race. **5** (**the Man**) black slang white people collectively regarded as a controlling group. **6** a figure or token used in a board game. ● v. (**manned**, **manning**) **1** provide (a place or machine) with the personnel to run, operate, or defend it. **2** archaic fortify the spirits or courage of. ● exclam. informal, chiefly N. Amer. used for emphasis or to express surprise, admiration, or delight.
– PHRASES **be someone's** (or **the**) **man** be the person perfectly suited to a requirement or task. **be man enough** be brave enough. **man about town** a fashionable and sociable man. **man and boy** from childhood. **the man in** (or US **on**) **the street** the average man. **man of the cloth** a clergyman. **man of God** a clergyman. ➤a holy man or saint. **man of the house** the male head of a household. **man of letters** a male scholar or author. **man of straw** (also **straw man**) **1** a person who is a sham. **2** a sham argument. **3** a person undertaking a financial commitment without adequate means. **man to man** **1** in a direct and frank way between two men. **2** denoting a defensive tactic in soccer or other sports in which each player is responsible for marking one opponent. **to a man** without exception.
– DERIVATIVES **manless** adj. **manlike** adj. **manned** adj.
– ORIGIN OE *man(n)*, (pl.) *menn* (n.), *mannian* (v.), of Gmc origin; rel. to Sanskrit *manu* 'mankind'.

**USAGE** man

The generic use of **man** to refer to 'human beings in general' has become problematic in modern use; it is now widely regarded as old-fashioned or sexist. Alternative terms such as **the human race** or **humankind** may be used in some contexts, but elsewhere there are no established alternatives, for example for the term **manpower** or the verb **man**.

**-man** ● comb. form **1** in nouns denoting a man of a specified nationality or origin: *Frenchman*. **2** in nouns denoting a person, especially a man, belonging to a specified group or having a specified occupation or role: *layman* | *oarsman*. **3** a ship of a specified kind: *merchantman*.

**mana** /ˈmɑːnə/ ● n. (especially in Polynesian, Melanesian, and Maori belief) pervasive supernatural or magical power.
– ORIGIN from Maori.

**manacle** /ˈmanək(ə)l/ ● n. a metal band, chain, or shackle for fastening someone's hands or ankles. ● v.

(usu. **be manacled**) fetter with a manacle or manacles.
– ORIGIN ME: from OFr. *manicle* 'handcuff', from L. *manicula*, dimin. of *manus* 'hand'.

**manage** • **v. 1** be in charge of; run. **2** supervise (staff). **3** be the manager of (a sports team or a performer). **4** administer and regulate (resources under one's control). **5** maintain control or influence over (a person or animal). **6** control the use or exploitation of (land). **7** succeed in surviving or in attaining one's aims; cope. **8** succeed in achieving or producing (something difficult). **9** succeed in withstanding. **10** be free to attend at (a certain time).
– DERIVATIVES **manageability** n. **manageable** adj. **manageableness** n. **manageably** adv. **managing** adj. & n.
– ORIGIN C16 (in the sense 'put (a horse) through the paces of the manège'): from Ital. *maneggiare*, based on L. *manus* 'hand'.

**managed care** • **n.** US a system of health care emphasizing preventative medicine and home treatment.

**managed currency** • **n.** a currency whose exchange rate is regulated or controlled by the government.

**managed economy** • **n.** an economy in which the framework and general policies are regulated or controlled by the government.

**managed fund** • **n.** an investment fund run on behalf of an investor by an agent (typically an insurance company).

**management** • **n. 1** the process of managing. **2** [treated as sing. or pl.] the people managing an organization. **3** Medicine & Psychiatry the treatment or control of diseases or disorders, or the care of patients who suffer them. **4** archaic trickery; deceit.

**management accounting** • **n.** the provision of financial data and advice to a company for use in the organization and development of its business.
– DERIVATIVES **management accountant** n.

**management company** • **n.** a company which is set up to manage a group of properties, a unit trust, an investment fund, etc.

**manager** • **n. 1** a person who manages an organization or group of staff. **2** a person who controls the professional activities of a performer, sports player, etc. **3** a person in charge of the activities, tactics, and training of a sports team. **4** Computing a program or system that controls or organizes a peripheral device or process. **5** Brit. a member of either House of Parliament appointed with others for some duty in which both Houses are concerned.
– DERIVATIVES **managerial** adj. **managerially** adv. **managership** n.

**manageress** • **n.** a female manager.

**managerialism** • **n.** belief in or reliance on the use of professional managers in administering or planning an activity.
– DERIVATIVES **managerialist** n. & adj.

**manakin** /ˈmanəkɪn/ • **n.** a small brightly coloured tropical American bird with a large head and small bill. [Family Pipridae: many species.]
– ORIGIN C17: var. of **MANIKIN**.

**mañana** /manˈjɑːnə/ • **adv. 1** tomorrow. **2** in the indefinite future.
– ORIGIN Sp., lit. 'tomorrow'.

**manat** /ˈmanat/ • **n.** (pl. same) the basic monetary unit of Azerbaijan and Turkmenistan, equal to 100 gopik in Azerbaijan and 100 tenge in Turkmenistan.

**man-at-arms** • **n.** (pl. **men-at-arms**) archaic a soldier.

**manatee** /ˌmanəˈtiː, ˈmanətiː/ • **n.** a sea cow of tropical Atlantic coasts and estuaries, with a rounded tail flipper. [Genus *Trichechus*: three species.]
– ORIGIN C16: from Sp. *manati*, from Carib *manáti*.

**Manchester** • **n.** Austral./NZ cotton textiles; household linen.
– ORIGIN from the name of the city *Manchester*, historically a centre of cotton manufacture.

**Manchester terrier** • **n.** a small terrier of a breed with a short black-and-tan coat.
– ORIGIN from the name of the city *Manchester*, where the breed was once popular.

**manchet** /ˈmantʃɪt/ • **n.** archaic a fine wheaten loaf.
– ORIGIN ME: perh. from obs. *maine* 'flour of the finest quality' + obs. *cheat*, denoting a kind of wheaten bread.

**manchineel** /ˌman(t)ʃɪˈniːl/ • **n.** a Caribbean tree which has acrid apple-like fruit and poisonous milky sap which can cause temporary blindness. [*Hippomane mancinella*.]
– ORIGIN C17: from Fr. *mancenille*, from Sp. *manzanilla*, dimin. of *manzana* 'apple'.

**Manchu** /manˈtʃuː/ • **n. 1** a member of a people originally living in Manchuria, who formed the last imperial dynasty of China (1644–1912). **2** the Tungusic language of the Manchus.
– ORIGIN the name in Manchu, lit. 'pure'.

**manciple** /ˈmansɪp(ə)l/ • **n.** chiefly archaic an officer who buys provisions for a college, an Inn of Court, or a monastery.
– ORIGIN ME: via Anglo-Norman Fr. and OFr. from L. *mancipium* 'purchase', from *manceps* 'buyer', from *manus* 'hand' + *capere* 'take'.

**Mancunian** /manˈkjuːnɪən/ • **n.** a native or inhabitant of Manchester. • **adj.** of or relating to Manchester or Mancunians.
– ORIGIN C20: from *Mancunium*, the L. name of Manchester, + **-AN**.

**-mancy** • **comb. form** divination by a specified means: *geomancy*.
– DERIVATIVES **-mantic** comb. form in corresponding adjectives.
– ORIGIN from OFr. *-mancie*, via late L. *-mantia* from Gk *manteia* 'divination'.

**Mandaean** /manˈdiːən/ (also **Mandean**) • **n. 1** a member of a Gnostic sect surviving in Iraq and SW Iran, who regard John the Baptist as the Messiah. **2** the language of this sect, a form of Aramaic. • **adj.** of or relating to the Mandaeans or their language.
– ORIGIN C19: from Mandaean Aramaic *mandaia* 'Gnostics, those who have knowledge'.

**mandala** /ˈmandələ, ˈmʌn-/ • **n.** a circular figure representing the universe in Hindu and Buddhist symbolism.
– DERIVATIVES **mandalic** adj.
– ORIGIN from Sanskrit *maṇḍala* 'disc'.

**mandamus** /manˈdeɪməs/ • **n.** Law a judicial writ issued as a command to an inferior court or ordering a person to perform a public or statutory duty.
– ORIGIN C16: from L., lit. 'we command'.

**Mandan** /ˈmand(ə)n/ • **n.** (pl. same or **Mandans**) **1** a member of an American Indian people formerly living along the northern reaches of the Missouri River. **2** the Siouan language of this people.
– ORIGIN from N. Amer. Fr. *Mandane*, prob. from Dakota Sioux *mawátãna*.

**mandarin**[1] /ˈmand(ə)rɪn/ • **n. 1** (**Mandarin**) the standard literary and official form of Chinese. **2** an official in any of the nine top grades of the former imperial Chinese civil service. **3** porcelain decorated with figures representing Chinese mandarins. **4** a powerful official or senior bureaucrat.
– DERIVATIVES **mandarinate** n.
– ORIGIN C16: from Port. *mandarim*, via Malay from Hindi *mantrī* 'counsellor'.

**mandarin**[2] /ˈmand(ə)rɪn/ (also **mandarine** /-riːn/) • **n. 1** a small flattish citrus fruit with a loose yellow-orange skin. **2** the citrus tree that yields this fruit. [*Citrus reticulata*.]
– ORIGIN C18: from Fr. *mandarine*; perh. rel. to **MANDARIN**[1], the colour of the fruit being likened to the official's yellow robes.

**mandarin collar** • **n.** a small, close-fitting upright collar.

**mandarin duck** • **n.** a small tree-nesting East Asian duck, the male of which has showy plumage with an orange ruff and sail-like feathers on each side of the body. [*Aix galericulata*.]

**mandarin jacket** • **n.** a plain jacket with a mandarin collar.

**mandatary** /ˈmandət(ə)ri/ • **n.** (pl. **-ies**) historical a person or state receiving a mandate.

**mandate** ● **n.** /ˈmandeɪt/ **1** an official order or commission to do something. **2** Law a commission by which a party is entrusted to perform a service, especially without payment and with indemnity against loss by that party. **3** a written authority enabling someone to carry out transactions on another's bank account. **4** historical a commission from the League of Nations to a member state to administer a territory. **5** the authority to carry out a policy or course of action, regarded as given by the electorate to a party or candidate that wins an election. ● **v.** /manˈdeɪt/ **1** give (someone) authority to act in a certain way. **2** make mandatory. **3** historical assign (territory) under a mandate of the League of Nations.
– DERIVATIVES **mandated** adj.
– ORIGIN C16: from L. *mandatum* 'something commanded', neut. past part. of *mandare*, from *manus* 'hand' + *dare* 'give'.

**mandatory** /ˈmandət(ə)ri/ ● **adj.** required by law or mandate; compulsory. ● **n.** variant spelling of **MANDATARY**.
– DERIVATIVES **mandatorily** adv.

**Mande** /ˈmɑːndeɪ/ ● **n.** (pl. same or **Mandes**) **1** a member of any of a large group of peoples of West Africa. **2** the group of Niger–Congo languages spoken by these peoples.
– ORIGIN the name in Mande.

**Mandean** ● **n. & adj.** variant spelling of **MANDAEAN**.

**Mandelbrot set** ● **n.** Mathematics a particular set of complex numbers which has a highly convoluted fractal boundary when plotted.
– ORIGIN 1980s: named after the Polish-born US mathematician Benoit B. *Mandelbrot*.

**mandible** /ˈmandɪb(ə)l/ ● **n.** Anatomy & Zoology **1** the jaw or a jawbone, especially the lower jawbone in mammals and fishes. **2** either of the upper and lower parts of a bird's beak. **3** either half of the crushing organ in an arthropod's mouthparts.
– DERIVATIVES **mandibular** adj. **mandibulate** adj.
– ORIGIN ME: from OFr., or from late L. *mandibula*, from *mandere* 'to chew'.

**Manding** /ˈmandɪŋ/ (also **Mandingo** /manˈdɪŋgəʊ/) ● **n. & adj.** another term for **MANDE**.

**Mandinka** /mənˈdɪŋkə/ ● **n.** (pl. same or **Mandinkas**) **1** a member of a West African people living mainly in Senegal, Gambia, and Sierra Leone. **2** the Mande language of this people.
– ORIGIN the name in Mandinka.

**mandola** /manˈdəʊlə/ ● **n.** **1** a large tenor or bass mandolin, used in ensembles and folk groups. **2** (also **mandora** /-ˈdɔːrə/) historical an early stringed instrument of the mandolin or cittern type.
– ORIGIN C18: from Ital.

**mandolin** ● **n.** **1** a musical instrument resembling a lute, having paired metal strings plucked with a plectrum. **2** (also **mandoline**) a kitchen utensil consisting of a flat frame with adjustable blades for slicing vegetables.
– DERIVATIVES **mandolinist** n.
– ORIGIN C18: from Fr. *mandoline*, from Ital. *mandolino*, dimin. of *mandola* (see **MANDOLA**).

**mandorla** /manˈdɔːlə/ ● **n.** another term for **VESICA PISCIS**.
– ORIGIN C19: from Ital., lit. 'almond'.

**mandragora** /manˈdragərə/ ● **n.** poetic/literary the mandrake, especially when used as a narcotic.
– ORIGIN OE, via med. L. from L. and Gk *mandragoras*.

**mandrake** ● **n.** a Mediterranean plant of the nightshade family, having a forked fleshy root which supposedly resembles the human form and was formerly alleged to shriek when pulled from the ground, widely used in medicine and magic. [*Mandragora officinarum*.]
– ORIGIN ME *mandrag(g)e*, from MDu. *mandrag(r)e*, from med. L. *mandragora*; assoc. with **MAN** (because of the shape of its root) + *drake* in the OE sense 'dragon'.

**Mandrax** /ˈmandraks/ ● **n.** trademark a sedative drug containing methaqualone and diphenhydramine.
– ORIGIN 1960s: of unknown origin.

**mandrel** /ˈmandr(ə)l/ ● **n.** **1** a shaft or spindle in a lathe to which work is fixed while being turned. **2** a cylindrical rod round which metal or other material is forged or shaped. **3** Brit. a miner's pick.
– ORIGIN C16: of unknown origin.

**mandrill** /ˈmandrɪl/ ● **n.** a large West African baboon with a brightly coloured red and blue face, the male having a blue rump. [*Mandrillus sphinx*.]
– ORIGIN C18: prob. from **MAN** + **DRILL**[3].

**manducate** /ˈmandjʊkeɪt/ ● **v.** formal chew or eat.
– DERIVATIVES **manducation** n. **manducatory** adj.
– ORIGIN C17 (earlier (C15) as *manducation*): from L. *manducat-*, *manducare* 'chew'.

**mane** ● **n.** a growth of long hair on the neck of a horse, lion, or other animal. ➤a person's long hair.
– DERIVATIVES **-maned** adj. **maneless** adj.
– ORIGIN OE *manu*, of Gmc origin.

**maneater** ● **n.** **1** an animal that has a propensity for killing and eating humans. **2** informal a dominant woman who has many sexual partners.
– DERIVATIVES **man-eating** adj.

**manège** /maˈnɛʒ/ ● **n.** **1** an arena or enclosed area in which horses and riders are trained. **2** the movements of a trained horse. **3** horsemanship.
– ORIGIN C17: Fr., from Ital. (see **MANAGE**).

**manes** /ˈmɑːneɪz, ˈmeɪniːz/ ● **pl. n.** (in Roman mythology) the deified souls of dead ancestors.
– ORIGIN from L.

**maneuver** ● **n. & v.** US spelling of **MANOEUVRE**.

**man Friday** ● **n.** a male helper or follower.
– ORIGIN from *Man Friday*, the name of a character in Defoe's novel *Robinson Crusoe* (1719).

**manful** ● **adj.** resolute or brave, especially in the face of adversity.
– DERIVATIVES **manfully** adv. **manfulness** n.

**manga** /ˈmaŋgə/ ● **n.** a Japanese genre of cartoons, comic books, and animated films, typically with a science-fiction or fantasy theme.
– ORIGIN Japanese, from *man* 'indiscriminate' + *ga* 'picture'.

**mangabey** /ˈmaŋgəbeɪ/ ● **n.** a medium-sized long-tailed monkey native to the forests of West and central Africa. [Genus *Cercocebus*: several species.]
– ORIGIN C18: by erroneous assoc. with *Mangabey*, a region of Madagascar.

**manganate** /ˈmaŋgənət, -neɪt/ ● **n.** Chemistry a salt in which the anion contains both manganese and oxygen.

**manganese** /ˈmaŋgəniːz/ ● **n.** the chemical element of atomic number 25, a hard grey metal used in special steels and magnetic alloys. (Symbol: **Mn**)
– DERIVATIVES **manganic** adj. **manganous** adj.
– ORIGIN C17: via Fr. from Ital. *manganese*, unexplained alt. of med. L. *magnesia* (see **MAGNESIA**).

**manganite** /ˈmaŋgənʌɪt/ ● **n.** a steel-grey or black mineral consisting of a basic manganese oxide.

**mange** /meɪn(d)ʒ/ ● **n.** a skin disease of mammals caused by parasitic mites and occasionally communicable to humans, typically causing severe itching and hair loss.
– ORIGIN ME: from OFr. *mangeue*, from *mangier* 'eat', from L. *manducare* 'to chew'.

**mangel** /ˈmaŋg(ə)l/ (also **mangel-wurzel** /-ˌwəːz(ə)l/) ● **n.** another term for **MANGOLD**.

**manger** ● **n.** a long trough for feeding horses or cattle.
– ORIGIN ME: from OFr. *mangeure*, based on L. *manducat-* (see **MANDUCATE**).

**mangetout** /ˈmɒ̃ʒtuː, -ˈtuː/ ● **n.** (pl. same or **mangetouts** pronunc. same) chiefly Brit. a pea of a variety with an edible pod, eaten when the pod is young and flat.
– ORIGIN C19: from Fr., lit. 'eat all'.

**mangey** ● **adj.** variant spelling of **MANGY**.

**mangle**[1] ● **n.** **1** chiefly Brit. a machine having two or more cylinders turned by a handle, between which wet laundry is squeezed (to remove excess moisture) and pressed. **2** US a large machine for ironing sheets or other fabrics, using heated rollers. ● **v.** press with a mangle.
– ORIGIN C17: from Du. *mangel*, from *mangelen* 'to mangle', from med. L. *mango*, *manga*, from Gk *manganon* 'axis, engine'.

**mangle**[2] ● **v.** severely mutilate or damage by tearing or

## Word *Formation*

**-mania** 'madness, obsessiveness'

➤ Some **-mania** words in current use (full entries and definitions to be found in this dictionary):

| | | |
|---|---|---|
| bibliomania | passionate enthusiasm for books | Gk *biblion* 'book' |
| dipsomania | a craving for alcohol; alcoholism | Gk *dipsa* 'thirst' |
| egomania | obsessive egotism | based on EGO |
| erotomania | excessive sexual desire | Gk *erōt-*, *erōs* 'sexual love' |
| kleptomania | an irresistible urge to steal | Gk *kleptēs* 'thief' |
| megalomania | obsession with power | MEGALO- (from Gk *megas* 'great') |
| monomania | obsession with one thing | Gk *monos* 'alone' |
| mythomania | an abnormal tendency to tell lies | based on MYTH |
| nymphomania | uncontrollable sexual desire in a woman | L. *nympha* 'nymph' |
| pyromania | obsessive desire to set things on fire | Gk *pur* 'fire' |

➤ Some more unusual **-mania** words:

| | | |
|---|---|---|
| anthomania | passion for flowers | Gk *anthos* 'flower' |
| decalcomania | a process for transferring paper designs on to porcelain | Fr. *décalquer* 'transfer a tracing' (with reference to the enthusiasm for the process in the 1860s) |
| dromomania | passion for running | Gk *dromos* 'course, running' |
| etheromania | craving for ether (as a stimulant) | based on ETHER |
| graphomania | passion for writing | Gk *graphos* 'writing' |
| islomania | obsession with islands | based on ISLE |
| micromania | obsessive tendency to belittle oneself | Gk *mikros* 'small' |

➤ Related words:

| | |
|---|---|
| -maniac | forming nouns, e.g. ***megalomaniac*** 'a person obsessed with power' |
| -maniacal | forming adjectives, e.g. ***egomaniacal*** 'of or relating to excessive egotism' |

The use of **-mane**, taken from or imitating French, to form nouns meaning 'a person who has a mania for . . .', is now relatively rare. It survives in only a few words, e.g. ***balletomane***, ***bibliomane***.

crushing.
– DERIVATIVES **mangler** n.
– ORIGIN ME: from Anglo-Norman Fr. *mahangler*, appar. a frequentative of *mahaignier* 'maim'.

**mango** • n. (pl. **-oes** or **-os**) **1** a fleshy yellowish-red tropical fruit which is eaten ripe or used green for pickles or chutneys. ➤the evergreen Indian tree which bears this fruit. [*Mangifera indica*.] **2** a tropical American hummingbird that typically has green plumage with purple feathers on the wings, tail, or head. [Genus *Anthracothorax*: several species.]
– ORIGIN C16: from Port. *manga*, from a Dravidian lang.

**mangold** • n. a beet of a variety with a large root, cultivated as stockfeed. [*Beta vulgaris* subsp. *crassa*.]
– ORIGIN C19: from Ger. *Mangoldwurzel*, from *Mangold* 'beet' + *Wurzel* 'root'.

**mangonel** /ˈmaŋgən(ə)l/ • n. historical a military device for throwing stones and other missiles.
– ORIGIN ME: from OFr. *mangonel(le)*, from med. L. *manganellus*, dimin. of late L. *manganum*, from Gk *manganon* 'axis of a pulley'.

**mangosteen** /ˈmaŋgəstiːn/ • n. **1** a tropical fruit with sweet juicy white segments of flesh inside a thick reddish-brown rind. **2** the slow-growing Malaysian tree which bears this fruit. [*Garcinia mangostana*.]
– ORIGIN C16: from Malay *manggustan*.

**mangrove** • n. a tree or shrub which grows in muddy, chiefly tropical, coastal swamps and has tangled roots that grow above ground and form dense thickets. [*Rhizophora*, *Avicennia*, and other genera.]
– ORIGIN C17: prob. from Port. *mangue*, Sp. *mangle*, from Taino; prob. also assoc. with **GROVE**.

**mangy** (also **mangey**) • adj. (**-ier**, **-iest**) **1** having mange. **2** in poor condition; shabby.
– DERIVATIVES **manginess** n.

**manhandle** • v. **1** move (a heavy object) with great effort. **2** handle roughly by dragging or pushing.

**manhattan** • n. a cocktail made of vermouth and a spirit.

**manhole** • n. a covered opening in a floor or pavement allowing access beneath, especially one leading to a sewer.

**manhood** • n. **1** the state or period of being a man rather than a child. **2** the men of a country or society regarded collectively. **3** archaic the condition of being human. **4** the qualities traditionally associated with men, such as strength and sexual potency. **5** (**one's manhood**) informal, euphemistic a man's penis.

**man-hour** • n. an hour regarded in terms of the amount of work that can be done by one person in this time.

**manhunt** • n. an organized search for a person, especially a criminal.

**mania** • n. **1** mental illness marked by periods of excitement, delusions, and overactivity. **2** an obsession.
– ORIGIN ME: via late L. from Gk, lit. 'madness'.

**-mania** • comb. form Psychology **1** denoting a specified type of mental abnormality or obsession: *kleptomania*. **2** denoting extreme enthusiasm or admiration: *Beatlemania*. See word-formation panel.
– DERIVATIVES **-maniac** comb. form in corresponding nouns.

**maniac** /ˈmeɪnɪak/ • n. **1** a person exhibiting extremely wild or violent behaviour. **2** informal an obsessive enthusiast. **3** Psychiatry, archaic a person suffering from mania.
– DERIVATIVES **maniacal** /məˈnʌɪək(ə)l/ adj. **maniacally** /məˈnʌɪək(ə)li/ adv.
– ORIGIN C16: via late L. from late Gk *maniakos*, from *mania* (see **MANIA**).

**manic** • adj. **1** Psychiatry relating to or affected by mania. **2** showing wild excitement and energy.
– DERIVATIVES **manically** adv.

**manic depression** • n. a mental disorder marked by

alternating periods of elation and depression.
– DERIVATIVES **manic-depressive** adj. & n.

**Manichaean** /ˌmanɪˈkiːən/ (also **Manichean**) ● **adj. 1** chiefly historical of or relating to Manichaeism. **2** of or characterized by dualistic contrast or conflict between opposites. ● **n.** an adherent of Manichaeism.
– DERIVATIVES **Manichaeanism** n.

**Manichaeism** /ˌmanɪˈkiːɪz(ə)m/ (also **Manicheism**) ● **n.** a dualistic religious system with Christian, Gnostic, and pagan elements, founded in Persia in the 3rd century by Manes (*c.*216–*c.*276) and based on a supposed primeval conflict between light and darkness.
– ORIGIN C17: from late L. *Manichaeus* (from the name *Manes*) + **-ISM**.

**Manichee** /ˌmanɪˈkiː/ ● **n. & adj.** archaic term for **MANICHAEAN**.

**manicou** /ˈmanɪkuː/ ● **n.** W. Indian an opossum.
– ORIGIN from an Amer. Ind. word.

**manicure** ● **n.** a cosmetic treatment of the hands and nails. ● **v. 1** give a manicure to. **2** [as adj. **manicured**] (of a lawn or garden) trimmed or neatly maintained.
– DERIVATIVES **manicurist** n.
– ORIGIN C19: from Fr., from L. *manus* 'hand' + *cura* 'care'.

**manifest**[1] ● **adj.** clear or obvious to the eye or mind. ● **v. 1** make manifest; demonstrate. **2** become apparent. **3** (of a ghost) appear.
– DERIVATIVES **manifestly** adv.
– ORIGIN ME: via OFr. from L. *manifestus*.

**manifest**[2] ● **n. 1** a document detailing a ship's contents and cargo and listing passengers and crew, for the use of customs officers. **2** a list of passengers or cargo in an aircraft. **3** a list of the wagons forming a freight train. ● **v.** record in a manifest.
– ORIGIN C16: from Ital. *manifesto* (see **MANIFESTO**).

**manifestation** ● **n. 1** an event, object, or symptom that clearly shows or embodies something. **2** a version or incarnation. **3** an appearance of a ghost or spirit.
– ORIGIN ME: from late L. *manifestatio(n-)*, from *manifestare* 'make public'.

**manifest destiny** ● **n.** the 19th-century belief that the expansion of the United States throughout the American continents was both justified and inevitable.

**manifesto** ● **n.** (pl. **-os**) a public declaration of policy and aims.
– ORIGIN C17: from Ital., from *manifestare*, from L., 'make public', from *manifestus* (see **MANIFEST**[1]).

**manifold** /ˈmanɪfəʊld/ ● **adj.** formal or poetic/literary **1** many and various. **2** having many different forms. ● **n. 1** a pipe or chamber branching into several openings. **2** (in an internal-combustion engine) the part conveying air and fuel from the carburettor to the cylinders or that leading from the cylinders to the exhaust pipe.
– DERIVATIVES **manifoldly** adv. **manifoldness** n.
– ORIGIN OE *manigfeald*.

**manikin** (also **mannikin**) ● **n. 1** a very small person. **2** a jointed model of the human body.
– ORIGIN C16: from Du. *manneken*, dimin. of *man* 'man'.

**Manila** /məˈnɪlə/ (also **Manilla**) ● **n. 1** (also **Manila hemp**) the strong fibre of a Philippine plant (*Musa textilis*), used for rope, matting, paper, etc. **2** strong brown paper, originally made from Manila hemp. **3** a cigar or cheroot made in Manila.
– ORIGIN C17: from *Manila*, capital of the Philippines.

**manilla** /məˈnɪlə/ ● **n.** a metal bracelet used by some African peoples as a medium of exchange.
– ORIGIN C16: from Sp., based on L. *manicula* (see **MANACLE**).

**manioc** /ˈmanɪɒk/ ● **n.** another term for **CASSAVA**.
– ORIGIN C16: from Fr., from Tupi *manioca*.

**maniple** /ˈmanɪp(ə)l/ ● **n. 1** a subdivision of a Roman legion, containing either 120 or 60 men. **2** (in church use) a vestment formerly worn by a priest celebrating the Eucharist, consisting of a strip hanging from the left arm.
– DERIVATIVES **manipular** adj.
– ORIGIN ME: from OFr. *maniple*, from L. *manipulus* 'handful, troop'.

**manipulate** /məˈnɪpjʊleɪt/ ● **v. 1** handle or control with dexterity. **2** examine or treat (a part of the body) by feeling or moving it with the hand. **3** control or influence cleverly or unscrupulously. **4** alter or present (data) so as to mislead.
– DERIVATIVES **manipulability** n. **manipulable** adj. **manipulatable** adj. **manipulation** n. **manipulator** n. **manipulatory** adj.
– ORIGIN C19: back-form. from earlier *manipulation* (C18), from L. *manipulus* 'handful'.

**manipulative** ● **adj. 1** tending to manipulate others cleverly or unscrupulously. **2** of or relating to manipulation of an object or part of the body.
– DERIVATIVES **manipulatively** adv. **manipulativeness** n.

**Manipuri** /ˌmʌnɪˈpʊəri/ ● **n.** (pl. same or **Manipuris**) **1** a native or inhabitant of Manipur. **2** the Tibeto-Burman official language of Manipur.

**Manit.** ● **abbrev.** Manitoba.

**Manitoban** /ˌmanɪˈtəʊbən/ ● **n.** a native or inhabitant of the Canadian province of Manitoba. ● **adj.** of or relating to Manitoba.

**manitou** /ˈmanɪtuː/ ● **n.** (among certain Algonquian North American Indians) a good or evil spirit as an object of reverence.
– ORIGIN C17: via Fr. from an Algonquian lang.

**mankind** ● **n. 1** human beings collectively; the human race. **2** men, as distinct from women.

**manky** ● **adj.** (**-ier**, **-iest**) Brit. informal **1** inferior; worthless. **2** grimy; dirty.
– ORIGIN 1950s: prob. from obs. *mank* 'mutilated, defective', from OFr. *manque*, from L. *mancus* 'maimed'.

**manly** ● **adj.** (**-ier**, **-iest**) **1** having or denoting those good qualities traditionally associated with men, such as courage and strength. **2** (of an activity) befitting a man.
– DERIVATIVES **manliness** n.

**man-made** ● **adj.** made or caused by human beings.

**manna** ● **n. 1** (in the Bible) the substance miraculously supplied as food to the Israelites in the wilderness (Exod. 16). **2** an unexpected or gratuitous benefit. **3** (in Christian contexts) spiritual nourishment, especially the Eucharist. **4** a sweet gum obtained from the manna ash or a similar plant, used as a mild laxative.
– ORIGIN OE, via late L. and Gk from Aramaic *mannā*, from Heb. *mān*, corresp. to Arab. *mann*, denoting an exudation of a tamarisk.

**manna ash** ● **n.** an ash tree which bears fragrant white flowers and exudes a sweet edible gum (manna) from its branches when they are damaged, native to southern Europe and SW Asia. [*Fraxinus ornus*.]

**mannequin** /ˈmanɪkɪn, -kwɪn/ ● **n.** a dummy used to display clothes in a shop window.
– ORIGIN C18: from Fr. (see **MANIKIN**).

**manner** ● **n. 1** a way in which something is done or happens. **2** a style in literature or art. **3** (**manner of**) chiefly poetic/literary a kind or sort. **4** a person's outward bearing or way of behaving towards others. **5** (**manners**) polite or well-bred social behaviour. ➤ social behaviour or habits.
– PHRASES **all manner of** many different kinds of. **in a manner of speaking** in some sense; so to speak. **to the manner born** naturally at ease in a specified job or situation. [with allusion to Shakespeare's *Hamlet* I. iv. 17.]
– DERIVATIVES **mannerless** adj.
– ORIGIN ME: from OFr. *maniere*, based on L. *manuarius* 'of the hand', from *manus* 'hand'.

**mannered** ● **adj. 1** [in combination] behaving in a specified way: *well-mannered*. **2** (of an artistic style) marked by idiosyncratic or exaggerated mannerisms.

**mannerism** ● **n. 1** a habitual gesture or way of speaking or behaving. **2** excessive or self-conscious use of a distinctive style in art, literature, or music. **3** (**Mannerism**) a style of 16th-century Italian art characterized by distortions in scale and perspective and the use of bright, often lurid colours.
– DERIVATIVES **mannerist** n. & adj. **manneristic** adj.

**mannerly** ● **adj.** well-mannered; polite.
– DERIVATIVES **mannerliness** n.

**mannikin** ● **n. 1** a small waxbill of the Old World tropics, typically brown, black, and white, popular as a cage bird. [Genus *Lonchura*: many species.] **2** variant spelling of

**MANIKIN.**

**mannish** ● **adj.** (of a woman) having an appearance and characteristics that are associated with men.
– DERIVATIVES **mannishly** adv. **mannishness** n.
– ORIGIN OE *mennisc* 'human' (see **MAN**, **-ISH**[1]); the current sense dates from ME.

**mannitol** /'manɪtɒl/ ● **n.** Chemistry a sweet-tasting crystalline alcohol found in many plants.
– ORIGIN C19: from *mannite*, in the same sense (from **MANNA** + **-ITE**[1]) + **-OL**.

**mannose** /'manəʊz, -s/ ● **n.** Chemistry a sugar of the hexose class which occurs as a component of many natural polysaccharides.
– ORIGIN C19: from *mannite* 'mannitol' + **-OSE**[2].

**manoeuvre** /mə'nuːvə/ (US **maneuver**) ● **n. 1** a physical movement or series of moves requiring skill and care. **2** a carefully planned scheme or action. **3** (**manoeuvres**) a large-scale military exercise. ● **v.** (**manoeuvred, manoeuvring**) **1** perform or carry out a manoeuvre. **2** carefully guide or manipulate (someone or something) in order to achieve an end.
– DERIVATIVES **manoeuvrability** n. **manoeuvrable** adj. **manoeuvrer** n.
– ORIGIN C18: from Fr. *manœuvre* (n.), *manœuvrer* (v.), from med. L. *manuoperare* from L. *manus* 'hand' + *operari* 'to work'.

**man-of-war** (also **man-o'-war**) ● **n.** (pl. **men-of-war** or **men-o'-war**) **1** historical an armed sailing ship. **2** another term for **FRIGATE BIRD**. **3** short for **PORTUGUESE MAN-OF-WAR**.

**manometer** /mə'nɒmɪtə/ ● **n.** an instrument for measuring the pressure acting on a column of fluid, especially one incorporating a U-shaped tube.
– DERIVATIVES **manometric** adj.
– ORIGIN C18: from Fr. *manomètre*, from Gk *manos* 'thin' + *-mètre* '(instrument) measuring'.

**ma non troppo** ● **adv.** Music but not too much: *allegro ma non troppo.*
– ORIGIN from Ital.

**manor** ● **n. 1** a large country house with lands. **2** chiefly historical (especially in England and Wales) a unit of land, originally a feudal lordship, consisting of a lord's demesne and lands rented to tenants. **3** Brit. informal one's home territory or area of operation.
– DERIVATIVES **manorial** adj.
– ORIGIN ME: from Anglo-Norman Fr. *maner* 'dwelling', from L. *manere* 'remain'.

**manpower** ● **n.** the number of people working or available for work or service.

**manqué** /'mɒ̃keɪ/ ● **adj.** [postpos.] having failed to become what one might have been; unfulfilled: *an actor manqué.*
– ORIGIN C18: Fr., past part. of *manquer* 'to lack'.

**mansard** /'mansɑːd, -səd/ ● **n. 1** a roof having four sides, in each of which the lower part of the slope is steeper than the upper part. **2** Brit. another term for **GAMBREL**.
– ORIGIN C18: from Fr. *mansarde*, named after the C17 Fr. architect François *Mansart*.

**manse** /mans/ ● **n.** the house occupied by a minister of a Scottish Presbyterian Church.
– ORIGIN C15: from med. L. *mansus* 'house, dwelling', from *manere* 'remain'.

**manservant** ● **n.** (pl. **menservants**) a male servant.

**-manship** ● **suffix** (forming nouns) denoting skill in a subject or activity: *marksmanship.*

**mansion** ● **n. 1** a large, impressive house. **2** (**mansion block**) Brit. a large block of flats. **3** (in names) a terrace or mansion block: *Carlyle Mansions.*
– ORIGIN ME (denoting the chief residence of a lord): via OFr. from L. *mansio(n-)* 'place where someone stays', from *manere* 'remain'.

**mansion house** ● **n.** Brit. **1** the house of a lord mayor or a landed proprietor. **2** (**the Mansion House**) the official residence of the Lord Mayor of London.

**manslaughter** ● **n.** the crime of killing a human being without malice aforethought, or otherwise in circumstances not amounting to murder.

**mansuetude** /'manswɪtjuːd/ ● **n.** archaic meekness; gentleness.
– ORIGIN ME: from OFr., or from L. *mansuetudo*, from *mansuetus* 'gentle, tame'.

**manta** /'mantə/ ● **n.** a devil ray that occurs in tropical seas and may reach very great size. [*Manta birostris*.]
– ORIGIN C17: from Latin Amer. Sp., lit. 'large blanket'.

**manteau** /'mantəʊ/ ● **n.** historical a loose gown or cloak worn by women.
– ORIGIN C17: from Fr.; cf. **MANTUA**.

**mantel** (also **mantle**) ● **n.** a mantelpiece or mantelshelf.
– ORIGIN C16: specialized use of **MANTLE**[1].

**mantelet** /'mant(ə)lɪt/ ● **n.** variant spelling of **MANTLET**.

**mantelletta** /ˌmantɪ'lɛtə/ ● **n.** (pl. **mantellettas** or **mantellette** /-teɪ/) a sleeveless vestment reaching to the knees, worn by cardinals, bishops, and other high-ranking Catholic ecclesiastics.
– ORIGIN C19: from Ital., from a dimin. of L. *mantellum* 'mantle'.

**mantelpiece** (also **mantlepiece**) ● **n. 1** a structure of wood, marble, or stone above and around a fireplace. **2** a mantelshelf.

**mantelshelf** (also **mantleshelf**) ● **n. 1** a shelf forming the top of a mantelpiece. **2** Climbing a projecting ledge of rock. ➤a move for climbing on such a ledge from below by pressing down on it with the hands to raise the upper body. ● **v.** Climbing perform such a move.

**manteltree** ● **n.** a beam or arch across the opening of a fireplace, supporting the masonry above.

**mantic** /'mantɪk/ ● **adj.** formal of or relating to divination or prophecy.
– ORIGIN C19: from Gk *mantikos*, from *mantis* 'prophet'.

**manticore** /'mantɪkɔː/ ● **n.** a mythical beast typically depicted as having the body of a lion, the face of a man, and the sting of a scorpion.
– ORIGIN ME: from OFr., via L. from Gk *mantikhōras*, corrupt reading in Aristotle for *martikhoras*, from an Old Pers. word meaning 'maneater'.

**mantid** ● **n.** another term for **MANTIS**.

**mantilla** /man'tɪlə/ ● **n.** (in Spain) a lace or silk scarf worn by women over the hair and shoulders.
– ORIGIN Sp., dimin. of *manta* 'mantle'.

**mantis** /'mantɪs/ (also **praying mantis**) ● **n.** (pl. same or **mantises**) a slender predatory insect with a triangular head, typically waiting motionless for prey with its forelegs folded like hands in prayer. [*Mantis religiosa* (southern Europe) and many other species, suborder Mantodea.]
– ORIGIN C17: mod. L., from Gk, lit. 'prophet'.

**mantissa** /man'tɪsə/ ● **n. 1** Mathematics the part of a logarithm after the decimal point. **2** Computing the part of a floating-point number which represents the significant digits of the number.
– ORIGIN C17: from L., lit. 'makeweight', perh. from Etruscan.

**mantle**[1] ● **n. 1** a woman's loose sleeveless cloak or shawl. **2** a covering: *a mantle of snow.* **3** (also **gas mantle**) a mesh cover fixed round a gas jet to give an incandescent light when heated. **4** Ornithology a bird's back, scapulars, and wing coverts. **5** Zoology an outer or enclosing layer of tissue, especially (in molluscs, cirripedes, and brachiopods) a fold of skin enclosing the viscera and secreting the shell. **6** an important role or responsibility that passes from one person to another. [with allusion to the passing of Elijah's cloak (mantle) to Elisha (2 Kings 2:13).] **7** Geology the region of the earth's interior between the crust and the core, believed to consist of hot, dense silicate rocks (mainly peridotite). ● **v. 1** poetic/literary cloak or envelop. **2** (of the face) glow with a blush. **3** (of a bird of prey on the ground) spread the wings and tail, especially so as to cover captured prey. **4** archaic (of a liquid) become covered with a head or froth.
– ORIGIN OE *mentel*, from L. *mantellum* 'cloak'.

**mantle**[2] ● **n.** variant spelling of **MANTEL**.

**mantlepiece** ● **n.** variant spelling of **MANTELPIECE**.

**mantleshelf** ● **n.** variant spelling of **MANTELSHELF**.

**mantlet** (also **mantelet**) ● **n. 1** historical a woman's short, loose sleeveless cloak or shawl. **2** a bulletproof screen on a military vehicle. ➤historical a movable shelter or screen

used to protect soldiers.
– ORIGIN ME: from OFr. *mantelet*, dimin. of *mantel* 'mantle'.

**mantling** • n. Heraldry a piece of ornamental drapery depicted issuing from a helmet and surrounding a shield.
– ORIGIN C16: from MANTLE[1] + -ING[1].

**Mantoux test** /'mɒ̃tuː, 'mantuː/ • n. Medicine a skin test for immunity to tuberculosis using injection of tuberculin.
– ORIGIN 1930s: named after the Fr. physician Charles *Mantoux*.

**mantra** /'mantrə/ • n. **1** (originally in Hinduism and Buddhism) a word or sound repeated to aid concentration in meditation. **2** a Vedic hymn.
– DERIVATIVES **mantric** adj.
– ORIGIN C18: Sanskrit, lit. 'instrument of thought', from *man* 'think'.

**mantrap** • n. a trap for catching people.

**mantua** /'mantjʊə/ • n. a woman's loose gown of a kind fashionable during the 17th and 18th centuries.
– ORIGIN alt. of Fr. *manteau*, influenced by the name of the Ital. town *Mantua*.

**manual** • adj. **1** of, done, or worked with the hands. **2** using or working with the hands. • n. **1** a book giving instructions or information. **2** an organ keyboard played with the hands not the feet. **3** a vehicle with manual transmission.
– DERIVATIVES **manually** adv.
– ORIGIN ME: from OFr. *manuel*, from (and later assimilated to) L. *manualis*, from *manus* 'hand'.

**manual alphabet** • n. another term for FINGER ALPHABET.

**manubrium** /mə'n(j)uːbrɪəm/ • n. (pl. **manubria** or **manubriums**) Anatomy & Zoology **1** the broad upper part of the sternum of mammals, with which the clavicles and first ribs articulate. **2** the tube which bears the mouth of a coelenterate.
– DERIVATIVES **manubrial** adj.
– ORIGIN C17: from L., 'haft'.

**Manueline** /'manjʊəlʌɪn/ • adj. denoting an ornate style of Portuguese architecture developed during the reign of Manuel I (1495–1521).

**manufactory** • n. (pl. **-ies**) archaic a factory.
– ORIGIN C17: from MANUFACTURE, on the pattern of *factory*.

**manufacture** • v. **1** make (something) on a large scale using machinery. **2** (of a living thing) produce (a substance) naturally. **3** make or produce (something abstract) in a merely mechanical way. **4** invent or fabricate (evidence or a story). • n. the process of manufacturing.
– DERIVATIVES **manufacturability** n. **manufacturable** adj. **manufacturer** n. **manufacturing** adj. & n.
– ORIGIN C16 (denoting something made by hand): from Fr. (re-formed by assoc. with L. *manu factum* 'made by hand'), from Ital. *manifattura*.

**manuka** /'mɑːnʊkə, ma'nuːkə/ • n. a small tree with aromatic leaves which are sometimes used for tea, native to New Zealand and Tasmania. [*Leptospermum scoparium*.]
– ORIGIN C19: from Maori.

**manumit** /ˌmanjʊ'mɪt/ • v. (**manumitted**, **manumitting**) historical release from slavery; set free.
– DERIVATIVES **manumission** n. **manumitter** n.
– ORIGIN ME: from L. *manumittere*, lit. 'send forth from the hand'.

**manure** • n. animal dung used for fertilizing land. • v. apply manure to.
– ORIGIN ME (in the sense 'cultivate (land)'): from Anglo-Norman Fr. *mainoverer*, OFr. *manouvrer* (see MANOEUVRE).

**manus** /'meɪnəs/ • n. (pl. same) chiefly Zoology the terminal segment of a forelimb.
– ORIGIN C19: from L., 'hand'.

**manuscript** • n. **1** a handwritten book, document, or piece of music. **2** a handwritten or typed text submitted for or awaiting printing and publication.
– ORIGIN C16: from med. L. *manuscriptus*, from *manu* 'by hand' + *scriptus* 'written'.

**manuscript paper** • n. paper printed with staves for writing music on.

**Manx** • n. the Celtic language formerly spoken in the Isle of Man, still used for some ceremonial purposes. • adj. of or relating to the Isle of Man or its people or language.
– DERIVATIVES **Manxman** n. (pl. **-men**). **Manxwoman** n. (pl. **-women**).
– ORIGIN from ON, from Old Ir. *Manu* 'Isle of Man' + *-skr* (equivalent of -ISH[1]).

**Manx cat** • n. a cat of a breed having no tail or an extremely short one.

**Manx Loghtan** /'lɒxt(ə)n/ • n. a sheep of a primitive breed with several pairs of horns and tawny red-brown wool.

**Manx shearwater** • n. a dark-backed shearwater that nests on islands in the NE Atlantic and Mediterranean. [*Puffinus puffinus*.]

**many** • det., pron., & adj. (**more**, **most**) a large number of. • n. [as pl. n. **the many**] the majority of people.
– PHRASES **a good** (or **great**) **many** a large number. **many a ——** a large number of.
– ORIGIN OE *manig*, of Gmc origin.

**manzanilla** /ˌmanzə'nɪlə, -'niːljə/ • n. a pale, very dry Spanish sherry.
– ORIGIN Sp., lit. 'chamomile' (because the flavour is said to be reminiscent of that of chamomile).

**manzanita** /ˌmanzə'niːtə/ • n. an evergreen dwarf shrub related to the bearberry, native to California. [*Arctostaphylos manzanita* and other species.]
– ORIGIN C19: from Sp., dimin. of *manzana* 'apple'.

**Mao** /maʊ/ • n. [as modifier] denoting a jacket or suit of a plain style with a mandarin collar, associated with communist China.
– ORIGIN 1960s: by assoc. with *Mao Zedong* (see MAOISM).

**Maoism** • n. the communist doctrines of Mao Zedong (1893–1976), Chinese head of state 1949–59, as formerly practised in China.
– DERIVATIVES **Maoist** n. & adj.

**Maori** /'maʊri/ • n. (pl. same or **Maoris**) **1** a member of the aboriginal people of New Zealand. **2** the Polynesian language of this people.
– ORIGIN the name in Maori.

**mao-tai** /maʊ'tʌɪ/ • n. a strong sorghum-based liquor distilled in SW China.
– ORIGIN named after a town in SW China.

**map** • n. **1** a diagrammatic representation of an area of land or sea showing physical features, cities, roads, etc. **2** a diagram or collection of data showing the spatial arrangement or distribution of something over an area. **3** Biology a representation of the sequence of genes on a chromosome or of bases in a DNA or RNA molecule. • v. (**mapped**, **mapping**) **1** represent or record on or in a map. **2** (**map something out**) plan a route or course of action in detail. **3** Mathematics & Linguistics associate each element of (a set) with an element of another set. ➤(**map on to**) be associated with or linked to.
– PHRASES **off the map** (of a place) very distant or remote. **put something on the map** bring something to prominence. **wipe something off the map** obliterate something totally.
– DERIVATIVES **mapless** adj. **mappable** adj. **mapper** n. **mapping** n.
– ORIGIN C16: from med. L. *mappa mundi*, lit. 'sheet of the world', from L. *mappa* 'sheet, napkin'.

**maple** • n. a tree or shrub with lobed leaves, winged fruits, and a syrupy sap. [*Acer campestre* (**field maple**, Europe), *A. saccharum* (**sugar maple**, N. America), and related species.]
– ORIGIN OE *mapel-* in *mapeltreow*, *mapulder* 'maple tree'.

**maple leaf** • n. the leaf of the maple, the emblem of Canada.

**maple sugar** • n. N. Amer. sugar produced by evaporating maple syrup.

**maple syrup** • n. syrup produced from the sap of certain maples, especially the sugar maple.

**map reference** • n. a set of numbers and letters specifying a location as represented on a map.

**Mapuche** /ma'pʊtʃi/ • n. (pl. same or **Mapuches**) **1** a member of an American Indian people of central Chile

and adjacent parts of Argentina. **2** the Araucanian language of this people.
– ORIGIN the name in Mapuche, from *mapu* 'land' + *che* 'people'.

**maquette** /ma'kɛt/ ● **n.** a sculptor's small preliminary model or sketch.
– ORIGIN C20: from Fr., from Ital. *machietta*, dimin. of *macchia* 'spot'.

**maquillage** /ˌmakɪ'jɑːʒ/ ● **n.** make-up; cosmetics.
– ORIGIN Fr., from *maquiller* 'to make up', from OFr. *masquiller* 'to stain'.

**maquis** /ma'kiː, French maki/ ● **n.** (pl. same) **1** (**the Maquis**) the French resistance movement during the German occupation (1940–5). ➤a member of this movement. **2** dense scrub vegetation consisting of hardy evergreen shrubs and small trees, characteristic of coastal regions in the Mediterranean.
– ORIGIN C19: from Fr., 'brushwood', from Corsican Ital. *macchia*.

**maquisard** /ˌmakɪ'zɑː, French makizaʀ/ ● **n.** a member of the Maquis.

**Mar.** ● **abbrev.** March.

**mar** ● **v.** (**marred**, **marring**) impair; spoil.
– ORIGIN OE *merran* 'hinder, damage', of Gmc origin.

**marabou** /'marəbuː/ ● **n.** **1** a large African stork with a massive bill and large neck pouch. [*Leptoptilos crumeniferus*.] **2** down from the wing or tail of the marabou used as a trimming for hats or clothing.
– ORIGIN C19: from Fr., from Arab. *murābiṭ* 'holy man' (see also MARABOUT), the stork being regarded as holy.

**marabout** /'marəbuːt/ ● **n.** **1** a Muslim hermit or monk, especially in North Africa. **2** a shrine marking the burial place of a Muslim hermit or monk.
– ORIGIN C17: via Fr. and Port. from Arab. *murābiṭ* 'holy man'.

**maraca** /mə'rakə/ ● **n.** a hollow gourd or gourd-shaped container filled with small beans, stones, etc., forming one of a pair and shaken as a percussion instrument.
– ORIGIN C17: from Port. *maracá*, from Tupi.

**maranta** /mə'rantə/ ● **n.** **1** a tropical American plant of a genus which includes the prayer plant and the arrowroot. [Genus *Maranta*.] **2** a calathea.
– ORIGIN mod. L., named after a C16 Ital. herbalist Bartollomeo *Maranta*.

**maraschino** /ˌmarə'skiːnəʊ, -'ʃiːnəʊ/ ● **n.** (pl. **-os**) **1** a strong, sweet liqueur made from small black Dalmatian cherries. **2** (also **maraschino cherry**) a cherry preserved in maraschino.
– ORIGIN Ital., from *marasca* (the name of the cherry), from *amaro* 'bitter'.

**marasmus** /mə'razməs/ ● **n.** Medicine undernourishment causing a child's weight to be significantly low for their age.
– DERIVATIVES **marasmic** adj.
– ORIGIN C17: mod. L., from Gk *marasmos* 'withering'.

**Maratha** /mə'rɑːtə, -'ratə/ (also **Mahratta**) ● **n.** a member of the princely and military castes of the former Hindu kingdom of Maharashtra in central India.
– ORIGIN via Hindi from Sanskrit *Mahārāṣtra* 'great kingdom'.

**Marathi** /mə'rɑːti, -'rati/ (also **Mahratti**) ● **n.** the Indic language of the Marathas.

**marathon** ● **n.** **1** a long-distance running race, strictly one of 26 miles 385 yards (42.195 km). **2** a long-lasting and difficult task. ➤[as modifier] of great duration or difficulty: *a marathon effort.*
– DERIVATIVES **marathoner** n.
– ORIGIN C19: from *Marathōn* in Greece, the scene of a victory over the Persians in 490 BC; the modern race is based on the tradition that a messenger ran from Marathon to Athens (22 miles) with the news.

**maraud** /mə'rɔːd/ ● **v.** [often as adj. **marauding**] attack and steal; raid.
– DERIVATIVES **marauder** n.
– ORIGIN C17: from Fr. *marauder*, from *maraud* 'rogue'.

**marble** ● **n.** **1** a hard crystalline metamorphic form of limestone, typically variegated or mottled, which may be polished and is used in sculpture and building. **2** a small ball of coloured glass used as a toy. ➤(**marbles**) [treated as sing.] a game in which marbles are rolled along the ground. **3** (**one's marbles**) informal one's mental faculties. ● **v.** give (something) the appearance of marble.
– DERIVATIVES **marbled** adj. **marbleize** (also **-ise**) v. **marbler** n. **marbly** adj.
– ORIGIN ME: via OFr. (var. of *marbre*), from L. *marmor*, from Gk *marmaros* 'shining stone'.

**marble cake** ● **n.** a cake with a mottled appearance, made of light and dark sponge.

**marbled white** ● **n.** a white butterfly with black markings which lives in rough grassland. [*Melanargia galathea* and other species.]

**marbling** ● **n.** **1** colouring or marking that resembles marble. **2** streaks of fat in lean meat.

**Marburg disease** ● **n.** an acute, often fatal, form of haemorrhagic fever caused by a filovirus (**Marburg virus**) which normally lives in African monkeys.

**marc** ● **n.** **1** the refuse of grapes that have been pressed for winemaking. **2** an alcoholic spirit distilled from this.
– ORIGIN C17: from Fr., from *marcher* in the early sense 'to tread or trample'.

**Marcan** /'mɑːk(ə)n/ ● **adj.** of or relating to St Mark or the Gospel ascribed to him.

**marcasite** /'mɑːkəsʌɪt, -ziːt/ ● **n.** **1** a semi-precious stone consisting of iron pyrites. **2** a bronze-yellow mineral consisting of iron disulphide but differing from pyrite in typically forming aggregates of tabular crystals. **3** a piece of polished steel or similar metal cut as a gem.
– ORIGIN ME: from med. L. *marcasita*, from Arab. *marḳašīṯa*, from Pers.

**marcato** /mɑː'kɑːtəʊ/ ● **adv. & adj.** Music played with emphasis.
– ORIGIN Ital., 'marked, accented', of Gmc origin.

**marcescent** /mɑː'sɛs(ə)nt/ ● **adj.** Botany (of leaves or fronds) withering but remaining attached to the stem.
– DERIVATIVES **marcescence** n.
– ORIGIN C18: from L. *marcescent-* 'beginning to wither', from *marcere* 'wither'.

**March** ● **n.** the third month of the year.
– ORIGIN ME: from an OFr. dial. var. of *marz*, from L. *Martius* (*mensis*) '(month) of Mars'.

**march**[1] ● **v.** **1** walk in a military manner with a regular measured tread. **2** walk or proceed quickly and with determination. ➤force (someone) to walk somewhere quickly. **3** walk along public roads in an organized procession to make a protest. ● **n.** **1** an act or instance of marching. **2** a piece of music composed to accompany or be suggestive of marching.
– PHRASES **on the march** engaged in marching or making progress.
– ORIGIN ME: from Fr. *marcher* 'to walk'.

**march**[2] ● **n.** (usu. **Marches**) an area of land on the border between two countries or territories. ● **v.** (**march with**) have a common frontier with.
– ORIGIN ME: from OFr. *marche* (n.), *marchir* (v.), of Gmc origin; rel. to MARK[1].

**marcher**[1] ● **n.** a person taking part in a protest march.

**marcher**[2] ● **n.** chiefly historical an inhabitant of a frontier or border district.

**March hare** ● **n.** informal a brown hare in the breeding season, noted for its leaping, boxing, and chasing in circles.

**marching order** ● **n.** Military equipment for marching.

**marching orders** ● **pl. n.** **1** instructions from a superior officer for troops to depart. **2** informal a dismissal.

**marchioness** /ˌmɑːʃə'nɛs, 'mɑːʃ(ə)nɪs/ ● **n.** **1** the wife or widow of a marquess. **2** a woman holding the rank of marquess in her own right.
– ORIGIN C16: from med. L. *marchionissa*, fem. of *marchio(n-)* 'ruler of a border territory'.

**marchpane** /'mɑːtʃpeɪn/ ● **n.** archaic marzipan.

**march past** ● **n.** chiefly Brit. a formal march by troops past a saluting point at a review.

**marcottage** /ˌmɑːkɒ'tɑːʒ, mɑː'kɒtɪdʒ/ ● **n.** a method of propagating plants in which an incision is made below a

joint or node and covered with a thick layer of moss or other substance into which new roots grow.
– ORIGIN C20: from Fr., lit. 'layering', from *marcotter.*

**Mardi Gras** /ˌmɑːdɪ ˈgrɑː, French maʀdi gʀa/ ● **n.** a carnival held in some countries on Shrove Tuesday.
– ORIGIN Fr., lit. 'fat Tuesday', alluding to the last day of feasting before the fast and penitence of Lent.

**mardy** ● **adj.** (**-ier**, **-iest**) N. English sulky and whining.
– ORIGIN C20: from dial. *mard* 'spoilt' (describing a child), alt. of *marred* (see **MAR**).

**mare**[1] /mɛː/ ● **n.** the female of a horse or other equine animal.
– ORIGIN OE *mearh* 'horse', *mere* 'mare', from a Gmc base.

**mare**[2] /ˈmɑːreɪ, -ri/ ● **n.** (pl. **maria** /ˈmɑːrɪə/) Astronomy a large, level basalt plain on the surface of the moon, appearing dark by contrast with highland areas.
– ORIGIN C19: special use of L. *mare* 'sea'; these areas were once thought to be seas.

**mare clausum** /ˌmɑːreɪ ˈklaʊsʊm, ˈklɔːzəm/ ● **n.** (pl. **maria clausa** /ˌmɑːrɪə ˈklaʊsə, ˈklɔːzə/) Law the sea under the jurisdiction of a particular country.
– ORIGIN L., 'closed sea'.

**mare liberum** /ˌmɑːreɪ ˈliːbərʊm, ˈlʌɪbərəm/ ● **n.** (pl. **maria libera** /ˌmɑːrɪə ˈliːbərə, ˈlʌɪbərə/) Law the sea open to all nations.
– ORIGIN L., lit. 'free sea'.

**maremma** /məˈrɛmə/ ● **n.** (pl. **maremme** /-mi/) (especially in Italy) an area of low marshy land near a seashore.
– ORIGIN C19: Ital., from L. *maritima*, fem. of *maritimus* (see **MARITIME**).

**mare's nest** ● **n.** **1** a complex and difficult situation; a muddle. **2** an illusory discovery.
– ORIGIN C16: formerly in the phr. *to have found* (or *spied*) *a mare's nest* (i.e. something that does not exist), used in the sense 'to have discovered something amazing'.

**mare's tail** ● **n.** **1** a widely distributed water plant with whorls of narrow leaves around a tall stout stem. [*Hippuris vulgaris.*] **2** (**mare's tails**) long straight streaks of cirrus cloud.

**Mareva injunction** /məˈreɪvə, məˈriːvə/ ● **n.** English Law a court order freezing a debtor's assets, usually in order to prevent them being taken abroad.
– ORIGIN named after *Mareva* Compania Naveria S. A., the first plaintiff to be granted such an injunction (1975).

**Marfan's syndrome** /ˈmɑːfɑ̃z/ ● **n.** Medicine a hereditary disorder of the connective tissue, resulting in abnormally long and thin digits and also frequently in optical and cardiovascular defects.
– ORIGIN 1930s: named after the Fr. paediatrician Antonin B. J. *Marfan.*

**margarine** /ˌmɑːdʒəˈriːn, ˈmɑːgəriːn/ ● **n.** a butter substitute made from vegetable oils or animal fats.
– ORIGIN C19: from Fr., from Gk *margaron* 'pearl' (because of the lustre of the crystals of esters from which it was first made) + **-INE**[4].

**margarita** /ˌmɑːgəˈriːtə/ ● **n.** a cocktail made with tequila and citrus fruit juice.
– ORIGIN Sp. equivalent of the given name *Margaret.*

**margate** /ˈmɑːgɪt/ ● **n.** a deep-bodied greyish fish which occurs in warm waters of the western Atlantic. [*Haemulon album* and *Anisotremus surinamesis* (**black margate**).]
– ORIGIN C18: of unknown origin.

**margay** /ˈmɑːgeɪ/ ● **n.** a small South American wild cat with large eyes and a yellowish coat with black spots and stripes. [*Felis wiedii.*]
– ORIGIN C18: via Fr. from Tupi *marakaya.*

**marge**[1] ● **n.** Brit. informal short for **MARGARINE**.

**marge**[2] ● **n.** poetic/literary a margin.

**margin** ● **n.** **1** an edge or border. ➤the blank border on each side of the print on a page. **2** the furthest reach or limit: *the margins of acceptability.* **3** an amount above (or below) an accepted or minimum point: *they won by a convincing 17-point margin.* ➤Finance a sum deposited with a broker to cover the risk of loss on a transaction on account. ➤Austral./NZ an increment to a basic wage. ● **v.** (**margined**, **margining**) **1** provide with a margin: *its leaves are margined with yellow.* **2** deposit a margin on (an account or transaction).
– PHRASES **margin of error** a small amount allowed for in case of miscalculation or change of circumstances.
– DERIVATIVES **margined** adj.
– ORIGIN ME: from L. *margo, margin-* 'edge'.

**marginal** ● **adj.** **1** of, relating to, or situated at the margin: *marginal notes.* ➤of or relating to water adjacent to the land's edge or coast: *marginal aquatics.* **2** (of a decision or distinction) very narrow. ➤(of costs or benefits) relating to or resulting from small or unit changes. ➤chiefly Brit. (of a parliamentary seat) having a small majority. **3** of secondary or minor importance. ● **n.** **1** chiefly Brit. a marginal parliamentary seat. **2** a plant that grows in water close to the edge of land.
– DERIVATIVES **marginality** n.

**marginalia** /ˌmɑːdʒɪˈneɪlɪə/ ● **pl. n.** marginal notes.
– ORIGIN C19: from med. L., neut. pl. of *marginalis*, from *margo, margin-* (see **MARGIN**).

**marginalize** (also **-ise**) ● **v.** treat as marginal or peripheral.
– DERIVATIVES **marginalization** n.

**marginally** ● **adv.** to only a limited extent; slightly.

**marginate** Biology ● **v.** /ˈmɑːdʒɪneɪt/ provide with a margin; form a margin to. ● **adj.** /ˈmɑːdʒɪnət/ having a distinct margin.
– DERIVATIVES **margination** n.

**margin call** ● **n.** Finance a demand by a broker that an investor deposit further cash or securities to cover possible losses.

**margrave** /ˈmɑːgreɪv/ ● **n.** historical the hereditary title of some princes of the Holy Roman Empire.
– DERIVATIVES **margravate** /ˈmɑːgrəvət/ n.
– ORIGIN C16, from MDu. *markgrave*, from *marke* 'boundary' + *grave* 'count'.

**margravine** /ˈmɑːgrəviːn/ ● **n.** historical the wife of a margrave.

**marguerite** /ˌmɑːgəˈriːt/ ● **n.** another term for **OX-EYE DAISY**.
– ORIGIN C17: Fr. equivalent of the given name *Margaret.*

**Mari** /ˈmɑːriː/ ● **n.** (pl. same or **Maris**) **1** a member of a people of the central Volga valley in Russia. **2** the Uralic language of this people.
– ORIGIN the name in Mari.

**maria** plural form of **MARE**[2].

**mariachi** /ˌmarɪˈɑːtʃi/ ● **n.** (pl. **mariachis**) [as modifier] denoting a traditional Mexican folk music performed by strolling musicians.
– ORIGIN Mex. Sp., 'street singer'.

**mariage blanc** /ˌmarɪɑːʒ ˈblɒ̃, French maʀjaʒ blɑ̃/ ● **n.** (pl. **mariages blancs** pronunc. same) an unconsummated marriage.
– ORIGIN Fr., lit. 'white marriage'.

**Marian** /ˈmɛːrɪən/ ● **adj.** **1** of or relating to the Virgin Mary. **2** of or relating to Queen Mary I of England.

**mariculture** /ˈmarɪˌkʌltʃə/ ● **n.** the cultivation of fish or other marine life for food.
– ORIGIN C20: from L. *mare, mari-* 'sea' + **CULTURE**.

**Marie Rose** ● **n.** a cold sauce made from mayonnaise and tomato purée and served with seafood.
– ORIGIN 1970s: origin unknown.

**marigold** ● **n.** a plant of the daisy family with yellow, orange, or copper-brown flowers, cultivated as an ornamental. [Genera *Calendula* and *Tagetes.*] ➤used in names of other plants with yellow flowers, e.g. **marsh marigold**.
– ORIGIN ME: from the given name *Mary* + dial. *gold*, denoting the corn or garden marigold in OE.

**marijuana** /ˌmarɪˈhwɑːnə/ (also **marihuana**) ● **n.** cannabis, especially as smoked in cigarettes.
– ORIGIN C19: from Latin Amer. Sp.

**marimba** /məˈrɪmbə/ ● **n.** a deep-toned xylophone of African origin.
– ORIGIN C18: from Kimbundu (a Bantu lang. of western Angola), perh. via Port.

**marina** ● **n.** a specially designed harbour with moorings

for pleasure yachts and small boats.
– ORIGIN C19: from Ital. or Sp., fem. of *marino*, from L. *marinus* (see **MARINE**).

**marinade** • n. /ˌmarɪˈneɪd, ˈmarɪneɪd/ a sauce, typically of oil, vinegar, and spices, in which meat, fish, or other food is soaked before cooking in order to flavour or soften it. • v. /ˈmarɪneɪd/ another term for **MARINATE**.
– ORIGIN C17: from Fr., from Sp. *marinada*, via *marinar* 'pickle in brine' from *marino* (see **MARINA**).

**marinara** /ˌmɑːrɪˈnɑːrə, ˈmar-/ • n. (in Italian cooking) a sauce made from tomatoes, onions, and herbs.
– ORIGIN from the Ital. phr. *alla marinara* 'sailor-style'.

**marinate** /ˈmarɪneɪt/ • v. soak in a marinade.
– DERIVATIVES **marination** n.
– ORIGIN C17: from Ital. *marinare* 'pickle in brine', or from Fr. *mariner* (from *marine* 'brine').

**marine** /məˈriːn/ • adj. **1** of, relating to, or produced by the sea. **2** of or relating to shipping or naval matters. • n. a member of a body of troops trained to serve on land or sea, in particular (in the UK) a member of the Royal Marines or (in the US) a member of the Marine Corps.
– PHRASES **tell that to the marines** a scornful expression of disbelief. [referring to the *horse marines*, an imaginary corps of cavalrymen employed to serve as marines (thus out of their element).]
– ORIGIN ME: from OFr. *marin, marine*, from L. *marinus*, from *mare* 'sea'.

**marine iguana** • n. a large lizard with webbed feet, native to the Galapagos Islands, which swims strongly and is the only marine lizard. [*Amblyrhynchus cristatus*.]

**mariner** • n. formal or poetic/literary a sailor.

**Mariolatry** /ˌmɛːrɪˈɒlətri/ • n. idolatrous worship of the Virgin Mary.

**Mariology** /ˌmɛːrɪˈɒlədʒi/ • n. the part of Christian theology concerned with the Virgin Mary.
– DERIVATIVES **Mariological** adj.

**marionette** /ˌmarɪəˈnɛt/ • n. a puppet worked by strings.
– ORIGIN C17: from Fr. *marionnette*, from *Marion*, dimin. of *Marie*.

**mariposa tulip** /ˌmarɪˈpəʊsə/ (also **mariposa lily**) • n. a North American lily with large brightly coloured cup-shaped flowers. [Genus *Calochortus*.]
– ORIGIN C19: *mariposa* from Sp., lit. 'butterfly'.

**Maris Piper** /ˈmarɪs/ • n. a potato of a variety with creamy flesh and smooth oval tubers.
– ORIGIN 1970s: named after *Maris* Lane, original site of the Plant Breeding Institute; *Piper* was chosen arbitrarily.

**Marist** /ˈmɛːrɪst, ˈmarɪst/ • n. **1** a member of the Society of Mary, a Roman Catholic missionary and teaching order. **2** a member of the Little Brothers of Mary, a Roman Catholic teaching order.
– ORIGIN C19: from Fr. *Mariste*, from *Marie*, equivalent of *Mary*.

**marital** • adj. of or relating to marriage or the relations between husband and wife.
– DERIVATIVES **maritally** adv.
– ORIGIN C16: from L. *maritalis*, from *maritus* 'husband'.

**maritime** • adj. **1** connected with the sea, especially in relation to seafaring commercial or military activity. **2** living or found in or near the sea. **3** denoting a climate that is moist and temperate owing to the influence of the sea.
– ORIGIN C16: from L. *maritimus*, from *mare* 'sea'.

**maritime pine** • n. a pine tree with long thick needles and clustered cones, native to the coasts of the Mediterranean and Iberia. [*Pinus pinaster*.]

**marjoram** /ˈmɑːdʒ(ə)rəm/ • n. **1** (also **sweet marjoram**) an aromatic southern European plant of the mint family, the leaves of which are used as a herb. [*Origanum majorana*.] **2** (also **wild marjoram**) another term for **OREGANO**.
– ORIGIN ME: from OFr. *majorane*, from med. L. *majorana*, of unknown ultimate origin.

**mark[1]** • n. **1** a small area on a surface having a different colour from its surroundings, typically one caused by accident or damage. **2** something that indicates position or acts as a pointer. ➤a competitor's starting point in a race. ➤Nautical a piece of material or a knot used to indicate a depth on a sounding line. ➤Telecommunications one of two possible states of a signal in certain systems. The opposite of **SPACE**. **3** a sign or indication: *a mark of respect*. ➤a written symbol made on a document in place of a signature by someone who cannot write. **4** a level or stage: *unemployment passed the two million mark*. **5** a point awarded for a correct answer or for proficiency in an examination. ➤a figure or letter representing the total of such points. ➤(also **handicap mark**) Horse Racing an official assessment of a horse's form, used as the basis for calculating the weight the horse has to carry in a race. **6** (followed by a numeral) a particular model or type of a vehicle or machine: *a Mark 10 Jaguar*. **7** a target. ➤informal, chiefly US a person who is easily deceived or taken advantage of: *they figure I'm an easy mark*. **8** Rugby Union the act of cleanly catching the ball direct from a kick, knock-on, or forward throw by an opponent, on or behind one's own 22-metre line, and exclaiming 'Mark', after which a free kick can be taken by the catcher. **9** Australian Rules an act of catching a ball that has been kicked at least ten metres before it reaches the ground, or the spot from which the subsequent kick is taken. • v. **1** make a mark on. ➤**(mark something up)** annotate or correct a text for printing, keying, or typesetting. ➤become stained. **2** identify using a mark or by writing something down. ➤separate or distinguish by means of a particular feature or characteristic. ➤**(mark someone out for)** select or destine someone for (a particular role). ➤**(mark someone down as)** judge someone to be. **3** indicate the position of. ➤acknowledge or celebrate (an event) with a particular action. ➤be an indication of (a significant event or phase). **4** (**mark something up** or **down**) (of a retailer) increase or reduce the indicated price of an item. **5** assess and give a mark to (written work). ➤**(mark someone/thing down)** reduce the number of marks awarded to a candidate or their work. **6** notice or pay careful attention to. **7** Brit. (in team games) stay close to (an opponent) in order to prevent them getting or passing the ball. ➤Australian Rules catch (the ball) from a kick of at least ten metres.
– PHRASES **be quick** (or **slow**) **off the mark** be fast (or slow) in responding. **get off the mark** get started. **leave** (or **make**) **its** (or **one's** or **a**) **mark** have a lasting or significant effect. **one's mark** Brit. something which is particularly typical of or suitable for someone: *'A motel! That's just about your mark!'* **mark time 1** (of troops) march on the spot without moving forward. **2** pass one's time in routine activities until a more favourable opportunity presents itself. **mark you** chiefly Brit. used to emphasize or draw attention. **near** (or **close**) **to the mark** almost accurate. **off** (or **wide of**) **the mark** incorrect or inaccurate. **of mark** dated having importance or distinction. **on the mark** correct; accurate. **on your marks** used to instruct competitors in a race to prepare themselves in the correct starting position. **up to the mark** up to the required standard or normal level.
– ORIGIN OE *mearc, gemerce* (n.), *mearcian* (v.), of Gmc origin.

**mark[2]** • n. **1** the basic monetary unit of Germany, equal to 100 pfennig. **2** a former English and Scottish money of account, equal to thirteen shillings and four pence in the currency of the day. **3** a denomination of weight for gold and silver, formerly used throughout western Europe and typically equal to 8 ounces (226.8 grams).
– ORIGIN OE *marc*, from ON *mǫrk*; prob. rel. to **MARK[1]**.

**markdown** • n. a reduction in price.

**marked** • adj. **1** having a visible mark. ➤(of playing cards) having distinctive marks on their backs to assist cheating. **2** Linguistics (of words or forms) distinguished by a particular feature. **3** clearly noticeable. **4** singled out, especially as a target for attack: *a marked man*.
– DERIVATIVES **markedly** adv. **markedness** n.

**marker** • n. **1** an object used to indicate a position, place, or route. ➤a thing serving as a standard of comparison. **2** a felt-tip pen with a broad tip. **3** (in team games) a player who marks an opponent. **4** a person who marks a test or examination. ➤a person who records the score in a game, especially in snooker or billiards. **5** N. Amer. informal a promissory note; an IOU.

**market** ● n. **1** a regular gathering of people for the purchase and sale of provisions, livestock, and other commodities. ➤an open space or covered building where vendors convene to sell their goods. **2** an area or arena in which commercial dealings are conducted: *the labour market.* **3** a demand for a particular commodity or service. ➤[often as modifier] the free market; the operation of supply and demand: *market forces.* **4** a stock market. ● v. (**marketed**, **marketing**) **1** advertise or promote. **2** dated buy or sell goods in a market.
– PHRASES **be in the market for** wish to buy. **make a market** Finance take part in active dealing in shares or other assets. **on the market** available for sale.
– DERIVATIVES **marketer** n.
– ORIGIN ME, via Anglo-Norman Fr. from L. *mercatus*, from *mercari* 'buy' (see also **MERCHANT**).

**marketable** ● adj. **1** able or fit to be sold or marketed. **2** in demand.
– DERIVATIVES **marketability** n.

**marketeer** ● n. **1** a person who sells goods or services in a market. **2** a person who works in or advocates a particular type of market.

**market garden** ● n. chiefly Brit. a place where vegetables and fruit are grown for sale.
– DERIVATIVES **market gardener** n. **market gardening** n.

**marketing** ● n. the action or business of promoting and selling products or services.

**marketization** (also **-isation**) ● n. **1** the exposure of an industry or service to market forces. **2** conversion from a planned to a market economy.
– DERIVATIVES **marketize** (also **-ise**) v.

**market-maker** ● n. a dealer in securities or other assets who undertakes to buy or sell at specified prices at all times.

**marketplace** ● n. **1** an open space where a market is held. **2** the arena of competitive or commercial dealings.

**market research** ● n. the activity of gathering information about consumers' needs and preferences.
– DERIVATIVES **market researcher** n.

**market share** ● n. the portion of a market controlled by a particular company or product.

**market town** ● n. (in the UK) a town of moderate size where a regular market is held.

**market value** ● n. the amount for which something can be sold on a given market. Often contrasted with **BOOK VALUE**.

**markhor** /ˈmɑːkɔː/ ● n. a large wild goat with very long twisted horns, native to central Asia. [*Capra falconeri*.]
– ORIGIN C19: from Pers. *mār-ḵwār*, from *mār* 'serpent' + *ḵwār* '-eating'.

**marking** ● n. (usu. **markings**) an identification mark. ➤a pattern of marks on an animal's fur, feathers, or skin.

**markka** /ˈmɑːkɑː, -kə/ ● n. the basic monetary unit of Finland, equal to 100 penniä.
– ORIGIN from Finnish.

**Markov model** /ˈmɑːkɒf/ (also **Markov chain**) ● n. Statistics a stochastic model describing a sequence of possible events in which the probability of each event depends only on the state attained in the previous event.
– ORIGIN C20: named after the Russ. mathematician Andrei A. *Markov.*

**marksman** ● n. (pl. **-men**) a person skilled in shooting.
– DERIVATIVES **marksmanship** n.

**mark-up** ● n. **1** the amount added to the cost price of goods to cover overheads and profit. **2** Computing a set of codes assigned to elements of a text to indicate their structural or logical relation to the rest of the text.

**marl**[1] ● n. an unconsolidated sedimentary rock or soil consisting of clay and lime, formerly used as fertilizer. ● v. apply marl to.
– DERIVATIVES **marly** adj.
– ORIGIN ME: from OFr. *marle*, from med. L. *margila*, from L. *marga*, of Celtic origin.

**marl**[2] ● n. a mottled yarn or fabric.
– DERIVATIVES **marled** adj.
– ORIGIN C19: shortening of *marbled*.

**marlin** /ˈmɑːlɪn/ ● n. a large edible billfish of warm seas, which is a highly prized game fish. [Genera *Makaira* and *Tetrapterus*: several species.]
– ORIGIN C20: from **MARLINSPIKE** (with ref. to its pointed snout).

**marline** /ˈmɑːlɪn/ ● n. Nautical light rope made of two strands.
– ORIGIN ME: from Mid. Low Ger. *marling*.

**marlinspike** (also **marlinespike**) ● n. a pointed metal tool used by sailors to separate strands of rope or wire.
– ORIGIN C17: from *marl* 'fasten with marline' (from Du. *marlen* 'keep binding') + **SPIKE**[1].

**marmalade** ● n. a preserve made from citrus fruit, especially bitter oranges.
– ORIGIN C15: from Port. *marmelada* 'quince jam', from *marmelo* 'quince', based on Gk *melimēlon* (from *meli* 'honey' + *mēlon* 'apple').

**Marmite** /ˈmɑːmʌɪt/ ● n. trademark a dark savoury spread made from yeast extract and vegetable extract.

**marmite** /ˈmɑːmʌɪt, mɑːˈmiːt/ ● n. an earthenware cooking container.
– ORIGIN C19: Fr., from OFr. *marmite* 'hypocritical', with ref. to the hidden contents of the lidded pot, from *marmotter* 'to mutter' + *mite* 'cat'.

**marmoreal** /mɑːˈmɔːrɪəl/ ● adj. poetic/literary made of or likened to marble.
– DERIVATIVES **marmoreally** adv.
– ORIGIN C18: from L. *marmoreus* (from *marmor* 'marble').

**marmoset** /ˈmɑːməzɛt/ ● n. a small tropical American monkey with a silky coat and a long tail. [Genera *Callithrix* and *Cebuella*: four species.]
– ORIGIN ME: from OFr. *marmouset* 'grotesque image', of unknown ultimate origin.

**marmot** /ˈmɑːmət/ ● n. a heavily built, gregarious burrowing rodent, typically living in mountainous country. [Genus *Marmota*: several species.]
– ORIGIN C17: from Fr. *marmotte*, prob. via Romansch *murmont* from late L. *mus montanus* 'mountain mouse'.

**marocain** /ˌmarəˈkeɪn/ ● n. a dress fabric of ribbed crêpe.
– ORIGIN 1920s: from Fr., lit. 'Moroccan'.

**Maronite** /ˈmarənʌɪt/ ● n. a member of a Christian sect of Syrian origin, living chiefly in Lebanon and in communion with the Roman Catholic Church.
– ORIGIN C16: from med. L. *Maronita*, from the name of John *Maro*, a C7 Syrian religious leader.

**Maroon** ● n. a member of a group of black people living in parts of Suriname and the West Indies, descended from runaway slaves.
– ORIGIN C17: from Fr. *marron* meaning 'feral', from Sp. *cimarrón* 'runaway slave'.

**maroon**[1] ● n. **1** a dark brownish-red colour. **2** chiefly Brit. a firework that makes a loud bang, used as a signal or warning.
– ORIGIN C17 (in the sense 'chestnut'): from Fr. *marron* 'chestnut'; sense 2 is so named because the firework makes the noise of a chestnut bursting in the fire.

**maroon**[2] ● v. (usu. **be marooned**) abandon (someone) alone in an inaccessible place, especially an island.
– ORIGIN C18: from **MAROON**.

**marque**[1] /mɑːk/ ● n. a make of car, as distinct from a specific model.
– ORIGIN C20: from Fr., back-form. from *marquer* 'to brand'.

**marque**[2] /mɑːk/ ● n. see **LETTER OF MARQUE**.

**marquee** /mɑːˈkiː/ ● n. **1** chiefly Brit. a large tent used for social or commercial functions. **2** N. Amer. a roof-like projection over the entrance to a theatre, hotel, or other building. **3** [as modifier] N. Amer. leading; pre-eminent: *a marquee player.*
– ORIGIN C17: from **MARQUISE**, taken as pl. and assimilated to **-EE**; sense 3 is with allusion to billing the name of an entertainer over the entrance to a theatre.

**Marquesan** /mɑːˈkeɪz(ə)n, -s(ə)n/ ● n. **1** a native or inhabitant of the Marquesas Islands in the South Pacific, especially a member of the aboriginal Polynesian people of these islands. **2** the Polynesian language of this people.

**marquess** /'mɑːkwɪs/ ● **n.** a British nobleman ranking above an earl and below a duke. Compare with **MARQUIS**.
– ORIGIN C16: var. of **MARQUIS**.

**marquetry** /'mɑːkɪtri/ (also **marquetery** or **marqueterie**) ● **n.** inlaid work made from small pieces of variously coloured wood, used chiefly for the decoration of furniture.
– ORIGIN C16: from Fr. *marqueterie*, from *marqueter* 'become variegated'.

**marquis** /'mɑːkwɪs/ ● **n. 1** (in some European countries) a nobleman ranking above a count and below a duke. Compare with **MARQUESS**. **2** variant spelling of **MARQUESS**.
– DERIVATIVES **marquisate** (also **marquessate**) n.
– ORIGIN ME: from OFr. *marchis*, from **MARCH**[2].

**marquise** /mɑː'kiːz/ ● **n. 1** the wife or widow of a marquis, or a woman holding the rank of marquis in her own right. **2** a finger ring set with a pointed oval gem or cluster of gems. **3** archaic term for **MARQUEE**. **4** a chilled dessert similar to a chocolate mousse.
– ORIGIN C17: Fr., fem. of **MARQUIS**.

**marquisette** /ˌmɑːkɪ'zɛt/ ● **n.** a fine, light, gauze fabric, now chiefly used for net curtains.
– ORIGIN C20: from Fr., dimin. of **MARQUISE**.

**marram grass** /'marəm/ ● **n.** a coarse grass of coastal sand dunes. [*Ammophila arenaria*.]
– ORIGIN C17: from ON *marálmr*, from *marr* 'sea' + *hálmr* 'haulm'.

**marriage** ● **n. 1** the formal union of a man and a woman, typically as recognized by law, by which they become husband and wife. **2** a combination of elements.
– PHRASES **by marriage** as a result of a marriage. **in marriage** as husband or wife.
– ORIGIN ME: from OFr. *mariage*, from *marier* 'marry'.

**marriageable** ● **adj.** fit or suitable for marriage, especially in being wealthy or of the right age.
– DERIVATIVES **marriageability** n.

**marriage guidance** ● **n.** (in the UK) counselling of married couples who have problems in their relationship.

**marriage of convenience** ● **n.** a marriage concluded primarily to achieve a practical purpose.

**married** ● **adj.** of, relating to, or united by marriage. ● **n.** (**marrieds**) married people.

**marron** /'marən/ ● **n.** (pl. same or **marrons**) a large Australian freshwater crayfish which lives on the sandy bottoms of rivers and streams. [*Cherax tenuimanus*.]
– ORIGIN 1940s: from Nyungar *marran*.

**marron glacé** /ˌmarɒ̃ 'glaseɪ/ ● **n.** (pl. **marrons glacés** pronunc. same) a chestnut preserved in and coated with sugar.
– ORIGIN Fr., 'iced chestnut'.

**marrow** ● **n. 1** Brit. a long white-fleshed gourd with thin green skin, eaten as a vegetable. **2** the plant of the gourd family which produces this. [*Cucurbita pepo*.] **3** (also **bone marrow**) a soft fatty substance in the cavities of bones, in which blood cells are produced. **4** the vital part: *such men were the marrow of the organization.*
– PHRASES **to the marrow** to one's innermost being.
– DERIVATIVES **marrowy** adj.
– ORIGIN OE *mearg*, *mærg*, of Gmc origin.

**marrowbone** ● **n.** a bone containing edible marrow.

**marrowfat pea** ● **n.** a pea of a large variety which is processed and sold in cans.

**marry**[1] ● **v.** (**-ies**, **-ied**) **1** join in marriage. ➤ take as one's wife or husband in marriage. ➤ (**marry into**) become a member of (a family) by marriage. ➤ (of a parent or guardian) give (a son or daughter) in marriage. **2** join together; combine harmoniously. **3** Nautical splice (rope ends) together without increasing their girth.
– ORIGIN ME: from OFr. *marier*, from L. *maritare*, from *maritus*, lit. 'married', 'husband'.

**marry**[2] ● **exclam.** archaic expressing surprise, indignation, or emphatic assertion.
– ORIGIN ME: var. of *Mary* (mother of Jesus).

**Mars** ● **n.** a small planet of the solar system which is fourth in order from the sun and the nearest to the earth.

**Marsala** /mɑː'sɑːlə/ ● **n.** a dark, sweet fortified dessert wine produced in Sicily.
– ORIGIN named after *Marsala*, a town in Sicily.

**marsh** ● **n.** an area of low-lying land which is flooded in wet seasons or at high tide, and typically remains waterlogged at all times.
– DERIVATIVES **marshiness** n. **marshy** adj.
– ORIGIN OE *mer(i)sc*, of W. Gmc origin.

**marshal** ● **n. 1** an officer of the highest rank in the armed forces of some countries. ➤ chiefly historical a high-ranking officer of state. **2** US a federal or municipal law officer. ➤ the head of a police department. ➤ N. Amer. the head of a fire department. **3** an official responsible for supervising public events, especially sports events or parades. **4** (in the UK) an official accompanying a judge on circuit, with secretarial and social duties. ● **v.** (**marshalled**, **marshalling**; US **marshaled**, **marshaling**) **1** assemble (a group of people, especially soldiers) in order. **2** bring together or arrange in order (facts, information, etc.). **3** direct the movement of (an aircraft) on the ground at an airport. **4** Heraldry combine (coats of arms) to indicate marriage, descent, or the bearing of office.
– DERIVATIVES **marshaller** n. **marshalship** n.
– ORIGIN ME: from OFr. *mareschal* 'farrier, commander', from late L. *mariscalcus*, from Gmc elements meaning 'horse' (cf. **MARE**[1]) and 'servant'.

**Marshallese** /ˌmɑːʃə'liːz/ ● **n.** (pl. same) **1** a native or inhabitant of the Marshall Islands. **2** the Micronesian language of the Marshall Islands.

**marshalling yard** ● **n.** a large railway yard in which freight wagons are organized into trains.

**Marshal of the Royal Air Force** ● **n.** the highest rank of officer in the RAF.

**marshalsea** /'mɑːʃ(ə)lsiː/ ● **n.** (in England) a court formerly held before the steward and the knight marshal of the royal household.
– ORIGIN ME: earlier spelling *marchalcy*.

**Marsh Arab** ● **n.** a member of a semi-nomadic Arab people inhabiting marshland in southern Iraq.

**marsh fever** ● **n.** another term for **MALARIA**.

**marsh gas** ● **n.** methane, especially as generated by decaying matter in marshes.

**marsh harrier** ● **n.** a large harrier that frequents marshes and reed beds. [*Circus aeruginosus* and related species.]

**marsh hawk** ● **n.** North American term for **HEN HARRIER**.

**marshland** ● **n.** (also **marshlands**) land consisting of marshes.

**marshmallow** ● **n.** a spongy item of confectionery made from a mixture of sugar, albumen, and gelatin.

**marsh mallow** ● **n.** a tall pink-flowered plant which grows in brackish marshes and whose roots were formerly used to make marshmallow. [*Althaea officinalis*.]

**marsh marigold** ● **n.** a plant of the buttercup family which has large yellow flowers and grows in damp ground and shallow water. [*Caltha palustris*.]

**marsh treader** ● **n.** North American term for **WATER MEASURER**.

**marshwort** ● **n.** a white-flowered plant of the parsley family which grows in boggy areas. [Genus *Apium*: several species, in particular *A. nodiflorum*.]

**marsupial** /mɑː'suːpɪəl/ ● **n.** a mammal of an order (Marsupialia) whose young are born incompletely developed and are carried and suckled in a pouch on the mother's belly.
– ORIGIN C17 (in the sense 'resembling a pouch'): from mod. L. *marsupialis*, via L. from Gk *marsupion* (see **MARSUPIUM**).

**marsupium** /mɑː'suːpɪəm/ ● **n.** (pl. **marsupia** /-pɪə/) Zoology a pouch that protects eggs, offspring, or reproductive structures, especially the pouch of a female marsupial mammal.
– ORIGIN C17: via L. from Gk *marsupion*, dimin. of

*marsipos* 'purse'.

**mart** ● n. a trade centre or market.
– ORIGIN ME: from MDu. *mart*, var. of *marct* 'market'.

**martagon lily** /ˈmɑːtəg(ə)n/ ● n. a lily that typically has small purple flowers said to resemble turbans. [*Lilium martagon*.]
– ORIGIN ME (as *mortagon*): from med. L. *martagon*, of uncertain origin; cf. Ottoman Turk. *martagān*, denoting a Turkish kind of turban.

**Martello** /mɑːˈtɛləʊ/ (also **Martello tower**) ● n. (pl. **-os**) any of numerous small circular forts that were erected for defence along the coasts of Britain during the Napoleonic Wars.
– ORIGIN alt. of Cape *Mortella* in Corsica, where such a tower proved difficult for the English to capture in 1794.

**marten** /ˈmɑːtɪn/ ● n. a weasel-like mammal of forests in Eurasia and North America, hunted for fur in some countries. [Genus *Martes*: several species.]
– ORIGIN ME: from OFr. *(peau) martrine* 'marten (fur)', from *martre*, of W. Gmc origin.

**martensite** /ˈmɑːtɪnzʌɪt/ ● n. Metallurgy a hard and very brittle solid solution of carbon in iron that is the main constituent of hardened steel.
– DERIVATIVES **martensitic** adj.
– ORIGIN C19: named after the Ger. metallurgist Adolf *Martens* + **-ITE**[1].

**martial** /ˈmɑːʃ(ə)l/ ● adj. of or appropriate to war; warlike.
– DERIVATIVES **martially** adv.
– ORIGIN ME: from OFr., or from L. *martialis*, from *Mars*, the name of the Roman god of war.

**martial arts** ● pl. n. various sports or skills, mainly of Japanese origin, which originated as forms of self-defence or attack, such as judo, karate, and kendo.
– DERIVATIVES **martial artist** n.

**martial eagle** ● n. a brown eagle with a brown-spotted white belly, the largest African eagle. [*Polmaetus bellicosus*.]

**martial law** ● n. military government, involving the suspension of ordinary law.

**Martian** ● adj. of or relating to the planet Mars or its supposed inhabitants. ● n. a hypothetical or fictional inhabitant of Mars.
– ORIGIN ME, via OFr. or L., from L. *Marti-*, *Mars*, the Roman god of war.

**martin** ● n. used in names of small short-tailed swallows, e.g. **house martin**.
– ORIGIN ME: prob. a shortening of obs. *martinet*, from Fr., prob. from the name of St *Martin* of Tours.

**martinet** /ˌmɑːtɪˈnɛt/ ● n. a strict disciplinarian, especially in the armed forces.
– DERIVATIVES **martinettish** (also **martinetish**) adj.
– ORIGIN C17: named after Jean *Martinet*, C17 Fr. drill master.

**martingale** /ˈmɑːtɪŋgeɪl/ ● n. **1** a strap or set of straps running from the noseband or reins to the girth of a horse, used to prevent the horse from raising its head too high. **2** a gambling system that involves a continual doubling of the stakes.
– ORIGIN C16: from Fr., from Sp. *almártaga*, from Arab. *al-marta'a* 'the fastening', influenced by *martingale*, from Occitan *martegal* 'inhabitant of Martigues (in Provence)'.

**Martini** /mɑːˈtiːni/ ● n. **1** trademark a type of vermouth produced in Italy. **2** a cocktail made from gin and dry vermouth.
– ORIGIN named after *Martini* and Rossi, an Ital. firm selling vermouth.

**Martiniquan** /ˌmɑːtɪˈniːkən, French maʀtinikən/ (also **Martinican**) ● n. a native or inhabitant of Martinique, a French island in the Lesser Antilles. ● adj. of or relating to Martinique.

**Martinist** ● n. an adherent of a form of mystical pantheism developed by the French philosopher L. C. de Saint-Martin (1743–1803).
– DERIVATIVES **Martinism** n.

**Martinmas** /ˈmɑːtɪnməs/ ● n. St Martin's Day, 11 November.

**martlet** /ˈmɑːtlɪt/ ● n. Heraldry a bird similar to a swallow but without feet, borne as a charge or a mark of cadency for a fourth son.
– ORIGIN ME (denoting a swift): from OFr. *merlet*, influenced by *martinet* (see **MARTIN**).

**martyr** ● n. **1** a person who is killed because of their religious or other beliefs. **2** a person who displays or exaggerates their suffering or discomfort in order to obtain sympathy or admiration. ● v. (usu. **be martyred**) kill as a martyr; make a martyr of.
– DERIVATIVES **martyrdom** n. **martyrization** (also **-isation**) n. **martyrize** (also **-ise**) v.
– ORIGIN OE *martir*, via eccles. L. from Gk *martur* 'witness' (in Christian use, 'martyr').

**martyrology** ● n. (pl. **-ies**) **1** the study of the lives of martyrs. **2** a list or register of martyrs.
– DERIVATIVES **martyrological** adj. **martyrologist** n.

**martyry** ● n. (pl. **-ies**) a shrine or church erected in honour of a martyr.

**marvel** ● v. (**marvelled**, **marvelling**; US **marveled**, **marveling**) be filled with wonder or astonishment. ● n. a wonderful or astonishing person or thing.
– DERIVATIVES **marveller** n.
– ORIGIN ME: from OFr. *merveille*, from late L. *mirabilia*, neut. pl. of L. *mirabilis* 'wonderful', from *mirari* 'wonder at'.

**marvellous** (US **marvelous**) ● adj. **1** causing great wonder; extraordinary. **2** extremely good or pleasing.
– DERIVATIVES **marvellously** adv. **marvellousness** n.

**marvel of Peru** ● n. a tropical American herbaceous plant with fragrant trumpet-shaped flowers which open late in the afternoon. [*Mirabilis jalapa*.]

**Marwari** /məːˈwɑːri/ ● n. an Indic language spoken in the Indian state of Rajasthan.
– ORIGIN from Hindi *Mārvār*, from Sanskrit *maru* 'desert'.

**Marxism** ● n. the political and economic theories of Karl Marx and Friedrich Engels, later developed by their followers to form the basis for the theory and practice of communism.
– DERIVATIVES **Marxist** n. & adj.

**Marxism–Leninism** ● n. the doctrines of Marx as interpreted and put into effect by Lenin in the Soviet Union and (at first) by Mao Zedong in China.
– DERIVATIVES **Marxist–Leninist** n. & adj.

**Mary Jane** ● n. **1** a flat, round-toed shoe for women and girls, with a single strap across the top. **2** informal marijuana.

**Marylander** ● n. a native or inhabitant of the US state of Maryland.

**marzipan** /ˈmɑːzɪpan, ˌmɑːzɪˈpan/ ● n. a sweet yellowish paste of ground almonds, sugar, and egg whites, used to coat large cakes or to make confectionery.
– DERIVATIVES **marzipanned** adj.
– ORIGIN C15 (as *marchpane*): from Ital. *marzapane*, perh. from Arab.

**masa** /ˈmasa/ ● n. (in Latin American cuisine) dough made from maize flour and used to make tortillas, tamales, etc.
– ORIGIN from Sp.

**Masai** /ˈmɑːsʌɪ, məˈsʌɪ, mɑːˈsʌɪ/ (also **Maasai**) ● n. (pl. same or **Masais**) **1** a member of a pastoral people living in Tanzania and Kenya. **2** the Nilotic language of this people.
– ORIGIN the name in Masai.

**masala** /məˈsɑːlə/ ● n. a spice mixture ground into a paste or powder for use in Indian cookery.
– ORIGIN from Urdu *maṣālaḥ*, based on Arab. *maṣāliḥ* 'ingredients, materials'.

**mascara** /maˈskɑːrə/ ● n. a cosmetic for darkening and thickening the eyelashes.
– DERIVATIVES **mascaraed** adj.
– ORIGIN C19: from Ital., lit. 'mask'.

**mascarpone** /ˌmaskəˈpəʊneɪ, -ˈpəʊni/ ● n. a soft, mild Italian cream cheese.
– ORIGIN from Ital.

**mascle** /ˈmɑːsk(ə)l/ ● n. Heraldry a lozenge voided, i.e. with a central lozenge-shaped aperture.
– ORIGIN ME: from Anglo-Norman Fr., from Anglo-Latin

*mascula* 'mesh'.

**mascon** /ˈmaskɒn/ ● **n.** Astronomy a concentration of denser material below the surface of the moon or other body, causing a local increase in gravitational pull.
– ORIGIN 1960s: from *mas(s) con(centration)*.

**mascot** ● **n.** a person or thing that is supposed to bring good luck, especially one linked to a particular event or organization.
– ORIGIN C19: from Fr. *mascotte*, from mod. Provençal *mascotto*, fem. dimin. of *masco* 'witch'.

**masculine** ● **adj. 1** having qualities or appearance traditionally associated with men. ➤male. **2** Grammar of or denoting a gender of nouns and adjectives conventionally regarded as male. ● **n.** (**the masculine**) the male sex or gender.
– DERIVATIVES **masculinely** adv. **masculinist** adj. or n. **masculinity** n.
– ORIGIN ME: via OFr. from L. *masculinus*, from *masculus* 'male'.

**masculine rhyme** ● **n.** Prosody a rhyme between final stressed syllables (e.g. *blow/flow, confess/redress*).

**masculinize** (also **-ise**) ● **v.** induce male physiological characteristics in. ➤cause to appear or seem masculine.
– DERIVATIVES **masculinization** n.

**maser** /ˈmeɪzə/ ● **n.** a form of laser generating a beam of microwaves.
– ORIGIN 1950s: acronym from *microwave amplification by the stimulated emission of radiation*.

**mash** ● **n. 1** a soft mass made by crushing a substance into a pulp. **2** bran mixed with hot water, given as a warm food to horses. **3** Brit. informal boiled and mashed potatoes. **4** (in brewing) a mixture of powdered malt and hot water, which is left standing until the sugars dissolve to form the wort. ● **v. 1** reduce or beat to a mash. **2** (in brewing) mix (powdered malt) with hot water to form wort. **3** Brit. informal (with reference to tea) brew or infuse. **4** US & W. Indian informal press forcefully on.
– DERIVATIVES **masher** n.
– ORIGIN OE *māsc* (used as a brewing term), of W. Gmc origin.

**mashie** /ˈmaʃi/ ● **n.** Golf, dated an iron used for lofting or for medium distances.
– ORIGIN C19: perh. from Fr. *massue* 'club'.

**mash note** ● **n.** N. Amer. informal a letter which expresses infatuation or gushing appreciation.
– ORIGIN C19: from sl. *mash* 'infatuation'.

**Mashona** /məˈʃəʊnə/ ● **n.** the Shona people collectively, particularly those of Zimbabwe.
– ORIGIN the name in Shona.

**masjid** /ˈmʌsdʒɪd, ˈmas-/ ● **n.** Arabic word for a mosque.

**mask** ● **n. 1** a covering for all or part of the face, worn as a disguise, for protection or hygiene, or for theatrical effect. **2** a likeness of a person's face moulded or sculpted in clay or wax. ➤the face or head of an animal, especially of a fox, as a hunting trophy. **3** a disguise or pretence: *she let her mask of respectability slip.* **4** Photography a piece of material such as card used to cover part of an image that is not required when exposing a print. ➤Electronics a patterned metal film used in the manufacture of microcircuits to allow selective modification of the underlying material. **5** a face pack. **6** a respirator used to filter inhaled air or to supply gas for inhalation. ● **v. 1** cover with a mask. **2** conceal from view; disguise: *brandy did not mask the bitter taste.* **3** cover so as to protect during a particular process, especially painting.
– DERIVATIVES **masked** adj. **masker** n.
– ORIGIN C16: from Fr. *masque*, from Ital. *maschera, mascara*, prob. from med. L. *masca* 'witch, spectre', but influenced by Arab. *maskara* 'buffoon'.

**masked ball** ● **n.** a ball at which participants wear masks to conceal their faces.

**masking tape** ● **n.** adhesive tape used in painting to cover areas on which paint is not wanted.

**maskinonge** /ˈmaskɪnɒn(d)ʒ, -ˈnɒn(d)ʒi/ ● **n.** another term for **MUSKELLUNGE**.

**masochism** /ˈmasəkɪz(ə)m/ ● **n.** the tendency to derive pleasure, especially sexual gratification, from one's own pain or humiliation.
– DERIVATIVES **masochist** n. **masochistic** adj. **masochistically** adv.
– ORIGIN C19: named after Leopold von Sacher-*Masoch*, the Austrian novelist who described it, + **-ISM**.

**mason** ● **n. 1** a builder and worker in stone. **2** (**Mason**) a Freemason. ● **v.** build from or strengthen with stone.
– ORIGIN ME: from OFr. *masson* (n.), *maçonner* (v.), prob. of Gmc origin.

**mason bee** ● **n.** a solitary bee which lays its eggs in cavities, constructing cells of sand and other particles. [*Osmia* and other genera.]

**Masonic** /məˈsɒnɪk/ ● **adj.** of or relating to Freemasons: *a Masonic lodge.*

**Masonite** ● **n.** trademark, chiefly N. Amer. fibreboard made from wood fibre pulped under steam at high pressure.
– ORIGIN 1920s: from the name of the *Mason* Fibre Co., Laurel, Mississippi.

**Mason jar** ● **n.** chiefly N. Amer. a wide-mouthed glass jar with an airtight screw top, used for preserving fruit and vegetables.
– ORIGIN C19: named after the Amer. inventor John L. *Mason*.

**masonry** ● **n. 1** stonework. ➤the work of a mason. **2** (**Masonry**) Freemasonry.

**mason's mark** ● **n.** a distinctive device carved on stone by the mason who dressed it.

**mason wasp** ● **n.** a solitary wasp that lays its eggs in a cavity which it seals with mud. [Family Eumenidae: many species.]

**masque** /mɑːsk/ ● **n.** a form of amateur dramatic entertainment, popular in 16th- and 17th-century England, which consisted of dancing and acting performed by masked players.
– DERIVATIVES **masquer** n.
– ORIGIN C16: prob. a back-form. (influenced by Fr. *masque* 'mask') from *masker* 'person wearing a mask'.

**masquerade** /ˌmɑːskəˈreɪd, ˌmas-/ ● **n. 1** a false show or pretence. **2** a masked ball. ➤the wearing of disguise. ● **v.** pretend to be someone that one is not. ➤be disguised or passed off as something else: *the idle gossip that masquerades as news.*
– DERIVATIVES **masquerader** n.
– ORIGIN C16: from Fr. *mascarade*, from Ital. *mascherata*, from *maschera* 'mask'.

**Mass** ● **n.** the Christian Eucharist or Holy Communion, especially in the Roman Catholic Church. ➤a musical setting of parts of the liturgy used in the Mass.
– PHRASES **hear Mass** attend a celebration of the Mass without taking communion.
– ORIGIN OE *mæsse*, from eccles. L. *missa*, from L. *miss-*, *mittere* 'dismiss', perh. from the last words of the service, *Ite, missa est* 'Go, it is the dismissal'.

**Mass.** ● **abbrev.** Massachusetts.

**mass** ● **n. 1** a coherent body of matter with no definite shape. ➤any of the main portions in a painting that each have some unity in colour, lighting, etc. **2** a large number of people or objects gathered together. ➤a large amount of material. **3** (**the mass of**) the majority of. ➤(**the masses**) the ordinary people. **4** Physics the quantity of matter which a body contains, as measured by its acceleration under a given force or by the force exerted on it by a gravitational field. ➤(in general use) weight. ● **adj.** relating to, done by, or affecting large numbers of people or things: *a mass exodus of refugees.* ● **v.** assemble or cause to assemble into a single body or mass.
– PHRASES **in mass** as a body. **in the mass** as a whole.
– DERIVATIVES **massy** adj. (poetic/literary).
– ORIGIN ME: from OFr. *masse*, from L. *massa*, from Gk *maza* 'barley cake'.

**massacre** ● **n. 1** an indiscriminate and brutal slaughter of people. **2** informal a very heavy defeat. ● **v. 1** deliberately and violently kill (a large number of people). **2** informal inflict a heavy defeat on.
– ORIGIN C16: from Fr., of unknown origin.

**massage** /ˈmasɑːʒ, məˈsɑːʒ, -dʒ/ ● **n.** the rubbing and kneading of muscles and joints of the body with the hands, especially to relieve tension or pain. ● **v. 1** give a massage to. ➤(**massage something in/into**) rub a sub-

stance into (the skin or hair). **2** manipulate (figures) to give a more acceptable result. **3** gently flatter (someone's ego).
– DERIVATIVES **massager** n.
– ORIGIN C19: from Fr., from *masser* 'knead, treat with massage', prob. from Port. *amassar* 'knead', from *massa* 'dough'.

**massage parlour** • n. an establishment providing massage.

**massasauga** /ˌmasəˈsɔːɡə/ • n. a small North American rattlesnake which favours damp habitats. [*Sistrurus catenatus*.]
– ORIGIN C19: formed from *Mississauga*, a town in southern Ontario, Canada.

**mass defect** • n. Physics the difference between the mass of an isotope and its mass number, representing binding energy.

**massé** /ˈmaseɪ/ • n. Billiards & Snooker a stroke made with an inclined cue, imparting swerve to the ball.
– ORIGIN C19: Fr., past part. of *masser* 'play a massé stroke'.

**mass energy** • n. Physics a body's mass regarded as energy, according to the laws of relativity.

**masseter** /maˈsiːtə/ • n. Anatomy a muscle which runs through the rear part of the cheek and acts to close the jaw in chewing.
– ORIGIN C16: from Gk *masētēr*, from *masasthai* 'to chew'.

**masseur** /maˈsəː/ • n. a person who provides massage professionally.
– ORIGIN Fr., from *masser* 'to massage'.

**masseuse** /maˈsəːz/ • n. a female masseur.
– ORIGIN from Fr.

**massicot** /ˈmasɪkɒt/ • n. a yellow form of lead monoxide, used as a pigment.
– ORIGIN C15: from Fr., ult. from Arab. *martak*.

**massif** /ˈmasɪf, maˈsiːf/ • n. a compact group of mountains.
– ORIGIN C16: Fr. 'massive', used as a noun.

**massive** • adj. **1** large and heavy or solid. **2** exceptionally large, intense, or severe. **3** Geology (of rocks or beds) having no discernible form or structure. ➤(of a mineral) not visibly crystalline. • n. Brit. informal a group of young people from a particular area with a common interest.
– DERIVATIVES **massively** adv. **massiveness** n.
– ORIGIN ME: from Fr. *massif*, *-ive*, from OFr. *massis*, based on L. *massa* (see **MASS**).

**mass market** • n. the market for goods that are produced in large quantities.

**mass noun** • n. Grammar a noun denoting something which cannot be counted, in English usually a noun which lacks a plural in ordinary usage and is not used with the indefinite article, e.g. *luggage*, *happiness*. Contrasted with **COUNT NOUN**.

**mass number** • n. Physics the total number of protons and neutrons in a nucleus.

**mass-produce** • v. produce large quantities of (a standardized article) by an automated mechanical process.
– DERIVATIVES **mass-produced** adj. **mass-producer** n. **mass production** n.

**mass spectrograph** • n. a mass spectrometer in which the particles are detected photographically.

**mass spectrometer** • n. an apparatus for separating isotopes, molecules, and molecular fragments according to mass by ionizing them and making them move in different paths by means of electric and magnetic fields.

**mass spectrum** • n. a distribution of ions shown by the use of a mass spectrograph or mass spectrometer.

**mast**[1] • n. **1** a tall upright post, spar, or other structure on a boat, in sailing vessels generally carrying a sail or sails. **2** any tall upright post, especially a flagpole or a television or radio transmitter.
– PHRASES **before the mast** historical serving as an ordinary seaman. **nail** (or **pin**) **one's colours to the mast** declare openly and firmly what one believes.
– DERIVATIVES **-masted** adj.
– ORIGIN OE *mæst*, of W. Gmc origin.

**mast**[2] • n. the fruit of beech, oak, chestnut, and other forest trees, especially as food for pigs.
– ORIGIN OE *mæst*, of W. Gmc origin.

**mastaba** /ˈmastəbə/ • n. **1** Archaeology an ancient Egyptian tomb consisting of an underground burial chamber with rooms above it. **2** (in Islamic countries) a bench attached to a house.
– ORIGIN from Arab. *maṣṭaba*.

**mast cell** • n. a cell filled with basophil granules, found in connective tissue and releasing histamine and other substances during inflammatory and allergic reactions.
– ORIGIN C19: *mast* from Ger. *Mast* 'fattening, feeding'.

**mastectomy** /maˈstɛktəmi/ • n. (pl. **-ies**) a surgical operation to remove a breast.
– ORIGIN 1920s: from Gk *mastos* 'breast' + **-ECTOMY**.

**master**[1] • n. **1** chiefly historical a man who has people working for him, especially servants or slaves. ➤dated a male head of a household. ➤the male owner of a dog, cat, etc. **2** a skilled practitioner of a particular art or activity. ➤a great artist, especially one belonging to the accepted canon. ➤a very strong chess player. ➤(**Masters**) [treated as sing.] (in some sports) a class for competitors over the usual age for the highest level of competition. **3** a person who has complete control of something: *he was master of the situation.* **4** a man in charge of an organization or group. ➤chiefly Brit. a male schoolteacher, especially at a public or prep school. ➤the head of a college or school. ➤the presiding officer of a livery company or Masonic lodge. ➤the captain of a merchant ship. ➤(in England and Wales) an official of the Supreme Court. **5** [usu. in titles] a person who holds a second or further degree: *a master's degree.* **6** a machine or device directly controlling another. Compare with **SLAVE**. **7** a title prefixed to the name of a boy. **8** an original film, recording, or document from which copies can be made. • adj. **1** having or showing very great skill or proficiency. ➤denoting a person skilled in a particular trade and able to teach others: *a master builder.* **2** main; principal. • v. **1** acquire complete knowledge or skill in. **2** gain control of; overcome. **3** make a master copy of (a film or record).
– DERIVATIVES **masterdom** n. **masterhood** n. **masterless** adj. **mastership** n.
– ORIGIN OE *mæg(i)ster*, from L. *magister*.

**master**[2] • n. a ship or boat with a specified number of masts: *a three-master.*

**Master Aircrew** • n. a generic RAF rank equivalent to warrant officer, only applied to members of an aircrew.

**master-at-arms** • n. (pl. **masters-at-arms**) a warrant officer appointed to carry out or supervise police duties on board a ship.

**master chief petty officer** • n. a rank in the US navy, above senior chief petty officer and below warrant officer.

**masterclass** • n. a class, especially in music, given by an expert to highly talented students.

**master corporal** • n. a rank in the Canadian army and air force, above corporal and below sergeant.

**masterful** • adj. **1** powerful and able to control others. **2** performed or performing very skilfully.
– DERIVATIVES **masterfully** adv. **masterfulness** n.

**master gunnery sergeant** • n. a rank of non-commissioned officer in the US marines, above master sergeant and below sergeant major.

**master key** • n. a key that opens several locks, each of which also has its own key.

**masterly** • adj. performed or performing very skilfully.

**mastermind** • n. a person with outstanding intellect. ➤a person who plans and directs a complex scheme or enterprise. • v. be the mastermind of.

**master of ceremonies** • n. a person in charge of procedure at a state occasion, formal event, or entertainment, introducing the speakers or performers.

**Master of the Rolls** • n. (in England and Wales) the judge who presides over the Court of Appeal and who was formerly in charge of the Public Record Office.

**masterpiece** • n. **1** a work of outstanding artistry, skill, or workmanship. **2** historical a piece of work by a craftsman accepted as qualification for membership of a guild as an acknowledged master.

**master seaman** • n. a rank in the Canadian navy, above leading seaman and below petty officer.

**master sergeant** • n. a high rank of non-commissioned officer in the US armed forces.

**master warrant officer** • n. a rank in the Canadian army and air force, above warrant officer and below chief warrant officer.

**masterwork** • n. a masterpiece.

**masterwort** • n. a plant of the parsley family with white or pinkish flowers, native to central and southern Europe. [Genera *Peucedanum* and *Astrantia*.]

**mastery** • n. **1** comprehensive knowledge or skill in a particular field. **2** the mastering of a subject or skill. **3** control or superiority over someone or something.

**masthead** • n. **1** the highest part of a ship's mast or of the lower section of a mast. **2** the name of a newspaper or magazine printed at the top of the first or editorial page. • v. **1** historical send (a sailor) to the masthead, especially as a punishment. **2** raise (a flag or sail) to the masthead.

**mastic** /'mastɪk/ • n. **1** an aromatic gum or resin exuded from the bark of a Mediterranean tree, used in making varnish and chewing gum and as a flavouring. **2** the bushy evergreen Mediterranean tree which yields mastic, closely related to the pistachio. [*Pistacia lentiscus*.] ➤ used in names of similar or related trees, e.g. **American mastic**. **3** a putty-like waterproof filler and sealant used in building.
– ORIGIN ME: via OFr. and L. from Gk *mastikhē* (perh. from *mastikhan* 'masticate').

**masticate** /'mastɪkeɪt/ • v. chew (food).
– DERIVATIVES **mastication** n. **masticator** n. **masticatory** adj.
– ORIGIN C17 (earlier (ME) as *mastication*): from late L. *masticat-*, *masticare* 'chew', from Gk *mastikhan* 'grind the teeth'.

**mastiff** /'mastɪf, 'mɑː-/ • n. a dog of a large, strong breed with drooping ears and pendulous lips.
– ORIGIN ME: from OFr. *mastin*, based on L. *mansuetus* 'tame'.

**mastiff bat** • n. **1** a heavily built free-tailed bat with a broad muzzle, found mainly in America and Australasia. [*Eumops*, *Molossus*, and other genera: several species.] **2** another term for **BULLDOG BAT**.

**mastitis** /ma'stʌɪtɪs/ • n. inflammation of the mammary gland in the breast or udder.
– ORIGIN C19: from Gk *mastos* 'breast' + **-ITIS**.

**mastodon** /'mastədɒn/ • n. a large extinct elephant-like mammal of the Miocene to Pleistocene epochs, having teeth of a relatively primitive form and number.
– ORIGIN C19: mod. L., from Gk *mastos* 'breast' + *odous*, *odont-* 'tooth' (with ref. to nipple-shaped tubercles on the crowns of its molar teeth).

**mastoid** /'mastɔɪd/ • adj. Anatomy of or relating to the mastoid process. • n. Anatomy the mastoid process. ➤ **(mastoids)** [treated as sing.] informal mastoiditis.
– ORIGIN C18: via Fr. and mod. L. from Gk *mastoeidēs* 'breast-shaped', from *mastos* 'breast'.

**mastoiditis** /ˌmastɔɪ'dʌɪtɪs/ • n. Medicine inflammation of the mastoid process.

**mastoid process** • n. a conical prominence of the temporal bone behind the ear, to which neck muscles are attached, and which has air spaces linked to the middle ear.

**masturbate** /'mastəbeɪt/ • v. stimulate one's genitals with one's hand for sexual pleasure.
– DERIVATIVES **masturbation** n. **masturbator** n. **masturbatory** adj.
– ORIGIN C19: from L. *masturbat-*, *masturbari* 'masturbate', of unknown ultimate origin.

**mat**[1] • n. **1** a thick piece of material placed on the floor and used as protection from dirt, for people to wipe their feet on, or as a decorative rug. ➤ a piece of resilient material for landing on in gymnastics, wrestling, or similar sports. **2** a small piece of cork, card, or similar material placed on a surface to protect it from the heat or moisture of an object placed on it. **3** (also **mouse mat**) a small piece of rigid or resilient material on which a computer mouse is moved. **4** a thick, untidy layer of hairy or woolly material. • v. **(matted, matting)** [usu. as adj. **matted**] tangle in a thick mass: *matted hair.*
– PHRASES **go to the mat** informal vigorously engage in an argument, especially on behalf of another. **on the mat** informal being reprimanded by someone in authority. [with military ref., in which an accused would stand on the orderly room mat.]
– ORIGIN OE *m(e)att(e)*, of W. Gmc origin.

**mat**[2] • n. short for **MATRIX** (in sense 2).

**mat**[3] • n. variant spelling of **MATT**.

**Matabele** /ˌmatə'biːli/ • n. the Ndebele people collectively, particularly those of Zimbabwe.
– ORIGIN from Sotho *matebele*, sing. *letebele*, the name given to this people.

**matador** /'matədɔː/ • n. **1** a bullfighter whose task is to kill the bull. **2** (in ombre, skat, and other card games) any of the highest trumps. **3** a domino game in which halves are matched so as to make a total of seven.
– ORIGIN Sp., lit. 'killer', from *matar* 'to kill', from Pers. *māt* 'dead'.

**matai**[1] /'matʌɪ/ • n. (pl. **matais**) a coniferous New Zealand tree yielding pale wood. [*Prumnopitys taxifolia*.]
– ORIGIN C19: from Maori.

**matai**[2] /mə'tʌɪ/ • n. (pl. same) (in a Samoan extended family or clan) a person who is chosen to succeed and be honoured as the head of the family.
– ORIGIN from Samoan.

**matamata** /ˌmatə'matə/ • n. a South American freshwater turtle that has a broad flat head and neck with irregular projections of skin. [*Chelus fimbriatus*.]
– ORIGIN C19: of unknown origin; prob. from a S. Amer. Ind. lang.

**match**[1] • n. **1** a contest in which people or teams compete against each other. **2** a person or thing able to contend with another as an equal. **3** a person or thing that resembles or corresponds to another. ➤ Computing a string that fulfils the specified conditions of a computer search. ➤ a pair that corresponds or is very similar. **4** a person viewed in regard to their eligibility for marriage. ➤ a marriage. • v. **1** correspond or cause to correspond in some essential respect; make or be harmonious. **2** be equal to in quality or strength. ➤ equalize (two coupled electrical impedances) so as to bring about the maximum transfer of power from one to the other. **3** place in contest or competition with another. **4** **(match someone with)** archaic bring about the marriage of someone to.
– DERIVATIVES **matchable** adj. **matching** adj.
– ORIGIN OE *gemæcca* 'mate, companion', of W. Gmc origin.

**match**[2] • n. **1** a short, thin piece of wood or cardboard used to light a fire, being tipped with a composition that ignites when rubbed against a rough surface. **2** historical a piece of wick or cord designed to burn at a uniform rate, used for firing a cannon or lighting gunpowder.
– ORIGIN ME: from OFr. *meche*, perh. from L. *myxa* 'spout of a lamp', later 'lamp wick'.

**matchboard** • n. interlocking boards joined together by tongue and groove.

**matchbook** • n. N. Amer. a small cardboard folder of matches.

**matchbox** • n. **1** a small box in which matches are sold. **2** [as modifier] very small: *her matchbox apartment.*

**matchless** • adj. unequalled; incomparable.
– DERIVATIVES **matchlessly** adv.

**matchlock** • n. historical a type of gun with a lock in which a piece of wick was used for igniting the powder. ➤ a lock of this kind.

**matchmaker** • n. a person who arranges marriages or initiates relationships between others.
– DERIVATIVES **matchmaking** n.

**match play** • n. play in golf in which the score is reckoned by counting the holes won by each side. Compare with **STROKE PLAY**.
– DERIVATIVES **match player** n.

**match point** • n. **1** (in tennis and other sports) a point which if won by one of the players will also win them the match. **2** (in duplicate bridge) a unit of scoring in matches and tournaments.

**matchstick** ● **n. 1** the stem of a match. **2** a long thin piece: *cut the vegetables into matchsticks.* ➤ [as modifier] (of a figure) drawn using thin straight lines.

**matchwood** ● **n. 1** very small pieces or splinters of wood. **2** light poor-quality wood.

**mate**[1] ● **n. 1** Brit. informal a friend or companion. **2** [in combination] a fellow member or joint occupant: *his table-mates.* **3** the sexual partner of a bird or other animal. **4** an assistant or deputy in some trades: *a plumber's mate.* **5** an officer on a merchant ship subordinate to the master. See also **FIRST MATE**. ● **v. 1** (with reference to animals or birds) come or bring together for breeding; copulate. **2** join or connect mechanically.
– DERIVATIVES **mateless** adj.
– ORIGIN ME: from Mid. Low Ger. *māt(e)* 'comrade', of W. Gmc origin.

**mate**[2] ● **n. & v.** Chess short for **CHECKMATE**.
– ORIGIN ME: from Anglo-Norman Fr. *mat*, from the phr. *eschec mat* (see **CHECKMATE**), and Anglo-Norman Fr. *mater* 'to checkmate'.

**maté** /'mateɪ/ (also **yerba maté**) ● **n. 1** (also **maté tea**) a bitter infusion made from the leaves of a South American shrub, which is high in caffeine. **2** the shrub of the holly family which produces these leaves. [*Ilex paraguariensis.*]
– ORIGIN C18: from Sp. *mate* 'calabash', from Quechua *mati*.

**matelassé** /ˌmat(ə)'laseɪ/ ● **n.** a fabric having a raised design like quilting.
– ORIGIN C19: Fr., past part. of *matelasser* 'to quilt', from *matelas* 'mattress'.

**matelot** /'matləʊ/ ● **n.** Brit. informal a sailor.
– ORIGIN C19: from Fr., var. of *matenot*, from MDu. *mattenoot* 'bed companion', because sailors had to share hammocks.

**matelote** /'mat(ə)ləʊt/ ● **n.** a dish of fish in a sauce of wine and onions.
– ORIGIN Fr., from *à la matelote*, lit. 'mariner-style'.

**mater** /'meɪtə/ ● **n.** Brit. informal, dated mother.
– ORIGIN from L.

**materfamilias** /ˌmeɪtəfə'mɪlɪas/ ● **n.** (pl. **matresfamilias**) the female head of a family or household.
– ORIGIN L., from *mater* 'mother' + *familias*, old genitive form of *familia* 'family'.

**material** ● **n. 1** the matter from which a thing is or can be made. ➤ items needed for an activity. **2** information or ideas for use in creating a book, performance, or other work. **3** cloth or fabric. **4** a person of a specified quality or suitability: *he's not really Olympic material.* ● **adj. 1** denoting or consisting of physical objects rather than the mind or spirit: *the material world.* **2** important; essential; relevant: *the insects did not do any material damage.* **3** Philosophy concerned with the matter of reasoning, not its form.
– DERIVATIVES **materiality** n.
– ORIGIN ME: from late L. *materialis*, from L. *materia* 'matter'.

**materialism** ● **n. 1** a tendency to consider material possessions and physical comfort as more important than spiritual values. **2** Philosophy the doctrine that nothing exists except matter and its movements and modifications.
– DERIVATIVES **materialist** n. & adj. **materialistic** adj. **materialistically** adv.

**materialize** (also **-ise**) ● **v. 1** become actual fact; happen. ➤ appear or be present: *the train failed to materialize.* **2** (of a ghost or spirit) appear in bodily form.
– DERIVATIVES **materialization** n.

**materially** ● **adv. 1** substantially; considerably. **2** in terms of material possessions.

**materia medica** /məˌtɪərɪə 'mɛdɪkə/ ● **n.** the body of remedial substances used in the practice of medicine. ➤ the study of the origin and properties of these substances.
– ORIGIN C17: mod. L., translation of Gk *hulē iatrikē* 'healing material'.

**materiel** /məˌtɪərɪ'ɛl/ ● **n.** military materials and equipment.
– ORIGIN C19: from Fr. *matériel*.

**maternal** ● **adj. 1** of or relating to a mother. ➤ denoting feelings associated with or typical of a mother; motherly. **2** related through the mother's side of the family: *maternal grandparents.*
– DERIVATIVES **maternalism** n. **maternalist** adj. **maternalistic** adj. **maternally** adv.
– ORIGIN C15: from Fr. *maternel*, from L. *maternus*, from *mater* 'mother'.

**maternity** ● **n. 1** motherhood. **2** [usu. as modifier] the period during pregnancy and shortly after childbirth: *maternity clothes.*

**mateship** ● **n.** Austral./NZ informal companionship or friendship.

**matey** (also **maty**) Brit. informal ● **adj.** (**-ier**, **-iest**) familiar and friendly: *a matey grin.* ● **n.** a familiar form of address to a male.
– DERIVATIVES **mateyness** (also **matiness**) n. **matily** adv.

**math** ● **n.** N. Amer. short for **MATHEMATICS**.

**mathematical** ● **adj. 1** of or relating to mathematics. **2** (of a proof or analysis) rigorously precise.
– DERIVATIVES **mathematically** adv.
– ORIGIN ME: from L. *mathematicalis*, from Gk *mathēmatikos*, from *mathēma*, *mathēmat-* 'science', from the base of *manthanein* 'learn'.

**mathematics** ● **pl. n.** [usu. treated as sing.] the branch of science concerned with number, quantity, and space, either as abstract concepts (**pure mathematics**) or as applied to physics, engineering, and other subjects (**applied mathematics**).
– DERIVATIVES **mathematician** n.

**mathematize** (also **-ise**) ● **v.** regard or treat in mathematical terms.
– DERIVATIVES **mathematization** n.

**maths** ● **pl. n.** Brit. short for **MATHEMATICS**.

**Matilda** ● **n.** Austral./NZ informal, archaic a bushman's bundle.
– PHRASES **waltz** (or **walk**) **Matilda** carry such a bundle.
– ORIGIN C19: from the given name *Matilda*.

**matinal** /'matɪn(ə)l/ ● **adj.** rare relating to or taking place in the morning.
– ORIGIN C19: from Fr., from *matin* 'morning'.

**matinee** /'matɪneɪ/ ● **n.** an afternoon performance in a theatre or cinema.
– ORIGIN C19: from Fr. *matinée*, lit. 'morning (as a period of activity)', from *matin* 'morning': performances were formerly also in the morning.

**matinee coat** ● **n.** Brit. a baby's short coat.

**matinee idol** ● **n.** informal, dated a handsome actor admired chiefly by women.

**matins** (also **mattins**) ● **n. 1** a service of morning prayer, especially in the Anglican Church. ➤ a service forming part of the traditional Divine Office of the Western Christian Church, originally said (or chanted) at or after midnight. **2** (also **matin**) poetic/literary the morning song of birds.
– ORIGIN ME: from OFr. *matines*, pl. of *matin* 'morning', from L. *matutinum*, neut. of *matutinus* 'early in the morning', from *Matuta*, the name of the dawn goddess.

**matriarch** /'meɪtrɪɑːk/ ● **n. 1** a woman who is the head of a family or tribe. **2** an older woman who is powerful within a family or organization.
– DERIVATIVES **matriarchal** /-'ɑːk(ə)l/ adj. **matriarchate** n.
– ORIGIN C17: from L. *mater* 'mother', on the false analogy of *patriarch*.

**matriarchy** ● **n.** (pl. **-ies**) **1** a system of society or government ruled by women. **2** a form of social organization in which descent and relationship are reckoned through the female line.

**matrices** plural form of **MATRIX**.

**matricide** /'matrɪsʌɪd, 'meɪtrɪ-/ ● **n.** the killing of one's mother. ➤ a person who kills their mother.
– DERIVATIVES **matricidal** adj.
– ORIGIN C16: from L. *matricidium*, from *mater*, *matr-* 'mother' + *-cidium* (see **-CIDE**).

**matriculate** /mə'trɪkjʊleɪt/ ● **v.** enrol or be enrolled at a

college or university.
– DERIVATIVES **matriculation** n.
– ORIGIN C16: from med. L. *matriculat-*, *matriculare* 'enrol', from late L. *matricula* 'register', dimin. of L. *matrix*.

**matrifocal** • adj. (of a society) based on the mother as the head of the household.

**matrilineal** • adj. of or based on kinship with the mother or the female line.
– DERIVATIVES **matrilineally** adv.

**matrilocal** • adj. of or denoting a custom in marriage whereby the husband goes to live with the wife's community.
– DERIVATIVES **matrilocality** n.

**matrimony** /ˈmatrɪməni/ • n. the state or ceremony of being married; marriage.
– DERIVATIVES **matrimonial** adj. **matrimonially** adv.
– ORIGIN ME: via OFr. from L. *matrimonium*, based on *mater, matr-* 'mother'.

**matrix** /ˈmeɪtrɪks/ • n. (pl. **matrices** /-siːz/ or **matrixes**) **1** an environment or material in which something develops. ➤ Biology the substance between cells or in which structures are embedded. **2** a mould in which something, such as a gramophone record or printing type, is cast or shaped. **3** Mathematics a rectangular array of quantities or expressions in rows and columns that is treated as a single entity and manipulated according to particular rules. ➤ a grid-like array of elements, especially of data items; a lattice. ➤ an organizational structure in which two or more lines of command, responsibility, or communication may run through the same individual. **4** a mass of fine-grained rock in which gems, crystals, or fossils are embedded. **5** fine material.
– ORIGIN ME (in the sense 'womb'): from L., 'breeding female', later 'womb', from *mater, matr-* 'mother'.

**matron** • n. **1** a woman in charge of domestic and medical arrangements at a boarding school or other establishment. **2** Brit. the woman in charge of the nursing in a hospital (official term now **senior nursing officer**). **3** chiefly US a female prison officer. **4** a married woman, typically one who is dignified or staid.
– DERIVATIVES **matronhood** n. **matronly** adj.
– ORIGIN ME: from OFr. *matrone*, from L. *matrona*, from *mater, matr-* 'mother'.

**matron of honour** • n. a married woman attending the bride at a wedding.

**matronymic** /ˌmatrəˈnɪmɪk/ (also **metronymic**) • n. a name derived from the name of a mother or female ancestor.
– ORIGIN C18: from L. *mater, matr-* 'mother', on the pattern of *patronymic*.

**matsuri** /matˈsuːri/ • n. a solemn festival celebrated periodically at Shinto shrines in Japan.
– ORIGIN from Japanese.

**Matt.** • abbrev. Matthew (especially in biblical references).

**matt** (also **matte** or **mat**) • adj. (of a colour or surface) dull and flat, without a shine. • n. **1** a matt colour, paint, or finish. **2** a sheet of cardboard placed on the back of a picture, as a mount or to form a border. • v. (**matted**, **matting**) give a matt appearance to.
– ORIGIN C17: from Fr. *mat*.

**mattar** /ˈmʌtəː/ • n. Indian term for **PEA**.

**matte**[1] /mat/ • n. an impure product of the smelting of sulphide ores, especially those of copper or nickel.
– ORIGIN C19: from Fr. (in OFr. meaning 'curds'), fem. of *mat* 'matt'.

**matte**[2] /mat/ • n. a mask used to obscure part of an image in a film and allow another image to be substituted.
– ORIGIN C19: from Fr.

**matte**[3] • adj., n., & v. variant spelling of **MATT**.

**matter** • n. **1** physical substance or material in general, as distinct from mind and spirit; (in physics) that which occupies space and possesses mass, especially as distinct from energy. **2** an affair or situation under consideration; a topic. ➤ (**matters**) the present state of affairs. **3** [usu. with neg. or in questions] (**the matter**) the reason for a problem: *what's the matter?* **4** written or printed material. ➤ Printing the body of a printed work, as distinct from titles, headings, etc. **5** Logic the particular content of a proposition, as distinct from its form. **6** Law something which is to be tried or proved in court; a case. • v. **1** be important or significant. **2** rare (of a wound) secrete or discharge pus.
– PHRASES **for that matter** used to indicate that a subject, though mentioned second, is as relevant as the first. **in the matter of** as regards. **a matter of 1** (of time) no more than: *they were shown the door in a matter of minutes.* **2** a question of. **a matter of course** the natural or expected thing. **a matter of record** a thing that is established as a fact through being officially recorded. **no matter 1** regardless of. **2** it is of no importance.
– ORIGIN ME: via OFr. from L. *materia* 'timber, substance', also 'subject of discourse', from *mater* 'mother'.

**matter of fact** • n. **1** a fact as distinct from an opinion or conjecture. **2** Law the part of a judicial inquiry concerned with the truth of alleged facts. Often contrasted with **MATTER OF LAW**. • adj. (**matter-of-fact**) **1** concerned only with factual content. **2** unemotional and practical.
– PHRASES **as a matter of fact** in reality; in fact.
– DERIVATIVES **matter-of-factly** adv. **matter-of-factness** n.

**matter of law** • n. Law the part of a judicial inquiry concerned with the interpretation of the law. Often contrasted with **MATTER OF FACT**.

**matting** • n. material used for mats, especially coarse fabric woven from a natural fibre.

**mattins** • n. variant spelling of **MATINS**.

**mattock** • n. an agricultural tool similar to a pickaxe, but with one arm of the head curved like an adze and the other like a chisel edge, used for breaking up hard ground, digging up roots, etc.
– ORIGIN OE *mattuc*, of uncertain origin.

**mattress** • n. **1** a fabric case filled with soft, firm, or springy material used for sleeping on. **2** Engineering a flat structure of brushwood, concrete, or other material used as strengthening for foundations, embankments, etc.
– ORIGIN ME: via OFr. and Ital. from Arab. *maṭraḥ* 'carpet or cushion'.

**maturate** /ˈmatjʊreɪt/ • v. Medicine (of a boil, abscess, etc.) form pus.

**maturation** • n. **1** the action or process of maturing. **2** the formation of pus in a boil, abscess, etc.
– DERIVATIVES **maturational** adj. **maturative** adj.

**mature** • adj. (**-er**, **-est**) **1** fully developed physically; full-grown. **2** having reached a stage of mental or emotional development characteristic of an adult; grown-up. **3** having reached the most fully developed stage in a process. ➤ denoting an economy or industry that has developed to a point where substantial expansion no longer takes place. **4** (of certain foodstuffs or drinks) ready for consumption; ripe. **5** (of thought or planning) careful and thorough. **6** (of a bill) due for payment. • v. **1** become mature. **2** (of an insurance policy, security, etc.) reach the end of its term and hence become payable.
– DERIVATIVES **maturely** adv.
– ORIGIN ME: from L. *maturus* 'timely, ripe'; perh. rel. to **MATINS**.

**mature student** • n. chiefly Brit. an adult student who is older than most other students, especially one who is over 25.

**maturity** • n. **1** the state, fact, or period of being mature. **2** the time when an insurance policy, security, etc. matures.

**matutinal** /ˌmatjʊˈtʌɪn(ə)l, məˈtjuːtɪn(ə)l/ • adj. formal of or occurring in the morning.
– ORIGIN C16: from late L. *matutinalis*, from L. *matutinus* 'early'.

**maty** • adj. & n. variant spelling of **MATEY**.

**matzo** /ˈmatsə, ˈmatsəʊ/ (also **matzoh** or **matzah**) • n. (pl. **matzos**, **matzohs**, or **matzoth** /-əʊt/) a crisp biscuit of unleavened bread, traditionally eaten by Jews during Passover.
– ORIGIN Yiddish, from Heb. *maṣṣāh*.

**mauby** /ˈməʊbi/ • n. a West Indian drink made from the

bark of trees of the buckthorn family.
– ORIGIN from Carib *mabi*, denoting a drink made from sweet potatoes.

**maudlin** /ˈmɔːdlɪn/ • **adj.** self-pityingly or tearfully sentimental.
– ORIGIN ME (denoting Mary Magdalen): from OFr. *Madeleine*, from eccles. L. *Magdalena*; the current sense derives from images of Mary Magdalen weeping.

**maul** • **v. 1** (of an animal) wound by scratching and tearing. **2** handle or treat savagely or roughly. **3** Rugby Union take part in a maul. • **n. 1** Rugby Union a loose scrum formed around a player with the ball off the ground. Compare with **RUCK**[1]. **2** another term for **BEETLE**[2] (in sense 1).
– DERIVATIVES **mauler** n.
– ORIGIN ME (in the senses 'hammer' and 'strike with a heavy weapon'): from OFr. *mail*, from L. *malleus* 'hammer'.

**maulana** /maʊˈlɑːnə/ • **n.** a Muslim man revered for his religious learning or piety.
– ORIGIN C19: from Arab. *mawlānā* 'our master'.

**maulstick** /ˈmɔːlstɪk/ (US also **mahlstick**) • **n.** a light stick with a padded leather ball at one end, held by a painter to support and steady the brush hand.
– ORIGIN C17: from Du. *maalstok*, from *malen* 'to paint' + *stok* 'stick'.

**maunder** /ˈmɔːndə/ • **v.** move, talk, or act in a rambling or aimless manner.
– ORIGIN C17: perh. from obs. *maunder* 'to beg'.

**Maundy** /ˈmɔːndi/ • **n.** (in the UK) a public ceremony on the Thursday before Easter (**Maundy Thursday**) at which the monarch distributes specially minted coins (**Maundy money**).
– ORIGIN ME: from OFr. *mande*, from L. *mandatum* 'mandate, commandment', from *mandatum novum* 'new commandment' (see John 13:34).

**Mauritanian** /ˌmɒrɪˈteɪnɪən/ • **n.** a native or inhabitant of Mauritania, a country in West Africa. • **adj.** of or relating to Mauritania.

**Mauritian** /məˈrɪʃ(ə)n/ • **n.** a native or inhabitant of the island of Mauritius in the Indian Ocean. • **adj.** of or relating to Mauritius.

**mausoleum** /ˌmɔːsəˈlɪəm, -z-/ • **n.** (pl. **mausolea** /-ˈlɪə/ or **mausoleums**) a building, especially a large and stately one, housing a tomb or tombs.
– ORIGIN C15: via L. from Gk *Mausōleion*, from *Mausōlos*, the name of a king of Caria (4th cent. BC), to whose tomb in Halicarnassus the name was orig. applied.

**mauve** /məʊv/ • **n. 1** a pale purple colour. **2** historical a pale purple synthetic dye.
– DERIVATIVES **mauvish** adj.
– ORIGIN C19: from Fr., lit. 'mallow', from L. *malva*.

**mauveine** /ˈməʊviːn/ • **n.** another term for **MAUVE** (in sense 2).

**maven** /ˈmeɪv(ə)n/ • **n.** N. Amer. informal an expert or connoisseur.
– ORIGIN 1960s: Yiddish.

**maverick** • **n. 1** [often as modifier] an unorthodox or independent-minded person: *a maverick politician.* **2** N. Amer. an unbranded calf or yearling.
– ORIGIN C19: from the name of Samuel A. *Maverick*, a Texas rancher who did not brand his cattle.

**mavis** /ˈmeɪvɪs/ • **n.** poetic/literary a song thrush.
– ORIGIN ME: from OFr. *mauvis*, of unknown origin.

**maw** • **n.** the jaws or throat, especially of a voracious animal.
– ORIGIN OE *maga* (in the sense 'stomach'), of Gmc origin.

**mawkish** • **adj. 1** sentimental in a feeble or sickly way. **2** archaic or dialect having a faint sickly flavour.
– DERIVATIVES **mawkishly** adv. **mawkishness** n.
– ORIGIN C17 (in the sense 'inclined to sickness'): from obs. *mawk* 'maggot', from ON *mathkr*, of Gmc origin.

**max** • **abbrev.** maximum. • **v.** N. Amer. informal reach or cause to reach a limit: *job growth will max out.*

**maxi** • **n.** (pl. **maxis**) **1** a skirt or coat reaching to the ankle. **2** a racing yacht of between approximately 15 and 20 metres in length. **3** [in combination] large or long: *a maxi-farm.*
– ORIGIN 1960s: abbrev. of **MAXIMUM**.

**maxilla** /makˈsɪlə/ • **n.** (pl. **maxillae** /-liː/) Anatomy & Zoology the jaw or jawbone, specifically the upper jaw in most vertebrates. ➤(in many arthropods) each of a pair of mouthparts used in chewing.
– DERIVATIVES **maxillary** adj.
– ORIGIN ME: from L., 'jaw'.

**maxim** • **n.** a short, pithy statement expressing a general truth or rule of conduct.
– ORIGIN ME: from Fr. *maxime*, from med. L. (*propositio*) *maxima* 'most important (proposition)'.

**maxima** plural form of **MAXIMUM**.

**maximal** • **adj.** of or constituting a maximum.
– DERIVATIVES **maximally** adv.

**maximalist** • **n.** a person who holds extreme views. • **adj.** of or relating to an extreme position.
– DERIVATIVES **maximalism** n.

**maximize** (also **-ise**) • **v. 1** make as large or great as possible. **2** make the best use of.
– DERIVATIVES **maximization** n. **maximizer** n.

**maximum** • **n.** (pl. **maxima** /-mə/ or **maximums**) the greatest amount, extent, or intensity possible or recorded. • **adj.** greatest in amount, extent, or intensity.
– ORIGIN C17: from mod. L., neut. of L. *maximus* 'greatest'.

**maxixe** /makˈsiːks, məˈʃiːʃə/ • **n.** a Brazilian dance for couples, resembling the polka and the local tango.
– ORIGIN C20: Port.

**maxwell** (abbrev.: **Mx**) • **n.** Physics a unit of magnetic flux in the c.g.s. system, equal to that induced through one square centimetre by a perpendicular magnetic field of one gauss.
– ORIGIN C20: named after the Sc. physicist J. C. *Maxwell* (1831–79).

**Maxwell–Boltzmann distribution** • **n.** Physics a formula describing the statistical distribution of particles in a system among different energy levels.
– ORIGIN 1920s: named after J. C. *Maxwell* and the Austrian physicist L. *Boltzmann*.

**Maxwell's demon** • **n.** Physics an imaginary being controlling a hole in a partition in a gas-filled container and allowing only fast-moving molecules to pass in one direction and slow-moving molecules in the other, thereby producing a temperature difference in violation of the second law of thermodynamics.

**May** • **n.** the fifth month of the year.
– ORIGIN OE, from OFr. *mai*, from L. *Maius* (*mensis*) '(month) of the goddess *Maia*'.

**may**[1] • **modal v.** (3rd sing. present **may**; past **might** /mʌɪt/) **1** expressing possibility. **2** expressing permission. **3** expressing a wish or hope.
– PHRASES **be that as it may** nevertheless. **that is as may be** that may or may not be so.
– ORIGIN OE *mæg*, of Gmc origin, from a base meaning 'have power'.

**may**[2] • **n.** the hawthorn or its blossom.
– ORIGIN ME: from **MAY**.

**Maya** /ˈmʌɪ(j)ə, ˈmeɪ(j)ə/ • **n.** (pl. same or **Mayas**) **1** a member of an American Indian people of Yucatán and other parts of Central America. **2** the language of this people.
– ORIGIN the name in Maya.

**maya** /ˈmɑːjə/ • **n.** Hinduism the supernatural power wielded by gods and demons. ➤Hinduism & Buddhism the power by which the universe becomes manifest; the illusion or appearance of the phenomenal world.
– ORIGIN from Sanskrit *māyā*, from *mā* 'create'.

**Mayan** /ˈmʌɪ(j)ən, ˈmeɪ(j)ən/ • **n.** a large family of American Indian languages spoken in Central America. • **adj. 1** denoting or relating to this family of languages. **2** denoting or relating to the Maya people.

**mayapple** • **n.** an American herbaceous plant of the barberry family, which bears a yellow egg-shaped fruit in May. [*Podophyllum peltatum.*]

**maybe** • **adv.** perhaps; possibly. • **n.** a mere possibility or probability.

**May bug** ● n. another term for COCKCHAFER.

**May Day** ● n. 1 May, celebrated in many countries as a traditional springtime festival or as an international day honouring workers.

**Mayday** ● n. an international radio distress signal used by ships and aircraft.
– ORIGIN 1920s: representing a pronunc. of Fr. *m'aider*, from *venez m'aider* 'come and help me'.

**mayest** /'meɪɪst/ archaic second person singular present of MAY[1].

**mayflower** ● n. the trailing arbutus.

**mayfly** ● n. (pl. **-flies**) a short-lived slender insect with delicate transparent wings which lives close to water. [Order Ephemeroptera: many species.]

**mayhap** ● adv. archaic perhaps; possibly.
– ORIGIN C16: from *it may hap*.

**mayhem** ● n. **1** violent or damaging disorder; chaos. **2** Law, chiefly historical the crime of maliciously injuring someone, originally so as to render the victim defenceless.
– ORIGIN C16: from OFr. *mayhem* (see MAIM).

**maying** ● n. archaic celebration of May Day.

**mayn't** ● contr. may not.

**mayonnaise** ● n. a thick creamy dressing consisting of egg yolks beaten with oil and vinegar.
– ORIGIN Fr., prob. from the fem. of *mahonnais* 'of or from Port *Mahon*', the capital of Minorca.

**mayor** ● n. the elected head of the municipal corporation of a city or borough.
– DERIVATIVES **mayoral** adj. **mayorship** n.
– ORIGIN ME: from OFr. *maire*, from L. *major* 'greater'.

**mayoralty** /'mɛːr(ə)lti/ ● n. (pl. **-ies**) the period or term of office of a mayor.

**mayoress** /'mɛːrɪs, ˌmɛː'rɛs/ ● n. **1** the wife of a mayor. **2** a woman holding the office of mayor.

**maypole** ● n. a decorated pole round which people traditionally dance on May Day holding long ribbons attached to the top.

**May queen** ● n. a pretty girl chosen and crowned in traditional celebrations of May Day.

**mayst** archaic second person singular present of MAY[1].

**mayweed** ● n. a wild chamomile typically found as a weed of waste ground. [*Anthemis cotula* (**stinking mayweed**), *Tripleurospermum inodorum* (**scentless mayweed**), and other species.]
– ORIGIN C16: from *maythe(n)*, an earlier name for this plant, + WEED.

**maze** ● n. **1** a network of paths and hedges designed as a puzzle through which one has to find a way. **2** a confusing mass of information. ● v. (**be mazed**) archaic or dialect be dazed and confused.
– DERIVATIVES **mazy** adj. (**-ier**, **-iest**).
– ORIGIN ME (denoting delirium or delusion): prob. from the base of AMAZE.

**mazel tov** /'maz(ə)l ˌtɔːv, ˌtɒf/ ● exclam. (among Jews) congratulations; good luck.
– ORIGIN from mod. Heb. *mazzāl ṭōḇ*, lit. 'good star'.

**mazer** /'meɪzə/ ● n. historical a hardwood drinking bowl.
– ORIGIN ME: from OFr. *masere*, of Gmc origin.

**mazuma** /mə'zuːmə/ ● n. informal, chiefly US money; cash.
– ORIGIN C20: Yiddish, from Heb. *mĕzummān*.

**mazurka** /mə'zəːkə, mə'zʊəkə/ ● n. a lively Polish dance in triple time.
– ORIGIN C19: via Ger. from Polish *mazurka*, denoting a woman of the province Mazovia.

**mazzard** /'mazəd/ ● n. another term for GEAN.
– ORIGIN C16: prob. an alt. of MAZER, in the sense 'hardwood'.

**MB** ● abbrev. **1** Bachelor of Medicine. [from L. *Medicinae Baccalaureus*.] **2** Manitoba (in official postal use). **3** (also **Mb**) Computing megabyte(s).

**MBA** ● abbrev. Master of Business Administration.

**mbaqanga** /ˌ(ə)mba'kɑːŋga/ ● n. a rhythmical popular music style of southern Africa.
– ORIGIN from Zulu *umbaqanga*, lit. 'steamed maize bread', with ref. to the notion of basic cultural sustenance.

**MBE** ● abbrev. (in the UK) Member of the Order of the British Empire.

**mbira** /(ə)m'bɪərə/ ● n. another term for THUMB PIANO.
– ORIGIN C19: from Shona, prob. an alt. of *rimba* 'a note'.

**MBO** ● abbrev. management buyout.

**Mbuti** /(ə)m'buːti/ ● n. (pl. same or **Mbutis**) a member of a pygmy people of western Uganda and parts of Zaire (Democratic Republic of Congo).
– ORIGIN the name in local langs.

**Mbyte** ● abbrev. megabyte(s).

**MC** ● abbrev. **1** Master of Ceremonies. **2** (in the US) Member of Congress. **3** (in the UK) Military Cross. **4** Monaco (international vehicle registration). **5** music cassette (of pre-recorded audio tape).

**Mc** ● abbrev. megacycle(s), a unit of frequency equal to one million cycles.

**MCB** ● abbrev. miniature circuit-breaker.

**MCC** ● abbrev. Marylebone Cricket Club.

**mcg** ● abbrev. microgram.

**MCh** (also **M Chir**) ● abbrev. Master of Surgery.
– ORIGIN from L. *Magister Chirurgiae*.

**mCi** ● abbrev. millicurie(s).

**McNaghten rules** /mək'nɔːt(ə)n/ (also **M'Naghten** or **McNaughten rules**) ● pl. n. Brit. rules or criteria for judging criminal responsibility where there is a question of insanity.
– ORIGIN established by the House of Lords, following the case of Regina v McNaghten (1843).

**MCom** ● abbrev. Master of Commerce.

**m-commerce** ● n. commercial transactions conducted electronically by mobile phone.

**MCR** ● abbrev. Brit. Middle Common Room.

**MD** ● abbrev. **1** Doctor of Medicine. [from L. *Medicinae Doctor*.] **2** Brit. Managing Director. **3** Maryland (in official postal use). **4** Medicine mentally deficient. **5** musical director.

**Md** ● symb. the chemical element mendelevium.

**Md.** ● abbrev. Maryland.

**MDF** ● abbrev. medium density fibreboard.

**MDMA** ● abbrev. methylenedioxymethamphetamine, the drug Ecstasy.

**MDT** ● abbrev. Mountain Daylight Time.

**ME** ● abbrev. **1** Maine (in official postal use). **2** Middle English. **3** Medicine myalgic encephalomyelitis.

**Me** ● abbrev. **1** Maine. **2** Maître (title of a French advocate).

**me**[1] ● pron. [first person sing.] **1** used by a speaker to refer to himself or herself as the object of a verb or preposition. ➤used after the verb 'to be' and after 'than' or 'as'. **2** N. Amer. informal to or for myself.
– PHRASES **me and mine** my relatives.
– ORIGIN OE *mē*, accusative and dative of I[2], of Gmc origin.

**me**[2] (also **mi**) ● n. Music (in tonic sol-fa) the third note of a major scale. ➤the note E in the fixed-doh system.
– ORIGIN ME *mi*, an arbitrary name for the note, taken from the first syllable of *mira*, from a Latin hymn.

**mea culpa** /ˌmeɪə 'kʊlpə, ˌmiːə 'kʌlpə/ ● n. an acknowledgement of one's fault or error.
– ORIGIN L., 'by my fault'.

**mead**[1] ● n. an alcoholic drink of fermented honey and water.
– ORIGIN OE *me(o)du*, of Gmc origin.

**mead**[2] ● n. poetic/literary a meadow.
– ORIGIN OE *mǣd*, of Gmc origin; rel. to MOW[1].

**meadow** ● n. **1** an area of grassland, especially one used for hay. **2** a piece of low ground near a river.
– DERIVATIVES **meadowy** adj.
– ORIGIN OE *mǣdwe*, oblique case of *mǣd* (see MEAD[2]).

**meadow brown** ● n. a common butterfly having brown and orange wings with small eyespots. [*Maniola jurtina*.]

**meadowlark** ● n. a ground-dwelling American songbird, typically brown with yellow and black underparts. [*Sturnella magna*, *S. neglecta*, and related species.]

**meadow rue** ● n. a plant of the buttercup family with heads of small fluffy yellow flowers. [*Thalictrum flavum* and related species.]

**meadow saffron** • n. a poisonous lilac-flowered autumn crocus. [*Colchicum autumnale.*]

**meadowsweet** • n. a tall plant with heads of creamy-white fragrant flowers, growing typically in damp meadows. [*Filipendula ulmaria.*]

**meagre** (US **meager**) • adj. **1** lacking in quantity or quality. **2** lean; thin.
– DERIVATIVES **meagrely** adv. **meagreness** n.
– ORIGIN ME: from OFr. *maigre*, from L. *macer*.

**meal**[1] • n. any of the regular daily occasions when food is eaten. ➤ the food eaten on such an occasion.
– PHRASES **make a meal of** Brit. informal carry out (a task) with unnecessary effort or thoroughness. **meals on wheels** meals delivered to old people or invalids who cannot cook for themselves.
– ORIGIN OE *mǣl* (also in the senses 'measure', 'fixed time'), of Gmc origin.

**meal**[2] • n. **1** the edible part of any grain or pulse ground to powder. **2** any powdery substance made by grinding: *herring meal.*
– ORIGIN OE *melu, meolo*, of Gmc origin.

**meal beetle** • n. a dark brown beetle which is a pest of stored grain and cereal products. [*Tenebrio molitor.*]

**mealie** (also **mielie**) • n. chiefly S. African a maize plant or cob.
– ORIGIN C19: from Afrik. *mielie*, from Port. *milho* 'maize, millet'.

**meal ticket** • n. a person or thing that is exploited as a source of regular income.

**mealtime** • n. the time at which a meal is eaten.

**mealworm** • n. the larva of the meal beetle, used as food for cage birds and other insectivorous animals.

**mealy** • adj. (**-ier, -iest**) **1** of, like, or containing meal. **2** pale in colour.
– DERIVATIVES **mealiness** n.

**mealy bug** • n. a small sap-sucking scale insect which is coated with a white powdery wax resembling meal and which can be a serious pest. [*Pseudococcus* and other genera.]

**mealy-mouthed** • adj. reluctant to speak frankly.
– ORIGIN C16: perh. from Ger. *Mehl im Maule behalten*, lit. 'carry meal in the mouth', i.e. be unstraightforward in speech, or rel. to L. *mel* 'honey'.

**mean**[1] • v. (past and past part. **meant**) **1** intend to convey or refer to. ➤ (of a word) have as its signification in the same language or its equivalent in another language. ➤ (**mean something to**) be of a specified degree of importance to. **2** intend to occur or be the case. ➤ (often **be meant for**) design or destine for a particular purpose. ➤ (**mean something by**) have as a motive or excuse in explanation. **3** have as a consequence or result.
– PHRASES **mean business** be in earnest. **mean well** have good intentions, but not always carry them out.
– ORIGIN OE *mǣnan*, of W. Gmc origin.

**mean**[2] • adj. **1** unwilling to give or share money. **2** unkind or unfair. ➤ vicious or aggressive. **3** poor in quality and appearance. ➤ (of a person's mental ability) inferior. **4** dated of low birth or social class. **5** informal excellent.
– PHRASES **no mean ——** very good of its kind: *it was no mean feat.*
– DERIVATIVES **meanly** adv. **meanness** n.
– ORIGIN ME (orig. in the sense 'common to two or more persons'), shortening of OE *gemǣne*, of Gmc origin.

**mean**[3] • n. **1** (also **arithmetic mean**) the average of a set of quantities. See also GEOMETRIC MEAN. **2** a condition, quality, or course of action equally removed from two opposite extremes. • adj. **1** calculated as a mean. **2** equally far from two extremes.
– ORIGIN ME: from OFr. *meien*, from L. *medianus* (see MEDIAN).

**meander** /mɪˈandə, miː-/ • v. **1** (of a river or road) follow a winding course. **2** wander aimlessly. • n. **1** a winding curve or bend of a river or road. **2** a circuitous journey. **3** an ornamental pattern of winding or interlocking lines, e.g. in a mosaic.
– ORIGIN C16: from L. *maeander*, from Gk *Maiandros, Menderes*, the name of a river of SW Turkey.

**meaning** • n. **1** what is meant by a word, text, concept, or action. **2** worthwhile quality; purpose. • adj. expressive: *she gave him a meaning look.*
– DERIVATIVES **meaningless** adj. **meaninglessly** adv. **meaninglessness** n. **meaningly** adv.

**meaningful** • adj. **1** having meaning. ➤ Logic having a recognizable function in a logical language or other sign system. **2** worthwhile. **3** expressive.
– DERIVATIVES **meaningfully** adv. **meaningfulness** n.

**means** • pl. n. **1** [treated as sing. or pl.] an action or system by which a result is achieved. **2** financial resources; income. ➤ substantial resources; wealth.
– PHRASES **by all means** of course. **by any means** [with neg.] at all. **by means of** by using. **by no means** (or **by no manner of means**) certainly not. **a means to an end** a thing that is not valued in itself but is useful in achieving an aim.
– ORIGIN ME: pl. of MEAN[3], the early sense being 'intermediary'.

**mean sea level** • n. the sea level halfway between the mean levels of high and low water.

**mean solar time** • n. Astronomy time reckoned by the motion of the mean sun (such as is shown by an ordinary clock). Compare with APPARENT TIME.

**means test** • n. an official investigation into a person's financial circumstances to determine their eligibility for state assistance. • v. (**means-test**) [usu. as adj. **means-tested**] make conditional on a means test.

**mean sun** • n. an imaginary sun conceived as moving at a constant speed equal to the mean rate of the real sun, used in calculating solar time.

**meant** past and past participle of MEAN[1].

**meantime** • adv. (also **in the meantime**) meanwhile.

**mean time** • n. Astronomy another term for MEAN SOLAR TIME.

**meanwhile** • adv. **1** (also **in the meanwhile**) in the intervening period of time. **2** at the same time.

**measles** • pl. n. [treated as sing.] **1** an infectious viral disease causing fever and a red rash, typically occurring in childhood. **2** a disease of pigs caused by encysted larvae of the human tapeworm.
– ORIGIN ME *maseles*, prob. from MDu. *masel* 'pustule'.

**measly** • adj. (**-ier, -iest**) informal contemptibly small or few.
– ORIGIN C16 (describing a pig or pork infected with measles): from MEASLES + -Y[1].

**measurable** • adj. able or large enough to be measured.
– DERIVATIVES **measurability** n. **measurably** adv.

**measure** • v. **1** ascertain the size, amount, or degree of (something) by comparison with a standard unit or with an object of known size. ➤ be of (a specified size or degree). ➤ (**measure something out**) take an exact quantity of something. ➤ assess the extent, quality, value, or effect of. ➤ (**measure up**) reach the required or expected standard. **2** archaic travel over (a certain distance or area). • n. **1** a means of achieving a purpose: *cost-cutting measures.* ➤ a legislative bill. **2** a standard unit used to express size, amount, or degree. ➤ an instrument such as a container, rod, or tape marked with standard units and used for measuring. **3** (**a measure of**) a certain amount or degree of. ➤ an indication of extent or quality. **4** the rhythm of a piece of poetry or a piece of music. ➤ a particular metrical unit or group. ➤ N. Amer. a bar of music or the time of a piece of music. **5** archaic a dance. **6** (**measures**) a group of rock strata. **7** Printing the width of a full line of type or print, typically expressed in picas.
– PHRASES **beyond measure** to a very great extent. **for good measure** as an amount or item beyond that which is strictly required. **get** (or **take** or **have**) **the measure of** assess or have assessed the character or abilities of. **in —— measure** to the degree specified.
– ORIGIN ME (also in the sense 'moderation'): from OFr. *mesure*, from L. *mensura*, from *mens-, metiri* 'measure'.

**measured** • adj. **1** having a slow, regular rhythm. **2** (of speech or writing) deliberate and restrained.
– DERIVATIVES **measuredly** adv.

**measureless** • adj. having no limits.

**measurement** • n. the action of measuring. ➤ an

amount, size, or extent as established by measuring. ➤ a unit or system of measuring.

**measuring worm** ● n. another term for LOOPER.

**meat** ● n. **1** the flesh of an animal (especially a mammal) as food. ➤ chiefly US the edible part of fruits, nuts, or eggs. ➤ archaic food of any kind. **2** (**the meat of**) the essence or chief part of.
– PHRASES **be meat and drink to** Brit. **1** be a source of great pleasure to. **2** be a routine matter for. **easy meat** informal a person or animal that is easily overcome or outwitted. **meat and potatoes** chiefly N. Amer. ordinary but fundamental things.
– DERIVATIVES **meatless** adj.
– ORIGIN OE *mete* 'food' or 'article of food', of Gmc origin.

**meatball** ● n. **1** a ball of minced or chopped meat. **2** N. Amer. informal a dull or stupid person.

**meathead** ● n. informal a stupid person.

**meat loaf** ● n. minced or chopped meat moulded into the shape of a loaf and baked.

**meat safe** ● n. Brit. historical a cupboard or cover of wire gauze or a similar material, used for storing meat.

**meatus** /mɪ'eɪtəs/ ● n. (pl. same or **meatuses**) Anatomy a passage or opening leading to the interior of the body.
– ORIGIN ME: from L., 'passage' from *meare* 'to flow, run'.

**meaty** ● adj. (**-ier**, **-iest**) **1** resembling or full of meat. **2** brawny. **3** full of substance.
– DERIVATIVES **meatily** adv. **meatiness** n.

**Mecca** ● n. (**a Mecca**) a place which attracts people of a particular group or with a particular interest.
– ORIGIN from the city of *Mecca* in Saudi Arabia, considered by Muslims to be the holiest city of Islam.

**mechanic** ● n. **1** a skilled worker who repairs and maintains machinery. **2** archaic a manual labourer or artisan.
– ORIGIN ME (as an adjective in the sense 'relating to manual labour'): via OFr. or L. from Gk *mēkhanikos*, from *mēkhanē* (see MACHINE).

**mechanical** ● adj. **1** working or produced by machines or machinery. ➤ of or relating to machines or machinery. **2** lacking thought or spontaneity. **3** relating to physical forces or motion. ➤ (of a theory) explaining phenomena in terms only of physical processes. ● n. **1** (**mechanicals**) the working parts of a machine, especially a car. **2** archaic a manual worker.
– DERIVATIVES **mechanically** adv. **mechanicalness** n.

**mechanical advantage** ● n. the ratio of the force produced by a machine to the force applied to it.

**mechanical drawing** ● n. a scale drawing of a mechanical or architectural structure done with precision instruments.

**mechanical engineering** ● n. the branch of engineering concerned with the design, construction, and use of machines.
– DERIVATIVES **mechanical engineer** n.

**mechanician** ● n. a person skilled in the design or construction of machinery.

**mechanics** ● pl. n. **1** [treated as sing.] the branch of applied mathematics concerned with motion and forces producing motion. ➤ machinery as a subject. **2** the machinery or working parts of something. ➤ the practicalities or details of something.

**mechanism** ● n. **1** a piece of machinery. **2** a process by which something takes place or is brought about. **3** Philosophy the doctrine that all natural phenomena allow mechanical explanation by physics and chemistry.
– DERIVATIVES **mechanist** n.
– ORIGIN C17: from mod. L. *mechanismus*, from Gk *mēkhanē* (see MACHINE).

**mechanistic** ● adj. Philosophy of or relating to mechanism.
– DERIVATIVES **mechanistically** adv.

**mechanize** (also **-ise**) ● v. introduce machines or automatic devices into. ➤ equip (a military force) with modern weapons and vehicles.
– DERIVATIVES **mechanization** n. **mechanizer** n.

**mechano-** /'mɛk(ə)nəʊ/ ● comb. form mechanical; relating to a mechanical source: *mechanoreceptor.*
– ORIGIN from Gk *mēkhanē* 'machine'.

**mechanoreceptor** ● n. Zoology a sense organ or cell that responds to mechanical stimuli such as touch or sound.
– DERIVATIVES **mechanoreceptive** adj.

**mechatronics** ● pl. n. [treated as sing.] technology combining electronics and mechanical engineering.
– ORIGIN 1980s: blend of MECHANICS and ELECTRONICS.

**Mechlin** /'mɛklɪn/ (also **Mechlin lace**) ● n. lace made at Mechelen (formerly known as Mechlin) in Belgium, characterized by patterns outlined in heavier thread.

**MEcon** ● abbrev. Master of Economics.

**meconium** /mɪ'kəʊnɪəm/ ● n. Medicine the dark green substance forming the first faeces of a newborn infant.
– ORIGIN C18: from L., lit. 'poppy juice'.

**MEd** ● abbrev. Master of Education.

**Med** ● n. (**the Med**) informal the Mediterranean Sea.

**med.** ● abbrev. **1** informal, chiefly N. Amer. medical. **2** medium.

**médaillon** /ˌmeɪdʌɪ'jɒ̃/ ● n. (pl. pronounced same) a small flat round or oval cut of meat or fish.
– ORIGIN Fr., lit. 'medallion'.

**medal** ● n. a metal disc with an inscription or design, awarded to acknowledge distinctive achievement or made to commemorate an event.
– DERIVATIVES **medalled** adj. **medallic** adj.
– ORIGIN C16: from Fr. *médaille*, from Ital. *medaglia*, from med. L. *medalia* 'half a denarius'.

**medallion** ● n. **1** a piece of jewellery in the shape of a medal, worn as a pendant. **2** an oval or circular painting, panel, or design used to decorate a building or textile.
– ORIGIN C17: from Fr. *médaillon*, from Ital. *medaglione*, augmentative of *medaglia* (see MEDAL).

**medallist** (US **medalist**) ● n. **1** an athlete or other person awarded a medal. **2** an engraver or designer of medals.

**medal play** ● n. Golf another term for STROKE PLAY.

**meddle** ● v. (usu. **meddle in/with**) interfere in something that is not one's concern.
– DERIVATIVES **meddler** n. **meddlesome** adj. **meddlesomely** adv. **meddlesomeness** n.
– ORIGIN ME (in the sense 'mix'): from OFr. *medler*, var. of *mesler*, based on L. *miscere* 'to mix'.

**Mede** /mi:d/ ● n. a member of an Indo-European people who inhabited ancient Media (present-day Azerbaijan, NW Iran, and NE Iraq), establishing an extensive empire during the 7th century BC.
– DERIVATIVES **Median** adj.

**medevac** /'mɛdɪvak/ (also **medivac**) N. Amer. ● n. the evacuation of military or other casualties to hospital by air. ● v. (**medevacked**, **medevacking**) transport to hospital in this way.
– ORIGIN 1960s: blend of MEDICAL and EVACUATION.

**medfly** ● n. (pl. **-flies**) chiefly N. Amer. a Mediterranean fruit fly whose larvae are a pest of citrus fruit in many parts of the world. [*Ceratitis capitata.*]

**media**[1] /'mi:dɪə/ ● n. **1** plural form of MEDIUM. **2** [treated as sing. or pl.] the main means of mass communication (especially television, radio, and newspapers) regarded collectively.

**USAGE media**

The word **media** comes from the Latin plural of **medium**. The traditional view is that it should therefore be treated as a plural noun in all its senses in English. In practice, in the sense 'television, radio, and the press collectively', it behaves as a collective noun (like **staff** or **clergy**, for example), which means that it is acceptable in standard English for it to take either a singular or a plural verb.

**media**[2] /'mi:dɪə/ ● n. (pl. **mediae** /-dɪi:/) Anatomy an intermediate layer, especially in the wall of a blood vessel.
– ORIGIN C19: shortening of mod. L. *tunica* (or *membrana*) *media* 'middle sheath (or layer)'.

**mediaeval** ● adj. variant spelling of MEDIEVAL.

**media event** ● n. an event intended primarily to attract publicity.

**mediagenic** /ˌmi:dɪə'dʒɛnɪk/ ● adj. chiefly US tending to convey a favourable impression when reported by the media, especially by television.

**medial** • adj. 1 situated in the middle. 2 Phonetics pronounced in the middle of the mouth.
– DERIVATIVES **medially** adv.
– ORIGIN C16 (in the sense 'relating to the average'): from late L. *medialis*, from L. *medius* 'middle'.

**median** /ˈmiːdɪən/ • adj. 1 technical, chiefly Anatomy situated in the middle, especially of the body. 2 denoting or relating to a value or quantity lying at the mid point of a frequency distribution of observed values or quantities, such that there is an equal probability of falling above or below it. ➤ denoting the middle term (or mean of the middle two terms) of a series arranged in order of magnitude. • n. 1 a median value. 2 (also **median strip**) North American term for **CENTRAL RESERVATION**. 3 Geometry a straight line drawn from any vertex of a triangle to the middle of the opposite side.
– DERIVATIVES **medianly** adv.
– ORIGIN ME: from med. L. *medianus*, from *medius* 'mid'.

**mediant** /ˈmiːdɪənt/ • n. Music the third note of the diatonic scale of any key.
– ORIGIN C18: from Fr. *médiante*, from Ital. *mediante* 'coming between'.

**mediastinum** /ˌmiːdɪəˈstʌɪnəm/ • n. (pl. **mediastina** /-nə/) Anatomy a membranous partition, especially that between the lungs.
– DERIVATIVES **mediastinal** adj.
– ORIGIN ME: neut. of med. L. *mediastinus* 'medial', based on L. *medius* 'middle'.

**mediate** • v. /ˈmiːdɪeɪt/ 1 intervene in a dispute to bring about an agreement or reconciliation. 2 technical be a medium for (a process or effect). • adj. /ˈmiːdɪət/ involving an intermediate agency.
– DERIVATIVES **mediately** adv. **mediation** n. **mediator** n. **mediatory** /ˈmiːdɪət(ə)ri/ adj.
– ORIGIN ME (as an adjective in the sense 'interposed'): from late L. *mediatus*, *mediare* 'place in the middle', from L. *medius* 'middle'.

**medic** /ˈmɛdɪk/ • n. informal a medical practitioner or student.
– ORIGIN C17: from L. *medicus* 'physician'.

**Medicaid** • n. (in the US) a federal system of health insurance for those requiring financial assistance.
– ORIGIN 1960s: from **MEDICAL** + **AID**.

**medical** • adj. of or relating to the science or practice of medicine. • n. an examination to assess a person's state of physical health or fitness.
– DERIVATIVES **medically** adv.
– ORIGIN C17: via Fr. from med. L. *medicalis*, from L. *medicus* 'physician'.

**medical certificate** • n. a doctor's certificate giving the state of a person's health with regard to their fitness or unfitness to work.

**medicalize** (also **-ise**) • v. treat as a medical problem, especially without justification.
– DERIVATIVES **medicalization** n.

**medical officer** • n. a doctor in charge of the health services of a civilian or military authority or other organization.

**medical practitioner** • n. a physician or surgeon.

**medicament** /mɪˈdɪkəm(ə)nt, ˈmɛdɪk-/ • n. a medicinal substance.
– ORIGIN ME: via Fr. from L. *medicamentum*, from *medicari* (see **MEDICATE**).

**Medicare** • n. (in the US) a federal system of health insurance for people over 65 years of age. ➤ (in Canada and Australia) a national health-care scheme financed by taxation.
– ORIGIN 1960s: from **MEDICAL** + **CARE**.

**medicate** • v. administer medicine or a drug to. ➤ add a medicinal substance to.
– DERIVATIVES **medicative** adj.
– ORIGIN C17 (earlier (ME) as *medication*): from L. *medicat-*, *medicari* 'administer remedies to'.

**medication** • n. a medicine or drug. ➤ treatment using drugs.

**Medicean** /ˌmɛdɪˈtʃiːən, -ˈsiːən, mɛˈdiːtʃɪən/ • adj. of or relating to the Medici, a powerful Italian family who effectively ruled Florence in the 15th century.

**medicinal** • adj. having healing properties. ➤ relating to medicines or drugs. • n. a medicinal substance.
– DERIVATIVES **medicinally** adv.

**medicine** • n. 1 the science or practice of the diagnosis, treatment, and prevention of disease (in technical use often taken to exclude surgery). 2 a drug or other preparation for the treatment or prevention of disease. 3 (among North American Indians and some other peoples) a spell, charm, or fetish believed to have healing or magical power.
– PHRASES **give someone a dose** (or **taste**) **of their own medicine** give someone the same bad treatment that they have given to others. **take one's medicine** submit to punishment as being deserved.
– ORIGIN ME: via OFr. from L. *medicina*, from *medicus* 'physician'.

**medicine ball** • n. a large, heavy solid ball thrown and caught for exercise.

**medicine man** • n. (among North American Indians and some other peoples) a shaman.

**medick** /ˈmiːdɪk/ • n. a yellow-flowered plant of the pea family related to alfalfa. [Genus *Medicago*.]
– ORIGIN ME: from L. *medica*, from Gk *Mēdikē* (*poa*) 'Median (grass)'.

**medico** • n. (pl. **-os**) informal a medical practitioner or student.
– ORIGIN C17: via Ital. from L. *medicus* 'physician'.

**medico-** • comb. form relating to the field of medicine: *medico-social*.
– ORIGIN from L. *medicus* 'physician'.

**medieval** /ˌmɛdɪˈiːv(ə)l, mɪː-/ (also **mediaeval**) • adj. of or relating to the Middle Ages. ➤ informal very old-fashioned or outdated.
– DERIVATIVES **medievalism** n. **medievalist** n. **medievalize** (also **-ise**) v. **medievally** adv.
– ORIGIN C19: from mod. L. *medium aevum* 'middle age' + **-AL**.

**medieval Latin** • n. Latin of about AD 600–1500.

**medina** /mɛˈdiːnə/ • n. the old quarter of a North African town.
– ORIGIN Arab., lit. 'town'.

**mediocracy** • n. (pl. **-ies**) a dominant class consisting of mediocre people.

**mediocre** /ˌmiːdɪˈəʊkə/ • adj. of only moderate or average quality.
– DERIVATIVES **mediocrely** adv. **mediocrity** n. (pl. **-ies**).
– ORIGIN C16: from Fr. *médiocre*, from L. *mediocris* 'of middle height or degree', lit. 'somewhat mountainous'.

**meditate** • v. 1 focus one's mind for a period of time for spiritual purposes or as a method of relaxation. 2 (often **meditate on/upon**) think carefully about.
– DERIVATIVES **meditative** adj. **meditatively** adv. **meditativeness** n. **meditator** n.
– ORIGIN C16 (earlier (ME) as *meditation*): from L. *meditat-*, *meditari* 'contemplate', from a base meaning 'measure'; rel. to **METE**[1].

**meditation** • n. 1 the action or practice of meditating. 2 a discourse expressing considered thoughts on a subject.

**Mediterranean** /ˌmɛdɪtəˈreɪnɪən/ • adj. of or characteristic of the Mediterranean Sea, the countries bordering it, or their inhabitants. • n. a native of a Mediterranean country.
– ORIGIN C16: from L. *mediterraneus* 'inland' (from *medius* 'middle' + *terra* 'land') + **-AN**.

**Mediterranean climate** • n. a climate distinguished by warm, wet winters under prevailing westerly winds and calm, hot, dry summers.

**medium** • n. (pl. **media** or **mediums**) 1 an agency or means of doing something. ➤ the material or form used by an artist, composer, or writer. 2 a substance through which sensory impressions are conveyed or physical forces are transmitted. 3 a particular form of storage material for computer files, such as magnetic tape or discs. 4 a liquid (e.g. oil) with which pigments are mixed to make paint. 5 (pl. **mediums**) a person claiming

to be able to communicate between the dead and the living. **6** the middle quality or state between two extremes. **7** the substance in which an organism lives or is cultured. • **adj.** between two extremes; average.
– DERIVATIVES **mediumism** n. **mediumistic** adj. **mediumship** n.
– ORIGIN C16: from L., lit. 'middle'.

**medium frequency** • **n.** a radio frequency between 300 kHz and 3 MHz.

**medium wave** • **n.** chiefly Brit. a radio wave of a frequency between 300 kHz and 3 MHz. ➤ broadcasting using such radio waves.

**medivac** • **n. & v.** variant spelling of **MEDEVAC**.

**medlar** • **n. 1** a small bushy tree of the rose family. [*Mespilus germanica*.] **2** the small brown apple-like fruit of this tree, edible once it has begun to decay.
– ORIGIN ME: from OFr. *medler*, from *medle* 'medlar fruit', from L. *mespila*, from Gk *mespilē*, *mespilon*.

**medley** • **n.** (pl. **-eys**) a varied mixture. ➤ a collection of songs or other musical items performed as a continuous piece. ➤ a swimming race in which contestants swim sections in different strokes. • **v.** (past and past part. **-eyed** or **-ied**) archaic make a medley of.
– ORIGIN ME (denoting hand-to-hand combat, also cloth made of variegated wool): from OFr. *medlee*, var. of *meslee* 'melee', based on med. L. *misculare* 'to mix'; cf. **MEDDLE**.

**Médoc** /meɪˈdɒk, French medɔk/ • **n.** (pl. same) a red wine produced in the Médoc area of SW France.

**medrese** /mɛˈdrɛseɪ/ • **n.** variant spelling of **MADRASA**.

**medulla** /mɛˈdʌlə/ • **n. 1** a distinct inner region of an organ or tissue, especially a kidney, the adrenal gland, or hair. **2** the soft internal tissue or pith of a plant.
– DERIVATIVES **medullary** adj.
– ORIGIN ME (in the sense 'bone marrow'): from L., 'pith or marrow'.

**medulla oblongata** /ˌɒblɒŋˈɡɑːtə/ • **n.** the continuation of the spinal cord within the skull, forming the lowest part of the brainstem.
– ORIGIN C17: mod. L., lit. 'elongated medulla'.

**medusa** /mɪˈdjuːzə, -sə/ • **n.** (pl. **medusae** /-ziː, -siː/ or **medusas**) Zoology the free-swimming sexual form of a jellyfish or other coelenterate, typically umbrella-shaped with stinging tentacles around the edge. Compare with **POLYP**.
– DERIVATIVES **medusoid** adj. & n.
– ORIGIN C18: named by assoc. with *Medusa*, the name of a gorgon in Gk mythology with snakes in her hair.

**meed** • **n.** archaic a deserved share or reward.
– ORIGIN OE *mēd*, of Gmc origin.

**meek** • **adj.** quiet, gentle, and submissive.
– DERIVATIVES **meekly** adv. **meekness** n.
– ORIGIN ME *me(o)c*, from ON *mjúkr* 'soft, gentle'.

**meerkat** /ˈmɪəkat/ • **n.** a small southern African mongoose. [*Suricata suricatta* (**grey meerkat**) and other species.]
– ORIGIN C18: from S. Afr. Du., from Du., appar. from *meer* 'sea' + *kat* 'cat'.

**meerschaum** /ˈmɪəʃɔːm, -ʃəm/ • **n.** a soft white clay-like material consisting of hydrated magnesium silicate, found chiefly in Turkey. ➤ a tobacco pipe with a bowl made from this.
– ORIGIN C18: from Ger., lit. 'sea-foam', translation of Pers. *kef-i-daryā* (alluding to its frothy appearance).

**meet[1]** • **v.** (past and past part. **met**) **1** arrange or happen to come into the presence or company of. ➤ make the acquaintance of for the first time. ➤ come together as opponents in a contest. ➤ experience (a particular situation or attitude). ➤ (**meet something with**) have (a particular reaction) to something: *the announcement was met with silence.* ➤ (**meet with**) receive (a particular reaction). **2** touch; join. **3** fulfil or satisfy (a requirement or condition). ➤ pay (a required amount). • **n. 1** a gathering of riders and hounds before a hunt begins. **2** an organized event at which a number of races or other sporting contests are held.
– PHRASES **meet the case** Brit. be adequate. **meet someone's eye** (or **eyes** or **ear**) be visible (or audible). **meet someone's eye** (or **eyes** or **gaze**) look directly at someone. **meet someone halfway** make a compromise with someone.
– ORIGIN OE *mētan* 'come upon', of Gmc origin.

**meet[2]** • **adj.** archaic suitable or proper.
– DERIVATIVES **meetly** adv. **meetness** n.
– ORIGIN ME (in the sense 'made to fit'): shortening of OE *gemǣte*, of Gmc origin; rel. to **METE[1]**.

**meeting** • **n. 1** an assembly of people for a particular purpose, especially for formal discussion. ➤ an organized event at which a number of races or other sporting contests are held. **2** an instance of two or more people meeting.

**meeting ground** • **n.** a common area of knowledge or interest.

**meeting house** • **n.** a Quaker place of worship.

**mefloquine** /ˈmɛfləkwiːn/ • **n.** Medicine an antimalarial drug consisting of a fluorinated derivative of quinoline.
– ORIGIN 1970s: from *me(thyl)* + *fl(uor)o* + *quin(olin)e*.

**mega** informal • **adj. 1** huge. **2** excellent. • **adv.** extremely.
– ORIGIN 1980s: independent usage of **MEGA-**.

**mega-** • **comb. form 1** large: *megalith*. **2** denoting a factor of one million ($10^6$): *megahertz*. **3** Computing denoting a factor of $2^{20}$.
– ORIGIN from Gk *megas* 'great'.

**megabit** • **n.** Computing a unit of data size or network speed, equal to one million or (strictly) 1,048,576 bits (per second).

**megabuck** • **n.** informal a million dollars. ➤ (**megabucks**) a huge sum of money.

**megabyte** (abbrev.: **Mb** or **MB**) • **n.** Computing a unit of information equal to one million or (strictly) 1,048,576 bytes.

**megadeath** • **n.** a unit used in quantifying the casualties of nuclear war, equal to the deaths of one million people.

**megafauna** • **n.** Zoology the large animals of a particular region, habitat, or geological period.
– DERIVATIVES **megafaunal** adj.

**megaflop** • **n.** Computing a unit of computing speed equal to one million or (strictly) 1,048,576 floating-point operations per second.

**megahertz** (abbrev.: **MHz**) • **n.** (pl. same) a unit of frequency equal to one million hertz.

**megalith** • **n.** Archaeology a large stone that forms a prehistoric monument or part of one.
– ORIGIN C19: back-form. from **MEGALITHIC**.

**megalithic** • **adj.** Archaeology made of, denoting, or marked by the use of megaliths.
– ORIGIN C19: from **MEGA-** + Gk *lithos* + **-IC**.

**megalo-** /ˈmɛɡələʊ/ • **comb. form** great: *megaloblast*.
– ORIGIN from Gk *megas*, *megal-* 'great'.

**megaloblast** /ˈmɛɡələ(ʊ)blast/ • **n.** Medicine a large, abnormal red blood cell typical of certain forms of anaemia.
– DERIVATIVES **megaloblastic** adj.

**megalomania** • **n.** obsession with the exercise of power. ➤ delusion about one's own power or importance (typically as a symptom of manic or paranoid disorder).
– DERIVATIVES **megalomaniac** n. & adj. **megalomaniacal** adj. **megalomanic** adj.

**megalopolis** /ˌmɛɡəˈlɒp(ə)lɪs/ • **n.** a very large, heavily populated city or urban complex.
– DERIVATIVES **megalopolitan** n. & adj.
– ORIGIN C19 (earlier (C17) as *megalopolitan*): from **MEGALO-** + Gk *polis* 'city'.

**megalosaurus** /ˌmɛɡ(ə)lə(ʊ)ˈsɔːrəs/ • **n.** a large carnivorous bipedal dinosaur of the mid Jurassic period.

**megamouth shark** • **n.** a rare shark with a very large wide mouth and tiny teeth. [*Megachasma pelagios*.]

**megaphone** • **n.** a large funnel-shaped device for amplifying and directing the voice.
– DERIVATIVES **megaphonic** adj.

**megapode** /ˈmɛɡəpəʊd/ • **n.** a large ground-dwelling Australasian or SE Asian bird that builds a large mound of plant debris to incubate its eggs. [Family Megapodiidae: several species.]
– ORIGIN C19: from mod. L. *Megapodius* (genus name), from **MEGA-** + Gk *pous*, *pod-* 'foot'.

**megaron** /ˈmɛɡər(ə)n/ ● **n.** Archaeology the central hall of a large Mycenaean house.
– ORIGIN from Gk.

**megaspore** ● **n.** Botany the larger of the two kinds of spores produced by some ferns. Compare with **MICROSPORE**.

**megastar** ● **n.** informal a very famous person in the world of entertainment or sport.
– DERIVATIVES **megastardom** n.

**megastore** ● **n.** a very large shop, typically one specializing in a particular type of product.

**megatherium** /ˌmɛɡəˈθɪərɪəm/ ● **n.** (pl. **megatheriums** or **megatheria**) an extinct giant ground sloth of the Pliocene and Pleistocene epochs.
– ORIGIN mod. L., from Gk *mega thērion* 'great animal'.

**megaton** ● **n.** a unit of explosive power equivalent to one million tons of TNT.

**megavolt** (abbrev.: **MV**) ● **n.** a unit of electromotive force equal to one million volts.

**megawatt** (abbrev.: **MW**) ● **n.** a unit of electrical or other power equal to one million watts.

**me generation** ● **n.** a generation of people characterized by selfish materialism.

**Megger** /ˈmɛɡə/ ● **n.** trademark an instrument for measuring the resistance of electrical insulation.
– ORIGIN C20: perh. from **MEGOHM**.

**Megillah** /məˈɡɪlə/ ● **n.** **1** each of the books of the Hebrew scriptures (the Song of Solomon, Ruth, Lamentations, Ecclesiastes, and Esther) appointed to be read on certain Jewish notable days. **2** (**the whole megillah**) N. Amer. informal something in its entirety.
– ORIGIN from Heb. *mĕḡillāh*, lit. 'scroll'.

**megilp** /məˈɡɪlp/ (also **magilp**) ● **n.** a mixture of mastic resin and linseed oil added to oil paints, widely used in the 19th century.
– ORIGIN C18: of unknown origin.

**megohm** /ˈmɛɡəʊm/ ● **n.** a unit of electrical resistance equal to one million ohms.

**megrim**[1] /ˈmiːɡrɪm/ ● **n.** archaic **1** (**megrims**) low spirits. **2** a whim or fancy.
– ORIGIN ME: var. of **MIGRAINE**.

**megrim**[2] /ˈmiːɡrɪm/ ● **n.** a deep-water flatfish of the European Atlantic coast. [*Lepidorhombus whiffiagonis*.] ➤ another term for **SCALDFISH**.
– ORIGIN C19: of unknown origin.

**meibomian** /mʌɪˈbəʊmɪən/ ● **adj.** Anatomy relating to or denoting large sebaceous glands of the human eyelid, whose infection results in inflammation and swelling.
– ORIGIN C19: from the name of the C18 Ger. anatomist Heinrich *Meibom*, + **-IAN**.

**Meiji** /ˈmeɪdʒi/ ● **n.** [as modifier] denoting the period (1868–1912) when Japan was ruled by the emperor Meiji Tenno, marked by modernization and westernization.
– ORIGIN Japanese, lit. 'enlightened government'.

**meiosis** /mʌɪˈəʊsɪs/ ● **n.** (pl. **meioses** /-siːz/) **1** Biology a type of cell division that results in daughter cells each with half the number of chromosomes of the parent cell. Compare with **MITOSIS**. **2** another term for **LITOTES**.
– DERIVATIVES **meiotic** adj. **meiotically** adv.
– ORIGIN C16: mod. L., from Gk *meiōsis*, from *meioun* 'lessen'.

**Meissen** /ˈmʌɪs(ə)n/ ● **n.** fine hard-paste porcelain produced at Meissen in Germany since 1710.

**-meister** /ˈmʌɪstə/ ● **comb. form** denoting a person regarded as skilled or prominent in a specified area of activity: *gag-meister*.
– ORIGIN from Ger. *Meister* 'master'.

**Meistersinger** /ˈmʌɪstəsɪŋə/ ● **n.** (pl. same) a member of one of the guilds of German lyric poets and musicians which flourished from the 12th to 17th century.
– ORIGIN Ger., from *Meister* 'master' + *Singer* 'singer'.

**meitnerium** /mʌɪtˈnɪərɪəm/ ● **n.** the chemical element of atomic number 109, a very unstable element made by high-energy atomic collisions. (Symbol: **Mt**)
– ORIGIN 1990s: mod. L., from the name of the Swed. physicist Lise *Meitner*.

**melamine** /ˈmɛləmiːn/ ● **n.** **1** Chemistry a white crystalline compound made by heating cyanamide. **2** a plastic made by polymerizing this with formaldehyde.
– ORIGIN C19: from Ger. *melam* (an arbitrary formation), denoting an insoluble amorphous organic substance, + **AMINE**.

**melancholia** /ˌmɛlənˈkəʊlɪə/ ● **n.** melancholy. ➤ dated a mental condition marked by persistent depression and ill-founded fears.
– ORIGIN ME (denoting black bile): from late L. (see **MELANCHOLY**).

**melancholy** ● **n.** **1** a deep and long-lasting sadness. ➤ another term for **MELANCHOLIA** (as a mental condition). **2** historical another term for **BLACK BILE**. ● **adj.** depressed or depressing.
– DERIVATIVES **melancholic** adj. **melancholically** adv.
– ORIGIN ME: from OFr. *melancolie*, via late L. from Gk *melankholia*, from *melas*, *melan-* 'black' + *kholē* 'bile', an excess of which was formerly believed to cause depression.

**Melanesian** /ˌmɛləˈniːzɪ(ə)n, -ʒ(ə)n/ ● **n.** **1** a native or inhabitant of any of the islands of Melanesia in the western Pacific. **2** any of the languages of Melanesia. ● **adj.** of or relating to Melanesia, its peoples, or their languages.

**melange** /meɪˈlɒ̃ʒ/ ● **n.** a varied mixture.
– ORIGIN from Fr. *mélange*, from *mêler* 'to mix'.

**melanin** /ˈmɛlənɪn/ ● **n.** a dark brown to black pigment occurring in the hair, skin, and iris of the eye, responsible for tanning of skin exposed to sunlight.
– ORIGIN C19: from Gk *melas*, *melan-* 'black' + **-IN**[1].

**melanism** /ˈmɛlənɪz(ə)m/ ● **n.** chiefly Zoology darkening of body tissues due to excessive production of melanin, especially as a form of colour variation in animals.
– DERIVATIVES **melanic** /mɪˈlanɪk/ adj.

**melanocyte** /ˈmɛlənə(ʊ)ˌsʌɪt, mɪˈlanə(ʊ)-/ ● **n.** Physiology a mature melanin-forming cell, especially in the skin.

**melanoma** /ˌmɛləˈnəʊmə/ ● **n.** Medicine a tumour of melanin-forming cells, especially a malignant tumour associated with skin cancer.
– ORIGIN C19: from Gk *melas*, *melan-* 'black' + **-OMA**.

**melanosis** /ˌmɛləˈnəʊsɪs/ ● **n.** Medicine excessive production of melanin in the skin or other tissue.
– DERIVATIVES **melanotic** adj.
– ORIGIN C19: mod. L., from Gk *melas*, *melan-* 'black' + **-OSIS**.

**melatonin** /ˌmɛləˈtəʊnɪn/ ● **n.** Biochemistry a hormone secreted by the pineal gland which inhibits melanin formation.
– ORIGIN 1950s: from Gk *melas* 'black' + **SEROTONIN**.

**Melba sauce** ● **n.** a sauce made from puréed raspberries thickened with icing sugar.
– ORIGIN from the name of the Austral. operatic soprano Dame Nellie *Melba* (1861–1931).

**Melba toast** ● **n.** very thin crisp toast.

**meld**[1] ● **v.** blend; combine. ● **n.** a thing formed by melding.
– ORIGIN 1930s: perh. a blend of **MELT** and **WELD**[1].

**meld**[2] ● **v.** (in rummy, canasta, and other card games) lay down or declare (a combination of cards) in order to score points. ● **n.** a completed set or run of cards in any of these games.
– ORIGIN C19 (orig. US): from Ger. *melden* 'announce'.

**melee** /ˈmɛleɪ/ ● **n.** a confused crowd or scuffle.
– ORIGIN C17: from Fr. *mêlée*, from an OFr. var. of *meslee* (see **MEDLEY**).

**melic** /ˈmɛlɪk/ ● **adj.** (of an ancient Greek lyric poem) meant to be sung.
– ORIGIN C17: via L. from Gk *melikos*, from *melos* 'song'.

**melick** ● **n.** a grass with purplish florets. [Genus *Melica*.]
– ORIGIN C18: from mod. L. *melica*, perh. from Ital. *melica* 'sorghum'.

**melilot** /ˈmɛlɪlɒt/ ● **n.** a fragrant plant of the pea family with small yellow or white flowers. [Genus *Melilotus*.]
– ORIGIN ME: from OFr., via L. from Gk *melilōtos* 'honey lotus'.

**meliorate** /ˈmiːlɪəreɪt/ ● **v.** formal another term for **AMELIORATE**.
– DERIVATIVES **melioration** n. **meliorative** adj.

– ORIGIN C16 (earlier (ME) as *melioration*): from late L. *meliorat-*, *meliorare* 'improve'.

**meliorism** /ˈmiːlɪərɪz(ə)m/ • **n.** Philosophy the belief that the world can be made better by human effort.
– DERIVATIVES **meliorist** n. & adj. **melioristic** adj.
– ORIGIN C19: from L. *melior* 'better' + **-ISM**.

**melisma** /mɪˈlɪzmə/ • **n.** (pl. **melismas** or **melismata** /-mətə/) Music a group of notes sung to one syllable of text.
– DERIVATIVES **melismatic** adj.
– ORIGIN C19: from Gk, lit. 'melody'.

**Melkite** /ˈmɛlkʌɪt/ • **n.** an Orthodox or Uniate Christian belonging to the patriarchate of Antioch, Jerusalem, or Alexandria. ➤an Eastern Christian adhering to the Orthodox faith as defined by the councils of Ephesus (AD 431) and Chalcedon (AD 451) and as accepted by the Byzantine emperor.
– ORIGIN C17: via eccles. L. from Byzantine Gk *Melkhitai*, pl. representing Syriac *malkāyā* 'royalists' (i.e. expressing agreement with the Byzantine emperor).

**melliferous** /mɛˈlɪf(ə)rəs/ • **adj.** yielding or producing honey.
– ORIGIN C17: from L. *mellifer* (from *mel* 'honey' + *-fer* 'bearing') + **-OUS**.

**mellifluous** /mɛˈlɪfluəs/ • **adj.** pleasingly smooth and musical to hear.
– DERIVATIVES **mellifluence** n. **mellifluent** adj. **mellifluously** adv. **mellifluousness** n.
– ORIGIN C15: from late L. *mellifluus* (from L. *mel* 'honey' + *fluere* 'to flow') + **-OUS**.

**mellophone** /ˈmɛləfəʊn/ • **n.** a brass instrument similar to the orchestral French horn, played mainly in military and concert bands.
– ORIGIN 1920s: from **MELLOW** + **-PHONE**.

**mellotron** /ˈmɛlətrɒn/ • **n.** an electronic keyboard instrument in which each key controls the playback of a single pre-recorded musical sound.
– ORIGIN 1960s: from **MELLOW** + *-tron*, element of **ELECTRONIC**.

**mellow** • **adj. 1** (especially of sound, taste, and colour) pleasantly smooth or soft. ➤archaic (of fruit) ripe, soft, sweet, and juicy. **2** (of a person's character) softened by maturity or experience. ➤relaxed and good-humoured. **3** (of earth) rich and loamy. • **v.** make or become mellow.
– DERIVATIVES **mellowly** adv. **mellowness** n.
– ORIGIN ME: perh. from attributive use of OE *melu*, *melw-* (see **MEAL**[2]).

**melodeon** /mɪˈləʊdɪən/ (also **melodion**) • **n. 1** a small accordion of German origin, played especially by folk musicians. **2** a small organ popular in the 19th century, similar to the harmonium.
– ORIGIN C19: prob. from **MELODY**, on the pattern of *accordion*; sense 2 is an alt. of earlier *melodium*.

**melodic** • **adj.** of, having, or producing melody. ➤pleasant-sounding.
– DERIVATIVES **melodically** adv.

**melodica** /məˈlɒdɪkə/ • **n.** a wind instrument with a small keyboard controlling a row of reeds, and a mouthpiece at one end.
– ORIGIN 1960s: from **MELODY**, on the pattern of *harmonica*.

**melodic minor** • **n.** Music a minor scale with the sixth and seventh degrees raised when ascending and lowered when descending.

**melodious** • **adj.** pleasant-sounding; tuneful. ➤relating to melody.
– DERIVATIVES **melodiously** adv. **melodiousness** n.

**melodist** • **n. 1** a composer of melodies. **2** archaic a singer.

**melodrama** • **n. 1** a sensational dramatic piece with exaggerated characters and exciting events. ➤language, behaviour, or events resembling such drama. **2** historical a play interspersed with songs and orchestral music accompanying the action.
– DERIVATIVES **melodramatist** n. **melodramatize** (also **-ise**) v.
– ORIGIN C19: from Fr. *mélodrame*, from Gk *melos* 'music' + Fr. *drame* 'drama'.

**melodramatic** • **adj.** of, relating to, or characteristic of melodrama. ➤exaggerated or overemotional.
– DERIVATIVES **melodramatically** adv. **melodramatics** pl. n.

**melody** • **n.** (pl. **-ies**) a sequence of single notes that is musically satisfying. ➤the principal part in harmonized music.
– ORIGIN ME: from OFr. *melodie*, via late L. from Gk *melōidia*, from *melos* 'song'.

**melon** • **n. 1** the large round fruit of a plant of the gourd family, with sweet pulpy flesh and many seeds. **2** the plant which yields this fruit. [*Cucumis melo* subsp. *melo*.] **3** Zoology a waxy mass in the head of some toothed whales, thought to focus acoustic signals.
– ORIGIN ME: via OFr. from late L. *melo*, *melon-*, contr. of L. *melopepo*, from Gk *mēlopepōn*, from *mēlon* 'apple' + *pepōn* 'gourd'.

**melt** • **v. 1** make or become liquefied by heating. ➤(**melt something down**) melt something, especially a metal article, so as to reuse the raw material. ➤dissolve in liquid. **2** become or make more tender or loving. **3** (often **melt away**) disappear or disperse. ➤(**melt into**) change or merge imperceptibly into (another form or state). • **n. 1** an act of melting. ➤metal or other material in a melted condition. ➤an amount melted at any one time. **2** chiefly N. Amer. a sandwich, hamburger, or other dish containing or topped with melted cheese.
– DERIVATIVES **meltable** adj. **melter** n. **melting** adj. **meltingly** adv.
– ORIGIN OE *meltan*, *mieltan*, of Gmc origin; rel. to **MALT**.

**meltdown** • **n. 1** an accident in a nuclear reactor in which the fuel overheats and melts the reactor core or shielding. **2** a disastrous collapse or breakdown.

**meltemi** /mɛlˈtɛmi/ • **n.** a dry north-westerly wind which blows during the summer in the eastern Mediterranean.
– ORIGIN from mod. Gk *meltémi*, Turk. *meltem*.

**melting point** • **n.** the temperature at which a given solid will melt.

**melting pot** • **n. 1** a pot in which metals or other materials are melted and mixed. ➤a place where different peoples, styles, etc., are mixed together. **2** a situation of constant change and uncertain outcome: *the railway's future is in the melting pot.*

**melton** • **n.** heavy woollen cloth with a close-cut nap, used for overcoats and jackets.
– ORIGIN C19: named after *Melton* Mowbray, a town in central England, formerly a centre of manufacture.

**meltwater** (also **meltwaters**) • **n.** water formed by the melting of snow and ice, especially from a glacier.

**member** • **n. 1** a person, country, or organization belonging to a group, society, or team. ➤(**Member**) a person formally elected to certain legislative bodies. ➤used in the title awarded to a person admitted to (usually the lowest grade of) certain honours. **2** a constituent piece of a complex structure. ➤a part of a sentence, equation, etc. **3** archaic a part of the body, especially a limb. ➤(also **male member**) a man's penis.
– DERIVATIVES **-membered** adj. (chiefly Chemistry). **membership** n.
– ORIGIN ME: via OFr. from L. *membrum* 'limb'.

**membrane** • **n. 1** Anatomy & Zoology a pliable sheet-like structure acting as a boundary, lining, or partition in an organism or cell. **2** a thin pliable sheet of material. **3** Biology a double layer of lipids and proteins forming the boundary of a cell or organelle.
– DERIVATIVES **membranaceous** adj. **membraneous** adj. **membranous** adj.
– ORIGIN ME: from L. *membrana*, from *membrum* 'limb'.

**membranous labyrinth** • **n.** see **LABYRINTH**.

**membrum virile** /ˌmɛmbrəm vɪˈrʌɪli, vɪˈriːli/ • **n.** archaic a man's penis.
– ORIGIN L., lit. 'male member'.

**meme** /miːm/ • **n.** Biology a cultural or behavioural element passed on by imitation or other non-genetic means.
– DERIVATIVES **memetic** adj.
– ORIGIN 1970s: from Gk *mimēma* 'that which is imitated', on the pattern of *gene*.

**memento** /mɪˈmɛntəʊ/ ● **n.** (pl. **-os** or **-oes**) an object kept as a reminder or souvenir.
– ORIGIN ME (denoting a prayer of commemoration): from L., lit. 'remember!', imper. of *meminisse.*

**memento mori** /mɪˌmɛntəʊ ˈmɔːri, -rʌɪ/ ● **n.** (pl. same) an object kept as a reminder that death is inevitable.
– ORIGIN L., lit. 'remember (that you have) to die'.

**memo** ● **n.** (pl. **-os**) informal a memorandum.

**memoir** ● **n. 1** a historical account or biography written from personal knowledge. ➤ **(memoirs)** an account written by a public figure of their life and experiences. **2** an essay on a learned subject. ➤ **(memoirs)** the proceedings of a learned society.
– DERIVATIVES **memoirist** n.
– ORIGIN C15 (denoting a memorandum): from Fr. *mémoire* (masc.), a special use of *mémoire* (fem.) 'memory'.

**memorabilia** /ˌmɛm(ə)rəˈbɪlɪə/ ● **pl. n.** objects kept or collected because of their associations with memorable people or events.
– ORIGIN C18: from L., neut. pl. of *memorabilis* 'memorable'.

**memorable** ● **adj.** worth remembering or easily remembered.
– DERIVATIVES **memorability** n. **memorably** adv.
– ORIGIN C15: from L. *memorabilis*, from *memorare* 'bring to mind'.

**memorandum** ● **n.** (pl. **memoranda** or **memorandums**) a written message in business or diplomacy. ➤ a note recording something. ➤ Law a document recording the terms of a transaction.
– ORIGIN ME: from L., lit. 'something to be brought to mind', gerundive of *memorare.*

**memorial** ● **n. 1** a structure or object established in memory of a person or event. ➤ [as modifier] intended to commemorate someone or something. **2** chiefly historical a statement of facts, especially as the basis of a petition. ➤ a written record.
– DERIVATIVES **memorialist** n. **memorialize** (also **-ise**) v.
– ORIGIN ME: from late L. *memoriale* 'record, memory', from L. *memorialis* 'serving as a reminder'.

**Memorial Day** ● **n.** (in the US) a day on which those who died on active service are remembered, usually the last Monday in May.

**memorize** (also **-ise**) ● **v.** learn by heart.
– DERIVATIVES **memorizable** adj. **memorization** n. **memorizer** n.

**memory** ● **n.** (pl. **-ies**) **1** the faculty by which the mind stores and remembers information. **2** something remembered. ➤ the remembering or commemoration of a dead person. ➤ the length of time over which a person or event continues to be remembered. **3** a computer's equipment or capacity for storing data or program instructions for retrieval.
– PHRASES **from memory** without reading or referring to notes. **in memory of** intended to remind people of. **take a trip** (or **walk**) **down memory lane** indulge in pleasant or sentimental memories.
– ORIGIN ME: from OFr. *memorie*, from L. *memoria* 'memory', from *memor* 'mindful, remembering'.

**memory book** ● **n.** US a scrapbook.

**memsahib** /ˈmɛmsʌˌhiːb, ˈmɛmsɑːb/ ● **n.** Indian dated a married white woman (used as a respectful form of address).
– ORIGIN from *mem* (representing an Ind. pronunc. of **MA'AM**) + **SAHIB**.

**men** plural form of **MAN**.

**menace** ● **n.** a threat or danger. ➤ a threatening quality. ● **v.** threaten (someone).
– DERIVATIVES **menacer** n. **menacing** adj. **menacingly** adv.
– ORIGIN ME: via OFr. from late L. *minacia*, from L. *minax, minac-* 'threatening', from *minae* 'threats'.

**ménage** /meɪˈnɑːʒ/ ● **n.** the members of a household.
– ORIGIN ME: from OFr. *menage*, from *mainer* 'to stay', influenced by OFr. *mesnie* 'household', both ult. based on L. *manere* 'remain'.

**ménage à trois** /meɪˌnɑːʒ ɑː ˈtrwʌ/ ● **n.** (pl. **ménages à trois** pronunc. same) an arrangement in which a married couple and the lover of one of them live together.
– ORIGIN Fr., 'household of three'.

**menagerie** /məˈnadʒ(ə)ri/ ● **n.** a collection of wild animals kept in captivity for exhibition.
– ORIGIN C17: from Fr. *ménagerie*, from *ménage* (see **MÉNAGE**).

**menaquinone** /ˌmɛnəˈkwɪnəʊn/ ● **n.** Biochemistry vitamin K, a compound produced by intestinal bacteria and essential for the blood-clotting process.
– ORIGIN 1940s: from the chemical name *me(thyl)-na(phtho)quinone.*

**menarche** /mɛˈnɑːki/ ● **n.** the first occurrence of menstruation.
– ORIGIN C19: mod. L., from Gk *mēn* 'month' + *arkhē* 'beginning'.

**mend** ● **v. 1** restore to a sound condition. ➤ return to health. ➤ improve: *mend your ways.* **2** add fuel to (a fire). ● **n.** a repair in a material.
– PHRASES **mend (one's) fences** make peace with a person. **on the mend** improving in health or condition.
– DERIVATIVES **mendable** adj. **mender** n.
– ORIGIN ME: shortening of **AMEND**.

**mendacious** /mɛnˈdeɪʃəs/ ● **adj.** untruthful.
– DERIVATIVES **mendaciously** adv. **mendacity** n.
– ORIGIN C17: from L. *mendax, mendac-* 'lying' + **-IOUS**.

**Mende** /ˈmɛndi/ ● **n.** (pl. same) **1** a member of a people inhabiting Sierra Leone in West Africa. **2** the language of this people, belonging to the Mande group.
– ORIGIN the name in Mende.

**mendelevium** /ˌmɛndəˈliːvɪəm, -ˈleɪvɪəm/ ● **n.** the chemical element of atomic number 101, an artificially made radioactive metal of the actinide series. (Symbol: **Md**)
– ORIGIN 1950s: mod. L., from the name of the Russ. chemist Dimitri *Mendeleev* (1834–1907).

**Mendelism** /ˈmɛnd(ə)lɪz(ə)m/ ● **n.** Biology the theory of heredity based on the recurrence of characteristics transmitted as genes, as formulated by the 19th-century Moravian botanist Gregor Johann Mendel.
– DERIVATIVES **Mendelian** adj. & n.

**mendicant** /ˈmɛndɪk(ə)nt/ ● **adj.** given to begging. ➤ of or denoting a religious order originally dependent on alms. ● **n.** a beggar. ➤ a member of a mendicant order.
– DERIVATIVES **mendicancy** n. **mendicity** n.
– ORIGIN ME: from L. *mendicant-, mendicare* 'beg', from *mendicus* 'beggar', from *mendum* 'fault'.

**mending** ● **n.** things to be repaired by sewing or darning.

**menfolk** (US also **menfolks**) ● **pl. n.** a group of men considered collectively.

**menhaden** /mɛnˈheɪd(ə)n/ ● **n.** a large deep-bodied fish of the herring family, found off the east coast of North America. [*Brevoortia tyrannus* and related species.]
– ORIGIN C18: from Algonquian.

**menhir** /ˈmɛnhɪə/ ● **n.** Archaeology a tall upright stone of a kind erected in prehistoric times in western Europe.
– ORIGIN C19: from Breton *men* 'stone' + *hir* 'long'.

**menial** /ˈmiːnɪəl/ ● **adj.** (of work) requiring little skill and lacking prestige. ➤ dated (of a servant) domestic. ● **n.** a person with a menial job.
– DERIVATIVES **menially** adv.
– ORIGIN ME: from OFr., from *mesnee* 'household'.

**Ménière's disease** /mɛnˈjɛː/ ● **n.** a disease of the inner ear causing progressive deafness, tinnitus, and vertigo.
– ORIGIN C19: named after the Fr. physician Prosper *Ménière.*

**meninges** /mɪˈnɪndʒiːz/ ● **pl. n.** (sing. **meninx**) Anatomy the three membranes (the dura mater, arachnoid, and pia mater) that line the skull and vertebral canal and enclose the brain and spinal cord.
– DERIVATIVES **meningeal** adj.
– ORIGIN mod. L., from Gk *mēninx, mēning-* 'membrane'.

**meningitis** /ˌmɛnɪnˈdʒʌɪtɪs/ ● **n.** a disease in which there is inflammation of the meninges, caused by viral or bacterial infection.
– DERIVATIVES **meningitic** adj.

**meningococcus** /mɪˌnɪŋgəʊˈkɒkəs, -ˌnɪndʒəʊ-/ ● **n.** (pl. **meningococci** /-ˈkɒk(s)ʌɪ, -ˈkɒk(s)iː/) a bacterium involved in some forms of meningitis. [*Neisseria*

*meningitidis.*]
– DERIVATIVES **meningococcal** adj.

**meninx** /ˈmiːnɪŋks/ singular form of **MENINGES**.

**meniscus** /mɪˈnɪskəs/ ● n. (pl. **menisci** /-sʌɪ/) **1** Physics the curved upper surface of a liquid in a tube. **2** a thin lens convex on one side and concave on the other. **3** Anatomy a thin fibrous cartilage between the surfaces of some joints.
– ORIGIN C17: mod. L., from Gk *mēniskos* 'crescent'.

**Mennonite** /ˈmɛnənʌɪt/ ● n. a member of a Protestant sect originating in Friesland in the 16th century, emphasizing adult baptism and rejecting Church organization, military service, and public office.
– ORIGIN from the name of its founder, *Menno* Simons (1496–1561), + **-ITE**[1].

**meno** /ˈmɛnəʊ/ ● adv. Music less.
– ORIGIN from Ital.

**meno-** ● comb. form relating to menstruation: *menopause*.
– ORIGIN from Gk *mēn* 'month'.

**Menominee** /mɪˈnɒmɪniː/ (also **Menomini**) ● n. (pl. same or **Menominees**) **1** a member of an American Indian people of NE Wisconsin. **2** the extinct Algonquian language of this people.
– ORIGIN from Ojibwa *manōminī*, lit. 'wild-rice person'.

**meno mosso** /ˌmɛnəʊ ˈmɒsəʊ/ ● adv. & adj. Music less quickly.
– ORIGIN from Ital.

**menopause** /ˈmɛnəpɔːz/ ● n. the ceasing of menstruation or the period in a woman's life (typically between 45 and 50) when this occurs.
– DERIVATIVES **menopausal** adj.
– ORIGIN C19: from mod. L. *menopausis* (see **MENO-**, **PAUSE**).

**menorah** /mɪˈnɔːrə/ ● n. **1** a holy candelabrum with seven branches, used in the ancient temple at Jerusalem. **2** a candelabrum used in Jewish worship, typically with eight branches.
– ORIGIN from Heb.

**menorrhagia** /ˌmɛnəˈreɪdʒɪə/ ● n. Medicine abnormally heavy bleeding at menstruation.
– ORIGIN C18: mod. L., from **MENO-** + *-rrhag-*, stem of Gk *rhēgnunai* 'to burst'.

**menorrhoea** /ˌmɛnəˈriːə/ ● n. Medicine the flow of blood at menstruation.
– ORIGIN C19: back-form. from **AMENORRHOEA**.

**mensch** /mɛnʃ/ ● n. N. Amer. informal a person of integrity and honour.
– ORIGIN 1930s: Yiddish *mensh*, from Ger. *Mensch*, lit. 'person'.

**menses** /ˈmɛnsiːz/ ● pl. n. **1** blood and other matter discharged from the uterus at menstruation. **2** [treated as sing.] the time of menstruation.
– ORIGIN C16: from L., pl. of *mensis* 'month'.

**Menshevik** /ˈmɛnʃɪvɪk/ ● n. a member of the non-Leninist wing of the Russian Social Democratic Workers' Party, defeated by the Bolsheviks in 1917.
– ORIGIN from Russ. *Men'shevik* 'a member of the minority', from *men'she* 'less'.

**men's movement** ● n. (chiefly in the US) a movement aimed at liberating men from traditional views about their character and role in society.

**mens rea** /ˌmɛnz ˈriːə/ ● n. Law the intention or knowledge of wrongdoing that constitutes part of a crime. Compare with **ACTUS REUS**.
– ORIGIN L., lit. 'guilty mind'.

**menstrual** ● adj. of or relating to the menses or menstruation.
– ORIGIN ME: from L. *menstrualis*, from *menstruum* 'menses', from *mensis* 'month'.

**menstrual cycle** ● n. the process of ovulation and menstruation in women and other female primates.

**menstruate** /ˈmɛnstrʊeɪt/ ● v. (of a non-pregnant woman) discharge blood and other material from the lining of the uterus at intervals of about one lunar month.
– DERIVATIVES **menstruation** n.
– ORIGIN C17 (earlier (ME) as *menstruous*): from late L. *menstruat-*, *menstruare* 'menstruate', from *menstrua* 'menses'.

**menstruous** ● adj. of, relating to, or in the process of menstruation.

**menstruum** /ˈmɛnstrʊəm/ ● n. (pl. **menstrua** /-strʊə/) **1** menses. **2** archaic a solvent.
– ORIGIN ME: from L., neut. of *menstruus* 'monthly', from *mensis* 'month'; sense 2 is by alchemical analogy between transmutation of metals into gold and the supposed action of menses on the ovum.

**mensurable** ● adj. able to be measured.
– ORIGIN ME (in the sense 'moderate'): from late L. *mensurabilis*, from *mensurare* 'to measure'.

**mensural** /ˈmɛnʃ(ə)r(ə)l, -sjə-/ ● adj. **1** of or involving measuring. **2** Music involving notes of definite duration and usually a regular metre.
– ORIGIN C16: from L. *mensuralis*, from *mensura* 'measure'.

**menswear** ● n. clothes for men.

**mensuration** ● n. measurement. ➤ the part of geometry concerned with ascertaining lengths, areas, and volumes.
– ORIGIN C16: from late L. *mensuratio(n-)*, from *mensurare* 'to measure'.

**-ment** ● suffix **1** forming nouns expressing the means or result of an action: *curtailment*. **2** forming nouns from adjectives (such as *merriment* from *merry*).
– ORIGIN from Fr., or from L. *-mentum*.

**mental** ● adj. **1** of, done by, or occurring in the mind. **2** of or relating to disorders or illnesses of the mind. ➤ informal mad.
– DERIVATIVES **mentally** adv.
– ORIGIN ME: from late L. *mentalis*, from L. *mens*, *ment-* 'mind'.

**mental age** ● n. a person's mental ability expressed as the age at which an average person reaches the same ability.

**mental block** ● n. an inability to recall something or to perform a mental action.

**mental defective** ● n. dated a person with a mental handicap.

**mental deficiency** ● n. dated the condition of having a mental handicap.

**mental handicap** ● n. a condition in which the intellectual capacity of a person is permanently lowered or underdeveloped to an extent which prevents normal function in society.

**mentalism** ● n. Philosophy the theory that physical and psychological phenomena are ultimately explicable only in terms of a creative and interpretative mind.
– DERIVATIVES **mentalist** n. & adj. **mentalistic** adj.

**mentality** ● n. (pl. **-ies**) **1** often derogatory a characteristic way of thinking. **2** the capacity for intelligent thought.

**mentally handicapped** ● adj. having very limited intellectual functions.

**mentation** ● n. technical mental activity.
– ORIGIN C19: from L. *mens*, *ment-* 'mind' + **-ATION**.

**menthol** ● n. a crystalline alcohol with a minty taste and odour, found in peppermint and other natural oils.
– DERIVATIVES **mentholated** adj.
– ORIGIN C19: from Ger., from L. *mentha* 'mint' + **-OL**.

**mention** ● v. refer to briefly. ➤ refer to (someone) by name. ● n. a reference to someone or something. ➤ a formal acknowledgement of something noteworthy.
– PHRASES **be mentioned in dispatches** Brit. be commended for one's actions by name in an official military report. **mention someone in one's will** leave a legacy to someone.
– DERIVATIVES **mentionable** adj.
– ORIGIN ME: via OFr. from L. *mentio(n-)*; rel. to **MIND**.

**mento** ● n. (pl. **-os**) a style of Jamaican folk music based on a traditional dance rhythm in duple time.
– ORIGIN C20: of unknown origin.

**mentor** ● n. an experienced and trusted adviser. ➤ an experienced person in an institution who trains and counsels new employees or students. ● v. be a mentor to.
– ORIGIN C18: via Fr. and L. from Gk *Mentōr*, the adviser of the young Telemachus in Homer's *Odyssey*.

**menu** ● n. **1** a list of dishes available in a restaurant. ➤ the food available or to be served in a restaurant or at a meal. **2** Computing a list of commands or facilities, especially one displayed on screen.
– ORIGIN C19: from Fr., 'detailed list'.

**menudo** /mɪˈnuːdəʊ/ ● n. (pl. **-os**) a spicy Mexican soup made from tripe.
– ORIGIN noun use of a Mex. Sp. adjective meaning 'small'.

**Meo** /mɪˈəʊ/ ● n. (pl. same or **-os**) & adj. another term for **HMONG**.

**meow** ● n. & v. variant spelling of **MIAOW**.

**MEP** ● abbrev. Member of the European Parliament.

**meperidine** /mɛˈpɛrɪdiːn/ ● n. another term for **PETHIDINE**.
– ORIGIN 1940s: blend of **METHYL** and **PIPERIDINE**.

**Mephistopheles** /ˌmɛfɪˈstɒfɪliːz/ ● n. an evil spirit to whom Faust, in the German legend, sold his soul.
– DERIVATIVES **Mephistophelean** /-ˈfiːlɪən, -fɪˈliːən/ (also **Mephistophelian**) adj.

**mephitic** /mɪˈfɪtɪk/ ● adj. (especially of a gas or vapour) foul-smelling; noxious.
– ORIGIN C17: from late L. *mephiticus*, from *mephitis* 'noxious exhalation'.

**-mer** ● comb. form denoting polymers and related kinds of molecule: *elastomer*.
– ORIGIN from Gk *meros* 'part'.

**meranti** /məˈranti/ ● n. white, red, or yellow hardwood from a SE Asian tree (genus *Shorea*).
– ORIGIN C18: from Malay.

**merbau** /ˈməːbəʊ/ ● n. the hardwood of a SE Asian tree (genus *Intsia*).
– ORIGIN C18: from Malay.

**mercado** /məːˈkɑːdəʊ/ ● n. (pl. **-os**) (in Spanish-speaking countries) a market.
– ORIGIN Sp., from L. *mercatus* 'market'.

**mercantile** /ˈməːk(ə)ntʌɪl/ ● adj. **1** of or relating to trade or commerce. **2** of or relating to mercantilism.
– ORIGIN C17: from Fr., from Ital., from *mercante* 'merchant'.

**mercantile marine** ● n. the merchant navy.

**mercantilism** /ˈməːk(ə)ntʌɪˌlɪz(ə)m/ ● n. chiefly historical the economic theory that trade generates wealth and is stimulated by the accumulation of profitable balances, which a government should encourage by means of protectionism.
– DERIVATIVES **mercantilist** n. & adj.

**mercaptan** /məˈkapt(ə)n/ ● n. Chemistry another term for **THIOL**.
– ORIGIN C19: from mod. L. *mercurium captans*, lit. 'capturing mercury'.

**Mercator projection** ● n. a world map projection made on to a cylinder in such a way that all parallels of latitude have the same length as the equator.
– ORIGIN from *Mercator*, Latinized name of the C16 Flemish geographer Gerhard Kremer.

**mercenary** /ˈməːsɪn(ə)ri/ ● adj. motivated primarily by the desire for gain. ● n. (pl. **-ies**) a professional soldier hired to serve in a foreign army.
– DERIVATIVES **mercenariness** n.
– ORIGIN ME: from L. *mercenarius* 'hireling', from *merces, merced-* 'reward'.

**mercer** ● n. Brit., chiefly historical a dealer in textile fabrics, especially silk and other fine materials.
– DERIVATIVES **mercery** n.
– ORIGIN ME: from OFr. *mercier*, based on L. *merx, merc-* 'goods'.

**mercerize** (also **-ise**) ● v. [often as adj. **mercerized**] treat (cotton fabric or thread) under tension with caustic alkali to impart strength and lustre.
– ORIGIN C19: from the name of John *Mercer*, said to have invented the process, + **-IZE**.

**merchandise** ● n. /ˈməːtʃ(ə)ndʌɪs, -z/ goods for sale. ➤ products used to promote a film, pop group, etc. ● v. /ˈməːtʃ(ə)ndʌɪz/ (also **-ize**) promote the sale of (goods). ➤ advertise or publicize (an idea or person). ➤ archaic trade or traffic in.
– DERIVATIVES **merchandisable** adj. **merchandiser** n. **merchandising** n.
– ORIGIN ME: from OFr. *marchandise*, from *marchand* 'merchant'.

**merchant** ● n. **1** a person involved in wholesale trade. ➤ chiefly N. Amer. a retail trader. **2** informal, chiefly derogatory a person with a partiality for a particular activity or viewpoint: *a speed merchant*. ● adj. (of ships, sailors, or shipping activity) involved with commerce.
– ORIGIN ME: from OFr. *marchant*, based on L. *mercari* 'to trade', from *merx, merc-* 'merchandise'.

**merchantable** ● adj. saleable.
– ORIGIN C15: from *merchant* 'haggle, trade as a merchant', from OFr. *marchander*, from *marchand* 'merchant'.

**merchant bank** ● n. chiefly Brit. a bank dealing in commercial loans and investment.
– DERIVATIVES **merchant banker** n.

**merchantman** ● n. (pl. **-men**) a ship conveying merchandise.

**merchant marine** ● n. chiefly US another term for **MERCHANT NAVY**.

**merchant navy** ● n. chiefly Brit. a country's commercial shipping.

**merchant prince** ● n. a merchant whose wealth is sufficient to confer political influence.

**Mercian** /ˈməːʃɪən, ˈməːsɪən/ ● n. a native or inhabitant of Mercia, a former kingdom of central England. ● adj. of or relating to Mercia.

**merciful** ● adj. showing mercy. ➤ coming as a mercy.
– DERIVATIVES **mercifulness** n.

**mercifully** ● adv. **1** in a merciful manner. **2** to one's great relief.

**merciless** ● adj. showing no mercy.
– DERIVATIVES **mercilessly** adv. **mercilessness** n.

**mercurial** /məːˈkjʊərɪəl/ ● adj. **1** subject to sudden changes of mood or mind. **2** of or containing the element mercury. **3** (**Mercurial**) of the planet Mercury. ● n. a drug containing mercury.
– DERIVATIVES **mercuriality** /-ˈalɪti/ n. **mercurially** adv.
– ORIGIN ME: from L. *mercurialis* 'relating to the god Mercury', from *Mercurius* 'Mercury'.

**Mercury** ● n. a small planet that is the closest to the sun in the solar system.
– DERIVATIVES **Mercurian** adj.

**mercury**[1] ● n. the chemical element of atomic number 80, a heavy silvery-white liquid metal used in some thermometers and barometers. (Symbol: **Hg**)
– DERIVATIVES **mercuric** adj. **mercurous** adj.
– ORIGIN ME: from L. *Mercurius*, the name of the Roman god of trading and messenger of the gods.

**mercury**[2] ● n. a plant of a genus which includes dog's mercury. [Genus *Mercurialis*.]
– ORIGIN C16: from the genus name, from L. *mercurialis* 'of the god Mercury'.

**mercury vapour lamp** ● n. a lamp in which light is produced by an electrical discharge through mercury vapour.

**mercy** ● n. (pl. **-ies**) **1** compassion or forgiveness shown towards an enemy or offender in one's power. **2** something to be grateful for. **3** [as modifier] (especially of a journey or mission) motivated by compassion. ● exclam. archaic used to express surprise or fear.
– PHRASES **at the mercy of** completely in the power of.
– ORIGIN ME: from OFr. *merci* 'pity' or 'thanks', from L. *merces, merced-* 'reward', in Christian L. 'pity, favour, heavenly reward'.

**mercy killing** ● n. the killing of someone suffering from an incurable and painful disease.

**mere**[1] /mɪə/ ● adj. **1** that is solely or no more or better than what is specified: *mere mortals*. **2** (**the merest**) the smallest or slightest: *the merest hint*.
– ORIGIN ME (in the senses 'pure' and 'sheer, downright'): from L. *merus* 'undiluted'.

**mere**[2] /mɪə/ ● n. chiefly poetic/literary a lake or pond.
– ORIGIN OE, of Gmc origin.

**mere**[3] /ˈmɛri/ ● n. a Maori war club, especially one of greenstone.

– ORIGIN from Maori.

**merely** ● adv. just; only.

**merengue** /mə'rɛŋgeɪ/ (also **meringue**) ● n. a Caribbean style of dance music typically in duple and triple time. ➤a dance style associated with such music, with alternating long and short stiff-legged steps.

– ORIGIN C19: prob. Amer. Sp.

**mere right** ● n. Law a right with no remedy.

**meretricious** /,mɛrɪ'trɪʃəs/ ● adj. **1** showily but falsely attractive. **2** archaic characteristic of a prostitute.

– DERIVATIVES **meretriciously** adv. **meretriciousness** n.

– ORIGIN C17: from L. *meretricius* (adj. from *meretrix*, *meretric-* 'prostitute', from *mereri* 'be hired') + **-ous**.

**merganser** /mə:'ganzə, -sə/ ● n. a fish-eating diving duck with a long, thin serrated and hooked bill. [*Mergus serrator* (**red-breasted merganser**) and related species.]

– ORIGIN C17: mod. L., from L. *mergus* 'diver' + *anser* 'goose'.

**merge** ● v. combine or be combined to form one. ➤blend or cause to blend gradually into something else. ➤(usu. **merge something in**) Law absorb (a title or estate) in another.

– ORIGIN C17 (in the sense 'immerse (oneself)'): from L. *mergere* 'to dip, plunge'; the legal sense is from Anglo-Norman Fr. *merger*.

**merger** ● n. the combining of two things, especially companies, into one. ➤Law the merging of one estate or title in another.

– ORIGIN C18: from Anglo-Norman Fr. *merger* (v. used as n.): see **MERGE**.

**meridian** /mə'rɪdɪən/ ● n. **1** a circle of constant longitude passing through a given place on the earth's surface and the poles. ➤Astronomy a circle passing through the celestial poles and the zenith of a given place on the earth's surface. **2** (in acupuncture and Chinese medicine) a pathway in the body along which vital energy is said to flow.

– ORIGIN ME: from OFr. *meridien*, from L. *meridianum* 'noon', from *medius* 'middle' + *dies* 'day'; the astronomy use is due to the fact that the sun crosses a meridian at noon.

**meridian circle** ● n. Astronomy a telescope mounted so as to move only on a North–South line, for observing the transit of celestial objects across the meridian.

**meridional** /mə'rɪdɪən(ə)l/ ● adj. **1** southern. ➤relating to or characteristic of the people of southern Europe. **2** of or relating to a meridian. ● n. an inhabitant of the south, especially of France.

– ORIGIN ME: via OFr. from late L. *meridionalis*, formed irregularly from L. *meridies* 'midday, south'.

**meringue**[1] /mə'raŋ/ ● n. an item of sweet food made from egg whites and sugar and baked until crisp.

– ORIGIN from Fr., of unknown origin.

**meringue**[2] /mə'raŋ/ ● n. variant spelling of **MERENGUE**.

**merino** /mə'ri:nəʊ/ ● n. (pl. **-os**) **1** a sheep of a breed with long, fine wool. **2** a soft woollen or wool-and-cotton material, originally of merino wool.

– ORIGIN C18: from Sp., of unknown origin.

**meristem** /'mɛrɪstɛm/ ● n. Botany a region of plant tissue consisting of actively dividing cells.

– DERIVATIVES **meristematic** /-stə'matɪk/ adj.

– ORIGIN C19: from Gk *meristos* 'divisible' + *-em* on the pattern of *xylem*.

**merit** ● n. **1** excellence; worth. ➤an examination grade denoting above-average performance. **2** (usu. **merits**) a good point or feature. ➤(**merits**) Theology good deeds entitling someone to a future reward. ➤(**merits**) chiefly Law the intrinsic rights and wrongs of a case. ● v. (**merited**, **meriting**) deserve or be worthy of.

– ORIGIN ME: via OFr. from L. *meritum* 'due reward', from *mereri* 'earn, deserve'.

**merit good** ● n. Brit. a commodity or service, such as education, regarded as good.

**meritocracy** /,mɛrɪ'tɒkrəsi/ ● n. (pl. **-ies**) government by people selected according to merit. ➤a society governed by meritocracy. ➤a ruling or influential class of educated people.

– DERIVATIVES **meritocratic** /-tə'kratɪk/ adj.

**meritorious** /,mɛrɪ'tɔ:rɪəs/ ● adj. **1** deserving reward or praise. **2** Law, chiefly N. Amer. (of an action) likely to succeed on the merits of the case.

– DERIVATIVES **meritoriously** adv. **meritoriousness** n.

– ORIGIN ME: from late L. *meritorius* (from *merit-*, *mereri* 'earn') + **-ous**.

**merkin** /'mə:kɪn/ ● n. an artificial covering of hair for the pubic area.

– ORIGIN C17: appar. a var. of dial. *malkin*, dimin. of *Malde* (early form of the given name *Maud*).

**merle** /mə:l/ ● n. Scottish or archaic a blackbird.

– ORIGIN ME: via OFr. from L. *merula*.

**merlin** ● n. a small dark falcon that hunts small birds. [*Falco columbarius*.]

– ORIGIN ME: from Anglo-Norman Fr. *merilun*, from OFr. *esmerillon*, augmentative of *esmeril*, of Gmc origin.

**merlon** /'mə:lən/ ● n. the solid part of an embattled parapet between two embrasures.

– ORIGIN C18: from Fr., from Ital. *merlone*, from *merlo* 'battlement'.

**Merlot** /'mə:ləʊ, -lɒt/ ● n. a variety of black wine grape originally from the Bordeaux region of France.

– ORIGIN from Fr.

**mermaid** ● n. a mythical sea creature with the head and trunk of a woman and the tail of a fish.

– DERIVATIVES **merman** n. (pl. **-men**).

– ORIGIN ME: from **MERE**[2] (in the obs. sense 'sea') + **MAID**.

**mermaid's purse** ● n. the horny egg case of a skate, ray, or small shark.

**mero-** ● comb. form partly; partial: *meronym*.

– ORIGIN from Gk *meros* 'part'.

**meronym** /'mɛrənɪm/ ● n. Linguistics a term denoting part of something but used to refer to the whole of it, e.g. *faces* used to mean *people* in *I see several familiar faces*.

– DERIVATIVES **meronymy** /mə'rɒnəmi/ n.

– ORIGIN from Gk *meros* 'part' + *onoma* 'name'.

**-merous** ● comb. form Biology having a specified number of parts: *pentamerous*.

– ORIGIN on the pattern of words such as *(di)merous* (see also **-MER**).

**Merovingian** /,mɛrə'vɪn(d)ʒɪən/ ● adj. of or relating to the Frankish dynasty reigning in Gaul and Germany *c.*500–750. ● n. a member of this dynasty.

– ORIGIN from Fr. *mérovingien*, from med. L. *Merovingi* 'descendants of Merovich' (a semi-legendary Frankish leader).

**merriment** ● n. gaiety and fun.

**merry** ● adj. (**-ier**, **-iest**) **1** cheerful and lively. ➤characterized by festivity. **2** Brit. informal slightly drunk.

– PHRASES **make merry** indulge in merriment.

– DERIVATIVES **merrily** adj. **merriness** n.

– ORIGIN OE *myrige* 'pleasing, delightful', of Gmc origin; rel. to **MIRTH**.

**merry andrew** ● n. archaic a clown or buffoon.

**merry-go-round** ● n. **1** a revolving machine with model horses or cars on which people ride for amusement. **2** a continuous cycle of activities or events.

**merrymaking** ● n. fun; festivity.

– DERIVATIVES **merrymaker** n.

**merrythought** ● n. dated, chiefly Brit. a bird's wishbone.

**merveille du jour** /mɛ:,veɪ d(j)u: 'ʒʊə/ ● n. a moth with greyish-green coloration that camouflages it on lichen-covered bark. [*Dichonia aprilina*.]

– ORIGIN C19: from Fr., lit. 'wonder of the day'.

**mesa** /'meɪsə/ ● n. an isolated flat-topped hill with steep sides, found in landscapes with horizontal strata.

– ORIGIN C18: Sp., lit. 'table', from L. *mensa*.

**mésalliance** /mɛ'zalɪəns/ ● n. a marriage to a person thought to be unsuitable.

– ORIGIN Fr., from *més-* 'wrong, misdirected' + *alliance* (see **ALLIANCE**).

**mescal** /'mɛskal, mɛ'skal/ ● n. **1** another term for **MAGUEY**. ➤an intoxicating liquor distilled from the sap of an agave. **2** another term for **PEYOTE**.

– ORIGIN C18: from Sp. *mezcal*, from Nahuatl *mexcalli*.

**mescaline** /'mɛskəlɪn, -li:n/ (also **mescalin** /-lɪn/) ● n. a hallucinogenic compound present in the peyote cactus.

**mesclun** /ˈmɛsklən/ ● **n.** a Provençal green salad having a mixture of edible leaves and flowers.
– ORIGIN Provençal, lit. 'mixture'.

**Mesdames** /meɪˈdɑːm, -ˈdam/ plural form of **MADAME**.

**Mesdemoiselles** /meɪd-, French med-/ plural form of **MADEMOISELLE**.

**mesembryanthemum** /mɪˌzɛmbrɪˈanθɪməm/ ● **n.** a succulent South African plant with brightly coloured daisy-like flowers. [Genus *Mesembryanthemum*.]
– ORIGIN mod. L., based on Gk *mesēmbria* 'noon' + *anthemon* 'flower'.

**mesencephalon** /ˌmɛsɛnˈsɛf(ə)lɒn, ˌmiːz-, -ˈkɛf-/ ● **n.** Anatomy another term for **MIDBRAIN**.
– DERIVATIVES **mesencephalic** adj.
– ORIGIN C19: from Gk *mesos* 'middle' + **ENCEPHALON**.

**mesenchyme** /ˈmɛsəŋkʌɪm, ˈmiːz-/ ● **n.** Embryology embryonic tissue which develops into connective and skeletal tissues.
– DERIVATIVES **mesenchymal** adj.
– ORIGIN C19: from Gk *mesos* 'middle' + *enkhuma* 'infusion'.

**mesenteron** /mɪˈsɛntərɒn/ ● **n.** Zoology the middle section of the intestine, especially in an embryo or arthropod.
– ORIGIN C19: from Gk *mesos* 'middle' + *enteron* 'intestine'.

**mesentery** /ˈmɛs(ə)nt(ə)ri/ ● **n.** (pl. **-ies**) Anatomy a fold of the peritoneum attaching the stomach, small intestine, and other organs to the posterior wall of the abdomen.
– DERIVATIVES **mesenteric** adj.
– ORIGIN ME: via med. L. from Gk *mesenterion*, from *mesos* 'middle' + *enteron* 'intestine'.

**mesh** ● **n. 1** material made of a network of wire or thread. **2** an interlaced structure. **3** a complex or constricting situation. **4** Computing a set of finite elements used to represent a geometric object. ● **v. 1** (of a gearwheel) lock together with another. ➤make or become entangled or entwined. ➤be or bring into harmony. **2** Computing represent by means of a mesh.
– PHRASES **in mesh** (of gearwheels) engaged.
– DERIVATIVES **meshed** adj.
– ORIGIN ME: prob. from an unrecorded OE word rel. to MDu. *maesche*, of Gmc origin.

**meshuga** /mɪˈʃʊɡə/ (also **meshugga**) ● **adj.** informal, chiefly N. Amer. mad.
– ORIGIN C19: from Yiddish *meshuge*, from Heb.

**mesial** /ˈmiːzɪəl, ˈmɛsɪəl/ ● **adj.** Anatomy of, in, or directed towards the midline of a body.
– DERIVATIVES **mesially** adv.
– ORIGIN C19: formed irregularly from Gk *mesos* 'middle' + **-IAL**.

**mesic**[1] /ˈmiːzɪk, ˈmɛzɪk/ ● **adj.** Ecology containing a moderate amount of moisture. Compare with **HYDRIC** and **XERIC**.
– ORIGIN 1920s: from Gk *mesos* 'middle' + **-IC**.

**mesic**[2] /ˈmiːzɪk, ˈmɛzɪk/ ● **adj.** Physics of or relating to a meson.

**mesmeric** /mɛzˈmɛrɪk/ ● **adj.** causing one to become transfixed and unaware of one's surroundings; hypnotic. ➤archaic relating to or produced by mesmerism.
– DERIVATIVES **mesmerically** adv.

**mesmerism** ● **n.** historical a therapeutic technique involving hypnotism.
– DERIVATIVES **mesmerist** n.
– ORIGIN C18: named after the Austrian physician Franz A. *Mesmer*.

**mesmerize** (also **-ise**) ● **v.** capture the whole attention of; fascinate or transfix. ➤archaic hypnotize.
– DERIVATIVES **mesmerization** n. **mesmerizer** n. **mesmerizing** adj. **mesmerizingly** adv.

**mesne** /miːn/ ● **adj.** Law intermediate.
– ORIGIN ME (as adv. and n.): from legal Fr., var. of Anglo-Norman Fr. *meen* (see **MEAN**[3]).

**mesne lord** ● **n.** Brit. historical a lord holding an estate from a superior feudal lord.

**mesne profits** ● **pl. n.** Law the profits of an estate received by a tenant in wrongful possession and recoverable by the landlord.

**meso-** /ˈmɛsəʊ, ˈmɛzəʊ, ˈmiːsəʊ, ˈmiːzəʊ/ ● **comb. form** middle; intermediate: *mesomorph*.
– ORIGIN from Gk *mesos* 'middle'.

**mesoblast** /ˈmɛsə(ʊ)blast, ˈmɛz-, ˈmiːs-, ˈmiːz-/ ● **n.** Embryology the mesoderm of an embryo in its earliest stages.

**mesocarp** ● **n.** Botany the middle layer of the pericarp of a fruit.

**mesocephalic** /ˌmɛsə(ʊ)sɪˈfalɪk, ˌmɛz-, ˌmiːs-, ˌmiːz-, -kɛ-/ ● **adj.** Anatomy having a medium-sized head.

**mesoderm** ● **n.** Embryology the middle layer of cells or tissues of an embryo, or the parts derived from this (e.g. cartilage, muscles, and bone).
– DERIVATIVES **mesodermal** adj.
– ORIGIN C19: from **MESO-** + Gk *derma* 'skin'.

**mesogastrium** ● **n.** (pl. **mesogastria**) Anatomy the middle region of the abdomen.
– DERIVATIVES **mesogastric** adj.
– ORIGIN C19: mod. L., from **MESO-** + Gk *gastēr, gastr-* 'stomach'.

**Mesolithic** ● **adj.** Archaeology relating to or denoting the middle part of the Stone Age, between the end of the glacial period and the beginnings of agriculture.
– ORIGIN C19: from **MESO-** + Gk *lithos* 'stone' + **-IC**.

**mesomerism** /mɪˈsɒmərɪz(ə)m, mɪˈzɒm-/ ● **n.** Chemistry old-fashioned term for **RESONANCE**.
– DERIVATIVES **mesomeric** adj.
– ORIGIN 1930s: from **MESO-** after *tautomerism*.

**mesomorph** ● **n.** Physiology a person with a compact and muscular body. Compare with **ECTOMORPH** and **ENDOMORPH**.
– DERIVATIVES **mesomorphic** adj.
– ORIGIN 1920s: *meso-* from *mesodermal* (being the layer of the embryo giving rise to these physical characteristics) + **-MORPH**.

**meson** /ˈmiːzɒn, ˈmɛzɒn/ ● **n.** Physics a subatomic particle, intermediate in mass between an electron and a proton, that transmits the strong interaction binding nucleons together.
– DERIVATIVES **mesonic** /mɪˈzɒnɪk/ adj.
– ORIGIN 1930s: from **MESO-** + **-ON**.

**mesopause** ● **n.** the boundary in the earth's atmosphere between the mesosphere and the thermosphere.

**mesopelagic** /ˌmɛsə(ʊ)pɪˈladʒɪk, ˌmɛz-, ˌmiːs-, ˌmiːz-/ ● **adj.** Biology inhabiting the intermediate depths of the sea.

**mesophyll** ● **n.** Botany the parenchyma of a leaf, containing many chloroplasts.
– ORIGIN C19: from **MESO-** + Gk *phullon* 'leaf'.

**mesophyte** ● **n.** Botany a plant needing only a moderate amount of water.
– DERIVATIVES **mesophytic** adj.

**Mesopotamian** /ˌmɛsəpəˈteɪmɪən/ ● **n.** a native or inhabitant of Mesopotamia, an ancient region of SW Asia. ● **adj.** of or relating to Mesopotamia.

**mesosaur** ● **n.** an extinct small aquatic reptile of the early Permian period, with an elongated body and a long, narrow snout with numerous teeth.
– ORIGIN 1950s: mod. L., from Gk *mesos* 'middle' + *sauros* 'lizard'.

**mesoscale** ● **n.** chiefly Meteorology an intermediate scale.

**mesosphere** ● **n.** the region of the earth's atmosphere above the stratosphere and below the thermosphere, between about 50 and 80 km in altitude.

**mesothelioma** /ˌmɛsə(ʊ)ˌθiːlɪˈəʊmə, ˌmɛz-, ˌmiːs-, ˌmiːz-/ ● **n.** Medicine cancer of mesothelial tissue, often associated with exposure to asbestos.

**mesothelium** /ˌmɛsə(ʊ)ˈθiːlɪəm, ˌmɛz-, ˌmiːs-, ˌmiːz-/ ● **n.** (pl. **mesothelia**) Anatomy the epithelium lining the pleurae, peritoneum, and pericardium, derived from the surface layer of the embryonic mesoderm.
– DERIVATIVES **mesothelial** adj.
– ORIGIN C19: from **MESO-** + a shortened form of **EPITHELIUM**.

**Mesozoic** /ˌmɛsə(ʊ)ˈzəʊɪk, ˌmɛz-, ˌmiːs-, ˌmiːz-/ ● **adj.** Geology relating to or denoting the era between the Palaeozoic and Cenozoic eras (comprising the Triassic, Jurassic, and Cretaceous periods, about 245 to 65 million years

ago).
– ORIGIN C19: from **MESO-** + Gk *zōion* 'animal' + **-IC**.

**mesquite** /ˈmɛskiːt, mɛˈskiːt/ ● n. a spiny tree native to the south-western US and Mexico, yielding wood, tanbark, medicinal products, and edible pods. [*Prosopis glandulosa* and related species.]
– ORIGIN C18: from Mex. Sp. *mezquite*.

**mesquite bean** ● n. an edible pod from the mesquite, used especially to produce flour or as fodder.

**mess** ● n. **1** a dirty or untidy state or condition. ➤ euphemistic a domestic animal's excrement. **2** a portion of semi-solid or pulpy food. **3** a confused and problematic situation. ➤ a person whose affairs are in such a situation. **4** a place in which members of the armed forces take their meals. ● v. **1** make untidy or dirty. ➤ (of a domestic animal) defecate. ➤ make dirty by defecating. **2** take one's meals.
– PHRASAL VERBS **mess about/around** behave in a silly or playful way. ➤ occupy oneself in a pleasantly desultory way. **mess someone about/around** Brit. informal cause someone inconvenience or problems. **mess up** informal mishandle a situation. **mess someone up** informal cause someone emotional or psychological problems. **mess with** informal meddle or interfere with.
– ORIGIN ME: from OFr. *mes* 'portion of food', from late L. *missum* 'something put on the table', past part. of *mittere* 'send, put'.

**message** ● n. **1** a verbal, written, or recorded communication sent by one person to another. **2** a significant point or central theme. ➤ a divinely inspired communication. **3** Scottish & Irish an errand. ➤ (**messages**) things bought; shopping. ● v. send a message to, especially by email.
– PHRASES **get the message** informal understand what is meant.
– ORIGIN ME: from OFr., based on L. *missus*, past part. of *mittere* 'send'.

**message stick** ● n. (among Australian Aboriginals) a stick carved with symbolic patterns, used to convey a message from one community to another.

**Messeigneurs** plural form of **MONSEIGNEUR**.

**messenger** ● n. a person who carries a message. ● v. chiefly US send by messenger.
– ORIGIN ME: from ONorth. Fr. *messanger*, var. of OFr. *messager*, from L. *missus* (see **MESSAGE**).

**messenger RNA** ● n. the form of RNA in which genetic information transcribed from DNA as a sequence of bases is transferred to a ribosome.

**mess hall** ● n. chiefly N. Amer. a place where people, especially soldiers, eat together.

**messiah** /mɪˈsʌɪə/ ● n. **1** (**the Messiah**) the promised deliverer of the Jewish nation prophesied in the Hebrew Bible. ➤ Jesus regarded by Christians as the Messiah of these prophecies. **2** a leader or saviour.
– DERIVATIVES **messiahship** n.
– ORIGIN OE *Messias*: via late L. and Gk from Heb. *māšīaḥ* 'anointed'.

**messianic** /ˌmɛsɪˈanɪk/ ● adj. **1** of or relating to the Messiah. **2** inspired by hope or belief in a messiah.
– DERIVATIVES **messianism** /mɪˈsʌɪənɪz(ə)m/ n.

**Messieurs** plural form of **MONSIEUR**.

**mess jacket** ● n. a short jacket worn by a military officer on formal occasions in the mess.

**mess kit** ● n. **1** military uniform worn on formal occasions in the mess. **2** a soldier's cooking and eating utensils.

**messmate** ● n. (in the navy) a person with whom one shares accommodation.

**Messrs** plural form of **MR**.
– ORIGIN C18: abbrev. of **MESSIEURS**.

**mess tin** ● n. Brit. a rectangular metal dish forming part of a mess kit.

**messuage** /ˈmɛswɪdʒ/ ● n. Law a house with outbuildings and land.
– ORIGIN ME: from Anglo-Norman Fr., based on L. *manere* 'dwell'.

**messy** ● adj. (**-ier**, **-iest**) **1** untidy or dirty. **2** confused and difficult to deal with.
– DERIVATIVES **messily** adv. **messiness** n.

**mestizo** /mɛˈstiːzəʊ, Spanish mesˈtiso, -ˈtiθo/ ● n. (fem. **mestiza** /mɛˈstiːzə, Spanish mesˈtisa, -ˈtiθa/) (pl. **-os** (or **-as**)) a Latin American of mixed race, especially the offspring of a Spaniard and an American Indian.
– ORIGIN Sp. 'mixed', based on L. *mixtus*.

**Met** ● abbrev. informal **1** meteorological. **2** metropolitan. **3** (**the Met**) [treated as sing. or pl.] the Metropolitan Police in London.

**met** past and past participle of **MEET**[1].

**meta-** (also **met-** before a vowel or h) ● comb. form **1** denoting a change of position or condition: *metamorphosis*. **2** denoting position behind, after, or beyond: *metacarpus*. **3** denoting something of a higher or second-order kind: *metalanguage*. **4** Chemistry denoting substitution at two carbon atoms separated by one other in a benzene ring: *metadichlorobenzene*. Compare with **ORTHO-** and **PARA-**[1].
– ORIGIN from Gk *meta* 'with, across, or after'.

**metabolism** /mɪˈtabəlɪz(ə)m/ ● n. the chemical processes that occur within a living organism to maintain life.
– DERIVATIVES **metabolic** /ˌmɛtəˈbɒlɪk/ adj. **metabolically** adv.
– ORIGIN C19: from Gk *metabolē* 'change' + **-ISM**.

**metabolite** /mɪˈtabəlʌɪt/ ● n. Biochemistry a substance formed in or necessary for metabolism.

**metabolize** (also **-ise**) ● v. process or undergo processing by metabolism.
– DERIVATIVES **metabolizable** adj. **metabolizer** n.

**metacarpus** ● n. (pl. **metacarpi**) the group of five bones of the hand between the wrist (carpus) and the fingers.
– DERIVATIVES **metacarpal** adj. & n.
– ORIGIN ME: mod. L., alt. of Gk *metakarpion*.

**metacentre** (US **metacenter**) ● n. the point of intersection between a vertical line through the centre of buoyancy of a floating vessel and a similar line through the new centre of buoyancy when the vessel is tilted.
– DERIVATIVES **metacentric** adj.

**metachrosis** /ˌmɛtəˈkrəʊsɪs/ ● n. Zoology the ability of some animals, e.g. chameleons, to change colour.
– ORIGIN C19: mod. L., from **META-** + Gk *khrōsis* 'colouring'.

**metadata** ● n. a set of data that describes and gives information about other data.

**metafiction** ● n. fiction in which the author self-consciously parodies or departs from novelistic conventions.
– DERIVATIVES **metafictional** adj.

**metage** /ˈmiːtɪdʒ/ ● n. the official weighing of loads of coal, grain, etc.
– ORIGIN C16: from **METE**[1] + **-AGE**.

**metagenesis** /ˌmɛtəˈdʒɛnɪsɪs/ ● n. Biology the alternation of generations between sexual and asexual reproduction.

**metal** ● n. **1** a solid material which is typically hard, shiny, malleable, fusible, and ductile, with good electrical and thermal conductivity, e.g. iron, copper, and silver. ➤ Heraldry gold and silver. **2** (also **road metal**) broken stone used in road-making. **3** (**metals**) the steel tracks of a railway. **4** molten glass before it is blown or cast. ● v. (**metalled**, **metalling**; N. Amer. **metaled**, **metaling**) [usu. as adj. **metalled**] **1** make from or coat with metal. **2** Brit. make or mend (a road) with road metal.
– DERIVATIVES **metalware** n.
– ORIGIN ME: from OFr. *metal* or L. *metallum*, from Gk *metallon* 'mine, quarry, or metal'.

**metalanguage** ● n. **1** a form of language or set of terms used for the description or analysis of another language. **2** Logic a system of propositions about propositions.

**metaldehyde** /mɪˈtaldɪhʌɪd/ ● n. Chemistry a solid made by polymerizing acetaldehyde, used in slug pellets and as fuel for portable stoves.

**metal detector** ● n. an electronic device that gives an audible signal when it is close to metal.

**metalinguistics** ● pl. n. [treated as sing.] the branch of linguistics concerned with metalanguages.
– DERIVATIVES **metalinguistic** adj.

**metallic** ● adj. of, relating to, or resembling metal. ➤ (of sound) sharp and ringing. ➤ having the sheen or lustre of

metal. ● **n.** a thing that is made of, contains, or resembles metal.
– DERIVATIVES **metallically** adv. **metallicity** n.
**metalliferous** ● **adj.** containing or producing metal.
**metallize** (also **-ise**, US also **metalize**) ● **v. 1** coat with metal. **2** make metallic.
– DERIVATIVES **metallization** n.
**metallography** /ˌmɛtəˈlɒɡrəfi/ ● **n.** the descriptive science of the structure and properties of metals.
– DERIVATIVES **metallographic** adj. **metallographical** adj. **metallographically** adv.
**metalloid** ● **n.** another term for **SEMIMETAL**.
**metallurgy** /mɪˈtalədʒi, ˈmɛt(ə)ˌləːdʒi/ ● **n.** the branch of science concerned with the properties, production, and purification of metals.
– DERIVATIVES **metallurgic** /ˌmɛtəˈləːdʒɪk/ adj. **metallurgical** adj. **metallurgically** adv. **metallurgist** n.
– ORIGIN C18: from Gk *metallon* 'metal' + *-ourgia* 'working'.
**metalwork** ● **n. 1** the art of making things from metal. **2** metal objects collectively.
– DERIVATIVES **metalworker** n. **metalworking** n.
**metamere** /ˈmɛtəmɪə/ ● **n.** Zoology another term for **SOMITE**.
– DERIVATIVES **metameric** adj. **metamerism** n.
– ORIGIN C19: from **META-** + Gk *meros* 'part'.
**metamessage** ● **n.** an underlying meaning or implicit message.
**metamorphic** ● **adj. 1** Geology (of rock) that has undergone transformation by heat, pressure, or other natural agencies. **2** of or marked by metamorphosis.
– DERIVATIVES **metamorphism** n.
– ORIGIN C19: from **META-** + Gk *morphē* 'form' + **-IC**.
**metamorphose** /ˌmɛtəˈmɔːfəʊz/ ● **v. 1** (of an insect or amphibian) undergo metamorphosis. **2** change or cause to change completely. **3** Geology subject (rock) to metamorphism.
**metamorphosis** /ˌmɛtəˈmɔːfəsɪs, ˌmɛtəmɔːˈfəʊsɪs/ ● **n.** (pl. **metamorphoses** /-siːz/) **1** Zoology (in an insect or amphibian) the process of transformation from an immature form to an adult form in two or more distinct stages. **2** a change in form or nature.
– ORIGIN ME: via L. from Gk *metamorphōsis*, from *metamorphoun* 'transform, change shape'.
**metanoia** /ˌmɛtəˈnɔɪə/ ● **n.** change in one's way of life resulting from penitence or spiritual conversion.
– ORIGIN C19: from Gk, from *metanoein* 'change one's mind'.
**metaphase** ● **n.** Biology the second stage of cell division, between prophase and anaphase, during which the chromosomes become attached to the spindle fibres.
**metaphor** ● **n.** a figure of speech in which a word or phrase is applied to something to which it is not literally applicable. ➤a thing regarded as symbolic of something else.
– DERIVATIVES **metaphoric** adj. **metaphorical** adj. **metaphorically** adv.
– ORIGIN C15: from Fr. *métaphore*, via L. from Gk *metaphora*, from *metapherein* 'to transfer'.
**metaphosphoric acid** ● **n.** Chemistry a glassy deliquescent polymeric solid obtained by heating orthophosphoric acid.
– DERIVATIVES **metaphosphate** n.
**metaphrase** ● **n.** a literal, word-for-word translation. ● **v.** alter the phrasing or language of.
– DERIVATIVES **metaphrastic** adj.
– ORIGIN C17: from Gk *metaphrazein*, lit. 'word differently'.
**metaphysic** ● **n.** a system of metaphysics.
**metaphysical** ● **adj. 1** of or relating to metaphysics. ➤based on abstract reasoning. ➤transcending physical matter or the laws of nature. **2** denoting certain 17th century English poets known for their subtlety of thought and complex imagery. ● **n.** (**the Metaphysicals**) the metaphysical poets.
– DERIVATIVES **metaphysically** adv.
**metaphysics** ● **pl. n.** [usu. treated as sing.] **1** the branch of philosophy concerned with the first principles of things, including abstract concepts such as being and knowing. **2** informal abstract talk; mere theory.
– DERIVATIVES **metaphysician** n.
– ORIGIN C16: representing med. L. *metaphysica* (neut. pl.), based on Gk *ta meta ta phusika* 'the things after the Physics', referring to the sequence of Aristotle's works.
**metaplasia** /ˌmɛtəˈpleɪzɪə/ ● **n.** Physiology abnormal change in the nature of a tissue.
– DERIVATIVES **metaplastic** adj.
– ORIGIN C19: mod. L., from Ger. *Metaplase*, based on Gk *metaplassein* 'mould into a new form'.
**metapsychology** ● **n.** the study of mental processes beyond what can be studied experimentally.
– DERIVATIVES **metapsychological** adj.
**metasomatism** /ˌmɛtəˈsəʊmətɪz(ə)m/ ● **n.** Geology change in the chemical composition of a rock.
– DERIVATIVES **metasomatic** adj. **metasomatize** (also **-ise**) v.
– ORIGIN C19: from **META-** + Gk *sōma*, *somat-* 'body' + **-ISM**.
**metastable** /ˌmɛtəˈsteɪb(ə)l/ ● **adj.** Physics **1** (of equilibrium) stable only under small disturbances. **2** (of a substance or particle) theoretically unstable but so long-lived as to be stable for practical purposes.
– DERIVATIVES **metastability** n.
**metastasis** /mɪˈtastəsɪs/ ● **n.** (pl. **metastases** /-siːz/) Medicine the development of secondary tumours at a distance from a primary site of cancer.
– DERIVATIVES **metastasize** (also **-ise**) v. **metastatic** adj.
– ORIGIN C16: from Gk, lit. 'removal or change'.
**metatarsus** ● **n.** (pl. **metatarsi**) the bones of the foot, between the ankle and the toes.
– DERIVATIVES **metatarsal** adj. & n.
**Metatheria** /ˌmɛtəˈθɪərɪə/ ● **pl. n.** Zoology a group of mammals which comprises the marsupials. Compare with **EUTHERIA**.
– DERIVATIVES **metatherian** n. & adj.
– ORIGIN mod. L., from **META-** + Gk *thēria*, pl. of *thērion* 'wild animal'.
**metathesis** /mɪˈtaθɪsɪs/ ● **n.** (pl. **metatheses** /-siːz/) **1** Grammar the transposition of sounds or letters in a word. **2** Chemistry another term for **DOUBLE DECOMPOSITION**.
– DERIVATIVES **metathetic** /ˌmɛtəˈθɛtɪk/ adj. **metathetical** adj.
– ORIGIN C16: from Gk, 'transposition'.
**Metazoa** /ˌmɛtəˈzəʊə/ ● **pl. n.** Zoology a major division of the animal kingdom, comprising all animals other than protozoans and sponges.
– DERIVATIVES **metazoan** n. & adj.
– ORIGIN mod. L., from **META-** (expressing change) + *zōia*, pl. of *zōion* 'animal'.
**mete**[1] /miːt/ ● **v. 1** (**mete something out**) dispense or allot justice, punishment, etc. **2** (in biblical use) measure out.
– ORIGIN OE *metan* 'measure', of Gmc origin; rel. to **MEET**[2].
**mete**[2] /miːt/ ● **n.** a boundary or boundary stone.
– ORIGIN ME: from OFr., from L. *meta* 'boundary, goal'.
**metempsychosis** /ˌmɛtɛmsʌɪˈkəʊsɪs/ ● **n.** (pl. **metempsychoses** /-siːz/) the supposed transmigration at death of the soul into a new body.
– ORIGIN C16: via late L. from Gk *metempsukhōsis*, from *meta-* (expressing change) + *en* 'in' + *psukhē* 'soul'.
**meteor** ● **n.** a small body of matter from outer space that becomes incandescent as a result of friction with the earth's atmosphere and appears as a streak of light.
– ORIGIN C16 (denoting any atmospheric phenomenon): from mod. L. *meteorum*, from Gk *meteōron*, neut. (used as n.) of *meteōros* 'lofty'.
**meteoric** ● **adj. 1** of or relating to meteors or meteorites. **2** (of change or development) very rapid. **3** chiefly Geology relating to or denoting water derived from the atmosphere.
– DERIVATIVES **meteorically** adv.
**meteorite** ● **n.** a piece of rock or metal that has fallen to the earth as a meteor.
– DERIVATIVES **meteoritic** adj.
**meteoroid** ● **n.** Astronomy a small body in the solar system

that would become a meteor if it entered the earth's atmosphere.
– DERIVATIVES **meteoroidal** adj.

**meteorology** /ˌmiːtɪəˈrɒlədʒi/ ● n. **1** the study of the processes and phenomena of the atmosphere, especially as a means of weather forecasting. **2** the climate and weather of a region.
– DERIVATIVES **meteorological** adj. **meteorologically** adv. **meteorologist** n.
– ORIGIN C16: from Gk *meteōrologia*, from *meteōron* (see **METEOR**).

**meter**[1] ● n. a device that measures and records the quantity, degree, or rate of something. ● v. [often as adj. **metered**] measure with a meter.
– ORIGIN ME (in the sense 'person who measures'): from **METE**[1] + **-ER**[1].

**meter**[2] ● n. US spelling of **METRE**[1], **METRE**[2].

**-meter** ● comb. form **1** in names of measuring instruments: *thermometer*. **2** Prosody in nouns denoting lines of poetry with a specified number of measures: *hexameter*.
– ORIGIN from Gk *metron* 'measure'.

**meth** (also **crystal meth**) ● n. informal the drug methamphetamine.

**methacrylic acid** ● n. Chemistry a low-melting solid acid which polymerizes when distilled, used to make synthetic resins.
– DERIVATIVES **methacrylate** n.

**methadone** /ˈmɛθədəʊn/ ● n. a powerful synthetic analgesic similar to morphine, used as a substitute drug in the treatment of morphine and heroin addiction.
– ORIGIN 1940s: from its chemical name, *(6-di)meth(yl)a(mino-4,4-)d(iphenyl-3-heptan)one.*

**methaemoglobin** /ˌmɛθiːməˈɡləʊbɪn, mɛtˌhiː-/ (US **methemoglobin**) ● n. Biochemistry a stable oxidized form of haemoglobin which is unable to release oxygen to the tissues.
– DERIVATIVES **methaemoglobinaemia** (US **methemoglobinemia**) n.

**methamphetamine** /ˌmɛθamˈfɛtəmiːn, -ɪn/ ● n. a synthetic drug with more rapid and lasting effects than amphetamine, used illegally as a stimulant.

**methanal** /ˈmɛθənal/ ● n. systematic chemical name for **FORMALDEHYDE**.
– ORIGIN C19: blend of **METHANE** and **ALDEHYDE**.

**methane** /ˈmiːθeɪn, ˈmɛθeɪn/ ● n. Chemistry a colourless, odourless flammable gas which is the main constituent of natural gas and the simplest member of the alkane series. [$CH_4$.]
– ORIGIN C19: from **METHYL** + **-ANE**[2].

**methanogen** /ˈmɛθənə(ʊ)dʒ(ə)n, mɛˈθanə(ʊ)-/ ● n. Biology a methane-producing bacterium.
– DERIVATIVES **methanogenesis** n. **methanogenic** adj.

**methanoic acid** /ˌmɛθəˈnəʊɪk/ ● n. systematic chemical name for **FORMIC ACID**.
– DERIVATIVES **methanoate** n.

**methanol** /ˈmɛθənɒl/ ● n. Chemistry a toxic flammable liquid alcohol, made chiefly by oxidizing methane. [$CH_3OH$.]

**methedrine** /ˈmɛθədrɪn, -driːn/ ● n. (trademark in the UK) another term for **METHAMPHETAMINE**.
– ORIGIN 1930s: blend of **METHYL** and **BENZEDRINE**.

**metheglin** /mɪˈθɛɡlɪn, ˈmɛθəɡlɪn/ ● n. historical a spiced variety of mead.
– ORIGIN C16: from Welsh *meddyglyn*, from *meddyg* 'medicinal' + *llyn* 'liquor'.

**methemoglobin** ● n. US spelling of **METHAEMOGLOBIN**.

**methicillin** /ˌmɛθɪˈsɪlɪn/ ● n. Medicine a semi-synthetic form of penicillin.
– ORIGIN 1960s: from *meth(yl)* and *(pen)icillin*.

**methinks** ● v. (past **methought**) archaic or humorous it seems to me.
– ORIGIN OE *mē thyncth*, from *mē* 'to me' + *thyncth* 'it seems' (from *thyncan* 'seem', rel. to **THINK**).

**methionine** /mɪˈθʌɪəniːn/ ● n. Biochemistry a sulphur-containing amino acid which is a constituent of most proteins and is essential to the diet of vertebrates.
– ORIGIN 1920s: from **METHYL** + Gk *theion* 'sulphur'.

**method** ● n. **1** a particular procedure for accomplishing or approaching something. **2** orderliness of thought or behaviour.
– ORIGIN ME: via L. from Gk *methodos* 'pursuit of knowledge', from *meta-* (expressing development) + *hodos* 'way'.

**method acting** ● n. a technique of acting in which an actor aspires to complete emotional identification with a part.
– DERIVATIVES **method actor** n.

**méthode champenoise** /meɪˌtəʊd ʃɒ̃pənˈwɑːz/ ● n. a method of making sparkling wine by allowing the last stage of fermentation to take place in the bottle. ➤ sparkling wine made in this way.
– ORIGIN Fr., lit. 'champagne method'.

**methodical** ● adj. characterized by method or order.
– DERIVATIVES **methodic** adj. **methodically** adv.

**Methodist** ● n. a member of a Christian Protestant denomination originating in the 18th-century evangelistic movement of Charles and John Wesley. ● adj. of or relating to Methodists or Methodism.
– DERIVATIVES **Methodism** n. **Methodistic** adj.
– ORIGIN prob. from the notion of following a specified 'method' of Bible study.

**methodize** (also **-ise**) ● v. rare arrange in an orderly or systematic manner.
– DERIVATIVES **methodizer** n.

**methodology** ● n. (pl. **-ies**) a system of methods used in a particular field.
– DERIVATIVES **methodological** adj. **methodologically** adv. **methodologist** n.

**methotrexate** /ˌmɛθəˈtrɛkseɪt, ˌmiːθə-/ ● n. Medicine a synthetic compound that interferes with cell growth, used to treat leukaemia and other cancers.
– ORIGIN 1950s: from *meth-* (denoting a substance containing methyl groups) + elements of unknown origin.

**methought** past of **METHINKS**.

**meths** ● n. Brit. informal methylated spirit.

**Methuselah** ● n. **1** a very old person. **2** (**methuselah**) a wine bottle of eight times the standard size.
– ORIGIN 1930s: from the name of the biblical patriarch *Methuselah*, said to have lived for 969 years (Gen. 5:27).

**methyl** /ˈmiːθʌɪl, ˈmɛθ-, -θɪl/ ● n. [as modifier] Chemistry of or denoting the alkyl radical $-CH_3$, derived from methane.
– ORIGIN C19: back-form. from **METHYLENE**.

**methyl alcohol** ● n. another term for **METHANOL**.

**methylate** /ˈmɛθɪleɪt/ ● v. [often as adj. **methylated**] **1** mix with methanol or methylated spirit. **2** Chemistry introduce a methyl group into.
– DERIVATIVES **methylation** n.

**methylated spirit** (also **methylated spirits**) ● n. alcohol for general use, made unfit for drinking by the addition of methanol and pyridine and a violet dye.

**methylbenzene** ● n. systematic chemical name for **TOLUENE**.

**methyl cyanide** ● n. another term for **ACETONITRILE**.

**methylene** /ˈmɛθɪliːn/ ● n. [as modifier] Chemistry of or denoting the divalent radical $-CH_2-$.
– ORIGIN C19: from Fr. *méthylène* (formed irregularly from Gk *methu* 'wine' + *hulē* 'wood') + **-ENE**.

**methylphenidate** /ˌmiːθʌɪlˈfɛnɪdeɪt, ˌmɛθ-, -θɪl-/ ● n. Medicine a synthetic drug that stimulates the nervous system, used to treat attention deficit disorder.

**metic** /ˈmɛtɪk/ ● n. a foreigner living in an ancient Greek city who had some of the privileges of citizenship.
– ORIGIN C19: formed irregularly from Gk *metoikos*, from *meta-* (expressing change) + *oikos* 'dwelling'.

**metical** /ˌmɛtɪˈkal/ ● n. (pl. **meticais**) the basic monetary unit of Mozambique, equal to 100 centavos.
– ORIGIN Port., based on Arab. *mitkāl*, from *takala* 'to weigh'.

**meticulous** /mɪˈtɪkjʊləs/ ● adj. very careful and precise.
– DERIVATIVES **meticulously** adv. **meticulousness** n.
– ORIGIN C16 (in the sense 'fearful or timid', later 'overcareful about detail'): from L. *meticulosus*, from *metus*

'fear'.

**métier** /ˈmɛtjeɪ/ ● **n.** **1** a trade, profession, or occupation. **2** an outstanding or advantageous characteristic.
– ORIGIN C18: Fr., based on L. *ministerium* 'service'.

**Metis** /meɪˈtiːs/ ● **n.** (pl. same) (in Canada) a person of mixed race, especially the offspring of a white person and an American Indian.
– ORIGIN from Fr. *métis*, from L. *mixtus* 'mixed'; rel. to **MESTIZO**.

**metol** /ˈmɛtɒl/ ● **n.** a soluble white compound used as a photographic developer.
– ORIGIN C19: from Ger., arbitrarily named by the inventor.

**Metonic cycle** /mɪˈtɒnɪk/ ● **n.** a period of 19 years (235 lunar months), after which the new and full moons return to the same day of the year.
– ORIGIN named after *Metōn*, an Athenian astronomer of the 5th cent. BC.

**metonym** /ˈmɛtənɪm/ ● **n.** a word or expression used as a substitute for something with which it is closely associated, e.g. *Washington* for the US government.
– DERIVATIVES **metonymic** adj. **metonymical** adj. **metonymically** adv. **metonymy** /mɪˈtɒnɪmi/ n.
– ORIGIN C19 (earlier (C16) as *metonymy*): via L. from Gk *metōnumia*, lit. 'change of name'.

**metope** /ˈmɛtəʊp, ˈmɛtəpi/ ● **n.** Architecture a square space between triglyphs in a Doric frieze.
– ORIGIN C16: via L. from Gk *metopē*, from *meta* 'between' + *opē* 'hole for a beam end'.

**metre**[1] (US **meter**) ● **n.** the fundamental unit of length in the metric system, equal to 100 centimetres (approx. 39.37 inches).
– DERIVATIVES **metreage** n.
– ORIGIN C18: from Fr. *mètre*, from Gk *metron* 'measure'.

**metre**[2] (US **meter**) ● **n.** **1** the rhythm of a piece of poetry, determined by the number and length of feet in a line. **2** the basic pulse and rhythm of a piece of music.
– ORIGIN OE, reinforced in ME by OFr. *metre*, from L. *metrum*, from Gk *metron* 'measure'.

**metric**[1] ● **adj.** of or based on the metre; relating to or using the metric system. ● **n.** **1** technical a system or standard of measurement. ➤Mathematics & Physics a topological function based on distances or on quantities analogous to distances. **2** informal the metric system.

**metric**[2] ● **adj.** relating to or composed in a poetic metre. ● **n.** the metre of a poem.

**-metric** ● **comb. form** in adjectives corresponding to nouns ending in *-meter* (such as *geometric* corresponding to *geometer* and *geometry*).
– DERIVATIVES **-metrically** comb. form in corresponding adverbs.

**metrical** ● **adj.** **1** of, relating to, or composed in poetic metre. **2** of or involving measurement.
– DERIVATIVES **metrically** adv.

**-metrical** ● **comb. form** equivalent to **-METRIC**.

**metricate** ● **v.** change or adapt to a metric system of measurement.
– DERIVATIVES **metrication** n.

**metric system** ● **n.** the decimal measuring system based on the metre, litre, and gram as units of length, capacity, and weight or mass.

**metric ton** (also **metric tonne**) ● **n.** a unit of weight equal to 1,000 kilograms (2,205 lb).

**metritis** /mɪˈtrʌɪtɪs/ ● **n.** Medicine inflammation of the womb.
– ORIGIN C19: from Gk *mētra* 'womb' + **-ITIS**.

**metro** ● **n.** (pl. **-os**) an underground railway system in a city, especially Paris.
– ORIGIN C20: from Fr. *métro*, abbrev. of *métropolitain* (from *Chemin de Fer Métropolitain* 'Metropolitan Railway').

**metrology** /mɪˈtrɒlədʒi/ ● **n.** the scientific study of measurement.
– DERIVATIVES **metrological** adj.
– ORIGIN C19: from Gk *metron* 'measure' + **-LOGY**.

**metronidazole** /ˌmɛtrəˈnʌɪdəzəʊl/ ● **n.** Medicine a synthetic drug used to treat trichomoniasis and similar infections.
– ORIGIN C20: from *me(thyl)* + *(ni)tro-* + *(im)idazole*.

**metronome** /ˈmɛtrənəʊm/ ● **n.** a musicians' device that marks time at a selected rate by giving a regular tick.
– DERIVATIVES **metronomic** adj. **metronomically** adv.
– ORIGIN C19: from Gk *metron* 'measure' + *nomos* 'law'.

**metronymic** /ˌmɛtrəˈnɪmɪk/ ● **adj. & n.** variant spelling of **MATRONYMIC**.

**metropole** /ˈmɛtrəpəʊl/ ● **n.** the parent state of a colony.
– ORIGIN C15: from OFr. *metropole*, based on Gk *mētēr, mētr-* + *polis* (see **METROPOLIS**).

**metropolis** /mɪˈtrɒp(ə)lɪs/ ● **n.** the capital city of a country. ➤a large and busy city.
– ORIGIN ME: via late L. from Gk *mētropolis* 'mother state', from *mētēr, mētr-* 'mother' + *polis* 'city'.

**metropolitan** ● **adj.** **1** relating to or denoting a metropolis. **2** relating to or denoting the parent state of a colony. **3** Christian Church relating to or denoting a metropolitan or his see. ● **n.** **1** Christian Church a bishop having authority over the bishops of a province, in particular (in Orthodox Churches) one ranking above archbishop and below patriarch. **2** an inhabitant of a metropolis.
– ORIGIN ME (in the eccles. sense): from late L. *metropolitanus*, from Gk *mētropolitēs* 'citizen of a mother state', from *mētropolis* (see **METROPOLIS**).

**metropolitan county** ● **n.** (in England) each of six units of local government centred on a large urban area (in existence since 1974, although their councils were abolished in 1986).

**metropolitan magistrate** ● **n.** (in the UK) a stipendiary magistrate who sits in petty sessional courts in London.

**metrorrhagia** /ˌmiːtrəˈreɪdʒɪə/ ● **n.** abnormal bleeding from the womb.
– ORIGIN C19: mod. L., from Gk *mētra* 'womb' + *-rrhag-*, stem of *rhēgnunai* 'to burst'.

**-metry** ● **comb. form** in nouns denoting procedures and systems corresponding to names of instruments ending in *-meter* (such as *calorimetry* corresponding to *calorimeter*).
– ORIGIN from Gk *-metria*, from *-metrēs* 'measurer'.

**mettle** ● **n.** a person's ability to cope with difficulties; spirit and resilience.
– PHRASES **be on one's mettle** be ready or forced to do one's best.
– DERIVATIVES **mettlesome** adj.
– ORIGIN C16: specialized spelling (for figurative senses) of **METAL**.

**meunière** /məːnˈjɛː/ ● **adj.** [usu. postpos.] cooked or served in lightly browned butter with lemon juice and parsley.
– ORIGIN from Fr. *(à la) meunière* '(in the manner of) a miller's wife'.

**Meursault** /məːˈsəʊ, ˈməː-/ ● **n.** (pl. same) a burgundy wine, typically white, produced near Beaune.
– ORIGIN named after a commune in the Côte d'Or region of France.

**MeV** ● **abbrev.** mega-electronvolt(s).

**mew**[1] ● **v.** (of a cat or gull) make a characteristic high-pitched crying noise. ● **n.** a mewing noise.
– ORIGIN ME: imitative.

**mew**[2] Falconry ● **n.** a cage or building for trained hawks, especially while they are moulting. ● **v.** **1** (of a trained hawk) moult. **2** confine (a moulting trained hawk) to a mew. **3** (often **mew someone up**) confine in a restricting place or situation.
– ORIGIN ME: from OFr. *mue*, from *muer* 'to moult', from L. *mutare* 'to change'.

**mew gull** ● **n.** chiefly N. Amer. a migratory northern gull with greenish-grey legs. [*Larus canus.*]

**mewl** ● **v.** [often as adj. **mewling**] **1** cry feebly or querulously. **2** (of a cat or bird) mew.
– ORIGIN ME: imitative; cf. **MIAUL**.

**mews** ● **n.** (pl. same) Brit. **1** a row of houses or flats converted from stables, or built to appear so. **2** a group of stables round a yard or along an alley.
– ORIGIN ME: pl. of **MEW**[2], orig. referring to the royal stables on the site of the hawk mews at Charing Cross, London.

**MEX** ● **abbrev.** Mexico (international vehicle registration).

**Mexican** ● **n.** a native or inhabitant of Mexico. ● **adj.** of or relating to Mexico.

**Mexicano** /ˌmɛksɪˈkɑːnəʊ/ ● **n. & adj.** informal, chiefly US another term for **MEXICAN**.
– ORIGIN from Sp.

**Mexican wave** ● **n.** an effect resembling a moving wave produced by successive sections of a stadium crowd standing up, raising their arms, lowering them, and sitting down again.
– ORIGIN so named because of the repeated practice of this at the 1986 soccer World Cup finals in Mexico City.

**meze** /ˈmeɪzeɪ/ ● **n.** (pl. same or **mezes**) (in Turkish, Greek, and Middle Eastern cookery) a selection of hot and cold hors d'oeuvres.
– ORIGIN from Turk., lit. 'appetizer'.

**mezereon** /mɪˈzɪərɪən/ ● **n.** a shrub with fragrant purplish-red flowers and poisonous red berries. [*Daphne mezereum*.]
– ORIGIN C15: from med. L., from Arab. *māzaryūn*.

**mezuzah** /mɛˈzuːzə/ ● **n.** (pl. **mezuzahs** or **mezuzoth** /-zəʊt/) a parchment inscribed with religious texts, attached in a case to the doorpost of a Jewish house as a sign of faith.
– ORIGIN C17: from Heb. *mĕzūzāh* 'doorpost'.

**mezzaluna** /ˌmɛtsəˈluːnə/ ● **n.** a utensil for chopping herbs, vegetables, etc., with a semi-circular blade and a handle at each end.
– ORIGIN Ital., lit. 'half moon'.

**mezzanine** /ˈmɛzəniːn, ˈmɛts-/ ● **n.** **1** a low storey between two others, typically between the ground and first floors. **2** N. Amer. the lowest balcony of a theatre or the front rows of the balcony. ● **adj.** Finance referring to unsecured, higher-yielding loans that are subordinate to bank loans and secured loans but rank above equity.
– ORIGIN C18: from Fr., from Ital. *mezzanino*, dimin. of *mezzano* 'middle', from L. *medianus* 'median'.

**mezza voce** /ˌmɛtsə ˈvəʊtʃeɪ, ˈvɒtʃi/ ● **adv. & adj.** Music using half the singer's vocal power.
– ORIGIN Ital., lit. 'half voice'.

**mezzo** /ˈmɛtsəʊ/ (also **mezzo-soprano**) ● **n.** (pl. **-os**) a female singer with a voice pitched between soprano and contralto.
– ORIGIN C18: Ital., from L. *medius* 'middle'.

**mezzo forte** ● **adv. & adj.** Music moderately loud or loudly.

**mezzo piano** ● **adv. & adj.** Music moderately soft or softly.

**mezzo-relievo** /ˌmɛtsəʊrɪˈljiːvəʊ/ ● **n.** (pl. **-os**) Sculpture another term for **HALF RELIEF**.
– ORIGIN C16: from Ital. *mezzo-rilievo*.

**mezzotint** /ˈmɛtsəʊtɪnt, ˈmɛzəʊ-/ ● **n.** a print made from an engraved copper or steel plate, the surface of which has been partially roughened, for shading, and partially smoothed, for light areas. ● **v.** engrave in mezzotint.
– DERIVATIVES **mezzotinter** n.
– ORIGIN from Ital. *mezzotinto*, from *mezzo* 'half' + *tinto* 'tint'.

**MF** ● **abbrev.** medium frequency.

**mf** ● **abbrev.** mezzo forte.

**MFH** ● **abbrev.** Master of Foxhounds.

**MG** ● **abbrev.** **1** machine gun. **2** historical Morris Garages.

**Mg** ● **symb.** the chemical element magnesium.

**mg** ● **abbrev.** milligram(s).

**Mgr** ● **abbrev.** **1** (**mgr**) manager. **2** Monseigneur. **3** Monsignor.

**MGy Sgt** ● **abbrev.** Master Gunnery Sergeant.

**MHK** ● **abbrev.** (in the Isle of Man) Member of the House of Keys.

**mho** /məʊ/ ● **n.** (pl. **-os**) the reciprocal of an ohm, a former unit of electrical conductance.
– ORIGIN C19: the word **OHM** reversed.

**MHR** ● **abbrev.** (in the US and Australia) Member of the House of Representatives.

**MHz** ● **abbrev.** megahertz.

**MI** ● **abbrev.** **1** Michigan (in official postal use). **2** Brit. historical Military Intelligence.

**mi** ● **n.** variant spelling of **ME**[2].

**mi.** ● **abbrev.** mile(s).

**MI5** ● **abbrev.** (in the UK) the governmental agency responsible for internal security and counter-intelligence on British territory (now officially named the Security Service).
– ORIGIN from *Military Intelligence section 5*.

**MI6** ● **abbrev.** (in the UK) the governmental agency responsible for matters of internal security and counter-intelligence overseas (now officially named the Secret Intelligence Service).
– ORIGIN from *Military Intelligence section 6*.

**MIA** ● **abbrev.** chiefly US missing in action.

**Miao** /mɪˈaʊ/ ● **n.** (pl. same) & **adj.** another term for **HMONG**.
– ORIGIN from Chin. *Miáo*, lit. 'tribes'.

**miaow** (also **meow**) ● **n.** the characteristic crying sound of a cat. ● **v.** (of a cat) make a miaow.
– ORIGIN C17: imitative.

**miasma** /mɪˈazmə, mʌɪ-/ ● **n.** (pl. **miasmas**) poetic/literary **1** an unpleasant or unhealthy vapour. **2** an oppressive or unpleasant atmosphere.
– DERIVATIVES **miasmal** adj. **miasmatic** adj. **miasmic** adj. **miasmically** adv.
– ORIGIN C17: from Gk, lit. 'defilement', from *miainein* 'pollute'.

**miaul** /mɪˈɔːl/ ● **v.** rare miaow.
– ORIGIN C17: from Fr. *miauler*, of imitative origin.

**Mic.** ● **abbrev.** Micah (in biblical references).

**mic** /mʌɪk/ ● **n.** informal a microphone.

**mica** /ˈmʌɪkə/ ● **n.** a silicate mineral found as minute shiny scales in granite and other rocks.
– DERIVATIVES **micaceous** /mɪˈkeɪʃəs/ adj.
– ORIGIN C18: from L., lit. 'crumb'.

**mica schist** ● **n.** a fissile metamorphic rock containing quartz and mica.

**mice** plural form of **MOUSE**.

**micelle** /mɪˈsɛl, mʌɪˈsɛl/ ● **n.** Chemistry an aggregate of molecules in a colloidal solution.
– DERIVATIVES **micellar** adj.
– ORIGIN C19: coined as a dimin. of L. *mica* 'crumb'.

**Mich.** ● **abbrev.** Michigan.

**Michaelmas** /ˈmɪk(ə)lməs/ ● **n.** the feast of St Michael, 29 September.
– ORIGIN OE *Sanct Michaeles mæsse* 'Saint Michael's Mass', referring to the Archangel.

**Michaelmas daisy** ● **n.** a North American aster with numerous pinkish-lilac daisy-like flowers which bloom around Michaelmas. [*Aster novi-belgii*.]

**Michaelmas term** ● **n.** Brit. (in some universities) the autumn term.

**Michigander** /mɪʃɪˈgandə/ ● **n.** a native or inhabitant of the US state of Michigan.

**Mick** ● **n.** informal, offensive **1** an Irishman. **2** a Roman Catholic.
– ORIGIN C19: familiar form of the given name *Michael*.

**mick** ● **n.** Austral./NZ (in the game of two-up) the reverse side of a coin.
– ORIGIN C20: of unknown origin.

**mickey** ● **n.** (in phr. **take the mickey**) informal, chiefly Brit. tease or ridicule someone.
– DERIVATIVES **mickey-taking** n.
– ORIGIN 1950s: of unknown origin.

**Mickey Finn** ● **n.** informal a surreptitiously drugged or doctored drink.
– ORIGIN 1920s: of unknown origin; sometimes said to be the name of a notorious Chicago saloon-keeper.

**Mickey Mouse** ● **adj.** informal ineffective or insignificant.
– ORIGIN the name of a character created by the Amer. cartoonist Walt Disney.

**mickle** (also **muckle**) archaic or Scottish & N. English ● **n.** a large amount. ● **adj.** very large.
– PHRASES **many a little makes a mickle** (also **many a mickle makes a muckle**) many small amounts accumulate to make a large amount.

– ORIGIN OE *micel* 'great, numerous, much', of Gmc origin.

**USAGE mickle**

The forms **mickle** and **muckle** are, by origin, merely variants of the same (now dialect) word meaning 'a large amount'. However, the alternative form of the proverb (originally a misquotation) has led to a misunderstanding that **mickle** means 'a small amount'.

**Micmac** /ˈmɪkmak/ (also **Mi'kmaq**) ● **n.** (pl. same or **Micmacs**) **1** a member of an American Indian people inhabiting the Maritime Provinces of Canada. **2** the Algonquian language of this people.
– ORIGIN via Fr. from Micmac.

**micro** ● **n.** (pl. **-os**) **1** a microcomputer. **2** a microprocessor. ● **adj.** extremely small.

**micro-** ● **comb. form 1** small: *microbrewery.* ➤ of reduced or restricted size: *microdot.* **2** denoting a factor of one millionth ($10^{-6}$): *microfarad.*
– ORIGIN from Gk *mikros* 'small'.

**microanalysis** ● **n.** the quantitative analysis of chemical compounds using a sample of a few milligrams.
– DERIVATIVES **microanalytical** adj.

**microbe** /ˈmʌɪkrəʊb/ ● **n.** a micro-organism, especially a bacterium causing disease or fermentation.
– DERIVATIVES **microbial** adj. **microbic** adj.
– ORIGIN C19: from Fr., from Gk *mikros* 'small' + *bios* 'life'.

**microbiology** ● **n.** the scientific study of micro-organisms.
– DERIVATIVES **microbiological** adj. **microbiologically** adv. **microbiologist** n.

**microbiota** /ˌmʌɪkrəʊbʌɪˈəʊtə/ ● **n.** the micro-organisms of a particular place or geological period.

**microbrew** ● **n.** chiefly N. Amer. a beer produced in a microbrewery.

**microbrewery** ● **n.** (pl. **-ies**) chiefly N. Amer. a brewery producing limited quantities of beer.

**microburst** ● **n.** a sudden, powerful, localized air current, especially a downdraught.

**microcellular** ● **adj.** containing or made up of minute cells.

**microcephaly** /ˌmʌɪkrəʊˈsɛfəli, -ˈkɛfəli/ ● **n.** Medicine abnormal smallness of the head.
– DERIVATIVES **microcephalic** adj. & n. **microcephalous** adj.

**microchip** ● **n.** a tiny wafer of semiconducting material used to make an integrated circuit.

**microcircuit** ● **n.** a minute electric circuit, especially an integrated circuit.
– DERIVATIVES **microcircuitry** n.

**microcirculation** ● **n.** circulation of the blood in the smallest blood vessels.

**microclimate** ● **n.** the climate of a very small or restricted area.
– DERIVATIVES **microclimatic** adj. **microclimatically** adv.

**microcline** /ˈmʌɪkrə(ʊ)klʌɪn/ ● **n.** a green, pink or brown mineral consisting of potassium-rich feldspar.
– ORIGIN C19: from Ger. *Microklin*, from Gk *mikros* 'small' + *klinein* 'to lean' (because its angle of cleavage is close to 90 degrees).

**microcode** ● **n.** Computing a very low-level instruction set controlling the operation of a computer.

**microcomputer** ● **n.** a small computer with a microprocessor as its central processor.

**microcopy** ● **n.** (pl. **-ies**) a copy of printed matter that has been reduced in size by microphotography. ● **v.** (**-ies**, **-ied**) make a microcopy of.

**microcosm** /ˈmʌɪkrə(ʊ)kɒz(ə)m/ ● **n. 1** a thing regarded as encapsulating in miniature the characteristics of something much larger. **2** humankind regarded as the epitome of the universe.
– DERIVATIVES **microcosmic** /-ˈkɒzmɪk/ adj. **microcosmically** /-ˈkɒzmɪk(ə)li/ adv.
– ORIGIN ME: from OFr. *microcosme* or med. L. *microcosmus*, from Gk *mikros kosmos* 'little world'.

**microcosmic salt** ● **n.** hydrated sodium ammonium hydrogen phosphate, obtained from human urine.

**microcredit** ● **n.** the lending of small amounts of money at low interest to new businesses in the developing world.

**microcrystalline** ● **adj.** formed of microscopic crystals.

**microcyte** /ˈmʌɪkrə(ʊ)sʌɪt, ˈmɪ-/ ● **n.** Medicine an unusually small red blood cell.
– DERIVATIVES **microcytic** adj.

**microdot** ● **n. 1** a microphotograph, especially of a printed document, of about 1 mm across. **2** a tiny tablet of LSD.

**microeconomics** ● **pl. n.** [treated as sing.] the part of economics concerned with single factors and the effects of individual decisions.
– DERIVATIVES **microeconomic** adj.

**microelectronics** ● **pl. n.** [usu. treated as sing.] the design, manufacture, and use of microchips and microcircuits.
– DERIVATIVES **microelectronic** adj.

**micro-environment** ● **n.** Biology the immediate small-scale environment of an organism.

**microevolution** ● **n.** Biology evolutionary change within a species or small group of organisms, especially over a short period.
– DERIVATIVES **microevolutionary** adj.

**microfarad** (abbrev: **μF**) ● **n.** one millionth of a farad.

**microfauna** ● **n.** Ecology microscopic animals living in the soil.

**microfibre** (US also **microfiber**) ● **n.** a very fine synthetic yarn.

**microfiche** /ˈmʌɪkrə(ʊ)fiːʃ/ ● **n.** a flat piece of film containing microphotographs of the pages of a newspaper, catalogue, etc.

**microfilaria** /ˌmʌɪkrəʊfɪˈlɛːrɪə/ ● **n.** (pl. **microfilariae**) Zoology the minute larva of a filaria.

**microfilm** ● **n.** a length of film containing microphotographs of a newspaper, catalogue, etc. ● **v.** make a microfilm of.

**microflora** ● **n.** Biology the micro-organisms of a particular habitat or host organism.

**microform** ● **n.** microphotographic reproduction on film or paper of a manuscript, map, etc.

**microfossil** ● **n.** a fossil that can only be seen with a microscope.

**microglia** /ˌmʌɪkrə(ʊ)ˈglʌɪə, ˌmɪ-/ ● **pl. n.** Anatomy glial cells that function as macrophages in the central nervous system.
– DERIVATIVES **microglial** adj.

**microgram** (abbrev: **μg**) ● **n.** one millionth of a gram.

**micrograph** ● **n.** a photograph taken using a microscope.
– DERIVATIVES **micrographic** adj. **micrographics** pl. n. **micrography** n.

**microgravity** ● **n.** very weak gravity, as in an orbiting spacecraft.

**microgroove** ● **n.** a very narrow groove on a long-playing record.

**microhabitat** ● **n.** Ecology a habitat of limited extent which differs in character from the surrounding habitat.

**microinject** ● **v.** Biology inject into a microscopic object.
– DERIVATIVES **microinjection** n.

**microinstruction** ● **n.** Computing a single instruction in microcode.

**microkernel** ● **n.** Computing a small modular part of an operating system kernel which implements its basic features.

**microlepidoptera** /ˌmʌɪkrə(ʊ)lɛpɪˈdɒpt(ə)rə/ ● **pl. n.** Entomology the numerous small moths which are of interest only to specialists.

**microlight** ● **n.** chiefly Brit. a very small, light, one- or two-seater aircraft.

**microlith** ● **n.** Archaeology a minute shaped flint, typically part of a composite tool.
– DERIVATIVES **microlithic** adj.

**microlitre** (US also **microliter**) (abbrev.: **µl**) ● **n.** one millionth of a litre.

**micromanage** ● **v.** N. Amer. control even the smallest part of.
– DERIVATIVES **micromanagement** n. **micromanager** n.

**micromesh** ● **n.** a material consisting of a very fine mesh.

**micrometer** /mʌɪˈkrɒmɪtə/ ● **n.** a gauge which measures small distances or thicknesses.
– DERIVATIVES **micrometry** n.

**micrometre** /ˈmʌɪkrə(ʊ)ˌmiːtə/ (US **micrometer**) (abbrev.: **µm**) ● **n.** one millionth of a metre.

**microminiaturization** (also **-isation**) ● **n.** the manufacture of extremely small electronic devices.

**micron** /ˈmʌɪkrɒn/ ● **n.** one millionth of a metre.
– ORIGIN C19: from Gk *mikron*, neut. of *mikros* 'small'.

**Micronesian** ● **n.** **1** a native of Micronesia, an island group in the western Pacific. **2** the group of Austronesian languages spoken in Micronesia. ● **adj.** of or relating to Micronesia.

**micronize** /ˈmʌɪkrənʌɪz/ (also **-ise**) ● **v.** break into very fine particles.
– DERIVATIVES **micronization** n. **micronizer** n.

**micronutrient** ● **n.** a chemical element or substance required in trace amounts by living organisms.

**micro-organism** ● **n.** a microscopic organism, especially a bacterium, virus, or fungus.

**microphagous** /mʌɪˈkrɒfəgəs/ ● **adj.** Zoology feeding on minute particles or micro-organisms.
– DERIVATIVES **microphagic** adj.

**microphone** ● **n.** an instrument for converting sound waves into electrical energy variations which may then be amplified, transmitted, or recorded.
– DERIVATIVES **microphonic** adj.

**microphotograph** ● **n.** a photograph reduced to a very small size.
– DERIVATIVES **microphotography** n.

**microphysics** ● **pl. n.** [treated as sing.] the branch of physics concerned with bodies and phenomena on a microscopic or smaller scale.
– DERIVATIVES **microphysical** adj.

**micropore** ● **n.** a very narrow pore.
– DERIVATIVES **microporous** adj.

**microprint** ● **n.** text reduced by microphotography.
– DERIVATIVES **microprinting** n.

**microprobe** ● **n.** an instrument in which a narrow beam of electrons is focused on to a sample and the resulting fluorescence is analysed to yield chemical information.

**microprocessor** ● **n.** an integrated circuit containing all the functions of a central processing unit of a computer.

**microprogram** ● **n.** a microinstruction program.

**micropropagation** ● **n.** Botany the propagation of plants by growing plantlets in tissue culture and then planting them out.

**micropterous** /mʌɪˈkrɒpt(ə)rəs/ ● **adj.** Entomology having small or reduced wings.

**micropyle** /ˈmʌɪkrə(ʊ)pʌɪl/ ● **n.** **1** Botany a small opening in the surface of an ovule, which the pollen tube penetrates. **2** Zoology a small opening for spermatozoa in the egg of a fish, insect, etc.
– ORIGIN C19: from **MICRO-** + Gk *pulē* 'gate'.

**microreader** ● **n.** a device producing an enlarged readable image from a microfilm or microprint.

**microscooter** ● **n.** a small two-wheeled foldable aluminium scooter for both children and adults.

**microscope** ● **n.** an optical instrument for viewing very small objects, typically magnifying by several hundred times.
– ORIGIN C17: from mod. L. *microscopium* (see **MICRO-**, **-SCOPE**).

**microscopic** ● **adj.** **1** so small as to be visible only with a microscope. ➤ informal extremely small. **2** concerned with minute detail. **3** of or relating to a microscope.
– DERIVATIVES **microscopical** adj. **microscopically** adv.

**microscopy** /mʌɪˈkrɒskəpi/ ● **n.** the use of a microscope.
– DERIVATIVES **microscopist** n.

**microsecond** (abbrev.: **µs**) ● **n.** one millionth of a second.

**microseism** /ˈmʌɪkrəʊˌsʌɪz(ə)m/ ● **n.** Geology an imperceptibly small earthquake.
– DERIVATIVES **microseismic** adj.

**microsome** /ˈmʌɪkrəsəʊm/ ● **n.** Biology a fragment of endoplasmic reticulum and attached ribosomes obtained by centrifugation of homogenized cells.
– DERIVATIVES **microsomal** adj.

**microspecies** ● **n.** (pl. **same**) Biology a species differing only in minor characteristics from others of its group, typically one of limited geographical range forming part of an aggregate species.

**microsphere** ● **n.** a microscopic hollow sphere, especially of a protein or synthetic polymer.

**microsporangium** /ˌmʌɪkrə(ʊ)spəˈrandʒɪəm/ ● **n.** (pl. **microsporangia** /-dʒɪə/) Botany a sporangium containing microspores.

**microspore** ● **n.** Botany the smaller of the two kinds of spore produced by some ferns. Compare with **MEGASPORE.**

**microstructure** ● **n.** the fine structure (in a metal or other material) which can be made visible and examined with a microscope.
– DERIVATIVES **microstructural** adj.

**microsurgery** ● **n.** intricate surgery performed using miniaturized instruments and a microscope.
– DERIVATIVES **microsurgical** adj.

**microswitch** ● **n.** an electric switch that can be operated rapidly by a small movement.

**microtechnology** ● **n.** technology that uses microelectronics.
– DERIVATIVES **microtechnological** adj.

**microtome** /ˈmʌɪkrə(ʊ)təʊm/ ● **n.** chiefly Biology an instrument for cutting extremely thin sections of material for examination under a microscope.

**microtone** ● **n.** Music an interval smaller than a semitone.
– DERIVATIVES **microtonal** adj. **microtonality** n. **microtonally** adv.

**microtubule** ● **n.** Biology a microscopic tubular structure present in numbers in the cytoplasm of cells, sometimes aggregating to form more complex structures.

**microvascular** ● **adj.** of or relating to the smallest blood vessels.

**microvillus** ● **n.** (pl. **microvilli**) Biology each of a large number of minute projections from the surface of some cells.
– DERIVATIVES **microvillar** adj.

**microwave** ● **n.** **1** an electromagnetic wave with a wavelength in the range 0.001–0.3 m, shorter than that of a normal radio wave but longer than those of infrared radiation. **2** (also **microwave oven**) an oven that uses microwaves to cook or heat food. ● **v.** cook (food) in a microwave oven.
– DERIVATIVES **microwaveable** (also **microwavable**) adj.

**microwave background** ● **n.** Astronomy a weak uniform microwave radiation which is detectable in nearly every direction of the sky, believed to be evidence of the big bang.

**micrurgy** /ˈmʌɪkrəːdʒi/ ● **n.** Biology the manipulation of individual cells under a microscope.
– DERIVATIVES **micrurgical** adj.
– ORIGIN 1920s: from **MICRO-** + Gk *-ourgia* 'work'.

**micturate** /ˈmɪktjʊreɪt/ ● **v.** formal urinate.
– DERIVATIVES **micturition** n.
– ORIGIN C19: back-form. from *micturition* (C18), from L. *micturit-*, *micturire* 'urinate'.

**mid**[1] ● **adj.** **1** of or in the middle part or position of a range. **2** Phonetics (of a vowel) pronounced with the tongue neither high nor low.

**mid**[2] ● **prep.** poetic/literary in the middle of; amid.
– ORIGIN shortening of **AMID.**

**mid-** ● **comb. form** denoting the middle of: *midsection*. ➤ in the middle; medium; half: *midway*.
– ORIGIN OE *midd*, of Gmc origin; rel. to L. *medius* and Gk

*mesos.*

**Midas touch** /ˈmʌɪdəs/ ● **n.** (**the Midas touch**) the ability to make a lot of money.
– ORIGIN from *Midas*, king of Phrygia, in Gk mythology given by Dionysus the power to turn everything he touched into gold.

**mid-Atlantic** ● **adj. 1** situated or occurring in the middle of the Atlantic ocean. **2** having characteristics of both Britain and America. **3** of or relating to states on the middle Atlantic coast of the United States.

**midbrain** ● **n.** Anatomy a small central part of the brainstem, developing from the middle of the primitive or embryonic brain.

**midday** ● **n.** the middle of the day; noon.

**midden** /ˈmɪd(ə)n/ ● **n. 1** a dunghill or refuse heap. **2** short for **KITCHEN MIDDEN**.
– ORIGIN ME *myddyng*, of Scand. origin.

**middle** ● **adj. 1** at an equal distance from the extremities of something; central. ➤(of a member of a group or series) placed so as to have the same number of members on each side. ➤intermediate in rank, quality, or ability. **2** Grammar denoting a voice of verbs in some languages, such as Greek, which expresses reciprocal or reflexive action. ● **n. 1** a middle point or position. **2** informal a person's waist and abdomen. **3** Grammar a middle form or voice of a verb. ● **v.** (in cricket, tennis, etc.) strike (the ball) with the middle of the bat, racket, or club.
– ORIGIN OE *middel*, of W. Gmc origin; rel. to **MID**.

**middle age** ● **n.** the period between youth and old age, about 45 to 60.
– DERIVATIVES **middle-aged** adj.

**middle-aged spread** (also **middle-age spread**) ● **n.** the fat that may accumulate in middle age around the waist and abdomen.

**Middle Ages** ● **pl. n.** the period of European history from the fall of the Roman Empire in the West (5th century) to the fall of Constantinople (1453), or, more narrowly, from *c.*1000 to 1453.

**Middle America** ● **n. 1** the conservative middle classes of the United States, regarded as characteristically inhabiting the Midwest. **2** Mexico and Central America.
– DERIVATIVES **Middle American** adj. & n.

**middlebrow** ● **adj.** informal, chiefly derogatory demanding or involving only a moderate degree of intellectual application; conventional rather than challenging.

**middle C** ● **n.** Music the C near the middle of the piano keyboard, written on the first leger line below the treble stave or the first leger line above the bass stave.

**middle class** ● **n.** [treated as sing. or pl.] the social group between the upper and working classes; professional and business people. ● **adj.** of, relating to, or characteristic of the middle class.
– DERIVATIVES **middle-classness** n.

**middle common room** ● **n.** Brit. a common room for the use of postgraduate students in a university or college.

**middle distance** ● **n. 1** the part of a real or painted landscape between the foreground and the background. **2** [as modifier] Athletics denoting or relating to a race distance of between 800 and 5,000 metres.

**Middle Dutch** ● **n.** the Dutch language from *c.*1100–1500.

**middle ear** ● **n.** the air-filled central cavity of the ear, behind the eardrum.

**Middle East** ● **n.** an area of SW Asia and northern Africa, stretching from the Mediterranean to Pakistan and including the Arabian Peninsula.
– DERIVATIVES **Middle Eastern** adj.

**middle eight** ● **n.** a short section (typically of eight bars) in the middle of a conventionally structured popular song, generally of a different character from the other parts of the song.

**Middle England** ● **n.** the conservative middle classes in England.
– DERIVATIVES **Middle Englander** n.

**Middle English** ● **n.** the English language from *c.*1150 to *c.*1470.

**middle ground** ● **n. 1** an area of compromise or possible agreement between two extreme positions. **2** the middle distance of a painting or photograph.

**Middle High German** ● **n.** the language of southern Germany from *c.*1200–1500.

**Middle Low German** ● **n.** the Low German language (spoken in northern Germany) from *c.*1200–1500.

**middleman** ● **n.** (pl. **-men**) **1** a person who buys goods from producers and sells them to retailers or consumers. **2** a person who arranges business or political deals between other people.

**middle name** ● **n. 1** a person's name placed after the first name and before the surname. **2** a quality for which a person is notable: *optimism is my middle name.*

**middle-of-the-road** ● **adj. 1** moderate. **2** conventional and unadventurous.

**middle passage** ● **n.** historical the sea journey undertaken by slave ships from West Africa to the West Indies.

**middle school** ● **n. 1** (in the UK) a school for children from about 9 to 13 years old. **2** (in the US and Canada) a junior high school.

**middle term** ● **n.** Logic the term common to both premises of a syllogism.

**middleware** ● **n.** Computing software that occupies a position in a hierarchy between the operating system and the applications.

**middle watch** ● **n.** the period from midnight to 4 a.m. on board a ship.

**middleweight** ● **n.** a weight in boxing and other sports intermediate between welterweight and light heavyweight.

**middling** ● **adj.** moderate or average in size, amount, or rank. ➤neither very good nor very bad. ● **n.** (**middlings**) bulk goods of medium grade, especially flour of medium fineness. ● **adv.** informal fairly or moderately: *middling rich.*
– DERIVATIVES **middlingly** adv.
– ORIGIN ME (orig. Scots): prob. from **MID-** + the adverbial suffix *-ling*.

**Middx** ● **abbrev.** Middlesex.

**middy** ● **n.** (pl. **-ies**) **1** informal a midshipman. **2** (also **middy blouse**) chiefly historical a woman's or child's loose blouse with a sailor collar.

**midfield** ● **n.** (chiefly in soccer) the central part of the field. ➤the players in a team who play in a central position between attack and defence.
– DERIVATIVES **midfielder** n.

**midge** ● **n. 1** a small two-winged fly that forms swarms near water or marshy areas, and of which many kinds feed on blood. [Families Ceratopogonidae (**biting midges**) and Chironomidae, many species.] ➤used in names of other small flies whose larvae are pests of plants, e.g. **gall midge**. **2** informal a small person.
– ORIGIN OE *mycg(e)*, of Gmc origin.

**midget** ● **n.** an extremely small person. ➤[as modifier] extremely small.
– ORIGIN C19: from **MIDGE** + **-ET**[1].

**midgut** ● **n.** Zoology the middle part of the alimentary canal, including (in vertebrates) the small intestine.

**midheaven** ● **n.** Astrology the point where the ecliptic intersects the meridian.

**MIDI** ● **n.** a standard for interconnecting electronic musical instruments and computers.
– ORIGIN 1980s: acronym from *musical instrument digital interface.*

**midi** ● **n.** (pl. **midis**) a woman's calf-length skirt, dress, or coat.
– ORIGIN 1960s: from **MID**, on the pattern of *mini.*

**midi-** ● **comb. form** medium-sized; of medium length: *midiskirt.*

**midinette** /ˌmɪdɪˈnɛt/ ● **n.** a seamstress in a Parisian fashion house.
– ORIGIN Fr., from *midi* 'midday' + *dînette* 'light dinner' (because only a short break was taken for lunch).

**midiron** ● **n.** Golf an iron with a medium degree of loft, such as a four-, five-, or six-iron.

**midi system** • n. Brit. a set of compact stacking hi-fi equipment components.

**midland** • n. the middle part of a country. ➤(**the Midlands**) the inland counties of central England. ➤(**Midland**) a part of the central United States, roughly bounded by Illinois, South Carolina, and Delaware. • adj. of or in a midland. ➤(**Midland**) of or in the English Midlands or the Midland of the United States.
– DERIVATIVES **midlander** n.

**midlife** • n. the central period of a person's life, between around 45 and 60 years old.

**midline** • n. a median line or plane of bilateral symmetry.

**midmost** • adj. & adv. poetic/literary in the most central position.

**midnight** • n. twelve o'clock at night; the middle of the night.

**midnight blue** • n. a very dark blue.

**midnight feast** • n. a secret meal eaten by children late at night.

**midnight sun** • n. the sun when seen at midnight during the summer in either the Arctic or Antarctic Circle.

**mid-ocean ridge** • n. Geology a long, seismically active submarine ridge system situated in the middle of an ocean basin.

**mid-off** • n. Cricket a fielding position on the off side near the bowler.

**mid-on** • n. Cricket a fielding position on the on side near the bowler.

**Midrash** /ˈmɪdraʃ, -rʌʃ/ • n. (pl. **Midrashim** /-ˈʃɪm/) an ancient commentary on part of the Hebrew scriptures, attached to the biblical text.
– ORIGIN from Heb. *midrāš* 'commentary', from *dāraš* 'expound'.

**midrib** • n. a large strengthened vein along the midline of a leaf.

**midriff** • n. the region of the front of the body between the chest and the waist.
– ORIGIN OE *midhrif*, from MID[1] + *hrif* 'belly'.

**midship** • n. the middle part of a ship or boat.

**midshipman** • n. (pl. **-men**) **1** a rank of officer in the Royal Navy, above naval cadet and below sub lieutenant. **2** a naval cadet in the US navy. **3** an American toadfish with dorsal and anal fins that run most of the length of the body and rows of light organs on the underside. [Genus *Porichthys*: two or three species.]

**midships** • adv. & adj. another term for AMIDSHIPS.

**mid shot** • n. Photography a shot taken at a medium distance.

**midst** archaic or poetic/literary • prep. in the middle of. • n. the middle point or part.
– PHRASES **in our** (or **your**, **their**, etc.) **midst** among us (or you or them).
– ORIGIN ME: from *in middes* 'in the middle'.

**midstream** • n. the middle of a stream or river.
– PHRASES **in midstream 1** in the middle of a stream or river. **2** part-way through an activity, speech, etc.

**midsummer** • n. **1** the middle part of summer. **2** the summer solstice.

**Midsummer Day** (also **Midsummer's Day**) • n. 24 June, a quarter day in England, Wales, and Ireland.

**midterm** • n. **1** the middle of a period of office, an academic term, or a pregnancy. **2** N. Amer. an exam in the middle of an academic term.

**midtown** • n. N. Amer. the central part of a city between the downtown and uptown areas.

**midway** • adv. & adj. in or towards the middle of something. • n. N. Amer. an area of sideshows or other amusements at a fair or exhibition.

**midweek** • n. the middle of the week. • adj. & adv. in the middle of the week.

**Midwest** • n. the region of northern states of the US from Ohio west to the Rocky Mountains.
– DERIVATIVES **Midwestern** adj.

**midwicket** • n. Cricket a fielding position on the leg side, level with the middle of the pitch.

**midwife** • n. (pl. **-wives**) a nurse who is trained to assist women in childbirth.
– DERIVATIVES **midwifery** /-ˈwɪf(ə)ri/ n.
– ORIGIN ME: prob. from the obs. prep. *mid* 'with' + WIFE (in the archaic sense 'woman').

**midwife toad** • n. a European toad, the male of which has a distinctive piping call in spring and carries the developing eggs wrapped around his hind legs. [*Alytes obstetricans*.]

**midwinter** • n. **1** the middle part of winter. **2** the winter solstice.

**mielie** • n. variant spelling of MEALIE.

**Mien** /mjɛn/ • n. another term for YAO.

**mien** /miːn/ • n. a person's look or manner.
– ORIGIN C16: prob. from Fr. *mine* 'expression', influenced by obs. *demean* 'bearing, demeanour' (from DEMEAN[2]).

**Miesian** /ˈmiːzɪən/ • adj. of or relating to the work of the German-born architect Ludwig Mies van der Rohe (1886–1969).

**mifepristone** /ˌmɪfɛˈprɪstəʊn/ • n. Medicine a synthetic steroid that inhibits the action of progesterone, given orally in early pregnancy to induce abortion.
– ORIGIN 1980s: prob. from Du. *mifepriston*, from *mife-* (representing *aminophenol*) + *-pr-* (representing *propyl*) + *-ist-* (representing OESTRADIOL) + -ONE.

**miff** • v. (usu. **be miffed**) informal offend or irritate.
– ORIGIN C17: perh. imitative.

**miffy** • adj. informal easily offended or irritated.

**might**[1] • modal v. (3rd sing. present **might**) past of MAY[1]. **1** used in reported speech to express possibility or permission. ➤expressing a possibility based on a condition not fulfilled. ➤expressing annoyance: *you might have told me!* **2** used politely or tentatively in questions and requests. ➤asking for information, especially condescendingly: *who might you be?* **3** used to express possibility or make a suggestion.

**might**[2] • n. great power or strength.
– PHRASES **with might and main** with all one's strength or power.
– ORIGIN OE *miht*, *mieht*, of Gmc origin; rel. to MAY[1].

**mightn't** • contr. might not.

**mighty** • adj. (**-ier**, **-iest**) **1** possessing great power or strength. **2** informal very large. • adv. informal, chiefly N. Amer. extremely.
– DERIVATIVES **mightily** adv. **mightiness** n.
– ORIGIN OE *mihtig* (see MIGHT[2], -Y[1]).

**migmatite** /ˈmɪgmətʌɪt/ • n. Geology a rock composed of two intermingled but distinguishable components, typically a granitic rock within a metamorphic host rock.
– ORIGIN C20: from Gk *migma*, *migmat-* 'mixture' + -ITE[1].

**mignonette** /ˌmɪnjəˈnɛt/ • n. a plant with spikes of small fragrant greenish flowers. [*Reseda lutea* and related species.]
– ORIGIN C18: from Fr. *mignonnette*, dimin. of *mignon* 'small and sweet'.

**migraine** /ˈmiːgreɪn, ˈmʌɪ-/ • n. a recurrent throbbing headache, typically affecting one side of the head and often accompanied by nausea and disturbed vision.
– DERIVATIVES **migrainous** adj.
– ORIGIN ME: from Fr., via late L. from Gk *hēmikrania*, from *hēmi-* 'half' + *kranion* 'skull'.

**migrant** • n. **1** an animal that migrates. **2** a worker who moves from place to place to do seasonal work. • adj. tending to migrate or having migrated.

**migrate** /mʌɪˈgreɪt, ˈmʌɪgreɪt/ • v. **1** (of an animal) move from one habitat to another according to the seasons. **2** (of a person) move to settle in a new area in order to find work. ➤move from one part of something to another. **3** Computing transfer or cause to transfer from one system to another.
– DERIVATIVES **migration** /-ˈgreɪʃ(ə)n/ n. **migrational** adj. **migrator** n. **migratory** /ˈmʌɪgrət(ə)ri, mʌɪˈgreɪt(ə)ri/ adj.
– ORIGIN C17: from L. *migrat-*, *migrare* 'move, shift'.

**mihrab** /ˈmiːrɑːb/ • n. a niche in the wall of a mosque, at the point nearest to Mecca, towards which the congregation faces to pray.
– ORIGIN from Arab. *miḥrāb* 'place for prayer'.

**mikado** /mɪˈkɑːdəʊ/ ● **n.** historical a title given to the emperor of Japan.
– ORIGIN Japanese, from *mi* 'august' + *kado* 'gate' (a transferred use of 'gate (to the Imperial palace)', an ancient place of audience).

**mike**[1] informal ● **n.** a microphone. ● **v.** place a microphone close to or in.

**mike**[2] Brit. informal, dated ● **v.** idle away one's time. ● **n.** a period of idleness.
– ORIGIN C19: of unknown origin.

**Mi'kmaq** ● **n.** variant spelling of **MICMAC**.

**mil**[1] ● **abbrev. 1** millilitres. **2** millimetres. **3** informal (used in sums of money) millions.

**mil**[2] ● **n.** one thousandth of an inch.
– ORIGIN C17: from L. *millesimum* 'thousandth', from *mille* 'thousand'.

**milady** /mɪˈleɪdi/ ● **n.** (pl. **-ies**) historical or humorous used to address or refer to an English noblewoman.
– ORIGIN C18: via Fr. from Engl. *my lady*.

**milage** ● **n.** variant spelling of **MILEAGE**.

**Milanese** /ˈmɪlaniːz/ ● **n.** (pl. same) a native or inhabitant of Milan. ● **adj.** of or relating to Milan or the Milanese.

**milch** /mɪltʃ/ ● **adj.** denoting a domestic mammal giving or kept for milk.
– ORIGIN ME: from OE *-milce* in *thrimilce* 'May' (when cows could be milked three times a day), from the Gmc base of **MILK**.

**milch cow** ● **n.** a person or organization that is a source of easy profit.

**mild** ● **adj. 1** gentle and not easily provoked. **2** of only moderate severity. ➤not keenly felt: *mild surprise*. ➤(of a medicine or cosmetic) acting gently. ➤not sharp or strong in flavour. **3** (of weather) moderately warm; less cold than expected. ● **n.** Brit. a kind of dark beer not strongly flavoured with hops.
– DERIVATIVES **mildish** adj. **mildly** adv. **mildness** n.
– ORIGIN OE *milde*, of Gmc origin.

**mildew** ● **n.** a coating of minute fungal hyphae, growing on plants or damp organic material such as paper or leather. ● **v.** affect or be affected with mildew.
– DERIVATIVES **mildewy** adj.
– ORIGIN OE *mildēaw* 'honeydew', of Gmc origin.

**mild steel** ● **n.** steel containing a small percentage of carbon, that is strong and tough but not readily tempered.

**mile** ● **n. 1** (also **statute mile**) a unit of linear measure equal to 1,760 yards (approximately 1.609 kilometres). **2** historical a Roman measure of 1,000 paces. **3** (**miles**) informal a very long way or a very great amount. ● **adv.** (**miles**) informal by a great amount or a long way: *it is miles better*.
– PHRASES **be miles away** informal be lost in thought. **go the extra mile** be especially assiduous in one's attempt to achieve something. **run a mile** informal run rapidly away; flee. **stand** (or **stick**) **out a mile** informal be very obvious or incongruous.
– ORIGIN OE *mīl*, based on L. *mil(l)ia*, pl. of *mille* 'thousand'.

**mileage** (also **milage**) ● **n. 1** a number of miles travelled or covered. **2** informal actual or potential benefit or advantage: *he was getting a lot of mileage out of the mix-up*.

**mileometer** ● **n.** variant spelling of **MILOMETER**.

**milepost** ● **n.** chiefly N. Amer. & Austral. **1** a marker or signpost indicating how distant a particular place is. **2** a post one mile from the finishing post of a race. **3** an event marking a significant new development or stage.

**miler** ● **n.** informal a person or horse trained specially to run a mile.
– DERIVATIVES **miling** n.

**milestone** ● **n. 1** a stone set up beside a road to mark the distance in miles to a particular place. **2** an event marking a significant new development or stage.

**milfoil** /ˈmɪlfɔɪl/ ● **n. 1** the common yarrow. **2** (also **water milfoil**) an aquatic plant with whorls of fine submerged leaves and wind-pollinated flowers. [Genus *Myriophyllum*.]
– ORIGIN ME: via OFr. from L. *millefolium*, from *mille* 'thousand' + *folium* 'leaf'.

**milia** plural form of **MILIUM**.

**miliaria** /ˌmɪlɪˈɛːrɪə/ ● **n.** medical term for **PRICKLY HEAT**.
– ORIGIN C19: mod. L., from L. *miliarius* (see **MILIARY**).

**miliary** /ˈmɪlɪəri/ ● **adj.** Medicine (of a disease) accompanied by a rash with lesions resembling millet seed.
– ORIGIN C17: from L. *miliarius*, from *milium* 'millet'.

**milieu** /ˈmiːljəː, mɪˈljəː/ ● **n.** (pl. **milieux** or **milieus** pronounced same or /-ljəːz/) a person's social environment.
– ORIGIN C19: Fr., from *mi* 'mid' + *lieu* 'place'.

**militant** ● **adj.** favouring confrontational methods in support of a cause. ● **n.** a militant person.
– DERIVATIVES **militancy** n. **militantly** adv.
– ORIGIN ME (in the sense 'engaged in warfare'): from OFr., or from L. *militant-*, *militare* (see **MILITATE**).

**militaria** /ˌmɪlɪˈtɛːrɪə/ ● **pl. n.** military articles of historical interest.

**militarism** ● **n.** the belief that a country should maintain and readily draw on a strong military capability for the defence or promotion of national interests.
– DERIVATIVES **militarist** n. & adj. **militaristic** adj.

**militarize** (also **-ise**) ● **v. 1** equip with military resources. **2** give a military character to.
– DERIVATIVES **militarization** n. **militarized** adj.

**military** ● **adj.** of, relating to, or characteristic of soldiers or armed forces. ● **n.** (**the military**) the armed forces of a country.
– DERIVATIVES **militarily** adv.
– ORIGIN ME: from Fr. *militaire* or L. *militaris*, from *miles*, *milit-* 'soldier'.

**military attaché** ● **n.** an army officer serving with an embassy or attached as an observer to a foreign army.

**military honours** ● **pl. n.** ceremonies performed by troops as a mark of respect at the burial of a member of the armed forces.

**military-industrial complex** ● **n.** a country's military establishment and those industries producing arms or other military materials, regarded as a powerful vested interest.

**military police** ● **n.** [treated as pl.] a military corps responsible for policing and disciplinary duties in an army.
– DERIVATIVES **military policeman** n. **military policewoman** n.

**militate** ● **v.** (**militate against**) (of a fact or circumstance) be a powerful or conclusive factor in preventing.
– ORIGIN C16: from L. *militat-*, *militare* 'serve as a soldier', from *miles*, *milit-* 'soldier'.

**militia** /mɪˈlɪʃə/ ● **n.** a military force that is raised from the civil population to supplement a regular army in an emergency. ➤a rebel force acting in opposition to a regular army. ➤(in the US) all able-bodied civilians eligible by law for military service.
– ORIGIN C16: from L., lit. 'military service'.

**militiaman** ● **n.** (pl. **-men**) a member of a militia.

**milium** /ˈmɪlɪəm/ ● **n.** (pl. **milia** /ˈmɪlɪə/) Medicine a small, hard, pale keratinous nodule formed on the skin, typically by a blocked sebaceous gland.
– ORIGIN C19: from L., lit. 'millet' (because of a resemblance to a millet seed).

**milk** ● **n.** an opaque white fluid rich in fat and protein, secreted by female mammals for the nourishment of their young. ➤the milk of cows as a food and drink for humans. ➤the milk-like juice of certain plants, such as the coconut. ➤a milk-like liquid with a particular ingredient or use: *cleansing milk*. ● **v. 1** draw milk from (a cow or other animal). ➤extract sap, venom, or other substances from. **2** exploit or defraud (someone) by taking small amounts of their money over a period of time. ➤get all possible advantage from (a situation).
– PHRASES **in milk** (of an animal) producing milk. **milk and honey** prosperity and abundance. [with biblical allusion to the prosperity of the Promised Land (Exod. 3:8).]
– ORIGIN OE *milc*, *milcian*, of Gmc origin.

**milk-and-water** ● **adj.** feeble; ineffective.

**milk bar** ● **n.** Brit. a snack bar that sells milk drinks and other refreshments.

**milk chocolate** ● n. solid chocolate made with the addition of milk.

**milker** ● n. **1** a cow or other animal that is kept for milk. **2** a person that milks cows.

**milk fever** ● n. **1** an acute illness in female cows or other animals that have just produced young, caused by calcium deficiency. **2** a fever in women caused by infection after childbirth, formerly supposed to be due to the swelling of the breasts with milk.

**milkfish** ● n. (pl. same or **-fishes**) a large active silvery fish of the Indo-Pacific region, farmed for food. [*Chanos chanos*.]

**milk float** ● n. Brit. an open-sided electrically powered van that is used for delivering milk to houses.

**milk glass** ● n. semi-translucent glass, whitened by the addition of various ingredients.

**milking stool** ● n. a short three-legged stool, of a kind traditionally used while milking cows.

**milk-leg** ● n. painful swelling of the leg after giving birth, caused by thrombophlebitis in the femoral vein.

**milk loaf** ● n. Brit. a loaf of bread made with milk instead of water.

**milkmaid** ● n. chiefly archaic a girl or woman who milks cows or does other work in a dairy.

**milkman** ● n. (pl. **-men**) a man who sells and delivers milk.

**Milk of Magnesia** ● n. Brit. trademark a white suspension of hydrated magnesium carbonate in water, used as an antacid or laxative.

**milk pudding** ● n. Brit. a baked pudding made of milk and a grain such as rice, sago, or tapioca.

**milk round** ● n. **1** Brit. a regular milk delivery along a fixed route. **2** a series of visits to universities and colleges by recruiting staff from large companies.

**milk run** ● n. a routine, uneventful journey.

**milkshake** ● n. a cold drink made from milk whisked with ice cream and fruit or other flavouring.

**milksop** ● n. a timid and indecisive person.

**milk stout** ● n. a kind of sweet stout made with lactose.

**milk sugar** ● n. another term for **LACTOSE**.

**milk thistle** ● n. **1** a thistle with a solitary purple flower and glossy marbled leaves, used in herbal medicine. [*Silybum marianum*.] **2** another term for **SOWTHISTLE**.

**milk tooth** ● n. any of a set of early, temporary (deciduous) teeth in children or young mammals.

**milk train** ● n. a train that runs very early in the morning to transport milk but also carries passengers.

**milk vetch** ● n. a yellow-flowered leguminous plant, grown in some regions for fodder. [*Astragalus glycyphyllos*.]

**milkweed** ● n. **1** a herbaceous American plant with milky sap. [Genus *Asclepias*.] **2** (also **milkweed butterfly**) another term for **MONARCH** (in sense 2).

**milkwort** ● n. a small plant with blue, pink, or white flowers, formerly supposed to increase a mother's milk production. [*Polygala vulgaris* and related species.]

**milky** ● adj. (**-ier**, **-iest**) **1** containing milk. **2** resembling milk; of a soft white colour or clouded appearance.
– DERIVATIVES **milkily** adv. **milkiness** n.

**Milky Way** ● n. a faint band of light crossing the night sky, made up of vast numbers of stars forming the bulk of the galaxy of which our solar system is a part.

**mill**[1] ● n. **1** a building equipped with machinery for grinding grain into flour. ➤a piece of machinery for grinding grain. **2** a domestic device for grinding a solid substance to powder or pulp: *a pepper mill.* **3** a building fitted with machinery for a manufacturing process: *a steel mill.* ➤a piece of manufacturing machinery. ● v. **1** grind in a mill. **2** cut or shape (metal) with a rotating tool. **3** produce regular ribbed markings on the edge of (a coin). **4** (**mill about/around**) (of people or animals) move around in a confused mass. **5** thicken (wool) by fulling it.
– PHRASES **go** (or **put someone**) **through the mill** undergo (or cause someone to undergo) an unpleasant experience.
– DERIVATIVES **millable** adj. **milled** adj.
– ORIGIN OE *mylen*, based on late L. *molinum*, from L. *mola* 'grindstone, mill', from *molere* 'to grind'.

**mill**[2] ● n. N. Amer. a monetary unit used only in calculations, worth one thousandth of a dollar.
– ORIGIN C18: from L. *millesimum* 'thousandth part'; cf. **CENT**.

**millboard** ● n. stiff grey pasteboard, used for the covers of books.

**mill dam** ● n. a dam built across a stream to raise the level of the water so that it will turn the wheel of a watermill.

**millefeuille** /miːlˈfəːi/ ● n. a rich cake consisting of thin layers of puff pastry filled with jam and cream.
– ORIGIN Fr., lit. 'thousand-leaf'.

**millefiori** /ˌmiːlɪfɪˈɔːri/ ● n. a kind of ornamental glass in which a number of rods of different colours are fused together and cut into sections which form various patterns, typically embedded in clear glass.
– ORIGIN C19: from Ital. *millefiore*, lit. 'a thousand flowers'.

**millefleurs** /ˈmiːlflәː/ ● n. a pattern of flowers and leaves used especially in tapestry and on porcelain.
– ORIGIN C19: Fr., lit. 'a thousand flowers'.

**millenarian** /ˌmɪlɪˈnɛːrɪən/ ● adj. **1** relating to or believing in Christian millenarianism. **2** denoting a religious or political group seeking rapid and radical change. ● n. a person who believes in millenarianism.
– ORIGIN C17: from late L. *millenarius* (see **MILLENARY**) + **-AN**.

**millenarianism** ● n. belief in a future thousand-year age of blessedness, beginning with or culminating in the Second Coming of Christ (central to the teaching of the Adventists, Mormons, and Jehovah's Witnesses).
– DERIVATIVES **millenarianist** n. & adj.

**millenary** /mɪˈlɛnəri, ˈmɪlɪnəri/ ● n. (pl. **-ies**) **1** a period of a thousand years. **2** a thousandth anniversary. ● adj. consisting of a thousand.
– ORIGIN C16: from late L. *millenarius* 'having a thousand'.

**millennialism** ● n. another term for **MILLENARIANISM**.
– DERIVATIVES **millennialist** n. & adj.

**millennium** /mɪˈlɛnɪəm/ ● n. (pl. **millennia** /-nɪə/ or **millenniums**) **1** a period of a thousand years, especially when calculated from the traditional date of the birth of Christ. ➤(**the millennium**) Christian Theology the prophesied thousand-year reign of Christ at the end of the age (Rev. 20:1–5). ➤a utopian period of peace, justice, and prosperity. **2** an anniversary of a thousand years. **3** (**the millennium**) the point at which one period of a thousand years ends and another begins.
– DERIVATIVES **millennial** adj.
– ORIGIN C17: mod. L., from L. *mille* 'thousand', on the pattern of *biennium*.

**USAGE** millennium

The correct spelling is **millennium**, with two **n**s. The spelling with one **n** is a common error (found in just over 10 per cent of citations in the British National Corpus), formed by analogy with other similar words correctly spelled with only one **n**, such as **millenarian** and **millenary**.

**millennium bug** ● n. an inability in older computing software to deal correctly with dates of 1 January 2000 or later.

**millepore** /ˈmɪlɪpɔː/ ● n. Zoology a fire coral.
– ORIGIN C18: from Fr. *millépore* or mod. L. *millepora*, from L. *mille* 'thousand' + *porus* 'pore'.

**miller** ● n. a person who owns or works in a grain mill.

**miller's thumb** ● n. a small freshwater fish with a broad flattened head. [*Cottus gobio*.]

**millesimal** /mɪˈlɛsɪm(ə)l/ ● adj. of or relating to division into thousandths; thousandth. ● n. a thousandth part.
– DERIVATIVES **millesimally** adv.
– ORIGIN C18: from L. *millesimus* (from *mille* 'thousand') + **-AL**.

**millet** ● n. a cereal which bears a large crop of small seeds, used to make flour or alcoholic drinks. [*Panicum miliaceum* and other species.]
– ORIGIN ME: from Fr., dimin. of dial. *mil*, from L. *milium*.

**millhand** ● n. a worker in a mill.

**milli-** ● comb. form a thousand, chiefly denoting a factor of one thousandth: *milligram.*
– ORIGIN from L. *mille* 'thousand'.

**milliammeter** /ˌmɪlɪ'amɪtə/ ● n. an instrument for measuring electric current in milliamperes.

**milliamp** ● n. short for **MILLIAMPERE**.

**milliampere** ● n. one thousandth of an ampere.

**milliard** /'mɪlɪɑːd/ ● n. Brit. one thousand million.
– ORIGIN C18: Fr., from *mille* 'thousand'.

**millibar** ● n. one thousandth of a bar, the cgs unit of atmospheric pressure equivalent to 100 pascals.

**millieme** /ˌmiː(l)'jɛm/ ● n. a monetary unit of Egypt, equal to one thousandth of a pound.
– ORIGIN from Fr. *millième* 'thousandth'.

**milligram** (also **milligramme**) (abbrev.: **mg**) ● n. one thousandth of a gram.

**millilitre** (US **milliliter**) (abbrev.: **ml**) ● n. one thousandth of a litre (0.002 pint).

**millimetre** (US **millimeter**) (abbrev.: **mm**) ● n. one thousandth of a metre (0.039 in.).

**milliner** ● n. a person who makes or sells women's hats.
– DERIVATIVES **millinery** n.
– ORIGIN ME (orig. in the sense 'native of Milan', later 'a vendor of fancy goods from Milan'): from the name of the Ital. city *Milan* + **-ER**[1].

**million** ● cardinal number (pl. **millions** or (with numeral or quantifying word) same) **1** (**a/one million**) the number equivalent to the product of a thousand and a thousand; 1,000,000 or $10^6$. **2** (also **millions**) informal a very large number or amount.
– DERIVATIVES **millionfold** adj. & adv. **millionth** ordinal number.
– ORIGIN ME: from OFr., prob. from Ital. *milione*, from *mille* 'thousand' + the augmentative suffix *-one*.

**millionaire** ● n. (fem. **millionairess**) a person whose assets are worth one million pounds or dollars or more.
– ORIGIN C19: from Fr. *millionnaire*, from *million* (see **MILLION**).

**millipede** /'mɪlɪpiːd/ ● n. an arthropod with an elongated body composed of many segments, most of which bear two pairs of legs. [Class Diplopoda: many species.]
– ORIGIN C17: from L. *millepeda* 'woodlouse', from *mille* 'thousand' + *pes, ped-* 'foot'.

**millisecond** ● n. one thousandth of a second.

**millivolt** ● n. one thousandth of a volt.

**millpond** ● n. the pool created by a mill dam, providing the head of water that powers a watermill.

**mill race** ● n. the channel carrying the swift current of water that drives a mill wheel.

**Mills bomb** ● n. historical an oval hand grenade.
– ORIGIN C20: named after the Engl. engineer Sir William *Mills*.

**millstone** ● n. **1** each of two circular stones used for grinding grain. **2** a burden of responsibility.

**millstone grit** ● n. a coarse sandstone of the British Carboniferous, occurring immediately below the coal measures.

**millstream** ● n. the flowing water that drives a mill wheel.

**mill wheel** ● n. a wheel used to drive a watermill.

**millwright** ● n. a person who designs or builds grain mills or who maintains mill machinery.

**milo** /'mʌɪləʊ/ ● n. sorghum of a drought-resistant variety which is an important cereal in the central US.
– ORIGIN C19: from Sesotho *maili*.

**milometer** /mʌɪ'lɒmɪtə/ (also **mileometer**) ● n. Brit. an instrument on a vehicle for recording the number of miles travelled.

**milord** ● n. historical or humorous used to address or refer to an English nobleman.
– ORIGIN C17: via Fr. from Engl. *my lord*.

**Milquetoast** /'mɪlktəʊst/ ● n. chiefly N. Amer. a person who is timid or submissive.
– ORIGIN 1930s: from the name of a cartoon character, Caspar *Milquetoast*, created by H. T. Webster in 1924.

**milt** ● n. the semen or sperm-filled reproductive gland of a male fish.
– ORIGIN OE *milte* 'spleen', of Gmc origin; perh. rel. to **MELT**.

**Miltonian** /mɪl'təʊnɪən/ ● n. an admirer or follower of the English poet John Milton (1608–74). ● adj. (also **Miltonic**) of or relating to Milton.

**mime** ● n. **1** the expression of action, character, or emotion by gesture and movement and without words, especially as a form of theatrical performance. **2** (in ancient Greece and Rome) a simple farcical drama including mimicry. ● v. **1** use mime to act out (a play or role). **2** pretend to sing or play an instrument as a recording is being played.
– DERIVATIVES **mimer** n.
– ORIGIN C17: from L. *mimus*, from Gk *mimos*.

**mimeograph** ● n. a duplicating machine which produces copies from a stencil, now superseded by the photocopier. ● v. make a copy of (a document) with a mimeograph.
– ORIGIN C19: formed irregularly from Gk *mimeomai* 'I imitate' + **-GRAPH**.

**mimesis** /mɪ'miːsɪs, mʌɪ-/ ● n. **1** imitative representation of the real world in art and literature. **2** the deliberate imitation of the behaviour of one group of people by another as a factor in social change. **3** Zoology mimicry of another animal or plant.
– DERIVATIVES **mimetic** adj. **mimetically** adv.
– ORIGIN C16: from Gk *mimēsis*, from *mimeisthai* 'to imitate'.

**mimic** ● v. (**mimicked**, **mimicking**) imitate in order to entertain or ridicule. ➤(of an animal or plant) take on the appearance of (another animal or plant) in order to deter predators or for camouflage. ➤replicate the effects of. ● n. **1** a person skilled in mimicking. **2** an animal or plant that mimics.
– DERIVATIVES **mimicker** n. **mimicry** n.
– ORIGIN C16: via L. from Gk *mimikos*, from *mimos* 'mime'.

**mimosa** /mɪ'məʊzə, -sə/ ● n. **1** an Australian acacia tree with delicate fern-like leaves and yellow flowers. [*Acacia dealbata*.] **2** a plant of a genus that includes the sensitive plant. [Genus *Mimosa*.] **3** N. Amer. a drink of champagne and orange juice.
– ORIGIN mod. L., appar. from L. *mimus* 'mime' (because the plant seemingly mimics the sensitivity of an animal) + the fem. suffix *-osa*.

**mimsy** ● adj. rather feeble and prim or over-restrained.
– ORIGIN 1871: nonsense word coined by Lewis Carroll; a blend of **MISERABLE** and **FLIMSY**.

**mimulus** /'mɪmjʊləs/ ● n. a plant of a genus which includes the musk plants and the monkey flower. [Genus *Mimulus*.]
– ORIGIN mod. L., appar. a dimin. of L. *mimus* 'mime', perh. with ref. to its mask-like flowers.

**Min** ● n. a dialect of Chinese spoken mainly in Fujian province, Hainan, and Taiwan.
– ORIGIN from Chin.

**min.** ● abbrev. **1** minim (fluid measure). **2** minimum. **3** minute(s).

**Minangkabau** /ˌmiːnaŋkə'baʊ/ ● n. an Indonesian language spoken in Sumatra and elsewhere.
– ORIGIN from Malay and Indonesian.

**minaret** /'mɪnərɛt, ˌmɪnə'rɛt/ ● n. a slender tower, especially that of a mosque, with a balcony from which a muezzin calls Muslims to prayer.
– DERIVATIVES **minareted** adj.
– ORIGIN C17: from Fr., or from Sp. *minarete*, Ital. *minaretto*, via Turk. from Arab. *manār(a)* 'lighthouse, minaret', based on *nār* 'fire or light'.

**minatory** /'mɪnəˌt(ə)ri/ ● adj. formal expressing or conveying a threat.
– ORIGIN C16: from late L. *minatorius*, from *minat-*, *minari* 'threaten'.

**mince** ● v. **1** [often as adj. **minced**] cut up or shred (meat) into very small pieces. **2** walk in an affected manner with short, quick steps and swinging hips. ● n. chiefly Brit. minced meat.
– PHRASES **mince words** (or **one's words**) [usu. with neg.]

voice one's disapproval delicately or gently.
– DERIVATIVES **mincer** n. **mincing** adj. **mincingly** adv.
– ORIGIN ME: from OFr. *mincier*, based on L. *minutia* 'smallness'.

**mincemeat** • n. a mixture of currants, raisins, apples, candied peel, sugar, spices, and suet.
– PHRASES **make mincemeat of** informal defeat decisively.

**mince pie** • n. chiefly Brit. a small pie containing mincemeat, typically eaten at Christmas.

**mind** • n. **1** the faculty of consciousness and thought. **2** the source of a person's thoughts; the intellect. ➤ a person's memory. ➤ a person identified with their intellectual faculties: *he was one of the greatest minds of his time.* **3** a person's attention. ➤ a person's will or determination. • v. **1** be distressed or annoyed by; object to. **2** remember or take care to do something: *mind you look after the children.* ➤ give attention to; watch out for: *mind your head!* **3** (also **mind you**) introducing a qualification to a previous statement: *mind you, he didn't seem bothered.* **4** take care of temporarily. **5** (**be minded**) be inclined to do a particular thing. **6** N. Amer. & Irish be obedient to.
– PHRASES **be in** (or **of**) **two minds** be unable to decide between alternatives. **be of one** (or **a different**) **mind** share the same (or hold a different) opinion. **give someone a piece of one's mind** rebuke someone. **have a** (or **a good** or **half a**) **mind to do something** be inclined to do something. **have someone/thing in mind 1** be thinking of someone or something. **2** intend to do something. **in one's mind's eye** in one's imagination. **mind over matter** the use of will power to overcome physical problems. **mind one's own business** refrain from prying or interfering. **mind one's Ps & Qs** be careful to be polite and avoid giving offence. [said by some to refer to the care a young pupil must pay in differentiating the tailed letters *p* and *q*.] **mind the shop** informal be in charge of something temporarily. **never mind 1** do not or let us not be concerned or distressed. **2** (also **never you mind**) used in refusing to answer a question: *never mind where I'm going.* **3** let alone: *he found it hard to think, never mind talk.* **out of one's mind** having lost control of one's mental faculties. **put one in mind of** remind one of. **put** (or **set**) **one's mind to** direct all one's attention to. **put someone/thing out of one's mind** stop thinking about someone or something. **to my mind** in my opinion.
– ORIGIN OE *gemynd* 'memory, thought', of Gmc origin; rel. to L. *mens* 'mind'.

**mind-bending** • adj. informal influencing or altering one's state of mind.
– DERIVATIVES **mind-bender** n. **mind-bendingly** adv.

**mind-blowing** • adj. informal overwhelmingly impressive.
– DERIVATIVES **mind-blowingly** adv.

**mind-boggling** • adj. informal overwhelming.
– DERIVATIVES **mind-bogglingly** adv.

**minded** • adj. [usu. in combination] inclined to think in a particular way: *liberal-minded scholars.*

**minder** • n. informal a person whose job it is to look after someone or something.

**mindful** • adj. **1** conscious or aware of something. **2** formal inclined or intending to do something.
– DERIVATIVES **mindfully** adv. **mindfulness** n.

**mind game** • n. a series of actions or responses planned for their psychological effect on another.

**mindless** • adj. **1** acting or done without justification and with no concern for the consequences. **2** (**mindless of**) not thinking of or concerned about. **3** (of an activity) simple and repetitive.
– DERIVATIVES **mindlessly** adv. **mindlessness** n.

**mind-numbing** • adj. so extreme or intense as to prevent normal thought.
– DERIVATIVES **mind-numbingly** adv.

**mind-reader** • n. a person who can supposedly discern what another person is thinking.
– DERIVATIVES **mind-reading** n.

**mindset** • n. a habitual way of thinking.

**mindshare** • n. consumer awareness of a product or brand, typically as opposed to market share.

**mind-your-own-business** • n. a creeping Mediterranean plant with masses of tiny leaves, grown as an indoor plant. [*Soleirolia soleirolia.*]

**mine**[1] • possess. pron. referring to a thing or things belonging to or associated with the speaker. • possess. det. archaic (used before a vowel) my.
– ORIGIN OE *mīn*, of Gmc origin; rel. to **ME**[1].

**mine**[2] • n. **1** an excavation in the earth for extracting coal or other minerals. **2** an abundant source of something: *a mine of information.* **3** a type of bomb placed on or in the ground or water, which detonates on contact. **4** historical a subterranean passage tunnelled under the wall of a besieged fortress, in which explosives were placed. • v. **1** obtain from a mine. ➤ excavate for coal or other minerals. **2** lay a mine or mines on or in. ➤ destroy by means of a mine or mines.
– DERIVATIVES **mineable** (also **minable**) adj. **mining** n.
– ORIGIN ME: from OFr. *mine* (n.), *miner* (v.), perh. of Celtic origin.

**minefield** • n. **1** an area planted with explosive mines. **2** a subject or situation presenting unseen hazards.

**minehunter** • n. Brit. a warship used for detecting and destroying explosive mines.
– DERIVATIVES **minehunting** n.

**minelayer** • n. a warship, aircraft, or land vehicle from which explosive mines are laid.
– DERIVATIVES **minelaying** n.

**miner** • n. a person who works in a mine. ➤ used in names of burrowing or tunnelling insects and birds, e.g. **leaf miner**.

**mineral** • n. **1** a solid inorganic substance of natural occurrence. ➤ a substance obtained by mining. ➤ an inorganic substance needed by the human body for good health. **2** (**minerals**) Brit. effervescent soft drinks. • adj. of or denoting a mineral.
– ORIGIN ME: from med. L. *minerale*, neut. (used as n.) of *mineralis*, from *minera* 'ore'.

**mineralize** (also **-ise**) • v. **1** convert (organic matter) wholly or partly into a mineral or inorganic material or structure. **2** impregnate (water or another liquid) with a mineral substance.
– DERIVATIVES **mineralization** n.

**mineralocorticoid** /ˌmɪn(ə)rələ(ʊ)ˈkɔːtɪkɔɪd/ • n. Biochemistry a corticosteroid which is involved with maintaining the salt balance in the body, such as aldosterone.

**mineralogy** • n. the scientific study of minerals.
– DERIVATIVES **mineralogical** adj. **mineralogically** adv. **mineralogist** n.

**mineral oil** • n. petroleum, or a distillation product of petroleum.

**mineral spirits** • n. North American term for **WHITE SPIRIT**.

**mineral water** • n. water having some dissolved salts naturally present.

**mineral wool** • n. a substance resembling matted wool and made from inorganic mineral material, used chiefly for packing or insulation.

**Minervois** /ˌmɪnɛːˈvwʌ, French minɛʀvwa/ • n. a wine produced in the district of Minervois in southern France.

**mineshaft** • n. a deep, narrow shaft that gives access to a mine.

**minestrone** /ˌmɪnɪˈstrəʊni/ • n. a soup containing vegetables and pasta.
– ORIGIN from Ital.

**minesweeper** • n. a warship equipped for detecting and removing or destroying tethered explosive mines.
– DERIVATIVES **minesweeping** n.

**Ming** • n. **1** the dynasty ruling China from 1368 to 1644. **2** [as modifier] denoting Chinese porcelain made during the Ming dynasty, characterized by elaborate designs and vivid colours.
– ORIGIN Chin., lit. 'clear or bright'.

**minge** /mɪn(d)ʒ/ • n. Brit. vulgar slang a woman's pubic hair or genitals.
– ORIGIN C19: of unknown origin.

**minger** /ˈmɪŋə/ • n. Brit. informal, derogatory an unattractive or unpleasant person or thing.

**minging** /ˈmɪŋɪŋ/ ● **adj.** Brit. informal foul-smelling. ➤ very bad or unpleasant.
– ORIGIN C20: perh. from Scots dial. *ming* 'excrement'.

**mingle** ● **v. 1** mix or cause to mix together. **2** move around and engage with others at a social function.
– ORIGIN ME: frequentative of obs. *meng* 'mix or blend' (rel. to **AMONG**), perh. influenced by MDu. *mengelen*.

**mingy** /ˈmɪn(d)ʒi/ ● **adj.** (**-ier**, **-iest**) informal mean; ungenerous.
– DERIVATIVES **mingily** adv.
– ORIGIN C20: perh. a blend of **MEAN²** and **STINGY**.

**mini** ● **adj.** denoting a miniature version of something. ● **n.** (pl. **minis**) **1** a very short skirt or dress. **2** short for **MINICOMPUTER**.

**mini-** ● **comb. form** very small or minor of its kind; miniature: *minibus*.
– ORIGIN from **MINIATURE**, reinforced by **MINIMUM**.

**miniature** ● **adj.** of a much smaller size than normal. ● **n. 1** a thing that is much smaller than normal. ➤ a plant or animal that is a smaller version of an existing variety or breed. ➤ a very small and minutely detailed painting, especially a portrait. **2** a picture or decorated letter in an illuminated manuscript.
– DERIVATIVES **miniaturist** n. **miniaturization** (also **-isation**) n. **miniaturize** (also **-ise**) v.
– ORIGIN C16: from Ital. *miniatura*, via med. L. from L. *miniare* 'rubricate', from *minium* 'red lead, vermilion' (used to mark particular words in manuscripts).

**minibar** ● **n.** a refrigerator in a hotel room containing a selection of drinks.

**minibus** ● **n.** a small bus for about ten to fifteen passengers.

**minicab** ● **n.** Brit. a car that is used as a taxi but which must be ordered in advance.

**minicam** ● **n.** a hand-held video camera.

**minicomputer** ● **n.** a computer of medium power, more than a microcomputer but less than a mainframe.

**minidisc** ● **n.** a disc having a format similar to a small CD but able to record sound or data as well as play it back.

**minidress** ● **n.** a very short dress.

**minigolf** ● **n.** an informal version of golf played on a series of short obstacle courses.

**minikin** ● **adj.** chiefly archaic small; insignificant.

**minim** ● **n. 1** Music, chiefly Brit. a note having the time value of two crotchets or half a semibreve, represented by a ring with a stem. **2** a small ancient Roman coin, typically of bronze. **3** one sixtieth of a fluid drachm, about one drop of liquid. **4** (in calligraphy) a short vertical stroke, as in the letters *i*, *m*, *n*, *u*.
– ORIGIN ME: from L. *minima*, from *minimus* 'smallest'.

**minima** plural form of **MINIMUM**.

**minimal** ● **adj. 1** of a minimum amount, quantity, or degree. **2** Art characterized by the use of simple or primary forms or structures. ➤ Music characterized by the repetition and gradual alteration of short phrases.
– DERIVATIVES **minimally** adv.
– ORIGIN C17: from L. *minimus* 'smallest' + **-AL**.

**minimalist** ● **n. 1** a person who practises or supports the theories of minimal art or music. **2** a person advocating moderate reform in politics. ● **adj. 1** relating to minimal art or music. **2** advocating moderate political reform.
– DERIVATIVES **minimalism** n.
– ORIGIN C20: first used with ref. to the Russ. Mensheviks; usage in art and music dates from the 1960s.

**minimart** ● **n.** N. Amer. a convenience store.

**minimax** ● **n.** Mathematics the lowest of a set of maximum values. ➤ [as modifier] (in game theory) denoting a strategy that minimizes the greatest possible risk.
– ORIGIN 1940s: blend of **MINIMUM** and **MAXIMUM**.

**minimize** (also **-ise**) ● **v. 1** reduce to the smallest possible amount or degree. **2** represent or estimate at less than the true value or importance.
– DERIVATIVES **minimization** n. **minimizer** n.

**minimum** ● **n.** (pl. **minima** or **minimums**) the least or smallest amount, extent, or intensity possible or recorded. ● **adj.** smallest or lowest in amount, extent, or intensity.
– ORIGIN C17: from L., neut. of *minimus* 'least'.

**minimum wage** ● **n.** the lowest wage permitted by law or by agreement.

**mining bee** ● **n.** a solitary bee that builds long underground tunnels containing nest chambers. [*Andrena* and other genera.]

**minion** /ˈmɪnjən/ ● **n.** a follower or underling of a powerful person, especially a servile or unimportant one.
– ORIGIN C15: from Fr. *mignon*, *mignonne*.

**mini-pill** ● **n.** a contraceptive pill containing a progestogen and not oestrogen.

**mini rugby** ● **n.** a simplified version of rugby with only nine players in a team.

**miniseries** ● **n.** (pl. same) a television drama shown in a small number of episodes.

**miniskirt** ● **n.** a very short skirt.

**minister** ● **n. 1** a head of a government department. **2** a diplomatic agent, usually ranking below an ambassador, representing a state or sovereign in a foreign country. **3** a member of the clergy, especially in the Presbyterian and Nonconformist Churches. **4** (also **minister general**) the superior of some religious orders. **5** archaic a person or thing used to achieve or convey something. ● **v. 1** (**minister to**) attend to the needs of. **2** archaic provide. **3** act as a minister of religion. **4** administer (a sacrament).
– DERIVATIVES **ministerial** adj. **ministerially** adv. **ministership** n.
– ORIGIN ME: from OFr. *ministre* (n.), *ministrer* (v.), from L. *minister* 'servant', from *minus* 'less'.

**Minister of State** ● **n.** (in the UK) a government minister ranking below a Secretary of State.

**Minister of the Crown** ● **n.** (in the UK and Canada) a member of the cabinet.

**Minister without Portfolio** ● **n.** a government minister who has cabinet status, but is not in charge of a specific department of state.

**ministration** ● **n. 1** (usu. **ministrations**) chiefly formal or humorous the provision of assistance or care. **2** the services of a minister of religion or of a religious institution. **3** the action of administering the sacrament.
– DERIVATIVES **ministrant** n.

**ministry** ● **n.** (pl. **-ies**) **1** a government department headed by a minister. **2** a period of government under one Prime Minister. **3** the work, vocation, or office of a minister of religion. ➤ spiritual service to others provided by the Christian Church. **4** the action of ministering to someone.

**minivan** ● **n.** a small van fitted with seats for passengers.

**miniver** /ˈmɪnɪvə/ ● **n.** white fur used for lining or trimming clothes.
– ORIGIN ME: from OFr. *menu vair* 'little vair' (see **VAIR**).

**mink** ● **n.** (pl. same or **minks**) a semiaquatic stoat-like carnivore widely farmed for its fur. [*Mustela vison* (N. America) and *M. lutreola* (Eurasia).] ➤ the thick brown fur of the mink.
– ORIGIN ME (denoting the animal's fur): from Swed.

**minke** /ˈmɪŋkə, -ki/ ● **n.** a small rorqual whale with a dark grey back and white underparts. [*Balaenoptera acutorostrata*.]
– ORIGIN 1930s: prob. from *Meincke*, the name of a Norw. whaler.

**Minn.** ● **abbrev.** Minnesota.

**minneola** /ˌmɪnɪˈəʊlə/ ● **n.** a deep reddish tangelo of a thin-skinned variety.
– ORIGIN C20: named after a town in Florida, US.

**Minnesinger** /ˈmɪnəsɪŋə/ ● **n.** a German lyric poet and singer of the 12th–14th centuries, who performed songs of courtly love.
– ORIGIN C19: from Ger. *Minnesinger* 'love singer'.

**Minnesotan** /ˌmɪnɪˈsəʊt(ə)n/ ● **n.** a native or inhabitant of the US state of Minnesota. ● **adj.** of or relating to Minnesota or Minnesotans.

**minnow** ● **n. 1** a small freshwater fish of the carp family, which typically forms large shoals. [*Phoxinus phoxinus*.] ➤ used in names of similar fishes, e.g. **mudminnow**.

➤ Fishing an artificial lure imitating a minnow. **2** a small or unimportant person or organization.
– ORIGIN ME: prob. rel. to Du. *meun* and Ger. *Münne*, influenced by Anglo-Norman Fr. *menu* 'small, minnow'.

**Minoan** /mɪˈnəʊən/ ● **adj.** relating to or denoting a Bronze Age civilization centred on Crete (*c.*3000–1050 BC). ● **n. 1** an inhabitant of Minoan Crete. **2** the language or scripts associated with the Minoans.
– ORIGIN named after the legendary Cretan king *Minos*, to whom a palace excavated at Knossos was attributed.

**minor** ● **adj. 1** having little importance, seriousness, or significance. **2** Music (of a scale) having intervals of a semitone between the second and third degrees, and (usually) the fifth and sixth, and the seventh and eighth. Contrasted with **MAJOR**. ➤ (of an interval) characteristic of a minor scale and less by a semitone than the equivalent major interval. ➤ [often postpos.] (of a key or mode) based on a minor scale: *Concerto in A minor.* **3** [postpos.] Brit. dated (appended to a surname in public schools) indicating the younger of two brothers: *Smith minor.* **4** Logic (of a term) occurring as the subject of the conclusion of a categorical syllogism. ➤ (of a premise) containing the minor term in a categorical syllogism. ● **n. 1** a person under the age of full legal responsibility. **2** Music a minor key, interval, or scale. **3** Bell-ringing a system of change-ringing using six bells. **4** (**minors**) N. Amer. the minor leagues in baseball or American football. **5** N. Amer. a student's subsidiary subject or course. **6** Logic a minor term or premise. **7** a small drab moth which has purplish caterpillars that feed on grass. [Genus *Oligia*.] ● **v.** (**minor in**) N. Amer. study or qualify in as a subsidiary subject.
– ORIGIN ME (orig. denoting a Franciscan friar, suggested by the Latin name *Fratres Minores*, 'Lesser Brethren', chosen by St Francis): from L., 'smaller, less'.

**minor axis** ● **n.** Geometry the shorter axis of an ellipse that is perpendicular to its major axis.

**Minorcan** /mɪˈnɔːkən/ ● **n.** a native or inhabitant of Minorca. ● **adj.** of or relating to Minorca or Minorcans.

**minor canon** ● **n.** a member of the Christian clergy who assists in the daily services of a cathedral but is not a member of the chapter.

**minor county** ● **n.** Brit. Cricket a county whose team does not take part in the County Championship.

**minority** ● **n.** (pl. **-ies**) **1** the smaller number or part; a number or part representing less than half of the whole. **2** a relatively small group of people, differing from others in race, religion, language, or political persuasion. **3** the state or period of being a minor.
– ORIGIN C15: from Fr. *minorité* or med. L. *minoritas*, from L. *minor* (see **MINOR**).

**minority government** ● **n.** a government in which the governing party has most seats but still less than half the total.

**minor league** ● **n.** N. Amer. a league below the level of the major league in baseball or American football.
– DERIVATIVES **minor-leaguer** n.

**minor orders** ● **pl. n.** chiefly historical the grades of Catholic or Orthodox clergy below the rank of deacon.

**minor piece** ● **n.** Chess a bishop or knight.

**minor planet** ● **n.** an asteroid.

**minor prophet** ● **n.** any of the twelve prophets after whom the shorter prophetic books of the Bible, from Hosea to Malachi, are named.

**minor suit** ● **n.** Bridge diamonds or clubs.

**Minotaur** /ˈmɪnətɔː, ˈmʌɪ-/ ● **n.** Greek Mythology a creature who was half-man and half-bull, kept in a labyrinth on Crete by king Minos and killed by Theseus.
– ORIGIN from OFr., via L. from Gk *Minōtauros*, lit. 'bull of Minos'.

**minotaur beetle** ● **n.** a black dung beetle with three horns on the thorax. [*Typhaeus typhoeus*.]

**minoxidil** /mɪˈnɒksɪdɪl/ ● **n.** Medicine a synthetic drug which is used as a vasodilator in the treatment of hypertension, and also in lotions to promote hair growth.
– ORIGIN 1970s: from *amino* (see **AMINO ACID**) + **OXIDE** + *-dil* (perh. representing **DILATE**).

**minster** ● **n.** a large or important church, typically one of cathedral status in the north of England that was built as part of a monastery.
– ORIGIN OE *mynster*, via eccles. L. from Gk *monastērion* (see **MONASTERY**).

**minstrel** ● **n.** a medieval singer or musician.
– ORIGIN ME: from OFr. *menestral* 'entertainer, servant', via Provençal from late L. *ministerialis*, from L. *minister* (see **MINISTER**).

**minstrelsy** ● **n.** the practice of performing as a minstrel.

**mint**[1] ● **n. 1** an aromatic plant with two-lipped, typically lilac flowers, several kinds of which are used as culinary herbs. [Genus *Mentha*: several species.] ➤ the flavour of mint, especially peppermint. **2** a peppermint sweet.
– DERIVATIVES **minted** adj. **minty** adj. (**-ier, -iest**).
– ORIGIN OE *minte*, of W. Gmc origin; ult. via L. from Gk *minthē*.

**mint**[2] ● **n. 1** a place where money is coined. **2** informal a large sum of money: *it cost a mint.* ● **adj.** in pristine condition; as new. ● **v. 1** make (a coin) by stamping metal. **2** [usu. as adj. **minted**] produce for the first time: *newly minted technology.*
– DERIVATIVES **mintage** n. **minter** n.
– ORIGIN OE *mynet* 'coin', of W. Gmc origin; from L. *moneta* 'money'.

**mint julep** ● **n.** a long drink consisting of bourbon, crushed ice, sugar, and fresh mint.

**Minton** ● **n.** pottery made at Stoke-on-Trent by Thomas Minton (1766–1836) or his factory.

**mint sauce** ● **n.** chopped spearmint in vinegar and sugar, traditionally eaten with lamb.

**minuend** /ˈmɪnjʊɛnd/ ● **n.** Mathematics a quantity or number from which another is to be subtracted.
– ORIGIN C18: from L. *minuendus*, gerundive of *minuere* 'diminish'.

**minuet** ● **n. 1** a stately ballroom dance in triple time, popular in the 18th century. **2** a piece of music in triple time in the style of such a dance, typically as a movement in a suite, sonata, or symphony. ● **v.** (**minueted, minueting**) dance a minuet.
– ORIGIN C17: from Fr. *menuet*, 'fine, delicate', dimin. (used as n.) of *menu* 'small'.

**minus** ● **prep. 1** with the subtraction of. **2** (of temperature) falling below zero by: *minus 40 degrees centigrade.* **3** informal lacking: *he was minus a finger.* ● **adj. 1** (before a number) below zero; negative. **2** (after a grade) rather worse than: *C minus.* **3** having a negative electric charge. ● **n. 1** short for **MINUS SIGN**. **2** informal a disadvantage.
– ORIGIN C15: from L., neut. of *minor* 'less'.

**minuscule** /ˈmɪnəskjuːl/ ● **adj. 1** extremely tiny. **2** of or in lower-case letters, as distinct from capitals or uncials. **3** of or in a small cursive script of the Roman alphabet, with ascenders and descenders, developed in the 7th century AD. ● **n. 1** minuscule script. **2** a small or lower-case letter.
– DERIVATIVES **minuscular** /mɪˈnʌskjʊlə/ adj.
– ORIGIN C18: from Fr., from L. *minuscula* (*littera*) 'somewhat smaller (letter)'.

**USAGE minuscule**

The correct spelling is **minuscule** rather than **miniscule**.

**minus sign** ● **n.** the symbol –, indicating subtraction or a negative value.

**minute**[1] /ˈmɪnɪt/ ● **n. 1** a period of time equal to sixty seconds or a sixtieth of an hour. **2** informal a very short time. **3** (also **arc minute** or **minute of arc**) a sixtieth of a degree of angular measurement. (Symbol: ′)
– PHRASES **at the minute** Brit. informal at the present time. **up to the minute** incorporating the very latest information or developments.
– ORIGIN ME: via OFr. from late L. *minuta*, fem. (used as n.) of *minutus* 'made small'; the senses 'period of sixty seconds' and 'sixtieth of a degree' derive from med. L. *pars minuta prima* 'first minute part'.

**minute**[2] /mʌɪˈnjuːt/ ● **adj.** (**-est**) **1** extremely small. **2** precise and meticulous: *a minute examination.*
– DERIVATIVES **minutely** adv. **minuteness** n.
– ORIGIN ME (in the sense 'lesser', with ref. to a tithe or tax): from L. *minutus* 'lessened', past part. of *minuere.*

**minute**[3] /ˈmɪnɪt/ ● **n.** **1** (**minutes**) a summarized record of the points discussed at a meeting. **2** an official memorandum. ● **v.** **1** record or note (the points discussed at a meeting). **2** send (someone) a minute.
– ORIGIN ME: from Fr. *minute*, from the notion of a rough copy in 'small writing' (L. *scriptura minuta*).

**minute gun** ● **n.** a gun fired at intervals of a minute, especially at a funeral.

**minuteman** /ˈmɪnɪtman/ ● **n.** (pl. **-men**) historical a member of a class of militiamen of the American revolutionary period who volunteered to be ready for service at a minute's notice.

**minute steak** ● **n.** a thin slice of steak cooked very quickly.

**minutiae** /mɪˈnjuːʃɪiː, mʌɪ-, -ʃɪʌɪ/ (also **minutia** /-ʃɪə/) ● **pl. n.** the small or precise details of something.
– ORIGIN C18: L., lit. 'trifles', from *minutia* 'smallness', from *minutus* (see **MINUTE**[2]).

**minx** ● **n.** humorous or derogatory an impudent, cunning, or boldly flirtatious girl or young woman.
– DERIVATIVES **minxish** adj.
– ORIGIN C16 (denoting a pet dog): of unknown origin.

**minyan** /ˈmɪnjən/ ● **n.** (pl. **minyanim** /ˈmɪnjənɪm/) a quorum of ten men over the age of 13 required for traditional Jewish public worship.
– ORIGIN C18: from Heb. *minyān*, lit. 'reckoning'.

**Miocene** /ˈmʌɪə(ʊ)siːn/ ● **adj.** Geology relating to or denoting the fourth epoch of the Tertiary period (between the Oligocene and Pliocene epochs, 23.3 to 5.2 million years ago), a time when the first apes appeared.
– ORIGIN C19: formed irregularly from Gk *meiōn* 'less' + *kainos* 'new'.

**miosis** /mʌɪˈəʊsɪs/ (also **myosis**) ● **n.** excessive constriction of the pupil of the eye.
– DERIVATIVES **miotic** adj.
– ORIGIN C19: from Gk *muein* 'shut the eyes' + **-OSIS**.

**MIPS** ● **n.** a unit of computing speed equivalent to a million instructions per second.
– ORIGIN 1970s: acronym.

**mirabelle** /ˌmɪrəˈbɛl/ ● **n.** **1** a sweet yellow plum-like fruit that is a variety of the greengage. ➤ the tree that bears such fruit. **2** a liqueur distilled from mirabelles.
– ORIGIN C18: from Fr.

**mirabile dictu** /mɪˌrɑːbɪleɪ ˈdɪktuː/ ● **adv.** wonderful to relate.
– ORIGIN from L.

**miracidium** /ˌmʌɪrəˈsɪdɪəm/ ● **n.** (pl. **miracidia**) Zoology a free-swimming ciliated larval stage in which a parasitic fluke passes from the egg to its first host, typically a snail.
– ORIGIN C19: from Gk *meirakidion*, dimin. of *meirakion* 'boy, stripling'.

**miracle** ● **n.** **1** an extraordinary and welcome event that is not explicable by natural or scientific laws, attributed to a divine agency. ➤ a remarkable and very welcome occurrence. **2** an amazing product or achievement, or an outstanding example of something: *a miracle of design.*
– ORIGIN ME: via OFr. from L. *miraculum* 'object of wonder', from *mirari* 'to wonder', from *mirus* 'wonderful'.

**miracle play** ● **n.** a mystery play.

**miraculous** ● **adj.** having the character of a miracle.
– DERIVATIVES **miraculously** adv. **miraculousness** n.

**mirador** /ˌmɪrəˈdɔː, ˈmɪrədɔː/ ● **n.** a turret or tower attached to a building and providing an extensive view.
– ORIGIN C17: from Sp., from *mirar* 'to look'.

**mirage** /ˈmɪrɑːʒ, mɪˈrɑːʒ/ ● **n.** an optical illusion caused by atmospheric conditions, especially the appearance of a sheet of water in a desert or on a hot road caused by the refraction of light from the sky by heated air.
– ORIGIN C19: from Fr., from *se mirer* 'be reflected', from L. *mirare* 'look at'.

**MIRAS** /ˈmʌɪrəs/ ● **abbrev.** (in the UK) mortgage interest relief at source.

**mirch** /mɪətʃ/ ● **n.** Indian term for **CHILLI** or **CHILLI POWDER**.

**mire** ● **n.** **1** a stretch of swampy or boggy ground. ➤ soft mud or dirt. ➤ Ecology a wetland area or ecosystem based on peat. **2** a state of difficulty from which it is hard to extricate oneself. ● **v.** **1** cause to become stuck in mud. ➤ cover or spatter with mud. **2** beset with difficulties.
– ORIGIN ME: from ON *mýrr*, of Gmc origin; rel. to **MOSS**.

**mirepoix** /ˈmɪəˌpwɑː/ ● **n.** a mixture of sautéed chopped vegetables used in various sauces.
– ORIGIN Fr., named after the C18 Fr. general Duc de *Mirepoix*.

**mirid** /ˈmɪrɪd, ˈmʌɪərɪd/ ● **n.** an active plant bug of a large family (Miridae) that includes numerous plant pests.
– ORIGIN 1940s: from mod. L. *Miridae*, from *mirus* 'wonderful'.

**mirin** /ˈmɪrɪn/ ● **n.** a rice wine used as a flavouring in Japanese cookery.
– ORIGIN from Japanese.

**mirk** ● **n. & adj.** archaic spelling of **MURK**.

**mirky** ● **adj.** archaic spelling of **MURKY**.

**mirliton** /ˈməːlɪtɒn/ ● **n.** **1** a musical instrument with a nasal tone produced by a vibrating membrane, resembling a kazoo. **2** chiefly US another term for **CHAYOTE** (in sense 1).
– ORIGIN C19: from Fr., 'reed pipe', of imitative origin.

**miro** /ˈmɪərəʊ/ ● **n.** (pl. **-os**) an evergreen coniferous New Zealand tree which yields useful wood. [*Prumnopitys ferruginea*.]
– ORIGIN C19: from Maori.

**mirror** ● **n.** **1** a surface, typically of glass coated with a metal amalgam, which reflects a clear image. **2** something regarded as accurately representing something else. **3** (also **mirror site**) Computing a site on a network which stores the contents copied from another site. ● **v.** **1** show a reflection of. **2** correspond to. **3** Computing copy the contents of (a network site) and store at another site. ➤ store copies of data in (two or more hard disks).
– DERIVATIVES **mirrored** adj.
– ORIGIN ME: from OFr. *mirour*, based on L. *mirare* 'look at'.

**mirrorball** ● **n.** a revolving ball covered with small mirrored facets, used to provide lighting effects at discos or dances.

**mirror carp** ● **n.** a common carp of an ornamental variety that has a row of large shiny plate-like scales along each side.

**mirror finish** ● **n.** a smooth reflective finish.

**mirror image** ● **n.** an identical image, but with the structure reversed, as in a mirror.

**mirror symmetry** ● **n.** symmetry about a plane, like that between an object and its reflection.

**mirror writing** ● **n.** reversed writing resembling ordinary writing reflected in a mirror.

**mirth** ● **n.** amusement; laughter.
– DERIVATIVES **mirthful** adj. **mirthfully** adv. **mirthless** adj. **mirthlessly** adv. **mirthlessness** n.
– ORIGIN OE *myrgth*, of Gmc origin; rel. to **MERRY**.

**MIRV** /məːv/ ● **n.** an intercontinental nuclear missile with several independent warheads.
– ORIGIN 1960s: acronym from *Multiple Independently targeted Re-entry Vehicle.*

**miry** /ˈmʌɪri/ ● **adj.** very muddy or boggy.

**MIS** ● **abbrev.** Computing management information systems.

**mis-**[1] ● **prefix** (added to verbs and their derivatives) wrongly: *misapply.* ➤ badly: *mismanage.* ➤ unsuitably: *misname.*
– ORIGIN OE, of Gmc origin.

**mis-**[2] ● **prefix** occurring in a few words adopted from French expressing a sense with negative force: *misadventure.*
– ORIGIN from OFr. *mes-* (based on L. *minus*), assimilated to **MIS-**[1].

**misadventure** ● **n.** **1** (also **death by misadventure**) Law death caused accidentally while performing a legal act without negligence or intent to harm. **2** a mishap.

**misaligned** ● **adj.** incorrectly aligned.
– DERIVATIVES **misalignment** n.

**misalliance** ● **n.** an unsuitable or unhappy alliance or marriage.

**misandry** /mɪˈsandri/ ● **n.** hatred of men.

– ORIGIN 1940s: from Gk *miso-* 'hating' + *aner, andr-* 'man', on the pattern of *misogyny*.

**misanthrope** /ˈmɪz(ə)nθrəʊp, mɪs-/ (also **misanthropist** /mɪˈzanθrəpɪst, mɪˈsan-/) ● n. a person who dislikes humankind.
– DERIVATIVES **misanthropic** adj. **misanthropical** adj. **misanthropically** adv. **misanthropy** n.
– ORIGIN C16: from Gk *misanthrōpos*, from *misein* 'to hate' + *anthrōpos* 'man'.

**misapply** ● v. (**-ies**, **-ied**) use for the wrong purpose or in the wrong way.
– DERIVATIVES **misapplication** n.

**misapprehension** ● n. a mistaken belief.
– DERIVATIVES **misapprehensive** adj.

**misappropriate** ● v. dishonestly or unfairly take for one's own use.
– DERIVATIVES **misappropriation** n.

**misbegotten** ● adj. **1** badly conceived, designed, or planned. ➤contemptible. **2** archaic (of a child) illegitimate.

**misbehave** ● v. behave badly.
– DERIVATIVES **misbehaviour** n.

**misbelief** ● n. **1** a wrong or false belief or opinion. **2** less common term for **DISBELIEF**.
– DERIVATIVES **misbeliever** n.

**misc.** ● abbrev. miscellaneous.

**miscalculate** ● v. calculate or assess wrongly.
– DERIVATIVES **miscalculation** n.

**miscall** ● v. **1** call by a wrong or inappropriate name. **2** archaic or dialect insult verbally.

**miscarriage** ● n. the spontaneous or unplanned expulsion of a fetus from the womb before it is able to survive independently.

**miscarriage of justice** ● n. a failure of a court or judicial system to attain the ends of justice.

**miscarry** ● v. (**-ies**, **-ied**) **1** have a miscarriage. **2** (of a plan) fail. **3** dated (of a letter) fail to reach its destination.

**miscast** ● v. (past and past part. **miscast**) (usu. **be miscast**) allot an unsuitable role to (an actor).

**miscegenation** /ˌmɪsɪdʒɪˈneɪʃ(ə)n/ ● n. the interbreeding of people of different races.
– ORIGIN C19: formed irregularly from L. *miscere* 'to mix' + *genus* 'race' + **-ATION**.

**miscellanea** /ˌmɪsəˈleɪnɪə/ ● pl. n. miscellaneous items collected together.
– ORIGIN C16: from L., neut. pl. of *miscellaneus* (see **MISCELLANEOUS**).

**miscellaneous** /ˌmɪsəˈleɪnɪəs/ ● adj. of various types. ➤composed of members or elements of different kinds.
– DERIVATIVES **miscellaneously** adv. **miscellaneousness** n.
– ORIGIN C17: from L. *miscellaneus* (from *miscellus* 'mixed', from *miscere* 'to mix') + **-OUS**.

**miscellany** /mɪˈsɛləni/ ● n. (pl. **-ies**) a mixture. ➤a collection of pieces of writing by different authors.
– ORIGIN C16: from Fr. *miscellanées* (fem. pl.), from L. *miscellanea* (see **MISCELLANEA**).

**mischance** ● n. bad luck. ➤an unlucky occurrence.

**mischief** ● n. **1** playful misbehaviour or troublemaking. **2** harm or injury caused by someone or something. ➤archaic a person responsible for this. **3** Law a wrong or hardship which it is the object of a statute to remove or for which the common law affords a remedy.
– PHRASES **do someone a mischief** informal injure someone.
– ORIGIN ME: from OFr. *meschief*, from *meschever* 'come to an unfortunate end'.

**mischievous** ● adj. **1** causing or disposed to mischief. **2** intended to cause harm or trouble.
– DERIVATIVES **mischievously** adv. **mischievousness** n.
– ORIGIN ME (orig. 'unfortunate or calamitous', later 'having harmful effects'): from Anglo-Norman Fr. *meschevous*, from OFr. *meschever* (see **MISCHIEF**).

**misch metal** /mɪʃ/ ● n. an alloy of cerium, lanthanum, and other rare-earth metals, used as an additive in various alloys.
– ORIGIN 1920s: from Ger. *Mischmetall*, from *mischen* 'to mix' + *Metall* 'metal'.

**miscible** /ˈmɪsɪb(ə)l/ ● adj. (of liquids) forming a homogeneous mixture when added together.
– DERIVATIVES **miscibility** n.
– ORIGIN C16: from med. L. *miscibilis*, from L. *miscere* 'to mix'.

**miscommunication** ● n. failure to communicate adequately.

**misconceive** ● v. **1** fail to understand correctly. **2** (usu. **be misconceived**) judge or plan badly.
– DERIVATIVES **misconceiver** n.

**misconception** ● n. a false or mistaken view or opinion.

**misconduct** ● n. **1** unacceptable or improper behaviour. **2** mismanagement. ● v. **1** (**misconduct oneself**) behave in an improper manner. **2** mismanage.

**misconstrue** ● v. (**misconstrues**, **misconstrued**, **misconstruing**) interpret wrongly.
– DERIVATIVES **misconstruction** n.

**miscount** ● v. count incorrectly. ● n. an incorrect count.

**miscreant** /ˈmɪskrɪənt/ ● n. **1** a person who behaves badly or unlawfully. **2** archaic a heretic. ● adj. **1** behaving badly or unlawfully. **2** archaic heretical.
– ORIGIN ME (as adj. meaning 'disbelieving'): from OFr. *mescreant*, pres. part. of *mescreire* 'disbelieve', from *mes-* 'mis-' + *creire* 'believe' (from L. *credere*).

**miscue**[1] ● n. (in billiards and snooker) a failure to cue the ball properly. ➤(in other sports) a faulty strike, kick, or catch. ● v. (**miscues**, **miscued**, **miscueing** or **miscuing**) perform a miscue.

**miscue**[2] ● n. Linguistics a reading error caused by failure to respond correctly to a phonetic or contextual cue.

**misdate** ● v. assign an incorrect date to.

**misdeal** ● v. (past and past part. **misdealt**) deal cards wrongly. ● n. a hand dealt wrongly.

**misdeed** ● n. a wicked or illegal act.

**misdemeanour** (US **misdemeanor**) ● n. a minor wrongdoing. ➤Law a non-indictable offence, regarded in the US (and formerly the UK) as less serious than a felony.

**misdescribe** ● v. describe inaccurately.
– DERIVATIVES **misdescription** n.

**misdiagnose** ● v. diagnose incorrectly.
– DERIVATIVES **misdiagnosis** n.

**misdial** ● v. (**misdialled**, **misdialling**; US **misdialed**, **misdialing**) dial a telephone number incorrectly.

**misdirect** ● v. **1** direct wrongly. **2** (of a judge) instruct (a jury) wrongly.
– DERIVATIVES **misdirection** n.

**misdoing** ● n. a misdeed.

**misdoubt** ● v. chiefly archaic or dialect have doubts about the truth or existence of. ➤be suspicious about.

**miseducate** ● v. educate wrongly.
– DERIVATIVES **miseducation** n.

**mise en place** /ˌmiːz ɒ̃ ˈplas, French miz ɑ̃ plas/ ● n. (in a professional kitchen) the preparation of dishes and ingredients before the beginning of service.
– ORIGIN Fr., lit. 'putting in place'.

**mise en scène** /ˌmiːz ɒ̃ ˈsɛn, French miz ɑ̃ sɛn/ ● n. **1** the arrangement of scenery and stage properties in a play. **2** the setting of an event.
– ORIGIN Fr., lit. 'putting on stage'.

**misemploy** ● v. employ or use wrongly.
– DERIVATIVES **misemployment** n.

**miser** ● n. a person who hoards wealth and spends very little.
– ORIGIN C15: from L., lit. 'wretched'.

**miserable** ● adj. **1** wretchedly unhappy or uncomfortable. ➤causing unhappiness or discomfort. ➤habitually morose. **2** pitiably small or inadequate. ➤contemptible. ➤Austral./NZ & Scottish miserly.
– DERIVATIVES **miserableness** n. **miserably** adv.
– ORIGIN ME: from Fr. *misérable*, from L. *miserabilis* 'pitiable', from *miserari* 'to pity', from *miser* 'wretched'.

**misère** /mɪˈzɛː/ ● n. (in solo whist) a bid by which a

player undertakes to win no tricks.
– ORIGIN C19: Fr., lit. 'poverty or misery'.

**miserere** /ˌmɪzəˈrɪəri, -ˈrɛː-/ ● **n.** **1** a psalm, prayer, or cry for mercy. **2** another term for **MISERICORD** (in sense 1).
– ORIGIN ME: from L., 'have mercy!', imper. of *misereri*, from *miser* 'wretched'.

**misericord** /mɪˈzɛrɪkɔːd/ ● **n.** **1** a ledge projecting from the underside of a hinged seat in a choir stall, giving support to someone standing when the seat is folded up. **2** historical an apartment in a monastery in which some relaxations of discipline were permitted. **3** historical a small dagger for delivering a death stroke to a wounded enemy.
– ORIGIN ME (denoting pity): from OFr. *misericorde*, from L. *misericordia*, from *misericors* 'compassionate', from the stem of *misereri* 'to pity' + *cor, cord-* 'heart'.

**miserly** ● **adj.** **1** of or characteristic of a miser. **2** (of a quantity) pitiably small.
– DERIVATIVES **miserliness** n.

**misery** ● **n.** (pl. **-ies**) wretched unhappiness or discomfort. ➤ a cause of this. ➤ Brit. informal a person who is constantly miserable.
– PHRASES **put someone/thing out of their misery** kill an animal in pain. ➤ informal release someone from suspense or anxiety.
– ORIGIN ME: from OFr. *miserie*, from L. *miseria*, from *miser* 'wretched'.

**misfeasance** /mɪsˈfiːz(ə)ns/ ● **n.** Law a transgression, especially the wrongful exercise of lawful authority.
– ORIGIN C17: from OFr. *mesfaisance*, from *mesfaire*, from *mes-* 'wrongly' + *faire* 'do'; cf. **MALFEASANCE**.

**misfield** ● **v.** (in cricket and rugby) field (a ball) badly. ● **n.** an instance of misfielding.

**misfire** ● **v.** **1** (of a gun) fail to fire properly. ➤ (of an internal-combustion engine) fail to ignite the fuel correctly or at all. **2** fail to produce the intended result. ● **n.** an instance of misfiring.

**misfit** ● **n.** **1** a person whose behaviour or attitude sets them apart from others. **2** something that does not fit or fits badly.

**misfit stream** ● **n.** Geography a stream which is too small to have eroded the valley which it occupies.

**misfortune** ● **n.** bad luck. ➤ an unfortunate event.

**misgive** ● **v.** (past **misgave**; past part. **misgiven**) poetic/literary (of the mind or heart) fill (someone) with doubt, apprehension, or foreboding.

**misgiving** ● **n.** a feeling of doubt or apprehension about something.

**misgovern** ● **v.** govern unfairly or poorly.
– DERIVATIVES **misgovernment** n.

**misguide** ● **v.** rare mislead.
– DERIVATIVES **misguidance** n.

**misguided** ● **adj.** showing faulty judgement or reasoning.
– DERIVATIVES **misguidedly** adv. **misguidedness** n.

**mishandle** ● **v.** handle wrongly or ineffectively.

**mishap** ● **n.** an unlucky accident.

**mishear** ● **v.** (past and past part. **misheard**) hear incorrectly.

**mishit** ● **v.** (**mishitting**; past and past part. **mishit**) hit or kick (a ball) badly. ● **n.** an instance of mishitting.

**mishmash** ● **n.** a confused mixture.
– ORIGIN C15: reduplication of **MASH**.

**Mishnah** /ˈmɪʃnə/ ● **n.** a collection of exegetical material embodying the oral tradition of Jewish law and forming part of the Talmud.
– DERIVATIVES **Mishnaic** /-ˈneɪɪk/ adj.
– ORIGIN from Heb. *mišnāh* '(teaching by) repetition'.

**misidentify** /mɪsʌɪˈdɛntɪfʌɪ/ ● **v.** (**-ies**, **-ied**) identify incorrectly.
– DERIVATIVES **misidentification** /-fɪˈkeɪʃ(ə)n/ n.

**misinform** ● **v.** give false or inaccurate information to.
– DERIVATIVES **misinformation** n.

**misinterpret** ● **v.** (**misinterpreted**, **misinterpreting**) interpret wrongly.
– DERIVATIVES **misinterpretation** n. **misinterpreter** n.

**misjudge** ● **v.** form an incorrect opinion of. ➤ judge wrongly.
– DERIVATIVES **misjudgement** (also **misjudgment**) n.

**miskey** ● **v.** (**-eys**, **-eyed**) key (words or data) wrongly.

**miskick** ● **v.** kick (a ball) badly. ● **n.** an instance of miskicking.

**Miskito** /mɪˈskiːtəʊ/ (also **Mosquito**) ● **n.** (pl. same or **-os**) **1** a member of an American Indian people of the Atlantic coast of Nicaragua and Honduras. **2** the language of this people.
– ORIGIN the name in Miskito.

**mislay** ● **v.** (past and past part. **mislaid**) unintentionally put (an object) where it cannot readily be found.

**mislead** ● **v.** (past and past part. **misled**) cause to have a wrong impression about someone or something.
– DERIVATIVES **misleader** n. **misleading** adj. **misleadingly** adv. **misleadingness** n.

**mislike** ● **v.** & **n.** archaic dislike.

**mismanage** ● **v.** manage badly or wrongly.
– DERIVATIVES **mismanagement** n.

**mismatch** ● **n.** **1** a failure to correspond or match. **2** an unequal sporting contest. ● **v.** [usu. as adj. **mismatched**] match unsuitably or incorrectly.

**mismated** ● **adj.** badly matched or not matching.

**mismeasure** ● **v.** measure or estimate incorrectly.
– DERIVATIVES **mismeasurement** n.

**misname** ● **v.** give a wrong or inappropriate name to.

**misnomer** ● **n.** a wrong or inaccurate name or term. ➤ the wrong use of a name or term.
– ORIGIN ME: from Anglo-Norman Fr., from the OFr. verb *mesnommer*, from *mes-* 'wrongly' + *nommer* 'to name' (based on L. *nomen* 'name').

**miso** /ˈmiːsəʊ/ ● **n.** paste made from fermented soya beans and barley or rice malt, used in Japanese cookery.
– ORIGIN from Japanese.

**misogamy** /mɪˈsɒgəmi, mʌɪ-/ ● **n.** rare hatred of marriage.
– DERIVATIVES **misogamist** n.
– ORIGIN C17: from Gk *misos* 'hatred' + *gamos* 'marriage'.

**misogynist** /mɪˈsɒdʒ(ə)nɪst, mʌɪ-/ ● **n.** a man who hates women.
– DERIVATIVES **misogynistic** adj.

**misogyny** /mɪˈsɒdʒ(ə)ni, mʌɪ-/ ● **n.** hatred of women.
– DERIVATIVES **misogynous** adj.
– ORIGIN C17: from Gk *misos* 'hatred' + *gunē* 'woman'.

**mispickel** /ˈmɪspɪk(ə)l/ ● **n.** another term for **ARSENOPYRITE**.
– ORIGIN C17: from Ger.

**misplace** ● **v.** put in the wrong place.
– DERIVATIVES **misplacement** n.

**misplaced** ● **adj.** incorrectly placed. ➤ unwise or inappropriate.

**misplay** ● **v.** play (a ball or card) wrongly or badly. ● **n.** an instance of misplaying.

**misprint** ● **n.** an error in printed text. ● **v.** print incorrectly.

**misprision**[1] /mɪsˈprɪʒ(ə)n/ (also **misprision of treason** or **felony**) ● **n.** Law, chiefly historical the deliberate concealment of one's knowledge of a crime.
– ORIGIN ME: from OFr. *mesprision* 'error', from *mesprendre*, from *mes-* 'wrongly' + *prendre* 'to take'.

**misprision**[2] /mɪsˈprɪʒ(ə)n/ ● **n.** rare erroneous judgement.
– ORIGIN C16: from **MISPRIZE**, influenced by **MISPRISION**[1].

**misprize** ● **v.** rare undervalue.
– ORIGIN C15: from OFr. *mesprisier*, from *mes-* 'wrongly' + *prisier* 'estimate the value of'.

**mispronounce** ● **v.** pronounce wrongly.
– DERIVATIVES **mispronunciation** n.

**misquote** ● **v.** quote inaccurately. ● **n.** an inaccurate quote.
– DERIVATIVES **misquotation** n.

**misread** ● **v.** (past and past part. **misread**) read or interpret wrongly.

**misreport** ● **v.** give a false or inaccurate report of.

**misrepresent** ● **v.** give a false or misleading account

of.
– DERIVATIVES **misrepresentation** n. **misrepresentative** adj.

**misrule** • n. unfair or inefficient government. ➤ disorder. • v. govern badly.

**Miss.** • abbrev. Mississippi.

**miss**[1] • v. **1** fail to hit, reach, or come into contact with. ➤ be too late to catch. ➤ fail to notice, hear, or understand. ➤ fail to attend, watch, or participate in. ➤ avoid. **2** (usu. **miss something out**) omit. **3** notice the loss or absence of. ➤ feel regret or sadness at the absence of. **4** (of an engine or vehicle) misfire. • n. an instance of missing something.
– PHRASES **give something a miss** Brit. informal decide not to do or have something. **miss the boat** (or **bus**) informal be too slow to take advantage of something. **not miss a trick** informal never fail to take advantage of a situation.
– DERIVATIVES **missable** adj.
– ORIGIN OE *missan*, of Gmc origin.

**miss**[2] • n. **1** (**Miss**) a title prefixed to the name of an unmarried woman or girl. ➤ the title of a beauty queen: *Miss World*. ➤ used to address a female shop assistant, teacher, etc. **2** often derogatory or humorous a girl or young woman, especially one regarded as silly.
– DERIVATIVES **missish** adj.
– ORIGIN C17: abbrev. of MISTRESS.

**miss**[3] • n. informal a miscarriage.

**missal** /ˈmɪs(ə)l/ • n. a book of the texts used in Catholic Mass throughout the year.
– ORIGIN ME: from med. L. *missale*, neut. of eccles. L. *missalis* 'relating to the Mass', from *missa* 'Mass'.

**missel thrush** • n. variant spelling of MISTLE THRUSH.

**misshape** • v. archaic give a bad or ugly shape to. • n. a misshapen sweet or biscuit sold cheaply.

**misshapen** • adj. not having the normal or natural shape.
– DERIVATIVES **misshapenly** adv. **misshapenness** n.

**missile** • n. **1** an object which is forcibly propelled at a target. **2** a weapon that is self-propelled or directed by remote control.
– ORIGIN C17 (as adj. meaning 'suitable for throwing'): from L. *missile*, neut. (used as n.) of *missilis*, from *miss-*, *mittere* 'send'.

**missilery** /ˈmɪsʌɪlri/ • n. **1** the study of missiles. **2** missiles collectively.

**missing** • adj. absent and of unknown whereabouts. ➤ not present when expected or supposed to be. ➤ not yet confirmed as alive, but not known to be dead.

**missing link** • n. a hypothetical fossil form intermediate between two living forms, especially between humans and apes.

**mission** • n. **1** an important assignment, typically involving travel abroad. ➤ [treated as sing. or pl.] a group of people sent on a mission. ➤ an organization or institution involved in a long-term assignment abroad. ➤ a military or scientific expedition. **2** the vocation of a religious organization to spread its faith. ➤ a strongly felt aim or calling.
– ORIGIN C16 (denoting the sending of the Holy Spirit into the world): from L. *missio(n-)*, from *mittere* 'send'.

**missionary** • n. (pl. **-ies**) a person sent on a religious mission. • adj. of or characteristic of a missionary or religious mission.

**missionary position** • n. informal a position for sexual intercourse in which a couple lie face to face with the woman underneath the man.
– ORIGIN said to be so named because early missionaries advocated the position as 'proper' to primitive peoples.

**missioner** • n. **1** a person in charge of a religious mission. **2** a missionary.

**mission statement** • n. a formal summary of the aims and values of an organization.

**missis** /ˈmɪsɪs, -ɪz/ • n. variant spelling of MISSUS.

**Mississippian** • adj. **1** of or relating to the US state of Mississippi. **2** Geology of or denoting the early part of the Carboniferous period in North America. **3** Archaeology of or denoting a settled culture of the south-eastern US, dated to AD 800–1300. • n. a native or inhabitant of Mississippi.

**missive** • n. **1** formal or humorous a letter. **2** Scots Law a document in the form of a letter interchanged by the parties to a contract.
– ORIGIN ME (as adj., orig. in the phr. LETTER MISSIVE): from med. L. *missivus*, from L. *mittere* 'send'.

**Missourian** /mɪˈzʊəriən/ • n. a native or inhabitant of the US state of Missouri. • adj. of or relating to Missouri.

**misspell** • v. (past and past part. **misspelt** or **misspelled**) spell wrongly.

**misspend** • v. (past and past part. **misspent**) [usu. as adj. **misspent**] spend (time or money) foolishly or wastefully.

**misstate** • v. make wrong or inaccurate statements about.
– DERIVATIVES **misstatement** n.

**misstep** • n. **1** a badly judged step. **2** a mistake.

**missus** /ˈmɪsəz/ (also **missis**) • n. informal or humorous a person's wife. ➤ informal a form of address to a woman.

**missy** • n. (pl. **-ies**) used as an affectionate or disparaging form of address to a young girl.

**mist** • n. a cloud of tiny water droplets in the atmosphere at or near the earth's surface, limiting visibility to a lesser extent than fog. ➤ a condensed vapour settling on a surface. ➤ a blurring of the sight, especially caused by tears. • v. cover or become covered with mist.
– ORIGIN OE, of Gmc origin.

**mistake** • n. a thing which is not correct. ➤ an error of judgement. • v. (past **mistook**; past part. **mistaken**) be wrong about. ➤ (**mistake someone/thing for**) wrongly identify someone or something as.
– DERIVATIVES **mistakable** (also **mistakeable**) adj. **mistakably** (also **mistakeably**) adv.
– ORIGIN ME (as v.): from ON *mistaka* 'take in error', prob. influenced in sense by OFr. *mesprendre*.

**mistaken** • adj. wrong. ➤ (especially of a belief) based on a misunderstanding or faulty judgement.
– DERIVATIVES **mistakenly** adv. **mistakenness** n.

**mister** • n. variant form of MR, often used humorously. ➤ informal a form of address to a man.

**mistime** • v. choose an inappropriate moment to do or say.

**mistitle** • v. give the wrong title or name to.

**mistle thrush** /ˈmɪs(ə)l/ (also **missel thrush**) • n. a large thrush with a spotted breast and harsh rattling call, having a fondness for mistletoe berries. [*Turdus viscivorus*.]
– ORIGIN C17: *mistle* from OE *mistel* (see MISTLETOE).

**mistletoe** • n. a leathery-leaved parasitic plant which grows on broadleaf trees and bears white berries in winter. [*Viscum album* (Eurasia), *Phoradendron flavescens* (N. America), and other species.]
– ORIGIN OE *misteltān*, from *mistel* 'mistletoe' (of Gmc origin) + *tān* 'twig'.

**mistook** past of MISTAKE.

**mistral** /ˈmɪstr(ə)l, mɪˈstrɑːl/ • n. a strong, cold north-westerly wind that blows through the Rhône valley and southern France towards the Mediterranean.
– ORIGIN C17: Fr., from Provençal, from L. *magistralis (ventus)*, lit. 'master wind'.

**mistranslate** • v. translate incorrectly.
– DERIVATIVES **mistranslation** n.

**mistreat** • v. treat badly or unfairly.
– DERIVATIVES **mistreatment** n.

**mistress** • n. **1** a woman in a position of authority or control. ➤ chiefly Brit. a female schoolteacher. ➤ the female owner of a dog, cat, etc. ➤ archaic a female head of a household. **2** a woman skilled in a particular subject or activity: *a mistress of the sound bite*. **3** a woman (other than a wife) having a sexual relationship with a married man. ➤ archaic or poetic/literary a woman loved and courted by a man. **4** (**Mistress**) archaic or dialect Mrs.
– ORIGIN ME: from OFr. *maistresse*, from *maistre* 'master'.

**Mistress of the Robes** • n. (in the English royal household) a woman of high rank in charge of the Queen's wardrobe.

**mistrial** ● **n.** a trial rendered invalid through an error in proceedings. ➤US an inconclusive trial.

**mistrust** ● **v.** have no trust in. ● **n.** lack of trust.
– DERIVATIVES **mistrustful** adj. **mistrustfully** adv. **mistrustfulness** n.

**misty** ● **adj.** (**-ier**, **-iest**) full of, covered with, or accompanied by mist. ➤indistinct or dim in outline.
– DERIVATIVES **mistily** adv. **mistiness** n.

**mistype** ● **v.** type incorrectly.

**misunderstand** ● **v.** (past and past part. **misunderstood** /-'stʊd/) fail to understand correctly.

**misunderstanding** ● **n.** a failure to understand something correctly. ➤a disagreement.

**misusage** ● **n.** archaic unjust treatment.

**misuse** ● **v. 1** use wrongly. **2** treat badly or unfairly. ● **n.** the action of misusing something.
– DERIVATIVES **misuser** n.

**MIT** ● **abbrev.** Massachusetts Institute of Technology.

**mitch** ● **v.** informal, chiefly Irish play truant from school.
– ORIGIN C15: appar. from OFr. *muchier* 'hide, lurk'.

**mite**[1] ● **n.** a minute arachnid with four pairs of legs, several kinds of which are parasitic. [Order Acari: many species.]
– ORIGIN OE *mīte*, of Gmc origin.

**mite**[2] ● **n. 1** a small child or animal. **2** a very small amount. ➤historical a small coin, in particular a small Flemish copper coin of very low face value. ● **adv.** (**a mite**) informal a little; slightly.
– ORIGIN ME (denoting a small Flemish copper coin): from MDu. *mīte*; prob. from the same Gmc word as MITE[1].

**miter** ● **n. & v.** US spelling of MITRE.

**mither** /'mʌɪðə/ ● **v.** dialect, chiefly N. English make a fuss. ➤pester or irritate.
– ORIGIN C17: of unknown origin; cf. Welsh *moedrodd* 'to worry, bother'.

**Mithraism** /'mɪθrəˌɪz(ə)m, 'mɪθreɪ-/ ● **n.** the cult of the ancient Persian god Mithras, a god of light, truth, and honour chiefly worshipped in the first three centuries AD.
– DERIVATIVES **Mithraic** /-'θreɪɪk/ adj. **Mithraist** n.

**mitigate** /'mɪtɪgeɪt/ ● **v.** [often as adj. **mitigating**] make less severe, serious, or painful.
– DERIVATIVES **mitigable** adj. **mitigation** n. **mitigator** n. **mitigatory** adj.
– ORIGIN ME: from L. *mitigat-*, *mitigare* 'soften, alleviate'.

**mitochondrion** /ˌmʌɪtə(ʊ)'kɒndrɪən/ ● **n.** (pl. **mitochondria** /-rɪə/) Biology a structure found in large numbers in most cells, in which respiration and energy production occur.
– DERIVATIVES **mitochondrial** adj.
– ORIGIN C20: mod. L., from Gk *mitos* 'thread' + *khondrion* (dimin. of *khondros* 'granule').

**mitogen** /'mʌɪtədʒ(ə)n/ ● **n.** Physiology a substance that induces or stimulates mitosis.
– DERIVATIVES **mitogenic** adj.

**mitosis** /mʌɪ'təʊsɪs/ ● **n.** (pl. **mitoses**) Biology a type of cell division that results in daughter cells each with the same number and kind of chromosomes as the parent nucleus. Compare with MEIOSIS.
– DERIVATIVES **mitotic** adj.
– ORIGIN C19: mod. L., from Gk *mitos* 'thread'.

**mitral** /'mʌɪtr(ə)l/ ● **adj.** Anatomy relating to or denoting the valve between the left atrium and the left ventricle of the heart.
– ORIGIN C17: from mod. L. *mitralis*, from L. *mitra* 'belt or turban' (from the valve's shape).

**mitre** (US **miter**) ● **n. 1** a tall cleft headdress that tapers to a point at front and back, worn by bishops and senior abbots. **2** (also **mitre joint**) a joint made between two pieces of wood or other material at an angle of 90°, such that the line of junction bisects this angle. ➤a diagonal seam of two pieces of fabric that meet at a corner. **3** (also **mitre shell**) a mollusc of warm seas which has a sharply pointed shell. [*Mitra* and other genera.] ● **v.** join by means of a mitre.
– DERIVATIVES **mitred** adj.
– ORIGIN ME: from OFr., via L. from Gk *mitra* 'belt or turban'.

**mitre box** (also **mitre block** or **mitre board**) ● **n.** a guide for a saw when cutting mitre joints.

**mitre wheel** ● **n.** each of a pair of bevelled cogwheels with teeth set at 45° and axes at right angles.

**mitt** ● **n. 1** a mitten. ➤a glove leaving the fingers and thumb-tip exposed. ➤(also **baseball mitt**) Baseball a large fingerless glove worn by the catcher or first baseman. **2** informal a hand.
– ORIGIN C18: abbrev. of MITTEN.

**mitten** ● **n.** a glove with two sections, one for the thumb and the other for all four fingers. ➤(**mittens**) informal boxing gloves.
– DERIVATIVES **mittened** adj.
– ORIGIN ME: from OFr. *mitaine*, perh. from *mite* pet name for a cat (because mittens were often made of fur).

**mitten crab** ● **n.** an olive-green crab with fur-covered pincers, native to Asia. [*Eriocheir sinensis.*]

**mitzvah** /'mɪtsvə/ ● **n.** (pl. **mitzvoth** /-vəʊt/) Judaism **1** a precept or commandment. **2** a good deed done from religious duty.
– ORIGIN C17: from Heb. *miṣwāh* 'commandment'.

**mix** ● **v. 1** combine or be able to be combined to form a whole. ➤make by mixing ingredients. ➤combine (signals or soundtracks) into one to produce a recording. **2** (**mix something up**) spoil the order or arrangement of something. ➤(**mix someone/thing up**) confuse someone or something with another. **3** associate with others socially. **4** (**mix it**) informal be belligerent. ● **n.** a mixture of two or more different people or things. ➤the proportion of different people or things constituting a mixture. ➤a version of a recording mixed in a different way from the original.
– PHRASES **be** (or **get**) **mixed up in** (or **with**) be (or become) involved in or with (dubious or dishonest actions or people). **mix and match** select and combine different but complementary items to form a coordinated set.
– DERIVATIVES **mixable** adj.
– ORIGIN ME: back-form. from MIXED (taken as a past part.).

**mixed** ● **adj.** consisting of different qualities or elements. ➤involving a mixture of races or social classes. ➤of or for members of both sexes.
– ORIGIN ME *mixt*: from OFr. *mixte*, from L. *mixtus*, past part. of *miscere* 'to mix'.

**mixed bag** (also **mixed bunch**) ● **n.** a diverse assortment.

**mixed blessing** ● **n.** a thing with advantages and disadvantages.

**mixed doubles** ● **pl. n.** [treated as sing.] (especially in tennis and badminton) a game involving sides each consisting of a man and a woman.

**mixed economy** ● **n.** an economic system combining private and state enterprise.

**mixed farming** ● **n.** farming of both crops and livestock.

**mixed grill** ● **n.** Brit. a dish of various grilled meats and vegetables.

**mixed marriage** ● **n.** a marriage between people of different races or religions.

**mixed media** ● **n.** the use of a variety of media in entertainment or art. ● **adj.** (**mixed-media**) another term for MULTIMEDIA.

**mixed metaphor** ● **n.** a combination of incompatible metaphors (e.g. *this tower of strength will forge ahead*).

**mixed number** ● **n.** a number consisting of an integer and a proper fraction.

**mixed-up** ● **adj.** informal suffering from psychological or emotional problems.

**mixer** ● **n. 1** a machine or device for mixing things. **2** a person considered in terms of their ability to mix socially: *a good mixer.* **3** a soft drink that can be mixed with alcohol. **4** (in recording and cinematography) a device for merging input signals to produce a combined output. ➤a person who operates this.

**mixer tap** ● **n.** Brit. a tap through which mixed hot and cold water can be drawn by means of separate controls.

**mixing desk** ● n. a console where sound signals are mixed.

**Mixtec** /'mɪstɛk/ ● n. (pl. same or **Mixtecs**) **1** a member of an American Indian people of southern Mexico. **2** the Otomanguean language of this people.
– ORIGIN Sp., from Nahuatl *mixtecah* 'person from a cloudy place'.

**mixture** ● n. a substance made by mixing other substances together. ➤ the process of mixing or being mixed. ➤ (**a mixture of**) a combination of different things in which the components are individually distinct. ➤ the charge of gas or vapour mixed with air admitted to the cylinder of an internal-combustion engine.
– ORIGIN ME: from Fr. *mixture* or L. *mixtura*, from *mixtus* (see MIXED).

**mix-up** ● n. informal a confusion or misunderstanding.

**mizuna** /mɪ'zu:nə/ (also **mizuna greens**) ● n. an oriental rape with leaves that are eaten as a salad vegetable. [*Brassica rapa* var. *nipposinica*.]
– ORIGIN 1990s: from Japanese.

**mizzen** /'mɪz(ə)n/ (also **mizen**) ● n. **1** (also **mizzenmast**) the mast aft of a ship's mainmast. **2** (also **mizzensail**) a sail on a mizzenmast.
– ORIGIN ME: from Ital. *mezzana* 'mizzensail', fem. (used as n.) of *mezzano* 'middle', from L. *medianus* (see MEDIAN).

**mizzle**[1] /'mɪz(ə)l/ chiefly dialect ● n. light rain; drizzle. ● v. (**it mizzles**, **it is mizzling**, etc.) rain lightly.
– DERIVATIVES **mizzly** adj.
– ORIGIN ME (as v.): prob. a frequentative from the base of MIST.

**mizzle**[2] /'mɪz(ə)l/ ● v. Brit. informal, dated vanish.
– ORIGIN C18: of unknown origin.

**Mk** ● abbrev. **1** the German mark. **2** (in biblical references) the Gospel of Mark. **3** (followed by a numeral) mark (of a vehicle or machine).

**mks** ● abbrev. metre-kilogram-second (denoting a system of measurement using these as basic units).

**Mkt** ● abbrev. Market (in place names).

**ml** ● abbrev. **1** mile(s). **2** millilitre(s).

**MLA** ● abbrev. **1** Member of the Legislative Assembly. **2** Modern Language Association (of America).

**MLC** ● abbrev. Member of the Legislative Council.

**MLD** ● abbrev. minimum lethal dose.

**MLF** ● abbrev. multilateral nuclear force.

**MLitt** ● abbrev. Master of Letters.
– ORIGIN from L. *Magister Litterarum*.

**Mlle** ● abbrev. (pl. **Mlles**) Mademoiselle.

**MM** ● abbrev. **1** Maelzel's metronome (an indication of tempo in music). [with ref. to the metronome invented by Johann *Maelzel*.] **2** Messieurs. **3** (in the UK) Military Medal.

**mm** ● abbrev. millimetre(s).

**Mme** ● abbrev. (pl. **Mmes**) Madame.

**m.m.f.** ● abbrev. magnetomotive force.

**MMR** ● abbrev. measles, mumps, and rubella (a vaccination given to children).

**MMus** ● abbrev. Master of Music.

**MN** ● abbrev. **1** (in the UK) Merchant Navy. **2** Minnesota (in official postal use).

**Mn** ● symb. the chemical element manganese.

**MNA** ● abbrev. (in Canada) Member of the National Assembly (of Quebec).

**mnemonic** /nɪ'mɒnɪk/ ● n. a pattern of letters or ideas which aids the memory. ● adj. aiding or designed to aid the memory. ➤ relating to the power of memory.
– DERIVATIVES **mnemonically** adv. **mnemonist** /'ni:mənɪst/ n.
– ORIGIN C18 (as adj.): via med. L. from Gk *mnēmonikos*, from *mnēmōn* 'mindful'.

**mnemonics** ● pl. n. [usu. treated as sing.] the study and development of systems for improving and aiding the memory.

**MO** ● abbrev. **1** Computing (of a disk or disk drive) magneto-optical. **2** Medical Officer. **3** Missouri (in official postal use). **4** modus operandi. **5** money order.

**Mo** ● symb. the chemical element molybdenum.

**mo** ● n. informal, chiefly Brit. a moment.

**mo.** ● abbrev. N. Amer. month.

**-mo** /məʊ/ ● suffix forming nouns denoting a book size by the number of leaves into which a sheet of paper has been folded: *twelvemo*.
– ORIGIN from the final syllable of L. ordinal numbers such as *duodecimo* (masc. ablative sing.).

**moa** /'məʊə/ ● n. a large extinct flightless bird resembling the emu, formerly found in New Zealand. [*Dinornis maximus* and other species.]
– ORIGIN C19: from Maori.

**Moabite** /'məʊəbʌɪt/ ● n. a member of a Semitic people living in Moab to the east of the Dead Sea during biblical times, traditionally descended from Lot.

**moan** ● n. **1** a long, low sound expressing suffering or sexual pleasure. ➤ a low sound made by the wind. **2** informal a trivial complaint. ● v. **1** utter or make a moan. ➤ poetic/literary lament. **2** informal complain or grumble.
– DERIVATIVES **moaner** n. **moanful** adj.
– ORIGIN ME: of unknown origin.

**moat** ● n. a deep, wide defensive ditch surrounding a castle or town, typically filled with water. ● v. [often as adj. **moated**] surround with a moat.
– ORIGIN ME: from OFr. *mote* 'mound'.

**mob** ● n. **1** a disorderly or violent crowd. **2** Brit. informal an associated group of people. ➤ (**the Mob**) N. Amer. the Mafia. ➤ (**the mob**) the ordinary people. **3** Austral./NZ a flock or herd of animals. ● v. (**mobbed**, **mobbing**) crowd round in an unruly and excitable way. ➤ N. Amer. crowd into.
– DERIVATIVES **mobber** n.
– ORIGIN C17: abbrev. of archaic *mobile*, short for L. *mobile vulgus* 'excitable crowd'.

**mob cap** ● n. a large, soft indoor hat covering the hair, worn by women in the 18th and early 19th centuries.
– ORIGIN C18 (orig. in the sense 'prostitute', later 'négligé'): *mob*, var. of obs. *mab* 'slut'.

**mobe** (also **mobey**) ● n. informal a mobile phone.

**mob-handed** ● adv. Brit. informal in considerable numbers.

**mobile** /'məʊbʌɪl/ ● adj. able to move or be moved freely or easily. ➤ (of a shop, library, etc.) accommodated in a vehicle so as to travel around. ➤ able or willing to move between occupations, places of residence, or social classes. ● n. **1** a decorative structure suspended so as to turn freely in the air. **2** a mobile phone.
– PHRASES **upwardly** (or **downwardly**) **mobile** moving to a higher (or lower) social class.
– DERIVATIVES **mobility** n.
– ORIGIN C15 (earlier (ME) as *mobility*): via Fr. from L. *mobilis*, from *movere* 'to move'.

**mobile home** ● n. a large caravan used as permanent living accommodation.

**mobile phone** ● n. a portable telephone using a cellular radio system.

**mobility allowance** ● n. Brit. a state travel benefit for disabled people.

**mobilize** (also **-ise**) ● v. **1** prepare and organize (troops) for active service. ➤ organize (people or resources) for a particular task. **2** make mobile. ➤ make transportable by or as a liquid.
– DERIVATIVES **mobilizable** adj. **mobilization** n. **mobilizer** n.

**Möbius strip** /'mə:bɪəs/ ● n. a surface with one continuous side formed by joining the ends of a rectangle after twisting one end through 180°.
– ORIGIN C20: named after the Ger. mathematician August F. *Möbius*.

**mobocracy** ● n. (pl. **-ies**) rule or domination by the masses.

**mob rule** ● n. political control imposed and enforced by a mob.

**mobster** ● n. informal a gangster.

**moccasin** ● n. **1** a soft leather slipper or shoe, having the sole turned up and sewn to the upper in a gathered seam, originally worn by North American Indians. **2** a venomous American pit viper. [Genus *Agkistrodon*: three species.]
– ORIGIN C17: from Virginia Algonquian *mockasin*.

**mocha** /ˈmɒkə/ ● **n.** **1** a fine-quality coffee. ➤a drink or flavouring made with this, typically with chocolate added. **2** a soft leather made from sheepskin.
– ORIGIN C18: named after *Mocha*, a port on the Red Sea, from where the coffee and leather were first shipped.

**mock** ● **v.** tease scornfully; ridicule. ➤mimic scornfully or contemptuously. ● **adj.** **1** not authentic or real. **2** (of an examination, battle, etc.) undertaken for training or practice. ● **n.** **1** (**mocks**) Brit. informal mock examinations. **2** dated an object of derision.
– DERIVATIVES **mockable** adj. **mocking** adj. **mockingly** adv.
– ORIGIN ME: from OFr. *mocquer* 'deride'.

**mocker** ● **n.** a person who mocks.
– PHRASES **put the mockers on** Brit. informal put an end to. ➤bring bad luck to.

**mockery** ● **n.** (pl. **-ies**) ridicule. ➤an absurd imitation.
– PHRASES **make a mockery of** cause to appear absurd.

**mock-heroic** ● **adj.** imitating the style of heroic literature to satirize a mundane subject. ● **n.** a burlesque imitation of the heroic character or literary style.

**mockingbird** ● **n.** a long-tailed American songbird with greyish plumage, noted for mimicking the calls of other birds. [*Mimus polyglottos* and other species.]

**mock moon** ● **n.** Astronomy a paraselene.

**mockney** ● **n.** Brit. informal an accent and form of speech affected by a middle-class speaker in imitation of cockney or other London speech.

**mock orange** ● **n.** a bushy shrub with strongly orange-scented white flowers. [*Philadelphus coronarius* and related species.]

**mock sun** ● **n.** Astronomy a parhelion.

**mock turtle soup** ● **n.** imitation turtle soup made from a calf's head.

**mockumentary** ● **n.** a television programme or film which takes the form of a serious documentary in order to satirize its subject.

**mock-up** ● **n.** an experimental replica or model of something.

**MOD** ● **abbrev.** (in the UK) Ministry of Defence.

**Mod** ● **n.** a Highland meeting for Gaelic literature and music.
– ORIGIN from Sc. Gaelic *mōd*.

**mod**[1] ● **adj.** informal modern. ● **n.** Brit. (especially in the 1960s) a young person of a group characterized by a stylish appearance and the riding of motor scooters.

**mod**[2] ● **prep.** Mathematics short for MODULO.

**modal** /ˈməʊd(ə)l/ ● **adj.** **1** of or relating to mode or form as opposed to substance. **2** Grammar of or denoting the mood of a verb. ➤relating to a modal verb. **3** Statistics occurring most frequently in a population. **4** Music of or denoting music using melodies or harmonies based on modes other than the ordinary major and minor scales. **5** Logic (of a proposition) in which the predicate is affirmed of the subject with some qualification or condition.
– DERIVATIVES **modally** adv.

**modalism** ● **n.** **1** Theology the doctrine that the persons of the Trinity represent only three modes or aspects of the divine nature. **2** Music the use of modal melodies and harmonies.

**modality** ● **n.** (pl. **-ies**) **1** modal quality. **2** a method or procedure. **3** a form of sensory perception.

**modal verb** ● **n.** Grammar an auxiliary verb expressing necessity or possibility, e.g. *must, shall, will.*

**mod cons** ● **pl. n.** Brit. informal modern conveniences.

**mode** ● **n.** **1** a way in which something occurs or is done. ➤Computing a way of operating a system. ➤Physics any of the kinds or patterns of vibration of an oscillating system. ➤Logic the character of a modal proposition. ➤Logic & Grammar another term for MOOD[2]. **2** a style in clothes, art, etc. **3** Statistics the value that occurs most frequently in a given data set. **4** Music a set of notes forming a scale, from which melodies and harmonies are constructed.
– ORIGIN ME (in the musical and grammatical senses): from L. *modus* 'measure'; cf. MOOD[2].

**model** ● **n.** **1** a three-dimensional representation of a person or thing, typically on a smaller scale. ➤(in sculpture) a figure in clay or wax, to be reproduced in a more durable material. **2** something used as an example. ➤a simplified description, especially a mathematical one, of a system or process, to assist calculations and predictions. ➤a person or thing that is an excellent example of a quality: *she was a model of self-control.* **3** a person employed to display clothes by wearing them. ➤a person employed to pose for an artist, sculptor, etc. **4** a particular version of a product. ➤a garment or a copy of a garment by a well-known designer. ● **v.** (**modelled**, **modelling**; US **modeled**, **modeling**) **1** fashion or shape (a figure) in clay, wax, etc. ➤Art cause to appear three-dimensional. ➤devise a mathematical model of. **2** (**model something on/after**) use as an example for something. **3** display (clothes) by wearing them. ➤work as a model.
– DERIVATIVES **modeller** n. **modelling** n.
– ORIGIN C16: from Fr. *modelle*, from Ital. *modello*, alt. of L. *modulus* (see MODULUS).

**modem** /ˈməʊdɛm/ ● **n.** a device for interconverting digital and analogue signals, especially to enable a computer to be connected to a telephone line. ● **v.** send (data) by modem.
– ORIGIN C20: blend of *modulator* and *demodulator.*

**moderate** ● **adj.** **1** average in amount, intensity, or degree. **2** not radical or excessively right- or left-wing. ● **n.** /ˈmɒd(ə)rət/ a person with moderate views. ● **v.** **1** make or become less extreme, intense, or violent. **2** review (examination papers or results) so as to ensure consistency of marking. **3** (in academic and ecclesiastical contexts) preside over (a deliberative body) or at (a debate). **4** Physics retard (neutrons) with a moderator.
– DERIVATIVES **moderately** adv. **moderatism** n.
– ORIGIN ME: from L. *moderat-*, *moderare* 'reduce, control'; rel. to MODEST.

**moderation** ● **n.** **1** the avoidance of excess or extremes, especially in one's behaviour or political opinions. **2** the process of moderating examination papers or results. ➤(**Moderations**) the first public examination in some faculties for the BA degree at Oxford University. **3** Physics the retardation of neutrons by a moderator.
– PHRASES **in moderation** within reasonable limits.

**moderato** /ˌmɒdəˈrɑːtəʊ/ ● **adv. & adj.** Music at a moderate pace.
– ORIGIN Ital., lit. 'moderate'.

**moderator** ● **n.** **1** an arbitrator or mediator. ➤a presiding officer, especially a chairman of a debate. ➤a Presbyterian minister presiding over an ecclesiastical body. **2** a person who moderates examination papers. **3** Physics a substance used in a nuclear reactor to retard neutrons.
– DERIVATIVES **moderatorship** n.

**modern** ● **adj.** of or relating to the present or recent times. ➤characterized by or using the most up-to-date techniques, equipment, etc. ➤denoting a recent style in art, architecture, etc. marked by a departure from traditional styles and values. ● **n.** a person who advocates a departure from traditional styles or values.
– DERIVATIVES **modernity** n. **modernly** adv. **modernness** n.
– ORIGIN ME: from late L. *modernus*, from L. *modo* 'just now'.

**modern English** ● **n.** English since about 1500.

**modern history** ● **n.** history from the end of the Middle Ages to the present day.

**modernism** ● **n.** modern ideas, methods, or styles. ➤a movement in the arts or religion that aims to break with traditional forms or ideas.
– DERIVATIVES **modernist** n. & adj. **modernistic** adj.

**modernize** (also **-ise**) ● **v.** adapt to modern needs or habits.
– DERIVATIVES **modernization** n. **modernizer** n.

**modern Latin** ● **n.** Latin since 1500, used especially in scientific terminology.

**modest** ● **adj.** **1** unassuming in the estimation of one's abilities. **2** relatively moderate, limited, or small. **3** decent; decorous.
– DERIVATIVES **modestly** adv. **modesty** n.
– ORIGIN C16: from Fr. *modeste*, from L. *modestus* 'keeping due measure', rel. to *modus* 'measure'.

**modicum** /ˈmɒdɪkəm/ ● n. a small quantity of something.
– ORIGIN C15: from L., neut. of *modicus* 'moderate', from *modus* 'measure'.

**modification** ● n. the action of modifying. ➤ a change made.

**modifier** ● n. **1** a person or thing that modifies something. **2** Grammar a word, especially an adjective or noun used attributively, that qualifies the sense of a noun (e.g. *good* and *family* in *a good family house*).

**modify** ● v. (**-ies**, **-ied**) **1** make partial changes to. ➤ Biology transform (a structure) during development or evolution. ➤ Phonetics pronounce (a speech sound) differently from the norm. **2** Grammar qualify the sense of (a noun).
– DERIVATIVES **modifiable** adj. **modificatory** adj.
– ORIGIN ME: from OFr. *modifier*, from L. *modificare*, from *modus* (see **MODE**).

**modillion** /məˈdɪljən/ ● n. Architecture a projecting bracket under the corona of a cornice in the Corinthian and other orders.
– ORIGIN C16: from Fr. *modillon*, from Ital. *modiglione*, based on L. *mutulus* 'mutule'.

**modish** /ˈməʊdɪʃ/ ● adj. fashionable.
– DERIVATIVES **modishly** adv. **modishness** n.

**modiste** /mɒˈdiːst/ ● n. dated a fashionable milliner or dressmaker.
– ORIGIN C19: Fr., from *mode* 'fashion'.

**Mods** ● pl. n. informal the Moderations examination at Oxford University.

**modular** ● adj. **1** employing or involving modules. **2** Mathematics of or relating to a modulus.
– DERIVATIVES **modularity** n.

**modulate** /ˈmɒdjʊleɪt/ ● v. **1** exert a modifying influence on; regulate. **2** vary the strength, tone, or pitch of (one's voice). ➤ alter the amplitude or frequency of (an oscillation or signal) in accordance with the variations of a second signal. **3** Music change from one key to another.
– DERIVATIVES **modulation** n. **modulator** n.
– ORIGIN C16 (earlier (ME) as *modulation*): from L. *modulat-*, *modulari* 'measure, make melody', from *modulus* (see **MODULUS**).

**module** ● n. each of a set of standardized parts or independent units that can be used to construct a more complex structure. ➤ each of a set of independent units of study or training forming part of a course. ➤ an independent self-contained unit of a spacecraft.
– ORIGIN C16: from Fr., or from L. *modulus* (see **MODULUS**).

**modulo** /ˈmɒdjʊləʊ/ ● prep. Mathematics with respect to or using a modulus of a specified number.
– ORIGIN C19: from L., ablative of **MODULUS**.

**modulus** /ˈmɒdjʊləs/ ● n. (pl. **moduli** /-lʌɪ, -liː/) Mathematics **1** another term for **ABSOLUTE VALUE** (in sense 1). ➤ the positive square root of the sum of the squares of the real and imaginary parts of a complex number. **2** a constant factor or ratio, especially one relating a physical effect to the force producing it. **3** a number used as a divisor for considering numbers in sets, numbers being considered congruent when giving the same remainder when divided by it.
– ORIGIN C16: from L., lit. 'measure', dimin. of *modus*.

**modus operandi** /ˌməʊdəs ɒpəˈrandiː, -dʌɪ/ ● n. (pl. **modi operandi** /ˌməʊdi/) a way of doing something. ➤ the way in which something works.
– ORIGIN L., lit. 'way of operating'.

**modus vivendi** /ˌməʊdəs vɪˈvɛndiː, -dʌɪ/ ● n. (pl. **modi vivendi** /ˌməʊdi/) **1** an arrangement allowing conflicting parties to coexist peacefully. **2** a way of living.
– ORIGIN L., lit. 'way of living'.

**Mogadon** /ˈmɒɡədɒn/ ● n. trademark for **NITRAZEPAM**.

**moggie** (also **moggy**) ● n. (pl. **-ies**) Brit. informal a cat.
– ORIGIN C17: var. of *Maggie*, familiar form of the given name *Margaret*.

**Mogul** /ˈməʊɡ(ə)l/ (also **Moghul** or **Mughal**) ● n. **1** a member of the Muslim dynasty of Mongol origin which ruled much of India in the 16th–19th centuries. ➤ (often **the Great Mogul**) the Mogul emperor of Delhi. **2** (**mogul**) informal an important or powerful person.
– ORIGIN from Pers. *muġul* 'Mongol'.

**mogul** /ˈməʊɡ(ə)l/ ● n. a bump on a ski slope formed by skiers turning.
– ORIGIN 1960s: prob. from Ger. dial. *Mugel, Mugl.*

**MOH** ● abbrev. **1** Ministry of Health. **2** Medical Officer of Health (chief health executive of a local authority).

**mohair** ● n. the hair of the angora goat. ➤ a yarn or fabric made from this.
– ORIGIN C16: from Arab. *mukayyar* 'cloth made of goat's hair' (lit. 'choice, select').

**Mohawk** ● n. (pl. same or **Mohawks**) **1** a member of an American Indian people originally inhabiting parts of what is now upper New York State. **2** the Iroquoian language of this people. **3** chiefly N. Amer. a Mohican haircut. **4** Skating a step from either edge of the skate to the same edge on the other foot in the opposite direction.
– ORIGIN from Narragansett *mohowawog*, lit. 'maneaters'.

**Mohegan** /məʊˈhiːɡ(ə)n/ (also **Mohican**) ● n. **1** a member of an American Indian people formerly inhabiting western parts of Connecticut and Massachusetts. Compare with **MAHICAN**. **2** the extinct Algonquian language of this people. ● adj. of or relating to the Mohegans or their language.
– ORIGIN from Mohegan, lit. 'people of the tidal waters'.

**mohel** /ˈməʊ(h)(ə)l/ ● n. a Jew who performs the rite of circumcision.
– ORIGIN C17: from Heb. *mōhēl.*

**Mohican**[1] /məʊˈhiːk(ə)n, ˈməʊɪk(ə)n/ ● n. a hairstyle with the head shaved except for a central strip of hair from the forehead to the back of the neck, typically made to stand erect.
– ORIGIN 1960s: erroneously assoc. with the Amer. Indian people; cf. **HURON**.

**Mohican**[2] /məʊˈhiːk(ə)n/ ● adj. & n. old-fashioned variant of **MAHICAN** or **MOHEGAN**.

**Moho** /ˈməʊhəʊ/ ● n. Geology the boundary surface between the earth's crust and the mantle.
– ORIGIN 1930s: abbrev. of *Mohorovičić discontinuity*, named after the Yugoslav seismologist Andrija *Mohorovičić.*

**Mohs' scale** /məʊz/ ● n. a scale of hardness used in classifying minerals.
– ORIGIN C19: named after the Ger. mineralogist F. *Mohs.*

**moidore** /ˈmɔɪdɔː/ ● n. a Portuguese gold coin, current in England in the early 18th century.
– ORIGIN from Port. *moeda d'ouro* 'money of gold'.

**moiety** /ˈmɔɪɪti/ ● n. (pl. **-ies**) formal or technical each of two parts into which a thing is or can be divided.
– ORIGIN ME: from OFr. *moite*, from L. *medietas* 'middle', from *medius* 'mid, middle'.

**moil** /mɔɪl/ archaic, dialect, or N. Amer. ● v. **1** work hard. **2** move around in confusion. ● n. **1** hard work. **2** confusion.
– ORIGIN ME (in the sense 'moisten'): from OFr. *moillier* 'paddle in mud, moisten', based on L. *mollis* 'soft'.

**moire** /mwɑː/ (also **moiré** /ˈmwɑːreɪ/) ● n. silk subjected to heat and pressure after weaving to give a rippled appearance. ● adj. (of silk) having a finish of this type. ➤ having a pattern of wavy lines like that of moire.
– ORIGIN C17: from Fr. *moire* 'mohair' (the original fabric); the var. *moiré* is from the past part. of *moirer* 'give a watered appearance'.

**moist** ● adj. **1** slightly wet; damp or humid. ➤ (of a climate) rainy. **2** Medicine marked by a fluid discharge.
– DERIVATIVES **moisten** v. **moistly** adv. **moistness** n.
– ORIGIN ME: from OFr. *moiste*, based on L. *mucidus* 'mouldy' (influenced by *musteus* 'fresh', from *mustum*: see **MUST**[2]).

**moisture** ● n. water or other liquid diffused in a small quantity as vapour, within a solid, or condensed on a surface.
– DERIVATIVES **moistureless** adj.

**moisturize** (also **-ise**) ● v. make (something, especially the skin) less dry.

**moisturizer** ● n. a cosmetic preparation for moisturizing the skin.

**mojo** /ˈməʊdʒəʊ/ ● n. (pl. **-os**) chiefly US a magic charm or spell. ➤ magic.
– ORIGIN C20: prob. of Afr. origin; cf. Gullah *moco* 'witch-

craft'.

**moke** ● n. Brit. informal a donkey. ➤ Austral./NZ a horse.
– ORIGIN C19: of unknown origin.

**moksha** /ˈmɒkʃə/ ● n. (in Hinduism and Jainism) release from the cycle of rebirth.
– ORIGIN from Sanskrit *mokṣa*.

**mol** /məʊl/ ● n. Chemistry short for **MOLE**[4].

**mola** /ˈməʊlə/ ● n. (pl. same or **molas**) another term for **SUNFISH** (in sense 1).
– ORIGIN C16: from L., lit. 'millstone', with ref. to the shape.

**molal** /ˈməʊləl/ ● adj. Chemistry (of a solution) containing one mole of solute per kilogram of solvent.
– DERIVATIVES **molality** n.

**molar**[1] (also **molar tooth**) ● n. a grinding tooth at the back of a mammal's mouth.
– ORIGIN ME: from L. *molaris*, from *mola* 'millstone'.

**molar**[2] ● adj. acting on or by means of large masses or units.
– ORIGIN C19: from L. *moles* 'mass' + **-AR**[1].

**molar**[3] ● adj. Chemistry of or relating to one mole of a substance. ➤ (of a solution) containing one mole of solute per litre of solvent.
– DERIVATIVES **molarity** n.

**molasses** ● n. **1** thick, dark brown juice obtained from raw sugar during the refining process. **2** N. Amer. golden syrup.
– ORIGIN C16: from Port. *melaço*, from late L. *mellacium* 'must', based on *mel* 'honey'.

**mold** ● n. & v. US spelling of **MOULD**[1], **MOULD**[2], and **MOULD**[3].

**Moldavian** ● n. **1** a native or national of Moldavia, a former principality of SE Europe. **2** the Romanian language as used in Moldavia. ● adj. of or relating to Moldavia.

**molder** ● v. & n. US spelling of **MOULDER**.

**molding** ● n. US spelling of **MOULDING**.

**Moldovan** /mɒlˈdəʊv(ə)n/ ● n. a native or inhabitant of Moldova, a country in SE Europe. ● adj. of or relating to Moldova.

**moldy** ● adj. US spelling of **MOULDY**.

**mole**[1] /məʊl/ ● n. **1** a small burrowing insectivorous mammal with dark velvety fur, a long muzzle, and very small eyes. [*Talpa europaea* and other species.] **2** a spy who gradually achieves an important position within the security defences of a country. ➤ a betrayer of confidential information.
– ORIGIN ME: from the Gmc base of MDu. and Mid. Low Ger. *mol*.

**mole**[2] /məʊl/ ● n. a small dark blemish on the skin caused by a high concentration of melanin.
– ORIGIN OE *māl* 'discoloured spot', of Gmc origin.

**mole**[3] /məʊl/ ● n. a large solid structure serving as a pier, breakwater, or causeway. ➤ a harbour formed by a mole.
– ORIGIN C16: from Fr. *môle*, from L. *moles* 'mass'.

**mole**[4] /məʊl/ ● n. Chemistry the SI unit of amount of substance, equal to the quantity containing as many elementary units as there are atoms in 0.012 kg of carbon-12.
– ORIGIN C20: from Ger. *Mol*, from *Molekul* 'molecule'.

**mole**[5] /məʊl/ ● n. Medicine an abnormal mass of tissue in the uterus.
– ORIGIN ME: from Fr. *môle*, from L. *mola* in the sense 'false conception'.

**mole**[6] /ˈməʊleɪ/ ● n. a highly spiced Mexican savoury sauce containing chilli peppers and chocolate.
– ORIGIN Mex. Sp., from Nahuatl *molli* 'sauce, stew'.

**mole cricket** ● n. a large burrowing nocturnal cricket-like insect. [Family Gryllotalpidae: many species.]

**molecular** /məˈlɛkjʊlə/ ● adj. of, relating to, or consisting of molecules.
– DERIVATIVES **molecularity** n. **molecularly** adv.

**molecular biology** ● n. the branch of biology concerned with the macromolecules (e.g. proteins and DNA) essential to life.

**molecular electronics** ● pl. n. [treated as sing.] a branch of electronics in which individual molecules perform the same function as microelectronic devices such as diodes.

**molecular sieve** ● n. a zeolite or other crystalline substance with pores large enough for small molecules to pass through.

**molecular weight** ● n. another term for **RELATIVE MOLECULAR MASS**.

**molecule** /ˈmɒlɪkjuːl/ ● n. a group of atoms bonded together, representing the smallest fundamental unit of a compound that can take part in a chemical reaction.
– ORIGIN C18: from Fr. *molécule*, from mod. L. *molecula*, dimin. of L. *moles* 'mass'.

**molehill** ● n. a small mound of earth thrown up by a burrowing mole.
– PHRASES **make a mountain out of a molehill** greatly exaggerate the importance of a minor problem.

**mole rat** ● n. a rat-like African rodent that lives underground, with long incisors used in digging. [Many species, mainly in the family Bathyergidae.]

**moleskin** ● n. **1** the skin of a mole used as fur. **2** a thick, strong cotton fabric with a shaved pile surface.

**molest** ● v. pester or harass in a hostile way. ➤ assault or abuse sexually.
– DERIVATIVES **molestation** n. **molester** n.
– ORIGIN ME: from OFr. *molester* or L. *molestare* 'annoy', from *molestus* 'troublesome'.

**moletronics** /ˌmɒlɪˈtrɒnɪks/ ● pl. n. [treated as sing.] short for **MOLECULAR ELECTRONICS**.

**moline** /məˈlʌɪn/ ● adj. [postpos.] Heraldry (of a cross) having each extremity broadened, split, and curved back.
– ORIGIN C16: prob. from Anglo-Norman Fr. *moliné*, from *molin* 'mill', because of a resemblance to the iron support of a millstone.

**moll** ● n. informal **1** a gangster's female companion. **2** a prostitute.
– ORIGIN C17: familiar form of the given name *Mary*.

**mollify** /ˈmɒlɪfʌɪ/ ● v. (**-ies**, **-ied**) appease the anger or anxiety of. ➤ rare reduce the severity of; soften.
– DERIVATIVES **mollification** n. **mollifier** n.
– ORIGIN ME: from Fr. *mollifier* or L. *mollificare*, from *mollis* 'soft'.

**mollisol** /ˈmɒlɪsɒl/ ● n. Soil Science a temperate grassland soil with a dark, humus-rich surface layer containing high concentrations of calcium and magnesium.
– ORIGIN C20: from L. *mollis* 'soft' + *solum* 'ground, soil'.

**mollusc** /ˈmɒləsk/ (US **mollusk**) ● n. Zoology an invertebrate of a large phylum (Mollusca) including snails, slugs, and mussels, with a soft unsegmented body and often an external shell.
– DERIVATIVES **molluscan** /məˈlʌskən/ adj.
– ORIGIN C18: from mod. L. *mollusca*, neut. pl. of L. *molluscus*, from *mollis* 'soft'.

**molluscum contagiosum** /məˌlʌskəm kənˌteɪdʒɪˈəʊsəm/ ● n. Medicine a chronic viral disorder of the skin characterized by groups of small, smooth, painless pinkish nodules.
– ORIGIN C19: from L. *molluscum*, neut. of *molluscus* + *contagiosum*, neut. of *contagiosus* 'contagious'.

**molly** (also **mollie**) ● n. a small live-bearing killifish which has been bred for aquaria in many colours, especially black. [Genus *Poecilia*: several species.]
– ORIGIN 1930s: from mod. L. *Mollienisia* (former genus name), from the name of Count *Mollien*, Fr. statesman.

**mollycoddle** ● v. treat indulgently or overprotectively. ● n. an effeminate man or boy.
– ORIGIN C19: from *molly* 'girl' (see **MOLL**) + **CODDLE**.

**mollymawk** ● n. chiefly Austral./NZ an albatross.
– ORIGIN C17: from Du. *mallemok*, from *mal* 'foolish' + *mok* 'gull'.

**moloch** /ˈməʊlɒk/ ● n. a harmless spiny lizard of grotesque appearance which feeds chiefly on ants, found in arid inland Australia. [*Moloch horridus*.]
– ORIGIN from the name of a Caananite idol to whom children were sacrificed.

**Molotov cocktail** ● n. a crude incendiary device, consisting of a bottle of flammable liquid ignited by means of a wick.
– ORIGIN named after the Soviet statesman Vyacheslav *Molotov*, who organized the production of similar devices in World War II.

**molt** ● v. & n. US spelling of MOULT.

**molten** /ˈməʊlt(ə)n/ ● adj. liquefied by heat.
– ORIGIN ME: archaic past part. of MELT.

**molto** /ˈmɒltəʊ/ ● adv. Music very.
– ORIGIN Ital., from L. *multus* 'much'.

**Moluccan** /məˈlʌkən/ ● n. a native or inhabitant of the Molucca Islands in Indonesia. ● adj. of or relating to the Molucca Islands.

**moly** /ˈməʊli/ ● n. 1 a plant related to the onions, with small yellow flowers. [*Allium moly.*] 2 a mythical magic herb with white flowers and black roots.
– ORIGIN C16: via L. from Gk *mōlu*.

**molybdate** /məˈlɪbdeɪt/ ● n. Chemistry a salt in which the anion contains both molybdenum and oxygen.

**molybdenite** /məˈlɪbdənʌɪt/ ● n. a blue-grey mineral consisting of molybdenum disulphide.

**molybdenum** /məˈlɪbdənəm/ ● n. the chemical element of atomic number 42, a brittle silver-grey metal. (Symbol: **Mo**)
– ORIGIN C19: mod. L., earlier *molybdena* (orig. denoting a salt of lead), from Gk *molubdaina* 'plummet', from *molubdos* 'lead'.

**mom** ● n. North American term for MUM¹.

**moment** ● n. 1 a brief period of time. ➤ an exact point in time. 2 formal importance. 3 Physics a turning effect produced by a force on an object, expressed as the product of the force and the distance from its line of action to a given point.
– PHRASES **(at) any moment** very soon. **for the moment** for now. **have one's** (or **its**) **moments** have periods that are better than others. **moment of truth** a time of crisis or test. [orig. the final sword-thrust in a bullfight.] **of the moment** currently popular, famous, or important.
– ORIGIN ME: from L. *momentum* (see MOMENTUM).

**momenta** plural form of MOMENTUM.

**momentarily** ● adv. 1 for a very short time. 2 N. Amer. very soon.

**momentary** ● adj. brief.
– DERIVATIVES **momentariness** n.

**momently** ● adv. archaic or poetic/literary 1 continually. 2 briefly.

**moment of inertia** ● n. Physics a quantity expressing a body's tendency to resist angular acceleration.

**momentous** ● adj. of great importance or significance.
– DERIVATIVES **momentously** adv. **momentousness** n.

**momentum** /məˈmɛntəm/ ● n. (pl. **momenta** /-tə/) 1 Physics the quantity of motion of a moving body, equal to the product of its mass and velocity. 2 impetus gained by movement or progress: *the investigation gathered momentum.*
– ORIGIN C17: from L., from *movimentum*, from *movere* 'to move'.

**momma** ● n. North American term for MAMA.

**mommy** ● n. (pl. **-ies**) North American term for MUMMY¹.

**mommy track** ● n. N. Amer. informal a career path for women who sacrifice some promotions and pay rises in order to devote more time to raising their children.
– DERIVATIVES **mommy tracker** n. **mommy tracking** n.

**Mon** /mɔːn/ ● n. (pl. same or **Mons**) 1 a member of a people inhabiting parts of SE Burma (Myanmar) and western Thailand. 2 the language of this people, related to Khmer.
– ORIGIN the name in Mon.

**Mon.** ● abbrev. Monday.

**mon-** ● comb. form variant spelling of MONO- shortened before a vowel (as in *monamine*).

**monad** /ˈmɒnad, ˈməʊ-/ ● n. 1 technical a single unit; the number one. 2 Philosophy (in the philosophy of Leibniz) an indivisible and hence ultimately simple entity, e.g. an atom or a person. 3 Biology, dated a single-celled organism or a single cell.
– DERIVATIVES **monadic** adj. **monadism** n. (Philosophy).
– ORIGIN C17: via late L. from Gk *monas, monad-* 'unit', from *monos* 'alone'.

**monadelphous** /ˌmɒnəˈdɛlfəs/ ● adj. Botany (of stamens) united by their filaments.
– ORIGIN C19: from Gk *monos* 'one' + *adelphos* 'brother' + **-OUS**.

**monadnock** /məˈnadnɒk/ ● n. an isolated hill or ridge of erosion-resistant rock rising above a peneplain.
– ORIGIN C19: named after Mount *Monadnock* in New Hampshire, US.

**monamine** ● n. variant spelling of MONOAMINE.

**monarch** /ˈmɒnək/ ● n. 1 a sovereign head of state, especially a king, queen, or emperor. 2 a large migratory orange and black butterfly, chiefly North American, whose caterpillars feed on milkweed. [*Danaus plexippus.*] 3 (also **monarch flycatcher**) a flycatcher of Africa, Asia, and Australasia, typically with bold plumage. [Family Monarchidae: many species.]
– DERIVATIVES **monarchal** adj. **monarchial** adj. **monarchic** adj. **monarchical** adj. **monarchically** adv.
– ORIGIN ME: from late L. *monarcha*, from Gk *monarkhēs*, from *monos* 'alone' + *arkhein* 'to rule'.

**monarchism** ● n. support for the principle of monarchy.
– DERIVATIVES **monarchist** n. & adj.

**monarchy** ● n. (pl. **-ies**) government by a monarch. ➤ a state with a monarch.
– ORIGIN ME: from OFr. *monarchie*, via late L. from Gk *monarkhia* 'the rule of one'.

**monastery** ● n. (pl. **-ies**) a community of monks living under religious vows.
– ORIGIN ME: via eccles. L. from eccles. Gk *monastērion*, from *monazein* 'live alone', from *monos* 'alone'.

**monastic** ● adj. of or relating to monks, nuns, etc., or the buildings in which they live. ➤ resembling monks or their way of life. ● n. a monk or other follower of a monastic rule.
– DERIVATIVES **monastically** adv. **monasticism** n.
– ORIGIN ME: from late L. *monasticus*, from Gk *monastikos*, from *monazein* 'live alone'.

**monatomic** /ˌmɒnəˈtɒmɪk/ ● adj. Chemistry consisting of one atom.

**monaural** /mɒnˈɔːr(ə)l/ ● adj. 1 of or involving one ear. 2 another term for MONOPHONIC (in sense 1).
– DERIVATIVES **monaurally** adv.

**monazite** /ˈmɒnəzʌɪt/ ● n. a brown mineral consisting of a phosphate of rare-earth elements and thorium.
– ORIGIN C19: from Ger. *Monazit*, from Gk *monazein* 'live alone' (because of its rare occurrence).

**mondaine** /mɒnˈdeɪn, French mɔ̃dɛn/ ● adj. of the fashionable world; worldly. ● n. dated a fashionable woman.
– ORIGIN Fr., fem. of *mondain* (see MUNDANE).

**Monday** ● n. the day of the week before Tuesday and following Sunday. ● adv. chiefly N. Amer. on Monday. ➤ **(Mondays)** on Mondays; each Monday.
– ORIGIN OE *Mōnandæg* 'day of the moon', translation of late L. *lunae dies*.

**mondial** /ˈmɒndɪəl/ ● adj. of or involving the whole world; worldwide.
– ORIGIN C20: Fr.

**mondo** /ˈmɒndəʊ/ ● adv. & adj. informal, chiefly US (often with a pseudo-Italian noun or adjective) very striking or remarkable: *mondo bizarro.*
– ORIGIN from Ital. *Mondo Cane*, lit. 'dog's world', the title of a film (1961) depicting bizarre behaviour.

**Monégasque** /ˌmɒneɪˈgask, French mɔnegask/ ● n. a native or national of Monaco. ● adj. of or relating to Monaco or its inhabitants.
– ORIGIN from Fr.

**Monel** /ˈməʊn(ə)l/ ● n. trademark a nickel-copper alloy with high tensile strength and resistance to corrosion.
– ORIGIN C20: named after the Amer. businessman Ambrose *Monell.*

**monetarism** ● n. the theory or practice of controlling the supply of money as the chief method of stabilizing the economy.
– DERIVATIVES **monetarist** n. & adj.

**monetary** ● adj. of or relating to money or currency.
– DERIVATIVES **monetarily** adv.

**monetize** /ˈmʌnɪtʌɪz/ (also **monetarize**, **-ise**) ● v. 1 convert into or express in the form of currency. 2 [usu. as adj. **monetized**] adapt (a society) to the use of money.
– DERIVATIVES **monetization** n.

## Word *Formation*

**-monger** 'a dealer or trader', from OE *mangere*, based on Latin *mango*

➤ Many **-monger** words are of very early origin, having come directly from Old English with the neutral sense 'trader':

| | |
|---|---|
| fishmonger | a dealer in fish |
| fleshmonger | (now obsolete: originally, a butcher) |
| ironmonger | a hardware retailer |
| woodmonger | (now obsolete: a timber merchant) |

➤ From the 16th century, the use of **-monger** acquired derogatory implications, as in the following (now mostly obsolete) terms:

| | | |
|---|---|---|
| costermonger | a market trader in fruit and vegetables; used as a general term of abuse from the 17th century (as recorded in Shakespeare's *Henry VI Part II*) | *Costard*, a variety of apple |
| fleshmonger | a pimp (as recorded in Shakespeare's *Measure for Measure*) | based on FLESH |
| massmonger | a Roman Catholic | the Roman Catholic 'Mass' |
| meritmonger | a person who seeks salvation through good works | 'merit' used in an early theological sense 'good works in return for favour from God' |
| moneymonger | a moneylender | based on MONEY |
| muttonmonger | a sexually promiscuous man | figurative use of 'mutton' |
| newsmonger | a gossip | based on NEWS |
| questmonger | a person involved in trials and inquests, especially a person benefiting from giving false information | *quest* in earlier sense 'an inquest, inquiry' |
| warmonger | a person or state encouraging war or warlike aggression | based on WAR |
| whoremonger | a fornicator | based on WHORE |

Recent **-monger** coinages include ***scaremonger***, ***rumour-monger***, and ***gossipmonger***.

**money** • **n.** a medium of exchange in the form of coins and banknotes. ➤(**moneys** or **monies**) formal sums of money. ➤wealth. ➤payment or financial gain.
– PHRASES **be in the money** informal have or win a lot of money. **for my money** informal in my opinion or judgement. **money for old rope** (or **money for jam**) Brit. informal money or reward earned for little or no effort. **on the money** informal, chiefly N. Amer. accurate; correct. **put one's money where one's mouth is** informal take action to support one's statements or opinions.
– DERIVATIVES **moneyless** adj.
– ORIGIN ME: from OFr. *moneie*, from L. *moneta* 'mint, money', orig. a title of the goddess Juno, in whose temple in Rome money was minted.

**moneybags** • **pl. n.** [treated as sing.] informal a wealthy person.

**moneyed** • **adj.** having much money; affluent.

**moneyer** • **n.** archaic a person who mints money.

**money-grubbing** • **adj.** informal overeager to make money; grasping.
– DERIVATIVES **money-grubber** n.

**moneylender** • **n.** a person whose business is lending money to others who pay interest.
– DERIVATIVES **moneylending** n. & adj.

**money market** • **n.** the trade in short-term loans between banks and other financial institutions.

**money order** • **n.** a printed order for payment of a specified sum, issued by a bank or Post Office.

**money spider** • **n.** a very small shiny black spider. [Family Linyphiidae.]
– ORIGIN so named because supposed to bring financial luck.

**money-spinner** • **n.** chiefly Brit. a thing that brings in a profit.
– DERIVATIVES **money-spinning** adj.

**money supply** • **n.** the total amount of money in circulation or in existence in a country.

**moneywort** • **n.** another term for CREEPING JENNY.
– ORIGIN C16: from a supposed resemblance of the plant's leaves to coins.

**-monger** • **comb. form 1** denoting a dealer or trader in a specified commodity: *fishmonger.* **2** chiefly derogatory denoting a person engaging in a particular activity: *rumourmonger.* See word-formation panel.
– ORIGIN OE *mangere*, from *mangian* 'to traffic', of Gmc origin, based on L. *mango* 'dealer'.

**mongo** /ˈmɒŋgəʊ/ • **n.** (pl. same or **-os**) a monetary unit of Mongolia, equal to one hundredth of a tugrik.
– ORIGIN from Mongolian *möngö* 'silver'.

**Mongol** /ˈmɒŋg(ə)l/ • **n. 1** a native or national of Mongolia; a Mongolian. **2** the Altaic language of this people; Mongolian. **3** (**mongol**) offensive a person with Down's syndrome. • **adj.** of or relating to the people of Mongolia or their language.
– DERIVATIVES **Mongolian** n. & adj. **mongolism** n. (offensive).

**Mongoloid** • **adj. 1** of or relating to the broad division of humankind including the indigenous peoples of east Asia, SE Asia, and the Arctic region of North America. **2** (**mongoloid**) offensive affected with Down's syndrome. • **n. 1** a person of a Mongoloid physical type. **2** offensive a person with Down's syndrome.

**USAGE** Mongoloid

The term **Mongoloid** belongs to a set of terms introduced by 19th-century anthropologists attempting to categorize human races. Such terms are associated with outdated notions of racial types, and so are now potentially offensive and best avoided.

**mongoose** • **n.** (pl. **mongooses**) a small carnivorous mammal with a long body and tail, native to Africa and Asia. [Family Herpestidae: many species.]
– ORIGIN C17: from Marathi *mangūs*.

**mongrel** • **n. 1** a dog of no definable type or breed. **2** offensive a person of mixed descent.
– DERIVATIVES **mongrelism** n. **mongrelization** (also **-isation**) n. **mongrelize** (also **-ise**) v.

– ORIGIN ME: of Gmc origin, appar. from a base meaning 'mix', and rel. to **MINGLE** and **AMONG**.

**monial** /ˈməʊnɪəl/ ● n. a mullion.
– ORIGIN ME: from OFr. *moinel* 'middle'.

**monic** /ˈmɒnɪk/ ● adj. Mathematics (of a polynomial) having the coefficient of the term of highest degree equal to one.
– ORIGIN from **MONO-** + **-IC**.

**monies** plural form of **MONEY**, as used in financial contexts.

**moniker** /ˈmɒnɪkə/ (also **monicker**) ● n. informal a name.
– DERIVATIVES **monikered** adj.
– ORIGIN C19: of unknown origin.

**moniliform** /məˈnɪlɪfɔːm/ ● adj. Zoology & Botany resembling a string of beads.
– ORIGIN C19: from Fr. *moniliforme* or mod. L. *moniliformis*, from L. *monile* 'necklace' + **-IFORM**.

**monism** /ˈmɒnɪz(ə)m, ˈməʊ-/ ● n. Philosophy & Theology **1** a theory or doctrine that denies the existence of a distinction or duality, such as that between matter and mind, or God and the world. **2** the doctrine that only one supreme being exists. Compare with **PLURALISM**.
– DERIVATIVES **monist** n. & adj. **monistic** adj.
– ORIGIN C19: from mod. L. *monismus*, from Gk *monos* 'single'.

**monition** /məˈnɪʃ(ə)n/ ● n. **1** rare a warning of impending danger. **2** a formal notice from a bishop or ecclesiastical court admonishing a person not to do something.
– ORIGIN ME: via OFr. from L. *monitio(n-)*, from *monere* 'warn'.

**monitor** ● n. **1** a person or device that monitors something. **2** a school pupil with disciplinary or other special duties. **3** a television receiver used in a studio to view the picture being transmitted from a particular camera. ➤a screen which displays an image generated by a computer. ➤a loudspeaker used by performers on stage to hear themselves or in a studio to hear what has been recorded. **4** (also **monitor lizard**) a large tropical Old World lizard with a long neck and a short body, formerly believed to warn of the approach of crocodiles. [Genus *Varanus*: many species.] **5** historical a shallow-draught warship mounting one or two heavy guns for bombardment. ● v. observe and check over a period of time. ➤maintain regular surveillance over. ➤listen to and report on (a radio broadcast or telephone conversation).
– DERIVATIVES **monitorial** adj. **monitorship** n.
– ORIGIN C16: from L., from *monit-*, *monere* 'warn'.

**monitory** ● adj. rare giving or serving as a warning. ● n. (pl. **-ies**) (in church use) a letter of admonition from the Pope or a bishop.

**monk** ● n. a member of a religious community of men typically living under vows of poverty, chastity, and obedience.
– DERIVATIVES **monkish** adj. **monkishly** adv. **monkishness** n.
– ORIGIN OE *munuc*, based on Gk *monakhos* 'solitary', from *monos* 'alone'.

**monkery** ● n. derogatory monasticism.

**monkey** ● n. (pl. **-eys**) **1** a small to medium-sized primate typically having a long tail and living in trees in tropical countries. [Families Cebidae and Callitrichidae (New World), and Cercopithecidae (Old World).] **2** a mischievous person, especially a child. **3** Brit. informal a sum of £500. **4** (also **monkey engine**) a piledriving machine consisting of a heavy hammer or ram working vertically in a groove. ● v. (**-eys**, **-eyed**) **1** (**monkey about/around**) behave in a silly or playful way. ➤(**monkey with**) tamper with. **2** archaic ape; mimic.
– PHRASES **make a monkey of** (or **out of**) make (someone) appear ridiculous. **a monkey on one's back** informal a burdensome problem. ➤a dependence on drugs. **not give a monkey's** informal not care at all.
– DERIVATIVES **monkeyish** adj.
– ORIGIN C16: of unknown origin, perh. from Low Ger.

**monkey bars** ● pl. n. a piece of playground equipment consisting of a horizontally mounted overhead ladder.

**monkey business** ● n. informal mischievous or deceitful behaviour.

**monkey flower** ● n. a plant of boggy ground, with yellow or red snapdragon-like flowers. [*Mimulus guttatus* and related species.]

**monkey jacket** ● n. a short, close-fitting jacket worn by sailors or waiters or by officers in their mess.

**monkey nut** ● n. Brit. a peanut.

**monkey puzzle** ● n. an evergreen coniferous tree with branches covered in spirals of tough spiny leaf-like scales, native to Chile. [*Araucaria araucana*.]

**monkeyshines** ● pl. n. informal North American term for **MONKEY TRICKS**.

**monkey suit** ● n. informal a man's evening dress or formal suit.

**monkey tricks** ● pl. n. Brit. informal mischievous behaviour.

**monkey wrench** ● n. an adjustable spanner with large jaws which has its adjusting screw contained in the handle. ● v. (**monkey-wrench**) informal sabotage, especially as a form of protest.
– PHRASES **a monkey wrench in the works** chiefly N. Amer. a person or thing that prevents the successful implementation of a plan.
– DERIVATIVES **monkey-wrencher** n.

**monkfish** ● n. (pl. same or **-fishes**) **1** an angel shark. [*Squatina squatina*.] **2** an anglerfish. [*Lophius piscatorius*.]

**Mon-Khmer** /ˈmɔːnˌkmɛː/ ● n. a family of Austro-Asiatic languages of SE Asia, of which the most important are Mon and Khmer.

**monk seal** ● n. a seal with a dark back and pale underside, occurring in warm waters of the northern hemisphere. [Genus *Monachus*.]

**monkshood** ● n. an aconite with blue or purple flowers. [*Aconitum napellus* (Europe), *A. uncinatum* (N. America), and related species.]

**mono** ● adj. **1** monophonic. **2** monochrome. ● n. (pl. **-os**) **1** monophonic reproduction. **2** monochrome reproduction. **3** N. Amer. short for **MONONUCLEOSIS**. **4** N. Amer. short for **MONOFILAMENT**.

**mono-** (also **mon-** before a vowel) ● comb. form **1** one; alone; single: *monocoque*. **2** Chemistry (forming names of compounds) containing one atom or group of a specified kind: *monoamine*.
– ORIGIN from Gk *monos* 'alone'.

**monoamine** /ˌmɒnəʊˈeɪmiːn/ (also **monamine**) ● n. Chemistry a compound having a single amine group in its molecule, especially one which is a neurotransmitter (e.g. serotonin, noradrenaline).

**monoamine oxidase** ● n. Biochemistry an enzyme (present in most tissues) which catalyses the oxidation and inactivation of monoamine neurotransmitters.

**monoamine oxidase inhibitor** ● n. Medicine any of a group of antidepressant drugs which inhibit the activity of monoamine oxidase (so allowing accumulation of serotonin and noradrenaline in the brain).

**monobasic** ● adj. Chemistry (of an acid) having one replaceable hydrogen atom.

**monobloc** ● adj. made as or contained in a single casting.
– ORIGIN C20: from Fr., from **MONO-** + *bloc* 'block'.

**monocarpic** /ˌmɒnə(ʊ)ˈkɑːpɪk/ ● adj. Botany (of a plant) flowering only once and then dying.
– ORIGIN C19: from **MONO-** + Gk *karpos* 'fruit' + **-IC**.

**monocausal** ● adj. in terms of a sole cause.

**monochasium** /ˌmɒnə(ʊ)ˈkeɪzɪəm/ ● n. (pl. **monochasia**) Botany a cyme in which each flowering branch gives rise to one lateral branch, so that the inflorescence is helicoid or asymmetrical.
– ORIGIN C19: mod. L., from **MONO-** + Gk *khasis* 'separation'.

**monochord** ● n. an instrument for comparing musical pitches, using a taut wire whose vibrating length can be adjusted with a movable bridge.
– ORIGIN ME: from OFr. *monacorde*, via late L. from Gk *monokhordon*, neut. (used as n.) of *monokhordos* 'having a single string'.

**monochromatic** ● adj. **1** containing or using only one

colour. **2** Physics (of light or other radiation) of a single wavelength or frequency.
– DERIVATIVES **monochromatically** adv.

**monochromatism** • **n.** complete colour blindness in which all colours appear as shades of one colour.

**monochromator** /ˈmɒnə(ʊ)krəˌmeɪtə, ˌmɒnə(ʊ)ˈkrɒmɪtə/ • **n.** Physics a device used to select radiation of (or very close to) a single wavelength or energy.

**monochrome** • **n.** representation or reproduction in black and white or in varying tones of only one colour. • **adj.** (of a photograph or picture, or a television screen) consisting of or displaying images in black and white or in varying tones of only one colour.
– DERIVATIVES **monochromic** adj.
– ORIGIN C17: based on Gk *monokhrōmatos* 'of a single colour'.

**monocle** /ˈmɒnək(ə)l/ • **n.** a single eyeglass kept in position by the muscles around the eye.
– DERIVATIVES **monocled** adj.
– ORIGIN C19: from Fr. (earlier in the sense 'one-eyed'), from late L. *monoculus* 'one-eyed'.

**monocline** /ˈmɒnə(ʊ)klʌɪn/ • **n.** Geology a bend in rock strata that are otherwise uniformly dipping or horizontal.
– DERIVATIVES **monoclinal** adj.
– ORIGIN C19: from **MONO-** + Gk *klinein* 'to lean'.

**monoclinic** • **adj.** denoting a crystal system with three unequal axes of which one is at right angles to the other two.

**monoclonal** /ˌmɒnə(ʊ)ˈkləʊn(ə)l/ • **adj.** Biology forming a clone which is derived asexually from a single individual or cell.

**monoclonal antibody** • **n.** an antibody produced by a single clone of cells or cell line and consisting of identical antibody molecules.

**monocoque** /ˈmɒnə(ʊ)kɒk/ • **n.** an aircraft or vehicle structure in which the chassis is integral with the body.
– ORIGIN C20: from Fr., from *mono-* 'single' + *coque* 'shell'.

**monocot** • **n.** Botany short for **MONOCOTYLEDON**.

**monocotyledon** /ˌmɒnə(ʊ)kɒtɪˈliːd(ə)n/ • **n.** Botany a plant with an embryo bearing a single cotyledon, such plants constituting the smaller (Monocotyledoneae) of the two classes of flowering species. Compare with **DICOTYLEDON**.
– DERIVATIVES **monocotyledonous** adj.

**monocracy** /məˈnɒkrəsi/ • **n.** (pl. **-ies**) a system of government by one person only.
– DERIVATIVES **monocrat** n. **monocratic** adj.

**monocrystalline** • **adj.** consisting of a single crystal.

**monocular** /məˈnɒkjʊlə/ • **adj.** with, for, or in one eye. • **n.** an optical instrument for viewing distant objects with one eye, like one half of a pair of binoculars.
– DERIVATIVES **monocularly** adv.
– ORIGIN C17: from late L. *monoculus* 'having one eye' + **-AR**[1].

**monoculture** • **n.** the cultivation of a single crop in a given area.

**monocycle** • **n.** a unicycle.

**monocyclic** /ˌmɒnə(ʊ)ˈsʌɪklɪk, -ˈsɪk-/ • **adj. 1** Chemistry having one ring of atoms in its molecule. **2** of or relating to a single cycle of activity.

**monocyte** /ˈmɒnə(ʊ)sʌɪt/ • **n.** Physiology a large phagocytic white blood cell with a simple oval nucleus and clear, greyish cytoplasm.

**monodactyl** /ˌmɒnə(ʊ)ˈdaktɪl/ • **adj.** Zoology having only one finger or toe on each hand or foot.
– DERIVATIVES **monodactyly** n.

**monodisperse** /ˌmɒnə(ʊ)ˈdɪspəːs/ • **adj.** Chemistry (of a colloid) containing particles of uniform size.

**monodrama** • **n.** a dramatic piece for one performer.

**monody** /ˈmɒnədi/ • **n.** (pl. **-ies**) **1** an ode sung by a single actor in a Greek tragedy. **2** a poem lamenting a person's death. **3** music with only one melodic line.
– DERIVATIVES **monodic** adj. **monodist** n.
– ORIGIN C17: via late L. from Gk *monōdia*, from *monōdos* 'singing alone'.

**monoecious** /məˈniːʃəs/ • **adj.** Biology (of a plant or invertebrate animal) having both the male and female reproductive organs in the same individual; hermaphrodite. Compare with **DIOECIOUS**.
– DERIVATIVES **monoecy** n.
– ORIGIN C18: from mod. L. *Monoecia* (denoting a class of such plants in Linnaeus's system), from Gk *monos* 'single' + *oikos* 'house'.

**monofilament** (also **monofil**) • **n.** a single strand of man-made fibre. ➤a type of fishing line using such a strand.

**monogamy** /məˈnɒgəmi/ • **n. 1** the practice of being married to or having a sexual relationship with only one person at a time. **2** Zoology the habit of having only one mate at a time.
– DERIVATIVES **monogamist** n. **monogamous** adj. **monogamously** adv.
– ORIGIN C17: from Fr. *monogamie*, via eccles. L. from Gk *monogamia*, from *monos* 'single' + *gamos* 'marriage'.

**monogenean** /ˌmɒnə(ʊ)dʒɪˈniːən, mɒnə(ʊ)ˈdʒɛnɪən/ • **adj.** Zoology relating to or denoting a group of parasitic flukes which only require a single host to complete their life cycle. Compare with **DIGENEAN**.
– ORIGIN 1960s: from mod. L. *Monogenea* (from Gk *monos* 'single' + *genea* 'generation') + **-AN**.

**monogenesis** /ˌmɒnə(ʊ)ˈdʒɛnɪsɪs/ (also **monogeny** /məˈnɒdʒəni/) • **n.** origination from a single source or place.
– DERIVATIVES **monogenetic** adj. **monogenism** n. **monogenist** n.

**monogenic** /ˌmɒnə(ʊ)ˈdʒɛnɪk/ • **adj.** Genetics involving or controlled by a single gene.
– DERIVATIVES **monogenically** adv.

**monoglot** /ˈmɒnə(ʊ)glɒt/ • **adj.** using or speaking only one language. • **n.** a monoglot person.
– ORIGIN C19: from Gk *monoglōttos*, from *monos* 'single' + *glōtta* 'tongue'.

**monogram** • **n.** a motif of two or more interwoven letters, typically a person's initials. • **v.** decorate with a monogram.
– DERIVATIVES **monogrammatic** adj.

**monograph** • **n.** a detailed written study of a single specialized subject. • **v.** write a monograph on.
– DERIVATIVES **monographer** n. **monographic** adj. **monographist** n.

**monohull** • **n.** a boat with only one hull, as opposed to a catamaran or multihull.

**monohybrid** • **n.** Genetics a hybrid that is heterozygous with respect to a specified gene.

**monohydrate** • **n.** Chemistry a hydrate containing one mole of water per mole of the compound.

**monohydric** • **adj.** Chemistry (of an alcohol) containing one hydroxyl group.

**monokini** • **n.** a woman's one-piece beach garment equivalent to the lower half of a bikini.

**monolatry** /məˈnɒlətri/ • **n.** the worship of one god without denial of the existence of other gods.
– DERIVATIVES **monolater** n. **monolatrist** n. **monolatrous** adj.

**monolayer** • **n. 1** Chemistry a layer one molecule thick. **2** Biology & Medicine a cell culture in a layer one cell thick.

**monolingual** • **adj.** speaking, using, or expressed in only one language.
– DERIVATIVES **monolingualism** n.

**monolith** • **n. 1** a large single upright block of stone or concrete, especially a pillar or monument. **2** a very large and indivisible organization or institution.
– ORIGIN C19: from Fr. *monolithe*, from Gk *monolithos*, from *monos* 'single' + *lithos* 'stone'.

**monolithic** • **adj. 1** formed of a single large block of stone. **2** very large and uniform or indivisible. **3** Electronics (of a solid-state circuit) composed of active and passive components formed in a single chip.

**monologue** • **n. 1** a long speech by one actor in a play or film. **2** a long, tedious speech by one person during a conversation.
– DERIVATIVES **monologic** adj. **monological** adj. **monologist** (also **-loguist**) n. **monologize** (also **-ise**) v.
– ORIGIN C17: from Fr., from Gk *monologos* 'speaking

alone'.

**monomania** ● n. obsessive preoccupation with one thing.
– DERIVATIVES **monomaniac** n. & adj. **monomaniacal** adj.

**monomer** /ˈmɒnəmə/ ● n. Chemistry a molecule that can be bonded to other identical molecules to form a polymer.
– DERIVATIVES **monomeric** adj.

**monometallic** ● adj. consisting of one metal only. ➤ of, involving, or using a standard of currency based on one metal.
– DERIVATIVES **monometallism** n. **monometallist** n. & adj.

**monometer** /məˈnɒmɪtə/ ● n. Prosody a line consisting of one metrical foot.
– DERIVATIVES **monometric** adj. **monometrical** adj.

**monomial** /məˈnəʊmɪəl/ Mathematics ● adj. (of an algebraic expression) consisting of one term. ● n. a monomial expression.
– ORIGIN C18: from MONO-, on the pattern of *binomial*.

**monomolecular** ● adj. Chemistry (of a layer) one molecule thick. ➤ consisting of or involving one molecule.

**monomorphemic** /ˌmɒnə(ʊ)mɔːˈfiːmɪk/ ● adj. Linguistics consisting of a single morpheme.

**monomorphic** /ˌmɒnə(ʊ)ˈmɔːfɪk/ ● adj. Biology (of a species or population) showing little or no variation in morphology or phenotype. ➤ (of an animal species) having sexes that are similar in size and appearance.
– DERIVATIVES **monomorphism** n. **monomorphous** adj.
– ORIGIN C19: from MONO- + Gk *morphē* 'form'.

**mononuclear** ● adj. Biology (of a cell) having one nucleus.

**mononucleosis** /ˌmɒnə(ʊ)njuːklɪˈəʊsɪs/ ● n. Medicine an abnormally high proportion of monocytes in the blood, especially associated with glandular fever.

**monophagous** /məˈnɒfəgəs/ ● adj. Zoology (of an animal) eating only one kind of food.

**monophonic** /ˌmɒnə(ʊ)ˈfɒnɪk/ ● adj. **1** (of sound reproduction) using only one channel of transmission. Compare with STEREOPHONIC. **2** Music having a single melodic line without harmonies or melody in counterpoint.
– DERIVATIVES **monophonically** adv. **monophony** n.

**monophthong** /ˈmɒnəfθɒŋ/ ● n. Phonetics a vowel that has a single perceived auditory quality.
– DERIVATIVES **monophthongal** adj.
– ORIGIN C17: from Gk *monophthongos*, from *monos* 'single' + *phthongos* 'sound'.

**monophyletic** /ˌmɒnə(ʊ)fʌɪˈlɛtɪk/ ● adj. Biology (of a group of organisms) descended from a common evolutionary ancestor or ancestral group, especially one not shared with any other group.

**Monophysite** /məˈnɒfɪsʌɪt/ ● n. Christian Theology a person who holds that there is only one inseparable nature (partly divine, partly and subordinately human) in the person of Christ.
– DERIVATIVES **Monophysitism** n.
– ORIGIN C17: via eccles. L. from eccles. Gk *monophusitēs*, from *monos* 'single' + *phusis* 'nature'.

**monoplane** ● n. an aircraft with one pair of wings.

**monoplegia** /ˌmɒnə(ʊ)ˈpliːdʒə/ ● n. paralysis of one limb or region of the body. Compare with PARAPLEGIA.
– DERIVATIVES **monoplegic** adj.

**monoploid** /ˈmɒnə(ʊ)plɔɪd/ ● adj. less common term for HAPLOID.

**monopod** ● n. a one-legged support for a camera or fishing rod.
– ORIGIN C19: via L. from Gk *monopodion*, from *monos* 'single' + *pous, pod-* 'foot'.

**monopodium** /ˌmɒnə(ʊ)ˈpəʊdɪəm/ ● n. (pl. **monopodia**) Botany a single continuous growth axis which extends at its apex and produces successive lateral shoots.
– DERIVATIVES **monopodial** adj.

**monopole**[1] ● n. **1** Physics a single electric charge or magnetic pole, especially a hypothetical isolated magnetic pole. **2** a radio aerial or pylon consisting of a single pole or rod.

**monopole**[2] ● n. a champagne that is exclusive to one shipper.
– ORIGIN C19: from Fr. 'monopoly'.

**monopolist** ● n. a person who has a monopoly.
– DERIVATIVES **monopolistic** adj. **monopolistically** adv.

**monopolize** (also **-ise**) ● v. hold or obtain a monopoly on.
– DERIVATIVES **monopolization** n. **monopolizer** n.

**monopoly** ● n. (pl. **-ies**) **1** the exclusive possession or control of the supply of or trade in a commodity or service. ➤ a company or group having a monopoly, or a commodity or service controlled by one. **2** exclusive possession or control of something: *men don't have a monopoly on unrequited love.* **3** (**Monopoly**) trademark a board game in which players engage in simulated property and financial dealings using imitation money.
– ORIGIN C16: via L. from Gk *monopōlion*, from *monos* 'single' + *pōlein* 'sell'.

**monopropellant** ● n. a substance used as rocket fuel without an additional oxidizing agent. ● adj. using such a substance.

**monopsony** /məˈnɒpsəni/ ● n. (pl. **-ies**) Economics a market situation in which there is only one buyer.
– ORIGIN 1930s: from MONO- + Gk *opsōnein* 'buy provisions' + -Y[3].

**monopteros** /məˈnɒptərɒs/ ● n. a classical temple consisting of a single circle of columns supporting a roof.
– DERIVATIVES **monopteral** adj.
– ORIGIN C17: from med. L., from Gk *monos* 'single' + *pteron* 'wing'.

**monorail** ● n. a railway in which the track consists of a single rail, typically elevated and with the trains suspended from it.

**monorchid** ● adj. having only one testicle. ● n. a monorchid person or animal.
– DERIVATIVES **monorchidism** n.
– ORIGIN C19: from mod. L. *monorchis, monorchid-*, from Gk *monos* 'single' + *orkhis* 'testicle'.

**monosaccharide** ● n. Chemistry any of the class of sugars (e.g. glucose) that cannot be hydrolysed to give a simpler sugar.

**monosemy** /ˈmɒnə(ʊ)ˌsiːmi/ ● n. Linguistics the property of having only one meaning.
– DERIVATIVES **monosemic** adj. **monosemous** adj.
– ORIGIN 1950s: from MONO- + Gk *sēma* 'sign' + -Y[3].

**monoski** ● n. a single broad ski attached to both feet.
– DERIVATIVES **monoskier** n. **monoskiing** n.

**monosodium glutamate** ● n. a compound which occurs naturally as a breakdown product of proteins and is used as a flavour enhancer in food.

**monosome** /ˈmɒnə(ʊ)səʊm/ ● n. Biology an unpaired (usually X) chromosome in a diploid chromosome complement.

**monosomy** /məˈnɒsəmi/ ● n. Biology the condition of having a diploid chromosome complement in which one (usually the X) chromosome lacks its homologous partner.
– DERIVATIVES **monosomic** adj.

**monospecific** ● adj. Biology **1** relating to or consisting of only one species. **2** (of an antibody) specific to one antigen.

**monostable** Electronics ● adj. (of a circuit or device) having only one stable position or state. ● n. a monostable device or circuit.

**monostrophic** /ˌmɒnə(ʊ)ˈstrɒfɪk, -ˈstrəʊf-/ ● adj. Prosody consisting of repetitions of the same strophic arrangement.

**monosyllabic** ● adj. **1** consisting of one syllable. **2** using brief words to signify reluctance to engage in conversation.
– DERIVATIVES **monosyllabically** adv. **monosyllable** n.

**monosynaptic** /ˌmɒnə(ʊ)sɪˈnaptɪk/ ● adj. Physiology (of a reflex pathway) involving a single synapse.

**monotechnic** ● adj. related to or teaching a single technical subject.

**monotheism** /ˈmɒnə(ʊ)ˌθiːɪz(ə)m/ ● n. the doctrine or belief that there is only one God.
– DERIVATIVES **monotheist** n. & adj. **monotheistic** adj. **monotheistically** adv.

– ORIGIN C17: from **MONO-** + Gk *theos* 'god' + **-ISM**.

**Monothelite** /mə'nɒθəlʌɪt/ (also **Monothelete** /-liːt/) ● **n.** Christian Theology an adherent of the 7th-century doctrine that Jesus had only one (i.e. divine) will.
– ORIGIN ME: via eccles. L. from eccles. Gk *monothelētēs*, from *monos* 'single' + *thelētēs* (from *thelein* 'to will').

**monotint** ● **n.** archaic term for **MONOCHROME**.

**monotone** /'mɒnətəʊn/ ● **n.** a continuing sound that is unchanging in pitch and lacks intonation.
– ORIGIN C17: from mod. L. *monotonus*, from late Gk *monotonos*.

**monotonic** ● **adj. 1** Mathematics (of a function or quantity) varying in such a way that it either never decreases or never increases. **2** speaking or uttered in a monotone.
– DERIVATIVES **monotonically** adv. **monotonicity** n.

**monotonous** ● **adj. 1** dull, tedious, and repetitious. **2** lacking in variation of tone or pitch.
– DERIVATIVES **monotonously** adv. **monotony** n.

**monotreme** /'mɒnə(ʊ)triːm/ ● **n.** Zoology a mammal of a small order (Monotremata) comprising the platypus and the echidnas, distinguished by laying eggs and having a common urogenital and digestive opening.
– ORIGIN C19: from **MONO-** + Gk *trēma* 'hole'.

**monotropy** /mə'nɒtrəpi/ ● **n.** Chemistry the existence of allotropes of an element, one of which is stable and the others metastable under all known conditions.
– DERIVATIVES **monotrope** n.
– ORIGIN C20: from **MONO-** + Gk *tropē* 'turning' + **-Y**³.

**monotype** ● **n. 1** (**Monotype**) Printing, trademark a typesetting machine which casts type in metal, one character at a time. **2** a single print taken from a design created in oil paint or printing ink on glass or metal.

**monotypic** /ˌmɒnə(ʊ)'tɪpɪk/ ● **adj.** chiefly Biology having only one type or representative, especially (of a genus) containing only one species.

**monounsaturated** ● **adj.** Chemistry (of an organic compound, especially a fat) saturated except for one multiple bond.

**monovalent** /ˌmɒnə(ʊ)'veɪl(ə)nt/ ● **adj.** Chemistry having a valency of one.

**monoxide** ● **n.** Chemistry an oxide containing one atom of oxygen in its molecule or empirical formula.

**monozygotic** /ˌmɒnə(ʊ)zʌɪ'gɒtɪk/ ● **adj.** (of twins) derived from a single ovum, and so identical.
– ORIGIN C20: from **MONO-** + **ZYGOTE** + **-IC**.

**monozygous** /ˌmɒnə(ʊ)'zʌɪgəs/ ● **adj.** another term for **MONOZYGOTIC**.
– DERIVATIVES **monozygosity** n.

**mons** /mɒnz/ ● **n.** short for **MONS PUBIS**.

**Monseigneur** /ˌmɒnsɛ'njəː, French mɔ̃sɛɲœʀ/ ● **n.** (pl. **Messeigneurs** /ˌmɛsɛn'jəː, French mesɛɲœʀ/) a title or form of address for a French-speaking prince, cardinal, archbishop, or bishop.
– ORIGIN Fr., from *mon* 'my' + *seigneur* 'lord'.

**Monsieur** /mə'sjəː, French məsjø/ ● **n.** (pl. **Messieurs** /mɛ'sjəː, French mesjø/) a title or form of address for a French-speaking man, corresponding to *Mr* or *sir*.
– ORIGIN Fr., from *mon* 'my' + *sieur* 'lord'.

**Monsignor** /mɒn'siːnjə, ˌmɒnsiː'njɔː/ ● **n.** (pl. **Monsignori** /-'njɔːri/) the title of various senior Roman Catholic posts, such as a prelate or an officer of the papal court.
– ORIGIN Ital., on the pattern of Fr. *Monseigneur*.

**monsoon** ● **n. 1** a seasonal prevailing wind in the region of the Indian subcontinent and SE Asia, bringing rain when blowing from the south-west. **2** the rainy season accompanying the SW monsoon.
– DERIVATIVES **monsoonal** adj.
– ORIGIN C16: from Port. *monção*, from Arab. *mawsim* 'season'.

**mons pubis** /ˌmɒnz 'pjuːbɪs/ ● **n.** the rounded mass of fatty tissue lying over the joint of the pubic bones.
– ORIGIN C19: L., lit. 'mount of the pubes'.

**monster** ● **n. 1** a large, ugly, and frightening imaginary creature. ➤an inhumanly cruel or wicked person. ➤humorous a rude or badly behaved person, typically a child. **2** a congenitally malformed or mutant animal or plant. **3** [as modifier] informal extraordinarily large.
– ORIGIN ME: from OFr. *monstre*, from L. *monstrum* 'portent or monster', from *monere* 'warn'.

**monstera** /mɒn'stɪərə/ ● **n.** a tropical American climbing plant of a genus including the Swiss cheese plant. [Genus *Monstera*.]
– ORIGIN mod. L., perh. from L. *monstrum* 'monster'.

**monstrance** /'mɒnstr(ə)ns/ ● **n.** (in the Roman Catholic Church) an open or transparent receptacle in which the consecrated Host is exposed for veneration.
– ORIGIN ME (also in the sense 'demonstration or proof'): from med. L. *monstrantia*, from L. *monstrare* 'to show'.

**monstrosity** ● **n.** (pl. **-ies**) **1** something very large and unsightly. ➤a grossly malformed animal, plant, or person. **2** something which is outrageously or offensively wrong.

**monstrous** ● **adj. 1** very large and ugly or frightening. **2** inhumanly or outrageously evil or wrong.
– DERIVATIVES **monstrously** adv. **monstrousness** n.

**mons Veneris** /ˌmɒnz 'vɛnərɪs/ ● **n.** (in women) the mons pubis.
– ORIGIN C17: L., lit. 'mount of Venus'.

**Mont.** ● **abbrev.** Montana.

**montage** /mɒn'tɑːʒ, 'mɒntɑːʒ/ ● **n.** the technique of producing a picture, film, etc. by piecing together separate sections. ➤a picture, film, etc. resulting from this.
– ORIGIN C20: Fr., from *monter* 'to mount'.

**Montagnais** /ˌmɒntan'jeɪ/ ● **n.** (pl. same) **1** a member of an American Indian people living in eastern Canada. **2** the Algonquian language of this people, closely related to Cree.
– ORIGIN from Fr., lit. 'of the mountains'.

**Montagnard** /ˌmɒntə'njɑː(d)/ ● **n. & adj.** former term for **HMONG**.
– ORIGIN Fr., from *montagne* 'mountain'.

**Montanan** /mɒn'tan(ə)n/ ● **n.** a native or inhabitant of the US state of Montana. ● **adj.** of or relating to Montana.

**montane** /'mɒnteɪn/ ● **adj.** of or inhabiting mountainous country.
– ORIGIN C19: from L. *montanus*, from *mons, mont-* 'mountain'.

**Montanism** /'mɒntənɪz(ə)m/ ● **n.** the tenets of a heretical millenarian Christian sect founded by the 2nd-century priest Montanus.
– DERIVATIVES **Montanist** n.

**montbretia** /mɒn(t)'briːʃə/ ● **n.** a plant of the iris family with bright orange-yellow trumpet-shaped flowers. [*Crocosmia* × *crocosmiflora*.]
– ORIGIN C19: mod. L., named after the Fr. botanist A. F. E. Coquebert de *Montbret*.

**monte** /'mɒnti/ ● **n.** (usu. **three-card monte**) a game of Mexican origin played with three cards, similar to three-card trick.
– ORIGIN C19: Sp., lit. 'mountain', also 'heap of cards left after dealing'.

**Monte Carlo method** ● **n.** Statistics a technique in which a large quantity of randomly generated numbers are studied using a probabilistic model to find an approximate solution to a numerical problem.

**Montenegrin** /ˌmɒntɪ'niːgrɪn/ ● **n.** a native or inhabitant of Montenegro, a republic in the Balkans.

**Montessori** /ˌmɒntɪ'sɔːri/ ● **n.** [usu. as modifier] a system of education for young children that seeks to develop natural interests and activities rather than use formal teaching methods.
– ORIGIN C20: from the name of the Ital. educationist Maria *Montessori*.

**Montezuma's revenge** /ˌmɒntɪ'z(j)uːməz/ ● **n.** informal diarrhoea suffered by visitors to Mexico.
– ORIGIN 1960s: from the name of *Montezuma* II, the last Aztec emperor.

**month** ● **n.** each of the twelve named periods into which a year is divided. ➤a period of time between the same dates in successive calendar months. ➤a period of 28 days or four weeks.
– PHRASES **a month of Sundays** informal a very long time.
– ORIGIN OE *mōnath*, of Gmc origin; rel. to **MOON**.

**monthly** • adj. done, produced, or occurring once a month. • adv. once a month; every month. • n. (pl. **-ies**) **1** a magazine that is published once a month. **2** (**monthlies**) informal a menstrual period.

**montmorillonite** /ˌmɒntməˈrɪlənʌɪt/ • n. an aluminium-rich clay mineral which undergoes reversible expansion on absorbing water.
– ORIGIN C19: from *Montmorillon*, the name of a town in France, + **-ITE**[1].

**Montserratian** /ˌmɒn(t)səˈraʃ(ə)n/ • n. a native or inhabitant of the Caribbean island of Montserrat. • adj. of or relating to Montserrat.

**monty** • n. (in phr. **the full monty**) Brit. informal the full amount expected, desired, or possible.
– ORIGIN of unknown origin; perh. from *the full Montague Burton*, appar. meaning 'Sunday-best three-piece suit' (from the name of a tailor), or in ref. to 'the full cooked English breakfast' insisted upon by Field Marshal *Montgomery*.

**monument** • n. **1** a statue, building, or other structure erected to commemorate a notable person or event. **2** a structure or site of historical importance or interest. **3** an enduring and memorable example or reminder: *the house was a monument to untutored taste.*
– ORIGIN ME (denoting a burial place): via Fr. from L. *monumentum*, from *monere* 'remind'.

**monumental** • adj. **1** great in importance, extent, or size. **2** of or serving as a monument.
– DERIVATIVES **monumentalism** n. **monumentality** n. **monumentalize** (also **-ise**) v. **monumentally** adv.

**monumental mason** • n. Brit. a person who makes tombstones and similar items.

**-mony** • suffix forming nouns often denoting an action, state, or quality: *ceremony.*
– ORIGIN from L. *-monia*, *-monium*.

**monzonite** /ˈmɒnzənʌɪt/ • n. Geology a granular igneous rock containing approximately equal amounts of orthoclase and plagioclase.
– ORIGIN C19: named after Mount *Monzoni* in the Tyrol, Italy, + **-ITE**[1].

**moo** • v. (**moos, mooed**) make the characteristic deep resonant vocal sound of cattle. • n. (pl. **moos**) **1** a sound of this kind. **2** Brit. informal an irritating or disliked woman.
– ORIGIN C16: imitative.

**mooch** informal • v. **1** (usu. **mooch about/around**) Brit. loiter in a bored or listless manner. **2** N. Amer. ask for or obtain (something) without paying for it. • n. **1** Brit. an instance of loitering in a bored or listless manner. **2** N. Amer. a beggar or scrounger.
– DERIVATIVES **moocher** n.
– ORIGIN ME (in the sense 'to hoard'): prob. from Anglo-Norman Fr. *muscher* 'hide, skulk'.

**moo-cow** • n. a child's name for a cow.

**mood**[1] • n. **1** a state of mind or feeling. ➤an angry, irritable, or sullen state of mind. **2** the atmosphere or pervading tone of a work of art. **3** [as modifier] inducing or suggestive of a particular mood: *mood music.*
– ORIGIN OE *mōd*, of Gmc origin.

**mood**[2] • n. **1** Grammar a form or category of a verb expressing fact (indicative mood), command (imperative mood), question (interrogative mood), wish (optative mood), or conditionality (subjunctive mood). **2** Logic any of the valid forms into which each of the figures of a categorical syllogism may occur.
– ORIGIN C16: var. of **MODE**, influenced by **MOOD**[1].

**moody** • adj. (**-ier, -iest**) **1** given to unpredictable changes of mood, especially sudden bouts of gloominess or sullenness. **2** giving an impression of melancholy or mystery.
– DERIVATIVES **moodily** adv. **moodiness** n.

**moolah** /ˈmuːlə/ • n. informal money.
– ORIGIN 1930s (orig. US): of unknown origin.

**mooli** /ˈmuːli/ • n. a radish of a variety with a large slender white root, used especially in Eastern cuisine.
– ORIGIN 1960s: from Hindi *mūlī*, from Sanskrit *mūla* 'root'.

**moon** • n. **1** (also **Moon**) the natural satellite of the earth, visible (chiefly at night) by reflected light from the sun. ➤a natural satellite of any planet. **2** poetic/literary or humorous a month: *many moons ago.* • v. **1** behave or move in a listless or dreamy manner. **2** informal expose one's buttocks to someone in order to insult or amuse them.
– PHRASES **over the moon** Brit. informal delighted.
– DERIVATIVES **moonless** adj. **moonlike** adj.
– ORIGIN OE *mōna*, of Gmc origin; rel. to **MONTH**.

**moonbeam** • n. a ray of moonlight.

**moon boot** • n. a warm, thickly padded boot with an outer surface of fabric or plastic.

**mooncalf** • n. (pl. **mooncalves**) a foolish person.

**moon daisy** • n. another term for **OX-EYE DAISY**.

**moon-faced** • adj. having a round face.

**moonfish** • n. (pl. same or **-fishes**) a deep-bodied, laterally compressed marine fish. [*Selene setapinnis* (Atlantic), and other species.]

**moonflower** • n. a tropical American climbing plant of the convolvulus family, with sweet-smelling trumpet-shaped white flowers which open at dusk and close at midday. [*Ipomoea alba*.]

**Moonie** • n. informal, often derogatory a member of the Unification Church.
– ORIGIN 1970s: from the name of its founder, Sun Myung *Moon*.

**moonlight** • n. the light of the moon. • v. (past and past part. **-lighted**) informal do a second job, especially secretly and at night, in addition to one's regular employment.
– DERIVATIVES **moonlighter** n. **moonlit** adj.

**moonraker** • n. **1** dialect a native of the county of Wiltshire. [with ref. to a story of men caught raking a pond, who claimed they were raking out the moon.] **2** a small square sail set above a skysail on a sailing ship.

**moonrat** • n. a rat-like mammal of the hedgehog family, native to SE Asia and China. [*Echinosorex gymnurus* and other species.]

**moonscape** • n. a landscape resembling the surface of the moon, especially in being rocky and barren.

**moonshee** /ˈmuːnʃiː/ • n. variant spelling of **MUNSHI**.

**moonshine** • n. **1** foolish talk or ideas. **2** informal, chiefly N. Amer. illicitly distilled or smuggled liquor.

**moonshiner** • n. informal, chiefly N. Amer. an illicit distiller or smuggler of liquor.

**moon shot** • n. the launching of a spacecraft to the moon.

**moonstomp** • n. an informal dance characterized by heavy rhythmic stamping. • v. perform such a dance.

**moonstone** • n. a pearly white semi-precious stone, especially one consisting of alkali feldspar.

**moonstruck** • adj. unable to think or act normally, especially because of being in love.

**moonwalk** • v. [usu. as noun **moonwalking**] **1** walk on the moon. **2** move or dance in a way reminiscent of the characteristic weightless movement of walking on the moon.
– DERIVATIVES **moonwalker** n.

**moonwort** /ˈmuːnwəːt/ • n. a fern with a single small frond of fan-shaped lobes and a separate spore-producing spike. [Genus *Botrychium*.]
– ORIGIN C15: so called because of the crescent-shaped segments of the fronds.

**moony** • adj. (**-ier, -iest**) dreamy and unaware of one's surroundings, especially through being in love.

**Moor** /mʊə, mɔː/ • n. a member of a NW African Muslim people of mixed Berber and Arab descent, that conquered the Iberian peninsula in the 8th century.
– DERIVATIVES **Moorish** adj.
– ORIGIN from OFr. *More*, via L. from Gk *Mauros* 'inhabitant of Mauretania' (an ancient region of N. Africa).

**moor**[1] /mʊə, mɔː/ • n. **1** a tract of open uncultivated upland, typically covered with heather. **2** US or dialect a fen.
– DERIVATIVES **moorish** adj. **moory** adj.
– ORIGIN OE *mōr*, of Gmc origin.

**moor**[2] /mʊə, mɔː/ • v. make fast (a boat) by attaching it by cable or rope to the shore or to an anchor.
– DERIVATIVES **moorage** n.
– ORIGIN C15: prob. from the Gmc base of Du. *meren*.

**moorcock** • n. Brit. a male red grouse.

**moorfowl** ● n. (pl. same) Brit. another term for RED GROUSE.

**moorhen** ● n. an aquatic bird of the rail family with mainly blackish plumage and a red and yellow bill. [*Gallinula chloropus* and other species.]

**mooring** (also **moorings**) ● n. **1** a place where a boat is moored. **2** the ropes or cables by which a boat is moored.

**Moorish idol** ● n. a disc-shaped fish with bold vertical black-and-white bands and a very tall tapering dorsal fin, of coral reefs in the Indo-Pacific region. [*Zanclus cornutus*.]

**moorland** ● n. (also **moorlands**) an extensive area of moor.

**moose** ● n. (pl. same) North American term for ELK.
– ORIGIN C17: from Abnaki *mos*.

**moot** ● adj. subject to debate, dispute, or uncertainty: *a moot point*. ● v. raise or suggest (a question or idea). ● n. **1** Brit. an assembly held for debate, especially in Anglo-Saxon and medieval times. **2** Law a mock trial set up to examine a hypothetical case as an academic exercise.
– ORIGIN OE *mōt* 'assembly or meeting' and *mōtian* 'to converse', of Gmc origin; rel. to MEET[1].

**mop[1]** ● n. **1** an implement consisting of a bundle of thick loose strings or a sponge attached to a handle, used for wiping floors. ➤ an act of wiping with a mop. **2** a thick mass of disordered hair. ● v. (**mopped**, **mopping**) **1** clean or soak up liquid by wiping. **2** (**mop something up**) put an end to or dispose of something.
– DERIVATIVES **moppy** adj.
– ORIGIN C15: perh. ult. rel. to L. *mappa* 'napkin'.

**mop[2]** ● n. Brit. historical an autumn fair or gathering at which farmhands and servants were hired.
– ORIGIN C17: prob. from the practice at the fair whereby a mop was carried by a maidservant seeking employment.

**mopboard** ● n. US term for SKIRTING.

**mope** ● v. (often **mope around/about**) be listless and apathetic because of unhappiness or boredom. ● n. informal a depressive or foolish person.
– DERIVATIVES **moper** n. **mopery** n. **mopey** (also **mopy**) adj. **mopily** adv. **mopiness** n. **mopish** adj.
– ORIGIN C16: perh. of Scand. origin; cf. Swed. dial. *mopa* 'to sulk'.

**moped** /ˈməʊpɛd/ ● n. a light motor cycle, especially one with an engine capacity of not more than 50 cc.
– ORIGIN 1950s: from Swed., from (*trampcykel med*) *mo(tor och) ped(aler)* 'pedal cycle with motor and pedals'.

**moppet** ● n. informal a small endearingly sweet child.
– ORIGIN C17: from obs. *moppe* 'baby or rag doll' + -ET[1].

**moquette** /mɒˈkɛt/ ● n. a thick pile fabric used for carpets and upholstery.
– ORIGIN 1930s: from Fr., perh. from obs. Ital. *mocaiardo* 'mohair'.

**MOR** ● abbrev. (of music) middle-of-the-road.

**mor** /mɔː/ ● n. Soil Science humus formed under acid conditions.
– ORIGIN 1930s: from Dan.

**moraine** /məˈreɪn/ ● n. Geology a mass of rocks and sediment carried down and deposited by a glacier.
– DERIVATIVES **morainal** adj. **morainic** adj.
– ORIGIN C18: from Fr., from Ital. dial. *morena*, from Fr. dial. *morre* 'snout'.

**moral** ● adj. **1** concerned with the principles of right and wrong behaviour and the goodness or badness of human character. **2** adhering to the code of behaviour that is considered right or acceptable. ● n. **1** a lesson that can be derived from a story or experience. **2** (**morals**) standards of behaviour, or principles of right and wrong.
– DERIVATIVES **morally** adv.
– ORIGIN ME: from L. *moralis*, from *mos*, *mor-* 'custom', (pl.) *mores* 'morals'.

**morale** /məˈrɑːl/ ● n. the confidence, enthusiasm, and discipline of a person or group at a particular time.
– ORIGIN C18: from Fr. *moral*, respelled to preserve the final stress in pronunc.

**moralist** ● n. **1** a person who moralizes, or who teaches or promotes morality. **2** a person who behaves morally.
– DERIVATIVES **moralism** n. **moralistic** adj. **moralistically** adv.

**morality** ● n. (pl. **-ies**) **1** principles concerning the distinction between right and wrong or good and bad behaviour. ➤ a system of values and moral principles. **2** the extent to which an action is right or wrong.

**morality play** ● n. a kind of drama presenting a moral lesson and having personified abstract qualities as the main characters.

**moralize** (also **-ise**) ● v. **1** comment on issues of right and wrong, typically with an unfounded air of superiority. **2** interpret or explain as giving moral lessons. **3** improve the morals of.
– DERIVATIVES **moralization** n. **moralizer** n. **moralizing** adj. **moralizingly** adv.

**moral law** ● n. (in some systems of ethics) an absolute principle defining the criteria of right action.

**moral majority** ● n. [treated as pl.] a majority of people regarded as favouring strict moral standards. ➤ (**Moral Majority**) a right-wing Christian movement in the US.

**moral philosophy** ● n. the branch of philosophy concerned with ethics.

**moral science** ● n. dated social sciences and/or philosophy.

**moral sense** ● n. the ability to distinguish between right and wrong.

**moral support** ● n. support or help of a psychological rather than physical nature.

**moral victory** ● n. a defeat that can be interpreted as a victory in terms of morals or principles.

**morass** /məˈras/ ● n. **1** an area of muddy or boggy ground. **2** a complicated or confused situation.
– ORIGIN C15: from Du. *moeras*, alt. (by assimilation to *moer* 'moor') of MDu. *marasch*, from OFr. *marais* 'marsh', from med. L. *mariscus*.

**moratorium** /ˌmɒrəˈtɔːrɪəm/ ● n. (pl. **moratoriums** or **moratoria** /-rɪə/) **1** a temporary prohibition of an activity. **2** Law a legal authorization to debtors to postpone payment.
– ORIGIN C19: mod. L., neut. (used as n.) of late L. *moratorius* 'delaying', from L. *morat-*, *morari* 'delay'.

**Moravian** ● n. **1** a native or inhabitant of the region of Moravia in the Czech Republic. **2** a member of a Protestant Church founded by emigrants from Moravia holding views derived from the Hussites and accepting the Bible as the only source of faith. ● adj. of or relating to Moravia or the Moravian Church.

**moray** /mɒˈreɪ, ˈmɒreɪ/ (also **moray eel**) ● n. an eel-like predatory fish of warm seas which typically hides in crevices. [Family Muraenidae: numerous species.]
– ORIGIN C17: from Port. *moréia*, via L. from Gk *muraina*.

**morbid** ● adj. **1** characterized by or appealing to an abnormal and unhealthy interest in unpleasant subjects, especially death and disease. **2** Medicine of the nature of or indicative of disease.
– DERIVATIVES **morbidity** n. **morbidly** adv. **morbidness** n.
– ORIGIN C17: from L. *morbidus*, from *morbus* 'disease'.

**morbid anatomy** ● n. the anatomy of diseased organs and tissues.

**morbific** /mɔːˈbɪfɪk/ ● adj. dated causing disease.

**morbilli** /mɔːˈbɪlʌɪ, -liː/ ● pl. n. technical term for MEASLES.
– ORIGIN C16: L., pl. of *morbillus* 'pustule', from *morbus* 'disease'.

**morbillivirus** /mɔːˈbɪlɪˌvʌɪrəs/ ● n. Medicine any of a group of paramyxoviruses which causes measles, rinderpest, and canine distemper.
– ORIGIN 1970s: from L. *morbilli* (pl. of *morbillus* 'pustule', from *morbus* 'disease') + VIRUS.

**morceau** /mɔːˈsəʊ/ ● n. (pl. **morceaux**) a short literary or musical composition.
– ORIGIN C18: Fr., lit. 'morsel, piece'.

**mordacious** /mɔːˈdeɪʃəs/ ● adj. formal **1** bitingly sarcastic or vituperative. **2** given to biting.
– ORIGIN C17: from L. *mordax*, *mordac-* 'biting' + -IOUS.

**mordant** /ˈmɔːd(ə)nt/ ● adj. (especially of humour) sharp or critical; biting. ● n. a substance that combines with a

dye or stain and thereby fixes it in a material. ➤an adhesive compound for fixing gold leaf. ➤a corrosive liquid used to etch the lines on a printing plate. ● **v.** impregnate or treat (a fabric) with a mordant.
– DERIVATIVES **mordancy** n. **mordantly** adv.
– ORIGIN C15: from Fr., pres. part. of *mordre* 'to bite', from L. *mordere*.

**mordent** /ˈmɔːd(ə)nt/ ● **n.** Music an ornament consisting of one rapid alternation of a written note with the note immediately below or above it in the scale.
– ORIGIN C19: via Ger. from Ital. *mordente*, pres. part. of *mordere* 'to bite'.

**Mordvin** /ˈmɔːdvɪn/ (also **Mordva** /ˈmɔːdvə/) ● **n. 1** a member of a non-Russian people inhabiting Mordvinia in European Russia. **2** the Finno-Ugric language of this people.

**more** ● **det. & pron.** a greater or additional amount or degree. ● **adv. 1** forming the comparative of adjectives and adverbs, especially those of more than one syllable. **2** to a greater extent. ➤(**more than**) extremely: *she is more than happy to oblige.* **3** again. **4** moreover.
– PHRASES **more and more** at a continually increasing rate. **more or less** speaking imprecisely; to a certain extent. **no more 1** nothing further. **2** no further. **3** (**be no more**) exist no longer. **4** never again. **5** neither.
– ORIGIN OE *māra*, of Gmc origin.

**moreen** /məˈriːn/ (also **morine**) ● **n.** a strong ribbed cotton fabric, used chiefly for curtains.
– ORIGIN C17: perh. a fanciful formation from MOIRE.

**moreish** ● **adj.** Brit. informal so pleasant to eat that one wants more.

**morel** /məˈrɛl/ ● **n.** an edible fungus having a brown oval or pointed fruiting body with an irregular honeycombed surface. [*Morchella esculenta* and related species.]
– ORIGIN C17: from Fr. *morille*, from Du. *morilje*.

**morello** /mɒˈrɛləʊ/ ● **n.** (pl. **-os**) a dark cherry of a sour kind used in cooking.
– ORIGIN C17: from Ital. *morello* 'blackish', from med. L. *morellus*, dimin. of L. *Maurus* 'Moor'.

**moreover** ● **adv.** as a further matter; besides.

**mores** /ˈmɔːreɪz, -riːz/ ● **pl. n.** the customs and conventions of a community.
– ORIGIN C19: from L., pl. of *mos, mor-* 'custom'.

**Moresco** /məˈrɛskəʊ/ ● **n. & adj.** variant spelling of MORISCO.

**Moresque** /məˈrɛsk, mɔː-/ ● **adj.** (of art or architecture) Moorish in style or design.
– ORIGIN ME (as a noun denoting arabesque ornament): from Fr., from Ital. *moresco*, from *Moro* 'Moor'.

**morganatic** /ˌmɔːgəˈnatɪk/ ● **adj.** of or denoting a marriage in which neither the spouse of lower rank, nor any children, have any claim to the possessions or title of the spouse of higher rank.
– DERIVATIVES **morganatically** adv.
– ORIGIN C18: from mod. L. *morganaticus*, from med. L. *matrimonium ad morganaticam* 'marriage with a morning gift' (because a gift given by a husband on the morning after the marriage was the wife's sole entitlement).

**morgen** /ˈmɔːg(ə)n/ ● **n. 1** a South African measure of land equal to about 0.8 hectare or two acres. **2** a Scandinavian and German measure of land equal to about 0.3 hectare or two thirds of an acre.
– ORIGIN C17: from Du., or from Ger. *Morgen* 'morning', appar. from the notion of 'an area of land that can be ploughed in a morning'.

**morgue** /mɔːg/ ● **n. 1** a mortuary. **2** informal a newspaper's collection of miscellaneous information for use in future obituaries.
– ORIGIN C19: from Fr., orig. the name of a building in Paris where bodies were kept until identified.

**moribund** /ˈmɒrɪbʌnd/ ● **adj. 1** at the point of death. **2** in terminal decline; lacking vitality or vigour.
– DERIVATIVES **moribundity** n.
– ORIGIN C18: from L. *moribundus*, from *mori* 'to die'.

**morine** ● **n.** variant spelling of MOREEN.

**morion** /ˈmɒrɪən/ ● **n.** a kind of helmet without beaver or visor, worn in the 16th and 17th centuries.
– ORIGIN Fr., from Sp. *morrión*, from *morro* 'round object'.

**Morisco** /məˈrɪskəʊ/ (also **Moresco**) ● **n.** (pl. **-os** or **-oes**) historical a Moor in Spain, especially one who had accepted Christian baptism.
– ORIGIN Sp., from *Moro* 'Moor'.

**Mormon** /ˈmɔːmən/ ● **n.** a member of the Church of Jesus Christ of Latter-Day Saints, a religion founded in the US in 1830 by Joseph Smith Jr.
– DERIVATIVES **Mormonism** n.
– ORIGIN the name of a prophet to whom Smith attributed *The Book of Mormon*, a collection of supposed revelations.

**morn** ● **n.** poetic/literary morning.
– ORIGIN OE *morgen*, of Gmc origin.

**mornay** /ˈmɔːneɪ/ ● **adj.** denoting or served in a cheese-flavoured white sauce.
– ORIGIN named after *Mornay*, the eldest son of the Fr. cook Joseph Voiron, the inventor of the sauce.

**morning** ● **n.** the period of time between midnight and noon, especially from sunrise to noon. ➤sunrise. ● **adv.** (**mornings**) informal every morning.
– ORIGIN ME: from MORN, on the pattern of *evening*.

**morning-after pill** ● **n.** a contraceptive pill that is effective within about thirty-six hours after intercourse.

**morning coat** ● **n.** a man's formal coat with a long back section cut into tails which curves up to join the waist at the front.

**morning dress** ● **n.** a man's formal dress of morning coat and striped trousers.

**morning glory** ● **n.** a climbing plant of the convolvulus family with trumpet-shaped flowers. [*Ipomoea purpureus* (tropical America) and related species.]

**morning sickness** ● **n.** nausea occurring in the first few months of pregnancy.

**morning star** ● **n.** (**the morning star**) a planet, especially Venus, when visible in the east before sunrise.

**Moro** /ˈmɔːrəʊ/ ● **n.** (pl. **-os**) a Muslim inhabitant of the Philippines.
– ORIGIN Sp., lit. 'Moor'.

**Moroccan** /məˈrɒkən/ ● **n.** a native or inhabitant of Morocco. ● **adj.** of or relating to Morocco.

**morocco** ● **n.** (pl. **-os**) fine flexible leather made (originally in Morocco) from goatskins tanned with sumac.

**moron** ● **n.** informal a stupid person.
– DERIVATIVES **moronic** adj. **moronically** adv.
– ORIGIN C20: from Gk *mōron*, neut. of *mōros* 'foolish'.

**morose** ● **adj.** sullen and ill-tempered.
– DERIVATIVES **morosely** adv. **moroseness** n.
– ORIGIN C16: from L. *morosus* 'peevish', from *mos, mor-* 'manner'.

**morph**[1] /mɔːf/ ● **n. 1** Biology each of several variant forms of an animal or plant. **2** Linguistics an actual linguistic form.
– ORIGIN 1940s: from Gk *morphē* 'form'.

**morph**[2] /mɔːf/ ● **v.** change smoothly and gradually from one image to another using computer animation techniques. ● **n.** an image processed in this way.
– ORIGIN 1990s: element from METAMORPHOSIS.

**-morph** ● **comb. form** denoting something having a specified form or character: *endomorph.* See word-formation panel.
– ORIGIN from Gk *morphē* 'form'.

**morpheme** /ˈmɔːfiːm/ ● **n.** Linguistics a meaningful morphological unit of a language that cannot be further divided (e.g. *in, come, -ing,* forming *incoming*).
– DERIVATIVES **morphemic** adj. **morphemically** adv.
– ORIGIN C19: from Fr. *morphème*, from Gk *morphē* 'form', on the pattern of Fr. *phonème* 'phoneme'.

**morphemics** /mɔːˈfiːmɪks/ ● **pl. n.** [treated as sing.] Linguistics the study of word structure in terms of morphemes.

**morphia** /ˈmɔːfɪə/ ● **n.** dated morphine.

**morphic resonance** ● **n.** a supposed paranormal influence by which a pattern of events or behaviour can facilitate subsequent occurrences of similar patterns.

**morphine** /ˈmɔːfiːn/ ● **n.** an analgesic and narcotic drug obtained from opium and used medicinally to relieve pain.
– ORIGIN C19: from Ger. *Morphin*, from the name of the

## Word *Formation*

**-morph** from Greek *morphē* 'form'

➤ Frequently also found as adjectives **-morphic** or **-morphous,** the **-morph** element gives rise to a variety of both technical and general words:

| | | |
|---|---|---|
| amorphous | having no clearly defined form | Gk *a-* 'without' |
| anthropomorphic | tending to attribute human characteristics to animals or objects | Gk *anthrōpos* 'human being' |
| biomorph | a decorative thing resembling a living organism | Gk *bios* 'life' |
| dimorphic | (of an organism) occurring in two different forms | Gk *di-* 'two' |
| geomorphology | the study of the physical features of the earth's surface | Gk *gē* 'earth' + -LOGY |
| isomorphic | similar in form or relation | Gk *isos* 'equal' |
| metamorphic | (of rock) having undergone transformation by heat, pressure, etc. | META- (denoting a change of condition) |
| morphology | the study of the forms of words | -LOGY (in the sense 'word') |
| zoomorphic | having an animal form | Gk *zōion* 'animal' |

Roman god of sleep, *Morpheus.*

**morphinism** /'mɔːfɪnɪz(ə)m/ ● **n.** Medicine dependence on or addiction to morphine.

**morpho** ● **n.** (pl. **-os**) a large tropical butterfly, the male of which has bright blue iridescent wings. [Genus *Morpho.*]
– ORIGIN mod. L., from Gk *Morphō*, an epithet of Aphrodite.

**morphogen** /'mɔːfədʒ(ə)n/ ● **n.** Biology a chemical agent able to cause or determine morphogenesis.

**morphogenesis** /,mɔːfə(ʊ)'dʒɛnɪsɪs/ ● **n.** **1** Biology the origin and development of morphological characteristics. **2** Geology the formation of landforms or other structures.
– DERIVATIVES **morphogenetic** adj. **morphogenic** adj.

**morpholine** /'mɔːfəliːn/ ● **n.** Chemistry a synthetic compound used as a solvent for resins and dyes and as an ingredient of emulsifying soaps used in floor polishes.
– ORIGIN C19: from **MORPHINE** + *-ol-* (see **-OL**).

**morphology** /mɔː'fɒlədʒi/ ● **n.** (pl. **-ies**) **1** the branch of biology concerned with the forms and structures of living organisms. **2** Linguistics the study of inflections and other forms of words.
– DERIVATIVES **morphologic** adj. **morphological** adj. **morphologically** adv. **morphologist** n.

**morphometrics** /,mɔːfə(ʊ)'mɛtrɪks/ ● **pl. n.** [usu. treated as sing.] chiefly Biology morphometry, especially of living organisms.

**morphometry** /mɔː'fɒmɪtri/ ● **n.** the process of measuring the external shape and dimensions of landforms, living organisms, or other objects.
– DERIVATIVES **morphometric** adj. **morphometrically** adv.

**Morris chair** ● **n.** a type of easy chair with open padded arms and an adjustable back.
– ORIGIN C19: named after the Engl. craftsman William *Morris.*

**morris dance** ● **n.** a traditional English dance performed outdoors by groups of dancers wearing costumes with small bells attached and carrying handkerchiefs or sticks.
– DERIVATIVES **morris dancer** n. **morris dancing** n.
– ORIGIN ME: *morris* from *morys,* var. of *Moorish* (see **MOOR**).

**Morrison shelter** ● **n.** a movable air-raid shelter, shaped like a table and used indoors during the Second World War.
– ORIGIN named after Herbert S. *Morrison*, UK Secretary of State for Home Affairs and Home Security 1940–5.

**morrow** ● **n.** (**the morrow**) archaic or poetic/literary the following day.
– ORIGIN ME *morwe*, from OE *morgen* (see **MORN**).

**Morse** ● **n.** (also **Morse code**) an alphabet or code in which letters are represented by combinations of long and short light or sound signals. ● **v.** signal with Morse code.
– ORIGIN C19: named after the Amer. inventor Samuel F. B. *Morse.*

**morsel** ● **n.** a small piece of food; a mouthful.
– ORIGIN ME: from OFr., dimin. of *mors* 'a bite', from L. *mors-*, *mordere* 'to bite'.

**mort** ● **n.** Hunting, archaic the note sounded on a horn when the quarry is killed.
– ORIGIN ME: via OFr. from L. *mors, mort-* 'death'.

**mortadella** /,mɔːtə'dɛlə/ ● **n.** a type of smooth-textured Italian sausage containing pieces of fat.
– ORIGIN Ital. dimin., formed irregularly from L. *murtatum* '(sausage) seasoned with myrtle berries'.

**mortal** ● **adj.** **1** (of a living creature) subject to death. **2** causing or liable to cause death; fatal. ➤ (of conflict or an enemy) admitting no reconciliation. ➤ Christian Theology denoting a grave sin that is regarded as depriving the soul of divine grace. Often contrasted with **VENIAL**. **3** (of a feeling, especially fear) very intense. **4** informal conceivable or imaginable: *every mortal thing.* ➤ very great: *a mortal hurry.* ● **n.** **1** a mortal being. **2** humorous a person contrasted with those of higher status or ability.
– DERIVATIVES **mortally** adv.
– ORIGIN ME: from OFr., or from L. *mortalis*, from *mors, mort-* 'death'.

**mortality** ● **n.** (pl. **-ies**) **1** the state of being mortal. **2** death, especially on a large scale. ➤ (also **mortality rate**) the number of deaths in a given area or period, or from a particular cause.

**mortar**[1] ● **n.** **1** a short smooth-bore gun for firing bombs at high angles. **2** a cup-shaped receptacle in which ingredients are crushed or ground in cooking or pharmacy. ● **v.** attack or bombard with bombs fired from a mortar.
– ORIGIN OE, from OFr. *mortier,* from L. *mortarium.*

**mortar**[2] ● **n.** a mixture of lime with cement, sand, and water, used in building to bond bricks or stones. ● **v.** fix or join using mortar.
– DERIVATIVES **mortarless** adj. **mortary** adj.
– ORIGIN ME: from OFr. *mortier,* from L. *mortarium,* prob. a transferred sense of the word denoting a container (see **MORTAR**[1]).

**mortar board** ● **n.** **1** an academic cap with a stiff, flat square top and a tassel. **2** a small square board with a handle on the underside, used by bricklayers for holding mortar.

**mortgage** /'mɔːgɪdʒ/ ● **n.** **1** the charging of property by a debtor to a creditor as security for a debt (especially one incurred by the purchase of the property), on the condition that it shall be returned on payment of the debt within a certain period. **2** a loan obtained through the conveyance of property as security. ● **v.** convey (a property) to a creditor as security on a loan.
– DERIVATIVES **mortgageable** adj.
– ORIGIN ME: from OFr., lit. 'dead pledge', from *mort* 'dead' + *gage* 'pledge'.

**mortgagee** ● **n.** the lender in a mortgage, typically a bank or building society.

**mortgage rate** ● n. the rate of interest charged by a mortgage lender.

**mortgagor** /ˌmɔːgɪˈdʒɔː/ ● n. the borrower in a mortgage, typically a person buying a house.

**mortice** ● n. & v. variant spelling of **MORTISE**.

**mortician** /mɔːˈtɪʃ(ə)n/ ● n. chiefly N. Amer. an undertaker.
– ORIGIN C19: from L. *mors, mort-* 'death' + **-ICIAN**.

**mortify** /ˈmɔːtɪfʌɪ/ ● v. (**-ies, -ied**) **1** (often **be mortified**) cause to feel embarrassed, ashamed, or humiliated. **2** subdue (physical urges) by self-denial or discipline. **3** (of flesh) be affected by gangrene or necrosis.
– DERIVATIVES **mortification** n. **mortifying** adj. **mortifyingly** adv.
– ORIGIN ME: from OFr. *mortifier*, from eccles. L. *mortificare* 'kill, subdue', from L. *mors, mort-* 'death'.

**mortise** /ˈmɔːtɪs/ (also **mortice**) ● n. a hole or recess designed to receive a corresponding projection (a tenon) so as to join or lock two parts together. ● v. join securely by means of a mortise and tenon. ➤ [often as adj. **mortised**] cut a mortise in or through.
– DERIVATIVES **mortiser** n.
– ORIGIN ME: from OFr. *mortaise*.

**mortise lock** ● n. a lock set within the body of a door in a recess or mortise, as opposed to one attached to the door surface.

**mortmain** /ˈmɔːtmeɪn/ ● n. Law the status of lands or tenements held inalienably by an ecclesiastical or other corporation.
– ORIGIN ME: from Anglo-Norman Fr., OFr. *mortemain*, from med. L. *mortua manus* 'dead hand' (prob. alluding to impersonal ownership).

**mortuary** /ˈmɔːtjʊəri, -tʃʊ-/ ● n. (pl. **-ies**) a room or building in which dead bodies are kept until burial or cremation. ● adj. of or relating to burial or tombs.
– ORIGIN ME (denoting a gift claimed by a parish priest from a deceased person's estate): from L. *mortuarius*, from *mortuus* 'dead'.

**morula** /ˈmɔːr(j)ʊlə/ ● n. (pl. **morulae** /-liː/) Embryology a solid ball of cells resulting from division of a fertilized ovum, and from which a blastula is formed.
– ORIGIN C19: mod. L., dimin. of L. *morum* 'mulberry'.

**morwong** /ˈmɔːwɒŋ/ ● n. a brightly coloured marine fish of Australian waters. [*Nemadactylus* and other genera.]
– ORIGIN C19: prob. from a New South Wales Aborig. lang.

**Mosaic** /məʊˈzeɪɪk/ ● adj. of or associated with Moses.
– ORIGIN C17: from Fr. *mosaïque* or mod. L. *Mosaicus*.

**mosaic** /mə(ʊ)ˈzeɪɪk/ ● n. **1** a picture or pattern produced by arranging together small variously coloured pieces of stone, tile, or glass. ➤ a colourful and variegated pattern. **2** Biology an individual (especially an animal) composed of cells of two genetically different types. **3** (also **mosaic disease**) a virus disease that results in leaf variegation in tobacco, maize, sugar cane, and other plants. **4** an arrangement of photosensitive elements in a television camera. ● v. (**mosaicked, mosaicking**) decorate with a mosaic.
– DERIVATIVES **mosaicist** n.
– ORIGIN ME: from Fr. *mosaïque*, based on L. *musi(v)um* 'decoration with small square stones', perh. ult. from Gk *mousa* 'a muse'.

**mosaic gold** ● n. an imitation gold pigment consisting of tin disulphide.

**mosaicism** /məʊˈzeɪɪsɪz(ə)m/ ● n. Biology the property or state of being composed of cells of two genetically different types.

**mosasaur** /ˈməʊzəsɔː/ ● n. a large fossil marine reptile with paddle-like limbs and a long flattened tail.
– ORIGIN C19: from mod. L. *Mosasaurus*, from L. *Mosa*, the river Meuse (near which it was first discovered) + Gk *sauros* 'lizard'.

**moscato** /mɒˈskɑːtəʊ/ ● n. a sweet Italian dessert wine.
– ORIGIN Ital.; rel. to **MUSCAT**.

**moschatel** /ˌmɒskəˈtɛl/ ● n. a small plant with pale green musk-scented flowers which grow at right angles to each other, forming five sides of a cube. [*Adoxa moschatellina*.]
– ORIGIN C18: from Fr. *moscatelle*, from Ital. *moscatella*, from *moscato* 'musk'.

**Moselle** /mə(ʊ)ˈzɛl/ (also **Mosel**) ● n. a light medium-dry white wine produced in the valley of the River Moselle.

**Moses basket** ● n. a carrycot or small portable cot made of wickerwork.
– ORIGIN with allusion to the biblical story of Moses being left in a basket among the bulrushes (Exod. 2:3).

**mosey** informal ● v. (**-eys, -eyed**) walk or move in a leisurely manner. ● n. a leisurely walk.
– ORIGIN C19: of unknown origin.

**MOSFET** ● n. Electronics a field-effect transistor in which there is a thin layer of silicon oxide between the gate and the channel.
– ORIGIN 1960s: acronym from *metal oxide semiconductor field-effect transistor*.

**mosh** ● v. dance to rock music in a violent manner involving jumping up and down and deliberately colliding with other dancers.
– ORIGIN 1980s: perh. from **MASH** or **MUSH**[1].

**moshav** /ˈməʊʃɑːv, məʊˈʃɑːv/ ● n. (pl. **moshavim**) a cooperative association of Israeli smallholders.
– ORIGIN from Heb. *mōšāḇ*, lit. 'dwelling'.

**Moslem** /ˈmɒzləm/ ● n. & adj. variant spelling of **MUSLIM**.

**Mosotho** /məˈsuːtuː/ singular form of **BASOTHO**.

**mosque** ● n. a Muslim place of worship.
– ORIGIN ME: from Fr. *mosquée*, via Ital. and Sp. from Egyptian Arab. *masgid*.

**Mosquito** ● n. (pl. **-os**) & adj. variant spelling of **MISKITO**.

**mosquito** ● n. (pl. **-oes**) a slender long-legged fly with aquatic larvae, some kinds of which transmit malaria and other diseases through the bite of the bloodsucking female. [Family Culicidae.]
– ORIGIN C16: from Sp. and Port., dimin. of *mosca*, from L. *musca* 'fly'.

**mosquito net** ● n. a fine net hung across a door or window or around a bed to keep mosquitoes away.

**moss** ● n. **1** a small flowerless green plant which grows in low carpets or rounded cushions in damp habitats and reproduces by means of spores. [Class Musci.] ➤ used in names of algae, lichens, and other low-growing plants, e.g. **reindeer moss**. **2** Scottish & N. English a peat bog. ● v. [usu. as adj. **mossed**] cover with moss.
– DERIVATIVES **mossiness** n. **mossy** adj. (**-ier, -iest**).
– ORIGIN OE *mos* 'bog or moss', of Gmc origin.

**moss agate** ● n. agate with moss-like dendritic markings.

**moss animal** ● n. a minute sedentary colonial aquatic animal found encrusting rocks or seaweed or forming stalked fronds. [Phylum Bryozoa.]

**mossback** ● n. N. Amer. informal an old-fashioned or extremely conservative person.
– DERIVATIVES **mossbacked** adj.

**Mössbauer effect** /ˈməːsbaʊə/ ● n. Chemistry an effect in which certain atomic nuclei bound in a crystal emit gamma rays of sharply defined frequency which can be used as a probe of energy levels in other nuclei.
– ORIGIN 1960s: named after the Ger. physicist Rudolf L. *Mössbauer*.

**moss hag** ● n. Scottish an area of broken ground or a hole from which peat has been taken.

**mossie** ● n. (pl. **-ies**) variant spelling of **MOZZIE**.

**moss stitch** ● n. alternate plain and purl stitches in knitting.

**mosstrooper** ● n. a person who lived by plundering property in the Scottish Borders in the 17th century.

**most** ● det. & pron. **1** greatest in amount or degree. **2** the majority of; nearly all of. ● adv. **1** to the greatest extent. **2** forming the superlative of adjectives and adverbs, especially those of more than one syllable. **3** extremely; very. **4** N. Amer. informal almost.
– PHRASES **at (the) most** not more than. **be the most** informal be the best of all. **for the most part** in most cases; usually. **make the most of** use or represent to the best advantage.
– ORIGIN OE *māst*, of Gmc origin.

**-most** • suffix forming superlative adjectives and adverbs from prepositions and other words indicating relative position: *innermost.*
– ORIGIN OE *-mest*, assimilated to **MOST**.

**most favoured nation** • n. a country which has been granted the most favourable trading terms available by another country.

**Most Honourable** • adj. (in the UK) a title given to marquesses, members of the Privy Council, and holders of the Order of the Bath.

**mostly** • adv. **1** as regards the greater part or number. **2** usually.

**Most Reverend** • adj. the title of an Anglican archbishop or an Irish Roman Catholic bishop.

**most significant bit** • n. Computing the bit in a binary number which is of the greatest numerical value.

**MOT** • n. (in the UK) a compulsory annual test for safety and exhaust emissions of motor vehicles of more than a specified age.
– ORIGIN abbrev. of *Ministry of Transport*, which introduced the original test.

**mot**[1] /məʊ, French mo/ • n. (pl. pronounced same or /məʊz/) short for **BON MOT**.

**mot**[2] /mɒt/ • n. Irish informal a girl or young woman; a man's girlfriend.
– ORIGIN C16: of unknown origin.

**mote** • n. a speck.
– ORIGIN OE *mot*, rel. to Du. *mot* 'dust, sawdust'.

**motel** • n. a roadside hotel designed primarily for motorists, typically having the rooms arranged in low blocks with parking directly outside.
– ORIGIN 1920s: blend of **MOTOR** and **HOTEL**.

**motet** /məʊ'tɛt/ • n. a short piece of sacred choral music.
– ORIGIN ME: from OFr., dimin. of *mot* 'word'.

**moth** • n. a chiefly nocturnal insect having two pairs of broad wings covered in microscopic scales, typically drably coloured and held flat when at rest, and lacking the clubbed antennae of butterflies. [Most superfamilies of the order Lepidoptera.]
– ORIGIN OE *moththe*, of Gmc origin.

**mothball** • n. a small pellet of naphthalene or camphor, placed among stored clothes and textiles to deter clothes moths. • v. **1** store (clothes) among or in mothballs. **2** put into storage or on hold for an indefinite period.
– PHRASES **in mothballs** in storage or on hold.

**moth-eaten** • adj. **1** damaged by moths. **2** old and disused.

**mother** /'mʌðə/ • n. **1** a woman in relation to a child or children to whom she has given birth. ➤a woman who has care of a child through adoption. ➤a female animal in relation to its offspring. **2** (**Mother**) (especially as a title or form of address) the head of a female religious community. **3** informal an extreme example or very large specimen: *the mother of all traffic jams.* **4** vulgar slang, chiefly N. Amer. short for **MOTHERFUCKER**. • v. **1** bring up (a child) with care and affection. **2** look after kindly and protectively, sometimes excessively so. **3** dated give birth to.
– DERIVATIVES **motherhood** n. **mothering** n. **motherless** adj. **motherlessness** n.
– ORIGIN OE *mōdor*, of Gmc origin.

**motherboard** • n. Computing a printed circuit board containing the principal components of a microcomputer or other device, with connectors for other circuit boards to be slotted into.

**mother country** • n. a country in relation to its colonies.

**motherfucker** • n. vulgar slang, chiefly N. Amer. a despicable or very unpleasant person or thing.
– DERIVATIVES **motherfucking** adj.

**Mothering Sunday** • n. Brit. the fourth Sunday in Lent, traditionally a day for honouring one's mother.

**mother-in-law** • n. (pl. **mothers-in-law**) the mother of one's husband or wife.

**mother-in-law's tongue** • n. a West African plant of the agave family, which has long slender leaves with yellow marginal stripes. [*Sansevieria trifasciata.*]

**motherland** • n. one's native country.

**mother lode** • n. Mining a principal vein of an ore or mineral.

**motherly** • adj. of, resembling, or characteristic of a mother, especially in being caring, protective, and kind.
– DERIVATIVES **motherliness** n.

**mother-of-pearl** • n. a smooth iridescent substance forming the inner layer of the shell of some molluscs, especially oysters and abalones, used as ornamentation.

**mother's boy** • n. a boy or man who is excessively influenced by or attached to his mother.

**Mother's Day** • n. a day of the year on which mothers are particularly honoured by their children (in North America the second Sunday in May; in Britain the fourth Sunday in Lent, Mothering Sunday).

**mother ship** • n. a large spacecraft or ship from which smaller craft are launched or maintained.

**mother's ruin** • n. Brit. informal gin.

**Mother Superior** • n. the head of a female religious community.

**mother-to-be** • n. (pl. **mothers-to-be**) a woman who is expecting a baby.

**mother tongue** • n. a person's native language.

**motherwort** • n. a tall strong-smelling plant of the mint family, used in herbal medicine, especially in the treatment of gynaecological disorders. [*Leonurus cardiaca.*]

**mothy** • adj. (**-ier**, **-iest**) infested with or damaged by moths.

**motif** /məʊ'tiːf/ • n. **1** a single or recurring image forming a design. **2** a distinctive or dominant theme in a work of art. **3** a decorative device applied to a garment or textile. **4** Biochemistry a distinctive sequence on a protein or DNA, having a three-dimensional structure that allows binding interactions to occur.
– ORIGIN C19: from Fr.

**motile** /'məʊtʌɪl/ • adj. **1** Zoology & Botany (of cells, gametes, and single-celled organisms) capable of motion. **2** Psychology of, relating to, or characterized by responses that involve muscular rather than audio-visual sensations.
– DERIVATIVES **motility** n.
– ORIGIN C19: from L. *motus* 'motion', on the pattern of *mobile.*

**motion** • n. **1** the action or process of moving or being moved. **2** a movement or gesture. **3** a piece of moving mechanism. **4** a formal proposal put to a legislature or committee. **5** Law an application for a rule or order of court. **6** Brit. an evacuation of the bowels. ➤a portion of excrement. • v. direct (someone) with a gesture.
– PHRASES **go through the motions 1** do something perfunctorily. **2** simulate an action.
– DERIVATIVES **motional** adj. **motionless** adj. **motionlessly** adv.
– ORIGIN ME: via OFr. from L. *motio(n-)*, from *movere* 'to move'.

**motion picture** • n. chiefly N. Amer. another term for **FILM** (in sense 3).

**motivate** • v. **1** provide with a motive. **2** stimulate the interest of.
– DERIVATIVES **motivator** n.

**motivation** • n. **1** a motive. **2** enthusiasm.
– DERIVATIVES **motivational** adj. **motivationally** adv.

**motive** • n. **1** a factor inducing a person to act in a particular way. **2** a motif. • adj. **1** producing physical or mechanical motion. **2** acting as a motive.
– DERIVATIVES **motiveless** adj. **motivelessly** adv. **motivelessness** n.
– ORIGIN ME: from OFr. *motif*, from late L. *motivus*, from *movere* 'to move'.

**motive power** • n. **1** the energy (in the form of steam, electricity, etc.) used to drive machinery. **2** the locomotive engines of a railway system collectively.

**motivic** /'məʊtɪvɪk/ • adj. Music of or relating to a motif or motifs.

**mot juste** /məʊ 'ʒuːst, French mo ʒyst/ • n. (pl. **mots justes** pronunc. same) (**the mot juste**) the exact, appropriate word.

**motley** /'mɒtli/ • adj. (**-ier**, **-iest**) varied in appearance or

character; disparate. ● **n.** **1** a varied mixture. **2** historical the particoloured costume of a jester.
– ORIGIN ME: of unknown origin.

**motmot** /ˈmɒtmɒt/ ● **n.** a colourful tropical American bird, typically with two long racket-like tail feathers. [Family Momotidae: numerous species.]
– ORIGIN C19: from Latin Amer. Sp., of imitative origin.

**motocross** ● **n.** cross-country racing on motorcycles.
– DERIVATIVES **motocrosser** n.
– ORIGIN C20: abbrev. of **MOTOR** + **CROSS**.

**motoneuron** /ˌməʊtə(ʊ)ˈnjʊərɒn/ ● **n.** a motor neuron.

**moto perpetuo** /ˌməʊtəʊ pəˈpɛtjʊəʊ/ ● **n.** (pl. **moto perpetui**) a piece of fast-moving instrumental music consisting mainly of notes of equal length.
– ORIGIN Ital., lit. 'perpetual motion'.

**motor** ● **n.** **1** a machine, especially one powered by electricity or internal combustion, that supplies motive power for a vehicle or other device. **2** Brit. informal a car. ● **adj.** **1** giving, imparting, or producing motion or action. **2** Physiology relating to muscular movement or the nerves activating it. ● **v.** informal, chiefly Brit. travel in a car.
– DERIVATIVES **motorable** adj. **motorization** (also **-isation**) n. **motorize** (also **-ise**) v.
– ORIGIN ME: from L., lit. 'mover', based on *movere* 'to move'.

**Motorail** ● **n.** a rail service in which cars are transported together with their drivers and passengers.

**motorbike** ● **n.** a motorcycle.

**motor boat** ● **n.** a boat powered by a motor.

**motorcade** /ˈməʊtəkeɪd/ ● **n.** a procession of motor vehicles.
– ORIGIN C20: from **MOTOR**, on the pattern of *cavalcade*.

**motor car** ● **n.** **1** chiefly Brit. a car. **2** US a self-propelled railway vehicle used to carry railway workers.

**motorcycle** ● **n.** a two-wheeled vehicle that is powered by a motor.
– DERIVATIVES **motorcycling** n. **motorcyclist** n.

**motor drive** ● **n.** a battery-driven motor in a camera, used to wind the film rapidly between exposures.

**motorhome** ● **n.** chiefly N. Amer. a motor vehicle that is fitted out as a caravan.

**motorist** ● **n.** the driver of a car.

**motor lodge** (also **motor hotel**) ● **n.** a motel.

**motorman** ● **n.** (pl. **-men**) the driver of a train or tram.

**motormouth** ● **n.** informal a person who talks quickly and incessantly.
– DERIVATIVES **motormouthed** adj.

**motor nerve** ● **n.** a nerve carrying impulses from the brain or spinal cord to a muscle or gland.

**motor neuron** ● **n.** a nerve cell forming part of a pathway along which impulses pass from the brain or spinal cord to a muscle or gland.

**motor neuron disease** ● **n.** a progressive disease involving degeneration of the motor neurons and wasting of the muscles.

**motor racing** ● **n.** the sport of racing in specially developed fast cars.

**motor scooter** ● **n.** see **SCOOTER**.

**motor sport** ● **n.** another term for **MOTOR RACING**.

**motor vehicle** ● **n.** a road vehicle powered by an internal-combustion engine.

**motorway** ● **n.** Brit. a road designed for fast traffic, typically with three lanes in each direction.

**motor yacht** ● **n.** a motor-driven boat equipped for cruising.

**motte** /mɒt/ ● **n.** historical a mound forming the site of a castle or camp.
– ORIGIN C19: from Fr., 'mound', from OFr. *mote* (see **MOAT**).

**mottle** ● **v.** mark with patches or spots of a different shade or colour. ● **n.** a mottled marking. ➤ a patch or spot forming part of such a marking.
– DERIVATIVES **mottled** adj.
– ORIGIN C18: prob. a back-form. from **MOTLEY**.

**motto** ● **n.** (pl. **-oes** or **-os**) **1** a short sentence or phrase encapsulating a belief or ideal. **2** Music a symbolically significant phrase which recurs throughout a musical work.
– ORIGIN C16: from Ital., 'word'.

**Motu** /ˈməʊtuː/ ● **n.** (pl. same) **1** a member of a Melanesian people of Papua New Guinea inhabiting the area around Port Moresby. **2** the language of this people.
– ORIGIN the name in Melanesian.

**moue** /muː/ ● **n.** a pout.
– ORIGIN C19: Fr., earlier having the sense 'lip'.

**mouflon** /ˈmuːflɒn/ (also **moufflon**) ● **n.** a small wild sheep with chestnut-brown wool, found in mountainous country from Iran to Asia Minor; it is the ancestor of the domestic sheep. [*Ovis orientalis*.]
– ORIGIN C18: from Fr., from Ital. *muflone*.

**mouillé** /ˈmuːjeɪ/ ● **adj.** Phonetics (of a consonant) palatalized.
– ORIGIN Fr., 'wetted'.

**mould**[1] (US **mold**) ● **n.** **1** a hollow container used to give shape to molten or hot liquid material (such as wax or metal) when it cools and hardens. **2** something made in this way, especially a dish such as a jelly or mousse. **3** a distinctive form, style, or character: *a superb striker in the same mould as Lineker.* **4** a frame or template for producing mouldings. ● **v.** **1** form (an object) out of a malleable substance. ➤ give a shape to (a malleable substance). **2** influence the formation or development of. **3** [as adj. **moulded**] (of an ornamental part of a building) shaped to a particular design: *a moulded cornice.*
– PHRASES **break the mould** end a restrictive pattern of events or behaviour by doing things differently.
– DERIVATIVES **mouldable** adj. **moulder** n.
– ORIGIN ME: appar. from OFr. *modle*, from L. *modulus* (see **MODULUS**).

**mould**[2] (US **mold**) ● **n.** a furry growth of minute fungi occurring typically in moist warm conditions on organic matter. ➤ a fungus of this kind.
– ORIGIN ME: prob. from obs. *mould*, past part. of *moul* 'grow mouldy', of Scand. origin.

**mould**[3] (US **mold**) ● **n.** chiefly Brit. soft loose earth, especially when rich in organic matter.
– ORIGIN OE *molde*, from a Gmc base meaning 'pulverize or grind'; rel. to **MEAL**[2].

**mouldboard** ● **n.** a board in a plough that turns the earth over.

**moulder** (US **molder**) ● **v.** [often as adj. **mouldering**] slowly decay.
– ORIGIN C16: perh. from **MOULD**[3], but cf. Norw. dial. *muldra* 'crumble'.

**moulding** (US **molding**) ● **n.** an ornamentally shaped outline as an architectural feature.

**mouldy** (US **moldy**) ● **adj.** (**-ier**, **-iest**) **1** covered with mould. **2** informal tediously old-fashioned. ➤ informal, chiefly Brit. dull or depressing.
– DERIVATIVES **mouldiness** n.

**moules marinière** /ˌmuːl marɪnˈjɛː/ (also **moules à la marinière**) ● **pl. n.** mussels served in their shells and cooked in a wine and onion sauce.
– ORIGIN Fr., lit. 'mussels in the marine style'.

**moulin** /ˈmuːlɪn/ ● **n.** a vertical shaft in a glacier, formed by surface water percolating through a crack in the ice.
– ORIGIN C19: Fr., lit. 'mill'.

**moult** (US **molt**) ● **v.** (of an animal) shed old feathers, hair, or skin, to make way for a new growth. ● **n.** a period of moulting.
– ORIGIN ME *moute*, from an OE verb based on L. *mutare* 'to change'.

**mound**[1] ● **n.** **1** a raised mass of earth or other compacted material, especially one created for purposes of defence or burial. ➤ Baseball a slight elevation from which the pitcher delivers the ball. **2** a small hill. **3** a heap or pile. **4** a large quantity. ● **v.** **1** heap up into a mound. **2** archaic enclose or fortify with an embankment.
– ORIGIN C16 (meaning 'boundary hedge or fence'): of obscure origin.

**mound**[2] ● **n.** archaic a ball representing the earth, typically of gold and surmounted by a cross, used as part of royal regalia.
– ORIGIN ME: from OFr. *monde*, from L. *mundus* 'world'.

**mound-builder** ● **n.** another term for **MEGAPODE**.

**mount**[1] • v. **1** climb up or on to; ascend. **2** get up on (an animal or bicycle) in order to ride it. ➤(often **be mounted**) set on horseback; provide with a horse. **3** (of a male animal) get on (a female) for the purpose of copulation. **4** grow larger, more numerous, or more intense: *the costs mount up when you buy a home.* **5** organize and initiate (a campaign or other course of action). **6** set up (a barrier, stall, checkpoint, etc.). **7** fix in position or on a support. **8** (with reference to a picture or photograph) set in or attach to a backing. **9** fix (a specimen) on a microscopic slide. • n. **1** a backing on which a picture or photograph is set for display. **2** a support for a piece of equipment. **3** a microscope slide. **4** a stamp hinge. **5** a horse used for riding.
– PHRASES **mount guard** keep watch.
– DERIVATIVES **mountable** adj. **mounted** adj. **mounter** n. **mounting** n.
– ORIGIN ME: from OFr. *munter*, based on L. *mons, mont-* 'mountain'.

**mount**[2] • n. archaic or in place names a mountain or hill: *Mount Everest.*
– ORIGIN OE *munt*, from L. *mons, mont-* 'mountain'.

**mountain** • n. **1** an elevation of the earth's surface rising abruptly and to a large height from the surrounding level. **2** a large pile or quantity of something. **3** a surplus stock of a commodity.
– PHRASES **move mountains** achieve spectacular and apparently impossible results.
– ORIGIN ME: from OFr. *montaigne*, based on L. *mons, mont-* 'mountain'.

**mountain ash** • n. **1** a rowan. [*Sorbus americana* (N. America) and related species.] **2** Austral. a tall eucalyptus tree used for wood. [*Eucalyptus regnans* and other species.]

**mountain avens** • n. a creeping arctic-alpine plant with white flowers and glossy leaves. See also **DRYAS**. [*Dryas octopetala*, family Rosaceae.]

**mountain beaver** • n. a burrowing forest-dwelling rodent of western North America. [*Aplodontia rufa*.]

**mountain bike** • n. a bicycle with a light sturdy frame, broad deep-treaded tyres, and multiple gears, originally designed for riding on mountainous terrain.
– DERIVATIVES **mountain biker** n. **mountain biking** n.

**mountain devil** • n. another term for **MOLOCH**.

**mountain dew** • n. informal illicitly distilled liquor, especially whisky or rum.

**mountaineering** • n. the sport or activity of climbing mountains.
– DERIVATIVES **mountaineer** n.

**mountain everlasting** • n. another term for **CAT'S FOOT**.

**mountain gem** • n. a green hummingbird found in the upland forests of Central America. [Genus *Lampornis*: several species.]

**mountain goat** • n. **1** (also **Rocky Mountain goat**) a goat-antelope with shaggy white hair and backward-curving horns, living in the Rocky Mountains of North America. [*Oreamnos americanus*.] **2** any goat that lives on mountains, proverbial for its agility.

**mountain laurel** • n. a North American kalmia which bears clusters of bright pink flowers. [*Kalmia latifolia*.]

**mountain lion** • n. North American term for **PUMA**.

**mountainous** • adj. **1** (of a region) having many mountains. **2** huge.

**mountain sickness** • n. altitude sickness.

**mountebank** /ˈmaʊntɪbaŋk/ • n. **1** a swindler. **2** historical a person who sold patent medicines in public places.
– DERIVATIVES **mountebankery** n.
– ORIGIN C16: from Ital. *montambanco*, from the imper. phr. *monta in banco!* 'climb on the bench!' (with allusion to the raised platform used to attract an audience).

**Mountie** • n. informal a member of the Royal Canadian Mounted Police.

**mounting block** • n. a block of stone or low wooden steps from which a rider mounts a horse.

**mourn** • v. feel deep sorrow following the death or loss of. ➤express this sorrow through conventions such as the wearing of black clothes.
– ORIGIN OE *murnan*, of Gmc origin.

**mourner** • n. a person who attends a funeral as a relative or friend of the dead person.

**mournful** • adj. feeling, expressing, or inducing sadness, regret, or grief.
– DERIVATIVES **mournfully** adv. **mournfulness** n.

**mourning** • n. **1** the experience or expression of deep sorrow for someone who has died. **2** black clothes conventionally worn in a period of mourning.

**mourning cloak** • n. North American term for **CAMBERWELL BEAUTY**.

**mourning dove** • n. a North and Central American dove with a long tail, a grey-brown back, and a plaintive call. [*Zenaida macroura*.]

**mouse** • n. (pl. **mice**) **1** a small rodent that typically has a pointed snout, relatively large ears and eyes, and a long tail. [Many species, especially in the family Muridae.] **2** a timid and quiet person. **3** (pl. also **mouses**) Computing a small hand-held device which is dragged across a flat surface to move the cursor on a computer screen, having buttons which are pressed to control computer functions. **4** informal a lump or bruise on or near the eye. • v. /also maʊz/ **1** hunt for or catch mice. **2** (**mouse about**) prowl about.
– DERIVATIVES **mouser** n.
– ORIGIN OE *mūs*, (pl.) *mȳs*, of Gmc origin.

**mousebird** • n. a small gregarious African bird with drab plumage, a crest, and a long tail. [Family Coliidae.]

**mouse deer** • n. another term for **CHEVROTAIN**.

**mouse-ear** (also **mouse-ear chickweed**) • n. a small white-flowered creeping chickweed with softly hairy leaves which supposedly resemble the ears of mice. [Genus *Cerastium*.]

**mouse hare** • n. another term for **PIKA**.

**mouse potato** • n. informal a person who spends large amounts of time operating a computer.
– ORIGIN 1990s: on the pattern of *couch potato*.

**mousetrap** • n. **1** a trap for catching mice (traditionally baited with cheese). **2** Brit. informal cheese of poor quality. • v. N. Amer. informal induce (someone) to do something by means of a trick.

**mousey** • adj. variant spelling of **MOUSY**.

**moussaka** /muːˈsɑːkə, ˌmuːsəˈkɑː/ • n. a Greek dish consisting of minced lamb, aubergines, and tomatoes, with a cheese sauce on top.
– ORIGIN from Turk. *musakka*.

**mousse** • n. **1** a sweet or savoury dish made as a smooth light mass in which the main ingredient is whipped with cream or egg white, typically served chilled. **2** a soft, light, or aerated preparation for the skin or hair. • v. style (hair) using mousse.
– ORIGIN C19: from Fr., 'moss or froth'.

**mousseline** /ˈmuːsliːn/ • n. **1** a fine, semi-opaque fabric. **2** a soft mousse or whipped sauce.
– ORIGIN C17: from Fr. (see **MUSLIN**).

**mousseron** /ˈmuːsərɒn/ • n. an edible mushroom with a flattish white cap, pink gills, and a mealy smell. [*Clitopilus prunulus*.]
– ORIGIN from OFr. (see **MUSHROOM**).

**mousseux** /muːˈsəː, French musø/ • adj. (of wine) sparkling. • n. (pl. same) sparkling wine.
– ORIGIN from Fr., from *mousse* 'froth'.

**moustache** (US also **mustache**) • n. a strip of hair left to grow above the upper lip.
– DERIVATIVES **moustached** adj.
– ORIGIN C16: from Fr., from Ital. *mostaccio*, from Gk *mustax, mustak-*.

**Mousterian** /muːˈstɪərɪən/ • adj. Archaeology relating to or denoting the main culture of the Middle Palaeolithic period in Europe, between the Acheulian and Aurignacian periods (chiefly 80,000–35,000 years ago).
– ORIGIN C19: from Fr. *moustiérien*, from *Le Moustier*, a cave in SW France where objects from this culture were found.

**mousy** (also **mousey**) • adj. (**-ier**, **-iest**) **1** of or like a

mouse. **2** (of hair) of a dull, light brown colour. **3** (of a person) timid and ineffectual.
– DERIVATIVES **mousiness** n.

**mouth** • n. (pl. **mouths**) **1** the opening and cavity in the lower part of the human face, surrounded by the lips, through which food and air are taken and vocal sounds are emitted. ➤the corresponding opening through which an animal takes in food. **2** informal talkativeness; impudence. **3** an opening or entrance to a structure that is hollow, concave, or almost completely enclosed. **4** the opening or entrance to a harbour or bay. ➤the place where a river enters the sea. • v. **1** say (something) in an insincere or pompous way. ➤(**mouth off**) informal talk in an opinionated or abusive way. **2** move the lips as if to form (words): *she mouthed a silent farewell.* **3** take in or touch with the mouth. **4** train the mouth of (a horse) so that it responds to a bit.
– PHRASES **be all mouth (and no trousers)** informal tend to talk boastfully but not to act on one's words. **give mouth** (of a dog) bark. **keep one's mouth shut** informal say nothing; avoid revealing a secret. **watch one's mouth** informal be careful about what one says.
– DERIVATIVES **-mouthed** adj. **mouther** /'maʊðə/ n. **mouthless** adj.
– ORIGIN OE *mūth*, of Gmc origin.

**mouthbrooder** • n. a freshwater cichlid fish which protects its eggs (and in some cases its young) by carrying them in its mouth. [*Sarotherodon* and other genera.]

**mouthful** • n. (pl. **-fuls**) **1** a quantity of food or drink that fills or can be put in the mouth. **2** a long or complicated word or phrase.
– PHRASES **give someone a mouthful** Brit. informal talk to someone in an angry or abusive way. **say a mouthful** N. Amer. informal say something noteworthy.

**mouth organ** • n. a harmonica.

**mouthpart** • n. Zoology any of the appendages surrounding the mouth of an insect or other arthropod and adapted for feeding.

**mouthpiece** • n. **1** a part of a musical instrument, telephone, etc. that is designed to be put in or against the mouth. **2** a gumshield. **3** a person who speaks on behalf of another person or an organization.

**mouth-to-mouth** • adj. denoting a method of artificial respiration in which a person breathes into someone's lungs through their mouth.

**mouthwash** • n. an antiseptic liquid used for rinsing the mouth or gargling.

**mouth-watering** • adj. **1** smelling or looking delicious. **2** highly attractive or tempting.

**mouthy** • adj. (**-ier, -iest**) informal inclined to talk a lot, especially in an impudent way.

**movable** (also **moveable**) • adj. **1** capable of being moved. **2** denoting a religious feast day that is variable in date from year to year (such as Easter). **3** Law (of property) of the nature of a chattel, as distinct from land or buildings. • n. (**movables**) property or possessions not including land or buildings.
– DERIVATIVES **movability** n. **movably** adv.
– ORIGIN ME: from OFr., from *moveir* 'to move'.

**movable-doh** • adj. denoting a system of solmization (such as tonic sol-fa) in which doh is the keynote of any major scale. Compare with **FIXED-DOH**.

**move** • v. **1** go or cause to go in a specified direction or manner. **2** change or cause to change position. ➤(**move up**) adjust one's position to be nearer to or make room for someone else. **3** change one's place of residence. ➤(**move in** or **out**) start (or cease) living or working in a place. **4** take a new job. **5** change or cause to change from one state, opinion, sphere, or activity to another. **6** take or cause to take action. **7** (usu. **be moved**) provoke a strong feeling, especially of sorrow or sympathy, in. **8** make progress: *they are anxious to get things moving.* **9** (**move in/within**) be socially active in (a particular sphere) or among (a particular group). **10** propose for discussion and resolution at a meeting or legislative assembly. **11** (with reference to the bowels) empty or be emptied. • n. **1** an instance of moving. **2** a change of state or opinion. **3** an action that initiates or advances a process or plan. **4** a manoeuvre in a sport or game. **5** a player's turn during a board game.
– PHRASES **get a move on** informal hurry up. **make a move 1** take action. **2** Brit. set off; leave somewhere. **make a move on** (or **put the moves on**) informal make a proposition of a sexual nature to.
– ORIGIN ME: from OFr. *moveir*, from L. *movere*.

**moveable** • adj. & n. variant spelling of **MOVABLE**.

**movement** • n. **1** an act of moving. **2** (**movements**) a person's activities during a particular period of time. **3** a group of people working together to advance a shared cause. ➤a cause of this type. **4** a change or development. **5** Music a principal division of a musical work, that is self-sufficient in terms of key, tempo, and structure. **6** the moving parts of a mechanism, especially a clock or watch.
– ORIGIN ME: via OFr. from med. L. *movimentum*, from L. *movere* 'to move'.

**mover** • n. **1** a person or thing that is moving. **2** a person who instigates or organizes something. **3** chiefly N. Amer. a person who transports furniture to new premises.
– PHRASES **a mover and shaker** a person who initiates events and influences people. [from *movers and shakers*, a phr. from O'Shaughnessy's *Music & Moonlight* (1874).]

**movie** • n. chiefly N. Amer. **1** a cinema film. **2** (**the movies**) films generally; the film industry.

**movie theatre** (also **movie house**) • n. N. Amer. a cinema.

**moving** • adj. **1** in motion. **2** arousing strong emotion.
– DERIVATIVES **movingly** adv.

**moving-coil** • adj. (of an electrical device such as a voltmeter or microphone) containing a wire coil suspended in a magnetic field, so that the coil either moves in response to a current or produces a current when it is made to move.

**moving pavement** • n. a travelator.

**moving staircase** • n. Brit. an escalator.

**mow**[1] • v. (past part. **mowed** or **mown**) **1** cut down or trim (grass or a cereal crop) with a machine or scythe. **2** (**mow someone down**) kill someone with a fusillade of bullets or other missiles. ➤recklessly knock someone down with a car.
– DERIVATIVES **mower** n.
– ORIGIN OE *māwan*, of Gmc origin; rel. to **MEAD**[2].

**mow**[2] • n. N. Amer. or dialect **1** a stack of hay, corn, or other crop. **2** a place in a barn where such a stack is kept.
– ORIGIN OE *mūga*; of unknown ult. origin.

**mowing** • n. **1** (**mowings**) loose mown grass. **2** US a field of grass grown for hay.

**MOX** • n. a type of nuclear fuel designed for use in breeder reactors, consisting of a blend of uranium and plutonium oxides.
– ORIGIN from *m(ixed) ox(ides)*.

**moxa** /'mɒksə/ • n. a downy substance obtained from the dried leaves of an Asian plant related to mugwort (*Crossostephium artemisioides*), burnt on or near the skin in Eastern medicine as a counterirritant.
– ORIGIN C17: from Japanese *mogusa*, from *moe kusa* 'burning herb'.

**moxibustion** /ˌmɒksɪ'bʌstʃ(ə)n/ • n. (in Eastern medicine) the burning of moxa as a counterirritant.

**moxie** /'mɒksi/ • n. N. Amer. informal force of character; determination or nerve.
– ORIGIN C20: from *Moxie*, the proprietary name of a soft drink.

**Mozambican** /ˌməʊzam'biːkən/ • n. a native or inhabitant of Mozambique. • adj. of or relating to Mozambique or Mozambicans.

**Mozarabic** /məʊ'zarabɪk/ • adj. historical of or relating to the Christian inhabitants of Spain under the Muslim Moorish kings.
– DERIVATIVES **Mozarab** n.
– ORIGIN C17: from Sp. *mozárabe* (from Arab. *musta'rib*, lit. 'making oneself an Arab') + **-IC**.

**Mozartian** /məʊt'sɑːtɪən/ • adj. of, relating to, or characteristic of the work of the Austrian composer Wolfgang Amadeus Mozart (1756–91). • n. a follower of Mozart.

**mozzarella** /ˌmɒtsəˈrɛlə/ ● **n.** a firm white Italian cheese made from buffalo's or cow's milk.
– ORIGIN Ital., dimin. of *mozza*, denoting a kind of cheese, from *mozzare* 'cut off'.

**mozzie** (also **mossie**) ● **n.** (pl. **-ies**) informal a mosquito.

**MP** ● **abbrev.** **1** Member of Parliament. **2** military police. **3** military policeman.

**mp** ● **abbrev.** mezzo piano.

**m.p.** ● **abbrev.** melting point.

**MPC** ● **abbrev.** multimedia personal computer.

**MPD** ● **abbrev.** multiple personality disorder.

**MPEG** /ˈɛmpɛg/ ● **n.** Computing an international standard for encoding and compressing video images.
– ORIGIN C20: from *Motion Pictures Experts Group.*

**mpg** ● **abbrev.** miles per gallon.

**mph** ● **abbrev.** miles per hour.

**MPhil** ● **abbrev.** Master of Philosophy.

**MP3** ● **n.** a means of compressing a sound sequence into a very small file, used as a way of downloading audio files from the Internet.
– ORIGIN from **MPEG** + *Audio Layer-3.*

**MPV** ● **abbrev.** multi-purpose vehicle.

**MR** ● **abbrev.** Master of the Rolls.

**Mr** ● **n.** **1** a title used before a man's surname or full name (especially when he holds no honorific or professional title). **2** a title used before the name of an office to address a man who holds it: *Mr President.*
– ORIGIN ME: orig. an abbrev. of **MASTER**[1]; cf. **MISTER**.

**MRBM** ● **abbrev.** medium-range ballistic missile.

**MRC** ● **abbrev.** (in the UK) Medical Research Council.

**MRCP** ● **abbrev.** Member of the Royal College of Physicians.

**MRCVS** ● **abbrev.** Member of the Royal College of Veterinary Surgeons.

**MRE** ● **abbrev.** (in the US) meal ready to eat.

**MRI** ● **abbrev.** magnetic resonance imaging.

**mRNA** ● **abbrev.** Biology messenger RNA.

**MRPhS** ● **abbrev.** Member of the Royal Pharmaceutical Society.

**Mr Right** ● **n.** informal a single woman's ideal partner or husband.

**Mrs** ● **n.** a title used before a married woman's surname or full name (especially when she holds no honorific or professional title).
– ORIGIN C17: abbrev. of **MISTRESS**; cf. **MISSUS**.

**MRSA** ● **abbrev.** methicillin-resistant *Staphylococcus aureus.*

**Mrs Grundy** ● **n.** (pl. **Mrs Grundys**) a person with very conventional standards of propriety.
– ORIGIN C19: a person repeatedly mentioned in T. Morton's comedy *Speed the Plough* (1798).

**MS** ● **abbrev.** **1** manuscript. **2** Master of Surgery. **3** Master of Science. **4** Mississippi (in official postal use). **5** multiple sclerosis.

**Ms** ● **n.** a title used before the surname or full name of a woman regardless of her marital status (a neutral alternative to **Mrs** or **Miss**).
– ORIGIN 1950s: combination of **MRS** and **MISS**[2].

**MSB** ● **abbrev.** most significant bit.

**MSC** ● **abbrev.** (in the UK) Manpower Services Commission.

**MSc** ● **abbrev.** Master of Science.

**MS-DOS** ● **abbrev.** Computing, trademark Microsoft disk operating system.

**MSF** ● **abbrev.** (in the UK) Manufacturing, Science, and Finance (a trade union representing skilled and professional workers).

**MSG** ● **abbrev.** monosodium glutamate.

**Msgr** ● **abbrev.** **1** Monseigneur. **2** Monsignor.

**MSgt** ● **abbrev.** Master Sergeant.

**MSP** ● **abbrev.** Member of the Scottish Parliament.

**MSS** /ɛmˈɛsɪz/ ● **abbrev.** manuscripts.

**MT** ● **abbrev.** **1** machine translation. **2** Montana (in official postal use).

**Mt** ● **abbrev.** **1** the Gospel of Matthew (in biblical references). **2** [in place names] Mount. ● **symb.** the chemical element meitnerium.

**MTB** ● **abbrev.** **1** motor torpedo boat. **2** mountain bike.

**MTBF** ● **abbrev.** mean time between failures.

**MTech** ● **abbrev.** Master of Technology.

**mu** /mjuː/ ● **n.** **1** the twelfth letter of the Greek alphabet (Μ, μ), transliterated as 'm'. **2** [as modifier] Physics relating to muons. ● **symb.** **1** (μ) micron. **2** (μ) 'micro-' in symbols for units.
– ORIGIN from Gk.

**much** ● **det. & pron.** (**more**, **most**) **1** a large amount. **2** [with neg.] indicating that someone or something is a poor specimen: *I'm not much of a gardener.* ● **adv.** **1** to a great extent; a great deal. **2** [usu. with neg. or in questions] often.
– PHRASES **a bit much** informal somewhat excessive or unreasonable. (**as**) **much as** even though. **how much** used to ask what a particular amount or cost is. **so much the better** (or **worse**) that is even better (or worse). **too much** too difficult or exhausting to tolerate.
– DERIVATIVES **muchly** adv. (humorous).
– ORIGIN ME: shortened from *muchel*, from OE *micel* (see **MICKLE**).

**muchness** ● **n.** (in phr. (**much**) **of a muchness**) informal very similar.

**mucho** /ˈmʊtʃəʊ, ˈmʌtʃəʊ/ informal, humorous ● **det.** much or many. ● **adv.** very.
– ORIGIN from Sp.

**mucilage** /ˈmjuːsɪlɪdʒ/ ● **n.** **1** a viscous secretion or bodily fluid. **2** a viscous or gelatinous solution extracted from plants, used in medicines and adhesives. **3** N. Amer. an adhesive solution; gum or glue.
– DERIVATIVES **mucilaginous** /-ˈladʒɪnəs/ adj.
– ORIGIN ME: via Fr. from late L. *mucilago* 'musty juice', from L. *mucus* (see **MUCUS**).

**mucin** /ˈmjuːsɪn/ ● **n.** Biochemistry a glycoprotein constituent of mucus.
– ORIGIN C19: from **MUCUS** + **-IN**[1].

**mucinous** ● **adj.** of, relating to, or covered with mucus.

**muck** ● **n.** **1** dirt or rubbish. **2** manure. ● **v.** **1** (**muck something up**) informal spoil something. **2** (**muck something out**) chiefly Brit. remove manure and other dirt from a stable etc. **3** (**muck about/around**) Brit. informal behave in a silly or aimless way. ➤(**muck about/around with something**) spoil something by interfering with it. **4** (**muck someone about/around**) Brit. informal treat someone inconsiderately, typically by disrupting their plans. **5** (**muck in**) Brit. informal share tasks or accommodation.
– PHRASES **Lord** (or **Lady**) **Muck** Brit. informal a socially pretentious man (or woman).
– DERIVATIVES **muckiness** n. **mucky** adj. (**-ier**, **-iest**).
– ORIGIN ME *muk*, prob. of Scand. origin: cf. ON *myki* 'dung', from a Gmc base meaning 'soft', shared by **MEEK**.

**muckamuck** /ˈmʌkəmʌk/ (also **mucky-muck**) ● **n.** N. Amer. informal a person of importance or self-importance.
– ORIGIN C19: from Chinook Jargon, shortening of **HIGH MUCK-A-MUCK**.

**mucker** ● **n.** **1** Brit. informal a friend or companion. [1940s: prob. from *muck in* (see **MUCK**).] **2** US informal, dated a rough or coarse person. [C19: prob. from Ger. *Mucker* 'sulky person'.] **3** a person who removes dirt and waste, especially from mines or stables.

**muckle** ● **n. & adj.** variant form of **MICKLE**.

**muckraking** ● **n.** the action of searching out and publicizing scandal about famous people.
– DERIVATIVES **muckrake** v. **muckraker** n.
– ORIGIN coined by President Theodore Roosevelt in a speech (1906) alluding to Bunyan's *Pilgrim's Progress* and the man with the *muck rake.*

**muco-** ● **comb. form** Biochemistry representing **MUCUS**.

**mucopolysaccharide** /ˌmjuːkəʊpɒlɪˈsakərʌɪd/ ● **n.** Biochemistry a substance occurring chiefly in connective tissue and consisting of complex polysaccharides containing amino groups.

**mucosa** /mjuːˈkəʊsə/ ● **n.** (pl. **mucosae** /-siː/) a mucous membrane.
– DERIVATIVES **mucosal** adj.
– ORIGIN C19: mod. L., fem. of *mucosus* 'mucous'.

**mucous membrane** • n. a mucus-secreting epithelial tissue lining many body cavities and tubular organs including the gut and respiratory passages.

**mucro** /ˈmjuːkrəʊ/ • n. (pl. **mucrones** /-ˈkrəʊniːz/ or **mucros**) Botany & Zoology a short sharp point at the end of a part or organ.
– DERIVATIVES **mucronate** adj.
– ORIGIN C17: from L., 'sharp point'.

**mucus** /ˈmjuːkəs/ • n. **1** a slimy substance secreted by the mucous membranes and glands of animals for lubrication, protection, etc. **2** mucilage from plants.
– DERIVATIVES **mucoid** adj. **mucosity** n. **mucous** adj.
– ORIGIN C17: from L.

**MUD** • n. a computer-based text or virtual reality game involving several players.
– ORIGIN C20: from *multi-user dungeon* or *dimension*.

**mud** • n. **1** soft, sticky matter consisting of mixed earth and water. **2** damaging information or allegations.
– PHRASES **drag someone through the mud** slander or denigrate someone publicly. **here's mud in your eye!** informal used as a toast. **one's name is mud** informal one is in disgrace or unpopular.
– ORIGIN ME: prob. from Mid. Low Ger. *mudde*.

**mudbank** • n. a bank of mud on the bed of a river or the bottom of the sea.

**mudbath** • n. **1** a bath in the mud of mineral springs, taken especially to relieve rheumatic complaints. **2** a muddy place.

**mudbug** • n. N. Amer. a freshwater crayfish.

**muddle** • v. **1** bring into a disordered or confusing state. ➤**(muddle something up)** confuse two or more things with each other. **2** confuse (a person). **3** busy oneself in a confused and ineffective way. ➤**(muddle along/through)** cope more or less satisfactorily. **4** US mix (a drink) or stir (an ingredient) into a drink. • n. a muddled state.
– DERIVATIVES **muddled** adj. **muddler** n. **muddling** adj. **muddlingly** adv. **muddly** adj.
– ORIGIN ME (in the sense 'wallow in mud'): perh. from MDu. *moddelen*, frequentative of *modden* 'dabble in mud'; cf. **MUD**.

**muddle-headed** • adj. disorganized or confused.
– DERIVATIVES **muddle-headedness** n.

**muddy** • adj. (**-ier**, **-iest**) **1** covered in, full of, or reminiscent of mud. **2** clouded; not bright or clear. • v. (**-ies**, **-ied**) **1** cause to become muddy. **2** make unclear: *an attempt to muddy the issue.*
– DERIVATIVES **muddily** adv. **muddiness** n.

**Mudejar** /muːˈdeɪhɑː/ • adj. **1** of or denoting a partly Gothic, partly Islamic style of architecture and art prevalent in Spain in the 12th to 15th centuries. **2** of or relating to Muslim subjects of Christian monarchs during the reconquest of the Iberian peninsula from the Moors. • n. (pl. **Mudejares** /-reɪz/) a Mudejar subject.
– ORIGIN via Sp. from Arab. *mudajjan* 'allowed to stay'.

**mudfish** • n. (pl. same or **-fishes**) **1** an elongated fish that can survive drought by burrowing in the mud. [*Protopterus annectens* (an African lungfish) and genus *Neochanna* (New Zealand).] **2** another term for **BOWFIN**.

**mudflap** • n. a flap that hangs behind the wheel of a vehicle, designed to prevent mud and stones thrown up from the road hitting the bodywork or other vehicles.

**mudflat** • n. a stretch of muddy land left uncovered at low tide.

**mudguard** • n. a curved strip or cover over a wheel of a bicycle or motorcycle, designed to protect the vehicle and rider from water and dirt thrown up from the road.

**mudlark** (also **mudlarker**) • n. a person who scavenges in river mud for objects of value.

**mudminnow** • n. a small stout-bodied freshwater fish that is able to survive low concentrations of oxygen and very low temperatures. [Genus *Umbra*: several species.]

**mud pack** • n. a paste of fuller's earth or a similar substance, applied thickly to the face to improve the condition of the skin.

**mud puppy** • n. a large neotenous salamander of the eastern US. [*Necturus maculosus*.]

**mudra** /ˈmʌdrə/ • n. **1** a symbolic hand gesture used in Hindu ceremonies and statuary, and in Indian dance. **2** a movement or pose in yoga.
– ORIGIN from Sanskrit *mudrā* 'sign or token'.

**mudskipper** • n. a small goby of tropical mangrove swamps which is able to move around out of water. [*Periopthalmodon schlosseri* and other species.]

**mud-slinging** • n. informal the casting of insults and accusations.
– DERIVATIVES **mud-sling** v. **mud-slinger** n.

**mudstone** • n. a dark sedimentary rock formed from consolidated mud and lacking the laminations of shale.

**mudwort** • n. a very small creeping plant that grows in mud and damp soils in north temperate regions. [*Limosella aquatica*.]

**muesli** /ˈm(j)uːzli/ • n. (pl. **mueslis**) a mixture of oats and other cereals, dried fruit, and nuts, typically eaten with milk at breakfast.
– ORIGIN from Swiss Ger.

**muezzin** /muːˈɛzɪn/ • n. a man who calls Muslims to prayer from the minaret of a mosque.
– ORIGIN C16: dial. var. of Arab. *mu'aḏḏin*, active part. of *aḏḏana'* 'proclaim'.

**muff**[1] • n. **1** a short tube made of fur or other warm material into which the hands are placed for warmth. **2** vulgar slang a woman's genitals.
– ORIGIN C16: from Du. *mof*, MDu. *muffel*, from med. L. *muff(u)la*, of unknown ult. origin.

**muff**[2] informal • v. handle clumsily; bungle. • n. a mistake or failure, especially a failure to catch a ball cleanly.
– ORIGIN C19: of unknown origin.

**muffin** • n. **1** (N. Amer. **English muffin**) a thick, flattened spongy bread roll made from yeast dough and eaten split, toasted, and buttered. **2** chiefly N. Amer. a small domed cake.
– ORIGIN C18: of unknown origin.

**muffle** • v. **1** wrap or cover for warmth. **2** wrap or cover (a source of sound) to reduce its loudness. ➤make (a sound) quieter or less distinct. • n. a receptacle in a furnace or kiln in which things can be heated without contact with combustion products.
– ORIGIN ME (as v.): perh. a shortening of OFr. *enmoufler*; the noun (C17) from OFr. *moufle* 'thick glove'.

**muffler** • n. **1** a wrap or scarf worn around the neck and face for warmth. **2** a device used to deaden the sound of a drum, bell, piano, or other instrument. **3** N. Amer. a silencer for a motor vehicle exhaust.

**mufti**[1] /ˈmʌfti/ • n. (pl. **muftis**) a Muslim legal expert who is empowered to give rulings on religious matters.
– ORIGIN C16: from Arab. *muftī*, active part. of *'aftā* 'decide a point of law'.

**mufti**[2] /ˈmʌfti/ • n. civilian clothes when worn by military or police staff.
– ORIGIN C19: perh. humorously from **MUFTI**[1].

**mug**[1] • n. **1** a large cup, typically cylindrical and with a handle and used without a saucer. **2** informal a person's face. **3** Brit. informal a stupid or gullible person. **4** US informal a hoodlum or thug. • v. (**mugged**, **mugging**) informal **1** attack and rob (someone) in a public place. **2** make faces before an audience or a camera.
– PHRASES **a mug's game** informal an activity likely to be unsuccessful or dangerous.
– DERIVATIVES **mugful** n. (pl. **-fuls**). **mugging** n.
– ORIGIN C16: prob. of Scand. origin.

**mug**[2] • v. (**mugged**, **mugging**) (**mug something up**) Brit. informal learn or study a subject quickly and intensively, especially for an exam.
– ORIGIN C19: of unknown origin.

**Muganda** /mʊˈgandə/ • n. singular form of **BAGANDA**.

**mugger**[1] • n. a person who attacks and robs another in a public place.

**mugger**[2] • n. a large short-snouted Indian crocodile, venerated by many Hindus. [*Crocodylus palustris*.]
– ORIGIN C19: from Hindi *magar*.

**muggins** • n. (pl. same or **mugginses**) Brit. informal a foolish and gullible person (often used to refer to oneself).
– ORIGIN C19: perh. a use of the surname *Muggins*, with allusion to **MUG**[1].

**muggy** ● **adj.** (**-ier**, **-iest**) (of the weather) unpleasantly warm and humid.
– DERIVATIVES **mugginess** n.
– ORIGIN C18: from dial. *mug* 'mist', from ON *mugga*.

**Mughal** /ˈmuːɡɑːl/ ● **n.** variant spelling of **MOGUL**.

**mugshot** ● **n.** informal a photograph of a person's face made for an official purpose, especially police records.

**mugwort** ● **n.** a plant of the daisy family, with aromatic divided leaves that are dark green above and whitish below. [*Artemisia vulgaris* and related species.]
– ORIGIN OE *mucgwyrt* (see **MIDGE**, **WORT**).

**mugwump** /ˈmʌɡwʌmp/ ● **n.** N. Amer. a person who remains aloof or independent, especially from party politics.
– ORIGIN C19: from Algonquian *mugquomp* 'great chief'.

**Muhammadan** /mʊˈhaməd(ə)n/ (also **Mohammedan**) ● **n. & adj.** archaic term for **MUSLIM** (not favoured by Muslims).
– DERIVATIVES **Muhammadanism** n.
– ORIGIN C17: from the name of the Arab prophet and founder of Islam *Muhammad* + **-AN**.

**mujahedin** /ˌmʊdʒɑːhɪˈdiːn/ (also **mujahidin**, **mujaheddin**, or **mujahideen**) ● **pl. n.** Islamic guerrilla fighters.
– ORIGIN from Pers. and Arab. *mujāhidīn*, colloq. pl. of *mujāhid*, denoting a person who fights a jihad.

**mujtahid** /mʊdʒˈtɑːhɪd/ ● **n.** (pl. **mujtahids** or **mujtahidūn**) a person accepted as an original authority in Islamic law.
– ORIGIN Pers., from Arab., active part. of *ijtahada* 'strive'.

**mukluk** /ˈmʌklʌk/ ● **n.** N. Amer. a high, soft boot that is worn in the American Arctic and is traditionally made from sealskin.
– ORIGIN C19: from Yupik *maklak* 'bearded seal'.

**mukti** /ˈmʌkti, ˈmʊkti/ ● **n.** another term for **MOKSHA**.
– ORIGIN Sanskrit, lit. 'release'.

**muktuk** /ˈmʌktʌk/ ● **n.** the skin and blubber of a whale, used as food by the Inuit.
– ORIGIN from Inuit *maktak*.

**mulatto** /m(j)uːˈlatəʊ/ ● **n.** (pl. **-oes** or **-os**) a person with one white and one black parent. ● **adj.** relating to or denoting a mulatto or mulattoes.
– ORIGIN C16: from Sp. *mulato* 'young mule or mulatto', formed irregularly from *mulo* 'mule'.

**mulberry** ● **n.** **1** a small tree with dark red or white loganberry-like fruit, native to the Far East and cultivated elsewhere. [*Morus alba* (**white mulberry**), *M. nigra* (**black mulberry**), and other species.] ➤the fruit of this tree. **2** a dark red or purple colour.
– ORIGIN OE *mōrberie*, from L. *morum* + **BERRY**.

**mulch** /mʌl(t)ʃ/ ● **n.** a mass of leaves, bark, or compost spread around or over a plant for protection or to enrich the soil. ● **v.** apply a mulch. ➤cover with mulch.
– ORIGIN C17: prob. from dial. *mulch* 'soft' used as a noun, from OE *melsc*, *mylsc*.

**mulct** /mʌlkt/ formal ● **v.** extract money from by fine or taxation. ➤(**mulct something of**) take money or possessions from (someone) by fraudulent means. ● **n.** a fine or compulsory payment.
– ORIGIN C15: from L. *mulctare*, *multare*, from *mulcta* 'a fine'.

**mule**[1] ● **n.** **1** the offspring of a male donkey and a female horse, typically sterile. Compare with **HINNY**[1]. **2** a hybrid plant or animal, especially a sterile one. **3** a stupid or obstinate person. **4** informal a courier for illegal drugs. **5** (also **spinning mule**) a kind of spinning machine producing yarn on spindles.
– ORIGIN OE *mūl*, prob. of Gmc origin, from L. *mulus*, *mula*.

**mule**[2] ● **n.** a slipper or light shoe without a back.
– ORIGIN C16: from Fr., 'slipper'.

**mule deer** ● **n.** a North American deer with long ears and black markings on the tail. [*Odocoileus hemionus*.]

**muleta** /məˈleɪtə/ ● **n.** a red cloth fixed to a stick, brandished by a matador during a bullfight.
– ORIGIN from Sp.

**muleteer** /ˌmjuːlɪˈtɪə/ ● **n.** a person who drives mules.
– ORIGIN C16: from Fr. *muletier*, from *mulet*, dimin. of OFr. *mul* 'mule'.

**mulga** /ˈmʌlɡə/ ● **n.** **1** a small Australian acacia tree or shrub with greyish foliage, which forms dense scrubby growth and is also grown for its wood. [*Acacia aneura*.] **2** an area of scrub or bush dominated by this plant. **3** (**the mulga**) Austral. informal the outback.
– ORIGIN C19: from Yuwaalaraay (an Aborig. lang. of New South Wales).

**mulgara** /məlˈɡɑːrə/ ● **n.** a rat-sized carnivorous marsupial with a pointed snout and a crested tail, native to central Australia. [*Dasycercus cristicauda*.]
– ORIGIN 1940s: prob. from Wangganguru (an Aborig. lang.) *mardagura*.

**muliebrity** /ˌmjuːlɪˈɛbrɪti/ ● **n.** poetic/literary womanly qualities; womanhood.
– ORIGIN C16: from late L. *muliebritas*, from L. *mulier* 'woman'.

**mulish** /ˈmjuːlɪʃ/ ● **adj.** stubborn (like a mule).
– DERIVATIVES **mulishly** adv. **mulishness** n.

**mull**[1] ● **v.** (usu. **mull over**) think about at length.
– ORIGIN C19: of uncertain origin.

**mull**[2] ● **v.** [usu. as adj. **mulled**] warm (wine or beer) and add sugar and spices to it.
– ORIGIN C17: of unknown origin.

**mull**[3] ● **n.** (in Scottish place names) a promontory: *the Mull of Kintyre.*
– ORIGIN ME: cf. Sc. Gaelic *maol* and Icelandic *múli*.

**mull**[4] ● **n.** humus formed under non-acid conditions.
– ORIGIN 1920s: from Dan. *muld* 'soil'.

**mull**[5] ● **n.** a thin muslin, used in bookbinding for joining the spine of a book to its cover.
– ORIGIN C17: abbrev., from Hindi *malmal*.

**mullah** /ˈmʌlə, ˈmʊlə/ ● **n.** a Muslim learned in Islamic theology and sacred law.
– ORIGIN C17: from Pers., Turk., and Urdu *mullā*, from Arab. *mawlā*.

**mullein** /ˈmʌlɪn/ ● **n.** a plant with woolly leaves and tall spikes of yellow flowers. [*Verbascum thapsus* (**great mullein**) and related species.]
– ORIGIN ME: from OFr. *moleine*, of Celtic origin.

**muller** /ˈmʌlə/ ● **n.** a stone used for grinding materials such as artists' pigments.
– ORIGIN ME: perh. from Anglo-Norman Fr. *moldre* 'to grind'.

**Müllerian mimicry** /mʊˈlɪərɪən/ ● **n.** Zoology a form of mimicry in which two or more noxious animals develop similar appearances as a shared protective device.
– ORIGIN C19: named after the Ger. zoologist J. F. T. *Müller*.

**mullet**[1] ● **n.** any of various chiefly marine fish that are widely caught for food. [Families Mullidae (red mullets) and Mugilidae (grey mullets): several species.]
– ORIGIN ME: from OFr. *mulet*, dimin. of L. *mullus* 'red mullet', from Gk *mullos*.

**mullet**[2] ● **n.** Heraldry a star with five (or more) straight-edged points or rays, as a charge or a mark of cadency for a third son.
– ORIGIN ME: from OFr. *molette* 'rowel', dimin. of *meule* 'millstone', from L. *mola* 'grindstone'.

**mullet**[3] ● **n.** a man's hairstyle in which the hair is cut short at the front and sides and left long at the back.
– ORIGIN 1990s: of unknown origin.

**mulligan** /ˈmʌlɪɡ(ə)n/ ● **n.** informal, chiefly N. Amer. **1** a stew made from odds and ends of food. **2** (in informal golf) an extra stroke allowed after a poor shot, not counted on the scorecard.
– ORIGIN C20: appar. from the surname *Mulligan*.

**mulligatawny** /ˌmʌlɪɡəˈtɔːni/ ● **n.** a spicy meat soup originally made in India.
– ORIGIN from Tamil *miḷaku-taṇṇi* 'pepper-water'.

**mullion** /ˈmʌljən/ ● **n.** a vertical bar between the panes of glass in a window. Compare with **TRANSOM**.
– DERIVATIVES **mullioned** adj.
– ORIGIN C16: prob. an alt. form of **MONIAL**.

**mullock** /ˈmʌlək/ ● **n.** **1** Austral./NZ or dialect rubbish or nonsense. **2** Austral./NZ rock which contains no gold or from which gold has been extracted.
– PHRASES **poke mullock at** Austral./NZ informal ridicule.

– ORIGIN ME: dimin. of earlier *mul* 'dust, rubbish', from MDu.

**mulloway** /'mʌləweɪ/ ● **n.** a large edible predatory fish of Australian coastal waters. [*Johnius antarctica*.]
– ORIGIN C19: from Yaralde (an Aborig. lang. of South Australia).

**multi-** ● **comb. form** more than one; many: *multicultural*.
– ORIGIN from L. *multus* 'much, many'.

**multi-access** ● **adj.** (of a computer system) allowing the simultaneous connection of a number of terminals.

**multiaxial** ● **adj.** involving or possessing several or many axes.

**multicast** ● **v.** (past and past part. **multicast**) send (data) across a computer network to several users at the same time. ● **n.** a set of multicast data.

**multicellular** ● **adj.** Biology (of an organism or part) having or consisting of many cells.
– DERIVATIVES **multicellularity** n.

**multicoloured** (also **multicolour**; US **-colored**, **-color**) ● **adj.** having many colours.

**multicultural** ● **adj.** of, relating to, or constituting several cultural or ethnic groups.
– DERIVATIVES **multiculturalism** n. **multiculturalist** n. & adj. **multiculturally** adv.

**multidimensional** ● **adj.** of or involving several dimensions.
– DERIVATIVES **multidimensionality** n. **multidimensionally** adv.

**multidisciplinary** ● **adj.** involving several academic disciplines or professional specializations.

**multi-ethnic** ● **adj.** of, relating to, or constituting several ethnic groups.

**multifaceted** ● **adj.** having many facets.

**multifactorial** ● **adj.** involving or dependent on a number of factors or causes.

**multi-faith** ● **adj.** involving or characterized by a variety of religions.

**multifarious** /ˌmʌltɪ'fɛːrɪəs/ ● **adj.** having great variety and diversity. ➤ many and various.
– DERIVATIVES **multifariously** adv. **multifariousness** n.
– ORIGIN C16: from L. *multifarius* + **-ous**.

**multifid** /'mʌltɪfɪd/ ● **adj.** Botany & Zoology divided into several or many parts by deep clefts or notches.
– ORIGIN C18: from L. *multifidus*, from *multus* 'much, many' + *-fid* from *fidus* 'cleft, split'.

**multifilament** ● **adj.** denoting a cord or yarn composed of a number of strands or filaments wound together.

**multiflora** ● **n.** an East Asian shrubby or climbing rose which bears clusters of small single pink or white flowers. [*Rosa multiflora*.]
– ORIGIN C19: from late L., fem. of *multiflorus* 'multiflorous'.

**multifocal** ● **adj.** chiefly Medicine & Optics having more than one focus.

**multifoil** ● **n.** Architecture an ornament consisting of more than five foils.

**multiform** ● **adj.** existing in many forms or kinds.
– DERIVATIVES **multiformity** n.

**multifunctional** (also **multifunction**) ● **adj.** having or fulfilling several functions.

**multigenerational** ● **adj.** of or relating to several generations.

**multigrade** ● **n. 1** an engine oil meeting the requirements of several standard grades. **2** (trademark in the US) a kind of photographic paper made with two emulsions of different sensitivities, from which prints with different levels of contrast can be made.

**multigrain** ● **adj.** (of bread) made from more than one kind of grain.

**multigravida** /ˌmʌltɪ'gravɪdə/ ● **n.** (pl. **multigravidae** /-diː/) Medicine & Zoology a woman (or female animal) that is or has been pregnant for at least a second time.
– ORIGIN C19: from **multi-**, on the pattern of *primigravida*.

**multigym** ● **n.** an apparatus on which a number of weightlifting and other exercises can be performed.

**multihull** ● **n.** a boat with two or more, especially three, hulls.

**multilateral** ● **adj.** agreed upon or participated in by three or more parties.
– DERIVATIVES **multilateralism** n. **multilateralist** adj. & n. **multilaterally** adv.

**multilayer** ● **adj.** relating to or consisting of several or many layers. ● **n.** a multilayer coating or deposit.
– DERIVATIVES **multilayered** adj.

**multilingual** ● **adj.** in or using several languages.
– DERIVATIVES **multilingualism** n. **multilingually** adv.

**multimedia** ● **adj.** using more than one medium of expression or communication. ● **n.** Computing an extension of hypertext allowing the provision of audio and video material cross-referenced to a text.

**multimeter** ● **n.** an instrument designed to measure electric current, voltage, and resistance.

**multimillion** ● **adj.** consisting of several million.

**multimillionaire** ● **n.** a person with assets worth several million pounds or dollars.

**multinational** ● **adj. 1** including or involving several countries or nationalities. **2** operating in several countries. ● **n.** a company operating in several countries.
– DERIVATIVES **multinationally** adv.

**multinomial** /ˌmʌltɪ'nəʊmɪəl/ ● **adj. & n.** Mathematics another term for **polynomial**.
– ORIGIN C17: from **multi-**, on the pattern of *binomial*.

**multipack** ● **n.** a package containing a number of similar or identical products sold at a discount compared to the price when bought separately.

**multipara** /mʌl'tɪp(ə)rə/ ● **n.** (pl. **multiparae** /-riː/) Medicine & Zoology a woman (or female animal) that has had more than one pregnancy resulting in viable offspring.
– DERIVATIVES **multiparous** adj.
– ORIGIN C19: mod. L., fem. of *multiparus* 'multiparous'.

**multipartite** /ˌmʌltɪ'pɑːtʌɪt/ ● **adj. 1** having several or many parts or divisions. **2** Biology (of a virus) existing as two or more separate but incomplete particles. **3** another term for **multiparty**.

**multiparty** ● **adj.** of or involving several political parties.

**multiphase** ● **adj. 1** in, of, or relating to more than one phase. **2** (of an electrical device or circuit) polyphase.

**multiplay** ● **adj.** denoting a compact disc player which can be stacked with a number of discs before needing to be reloaded.

**multiplayer** ● **n. 1** a compact disc player which can play a number of discs in succession. **2** a multimedia computer and home entertainment system integrating conventional and interactive audio and video functions with those of a personal computer. ● **adj.** denoting a computer game for or involving several players.

**multiple** ● **adj. 1** having or involving several parts or elements. **2** numerous. **3** (of a disease or injury) complex in its nature or effect; affecting several parts of the body. ● **n. 1** a number that may be divided by another a certain number of times without a remainder. **2** chiefly Brit. a shop with branches.
– ORIGIN C17: from Fr., from late L. *multiplus*, alt. of L. *multiplex* (see **multiplex**).

**multiple-choice** ● **adj.** (of a question in an examination) accompanied by several possible answers from which the candidate must try to choose the correct one.

**multiple fruit** ● **n.** Botany a fruit formed from carpels derived from several flowers, such as a pineapple.

**multiple sclerosis** ● **n.** see **sclerosis**.

**multiple star** ● **n.** a group of stars very close together as seen from the earth, especially one whose members are in fact close together and rotate around a common centre.

**multiplet** ● **n.** Physics a group of closely associated things, especially closely spaced spectrum lines or atomic energy levels, or subatomic particles differing only in a single property.
– ORIGIN 1920s: from **multiple**, on the pattern of words such as *doublet* and *triplet*.

**multiple unit** ● **n.** a passenger train of two or more carriages powered by integral motors which drive a number of axles.

**multiplex** • adj. **1** consisting of many elements in a complex relationship. **2** involving simultaneous transmission of several messages along a single channel of communication. **3** (of a cinema) having several separate screens within one building. • n. **1** a multiplex system or signal. **2** a multiplex cinema. • v. incorporate into a multiplex signal or system.
– DERIVATIVES **multiplexer** (also **multiplexor**) n.
– ORIGIN ME in the mathematical sense 'multiple': from L.

**multiplicand** /ˌmʌltɪplɪˈkand, ˈmʌltɪplɪˌkand/ • n. a quantity which is to be multiplied by another (the multiplier).

**multiplication** • n. **1** the process of multiplying. **2** Mathematics the process of combining matrices, vectors, or other quantities under specific rules to obtain their product.

**multiplication sign** • n. the sign ×, used to indicate that one quantity is to be multiplied by another.

**multiplication table** • n. a list of multiples of a particular number, typically from 1 to 12.

**multiplicative** /ˈmʌltɪˌplɪkətɪv/ • n. subject to or of the nature of multiplication.

**multiplicity** • n. (pl. **-ies**) a large number or variety.

**multiplier** • n. **1** a quantity by which a given number (the multiplicand) is to be multiplied. **2** Economics a factor by which an increment of income exceeds the resulting increment of saving or investment. **3** a device for increasing by repetition the intensity of an electric current, force, etc. to a measurable level. **4** a type of fishing reel with a geared spool.

**multiply**[1] /ˈmʌltɪplʌɪ/ • v. (**-ies**, **-ied**) **1** obtain from (a number) another which contains the first number a specified number of times. **2** increase or cause to increase in number or quantity. **3** increase in number by reproducing. **4** propagate (plants).
– DERIVATIVES **multipliable** adj. **multiplicable** adj.
– ORIGIN ME: from OFr. *multiplier*, from L. *multiplicare*.

**multiply**[2] /ˈmʌltɪpli/ • adv. in different ways or respects.

**multipolar** • adj. **1** having many poles or extremities. **2** polarized in several ways or directions.
– DERIVATIVES **multipolarity** n. **multipole** n.

**multiprocessing** (also **multiprogramming**) • n. Computing another term for **MULTITASKING**.

**multiprocessor** • n. a computer with more than one central processor.

**multi-purpose** • adj. having several purposes.

**multiracial** • adj. consisting of or relating to people of many races.
– DERIVATIVES **multiracialism** n. **multiracialist** adj. & n. **multiracially** adv.

**multisession** • adj. Computing denoting a format for recording digital information on to a CD-ROM disc over two or more separate sessions.

**multispectral** • adj. operating in or involving several regions of the electromagnetic spectrum.

**multistage** • adj. **1** consisting of or relating to several stages or processes. **2** (of a rocket) having at least two sections which contain their own motor and are jettisoned as their fuel runs out. **3** (of a pump, turbine, or similar device) having more than one rotor.

**multi-storey** • adj. (of a building) having several storeys. • n. Brit. informal a multi-storey car park.

**multitasking** • n. Computing the execution of more than one program or task simultaneously by sharing the resources of the computer processor between them.
– DERIVATIVES **multitask** v.

**multithreading** • n. Computing a technique by which a single set of code can be used by several processors at different stages of execution.
– DERIVATIVES **multithreaded** adj.

**multi-track** • adj. relating to or made by the mixing of several separately recorded tracks of sound. • n. a multi-track recording. • v. record using multi-track recording.
– DERIVATIVES **multi-tracked** adj.

**multitude** • n. **1** a large number of people or things. **2** (**the multitude**) the mass of ordinary people.
– ORIGIN ME: via OFr. from L. *multitudo*, from *multus* 'many'.

**multitudinous** /ˌmʌltɪˈtjuːdɪnəs/ • adj. **1** very numerous. ➤consisting of many individuals or elements. **2** poetic/literary (of a body of water) vast.
– DERIVATIVES **multitudinously** adv. **multitudinousness** n.
– ORIGIN C17: from L. *multitudo* (see **MULTITUDE**) + **-OUS**.

**multi-utility** • n. Brit. a privatized utility which has extended or combined its business to offer its customers additional services (especially those of another privatized utility).

**multivalent** /ˌmʌltɪˈveɪl(ə)nt/ • adj. **1** having many applications, interpretations, or values. **2** Medicine having several sites of possible attachment to an antibody or antigen. **3** Chemistry another term for **POLYVALENT**.
– DERIVATIVES **multivalence** n. **multivalency** n.

**multivalve** • adj. (of an internal-combustion engine) having more than two valves per cylinder, typically four.

**multivariate** /ˌmʌltɪˈvɛːrɪət/ • adj. Statistics involving two or more variable quantities.

**multivendor** • adj. denoting or relating to computer hardware or software products or network services from more than one supplier.

**multiverse** • n. an infinite realm of being or potential being of which the universe is regarded as a part.

**multiway** • adj. having several paths, routes, or channels.

**multum in parvo** /ˌmʌltəm ɪn ˈpɑːvəʊ/ • n. a great deal in a small space.
– ORIGIN L., lit. 'much in little'.

**mum**[1] • n. Brit. informal one's mother.

**mum**[2] • adj. (in phr. **keep mum**) informal remain silent so as not to reveal a secret.
– PHRASES **mum's the word** do not reveal a secret.
– ORIGIN ME: imitative of a sound made with closed lips.

**mum**[3] • v. (**mummed**, **mumming**) act in a mummers' play.
– ORIGIN ME: cf. **MUM**[2] and Mid. Low Ger. *mummen*.

**mumble** • v. **1** say something indistinctly and quietly. **2** bite or chew with toothless gums. • n. a quiet and indistinct utterance.
– DERIVATIVES **mumbler** n. **mumbling** adj. **mumblingly** adv.
– ORIGIN ME: frequentative of **MUM**[2].

**mumblety-peg** /ˈmʌmb(ə)lti/ • n. chiefly US a game in which each player in turn throws a knife or pointed stick from a series of positions, continuing until it fails to stick in the ground.
– ORIGIN C17: from *mumble* in the sense 'bite as if with toothless gums', from the requirement of the game that an unsuccessful player withdraw a peg from the ground using the mouth.

**mumbo-jumbo** • n. informal language or ritual causing or intended to cause confusion or bewilderment.
– ORIGIN C18 (as *Mumbo Jumbo*, denoting a supposed African idol): of unknown origin.

**mu-meson** • n. another term for **MUON**.

**mummer** • n. an actor in a mummers' play. ➤archaic or derogatory an actor in the theatre.
– ORIGIN ME: from OFr. *momeur*, from *momer* 'act in a mime'.

**mummers' play** (also **mumming play**) • n. a traditional English folk play of a type often associated with Christmas and popular in the 18th and early 19th centuries.

**mummery** • n. (pl. **-ies**) **1** a performance by mummers. **2** ridiculous ceremony.

**mummichog** /ˈmʌmɪtʃɒg/ • n. a small marine fish of sheltered shores and estuaries of eastern North America, popular in aquaria and also used as bait. [*Fundulus heteroclitus*.]
– ORIGIN C18: from Narragansett *moamitteaug*.

**mummify** ● v. (**-ies**, **-ied**) [usu. as adj. **mummified**] **1** (especially in ancient Egypt) preserve (a body) as a mummy. **2** dry up (a body) and so preserve it.
– DERIVATIVES **mummification** n.

**mummy**[1] ● n. (pl. **-ies**) Brit. informal one's mother.
– ORIGIN C18: perh. an alt. of earlier **MAMMY**.

**mummy**[2] ● n. (pl. **-ies**) (especially in ancient Egypt) a body that has been preserved for burial by embalming and wrapping in bandages.
– ORIGIN ME: from Fr. *momie*, from med. L. *mumia* and Arab. *mūmiyā* 'embalmed body'.

**mumps** ● pl. n. [treated as sing.] a viral disease mainly affecting children, causing swelling of the parotid salivary glands of the face.
– ORIGIN C16: from obs. *mump* 'grimace'.

**mumsy** Brit. informal ● adj. (of a woman) homely and unfashionable. ● n. chiefly humorous one's mother.
– ORIGIN C19: humorous var. of **MUMMY**[1].

**mun** /mʌn/ ● modal v. dialect form of **MUST**[1].
– ORIGIN ME: from ON *muna*, from the Gmc base of **MIND**.

**munch** ● v. eat steadily and audibly.
– DERIVATIVES **muncher** n.
– ORIGIN ME: imitative; cf. **CRUNCH**.

**Munchausen's syndrome** /ˈmʌn(t)ʃˌaʊz(ə)nz/ ● n. Psychiatry a mental disorder in which a person feigns severe illness so as to obtain medical attention.
– ORIGIN from the name of Baron *Munchausen*, the hero of a book of fantastic tales (1785).

**munchies** ● pl. n. informal **1** snacks or small items of food. **2** (**the munchies**) a sudden strong desire for food.

**Munda** /ˈmʊndə/ ● n. (pl. same or **Mundas**) **1** a member of a group of indigenous peoples living scattered in a region from east central India to Nepal and Bangladesh. **2** a family of languages spoken by these peoples, distantly related to the Mon-Khmer family.
– ORIGIN the name in Munda.

**mundane** /ˈmʌndeɪn, mʌnˈdeɪn/ ● adj. **1** lacking interest or excitement. **2** of this earthly world rather than a heavenly or spiritual one.
– DERIVATIVES **mundanely** adv. **mundaneness** n. **mundanity** /-ˈdanɪti/ n. (pl. **-ies**).
– ORIGIN ME: from OFr. *mondain*, from late L. *mundanus*, from L. *mundus* 'world'.

**mung bean** /mʌŋ, muːŋ/ ● n. **1** a small round green bean grown in the tropics. **2** the plant that produces these beans, chiefly grown as a source of bean sprouts. [*Vigna radiata*.]
– ORIGIN C19: from Hindi *mūng*.

**mungo** /ˈmʌŋgəʊ/ ● n. cloth made from recycled woven or felted material.
– ORIGIN C19: of unknown origin.

**muni** /ˈmjuːni/ ● n. (pl. **munis**) US short for **MUNICIPAL BOND**.

**municipal** /mjʊˈnɪsɪp(ə)l/ ● adj. of or relating to a municipality.
– DERIVATIVES **municipalization** (also **-isation**) n. **municipalize** (also **-ise**) v. **municipally** adv.
– ORIGIN C16 (orig. relating to the internal affairs of a state): from L. *municipalis* (from *municipium* 'free city') + *capere* 'take'.

**municipal bond** ● n. (chiefly in the US) a security issued by or on behalf of a local authority.

**municipality** ● n. (pl. **-ies**) a town or district that has local government. ➤the governing body of such an area.

**munificent** /mjʊˈnɪfɪs(ə)nt/ ● adj. very generous.
– DERIVATIVES **munificence** n. **munificently** adv.
– ORIGIN C16: from L. *munificent-*, *munificentior*, compar. of *munificus* 'bountiful'.

**muniments** /ˈmjuːnɪm(ə)nts/ ● pl. n. chiefly Law title deeds or other documents proving a person's title to land.
– ORIGIN ME: via OFr. from L. *munimentum* 'defence' (in med. L. 'title deed'), from *munire* 'fortify'.

**munition** /mjʊˈnɪʃ(ə)n/ ● n. (**munitions**) military weapons, ammunition, equipment, and stores. ● v. supply with munitions.
– DERIVATIVES **munitioner** n. (rare).
– ORIGIN ME: from Fr., from L. *munitio(n-)* 'fortification', from *munire* 'fortify'.

**Munro** /mʌnˈrəʊ/ ● n. (pl. **-os**) any of the 277 mountains in Scotland that are at least 3,000 feet high (approximately 914 metres).
– ORIGIN C20: named after Sir Hugh Thomas *Munro*, who published a list of all such mountains in 1891.

**munshi** /ˈmuːnʃiː/ (also **moonshee**) ● n. (pl. **munshis**) a secretary or language teacher in the Indian subcontinent.
– ORIGIN Pers. and Urdu *munšī* from Arab. *munšiʾ* 'writer, author'.

**munt** /mʊnt/ ● n. S. African informal, offensive a black African.
– ORIGIN shortening of Zulu *umuntu* 'person'.

**muntjac** /ˈmʌntdʒak/ ● n. a small SE Asian deer with a doglike bark and small tusks. [Genus *Muntiacus*: several species.]
– ORIGIN C18: from Sundanese *minchek*.

**Muntz metal** /mʌnts/ ● n. a form of brass used for casting and working at high temperatures.
– ORIGIN C19: named after the Engl. manufacturer George F. *Muntz*.

**muon** /ˈmjuːɒn/ ● n. Physics an unstable meson with a mass around 200 times that of the electron.
– DERIVATIVES **muonic** adj.
– ORIGIN 1950s: contr. of **MU-MESON**.

**murage** /ˈmjʊərɪdʒ/ ● n. Brit. historical tax levied for building or repairing the walls of a town.
– ORIGIN ME: from OFr. from *mur* 'wall', from L. *murus*.

**mural** /ˈmjʊər(ə)l/ ● n. a painting executed directly on a wall. ● adj. **1** of, like, or relating to a wall. **2** Medicine of or relating to the wall of a body cavity or blood vessel.
– DERIVATIVES **muralist** n.
– ORIGIN ME: from Fr., from L. *muralis*, from *murus* 'wall'.

**mural crown** ● n. **1** Heraldry a representation of a city wall in the form of a crown, borne above the shield in the arms of distinguished soldiers and of some civic authorities. **2** (in ancient Roman times) a crown or garland given to the soldier who was first to scale the wall of a besieged town.

**murder** ● n. **1** the unlawful premeditated killing of one person by another. **2** informal a very difficult or unpleasant situation or experience. ● v. **1** kill unlawfully and with premeditation. **2** informal punish severely. **3** informal, chiefly Brit. consume (food or drink) with relish.
– PHRASES **get away with** (**blue**) **murder** informal succeed in doing whatever one chooses without being punished. **murder will out** murder cannot remain undetected. **scream** (or **yell**) **blue** (or N. Amer. **bloody**) **murder** informal make an extravagant and noisy protest.
– DERIVATIVES **murderer** n. **murderess** n.
– ORIGIN OE *morthor*, of Gmc origin.

**murderous** ● adj. **1** capable of, intending, or involving murder or extreme violence. **2** informal extremely arduous or unpleasant.
– DERIVATIVES **murderously** adv. **murderousness** n.

**mure** /mjʊə/ ● v. archaic confine in or as in a prison.
– ORIGIN ME: from OFr. *murer*, from L. *murare*, from *murus* 'wall'.

**murex** /ˈmjʊərɛks/ ● n. (pl. **murices** /-rɪsiːz/ or **murexes**) a predatory tropical marine mollusc with a spiny shell. [Genus *Murex*.]
– ORIGIN C16: from L.

**muriatic acid** /ˌmjʊərɪˈatɪk/ ● n. archaic term for **HYDROCHLORIC ACID**.
– DERIVATIVES **muriate** n.
– ORIGIN C17: *muriatic* from L. *muriaticus*, from *muria* 'brine'.

**murine** /ˈmjʊərʌɪn, -rɪn/ ● adj. Zoology of or relating to mice or related rodents.
– ORIGIN C17: from L. *murinus*, from *mus*, *mur-* 'mouse'.

**murk** ● n. darkness or fog causing poor visibility. ● adj. archaic or Scottish dark or gloomy.
– ORIGIN OE *mirce*, of Gmc origin.

**murky** ● adj. (**-ier**, **-iest**) **1** dark and gloomy. ➤(of water) dirty or cloudy. **2** deliberately obscure so as to conceal dishonesty or immorality.

– DERIVATIVES **murkily** adv. **murkiness** n.

**murmur** ● n. **1** a low continuous background noise. **2** a quietly spoken utterance. ➤ the quiet or subdued expression of a feeling. **3** Medicine a recurring sound heard in the heart through a stethoscope that is usually a sign of disease or damage. ● v. **1** say something in a murmur. **2** make a low continuous sound.
– PHRASES **without a murmur** without complaining.
– DERIVATIVES **murmurer** n. **murmurous** adj.
– ORIGIN ME: from OFr. *murmure*, from *murmurer* 'to murmur', from L. *murmurare*, from *murmur* 'a murmur'.

**murmuring** ● n. **1** a low continuous sound. **2** a subdued or private expression of discontent.
– DERIVATIVES **murmuringly** adv.

**murphy** ● n. (pl. **-ies**) informal a potato.
– ORIGIN C19: from *Murphy*, an Ir. surname.

**Murphy's Law** ● n. a supposed law of nature, to the effect that anything that can go wrong will go wrong.

**murrain** /ˈmʌrɪn/ ● n. **1** redwater fever or a similar infectious disease affecting cattle or other animals. **2** archaic a plague or crop blight.
– ORIGIN ME: from OFr. *morine*, based on L. *mori* 'to die'.

**murre** /məː/ ● n. N. Amer. a guillemot with a white breast. [Genus *Uria*: two species.]
– ORIGIN C16: of unknown origin.

**murrelet** /ˈməːlɪt/ ● n. a small North Pacific auk, typically having a grey back and white underparts. [Genera *Brachyramphus* and *Synthliboramphus*: six species.]

**murrey** /ˈmʌri/ ● n. archaic the deep purple-red colour of a mulberry. ➤ Heraldry another term for **SANGUINE**.
– ORIGIN ME: via OFr. from med. L. *moratus*, from *morum* 'mulberry'.

**murther** /ˈməːðə/ ● n. & v. archaic spelling of **MURDER**.

**MusB** (also **Mus Bac**) ● abbrev. Bachelor of Music.
– ORIGIN from L. *Musicae Baccalaureus*.

**Muscadelle** /ˌmʌskəˈdɛl/ ● n. a variety of white grape grown mainly for sweet white wines in Bordeaux and Australia.
– ORIGIN Fr., from **MUSCAT** + **-EL**.

**Muscadet** /ˈmʌskədeɪ, ˈmʊsk-, French myskadɛ/ ● n. a dry white wine from the Loire region of France.
– ORIGIN Fr., from *muscade* 'nutmeg'.

**muscadine** /ˈmʌskədɪn, -ʌɪn/ ● n. a wine grape with a musky flavour, native to Mexico and the south-eastern US. [*Vitis rotundifolia*.]
– ORIGIN prob. an alt. of **MUSCATEL**.

**muscarine** /ˈmʌskəriːn, -ɪn/ ● n. Chemistry a poisonous compound present in fly agaric and other fungi.
– DERIVATIVES **muscarinic** adj. (Physiology).
– ORIGIN C19: based on L. *musca* 'fly'.

**muscat** /ˈmʌskat/ ● n. a variety of white, red, or black grape with a musky scent, grown for wine or eating as fruit or raisins. ➤ a sweet or fortified white wine made from these grapes.
– ORIGIN Fr., from Provençal, from *musc* 'musk'.

**muscatel** /ˌmʌskəˈtɛl/ ● n. a muscat grape or a raisin made from such a grape. ➤ a sweet wine made from muscat grapes.
– ORIGIN via OFr. from Provençal, dimin. of *muscat* (see **MUSCAT**).

**muscle** ● n. **1** a band of fibrous tissue in the body that has the ability to contract, producing movement in or maintaining the position of a part of the body. **2** physical power. ➤ political or economic power. ● v. informal **1** N. Amer. move (an object) by use of physical strength. **2** (**muscle in/into**) force one's way into (another's affairs).
– DERIVATIVES **-muscled** adj. **muscleless** adj. **muscly** adj.
– ORIGIN ME: from Fr., from L. *musculus*, dimin. of *mus* 'mouse' (some muscles being thought to be mouse-like in form).

**muscle-bound** ● adj. having well-developed or overdeveloped muscles.

**muscleman** ● n. (pl. **-men**) a large, strong man, especially one employed to protect someone or intimidate people.

**muscovado** /ˌmʌskəˈvɑːdəʊ/ (also **muscovado sugar**) ● n. unrefined sugar made from evaporating the juice of sugar cane and draining off the molasses.
– ORIGIN C17: from Port. *mascabado (açúcar)* '(sugar) of the lowest quality'.

**Muscovite** /ˈmʌskəvʌɪt/ ● n. a native or citizen of Moscow. ➤ archaic a Russian. ● adj. of or relating to Moscow. ➤ archaic of or relating to Russia.

**muscovite** /ˈmʌskəvʌɪt/ ● n. a silver-grey form of mica occurring in many igneous and metamorphic rocks.
– ORIGIN C19: from obs. *Muscovy glass* (in the same sense) + **-ITE**[1].

**Muscovy** /ˈmʌskəvi/ ● n. archaic Russia.
– ORIGIN from obs. Fr. *Muscovie*, from mod. L *Moscovia*, from Russ. *Moskva* 'Moscow'.

**Muscovy duck** ● n. a large tropical American duck with glossy greenish-black plumage. [*Cairina moschata*.]

**muscular** ● adj. of or affecting the muscles. ➤ having well-developed muscles.
– DERIVATIVES **muscularity** n. **muscularly** adv.

**muscular Christianity** ● n. a Christian life of cheerful physical activity, especially as popularly associated with boys' public schools of the Victorian British Empire.

**muscular dystrophy** ● n. a hereditary condition marked by progressive weakening and wasting of the muscles.

**muscular rheumatism** ● n. aching pain in the muscles and joints.

**musculature** /ˈmʌskjʊlətʃə/ ● n. the muscular system or arrangement of a body or an organ.
– ORIGIN C19: from Fr., from L. *musculus* (see **MUSCLE**).

**musculoskeletal** /ˌmʌskjʊləʊˈskɛlɪt(ə)l/ ● adj. relating to or denoting the musculature and skeleton together.

**MusD** (also **Mus Doc**) ● abbrev. Doctor of Music.
– ORIGIN from L. *Musicae Doctor*.

**muse**[1] ● n. (**Muse**) (in Greek and Roman mythology) each of nine goddesses who preside over the arts and sciences. ➤ a woman, or a force personified as a woman, who is the source of inspiration for a creative artist.
– ORIGIN ME: from OFr., or from L. *musa*, from Gk *mousa*.

**muse**[2] ● v. (often **muse on**) be absorbed in thought. ➤ say to oneself in a thoughtful manner.
– DERIVATIVES **musing** adj. **musingly** adv.
– ORIGIN ME: from OFr. *muser* 'meditate, waste time'.

**museology** /ˌmjuːzɪˈɒlədʒi/ ● n. the science or practice of organizing and managing museums.
– DERIVATIVES **museological** adj. **museologist** n.

**musette** /mjuːˈzɛt/ ● n. **1** a kind of small bagpipe played with bellows, popular in France in the 17th–18th centuries and in later folk music. ➤ a tune or piece of music imitating the sound of this, typically with a drone. **2** a small simple variety of oboe, used chiefly in 19th-century France. **3** (also **musette bag**) US a small knapsack.
– ORIGIN ME: from OFr., dimin. of *muse* 'bagpipe'.

**museum** ● n. a building in which objects of historical, scientific, artistic, or cultural interest are stored and exhibited.
– ORIGIN C17 (denoting a university building): via L. from Gk *mouseion* 'seat of the Muses'.

**museum beetle** ● n. a small beetle whose larvae can cause severe damage to carpets, stored goods, etc. [*Anthrenus museorum* and related species.]

**museum piece** ● n. Brit. a person or object regarded as old-fashioned or useless.

**mush**[1] /mʌʃ/ ● n. **1** a soft, wet, pulpy mass. ➤ N. Amer. thick maize porridge. **2** cloying sentimentality. **3** Brit. informal a person's mouth or face. ● v. [usu. as adj. **mushed**] reduce to mush.
– DERIVATIVES **mushily** adv. **mushiness** n. **mushy** adj. (**-ier**, **-iest**).
– ORIGIN C17: appar. a var. of **MASH**.

**mush**[2] /mʌʃ/ N. Amer. ● v. travel across snow with a dog sled. ● exclam. a command urging on dogs during such a journey.
– DERIVATIVES **musher** n.
– ORIGIN C19: prob. an alt. of Fr. *marchez!* or *marchons!*, imper. of *marcher* 'to advance'.

**mush**[3] /mʊʃ/ ● n. Brit. used as an informal term of address.
– ORIGIN 1930s: of unknown origin.

**mushroom** ● n. **1** a spore-producing fungal growth, often edible and typically having a domed cap with gills on the underside. **2** a pale pinkish-brown colour. ● v. **1** increase or develop rapidly. **2** form a shape resembling that of a mushroom. **3** [usu. as noun **mushrooming**] gather mushrooms.
– DERIVATIVES **mushroomy** adj.
– ORIGIN ME: from OFr. *mousseron*, from late L. *mussirio(n-)*.

**mushroom cloud** ● n. a mushroom-shaped cloud of dust and debris formed after a nuclear explosion.

**mushroom growth** ● n. a sudden development or expansion.

**music** ● n. **1** the art or science of combining vocal or instrumental sounds (or both) to produce beauty of form, harmony, and expression of emotion. ➤the sound so produced. **2** the written or printed signs representing such sound.
– PHRASES **music to one's ears** something that is very pleasant to hear or learn.
– ORIGIN ME: from OFr. *musique*, via L. from Gk *mousikē (tekhnē)* '(art) of the Muses', from *mousa* 'muse'.

**musical** ● adj. **1** of, relating to, or accompanied by music. ➤fond of or skilled in music. **2** pleasant-sounding. ● n. a play or film in which singing and dancing play an essential part.
– DERIVATIVES **musicality** n. **musicalize** (also **-ise**) v. **musically** adv.

**musical box** ● n. Brit. a small box which plays a tune when the lid is opened.

**musical chairs** ● n. **1** a party game in which players compete for a decreasing number of chairs, the losers in successive rounds being those unable to find a chair to sit on when the accompanying music is stopped. **2** a situation in which people frequently exchange jobs or positions.

**musical comedy** ● n. a musical.

**musicale** /ˌmjuːzɪˈkɑːl/ ● n. N. Amer. a musical gathering or concert.
– ORIGIN C19: Fr., from *soirée musicale* 'evening of music'.

**musical glasses** ● pl. n. a graduated series of glass bowls or tubes played as a musical instrument by rubbing with the fingers.

**musical instrument** ● n. see **INSTRUMENT** (sense 3).

**musical saw** ● n. a saw, typically held between the knees and played with a bow like a cello.

**music box** ● n. a musical box.

**music centre** ● n. Brit. a combined radio, cassette player, and record or compact disc player.

**music drama** ● n. an opera governed by considerations of dramatic effectiveness, rather than by having a series of formal arias.

**music hall** ● n. a form of variety entertainment popular in Britain *c.*1850–1918, consisting of singing, dancing, comedy, and novelty acts. ➤a theatre where such entertainment took place.

**musician** ● n. a person who plays a musical instrument or is otherwise musically gifted.
– DERIVATIVES **musicianly** adj. **musicianship** n.
– ORIGIN ME: from OFr. *musicien*, from L. *musica* (see **MUSIC**).

**musicology** ● n. the study of music as an academic subject.
– DERIVATIVES **musicological** adj. **musicologist** n.
– ORIGIN C20: from Fr. *musicologie*.

**music theatre** ● n. a combination of music and drama in modern form distinct from traditional opera, typically for a small group of performers.

**musique concrète** /mjuːˌziːk kɔ̃ˈkrɛt/ ● n. music constructed by mixing recorded sounds.
– ORIGIN 1940s: Fr., lit. 'concrete music'.

**musk** ● n. **1** a strong-smelling reddish-brown substance secreted by the male musk deer, used as an ingredient in perfumery. **2** (also **musk plant**) a musk-scented plant related to the monkey flower. [*Mimulus moschatus* and related species.]
– DERIVATIVES **muskiness** n. **musky** adj. (**-ier**, **-iest**).
– ORIGIN ME: from late L. *muscus*, from Pers. *mušk*, perh. from Sanskrit *muṣka* 'scrotum' (because of the similarity in shape of a musk deer's musk bag).

**musk deer** ● n. a small East Asian deer without antlers, the male of which produces musk in an abdominal sac. [Genus *Moschus*: several species.]

**muskeg** /ˈmʌskɛg/ ● n. a swamp or bog in northern North America.
– ORIGIN C19: from Cree.

**muskellunge** /ˈmʌskəˌlʌn(d)ʒ/ ● n. a large pike that occurs only in the Great Lakes region of North America. [*Esox masquinongy.*]
– ORIGIN C18: based on Ojibwa, 'great fish'.

**musket** ● n. historical an infantryman's light gun with a long barrel, typically smooth-bored and fired from the shoulder.
– ORIGIN C16: from Fr. *mousquet*, from Ital. *moschetto* 'crossbow bolt'.

**musketeer** ● n. historical **1** a soldier armed with a musket. **2** a member of the household troops of the French king in the 17th and 18th centuries.

**musketry** ● n. **1** musket fire. **2** musketeers collectively. **3** the art or technique of handling a musket.

**musk melon** ● n. a yellow or green melon of a variety which has a raised network of markings on the skin.

**Muskogean** /ˌmʌskəˈgiːən, mʌˈskəʊgɪən/ ● n. a family of American Indian languages spoken in SE North America, including Creek and Choctaw.

**Muskogee** /mʌˈskəʊgi/ ● n. (pl. same or **Muskogees**) **1** a member of an American Indian people of SE North America. **2** the Muskogean language of this people.
– ORIGIN from Creek *ma:skó:ki*.

**musk ox** ● n. a large heavily built goat-antelope with a thick shaggy coat and a horny boss on the head, native to the tundra of North America and Greenland. [*Ovibos moschatus.*]

**muskrat** ● n. a large semiaquatic North American rodent with a musky smell, valued for its fur. [*Ondatra zibethicus.*] ➤the fur of the muskrat.

**Muslim** /ˈmʊzlɪm, ˈmʌz-, -s-/ (also **Moslem**) ● n. a follower of Islam. ● adj. of or relating to the Muslims or Islam.
– ORIGIN C17: from Arab., active part. of *'aslama* (see **ISLAM**).

**muslin** ● n. lightweight cotton cloth in a plain weave.
– DERIVATIVES **muslined** adj.
– ORIGIN C17: from Fr. *mousseline*, from Ital. *mussolina*, from *Mussolo* 'Mosul' (the place of manufacture in Iraq).

**muso** /ˈmjuːzəʊ/ ● n. (pl. **-os**) Brit. informal **1** a musician, especially one over-concerned with technique. **2** a keen music fan.

**musquash** /ˈmʌskwɒʃ/ ● n. archaic term for **MUSKRAT**.
– ORIGIN C17: from Abnaki *mòskwas*.

**muss** informal, chiefly N. Amer. ● v. make untidy or messy. ● n. a mess or muddle.
– DERIVATIVES **mussy** adj. (dated).
– ORIGIN C19: appar. a var. of **MESS**.

**mussel** ● n. **1** a marine bivalve mollusc with a dark brown or purplish-black shell. [*Mytilus edulis* (**edible mussel**) and other species, family Mytilidae.] **2** a freshwater bivalve mollusc, some kinds of which produce small pearls. [Family Unionidae.]
– ORIGIN OE *mus(c)le*; ult. from late L. *muscula*, from L. *musculus* (see **MUSCLE**).

**Mussulman** /ˈmʌs(ə)lmən/ ● n. (pl. **Mussulmans** or **Mussulmen**) & adj. archaic term for **MUSLIM**.
– ORIGIN C16: from Pers. *musulmān*, from *muslim* (see **MUSLIM**).

**must**[1] ● modal v. (past **had to** or in reported speech **must**) **1** be obliged to; should. ➤expressing insistence. **2** expressing an opinion about something that is very likely. ● n. informal something that should not be overlooked or missed.
– ORIGIN OE *mōste*, past tense of *mōt* 'may', of Gmc

origin.

**must²** ● n. grape juice before or during fermentation.
– ORIGIN OE, from L. *mustum*, neut. (used as n.) of *mustus* 'new'.

**must³** ● n. mustiness or mould.
– ORIGIN C17: back-form. from **MUSTY**.

**must⁴** (also **musth**) ● n. the frenzied state of a rutting male elephant or camel.
– ORIGIN C19: via Urdu from Pers. *mast* 'intoxicated'.

**mustache** ● n. US spelling of **MOUSTACHE**.

**mustachios** /mə'stɑːʃɪəʊz/ ● pl. n. a long or elaborate moustache.
– DERIVATIVES **mustachioed** adj.
– ORIGIN C16: from Sp. *mostacho* (sing.), from Ital. *mostaccio* (see **MOUSTACHE**).

**mustang** /'mʌstaŋ/ ● n. a small and lightly built feral horse of the south-western US.
– ORIGIN C19: from a blend of Sp. *mestengo* and *mostrenco*, both meaning 'wild or masterless cattle'.

**mustard** ● n. **1** a hot-tasting yellow or brown paste made from the crushed seeds of certain plants, eaten with meat or used as a cooking ingredient. **2** a plant of the cabbage family whose seeds are used to make this paste. [*Brassica nigra* (**black mustard**), *Sinapis alba* (**white mustard**, eaten as a seedling with cress), and other species.] **3** a brownish yellow colour.
– DERIVATIVES **mustardy** adj.
– ORIGIN ME: from OFr. *moustarde*, from L. *mustum* 'must' (the condiment being orig. prepared with grape must).

**mustard gas** ● n. a liquid whose vapour is a powerful irritant and vesicant, used in chemical weapons.

**mustard greens** ● pl. n. chiefly US the leaves of the mustard plant used in salads.

**mustard plaster** ● n. dated a poultice made with mustard.

**mustelid** /'mʌstɪlɪd, mʌ'stɛlɪd/ ● n. Zoology a mammal of a family (Mustelidae) including the weasels, martens, skunks, and otters.
– ORIGIN C20: from mod. L. *Mustelidae*, from L. *mustela* 'weasel'.

**muster** ● v. **1** come or bring (troops) together, especially for inspection or in preparation for battle. ➤(of a group of people) gather together. ➤Austral./NZ round up (livestock). **2** summon up (a feeling, attitude, or response). **3** (**muster someone in** or **out**) US enrol someone into (or discharge someone from) military service. ● n. **1** an instance of mustering troops. ➤Austral./NZ a rounding up of livestock. **2** Austral. informal the number of people attending a meeting.
– PHRASES **pass muster** be accepted as satisfactory.
– DERIVATIVES **musterer** n. (Austral./NZ).
– ORIGIN ME: from OFr. *moustrer* (v.), *moustre* (n.), from L. *monstrare* 'to show'.

**muster roll** ● n. an official list of officers and men in a military unit or ship's company.

**musth** ● n. variant spelling of **MUST⁴**.

**must-have** informal ● n. an essential or highly desirable item: *these belts are a must-have this season.* ● adj. essential or highly desirable.

**mustn't** ● contr. must not.

**musty** ● adj. (**-ier**, **-iest**) **1** having a stale or mouldy smell or taste. **2** unoriginal or outdated.
– DERIVATIVES **mustily** adv. **mustiness** n.
– ORIGIN C16: perh. an alt. of *moisty* 'moist'.

**mutable** /'mjuːtəb(ə)l/ ● adj. liable to change. ➤poetic/literary inconstant in one's affections.
– DERIVATIVES **mutability** n.
– ORIGIN ME: from L. *mutabilis*, from *mutare* 'to change'.

**mutagen** /'mjuːtədʒ(ə)n/ ● n. a substance which causes genetic mutation.
– DERIVATIVES **mutagenesis** n. **mutagenic** adj.
– ORIGIN 1940s: from **MUTATION** + **-GEN**.

**mutant** ● adj. resulting from or showing the effect of mutation. ● n. a mutant form.
– ORIGIN C20: from L. *mutant-*, *mutare* 'to change'.

**mutate** ● v. undergo or cause to undergo mutation.
– DERIVATIVES **mutator** n.
– ORIGIN C19: back-form. from **MUTATION**.

**mutation** ● n. **1** the action or process of changing. ➤a change. **2** a change in the structure of a gene resulting in a variant form which may be transmitted to subsequent generations. ➤a distinct form resulting from such a change. **3** Linguistics (in Celtic languages) change of an initial consonant in a word caused by the preceding word. ➤(in Germanic languages) umlaut.
– DERIVATIVES **mutational** adj. **mutationally** adv. **mutative** adj.
– ORIGIN ME: from L. *mutatio(n-)*, from *mutare* 'to change'.

**mutatis mutandis** /muː,tɑːtɪs muː'tandɪs, mjuː-, -iːs/ ● adv. (used when comparing two or more cases) making necessary alterations while not affecting the main point.
– ORIGIN L., lit. 'things being changed that have to be changed'.

**mutch** ● n. historical a linen cap worn by old women or children.
– ORIGIN ME: from MDu. *mutse*, from med. L. *almucia* 'amice'.

**mute** /mjuːt/ ● adj. **1** refraining from speech or temporarily speechless. ➤dated lacking the faculty of speech. ➤(of hounds) not giving tongue while hunting. **2** (of a letter) not pronounced. ● n. **1** dated a person without the power of speech. ➤historical (in some Asian countries) a servant who was deprived of the power of speech. **2** historical a professional attendant or mourner at a funeral. **3** a clamp placed over the bridge of a stringed instrument to deaden the resonance without affecting the vibration of the strings. **4** a pad or cone placed in the opening of a brass or other wind instrument. ● v. **1** (usu. **be muted**) deaden or muffle the sound of. **2** reduce the strength or intensity of. ➤[as adj. **muted**] (of colour or lighting) not bright; subdued.
– DERIVATIVES **mutely** adv. **muteness** n.
– ORIGIN ME: from OFr. *muet*, dimin. of *mu*, from L. *mutus*.

**mute swan** ● n. the common non-migratory Eurasian swan, with an orange-red bill with a black knob at the base. [*Cygnus olor*.]

**muti** /'muːti/ ● n. S. African informal traditional African medicine, especially that based on the use of herbs or parts of animals.
– ORIGIN from Zulu *umuthi* 'plant or medicine'.

**mutilate** ● v. injure or damage severely, typically so as to disfigure.
– DERIVATIVES **mutilation** n. **mutilator** n.
– ORIGIN C16: from L. *mutilat-*, *mutilare* 'maim'.

**mutineer** ● n. a person who mutinies.
– ORIGIN C17: from Fr. *mutinier*, from *mutin* 'rebellious'.

**mutinous** ● adj. tending to mutiny; rebellious.
– DERIVATIVES **mutinously** adv.

**mutiny** ● n. (pl. **-ies**) an open rebellion against the proper authorities, especially by soldiers or sailors against their officers. ● v. (**-ies**, **-ied**) engage in mutiny; rebel.
– ORIGIN C16: from obs. *mutine* 'rebellion', from Fr. *mutin* 'mutineer'.

**mutism** /'mjuːtɪz(ə)m/ ● n. inability or unwillingness to speak, especially as a result of congenital deafness or brain damage.

**mutt** ● n. informal **1** humorous or derogatory a dog, especially a mongrel. **2** a person regarded as stupid or incompetent.
– ORIGIN C19: abbrev. of **MUTTONHEAD**.

**mutter** ● v. say in a barely audible voice. ➤talk or grumble in secret or in private. ● n. a barely audible utterance.
– DERIVATIVES **mutterer** n. **muttering** adj. **mutteringly** adv.
– ORIGIN ME: imitative.

**mutton** ● n. the flesh of mature sheep used as food.
– PHRASES **mutton dressed as lamb** Brit. informal, derogatory a middle-aged or old woman dressed in a style suitable for a much younger woman.
– DERIVATIVES **muttony** adj.
– ORIGIN ME: from OFr. *moton*, from med. L. *multo(n-)*, prob. of Celtic origin.

**mutton bird** ● n. a shearwater or petrel of the southern oceans. [*Puffinus tenuirostris* and other species.]
– ORIGIN C19: because when cooked, the flesh of some species resembles mutton in flavour.

**mutton chop whiskers** ● pl. n. the whiskers on a man's cheek when shaped like a meat chop, narrow at the top and broad and rounded at the bottom.

**muttonhead** ● n. informal, dated a dull or stupid person.
– DERIVATIVES **muttonheaded** adj.

**mutual** /ˈmjuːtʃʊəl, -tjʊəl/ ● adj. **1** experienced or done by each of two or more parties towards the other or others: *mutual respect.* ➤(of two or more parties) having the same specified relationship to each other. **2** held in common by two or more parties: *a mutual friend.* **3** denoting a building society or insurance company owned by its members and dividing some or all of its profits between them.
– DERIVATIVES **mutuality** n. **mutually** adv.
– ORIGIN C15: from OFr. *mutuel*, from L. *mutuus* 'mutual, borrowed'.

**mutual fund** ● n. N. Amer. a unit trust.

**mutual induction** ● n. Physics the production of an electromotive force in a circuit by a change in the current in an adjacent circuit linked to the first by a magnetic field.
– DERIVATIVES **mutual inductance** n.

**mutualism** ● n. **1** the doctrine that mutual dependence is necessary to social well-being. **2** Biology symbiosis which is beneficial to both organisms involved.
– DERIVATIVES **mutualist** n. & adj. **mutualistic** adj. **mutualistically** adv.

**mutualize** (also **-ise**) ● v. organize (a business) on mutual principles.

**mutuel** /ˈmjuːtʃʊəl, -tjʊəl/ ● n. chiefly US (in betting) a pari-mutuel.

**mutule** /ˈmjuːtjuːl/ ● n. Architecture a stone block projecting under a cornice in the Doric order.
– ORIGIN C17: from Fr., from L. *mutulus*.

**muumuu** /ˈmuːmuː/ ● n. a loose, brightly coloured dress as traditionally worn by Hawaiian women.
– ORIGIN C20: from Hawaiian *mu'u mu'u*, lit. 'cut off'.

**mux** ● n. a multiplexer. ● v. short for **MULTIPLEX**.

**muzak** /ˈmjuːzak/ ● n. trademark recorded light background music played through speakers in public places.
– ORIGIN 1930s: alt. of **MUSIC**.

**muzhik** /muːˈʒɪk, ˈmuːʒɪk/ ● n. historical a Russian peasant.
– ORIGIN from Russ.

**muzzle** ● n. **1** the projecting part of the face, including the nose and mouth, of an animal such as a dog or horse. ➤a guard fitted over an animal's muzzle to stop it biting or feeding. **2** the open end of the barrel of a firearm. ● v. **1** put a muzzle on (an animal). **2** prevent from freedom of expression.
– ORIGIN ME: from OFr. *musel*, dimin. of med. L. *musum*.

**muzzy** ● adj. (**-ier**, **-iest**) **1** confused. **2** (of a visual image) blurred. ➤(of a sound) indistinct.
– DERIVATIVES **muzzily** adv. **muzziness** n.
– ORIGIN C18: of unknown origin.

**MV** ● abbrev. **1** megavolt(s). **2** motor vessel. **3** muzzle velocity.

**MVO** ● abbrev. Member of the Royal Victorian Order.

**MVP** ● abbrev. N. Amer. most valuable player.

**MW** ● abbrev. **1** Malawi (international vehicle registration). **2** medium wave. **3** megawatt(s).

**mW** ● abbrev. milliwatt(s).

**Mx** ● abbrev. **1** maxwell(s). **2** Middlesex (a former county in England).

**MY** ● abbrev. motor yacht.

**my** ● possess. det. **1** belonging to or associated with the speaker. ➤used with forms of address in affectionate, sympathetic, humorous, or patronizing contexts. **2** used in various expressions of surprise.
– PHRASES **My Lady** (or **Lord**) a polite form of address to certain titled people.
– ORIGIN ME *mi*, reduced from *min*, from OE *mīn* (see **MINE**[1]).

**my-** ● comb. form variant spelling of **MYO-** shortened before a vowel (as in *myalgia*).

**myalgia** /mʌɪˈaldʒə/ ● n. pain in a muscle or group of muscles.
– DERIVATIVES **myalgic** adj.
– ORIGIN C19: mod. L., from Gk *mus* 'muscle' + **-ALGIA**.

**myalgic encephalomyelitis** (abbrev.: **ME**) ● n. another term for **CHRONIC FATIGUE SYNDROME**.

**myalism** /ˈmʌɪəlɪz(ə)m/ ● n. a Jamaican folk religion focused on the power of ancestors, typically involving drumming, dancing, spirit possession, ritual sacrifice, and herbalism.
– ORIGIN C19: from *myal*, in the same sense (perh. from Hausa *mayl* 'sorcerer'), + **-ISM**.

**myall** /ˈmʌɪəl/ ● n. **1** an Australian acacia tree with hard scented wood, used for tobacco pipes and other decorative work. [*Acacia pendula* and other species.] **2** Austral. an Australian Aboriginal living in a traditional way.
– ORIGIN C19: sense 1 is perh. a transferred use of sense 2, with ref. to trade in wood between Dharuk-speakers and Kamilaroi-speakers; sense 2 is from Dharuk *mayal, miyal* 'person of another tribe'.

**myasthenia** /ˌmʌɪəsˈθiːnɪə/ (also **myasthenia gravis** /ˈgrɑːvɪs, ˈgravɪs/) ● n. a rare chronic autoimmune disease marked by muscular weakness without atrophy.
– ORIGIN C19: mod. L., from Gk *mus* 'muscle' + **ASTHENIA**.

**mycelium** /mʌɪˈsiːlɪəm/ ● n. (pl. **mycelia** /-lɪə/) Botany a network of fine white filaments (hyphae) constituting the vegetative part of a fungus.
– DERIVATIVES **mycelial** adj.
– ORIGIN C19: mod. L., from Gk *mukēs* 'fungus', on the pattern of *epithelium*.

**Mycenaean** /ˌmʌɪsɪˈniːən/ (also **Mycenean**) Archaeology ● adj. relating to or denoting a late Bronze Age civilization in Greece represented by finds at Mycenae and other ancient cities of the Peloponnese. ● n. an inhabitant of Mycenae or member of the Mycenaean people.

**-mycin** ● comb. form in names of antibiotic compounds derived from fungi: *streptomycin.*
– ORIGIN based on **MYCO-**.

**myco-** ● comb. form relating to fungi: *mycoprotein.*
– ORIGIN formed irregularly from Gk *mukēs* 'fungus, mushroom'.

**mycobacterium** /ˌmʌɪkə(ʊ)bakˈtɪərɪəm/ ● n. (pl. **mycobacteria** /-rɪə/) a bacterium of a group which includes the causative agents of leprosy and tuberculosis.
– DERIVATIVES **mycobacterial** adj.

**mycology** /mʌɪˈkɒlədʒi/ ● n. the scientific study of fungi.
– DERIVATIVES **mycological** adj. **mycologically** adv. **mycologist** n.

**mycoplasma** /ˌmʌɪkə(ʊ)ˈplazmə/ ● n. (pl. **mycoplasmas** or **mycoplasmata** /-mətə/) a small, typically parasitic bacterium lacking cell walls. [Order Mycoplasmatales.]

**mycoprotein** ● n. protein derived from fungi, especially as produced for human consumption.

**mycorrhiza** /ˌmʌɪkə(ʊ)ˈrʌɪzə/ ● n. (pl. **mycorrhizae** /-ziː/) Botany a fungus which grows in association with the roots of a plant.
– DERIVATIVES **mycorrhizal** adj.
– ORIGIN C19: mod. L., from **MYCO-** + Gk *rhiza* 'root'.

**mycosis** /mʌɪˈkəʊsɪs/ ● n. (pl. **mycoses** /-siːz/) a disease caused by infection with a fungus, such as thrush.
– DERIVATIVES **mycotic** /-ˈkɒtɪk/ adj.

**mycotoxin** ● n. any toxic substance produced by a fungus.

**mydriasis** /ˌmɪdrɪˈeɪsɪs, mɪˈdrʌɪəsɪs/ ● n. Medicine dilation of the pupil of the eye.
– ORIGIN C19: via L. from Gk *mudriasis*.

**myelin** /ˈmʌɪəlɪn/ ● n. Anatomy & Physiology a whitish fatty substance forming a sheath around many nerve fibres.
– DERIVATIVES **myelinated** adj. **myelination** n.
– ORIGIN C19: from Gk *muelos* 'marrow' + **-IN**[1].

**myelitis** /ˌmʌɪəˈlʌɪtɪs/ ● n. Medicine inflammation of the spinal cord.
– ORIGIN C19: mod. L., from Gk *muelos* 'marrow' + **-ITIS**.

**myeloid** /ˈmʌɪəlɔɪd/ ● **adj. 1** of or relating to bone marrow. **2** of or relating to the spinal cord.
– ORIGIN C19: from Gk *muelos* 'marrow' + **-OID**.

**myeloma** /ˌmʌɪəˈləʊmə/ ● **n.** (pl. **myelomas** or **myelomata** /-mətə/) Medicine a malignant tumour of the bone marrow.
– ORIGIN C19: mod. L., from Gk *muelos* 'marrow' + **-OMA**.

**Mylar** /ˈmʌɪlɑː/ ● **n.** trademark a form of polyester resin made by copolymerizing ethylene glycol and terephthalic acid and used to make heat-resistant plastic films and sheets.
– ORIGIN 1950s: an arbitrary formation.

**mylonite** /ˈmʌɪlənʌɪt/ ● **n.** Geology a fine-grained metamorphic rock, typically banded, resulting from the grinding or crushing of other rocks.
– ORIGIN C19: from Gk *mulōn* 'mill' + **-ITE**[1].

**mynah** /ˈmʌɪnə/ (also **mynah bird**) (also **myna**) ● **n.** a southern Asian or Australasian starling with a loud call, some kinds of which can mimic human speech. [*Gracula religiosa* (**hill mynah**) and other species.]
– ORIGIN C18: from Hindi *mainā*.

**myo-** (also **my-** before a vowel) ● **comb. form** of muscle; relating to muscles: *myocardium*.
– ORIGIN from Gk *mus, mu-* 'mouse or muscle'.

**myocardium** /ˌmʌɪə(ʊ)ˈkɑːdɪəm/ ● **n.** Anatomy the muscular tissue of the heart.
– DERIVATIVES **myocardial** adj. **myocarditis** n.
– ORIGIN C19: mod. L., from **MYO-** + Gk *kardia* 'heart'.

**myoclonus** /ˌmʌɪə(ʊ)ˈkləʊnəs/ ● **n.** Medicine spasmodic jerky contraction of groups of muscles.
– DERIVATIVES **myoclonic** adj.

**myofibril** /ˌmʌɪə(ʊ)ˈfʌɪbrɪl/ ● **n.** any of the elongated contractile threads found in striated muscle cells.

**myogenic** /ˌmʌɪə(ʊ)ˈdʒɛnɪk/ ● **adj.** Physiology originating in muscle tissue (rather than from nerve impulses).

**myoglobin** /ˌmʌɪə(ʊ)ˈgləʊbɪn/ ● **n.** Biochemistry a red protein containing haem, which carries and stores oxygen in muscle cells.

**myology** /mʌɪˈɒlədʒi/ ● **n.** the study of the structure, arrangement, and action of muscles.
– DERIVATIVES **myological** adj. **myologist** n.

**myopathy** /mʌɪˈɒpəθi/ ● **n.** (pl. **-ies**) Medicine a disease of muscle tissue.
– DERIVATIVES **myopathic** adj.

**myope** /ˈmʌɪəʊp/ ● **n.** a short-sighted person.
– ORIGIN C18: from Fr., via late L. from Gk *muōps*, from *muein* 'to shut' + *ōps* 'eye'.

**myopia** /mʌɪˈəʊpɪə/ ● **n. 1** short-sightedness. **2** lack of foresight or intellectual insight.
– DERIVATIVES **myopic** /-ˈɒpɪk/ adj. **myopically** /-ˈɒpɪk(ə)li/ adv.
– ORIGIN C18: mod. L., from late Gk *muōpia*, from Gk *muōps* (see **MYOPE**).

**myosin** /ˈmʌɪə(ʊ)sɪn/ ● **n.** Biochemistry a fibrous protein which forms (together with actin) the contractile filaments of muscle cells.

**myosis** ● **n.** variant spelling of **MIOSIS**.

**myositis** /ˌmʌɪə(ʊ)ˈsʌɪtɪs/ ● **n.** Medicine inflammation and degeneration of muscle tissue.
– ORIGIN C19: formed irregularly from Gk *mus, mu-* 'muscle' + **-ITIS**.

**myosotis** /ˌmʌɪə(ʊ)ˈsəʊtɪs/ ● **n.** a plant of a genus which includes the forget-me-nots. [Genus *Myosotis*.]
– ORIGIN mod. L., from Gk *muosōtis*, from *mus, mu-* 'mouse' + *ous, ōt-* 'ear'.

**myotonia** /ˌmʌɪə(ʊ)ˈtəʊnɪə/ ● **n.** inability to relax voluntary muscle after vigorous effort.
– DERIVATIVES **myotonic** adj.
– ORIGIN C19: from **MYO-** + Gk *tonos* 'tone'.

**myriad** /ˈmɪrɪəd/ poetic/literary ● **n. 1** an indefinitely great number. **2** (chiefly in classical history) a unit of ten thousand. ● **adj.** innumerable. ➤having innumerable elements: *the myriad political scene*.
– ORIGIN C16: via late L. from Gk *murias, muriad-*, from *murioi* '10,000'.

**myriapod** /ˈmɪrɪəpɒd/ ● **n.** Zoology a centipede, millipede, or other arthropod having an elongated body with numerous leg-bearing segments.
– ORIGIN C19: from mod. L. *Myriapoda* (former class name), from Gk *murias* (see **MYRIAD**) + *pous, pod-* 'foot'.

**myrmecology** /ˌməːmɪˈkɒlədʒi/ ● **n.** the branch of entomology concerned with ants.
– DERIVATIVES **myrmecological** adj. **myrmecologist** n.
– ORIGIN C19: from Gk *murmēx, murmēk-* 'ant' + **-LOGY**.

**myrmecophile** /ˈməːmɪkə(ʊ)fʌɪl, məˈmiːkə(ʊ)-/ ● **n.** Biology an invertebrate or plant which has a symbiotic relationship with ants, such as living inside an ants' nest.
– DERIVATIVES **myrmecophilous** adj. **myrmecophily** n.
– ORIGIN C19: from Gk *murmēx, murmēk-* 'ant' + **-PHILE**.

**myrmidon** /ˈməːmɪd(ə)n/ ● **n.** a hired ruffian or unscrupulous subordinate.
– ORIGIN ME: from L. *Myrmidones* (pl.), from Gk *Murmidones*, a warlike people of Thessaly who accompanied Achilles to Troy.

**myrobalan** /mʌɪˈrɒbələn/ ● **n. 1** (also **myrobalan plum**) another term for **CHERRY PLUM**. **2** a tropical tree of a characteristic pagoda shape. [*Terminalia chebula* and related species.] ➤(also **myrobalan nut**) the fruit of this tree, used in tanning.
– ORIGIN ME: from Fr. *myrobolan* or L. *myrobalanum*, from Gk *murobalanos*, from *muron* 'unguent' + *balanos* 'acorn'.

**myrrh**[1] /məː/ ● **n.** a fragrant gum resin obtained from certain trees and used, especially in the Near East, in perfumery, medicines, and incense.
– DERIVATIVES **myrrhy** adj.
– ORIGIN OE *myrra, myrre*, via L. from Gk *murra*, of Semitic origin.

**myrrh**[2] /məː/ ● **n.** another term for **SWEET CICELY**.
– ORIGIN C16: from L. *myrris*, from Gk *murris*.

**myrtaceous** /məːˈteɪʃəs/ ● **adj.** Botany relating to or denoting plants of the myrtle family (Myrtaceae).
– ORIGIN C19: from mod. L. *Myrtaceae* (pl.), from the genus name *Myrtus* (see **MYRTLE**), + **-OUS**.

**myrtle** ● **n. 1** an evergreen shrub with glossy aromatic foliage and white flowers followed by purple-black oval berries. [*Myrtus communis*.] **2** N. Amer. the lesser periwinkle. [*Vinca minor*.]
– ORIGIN ME: from med. L. *myrtilla, myrtillus*, dimin. of L. *myrta, myrtus*, from Gk *murtos*.

**myself** ● **pron.** [first person sing.] **1** [reflexive] used by a speaker to refer to himself or herself as the object of a verb or preposition when he or she is the subject of the clause. **2** [emphatic] I or me personally. **3** poetic/literary term for **I**[2].
– ORIGIN OE *me self*, from **ME**[1] + **SELF**.

**Mysian** /ˈmɪsɪən/ ● **n.** a native or inhabitant of Mysia, an ancient region of NW Asia Minor. ● **adj.** of or relating to Mysia.

**mysid** /ˈmʌɪsɪd/ ● **n.** Zoology a crustacean of an order (Mysidacea) that comprises the opossum shrimps.
– ORIGIN C20: from mod. L. *Mysis* (genus name) + **-ID**[3].

**mystagogue** /ˈmɪstəgɒg/ ● **n.** a teacher or propounder of mystical doctrines.
– DERIVATIVES **mystagogy** n.
– ORIGIN C16: from Fr., or via L. from Gk *mustagōgos*, from *mustēs* 'initiated person' + *agōgos* 'leading'.

**mystery**[1] ● **n.** (pl. **-ies**) **1** something that is difficult or impossible to understand or explain. ➤secrecy or obscurity. ➤a person or thing whose identity or nature is puzzling or unknown. **2** a novel, play, or film dealing with a puzzling crime. **3** (**mysteries**) the secret rites of an ancient or tribal religion, to which only initiates are admitted. ➤archaic the Christian Eucharist. **4** chiefly Christian Theology a religious belief based on divine revelation and regarded as beyond human understanding. **5** an incident in the life of Jesus or of a saint as a focus of devotion in the Roman Catholic Church, especially each of those commemorated by one of the decades of the rosary.
– DERIVATIVES **mysterious** adj. **mysteriously** adv. **mysteriousness** n.
– ORIGIN ME: from OFr. *mistere* or L. *mysterium*, from Gk *mustērion*; rel. to **MYSTIC**.

**mystery**[2] ● **n.** (pl. **-ies**) archaic a handicraft or trade.
– ORIGIN ME: from med. L. *misterium*, contr. of *ministerium* 'ministry', by assoc. with *mysterium* (see **MYSTERY**[1]).

**mystery play** ● n. a popular medieval play based on biblical stories or the lives of the saints.

**mystery tour** ● n. Brit. a pleasure excursion to an unspecified destination.

**mystic** ● n. a person who seeks by contemplation and self-surrender to attain unity with the Deity or the absolute, and so reach truths beyond human understanding. ● adj. another term for **MYSTICAL**.
– ORIGIN ME: from OFr. *mystique*, or via L. from Gk *mustikos*, from *mustēs* 'initiated person' from *muein* 'close the eyes or lips', also 'initiate'.

**mystical** ● adj. **1** of or relating to mystics or mysticism. ➤ having a spiritual symbolic or allegorical significance that transcends human understanding. ➤ of or relating to ancient religious mysteries or other occult rites. **2** inspiring a sense of spiritual mystery, awe, and fascination.
– DERIVATIVES **mystically** adv.

**mysticism** ● n. **1** the beliefs or state of mind characteristic of mystics. **2** vague or ill-defined religious or spiritual belief, especially as associated with a belief in the occult.

**mystify** ● v. (**-ies**, **-ied**) utterly bewilder. ➤ make obscure or mysterious.
– DERIVATIVES **mystification** n. **mystifier** n. **mystifying** adj. **mystifyingly** adv.
– ORIGIN C19: from Fr. *mystifier*, formed irregularly from *mystique* 'mystic' or from *mystère* 'mystery'.

**mystique** ● n. a fascinating aura of mystery, awe, and power. ➤ an air of secrecy surrounding an activity or subject, making it impressive or baffling to the layperson.
– ORIGIN C19: from Fr., from OFr. (see **MYSTIC**).

**myth** ● n. **1** a traditional story concerning the early history of a people or explaining a natural or social phenomenon, and typically involving supernatural beings or events. **2** a widely held but false belief. ➤ a fictitious person or thing. ➤ an exaggerated or idealized conception of a person or thing.
– DERIVATIVES **mythic** adj. **mythical** adj. **mythically** adv.
– ORIGIN C19 (earlier (C17) as *mythic*): from mod. L. *mythus*, via late L. from Gk *muthos*.

**mythi** plural form of **MYTHUS**.

**mythicize** (also **-ise**) ● v. treat as a myth; interpret mythically.
– DERIVATIVES **mythicism** n. **mythicist** n.

**mytho-** ● comb. form of or relating to myth: *mythography*.
– ORIGIN from Gk *muthos*, or from **MYTH**.

**mythography** ● n. **1** the representation of myths, especially in the plastic arts. **2** the creation or collection of myths.
– DERIVATIVES **mythographer** n.

**mythology** ● n. (pl. **-ies**) **1** a collection of myths, especially one belonging to a particular religious or cultural tradition. **2** a set of widely held but exaggerated or fictitious stories or beliefs. **3** the study of myths.
– DERIVATIVES **mythologer** n. **mythologic** adj. **mythological** adj. **mythologically** adv. **mythologist** n. **mythologize** (also **-ise**) v. **mythologizer** (also **-iser**) n.
– ORIGIN ME: from Fr. *mythologie*, or via late L. from Gk *muthologia*, from *muthos* 'myth' + *-logia* (see **-LOGY**).

**mythomania** ● n. an abnormal or pathological tendency to exaggerate or tell lies.
– DERIVATIVES **mythomaniac** n. & adj.

**mythopoeia** /ˌmɪθə(ʊ)ˈpiːə/ ● n. the making of a myth or myths.
– DERIVATIVES **mythopoeic** adj. **mythopoetic** adj.
– ORIGIN 1950s: from Gk *muthopoiia*.

**mythos** /ˈmʌɪθɒs, ˈmɪθɒs/ ● n. (pl. **mythoi** /-θɔɪ/) technical **1** a myth or mythology. **2** an ideology.
– ORIGIN C18: from Gk.

**mythus** /ˈmʌɪθəs, ˈmɪθəs/ ● n. (pl. **mythi** /-θʌɪ/) a myth or mythos.
– ORIGIN C19: mod. L.

**myxo-** (also **myx-**) ● comb. form relating to mucus: *myxovirus*.
– ORIGIN from Gk *muxa* 'slime, mucus'.

**myxoedema** /ˌmɪksɪˈdiːmə/ (US **myxedema**) ● n. Medicine a condition caused by hyperthyroidism, marked by swelling of the skin and underlying tissues.

**myxoma** /mɪkˈsəʊmə/ ● n. (pl. **myxomas** or **myxomata** /-mətə/) Medicine a benign tumour of connective tissue containing mucous or gelatinous material.
– DERIVATIVES **myxomatous** adj.

**myxomatosis** /ˌmɪksəməˈtəʊsɪs/ ● n. a highly infectious and usually fatal viral disease of rabbits, causing swelling of the mucous membranes and inflammation and discharge around the eyes.

**myxovirus** /ˈmɪksə(ʊ)ˌvʌɪrəs/ ● n. any of a group of RNA viruses including the influenza virus.

**N**[1] (also **n**) ● n. (pl. **Ns** or **N's**) **1** the fourteenth letter of the alphabet. **2** denoting the next after M in a set of items, categories, etc.

**N**[2] ● abbrev. **1** (used in recording moves in chess) knight. [representing the pronunc. of *kn-*, since the initial letter *k-* represents 'king'.] **2** (chiefly in place names) New. **3** Physics newton(s). **4** Chemistry (with reference to solutions) normal. **5** North or Northern. **6** Norway (international vehicle registration). **7** nuclear. ● symb. the chemical element nitrogen.

**n** ● abbrev. **1** nano- ($10^{-9}$). **2** Grammar neuter. **3** (***n-***) Chemistry normal (denoting straight-chain hydrocarbons). **4** note (used in a book's index to refer to a footnote). **5** Grammar noun. ● symb. an unspecified or variable number.

**'n** (also **'n'**) ● contr. and (used in informal contexts to coordinate two closely connected elements): *rock 'n roll.*

**-n**[1] ● suffix variant spelling of **-EN**[2].

**-n**[2] ● suffix variant spelling of **-EN**[3].

**Na** ● symb. the chemical element sodium.
– ORIGIN from mod. L. *natrium.*

**n/a** ● abbrev. **1** not applicable. **2** not available.

**NAACP** ● abbrev. National Association for the Advancement of Colored People.

**NAAFI** /ˈnafi/ ● abbrev. Navy, Army, and Air Force Institutes. ● n. (usu. **Naafi**) a canteen or shop run by the NAAFI.

**naan** ● n. variant spelling of **NAN**[2].

**nab** ● v. (**nabbed**, **nabbing**) informal **1** catch (someone) doing something wrong. **2** take or grab suddenly.
– ORIGIN C17 (also as *napp*; cf. **KIDNAP**): of unknown origin.

**Nabataean** /ˌnabəˈtiːən/ (also **Nabatean**) ● n. **1** a member of an ancient Arabian people having a kingdom with its capital at Petra (now in Jordan). **2** the extinct language of this people, a form of Aramaic strongly influenced by Arabic. ● adj. of or relating to the Nabataeans or their language.
– ORIGIN from L. *Nabat(h)aeus*, Gk *Nabat(h)aios* (cf. Arab. *Nabaṭī* 'relating to the Nabataeans)' + **-AN**.

**nabe** ● n. US informal a neighbourhood. ➤ a neighbour.

**nabob** /ˈneɪbɒb/ ● n. historical **1** a Muslim official or governor under the Mogul empire. **2** a person who returned from India to Europe with a fortune.
– ORIGIN from Port. *nababo* or Sp. *nabab*, from Urdu; see also **NAWAB**.

**nacelle** /nəˈsɛl/ ● n. **1** the outer casing of an aircraft engine. **2** chiefly historical the car of an airship.
– ORIGIN C20: from Fr., from late L. *navicella*, dimin. of L. *navis* 'ship'.

**naches** /ˈnʌxəs/ (also **nachas** pronunc. same) ● n. US pride at the achievements of one's children.
– ORIGIN C20: from Yiddish *nakhes*, from Heb. *naḥaṯ* 'contentment'.

**nacho** /ˈnatʃəʊ/ ● n. (pl. **-os**) a small piece of tortilla topped with melted cheese, peppers, etc.
– ORIGIN perh. from Mex. Sp. *Nacho*, familiar form of *Ignacio*, first name of the chef credited with creating the dish, or from Sp. *nacho* 'flat-nosed'.

**NACODS** /ˈneɪkɒds/ ● abbrev. (in the UK) National Association of Colliery Overmen, Deputies, and Shotfirers.

**nacre** /ˈneɪkə/ ● n. mother-of-pearl.
– DERIVATIVES **nacreous** adj.
– ORIGIN C16: from Fr., of unknown origin.

**NAD** ● abbrev. Biochemistry nicotinamide adenine dinucleotide, a coenzyme important in many biological oxidation reactions.

**nada** /ˈnɑːdə, ˈnadə/ ● pron. N. Amer. informal nothing.
– ORIGIN from Sp.

**Na-Dene** /nɑːˈdɛneɪ, -ni/ ● n. a postulated phylum of North American Indian languages including the Athabaskan family, Tlingit, and (in some classifications) Haida.
– ORIGIN C20: from Tlingit *naa* 'tribe' + N. Athabaskan *dene* 'tribe'.

**nadir** /ˈneɪdɪə, ˈnadɪə/ ● n. **1** Astronomy the point on the celestial sphere directly below an observer. The opposite of **ZENITH**. **2** the lowest or most unsuccessful point: *his fortunes reached their nadir.*
– ORIGIN ME: via Fr. from Arab. *naẓīr* (*as-samt*) 'opposite (to the zenith)'.

**naevus** /ˈniːvəs/ (US **nevus**) ● n. (pl. **naevi** /-vʌɪ, -viː/) a birthmark or a mole on the skin, especially a birthmark in the form of a raised red patch.
– ORIGIN C19: from L.

**naff**[1] ● v. **1** (**naff off**) Brit. informal go away. **2** [as adj. **naffing**] used to emphasize annoyance.
– ORIGIN 1950s: euphemism for **FUCK**; cf. **EFF**.

**naff**[2] ● adj. Brit. informal lacking taste or style.
– DERIVATIVES **naffness** n.
– ORIGIN 1960s: of unknown origin.

**NAFTA** (also **Nafta**) ● abbrev. North American Free Trade Agreement.

**nag**[1] ● v. (**nagged**, **nagging**) **1** harass (someone) constantly to do something to which they are averse. **2** [often as adj. **nagging**] be persistently painful or worrying to. ● n. **1** a person who nags. **2** a persistent feeling of anxiety: *he felt a little nag of doubt.*
– DERIVATIVES **nagger** n. **naggingly** adv. **naggy** adj.
– ORIGIN C19 (orig. dial. in the sense 'gnaw'): perh. of Scand. or Low Ger. origin.

**nag**[2] ● n. informal, often derogatory a horse, especially one that is old or in poor health. ➤ archaic a horse suitable for riding rather than as a draught animal.
– ORIGIN ME: of unknown origin.

**Naga** /ˈnɑːgə/ ● n. **1** a member of a group of peoples living in or near the Naga Hills of Burma (Myanmar) and NE India. **2** any of the Tibeto-Burman languages of these peoples.
– ORIGIN perh. from Sanskrit *nagna* 'naked' or *naga* 'mountain'.

**naga** /ˈnɑːgə/ ● n. (in Indian mythology) a member of a semi-divine race, part human, part cobra in form, associated with water and sometimes with mystical initiation.
– ORIGIN from Sanskrit *nāga* 'serpent'.

**Nah.** ● abbrev. Nahum (in biblical references).

**Nahuatl** /ˈnɑːwɑːt(ə)l, nɑːˈwɑːt(ə)l/ ● n. **1** a member of a group of peoples native to southern Mexico and Central America, including the Aztecs. **2** the Uto-Aztecan language of these peoples.
– ORIGIN via Sp. from Nahuatl.

**naiad** /ˈnʌɪad/ ● n. (pl. **naiads** or **naiades** /ˈnʌɪəˌdiːz/) **1** (in classical mythology) a nymph inhabiting a river, spring, or waterfall. **2** the aquatic larva of a dragonfly, mayfly, or stonefly. **3** an aquatic plant with narrow leaves and minute flowers. [Genus *Najas*.]
– ORIGIN via L. from Gk *Naias*, *Naiad-*, from *naein* 'to flow'.

**naiant** /ˈneɪənt/ ● adj. [postpos.] Heraldry (of a fish or marine creature) swimming horizontally.
– ORIGIN C16: from Anglo-Norman Fr., var. of OFr. *noiant*,

*noier* 'to swim'.

**naif** /nʌɪ'iːf, nɑː'iːf/ ● **adj.** naive. ● **n.** a naive person.
– ORIGIN from Fr. *naïf.*

**nail** ● **n. 1** a small metal spike with a broadened flat head, driven typically into wood to join things together or to serve as a hook. **2** a horny covering on the upper surface of the tip of the finger and toe in humans and other primates. ➤a hard growth on the upper mandible of some soft-billed birds. **3** a former measure of length for cloth, equal to 2¼ inches. **4** a former measure of wool, beef, or other commodity, roughly equal to 7 or 8 pounds. ● **v. 1** fasten with a nail or nails. **2** informal detect or catch (someone, especially a suspected criminal). **3** informal (in sport) strike (a ball) forcefully and successfully. ➤Baseball (of a fielder) put (a runner) out by throwing to a base. ➤chiefly N. Amer. (of a player) defeat or outwit (an opponent). **4** (**nail someone down**) elicit a firm commitment from someone. **5** (**nail something down**) identify something precisely.
– PHRASES **a nail in the coffin** an action or event likely to have a detrimental or destructive effect. **on the nail** (N. Amer. also **on the barrelhead**) (of payment) without delay.
– DERIVATIVES **-nailed** adj. **nailless** adj.
– ORIGIN OE *nægel* (n.), *næglan* (v.), of Gmc origin.

**nail-biting** ● **adj.** causing great anxiety or tension.

**nail enamel** ● **n.** N. Amer. nail polish.

**nailer** ● **n. 1** chiefly historical a maker of nails. **2** a power tool for inserting nails.
– DERIVATIVES **nailery** n.

**nail file** ● **n.** a small file or emery board used for smoothing and shaping the fingernails and toenails.

**nail head** ● **n.** an ornament resembling the head of a nail, used chiefly in architecture and on clothing.

**nail polish** ● **n.** varnish applied to the fingernails or toenails to colour them or make them shiny.

**nail punch** (also **nail set**) ● **n.** a tool hit with a hammer to sink the head of a nail below a surface.

**nail sickness** ● **n.** the condition of a structure which is held together with corroded nails.

**nail varnish** ● **n.** Brit. nail polish.

**nainsook** /'neɪnsʊk/ ● **n.** a fine, soft cotton fabric, originally from the Indian subcontinent.
– ORIGIN C18: from Hindi *nainsukh*, from *nain* 'eye' + *sukh* 'pleasure'.

**naira** /'nʌɪrə/ ● **n.** the basic monetary unit of Nigeria, equal to 100 kobo.
– ORIGIN contr. of *Nigeria.*

**naissant** /'neɪs(ə)nt/ ● **adj.** Heraldry (of a charge, especially an animal) issuing from the middle of an ordinary, especially a fess.
– ORIGIN C16: from Fr., lit. 'being born', pres. part. of *naître.*

**naive** /nʌɪ'iːv, nɑː'iːv/ (also **naïve**) ● **adj. 1** lacking experience, wisdom, or judgement. **2** natural and unaffected. ➤of or denoting art produced in a style which deliberately rejects sophisticated artistic techniques and has a bold directness resembling a child's work.
– DERIVATIVES **naively** adv. **naiveness** n. **naivety** n.
– ORIGIN C17: from Fr. *naïve*, fem. of *naïf*, from L. *nativus* 'native, natural'.

**naked** ● **adj. 1** without clothes. ➤(of an object) without the usual covering or protection. ➤(of a tree, plant, or animal) without leaves, hairs, etc. **2** exposed to harm; vulnerable. **3** (of feelings or behaviour) undisguised.
– PHRASES **naked of** devoid of.
– DERIVATIVES **nakedly** adv. **nakedness** n.
– ORIGIN OE *nacod*, of Gmc origin.

**naked eye** ● **n.** (**the naked eye**) unassisted vision, without a telescope, microscope, or other device.

**naked ladies** (also **naked boys**) ● **pl. n.** the meadow saffron.

**naker** /'neɪkə/ ● **n.** historical a kettledrum.
– ORIGIN ME: from OFr. *nacaire*, from Arab. *naḳḳāra* 'drum'.

**naloxone** /nə'lɒksəʊn/ ● **n.** Medicine a synthetic drug, similar to morphine, which blocks opiate receptors in the nervous system.
– ORIGIN 1960s: contr. of *N-allylnoroxymorphone.*

**naltrexone** /nal'trɛksəʊn/ ● **n.** Medicine a synthetic drug, similar to morphine, which blocks opiate receptors in the nervous system and is used chiefly in the treatment of heroin addiction.
– ORIGIN 1970s: from a contr. of *N-al(lylnoroxymorph)one* (see **NALOXONE**), with the insertion of the arbitrary element *-trex-*.

**Nama** /'nɑːmə/ ● **n.** (pl. same or **Namas**) **1** a member of one of the Khoikhoi peoples of South Africa and SW Namibia. **2** the Khoisan language of this people.
– ORIGIN the name in Nama.

**USAGE** Nama

**Nama** is the standard accepted term in this context. The word **Hottentot**, an older term with a somewhat broader meaning, is obsolete and may now cause offence.

**namaskar** /ˌnʌmʌs'kɑː/ ● **n.** a traditional Indian gesture of greeting, made by bringing the palms together before the face or chest and bowing.
– ORIGIN via Hindi from Sanskrit *namaskāra*, from *namas* 'bowing' + *kāra* 'action'.

**namaste** /'nʌməsteɪ/ ● **exclam.** (in India) a respectful greeting said when giving a namaskar. ● **n.** another term for **NAMASKAR**.
– ORIGIN via Hindi from Sanskrit *namas* 'bowing' + *te* 'to you'.

**namby-pamby** derogatory ● **adj.** lacking courage or vigour; feeble. ● **n.** (pl. **-ies**) a namby-pamby person.
– ORIGIN C18: fanciful formation based on the given name of *Ambrose* Philips, an Engl. writer whose pastorals were ridiculed as insipid.

**name** ● **n. 1** a word or set of words by which someone or something is known, addressed, or referred to. **2** a famous person. ➤a reputation, especially a good one. **3** (in the UK) an insurance underwriter belonging to a Lloyd's syndicate. ● **v. 1** give a name to. ➤identify or mention by name. ➤(**name someone/thing after** or N. Amer. also **for**) call someone or something by the same name as. ➤chiefly Brit. (of the Speaker) mention (an MP) by name as disobedient to the chair and thereby subject to a ban from the House. **2** specify (a sum, time, or place). ● **adj.** (of a person or product) having a well-known name.
– PHRASES **by** (or **of**) **the name of** called. **call someone names** insult someone verbally. **have to one's name** [often with neg.] in one's possession. **in all but name** existing in a particular state but not formally recognized as such. **in someone's name 1** formally registered as belonging to or reserved for someone. **2** on behalf of someone. **in the name of** for the sake of. **make a name for oneself** become famous. **name the day** arrange the date for a specific occasion, especially a wedding. **name names** mention specific names, especially in accusation. **the name of the game** informal the main purpose or most important aspect of a situation.
– DERIVATIVES **nameable** adj.
– ORIGIN OE *nama*, *noma* (n.), *(ge)namian* (v.), of Gmc origin.

**namecheck** ● **n.** a public mention of the name of a person or thing, especially in acknowledgement or for publicity purposes. ● **v.** mention in this way.

**name day** ● **n.** the feast day of a saint after whom a person is named.

**name-dropping** ● **n.** the practice of casually mentioning the names of famous people one knows in order to impress.
– DERIVATIVES **name-drop** v. **name-dropper** n.

**nameless** ● **adj. 1** having no name or no known name. **2** difficult to describe. ➤too horrific to be described. **3** archaic (of a child) illegitimate.
– DERIVATIVES **namelessly** adv. **namelessness** n.

**namely** ● **adv.** that is to say.

**nameplate** ● **n.** a plate attached to something and bearing the name of the owner, occupier, or the thing itself.

**namesake** ● **n.** a person or thing that has the same name as another.
– ORIGIN C17: from the phr. *for the name's sake.*

**Namibian** /nə'mɪbɪən/ ● **n.** a native or inhabitant of Namibia. ● **adj.** of or relating to Namibia.

**nan**[1] /nan/ ● **n.** Brit. informal one's grandmother.
– ORIGIN 1940s: abbrev. of **NANNY**, or a child's pronunc. of **GRAN**.

**nan**[2] /nɑːn/ (also **naan**) ● **n.** (in Indian cookery) a type of leavened bread, typically of a flattened teardrop shape.
– ORIGIN from Urdu and Pers. *nān*.

**nana**[1] /'nɑːnə/ ● **n.** Brit. informal a silly person; a fool.
– ORIGIN 1960s: perh. a shortening of **BANANA**.

**nana**[2] /'nanə/ (Brit. also **nanna**) ● **n.** informal one's grandmother.
– ORIGIN C19: child's pronunc. of **NANNY** or **GRAN**.

**nancy** (also **nance**, **nancy boy**) ● **n.** (pl. **-ies**) informal, derogatory an effeminate or homosexual man.
– ORIGIN C20: familiar form of the given name *Ann*.

**nancy story** ● **n.** W. Indian **1** a traditional African folk tale about Anancy the spider, who overcomes others by cunning. **2** an elaborate evasive story or lie.
– ORIGIN *nancy*, from *Anancy*, from Twi *ananse* 'spider'.

**NAND** ● **n.** [as modifier] Electronics denoting a gate circuit which produces an output signal unless there are signals on all of its inputs.
– ORIGIN 1950s: from *not and*.

**nandrolone** /'nandrələʊn/ ● **n.** an anabolic steroid with tissue-building properties, used unlawfully to enhance performance in sport.
– ORIGIN shortened form of its chemical name.

**nankeen** /naŋ'kiːn, nan-/ ● **n.** a yellowish cotton cloth. ➤ **(nankeens)** historical trousers made of this cloth.
– ORIGIN C18: from the name of the city of *Nanking* in China, where it was first made.

**nanna** ● **n.** variant spelling of **NANA**[2].

**nanny** ● **n.** (pl. **-ies**) **1** a person, typically a woman, employed to look after a child in its own home. **2** a person or institution regarded as interfering and overprotective. **3** (also **nanny goat**) a female goat. ● **v.** (**-ies**, **-ied**) [usu. as noun **nannying**] be overprotective towards.
– ORIGIN C18: familiar form of the given name *Ann*.

**nano-** /'nanəʊ/ ● **comb. form** denoting a factor of $10^{-9}$: *nanosecond*. ➤ submicroscopic: *nanotube*.
– ORIGIN via L. from Gk *nanos* 'dwarf'.

**nanobacterium** ● **n.** a kind of micro-organism about a tenth the size of the smallest normal bacteria, claimed to have been discovered in living tissue and in rock.

**nanobe** /'nanəʊb/ ● **n.** another term for **NANOBACTERIUM**.

**nanometre** /'nanə(ʊ),miːtə/ (US **nanometer**) (abbrev.: **nm**) ● **n.** one thousand millionth of a metre.

**nanosecond** (abbrev.: **ns**) ● **n.** one thousand millionth of a second.

**nanotechnology** ● **n.** technology on an atomic or molecular scale, concerned with dimensions of less than 100 nanometres.
– DERIVATIVES **nanotechnological** adj. **nanotechnologist** n.

**nanotube** ● **n.** Chemistry a cylindrical molecule of a fullerene.

**naos** /'neɪɒs/ ● **n.** (pl. **naoi** /'neɪɔɪ/) **1** the inner chamber or sanctuary of a Greek or other ancient temple. **2** the main body or nave of a Byzantine church.
– ORIGIN Gk, lit. 'temple'.

**nap**[1] ● **v.** (**napped**, **napping**) sleep lightly or briefly, especially during the day. ● **n.** a short sleep of this type.
– ORIGIN OE *hnappian*, prob. of Gmc origin.

**nap**[2] ● **n. 1** the raised hairs, threads, or similar small projections on the surface of fabric or suede leather. **2** Austral. informal a bedroll used for sleeping on in the open.
– DERIVATIVES **napless** adj.
– ORIGIN ME *noppe*, from MDu., Mid. Low Ger. *noppe* 'nap', *noppen* 'trim the nap from'.

**nap**[3] ● **n. 1** a card game resembling whist in which players declare the number of tricks they expect to take, up to five. **2** Brit. the betting of all one's money on one prospective winner. ➤ a tipster's choice for this. ● **v.** (**napped**, **napping**) Brit. name (a horse or greyhound) as a probable winner of a race.
– PHRASES **go nap** attempt to take all five tricks in nap. ➤ score or win five times. ➤ risk everything in one attempt.
– ORIGIN C19: abbrev. of *napoleon*, the orig. name of the card game.

**napa** ● **n.** variant spelling of **NAPPA**.

**napalm** /'neɪpɑːm/ ● **n.** a highly flammable sticky jelly consisting of petrol thickened with special soaps, used in incendiary bombs and flame-throwers. ● **v.** attack with bombs containing napalm.
– ORIGIN 1940s: from *na(phthenic)* and *palm(itic acid)*.

**nape** ● **n.** the back of a person's neck.
– ORIGIN ME: of unknown origin.

**napery** /'neɪp(ə)ri/ ● **n.** archaic household linen, especially tablecloths and napkins.
– ORIGIN ME: from OFr. *naperie*, from *nape* 'tablecloth'.

**nap hand** ● **n.** informal a series of five winning points, victories, etc. in a game or sport.

**naphtha** /'nafθə/ ● **n.** Chemistry a flammable oil containing various hydrocarbons, obtained by the dry distillation of organic substances such as coal, shale, or petroleum.
– ORIGIN ME *napte*, from L. *naphtha* from Gk.

**naphthalene** /'nafθəliːn/ ● **n.** Chemistry a volatile white crystalline compound produced by the distillation of coal tar, used in mothballs and for chemical manufacture.
– DERIVATIVES **naphthalic** adj.

**naphthene** /'nafθiːn/ ● **n.** Chemistry any of a group of cyclic aliphatic hydrocarbons (e.g. cyclohexane) obtained from petroleum.
– DERIVATIVES **naphthenic** adj.

**naphthol** /'nafθɒl/ ● **n.** Chemistry a crystalline solid derived from naphthalene, used in antiseptics and dyes.

**Napierian logarithm** /neɪ'pɪərɪən/ ● **n.** another term for **NATURAL LOGARITHM**.
– ORIGIN C19: named after the Sc. mathematician John *Napier* (1550–1617).

**Napier's bones** ● **pl. n.** Mathematics slips of ivory or other material divided into sections marked with digits, formerly used to facilitate multiplication and division.

**napkin** ● **n. 1** a square piece of cloth or paper used at a meal to wipe the fingers or lips and to protect garments. **2** Brit. dated a baby's nappy. **3** (also **sanitary napkin**) chiefly N. Amer. another term for **SANITARY TOWEL**.
– ORIGIN ME: from OFr. *nappe* 'tablecloth' (from L. *mappa*: see **MAP**) + **-KIN**.

**napoleon** ● **n. 1** a gold twenty-franc French coin minted in the reign of Napoleon I. **2** a high boot worn by men in the 19th century. **3** N. Amer. a flaky rectangular pastry with a sweet filling.

**Napoleonic** /nəpəʊlɪ'ɒnɪk/ ● **adj.** of, relating to, or characteristic of Napoleon I or his time.

**nappa** /'napə/ (also **napa**) ● **n.** a soft leather made by a special tawing process from the skin of sheep or goats.
– ORIGIN C19: from *Napa*, a valley in California.

**nappe** /nap/ ● **n.** Geology a sheet of rock that has moved sideways over neighbouring strata as a result of an overthrust or folding.
– ORIGIN C19: from Fr. *nappe* 'tablecloth'.

**napped**[1] ● **adj.** (of a textile) having a nap.

**napped**[2] ● **adj.** (of food) served in a sauce.
– ORIGIN 1970s: from Fr. *napper* 'coat with (a sauce)', from *nappe* 'cloth', figuratively 'pool of liquid', + **-ED**[2].

**napper** ● **n.** Brit. informal a person's head.
– ORIGIN C18: from thieves' sl., of unknown origin.

**nappy**[1] ● **n.** (pl. **-ies**) Brit. a piece of absorbent material wrapped round a baby's bottom and between its legs to absorb and retain urine and faeces.
– ORIGIN C20: abbrev. of **NAPKIN**.

**nappy**[2] ● **adj.** US informal (of a black person's hair) frizzy.
– ORIGIN C15 (in the sense 'shaggy'): from MDu. *noppigh*, Mid. Low Ger. *noppich*, from *noppe* (see **NAP**[2]).

**nappy rash** ● **n.** Brit. inflammation of a baby's skin caused by prolonged contact with a damp nappy.

**narc** ● **n.** informal, chiefly N. Amer. an official narcotics agent.

**narcissism** /'nɑːsɪsɪz(ə)m, nɑː'sɪs-/ ● **n.** excessive or erotic interest in oneself and one's physical appearance.
– DERIVATIVES **narcissist** n. **narcissistic** adj. **narcissis-**

**tically** adv.
– ORIGIN C19: from *Narcissus*, the name of a beautiful youth in Gk mythology who fell in love with his own reflection in a pool, + **-ISM**.

**narcissus** /nɑːˈsɪsəs/ ● **n.** (pl. **narcissi** /-sʌɪ/ or **narcissuses**) a daffodil with a flower that has white or pale outer petals and a shallow orange or yellow centre. [*Narcissus poeticus* and related species.]
– ORIGIN via L. from Gk *narkissos*, perh. from *narkē* 'numbness', with ref. to its narcotic effects.

**narco** ● **n.** (pl. **-os**) US informal short for **NARCOTIC**.

**narco-** ● **comb. form 1** relating to a state of insensibility: *narcolepsy*. **2** relating to narcotic drugs or their use: *narcoterrorism*.
– ORIGIN from Gk *narkē* 'numbness'.

**narcolepsy** /ˈnɑːkə(ʊ)lɛpsi/ ● **n.** Medicine a condition characterized by an extreme tendency to fall asleep whenever in relaxing surroundings.
– DERIVATIVES **narcoleptic** adj. & n.
– ORIGIN C19: from Gk *narkē* 'numbness', on the pattern of *epilepsy*.

**narcosis** /nɑːˈkəʊsɪs/ ● **n.** Medicine a state of stupor, drowsiness, or unconsciousness produced by drugs.
– ORIGIN C17: from Gk *narkōsis*, from *narkoun* 'make numb'.

**narcoterrorism** ● **n.** terrorism associated with the trade in illicit drugs.
– DERIVATIVES **narcoterrorist** n.

**narcotic** ● **n.** an addictive drug, especially an illegal one, affecting mood or behaviour. ➤Medicine a drug which induces drowsiness, stupor, or insensibility, and relieves pain. ● **adj.** relating to narcotics.
– DERIVATIVES **narcotically** adv. **narcotism** n. **narcotization** (also **-isation**) n. **narcotize** (also **-ise**) v.
– ORIGIN ME: from OFr. *narcotique*, via med. L. from Gk *narkōtikos*, from *narkoun* 'make numb'.

**nard** ● **n.** the Himalayan spikenard.
– ORIGIN OE, via L. from Gk *nardos*; rel. to Sanskrit *nalada, narada*.

**nardoo** /nɑːˈduː, ˈnɑːduː/ ● **n.** an Australian fern with long stalks bearing either silvery-green lobes or woody cases containing spores. [*Marsilea drummondii*.]
– ORIGIN C19: from an Aborig. lang.

**nares** /ˈnɛːriːz/ ● **pl. n.** (sing. **naris**) Anatomy the nostrils.
– DERIVATIVES **narial** adj.
– ORIGIN C17: pl. of L. *naris* 'nostril, nose'.

**narghile** /ˈnɑːgɪleɪ, -li/ ● **n.** a hookah.
– ORIGIN C18: from Pers. *nārgīl* 'coconut, hookah', from Sanskrit *nārikela* 'coconut'.

**nariyal** /ˈnɑːrɪəl/ ● **n.** Indian term for **COCONUT**.
– ORIGIN from Hindi *nāriyal*.

**nark** informal ● **n. 1** chiefly Brit. a police informer. **2** Austral./NZ an annoying person or thing. ● **v.** chiefly Brit. annoy.
– ORIGIN C19: from Romany *nāk* 'nose'.

**narky** ● **adj.** (**-ier**, **-iest**) Brit. informal irritable.

**Narragansett** /ˌnarəˈgansət/ (also **Narraganset**) ● **n.** (pl. same or **Narragansetts**) **1** a member of an American Indian people originally of Rhode Island. **2** the extinct Algonquian language of this people.
– ORIGIN the name in Narragansett, lit. 'people of the promontory'.

**narrate** ● **v.** give a spoken or written account of. ➤provide a commentary to accompany (a film, story, etc.).
– DERIVATIVES **narratable** adj. **narration** n. **narrator** n. **narratorial** adj.
– ORIGIN C17 (ME as *narration*): from L. *narrat-*, *narrare* 'relate'.

**narrative** ● **n.** a spoken or written account of connected events; a story. ➤the narrated part of a literary work, as distinct from dialogue. ➤the practice or art of narration. ● **adj.** in the form of or concerned with narration.
– DERIVATIVES **narratively** adv. **narrativity** n. **narrativize** (also **-ise**) v.

**narratology** ● **n.** the branch of knowledge or criticism concerned with the structure and function of narrative.
– DERIVATIVES **narratological** adj. **narratologist** n.

**narrow** ● **adj.** (**-er**, **-est**) **1** of small width in comparison to length. **2** limited in extent, amount, or scope. **3** barely achieved: *a narrow escape*. **4** Phonetics denoting a vowel pronounced with the root of the tongue drawn back so as to narrow the pharynx. ● **v.** become or make narrower. ➤(**narrow something down**) reduce the number of possibilities or options. ● **n.** (**narrows**) a narrow channel connecting two larger areas of water.
– DERIVATIVES **narrowish** adj. **narrowly** adv. **narrowness** n.
– ORIGIN OE *nearu*, of Gmc origin.

**narrowband** ● **adj.** of or involving signals over a narrow range of frequencies.

**narrowboat** ● **n.** Brit. a canal boat less than 7 ft (2.1 metres) wide with a maximum length of 70 ft (21.3 metres) and steered with a tiller rather than a wheel.

**narrowcast** ● **v.** (past and past part. **narrowcast** or **narrowcasted**) transmit a television programme, especially by cable, to a comparatively small or specialist audience. ● **n.** transmission of this type.
– DERIVATIVES **narrowcaster** n.

**narrow circumstances** ● **pl. n.** poverty.

**narrow gauge** ● **n.** a railway gauge which is narrower than the standard gauge of 4 ft 8½ inches (1.435 m).

**narrow-minded** ● **adj.** not willing to listen to or tolerate other people's views; prejudiced.
– DERIVATIVES **narrow-mindedly** adv. **narrow-mindedness** n.

**narrow money** ● **n.** Economics money in forms that can be used as a medium of exchange, generally notes and coins.

**narrow squeak** ● **n.** Brit. informal an escape or victory that is narrowly achieved.

**narthex** /ˈnɑːθɛks/ ● **n.** an antechamber, porch, or distinct area at the western entrance of some early Christian churches. ➤an antechamber or large porch in a modern church.
– ORIGIN C17: via L. from Gk *narthēx*.

**narwhal** /ˈnɑːw(ə)l/ ● **n.** a small Arctic whale, the male of which has a long forward-pointing spirally twisted tusk developed from one of its teeth. [*Monodon monoceros*.]
– ORIGIN C17: from Du. *narwal*, Dan. *narhval*, based on ON *nár* 'corpse', with ref. to skin colour.

**nary** /ˈnɛːri/ ● **adj.** informal or dialect form of **NOT**.
– ORIGIN C18: from the phr. *ne'er a*.

**NASA** /ˈnasə/ ● **abbrev.** (in the US) National Aeronautics and Space Administration.

**nasal** /ˈneɪz(ə)l/ ● **adj. 1** of or relating to the nose. **2** (of a speech sound) pronounced by the breath resonating in the nose, e.g. *m, n, ng*, or French *en, un*. ➤(of speech) characterized by resonance in the nose as well as the mouth. ● **n. 1** a nasal speech sound. **2** historical a nosepiece on a helmet.
– DERIVATIVES **nasality** n. **nasally** adv.
– ORIGIN ME: from med. L. *nasalis*, from L. *nasus* 'nose'.

**nasalize** (also **-ise**) ● **v.** pronounce or utter (a speech sound) with the breath resonating in the nose.
– DERIVATIVES **nasalization** n.

**nascent** /ˈnas(ə)nt, ˈneɪ-/ ● **adj. 1** just coming into existence and beginning to display signs of future potential. **2** Chemistry (chiefly of hydrogen) freshly generated in a reactive form.
– DERIVATIVES **nascency** /ˈnas(ə)nsi, ˈneɪ-/ n.
– ORIGIN C17: from L. *nascent-*, *nasci* 'to be born'.

**naseberry** /ˈneɪzb(ə)ri, -bɛri/ ● **n.** another term for **SAPODILLA** or ***sapodilla plum***.
– ORIGIN C17: from Sp. and Port. *néspera* 'medlar' + **BERRY**.

**naso-** /ˈneɪzəʊ/ ● **comb. form** relating to the nose.
– ORIGIN from L. *nasus* 'nose'.

**nasogastric** ● **adj.** reaching or supplying the stomach via the nose.

**nasopharynx** ● **n.** Anatomy the upper part of the pharynx, connecting with the nasal cavity above the soft palate.
– DERIVATIVES **nasopharyngeal** adj.

**nastic** /ˈnastɪk/ ● **adj.** Botany (of the movement of plant parts) caused by an external stimulus but unaffected in direction by it.

– ORIGIN C20: from Gk *nastos* 'squeezed together' + **-IC**.

**nasturtium** /nəˈstəːʃ(ə)m/ ● **n.** a South American trailing plant with round leaves and bright orange, yellow, or red flowers, widely grown as an ornamental. [*Tropaeolum majus*.]
– ORIGIN OE, from L., appar. from *naris* 'nose' + *torquere* 'to twist'.

**nasty** ● **adj.** (**-ier**, **-iest**) **1** highly unpleasant or repugnant. **2** unpleasant or spiteful in behaviour. ➤annoying or unwelcome. **3** physically or mentally damaging or harmful. ● **n.** (pl. **-ies**) informal a nasty person or thing.
– DERIVATIVES **nastily** adv. **nastiness** n.
– ORIGIN ME: of unknown origin.

**NASUWT** ● **abbrev.** (in the UK) National Association of Schoolmasters and Union of Women Teachers.

**Nat.** ● **abbrev. 1** national. **2** nationalist. **3** natural.

**natal**[1] /ˈneɪt(ə)l/ ● **adj.** of or relating to the place or time of one's birth.
– ORIGIN ME: from L. *natalis*, from *nat-*, *nasci* 'be born'.

**natal**[2] /ˈneɪt(ə)l/ ● **adj.** Anatomy relating to the buttocks.
– ORIGIN C19: from **NATES** + **-AL**.

**natality** /nəˈtalɪti/ ● **n.** birth rate.

**natant** /ˈneɪt(ə)nt/ ● **adj.** formal, rare swimming or floating.
– DERIVATIVES **natation** /nəˈteɪʃ(ə)n/ n. **natatorial** /ˌneɪtəˈtɔːrɪəl/ adj. **natatory** /ˈneɪtət(ə)ri, nəˈteɪt(ə)ri/ adj.
– ORIGIN C18 (C16 as *natation*): from L. *natant-*, *natare* 'swim'.

**natatorium** /ˌneɪtəˈtɔːrɪəm/ ● **n.** N. Amer. a swimming pool.
– ORIGIN C19: from late L., neut. (used as n.) of *natatorius* 'relating to a swimmer', from *natare* 'to swim'.

**natch** ● **adv.** informal naturally.

**nates** /ˈneɪtiːz/ ● **pl. n.** Anatomy the buttocks.
– ORIGIN C17: L., pl. of *natis* 'buttock, rump'.

**NATFHE** ● **abbrev.** (in the UK) National Association of Teachers in Further and Higher Education.

**natheless** /ˈneɪθlɪs/ (also **nathless**) ● **adv.** archaic nevertheless.
– ORIGIN OE.

**nation** ● **n.** a large aggregate of people united by common descent, culture, or language, inhabiting a particular state or territory. ➤a North American Indian people or confederation of peoples.
– DERIVATIVES **nationhood** n.
– ORIGIN ME: via OFr. from L. *natio(n-)*, from *nat-*, *nasci* 'be born'.

**national** ● **adj. 1** of, relating to, or characteristic of a nation. **2** owned, controlled, or financially supported by the state. ● **n. 1** a citizen of a particular country. **2** a national newspaper as opposed to a local one.
– DERIVATIVES **nationally** adv.
– ORIGIN C16: from Fr., from L. *natio(n-)* (see **NATION**).

**National Assembly** ● **n.** an elected legislature in various countries. ➤the elected legislature in France during the first part of the Revolution, 1789–91.

**National Assistance** ● **n.** welfare payment made to people on low incomes in Britain from 1948–1965.

**national bank** ● **n.** another term for **CENTRAL BANK**. ➤(in the US) a commercial bank which is chartered under the federal government and is a member of the Federal Reserve System.

**national curriculum** ● **n.** a curriculum of study laid down to be taught in state schools.

**national debt** ● **n.** the total amount of money which a country's government has borrowed.

**national football** ● **n.** Austral. Australian Rules football.

**national grid** ● **n.** Brit. **1** the network of high-voltage power lines between major power stations. **2** the metric system of geographical coordinates used in maps of the British Isles.

**National Guard** ● **n.** (in the US) the primary reserve military force partly maintained by the states but also available for federal use.

**national income** ● **n.** the total amount of money earned within a country.

**National Insurance** ● **n.** (in the UK) a system of compulsory payments by employees and employers to provide state assistance for people who are sick, unemployed, or retired.

**nationalism** ● **n. 1** patriotic feeling, principles, or efforts. ➤an extreme form of this marked by a feeling of superiority over other countries. **2** advocacy of political independence for a particular country.
– DERIVATIVES **nationalist** n. & adj. **nationalistic** adj. **nationalistically** adv.

**nationality** ● **n.** (pl. **-ies**) **1** the status of belonging to a particular nation. **2** an ethnic group forming a part of one or more political nations.

**nationalize** (also **-ise**) ● **v. 1** transfer (a major branch of industry or commerce) from private to state ownership or control. **2** make distinctively national. **3** [usu. as adj. **nationalized**] naturalize (a foreigner).
– DERIVATIVES **nationalization** n. **nationalizer** n.

**national park** ● **n.** an area of countryside protected by the state for the enjoyment of the general public or the preservation of wildlife.

**national service** ● **n.** a period of compulsory service in the armed forces during peacetime.

**National Socialism** ● **n.** historical the political doctrine of the Nazi Party of Germany.
– DERIVATIVES **National Socialist** n.

**nation state** ● **n.** a sovereign state of which most of the citizens or subjects are united also by factors which define a nation, such as language or common descent.

**nationwide** ● **adj. & adv.** throughout the whole nation.

**native** ● **n. 1** a person born in a specified place or associated with a place by birth. ➤a local inhabitant. **2** an animal or plant indigenous to a place. **3** dated, chiefly offensive a non-white original inhabitant of a country as regarded by European colonists or travellers. ● **adj. 1** associated with the place or circumstances of a person's birth. ➤of the indigenous inhabitants of a place. **2** (of a plant or animal) of indigenous origin or growth. **3** innate; in a person's character: *native wit*. **4** (of a metal or other mineral) found in a pure or uncombined state.
– PHRASES **go native** derogatory (of a person living abroad) adopt the way of life of the country one is living in.
– DERIVATIVES **natively** adv. **nativeness** n.
– ORIGIN ME: from L. *nativus*, from *nat-*, *nasci* 'be born'.

**Native American** ● **n.** a member of any of the indigenous peoples of North and South America and the Caribbean Islands. ● **adj.** of or relating to these peoples.

**USAGE** Native American

In the US, **Native American** is now the current accepted term in many contexts. See also **AMERICAN INDIAN**.

**native bear** ● **n.** Australian term for **KOALA**.

**native cat** ● **n.** Australian term for **QUOLL**.

**native hen** ● **n.** an Australian moorhen, with a greenish bill. [*Gallinula ventralis* and *G. mortierii*.]

**native rock** ● **n.** rock in its original place, i.e. that has not been moved or quarried.

**native speaker** ● **n.** a person who has spoken the language in question from earliest childhood.

**nativism** /ˈneɪtɪvɪz(ə)m/ ● **n. 1** the theory or doctrine that concepts and ways of thinking are innate rather than acquired or learned. **2** historical, chiefly US the policy of protecting the interests of native-born or established inhabitants against those of immigrants. **3** a return to or emphasis on traditional or local customs.
– DERIVATIVES **nativist** n. & adj. **nativistic** adj.

**nativity** ● **n.** (pl. **-ies**) **1** the occasion of a person's birth. **2** (usu. **the Nativity**) the birth of Jesus Christ. ➤the Christian festival of Christ's birth; Christmas.
– ORIGIN ME: from OFr. *nativite*, from late L. *nativitas*, from L. *nativus* (see **NATIVE**).

**nativity play** ● **n.** a play performed at Christmas based on the events surrounding the birth of Jesus Christ.

**NATO** (also **Nato**) ● **abbrev.** North Atlantic Treaty Organization.

**natriuresis** /ˌneɪtrɪjʊ(ə)ˈriːsɪs, ˌnat-/ ● **n.** Physiology excretion of sodium in the urine.
– DERIVATIVES **natriuretic** adj.
– ORIGIN 1950s: from **NATRON** + Gk *ourēsis* 'urination'.

**natron** /ˈneɪtr(ə)n, ˈnat-/ ● **n.** a mineral salt found in dried lake beds, consisting of hydrated sodium carbonate.
– ORIGIN C17: from Fr., from Sp. *natrón*, via Arab. from Gk *nitron* (see **NITRE**).

**natter** informal, chiefly Brit. ● **v.** chat casually. ● **n.** a chat.
– DERIVATIVES **natterer** n.
– ORIGIN C19 (in the dial. sense 'grumble, fret'): imitative.

**natterjack toad** ● **n.** a small toad with a bright yellow stripe down its back. [*Bufo calamita*.]
– ORIGIN C18: perh. from **NATTER** (because of its loud croak) + **JACK**[1].

**natty** ● **adj.** (**-ier, -iest**) informal (of a person or their clothing) smart and fashionable.
– DERIVATIVES **nattily** adv. **nattiness** n.
– ORIGIN C18 (orig. sl.): perh. rel. to **NEAT**[1].

**natty dread** ● **n.** black English **1** (**natty dreads**) dreadlocks. **2** a Rastafarian man with dreadlocks.
– ORIGIN *natty* a var. of **KNOTTY**.

**Natufian** /nɑːˈtuːfɪən/ ● **adj.** Archaeology relating to or denoting a late Mesolithic culture of the Middle East, dated to about 12,500–10,000 years ago.
– ORIGIN 1930s: from Wadi *an-Natuf*, the type site (a cave north-west of Jerusalem), + **-IAN**.

**natural** ● **adj. 1** existing in or derived from nature; not made, caused by, or processed by humankind. ➤(of fabric) unbleached and undyed; off-white. **2** in accordance with nature; normal. ➤relaxed and unaffected. ➤inevitable: *the natural choice.* ➤(of law or justice) based on innate moral sense. **3** (of a parent or child) related by blood. ➤chiefly archaic illegitimate. **4** Music (of a note) not sharpened or flattened. ➤(of a brass instrument) having no valves and able to play only the notes of the harmonic series above a fundamental note. ➤of or relating to the notes and intervals of the harmonic series. **5** Christian Theology relating to human or physical nature as distinct from the spiritual or supernatural realm. **6** Bridge (of a bid) straightforwardly reflecting one's holding of cards. Often contrasted with **CONVENTIONAL** or **ARTIFICIAL**. ● **n. 1** a person with an innate gift or talent for a particular task or activity. **2** Music a natural note, or a sign (♮) denoting one when a previous sign or the key signature would otherwise demand a sharp or a flat. ➤any of the longer, lower keys on a keyboard instrument that are normally white. **3** an off-white colour. **4** a hand of cards, throw of dice, or other result which wins immediately. **5** Fishing an insect or other small creature used as bait, rather than an artificial imitation. **6** archaic a person mentally handicapped from birth.
– DERIVATIVES **naturalness** n.

**natural-born** ● **adj.** having a specified innate characteristic or ability. ➤archaic having a position by birth.

**natural classification** ● **n.** a scientific classification according to features which are held to be objectively significant, rather than being selected for convenience.

**natural frequency** ● **n.** Physics a frequency at which a system oscillates when not subjected to a continuous or repeated external force.

**natural gas** ● **n.** flammable gas, consisting largely of methane and other hydrocarbons, occurring naturally underground and used as fuel.

**natural history** ● **n. 1** the scientific study of animals or plants, especially as concerned with observation rather than experiment and presented in popular form. **2** Medicine the usual course of development of a disease or condition, especially in the absence of treatment.
– DERIVATIVES **natural historian** n.

**naturalism** ● **n. 1** (in art and literature) a style and theory of representation based on the accurate depiction of detail. **2** a philosophical viewpoint according to which everything arises from natural properties and causes, and supernatural or spiritual explanations are excluded or discounted. ➤(in moral philosophy) the theory that ethical statements can be derived from non-ethical ones.

**naturalist** ● **n. 1** an expert in or student of natural history. **2** an exponent or practitioner of naturalism.

**naturalistic** ● **adj. 1** derived from or imitating real life or nature. **2** based on the theory of naturalism.
– DERIVATIVES **naturalistically** adv.

**naturalize** (also **-ise**) ● **v. 1** admit (a foreigner) to the citizenship of a country. ➤alter (an adopted foreign word) so that it conforms more closely to the phonology or orthography of the adopting language. **2** [usu. as adj. **naturalized**] Biology establish (a plant or animal) so that it lives wild in a region where it is not indigenous. **3** regard as or cause to appear natural. ➤explain (a phenomenon) in a naturalistic way.
– DERIVATIVES **naturalization** n.

**natural language** ● **n.** a language that has developed naturally in use, as opposed to an artificial language or computer code.

**natural law** ● **n. 1** a body of unchanging moral principles regarded as a basis for all human conduct. **2** an observable law or laws relating to natural phenomena.

**natural life** ● **n.** the expected span of a person's or animal's life under normal circumstances.

**natural logarithm** ● **n.** Mathematics a logarithm to the base *e* (2.71828 ...).

**naturally** ● **adv. 1** in a natural manner. **2** of course.

**natural magic** ● **n.** (in the Middle Ages) magic practised for beneficial purposes, involving the making of images, healing, and the use of herbs.

**natural numbers** ● **pl. n.** the positive integers (whole numbers) 1, 2, 3, etc., and sometimes zero as well.

**natural philosophy** ● **n.** archaic natural science, especially physical science.
– DERIVATIVES **natural philosopher** n.

**natural religion** ● **n.** religion based on reason rather than divine revelation, especially deism.

**natural resources** ● **pl. n.** materials or substances occurring in nature which can be exploited for economic gain.

**natural science** ● **n.** a branch of science which deals with the physical world, e.g. physics, chemistry, geology, biology. ➤the branch of knowledge which deals with the study of the physical world.

**natural selection** ● **n.** Biology the evolutionary process whereby organisms better adapted to their environment tend to survive and produce more offspring.

**natural theology** ● **n.** theology or knowledge of God based on observed facts and experience apart from divine revelation.

**natural virtues** ● **pl. n.** the traditional chief moral virtues of justice, prudence, temperance, and fortitude. Often contrasted with **THEOLOGICAL VIRTUE**.

**natural year** ● **n.** the tropical or solar year.

**nature** ● **n. 1** the phenomena of the physical world collectively, including plants, animals, and the landscape, as opposed to humans or human creations. ➤the physical force regarded as causing and regulating these phenomena. ➤archaic a living thing's vital functions or needs. **2** the basic or inherent features, qualities, or character of a person or thing. ➤inborn or hereditary characteristics as an influence on or determinant of personality. Often contrasted with **NURTURE**. ➤archaic a person of a specified character.
– PHRASES **someone's better nature** a person's capacity for tolerance, generosity, or sympathy. **in the nature of things** inevitable or inevitably. **in a state of nature 1** in an uncivilized or uncultivated state. **2** totally naked. **3** Christian Theology in a morally unregenerate condition, unredeemed by divine grace. **the nature of the beast** informal the inherent or essential character of something.
– DERIVATIVES **-natured** adj.
– ORIGIN ME: from OFr., from L. *natura* 'birth, nature, quality', from *nat-*, *nasci* 'be born'.

**nature cure** ● **n.** another term for **NATUROPATHY**.

**nature reserve** ● **n.** a tract of land managed so as to preserve its flora, fauna, and physical features.

**nature study** ● **n.** the practical study of plants, animals, and natural phenomena as a school subject.

**nature trail** ● **n.** a signposted path through the countryside designed to draw attention to natural features.

**naturism** ● **n. 1** nudism. **2** the worship of nature or natural objects.

– DERIVATIVES **naturist** n. & adj.

**naturopathy** /ˌneɪtʃəˈrɒpəθi/ ● n. a system of alternative medicine based on the theory that diseases can be successfully treated or prevented without the use of drugs, by techniques such as control of diet, exercise, and massage.
– DERIVATIVES **naturopath** n. **naturopathic** adj.

**Naugahyde** /ˈnɔːɡəhʌɪd/ ● n. N. Amer. (trademark in the US) an artificial material designed to resemble leather.
– ORIGIN C20: from *Nauga(tuck)*, the name of a town in Connecticut + *-hyde* (alt. of **HIDE**²).

**naught** ● pron. archaic nothing. ● n. N. Amer. variant spelling of **NOUGHT**.
– PHRASES **come to naught** be ruined or foiled. **set at naught** archaic disregard; despise.
– ORIGIN OE *nāwiht*, *-wuht*, from *nā* 'no' + *wiht* 'thing' (see **WIGHT**).

**naughty** ● adj. (-ier, -iest) **1** (especially of a child) disobedient; badly behaved. **2** informal mildly rude or indecent. **3** archaic wicked.
– DERIVATIVES **naughtily** adv. **naughtiness** n.
– ORIGIN ME: from **NAUGHT** + **-Y**¹.

**nauplius** /ˈnɔːplɪəs/ ● n. (pl. **nauplii** /-plɪʌɪ, -plɪiː/) Zoology the first larval stage of many crustaceans, having an unsegmented body and a single eye.
– ORIGIN C19: from L., denoting a kind of shellfish, or from the Gk name *Nauplios*, the son of the sea god Poseidon in Gk mythology.

**nausea** /ˈnɔːsɪə, -z-/ ● n. a feeling of sickness with an inclination to vomit.
– ORIGIN ME: via L. from Gk *nausia*, from *naus* 'ship'.

**nauseate** ● v. [often as adj. **nauseating**] affect with nausea.
– DERIVATIVES **nauseatingly** adv.

**nauseous** ● adj. **1** affected with nausea. **2** causing nausea; offensive to the taste or smell.
– DERIVATIVES **nauseously** adv. **nauseousness** n.
– ORIGIN C17: from L. *nauseosus* (from *nausea* 'seasickness').

**nautch** /nɔːtʃ/ ● n. (in the Indian subcontinent) a traditional dance performed by professional dancing girls.
– ORIGIN from Hindi *nāc*, from Prakrit *nachcha*, from Sanskrit *nṛtya* 'dancing'.

**nautical** ● adj. of or concerning sailors or navigation; maritime.
– DERIVATIVES **nautically** adv.
– ORIGIN C16: from Fr. *nautique*, or via L. from Gk *nautikos*, from *nautēs* 'sailor'.

**nautical almanac** ● n. a yearbook containing astronomical and tidal information for navigators.

**nautical mile** ● n. a unit used in measuring distances at sea, equal to 1,852 metres (approximately 2,025 yards).

**nautilus** /ˈnɔːtɪləs/ ● n. (pl. **nautiluses** or **nautili** /-lʌɪ, -liː/) a cephalopod mollusc with a light external spiral shell and numerous short tentacles around the mouth. [Genus *Nautilus*: several species.]
– DERIVATIVES **nautiloid** n.
– ORIGIN mod. L., from L., from Gk *nautilos*, lit. 'sailor'.

**NAV** ● abbrev. net asset value.

**navaid** /ˈnaveɪd/ ● n. a navigational device in an aircraft, ship, or other vehicle.

**Navajo** /ˈnavəhəʊ/ (also **Navaho**) ● n. (pl. same or **-os**) **1** a member of an American Indian people of New Mexico and Arizona. **2** the Athabaskan language of this people.
– ORIGIN from Sp. *Apaches de Navajó* 'apaches from Navajo', from Tewa *navahu:* 'fields adjoining an arroyo'.

**naval** ● adj. of, in, or relating to a navy or navies.
– ORIGIN ME: from L. *navalis*, from *navis* 'ship'.

**naval architecture** ● n. the designing of ships.
– DERIVATIVES **naval architect** n.

**naval stores** ● pl. n. materials used in shipping.

**Navaratri** /ˌnʌvəˈrʌtri/ (also **Navaratra**) ● n. a Hindu autumn festival extending over the nine nights before Dussehra.
– ORIGIN Sanskrit, lit. 'nine nights'.

**navarin** /ˈnav(ə)rɪn, -rã/ ● n. a casserole of lamb or mutton with vegetables.
– ORIGIN from Fr.

**nave**¹ ● n. the central part of a church building, usually separated from the chancel by a step or rail and from adjacent aisles by pillars.
– ORIGIN C17: from L. *navis* 'ship'.

**nave**² ● n. the hub of a wheel.
– ORIGIN OE *nafu*, *nafa*, of Gmc origin.

**navel** ● n. **1** a rounded knotty depression in the centre of a person's belly caused by the detachment of the umbilical cord after birth; the umbilicus. **2** the central point of a place.
– ORIGIN OE *nafela*, of Gmc origin.

**navel-gazing** ● n. complacent self-absorption or narrow concentration on a single issue.

**navel orange** ● n. a large seedless orange of a variety which has a navel-like depression at the top containing a small secondary fruit.

**navelwort** ● n. another term for **PENNYWORT**.

**navicular** /nəˈvɪkjʊlə/ ● adj. chiefly archaic boat-shaped. ● n. **1** (also **navicular bone**) a boat-shaped bone in the ankle or wrist, especially that in the ankle, between the talus and the cuneiform bones. **2** (also **navicular disease** or **navicular syndrome**) a chronic disorder of the navicular bone in horses, causing lameness in the front feet.
– ORIGIN ME: from Fr. *naviculaire* or late L. *navicularis*, from L. *navicula* 'little ship'.

**navigable** ● adj. (of a waterway or sea) able to be sailed on by ships or boats.
– DERIVATIVES **navigability** n.

**navigate** ● v. **1** plan and direct the route or course of a ship, aircraft, or other form of transport, especially by using instruments or maps. **2** sail or travel over (a stretch of water or terrain). ➤ guide (a vessel or vehicle) over a specified route or terrain.
– ORIGIN C16: from L. *navigat-*, *navigare* 'to sail'.

**navigation** ● n. **1** the process or activity of navigating. **2** the passage of ships. **3** chiefly dialect a navigable inland waterway, especially a canal.
– DERIVATIVES **navigational** adj. **navigationally** adv.

**navigation lights** ● pl. n. a set of lights shown by a ship or aircraft at night to indicate its position and orientation.

**navigator** ● n. **1** a person who navigates a ship, aircraft, etc. **2** historical a person who explores by sea. **3** Computing a browser program for accessing data on the World Wide Web or another information system.

**navvy** ● n. (pl. **-ies**) Brit. dated a labourer employed in the excavation and construction of a road, railway, or canal.
– ORIGIN C19: abbrev. of **NAVIGATOR**.

**navy** ● n. (pl. **-ies**) **1** [treated as sing. or pl.] the branch of a state's armed services which conducts military operations at sea. ➤ poetic/literary a fleet of ships. **2** (also **navy blue**) a dark blue colour.
– ORIGIN ME: from OFr. *navie* 'ship, fleet', from pop. L. *navia* 'ship', from L. *navis* 'ship'.

**navy bean** ● n. chiefly N. Amer. another term for **HARICOT**.

**navy yard** ● n. US a shipyard for the construction, repair, and equipping of naval vessels.

**nawab** /nʌˈwɑːb/ ● n. Indian **1** a native governor during the time of the Mogul empire. **2** a Muslim nobleman or person of high status.
– ORIGIN from Urdu *nawwāb*, var. of Arab. *nuwwāb*, pl. (used as sing.) of *nā'ib* 'deputy'; cf. **NABOB**.

**Naxalite** /ˈnaksəlʌɪt/ ● n. (in the Indian subcontinent) a member of an armed revolutionary group advocating Maoist communism.
– ORIGIN 1960s: from *Naxal(bari)*, a place name in West Bengal + **-ITE**¹.

**nay** ● adv. **1** or rather; and more than that. **2** archaic or dialect no. ● n. a negative answer.
– ORIGIN ME: from ON *nei*, from *ne* 'not' + *ei* 'ever' (cf. **AYE**²).

**naysay** ● v. (past and past part. **-said**) chiefly US say no to; deny or oppose.
– DERIVATIVES **naysayer** n.

**Nazarene** /ˈnazəriːn, ˌnazəˈriːn/ ● n. **1** a native or inhabitant of Nazareth. ➤ (**the Nazarene**) Jesus Christ.

➤(chiefly in Jewish or Muslim use) a Christian. ➤a member of an early sect or faction of Jewish Christians. **2** a member of a group of 19th-century German painters who sought to revive the art and techniques of medieval Germany and early Renaissance Italy. ● **adj.** of or relating to Nazareth or Nazarenes.

**Nazi** /ˈnɑːtsi, ˈnɑːzi/ ● **n.** (pl. **Nazis**) **1** historical a member of the National Socialist German Workers' Party. **2** derogatory a person with extreme racist or authoritarian views.
– DERIVATIVES **Nazidom** n. **Nazify** v. (**-ies, -ied**). **Naziism** n. **Nazism** n.
– ORIGIN Ger., abbrev. representing the pronunc. of *Nati-* in *Nationalsozialist* 'national socialist', prob. by analogy with *Sozi* from *Sozialist* 'socialist'.

**Nazirite** /ˈnazərʌɪt/ (also **Nazarite**) ● **n.** an ancient Israelite who had taken certain vows of abstinence.
– ORIGIN from Heb. *nāzīr* 'consecrated one' + **-ITE**[1].

**NB** ● **abbrev. 1** New Brunswick (in official postal use). **2** nota bene.

**Nb** ● **symb.** the chemical element niobium.

**nb** ● **abbrev.** Cricket no-ball.

**NBA** ● **abbrev. 1** (in North America) National Basketball Association. **2** (in the US) National Boxing Association. **3** Net Book Agreement.

**NBC** ● **abbrev. 1** (in the US) National Broadcasting Company. **2** (of weapons or warfare) nuclear, biological, and chemical.

**NBG** ● **abbrev.** informal no bloody good.

**NC** ● **abbrev. 1** network computer. **2** North Carolina (in official postal use). **3** numerical control.

**NC-17** ● **symb.** (in the US) films classified as suitable for adults only.
– ORIGIN representing *no children* (*under*) *17*.

**NCO** ● **abbrev.** non-commissioned officer.

**NCT** ● **abbrev.** (in the UK) National Childbirth Trust.

**NCU** ● **abbrev.** (in the UK) National Communications Union.

**ND** ● **abbrev.** North Dakota (in official postal use).

**Nd** ● **symb.** the chemical element neodymium.

**n.d.** ● **abbrev.** no date.

**-nd** ● **suffix** variant spelling of **-AND, -END**.

**N. Dak.** ● **abbrev.** North Dakota.

**Ndebele** /ˌ(ə)ndəˈbiːli, -ˈbeɪli/ ● **n.** (pl. same or **Ndebeles**) **1** a member of a people of Zimbabwe and NE South Africa. **2** the Bantu language of this people.
– ORIGIN the name in the Nguni langs.

**NE** ● **abbrev. 1** Nebraska (in official postal use). **2** New England. **3** north-east or north-eastern.

**Ne** ● **symb.** the chemical element neon.

**né** /neɪ/ masc. of **NÉE**.

**Neanderthal** /nɪˈandətɑːl/ ● **n. 1** (also **Neanderthal man**) an extinct human that was widely distributed in ice age Europe between *c.*120,000–35,000 years ago, with a receding forehead and prominent brow ridges. **2** informal an uncivilized or uncouth man.
– ORIGIN C19: from *Neanderthal*, a region in Germany where remains of Neanderthal man were found.

**neap** /niːp/ ● **n.** (also **neap tide**) a tide just after the first or third quarters of the moon when there is least difference between high and low water. ● **v. 1** (**be neaped**) (of a boat) be kept aground or in harbour by a neap tide. **2** archaic (of a tide) tend towards or reach the highest point of a neap tide.
– ORIGIN ME, from OE *nēp-* in *nēpflōd* 'neap flood', of unknown origin.

**Neapolitan** /nɪəˈpɒlɪt(ə)n/ ● **n.** a native or citizen of Naples. ● **adj. 1** of or relating to Naples. **2** (of ice cream) made in layers of different colours.

**near** ● **adv. 1** at or to a short distance away. **2** a short time away in the future. **3** almost. ● **prep.** (also **near to**) **1** at or to a short distance away from (a place). **2** a short period of time from. **3** almost. **4** similar to. ● **adj. 1** located a short distance away. **2** only a short time ahead. **3** similar. ➤close to being (the thing mentioned). ➤having a close family connection. **4** located on the nearside of a vehicle. Compare with **OFF** (in sense 3). **5** archaic mean; miserly. ● **v.** approach.
– DERIVATIVES **nearish** adj. **nearness** n.
– ORIGIN ME: from ON *nœr* 'nearer', compar. of *ná*, corresp. to OE *nēah* 'nigh'.

**nearby** ● **adj.** not far away. ● **adv.** (also **near by**) close by.

**Nearctic** /nɪˈɑːktɪk/ ● **adj.** Zoology relating to or denoting a zoogeographical region comprising North America as far south as northern Mexico, together with Greenland.
– ORIGIN C19: from **NEO-** + **ARCTIC**.

**near-death experience** ● **n.** an unusual experience taking place on the brink of death and recounted by a person on recovery, typically an out-of-body experience or a vision of a tunnel of light.

**Near East** ● **n.** the countries of SW Asia between the Mediterranean and India (including the Middle East).
– DERIVATIVES **Near Eastern** adj.

**near go** ● **n.** Brit. informal, dated a narrow avoidance of something unpleasant.

**nearly** ● **adv. 1** very close to; almost. **2** closely.
– PHRASES **not nearly** nothing like; far from.

**near miss** ● **n. 1** a narrowly avoided collision. **2** a bomb or shot that just misses its target.

**near money** ● **n.** Finance assets which can readily be converted into cash, such as bills of exchange.

**nearside** ● **n.** (usu. **the nearside**) chiefly Brit. the side of a vehicle nearest the kerb. Compare with **OFFSIDE**. ➤the left side of a horse.

**near-sighted** ● **adj.** another term for **SHORT-SIGHTED**.
– DERIVATIVES **near-sightedly** adv. **near-sightedness** n.

**neat**[1] ● **adj. 1** in good order; tidy or carefully arranged. **2** done with or demonstrating skill or efficiency. **3** (of a drink of spirits) not diluted or mixed with anything else. **4** informal, chiefly N. Amer. excellent.
– DERIVATIVES **neaten** v. **neatly** adv. **neatness** n.
– ORIGIN C15: from Fr. *net*, from L. *nitidus* 'shining'; rel. to **NET**[2].

**neat**[2] ● **n.** archaic a bovine animal or animals.
– ORIGIN OE, of Gmc origin.

**neath** ● **prep.** chiefly poetic/literary beneath.

**neat's-foot oil** ● **n.** oil obtained by boiling the feet of cattle, used to dress leather.

**NEB** ● **abbrev. 1** (in the UK) National Enterprise Board. **2** New English Bible.

**Neb.** ● **abbrev.** Nebraska.

**neb** ● **n.** Scottish & N. English a nose, snout, or bird's beak.
– ORIGIN OE *nebb*, of Gmc origin.

**nebbish** ● **n.** informal, chiefly N. Amer. a pitifully ineffectual or timid man.
– DERIVATIVES **nebbishy** adj.
– ORIGIN C19: from Yiddish *nebekh* 'poor thing'.

**Nebr.** ● **abbrev.** Nebraska.

**Nebraskan** /nɪˈbrask(ə)n/ ● **n.** a native or inhabitant of the US state of Nebraska. ● **adj.** of or relating to Nebraska.

**Nebuchadnezzar** /ˌnɛbjʊkədˈnɛzə/ ● **n.** a very large wine bottle, equivalent in capacity to about twenty regular bottles.
– ORIGIN C20: from *Nebuchadnezzar* II, king of Babylon in the 6th cent. BC.

**nebula** /ˈnɛbjʊlə/ ● **n.** (pl. **nebulae** /-liː/ or **nebulas**) **1** Astronomy a visible cloud of gas or dust in outer space. ➤old-fashioned term for **GALAXY**. **2** Medicine a clouded spot on the cornea causing defective vision.
– DERIVATIVES **nebular** adj.
– ORIGIN C17: from L., lit. 'mist'.

**nebulizer** /ˈnɛbjʊlʌɪzə/ (also **-iser**) ● **n.** a device for producing a fine spray of liquid, used e.g. for inhaling a medicinal drug.
– DERIVATIVES **nebulize** (also **-ise**) v.

**nebulous** /ˈnɛbjʊləs/ ● **adj. 1** in the form of a cloud or haze; hazy. **2** (of a concept or idea) vague or ill-defined. **3** Astronomy relating to a nebula or nebulae.
– DERIVATIVES **nebulosity** n. **nebulously** adv. **nebulousness** n.
– ORIGIN ME (in the sense 'cloudy'): from Fr. *nébuleux* or L. *nebulosus*, from *nebula* 'mist'.

**nebuly** /ˈnɛbjʊli/ ● **adj.** Heraldry divided or edged with a line formed of deeply interlocking curves.

– ORIGIN C16: from Fr. *nébulé*, from med. L. *nebulatus* 'clouded', from L. *nebula* 'mist'.

**NEC** • abbrev. **1** National Executive Committee. **2** (in the UK) National Exhibition Centre.

**nécessaire** /ˌnɛsɛˈsɛː/ • n. a small ornamental case for pencils, scissors, and other small items.
– ORIGIN C19: Fr., lit. 'necessary (thing)'.

**necessarian** /ˌnɛsɪˈsɛːrɪən/ • n. & adj. another term for NECESSITARIAN.
– DERIVATIVES **necessarianism** n.

**necessarily** /ˈnɛsəs(ə)rɪli, ˌnɛsəˈsɛrɪli/ • adv. as a necessary result; inevitably.

**necessary** • adj. **1** required to be done, achieved, or present; needed. **2** inevitable: *a necessary consequence*. ➤ Philosophy inevitably resulting from the nature of things, so that the contrary is impossible. ➤ Philosophy (of an agent) having no independent volition. • n. **1** (**necessaries**) the basic requirements of life, such as food and warmth. **2** (**the necessary**) informal the action or item needed. ➤ Brit. informal the money required.
– ORIGIN ME: from L. *necessarius*, from *necesse* 'be needful'.

**necessitarian** /nəˌsɛsɪˈtɛːrɪən/ • n. Philosophy another term for ***determinist*** (see DETERMINISM).
– DERIVATIVES **necessitarianism** n.

**necessitate** • v. make necessary as a result or consequence. ➤ force or compel to do something.

**necessitous** • adj. (of a person) poor; needy.

**necessity** • n. (pl. **-ies**) **1** the state or fact of being necessary. **2** an indispensable thing.
– ORIGIN ME: from OFr. *necessite*, from L. *necessitas*, from *necesse* 'needful'.

**neck** • n. **1** the part of a person's or animal's body connecting the head to the rest of the body. **2** a narrow connecting or end part. ➤ the part of a bottle or other container near the mouth. ➤ a narrow piece of terrain or sea. **3** the length of a horse's head and neck as a measure of its lead in a race. **4** the part of a violin, guitar, or other instrument that bears the fingerboard. **5** (usu. in phr. **have the neck to do something**) informal impudence or nerve. **6** Geology a column of igneous rock occupying the site of a volcanic vent. • v. **1** informal kiss and caress amorously. **2** Brit. informal swallow (a drink). **3** become narrow at a particular point when subjected to tension.
– PHRASES **get** (or **catch**) **it in the neck** informal be severely criticized or punished. **neck and neck** level in a race, competition, or comparison. **neck of the woods** informal a particular area or locality. **up to one's neck in** informal heavily, deeply, or busily involved in.
– DERIVATIVES **-necked** adj. **necker** n. **neckless** adj.
– ORIGIN OE *hnecca* 'back of the neck', of Gmc origin.

**neckband** • n. a strip of material round the neck of a garment.

**neckcloth** • n. a cravat.

**neckerchief** • n. a square of cloth worn round the neck.

**necking** • n. Architecture a short plain concave section between the capital and the shaft of a classical Doric or Tuscan column.

**necklace** • n. **1** an ornamental chain or string of beads, jewels, or links worn round the neck. **2** (in South Africa) a tyre doused or filled with petrol, placed round a victim's neck and set alight. • v. kill with a tyre necklace.

**necklet** • n. a close-fitting, typically rigid ornament worn around the neck.

**neckline** • n. the edge of a woman's garment at or below the neck.

**necktie** • n. N. Amer. or dated a tie worn around the neck.

**necktie party** • n. N. Amer. informal a lynching or hanging.

**necro-** • comb. form relating to a corpse or death.
– ORIGIN from Gk *nekros* 'corpse'.

**necrobiosis** /ˌnɛkrə(ʊ)bʌɪˈəʊsɪs/ • n. Medicine gradual degeneration and death of cells in the body tissues.
– DERIVATIVES **necrobiotic** /-ˈɒtɪk/ adj.

**necrology** /nɛˈkrɒlədʒi/ • n. (pl. **-ies**) formal **1** an obituary notice. **2** a list of deaths.
– DERIVATIVES **necrological** adj. **necrologist** n.

**necromancy** /ˈnɛkrə(ʊ)ˌmansi/ • n. the supposed practice of communicating with the dead, especially in order to predict the future. ➤ witchcraft, sorcery, or black magic in general.
– DERIVATIVES **necromancer** n. **necromantic** adj.

**necrophilia** /ˌnɛkrə(ʊ)ˈfɪlɪə/ • n. sexual intercourse with or attraction towards corpses.
– DERIVATIVES **necrophile** n. **necrophiliac** n. **necrophilic** adj. **necrophilism** n. **necrophilist** n.

**necrophobia** • n. extreme or irrational fear of death or dead bodies.

**necropolis** /nɛˈkrɒpəlɪs/ • n. a cemetery, especially a large ancient one.
– ORIGIN C19: from Gk, from *nekros* 'dead person' + *polis* 'city'.

**necropsy** /ˈnɛkrɒpsi, nɛˈkrɒpsi/ • n. (pl. **-ies**) another term for AUTOPSY.

**necrosis** /nɛˈkrəʊsɪs/ • n. Medicine the death of most or all of the cells in an organ or tissue due to disease, injury, or failure of the blood supply.
– DERIVATIVES **necrotic** adj.
– ORIGIN C17: mod. L., from Gk *nekrōsis* (see NECRO-, -OSIS).

**necrotizing** /ˈnɛkrəˌtʌɪzɪŋ/ (also **-ising**) • adj. causing or accompanied by necrosis.
– DERIVATIVES **necrotized** adj.

**necrotizing fasciitis** • n. Medicine an acute disease in which inflammation of the fasciae of muscles or other organs results in rapid destruction of overlying tissues.

**nectar** • n. **1** a sugary fluid secreted within flowers to encourage pollination by insects, collected by bees to make into honey. **2** (in Greek and Roman mythology) the drink of the gods. ➤ a delicious drink.
– DERIVATIVES **nectarean** adj. **nectareous** adj. **nectariferous** adj. **nectarivorous** adj. **nectarous** adj.
– ORIGIN C16: via L. from Gk *nektar*.

**nectarine** /ˈnɛktərɪn, -iːn/ • n. **1** a peach of a variety with smooth, thin, brightly coloured skin and rich firm flesh. **2** the tree bearing this fruit.
– ORIGIN C17: from NECTAR + -INE[4].

**nectary** • n. (pl. **-ies**) Botany a nectar-secreting glandular organ in a flower or on a leaf or stem.

**ned** • n. Scottish informal a hooligan or petty criminal. ➤ a stupid or loutish boy or man.
– ORIGIN perh. from *Ned* (see NEDDY).

**neddy** • n. (pl. **-ies**) informal **1** Brit. a child's word for a donkey. **2** Austral. a horse, especially a racehorse.
– ORIGIN C16: dimin. of *Ned*, familiar form of the given name *Edward*.

**née** /neɪ/ (masc. **né**) • adj. originally called; born (used in citing a person's former name, especially a married woman's maiden name).
– ORIGIN C18: Fr., lit. 'born', past part. of *naître*.

**need** • v. **1** require (something) because it is essential or very important rather than just desirable. **2** [usu. with neg. or in questions] expressing necessity or obligation: *need I say more?* **3** archaic be necessary. • n. **1** circumstances in which something is necessary; necessity. **2** a thing that is wanted or required. **3** the state of lacking basic necessities such as food, or of requiring help. • adv. (**needs**) archaic of necessity.
– PHRASES **needs must** (or **must needs**) it is or was necessary or unavoidable.
– ORIGIN OE *nēodian* (v.), *nēod*, *nēd* (n.), of Gmc origin.

**need-blind** • adj. US of or denoting a university admissions policy in which applicants are judged solely on their own merits, irrespective of their ability to pay for tuition.

**needful** • adj. **1** formal necessary; requisite. **2** archaic needy.
– DERIVATIVES **needfully** adv. **needfulness** n.

**needle** • n. **1** a very fine slender piece of metal with a point at one end and a hole or eye for thread at the other, used in sewing. ➤ a similar, larger instrument used in crochet, knitting, etc. **2** the pointed hollow end of a hypodermic syringe. **3** a stylus used to play records. **4** a thin pointer on a dial, compass, etc. **5** Brit. informal hostility or

antagonism provoked by rivalry. **6** the slender, sharp, stiff leaf of a fir or pine tree. **7** a steel pin exploding the cartridge of a breech-loading gun. **8** a beam used as a temporary support during underpinning. ● **v.** **1** prick or pierce with a needle. **2** informal provoke or annoy by continual criticism or questioning.
– DERIVATIVES **needler** n.
– ORIGIN OE *nǣdl*, of Gmc origin.

**needlecord** ● **n.** Brit. fine-ribbed corduroy fabric.

**needlecraft** ● **n.** needlework.

**needlefish** ● **n.** (pl. same or **-fishes**) North American term for **GARFISH**.

**needlepoint** ● **n.** **1** closely stitched embroidery worked over canvas. **2** (also **needlelace**) lace made by hand using a needle rather than bobbins.

**needless** ● **adj.** unnecessary; avoidable.
– PHRASES **needless to say** of course.
– DERIVATIVES **needlessly** adv. **needlessness** n.

**needle valve** ● **n.** a valve closed by a thin tapering part.

**needlewoman** ● **n.** (pl. **-women**) a woman who has particular sewing skills.

**needlework** ● **n.** the art or practice of sewing or embroidery. ➤ sewn or embroidered items collectively.
– DERIVATIVES **needleworker** n.

**needn't** ● **contr.** need not.

**needy** ● **adj.** (**-ier**, **-iest**) **1** lacking the necessities of life; very poor. **2** needing emotional support; insecure.
– DERIVATIVES **neediness** n.

**neem** /niːm/ ● **n.** a tropical Old World tree which yields mahogany-like wood, oil, medicinal products, and insecticide. [*Azadirachta indica*.]
– ORIGIN C19: via Hindi from Sanskrit *nimba*.

**neep** ● **n.** Scottish & N. English a turnip.
– ORIGIN OE *nǣp*, from L. *napus*.

**ne'er** /nɛː/ ● **contr.** poetic/literary or dialect never.

**ne'er-do-well** ● **n.** a person who is lazy and irresponsible. ● **adj.** lazy and irresponsible.

**nefarious** /nɪˈfɛːrɪəs/ ● **adj.** wicked or criminal.
– DERIVATIVES **nefariously** adv. **nefariousness** n.
– ORIGIN C17: from L. *nefarius*, from *nefas*, *nefar-* 'wrong' + **-OUS**.

**neg** ● **n.** informal a photographic negative.

**neg.** ● **abbrev.** negative.

**nega-** ● **comb. form** informal denoting the negative counterpart of a unit of measurement, in particular a unit of energy saved as a result of conservation measures.

**negate** /nɪˈgeɪt/ ● **v.** **1** nullify; make ineffective. **2** Logic & Grammar make (a clause, sentence, or proposition) negative in meaning. **3** deny the existence of.
– ORIGIN C17 (earlier (ME) as *negation*): from L. *negat-*, *negare* 'deny'.

**negation** ● **n.** **1** the contradiction or denial of something. ➤ Logic a proposition whose assertion specifically denies the truth of another proposition. **2** the absence or opposite of something actual or positive. **3** Mathematics inversion.
– DERIVATIVES **negatory** /nɪˈgeɪt(ə)ri, ˈnɛgət(ə)ri/ adj.

**negative** ● **adj.** **1** consisting in or characterized by the absence rather than the presence of distinguishing features. ➤ expressing or implying denial, disagreement, or refusal. ➤ Grammar & Logic stating that something is not the case. Contrasted with **AFFIRMATIVE** and **INTERROGATIVE**. ➤ [as exclam.] (especially in a military context) no. **2** pessimistic, undesirable, or unwelcome. **3** (of a quantity) less than zero. **4** of, containing, producing, or denoting the kind of electric charge carried by electrons. **5** (of a photographic image) showing light and shade or colours reversed from those of the original. **6** Brit. relating to or denoting proposed legislation which will come into force after a specified period unless explicitly rejected in a parliamentary vote. ● **n.** **1** a word or statement expressing denial, refusal, or negation. ➤ a bad or unwelcome quality or aspect. **2** a negative photographic image from which positive prints may be made. ● **v.** **1** reject, veto, or contradict. **2** render ineffective; neutralize.
– DERIVATIVES **negatively** adv. **negativeness** n. **negativism** n. **negativist** n. & adj. **negativistic** adj. **negativity** n.
– ORIGIN ME: from late L. *negativus*, from *negare* (see **NEGATE**).

**negative equity** ● **n.** potential indebtedness arising when the market value of a property falls below the outstanding amount of a mortgage secured on it.

**negative feedback** ● **n.** feedback that tends to reduce the effect by which it is produced.

**negative geotropism** ● **n.** the tendency of plant stems and other parts to grow upwards.

**negative pole** ● **n.** the south-seeking pole of a magnet.

**negative sign** ● **n.** another term for **MINUS SIGN**.

**negator** /nɪˈgeɪtə/ ● **n.** Grammar a word expressing negation, especially (in English) the word *not*.

**neglect** ● **v.** fail to give proper care or attention to. ➤ fail to do something. ● **n.** the state or process of neglecting or being neglected. ➤ failure to do something.
– DERIVATIVES **neglectful** adj. **neglectfully** adv. **neglectfulness** n.
– ORIGIN C16 (earlier (ME) as *negligence*, *negligent*): from L. *neglect-*, *neglegere* 'disregard'.

**negligee** /ˈnɛglɪʒeɪ/ ● **n.** a woman's light, filmy dressing gown.
– ORIGIN C18 (denoting a woman's loose gown): from Fr., lit. 'given little thought or attention', fem. past part. of *négliger* 'to neglect'.

**negligence** ● **n.** failure to take proper care over something. ➤ Law breach of a duty of care which results in damage.
– DERIVATIVES **negligent** adj. **negligently** adv.
– ORIGIN ME: from OFr., or from L. *negligentia*, from *negligere*, var. of *neglegere* (see **NEGLECT**).

**negligible** ● **adj.** so small or unimportant as to be not worth considering; insignificant.
– DERIVATIVES **negligibility** /-ˈbɪlɪti/ n. **negligibly** adv.
– ORIGIN C19: from obs. Fr., from *négliger* 'to neglect'.

**negotiable** ● **adj.** **1** open to discussion or modification. **2** able to be traversed; passable. **3** able to be transferred or assigned to the legal ownership of another person.
– DERIVATIVES **negotiability** n.

**negotiate** ● **v.** **1** try to reach an agreement or compromise by discussion with others. ➤ obtain or bring about by negotiating. **2** find a way over or through (an obstacle or difficult path). **3** transfer (a cheque, bill, etc.) to the legal ownership of another. ➤ convert (a cheque) into cash or notes.
– DERIVATIVES **negotiant** n. (archaic). **negotiation** n. **negotiator** n.
– ORIGIN C17 (earlier (C15) as *negotiation*): from L. *negotiat-*, *negotiari* 'do in the course of business', from *negotium* 'business'.

**Negress** /ˈniːgrɪs, -grɛs/ ● **n.** a woman or girl of black African origin. See **NEGRO**.

**Negrillo** /nɪˈgrɪləʊ/ ● **n.** (pl. **-os**) a member of a black people of short stature native to central and southern Africa.
– ORIGIN Sp., dimin. of *negro* (see **NEGRO**).

**Negrito** /nɪˈgriːtəʊ/ ● **n.** (pl. **-os**) a member of a black people of short stature native to the Austronesian region.
– ORIGIN Sp., dimin. of *negro* (see **NEGRO**).

**Negritude** /ˈnɛgrɪtjuːd/ ● **n.** the quality, fact, or awareness of being of black African origin.

**Negro** /ˈniːgrəʊ/ ● **n.** (pl. **-oes**) a member of a dark-skinned group of peoples originally native to Africa south of the Sahara.
– ORIGIN via Sp. and Port. from L. *niger*, *nigr-* 'black'.

**USAGE** Negro

Since the 1960s, when the term **black** was favoured as the term to express racial pride, **Negro** (together with related words such as **Negress**) has dropped out of favour. It is now regarded as old-fashioned or even offensive in both British and US English.

**Negroid** ● **adj.** of or relating to the division of humankind represented by the indigenous peoples of central and southern Africa.

**USAGE** Negroid

The term **Negroid** belongs to a set of terms introduced by 19th-century anthropologists attempting to categorize human races. Such terms are associated with outdated notions of racial types, and so are now potentially offensive and best avoided.

**negroni** /nɪˈɡrəʊni/ ● **n.** a cocktail made from gin, vermouth, and Campari.
– ORIGIN from Ital.

**Negrophobia** ● **n.** intense or irrational dislike or fear of black people.
– DERIVATIVES **Negrophobe** n.

**Negus** /ˈniːɡəs/ ● **n.** historical a ruler, or the supreme ruler, of Ethiopia.
– ORIGIN from Amharic *n'gus* 'king'.

**negus** /ˈniːɡəs/ ● **n.** historical a hot drink of port, sugar, lemon, and spice.
– ORIGIN C18: named after Colonel Francis *Negus*, who created it.

**Neh.** ● **abbrev.** Nehemiah (in biblical references).

**neigh** /neɪ/ ● **n.** a characteristic high whinnying sound made by a horse. ● **v.** (of a horse) utter a neigh.
– ORIGIN OE *hnǣgan* (v.), of imitative origin.

**neighbour** (US **neighbor**) ● **n.** a person living next door to or very near to another. ➤ a person or place in relation to others next to it. ● **v.** [usu. as adj. **neighbouring**] be situated next to or very near (another).
– DERIVATIVES **neighbourless** adj. **neighbourliness** n. **neighbourly** adj.
– ORIGIN OE *nēahgebūr*, from *nēah* 'nigh, near' + *gebūr* 'inhabitant, peasant, farmer' (cf. **BOOR**).

**neighbourhood** (US **neighborhood**) ● **n.** a district or community within a town or city. ➤ the area surrounding a particular place, person, or object.
– PHRASES **in the neighbourhood of** approximately; about.

**neighbourhood watch** ● **n.** a scheme of systematic local vigilance by householders to discourage crime, especially burglary.

**neither** /ˈnʌɪðə, ˈniː-/ ● **det. & pron.** not the one nor the other of two people or things; not either. ● **adv. 1** used before the first of two (or occasionally more) alternatives (the others being introduced by 'nor') to indicate that they are each untrue or each do not happen. **2** used to introduce a further negative statement.
– ORIGIN ME: alt. (by assoc. with **EITHER**) of OE *nawther*, contr. of *nāhwæther* (from *nā* 'no' + *hwæther* 'whether').

**nekton** /ˈnɛkt(ə)n, -tɒn/ ● **n.** Zoology aquatic animals that are able to swim and move independently of water currents, as distinct from plankton.
– DERIVATIVES **nektonic** adj.
– ORIGIN C19: via Ger. from Gk *nēkton*, neut. of *nēktos* 'swimming', from *nēkhein* 'to swim'.

**nelly** ● **n.** (pl. **-ies**) informal **1** a silly person. **2** derogatory an effeminate homosexual man.
– PHRASES **not on your nelly** Brit. certainly not. [orig. as *not on your Nelly Duff*, rhyming sl. for 'puff' (i.e. breath of life); modelled on the phr. *not on your life*.]
– ORIGIN C20: from the given name *Nelly*.

**nelson** ● **n.** a wrestling hold in which one arm is passed under the opponent's arm from behind and the hand is applied to the neck (**half nelson**), or both arms and hands are applied (**full nelson**).
– ORIGIN C19: appar. from the surname *Nelson*.

**nematic** /nɪˈmatɪk/ ● **adj.** relating to or denoting a state of a liquid crystal in which the molecules are oriented in parallel but not arranged in well-defined planes. Compare with **SMECTIC**.
– ORIGIN C20: from Gk *nēma*, *nēmat-* 'thread' + **-IC**.

**nemato-** /nɪˈmatəʊ, ˈnɛmətəʊ/ (also **nemat-** before a vowel) ● **comb. form 1** denoting something thread-like in shape: *nematocyst*. **2** relating to Nematoda.
– ORIGIN from Gk *nēma*, *nēmat-* 'thread'.

**nematocyst** /nɪˈmatə(ʊ)sɪst, ˈnɛmət-/ ● **n.** Zoology a specialized cell in the tentacles of a jellyfish or other coelenterate, containing a barbed or venomous coiled thread that can be projected in self-defence or to capture prey.

**Nematoda** /ˌnɛməˈtəʊdə/ ● **pl. n.** Zoology a large phylum of worms with slender, unsegmented, cylindrical bodies, including the roundworms, threadworms, and eelworms.
– DERIVATIVES **nematode** /ˈnɛmətəʊd/ n.

**nematology** /ˌnɛməˈtɒlədʒi/ ● **n.** the scientific study of nematode worms.
– DERIVATIVES **nematologist** n.

**Nembutal** /ˈnɛmbjʊt(ə)l, -tɑːl/ ● **n.** (trademark in the US) the drug sodium pentobarbitone.
– ORIGIN C20: from *N(a)* (symbol for sodium) + *e(thyl)*, *m(ethyl)*, *but(yl)*, elements of the systematic name, + **-AL**.

**nem. con.** ● **adv.** with no one dissenting; unanimously.
– ORIGIN L. *nemine contradicente*.

**Nemertea** /ˌnɛməˈtiːə, nɪˈməːtɪə/ ● **pl. n.** Zoology a small phylum that comprises the ribbon worms.
– DERIVATIVES **nemertean** adj. & n. **nemertine** /ˈnɛmətiːn, ˈnɛmətʌɪn/ adj. & n.
– ORIGIN mod. L., from Gk *Nēmertēs*, the name of a sea nymph.

**nemesia** /nɪˈmiːʒə/ ● **n.** a plant related to the snapdragon, cultivated for its colourful, funnel-shaped flowers. [Genus *Nemesia*.]
– ORIGIN mod. L., from Gk *nemesion*, denoting various similar plants.

**nemesis** /ˈnɛmɪsɪs/ ● **n.** (pl. **nemeses** /-siːz/) the inescapable agent of someone's downfall, especially when deserved. ➤ a downfall caused by such an agent.
– ORIGIN C16: Gk, lit. 'retribution', personified as the goddess of divine punishment.

**nene** /ˈneɪneɪ/ (also **ne-ne**) ● **n.** a rare goose native to Hawaii, now breeding chiefly in captivity. [*Branta sandvicensis*.]
– ORIGIN C20: from Hawaiian.

**Nenets** /ˈnɛnɛts/ ● **n.** (pl. same or **Nentsy** or **Nentsi**) **1** a member of a nomadic people of Siberia. **2** the Samoyedic language of this people.
– ORIGIN the name in Russ.

**neo-** /ˈniːəʊ/ ● **comb. form 1** new: *neonate*. **2** a new or revived form of: *neo-Darwinian*.
– ORIGIN from Gk *neos* 'new'.

**neoclassicism** ● **n.** the revival of a classical style or treatment in art, literature, architecture, or music.
– DERIVATIVES **neoclassic** adj. **neoclassical** adj. **neoclassicist** n. & adj.

**neocolonialism** ● **n.** the use of economic, political, or cultural pressures to control or influence other countries, especially former dependencies.
– DERIVATIVES **neocolonial** adj. **neocolonialist** n. & adj.

**neocortex** ● **n.** (pl. **neocortices**) Anatomy a part of the cerebral cortex concerned with sight and hearing in mammals, regarded as the most recently evolved part of the cortex.
– DERIVATIVES **neocortical** adj.

**neo-Darwinian** ● **adj.** Biology of or relating to the modern version of Darwin's theory of evolution by natural selection, incorporating the findings of genetics.
– DERIVATIVES **neo-Darwinism** n. **neo-Darwinist** n.

**neodymium** /ˌniːə(ʊ)ˈdɪmɪəm/ ● **n.** the chemical element of atomic number 60, a silvery-white metal of the lanthanide series. (Symbol: **Nd**)
– ORIGIN C19: from **NEO-** + a shortened form of **DIDYMIUM**.

**Neogene** /ˈniːə(ʊ)dʒiːn/ ● **adj.** Geology relating to or denoting the later division of the Tertiary period (comprising the Miocene and Pliocene epochs, from 23.3 to 1.64 million years ago).
– ORIGIN C19: from **NEO-** + Gk *-genēs* (see **-GEN**).

**neo-Impressionism** ● **n.** a late 19th-century movement in French painting which sought to improve on Impressionism through a systematic approach to form and colour, particularly using pointillist technique.
– DERIVATIVES **neo-Impressionist** adj. & n.

**Neolithic** /ˌniːə(ʊ)ˈlɪθɪk/ ● **adj.** Archaeology relating to or denoting the later part of the Stone Age, when ground or polished stone weapons and implements prevailed.
– ORIGIN C19: from **NEO-** + Gk *lithos* 'stone' + **-IC**.

**neologism** /nɪˈɒlədʒɪz(ə)m/ ● **n.** a newly coined word or expression.
– DERIVATIVES **neologist** n. **neologize** (also **-ise**) v.

– ORIGIN C19: from Fr. *néologisme.*

**Neo-Melanesian** ● n. another term for **TOK PISIN**.

**neomycin** /ˌniːə(ʊ)ˈmʌɪsɪn/ ● n. Medicine an antibiotic related to streptomycin, active against a wide variety of bacterial infections.

**neon** ● n. **1** the chemical element of atomic number 10, an inert gaseous element of the noble gas group. (Symbol: **Ne**) **2** fluorescent lighting and signs using neon or another gas. ➤[as modifier] very bright or fluorescent in colour.

– ORIGIN C19: from Gk, lit. 'something new', neut. of the adj. *neos.*

**neonatal** /ˌniːə(ʊ)ˈneɪt(ə)l/ ● adj. of or relating to newborn children (or mammals).

– DERIVATIVES **neonatologist** n. **neonatology** n.

**neonate** /ˈniːə(ʊ)neɪt/ ● n. a newborn child or mammal. ➤Medicine an infant less than four weeks old.

– ORIGIN 1930s: from mod. L. *neonatus*, from Gk *neos* 'new' + L. *nat-*, *nasci* 'be born'.

**neon tetra** ● n. see **TETRA**.

**neophobia** ● n. extreme or irrational fear or dislike of anything new, novel, or unfamiliar.

– DERIVATIVES **neophobic** adj.

**neophyte** /ˈniːə(ʊ)fʌɪt/ ● n. **1** a person who is new to a subject, skill, or belief. **2** a novice in a religious order, or a newly ordained priest.

– ORIGIN ME: via eccles. L. from Gk *neophutos*, lit. 'newly planted'.

**neoplasia** /ˌniːə(ʊ)ˈpleɪzɪə/ ● n. Medicine the presence or formation of new, abnormal growth of tissue.

– ORIGIN C19: from **NEO-** + Gk *plasis* 'formation'.

**neoplasm** ● n. a new and abnormal growth of tissue in some part of the body, especially as a characteristic of cancer.

**neoplastic[1]** ● adj. Medicine of or relating to a neoplasm or neoplasia.

**neoplastic[2]** ● adj. Art of or relating to neoplasticism.

**neoplasticism** ● n. a style of abstract painting characterized by the use of rectangular shapes and primary colours.

**Neoplatonism** /ˌniːəʊˈpleɪt(ə)nɪz(ə)m/ ● n. a philosophical and religious system developed in the 3rd century AD, combining Platonic and other Greek thought with oriental mysticism.

– DERIVATIVES **Neoplatonic** adj. **Neoplatonist** n.

**neoprene** /ˈniːə(ʊ)priːn/ ● n. a synthetic polymer resembling rubber.

– ORIGIN 1930s: from **NEO-** + *prene* (perh. from **PROPYL** + **-ENE**), on the pattern of words such as *isoprene.*

**neo-realism** ● n. a naturalistic movement in Italian literature and cinema that emerged in the 1940s.

– DERIVATIVES **neo-realist** n. & adj.

**neostigmine** /ˌniːə(ʊ)ˈstɪgmiːn/ ● n. Medicine a synthetic compound with the property of inhibiting cholinesterase and used to treat ileus, glaucoma, and myasthenia gravis.

– ORIGIN 1940s: from **NEO-**, on the pattern of *physostigmine.*

**neoteny** /niːˈɒt(ə)ni/ ● n. Zoology **1** the retention of juvenile features in the adult animal. **2** the sexual maturity of an animal while it is still in a mainly larval state, as in the axolotl.

– DERIVATIVES **neotenic** adj. **neotenous** adj.

– ORIGIN C19: coined in Ger. as *Neotenie*, from Gk *neos* 'new' (in the sense 'juvenile') + *teinein* 'extend'.

**neoteric** /ˌniːə(ʊ)ˈtɛrɪk/ ● adj. recent; new; modern.

– ORIGIN C16: via late L. from Gk *neōterikos*, from *neōteros* 'newer', compar. of *neos.*

**Neotropical** ● adj. Zoology relating to or denoting a zoogeographical region comprising Central and South America and the Caribbean.

– DERIVATIVES **neotropics** pl. n.

**Nepalese** /nɛpəˈliːz/ ● n. a native or inhabitant of Nepal. ● adj. of or relating to Nepal.

**Nepali** /nɪˈpɔːli/ ● n. (pl. same or **Nepalis**) **1** a native or national of Nepal. **2** the Indic official language of Nepal.

**nepenthes** /nɪˈpɛnθiːz/ ● n. **1** (also **nepenthe**) a drug described in Homer's *Odyssey* as banishing grief or trouble from a person's mind. **2** a plant of a genus that comprises the Old World pitcher plants. [Genus *Nepenthes.*]

– ORIGIN via L. from Gk *nēpenthēs* 'dispelling pain'.

**neper** /ˈniːpə, ˈneɪ-/ ● n. Physics a logarithmic unit used in comparing voltages, currents, or power levels.

– ORIGIN C20: from *Neperus*, Latinized form of the name of the Sc. mathematician John *Napier.*

**nepeta** /nɪˈpiːtə/ ● n. a plant of a genus that includes catmint and several kinds with spikes of blue or violet flowers. [Genus *Nepeta.*]

– ORIGIN mod. L., from L. *nepeta* 'calamint' (formerly in this genus).

**nepheline** /ˈnɛf(ə)lɪn/ ● n. a colourless, greenish, or brownish aluminosilicate mineral occurring in igneous rocks.

– ORIGIN C19: from Fr. *néphéline*, from Gk *nephelē* 'cloud' (because its fragments become cloudy on immersion in nitric acid) + **-INE[2]**.

**nephelometer** /ˌnɛfəˈlɒmɪtə/ ● n. an instrument for measuring the size and concentration of suspended particles by means of light scattering.

– ORIGIN C19: from Gk *nephelē* 'cloud' + **-METER**.

**nephew** ● n. a son of one's brother or sister, or of one's brother-in-law or sister-in-law.

– ORIGIN ME: from OFr. *neveu*, from L. *nepos* 'grandson, nephew'.

**nephology** /nɪˈfɒlədʒi/ ● n. the study or contemplation of clouds.

– ORIGIN C19: from Gk *nephos* 'cloud' + **-LOGY**.

**nephr-** /nɪfr/ ● comb. form variant spelling of **NEPHRO-** shortened before a vowel (as in *nephrectomy*).

**nephrectomy** /nɪˈfrɛktəmi/ ● n. (pl. **-ies**) surgical removal of one or both kidneys.

**nephridiopore** /nɪˈfrɪdɪəpɔː/ ● n. Zoology the external opening of a nephridium.

**nephridium** /nɪˈfrɪdɪəm/ ● n. (pl. **nephridia**) Zoology (in many invertebrates) a minute tube open to the exterior for excretion or osmoregulation.

– DERIVATIVES **nephridial** adj.

– ORIGIN C19: mod. L., from Gk *nephrion* (dimin. of *nephros* 'kidney') + the dimin. ending *-idium.*

**nephrite** /ˈnɛfrʌɪt/ ● n. a pale green or white silicate mineral which is one of the forms of jade.

– ORIGIN C18: from Ger. *Nephrit*, from Gk *nephros* 'kidney' (with ref. to its supposed efficacy in treating kidney disease).

**nephritic** /nɪˈfrɪtɪk/ ● adj. renal. ➤of or relating to nephritis.

– ORIGIN C19: via late L. from Gk *nephritikos* (see **NEPHRITIS**).

**nephritis** /nɪˈfrʌɪtɪs/ ● n. Medicine inflammation of the kidneys.

– ORIGIN C16: via late L. from Gk, from *nephros* 'kidney'.

**nephro-** (also **nephr-** before a vowel) ● comb. form of or relating to the kidneys: *nephrotoxic.*

– ORIGIN from Gk *nephros* 'kidney'.

**nephrology** /nɛˈfrɒlədʒi/ ● n. the branch of medicine concerned with the physiology and diseases of the kidneys.

– DERIVATIVES **nephrological** adj. **nephrologist** n.

**nephron** /ˈnɛfrɒn/ ● n. Anatomy a functional unit within the kidney, consisting of a glomerulus and an associated tubule.

– ORIGIN 1930s: via Ger. from Gk *nephros* 'kidney'.

**nephrosis** /nɪˈfrəʊsɪs/ ● n. Medicine kidney disease, especially with oedema and proteinuria.

– DERIVATIVES **nephrotic** adj.

**ne plus ultra** /ˌneɪ plʊs ˈʊltrɑː/ ● n. (**the ne plus ultra**) the perfect or most extreme example.

– ORIGIN L., lit. 'not further beyond', the supposed inscription on the Pillars of Hercules prohibiting passage by ships.

**nepotism** /ˈnɛpətɪz(ə)m/ ● n. the favouring of relatives or friends, especially by giving them jobs.

– DERIVATIVES **nepotist** n. **nepotistic** adj.

– ORIGIN C17: from Fr. *népotisme*, from Ital. *nepotismo*, from *nipote* 'nephew' (with ref. to privileges bestowed on the 'nephews' of popes, often really their illegitimate sons).

**Neptune** ● n. a planet of the solar system, eighth in order from the sun.

**Neptunian** ● adj. 1 relating to the Roman sea god Neptune or to the sea. 2 relating to the planet Neptune.

**neptunium** /nɛp'tjuːnɪəm/ ● n. the chemical element of atomic number 93, a radioactive metal of the actinide series. (Symbol: **Np**)
– ORIGIN C19: from NEPTUNE, on the pattern of *uranium* (Neptune being the next planet beyond Uranus).

**NERC** ● abbrev. (in the UK) Natural Environment Research Council.

**nerd** ● n. informal, chiefly US a person who lacks social skills or is boringly studious.
– DERIVATIVES **nerdish** adj. **nerdishness** n. **nerdy** adj.
– ORIGIN 1950s: of unknown origin.

**Nereid** /'nɪərɪɪd/ ● n. Greek Mythology any of the sea nymphs, daughters of the old sea god Nereus.

**nereid** ● n. Zoology a bristle worm of the ragworm family (Nereidae).

**nerine** /nɪ'rʌɪni, nə'riːnə/ ● n. a bulbous South African plant with narrow strap-shaped petals that are typically crimped and twisted. [Genus *Nerine*.]
– ORIGIN mod. L., deriv. of Gk *Nērēis, Nērēid-* 'Nereid'.

**nerite** /'nɪərʌɪt/ ● n. a mollusc with a globe-shaped and brightly marked shell, chiefly tropical and aquatic. [*Theodoxus fluviatilis* and other species.]
– ORIGIN C18: from L. *nerita*, from Gk *nēritēs* 'sea mussel', from the name of the sea god *Nereus*.

**neritic** /nɪ'rɪtɪk/ ● adj. Ecology of or denoting the shallow waters overlying the continental shelf.
– ORIGIN C19: from NERITE + -IC.

**neroli** /'nɪərəli/ (also **neroli oil**) ● n. an essential oil distilled from the flowers of the Seville orange.
– ORIGIN C17: via Fr. from Ital. *neroli*, said to be the name of an Ital. princess.

**nervation** ● n. Botany the arrangement of nerves in a leaf.
– ORIGIN C18: from Fr., based on *nerf* 'nerve'.

**nerve** ● n. 1 a whitish fibre or bundle of fibres in the body that transmits impulses of sensation between the brain or spinal cord and other parts of the body. 2 (**nerves**) bravery; assurance. ➤(**one's nerve**) one's steadiness and courage. 3 (**nerves**) nervousness. 4 informal cheek. 5 Botany a prominent unbranched rib in a leaf, especially the midrib of the leaf of a moss. ● v. (**nerve oneself**) brace oneself for a demanding situation.
– PHRASES **a bag** (or **bundle**) **of nerves** informal someone who is extremely nervous. **get on someone's nerves** informal irritate someone. **touch** (or **hit**) **a** (**raw**) **nerve** refer to a sensitive topic.
– DERIVATIVES **-nerved** adj.
– ORIGIN ME: from L. *nervus*; rel. to Gk *neuron* 'nerve' (see NEURON).

**nerve cell** ● n. a neuron.

**nerve centre** ● n. 1 a group of connected nerve cells performing a particular function. 2 the control centre of an organization or operation.

**nerve fibre** ● n. the axon of a neuron.

**nerve gas** ● n. a poisonous vapour which disrupts the transmission of nerve impulses, causing death or disablement.

**nerveless** ● adj. 1 lacking vigour or feeling. 2 confident. 3 Anatomy & Biology lacking nerves or nervures.
– DERIVATIVES **nervelessly** adv. **nervelessness** n.

**nerve net** ● n. Zoology (in some invertebrates) a diffuse network of neurons conducting impulses in all directions from a point of stimulus.

**nerve-racking** (also **nerve-wracking**) ● adj. stressful; frightening.

**nervine** /'nəːvʌɪn, -iːn/ ● adj. (of a medicine) used to calm the nerves. ● n. a nervine medicine.
– ORIGIN C17: from med. L. *nervinus* 'of the nerves or sinews', or suggested by Fr. *nervin*.

**nervous** ● adj. 1 easily agitated or alarmed. ➤apprehensive. ➤resulting from anxiety or anticipation. 2 relating to or affecting the nerves.
– DERIVATIVES **nervously** adv. **nervousness** n.
– ORIGIN ME: from L. *nervosus* 'sinewy, vigorous', from L. *nervus* (see NERVE).

**nervous breakdown** ● n. a period of mental illness resulting from severe depression or stress.

**nervous system** ● n. the network of nerve cells and fibres which transmits nerve impulses between parts of the body.

**nervous wreck** ● n. informal a stressed or emotionally exhausted person.

**nervure** /'nəːvjʊə/ ● n. 1 Entomology each of the hollow veins forming the framework of an insect's wing. 2 Botany the principal vein of a leaf.
– ORIGIN C19: from Fr., from *nerf* 'nerve'.

**nervy** ● adj. (**-ier**, **-iest**) 1 chiefly Brit. nervous. ➤characterized or produced by nervousness. 2 N. Amer. informal bold or impudent. 3 archaic or poetic/literary sinewy or strong.
– DERIVATIVES **nervily** adv. **nerviness** n.

**nescient** /'nɛsɪənt/ ● adj. poetic/literary ignorant.
– DERIVATIVES **nescience** n.
– ORIGIN ME: from L. *nescient-*, *nescire* 'to not know', from *ne-* 'not' + *scire* 'know'.

**nesh** ● adj. dialect weak; feeble.
– DERIVATIVES **neshness** n.
– ORIGIN OE *hnesce*, of Gmc origin.

**ness** ● n. a headland and promontory.
– ORIGIN OE *næs*, perh. reinforced in ME by ON *nes*; rel. to OE *nasu* 'nose'.

**-ness** ● suffix forming nouns chiefly from adjectives: 1 denoting a state or condition: *liveliness*. ➤an instance of this: *a kindness*. 2 something in a certain state: *wilderness*.
– ORIGIN OE *-nes*, *-ness*, of Gmc origin.

**nest** ● n. 1 a structure or place made or chosen by a bird for laying eggs and sheltering its young. ➤a place where an animal or insect breeds or shelters. ➤a snug or secluded retreat. ➤a bowl-shaped object likened to a bird's nest. 2 a place filled with undesirable people or things: *a nest of spies*. 3 a set of similar objects of graduated sizes, fitting together for storage. ● v. 1 use or build a nest. 2 fit (an object or objects) inside a larger one. 3 (especially in computing and linguistics) place in a hierarchical arrangement, typically in a lower position.
– DERIVATIVES **nestful** n. (pl. **-fuls**).
– ORIGIN OE *nest*, of Gmc origin.

**nest box** (also **nesting box**) ● n. a box provided for a bird to nest in.

**nest egg** ● n. 1 a sum of money saved for the future. 2 a real or artificial egg left in a nest to induce hens to lay there.

**nester** ● n. a bird nesting in a specified manner or place: *a scarce nester in Britain*.

**nestle** ● v. 1 settle comfortably within or against something. 2 (of a place) lie in a sheltered position.
– ORIGIN OE *nestlian*, from NEST.

**nestling** ● n. a bird that is too young to leave the nest.

**Nestorianism** /nɛ'stɔːrɪənɪz(ə)m/ ● n. the Christian doctrine that there were two separate persons in Christ, one human and one divine, maintained by some ancient Churches of the Middle East.
– DERIVATIVES **Nestorian** adj. & n.
– ORIGIN named after *Nestorius*, patriarch of Constantinople (428–31).

**net**[1] ● n. 1 a length of open-meshed material of twine, cord, etc., used typically for catching fish. ➤a net supported by a frame at the end of a handle, used for catching fish or insects. 2 a structure with a net used in various games, e.g. as a goal in football, to divide a tennis court, or to enclose a cricket practice area. 3 a fine fabric with a very open weave. ➤(**nets**) Brit. informal net curtains. 4 a trap. ➤a system for selecting or recruiting someone. 5 a communications or broadcasting network. ➤a network of interconnected computers. ➤(**the Net**) the Internet. ● v. (**netted**, **netting**) 1 catch or obtain with or as with a net. 2 (in sport) hit (a ball) into the net; score (a goal). 3 cover with a net.
– DERIVATIVES **netful** n. (pl. **-fuls**). **netter** n.

– ORIGIN OE *net*, *nett*, of Gmc origin.

**net**[2] (Brit. also **nett**) • **adj.** **1** (of an amount, value, or price) remaining after a deduction of tax or other contributions. Often contrasted with **GROSS**. ➤(of a price) to be paid in full. ➤(of a weight) excluding that of the packaging. **2** (of an effect or result) overall. • **v.** (**netted**, **netting**) acquire (a sum) as clear profit. ➤(**net something down/off/out**) exclude a non-net amount when making a calculation, to reduce the amount left to a net sum.

– ORIGIN ME (in the senses 'clean' and 'smart', also 'free from deductions'): from Fr. *net*; see **NEAT**[1].

**netball** • **n.** a seven-a-side game in which goals are scored by throwing a ball through a netted hoop.

**nether** /ˈnɛðə/ • **adj.** lower in position.

– DERIVATIVES **nethermost** adj.

– ORIGIN OE *nithera*, *neothera*, of Gmc origin.

**Netherlander** • **n.** a native or inhabitant of the Netherlands.

– DERIVATIVES **Netherlandish** adj.

**nether regions** • **pl. n.** **1** hell; the underworld. **2** euphemistic a person's genitals and bottom.

**netherworld** • **n.** the underworld; hell.

**net national product** • **n.** the total value of goods produced and services provided in a country during one year, after depreciation of capital goods has been allowed for.

**net profit** • **n.** the actual profit after working expenses have been paid.

**netsuke** /ˈnɛtski, ˈnɛtsʊki/ • **n.** (pl. same or **netsukes**) a carved button-like Japanese ornament of wood or ivory, formerly worn tucked into the sash of a kimono.

– ORIGIN C19: from Japanese.

**nett** • **adj.** & **v.** Brit. variant spelling of **NET**[2].

**netting** • **n.** netted fabric.

**nettle** • **n.** a herbaceous plant having jagged leaves covered with stinging hairs. [*Urtica dioica* and other species.] ➤used in names of plants of a similar appearance, e.g. **dead-nettle**. • **v.** **1** annoy. **2** sting with nettles.

– PHRASES **grasp the nettle** Brit. tackle a difficulty boldly.

– ORIGIN OE *netle*, *netele*, of Gmc origin.

**nettlerash** • **n.** another term for **URTICARIA**.

– ORIGIN from its resemblance to a nettle sting.

**nettlesome** • **adj.** chiefly US causing annoyance or difficulty.

**net ton** • **n.** another term for **TON**[1] (in sense 6).

**network** • **n.** **1** an arrangement of intersecting horizontal and vertical lines. **2** a complex system of railways, roads, etc. **3** a group or system of interconnected people or things. ➤a group of broadcasting stations that connect for the simultaneous broadcast of a programme. ➤a number of interconnected computers, machines, or operations. ➤a system of connected electrical conductors. • **v.** **1** connect as or operate with a network. ➤Brit. broadcast on a network. ➤link (machines) to operate interactively. **2** [often as noun **networking**] interact with others to exchange information and develop useful contacts.

– DERIVATIVES **networkable** adj.

**network appliance** • **n.** a relatively low-cost computer designed chiefly to provide Internet access and without the full capabilities of a standard personal computer.

**networker** • **n.** **1** Computing a person who operates from home or an external office via a computer network. **2** a person who networks with others in a similar field.

**neume** /njuːm/ (also **neum**) • **n.** Music (in plainsong) a note or group of notes to be sung to a single syllable.

– ORIGIN ME: from OFr. *neume*, from med. L. *neu(p)ma*, from Gk *pneuma* 'breath'.

**neural** • **adj.** of or relating to a nerve or the nervous system.

– DERIVATIVES **neurally** adv.

– ORIGIN C19: from Gk *neuron* in the sense 'nerve' + **-AL**.

**neuralgia** /ˌnjʊəˈraldʒə/ • **n.** intense pain along the course of a nerve, especially in the head or face.

– DERIVATIVES **neuralgic** adj.

**neural network** (also **neural net**) • **n.** a computer system modelled on the human brain and nervous system.

**neural tube** • **n.** Zoology & Medicine (in an embryo) a hollow structure from which the brain and spinal cord form.

**neurasthenia** /ˌnjʊərəsˈθiːnɪə/ • **n.** Medicine, dated a condition of lassitude, fatigue, headache, and irritability, typically ascribed to emotional disturbance.

– DERIVATIVES **neurasthenic** adj. & n.

**neuritis** /ˌnjʊəˈrʌɪtɪs/ • **n.** Medicine inflammation of a peripheral nerve or nerves.

– DERIVATIVES **neuritic** adj.

**neuro-** • **comb. form** relating to nerves or the nervous system: *neuroanatomy*.

– ORIGIN from Gk *neuron* 'nerve, sinew, tendon'.

**neuroanatomy** • **n.** the anatomy of the nervous system.

– DERIVATIVES **neuroanatomical** adj. **neuroanatomist** n.

**neurobiology** • **n.** the biology of the nervous system.

– DERIVATIVES **neurobiological** adj. **neurobiologist** n.

**neurofibril** /ˌnjʊərə(ʊ)ˈfʌɪbrɪl/ • **n.** Anatomy a fibril in the cytoplasm of a nerve cell.

– DERIVATIVES **neurofibrillary** adj.

**neurofibroma** /ˌnjʊərə(ʊ)fʌɪˈbrəʊmə/ • **n.** (pl. **neurofibromas** or **neurofibromata** /-mətə/) Medicine a tumour formed on a nerve cell sheath, frequently symptomless but occasionally malignant.

**neurofibromatosis** /ˌnjʊərə(ʊ)fʌɪˌbrəʊməˈtəʊsɪs/ • **n.** Medicine a disease in which neurofibromas form throughout the body.

**neurogenesis** /ˌnjʊərə(ʊ)ˈdʒɛnɪsɪs/ • **n.** Physiology the growth and development of nervous tissue.

**neurogenic** /ˌnjʊərə(ʊ)ˈdʒɛnɪk/ • **adj.** Physiology caused by or arising in the nervous system.

**neurohormone** • **n.** Physiology a hormone (such as noradrenaline) produced by nerve cells and secreted into the circulation.

**neuroleptic** /ˌnjʊərə(ʊ)ˈlɛptɪk/ Medicine • **adj.** tending to reduce nervous tension by depressing nerve functions. • **n.** a neuroleptic drug.

– ORIGIN C20: from **NEURO-** + Gk *lēpsis* 'seizing' + **-IC**.

**neurolinguistic programming** • **n.** a system of alternative therapy intended to improve self-awareness and change patterns of mental and emotional behaviour.

**neurolinguistics** • **pl. n.** [treated as sing.] the branch of linguistics concerned with the relationship between language and the brain.

– DERIVATIVES **neurolinguistic** adj.

**neurology** /ˌnjʊəˈrɒlədʒi/ • **n.** the branch of medicine and biology concerned with the nervous system.

– DERIVATIVES **neurological** adj. **neurologically** adv. **neurologist** n.

– ORIGIN C17: from mod. L. *neurologia*, from **NEURO-** + **-LOGY**.

**neuroma** /ˌnjʊəˈrəʊmə/ • **n.** (pl. **neuromas** or **neuromata** /-mətə/) another term for **NEUROFIBROMA**.

**neuromuscular** • **adj.** of or relating to nerves and muscles.

**neuron** /ˈnjʊərɒn/ (also **neurone** /-rəʊn/) • **n.** a specialized cell transmitting nerve impulses.

– DERIVATIVES **neuronal** /-ˈrəʊn(ə)l/ adj. **neuronic** /-ˈrɒnɪk/ adj.

– ORIGIN C19: from Gk *neuron* 'sinew, tendon'; cf. **NERVE**.

**USAGE** neuron

In scientific sources the standard spelling is **neuron**. The spelling **neurone** is found only in non-technical sources.

**neuropathology** • **n.** the pathology of the nervous system.

– DERIVATIVES **neuropathological** adj. **neuropathologist** n.

**neuropathy** /ˌnjʊəˈrɒpəθi/ • **n.** Medicine disease or dysfunction of peripheral nerves.

– DERIVATIVES **neuropathic** adj.

**neuropeptide** • **n.** Biochemistry any of a group of polypeptide compounds which act as neurotransmitters.

**neurophysiology** • **n.** the physiology of the nervous system.

– DERIVATIVES **neurophysiological** adj. **neurophysiologist** n.

**neuropsychiatry** ● n. psychiatry relating mental disturbance to disordered brain function.
– DERIVATIVES **neuropsychiatric** adj. **neuropsychiatrist** n.

**neuropsychology** ● n. the study of the relationship between behaviour and brain function.
– DERIVATIVES **neuropsychological** adj. **neuropsychologist** n.

**Neuroptera** /ˌnjʊəˈrɒpt(ə)rə/ ● pl. n. Entomology an order of predatory flying insects, including the lacewings, alderflies, and snake flies, having four finely veined membranous wings.
– DERIVATIVES **neuropteran** n. & adj. **neuropterous** adj.
– ORIGIN mod. L., from **NEURO-** in the sense 'veined' + Gk *pteron* 'wing'.

**neuroscience** ● n. any or all of the sciences concerned with the nervous system and brain.
– DERIVATIVES **neuroscientist** n.

**neurosis** /ˌnjʊəˈrəʊsɪs/ ● n. (pl. **neuroses** /-siːz/) Medicine a relatively mild mental illness not caused by organic disease, involving depression, anxiety, obsessive behaviour, etc. but not a radical loss of touch with reality.
– ORIGIN C18: mod. L., from **NEURO-** + **-OSIS**.

**neurosurgery** ● n. surgery performed on the nervous system.
– DERIVATIVES **neurosurgeon** n. **neurosurgical** adj.

**neurotic** ● adj. **1** Medicine having, caused by, or relating to neurosis. **2** abnormally sensitive and obsessive. ● n. a neurotic person.
– DERIVATIVES **neurotically** adv. **neuroticism** n.

**neurotomy** /ˌnjʊəˈrɒtəmi/ ● n. the surgical cutting of a nerve to produce relief of pain or to suppress involuntary movements.

**neurotoxin** /ˌnjʊərəʊˈtɒksɪn/ ● n. a poison which acts on the nervous system.
– DERIVATIVES **neurotoxic** adj. **neurotoxicity** n.

**neurotransmitter** ● n. Physiology a chemical substance released from a nerve fibre and effecting the transfer of an impulse to another nerve, muscle, etc.
– DERIVATIVES **neurotransmission** n.

**neurotrophic** /ˌnjʊərə(ʊ)ˈtrəʊfɪk, -ˈtrɒfɪk/ ● adj. Physiology of or relating to the growth of nervous tissue.

**neurotropic** /ˌnjʊərə(ʊ)ˈtrəʊpɪk, -ˈtrɒpɪk/ ● adj. Medicine tending to attack or affect the nervous system.
– DERIVATIVES **neurotropism** n.

**neuston** /ˈnjuːstɒn/ ● n. Biology the small organisms living in or on the surface of water.
– DERIVATIVES **neustonic** adj.
– ORIGIN C20: via Ger. from Gk, neut. of *neustos* 'swimming', on the pattern of *plankton*.

**neuter** ● adj. **1** of or denoting a gender of nouns typically contrasting with masculine and feminine or common. **2** (of an animal) lacking developed sexual organs; castrated or spayed. ➤(of a plant or flower) having neither functional pistils nor stamens. ● n. **1** Grammar a neuter word. **2** a non-fertile caste of social insect, especially a worker bee or ant. ➤a castrated or spayed domestic animal. ● v. **1** castrate or spay. **2** render ineffective.
– ORIGIN ME: via OFr. from L. *neuter* 'neither', from *ne-* 'not' + *uter* 'either'.

**neutral** ● adj. **1** impartial. ➤belonging to an impartial state or group. ➤unbiased. **2** having no strongly marked characteristics. **3** Chemistry neither acid nor alkaline; having a pH of about 7. **4** electrically neither positive nor negative. ● n. **1** an impartial or unbiased state or person. **2** a neutral colour or shade. **3** a disengaged position of gears. **4** an electrically neutral point, terminal, etc.
– DERIVATIVES **neutrality** n. **neutrally** adv.
– ORIGIN ME (as n.): from L. *neutralis* 'of neuter gender', from L. *neuter* (see **NEUTER**).

**neutralism** ● n. a policy of political neutrality.
– DERIVATIVES **neutralist** n.

**neutralize** (also **-ise**) ● v. **1** render ineffective by applying an opposite force or effect. **2** make chemically neutral. **3** disarm (a bomb). **4** euphemistic kill; destroy.
– DERIVATIVES **neutralization** n. **neutralizer** n.

**neutrino** /njuːˈtriːnəʊ/ ● n. (pl. **-os**) a neutral subatomic particle with a mass close to zero, rarely interacting with normal matter.
– ORIGIN C20: from Ital., dimin. of *neutro* 'neutral'.

**neutron** ● n. a subatomic particle of about the same mass as a proton but without an electric charge, present in all atomic nuclei except those of ordinary hydrogen.
– ORIGIN C20: from **NEUTRAL** + **-ON**.

**neutron bomb** ● n. a nuclear weapon that produces large numbers of neutrons, rather than heat or blast.

**neutron star** ● n. Astronomy a celestial object of great density composed predominantly of neutrons, believed to be formed by the gravitational collapse of a star.

**neutropenia** /ˌnjuːtrə(ʊ)ˈpiːniə/ ● n. Medicine the presence of abnormally few neutrophils in the blood, leading to increased susceptibility to infection.
– DERIVATIVES **neutropenic** adj.
– ORIGIN C20: from **NEUTRAL** + Gk *penia* 'poverty, lack'.

**neutrophil** /ˈnjuːtrə(ʊ)fɪl/ ● n. Physiology a neutrophilic white blood cell.

**neutrophilic** ● adj. Physiology (of a cell or its contents) stained only by neutral dyes.

**Nev.** ● abbrev. Nevada.

**Nevadan** /nɪˈvɑːd(ə)n/ ● n. a native or inhabitant of the US state of Nevada. ● adj. of or relating to Nevada.

**névé** /ˈnɛveɪ/ ● n. uncompressed granular snow, especially at the head of a glacier.
– ORIGIN C19: from Swiss Fr., lit. 'glacier'.

**never** ● adv. **1** not ever. **2** not at all. ➤Brit. informal definitely or surely not.
– PHRASES **never a one** not one. **well I never!** informal expressing great surprise.
– ORIGIN OE *nǣfre*, from *ne* 'not' + *ǣfre* 'ever'.

**nevermore** ● adv. poetic/literary never again.

**never-never** ● n. (**the never-never**) Brit. informal hire purchase.

**never-never land** ● n. an imaginary utopian place.
– ORIGIN often with allusion to the ideal country in J. M. Barrie's *Peter Pan*.

**nevertheless** ● adv. in spite of that.

**nevus** ● n. (pl. **nevi**) US spelling of **NAEVUS**.

**new** ● adj. **1** not existing before; made, introduced, or discovered recently or now for the first time. ➤not previously used or owned. **2** (of vegetables) harvested early in the season. **3** seen, experienced, or acquired recently or now for the first time. ➤(**new to**) unfamiliar or strange to. ➤(**new to/at**) inexperienced at or unaccustomed to. ➤(in place names) discovered or founded later than and named after. **4** reinvigorated, restored, or reformed. ➤superseding and more advanced than others of the same kind: *the new architecture*. ● adv. newly.
– DERIVATIVES **newish** adj. **newness** n.
– ORIGIN OE *nīwe*, *nēowe*, of Gmc origin.

**New Age** ● n. a broad movement characterized by alternative approaches to traditional Western culture, with an interest in spirituality, mysticism, holism, and environmentalism.
– DERIVATIVES **New Ager** n. **New Agey** adj.

**New Age music** ● n. a style of chiefly instrumental music characterized by light melodic harmonies and sounds reproduced from the natural world, intended to promote serenity.

**newbie** ● n. (pl. **-ies**) informal an inexperienced newcomer.

**newborn** ● adj. recently born. ➤regenerated. ● n. a newborn child or animal.

**Newcastle disease** ● n. an acute infectious viral fever affecting birds, especially poultry.
– ORIGIN 1920s: so named because it was first recorded near Newcastle upon Tyne in 1927.

**newcomer** ● n. **1** a person who has recently arrived. **2** a novice.

**newel** /ˈnjuːəl/ ● n. the central supporting pillar of a spiral or winding staircase. ➤(also **newel post**) the top or bottom supporting post of a stair rail.
– ORIGIN ME: from OFr. *nouel* 'knob', from med. L. *nodellus*, dimin. of L. *nodus* 'knot'.

**New Englander** • n. a native or inhabitant of New England, an area on the NE coast of the US.

**newfangled** • adj. derogatory newly developed and unfamiliar.
– ORIGIN ME: from *newfangle* (now dial.) 'liking what is new', from the adv. **NEW** + a second element rel. to an OE word meaning 'to take'.

**Newfoundland** /ˈnjuːf(ə)n(d)lənd, -land, njuːˈfaʊnd lənd/ • n. a dog of a very large breed with a thick coarse coat.

**Newfoundlander** /ˈnjuːfəndləndə, -landə, -ˈfaʊndləndə/ • n. a native or inhabitant of Newfoundland.

**New Guinean** • n. a native or inhabitant of New Guinea. • adj. of or relating to New Guinea.

**New Hampshirite** • n. a native or inhabitant of the US state of New Hampshire.

**newie** • n. (pl. **-ies**) informal, chiefly Brit. a new person or thing.

**New Jerseyan** • n. a native or inhabitant of the US state of New Jersey. • adj. of or relating to New Jersey.

**new-laid** • adj. (of an egg) freshly laid.

**New Look** • n. a style of women's clothing introduced in 1947, featuring calf-length full skirts.

**newly** • adv. **1** recently. **2** again. ➤ in a new or different manner.

**newly-wed** • n. a recently married person.

**new man** • n. a man who rejects sexist attitudes and the traditional male role.

**Newmarket** • n. a card game in which players put down cards in sequence, hoping to play cards on which bets have been placed.

**new maths** (N. Amer. **new math**) • pl. n. [treated as sing.] a system of teaching mathematics to children, with emphasis on investigation by them and on set theory.

**New Mexican** • n. a native or inhabitant of the US state of New Mexico. • adj. of or relating to New Mexico.

**new moon** • n. **1** the phase of the moon when it first appears as a slender crescent. **2** Astronomy the time at which the moon is in conjunction with the sun and not visible from the earth.

**news** • n. **1** newly received or noteworthy information, especially about recent events. **2** (**the news**) a broadcast or published news report. **3** (**news to**) informal information not previously known to.
– ORIGIN ME: pl. of **NEW**, translating OFr. *noveles* or med. L. *nova* 'new things'.

**news agency** • n. an organization that collects and distributes news items.

**newsagent** • n. Brit. a person or shop selling newspapers, magazines, etc.

**newsboy** • n. a boy who sells or delivers newspapers.

**newscast** • n. a broadcast news report.

**newscaster** • n. a newsreader.

**news conference** • n. a press conference.

**newsflash** • n. a single item of important news broadcast separately and often interrupting other programmes.

**newsgroup** • n. a group of Internet users who exchange email on a topic of mutual interest.

**news hound** • n. informal a newspaper reporter.

**newsie** • n. (pl. **-ies**) variant spelling of **NEWSY**.

**newsletter** • n. a bulletin issued periodically to those in a particular group.

**newsman** • n. (pl. **-men**) a male reporter or journalist.

**newspaper** • n. a printed publication, typically issued daily or weekly, consisting of folded unstapled sheets and containing news, articles, and advertisements.

**newspaperman** (or **newspaperwoman**) • n. (pl. **-men** (or **-women**)) a male (or female) newspaper journalist.

**newspeak** • n. ambiguous euphemistic language used chiefly in political propaganda.
– ORIGIN 1949: the name of an artificial official lang. in George Orwell's *Nineteen Eighty-Four*.

**newsprint** • n. cheap, low-quality absorbent printing paper, used chiefly for newspapers.

**newsreader** • n. Brit. a person who reads out broadcast news bulletins.

**newsreel** • n. a short cinema film of news and current affairs.

**newsroom** • n. the area in a newspaper or broadcasting office where news is processed.

**news-sheet** • n. a simple form of newspaper.

**news-stand** • n. a stand for the sale of newspapers.

**New Stone Age** • n. the Neolithic period.

**New Style** • n. the calculation of dates using the Gregorian calendar.

**newsvendor** • n. Brit. a newspaper seller.

**news wire** • n. an up-to-date Internet news service.

**newsworthy** • adj. noteworthy as news.
– DERIVATIVES **newsworthiness** n.

**newsy** informal • adj. (**-ier**, **-iest**) full of news. • n. (also **newsie**) (pl. **-ies**) **1** chiefly US a reporter. **2** chiefly US & Austral. a newsboy.

**newt** • n. a small slender-bodied amphibian with a well-developed tail. [*Triturus* and other genera.]
– ORIGIN ME: from *an ewt* (*ewt* from OE *efeta*: see **EFT**), interpreted (by wrong division) as *a newt*.

**New Testament** • n. the second part of the Christian Bible, recording the life and teachings of Christ and his earliest followers.

**newton** (abbrev.: **N**) • n. Physics the SI unit of force, equal to the force that would give a mass of one kilogram an acceleration of one metre per second per second.
– ORIGIN C20: named after Sir Isaac *Newton*.

**Newtonian** • adj. **1** Physics relating to or arising from the work of the English scientist Sir Isaac Newton (1642–1727). **2** Astronomy denoting a reflecting telescope with a secondary mirror set at 45° to deflect the light from the main mirror to the eyepiece.

**Newton's rings** • pl. n. Optics circular interference fringes seen around the point of contact of a convex lens and a plane surface.

**new town** • n. a planned urban centre created in an undeveloped or rural area.

**new wave** • n. **1** another term for **NOUVELLE VAGUE**. **2** a style of rock music popular in the late 1970s, deriving from punk.

**New World** • n. North and South America regarded collectively, in contrast to Europe, Asia, and Africa.

**new year** • n. the calendar year just begun or about to begin. ➤ the period immediately before and after 31 December.
– PHRASES **New Year's** informal, chiefly N. Amer. New Year's Eve or New Year's Day.

**New Year's Day** • n. 1 January.

**New Year's Eve** • n. 31 December.

**New Yorker** • n. a native or inhabitant of the state or city of New York.

**New Zealander** • n. a native or inhabitant of New Zealand.

**New Zealand flax** • n. another term for **FLAX-LILY**.

**next** • adj. **1** coming immediately after the time of writing or speaking. ➤ (of a day of the week) nearest (or the nearest but one) after the present. ➤ (of an event) occurring directly after the present one in time. **2** coming immediately after the present one in space, order, or rank. • adv. immediately afterwards. ➤ following in the specified order. • n. the next person or thing. • prep. archaic next to. • det. (**a next**) W. Indian another.
– PHRASES **next to 1** beside. **2** following in order or importance. **3** almost. **4** in comparison with. **the next world** (according to some religious beliefs) the place where one goes after death.
– ORIGIN OE *nēhsta* 'nearest', superlative of *nēah* 'nigh'.

**next door** • adv. & adj. (**next-door**) in or to the next house or room. • n. the building, room, or people next door.
– PHRASES **next door to 1** in the next house or room to. **2** almost.

**next of kin** • n. [treated as sing. or pl.] a person's closest living relative or relatives.

**nexus** /ˈnɛksəs/ • n. (pl. same or **nexuses**) **1** a connection. ➤ a connected group or series. **2** the central and

most important point.
– ORIGIN C17: from L., 'a binding together', from *nex-*, *nectere* 'bind'.

**Nez Percé** /nɛz 'pəːs, 'pɛːseɪ/ ● **n.** (pl. same or **Nez Percés**) **1** a member of an American Indian people of central Idaho. **2** the Penutian language of this people.
– ORIGIN Fr., lit. 'pierced nose'.

**NF** ● **abbrev. 1** National Front. **2** Newfoundland (in official postal use).

**NFL** ● **abbrev.** National Football League (the top professional league for American football in the US).

**Nfld** ● **abbrev.** Newfoundland.

**NFU** ● **abbrev.** (in the UK) National Farmers' Union.

**ngaio** /'nʌɪəʊ/ ● **n.** (pl. **-os**) a small New Zealand tree with edible fruit and light white wood. [*Myoporum laetum*.]
– ORIGIN C19: from Maori.

**Ngbandi** /(ə)ŋ'bandi/ ● **n.** a Bantu language of northern Zaire (Democratic Republic of Congo). ● **adj.** of or relating to this language.
– ORIGIN the name in Ngbandi.

**NGO** ● **abbrev.** non-governmental organization.

**Ngoni** /(ə)ŋ'gəʊni/ ● **n.** (pl. same or **Ngonis**) **1** a member of a people living chiefly in Malawi. **2** (**ngoni**) a kind of traditional African drum.
– ORIGIN a local name.

**ngultrum** /(ə)ŋ'gʊltrəm/ ● **n.** (pl. same) the basic monetary unit of Bhutan, equal to 100 chetrum.
– ORIGIN from Dzongkha.

**Nguni** /(ə)ŋ'guːni/ ● **n.** (pl. same) **1** a member of a group of Bantu-speaking peoples living mainly in southern Africa. **2** the Bantu languages spoken by these peoples.
– ORIGIN from Zulu.

**ngwee** /(ə)ŋ'gweɪ/ ● **n.** (pl. same) a monetary unit of Zambia, equal to one hundredth of a kwacha.
– ORIGIN a local word.

**NH** ● **abbrev.** New Hampshire (in official postal use).

**NHS** ● **abbrev.** (in the UK) National Health Service.

**NI** ● **abbrev. 1** (in the UK) National Insurance. **2** Northern Ireland. **3** NZ North Island.

**Ni** ● **symb.** the chemical element nickel.

**niacin** /'nʌɪəsɪn/ ● **n.** another term for **NICOTINIC ACID**.

**nib** ● **n. 1** the pointed end part of a pen, which distributes the ink. ➤a pointed or projecting part of an object. **2** (**nibs**) shelled and crushed coffee or cocoa beans.
– DERIVATIVES **nibbed** adj.
– ORIGIN C16 (in the sense 'beak, nose'): prob. from MDu. *nib* or Mid. Low Ger. *nibbe*, var. of *nebbe* (see **NEB**).

**nibble** ● **v. 1** take small bites out of. ➤eat in small amounts. ➤gently bite at. **2** gradually erode. **3** show cautious interest in a project. ● **n. 1** an instance of nibbling. **2** a small piece of food bitten off. ➤(**nibbles**) informal small savoury snacks.
– DERIVATIVES **nibbler** n.
– ORIGIN C15: prob. of Low Ger. or Du. origin.

**niblet** ● **n.** a small piece of food.
– ORIGIN C19: from **NIBBLE** + **-LET**.

**niblick** /'nɪblɪk/ ● **n.** Golf, dated an iron with a heavy, lofted head, used especially for playing out of bunkers.
– ORIGIN C19: of unknown origin.

**nibs** ● **n.** (**his nibs**) informal a mock title used to refer to a self-important man.
– ORIGIN C19: of unknown origin.

**NIC** ● **abbrev. 1** (in the UK) National Insurance contribution. **2** newly industrialized country. **3** Nicaragua (international vehicle registration).

**NiCad** /'nʌɪkad/ (also US trademark **Nicad**) ● **n.** a battery or cell with a nickel anode, a cadmium cathode, and a potassium hydroxide electrolyte.
– ORIGIN 1950s: blend of **NICKEL** and **CADMIUM**.

**Nicam** /'nʌɪkam/ (also **NICAM**) ● **n.** a digital system used in British television to provide video signals with high-quality stereo sound.
– ORIGIN 1980s: acronym from *near instantaneously companded* (i.e. compressed and expanded) *audio multiplex*.

**Nicaraguan** /ˌnɪkə'ragjʊən, -'ragwən/ ● **n.** a native or inhabitant of Nicaragua. ● **adj.** of or relating to Nicaragua.

**nice** ● **adj. 1** pleasant; agreeable; satisfactory. ➤(of a person) good-natured; kind. **2** fine or subtle. ➤requiring careful attention. **3** archaic fastidious.
– PHRASES **nice and** —— satisfactory in terms of the quality described. **nice one** informal expressing approval.
– DERIVATIVES **nicely** adv. **niceness** n.
– ORIGIN ME (orig. meaning 'stupid', also 'coy, reserved', hence 'fine, subtle'): from OFr., from L. *nescius* 'ignorant', from *nescire* 'not know'.

**Nicene Creed** /nʌɪ'siːn, 'nʌɪ-/ ● **n.** a formal statement of Christian belief, widely used in liturgies and based on that adopted at the first Council of Nicaea in 325.

**nicety** /'nʌɪsɪti/ ● **n.** (pl. **-ies**) (usu. **niceties**) a fine detail or distinction. ➤accuracy. ➤a detail of etiquette.
– PHRASES **to a nicety** precisely.
– ORIGIN ME (in the sense 'folly, foolish conduct'): from OFr. *nicete*, based on L. *nescius* (see **NICE**).

**niche** /niːʃ, nɪtʃ/ ● **n. 1** a shallow recess, especially one in a wall to display an ornament. **2** (**one's niche**) a comfortable or suitable position in life. **3** a specialized but profitable corner of the market. **4** Ecology a role taken by a type of organism within its community. ● **v.** place or position in a niche.
– ORIGIN C17: from Fr., lit. 'recess', from *nicher* 'make a nest', based on L. *nidus* 'nest'.

**Nichiren** /'nɪʃərən/ (also **Nichiren Buddhism**) ● **n.** a Japanese Buddhist sect founded by the religious teacher Nichiren (1222–82).

**nichrome** /'nʌɪkrəʊm/ ● **n.** trademark an alloy of nickel and chromium, used chiefly in electrical heating elements.
– ORIGIN C20: blend of **NICKEL** and **CHROME**.

**nick**[1] ● **n. 1** a small cut or notch. **2** (**the nick**) Brit. informal prison. ➤a police station. **3** the junction between the floor and side walls in a squash court. ● **v. 1** make a nick or nicks in. **2** Brit. informal steal. ➤(**nick someone for**) N. Amer. informal cheat someone of. **3** Brit. informal arrest.
– PHRASES **in —— nick** Brit. informal in a specified condition. **in the nick of time** only just in time.
– ORIGIN ME: of unknown origin.

**nick**[2] ● **v.** Austral./NZ informal go quickly or surreptitiously. ➤(**nick off**) depart; go away.
– ORIGIN C19: prob. a figurative use of **NICK**[1] in the sense 'to steal'.

**nickel** ● **n. 1** a silvery-white metal resembling iron, the chemical element of atomic number 28. (Symbol: **Ni**) **2** N. Amer. informal a five-cent coin. ● **v.** (**nickelled**, **nickelling**; US **nickeled**, **nickeling**) coat with nickel.
– ORIGIN C18: shortening of Ger. *Kupfernickel*, the copper-coloured ore from which nickel was first obtained, from *Kupfer* 'copper' + *Nickel* 'demon' (with ref. to the ore's failure to yield copper).

**nickel-and-dime** N. Amer. ● **v.** spend or charge small amounts of money. ● **adj.** unimportant.
– ORIGIN 1970s: orig. denoting a store selling articles at five or ten cents.

**nickel brass** ● **n.** an alloy of copper, zinc, and nickel.

**nickelodeon** /ˌnɪkə'ləʊdɪən/ ● **n.** N. Amer. **1** informal, dated a jukebox, originally one operated by the insertion of a nickel. **2** historical a cinema charging one nickel.
– ORIGIN C20: from **NICKEL** (the coin) + a shortened form of **MELODEON**.

**nickel silver** ● **n.** another term for **GERMAN SILVER**.

**nickel steel** ● **n.** stainless steel containing chromium and nickel.

**nicker**[1] ● **n.** (pl. same) Brit. informal a pound sterling.
– ORIGIN C20: of unknown origin.

**nicker**[2] ● **v.** (of a horse) give a soft breathy whinny. ● **n.** a nickering sound.
– ORIGIN C16: imitative.

**nick-nack** ● **n.** variant spelling of **KNICK-KNACK**.

**nickname** ● **n.** a familiar or humorous name for a person or thing. ● **v.** give a nickname to.
– ORIGIN ME: from *an eke-name* (*eke* meaning 'addition': see **EKE**[2]), misinterpreted (by wrong division) as *a neke name*.

**Niçois** /niː'swɑː/ ● **n.** (fem. **Niçoise** /niː'swɑːz/) a native or inhabitant of the French city of Nice. ● **adj.** of, relating to, or characteristic of Nice or its inhabitants. ➤[postpos.] denoting food garnished with tomatoes, capers, and anchovies: *salade Niçoise.*

**Nicol prism** /ˈnɪk(ə)l/ ● **n.** a prism for producing plane-polarized light, consisting of two pieces of optically clear calcite cemented together with Canada balsam.
– ORIGIN C19: named after the Sc. physicist William *Nicol.*

**nicotiana** /ˌnɪkɒtɪˈɑːnə, -kəʊʃ-/ ● **n.** an ornamental plant related to tobacco, with tubular flowers that are particularly fragrant at night. [*Nicotiana alata* and other species.]
– ORIGIN from mod. L. *nicotiana* (*herba*) 'tobacco (plant)', named after Jaques *Nicot,* a C16 diplomat who introduced tobacco to France.

**nicotinamide** /ˌnɪkəˈtɪnəmʌɪd/ ● **n.** Biochemistry the amide of nicotinic acid, found widely in living cells.

**nicotinamide adenine dinucleotide** ● **n.** see **NAD**.

**nicotine** ● **n.** a toxic oily liquid which is the chief active constituent of tobacco.
– ORIGIN C19: from Fr., from **NICOTIANA** + **-INE**[4].

**nicotine patch** ● **n.** a patch impregnated with nicotine, worn on the skin by a person trying to reduce their craving for cigarettes.

**nicotinic acid** ● **n.** Biochemistry a vitamin of the B complex which occurs in milk, wheat germ, meat, and other foods and is involved in many metabolic processes.
– DERIVATIVES **nicotinate** n.

**nictation** ● **n.** technical blinking.
– ORIGIN C18: from L. *nictatio(n-),* from *nictare* 'to blink'.

**nictitating membrane** ● **n.** Zoology a whitish membrane forming an inner eyelid in birds, reptiles, and some mammals.
– ORIGIN C18: *nictitating* based on med. L. *nictitat-* 'blinked', frequentative of *nictare.*

**nidation** /nʌɪˈdeɪʃ(ə)n/ ● **n.** Medicine & Zoology implantation of a fertilized egg.
– ORIGIN C19: from L. *nidus* 'nest' + **-ATION**.

**nide** /nʌɪd/ ● **n.** archaic a brood or nest of pheasants.
– ORIGIN C17: from Fr. *nid* or L. *nidus* 'nest'.

**nidicolous** /nɪˈdɪk(ə)ləs/ ● **adj.** another term for **ALTRICIAL**.
– ORIGIN C20: from L. *nidus* 'nest' + *-colus* 'inhabiting' (from *colere* 'live in, cultivate').

**nidification** /ˌnɪdɪfɪˈkeɪʃ(ə)n/ ● **n.** Zoology nest-building.
– ORIGIN C17: from L. *nidificat-, nidificare* 'make into a nest', from *nidus* 'nest' + **-ATION**.

**nidifugous** /nɪˈdɪfjʊgəs/ ● **adj.** another term for **PRECOCIAL**.
– ORIGIN C20: from L. *nidus* 'nest' + *fugere* 'flee' + **-OUS**.

**nidus** /ˈnʌɪdəs/ ● **n.** (pl. **nidi** /-dʌɪ/ or **niduses**) **1** a place in which something is formed or deposited; a site of origin. **2** Medicine a place in which bacteria have multiplied or may multiply; a focus of infection.
– ORIGIN C18: from L., lit. 'nest'.

**niece** ● **n.** a daughter of one's brother or sister, or of one's brother-in-law or sister-in-law.
– ORIGIN ME: from OFr., based on L. *neptis* 'granddaughter', fem. of *nepos* (see **NEPHEW**).

**niello** /nɪˈɛləʊ/ ● **n.** a black compound of sulphur with silver, lead, or copper, used for filling in engraved designs in silver or other metals. ➤objects decorated with this.
– DERIVATIVES **nielloed** adj.
– ORIGIN C19: from Ital., from L. *nigellus,* dimin. of *niger* 'black'.

**niente** /nɪˈɛnteɪ/ ● **adv. & adj.** Music with the sound or tone gradually fading to nothing.
– ORIGIN Ital., lit. 'nothing'.

**Niersteiner** /ˈnɪəˌʃtʌɪnə, German ˈniːɐˌʃtaɪnɐ/ ● **n.** a white Rhine wine produced around Nierstein, a town in Germany.

**Nietzschean** /ˈniːtʃɪən/ ● **n.** a follower of the German philosopher Friedrich Wilhelm Nietzsche (1844–1900), especially a supporter of his theories of the superman able to rise above the restrictive morality of ordinary men. ● **adj.** of, relating to, or characteristic of Nietzsche or his views.
– DERIVATIVES **Nietzscheanism** n.

**niff** Brit. informal ● **n.** an unpleasant smell. ● **v.** stink.
– DERIVATIVES **niffy** adj. (**-ier, -iest**).
– ORIGIN C20 (orig. dial.): perh. from **SNIFF**.

**nifty** ● **adj.** (**-ier, -iest**) informal particularly good, skilful, or effective. ➤stylish.
– DERIVATIVES **niftily** adv. **niftiness** n.
– ORIGIN C19: of unknown origin.

**nigella** /nʌɪˈdʒɛlə/ ● **n.** a plant of a genus which includes love-in-a-mist. [Genus *Nigella.*]
– ORIGIN mod. L., fem. of L. *nigellus,* dimin. of *niger* 'black'.

**Niger–Congo** ● **adj.** denoting or belonging to a large phylum of languages in Africa, named after the Rivers Niger and Congo and comprising the Bantu, Mande, Gur, and Kwa families.

**Nigerian** /nʌɪˈdʒɪərɪən/ ● **n.** a native or inhabitant of Nigeria. ● **adj.** of or relating to Nigeria.

**niggard** /ˈnɪgəd/ ● **n.** a mean or stingy person. ● **adj.** archaic niggardly.
– ORIGIN ME: alt. of earlier *nigon.*

**niggardly** ● **adj.** ungenerous. ➤meagre. ● **adv.** archaic in a mean or meagre manner.
– DERIVATIVES **niggardliness** n.

**nigger** ● **n.** offensive a black person.
– ORIGIN C17 (as adj.): from earlier *neger,* from Fr. *nègre,* from Sp. *negro* (see **NEGRO**).

**niggle** ● **v. 1** cause slight but persistent annoyance, discomfort, or anxiety. **2** find fault with in a petty way. ● **n.** a trifling worry, dispute, or criticism.
– DERIVATIVES **niggling** adj. **nigglingly** adv. **niggly** adj.
– ORIGIN C17: appar. of Scand. origin.

**nigh** ● **adv., prep., & adj.** archaic near. ➤almost.
– ORIGIN OE *nēh, nēah,* of Gmc origin; cf. **NEAR**.

**night** ● **n. 1** the time from sunset to sunrise. ➤this as the interval between two days. **2** the darkness of night. ➤poetic/literary nightfall. **3** an evening. ● **adv.** (**nights**) informal at night. ● **exclam.** informal short for **GOODNIGHT**.
– DERIVATIVES **nightless** adj.
– ORIGIN OE *neaht, niht,* of Gmc origin.

**nightbird** ● **n.** another term for **NIGHT OWL**.

**night blindness** ● **n.** less technical term for **NYCTALOPIA**.

**nightcap** ● **n. 1** historical a cap worn in bed. **2** a hot or alcoholic drink taken at bedtime.

**nightclothes** ● **pl. n.** clothes worn in bed.

**nightclub** ● **n.** a club that is open at night, typically having a bar and disco or other entertainment.
– DERIVATIVES **nightclubber** n. **nightclubbing** n.

**night crawler** ● **n.** chiefly N. Amer. an earthworm that comes to the surface at night, often used as fishing bait.

**nightdress** ● **n.** a light, loose garment worn by a woman or girl in bed.

**nightfall** ● **n.** dusk.

**nightgown** ● **n. 1** a nightdress. **2** archaic a dressing gown.

**nighthawk** ● **n. 1** an American nightjar with pointed wings. [*Chordeiles minor* and other species.] **2** North American term for **NIGHT OWL**.

**night heron** ● **n.** a small short-necked heron that is active mainly at night. [Genus *Nycticorax*: several species.]

**nightie** ● **n.** informal a nightdress.

**nightingale** ● **n.** a small migratory thrush with drab brownish plumage, noted for its rich melodious song which can often be heard at night. [*Luscinia megarhynchos,* family Turdidae.]
– ORIGIN OE *nihtegala,* of Gmc origin, from the base of **NIGHT** and a base meaning 'sing'.

**nightjar** ● **n.** a nocturnal insectivorous bird with grey-brown camouflaged plumage, large eyes and gape, and a distinctive call. [*Caprimulgus europaeus* and other species, family Caprimulgidae.]

**nightlife** ● **n.** social activities or entertainment available at night.

**night light** ● **n.** a lamp or candle providing a dim light during the night.

**nightly** ● adj. **1** happening or done every night. **2** happening, done, or existing in the night. ● adv. every night.

**nightmare** ● n. **1** a frightening or unpleasant dream. **2** a very unpleasant experience or prospect.
– DERIVATIVES **nightmarish** adj. **nightmarishly** adv.
– ORIGIN ME (denoting a female evil spirit thought to lie upon and suffocate sleepers): from **NIGHT** + OE *mære* 'incubus'.

**night owl** ● n. informal a person who is habitually active or wakeful at night.

**night safe** ● n. Brit. a safe with access from the outer wall of a bank, used for deposits when the bank is closed.

**night school** ● n. an institution providing evening classes.

**nightshade** ● n. used in the names of a group of poisonous or narcotic plants, e.g. **deadly nightshade**.
– ORIGIN OE *nihtscada*, appar. from **NIGHT** + **SHADE**, prob. with ref. to dark and poisonous berries.

**nightshirt** ● n. a long shirt worn in bed, especially by boys or men.

**nightside** ● n. Astronomy the side of a planet or moon facing away from the sun and therefore in darkness.

**night soil** ● n. human excrement collected at night from cesspools and privies, sometimes used as manure.

**nightspot** ● n. informal a nightclub.

**nightstick** ● n. N. Amer. a police officer's truncheon.

**night table** (also **nightstand**) ● n. N. Amer. a small low bedside table.

**night-time** ● n. the time between evening and morning.

**nightwatchman** ● n. (pl. **-men**) **1** a person who guards a building at night. **2** Cricket an inferior batsman sent in to bat near the end of a day's play.

**nightwear** ● n. clothing worn in bed.

**nigrescent** /nɪ'grɛs(ə)nt, nʌɪ-/ ● adj. rare blackish.
– DERIVATIVES **nigrescence** n.
– ORIGIN C18: from L. *nigrescent-*, *nigrescere* 'grow black', from *niger*, *nigr-* 'black'.

**nigritude** /'nɪgrɪtjuːd/ ● n. rare blackness.
– ORIGIN C17: from L. *nigritudo* 'blackness', from *niger*, *nigr-* 'black'.

**nihilism** /'nʌɪ(h)ɪlɪz(ə)m/ ● n. **1** the rejection of all religious and moral principles, often in the belief that life is meaningless. **2** Philosophy extreme scepticism, maintaining that nothing has a real existence.
– DERIVATIVES **nihilist** n. **nihilistic** adj.
– ORIGIN C19: from L. *nihil* 'nothing' + **-ISM**.

**nihility** /nʌɪ'hɪlɪti, nɪ-/ ● n. rare nothingness.
– ORIGIN C17: from med. L. *nihilitas*, from L. *nihil* 'nothing'.

**nihil obstat** /ˌnʌɪhɪl 'ɒbstat, ˌnɪhɪl/ ● n. (in the Roman Catholic Church) a certificate affirming that a book is not open to objection on doctrinal or moral grounds.
– ORIGIN L., lit. 'nothing hinders'.

**-nik** ● suffix (forming nouns) denoting a person associated with a specified thing or quality: *beatnik*.
– ORIGIN from Russ. (on the pattern of *sputnik*) and Yiddish.

**Nikkei index** /'nɪkeɪ/ (also **Nikkei average**) ● n. a figure indicating the relative price of representative shares on the Tokyo Stock Exchange.
– ORIGIN 1970s: *Nikkei*, abbrev. of *Ni(hon) Kei(zai Shimbun)* 'Japanese Economic Journal'.

**nil** ● n. nothing; zero. ● adj. non-existent.
– ORIGIN C19: from L., contr. of *nihil* 'nothing'.

**nil desperandum** /ˌdɛspə'randəm/ ● exclam. do not despair; never despair.
– ORIGIN from L. *nil desperandum Teucro duce* 'no need to despair with Teucer as your leader', from Horace's *Odes* 1.vii.27.

**Nile green** (or **Nile blue**) ● n. a pale bluish green.
– ORIGIN C19: suggested by Fr. *eau de Nil* (see **EAU DE NIL**.)

**Nile perch** ● n. a large predatory fish found in lakes and rivers in NE and central Africa, widely caught for food. [*Lates niloticus*.]

**nilgai** /'nɪlgʌɪ/ ● n. a large Indian antelope, the male of which has a blue-grey coat and short horns. [*Boselaphus tragocamelus*.]
– ORIGIN C18: from Hindi *nīlgāī*, from *nīl* 'blue' + *gāī* 'cow'.

**Nilo-Saharan** /ˌnʌɪləʊsə'hɑːrən/ ● adj. denoting or belonging to a phylum of languages including the Nilotic family and other languages of northern and eastern Africa.

**Nilotic** /nʌɪ'lɒtɪk/ ● adj. **1** of or relating to the River Nile or to the Nile region of Africa. **2** denoting or belonging to a family of languages spoken in Egypt, Sudan, Kenya, and Tanzania.
– ORIGIN via L. from Gk *Neilōtikos*, from *Neilos* 'Nile'.

**nilpotent** /nɪl'pəʊt(ə)nt/ ● adj. Mathematics becoming zero when raised to some positive integral power.
– ORIGIN C19: from **NIL** + L. *potens*, *potent-* 'power'.

**nim** ● n. a game in which two players alternately take one or more objects from one of a number of heaps, each trying to take, or to compel the other to take, the last remaining object.
– ORIGIN C20: appar. from archaic *nim* 'to take' or from Ger. *nimm!* 'take!', imper. of *nehmen*.

**nimble** ● adj. (**-er**, **-est**) quick and light in movement or action.
– DERIVATIVES **nimbleness** n. **nimbly** adv.
– ORIGIN OE *nǣmel* 'quick to seize or comprehend', rel. to *niman* 'take', of Gmc origin; the *-b-* was added for ease of pronunc.

**nimbostratus** /ˌnɪmbə(ʊ)'strɑːtəs, -'streɪtəs/ ● n. cloud forming a low thick grey layer, from which rain or snow often falls.
– ORIGIN C19: mod. L., from **NIMBUS** + **STRATUS**.

**nimbus** /'nɪmbəs/ ● n. (pl. **nimbi** /-bʌɪ/ or **nimbuses**) **1** a large grey rain cloud. **2** a luminous cloud or a halo surrounding a supernatural being or saint.
– ORIGIN C17: from L., lit. 'cloud, aureole'.

**Nimby** /'nɪmbi/ ● n. (pl. **Nimbys**) a person who objects to the siting of unpleasant developments in their neighbourhood.
– ORIGIN 1980s: acronym from *not in my back yard*.

**niminy-piminy** ● adj. affectedly prim or refined.
– ORIGIN C18: fanciful coinage; cf. **NAMBY-PAMBY**.

**nimrod** /'nɪmrɒd/ ● n. a skilful hunter.
– ORIGIN C16: from Heb. *Nimrōd*, the name of the great-grandson of Noah, known for his skill as a hunter (see Gen. 10:8-9).

**nincompoop** /'nɪŋkəmpuːp/ ● n. a stupid person.
– ORIGIN C17: perh. from the given name *Nicholas* or from *Nicodemus* (by assoc. with the Pharisee of this name, and his naive questioning of Christ).

**nine** ● cardinal number **1** equivalent to the product of three and three; one less than ten; 9. (Roman numeral: **ix** or **IX**.) **2** (**the Nine**) Greek Mythology the nine Muses.
– PHRASES **dressed to** (or Brit. **up to**) **the nines** dressed very smartly or fancily.
– DERIVATIVES **ninefold** adj. & adv.
– ORIGIN OE *nigon*, of Gmc origin.

**ninepins** ● pl. n. [usu. treated as sing.] the traditional form of the game of skittles, using nine pins.
– PHRASES **go down** (or **drop** or **fall**) **like ninepins** succumb in large numbers.

**nineteen** ● cardinal number one more than eighteen; nine more than ten; 19. (Roman numeral: **xix** or **XIX**.)
– DERIVATIVES **nineteenth** ordinal number.
– ORIGIN OE *nigontȳne* (see **NINE**, **-TEEN**).

**nineteenth hole** ● n. informal, humorous the bar in a golf clubhouse, as reached after a round of eighteen holes.

**nine-to-five** ● adj. of or involving typical office hours. ● n. a nine-to-five job.
– DERIVATIVES **nine-to-fiver** n.

**ninety** ● cardinal number (pl. **-ies**) equivalent to the product of nine and ten; ten less than one hundred; 90. (Roman numeral: **xc** or **XC**.)
– DERIVATIVES **ninetieth** ordinal number. **ninetyfold** adj. & adv.
– ORIGIN OE *nigontig* (see **NINE**, **-TY**[2]).

**ning-nong** ● n. Austral./NZ informal a fool.
– ORIGIN C19: of unknown origin.

**ninja** /'nɪndʒə/ ● n. a person skilled in ninjutsu.
– ORIGIN Japanese, lit. 'spy'.

**ninjutsu** /nɪn'dʒʌtsuː/ ● **n.** the traditional Japanese technique of espionage, characterized by stealth and camouflage.
– ORIGIN Japanese, from *nin* 'stealth' + *jutsu* 'art, science'.

**ninny** ● **n.** (pl. **-ies**) informal a foolish and weak person.
– ORIGIN C16: perh. from **INNOCENT**.

**ninon** /'niːnɒn/ ● **n.** a lightweight silk dress fabric.
– ORIGIN C20: from Fr.

**ninth** ● **ordinal number 1** constituting number nine in a sequence; 9th. **2** (**a ninth/one ninth**) each of nine equal parts into which something is or may be divided. **3** Music an interval spanning nine consecutive notes in a diatonic scale. ➤the note which is higher by this interval than the tonic of a diatonic scale or root of a chord. ➤a chord in which the ninth note of the scale forms an important component.
– DERIVATIVES **ninthly** adv.

**niobium** /nʌɪ'əʊbɪəm/ ● **n.** the chemical element of atomic number 41, a silver-grey metal used in superconducting alloys. (Symbol: **Nb**)
– ORIGIN C19: mod. L., from *Niobe*, daughter of Tantalus in Gk mythology (because the element was first found in **TANTALITE**).

**Nip** ● **n.** informal, offensive a Japanese person.
– ORIGIN C20: abbrev. of *Nipponese*, from *Nippon* (the Japanese name for Japan).

**nip**[1] ● **v.** (**nipped**, **nipping**) **1** pinch, squeeze, or bite sharply. ➤(**nip something off**) remove something by pinching or squeezing sharply. **2** (of the cold or frost) cause pain or harm to. **3** Brit. informal go quickly. **4** US informal steal or snatch. ● **n. 1** an act of nipping. **2** a feeling of biting cold.
– PHRASES **nip something in the bud** suppress or destroy something at an early stage.
– ORIGIN ME: prob. of Low Ger. or Du. origin.

**nip**[2] ● **n.** a small quantity or sip of spirits. ● **v.** (**nipped**, **nipping**) take a sip of spirits.
– ORIGIN C18: prob. an abbrev. of the rare term *nipperkin* 'small measure'.

**nipa** /'niːpə, 'nʌɪpə/ ● **n.** a palm tree with creeping roots, characteristic of mangrove swamps in India and the Pacific islands. [*Nypa fruticans*.]
– ORIGIN C16: via Sp. or Port. from Malay *nīpah*.

**nip and tuck** ● **adv. & adj.** neck and neck. ● **n.** informal a cosmetic surgical operation.

**nipper** ● **n. 1** informal a child. **2** (**nippers**) pliers, pincers, or a similar tool. **3** a creature that nips. ➤the claw of a crab or lobster. **4** Austral. a burrowing marine prawn used as fishing bait.

**nipple** ● **n. 1** the small projection in which the mammary ducts of female mammals terminate and from which milk can be secreted. ➤the corresponding vestigial structure in a male. ➤N. Amer. the teat of a feeding bottle. **2** a small projection on a machine, especially one from which oil or other fluid is dispensed. ➤a short section of pipe with a screw thread at each end for coupling. ● **v.** provide with a projection like a nipple.
– ORIGIN C16 (also as *neble*, *nible*): perh. a dimin. of **NEB**.

**nipplewort** /'nɪp(ə)lwəːt/ ● **n.** a yellow-flowered plant of the daisy family, found in woods and on wasteland. [*Lapsana communis*.]

**nippy** ● **adj.** (**-ier**, **-iest**) informal **1** quick; nimble. **2** chilly.
– DERIVATIVES **nippily** adv.

**NIREX** /'nʌɪrɛks/ ● **abbrev.** (in the UK) Nuclear Industry Radioactive Waste Executive.

**nirvana** /nɪə'vɑːnə/ ● **n.** Buddhism a transcendent state in which there is no suffering or desire, and no sense of self. ➤a state of perfect happiness.
– ORIGIN from Sanskrit *nirvāṇa*, from *nirvā* 'be extinguished', from *nis* 'out' + *vā-* 'to blow'.

**Nisan** /'nɪs(ə)n, 'niːsɑːn/ ● **n.** (in the Jewish calendar) the seventh month of the civil and first of the religious year, usually coinciding with parts of March and April.
– ORIGIN from Heb. *nīsān*.

**nisei** /'niːseɪ, niː'seɪ/ ● **n.** (pl. same or **niseis**) N. Amer. an American or Canadian whose parents immigrated from Japan. Compare with **ISSEI** and **SANSEI**.
– ORIGIN 1940s: from Japanese, lit. 'second generation'.

**nisi** /'nʌɪsʌɪ/ ● **adj.** [postpos.] Law (of a decree, order, or rule) valid or taking effect only after certain conditions are met.
– ORIGIN C19: from L., lit. 'unless'.

**Nissen hut** /'nɪs(ə)n/ ● **n.** chiefly Brit. a tunnel-shaped hut of corrugated iron with a cement floor.
– ORIGIN C20: after the Brit. engineer Peter N. *Nissen*.

**nit**[1] ● **n.** informal **1** the egg or young form of a louse or other parasitic insect, especially the egg of a human head louse. **2** Brit. a stupid person.
– DERIVATIVES **nitty** adj.
– ORIGIN OE *hnitu*, of W. Gmc origin.

**nit**[2] ● **exclam.** Austral. informal used as a warning that someone is approaching.
– PHRASES **keep nit** keep watch.
– ORIGIN C19: prob. from **NIX**.

**niter** ● **n.** US spelling of **NITRE**.

**niterie** /'nʌɪtəri/ ● **n.** (pl. **-ies**) informal a nightclub.

**nitinol** /'nɪtɪnɒl/ ● **n.** an alloy of nickel and titanium.
– ORIGIN 1960s: from the chemical symbols **Ni** and **Ti** + the initial letters of *Naval Ordnance Laboratory* (in Maryland, US).

**nit-picking** ● **n.** informal fussy or pedantic fault-finding.
– DERIVATIVES **nit-pick** v. **nit-picker** n.

**nitrate** Chemistry ● **n.** /'nʌɪtreɪt/ a salt or ester of nitric acid. ● **v.** /nʌɪ'treɪt/ treat with nitric acid, especially so as to introduce the group $-NO_2$.
– DERIVATIVES **nitration** n.
– ORIGIN C18: from Fr. (see **NITRE**, **-ATE**[1]).

**nitrazepam** /nʌɪ'treɪzɪpam, -'trazə-/ ● **n.** Medicine a short-acting drug used to treat insomnia.
– ORIGIN 1960s: from *nitr(o)* + *az(o-)* + *ep(ine)* + *am(ide)*.

**nitre** /'nʌɪtə/ (US **niter**) ● **n.** potassium nitrate; saltpetre.
– ORIGIN ME: from OFr., from L. *nitrum*, from Gk *nitron*.

**nitric acid** ● **n.** Chemistry a colourless or pale yellow acid with strong corrosive and oxidizing properties. [$HNO_3$.]

**nitric oxide** ● **n.** Chemistry a colourless toxic gas made by reduction of nitric acid, reacting immediately with oxygen to form nitrogen dioxide. [NO.]

**nitride** /'nʌɪtrʌɪd/ ● **n.** Chemistry a compound of nitrogen with another element or group.

**nitrify** /'nʌɪtrɪfʌɪ/ ● **v.** (**-ies**, **-ied**) Chemistry convert (ammonia or another nitrogen compound) into nitrites or nitrates.
– DERIVATIVES **nitrification** n.
– ORIGIN C19: from Fr. *nitrifier*.

**nitrile** /'nʌɪtrʌɪl/ ● **n.** Chemistry an organic compound containing a cyanide group −CN bound to an alkyl group.
– ORIGIN C19: from **NITRE** + *-ile* (alt. of **-YL**).

**nitrite** /'nʌɪtrʌɪt/ ● **n.** Chemistry a salt or ester of nitrous acid.

**nitro** ● **n.** short for **NITROGLYCERINE**.

**nitro-** /'nʌɪtrəʊ/ ● **comb. form 1** of or containing nitric acid, nitrates, or nitrogen: *nitrogenous*. **2** Chemistry containing the group $-NO_2$: *nitrobenzene*.

**nitrobenzene** ● **n.** Chemistry a yellow oily liquid made by nitrating benzene, used in chemical synthesis.

**nitrocellulose** ● **n.** Chemistry a highly flammable material made by treating cellulose with concentrated nitric acid, used to make explosives and celluloid.

**nitrochalk** ● **n.** a mixture of chalk and ammonium nitrate, used as fertilizer.

**nitrogen** /'nʌɪtrədʒ(ə)n/ ● **n.** the chemical element of atomic number 7, a colourless, odourless unreactive gas that forms about 78 per cent of the earth's atmosphere. (Symbol: **N**)
– DERIVATIVES **nitrogenous** adj.
– ORIGIN C18: from Fr. *nitrogène* (see **NITRO-**, **-GEN**).

**nitrogen cycle** ● **n.** Ecology the series of processes by which nitrogen and its compounds are interconverted in the environment and in living organisms.

**nitrogen dioxide** ● **n.** Chemistry a reddish-brown poisonous gas formed when many metals dissolve in nitric acid. [$NO_2$.]

**nitrogen fixation** ● **n.** Biology the chemical processes by which atmospheric nitrogen is assimilated into organic compounds, especially by certain micro-organisms as part of the nitrogen cycle.

**nitrogen narcosis** • **n.** Medicine a drowsy state induced by breathing air under pressure, e.g. in deep-sea diving.

**nitroglycerine** (also **nitroglycerin**) • **n.** an explosive yellow liquid made by nitrating glycerol, used in dynamite.

**nitrosamine** /nʌɪˈtrəʊsəmiːn/ • **n.** Chemistry a compound containing the group =NNO attached to two organic groups.
– ORIGIN C19: from *nitroso-* (relating to nitric oxide in combination) + **AMINE**.

**nitrous** /ˈnʌɪtrəs/ • **adj.** of or containing nitrogen.
– ORIGIN C17: from L. *nitrosus* 'nitrous'.

**nitrous acid** • **n.** Chemistry an unstable, weak acid made by the action of acids on nitrites. [$HNO_2$.]

**nitrous oxide** • **n.** Chemistry a colourless gas with a sweetish odour which produces exhilaration or anaesthesia when inhaled and is used as an anaesthetic. [$N_2O$.]

**nitty-gritty** • **n.** informal the most important aspects or practical details of a matter.
– ORIGIN 1960s: of unknown origin.

**nitwit** • **n.** informal a silly or foolish person.
– DERIVATIVES **nitwitted** adj. **nitwittedness** n. **nitwittery** n.
– ORIGIN C20: appar. from **NIT**[1] + **WIT**[1].

**NIV** • **abbrev.** New International Version (of the Bible)

**nival** /ˈnʌɪv(ə)l/ • **adj.** of or relating to regions of perpetual snow.
– ORIGIN C17: from L. *nivalis*, from *nix, niv-* 'snow'.

**nivation** /nʌɪˈveɪʃ(ə)n/ • **n.** Geography erosion beneath or beside a snow bank, mainly as a result of alternate freezing and thawing.
– ORIGIN C20: from L. *nix, niv-* 'snow' + **-ATION**.

**niveous** /ˈnɪvɪəs/ • **adj.** poetic/literary snowy; like snow.
– ORIGIN C17: from L. *niveus* (from *nix, niv-* 'snow') + **-OUS**.

**nix** informal • **pron.** nothing. • **exclam. 1** expressing denial or refusal. **2** Brit. dated used as a warning that a person in authority is approaching. [perh. from the obs. phr. *keep nix* 'to watch, guard'.] • **v.** put an end to; cancel: *he nixed the deal.*
– ORIGIN C18: from Ger., colloq. var. of *nichts* 'nothing'.

**nixie** • **n.** a female water sprite.
– ORIGIN C19: from Ger.; rel. to the archaic Engl. word *nicker*, denoting a water demon.

**Nizam** /nɪˈzɑːm/ • **n.** historical **1** the title of the hereditary ruler of Hyderabad. [abbrev. of Urdu *nizām-al-mulk* 'administrator of the realm'.] **2** (**the nizam**) the Turkish regular army. [abbrev. of Turk. *nizām askeri* 'regular soldier'.]

**Nizari** /nɪˈzɑːri/ • **n.** a member of an Ismaili Muslim sect led by the Aga Khan.
– ORIGIN named after the C12 Egyptian Ismaili imam *Nizar*.

**NJ** • **abbrev.** New Jersey (in official postal use).

**NL** • **abbrev.** the Netherlands (international vehicle registration).

**NLP** • **abbrev. 1** natural language processing. **2** neurolinguistic programming.

**NM** • **abbrev.** New Mexico (in official postal use).

**nm** • **abbrev. 1** nanometre. **2** (also **n.m.**) nautical mile.

**NMR** • **abbrev.** Physics nuclear magnetic resonance.

**NNE** • **abbrev.** north-north-east.

**NNP** • **abbrev.** net national product.

**NNW** • **abbrev.** north-north-west.

**No**[1] • **symb.** the chemical element nobelium.

**No**[2] • **n.** variant spelling of **NOH**.

**No.** • **abbrev. 1** US North. **2** (also **no.**) number. [from L. *numero*, ablative of *numerus*.]

**no** • **det. 1** not any. **2** quite the opposite of: *it was no easy task.* **3** hardly any. • **exclam.** used to give a negative response. • **adv. 1** [with comparative] not at all: *they were no more able to do it than I was.* **2** Scottish not. • **n.** (pl. **noes**) a negative answer or decision, especially in voting.
– PHRASES **no can do** informal I am unable to do it. **no longer** not now as formerly. **no place** N. Amer. nowhere. **no through road** an indication that passage along a street is blocked or prohibited. **not take no for an answer** persist in spite of refusals. **no two ways about it** no possible doubt about something. **no way** informal under no circumstances; not at all. **no worries** informal, chiefly Austral. all right; fine. **or no** or not.
– ORIGIN OE *nō, nā* (adv.), from *ne* 'not' + *ō, ā* 'ever'.

**n.o.** • **abbrev.** Cricket not out.

**no-account** • **adj.** informal, chiefly N. Amer. unimportant or worthless.

**Noachian** /nəʊˈeɪkɪən/ • **adj.** of or relating to the biblical patriarch Noah or his time.

**noah** • **n.** Austral. informal a shark.
– ORIGIN 1940s: from rhyming sl. *Noah's ark*.

**nob**[1] • **n.** Brit. informal a person of wealth or high social position.
– DERIVATIVES **nobby** adj.
– ORIGIN C17 (orig. Scots as *knab*): of unknown origin.

**nob**[2] • **n.** informal a person's head.
– ORIGIN C17: appar. a var. of **KNOB**.

**no-ball** Cricket • **n.** an unlawfully delivered ball, counting as an extra run to the batting side if not scored from. • **v.** (of an umpire) declare (a bowler) to have bowled a no-ball.

**nobble** • **v.** Brit. informal **1** try to influence or thwart by underhand or unfair methods. ➤tamper with (a racehorse) to prevent it from winning a race. **2** accost (someone). **3** obtain dishonestly; steal. ➤seize.
– ORIGIN C19: prob. a var. of dial. *knobble, knubble* 'knock, strike with the knuckles'.

**nobbler** • **n.** informal **1** Brit. a person who nobbles someone or something. **2** Austral./NZ a drink of liquor.

**Nobelist** /nəʊˈbɛlɪst/ • **n.** chiefly N. Amer. a winner of a Nobel Prize.

**nobelium** /nə(ʊ)ˈbiːlɪəm, -ˈbɛl-/ • **n.** the chemical element of atomic number 102, an artificial radioactive metal of the actinide series. (Symbol: **No**)
– ORIGIN 1950s: from the name of Alfred *Nobel* + **-IUM**.

**Nobel Prize** • **n.** any of six international prizes awarded annually for outstanding work in physics, chemistry, physiology or medicine, literature, economics, and the promotion of peace.
– ORIGIN named after the C19 Swed. chemist and engineer Alfred *Nobel*, who endowed the prizes.

**nobiliary** /nə(ʊ)ˈbɪljəri/ • **adj.** of or relating to the nobility.
– ORIGIN C18: from Fr. *nobiliaire*, based on L. *nobilis* (see **NOBLE**).

**nobility** • **n.** (pl. **-ies**) **1** the quality of being noble. **2** the aristocracy.

**noble** • **adj.** (**-er, -est**) **1** belonging by rank, title, or birth to the aristocracy. **2** having fine personal qualities or high moral principles. **3** imposing; magnificent. • **n. 1** (especially in former times) a person of noble rank or birth. **2** historical a former English gold coin.
– PHRASES **the noble art** (or **science**) (**of self-defence**) chiefly archaic boxing.
– DERIVATIVES **nobleness** n. **nobly** adv.
– ORIGIN ME: from OFr., from L. *(g)nobilis* 'noted, high-born'.

**noble gas** • **n.** Chemistry any of the gaseous elements helium, neon, argon, krypton, xenon, and radon, which form compounds with difficulty or not at all.

**nobleman** (or **noblewoman**) • **n.** (pl. **-men** or **-women**) a man (or woman) who belongs to the aristocracy; a peer (or peeress).

**noble metal** • **n.** Chemistry a metal (e.g. gold, silver, or platinum) that resists attack by acids and other reagents and does not corrode.

**noble rot** • **n.** a grey mould (*Botrytis cinerea*) cultivated on grapes in order to perfect certain wines.
– ORIGIN 1930s: translation of Fr. *pourriture noble*.

**noble savage** • **n.** a representative of primitive mankind as idealized in Romantic literature.

**noblesse** /nəʊˈblɛs/ • **n.** the nobility of a foreign country.

– PHRASES **noblesse oblige** /ɒ'bliːʒ/ privilege entails responsibility.
– ORIGIN Fr., lit. 'nobility'.

**nobody** ● pron. no person; no one. ● n. (pl. **-ies**) a person of no importance or authority.
– ORIGIN ME: orig. as *no body*.

**no-brainer** ● n. N. Amer. informal something that involves little or no mental effort.

**nociceptor** /'nəʊsɪˌsɛptə/ ● n. Physiology a sensory receptor that reacts to painful stimuli.
– DERIVATIVES **nociceptive** adj.
– ORIGIN C20: from L. *nocere* 'to harm' + **RECEPTOR**.

**nock** ● n. Archery a notch at either end of a bow or at the end of an arrow, for receiving the bowstring. ● v. fit (an arrow) to the bowstring.
– ORIGIN ME: perh. from MDu. *nocke* 'point, tip'.

**no-claims bonus** (also **no-claims discount**) ● n. Brit. a reduction in an insurance premium when no claim has been made during an agreed preceding period.

**noctambulist** /nɒk'tambjʊlɪst/ ● n. rare a sleepwalker.
– DERIVATIVES **noctambulism** n.
– ORIGIN C18: from L. *nox, noct-* 'night' + *ambulare* 'walk' + **-IST**.

**noctiluca** /ˌnɒktɪ'luːkə/ ● n. (pl. **noctilucae** /-kiː/) a roughly spherical phosphorescent marine dinoflagellate. [Genus *Noctiluca*.]
– ORIGIN mod. L., from L., lit. 'night light, lantern'.

**noctilucent cloud** /ˌnɒktɪ'luːs(ə)nt/ ● n. a high, luminous cloud seen at night, especially in summer in high latitudes.
– ORIGIN C19: from L. *nox, noct-* 'night' + *lucere* 'to shine' + **-ENT**.

**noctuid** /'nɒktjʊɪd/ ● n. Entomology a moth of a large family (Noctuidae), whose members typically have pale or colourful hindwings.
– ORIGIN C19: from mod. L. *Noctuidae*, based on L. *noctua* 'night owl'.

**noctule** /'nɒktjuːl/ ● n. a large golden-brown bat with long slender wings, rounded ears, and a short muzzle. [*Nyctalus noctula*.]
– ORIGIN C18: from Fr., from Ital. *nottola* 'bat', lit. 'small night creature'.

**nocturn** ● n. (in the Roman Catholic Church) a part of matins originally said at night.
– ORIGIN ME: from OFr. *nocturne* or eccles. L. *nocturnum*, neut. of L. *nocturnus* 'of the night'.

**nocturnal** ● adj. done, occurring, or active at night.
– DERIVATIVES **nocturnally** adv.
– ORIGIN C15: from late L. *nocturnalis*, from L. *nocturnus* 'of the night', from *nox, noct-* 'night'.

**nocturnal emission** ● n. an involuntary ejaculation of semen during sleep.

**nocturne** /'nɒktəːn/ ● n. **1** Music a short composition of a romantic nature. **2** Art a picture of a night scene.
– ORIGIN C19: Fr., from L. *nocturnus* 'of the night'.

**nocuous** /'nɒkjʊəs/ ● adj. poetic/literary noxious.
– ORIGIN C17: from L. *nocuus* (from *nocere* 'to hurt') + **-OUS**.

**nod** ● v. (**nodded, nodding**) **1** lower and raise one's head slightly and briefly, especially in greeting, assent, or understanding, or as a signal. ➤ signify or express in this way: *he nodded his consent.* ➤ move one's head up and down repeatedly. **2** let one's head fall forward when drowsy or asleep. ➤ (**nod off**) informal fall asleep. ➤ make a mistake due to a momentary lack of attention. [with allusion to L. *dormitat Homerus* 'even Homer nods' (Horace *Ars Poet. 359*).] **3** Soccer head (the ball) in a specified direction without great force. **4** (**nod something through**) informal approve something by general agreement and without discussion. ● n. an act of nodding. ➤ a gesture of acknowledgement or concession.
– PHRASES **a nodding acquaintance** a slight acquaintance. **be on nodding terms** know someone slightly. **give someone/thing the nod 1** select or approve someone or something. **2** give someone a signal. **on the nod** Brit. informal **1** by general agreement and without discussion. **2** dated on credit.
– ORIGIN ME: perh. of Low Ger. origin.

**noddle¹** ● n. informal, dated a person's head.
– ORIGIN ME (denoting the back of the head): of unknown origin.

**noddle²** ● v. archaic, informal nod or wag (one's head).
– ORIGIN C18: frequentative of **NOD**.

**noddy** ● n. (pl. **-ies**) **1** dated a silly or foolish person. **2** a tropical tern with mainly dark-coloured plumage. [Genera *Anous* and *Procelsterna*.]
– ORIGIN prob. from **NOD** + **-Y¹**; in sense 2 perh. with ref. to the birds' nodding during courtship.

**node** ● n. technical **1** a point in a network at which lines intersect or branch. ➤ a piece of equipment, such as a computer or peripheral, attached to a network. ➤ Mathematics a point at which a curve intersects itself. ➤ Astronomy either of the two points at which a planet's orbit intersects the plane of the ecliptic or the celestial equator. **2** Botany the part of a plant stem from which one or more leaves emerge. **3** Anatomy a lymph node or other structure consisting of a small mass of differentiated tissue. **4** Physics & Mathematics a point at which the amplitude of vibration in a standing wave system is zero. ➤ a point of zero current or voltage.
– DERIVATIVES **nodal** adj. **nodical** adj.
– ORIGIN ME (denoting a knotty swelling or a protuberance): from L. *nodus* 'knot'.

**node of Ranvier** /'rɑːnvɪeɪ, French rɑ̃vje/ ● n. Anatomy a gap in the myelin sheath of a nerve, between adjacent Schwann cells.
– ORIGIN C19: named after the Fr. histologist Louis Antoine *Ranvier*.

**nodose** /nəʊ'dəʊs/ ● adj. technical characterized by hard or tight lumps; knotty.
– DERIVATIVES **nodosity** n.
– ORIGIN C18: from L. *nodosus*.

**nodule** ● n. **1** a small swelling or aggregation of cells, especially an abnormal one. **2** (usu. **root nodule**) a swelling on a root of a leguminous plant, containing nitrogen-fixing bacteria. **3** a small rounded lump of matter distinct from its surroundings.
– DERIVATIVES **nodular** adj. **nodulated** adj. **nodulation** n. **nodulose** adj. **nodulous** adj.
– ORIGIN ME: from L. *nodulus*, dimin. of *nodus* 'knot'.

**Noel** ● n. Christmas, especially as a refrain in carols and on Christmas cards.
– ORIGIN C19: Fr. *Noël*, based on L. *natalis* (see **NATAL¹**).

**noetic** /nəʊ'ɛtɪk/ ● adj. of or relating to mental activity or the intellect.
– ORIGIN C17: from Gk *noētikos*, from *noētos* 'intellectual', from *noein* 'perceive'.

**nog** ● n. archaic a small block or peg of wood.
– ORIGIN C17: of unknown origin.

**noggin** ● n. informal **1** a person's head. **2** a small quantity of alcoholic drink, typically a quarter of a pint.
– ORIGIN C17 (in the sense 'small drinking cup'): of unknown origin.

**nogging** ● n. Building **1** brickwork in a timber frame. **2** a horizontal piece of wood fixed to a framework to strengthen it.
– ORIGIN C19: from **NOG** + **-ING¹**.

**no-go area** ● n. Brit. an area to which entry is dangerous, impossible, or forbidden.

**Noh** /nəʊ/ (also **No**) ● n. traditional Japanese masked drama with dance and song, evolved from Shinto rites.
– ORIGIN from Japanese.

**no-hitter** ● n. Baseball a game in which a pitcher yields no hits to the opposing team.

**no-hoper** ● n. informal a person who is not expected to be successful.

**nohow** ● adv. informal **1** chiefly US used to emphasize a negative. **2** archaic not attractive, well, or in good order.

**noil** /nɔɪl/ ● n. (usu. **noils**) short strands and knots combed out of wool fibre before spinning.
– ORIGIN C17: prob. from OFr. *noel*, from med. L. *nodellus*, dimin. of L. *nodus* 'knot'.

**noise** ● n. **1** a sound, especially one that is loud, unpleasant, or disturbing. ➤ continuous or repeated loud, confused sounds. **2** (**noises**) conventional remarks expressing some emotion or purpose: *the government*

*made tough noises about defending sterling.* **3** technical irregular fluctuations accompanying and tending to obscure an electrical signal or other significant phenomenon. ● **v. 1** (usu. **be noised about**) dated talk about or make known publicly. **2** poetic/literary make much noise.
– PHRASES **make a noise** speak or act in a way designed to attract attention. **noises off 1** sounds made offstage to be heard by the audience of a play. **2** distracting or intrusive background noise.
– DERIVATIVES **noiseless** adj. **noiselessly** adv. **noiselessness** n.
– ORIGIN ME: from OFr., from L. *nausea* (see **NAUSEA**).

**noisette** /nwʌˈzɛt/ ● **n. 1** a small round piece of meat, especially lamb. **2** a chocolate made with hazelnuts.
– ORIGIN C19: Fr., dimin. of *noix* 'nut'.

**noisome** /ˈnɔɪs(ə)m/ ● **adj.** poetic/literary having an extremely offensive smell. ➤ disagreeable; unpleasant.
– DERIVATIVES **noisomeness** n.
– ORIGIN ME: from obs. *noy* (shortened form of **ANNOY**) + **-SOME**[1].

**noisy** ● **adj.** (**-ier, -iest**) **1** full of or making a lot of noise. **2** technical accompanied by random fluctuations that obscure information.
– DERIVATIVES **noisily** adv. **noisiness** n.

**nolens volens** /ˌnəʊlɛnz ˈvəʊlɛnz/ ● **adv.** formal whether a person wants or likes something or not.
– ORIGIN L., from *nolens* 'not willing' and *volens* 'willing'.

**nolle pros** /ˌnɒlɪ ˈprɒs, ˈprəʊs/ ● **v.** (**prossed, prossing**) US Law abandon or dismiss (a suit) by issuing a nolle prosequi.

**nolle prosequi** /ˌnɒlɪ ˈprɒsɪkwʌɪ/ ● **n.** Law a formal notice of abandonment by a plaintiff or prosecutor of all or part of a suit.
– ORIGIN L., lit. 'refuse to pursue'.

**no-load** ● **adj.** N. Amer. (of shares in a mutual fund) sold directly to a buyer without a commission being charged.

**nolo contendere** /ˌnəʊləʊ kɒnˈtɛndəri/ ● **n.** US Law a plea by which a defendant accepts conviction as in the case of a plea of guilty but does not admit guilt.
– ORIGIN L., lit. 'I do not wish to contend'.

**nom.** ● **abbrev.** nominal.

**nomad** ● **n.** a member of a people continually moving to find fresh pasture for its animals and having no permanent home. ➤ a wanderer.
– DERIVATIVES **nomadic** adj. **nomadically** adv. **nomadism** n.
– ORIGIN C16: from Fr. *nomade*, via L. from Gk *nomas, nomad-* (adj.), from the base of *nemein* 'to pasture'.

**no-man's-land** ● **n. 1** disputed ground between two opposing armies. **2** a piece of unowned land or wasteland.

**nombril** /ˈnɒmbrɪl/ ● **n.** Heraldry the point halfway between fess point and the base of the shield.
– ORIGIN C16: from Fr., lit. 'navel'.

**nom de guerre** /ˌnɒm də ˈgɛː/ ● **n.** (pl. **noms de guerre** pronunc. same) an assumed name under which a person engages in combat.
– ORIGIN Fr., lit. 'war name'.

**nom de plume** /ˌnɒm də ˈpluːm/ ● **n.** (pl. **noms de plume** pronunc. same) a pen name.
– ORIGIN C19: formed in Engl. from Fr. words, on the pattern of *nom de guerre.*

**nome** /nəʊm/ ● **n. 1** a territorial division of ancient Egypt. **2** an administrative division of modern Greece.
– ORIGIN C18: from Gk *nomos* 'division', from *nemein* 'to divide'.

**nomen** /ˈnəʊmən/ ● **n.** the second personal name of a citizen of ancient Rome, indicating their gens, e.g. Marcus *Tullius* Cicero.
– ORIGIN L., lit. 'name'.

**nomenclature** /nə(ʊ)ˈmɛŋklətʃə, ˈnəʊmənˌkleɪtʃə/ ● **n.** the selecting of names for things in a particular field. ➤ a body or system of names. ➤ formal the term or terms applied to someone or something.
– DERIVATIVES **nomenclator** n. **nomenclatural** /-ˈklatʃ(ə)r(ə)l, -kləˈtʃʊər(ə)l/ adj.
– ORIGIN C17: from Fr., from L. *nomenclatura*, from *nomen* 'name' + *clatura* 'calling, summoning' (from *calare* 'to call').

**nomenklatura** /nɒˌmɛnkləˈtjʊərə/ ● **n.** (in the former Soviet Union) a list of influential public positions to be filled by Party appointees.
– ORIGIN Russ., from L. *nomenclatura* (see **NOMENCLATURE**).

**nominal** ● **adj. 1** existing in name only. ➤ relating to or consisting of names. **2** Grammar headed by or having the function of a noun. **3** (of a sum of money) very small; far below the real value or cost: *a nominal fee.* **4** (of a quantity or dimension) stated but not necessarily corresponding exactly to the real value. **5** informal functioning normally or acceptably.
– DERIVATIVES **nominally** adv.
– ORIGIN C15: from L. *nominalis*, from *nomen, nomin-* 'name'.

**nominal definition** ● **n.** Logic a definition that describes something sufficiently to distinguish it from other things, but without describing its essence.

**nominalism** ● **n.** Philosophy the doctrine that universals or general ideas are mere names without any corresponding reality. Often contrasted with **REALISM** (sense 3).
– DERIVATIVES **nominalist** n. **nominalistic** adj.

**nominalize** (also **-ise**) ● **v.** Grammar form a noun from (a verb or adjective), e.g. *output, truth,* from *put out, true.*
– DERIVATIVES **nominalization** n.

**nominal value** ● **n.** Economics the value stated on a coin, note, etc.; face value.

**nominate** ● **v. 1** put forward as a candidate for election or for an honour or award. ➤ appoint to a job or position. **2** specify formally. ● **adj.** Zoology & Botany denoting a race or subspecies having the same epithet as the species to which it belongs, e.g. *Homo sapiens sapiens.*
– DERIVATIVES **nomination** n. **nominator** n.
– ORIGIN ME (as an adj. in the sense 'named'): from L. *nominat-, nominare* 'to name', from *nomen, nomin-* 'a name'.

**nominative** /ˈnɒmɪnətɪv/ ● **adj. 1** Grammar denoting a case of nouns, pronouns, and adjectives expressing the subject of a verb. **2** /ˈnɒmɪˌneɪtɪv/ of or appointed by nomination as distinct from election. ● **n.** Grammar a word in the nominative case.
– ORIGIN ME: from L. *nominativus*, translating Gk *onomastikē* (*ptōsis*) 'naming (case)'.

**nominee** ● **n. 1** a person who is nominated. **2** a person or company, not the owner, in whose name a company, stock, etc. is registered.

**nomogram** /ˈnɒməgram, ˈnəʊm-/ (also **nomograph**) ● **n.** a diagram representing the relations between three or more variable quantities by means of a number of scales, so arranged that the value of one variable can be found geometrically.
– DERIVATIVES **nomographic** adj. **nomographically** adv. **nomography** /nəˈmɒgrəfi/ n.
– ORIGIN C20: from Gk *nomos* 'law' + **-GRAM**[1].

**nomological** /ˌnɒməˈlɒdʒɪkəl/ ● **adj.** relating to or denoting natural laws which are neither logically necessary nor theoretically explicable, but just are so.
– DERIVATIVES **nomologically** adv.
– ORIGIN C19: from Gk *nomos* 'law' + *-logical* (see **-LOGY**).

**nomothetic** /ˌnɒməˈθɛtɪk, ˌnəʊm-/ ● **adj.** of or relating to general scientific laws.
– ORIGIN C17: from obs. *nomothete* 'legislator' (from Gk *nomothetēs*) + **-IC**.

**-nomy** ● **comb. form** denoting a specified area of knowledge or its laws: *astronomy.* See word-formation panel.
– ORIGIN from Gk *-nomia*; rel. to *nomos* 'law' and *nemein* 'distribute'.

**non-** ● **prefix** expressing negation or absence: *non-recognition.* ➤ not of the kind or class described: *non-believer.* ➤ expressing a neutral negative sense where *in-* or *un-* has a special connotation (such as *non-human* compared with *inhuman*).
– ORIGIN from L. *non* 'not'.

**nona-** /ˈnɒnə, ˈnəʊnə/ ● **comb. form** nine; having nine: *nonagon.*

## Word *Formation*

**-nomy** 'an area of knowledge' from Greek *-nomia*

➤ The Greek root *-nomia* is related to *nomos* 'law' and *nemein* 'distribute, manage'. It has given rise to a small and rather diverse group of words in English:

| | | |
|---|---|---|
| agronomy | the science of agriculture | Gk *agros* 'field' |
| antinomy | a paradox | Gk *anti* 'against' |
| astronomy | the science of space and celestial objects | Gk *astron* 'star' |
| autonomy | freedom of independent action | Gk *autos* 'self' |
| economy | overall production and consumption and supply of money within a region | Gk *oikonomia* 'household management' (from *oikos* 'house') |
| gastronomy | the art of cooking (and serving etc.) good food | Gk *gaster, gastr-* 'stomach' |
| taxonomy | the science of classification | Gk *taxis* 'arrangement' |

The word ***physiognomy***, which is superficially similar in form to the other **-nomy** words, is not etymologically related. It is formed on Gk *phusis* 'nature' + *gnōmōn* 'interpreter', giving rise to the current sense: 'facial features or expression'.

The oldest English **-nomy** word in current use is ***astronomy***, which has a first recorded date of 1205.

– ORIGIN from L. *nonus* 'ninth'.

**nonage** /ˈnəʊnɪdʒ, ˈnɒn-/ ● **n.** formal the period of immaturity or youth.
– ORIGIN ME: from OFr. *nonage*, from *non-* 'non-' + *age* 'age'.

**nonagenarian** /ˌnɒnədʒɪˈnɛːrɪən, ˌnəʊn-/ ● **n.** a person between 90 and 99 years old.
– ORIGIN C19: from L. *nonagenarius* (based on *nonaginta* 'ninety') + **-AN**.

**nonagon** /ˈnɒnəg(ə)n/ ● **n.** a plane figure with nine straight sides and angles.
– DERIVATIVES **nonagonal** adj.
– ORIGIN C17: formed irregularly from L. *nonus* 'ninth', on the pattern of words such as *hexagon*.

**non-alcoholic** ● **adj.** (of a drink) not containing alcohol.

**non-aligned** ● **adj.** (chiefly during the cold war) of or denoting countries pursuing a policy of neutrality towards the superpowers.
– DERIVATIVES **non-alignment** n.

**non-allergenic** ● **adj.** not causing an allergic reaction.

**non-allergic** ● **adj.** another term for **NON-ALLERGENIC**.

**nonane** /ˈnəʊneɪn, ˈnɒn-/ ● **n.** Chemistry a colourless liquid hydrocarbon of the alkane series, present in petroleum spirit. [$C_9H_{20}$.]
– ORIGIN C19: from **NONA-** 'nine' (denoting nine carbon atoms) + **-ANE**[2].

**non-attributable** ● **adj.** not able to be attributed to a particular source or cause.
– DERIVATIVES **non-attributably** adv.

**non-being** ● **n.** the state of not being; non-existence.

**non-believer** ● **n.** a person who does not believe in something, especially one who has no religious faith.

**non-belligerent** ● **adj.** not engaged in a war or conflict. ● **n.** a non-belligerent nation or person.
– DERIVATIVES **non-belligerence** n.

**non-capital** ● **adj.** Law (of an offence) not punishable by death.

**nonce**[1] /nɒns/ ● **adj.** denoting a word or expression coined for one occasion.
– PHRASES **for the nonce** for the present; temporarily.
– ORIGIN ME: from *then anes* 'the one (purpose)' (from *then*, obs. oblique form of **THE** + *ane* 'one' + **-S**[3]), alt. by misdivision; cf. **NEWT** and **NICKNAME**.

**nonce**[2] /nɒns/ ● **n.** Brit. informal a sexual deviant, especially a child molester.
– ORIGIN 1970s (orig. prison sl.): of unknown origin.

**nonchalant** /ˈnɒnʃ(ə)l(ə)nt/ ● **adj.** casually calm and relaxed.
– DERIVATIVES **nonchalance** n. **nonchalantly** adv.
– ORIGIN C18: from Fr., lit. 'not being concerned', from the verb *nonchaloir*.

**non-classified** ● **adj.** not designated as officially secret.

**non-collegiate** ● **adj. 1** (of a university) not composed of different colleges. **2** not belonging to a particular college.

**non-com** ● **n.** Military, informal a non-commissioned officer.

**non-combatant** ● **n.** a person who is not engaged in fighting during a war, especially a civilian, army chaplain, or army doctor.

**non-commissioned** ● **adj.** (of an officer in the army, navy, or air force) not holding a rank conferred by a commission.

**non-committal** ● **adj.** not displaying commitment to a definite opinion or policy.
– DERIVATIVES **non-committally** adv.

**non-communicant** ● **n.** a person who does not receive Holy Communion.

**non compos mentis** /ˌnɒn ˌkɒmpɒs ˈmɛntɪs/ ● **adj.** not in one's right mind.
– ORIGIN L., lit. 'not having control of one's mind'.

**non-conductor** ● **n.** a substance that does not conduct heat or electricity.
– DERIVATIVES **non-conducting** adj.

**nonconformist** ● **n.** a person who does not conform to prevailing ideas or established practice. ➤**(Nonconformist)** a member of a Protestant Church which dissents from the established Church of England. ● **adj.** not conforming to prevailing ideas or established practice.
– DERIVATIVES **nonconformism** n. **nonconformity** n.

**non-content** ● **n.** a member of the House of Lords who votes against a particular motion.

**non-contributory** ● **adj. 1** (of a pension) funded by regular payments by the employer, not the employee. **2** (of a state benefit) paid irrespective of taxes or other contributions made by recipients.

**non-controversial** ● **adj.** not controversial (less forceful in meaning than **uncontroversial**).

**non-cooperation** ● **n.** failure to cooperate, especially as a form of protest.

**nonda** /ˈnɒndə/ ● **n.** a tropical Australian tree with an edible, yellow plum-like fruit, growing on sand ridges. [*Parinari nonda*.]
– ORIGIN C19: prob. from a Queensland Aborig. lang.

**non-delivery** ● **n.** chiefly Law failure to provide or deliver goods.

**non-denominational** ● **adj.** open or acceptable to people of any Christian denomination.

**nondescript** /ˈnɒndɪskrɪpt/ ● **adj.** lacking distinctive or interesting characteristics. ● **n.** a nondescript person or thing.
– DERIVATIVES **nondescriptly** adv. **nondescriptness** n.
– ORIGIN C17 (in the sense 'not previously described scien-

tifically'): from **NON-** + obs. *descript* 'described, engraved'.

**non-destructive** ● **adj.** technical (chiefly of methods of testing) not involving damage to the specimen.

**non-disjunction** ● **n.** Genetics failure of a pair of homologous chromosomes to separate normally during nuclear division.

**non-drinker** ● **n.** a person who does not drink alcohol.

**non-drip** ● **adj.** (of paint) formulated so that it does not drip when wet.

**none**[1] /nʌn/ ● **pron.** not any. ➤no person; no one. ● **adv.** (**none the**) [with comparative] by no amount; not at all.
– PHRASES **none other than** used to emphasize the surprising identity of a person or thing. **will have** (or **want**) **none of something** refuse to approve or take part in something.
– ORIGIN OE *nān*, from *ne* 'not' + *ān* 'one', of Gmc origin.

**none**[2] /nəʊn/ (also **nones**) ● **n.** a service forming part of the Divine Office of the Western Christian Church, traditionally said at the ninth hour of the day (3 p.m.).
– ORIGIN C19: from Fr., from L. *nona*, fem. sing. of *nonus* 'ninth'; cf. **NOON**.

**nonentity** /nɒˈnɛntɪti/ ● **n.** (pl. **-ies**) **1** an unimportant person or thing. **2** non-existence.
– ORIGIN C16: from med. L. *nonentitas* 'non-existence'.

**nones** /nəʊnz/ ● **pl. n. 1** (in the ancient Roman calendar) the ninth day before the ides by inclusive reckoning, i.e. the 7th day of March, May, July, October, the 5th of other months. **2** variant spelling of **NONE**[2].
– ORIGIN via OFr. from L. *nonas*, fem. accusative pl. of *nonus* 'ninth'.

**non-essential** ● **adj.** not absolutely necessary. ● **n.** a non-essential thing.

**non est factum** /ˌnɒn ɛst ˈfaktəm/ ● **n.** Law a plea that a written agreement is invalid because the defendant was mistaken about its character when signing it.
– ORIGIN L., lit. 'it was not done'.

**nonesuch** ● **n.** variant spelling of **NONSUCH**.

**nonet** /nəʊˈnɛt, nɒˈnɛt/ ● **n. 1** a group of nine. **2** a musical composition for nine voices or instruments.
– ORIGIN C19: from Ital. *nonetto*, from *nono* 'ninth'.

**nonetheless** (also **none the less**) ● **adv.** in spite of that; nevertheless.

**non-Euclidean** ● **adj.** denoting systems of geometry that do not obey Euclidean postulates, especially that only one line through a given point can be parallel to a given line.

**non-event** ● **n.** an unexpectedly insignificant or uninteresting occasion. ➤an event that did not happen.

**non-existent** ● **adj.** not existing or not real or present.
– DERIVATIVES **non-existence** n.

**non-factive** ● **adj.** Linguistics denoting a verb that takes a clausal object which may or may not designate a true fact, e.g. *believe*. Contrasted with **CONTRAFACTIVE**, **FACTIVE**.

**nonfeasance** /nɒnˈfiːz(ə)ns/ ● **n.** Law failure to perform an act required by law.
– ORIGIN C17: from **NON-** + *feasance* (see **MALFEASANCE**).

**non-ferrous** ● **adj.** relating to or denoting a metal other than iron or steel.

**non-fiction** ● **n.** prose writing that is informative or factual rather than fictional.
– DERIVATIVES **non-fictional** adj.

**non-figurative** ● **adj.** Art abstract.

**non-finite** ● **adj. 1** not limited in size or extent. **2** Grammar (of a verb form) not limited by tense, person, or number.

**non-flam** ● **adj.** short for **NON-FLAMMABLE**.

**non-flammable** ● **adj.** not catching fire easily.

**non-fulfilment** ● **n.** failure to fulfil or carry out something.

**non-functional** ● **adj. 1** having no function. **2** not in working order.

**nong** /nɒŋ/ ● **n.** Austral./NZ informal a foolish or stupid person.
– ORIGIN 1940s: of unknown origin.

**non-governmental** ● **adj.** not belonging to or associated with any government.

**non-Hodgkin's lymphoma** ● **n.** Medicine a form of malignant lymphoma differing from Hodgkin's disease only by the absence of characteristic giant cells.

**non-human** ● **adj.** not human.

**non-infectious** ● **adj. 1** (of a disease) not liable to be transmitted through the environment. **2** not liable to spread infection.

**non-inflammable** ● **adj.** not catching fire easily.

**non-interference** ● **n.** failure or refusal to intervene without invitation or necessity.

**non-intervention** ● **n.** the policy of not becoming involved in the affairs of others.
– DERIVATIVES **non-interventionism** n. **non-interventionist** adj. & n.

**non-invasive** ● **adj. 1** (of medical procedures) not involving the introduction of instruments into the body. **2** (chiefly of disease) not tending to spread undesirably.

**non-judgemental** ● **adj.** avoiding moral judgements.

**Nonjuror** ● **n.** historical a member of the clergy who refused to take the oath of allegiance to William and Mary in 1689.

**non-linear** ● **adj. 1** not linear. **2** Mathematics designating or involving an equation including terms not of the first degree.
– DERIVATIVES **non-linearity** n. **non-linearly** adv.

**non-logical** ● **adj.** not according to the rules of logic (less forceful in meaning than **illogical**).
– DERIVATIVES **non-logically** adv.

**non-member** ● **n.** a person, country, etc. that is not a member of a particular organization.
– DERIVATIVES **non-membership** n.

**non-metal** ● **n.** an element or substance that is not a metal.
– DERIVATIVES **non-metallic** adj.

**non-moral** ● **adj.** not holding or manifesting moral principles.

**non-native** ● **adj. 1** not native to a particular place. **2** (of a speaker) not having spoken the language in question from earliest childhood.

**non-natural** ● **adj.** not produced by or involving natural processes. ➤Philosophy existing but not part of the natural world.

**non-negative** ● **adj.** Mathematics either positive or equal to zero.

**non-negotiable** ● **adj. 1** not open to discussion or modification. **2** not able to be transferred or assigned to the legal ownership of another person.

**no-no** ● **n.** (pl. **-os**) informal a thing that is not possible or acceptable.

**non-objective** ● **adj. 1** not objective. **2** Art abstract.

**non-observance** ● **n.** failure to observe an obligation, rule, or custom.

**no-nonsense** ● **adj.** simple and straightforward; sensible.

**non-operational** ● **adj. 1** not involving active duties. **2** not working or in use.

**nonpareil** /ˌnɒnpəˈreɪl/ ● **adj.** unrivalled. ● **n. 1** an unrivalled person or thing. **2** US a flat round confection made of chocolate covered with white sugar sprinkles. **3** Printing an old type size equal to six points.
– ORIGIN ME: from Fr., from *non-* 'not' + *pareil* 'equal'.

**non-person** ● **n.** a person regarded as non-existent or unimportant, or as having no rights.

**non placet** /nɒn ˈpleɪsɛt/ ● **n.** a negative vote in a Church or university assembly.
– ORIGIN L., lit. 'it does not please'.

**nonplus** /nɒnˈplʌs/ ● **v.** (**nonplussed**, **nonplussing**) **1** (usu. **be nonplussed**) surprise and confuse; flummox. **2** [as adj. **nonplussed**] N. Amer. informal unperturbed. ● **n.** a state of being nonplussed.
– ORIGIN C16: from L. *non plus* 'not more'.

**non possumus** /nɒn ˈpɒsjʊməs/ ● **n.** used as a statement expressing inability to act in a matter.
– ORIGIN L., lit. 'we cannot'.

**non-prescription** • adj. of or denoting medicines available for sale without a prescription.

**non-productive** • adj. not producing or able to produce (tending to be less forceful in meaning than **unproductive**).

– DERIVATIVES **non-productively** adv.

**non-professional** • adj. not professional. • n. a non-professional person.

**non-profit** • adj. not making or intended to make a profit.

**non-proliferation** • n. the prevention of an increase or spread of something, especially possession of nuclear weapons.

**non-proprietary** • adj. not registered or protected as a trademark or restricted to one manufacturer.

**non-resident** • adj. **1** not living in a particular country or a place of work. ➤(of a job or course) not requiring residence at the place of work or instruction. **2** Computing (of software) not kept permanently in memory. • n. a person not living in a particular place.

– DERIVATIVES **non-residence** n.

**non-residential** • adj. **1** not requiring or providing facilities for people to live on the premises. **2** containing or suitable for commercial premises rather than private houses.

**non-resistance** • n. the policy of not resisting authority.

**non-restrictive** • adj. **1** not involving restrictions or limitations. **2** Grammar (of a clause or phrase) giving additional information about a noun phrase whose particular reference has already been specified.

**non-return** • adj. permitting the flow of air or liquid in one direction only.

**non-returnable** • adj. **1** (especially of a deposit) not repayable in any circumstances. **2** (of bottles) not intended to be returned empty to the suppliers.

**non-rigid** • adj. not rigid. ➤denoting an airship whose shape is maintained solely by the pressure of the gas inside.

**non-scientific** • adj. not involving or relating to science or scientific methods.

– DERIVATIVES **non-scientist** n.

**nonsense** • n. **1** words that make no sense. **2** foolish or unacceptable behaviour. ➤an absurd or unthinkable scheme, situation, etc.

– PHRASES **make (a) nonsense of** reduce the value or relevance of (something) to a ridiculous degree.

– DERIVATIVES **nonsensical** adj. **nonsensicality** n. **nonsensically** adv.

**non sequitur** /nɒn 'sɛkwɪtə/ • n. a conclusion or statement that does not logically follow from the previous argument or statement.

– ORIGIN L., lit. 'it does not follow'.

**non-smoker** • n. a person who does not smoke tobacco.

– DERIVATIVES **non-smoking** adj.

**non-solid colour** • n. Computing a colour simulated by a pattern of dots of other colours.

**non-specific** • adj. not specific. ➤Medicine not assignable to a particular cause, condition, or category.

**non-specific urethritis** • n. Medicine urethritis due to infection by chlamydiae or other organisms (other than gonococci).

**non-standard** • adj. not average, normal, or usual. ➤(of language) not of the form that is accepted as standard.

**non-starter** • n. **1** a person or animal that fails to take part in a race. **2** informal something that has no chance of succeeding or being effective.

**non-stick** • adj. (of a pan or surface) covered with a substance that prevents food sticking to it during cooking.

**non-stop** • adj. continuing without stopping or pausing. ➤(of a passenger vehicle or journey) having no intermediate stops on the way to a destination. • adv. without stopping or pausing. • n. a non-stop flight or train.

**nonsuch** /'nʌnsʌtʃ/ • n. **1** (also **nonesuch**) archaic a person or thing regarded as perfect or excellent. **2** a small medick grown as a constituent of grazing pasture. [*Medicago lupulina*.]

– ORIGIN C17: coined on the pattern of *nonpareil*.

**nonsuit** Law • v. subject (a plaintiff) to the stoppage of their suit on the grounds of failure to make a legal case or bring sufficient evidence. • n. the stoppage of a suit on such grounds.

**non-technical** • adj. not relating to or involving science or technology. ➤not using technical terms or requiring specialized knowledge.

**non-transferable** • adj. not able to be transferred to the possession of another person.

**non-trivial** • adj. **1** not trivial; significant. **2** Mathematics having some terms not equal to zero.

**non-U** • adj. informal, chiefly Brit. (of language or social behaviour) not characteristic of the upper social classes.

**non-uniform** • adj. not uniform; varying.

– DERIVATIVES **non-uniformity** n. **non-uniformly** adv.

**non-union** • adj. not belonging to or connected with a trade union.

**non-use** • n. the refusal or failure to use something.

– DERIVATIVES **non-usage** n. **non-user** n.

**non-verbal** • adj. not involving or using words or speech.

– DERIVATIVES **non-verbally** adv.

**non-violent** • adj. (especially of political or social opposition) not using violence.

– DERIVATIVES **non-violence** n. **non-violently** adv.

**non-white** • adj. denoting or relating to a person who is not white or whose origin is not predominantly European. • n. a non-white person.

**non-word** • n. a group of letters or speech sounds that looks or sounds like a word but is not accepted as such by native speakers.

**nonyl** /'nɒnʌɪl, -nɪl, 'nəʊn-/ • n. [as modifier] Chemistry of or denoting an alkyl radical $-C_9H_{19}$, derived from nonane.

**noodle**[1] • n. (usu. **noodles**) a very thin, long strip of pasta or a similar flour paste.

– ORIGIN C18: from Ger. *Nudel*, of unknown origin.

**noodle**[2] • n. informal **1** a stupid or silly person. **2** a person's head.

– ORIGIN C18: of unknown origin.

**noodle**[3] • v. Austral. informal search (an old working) for opals.

– ORIGIN C20: of unknown origin.

**nook** • n. a corner or recess, especially one offering seclusion or security.

– PHRASES **every nook and cranny** every part of something.

– ORIGIN ME: of unknown origin.

**nooky** (also **nookie**) • n. informal sexual activity or intercourse.

– ORIGIN C20: perh. from NOOK.

**noon** • n. twelve o'clock in the day; midday.

– ORIGIN OE *nōn* 'the ninth hour from sunrise, i.e. approximately 3 p.m.', from L. *nona* (*hora*) 'ninth hour'; cf. NONE[2].

**noonday** • n. the middle of the day.

**no one** • pron. no person; not a single person.

**noontide** (also **noontime**) • n. poetic/literary noon.

**noose** • n. a loop with a running knot which tightens as the rope or wire is pulled, used especially to hang offenders or trap animals. • v. apply a noose to; catch with a noose. ➤form (a rope) into a noose.

– PHRASES **put one's head in a noose** bring about one's own downfall.

– ORIGIN ME: prob. via OFr. *no(u)s* from L. *nodus* 'knot'.

**Nootka** /'nuːtkə, 'nʊt-/ • n. (pl. same or **Nootkas**) **1** a member of an American Indian people of Vancouver Island, Canada. **2** the Wakashan language of this people.

– ORIGIN named after *Nootka* Sound, an inlet on the coast of Vancouver Island.

**nootropic** /ˌnəʊə'trəʊpɪk, -'trɒpɪk/ • adj. denoting drugs used to enhance memory or other cognitive functions.

– ORIGIN 1970s: from Fr. *nootrope* (from Gk *noos* 'mind' + *tropē* 'turning') + -IC.

**nopal** /'nəʊp(ə)l, 'nəʊpal/ • n. a Mexican cactus which is a major food plant of the cochineal insect. [Genus *Nopalea*.] ➤(**nopales** /nəʊ'pɑːlɛz/) the edible fleshy pads

of this cactus, used in Mexican cuisine.
– ORIGIN C18: via Fr. and Sp. from Nahuatl *nopalli.*

**nope** ● **exclam.** informal variant of **NO**.

**nor** ● **conj. & adv. 1** and not; and not either: *they were neither cheap nor convenient.* ➤neither: *nor can I.* **2** archaic or dialect than. ● **n.** (**NOR**) Electronics **1** a logical operation which gives the value one if and only if all the operands have a value of zero, and otherwise has a value of zero. **2** [as modifier] denoting a gate circuit which produces an output only when there are no signals on any of the input connections.
– ORIGIN ME: contr. of OE *nother* 'neither'.

**nor'** ● **abbrev.** (especially in compounds) north: *nor'west.*

**nor-** ● **prefix** Chemistry denoting an organic compound derived from another by shortening or contraction of a chain or ring by one carbon atom: *noradrenaline.*
– ORIGIN from *nor(mal)*, orig. used to refer to a compound without methyl substituents.

**noradrenaline** /ˌnɔːrəˈdrɛn(ə)lɪn/ ● **n.** Biochemistry an adrenal hormone which functions as a neurotransmitter and is also used as a drug to raise blood pressure.
– ORIGIN 1930s: from **NOR-** + **ADRENALIN**.

**Norbertine** /ˈnɔːbətɪn, -ʌɪn/ ● **n. & adj.** another term for **PREMONSTRATENSIAN**.
– ORIGIN C17: named after St *Norbert*, C12 founder of the order.

**Nordic** ● **adj. 1** of or relating to Scandinavia, Finland, and Iceland. **2** denoting a physical type of northern European peoples characterized by tall stature, a bony frame, light colouring, and a dolichocephalic head. **3** (in skiing) denoting the disciplines of cross-country skiing and ski jumping. ● **n.** a native of Scandinavia, Finland, or Iceland.
– ORIGIN from Fr. *nordique*, from *nord* 'north'.

**norepinephrine** /ˌnɔːrɛpɪˈnɛfrɪn, -riːn/ ● **n.** another term for **NORADRENALINE**.

**Norfolk jacket** ● **n.** a loose belted jacket with box pleats, typically made of tweed.

**nori** /ˈnɔːri/ ● **n.** (in Japanese cuisine) seaweed, eaten fresh or dried in sheets.
– ORIGIN from Japanese.

**noria** /ˈnɔːrɪə/ ● **n.** a device for raising water from a stream, consisting of a chain of buckets revolving round a wheel driven by the current.
– ORIGIN via Sp. from Arab. *nā'ūra.*

**norite** /ˈnɔːrʌɪt/ ● **n.** Geology a coarse-grained plutonic rock similar to gabbro but containing hypersthene.
– ORIGIN C19: from *Norway* + **-ITE**[1].

**nork** ● **n.** Austral. informal a woman's breast.
– ORIGIN 1960s: of unknown origin.

**norm** ● **n. 1** the usual, typical, or standard thing. ➤a required or acceptable standard: *the norms of good behaviour.* **2** Mathematics the sum of the squares of the real and imaginary components of a complex number, or the positive square root of this sum.
– ORIGIN C19: from L. *norma* 'precept, rule, carpenter's square'.

**normal** ● **adj. 1** conforming to a standard; usual, typical, or expected. **2** technical intersecting a given line or surface at right angles. **3** Medicine containing the same salt concentration as the blood. ➤Chemistry, dated (of a solution) containing one gram-equivalent of solute per litre. **4** Geology denoting a fault in which a relative downward movement occurred in the strata on the upper side of the fault plane. ● **n. 1** the normal state or condition: *her temperature was above normal.* **2** technical a line at right angles to a given line or surface.
– DERIVATIVES **normalcy** n. (chiefly N. Amer.). **normality** n.
– ORIGIN C17: from L. *normalis*, from *norma* (see **NORM**).

**normal distribution** ● **n.** Statistics a function that represents the distribution of many random variables as a symmetrical bell-shaped graph.

**normalize** (also **-ise**) ● **v. 1** bring to a normal or standard state. **2** Mathematics multiply by a factor that makes the norm equal to a desired value (usually 1).
– DERIVATIVES **normalization** n. **normalizer** n.

**normally** ● **adv. 1** in a normal manner; in the usual way. **2** as a rule. **3** technical at right angles to a given line or surface.

**normal school** ● **n.** (especially in North America and France) a college for the training of teachers.

**Norman** ● **n. 1** a member of a people of mixed Frankish and Scandinavian origin who settled in Normandy in the 10th century; in particular, any of the Normans who conquered England in 1066 or their descendants. ➤a native or inhabitant of modern Normandy. **2** (also **Norman French**) the northern form of Old French spoken by the Normans. ➤the French dialect of modern Normandy. ● **adj.** of or relating to the Normans or Normandy. ➤denoting the style of Romanesque architecture used in Britain under the Normans.
– DERIVATIVES **Normanesque** adj. **Normanism** n. **Normanize** (also **-ise**) v.
– ORIGIN ME: from OFr. *Normans*, pl. of *Normant*, from ON *Northmathr* 'Northman'.

**normative** ● **adj.** formal relating to or deriving from a standard or norm.
– DERIVATIVES **normatively** adv. **normativeness** n.
– ORIGIN C19: from Fr. *normatif, -ive*, from L. *norma* (see **NORM**).

**normotensive** /ˌnɔːmə(ʊ)ˈtɛnsɪv/ ● **adj.** Medicine having or denoting a normal blood pressure.

**Norn** /nɔːn/ ● **n.** a form of Norse formerly spoken in Orkney and Shetland.
– ORIGIN from ON *norrœn*, from *northr* 'north'.

**Norplant** ● **n.** trademark a contraceptive implant for women which gradually releases the hormone levonorgestrel.
– ORIGIN 1980s: from *(levo)nor(gestrel) (im)plant.*

**Norse** /nɔːs/ historical ● **n. 1** an ancient or medieval form of Norwegian or a related Scandinavian language. **2** [treated as pl.] Norwegians or Scandinavians. ● **adj.** of or relating to Norway or Scandinavia, or their inhabitants or language.
– DERIVATIVES **Norseman** n. (pl. **-men**).
– ORIGIN from Du. *noor(d)sch*, from *noord* 'north'.

**north** ● **n.** (usu. **the north**) **1** the direction in which a compass needle normally points, towards the horizon on the left-hand side of a person facing east. **2** the northern part of a country, region, or town. ➤(**the North**) the NE states of the United States. ● **adj. 1** lying towards, near, or facing the north. **2** (of a wind) blowing from the north. ● **adv.** to or towards the north.
– PHRASES **north by east** (or **west**) between north and north-north-east (or north-north-west).
– DERIVATIVES **northbound** adj. & adv.
– ORIGIN OE, of Gmc origin.

**North American** ● **n.** a native or inhabitant of North America, especially a citizen of the US or Canada. ● **adj.** of or relating to North America.

**Northants** /nɔːˈθants/ ● **abbrev.** Northamptonshire.

**north-east** ● **n.** (usu. **the north-east**) **1** the point of the horizon midway between north and east. **2** the north-eastern part of a country, region, or town. ● **adj. 1** lying towards, near, or facing the north-east. **2** (of a wind) from the north-east. ● **adv.** to or towards the north-east.
– DERIVATIVES **north-eastern** adj.

**northeaster** ● **n.** a wind blowing from the north-east.

**north-easterly** ● **adj. & adv.** in a north-eastward position or direction. ● **n.** another term for **NORTHEASTER**.

**north-eastward** ● **adv.** (also **north-eastwards**) towards the north-east. ● **adj.** situated in, directed towards, or facing the north-east.

**norther** ● **n.** US a strong cold north wind blowing over Texas, Florida, and the Gulf of Mexico.

**northerly** ● **adj. & adv. 1** in a northward position or direction. **2** (of a wind) blowing from the north. ● **n.** (often **northerlies**) a wind blowing from the north.

**northern** ● **adj. 1** situated in, directed towards, or facing the north. **2** (usu. **Northern**) living in, coming from, or characteristic of the north.
– DERIVATIVES **northernmost** adj.

**northerner** ● **n.** a native or inhabitant of the north of a particular region or country.

**Northern Lights** • pl. n. the aurora borealis (see **AURORA**).

**North Germanic** • n. a subdivision of the Germanic group of languages, comprising the Scandinavian languages. • adj. of or relating to North Germanic.

**northing** • n. **1** distance travelled or measured northward, especially at sea. **2** a figure or line representing northward distance on a map.

**North Korean** • n. a native or inhabitant of North Korea. • adj. of or relating to North Korea.

**northland** • n. (also **northlands**) poetic/literary the northern part of a country or region.

**north light** • n. good natural light without direct sun.

**Northman** • n. (pl. **-men**) archaic a native or inhabitant of Scandinavia, especially Norway.

**north-north-east** • n. the compass point or direction midway between north and north-east.

**north-north-west** • n. the compass point or direction midway between north and north-west.

**North Star** • n. the Pole Star.

**Northumb.** • abbrev. Northumberland.

**Northumbrian** /nɔːˈθʌmbrɪən/ • n. a native or inhabitant of Northumbria, an area of NE England. • adj. of or relating to Northumbria.

**northward** • adj. in a northerly direction. • adv. (also **northwards**) towards the north. • n. (**the northward**) the direction or region to the north.
– DERIVATIVES **northwardly** adj. & adv.

**north-west** • n. (usu. **the north-west**) **1** the point of the horizon midway between north and west. **2** the north-western part of a country, region, or town. • adj. **1** lying towards, near, or facing the north-west. **2** (of a wind) blowing from the north-west. • adv. to or towards the north-west.
– DERIVATIVES **north-western** adj.

**northwester** • n. a wind blowing from the north-west.

**north-westerly** • adj. & adv. in a north-westward position or direction. • n. another term for **NORTHWESTER**.

**north-westward** • adv. (also **north-westwards**) towards the north-west. • adj. situated in, directed towards, or facing the north-west.

**Norway lobster** • n. a small, slender, commercially important European lobster. [*Nephrops norvegicus*.]

**Norway rat** • n. another term for **BROWN RAT**.

**Norwegian** /nɔːˈwiːdʒ(ə)n/ • n. **1** a native or national of Norway, or a person of Norwegian descent. **2** the Scandinavian language spoken in Norway. • adj. of or relating to Norway or its people or language.
– ORIGIN from med. L. *Norvegia* 'Norway' (from ON *Norvegr*, lit. 'north way') + **-AN**.

**nor'wester** • n. **1** short for **NORTHWESTER**. **2** an oilskin jacket or sou'wester.

**nos** • abbrev. numbers.
– ORIGIN pl. of **No.**

**nose** • n. **1** the part projecting above the mouth on the face of a person or animal, containing the nostrils and used in breathing and smelling. **2** the sense of smell. ➤ the aroma of a particular substance, especially wine. **3** the front end of an aircraft, car, or other vehicle. ➤ a projecting part. **4** an instinctive talent for detecting something: *he has a nose for a good script.* **5** an act of looking around or prying: *she wanted a good nose round the house.* ➤ informal a police informer. • v. **1** (of an animal) thrust its nose against or into something. ➤ smell or sniff (something). **2** look around or pry into something. **3** make one's way slowly ahead, especially in a vehicle.
– PHRASES **by a nose** (of a victory) by a very narrow margin. **cut off one's nose to spite one's face** disadvantage oneself through a wilful attempt to gain an advantage or assert oneself. **get one's nose in front** manage to achieve a winning or leading position. **get up someone's nose** informal irritate or annoy someone. **give someone a bloody nose** inflict a resounding defeat on someone. **keep one's nose clean** informal stay out of trouble. **keep one's nose out of** refrain from interfering in. **nose to tail** (of vehicles) moving or standing close behind one another. **not see further than one's (or the end of one's) nose** fail to consider different possibilities or to foresee consequences. **on the nose 1** to a person's sense of smell. **2** informal, chiefly N. Amer. precisely. **3** Austral./NZ informal distasteful; offensive. **4** informal (of betting) on a horse to win (as opposed to being placed). **put someone's nose out of joint** informal offend someone or hurt their pride. **turn one's nose up at** informal show distaste or contempt for. **under someone's nose** informal directly in front of someone. **with one's nose in the air** haughtily.
– DERIVATIVES **-nosed** adj. **noseless** adj.
– ORIGIN OE *nosu*, of W. Gmc origin.

**nosebag** • n. a bag containing fodder, hung from a horse's head and into which it can reach to eat.

**noseband** • n. the strap of a bridle that passes over the horse's nose and under its chin.

**nosebleed** • n. **1** an instance of bleeding from the nose. **2** [as modifier] N. Amer. informal denoting seats in an extremely high position in a stadium, theatre, etc.

**nose candy** • n. N. Amer. informal cocaine.

**nosedive** • n. **1** a steep downward plunge by an aircraft. **2** a sudden dramatic deterioration. • v. make a nosedive.

**no-see-um** /nəʊˈsiːəm/ • n. N. Amer. a minute biting insect.

**nose flute** • n. a flute played by blowing through the nose rather than the mouth.

**nosegay** • n. a small sweet-scented bunch of flowers.
– ORIGIN ME: from **NOSE** + **GAY** in the obs. sense 'ornament'.

**nose guard** • n. American Football a nose tackle.

**nose job** • n. informal an operation involving rhinoplasty or cosmetic surgery on a person's nose.

**nose leaf** • n. a fleshy leaf-shaped structure on the nose of a bat, involved in echolocation.

**nosema** /nəʊˈsiːmə/ • n. a spore-forming parasitic protozoan that causes disease in honeybees. [Genus *Nosema*.]
– ORIGIN mod. L., from Gk *nosēma* 'disease'.

**nosepiece** • n. **1** the part of a helmet or headdress that protects a person's nose. ➤ chiefly N. Amer. another term for **NOSEBAND**. **2** the part of a microscope to which the objective lenses are attached.

**nose tackle** • n. American Football a defensive lineman positioned opposite the offensive centre.

**nosey** • adj. & v. variant spelling of **NOSY**.

**nosh** informal • n. food. • v. eat enthusiastically or greedily.
– ORIGIN C20 (denoting a snack bar): Yiddish.

**noshery** • n. (pl. **-ies**) informal a restaurant or snack bar.

**no-show** • n. a person who has made a reservation, booking, or appointment but neither keeps nor cancels it.

**nosh-up** • n. Brit. informal a large meal.

**no side** • n. Rugby the end of a game.

**nosing** • n. a rounded edge of a step or moulding. ➤ a metal shield for such an edge.

**nosocomial** /ˌnɒsə(ʊ)ˈkəʊmɪəl/ • adj. Medicine (of a disease) originating in a hospital.
– ORIGIN C19: from Gk *nosokomos* 'person who tends the sick' + **-IAL**.

**nosode** /ˈnɒsəʊd/ • n. a preparation of substances secreted in the course of a disease, used in homeopathy.
– ORIGIN C19: from Gk *nosos* 'disease' + **-ODE**[1].

**nosology** /nɒˈsɒlədʒi/ • n. the branch of medical science concerned with the classification of diseases.
– DERIVATIVES **nosological** adj. **nosologist** n.
– ORIGIN C18: from Gk *nosos* 'disease' + **-LOGY**.

**nostalgia** • n. sentimental longing or wistful affection for a period in the past.
– DERIVATIVES **nostalgic** adj. **nostalgically** adv. **nostalgist** n.
– ORIGIN C18 (in the sense 'acute homesickness'): mod. L. (translating Ger. *Heimweh*), from Gk *nostos* 'return home' + *algos* 'pain'.

**nostalgie de la boue** /ˌnɒstalˈ(d)ʒiː də la ˌbuː/ • n. a desire for degradation and depravity.
– ORIGIN Fr., lit. 'mud nostalgia'.

**nostoc** /ˈnɒstɒk/ ● **n.** Biology a single-celled aquatic blue-green alga which aggregates to form a gelatinous mass. [Genus *Nostoc*.]
– ORIGIN name invented by the C16 Swiss physician Paracelsus.

**Nostratic** /nɒˈstratɪk/ ● **adj.** relating to or denoting a hypothetical phylum of languages including the Indo-European, Semitic, Altaic, and Dravidian families.
– ORIGIN 1960s: from Ger. *nostratisch*, based on L. *nostras, nostrat-* 'of our country'.

**nostril** ● **n.** either of two external openings of the nasal cavity in vertebrates that admit air to the lungs and smells to the olfactory nerves.
– DERIVATIVES **-nostrilled** adj.
– ORIGIN OE *nosterl, nosthyrl*, from *nosu* 'nose' + *thȳr(e)l* 'hole'.

**nostrum** /ˈnɒstrəm/ ● **n.** **1** a quack medicine. **2** a favourite method for bringing about social or political reform.
– ORIGIN C17: from L., used in the sense '(something) of our own making', neut. of *noster* 'our'.

**nosy** (also **nosey**) ● **adj.** (**-ier**, **-iest**) informal showing too much curiosity about other people's affairs.
– DERIVATIVES **nosily** adv. **nosiness** n.

**nosy parker** ● **n.** informal, chiefly Brit. an overly inquisitive person.
– ORIGIN C20: from the picture postcard caption, 'The adventures of Nosey Parker', referring to a peeping Tom.

**not** ● **adv.** **1** (also **n't** joined to a preceding verb) used chiefly with an auxiliary verb or 'be' to form the negative. **2** used as a short substitute for a negative clause. **3** used to express the negative of other words. ➤used with a quantifier to exclude a person or part of a group. ➤less than. **4** used in understatements to suggest that the opposite of a following word or phrase is true. ➤informal, humorous following and emphatically negating a statement: *that sounds like quality entertainment—not!* ● **n.** (**NOT**) **1** a logical operation which gives the value zero if the operand is one, and vice versa. **2** [as modifier] Electronics denoting a gate circuit which produces an output only when there is no input signal. ● **adj.** (often **Not**) Art (of paper) not hot-pressed, and having a slightly textured surface.
– ORIGIN ME: contr. of **NOUGHT**.

**nota bene** /ˌnəʊtə ˈbɛneɪ/ ● **v.** formal observe carefully; take special note.
– ORIGIN L., lit. 'note well!'

**notability** ● **n.** (pl. **-ies**) a famous or important person.

**notable** ● **adj.** worthy of attention or notice. ● **n.** a famous or important person.

**notably** ● **adv.** **1** in particular. **2** in a notable way.

**notam** /ˈnəʊtəm/ ● **n.** a written notification issued to pilots before a flight, advising them of relevant circumstances or precautions.
– ORIGIN 1940s: from *no(tice) t(o) a(ir)m(en)*.

**notaphily** /nəʊˈtafɪli/ ● **n.** the collecting of banknotes as a hobby.
– DERIVATIVES **notaphilic** adj. **notaphilist** n.

**notarize** (also **-ise**) ● **v.** have (a document) legalized by a notary.

**notary** /ˈnəʊt(ə)ri/ (in full **notary public**) ● **n.** (pl. **-ies**) a person authorized to perform certain legal formalities, especially to draw up or certify contracts, deeds, etc.
– DERIVATIVES **notarial** adj.
– ORIGIN ME (in the sense 'clerk or secretary'): from L. *notarius* 'secretary', from *nota* 'mark'.

**notation** ● **n.** **1** a system of written symbols used to represent numbers, amounts, or elements in a field such as music or mathematics. **2** an annotation.
– DERIVATIVES **notate** v. **notational** adj. **notator** n.
– ORIGIN C16: from L. *notatio(n-)*, from *notare* (v.), from *nota* 'mark'.

**notch** ● **n.** **1** an indentation or incision on an edge or surface. ➤each of a series of holes for the tongue of a buckle. ➤a nick made on something to keep a record. ➤a point or degree in a scale. **2** N. Amer. a deep, narrow mountain pass. ● **v.** **1** make notches in. ➤secure or insert by means of notches. **2** score or achieve.
– DERIVATIVES **notcher** n.
– ORIGIN C16: prob. from Anglo-Norman Fr. *noche*, var. of OFr. *osche*.

**notchback** ● **n.** a car with a back that extends approximately horizontally from the bottom of the rear window so as to make a distinct angle with it.

**notch filter** ● **n.** Electronics a filter that attenuates signals within a very narrow band of frequencies.

**notchy** ● **adj.** (**-ier**, **-iest**) (of a manual gear-changing mechanism) difficult to use because the lever has to be moved accurately (as if into a narrow notch).

**note** ● **n.** **1** a brief written record of facts, topics, or thoughts, used as an aid to memory. ➤an annotation. **2** a short informal written message. ➤an official letter sent from the representative of one government to another. ➤a short official document of certification. **3** Brit. a banknote. ➤a written promise or notice of payment of various kinds. **4** a single tone of definite pitch made by a musical instrument or the human voice. ➤a written sign representing the pitch and duration of such a sound. ➤a key of a piano or similar instrument. **5** a bird's song or call, or a single tone in this. **6** a particular quality or tone expressing a mood or attitude. **7** any of the basic components of a fragrance or flavour. ● **v.** **1** pay attention to. **2** record in writing.
– PHRASES **hit** (or **strike**) **the right** (or **wrong**) **note** say or do something in the right (or wrong) way. **of note** important. **strike** (or **sound**) **a note of** express (a particular feeling or view). **take note** pay attention.
– ORIGIN ME: from OFr. *note* (n.), *noter* (v.), from L. *nota* 'a mark', *notare* 'to mark'.

**notebook** ● **n.** **1** a small book for writing notes in. **2** a portable computer that is smaller than a laptop.

**notecase** ● **n.** Brit. dated a small flat folding case or wallet for banknotes.

**note cluster** ● **n.** Music a chord containing a number of closely adjacent notes.

**noted** ● **adj.** well known.

**notelet** ● **n.** a small folded sheet of paper with a decorative design on the front, for an informal letter.

**notepad** ● **n.** **1** a pad of paper for writing notes on. **2** a pocket-sized personal computer in which text is input using a stylus.

**notepaper** ● **n.** paper for writing letters on.

**noteworthy** ● **adj.** interesting or significant.
– DERIVATIVES **noteworthiness** n.

**nothing** ● **pron.** not anything. ➤something of no importance or concern. ➤(in calculations) nought. ● **adj.** informal of no value or significance. ● **adv.** not at all. ➤[postpos.] N. Amer. informal used to contradict something emphatically.
– PHRASES **for nothing 1** without payment or charge. **2** to no purpose. **nothing but** only. **nothing doing** informal **1** there is no prospect of success or agreement. **2** nothing is happening. **nothing** (or **nothing else**) **for it** Brit. no alternative. **nothing less than** used to emphasize how extreme something is. **there is nothing to it** there is no difficulty involved. **sweet nothings** words of affection exchanged by lovers. **think nothing of it** do not apologize or feel bound to show gratitude.
– ORIGIN OE *nān thing* (see **NO**, **THING**).

**nothingness** ● **n.** **1** the absence or cessation of existence. **2** worthlessness; insignificance.

**notice** ● **n.** **1** attention; observation. **2** advance notification or warning. ➤a formal declaration of one's intention to end an agreement, typically one concerning employment or tenancy, at a specified time. **3** a displayed sheet or placard giving news or information. ➤a small advertisement or announcement in a newspaper or magazine. **4** a short published review of a new film, play, or book. ● **v.** **1** become aware of. ➤archaic remark upon. **2** (**be noticed**) be treated or recognized as noteworthy.
– PHRASES **at short** (or **a moment's**) **notice** with little warning. **put someone on notice** (or **serve notice**) warn someone of something about or likely to occur. **take** (**no**) **notice** (**of**) pay (no) attention (to).
– ORIGIN ME: from OFr., from L. *notitia* 'being known', from *notus* (see **NOTION**).

**noticeable** ● **adj.** easily seen or noticed; clear.
– DERIVATIVES **noticeably** adv.

**notifiable** • adj. denoting something, especially a serious infectious disease, that must be reported to the appropriate authorities.

**notify** • v. (**-ies**, **-ied**) inform, typically in a formal or official manner. ➤ report formally or officially.
– DERIVATIVES **notification** n.
– ORIGIN ME: from OFr. *notifier*, from L. *notificare* 'make known'.

**notion** • n. **1** a concept or belief. ➤ a vague awareness or understanding. **2** an impulse or desire. **3** (**notions**) chiefly N. Amer. items used in sewing, such as buttons and pins.
– ORIGIN ME: from L. *notio(n-)* 'idea', from *notus* 'known', past part. of *noscere*.

**notional** • adj. **1** hypothetical or imaginary. **2** Linguistics denoting or relating to an approach to grammar which is dependent on the definition of terminology (e.g. 'a verb is a doing word').
– DERIVATIVES **notionally** adv.

**notochord** /ˈnəʊtə(ʊ)kɔːd/ • n. Zoology a cartilaginous skeletal rod supporting the body in all embryonic and some adult chordate animals.
– ORIGIN C19: from Gk *nōton* 'back' + **CHORD**[2].

**notorious** • adj. famous for some bad quality or deed.
– DERIVATIVES **notoriety** n. **notoriously** adv.
– ORIGIN C15: from med. L. *notorius* (from L. *notus* 'known') + **-OUS**.

**notornis** /nə(ʊ)ˈtɔːnɪs/ • n. another term for **TAKAHE**.
– ORIGIN C19: from Gk *notos* 'south' + *ornis* 'bird'.

**no-trumper** • n. Bridge a hand on which a no-trump bid can suitably be made or has been made.

**no trumps** • n. Bridge a situation in which no suit is designated as trumps.

**Nottingham lace** • n. a type of machine-made flat lace.

**Notts.** • abbrev. Nottinghamshire.

**notwithstanding** • prep. in spite of. • adv. nevertheless. • conj. although.
– ORIGIN ME: from **NOT** + *withstanding*, pres. part. of **WITHSTAND**.

**nougat** /ˈnuːgɑː, ˈnʌgət/ • n. a sweet made from sugar or honey, nuts, and egg white.
– ORIGIN C19: from Fr., from Provençal *nogat*, from *noga* 'nut'.

**nougatine** /ˌnuːgəˈtiːn/ • n. nougat covered with chocolate.
– ORIGIN C19: from **NOUGAT** + **-INE**[1].

**nought** • n. the digit 0. • pron. variant spelling of **NAUGHT**.

**noughts and crosses** • pl. n. chiefly Brit. a game in which two players seek to complete a row of either three noughts or three crosses drawn alternately in the spaces of a grid of nine squares.

**noumenon** /ˈnaʊmənɒn/ • n. (pl. **noumena**) (in Kantian philosophy) a thing as it is in itself, as distinct from a thing as it is knowable by the senses through phenomenal attributes.
– DERIVATIVES **noumenal** adj.
– ORIGIN C18: via Ger. from Gk, lit. '(something) conceived'.

**noun** • n. Grammar a word (other than a pronoun) used to identify any of a class of people, places, or things (**common noun**), or to name a particular one of these (**proper noun**).
– DERIVATIVES **nounal** adj.
– ORIGIN ME: from Anglo-Norman Fr., from L. *nomen* 'name'.

**noun phrase** • n. Grammar a word or group of words that function in a sentence as subject, object, or prepositional object.

**nourish** • v. **1** provide with the food or other substances necessary for growth and health. ➤ enhance the fertility of (soil). **2** keep (a feeling or belief) in one's mind for a long time.
– DERIVATIVES **nourisher** n. **nourishing** adj. **nourishingly** adv. **nourishment** n.
– ORIGIN ME: from OFr. *noriss-*, lengthened stem of *norir*, from L. *nutrire* 'feed, cherish'.

**nous** /naʊs/ • n. **1** Brit. informal practical intelligence. **2** Philosophy the mind or intellect.
– ORIGIN C17: from Gk, 'mind, intelligence'.

**nouveau** /ˈnuːvəʊ, French nuvo/ • adj. informal **1** short for **NOUVEAU RICHE**. **2** up to date.

**nouveau riche** /ˌnuːvəʊ ˈriːʃ, French nuvo ʀiʃ/ • n. [treated as pl.] people who have recently acquired wealth, typically those perceived as lacking good taste. • adj. of, relating to, or characteristic of such people.
– ORIGIN Fr., lit. 'new rich'.

**nouveau roman** /ˌnuːvəʊ rəʊˈmɑːn, French nuvo ʀɔmɑ̃/ • n. a style of avant-garde French novel which rejected traditional novelistic conventions in an attempt to reflect the sometimes random nature of experience.
– ORIGIN Fr., lit. 'new novel'.

**nouvelle** /nuːˈvɛl/ • adj. of or relating to nouvelle cuisine.

**nouvelle cuisine** /kwɪˈziːn/ • n. a modern style of cookery that avoids rich foods and emphasizes the freshness of the ingredients and the presentation of the dishes.
– ORIGIN Fr., lit. 'new cookery'.

**nouvelle vague** /nuːˌvɛl ˈvɑːg, French nuvɛl vag/ • n. a grouping of French film directors in the late 1950s and 1960s who sought to make stylistically innovative films.
– ORIGIN Fr., lit. 'new wave'.

**Nov.** • abbrev. November.

**nova** /ˈnəʊvə/ • n. (pl. **novae** /-viː/ or **novas**) Astronomy a star showing a sudden large increase in brightness and then slowly returning to normal.
– ORIGIN C19: from L., fem. of *novus* 'new' (because such stars were thought to be newly formed).

**novaculite** /nə(ʊ)ˈvakjʊlʌɪt/ • n. Geology a hard, dense, fine-grained siliceous rock resembling chert, with a high content of microcrystalline quartz.
– ORIGIN C18: from L. *novacula* 'razor' + **-ITE**[1].

**Nova Scotian** /ˌnəʊvə ˈskəʊʃ(ə)n/ • n. a native or inhabitant of the Canadian province or peninsula of Nova Scotia. • adj. of or relating to Nova Scotia.

**novation** /nə(ʊ)ˈveɪʃ(ə)n/ • n. Law the substitution of a new contract in place of an old one.
– DERIVATIVES **novate** v.
– ORIGIN C16: from late L. *novatio(n-)*, from *novare* 'make new'.

**novel**[1] • n. a fictitious prose narrative of book length.
– ORIGIN C16: from Ital. *novella (storia)* 'new (story)'.

**novel**[2] • adj. interestingly new or unusual.
– DERIVATIVES **novelly** adv.
– ORIGIN ME: from OFr., from L. *novellus*, from *novus* 'new'.

**novelette** • n. chiefly derogatory a short novel, typically a light romantic one.
– DERIVATIVES **novelettish** adj.

**novelist** • n. a writer of novels.

**novelistic** • adj. of or characteristic of novels.

**novelize** (also **-ise**) • v. [usu. as adj. **novelized**] convert (a story, typically one in the form of a film) into a novel.
– DERIVATIVES **novelization** n.

**novella** /nəˈvɛlə/ • n. a short novel or long short story.
– ORIGIN C20: from Ital., 'novel'.

**novelty** • n. (pl. **-ies**) **1** the quality of being novel. ➤ a new or unfamiliar thing or experience. ➤ [as modifier] denoting something intended to be amusing as a result of its originality or unusualness. **2** a small and inexpensive toy or ornament.

**November** • n. **1** the eleventh month of the year. **2** a code word representing the letter N, used in radio communication.
– ORIGIN OE, from L., from *novem* 'nine' (being orig. the ninth month of the Roman year).

**novena** /nə(ʊ)ˈviːnə/ • n. (in the Roman Catholic Church) a form of worship consisting of special prayers or services on nine successive days.
– ORIGIN C19: from med. L., from L. *novem* 'nine'.

**novice** /ˈnɒvɪs/ • n. **1** a person new to and inexperienced in a job or situation. **2** a person who has entered a religious order and is under probation, before taking vows.

**3** a racehorse that has not yet won a major prize or reached a level of performance to qualify for important events.
– ORIGIN ME: from OFr., from late L. *novicius*, from *novus* 'new'.

**novitiate** /nə(ʊ)'vɪʃɪət, -ɪeɪt/ (also **noviciate**) ● **n. 1** the period or state of being a novice. **2** a novice, especially in a religious order. **3** a place housing religious novices.
– ORIGIN C17: from eccles. L. *noviciatus*, from L. *novicius* (see **NOVICE**).

**novocaine** /'nəʊvəkeɪn/ ● **n.** another term for **PROCAINE**.
– ORIGIN C20: from L. *novus* 'new' + *-caine* (from **COCAINE**).

**now** ● **adv. 1** at the present time. ➤at or from this precise moment. ➤under the present circumstances. **2** used, especially in conversation, to draw attention to something. **3** used in a request, instruction, or question. ● **conj.** as a consequence of the fact. ● **adj.** informal fashionable.
– PHRASES **now and again** (or **then**) from time to time. **now or never** used to convey urgency. **now you're talking** an expression of enthusiastic agreement or approval.
– DERIVATIVES **nowness** n.
– ORIGIN OE *nū*, of Gmc origin.

**nowadays** ● **adv.** at the present time, in contrast with the past.

**noway** (also **noways**) ● **adv.** chiefly archaic or N. Amer. not at all.

**Nowel** (also **Nowell**) ● **n.** archaic spelling of **NOEL**.

**nowhere** ● **adv.** not in or to any place. ● **pron. 1** no place. **2** a place that is remote or uninteresting. ● **adj.** informal having no prospect of progress or success.
– PHRASES **be** (or **come**) **nowhere** be badly defeated in a race or competition. **from** (or **out of**) **nowhere** appearing or happening suddenly and unexpectedly. **get** (or **go**) **nowhere** make no progress. **get someone nowhere** be of no benefit to someone. **nowhere near** not nearly.
– ORIGIN OE *nāhwǣr* (see **NO**, **WHERE**).

**nowise** ● **adv.** archaic not at all.

**nowt** /naʊt/ ● **pron. & adv.** N. English nothing.

**NOx** ● **n.** oxides of nitrogen, especially as atmospheric pollutants.

**noxious** /'nɒkʃəs/ ● **adj.** harmful, poisonous, or very unpleasant.
– DERIVATIVES **noxiously** adv. **noxiousness** n.
– ORIGIN C15: from L. *noxius* (from *noxa* 'harm') + **-OUS**.

**noyau** /nwʌ'jəʊ/ ● **n.** (pl. **noyaux** /-jəʊz/) a liqueur made of brandy flavoured with fruit kernels.
– ORIGIN Fr., lit. 'kernel'.

**nozzle** ● **n.** a spout at the end of a pipe, hose, or tube used to control a jet of liquid or gas.
– ORIGIN C17: from **NOSE** + **-LE**[2].

**NP** ● **abbrev.** notary public.

**Np** ● **symb.** the chemical element neptunium.

**n.p.** ● **abbrev. 1** new paragraph. **2** (in book classification) no place of publication.

**NPV** ● **abbrev.** net present value.

**nr** ● **abbrev.** near.

**NRA** ● **abbrev. 1** (in the US) National Rifle Association. **2** (in the UK) National Rivers Authority.

**NRSV** ● **abbrev.** New Revised Standard Version (of the Bible).

**NS** ● **abbrev. 1** (in calculating dates) New Style. **2** Nova Scotia (in official postal use).

**ns** ● **abbrev.** nanosecond.

**n/s** ● **abbrev.** (in personal advertisements) non-smoker; non-smoking.

**NSA** ● **abbrev.** (in the US) National Security Agency.

**NSB** ● **abbrev.** (in the UK) National Savings Bank.

**NSC** ● **abbrev.** (in the US) National Security Council.

**NSF** ● **abbrev.** (in the US) National Science Foundation.

**NSPCC** ● **abbrev.** (in the UK) National Society for the Prevention of Cruelty to Children.

**NSU** ● **abbrev.** Medicine non-specific urethritis.

**NSW** ● **abbrev.** New South Wales.

**NT** ● **abbrev. 1** National Trust. **2** New Testament. **3** Northern Territory. **4** Northwest Territories (in official postal use). **5** Bridge no trump(s).

**-n't** ● **contr.** not, used with auxiliary verbs (e.g. *can't*).

**Nth** ● **abbrev.** North.

**nth** /ɛnθ/ ● **adj. 1** Mathematics denoting an unspecified member of a series of numbers or enumerated items. **2** denoting the last or latest item or instance in a long series.
– PHRASES **to the nth degree** to the utmost.

**NTP** ● **abbrev.** Chemistry normal temperature and pressure.

**NTSC** ● **n.** the television broadcasting system used in North America and Japan.
– ORIGIN 1950s: acronym from *National Television Standard Committee.*

**n-type** ● **adj.** Electronics denoting a region in a semiconductor in which electrical conduction is due chiefly to the movement of electrons. Compare with **P-TYPE**.

**nu** /njuː/ ● **n.** the thirteenth letter of the Greek alphabet (N, ν), transliterated as 'n'. ● **symb.** (ν) frequency.
– ORIGIN from Gk.

**nuance** /'njuːɑːns/ ● **n.** a subtle difference in or shade of meaning, expression, colour, etc. ● **v.** (usu. **be nuanced**) give nuances to.
– ORIGIN C18: from Fr., 'shade, subtlety'.

**nub** ● **n. 1** (**the nub**) the crux or central point of a matter. **2** a small lump or protuberance. ➤a small chunk or nugget of metal or rock.
– ORIGIN C17: appar. a var. of dial. *knub* 'protuberance'.

**Nuba** /'nuːbə/ ● **n.** (pl. same or **Nubas**) a member of a Nilotic people inhabiting southern Kordofan in Sudan.
– ORIGIN from L. *Nubae* 'Nubians'.

**nubbin** /'nʌbɪn/ ● **n.** a small lump or residual part.
– ORIGIN C17: dimin. of **NUB**.

**nubby** (also **nubbly**) ● **adj.** chiefly US **1** (of fabric) coarse or knobbly in texture. **2** stubby or lumpy.
– ORIGIN C19: derivative of *nubble* 'small lump'.

**Nubian** ● **n. 1** a native or inhabitant of an area of southern Egypt and northern Sudan corresponding to the ancient region of Nubia. **2** the Nilo-Saharan language spoken by the Nubians. **3** a goat of a short-haired breed with long pendant ears and long legs, originally from Africa. ● **adj.** of or relating to the Nubians or their language, or ancient Nubia.

**nubile** /'njuːbʌɪl/ ● **adj.** (of a girl or woman) youthful but sexually mature and attractive.
– DERIVATIVES **nubility** n.
– ORIGIN C17: from L. *nubilis* 'marriageable'.

**nubuck** /'njuːbʌk/ ● **n.** cowhide leather which has been rubbed on the flesh side to give a suede-like effect.
– ORIGIN 1970s: perh. respelling of **NEW** + **BUCK**[1].

**nucellus** /njuː'sɛləs/ ● **n.** (pl. **nucelli**) Botany the central part of an ovule, containing the embryo sac.
– DERIVATIVES **nucellar** adj.
– ORIGIN C19: mod. L., appar. an irregular dimin. of **NUCLEUS**.

**nuchal** /'njuːk(ə)l/ ● **adj.** Anatomy of or relating to the nape of the neck.
– ORIGIN C19: from obs. *nucha* 'nape' (from med. L. *nucha* 'medulla oblongata') + **-AL**.

**nuci-** /'njuːsi/ ● **comb. form** of a nut or nuts: *nuciferous.*
– ORIGIN from L. *nux*, *nuc-* 'nut'.

**nuciferous** /njuː'sɪf(ə)rəs/ ● **adj.** Botany bearing nuts.

**nuclear** ● **adj. 1** of or relating to a nucleus. **2** relating to or using energy released in nuclear fission or fusion. ➤possessing or involving nuclear weapons.

**nuclear family** ● **n.** a couple and their dependent children, regarded as a basic social unit.

**nuclear force** ● **n.** Physics the strong attractive force that holds nucleons together in the atomic nucleus.

**nuclear fuel** ● **n.** a substance that will sustain a fission chain reaction so that it can be used as a source of nuclear energy.

**nuclear isomer** ● **n.** another term for **ISOMER** (in sense 2).

**nuclear magnetic resonance** ● **n.** the absorption of electromagnetic radiation by certain nuclei (especially protons) in an external magnetic field, used as an analytical and imaging technique.

**nuclear medicine** • n. the branch of medicine concerned with the use of radioactive substances in research, diagnosis, and treatment.

**nuclear physics** • pl. n. [treated as sing.] the physics of atomic nuclei and their interactions, especially in the generation of nuclear energy.

**nuclear power** • n. **1** electric or motive power generated by a nuclear reactor. **2** a country that has nuclear weapons.
– DERIVATIVES **nuclear-powered** adj.

**nuclear threshold** • n. a point in a conflict at which nuclear weapons are or would be brought into use.

**nuclear umbrella** • n. the supposed protection gained from an alliance with a country possessing nuclear weapons.

**nuclear waste** • n. radioactive waste material, for example from the use or reprocessing of nuclear fuel.

**nuclear winter** • n. a period of abnormal cold and darkness predicted to follow a nuclear war, caused by a layer of smoke and dust in the atmosphere blocking the sun's rays.

**nuclease** /ˈnjuːklɪeɪz/ • n. Biochemistry an enzyme that cleaves nucleic acid chains into smaller units.

**nucleate** • adj. /ˈnjuːklɪət/ chiefly Biology having a nucleus. • v. /ˈnjuːklɪeɪt/ [usu. as adj. **nucleated**] **1** form a nucleus. **2** form around a central area.
– DERIVATIVES **nucleation** n.

**nuclei** plural form of **NUCLEUS**.

**nucleic acid** /njuːˈkliːɪk, -ˈkleɪɪk/ • n. Biochemistry a complex organic substance, especially DNA or RNA, whose molecules consist of long chains of nucleotides.

**nucleo-** • comb. form representing **NUCLEUS**, **NUCLEAR**, or **NUCLEIC ACID**.

**nucleolus** /ˌnjuːklɪˈəʊləs/ • n. (pl. **nucleoli** /-lʌɪ/) Biology a small dense spherical structure in a cell nucleus during interphase.
– DERIVATIVES **nucleolar** adj.
– ORIGIN C19: from late L., dimin. of L. *nucleus* (see **NUCLEUS**).

**nucleon** /ˈnjuːklɪɒn/ • n. Physics a proton or neutron.

**nucleonics** /ˌnjuːklɪˈɒnɪks/ • pl. n. [treated as sing.] the branch of science and technology concerned with atomic nuclei and nuclear power.
– DERIVATIVES **nucleonic** adj.
– ORIGIN 1940s: from **NUCLEAR**, on the pattern of *electronics*.

**nucleophilic** /ˌnjuːklɪə(ʊ)ˈfɪlɪk/ • adj. Chemistry having a tendency to donate electrons or react with protons. Often contrasted with **ELECTROPHILIC**.
– DERIVATIVES **nucleophile** n.

**nucleoside** • n. Biochemistry an organic compound consisting of a purine or pyrimidine base linked to a sugar, e.g. adenosine.

**nucleosynthesis** • n. Astronomy the cosmic formation of atoms more complex than the hydrogen atom.
– DERIVATIVES **nucleosynthetic** adj.

**nucleotide** • n. Biochemistry a compound consisting of a nucleoside linked to a phosphate group, forming the basic structural unit of nucleic acids.

**nucleus** /ˈnjuːklɪəs/ • n. (pl. **nuclei** /-lɪʌɪ/) **1** the central and most important part of an object or group. **2** Physics the positively charged central core of an atom, containing nearly all its mass. **3** Biology a structure present in most cells, containing the genetic material. **4** a discrete mass of grey matter in the central nervous system.
– ORIGIN C18: from L., lit. 'kernel, inner part', dimin. of *nux, nuc-* 'nut'.

**nuclide** /ˈnjuːklʌɪd/ • n. Physics a distinct kind of atom or nucleus characterized by a specific number of protons and neutrons.
– DERIVATIVES **nuclidic** adj.
– ORIGIN 1940s: from **NUCLEUS** + *-ide* (from Gk *eidos* 'form').

**nuddy** • n. (in phr. **in the nuddy**) informal in the nude.

**nude** • adj. wearing no clothes. • n. a naked human figure as a subject in art or photography.
– DERIVATIVES **nudity** n.
– ORIGIN ME (in the sense 'plain, explicit'): from L. *nudus*.

**nudge** • v. **1** prod gently with one's elbow to attract attention. **2** touch or push gently or gradually. **3** give gentle encouragement to. • n. a light touch or push.
– DERIVATIVES **nudger** n.
– ORIGIN C17: of unknown origin; cf. Norw. dial. *nugga*, *nyggja* 'to push, rub'.

**Nudibranchia** /ˌnjuːdɪˈbraŋkɪə/ • pl. n. Zoology an order of shell-less marine molluscs comprising the sea slugs.
– DERIVATIVES **nudibranch** /ˈnjuːdɪbraŋk/ n.
– ORIGIN mod. L., from L. *nudus* 'nude' + **BRANCHIA**.

**nudist** • n. a person who goes naked wherever possible.
– DERIVATIVES **nudism** n.

**nudnik** /ˈnʊdnɪk/ (also **nudnick**) • n. N. Amer. informal a pestering or irritating person.
– ORIGIN C20: Yiddish, from Russ. *nudnyĭ* 'tedious'.

**nuée ardente** /ˌnjʊeɪ ɑːˈdɒ̃t/ • n. Geology an incandescent cloud of gas, ash, and lava fragments ejected from a volcano, typically as part of a pyroclastic flow.
– ORIGIN Fr., lit. 'burning cloud'.

**Nuer** /ˈnuːə/ • n. (pl. same or **Nuers**) **1** a member of an African people of SE Sudan and Ethiopia. **2** the Nilotic language of this people.
– ORIGIN the name in Dinka.

**nuevo sol** /ˌnweɪvəʊ ˈsɒl, Spanish ˌnweβo ˈsol/ • n. another term for **SOL**[3].
– ORIGIN Sp., 'new sol'.

**nuff** • det., pron., & adv. non-standard spelling of **ENOUGH**, representing informal speech. • det. black English much.

**nugatory** /ˈnjuːgət(ə)ri, ˈnuː-/ • adj. **1** worthless. **2** useless or invalid.
– ORIGIN C17: from L. *nugatorius*, from *nugari* 'to trifle'.

**nugget** • n. **1** a small lump of gold or other precious metal found ready-formed in the earth. **2** a small but valuable fact.
– DERIVATIVES **nuggety** adj. (chiefly Austral./NZ).
– ORIGIN C19: appar. from dial. *nug* 'lump', of unknown origin.

**nuisance** • n. a person or thing causing inconvenience or annoyance. ➤ Law an act which is harmful or offensive to the public or a member of it and for which there is a legal remedy.
– ORIGIN ME (in the sense 'injury'): from OFr., 'hurt', based on L. *nocere* 'to harm'.

**nuisance grounds** • pl. n. Canadian a rubbish dump.

**Nuits St George** /ˌnwiː sã ˈʒɔːʒ, French nɥi sɛ̃ ʒɔʀʒ/ • n. a red burgundy wine, produced in the district of Nuits St Georges, France.

**NUJ** • abbrev. (in the UK) National Union of Journalists.

**nuke** informal • n. a nuclear weapon. • v. **1** attack or destroy with nuclear weapons. **2** N. Amer. cook or heat up (food) in a microwave oven.

**null** • adj. **1** (usu. in phr. **null and void**) having no legal force; invalid. **2** having or associated with the value zero. ➤ Mathematics (of a set or matrix) having no elements, or only zeros as elements. **3** having no positive substance. • n. **1** a dummy letter in a cipher. **2** Electronics a condition in which no signal is generated; something generating no signal. • v. Electronics cancel out, creating a null.
– ORIGIN ME: from Fr. *nul, nulle*, from L. *nullus* 'none', from *ne* 'not' + *ullus* 'any'.

**nullah** /ˈnʌlə/ • n. Indian a dry river bed or ravine.
– ORIGIN C18: from Hindi *nālā*.

**nulla-nulla** /ˈnʌlənʌlə/ (also **nulla**) • n. a hardwood club used as a weapon by Australian Aboriginals.
– ORIGIN from Dharuk *ngalla-ngalla*.

**null hypothesis** • n. (in a statistical test) the hypothesis that any observed differences between two populations are due to sampling or experimental error.

**nullify** /ˈnʌlɪfʌɪ/ • v. (**-ies**, **-ied**) make null and void. ➤ cancel out.
– DERIVATIVES **nullification** n. **nullifier** n.

**nullipara** /nʌˈlɪp(ə)rə/ • n. (pl. **nulliparae** /nʌˈlɪp(ə)riː/) Medicine & Zoology a woman (or female animal) that has

never given birth.
– DERIVATIVES **nulliparous** adj.
– ORIGIN C19: mod. L., from L. *nullus* 'none' + *-para*, from *parere* 'bear children'.

**nullity** • n. (pl. **-ies**) **1** Law a thing that is legally void. ➤ the state of being legally void. **2** a thing of no importance or worth. ➤ nothingness.

**NUM** • abbrev. (in the UK) National Union of Mineworkers.

**Num.** • abbrev. Numbers (in biblical references).

**numb** • adj. deprived of the power of sensation. • v. make numb.
– DERIVATIVES **numbly** adv. **numbness** n.
– ORIGIN ME *nome(n)*, past part. of obs. *nim* 'take'.

**numbat** /'nʌmbat/ • n. a small termite-eating Australian marsupial with a black-and-white-striped back and a bushy tail. [*Myrmecobius fasciatus*.]
– ORIGIN C20: from Nyungar.

**number** • n. **1** an arithmetical value, expressed by a word, symbol, or figure, representing a particular quantity. **2** a quantity or amount. ➤ (**a number of**) several. ➤ (**numbers**) a large quantity or amount; numerical preponderance. **3** a single issue of a magazine. **4** a song, dance, or other musical item. **5** informal an item of clothing of a particular type: *a little black number.* **6** a grammatical classification of words that consists typically of singular and plural. • v. **1** amount to. **2** assign a number to. ➤ count. **3** include as a member of a group.
– PHRASES **by numbers** following simple instructions identified or as if identified by numbers. **someone's** (or **something's**) **days are numbered** someone or something will not survive or remain in power for much longer. **do a number on** N. Amer. informal deceive or disparage. **have someone's number** informal understand a person's real motives or character. **someone's number is up** informal someone is finished or doomed to die. [with ref. to a lottery number or a number by which one may be identified.] **without number** too many to count.
– DERIVATIVES **numberless** adj.
– ORIGIN ME: from OFr. *nombre* (n.), *nombrer* (v.), from L. *numerus*.

**number cruncher** • n. informal **1** a computer or program capable of performing rapid calculations with large amounts of data. **2** often derogatory a statistician or other person dealing with large amounts of numerical data.
– DERIVATIVES **number crunching** n.

**numbered account** • n. a bank account, especially in a Swiss bank, identified only by a number and not bearing the owner's name.

**number one** informal • n. **1** oneself. **2** a person or thing that is foremost in an activity or area. **3** euphemistic urine. **4** a first lieutenant in the navy. • adj. most important; foremost.
– PHRASES **number one, number two, etc.** the shortest, or next shortest, etc., cropped men's haircut produced with electric hair clippers.

**number plate** • n. Brit. a sign affixed to the front and rear of a vehicle displaying its registration number.

**numbers game** • n. **1** often derogatory the use or manipulation of statistics or figures. **2** (also **numbers racket**) N. Amer. a lottery based on the occurrence of unpredictable numbers in the results of races, a lottery, etc.

**number two** • n. informal **1** a second in command. **2** euphemistic faeces.

**numbles** (also **umbles**) • pl. n. Brit. archaic an animal's entrails, especially those of a deer, as used for food.
– ORIGIN ME (denoting the back and loins of a deer): from OFr., from L. *lumbulus*, dimin. of *lumbus* 'loin'.

**numbskull** (also **numskull**) • n. informal a stupid person.

**numdah** /'nʌmdə/ • n. (in the Indian subcontinent and the Middle East) an embroidered felt or woollen rug.
– ORIGIN from Urdu *namdā*, from Pers. *namad* 'carpet'.

**numen** /'nju:mən/ • n. (pl. **numina** /-mɪnə/) a presiding spirit or deity.
– ORIGIN C17: from L.

**numerable** • adj. able to be counted.
– ORIGIN C16: from L. *numerabilis*, from *numerare* 'to number'.

**numeraire** /'nju:mərɛ:/ • n. Economics an item or commodity acting as a measure of value or as a standard for currency exchange.
– ORIGIN 1960s: from Fr. *numéraire*, from late L. *numerarius*, from L. *numerus* 'a number'.

**numeral** • n. a figure, word, or group of figures denoting a number. • adj. of or denoting a number.
– ORIGIN ME: from late L. *numeralis*, from L. *numerus* (see **NUMBER**).

**numerate** /'nju:m(ə)rət/ • adj. having a good basic knowledge of arithmetic.
– DERIVATIVES **numeracy** n.
– ORIGIN 1950s: from L. *numerus* 'a number', on the pattern of *literate*.

**numeration** • n. the action or process of numbering or calculating. ➤ a method of numbering or computing.
– ORIGIN ME: from L. *numeratio(n-)* 'payment' (in late L. 'numbering'), from *numerare* 'to number'.

**numerator** • n. the number above the line in a vulgar fraction showing how many of the parts indicated by the denominator are taken, e.g. 2 in ⅔.

**numerical** • adj. of, relating to, or expressed as a number or numbers.
– DERIVATIVES **numerically** adv.
– ORIGIN C17: from med. L. *numericus* (from L. *numerus* 'a number') + **-AL**.

**numerical analysis** • n. the branch of mathematics concerned with the development and use of numerical methods for solving problems.

**numerology** /ˌnju:mə'rɒlədʒi/ • n. the branch of knowledge concerned with the occult significance of numbers.
– DERIVATIVES **numerological** adj. **numerologist** n.
– ORIGIN C20: from L. *numerus* 'a number' + **-LOGY**.

**numero uno** /ˌnju:mərəʊ 'u:nəʊ/ • n. (pl. **-os**) informal the best or most important person or thing.
– ORIGIN Ital., lit. 'number one'.

**numerous** • adj. many. ➤ consisting of many members.
– DERIVATIVES **numerously** adv. **numerousness** n.
– ORIGIN ME: from L. *numerosus*, from *numerus* 'a number'.

**numerus clausus** /ˌnju:mərəs 'klaʊsəs/ • n. a fixed maximum number of entrants admissible to an academic institution.
– ORIGIN L., lit. 'closed number'.

**Numidian** /nju:'mɪdɪən/ • n. a native or inhabitant of the ancient region of Numidia in North Africa. • adj. of or relating to Numidia.

**numina** plural form of **NUMEN**.

**numinous** /'nju:mɪnəs/ • adj. having a strong religious or spiritual quality.
– ORIGIN C17: from L. *numen*, *numin-* 'divine will' + **-OUS**.

**numismatic** /ˌnju:mɪz'matɪk/ • adj. of or relating to coins or medals.
– DERIVATIVES **numismatically** adv.
– ORIGIN C18: from Fr. *numismatique*, via L. from Gk *nomisma*, *nomismat-* 'current coin'.

**numismatics** • pl. n. [usu. treated as sing.] the study or collection of coins, banknotes, and medals.
– DERIVATIVES **numismatist** /nju:'mɪzmətɪst/ n.

**numismatology** /ˌnju:mɪzmə'tɒlədʒi, nju:ˌmɪz-/ • n. numismatics.

**nummulite** /'nʌmjʊlʌɪt/ • n. Palaeontology the fossilized disc-shaped calcareous shell of a foraminifer.
– ORIGIN C19: from L. *nummulus* (dimin. of *nummus* 'coin') + **-ITE**[1].

**numnah** /'nʌmnə/ • n. a pad placed under a saddle.
– ORIGIN C19: from Urdu *namdā*.

**numpty** • n. (pl. **-ies**) Scottish informal a stupid or ineffectual person.
– ORIGIN from obs. *numps* 'a stupid person'.

**numskull** • n. variant spelling of **NUMBSKULL**.

**nun** • n. **1** a member of a female religious community, living under vows of poverty, chastity, and obedience. **2** a pigeon of a breed with a crest on its neck.
– DERIVATIVES **nunlike** adj. **nunnish** adj.
– ORIGIN OE *nonne*, from eccles. L. *nonna*, fem. of *nonnus*

'monk'.

**nunatak** /'nʌnətak/ ● **n.** an isolated peak of rock projecting above a surface of inland ice or snow.
– ORIGIN C19: from Eskimo *nunataq*.

**Nunc Dimittis** /ˌnʌŋk dɪ'mɪtɪs/ ● **n.** the Song of Simeon (Luke 2:29–32) used as a canticle in Christian liturgy.
– ORIGIN L., the opening words of the canticle, '(Lord), now you let (your servant) depart'.

**nunchaku** /nʌn'tʃaku:/ ● **n.** (pl. same or **nunchakus**) a Japanese martial arts weapon consisting of two hardwood sticks joined together by a chain, rope, or thong.
– ORIGIN from Japanese.

**nuncio** /'nʌnsɪəʊ, 'nʌnʃɪəʊ/ ● **n.** (pl. **-os**) (in the Roman Catholic Church) a papal ambassador to a foreign government or court.
– DERIVATIVES **nunciature** n.
– ORIGIN C16: from Ital., from L. *nuntius* 'messenger'.

**nuncupative** /'nʌŋkjʊˌpətɪv/ ● **adj.** Law (of a will or testament) declared orally, especially by a mortally wounded soldier or sailor.
– ORIGIN C16: from late L. *nuncupativus*, from L. *nuncupat-*, *nuncupare* 'declare'.

**nunnery** ● **n.** (pl. **-ies**) a religious house of nuns.

**nuoc mam** /nwɒk 'mɑ:m/ ● **n.** a spicy Vietnamese fish sauce.
– ORIGIN from Vietnamese.

**nuptial** /'nʌpʃ(ə)l/ ● **adj.** **1** of or relating to marriage or weddings. **2** Zoology of or denoting characteristic breeding coloration or behaviour. ● **n.** (**nuptials**) a wedding.
– ORIGIN C15: from OFr., or from L. *nuptialis*, from *nuptiae* 'wedding'.

**nuptiality** ● **n.** the frequency or incidence of marriage within a population.

**nuragh** /'nʊərag/ (also **nuraghe** /-gi/) ● **n.** (pl. **nuraghi** /-gi/) a type of massive stone tower found in Sardinia, dating from the Bronze and Iron Ages.
– ORIGIN from Sardinian.

**Nurofen** /'njʊərəfɛn/ ● **n.** trademark for **IBUPROFEN**.
– ORIGIN invented word on the pattern of *ibuprofen*.

**nurse**[1] ● **n.** **1** a person trained to care for the sick or infirm. ➤ dated a person employed or trained to take charge of young children. **2** Entomology a worker bee or other social insect that cares for a young brood. **3** Forestry a tree or crop planted as a shelter to others. ● **v.** **1** give medical and other attention to. ➤ work as a nurse. **2** feed or be fed at the breast. **3** treat or hold carefully or protectively. ➤ hold (a cup or glass), drinking from it occasionally. **4** harbour (a belief or feeling) for a long time. **5** Billiards & Snooker try to play strokes which keep (the balls) close together.
– DERIVATIVES **nursing** n.
– ORIGIN ME: contr. of earlier *nourice*, from OFr., from late L. *nutricia*, fem. of L. *nutricius* '(person) that nourishes', from *nutrix*, *nutric-* 'nurse', from *nutrire* 'nourish'.

**nurse**[2] (also **grey nurse**) ● **n.** a greyish Australian shark of shallow inshore waters. [*Odontaspis arenarius*.]
– ORIGIN C15: orig. as *nusse*, perh. derived (by wrong division) from *an huss* (see **HUSS**).

**nurse hound** ● **n.** a large spotted dogfish of the NE Atlantic, which is caught for food. [*Scyliorhinus stellaris*.]

**nurseling** ● **n.** archaic spelling of **NURSLING**.

**nursemaid** ● **n.** a woman or girl employed to look after a young child or children. ● **v.** look after or be overprotective towards.

**nursery** ● **n.** (pl. **-ies**) **1** a room in a house for the special use of young children. ➤ (also **day nursery**) a nursery school. **2** a place where young plants and trees are grown for sale or for planting elsewhere. **3** a place or natural habitat which breeds or supports animals. **4** [as modifier] denoting a race for two-year-old horses.

**nursery cannon** ● **n.** Billiards a cannon which keeps the balls close together.

**nursery class** ● **n.** a class for the education of children mainly between the ages of three and five.

**nurseryman** ● **n.** (pl. **-men**) a worker in or owner of a plant or tree nursery.

**nursery nurse** ● **n.** Brit. a person trained to look after young children and babies in nurseries, crèches, etc.

**nursery rhyme** ● **n.** a simple traditional song or poem for children.

**nursery school** ● **n.** a school for young children, mainly between the ages of three and five.

**nursery slope** ● **n.** Brit. Skiing a gentle slope suitable for beginners.

**nurse shark** ● **n.** a slow-moving shark with barbels on the snout. [*Ginglymostoma cirratum* (Atlantic) and other species.]

**nursing home** ● **n.** a small private institution for the elderly providing residential accommodation with health care.

**nursing officer** ● **n.** Brit. a senior nurse with administrative responsibility.

**nursling** ● **n.** dated a baby that is being breastfed.

**nurture** /'nə:tʃə/ ● **v.** **1** rear and encourage the development of (a child). **2** cherish (a hope, belief, or ambition). ● **n.** **1** the action or process of nurturing. **2** upbringing, education, and environment as an influence on or determinant of personality. Often contrasted with **NATURE**.
– DERIVATIVES **nurturance** n. **nurturant** adj. **nurturer** n.
– ORIGIN ME: from OFr. *noureture* 'nourishment', based on L. *nutrire* 'feed, cherish'.

**NUS** ● **abbrev.** (in the UK) National Union of Students.

**NUT** ● **abbrev.** (in the UK) National Union of Teachers.

**nut** ● **n.** **1** a fruit consisting of a hard or tough shell around an edible kernel. ➤ the hard kernel of such a fruit. **2** a small flat piece of metal or other material, typically square or hexagonal, with a threaded hole through it for screwing on to a bolt. ➤ the part at the lower end of a violin bow with a screw for adjusting the tension of the hair. **3** informal a crazy or eccentric person. ➤ an obsessive enthusiast or devotee. **4** informal a person's head. **5** a small lump of coal. **6** (**nuts**) vulgar slang a man's testicles. **7** the fixed ridge on the neck of a stringed instrument over which the strings pass. ● **v.** (**nutted**, **nutting**) **1** informal butt with one's head. **2** [usu. as noun **nutting**] archaic gather nuts.
– PHRASES **do one's nut** Brit. informal be extremely angry or agitated. **nuts and bolts** informal the basic practical details. **a tough** (or **hard**) **nut to crack** informal a problem or an opponent that is hard to solve or overcome. **use** (or **take**) **a sledgehammer to crack a nut** informal use disproportionately drastic measures to deal with a simple problem.
– ORIGIN OE *hnutu*, of Gmc origin.

**nutation** /nju:'teɪʃ(ə)n/ ● **n.** **1** a periodic variation in the inclination of an axis of rotation, especially that causing the earth's precession to follow a wavy rather than a circular path. **2** Botany the circular swaying movement of the tip of a growing shoot.
– ORIGIN C17 (denoting nodding of the head): from L. *nutatio(n-)*, from *nutare* 'to nod'.

**nutcase** ● **n.** informal a mad or foolish person.

**nutcracker** ● **n.** **1** (**nutcrackers**) a device for cracking nuts. **2** a bird of the crow family that feeds on the seeds of conifers. [Genus *Nucifraga*: two species.]

**nutgall** ● **n.** **1** another term for **ALEPPO GALL**. **2** a gall which forms inside hazel buds.

**nuthatch** ● **n.** a small songbird, typically grey-backed with pale underparts, which climbs up and down tree trunks. [*Sitta europaea* and related species.]
– ORIGIN ME: from **NUT** + obs. *hatch* (rel. to **HACK**[1]).

**nutlet** ● **n.** Botany a small nut, especially an achene.

**nut loaf** ● **n.** a baked vegetarian dish made from ground or chopped nuts, vegetables, and herbs.

**nutmeg** ● **n.** **1** the hard, aromatic, almost spherical seed of a tropical tree, used as a spice. **2** the evergreen tree that bears these seeds, native to the Moluccas. [*Myristica fragrans*.]
– ORIGIN ME *notemuge*, partial translation of OFr. *nois muguede*, based on L. *nux* 'nut' + late L. *muscus* 'musk'.

**nutria** /'nju:trɪə/ ● **n.** the skin or fur of the coypu.
– ORIGIN C19: from Sp., lit. 'otter'.

**nutrient** ● **n.** a substance that provides nourishment essential for the maintenance of life and for growth.

– ORIGIN C17: from L. *nutrient-*, *nutrire* 'nourish'.

**nutriment** ● **n.** nourishment; sustenance.
– DERIVATIVES **nutrimental** /-'mɛnt(ə)l/ adj.
– ORIGIN ME: from L. *nutrimentum*, from *nutrire* 'nourish'.

**nutrition** ● **n. 1** the process of ingesting and assimilating nutrients. ➤food; nourishment. **2** the branch of science concerned with nutrients and their ingestion.
– DERIVATIVES **nutritional** adj. **nutritionally** adv. **nutritionist** (also **nutritionalist**) n.
– ORIGIN ME: from late L. *nutritio(n-)*, from *nutrire* 'nourish'.

**nutritious** ● **adj.** full of nutrients; nourishing.
– DERIVATIVES **nutritiously** adv. **nutritiousness** n.
– ORIGIN C17: from L. *nutritius* 'that nourishes' + **-OUS**.

**nutritive** ● **adj. 1** of or relating to nutrition. **2** nutritious.
– ORIGIN ME: from med. L. *nutritivus*, from *nutrire* 'nourish'.

**nuts** ● **adj.** informal mad.

**nutshell** ● **n.** the hard woody covering around the kernel of a nut.
– PHRASES **in a nutshell** in the fewest possible words.

**nutso** N. Amer. informal ● **adj.** mad. ● **n.** (pl. **-os**) a mad or eccentric person.

**nutter** ● **n.** Brit. informal a mad or eccentric person.

**nutty** ● **adj.** (**-ier**, **-iest**) **1** tasting like nuts. ➤containing a lot of nuts. **2** informal mad.
– DERIVATIVES **nuttiness** n.

**nux vomica** /nʌks 'vɒmɪkə/ ● **n.** a spiny southern Asian tree with berry-like fruit and toxic seeds that contain strychnine. [*Strychnos nux-vomica*.]
– ORIGIN ME: from med. L., from L. *nux* 'nut' + *vomica* 'causing vomiting'.

**nuzzle** ● **v.** rub or push against gently with the nose and mouth.
– ORIGIN ME (in the sense 'grovel'): frequentative from **NOSE**, reinforced by Du. *neuzelen* 'poke with the nose'.

**NV** ● **abbrev.** Nevada (in official postal use).

**NVQ** ● **abbrev.** (in the UK) National Vocational Qualification.

**NW** ● **abbrev. 1** north-west. **2** north-western.

**NY** ● **abbrev.** New York (in official postal use).

**nyaff** /njaf/ ● **n.** Scottish informal a stupid, irritating, or insignificant person.
– ORIGIN C19: from Sc. dial. *nyaff* 'yelp, complain'.

**nyala** /'njɑːlə/ ● **n.** (pl. same) a southern African antelope with a conspicuous crest on the neck and back and lyre-shaped horns. [*Tragelaphus angasi*.]
– ORIGIN C19: from Zulu.

**Nyanja** /'njandʒə/ ● **n.** (pl. same or **Nyanjas**) **1** a member of a people of Malawi and eastern and central Zambia. **2** the Bantu language of this people.
– ORIGIN a local name, lit. 'lake'.

**NYC** ● **abbrev.** New York City.

**nyctalopia** /ˌnɪktə'ləʊpɪə/ ● **n.** a condition marked by inability to see in dim light or at night.
– ORIGIN C17: via late L. from Gk *nuktalōps*, from *nux*, *nukt-* 'night' + *alaos* 'blind' + *ōps* 'eye'.

**nyctophobia** /ˌnɪktə(ʊ)'fəʊbɪə/ ● **n.** extreme or irrational fear of the night or of darkness.
– ORIGIN C20: from Gk *nux*, *nukt-* 'night' + **PHOBIA**.

**nylon** ● **n. 1** a tough, lightweight, elastic synthetic polymer with a protein-like chemical structure. **2** nylon fabric or yarn. ➤(**nylons**) stockings or tights made of nylon.
– ORIGIN 1930s: an invented word, on the pattern of *cotton* and *rayon*.

**nymph** ● **n. 1** a mythological spirit of nature imagined as a beautiful maiden. ➤poetic/literary a beautiful young woman. **2** an immature form of a dragonfly or other insect that does not undergo complete metamorphosis.
– DERIVATIVES **nymphal** adj. **nymphean** adj.
– ORIGIN ME: from OFr. *nimphe*, from L. *nympha*, from Gk *numphē* 'nymph, bride'.

**nymphaeum** /nɪm'fiːəm/ ● **n.** (pl. **nymphaea**) a grotto or shrine dedicated to a nymph or nymphs.
– ORIGIN via L. from Gk.

**nymphet** /'nɪmfɛt, nɪm'fɛt/ (also **nymphette**) ● **n.** an attractive and sexually mature young girl.
– ORIGIN 1950s: from **NYMPH** + **-ET**[1].

**nympho** ● **n.** informal a nymphomaniac.

**nympholepsy** /'nɪmfə(ʊ)ˌlɛpsi/ ● **n.** poetic/literary frenzy caused by desire for the unattainable.
– DERIVATIVES **nympholept** n. **nympholeptic** adj.
– ORIGIN C18: from Gk *numpholēptos* 'caught by nymphs', on the pattern of *epilepsy*.

**nymphomania** ● **n.** uncontrollable or excessive sexual desire in a woman.
– DERIVATIVES **nymphomaniac** n. & adj. **nymphomaniacal** adj.
– ORIGIN C18: mod. L., from L. *nympha* (see **NYMPH**) + **-MANIA**.

**Nynorsk** /'njuːnɔːsk/ ● **n.** a literary form of the Norwegian language, serving as a national language more clearly distinct from Danish than Bokmål.
– ORIGIN Norw., from *ny* 'new' + *Norsk* 'Norwegian'.

**NYSE** ● **abbrev.** New York Stock Exchange.

**nystagmus** /nɪ'stagməs/ ● **n.** rapid involuntary movements of the eyes.
– DERIVATIVES **nystagmic** adj.
– ORIGIN C19: from Gk *nustagmos* 'nodding, drowsiness'.

**nystatin** /'nʌɪstətɪn, 'nɪs-/ ● **n.** an antibiotic used chiefly to treat fungal infections.
– ORIGIN 1950s: from *N(ew) Y(ork) Stat(e)* (where it was developed) + **-IN**[1].

**Nyungar** /'njʊŋə/ ● **n.** an Aboriginal language of SW Australia, now extinct.
– ORIGIN the name in Nyungar, lit. 'man'.

**NZ** ● **abbrev.** New Zealand.

**O**[1] (also **o**) ● n. (pl. **Os** or **O's**) **1** the fifteenth letter of the alphabet. **2** denoting the next after N in a set of items, categories, etc. **3** a human blood type (in the ABO system) lacking both the A and B antigens. **4** (also **oh**) zero (in a sequence of numerals, especially when spoken).

**O**[2] ● abbrev. **1** US Ohio. **2** Cricket (on scorecards) over(s). ● symb. the chemical element oxygen.

**O**[3] ● exclam. **1** archaic spelling of **OH**[1]. **2** used before a name in the vocative.

**O'** ● prefix in Irish patronymic names such as *O'Neill*.
– ORIGIN C18: from Ir. *ó*, *ua* 'descendant'.

**o** ● abbrev. (**o-**) Chemistry ortho-: o-*xylene*.

**o'** ● prep. short for **OF**, used to represent an informal pronunciation.

**-o** ● suffix forming chiefly informal or slang variants or derivatives such as *beano*.
– ORIGIN perh. from **OH**[1], reinforced by abbreviated forms such as *hippo*.

**-o-** ● suffix used as the terminal vowel of combining forms (often elided before a vowel, as in *neuralgia*): *chemico-*.
– ORIGIN from Gk.

**oaf** ● n. a stupid, boorish, or clumsy man.
– DERIVATIVES **oafish** adj. **oafishly** adv. **oafishness** n.
– ORIGIN C17 (orig. in the sense 'elf's child', later 'idiot child'): var. of obs. *auf*, from ON *álfr* 'elf'.

**oak** ● n. **1** a large tree which bears acorns and typically has lobed leaves and hard durable wood. [Genus *Quercus*: many species.] ➤ used in names of other trees or plants resembling this, e.g. **poison oak**. **2** a smoky flavour or nose characteristic of wine aged in oak barrels.
– PHRASES **sport the** (or **one's**) **oak** Brit. (in certain universities) shut the outer door of one's room as a sign that one does not wish to be disturbed. [such doors were often formerly of oak.]
– DERIVATIVES **oaken** adj. (archaic). **oaky** adj.
– ORIGIN OE *āc*, of Gmc origin.

**oak apple** ● n. a spongy spherical gall which forms on oak trees, caused by wasp larvae.

**oak leaf** ● n. a red or green variety of lettuce which has leaves with serrated edges and a slightly bitter taste.

**oakum** ● n. chiefly historical loose fibre obtained by untwisting old rope, used especially in caulking wooden ships.
– ORIGIN OE *ācumbe*, lit. 'off-combings', of Gmc origin.

**OAP** ● abbrev. Brit. old-age pensioner.

**OAPEC** /ˈəʊpɛk/ ● abbrev. Organization of Arab Petroleum Exporting Countries.

**oar** ● n. a pole with a flat blade, used to row or steer a boat through the water. ➤ a rower.
– PHRASES **put** (or **stick**) **one's oar in** informal give an opinion without being asked.
– DERIVATIVES **oared** adj. **oarless** adj.
– ORIGIN OE *ār*, of Gmc origin.

**oarfish** ● n. (pl. same or **-fishes**) a very long, narrow silvery fish of the deep ocean. [*Regalecus glesne*.]

**oarlock** ● n. N. Amer. a rowlock.

**oarsman** (or **oarswoman**) ● n. (pl. **-men** or **-women**) a rower.
– DERIVATIVES **oarsmanship** n.

**oarweed** ● n. a large brown kelp with a long hard stalk and a large oar-shaped frond divided into ribbon-like strips, growing on rocky shores. [Genus *Laminaria*.]

**OAS** ● abbrev. Organization of American States.

**oasis** /əʊˈeɪsɪs/ ● n. (pl. **oases** /-siːz/) **1** a fertile spot in a desert where the water table rises to ground level. **2** an area or period of calm in the midst of a difficult or hectic place or situation.
– ORIGIN C17: via late L. from Gk.

**oast** /əʊst/ ● n. a kiln for drying hops.
– ORIGIN OE *āst*, of Gmc origin.

**oast house** ● n. a building containing an oast, typically conical in shape with a cowl on top.

**oat** ● n. a cereal plant with a loose branched cluster of florets, cultivated in cool climates. [*Avena sativa* and related species.]
– PHRASES **feel one's oats** N. Amer. informal feel lively and energetic. **get one's oats** Brit. informal have sexual intercourse. **sow one's wild oats** go through a period of wild or promiscuous behaviour while young.
– DERIVATIVES **oaten** adj. (archaic). **oaty** adj.
– ORIGIN OE *āte*, pl. *ātan*, of unknown origin.

**oatcake** ● n. a thin savoury oatmeal biscuit, traditionally made in Scotland.

**oater** ● n. informal, chiefly US a western film.
– ORIGIN 1950s: derivative of **OAT**, with allusion to horse feed.

**oat grass** ● n. a wild grass which resembles the oat. [*Avenula* and other genera.]

**oath** ● n. (pl. **oaths**) **1** a solemn promise, often invoking a divine witness, as to the truth of something or as a commitment to future action. **2** a profane or offensive expression of anger or other strong emotions.
– PHRASES **my oath** Austral./NZ an exclamation of agreement. **under** (or Brit. **on**) **oath** having sworn to tell the truth, especially in a court of law.
– ORIGIN OE *āth*, of Gmc origin.

**oatmeal** ● n. **1** meal made from ground oats and chiefly used in porridge or oatcakes. **2** a greyish-fawn colour flecked with brown.

**OAU** ● abbrev. Organization of African Unity.

**OB** ● abbrev. Brit. outside broadcast.

**ob.** ● abbrev. he or she died.
– ORIGIN from L. *obiit*.

**ob-** (also **oc-** before *c*; **of-** before *f*; **op-** before *p*) ● prefix forming words of mainly Latin origin, meaning: **1** to, towards: *obverse*. **2** against; blocking: *opponent*. ➤ concealment: *occult*. **3** finality or completeness: *obsolete*. **4** technical in a direction or manner contrary to the usual: *obconical*.
– ORIGIN from L. *ob* 'towards, against, in the way of'.

**Obad.** ● abbrev. Obadiah (in biblical references).

**obbligato** /ˌɒblɪˈɡɑːtəʊ/ (US also **obligato**) ● n. (pl. **obbligatos** or **obbligati**) an instrumental part integral to a piece of music and not to be omitted in performance.
– ORIGIN Ital., lit. 'obligatory'.

**obconical** /ɒbˈkɒnɪk(ə)l/ ● adj. Botany in the form of an inverted cone.

**obcordate** /ɒbˈkɔːdeɪt/ ● adj. Botany (of a leaf) in the shape of a heart with the pointed end at the base.

**obdurate** /ˈɒbdjʊrət/ ● adj. stubbornly refusing to change one's opinion or course of action.
– DERIVATIVES **obduracy** n. **obdurately** adv. **obdurateness** n.
– ORIGIN ME (orig. in the sense 'impenitent'): from L. *obduratus*, past part. of *obdurare*, from *ob-* 'in opposition' + *durare* 'harden'.

**OBE** ● abbrev. Officer of the Order of the British Empire.

**obeah** /ˈəʊbɪə/ (also **obi**) ● n. a kind of sorcery practised especially in the Caribbean.
– ORIGIN Twi, from *bayi* 'sorcery'.

**obeche** /əʊˈbiːtʃi/ ● **n.** a tropical African tree whose pale wood is used for plywood and veneers. [*Triplochiton scleroxylon*.]
– ORIGIN C20: a term used in Nigeria.

**obedience** ● **n.** **1** compliance with an order or law or submission to another's authority. **2** observance of a monastic rule.
– DERIVATIVES **obedient** adj. **obediently** adv.
– ORIGIN ME: via OFr. from L. *oboedientia*, from *oboedire* (see **OBEY**).

**obeisance** /ə(ʊ)ˈbeɪs(ə)ns/ ● **n.** deferential respect. ➤a gesture expressing this, such as a bow.
– DERIVATIVES **obeisant** adj.
– ORIGIN ME: from OFr. *obeissance*, from *obeissant*, *obeir* 'obey'.

**obeli** plural form of **OBELUS**.

**obelisk** /ˈɒb(ə)lɪsk/ ● **n.** **1** a tapering stone pillar of square or rectangular cross section, set up as a monument or landmark. **2** another term for **OBELUS**.
– ORIGIN C16: via L. from Gk *obeliskos*, dimin. of *obelos* 'pointed pillar'.

**obelize** /ˈɒb(ə)lʌɪz/ (also **-ise**) ● **v.** mark (a spurious or doubtful word or passage) with an obelus.
– ORIGIN C17: from Gk *obelizein*, in the same sense.

**obelus** /ˈɒb(ə)ləs/ ● **n.** (pl. **obeli** /-lʌɪ, -liː/) **1** a symbol (†) used as a reference mark in printed matter, or to indicate that a person is deceased. **2** a mark (– or ÷) used in ancient manuscripts to mark a word or passage as spurious or doubtful.
– ORIGIN ME: via L. from Gk *obelos* 'pointed pillar', also 'critical mark'.

**obese** ● **adj.** grossly fat or overweight.
– DERIVATIVES **obesity** n.
– ORIGIN C17: from L. *obesus* 'having eaten until fat'.

**obey** ● **v.** submit to the authority of. ➤carry out (a command or instruction). ➤behave in accordance with (a general principle, natural law, etc.).
– DERIVATIVES **obeyer** n.
– ORIGIN ME: from OFr. *obeir*, from L. *oboedire*, from *ob-* 'in the direction of' + *audire* 'hear'.

**obfuscate** /ˈɒbfʌskeɪt/ ● **v.** **1** make unclear or unintelligible. **2** bewilder.
– DERIVATIVES **obfuscation** n. **obfuscatory** adj.
– ORIGIN ME: from late L. *obfuscat-*, *obfuscare* 'darken'.

**obi**[1] /ˈəʊbi/ ● **n.** variant form of **OBEAH**.

**obi**[2] /ˈəʊbi/ ● **n.** (pl. **obis**) a broad sash worn round the waist of a Japanese kimono.
– ORIGIN Japanese, lit. 'belt'.

**obit** /ˈɒbɪt, ˈəʊ-/ ● **n.** informal an obituary.

**obiter** /ˈɒbɪtə/ ● **adv. & adj.** (chiefly in legal contexts) made or said in passing. ● **n.** short for **OBITER DICTUM**.
– ORIGIN L., orig. as the phr. *ob itur* 'by the way'.

**obiter dictum** /ˈdɪktəm/ ● **n.** (pl. **obiter dicta** /ˈdɪktə/) **1** Law a judge's expression of opinion uttered in court or giving judgement, but not essential to the decision and therefore without binding authority. **2** an incidental remark.
– ORIGIN L. *obiter* 'in passing' + *dictum* 'something that is said'.

**obituary** /ə(ʊ)ˈbɪtʃʊəri, -tʃəri, -tjʊəri/ ● **n.** (pl. **-ies**) a notice of a person's death in a newspaper or periodical, typically including a brief biography.
– DERIVATIVES **obituarist** n.
– ORIGIN C18: from med. L. *obituarius*, from L. *obitus* 'death'.

**object** ● **n.** /ˈɒbdʒɪkt, -dʒɛkt/ **1** a material thing that can be seen and touched. ➤Philosophy a thing external to the thinking mind or subject. **2** a person or thing to which an action or feeling is directed: *she was the object of attention.* **3** a goal or purpose. **4** Grammar a noun phrase governed by an active transitive verb or by a preposition. **5** Computing a data construct that provides a description of something known to a computer. ● **v.** /əbˈdʒɛkt/ express disapproval or opposition.
– PHRASES **no object** not influencing or restricting choices or decisions: *a tycoon for whom money is no object.*
– DERIVATIVES **objectless** adj. **objector** n.
– ORIGIN ME: from med. L. *objectum* 'thing presented to the mind', neut. past part. of L. *obicere*, from *ob-* 'in the way of' + *jacere* 'to throw'.

**object ball** ● **n.** Billiards & Snooker the ball at which a player aims the cue ball.

**object choice** ● **n.** Psychoanalysis a person or thing external to the ego chosen as a focus of desire or sexual activity.

**object glass** ● **n.** old-fashioned term for **OBJECTIVE** (in sense 2).

**objectify** ● **v.** (**-ies**, **-ied**) **1** express in a concrete form. **2** degrade to the status of an object: *a sexist attitude that objectifies women.*
– DERIVATIVES **objectification** n.

**objection** ● **n.** the action of challenging or disagreeing with something. ➤an expression of disapproval or opposition.

**objectionable** ● **adj.** arousing distaste or opposition.
– DERIVATIVES **objectionableness** n. **objectionably** adv.

**objective** ● **adj.** **1** not influenced by personal feelings or opinions in considering and representing facts. **2** not dependent on the mind for existence; actual. **3** Grammar relating to or denoting a case of nouns and pronouns used for the object of a transitive verb or a preposition. ● **n.** **1** a goal or aim. **2** the lens in a telescope or microscope nearest to the object observed.
– DERIVATIVES **objectively** adv. **objectiveness** n. **objectivity** n. **objectivization** (also **-isation**) n. **objectivize** (also **-ise**) v.

**objective danger** ● **n.** Climbing a danger, such as a rock fall, that does not arise from a climber's lack of skill.

**objectivism** ● **n.** **1** the tendency to emphasize what is external to or independent of the mind. **2** Philosophy the belief that moral truths exist independently of human knowledge or perception of them.
– DERIVATIVES **objectivist** n. & adj. **objectivistic** adj.

**object language** ● **n.** **1** a language described by means of another language. **2** Computing a language into which a program is translated by means of a compiler or assembler.

**object lesson** ● **n.** a striking practical example of a principle or ideal.

**objet d'art** /ˌɒbʒeɪ ˈdɑː/ ● **n.** (pl. **objets d'art** pronunc. same) a small decorative or artistic object.
– ORIGIN Fr., lit. 'object of art'.

**objet trouvé** /ˌɒbʒeɪ ˈtruːveɪ/ ● **n.** (pl. **objets trouvés** pronunc. same) an ordinary object found at random and considered as a work of art.
– ORIGIN Fr., lit. 'found object'.

**objurgate** /ˈɒbdʒəgeɪt/ ● **v.** rare rebuke severely.
– DERIVATIVES **objurgation** n. **objurgatory** adj.
– ORIGIN C17: from L. *objurgat-*, *objurgare* 'chide'.

**oblast** /ˈɒblast/ ● **n.** an administrative division or region of Russia and the former Soviet Union.
– ORIGIN from Russ.

**oblate**[1] /ˈɒbleɪt/ ● **n.** a person dedicated to a religious life, but typically not having taken full monastic vows.
– ORIGIN C17: from Fr., from med. L. *oblatus*, past part. of L. *offerre* 'to offer'.

**oblate**[2] /ˈɒbleɪt/ ● **adj.** Geometry (of a spheroid) flattened at the poles. Often contrasted with **PROLATE**.
– ORIGIN C18: from mod. L. *oblatus*, from *ob-* 'inversely' + *-latus* 'carried'.

**oblation** ● **n.** a thing presented or offered to God or a god. ➤Christian Church the presentation of bread and wine to God in the Eucharist.
– DERIVATIVES **oblational** adj. **oblatory** adj.
– ORIGIN ME: from OFr., or from late L. *oblatio(n-)*, from L. *offerre* 'to offer'.

**obligate** ● **v.** **1** compel legally or morally. **2** US commit (assets) as security. ● **adj.** Biology restricted to a particular function or mode of life: *an obligate parasite.*
– DERIVATIVES **obligator** n.
– ORIGIN ME (as adj. in the sense 'bound by law'): from L. *obligat-*, *obligare* (see **OBLIGE**).

**obligation** ● **n.** **1** an act or course of action to which a person is morally or legally bound. ➤the condition of

being so bound. **2** a debt of gratitude for a service or favour.
– PHRASES **day of obligation** (in the Roman Catholic Church) a day on which all are required to attend Mass.
– DERIVATIVES **obligational** adj.

**obligato** ● n. US variant spelling of **OBBLIGATO**.

**obligatory** /ə'blɪgət(ə)ri/ ● adj. compulsory. ➤(of a ruling) having binding force.
– DERIVATIVES **obligatorily** adv.

**oblige** ● v. **1** (usu. **be obliged to do something**) compel legally or morally. **2** perform a service or favour for. ➤(**be obliged**) be indebted or grateful.
– DERIVATIVES **obliger** n.
– ORIGIN ME: from OFr. *obliger*, from L. *obligare*, from *ob-* 'towards' + *ligare* 'to bind'.

**obligee** /ˌɒblɪ'dʒiː/ ● n. Law a person to whom another is bound by contract or other legal procedure. Compare with **OBLIGOR**.

**obligement** ● n. chiefly Scottish a favour.

**obliging** ● adj. willing to do a service or kindness; helpful.
– DERIVATIVES **obligingly** adv. **obligingness** n.

**obligor** /'ɒblɪgɔː, ˌɒblɪ'gɔː/ ● n. Law a person who is bound to another by contract or other legal procedure. Compare with **OBLIGEE**.

**oblique** /ə'bliːk/ ● adj. **1** neither parallel nor at right angles; slanting. **2** not explicit or direct. **3** Geometry (of a line, plane figure, or surface) inclined at other than a right angle. ➤(of an angle) acute or obtuse. ➤(of a cone, cylinder, etc.) with an axis not perpendicular to the plane of its base. **4** Anatomy (especially of a muscle) neither parallel nor perpendicular to the long axis of a body or limb. **5** Grammar denoting any case other than the nominative or vocative. ● n. **1** Brit. another term for **SLASH** (in sense 3). **2** an oblique muscle.
– DERIVATIVES **obliquely** adv. **obliqueness** n. **obliquity** /ə'blɪkwɪti/ n.
– ORIGIN ME: from L. *obliquus*.

**obliterate** /ə'blɪtəreɪt/ ● v. **1** destroy utterly; wipe out. **2** blot out; erase.
– DERIVATIVES **obliteration** n. **obliterative** /-rətɪv/ adj. **obliterator** n.
– ORIGIN C16: from L. *obliterat-*, *obliterare* 'strike out, erase', based on *littera* 'letter, something written'.

**oblivion** ● n. **1** the state of being unaware of what is happening around one. **2** the state of being forgotten. **3** destruction or extinction. **4** Law, historical amnesty or pardon.
– ORIGIN ME: via OFr. from L. *oblivio(n-)*, from *oblivisci* 'forget'.

**oblivious** ● adj. not aware of what is happening around one.
– DERIVATIVES **obliviously** adv. **obliviousness** n.

**oblong** ● adj. having a rectangular shape. ● n. an oblong object or flat figure.
– ORIGIN ME: from L. *oblongus* 'longish'.

**obloquy** /'ɒbləkwi/ ● n. strong public condemnation.
– ORIGIN ME: from late L. *obloquium* 'contradiction', from L. *obloqui*, from *ob-* 'against' + *loqui* 'speak'.

**obnoxious** /əb'nɒkʃəs/ ● adj. extremely unpleasant.
– DERIVATIVES **obnoxiously** adv. **obnoxiousness** n.
– ORIGIN C16 (in the sense 'vulnerable (to harm)'): from L. *obnoxiosus*, from *obnoxius* 'exposed to harm', from *ob-* 'towards' + *noxa* 'harm'.

**oboe** /'əʊbəʊ/ ● n. a woodwind instrument of treble pitch, played with a double reed and having an incisive tone.
– DERIVATIVES **oboist** n.
– ORIGIN C18: from Ital., or from Fr. *hautbois*, from *haut* 'high' + *bois* 'wood'.

**oboe d'amore** /da'mɔːreɪ/ ● n. a type of oboe with a bulbous bell, sounding a minor third lower than the ordinary oboe and used in baroque music.
– ORIGIN C19: from Ital., lit. 'oboe of love'.

**obol** /'ɒb(ə)l/ ● n. an ancient Greek coin worth one sixth of a drachma.
– ORIGIN via L. from Gk *obolos*, var. of *obelos* (see **OBELUS**).

**O-Bon** /əʊ'bɒn/ ● n. another name for **BON**.

**obovate** /ɒb'əʊveɪt/ ● adj. Botany (of a leaf) ovate, with the narrower end at the base.

**obscene** ● adj. **1** offensive or disgusting by accepted standards of morality and decency. **2** repugnant.
– DERIVATIVES **obscenely** adv.
– ORIGIN C16: from Fr. *obscène* or L. *obscaenus* 'ill-omened or abominable'.

**obscenity** ● n. (pl. **-ies**) **1** the state or quality of being obscene. **2** an obscene action, image, or expression.

**obscurantism** /ˌɒbskjʊ'rantɪz(ə)m/ ● n. the practice of preventing the facts or full details of something from becoming known.
– DERIVATIVES **obscurant** n. & adj. **obscurantist** n. & adj.
– ORIGIN C19: from earlier *obscurant*, denoting a person who obscures something, via Ger. from L. *obscurant-*, *obscurare* 'make dark'.

**obscure** ● adj. (**-er**, **-est**) **1** not discovered or known about; uncertain. ➤not important or well known. **2** not clearly expressed or easily understood. **3** hard to make out; indistinct. ● v. **1** keep from being seen; conceal. **2** make unclear.
– DERIVATIVES **obscuration** n. **obscurely** adv. **obscurity** n.
– ORIGIN ME: from OFr. *obscur*, from L. *obscurus* 'dark'.

**obsequies** /'ɒbsɪkwɪz/ ● pl. n. funeral rites.
– ORIGIN ME: pl. of obs. *obsequy*, from Anglo-Norman Fr., from the med. L. pl. *obsequiae* (from L. *exsequiae* 'funeral rites', influenced by *obsequium* 'dutiful service').

**obsequious** /əb'siːkwɪəs/ ● adj. obedient or attentive to an excessive or servile degree.
– DERIVATIVES **obsequiously** adv. **obsequiousness** n.
– ORIGIN C15: from L. *obsequiosus*, from *obsequium* 'compliance', from *obsequi* 'follow, comply with'.

**observance** ● n. **1** the practice of observing the requirements of law, morality, or ritual. **2** (usu. **observances**) an act performed for religious or ceremonial reasons. ➤a rule to be followed by a religious order. **3** archaic respect; deference.

**observant** ● adj. **1** quick to notice things. **2** observing the rules of a religion. ● n. (**Observant**) historical a member of a branch of the Franciscan order that followed a strict rule.

**observation** ● n. **1** the action or process of closely observing or monitoring. **2** the ability to notice significant details. **3** the taking of the sun's or another celestial body's altitude to find a latitude or longitude. **4** a comment based on something one has seen, heard, or noticed.
– DERIVATIVES **observational** adj. **observationally** adv.

**observatory** ● n. (pl. **-ies**) a room or building housing an astronomical telescope or other scientific equipment for the study of natural phenomena.

**observe** ● v. **1** notice; perceive. ➤watch attentively. ➤detect in the course of a scientific study. **2** say; remark: *'It's chilly,' she observed.* **3** fulfil or comply with.
– DERIVATIVES **observable** adj. **observably** adv. **observer** n.
– ORIGIN ME: from OFr. *observer*, from L. *observare* 'to watch'.

**obsess** ● v. **1** (usu. **be obsessed**) preoccupy continually or to a troubling extent. **2** be preoccupied in this way.
– DERIVATIVES **obsessive** adj. & n. **obsessively** adv. **obsessiveness** n.
– ORIGIN ME: from L. *obsess-*, *obsidere* 'besiege'.

**obsession** ● n. **1** the state of being obsessed. **2** an idea or thought that obsesses someone.
– DERIVATIVES **obsessional** adj. **obsessionally** adv.

**obsessive–compulsive** ● adj. Psychiatry denoting or relating to a disorder in which a person feels compelled to perform certain actions repeatedly to alleviate persistent fears or intrusive thoughts.

**obsidian** /əb'sɪdɪən/ ● n. a hard, dark, glass-like volcanic rock formed by the rapid solidification of lava without crystallization.
– ORIGIN C17: from L. *obsidianus*, error for *obsianus*, from *Obsius*, the name (in Pliny) of the discoverer of a similar stone.

**obsolescent** /ˌɒbsə'lɛs(ə)nt/ ● adj. becoming obsolete.
– DERIVATIVES **obsolesce** v. **obsolescence** n.

– ORIGIN C18: from L. *obsolescent-*, *obsolescere* 'fall into disuse'.

**obsolete** • **adj. 1** no longer produced or used; out of date. **2** Biology less developed than formerly or in a related species; rudimentary; vestigial. • **v.** chiefly US cause (a product or idea) to become obsolete by replacing it with something new.
– DERIVATIVES **obsoletely** adv. **obsoleteness** n. **obsoletism** n.
– ORIGIN C16: from L. *obsoletus* 'grown old, worn out', past part. of *obsolescere* 'fall into disuse'.

**obstacle** • **n.** a thing that blocks one's way or hinders progress.
– ORIGIN ME: via OFr. from L. *obstaculum*, from *obstare* 'impede'.

**obstacle race** • **n.** a race in which various obstacles, such as fences and pits, have to be negotiated.

**obstetric** • **adj.** of or relating to childbirth and the processes associated with it.
– DERIVATIVES **obstetrical** adj. (chiefly N. Amer.). **obstetrically** adv. **obstetrics** pl. n.
– ORIGIN C18: from mod. L. *obstetricus* from L. *obstetricius* (based on *obstetrix* 'midwife'), from *obstare* 'be present'.

**obstetrician** /ˌɒbstəˈtrɪʃ(ə)n/ • **n.** a physician or surgeon qualified to practise in obstetrics.

**obstinate** • **adj. 1** stubbornly refusing to change one's opinion or chosen course of action. **2** unyielding: *an obstinate problem.*
– DERIVATIVES **obstinacy** n. **obstinately** adv.
– ORIGIN ME: from L. *obstinatus*, *obstinare* 'persist'.

**obstreperous** /əbˈstrɛp(ə)rəs/ • **adj.** noisy and difficult to control.
– DERIVATIVES **obstreperously** adv. **obstreperousness** n.
– ORIGIN C16: from L. *obstreperus* (from *obstrepere*, from *ob-* 'against' + *strepere* 'make a noise') + **-OUS**.

**obstruct** • **v. 1** block; be in the way of. **2** prevent or hinder.
– DERIVATIVES **obstructive** adj. **obstructively** adv. **obstructiveness** n. **obstructor** n.
– ORIGIN C16: from L. *obstruct-*, *obstruere* 'block up'.

**obstruction** • **n. 1** the action of obstructing or the state of being obstructed. **2** a thing that obstructs.

**obstructionism** • **n.** the practice of deliberately impeding or delaying the course of legal, legislative, or other procedures.
– DERIVATIVES **obstructionist** n. & adj.

**obstruent** /ˈɒbstrʊənt/ • **n.** Phonetics a fricative or plosive speech sound.
– ORIGIN C17: from L. *obstruent-*, *obstruere* 'block up'.

**obtain** • **v. 1** acquire or secure. **2** formal be prevalent, customary, or established.
– DERIVATIVES **obtainability** n. **obtainable** adj. **obtainer** n. **obtainment** n. **obtention** n.
– ORIGIN ME: from OFr. *obtenir*, from L. *obtinere* 'obtain, gain'.

**obtrude** • **v. 1** become obtrusive. **2** impose or force on someone.
– DERIVATIVES **obtruder** n. **obtrusion** n.
– ORIGIN C16: from L. *obtrudere*, from *ob-* 'towards' + *trudere* 'to push'.

**obtrusive** • **adj.** noticeable or prominent in an unwelcome or intrusive way.
– DERIVATIVES **obtrusively** adv. **obtrusiveness** n.
– ORIGIN C17: from L. *obtrus-*, *obtrudere* (see **OBTRUDE**).

**obturator** /ˈɒbtjʊəreɪtə/ • **n.** Anatomy either of two muscles covering the outer front part of the pelvis on each side and involved in movements of the thigh and hip.
– ORIGIN C18: from med. L., lit. 'obstructor', from *obturare* 'stop up'.

**obturator foramen** • **n.** Anatomy a large opening in the hip bone between the pubis and the ischium.

**obtuse** • **adj. 1** annoyingly insensitive or slow to understand. **2** (of an angle) more than 90° and less than 180°. **3** not sharp-pointed or sharp-edged; blunt.
– DERIVATIVES **obtusely** adv. **obtuseness** n. **obtusity** n.
– ORIGIN ME: from L. *obtusus*, *obtundere*, from *ob-* 'against' + *tundere* 'to beat'.

**Ob-Ugrian** /ɒbˈuːgrɪən, -ˈjuː-/ (also **Ob-Ugric**) • **adj.** of or denoting a branch of the Finno-Ugric language family containing two languages of western Siberia, related to Hungarian. • **n.** this group of languages.
– ORIGIN 1930s: from *Ob*, the name of a Siberian river, + **UGRIAN**.

**obverse** • **n. 1** the side of a coin or medal bearing the head or principal design. **2** the opposite or counterpart of a fact or truth. • **adj. 1** of or denoting the obverse of a coin or medal. **2** corresponding to something as its opposite or counterpart.
– DERIVATIVES **obversely** adv.
– ORIGIN C17: from L. *obversus*, *obvertere* (see **OBVERT**).

**obvert** • **v.** Logic alter (a proposition) so as to infer another proposition with a contradictory predicate, e.g. *'no men are immortal'* to *'all men are mortal'*.
– DERIVATIVES **obversion** n.
– ORIGIN C17: from L. *obvertere*, from *ob-* 'towards' + *vertere* 'to turn'.

**obviate** /ˈɒbvɪeɪt/ • **v. 1** remove (a need or difficulty). **2** avoid; prevent.
– DERIVATIVES **obviation** n.
– ORIGIN C16: from late L. *obviat-*, *obviare* 'prevent'.

**obvious** • **adj. 1** easily perceived or understood; clear. **2** derogatory predictable and lacking in subtlety.
– DERIVATIVES **obviously** adv. **obviousness** n.
– ORIGIN C16 (in the sense 'frequently encountered'): from L. *obvius* (from the phr. *ob viam* 'in the way') + **-OUS**.

**OC** • **abbrev. 1** Officer Commanding. **2** Officer of the Order of Canada.

**oc-** • **prefix** variant spelling of **OB-** assimilated before *c* (as in *occasion*, *occlude*).

**oca** /ˈəʊkə/ • **n.** a South American plant related to wood sorrel, long cultivated in Peru for its edible tubers. [*Oxalis tuberosa*.]
– ORIGIN C17: from Amer. Sp., from Quechua *ócca*.

**ocarina** /ˌɒkəˈriːnə/ • **n.** a small wind instrument with holes for the fingers, typically having the shape of a bird.
– ORIGIN C19: from Ital., from *oca* 'goose' (from its shape).

**OCAS** • **abbrev.** Organization of Central American States.

**Occam's razor** (also **Ockham's razor**) • **n.** the scientific principle that in explaining a thing no more assumptions should be made than are necessary.
– ORIGIN C19: named after the C13 Engl. philosopher William of *Occam*.

**occasion** • **n. 1** a particular event, or the time at which it takes place. ➤a suitable or opportune time. **2** a special event or celebration. **3** formal reason; cause: *we have occasion to rejoice.* • **v.** formal cause.
– PHRASES **on occasion** from time to time. **rise to the occasion** perform well in response to a special situation. **take occasion** make use of an opportunity to do something.
– ORIGIN ME: from L. *occasio(n-)* 'juncture, reason', from *occidere* 'go down, set'.

**occasional** • **adj. 1** occurring infrequently or irregularly. **2** produced on or intended for particular occasions: *occasional verse.*
– DERIVATIVES **occasionality** n. **occasionally** adv.

**Occident** /ˈɒksɪd(ə)nt/ • **n.** (**the Occident**) formal or poetic/literary the countries of the West, especially Europe and America.
– ORIGIN ME: via OFr. from L. *occident-*, *occidere* 'go down, set'.

**occidental** • **adj.** of or relating to the countries of the West. • **n.** (**Occidental**) a native or inhabitant of the West.
– DERIVATIVES **occidentalism** n. **occidentalize** (also **-ise**) v.

**occipital lobe** • **n.** Anatomy the rearmost lobe in each cerebral hemisphere of the brain.

**occiput** /ˈɒksɪpʌt/ • **n.** Anatomy the back of the head.
– DERIVATIVES **occipital** adj.
– ORIGIN ME: from L. *occiput*, from *ob-* 'against' + *caput* 'head'.

**Occitan** /ˈɒksɪt(ə)n/ ● **n.** the medieval or modern language of Languedoc (southern France), including literary Provençal of the 12th–14th centuries. ● **adj.** of or relating to Occitan.
– DERIVATIVES **Occitanian** n. & adj.
– ORIGIN from Fr.

**occlude** /əˈkluːd/ ● **v. 1** stop, close up, or obstruct. **2** Chemistry (of a solid) absorb and retain (a gas or impurity). **3** (of a tooth) come into contact with another in the opposite jaw.
– ORIGIN C16: from L. *occludere* 'shut up'.

**occluded front** ● **n.** Meteorology a composite front produced by occlusion.

**occlusal** ● **adj.** Dentistry of, relating to, or involved in the occlusion of teeth.

**occlusion** ● **n. 1** Medicine the blockage or closing of a blood vessel or hollow organ. **2** Meteorology a process by which the cold front of a rotating low-pressure system catches up the warm front, so that the warm air between them is forced upwards. **3** Dentistry the position of the teeth when the jaws are closed.
– DERIVATIVES **occlusive** adj.

**occult** /ɒˈkʌlt, ˈɒkʌlt/ ● **n.** (**the occult**) supernatural beliefs, practices, or phenomena. ● **adj. 1** of, involving, or relating to the occult. **2** esoteric. **3** Medicine (of a disease or process) not accompanied by readily discernible signs or symptoms. ➤(of blood) abnormally present, but detectable only chemically or microscopically. ● **v.** /ɒˈkʌlt/ **1** cut off from view by interposing something. **2** Astronomy (of a celestial body) conceal (an apparently smaller body) from view by passing or being in front of it.
– DERIVATIVES **occultation** n. **occultism** n. **occultist** n. **occultly** adv. **occultness** n.
– ORIGIN C15: from L. *occultare* 'secrete', frequentative of *occult-*, *occulere* 'conceal'.

**occulting light** ● **n.** a light in a lighthouse or buoy which shines for a longer period than that for which it is cut off.

**occupancy** ● **n. 1** the action or fact of occupying a place. **2** the proportion of hotel or office accommodation occupied or used.

**occupant** ● **n. 1** a person who occupies a place at a given time. ➤Law a person holding property, especially land, in actual possession. **2** the holder of a position or office.

**occupation** ● **n. 1** the action, state, or period of occupying or being occupied. **2** a job or profession. **3** a way of spending time.
– DERIVATIVES **occupational** adj. **occupationally** adv.

**occupational hazard** ● **n.** a risk accepted as a consequence of a particular occupation.

**occupational psychology** ● **n.** the study of human behaviour at work.
– DERIVATIVES **occupational psychologist** n.

**occupational therapy** ● **n.** the use of particular activities as an aid to recuperation from physical or mental illness.
– DERIVATIVES **occupational therapist** n.

**occupy** ● **v.** (**-ies**, **-ied**) **1** reside or have one's place of business in. ➤take control of (a place) by military conquest or settlement. ➤enter and stay in (a building) without authority, especially as a form of protest. **2** fill or take up (a space or time). **3** hold (a position or job). **4** keep (someone) busy, active, or preoccupied.
– DERIVATIVES **occupier** n.
– ORIGIN ME: formed irregularly from OFr. *occuper*, from L. *occupare* 'seize'.

**occur** ● **v.** (**occurred**, **occurring**) **1** happen; take place. **2** exist or be found to be present in a place or under a particular set of conditions. **3** (**occur to**) come into the mind of.
– ORIGIN C15: from L. *occurrere* 'go to meet, present itself', from *ob-* 'against' + *currere* 'to run'.

**occurrence** /əˈkʌr(ə)ns/ ● **n. 1** the fact or frequency of something occurring. **2** a thing that occurs; an incident or event.

**occurrent** ● **adj.** actually occurring or observable, not potential or hypothetical.

**OCD** ● **abbrev.** obsessive–compulsive disorder.

**ocean** ● **n.** a very large expanse of sea; in particular, each of the Atlantic, Pacific, Indian, Arctic, and Antarctic Oceans. ➤(**the ocean**) chiefly N. Amer. the sea.
– DERIVATIVES **oceanward** adv. & adj. **oceanwards** adv.
– ORIGIN ME: from OFr. *occean*, via L. from Gk *ōkeanos* 'great stream encircling the earth's disc'.

**oceanarium** /ˌəʊʃəˈnɛːrɪəm/ ● **n.** (pl. **oceanariums** or **oceanaria** /-rɪə/) a large seawater aquarium.
– ORIGIN 1940s: from OCEAN, on the pattern of *aquarium*.

**Oceanian** /ˌəʊsɪˈɑːnɪən, -ʃɪ-/ ● **adj.** of or relating to Oceania, the islands of the Pacific Ocean and adjacent seas. ● **n.** a native or inhabitant of Oceania; a Polynesian.

**oceanic** /ˌəʊsɪˈanɪk, -ʃɪ-/ ● **adj. 1** of or relating to the ocean. **2** (**Oceanic**) another term for OCEANIAN.

**oceanic bonito** ● **n.** a skipjack tuna.

**Oceanid** /əʊˈsiːənɪd, ˈəʊʃ(ə)nɪd/ ● **n.** (pl. **Oceanids** or **Oceanides** /ˌəʊsɪˈanɪdiːz, ˌəʊʃɪ-/) Greek Mythology a sea nymph.
– ORIGIN from Fr. *Océanide*, from Gk *ōkeanis*, *ōkeanid-*.

**oceanography** ● **n.** the branch of science concerned with the physical and biological properties and phenomena of the sea.
– DERIVATIVES **oceanographer** n. **oceanographic** adj. **oceanographical** adj.

**oceanology** ● **n. 1** another term for OCEANOGRAPHY. **2** the branch of technology and economics concerned with human use of the sea.
– DERIVATIVES **oceanological** adj. **oceanologist** n.

**ocellated** /ˈɒsɪleɪtɪd/ ● **adj.** (of an animal, or its plumage or body surface) having eye-like markings.

**ocellus** /əˈsɛləs/ ● **n.** (pl. **ocelli** /-lʌɪ, -liː/) Zoology **1** another term for SIMPLE EYE. **2** another term for EYESPOT (in senses 1 and 2).
– DERIVATIVES **ocellar** adj.
– ORIGIN C19: from L., dimin. of *oculus* 'eye'.

**ocelot** /ˈɒsɪlɒt, ˈəʊs-/ ● **n.** a medium-sized wild cat that has an orange-yellow coat marked with black stripes and spots, native to South and Central America. [*Felis pardalis*.]
– ORIGIN C18: from Fr., from Nahuatl *tlatlocelotl*, lit. 'field tiger'.

**och** /ɒk, ɒx/ ● **exclam.** Scottish & Irish used to express a range of emotions, typically surprise, regret, or disbelief.

**oche** /ˈɒki/ (also **hockey**) ● **n.** Brit. the line behind which darts players stand when throwing.
– ORIGIN C20: perh. rel. to OFr. *ocher* 'cut a notch in'.

**ochlocracy** /ɒkˈlɒkrəsi/ ● **n.** formal government by the populace; mob rule.
– DERIVATIVES **ochlocrat** n. **ochlocratic** adj.
– ORIGIN C16: via Fr. from Gk *okhlokratia*, from *okhlos* 'mob' + *-kratia* 'power'.

**ochone** /əʊˈhəʊn, ɒˈxəʊn/ (also **ohone**) ● **exclam.** Irish & Scottish poetic/literary used to express regret or sorrow.
– ORIGIN from Sc. Gaelic *ochòin*, Ir. *ochón*.

**ochre** /ˈəʊkə/ (US also **ocher**) ● **n.** an earthy pigment containing ferric oxide, varying from light yellow to brown or red.
– DERIVATIVES **ochreish** adj. **ochreous** /ˈəʊkrɪəs/ adj. **ochroid** adj. **ochrous** adj. **ochry** adj.
– ORIGIN ME: from OFr. *ocre*, via L. from Gk *ōkhra* 'yellow ochre'.

**ochrea** /ˈɒkrɪə/ ● **n.** (pl. **ochreas** or **ochreae** /ˈɒkrɪiː/) Botany a dry sheath round a stem formed by the cohesion of two or more stipules, characteristic of the dock family.
– ORIGIN C19: from L., lit. 'protective legging'.

**-ock** ● **suffix** forming nouns originally with diminutive sense: *haddock*. ➤also occasionally forming words from other sources: *bannock*.
– ORIGIN OE *-uc*, *-oc*.

**ocker** ● **n.** Austral. informal a boorish or uncultivated Australian.
– ORIGIN alt. of *Oscar*, the name of an Austral. TV character.

**Ockham's razor** ● **n.** variant spelling of OCCAM'S RAZOR.

**o'clock** ● **adv.** used to specify the hour when telling the time.

– ORIGIN contr. of *of the clock*.

**ocotillo** /ˌəʊkə'tiːjəʊ, -'tiːjəʊ/ • **n.** (pl. **-os**) chiefly US a spiny scarlet-flowered desert shrub of the south-western US and Mexico. [*Fouquieria splendens*.]
– ORIGIN C19: via Amer. Sp. (dimin. form) from Nahuatl *ocotl* 'torch'.

**OCR** • **abbrev.** optical character recognition.

**-ocracy** • **comb. form** see **-CRACY**.

**Oct.** • **abbrev.** October.

**oct.** • **abbrev.** octavo.

**oct-** • **comb. form** variant spelling of **OCTA-** and **OCTO-** assimilated before a vowel (as in *octennial*).

**octa-** (also **oct-** before a vowel) • **comb. form** eight; having eight: *octahedron*.
– ORIGIN from Gk *oktō* 'eight'.

**octad** /'ɒktad/ • **n.** a group or set of eight.
– ORIGIN C19: via late L. from Gk *oktas, oktad-*, from *oktō* 'eight'.

**octagon** • **n.** a plane figure with eight straight sides and eight angles.
– DERIVATIVES **octagonal** adj. **octagonally** adv.
– ORIGIN C16: via L. from Gk *octagōnos* 'eight-angled'.

**octahedron** /ˌɒktə'hiːdrən, -'hɛd-/ • **n.** (pl. **octahedra** /-drə/ or **octahedrons**) a three-dimensional shape having eight plane faces, in particular a regular solid figure with eight equal triangular faces.
– DERIVATIVES **octahedral** adj.
– ORIGIN C16: from Gk *oktaedron*, neut. (used as n.) of *oktaedros* 'eight-faced'.

**octal** /'ɒkt(ə)l/ • **adj.** relating to or using a system of numerical notation that has 8 rather than 10 as a base. • **n.** the octal system; octal notation.

**octamerous** /ɒk'tam(ə)rəs/ • **adj.** Botany & Zoology **1** having parts arranged in groups of eight. **2** consisting of eight joints or parts.

**octameter** /ɒk'tamɪtə/ • **n.** Prosody a line of verse consisting of eight metrical feet.

**octane** • **n.** Chemistry a liquid hydrocarbon of the alkane series, present in petroleum spirit. [$C_8H_{18}$.]
– ORIGIN C19: from **OCTO-** 'eight' (denoting eight carbon atoms) + **-ANE**[2].

**octane number** (also **octane rating**) • **n.** a figure indicating the anti-knock properties of a fuel, based on a comparison with a mixture of isooctane and heptane.

**octangular** • **adj.** having eight angles.

**octant** /'ɒkt(ə)nt/ • **n. 1** an arc of a circle equal to one eighth of its circumference, or the area enclosed by such an arc with two radii of the circle. **2** each of eight parts into which a space or solid body is divided by three planes which intersect (especially at right angles) at a single point. **3** an obsolete instrument in the form of a graduated eighth of a circle, used in astronomy and navigation.
– ORIGIN C17: from L. *octans, octant-* 'half-quadrant', from *octo* 'eight'.

**octastyle** • **adj.** (of a building or portico) having eight columns at the end or in front. • **n.** a portico or building in this style.
– ORIGIN C18: via L. from Gk *oktastulos*, from *okta-* 'eight' + *stulos* 'pillar'.

**octavalent** /ˌɒktə'veɪl(ə)nt/ • **adj.** Chemistry having a valency of eight.

**octave** /'ɒktɪv/ • **n. 1** Music a series of eight notes occupying the interval between (and including) two notes, one having twice or half the frequency of vibration of the other. ➤the interval between these two notes. ➤each of the two notes at the extremes of this interval. ➤these two notes sounding together. **2** a group or stanza of eight lines. **3** the seventh day after a Church festival. ➤a period of eight days beginning with the day of such a festival. **4** Fencing the last of eight parrying positions. **5** Brit. a wine cask holding an eighth of a pipe.
– ORIGIN ME (in sense 3): via OFr. from L. *octava dies* 'eighth day'.

**octavo** /ɒk'tɑːvəʊ, -'teɪ-/ (abbrev.: **8vo**) • **n.** (pl. **-os**) a size of book page that results from folding each printed sheet into eight leaves (sixteen pages).
– ORIGIN C16: from L. *in octavo* 'in an eighth', from *octavus* 'eighth'.

**octennial** • **adj.** lasting for or recurring every eight years.
– ORIGIN C17: from late L. *octennium* 'period of eight years' + **-AL**.

**octet** /ɒk'tɛt/ • **n. 1** a group of eight musicians. ➤a musical composition for eight voices or instruments. **2** a group of eight lines of verse. **3** Chemistry a stable group of eight electrons occupying a single shell in an atom.
– ORIGIN C19: from Ital. *ottetto* or Ger. *Oktett*, on the pattern of *duet* and *quartet*.

**octo-** (also **oct-** before a vowel) • **comb. form** eight; having eight: *octosyllabic*.
– ORIGIN from L. *octo* or Gk *oktō* 'eight'.

**October** • **n.** the tenth month of the year.
– ORIGIN OE, from L., from *octo* 'eight' (being orig. the eighth month of the Roman year).

**octocentenary** • **n.** (pl. **-ies**) an eight-hundredth anniversary.

**octodecimo** /ˌɒktəʊ'dɛsɪməʊ/ • **n.** (pl. **-os**) a size of book page resulting from folding each printed sheet into eighteen leaves (thirty-six pages).
– ORIGIN C19: from L. *in octodecimo* 'in an eighteenth', from *octodecimus* 'eighteenth'.

**octofoil** • **adj.** having or consisting of eight leaves or lobes. • **n.** an octofoil ornamental or heraldic figure.

**octogenarian** /ˌɒktə(ʊ)dʒɪ'nɛːrɪən/ • **n.** a person who is between 80 and 89 years old.
– ORIGIN C19: from L. *octogenarius* (based on *octoginta* 'eighty') + **-AN**.

**Octopoda** /ˌɒktə'pəʊdə/ • **pl. n.** Zoology an order of cephalopod molluscs that comprises the octopuses.
– DERIVATIVES **octopod** n.
– ORIGIN mod. L., from Gk *oktōpous, oktōpod-*, from *oktō* 'eight' + *pous, pod-* 'foot'.

**octopus** • **n.** (pl. **octopuses**) a cephalopod mollusc with eight sucker-bearing arms, a soft sac-like body, strong beak-like jaws, and no internal shell. [Order Octopoda: many species.]
– DERIVATIVES **octopoid** adj.
– ORIGIN C18: from Gk *oktōpous* (see **OCTOPODA**).

**USAGE** octopus

The standard plural in English of **octopus** is **octopuses**. However, since the word comes from Greek, the Greek plural form **octopodes** is still occasionally used. The plural form **octopi**, formed according to rules for Latin plurals, is incorrect.

**octoroon** /ˌɒktə'ruːn/ • **n.** archaic a person whose parents are a quadroon and a white person and who is therefore one-eighth black by descent.
– ORIGIN C19: from **OCTO-**, on the pattern of *quadroon*.

**octosyllable** • **n.** a word or line of verse with eight syllables.
– DERIVATIVES **octosyllabic** adj. & n.

**octothorp** /'ɒktə(ʊ)θɔːp/ (also **octothorpe**) • **n.** chiefly N. Amer. another term for the symbol #.
– ORIGIN 1970s: of uncertain origin; prob. from **OCTO-** (referring to the eight points on the symbol) + the surname *Thorpe*.

**octroi** /'ɒktrwɑː/ • **n.** a duty levied in some countries on various goods entering a town or city.
– ORIGIN C16: from Fr. *octroyer* 'to grant', based on med. L. *auctorizare* (see **AUTHORIZE**).

**octuple** /'ɒktjʊp(ə)l, ɒk'tjuːp(ə)l/ • **adj. 1** consisting of eight parts or things. **2** eight times as many or as much. • **v.** make or become eight times as numerous or as large.
– ORIGIN C17: from Fr. *octuple* or L. *octuplus*, from *octo* 'eight' + *-plus* (as in *duplus* 'double').

**octuplet** • **n.** each of eight children born at one birth.

**octyl** /'ɒktʌɪl, -tɪl/ • **n.** [as modifier] Chemistry of or denoting an alkyl radical $-C_8H_{17}$, derived from octane.

**ocular** /'ɒkjʊlə/ • **adj.** Medicine of or connected with the eyes or vision. • **n.** another term for **EYEPIECE**.
– DERIVATIVES **ocularly** adv.

– ORIGIN C16: from late L. *ocularis*, from L. *oculus* 'eye'.

**ocularist** ● n. a person who makes artificial eyes.

**oculist** /ˈɒkjʊlɪst/ ● n. a person who specializes in the medical treatment of diseases or defects of the eye; an ophthalmologist.
– ORIGIN C16: from Fr. *oculiste*, from L. *oculus* 'eye'.

**oculo-** /ˈɒkjʊləʊ/ ● comb. form relating to the eye or the power of vision: *oculomotor.*
– ORIGIN from L. *oculus* 'eye'.

**oculomotor** /ˈɒkjʊlə(ʊ),məʊtə/ ● adj. of or relating to the motion of the eye.

**oculomotor nerves** ● pl. n. Anatomy the pair of cranial nerves supplying muscles in and around the eyeballs.

**oculus** /ˈɒkjʊləs/ ● n. (pl. **oculi** /-lʌɪ, -liː/) Architecture **1** a circular window. **2** the central boss of a volute. **3** an opening at the apex of a dome.
– ORIGIN C19: from L., lit. 'eye'.

**OD**[1] ● abbrev. ordnance datum.

**OD**[2] informal ● v. (**OD's**, **OD'd**, **OD'ing**) take an overdose of a drug. ● n. an overdose.

**od** ● n. a hypothetical power once thought to pervade nature and account for various scientific phenomena.
– ORIGIN C19: arbitrary term coined in Ger. by Baron von Reichenbach, Ger. scientist.

**odalisque** /ˈəʊd(ə)lɪsk/ ● n. historical a female slave or concubine in a harem, especially one in the seraglio of the Sultan of Turkey.
– ORIGIN C17: from Fr., from Turk. *odalık*, from *oda* 'chamber' + *lık* 'function'.

**odd** ● adj. **1** unusual or unexpected; strange. **2** (of whole numbers such as 3 and 5) having one left over as a remainder when divided by two. ➤denoting a single goal by which one side defeats another in a game where three or more goals are scored. **3** [in combination] in the region of: *fifty-odd years.* **4** occasional: *we have the odd drink together.* ➤spare; unoccupied: *an odd five minutes.* **5** detached from a pair or set.
– PHRASES **odd one out** a person or thing differing in some way from the other members of a group or set.
– DERIVATIVES **oddish** adj. **oddly** adv. **oddness** n.
– ORIGIN ME: from ON *odda-*, found in combinations such as *odda-mathr* 'third or odd man', from *oddi* 'angle'.

**oddball** informal ● n. a strange or eccentric person. ● adj. strange; bizarre.

**Oddfellow** ● n. a member of a fraternity similar to the Freemasons.

**oddity** ● n. (pl. **-ies**) **1** the quality of being strange. **2** a strange person or thing.

**odd job** ● n. a casual or isolated piece of work, especially one of a routine domestic or manual nature.
– DERIVATIVES **odd-jobber** n. **odd-jobbing** n.

**odd-job man** ● n. a man who does odd jobs.

**odd lot** ● n. **1** an incomplete set or random mixture of things. **2** US Finance a transaction involving an unusually small number of shares.

**oddment** ● n. (usu. **oddments**) an item or piece of something left over from a larger piece or set.

**odds** ● pl. n. **1** the ratio between the amounts staked by the parties to a bet, based on the expected probability either way. **2** (**the odds**) the chances of something happening or being the case. **3** (**the odds**) the balance of advantage; superiority in strength, power, or resources: *she clung to the lead against all the odds.*
– PHRASES **at odds** in conflict or at variance. **by all odds** N. Amer. certainly. **it makes no odds** informal, chiefly Brit. it does not matter. [from an earlier use of *odds* in the sense 'difference in advantage or effect'.] **lay** (or **give**) **odds** offer a bet with odds favourable to the other better. **over the odds** Brit. (especially of a price) above what is generally considered acceptable. **take odds** offer a bet with odds unfavourable to the other better.
– ORIGIN C16: appar. the pl. of the obs. noun *odd* 'odd number or odd person'.

**odds and ends** ● pl. n. miscellaneous articles or remnants.

**odds and sods** ● pl. n. informal, chiefly Brit. miscellaneous people or articles.

**odds-on** ● adj. **1** (especially of a horse) rated at evens or less to win. **2** very likely to happen or succeed.

**ode** ● n. **1** a lyric poem, typically in the form of an address, written in varied or irregular metre. **2** a classical poem of a kind originally meant to be sung.
– ORIGIN C16: from Fr., from late L. *oda*, from Gk *ōidē*, Attic form of *aoidē* 'song', from *aeidein* 'sing'.

**-ode**[1] ● comb. form of the nature of a specified thing: *geode.*
– ORIGIN from Gk adjectival ending *-ōdēs*.

**-ode**[2] ● comb. form in names of electrodes, or devices having them: *diode.*
– ORIGIN from Gk *hodos* 'way'.

**odeum** /ˈəʊdɪəm/ (also **odeon** /ˈəʊdɪən/) ● n. (pl. **odeums** or **odea** /-dɪə/) (in ancient Greece or Rome) a building used for musical performances.
– ORIGIN from Fr. *odéum* or L. *odeum*, from Gk *ōideion* (see **ODE**).

**odiferous** /əʊˈdɪf(ə)rəs/ ● adj. variant spelling of **ODORIFEROUS**.

**odious** ● adj. extremely unpleasant; repulsive.
– DERIVATIVES **odiously** adv. **odiousness** n.
– ORIGIN ME: from OFr. *odieus*, from L. *odiosus*, from *odium* 'hatred'.

**odium** /ˈəʊdɪəm/ ● n. general or widespread hatred or disgust.
– ORIGIN C17: from L., 'hatred', from the verb stem *od-* 'hate'.

**odometer** /əʊˈdɒmɪtə/ ● n. chiefly N. Amer. an instrument for measuring the distance travelled by a wheeled vehicle.
– ORIGIN C18: from Fr. *odomètre*, from Gk *hodos* 'way' + **-METER**.

**Odonata** /,əʊdəˈnɑːtə/ ● pl. n. Entomology an order of insects that comprises the dragonflies and damselflies.
– DERIVATIVES **odonate** n. & adj.
– ORIGIN mod. L., formed irregularly from Gk *odōn* (var. of *odous*) 'tooth', with ref. to the insect's mandibles.

**odonto-** ● comb. form relating to a tooth or teeth: *odontology.*
– ORIGIN from Gk *odous*, *odont-* 'tooth'.

**odontoid** /ə(ʊ)ˈdɒntɔɪd/ (also **odontoid process**) ● n. Anatomy a projection from the second cervical vertebra (axis) on which the first (atlas) can pivot.
– ORIGIN C19: from Gk *odontoeidēs*, from *odous*, *odont-* 'tooth' + *eidos* 'form'.

**odontology** /,ɒdɒnˈtɒlədʒi, ,əʊdɒn-/ ● n. the scientific study of the structure and diseases of teeth.
– DERIVATIVES **odontological** adj. **odontologist** n.

**odor** ● n. US spelling of **ODOUR**.

**odorant** ● n. a substance used to give a particular scent or odour to a product.
– ORIGIN ME: from OFr., pres. part. of *odorer*, from L. *odorare* 'give an odour to'.

**odoriferous** /,əʊdəˈrɪf(ə)rəs/ ● adj. having an odour.
– DERIVATIVES **odoriferously** adv.
– ORIGIN ME: from L. *odorifer* 'odour-bearing' + **-OUS**.

**odour** (US **odor**) ● n. a distinctive smell. ➤a lingering quality or impression.
– PHRASES **be in good** (or **bad**) **odour** informal be in or out of favour.
– DERIVATIVES **odorize** (also **-ise**) v. **odorizer** (also **-iser**) n. **odorous** adj. **odourless** adj.
– ORIGIN ME: from Anglo-Norman Fr., from L. *odor* 'smell, scent'.

**odyssey** /ˈɒdɪsi/ ● n. (pl. **-eys**) a long and eventful or adventurous journey or process.
– DERIVATIVES **odyssean** /,ɒdɪˈsiːən/ adj.
– ORIGIN C19: from *Odyssey*, the title of a Gk epic poem attributed to Homer describing the adventures of Odysseus (Ulysses) on his journey home from Troy; via L. from Gk *Odusseia*.

**OE** ● abbrev. Old English.

**Oe** ● abbrev. oersted(s).

**OECD** ● abbrev. Organization for Economic Cooperation and Development.

**OED** ● abbrev. Oxford English Dictionary.

**oedema** /ɪˈdiːmə/ (US **edema**) ● n. a condition character-

ized by an excess of watery fluid collecting in the cavities or tissues of the body.
– DERIVATIVES **oedematous** adj.
– ORIGIN ME: mod. L., from Gk *oidēma*, from *oidein* 'to swell'.

**Oedipus complex** • n. (in Freudian theory) the complex of emotions aroused in a young child by an unconscious sexual desire for the parent of the opposite sex.
– DERIVATIVES **Oedipal** adj.
– ORIGIN C20: by assoc. with *Oedipus*, who, in Gk mythology, unwittingly killed his father and married his mother.

**OEM** • abbrev. original equipment manufacturer.

**oenology** /iːˈnɒlədʒi/ (US also **enology**) • n. the study of wines.
– DERIVATIVES **oenological** adj. **oenologist** n.
– ORIGIN C19: from Gk *oinos* 'wine' + **-LOGY**.

**oenophile** /ˈiːnə(ʊ)fʌɪl/ (US also **enophile**) • n. a connoisseur of wines.
– DERIVATIVES **oenophilist** /iːˈnɒfɪlɪst/ n.

**o'er** • adv. & prep. archaic or poetic/literary form of **OVER**.

**oersted** (abbrev.: **Oe**) • n. Physics a unit of magnetic field strength equivalent to 79.58 amperes per metre.
– ORIGIN C19: named after Dan. physicist H. C. *Oersted*.

**oesophagitis** /ɪˌsɒfəgəˈdʒʌɪtɪs/ (US **esophagitis**) • n. Medicine inflammation of the oesophagus.

**oesophagoscope** /ɪˈsɒfəgəˌskəʊp/ (US **esophagoscope**) • n. an instrument for the inspection or treatment of the oesophagus.

**oesophagus** /ɪˈsɒfəgəs/ (US **esophagus**) • n. (pl. **oesophagi** /-dʒʌɪ/ or **oesophaguses**) the part of the alimentary canal which connects the throat to the stomach.
– DERIVATIVES **oesophageal** /ɪˌsɒfəˈdʒiːəl, ˌiːsəˈfadʒɪəl/ adj.
– ORIGIN ME: mod. L., from Gk *oisophagos*.

**oestradiol** /ˌiːstrəˈdʌɪɒl, ˌɛstrə-/ (US **estradiol**) • n. Biochemistry a major oestrogen produced in the ovaries.
– ORIGIN 1930s: from **OESTRUS** + **DI-**[1] + **-OL**.

**oestriol** /ˈiːstrɪɒl, ˈɛstrɪɒl/ (US also **estriol**) • n. Biochemistry an oestrogen which is one of the metabolic products of oestradiol.
– ORIGIN 1930s: from *oestrane* (the parent molecule of most oestrogens) + **TRI-** + **-OL**.

**oestrogen** /ˈiːstrədʒ(ə)n, ˈɛstrə-/ (US **estrogen**) • n. any of a group of steroid hormones which promote the development and maintenance of female characteristics of the body.
– DERIVATIVES **oestrogenic** adj.
– ORIGIN 1920s: from **OESTRUS** + **-GEN**.

**oestrone** /ˈiːstrəʊn, ˈɛstrəʊn/ (US **estrone**) • n. Biochemistry an oestrogen similar to but less potent than oestradiol.
– ORIGIN 1930s: from *oestrane* (parent molecule of most oestrogens) + **-ONE**.

**oestrus** /ˈiːstrəs, ˈɛstrəs/ (US **estrus**) • n. a recurring period of sexual receptivity and fertility in many female mammals; heat.
– DERIVATIVES **oestrous** adj.
– ORIGIN C17: from Gk *oistros* 'gadfly or frenzy'.

**oeuvre** /ˈəːvr(ə)/ • n. the body of work of a painter, composer, or author.
– ORIGIN C19: Fr., lit. 'work'.

**of** • prep. **1** expressing the relationship between a part and a whole. **2** expressing the relationship between a scale or measure and a value. ➤ expressing an age. **3** indicating an association between two entities, typically one of belonging. **4** expressing the relationship between a direction and a point of reference. **5** expressing the relationship between a general category and something which belongs to such a category. **6** expressing the relationship between an abstract concept and a noun denoting the subject or object of the underlying verb. **7** indicating the relationship between a verb and an indirect object. **8** indicating the material constituting something. **9** N. Amer. expressing time in relation to the following hour.
– PHRASES **be of** possess intrinsically or give rise to.
– ORIGIN OE, of Gmc origin.

**of-** • prefix variant spelling of **OB-** assimilated before *f* (as in *offend*).

**ofay** /ˈəʊfeɪ/ • n. US a derogatory term for a white person used by black people.
– ORIGIN 1920s: from **AU FAIT**, in the sense 'genteel'.

**Off.** • abbrev. **1** Office. **2** Officer.

**off** • adv. **1** away from the place in question. **2** so as to be removed or separated. **3** starting a journey or race. **4** so as to bring to an end or be discontinued. **5** (of an electrical appliance or power supply) not functioning or so as to cease to function. **6** having specified material goods or wealth: *how are you off for money?* • prep. **1** moving away and often down from. **2** situated or leading in a direction away from. **3** so as to be removed or separated from. **4** informal having a temporary dislike of. • adj. **1** unsatisfactory or inadequate. **2** (of food) no longer fresh. **3** located on the side of a vehicle that is normally furthest from the kerb. Compare with **NEAR** (in sense 4). **4** Brit. informal annoying or unfair. **5** Brit. informal unwell. • n. **1** (also **off side**) Cricket the half of the field towards which the batsman's feet are pointed when standing to receive the ball. The opposite of **LEG**. **2** Brit. informal the start of a race or journey. • v. informal **1** leave. **2** N. Amer. kill; murder.
– PHRASES **off and on** intermittently.
– ORIGIN OE, orig. a var. of **OF** (which combined the senses of 'of' and 'off').

**offal** • n. **1** the entrails and internal organs of an animal used as food. **2** decaying or waste matter.
– ORIGIN ME: prob. suggested by MDu. *afval*, from *af* 'off' + *vallen* 'to fall'.

**offbeat** • adj. **1** Music not coinciding with the beat. **2** informal unconventional; unusual. • n. Music any of the normally unaccented beats in a bar.

**off-brand** N. Amer. • adj. denoting or relating to an item of goods of an unknown, unpopular, or inferior brand. • n. an unknown, unpopular, or inferior brand.

**off break** • n. Cricket a ball which spins from the off side towards the leg side after pitching.

**off-colour** • adj. **1** Brit. slightly unwell. **2** slightly indecent or obscene.

**offcut** • n. a piece of waste material that is left behind after cutting a larger piece.

**off-cutter** • n. Cricket a fast off break.

**off drive** Cricket • n. a drive to the off side. • v. (**off-drive**) drive (the ball) to the off side; drive a ball from (a bowler) to the off side.

**off-dry** • adj. (of wine) having an almost dry flavour, with just a trace of sweetness.

**offence** (US **offense**) • n. **1** an act or instance of offending. **2** resentment or hurt. **3** the action of making a military attack. **4** N. Amer. the attacking team in a sport.

**offend** • v. **1** cause to feel hurt or resentful. **2** be displeasing to. **3** commit an illegal act. ➤ break a commonly accepted rule or principle.
– DERIVATIVES **offended** adj. **offendedly** adv. **offender** n.
– ORIGIN ME: from OFr. *offendre*, from L. *offendere* 'strike against'.

**offense** • n. US spelling of **OFFENCE**.

**offensive** • adj. **1** causing offence. **2** (of a military operation or weapon) involved or used in active attack. **3** chiefly N. Amer. of or relating to the team in possession of the ball or puck in a game. • n. **1** a military campaign of attack. **2** a forceful campaign.
– PHRASES **be on the offensive** be ready to act aggressively.
– DERIVATIVES **offensively** adv. **offensiveness** n.

**OFFER** • abbrev. (in the UK) Office of Electricity Regulation.

**offer** • v. **1** present or proffer. **2** express readiness to do something for or on behalf of someone. **3** provide (access or opportunity). **4** (often **offer something up**) present (a prayer or sacrifice) to a deity. **5** (**offer something up**) place something in juxtaposition with something else. • n. **1** an expression of readiness to do or give something. **2** an amount of money that someone is willing to pay for something. **3** a specially reduced price. **4** a proposal of marriage.

– PHRASES **on offer 1** available. **2** for sale at a reduced price.
– DERIVATIVES **offerer** (or **offeror**) n.
– ORIGIN OE *offrian* 'sacrifice to a deity', of Gmc origin, from L. *offerre* 'bestow, present', reinforced by Fr. *offrir*.

**offer document** ● n. a document containing details of a takeover bid which is sent to the shareholders of the target company.

**offering** ● n. a thing offered, especially as a gift or contribution. ➤something offered as a religious sacrifice or token of devotion.

**offertory** /'ɒfət(ə)ri/ ● n. (pl. **-ies**) Christian Church **1** the offering of the bread and wine at the Eucharist. ➤an anthem accompanying this. **2** a collection of money made at a religious service.
– ORIGIN ME: from eccles. L. *offertorium* 'offering', from late L. *offert-* (which replaced L. *oblat-*) 'offered', from *offerre* (see **OFFER**).

**off-gas** ● n. a gas which is given off, especially one emitted as the by-product of a chemical process. ● v. give off a chemical, especially a harmful one, in the form of a gas.

**offhand** ● adj. ungraciously nonchalant or cool in manner. ● adv. without previous consideration.
– DERIVATIVES **offhanded** adj. **offhandedly** adv. **offhandedness** n.

**office** ● n. **1** a room, set of rooms, or building used as a place of business for non-manual work. **2** a position of authority or service. ➤tenure of an official position. **3** (usu. **offices**) a service done for others. **4** (also **Divine Office**) Christian Church the services of prayers and psalms said daily by Catholic priests or other clergy. **5** (**offices**) Brit. dated the parts of a house given over to household work or to storage.
– ORIGIN ME: via OFr. from L. *officium* 'performance of a task' (in med. L. also 'office, divine service'), based on *opus* 'work' + *facere* 'do'.

**office boy** (or **office girl**) ● n. a young man (or woman) employed in an office to carry out routine tasks.

**office of arms** ● n. Heraldry the College of Arms, or a similar body in another country.

**officer** ● n. **1** a person holding a position of authority, especially a member of the armed forces who holds a commission or a member of the police force. ➤a bailiff. **2** a holder of a post, especially of a public, civil, or ecclesiastical office. **3** a member of a certain grade in some honorary orders, such as the grade next below commander in the Order of the British Empire. ● v. provide with an officer or officers.

**officer of arms** ● n. Heraldry a heraldic official; a herald or pursuivant.

**official** ● adj. **1** of or relating to an authority or public body and its activities and responsibilities. **2** having the approval or authorization of such a body. ● n. a person holding public office or having official duties.
– DERIVATIVES **officialdom** n. **officialism** n. **officialize** (also **-ise**) v. **officially** adv.

**official birthday** ● n. (in the UK) a day in June chosen for the observance of the sovereign's birthday.

**officialese** ● n. the formal and typically verbose style of writing considered to be characteristic of official documents.

**official secret** ● n. Brit. a piece of information that is important for national security and is officially classified as confidential.

**officiant** /ə'fɪʃɪənt, -ʃ(ə)nt/ ● n. a priest or minister who performs a religious service or ceremony.
– ORIGIN C19: from med. L. *officiant-*, *officiare* 'perform divine service'.

**officiate** /ə'fɪʃɪeɪt/ ● v. **1** act as an official. **2** perform a religious service or ceremony.
– DERIVATIVES **officiation** n. **officiator** n.
– ORIGIN C17: from med. L. *officiare* 'perform divine service', from *officium* (see **OFFICE**).

**officinal** /ə'fɪsɪn(ə)l, ɒfɪ'siːn(ə)l/ ● adj. (of a herb or drug) used in medicine.
– DERIVATIVES **officinally** adv.
– ORIGIN C17: from med. L. *officinalis* 'storeroom for medicines', from L. *officina* 'workshop'.

**officious** ● adj. asserting authority or interfering in an annoyingly domineering way.
– DERIVATIVES **officiously** adv. **officiousness** n.

**offie** (also **offy**) ● n. (pl. **-ies**) Brit. informal an off-licence.

**offing** ● n. the more distant part of the sea in view.
– PHRASES **in the offing** likely to happen or appear soon.
– ORIGIN C17: perh. from **OFF** + **-ING**[1].

**offish** ● adj. informal aloof or distant in manner.
– DERIVATIVES **offishly** adv. **offishness** n.

**off-key** ● adj. & adv. **1** Music not in the correct key or of the correct pitch. **2** inappropriate.

**off-licence** ● n. Brit. a shop selling alcoholic drink for consumption elsewhere.

**off-limits** ● adj. out of bounds.

**off-line** Computing ● adj. not controlled by or directly connected to a computer. ● adv. while off-line. ➤with a delay between the production of data and its processing.

**offload** ● v. **1** unload (a cargo). **2** rid oneself of. **3** Computing move (data or a task) from one processor to another.

**off-message** ● adj. (of a politician) departing from the official party line.

**off-peak** ● adj. & adv. at a time when demand is less.

**off-piste** ● adj. & adv. Skiing away from prepared ski runs.

**off-pitch** ● adj. Music not of the correct pitch.

**off-plan** ● adv. & adj. (of the selling or purchasing of property) before the property is built and with only the plans available for inspection.

**off-price** ● adj. & adv. N. Amer. denoting the retailing of branded goods at a discount.

**offprint** ● n. a printed copy of an article that originally appeared as part of a larger publication.

**off-putting** ● adj. unpleasant or disconcerting.
– DERIVATIVES **off-puttingly** adv.

**off-ramp** ● n. N. Amer. an exit road from a motorway.

**off-road** ● adv. away from the road; on rough terrain. ● adj. denoting a vehicle or bicycle for use off-road.
– DERIVATIVES **off-roader** n. **off-roading** n.

**off-sale** ● n. the sale of alcoholic drink for consumption elsewhere than at the place of sale.

**off season** ● n. a time of year when a particular activity is not engaged in or a business is quiet.

**offset** ● n. **1** a consideration or amount that diminishes or balances the effect of a contrary one. **2** the amount by which something is out of line. **3** Surveying a short distance measured perpendicularly from the main line of measurement. **4** a side shoot from a plant serving for propagation. **5** a spur in a mountain range. **6** Architecture a sloping ledge in a wall or other feature where the thickness of the part above is diminished. **7** a bend in a pipe to carry it past an obstacle. **8** a method of printing in which ink is transferred from a plate or stone to a uniform rubber surface and from that to the paper. ● v. (**-setting**; past and past part. **-set**) **1** (often **be offset**) counterbalance; compensate for. **2** place out of line. **3** transfer an impression by means of offset printing.

**offshoot** ● n. **1** a side shoot on a plant. **2** a thing that develops from something else.

**offshore** ● adj. & adv. **1** situated at sea some distance from the shore. **2** (of the wind) blowing towards the sea from the land. **3** of or relating to the business of extracting oil or gas from the seabed. **4** made, situated, or registered abroad. **5** of, relating to, or from a foreign country.

**offside** ● adj. & adv. (in games such as football) occupying a position on the field where playing the ball or puck is not allowed, generally through being between the ball and the opponents' goal. ● n. **1** the fact of being offside. **2** (usu. **the off side**) chiefly Brit. the side of a vehicle furthest from the kerb. Compare with **NEARSIDE**. ➤the right side of a horse.

**off spin** ● n. Cricket a type of spin bowling that causes the ball to deviate from the off side towards the leg side after pitching; off breaks.
– DERIVATIVES **off-spinner** n.

**offspring** ● n. (pl. same) a person's child or children, or

the young of an animal.
– ORIGIN OE *ofspring* (see **OFF**, **SPRING**).

**offstage** • **adj. & adv.** (in a theatre) not on the stage and so not visible to the audience.

**off stump** • **n.** Cricket the stump on the off side of a wicket.

**off-tackle** • **adj.** American Football of, directed towards, or occurring in a part of the offensive line immediately to the outside of either of the tackles.

**offtake** • **n.** the removal of oil from a reservoir or supply.

**off-trade** • **n.** the part of the market in alcoholic drinks which is made up of off-sales.

**off-white** • **n.** a white colour with a grey or yellowish tinge.

**off-width** • **adj.** Climbing (of a crack in the rock) too wide to be a jam and too narrow to be a chimney.

**offy** • **n.** (pl. **-ies**) variant spelling of **OFFIE**.

**Ofgas** /ˈɒfgas/ • **abbrev.** (in the UK) Office of Gas Supply.

**Ofsted** /ˈɒfstɛd/ • **abbrev.** (in the UK) Office for Standards in Education.

**OFT** • **abbrev.** (in the UK) Office of Fair Trading.

**oft** • **adv.** archaic or poetic/literary often.
– ORIGIN OE, of Gmc origin.

**Oftel** /ˈɒftɛl/ • **abbrev.** (in the UK) Office of Telecommunications.

**often** /ˈɒf(ə)n, ˈɒft(ə)n/ • **adv.** (**oftener**, **oftenest**) **1** frequently. **2** in many instances.
– ORIGIN ME: extended form of **OFT**, prob. influenced by *selden* 'seldom'.

**oftentimes** • **adv.** archaic or N. Amer. often.
– ORIGIN ME: extended form of **OFT-TIMES**, influenced by **OFTEN**.

**oft-times** • **adv.** archaic or poetic/literary often.

**Ofwat** /ˈɒfwɒt/ • **abbrev.** (in the UK) Office of Water Services.

**ogam** • **n.** variant spelling of **OGHAM**.

**ogee** /ˈəʊdʒiː, əʊˈdʒiː/ Architecture • **adj.** showing in section an S-shaped curve. • **n.** an S-shaped line or moulding.
– ORIGIN ME: appar. from **OGIVE** (with which it was orig. synonymous).

**ogee arch** • **n.** Architecture an arch with two ogee curves meeting at the apex.

**Ogen** /ˈəʊgɛn/ • **n.** a small melon with pale orange flesh and an orange skin ribbed with green.
– ORIGIN 1960s: from the name of a kibbutz in Israel.

**ogham** /ˈɒgəm/ (also **ogam**) • **n.** an ancient British and Irish alphabet, consisting of twenty characters formed by parallel strokes on either side of or across a continuous line. ➤an inscription in or character from this alphabet.
– ORIGIN C18: from Ir. *ogam*, connected with *Ogma*, the name of its mythical inventor.

**ogive** /ˈəʊdʒʌɪv, əʊˈdʒʌɪv/ • **n.** Architecture **1** a pointed or Gothic arch. **2** one of the diagonal groins or ribs of a vault.
– DERIVATIVES **ogival** adj.
– ORIGIN ME: from Fr., of unknown origin.

**ogle** • **v.** stare at lecherously. • **n.** a lecherous look.
– DERIVATIVES **ogler** n.
– ORIGIN C17: prob. from Low Ger. or Du.

**O grade** • **n.** short for **ORDINARY GRADE**.

**ogre** • **n.** (fem. **ogress**) **1** (in folklore) a man-eating giant. **2** a cruel or terrifying person.
– DERIVATIVES **ogreish** (also **ogrish**) adj.
– ORIGIN C18: from Fr.

**OH** • **abbrev.** Ohio (in official postal use).

**oh**[1] • **exclam.** **1** expressing surprise, disappointment, joy, or other emotion. **2** used when responding to something that has just been said.

**oh**[2] • **n.** variant spelling of **O**[1] (in sense 4).

**OHC** • **abbrev.** overhead camshaft.

**Ohioan** /əʊˈhʌɪəʊən/ • **n.** a native or inhabitant of the US state of Ohio. • **adj.** of or relating to Ohio or Ohioans.

**ohm** • **n.** the SI unit of electrical resistance, transmitting a current of one ampere when subjected to a potential difference of one volt. (Symbol: Ω)
– DERIVATIVES **ohmic** adj. **ohmically** adv.
– ORIGIN C19: named after the Ger. physicist G. S. *Ohm*.

**ohmmeter** /ˈəʊmˌmiːtə/ • **n.** an instrument for measuring electrical resistance.

**OHMS** • **abbrev.** on Her (or His) Majesty's Service.

**Ohm's law** • **n.** Physics a law stating that electric current is proportional to voltage and inversely proportional to resistance.

**ohnosecond** • **n.** Computing, informal a moment in which one realizes that one has made an error, typically by pressing the wrong button.

**oho** • **exclam.** expressing pleased surprise or recognition.
– ORIGIN ME: from **O**[3] + **HO**[1].

**-oholic** • **suffix** variant spelling of **-AHOLIC**.

**ohone** • **exclam.** variant spelling of **OCHONE**.

**OHP** • **abbrev.** Brit. overhead projector.

**OHV** • **abbrev.** overhead valve.

**oi** • **exclam.** (also **oy**) informal used to attract someone's attention, especially in a rough or angry way. • **n.** a type of harsh, aggressive punk music originally popular in the late 1970s and early 1980s.
– ORIGIN 1930s: var. of **HOY**[1].

**-oid** • **suffix** forming adjectives and nouns: **1** Zoology denoting an animal belonging to a higher taxon with a name ending in *-oidea*: *hominoid*. **2** denoting form or resemblance: *asteroid*. See word-formation panel.
– DERIVATIVES **-oidal** suffix forming corresponding adjectives. **-oidally** suffix forming corresponding adverbs.
– ORIGIN from mod. L. *-oides*, from Gk *-oeidēs*; rel. to *eidos* 'form'.

**oidium** /əʊˈɪdɪəm/ • **n.** (pl. **oidia** /-dɪə/) **1** Botany a fungal spore formed by the breaking up of hyphae into cells. **2** a disease of vines caused by a powdery mildew.
– ORIGIN C19: mod. L., from Gk *ōion* 'egg' + the dimin. suffix *-idion*.

**OIEO** • **abbrev.** Brit. offers in excess of.

**oik** (also **oick**) • **n.** informal an uncouth or obnoxious person.
– ORIGIN 1930s: of unknown origin.

**oil** • **n.** **1** a viscous liquid derived from petroleum, used especially as a fuel or lubricant. ➤petroleum. **2** any of various viscous liquids which are insoluble in water but soluble in organic solvents and are obtained from animals or plants. **3** Chemistry any of a group of natural esters of glycerol and various fatty acids, which are liquid at room temperature. Compare with **FAT**. **4** oil paint. • **v.** **1** lubricate, coat, or impregnate with oil. **2** supply with oil as fuel.
– DERIVATIVES **oiled** adj.
– ORIGIN ME: from ONorth. Fr. *olie*, OFr. *oile*, from L. *oleum* '(olive) oil'; cf. *olea* 'olive'.

**oil beetle** • **n.** a slow-moving flightless beetle that releases a foul-smelling oily secretion when disturbed. [*Meloe* and other genera.]

**oilbird** • **n.** a large nocturnal fruit-eating bird that resembles a nightjar, living in caves in Central and South America. [*Steatornis caripensis*.]

**oilcake** • **n.** a mass of compressed linseed or other plant material left after oil has been extracted, used as fodder or fertilizer.

**oilcan** • **n.** a can with a long nozzle used for applying oil to machinery.

**oilcloth** • **n.** cotton fabric treated with oil to make it waterproof.

**oil engine** • **n.** an internal-combustion engine in which the fuel enters the cylinder as a liquid.

**oiler** • **n.** **1** an oil tanker. **2** an oilcan. **3** N. Amer. informal an oil well. **4** (**oilers**) N. Amer. informal oilskin garments.

**oilfield** • **n.** an area of land or seabed underlain by strata yielding significant quantities of mineral oil.

**oil-fired** • **adj.** (especially of a heating system or power station) using oil as fuel.

**oilfish** • **n.** (pl. same or **-fishes**) a large violet or purple-brown escolar, the flesh of which is oily and unpalatable. [*Ruvettus pretiosus*.]

**oil gilding** • **n.** gilding in which gold leaf is laid on a

## Word *Formation*

**-oid** 'form or resemblance', from Greek *-oeidēs*, related to *eidos* 'form'

➤ Many technical and semi-technical words are formed using **-oid**:

| | | |
|---|---|---|
| amoeboid | resembling an amoeba | based on AMOEBA |
| android | a robot with a human appearance | Gk *anēr, andr-* 'man' |
| crinoid | a marine invertebrate of a class including the sea lilies | Gk *krinon* 'lily' |
| dendroid | tree-shaped | Gk *dendron* 'tree' |
| diploid | having two complete sets of chromosomes | Gk *diplous* 'double' |
| elephantoid | resembling an elephant | based on ELEPHANT |
| fibroid | a benign tumour of fibrous tissue | based on FIBRE |
| gadoid | a fish of an order including cod and hake | Gk *gados* 'cod' |
| haploid | having a single set of unpaired chromosomes | Gk *haploos* 'single' |
| hominoid | a primate of a group that includes humans | L. *homo, homin-* 'man' |
| humanoid | a being resembling a human | based on HUMAN |
| paranoid | relating to paranoia | Gk *para* 'irregular' + *noos* 'mind' |
| Polaroid | (trademark) a composite material with the property of polarizing light, used in sunglasses etc. | based on POLARIZE |
| rheumatoid | relating to rheumatism | based on RHEUMATISM |
| thyroid | a gland in the neck secreting hormones regulating growth and metabolism | Gk *thureos* 'oblong shield' (with reference to its shape) |

The word ***tabloid***, which is first recorded with its current sense in the early 20th century, is formed on TABLET + -OID. In its earliest uses it denoted a medicine sold in tablet form; the current sense of a 'popular newspaper' reflects the notion of something that is 'concentrated' and 'easily assimilated'.

surface formed of linseed oil mixed with a yellow pigment.

**oil gland** ● n. Botany & Zoology a gland which secretes oil. ➤ Ornithology another term for **PREEN GLAND**.

**oil lamp** ● n. a lamp using oil as fuel.

**oilman** ● n. (pl. **-men**) an owner or employee of an oil company.

**oil meal** ● n. ground oilcake.

**oil paint** ● n. a paste made with ground pigment and a drying oil such as linseed oil, used chiefly by artists.

**oil painting** ● n. **1** the art of painting in oils. **2** a picture painted in oils.
– PHRASES **be no oil painting** Brit. informal be rather unattractive.

**oil palm** ● n. a tropical West African palm which is the chief source of palm oil. [*Elaeis guineensis*: several cultivars.]

**oil pan** ● n. an engine sump.

**oil platform** ● n. a structure designed to stand on the seabed to provide a stable base above water for the drilling and regulation of oil wells.

**oil rig** ● n. a structure with equipment for drilling an oil well; an oil platform.

**oil sand** ● n. a deposit of loose sand or partially consolidated sandstone containing bitumen.

**oilseed** ● n. any of a number of seeds from cultivated crops yielding oil, e.g. rape, peanut, or cotton.

**oil shale** ● n. fine-grained sedimentary rock from which oil can be extracted.

**oilskin** ● n. heavy cotton cloth waterproofed with oil. ➤ (**oilskins**) a set of garments made of oilskin.

**oil slick** ● n. a film or layer of oil floating on an expanse of water.

**oilstone** ● n. a fine-grained flat stone used with oil for sharpening chisels, planes, or other tools.

**oil well** ● n. an artificially made well or shaft in rock from which mineral oil is drawn.

**oily** ● adj. (**-ier**, **-iest**) **1** containing, covered with, or soaked in oil. **2** resembling oil. **3** (of a person) unpleasantly smooth and ingratiating.
– DERIVATIVES **oilily** adv. **oiliness** n.

**oink** ● n. the characteristic grunting sound of a pig. ● v. make such a sound.
– ORIGIN 1940s: imitative.

**ointment** ● n. a smooth oily substance that is rubbed on the skin for medicinal purposes or as a cosmetic.
– ORIGIN ME: alt. of OFr. *oignement*, from a pop. L. form of L. *unguentum* (see **UNGUENT**); influenced by obs. *oint* 'anoint' (from OFr., past part. of *oindre* 'anoint').

**OIRO** ● abbrev. Brit. offers in the region of.

**Ojibwa** /ə(ʊ)'dʒɪbweɪ/ ● n. (pl. same or **Ojibwas**) **1** a member of an American Indian people inhabiting a wide area around Lake Superior. **2** the Algonquian language of this people.
– ORIGIN from Ojibwa *ojibwe*, said to mean 'puckered', with ref. to their moccasins.

**OK¹** (also **okay**) informal ● exclam. **1** expressing agreement or acquiescence. **2** introducing an utterance. ● adj. **1** satisfactory, but not especially good. **2** permissible. ● adv. in a satisfactory manner or to a satisfactory extent. ● n. an authorization or approval. ● v. (**OK's**, **OK'd**, **OK'ing**) give approval to.
– ORIGIN C19 (orig. US): prob. an abbrev. of *orl korrect*, humorous form of *all correct*, popularized as a slogan during President Van Buren's re-election campaign of 1840 in the US; his nickname *Old Kinderhook* (derived from his birthplace) provided the initials.

**OK²** ● abbrev. Oklahoma (in official postal use).

**okapi** /ə(ʊ)'kɑːpi/ ● n. (pl. same or **okapis**) a large browsing mammal of the giraffe family that lives in the rainforests of northern Zaire (Democratic Republic of Congo), having a dark chestnut coat with stripes on the hindquarters and upper legs. [*Okapia johnstoni*.]
– ORIGIN C20: a local word.

**okay** ● exclam., adj., adv., n., & v. variant spelling of **OK¹**.

**okey-dokey** (also **okey-doke**) ● exclam. variant form of **OK¹**.

**Okie** ● n. (pl. **-ies**) US informal a native or inhabitant of Oklahoma. ➤ historical, derogatory a migrant agricultural worker from Oklahoma who had been forced to leave a farm during the depression of the 1930s.

**Okla** ● abbrev. Oklahoma.

**Oklahoman** /ˌəʊklə'həʊm(ə)n/ ● n. a native or inhabitant of the US state of Oklahoma. ● adj. of or relating to Oklahoma or Oklahomans.

**okra** /'ɒkrə, 'əʊkrə/ ● n. a plant of the mallow family with long ridged seed pods, native to the Old World tropics. [*Abelmoschus esculentus*.] ➤ the immature seed pods of

this plant, eaten as a vegetable.
– ORIGIN C18: a W. Afr. word.

**okta** /ˈɒktə/ • n. (pl. same or **oktas**) Meteorology a unit used in expressing the extent of cloud cover, equal to one eighth of the sky.
– ORIGIN 1950s: alt. of **OCTA-**.

**-ol** • suffix Chemistry forming names of organic compounds. **1** denoting alcohols and phenols: *retinol.* **2** denoting oils and oil-derived compounds: *benzol.*
– ORIGIN sense 1 from *(alcoh)ol*; sense 2 from L. *oleum* 'oil'. See also **-OLE**.

**old** • adj. (**-er**, **-est**) **1** having lived for a long time; no longer young. ➤made or built long ago. ➤possessed or used for a long time. **2** former; previous. **3** dating from far back; long-established or known: *old friends.* **4** of a specified age: *he was fourteen years old.* ➤[as noun] a person or animal of the age specified. **5** informal expressing affection, familiarity, or contempt: *good old mum.*
– PHRASES **of old 1** in or belonging to the past. **2** for a long time. **the old days** a period in the past.
– DERIVATIVES **oldish** adj. **oldness** n.
– ORIGIN OE *ald*, of W. Gmc origin.

**old age** • n. **1** the later part of normal life. **2** the state of being old.

**old-age pension** • n. another term for **RETIREMENT PENSION**.
– DERIVATIVES **old-age pensioner** n.

**old boy** • n. **1** a former male pupil of a school. **2** informal an elderly man. ➤an affectionate form of address for a man or boy.

**old boy network** (also **old boys' network**) • n. an informal system through which men are thought to use their positions of influence to help others who went to the same school or university, or who share a similar social background.

**Old Church Slavonic** • n. the oldest recorded Slavic language, as used by the apostles Cyril and Methodius and surviving in texts from the 9th–12th centuries.

**old country** • n. (**the old country**) the native country of a person who has gone to live abroad.

**olde** /əʊld, ˈəʊldi/ (also **olde worlde**) • adj. pseudo-archaic old-fashioned in a way that is intended to be attractively quaint: *Ye Olde Tea Shoppe.*

**olden** • adj. of a former age: *the olden days.*

**Old English** • n. the language of the Anglo-Saxons (up to about 1150), an inflected language with a Germanic vocabulary.

**Old English sheepdog** • n. a large sheepdog of a breed with a shaggy blue-grey and white coat.

**old-fashioned** • adj. according to or favouring styles or views that are no longer current. • n. N. Amer. a cocktail consisting chiefly of whisky, bitters, water, and sugar.
– DERIVATIVES **old-fashionedness** n.

**Old French** • n. the French language up to *c.*1400.

**Old Frisian** • n. the Frisian language up to *c.*1400, closely related to both Old English and Old Saxon.

**old fruit** • n. Brit. informal, dated a friendly form of address to a man.

**old girl** • n. **1** a former female pupil of a school, college, or university. **2** informal an elderly woman. ➤an affectionate term of address to a girl or woman.

**Old Glory** • n. US informal the US national flag.

**old gold** • n. a dull brownish-gold colour.

**old-growth** • adj. (of a tree, forest, etc.) never felled; mature.

**old guard** • n. the original or long-standing members of a group seen as being unwilling to accept change.

**old hand** • n. a person with a lot of experience.

**old hat** • adj. informal tediously familiar or out of date.

**Old High German** • n. the language of southern Germany up to *c.*1200, from which modern standard German is derived.

**Old Icelandic** • n. Icelandic up to the 16th century, a form of Old Norse in which the medieval sagas were composed.

**oldie** • n. informal an old person or thing, in particular an old song or film that is still well known or popular.

**Old Irish** • n. the Irish Gaelic language up to *c.*1000, from which modern Irish and Scottish Gaelic are derived.

**old lady** • n. **1** an elderly woman. ➤(**one's old lady**) informal one's mother, wife, or girlfriend. **2** a brownish moth with a creamy pattern on the wings. [*Mormo maura.*]

**Old Latin** • n. Latin before about 100 BC.

**old-line** • adj. N. Amer. **1** holding conservative views. **2** well established.
– DERIVATIVES **old-liner** n.

**Old Low German** • n. the language of northern Germany and the Netherlands up to *c.*1200, from which modern Dutch and modern Low German are derived.

**old maid** • n. **1** derogatory a single woman regarded as too old for marriage. ➤a prim and fussy person. **2** a card game in which players collect pairs and try not to be left with an odd penalty card, typically a queen.
– DERIVATIVES **old-maidish** adj.

**old man** • n. an elderly man. ➤(**one's old man**) informal one's father, husband, or male partner. ➤Brit. informal an affectionate form of address between men or boys.

**old man's beard** • n. **1** a wild clematis with grey fluffy hairs around the seeds. [*Clematis vitalba* (traveller's joy) and other species.] **2** a lichen forming shaggy greyish growths on trees. [*Usnea barbata* and related species.]

**old master** • n. a great artist of former times, especially of the 13th–17th century in Europe.

**old moon** • n. the moon in its last quarter, before the new moon.

**Old Nick** • n. an informal name for the Devil.

**Old Norse** • n. the North Germanic language of medieval Norway, Iceland, Denmark, and Sweden, from which the modern Scandinavian languages are derived.

**Oldowan** /ˈɒldə(ʊ)wən/ • adj. Archaeology relating to or denoting an early Lower Palaeolithic culture of Africa, dated to about 2.0–1.5 million years ago.
– ORIGIN 1930s: from *Oldoway*, alt. of *Olduvai Gorge* in Tanzania, + **-AN**.

**Old Pals Act** • n. Brit. informal the tendency of people to use a position of influence to help their friends.

**Old Persian** • n. the Persian language up to the 3rd century BC, written in cuneiform.

**Old Prussian** • n. a Baltic language, related to Lithuanian, spoken in Prussia until the 17th century.

**Old Saxon** • n. the dialect of Old Low German spoken in Saxony up to *c.*1200.

**old school** • n. the traditional form or type: *a gentleman of the old school.*

**Old Slavonic** • n. another name for **CHURCH SLAVONIC**.

**old stager** • n. informal a very experienced or long-serving person.

**oldster** • n. informal, chiefly N. Amer. an older person.

**Old Stone Age** • n. the Palaeolithic period.

**Old Style** • n. the method of calculating dates using the Julian calendar.

**old sweat** • n. informal a veteran soldier.

**Old Testament** • n. the first part of the Christian Bible, comprising thirty-nine books and corresponding approximately to the Hebrew Bible.

**old thing** • n. informal a familiar form of address.

**old-time** • adj. pleasingly traditional or old-fashioned.

**old-timer** • n. informal a very experienced or long-serving person. ➤N. Amer. an old person.

**Old Welsh** • n. the Welsh language up to *c.*1150.

**old wives' tale** • n. a widely held traditional belief that is now thought to be unscientific or incorrect.

**old woman** • n. **1** an elderly female person. ➤(**one's old woman**) informal one's mother, wife, or female partner. **2** derogatory a fussy or timid person.
– DERIVATIVES **old-womanish** adj.

**Old World** ● n. Europe, Asia, and Africa, regarded collectively as the part of the world known before the discovery of the Americas.

**OLE** ● abbrev. Computing object linking and embedding.

**ole** ● adj. US informal old.

**-ole** ● comb. form in names of organic compounds, especially heterocyclic compounds: *thiazole.*
– ORIGIN from L. *oleum* 'oil' (cf. **-OL**).

**olé** /əʊ'leɪ/ ● exclam. bravo!
– ORIGIN from Sp.

**oleaceous** /ˌəʊlɪ'eɪʃəs/ ● adj. Botany relating to or denoting plants of the olive family (Oleaceae).
– ORIGIN C19: from mod. L. *Oleaceae*, based on L. *olea* 'olive tree', + **-OUS**.

**oleaginous** /ˌəʊlɪ'adʒɪnəs/ ● adj. **1** oily or greasy. **2** exaggeratedly complimentary; obsequious.
– ORIGIN ME: from Fr. *oléagineux*, from L. *oleaginus* 'of the olive tree'.

**oleander** /ˌəʊlɪ'andə/ ● n. a poisonous evergreen shrub grown in warm countries for its clusters of white, pink, or red flowers. [*Nerium oleander.*]
– ORIGIN C16: from med. L., of unknown ultimate origin.

**oleaster** /ˌəʊlɪ'astə/ ● n. a shrub or small tree with fruit resembling an olive. [*Elaeagnus angustifolia* (SE Europe and western Asia) and related species.]
– ORIGIN ME: from L., from *olea* 'olive tree'.

**olecranon** /əʊ'lɛkrənɒn, ˌəʊlɪ'kreɪnən/ ● n. Anatomy a bony prominence at the elbow, on the upper end of the ulna.
– ORIGIN C18: from Gk *ōle(no)kranon*, from *ōlenē* 'elbow' + *kranion* 'head'.

**olefin** /'əʊlɪfɪn/ (also **olefine**) ● n. Chemistry another term for **ALKENE**.
– DERIVATIVES **olefinic** adj.
– ORIGIN C19: from Fr. *oléfiant* 'oil-forming' (with ref. to oily ethylene dichloride).

**oleic acid** /əʊ'liːɪk/ ● n. Chemistry an unsaturated fatty acid present in many fats and soaps.
– DERIVATIVES **oleate** /'əʊlɪət/ n.
– ORIGIN C19: *oleic* from L. *oleum* 'oil'.

**oleiferous** /ˌəʊlɪ'ɪf(ə)rəs/ ● adj. Botany (of seeds, glands, etc.) producing oil.

**oleo-** /'əʊlɪəʊ, 'ɒlɪəʊ/ ● comb. form relating to or containing oil: *oleomargarine.*
– ORIGIN from L. *oleum* 'oil'.

**oleograph** ● n. a print textured to resemble an oil painting.
– DERIVATIVES **oleographic** adj. **oleography** n.

**oleomargarine** ● n. a fatty substance extracted from beef fat and widely used in the manufacture of margarine. ➤ N. Amer. dated margarine.

**oleoresin** ● n. a natural or artificial mixture of essential oils and a resin, e.g. balsam.
– DERIVATIVES **oleoresinous** adj.

**Olestra** /ɒ'lɛstrə/ ● n. trademark a synthetic calorie-free substitute for fat in foods, able to pass through the body without being absorbed.
– ORIGIN 1980s: from *(p)ol(y)est(e)r* + the suffix *-a*.

**oleum** /'əʊlɪəm/ ● n. a dense, corrosive liquid consisting of concentrated sulphuric acid containing excess sulphur trioxide in solution.
– ORIGIN C20: from L., lit. 'oil'.

**O level** ● n. short for **ORDINARY LEVEL**.

**olfaction** /ɒl'fakʃ(ə)n/ ● n. technical the action or capacity of smelling; the sense of smell.
– DERIVATIVES **olfactive** adj.
– ORIGIN C19: from L. *olfactus* 'a smell' + **-ION**.

**olfactometer** /ˌɒlfak'tɒmɪtə/ ● n. an instrument for measuring the intensity of an odour or sensitivity to an odour.
– DERIVATIVES **olfactometry** n.

**olfactory** /ɒl'fakt(ə)ri/ ● adj. of or relating to the sense of smell.
– ORIGIN C17: from L. *olfactare* (frequentative of *olfacere* 'to smell') + **-ORY**[2].

**olfactory nerves** ● pl. n. Anatomy the pair of cranial nerves supplying the smell receptors in the nose.

**olibanum** /ɒ'lɪbənəm/ ● n. frankincense.
– ORIGIN ME: from med. L., from late L. *libanus*, from Gk *libanos* 'frankincense'.

**oligaemia** /ˌɒlɪ'giːmɪə/ (US **oligemia**) ● n. another term for **HYPOVOLAEMIA**.
– DERIVATIVES **oligaemic** adj.
– ORIGIN C19: from Fr. *oligaimie*, from Gk *oligaimia*.

**oligarch** /'ɒlɪgɑːk/ ● n. a ruler in an oligarchy.

**oligarchy** ● n. (pl. **-ies**) a small group of people having control of a state. ➤ a state governed by such a group.
– DERIVATIVES **oligarchic** adj. **oligarchical** adj. **oligarchically** adv.
– ORIGIN C15: from Gk *oligarkhia*, from *oligoi* 'few' + *arkhein* 'to rule'.

**oligo-** ● comb. form having few; containing a relatively small number of units: *oligopoly.*
– ORIGIN from Gk *oligos* 'small', *oligoi* 'few'.

**Oligocene** /'ɒlɪgə(ʊ)siːn/ ● adj. Geology relating to or denoting the third epoch of the Tertiary period (between the Eocene and Miocene epochs, 35.4 to 23.3 million years ago), a time when the first primates appeared.
– ORIGIN C19: from **OLIGO-** + Gk *kainos* 'new'.

**Oligochaeta** /ˌɒlɪgə(ʊ)'kiːtə/ ● pl. n. Zoology a class of annelid worms which includes the earthworms.
– DERIVATIVES **oligochaete** n.
– ORIGIN mod. L., from **OLIGO-** + Gk *khaitē* 'long hair' (taken to mean 'bristle'), because they have fewer setae than polychaetes.

**oligoclase** /'ɒlɪgə(ʊ)kleɪz/ ● n. a feldspar mineral common in siliceous igneous rocks, consisting of a sodium-rich plagioclase.
– ORIGIN C19: from **OLIGO-** + Gk *klasis* 'breaking' (because thought to have a less perfect cleavage than albite).

**oligodendrocyte** /ˌɒlɪgə(ʊ)'dɛndrəsʌɪt/ ● n. Anatomy a glial cell resembling an astrocyte but with fewer protuberances, concerned with the production of myelin.
– ORIGIN 1930s: from **OLIGODENDROGLIA** + **-CYTE**.

**oligodendroglia** /ˌɒlɪgə(ʊ)dɛndrə'glʌɪə/ ● pl. n. Anatomy oligodendrocytes collectively.
– DERIVATIVES **oligodendroglial** adj.
– ORIGIN 1920s: from **OLIGO-** + **DENDRO-** + **GLIA**.

**oligodendroglioma** /ˌɒlɪgə(ʊ)ˌdɛndrə(ʊ)glɪ'əʊmə/ ● n. (pl. **oligodendrogliomas** or **oligodendrogliomata** /-mətə/) Medicine a tumour derived from oligodendroglia.

**oligomer** /ə'lɪgəmə, 'ɒlɪg-/ ● n. Chemistry a polymer whose molecules consist of relatively few repeating units.

**oligomerize** /ə'lɪgəmərʌɪz/ (also **-ise**) ● v. Chemistry join a number of molecules of (a monomer) together to form an oligomer.
– DERIVATIVES **oligomerization** n.

**oligomerous** /ˌɒlɪ'gɒmərəs/ ● adj. Biology having a small number of segments or parts.

**oligonucleotide** /ˌɒlɪgə(ʊ)'njuːklɪətʌɪd/ ● n. Biochemistry a polynucleotide whose molecules contain a relatively small number of nucleotides.

**oligopeptide** /ˌɒlɪgə(ʊ)'pɛptʌɪd/ ● n. Biochemistry a peptide whose molecules contain a relatively small number of amino-acid residues.

**oligopoly** /ˌɒlɪ'gɒp(ə)li/ ● n. (pl. **-ies**) a state of limited competition, in which a market is shared by a small number of producers or sellers.
– DERIVATIVES **oligopolist** n. **oligopolistic** adj.
– ORIGIN C19: from **OLIGO-**, on the pattern of *monopoly.*

**oligopsony** /ɒlɪ'gɒps(ə)ni/ ● n. (pl. **-ies**) a state of the market in which only a small number of buyers exists for a product.
– DERIVATIVES **oligopsonistic** adj.
– ORIGIN 1940s: from **OLIGO-**, on the pattern of *monopsony.*

**oligosaccharide** /ˌɒlɪgə(ʊ)'sakərʌɪd/ ● n. Biochemistry a carbohydrate whose molecules are composed of a relatively small number of monosaccharide units.

**oligospermia** /ˌɒlɪgə(ʊ)'spəːmɪə/ ● n. Medicine deficiency of sperm cells in the semen.

**oligotrophic** /ˌɒlɪgə(ʊ)'trəʊfɪk, -'trɒfɪk/ ● adj. Ecology (of a body of water) relatively poor in plant nutrients and containing abundant oxygen in the deeper parts.
– DERIVATIVES **oligotrophy** n.

**oliguria** /ɒlɪˈgjʊərɪə/ • **n.** Medicine the production of abnormally small amounts of urine.
– DERIVATIVES **oliguric** adj.

**olingo** /ɒˈlɪŋgəʊ/ • **n.** (pl. **-os**) a small nocturnal mammal resembling the kinkajou but with a bushy non-prehensile tail, living in tropical American rainforests. [Genus *Bassaricyon*.]
– ORIGIN 1920s: via Amer. Sp. from Mayan.

**olio** /ˈəʊlɪəʊ/ • **n.** (pl. **-os**) **1** a highly spiced stew from Spain and Portugal. **2** a collection or miscellany. **3** a variety act or show.
– ORIGIN C17: from Sp. *olla* 'stew'.

**olivaceous** /ˌɒlɪˈveɪʃəs/ • **adj.** technical of a dusky yellowish green colour; olive green.

**olivary** /ˈɒlɪv(ə)ri/ • **adj.** Anatomy relating to or denoting the nucleus situated in the olive of the medulla oblongata in the brain.

**olive** • **n. 1** a small oval fruit with a hard stone and bitter flesh, green when unripe and bluish black when ripe, used as food and as a source of oil. **2** (also **olive tree**) the small evergreen tree which yields this fruit, native to warm regions of the Old World. [*Olea europaea*.] **3** (also **olive green**) a greyish-green colour like that of an unripe olive. ➤[as modifier] (of the complexion) yellowish brown; sallow. **4** a slice of beef or veal made into a roll with stuffing inside and stewed. **5** (also **olive shell**) a marine mollusc with a smooth, roughly cylindrical shell. [Genus *Oliva*.] **6** Anatomy each of a pair of smooth, oval swellings in the medulla oblongata. **7** a metal ring or fitting tightened under a threaded nut to form a seal.
– ORIGIN ME: via OFr. from L. *oliva*, from Gk *elaia*, from *elaion* 'oil'.

**olive branch** • **n.** an offer of reconciliation.
– ORIGIN in allusion to the story of Noah in Gen. 8:1, in which a dove returns with an olive branch after the Flood.

**olive drab** • **n.** a dull olive-green colour, used in some military uniforms.

**olive oil** • **n.** an oil obtained from olives, used in cookery and salad dressings.

**olivine** /ˈɒlɪviːn, -ʌɪn/ • **n.** a green or brown silicate mineral occurring in basalt and other igneous rocks.

**olla podrida** /ˌɒlə pə(ʊ)ˈdriːdə, Spanish ˌoja poˈðriða/ • **n.** another term for **OLIO** (in sense 1).
– ORIGIN Sp., lit. 'rotten pot'.

**olm** /əʊlm, ɒlm/ • **n.** a pale-skinned blind salamander with external gills which lives in limestone caves in SE Europe. [*Proteus anguinus*.]
– ORIGIN C19: from Ger.

**Olmec** /ˈɒlmɛk/ • **n.** (pl. same or **Olmecs**) **1** a member of a prehistoric people who lived on the Gulf of Mexico. **2** a native people inhabiting this area during the 15th and 16th centuries.
– ORIGIN from Nahuatl *Olmecatl*, (pl.) *Olmeca*, lit. 'inhabitants of the rubber country'.

**-ology** • **comb. form** common form of **-LOGY**.

**oloroso** /ˌɒləˈrəʊsəʊ/ • **n.** a heavy, dark, medium-sweet sherry.
– ORIGIN Sp., lit. 'fragrant'.

**Olympiad** /əˈlɪmpɪad/ • **n. 1** a celebration of the ancient or modern Olympic Games. **2** a period of four years between Olympic Games, used by the ancient Greeks in dating events.

**Olympian** • **adj. 1** associated with Mount Olympus in NE Greece, traditional home of the Greek gods. ➤resembling or appropriate to a god, especially in superiority and aloofness. **2** relating to the ancient or modern Olympic Games. • **n. 1** any of the twelve Greek gods regarded as living on Olympus. ➤a very superior or exalted person. **2** a competitor in the Olympic Games.

**Olympic** • **adj.** of or relating to ancient Olympia or the Olympic Games. • **n.** (**the Olympics**) the Olympic Games.

**Olympic Games** • **pl. n. 1** a sports festival held every four years in different countries, instigated in 1896. **2** an ancient Greek festival with athletic, literary, and musical competitions, held at Olympia every four years.

**OM** • **abbrev.** (in the UK) Order of Merit.

**om** /əʊm/ • **n.** Hinduism & Tibetan Buddhism a mystic syllable, considered the most sacred mantra.
– ORIGIN Sanskrit, sometimes regarded as three sounds, *a-u-m*, symbolic of the three major Hindu deities.

**-oma** • **suffix** (forming nouns) denoting tumours and other abnormal growths: *carcinoma*.
– DERIVATIVES **-omatous** suffix forming corresponding adjectives.
– ORIGIN mod. L., from a Gk suffix denoting the result of verbal action.

**omadhaun** /ˈɒmədɔːn/ (also **omadawn** or **omadhawn**) • **n.** Irish a foolish person.
– ORIGIN C19: from Ir. *amadán*.

**Omaha** /ˈəʊməhɑː/ • **n.** (pl. same or **Omahas**) **1** a member of an American Indian people of NE Nebraska. **2** the Siouan language of this people.
– ORIGIN from Omaha *umonhon* 'upstream people'.

**Omani** /əʊˈmɑːni/ • **n.** a native or inhabitant of Oman. • **adj.** of or relating to Oman.

**omasum** /əʊˈmeɪsəm/ • **n.** (pl. **omasa** /-sə/) Zoology the muscular third stomach of a ruminant animal, between the reticulum and the abomasum.
– ORIGIN C18: from L., lit. 'bullock's tripe'.

**ombre** /ˈɒmbə, ˈɒmbreɪ/ • **n.** a trick-taking card game for three people using a pack of forty cards, popular in the 17th–18th centuries.
– ORIGIN from Sp. *hombre* 'man', with ref. to one player seeking to win the pool.

**ombré** /ˈɒmbreɪ/ • **adj.** (of a fabric) having a design in which the colour is graduated from light to dark.
– ORIGIN Fr., past part. of *ombrer* 'to shade'.

**ombro-** • **comb. form** relating to rain: *ombrotrophic*.
– ORIGIN from Gk *ombros* 'rain shower'.

**ombrotrophic** /ˌɒmbrə(ʊ)ˈtrəʊfɪk, -ˈtrɒfɪk/ • **adj.** Ecology (of a bog or its vegetation) dependent on atmospheric moisture for its nutrients.

**ombudsman** /ˈɒmbʊdzmən/ • **n.** (pl. **-men**) an official appointed to investigate individuals' complaints against maladministration, especially that of public authorities.
– ORIGIN 1950s: from Swed., 'legal representative'.

**-ome** • **suffix** chiefly Biology forming nouns denoting objects or parts having a specified nature: *rhizome*.
– ORIGIN var. form of **-OMA**.

**omega** /ˈəʊmɪgə/ • **n. 1** the last letter of the Greek alphabet (Ω, ω), transliterated as 'o' or 'ō'. **2** the last of a series; the final development. • **symb.** (Ω) ohm(s).
– ORIGIN from Gk *ō mega* 'the great O'.

**omelette** (US also **omelet**) • **n.** a dish of beaten eggs cooked in a frying pan and usually served with a savoury topping or filling.
– ORIGIN Fr., earlier *amelette* (alt. of *alumette*), var. of *alumelle*, from *lemele* 'knife blade'.

**omen** • **n.** an event regarded as a portent of good or evil.
– ORIGIN C16: from L.

**omentum** /əʊˈmɛntəm/ • **n.** (pl. **omenta** /-tə/) Anatomy a fold of peritoneum connecting the stomach with other abdominal organs.
– DERIVATIVES **omental** adj.
– ORIGIN ME: from L.

**omertà** /ˌəʊmɛːˈtɑː, Italian omerˈta/ • **n.** a code of silence about criminal activity, practised by the Mafia.
– ORIGIN Ital. dial., var. of *umiltà* 'humility'.

**omicron** /ə(ʊ)ˈmʌɪkrɒn/ • **n.** the fifteenth letter of the Greek alphabet (Ο, ο), transliterated as 'o'.
– ORIGIN from Gk *o mikron* 'small o'.

**ominous** • **adj.** giving the worrying impression that something bad is going to happen.
– DERIVATIVES **ominously** adv. **ominousness** n.
– ORIGIN C16: from L. *ominosus*, from *omen*, *omin-* 'omen'.

**omit** • **v.** (**omitted**, **omitting**) leave out or exclude. ➤fail to do.
– DERIVATIVES **omissible** adj. **omission** n. **omissive** adj.
– ORIGIN ME: from L. *omittere*, from *ob-* 'down' + *mittere* 'let go'.

**ommatidium** /ˌɒməˈtɪdɪəm/ • **n.** (pl. **ommatidia** /-dɪə/)

Entomology each of the optical units that make up the compound eye of an insect.
– ORIGIN C19: mod. L., from Gk *ommatidion*, dimin. of *omma*, *ommat-* 'eye'.

**omni-** ● **comb. form** all; of all things: *omnifarious*. ➤ in all ways or places: *omnipresent*.
– ORIGIN from L. *omnis* 'all'.

**omnibus** ● **n. 1** a volume containing several works previously published separately. ➤ chiefly Brit. a single edition of two or more consecutive programmes previously broadcast separately. **2** dated a bus.
– ORIGIN C19: via Fr. from L., lit. 'for all', dative pl. of *omnis*.

**omnicompetent** ● **adj.** able to deal with all matters or solve all problems. ➤ (of a legislative body) having powers to legislate on all matters.
– DERIVATIVES **omnicompetence** n.

**omnidirectional** ● **adj.** Telecommunications receiving signals from or transmitting in all directions.

**omnifarious** /ˌɒmnɪˈfɛːrɪəs/ ● **adj.** formal comprising or relating to all sorts or varieties.
– ORIGIN C17: from late L. *omnifarius* + **-OUS**; cf. **MULTIFARIOUS**.

**omnipotent** /ɒmˈnɪpət(ə)nt/ ● **adj.** (especially of a deity) having unlimited or very great power.
– DERIVATIVES **omnipotence** n. **omnipotently** adv.
– ORIGIN ME: via OFr. from L. *omnipotent-* 'all-powerful'.

**omnipresent** ● **adj. 1** (of God) present everywhere at the same time. **2** widely or constantly encountered.
– DERIVATIVES **omnipresence** n.
– ORIGIN C17: from med. L. *omnipraesent-*.

**omniscient** /ɒmˈnɪsɪənt/ ● **adj.** knowing everything.
– DERIVATIVES **omniscience** n. **omnisciently** adv.
– ORIGIN C17: from med. L. *omniscient-* 'all-knowing'.

**omnisexual** ● **adj.** involving or characterized by a diverse sexual propensity.
– DERIVATIVES **omnisexuality** n.

**omnium gatherum** /ˌɒmnɪəm ˈɡaðərəm/ ● **n.** a collection of miscellaneous people or things.
– ORIGIN C16: mock L., from L. *omnium* 'of all' and **GATHER** + the L. suffix *-um*.

**omnivore** /ˈɒmnɪvɔː/ ● **n.** an omnivorous animal.

**omnivorous** /ɒmˈnɪv(ə)rəs/ ● **adj. 1** (of an animal) feeding on a variety of food of both plant and animal origin. **2** indiscriminate in taking in or using whatever is available.
– DERIVATIVES **omnivorously** adv. **omnivorousness** n.
– ORIGIN C17: from L. *omnivorus* + **-OUS**.

**omophagy** /ə(ʊ)ˈmɒfədʒi/ (also **omophagia**) ● **n.** the eating of raw food, especially raw meat.
– DERIVATIVES **omophagic** adj. **omophagous** adj.
– ORIGIN C18: from Gk *ōmophagia*, from *ōmos* 'raw' + *-phagia*.

**Omotic** /əʊˈmɒtɪk/ ● **n.** a subfamily of Afro-Asiatic languages spoken in Ethiopia. ● **adj.** denoting or belonging to this subfamily.
– ORIGIN 1970s: from *Omo*, the name of a river in SW Ethiopia, + **-OTIC**.

**omphalo-** /ˈɒmfələʊ/ ● **comb. form** relating to the navel: *omphalocele*.
– ORIGIN from Gk *omphalos* 'navel'.

**omphalos** /ˈɒmfəlɒs/ ● **n.** (pl. **omphaloi** /-lɔɪ/) **1** (in ancient Greece) a conical stone, especially that at Delphi, representing the navel of the earth. **2** a boss on an ancient Greek shield.
– ORIGIN Gk, lit. 'navel, boss'.

**ON**[1] ● **abbrev.** Ontario (in official postal use).

**ON**[2] ● **abbrev.** Old Norse.

**on** ● **prep. 1** physically in contact with and supported by (a surface). ➤ located somewhere in the general surface area of (a place). ➤ on to. ➤ in the possession of. **2** forming a distinctive or marked part of the surface of. **3** about; concerning. ➤ having (the thing mentioned) as a basis. **4** as a member of (a committee, jury, etc.). **5** having (the thing mentioned) as a target, aim, or focus. **6** having (the thing mentioned) as a medium for transmitting or storing information. ➤ being broadcast by (a radio or television channel). **7** in the course of (a journey). ➤ while travelling in (a public service vehicle). **8** indicating the day or part of a day during which an event takes place. ➤ at the time of. **9** engaged in. **10** regularly taking (a drug or medicine). **11** paid for by. **12** added to. ● **adv. 1** physically in contact with and supported by a surface. ➤ (of clothing) being worn by a person. **2** indicating continuation of a movement or action. ➤ further forward; in an advanced state. **3** (of an event) taking place or being presented. ➤ due to take place as planned. **4** (of an electrical appliance or power supply) functioning. **5** (of an actor) on stage. ➤ (of an employee) on duty. ● **n.** (also **on side**) Cricket the leg side.
– PHRASES **be on about** Brit. informal talk about tediously and at length. **be on at** Brit. informal nag or grumble at. **be on to** informal **1** be close to uncovering an illegal or undesirable activity engaged in by (someone). **2** (**be on to something**) have an idea that is likely to lead to an important discovery. **on and on** continually; at tedious length. **on to** moving to a location on the surface of (something) or aboard (a public service vehicle).
– ORIGIN OE *on*, *an*, of Gmc origin.

**-on** ● **suffix** Physics, Biochemistry, & Chemistry forming nouns: **1** denoting subatomic particles or quanta: *neutron*. **2** denoting molecular units: *codon*. **3** denoting substances: *interferon*.
– ORIGIN sense 1 orig. in *electron*, from **ION**, influenced (as in sense 2) by Gk *on* 'being'; sense 3 is on the pattern of words such as *cotton* or from Ger. *-on*.

**onager** /ˈɒnəɡə/ ● **n.** an animal of a race of the Asian wild ass native to northern Iran. [*Equus hemionus onager*.]
– ORIGIN ME: via L. from Gk *onagros*, from *onos* 'ass' + *agrios* 'wild'.

**onanism** /ˈəʊnənɪz(ə)m/ ● **n.** formal **1** masturbation. **2** coitus interruptus.
– DERIVATIVES **onanist** n. **onanistic** adj.
– ORIGIN C18: from Fr. *onanisme* or mod. L. *onanismus*, from the name *Onan* (Gen. 38:9).

**on-board** ● **adj. 1** situated on board a ship, aircraft, or other vehicle. **2** Computing incorporated into the main circuit board of a computer or computerized device.

**ONC** ● **abbrev.** historical (in the UK) Ordinary National Certificate.

**once** ● **adv. 1** on one occasion or for one time only. ➤ [usu. with neg.] at all; on even one occasion. **2** formerly. **3** multiplied by one. ● **conj.** as soon as; when.
– PHRASES **all at once 1** suddenly. **2** all at the same time. **at once 1** immediately. **2** simultaneously. **for once** (or **this once**) on this occasion only. **once again** (or **more**) one more time. **once and for all** (or **once for all**) now and for the last time; finally. **once** (or **every once**) **in a while** occasionally. **once or twice** a few times. **once upon a time** at some time in the past.
– ORIGIN ME *ones*, genitive of **ONE**.

**once-over** ● **n.** informal a rapid inspection, search, or piece of work.

**oncer** ● **n.** Brit. informal **1** historical a one-pound note. **2** a person who does a particular thing only once.

**onchocerciasis** /ˌɒŋkəʊsəːˈsʌɪəsɪs, -ˈkʌɪəsɪs/ ● **n.** technical term for **RIVER BLINDNESS**.
– ORIGIN C20: from mod. L. *Onchocerca* (genus name of the filarial parasite causing the disease, from Gk *onkos* 'barb' + *kerkos* 'tail') + **-IASIS**.

**onco-** ● **comb. form** of or relating to tumours: *oncology*.
– ORIGIN from Gk *onkos* 'mass'.

**oncogene** /ˈɒŋkə(ʊ)dʒiːn/ ● **n.** Medicine a gene which in certain circumstances can transform a cell into a tumour cell.

**oncogenic** /ˌɒŋkə(ʊ)ˈdʒɛnɪk/ ● **adj.** Medicine causing development of a tumour or tumours.
– DERIVATIVES **oncogenesis** n. **oncogenicity** n.

**oncology** /ɒŋˈkɒlədʒi/ ● **n.** Medicine the study and treatment of tumours.
– DERIVATIVES **oncological** adj. **oncologist** n.

**oncoming** ● **adj.** approaching from the front; moving towards one. ● **n.** the approach or onset of something.

**oncost** ● **n.** Brit. an overhead expense.

**OND** ● **abbrev.** historical (in the UK) Ordinary National Diploma.

**ondes martenot** /ɒ̃d 'mɑːt(ə)nəʊ, French ɔ̃d martəno/ • **n.** (pl. same) Music an electronic keyboard producing one note of variable pitch.
– ORIGIN 1950s: from Fr. *ondes musicales*, lit. 'musical waves' (the orig. name of the instrument) and the name of Maurice *Martenot*, its inventor.

**on dit** /ɒ̃ 'diː/ • **n.** (pl. **on dits** pronunc. same) a piece of gossip; a rumour.
– ORIGIN Fr., lit. 'they say'.

**on drive** • **n.** Cricket a drive to the on side.

**one** • **cardinal number 1** the lowest cardinal number; half of two; 1. (Roman numeral: **i** or **I**.) **2** single, or a single person or thing. ➤denoting a particular item of a pair or number of items. ➤(before a person's name) a certain. ➤informal, chiefly N. Amer. a noteworthy example of. ➤identical; the same. **3** informal a joke or story. • **pron. 1** used to refer to a person or thing previously mentioned or easily identified. **2** a person of a specified kind. **3** [third person sing.] used to refer to the speaker, or any person, as representing people in general.
– PHRASES **at one** in agreement or harmony. **one after another** (or **the other**) following one another in quick succession. **one and all** everyone. **one and only** unique; single. **one another** each other. **one by one** separately and in succession. **one day** at a particular but unspecified time in the past or future. **one or another** (or **the other**) a particular but unspecified one out of a set of items. **one or two** informal a few.
– DERIVATIVES **onefold** adj.
– ORIGIN OE *ān*, of Gmc origin.

**-one** • **suffix** Chemistry forming nouns denoting various compounds, especially ketones: *acetone*.
– ORIGIN from Gk patronymic *-ōnē*.

**one-armed bandit** • **n.** informal a fruit machine operated by pulling a long handle at the side.

**one-dimensional** • **adj. 1** having or relating to a single dimension. **2** lacking depth; superficial.
– DERIVATIVES **one-dimensionality** n.

**one-horse race** • **n.** a contest in which one competitor is clearly superior to all the others.

**one-horse town** • **n.** informal a small town with few and poor facilities.

**Oneida** /əʊ'nʌɪdə/ • **n.** (pl. same or **Oneidas**) **1** a member of an American Indian people formerly inhabiting upper New York State. **2** the extinct Iroquoian language of this people.
– ORIGIN from a local word meaning 'erected stone', the name of successive principal Oneida settlements, near which a large boulder was traditionally erected.

**oneiric** /ə(ʊ)'nʌɪrɪk/ • **adj.** formal of or relating to dreams or dreaming.

**oneiro-** /ə(ʊ)'nʌɪrəʊ/ • **comb. form** relating to dreams or dreaming: *oneiromancy*.
– ORIGIN from Gk *oneiros* 'dream'.

**oneiromancy** /ə'nʌɪrə(ʊ),mansi/ • **n.** the interpretation of dreams in order to foretell the future.

**one-liner** • **n.** informal a short joke or witty remark.

**one-man band** • **n. 1** a street entertainer who plays many instruments at the same time. **2** a person who runs a business alone.

**oneness** • **n. 1** the state of being unified, whole, or in harmony. **2** the state of being one in number.

**one-night stand** (also **one-nighter**) • **n. 1** informal a sexual relationship lasting only one night. **2** a single performance of a play or show in a particular place.

**one-off** informal, chiefly Brit. • **adj.** done, made, or happening only once. • **n.** something done, made, or happening only once. ➤a unique or remarkable person.

**oner** • **n.** Brit. informal **1** something denoted by the number one. **2** archaic a remarkable person or thing.

**onerous** /'əʊn(ə)rəs, 'ɒn-/ • **adj.** involving an oppressively burdensome amount of effort and difficulty. ➤Law involving heavy obligations.
– DERIVATIVES **onerously** adv. **onerousness** n.
– ORIGIN ME: from OFr. *onereus*, from L. *onerosus*, from *onus, oner-* 'burden'.

**oneself** • **pron.** [third person sing.] **1** [reflexive] used as the object of a verb or preposition when this is the same as the subject of the clause and the subject is 'one'. **2** [emphatic] used to emphasize that one does something individually or unaided. **3** in one's normal and individual state of body or mind.

**one-sided** • **adj. 1** unfairly dealing with or biased towards only one side of a contentious issue. ➤(of a contest or conflict) grossly unequal. **2** occurring on or having one side only.
– DERIVATIVES **one-sidedly** adv. **one-sidedness** n.

**one-step** • **n.** a vigorous kind of foxtrot in duple time.

**one-tailed** • **adj.** Statistics denoting a test for deviation from the null hypothesis in one direction only.

**one-time** • **adj.** former.

**one-track mind** • **n.** informal a mind preoccupied with one subject, especially sex.

**one-trick pony** • **n.** a person or thing with only one special feature, talent, or area of expertise.

**one-two** • **n. 1** a pair of punches in quick succession, especially with alternate hands. **2** chiefly Soccer a move in which a player plays a short pass to a teammate and moves forward to receive an immediate return pass.

**one-up** • **adj.** informal having a psychological advantage over someone.

**one-upmanship** • **n.** informal the technique of gaining an advantage or feeling of superiority over another.

**one-way** • **adj.** moving or allowing movement in one direction only.

**one-world** • **adj.** relating to or holding the view that the world's inhabitants are interdependent and should behave accordingly.
– DERIVATIVES **one-worlder** n. **one-worldism** n.

**ongoing** • **adj.** continuing; still in progress.
– DERIVATIVES **ongoingness** n.

**onion** • **n. 1** an edible bulb used as a vegetable, having a pungent taste and smell and composed of several concentric layers. **2** the plant that produces this bulb, with spherical heads of greenish-white flowers. [*Allium cepa*.]
– PHRASES **know one's onions** informal be very knowledgeable.
– DERIVATIVES **oniony** adj.
– ORIGIN ME: from OFr. *oignon*, based on L. *unio(n-)*, denoting a kind of onion.

**onion dome** • **n.** a dome which bulges in the middle and rises to a point, used especially in Russian church architecture.
– DERIVATIVES **onion-domed** adj.

**onion set** • **n.** a small onion bulb planted instead of seed to yield a mature bulb.

**onion-skin paper** • **n.** very fine smooth translucent paper.

**online** • **adj. & adv. 1** controlled by or connected to a computer. **2** in or into operation or existence.

**onlooker** • **n.** a non-participating observer; a spectator.
– DERIVATIVES **onlooking** adj.

**only** • **adv. 1** and no one or nothing more besides. ➤no longer ago than. ➤not until. **2** with the negative or unfortunate result that. • **adj.** alone of its or their kind; single or solitary. ➤alone deserving consideration. • **conj.** informal except that.
– PHRASES **only just 1** by a very small margin. **2** very recently. **only too** —— to an extreme or regrettable extent.
– ORIGIN OE *ānlic* (see ONE, -LY[1]).

**on-message** • **adj.** (of a politician) stating the official party line.

**o.n.o.** • **abbrev.** Brit. or nearest offer (used in advertisements).

**onomasiology** /,ɒnə(ʊ)meɪsɪ'ɒlədʒi/ • **n.** the branch of knowledge concerned with terminology, in particular contrasting terms for similar concepts, as in a thesaurus.
– DERIVATIVES **onomasiological** adj.
– ORIGIN C20: from Gk *onomasia* 'term' + -LOGY.

**onomast** /'ɒnəmast/ • **n.** a person who studies proper names, especially personal names.

**onomastic** /ɒnəˈmastɪk/ ● **adj.** of or relating to onomastics.
– ORIGIN C16 (as n.): from Gk *onomastikos*, from *onoma* 'name'.

**onomastics** ● **pl. n.** [usu. treated as sing.] the study of the history and origin of proper names, especially personal names.

**onomatopoeia** /ˌɒnə(ʊ)matəˈpiːə/ ● **n.** the formation of a word from a sound associated with what is named (e.g. *cuckoo, sizzle*). ➤ the use of such words for rhetorical effect.
– DERIVATIVES **onomatopoeic** adj. **onomatopoeically** adv.
– ORIGIN C16: via late L. from Gk *onomatopoiia* 'word-making', from *onoma, onomat-* 'name' + *-poios* 'making'.

**Onondaga** /ˌɒnənˈdɑːɡə/ ● **n.** (pl. same or **Onondagas**) **1** a member of an Iroquois people formerly inhabiting an area near Syracuse, New York. **2** the extinct Iroquoian language of this people.
– ORIGIN from the Iroquoian name of their main settlement, lit. 'on the hill'.

**onrush** ● **n.** a surging rush forward. ● **v.** [usu. as adj. **onrushing**] move forward in a surging rush.

**onset** ● **n. 1** the beginning of something, especially something unpleasant. **2** archaic a military attack.

**onshore** ● **adj. & adv.** situated or occurring on land. ➤ (of the wind) blowing from the sea towards the land.

**onside** ● **adj. & adv. 1** (in sport) not offside. **2** informal in or into a position of agreement.

**onslaught** ● **n.** a fierce or destructive attack. ➤ an overwhelmingly large quantity of people or things.
– ORIGIN C17 (also as *anslaight*): from MDu. *aenslag*, from *aen* 'on' + *slag* 'blow', assoc. with obs. *slaught* 'slaughter'.

**onstage** ● **adj. & adv.** (in a theatre) on the stage and so visible to the audience.

**on-stream** ● **adv. & adj.** in or into industrial production or useful operation.

**Ont.** ● **abbrev.** Ontario.

**-ont** ● **comb. form** Biology denoting an individual or cell of a specified type: *schizont*.
– ORIGIN from Gk *ont-* 'being', pres. part. of *eimi* 'be'.

**Ontarian** /ɒnˈtɛːrɪən/ ● **n.** a native or inhabitant of the Canadian province of Ontario. ● **adj.** of or relating to Ontario.

**ontic** /ˈɒntɪk/ ● **adj.** Philosophy of or relating to entities and the facts about them.
– ORIGIN 1940s: from Gk *ōn, ont-* 'being' + **-IC**.

**onto** ● **prep.** variant form of ***on to*** (see **ON**).

> **USAGE** onto
>
> The preposition **onto** written as one word (instead of **on to**) is widely used, but is still not wholly accepted as part of standard British English (unlike **into**, for example). However, in US English, **onto** is standard.

**ontogenesis** /ˌɒntə(ʊ)ˈdʒɛnɪsɪs/ ● **n.** Biology the development of an individual organism or anatomical or behavioural feature from the earliest stage to maturity.
– DERIVATIVES **ontogenetic** adj. **ontogenetically** adv.
– ORIGIN C19: from Gk *ōn, ont-* 'being' + *genesis* 'birth'.

**ontogeny** /ɒnˈtɒdʒəni/ ● **n.** the branch of biology concerned with ontogenesis. Compare with **PHYLOGENY**. ➤ another term for **ONTOGENESIS**.
– DERIVATIVES **ontogenic** adj. **ontogenically** adv.

**ontology** /ɒnˈtɒlədʒi/ ● **n.** the branch of metaphysics concerned with the nature of being.
– DERIVATIVES **ontological** adj. **ontologically** adv. **ontologist** n.
– ORIGIN C18: from mod. L. *ontologia*, from Gk *ōn, ont-* 'being' + **-LOGY**.

**onus** /ˈəʊnəs/ ● **n.** a burden, duty, or responsibility.
– ORIGIN C17: from L., lit. 'load or burden'.

**onward** ● **adv.** (also **onwards**) **1** in a continuing forward direction; ahead. ➤ forward in time. **2** so as to make progress or become more successful. ● **adj.** (of a journey) moving forward.

**Onychophora** /ˌɒnɪˈkɒf(ə)rə/ ● **pl. n.** Zoology a small phylum of terrestrial invertebrates which comprises the velvet worms.
– DERIVATIVES **onychophoran** adj. & n.
– ORIGIN mod. L., from Gk *onux, onukh-* 'nail, claw' + *-phoros* 'bearing'.

**-onym** ● **comb. form** forming nouns: **1** denoting a type of name: *pseudonym*. **2** denoting a word having a specified relationship to another: *antonym*. See word-formation panel.
– ORIGIN from Gk *-ōnumon*, neut. of *-ōnumos*, comb. form of *onoma* 'name'.

**onyx** /ˈɒnɪks, ˈəʊnɪks/ ● **n.** a semi-precious variety of agate with different colours in layers.
– ORIGIN ME: from OFr. *oniche, onix*, via L. from Gk *onux* 'fingernail or onyx'.

**onyx marble** ● **n.** banded calcite or other stone used as a decorative material.

**oo-** /ˈəʊə/ ● **comb. form** Biology relating to or denoting an egg or ovum: *oogenesis*.
– ORIGIN from Gk *ōion* 'egg'.

**oocyte** /ˈəʊəsʌɪt/ ● **n.** Biology a cell in an ovary which may undergo meiotic division to form an ovum.

**oodles** ● **pl. n.** informal a very great number or amount.
– ORIGIN C19 (orig. US): of unknown origin.

**oo-er** ● **exclam.** expressing surprise or alarm.

**oogamous** /əʊˈɒɡəməs/ ● **adj.** Biology relating to or denoting reproduction by the union of mobile male and immobile female gametes.
– DERIVATIVES **oogamously** adv. **oogamy** n.
– ORIGIN C19: from **oo-** + Gk *gamos* 'marriage' + **-OUS**.

**oogenesis** /əʊəˈdʒɛnɪsɪs/ ● **n.** Biology the production or development of an ovum.

**oogonium** /ˌəʊəˈɡəʊnɪəm/ ● **n.** (pl. **oogonia**) **1** Botany the female sex organ of certain algae and fungi. **2** Biology an immature female reproductive cell that gives rise to primary oocytes by mitosis.
– ORIGIN C19: from **oo-** + Gk *gonos* 'generation' + **-IUM**.

**ooh** ● **exclam.** used to express a range of emotions including surprise, delight, or pain. ● **v.** (**oohed, oohing**) (usu. in phr. **ooh and aah**) utter such an exclamation.

**oojah** /ˈuːdʒɑː/ (also **oojamaflip** /ˈuːdʒəməflɪp/) ● **n.** informal something that one cannot or does not want to name.
– ORIGIN C20: of unknown origin.

**oolite** /ˈəʊəlʌɪt/ ● **n.** Geology limestone consisting of a mass of rounded grains (ooliths) made up of concentric layers.
– DERIVATIVES **oolitic** adj.
– ORIGIN C19: from Fr. *oölithe*, mod. L. *oolites* (see **oo-**, **-LITE**).

**oolith** /ˈəʊəlɪθ/ ● **n.** Geology any of the rounded grains making up oolite.

**oology** /əʊˈɒlədʒi/ ● **n.** the study or collecting of birds' eggs.
– DERIVATIVES **oological** adj. **oologist** n.

**oolong** /ˈuːlɒŋ/ ● **n.** a kind of dark-coloured partly fermented China tea.
– ORIGIN C19: from Chin. *wūlóng*, lit. 'black dragon'.

**oompah** ● **n.** informal the rhythmical sound of deep-toned brass instruments in a band.
– ORIGIN C19: imitative.

**oomph** (also **umph**) ● **n.** informal the quality of being exciting, energetic, or sexually attractive.
– ORIGIN 1930s: perh. imitative.

**-oon** ● **suffix** forming nouns, originally from French words having the final stressed syllable *-on*: *balloon*.
– ORIGIN from L. *-onis*, sometimes via Ital. *-one*.

**oophorectomy** /ˌəʊəfəˈrɛktəmi/ ● **n.** (pl. **-ies**) surgical removal of one or both ovaries; ovariectomy.
– ORIGIN C19: from mod. L. *oophoron* 'ovary' + **-ECTOMY**.

**oophoritis** /ˌəʊəfəˈrʌɪtɪs/ ● **n.** Medicine inflammation of an ovary.

**oops** ● **exclam.** informal used to show recognition of a mistake or minor accident.

**oops-a-daisy** ● **exclam.** variant spelling of **UPSY-DAISY**.

**ooze**[1] ● **v. 1** (of a fluid) slowly trickle or seep out. ➤ slowly exude or discharge (a viscous fluid). **2** give a powerful

## Word *Formation*

**-onym** from Greek *onoma* 'name'

**➤ 1.** Types of name:

| | | |
|---|---|---|
| anonym | an anonymous person or thing | Gk *anōnumos* 'nameless' (from *an-* 'without') |
| cryptonym | a code name | Gk *kruptos* 'hidden' |
| eponym | a name or word taken from a person's name | Gk *epōnumos* 'given as a name' (from *epi* 'upon') |
| pseudonym | a fictitious name, as used by an author | Gk *pseudēs* 'false' |
| toponym | a place name | Gk *topos* 'place' |

**➤ 2.** Words having a specific relationship to another word or words:

| | | |
|---|---|---|
| acronym | a word formed from the initial letters of other words | Gk *akron* 'end, tip' |
| antonym | a word opposite in meaning to another | Gk *anti-* 'against' |
| homonym | each of two words with the same written form but different meanings and origin | Gk *homos* 'same' |
| meronym | a term denoting part of something used to refer to the whole | Gk *meros* 'part' |
| metonym | a word used to substitute for another | Gk *metōnumia* 'change of name' |
| synonym | a word or phrase with the same (or similar) meaning as another | Gk *sun-* 'with' |

**➤** Related words:

| | |
|---|---|
| -onymous | forming adjectives, e.g. ***synonymous*** 'meaning the same as'. Some **-onymous** forms are more common than their counterparts in **-onym**, as ***anonymous*** 'of unknown identity or authorship'. |

impression of (a quality): *she oozes sex appeal.* ● **n. 1** the sluggish flow of a fluid. **2** an infusion of oak bark or other vegetable matter, used in tanning.
– DERIVATIVES **oozy** adj.
– ORIGIN OE *wōs* 'juice or sap'.

**ooze**[2] ● **n.** wet mud or slime, especially that found at the bottom of a river, lake, or sea.
– DERIVATIVES **oozy** adj.
– ORIGIN OE *wāse*; rel. to ON *veisa* 'stagnant pool', influenced by **OOZE**[1].

**OP** ● **abbrev. 1** observation post. **2** (in the theatre) opposite prompt, the offstage area to the right of an actor. **3** organophosphate(s). **4** (in the Roman Catholic Church) Order of Preachers (Dominican). [L. *Ordo Praedicatorum*.]

**Op.** (also **op.**) ● **abbrev.** Music (before a number given to each work of a particular composer) opus.

**op** ● **n.** informal **1** a surgical operation. **2** (**ops**) military operations. **3** a radio or telephone operator.

**op-** ● **prefix** variant spelling of **OB-** assimilated before *p* (as in *oppress*, *oppugn*).

**o.p.** ● **abbrev. 1** (of a book) out of print. **2** (of alcohol) overproof.

**opacify** /ə(ʊ)ˈpasɪfʌɪ/ ● **v.** (**-ies**, **-ied**) technical make or become opaque.
– DERIVATIVES **opacifier** n.

**opacity** /ə(ʊ)ˈpasɪti/ ● **n.** the condition of being opaque.

**opah** /ˈəʊpə/ ● **n.** a large deep-bodied fish with a deep blue back, silvery belly, and crimson fins, living in deep oceanic waters. [*Lampris guttatus*.]
– ORIGIN C18: a W. Afr. word.

**opal** ● **n.** a gemstone consisting of a quartz-like form of hydrated silica, typically semi-transparent and showing many small points of shifting colour against a pale or dark ground.
– ORIGIN C16: from Fr. *opale* or L. *opalus*, prob. based on Sanskrit *upala* 'precious stone'.

**opalescent** ● **adj.** showing many small points of shifting colour against a pale or dark ground.
– DERIVATIVES **opalescence** n.

**opal glass** ● **n.** a type of semi-translucent white glass.

**opaline** /ˈəʊp(ə)lʌɪn, -lɪn/ ● **adj.** opalescent. ● **n.** translucent or semi-translucent glass such as milk glass.

**op-amp** ● **abbrev.** operational amplifier.

**opaque** /ə(ʊ)ˈpeɪk/ ● **adj.** (**-er**, **-est**) **1** not able to be seen through; not transparent. **2** difficult or impossible to understand. ● **n.** an opaque thing. ➤Photography a substance for producing opaque areas on negatives.
– DERIVATIVES **opaquely** adv. **opaqueness** n.
– ORIGIN ME *opake*, from L. *opacus* 'darkened'.

**op art** ● **n.** a form of abstract art that gives the illusion of movement by its use of pattern and colour.
– ORIGIN 1960s: abbrev. of *optical art* on the pattern of *pop art*.

**op. cit.** ● **adv.** in the work already cited.
– ORIGIN from L. *opere citato*.

**ope** ● **adj. & v.** poetic/literary or archaic form of **OPEN**.

**OPEC** ● **abbrev.** Organization of the Petroleum Exporting Countries.

**Op-Ed** ● **adj.** N. Amer. relating to or denoting a newspaper page opposite the editorial page, devoted to personal comment, feature articles, etc.

**open** ● **adj. 1** allowing access, passage, or view; not closed, fastened, or restricted. ➤(of the bowels) not constipated. **2** exposed to the air or to view or attack; not covered or protected. ➤(**open to**) vulnerable or subject to. ➤(of land) not covered with buildings or trees. ➤(of a town or city) officially declared to be undefended, and so immune under international law from bombardment. **3** spread out or unfolded. ➤(of a book) with the covers parted and able to be read. **4** officially admitting customers or visitors; available for business. ➤(of an offer or opportunity) still available. **5** frank and communicative. ➤not concealed; manifest. **6** not finally settled; still admitting of debate. ➤(often **open to**) accessible to new ideas; receptive. ➤freely available or accessible. ➤(**open to**) admitting of; making possible. **7** Music (of a string) allowed to vibrate along its whole length. ➤(of a pipe) unstopped at each end. **8** Phonetics (of a vowel) produced with a relatively wide opening of the mouth and the

tongue kept low. ➤(of a syllable) ending in a vowel. **9** (of an electric circuit) having a break in the conducting path. ● **v. 1** move (a door, window, etc.) so that it is open. ➤undo or remove the cover or fastening of. ➤(**open on to/into**) (of a door, window, etc.) give access to. **2** spread out; unfold or be unfolded. ➤part the covers of (a book) to read it. ➤(of a prospect) come into view; spread out. **3** make or become officially ready for customers or visitors. ➤ceremonially declare (a building, road, etc.) to be completed and ready for use. **4** formally begin or establish. ➤(**open up** or **open fire**) begin shooting. ➤(of a counsel in a law court) make a preliminary statement in (a case) before calling witnesses. ➤Bridge make (the first bid) in the auction. **5** make available or more widely known. ➤(**open out/up**) become more communicative or confiding. **6** break the conducting path of (an electric circuit). **7** Nautical achieve a clear view of (a place) by sailing past a headland or other obstruction. ● **n. 1** (**the open**) fresh air or open countryside. ➤(usu. in phr. **bring in/into the open**) a lack of concealment or secrecy. **2** (**Open**) a championship or competition with no restrictions on who may compete. **3** an accidental break in the conducting path for an electric current.
– PHRASES **the open air** a free or unenclosed space outdoors. **in open court** in a court of law, before the judge and the public. **open-and-shut** (of a case or argument) admitting no doubt or dispute; straightforward.
– DERIVATIVES **openable** adj. **openness** n.
– ORIGIN OE *open* (adj.), *openian* (v.), of Gmc origin, from the root of the adv. UP.

**Open Brethren** ● **pl. n.** one of the two principal divisions of the Plymouth Brethren (the other being the Exclusive Brethren).

**opencast** ● **adj.** Brit. denoting a method of mining in which coal or ore is extracted at or from a level near the earth's surface, rather than from shafts.

**open chain** ● **n.** Chemistry a molecular structure consisting of a chain of atoms with no closed rings.

**open cluster** ● **n.** Astronomy a loose grouping of stars.

**open college** ● **n.** (in the UK) an organization established to provide retraining opportunities, chiefly for the staff of companies.

**open communion** ● **n.** Christian Church communion administered to any Christian believer.

**open day** ● **n.** Brit. a day when members of the public may visit a place or institution to which they do not usually have access.

**open-ended** ● **adj.** having no predetermined limit or boundary.
– DERIVATIVES **open-endedness** n.

**opener** ● **n. 1** a device for opening something. **2** a person or thing that opens or begins, in particular the first goal in a match or a cricketer who opens the batting.
– PHRASES **for openers** informal to start with; first of all.

**open-faced** ● **adj. 1** having a frank or ingenuous expression. **2** (of a watch) having no cover other than the glass. **3** (also **open-face**) chiefly N. Amer. (of a sandwich or pie) without an upper layer of bread or pastry.

**open-field system** ● **n.** the medieval system of farming in England, in which land was divided into strips and available for grazing outside the growing season.

**open-handed** ● **adj. 1** (of a blow) delivered with the palm of the hand. **2** generous.
– DERIVATIVES **open-handedly** adv. **open-handedness** n.

**open-hearted** ● **adj.** unrestrainedly warm and kindly.
– DERIVATIVES **open-heartedness** n.

**open-hearth process** ● **n.** a steel-making process in which scrap iron or steel, limestone, and pig iron are melted together in a shallow reverberatory furnace.

**open-heart surgery** ● **n.** surgery in which the heart is exposed and the blood made to bypass it.

**open house** ● **n. 1** a place or situation in which all visitors are welcome. **2** N. Amer. an open day.

**opening** ● **n. 1** an aperture or gap. **2** a beginning; an initial part. ➤a ceremony at which a building, show, etc. is declared to be open. **3** an opportunity to achieve something. ➤an available job or position. ● **adj.** coming at the beginning; initial.

**open letter** ● **n.** a letter addressed to a particular person but intended for publication in a newspaper or journal.

**openly** ● **adv.** without concealment, deception, or prevarication; frankly or honestly.
– ORIGIN OE *openlīce* (see OPEN, -LY[2]).

**open market** ● **n.** an unrestricted market with free access by and competition of buyers and sellers.

**open marriage** ● **n.** a marriage in which both partners agree that each may have sexual relations with others.

**open mind** ● **n.** a mind willing to consider new ideas.
– DERIVATIVES **open-minded** adj. **open-mindedly** adv. **open-mindedness** n.

**open-necked** ● **adj.** (of a shirt) worn with the collar unbuttoned and without a tie.

**open outcry** ● **n.** a system of financial trading in which dealers shout their bids and contracts aloud.

**open-pit** ● **adj.** North American term for OPENCAST.

**open-plan** ● **adj.** (of a room or building) having large rooms with few or no internal dividing walls.

**open prison** ● **n.** Brit. a prison with the minimum of restrictions on prisoners' movements and activities.

**open question** ● **n.** a matter that is not yet decided or is unable to be decided.

**open range** ● **n.** N. Amer. a tract of land without fences or other barriers.

**open-reel** ● **adj.** another term for REEL-TO-REEL.

**open sandal** ● **n.** a sandal that does not cover the toes.

**open sandwich** ● **n.** a sandwich without a top slice of bread.

**open season** ● **n.** the annual period when restrictions on the killing of certain types of wildlife, especially for sport, are lifted.

**open secret** ● **n.** a supposed secret that is in fact known to many people.

**open shop** ● **n.** a place of work where employees do not have to join a trade union.

**open side** ● **n.** Rugby the side of the scrum on which the main line of the opponents' backs is ranged.

**open society** ● **n.** a society characterized by a flexible structure, freedom of belief, and wide dissemination of information.

**open-toed** ● **adj.** (of a shoe) not covering the toes.

**open-topped** (also **open-top**) ● **adj.** (of a vehicle) not having a roof or having a folding or detachable roof.

**open verdict** ● **n.** Law a verdict of a coroner's jury affirming the occurrence of a suspicious death but not specifying the cause.

**openwork** ● **n.** ornamental work in cloth, leather, etc. with regular patterns of openings and holes.

**opera**[1] ● **n.** a dramatic work in one or more acts that is set to music for singers and instrumentalists. ➤a building for the performance of opera.
– ORIGIN C17: from Ital., from L., lit. 'labour, work'.

**opera**[2] plural form of OPUS.

**operable** ● **adj. 1** able to be operated. **2** able to be treated by means of a surgical operation.
– DERIVATIVES **operability** n.

**opéra bouffe** /ˌɒp(ə)rə ˈbuːf, French ɔpeʀa buf/ ● **n.** (pl. **opéras bouffes**) a French comic opera.
– ORIGIN Fr., from Ital. (see OPERA BUFFA).

**opera buffa** /ˌɒp(ə)rə ˈbuːfə/ ● **n.** a comic opera, especially in Italian.
– ORIGIN from Ital.

**opera cloak** ● **n.** a cloak of rich material worn over evening clothes, especially by women.

**opéra comique** /ˌɒp(ə)rə kɒˈmiːk, French ɔpeʀa kɔmik/ ● **n.** a comic opera, especially one in French, with spoken dialogue.

**opera glasses** ● **pl. n.** small binoculars for use at the opera or theatre.

**opera hat** ● **n.** a collapsible top hat.

**opera house** ● **n.** a theatre for the performance of opera.

**operand** /ˈɒpərand/ ● **n.** Mathematics the quantity on which an operation is to be done.
– ORIGIN C19: from L. *operandum*, neut. gerundive of

*operari* (see **OPERATE**).

**operant** /ˈɒp(ə)r(ə)nt/ Psychology ● **adj.** involving the modification of behaviour by the reinforcing or inhibiting effect of its own consequences. ● **n.** an item of behaviour that is not a response to a prior stimulus but something which is initially spontaneous.
– ORIGIN ME: from L. *operant-*, *operari* 'to be at work'.

**opera seria** /ˈsɪərɪə/ ● **n.** an opera, especially one of the 18th century in Italian, on a serious theme.
– ORIGIN Ital., lit. 'serious opera'.

**operate** ● **v. 1** (with reference to a machine, process, etc.) function or control the functioning of. **2** (with reference to an organization) manage or be managed and run. ➤(of an armed force) conduct military activities. **3** be in effect. **4** perform a surgical operation.
– ORIGIN C17: from L. *operat-*, *operari*, from *opus*, *oper-* 'work'.

**operatic** ● **adj.** of, relating to, or characteristic of opera. ➤extravagantly theatrical.
– DERIVATIVES **operatically** adv.

**operatics** ● **pl. n.** [often treated as sing.] the production or performance of operas.

**operating profit** ● **n.** a gross profit before deduction of expenses.

**operating system** ● **n.** the low-level software that supports a computer's basic functions.

**operating table** ● **n.** a table on which a patient is placed during a surgical operation.

**operating theatre** (N. Amer. **operating room**) ● **n.** a room in which surgical operations are performed.

**operation** ● **n. 1** the action or process of operating. **2** an act of surgery performed on a patient. **3** a concerted action involving a number of people, especially members of the armed forces or the police. **4** a business organization; a company. **5** Mathematics a process in which a number, quantity, expression, etc., is altered or manipulated according to set formal rules.

**operational** ● **adj. 1** in or ready for use. **2** relating to the operation of an organization. **3** Philosophy of, relating to, or in accordance with operationalism.
– DERIVATIVES **operationally** adv.

**operational amplifier** ● **n.** Electronics an amplifier with high gain and high input impedance, used especially in circuits for performing mathematical operations on an input voltage.

**operationalism** ● **n.** Philosophy a form of positivism which defines scientific concepts in terms of the operations used to determine or prove them.
– DERIVATIVES **operationalist** n. & adj.

**operationalize** (also **-ise**) ● **v. 1** put into operation or use. **2** Philosophy express or define operationally.

**operational research** (also **operations research**) ● **n.** a method of mathematically based analysis for providing a quantitive basis for management decisions.

**operations room** ● **n.** a room from which military or police operations are directed.

**operative** ● **adj. 1** functioning; having effect. ➤(of a word) having the most relevance or significance in a phrase. **2** of or relating to surgery. ● **n. 1** a worker, especially a skilled one. **2** a private detective or secret agent.
– DERIVATIVES **operatively** adv. **operativeness** n.

**operator** ● **n. 1** a person who operates equipment or a machine. ➤a person who works at the switchboard of a telephone exchange. **2** a person or company that runs a business or enterprise: *a tour operator.* **3** informal a person who acts in a specified, especially manipulative, way: *a smooth operator.* **4** Mathematics a symbol or function denoting an operation (e.g. ×, +).

**opera window** ● **n.** chiefly US a small window behind the rear side window of a motor car.

**operculum** /ə(ʊ)ˈpəːkjʊləm/ ● **n.** (pl. **opercula** /-lə/) **1** technical term for **GILL COVER**. **2** a plate that closes the aperture of a gastropod mollusc's shell when the animal is retracted. **3** a lid-like structure of the spore-containing capsule of a moss.
– DERIVATIVES **opercular** adj. **operculate** adj. **operculi-** comb. form.
– ORIGIN C18: from L., lit. 'lid, covering'.

**operetta** ● **n.** a short opera, usually on a light or humorous theme and having spoken dialogue.
– ORIGIN C18: from Ital., dimin. of *opera* (see **OPERA**[1]).

**operon** /ˈɒpərɒn/ ● **n.** Biology a unit made up of linked genes which is thought to regulate other genes responsible for protein synthesis.
– ORIGIN 1960s: from Fr. *opérer* 'to effect, work' + **-ON**.

**ophicleide** /ˈɒfɪklʌɪd/ ● **n.** an obsolete bass brass instrument with keys.
– ORIGIN C19: from Fr. *ophicléide*, from Gk *ophis* 'serpent' + *kleis*, *kleid-* 'key'.

**Ophidia** /ɒˈfɪdɪə/ ● **pl. n.** Zoology a group of reptiles which comprises the snakes.
– DERIVATIVES **ophidian** n. & adj.
– ORIGIN mod. L., from Gk *ophis*, *ophid-* 'snake'.

**ophiolite** /ˈɒfɪəlʌɪt/ ● **n.** Geology an igneous rock consisting largely of serpentine.
– DERIVATIVES **ophiolitic** adj.
– ORIGIN C19: from Gk *ophis* 'snake' + **-LITE**.

**Ophiuroidea** /ˌɒfɪ(j)ʊəˈrɔɪdɪə/ ● **pl. n.** Zoology a class of echinoderms that comprises the brittlestars.
– DERIVATIVES **ophiuroid** n. & adj.
– ORIGIN mod. L., from *Ophiura* (genus name), from Gk *ophis* 'snake' + *oura* 'tail'.

**ophthalmia** /ɒfˈθalmɪə/ ● **n.** Medicine inflammation of the eye, especially conjunctivitis.
– ORIGIN ME: via late L. from Gk, from *ophthalmos* 'eye'.

**ophthalmic** ● **adj.** of or relating to the eye and its diseases.

**ophthalmic optician** ● **n.** Brit. an optician qualified to prescribe and dispense glasses and contact lenses and to detect eye diseases.

**ophthalmitis** /ˌɒfθalˈmʌɪtɪs/ ● **n.** Medicine inflammation of the eye.

**ophthalmo-** ● **comb. form** Medicine relating to the eyes: *ophthalmoscope.*
– ORIGIN from Gk *ophthalmos* 'eye'.

**ophthalmology** /ˌɒfθalˈmɒlədʒi/ ● **n.** the branch of medicine concerned with the study and treatment of disorders and diseases of the eye.
– DERIVATIVES **ophthalmological** adj. **ophthalmologist** n.

**ophthalmoplegia** /ɒfˌθalmə(ʊ)ˈpliːdʒə/ ● **n.** Medicine paralysis of the muscles within or surrounding the eye.
– DERIVATIVES **ophthalmoplegic** adj.

**ophthalmoscope** /ɒfˈθalməskəʊp/ ● **n.** an instrument for inspecting the retina and other parts of the eye.
– DERIVATIVES **ophthalmoscopic** adj. **ophthalmoscopy** n.

**-opia** ● **comb. form** denoting a visual disorder: *myopia.*
– ORIGIN from Gk *ōps*, *ōp-* 'eye, face'.

**opiate** ● **adj.** /ˈəʊpɪət/ relating to, resembling, or containing opium. ● **n.** /ˈəʊpɪət/ **1** a drug derived from or related to opium. **2** something inducing a false and unrealistic sense of contentment. ● **v.** /ˈəʊpɪeɪt/ [often as adj. **opiated**] impregnate with opium.

**opine** ● **v.** formal hold and state as one's opinion.
– ORIGIN ME: from L. *opinari* 'think, believe'.

**opinion** ● **n. 1** a view or judgement not necessarily based on fact or knowledge. ➤the beliefs or views of a large number of people: *the changing climate of opinion.* ➤an estimation of quality or worth: *he had a high opinion of himself.* **2** Law a formal statement of reasons for a judgement given. ➤a barrister's advice on the merits of a case.
– PHRASES **be of the opinion that** believe or maintain that. **a matter of opinion** something not capable of being proven either way.
– ORIGIN ME: via OFr. from L. *opinio(n-)*, from the stem of *opinari* 'think, believe'.

**opinionated** ● **adj.** assertively dogmatic in one's views.

**opinion poll** ● **n.** an assessment of public opinion by questioning of a representative sample, especially to forecast the results of voting.

**opioid** /ˈəʊpɪɔɪd/ Biochemistry ● **n.** a compound resembling opium in addictive properties or physiological effects. ● **adj.** relating to or denoting such compounds.

**opistho-** /əˈpɪsθəʊ/ ● **prefix** behind; to the rear: *opisthosoma*.
– ORIGIN from Gk *opisthen* 'behind'.

**Opisthobranchia** /əˌpɪsθə(ʊ)ˈbraŋkɪə/ ● **pl. n.** Zoology a group of molluscs including the sea slugs and sea hares.
– DERIVATIVES **opisthobranch** /əˈpɪsθə(ʊ)braŋk/ n.
– ORIGIN mod. L., from **OPISTHO-** + *brankhia* 'gills'.

**opisthosoma** /əˌpɪsθəˈsəʊmə/ ● **n.** Zoology the abdomen of a spider or other arachnid.

**opium** ● **n. 1** an addictive drug prepared from the juice of a poppy (*Papaver somniferum*), used illicitly as a narcotic and occasionally in medicine as an analgesic. **2** something inducing a false and unrealistic sense of contentment.
– ORIGIN ME: via L. from Gk *opion* 'poppy juice'.

**opopanax** /ə(ʊ)ˈpɒpənaks/ (also **opoponax**) ● **n. 1** an American acacia with violet-scented flowers that yield an essential oil used in perfumery. [*Acacia farnesiana*.] **2** a yellow-flowered Mediterranean plant of the parsley family. [*Opopanax chironium*.] **3** a fragrant gum resin obtained from these or other plants, used in perfumery.
– ORIGIN ME: via L. from Gk, from *opos* 'juice' + *panax* 'all-healing'; cf. **PANACEA**.

**opossum** /əˈpɒs(ə)m/ ● **n. 1** an American marsupial which has a naked prehensile tail and hind feet with an opposable thumb. [Family Didelphidae: numerous species.] **2** Austral./NZ a possum.
– ORIGIN C17: from Virginia Algonquian *opassom*, from *op* 'white' + *assom* 'dog'.

**opossum shrimp** ● **n.** a shrimp-like crustacean whose eggs and young are carried in a ventral brood pouch. [Order Mysidacea.]

**opp.** ● **abbrev.** opposite.

**oppo** ● **n.** (pl. **-os**) Brit. informal a colleague or friend.
– ORIGIN 1930s: abbrev. of *opposite number*.

**opponent** ● **n.** a person who opposes.
– ORIGIN C16: from L. *opponent-*, *opponere* 'set against'.

**opponent muscle** ● **n.** Anatomy any of several muscles enabling the thumb to be placed front to front against a finger of the same hand.

**opportune** /ˈɒpətjuːn, ˌɒpəˈtjuːn/ ● **adj.** (of a time) especially convenient or appropriate. ➤ appropriately timed.
– DERIVATIVES **opportunely** adv. **opportuneness** n.
– ORIGIN ME: from OFr. *opportun(e)*, from L. *opportunus*, from *ob-* 'in the direction of' + *portus* 'harbour', orig. describing the wind driving towards the harbour.

**opportunist** ● **n.** a person who takes advantage of opportunities as and when they arise, regardless of planning or principle. ● **adj.** opportunistic.
– DERIVATIVES **opportunism** n.

**opportunistic** ● **adj. 1** exploiting immediate opportunities, especially in an unplanned or selfish way. **2** Medicine (of an infection) occurring when the immune system is depressed.
– DERIVATIVES **opportunistically** adv.

**opportunity** ● **n.** (pl. **-ies**) a favourable time or set of circumstances for doing something.
– ORIGIN ME: from OFr. *opportunite*, from L. *opportunitas*, from *opportunus* (see **OPPORTUNE**).

**opportunity cost** ● **n.** Economics the loss of other alternatives when one alternative is chosen.

**opportunity shop** ● **n.** Austral./NZ a charity shop.

**opposable** ● **adj.** Zoology (of the thumb of a primate) capable of facing and touching the other digits on the same hand.

**oppose** ● **v. 1** (also **be opposed to**) disapprove of, resist, or be hostile to. ➤ compete with or fight. **2** [as adj. **opposed**] (of two or more things) contrasting or conflicting. **3** [as adj. **opposing**] opposite.
– DERIVATIVES **opposer** n.
– ORIGIN ME: from OFr. *opposer*, from L. *opponere* (see **OPPONENT**).

**opposite** ● **adj. 1** situated on the other or further side; facing. ➤ (of angles) between opposite sides of the intersection of two lines. ➤ Botany (of leaves or shoots) arising in pairs at the same level on opposite sides of the stem. **2** completely different. ➤ being the other of a contrasted pair: *the opposite ends of the price range*. ● **n.** an opposite person or thing. ● **adv.** in an opposite position. ● **prep. 1** in a position opposite to. **2** co-starring beside.
– PHRASES **the opposite sex** women in relation to men or vice versa.
– DERIVATIVES **oppositely** adv. **oppositeness** n.
– ORIGIN ME: via OFr. from L. *oppositus*, *opponere* 'set against'.

**opposite number** ● **n.** a person's counterpart in another organization or country.

**opposition** ● **n. 1** resistance or dissent. ➤ (often **the opposition**) a group of opponents. ➤ (**the Opposition**) Brit. the principal parliamentary party opposed to that in office. **2** a contrast or antithesis. **3** Astronomy & Astrology the apparent position of two celestial objects that are directly opposite each other in the sky, especially the position of a planet when opposite the sun.
– DERIVATIVES **oppositional** adj.

**oppress** ● **v. 1** keep in subjection and hardship. **2** cause to feel distressed or anxious.
– DERIVATIVES **oppression** n. **oppressor** n.
– ORIGIN ME: from OFr. *oppresser*, from med. L. *oppressare*, from L. *oppress-*, *opprimere* 'press against'.

**oppressive** ● **adj. 1** harsh and authoritarian. **2** weighing heavily on the mind or spirits. **3** (of weather) close and sultry.
– DERIVATIVES **oppressively** adv. **oppressiveness** n.

**opprobrious** /əˈprəʊbrɪəs/ ● **adj.** highly scornful.
– DERIVATIVES **opprobriously** adv.

**opprobrium** /əˈprəʊbrɪəm/ ● **n. 1** harsh criticism or scorn. **2** public disgrace arising from shameful conduct.
– ORIGIN C17 (earlier (ME) as *opprobrious*): from L., lit. 'infamy'.

**oppugn** /əˈpjuːn/ ● **v.** archaic dispute the truth or validity of.
– DERIVATIVES **oppugner** n.
– ORIGIN ME: from L. *oppugnare* 'attack, besiege'.

**oppugnant** /əˈpʌgnənt/ ● **adj.** rare opposing; antagonistic.
– DERIVATIVES **oppugnancy** n.
– ORIGIN C16: from L. *oppugnant-*, *oppugnare* 'fight against' (see **OPPUGN**).

**opsimath** /ˈɒpsɪmaθ/ ● **n.** poetic/literary a person who begins to learn or study only late in life.
– ORIGIN C19: from Gk *opsimathēs*, from *opse* 'late' + the stem *math-* 'learn'.

**opsonin** /ˈɒpsənɪn/ ● **n.** Biochemistry an antibody or other substance which binds to foreign micro-organisms or cells making them more susceptible to phagocytosis.
– DERIVATIVES **opsonic** adj.
– ORIGIN C20: from L. *opsonare* 'buy provisions' (from Gk *opsōnein*) + **-IN**[1].

**opt** ● **v.** make a choice. ➤ (**opt out**) choose not to participate. ➤ (**opt out**) Brit. (of a school or hospital) decide to withdraw from local authority control.
– ORIGIN C19: from Fr. *opter*, from L. *optare* 'choose, wish'.

**optative** /ˈɒptətɪv, ɒpˈteɪtɪv/ ● **adj.** Grammar relating to or denoting a mood of verbs in Greek and certain other languages, expressing a wish, equivalent in meaning to English *let's* or *if only*.
– DERIVATIVES **optatively** adv.
– ORIGIN C16: from Fr. *optatif*, *-ive*, from late L. *optativus*, from *optat-*, *optare* (see **OPT**).

**optic** ● **adj.** of or relating to the eye or vision. ● **n. 1** a lens or other optical component in an optical instrument. **2** archaic or humorous the eye. **3** Brit. trademark a device fastened to the neck of an inverted bottle for measuring out spirits.
– ORIGIN ME: from Fr. *optique* or med. L. *opticus*, from Gk *optikos*, from *optos* 'seen'.

**optical** ● **adj. 1** of or relating to vision, light, or optics. **2** of or using visible light (as opposed to other electromagnetic radiation).
– DERIVATIVES **optically** adv.

**optical activity** ● **n.** Chemistry the property of rotating the plane of polarization of plane-polarized light.

– DERIVATIVES **optically active** adj.

**optical bench** • n. a straight rigid graduated bar to which supports for lenses, light sources, and other optical components can be attached.

**optical brightener** • n. a fluorescent substance added to detergents to produce a whitening effect on laundry.

**optical character recognition** • n. the identification of printed characters using photoelectric devices and computer software.

**optical density** • n. Physics the degree to which a refractive medium retards transmitted rays of light.

**optical fibre** • n. a thin glass fibre through which light can be transmitted.

**optical glass** • n. a very pure kind of glass used for lenses.

**optical illusion** • n. a thing that deceives the eye by appearing to be other than it is.

**optical isomer** • n. Chemistry each of two or more isomers with molecules which are mirror images of each other and typically differ in optical activity.
– DERIVATIVES **optical isomerism** n.

**optic angle** • n. the angle formed by lines from the extremities of an object to the eye, or from the eyes to a given point.

**optic chiasma** • n. see **CHIASMA** (sense 1).

**optician** • n. a person qualified to prescribe and dispense glasses and contact lenses, and to detect eye diseases (**ophthalmic optician**), or to make and supply glasses and contact lenses (**dispensing optician**).
– ORIGIN C17: from Fr. *opticien.*

**optic lobe** • n. Anatomy a lobe in the midbrain from which the optic nerve partly arises.

**optic nerves** • pl. n. Anatomy the pair of cranial nerves transmitting retinal impulses to the brain from the eyes.

**optics** • pl. n. [usu. treated as sing.] the branch of science concerned with vision and the behaviour of light.

**optima** plural form of **OPTIMUM**.

**optimal** • adj. best or most favourable.
– DERIVATIVES **optimality** n. **optimally** adv.
– ORIGIN C19: from L. *optimus* 'best' + **-AL**.

**optimism** • n. **1** hopefulness and confidence about the future or the success of something. **2** Philosophy the doctrine, especially as set forth by Leibniz, that this world is the best of all possible worlds. ➤ the belief that good must ultimately prevail over evil in the universe.
– DERIVATIVES **optimist** n. **optimistic** adj. **optimistically** adv.
– ORIGIN C18: from Fr. *optimisme*, from L. *optimum* (see **OPTIMUM**).

**optimize** (also **-ise**) • v. make the best or most effective use of (a situation or resource).
– DERIVATIVES **optimization** n. **optimizer** n.
– ORIGIN C19: from L. *optimus* 'best' + **-IZE**.

**optimum** • adj. most conducive to a favourable outcome. • n. (pl. **optima** or **optimums**) the optimum conditions for growth, reproduction, or success.
– ORIGIN C19: from L., neut. of *optimus* 'best'.

**option** • n. **1** a thing that is or may be chosen. ➤ the freedom or right to choose. **2** a right to buy or sell a particular thing at a specified price within a set time. • v. buy or sell an option on.
– PHRASES **keep** (or **leave**) **one's options open** not commit oneself.
– ORIGIN C16: from Fr., or from L. *optio(n-)*, from the stem of *optare* 'choose'.

**optional** • adj. available to be chosen but not obligatory: *optional extras.*
– DERIVATIVES **optionality** n. **optionally** adv.

**optocoupler** • n. Electronics a device containing light-emitting and light-sensitive components, used to couple isolated circuits.

**optoelectronics** • pl. n. [treated as sing.] the branch of technology concerned with the combined use of electronics and light.
– DERIVATIVES **optoelectronic** adj.

**optometer** /ɒp'tɒmɪtə/ • n. an instrument for testing the refractive power of the eye.
– ORIGIN C18: from Gk *optos* 'seen' + **-METER**.

**optometry** • n. the occupation of measuring eyesight, prescribing corrective lenses, and detecting eye disease.
– DERIVATIVES **optometric** adj. **optometrist** n. (chiefly N. Amer.).

**opulent** • adj. ostentatiously rich and luxurious. ➤ wealthy.
– DERIVATIVES **opulence** n. **opulently** adv.
– ORIGIN C16: from L. *opulent-* 'wealthy, splendid'.

**opuntia** /ɒ'pʌnʃɪə, ə(ʊ)-/ • n. a cactus of a genus that comprises the prickly pears. [Genus *Opuntia.*]
– ORIGIN C17: from L., a name given to a plant growing around *Opus* (stem *Opunt-*), a city in ancient Greece.

**opus** /'əʊpəs, 'ɒp-/ • n. (pl. **opuses** or **opera** /'ɒp(ə)rə/) **1** Music a separate composition or set of compositions. **2** an artistic work, especially one on a large scale.
– ORIGIN C18: from L., lit. 'work'.

**opuscule** /ə'pʌskju:l/ (also **opusculum** /ə'pʌskjʊləm/) • n. (pl. **opuscules** or **opuscula** /-lə/) rare a small or minor opus.
– ORIGIN C17: from Fr., from L. *opusculum*, dimin. of *opus* 'work'.

**opus Dei** /ˌəʊpəs 'deɪi:, 'ɒpəs/ • n. **1** Christian Church liturgical worship regarded as humankind's primary duty to God. **2** (**Opus Dei**) a Roman Catholic organization of laymen and priests founded in 1928 with the aim of re-establishing Christian ideals in society.
– ORIGIN C19: from med. L., lit. 'work of God'.

**OR** • abbrev. **1** operational research. **2** Oregon (in official postal use). **3** Brit. Military other ranks (as opposed to commissioned officers).

**or**[1] • conj. **1** used to link alternatives. **2** introducing a synonym or explanation of a preceding word or phrase. **3** otherwise. **4** poetic/literary either. • n. (**OR**) a logical operation which gives the value one if at least one operand has the value one, and otherwise gives a value of zero. ➤ [as modifier] Electronics denoting a gate circuit which produces an output if there is a signal on any of its inputs.
– PHRASES **or so** (after a quantity) approximately.
– ORIGIN ME: a reduced form of the obs. conjunction *other* (which superseded OE *oththe* 'or').

**or**[2] • n. gold or yellow, as a heraldic tincture.
– ORIGIN C16: from Fr., from L. *aurum* 'gold'.

**-or**[1] • suffix (forming nouns) denoting a person or thing performing the action of a verb, or denoting another agent: *escalator.*
– ORIGIN from L., sometimes via Anglo-Norman Fr. *-eour* or OFr. *-eor* (see also **-ATOR**).

**-or**[2] • suffix forming nouns denoting a state or condition: *terror.*
– ORIGIN from L., sometimes via OFr. *-or, -ur.*

**-or**[3] • suffix forming adjectives expressing a comparative sense: *junior.*
– ORIGIN via Anglo-Norman Fr. from L.

**-or**[4] • suffix US form of **-OUR**[1].

**orache** /'ɒrətʃ/ (also **orach**) • n. a plant with red, yellow, or green leaves sometimes eaten as a vegetable. [*Atriplex hortensis* and related species.]
– ORIGIN ME *orage*, from Anglo-Norman Fr. *arasche*, from L. *atriplex*, from Gk *atraphaxus.*

**oracle** • n. **1** a priest or priestess acting as a medium for divine advice or prophecy in classical antiquity. **2** an infallible authority. **3** archaic a response or message given by an oracle, especially an ambiguous one.
– ORIGIN ME: via OFr. from L. *oraculum*, from *orare* 'speak'.

**oracular** /ɒ'rakjʊlə/ • adj. **1** of or relating to an oracle. **2** hard to interpret. **3** holding or claiming the authority of an oracle.
– DERIVATIVES **oracularity** n. **oracularly** adv.

**oracy** /'ɔ:rəsi/ • n. Brit. the ability to express oneself fluently and grammatically in speech.
– ORIGIN 1960s: from L. *os, or-* 'mouth', on the pattern of *literacy.*

**oral** • adj. **1** spoken rather than written. **2** of or relating to the mouth. ➤ done or taken by the mouth. ➤ Psychoanalysis relating to or denoting a stage of infantile psychosexual

development in which the mouth is the main source of sensuous experience. ● n. a spoken examination or test.
– DERIVATIVES **orally** adv.
– ORIGIN C17: from late L. *oralis*, from L. *os, or-* 'mouth'.

**oral history** ● n. the collection and study of tape-recorded historical information drawn from the speaker's personal knowledge of past events.

**oralism** ● n. the system of teaching profoundly deaf people to communicate by the use of speech and lip-reading rather than sign language.
– DERIVATIVES **oralist** adj. & n.

**orality** ● n. **1** the quality of being verbally communicated. **2** Psychoanalysis the focusing of sexual energy and feeling on the mouth.

**Oral Law** ● n. Judaism the part of Jewish religious law believed to have been passed down by oral tradition before being collected in the Mishnah.

**oral sex** ● n. sexual activity in which the genitals of one partner are stimulated by the mouth of the other.

**Orang Asli** /ˌɒrəŋ 'azli/ ● n. [treated as pl.] a collective term for the indigenous peoples of Malaysia.
– ORIGIN Malay, from *orang* 'person' and *as(a)li* 'of ancient origin'.

**Orange** ● adj. of or relating to Orangemen or their Order.
– DERIVATIVES **Orangeism** n.
– ORIGIN after the Protestant William of *Orange* (William III).

**orange** ● n. **1** a large round citrus fruit with a tough bright reddish-yellow rind. ➤a drink made from or flavoured with orange juice. **2** the evergreen tree which produces this fruit, native to warm regions of south and SE Asia. [*Citrus sinensis* and related species.] ➤used in names of other plants with similar fruit or flowers, e.g. **Osage orange**. **3** a bright reddish-yellow colour. ● adj. reddish yellow.
– DERIVATIVES **orangey** (also **orangy**) adj. **orangish** adj.
– ORIGIN ME: from OFr. *orenge*, based on Arab. *nāranj*, from Pers. *nārang*.

**orangeade** ● n. Brit. a fizzy soft drink flavoured with orange.

**orange flower water** ● n. a solution of neroli in water, used in perfumery and as a food flavouring.

**Orangeman** ● n. (pl. **-men**) a member of the Orange Order, a Protestant political society in Ireland, especially in Northern Ireland.

**orange pekoe** ● n. a type of black tea made from young leaves.

**orangery** ● n. (pl. **-ies**) a building like a large conservatory where orange trees are grown.

**orange stick** ● n. a thin stick, pointed at one end and typically made of orange wood, used for manicuring the fingernails.

**orang-utan** /ɔːˌraŋuː'tan, ə'raŋuːtan/ (also **-utang** /-uː'taŋ/) ● n. a large arboreal ape with long red hair, long arms, and hooked hands and feet, native to Borneo and Sumatra. [*Pongo pygmaeus*.]
– ORIGIN C17: from Malay *orang huan* 'forest person'.

**oration** ● n. a formal speech, especially one given on a ceremonial occasion.
– DERIVATIVES **orate** v.
– ORIGIN ME (denoting a prayer): from L. *oratio(n-)* 'discourse, prayer', from *orare* 'speak, pray'.

**orator** ● n. a proficient public speaker. ➤(also **public orator**) an official speaking for a university on ceremonial occasions.
– DERIVATIVES **oratorial** adj.
– ORIGIN ME: from Anglo-Norman Fr. *oratour*, from L. *orator* 'speaker, pleader'.

**oratorio** /ˌɒrə'tɔːrɪəʊ/ ● n. (pl. **-os**) a large-scale semi-dramatic musical work for orchestra and voices on a sacred theme, performed without costume, scenery, or action.
– ORIGIN Ital., from eccles. L. *oratorium* 'oratory', from the musical services held in the church of the Oratory of St Philip Neri in Rome.

**oratory¹** /'ɒrət(ə)ri/ ● n. (pl. **-ies**) **1** a small chapel for private worship. **2** (**Oratory**) (in the Roman Catholic Church) a religious society of secular priests founded to provide plain preaching and popular services.
– DERIVATIVES **Oratorian** n. & adj.
– ORIGIN ME: from Anglo-Norman Fr. *oratorie*, from eccles. L. *oratorium*, based on L. *orare* 'pray, speak'; sense 2 is from *Congregation of the Fathers of the Oratory*.

**oratory²** ● n. **1** the art or practice of formal public speaking. **2** rhetorical or eloquent language.
– DERIVATIVES **oratorical** /-'tɒrɪk(ə)l/ adj.
– ORIGIN C16: from L. *oratoria*, fem. of *oratorius* 'relating to an orator'.

**orb** ● n. a spherical object or shape. ➤a golden globe surmounted by a cross, forming part of the regalia of a monarch. ➤poetic/literary a celestial body. ➤poetic/literary an eye.
– ORIGIN ME: from L. *orbis* 'ring'.

**orbicular** /ɔː'bɪkjʊlə/ ● adj. **1** technical having the shape of a flat ring or disc. **2** poetic/literary spherical or rounded. **3** Geology (of a rock) containing spheroidal igneous inclusions.
– DERIVATIVES **orbicularity** n. **orbicularly** adv.

**orbit** ● n. **1** the regularly repeated elliptical course of a celestial object or spacecraft about a star or planet. **2** a field of activity or influence: *they brought many friends within the orbit of our lives.* **3** the path of an electron round an atomic nucleus. **4** Anatomy the eye socket. ● v. (**orbited**, **orbiting**) move in orbit round (a star or planet). ➤put (a satellite) into orbit.
– PHRASES **into orbit** informal into a state of heightened activity, anger, or excitement.
– ORIGIN C16: from L. *orbita* 'course, track', fem. of *orbitus* 'circular'.

**orbital** ● adj. **1** of or relating to an orbit or orbits. **2** Brit. (of a road) passing round the outside of a town. ● n. Physics a pattern of electron density representing the possible behaviour of one or more electrons in an atom or molecule.

**orbital sander** ● n. a sander in which the sanding surface has a minute circular motion without rotating relative to the workpiece.

**orbiter** ● n. a spacecraft designed to go into orbit, especially one that does not subsequently land.

**orb web** ● n. a circular vertical spider's web formed of threads radiating from a central point, crossed by radial links that spiral in from the edge.

**orc** ● n. (in fantasy literature and games) a member of an imaginary race of ugly, warlike human-like creatures.
– ORIGIN C16 (denoting an ogre): perh. from L. *orcus* 'hell' or Ital. *orco* 'monster'; the word was popularized by Tolkien's fantasy adventures.

**orca** /'ɔːkə/ ● n. another term for **KILLER WHALE**.
– ORIGIN C19: from Fr. *orque* or L. *orca*, denoting a kind of whale.

**Orcadian** /ɔː'keɪdɪən/ ● adj. of or relating to the Orkney Islands or their inhabitants. ● n. a native or inhabitant of the Orkney Islands.
– ORIGIN from *Orcades*, the L. name for the Orkney Islands, + **-IAN**.

**orch.** ● abbrev. **1** orchestra. **2** orchestrated by.

**orchard** ● n. a piece of enclosed land planted with fruit trees.
– DERIVATIVES **orchardist** n.
– ORIGIN OE *ortgeard*; the first element from L. *hortus* 'garden', the second representing **YARD²**.

**orchestra** ● n. **1** [treated as sing. or pl.] a group of instrumentalists, especially one combining string, woodwind, brass, and percussion sections. **2** (also **orchestra pit**) the part of a theatre where the orchestra plays, typically in front of the stage and on a lower level. **3** N. Amer. the stalls in a theatre. **4** the semicircular space in front of an ancient Greek theatre stage where the chorus danced and sang.
– DERIVATIVES **orchestral** adj. **orchestrally** adv.
– ORIGIN C17: via L. from Gk *orkhēstra*, from *orkheisthai* 'to dance'.

**orchestra stalls** ● pl. n. Brit. the front part of the stalls in a theatre.

**orchestrate** ● v. **1** arrange or score (music) for orchestral performance. **2** direct (a situation) to produce a de-

sired effect.
– DERIVATIVES **orchestration** n. **orchestrator** n.

**orchid** • n. a plant of a large family (Orchidaceae) distinguished by complex showy flowers with a labellum and frequently a spur.
– DERIVATIVES **orchidaceous** adj. **orchidist** n.
– ORIGIN C19: from mod. L. *Orchid(ac)eae*, formed irregularly from L. **ORCHIS**.

**orchidectomy** • n. surgical removal of one or both testicles.
– ORIGIN C19: from mod. L. *orchido-* (from a Latinized stem of Gk *orkhis* 'testicle') + **-ECTOMY**.

**orchil** /'ɔːtʃɪl/ • n. **1** a red or violet dye obtained from lichen, used as a source of litmus. **2** a lichen which produces this dye. [*Roccella* and other genera.]
– ORIGIN C15: from OFr. *orcheil*, rel. to Sp. *urchilla*.

**orchis** /'ɔːkɪs/ • n. an orchid of north temperate regions, with a tuberous root and a spike of typically purple or pinkish flowers. [*Orchis* and other genera: many species.]
– ORIGIN mod. L., based on Gk *orkhis*, lit. 'testicle' (with ref. to the shape of its tuber).

**orchitis** /ɔː'kʌɪtɪs/ • n. Medicine inflammation of one or both of the testicles.
– ORIGIN C18: mod. L., from Gk *orkhis* 'testicle' + **-ITIS**.

**orcinol** /'ɔːsɪnɒl/ • n. Chemistry a crystalline compound extracted from orchil, used to make dyes.
– ORIGIN C19: from mod. L. *orcina*, from Ital. *orcello* 'orchil'.

**ord.** • abbrev. **1** order. **2** ordinary.

**ordain** • v. **1** confer holy orders on. **2** order officially. ➤(of God or fate) decide in advance.
– DERIVATIVES **ordainer** n. **ordainment** n.
– ORIGIN ME: from Anglo-Norman Fr. *ordeiner*, from L. *ordinare*, from *ordo, ordin-* (see **ORDER**).

**ordeal** • n. **1** a prolonged painful or horrific experience. **2** an ancient test of guilt or innocence by subjection of the accused to severe pain, survival of which was taken as divine proof of innocence.
– ORIGIN OE *ordāl, ordēl*, of Gmc origin, from a base meaning 'share out'.

**order** • n. **1** the arrangement or disposition of people or things according to a particular sequence or method. ➤a state in which everything is in its correct place. ➤a state in which the laws and rules regulating public behaviour are observed. ➤the prescribed procedure followed by a meeting, legislative assembly, or court of law. ➤a prescribed form of liturgical service. **2** an authoritative command or direction. ➤a verbal or written request for something to be made, supplied, or served. **3** a social class. ➤a particular social, political, or economic system. ➤a rank in the Christian ministry, especially that of bishop, priest, or deacon. ➤(**orders**) the rank of an ordained minister of the Church. See also **HOLY ORDERS**. ➤Theology any of the nine grades of angelic beings in the celestial hierarchy. **4** Biology a principal taxonomic category that ranks below class and above family. **5** a society of monks, nuns, or friars living under the same rule. ➤historical a society of knights constituted in a similar way to a monastic order. ➤an institution founded by a monarch along the lines of such an order of knights for the purpose of honouring meritorious conduct. ➤a Masonic or similar fraternity. **6** the quality or nature of something: *poetry of the highest order.* **7** any of the five classical styles of architecture (Doric, Ionic, Corinthian, Tuscan, and Composite) based on proportions of columns and the style of their decoration. **8** Military equipment or uniform for a specified purpose or of a specified type: *drill order.* **9** Mathematics the degree of complexity of an equation, expression, etc. ➤the number of elements in a finite group. ➤the number of rows or columns in a square matrix. • v. **1** give an order. **2** request (something) to be made, supplied, or served. **3** arrange methodically.
– PHRASES **in order 1** in the correct condition for operation or use. **2** appropriate in the circumstances. **in order for** (or **that**) so that. **in order to** with the purpose of doing. **of** (or **on**) **the order of** approximately. **on order** (of goods) requested but not yet received. **order arms** Military hold a rifle with its butt on the ground close to one's right side. **order of battle** the units, formations, and equipment of a military force. **the order of the day 1** the prevailing or required custom or state of affairs. **2** (in a legislature) the business to be considered on a particular day. **out of order 1** (of an electrical or mechanical device) not working properly or at all. **2** Brit. informal unacceptable or wrong.
– ORIGIN ME: from OFr. *ordre*, from L. *ordo, ordin-* 'row, series'.

**Order in Council** • n. Brit. a sovereign's order on an administrative matter, given on the advice of the Privy Council.

**orderly** • adj. **1** neatly and methodically arranged. **2** well behaved. **3** Military charged with the conveyance or execution of orders. • n. (pl. **-ies**) **1** an attendant in a hospital responsible for cleaning and other non-medical tasks. **2** a soldier who carries orders or performs minor tasks for an officer.
– DERIVATIVES **orderliness** n.

**orderly officer** • n. Brit. Military the officer in charge of the security and administration of a unit or establishment for a day at a time.

**orderly room** • n. Military the room in a barracks used for regimental or company business.

**order of magnitude** • n. **1** a class in a system of classification determined by size, typically in powers of ten. **2** size or quantity.

**Order Paper** • n. Brit. a paper on which the day's business for a legislative assembly is entered.

**ordinal** • n. Christian Church, chiefly historical a service book, especially one with the forms of service used at ordinations. • adj. **1** of or relating to order in a series. **2** Biology of or relating to a taxonomic order.
– ORIGIN ME: the noun from med. L. *ordinale*; the adjective from late L. *ordinalis* 'relating to order', from L. *ordo, ordin-* (see **ORDER**).

**ordinal number** • n. a number defining a thing's position in a series, such as 'first' or 'second'.

**ordinance** • n. formal **1** an authoritative order. ➤N. Amer. a by-law. **2** a religious rite. **3** archaic ordonnance.
– ORIGIN ME: from OFr. *ordenance*, from med. L. *ordinantia*, from L. *ordinare* (see **ORDAIN**).

**ordinand** /'ɔːdɪnand/ • n. a person who is training to be ordained as a priest or minister.
– ORIGIN C19: from L. *ordinandus*, gerundive of *ordinare* (see **ORDAIN**).

**ordinary** • adj. **1** with no distinctive features; normal or usual. **2** (of a judge, archbishop, or bishop) exercising authority by virtue of office and not by deputation. • n. (pl. **-ies**) **1** Brit. Law a judge exercising authority by virtue of office and not by deputation. **2** (**the Ordinary**) an ecclesiastic, such as an archbishop in a province, with immediate jurisdiction. **3** (**Ordinary**) those parts of a Roman Catholic service, especially the Mass, which do not vary from day to day. ➤a rule or book laying down the order of divine service. **4** Heraldry any of the simplest principal charges used in coats of arms. **5** Brit. archaic a meal provided at a fixed time and price at an inn. **6** historical, chiefly N. Amer. a penny-farthing bicycle.
– PHRASES **in ordinary** Brit. (in titles) by permanent appointment, especially to the royal household. **out of the ordinary** unusual.
– DERIVATIVES **ordinarily** adv. **ordinariness** n.
– ORIGIN ME: the noun partly via OFr.; the adjective from L. *ordinarius* 'orderly', from *ordo, ordin-* 'order'.

**ordinary grade** • n. (in Scotland) the lower of the two main levels of the Scottish Certificate of Education examination. Compare with **HIGHER**.

**ordinary level** • n. historical (in the UK except Scotland) the lower of the two main levels of the GCE examination.

**ordinary ray** • n. Optics (in double refraction) the light ray that obeys the ordinary laws of refraction.

**ordinary seaman** • n. the lowest rank of sailor in the Royal Navy, below able seaman.

**ordinary share** • n. Brit. a share entitling its holder to dividends which vary in amount depending on the fortunes of the company. Compare with **PREFERENCE**

**SHARE**.

**ordinate** /ˈɔːdɪnət/ ● **n.** Mathematics a straight line from a point on a graph drawn parallel to the vertical axis and meeting the other; the *y*-coordinate. Compare with **ABSCISSA**.
– ORIGIN C17: from L. *linea ordinata applicata* 'line applied parallel'.

**ordination** ● **n.** the action of ordaining someone in holy orders.

**ordnance** /ˈɔːdnəns/ ● **n. 1** mounted guns; cannon. ➤ US munitions. **2** a government department dealing especially with military stores and materials.
– ORIGIN ME: var. of **ORDINANCE**.

**ordnance datum** ● **n.** Brit. the mean sea level as defined for Ordnance Survey.

**Ordnance Survey** ● **n.** (in the UK) an official survey organization, originally under the Master of the Ordnance, preparing large-scale detailed maps of the whole country.

**ordonnance** /ˈɔːdənəns/ ● **n.** the systematic arrangement of elements in art and architecture.
– ORIGIN C17: from Fr., alt. of OFr. *ordenance* (see **ORDINANCE**).

**Ordovician** /ˌɔːdəˈvɪʃɪən/ ● **adj.** Geology relating to or denoting the second period of the Palaeozoic era (between the Cambrian and Silurian periods, about 510 to 439 million years ago), a time when the first vertebrates appeared.
– ORIGIN C19: from *Ordovices*, the L. name of an ancient Brit. tribe, + **-IAN**.

**ordure** /ˈɔːdjʊə/ ● **n.** excrement; dung.
– ORIGIN ME: from OFr., from *ord* 'foul', from L. *horridus* (see **HORRID**).

**Ore.** ● **abbrev.** Oregon.

**ore** ● **n.** a naturally occurring solid material from which a metal or valuable mineral can be extracted profitably.
– ORIGIN OE *ōra* 'unwrought metal', of W. Gmc origin.

**øre** /ˈəːrə/ ● **n.** (pl. same) a monetary unit of Denmark and Norway, equal to one hundredth of a krone.
– ORIGIN from Dan. and Norw.

**öre** /ˈəːrə/ ● **n.** (pl. same) a monetary unit of Sweden, equal to one hundredth of a krona.
– ORIGIN from Swed.

**oread** /ˈɔːrɪad/ ● **n.** Greek & Roman Mythology a nymph believed to inhabit mountains.
– ORIGIN from L. *Oreas, Oread-*, from Gk *Oreias*, from *oros* 'mountain'.

**orectic** /ɒˈrɛktɪk/ ● **adj.** technical, rare of or concerning desire or appetite.
– ORIGIN C17 (as a noun in the sense 'stimulant for the appetite'): from Gk *orektikos*, from *oregein* 'reach for'.

**Oreg.** ● **abbrev.** Oregon.

**oregano** /ˌɒrɪˈgɑːnəʊ, əˈrɛgənəʊ/ ● **n.** an aromatic plant related to marjoram, with small purple flowers and leaves used as a culinary herb. [*Origanum vulgare*.]
– ORIGIN C18: from Sp., var. of **ORIGANUM**.

**Oregonian** /ˌɒrɪˈgəʊnɪən/ ● **n.** a native or inhabitant of the US state of Oregon. ● **adj.** of or relating to Oregon.

**Oreo** /ˈɔːrɪəʊ/ ● **n.** (pl. **-os**) **1** US trademark a chocolate biscuit with a white cream filling. **2** US informal, derogatory an American black who is seen, especially by other blacks, as wishing to be part of the white establishment.

**orf** ● **n.** an infectious disease of sheep and goats caused by a poxvirus, characterized by skin lesions and secondary bacterial infection.
– ORIGIN C19: prob. from ON *hrufa*.

**orfe** /ɔːf/ ● **n.** a silvery freshwater fish of the carp family, fished commercially in eastern Europe. [*Leuciscus idus*.]
– ORIGIN C19: from Ger.; perh. rel. to Fr. *orphe*, L. *orphus*, and Gk *orphos* 'sea perch'.

**organ** ● **n. 1** a large musical instrument having rows of pipes supplied with air from bellows and arranged in ranks, each controlled by a stop, and played using a keyboard or by an automatic mechanism. ➤ a smaller instrument without pipes, producing similar sounds electronically. **2** a part of an organism which is typically self-contained and has a specific vital function. ➤ euphemistic a man's penis. **3** a department or organization that performs a specified function. **4** a newspaper or periodical which puts forward the views of a political party or movement.
– DERIVATIVES **organist** n.
– ORIGIN OE, via L. from Gk *organon* 'tool, sense organ', reinforced in ME by OFr. *organe*.

**organ-blower** ● **n.** a person or mechanism working the bellows of an organ.

**organdie** /ˈɔːg(ə)ndi, ɔːˈgandi/ (US also **organdy**) ● **n.** (pl. **-ies**) a fine, translucent, stiff cotton muslin, used chiefly for dresses.
– ORIGIN C19: from Fr. *organdi*, of unknown origin.

**organelle** /ˌɔːgəˈnɛl/ ● **n.** Biology any of a number of organized or specialized structures within a living cell.
– ORIGIN C20: from mod. L. *organella*, dimin. of *organum* (see **ORGAN**).

**organ-grinder** ● **n.** a street musician who plays a barrel organ.

**organic** ● **adj. 1** relating to or derived from living matter. ➤ Chemistry relating to or denoting compounds containing carbon and chiefly or ultimately of biological origin. Compare with **INORGANIC**. **2** Physiology of or relating to a bodily organ or organs. ➤ Medicine (of a disease) affecting the structure of an organ. **3** produced or involving production without the use of chemical fertilizers or other artificial chemicals. **4** denoting a harmonious relationship between the elements of a whole. ➤ characterized by natural development.
– DERIVATIVES **organically** adv.

**organicism** ● **n.** the doctrine that everything in nature has an organic basis or is part of an organic whole.
– DERIVATIVES **organicist** adj. & n. **organicistic** adj.

**organic law** ● **n.** a law stating the formal constitution of a nation.

**organism** ● **n.** an individual animal, plant, or single-celled life form. ➤ a whole with interdependent parts, compared to a living being.
– DERIVATIVES **organismal** adj. **organismic** adj.
– ORIGIN C18 (in the sense 'organization'): current senses derive from Fr. *organisme*.

**organization** (also **-isation**) ● **n. 1** the action of organizing. ➤ systematic arrangement of elements. ➤ a systematic approach to tasks. **2** an organized body of people with a particular purpose, such as a business or government department.
– DERIVATIVES **organizational** adj. **organizationally** adv.

**organization man** ● **n.** a man who lets his personal life be dominated by the organization he serves.

**organize** (also **-ise**) ● **v. 1** arrange systematically; order. **2** Brit. make arrangements or preparations for. **3** form (people) into a trade union or other political group.
– DERIVATIVES **organizable** adj. **organizer** n.
– ORIGIN ME: from med. L. *organizare*, from L. *organum* (see **ORGAN**).

**organo-** /ˈɔːg(ə)nəʊ, ɔːˈganəʊ/ ● **comb. form 1** chiefly Biology relating to bodily organs: *organogenesis*. **2** Chemistry (forming names of classes of organic compounds containing a particular element or group) organic: *organophosphate*.
– ORIGIN from Gk *organon* 'organ'; sense 2 from **ORGANIC**.

**organ of Corti** ● **n.** Anatomy a structure in the cochlea of the inner ear which produces nerve impulses in response to sound vibrations.
– ORIGIN C19: named after the Ital. anatomist Alfonso *Corti*.

**organogenesis** /ˌɔːg(ə)nə(ʊ)ˈdʒɛnɪsɪs, ɔːˌgan(ə)-/ ● **n.** Biology the production and development of the organs of an animal or plant.

**organoleptic** /ˌɔːg(ə)nə(ʊ)ˈlɛptɪk/ ● **adj.** acting on, or involving the use of, the sense organs.
– ORIGIN C19: from Fr. *organoleptique*, from Gk *organon* 'organ' + *lēptikos* 'disposed to take'.

**organometallic** ● **adj.** Chemistry (of a compound) containing a metal atom bonded to an organic group or groups.

**organon** /ˈɔːg(ə)nɒn/ ● **n.** a means of reasoning or a system of logic.
– ORIGIN C16: from Gk, lit. 'instrument, organ'; *Organon*

was the title of Aristotle's logical treatises.

**organophosphorus** /ˌɔːg(ə)nəʊˈfɒsf(ə)rəs/ ● **adj.** denoting synthetic organic compounds containing phosphorus.
– DERIVATIVES **organophosphate** n.

**organotherapy** ● **n.** the treatment of disease with extracts from animal organs, especially glands.
– DERIVATIVES **organotherapeutic** adj.

**organ screen** ● **n.** an ornamental screen between the choir and the nave in some cathedrals and large churches, above which the organ is placed.

**organum** /ˈɔːg(ə)nəm/ ● **n.** (pl. **organa** /-nə/) an early type of polyphonic music based on plainsong with an accompaniment sung below or above the melody.
– ORIGIN L., from Gk *organon*, lit. 'instrument, organ'.

**organza** /ɔːˈganzə/ ● **n.** a thin, stiff, transparent dress fabric made of silk or a synthetic yarn.
– ORIGIN C19: prob. from *Lorganza*, a US trademark.

**organzine** /ˈɔːg(ə)nziːn, -ˈganziːn/ ● **n.** a silk thread made of strands twisted together in the contrary direction to that of each individual strand.
– ORIGIN C17: from Fr. *organsin*, from Ital. *organzino*.

**orgasm** ● **n.** the climax of sexual excitement, characterized by intensely pleasurable sensations centred in the genitals. ● **v.** have an orgasm.
– ORIGIN C17: from Fr. *orgasme*, or from mod. L. *orgasmus*, from Gk *orgasmos*, from *organ* 'swell or be excited'.

**orgasmic** ● **adj. 1** of or relating to orgasm. ➤able to achieve orgasm. **2** informal very enjoyable.
– DERIVATIVES **orgasmically** adv. **orgastic** adj. **orgastically** adv.

**orgeat** /ˈɔːdʒɪət/ ● **n.** a cooling drink made from orange flower water and either barley or almonds.
– ORIGIN Fr., from Provençal *orjat*, from *ordi* 'barley'.

**orgone** /ˈɔːgəʊn/ ● **n.** a supposed excess sexual energy or life force distributed throughout the universe which can be collected and stored for subsequent therapeutic use.
– ORIGIN 1940s: coined by the psychoanalyst Wilhelm Reich, from **ORGANISM** or **ORGANIC** + *-one*, after **HORMONE**.

**orgulous** /ˈɔːgjʊləs/ ● **adj.** poetic/literary haughty.
– ORIGIN ME: from OFr. *orguillus*, from *orguill* 'pride'.

**orgy** ● **n.** (pl. **-ies**) **1** a wild party characterized by excessive drinking and indiscriminate sexual activity. **2** excessive indulgence in a specified activity. **3** secret rites used particularly in the worship of Bacchus and Dionysus, celebrated with dancing, drunkenness, and singing.
– DERIVATIVES **orgiastic** adj. **orgiastically** adv.
– ORIGIN C16: orig. pl., from Fr. *orgies*, via L. from Gk *orgia* 'secret rites or revels'.

**oribi** /ˈɒrɪbi/ ● **n.** (pl. same or **oribis**) a small antelope of the African savannah, having a reddish-fawn back, white underparts, and short vertical horns. [*Ourebia ourebi*.]
– ORIGIN C18: from Afrik., from Khoikhoi.

**oriel** /ˈɔːrɪəl/ ● **n.** a large upper-storey bay with a window (**oriel window**), supported by brackets or on corbels.
– ORIGIN ME: from OFr. *oriol* 'gallery'.

**orient** ● **n.** /ˈɔːrɪənt, ˈɒr-/ **1** (**the Orient**) poetic/literary the countries of the East, especially east Asia. **2** the special lustre of a pearl of the finest quality (with reference to fine pearls from the East). ● **adj.** /ˈɔːrɪənt, ˈɒr-/ poetic/literary oriental. ● **v.** /ˈɔːrɪɛnt, ˈɒr-/ **1** align or position relative to the points of a compass or other specified positions. ➤(**orient oneself**) find one's position in relation to unfamiliar surroundings. **2** tailor to specified circumstances.
– ORIGIN ME: via OFr. from L. *orient-* 'rising or east', from *oriri* 'to rise'.

**oriental** (also **Oriental**) ● **adj. 1** of, from, or characteristic of the Far East. ➤(**Oriental**) Zoology relating to or denoting a zoogeographical region comprising Asia south of the Himalayas and western Indonesia. **2** (of a pearl or other jewel) orient. ● **n.** often offensive a person of Far Eastern descent.
– DERIVATIVES **orientalism** n. **orientalist** n. **orientalize** (also **-ise**) v. **orientally** adv.

USAGE **oriental**

The term **oriental** is now regarded as old-fashioned and potentially offensive as a term denoting people from the Far East. In US English, **Asian** is the standard accepted term in modern use; in British English, where **Asian** tends to denote people from the Indian subcontinent, specific terms such as **Chinese** or **Japanese** are more likely to be used.

**orientalia** /ˌɔːrɪɛnˈteɪlɪə, ɒr-/ ● **pl. n.** books and other items relating to or characteristic of the Orient.
– ORIGIN C20: from L., neut. pl. of *orientalis* 'oriental'.

**orientation** ● **n. 1** the action of orienting. ➤a relative position. **2** the direction of someone's interest or attitude, especially political or sexual.
– DERIVATIVES **orientate** v. **orientational** adj.
– ORIGIN C19: appar. from **ORIENT**.

**orientation course** ● **n.** chiefly N. Amer. a course giving information to newcomers to a university or other organization.

**orienteering** ● **n.** a competitive sport in which runners have to find their way across rough country with the aid of a map and compass.
– DERIVATIVES **orienteer** n. & v.
– ORIGIN 1940s: from Swed. *orientering*.

**orifice** /ˈɒrɪfɪs/ ● **n.** an opening, particularly one in the body such as a nostril.
– ORIGIN ME: from Fr., from late L. *orificium*, from *os, or-* 'mouth' + *facere* 'make'.

**oriflamme** /ˈɒrɪflam/ ● **n.** the sacred scarlet banner of St Denis, given to early French kings on setting out for war.
– ORIGIN ME: from OFr., from L. *aurum* 'gold' + *flamma* 'flame'.

**origami** /ˌɒrɪˈgɑːmi/ ● **n.** the Japanese art of folding paper into decorative shapes and figures.
– ORIGIN Japanese, from *oru, -ori* 'fold' + *kami* 'paper'.

**origanum** /ɒˈrɪg(ə)nəm/ ● **n.** an aromatic plant of a genus that includes marjoram and oregano. [Genus *Origanum*.]
– ORIGIN L., from Gk *origanon*, perh. from *oros* 'mountain' + *ganos* 'brightness'.

**origin** ● **n. 1** the point where something begins or arises. ➤Anatomy the more fixed end or attachment of a muscle. **2** a person's social background or ancestry. **3** Mathematics a fixed point from which coordinates are measured.
– ORIGIN C16: from Fr. *origine*, from L. *origo, origin-*, from *oriri* 'to rise'.

**original** ● **adj. 1** existing from the beginning; first or earliest. **2** produced first-hand; not a copy. **3** inventive or novel. ● **n. 1** the earliest form of something, from which copies can be made. ➤(**the original**) the language in which something was first written. **2** an eccentric or unusual person.
– DERIVATIVES **originality** n. **originally** adv.
– ORIGIN ME: from OFr., or from L. *originalis*, from *origin-* (see **ORIGIN**).

**original gravity** ● **n.** (in brewing) the relative density of the wort before it is fermented to produce beer, chiefly dependent on the quantity of fermentable sugars in solution.

**original print** ● **n.** a print made directly from an artist's own woodcut, etching, etc., and printed under the artist's supervision.

**original sin** ● **n.** Christian Theology the tendency to evil supposedly innate in all human beings, held to be inherited from Adam in consequence of the Fall.

**originate** ● **v.** have a specified beginning. ➤create or initiate.
– DERIVATIVES **origination** n. **originative** adj. **originator** n.

**Orimulsion** /ˌɒrɪˈmʌlʃ(ə)n/ ● **n.** trademark a fuel consisting of an emulsion of bitumen in water.
– ORIGIN 1980s: blend of *Orinoco* (an oil belt in Venezuela where the bitumen was orig. extracted) and **EMULSION**.

**O-ring** ● **n.** a gasket in the form of a ring with a circular cross section.

**oriole** /ˈɔːrɪəʊl, ˈɔːrɪəl/ ● **n. 1** a brightly coloured arboreal bird with a musical call. [*Oriolus oriolus* (**golden oriole**)

and related species.] **2** an American songbird with black and orange or yellow plumage. [Genus *Icterus*: many species.]
– ORIGIN C18: from med. L. *oriolus*, from L. *aureolus*, dimin. of *aureus* 'golden'.

**Orisha** /ə'rɪʃə/ ● n. (pl. same or **Orishas**) (in southern Nigeria and among certain black religious cults of South America and the Caribbean) any of several minor gods.
– ORIGIN from Yoruba.

**orison** /'ɒrɪz(ə)n, -s(ə)n/ ● n. archaic a prayer.
– ORIGIN ME: from OFr. *oreison*, from L. *oratio(n-)* (see **ORATION**).

**-orium** ● suffix forming nouns denoting a place for a particular function: *sanatorium*.
– ORIGIN from L.; cf. **-ORY**[1].

**Oriya** /ɒ'riːjə/ ● n. (pl. same or **Oriyas**) **1** a native or inhabitant of the modern state of Orissa or the ancient region of Odra in India. **2** the Indic language of these people.
– ORIGIN from Hindi *Uṛiyā*.

**orle** /ɔːl/ ● n. Heraldry a narrow border of charges inset from the edge of a shield.
– ORIGIN C16: from Fr. *ourle*, from *ourler* 'to hem'.

**Orlon** /'ɔːlɒn/ ● n. trademark a synthetic acrylic fibre and fabric used for clothing, knitwear, etc.
– ORIGIN 1950s: invented word, on the pattern of *nylon*.

**orlop** /'ɔːlɒp/ (also **orlop deck**) ● n. the lowest deck of a wooden sailing ship with three or more decks.
– ORIGIN ME: from Du. *overloop* 'covering', from *overlopen* 'run over'.

**ormer** /'ɔːmə/ ● n. an abalone, especially one used as food in the Channel Islands. [*Haliotis tuberculata* and other species.]
– ORIGIN C17: Channel Islands Fr., from Fr. *ormier*, from L. *auris maris* 'ear of the sea' (because of its ear-like shape).

**ormolu** /'ɔːməluː/ ● n. a gold-coloured alloy of copper, zinc, and tin used in decoration and making ornaments.
– ORIGIN C18: from Fr. *or moulu* 'powdered gold'.

**ornament** ● n. /'ɔːnəm(ə)nt/ **1** an object designed to add beauty to something. ➤ decorative items collectively; decoration. ➤ (**ornaments**) Music embellishments made to a melody. **2** (**ornaments**) Christian Church the accessories of worship, such as the chalice. ● v. /'ɔːnəmɛnt/ beautify.
– DERIVATIVES **ornamentation** n.
– ORIGIN ME: from OFr. *ournement*, from L. *ornamentum* 'equipment, ornament', from *ornare* 'adorn'.

**ornamental** ● adj. serving or intended as an ornament. ● n. a plant grown for its attractive appearance.
– DERIVATIVES **ornamentalism** n. **ornamentalist** n. **ornamentally** adv.

**ornate** ● adj. **1** elaborately or highly decorated. **2** (of literary style) using unusual words and complex constructions.
– DERIVATIVES **ornately** adv. **ornateness** n.
– ORIGIN ME: from L. *ornatus*, *ornare* 'adorn'.

**ornery** /'ɔːnəri/ ● adj. N. Amer. informal bad-tempered.
– DERIVATIVES **orneriness** n.
– ORIGIN C19: var. of **ORDINARY**, representing a dial. pronunc.

**ornithine** /'ɔːnɪθiːn/ ● n. Biochemistry an amino acid which is produced by the body and is important in protein metabolism.
– ORIGIN C19: from **ORNITHO-** (with ref. to a constituent found in bird excrement) + **-INE**[4].

**ornithischian** /ˌɔːnɪ'θɪskɪən, -'θɪʃɪən/ ● n. Palaeontology a herbivorous dinosaur of a group with a pelvic structure resembling that of birds. Compare with **SAURISCHIAN**.
– ORIGIN C20: from mod. L. *Ornithischia* (name of an order), from Gk *ornis*, *ornith-* 'bird' + *iskhion* 'hip joint'.

**ornitho-** ● comb. form relating to or resembling a bird or birds: *ornithology*.
– ORIGIN from Gk *ornis*, *ornith-* 'bird'.

**ornithology** /ˌɔːnɪ'θɒlədʒi/ ● n. the scientific study of birds.
– DERIVATIVES **ornithological** adj. **ornithologically** adv. **ornithologist** n.
– ORIGIN C17: from mod. L. *ornithologia*, from Gk *ornithologos* 'treating of birds'.

**ornithopter** /'ɔːnɪˌθɒptə/ ● n. chiefly historical a machine designed to achieve flight by means of flapping wings.
– ORIGIN C20: coined in Fr. as *ornithoptère*.

**ornithosis** /ˌɔːnɪ'θəʊsɪs/ ● n. another term for **PSITTACOSIS**.

**oro-** ● comb. form of or relating to mountains: *orogeny*.
– ORIGIN from Gk *oros* 'mountain'.

**orogeny** /ɒ'rɒdʒəni/ ● n. Geology a process in which a section of the earth's crust is folded and deformed by lateral compression to form a mountain range.
– DERIVATIVES **orogenesis** n. **orogenic** adj.

**orographic** /ˌɒrə'grafɪk/ ● adj. of or relating to mountains, especially as regards their position and form. ➤ (of clouds or rainfall) resulting from the effects of mountains in forcing moist air to rise.
– DERIVATIVES **orographical** adj.

**Oromo** /'ɒrəməʊ/ ● n. (pl. same or **-os**) **1** a member of an East African people, the largest ethnic group in Ethiopia. **2** the Cushitic language of this people.
– ORIGIN the name in Oromo.

**oropendola** /ˌɒrə'pɛndələ/ ● n. a large gregarious tropical American bird which has brown or black plumage with yellow outer tail feathers, and constructs a pendulous nest. [Genus *Psarocolius*: several species.]
– ORIGIN C19: from Sp., lit. 'golden oriole'.

**oropharynx** /ˌɔːrə(ʊ)'farɪŋks/ ● n. (pl. **oropharynges** or **oropharynxes**) Anatomy the part of the pharynx that lies between the soft palate and the hyoid bone.
– DERIVATIVES **oropharyngeal** adj.
– ORIGIN C19: formed irregularly from L. *os*, *-or* 'mouth' + **PHARYNX**.

**orotund** /'ɒrə(ʊ)tʌnd, 'ɔː-/ ● adj. **1** (of the voice) resonant and impressive. **2** (of writing or style) pompous.
– DERIVATIVES **orotundity** n.
– ORIGIN C18: from L. *ore rotundo* 'with rounded mouth'.

**orphan** ● n. **1** a child whose parents are dead. **2** Printing the first line of a paragraph set as the last line of a page or column, considered undesirable. ● v. (usu. **be orphaned**) make an orphan.
– DERIVATIVES **orphanhood** n.
– ORIGIN ME: via late L. from Gk *orphanos* 'bereaved'.

**orphanage** ● n. a residential institution for the care and education of orphans.

**orphan drug** ● n. a synthetic pharmaceutical which remains commercially undeveloped.

**Orphic** ● adj. **1** of or concerning Orpheus, a legendary Greek poet and lyre-player, or the cult of Orphism. **2** of or relating to the artistic movement of Orphism.
– ORIGIN C17: via L. from Gk *Orphikos*, from *Orpheus*.

**Orphism** /'ɔːfɪz(ə)m/ ● n. **1** a mystic religion of ancient Greece, said to have been based on poems by Orpheus, characterized by rites of purification, death, and rebirth. **2** a short-lived art movement (*c.*1912) within cubism, characterized by a more lyrical use of colour than is found in other cubist works.

**orphrey** /'ɔːfri/ ● n. (pl. **-eys**) an ornamental stripe or border on an ecclesiastical vestment.
– ORIGIN ME: from OFr. *orfreis*, from a med. L. alt. of *auriphrygium*, from L. *aurum* 'gold' + *Phrygius* 'Phrygian'.

**orpiment** /'ɔːpɪm(ə)nt/ ● n. a bright yellow mineral consisting of arsenic trisulphide, formerly used as a dye and artist's pigment.
– ORIGIN ME: via OFr. from L. *auripigmentum*, from *aurum* 'gold' + *pigmentum* 'pigment'.

**orpine** /'ɔːpɪn/ (also **orpin**) ● n. a purple-flowered stonecrop. [*Sedum telephium*.]
– ORIGIN ME: from OFr. *orpine*, prob. an alt. of **ORPIMENT**, orig. applied to a yellow-flowered sedum.

**orra** /'ɒrə/ ● adj. Scottish **1** separated from a usual pair; odd. **2** occasional; superfluous.
– ORIGIN C16: of unknown origin.

**orrery** /'ɒrəri/ ● n. (pl. **-ies**) a clockwork model of the solar system, or of just the sun, earth, and moon.
– ORIGIN C18: named after the fourth Earl of *Orrery*, for whom one was made.

**orris** /ˈɒrɪs/ (also **orris root**) ● **n.** a preparation of the fragrant rootstock of an iris, used in perfumery and formerly in medicine.
– ORIGIN C16: appar. an unexplained alt. of **IRIS**.

**ortanique** /ˌɔːtəˈniːk/ ● **n.** a citrus fruit which is a cross between an orange and a tangerine. [*Citrus sinensis* × *reticulata*.]
– ORIGIN blend of **ORANGE**, **TANGERINE**, and **UNIQUE**.

**ortho-** ● **comb. form 1** straight; rectangular; upright: *orthodontics*. ➤ correct: *orthoepy*. **2** Chemistry denoting substitution at two adjacent carbon atoms in a benzene ring: *orthodichlorobenzene*. Compare with **META-** and **PARA-**[1]. **3** Chemistry denoting a compound from which a *meta-*compound is formed by dehydration: *orthophosphoric acid*.
– ORIGIN from Gk *orthos* 'straight, right'.

**orthochromatic** ● **adj.** denoting black-and-white photographic film sensitive to all visible light except red.

**orthoclase** /ˈɔːθəkleɪz/ ● **n.** a potassium-rich mineral of the feldspar group, typically white or pink.
– ORIGIN C19: from **ORTHO-** + Gk *klasis* 'breaking' (because of the characteristic two cleavages at right angles).

**orthodontics** /ˌɔːθəˈdɒntɪks/ (also **orthodontia** /-ˈdɒntɪə/) ● **pl. n.** [treated as sing.] the treatment of irregularities in the teeth and jaws.
– DERIVATIVES **orthodontic** adj. **orthodontically** adv. **orthodontist** n.
– ORIGIN C20: from **ORTHO-** + Gk *odous, odont-* 'tooth'.

**orthodox** ● **adj. 1** conforming with traditional or generally accepted beliefs. **2** conventional; normal. **3** (usu. **Orthodox**) of or relating to Orthodox Judaism or the Orthodox Church.
– DERIVATIVES **orthodoxly** adv.
– ORIGIN ME: from Gk *orthodoxos*, from *orthos* 'straight or right' + *doxa* 'opinion'.

**Orthodox Church** ● **n.** a Christian Church or federation of Churches acknowledging the authority of the patriarch of Constantinople and originating in the Greek-speaking Church of the Byzantine Empire.

**Orthodox Judaism** ● **n.** a major branch within Judaism which teaches strict adherence to rabbinical interpretation of Jewish law and its traditional observances.

**orthodoxy** ● **n.** (pl. **-ies**) **1** orthodox theory, doctrine, or practice. ➤ the state of being orthodox. **2** the whole community of Orthodox Jews or Orthodox Christians.

**orthodromic** /ˌɔːθəˈdrəʊmɪk/ ● **adj.** Physiology (of an impulse) travelling in the normal direction in a nerve fibre. The opposite of **ANTIDROMIC**.
– ORIGIN 1940s: from **ORTHO-** + Gk *dromos* 'running' + **-IC**.

**orthoepy** /ˈɔːθəʊɛpi, -iːpi, ɔːˈθəʊɪpi/ ● **n.** the study of correct or accepted pronunciation.
– DERIVATIVES **orthoepic** /-ˈɛpɪk/ adj. **orthoepist** n.
– ORIGIN C17: from Gk *orthoepeia* 'correct speech'.

**orthogenesis** /ˌɔːθə(ʊ)ˈdʒɛnɪsɪs/ ● **n.** Biology, chiefly historical evolution in which variations follow a particular direction and are not merely sporadic and fortuitous.
– DERIVATIVES **orthogenesist** n. **orthogenetic** adj. **orthogenetically** adv.

**orthogonal** /ɔːˈθɒg(ə)n(ə)l/ ● **adj. 1** of or involving right angles; at right angles to each other. **2** Statistics (of variates) statistically independent.
– DERIVATIVES **orthogonality** n. **orthogonally** adv.
– ORIGIN C16: from Fr., based on Gk *orthogōnios* 'right-angled'.

**orthographic projection** ● **n.** Engineering a method of projection in which an object is depicted using parallel lines to project its outline on to a plane.

**orthography** /ɔːˈθɒgrəfi/ ● **n.** (pl. **-ies**) **1** the conventional spelling system of a language. ➤ the study of spelling and how letters combine to represent sounds and form words. **2** orthographic projection.
– DERIVATIVES **orthographer** n. **orthographic** adj. **orthographical** adj. **orthographically** adv.
– ORIGIN ME: via OFr. and L. from Gk *orthographia*, from *orthos* 'correct' + *-graphia* 'writing'.

**orthopaedics** /ˌɔːθəˈpiːdɪks/ (US **-pedics**) ● **pl. n.** [treated as sing.] the branch of medicine concerned with the correction of deformities of bones or muscles.
– DERIVATIVES **orthopaedic** adj. **orthopaedically** adv. **orthopaedist** n.
– ORIGIN C19: from Fr. *orthopédie*, from Gk *orthos* 'right or straight' + *paideia* 'rearing of children'.

**orthophosphoric acid** /ˌɔːθə(ʊ)fɒsˈfɒrɪk/ ● **n.** another term for **PHOSPHORIC ACID**.
– DERIVATIVES **orthophosphate** n.

**Orthoptera** /ɔːˈθɒpt(ə)rə/ ● **pl. n.** Entomology an order of insects that includes the grasshoppers and crickets.
– DERIVATIVES **orthopteran** n. & adj. **orthopterous** adj.
– ORIGIN mod. L., from **ORTHO-** + Gk *pteros* 'wing'.

**orthoptics** ● **pl. n.** [treated as sing.] the study or treatment of irregularities of the eyes, especially those of the eye muscles that prevent normal binocular vision.
– DERIVATIVES **orthoptic** adj. **orthoptist** n.
– ORIGIN C19: from **ORTHO-** + Gk *optikos* (see **OPTIC**).

**orthorhombic** /ˌɔːθə(ʊ)ˈrɒmbɪk/ ● **adj.** denoting a crystal system with three unequal axes at right angles.

**orthostat** /ˈɔːθə(ʊ)stat/ ● **n.** Archaeology an upright stone or slab forming part of a structure or set in the ground.
– ORIGIN C20: from Gk *orthostatēs*, from *orthos* 'right or straight' + *statos* 'standing'.

**orthostatic** ● **adj. 1** Medicine relating to or caused by an upright posture. **2** Archaeology (of a structure) built of orthostats.

**orthotic** ● **adj.** relating to orthotics. ● **n.** an artificial support or brace for the limbs or spine.

**orthotics** /ɔːˈθɒtɪkz/ ● **pl. n.** [treated as sing.] the branch of medicine concerned with the provision and use of artificial supports or braces.
– DERIVATIVES **orthotist** n.

**ortolan** /ˈɔːt(ə)lən/ (also **ortolan bunting**) ● **n.** a small songbird formerly eaten as a delicacy, the male having an olive-green head and yellow throat. [*Emberiza hortulana*.]
– ORIGIN C16: from Fr., from Provençal, lit. 'gardener'.

**Ortonesque** ● **adj.** of or characteristic of the work of the English dramatist Joe Orton (1933–67).

**orts** /ɔːtz/ ● **pl. n.** archaic or dialect scraps; remains.
– ORIGIN ME: from Mid. Low Ger. *orte* 'food remains'.

**Orwellian** ● **adj.** of or characteristic of the work of the British novelist George Orwell (1903–50), especially with reference to the totalitarian state as depicted in *Nineteen Eighty-four*.

**-ory**[1] ● **suffix** (forming nouns) denoting a place for a particular function: *dormitory*.
– DERIVATIVES **-orial** suffix forming corresponding adjectives.
– ORIGIN from L. *-oria, -orium*, sometimes via Anglo-Norman Fr. *-orie*, OFr. *-oire*.

**-ory**[2] ● **suffix** forming adjectives (and occasionally nouns) relating to or involving a verbal action: *compulsory*.
– ORIGIN from L. *-orius*, sometimes via Anglo-Norman Fr. *-ori(e)*.

**oryx** /ˈɒrɪks/ ● **n.** a large long-horned antelope of arid regions of Africa and Arabia. [Genus *Oryx*: three species.]
– ORIGIN ME: via L. from Gk *orux* 'stonemason's pickaxe' (because of its pointed horns).

**orzo** /ˈɔːtsəʊ/ ● **n.** small pieces of pasta, shaped like grains of barley or rice.
– ORIGIN Ital., lit. 'barley'.

**OS** ● **abbrev. 1** (in calculating dates) Old Style. **2** Computing operating system. **3** Ordinary Seaman. **4** (in the UK) Ordnance Survey. **5** (as a size of clothing) outsize. **6** out of stock.

**Os** ● **symb.** the chemical element osmium.

**Osage** /əʊˈseɪdʒ, ˈəʊseɪdʒ/ ● **n.** (pl. same or **Osages**) **1** a member of an American Indian people formerly inhabiting the Osage River valley in Missouri. **2** the Siouan language of this people.
– ORIGIN alt. of Osage *Wazhazhe*, the name of one of the three groups that compose this people.

**Osage orange** ● **n.** a small spiny North American tree with inedible green orange-like fruit and durable wood (used by the Osage for their bows). [*Maclura pomifera*.]

**Oscan** /ˈɒsk(ə)n/ ● **n.** an extinct Italic language of southern Italy, related to Umbrian and surviving in inscriptions mainly of the 4th to 1st centuries BC. ● **adj.** of or relating to this language.
– ORIGIN C16: from L. *Oscus* 'Oscan' + **-AN**.

**Oscar** ● **n.** **1** (trademark in the US) the nickname for a gold statuette given as an Academy award. **2** a code word representing the letter O, used in radio communication.
– ORIGIN one of the several speculative explanations of sense 1 claims that the statuette reminded an executive director of the Academy of Motion Picture Arts and Sciences of her uncle Oscar.

**oscar** (also **oscar cichlid**) ● **n.** a South American cichlid fish with velvety brown young and multicoloured adults, popular in aquaria. [*Astronotus ocellatus*.]

**oscillate** /ˈɒsɪleɪt/ ● **v.** **1** move or swing back and forth at a regular speed. ➤ waver between extremes of opinion or emotion. **2** Physics move or vary with periodic regularity. ➤ cause an electric current or voltage to behave thus.
– DERIVATIVES **oscillation** n. **oscillator** n. **oscillatory** /ɒˈsɪlət(ə)ri, ˈɒsɪləˌt(ə)ri/ adj.
– ORIGIN C18 (earlier (C17) as *oscillation*): from L. *oscillat-*, *oscillare* 'swing'.

**oscillo-** /əˈsɪləʊ/ ● **comb. form** relating to oscillation, especially of electric current: *oscilloscope*.

**oscillograph** ● **n.** a device for recording oscillations, especially those of an electric current.
– DERIVATIVES **oscillogram** n. **oscillographic** adj. **oscillography** n.

**oscilloscope** ● **n.** a device for viewing oscillations by a display on the screen of a cathode ray tube.
– DERIVATIVES **oscilloscopic** adj.

**oscine** /ˈɒsʌɪn, -sɪn/ ● **adj.** Ornithology relating to or denoting birds of a large suborder (Oscines) that includes nearly all passerine birds.
– ORIGIN C19: from L. *oscen, oscin-* 'songbird' + **-INE**[1].

**Osco-Umbrian** ● **n.** **1** a group of ancient Italic languages including Oscan and Umbrian, spoken in Italy in the 1st millennium BC. **2** a member of any of the peoples who spoke a language in this group. ● **adj.** of or relating to these peoples or their languages.

**oscula** plural form of **OSCULUM**.

**oscular** /ˈɒskjʊlə/ ● **adj.** **1** humorous of or relating to kissing. **2** Zoology of or relating to an osculum.
– ORIGIN C19: from L. *osculum* 'mouth, kiss' (dimin. of *os* 'mouth') + **-AR**[1].

**osculate** /ˈɒskjʊleɪt/ ● **v.** **1** Mathematics (of curves or surfaces) touch so as to have a common tangent at the point of contact. **2** humorous kiss.
– DERIVATIVES **osculant** adj. **osculation** n. **osculatory** adj.
– ORIGIN C17: from L. *osculat-*, *osculari* 'kiss'.

**osculum** /ˈɒskjʊləm/ ● **n.** (pl. **oscula** /-lə/) Zoology a large aperture in a sponge through which water is expelled.
– ORIGIN C17: from L. 'little mouth'.

**-ose**[1] ● **suffix** (forming adjectives) having a specified quality: *bellicose*.
– DERIVATIVES **-osely** suffix forming corresponding adverbs. **-oseness** suffix forming corresponding nouns.
– ORIGIN from L. *-osus*.

**-ose**[2] ● **suffix** Chemistry forming names of sugars and other carbohydrates: *cellulose*.
– ORIGIN on the pattern of *(gluc)ose*.

**OSHA** ● **abbrev.** (in the US) Occupational Safety and Health Administration.

**osier** /ˈəʊzɪə/ ● **n.** a small willow of damp habitats with long flexible shoots used in basketwork. [*Salix viminalis*.] ➤ a willow shoot.
– ORIGIN ME: from OFr.; cf. med. L. *auseria* 'osier bed'.

**-osis** ● **suffix** (pl. **-oses**) denoting a process, condition, or pathological state: *metamorphosis*.
– ORIGIN via L. from Gk *-ōsis*, verbal noun ending.

**-osity** ● **suffix** forming nouns from adjectives ending in *-ose* (such as *verbosity* from *verbose*) and from adjectives ending in *-ous* (such as *pomposity* from *pompous*).
– ORIGIN from Fr. *-osité* or L. *-ositas*.

**Osmanli** /ɒzˈmanli/ ● **adj. & n.** (pl. same or **Osmanlis**) old-fashioned term for **OTTOMAN**.
– ORIGIN Turk., from the name *Osman*, from Arab. *ʿuṯmān* (see **OTTOMAN**) + the adjectival suffix *-li*.

**osmic** /ˈɒzmɪk/ ● **adj.** relating to odours or the sense of smell.
– DERIVATIVES **osmically** adv.
– ORIGIN C20: from Gk *osmē* 'odour' + **-IC**.

**osmic acid** ● **n.** Chemistry a solution of osmium tetroxide, a poisonous yellow compound used as a biological stain.
– ORIGIN C19: *osmic* from **OSMIUM** + **-IC**.

**osmium** /ˈɒzmɪəm/ ● **n.** the chemical element of atomic number 76, a hard, dense silvery-white metal. (Symbol: **Os**)
– ORIGIN C19: mod. L., from Gk *osmē* 'smell' (from the pungent smell of one of its oxides).

**osmo-** ● **comb. form** representing **OSMOSIS**.

**osmolality** /ˌɒzmə(ʊ)ˈlalɪti/ ● **n.** Chemistry the concentration of a solution expressed as the total number of solute particles per kilogram.
– ORIGIN 1950s: blend of *osmotic* (see **OSMOSIS**) and **MOLAL**, + **-ITY**.

**osmolarity** /ˌɒzmə(ʊ)ˈlarɪti/ ● **n.** Chemistry the concentration of a solution expressed as the total number of solute particles per litre.
– ORIGIN 1950s: blend of *osmotic* (see **OSMOSIS**) and **MOLAR**[3], + **-ITY**.

**osmoregulation** ● **n.** Biology the maintenance of constant osmotic pressure in the fluids of an organism by the control of water and salt concentrations.
– DERIVATIVES **osmoregulatory** adj.

**osmose** /ˈɒzməʊs/ ● **v.** rare pass by or as if by osmosis.

**osmosis** /ɒzˈməʊsɪs/ ● **n.** **1** Biology & Chemistry a process by which solvent molecules pass through a semipermeable membrane from a less concentrated solution into a more concentrated one. **2** the process of gradual or unconscious assimilation of ideas or knowledge.
– DERIVATIVES **osmotic** adj. **osmotically** adv.
– ORIGIN C19: Latinized form of earlier *osmose*, from Gk *ōsmos* 'a push'.

**osmotic pressure** /ɒzˈmɒtɪk/ ● **n.** Chemistry the pressure that would have to be applied to a pure solvent to prevent it from passing into a given solution by osmosis.

**osmunda** /ɒzˈmʌndə/ ● **n.** a plant of a genus that includes the royal and cinnamon ferns. [Genus *Osmunda*.]
– ORIGIN Anglo-Latin, from Anglo-Norman Fr. *osmunde*.

**osnaburg** /ˈɒznəbəːg/ ● **n.** a kind of coarse linen or cotton used chiefly for furnishings and sacks.
– ORIGIN ME: alt. of *Osnabrück*, the name of a city in Germany where the cloth was orig. produced.

**osprey** /ˈɒspri, -preɪ/ ● **n.** (pl. **-eys**) a large fish-eating bird of prey with long, narrow wings and a white underside and crown. [*Pandion haliaetus*.]
– ORIGIN ME: from OFr. *ospres*, appar. based on L. *ossifraga*, from *os* 'bone' + *frangere* 'to break'.

**OSS** ● **abbrev.** (in the US) Office of Strategic Services, an intelligence organization.

**osseous** /ˈɒsɪəs/ ● **adj.** chiefly Zoology & Medicine consisting of or turned into bone.
– ORIGIN ME: from L. *osseus* 'bony' + **-OUS**.

**Ossete** /ˈɒsiːt/ ● **n.** **1** a native or inhabitant of Ossetia in the Caucasus. **2** another term for **OSSETIAN** (in sense 1).

**Ossetian** ● **n.** **1** the language of the Ossetes, belonging to the Iranian group. **2** a native or inhabitant of Ossetia. ● **adj.** of or relating to the Ossetes or their language.
– DERIVATIVES **Ossetic** adj. & n.

**Ossi** /ˈɒsi/ ● **n.** (pl. **Ossies** or **Ossis**) informal, often derogatory (in Germany) a citizen of the former German Democratic Republic.
– ORIGIN Ger., prob. an abbrev. of *Ostdeutsche* 'East German'.

**ossicle** /ˈɒsɪk(ə)l/ ● **n.** **1** Anatomy & Zoology a very small bone, especially one of those in the middle ear. **2** Zoology a small piece of calcified material forming part of the skeleton of an invertebrate animal such as an echinoderm.
– ORIGIN C16: from L. *ossiculum*, dimin. of *os* 'bone'.

**ossify** /ˈɒsɪfʌɪ/ ● **v.** (**-ies**, **-ied**) **1** turn into bone or bony

tissue. **2** [often as adj. **ossified**] cease developing; become inflexible.
– DERIVATIVES **ossification** n.
– ORIGIN C18: from Fr. *ossifier*, from L. *os, oss-* 'bone'.

**osso bucco** /ˌɒsəʊ ˈbuːkəʊ/ ● **n.** an Italian dish made of shin of veal containing marrowbone, stewed in wine with vegetables.
– ORIGIN Ital., lit. 'marrowbone'.

**ossuary** /ˈɒsjʊəri/ ● **n.** (pl. **-ies**) a container or room for the bones of the dead.
– ORIGIN C17: from late L. *ossuarium*, formed irregularly from L. *os, oss-* 'bone'.

**osteitis** /ˌɒstɪˈʌɪtɪs/ ● **n.** Medicine inflammation of the substance of a bone.
– ORIGIN C19: from Gk *osteon* 'bone' + **-ITIS**.

**ostensible** /ɒˈstɛnsɪb(ə)l/ ● **adj.** apparently true, but not necessarily so.
– DERIVATIVES **ostensibly** adv.
– ORIGIN C18: from Fr., from med. L. *ostensibilis*, *ostendere* 'stretch out to view'.

**ostensive** ● **adj.** Linguistics denoting a way of defining by direct demonstration, e.g. pointing.
– DERIVATIVES **ostensively** adv. **ostensiveness** n.
– ORIGIN C16: from late L. *ostensivus*, from *ostens-* (see **OSTENSIBLE**).

**ostensory** /ɒˈstɛns(ə)ri/ ● **n.** (pl. **-ies**) a monstrance.
– ORIGIN C18: from med. L. *ostensorium*, from *ostens-* (see **OSTENSIBLE**).

**ostentation** ● **n.** the pretentious display of wealth, skill, or knowledge, designed to impress.
– DERIVATIVES **ostentatious** adj. **ostentatiously** adv. **ostentatiousness** n.
– ORIGIN ME: via OFr. from L. *ostentatio(n-)*, from *ostentare*, frequentative of *ostendere* 'stretch out to view'.

**osteo-** ● **comb. form** of or relating to the bones: *osteoporosis.*
– ORIGIN from Gk *osteon* 'bone'.

**osteoarthritis** ● **n.** Medicine degeneration of joint cartilage and the underlying bone, most common from middle age onward, causing pain and stiffness.
– DERIVATIVES **osteoarthritic** adj.

**osteogenesis** /ˌɒstɪə(ʊ)ˈdʒɛnɪsɪs/ ● **n.** the formation of bone.
– DERIVATIVES **osteogenetic** adj. **osteogenic** adj.

**osteogenesis imperfecta** /ˌɪmpəːˈfɛktə/ ● **n.** Medicine an inherited disorder characterized by extreme fragility of the bones.

**osteology** /ˌɒstɪˈɒlədʒi/ ● **n.** the study of the structure and function of the skeleton and bony structures.
– DERIVATIVES **osteological** adj. **osteologically** adv. **osteologist** n.

**osteomalacia** /ˌɒstɪəʊməˈleɪʃɪə/ ● **n.** softening of the bones, typically through a deficiency of vitamin D or calcium.
– DERIVATIVES **osteomalacic** /-ˈlasɪk/ adj.
– ORIGIN C19: mod. L., from **OSTEO-** + Gk *malakos* 'soft'.

**osteomyelitis** /ˌɒstɪəʊmʌɪˈlʌɪtɪs/ ● **n.** Medicine inflammation of bone or bone marrow.

**osteopathy** /ˌɒstɪˈɒpəθi/ ● **n.** a system of complementary medicine involving the treatment of medical disorders through the manipulation and massage of the skeleton and musculature.
– DERIVATIVES **osteopath** n. **osteopathic** adj. **osteopathically** adv.

**osteophyte** /ˈɒstɪə(ʊ)fʌɪt/ ● **n.** Medicine a bony projection associated with the degeneration of cartilage at joints.
– DERIVATIVES **osteophytic** adj.

**osteoporosis** /ˌɒstɪəʊpəˈrəʊsɪs/ ● **n.** a medical condition in which the bones become brittle and fragile from loss of tissue, typically as a result of hormonal changes, or deficiency of calcium or vitamin D.
– DERIVATIVES **osteoporotic** adj.
– ORIGIN C19: from **OSTEO-** + Gk *poros* 'passage, pore' + **-OSIS**.

**ostinato** /ˌɒstɪˈnɑːtəʊ/ ● **n.** (pl. **ostinatos** or **ostinati** /-ti/) a continually repeated musical phrase or rhythm.
– ORIGIN Ital., lit. 'obstinate'.

**ostium** /ˈɒstɪəm/ ● **n.** (pl. **ostia** /ˈɒstɪə/) **1** Anatomy & Zoology an opening into a vessel or cavity of the body. **2** Zoology each of a number of pores in the wall of a sponge, through which water is drawn in.
– ORIGIN C17: from L., 'door, opening'.

**ostler** /ˈɒslə/ (also **hostler**) ● **n.** historical a man employed to look after the horses of people staying at an inn.
– ORIGIN ME: from OFr. *hostelier* 'innkeeper', from *hostel* (see **HOSTEL**).

**Ostmark** /ˈɒstmɑːk/ ● **n.** the basic monetary unit of the former German Democratic Republic, equal to 100 pfennigs.
– ORIGIN Ger., lit. 'east mark' (see **MARK**[2]).

**Ostpolitik** /ˈɒstpɒlɪˌtiːk/ ● **n.** historical the foreign policy of détente of western European countries with reference to the former communist bloc.
– ORIGIN Ger., from *Ost* 'east' + *Politik* 'politics'.

**ostracize** /ˈɒstrəsʌɪz/ (also **-ise**) ● **v.** exclude from a society or group. ➤(in ancient Greece) banish (a citizen) from a city for five or ten years by popular vote.
– DERIVATIVES **ostracism** n.
– ORIGIN C17: from Gk *ostrakizein*, from *ostrakon* 'shell or potsherd' (on which names were written in voting to banish unpopular citizens).

**Ostracoda** /ˌɒstrəˈkəʊdə/ ● **pl. n.** Zoology a class of minute aquatic crustaceans with a hinged shell from which the antennae protrude.
– DERIVATIVES **ostracod** /ˈɒstrəkɒd/ n.
– ORIGIN mod. L., from Gk *ostrakōdēs* 'testaceous', from *ostrakon* 'shell'.

**ostracoderm** /ɒˈstrakədəːm/ ● **n.** an early jawless fossil fish of the Cambrian to Devonian periods, with a heavily armoured body.
– ORIGIN C19: from mod. L. *Ostracodermi* (former taxonomic name), from Gk *ostrakon* 'shell' + *derma* 'skin'.

**ostrich** ● **n. 1** a large flightless swift-running African bird with a long neck, long legs, and two toes on each foot. [*Struthio camelus.*] **2** a person who refuses to accept facts.
– ORIGIN ME: from OFr. *ostriche*, from L. *avis* 'bird' + late L. *struthio* (from Gk *strouthiōn* 'ostrich', from *strouthos* 'sparrow or ostrich'); sense 2 is from the popular belief that ostriches bury their heads in the sand if pursued.

**Ostrogoth** /ˈɒstrəgɒθ/ ● **n.** a member of the eastern branch of the Goths, who conquered Italy in the 5th–6th centuries AD.
– DERIVATIVES **Ostrogothic** adj.
– ORIGIN from late L. *Ostrogothi* (pl.), from the Gmc base of **EAST** + late L. *Gothi* 'Goths'.

**OT** ● **abbrev. 1** occupational therapist; occupational therapy. **2** Old Testament.

**-ot**[1] ● **suffix** forming nouns which were originally diminutives: *parrot.*
– ORIGIN from Fr.

**-ot**[2] ● **suffix** (forming nouns) denoting a person of a particular type: *idiot.* ➤denoting a native of a place: *Cypriot.*
– ORIGIN via Fr. and L. from Gk *ōtēs*.

**otalgia** /əʊˈtaldʒə/ ● **n.** Medicine earache.
– ORIGIN C17: from Gk *ōtalgia*, from *ous, ōt-* 'ear' + *algos* 'pain'.

**OTC** ● **abbrev. 1** (in the UK) Officers' Training Corps. **2** over the counter.

**other** ● **adj. & pron. 1** used to refer to a person or thing that is different from one already mentioned or known. ➤alternative of two. ➤those not already mentioned. **2** additional. **3** (**the other**) informal, euphemistic sexual intercourse. **4** (usu. **the Other**) Philosophy & Sociology that which is distinct from, different from, or opposite to something or oneself.
– PHRASES **no other** archaic nothing else. **the other day** (or **night**, **week**, etc.) a few days (or nights, weeks, etc.) ago. **the other thing** Brit., chiefly humorous an unexpressed alternative.
– ORIGIN OE *ōther*, of Gmc origin.

**other half** ● **n.** Brit. informal one's wife, husband, or partner.

**otherness** ● **n.** the quality or fact of being different.

**other place** ● **n.** (**the other place**) Brit. humorous **1** hell, as opposed to heaven. **2** Oxford University as regarded by Cambridge, and vice versa. **3** the House of Lords as regarded by the House of Commons, and vice versa.

**other ranks** • **pl. n.** Brit. (in the armed forces) all those who are not commissioned officers.

**otherwhere** • **adv. & pron.** archaic or poetic/literary elsewhere.

**otherwise** • **adv. 1** in different circumstances; or else. **2** in other respects. **3** in a different way. ➤alternatively. • **adj.** in a different state or situation.
– PHRASES **or** (or **and**) **otherwise** indicating the opposite of something stated.
– ORIGIN OE *on ōthre wisan* (see **OTHER**, **WISE**[2]).

**other woman** • **n.** (**the other woman**) the mistress of a married man.

**other world** • **n.** the spiritual world or afterlife.

**other-worldly** • **adj. 1** of or relating to an imaginary or spiritual world. **2** unworldly.
– DERIVATIVES **other-worldliness** n.

**otic** /ˈəʊtɪk, ˈɒtɪk/ • **adj.** Anatomy of or relating to the ear.
– ORIGIN C17: from Gk *ōtikos*, from *ous*, *ōt-* 'ear'.

**-otic** • **suffix** forming adjectives and nouns corresponding to nouns ending in *-osis* (e.g. *neurotic* corresponding to *neurosis*).
– DERIVATIVES **-otically** suffix forming corresponding adverbs.
– ORIGIN from Fr. *-otique*, via L. from the Gk adjectival ending *-ōtikos*.

**otiose** /ˈəʊtɪəʊs, ˈəʊʃɪ-, -z/ • **adj.** serving no practical purpose. ➤archaic idle.
– DERIVATIVES **otiosely** adv.
– ORIGIN C18: from L. *otiosus*, from *otium* 'leisure'.

**otitis** /ə(ʊ)ˈtʌɪtɪs/ • **n.** Medicine inflammation of part of the ear, especially the middle ear (**otitis media**).
– ORIGIN C18: mod. L., from Gk *ous*, *ōt-* 'ear' + **-ITIS**.

**oto-** /ˈəʊtəʊ/ • **comb. form** of or relating to the ears: *otoscope*.
– ORIGIN from Gk *ous*, *ōt-* 'ear'.

**otolaryngology** /ˌəʊtə(ʊ)larɪŋˈgɒlədʒi/ • **n.** the study of diseases of the ear and throat.
– DERIVATIVES **otolaryngological** adj. **otolaryngologist** n.

**otolith** • **n.** Zoology each of three small oval calcareous bodies in the inner ear of vertebrates, involved in the sensing of gravity and movement.
– DERIVATIVES **otolithic** adj.

**otology** /əʊˈtɒlədʒi/ • **n.** the study of the anatomy and diseases of the ear.
– DERIVATIVES **otological** adj. **otologist** n.

**Otomanguean** /ˌəʊtə(ʊ)ˈmaŋgɪən, -ˈmaŋgwɪən/ • **adj.** relating to or denoting a family of American Indian languages of central and southern Mexico.
– ORIGIN 1940s: from **OTOMI** + *Mangue* (an extinct lang. of Costa Rica) + **-AN**.

**Otomi** /ˌəʊtəˈmiː/ • **n.** (pl. same) **1** a member of an American Indian people inhabiting parts of central Mexico. **2** the Otomanguean language of this people.
– ORIGIN via Amer. Sp. from Nahuatl *otomih*, lit. 'unknown'.

**otoplasty** /ˈəʊtə(ʊ)ˌplasti/ • **n.** (pl. **-ies**) Medicine a surgical operation to enhance the appearance of an ear.

**otorhinolaryngology** /ˌəʊtə(ʊ)ˌrʌɪnəʊˌlarɪŋˈgɒlədʒi/ • **n.** the study of diseases of the ear, nose, and throat.
– DERIVATIVES **otorhinolaryngologist** n.

**otoscope** • **n.** an instrument for visual examination of the eardrum and passage of the outer ear.
– DERIVATIVES **otoscopic** adj.

**OTT** • **abbrev.** Brit. informal over the top.

**ottava rima** /ɒˌtɑːvə ˈriːmə/ • **n.** a form of poetry consisting of stanzas of eight lines of ten or eleven syllables, rhyming *abababcc*.
– ORIGIN C18: from Ital., lit. 'eighth rhyme'.

**otter** • **n. 1** a semiaquatic fish-eating mammal of the weasel family, with an elongated body, dense fur, and webbed feet. [*Lutra lutra* and other species.] **2** a piece of board used to carry fishing bait in water.
– ORIGIN OE *otr*, *ot(t)or*, of Gmc origin.

**otter board** • **n.** either of a pair of boards attached to each side of the mouth of a trawl net, keeping it open as it is pulled through the water.

**otter dog** (also **otter hound**) • **n.** a large hound of a breed with a long rough coat, used in otter hunting.

**otto** • **n.** another term for **ATTAR**.

**Ottoman** /ˈɒtəmən/ • **adj.** historical **1** of or relating to the Turkish dynasty of Osman I (Othman I), founded in *c.*1300. ➤of or relating to the branch of the Turks to which Osman belonged. ➤of or relating to the Ottoman Empire ruled by his successors. **2** Turkish. • **n.** (pl. **Ottomans**) a Turk, especially of the Ottoman period.
– ORIGIN based on Arab. *'uṯmānī* (adj.), from *'Uṯmān* 'Othman'.

**ottoman** • **n.** (pl. **ottomans**) **1** a low upholstered seat without a back or arms, typically serving also as a box, with the seat hinged to form a lid. **2** a heavy ribbed fabric made from silk and either cotton or wool.
– ORIGIN C19: from Fr. *ottomane*, fem. of *ottoman* 'Ottoman'.

**OU** • **abbrev.** (in the UK) Open University.

**ou**[1] /əʊ/ • **n.** (pl. **ouens** /ˈəʊənz/ or **ous**) S. African informal a man; a person.
– ORIGIN Afrik., prob. from Du. *ouwe* 'old man'.

**ou**[2] /ˈəʊuː/ • **n.** a fruit-eating Hawaiian honeycreeper with a stout bill and green and yellow plumage. [*Psittirostra psittacea*.]
– ORIGIN C19: the name in Hawaiian.

**ouabain** /ˈuːəbeɪn/ • **n.** Chemistry a toxic compound used as a very rapid cardiac stimulant.
– ORIGIN C19: via Fr. from Somali *wabayo*, denoting a tree that yields ouabain.

**ouananiche** /ˌwanəˈniːʃ/ • **n.** (pl. same) Canadian an Atlantic salmon of landlocked populations living in lakes in Labrador and Newfoundland.
– ORIGIN C19: via Canad. Fr. from Algonquian.

**oubliette** /ˌuːblɪˈɛt/ • **n.** a secret dungeon with access only through a trapdoor in its ceiling.
– ORIGIN C18: from Fr., from *oublier* 'forget'.

**ouch** • **exclam.** used to express pain.
– ORIGIN natural exclamation.

**oud** /uːd/ • **n.** a form of lute or mandolin played in Arab countries.
– ORIGIN C18: from Arab. *al-'ūd*.

**ouens** plural form of **OU**[1].

**ought**[1] • **modal v.** (3rd sing. present and past **ought**) **1** used to indicate duty or correctness. ➤used to indicate a desirable or expected state. ➤used to give or ask advice. **2** used to indicate something that is probable.
– ORIGIN OE *āhte*, past tense of *āgan* 'owe' (see **OWE**).

**ought**[2] (also **aught**) • **n.** archaic term for **NOUGHT**.
– ORIGIN C19: perh. from *an ought*, by wrong division of *a nought*.

**ought**[3] • **pron.** variant spelling of **AUGHT**[1].

**oughtn't** • **contr.** ought not.

**ouguiya** /uːˈgiːjə/ (also **ougiya**) • **n.** the basic monetary unit of Mauritania, equal to five khoums.
– ORIGIN via Fr. from Mauritanian Arab., from Arab. *'ūḳiyya*, from Gk *ounkia*, from L. *uncia* 'ounce'.

**Ouija board** /ˈwiːdʒə/ • **n.** trademark a board with letters, numbers, and other signs around its edge, to which a planchette or other pointer moves, supposedly in answer to questions from people at a seance.
– ORIGIN C19: *Ouija* from Fr. *oui* 'yes' + Ger. *ja* 'yes'.

**ounce**[1] • **n. 1** (abbrev.: **oz**) a unit of weight of one sixteenth of a pound avoirdupois (approximately 28 grams). ➤a unit of one twelfth of a pound troy or apothecaries' measure, equal to 480 grains (approximately 31 grams). **2** a very small amount.
– ORIGIN ME: from OFr. *unce*, from L. *uncia* 'twelfth part (of a pound or foot)'; cf. **INCH**[1].

**ounce**[2] • **n.** a snow leopard.
– ORIGIN ME: from OFr. *once*, earlier *lonce* (the *l-* being misinterpreted as the definite article), based on L. *lynx*, *lync-* (see **LYNX**).

**our** • **possess. det. 1** belonging to or associated with the speaker and one or more others previously mentioned or easily identified. ➤belonging to or associated with

people in general. **2** used in formal contexts by a royal person or a writer to refer to something belonging to himself or herself. **3** informal, chiefly N. English used with a name to refer to a relative or friend of the speaker.
– ORIGIN OE *ūre*, of Gmc origin.

**-our**[1] • **suffix** variant spelling of **-OR**[2] surviving in some nouns such as *ardour, colour.*

**-our**[2] • **suffix** variant spelling of **-OR**[1] (as in *saviour*).

**Our Father** • **n. 1** God. **2** the Lord's Prayer.

**Our Lady** • **n.** the Virgin Mary.

**Our Lord** • **n.** God or Jesus.

**ouroboros** /ˌjʊərəʊˈbɒrəs/ • **n.** variant spelling of **UROBOROS**.

**ours** • **possess. pron.** used to refer to something belonging to or associated with the speaker and one or more others previously mentioned or easily identified.

**ourself** • **pron.** [first person pl.] **1** used instead of 'ourselves' typically when 'we' refers to people in general. **2** archaic used instead of 'myself' by a sovereign.

**ourselves** • **pron.** [first person pl.] **1** used as the object of a verb or preposition when this is the same as the subject of the clause and the subject is the speaker and one or more other people considered together. **2** [emphatic] we or us personally.

**-ous** • **suffix** forming adjectives: **1** characterized by: *mountainous.* **2** Chemistry denoting an element in a lower valency: *sulphurous.* Compare with **-IC**.
– DERIVATIVES **-ously** suffix forming corresponding adverbs. **-ousness** suffix forming corresponding nouns.
– ORIGIN from Anglo-Norman Fr., or OFr. *-eus*, from L. *-osus.*

**ousel** • **n.** variant spelling of **OUZEL**.

**oust** /aʊst/ • **v. 1** drive out or expel from a position or place. **2** Law deprive of or exclude from possession of something. ➤take away (a court's jurisdiction) in a matter.
– ORIGIN ME: from Anglo-Norman Fr. *ouster* 'take away', from L. *obstare* 'oppose, hinder'.

**ouster** • **n. 1** Law ejection from a freehold or other possession; deprivation of an inheritance. ➤removal from the jurisdiction of the courts. ➤a clause that is or is claimed to be outside the jurisdiction of the courts. **2** chiefly N. Amer. dismissal from a position.

**out** • **adv. 1** moving away from a place, especially from one that is enclosed to one that is open. ➤outdoors. ➤no longer in prison. **2** away from one's usual base or residence. **3** to sea, away from the land. ➤(of the tide) falling or at its lowest level. **4** so as to be revealed, heard, or known. **5** at or to an end. ➤so as to no longer exist. **6** at a specified distance away from the goal or a finishing line. • **prep.** non-standard contraction of **OUT OF**. • **adj. 1** not at home or one's place of work. **2** revealed. ➤published. ➤informal in existence or use. ➤open about one's homosexuality. **3** no longer existing. ➤informal no longer in fashion. **4** not possible or worth considering. **5** unconscious. **6** mistaken. **7** (of the ball in tennis, squash, etc.) outside the playing area. **8** Cricket & Baseball no longer batting. **9** (of a flower) open. • **n. 1** informal a form of escape. **2** Baseball an act of putting a player out. • **v. 1** informal reveal the homosexuality of. **2** knock out. **3** W. Indian extinguish. **4** dated expel, reject, or dismiss.
– PHRASES **at outs** (N. Amer. **on the outs**) in dispute. **out and about** engaging in normal activity after an illness. **out for** intent on having. **out of 1** from. **2** not having (something). **out of it** informal **1** not included. **2** unaware of what is happening. ➤Brit. drunk. **out to do something** keenly striving to do something. **out with it** say what you are thinking.
– ORIGIN OE *ūt* (adv.), *ūtian* (v.), of Gmc origin.

**out-** • **prefix 1** to the point of surpassing or exceeding: *outperform.* **2** external; separate; from outside: *outbuildings.* **3** away from; outward: *outpost.*

**outage** /ˈaʊtɪdʒ/ • **n.** a period when a power supply or other service is not available.

**out and out** • **adj.** absolute. • **adv.** completely.

**out-and-outer** • **n.** archaic, informal an out-and-out possessor of a particular quality.

**outback** • **n.** (**the outback**) a remote or sparsely populated inland area, especially in Australia.
– DERIVATIVES **outbacker** n.

**outbalance** • **v.** be more valuable or important than.

**outbid** • **v.** (**-bidding**; past and past part. **-bid**) bid more for something than.

**outboard** • **adj. & adv.** on, towards, or near the outside of a ship or aircraft. ➤(of a motor) portable and attachable to the outside of the stern of a boat. • **n.** an outboard motor. ➤a boat with such a motor.

**outbound** • **adj. & adv.** outward bound.

**outbrave** • **v.** archaic **1** outdo in bravery. **2** face with brave defiance.

**outbreak** • **n.** a sudden or violent occurrence of war, disease, etc.

**outbreed** • **v.** (past and past part. **-bred**) [usu. as noun **outbreeding**] breed from parents not closely related.

**outbuilding** • **n.** a smaller detached building in the grounds of a main building.

**outburst** • **n.** a sudden violent occurrence or release of something, especially angry words.

**outcall** • **n.** a house call made by a prostitute.

**outcast** • **n.** a person rejected by their society or social group. • **adj.** rejected or cast out.

**outcaste** • **n.** (in Hindu society) a person with no caste, or one expelled from their caste. • **v.** cause (someone) to lose their caste.

**outclass** • **v.** be far superior to.

**outcome** • **n.** a consequence.

**outcrop** • **n.** a rock formation that is visible on the surface. • **v.** (**-cropped**, **-cropping**) [often as noun **outcropping**] appear as an outcrop.

**outcross** • **v.** breed (an animal or plant) with one not closely related. • **n.** an animal or plant resulting from outcrossing.

**outcry** • **n.** (pl. **-ies**) a strong expression of public disapproval. ➤an exclamation or shout.

**outdated** • **adj.** obsolete.
– DERIVATIVES **outdatedness** n.

**outdistance** • **v.** leave (a competitor or pursuer) far behind.

**outdo** • **v.** (**-does**, **-doing**; past **-did**; past part. **-done**) be superior to in action or performance.

**outdoor** • **adj.** done, situated, or used outdoors. ➤liking the outdoors.

**outdoor pursuits** • **pl. n.** Brit. outdoor sporting or leisure activities.

**outdoors** • **adv.** in or into the open air. • **n.** any area outside buildings or shelter.
– DERIVATIVES **outdoorsman** n. (pl. **-men**). **outdoorsy** adj. (informal).

**outdrive** • **v.** (past **-drove**; past part. **-driven**) drive better or faster than. • **n.** an outboard motor.

**outer** • **adj. 1** outside; external. ➤further from the centre or the inside. **2** objective or physical. • **n. 1** Brit. the division of a target furthest from the bullseye. **2** Brit. an outer garment or part of one. **3** Brit. a container for transport or display of packaged items. **4** Austral. informal the part of a racecourse outside the enclosure.

**outer bar** • **n.** (**the outer bar**) (in the UK) barristers who are not Queen's or King's Counsels.

**Outer House** (in full **the Outer House of the Court of Session**) • **n.** (in Scotland) a law court that hears cases in the first instance.

**outermost** • **adj.** furthest from the centre.

**outer space** • **n.** the physical universe beyond the earth's atmosphere.

**outerwear** • **n.** clothes worn over other clothes.

**outface** • **v.** disconcert or defeat by bold confrontation.

**outfall** • **n.** the place where a river, drain, etc. empties into the sea, a river, or a lake.

**outfield** • **n. 1** Cricket the part of the field furthest from the wicket. **2** Baseball the grassy area beyond the infield. **3** the outlying land of a farm.
– DERIVATIVES **outfielder** n.

**outfight** • **v.** (past and past part. **-fought**) beat in a fight.

**outfit** • **n. 1** a set of clothes worn together. **2** informal a group of people undertaking a particular activity together. **3** a complete set of equipment needed for a particular purpose. ● v. (**-fitted**, **-fitting**) (usu. **be outfitted**) provide with an outfit of clothes or equipment.

**outfitter** (also **outfitters**) ● n. **1** Brit. dated a shop selling men's clothing. **2** N. Amer. a shop selling equipment, typically for outdoor pursuits.

**outflank** ● v. **1** move round the side of (an enemy) so as to outmanoeuvre them. **2** outwit.

**outflow** ● n. **1** the action of flowing or moving out. **2** something, such as water, money, etc., that flows or moves out.

**outfox** ● v. informal defeat with cunning.

**outgas** ● v. (**-gases**, **-gassing**, **-gassed**) release or give off as a gas or vapour.

**outgeneral** ● v. (**-generalled**, **-generalling**; US **-generaled**, **-generaling**) defeat by superior strategy or tactics.

**outgo** archaic ● v. (**-goes**; past **-went**; past part. **-gone**) go faster than. ● n. expenditure.

**outgoing** ● adj. **1** friendly and confident. **2** leaving an office or position. ➤ going out or away from a place. ● n. Brit. **1** (**outgoings**) one's regular expenditure. **2** an instance of going out.

**outgross** ● v. surpass in gross takings or profit.

**out-group** ● n. those who do not belong to an in-group.

**outgrow** ● v. (past **-grew**; past part. **-grown**) **1** grow too big for. **2** leave behind as one matures. **3** grow faster or taller than.

– PHRASES **outgrow one's strength** Brit. become lanky and weak through too rapid growth.

**outgrowth** ● n. **1** something that grows out of something else. **2** a natural development or result. **3** the process of growing out.

**outguess** ● v. guess correctly what is intended by.

**outgun** ● v. (**-gunned**, **-gunning**) [often **be outgunned**] have more or better weaponry than. ➤ shoot better than.

**out-half** ● n. Rugby another term for **STAND-OFF HALF**.

**outhaul** ● n. Sailing a rope used to haul out the clew of a sail.

**outhouse** ● n. a smaller building built on to or in the grounds of a house. ➤ an outside toilet. ● v. store away from the main storage area.

**outie** /'aʊti/ ● n. (pl. **-ies**) S. African informal a homeless person.

**outing** ● n. **1** a short trip taken for pleasure. ➤ a brief journey from home. ➤ informal a public appearance in something. **2** the practice of revealing the homosexuality of a prominent person.

**out island** ● n. an island away from the mainland.

**outjockey** ● v. (**-eys**, **-eyed**) dated outwit by deception.

**outlander** ● n. chiefly N. Amer. a foreigner or stranger.

**outlandish** ● adj. **1** bizarre or unfamiliar. **2** archaic foreign.

– DERIVATIVES **outlandishly** adv. **outlandishness** n.

– ORIGIN OE *ūtlendisc* 'not native', from *ūtland* 'foreign country'.

**outlast** ● v. outlive.

**outlaw** ● n. **1** a fugitive from the law. **2** historical a person deprived of the benefit and protection of the law. ● v. **1** ban. **2** historical deprive of the benefit and protection of the law.

– DERIVATIVES **outlawry** n.

– ORIGIN OE *ūtlaga* (n.), *ūtlagian* (v.), from ON *útlagi* (n.) from *útlagr* 'outlawed or banished'.

**outlay** ● n. an amount of money spent.

**outlet** ● n. **1** a pipe or hole through which water or gas may escape. **2** the mouth of a river. **3** an output socket in an electrical device. **4** a point from which goods are sold or distributed. **5** a means of expressing one's talents, energy, or emotions.

**outlier** /'aʊtlʌɪə/ ● n. **1** a person or thing away or detached from the main body or system. **2** Geology a younger rock formation among older rocks. **3** Statistics a result differing greatly from others in the same sample.

**outline** ● n. **1** a line or lines enclosing or indicating the shape of an object in a sketch or diagram. ➤ the contours or bounds of an object. **2** a word in shorthand. **3** a general plan showing essential features but no detail. ➤ the main features of something. ● v. **1** draw or define the outer edge or shape of. **2** give a summary of.

**outliner** ● n. a z program allowing editing of an outline of the structure of a document.

**outlive** ● v. **1** live longer than. ➤ survive or last beyond. **2** archaic live through (an experience).

**outlook** ● n. **1** a person's point of view or attitude to life. **2** a view. **3** the prospect for the future.

**outlying** ● adj. remote.

**outmanoeuvre** ● v. evade by moving faster or more skilfully. ➤ use skill and cunning to beat.

**outmatch** ● v. be superior to.

**outmeasure** ● v. archaic exceed in quantity or extent.

**outmigration** ● n. migration from one place to another, especially within a country.

**outmoded** ● adj. old-fashioned.

– DERIVATIVES **outmodedness** n.

**outmost** ● adj. chiefly archaic furthest away.

– ORIGIN ME: var. of *utmest* 'utmost'.

**outnumber** ● v. be more numerous than.

**out-of-body experience** ● n. a sensation of being outside one's body, typically of floating and observing oneself from a distance.

**out-of-court** ● adj. (of a settlement) made without the intervention of a court.

**out of date** ● adj. **1** old-fashioned. **2** no longer valid.

**outpace** ● v. go faster than.

**outpatient** ● n. a patient attending a hospital for treatment without staying overnight.

**outperform** ● v. **1** perform better than. **2** be more profitable than.

– DERIVATIVES **outperformance** n.

**outplacement** ● n. the provision of assistance to redundant employees in finding new employment.

**outplay** ● v. play better than.

**outpoint** ● v. Boxing defeat on points.

**outport** ● n. **1** a subsidiary port. ➤ Brit. any British port other than London. **2** Canadian (especially in Newfoundland) a remote fishing village.

**outpost** ● n. a small military camp at a distance from the main army. ➤ a remote part of a country or empire. ➤ an isolated or remote branch of something.

**outpouring** ● n. **1** something that streams out rapidly. **2** an outburst of strong emotion.

**output** ● n. **1** the amount of something produced by a person, machine, or industry. ➤ the process of producing something. ➤ the power, energy, etc. supplied by a device or system. **2** Electronics a place where power or information leaves a system. ● v. (**-putting**; past and past part. **-put** or **-putted**) (of a computer) produce or supply (data).

**outrage** ● n. an extremely strong reaction of anger or indignation. ➤ a cause of outrage. ● v. **1** arouse outrage in. **2** violate or infringe flagrantly.

– ORIGIN ME: from OFr. *ou(l)trage*, based on L. *ultra* 'beyond'; influenced by the belief that the word is a compound of **OUT** and **RAGE**.

**outrageous** ● adj. **1** shockingly bad or excessive. **2** very bold and unusual.

– DERIVATIVES **outrageously** adv. **outrageousness** n.

**outran** past of **OUTRUN**.

**outrank** ● v. have a higher rank than. ➤ be better or more important than.

**outré** /'u:treɪ/ ● adj. unusual and typically rather shocking.

– ORIGIN Fr., lit. 'exceeded', past part. of *outrer* (see **OUTRAGE**).

**outreach** ● v. /aʊt'ri:tʃ/ reach further than. ➤ poetic/literary reach out. ● n. /'aʊtri:tʃ/ **1** the extent or length of reaching out. **2** an organization's involvement with or influence in the community.

**out relief** ● n. Brit. historical assistance for very poor people not living in a workhouse.

**outride** ● v. (past **-rode**; past part. **-ridden**) **1** ride better, faster, or further than. **2** archaic (of a ship) come safely through (a storm).

**outrider** • **n.** a person in a vehicle or on horseback who escorts or guards another vehicle. ➤ US a mounted official who escorts racehorses to the starting post. ➤ US a mounted herdsman who prevents cattle from straying.
– DERIVATIVES **outriding** n.

**outrigger** • **n.** a beam, spar, or framework projecting from or over a boat's side. ➤ a stabilizing float or secondary hull fixed parallel to a canoe or small ship. ➤ a boat fitted with such a structure. ➤ a similar projecting support in another structure.
– DERIVATIVES **outrigged** adj.
– ORIGIN C18: perh. influenced by the obs. naut. term *outligger*, in the same sense.

**outright** • **adv. 1** altogether. **2** openly. **3** immediately. ➤ not by degrees or instalments. • **adj. 1** open and direct. **2** complete.

**outro** • **n.** (pl. **-os**) informal the concluding section of a piece of music or a radio or television programme.
– ORIGIN 1970s: from **OUT**, on the pattern of *intro*.

**outrode** past of **OUTRIDE**.

**outrun** • **v.** (**-running**; past **-ran**; past part. **-run**) **1** run or travel faster or further than. ➤ escape from. **2** exceed.

**outsell** • **v.** (past and past part. **-sold**) be sold in greater quantities than. ➤ sell more of something than.

**outset** • **n.** the start or beginning.

**outshine** • **v.** (past and past part. **-shone**) **1** shine more brightly than. **2** be much better than.

**outside** • **n.** the external side or surface of something. ➤ the part of a path nearer to a road. ➤ the side of a bend or curve where the edge is longer. ➤ (**outsides**) the outer sheets of a ream of paper. ➤ the external appearance of someone or something. • **adj. 1** situated on or near the outside. ➤ (in hockey, soccer, etc.) denoting positions nearer to the sides of the field. **2** not of or belonging to a particular group. ➤ beyond one's immediate personal concerns. • **prep. & adv. 1** situated or moving beyond the boundaries of. ➤ not being a member of. ➤ (in hockey, soccer, etc.) closer to the side of the field than. **2** beyond the limits or scope of.
– PHRASES **at the outside** at the most. **get outside of** informal eat or drink. **an outside chance** a remote possibility. **outside of** informal, chiefly N. Amer. beyond the boundaries of. ➤ apart from.

**outside broadcast** • **n.** Brit. a radio or television programme recorded or broadcast live on location.

**outside interest** • **n.** an interest not connected with one's work or studies.

**outsider** • **n. 1** a person who does not belong to a particular group. ➤ a person not accepted by or isolating themselves from society. **2** a competitor thought to have little chance of success.

**outsize** • **adj.** (also **outsized**) exceptionally large. • **n.** an outsize person or thing.

**outskirts** • **pl. n.** the outer parts of a town or city.

**outsmart** • **v.** outwit.

**outsold** past and past participle of **OUTSELL**.

**outsole** • **n.** the outer sole of a boot or shoe.

**outsource** • **v.** obtain by contract from an outside supplier. ➤ contract (work) out.

**outspan** S. African • **v.** (**-spanned**, **-spanning**) unharness (an animal) from a wagon. • **n.** a place for grazing or camping on a wagon journey.
– ORIGIN C19: from Du. *uitspannen* 'unyoke'.

**outspoken** • **adj.** frank in stating one's opinions.
– DERIVATIVES **outspokenly** adv. **outspokenness** n.

**outspread** • **adj.** fully extended or expanded. • **v.** (past and past part. **-spread**) poetic/literary spread out.

**outstanding** • **adj. 1** exceptionally good. **2** clearly noticeable. **3** not yet done. ➤ (of a debt) unpaid.
– DERIVATIVES **outstandingly** adv.

**outstare** • **v.** stare at (someone) for longer than they can stare back.

**outstation** • **n.** a branch of an organization situated far from its headquarters. ➤ Austral./NZ a part of a farming estate that is separate from the main estate. ➤ Austral. an autonomous Aboriginal community situated far from a centre on which it depends.

**outstay** • **v. 1** stay beyond the limit of (one's expected or permitted time). **2** last longer than (another competitor).

**outstretch** • **v.** [usu. as adj. **outstretched**] **1** extend or stretch out. **2** go beyond the limit of.

**outstrip** • **v.** (**-stripped**, **-stripping**) move faster than and overtake. ➤ exceed.

**outswinger** • **n.** Cricket a ball bowled with a swerve or swing from the leg to the off side.
– DERIVATIVES **outswing** n. **outswinging** adj.

**out-take** • **n.** a sequence filmed or recorded for a film, programme, etc. but cut from the final version.

**out-thrust** • **adj.** extended outward. • **n.** a thing which projects outward.

**out-top** • **v.** rare surpass in number, amount, height, etc.

**out tray** • **n.** a tray on a desk for letters and documents that have been dealt with.

**out-turn** • **n. 1** the amount of something produced. **2** a result or consequence.

**outvote** • **v.** defeat by gaining more votes.

**outwait** • **v.** wait longer than.

**outward** • **adj. 1** of, on, or from the outside. ➤ relating to the external appearance of something rather than its true nature. ➤ archaic outer. **2** going out or away from a place. • **adv.** outwards.
– DERIVATIVES **outwardly** adv. **outwardness** n.

**outward bound** • **adj.** going away from home. • **n.** (**Outward Bound**) trademark an organization providing naval and adventure training and other outdoor activities for young people.

**outwards** • **adv.** towards the outside; away from the centre or a place.

**outwash** • **n.** material carried away from a glacier by meltwater and deposited beyond the moraine.

**outwatch** • **v.** archaic watch (something) until it disappears. ➤ keep awake beyond the end of.

**outwear** • **v.** (past **-wore**; past part. **-worn**) last longer than.

**outweigh** • **v.** be heavier, greater, or more significant than.

**outwent** past of **OUTGO**.

**outwit** • **v.** (**-witted**, **-witting**) deceive by greater ingenuity.

**outwith** • **prep.** Scottish outside; beyond.

**outwore** past of **OUTWEAR**.

**outwork** • **n. 1** an outer section of a fortification or system of defence. **2** Brit. work done outside the factory or office which provides it.
– DERIVATIVES **outworker** n. **outworking** n.

**outworn** past participle of **OUTWEAR**. • **adj. 1** out of date. **2** worn out.

**ouzel** /ˈuːz(ə)l/ (also **ousel**) • **n.** used in names of birds resembling the blackbird, e.g. **ring ouzel**.
– ORIGIN OE *ōsle* 'blackbird', of Gmc origin.

**ouzo** /ˈuːzəʊ/ • **n.** a Greek aniseed-flavoured spirit.
– ORIGIN from mod. Gk.

**ova** plural form of **OVUM**.

**oval** • **adj.** having a rounded and slightly elongated outline; egg-shaped. • **n.** an oval body, object, or design. ➤ an oval sports field or track. ➤ a ground for Australian Rules football.
– DERIVATIVES **ovality** n. **ovalness** n.
– ORIGIN C16: from Fr., or mod. L. *ovalis*, from L. *ovum* 'egg'.

**ovalbumin** /əʊˈvalbjʊmɪn/ • **n.** Biochemistry albumin from the white of eggs.
– ORIGIN C19: from L. *ovi albumen* 'albumen of egg', alt. on the pattern of *albumin*.

**Oval Office** • **n.** the office of the US President in the White House.

**Ovambo** /əʊˈvambəʊ/ • **n.** (pl. same or **-os**) **1** a member of a people of northern Namibia. **2** the Bantu language of this people.
– ORIGIN a local name, from *ova-* (prefix denoting a pl.) +

*ambo* 'man of leisure'.

**ovarian** /əʊˈvɛːrɪən/ ● **adj.** of or relating to an ovary or the ovaries.

**ovariectomy** /ˌəʊvərɪˈɛktəmi/ ● **n.** (pl. **-ies**) surgical removal of one or both ovaries.

**ovariotomy** /ˌəʊvərɪˈɒtəmi/ ● **n.** another term for **OVARIECTOMY**.

**ovary** /ˈəʊv(ə)ri/ ● **n.** (pl. **-ies**) **1** a female reproductive organ in which ova or eggs are produced. **2** Botany the base of the carpel of a flower, containing one or more ovules.
– DERIVATIVES **ovaritis** n.
– ORIGIN C17: from mod. L. *ovarium*, from L. *ovum* 'egg'.

**ovate**[1] /ˈəʊveɪt/ ● **adj.** chiefly Biology oval; egg-shaped.
– ORIGIN C18: from L. *ovatus* 'egg-shaped'.

**ovate**[2] /ˈɒvət/ ● **n.** a member of an order of Welsh bards recognized at an Eisteddfod. ➤historical an ancient Celtic priest or natural philosopher.
– ORIGIN C18: from the Gk pl. *ouateis* 'soothsayers'.

**ovation** ● **n.** **1** a sustained show of appreciation, especially applause, from an audience. **2** a processional entrance into ancient Rome by a victorious commander, of lesser honour than a triumph.
– ORIGIN C16: from L. *ovatio(n-)*, from *ovare* 'exult'.

**oven** ● **n.** **1** an enclosed compartment, usually part of a cooker, for cooking food. **2** a small furnace or kiln.
– ORIGIN OE *ofen*, of Gmc origin.

**ovenbird** ● **n.** **1** a small, drab tropical American bird which makes a domed oven-like nest of mud. [Family Furnariidae: numerous species.] **2** a brown North American warbler that builds a domed nest of vegetation on the ground. [*Seiurus aurocapillus*.]

**oven glove** ● **n.** a padded glove for handling hot dishes from an oven.

**ovenproof** ● **adj.** suitable for use in an oven.

**oven-ready** ● **adj.** (of food) prepared before sale for cooking in an oven.

**ovenware** ● **n.** ovenproof dishes.

**over** ● **prep.** **1** extending upwards from or above. ➤above so as to cover or protect. **2** beyond. **3** expressing passage or trajectory across. ➤beyond and falling or hanging from. **4** expressing duration. **5** by means of. **6** at a higher level or layer than. ➤expressing authority or control. ➤expressing preference. ➤expressing majority. **7** higher or more than (a specified number or quantity). **8** on the subject of. ● **adv.** **1** expressing passage or trajectory across an area. ➤beyond and falling or hanging from a point. **2** in or to the place indicated. **3** used to express action and result. ➤finished. **4** used to express repetition of a process. ● **n.** Cricket a sequence of six balls bowled by a bowler from one end of the pitch.
– PHRASES **be over** be no longer affected by. **over against** adjacent to. ➤in contrast with. **over and above** in addition to. **over and out** indicating that a message on a two-way radio has finished.
– ORIGIN OE *ofer*, of Gmc origin.

**over-** ● **prefix** **1** excessively: *overambitious*. ➤completely: *overjoyed*. **2** upper; outer; extra: *overcoat*. ➤over; above: *overcast*.

**over-abundant** ● **adj.** excessive in quantity.
– DERIVATIVES **over-abundance** n. **over-abundantly** adv.

**overachieve** ● **v.** do better than expected, especially at school.
– DERIVATIVES **overachievement** n. **overachiever** n.

**overact** ● **v.** act a role in an exaggerated manner.

**overactive** ● **adj.** excessively active.
– DERIVATIVES **overactivity** n.

**overage** ● **n.** an excess or surplus, especially an amount greater than estimated.

**over age** ● **adj.** over a certain age limit.

**overall** ● **adj.** total. ➤taking everything into account. ● **adv.** taken as a whole. ● **n.** **1** (also **overalls**) Brit. a loose-fitting coat or pair of dungarees worn over ordinary clothes for protection. **2** (**overalls**) Brit. close-fitting trousers worn as part of an army uniform on formal occasions.
– DERIVATIVES **overalled** adj.

**overambitious** ● **adj.** excessively ambitious.
– DERIVATIVES **overambition** n. **overambitiously** adv.

**overanxious** ● **adj.** excessively anxious.
– DERIVATIVES **overanxiety** n. **overanxiously** adv.

**overarch** ● **v.** **1** form an arch over. **2** [as adj. **overarching**] all-embracing.

**overarm** ● **adj.** & **adv.** (of a throw, stroke with a racket, etc.) made with the hand or arm above shoulder-level.

**overate** past of **OVEREAT**.

**overawe** ● **v.** (usu. **be overawed**) subdue or inhibit with a sense of awe.

**overbalance** ● **v.** chiefly Brit. **1** fall or cause to fall due to loss of balance. **2** outweigh. ● **n.** archaic excess of weight, value, or amount.

**overbear** ● **v.** (past **-bore**; past part. **-borne**) overcome by emotional pressure or physical force.

**overbearing** ● **adj.** unpleasantly overpowering.
– DERIVATIVES **overbearingly** adv. **overbearingness** n.

**overbid** ● **v.** (**-bidding**; past and past part. **-bid**) **1** (in an auction) make a higher bid than a previous bid. **2** Bridge bid more than is warranted or manageable. ● **n.** a bid higher than another or higher than is justified.
– DERIVATIVES **overbidder** n.

**overbite** ● **n.** Dentistry the overlapping of the lower teeth by the upper.

**overblouse** ● **n.** a blouse designed to be worn without being tucked into a skirt or trousers.

**overblown** ● **adj.** **1** excessively inflated or pretentious. **2** (of a flower) past its prime.

**overboard** ● **adv.** from a ship into the water.
– PHRASES **go overboard** **1** be very enthusiastic. **2** go too far.

**overbook** ● **v.** accept more reservations for (a flight or hotel) than there is room for.

**overboot** ● **n.** a boot worn over another boot or shoe for protection or warmth.

**overbore** past of **OVERBEAR**.

**overborne** past participle of **OVERBEAR**.

**overbought** past and past participle of **OVERBUY**.

**overbridge** ● **n.** a bridge over a railway or road.

**overbrim** ● **v.** archaic flow over the brim of.

**overbrimming** ● **adj.** abundant.

**overbuild** ● **v.** (past and past part. **-built**) **1** put up too many buildings in. ➤build too many of. ➤build elaborately. **2** [often as noun **overbuilding**] build on top of.

**overburden** ● **v.** burden excessively. ● **n.** **1** rock or soil overlying a mineral deposit, archaeological site, etc. **2** an excessive burden.
– DERIVATIVES **overburdensome** /əʊvəˈbəːd(ə)ns(ə)m/ adj.

**overbuy** ● **v.** (past and past part. **-bought**) buy too many or too much of.

**overcall** Bridge ● **v.** bid higher than an opponent. ● **n.** an act of overcalling.

**overcame** past of **OVERCOME**.

**overcapacity** ● **n.** an excess of productive capacity.

**overcapitalize** (also **-ise**) ● **v.** [usu. as adj. **overcapitalized**] provide with an excessive amount of capital. ➤overestimate the capital value of (a company).

**overcareful** ● **adj.** excessively careful.
– DERIVATIVES **overcarefully** adv.

**overcast** ● **adj.** **1** (of the sky or weather) cloudy; dull. **2** edged with stitching to prevent fraying. ● **n.** cloud covering a large part of the sky. ● **v.** (past and past part. **-cast**) **1** cover with clouds or shade. **2** stitch over (a raw edge) to prevent fraying.

**overcautious** ● **adj.** excessively cautious.
– DERIVATIVES **overcaution** n. **overcautiously** adv. **overcautiousness** n.

**overcharge** ● **v.** **1** charge too high a price. **2** put too much electric charge into (a battery).

**overcheck**[1] ● **n.** a check pattern superimposed on a colour or design.

**overcheck**[2] ● **n.** a strap passing over a horse's head between the ears, to pull up on the bit and make breathing easier.

**overclass** ● **n.** a privileged, wealthy, or powerful section of society.

**overcloud** ● v. mar, dim, or obscure.

**overcoat** ● n. **1** a long warm coat. **2** a top, final layer of paint or varnish.

**overcome** ● v. (past **-came**; past part. **-come**) succeed in dealing with (a problem). ➤ defeat. ➤ (usu. **be overcome**) (of an emotion) overwhelm.

**overcommit** ● v. (**-committed**, **-committing**) oblige to do more than is possible. ➤ allocate more (resources) than can be provided.

– DERIVATIVES **overcommitment** n.

**overcompensate** ● v. take excessive measures to compensate for something.

– DERIVATIVES **overcompensating** adj. **overcompensatingly** adv. **overcompensation** n. **overcompensatory** adj.

**overconfident** ● adj. excessively confident.

– DERIVATIVES **overconfidence** n. **overconfidently** adv.

**overcook** ● v. cook too much or for too long.

**overcritical** ● adj. inclined to find fault too readily.

**overcrop** ● v. (**-cropped**, **-cropping**) [usu. as noun **overcropping**] exhaust (land) by the continuous growing of crops.

**overcrowd** ● v. [often as noun **overcrowding**] fill beyond what is usual or comfortable.

**overcurious** ● adj. excessively curious.

– DERIVATIVES **overcuriosity** /ˌəʊvəkjʊərɪˈɒsɪti/ n.

**overdelicate** ● adj. excessively delicate.

– DERIVATIVES **overdelicacy** n.

**overdetermine** ● v. technical determine, account for, or cause in more than one way or with more conditions than are necessary.

– DERIVATIVES **overdetermination** n.

**overdevelop** ● v. (**-developed**, **-developing**) develop to excess.

– DERIVATIVES **overdevelopment** n.

**overdo** ● v. (**-does**; past **-did**; past part. **-done**) exaggerate. ➤ use too much of. ➤ (**overdo it/things**) exhaust oneself. ➤ [often as adj. **overdone**] overcook.

– DERIVATIVES **overdoer** n.

– ORIGIN OE *oferdōn* (see OVER-, DO[1]).

**overdose** ● n. an excessive and dangerous dose of a drug. ● v. take an overdose. ➤ give an overdose to.

– DERIVATIVES **overdosage** /ˈəʊvəˈdəʊsɪdʒ/ n.

**overdraft** ● n. a deficit in a bank account caused by drawing more money than the account holds.

**overdramatize** (also **-ise**) ● v. react to or portray in an excessively dramatic way.

– DERIVATIVES **overdramatic** adj.

**overdraw** ● v. (past **-drew**; past part. **-drawn**) **1** (usu. **be overdrawn**) draw more money from (a bank account) than it holds. ➤ (**be overdrawn**) have taken more money from an account than it holds. **2** exaggerate.

**overdress** ● v. (usu. **be overdressed**) dress too elaborately or formally. ● n. chiefly Brit. a dress worn over other clothing.

**overdrive** ● n. **1** a gear in a motor vehicle providing a gear ratio higher than that of the usual top gear. **2** a state of high or excessive activity. **3** a mechanism allowing the exceeding of a normal operating level in equipment, especially the amplifier of an electric guitar. ● v. [usu. as adj. **overdriven**] **1** drive or work to exhaustion. **2** give (an electric guitar) a distorted sound.

**overdub** ● v. (**-dubbed**, **-dubbing**) record (additional sounds) on an existing recording. ● n. an instance of overdubbing.

**overdue** ● adj. past the time when due. ➤ not having arrived, been born, etc. at the expected time. ➤ (of a library book) retained longer than allowed.

**overeager** ● adj. excessively eager.

– DERIVATIVES **overeagerly** adv. **overeagerness** n.

**over easy** ● adj. N. Amer. (of an egg) fried on both sides, with the yolk remaining slightly liquid.

**overeat** ● v. (past **-ate**; past part. **-eaten**) [usu. as noun **overeating**] eat too much.

– DERIVATIVES **overeater** n.

**over-egg** ● v. (in phr. **over-egg the pudding**) go too far in doing something; exaggerate.

**over-elaborate** ● adj. excessively elaborate. ● v. explain or treat in excessive detail.

– DERIVATIVES **over-elaborately** adv. **over-elaborateness** n. **over-elaboration** n.

**overemotional** ● adj. excessively emotional.

– DERIVATIVES **overemotionally** adv.

**overemphasize** (also **-ise**) ● v. place excessive emphasis on.

– DERIVATIVES **overemphasis** n.

**overenthusiasm** ● n. excessive enthusiasm.

– DERIVATIVES **overenthusiastic** adj. **overenthusiastically** adv.

**overestimate** ● v. form too high an estimate of. ● n. an excessively high estimate.

– DERIVATIVES **overestimation** n.

**overexcite** ● v. [usu. as adj. **overexcited**] excite excessively.

– DERIVATIVES **overexcitable** adj. **overexcitement** n.

**over-exercise** ● v. exercise to excess. ● n. excessive exercise.

**overexert** ● v. (**overexert oneself**) exert oneself excessively.

– DERIVATIVES **overexertion** n.

**overexpose** ● v. expose too much.

– DERIVATIVES **overexposure** n.

**overextend** ● v. (usu. **be overextended**) **1** make too long. **2** impose an excessive burden on.

– DERIVATIVES **overextension** n.

**overfall** ● n. **1** a turbulent stretch of open water caused by a strong current or tide over a submarine ridge, or by a meeting of currents. **2** a place where surplus water overflows from a dam, pool, etc.

**overfamiliar** ● adj. **1** too well known. ➤ (**overfamiliar with**) too well acquainted with. **2** inappropriately informal.

– DERIVATIVES **overfamiliarity** n.

**overfeed** ● v. (past and past part. **-fed**) feed too much.

**overfill** ● v. fill to excess.

**overfine** ● adj. excessively fine.

**overfish** ● v. deplete (a body of water, stock of fish, etc.) by too much fishing.

**overflow** ● v. **1** flow over the brim of a receptacle. ➤ spread over or cover. **2** be excessively full or crowded. **3** (**overflow with**) be very full of (an emotion). ● n. **1** the overflowing of a liquid. ➤ the excess not able to be accommodated by a space. **2** (also **overflow pipe**) an outlet for excess water. **3** Computing the generation of a number which is too large for the assigned location.

**overfly** ● v. (**-flies**; past **-flew**; past part. **-flown**) fly over or beyond.

– DERIVATIVES **overflight** n.

**overfold** ● n. **1** a part of something folded over another part. **2** Geology a fold in which both the limbs dip in the same direction.

**overfond** ● adj. excessively fond.

– DERIVATIVES **overfondly** adv. **overfondness** n.

**overfull** ● adj. excessively full.

**overgarment** ● n. a garment worn over others.

**overgeneralize** (also **-ise**) ● v. generalize more widely than is justified.

– DERIVATIVES **overgeneralization** n.

**overgenerous** ● adj. excessively generous.

– DERIVATIVES **overgenerously** adv.

**overglaze** ● n. decoration or a second glaze applied to glazed ceramic. ● adj. (of decoration) applied on a glazed surface.

**overgraze** ● v. graze (grassland) too heavily.

**overground** ● adv. & adj. on or above the ground.

**overgrow** ● v. (past **-grew**; past part. **-grown**) grow or spread over.

**overgrown** ● adj. **1** grown over with vegetation. **2** grown too large. ➤ chiefly derogatory used in likening an adult to a child.

**overgrowth** ● n. excessive growth.

**overhand** • adj. & adv. **1** overarm. **2** with the palm downward or inward.

**overhand knot** • n. a simple knot made by forming a loop and passing a free end through it.

**overhang** • v. (past and past part. **-hung**) **1** hang over. **2** loom over. • n. an overhanging part.

**overhaul** • v. **1** examine (machinery or equipment) and repair it if necessary. **2** Brit. overtake. • n. an act of overhauling.
– ORIGIN C17 (orig. in naut. use in the sense 'release (rope tackle) by slackening'): from **OVER-** + **HAUL**.

**overhead** • adv. above one's head; in the sky. • adj. **1** situated overhead. **2** (of a driving mechanism) above the object driven. **3** (of an expense) incurred in the upkeep or running of premises or a business. • n. **1** an overhead cost or expense. **2** a transparency for use with an overhead projector.

**overhead projector** • n. a device that projects an enlarged image of a transparency by means of an overhead mirror.

**overhear** • v. (past and past part. **-heard**) hear accidentally or secretly.

**overheat** • v. **1** make or become too hot. **2** Economics (of an economy) show marked inflation when increased demand results in rising prices.

**overindulge** • v. **1** indulge to excess. **2** gratify the wishes of to an excessive extent.
– DERIVATIVES **overindulgence** n. **overindulgent** adj.

**overinflated** • adj. **1** (of a price or value) excessive. ➤ exaggerated. **2** filled with too much air.

**overissue** • v. (**-issues**, **-issued**, **-issuing**) issue (banknotes, shares, etc.) beyond the authorized amount or the issuer's ability to pay. • n. the action of overissuing.

**overjoyed** • adj. extremely happy.

**overkill** • n. the amount by which destruction or the capacity for destruction exceeds what is necessary. ➤ excessive use, treatment, or action.

**overladen** • adj. bearing too large a load.

**overlaid** past and past participle of **OVERLAY**[1].

**overlain** past participle of **OVERLIE**.

**overland** • adj. & adv. by land. • v. Austral./NZ historical drive (livestock) over a long distance. ➤ travel a long distance by land.

**overlander** • n. Austral./NZ historical **1** a person who overlands livestock. **2** informal a tramp.

**overlap** • v. (**-lapped**, **-lapping**) extend over so as to cover partly. ➤ partly coincide. • n. an overlapping part or amount. ➤ an instance of overlapping.

**overlarge** • adj. too large.

**overlay**[1] • v. (past and past part. **-laid**) (often **be overlaid with**) **1** coat the surface of. **2** lie on top of. **3** (of a quality or feeling) become more prominent than (a previous one). • n. **1** a covering. ➤ a transparent sheet over artwork or a map, giving additional detail. ➤ a graphical computer display which can be superimposed on another. **2** Computing replacement of a block of stored instructions or data with another.

**overlay**[2] past of **OVERLIE**.

**overleaf** • adv. on the other side of the page.

**overleap** • v. (past and past part. **-leaped** or **-leapt**) archaic **1** jump over or across. **2** omit; ignore.

**overlie** • v. (**-lying**; past **-lay**; past part. **-lain**) lie on top of.

**overload** • v. **1** load excessively. **2** put too great a demand on (an electrical system). • n. an excessive amount.

**overlock** • v. prevent fraying of (an edge of cloth) by oversewing it.
– DERIVATIVES **overlocker** n.

**overlong** • adj. & adv. too long.

**overlook** • v. **1** fail to notice. ➤ ignore or disregard. ➤ pass over in favour of another. **2** have a view of from above. **3** archaic supervise. **4** archaic bewitch with the evil eye. • n. N. Amer. a commanding position or view.

**overlooker** • n. a supervisor.

**overlord** • n. a ruler, especially a feudal lord.
– DERIVATIVES **overlordship** n.

**overly** • adv. excessively.

**overlying** present participle of **OVERLIE**.

**overman** • v. (**-manned**, **-manning**) provide with more people than necessary. • n. (pl. **-men**) **1** an overseer in a colliery. **2** Philosophy another term for **SUPERMAN**. [translation of Nietzsche's *Übermensch*.]

**overmantel** • n. an ornamental structure over a mantelpiece.

**overmaster** • v. poetic/literary overcome.

**overmatch** • v. [usu. as adj. **overmatched**] chiefly N. Amer. be stronger, better armed, or more skilful than.

**overmighty** • adj. Brit. excessively powerful.

**overmuch** • adv., det., & pron. too much.

**overnice** • adj. dated excessively fussy or fastidious.

**overnight** • adv. **1** for the duration of a night. ➤ during the course of a night. **2** suddenly. • adj. **1** for use overnight. ➤ done or happening overnight. **2** sudden. • v. stay overnight. ➤ N. Amer. convey (goods) overnight. • n. a stop or stay lasting one night.

**overnighter** • n. **1** a person who stays overnight. ➤ N. Amer. an overnight trip or stay. **2** an overnight bag.

**overpaid** past and past participle of **OVERPAY**.

**overpaint** • v. cover with paint. • n. paint added as a covering layer.

**overparted** • adj. (of an actor or singer) having too difficult a part or too many parts to play.

**over-particular** • adj. fussy.

**overpass** • n. a bridge by which a road or railway line passes over another. • v. **1** rare surpass. **2** archaic come to the end of.

**overpay** • v. (past and past part. **-paid**) pay too much.
– DERIVATIVES **overpayment** n.

**overpitch** • v. [often as adj. **overpitched**] **1** Cricket bowl (a ball) so that it pitches or would pitch too far. **2** Brit. exaggerate.

**overplay** • v. overemphasize.
– PHRASES **overplay one's hand** spoil one's chance of success through excessive confidence.

**overplus** • n. dated a surplus.
– ORIGIN ME: partial translation of Fr. *surplus* or med. L. *superplus*.

**overpopulate** • v. [usu. as adj. **overpopulated**] populate (an area) in too large numbers.
– DERIVATIVES **overpopulation** n.

**overpower** • v. defeat with superior strength. ➤ overwhelm.
– DERIVATIVES **overpowering** adj. **overpoweringly** adv.

**overprice** • v. [often as adj. **overpriced**] charge too high a price for.

**overprint** • v. **1** print additional matter on. ➤ print with (additional matter). **2** print too many or too much of. **3** Photography make (a print) darker than intended. • n. additional matter overprinted. ➤ an overprinted postage stamp.

**overproduce** • v. **1** produce an excess of. **2** record or produce (a song or film) in an excessively elaborate way.
– DERIVATIVES **overproduction** n.

**overproof** • adj. containing more alcohol than proof spirit does.

**overprotective** • adj. excessively protective.
– DERIVATIVES **overprotect** v. **overprotection** n. **overprotectiveness** n.

**overqualified** • adj. too highly qualified.

**overran** past of **OVERRUN**.

**overrate** • v. [often as adj. **overrated**] rate more highly than is deserved.

**overreach** • v. **1** reach too far. ➤ (**overreach oneself**) try to do more than is possible. **2** (of a horse, dog, etc.) bring the hind feet so far forward that they fall alongside or strike the forefeet. **3** outwit. • n. an injury to a horse's forefoot due to overreaching.

**overreacher** • n. N. Amer. a fraudster.

**overreact** • v. react more emotionally or forcibly than is justified.
– DERIVATIVES **overreaction** n.

**over-refine** • v. refine too much.

– DERIVATIVES **over-refinement** n.

**override** ● v. (past **-rode**; past part. **-ridden**) **1** use one's authority to reject or cancel. **2** interrupt the action of (an automatic function). **3** be more important than. **4** overlap. **5** travel or move over. ● n. **1** the action or process of overriding. **2** a device on a machine for overriding an automatic function. **3** an excess or increase on a budget, salary, or cost.

**overrider** ● n. Brit. either of a pair of projecting pieces on the bumper of a car.

**overriding** ● adj. **1** more important than any other considerations. **2** extending or moving over.

**overripe** ● adj. too ripe.

**overrode** past of **OVERRIDE**.

**overruff** ● v. (in card games) play a trump that is higher than one already played in the same trick. ● n. an act of overruffing.

**overrule** ● v. reject or disallow by exercising one's superior authority.

**overrun** ● v. (**-running**; past **-ran**; past part. **-run**) **1** spread over or occupy (a place) in large numbers. **2** move or extend over or beyond. **3** exceed (an expected or allowed time or cost). **4** rotate faster than (another part of a machine). ● n. **1** an instance of overrunning. **2** a clear area beyond the end of a runway. **3** the movement of a vehicle at a speed greater than is imparted by the engine.

– ORIGIN OE *oferyrnan* (see **OVER-**, **RUN**).

**oversail** ● v. (of a part of a building) project beyond (a lower part).

– ORIGIN C17 (orig. Scots): from **OVER** + Fr. *saillir* 'jut out'.

**oversampling** ● n. Electronics the technique of increasing the apparent sampling frequency of a digital signal by repeating each digit a number of times, in order to facilitate the subsequent filtering of unwanted noise.

**oversaw** past of **OVERSEE**.

**overscan** ● n. the facility on some computer screens or televisions to enlarge the picture size so that the edges of the picture are lost.

**overseas** ● adv. in or to a foreign country. ● adj. from, to, or relating to a foreign country. ● n. foreign countries regarded collectively.

**oversee** ● v. (**-sees**; past **-saw**; past part. **-seen**) supervise.

– DERIVATIVES **overseer** n.

– ORIGIN OE *oferséon* 'look at from above'.

**oversell** ● v. (past and past part. **-sold**) **1** sell more of (something) than exists or can be delivered. **2** exaggerate the merits of.

**oversensitive** ● adj. excessively sensitive.

– DERIVATIVES **oversensitiveness** n. **oversensitivity** n.

**overset** ● v. (**-setting**; past and past part. **-set**) **1** upset emotionally. **2** archaic overturn.

**oversew** ● v. (past part. **-sewn** or **-sewed**) sew (the edges of two pieces of fabric) with every stitch passing over the join. ➤join the sections of (a book) in such a way.

**oversexed** ● adj. having unusually strong sexual desires.

**overshadow** ● v. **1** tower above and cast a shadow over. **2** cast a gloom over. **3** appear more prominent or important than. **4** be more impressive or successful than.

– ORIGIN OE *ofersceadwian*.

**overshoe** ● n. a shoe worn over a normal shoe, typically made either of rubber to protect the normal shoe or of felt to protect a floor surface.

**overshoot** ● v. (past and past part. **-shot**) **1** go past (a point) unintentionally. **2** exceed (a financial target or limit). ● n. an act of overshooting.

**overshot** past and past participle of **OVERSHOOT**. ● adj. **1** (of a waterwheel) turned by water falling on to it from a channel. **2** denoting an upper jaw which projects beyond the lower jaw.

**overside** ● adv. over the side of a ship.

**oversight** ● n. **1** an unintentional failure to notice or do something. **2** the action of overseeing.

**oversimplify** ● v. (**-ies**, **-ied**) [often as adj. **oversimplified**] simplify (something) so much that a distorted impression of it is given.

– DERIVATIVES **oversimplification** n.

**oversite** ● n. a layer of concrete used to seal the earth under the ground floor of a house.

**oversized** (also **oversize**) ● adj. bigger than the usual size.

**overskirt** ● n. an outer skirt forming a second layer over a skirt or dress.

**overslaugh** /ˈəʊvəslɔː/ ● v. US pass over (someone) in favour of another.

– ORIGIN C18: from Du. *overslag* (n.), from *overslaan* 'pass over'.

**oversleep** ● v. (past and past part. **-slept**) sleep longer or later than one has intended.

**oversleeve** ● n. a protective sleeve covering an ordinary sleeve.

**oversold** past and past participle of **OVERSELL**.

**oversoul** ● n. (in Transcendentalism) a divine spirit supposed to pervade the universe and to encompass all human souls.

**overspend** ● v. (past and past part. **-spent**) spend too much. ● n. an act of overspending.

**overspill** ● n. **1** an instance of something spilling over. **2** Brit. a surplus population moving from an overcrowded area to live elsewhere.

**overspread** ● v. (past and past part. **-spread**) cover the surface of; spread over.

– ORIGIN OE *ofersprǣdan*.

**overstaff** ● v. provide with more members of staff than are necessary.

**overstate** ● v. state too emphatically; exaggerate.

– DERIVATIVES **overstatement** n.

**overstay** ● v. stay longer than the duration or limits of.

– DERIVATIVES **overstayer** n.

**oversteer** ● v. turn or cause to turn more sharply than is desirable. ● n. the tendency of a vehicle to oversteer.

**overstep** ● v. (**-stepped**, **-stepping**) go beyond (a prescribed or generally accepted limit).

– PHRASES **overstep** (or **overshoot**) **the mark** go beyond what is intended or acceptable.

**overstimulate** ● v. stimulate excessively.

– DERIVATIVES **overstimulation** n.

**overstitch** ● n. a stitch made over an edge or over another stitch. ● v. sew with an overstitch.

**overstock** ● v. stock with more than is necessary or required. ➤put more animals in (an area) than it is capable of supporting in terms of food or space. ● n. chiefly N. Amer. a supply or quantity in excess of demand.

**overstrain** ● v. subject to an excessive demand on strength, resources, or abilities. ● n. the action or result of overstraining.

**overstress** ● v. **1** subject to too much stress. **2** lay too much emphasis on. ● n. excessive stress.

**overstretch** ● v. [often as adj. **overstretched**] stretch too much.

**overstrike** ● n. the superimposing of one printed character or one coin design on another.

– DERIVATIVES **overstriking** n.

**overstrung** ● adj. (of a piano) with strings in sets crossing each other obliquely.

**overstuff** ● v. [usu. as adj. **overstuffed**] cover (furniture) completely with a thick layer of stuffing.

**oversubscribed** ● adj. **1** (of something for sale) applied for in greater quantities than are available. **2** (of a course or institution) having more applications than available places.

**oversubtle** ● adj. making excessively fine distinctions.

**overt** /əʊˈvəːt, ˈəʊvət/ ● adj. done or shown openly.

– DERIVATIVES **overtly** adv. **overtness** n.

– ORIGIN ME: from OFr., past part. of *ovrir* 'to open', from L. *aperire*.

**overtake** ● v. (past **-took**; past part. **-taken**) **1** catch up with and pass while travelling in the same direction. **2** become greater or more successful than. **3** come suddenly or unexpectedly upon.

**overtask** ● v. impose too much work on.

**overtax** ● v. tax excessively.

– DERIVATIVES **overtaxation** n.

**overthrow** • v. (past **-threw**; past part. **-thrown**) **1** remove forcibly from power. **2** put an end to through force. **3** throw (a ball) further than the intended distance. ➤ chiefly N. Amer. throw a ball beyond (a receiving player). • n. **1** a removal from power; a defeat or downfall. **2** (in cricket, baseball, etc.) a throw which sends a ball past its intended recipient or target. ➤ a score made because the ball has been overthrown. **3** a panel of wrought-iron work above an arch or gateway.

**overthrust** • v. (past and past part. **-thrust**) Geology force (a body of rock) over another formation.

**overtime** • n. **1** time worked in addition to one's normal working hours. **2** N. Amer. extra time played at the end of a tie game. • adv. in addition to normal working hours.

**overtire** • v. exhaust.

– DERIVATIVES **overtired** adj.

**overtone** • n. **1** a musical tone which is a part of the harmonic series above a fundamental note, and may be heard with it. **2** a subtle or subsidiary quality, implication, or connotation. **3** Physics a component of any oscillation whose frequency is an integral multiple of the fundamental frequency.

– ORIGIN C19: from **OVER-** + **TONE**, suggested by Ger. *Oberton*.

**overtop** • v. (**-topped**, **-topping**) **1** exceed in height. **2** (especially of water) rise over the top of. • adv. & prep. chiefly Canadian over.

**overtrain** • v. train or cause to train too much.

**overtrick** • n. Bridge a trick taken by the declarer in excess of the contract.

**overtrousers** • pl. n. protective or waterproof trousers worn over other trousers.

**overtrump** • v. another term for **OVERRUFF**.

**overture** • n. **1** an orchestral piece at the beginning of a musical work. ➤ an independent orchestral composition in one movement. **2** an introduction to something more substantial. **3** an approach made with the aim of opening negotiations or establishing a relationship.

– ORIGIN ME (in the sense 'aperture'): from OFr., from L. *apertura* 'aperture'.

**overturn** • v. **1** turn over or cause to turn over and come to rest upside down. **2** abolish, invalidate, or reverse (an established fact or system, legal decision, etc.). • n. **1** an act of overturning. **2** Ecology the occasional mixing of the water of a thermally stratified lake.

**overtype** • v. type over (another character) on a computer screen. • n. a facility allowing overtyping.

**overuse** • v. use too much. • n. excessive use.

**overvalue** • v. (**-values**, **-valued**, **-valuing**) **1** overestimate the importance of. **2** fix the value of (something, especially a currency) at too high a level.

– DERIVATIVES **overvaluation** n.

**overview** • n. a general review or summary. • v. give an overview of.

**overwater** • v. apply too much water to. • adj. situated or taking place above water.

**overweening** • adj. showing excessive confidence or pride.

– DERIVATIVES **overweeningly** adv.

**overweight** • adj. above a normal, desirable, or permitted weight. • n. excessive or extra weight. • v. [usu. as adj. **overweighted**] overload.

**overwhelm** • v. **1** bury or drown beneath a huge mass. ➤ give too much of something to: *they were overwhelmed by letters*. **2** defeat completely; overpower. **3** (usu. **be overwhelmed**) have a strong emotional effect on.

– DERIVATIVES **overwhelming** adj. **overwhelmingly** adv. **overwhelmingness** n.

**overwind** • v. (past and past part. **-wound**) wind (a mechanism) beyond the proper stopping point.

**overwinter** • v. **1** spend the winter in a specified place. **2** (with reference to an insect, plant, etc.) live or maintain through the winter.

**overwork** • v. **1** work or cause to work too hard. **2** [usu. as adj. **overworked**] use (a word or idea) too much and so make it weaker in effect. • n. excessive work.

**overwound** past and past participle of **OVERWIND**.

**overwrite** • v. (past **-wrote**; past part. **-written**) **1** write on top of (other writing). ➤ another term for **OVERTYPE**. **2** Computing destroy (data) or the data in (a file) by entering new data in its place. **3** write too elaborately or ornately. **4** (in insurance) accept more risk than the premium income limits allow.

– DERIVATIVES **overwriting** n.

**overwrought** • adj. **1** in a state of nervous excitement or anxiety. **2** (of a piece of writing or a work of art) too elaborate or complicated in design or construction.

– ORIGIN ME: archaic past part. of **OVERWORK**.

**overzealous** • adj. too zealous.

– DERIVATIVES **overzealously** adv. **overzealousness** n.

**ovi-** • comb. form chiefly Zoology of or relating to eggs or ova: *oviparous*.

– ORIGIN from L. *ovum* 'egg'.

**oviduct** /'əʊvɪdʌkt/ • n. Anatomy & Zoology the tube through which an ovum or egg passes from an ovary.

– DERIVATIVES **oviducal** /-'dju:k(ə)l/ adj. **oviductal** adj.

**oviform** /'əʊvɪfɔ:m/ • adj. egg-shaped.

**ovine** /'əʊvʌɪn/ • adj. of, relating to, affecting, or resembling sheep.

– ORIGIN C19: from late L. *ovinus*, from L. *ovis* 'sheep'.

**oviparous** /əʊ'vɪp(ə)rəs/ • adj. Zoology (of an animal) producing young by means of eggs which are hatched after they have been laid by the parent, as in birds. Compare with **VIVIPAROUS** and **OVOVIVIPAROUS**.

– DERIVATIVES **oviparity** n.

**oviposit** /ˌəʊvɪ'pɒzɪt/ • v. (**oviposited**, **ovipositing**) Zoology (especially of an insect) lay an egg or eggs.

– DERIVATIVES **oviposition** n.

– ORIGIN C19: from **OVI-** + L. *posit-*, *ponere* 'place'.

**ovipositor** /ˌəʊvɪ'pɒzɪtə/ • n. Zoology a tubular organ through which a female insect or fish deposits eggs.

**ovoid** /'əʊvɔɪd/ • adj. **1** (of a solid or a three-dimensional surface) more or less egg-shaped. **2** (of a plane figure) oval. • n. an ovoid body or surface.

– ORIGIN C19: from Fr. *ovoïde*, from mod. L. *ovoides*, from L. *ovum* 'egg'.

**ovolo** /'əʊvələʊ/ • n. (pl. **ovoli** /-li:/) Architecture a rounded convex moulding.

– ORIGIN C17: from Ital., dimin. of *ovo* 'egg', from L. *ovum*.

**ovotestis** /ˌəʊvəʊ'tɛstɪs/ • n. (pl. **ovotestes** /-ti:z/) Zoology an organ producing both ova and spermatozoa, especially in some gastropod molluscs.

– ORIGIN C19: from **OVUM** + **TESTIS**.

**ovoviviparous** /ˌəʊvəʊvɪ'vɪp(ə)rəs/ • adj. Zoology (of an animal) producing young by means of eggs which are hatched within the body of the parent, as in some snakes. Compare with **OVIPAROUS** and **VIVIPAROUS**.

– DERIVATIVES **ovoviviparity** n.

**ovulate** /'ɒvjʊleɪt/ • v. discharge ova or ovules from the ovary.

– DERIVATIVES **ovulation** n. **ovulatory** adj.

– ORIGIN C19: back-form. from *ovulation*, or from med. L. *ovulum* (see **OVULE**) + **-ATE**[3].

**ovule** /'ɒvju:l, 'əʊ-/ • n. Botany the part of the ovary of seed plants that contains the female germ cell and after fertilization becomes the seed.

– DERIVATIVES **ovular** adj.

– ORIGIN C19: from Fr., from med. L. *ovulum*, dimin. of **OVUM**.

**ovum** /'əʊvəm/ • n. (pl. **ova** /'əʊvə/) Biology a mature female reproductive cell, which can divide to give rise to an embryo usually only after fertilization by a male cell.

– ORIGIN C18: from L., lit. 'egg'.

**ow** • exclam. used to express sudden pain.

– ORIGIN C19: natural exclam.

**owe** • v. **1** have an obligation to pay (money or goods) to (someone) in return for something received. **2** be under a moral obligation to show (gratitude, respect, etc.) or to offer (an explanation) to (someone). **3** (**owe something to**) have something because of. **4** be indebted to (someone or something) for (something).

– ORIGIN OE *āgan* 'own, have it as an obligation', of Gmc origin; cf. **OUGHT**[1].

**owing** ● adj. yet to be paid or supplied.
– PHRASES **owing to** because of or on account of.

**owl** ● n. a nocturnal bird of prey with large eyes, a hooked beak, and typically a loud hooting call. [Order Strigiformes: many species.]
– ORIGIN OE *ūle*, of Gmc origin, from a base imitative of the bird's call.

**owl butterfly** ● n. a very large South American butterfly which flies at dusk, with a large eye-like marking on the underside of each hindwing. [Genus *Caligo*.]

**owlet** ● n. **1** a young or small owl. **2** a noctuid moth.

**owlet-nightjar** ● n. a nocturnal Australasian bird resembling a small nightjar, with an owl-like face and a large gape. [Genus *Aegotheles*: several species.]

**owlish** ● adj. **1** like an owl, especially in being wise or solemn. **2** (of glasses or eyes) resembling the large round eyes of an owl.
– DERIVATIVES **owlishly** adv. **owlishness** n.

**owl light** ● n. dusk; twilight.

**owl monkey** ● n. another term for **DOUROUCOULI**.

**owl parrot** ● n. another term for **KAKAPO**.

**own** ● adj. & pron. (with a possessive) belonging or relating to the person specified. ➤done or produced by the person specified. ➤particular to the person or thing specified; individual. ● v. **1** possess. **2** formal admit or acknowledge that something is the case. **3** (**own up**) admit to having done something wrong or embarrassing.
– PHRASES **be one's own man** (or **woman**) act independently. ➤archaic be in full possession of one's faculties. **come into its** (or **one's**) **own** become fully effective. **hold one's own** retain a position of strength in a challenging situation.
– DERIVATIVES **-owned** adj. **owner** n. **ownerless** adj. **ownership** n.
– ORIGIN OE *āgen* 'owned, possessed', past part. of *āgan* 'owe'.

**own brand** ● n. Brit. a product manufactured specially for a retailer and bearing the retailer's name.

**owner-occupier** ● n. Brit. a person who owns the house, flat, etc. in which they live.
– DERIVATIVES **owner-occupied** adj.

**own goal** ● n. (in soccer) a goal scored when a player inadvertently strikes or deflects the ball into their own team's goal.

**owt** /aʊt/ ● pron. N. English anything.
– ORIGIN C19: var. of **AUGHT**[1].

**ox** ● n. (pl. **oxen** /ˈɒks(ə)n/) a domesticated bovine animal kept for milk or meat; a cow or bull. See also **CATTLE**. ➤used in names of wild animals related to or resembling this, e.g. **musk ox**. ➤a castrated bull, especially as a draught animal.
– ORIGIN OE *oxa*, of Gmc origin.

**ox-** ● comb. form variant spelling of **OXY-**[2] reduced before a vowel (as in *oxic*).

**oxalic acid** /ɒkˈsalɪk/ ● n. Chemistry a poisonous crystalline organic acid, present in rhubarb leaves, wood sorrel, and other plants.
– DERIVATIVES **oxalate** /ˈɒksəleɪt/ n.
– ORIGIN C18: from Fr. *oxalique*, via L. from Gk *oxalis* 'wood sorrel'.

**oxalis** /ˈɒksəlɪs, ɒkˈsɑːlɪs/ ● n. a plant of a genus which includes the wood sorrel, typically having three-lobed leaves and white, yellow, or pink flowers. [Genus *Oxalis*.]
– ORIGIN C17: via L. from Gk, from *oxus* 'sour' (because of its sharp-tasting leaves).

**oxbow** /ˈɒksbəʊ/ ● n. **1** a loop formed by a horseshoe bend in a river. **2** the U-shaped collar of an ox-yoke.

**oxbow lake** ● n. a curved lake formed from a horseshoe bend in a river where the main stream has cut across the neck and no longer flows around the loop of the bend.

**Oxbridge** ● n. Oxford and Cambridge universities regarded together.

**oxen** plural form of **ox**.

**oxer** ● n. **1** an ox-fence. **2** (in showjumping) a jump consisting of a brush fence with a guard rail on one or both sides.

**ox-eye** ● n. a yellow-flowered North American plant of the daisy family. [*Heliopsis helianthoides*.]

**ox-eye daisy** ● n. a daisy which has large white flowers with yellow centres. [*Leucanthemum vulgare*.]

**Oxf.** ● abbrev. Oxford.

**ox fence** ● n. a strong fence for confining cattle, consisting of a hedge with a strong guard rail on one side, and usually a ditch on the other.

**Oxford** ● n. a type of lace-up shoe with a low heel.
– ORIGIN C19: named after the city of *Oxford*.

**Oxford bags** ● pl. n. Brit. wide baggy trousers.
– ORIGIN 1920s: named after the city of *Oxford*.

**Oxford blue** ● n. Brit. **1** a dark blue, typically with a purple tinge, adopted as the colour of Oxford University. **2** a person who has represented Oxford University in a particular sport.

**Oxford Movement** ● n. another name for **TRACTARIANISM**.

**oxhide** ● n. leather made from the hide of an ox.

**oxic** /ˈɒksɪk/ ● adj. involving or containing oxygen.

**oxidant** /ˈɒksɪd(ə)nt/ ● n. an oxidizing agent.

**oxidase** /ˈɒksɪdeɪz/ ● n. Biochemistry an enzyme which promotes the transfer of a hydrogen atom from a particular substrate to an oxygen molecule.

**oxidation** ● n. Chemistry the process or result of oxidizing or being oxidized.
– DERIVATIVES **oxidational** adj. **oxidative** adj.
– ORIGIN C18: from Fr. (mod. Fr. *oxydation*), from *oxider* 'oxidize'.

**oxidation number** (also **oxidation state**) ● n. Chemistry a number representing the number of electrons lost or gained by an atom of a particular element when chemically combined.

**oxide** /ˈɒksʌɪd/ ● n. Chemistry a compound of oxygen with another element or group.
– ORIGIN C18: from Fr., from *oxygène* 'oxygen' + *-ide* (as in *acide* 'acid').

**oxidize** /ˈɒksɪdʌɪz/ (also **-ise**) ● v. combine or cause to combine with oxygen. ➤Chemistry undergo or cause to undergo a reaction in which electrons are lost to another substance or molecule. The opposite of **REDUCE**.
– DERIVATIVES **oxidizable** adj. **oxidization** n. **oxidizer** n.

**oxidizing agent** ● n. Chemistry a substance that tends to bring about oxidation by being reduced and gaining electrons.

**oximeter** /ɒkˈsɪmɪtə/ ● n. an instrument for measuring the proportion of oxygenated haemoglobin in the blood.
– DERIVATIVES **oximetry** n.

**oxisol** /ˈɒksɪsɒl/ ● n. Soil Science a stable, highly weathered, tropical mineral soil with oxidized subsurface horizons.
– ORIGIN 1960s: from **OXIC** + **-SOL**.

**oxlip** ● n. **1** a woodland primula with yellow flowers that hang down one side of the stem. [*Primula elatior*.] **2** (also **false oxlip**) a natural hybrid between a primrose and a cowslip.
– ORIGIN OE *oxanslyppe*, from *oxa* 'ox' + *slyppe* 'slime'; cf. **COWSLIP**.

**Oxon** /ˈɒks(ə)n, -sɒn/ ● abbrev. **1** Oxfordshire. **2** (in degree titles) of Oxford University.
– ORIGIN from med. L. *Oxoniensis*, from *Oxonia* (see **OXONIAN**).

**Oxonian** /ɒkˈsəʊnɪən/ ● adj. of or relating to Oxford or Oxford University. ● n. **1** a native or inhabitant of Oxford. **2** a member of Oxford University.
– ORIGIN C16: from *Oxonia* (Latinized name of Oxford, from its old form *Oxenford*) + **-AN**.

**oxpecker** ● n. a brown African bird related to the starlings, feeding on parasites that infest the skins of large grazing mammals. [Genus *Buphagus*: two species.]

**oxtail** ● n. the tail of an ox (used in making soup).

**oxter** /ˈɒkstə/ ● n. Scottish & N. English a person's armpit.
– ORIGIN OE *ōhsta*, *ōxta*.

**ox-tongue** ● n. **1** the tongue of an ox (used as meat). **2** a plant of the daisy family, with yellow dandelion-like flowers and prickly hairs on the stem and leaves. [Genus *Picris*.]

**oxy-**[1] ● comb. form denoting sharpness: *oxytone*.

– ORIGIN from Gk *oxus* 'sharp'.

**oxy-**[2] (also **ox-**) ● **comb. form** Chemistry representing OXYGEN.

**oxyacetylene** ● **adj.** of or denoting welding or cutting techniques using a very hot flame produced by mixing acetylene and oxygen.

**oxyacid** ● **n.** Chemistry an inorganic acid whose molecules contain oxygen.

**oxyanion** /ˌɒksɪ'anʌɪən/ ● **n.** Chemistry an anion containing one or more oxygen atoms bonded to another element.

**oxygen** ● **n.** the chemical element of atomic number 8, a colourless, odourless reactive gas that forms about 20 per cent of the earth's atmosphere and is essential to plant and animal life. (Symbol: **O**)
– DERIVATIVES **oxygenous** adj.
– ORIGIN C18: from Fr. (*principe*) *oxygène* 'acidifying constituent' (because at first it was held to be the essential component of acids).

**oxygenate** /'ɒksɪdʒəneɪt, ɒk'sɪdʒ-/ ● **v.** supply, treat, charge, or enrich with oxygen.
– DERIVATIVES **oxygenated** adj. **oxygenation** n.

**oxygenator** ● **n.** Medicine **1** an apparatus for oxygenating the blood. **2** an aquatic plant which enriches the surrounding water with oxygen.

**oxygen bar** ● **n.** an establishment where people pay to inhale pure oxygen for its reputedly therapeutic effects.

**oxyhaemoglobin** ● **n.** Biochemistry a bright red substance formed by the combination of haemoglobin with oxygen, present in oxygenated blood.

**oxymoron** /ˌɒksɪ'mɔːrɒn/ ● **n.** a figure of speech or expressed idea in which apparently contradictory terms appear in conjunction.
– DERIVATIVES **oxymoronic** adj.
– ORIGIN C17: from Gk *oxumōron*, neut. (used as n.) of *oxumōros* 'pointedly foolish', from *oxus* 'sharp' + *mōros* 'foolish'.

**oxyntic** /ɒk'sɪntɪk/ ● **adj.** of or denoting the secretory cells which produce hydrochloric acid in the main part of the stomach, or the glands which they compose.
– ORIGIN C19: from Gk *oxunteos* (verbal noun from *oxunein* 'sharpen') + **-IC**.

**oxytetracycline** /ˌɒksɪtɛtrə'sʌɪkliːn, -lɪn/ ● **n.** Medicine an antibiotic related to tetracycline.

**oxytocin** /ˌɒksɪ'təʊsɪn/ ● **n.** Biochemistry a hormone released by the pituitary gland that causes increased contraction of the womb during labour and stimulates the ejection of milk into the ducts of the breasts.
– ORIGIN 1920s: from Gk *oxutokia* 'sudden delivery' (from *oxus* 'sharp' + *tokos* 'childbirth') + **-IN**[1].

**oxytone** /'ɒksɪtəʊn/ ● **adj.** (especially in ancient Greek) having an acute accent on the last syllable. ● **n.** an oxytone word.
– ORIGIN C18: from Gk *oxutonos*, from *oxus* 'sharp' + *tonos* 'tone'.

**oy** ● **exclam. 1** variant spelling of **OI**. **2** variant of **OY VEY**.

**oyez** /əʊ'jɛs, -'jɛz, -'jeɪ/ (also **oyes**) ● **exclam.** a call given by a public crier or a court officer to command silence and attention before an announcement.
– ORIGIN ME: from OFr. *oiez!*, *oyez!* 'hear!', imper. pl. of *oir*, from L. *audire* 'hear'.

**oyster** ● **n. 1** a bivalve marine mollusc with a rough, flattened, irregularly oval shell, several kinds of which are farmed for food or pearls. [*Ostrea edulis* (Europe), *Crassostrea virginica* (America), and other species.] **2** a shade of greyish white. **3** an oval morsel of meat on each side of the backbone in poultry.
– PHRASES **the world is one's oyster** one is able to enjoy a broad range of opportunities. [from Shakespeare's *Merry Wives of Windsor* (II. ii. 5).]
– ORIGIN ME: from OFr. *oistre*, via L. from Gk *ostreon*; rel. to *osteon* 'bone' and *ostrakon* 'shell or tile'.

**oystercatcher** ● **n.** a wading bird with black-and-white or all-black plumage and a strong orange-red bill, feeding chiefly on shellfish. [*Haematopus ostralegus* and related species.]

**oyster mushroom** ● **n.** an edible fungus with a greyish-brown oyster-shaped cap and a very short or absent stem. [*Pleurotus ostreatus*.]

**oyster plant** ● **n. 1** another term for **SALSIFY**. **2** a blue-flowered thick-leaved creeping plant of the borage family, growing chiefly on stony beaches in northern Europe. [*Mertensia maritima*.]

**oyster sauce** ● **n.** a sauce made with oysters and soy sauce, used especially in oriental cookery.

**oy vey** /ɔɪ 'veɪ/ (also **oy**) ● **exclam.** indicating dismay or grief (used mainly by Yiddish-speakers).
– ORIGIN C19: Yiddish, lit. 'oh woe'.

**Oz** ● **n. & adj.** informal Australia or Australian.
– ORIGIN 1940s: representing a pronunc. of an abbrev. of *Australia*.

**oz** ● **abbrev.** ounce(s).
– ORIGIN from Ital. *onza* 'ounce'.

**Ozalid** /'əʊzəlɪd, 'ɒz-/ ● **n.** trademark a photocopy made by a process in which a diazonium salt and coupler are present in the paper coating, so that the image develops in the presence of ammonia.
– ORIGIN 1920s: by reversal of **DIAZO** and insertion of *-l*.

**ozokerite** /əʊ'zəʊkərʌɪt, -sərʌɪt, ˌəʊzə(ʊ)'sɪərʌɪt/ ● **n.** a brown or black paraffin wax occurring naturally in some shales and sandstones and formerly used in candles, polishes, and electrical insulation.
– ORIGIN C19: from Ger. *Ozokerit*, from Gk *ozein* 'to smell' + *kēros* 'wax'.

**ozone** ● **n. 1** an unstable, pungent, toxic form of oxygen with three atoms in its molecule, formed in electrical discharges or by ultraviolet light. **2** informal fresh invigorating air.
– DERIVATIVES **ozonic** adj.
– ORIGIN C19: from Ger. *Ozon*, from Gk *ozein* 'to smell'.

**ozone-friendly** ● **adj.** (of manufactured products) not containing chemicals that are destructive to the ozone layer.

**ozone hole** ● **n.** a region of marked thinning of the ozone layer in high latitudes, chiefly in winter, due to CFCs and other atmospheric pollutants.

**ozone layer** ● **n.** a layer in the earth's stratosphere at an altitude of about 10 km (6.2 miles) containing a high concentration of ozone, which absorbs most of the ultraviolet radiation reaching the earth from the sun.

**ozonize** /'əʊzənʌɪz/ (also **-ise**) ● **v.** convert into or treat with ozone.
– DERIVATIVES **ozonization** n. **ozonizer** n.

**Ozzie** ● **n.** variant spelling of **AUSSIE**.

# P p

**P**[1] (also **p**) ● n. (pl. **Ps** or **P's**) **1** the sixteenth letter of the alphabet. **2** denoting the next after O in a set of items, categories, etc.

**P**[2] ● abbrev. **1** (in tables of sports results) games played. **2** (on an automatic gear shift) park. **3** (on road signs and street plans) parking. **4** peta- ($10^{15}$). **5** Physics poise (unit of viscosity). **6** Portugal (international vehicle registration). **7** proprietary. ● symb. the chemical element phosphorus.

**p** ● abbrev. **1** page. **2** (***p-***) Chemistry para-. **3** Brit. penny or pence. **4** Music piano (softly). **5** pico- ($10^{-12}$). **6** Chemistry denoting electrons and orbitals possessing one unit of angular momentum. [from *principal*, orig. applied to lines in atomic spectra.] ● symb. **1** Physics pressure. **2** Statistics probability.

**PA** ● abbrev. **1** Panama (international vehicle registration). **2** Pennsylvania (in official postal use). **3** Brit. personal assistant. **4** Press Association. **5** public address.

**Pa** ● abbrev. pascal(s). ● symb. the chemical element protactinium.

**pa** ● n. informal father.
– ORIGIN C19: abbrev. of **PAPA**.

**p.a.** ● abbrev. per annum.

**paan** /pɑːn/ (also **pan**) ● n. Indian betel leaves prepared and used as a stimulant.
– ORIGIN via Hindi from Sanskrit *parṇa* 'feather, leaf'.

**pa'anga** /pɑː'ɑːŋgə/ ● n. (pl. same) the basic monetary unit of Tonga, equal to 100 seniti.
– ORIGIN from Tongan.

**pabulum** /'pabjʊləm/ (also **pablum**) ● n. bland intellectual matter or entertainment.
– ORIGIN C17 (in the sense 'food'): from L., from the stem of *pascere* 'to feed'.

**PABX** ● abbrev. private automatic branch exchange.

**PAC** ● abbrev. Pan-Africanist Congress.

**paca** /'pakə/ ● n. a robust nocturnal South American rodent that has a reddish-brown coat patterned with rows of white spots, hunted for its flesh. [Genus *Agouti*: two species, in particular *A. paca*.]
– ORIGIN C17: via Sp. and Port. from Tupi.

**pacamac** ● n. variant spelling of **PAKAMAC**.

**pacarana** /ˌpakə'rɑːnə/ ● n. a slow-moving South American cavy-like rodent that has coarse dark hair with white stripes along the back and a short tail. [*Dinomys branickii*.]
– ORIGIN from Tupi, lit. 'false paca'.

**PACE** ● abbrev. Brit. Police and Criminal Evidence Act.

**pace**[1] /peɪs/ ● n. **1** a single step taken when walking or running. **2** a gait of a horse, especially one of the recognized trained gaits. **3** speed or rate of motion, development, or change. **4** Cricket the state of a wicket as affecting the speed of the ball. ● v. **1** measure (a distance) by walking it and counting the number of steps taken. **2** walk at a steady speed, especially without a particular destination and as an expression of anxiety. **3** (of a trained horse) move with a distinctive lateral gait in which both legs on the same side are lifted together. **4** lead (another runner in a race) in order to establish a competitive speed. **5** (**pace oneself**) do something at a restrained and steady rate or speed. **6** move or develop (something) at a particular rate or speed.
– PHRASES **keep pace with** move, develop, or progress at the same speed as. **off the pace** behind the leader or leading group in a race or contest. **put someone through their paces** make someone demonstrate their abilities. **stand** (or **stay**) **the pace** be able to keep up with another or others.
– DERIVATIVES **-paced** adj.
– ORIGIN ME: from OFr. *pas*, from L. *passus* 'stretch (of the leg)'.

**pace**[2] /'pɑːtʃeɪ, 'peɪsi/ ● prep. with due respect to.
– ORIGIN L., lit. 'in peace', ablative of *pax*.

**pace bowler** ● n. Cricket a fast bowler.

**pace car** ● n. Motor Racing a car that sets the pace for the warm-up lap before a race but does not take part in it, or one that controls the pace in temporarily hazardous conditions.

**pacemaker** ● n. **1** a competitor who sets the pace at the beginning of a race or competition. **2** a person who sets standards of achievement for others. **3** an artificial device for stimulating and regulating the heart muscle. **4** a part of an organ or of the body which controls rhythmic physiological activity.
– DERIVATIVES **pacemaking** adj. & n.

**paceman** ● n. (pl. **-men**) Cricket a fast bowler.

**pace notes** ● pl. n. (in rally driving) notes made before a race by a competitor about the characteristics of a particular course.

**pacer** ● n. **1** a pacemaker. **2** chiefly US a horse bred or trained to pace.

**pacesetter** ● n. another term for **PACEMAKER** (in sense 1).
– DERIVATIVES **pacesetting** adj. & n.

**pacey** ● adj. variant spelling of **PACY**.

**pacha** ● n. variant spelling of **PASHA**.

**pachinko** /pə'tʃɪŋkəʊ/ ● n. a Japanese form of pinball.
– ORIGIN from Japanese.

**pachuco** /pə'tʃuːkəʊ/ ● n. (pl. **-os** /-əʊz/) chiefly US a member of a gang of young Mexican-Americans.
– ORIGIN Mex. Sp., lit. 'flashily dressed'.

**pachyderm** /'pakɪdəːm/ ● n. a very large mammal with thick skin, especially an elephant, rhinoceros, or hippopotamus.
– DERIVATIVES **pachydermal** adj. **pachydermatous** adj. **pachydermic** adj.
– ORIGIN C19: from Fr. *pachyderme*, from Gk *pakhudermos*, from *pakhus* 'thick' + *derma* 'skin'.

**pachysandra** /ˌpakɪ'sandrə/ ● n. an evergreen creeping shrubby plant of the box family. [Genus *Pachysandra*.]
– ORIGIN formed irregularly from Gk *pakhus* 'thick' + *anēr*, *andr-* 'male' (with ref. to the thick stamens).

**pachytene** /'pakɪtiːn/ ● n. Biology the third stage of the prophase of meiosis, following zygotene, during which the paired chromosomes shorten and thicken, the two chromatids of each separate, and exchange of segments between chromatids may occur.
– ORIGIN C20: from Gk *pakhus* 'thick' + *tainia* 'band'.

**pacific** ● adj. **1** peaceful in character or intent. **2** (**Pacific**) of or relating to the Pacific Ocean. ● n. (**the Pacific**) the Pacific Ocean.
– DERIVATIVES **pacifically** adv.
– ORIGIN C16: from Fr. *pacifique* or L. *pacificus* 'peacemaking', from *pax*, *pac-* 'peace'.

**Pacific Islander** ● n. a native or inhabitant of any of the islands in the South Pacific, especially an aboriginal native of Polynesia.

**pacifier** ● n. **1** a person or thing that pacifies. **2** N. Amer. a baby's dummy.

**pacifism** ● n. the belief that disputes should be settled by peaceful means and that war and violence are unjustifiable.

– DERIVATIVES **pacifist** n. & adj.
– ORIGIN C20: from Fr. *pacifisme*, from *pacifier* 'pacify'.

**pacify** ● v. (**-ies, -ied**) **1** quell the anger or agitation of. **2** bring peace to (a country or warring factions).
– DERIVATIVES **pacification** n. **pacificatory** adj.
– ORIGIN C15 (earlier (ME) as *pacification*): from OFr. *pacefier*, from L. *pacificare*, based on *pax, pac-* 'peace'.

**Pacinian corpuscle** /pəˈsɪnɪən/ ● n. Anatomy an encapsulated ending of a sensory nerve that acts as a receptor for pressure and vibration.
– ORIGIN C19: named after the Ital. anatomist Filippo *Pacini*.

**pack**[1] ● n. **1** a cardboard or paper container and the items contained within it. **2** a collection of related documents. **3** Brit. a set of playing cards. **4** a rucksack. **5** a quantity of foods packed or canned in a particular season. **6** a group of wild animals, especially wolves, living and hunting together. ➤a group of hounds kept for hunting. **7** (**Pack**) an organized group of Cub Scouts or Brownies. **8** Rugby a team's forwards considered as a group. **9** (**the pack**) the main body of competitors following the leader in a race or competition. **10** chiefly derogatory a group or set of similar things or people: *a pack of lies*. **11** pack ice. **12** a hot or cold pad of absorbent material, used for treating an injury. ● v. **1** fill (a suitcase or bag) with clothes and other items needed for travel. **2** place in a container for transport or storage. ➤be capable of being folded up for transport or storage. **3** informal carry (a gun). **4** cram a large number of things into. ➤[often as adj. **packed**] (of a large number of people) crowd into and fill (a place). **5** cover, surround, or fill. **6** Rugby (of players) form a scrum.
– PHRASES **pack heat** N. Amer. informal carry a gun. **pack a punch 1** hit with skill or force. **2** have a powerful effect. **packed out** Brit. informal very crowded. **send someone packing** informal dismiss someone peremptorily.
– PHRASAL VERBS **pack something in** informal give up an activity or job. **pack someone off** informal send someone somewhere peremptorily or without much notice. **pack something out** N. Amer. pack something up and take it away. **pack up** Brit. informal (of a machine) break down.
– DERIVATIVES **packable** adj. **packer** n.
– ORIGIN ME: from MDu., Mid. Low Ger. *pak* (n.), *pakken* (v.).

**pack**[2] ● v. fill (a jury or committee) with people likely to support a particular verdict or decision.
– ORIGIN C16 (in the sense 'enter into a private agreement'): prob. from the obs. verb *pact* 'enter into an agreement with', the final *-t* being interpreted as an inflection of the past tense.

**package** ● n. **1** an object or group of objects wrapped in paper or packed in a box. ➤N. Amer. a packet. **2** (also **package deal**) a set of proposals or terms offered or agreed as a whole. **3** informal a package holiday. **4** Computing a collection of programs or subroutines with related functionality. ● v. **1** put into a box or wrapping. **2** (usu. **be packaged**) present in a particular and advantageous way. **3** combine (various products) for sale as one unit. **4** commission and produce (an illustrated book) to sell as a complete product to publishers.
– DERIVATIVES **packaged** adj. **packager** n. **packaging** n.
– ORIGIN C16: from PACK[1] + -AGE; cf. Anglo-Latin *paccagium*.

**package holiday** (also **package tour**) ● n. a holiday organized by a travel agent, with arrangements for transport and accommodation made at an inclusive price.

**pack animal** ● n. **1** an animal used to carry packs. **2** an animal that lives and hunts in a pack.

**pack drill** ● n. a military punishment of marching up and down carrying full equipment.
– PHRASES **no names, no pack drill** punishment will be prevented if names and details are not mentioned.

**packed lunch** ● n. a cold lunch carried in a bag or box to work or school or on an excursion.

**packet** ● n. **1** a paper or cardboard container. **2** Computing a block of data transmitted across a network. **3** (**a packet**) informal, chiefly Brit. a large sum of money. **4** dated a boat travelling at regular intervals between two ports, originally for the conveyance of mail. ● v. (**packeted, packeting**) [often as adj. **packeted**] wrap up in a packet.
– ORIGIN C16: dimin. of PACK[1], perh. from Anglo-Norman Fr.; cf. Anglo-Latin *paccettum*.

**packetize** ● v. Computing partition or separate (data) into units for transmission in a packet-switching network.

**packet radio** ● n. a method of broadcasting that makes use of radio signals carrying packets of data.

**packet switching** ● n. Computing & Telecommunications a mode of data transmission in which a message is broken into a number of parts which are sent independently, over whatever route is optimum for each packet, and reassembled at the destination.

**packhorse** ● n. a horse used to carry loads.

**pack ice** ● n. (in polar seas) an expanse of large pieces of floating ice driven together into a mass.

**packing** ● n. **1** material used to protect fragile goods in transit. **2** material used to seal a join or assist in lubricating an axle.

**packing case** ● n. a large, strong box used for transportation or storage.

**packing density** ● n. Computing the density of stored information in terms of bits per unit occupied of its storage medium.

**packman** ● n. (pl. **-men**) archaic a pedlar.

**pack rat** ● n. **1** another term for WOODRAT. **2** N. Amer. derogatory a person who hoards things.

**packsack** ● n. N. Amer. a rucksack.

**packsaddle** ● n. chiefly N. Amer. a saddle adapted for securing the loads carried by a pack animal.

**pact** ● n. a formal agreement between individuals or parties.
– ORIGIN ME: from OFr., from L. *pactum* 'something agreed'.

**pacy** (also **pacey**) ● adj. (**-ier, -iest**) fast-moving.

**pad**[1] ● n. **1** a thick piece of soft or absorbent material. **2** the fleshy underpart of an animal's foot or of a human finger. **3** a protective guard worn over a part of the body by a sports player. **4** a number of sheets of blank paper fastened together at one edge. **5** a flat-topped structure or area used for helicopter take-off and landing or for rocket-launching. **6** Electronics a flat area on a track of a printed circuit or on the edge of an integrated circuit to which wires or component leads can be attached to make an electrical connection. **7** informal a person's home. ● v. (**padded, padding**) **1** [often as adj. **padded**] fill or cover with a pad. **2** (**pad up**) (in cricket) put on protective pads. ➤(of a batsman) deliberately use one's pads to block a ball. **3** (**pad something out**) lengthen a speech or piece of writing with unnecessary material. **4** chiefly N. Amer. defraud by adding false items to (an expenses claim or bill).
– DERIVATIVES **padding** n.
– ORIGIN C16 (in the sense 'bundle of straw to lie on'): the senses may not be of common origin; the meaning 'underpart of an animal's foot' is perh. rel. to Low Ger. *pad* 'sole of the foot'; the history remains obscure.

**pad**[2] ● v. (**padded, padding**) walk with steady steps making a soft, dull sound. ● n. the sound of such steps.
– ORIGIN C16: from Low Ger. *padden* 'to tread, go along a path', partly imitative.

**padauk** /paˈdaʊk/ (also **padouk**) ● n. **1** a hard wood from a tropical tree, resembling rosewood. **2** the tree which produces this wood. [*Pterocarpus soyauxii* (W. Africa) and related species.]
– ORIGIN C19: from Burmese.

**paddle**[1] ● n. **1** a short pole with a broad blade at one or both ends, used to move a small boat or canoe through the water. **2** a short-handled bat such as that used in table tennis. **3** any of various paddle-shaped instruments used for stirring or mixing. **4** N. Amer. informal a paddle-shaped instrument used for administering corporal punishment. **5** each of the boards fitted round the circumference of a paddle wheel or mill wheel. **6** the fin or flipper of an aquatic mammal or bird. **7** a flat array of solar cells projecting from a spacecraft. **8** Medicine a plastic-covered electrode used in cardiac stimulation. **9** an act of paddling. ● v. **1** propel (a boat or canoe) with a paddle or paddles. **2** (of a bird or other animal) swim with short fast strokes. **3**

informal, chiefly N. Amer. beat with a paddle as a punishment.
– DERIVATIVES **paddler** n.
– ORIGIN ME: of unknown origin.

**paddle²** ● v. walk with bare feet in shallow water. ● n. an act of paddling.
– DERIVATIVES **paddler** n.
– ORIGIN C16: of obscure origin; cf. Low Ger. *paddeln* 'tramp about'.

**paddleball** ● n. a game played with a light ball and wooden bat in a four-walled handball court.

**paddlefish** ● n. (pl. same or **-fishes**) a large fish related to the sturgeon, with an elongated snout. [*Polyodon spathula* (Mississippi basin) and *Psephurus gladius* (Yangtze River).]

**paddle steamer** (also **paddle boat**) ● n. a boat powered by steam and propelled by paddle wheels.

**paddle tennis** ● n. a type of tennis played in a small court with a paddle and lightweight ball.

**paddle wheel** ● n. a large steam-driven wheel with paddles round its circumference, attached to the side or stern of a ship and propelling the ship by its rotation.

**paddling pool** ● n. a shallow artificial pool for children to paddle in.

**paddock** ● n. **1** a small field or enclosure where horses are kept or exercised. **2** an enclosure adjoining a racecourse or track where horses or cars are gathered and displayed before a race. **3** Austral./NZ a field or plot of land enclosed by fencing or defined by natural boundaries. ● v. keep or enclose (a horse) in a paddock.
– ORIGIN C17: appar. a var. of dial. *parrock*, of unknown ultimate origin.

**Paddy** ● n. (pl. **-ies**) informal, chiefly offensive an Irishman.
– ORIGIN C18: familiar form of the Ir. given name *Padraig*.

**paddy¹** ● n. (pl. **-ies**) **1** a field where rice is grown. **2** rice still in the husk.
– ORIGIN C17: from Malay *pādī*.

**paddy²** ● n. Brit. informal a fit of temper.
– ORIGIN C19: from **PADDY**, assoc. with obs. *paddywhack* 'Irishman (given to brawling)'.

**paddymelon¹** ● n. Austral. a naturalized trailing or climbing plant with melon-like fruit, native to Africa. [*Cucumis myriocarpus*.]
– ORIGIN C19: prob. by erroneous assoc. with **PADDYMELON²**.

**paddymelon²** ● n. variant spelling of **PADEMELON**.

**paddy wagon** ● n. N. Amer. informal a police van.
– ORIGIN 1930s: *paddy* from **PADDY**.

**pademelon** /ˈpadɪˌmɛlən/ (also **paddymelon**) ● n. a small wallaby inhabiting the coastal scrub of Australia and New Guinea. [Genus *Thylogale*: three species.]
– ORIGIN C19 (earlier as *paddymelon*): prob. an alt. of Dharuk *badimalion*.

**padlock** ● n. a detachable lock hanging by a pivoted hook on the object fastened. ● v. [usu. as adj. **padlocked**] secure with a padlock.
– ORIGIN C15: from *pad-* (of unknown origin) + **LOCK¹**.

**padloper** /ˈpatˌlʊəpə/ ● n. S. African a small tortoise native to southern Africa, often seen on roads and paths. [Genus *Homopus*: several species.]
– ORIGIN Afrik., lit. 'vagabond', from *pad* 'path' + *loper* 'runner'.

**padouk** /pəˈduːk/ ● n. variant spelling of **PADAUK**.

**padre** /ˈpɑːdreɪ, -dri/ ● n. informal a chaplain in the armed services.
– ORIGIN C16: from Ital., Sp., and Port., lit. 'father, priest', from L. *pater, patr-* 'father'.

**padrino** /paˈdriːnəʊ/ ● n. (pl. **-os**) US a godfather; a patron.
– ORIGIN from Sp.

**padrone** /paˈdrəʊneɪ, -ni/ ● n. a patron or master, especially a Mafia boss.
– ORIGIN from Ital.

**padsaw** ● n. a small saw with a narrow blade, for cutting curves.

**pad thai** /pad ˈtʌɪ/ ● n. a Thai dish based on rice noodles.
– ORIGIN from Thai.

**paean** /ˈpiːən/ ● n. a song of praise or triumph.
– ORIGIN C16: via L. from Gk *paian* 'hymn of thanksgiving to Apollo' (invoked by the name *Paian*, orig. the Homeric name for the physician of the gods).

**paederasty** ● n. variant spelling of **PEDERASTY**.

**paediatrics** /ˌpiːdɪˈatrɪks/ (US **pediatrics**) ● pl. n. [treated as sing.] the branch of medicine concerned with children and their diseases.
– DERIVATIVES **paediatric** adj. **paediatrician** n.
– ORIGIN C19: from **PAEDO-** + Gk *iatros* 'physician' + **-ICS**.

**paedo-** (US **pedo-**) ● comb. form of a child; relating to children: *paedophile*.
– ORIGIN from Gk *pais, paid-* 'child, boy'.

**paedodontics** /ˌpiːdəʊˈdɒntɪks/ (US **pedodontics**) ● pl. n. [treated as sing.] the branch of dentistry concerned with children's teeth.
– DERIVATIVES **paedodontic** adj. **paedodontist** n.

**paedogenesis** /ˌpiːdə(ʊ)ˈdʒɛnɪsɪs/ ● n. Zoology another term for **NEOTENY** (in sense 2).
– DERIVATIVES **paedogenetic** adj.

**paedomorphosis** /ˌpiːdə(ʊ)ˈmɔːfəsɪs, -mɔːˈfəʊsɪs/ ● n. Zoology another term for **NEOTENY** (in sense 1).
– DERIVATIVES **paedomorphic** adj.

**paedophile** (US **pedophile**) ● n. a person who is sexually attracted to children.
– DERIVATIVES **paedophilia** n. **paedophiliac** adj. & n.

**paella** /pʌɪˈɛlə/ ● n. a Spanish dish of rice, saffron, chicken, seafood, etc., cooked and served in a large shallow pan.
– ORIGIN Catalan, from OFr. *paele*, from L. *patella* 'pan'.

**paeon** /ˈpiːən/ ● n. a metrical foot of one long syllable and three short syllables in any order.
– DERIVATIVES **paeonic** /piːˈɒnɪk/ adj.
– ORIGIN C17: via L. from Gk *paiōn*, the Attic form of *paian* (see **PAEAN**).

**paeony** ● n. variant spelling of **PEONY**.

**pagan** /ˈpeɪg(ə)n/ ● n. a person holding religious beliefs other than those of the main world religions. ● adj. of or relating to pagans or their beliefs.
– DERIVATIVES **paganish** adj. **paganism** n. **paganize** (also **-ise**) v.
– ORIGIN ME: from L. *paganus* 'villager, rustic', from *pagus* 'country district'; L. *paganus* also meant 'civilian', becoming, in Christian L., 'heathen'.

**page¹** ● n. **1** one side of a leaf of a book, magazine, or newspaper, or the material written or printed on it. **2** both sides of such a leaf considered as a single unit. **3** Computing a section of stored data, especially that which can be displayed on a screen at one time. **4** a particular episode considered as part of a longer history. ● v. **1** (**page through**) leaf through. ➤ Computing move through and display (text) one page at a time. **2** [usu. as noun **paging**] Computing divide (a piece of software or data) into sections, keeping the most frequently accessed in main memory and storing the rest in virtual memory. **3** paginate (a book).
– PHRASES **on the same page** US in agreement.
– DERIVATIVES **-paged** adj.
– ORIGIN C16: from Fr., from L. *pagina*, from *pangere* 'fasten'.

**page²** ● n. **1** a boy or young man employed in a hotel or club to run errands, open doors, etc. **2** a young boy attending a bride at a wedding. **3** historical a boy in training for knighthood, ranking next below a squire in the personal service of a knight. **4** historical a man or boy employed as the personal attendant of a person of rank. ● v. **1** summon over a public address system. **2** contact by means of a pager.
– ORIGIN ME: from OFr., perh. from Ital. *paggio*, from Gk *paidion*, dimin. of *pais, paid-* 'boy'.

**pageant** /ˈpadʒ(ə)nt/ ● n. **1** an entertainment consisting of a procession of people in elaborate costumes, or an outdoor performance of a historical scene. **2** (also **beauty pageant**) N. Amer. a beauty contest. **3** historical a scene erected on a fixed stage or moving vehicle as a public show.
– ORIGIN ME *pagyn*, of unknown origin.

**pageantry** ● n. elaborate display or ceremony.

**pageboy** • n. **1** a page in a hotel or attending a bride at a wedding. **2** a woman's hairstyle consisting of a shoulder-length bob with the ends rolled under.

**pager** • n. a small radio device which bleeps or vibrates to inform the wearer that someone wishes to contact them or that it has received a short text message.

**Page Three** • n. Brit. trademark [as modifier] characteristic of a feature which formerly appeared daily on page three of the *Sun* newspaper, comprising a picture of a topless young woman.

**Paget's disease** /'padʒɪts/ • n. **1** a chronic disease of the elderly characterized by alteration of bone tissue, especially in the spine, skull, or pelvis. **2** an inflammation of the nipple associated with breast cancer.
– ORIGIN C19: named after the Engl. surgeon Sir James *Paget*.

**page-turner** • n. informal an exciting book.
– DERIVATIVES **page-turning** adj. **page-turningly** adv.

**paginal** /'padʒɪn(ə)l/ • adj. of or relating to the pages of a book or periodical.

**paginate** /'padʒɪneɪt/ • n. assign numbers to the pages of a book, journal, etc.
– DERIVATIVES **pagination** n.

**pagoda** /pə'gəʊdə/ • n. a Hindu or Buddhist temple or sacred building, typically having a many-tiered tower.
– ORIGIN C16: from Port. *pagode*, perh. based on Pers. *butkada* 'temple of idols'.

**pagoda tree** • n. a SE Asian leguminous tree with hanging clusters of cream flowers, cultivated as an ornamental. [*Sophora japonica*.]

**pah** • exclam. used to express disgust or contempt.
– ORIGIN C16: natural utterance.

**Pahlavi** /'pɑːləvi/ (also **Pehlevi**) • n. an Aramaic-based writing system used in Persia from the 2nd century BC to the advent of Islam in the 7th century AD.
– ORIGIN from Pers. *pahlawī*, from *pahlav*, from *parthava* 'Parthia', an ancient kingdom SE of the Caspian Sea.

**pahoehoe** /pə'həʊɪhəʊi/ • n. Geology basaltic lava forming smooth undulating or ropy masses. Often contrasted with **AA**.
– ORIGIN C19: from Hawaiian.

**paid** past and past participle of **PAY**[1].
– PHRASES **put paid to** informal stop abruptly; destroy.

**paideia** /pʌɪ'dʌɪə/ • n. **1** (in ancient Greece) a system of broad cultural education. **2** the culture of a society.
– ORIGIN from Gk.

**paid-up** • adj. **1** with all subscriptions or charges paid in full. **2** fully committed to a cause, group, etc.: *a fully paid-up postmodernist*.

**pail** • n. a bucket.
– DERIVATIVES **pailful** n. (pl. **-fuls**).
– ORIGIN ME: origin uncertain; cf. OE *pægel* 'gill, small measure' and OFr. *paelle* 'pan, liquid measure, brazier'.

**paillasse** • n. variant spelling of **PALLIASSE**.

**paillette** /pal'jɛt, pʌɪ'jɛt/ • n. a spangle.
– ORIGIN C19: from Fr., dimin. of *paille*, from L. *palea* 'straw, chaff'.

**pain** • n. **1** a strongly unpleasant bodily sensation such as is caused by illness or injury. **2** mental suffering or distress. **3** (also **pain in the neck** or vulgar slang **arse**) informal an annoying or tedious person or thing. **4** (**pains**) careful effort. • v. cause mental or physical pain to. ➤ chiefly N. Amer. (of a part of the body) hurt.
– PHRASES **on** (or **under**) **pain of** on penalty of.
– DERIVATIVES **pained** adj.
– ORIGIN ME: from OFr. *peine*, from L. *poena* 'penalty', later 'pain'.

**painful** • adj. **1** affected with or causing pain. **2** informal very bad.
– DERIVATIVES **painfully** adv. **painfulness** n.

**painkiller** • n. a medicine for relieving pain.
– DERIVATIVES **painkilling** adj.

**painless** • adj. **1** not causing physical pain. **2** involving little effort or stress.
– DERIVATIVES **painlessly** adv. **painlessness** n.

**painstaking** • adj. done with or employing great care and thoroughness.
– DERIVATIVES **painstakingly** adv. **painstakingness** n.

**paint** • n. **1** a substance which is spread over a surface and dries to leave a thin decorative or protective coating. **2** an act of painting. **3** informal cosmetic make-up. **4** Basketball a rectangular area marked near the basket at each end of a court. **5** Computing the function or capability of producing graphics. **6** N. Amer. a piebald horse. • v. **1** apply paint to. ➤ apply (a liquid) to a surface with a brush. ➤ (**paint something out**) efface something with paint. **2** depict or produce with paint. ➤ give a description of (something). **3** Computing create (a graphic or screen display) using a paint program. **4** display a mark representing (an aircraft or vehicle) on a radar screen.
– PHRASES **paint the town red** informal go out and enjoy oneself flamboyantly.
– DERIVATIVES **paintable** adj. **painty** adj. (**-ier**, **-iest**).
– ORIGIN ME: from *peint* 'painted', past part. of OFr. *peindre*, from L. *pingere* 'to paint'.

**paintball** • n. **1** a game in which participants simulate military combat, shooting capsules of paint at each other with air guns. **2** such a capsule of paint.
– DERIVATIVES **paintballer** n.

**paintbox** • n. a box holding a palette of dry paints for painting pictures.

**paintbrush** • n. **1** a brush for applying paint. **2** [with modifier] a North American plant with brightly coloured brush-like flowering spikes. [*Castilleja coccinea* (**Indian paintbrush**) and related species.]

**painted lady** • n. a migratory butterfly with predominantly orange-brown wings and darker markings. [*Cynthia cardui* and related species.]

**painter**[1] • n. **1** an artist who paints pictures. **2** a person who paints buildings.
– ORIGIN ME: from Anglo-Norman Fr. *peintour*, based on L. *pictor*, from *pingere* 'to paint'.

**painter**[2] • n. a rope attached to the bow of a boat for tying it to a quay.
– ORIGIN ME: of uncertain origin; cf. OFr. *pentoir* 'something from which to hang things'.

**painterly** • adj. **1** of or appropriate to a painter; artistic. **2** demonstrating effective use of paint.
– DERIVATIVES **painterliness** n.

**painting** • n. **1** the action or process of painting. **2** a painted picture.

**paint shop** • n. the part of a factory where goods are painted, typically by spraying.

**paintwork** • n. chiefly Brit. painted surfaces in a building or on a vehicle.

**pair** • n. **1** a set of two things used together or regarded as a unit. **2** an article consisting of two joined or corresponding parts. **3** two people or animals related in some way or considered together. ➤ two members of a legislative assembly on opposing sides who absent themselves from voting by mutual arrangement, in order to maintain the relative position of the parties. • v. join or connect to form a pair. ➤ (**pair off/up**) form a couple.
– DERIVATIVES **paired** adj. **pairing** n. **pairwise** adj. & adv.
– ORIGIN ME: from OFr. *paire*, from L. *paria* 'equal things', neut. pl. of *par* 'equal'.

**pair production** • n. Physics the conversion of a gamma ray into an electron and a positron.

**paisa** /'pʌɪsɑː, -sə/ • n. (pl. **paise** /-seɪ or -sə/) a monetary unit of India, Pakistan, and Nepal, equal to one hundredth of a rupee.
– ORIGIN from Hindi *paisā*.

**paisley** /'peɪzli/ • n. a distinctive intricate pattern of curved feather-shaped figures based on an Indian pine cone design.
– ORIGIN C19: named after the town of *Paisley* in Scotland, place of manufacture of a woven woollen cloth orig. incorporating this design.

**Paiute** /'pʌɪuːt/ • n. (pl. same or **Paiutes**) **1** a member of either of two linguistically distinct American Indian peoples (the **Southern Paiute** and the **Northern Paiute**) of the western US. **2** either of the Uto-Aztecan languages of these peoples.
– ORIGIN from Sp. *Payuchi*, *Payuta*, influenced by **UTE**.

**pajamas** • pl. n. US spelling of **PYJAMAS**.

**pakamac** /ˈpakəmak/ (also **pacamac**) ● **n.** Brit. a lightweight plastic mackintosh that can be folded up into a small pack when not required.
– ORIGIN 1950s: phonetic respelling of *pack a mac*.

**pak choi** /pak ˈtʃɔɪ/ (also N. Amer. **bok choy**) ● **n.** a Chinese cabbage of a variety with smooth-edged tapering leaves.
– ORIGIN from Chin. (Cantonese dial.) *paâk ts'oì* 'white vegetable'.

**Pakeha** /ˈpɑːkɪhɑː/ ● **n.** NZ a white New Zealander, as opposed to a Maori.
– ORIGIN from Maori.

**Paki** ● **n.** (pl. **Pakis**) Brit. informal, offensive a Pakistani.
– ORIGIN 1960s: abbrev.

**Pakistani** /ˌpɑːkɪˈstɑːni, ˌpakɪ-, -ˈstani/ ● **n.** a native or inhabitant of Pakistan. ● **adj.** of or relating to Pakistan or Pakistanis.

**pakora** /pəˈkɔːrə/ ● **n.** (in Indian cookery) a piece of battered and deep-fried vegetable or meat.
– ORIGIN from Hindi *pakoṛā*, denoting a dish of vegetables in gram flour.

**pa kua** ● **n.** variant spelling of **BA GUA**.

**PAL** ● **n.** the television broadcasting system used in most of Europe.
– ORIGIN acronym from *Phase Alternate Line* (so named because the colour information in alternate lines is inverted in phase).

**pal** informal ● **n.** a friend. ● **v.** (**palled, palling**) (**pal up**) form a friendship.
– ORIGIN C17: from Romany, 'brother, mate', based on Sanskrit *bhrātṛ* 'brother'.

**palace** ● **n.** a large, impressive building forming the official residence of a sovereign, president, archbishop, etc.
– ORIGIN ME: from OFr. *paleis*, from L. *Palatium*, the name of the Palatine hill in Rome, where the house of the emperor was situated.

**palace revolution** (also **palace coup**) ● **n.** the non-violent overthrow of a sovereign or government by senior officials within the ruling group.

**paladin** /ˈpalədɪn/ ● **n.** historical **1** any of the twelve peers of Charlemagne's court. **2** a knight renowned for heroism and chivalry.
– ORIGIN C16: from Fr. *paladin*, from Ital. *paladino*, from L. *palatinus* (see **PALATINE**[1]).

**Palaearctic** /ˌpalɪˈɑːktɪk, ˌpeɪ-/ (also chiefly US **Palearctic**) ● **adj.** Zoology of or denoting a region comprising Eurasia north of the Himalayas, together with North Africa and the temperate part of the Arabian peninsula.

**palaeo-** /ˈpalɪəʊ, ˈpeɪlɪəʊ/ (US **paleo-**) ● **comb. form** older or ancient, especially relating to the geological past: *Palaeolithic*.
– ORIGIN from Gk *palaios* 'ancient'.

**palaeoanthropology** (US **paleoanthropology**) ● **n.** the branch of anthropology concerned with fossil hominids.
– DERIVATIVES **palaeoanthropological** adj. **palaeoanthropologist** n.

**palaeobiology** (US **paleobiology**) ● **n.** the biology of fossil animals and plants.
– DERIVATIVES **palaeobiological** adj. **palaeobiologist** n.

**palaeobotany** (US **paleobotany**) ● **n.** the study of fossil plants.
– DERIVATIVES **palaeobotanical** adj. **palaeobotanist** n.

**Palaeocene** /ˈpalɪə(ʊ)siːn, ˈpeɪ-/ (US **Paleocene**) ● **adj.** Geology relating to or denoting the earliest epoch of the Tertiary period (between the Cretaceous period and the Eocene epoch, about 65 to 56.5 million years ago), a time of rapid development of mammals.
– ORIGIN C19: from **PALAEO-** + Gk *kainos* 'new'.

**palaeoclimate** (US **paleoclimate**) ● **n.** a climate prevalent at a particular time in the geological past.
– DERIVATIVES **palaeoclimatic** adj. **palaeoclimatologist** n. **palaeoclimatology** n.

**palaeoecology** (US **paleoecology**) ● **n.** the ecology of fossil animals and plants.
– DERIVATIVES **palaeoecological** adj. **palaeoecologist** n.

**Palaeo-Eskimo** (US **Paleo-Eskimo**) ● **adj.** relating to or denoting the earliest prehistoric Inuit people, inhabiting the Arctic from Greenland to Siberia.

**Palaeogene** /ˈpalɪə(ʊ)dʒiːn, ˈpeɪ-/ (US **Paleogene**) ● **adj.** Geology relating to or denoting the earlier division of the Tertiary period (comprising the Palaeocene, Eocene, and Oligocene epochs, from about 65 to 23.3 million years ago).
– ORIGIN C19: from **PALAEO-** + Gk *genēs* (see **-GEN**).

**palaeogeography** (US **paleogeography**) ● **n.** the study of geographical features at periods in the geological past.
– DERIVATIVES **palaeogeographer** n. **palaeogeographical** adj.

**palaeography** /ˌpalɪˈɒgrəfi, peɪ-/ (US **paleography**) ● **n.** the study of ancient writing systems and the deciphering and dating of historical manuscripts.
– DERIVATIVES **palaeographer** n. **palaeographic** adj. **palaeographical** /-əˈgrafɪk(ə)l/ adj. **palaeographically** adv.

**Palaeo-Indian** (US **Paleo-Indian**) ● **adj.** relating to or denoting the earliest human inhabitants of the Americas, to *c.*5000 BC.

**Palaeolithic** /ˌpalɪə(ʊ)ˈlɪθɪk, ˌpeɪ-/ (US **Paleolithic**) ● **adj.** Archaeology relating to or denoting the early phase of the Stone Age, up to the end of the glacial period.
– ORIGIN C19: from **PALAEO-** + Gk *lithos* 'stone' + **-IC**.

**palaeomagnetism** (US **paleomagnetism**) ● **n.** the branch of geophysics concerned with the magnetism in rocks that was induced by the earth's magnetic field at the time of their formation.
– DERIVATIVES **palaeomagnetic** adj.

**palaeontology** /ˌpalɪɒnˈtɒlədʒi, ˌpeɪ-/ (US **paleontology**) ● **n.** the branch of science concerned with fossil animals and plants.
– DERIVATIVES **palaeontological** adj. **palaeontologist** n.
– ORIGIN C19: from **PALAEO-** + Gk *onta* 'beings' + **-LOGY**.

**Palaeo-Siberian** ● **adj.** of or denoting a group of languages spoken in eastern Siberia, including Chukchi.

**palaeosol** /ˈpalɪə(ʊ)sɒl, ˈpeɪ-/ (US **paleosol**) ● **n.** Geology a stratum or soil horizon which was formed as a soil in a past geological age.

**Palaeotropical** (US **Paleotropical**) ● **adj.** Botany & Zoology relating to or denoting a region including the tropical parts of the Old World.

**Palaeozoic** /ˌpalɪə(ʊ)ˈzəʊɪk, ˌpeɪ-/ (US **Paleozoic**) ● **adj.** Geology relating to or denoting the era between the Precambrian aeon and the Mesozoic era, about 570 to 245 million years ago.
– ORIGIN C19: from **PALAEO-** + Gk *zōē* 'life' + **-IC**.

**palaestra** /pəˈliːstrə, -ˈlʌɪstrə/ (also **palestra**) ● **n.** (in ancient Greece and Rome) a wrestling school or gymnasium.
– ORIGIN via L. from Gk *palaistra*, from *palaiein* 'wrestle'.

**palais** /ˈpaleɪ/ ● **n.** Brit. a public hall for dancing.
– ORIGIN C20: from Fr. *palais* (*de danse*) '(dancing) hall'.

**palanquin** /ˌpalənˈkiːn/ (also **palankeen**) ● **n.** (in India and the East) a covered litter for one passenger, carried on two horizontal poles by four or six bearers.
– ORIGIN C16: from Port. *palanquim*, from Oriya *pālaṅki*, based on Sanskrit *palyanka* 'bed, couch'.

**palapa** /pəˈlapə/ ● **n.** a traditional Mexican shelter roofed with palm leaves or branches.
– ORIGIN Mex. Sp., denoting the palm *Orbignya cohune*.

**palatable** /ˈpalətəb(ə)l/ ● **adj. 1** pleasant to taste. **2** (of an action or proposal) acceptable.
– DERIVATIVES **palatability** n. **palatably** adv.

**palatal** /ˈpalət(ə)l/ ● **adj. 1** of or relating to the palate. **2** Phonetics (of a speech sound) made by placing the blade of the tongue against or near the hard palate (e.g. *y* in *yes*). ● **n.** Phonetics a palatal sound.
– DERIVATIVES **palatalization** (also **-isation**) n. **palatalize** (also **-ise**) v. **palatally** adv.

**palate** ● **n. 1** the roof of the mouth, separating the cavities of the mouth and nose in vertebrates. **2** a person's ability to distinguish between and appreciate different flavours. **3** the flavour of a wine or beer.
– ORIGIN ME: from L. *palatum*.

**palatial** ● adj. resembling a palace, especially in being spacious or grand.
– DERIVATIVES **palatially** adv.
– ORIGIN C18: from L. *palatium* (see **PALACE**) + **-AL**.

**palatinate** /pə'latɪnət/ ● n. historical **1** a territory under the jurisdiction of a Count Palatine. **2** (**the Palatinate**) the territory of the German Empire ruled by the Count Palatine of the Rhine.

**palatine**[1] /'palətʌɪn, -tɪn/ ● adj. chiefly historical (of an official or feudal lord) having local authority that elsewhere belongs only to a sovereign. ➤(of a territory) subject to such authority.
– ORIGIN ME: from Fr. *palatin(e)*, from L. *palatinus* 'of the palace'.

**palatine**[2] /'palətʌɪn, -tɪn/ chiefly Anatomy ● adj. of or relating to the palate or the palatine bone. ● n. (also **palatine bone**) each of two bones within the skull forming parts of the eye socket, the nasal cavity, and the hard palate.
– ORIGIN C17: from Fr. *palatin(e)*, from L. *palatum* 'palate'.

**Palaung** /pə'laʊŋ/ ● n. (pl. same or **Palaungs**) **1** a member of an indigenous people of the northern Shan states of Burma (Myanmar). **2** the Mon-Khmer language of this people.
– ORIGIN the name in Palaung.

**palaver** /pə'lɑːvə/ informal ● n. **1** prolonged and tedious fuss or discussion. **2** dated a parley or improvised conference between two sides. ● v. talk unnecessarily at length.
– ORIGIN C18: from Port. *palavra* 'word'.

**palazzo** /pə'latsəʊ/ ● n. (pl. **palazzos** or **palazzi** /-tsi/) a palatial building, especially in Italy.
– ORIGIN Ital., 'palace'.

**palazzo pants** ● pl. n. women's loose wide-legged trousers.

**pale**[1] ● adj. **1** containing little colour or pigment; light in colour or shade. ➤(of a person's face) having little colour, typically as a result of shock, fear, or ill health. **2** unimpressive or inferior: *a pale imitation*. ● v. **1** become pale in one's face. **2** seem or become less important.
– DERIVATIVES **palely** adv. **paleness** n. **palish** adj.
– ORIGIN ME: from OFr. *pale*, from L. *pallidus*.

**pale**[2] ● n. **1** a wooden stake used with others to form a fence. **2** a boundary: *within the pale of decency*. **3** archaic or historical an area within determined bounds or subject to a particular jurisdiction. **4** Heraldry a broad vertical stripe down the middle of a shield.
– PHRASES **beyond the pale** outside the bounds of acceptable behaviour.
– ORIGIN ME: from OFr. *pal*, from L. *palus* 'stake'.

**palea** /'peɪlɪə/ ● n. (pl. **paleae** /-lɪiː/) Botany the upper bract of the floret of a grass. Compare with **LEMMA**[2].
– ORIGIN C18: from L., lit. 'chaff'.

**Palearctic** ● adj. chiefly US variant spelling of **PALAEARCTIC**.

**paleface** ● n. a name supposedly used by North American Indians for a white person.

**Palekh** /'pɑːlɛk/ ● n. [as modifier] denoting a type of Russian iconography or a style of miniature painting on boxes and other small items.
– ORIGIN from the name of a town north-east of Moscow renowned for this type of work.

**paleo-** ● comb. form US spelling of **PALAEO-**.

**Palestinian** /ˌpalɪ'stɪnɪən/ ● adj. of or relating to Palestine or its peoples. ● n. a member of the native Arab population of Palestine.

**palestra** /pə'lɛstrə/ ● n. variant spelling of **PALAESTRA**.

**palette** /'palɪt/ ● n. **1** a thin board or other surface on which an artist lays and mixes colours. **2** the range of colours used by a particular artist or at a particular time. **3** the range or variety of tonal or instrumental colour in a musical piece.
– ORIGIN C18: from Fr., dimin. of *pale* 'shovel', from L. *pala* 'spade'.

**palette knife** ● n. **1** a thin steel blade with a handle for mixing colours or applying or removing paint. **2** Brit. a kitchen knife or spatula with a long, blunt, flexible, round-ended blade.

**palfrey** /'pɔːlfri, 'pal-/ ● n. (pl. **-eys**) archaic a docile horse used for ordinary riding, especially by women.
– ORIGIN ME: from OFr. *palefrei*, from med. L. *palefredus*, alt. of late L. *paraveredus*, from Gk *para* 'beside, extra' + L. *veredus* 'light horse'.

**Pali** /'pɑːliː/ ● n. an Indic language, closely related to Sanskrit, which developed in northern India in the 5th–2nd centuries BC.
– ORIGIN from Pali *pāli(-bhāsā)* 'canonical texts'.

**palilalia** /ˌpalɪ'leɪlɪə/ ● n. Medicine a speech disorder characterized by involuntary repetition of words or sentences.
– ORIGIN C20: from Fr. *palilalie*, from Gk *palin* 'again' + *lalia* 'speech, chatter'.

**palimony** /'palɪməni/ ● n. informal, chiefly N. Amer. compensation made by one member of an unmarried couple to the other after separation.
– ORIGIN 1970s: from **PAL** + a shortened form of **ALIMONY**.

**palimpsest** /'palɪm(p)sɛst/ ● n. **1** a parchment or other surface in which later writing has been superimposed on effaced earlier writing. **2** something bearing visible traces of an earlier form.
– DERIVATIVES **palimpsestic** adj.
– ORIGIN C17: via L. from Gk *palimpsēstos*, from *palin* 'again' + *psēstos* 'rubbed smooth'.

**palindrome** /'palɪndrəʊm/ ● n. a word or sequence that reads the same backwards as forwards, e.g. *madam*.
– DERIVATIVES **palindromic** /-'drɒmɪk/ adj. **palindromist** n.
– ORIGIN C17: from Gk *palindromos* 'running back again'.

**paling** /'peɪlɪŋ/ ● n. a fence made from stakes. ➤a stake used in such a fence.

**palingenesis** /ˌpalɪn'dʒɛnɪsɪs/ ● n. Biology the exact reproduction of ancestral characteristics in ontogenesis.
– DERIVATIVES **palingenetic** adj.
– ORIGIN C19: from Gk *palin* 'again' + *genesis* 'birth'.

**palinode** /'palɪnəʊd/ ● n. a poem in which the poet retracts a view or sentiment expressed in a former poem.
– ORIGIN C16: via L. from Gk *palinōidia*, from *palin* 'again' + *ōidē* 'song'.

**palisade** /ˌpalɪ'seɪd/ ● n. **1** a fence of stakes or iron railings, forming an enclosure or defence. **2** (**palisades**) US a line of high cliffs. ● v. [usu. as adj. **palisaded**] enclose or provide with a palisade.
– ORIGIN C17: from Fr. *palissade*, from Provençal *palissada*, from *palissa* 'paling'.

**palisade layer** ● n. Botany a layer of parallel elongated cells below the epidermis of a leaf.

**pall**[1] /pɔːl/ ● n. **1** a cloth spread over a coffin, hearse, or tomb. **2** a dark cloud of smoke, dust, etc. **3** an enveloping air of gloom or fear. **4** an ecclesiastical pallium. ➤Heraldry a Y-shaped charge representing the front of an ecclesiastical pallium.
– ORIGIN OE *pæll* 'rich (purple) cloth', 'cloth cover for a chalice', from L. *pallium* 'covering, cloak'.

**pall**[2] /pɔːl/ ● v. become less appealing or interesting through familiarity.
– ORIGIN ME: shortening of **APPAL**.

**Palladian** /pə'leɪdɪən/ ● adj. in or denoting the neoclassical style of the 16th-century Italian architect Andrea Palladio, influential also in the 18th century.
– DERIVATIVES **Palladianism** n.

**palladium**[1] /pə'leɪdɪəm/ ● n. the chemical element of atomic number 46, a rare silvery-white metal resembling platinum. (Symbol: **Pd**)
– ORIGIN C19: mod. L., from *Pallas*, an asteroid discovered (1803) just before the element.

**palladium**[2] /pə'leɪdɪəm/ ● n. (pl. **palladia** /-dɪə/) archaic a safeguard or source of protection.
– ORIGIN ME: via L. from Gk *palladion*, denoting an image of the goddess Pallas (Athene), on which the safety of Troy was believed to depend.

**pall-bearer** ● n. a person helping to carry or officially escorting a coffin at a funeral.

**pallet**[1] ● n. **1** a straw mattress. **2** a crude or makeshift bed.
– ORIGIN ME: from Anglo-Norman Fr. *paillete*, from *paille* 'straw'.

**pallet²** ● n. **1** a portable platform on which goods can be moved, stacked, and stored. **2** a flat wooden blade with a handle, used to shape clay or plaster. **3** an artist's palette. **4** a projection on a machine part, serving to change the mode of motion of a wheel. ➤(in a clock or watch) a projection transmitting motion from an escapement to a pendulum or balance wheel.
– DERIVATIVES **palletize** (also **-ise**) v.
– ORIGIN ME: from Fr. *palette* 'little blade', from L. *pala* 'spade'.

**pallet³** ● n. Heraldry a narrow vertical strip usually borne in groups of two or three.
– ORIGIN C15: dimin. of **PALE²**.

**pallia** plural form of **PALLIUM**.

**palliasse** /'palɪas/ (also **paillasse**) ● n. a straw mattress.
– ORIGIN C16: from Fr. *paillasse*.

**palliate** /'palɪeɪt/ ● v. **1** make (the symptoms of a disease) less severe without removing the cause. **2** mitigate or disguise (something bad).
– DERIVATIVES **palliation** n. **palliator** n.
– ORIGIN ME: from late L. *palliat-*, *palliare* 'to cloak', from *pallium* 'cloak'.

**palliative** /'palɪətɪv/ ● adj. relieving pain or alleviating a problem without dealing with the cause. ● n. a palliative remedy or medicine.
– DERIVATIVES **palliatively** adv.

**pallid** ● adj. **1** pale, especially because of poor health. **2** feeble or insipid.
– DERIVATIVES **pallidly** adv. **pallidness** n.
– ORIGIN C16: from L. *pallidus* 'pale'.

**pallium** /'palɪəm/ ● n. (pl. **pallia** /-lɪə/ or **palliums**) **1** a woollen vestment conferred by the Pope on an archbishop, consisting of a narrow circular band placed round the shoulders with a short lappet hanging from front and back. **2** a man's large rectangular cloak worn in antiquity. **3** Zoology the mantle of a mollusc or brachiopod. **4** Anatomy the outer wall of the mammalian cerebrum, corresponding to the cerebral cortex.
– DERIVATIVES **pallial** adj.
– ORIGIN ME: from L., lit. 'covering'.

**pall-mall** /pal'mal/ ● n. a 16th- and 17th-century game in which a ball was driven through an iron ring suspended at the end of a long alley.
– ORIGIN from obs. Fr. *pallemaille*, from Ital. *pallamaglio*, from *palla* 'ball' + *maglio* 'mallet'.

**pallor** ● n. an unhealthy pale appearance.
– ORIGIN ME: from L., from *pallere* 'be pale'.

**pally** ● adj. (**-ier**, **-iest**) informal having a close, friendly relationship.

**palm¹** ● n. **1** (also **palm tree**) an unbranched evergreen tree with a crown of very long feathered or fan-shaped leaves, growing in tropical and warm regions. [Family Palmae: numerous species.] **2** a leaf of a palm awarded as a prize or viewed as a symbol of victory.
– ORIGIN OE *palm(a)*, of Gmc origin, from L. *palma* 'palm (of a hand)', its leaf being likened to a spread hand.

**palm²** ● n. **1** the inner surface of the hand between the wrist and fingers. **2** the palmate part of a deer's antler. ● v. **1** conceal (a small object) in the hand, especially as part of a trick. ➤(**palm something off**) sell or dispose of something by misrepresentation or fraud. ➤(**palm someone off**) informal persuade someone to accept something by deception. **2** deflect (a ball) with the palm of the hand.
– PHRASES **in the palm of one's hand** under one's control or influence. **read someone's palm** tell someone's fortune by looking at the lines on their palm.
– DERIVATIVES **palmar** /'palmə/ adj. **-palmed** adj. **palmful** n. (pl. **-fuls**).
– ORIGIN ME: from OFr. *paume*, from L. *palma*.

**palmate** /'palmeɪt/ ● adj. chiefly Botany & Zoology shaped like an open hand with a number of lobes resembling fingers.
– DERIVATIVES **palmated** adj.
– ORIGIN C18: from L. *palmatus*, from *palma* (see **PALM²**).

**palmate newt** ● n. a small olive-brown smooth-skinned newt, with partially webbed feet. [*Triturus helveticus*.]

**palmcorder** ● n. a small, hand-held camcorder.

**palmer** ● n. **1** historical a pilgrim, especially one who had returned from the Holy Land with a palm branch or leaf as a sign of having undertaken the pilgrimage. ➤an itinerant monk travelling from shrine to shrine under a vow of poverty. **2** a hairy artificial fly used in angling.
– ORIGIN ME: from Anglo-Norman Fr., from med. L. *palmarius* 'pilgrim', from L. *palma* 'palm'.

**palmette** /pal'mɛt/ ● n. Archaeology an ornament of radiating petals like a palm leaf.

**palmetto** /pal'mɛtəʊ/ ● n. (pl. **-os**) an American fan palm. [*Sabal palmetto* (south-eastern US) and other species.]
– ORIGIN C16: from Sp. *palmito*, lit. 'small palm'.

**palmier** /'palmɪeɪ/ ● n. (pl. pronounced same) a sweet crisp pastry shaped like a palm leaf.
– ORIGIN Fr., lit. 'palm tree'.

**palmistry** ● n. the art or practice of supposedly interpreting a person's character or predicting their future by examining the hand.
– DERIVATIVES **palmist** n.
– ORIGIN ME: from **PALM²** + *-estry* (of unknown origin), later alt. to *-istry*, perh. on the pattern of *sophistry*.

**palmitic acid** /pal'mɪtɪk/ ● n. Chemistry a solid saturated fatty acid obtained from palm oil and other vegetable and animal fats.
– DERIVATIVES **palmitate** /'palmɪteɪt/ n.
– ORIGIN C19: from Fr. *palmitique*, from *palme* (see **PALM¹**).

**Palm Sunday** ● n. the Sunday before Easter, on which Christ's entry into Jerusalem is celebrated in many Christian churches by processions in which branches of palms are carried.

**palmtop** ● n. a computer small and light enough to be held in one hand.

**palm wine** ● n. an alcoholic drink made from fermented palm sap.

**palmy** ● adj. (**-ier**, **-iest**) **1** comfortable and prosperous: *the palmy days of the 1970s*. **2** covered with palms.

**palmyra** ● n. an Asian fan palm which yields wood, fibre, and fruit. [*Borassus flabellifer*.]
– ORIGIN C17: from Port. *palmeira* 'palm tree', assoc. with the name of the ancient city of *Palmyra*.

**palomino** /ˌpalə'miːnəʊ/ ● n. **1** (pl. **-os**) a pale golden or tan-coloured horse with a white mane and tail, originally bred in the south-western US. **2** a variety of white grape used to make sherry and fortified wines.
– ORIGIN C20: from Latin Amer. Sp., from Sp. *palomino* 'young pigeon'.

**palooka** /pə'luːkə/ ● n. N. Amer. informal a lout.
– ORIGIN 1920s: of unknown origin.

**Palouse** /pə'luːz/ ● n. (pl. same or **Palouses**) a member of an American Indian people inhabiting the Palouse River valley in SW Washington and NW Idaho.
– ORIGIN the name in their own lang.

**paloverde** /ˌpaləʊ'vəːdi/ ● n. a thorny yellow-flowered tree that grows along water courses in the warm desert areas of America. [Genus *Cercidium*.]
– ORIGIN C19: from Latin Amer. Sp., lit. 'green tree'.

**palp** /palp/ ● n. Zoology each of a pair of elongated segmented appendages near the mouth of an arthropod, usually concerned with the senses of touch and taste.
– DERIVATIVES **palpal** adj.
– ORIGIN C19: from L. *palpus*, from *palpare* 'to feel'.

**palpable** /'palpəb(ə)l/ ● adj. **1** able to be touched or felt. **2** plain to see or comprehend: *a palpable sense of loss*.
– DERIVATIVES **palpability** n. **palpably** adv.
– ORIGIN ME: from late L. *palpabilis*, from L. *palpare* 'feel, touch gently'.

**palpate** /pal'peɪt/ ● v. examine (a part of the body) by touch, especially for medical purposes.
– DERIVATIVES **palpation** n.
– ORIGIN C19 (earlier (C15) as *palpation*): from L. *palpat-*, *palpare* 'touch gently'.

**palpebral** /'palpɪbr(ə)l/ ● adj. Anatomy of or relating to the eyelids.
– ORIGIN C19: from late L. *palpebralis*, from L. *palpebra* 'eyelid'.

**palpitant** • adj. rare palpitating.

**palpitate** /ˈpalpɪteɪt/ • v. [often as adj. **palpitating**] **1** (of the heart) beat rapidly, strongly, or irregularly. **2** shake; tremble.
– ORIGIN C17 (earlier (ME) as *palpitation*): from L. *palpitat-*, *palpitare*, frequentative of *palpare* 'touch gently'.

**palpitation** • n. (usu. **palpitations**) a noticeably rapid, strong, or irregular heartbeat due to agitation, exertion, or illness.

**palpus** /ˈpalpəs/ • n. (pl. **palpi** /-pʌɪ, -piː/) another term for **PALP**.

**palsgrave** /ˈpɔːlzgreɪv/ • n. historical a Count Palatine.
– ORIGIN C16: from early mod. Du. *paltsgrave*, from *palts* 'palatinate' + *grave* 'count'.

**palstave** /ˈpɔːlsteɪv/ • n. Archaeology a type of chisel shaped to fit into a split handle rather than having a socket for the handle.
– ORIGIN C19: from Dan. *paalstav*, from ON *pálstavr*, from *páll* 'hoe' + *stafr* 'staff'.

**palsy** /ˈpɔːlzi, ˈpɒl-/ • n. (pl. **-ies**) **1** dated paralysis, especially when accompanied by involuntary tremors. **2** archaic a condition of incapacity or helplessness. • v. (**be palsied**) be affected with palsy.
– ORIGIN ME: from OFr. *paralisie*, from an alt. of L. *paralysis* (see **PARALYSIS**).

**palsy-walsy** • adj. informal very friendly or intimate.
– ORIGIN 1930s: from **PAL** + **-SY**, by reduplication.

**palter** /ˈpɔːltə, ˈpɒl-/ • v. archaic **1** equivocate or prevaricate. **2** (**palter with**) trifle with.
– DERIVATIVES **palterer** n.
– ORIGIN C16 (in the sense 'mumble or babble'): of unknown origin.

**paltry** • adj. (**-ier**, **-iest**) **1** (of an amount) very small or meagre. **2** petty; trivial.
– DERIVATIVES **paltriness** n.
– ORIGIN C16: appar. based on dial. *pelt* 'rubbish'; cf. Low Ger. *paltrig* 'ragged'.

**paludal** /pəˈl(j)uːd(ə)l, ˈpal(j)ʊd(ə)l/ • adj. Ecology living or occurring in a marshy habitat.
– ORIGIN C19: from L. *palus*, *palud-* 'marsh' + **-AL**.

**paly** /ˈpeɪli/ • adj. Heraldry divided into equal vertical stripes.
– ORIGIN ME: from OFr. *pale* 'divided by stakes', from *pal* 'pale, stake'.

**palynology** /ˌpalɪˈnɒlədʒi/ • n. the study of pollen grains and other spores, especially as found in archaeological or geological deposits.
– DERIVATIVES **palynological** adj. **palynologist** n.
– ORIGIN 1940s: from Gk *palunein* 'sprinkle' + **-LOGY**.

**Pama-Nyungan** /ˌpɑːməˈnjʌŋgən/ • adj. relating to or denoting the main family of Australian Aboriginal languages, covering much of the continent except for a northern fringe.

**pampas** /ˈpampəs, -z/ • n. [treated as sing. or pl.] large treeless plains in South America.
– ORIGIN C18: via Sp. from Quechua *pampa* 'plain'.

**pampas grass** • n. a tall South American grass with silky flowering plumes. [*Cortaderia selloana*.]

**pamper** • v. indulge (someone) with a great deal of attention and comfort; spoil.
– ORIGIN ME (in the sense 'cram with food'): prob. of Low Ger. or Du. origin.

**pampero** /pamˈpɛːrəʊ/ • n. (pl. **-os**) a strong, cold southwesterly wind in South America, blowing from the Andes across the pampas towards the Atlantic.
– ORIGIN C18: from Sp. *pampas* 'plain'.

**pamphlet** /ˈpamflɪt/ • n. a small booklet or leaflet containing information or arguments about a single subject. • v. (**pamphleted**, **pamphleting**) distribute pamphlets to.
– ORIGIN ME: from *Pamphilet*, the familiar name of the C12 L. love poem *Pamphilus, seu de Amore*.

**pamphleteer** • n. a writer of pamphlets, especially controversial political ones.
– DERIVATIVES **pamphleteering** n.

**Pamphylian** /pamˈfɪlɪən/ • n. a native or inhabitant of the ancient region of Pamphylia in southern Asia Minor. • adj. of or relating to Pamphylia.

**pan**[1] /pan/ • n. **1** a metal container for cooking food in. **2** a bowl fitted at either end of a pair of scales. **3** a shallow bowl in which gravel and mud is shaken and washed by people seeking gold. **4** Brit. the bowl of a toilet. **5** a hollow in the ground in which water collects or in which a deposit of salt remains after evaporation. **6** a part of the lock that held the priming in old types of gun. **7** a hard stratum of compacted soil. **8** a steel drum. **9** US informal a face. • v. (**panned**, **panning**) **1** informal criticize severely. **2** wash gravel in a pan to separate out (gold). **3** (**pan out**) end up or conclude, especially in a good way.
– PHRASES **go down the pan** informal reach a stage of abject failure or uselessness.
– DERIVATIVES **panful** n. (pl. **-fuls**). **pan-like** adj.
– ORIGIN OE *panne*, of W. Gmc origin, perh. based on L. *patina* 'dish'.

**pan**[2] /pan/ • v. (**panned**, **panning**) swing (a video or film camera) in a horizontal or vertical plane to give a panoramic effect or follow a subject. • n. a panning movement.
– PHRASES **pan and scan** a technique for narrowing the aspect ratio of a widescreen film to fit a television screen by continuously selecting the most significant portion of the original picture.
– ORIGIN C20: abbrev. of **PANORAMA**.

**pan**[3] /pɑːn/ • n. variant spelling of **PAAN**.

**pan-** • comb. form including everything or everyone, especially in relation to the whole of a continent, people, etc.: *pan-African*.
– ORIGIN from Gk *pan*, neut. of *pas* 'all'.

**panacea** /ˌpanəˈsiːə/ • n. a solution or remedy for all difficulties or diseases.
– DERIVATIVES **panacean** adj.
– ORIGIN C16: via L. from Gk *panakeia*, from *panakēs* 'all-healing'.

**panache** /pəˈnaʃ/ • n. **1** flamboyant confidence of style or manner. **2** historical a tuft or plume of feathers, especially as a headdress or on a helmet.
– ORIGIN C16: from Fr., from Ital. *pennacchio*, from late L. *pinnaculum*, dimin. of *pinna* 'feather'.

**panada** /pəˈnɑːdə/ • n. a simple dish consisting of bread boiled to a pulp and flavoured.
– ORIGIN C16: from Sp. and Port., based on L. *panis* 'bread'.

**pan-Africanism** • n. the principle or advocacy of the political union of all the indigenous inhabitants of Africa.
– DERIVATIVES **pan-African** adj.

**panama** • n. a man's wide-brimmed hat of straw-like material, originally made from the leaves of a tropical palm tree.
– ORIGIN C19: named after the country of *Panama*.

**Panamanian** /ˈpanəmeɪnɪən/ • n. a native or inhabitant of Panama. • adj. of or relating to Panama.

**pan-Americanism** • n. the principle or advocacy of co-operation among all the countries of North and South America.
– DERIVATIVES **pan-American** adj.

**pan-Arabism** • n. the principle or advocacy of political alliance or union of all the Arab states.
– DERIVATIVES **pan-Arab** adj.

**panatella** /ˌpanəˈtɛlə/ • n. a long thin cigar.
– ORIGIN C19: from Latin Amer. Sp. *panatela*, denoting a long thin biscuit.

**pancake** • n. **1** a thin, flat cake of batter, fried and turned in a pan and typically rolled up with a sweet or savoury filling. **2** theatrical make-up consisting of a flat solid layer of compressed powder. • v. **1** (of an aircraft) make a pancake landing. **2** informal flatten or become flattened.
– PHRASES (**as**) **flat as a pancake** completely flat.

**Pancake Day** • n. Shrove Tuesday, when pancakes are traditionally eaten.

**pancake landing** • n. an emergency landing in which an aircraft levels out close to the ground and drops vertically with its undercarriage still retracted.

**pancake race** • n. a race in which each competitor

must toss a pancake from a pan as they run.

**pancetta** /pan'(t)ʃɛtə/ ● **n.** Italian cured belly of pork.
– ORIGIN Ital., dimin. of *pancio* 'belly'.

**panchakarma** /ˌpʌntʃə'kɑːmə/ ● **n.** (in Ayurvedic medicine) a fivefold detoxification treatment involving massage, herbal therapy, and other procedures.
– ORIGIN from Sanskrit *panca* 'five' + *karman* 'action'.

**panchayat** /pʌn'tʃʌɪjət/ ● **n.** Indian a village council.
– ORIGIN from Hindi (orig. denoting a council consisting of five members), from Sanskrit *panca* 'five' + *āyatta* 'depending upon'.

**Panchen Lama** /ˌpantʃ(ə)n 'lɑːmə/ ● **n.** a Tibetan lama ranking next after the Dalai Lama.
– ORIGIN Tibetan *panchen*, abbrev. of *pandi-tachen-po* 'great learned one'; cf. **PUNDIT**.

**panchromatic** ● **adj.** denoting black-and-white photographic film sensitive to all colours of the spectrum.

**pancreas** /'paŋkrɪəs/ ● **n.** (pl. **pancreases**) a large gland behind the stomach which secretes digestive enzymes into the duodenum.
– DERIVATIVES **pancreatic** adj.
– ORIGIN C16: mod. L., from Gk *pankreas*, from *pan* 'all' + *kreas* 'flesh'.

**pancreatectomy** /ˌpaŋkrɪə'tɛktəmi/ ● **n.** (pl. **-ies**) surgical removal of the pancreas.

**pancreatin** /'paŋkrɪətɪn/ ● **n.** a mixture of pancreatic enzymes obtained from animals, given as a medicine to aid digestion.

**pancreatitis** /ˌpaŋkrɪə'tʌɪtɪs/ ● **n.** Medicine inflammation of the pancreas.

**pancytopenia** /ˌpansʌɪtə(ʊ)'piːniə/ ● **n.** Medicine deficiency of all three cellular components of the blood (red cells, white cells, and platelets).
– ORIGIN C20: from **PAN-** + **CYTO-** + Gk *penia* 'lack'.

**panda**[1] /'pandə/ ● **n. 1** (also **giant panda**) a large bear-like black-and-white mammal native to bamboo forests in China. [*Ailuropoda melanoleuca.*] **2** (also **red panda**) a Himalayan raccoon-like mammal with thick reddish-brown fur and a bushy tail. [*Ailurus fulgens.*]
– ORIGIN C19: from Nepali.

**panda**[2] /'pʌndə/ ● **n.** a Brahmin expert in genealogy, who provides religious guidance and acts as a family priest.
– ORIGIN via Hindi from Sanskrit *paṇḍita* 'learned, wise'.

**panda car** ● **n.** Brit. informal a small police patrol car (originally black and white or blue and white).

**pandanus** /pan'deɪnəs, -'dan-/ (also **pandan**) ● **n.** a tropical tree or shrub with a twisted stem, long, spiny leaves, and fibrous edible fruit. [Genus *Pandanus.*]
– ORIGIN mod. L., from Malay *pandan*.

**pandect** /'pandɛkt/ ● **n.** chiefly historical a complete body of the laws of a country. ➤ **(the Pandects)** a 6th-century compendium of the Roman civil law.
– DERIVATIVES **pandectist** n.
– ORIGIN C16: from Fr. *pandecte*, from L. *pandecta*, from Gk *pandektēs* 'all-receiver'.

**pandemic** /pan'dɛmɪk/ ● **adj.** (of a disease) prevalent over a whole country or large part of the world. ● **n.** an outbreak of such a disease.
– ORIGIN C17: from Gk *pandēmos* (from *pan* 'all' + *dēmos* 'people') + **-IC**.

**pandemonium** /ˌpandɪ'məʊnɪəm/ ● **n.** wild and noisy disorder or confusion; uproar.
– ORIGIN C17: mod. L. (denoting the place of all demons, in Milton's *Paradise Lost*), from **PAN-** + Gk *daimōn* 'demon'.

**pander** ● **v.** (**pander to**) gratify or indulge (an immoral or distasteful desire or habit). ● **n. 1** dated a pimp. **2** archaic a person who panders to the desires of another.
– ORIGIN ME (as n.): from *Pandare*, the name of a character in Chaucer's *Troilus and Criseyde*.

**pandit** (also **pundit**) ● **n.** a Hindu scholar learned in Sanskrit and Hindu philosophy and religion.

**P & L** ● **abbrev.** profit and loss account.

**P. & O.** ● **abbrev.** Peninsular and Oriental Shipping Company (or Line).

**Pandora's box** ● **n.** a process that once begun generates many complicated problems.
– ORIGIN from *Pandora* in Gk mythology, who was sent to earth with a jar or box of evils and contrary to instructions opened it, letting out all the evils to infect the earth; hope alone remained.

**pandowdy** /pan'daʊdi/ ● **n.** (pl. **-ies**) N. Amer. a kind of spiced apple pudding baked in a deep dish.
– ORIGIN of unknown origin.

**p. & p.** ● **abbrev.** Brit. postage and packing.

**pane** ● **n. 1** a single sheet of glass in a window or door. **2** a sheet or page of stamps.
– ORIGIN ME: from OFr. *pan*, from L. *pannus* 'piece of cloth'.

**paneer** /pa'nɪə/ (also **panir**) ● **n.** a type of milk curd cheese used in Indian, Iranian, and Afghan cooking.
– ORIGIN from Hindi or Pers. *panīr* 'cheese'.

**panegyric** /ˌpanɪ'dʒɪrɪk/ ● **n.** a speech or text in praise of someone or something.
– DERIVATIVES **panegyrical** adj.
– ORIGIN C17: from Fr. *panégyrique*, via L. from Gk *panēgurikos* 'of public assembly'.

**panegyrize** /'panɪdʒɪrʌɪz/ (also **-ise**) ● **v.** speak or write in praise of; eulogize.
– DERIVATIVES **panegyrist** n.

**panel** ● **n. 1** a distinct section, typically rectangular, forming part of or set into a door, vehicle, garment, etc. ➤ a decorated area within a larger design containing a separate subject. **2** a flat board on which instruments or controls are fixed. **3** a small group of people brought together to investigate or decide upon a particular matter. ➤ Brit. a list of medical practitioners registered as accepting patients under the National Health Service. ➤ chiefly N. Amer. a list of available jurors or a jury. ➤ Scots Law a person or people charged with a crime or offence. ● **v.** (**panelled**, **panelling**; US **paneled**, **paneling**) [usu. as adj. **panelled**] cover (a wall or other surface) with panels.
– DERIVATIVES **panelling** n.
– ORIGIN ME (in sense 'piece of parchment', later 'list'): from OFr., based on L. *pannus* '(piece of) cloth'.

**panel beater** ● **n.** Brit. a person whose job is to beat out the bodywork of motor vehicles.

**panel game** ● **n.** Brit. a broadcast quiz played by a panel or team of people.

**panel heating** ● **n.** a system of heating rooms by panels in the walls and ceiling that contain hot-water pipes or a similar heat source.

**panellist** (US **panelist**) ● **n.** a member of a panel, especially in a broadcast game or discussion.

**panel pin** ● **n.** Brit. a light, thin nail with a very small head.

**panel saw** ● **n.** Brit. a light saw with small teeth, for cutting thin wood.

**panel truck** ● **n.** N. Amer. a small enclosed delivery truck.

**panentheism** /pan'ɛnθiːɪz(ə)m/ ● **n.** the belief or doctrine that God is greater than the universe and includes and interpenetrates it.
– DERIVATIVES **panentheistic** adj.

**panettone** /ˌpanɪ'təʊneɪ, -ni/ ● **n.** (pl. **panettoni** /ˌpanɪ'təʊni/) a rich Italian bread made with eggs, fruit, and butter, eaten at Christmas.
– ORIGIN Ital., from *panetto* 'cake', dimin. of *pane* 'bread'.

**panforte** /pan'fɔːteɪ, -ti, Italian pan'forte/ ● **n.** a hard, spicy Italian cake containing nuts, candied peel, and honey.
– ORIGIN Ital., from *pane* 'bread' + *forte* 'strong'.

**pan-fry** ● **v.** fry in a pan in shallow fat.

**pang** ● **n.** a sudden sharp pain or painful emotion.
– ORIGIN C15: perh. an alt. of **PRONG**.

**panga** /'paŋgə/ ● **n.** a bladed African tool like a machete.
– ORIGIN from Kiswahili.

**pan-Germanism** ● **n.** the principle or advocacy of a political unification of all Europeans speaking German or a Germanic language.
– DERIVATIVES **pan-German** adj. **pan-Germanic** adj.

**Pangloss** /'paŋglɒs/ ● **n.** a person who is optimistic regardless of the circumstances.

– DERIVATIVES **Panglossian** adj.
– ORIGIN C19: from the name of the tutor and philosopher in Voltaire's *Candide* (1759).

**pangolin** /paŋ'gə(ʊ)lɪn/ • **n.** an insectivorous mammal whose body is covered with horny overlapping scales. [Genera *Manis* (Asia) and *Phataginus* (Africa).]
– ORIGIN C18: from Malay *peng-guling*, lit. 'roller' (from its habit of rolling into a ball).

**panhandle** N. Amer. • **n.** a narrow strip of territory projecting from the main territory of one state into another. • **v.** informal beg in the street.
– DERIVATIVES **panhandler** n.

**Panhellenism** /ˌpan'hɛlənɪzm, -hɛ'liː-/ • **n.** the principle or advocacy of the political union of all Greeks.
– DERIVATIVES **Panhellenic** adj.

**pani** /'pɑːni/ • **n.** Indian water.
– ORIGIN from Hindi *pānī*.

**panic[1]** • **n.** sudden uncontrollable fear or anxiety. ➤ informal frenzied hurry to do something. • **v.** (**panicked**, **panicking**) be affected by or cause to feel panic. ➤(**panic someone into**) drive someone through panic into (hasty or rash action).
– PHRASES **panic stations** Brit. informal a state of alarm or emergency.
– DERIVATIVES **panicky** adj.
– ORIGIN C17: from Fr. *panique*, from mod. L. *panicus*, from Gk *panikos*, from the name of the Gk god *Pan*, noted for causing terror.

**panic[2]** (also **panic grass**) • **n.** a cereal or fodder grass of a group including millet. [*Panicum* and other genera.]
– ORIGIN ME: from L. *panicum*, from *panus* 'ear of millet' (lit. 'thread wound on a bobbin'), based on Gk *pēnos* 'web', *pēnion* 'bobbin'.

**panic attack** • **n.** a sudden overwhelming feeling of acute and disabling anxiety.

**panic button** • **n.** a button for summoning help in an emergency.

**panicle** /'panɪk(ə)l/ • **n.** Botany a loose branching cluster of flowers, as in oats.
– DERIVATIVES **panicled** adj.
– ORIGIN C16: from L. *panicula*, dimin. of *panus* (see **PANIC[2]**).

**panino** /pa'niːnəʊ/ • **n.** (pl. **panini** /-ni/) a sandwich made with a baguette or with Italian bread, typically one that is toasted.
– ORIGIN Ital., lit. 'bread roll'.

**pani puri** /'pɑːnɪ ˌpuːri/ • **n.** (in Indian cookery) a puff-pastry ball filled with spiced mashed potato and tamarind juice and fried.
– ORIGIN from Hindi *pānī* 'water' and *pūrī* from Sanskrit *pūrikā* 'fried wheaten cake'.

**panir** • **n.** variant spelling of **PANEER**.

**Panjabi** • **n.** (pl. **Panjabis**) & **adj.** variant spelling of **PUNJABI**.

**panjandrum** /pan'dʒandrəm/ • **n.** a person who has or claims to have a great deal of authority or influence.
– ORIGIN C19: from *Grand Panjandrum*, an invented phr. in a nonsense verse (1755) by Samuel Foote.

**pannage** /'panɪdʒ/ • **n.** chiefly historical the right of feeding pigs or other animals in a wood.
– ORIGIN ME: from OFr. *pasnage*, from med. L. *pastionaticum*, from *pastio(n-)* 'pasturing'.

**panne** /pan/ • **n.** a shining fabric resembling velvet, made of silk or rayon and having a flattened pile.
– ORIGIN C18: from Fr., of unknown origin.

**pannier** • **n. 1** a basket, especially one of a pair carried by a beast of burden. ➤a bag or box fitted on either side of the rear wheel of a bicycle or motorcycle. **2** historical part of a skirt looped up round the hips and supported on a frame.
– ORIGIN ME: from OFr. *panier*, from L. *panarium* 'bread basket'.

**pannikin** • **n.** a small metal drinking cup.
– ORIGIN C19: from **PAN[1]** + **-KIN**.

**pannist** • **n.** W. Indian a person who plays in a steel band.

**pannus** /'panəs/ • **n.** Medicine a condition in which a layer of vascular fibrous tissue covers an organ.
– ORIGIN ME: perh. from L., lit. 'cloth'.

**panoply** /'panəpli/ • **n. 1** a complete or impressive collection or display of something. **2** historical or poetic/literary a complete set of arms or suit of armour.
– DERIVATIVES **panoplied** adj.
– ORIGIN C16: from Fr. *panoplie* or mod. L. *panoplia* 'full armour', from Gk.

**panoptic** /pan'ɒptɪk/ • **adj.** showing or seeing the whole at one view.
– ORIGIN C19: from Gk *panoptos* 'seen by all' + **-IC**.

**panopticon** /pan'ɒptɪk(ə)n/ • **n.** historical a circular prison with cells arranged around a central well, from which prisoners could at all times be observed.
– ORIGIN C18: from **PAN-** + Gk *optikon*, neut. of *optikos* 'optic'.

**panorama** • **n. 1** an unbroken view of a surrounding region. **2** a complete survey of a subject or sequence of events.
– DERIVATIVES **panoramic** adj. **panoramically** adv.
– ORIGIN C18: from **PAN-** + Gk *horama* 'view'.

**pan-pan** • **n.** an international radio distress signal, of less urgency than a mayday signal.
– ORIGIN 1920s: *pan* from Fr. *panne* 'breakdown'.

**pan pipes** • **pl. n.** a musical instrument made from a row of short pipes of varying length fixed together and played by blowing across the top.
– ORIGIN orig. assoc. with the Gk rural god *Pan*.

**panpsychism** /pan'sʌɪkɪz(ə)m/ • **n.** the doctrine or belief that everything material, however small, has an element of individual consciousness.
– DERIVATIVES **panpsychist** adj. & n.

**pansexual** • **adj.** not limited or inhibited in sexual choice with regard to gender or activity. • **n.** a person who is sexually inclusive in this way.
– DERIVATIVES **pansexuality** n.

**panslavism** /pan'slɑːvɪz(ə)m/ • **n.** the principle or advocacy of the political union of all Slavs or all Slavic peoples.
– DERIVATIVES **panslavist** adj. & n.

**panspermia** /pan'spəːmɪə/ • **n.** the theory that life on the earth originated from micro-organisms or substances present in outer space.
– ORIGIN C19: from Gk, from *panspermos* 'containing all kinds of seed'.

**panstick** • **n.** a kind of matt cosmetic foundation in stick form, used in theatrical make-up.
– ORIGIN 1940s: from **PANCAKE** + **STICK[1]**.

**pansy** • **n. 1** a viola with flowers in rich colours, especially of a cultivated variety. [*Viola tricolor* (**wild pansy**) and related species and hybrids.] **2** informal, derogatory an effeminate or homosexual man.
– DERIVATIVES **pansified** adj. (informal, derogatory).
– ORIGIN ME: from Fr. *pensée* 'thought, pansy', from *penser* 'think'.

**pant** • **v. 1** breathe with short, quick breaths, typically from exertion or excitement. ➤long for or to do something. **2** poetic/literary (of the heart or chest) throb violently from strong emotions. • **n.** a short, quick breath.
– DERIVATIVES **panting** adj. **pantingly** adv.
– ORIGIN ME: rel. to OFr. *pantaisier* 'be agitated, gasp', based on Gk *phantasioun* 'cause to imagine', from *phantasia* (see **FANTASY**).

**Pantagruelian** /ˌpantəgruː'ɛlɪən/ • **adj.** rare enormous.
– ORIGIN C17: from *Pantagruel* (the name of a giant in Rabelais' *Gargantua and Pantagruel*) + **-IAN**.

**pantalettes** (chiefly N. Amer. also **pantalets**) • **pl. n.** long underpants with a frill at the bottom of each leg, worn by women and girls in the 19th century.

**pantaloon** • **n. 1** (**pantaloons**) women's baggy trousers gathered at the ankles. ➤historical men's close-fitting breeches fastened below the calf or at the foot. **2** (**Pantaloon**) a character in Italian commedia dell'arte represented as a foolish old man wearing pantaloons.
– ORIGIN C16: from Fr. *pantalon*, from the Ital. name *Pantalone* 'Pantaloon'.

**pantechnicon** /pan'tɛknɪk(ə)n/ • **n.** Brit. a large van for transporting furniture.

– ORIGIN C19: from **PAN-** + *tekhnikon* 'piece of art', orig. the name of a London bazaar selling artistic work, later converted into a furniture warehouse.

**pantheism** /ˈpanθiːɪz(ə)m/ ● **n. 1** a doctrine or belief which identifies God with the universe, or regards the universe as a manifestation of God. **2** rare worship that admits or tolerates all gods.

– DERIVATIVES **pantheist** n. **pantheistic** adj. **pantheistical** adj. **pantheistically** adv.

– ORIGIN C18: from **PAN-** + Gk *theos* 'god' + **-ISM**.

**pantheon** /ˈpanθɪən/ ● **n. 1** all the gods of a people or religion collectively. **2** an ancient temple dedicated to all the gods. **3** a collection of particularly famous or important people.

– ORIGIN ME (referring especially to a circular temple in Rome): via L. from Gk *pantheion*, from *pan* 'all' + *theion* 'holy' (from *theos* 'god').

**panther** ● **n. 1** a leopard, especially a black one. **2** N. Amer. a puma or a jaguar.

– ORIGIN ME: from OFr. *pantere*, from L. *panthera*, from Gk *panthēr*.

**panties** ● **pl. n.** informal legless underpants worn by women and girls; knickers.

**pantihose** ● **pl. n.** variant spelling of **PANTYHOSE**.

**pantile** /ˈpantʌɪl/ ● **n.** a roof tile curved to form an S-shaped section, fitted to overlap its neighbour.

– DERIVATIVES **pantiled** adj.

– ORIGIN C17: from **PAN¹** + **TILE**.

**Pantisocracy** /ˌpantɪˈsɒkrəsi/ ● **n.** a form of utopian social organization in which all are equal in social position and responsibility.

– DERIVATIVES **Pantisocratic** adj.

– ORIGIN C18: from **PANTO-** + Gk *isokratia* 'equality of power'.

**panto** ● **n.** (pl. **-os**) Brit. informal a pantomime.

**panto-** ● **comb. form** all; universal: *pantomime*.

– ORIGIN from Gk *pas*, *pant-* 'all'.

**Pantocrator** /panˈtɒkrətə/ ● **n.** a title of Christ represented as the ruler of the universe, especially in Byzantine church decoration.

– ORIGIN C19: via L. from Gk, 'ruler over all'.

**pantograph** ● **n. 1** an instrument for copying a plan or drawing on a different scale by a system of hinged and jointed rods. **2** a jointed framework conveying a current to an electric train or tram from overhead wires.

– DERIVATIVES **pantographic** adj.

– ORIGIN C18: from **PANTO-** + Gk *-graphos* 'writing'.

**pantomime** ● **n. 1** Brit. a theatrical entertainment involving music, topical jokes, and slapstick comedy, usually produced around Christmas. **2** a dramatic entertainment in which performers express meaning through gestures accompanied by music. **3** informal a ridiculous or confused action or situation. ● **v.** express or represent by extravagant and exaggerated mime.

– DERIVATIVES **pantomimic** adj.

– ORIGIN C16: from Fr. *pantomime* or L. *pantomimus*, from Gk *pantomimos* (see **PANTO-**, **MIME**).

**pantothenic acid** /ˌpantəˈθɛnɪk/ ● **n.** Biochemistry a vitamin of the B complex, found in rice, bran, etc., and essential for the oxidation of fats and carbohydrates.

– DERIVATIVES **pantothenate** n.

– ORIGIN 1930s: from Gk *pantothen* 'from every side' (with allusion to its widespread occurrence).

**pantry** ● **n.** (pl. **-ies**) a small room or cupboard in which food, crockery, and cutlery are kept.

– ORIGIN ME: from Anglo-Norman Fr. *panterie*, from *paneter* 'baker', based on L. *panis* 'bread'.

**pants** ● **pl. n. 1** Brit. underpants or knickers. **2** chiefly N. Amer. trousers. **3** Brit. informal rubbish; nonsense.

– PHRASES **catch someone with their pants** (or **trousers**) **down** informal catch someone in an embarrassingly unprepared state. **fly** (or **drive**) **by the seat of one's pants** informal rely on instinct rather than logic or knowledge. **scare** (or **bore** etc.) **the pants off someone** informal make someone extremely scared, bored, etc.

– ORIGIN C19: abbrev. of *pantaloons* (see **PANTALOON**).

**pantsuit** (also **pants suit**) ● **n.** chiefly N. Amer. a trouser suit.

**panty girdle** (also **pantie girdle**) ● **n.** a woman's control undergarment with a crotch shaped like pants.

**pantyhose** (also **pantihose**) ● **pl. n.** N. Amer. women's thin nylon tights.

**pantywaist** ● **n.** N. Amer. informal a feeble or effeminate person.

– ORIGIN 1930s: extended use of the literal sense 'child's garment consisting of panties attached to a bodice'.

**panzer** /ˈpanzə/ ● **n.** a German armoured unit.

– ORIGIN from Ger. *Panzer*, lit. 'coat of mail'.

**pap¹** ● **n. 1** bland soft or semi-liquid food such as that suitable for babies or invalids. **2** (in Africa and the Caribbean) maize porridge. **3** worthless or trivial reading matter or entertainment.

– ORIGIN ME: prob. from Mid. Low Ger., MDu. *pappe*, prob. based on L. *pappare* 'eat'.

**pap²** ● **n.** archaic or dialect a woman's breast or nipple.

– ORIGIN ME: prob. of Scand. origin, from a base imitative of the sound of sucking.

**papa** /pəˈpɑː, ˈpɑːpə/ ● **n. 1** N. Amer. or dated one's father. **2** a code word representing the letter P, used in radio communication.

– ORIGIN C17: from Fr., via late L. from Gk *papas*.

**papacy** /ˈpeɪpəsi/ ● **n.** (pl. **-ies**) **1** the office or authority of the Pope. **2** the tenure of office of a pope.

– ORIGIN ME: from med. L. *papatia*, from *papa* 'pope'.

**Papago** /ˈpapəgəʊ, ˈpɑː-/ ● **n.** (pl. same or **-os**) **1** a member of an American Indian people of the south-western US and northern Mexico. **2** the Uto-Aztecan language of this people.

– ORIGIN via Sp. from an Amer. Ind. word.

**papain** /pəˈpeɪɪn, pəˈpʌɪɪn/ ● **n.** a protein-digesting enzyme obtained from unripe papaya fruit, used to tenderize meat and as a food supplement to aid digestion.

– ORIGIN C19: from **PAPAYA** + **-IN¹**.

**papal** /ˈpeɪp(ə)l/ ● **adj.** of or relating to a pope or the papacy.

– DERIVATIVES **papally** adv.

– ORIGIN ME: from OFr., from med. L. *papalis*, from eccles. L. *papa* 'bishop (of Rome)'.

**papalist** chiefly historical ● **n.** a supporter of the papacy, especially an advocate of papal supremacy. ● **adj.** supporting the papacy.

**paparazzo** /ˌpapəˈratsəʊ/ ● **n.** (pl. **paparazzi** /-tsi/) (usu. **paparazzi**) a freelance photographer who pursues celebrities to get photographs of them.

– ORIGIN C20: from Ital., from the name of a character in Fellini's film *La Dolce Vita* (1960).

**papaveraceous** /pəˌpeɪvəˈreɪʃəs, -ˌpav-/ ● **adj.** Botany relating to or denoting plants of the poppy family (Papaveraceae).

– ORIGIN C19: from mod. L. *Papaveraceae*, based on L. *papaver* 'poppy', + **-OUS**.

**papaverine** /pəˈpeɪvərʌɪn, -ˈpav-, -iːn/ ● **n.** Chemistry a compound present in opium, used medicinally to alleviate muscle spasm and asthma.

**papaw** /pəˈpɔː/ ● **n.** variant spelling of **PAWPAW**.

**papaya** /pəˈpʌɪə/ ● **n. 1** a fruit shaped like an elongated melon, with edible orange flesh and small black seeds. **2** the fast-growing tree which bears this fruit, native to warm regions of America. [*Carica papaya*.]

– ORIGIN C16: from Sp. and Port. (see **PAWPAW**).

**paper** ● **n. 1** material manufactured in thin sheets from the pulp of wood or other fibrous substances, used for writing or printing on or as wrapping material. ➤ (**papers**) sheets of paper covered with writing or printing; documents. ➤ [as modifier] officially documented but having no real existence or use: *a paper profit*. **2** a newspaper. **3** a government report or policy document. **4** an essay or dissertation read at a seminar or published in a journal. **5** a set of examination questions to be answered at one session. ➤ the written answers to such questions. **6** theatrical slang free passes of admission to a theatre or other entertainment. ● **v. 1** cover with wallpaper. ➤ (**paper over**) cover (a hole or blemish) with wallpaper. ➤ (**paper over**) disguise (an awkward problem) instead of resolving it. **2** theatrical slang fill (a theatre) by giving out free tickets.

– PHRASES **on paper 1** in writing. **2** in theory rather than in reality.
– DERIVATIVES **paperer** n. **paperless** adj. **papery** n.
– ORIGIN ME: from Anglo-Norman Fr. *papir*, from L. *papyrus* (see **PAPYRUS**).

**paperback** • n. a book bound in stiff paper or flexible card.

**paperbark** • n. a cajuput or other tree with peeling papery bark.

**paperboard** • n. cardboard or pasteboard.

**paper boy** (or **paper girl**) • n. a boy (or girl) who delivers newspapers to people's homes.

**paperchase** • n. **1** Brit. a cross-country race in which the runners follow a trail marked by torn-up paper. **2** informal an excessively bureaucratic procedure.

**paper clip** • n. a piece of bent wire or plastic used for holding several sheets of paper together.

**paperhanger** • n. a person who decorates with wallpaper, especially professionally.

**paperknife** • n. (pl. **paperknives**) a blunt knife used for opening envelopes.

**paper money** • n. money in the form of banknotes.

**paper mulberry** • n. a mulberry tree whose inner bark is used for making paper and tapa cloth. [*Broussonetia papyrifera*.]

**paper nautilus** • n. a small floating octopus, the female of which secretes a thin coiled papery shell in which its eggs are laid. [Genus *Argonauta*.]

**paper-pusher** • n. informal, chiefly N. Amer. a bureaucrat or menial clerical worker.
– DERIVATIVES **paper-pushing** n. & adj.

**paper round** (N. Amer. **paper route**) • n. a job of regularly delivering newspapers.

**paper taffeta** • n. a lightweight taffeta with a crisp papery finish.

**paper tape** • n. paper in the form of a long narrow strip with holes punched in it, used in older computer systems for conveying data or instructions.

**paper-thin** • adj. very thin or insubstantial.

**paper tiger** • n. a person or thing that appears threatening but is ineffectual.

**paper trail** • n. chiefly N. Amer. the total amount of written evidence of someone's activities.

**paperweight** • n. a small, heavy object for keeping loose papers in place.

**paperwork** • n. routine work involving written documents such as forms, records, or letters.

**papier collé** /ˌpapɪeɪ ˈkɒleɪ/ • n. (pl. **papiers collés** pronunc. same) the technique of using paper for collage.
– ORIGIN Fr., lit. 'glued paper'.

**papier mâché** /ˌpapɪeɪ ˈmaʃeɪ/ • n. a malleable mixture of paper and glue that becomes hard when dry, used to make boxes, ornaments, etc.
– ORIGIN Fr., lit. 'chewed paper'.

**papilla** /pəˈpɪlə/ • n. (pl. **papillae** /-liː/) **1** a small rounded protuberance on a part or organ of the body. **2** a small fleshy projection on a plant.
– DERIVATIVES **papillary** adj. **papillate** /ˈpapɪleɪt, pəˈpɪlət/ adj. **papillose** /ˈpapɪləʊs/ adj.
– ORIGIN C17: from L., lit. 'nipple', dimin. of *papula* 'small protuberance'.

**papilloma** /ˌpapɪˈləʊmə/ • n. (pl. **papillomas** or **papillomata** /-mətə/) Medicine a small wart-like growth on the skin or on a mucous membrane, derived from the epidermis and usually benign.

**papillon** /ˈpapɪlɒn, ˈpapɪjɒ̃/ • n. a dog of a toy breed with ears suggesting the form of a butterfly.
– ORIGIN C20: from Fr., lit. 'butterfly', from L. *papilio(n-)*.

**papist** /ˈpeɪpɪst/ chiefly derogatory • n. **1** a Roman Catholic. **2** another term for **PAPALIST**. • adj. Roman Catholic or papalist.
– DERIVATIVES **papism** n. **papistical** adj. (archaic). **papistry** n.
– ORIGIN C16: from Fr. *papiste* or mod. L. *papista*, from eccles. L. *papa* 'bishop (of Rome)'.

**papoose** /pəˈpuːs/ • n. chiefly offensive a young North American Indian child.
– ORIGIN C17: from Algonquian *papoos*.

**pappardelle** /ˌpapɑːˈdɛleɪ, Italian ˌpaparˈdelle/ • pl. n. pasta in the form of broad flat ribbons.
– ORIGIN Ital., from *pappare* 'eat hungrily'.

**pappus** /ˈpapəs/ • n. (pl. **pappi** /-pʌɪ, -piː/) Botany a tuft of hairs on a seed which assists dispersal by the wind.
– DERIVATIVES **pappose** adj.
– ORIGIN C18: via L. from Gk *pappos*.

**pappy**[1] • n. (pl. **-ies**) a child's word for father.

**pappy**[2] • adj. of the nature of pap.

**paprika** /ˈpaprɪkə, pəˈpriːkə/ • n. a powdered spice with a deep orange-red colour and a mildly pungent flavour, made from certain varieties of sweet pepper.
– ORIGIN C19: from Hungarian.

**Pap test** /pap/ • n. a test carried out on a cervical smear to detect cancer of the cervix or womb.
– ORIGIN 1960s: named after the Amer. scientist George N. *Papanicolaou*.

**Papuan** • n. **1** a native or inhabitant of Papua, or of Papua New Guinea. **2** a heterogeneous group of around 750 languages spoken in Papua New Guinea and neighbouring islands. • adj. of or relating to Papua or its people or their languages.

**papule** /ˈpapjuːl/ (also **papula** /-jʊlə/) • n. (pl. **papules** or **papulae** /-jʊliː/) Medicine a small pimple or swelling on the skin, often forming part of a rash.
– DERIVATIVES **papular** adj. **papulose** adj. **papulous** adj.
– ORIGIN C18: from L. *papula*.

**papyrus** /pəˈpʌɪrəs/ • n. (pl. **papyri** /-rʌɪ, -riː/ or **papyruses**) **1** a material prepared in ancient Egypt from the pithy stem of a water plant and used in the ancient Mediterranean world for writing or painting on. **2** the tall aquatic sedge from which this material is obtained. [*Cyperus papyrus*.]
– DERIVATIVES **papyrological** adj. **papyrologist** n. **papyrology** n.
– ORIGIN ME: via L. from Gk *papuros*.

**par** • n. **1** Golf the number of strokes a first-class player should normally require for a particular hole or course. ➤a score of this number of strokes at a hole. **2** (usu. in phr. **above** or **below** or **under par**, or **on a par with**) the usual or expected level or amount. **3** Stock Exchange the face value of a share or other security, as distinct from its market value. ➤(also **par of exchange**) the recognized value of one country's currency in terms of another's. • v. (**parred**, **parring**) Golf play (a hole) in par.
– PHRASES **par for the course** what is normal or expected in any given circumstances.
– ORIGIN C16 (in the sense 'equality of value or standing'): from L., 'equal', also 'equality'.

**par.** (also **para.**) • abbrev. paragraph.

**par-** • comb. form variant spelling of **PARA-**[1] shortened before a vowel or *h* (as in *paraldehyde, parody, parhelion*).

**para**[1] /ˈparə/ • n. informal a paratrooper.

**para**[2] /ˈpɑːrə/ • n. (pl. same or **paras**) a monetary unit of Bosnia–Herzegovina, Montenegro, and Serbia, equal to one hundredth of a dinar.
– ORIGIN Turk., from Pers. *pāra* 'piece, portion'.

**para-**[1] (also **par-**) • prefix **1** beside; adjacent to: *parathyroid*. **2** beyond or distinct from, but analogous to: *paramilitary*. **3** Chemistry denoting substitution at diametrically opposite carbon atoms in a benzene ring: *paradichlorobenzene*. Compare with **META-** and **ORTHO-**.
– ORIGIN from Gk *para* 'beside, beyond'.

**para-**[2] • comb. form denoting something that protects or wards off: *parachute*.
– ORIGIN from Fr., from the Ital. imper. sing. of *parare* 'defend, shield'.

**parabasis** /pəˈrabəsɪs/ • n. (pl. **parabases** /-siːz/) (in ancient Greek comedy) a direct address to the audience, sung or chanted by the chorus on behalf of the author.
– ORIGIN C19: from Gk, from *parabainein* 'go aside'.

**parabiosis** /ˌparəbʌɪˈəʊsɪs/ • n. Biology the anatomical joining of two individuals, especially artificially in physiological research.
– DERIVATIVES **parabiotic** adj.
– ORIGIN C20: mod. L., from **PARA-**[1] + Gk *biōsis* 'mode of life'.

**parable** ● **n.** a simple story used to illustrate a moral or spiritual lesson.
– ORIGIN ME: from OFr. *parabole*, from an eccles. L. sense 'discourse, allegory' of L. *parabola* 'comparison', from Gk *parabolē* (see **PARABOLA**).

**parabola** /pəˈrab(ə)lə/ ● **n.** (pl. **parabolas** or **parabolae** /-liː/) a symmetrical open plane curve of the kind formed by the intersection of a cone with a plane parallel to its side.
– ORIGIN C16: mod. L., from Gk *parabolē* 'placing side by side, application', based on *ballein* 'to throw'.

**parabolic** /ˌparəˈbɒlɪk/ ● **adj. 1** of or like a parabola or part of one. **2** of or expressed in parables.
– DERIVATIVES **parabolical** adj. **parabolically** adv.

**paraboloid** /pəˈrab(ə)lɔɪd/ ● **n. 1** a solid generated by rotating a parabola about its axis of symmetry. **2** a solid with two or more non-parallel parabolic cross sections.
– DERIVATIVES **paraboloidal** adj.

**paracellular** ● **adj.** Biology passing or situated beside or between cells.

**paracetamol** /ˌparəˈsiːtəmɒl, -ˈsɛt-/ ● **n.** (pl. same or **paracetamols**) Brit. a synthetic compound used to relieve pain and reduce fever.
– ORIGIN 1950s: abbrev. of its chemical name *para-acetylaminophenol*.

**parachronism** /pəˈrakrənɪz(ə)m/ ● **n.** an error in chronology, especially by assigning too late a date.
– ORIGIN C17: from **PARA-**[1] + Gk *khronos* 'time' + **-ISM**, perh. suggested by **ANACHRONISM**.

**parachute** ● **n.** a cloth canopy which fills with air and allows a person or heavy object attached to it to descend slowly when dropped from a high position, especially in an aircraft. ● **v.** drop or cause to drop by parachute.
– DERIVATIVES **parachutist** n.
– ORIGIN C18: from Fr. *para-* 'protection against' + *chute* 'fall'.

**Paraclete** /ˈparəkliːt/ ● **n.** (in Christian theology) the Holy Spirit as advocate or counsellor (John 14:16, 26).
– ORIGIN via late L. from Gk *paraklētos* 'called in aid'.

**paracrine** /ˈparəkrʌɪn/ ● **adj.** Physiology relating to or denoting a hormone which has an effect only in the vicinity of the gland secreting it.
– ORIGIN 1970s: from **PARA-**[1] + *krinein* 'to separate'.

**parade** ● **n. 1** a public procession, especially one celebrating a special day or event. **2** a formal march or gathering of troops for inspection or display. **3** a series or succession: *a parade of celebrities trooped on to his show.* **4** a boastful or ostentatious display. **5** Brit. a public square, promenade, or row of shops. ● **v. 1** walk, march, or display in a parade. **2** display (something) publicly in order to impress or attract attention: *he paraded his knowledge.* **3** (**parade as**) masquerade as.
– DERIVATIVES **parader** n.
– ORIGIN C17: from Fr., lit. 'a showing', from Sp. *parada* and Ital. *parata*, based on L. *parare* 'prepare'.

**parade ground** ● **n.** a place where troops gather for parade.

**paradiddle** /ˈparəˌdɪd(ə)l/ ● **n.** Music one of the rudiments of drumming, consisting of four even strokes played in the order 'left right left left' or 'right left right right'.
– ORIGIN 1920s: imitative.

**paradigm** /ˈparədʌɪm/ ● **n. 1** technical a typical example, pattern, or model of something. **2** a world view underlying the theories and methodology of a scientific subject. **3** Linguistics a set of items that form mutually exclusive choices in particular syntactic roles. Often contrasted with **SYNTAGM**. **4** Grammar a table of all the inflected forms of a word.
– DERIVATIVES **paradigmatic** /parədɪgˈmatɪk/ adj. **paradigmatically** adv.
– ORIGIN C15: via late L. from Gk *paradeigma*, from *paradeiknunai* 'show side by side'.

**paradigm shift** ● **n.** a fundamental change in approach or underlying assumptions.

**paradise** /ˈparədʌɪs/ ● **n. 1** (in some religions) heaven as the ultimate abode of the just. ➤(**Paradise**) the Garden of Eden. **2** an ideal or idyllic place or state.
– DERIVATIVES **paradisal** adj. **paradisiacal** /-dɪˈsʌɪək(ə)l/ (also **paradisaical** /-dɪˈseɪɪk(ə)l/ or **paradisical** /-ˈdɪsɪk(ə)l/) adj.
– ORIGIN ME: from OFr. *paradis*, via eccles. L. from Gk *paradeisos* 'royal (enclosed) park'.

**parador** /ˈparədɔː, ˌparəˈdɔː/ ● **n.** (pl. **paradors** or **paradores** /-ˈdɔːreɪz/) a hotel in Spain owned and administered by the government.
– ORIGIN from Sp.

**parados** /ˈparədɒs/ ● **n.** an elevation of earth behind a fortified place as a protection against attack from the rear.
– ORIGIN C19: from Fr., from *para-* 'protection against' + *dos* 'back'.

**paradox** ● **n. 1** a seemingly absurd or self-contradictory statement or proposition that may in fact be true. ➤an apparently sound statement or proposition which leads to a logically unacceptable conclusion. **2** a person or thing that combines contradictory features or qualities.
– DERIVATIVES **paradoxical** adj. **paradoxically** adv.
– ORIGIN C16 (orig. denoting a statement contrary to accepted opinion): via late L. from Gk *paradoxon* 'contrary (opinion)'.

**paraesthesia** /ˌparɪsˈθiːzɪə/ (US **paresthesia**) ● **n.** (pl. **paraesthesiae** /-zɪiː/ or **paraesthesias**) Medicine an abnormal sensation, especially 'pins and needles', caused by pressure on or damage to peripheral nerves.
– ORIGIN C19: from **PARA-**[1] + Gk *aisthēsis* 'sensation' + **-IA**[1].

**paraffin** ● **n. 1** (Brit. **paraffin wax**) a flammable waxy solid obtained by distilling petroleum or shale and used for sealing and waterproofing and in candles. **2** (also **paraffin oil** or **liquid paraffin**) Brit. a liquid fuel made similarly, especially kerosene. **3** Chemistry old-fashioned term for **ALKANE**.
– ORIGIN C19: from Ger., from L. *parum* 'little' + *affinis* 'related' (from its low reactivity).

**paragliding** ● **n.** a sport in which a person glides through the air by means of a wide parachute after jumping from or being hauled to a height.
– DERIVATIVES **paraglide** v. **paraglider** n.

**paragon** ● **n. 1** a person or thing regarded as a model of excellence or of a particular quality. **2** a perfect diamond of 100 carats or more.
– ORIGIN C16: from obs. Fr., from Ital. *paragone* 'touchstone', from med. Gk *parakonē* 'whetstone'.

**paragraph** ● **n.** a distinct section of a piece of writing, indicated by a new line, indentation, or numbering. ● **v.** arrange in paragraphs.
– DERIVATIVES **paragraphic** adj.
– ORIGIN C15: from Fr. *paragraphe*, via med. L. from Gk *paragraphos* 'short stroke marking a break in sense'.

**paragraph mark** ● **n.** a symbol (usually ¶) used in printed text to mark a new paragraph or as a reference mark.

**Paraguayan** /ˈparəgwʌɪən/ ● **n.** a native or inhabitant of Paraguay. ● **adj.** of or relating to Paraguay.

**parakeet** /ˈparəkiːt/ (also **parrakeet**) ● **n.** a small parrot with predominantly green plumage and a long tail. [*Psittacula*, *Cyanoramphus*, and other genera.]
– ORIGIN C16: from OFr. *paroquet*, Ital. *parrocchetto*, and Sp. *periquito*, perh. based on a dimin. meaning 'little wig', referring to head plumage, or based on a dimin. of the given name *Pedro*.

**paralanguage** ● **n.** the non-lexical component of communication by speech, for example intonation, hesitation noises, gesture, and facial expression.

**paraldehyde** /pəˈraldɪhʌɪd/ ● **n.** Chemistry a liquid made by treating acetaldehyde with acid, used medicinally as a sedative, hypnotic, and anticonvulsant.

**paralegal** chiefly N. Amer. ● **adj.** of or relating to auxiliary aspects of the law. ● **n.** a person trained in subsidiary legal matters but not fully qualified as a lawyer.

**paralinguistic** ● **adj.** relating to or denoting paralanguage.

**paralipomena** /ˌparəlɪˈpɒmɪnə/ (also **paraleipomena** /-lʌɪ-/) ● **pl. n.** (sing. **paralipomenon**) formal things omitted from a work and added as a supplement.
– ORIGIN ME: via eccles. L. from Gk *paraleipomena*, from

*paraleipein* 'omit'.

**paralipsis** /ˌparəˈlɪpsɪs/ ● **n.** Rhetoric the device of giving emphasis by professing to say little or nothing of a subject, as in *not to mention their unpaid debts.*
– ORIGIN C16: via late L. from Gk *paraleipsis* 'passing over', from *paraleipein* 'omit'.

**parallax** /ˈparəlaks/ ● **n. 1** the apparent difference in the position of an object when viewed from different positions, e.g. through the viewfinder and the lens of a camera. **2** Astronomy the angular difference in the apparent positions of a star observed from opposite sides of the earth's orbit.
– DERIVATIVES **parallactic** adj.
– ORIGIN C16: from Fr. *parallaxe*, from Gk *parallaxis* 'a change', from *parallassein* 'to alternate'.

**parallel** ● **adj. 1** (of lines, planes, or surfaces) side by side and having the same distance continuously between them. **2** occurring or existing at the same time or in a similar way; corresponding. ➤Computing involving the simultaneous performance of operations. **3** of or denoting electrical components connected in parallel. ● **n. 1** a person or thing that is similar or analogous to another. **2** a similarity or comparison. **3** (also **parallel of latitude**) each of the imaginary parallel circles of constant latitude on the earth's surface. **4** Printing two parallel lines (||) as a reference mark. ● **v.** (**paralleled**, **paralleling**) **1** run or lie parallel to. **2** be similar or corresponding to.
– PHRASES **in parallel 1** taking place at the same time and having some connection. **2** (of electrical components or circuits) connected to common points at each end, so that the current is divided between them.
– DERIVATIVES **parallelism** n. **parallelistic** adj. **parallelization** (also **-isation**) n. (Computing). **parallelize** (also **-ise**) v. (Computing).
– ORIGIN C16: from Fr. *parallèle*, via L. from Gk *parallēlos*, from *para-* 'alongside' + *allēlos* 'one another'.

**parallel bars** ● **pl. n.** a pair of parallel rails on posts, used in gymnastics.

**parallel cousin** ● **n.** a first cousin.

**parallel distributed processing** ● **n.** another term for CONNECTIONISM.

**parallelepiped** /ˌparəlɛləˈpʌɪpɛd, ˌparəlɛˈlɛpɪpɛd/ ● **n.** Geometry a solid body of which each face is a parallelogram.
– ORIGIN C16: from Gk *parallēlepipedon*, from *parallēlos* 'beside another' + *epipedon* 'plane surface'.

**parallel imports** ● **pl. n.** goods imported by unlicensed distributors for sale at less than the manufacturer's official retail price.
– DERIVATIVES **parallel importing** n.

**parallelogram** /ˌparəˈlɛləgram/ ● **n.** a four-sided plane rectilinear figure with opposite sides parallel.
– ORIGIN C16: from Fr. *parallélogramme*, via late L. from Gk *parallēlogrammon*, from *parallēlos* 'alongside another' + *grammē* 'line'.

**parallel processing** ● **n.** a mode of computer operation in which a process is split into parts, which are executed simultaneously on different processors.

**parallel ruler** ● **n.** an instrument for drawing parallel lines, consisting of two or more rulers connected by jointed crosspieces so as to be always parallel.

**paralogism** /pəˈralədʒɪz(ə)m/ ● **n.** Logic a piece of illogical or fallacious reasoning, especially one which appears superficially logical.
– DERIVATIVES **paralogical** adj. **paralogically** adv. **paralogist** n.
– ORIGIN C16: from Fr. *paralogisme*, via late L. from Gk *paralogismos*, from *paralogizesthai* 'reason falsely'.

**Paralympics** ● **pl. n.** [usu. treated as sing.] an international athletic competition for disabled athletes.
– DERIVATIVES **Paralympic** adj.
– ORIGIN 1950s: blend of *paraplegic* and *Olympics*.

**paralyse** (chiefly US also **paralyze**) ● **v. 1** cause (a person or part of the body) to become incapable of movement. **2** bring to a standstill by causing disruption.
– ORIGIN C19: from Fr. *paralyser*, from *paralysie* 'paralysis'.

**paralysis** /pəˈralɪsɪs/ ● **n.** (pl. **paralyses** /-siːz/) **1** the loss of the ability to move part or most of the body. **2** inability to act or function.
– ORIGIN OE, via L. from Gk *paralusis*, from *paraluesthai* 'be disabled at the side'.

**paralytic** ● **adj. 1** relating to paralysis. **2** informal, chiefly Brit. extremely drunk. ● **n.** a person with paralysis.
– DERIVATIVES **paralytically** adv.

**paramagnetic** ● **adj.** (of a substance or body) very weakly attracted by the poles of a magnet, but not retaining any permanent magnetism.
– DERIVATIVES **paramagnetism** n.

**paramatta** ● **n.** variant spelling of PARRAMATTA.

**paramecium** /ˌparəˈmiːsɪəm/ ● **n.** Zoology a single-celled freshwater animal which has a characteristic slipper-like shape and is covered with cilia. [Genus *Paramecium*.]
– ORIGIN C18: mod. L., from Gk *paramēkēs* 'oval'.

**paramedic** ● **n.** a person who is trained to do medical work, especially emergency first aid, but is not a fully qualified doctor.
– DERIVATIVES **paramedical** adj.

**parameter** /pəˈramɪtə/ ● **n. 1** a measurable or quantifiable characteristic of a system. **2** Mathematics a quantity which is fixed for the case in question but may vary in other cases. **3** a limit or boundary which defines the scope of a particular process or activity.
– DERIVATIVES **parameterization** (also **-isation**) n. **parameterize** (also **-ise**) v. **parametric** adj. **parametrically** adv.
– ORIGIN C17: mod. L., from Gk *para-* 'beside' + *metron* 'measure'.

**parametric equalizer** ● **n.** an electronic device or computer program which allows any specific part of the frequency range of a signal to be selected and altered in strength.

**paramilitary** ● **adj.** organized on similar lines to a military force. ● **n.** (pl. **-ies**) a member of a paramilitary organization.

**paramnesia** /ˌparəmˈniːzɪə/ ● **n.** Psychiatry a condition involving distorted memory or confusions of fact and fantasy, e.g. déjà vu.

**paramo** /ˈparəməʊ/ ● **n.** (pl. **-os**) a high treeless plateau in tropical South America.
– ORIGIN Sp. and Port., from L. *paramus*.

**paramotor** ● **n.** (trademark in the US) a motorized steerable parachute, powered by a motor and propeller strapped to the pilot's back.
– DERIVATIVES **paramotoring** n.

**paramount** ● **adj. 1** more important than anything else; supreme. **2** having supreme power.
– DERIVATIVES **paramountcy** n. **paramountly** adv.
– ORIGIN C16: from Anglo-Norman Fr. *paramont*, from OFr. *par* 'by' + *amont* 'above'.

**paramour** ● **n.** archaic or derogatory a lover, especially the illicit partner of a married person.
– ORIGIN ME: from OFr. *par amour* 'by love'.

**paramyxovirus** /ˌparəˈmɪksə(ʊ)ˌvʌɪrəs/ ● **n.** Medicine any of a group of RNA viruses including those causing mumps and measles.

**parang**[1] /ˈpɑːraŋ, ˈpa-/ ● **n.** a Malayan machete.
– ORIGIN from Malay.

**parang**[2] /paˈraŋ/ ● **n.** a variety of Trinidadian folk music, traditionally played at Christmas by groups which travel from house to house.
– ORIGIN Sp. creole, based on Sp. *parranda* 'spree, binge'.

**paranoia** /ˌparəˈnɔɪə/ ● **n. 1** a mental condition characterized by delusions of persecution, unwarranted jealousy, or exaggerated self-importance. **2** unjustified suspicion and mistrust of others.
– DERIVATIVES **paranoiac** adj. & n. **paranoiacally** adv. **paranoic** /-ˈnəʊɪk, -ˈnɔɪɪk/ adj. **paranoically** /-ˈnəʊɪk(ə)li, -ˈnɔɪɪk(ə)li/ adv.
– ORIGIN C19: mod. L., from Gk, from *paranoos* 'distracted', from *para* 'irregular' + *noos* 'mind'.

**paranoid** ● **adj.** of, characterized by, or suffering from paranoia. ● **n.** a person who is paranoid.

**paranormal** ● **adj.** (of events or phenomena) supposedly beyond the scope of normal scientific understanding.
– DERIVATIVES **paranormally** adv.

**paraparesis** /ˌparəpəˈriːsɪs/ ● **n.** partial paralysis of the lower limbs.
– DERIVATIVES **paraparetic** adj.

**parapente** /ˈparəpɒnt/ ● **v.** [usu. as noun **parapenting**] take part in the sport of gliding by means of an aerofoil parachute launched from high ground. ● **n.** a parachute used for this purpose.
– DERIVATIVES **parapenter** n.
– ORIGIN 1980s: from Fr., from *para(chute)* + *pente* 'slope'.

**parapet** /ˈparəpɪt/ ● **n. 1** a low protective wall along the edge of a roof, bridge, or balcony. **2** a protective wall or earth defence along the top of a military trench.
– DERIVATIVES **parapeted** adj.
– ORIGIN C16: from Fr., or from Ital. *parapetto* 'chest-high wall', based on L. *pectus* 'chest'.

**paraph** /ˈparaf/ ● **n.** a flourish after a signature, originally as a precaution against forgery.
– ORIGIN ME (denoting a paragraph): from Fr. *paraphe*, based on med. L. *paragraphus* (see **PARAGRAPH**).

**paraphasia** /ˌparəˈfeɪzɪə/ ● **n.** Psychology speech disturbance in which words are jumbled and sentences meaningless, resulting from brain damage.
– DERIVATIVES **paraphasic** adj.

**paraphernalia** /ˌparəfəˈneɪlɪə/ ● **n.** [treated as sing. or pl.] miscellaneous articles, especially the equipment needed for a particular activity.
– ORIGIN C17 (denoting property owned by a married woman): from med. L., based on Gk *parapherna* 'property apart from a dowry'.

**paraphilia** /ˌparəˈfɪlɪə/ ● **n.** Psychiatry a condition characterized by abnormal sexual desires involving extreme or dangerous activities.
– DERIVATIVES **paraphiliac** adj. & n.

**paraphrase** ● **v.** express the meaning of (something) using different words, especially to achieve greater clarity. ● **n.** a rewording of a passage.
– DERIVATIVES **paraphrasable** adj. **paraphrastic** adj.
– ORIGIN C16: via L. from Gk *paraphrasis*, from *paraphrazein*, from *para-* (expressing modification) + *phrazein* 'tell'.

**paraplegia** /ˌparəˈpliːdʒə/ ● **n.** paralysis of the legs and lower body, typically caused by spinal injury or disease. Compare with **MONOPLEGIA**.
– DERIVATIVES **paraplegic** adj. & n.
– ORIGIN C17: mod. L., from Gk *paraplēgia*, from *paraplēssein* 'strike at the side'.

**parapsychic** ● **adj.** relating to or denoting mental phenomena for which no adequate scientific explanation exists.

**parapsychology** ● **n.** the study of mental phenomena which are excluded from or inexplicable by orthodox scientific psychology (such as hypnosis, telepathy, etc.).
– DERIVATIVES **parapsychological** adj. **parapsychologist** n.

**paraquat** /ˈparəkwɒt, -kwat/ ● **n.** a toxic fast-acting herbicide, which becomes deactivated in the soil.
– ORIGIN 1960s: from **PARA-**[1] + **QUATERNARY**.

**pararhyme** ● **n.** partial rhyme between words with the same pattern of consonants but different vowels.

**parasail** ● **v.** [often as noun **parasailing**] glide through the air wearing an open parachute while being towed by a motor boat. ● **n.** a parachute designed for parasailing.

**parascending** ● **n.** Brit. the sport or activity of paragliding or parasailing.
– DERIVATIVES **parascend** v. **parascender** n.

**paraselene** /ˌparəsɪˈliːni/ ● **n.** (pl. **paraselenae** /-niː/) a bright spot in the sky similar to a parhelion but formed by moonlight.
– ORIGIN C17: mod. L., from Gk *para-* 'beside' + *selēnē* 'moon'.

**parasitaemia** /ˌparəsɪˈtiːmɪə/ (US **parasitemia**) ● **n.** Medicine the presence of parasites in the blood.

**parasite** ● **n. 1** an organism which lives in or on another organism and benefits by deriving nutrients at the other's expense. **2** derogatory a person who habitually relies on or exploits others and gives nothing in return.
– DERIVATIVES **parasitic** adj. **parasitical** adj. **parasitically** adv. **parasiticide** n. **parasitism** n. **parasitological** adj. **parasitologist** n. **parasitology** n.
– ORIGIN C16: via L. from Gk *parasitos* '(person) eating at another's table', from *para-* 'alongside' + *sitos* 'food'.

**parasitize** /ˈparəsʌɪtʌɪz, -sɪ-/ (also **-ise**) ● **v.** infest or exploit as a parasite.
– DERIVATIVES **parasitization** n.

**parasitoid** /ˈparəsɪtɔɪd/ ● **n.** Entomology an insect whose larvae live as parasites which eventually kill their hosts, e.g. an ichneumon wasp.

**parasol** ● **n. 1** a light umbrella used to give shade from the sun. **2** (also **parasol mushroom**) a tall mushroom with a broad scaly greyish-brown cap. [*Lepiota procera* and related species.]
– ORIGIN C17: from Fr., from Ital. *parasole*, from *para-* 'protecting against' + *sole* 'sun'.

**parastatal** /ˌparəˈsteɪt(ə)l/ ● **adj.** (of an organization or industry) having some political authority and serving the state indirectly. ● **n.** a parastatal organization.

**parasternal** /ˌparəˈstəːnəl/ ● **adj.** Anatomy situated beside the sternum.

**parasuicide** ● **n.** Psychiatry apparent attempted suicide without the actual intention of killing oneself.

**parasympathetic** ● **adj.** Physiology relating to or denoting the part of the autonomic nervous system consisting of nerves arising from the brain and the lower end of the spinal cord and supplying the internal organs, blood vessels, and glands.

**parasynthesis** ● **n.** Linguistics a process by which a term is formed by adding a bound morpheme (e.g. *-ed*) to a combination of existing words (e.g. *black-eyed* from *black eye(s)* + *-ed*).
– DERIVATIVES **parasynthetic** adj. **parasynthetically** adv.

**paratha** /pəˈrɑːtə/ ● **n.** (in Indian cookery) a flat, thick piece of unleavened bread fried on a griddle.
– ORIGIN from Hindi *parāṭhā*.

**parathion** /ˌparəˈθʌɪən/ ● **n.** a highly toxic synthetic insecticide containing phosphorus and sulphur.
– ORIGIN 1940s: from **PARA-**[1] (in sense 2) + **THIO-** + **-ON**.

**parathyroid** ● **n.** Anatomy a gland next to the thyroid which secretes a hormone that regulates calcium levels in a person's body.

**paratroops** ● **pl. n.** troops equipped to be dropped by parachute from aircraft.
– DERIVATIVES **paratrooper** n.

**paratyphoid** ● **n.** a fever resembling typhoid, caused by related bacteria.

**paravane** ● **n.** a device towed behind a boat at a depth regulated by its vanes or planes, used to cut the moorings of submerged mines.

**par avion** /pɑː(r) aˈvjɒ̃, French par avjɔ̃/ ● **adv.** by airmail.
– ORIGIN Fr., lit. 'by aeroplane'.

**parboil** ● **v.** partly cook by boiling.
– ORIGIN ME: from OFr. *parbouillir*, from late L. *perbullire* 'boil thoroughly', from L. *per-* 'through, thoroughly' (later confused with **PART**) + *bullire* 'to boil'.

**parbuckle** /ˈpɑːbʌk(ə)l/ ● **n.** a loop of rope arranged like a sling, used for raising or lowering casks and other cylindrical objects. ● **v.** raise or lower with such a device.
– ORIGIN C17: from earlier *parbunkle*, of unknown origin.

**parcel** ● **n. 1** an object or collection of objects wrapped in paper in order to be carried or sent by post. **2** a quantity or amount of something, in particular land. ● **v.** (**parcelled**, **parcelling**; US **parceled**, **parceling**) **1** make (something) into a parcel by wrapping it. **2** (**parcel something out**) divide something into portions and then distribute it. **3** Nautical wrap (rope) with strips of tarred canvas to reduce chafing.
– ORIGIN ME: from OFr. *parcelle*, from L. *particula* 'small part'.

**parcel-gilt** ● **adj.** (of furniture, silverware, etc.) partly gilded, especially on the inner surface only.

**parch** ● **v. 1** make or become dry through intense heat. ➤ roast (corn, peas, etc.) lightly. **2** [as adj. **parched**] informal extremely thirsty.
– ORIGIN ME: of unknown origin.

**parchment** ● **n.** **1** a stiff material made from the prepared skin of a sheep or goat, formerly used as a writing surface. **2** (also **parchment paper**) stiff translucent paper treated to resemble parchment. **3** informal a diploma or other formal document.
– ORIGIN ME: from OFr. *parchemin*, from a blend of late L. *pergamina* 'writing material from Pergamum' and *Parthica pellis* 'Parthian skin' (a kind of scarlet leather).

**parclose** /ˈpɑːkləʊz/ ● **n.** a screen or railing in a church enclosing a tomb or altar or separating off a side chapel.
– ORIGIN ME: from OFr. *parclos(e)*, past part. of *parclore* 'enclose'.

**pard** ● **n.** archaic or poetic/literary a leopard.
– ORIGIN ME: from OFr., via L. from Gk *pardos*.

**pardalote** /ˈpɑːdələʊt/ ● **n.** a small white-spotted Australian songbird related to the flowerpeckers. [Genus *Pardalotus*: several species.]
– ORIGIN C19: from mod. L. *Pardalotus*, from Gk *pardalōtos* 'spotted like a leopard'.

**pardon** ● **n.** **1** the action of forgiving or being forgiven for an error or offence. **2** a remission of the legal consequences of an offence or conviction. **3** Christian Church, historical an indulgence. ● **v.** **1** forgive or excuse (a person, error, or offence). **2** release (an offender) from the legal consequences of an offence or conviction. ● **exclam.** used to ask a speaker to repeat something because one did not hear or understand it.
– PHRASES **I beg your pardon** (or **pardon me**) used to express polite apology or to indicate that one has not heard or understood something.
– DERIVATIVES **pardonable** adj. **pardonably** adv.
– ORIGIN ME: from OFr. *pardun* (n.), *pardoner* (v.), from med. L. *perdonare* 'concede, remit', from *per-* 'completely' + *donare* 'give'.

**pardoner** ● **n.** historical a person licensed to sell papal pardons or indulgences.

**pare** ● **v.** **1** trim by cutting away the outer edges of. **2** (often **pare something away/down**) reduce or diminish in a number of small successive stages.
– DERIVATIVES **parer** n.
– ORIGIN ME: from OFr. *parer* 'adorn, prepare', also 'peel, trim', from L. *parare* 'prepare'.

**paregoric** /ˌparɪˈɡɒrɪk/ ● **n.** a medicine containing opium and camphor, formerly used to treat diarrhoea and coughing in children.
– ORIGIN C17: via late L. from Gk *parēgorikos* 'soothing'.

**paren** /pəˈrɛn/ ● **n.** Printing a round bracket.
– ORIGIN C20: abbrev. of **PARENTHESIS**.

**parenchyma** /pəˈrɛŋkɪmə/ ● **n.** **1** Anatomy the functional tissue of an organ as distinguished from the connective and supporting tissue. **2** Botany the cellular tissue found in the softer parts of leaves, pulp of fruits, bark and pith of stems, etc.
– DERIVATIVES **parenchymal** adj. (chiefly Anatomy). **parenchymatous** adj. (chiefly Botany).
– ORIGIN C17: from Gk *parenkhuma* 'something poured in besides', from *para-* 'beside' + *enkhuma* 'infusion'.

**parent** ● **n.** **1** a father or mother. ➤ an animal or plant from which younger ones are derived. **2** an organization or company which owns or controls a number of subsidiaries. **3** archaic a forefather or ancestor. ● **v.** [often as noun **parenting**] be or act as a parent to.
– DERIVATIVES **parentage** n. **parental** adj. **parentally** adv. **parentcraft** n. **parenthood** n.
– ORIGIN ME: from OFr., from L. *parent-*, *parere* 'bring forth'.

**parenteral** /pəˈrɛnt(ə)r(ə)l/ ● **adj.** Medicine (chiefly of nutrition) involving another part of the body than the mouth and alimentary canal. Often contrasted with **ENTERAL**.
– DERIVATIVES **parenterally** adv.
– ORIGIN C20: from **PARA-**[1] + Gk *enteron* 'intestine' + **-AL**.

**parenthesis** /pəˈrɛnθɪsɪs/ ● **n.** (pl. **parentheses** /-siːz/) **1** a word or phrase inserted as an explanation or afterthought, in writing usually marked off by brackets, dashes, or commas. **2** (**parentheses**) a pair of round brackets () used to include such a word or phrase.
– DERIVATIVES **parenthesize** (also **-ise**) v. **parenthetic** /ˌpar(ə)nˈθɛtɪk/ adj. **parenthetical** adj. **parenthetically** adv.
– ORIGIN C16: via late L. from Gk, from *parentithenai* 'put in beside'.

**parergon** /pəˈrəːɡɒn/ ● **n.** (pl. **parerga** /-ɡə/) formal a supplementary or subsidiary piece of work.
– ORIGIN C17: via L. from Gk *parergon*, from *para-* 'beside, additional' + *ergon* 'work'.

**paresis** /pəˈriːsɪs, ˈparɪsɪs/ ● **n.** (pl. **pareses** /-siːz/) Medicine **1** muscular weakness or partial paralysis caused by nerve damage or disease. **2** (also **general paresis**) inflammation of the brain in the later stages of syphilis, causing progressive dementia and paralysis.
– DERIVATIVES **paretic** adj.
– ORIGIN C17: mod. L., from Gk *parienai* 'let go'.

**paresthesia** ● **n.** US spelling of **PARAESTHESIA**.

**pareu** /ˈpɑːreɪuː/ ● **n.** a kind of Polynesian sarong.
– ORIGIN from Tahitian.

**par excellence** /pɑːr ˈɛks(ə)l(ə)ns, French paʀ ɛksɛlɑ̃s/ ● **adj.** [postpos.] better or more than all others of the same kind: *Nash is the Regency architect par excellence.*
– ORIGIN Fr., lit. 'by excellence'.

**parfait** /ˈpɑːfeɪ/ ● **n.** **1** a rich cold dessert made with whipped cream, eggs, and fruit. **2** a dessert consisting of layers of ice cream, meringue, and fruit, served in a tall glass.
– ORIGIN from Fr. *parfait*, lit. 'perfect'.

**parfleche** /ˈpɑːflɛʃ/ ● **n.** (in American Indian culture) a buffalo's hide dried by being stretched on a frame.
– ORIGIN from Canad. Fr. *parflèche*, from Fr. *parer* 'ward off' + *flèche* 'arrow'.

**parfumerie** /pɑːˈfjuːm(ə)ri/ ● **n.** (pl. **-ies**) a place where perfume is sold or made.
– ORIGIN from Fr.

**pargana** /pəˈɡʌnə/ ● **n.** a group of villages or a subdivision of a district in India.
– ORIGIN Urdu, lit. 'district'.

**parget** /ˈpɑːdʒɪt/ (also **parge** /pɑːdʒ/) ● **v.** (**pargeted**, **pargeting**) cover with a patterned or decorative layer of plaster or mortar. ● **n.** plaster or mortar applied in this way.
– ORIGIN ME: from OFr. *parjeter*, from *par-* 'all over' + *jeter* 'to throw'.

**parhelion** /pɑːˈhiːlɪən/ ● **n.** (pl. **parhelia** /-lɪə/) a bright spot in the sky on either side of the sun, formed by refraction.
– DERIVATIVES **parhelic** adj.
– ORIGIN C17: from L. *parelion*, from Gk *para-* 'beside' + *hēlios* 'sun'.

**pariah** /pəˈrʌɪə/ ● **n.** **1** an outcast. **2** historical a member of a low caste or of no caste in southern India.
– ORIGIN C17: from Tamil *paṛaiyar* (pl.), '(hereditary) drummers', from *paṛai* 'a drum' (pariahs not being allowed to join in with a religious procession).

**pariah dog** ● **n.** another term for **PYE-DOG**.

**Parian** /ˈpɛːrɪən/ ● **adj.** **1** of or relating to the Greek island of Paros. **2** denoting fine white unglazed hard-paste porcelain likened to Parian marble.

**parietal** /pəˈrʌɪɪt(ə)l/ ● **adj.** **1** Anatomy & Biology of, relating to, or denoting the wall of the body or of a body cavity. **2** N. Amer. relating to residence within a college and especially to visits from members of the opposite sex. **3** Archaeology denoting prehistoric art found on rock walls. ● **n.** Anatomy & Zoology a parietal bone or other parietal structure.
– ORIGIN ME: from late L. *parietalis*, from L. *paries*, *pariet-* 'wall'.

**parietal bone** ● **n.** a bone forming the central side and upper back part of each side of the skull.

**parietal lobe** ● **n.** either of the paired lobes of the brain at the top of the head.

**pari-mutuel** /ˌpɑːrɪˈmjuːtʃʊəl, -ˈtjʊəl/ ● **n.** a form of betting in which those backing the first three places divide the losers' stakes.
– ORIGIN Fr., lit. 'mutual stake'.

**parings** ● **pl. n.** thin strips pared off from something.

**pari passu** /ˌpɑːrɪ ˈpasuː, ˌparɪ/ ● **adv.** side by side; equally or equivalently.
– ORIGIN L., lit. 'with equal step'.

**Paris green** ● **n.** a vivid green toxic salt of copper and arsenic, used as a preservative, pigment, and insecticide.

**parish** ● **n. 1** (in the Christian Church) a small administrative district with its own church and clergy. **2** (also **civil parish**) Brit. the smallest unit of local government in rural areas. **3** US (in Louisiana) a territorial division corresponding to a county in other states.
– ORIGIN ME: from Anglo-Norman Fr. and OFr. *paroche*, from late L. *parochia*, from Gk *paroikia* 'sojourning', based on *para-* 'beside, subsidiary' + *oikos* 'dwelling'.

**parish council** ● **n.** (in the UK) the administrative body in a civil parish.

**parishioner** ● **n.** a person who lives in a particular Church parish.

**parish-pump** ● **adj.** Brit. of local importance only; parochial.

**parish register** ● **n.** a book recording christenings, marriages, and burials at a parish church.

**Parisian** /pəˈrɪzɪən/ ● **adj.** of or relating to Paris. ● **n.** a native or inhabitant of Paris.

**Parisienne** /paˌrɪzɪˈɛn, French paʀizjɛn/ ● **n.** a Parisian girl or woman.

**parison** /ˈparɪs(ə)n/ ● **n.** a rounded mass of glass formed by rolling immediately after removal from the furnace.
– ORIGIN C19: from Fr. *paraison*, from *parer* 'prepare'.

**parity**[1] /ˈparɪti/ ● **n. 1** equality or equivalence, especially as regards status, pay, or value. **2** Mathematics the fact of being an even or an odd number. **3** Physics the property of a spatial wave equation that either remains the same or changes sign under a given transformation.
– ORIGIN C16: from late L. *paritas*, from *par* 'equal'.

**parity**[2] /ˈparɪti/ ● **n.** Medicine the fact or condition of having borne a specified number of children.
– ORIGIN C19: from *parous* 'having borne offspring' (back-form. from adjs. ending in **-PAROUS**) + **-ITY**.

**park** ● **n. 1** a large public garden in a town, used for recreation. **2** a large enclosed area, typically with woodland and pasture, attached to a country house. **3** an area devoted to a specified purpose: *a wildlife park*. **4** an area in which vehicles may be parked: *a coach park*. ● **v. 1** bring (a vehicle) to a halt and leave it temporarily, typically in a car park or by the side of the road. **2** informal deposit and leave in a convenient place until required: *park your bag by the door.* **3** (**park oneself**) informal sit down.
– ORIGIN ME: from OFr. *parc*, from med. L. *parricus*, of Gmc origin; rel. to **PADDOCK**.

**parka** ● **n. 1** a large windproof hooded jacket for use in cold weather. **2** a hooded jacket made of animal skin, worn by Eskimos.
– ORIGIN C18: via Aleut from Russ.

**parkerizing** (also **-ising**) ● **n.** a rustproofing process involving immersion in a hot acidic solution of a metal phosphate.
– DERIVATIVES **parkerized** adj.
– ORIGIN 1920s: from the *Parker* Rust-Proof Company of America + **-IZE** + **-ING**[1].

**parkie** (also **parky**) ● **n.** (pl. **-ies**) informal a park-keeper.

**parkin** ● **n.** Brit. soft, dark gingerbread made with oatmeal and treacle or molasses, especially in Yorkshire.
– ORIGIN C19: perh. from the family name *Parkin*.

**parking meter** ● **n.** a coin-operated machine next to a parking space in a street, for receiving a parking fee and indicating the time available.

**parking ticket** ● **n.** a notice informing a driver of a fine imposed for parking illegally.

**Parkinson's disease** ● **n.** a progressive disease of the brain and nervous system marked by tremor, muscular rigidity, and slow, imprecise movement.
– DERIVATIVES **Parkinsonian** adj. **Parkinsonism** n.
– ORIGIN C19: named after the Engl. surgeon James *Parkinson*.

**Parkinson's law** ● **n.** the notion that work expands so as to fill the time available for its completion.
– ORIGIN 1950s: named after the Engl. writer Cyril Northcote *Parkinson*.

**parkland** ● **n.** (also **parklands**) open grassy land with scattered groups of trees.

**parkway** ● **n. 1** N. Amer. an open landscaped highway. **2** Brit. used in names of railway stations with extensive parking facilities.

**parky**[1] ● **adj.** (**-ier**, **-iest**) Brit. informal chilly.
– ORIGIN C19: of unknown origin.

**parky**[2] ● **n.** variant spelling of **PARKIE**.

**Parl.** ● **abbrev.** Brit. **1** Parliament. **2** Parliamentary.

**parlance** /ˈpɑːl(ə)ns/ ● **n.** a particular way of using words, especially one common to those in a subject: *medical parlance*.
– ORIGIN C16 (denoting speech or debate): from OFr., from *parler* 'speak', from L. *parabola* 'comparison' (in late L. 'speech').

**parlando** /pɑːˈlandəʊ/ ● **adv. & adj.** Music (with reference to singing) expressive or declamatory in the manner of speech.
– ORIGIN Ital., lit. 'speaking'.

**parlay** /ˈpɑːleɪ/ N. Amer. ● **v.** (**parlay something into**) turn an initial stake or winnings into (a greater amount) by further gambling. ● **n.** a cumulative series of bets.
– ORIGIN C19: from Fr. *paroli*, from Ital., from *paro* 'like', from L. *par* 'equal'.

**parley** /ˈpɑːli/ ● **n.** (pl. **-eys**) a conference between opposing sides in a dispute, especially regarding an armistice. ● **v.** (**-eys**, **-eyed**) hold a parley.
– ORIGIN ME: perh. from OFr. *parlee* 'spoken'.

**parliament** /ˈpɑːləm(ə)nt/ ● **n. 1** (**Parliament**) (in the UK) the highest legislature, consisting of the Sovereign, the House of Lords, and the House of Commons. ➤ the members of this legislature for the period between dissolutions. **2** a similar body in other nations and states.
– DERIVATIVES **parliamentary** adj.
– ORIGIN ME: from OFr. *parlement* 'speaking'.

**parliamentarian** ● **n. 1** a member of a parliament, especially a person well versed in its procedure and debates. **2** historical a supporter of Parliament in the English Civil War; a Roundhead. ● **adj.** of or relating to parliament or parliamentarians.
– DERIVATIVES **parliamentarianism** n.

**Parliamentary Commissioner for Administration** ● **n.** official term in the UK for **OMBUDSMAN**.

**parliamentary private secretary** ● **n.** (in the UK) a Member of Parliament assisting a government minister.

**parlour** (US **parlor**) ● **n. 1** dated a sitting room in a private house. **2** a room in a public building, hotel, monastery, etc. for receiving guests or private conversation. **3** a shop or business providing specified goods or services: *an ice-cream parlour.* **4** a room or building equipped for milking cows. ● **adj.** derogatory, dated denoting a person who professes but does not actively support a particular political view: *a parlour socialist*.
– ORIGIN ME: from Anglo-Norman Fr. *parlur* 'place for speaking', from L. *parlare* 'speak'.

**parlour car** ● **n.** N. Amer. a luxuriously fitted railway carriage.

**parlour game** ● **n.** an indoor game, especially a word game.

**parlourmaid** ● **n.** historical a maid employed to wait at table.

**parlous** /ˈpɑːləs/ ● **adj.** archaic or humorous full of uncertainty; precarious: *the parlous state of the economy.*
– DERIVATIVES **parlously** adv. **parlousness** n.
– ORIGIN ME: contr. of ***perilous*** (see **PERIL**).

**Parma ham** ● **n.** a strongly flavoured Italian cured ham, eaten uncooked and thinly sliced.
– ORIGIN named after the city of *Parma* in Italy.

**Parma violet** ● **n.** a scented sweet violet, crystallized and used for food decoration.

**Parmentier** /ˈpɑːmɒ̃tɪeɪ/ ● **adj.** [postpos.] cooked or served with potatoes.
– ORIGIN from the name of the C18 Fr. agriculturalist An-

toine A. *Parmentier.*

**Parmesan** /pɑːmɪ'zan/ ● **n.** a hard, dry Italian cheese used chiefly in grated form.
– ORIGIN C16: from Fr., from Ital. *Parmigiano* 'of Parma'.

**Parmigiana** /ˌpɑːmɪ'dʒɑːnə, Italian ˌparmi'dʒana/ ● **adj.** [postpos.] cooked or served with Parmesan cheese.

**Parnassian** /pɑː'nasɪən/ ● **adj. 1** relating to poetry; poetic. **2** denoting a group of French poets who emphasized strictness of form, named from the anthology *Le Parnasse contemporain* (1866).

**parochial** /pə'rəʊkɪəl/ ● **adj. 1** of or relating to a Church parish. **2** having a narrow outlook or scope: *parochial attitudes.*
– DERIVATIVES **parochialism** n. **parochiality** n. **parochially** adv.
– ORIGIN ME: from OFr., from eccles. L. *parochialis*, from *parochia* (see **PARISH**).

**parochial school** ● **n.** North American term for **CHURCH SCHOOL**.

**parody** ● **n.** (pl. **-ies**) **1** an imitation of the style of a particular writer, artist, or genre with deliberate exaggeration for comic effect. **2** a travesty: *a parody of a smile.* ● **v.** (**-ies**, **-ied**) produce a parody of.
– DERIVATIVES **parodic** adj. **parodist** n.
– ORIGIN C16: via late L. from Gk *parōidia*, from *para-* 'beside' (expressing alteration) + *ōidē* 'ode'.

**parol** /pə'rəʊl, 'par(ə)l/ ● **adj.** Law expressed or agreed orally, or in writing but not under seal.
– PHRASES **by parol** by oral declaration.
– ORIGIN C15 (as n.): from OFr. *parole* (see **PAROLE**).

**parole** ● **n. 1** the temporary or permanent release of a prisoner before the expiry of a sentence, on the promise of good behaviour. **2** historical a prisoner of war's word of honour to return or act as a non-belligerent if released. **3** Linguistics the actual language used by people. Contrasted with **LANGUE**. ● **v.** release (a prisoner) on parole.
– DERIVATIVES **parolee** n.
– ORIGIN C15: from OFr., lit. 'word', from eccles. L. *parabola* 'speech'.

**paronomasia** /ˌparənə'meɪzɪə/ ● **n.** a play on words; a pun.
– ORIGIN C16: via L. from Gk *paronomasia*, from *para-* 'beside' (expressing alteration) + *onomasia* 'naming'.

**parotid** /pə'rɒtɪd/ ● **adj.** Anatomy relating to or denoting a pair of large salivary glands situated just in front of each ear.
– ORIGIN C17: via L. from Gk *parōtis, parōtid-*, from *para-* 'beside' + *ous, ōt-* 'ear'.

**parotitis** /ˌparə'tʌɪtɪs/ ● **n.** Medicine inflammation of a parotid gland, especially (**infectious parotitis**) mumps.

**-parous** ● **comb. form** Biology bearing offspring of a specified number or in a specified way: *multiparous* | *viviparous.*
– ORIGIN from L. *-parus* '-bearing' (from *parere* 'bring forth, produce') + **-ous**.

**Parousia** /pə'ruːzɪə/ ● **n.** Christian Theology the Second Coming.
– ORIGIN Gk, lit. 'being present'.

**paroxysm** /'parəksɪz(ə)m/ ● **n.** a sudden attack or violent expression of something: *a paroxysm of weeping.*
– DERIVATIVES **paroxysmal** adj.
– ORIGIN ME: from Fr. *paroxysme*, via med. L. from Gk *paroxusmos*, from *paroxunein* 'exasperate', from *para-* 'beyond' + *oxunein* 'sharpen'.

**paroxytone** /pə'rɒksɪtəʊn/ ● **n.** a word with an acute accent on the last syllable but one, especially in ancient Greek.
– ORIGIN C18: from mod. L. *paroxytonus* (adj.), from Gk *paroxutonos*, from *para-* 'alongside' + *oxutonos* 'sharp pitch'.

**parp** informal ● **n.** the honking sound of a car horn. ● **v.** make such a sound.
– ORIGIN 1950s: imitative.

**parpen** /'pɑːp(ə)n/ ● **n.** a stone passing through a wall, with two smooth vertical faces.
– ORIGIN ME: from OFr. *parpain* 'length of a stone', prob. based on L. *perpes* 'continuous'.

**parquet** /'pɑːki, 'pɑːkeɪ/ ● **n. 1** flooring composed of wooden blocks arranged in a geometric pattern. **2** N. Amer. the orchestra pit or ground floor of an auditorium.
– DERIVATIVES **parquetry** n.
– ORIGIN C17 (as v.): from Fr., lit. 'small park' (i.e. delineated area).

**parr** ● **n.** (pl. same) a young salmon or trout between the stages of fry and smolt, with dark rounded patches along its sides.
– ORIGIN C18: of unknown origin.

**parrakeet** ● **n.** variant spelling of **PARAKEET**.

**parramatta** /ˌparə'matə/ (also **paramatta**) ● **n.** a fine-quality twill fabric with a weft of worsted and a warp of cotton or silk.
– ORIGIN C19: named after *Parramatta* in Australia, site of a prison whose inmates manufactured this cloth.

**parricide** /'parɪsʌɪd/ ● **n. 1** the killing of a parent or near relative. **2** a person who commits parricide.
– DERIVATIVES **parricidal** adj.
– ORIGIN C16: from Fr., from L. *parricidium*, with unknown first elem. assoc. with L. *pater* 'father' and *parens* 'parent'.

**parrot** ● **n.** a mainly tropical bird, typically brightly coloured, with a strong downcurved hooked bill and a raucous voice, some kinds of which are able to mimic human speech. [Order Psittaciformes: many species.] ● **v.** (**parroted**, **parroting**) repeat mechanically.
– ORIGIN C16: prob. from dial. Fr. *perrot*, dimin. of the male given name *Pierre* 'Peter'.

**parrotbill** ● **n.** a titmouse-like songbird with brown and grey plumage and a short arched bill. [Family Panuridae: several species.]

**parrot-fashion** ● **adv.** (of repetition) without thought or understanding.

**parrotfish** ● **n.** (pl. same or **-fishes**) **1** a brightly coloured sea fish with a parrot-like beak. [*Scarus* and other genera.] **2** Austral./NZ a brightly coloured wrasse.

**parry** ● **v.** (**-ies**, **-ied**) **1** ward off (a weapon or attack) with a countermove. **2** answer (a question or accusation) evasively. ● **n.** (pl. **-ies**) an act of parrying.
– ORIGIN C17: prob. representing Fr. *parez!* 'ward off!', imper. of *parer.*

**parse** /pɑːz/ ● **v. 1** resolve (a sentence) into its component parts and describe their syntactic roles. **2** Computing analyse (text) into logical syntactic components.
– DERIVATIVES **parser** n.
– ORIGIN C16: perh. from ME *pars* 'parts of speech', from OFr. *pars* 'parts'.

**parsec** /'pɑːsɛk/ ● **n.** Astronomy a unit of distance equal to about 3.25 light years ($3.08 \times 10^{16}$ metres), corresponding to the distance at which the mean radius of the earth's orbit subtends an angle of one second of arc.
– ORIGIN C20: blend of **PARALLAX** and **SECOND**[2].

**Parsee** /pɑː'siː, 'pɑːsiː/ ● **n.** an adherent of Zoroastrianism, especially a descendant of those who fled to India from Persia during the 7th–8th centuries.
– ORIGIN from Pers. *pārsī* 'Persian', from *pārs* 'Persia'.

**parsimony** /'pɑːsɪməni/ ● **n.** extreme unwillingness to spend money or use resources.
– PHRASES **principle** (or **law**) **of parsimony** the scientific principle that things are usually connected in the simplest or most economical way.
– DERIVATIVES **parsimonious** adj. **parsimoniously** adv. **parsimoniousness** n.
– ORIGIN ME: from L. *parsimonia, parcimonia*, from *parcere* 'be sparing'.

**parsley** ● **n.** a plant with white flowers and crinkly or flat leaves used as a culinary herb and garnish. [*Petroselinum crispum.*]
– ORIGIN OE *petersilie*, via late L. based on Gk *petroselinon*, from *petra* 'rock' + *selinon* 'parsley', influenced in ME by OFr. *peresil*, of the same origin.

**parsley piert** /ˌpɑːslɪ 'pɪət/ ● **n.** a small hairy plant with divided leaves, growing as a weed of fields and waste places. [*Aphanes arvensis.*]
– ORIGIN C16: prob. an alt. form of Fr. *perce-pierre*, lit. 'pierce stone', used to denote various plants living in crevices.

**parsnip** ● **n. 1** a long tapering cream-coloured root with a

sweet flavour. **2** the plant of the parsley family which yields this root. [*Pastinaca sativa*.]
– ORIGIN ME: from OFr. *pasnaie*, from L. *pastinaca* (rel. to *pastinare* 'dig and trench the ground'); ending assimilated to **NEEP**.

**parson** ● **n.** a beneficed member of the Anglican clergy; a rector or vicar. ➤ informal any clergyman, especially a Protestant one.
– DERIVATIVES **parsonic** adj. **parsonical** adj.
– ORIGIN ME: from OFr. *persone*, from L. *persona* 'person' (in med. L. 'rector').

**parsonage** ● **n.** a church house provided for a parson.

**parson's nose** ● **n.** informal the fatty extremity of the rump of a cooked fowl.

**pars pro toto** /ˌpɑːz prəʊ 'təʊtəʊ/ ● **n.** formal a part taken as representative of the whole.
– ORIGIN L., lit. 'part on behalf of the whole'.

**part** ● **n. 1** a piece or segment of something which combined with others makes up the whole. ➤ a component of a machine: *aircraft parts*. **2** a measure allowing comparison between the amounts of different ingredients used in a mixture. ➤ a specified fraction of a whole. **3** some but not all of something. **4** (**parts**) informal a region, especially one not clearly specified or delimited. **5** a role played by an actor or actress. ➤ Music a melody or other constituent of harmony assigned to a particular voice or instrument. ➤ the contribution made by someone to an action or situation. **6** (**parts**) archaic abilities. **7** N. Amer. a parting in the hair. ● **v. 1** move apart or divide to leave a central space. ➤ leave someone's company. ➤ (**be parted**) leave the company of someone. **2** (**part with**) give up possession of; hand over. **3** separate (the hair on either side of a parting) with a comb. ● **adv.** partly (often used to contrast different parts of something): *part jazz, part blues*.
– PHRASES **be part and parcel of** be an essential element of. **for my** (or **his**, **her**, etc.) **part** as far as I am (or he, she, etc. is) concerned. **in part** to some extent though not entirely. **look the part** have an appearance or style of dress appropriate to a particular role or situation. **a man of** (**many**) **parts** a man showing great ability in many different areas. **on the part of** (or **on my**, **their**, etc. **part**) used to ascribe responsibility for something to someone. **part company** cease to be together; go in different directions. **take part** join in or be involved in an activity. **take the part of** give support and encouragement to (someone) in a dispute.
– ORIGIN OE (denoting a part of speech), from L. *pars*, *part-*; the verb is from OFr. *partir*, from L. *partire*, *partiri* 'divide, share'.

**partake** ● **v.** (past **partook**; past part. **partaken**) **1** (**partake in**) formal join in (an activity). **2** (**partake of**) be characterized by. **3** (**partake of**) eat or drink.
– DERIVATIVES **partaker** n.
– ORIGIN C16: back-form. from earlier *partaker* 'person who takes a part'.

**parterre** /pɑː'tɛː/ ● **n. 1** a level space in a garden occupied by an ornamental arrangement of flower beds. **2** chiefly N. Amer. the ground floor of a theatre auditorium behind the orchestra pit, especially the part beneath the balconies.
– ORIGIN C17: from Fr., from *par terre* 'on the ground'.

**part exchange** Brit. ● **n.** a method of buying something in which an article that one already owns is given as part of the payment for another, more expensive, article. ● **v.** (**part-exchange**) give or take in part exchange.

**parthenogenesis** /ˌpɑːθɪnə(ʊ)'dʒɛnɪsɪs/ ● **n.** Biology reproduction from an ovum without fertilization, especially in some invertebrates and lower plants.
– DERIVATIVES **parthenogenetic** adj. **parthenogenetically** adv.
– ORIGIN C19: mod. L., from Gk *parthenos* 'virgin' + *genesis* 'creation'.

**Parthian** /'pɑːθɪən/ ● **n.** a native or inhabitant of Parthia, an ancient kingdom which lay SE of the Caspian Sea. ● **adj.** of or relating to Parthia.

**Parthian shot** ● **n.** another term for **PARTING SHOT**.
– ORIGIN C19: so named because of the trick used by Parthians of shooting arrows backwards while fleeing.

**partial** ● **adj. 1** existing only in part; incomplete. **2** favouring one side in a dispute above the other; biased. **3** (**partial to**) having a liking for. ● **n.** Music an overtone or harmonic.
– DERIVATIVES **partiality** n. **partially** adv. **partialness** n.
– ORIGIN ME: from OFr. *parcial* (sense 2), Fr. *partiel* (sense 1), from late L. *partialis*, from *pars*, *part-* 'part'.

**partial derivative** ● **n.** Mathematics a derivative of a function of two or more variables with respect to one variable, the other(s) being treated as constant.

**partial differential equation** ● **n.** Mathematics an equation containing one or more partial derivatives.

**partial eclipse** ● **n.** an eclipse in which only part of the luminary is obscured or darkened.

**partial pressure** ● **n.** Chemistry the pressure that would be exerted by one of the gases in a mixture if it occupied the same volume on its own.

**partible** ● **adj.** denoting a system of inheritance in which a deceased person's estate is divided equally among the heirs.
– DERIVATIVES **partibility** n.

**participate** ● **v. 1** take part. **2** (**participate of**) archaic partake of (a quality).
– DERIVATIVES **participant** n. **participation** n. **participative** adj. **participator** n. **participatory** adj.
– ORIGIN C16: from L. *participat-*, *participare* 'share in', based on *pars*, *part-* 'part' + *capere* 'take'.

**participle** /'pɑːtɪsɪp(ə)l/ ● **n.** Grammar a word formed from a verb (e.g. *going*, *gone*, *being*, *been*) and used as an adjective or noun (as in *burnt toast*, *good breeding*) or used to make compound verb forms (*is going*, *has been*).
– DERIVATIVES **participial** /-'sɪpɪəl/ adj. **participially** /-'sɪpɪəli/ adv.
– ORIGIN ME: from OFr., by-form of *participe*, from L. *participium* 'sharing'.

**particle** ● **n. 1** a minute portion of matter. **2** Physics a subatomic constituent of the physical world, e.g. an electron, proton, neutrino, or photon. **3** Grammar a minor function word that has comparatively little meaning and does not inflect, e.g. *in*, *up*, *off*, or *over* used with verbs to make phrasal verbs.
– ORIGIN ME: from L. *particula* 'little part', dimin. of *pars*, *part-*.

**particle board** ● **n.** another term for **CHIPBOARD**.

**particle physics** ● **pl. n.** [treated as sing.] the branch of physics concerned with the properties, relationships, and interactions of subatomic particles.

**particoloured** (US **particolored**) ● **adj.** having or consisting of two or more different colours.
– ORIGIN C16: from **PARTY**[2] + **COLOURED**.

**particular** ● **adj. 1** denoting an individual member of a specified group or class. **2** especially great or intense: *exercise particular care when checking cash*. **3** fastidious about something. **4** Logic denoting a proposition in which something is asserted of some but not all of a class. Contrasted with **UNIVERSAL**. ● **n. 1** a detail. **2** Philosophy an individual item, as contrasted with a universal quality.
– PHRASES **in particular** used to show that a statement applies to one person or thing more than any other.
– ORIGIN ME: from OFr. *particuler*, from L. *particularis*, from *particula* 'small part'.

**particularism** ● **n. 1** exclusive attachment to one's own group, nation, etc. **2** the principle of leaving each state in an empire or federation free to govern itself and promote its own interests. **3** Theology the doctrine that some but not all people are elected and redeemed.
– DERIVATIVES **particularist** n. & adj. **particularistic** adj.

**particularity** ● **n.** (pl. **-ies**) **1** the quality of being individual. **2** fullness or minuteness of detail. ➤ (**particularities**) small details. **3** Christian Theology the doctrine of God's incarnation as Jesus as a particular person at a particular time and place.

**particularize** (also **-ise**) ● **v.** formal treat individually or in detail.
– DERIVATIVES **particularization** n.

**particularly** ● **adv. 1** to a higher degree than is usual or average. **2** in particular; specifically.

**particulate** /pɑː'tɪkjʊlət, -eɪt, pə-/ ● **adj.** of, relating to,

or in the form of minute particles. ● n. (**particulates**) matter in such a form.
– ORIGIN C19: from L. *particula* 'particle' + **-ATE**[2].

**parting** ● n. **1** the action of moving away or being separated from someone. **2** the action of dividing something into parts. **3** Brit. a line of scalp revealed in a person's hair by combing the hair away in opposite directions on either side.
– PHRASES **a** (or **the**) **parting of the ways** a point at which two people must separate or at which a decision must be taken.

**parting shot** ● n. a cutting remark made at the moment of departure.

**parti pris** /ˌpɑːtɪ ˈpriː/ ● n. (pl. **partis pris** pronunc. same) a preconceived view; a bias. ● adj. prejudiced; biased.
– ORIGIN Fr., lit. 'side taken'.

**partisan** /ˈpɑːtɪzan, ˌpɑːtɪˈzan/ ● n. **1** a strong supporter of a party, cause, or person. **2** a member of an armed group fighting secretly against an occupying force. ● adj. prejudiced in favour of a particular cause.
– DERIVATIVES **partisanship** n.
– ORIGIN C16: from Fr., via Ital. dial. from Ital. *partigiano*, from *parte* 'part'.

**partita** /pɑːˈtiːtə/ ● n. (pl. **partitas** or **partite** /-teɪ, -ti/) Music a suite, typically for a solo instrument or chamber ensemble.
– ORIGIN C19: from Ital., lit. 'divided off', fem. past part. of *partire*.

**-partite** /ˈpɑːtʌɪt/ ● suffix (forming adjectives) divided into a specified number of parts: *tripartite*.
– ORIGIN ME: from L. *partit-*, *partiri* 'divide up'.

**partition** ● n. **1** (especially with reference to a country) the action or state of dividing or being divided into parts. **2** a structure dividing a space into two parts, especially a light interior wall. **3** Chemistry the distribution of a solute between two immiscible solvents in contact with one another, in accordance with its differing solubility in each. **4** Computing each of a number of portions into which some operating systems divide memory or storage. ● v. **1** divide into parts. **2** divide or separate by erecting a partition.
– DERIVATIVES **partitioner** n. **partitionist** n.
– ORIGIN ME: from L. *partitio(n-)*, from *partiri* 'divide into parts'.

**partitive** /ˈpɑːtɪtɪv/ Grammar ● adj. denoting a grammatical construction indicating that only a part of a whole is referred to, for example *a slice of bacon, some of the children*. ● n. a noun or pronoun used as the first term in such a construction.
– DERIVATIVES **partitively** adv.

**partitive genitive** ● n. Grammar a genitive used to indicate a whole divided into or regarded in parts, expressed in English by *of* as in *most of us*.

**partly** ● adv. to some extent; not completely.

**partner** ● n. **1** a person who takes part in an undertaking with another or others, especially in a business or firm with shared risks and profits. **2** either of two people doing something as a couple or pair. **3** either member of a married couple or of an established unmarried couple. **4** US dated or dialect a friendly form of address by one man to another. ● v. **1** be the partner of. **2** N. Amer. associate as partners.
– DERIVATIVES **partnerless** adj.
– ORIGIN ME: alt. of *parcener* 'partner, joint heir', from Anglo-Norman Fr. *parcener*, based on L. *partitio(n-)* 'partition'.

**partners' desk** (also **partnership desk**) ● n. a large flat-topped pedestal desk with space for two people to sit opposite each other.

**partnership** ● n. **1** the state of being a partner or partners. **2** an association of two or more people as partners. **3** Cricket the number of runs added by a pair of batsmen before one of them is dismissed or the innings ends.

**part of speech** ● n. a category to which a word is assigned in accordance with its syntactic functions, e.g. noun, pronoun, adjective, determiner, verb, adverb, preposition, conjunction, and interjection.

**partook** past of **PARTAKE**.

**partridge** ● n. (pl. same or **partridges**) a short-tailed game bird with mainly brown plumage. [*Perdix perdix* (**grey partridge**) and other species.]
– ORIGIN ME *partrich*, from OFr. *pertriz*, *perdriz*, from L. *perdix*.

**partridgeberry** ● n. (pl. **-ies**) **1** a North American plant with edible red berries eaten by game birds. [*Mitchella repens* and *Vaccinium vitis-idaea* (cowberry).] **2** the fruit of this plant.

**part song** ● n. a secular song with three or more voice parts, typically unaccompanied, and homophonic rather than contrapuntal in style.

**part-time** ● adj. & adv. for only part of the usual working day or week.
– DERIVATIVES **part-timer** n.

**parturient** /pɑːˈtjʊərɪənt/ ● adj. technical about to give birth; in labour.
– ORIGIN C16: from L. *parturient-*, *parturire* 'to be in labour', inceptive of *parere* 'bring forth'.

**parturition** /ˌpɑːtjʊˈrɪʃ(ə)n/ ● n. formal or technical the action of giving birth to young; childbirth.
– ORIGIN C17: from late L. *parturitio(n-)*, from *parturire* (see **PARTURIENT**).

**part-way** ● adv. part of the way.

**part-work** ● n. Brit. a publication appearing in several parts over a period of time.

**party**[1] ● n. (pl. **-ies**) **1** a social gathering of invited guests, typically involving eating, drinking, and entertainment. **2** a formally constituted political group that contests elections and attempts to take part in government. **3** a group of people taking part in a particular activity or trip. **4** a person or group forming one side in an agreement or dispute. **5** informal a person, especially one with specified characteristics. ● v. (**-ies**, **-ied**) informal enjoy oneself at a party or other lively gathering.
– PHRASES **be party** (or **a party**) **to** be involved in.
– ORIGIN ME: from OFr. *partie*, based on L. *partiri* 'divide into parts'.

**party**[2] ● adj. Heraldry divided into parts of different tinctures.
– ORIGIN ME: from OFr. *parti* 'parted'.

**party line** ● n. **1** a policy, or the policies collectively, officially adopted by a political party. **2** a telephone line shared by two or more subscribers.

**party list** ● n. a proportional representation system in which people vote for a party and seats are filled from lists of candidates according to each party's share of the vote.

**party piece** ● n. Brit. a poem, song, or trick regularly performed by someone in order to entertain others.

**party politics** ● pl. n. [also treated as sing.] politics that relate to political parties rather than to the public good.
– DERIVATIVES **party political** adj.

**party-pooper** ● n. informal a person who throws gloom over social enjoyment.
– DERIVATIVES **party-pooping** n.

**party popper** ● n. a device which explosively ejects thin paper streamers when a string is pulled.

**party wall** ● n. a wall common to two adjoining buildings or rooms.

**parure** /pəˈrʊə/ ● n. a set of jewels intended to be worn together.
– ORIGIN C19: from Fr., from *parer* 'adorn'.

**parvenu** /ˈpɑːvənuː, -njuː/ often derogatory ● n. a person of obscure origin who has gained wealth, influence, or celebrity. ● adj. relating to or denoting such persons.
– ORIGIN C19: from Fr., lit. 'arrived', past part. of *parvenir*.

**parvis** /ˈpɑːvɪs/ (also **parvise**) ● n. an enclosed area in front of a church, typically surrounded with colonnades or porticoes.
– ORIGIN ME: from OFr., based on late L. *paradisus* 'paradise', in the Middle Ages denoting a court in front of St Peter's, Rome.

**parvovirus** /ˈpɑːvəʊˌvʌɪrəs/ ● n. Medicine any of a class of very small viruses causing contagious disease in dogs and other animals.
– ORIGIN 1960s: from L. *parvus* 'small' + **VIRUS**.

**PAS** ● **abbrev.** power-assisted steering.

**pas** /pɑː/ ● **n.** (pl. same) a step in dancing, especially in classical ballet.
– ORIGIN from Fr.

**pascal** /ˈpask(ə)l/ ● **n. 1** (abbrev.: **Pa**) the SI unit of pressure, equal to one newton per square metre. **2** (**Pascal**) a high-level structured computer programming language.
– ORIGIN 1950s: named after the C17 Fr. scientist Blaise *Pascal*.

**Pascal's triangle** ● **n.** Mathematics a triangular array of numbers in which those at the ends of the rows are 1 and each of the others is the sum of the nearest two numbers in the row above (the apex, 1, being at the top).

**paschal** /ˈpask(ə)l, ˈpɑːs-/ ● **adj.** formal **1** of or relating to Easter. **2** of or relating to the Jewish Passover.
– ORIGIN ME: from OFr., from eccles. L. *paschalis*, from *pascha* 'feast of Passover', via Gk and Aramaic from Heb. *Pesaḥ*.

**pas de chat** /ˌpɑː də ˈʃa/ ● **n.** (pl. same) Ballet a jump in which each foot in turn is raised to the opposite knee.
– ORIGIN Fr., lit. 'step of a cat'.

**pas de deux** /ˌpɑː də ˈdəː/ ● **n.** (pl. same) a dance for a couple.
– ORIGIN Fr., lit. 'step of two'.

**pash** ● **n.** informal, dated a brief infatuation.
– ORIGIN C20: abbrev. of **PASSION**.

**pasha** /ˈpaʃə/ (also **pacha**) ● **n.** historical the title of a Turkish officer of high rank.
– ORIGIN C17: from Turk. *paşa*, from Pahlavi *pati* 'lord' + *šāh* 'shah'.

**pashka** /ˈpaʃkə/ (also **paskha**) ● **n.** a rich Russian dessert made with curd cheese, dried fruit, nuts, and spices, traditionally eaten at Easter.
– ORIGIN Russ., lit. 'Easter'.

**pashmina** /pʌʃˈmiːnə/ ● **n.** a shawl made from fine-quality goat's wool.
– ORIGIN Pers., from *pašm* 'wool, down'.

**Pashto** /ˈpʌʃtəʊ/ ● **n.** the language of the Pathans, spoken in Afghanistan and northern Pakistan.
– ORIGIN the name in Pashto.

**paso doble** /ˌpasə(ʊ) ˈdəʊbleɪ/ ● **n.** (pl. **paso dobles**) a fast-paced ballroom dance based on a Latin American marching style. ➤ a piece of music for such a dance.
– ORIGIN 1920s: from Sp., lit. 'double step'.

**paspalum** /ˈpasp(ə)ləm/ ● **n.** a pasture grass of warm and tropical regions. [Genus *Paspalum*.]
– ORIGIN mod. L., from Gk *paspalos*, denoting a kind of millet.

**pasque flower** /pask, pɑːsk/ ● **n.** a spring-flowering plant related to the anemones, with purple flowers and fern-like foliage. [*Pulsatilla vulgaris*.]
– ORIGIN C16: from Fr. *passe-fleur*; later assoc. with archaic *pasque* 'Easter'.

**pasquinade** /ˌpaskwɪˈneɪd/ ● **n.** a satire or lampoon, originally one displayed or delivered in a public place.
– ORIGIN C16: from Ital. *pasquinata*, from *Pasquino*, a statue in Rome on which abusive Latin verses were posted.

**pass¹** ● **v. 1** move or cause to move in a specified direction. ➤ change from one state or condition to another. ➤ euphemistic die: *she passed away peacefully*. **2** go past or across; leave behind or on one side in proceeding. ➤ surpass; exceed. ➤ Tennis hit a winning shot past (an opponent). **3** (of time) elapse; go by. ➤ happen; be done or said. ➤ spend or use up (time). ➤ come to an end. **4** transfer (something) to someone, especially by handing or bequeathing it to the next person in a series. ➤ (in ball games) kick, hit, or throw (the ball) to a teammate. **5** be successful in (an examination, test, or course). ➤ judge the performance or standard of (someone or something) to be satisfactory. ➤ (**pass as/for**) be accepted as. **6** approve or put into effect (a proposal or law) by voting on it. **7** pronounce (a judgement or sentence). ➤ utter (remarks, especially criticism). ➤ (**pass on/upon**) archaic give a judgement on. **8** discharge (urine or faeces) from the body. **9** forgo one's turn or an opportunity to do or have something. ➤ [as exclam.] (in response to a question) I do not know. ➤ (of a company) not declare or pay (a dividend). ● **n. 1** an act or instance of moving past or through something. ➤ informal an amorous or sexual advance. ➤ a thrust in fencing. ➤ a juggling trick. ➤ Bridge an act of refraining from bidding during the auction. ➤ Computing a single scan through a set of data or a program. **2** a success in an examination. ➤ Brit. the achievement of a university degree without honours. **3** a card, ticket, or permit giving authorization for the holder to enter or have access to a place, form of transport, or event. **4** (in ball games) an act of passing the ball to a teammate. **5** a state or situation of a specified (usually bad) nature.
– PHRASES **come to a pretty pass** reach a regrettable state of affairs. **pass one's eye over** read cursorily. **pass water** urinate.
– PHRASAL VERBS **pass someone by** happen without being noticed or fully experienced by someone. **pass off** happen or be carried through in a specified (usually satisfactory) way. **pass something off** evade or lightly dismiss an awkward remark. **pass something off as** falsely represent something as. **pass out 1** become unconscious. **2** Brit. complete one's initial training in the armed forces. **pass someone over** ignore the claims of someone to advancement. **pass something over** avoid mentioning or considering something. **pass something up** refrain from taking up an opportunity.
– DERIVATIVES **passer** n.
– ORIGIN ME: from OFr. *passer*, based on L. *passus* 'pace'.

**pass²** ● **n.** a route over or through mountains.
– PHRASES **sell the pass** Brit. betray a cause.
– ORIGIN ME (in the sense 'division of a text, passage through'): var. of **PACE¹**, influenced by **PASS¹** and Fr. *pas*.

**passable** ● **adj. 1** good enough to be acceptable. **2** clear of obstacles and able to be travelled along or on.
– DERIVATIVES **passably** adv.

**passacaglia** /ˌpasəˈkɑːlɪə/ ● **n.** Music a composition similar to a chaconne, typically in slow triple time with variations over a ground bass.
– ORIGIN Ital., from Sp. *pasacalle*, from *pasar* 'to pass' + *calle* 'street' (because orig. with ref. to a street dance).

**passage¹** /ˈpasɪdʒ/ ● **n. 1** the action or process of moving through, under, over, or past something on the way from one place to another. ➤ the action or process of moving forward. ➤ the right to pass through somewhere. ➤ a journey by sea or air. **2** a way through something; a passageway. **3** the process of transition from one state to another. ➤ the passing of a bill into law. **4** a short section or episode from a text, musical composition, game, etc. **5** Medicine & Biology /paˈsɑːʒ/ the process of propagating micro-organisms or cells in a series of host organisms or culture media. ● **v.** /paˈsɑːʒ/ Medicine & Biology subject (micro-organisms or cells) to a passage.
– PHRASES **passage of** (or **at**) **arms** a fight or dispute. **work one's passage** work in return for a free place on a voyage.
– ORIGIN ME: from OFr., based on L. *passus* 'pace'.

**passage²** /paˈsɑːʒ/ ● **n.** a riding movement in which a horse executes a slow elevated trot, giving the impression of dancing.
– ORIGIN C18: from Fr. *passage*, from an alt. of Ital. *passeggiare* 'to walk, pace'.

**passage grave** ● **n.** Archaeology a prehistoric megalithic burial chamber inside a mound, with a passage leading to the exterior.

**passageway** ● **n.** a corridor or other narrow passage between buildings or rooms.

**passagework** ● **n.** music affording scope for virtuoso playing.

**passant** /ˈpas(ə)nt/ ● **adj.** Heraldry (of an animal) represented as walking towards the dexter side, with the right front foot raised.
– ORIGIN ME: from OFr., lit. 'proceeding', pres. part. of *passer*.

**passata** /pəˈsɑːtə/ ● **n.** a thick paste made from sieved tomatoes.
– ORIGIN from Ital.

**passband** ● **n.** a frequency band within which signals are transmitted by a filter without attenuation.

**passbook** ● **n. 1** a book issued by a bank or building

society to an account holder, recording transactions. **2** historical (in South Africa under apartheid) a black person's identity book, used to control travel and residence.

**passé** /ˈpaseɪ/ • **adj. 1** no longer fashionable; out of date. **2** archaic past one's prime.
– ORIGIN Fr., lit. 'gone by', past part. of *passer.*

**passed pawn** • **n.** Chess a pawn that no enemy pawn can stop from queening.

**passel** /ˈpas(ə)l/ • **n.** informal, chiefly US a large group: *a passel of journalists.*
– ORIGIN C19: representing a pronunc. of **PARCEL**.

**passementerie** /ˈpasm(ə)ntri/ • **n.** decorative textile trimming consisting of gold or silver lace, gimp, or braid.
– ORIGIN C17: from Fr., from *passement* 'gold lace'.

**passenger** • **n. 1** a traveller on a public or private conveyance other than the driver, pilot, or crew. **2** a member of a team who does very little effective work.
– ORIGIN ME: from the OFr. adj. *passager* 'passing, transitory', from *passage* (see **PASSAGE[1]**).

**passenger mile** • **n.** one mile travelled by one passenger, as a unit of traffic.

**passenger pigeon** • **n.** a migratory long-tailed North American pigeon, hunted to extinction by 1914. [*Ectopistes migratorius.*]

**passepartout** /ˌpaspɑːˈtuː, ˌpɑːs-/ • **n. 1** a simple picture frame consisting of pieces of glass and card taped together at the edges. **2** adhesive tape used in making such a frame. **3** archaic a master key.
– ORIGIN C17: from Fr., lit. 'passes everywhere'.

**passer-by** • **n.** (pl. **passers-by**) a person who happens to be going past something, especially on foot.

**passerine** /ˈpasərʌɪn, -riːn/ Ornithology • **adj.** denoting birds of a large order (Passeriformes) distinguished by having feet adapted for perching and including all songbirds. • **n.** a passerine bird.
– ORIGIN C18: from L. *passer* 'sparrow' + **-INE[1]**.

**pas seul** /pɑː ˈsəːl/ • **n.** a dance for one person.
– ORIGIN Fr., lit. 'single step'.

**passible** /ˈpasɪb(ə)l/ • **adj.** Christian Theology capable of feeling or suffering.
– DERIVATIVES **passibility** n.
– ORIGIN ME: from OFr., from late L. *passibilis*, from L. *pass-*, *pati* 'suffer'.

**passim** /ˈpasɪm/ • **adv.** (of references) at various places throughout the text.
– ORIGIN L., from *passus*, *pandere* 'scatter'.

**passing** • **adj. 1** going past. **2** (of a period of time) going by. **3** carried out quickly and lightly: *a passing glance.* **4** (of a resemblance or similarity) slight. • **n. 1** the passage of something, especially time. **2** the action of kicking, hitting, or throwing a ball to another team member during a sports match. **3** the end of something. ➤ euphemistic a person's death.
– PHRASES **in passing** briefly and casually.
– DERIVATIVES **passingly** adv.

**passing bell** • **n.** a bell rung immediately after a death as a signal for prayers.

**passing note** • **n.** Music a note not belonging to the harmony but interposed to secure a smooth transition.

**passing shot** • **n.** Tennis a shot aiming the ball beyond and out of reach of one's opponent.

**passion** • **n. 1** strong and barely controllable emotion. ➤ an outburst of such emotion. **2** intense sexual love. **3** an intense enthusiasm for something. **4** (**the Passion**) the suffering and death of Jesus. ➤ a musical setting of this.
– DERIVATIVES **passional** adj. (rare). **passionless** adj.
– ORIGIN ME: from OFr., from late L. *passio(n-)*, from L. *pati* 'suffer'.

**passionate** • **adj.** showing or caused by passion.
– DERIVATIVES **passionately** adv. **passionateness** n.

**passion flower** • **n.** an evergreen climbing plant of warm regions, with a complex flower said to suggest things associated with Christ's Crucifixion. [Genus *Passiflora.*]

**passion fruit** • **n.** the edible purple fruit of a passion flower (*Passiflora edulis*), grown chiefly in tropical America and the Caribbean.

**passion play** • **n.** a dramatic performance representing Christ's Passion.

**Passion Sunday** • **n.** the fifth Sunday in Lent.

**Passiontide** • **n.** the last two weeks of Lent.

**Passion Week** • **n. 1** the week between Passion Sunday and Palm Sunday. **2** older name for **HOLY WEEK**.

**passivate** /ˈpasɪveɪt/ • **v.** [usu. as adj. **passivated**] make (a metal or other substance) unreactive by coating or otherwise altering its surface.
– DERIVATIVES **passivation** n.

**passive** • **adj. 1** accepting or allowing what happens or what others do, without active response or resistance. **2** Grammar denoting a voice of verbs in which the subject undergoes the action of the verb (e.g. *they were killed* as opposed to *he killed them*). The opposite of **ACTIVE**. **3** denoting a circuit or device containing no source of energy or electromotive force. ➤ (of radar or a satellite) receiving or reflecting radiation rather than generating its own signal. **4** Chemistry unreactive because of a thin inert surface layer of oxide. • **n.** Grammar a passive form of a verb.
– DERIVATIVES **passively** adv. **passiveness** n. **passivity** n.
– ORIGIN ME: from L. *passivus*, from *pass-*, *pati* 'suffer'.

**passive immunity** • **n.** Physiology short-term immunity resulting from the introduction of antibodies from another person or animal.

**passive resistance** • **n.** non-violent opposition to authority, especially a refusal to cooperate with legal requirements.

**passive smoking** • **n.** the involuntary inhaling of smoke from other people's cigarettes, cigars, or pipes.

**passivize** (also **-ise**) • **v.** Grammar convert into the passive.
– DERIVATIVES **passivizable** adj. **passivization** n.

**pass key** • **n. 1** a key given only to those who are officially allowed access. **2** a master key.

**pass laws** • **pl. n.** laws formerly in operation in South Africa controlling the rights of black people to residence and travel.

**Passover** • **n.** the major Jewish spring festival, commemorating the liberation of the Israelites from Egyptian bondage.
– ORIGIN from *pass over*, with ref. to the exemption of the Israelites from the death of their firstborn (Exod. 12).

**passport** • **n.** an official document issued by a government, certifying the holder's identity and citizenship and entitling them to travel abroad under its protection.
– ORIGIN C15 (denoting authorization to depart from a port): from Fr. *passeport*, from *passer* 'to pass' + *port* 'seaport'.

**password** • **n.** a secret word or phrase used to gain admission to something.

**past** • **adj. 1** gone by in time and no longer existing. ➤ recently elapsed: *the past twelve months.* **2** Grammar (of a tense) expressing a past action or state. • **n. 1** (usu. **the past**) a past period or the events in it. ➤ a person's or thing's history or earlier life: *the country's colourful past.* **2** Grammar a past tense or form of a verb. • **prep. 1** to or on the further side of. **2** in front of or from one side to the other of. **3** beyond in time; later than. **4** no longer capable of. **5** beyond the scope of. • **adv. 1** so as to pass from one side of something to the other. **2** used to indicate the passage of time: *a week went past.*
– PHRASES **not put it past someone** believe someone to be capable of doing something wrong or rash. **past it** informal too old to be any good at anything.
– DERIVATIVES **pastness** n.
– ORIGIN ME: var. of *passed*, past part. of **PASS[1]**.

**pasta** • **n.** dough extruded or stamped into various shapes (e.g. spaghetti, lasagne) for cooking in boiling water and eating, typically with a savoury sauce.
– ORIGIN C19: from Ital., lit. 'paste'.

**paste** • **n. 1** a thick, soft, moist substance, typically produced by mixing dry ingredients with a liquid. **2** an adhesive of this kind. **3** a mixture of kaolin and water of low plasticity, used for making porcelain. **4** a hard vit-

reous composition used in making imitation gems. ● v. **1** coat or stick with paste. **2** Computing insert (a section of text) into a document. **3** [often as noun **pasting**] informal beat or defeat severely.
– ORIGIN ME: from OFr., from late L. *pasta* 'medicinal preparation in the shape of a small square', prob. from Gk *pastē*, (pl.) *pasta* 'barley porridge', from *pastos* 'sprinkled'.

**pasteboard** ● n. thin board made by pasting together sheets of paper.

**pastel** ● n. **1** a crayon made of powdered pigments bound with gum or resin. ➤a work of art created using pastels. **2** a soft and delicate shade of a colour. ● adj. of or denoting such a shade: *pastel blue curtains.*
– DERIVATIVES **pastellist** (also **pastelist**) n.
– ORIGIN C17: via Fr. from Ital. *pastello*, dimin. of *pasta* 'paste'.

**pastern** /'past(ə)n/ ● n. the sloping part of a horse's or other animal's foot between the fetlock and the hoof.
– ORIGIN ME: from OFr. *pasturon*, from *pasture*, orig. 'strap for hobbling a horse'.

**paste-up** ● n. a document prepared by combining and pasting various sections on a backing.

**pasteurellosis** /ˌpɑːstərɛ'ləʊsɪs, ˌpastərɛ'ləʊsɪs/ ● n. a bacterial infection commonly affecting animals and sometimes transferred to humans through bites and scratches.
– ORIGIN C20: from Fr. *pasteurellose*, from mod. L. *Pasteurella* genus name of the bacterium responsible (named after the C19 Fr. chemist and bacteriologist Louis *Pasteur*) + **-OSIS**.

**pasteurize** /'pɑːstʃərʌɪz, -stjə-, 'pas-/ (also **-ise**) ● v. [often as adj. **pasteurized**] subject (milk, wine, etc.) to a process of partial sterilization, especially by heating.
– DERIVATIVES **pasteurization** n. **pasteurizer** n.

**pasticcio** /pa'stɪtʃəʊ/ ● n. (pl. **-os**) another term for **PASTICHE**.
– ORIGIN from Ital.

**pastiche** /pa'stiːʃ/ ● n. an artistic work in a style that imitates that of another work, artist, or period. ● v. create a pastiche of (an artist or work).
– DERIVATIVES **pasticheur** n.
– ORIGIN C19: from Fr., from Ital. *pasticcio*, based on late L. *pasta* 'paste'.

**pastille** /'past(ə)l, -tɪl/ ● n. **1** a small sweet or lozenge. **2** a small pellet of aromatic paste burnt as a perfume or deodorizer.
– ORIGIN C17: from Fr., from L. *pastillus* 'little loaf, lozenge', from *panis* 'loaf'.

**pastime** ● n. an activity that someone does regularly for enjoyment; a hobby.
– ORIGIN C15: from **PASS**[1] + **TIME**, translating Fr. *passe-temps*.

**pastis** /'pastɪs, pa'stiːs/ ● n. (pl. same) an aniseed-flavoured aperitif.
– ORIGIN from Fr.

**past master** ● n. an experienced person particularly skilled at a specified activity.

**pastor** /'pɑːstə/ ● n. a minister in charge of a Christian church or congregation, especially in some non-episcopal churches. ● v. be the pastor of.
– DERIVATIVES **pastorate** n. **pastorship** n.
– ORIGIN ME: from Anglo-Norman Fr. *pastour*, from L. *pastor* 'shepherd', from *past-*, *pascere* 'feed, graze'.

**pastoral** /'pɑːst(ə)r(ə)l/ ● adj. **1** used for or relating to the farming or grazing of sheep or cattle. **2** portraying country life, especially in an idealized or romanticized form. **3** of or relating to the giving of spiritual guidance. **4** of or denoting a teacher's responsibility for the general well-being of pupils or students. ● n. a pastoral poem, picture, etc.
– DERIVATIVES **pastoralism** n. **pastorally** adv.

**pastorale** /ˌpastə'rɑːl/ ● n. (pl. **pastorales** or **pastorali** /-liː/) **1** a slow instrumental composition in compound time, usually with drone notes in the bass. **2** a simple musical play with a rural subject.
– ORIGIN C18: from Ital., lit. 'pastoral'.

**pastoralist** ● n. **1** (especially in Australia) a sheep or cattle farmer. **2** archaic a writer of pastorals.

**pastoral staff** ● n. a bishop's crozier.

**past perfect** ● adj. & n. another term for **PLUPERFECT**.

**pastrami** /pa'strɑːmi/ ● n. highly seasoned smoked beef, typically served in thin slices.
– ORIGIN from Yiddish.

**pastry** ● n. (pl. **-ies**) **1** a dough of flour, fat, and water, used as a base and covering in baked dishes such as pies. **2** an item of food consisting of sweet pastry with a cream, jam, or fruit filling.
– ORIGIN ME: from **PASTE**, influenced by OFr. *pastaierie.*

**pastry cream** ● n. a thick, creamy custard used as a filling for cakes or flans.

**pasturage** ● n. **1** land used for pasture. **2** the occupation or process of pasturing animals.

**pasture** ● n. **1** land covered mainly with grass, suitable for grazing cattle or sheep. **2** grass and herbage growing on such land. ● v. put (animals) to graze in a pasture.
– PHRASES **pastures new** somewhere offering new opportunities. [suggested by 'Tomorrow to fresh woods and pastures new' (Milton's *Lycidas*).] **put out to pasture** force to retire.
– ORIGIN ME: from OFr., from late L. *pastura* 'grazing', from *past-*, *pascere* 'graze'.

**pasty**[1] /'pasti/ (also **pastie**) ● n. (pl. **-ies**) chiefly Brit. a folded pastry case filled with seasoned meat and vegetables.
– ORIGIN ME: from OFr. *paste(e)*, based on late L. *pasta* 'paste'.

**pasty**[2] /'peɪsti/ ● adj. (**-ier**, **-iest**) **1** of or like paste. **2** (of a person's face) unhealthily pale.
– DERIVATIVES **pastiness** n.

**Pat** ● n. Brit. informal, often offensive an Irishman.
– ORIGIN C19: abbrev. of the given name *Patrick*.

**Pat.** ● abbrev. Patent.

**pat**[1] ● v. (**patted**, **patting**) **1** touch quickly and gently with the flat of the hand. **2** mould or position with gentle taps. ● n. **1** a light stroke with the hand. **2** a compact mass of soft material.
– PHRASES **a pat on the back** an expression of congratulation or encouragement.
– ORIGIN ME: prob. imitative.

**pat**[2] ● adj. simple and somewhat glib or unconvincing: *a pat answer.* ● adv. conveniently or opportunely.
– PHRASES **have something off** (or **down**) **pat** have something memorized perfectly. **stand pat** chiefly N. Amer. **1** stick stubbornly to one's opinion or decision. **2** (in poker and blackjack) retain one's hand as dealt.
– DERIVATIVES **patly** adv. **patness** n.
– ORIGIN C16: rel. to **PAT**[1]; appar. orig. 'as if with a pat'.

**pataca** /pə'tɑːkə/ ● n. the basic monetary unit of Macao, equivalent to 100 avos.
– ORIGIN from Sp. and Port.

**pat-a-cake** ● n. a children's game with gentle patting in time to the words of a rhyme.

**patagium** /ˌpatə'dʒʌɪəm/ ● n. (pl. **patagia** /-'dʒʌɪə/) **1** Zoology a membrane between the forelimbs and hindlimbs on each side of a bat or gliding mammal. **2** Entomology a lobe that covers the wing joint in many moths.
– ORIGIN C19: from L., denoting gold edging on a Roman lady's tunic, from Gk *patageion.*

**Patagonian** /ˌpatə'gəʊnɪən/ ● n. a native or inhabitant of the South American region of Patagonia. ● adj. of or relating to Patagonia.

**pataphysics** /ˌpatə'fɪzɪks/ ● pl. n. [usu. treated as sing.] a supposed branch of philosophy concerned with an imaginary realm additional to metaphysics.
– ORIGIN 1940s: from Gk *ta epi ta metaphusika*, lit. 'the (works) imposed on the metaphysics', introduced by the Fr. absurdist writer Alfred Jarry.

**patas monkey** /pə'tɑː/ ● n. a central African guenon with reddish-brown fur, a black face, and a white moustache. [*Erythrocebus patas.*]
– ORIGIN C18: *patas* from Senegalese Fr., from Wolof *pata.*

**Patau's syndrome** /'patаʊz/ ● n. Medicine a congenital chromosomal disorder resulting in brain, heart, and kidney defects, usually fatal soon after birth.
– ORIGIN 1960s: named after the Ger. physician Klaus

*Patau.*

**patball** ● n. Brit. a simple game in which a ball is hit back and forth between two players.

**patch** ● n. **1** a piece of material used to cover a torn or weak point. ➤a shield worn over a sightless or injured eye. ➤a piece of cloth sewn on to clothing as a badge. ➤an adhesive piece of drug-impregnated material worn on the skin so that the drug may be gradually absorbed. ➤historical a small black silk disc worn on the face, especially by women in the 17th and 18th centuries. **2** a small area differently coloured or otherwise distinct. **3** a small piece of ground, especially one used for gardening. ➤Brit. informal an area for which someone is responsible or in which they operate. **4** Brit. informal a period of time regarded as distinct: *a bad patch.* **5** a temporary electrical or telephone connection. **6** Computing a small piece of code inserted to correct or enhance a program. ● v. **1** mend, strengthen, or protect by means of a patch. ➤(usu. **be patched with**) cause to become variegated. ➤(**patch someone/thing up**) informal treat someone's injuries or repair the damage to something, especially hastily. ➤(**patch something together**) construct something hastily from unsuitable components. ➤(**patch up**) informal restore peaceful or friendly relations after (a quarrel or dispute). **2** connect by a temporary electrical, radio, or telephonic connection.
– PHRASES **not a patch on** Brit. informal greatly inferior to.
– DERIVATIVES **patcher** n.
– ORIGIN ME: perh. from a var. of OFr. *pieche*, dial. var. of *piece* 'piece'.

**patchboard** ● n. a board in a switchboard, computer, etc. with a number of sockets that can be connected in various combinations.

**patch cord** (also **patch lead**) ● n. an insulated lead with a plug at each end, for use with a patchboard.

**patchouli** /ˈpatʃʊli, pəˈtʃuːli/ ● n. **1** an aromatic oil used in perfumery, insecticides, and medicine. **2** the strongly scented SE Asian shrub of the mint family which yields this. [*Pogostemon cablin.*]
– ORIGIN C19: from Tamil *paççuli.*

**patch panel** ● n. another term for **PATCHBOARD**.

**patch pocket** ● n. a pocket made of a separate piece of cloth sewn on to the outside of a garment.

**patch test** ● n. an allergy test in which a range of substances are applied to the skin in light scratches or under a plaster.

**patchwork** ● n. **1** needlework in which small pieces of cloth in different designs are sewn together. **2** a thing composed of many different elements so as to appear variegated.

**patchy** ● adj. (**-ier, -iest**) **1** existing or happening in small, isolated areas. **2** not of the same quality throughout; inconsistent.
– DERIVATIVES **patchily** adv. **patchiness** n.

**pate** /peɪt/ ● n. archaic or humorous a person's head.
– ORIGIN ME: of unknown origin.

**pâte** /pɑːt/ ● n. the paste of which porcelain is made.
– ORIGIN C19: Fr., lit. 'paste'.

**pâté** /ˈpateɪ/ ● n. a rich savoury paste made from finely minced or mashed meat, fish, or other ingredients.
– ORIGIN Fr., from OFr. *paste* 'pie of seasoned meat'.

**pâté de foie gras** /ˌpateɪ də fwɑː ˈɡrɑː/ ● n. a smooth rich paste made from fatted goose liver.
– ORIGIN from Fr.

**patella** /pəˈtɛlə/ ● n. (pl. **patellae** /-liː/) Anatomy the kneecap.
– DERIVATIVES **patellar** adj. **patellate** /-lət/ adj.
– ORIGIN C16: from L., dimin. of *patina* 'shallow dish'.

**paten** /ˈpat(ə)n/ ● n. **1** a plate for holding the bread during the Eucharist. **2** a shallow metal plate or dish.
– ORIGIN ME: from OFr. *patene*, from L. *patina* 'shallow dish', from Gk *patanē* 'a plate'.

**patent** /ˈpat(ə)nt, ˈpeɪt-/ ● n. a government licence to an individual or body conferring a right or title for a set period, especially the sole right to make, use, or sell an invention. ● adj. /ˈpeɪt(ə)nt/ **1** easily recognizable; obvious. ➤Medicine (of a parasitic infection) showing detectable parasites in the tissues or faeces. **2** Medicine (of a duct or aperture) open and unobstructed. **3** made and marketed under a patent. ● v. obtain a patent for (an invention).
– DERIVATIVES **patency** n. **patentable** adj. **patently** /ˈpeɪt(ə)ntli/ adv.
– ORIGIN ME: from OFr., from L. *patent-*, *patere* 'lie open'; cf. **LETTERS PATENT**.

**patentee** /ˌpeɪt(ə)nˈtiː, ˌpat-/ ● n. a person or body that obtains or holds a patent for something.

**patent leather** ● n. glossy varnished leather, used chiefly for shoes, belts, and handbags.

**patent medicine** ● n. a medicine made and marketed under a patent and available without prescription.

**patent office** ● n. an office from which patents are issued.

**Patent Roll** ● n. historical (in the UK) a parchment roll listing the patents issued in a particular year.

**pater** /ˈpeɪtə/ ● n. **1** Brit. informal, dated father. **2** Anthropology a person's legal father. Often contrasted with **GENITOR**.
– ORIGIN from L.

**patera** /ˈpat(ə)rə/ ● n. (pl. **paterae** /-riː/) **1** a broad shallow dish of a kind used in ancient Rome for pouring libations. **2** a flat, round ornamental design resembling a shallow dish. **3** a broad, shallow bowl-shaped feature on a planet's surface.
– ORIGIN L., from *patere* 'be or lie open'.

**paterfamilias** /ˌpeɪtəfəˈmɪlɪas, ˌpatə-/ ● n. (pl. **patresfamilias** /ˌpeɪtriːz-, ˌpatriːz-/) the male head of a family or household.
– ORIGIN L., lit. 'father of the family'.

**paternal** ● adj. **1** of or appropriate to a father. **2** related through the father: *his paternal grandfather.*
– DERIVATIVES **paternally** adv.
– ORIGIN ME: from late L. *paternalis*, from L. *paternus*, from *pater* 'father'.

**paternalism** ● n. the policy of restricting the freedom and responsibilities of one's subordinates or dependents in their supposed best interest.
– DERIVATIVES **paternalist** n. & adj. **paternalistic** adj. **paternalistically** adv.

**paternity** ● n. **1** (especially in legal contexts) the state of being someone's father. **2** paternal origin.

**paternity suit** ● n. chiefly N. Amer. a court case held to establish the identity of a child's father.

**paternity test** ● n. a medical test to determine whether a man could be the father of a particular child.

**paternoster** /ˌpatəˈnɒstə/ ● n. **1** (in the Roman Catholic Church) the Lord's Prayer, especially in Latin. ➤a special rosary bead indicating that the Lord's Prayer is to be recited. **2** a lift consisting of a series of linked doorless compartments moving continuously on an endless belt. **3** a fishing line to which hooks or weights are attached at intervals.
– ORIGIN OE, from L. *pater noster* 'our father', the first words of the Lord's Prayer.

**path** ● n. (pl. **paths**) **1** a way or track laid down for walking or made by continual treading. **2** the direction in which a person or thing moves. **3** a course of action or conduct.
– DERIVATIVES **pathless** adj.
– ORIGIN OE *pæth*, of W. Gmc origin.

**-path** ● comb. form **1** denoting a practitioner of curative treatment: *homeopath.* **2** denoting a person who suffers from a disease: *psychopath.*
– ORIGIN back-form. from **-PATHY**, or from Gk *-pathēs* '-sufferer'.

**Pathan** /pəˈtɑːn/ ● n. a member of a Pashto-speaking people inhabiting NW Pakistan and SE Afghanistan.
– ORIGIN from Hindi *Paṭhān.*

**path-breaking** ● adj. pioneering; innovative.
– DERIVATIVES **path-breaker** n.

**pathetic** ● adj. **1** arousing pity, especially through vulnerability or sadness. **2** informal miserably inadequate. **3** archaic relating to the emotions.
– DERIVATIVES **pathetically** adv.
– ORIGIN C16: via late L. from Gk *pathētikos* 'sensitive', based on *pathos* 'suffering'.

## Word *Formation*

**-pathy** from Greek *patheia* 'suffering, feeling'

➤ Some **-pathy** words relate directly to the general sense 'feeling':

| | | |
|---|---|---|
| antipathy | feeling of aversion | Gk *antipathēs* 'opposed in feeling' |
| apathy | lack of interest or concern | Gk *apathēs* 'without feeling' |
| empathy | understanding and sharing the feelings of others | Gk *empatheia* (from *em-* 'in') |
| sympathy | feeling of concern and pity for another's misfortune | Gk *sumpatheia* (from *sun-* 'with') |
| telepathy | communication of thoughts by means other than the known senses | Gk *tēle-* 'far off' |

➤ Other **-pathy** words relate to medical disorders and treatments:

| | | |
|---|---|---|
| allopathy | treatment of disease by using drugs with effects opposite to the symptoms (cf. ***homeopathy***) | Gk *allos* 'other' |
| encepalopathy | a disease affecting the brain | Gk *enkephalos* 'brain' |
| homeopathy | a system of complementary medicine using minute doses of a substance which would normally produce symptoms of a disease | Gk *homoios* 'same' |
| idiopathy | a disease arising spontaneously without known cause | Gk *idios* 'own' |
| myopathy | a disease of muscle tissue | Gk *mus* 'muscle' |
| osteopathy | a system of complementary medicine using manipulation of the skeleton and musculature | Gk *osteon* 'bone' |
| psychopathy | mental illness or disorder | PSYCHO- |
| sociopathy | personality disorder involving extreme antisocial behaviour | SOCIO- |

➤ Related words:

-path forming nouns, e.g. ***osteopath*** 'a practitioner in osteopathy'

Certain **-path** nouns are more established than their **-pathy** counterparts, in particular ***sociopath*** and ***psychopath***. The latter typically has a more restricted use than ***psychopathy***, implying 'a person having extreme abnormal and violent social behaviour'.

-pathic forming adjectives, e.g. ***telepathic*** 'of or relating to telepathy'

**pathetic fallacy** ● **n.** the attribution of human feelings and responses to inanimate things or animals.

**pathfinder** ● **n.** a person who goes ahead and discovers or shows others a path or way.

**pathname** ● **n.** Computing a description of where an item is to be found in a hierarchy of directories.

**patho-** ● **comb. form** relating to disease: *pathology.*
– ORIGIN from Gk *pathos* 'suffering, disease'.

**pathogen** /ˈpaθədʒ(ə)n/ ● **n.** Medicine a bacterium, virus, or other micro-organism that can cause disease.
– DERIVATIVES **pathogenic** adj. **pathogenicity** n. **pathogenous** /-ˈθɒdʒɪnəs/ adj.

**pathogenesis** /ˌpaθə(ʊ)ˈdʒɛnɪsɪs/ ● **n.** Medicine the manner of development of a disease.
– DERIVATIVES **pathogenetic** adj.

**pathognomonic** /ˌpaθəgnə(ʊ)ˈmɒnɪk/ ● **adj.** Medicine indicative of a particular disease or condition.
– ORIGIN C17: from Gk *pathognōmonikos* 'skilled in diagnosis', from *pathos* 'suffering' + *gnōmōn* 'judge'.

**pathography** /pəˈθɒgrəfi/ ● **n.** (pl. **-ies**) a history or biography written with regard to the influence of a particular disease or disorder.

**pathological** (US **pathologic**) ● **adj. 1** involving, caused by, or of the nature of a disease. **2** informal compulsive: *a pathological gambler.* **3** of or relating to pathology.
– DERIVATIVES **pathologically** adv.

**pathology** ● **n. 1** the branch of medicine concerned with the causes and effects of diseases. **2** Medicine the typical behaviour of a specified disease.
– DERIVATIVES **pathologist** n.
– ORIGIN C17: from mod. or med. L. *pathologia* (see **PATHO-**, **-LOGY**).

**pathophysiology** ● **n.** Medicine the disordered physiological processes associated with disease or injury.
– DERIVATIVES **pathophysiologic** adj. **pathophysiological** adj. **pathophysiologically** adv. **pathophysiologist** n.

**pathos** /ˈpeɪθɒs/ ● **n.** a quality that evokes pity or sadness.
– ORIGIN C17: from Gk *pathos* 'suffering'.

**pathway** ● **n. 1** a path or its course. **2** a sequence of changes or events constituting a progression.

**-pathy** ● **comb. form 1** denoting feelings: *telepathy.* **2** denoting disorder in a particular part of the body: *neuropathy.* **3** denoting curative treatment of a specified kind: *hydropathy.* See word-formation panel.
– ORIGIN from Gk *patheia* 'suffering, feeling'.

**patience** ● **n. 1** the capacity to tolerate delay, trouble, or suffering without becoming angry or upset. **2** chiefly Brit. a card game for one player, the object of which is to use up all one's cards by forming particular arrangements and sequences.
– PHRASES **lose patience** (or **lose one's patience**) become unable to keep one's temper.
– ORIGIN ME: from OFr., from L. *patientia*, from *patient-*, *pati* 'suffer'.

**patient** ● **adj.** having or showing patience. ● **n.** a person receiving or registered to receive medical treatment.
– DERIVATIVES **patiently** adv.
– ORIGIN ME: from OFr., from L. *patient-*, *pati* 'suffer'.

**patina** /ˈpatɪnə/ ● **n. 1** a green or brown film on the surface of old bronze. **2** a sheen on wooden furniture produced by age and polishing. **3** any distinctive surface appearance acquired over time.
– DERIVATIVES **patinated** adj. **patination** n.
– ORIGIN C18: from Ital., from L. *patina* 'shallow dish'.

**patio** ● **n.** (pl. **-os**) **1** a paved outdoor area adjoining a house. **2** a roofless inner courtyard in a Spanish or Spanish-American house.

– ORIGIN C19: from Sp.

**patio door** ● **n.** a large glass sliding door leading to a patio, garden, or balcony.

**patio rose** ● **n.** a miniature floribunda rose.

**patisserie** /pəˈtiːs(ə)ri, -ˈtɪs-/ ● **n.** **1** a shop where pastries and cakes are sold. **2** pastries and cakes collectively.

– ORIGIN C16: from Fr. *pâtisserie*, from med. L. *pasticium* 'pastry'.

**Pat Malone** ● **n.** (in phr. **on one's Pat Malone**) Austral./NZ informal on one's own.

– ORIGIN C20: rhyming sl.

**Patna rice** ● **n.** rice of a variety with long firm grains, originally produced at Patna in India.

**patois** /ˈpatwɑː/ ● **n.** (pl. same /-wɑːz/) the dialect of the common people of a region, differing in various respects from the standard language of the country.

– ORIGIN C17: Fr., lit. 'rough speech', perh. from OFr. *patoier* 'treat roughly', from *patte* 'paw'.

**patootie** /pəˈtuːti/ ● **n.** (pl. **-ies**) N. Amer. informal **1** dated a girlfriend or an attractive girl. **2** a person's or animal's buttocks.

– ORIGIN 1920s: perh. an alt. of **POTATO**.

**patresfamilias** plural form of **PATERFAMILIAS**.

**patrial** /ˈpeɪtrɪəl/ ● **n.** Brit. historical a person with the right to live in the UK through the British birth of a parent or grandparent.

– DERIVATIVES **patriality** /-ˈalɪti/ n.

– ORIGIN C17: from Fr., or from med. L. *patrialis*, from L. *patria* 'fatherland', from *pater* 'father'.

**patriarch** /ˈpeɪtrɪɑːk/ ● **n.** **1** the male head of a family or tribe. ➤ an older man who is powerful within a family or organization. ➤ a founder. **2** a biblical figure regarded as a father of the human race, especially Abraham, Isaac, and Jacob, and their forefathers, or the sons of Jacob. **3** a bishop of one of the most ancient Christian sees (Alexandria, Antioch, Constantinople, Jerusalem, and formerly Rome). ➤ the head of an autocephalous Orthodox Church. ➤ a Roman Catholic bishop ranking above primates and metropolitans and immediately below the Pope.

– DERIVATIVES **patriarchal** adj. **patriarchally** adv. **patriarchate** n.

– ORIGIN ME: from OFr. *patriarche*, via eccles. L. from Gk *patriarkhēs*, from *patria* 'family' + *arkhēs* 'ruling'.

**patriarchy** ● **n.** (pl. **-ies**) **1** a form of social organization in which the father or eldest male is the head of the family and descent is reckoned through the male line. **2** a system of society or government ruled by men.

**patriate** /ˈpatrɪeɪt, ˈpeɪtrɪeɪt/ ● **v.** transfer control over (a constitution) from a mother country to its former dependency.

**patrician** /pəˈtrɪʃ(ə)n/ ● **n.** **1** an aristocrat or nobleman. **2** a member of the noble class in ancient Rome. **3** N. Amer. a member of a long-established wealthy family. ● **adj.** belonging to or characteristic of patricians.

– ORIGIN ME: from OFr. *patricien*, from L. *patricius* 'having a noble father', from *pater, patr-* 'father'.

**patriciate** ● **n.** **1** a noble order or class. **2** the position or rank of patrician in ancient Rome.

**patricide** /ˈpatrɪsʌɪd/ ● **n.** the killing of one's father. ➤ a person who kills their father.

– DERIVATIVES **patricidal** adj.

– ORIGIN C17: from late L. *patricidium*, alt. of L. *parricidium* (see **PARRICIDE**).

**patrilineal** ● **adj.** of, relating to, or based on relationship to the father or descent through the male line.

– ORIGIN C20: from L. *pater, patr-* 'father' + **LINEAL**.

**patrilocal** ● **adj.** of or denoting a custom in marriage whereby the wife goes to live with the husband's community.

– DERIVATIVES **patrilocality** n.

**patrimony** /ˈpatrɪməni/ ● **n.** (pl. **-ies**) **1** property inherited from one's father or male ancestor. **2** heritage. **3** chiefly historical property belonging by ancient endowment or right to a church or other institution.

– DERIVATIVES **patrimonial** /-ˈməʊnɪəl/ adj.

– ORIGIN ME: from OFr. *patrimoine*, from L. *patrimonium*, from *pater, patr-* 'father'.

**patriot** /ˈpatrɪət, ˈpeɪt-/ ● **n.** a person who vigorously supports their country and is prepared to defend it.

– DERIVATIVES **patriotic** adj. **patriotically** adv. **patriotism** n.

– ORIGIN C16: from Fr. *patriote*, from late L. *patriota* 'fellow countryman', from Gk *patriōtēs*, from *patrios* 'of one's fathers', from *patris* 'fatherland'.

**patristic** /pəˈtrɪstɪk/ ● **adj.** of or relating to the early Christian theologians or their writings.

– DERIVATIVES **patristics** pl. n.

– ORIGIN C19: from Ger. *patristisch*, from L. *pater, patr-* 'father'.

**patrol** ● **n.** **1** a person or group sent to keep watch over an area, especially a detachment of guards or police. **2** the action of patrolling an area. **3** an expedition to carry out reconnaissance. **4** a routine operational voyage of a ship or aircraft. ● **v.** (**patrolled**, **patrolling**) keep watch over (an area) by regularly walking or travelling around it.

– DERIVATIVES **patroller** n.

– ORIGIN C17: from Ger. *Patrolle*, from Fr. *patrouille*, from *patrouiller* 'paddle in mud', from *patte* 'paw' + dial. *(gad)rouille* 'dirty water'.

**patrolman** ● **n.** (pl. **-men**) N. Amer. a patrolling police officer.

**patrology** /pəˈtrɒlədʒi/ ● **n.** patristic theology.

– DERIVATIVES **patrologist** n.

– ORIGIN C17: from Gk *patēr, patr-* 'father' + **-LOGY**.

**patron** ● **n.** **1** a person who gives financial or other support to a person, organization, cause, etc. **2** a distinguished person who takes an honorary position in a charity. **3** a customer of a restaurant, hotel, etc., especially a regular one. **4** (in ancient Rome) a patrician in relation to a client. **5** (in ancient Rome) the former owner of a freed slave. **6** Brit., chiefly historical a person or institution with the right to grant a benefice to a member of the clergy.

– DERIVATIVES **patroness** n.

– ORIGIN ME: from OFr., from L. *patronus* 'protector of clients, defender', from *pater, patr-* 'father'.

**patronage** /ˈpatr(ə)nɪdʒ, ˈpeɪt-/ ● **n.** **1** the support given by a patron. **2** the power to control appointments to office or the right to privileges. **3** a patronizing manner. **4** the regular custom attracted by a restaurant, hotel, etc. **5** (in ancient Rome) the position of a patron.

**patronal** /pəˈtrəʊn(ə)l/ ● **adj.** of or relating to a patron saint.

**patronize** (also **-ise**) ● **v.** **1** [often as adj. **patronizing**] treat with an apparent kindness which betrays a feeling of superiority. **2** frequent (an establishment) as a customer. **3** act as a patron towards (a person, organization, etc.).

– DERIVATIVES **patronization** n. **patronizer** n. **patronizingly** adv.

**patron saint** ● **n.** the protecting or guiding saint of a person or place.

**patronymic** /ˌpatrəˈnɪmɪk/ ● **n.** a name derived from the name of a father or ancestor, e.g. *Johnson*, *O'Brien*, *Ivanovich*.

– ORIGIN C17: via late L. from Gk *patrōnumikos*, from *patrōnumos*, from *patēr, patr-* 'father' + *onoma* 'name'.

**patsy** ● **n.** (pl. **-ies**) informal, chiefly N. Amer. a person who is taken advantage of, especially by being cheated or blamed for something.

– ORIGIN C20: of unknown origin.

**pattée** /ˈpateɪ, -ti/ ● **adj.** [postpos.] (of a cross) having almost triangular arms, very narrow at the centre and broadening to squared ends.

– ORIGIN C15: from Fr., from *patte* 'paw'.

**patten** /ˈpat(ə)n/ ● **n.** historical a shoe or clog with a raised sole or set on an iron ring, worn to raise the feet above wet ground.

– ORIGIN ME: from OFr. *patin*, perh. from *patte* 'paw'.

**patter**[1] ● **v.** **1** make a repeated light tapping sound. **2** run with quick light steps. ● **n.** a repeated light tapping.

– ORIGIN C17: frequentative of **PAT**[1].

**patter**[2] ● **n.** rapid continuous talk, such as that used by a comedian or salesman. ➤ rapid speech included in a comic song. ➤ the jargon of a profession or other group. ● **v.** talk trivially at length.

– ORIGIN ME (as v. in the sense 'recite rapidly'): from **PATERNOSTER**.

**pattern** ● n. **1** a repeated decorative design. ➤an arrangement or sequence regularly found in comparable objects or events. **2** a model or design used as a guide in needlework and other crafts. ➤a set of instructions to be followed in making a sewn or knitted item. ➤a model from which a mould is made for a casting. **3** an example for others to follow. **4** a sample of cloth or wallpaper. ● v. **1** decorate with a pattern. **2** give a regular or intelligible form to. ➤(**pattern something on/after**) give something a form based on that of (something else).
– DERIVATIVES **patternless** adj.
– ORIGIN ME *patron* 'something serving as a model', from OFr. (see **PATRON**).

**patterned ground** ● n. Geology stony ground showing a pattern of polygons, rings, or stripes caused by repeated freezing and thawing.

**patty** ● n. (pl. **-ies**) **1** a small flat cake of minced food, especially meat. **2** a small pie or pasty. **3** N. Amer. a small round, flat chocolate-covered peppermint sweet.
– ORIGIN C17: alt. of Fr. *pâté*, by assoc. with **PASTY**[1].

**patulous** /'patjʊləs/ ● adj. rare spreading wide, like the branches of a tree.
– ORIGIN C17: from L. *patulus* (from *patere* 'be or lie open') + **-OUS**.

**patzer** /'pɑːtsə, 'pat-/ ● n. informal a poor player at chess.
– ORIGIN 1940s: perh. rel. to Ger. *patzen* 'to bungle'.

**paua** /'pɑːwə, 'paʊə/ ● n. **1** a large New Zealand abalone or its shell. **2** a Maori fish hook made from an abalone shell.
– ORIGIN C19: from Maori.

**paucity** /'pɔːsɪti/ ● n. the presence of something in only small or insufficient amounts.
– ORIGIN ME: from OFr. *paucite* or L. *paucitas*, from *paucus* 'few'.

**Pauli exclusion principle** ● n. Physics the assertion that no two fermions can have the same quantum number.
– ORIGIN 1920s: named after the Amer. physicist Wolfgang *Pauli*.

**Pauline** /'pɔːlʌɪn/ ● adj. Christian Theology relating to or characteristic of St Paul.

**Paul Jones** ● n. a ballroom dance in which the dancers change partners after circling in concentric rings.
– ORIGIN 1920s: named after the Amer. admiral John *Paul Jones* (1747–92).

**paulownia** /pɔː'ləʊnɪə, -'lɒvnɪə/ ● n. a small SE Asian tree with heart-shaped leaves and fragrant lilac flowers. [Genus *Paulownia*.]
– ORIGIN mod. L., named after the Russ. princess Anna *Pavlovna* (1795–1865).

**paunch** ● n. **1** a large or protruding abdomen or stomach. **2** Nautical, archaic a thick strong mat used to give protection from chafing on a mast or spar. ● v. disembowel (an animal).
– DERIVATIVES **paunchiness** n. **paunchy** adj.
– ORIGIN ME: from Anglo-Norman Fr. *pa(u)nche*, based on L. *pantex*, *pantic-* 'intestines'.

**pauper** ● n. **1** a very poor person. **2** historical a recipient of poor-law relief.
– DERIVATIVES **pauperdom** n. **pauperism** n. **pauperization** (also **-isation**) n. **pauperize** (also **-ise**) v.
– ORIGIN C15: from L., lit. 'poor'.

**paupiette** /pɔː'pjɛt/ ● n. a long, thin slice of fish or meat, rolled and stuffed with a filling.
– ORIGIN Fr., prob. from Ital. *polpetta*, from L. *pulpa* 'pulp'.

**pause** ● n. **1** a temporary stop in action or speech. **2** Music a mark (𝄐) over a note or rest that is to be lengthened by an unspecified amount. **3** a control allowing the temporary interruption of recording, playback, or other process. ● v. **1** have a pause; stop temporarily. **2** temporarily interrupt (a process or device).
– PHRASES **give pause to someone** (or **give pause for thought**) cause someone to think carefully or hesitate before doing something.
– ORIGIN ME: from OFr., from L. *pausa*, from Gk *pausis*, from *pausein* 'to stop'.

**pavage** /'peɪvɪdʒ/ ● n. historical a tax or toll to cover the paving of streets.
– ORIGIN ME: from OFr., from *paver* 'to pave'.

**pavane** /pə'van, -'vɑːn/ (also **pavan** /'pav(ə)n/) ● n. a stately dance in slow duple time, popular in the 16th and 17th centuries and performed in elaborate clothing. ➤a piece of music for this dance.
– ORIGIN C16: from Fr., from Ital. *pavana*, fem. adj. from *Pavo*, dial. name of the city of *Padua*.

**pave** ● v. (often **be paved with**) cover (a piece of ground) with flat stones or bricks.
– PHRASES **pave the way for** create the circumstances to enable (something) to happen or be done.
– DERIVATIVES **paver** n. **paving** n.
– ORIGIN ME: from OFr. *paver* 'pave'.

**pavé** /'paveɪ/ ● n. **1** a setting of precious stones placed so closely together that no metal shows. **2** a paved street, road, or path.
– ORIGIN Fr., lit. 'paved', past part. of *paver*.

**pavement** ● n. **1** Brit. a raised paved or asphalted path for pedestrians at the side of a road. **2** N. Amer. the hard surface of a road or street. **3** Geology a horizontal expanse of bare rock with cracks or joints: *a limestone pavement*.
– ORIGIN ME: from OFr., from L. *pavimentum* 'trodden down floor', from *pavire* 'beat, tread down'.

**pavement artist** ● n. Brit. an artist who draws with coloured chalks on paving stones to earn money from passers-by.

**pavilion** ● n. **1** Brit. a building at a cricket ground or other sports ground used for changing and taking refreshments. **2** a summer house or other decorative shelter in a park or large garden. **3** a detached or semi-detached block at a hospital or other building complex. **4** a marquee with a peak and crenellated decorations, used at a show or fair. **5** a temporary stand or other structure in which items are displayed at a trade exhibition.
– ORIGIN ME: from OFr. *pavillon*, from L. *papilio(n-)* 'butterfly or tent'.

**paviour** /'peɪvɪə/ (also **pavior**) ● n. **1** a paving stone. **2** archaic a person who lays paving stones.
– ORIGIN ME: from OFr. *paveur*, from *paver* 'pave'.

**pavlova** ● n. a dessert consisting of a meringue base or shell filled with whipped cream and fruit.
– ORIGIN 1920s: named after the Russ. ballerina Anna *Pavlova*.

**Pavlovian** /pav'ləʊvɪən/ ● adj. relating to or denoting classical conditioning as described by the Russian physiologist Ivan P. Pavlov (1849–1936).

**pavonine** /'pavənʌɪn/ ● adj. poetic/literary of or like a peacock.
– ORIGIN C17: from L. *pavoninus*, from *pavo*, *pavon-* 'peacock'.

**paw** ● n. **1** an animal's foot having claws and pads. **2** informal a person's hand. ● v. **1** feel or scrape with a paw or hoof. **2** informal touch or handle clumsily or lasciviously.
– ORIGIN ME: from OFr. *poue*, prob. of Gmc origin.

**pawky** ● adj. (**-ier**, **-iest**) chiefly Scottish & N. English drily humorous; sardonic.
– DERIVATIVES **pawkily** adv. **pawkiness** n.
– ORIGIN C17: from Scots and north. Engl. *pawk* 'trick'.

**pawl** /pɔːl/ ● n. **1** a pivoted curved bar or lever whose free end engages with the teeth of a cogwheel or ratchet so that the wheel or ratchet can only turn or move one way. **2** each of a set of short stout bars that by engaging with the whelps prevent a capstan, windlass, or winch from recoiling.
– ORIGIN C17: perh. from Low Ger. and Du. *pal* (rel. to *pal* 'fixed').

**pawn**[1] ● n. **1** a chess piece of the smallest size and value. **2** a person used by others for their own purposes.
– ORIGIN ME: from Anglo-Norman Fr. *poun*, from med. L. *pedo*, *pedon-* 'foot soldier', from L. *pes*, *ped-* 'foot'.

**pawn**[2] ● v. deposit (an object) with a pawnbroker as security for money lent. ● n. (usu. **in pawn**) the state of being pawned.
– ORIGIN C15: from OFr. *pan* 'pledge, security'.

**pawnbroker** ● n. a person who lends money at interest

on the security of an article pawned.
– DERIVATIVES **pawnbroking** n.

**Pawnee** /pɔːˈniː/ ● n. (pl. same or **Pawnees**) **1** a member of an American Indian confederacy formerly living in Nebraska, and now mainly in Oklahoma. **2** the language of these people, belonging to the Caddoan family.
– ORIGIN from Canad. Fr. *Pani*, from a N. Amer. Ind. lang.

**pawnshop** ● n. a pawnbroker's shop.

**pawpaw** /ˈpɔːpɔː/ (also **papaw**) ● n. **1** another term for **PAPAYA**. **2** US a North American tree with purple flowers and edible oblong yellow fruit with sweet pulp. [*Asimina triloba*.] ➤ the fruit of this tree.
– ORIGIN C17: from Sp. and Port. *papaya*, of Carib origin.

**pax** ● n. (in the Christian Church) the kiss of peace. ● exclam. Brit. informal, dated a call for a truce, used especially by schoolchildren when playing.
– ORIGIN L., lit. 'peace'.

**pay**[1] ● v. (past and past part. **paid**) **1** give (someone) money due for work, goods, or a debt incurred. ➤ give (a sum of money) thus owed. ➤ (**pay someone off**) dismiss someone with a final payment. **2** be profitable or advantageous. ➤ (**pay off**) informal yield good results. **3** suffer a loss or misfortune as a consequence of an action. ➤ give what is due or deserved to. ➤ (**pay someone back**) take revenge on someone. **4** give (attention, respect, or a compliment) to. ➤ make (a visit or a call) to. **5** (**pay something out**) let out a rope by slackening it. ● n. money paid for work.
– PHRASES **in the pay of** employed by. **pay dearly** suffer for a misdemeanour or failure. **pay its** (or **one's**) **way** earn enough to cover its or one's costs. **pay one's last respects** show respect towards a dead person by attending their funeral. **pay one's respects** make a polite visit to someone. **pay through the nose** informal pay much more than a fair price.
– DERIVATIVES **payee** n. **payer** n.
– ORIGIN ME (in the sense 'pacify'): from OFr. *paie* (n.), *payer* (v.), from L. *pacare* 'appease', from *pax*, *pac-* 'peace'.

**pay**[2] ● v. (past and past part. **payed**) Nautical seal (the deck or seams of a wooden ship) with pitch or tar to prevent leakage.
– ORIGIN C17: from ONorth. Fr. *peier*, from L. *picare*, from *pix*, *pic-* 'pitch'.

**payable** ● adj. **1** required to be paid. **2** able to be paid. ● n. (**payables**) debts owed by a business.

**payback** ● n. **1** profit from an investment equal to the initial outlay. **2** informal an act of revenge.

**pay bed** ● n. (in the UK) a hospital bed for private patients in a National Health Service hospital.

**pay channel** ● n. a television channel for which viewers pay a subscription fee additional to that already paid for the basic provision of a cable or satellite service.

**pay dirt** ● n. N. Amer. ground containing ore in sufficient quantity to be profitably extracted.
– PHRASES **hit** (or **strike**) **pay dirt** informal find or reach a source of profit.

**PAYE** ● abbrev. (in the UK) pay as you earn, the deduction of income tax from an employee's wages by an employer to be paid directly to the government.

**payess** /ˈpeɪɛs/ ● pl. n. chiefly N. Amer. uncut locks of hair at the side of the head worn by male Orthodox Jews.
– ORIGIN C20: Yiddish, from Heb. *pē'ōṯ* 'corners' (see Lev. 19:27).

**paying guest** ● n. a lodger.

**payload** ● n. **1** the part of a vehicle's load from which revenue is derived; passengers and cargo. **2** an explosive warhead carried by an aircraft or missile. **3** equipment, personnel, or satellites carried by a spacecraft.

**paymaster** ● n. **1** a person who pays another to do something and therefore controls them. **2** an official who pays troops or workers. **3** (in full **Paymaster General**) Brit. the minister at the head of the Treasury department responsible for payments.

**payment** ● n. **1** the action of paying or the process of being paid. **2** an amount paid or payable.

**paynim** /ˈpeɪnɪm/ ● n. archaic a non-Christian, especially a Muslim.
– ORIGIN ME: from OFr. *paienime*, from eccles. L. *paganismus* 'heathenism', from *paganus* (see **PAGAN**).

**pay-off** ● n. informal **1** a payment, especially one made as a bribe or on leaving a job. **2** the return on investment or on a bet. **3** informal a final outcome.

**payola** /peɪˈəʊlə/ ● n. chiefly N. Amer. bribery in return for the unofficial promotion of a product in the media.
– ORIGIN 1930s: from **PAY**[1] + *-ola* as in *Victrola*, the name of a make of gramophone.

**payout** ● n. a large payment of money, especially as compensation or a dividend.

**payphone** ● n. a public telephone that is operated by coins or by a credit or prepaid card.

**payroll** ● n. a list of a company's employees and the amount of money they are to be paid.

**paysage** /peɪˈzɑːʒ/ ● n. a landscape, especially as represented in art.
– DERIVATIVES **paysagist** /ˈpeɪzədʒɪst/ n.
– ORIGIN Fr., lit. 'countryside'.

**payslip** ● n. a note given to an employee, detailing the amount of pay given and any deductions.

**pay TV** ● n. television broadcasting in which viewers pay by subscription to watch a particular channel.

**Pb** ● symb. the chemical element lead.
– ORIGIN from L. *plumbum*.

**pb** ● abbrev. paperback.

**PBS** ● abbrev. (in the US) Public Broadcasting System (or Service).

**PBX** ● abbrev. private branch exchange, a private telephone switchboard.

**PC** ● abbrev. **1** personal computer. **2** police constable. **3** (also **pc**) politically correct; political correctness. **4** Privy Counsellor.

**p.c.** ● abbrev. **1** per cent. **2** postcard.

**PCB** ● abbrev. **1** Electronics printed circuit board. **2** Chemistry polychlorinated biphenyl.

**P-Celtic** ● n. & adj. another term for **BRYTHONIC**.
– ORIGIN *P*, from the development of the Indo-Eur. *kw* sound into *p* in this group of langs.

**PCI** ● abbrev. Peripheral Component Interconnect, a standard for connecting computers and their peripherals.

**PCM** ● abbrev. pulse code modulation.

**PCMCIA** ● abbrev. Personal Computer Memory Card International Association, denoting a standard specification for memory cards and interfaces in personal computers.

**PCP** ● abbrev. **1** pentachlorophenol. **2** phencyclidine. **3** pneumocystis carinii pneumonia.

**PCS** ● abbrev. personal communications services, a digital mobile telephony system.

**pct.** ● abbrev. N. Amer. per cent.

**PCV** ● abbrev. Brit. passenger-carrying vehicle.

**PD** ● abbrev. **1** US Police Department. **2** public domain.

**Pd** ● symb. the chemical element palladium.

**pd** ● abbrev. paid.

**PDA** ● abbrev. personal digital assistant, a basic palmtop computer.

**PDP** ● abbrev. parallel distributed processing.

**PDQ** ● abbrev. informal pretty damn quick.

**PDSA** ● abbrev. (in the UK) People's Dispensary for Sick Animals.

**PDT** ● abbrev. Pacific Daylight Time.

**PE** ● abbrev. **1** Peru (international vehicle registration). **2** physical education. **3** Prince Edward Island (in official postal use).

**pea** ● n. **1** a spherical green seed eaten as a vegetable. **2** the hardy climbing leguminous plant which yields pods containing peas. [*Pisum sativum*.] **3** used in names of similar or related plants or seeds. e.g. **chick pea**.
– ORIGIN C17: back-form. from **PEASE** (interpreted as pl.).

**pea-brain** ● n. informal a stupid person.
– DERIVATIVES **pea-brained** adj.

**peace** ● n. **1** freedom from disturbance; tranquillity. **2** freedom from or the cessation of war. **3** (**the peace**) Christian Church an action such as a handshake taking the place of the kiss of peace.

– PHRASES **at peace 1** free from anxiety or distress. **2** euphemistic dead. **hold one's peace** remain silent. **keep the peace** refrain or prevent others from disturbing civil order. **make (one's) peace** become reconciled.
– ORIGIN ME: from OFr. *pais*, from L. *pax, pac-* 'peace'.

**peaceable** • **adj. 1** inclined to avoid war. **2** free from conflict; peaceful.
– DERIVATIVES **peaceableness** n. **peaceably** adv.
– ORIGIN ME: from OFr. *peisible*, alt. of *plaisible*, from late L. *placibilis* 'pleasing', from L. *placere* 'to please'.

**peace dividend** • **n.** a sum of public money available for other purposes when spending on defence is reduced.

**peaceful** • **adj. 1** free from disturbance; calm. **2** not involving war or violence. **3** inclined to avoid conflict.
– DERIVATIVES **peacefully** adv. **peacefulness** n.

**peacekeeping** • **n.** the active maintenance of a truce, especially by an international military force.
– DERIVATIVES **peacekeeper** n.

**peacenik** • **n.** informal, often derogatory a member of a pacifist movement.
– ORIGIN 1960s.

**peace offering** • **n. 1** a conciliatory gift. **2** (in biblical use) an offering presented as a thanksgiving to God.

**peace officer** • **n.** N. Amer. a civil officer appointed to preserve law and order, such as a sheriff.

**peace pipe** • **n.** a tobacco pipe offered and smoked as a token of peace among North American Indians.

**peace sign** • **n.** a sign of peace made by holding up the hand with palm out-turned and the first two fingers extended in a V-shape.

**peacetime** • **n.** a period when a country is not at war.

**peach**[1] • **n. 1** a round stone fruit with juicy yellow flesh and downy yellow skin flushed with red. **2** the Chinese tree which bears this fruit. [*Prunus persica*.] **3** a pinkish-orange colour like that of a peach. **4** informal an exceptionally good or attractive person or thing.
– PHRASES **peaches and cream** (of a person's complexion) of a cream colour with downy pink cheeks.
– DERIVATIVES **peachiness** n. **peachy** adj. **(-ier, -iest)**.
– ORIGIN ME: from OFr. *pesche*, from med. L. *persica*, from L. *persicum (malum)*, lit. 'Persian apple'.

**peach**[2] • **v. (peach on)** informal inform on.
– ORIGIN ME: shortening of archaic *appeach*, from OFr. *empechier* (see **IMPEACH**).

**peach bloom** • **n.** a matt glaze of reddish pink mottled with green and brown, used on Chinese porcelain.

**peach blow** • **n. 1** another term for **PEACH BLOOM**. **2** a type of late 19th-century American purplish-pink glass.

**peach fuzz** • **n.** N. Amer. informal the down on the chin of an adolescent boy whose beard has not yet developed.

**peachick** • **n.** a young peafowl.

**peach Melba** • **n.** a dish of ice cream and peaches with Melba sauce.
– ORIGIN from the name of the Austral. operatic soprano Dame Nellie *Melba* (1861–1931).

**peachy-keen** • **adj.** N. Amer. informal pleasing; excellent.

**pea coat** • **n.** another term for **PEA JACKET**.

**peacock** • **n.** a male peafowl, having very long tail feathers with eye-like markings that can be erected and fanned out in display.
– ORIGIN ME: from OE *pēa* (from L. *pavo*) 'peacock' + **COCK**[1].

**peacock blue** • **n.** a greenish-blue colour like that of a peacock's neck.

**peacock butterfly** • **n.** a brightly coloured butterfly with conspicuous eyespots on its wings. [*Inachis io*.]

**peacock ore** • **n.** another term for **BORNITE**.

**peafowl** • **n.** a large crested pheasant of which the male is the peacock and the female the peahen. [*Pavo cristatus* (southern Asia) and other species.]

**pea green** • **n.** a bright green colour.

**peahen** • **n.** a female peafowl, which has drabber colours and a shorter tail than the male.

**pea jacket** • **n.** a short double-breasted overcoat of coarse woollen cloth, formerly worn by sailors.
– ORIGIN C18: prob. from Du. *pijjakker*, from *pij* 'coat of coarse cloth' + *jekker* 'jacket'.

**peak**[1] • **n. 1** the pointed top of a mountain. ➤a mountain with a peak. **2** a stiff brim at the front of a cap. **3** a point in a curve or on a graph, or a value of a physical quantity, which is higher than those around it. ➤the point of highest activity or achievement. **4** the upper, outer corner of a sail extended by a gaff. • **v.** reach a highest point. • **adj.** maximum. ➤characterized by maximum activity or demand: *peak hours*.
– ORIGIN C16: prob. a back-form. from *peaked*, var. of dial. *picked* 'pointed'.

**peak**[2] • **v.** archaic decline in health and spirits.
– ORIGIN C17: of unknown origin.

**peaked**[1] • **adj.** (of a cap) having a peak.

**peaked**[2] • **adj.** gaunt and pale from illness or fatigue.

**peak flow meter** • **n.** Medicine an instrument used to measure lung capacity in monitoring breathing disorders such as asthma.

**peak load** • **n.** the maximum of electrical power demand.

**peaky** • **adj. (-ier, -iest)** pale from illness or fatigue.

**peal** • **n. 1** a loud ringing of a bell or bells. ➤Bell-ringing a series of changes rung on a set of bells. ➤a set of bells. **2** a loud repeated or reverberating sound of thunder or laughter. • **v. 1** ring loudly or in a peal. **2** (of laughter or thunder) sound in a peal.
– ORIGIN ME: shortening of **APPEAL**.

**pean** /piːn/ • **n.** Heraldry fur resembling ermine but with gold spots on a black ground.
– ORIGIN C16: of unknown origin.

**peanut** • **n. 1** the oval seed of a South American plant, eaten as a snack or used for making oil or animal feed. **2** the leguminous plant that bears these seeds, which develop in underground pods. [*Arachis hypogaea*.] **3 (peanuts)** informal a paltry sum of money.

**peanut butter** • **n.** a spread made from ground roasted peanuts.

**peanut gallery** • **n.** N. Amer. informal the top gallery in a theatre where the cheaper seats are located.

**peanut worm** • **n.** a burrowing marine worm with a stout body and a slender retractable part bearing a mouth surrounded by tentacles. [Phylum Sipuncula.]

**pear** • **n. 1** a yellowish- or brownish-green edible fruit, narrow at the stalk and wider towards the tip. **2** the tree which bears this fruit. [*Pyrus communis* and related species.]
– ORIGIN OE *pere, peru*, of W. Gmc origin, from L. *pirum*.

**pear drop** • **n.** a boiled sweet in the shape of a pear, with a pungently sweet flavour.

**pearl**[1] • **n. 1** a hard, lustrous spherical mass, typically white or bluish-grey, formed within the shell of an oyster or other bivalve mollusc and highly prized as a gem. ➤an artificial imitation of this. **2** a thing of great worth: *pearls of wisdom*. **3** a very pale bluish grey or white colour. • **v. 1** poetic/literary form pearl-like drops. **2** [usu. as noun **pearling**] dive or fish for pearl oysters.
– PHRASES **cast pearls before swine** offer valuable things to people who do not appreciate them.
– DERIVATIVES **pearler** n.
– ORIGIN ME: from OFr. *perle*, perh. based on L. *perna* 'leg', extended to denote a leg-of-mutton-shaped bivalve.

**pearl**[2] • **n.** Brit. another term for **PICOT**.
– ORIGIN var. of **PURL**[1].

**pearl ash** • **n.** archaic commercial potassium carbonate.

**pearl barley** • **n.** barley reduced to small round grains by grinding.

**pearl button** • **n.** a button made of real or imitation mother-of-pearl.

**pearled** • **adj.** poetic/literary **1** adorned with pearls. **2** bluish-grey.

**pearlescent** • **adj.** having a lustre resembling that of mother-of-pearl.

**pearl everlasting** • **n.** variant of **PEARLY EVERLASTING**.

**pearlite** • **n.** Metallurgy a finely laminated mixture of ferrite and cementite present in cast iron and steel.
– ORIGIN C19: from **PEARL**[1] + **-ITE**[1].

**pearlized** (also **-ised**) ● **adj.** made to have a lustre like that of mother-of-pearl.

**pearl millet** ● **n.** a cereal with long cylindrical ears, cultivated in the driest areas of Africa and the Indian subcontinent. [*Pennisetum glaucum.*]

**pearl onion** ● **n.** a very small onion used for pickling.

**pearlware** ● **n.** fine glazed earthenware pottery, typically white.

**pearlwort** ● **n.** a small plant of the pink family, with inconspicuous white flowers. [Genus *Sagina.*]

**pearly** ● **adj.** (**-ier**, **-iest**) resembling a pearl in lustre or colour. ● **n.** (pl. **-ies**) (**pearlies**) Brit. **1** a pearly king's or queen's clothes or pearl buttons. **2** (also **pearly whites**) informal a person's teeth.
– DERIVATIVES **pearliness** n.

**pearly everlasting** (also **pearl everlasting**) ● **n.** an ornamental North American plant with grey-green foliage and pearly white flower heads. [*Anaphalis margaritacea.*]

**Pearly Gates** ● **pl. n.** informal the gates of heaven.

**pearly king** (or **pearly queen**) ● **n.** a London costermonger (or his wife) wearing traditional ceremonial clothes covered with pearl buttons.

**Pearmain** /ˈpɛːmeɪn, ˈpəː-, pəˈmeɪn/ ● **n.** a pear-shaped dessert apple of a variety with firm white flesh.
– ORIGIN ME (denoting an old variety of baking pear): from OFr. *parmain*, prob. based on L. *parmensis* 'of Parma'.

**pear-shaped** ● **adj.** having hips that are disproportionately wide in relation to the upper part of the body.
– PHRASES **go pear-shaped** Brit. informal go wrong. [orig. RAF sl.]

**peart** /pɪət, pjəːt/ ● **adj.** US dialect lively; cheerful.
– ORIGIN C15: var. of **PERT**.

**peasant** ● **n. 1** a poor smallholder or agricultural labourer of low social status. **2** informal an ignorant, rude, or unsophisticated person.
– DERIVATIVES **peasantry** n. **peasanty** adj.
– ORIGIN ME: from OFr. *paisent* 'country dweller', from *pais* 'country', based on L. *pagus* 'country district'.

**peasant economy** ● **n.** an agricultural economy in which the family is the basic unit of production.

**pease** /piːz/ ● **pl. n.** archaic peas.
– ORIGIN OE *pise* 'pea', (pl.) *pisan*, via L. from Gk *pison*.

**pease pudding** ● **n.** chiefly Brit. a dish of split peas boiled with onion and carrot and mashed to a pulp.

**pea-shooter** ● **n.** a toy weapon consisting of a small tube out of which dried peas are blown.

**pea-souper** ● **n.** Brit. informal a very thick yellowish fog.

**peat** ● **n.** partly decomposed vegetable matter forming a deposit on acidic, boggy ground, dried for use in gardening and as fuel.
– DERIVATIVES **peaty** adj.
– ORIGIN ME: from Anglo-Latin *peta*.

**peatland** ● **n.** (also **peatlands**) land consisting largely of peat or peat bogs.

**peat moss** ● **n. 1** a large absorbent moss which grows in dense masses on boggy ground. [Genus *Sphagnum.*] **2** a peat bog.

**peau-de-soie** /ˌpəʊdəˈswɑː/ ● **n.** a smooth, finely ribbed satin fabric of silk or rayon.
– ORIGIN C19: Fr., lit. 'skin of silk'.

**peau d'orange** /ˌpəʊ dɒˈrɒ̃ʒ/ ● **n.** a pitted or dimpled appearance of the skin, especially as characteristic of some cases of breast cancer or due to cellulite.
– ORIGIN Fr., lit. 'orange skin'.

**pebble** ● **n.** a small stone made smooth and round by the action of water or sand. ● **adj.** informal (of a spectacle lens) very thick and convex.
– DERIVATIVES **pebbled** adj. **pebbly** adj.
– ORIGIN OE, recorded as the first element of *papel-stān* 'pebble-stone', *pyppelrīpig* 'pebble-stream'.

**pebble-dash** ● **n.** chiefly Brit. mortar with pebbles in it, used as a coating for external walls.
– DERIVATIVES **pebble-dashed** adj.

**pec** ● **n.** informal a pectoral muscle.

**pecan** /ˈpiːk(ə)n, pɪˈkan, pɪˈkɑːn/ ● **n. 1** a smooth pinkish-brown nut resembling a walnut. **2** a hickory tree of the southern US, which produces these nuts. [*Carya illinoensis.*]
– ORIGIN C18: from Fr. *pacane*, from Illinois (an Amer. Ind. lang.).

**peccable** /ˈpɛkəb(ə)l/ ● **adj.** formal capable of sinning.
– DERIVATIVES **peccability** n.
– ORIGIN C17: from Fr., from med. L. *peccabilis*, from L. *peccare* 'to sin'.

**peccadillo** /ˌpɛkəˈdɪləʊ/ ● **n.** (pl. **-oes** or **-os**) a minor sin or fault.
– ORIGIN C16: from Sp. *pecadillo*, dimin. of *pecado* 'sin'.

**peccant** /ˈpɛk(ə)nt/ ● **adj.** archaic **1** having committed a fault or sin. **2** diseased or causing disease.
– DERIVATIVES **peccancy** n.
– ORIGIN C16: from L. *peccant-*, *peccare* 'to sin'.

**peccary** /ˈpɛk(ə)ri/ ● **n.** (pl. **-ies**) a gregarious piglike mammal found from the south-western US to Paraguay. [Family Tayassuidae: three species.]
– ORIGIN C17: from Carib *pakira*.

**peccavi** /pɛˈkɑːviː/ ● **exclam.** archaic used to express one's guilt.
– ORIGIN L., lit. 'I have sinned'.

**peck**[1] ● **v. 1** (of a bird) strike or bite with its beak. **2** kiss lightly or perfunctorily. **3** (**peck at**) informal eat (food) listlessly or daintily. **4** type slowly and laboriously. **5** archaic strike with a pick or other tool. ● **n. 1** an act of pecking. **2** a light or perfunctory kiss. **3** archaic informal food.
– ORIGIN ME: of unknown origin; cf. Mid. Low Ger. *pekken* 'peck'.

**peck**[2] ● **n. 1** a measure of capacity for dry goods, equal to a quarter of a bushel (2 imperial gallons = 9.092 l, or 8 US quarts = 8.81 l). **2** archaic a large number or amount of something.
– ORIGIN ME: from Anglo-Norman Fr. *pek*.

**peck**[3] ● **v.** (of a horse) stumble as a result of striking the ground with the front rather than the flat of the hoof.
– ORIGIN var. of obs. *pick* 'fix (something pointed) in the ground'.

**pecker** ● **n.** N. Amer. vulgar slang a man's penis.
– PHRASES **keep your pecker up** Brit. informal remain cheerful. [*pecker* prob. in the sense 'beak'.]

**peckerwood** ● **n.** US informal, often derogatory a white person, especially a poor one.
– ORIGIN 1920s: from a reversal of the elements of *woodpecker*, orig. a dial. word for the bird.

**pecking order** (also **peck order**) ● **n.** a hierarchy of status among members of a group, originally as observed among hens.

**peckish** ● **adj.** informal, chiefly Brit. hungry.

**Pecksniffian** /pɛkˈsnɪfɪən/ ● **adj.** hypocritical.
– ORIGIN C19: from Mr *Pecksniff*, the name of a character in Dickens's *Martin Chuzzlewit*, + **-IAN**.

**pecorino** /ˌpɛkəˈriːnəʊ/ ● **n.** (pl. **-os**) an Italian cheese made from ewes' milk.
– ORIGIN Ital., from *pecorino* 'of ewes'.

**pecten** /ˈpɛktɛn/ ● **n.** (pl. **pectens** or **pectines** /-tɪniːz/) Zoology **1** a comb-like structure or appendage. **2** a scallop. [Genus *Pecten.*]
– DERIVATIVES **pectinate** /-nət/ adj. **pectinated** adj. **pectination** n.
– ORIGIN ME (denoting the metacarpus): from L. *pecten*, *pectin-* 'a comb'.

**pectin** ● **n.** a soluble gelatinous polysaccharide present in ripe fruits, used as a setting agent in jams and jellies.
– DERIVATIVES **pectic** adj.
– ORIGIN C19: from Gk *pektos* 'congealed' + **-IN**[1].

**pectoral** /ˈpɛkt(ə)r(ə)l/ ● **adj.** of, on, or relating to the breast or chest. ● **n. 1** a pectoral muscle. **2** an ornamental breastplate.
– ORIGIN ME: from L. *pectorale* 'breastplate', *pectoralis* 'of the breast', from *pectus*, *pector-* 'breast, chest'.

**pectoral fin** ● **n.** Zoology each of a pair of fins situated on either side just behind a fish's head.

**pectoral muscle** ● **n.** each of four large paired muscles which cover the front of the ribcage.

**peculation** /pɛkjʊˈleɪʃ(ə)n/ ● **n.** formal the embezzlement of public funds.

– DERIVATIVES **peculate** v. **peculator** n.
– ORIGIN C17: from L. *peculat-*, *peculari* 'peculate'.

**peculiar** ● adj. **1** strange or odd. **2** (**peculiar to**) belonging exclusively to. **3** formal particular. ● n. chiefly Brit. a parish or church exempt from the jurisdiction of the diocese in which it lies, though subject to the jurisdiction of the monarch or an archbishop.
– DERIVATIVES **peculiarly** adv.
– ORIGIN ME: from L. *peculiaris* 'of private property', from *peculium* 'property', from *pecu* 'cattle'.

**peculiarity** ● n. (pl. **-ies**) **1** an unusual or distinctive feature or habit. **2** the state of being peculiar.

**pecuniary** /pɪˈkjuːnɪəri/ ● adj. formal of, relating to, or consisting of money.
– DERIVATIVES **pecuniarily** adv.
– ORIGIN C16: from L. *pecuniarius*, from *pecunia* 'money'.

**pedagogic** /ˌpɛdəˈgɒgɪk, -ˈgɒdʒ-/ ● adj. of or relating to teaching. ● n. (**pedagogics**) [treated as sing.] old-fashioned term for **PEDAGOGY**.
– DERIVATIVES **pedagogical** adj. **pedagogically** adv.

**pedagogue** /ˈpɛdəgɒg/ ● n. formal or humorous a teacher, especially a strict or pedantic one.
– ORIGIN ME: via L. from Gk *paidagōgos*, denoting a slave who accompanied a child to school (from *pais, paid-* 'boy' + *agōgos* 'guide').

**pedagogy** /ˈpɛdəgɒgi, -gɒdʒi/ ● n. (pl. **-ies**) the profession, science, or theory of teaching.

**pedal**[1] /ˈpɛd(ə)l/ ● n. **1** each of a pair of foot-operated levers for powering a bicycle or other vehicle propelled by leg power. **2** a foot-operated throttle, brake, or clutch control in a motor vehicle. **3** each of a set of two or three foot-operated levers on a piano, for sustaining or softening the tone. ➤ a foot-operated lever on other musical instruments, such as a harp or organ. **4** Music short for **PEDAL NOTE** (in sense 2). ● v. (**pedalled**, **pedalling**; US **pedaled**, **pedaling**) **1** move (a bicycle, pedalo, etc.) by working the pedals. **2** use the pedals of a piano, organ, etc.
– PHRASES **with the pedal to the metal** N. Amer. informal at full speed.
– DERIVATIVES **pedaller** (US **pedaler**) n.
– ORIGIN C17: from Fr. *pédale*, from Ital. *pedale*, from L. *pedalis* (see **PEDAL**[2]).

**pedal**[2] /ˈpɛd(ə)l, ˈpiː-/ ● adj. chiefly Medicine & Zoology of or relating to the foot or feet.
– ORIGIN C17: from L. *pedalis*, from *pes, ped-* 'foot'.

**pedal note** ● n. Music **1** the lowest or fundamental note of a harmonic series in some brass and wind instruments. **2** (also **pedal point**) a note sustained in one part (usually the bass) through successive harmonies, some of which are independent of it.

**pedalo** /ˈpɛdələʊ/ ● n. (pl. **-os** or **-oes**) Brit. a small pedal-operated pleasure boat.
– ORIGIN 1950s: from **PEDAL**[1] + **-O**.

**pedal pusher** ● n. **1** (**pedal pushers**) women's calf-length trousers. **2** informal a cyclist.

**pedal steel guitar** ● n. a musical instrument played like the Hawaiian guitar, but set on a stand with pedals to adjust the tension of the strings.

**pedant** /ˈpɛd(ə)nt/ ● n. a person who is excessively concerned with minor detail or with displaying technical knowledge.
– DERIVATIVES **pedantic** adj. **pedantically** adv. **pedantry** n.
– ORIGIN C16: from Fr. *pédant*, from Ital. *pedante*, perh. from the first element of L. *paedogogus* (see **PEDAGOGUE**).

**peddle** ● v. **1** sell (goods, especially small items) by going from place to place. **2** sell (an illegal drug or stolen item). **3** derogatory promote (an idea or view) persistently or widely.
– ORIGIN C16: back-form. from **PEDLAR**.

**peddler** ● n. variant spelling of **PEDLAR**.

**pederasty** (also **paederasty**) ● n. sexual intercourse between a man and a boy.
– DERIVATIVES **pederast** n. **pederastic** adj.
– ORIGIN C17: from mod. L. *paederastia*, from Gk *paiderastia*, from *pais, paid-* 'boy' + *erastēs* 'lover'.

**pedestal** ● n. **1** the base or support on which a statue, obelisk, or column is mounted. ➤ a position in which one is greatly or uncritically admired: *you shouldn't put him on a pedestal.* **2** each of the two supports of a kneehole desk or table. **3** the supporting column or base of a washbasin or toilet pan.
– ORIGIN C16: from Fr. *piédestal*, from Ital. *piedestallo*, from *piè* 'foot' + *di* 'of' + *stallo* 'stall'.

**pedestrian** ● n. a person walking rather than travelling in a vehicle. ● adj. dull; uninspired.
– DERIVATIVES **pedestrianly** adv.
– ORIGIN C18: from Fr. *pédestre* or L. *pedester* 'going on foot', also 'written in prose'.

**pedestrianize** ● v. make (a street or area) accessible only to pedestrians.
– DERIVATIVES **pedestrianization** n.

**pediatrics** ● pl. n. US spelling of **PAEDIATRICS**.

**pedicab** /ˈpɛdɪkab/ ● n. a small pedal-operated vehicle serving as a taxi.

**pedicel** /ˈpɛdɪs(ə)l/ ● n. **1** Botany a small stalk bearing an individual flower in an inflorescence. **2** Anatomy & Zoology another term for **PEDICLE**.
– DERIVATIVES **pedicellate** /-ˈdɪs(ə)leɪt/ adj.
– ORIGIN C17: from mod. L. *pedicellus* 'small foot', dimin. of *pes, ped-* 'foot'.

**pedicle** /ˈpɛdɪk(ə)l/ ● n. **1** Anatomy & Zoology a small stalk-like connecting structure. **2** Medicine part of a skin graft left temporarily attached to its original site.
– ORIGIN C17: from L. *pediculus* 'small foot', dimin. of *pes, ped-*.

**pediculosis** /pɪˌdɪkjʊˈləʊsɪs/ ● n. Medicine infestation with lice.
– ORIGIN C19: from L. *pediculus* 'louse' + **-OSIS**.

**pedicure** ● n. a cosmetic treatment of the feet and toenails. ● v. [usu. as adj. **pedicured**] give a pedicure to.
– ORIGIN C19: from Fr. *pédicure*, from L. *pes, ped-* 'foot' + *curare* 'attend to'.

**pedigree** ● n. **1** the record of descent of an animal, showing it to be pure-bred. **2** a person's lineage or ancestry. ➤ a genealogical table. **3** the history or provenance of a person or thing.
– DERIVATIVES **pedigreed** adj.
– ORIGIN ME: from Anglo-Norman Fr. *pé de grue* 'crane's foot', a mark used to denote succession in pedigrees.

**pediment** ● n. **1** Architecture the triangular upper part of the front of a classical building, typically surmounting a portico. **2** Geology a broad expanse of rock debris extending outwards from the foot of a slope.
– DERIVATIVES **pedimental** adj. **pedimented** adj.
– ORIGIN C16 (as *periment*): perh. an alt. of **PYRAMID**.

**pedipalp** /ˈpɛdɪpalp, ˈpiːdɪpalp/ ● n. Zoology each of the second pair of appendages attached to the cephalothorax of most arachnids.
– ORIGIN C19: from mod. L. *pedipalpi* (pl.), from L. *pes, ped-* 'foot' + *palpus* 'palp'.

**pedlar** (also **peddler**) ● n. **1** an itinerant trader in small goods. **2** a person who sells illegal drugs or stolen goods. **3** a person who peddles an idea or view.
– DERIVATIVES **pedlary** n. (archaic).
– ORIGIN ME: perh. an alt. of synonymous dial. *pedder*, appar. from dial. *ped* 'pannier'.

**pedo-**[1] ● comb. form US spelling of **PAEDO-**.

**pedo-**[2] /ˈpɛdəʊ/ ● comb. form relating to soil or soil types: *pedogenic.*
– ORIGIN from Gk *pedon* 'ground'.

**pedogenic** /ˌpɛdə(ʊ)ˈdʒɛnɪk/ ● adj. relating to or denoting processes occurring in soil or leading to the formation of soil.

**pedology** /pɪˈdɒlədʒi, pɛ-/ ● n. another term for **SOIL SCIENCE**.
– DERIVATIVES **pedological** /ˌpɛdəˈlɒdʒɪk(ə)l/ adj. **pedologist** n.

**pedometer** /pɪˈdɒmɪtə, pɛ-/ ● n. an instrument for estimating the distance travelled on foot by recording the number of steps taken.
– ORIGIN C18: from Fr. *pédomètre*, from L. *pes, ped-* 'foot'.

**peduncle** /pɪˈdʌŋk(ə)l/ ● n. **1** Botany the stalk bearing a flower or fruit, or the main stalk of an inflorescence. **2** Zoology a stalk-like connecting structure.

– DERIVATIVES **peduncular** adj. **pedunculate** adj.
– ORIGIN C18: from mod. L. *pedunculus*, from L. *pes, ped-* 'foot'.

**pedunculate oak** ● n. the common or English oak. [*Quercus robur.*]

**pee** informal ● v. (**pees**, **peed**, **peeing**) urinate. ● n. **1** an act of urinating. **2** urine.
– ORIGIN C18: euphemistic use of the initial letter of **PISS**.

**peek** ● v. **1** look quickly or furtively. **2** protrude slightly so as to be just visible. ● n. a quick or furtive look.
– ORIGIN ME *pike, pyke*, of unknown origin.

**peekaboo** (also **peek-a-boo**) ● n. a game played with a young child, which involves hiding and suddenly re-appearing, saying 'peekaboo'. ● adj. **1** (of a garment) made of transparent fabric or having a pattern of small holes. **2** (of a hairstyle) concealing one eye with a fringe or wave.
– ORIGIN C16: from **PEEK** + **BOO**.

**peel**[1] ● v. **1** remove the outer covering or skin from (a fruit, vegetable, etc.). **2** (of a surface) lose parts of its outer layer or covering in small strips or pieces. ➤ come off in strips or small pieces. **3** (**peel something away/off**) remove a thin outer covering. ➤ (**peel something off** or Brit. **peel off**) remove an article of clothing. **4** (**peel off**) leave a formation or group by veering away. **5** (**peel out**) N. Amer. informal leave quickly. ● n. the outer covering or rind of a fruit or vegetable.
– DERIVATIVES **peelings** pl. n.
– ORIGIN ME (in the sense 'to plunder'): var. of dial. *pill*, from L. *pilare* 'to strip hair from', from *pilus* 'hair'.

**peel**[2] ● n. archaic a shovel, especially a baker's shovel for carrying loaves into or out of an oven.
– ORIGIN ME: from OFr. *pele*, from L. *pala*, from the base of *pangere* 'to fix'.

**peel**[3] (also **pele** or **peel tower**) ● n. a small square defensive tower of a kind built in the 16th century in the border counties of England and Scotland.
– ORIGIN prob. short for synonymous *peel-house*: *peel* from Anglo-Norman Fr. *pel* 'stake, palisade'.

**peel**[4] ● v. Croquet send (another player's ball) through a hoop.
– ORIGIN C19: from the name of Walter H. *Peel*, founder of the All England Croquet Association.

**peeler**[1] ● n. a knife or device for peeling fruit and vegetables.

**peeler**[2] ● n. Brit. informal, archaic a police officer.
– ORIGIN C19: from the name of the Brit. Prime Minister Sir Robert *Peel* who established the Metropolitan Police.

**peely-wally** /'pi:lɪwɒli, ˌpi:lɪ'wali/ ● adj. Scottish pale and sickly.
– ORIGIN C19: prob. imitative of a whining sound.

**peen** /pi:n/ (also **pein**) ● n. the end of a hammer head opposite the face, typically wedge-shaped or rounded. ● v. **1** strike with a peen. **2** another term for **SHOT-PEEN**.
– ORIGIN C16: prob. of Scand. origin.

**peep**[1] ● v. **1** look quickly and furtively. **2** (**peep out**) come slowly or partially into view. ● n. **1** a quick or furtive look. **2** a momentary or partial view of something.
– ORIGIN C15: symbolic; cf. **PEEK**.

**peep**[2] ● n. **1** a weak, high-pitched sound made by a young bird or mammal. ➤ a brief, high-pitched electronic sound. **2** [with neg.] a slight utterance or complaint. ● v. make a peep.
– ORIGIN ME: imitative; cf. **CHEEP**.

**peep-bo** ● n. another term for **PEEKABOO**.

**pee-pee** ● n. N. Amer. informal **1** a child's word for an act of urinating. ➤ urine. **2** a penis.

**peeper**[1] ● n. **1** a person who peeps, especially in a voyeuristic way. **2** (**peepers**) informal a person's eyes.

**peeper**[2] (also **spring peeper**) ● n. a small North American tree frog, the males of which sing in early spring. [*Hyla crucifer.*]

**peephole** ● n. a small hole in a door through which callers may be identified before the door is opened.

**peeping Tom** ● n. a furtive voyeur.
– ORIGIN from the name of the person said to have watched Lady Godiva ride naked through Coventry.

**peep show** ● n. **1** a sequence of pictures viewed through a lens or hole set into a box, formerly offered as a public entertainment. **2** an erotic or pornographic film viewed from a coin-operated booth.

**peep sight** ● n. a backsight for rifles with a circular hole through which the foresight is brought into line with the object aimed at.

**peep-toe** ● adj. Brit. (of a shoe) having the tip cut away to leave the large toe partially exposed.

**peepul** /'pi:pʌl/ (also **pipal**) ● n. another term for **BO TREE**.
– ORIGIN C18: via Hindi from Sanskrit *pippala*.

**peer**[1] ● v. **1** look with difficulty or concentration. **2** be just visible.
– ORIGIN C16: perh. a var. of dial. *pire* or perh. partly from a shortening of **APPEAR**.

**peer**[2] ● n. **1** a member of the nobility in Britain or Ireland, comprising the ranks of duke, marquess, earl, viscount, and baron. **2** a person of the same age, status, or ability as another specified person. ● v. archaic make or become equal.
– PHRASES **without peer** unrivalled.
– DERIVATIVES **peerless** adj. **peerlessly** adv.
– ORIGIN ME: from OFr. *peer*, from L. *par* 'equal'.

**peerage** ● n. **1** the title and rank of peer or peeress. **2** (**the peerage**) peers collectively. **3** a book containing a full listing of peers and peeresses.

**peeress** /'pɪərɪs, -rɛs/ ● n. **1** a woman holding the rank of a peer in her own right. **2** the wife or widow of a peer.

**peer group** ● n. a group of people of approximately the same age, status, and interests.

**peerie** /'pi:ri/ ● adj. Scottish tiny; insubstantial.
– ORIGIN C19: of unknown origin.

**peer of the realm** ● n. a member of the class of peers who has the right to sit in the House of Lords.

**peer-to-peer** ● adj. Computing denoting a network in which each computer can act as a server for the others.

**peery** /'pɪəri/ ● n. (pl. **-ies**) Scottish & N. English a child's spinning top.
– ORIGIN C17: from *peer* (Scots spelling of **PEAR**) + **-Y**[1].

**peeve** informal ● v. annoy; irritate: *he was peeved at being left out.* ● n. a cause of annoyance.
– ORIGIN C20: back-form. from **PEEVISH**.

**peever** ● n. (often **peevers**) Scottish term for **HOPSCOTCH**.
– ORIGIN C19 (denoting the stone or piece of pottery used in the game): of unknown origin.

**peevish** ● adj. irritable.
– DERIVATIVES **peevishly** adv. **peevishness** n.
– ORIGIN ME (in the sense 'perverse, coy'): of unknown origin.

**peewee** ● n. **1** Scottish the lapwing. **2** N. Amer. variant spelling of **PEWEE**. **3** [as modifier] N. Amer. denoting a level of amateur sport for children aged eight or nine (in the US) or twelve or thirteen (in Canada).
– ORIGIN C19: senses 1 and 2 imitative; sense 3 reduplication of **WEE**[1].

**peewit** (also **pewit**) ● n. Brit. the lapwing.
– ORIGIN C16: imitative of the bird's call.

**peg** ● n. **1** a short projecting pin or bolt used for hanging things on, securing something in place, or marking a position. ➤ a clip for holding things together or hanging up clothes. **2** chiefly Indian a measure of spirits. **3** a point or limit on a scale, especially of exchange rates. **4** chiefly Baseball a strong throw. **5** informal a person's leg. **6** a place marked by a peg and allotted to a competitor to fish or shoot from. ● v. (**pegged**, **pegging**) **1** fix, attach, or mark with a peg or pegs. **2** fix (a price, rate, or amount) at a particular level. **3** N. Amer. informal form a fixed opinion of: *the officer probably has us pegged as anarchists.* **4** chiefly Baseball throw (a ball) hard and low.
– PHRASES **off the peg** chiefly Brit. (of clothes) ready-made. **a peg to hang a matter on** something used as a pretext or occasion for the treatment of a wider subject. **a square peg in a round hole** a person in a situation unsuited to their abilities or character. **take someone down a peg or two** make someone less arrogant.
– PHRASAL VERBS **peg away** informal work hard over a long

period. **peg out 1** informal, chiefly Brit. die. **2** score the winning point at cribbage. **3** Croquet hit the peg with the ball as the final stroke in a game.
– ORIGIN ME: prob. of Low Ger. origin.

**pegboard** • **n.** a board having a regular pattern of small holes for pegs, used chiefly for games or the display of information.

**pegbox** • **n.** a structure at the head of a stringed instrument where the strings are attached to the tuning pegs.

**pegged** • **adj.** North American term for **PEGTOP**.

**peggy** • **n.** (pl. **-ies**) nautical slang a steward in a ship's mess.
– ORIGIN C20 (earlier denoting a man of feminine habits): alt. of *Meggy*, familiar form of the given name *Margaret*.

**peg leg** • **n.** informal an artificial leg, especially a wooden one.

**pegmatite** /ˈpɛgmətʌɪt/ • **n.** Geology a coarsely crystalline granite or other igneous rock with crystals several centimetres in length.
– ORIGIN C19: from Gk *pēgma, pēgmat-* 'thing joined together' + **-ITE**[1].

**pegtop** • **n.** a pear-shaped spinning top with a central metal pin forming the point. • **adj.** dated (of a garment) wide at the top and narrow at the bottom.

**Pehlevi** /ˈpeɪləvi/ • **n.** variant spelling of **PAHLAVI**.

**PEI** • **abbrev.** Prince Edward Island.

**Peigan** /ˈpiːg(ə)n/ (also **Piegan**) • **n.** (pl. same or **Peigans**) a member of a North American Indian people of the Blackfoot confederacy.
– ORIGIN from Blackfoot *Piikániwa*.

**peignoir** /ˈpeɪnwɑː/ • **n.** a woman's light dressing gown or negligee.
– ORIGIN Fr., from *peigner* 'to comb' (because the garment was orig. worn while combing the hair).

**pein** • **n. & v.** variant spelling of **PEEN**.

**peine forte et dure** /pɛn ˌfɔːt eɪ ˈd(j)ʊə/ • **n.** a medieval form of torture in which the body was pressed with heavy weights.
– ORIGIN Fr., lit. 'strong and hard suffering'.

**pejorative** /pɪˈdʒɒrətɪv/ • **adj.** expressing contempt or disapproval.
– DERIVATIVES **pejoratively** adv.
– ORIGIN C19: from Fr. *péjoratif, -ive*, from late L. *pejorare* 'make worse'.

**pekan** /ˈpɛk(ə)n/ • **n.** N. Amer. the fisher (marten).
– ORIGIN C18: from Canad. Fr., from Algonquian.

**Pekinese** /ˌpiːkɪˈniːz/ (also **Pekingese**) • **n.** (pl. same) a lapdog of a short-legged breed with long hair and a snub nose. • **adj.** of or relating to Beijing (Peking), its citizens, or their culture or cuisine.

**Peking duck** • **n.** a Chinese dish consisting of strips of roast duck served with shredded vegetables and a sweet sauce.

**pekoe** /ˈpiːkəʊ, ˈpɛ-/ • **n.** a high-quality black tea made from young leaves.
– ORIGIN C18: from Chin. dial. *pekho*, from *pek* 'white' + *ho* 'down' (the leaves being picked when covered with down).

**pelage** /ˈpɛlɪdʒ/ • **n.** Zoology the fur, hair, or wool of a mammal.
– ORIGIN C19: from Fr., from OFr. *pel* 'hair'.

**Pelagian** /pɪˈleɪdʒɪən/ • **adj.** of or relating to the British or Irish monk Pelagius (*c.*360–*c.*420), or to his theory denying the doctrines of original sin and predestination. • **n.** a follower of Pelagius.
– DERIVATIVES **Pelagianism** n.

**pelagic** /pɪˈladʒɪk/ • **adj. 1** of or relating to the open sea. **2** (chiefly of fish) inhabiting the upper layers of the open sea.
– ORIGIN C17: via L. from Gk *pelagikos*, from *pelagios* 'of the sea'.

**pelargonium** /ˌpɛləˈgəʊnɪəm/ • **n.** a shrubby plant cultivated for its red, pink, or white flowers. See also **GERANIUM**. [Genus *Pelargonium*: many species.]
– ORIGIN mod. L., from Gk *pelargos* 'stork', appar. on the pattern of *geranium*.

**Pelasgian** /pɪˈlazgɪən/ • **n.** a member of an ancient people inhabiting the coasts and islands of the eastern Mediterranean and Aegean before the arrival of Greek-speaking peoples. • **adj.** of or relating to this people.
– ORIGIN C15: via L. from Gk *Pelasgos* + **-IAN**.

**pele** • **n.** variant spelling of **PEEL**[3].

**pelf** • **n.** archaic money, especially when gained dishonestly.
– ORIGIN ME (in the sense 'booty'): from a var. of OFr. *pelfre* 'spoils', of unknown origin; cf. **PILFER**.

**pelham** • **n.** a horse's bit which combines the action of a curb bit and a snaffle.
– ORIGIN C19: from the surname *Pelham*.

**pelican** • **n.** a large gregarious waterbird with a long bill and an extensible throat pouch for scooping up fish. [Genus *Pelecanus*: several species.]
– ORIGIN OE *pellicane*, via late L. from Gk *pelekan*, prob. based on *pelekus* 'axe' (with ref. to its bill).

**pelican crossing** • **n.** (in the UK) a pedestrian crossing with traffic lights operated by pedestrians.
– ORIGIN 1960s: *pelican* from *pe(destrian) li(ght) con(trolled)*, alt. to conform with the bird's name.

**Pelion** /ˈpiːlɪən/ • **n.** (in phr. **pile** or **heap Pelion on Ossa**) add an extra difficulty to something which is already onerous.
– ORIGIN the name of a mountain in Greece; the giants of Greek mythology were said to have piled Mounts Olympus and Ossa on its summit in their attempt to reach heaven and destroy the gods.

**pelisse** /pɪˈliːs/ • **n.** historical **1** a woman's ankle-length cloak with armholes or sleeves. **2** a fur-lined cloak, especially as part of a hussar's uniform.
– ORIGIN C18: from Fr., from med. L. *pellicia* (*vestis*) '(garment) of fur'.

**pelite** /ˈpiːlʌɪt/ • **n.** Geology a sediment or sedimentary rock composed of very fine clay or mud particles.
– ORIGIN C19: from Gk *pēlos* 'clay, mud' + **-ITE**[1].

**pellagra** /pɛˈlagrə, -ˈleɪgrə/ • **n.** a disease characterized by dermatitis, diarrhoea, and mental disturbance, caused by a deficiency of nicotinic acid or tryptophan in the diet.
– DERIVATIVES **pellagrous** adj.
– ORIGIN C19: from Ital., from *pelle* 'skin', on the pattern of *podagra*.

**pellet** • **n. 1** a small, rounded, compressed mass of a substance. **2** a piece of small shot or other lightweight bullet. **3** Ornithology a small mass of bones and feathers regurgitated by a bird of prey. • **v.** (**pelleted**, **pelleting**) **1** form into pellets. **2** hit with or as if with pellets.
– DERIVATIVES **pelletize** (also **-ise**) v.
– ORIGIN ME: from OFr. *pelote* 'metal ball', from a dimin. of L. *pila* 'ball'.

**pellicle** /ˈpɛlɪk(ə)l/ • **n.** technical a thin skin, cuticle, membrane, or film.
– DERIVATIVES **pellicular** /-ˈlɪkjʊlə/ adj.
– ORIGIN ME: from Fr. *pellicule*, from L. *pellicula* 'small piece of skin', dimin. of *pellis*.

**pellitory** /ˈpɛlɪtəri/ (also **pellitory of the wall**) • **n.** a plant of the nettle family with greenish flowers, which grows among stones or on walls. [*Parietaria judaica*.]
– ORIGIN ME: alt. of obs. *parietary*, from OFr. *paritaire*, based on L. *paries, pariet-* 'wall'.

**pell-mell** • **adj. & adv.** in a confused, rushed, or disorderly way. • **n.** a confused mixture; disorder.
– ORIGIN C16: from Fr. *pêle-mêle*, from earlier *pesle mesle, mesle pesle*, reduplication from *mesler* 'to mix'.

**pellucid** /pɪˈluːsɪd, pɛ-, -ˈljuːsɪd/ • **adj. 1** translucently clear. **2** easily understood.
– DERIVATIVES **pellucidly** adv.
– ORIGIN C17: from L. *pellucidus*, from *perlucere* 'shine through'.

**Pelmanism** /ˈpɛlmənɪz(ə)m/ • **n. 1** a system of memory training originally devised by the Pelman Institute for the Scientific Development of Mind, Memory, and Personality. **2** a card game in which matching pairs must be selected from memory from cards laid face down.

**pelmet** • **n.** a narrow border of cloth or wood, fitted across the top of a door or window to conceal the curtain

fittings.
– ORIGIN C20: prob. an alt. of Fr. *palmette*, lit. 'small palm' (see **PALMETTE**).

**pelorus** /pɪˈlɔːrəs/ ● **n.** a sighting device on a ship for taking the relative bearings of a distant object.
– ORIGIN C19: perh. from *Pelorus*, said to be the name of Hannibal's pilot.

**pelota** /pɪˈlɒtə, -ˈləʊtə/ ● **n. 1** a Basque or Spanish ball game played in a walled court with basket-like rackets attached to the hand. **2** the ball used in pelota.
– ORIGIN Sp., lit. 'ball'.

**peloton** /ˈpɛlətɒn/ ● **n.** the main group of cyclists in a race.
– ORIGIN 1950s: from Fr., lit. 'small ball' (because of the concentrated grouping of the pack).

**pelt**[1] ● **v. 1** hurl missiles at. **2** (**pelt down**) (of rain, hail, or snow) fall very heavily. **3** run very quickly. ● **n.** archaic an act of pelting.
– PHRASES (**at**) **full pelt** as fast as possible.
– ORIGIN C15: of unknown origin.

**pelt**[2] ● **n. 1** the skin of an animal with the fur, wool, or hair still on it. **2** the raw skin of a sheep or goat, stripped and ready for tanning.
– ORIGIN ME: either from obs. *pellet* 'skin', from an OFr. dimin. of *pel* 'skin', from L. *pellis* 'skin', or a back-form. from **PELTRY**.

**pelta** /ˈpɛltə/ ● **n.** (pl. **peltae** /-tiː/) a small light shield, as used by the ancient Greeks and Romans.
– ORIGIN from L., from Gk *peltē*.

**peltate** /ˈpɛlteɪt/ ● **adj.** chiefly Botany shield-shaped; more or less circular with a stalk underneath.

**Peltier effect** /ˈpɛltɪeɪ/ ● **n.** Physics an effect whereby heat is given out or absorbed when an electric current passes across a junction between two materials.
– ORIGIN C19: named after the Fr. scientist Jean *Peltier*.

**peltry** ● **n.** (also **peltries**) animal pelts collectively.
– ORIGIN ME: from Anglo-Norman Fr. *pelterie*, based on OFr. *pel* 'skin', from L. *pellis*.

**pelvic** ● **adj.** of or relating to the pelvis.

**pelvic fin** ● **n.** Zoology each of a pair of fins on the underside of a fish's body, attached to the pelvic girdle.

**pelvic floor** ● **n.** the muscular base of the abdomen, attached to the pelvis.

**pelvic girdle** ● **n.** (in vertebrates) the enclosing structure formed by the pelvis.

**pelvic inflammatory disease** ● **n.** inflammation of the female genital tract, accompanied by fever and lower abdominal pain.

**pelvis** ● **n.** (pl. **pelvises** or **pelves** /-viːz/) **1** the large bony frame at the base of the spine to which the lower or hindlimbs are attached. **2** (also **renal pelvis**) the broadened top part of the ureter into which the kidney tubules drain.
– ORIGIN C17: from L., lit. 'basin'.

**pelycosaur** /ˈpɛlɪkəsɔː/ ● **n.** a fossil reptile of the late Carboniferous and Permian periods, typically having a spiny sail-like crest on the back.
– ORIGIN C20: from Gk *pelux*, *peluk-* 'bowl' + *sauros* 'lizard'.

**Pembroke table** ● **n.** a small table with fixed legs and a drop-leaf on each side.

**Pembs.** ● **abbrev.** Pembrokeshire.

**pemmican** /ˈpɛmɪk(ə)n/ ● **n.** a pressed cake made from pounded dried meat mixed to a paste with melted fat and other ingredients, originally made by North American Indians and later adapted by Arctic explorers.
– ORIGIN from Cree *pimecan*, from *pime* 'fat'.

**pemphigus** /ˈpɛmfɪgəs/ ● **n.** Medicine a skin disease in which watery blisters form on the skin.
– DERIVATIVES **pemphigoid** adj.
– ORIGIN C18: mod. L., from Gk *pemphix*, *pemphig-* 'bubble'.

**PEN** ● **abbrev.** International Association of Poets, Playwrights, Editors, Essayists, and Novelists.

**Pen.** ● **abbrev.** Peninsula.

**pen**[1] ● **n. 1** an instrument for writing or drawing with ink, typically consisting of a metal nib or ball, or a nylon tip, fitted into a metal or plastic holder. ➤(**the pen**) writing as an occupation. ➤an electronic device used in conjunction with a writing surface to enter commands or data into a computer. **2** Zoology the tapering cartilaginous internal shell of a squid. ● **v.** (**penned**, **penning**) write or compose.
– PHRASES **pen and ink** Brit. rhyming slang a stink.
– ORIGIN ME (orig. denoting a feather with a sharpened quill): from OFr. *penne*, from L. *penna* 'feather'.

**pen**[2] ● **n. 1** a small enclosure in which sheep, pigs, or other farm animals are kept. **2** a covered dock for a submarine or other warship. **3** (in the West Indies) a farm or plantation. ● **v.** (**penned**, **penning**) **1** put or keep in a pen. **2** (**pen someone up/in**) confine someone in a restricted space.
– ORIGIN OE *penn*, of unknown origin.

**pen**[3] ● **n.** a female swan.
– ORIGIN C16: of unknown origin.

**pen**[4] ● **n.** N. Amer. informal short for **PENITENTIARY** (in sense 1).

**penal** ● **adj. 1** of, relating to, or prescribing the punishment of offenders under the legal system. ➤(of an act or offence) punishable by law. **2** (especially of taxation or interest rates) extremely severe.
– DERIVATIVES **penally** adv.
– ORIGIN ME: from OFr. *penal*, from L. *poenalis*, from *poena* 'pain, penalty'.

**penalize** (also **-ise**) ● **v. 1** subject to a penalty or punishment. ➤put at an unfair disadvantage. **2** Law make or declare (an action) legally punishable.
– DERIVATIVES **penalization** n.

**penal servitude** ● **n.** imprisonment with hard labour.

**penalty** ● **n.** (pl. **-ies**) **1** a punishment imposed for breaking a law, rule, or contract. **2** (in sports and games) a handicap imposed on a player or team for infringement of rules, especially a penalty kick. ➤Bridge points won by the defenders when the declarer fails to make the contract.
– PHRASES **under** (or **on**) **penalty of** under the threat of.
– ORIGIN C16: prob. via Anglo-Norman Fr., from med. L. *poenalitas*, based on *poena* 'pain'.

**penalty area** ● **n.** Soccer the rectangular area marked out in front of each goal, within which a foul by a defender involves the award of a penalty kick.

**penalty box** ● **n. 1** Soccer another term for **PENALTY AREA**. **2** Ice Hockey an area beside the rink reserved for penalized players and an official who records penalties.

**penalty kick** ● **n. 1** Soccer a free kick at the goal from the penalty spot, awarded to the attacking team after a foul within the penalty area. **2** Rugby a place kick awarded to a team after an offence by an opponent.

**penalty killer** ● **n.** Ice Hockey a player specializing in preventing the opposing side from scoring while their own team's strength is reduced through penalties.
– DERIVATIVES **penalty killing** n.

**penalty point** ● **n.** (in the UK) a punishment awarded by the courts for a driving offence and recorded cumulatively on a person's driving licence.

**penalty rate** ● **n.** Austral./NZ historical an increased rate of pay for overtime or for work performed under abnormal conditions.

**penalty spot** ● **n.** Soccer the point within the penalty area from which penalty kicks are taken.

**penalty try** ● **n.** Rugby a try awarded to a side when a touchdown is prevented by an offence by the opposition.

**penance** ● **n. 1** voluntary self-punishment as an open expression of repentance for wrongdoing. **2** a sacrament in which a member of the Church confesses sins to a priest and is given absolution. ➤a religious observance or other duty imposed as part of this sacrament. ● **v.** archaic impose a penance on.
– ORIGIN ME: from OFr., from L. *paenitentia* 'repentance', from *paenitere* 'be sorry'.

**penannular** /pɛˈnanjʊlə/ ● **adj.** Archaeology circular with a small part of the circumference missing.
– ORIGIN C19: from L. *paene* 'almost' + **ANNULAR**.

**penates** /pɪˈnɑːtiːz, -ˈneɪt-/ ● **pl. n.** household gods worshipped in conjunction with Vesta and the lares by the

ancient Romans.
– ORIGIN L., from *penus* 'provision of food'; rel. to *penes* 'within'.

**pence** plural form of **PENNY** (used for sums of money).

**penchant** /'pɒ̃ʃɒ̃/ ● **n.** a strong liking or inclination: *she has a penchant for champagne.*
– ORIGIN C17: from Fr., 'leaning, inclining', pres. part. of *pencher.*

**pencil** ● **n. 1** an instrument for writing or drawing, typically consisting of a thin stick of graphite enclosed in a long thin piece of wood or fixed in a thin cylindrical case. **2** Physics & Geometry a set of light rays, lines, etc. converging to or diverging narrowly from a point. ● **v.** (**pencilled, pencilling**; US **penciled, penciling**) **1** write, draw, or colour with a pencil. **2** (**pencil something in**) arrange or note down something provisionally.
– DERIVATIVES **penciller** n.
– ORIGIN ME (denoting a fine paintbrush): from OFr. *pincel*, from a dimin. of L. *peniculus* 'brush', dimin. of *penis* 'tail'.

**pencil moustache** ● **n.** a very thin moustache.

**pencil-pusher** ● **n.** N. Amer. another term for **PEN-PUSHER**.

**pencil skirt** ● **n.** a very narrow straight skirt.

**pendant** ● **n. 1** a piece of jewellery that hangs from a necklace chain. **2** a light designed to hang from the ceiling. **3** the part of a pocket watch by which it is suspended. **4** a short rope hanging from the head of a ship's mast, yardarm, or clew of a sail, used for attaching tackles. **5** Nautical a tapering flag. **6** /'pɛnd(ə)nt, 'pɒ̃dɒ̃/ a complementary or matching artistic, literary, or musical work. ● **adj.** pendent.
– ORIGIN ME: from OFr., lit. 'hanging', pres. part. of *pendre*, from L. *pendent-*, *pendere.*

**pendent** ● **adj. 1** hanging down. **2** pending. **3** Grammar (of a sentence) incomplete, especially in not having a finite verb.
– DERIVATIVES **pendency** n.

**pendente lite** /pɛn,dɛnteɪ 'lʌɪti, -,dɛnti/ ● **adv.** Law during litigation.
– ORIGIN L., lit. 'with the lawsuit pending'.

**pendentive** /pɛn'dɛntɪv/ ● **n.** Architecture a curved triangle of vaulting formed by the intersection of a dome with its supporting arches.
– ORIGIN C18: from the Fr. adjective *pendentif, -ive*, from L. *pendent-*, *pendere* 'hang down'.

**pending** ● **adj. 1** awaiting decision or settlement. **2** about to happen. ● **prep.** until.
– ORIGIN C17: anglicized spelling of Fr. *pendant* 'hanging'.

**Pendragon** /pɛn'drag(ə)n/ ● **n.** a title given to an ancient British or Welsh prince claiming supreme power.
– ORIGIN Welsh, lit. 'chief war-leader', from *pen* 'head' + *dragon* 'standard'.

**penduline tit** /'pɛndjʊlʌɪn/ ● **n.** a small titmouse that builds a nest suspended from a branch. [*Remiz pendulinus* (Eurasia) and other species.]
– ORIGIN C19: *penduline* from Fr. or mod. L. *pendulinus*, from L. *pendulus* 'hanging down'.

**pendulous** /'pɛndjʊləs/ ● **adj.** hanging down; drooping.
– DERIVATIVES **pendulously** adv.
– ORIGIN C17: from L. *pendulus* 'hanging down'.

**pendulum** /'pɛndjʊləm/ ● **n. 1** a weight hung from a fixed point so that it can swing freely, especially a rod with a weighted end that regulates the mechanism of a clock. **2** the tendency of a situation to oscillate between extremes: *the pendulum of fashion.*
– DERIVATIVES **pendular** adj.
– ORIGIN C17: from L., neut. of *pendulus* 'hanging down'.

**penectomy** /pɛ'nɛktəmi/ ● **n.** surgical amputation of the penis.

**peneplain** /'pi:nɪpleɪn/ ● **n.** Geology a level land surface produced by erosion over a long period.
– ORIGIN C19: from L. *paene* 'almost' + **PLAIN**[1].

**penetralia** /,pɛnɪ'treɪlɪə/ ● **pl. n.** the innermost parts of a building.
– ORIGIN C17: from L., lit. 'innermost things'.

**penetrant** /'pɛnɪtr(ə)nt/ ● **n.** a substance which can penetrate cracks, pores, and other surface defects. ● **adj.** Genetics (of genes) producing characteristic effects in the phenotypes of individuals possessing them.
– DERIVATIVES **penetrance** n. (Genetics).

**penetrate** ● **v. 1** force a way into or through. ➤ [as adj. **penetrating**] (of a sound) clearly heard through or above other sounds. **2** infiltrate (an enemy organization or a competitor's market). **3** understand or gain insight into (something complex or mysterious). **4** (of a man) insert the penis into the vagina or anus of (a sexual partner).
– DERIVATIVES **penetrability** n. **penetrable** adj. **penetratingly** adv. **penetration** n. **penetrator** n.
– ORIGIN C16 (earlier (ME) as *penetration*): from L. *penetrat-*, *penetrare* 'go into'.

**penetrative** ● **adj. 1** able to penetrate. **2** having or showing deep understanding and insight. **3** (of sexual activity) involving penetration.

**penetrometer** /,pɛnɪ'trɒmɪtə/ ● **n.** an instrument for determining the hardness of a substance by measuring the depth or rate of penetration of a rod or needle driven into it by a known force.

**penfriend** ● **n.** chiefly Brit. a person with whom one becomes friendly by exchanging letters.

**penguin** ● **n.** a flightless black and white seabird of the southern hemisphere, with wings used as flippers. [Family Spheniscidae: several species.]
– ORIGIN C16 (orig. denoting the great auk): of unknown origin.

**penicillate** /'pɛnɪsɪlət, -'sɪlət/ ● **adj.** Biology having, forming, or resembling a small tuft or tufts of hair.
– ORIGIN C19: from L. *penicillus* 'paintbrush' + **-ATE**[2].

**penicillin** ● **n.** an antibiotic produced naturally by certain blue moulds, now usually prepared synthetically.
– ORIGIN 1920s: from the mod. L. genus name *Penicillium* (from L. *penicillum* 'paintbrush') + **-IN**[1].

**penile** /'pi:nʌɪl/ ● **adj.** of or relating to the penis.
– ORIGIN C19: from mod. L. *penilis*, from *penis* 'tail, penis'.

**peninsula** /pɪ'nɪnsjʊlə/ ● **n.** a long, narrow piece of land projecting out into a sea or lake.
– DERIVATIVES **peninsular** adj.
– ORIGIN C16: from L. *paeninsula*, from *paene* 'almost' + *insula* 'island'.

**penis** /'pi:nɪs/ ● **n.** (pl. **penises** or **penes** /-ni:z/) the male copulatory organ, in mammals used also for urination.
– ORIGIN C17: from L., 'tail, penis'.

**penitent** ● **adj.** feeling or showing sorrow and regret for having done wrong. ● **n.** a person who repents their sins. ➤ (in the Roman Catholic Church) a person who confesses their sins to a priest and submits to the penance that he imposes.
– DERIVATIVES **penitence** n. **penitential** adj. **penitently** adv.
– ORIGIN ME: from OFr., from L. *paenitent-*, *paenitere* 'repent'.

**Penitential Psalms** ● **pl. n.** seven psalms (6, 32, 38, 51, 102, 130, 143) which express penitence.

**penitentiary** /,pɛnɪ'tɛnʃ(ə)ri/ ● **n.** (pl. **-ies**) **1** N. Amer. a prison for people convicted of serious crimes. **2** (in the Roman Catholic Church) a priest appointed to administer penance. ➤ an office in the papal court deciding questions relating to penance, dispensations, etc.
– ORIGIN ME: from med. L. *paenitentiarius*, from L. *paenitentia* 'repentance'.

**penknife** ● **n.** (pl. **penknives**) a small knife with a blade which folds into the handle.

**penlight** ● **n.** a small electric torch shaped like a pen.

**penman** ● **n.** (pl. **-men**) **1** historical a person, such as a clerk, employed to write by hand on behalf of others. **2** dated a person with a specified ability in handwriting. **3** an author.
– DERIVATIVES **penmanship** n.

**Penn.** (also **Penna.**) ● **abbrev.** Pennsylvania.

**pen name** ● **n.** a literary pseudonym.

**pennant** ● **n. 1** a tapering flag on a ship, especially one flown at the masthead of a vessel in commission. **2** a long triangular or swallow-tailed flag, especially as the military ensign of lancer regiments. **3** N. Amer. a flag denoting a sports championship or identifying a team, club, etc. **4** another term for **PENDANT** (in sense 4).

– ORIGIN C17: blend of **PENDANT** and **PENNON**.

**pennate** /ˈpɛnət/ ● **adj.** Botany (of a diatom) bilaterally symmetrical. Compare with **CENTRIC**.
– ORIGIN C19: from L. *pennatus* 'feathered, winged'.

**penne** /ˈpɛneɪ, ˈpɛni/ ● **pl. n.** pasta in the form of short wide tubes.
– ORIGIN Ital., pl. of *penna* 'quill'.

**penni** /ˈpɛni/ ● **n.** (pl. **penniä** /ˈpɛnɪɑː/) a monetary unit of Finland, equal to one hundredth of a markka.
– ORIGIN from Finnish.

**penniless** ● **adj.** without money; destitute.
– DERIVATIVES **pennilessness** n.

**pennon** /ˈpɛnən/ ● **n.** less common term for **PENNANT**.
– DERIVATIVES **pennoned** adj.
– ORIGIN ME: from OFr., from a derivative of L. *penna* 'feather'.

**penn'orth** /ˈpɛnəθ/ ● **n.** variant spelling of **PENNYWORTH**.

**Pennsylvania Dutch** (also **Pennsylvania German**) ● **n.** a dialect of High German spoken in parts of Pennsylvania.
– ORIGIN *Dutch* from Ger. *Deutsch* 'German'.

**Pennsylvanian** ● **n.** a native or inhabitant of the US state of Pennsylvania. ● **adj. 1** of or relating to Pennsylvania. **2** Geology of or denoting the later part of the Carboniferous period in North America.

**penny** ● **n.** (pl. **pennies** (for separate coins); **pence** (for a sum of money)) **1** (abbrev.: **p.**) a British bronze coin and monetary unit equal to one hundredth of a pound. **2** (abbrev.: **d.**) a former British coin and monetary unit equal to one twelfth of a shilling and 240th of a pound. **3** N. Amer. informal a one-cent coin. **4** [with neg.] (**a penny**) no money at all. **5** (in biblical use) a denarius.
– PHRASES **be two** (or **ten**) **a penny** chiefly Brit. be plentiful and thus of little value. **in for a penny, in for a pound** expressing an intention to see an undertaking through, however much time, effort, or money this entails. **pennies from heaven** unexpected benefits. **the penny dropped** informal, chiefly Brit. someone has finally realized something. **a penny for your thoughts** a request to someone to say what they are thinking about.
– ORIGIN OE *penig*, *penning* of Gmc origin; perh. rel. to **PAWN**[2] and (with ref. to shape) **PAN**[1].

**-penny** ● **comb. form** Brit. costing a specified number of pence (especially in pre-decimal currency): *threepenny*.

**penny ante** ● **n.** chiefly N. Amer. **1** poker played for very small stakes. **2** [as modifier] informal trivial or contemptible.

**penny black** ● **n.** the world's first adhesive postage stamp, issued in Britain in 1840.

**penny bun** ● **n.** another term for **CEP**.

**pennycress** ● **n.** a plant of the cabbage family with small white flowers and flat round pods. [*Thlaspi arvense*.]

**penny dreadful** ● **n.** historical or humorous a cheap, sensational comic or storybook.

**penny-farthing** ● **n.** Brit. an early type of bicycle with a very large front wheel and a small rear wheel.

**penny loafer** ● **n.** a casual leather shoe with a decorative slotted leather strip over the upper.

**penny-pinching** ● **adj.** unwilling to spend money; miserly. ● **n.** miserliness.
– DERIVATIVES **penny-pincher** n.

**penny plain** ● **adj.** plain and simple.
– ORIGIN C19: with ref. to prints of characters sold for toy theatres, costing one penny for black-and-white ones, and two pennies for coloured ones.

**penny post** ● **n.** historical a system established in the UK in 1840 of carrying letters at a standard charge of one penny each regardless of distance.

**pennyroyal** ● **n.** a small-leaved plant of the mint family, used in herbal medicine. [*Mentha pulegium* (Eurasia) and *Hedeoma pulegioides* (N. America).]
– ORIGIN C16: from Anglo-Norman Fr. *puliol* (based on L. *pulegium* 'thyme') + *real* 'royal'.

**penny share** (N. Amer. **penny stock**) ● **n.** a low-priced share in a small company.

**pennyweight** ● **n.** a unit of weight, 24 grains or one twentieth of an ounce troy.

**penny whistle** ● **n.** another term for **TIN WHISTLE**.

**penny wise** ● **adj.** careful to save small amounts of money.
– PHRASES **penny wise and pound foolish** economical in small matters but extravagant in large ones.

**pennywort** /ˈpɛnɪwəːt/ ● **n.** a plant with small rounded leaves, growing in crevices or marshy places. [*Umbilicus rupestris* (**wall pennywort**) and *Hydrocotyle vulgaris* (**marsh** or **water pennywort**).]

**pennyworth** (also **penn'orth**) ● **n. 1** an amount of something that may be bought for a penny. **2** (**one's pennyworth**) Brit. one's contribution to a discussion. **3** archaic a bargain.

**penology** /piːˈnɒlədʒi, pɪ-/ ● **n.** the study of the punishment of crime and of prison management.
– DERIVATIVES **penological** adj. **penologist** n.
– ORIGIN C19: from L. *poena* 'penalty' + **-LOGY**.

**pen pal** ● **n.** North American term for **PENFRIEND**.

**pen-pusher** ● **n.** informal a person with a clerical job involving routine paperwork.

**pensée** /pɒ̃ˈseɪ/ ● **n.** a thought or reflection put into literary form; an aphorism.
– ORIGIN from Fr.

**pensile** /ˈpɛnsʌɪl/ ● **adj.** pendulous.
– ORIGIN C17: from L. *pensilis*, from *pendere* 'hang'.

**pension**[1] /ˈpɛnʃ(ə)n/ ● **n. 1** a regular payment made by the state to people of or above the official retirement age and to some widows and disabled people. **2** a regular payment made during a person's retirement from an investment fund to which that person or their employer has contributed during their working life. **3** chiefly historical a regular payment as a reward made to a royal favourite or to enable an artist or scholar to continue their work. ● **v.** (**pension someone off**) dismiss someone from employment and pay them a pension.
– DERIVATIVES **pensionability** n. **pensionable** adj. **pensionless** adj.
– ORIGIN ME: from OFr., from L. *pensio(n-)* 'payment', from *pendere* 'to pay'.

**pension**[2] /pɒ̃ˈsjɒ̃/ ● **n.** a small hotel or boarding house in France and other European countries.
– ORIGIN from Fr.

**pensione** /ˌpɛnsɪˈəʊneɪ/ ● **n.** (pl. **pensioni** /-ni/) a small hotel or boarding house in Italy.
– ORIGIN from Ital.

**pensioner** ● **n.** a person receiving a pension.

**pensive** ● **adj.** engaged in deep thought.
– DERIVATIVES **pensively** adv. **pensiveness** n.
– ORIGIN ME: from OFr. *pensif*, *-ive*, from *penser* 'think', from L. *pensare* 'ponder'.

**penstemon** /pɛnˈstiːmən, -ˈstɛmən, ˈpɛnstɪmən/ (also **pentstemon**) ● **n.** a North American plant with stems of showy snapdragon-like flowers. [Genus *Penstemon*.]
– ORIGIN mod. L., formed irregularly from **PENTA-** + Gk *stēmōn* 'warp', used to mean 'stamen'.

**penstock** ● **n. 1** a sluice for controlling or directing the flow of water. **2** a channel for conveying water to a hydroelectric station.
– ORIGIN C17: from **PEN**[2] (meaning 'mill dam') + **STOCK**.

**pent** ● **adj.** chiefly poetic/literary another term for **PENT-UP**.

**penta-** ● **comb. form** five; having five: *pentadactyl*.
– ORIGIN from Gk *pente* 'five'.

**pentachlorophenol** /ˌpɛntəˌklɔːrəʊˈfiːnɒl/ ● **n.** Chemistry a crystalline synthetic compound used in insecticides, fungicides, wood preservatives, etc.

**pentachord** ● **n. 1** a musical instrument with five strings. **2** a series of five musical notes.

**pentacle** /ˈpɛntək(ə)l/ ● **n. 1** a pentagram, or a symbolic figure inscribed with one. **2** (**pentacles**) one of the suits in some tarot packs, corresponding to coins in others.
– ORIGIN C16: from med. L. *pentaculum*, appar. based on Gk *penta-* 'five'.

**pentad** /ˈpɛntad/ ● **n.** a group or set of five.
– ORIGIN C17: from Gk *pentas*, *pentad-*, from *pente* 'five'.

**pentadactyl** /ˌpɛntəˈdaktɪl/ ● **adj.** Zoology having five toes or fingers.
– DERIVATIVES **pentadactyly** n.

**pentagon** ● n. 1 a plane figure with five straight sides and five angles. 2 (**the Pentagon**) the headquarters of the US Department of Defense, near Washington DC.
– DERIVATIVES **pentagonal** adj.
– ORIGIN C16: via L. from Gk *pentagōnon*, neut. (used as n.) of *pentagōnos* 'five-angled'.

**Pentagonese** /ˌpɛntəgəˈniːz/ ● n. US informal the euphemistic or cryptic language supposedly used among high-ranking US military personnel.

**pentagram** ● n. a five-pointed star formed by drawing a continuous line in five straight segments, often used as a mystic and magical symbol.
– ORIGIN C19: from Gk *pentagrammon* (see **PENTA-**, **-GRAM**[1]).

**pentahedron** /ˌpɛntəˈhiːdr(ə)n, -ˈhɛd-/ ● n. (pl. **pentahedra** /-drə/ or **pentahedrons**) a solid figure with five plane faces.
– DERIVATIVES **pentahedral** adj.
– ORIGIN C18: from **PENTA-** + **-HEDRON**.

**pentamer** /ˈpɛntəmə/ ● n. Chemistry a polymer comprising five monomer units.
– DERIVATIVES **pentameric** /ˌpɛntəˈmɛrɪk/ adj.

**pentameral** /pɛnˈtamərəl/ ● adj. Zoology (of symmetry) fivefold, as typical of many echinoderms.
– DERIVATIVES **pentamerally** adv. **pentamery** n.

**pentamerous** /pɛnˈtam(ə)rəs/ ● adj. Botany & Zoology having parts arranged in groups of five. ➤ consisting of five joints or parts.

**pentameter** /pɛnˈtamɪtə/ ● n. Prosody a line of verse consisting of five metrical feet, or (in Greek and Latin verse) of two halves each of two feet and a long syllable.
– ORIGIN C16: via L. from Gk *pentametros* (see **PENTA-**, **-METER**).

**pentamidine** /pɛnˈtamɪdiːn/ ● n. Medicine a synthetic antibiotic drug used chiefly to treat PCP infection.
– ORIGIN 1940s: from **PENTANE** + **AMIDE** + **-INE**[4].

**pentane** /ˈpɛnteɪn/ ● n. Chemistry a volatile liquid hydrocarbon of the alkane series, present in petroleum spirit. [$C_5H_{12}$.]
– ORIGIN C19: from Gk *pente* 'five' (denoting five carbon atoms) + **-ANE**[2].

**pentangle** ● n. another term for **PENTAGRAM**.
– ORIGIN ME: perh. from med. L. *pentaculum* 'pentacle' (*-aculum* assimilated to L. *angulus* 'an angle').

**pentaploid** /ˈpɛntəplɔɪd/ ● adj. Genetics having or denoting cells or nuclei containing five homologous sets of chromosomes.

**pentaprism** ● n. a prism having a five-sided cross section with two silvered surfaces, giving a constant deviation of all rays of light through 90°.

**Pentateuch** /ˈpɛntətjuːk/ ● n. the first five books of the Old Testament and Hebrew Scriptures (Genesis, Exodus, Leviticus, Numbers, and Deuteronomy).
– DERIVATIVES **Pentateuchal** adj.
– ORIGIN via eccles. L. from eccles. Gk *pentateukhos*, from *penta-* 'five' + *teukhos* 'implement, book'.

**pentathlon** ● n. an athletic event comprising five different events for each competitor, in particular (also **modern pentathlon**) a men's event involving fencing, shooting, swimming, riding, and cross-country running.
– DERIVATIVES **pentathlete** n.
– ORIGIN C17: from Gk, from *pente* 'five' + *athlon* 'contest'.

**pentatonic** /ˌpɛntəˈtɒnɪk/ ● adj. Music relating to, based on, or denoting a scale of five notes.
– DERIVATIVES **pentatonicism** n.

**pentavalent** /ˌpɛntəˈveɪl(ə)nt/ ● adj. Chemistry having a valency of five.

**Pentecost** /ˈpɛntɪkɒst/ ● n. 1 the Christian festival celebrating the descent of the Holy Spirit on the disciples of Jesus after his Ascension, held on Whit Sunday. 2 the Jewish festival of Shavuoth.
– ORIGIN OE *pentecosten*, via eccles. L. from Gk *pentēkostē* (*hēmera*) 'fiftieth (day)' (because the Jewish festival is held on the fiftieth day after the second day of Passover).

**Pentecostal** ● adj. 1 of or relating to Pentecost. 2 (in Christian use) emphasizing baptism in the Holy Spirit, evidenced by 'speaking in tongues', prophecy, healing, and exorcism. ● n. a member of a Pentecostal sect.
– DERIVATIVES **Pentecostalism** n. **Pentecostalist** adj. & n.

**penthouse** ● n. 1 a flat on the top floor of a tall building, typically luxuriously fitted and offering fine views. 2 archaic an outhouse with a sloping roof, built on the side of a building.
– ORIGIN ME *pentis*, shortening of OFr. *apentis*, based on late L. *appendicium* 'appendage'; later assoc. with Fr. *pente* 'slope' and **HOUSE**.

**pentimento** /ˌpɛntɪˈmɛntəʊ/ ● n. (pl. **pentimenti** /-tiː/) a visible trace of earlier painting beneath the paint on a canvas.
– ORIGIN C20: from Ital., lit. 'repentance'.

**pentlandite** /ˈpɛntləndʌɪt/ ● n. a bronze-yellow mineral consisting of a sulphide of iron and nickel.
– ORIGIN C19: from the name of the Ir. traveller Joseph B. *Pentland* + **-ITE**[1].

**pentobarbitone** /ˌpɛntə(ʊ)ˈbɑːbɪtəʊn/ (US **pentobarbital**) ● n. Medicine a narcotic and sedative barbiturate drug formerly used to relieve insomnia.
– ORIGIN 1930s: from **PENTANE** + **BARBITONE** (or **BARBITAL**).

**pentode** /ˈpɛntəʊd/ ● n. Electronics a thermionic valve having five electrodes.
– ORIGIN C20: from Gk *pente* 'five' + *hodos* 'way'.

**pentose** /ˈpɛntəʊz, -s/ ● n. Chemistry any of the class of simple sugars whose molecules contain five carbon atoms (e.g. ribose).

**Pentothal** /ˈpɛntəθal/ ● n. trademark for **THIOPENTONE**.

**pent roof** ● n. a roof consisting of a single sloping surface.
– ORIGIN C19: from **PENTHOUSE** + **ROOF**.

**pentstemon** ● n. variant spelling of **PENSTEMON**.

**pent-up** ● adj. closely confined or held back.

**pentyl** /ˈpɛntʌɪl, -tɪl/ ● n. [as modifier] Chemistry of or denoting an alkyl radical $-C_5H_{11}$, derived from pentane.

**penult** /pɪˈnʌlt, ˈpɛnʌlt/ ● n. Linguistics the penultimate syllable of a word. ● adj. archaic term for **PENULTIMATE**.

**penultimate** ● adj. last but one.
– ORIGIN C17: from L. *paenultimus*, from *paene* 'almost' + *ultimus* 'last', on the pattern of *ultimate*.

**penumbra** /pɪˈnʌmbrə/ ● n. (pl. **penumbrae** /-briː/ or **penumbras**) 1 the partially shaded outer region of the shadow cast by an opaque object, especially the area of the earth or moon experiencing a partial eclipse. 2 Astronomy the less dark outer part of a sunspot.
– DERIVATIVES **penumbral** adj.
– ORIGIN C17: mod. L., from L. *paene* 'almost' + *umbra* 'shadow'.

**penurious** /pɪˈnjʊərɪəs/ ● adj. formal 1 extremely poor. 2 parsimonious.
– DERIVATIVES **penuriously** adv. **penuriousness** n.

**penury** /ˈpɛnjʊri/ ● n. extreme poverty.
– ORIGIN ME: from L. *penuria* 'need, scarcity'; perh. rel. to *paene* 'almost'.

**Penutian** /pəˈnuːʃ(ə)n, -ˈnuːtɪən/ ● n. a proposed superfamily or phylum of American Indian languages, most of which are now extinct or nearly so. ● adj. relating to or denoting these languages or any of the peoples speaking them.
– ORIGIN from *pen* and *uti*, words for 'two' in two groups of Penutian langs + **-AN**.

**peon** /ˈpiːən/ ● n. 1 /also peɪˈɒn/ a Spanish-American day labourer or unskilled farm worker. ➤ chiefly N. Amer. a person who does menial work. 2 /also pjuːn/ (in the Indian subcontinent and SE Asia) someone of low rank. 3 (pl. **peones** /peɪˈəʊneɪz/) another term for **BANDERILLERO**.
– DERIVATIVES **peonage** n.
– ORIGIN from Port. *peão* and Sp. *peón*, from med. L. *pedo*, *pedon-* 'walker, foot soldier'; cf. **PAWN**[1].

**peony** /ˈpiːəni/ (also **paeony**) ● n. a herbaceous or shrubby plant of north temperate regions, long cultivated for its showy flowers. [Genus *Paeonia*.]
– ORIGIN OE *peonie*, via L. from Gk *paiōnia*, from *Paiōn*, the name of the physician of the gods.

**people** ● pl. n. 1 human beings in general or considered

collectively. ➤(**the people**) the mass of citizens in a country; the populace. **2** (**one's people**) one's parents or relatives. **3** (**one's people**) one's employees or supporters. **4** (pl. **peoples**) [treated as sing. or pl.] the members of a particular nation, community, or ethnic group: *the native peoples of Canada.* ●v. **1** (usu. **be peopled**) (of a particular group of people) inhabit. ➤fill or be present in. **2** fill (an area or place) with a particular group of inhabitants.
– DERIVATIVES **peoplehood** n.
– ORIGIN ME: from Anglo-Norman Fr. *poeple*, from L. *populus* 'populace'.

**people carrier** ●n. a motor vehicle with three rows of seats.

**people person** ●n. informal a person who enjoys or is particularly good at interacting with others.

**PEP** ●abbrev. Brit. **1** personal equity plan. **2** Political and Economic Planning.

**pep** informal ●n. liveliness. ●v. (**pepped**, **pepping**) (**pep someone/thing up**) make someone or something more lively.
– ORIGIN C20: abbrev. of **PEPPER**.

**peperoni** ●n. variant spelling of **PEPPERONI**.

**peplum** /'pɛpləm/ ●n. a short flared, gathered, or pleated strip of fabric attached at the waist of a woman's jacket, dress, or blouse.
– ORIGIN C17: via L. from Gk *peplos* 'outer robe or shawl'.

**pepo** /'pi:pəʊ/ ●n. (pl. **-os**) any fleshy watery fruit of the melon or cucumber type, with numerous seeds and a firm rind.
– ORIGIN C19: from L., lit. 'pumpkin'.

**pepper** ●n. **1** a pungent, hot-tasting powder prepared from dried and ground peppercorns, used to flavour food. **2** a climbing vine with berries that are dried as black or white peppercorns. [*Piper nigrum.*] ➤used in names of related plants having hot-tasting leaves, or fruits used as a pungent spice, e.g. **Jamaica pepper**, **water pepper**. **3** a capsicum, especially a sweet pepper. ➤a reddish and typically hot-tasting spice prepared from various forms of capsicum. **4** Baseball a practice game in which a fielder throws at close range to a batter who hits back to the fielder. ●v. **1** sprinkle or season with pepper. **2** (usu. **be peppered with**) scatter liberally over or through. **3** hit repeatedly with small missiles or gunshot. **4** archaic inflict severe punishment or suffering upon.
– ORIGIN OE *piper*, *pipor*, of W. Gmc origin; via L. from Gk *peperi*, from Sanskrit *pippalī* 'berry, peppercorn'.

**pepper-and-salt** ●adj. flecked or speckled with intermingled dark and light shades.

**pepperbox** ●n. **1** a gun or piece of artillery with a revolving set of barrels. **2** archaic a pepper pot.

**peppercorn** ●n. the dried berry of a climbing vine, used whole as a spice or crushed or ground to make pepper.

**peppercorn rent** ●n. Brit. a very low or nominal rent.
– ORIGIN from the (formerly common) practice of stipulating the payment of a peppercorn as a nominal rent.

**pepper mill** ●n. a device for grinding peppercorns by hand to make pepper.

**peppermint** ●n. **1** the aromatic leaves of a plant of the mint family, or an oil obtained from them, used as a flavouring in food. **2** the plant which yields these leaves or oil. [*Mentha × piperita.*] **3** a sweet flavoured with peppermint oil. **4** Austral. a eucalyptus or myrtle with peppermint-scented foliage.
– DERIVATIVES **pepperminty** adj.

**pepperoni** /,pɛpə'rəʊni/ (also **peperoni**) ●n. beef and pork sausage seasoned with pepper.
– ORIGIN from Ital. *peperone* 'chilli'.

**pepper pot** ●n. **1** (N. Amer. **pepper shaker**) Brit. a container with a perforated top for sprinkling pepper. **2** a West Indian dish consisting of stewed meat or fish with vegetables, typically flavoured with cassareep.

**pepper spray** ●n. an aerosol spray containing oils derived from cayenne pepper, irritant to the eyes and respiratory passages and used as a disabling weapon.

**pepperwort** ●n. a wild cress with pungent leaves. [Genus *Lepidium.*]

**peppery** ●adj. **1** strongly flavoured with pepper or other hot spices. **2** irritable and sharp-tongued.
– DERIVATIVES **pepperiness** n.

**pep pill** ●n. informal a pill containing a stimulant drug.

**peppy** ●adj. (**-ier**, **-iest**) informal, chiefly N. Amer. lively.
– DERIVATIVES **peppily** adv. **peppiness** n.

**pepsin** ●n. Biochemistry the chief digestive enzyme in the stomach, which breaks down proteins into polypeptides.
– ORIGIN C19: from Gk *pepsis* 'digestion' + **-IN**[1].

**pep talk** ●n. informal a talk intended to make someone feel more courageous or enthusiastic.

**peptic** ●adj. of or relating to digestion.
– ORIGIN C17: from Gk *peptikos* 'able to digest'.

**peptic ulcer** ●n. a lesion in the lining of the digestive tract, typically in the stomach or duodenum, caused by the digestive action of pepsin and stomach acid.

**peptide** /'pɛptʌɪd/ ●n. Biochemistry a compound consisting of two or more amino acids linked in a chain.
– ORIGIN C20: from Ger. *Peptid*, back-form. from *Polypeptid* 'polypeptide'.

**peptone** /'pɛptəʊn/ ●n. Biochemistry a soluble protein formed in the early stage of protein digestion.
– ORIGIN C19: from Ger. *Pepton*, from Gk *pepton*, neut. of *peptos* 'cooked, digested'.

**Pequot** /'pi:kwɒt/ ●n. (pl. same or **Pequots**) **1** a member of an American Indian people of southern New England. **2** the extinct Algonquian language of this people.
– ORIGIN from Narragansett *paquatanog* 'destroyers'.

**per** ●prep. **1** for each: *£2 per square yard.* **2** by means of. **3** (**as per**) in accordance with. **4** Heraldry divided by a line in the direction of.
– PHRASES **as per usual** as usual.
– ORIGIN L., 'through, by means of'; partly via OFr.

**per-** ●prefix **1** through; all over: *pervade.* ➤completely; very: *perfect.* ➤to destruction; to ill effect: *perdition.* **2** Chemistry having the maximum proportion of some element in combination: *peroxide.*
– ORIGIN from L. (see **PER**).

**peradventure** archaic or humorous ●adv. perhaps. ●n. uncertainty or doubt.
– ORIGIN ME: from OFr. *per* (or *par*) *auenture* 'by chance'.

**perambulate** /pə'rambjʊleɪt/ ●v. **1** formal walk or travel from place to place. **2** Brit. historical walk round (a parish, forest, etc.) in order to officially assert and record its boundaries.
– DERIVATIVES **perambulation** n. **perambulatory** adj.
– ORIGIN ME: from L. *perambulat-*, *perambulare* 'walk about'.

**perambulator** ●n. formal term for **PRAM**[1].

**per annum** ●adv. for each year.
– ORIGIN C17: L.

**perborate** /pə'bɔ:reɪt/ ●n. Chemistry a salt which is an oxidized borate containing a peroxide linkage, especially a sodium salt of this kind used as a bleach.

**percale** /pə'keɪl/ ●n. a closely woven fine cotton fabric.
– ORIGIN C17: from Fr., of unknown origin.

**per capita** /pə: 'kapɪtə/ (also **per caput** /'kapʊt/) ●adv. & adj. for each person; in relation to people taken individually.
– ORIGIN C17: L., lit. 'by heads'.

**perceive** ●v. **1** become aware or conscious of. **2** regard as.
– DERIVATIVES **perceivable** adj. **perceiver** n.
– ORIGIN ME: from a var. of OFr. *perçoivre*, from L. *percipere* 'seize, understand'.

**per cent** ●adv. by a specified amount in or for every hundred. ●n. one part in every hundred. ➤the rate, number, or amount in each hundred.
– ORIGIN C16: from **PER** + **CENT**.

**percentage** ●n. **1** a rate, number, or amount in each hundred. **2** a proportion of a larger sum of money granted as an allowance or commission. **3** any proportion or share in relation to a whole.

**percentile** /pə'sɛntʌɪl/ ●n. Statistics each of the 100 equal groups into which a population can be divided according to the distribution of values of a particular variable. ➤each of the 99 intermediate values of a random variable which divide a frequency distribution into 100 such groups.

**percept** /ˈpəːsɛpt/ ● **n.** Philosophy something that is perceived. ➤a mental concept that is developed as a consequence of the process of perception.
– ORIGIN C19: from L. *perceptum* 'something perceived', neut. past part. of *percipere* 'seize, understand', on the pattern of *concept*.

**perceptible** ● **adj.** (especially of a slight movement or change of state) able to be perceived.
– DERIVATIVES **perceptibility** n. **perceptibly** adv.

**perception** ● **n. 1** the ability to see, hear, or become aware of something through the senses. ➤the state of being or process of becoming aware of something in such a way. **2** a way of regarding, understanding, or interpreting something. ➤intuitive understanding and insight. **3** Psychology & Zoology the neurophysiological processes, including memory, by which an organism becomes aware of and interprets external stimuli.
– DERIVATIVES **perceptional** adj.
– ORIGIN ME: from L. *perceptio(n-)*, from *percipere* (see **PERCEIVE**).

**perceptive** ● **adj.** having or showing acute insight.
– DERIVATIVES **perceptively** adv. **perceptiveness** n. **perceptivity** /-ˈtɪvɪti/ n.

**perceptual** ● **adj.** of or relating to the ability to interpret or become aware of something through the senses.
– DERIVATIVES **perceptually** adv.

**perch**[1] ● **n. 1** a thing on which a bird alights or roosts. **2** a high or narrow seat or resting place. ● **v. 1** alight, sit, or rest on a perch. **2** (**be perched**) (of a building) be situated above or on the edge of something. **3** (**perch someone/thing on**) set or balance someone or something on.
– ORIGIN ME: the noun from **PERCH**[3]; the verb from OFr. *percher*.

**perch**[2] ● **n.** (pl. same or **perches**) a freshwater fish with a high spiny dorsal fin, dark vertical bars on the body, and orange lower fins. [*Perca fluviatilis* (Europe), *P. flavescens* (**yellow perch**, N. America), and other species.] ➤used in names of similar or related fishes, e.g. **climbing perch**.
– ORIGIN ME: from OFr. *perche*, via L. from Gk *perkē*.

**perch**[3] ● **n.** historical, chiefly Brit. **1** a measure of length equal to a quarter of a chain or 5½ yards (approximately 5.029 m). **2** (also **square perch**) a measure of area equal to 160th of an acre or 30¼ square yards (approximately 25.29 sq. metres).
– ORIGIN ME (in the sense 'pole, stick'): from OFr. *perche*, from L. *pertica* 'measuring rod, pole'.

**perchance** ● **adv.** archaic or poetic/literary by some chance.
– ORIGIN ME: from OFr. *par cheance* 'by chance'.

**percheron** /ˈpəːʃ(ə)rɒn/ ● **n.** a powerful draught horse of a grey or black breed, originally from France.
– ORIGIN C19: from Fr., orig. bred in le *Perche*, the name of a district of northern France.

**perchloric acid** /pəˈklɔːrɪk/ ● **n.** Chemistry a fuming toxic liquid with powerful oxidizing properties. [$HClO_4$.]
– DERIVATIVES **perchlorate** n.

**perchloroethylene** /pəˌklɔːrəʊˈɛθɪliːn/ ● **n.** a toxic volatile solvent used as a dry-cleaning fluid. [$C_2Cl_4$.]

**perciform** /ˈpəːsɪfɔːm/ ● **adj.** Zoology relating to or denoting fish of a very large order (Perciformes) comprising the perches and their relatives.
– ORIGIN C19: from mod. L. *Perciformes*, from L. *perca* 'perch' + *forma* 'shape'.

**percipient** /pəˈsɪpɪənt/ ● **adj.** having a perceptive understanding of things. ● **n.** (especially in philosophy or with reference to psychic phenomena) a person who is able to perceive things.
– DERIVATIVES **percipience** n. **percipiently** adv.
– ORIGIN C17: from L. *percipient-*, *percipere* 'seize, understand'.

**percoid** /ˈpəːkɔɪd/ ● **n.** Zoology a fish of a large group (superfamily Percoidea) that includes the perches, basses, jacks, snappers, sea breams, etc.
– ORIGIN C19: from mod. L. *Percoïdes* (pl.), from L. *perca* 'perch'.

**percolate** ● **v. 1** filter through a porous surface or substance. **2** (of information etc.) spread gradually through a group of people. **3** (with reference to coffee) prepare or be prepared in a percolator. **4** US be or become full of lively activity or excitement.
– DERIVATIVES **percolated** adj. **percolation** n.
– ORIGIN C17: from L. *percolat-*, *percolare* 'strain through'.

**percolator** ● **n.** a machine for making coffee, consisting of a pot in which boiling water is circulated through a small chamber that holds the ground beans.

**per contra** /pəː ˈkɒntrə/ ● **adv.** on the other hand. ● **n.** the opposite side of an account or an assessment.
– ORIGIN C16: from Ital.

**percuss** /pəˈkʌs/ ● **v.** Medicine gently tap (a part of the body) as part of a diagnosis.
– ORIGIN C16: from L. *percuss-*, *percutere* 'strike through'.

**percussion** ● **n. 1** the action of playing a musical instrument by striking or shaking it. ➤[as modifier] denoting musical instruments played in this way. ➤percussion instruments forming a band or section of an orchestra. **2** the striking of one solid object with or against another with some degree of force. **3** Medicine the action of percussing a part of the body.
– DERIVATIVES **percussionist** n. **percussive** adj. **percussively** adv. **percussiveness** n.

**percussion cap** ● **n.** a small amount of explosive powder contained in metal or paper and exploded by striking.

**percussion drill** ● **n.** a hammer drill.

**percutaneous** /ˌpəːkjʊˈteɪnɪəs/ ● **adj.** Medicine made, done, or effected through the skin.
– DERIVATIVES **percutaneously** adv.
– ORIGIN C19: from L. *per cutem* 'through the skin' + **-ANEOUS**.

**per diem** /pəː ˈdiːɛm, ˈdʌɪɛm/ ● **adv. & adj.** for each day. ● **n.** an allowance or payment made for each day.
– ORIGIN C16: L.

**perdition** /pəˈdɪʃ(ə)n/ ● **n.** (in Christian theology) a state of eternal damnation into which a sinful and unpenitent person passes after death.
– ORIGIN ME: from OFr. *perdiciun*, from eccles. L. *perditio(n-)*, from L. *perdere* 'destroy'.

**perdurable** /pəˈdjʊərəb(ə)l/ ● **adj.** formal enduring continuously; permanent.
– DERIVATIVES **perdurability** n. **perdurably** adv.
– ORIGIN ME: via OFr. from late L. *perdurabilis*, from L. *perdurare* 'endure'.

**père** /pɛː/ ● **n.** used after a surname to distinguish a father from a son of the same name.
– ORIGIN Fr., 'father'.

**Père David's deer** ● **n.** a large deer with a red summer coat that turns dark grey in winter, and long antlers with backward pointing tines, now found only in captivity. [*Elaphurus davidianus*.]
– ORIGIN C19: named after the Fr. naturalist Father Armand *David*.

**peregrinate** /ˈpɛrɪgrɪˌneɪt/ ● **v.** archaic or humorous travel or wander from place to place.
– DERIVATIVES **peregrination** n. **peregrinator** n.
– ORIGIN C16 (earlier (ME) as *peregrination*): from L. *peregrinat-*, *peregrinari* 'travel abroad'.

**peregrine** /ˈpɛrɪgrɪn/ ● **n.** a powerful falcon that breeds chiefly on mountains and coastal cliffs. [*Falco peregrinus*.] ● **adj.** archaic foreign.
– ORIGIN ME: from L. *peregrinus* 'foreign'; the noun is a translation of the mod. L. taxonomic name, lit. 'pilgrim falcon', because falconers' birds were caught full-grown on migration, not taken from the nest.

**peremptory** /pəˈrɛm(p)t(ə)ri, ˈpɛrɪm-/ ● **adj. 1** insisting on immediate attention or obedience; brusque and imperious. **2** Law not open to appeal or challenge; final.
– DERIVATIVES **peremptorily** adv. **peremptoriness** n.
– ORIGIN ME: via Anglo-Norman Fr. from L. *peremptorius* 'deadly, decisive', from *perempt-*, *perimere* 'destroy, cut off'.

**peremptory challenge** ● **n.** Law a defendant's or lawyer's objection to a proposed juror, made without needing to give a reason.

**perennial** ● **adj.** **1** lasting through a year or several years. **2** (of a plant) living for several years. Compare with **ANNUAL**, **BIENNIAL**. **3** lasting for a long time; enduring or continually recurring. ➤ continually engaged in a specified activity: *a perennial student.* ● **n.** a perennial plant.
– DERIVATIVES **perennially** adv.
– ORIGIN C17 (in the sense 'remaining leafy throughout the year, evergreen'): from L. *perennis* 'lasting the year through' + **-IAL**.

**perestroika** /ˌpɛrɪˈstrɔɪkə/ ● **n.** (in the former Soviet Union) the policy or practice of reforming the economic and political system, practised in the 1980s under Mikhail Gorbachev.
– ORIGIN Russ., lit. 'restructuring'.

**perfect** ● **adj.** /ˈpəːfɪkt/ **1** having all the required elements, qualities, or characteristics. **2** free from any flaw; faultless. **3** complete; absolute: *it made perfect sense.* **4** Mathematics (of a number) equal to the sum of its positive divisors, e.g. the number 6, whose divisors (1, 2, 3) also add up to 6. **5** Grammar (of a tense) denoting a completed action or a state or habitual action which began in the past, formed in English with *have* or *has* and the past participle, as in *they have eaten.* **6** Botany (of a flower) having both stamens and carpels present and functional. **7** Botany denoting the stage or state of a fungus in which the sexually produced spores are formed. **8** Entomology (of an insect) fully adult and (typically) winged. ● **v.** /pəˈfɛkt/ **1** make perfect. **2** bring to completion. ● **n.** /ˈpəːfɪkt/ (**the perfect**) Grammar the perfect tense.
– DERIVATIVES **perfecter** n. **perfectibility** n. **perfectible** adj. **perfectly** adv. **perfectness** n.
– ORIGIN ME: from OFr. *perfet*, from L. *perfectus*, *perficere* 'complete'.

**perfecta** /pəˈfɛktə/ ● **n.** N. Amer. a bet in which the first two places in a race must be predicted in the correct order. Compare with **QUINELLA**.
– ORIGIN 1970s: from Latin Amer. Sp. *quiniela perfecta* 'perfect quinella'.

**perfect binding** ● **n.** a form of bookbinding in which the leaves are bound by gluing, after the back folds have been cut off, rather than sewing.

**perfect cadence** ● **n.** Music a cadence in which the chord of the dominant immediately precedes that of the tonic.

**perfect gas** ● **n.** another term for **IDEAL GAS**.

**perfection** ● **n.** **1** the action, process, or condition of perfecting or being perfect. **2** a perfect person or thing.

**perfectionism** ● **n.** **1** refusal to accept any standard short of perfection. **2** Philosophy a doctrine holding that religious, moral, social, or political perfection is attainable.
– DERIVATIVES **perfectionist** n. & adj. **perfectionistic** adj.

**perfective** Grammar ● **adj.** relating to or denoting an aspect of verbs in Slavic languages that expresses completed action. The opposite of **IMPERFECTIVE**. ● **n.** the perfective aspect, or a perfective form of a verb.

**perfecto** ● **n.** (pl. **-os**) a type of cigar that is thick in the centre and tapered at each end.
– ORIGIN C19: from Sp., lit. 'perfect'.

**perfect pitch** ● **n.** the ability to recognize the pitch of a note or produce any given note.

**perfect square** ● **n.** another term for **SQUARE NUMBER**.

**perfervid** /pəˈfəːvɪd/ ● **adj.** poetic/literary intense and impassioned.
– DERIVATIVES **perfervidly** adv.
– ORIGIN C19: from mod. L. *perfervidus*, from L. *per-* 'utterly' + *fervidus* 'glowing hot, fiery'.

**perfidy** /ˈpəːfɪdi/ ● **n.** poetic/literary deceitfulness; untrustworthiness.
– DERIVATIVES **perfidious** adj. **perfidiously** adv. **perfidiousness** n.
– ORIGIN C16: via Fr. from L. *perfidia*, from *perfidus* 'treacherous'.

**perfin** /ˈpəːfɪn/ ● **n.** Philately a postage stamp perforated with the initials or insignia of an organization.
– ORIGIN 1950s: from *perf(orated) in(itials)*.

**perfoliate** /pəˈfəʊlɪət/ ● **adj.** Botany (of a stalkless leaf or bract) extended at the base to encircle the node (so that the stem appears to pass through it). ➤ (of a plant) having such leaves.
– ORIGIN C17: from mod. L. *perfoliatus*, from L. *per-* 'through' + *foliatus* 'leaved'.

**perforate** ● **v.** /ˈpəːfəreɪt/ pierce and make a hole or holes in. ● **adj.** /ˈpəːf(ə)rət/ Biology & Medicine perforated.
– DERIVATIVES **perforated** adj. **perforation** n. **perforator** n.
– ORIGIN ME: from L. *perforat-*, *perforare* 'pierce through'.

**perforce** ● **adv.** formal necessarily; inevitably.
– ORIGIN ME: from OFr. *par force* 'by force'.

**perforin** /ˈpəːfərɪn/ ● **n.** Biochemistry a protein, released by killer cells of the immune system, which destroys targeted cells by creating lesions like pores in their membranes.
– ORIGIN 1980s: from **PERFORATE** + **-IN**[1].

**perform** ● **v.** **1** carry out, accomplish, or fulfil (an action, task, or function). **2** work, function, or do something to a specified standard: *the car performs well at low speeds.* **3** (of an investment) yield a profitable return. **4** present (a form of entertainment) to an audience.
– DERIVATIVES **performability** n. **performable** adj. **performer** n.
– ORIGIN ME: from Anglo-Norman Fr. *parfourmer*, alt. (by assoc. with *forme* 'form') of OFr. *parfournir*, from *par* 'through, to completion' + *fournir* 'furnish, provide'.

**performance** ● **n.** **1** an act of performing a play, concert, or other form of entertainment. **2** a person's rendering of a dramatic role, song, or piece of music. **3** informal a display of exaggerated behaviour; an elaborate fuss. **4** the action or process of performing a task or function. **5** the capabilities of a machine or product. **6** the extent to which an investment is profitable. **7** Linguistics an individual's actual use of a language, including hesitations and errors. Often contrasted with **COMPETENCE**.

**performance art** ● **n.** an art form that combines visual art with dramatic performance.
– DERIVATIVES **performance artist** n.

**performance bond** ● **n.** a bond issued by a bank or other financial institution, guaranteeing the fulfilment of a particular contract.

**performance poetry** ● **n.** a form of poetry that is performed as a dramatic monologue or exchange and frequently involves extemporization.
– DERIVATIVES **performance poet** n.

**performative** Linguistics & Philosophy ● **adj.** denoting a statement by means of which the speaker performs a particular act (e.g. *I apologize*). ● **n.** a performative verb, sentence, or utterance.

**performing arts** ● **pl. n.** forms of creative activity that are performed in front of an audience.

**perfume** /ˈpəːfjuːm/ ● **n.** **1** a fragrant liquid typically made from essential oils, used to impart a pleasant smell to one's body or clothes. **2** a pleasant smell. ● **v.** /also pəˈfjuːm/ **1** impart a pleasant smell to. **2** (usu. **be perfumed**) impregnate with perfume or a sweet-smelling ingredient. **3** apply perfume to.
– DERIVATIVES **perfumed** adj. **perfumy** adj.
– ORIGIN C16 (orig. denoting pleasant-smelling smoke from a substance used in fumigation): from Fr. *parfum* (n.), *parfumer* (v.), from obs. Ital. *parfumare*, lit. 'to smoke through'.

**perfumery** ● **n.** (pl. **-ies**) **1** the process of producing and selling perfumes. **2** a shop that sells perfumes.
– DERIVATIVES **perfumer** n.

**perfunctory** /pəˈfʌŋ(k)t(ə)ri/ ● **adj.** carried out with a minimum of effort or reflection.
– DERIVATIVES **perfunctorily** adv. **perfunctoriness** n.
– ORIGIN C16: from late L. *perfunctorius* 'careless', from L. *perfunct-*, *perfungi* 'have done with, discharge'.

**perfuse** ● **v.** **1** permeate or suffuse with a liquid, colour, quality, etc. **2** Medicine supply (an organ, tissue, or body) with a fluid, typically treated blood or a blood substitute, by circulating it through blood vessels or other natural channels.
– DERIVATIVES **perfusate** n. **perfusion** n. **perfusionist** n.

– ORIGIN ME: from L. *perfus-*, *perfundere* 'pour through'.

**pergola** /ˈpəːɡələ/ ● **n.** an arched structure forming a framework for climbing or trailing plants.
– ORIGIN C17: from Ital., from L. *pergula* 'projecting roof'.

**perhaps** ● **adv. 1** expressing uncertainty or possibility. **2** used when making a polite request or suggestion.
– ORIGIN C15: from **PER** + **HAP**.

**peri** /ˈpɪəri/ ● **n.** (pl. **peris**) (in Persian mythology) a genie or fairy.
– ORIGIN from Pers. *perī*.

**peri-** ● **prefix 1** round; about: *pericardium*. **2** Astronomy denoting the point nearest to a specified celestial body: *perihelion*. Compare with **APO-**.
– ORIGIN from Gk *peri* 'about, around'.

**perianth** /ˈpɛrɪanθ/ ● **n.** Botany the outer part of a flower, consisting of the calyx (sepals) and corolla (petals).
– ORIGIN C18: from Fr. *périanthe*, from mod. L. *perianthium*, from Gk *peri* 'around' + *anthos* 'flower'.

**periapsis** /ˌpɛrɪˈapsɪs/ ● **n.** (pl. **periapses** /-siːz/) Astronomy the point in the path of an orbiting body at which it is nearest to the body that it orbits.

**periapt** /ˈpɛrɪapt/ ● **n.** archaic an item worn as a charm or amulet.
– ORIGIN C16: from Fr. *périapte*, from Gk *periapton*, from *peri* 'around' + *haptein* 'fasten'.

**pericardium** /ˌpɛrɪˈkɑːdɪəm/ ● **n.** (pl. **pericardia** /-dɪə/) Anatomy the membrane enclosing the heart.
– DERIVATIVES **pericardial** adj. **pericarditis** n.
– ORIGIN ME: mod. L., from Gk *perikardion*, from *peri* 'around' + *kardia* 'heart'.

**pericarp** ● **n.** Botany the part of a fruit formed from the wall of the ripened ovary.
– ORIGIN C17: from Fr. *péricarpe*, from Gk *perikarpion* 'pod, shell', from *peri-* 'around' + *karpos* 'fruit'.

**perichondrium** /ˌpɛrɪˈkɒndrɪəm/ ● **n.** Anatomy the connective tissue that envelops cartilage where it is not at a joint.
– ORIGIN C18: mod. L., from **PERI-** + Gk *khondros* 'cartilage'.

**periclase** /ˈpɛrɪkleɪz, -s/ ● **n.** a colourless mineral consisting of magnesium oxide, occurring chiefly in marble and limestone.
– ORIGIN C19: from mod. L. *periclasia*, erroneously from Gk *peri* 'utterly' + *klasis* 'breaking' (because it cleaves perfectly).

**periclinal** /ˌpɛrɪˈklʌɪn(ə)l/ ● **adj.** Botany **1** (of a cell wall) parallel to the surface of the meristem. **2** (of cell division) taking place by the formation of periclinal walls.
– DERIVATIVES **periclinally** adv.
– ORIGIN C19: from Gk *periklinēs* 'sloping on all sides'.

**pericope** /pəˈrɪkəpi/ ● **n.** an extract from a text, especially a passage from the Bible.
– ORIGIN C17: via late L. from Gk *perikopē* 'section'.

**pericranium** ● **n.** Anatomy the periosteum enveloping the skull.
– ORIGIN ME: mod. L., from Gk *peri-* 'around' + *kranion* 'skull'.

**pericycle** ● **n.** Botany a thin layer of plant tissue between the endodermis and the phloem.
– DERIVATIVES **pericyclic** adj.
– ORIGIN C19: from Gk *perikuklos* 'spherical'.

**periderm** ● **n.** Botany the corky outer layer of a plant stem formed by the cambium or as a response to injury or infection.
– DERIVATIVES **peridermal** adj.
– ORIGIN C19: from **PERI-** + Gk *derma* 'skin'.

**peridium** /pɪˈrɪdɪəm/ ● **n.** (pl. **peridia** /-dɪə/) Botany the outer skin of a sporangium or other fruiting body of a fungus.
– ORIGIN C19: from Gk *pēridion*, lit. 'small wallet'.

**peridot** /ˈpɛrɪdɒt/ ● **n.** a green semi-precious variety of forsterite (olivine).
– ORIGIN C18: from Fr., from OFr. *peritot*, of unknown origin.

**peridotite** /ˈpɛrɪdɒtʌɪt/ ● **n.** Geology a dense, coarse-grained plutonic rock containing a large amount of olivine, believed to be the main constituent of the earth's mantle.
– DERIVATIVES **peridotitic** adj.

**perigee** /ˈpɛrɪdʒiː/ ● **n.** Astronomy the point in the orbit of the moon or a satellite at which it is nearest to the earth. The opposite of **APOGEE**.
– ORIGIN C16: from Fr. *périgée*, via mod. L. from Gk *perigeion* 'close round the earth'.

**periglacial** ● **adj.** Geology relating to or denoting an area adjacent to a glacier or ice sheet or otherwise subject to repeated freezing and thawing.

**perigynous** /pəˈrɪdʒɪnəs/ ● **adj.** Botany (of a plant or flower) having the stamens and other floral parts at the same level as the carpels. Compare with **EPIGYNOUS** and **HYPOGYNOUS**.
– DERIVATIVES **perigyny** n.

**perihelion** /ˌpɛrɪˈhiːlɪən/ ● **n.** (pl. **perihelia** /-lɪə/) Astronomy the point in the orbit of a planet, asteroid, or comet at which it is closest to the sun. The opposite of **APHELION**.
– ORIGIN C17: alt. of mod. L. *perihelium* (by substitution of the Gk inflection *-on*), from Gk *peri-* 'around' + *hēlios* 'sun'.

**peril** ● **n.** a situation of serious and immediate danger. ● **v.** (**perilled**, **perilling**; US **periled**, **periling**) archaic expose to danger.
– PHRASES **at one's peril** at one's own risk. **in** (or **at**) **peril of 1** very likely to suffer from. **2** at risk of losing or injuring: *they would be in peril of their life.*
– DERIVATIVES **perilous** adj. **perilously** adv. **perilousness** n.
– ORIGIN ME: from OFr., from L. *peric(u)lum* 'danger', from the base of *experiri* 'to try'.

**perilune** /ˈpɛrɪluːn/ ● **n.** the point at which a spacecraft in lunar orbit is closest to the moon. The opposite of **APOLUNE**.
– ORIGIN 1960s: from **PERI-** + L. *luna* 'moon', on the pattern of *perigee*.

**perilymph** ● **n.** Anatomy the fluid between the membraneous labyrinth of the ear and the bone which encloses it.
– DERIVATIVES **perilymphatic** adj.

**perimeter** ● **n. 1** the continuous line forming the boundary of a closed geometrical figure. **2** the outermost parts or boundary of an area or object. **3** Basketball an area away from the basket, beyond the reach of the defensive team. **4** an instrument for measuring the extent and characteristics of a person's field of vision.
– DERIVATIVES **perimetric** adj. **perimetry** n.
– ORIGIN ME: via L. from Gk *perimetros*, based on *peri-* 'around' + *metron* 'measure'.

**perimysium** /ˌpɛrɪˈmɪsɪəm/ ● **n.** Anatomy the sheath of connective tissue surrounding a bundle of muscle fibres.
– DERIVATIVES **perimysial** adj.
– ORIGIN C19: mod. L., from Gk *peri-* 'around' + *mus* 'muscle'.

**perinatal** ● **adj.** Medicine of or relating to the time immediately before and after a birth.
– DERIVATIVES **perinatally** adv. **perinatologist** n. **perinatology** n.

**per incuriam** /ˌpə(r) ɪnˈkjʊərɪam/ ● **adv.** Law through lack of due regard to the law or the facts.
– ORIGIN L., lit. 'through lack of care'.

**perineum** /ˌpɛrɪˈniːəm/ ● **n.** (pl. **perinea**) Anatomy the area between the anus and the scrotum or vulva.
– DERIVATIVES **perineal** adj.
– ORIGIN ME: from late L., from Gk *perinaion*.

**perineurium** /ˌpɛrɪˈnjʊərɪəm/ ● **n.** Anatomy the sheath of connective tissue surrounding a bundle of nerve fibres within a nerve.
– DERIVATIVES **perineurial** adj.
– ORIGIN C19: mod. L., from Gk *peri-* 'around' + *neuron* 'sinew'.

**period** ● **n. 1** a length or portion of time. **2** a portion of time characterized by the same prevalent features or conditions. **3** a major division of geological time that is a subdivision of an era and is itself subdivided into epochs. **4** each of the set divisions of the day in a school. **5** (also **menstrual period**) a monthly flow of blood and other material from the lining of the uterus, occurring in

women of child-bearing age when not pregnant. **6** chiefly N. Amer. a full stop. **7** Physics the interval of time between successive occurrences of the same state in an oscillatory or cyclic phenomenon. **8** Mathematics the interval between successive equal values of a periodic function. **9** Chemistry a set of elements occupying a horizontal row in the periodic table. **10** Astronomy the time taken by a celestial object to rotate about its axis, or to make one circuit of its orbit. **11** Rhetoric a complex sentence, especially one consisting of several clauses, constructed as part of a formal speech or oration. ● **adj.** belonging to or characteristic in style of a past historical time: *period furniture.*
– DERIVATIVES **periodization** (also **-isation**) n. **periodize** (also **-ise**) v.
– ORIGIN ME: from OFr. *periode*, via L. from Gk *periodos* 'orbit, recurrence, course'.

**periodic** /ˌpɪərɪˈɒdɪk/ ● **adj. 1** appearing or occurring at intervals. **2** Chemistry relating to the periodic table of the elements or the pattern of chemical properties which underlies it. **3** of or relating to a rhetorical period.
– DERIVATIVES **periodicity** n.

**periodic acid** /ˌpəːrʌɪˈɒdɪk/ ● **n.** Chemistry a hygroscopic solid acid with strong oxidizing properties.
– DERIVATIVES **periodate** /pəˈrʌɪədeɪt/ n.
– ORIGIN C19: from sense 2 of **PER-** + **IODIC ACID**.

**periodical** ● **adj.** occurring or appearing at intervals. ➤(of a magazine or newspaper) published at regular intervals. ● **n.** a periodical magazine or newspaper.
– DERIVATIVES **periodically** adv.

**periodic function** ● **n.** Mathematics a function returning to the same value at regular intervals.

**periodic table** ● **n.** Chemistry a table of the chemical elements arranged in order of atomic number, usually in rows, so that elements with similar atomic structure (and hence similar chemical properties) appear in vertical columns.

**periodontics** /ˌpɛrɪəˈdɒntɪks/ ● **pl. n.** [treated as sing.] the branch of dentistry concerned with the structures surrounding and supporting the teeth.
– DERIVATIVES **periodontal** adj. **periodontist** n.
– ORIGIN 1940s: from **PERI-** + Gk *odous*, *odont-* 'tooth' + **-ICS**.

**periodontitis** /ˌpɛrɪədɒnˈtʌɪtɪs/ ● **n.** Medicine inflammation of the tissue around the teeth.

**periodontology** /ˌpɛrɪədɒnˈtɒlədʒi/ ● **n.** another term for **PERIODONTICS**.

**period piece** ● **n.** an object or work that is set in or reminiscent of an earlier historical period.

**perioperative** ● **adj.** Medicine (of a process or treatment) occurring or performed at or around the time of an operation.

**periosteum** /ˌpɛrɪˈɒstɪəm/ ● **n.** (pl. **periostea** /-tɪə/) Anatomy a dense layer of vascular connective tissue enveloping the bones except at the surfaces of the joints.
– DERIVATIVES **periosteal** adj. **periostitis** n.
– ORIGIN C16: mod. L., from Gk *periosteon*, from *peri-* 'around' + *osteon* 'bone'.

**peripatetic** /ˌpɛrɪpəˈtɛtɪk/ ● **adj. 1** travelling from place to place. ➤working or based in a succession of places each for a short period. ➤(of a teacher) working in more than one school or college. **2** (**Peripatetic**) Aristotelian. [with ref. to Aristotle's practice of walking to and fro while teaching.] ● **n. 1** a peripatetic teacher. **2** (**Peripatetic**) an Aristotelian philosopher.
– DERIVATIVES **peripatetically** adv. **peripateticism** n.
– ORIGIN ME: from OFr. *peripatetique*, via L. from Gk *peripatētikos* 'walking up and down'.

**peripeteia** /ˌpɛrɪpɪˈtʌɪə, -ˈtiːə/ ● **n.** formal a sudden reversal of fortune or change in circumstances.
– ORIGIN C16: from Gk *peripeteia* 'sudden change', from *peri-* 'around' + the stem of *piptein* 'to fall'.

**peripheral** ● **adj. 1** of, relating to, or situated on the periphery. **2** marginal. **3** (of a device) able to be attached to and used with a computer, though not an integral part of it. **4** Anatomy near the surface of the body. ● **n.** Computing a peripheral device.
– DERIVATIVES **peripherality** n. **peripheralization** (also **-isation**) n. **peripheralize** (also **-ise**) v. **peripherally** adv.

**peripheral nervous system** ● **n.** Anatomy the nervous system outside the brain and spinal cord.

**periphery** /pəˈrɪf(ə)ri/ ● **n.** (pl. **-ies**) **1** the outer limits or edge of an area or object. **2** a marginal or secondary position, part, or aspect.
– ORIGIN C16: via late L. from Gk *periphereia* 'circumference'.

**periphrasis** /pəˈrɪfrəsɪs/ ● **n.** (pl. **periphrases** /-siːz/) **1** the use of indirect and circumlocutory speech or writing. **2** Grammar the use of separate words to express a grammatical relationship that is otherwise expressed by inflection, e.g. *did go* as opposed to *went.*
– DERIVATIVES **periphrastic** adj. **periphrastically** adv.
– ORIGIN C16: via L. from Gk, from *periphrazein*, from *peri-* 'around' + *phrazein* 'declare'.

**periphyton** /pəˈrɪfɪtɒn/ ● **n.** Ecology freshwater organisms attached to or clinging to plants and other objects projecting above the bottom sediments.
– DERIVATIVES **periphytic** adj.
– ORIGIN 1960s: from Gk *peri-* 'around' + *phuton* 'plant'.

**peripteral** /pəˈrɪpt(ə)r(ə)l/ ● **adj.** Architecture (of a building) having a single row of pillars on all sides in the style of the temples of ancient Greece.
– ORIGIN C19: from Gk *peripteron* (from *peri-* 'around' + *pteron* 'wing') + **-AL**.

**perique** /pɛˈriːk/ ● **n.** a strong dark tobacco from Louisiana.
– ORIGIN C19: Louisiana Fr., appar. from the nickname of Pierre Chenet, who first grew it.

**periscope** ● **n.** an apparatus consisting of a tube attached to a set of mirrors or prisms, by which an observer (typically in a submerged submarine or behind a high obstacle) can see things that are otherwise out of sight.
– DERIVATIVES **periscopic** adj. **periscopically** adv.

**perish** ● **v. 1** die, especially in large numbers. **2** suffer complete ruin or destruction. **3** rot or decay. **4** (**be perished**) Brit. be suffering from extreme cold.
– PHRASES **perish the thought** informal may the thought or idea prove unfounded.
– DERIVATIVES **perishable** adj.
– ORIGIN ME: from OFr. *periss-*, lengthened stem of *perir*, from L. *perire* 'pass away'.

**perishable** ● **adj. 1** (of food) likely to rot quickly. **2** having a brief life or significance: *ballet is the most perishable of arts.* ● **n.** (**perishables**) things, especially foodstuffs, likely to rot quickly.
– DERIVATIVES **perishability** n.

**perisher** ● **n.** Brit. informal a mischievous or awkward person, especially a child.

**perishing** ● **adj.** Brit. informal **1** extremely cold. **2** dated used for emphasis or to express annoyance.
– DERIVATIVES **perishingly** adv.

**perisperm** ● **n.** Botany (in some seeds) a mass of nutritive material outside the embryo sac.
– ORIGIN C19: from **PERI-** + Gk *sperma* 'seed'.

**Perissodactyla** /ˌpərɪsə(ʊ)ˈdaktɪlə/ ● **pl. n.** Zoology an order of mammals that comprises the horses, rhinoceroses, and tapirs (the odd-toed ungulates).
– DERIVATIVES **perissodactyl** n. & adj.
– ORIGIN mod. L., from Gk *perissos* 'uneven' + *daktulos* 'finger, toe'.

**peristalsis** /ˌpɛrɪˈstalsɪs/ ● **n.** Physiology the involuntary constriction and relaxation of the muscles of the intestine or another canal, creating wave-like movements which push the contents of the canal forward.
– DERIVATIVES **peristaltic** adj. **peristaltically** adv.
– ORIGIN C19: mod. L., from Gk *peristallein* 'wrap around'.

**peristaltic pump** ● **n.** a mechanical pump in which pressure is provided by the movement of a constriction along a tube, similar to biological peristalsis.

**peristome** /ˈpɛrɪstəʊm/ ● **n. 1** Zoology the parts surrounding the mouth of various invertebrates. **2** Botany a fringe of small projections around the mouth of a capsule in mosses and certain fungi.
– ORIGIN C18: from mod. L. *peristoma*, from Gk *peri-* 'around' + *stoma* 'mouth'.

**peristyle** ● n. Architecture a row of columns surrounding a space within a building such as a court or internal garden or edging a veranda or porch.
– ORIGIN C17: from Fr. *péristyle*, from L. *peristylum*, from Gk *peristulon*, from *peri-* 'around' + *stulos* 'pillar'.

**peritoneum** /ˌpɛrɪtəˈniːəm/ ● n. (pl. **peritoneums** or **peritonea** /-ˈniːə/) Anatomy the serous membrane lining the cavity of the abdomen and covering the abdominal organs.
– DERIVATIVES **peritoneal** adj.
– ORIGIN ME: via late L. from Gk *peritonaion*, from *peritonos* 'stretched round'.

**peritonitis** /ˌpɛrɪtəˈnʌɪtɪs/ ● n. Medicine inflammation of the peritoneum, typically caused by bacterial infection either via the blood or after rupture of an abdominal organ.

**peri-track** ● n. another term for **TAXIWAY**.
– ORIGIN contr. of *perimeter track*.

**periwig** ● n. a highly styled wig worn formerly as a fashionable headdress by both women and men and retained by judges and barristers as part of their professional dress.
– DERIVATIVES **periwigged** adj.
– ORIGIN C16: alt. of **PERUKE**, with *-wi-* representing the Fr. *-u-* sound.

**periwinkle**[1] ● n. a plant with flat five-petalled flowers and glossy leaves, some kinds of which contain alkaloids used in medicine. [Genera *Vinca* and *Catharanthus*.]
– ORIGIN OE *peruince*, from late L. *pervinca*, reinforced in ME by Anglo-Norman Fr. *pervenke*.

**periwinkle**[2] ● n. another term for **WINKLE**.
– ORIGIN C16: of unknown origin.

**perjure** ● v. (**perjure oneself**) Law commit perjury.
– DERIVATIVES **perjurer** n.
– ORIGIN ME (as *perjured* in the sense 'guilty of perjury'): from OFr. *parjurer*, from L. *perjurare* 'swear falsely'.

**perjured** ● adj. Law (of evidence) involving wilfully told untruths. ➤ guilty of perjury.

**perjury** /ˈpəːdʒ(ə)ri/ ● n. (pl. **-ies**) Law the offence of wilfully telling an untruth in a court after having taken an oath or affirmation.
– DERIVATIVES **perjurious** /-ˈdʒʊərɪəs/ adj.

**perk**[1] ● v. (**perk someone up** or **perk up**) make or become more cheerful or lively. ● adj. dialect perky; pert.
– ORIGIN ME (in the senses 'perch' and 'be lively'): perh. from an OFr. dial. var. of *percher* 'to perch'.

**perk**[2] ● n. informal a benefit to which one is entitled as an employee or shareholder of a company. ➤ an advantage or benefit following from a particular situation.
– ORIGIN C19: abbrev. of **PERQUISITE**.

**perk**[3] ● v. informal (with reference to coffee) percolate.

**perky** ● adj. (**-ier**, **-iest**) **1** cheerful and lively. **2** cheeky.
– DERIVATIVES **perkily** adv. **perkiness** n.

**perlé** /pəːˈleɪ/ ● n. a semi-sweet, slightly sparkling wine produced in South Africa.
– ORIGIN Fr., lit. 'beaded', perh. from an abbrev. of Ger. *Perlwein*, denoting a slightly sparkling wine.

**perlite** /ˈpəːlʌɪt/ ● n. a form of obsidian consisting of glassy globules, used as insulation or in plant growth media.
– ORIGIN C19: from Fr., from *perle* 'pearl'.

**perlocution** ● n. Philosophy & Linguistics an act of speaking or writing which has an action as its aim but which in itself does not effect or constitute the action, for example persuading or convincing.
– DERIVATIVES **perlocutionary** adj.

**perm**[1] ● n. (also **permanent wave**) a method of setting the hair in waves or curls and treating it with chemicals so that the style lasts for several months. ● v. treat (the hair) in such a way.
– ORIGIN 1920s: abbrev. of **PERMANENT**.

**perm**[2] Brit. informal ● n. a permutation, especially a selection of a specified number of matches in a football pool. ● v. make a selection of (so many) from a larger number.
– ORIGIN 1950s: abbrev. of **PERMUTATION**.

**permaculture** ● n. the development of agricultural ecosystems intended to be sustainable and self-sufficient.
– ORIGIN 1970s: blend of **PERMANENT** and **AGRICULTURE**.

**permafrost** ● n. a thick subsurface layer of soil that remains below freezing point throughout the year.
– ORIGIN 1940s: from **PERMANENT** + **FROST**.

**permalloy** /ˈpəːməlɔɪ/ ● n. an alloy of nickel and iron that is easily magnetized and demagnetized, used in electrical equipment.
– ORIGIN 1920s: from **PERMEABLE** + **ALLOY**.

**permanent** ● adj. lasting or remaining unchanged indefinitely, or intended to be so; not temporary. ● n. N. Amer. a perm for the hair.
– DERIVATIVES **permanence** n. **permanency** n. **permanentize** (also **-ise**) v. (rare). **permanently** adv.
– ORIGIN ME: from L. *permanent-* 'remaining to the end' (perh. via OFr.), from *per-* 'through' + *manere* 'remain'.

**permanent hardness** ● n. the presence in water of mineral salts (chiefly calcium sulphate) that are not removed by boiling.

**permanent magnet** ● n. a magnet that retains its magnetic properties in the absence of an inducing field or current.

**permanent set** ● n. an irreversible deformation that remains in a structure or material after it has been subjected to stress.

**permanent tooth** ● n. a tooth in a mammal that replaces a temporary milk tooth and lasts for most of the mammal's life.

**Permanent Undersecretary** (also **Permanent Secretary**) ● n. (in the UK) a senior civil servant who is a permanent adviser to a Secretary of State.

**permanent wave** ● n. see **PERM**[1].

**permanent way** ● n. Brit. the finished roadbed of a railway together with the track and other permanent equipment.

**permanganate** /pəˈmaŋɡənət, -eɪt/ ● n. Chemistry a salt containing the anion $MnO_4^-$, typically deep purplish-red and with strong oxidizing properties.

**permeability** ● n. **1** the state or quality of being permeable. **2** Physics a quantity measuring the influence of a substance on the magnetic flux in the region it occupies.

**permeable** ● adj. (of a material or membrane) allowing liquids or gases to pass through it.
– DERIVATIVES **permeabilization** (also **-isation**) n. **permeabilize** (also **-ise**) v.
– ORIGIN ME: from L. *permeabilis*, from *permeare* (see **PERMEATE**).

**permeance** /ˈpəːmɪəns/ ● n. Physics the property of allowing the passage of lines of magnetic flux.

**permeate** ● v. spread throughout; pervade.
– DERIVATIVES **permeation** n. **permeator** n.
– ORIGIN C17: from L. *permeat-*, *permeare* 'pass through'.

**permethrin** /pəˈmiːθrɪn/ ● n. a synthetic insecticide of the pyrethroid class, used chiefly against disease-carrying insects.
– ORIGIN 1970s: from sense 2 of **PER-** + *(res)methrin*, denoting a synthetic pyrethroid.

**Permian** /ˈpəːmɪən/ ● adj. Geology relating to or denoting the last period of the Palaeozoic era (between the Carboniferous and Triassic periods, about 290 to 245 million years ago), a time when reptiles proliferated and many marine animals became extinct.
– ORIGIN C16: from *Perm*, a Russ. province with extensive deposits from this period.

**per mille** /pəː ˈmɪleɪ, ˈmɪli/ (also **per mil** /mɪl/) ● adv. by a specified amount in or for every thousand.
– ORIGIN C17: from L.

**permissible** ● adj. allowable; permitted.
– DERIVATIVES **permissibility** n. **permissibly** adv.

**permission** ● n. authorization.
– ORIGIN ME: from L. *permissio(n-)*, from *permittere* (see **PERMIT**[1]).

**permissive** ● adj. **1** allowing or characterized by freedom of behaviour. **2** Law allowed but not obligatory; optional. ➤ denoting a path available for public use by the landowner's consent, not as a legal right of way.
– DERIVATIVES **permissively** adv. **permissiveness** n.

**permit**[1] ● v. /pəˈmɪt/ (**permitted**, **permitting**) **1** give permission to (someone) or for (something). **2** make possible. **3** (**permit of**) formal allow for; admit of. ● n. /ˈpəːmɪt/ an official document giving permission to do something.
– DERIVATIVES **permittee** n. **permitter** n.
– ORIGIN ME: from L. *permittere*, from *per-* 'through' + *mittere* 'send, let go'.

**permit**[2] /ˈpəːmɪt/ ● n. a deep-bodied fish of the jack family, found in warm waters of the western Atlantic and Caribbean and caught for food and sport. [*Trachinotus falcatus*.]
– ORIGIN alt. of Sp. *palometa* 'little dove'.

**permittivity** /ˌpəːmɪˈtɪvɪti/ ● n. Physics the ability of a substance to store electrical energy in an electric field.

**permutate** /ˈpəːmjʊteɪt/ ● v. change the order or arrangement of.
– ORIGIN C19: regarded as a back-form. from **PERMUTATION**.

**permutation** ● n. **1** a way, especially one of several possible variations, in which a set or number of things can be ordered or arranged. **2** Mathematics the action of changing the arrangement of a set of items. **3** Brit. a selection of a specified number of matches in a football pool.
– DERIVATIVES **permutational** adj.
– ORIGIN ME (in the sense 'exchange, barter'): via OFr. from L. *permutatio(n-)*, from *permutare* (see **PERMUTE**).

**permute** ● v. submit to a process of alteration, rearrangement, or permutation.
– ORIGIN ME: from L. *permutare* 'change completely'.

**pernambuco** ● n. the hard reddish wood of a Brazilian tree (*Caesalpinia echinata*), used for making violin bows and as a source of red dye.
– ORIGIN C16: from the name of the Brazilian state *Pernambuco*.

**pernicious** /pəˈnɪʃəs/ ● adj. having a harmful effect, especially in a gradual or subtle way.
– DERIVATIVES **perniciously** adv. **perniciousness** n.
– ORIGIN ME: from L. *perniciosus* 'destructive', from *pernicies* 'ruin', based on *nex*, *nec-* 'death'.

**pernicious anaemia** ● n. a deficiency in the production of red blood cells through a lack of vitamin $B_{12}$.

**pernickety** ● adj. informal, chiefly Brit. **1** fussy. **2** requiring a precise or careful approach.
– ORIGIN C19 (orig. Scots): of unknown origin.

**pernoctate** /ˈpəːnɒkteɪt, pəˈnɒkteɪt/ ● v. formal pass the night somewhere.
– DERIVATIVES **pernoctation** n.
– ORIGIN C17: from L. *pernoctat-*, *pernoctare* 'spend the night'.

**Pernod** /ˈpəːnəʊ/ ● n. trademark an aniseed-flavoured aperitif.
– ORIGIN named after the manufacturing firm *Pernod Fils*.

**peroneal** /ˌpɛrəˈniːəl/ ● adj. Anatomy relating to or situated in the outer side of the calf of the leg.
– ORIGIN C19: from mod. L. *peronaeus* 'peroneal muscle' (based on Gk *peronē* 'pin, fibula') + **-AL**.

**Peronist** /ˈpɛrənɪst/ ● adj. of or relating to the activities and social reforms of the Argentinian statesman Juan Domingo Péron (1895–1974). ● n. a supporter of Péron.

**perorate** /ˈpɛrəreɪt/ ● v. formal **1** speak at length. **2** sum up and conclude a speech.
– ORIGIN C17: from L. *perorat-*, *perorare* 'speak at length'.

**peroration** ● n. the concluding part of a speech; the summing up.

**perovskite** /pəˈrɒfskʌɪt/ ● n. a yellow, brown, or black mineral consisting largely of calcium titanate, with a crystal structure typical of many minerals and ceramics.
– ORIGIN C19: from the name of the Russ. mineralogist L. A. *Perovsky* + **-ITE**[1].

**peroxidase** /pəˈrɒksɪdeɪz/ ● n. Biochemistry an enzyme that catalyses the oxidation of a particular substrate by hydrogen peroxide.

**peroxide** ● n. **1** Chemistry a compound containing two oxygen atoms bonded together in its molecule or as the anion $O_2^{2-}$. **2** hydrogen peroxide, especially as used as a bleach for the hair. ● v. bleach (hair) with peroxide.
– ORIGIN C19: from sense 2 of **PER-** + **OXIDE**.

**perp** ● n. N. Amer. informal the perpetrator of a crime.

**perpend** /ˈpəːpɛnd/ ● n. a vertical layer of mortar between two bricks.

**perpendicular** /ˌpəːp(ə)nˈdɪkjʊlə/ ● adj. **1** at an angle of 90° to a given line, plane, or surface. **2** at an angle of 90° to the ground; vertical. **3** (**Perpendicular**) denoting the latest stage of English Gothic church architecture, prevalent from the late 14th to mid 16th centuries, characterized by broad arches and elaborate fan vaulting. ● n. a perpendicular line.
– DERIVATIVES **perpendicularity** n. **perpendicularly** adv.
– ORIGIN ME: via OFr. from L. *perpendicularis*, from *perpendiculum* 'plumb line'.

**perpetrate** /ˈpəːpɪtreɪt/ ● v. carry out or commit (a harmful, illegal, or immoral action).
– DERIVATIVES **perpetration** n. **perpetrator** n.
– ORIGIN C16: from L. *perpetrat-*, *perpetrare* 'perform'; in Engl. the verb was first used in the statutes referring to crime, hence the negative assoc.

**perpetual** /pəˈpɛtʃʊəl, -tjʊəl/ ● adj. **1** never ending or changing. ➤ denoting or having a position or trophy held for life rather than a limited period. ➤ (of an investment) having no fixed maturity date. **2** occurring repeatedly. **3** (of a plant) blooming or fruiting several times in one season.
– DERIVATIVES **perpetually** adv.
– ORIGIN ME: from OFr. *perpetuel*, from L. *perpetualis*, from *perpetuus* 'continuing throughout'.

**perpetual calendar** ● n. a calendar in which the day, the month, and the date are adjusted independently to show any combination of the three.

**perpetual check** ● n. Chess the situation of play when a draw is obtained by repeated checking of the king.

**perpetual motion** ● n. the motion of a hypothetical machine which, once activated, would run forever unless subject to an external force or to wear.

**perpetual spinach** ● n. another term for **SPINACH BEET**.

**perpetuate** /pəˈpɛtʃʊeɪt, -tjʊ-/ ● v. cause to continue indefinitely.
– DERIVATIVES **perpetuance** n. **perpetuation** n. **perpetuator** n.
– ORIGIN C16: from L. *perpetuat-*, *perpetuare* 'make permanent', from *perpetuus* (see **PERPETUAL**).

**perpetuity** ● n. (pl. **-ies**) **1** the state or quality of lasting forever. **2** a bond or other security with no fixed maturity date. **3** Law a restriction making an estate inalienable perpetually or for a period beyond certain limits fixed by law.

**perpetuum mobile** /pəːˌpɛtjʊəm ˈməʊbɪleɪ, ˈməʊbɪli/ ● n. **1** another term for **PERPETUAL MOTION**. **2** Music another term for **MOTO PERPETUO**.
– ORIGIN L., lit. 'continuously moving (thing)', on the pattern of *primum mobile*.

**perplex** ● v. cause to feel baffled.
– DERIVATIVES **perplexed** adj. **perplexedly** adv. **perplexing** adj. **perplexingly** adv. **perplexity** n.
– ORIGIN C15: from the obs. adj. *perplex* 'bewildered', from L. *perplexus* 'entangled'.

**per pro.** /pəː ˈprəʊ/ ● abbrev. per procurationem (used when signing a letter on someone else's behalf); now usually abbreviated to **pp**.
– ORIGIN from L.

**perquisite** /ˈpəːkwɪzɪt/ ● n. **1** formal a special right or privilege enjoyed as a result of one's position. **2** historical a thing which has served its primary use and to which a subordinate or employee has a customary right.
– ORIGIN ME: from med. L. *perquisitum* 'acquisition', from L. *perquirere* 'search diligently for'.

**perron** /ˈpɛrən/ ● n. Architecture an exterior set of steps and a platform at the main entrance to a large building such as a church or mansion.
– ORIGIN ME: from OFr., lit. 'large stone', from L. *petra* 'stone'.

**perry** ● n. (pl. **-ies**) an alcoholic drink made from the fermented juice of pears.

– ORIGIN ME: from OFr. *pere*, from an alt. of L. *pirum* 'pear'.

**per se** /pəː 'seɪ/ ● **adv.** by or in itself or themselves.
– ORIGIN from L.

**persecute** ● **v. 1** subject to prolonged hostility and ill-treatment. **2** persistently harass or annoy.
– DERIVATIVES **persecution** n. **persecutor** n. **persecutory** adj.
– ORIGIN ME: from OFr. *persecuter*, from L. *persecut-*, *persequi* 'follow with hostility'.

**persecution complex** ● **n.** an irrational and obsessive feeling that one is the object of collective hostility or ill-treatment on the part of others.

**perseverate** /pə'sɛvəreɪt/ ● **v.** Psychology repeat or prolong an action, thought, or utterance after the stimulus that prompted it has ceased.
– DERIVATIVES **perseveration** n.
– ORIGIN C20: from L. *perseverat-* 'strictly abided by', from *perseverare* (see **PERSEVERE**).

**persevere** ● **v.** continue in a course of action in spite of difficulty or with little or no indication of success.
– DERIVATIVES **perseverance** n. **persevering** adj. **perseveringly** adv.
– ORIGIN ME: from OFr. *perseverer*, from L. *perseverare* 'abide by strictly', from *perseverus* 'very strict'.

**Persian** ● **n. 1** a native or national of ancient or modern Persia (or Iran), or a person of Persian descent. **2** the language of modern Iran, an Indo-European language written in Arabic script. ➤an earlier form of this language spoken in ancient or medieval Persia. **3** a long-haired domestic cat of a breed originating in Persia, having a broad round head and stocky body. ● **adj.** of or relating to ancient Persia or modern Iran or its people or language.

**Persian blue** ● **n.** a shade of bright pale blue.

**Persian carpet** ● **n.** a carpet or rug woven in Iran in a traditional design incorporating stylized symbolic imagery, or made elsewhere in such a style.

**Persian lamb** ● **n.** the silky, tightly curled fleece of the karakul, used to make clothing.

**persiflage** /'pəːsɪflɑːʒ/ ● **n.** formal light mockery or banter.
– ORIGIN C18: from Fr. *persifler* 'to banter'.

**persimmon** /pə'sɪmən/ ● **n. 1** an edible fruit resembling a large tomato, with very sweet flesh. **2** the tree which yields this fruit. [*Diospyros virginiana* (America) and *D. kaki* (Japan).]
– ORIGIN C17: alt. of Algonquian *pessemmins*.

**persist** ● **v. 1** continue firmly or obstinately in an opinion or a course of action in spite of difficulty or opposition. **2** continue to exist.
– ORIGIN C16: from L. *persistere*, from *per-* 'through, steadfastly' + *sistere* 'to stand'.

**persistent** ● **adj. 1** persisting or having a tendency to persist. **2** continuing or recurring; prolonged. **3** Botany & Zoology (of a part of an animal or plant, such as a horn, leaf, etc.) remaining attached instead of falling off in the normal manner.
– DERIVATIVES **persistence** n. **persistency** n. **persistently** adv.

**persistent vegetative state** ● **n.** a condition in which a patient is completely unresponsive to stimuli and displays no sign of higher brain function, being kept alive only by medical intervention.

**persnickety** ● **adj.** North American term for **PERNICKETY**.

**person** ● **n.** (pl. **people** (in most general contexts) or **persons** (chiefly in official and formal contexts)) **1** a human being regarded as an individual. **2** an individual characterized by a preference or liking for a specified thing: *she's not a cat person.* **3** an individual's body: *concealed on his person.* **4** a character in a play or story. **5** Grammar a category used in the classification of pronouns, possessive determiners, and verb forms, according to whether they indicate the speaker (**first person**), the addressee (**second person**), or a third party (**third person**). **6** Christian Theology each of the three modes of being of God, namely the Father, the Son, and the Holy Ghost.
– PHRASES **in person** with the personal presence or action of the individual specified.
– ORIGIN ME: from OFr. *persone*, from L. *persona* 'actor's mask, character in a play', later 'human being'.

**-person** ● **comb. form** used as a neutral alternative to *-man* in nouns denoting professional status, a position of authority, etc.: *salesperson.*

**persona** /pə'səʊnə, pəː-/ ● **n.** (pl. **personas** or **personae** /-niː/) **1** the aspect of a person's character that is presented to or perceived by others. Compare with **ANIMA**. **2** a role or character adopted by an author or actor.
– ORIGIN C20: L., lit. 'mask, character played by an actor'.

**personable** ● **adj.** having a pleasant appearance and manner.
– DERIVATIVES **personableness** n. **personably** adv.

**personage** ● **n.** a person (expressing their importance or elevated status).
– ORIGIN ME: from OFr., reinforced by med. L. *personagium* 'effigy'.

**persona grata** /pə,səʊnə 'grɑːtə, pəː-/ ● **n.** (pl. **personae gratae** /-niː, -tiː/) a person who is acceptable to others.
– ORIGIN L., from *persona* (see **PERSONA**) + *grata*, fem. of *gratus* 'pleasing'.

**personal** ● **adj. 1** of, affecting, or belonging to a particular person. **2** involving the presence or action of a particular individual. **3** of or concerning a person's private rather than professional life. **4** making inappropriate or offensive reference to a person's character or appearance: *personal remarks.* **5** of or relating to a person's body: *personal hygiene.* **6** Grammar of or denoting one of the three persons. **7** existing as a self-aware entity, not as an abstraction or an impersonal force: *a personal God.* ● **n.** (**personals**) chiefly N. Amer. advertisements or messages in the personal column of a newspaper.
– DERIVATIVES **personally** adv.

**personal action** ● **n.** Law an action brought for compensation or damages for loss of a thing from the person responsible, rather than for recovery of the thing itself.

**personal ad** ● **n.** informal an advertisement or message placed in the personal column of a newspaper.

**personal assistant** ● **n.** a secretary or administrative assistant working for one particular person.

**personal column** ● **n.** a section of a newspaper devoted to private advertisements or messages.

**personal computer** ● **n.** a microcomputer designed for use by one person at a time.

**personal equity plan** ● **n.** (in the UK) an investment scheme whereby personal investors may invest a limited sum each year in shares or unit trusts in British companies without liability for tax on dividends or capital gains.

**personal estate** ● **n.** Law another term for **PERSONAL PROPERTY**.

**personal identification number** (abbrev.: **PIN**) ● **n.** a number allocated to an individual and used to validate electronic transactions.

**personalism** ● **n. 1** the quality of being personal; subjectivity. **2** allegiance to a particular political leader, rather than to a party or ideology.
– DERIVATIVES **personalist** n. **personalistic** adj.

**personality** ● **n.** (pl. **-ies**) **1** the combination of characteristics or qualities that form an individual's distinctive character. **2** the qualities that make someone interesting or popular. **3** a celebrity.

**personality disorder** ● **n.** Psychiatry a deeply ingrained and maladaptive pattern of behaviour, typically causing long-term difficulties in social relationships.

**personalize** (also **-ise**) ● **v. 1** design or produce (something) to meet someone's individual requirements. **2** make (something) identifiable as belonging to a particular person. **3** cause (an issue or argument) to become concerned with personalities or feelings rather than with general or abstract matters. **4** personify.
– DERIVATIVES **personalization** n.

**personal organizer** ● **n.** a loose-leaf notebook consisting of separate sections including a diary and address book. ➤a hand-held microcomputer serving the same purpose.

**personal pension** ● **n.** a pension scheme that is independent of the contributor's employer.

**personal pronoun** ● **n.** each of the pronouns in English (*I, you, he, she, it, we, they, me, him, her, us,* and *them*) comprising a set that shows contrasts of person, gender, number, and case.

**personal property** ● **n.** Law all of someone's property except land and those interests in land that pass to their heirs. Compare with **REAL PROPERTY**.

**personal stereo** ● **n.** a small portable audio cassette or compact disc player, used with lightweight headphones.

**personalty** /ˈpəːs(ə)n(ə)lti/ ● **n.** Law a person's personal property. Compare with **REALTY**.
– ORIGIN C16 (in the legal phr. *in the personalty* 'for damages'): from Anglo-Norman Fr. *personaltie*, from med. L. *personalitas*, from L. *personalis* 'of a person', from *persona* (see **PERSON**).

**persona non grata** ● **n.** (pl. **personae non gratae**) an unacceptable or unwelcome person.
– ORIGIN L., from *persona* (see **PERSONA**) + *non* 'not' + *grata*, fem. of *gratus* 'pleasing'.

**personate** ● **v.** formal play the part of or pretend to be.
– DERIVATIVES **personation** n. **personator** n.

**personify** ● **v.** (**-ies**, **-ied**) **1** represent (a quality or concept) by a figure in human form. **2** (usu. **be personified**) attribute a personal nature or human characteristics to. **3** represent or embody (a quality or concept) in a physical form.
– DERIVATIVES **personification** n. **personifier** n.

**personnel** ● **pl. n.** people employed in an organization or engaged in an organized undertaking.
– ORIGIN C19: from Fr. (adj. used as n.).

**personnel carrier** ● **n.** an armoured vehicle for transporting troops.

**person of colour** ● **n.** a non-white person.

**perspective** ● **n. 1** the art of representing three-dimensional objects on a two-dimensional surface so as to convey the impression of height, width, depth, and relative distance. **2** a view or prospect. **3** a particular way of regarding something. **4** understanding of the relative importance of things: *we must keep a sense of perspective about what he's done.* **5** an apparent spatial distribution in perceived sound.
– DERIVATIVES **perspectival** adj.
– ORIGIN ME (in the sense 'optics'): from med. L. *perspectiva* (*ars*) '(science of) optics', from *perspect-*, *perspicere* 'look at closely'.

**perspectivism** ● **n. 1** Philosophy the theory that knowledge of a subject is inevitably partial and limited by the individual perspective from which it is viewed. See also **RELATIVISM**. **2** the practice of regarding and analysing a situation or work of art from different points of view.
– DERIVATIVES **perspectivist** n.

**perspex** ● **n.** trademark a tough transparent plastic made of an acrylic resin, used as a substitute for glass.
– ORIGIN 1930s: formed irregularly from L. *perspicere* 'look through'.

**perspicacious** /ˌpəːspɪˈkeɪʃəs/ ● **adj.** having a ready insight into and understanding of things.
– DERIVATIVES **perspicaciously** adv. **perspicacity** n.
– ORIGIN C17: from L. *perspicax*, *perspicac-* 'seeing clearly' + **-ACIOUS**.

**perspicuous** /pəˈspɪkjʊəs/ ● **adj. 1** (of an account or representation) clearly expressed and easily understood; lucid. **2** (of a person) expressing things clearly.
– DERIVATIVES **perspicuity** n. **perspicuously** adv.
– ORIGIN C15 (in the sense 'transparent'): from L. *perspicuus* 'transparent, clear' + **-OUS**.

**perspire** ● **v.** give out sweat through the pores of the skin as a result of heat, physical exertion, or stress.
– DERIVATIVES **perspiration** n. **perspiratory** adj.
– ORIGIN C17: from Fr. *perspirer*, from L. *perspirare*, from *per-* 'through' + *spirare* 'breathe'.

**persuade** ● **v. 1** cause to do something through reasoning or argument. **2** cause to believe something. **3** (of a situation or event) provide a sound reason for (someone) to do something.
– DERIVATIVES **persuadability** n. **persuadable** adj. **persuader** n. **persuasible** adj.
– ORIGIN C15: from L. *persuadere*, from *per-* 'through, to completion' + *suadere* 'advise'.

**persuasion** ● **n. 1** the process of persuading or of being persuaded. **2** a belief or set of beliefs. **3** a group or sect holding a particular belief.

**persuasive** ● **adj. 1** good at persuading someone to do or believe something. **2** providing sound reasoning or argument.
– DERIVATIVES **persuasively** adv. **persuasiveness** n.

**pert** ● **adj. 1** attractively lively or cheeky. **2** (of a bodily feature or garment) neat and jaunty.
– DERIVATIVES **pertly** adv. **pertness** n.
– ORIGIN ME (in the sense 'manifest'): from OFr. *apert*, from L. *apertus* 'opened', past part. of *aperire*, reinforced by OFr. *aspert*, from L. *expertus* (see **EXPERT**).

**pertain** ● **v. 1** be appropriate, related, or applicable. **2** chiefly Law belong to something as a part, appendage, or accessory. **3** be in effect or existence in a specified place or at a specified time: *none of these circumstances pertained during the Jurassic.*
– ORIGIN ME: from OFr. *partenir*, from L. *pertinere* 'extend to, have reference to'.

**pertinacious** /ˌpəːtɪˈneɪʃəs/ ● **adj.** formal stubborn; persistent.
– DERIVATIVES **pertinaciously** adv. **pertinaciousness** n. **pertinacity** n.
– ORIGIN C17: from L. *pertinax*, *pertinac-* 'holding fast' + **-OUS**.

**pertinent** ● **adj.** relevant; appropriate.
– DERIVATIVES **pertinence** n. **pertinency** n. **pertinently** adv.
– ORIGIN ME: from OFr., or from L. *pertinent-*, *pertinere* (see **PERTAIN**).

**perturb** ● **v. 1** (usu. **be perturbed**) make anxious or unsettled. **2** alter the normal or regular state or path of (a system, moving object, or process).
– DERIVATIVES **perturbable** adj. **perturbative** /pəˈtəːbətɪv, ˈpəːtəbeɪtɪv/ adj. **perturbing** adj. **perturbingly** adv.
– ORIGIN ME: from OFr. *pertourber*, from L. *perturbare*, from *per-* 'completely' + *turbare* 'disturb'.

**perturbation** ● **n. 1** anxiety; uneasiness. ➤a cause of this. **2** the action of perturbing a system, moving object, or process.

**pertussis** /pəˈtʌsɪs/ ● **n.** medical term for **WHOOPING COUGH**.
– ORIGIN C18: mod. L., from **PER-** + L. *tussis* 'a cough'.

**peruke** /pəˈruːk/ ● **n.** archaic a wig or periwig.
– ORIGIN C16: from Fr. *perruque*, from Ital. *perrucca*, of unknown origin.

**peruse** /pəˈruːz/ ● **v.** formal read or examine thoroughly or carefully.
– DERIVATIVES **perusal** n. **peruser** n.
– ORIGIN C15 (in the sense 'use up, wear out'): perh. from **PER-** + **USE**, but cf. Anglo-Norman Fr. *peruser* 'examine'.

**Peruvian** /pəˈruːvɪən/ ● **n.** a native or inhabitant of Peru. ● **adj.** of or relating to Peru.

**Peruvian bark** ● **n.** archaic cinchona bark.

**perv** (also **perve**) informal ● **n. 1** a sexual pervert. **2** Austral./NZ a lecherous look. ● **v.** Austral./NZ gaze lecherously.
– DERIVATIVES **pervy** adj. (**-ier**, **-iest**).

**pervade** ● **v.** spread or be present throughout; suffuse.
– DERIVATIVES **pervader** n. **pervasion** n.
– ORIGIN C17: from L. *pervadere*, from *per-* 'throughout' + *vadere* 'go'.

**pervasive** ● **adj.** widespread.
– DERIVATIVES **pervasively** adv. **pervasiveness** n.

**perverse** ● **adj. 1** showing a deliberate and obstinate desire to behave unacceptably. ➤sexually perverted. **2** contrary to that which is accepted or expected. ➤Law (of a verdict) against the weight of evidence or the direction of the judge.
– DERIVATIVES **perversely** adv. **perverseness** n. **perversity** n. (pl. **-ies**).
– ORIGIN ME: from OFr. *pervers(e)*, from L. *perversus*, *pervertere* (see **PERVERT**).

**perversion** ● **n.** the action of perverting. ➤abnormal or unacceptable sexual behaviour.

**pervert** ● v. **1** alter from its original meaning or state to a corruption of what was first intended. **2** lead away from what is right, natural, or acceptable. ● n. a person with abnormal or unacceptable sexual behaviour.
– DERIVATIVES **perverter** n.
– ORIGIN ME: from OFr. *pervertir*, from L. *pervertere*, from *per-* 'thoroughly, to ill effect' + *vertere* 'to turn'.

**perverted** ● adj. characterized by sexually abnormal and unacceptable tendencies.
– DERIVATIVES **pervertedly** adv.

**pervious** /ˈpəːvɪəs/ ● adj. permeable.
– DERIVATIVES **perviousness** n.
– ORIGIN C17: from L. *pervius* 'having a passage through' (based on *via* 'way') + **-ous**.

**Pesach** /ˈpeɪsɑːx/ ● n. the Passover festival.
– ORIGIN from Heb. *Pesaḥ*.

**peseta** /pəˈseɪtə/ ● n. **1** the basic monetary unit of Spain, equal to 100 centimos. **2** historical a silver coin.
– ORIGIN Sp., dimin. of *pesa* 'weight', from L. *pensa* 'things weighed', from *pendere* 'weigh'.

**pesewa** /pɛˈsiːwə/ ● n. a monetary unit of Ghana, equal to one hundredth of a cedi.
– ORIGIN Akan, lit. 'penny'.

**pesky** ● adj. (**-ier**, **-iest**) informal annoying.
– DERIVATIVES **peskily** adv. **peskiness** n.
– ORIGIN C18: perh. rel. to **PEST**.

**peso** /ˈpeɪsəʊ/ ● n. (pl. **-os**) the basic monetary unit of several Latin American countries and of the Philippines, equal to 100 centésimos in Uruguay and 100 centavos elsewhere.
– ORIGIN Sp., lit. 'weight', from L. *pensum* 'something weighed', from *pendere* 'weigh'.

**pessary** /ˈpɛs(ə)ri/ ● n. (pl. **-ies**) **1** a small medicinal or contraceptive soluble block inserted into the vagina. **2** a device inserted into the vagina to support the uterus.
– ORIGIN ME: from late L. *pessarium*, based on Gk *pessos* 'oval stone'.

**pessimism** ● n. **1** lack of hope or confidence in the future. **2** Philosophy a belief that this world is as bad as it could be or that evil will ultimately prevail over good.
– DERIVATIVES **pessimist** n. **pessimistic** adj. **pessimistically** adv.
– ORIGIN C18: from L. *pessimus* 'worst', on the pattern of *optimism*.

**pest** ● n. **1** a destructive insect or other animal that attacks crops, food, or livestock. **2** informal an annoying person or thing. **3** (**the pest**) archaic bubonic plague.
– ORIGIN C15: from Fr. *peste* or L. *pestis* 'plague'.

**pester** ● v. trouble or annoy with persistent requests or interruptions.
– DERIVATIVES **pesterer** n.
– ORIGIN C16: from Fr. *empestrer* 'encumber', influenced by **PEST**.

**pest-house** ● n. historical a hospital for those with infectious diseases, especially the plague.

**pesticide** ● n. a substance for destroying insects or other pests of plants or animals.
– DERIVATIVES **pesticidal** adj.

**pestiferous** ● adj. **1** poetic/literary harbouring infection and disease. **2** humorous annoying.
– ORIGIN ME: from L. *pestifer* 'bringing pestilence' + **-ous**.

**pestilence** ● n. archaic a fatal epidemic disease, especially bubonic plague.
– ORIGIN ME: from OFr., from L. *pestilentia*, based on *pestis* 'a plague'.

**pestilent** ● adj. **1** deadly. **2** informal, dated annoying. **3** archaic harmful to morals or public order.
– DERIVATIVES **pestilently** adv.
– ORIGIN ME: from L. *pestilens*, *pestilent-* 'unhealthy, destructive', from *pestis* 'plague'.

**pestilential** ● adj. **1** of, relating to, or tending to cause infectious diseases. **2** of the nature of a pest. ➤ informal annoying.
– DERIVATIVES **pestilentially** adv.

**pestle** /ˈpɛs(ə)l/ ● n. a heavy tool with a rounded end, used for crushing and grinding substances in a mortar. ➤ a mechanical device for grinding, pounding, or stamping. ● v. crush or grind with a pestle.
– ORIGIN ME: from OFr. *pestel*, from L. *pistillum*, from *pist-*, *pinsere* 'to pound'.

**pesto** /ˈpɛstəʊ/ ● n. a sauce of crushed basil leaves, pine nuts, garlic, Parmesan cheese, and olive oil, typically served with pasta.
– ORIGIN Ital., from *pestare* 'pound, crush'.

**PET** ● abbrev. **1** polyethylene terephthalate. **2** positron emission tomography.

**Pet.** ● abbrev. Peter (in biblical references).

**pet**[1] ● n. **1** a domestic or tamed animal or bird kept for companionship or pleasure. **2** a person treated with special favour. **3** used as an affectionate form of address. ● adj. **1** of, relating to, or kept as a pet. **2** favourite or particular: *my pet hate is woodwork.* ● v. (**petted**, **petting**) **1** stroke or pat (an animal). **2** caress sexually.
– DERIVATIVES **petter** n.
– ORIGIN C16 (orig. Scots and north. Engl.): of unknown origin.

**pet**[2] ● n. a fit of sulking or ill humour.
– ORIGIN C16: of unknown origin.

**peta-** /ˈpɛtə/ ● comb. form denoting a factor of $10^{15}$: *petabytes.*
– ORIGIN from *pe(n)ta-* (see **PENTA-**), based on the supposed analogy of *tera-* and *tetra-*.

**petal** ● n. each of the segments of the corolla of a flower.
– DERIVATIVES **petaline** adj. **-petalled** adj. **petal-like** adj. **petaloid** adj.
– ORIGIN C18: from mod. L. *petalum* (in late L. 'metal plate'), from Gk *petalon* 'leaf', neut. (used as n.) of *petalos* 'outspread'.

**pétanque** /pəˈtaŋk, French petɑ̃k/ ● n. a game similar to boule played chiefly in Provence.
– ORIGIN Fr., from Provençal *pèd tanco*, lit. 'foot fixed (to the ground)', describing the start position.

**petard** /pɪˈtɑːd/ ● n. historical a small bomb made of a metal or wooden box filled with powder. ➤ a kind of firework that explodes with a sharp report.
– PHRASES **hoist with** (or **by**) **one's own petard** having one's schemes against others backfiring on one.
– ORIGIN C16: from Fr. *pétard*, from *péter* 'break wind'.

**petasus** /ˈpɛtəsəs/ ● n. a hat with a low crown and broad brim, worn in ancient Greece. ➤ Greek Mythology a winged hat of this type worn by the god Hermes.
– ORIGIN via L. from Gk *petasos*.

**petcock** ● n. a small valve in a pipe or cylinder for drainage or testing.

**petechia** /pɪˈtiːkɪə/ ● n. (pl. **petechiae** /-kɪiː/) Medicine a small red or purple spot caused by bleeding into the skin.
– DERIVATIVES **petechial** adj.
– ORIGIN C18: mod. L., from Ital. *petecchia* (a freckle or spot on the face), from L. *petigo* 'scab, eruption'.

**peter**[1] ● v. (usu. **peter out**) diminish or come to an end gradually.
– ORIGIN C19: of unknown origin.

**peter**[2] ● n. informal **1** a man's penis. **2** Austral./NZ a prison cell. **3** a safe.
– ORIGIN ME: from the given name *Peter*.

**peter**[3] ● n. & v. Bridge another term for **ECHO** (in sense 5).
– ORIGIN C19: from **BLUE PETER** (the action being likened to the raising of this flag).

**peterman** ● n. (pl. **-men**) archaic a safe-breaker.

**Peter Pan** ● n. a person who retains youthful features, or who is immature.
– ORIGIN the hero of J. M. Barrie's play of the same name (1904).

**Peter Principle** ● n. the principle that members of a hierarchy are promoted until they reach the level at which they are no longer competent.
– ORIGIN 1960s: named after the Amer. educationalist Laurence J. *Peter*.

**petersham** ● n. a corded tape used in dressmaking and millinery for stiffening.
– ORIGIN C19: named after the Engl. army officer Lord *Petersham*.

**Peter's pence** ● pl. n. **1** historical an annual tax of one

penny from householders with land of a certain value, paid to the papal see. **2** (since 1860) a voluntary payment by Roman Catholics to the papal treasury.
– ORIGIN named after St *Peter*, the first Pope.

**Peters projection** ● n. a world map projection in which areas are shown in correct proportion at the expense of distorted shape.
– ORIGIN named after the Ger. historian Arno *Peters*.

**pethidine** /ˈpɛθɪdiːn/ ● n. Medicine a synthetic compound used as a painkiller, especially for women in labour.
– ORIGIN 1940s: from *p(iper)idine* (from which the drug is derived), with the insertion of *eth(yl)*.

**pétillant** /ˈpɛtɪjɒ̃/ ● adj. (of wine) slightly sparkling.
– ORIGIN from Fr.

**petiole** /ˈpɛtɪəʊl/ ● n. **1** Botany the stalk that joins a leaf to a stem. **2** Zoology a slender stalk between two structures, e.g. the abdomen and thorax of an insect.
– DERIVATIVES **petiolar** adj. **petiolate** /-lət/ adj.
– ORIGIN C18: from Fr. *pétiole*, from L. *petiolus* 'little foot, stalk'.

**petit** /ˈpɛti/ ● adj. Law (of a crime) petty.
– ORIGIN ME: from OFr., 'small'.

**petit bourgeois** ● adj. of or characteristic of the lower middle class, especially in being conventional and conservative. ● n. (pl. **petits bourgeois** pronunc. same) a petit bourgeois person.
– ORIGIN Fr., lit. 'little citizen'.

**petite** ● adj. (of a woman) attractively small and dainty.
– ORIGIN C18: Fr., fem. of *petit* 'small'.

**petite bourgeoisie** (also **petit bourgeoisie**) ● n. [treated as sing. or pl.] the lower middle class.
– ORIGIN Fr., lit. 'little townsfolk'.

**petit four** /ˌpətɪ ˈfɔː, ˌpɛtɪ/ ● n. (pl. **petits fours** /ˈfɔːz/) a very small fancy cake, biscuit, or sweet.
– ORIGIN Fr., lit. 'little oven'.

**petitgrain** /ˈpɛtɪɡreɪn/ ● n. an essential oil with a floral scent, distilled from parts of the orange tree and other citrus plants and used in perfumery.
– ORIGIN from Fr. *petit grain* 'little grain' (from the small green fruits orig. used).

**petition** ● n. **1** a formal written request, typically signed by many people, appealing to authority in respect of a cause. ➤an appeal or request. **2** Law an application to a court for a writ, judicial action in a suit, etc. ● v. make or present a petition to.
– DERIVATIVES **petitionary** adj. **petitioner** n.
– ORIGIN ME: from L. *petitio(n-)*, from *petit-*, *petere* 'aim at, seek, lay claim to'.

**Petition of Right** ● n. **1** Brit. historical a parliamentary declaration of rights and liberties of the people assented to by Charles I in 1628. **2** English Law, chiefly historical a common-law remedy against the Crown for the recovery of property.

**petitio principii** /pɪˌtɪʃɪəʊ prɪnˈsɪpɪʌɪ, prɪŋˈkɪp-/ ● n. Logic a fallacy in which a conclusion is taken for granted in the premises.
– ORIGIN L., lit. 'laying claim to a principle'.

**petit mal** /mal/ ● n. a mild form of epilepsy characterized by brief spells of unconsciousness without loss of posture. Compare with **GRAND MAL**.
– ORIGIN C19: from Fr., lit. 'little sickness'.

**petit point** /pɔɪnt, pwã/ ● n. embroidery on canvas, using small, diagonal, adjacent stitches.
– ORIGIN C19: from Fr., lit. 'little stitch'.

**petits pois** /ˌpətɪ ˈpwɑː/ ● pl. n. small, fine peas.
– ORIGIN Fr., lit. 'small peas'.

**pet name** ● n. a name used to express fondness or familiarity.

**Petrarchan** /pɪˈtrɑːk(ə)n/ ● adj. denoting a sonnet of the kind used by the Italian poet Petrarch (1304–74), with an octave rhyming *abbaabba*, and a sestet typically rhyming *cdcdcd* or *cdecde*.

**petrel** /ˈpɛtr(ə)l/ ● n. a seabird related to the shearwaters, typically flying far from land. [Many species, chiefly in the family Procellariidae.]
– ORIGIN C17: assoc. with St Peter, from the bird's habit of flying low with legs dangling, and so appearing to walk on the water (see Matt. 14:30).

**Petri dish** /ˈpɛtri, ˈpiːtri/ ● n. a shallow, circular, transparent dish with a flat lid, used for the culture of microorganisms.
– ORIGIN C19: named after the Ger. bacteriologist Julius R. *Petri*.

**petrify** ● v. (**-ies**, **-ied**) **1** [often as adj. **petrified**] paralyse with fear. **2** change (organic matter) into stone by encrusting or replacing its original substance with a mineral deposit. **3** deprive or become deprived of vitality.
– DERIVATIVES **petrifaction** n. **petrification** n.
– ORIGIN ME: from Fr. *pétrifier*, from med. L. *petrificare*, from L. *petra* 'rock', from Gk.

**Petrine** /ˈpiːtrʌɪn/ ● adj. **1** Christian Theology of or relating to St Peter. ➤of or relating to the authority of the Pope, in his role as the successor of St Peter. **2** of or relating to Peter I of Russia.

**petro-** /ˈpɛtrəʊ/ ● comb. form **1** of rock; relating to rocks: *petrography*. **2** relating to petroleum: *petrodollar*.
– ORIGIN sense 1 from Gk *petros* 'stone', *petra* 'rock'; sense 2 from **PETROLEUM**.

**petrochemical** ● adj. **1** of or relating to the chemical properties and processing of petroleum and natural gas. **2** of or relating to the chemistry of rocks. ● n. a chemical obtained from petroleum and natural gas.
– DERIVATIVES **petrochemistry** n.

**petrodollar** ● n. a notional unit of currency earned from the export of petroleum.

**petroglyph** /ˈpɛtrə(ʊ)ɡlɪf/ ● n. a rock carving.
– ORIGIN C19: from **PETRO-** + Gk *glyphē* 'carving'.

**petrography** /pɛˈtrɒɡrəfi/ ● n. the study of the composition and properties of rocks.
– DERIVATIVES **petrographer** n. **petrographic** adj. **petrographical** adj.

**petrol** ● n. Brit. refined petroleum used as fuel in motor vehicles.
– ORIGIN C19: from Fr. *pétrole*, from med. L. *petroleum* (see **PETROLEUM**).

**petrolatum** /ˌpɛtrəˈleɪtəm/ ● n. another term for **PETROLEUM JELLY**.
– ORIGIN C19: mod. L., from **PETROL** + the L. suffix *-atum*.

**petrol bomb** ● n. Brit. a crude bomb consisting of a bottle containing petrol and a cloth wick.

**petroleum** ● n. a hydrocarbon oil found in suitable rock strata and extracted and refined to produce fuels including petrol, paraffin, and diesel oil; oil.
– ORIGIN ME: from med. L., from L. *petra* 'rock' (from Gk) + L. *oleum* 'oil'.

**petroleum ether** ● n. a volatile liquid distilled from petroleum.

**petroleum jelly** ● n. a translucent solid mixture of hydrocarbons, used as a lubricant or ointment.

**petrology** /pɪˈtrɒlədʒi/ ● n. the study of the origin, structure, and composition of rocks.
– DERIVATIVES **petrologic** adj. **petrological** adj. **petrologist** n.

**petrol station** ● n. Brit. an establishment selling petrol for motor vehicles.

**petrosal** /pɪˈtrəʊs(ə)l/ ● adj. Anatomy relating to or denoting the dense part of the temporal bone surrounding the inner ear.
– ORIGIN C18: from L. *petrosus* 'stony, rocky' (from *petra* 'rock') + **-AL**.

**petrous** /ˈpɛtrəs/ ● adj. Anatomy another term for **PETROSAL**.
– ORIGIN ME: from L. *petrosus* (see **PETROSAL**).

**petticoat** ● n. **1** a woman's light, loose undergarment in the form of a skirt or dress. **2** [as modifier] informal, often derogatory associated with women: *petticoat government*.
– DERIVATIVES **petticoated** adj.
– ORIGIN ME: from *petty coat*, lit. 'small coat'.

**pettifog** ● v. (**pettifogged**, **pettifogging**) archaic **1** quibble about petty points. **2** practise legal deception or trickery.
– DERIVATIVES **pettifoggery** n.
– ORIGIN C17: back-form. from **PETTIFOGGER**.

**pettifogger** ● n. archaic an inferior legal practitioner.
– ORIGIN C16: from **PETTY** + obs. *fogger* 'underhand dealer',

prob. from *Fugger*, the name of a family of merchants in Augsburg in the 15th and 16th cents.

**pettifogging** ● adj. petty; trivial.

**pettish** ● adj. petulant.
– DERIVATIVES **pettishly** adv. **pettishness** n.

**petty** ● adj. (-ier, -iest) **1** trivial. **2** mean; small-minded. **3** minor. ➤ Law (of a crime) of lesser importance. Compare with **GRAND** (in sense 2).
– DERIVATIVES **pettily** adv. **pettiness** n.
– ORIGIN ME: from a phonetic spelling of the pronunc. of Fr. *petit* 'small'.

**petty bourgeois** ● n. variant of **PETIT BOURGEOIS**.

**petty bourgeoisie** ● n. variant of **PETITE BOURGEOISIE**.

**petty cash** ● n. an accessible store of money for expenditure on small items.

**petty larceny** ● n. Law (in many US states and formerly in Britain) theft of personal property having a value less than a specified amount.

**petty officer** ● n. a rank of non-commissioned officer in the navy, above leading seaman or seaman and below chief petty officer.

**petty sessions** ● n. (in the UK) a magistrates' court for the summary trial of certain offences.

**petty treason** ● n. see **TREASON**.

**petulant** /'pɛtjʊl(ə)nt/ ● adj. childishly sulky or bad-tempered.
– DERIVATIVES **petulance** n. **petulantly** adv.
– ORIGIN C16 (in the sense 'immodest'): from Fr. *pétulant*, from L. *petulant-* 'impudent'.

**petunia** ● n. a South American plant of the nightshade family, with white, purple, or red funnel-shaped flowers. [*Petunia* × *hybrida*.]
– ORIGIN mod. L., from Fr. *petun*, from Guarani *petÿ* 'tobacco' (to which these plants are related).

**petuntse** /peɪ'tʊntsə, pɪ'tʌntsə/ ● n. a type of fine china stone used to make porcelain.
– ORIGIN C18: from Chin. (Mandarin dial.) *báidūnzi*, from *bái* 'white' + *dūn* 'stone' + the suffix *-zi*.

**pew** ● n. a long bench with a back, placed in rows in churches for the congregation. ➤ Brit. informal a seat.
– ORIGIN ME (orig. a raised, enclosed place for particular worshippers): from OFr. *puye* 'balcony', from L. *podia*, pl. of *podium* 'elevated place'.

**pewee** /'piːwiː/ (also **peewee**) ● n. a North American tyrant flycatcher with dark olive-grey plumage. [Genus *Contopus*: several species.]
– ORIGIN C18: imitative.

**pewit** ● n. variant spelling of **PEEWIT**.

**pewter** ● n. a grey alloy of tin with copper and antimony (formerly, tin and lead). ➤ utensils made of this.
– DERIVATIVES **pewterer** n.
– ORIGIN ME: from OFr. *peutre*, of unknown origin.

**peyote** /peɪ'əʊti/ ● n. **1** a small, soft, blue-green spineless cactus, native to Mexico and the southern US. [*Lophophora williamsii*.] **2** a hallucinogenic drug prepared from this, containing mescaline.
– ORIGIN C19: from Latin Amer. Sp., from Nahuatl *peyotl*.

**Pf.** ● abbrev. pfennig.

**Pfc.** ● abbrev. Private First Class.

**pfennig** /'(p)fɛnɪɡ/ ● n. a monetary unit of Germany, equal to one hundredth of a mark.
– ORIGIN from Ger. *Pfennig*; rel. to **PENNY**.

**PFI** ● abbrev. (in the UK) Private Finance Initiative, a scheme whereby public services such as the National Health Service raise funds for capital projects from commercial organizations.

**PG** ● abbrev. **1** (in film classification) parental guidance, indicating that some scenes may be considered unsuitable for children. **2** paying guest.

**PGA** ● abbrev. Professional Golfers' Association.

**pH** ● n. Chemistry a figure expressing acidity or alkalinity on a logarithmic scale on which 7 is neutral, lower values are more acid and higher values more alkaline.
– ORIGIN C20: from *p* representing Ger. *Potenz* 'power' + *H*, the symbol for hydrogen (the pH being derived from the reciprocal of the hydrogen-ion concentration).

**phaeton** /'feɪt(ə)n/ ● n. **1** historical a light, open four-wheeled horse-drawn carriage. **2** US a vintage touring car.
– ORIGIN C18: from Fr. *phaéton*, via L. from *Phaethōn*, son of the sun god Helios in Greek mythology.

**phage** /feɪdʒ, fɑːʒ/ ● n. short for **BACTERIOPHAGE**.

**phagocyte** /'faɡə(ʊ)sʌɪt/ ● n. Physiology a type of body cell which engulfs and absorbs bacteria and other small particles.
– DERIVATIVES **phagocytic** adj.
– ORIGIN C19: from Gk *phago-* 'eating' (from *phagein*) + **-CYTE**.

**phagocytosis** /ˌfaɡə(ʊ)sʌɪ'təʊsɪs/ ● n. Biology the ingestion of bacteria or other particles by phagocytes and amoeboid protozoans.
– DERIVATIVES **phagocytize** (also **-ise**) v. **phagocytose** v.

**-phagous** ● comb. form feeding or subsisting on a specified food: *coprophagous*.
– ORIGIN from L. *-phagus*, Gk *-phagos* (from *phagein* 'eat') + **-OUS**.

**-phagy** ● comb. form denoting the practice of eating a specified food: *anthropophagy*.
– ORIGIN from Gk *-phagia*, from *phagein* 'eat'.

**phalange** /'falan(d)ʒ/ ● n. **1** Anatomy another term for **PHALANX** (in sense 3). **2** (**Phalange**) a right-wing Maronite party in Lebanon. [C20: abbrev. of Fr. *Phalanges Libanaises* 'Lebanese phalanxes'.]
– DERIVATIVES **Phalangist** n. & adj.

**phalangeal** ● adj. Anatomy of or relating to a phalanx or the phalanges.

**phalanger** ● n. a lemur-like tree-dwelling marsupial native to Australia and New Guinea. [*Phalanger* and other genera.]
– ORIGIN C18: from Fr., from Gk *phalangion* 'spider's web' (because of their webbed toes).

**phalanx** /'falaŋks/ ● n. **1** (pl. **phalanxes**) a group of similar people or things. **2** a body of troops or police officers in close formation. ➤ (in ancient Greece) a body of Macedonian infantry with shields touching and spears overlapping. **3** (pl. **phalanges** /fə'lan(d)ʒiːz/) Anatomy a bone of the finger or toe.
– ORIGIN C16: via L. from Gk.

**phalarope** /'falərəʊp/ ● n. a small wading or swimming bird with a straight bill and lobed feet. [Genus *Phalaropus*: three species.]
– ORIGIN C18: from Fr., from mod. L. *Phalaropus*, formed irregularly from Gk *phalaris* 'coot' + *pous, pod-* 'foot'.

**phallic** ● adj. **1** of, relating to, or resembling a phallus or erect penis. **2** Psychoanalysis of or denoting the genital phase of psychosexual development, especially in males.
– DERIVATIVES **phallically** adv.

**phallocentric** /ˌfalə(ʊ)'sɛntrɪk/ ● adj. focused on the phallus as a symbol of male dominance.
– DERIVATIVES **phallocentricity** n. **phallocentrism** n.

**phallus** /'faləs/ ● n. (pl. **phalli** /-lʌɪ, -liː/ or **phalluses**) a penis, especially when erect. ➤ a representation of this, symbolizing fertility or potency.
– DERIVATIVES **phallicism** n. **phallism** n.
– ORIGIN C17: via late L. from Gk *phallos*.

**Phanariot** /fə'narɪət/ ● n. a Greek official in Constantinople under the Ottoman Empire.
– ORIGIN from mod. Gk *phanariōtēs*, from *Phanar*, Greek quarter of Istanbul, from Gk *phanarion* 'lighthouse' (one being situated in this area).

**phanerogam** /'fan(ə)rə(ʊ)ɡam/ ● n. Botany old-fashioned term for **SPERMATOPHYTE**.
– ORIGIN C19: from Fr. *phanérogame*, from Gk *phaneros* 'visible' + *gamos* 'marriage'.

**Phanerozoic** /ˌfan(ə)rə(ʊ)'zəʊɪk/ ● adj. Geology relating to or denoting the aeon covering the whole of time since the beginning of the Cambrian period about 570 million years ago (comprising the Palaeozoic, Mesozoic, and Cenozoic eras).
– ORIGIN C19: from Gk *phaneros* 'visible, evident' + *zōion* 'animal' + **-IC**.

**phantasize** • v. chiefly archaic variant spelling of **FANTASIZE**.

**phantasm** /ˈfantaz(ə)m/ • n. poetic/literary an illusion or apparition.
– DERIVATIVES **phantasmal** adj. **phantasmic** adj.
– ORIGIN ME: from OFr. *fantasme*, via L. from Gk *phantasma*, from *phantazein* 'make visible', from *phainein* 'to show'.

**phantasmagoria** /ˌfantazməˈgɒrɪə, -ˈgɔːrɪə/ • n. a sequence of dreamlike real or imaginary images.
– DERIVATIVES **phantasmagoric** adj. **phantasmagorical** adj.
– ORIGIN C19 (orig. the name of a London exhibition (1802) of optical illusions): prob. from Fr. *fantasmagorie*, from *fantasme* 'phantasm' + a fanciful suffix.

**phantast** • n. variant spelling of **FANTAST**.

**phantasy** • n. chiefly archaic variant spelling of **FANTASY**.

**phantom** • n. a ghost. ➤a figment of the imagination. ➤[as modifier] not real; illusory: *a phantom conspiracy.*
– ORIGIN ME: from OFr. *fantosme*, based on Gk *phantasma* (see **PHANTASM**).

**phantom circuit** • n. an arrangement of telegraph or other electric wires equivalent to an extra circuit.

**phantom limb** • n. a sensation experienced by an amputee that the limb is still there.

**phantom pregnancy** • n. a condition in which signs of pregnancy are present in a woman who is not pregnant.

**pharaoh** /ˈfɛːrəʊ/ • n. a ruler in ancient Egypt.
– DERIVATIVES **pharaonic** /ˌfɛːreɪˈɒnɪk/ adj.
– ORIGIN ME: via eccles. L. from Gk *Pharaō*, from Heb. *par'ōh*, from Egyptian *pr-'o* 'great house'.

**pharaoh ant** • n. a small yellowish ant, native to Africa and a pest of heated buildings worldwide. [*Monomorium pharaonis*.]

**Pharaoh's serpent** • n. an indoor firework producing ash in a coiled, serpentine form as it burns.
– ORIGIN named by assoc. with Aaron's staff which turned into a serpent before the Pharaoh (Exod. 7:9).

**Pharisee** /ˈfarɪsiː/ • n. **1** a member of an ancient Jewish sect, distinguished by strict observance of the traditional and written law, and commonly held to have pretensions to superior sanctity. **2** a self-righteous person.
– DERIVATIVES **Pharisaic** /ˌfarɪˈseɪɪk/ adj. **Pharisaical** adj. **Pharisaism** /ˈfarɪseɪˌɪz(ə)m/ n.
– ORIGIN OE *fariseus*, via eccles. L. from Gk *Pharisaios*, from Aramaic *prīšayyā* 'separated ones'.

**pharmaceutical** /ˌfɑːməˈsjuːtɪk(ə)l/ • adj. of or relating to medicinal drugs, or their preparation, use, or sale. • n. a compound manufactured for use as a medicinal drug.
– DERIVATIVES **pharmaceutically** adv. **pharmaceutics** pl. n.
– ORIGIN C17: via late L. from Gk *pharmakeutikos* (from *pharmakeutēs* 'druggist', from *pharmakon* 'drug') + **-AL**.

**pharmacist** • n. a person qualified to prepare and dispense medicinal drugs.

**pharmaco-** /ˈfɑːməkəʊ/ • comb. form relating to drugs.
– ORIGIN from Gk *pharmakon* 'drug, medicine'.

**pharmacodynamics** • pl. n. [treated as sing.] the branch of pharmacology concerned with the actions and effects of drugs.
– DERIVATIVES **pharmacodynamic** adj.

**pharmacogenomics** /ˌfɑːməkəʊdʒɛˈnɒmɪks/ • pl. n. [treated as sing.] the branch of genetics concerned with determining the likely response of an individual to therapeutic drugs.
– DERIVATIVES **pharmacogenomicist** n.

**pharmacognosy** /ˌfɑːməˈkɒgnəsi/ • n. the branch of knowledge concerned with medicinal drugs obtained from plants or other natural sources.
– DERIVATIVES **pharmacognosist** n.
– ORIGIN C19: from **PHARMACO-** + *gnōsis* 'knowledge'.

**pharmacokinetics** • pl. n. [treated as sing.] the branch of pharmacology concerned with the movement of drugs within the body.
– DERIVATIVES **pharmacokinetic** adj.

**pharmacology** • n. the branch of medicine concerned with the uses, effects, and action of drugs.
– DERIVATIVES **pharmacologic** adj. **pharmacological** adj. **pharmacologically** adv. **pharmacologist** n.
– ORIGIN C18: from mod. L. *pharmacologia*, from Gk *pharmakon* 'drug'.

**pharmacopoeia** /ˌfɑːməkəˈpiːə/ (US also **pharmacopeia**) • n. **1** a book containing a list of medicinal drugs with their effects and directions for use. **2** a stock of medicinal drugs.
– ORIGIN C17: mod. L., from Gk *pharmakopoiia* 'art of preparing drugs'.

**pharmacy** • n. (pl. **-ies**) **1** a place where medicinal drugs are prepared or sold. **2** the science or practice of preparing and dispensing medicinal drugs.
– ORIGIN ME: from OFr. *farmacie*, via med. L. from Gk *pharmakeia* 'practice of the druggist', based on *pharmakon* 'drug'.

**pharos** /ˈfɛːrɒs/ • n. archaic a lighthouse.
– ORIGIN via L. from Gk *Pharos*, the name of an island off Alexandria where a famous lighthouse stood.

**pharyngeal** /fəˈrɪn(d)ʒɪəl, ˌfarɪnˈdʒiːəl/ • adj. of or relating to the pharynx. ➤Phonetics (of a speech sound) produced by articulating the root of the tongue with the pharynx.
– ORIGIN C19: from mod. L. *pharyngeus* (from Gk *pharunx*, *pharung-* 'throat') + **-AL**.

**pharyngitis** /ˌfarɪŋˈdʒʌɪtɪs/ • n. Medicine inflammation of the pharynx.

**pharyngo-** /fəˈrɪŋgəʊ/ • comb. form of or relating to the pharynx: *pharyngotomy.*
– ORIGIN from mod. L. *pharynx*, *pharyng-*.

**pharyngotomy** /ˌfarɪŋˈgɒtəmi/ • n. (pl. **-ies**) a surgical incision into the pharynx.

**pharynx** /ˈfarɪŋks/ • n. (pl. **pharynges** /-ˈrɪn(d)ʒiːz/) Anatomy & Zoology the membrane-lined cavity behind the nose and mouth, connecting them to the oesophagus. ➤(in invertebrates) the part of the alimentary canal immediately behind the mouth.
– ORIGIN C17: mod. L., from Gk *pharunx*, *pharung-*.

**phase** /feɪz/ • n. **1** a distinct period or stage in a process of change or development. ➤each of the aspects of the moon or a planet, according to the amount of its illumination. **2** Zoology a genetic or seasonal variety of an animal's coloration. **3** Chemistry a distinct and homogeneous form of matter separated by its surface from other forms. **4** Physics the relationship in time between the cycles of an oscillating or repeating system and a fixed reference point or a different system. • v. (usu. **be phased**) **1** carry out in gradual stages. ➤(**phase something in/out**) introduce something into (or withdraw something from) use in gradual stages. **2** Physics adjust the phase of (something), especially so as to synchronize it with something else.
– PHRASES **in** (or **out of**) **phase** in (or out of) synchrony or harmony.
– ORIGIN C19: from Fr. *phase*, based on Gk *phasis* 'appearance'.

**phase angle** • n. **1** Physics a phase difference expressed as an angle, 360 degrees corresponding to one complete cycle. **2** Astronomy the angle between the lines joining a given planet to the sun and to the earth.

**phase contrast** • n. a technique in microscopy of introducing a phase difference in the illumination so as to enhance the outlines of the sample.

**phase-lock** • v. Electronics fix the frequency of (an oscillator or a laser) relative to a stable lower frequency.

**phase shift** • n. Physics a change in the phase of a waveform.

**phase space** • n. Physics a multidimensional space in which the axes correspond to the coordinates required to specify any state of a system.

**phasic** /ˈfeɪzɪk/ • adj. of or relating to a phase or phases. ➤chiefly Physiology occurring in phases.

**phasing** • n. **1** division into phases, or the relationship between phases. **2** the modification of a sound signal from an electric guitar or other electronic instrument by combining it with a phase-shifted copy.

**phat** /fat/ • adj. black slang excellent.
– ORIGIN 1970s (orig. used to describe a woman, in the sense 'sexy, attractive'): of uncertain origin.

**phatic** /ˈfatɪk/ ● **adj.** (of language) used for general social interaction rather than to convey specific meaning, e.g. *nice morning, isn't it?*
– ORIGIN 1920s: from Gk *phatos* 'spoken' or *phatikos* 'affirming'.

**PhD** ● **abbrev.** Doctor of Philosophy.
– ORIGIN from L. *philosophiae doctor.*

**pheasant** ● **n.** a large long-tailed game bird native to Asia, the male of which typically has showy plumage. [*Phasianus colchicus* and other species.]
– ORIGIN ME: from OFr. *fesan*, via L. from Gk *phasianos* '(bird) of *Phasis*', the name of a river in the Caucasus.

**pheasantry** ● **n.** (pl. **-ies**) a place where pheasants are reared or kept.

**pheasant's eye** ● **n.** a plant of the buttercup family which has scarlet flowers with dark centres. [*Adonis annua.*]

**phen-** ● **comb. form** variant spelling of **PHENO-** shortened before a vowel (as in *phencyclidine*).

**phencyclidine** /fɛnˈsʌɪklɪdiːn/ ● **n.** a synthetic compound used as a veterinary anaesthetic and in hallucinogenic drugs such as angel dust.
– ORIGIN 1950s: from **PHENO-** + **CYCLO-** + a shortened form of **PIPERIDINE**.

**pheno-** (also **phen-** before a vowel) ● **comb. form 1** Chemistry derived from benzene: *phenobarbitone.* **2** showing: *phenotype.*
– ORIGIN sense 1 from Fr. *phényle* 'phenyl', from Gk *phaino-* 'shining'; both senses from Gk *phainein* 'to show'.

**phenobarbital** /ˌfiːnə(ʊ)ˈbɑːbɪt(ə)l, ˌfɛn-/ ● **n.** US term for **PHENOBARBITONE**.

**phenobarbitone** /ˌfiːnə(ʊ)ˈbɑːbɪtəʊn, ˌfɛn-/ ● **n.** Medicine a narcotic and sedative barbiturate drug used chiefly to treat epilepsy.

**phenocryst** /ˈfiːnə(ʊ)krɪst, ˈfɛn-/ ● **n.** Geology a large or conspicuous crystal in a porphyritic rock.
– ORIGIN C19: from Fr. *phénocryste*, from Gk *phainein* 'to show' + *krustallos* 'crystal'.

**phenol** /ˈfiːnɒl/ ● **n.** Chemistry a mildly acidic toxic white crystalline solid obtained from coal tar and used in chemical manufacture. See also **CARBOLIC ACID**. ➤any compound with a hydroxyl group linked directly to a benzene ring.
– DERIVATIVES **phenolic** adj.
– ORIGIN C19: from Fr. *phénole*, based on *phène* 'benzene'.

**phenology** /fɪˈnɒlədʒi/ ● **n.** the study of cyclic and seasonal natural phenomena, especially in relation to climate and plant and animal life.
– DERIVATIVES **phenological** adj.
– ORIGIN C19: from **PHENOMENON** + **-LOGY**.

**phenolphthalein** /ˌfiːnɒlˈ(f)θaliːn, -ˈ(f)θeɪl-/ ● **n.** Chemistry a colourless crystalline solid (pink in alkaline solution) used as an acid–base indicator and medicinally as a laxative. [$C_{20}H_{14}O_4$.]
– ORIGIN C19: from **PHENOL** + *-phthal-* (from **NAPHTHALENE**) + **-IN**[1].

**phenom** ● **n.** N. Amer. informal an unusually gifted person.
– ORIGIN C19: abbrev. of **PHENOMENON**.

**phenomena** plural form of **PHENOMENON**.

**phenomenal** ● **adj. 1** extraordinary. **2** perceptible by the senses or through immediate experience.
– DERIVATIVES **phenomenalize** (also **-ise**) v. **phenomenally** adv.

**phenomenalism** ● **n.** Philosophy the doctrine that human knowledge is confined to the appearances presented to the senses.
– DERIVATIVES **phenomenalist** n. & adj. **phenomenalistic** adj.

**phenomenology** /fɪˌnɒmɪˈnɒlədʒi/ ● **n.** Philosophy **1** the science of phenomena as distinct from that of the nature of being. **2** an approach that concentrates on the study of consciousness and the objects of direct experience.
– DERIVATIVES **phenomenological** adj. **phenomenologically** adv. **phenomenologist** n.

**phenomenon** ● **n.** (pl. **phenomena**) **1** a fact or situation that is observed to exist or happen, especially one whose cause is in question. **2** Philosophy the object of a person's perception. **3** a remarkable person or thing.
– ORIGIN C16: via late L. from Gk *phainomenon* 'thing appearing to view', based on *phainein* 'to show'.

**USAGE** phenomenon

The word **phenomenon** comes from Greek, and its plural form is **phenomena**. In standard English it is a mistake to treat **phenomena** as if it were a singular form.

**phenothiazine** /ˌfiːnəʊˈθʌɪəziːn, ˌfɛnəʊ-/ ● **n.** Chemistry a synthetic compound used to treat parasitic infestations of animals, or one of its derivatives, used as tranquillizers.

**phenotype** /ˈfiːnə(ʊ)tʌɪp/ ● **n.** Biology the observable characteristics of an individual resulting from the interaction of its genotype with the environment.
– DERIVATIVES **phenotypic** adj. **phenotypical** adj. **phenotypically** adv.
– ORIGIN C20: from Ger. *Phaenotypus* (see **PHENO-**, **TYPE**).

**phenyl** /ˈfiːnʌɪl, ˈfɛnɪl/ ● **n.** [as modifier] Chemistry of or denoting the radical $-C_6H_5$, derived from benzene.
– ORIGIN C19: from Fr. *phényle*, from Gk *phaino-* 'shining' (because first used in names of by-products of the manufacture of gas for illumination).

**phenylalanine** /ˌfiːnʌɪlˈaləniːn, ˌfɛnɪl-/ ● **n.** Biochemistry an amino acid widely distributed in plant proteins, an essential nutrient in the diet of vertebrates.

**phenylketonuria** /ˌfiːnʌɪlˌkiːtə(ʊ)ˈnjʊərɪə, ˌfɛnɪl-/ ● **n.** Medicine an inherited inability to metabolize phenylalanine which can result in brain and nerve damage.

**phenytoin** /fɛˈnɪtəʊɪn/ ● **n.** Medicine a synthetic compound used as an anticonvulsant in the treatment of epilepsy.
– ORIGIN 1940s: blend of **PHENYL** and **HYDANTOIN**.

**pheromone** /ˈfɛrəməʊn/ ● **n.** Zoology a chemical substance produced and released by an animal, affecting the behaviour or physiology of others of its species.
– DERIVATIVES **pheromonal** adj.
– ORIGIN 1950s: from Gk *pherein* 'convey' + **HORMONE**.

**phew** ● **exclam.** informal expressing relief.
– ORIGIN C17: imitative of puffing.

**phi** /fʌɪ/ ● **n.** the twenty-first letter of the Greek alphabet (Φ, φ), transliterated as 'ph' or (in modern Greek) 'f'. ● **symb. 1** (φ) a plane angle. **2** (φ) a polar coordinate. Often coupled with θ.
– ORIGIN from Gk.

**phial** /ˈfʌɪəl/ ● **n.** a small cylindrical glass bottle, typically for medical samples or medicines.
– ORIGIN ME: from OFr. *fiole*, via L. from Gk *phialē*, denoting a broad flat container; cf. **VIAL**.

**Phi Beta Kappa** /ˌfʌɪ ˌbiːtə ˈkapə/ ● **n.** (in the US) an honorary society of undergraduates and some graduates, to which members are elected on the basis of high academic achievement. ➤a member of this society.
– ORIGIN from the initial letters of a Greek motto *philosophia biou kubernētēs* 'philosophy is the guide to life'.

**Phil.** ● **abbrev. 1** Epistle to the Philippians (in biblical references). **2** Philadelphia. **3** Philharmonic.

**phil-** ● **comb. form** variant spelling of **PHILO-** shortened before a vowel or *h* (as in *philanthrope*).

**-phil** ● **comb. form** having a chemical affinity for a substance: *neutrophil.*
– ORIGIN see **-PHILE**.

**Philadelphian** /ˌfɪləˈdɛlfɪən/ ● **n.** a native or inhabitant of Philadelphia. ● **adj.** of or relating to Philadelphia.

**philadelphus** /ˌfɪləˈdɛlfəs/ ● **n.** a mock orange.
– ORIGIN C18: mod. L. (adopted by Linnaeus as a genus name), from Gk *philadelphos* 'loving one's brother'.

**philander** /fɪˈlandə/ ● **v.** (of a man) readily or frequently enter into casual sexual relationships with women.
– DERIVATIVES **philanderer** n.
– ORIGIN C18: from earlier n. *philander* 'man, husband', often used in literature as the given name of a lover, from Gk *philandros* 'fond of men'.

**philanthrope** /ˈfɪlənˌθrəʊp/ ● **n.** archaic a philanthropist.
– ORIGIN C18: from Gk *philanthrōpos*, from *philein* 'to love' + *anthrōpos* 'human being'.

**philanthropist** ● **n.** a person who seeks to promote the welfare of others, especially by donating money to good

**Word *Formation***

**-phile** 'a person or organism with a fondness for or tendency towards', from Greek *philos* 'loving'

➤ Some **-phile** words in current use (full entries and definitions to be found in this dictionary):

| | | |
|---|---|---|
| audiophile | a hi-fi enthusiast | AUDIO- |
| bibliophile | a person who loves books | Gk *biblion* 'book' |
| cinephile | a cinema enthusiast | CINE- |
| electrophile | (in chemistry) a substance that attracts electrons | ELECTRO- |
| extremophile | an organism that lives in extreme environmental conditions | based on EXTREME |
| Francophile | a person who loves France or the French | L. *Francus* 'Frank' |
| halophile | an organism that thrives in salty conditions | Gk *hals, halo-* 'salt' |
| logophile | a word lover | Gk *logos* 'word' |
| necrophile | a person who is sexually attracted to dead bodies | Gk *nekros* 'corpse' |
| oenophile | a wine connoisseur | Gk *oinos* 'wine' |
| paedophile | a person who is sexually attracted to children | Gk *pais, paid-*, 'child' |
| technophile | an enthusiast for new technology | Gk *tekhnē* 'art, craft' |
| thermophile | an organism that thrives in hot temperatures | Gk *thermos* 'hot' |

➤ Related words:

-philia forming nouns, e.g. ***coprophilia*** 'excessive interest in faeces and defecation' (Gk *kopros* 'dung')
-philiac forming adjectives (and sometimes nouns), e.g. ***haemophiliac*** 'of or having haemophilia' or 'a person with haemophilia'

Most **-phile** and **-philia** words are of recent origin: ***paedophile***, for example, is first recorded in 1906, while ***Francophile*** and ***bibliophile*** first appear in the 19th century.

causes.
– DERIVATIVES **philanthropic** adj. **philanthropically** adv. **philanthropism** n. **philanthropize** (also **-ise**) v. **philanthropy** n.

**philately** /fɪˈlat(ə)li/ ● **n.** the collection and study of postage stamps.
– DERIVATIVES **philatelic** adj. **philatelically** adv. **philatelist** n.
– ORIGIN C19: from Fr. *philatélie*, from *philo-* 'loving' + Gk *ateleia* 'exemption from payment', used to mean a franking mark or postage stamp exempting the recipient from payment.

**-phile** ● **comb. form** denoting a person or thing having a fondness for or tendency towards a specified thing: *bibliophile*. See word-formation panel.
– ORIGIN from Gk *philos* 'loving'.

**Philem.** ● **abbrev.** Philemon (in biblical references).

**philharmonic** ● **adj.** devoted to music (chiefly used in the names of orchestras).

**philhellene** /ˈfɪlhɛˌliːn, fɪlˈhɛliːn/ ● **n. 1** a lover of Greece and Greek culture. **2** historical a supporter of Greek independence.
– DERIVATIVES **philhellenic** adj. **philhellenism** n.

**-philia** ● **comb. form** denoting fondness, especially an abnormal love for or inclination towards a specified thing: *paedophilia*.
– DERIVATIVES **-philiac** comb. form in corresponding nouns and adjectives. **-philic** comb. form in corresponding adjectives. **-philous** comb. form in corresponding adjectives.
– ORIGIN from Gk *philia* 'fondness'.

**philibeg** /ˈfɪləbɛg/ ● **n.** variant spelling of FILIBEG.

**philippic** /fɪˈlɪpɪk/ ● **n.** poetic/literary a bitter verbal attack or denunciation.
– ORIGIN C16: via L. from Gk *philippikos*, the name given to Demosthenes' speeches against Philip II of Macedon, and Cicero's against Mark Antony.

**Philippine** /ˈfɪlɪpiːn/ ● **adj.** of or relating to the Philippines.

**Philistine** /ˈfɪlɪstʌɪn/ ● **n. 1** a member of a non-Semitic people of ancient Palestine who came into conflict with the Israelites. **2** (**philistine**) a person who is hostile or indifferent to culture and the arts.
– DERIVATIVES **philistinism** /-stɪnɪz(ə)m/ n.
– ORIGIN from Fr. *Philistin*, via late L. from Gk *Philistinos*, from Heb. *pĕlištī*.

**Phillips** ● **adj.** trademark denoting a screw with a cross-shaped slot for turning, or a corresponding screwdriver.
– ORIGIN 1930s: from the name of the Amer. manufacturer Henry F. *Phillips*.

**Phillips curve** ● **n.** Economics a supposed inverse relationship between the level of unemployment and the rate of inflation.
– ORIGIN 1960s: named after the NZ economist Alban W. H. *Phillips*.

**phillumenist** /fɪˈluːmənɪst/ ● **n.** a collector of matchbox or matchbook labels.
– DERIVATIVES **phillumeny** n.
– ORIGIN 1940s: from PHIL- + L. *lumen* 'light' + -IST.

**Philly** ● **n.** US informal Philadelphia.

**philo-** (also **phil-** before a vowel or *h*) ● **comb. form** denoting a liking for a specified thing: *philopatric*.
– ORIGIN from Gk *philein* 'to love' or *philos* 'loving'.

**philodendron** /ˌfɪləˈdɛndrən/ ● **n.** (pl. **philodendrons** or **philodendra** /-drə/) a tropical American climbing plant grown as a greenhouse or indoor plant. [Genus *Philodendron*.]
– ORIGIN C19: from PHILO- + Gk *dendron* 'tree'.

**philogynist** /fɪˈlɒdʒɪnɪst/ ● **n.** formal a person who likes or admires women.
– DERIVATIVES **philogyny** n.
– ORIGIN C19: from PHILO- + Gk *gunē* 'woman' + -IST.

**philology** ● **n. 1** the study of the structure, historical development, and relationships of a language or languages. **2** chiefly N. Amer. literary or classical scholarship.
– DERIVATIVES **philologian** n. **philological** adj. **philologically** adv. **philologist** n.
– ORIGIN ME (in the sense 'love of learning'): from Fr. *philologie*, via L. from Gk *philologia* (see PHILO-, -LOGY).

**philopatric** /ˌfɪlə(ʊ)ˈpatrɪk/ ● **adj.** Zoology (of an animal or species) tending to return to or remain near a particular site.
– DERIVATIVES **philopatry** n.
– ORIGIN 1940s: from PHILO- + Gk *patra* 'fatherland' + -IC.

**philoprogenitive** /ˌfɪlə(ʊ)prə(ʊ)ˈdʒɛnɪtɪv/ ● **adj.** formal **1** having many offspring. **2** loving one's offspring.
– DERIVATIVES **philoprogenitiveness** n.

**philosopher** ● n. a person engaged or learned in philosophy.

**philosopher's stone** ● n. a mythical substance supposed to change any metal into gold or silver, the discovery of which was the supreme object of alchemy.

**philosophical** ● adj. **1** of, relating to, or devoted to the study of philosophy. **2** calm in adverse circumstances.
– DERIVATIVES **philosophic** adj. **philosophically** adv.

**philosophize** (also **-ise**) ● v. theorize about fundamental or serious issues, especially tediously. ➤explain or argue in terms of one's philosophical theories.
– DERIVATIVES **philosophizer** n.

**philosophy** ● n. (pl. **-ies**) **1** the study of the fundamental nature of knowledge, reality, and existence. ➤a set of theories of a particular philosopher. **2** the study of the theoretical basis of a branch of knowledge or experience. **3** a theory or attitude that guides one's behaviour.
– ORIGIN ME: from OFr. *philosophie*, via L. from Gk *philosophia* 'love of wisdom'.

**philtre** /'fɪltə/ (US **philter**) ● n. a love potion.
– ORIGIN C16: from Fr. *philtre*, via L. from Gk *philtron*, from *philein* 'to love'.

**-phily** ● comb. form equivalent to **-PHILIA**.

**phimosis** /fʌɪ'məʊsɪs/ ● n. Medicine a congenital narrowing of the opening of the foreskin so that it cannot be retracted.
– DERIVATIVES **phimotic** adj.
– ORIGIN C17: mod. L., from Gk, lit. 'muzzling'.

**phiz** /fɪz/ (also **phizog**, **fizzog** /'fɪzɒg/) ● n. Brit. informal one's face or expression.
– ORIGIN C17: abbrev. of **PHYSIOGNOMY**.

**phlebitis** /flɪ'bʌɪtɪs/ ● n. Medicine inflammation of the walls of a vein.
– DERIVATIVES **phlebitic** adj.
– ORIGIN C19: mod. L., from Gk, from *phleps*, *phleb-* 'vein'.

**phlebotomy** /flɪ'bɒtəmi/ ● n. (pl. **-ies**) the surgical opening or puncture of a vein to withdraw blood or introduce a fluid.
– DERIVATIVES **phlebotomist** n. **phlebotomize** (also **-ise**) v. (archaic).
– ORIGIN ME: via OFr. from late L. *phlebotomia* from Gk, from *phleps*, *phleb-* 'vein' + *-tomia* 'cutting'.

**phlegm** /flɛm/ ● n. **1** the thick viscous substance secreted by the mucous membranes of the respiratory passages, especially when produced in excessive quantities during a cold. **2** (in medieval science and medicine) one of the four bodily humours, believed to be associated with a calm or apathetic temperament. ➤calmness of temperament.
– DERIVATIVES **phlegmy** adj.
– ORIGIN ME *fleem*, *fleume*, from OFr. *fleume*, from late L. *phlegma* 'clammy moisture (of the body)', from Gk *phlegma* 'inflammation', from *phlegein* 'to burn'.

**phlegmatic** /flɛg'matɪk/ ● adj. unemotional and stolidly calm.
– DERIVATIVES **phlegmatically** adv.

**phloem** /'fləʊɛm/ ● n. Botany the vascular tissue in plants which conducts sugars and other metabolic products downwards from the leaves.
– ORIGIN C19: from Gk *phloos* 'bark' + the suffix *-ēma*.

**phlogiston** /flə'dʒɪst(ə)n, -'gɪst-/ ● n. a substance supposed by 18th-century chemists to exist in all combustible bodies, and to be released in combustion.
– ORIGIN C18: mod L., from Gk *phlogizein* 'set on fire'.

**phlox** /flɒks/ ● n. a North American plant with dense clusters of colourful scented flowers, grown as an alpine or border plant. [Genus *Phlox*.]
– ORIGIN mod. L., from L., denoting a flame-coloured flower, from Gk, lit. 'flame'.

**-phobe** ● comb. form denoting a person having a fear or dislike of a specified thing: *homophobe*.
– ORIGIN from Fr., via L. *-phobus* from Gk *-phobos* 'fearing', from *phobos* 'fear'.

**phobia** /'fəʊbɪə/ ● n. an extreme or irrational fear of something.
– DERIVATIVES **phobic** adj. & n.

**-phobia** ● comb. form extreme or irrational fear or dislike of a specified thing: *arachnophobia*. See word-formation panel.
– DERIVATIVES **-phobic** comb. form in corresponding adjectives.
– ORIGIN via L. from Gk.

**phocine** /'fəʊsʌɪn/ ● adj. Zoology of or relating to the true seals (family Phocidae).
– ORIGIN C19: from mod. L. *Phocinae* (subfamily name), from Gk *phōkē* 'seal'.

**phoebe** /'fiːbi/ ● n. an American tyrant flycatcher with mainly grey-brown or blackish plumage. [Genus *Sayornis*: three species.]
– ORIGIN C18: imitative; influenced by the name *Phoebe*.

**Phoenician** /fə'nɪʃ(ə)n, -'niː-/ ● n. **1** a member of an ancient Semitic people inhabiting Phoenicia in the eastern Mediterranean. **2** the Semitic language of this people. ● adj. of or relating to Phoenicia, its people, or its language.

**phoenix** /'fiːnɪks/ ● n. **1** (in classical mythology) a unique bird of the Arabian desert that burned itself on a funeral pyre every five or six centuries and rose from the ashes with renewed youth. **2** a uniquely remarkable person or thing.
– ORIGIN from OFr. *fenix*, via L. from Gk *phoinix* 'Phoenician, reddish purple, or phoenix'.

**Pholidota** /ˌfɒlɪ'dəʊtə/ ● pl. n. Zoology a small order of mammals that comprises the pangolins.
– ORIGIN mod. L., from Gk *pholidōtos* 'scaly', from *pholis*, *pholid-* 'scale'.

**phon** /fɒn/ ● n. a unit of the perceived loudness of sounds.
– ORIGIN 1930s: from Gk *phōnē* 'sound'.

**phonaesthesia** /ˌfəʊnəs'θiːzɪə/ (US also **phonesthesia**) ● n. attribution of common elements of meaning to certain sound sequences, e.g. initial *sl-*, as in *slow, sleep, slide*.
– DERIVATIVES **phonaesthetic** adj. **phonaesthetics** pl. n.
– ORIGIN C20: mod. L., from Gk *phōnē* 'sound' + *aesthesthai* 'perceive'.

**phonation** /fə(ʊ)'neɪʃ(ə)n/ ● n. Phonetics the production of speech sounds.
– DERIVATIVES **phonate** /fə(ʊ)'neɪt/ v. **phonatory** /'fəʊnət(ə)ri/ adj.
– ORIGIN C19: from Gk *phōnē* 'sound, voice' + **-ATION**.

**phone**[1] ● n. **1** a telephone. **2** (**phones**) informal headphones or earphones. ● v. telephone.

**phone**[2] ● n. Phonetics a speech sound.
– ORIGIN C19: from Gk *phōnē* 'sound, voice'.

**-phone** ● comb. form **1** denoting an instrument using or connected with sound: *megaphone*. **2** denoting a person who uses a specified language: *francophone*. See word-formation panel.
– DERIVATIVES **-phonic** comb. form in corresponding adjectives. **-phony** comb. form in corresponding nouns.
– ORIGIN from Gk *phōnē* 'sound, voice'.

**phone book** ● n. a telephone directory.

**phonecard** ● n. a prepaid card allowing the user to make calls up to a specified number of units on a public telephone.

**phone-in** ● n. a radio or television programme during which listeners or viewers telephone the studio and participate.

**phoneme** /'fəʊniːm/ ● n. Phonetics any of the distinct units of sound that distinguish one word from another, e.g. *p*, *b*, *d*, and *t* in *pad*, *pat*, *bad*, and *bat*.
– DERIVATIVES **phonemic** /-'niːmɪk/ adj. **phonemics** pl. n.
– ORIGIN C19: from Fr. *phonème*, from Gk *phōnēma* 'sound, speech', from *phōnein* 'speak'.

**phonetic** /fə'nɛtɪk/ ● adj. Phonetics of or relating to speech sounds. ➤(of a system of writing) having a direct correspondence between symbols and sounds. ➤of or relating to phonetics.
– DERIVATIVES **phonetically** adv. **phoneticism** n. **phoneticist** n. **phoneticize** (also **-ise**) v.
– ORIGIN C19: from mod. L. *phoneticus*, from Gk *phōnētikos*, from *phōnein* 'speak'.

## Word *Formation*

**-phobia** 'extreme or irrational fear or dislike', from Greek

➤ Some of the commonest phobias (full entries and definitions to be found in this dictionary):

| | | |
|---|---|---|
| acrophobia | fear of heights | Gk *akron* 'summit' |
| agoraphobia | fear of open or public places | Gk *agora* 'place of assembly' |
| ailurophobia | fear of cats | Gk *ailuros* 'cat' |
| arachnophobia | fear of spiders | Gk *arakhnē* 'spider' |
| claustrophobia | fear of confined places | L. *claustrum* 'lock, bolt' |
| cyberphobia | fear of computer technology | CYBER- (from Gk *kubernētēs* 'steersman') |
| gynophobia | fear of women | Gk *gunē* 'woman' |
| homophobia | fear of homosexuality | Gk *homos* 'same' |
| hydrophobia | fear of water | Gk *hudōr* 'water' |
| necrophobia | fear of death or dead bodies | Gk *nekros* 'corpse' |
| neophobia | fear of the new or unfamiliar | Gk *neos* 'new' |
| nyctophobia | fear of night or darkness | Gk *nux, nukt-* 'night' |
| photophobia | extreme sensitivity to light | Gk *phōs, phōt-* 'light' |
| technophobia | fear of new technology | Gk *tekhnē* 'art, craft' |
| xenophobia | fear or dislike of people from other countries | Gk *xenos* 'stranger' |

➤ Unusual or interesting phobias (mostly rare or obsolete words):

| | | |
|---|---|---|
| Anglophobia | fear of England | L. *Anglus* 'England' |
| arachibutyrophobia | fear of peanut butter sticking to the roof of one's mouth | L. *arachis* 'peanut' + *butyrum* 'butter' |
| batrachophobia | fear of frogs | Gk *batrakhos* 'frog' |
| bibliophobia | fear or dread of books | Gk *biblion* 'book' |
| brontophobia | fear of thunderstorms | Gk *brontē* 'thunder' |
| deipnophobia | fear of dinner parties | Gk *deipnos* 'dinner' |
| ergophobia | fear of work | Gk *ergon* 'work' |
| erythrophobia | intolerance of the colour red | Gk *eruthros* 'red' |
| hippophobia | fear of horses | Gk *hippos* 'horse' |
| logophobia | fear of words | Gk *logos* 'word' |
| mycophobia | fear of mushrooms | Gk *mukēs* 'mushroom' |
| panophobia | terror; excessive panic | Gk *pan* 'all' |
| symmetrophobia | dread of symmetry | based on SYMMETRY |
| thalassophobia | fear of the sea | Gk *thalassa* 'sea' |
| triskaidekaphobia | superstition regarding the number 13 | Gk *treiskaideka* 'thirteen' |

➤ Related words:

| | |
|---|---|
| -phobe | forming nouns, e.g. ***technophobe*** 'a person with an irrational fear of technology' |
| -phobic | forming adjectives, e.g. ***xenophobic*** 'of or relating to xenophobia' |

➤ Oldest phobias:

| | |
|---|---|
| hydrophobia | aversion to water (first recorded example from 1547, spelled *hidroforbia*) |
| tyrannophobia | fear of tyrants (first recorded in 1651) |
| psychrophobia | fear of cold things (first recorded in 1727) |

➤ New phobias:

| | |
|---|---|
| Europhobia | hatred of Europe and the European Union (1990s) |
| islamophobia | irrational hatred or fear of Islam (1990s) |

**phonetics** ● **pl. n.** [treated as sing.] the study and classification of speech sounds.
– DERIVATIVES **phonetician** n.

**phoney** (also **phony**) informal ● **adj.** (**-ier**, **-iest**) not genuine. ● **n.** (pl. **-eys** or **-ies**) a fraudulent person or thing.
– DERIVATIVES **phonily** adv. **phoniness** n.
– ORIGIN C19: of unknown origin.

**phonic** /ˈfəʊnɪk, ˈfɒnɪk/ ● **adj.** of or relating to speech sounds. ➤ of or relating to phonics.
– DERIVATIVES **phonically** adv.
– ORIGIN C19: from Gk *phōnē* 'voice' + **-IC**.

**phonics** ● **pl. n.** [treated as sing.] a method of teaching people to read by correlating sounds with alphabetic symbols.

**phono** ● **adj.** denoting a type of plug, and the corresponding socket, used with audio and video equipment, in which one conductor is cylindrical and the other is a central prong that extends beyond it.
– ORIGIN 1940s: abbrev. of **PHONOGRAPH**.

**phono-** /ˈfəʊnəʊ, ˈfɒn-/ ● **comb. form** relating to sound: *phonograph*.
– ORIGIN from Gk *phōnē* 'sound, voice'.

**phonocardiogram** ● **n.** Medicine a record of the sounds made by the heart.

**phonograph** ● **n. 1** Brit. an early form of gramophone able to record and reproduce sound. **2** N. Amer. a record player.
– DERIVATIVES **phonographic** adj.

**phonolite** /ˈfəʊnəlʌɪt/ ● **n.** Geology a fine-grained volcanic rock composed of alkali feldspars and nepheline.
– ORIGIN C19: from **PHONO-** 'relating to sound' (because of its resonance when struck) + **-ITE**[1].

**phonology** /fəˈnɒlədʒi/ ● **n.** the system of contrastive re-

## Word *Formation*

### **-phone** from Greek *phōnē* 'sound, voice'

**➤ 1.** Instruments connected with sound:

| | | |
|---|---|---|
| aerophone | technical term for a wind instrument | Gk *aēr* 'air' |
| diaphone | type of fog signal | Gk *dia* 'through' |
| earphone | device worn on the ear to listen to recorded or broadcast sound | based on EAR |
| gramophone | old-fashioned term for a record player | reversed use of -GRAM 'something written or recorded' |
| headphones | pair of earphones | based on HEAD |
| megaphone | funnel-shaped device for amplifying the voice | Gk *megas* 'great' |
| microphone | device for picking up sound for amplification, recording, etc. | Gk *mikros* 'small' |
| saxophone | a metal wind instrument | from the name of the instrument-maker Adolphe *Sax* |
| sousaphone | a type of tuba | from the name of the composer J. P. *Sousa* |
| telephone | device used for transmitting the voice over long distance | Gk *tēle-* 'far off' |

**➤ 2.** A person speaking a particular language:

| | | |
|---|---|---|
| anglophone | English | L. *Anglus* 'English' |
| francophone | French | L. *Francus* 'Frank' |
| lusophone | Portuguese | from *Lusitania*, ancient Roman province occupying modern-day Portugal |

The word ***telephone*** (shortened to ***phone***) has given rise to words denoting types of telephone or related devices, as: ***answerphone***, ***cellphone***, ***entryphone***, ***mobile phone***, ***payphone***, ***videophone***.

**➤** Related words:

-phony forming nouns, e.g. ***cacophony*** 'harsh discordant sounds' (from Gk *kakos* 'bad'); ***euphony*** 'pleasing sounds' (from Gk *eu* 'well')

-phonic forming adjectives, e.g. ***polyphonic*** 'having two or more vocal parts' (from Gk *polu-* 'many'); ***quadraphonic*** 'through four channels' (from L. *quattuor* 'four')

lationships among the fundamental speech sounds of a language. ➤ the study of these relationships within or between languages.
– DERIVATIVES **phonological** adj. **phonologically** adv. **phonologist** n.

**phonon** /ˈfəʊnɒn/ ● **n.** Physics a quantum of energy associated with a compressional wave such as a vibration of a crystal lattice.
– ORIGIN 1930s: from Gk *phōnē* 'sound', on the pattern of *photon*.

**phonotactics** /ˌfəʊnə(ʊ)ˈtaktɪks/ ● **pl. n.** [treated as sing.] the study of the rules governing possible phoneme sequences in a language.
– DERIVATIVES **phonotactic** adj.

**phony** ● **adj. & n.** variant spelling of **PHONEY**.

**phooey** informal ● **exclam.** used to express disdain or disbelief. ● **n.** nonsense.
– ORIGIN 1920s: imitative.

**-phore** ● **comb. form** denoting an agent or bearer of a specified thing: *semaphore*.
– DERIVATIVES **-phorous** comb. form in corresponding adjectives.
– ORIGIN from mod. L. *-phorus*, from Gk *-phoros*, *-phoron* 'bearing, bearer', from *pherein* 'to bear'.

**phoresy** /fəˈriːsi, ˈfɒrəsi/ ● **n.** Zoology an association in which one organism travels on the body of another, without being a parasite.
– DERIVATIVES **phoretic** /fəˈrɛtɪk/ adj.
– ORIGIN 1920s: from Fr. *phorésie*, from Gk *phorēsis* 'being carried'.

**phormium** /ˈfɔːmɪəm/ ● **n.** the flax-lily of New Zealand.
– ORIGIN C19: mod. L., from Gk *phormion* 'small basket' (with ref. to the use made of the fibres).

**phosgene** /ˈfɒzdʒiːn/ ● **n.** Chemistry a poisonous gas formerly used in warfare. [$COCl_2$.]
– ORIGIN C19: from Gk *phōs* 'light' + **-GEN**, with ref. to its original production by the action of sunlight on chlorine and carbon monoxide.

**phosphatase** /ˈfɒsfəteɪz/ ● **n.** Biochemistry an enzyme that promotes the hydrolysis of organic phosphates.

**phosphate** /ˈfɒsfeɪt/ ● **n.** Chemistry a salt or ester of phosphoric acid, typically containing the anion $PO_4^{3-}$ or the group $-OPO(OH)_2$.
– DERIVATIVES **phosphatic** adj.
– ORIGIN C18: from Fr., from *phosphore* 'phosphorus'.

**phosphene** /ˈfɒsfiːn/ ● **n.** a sensation of a ring or spot of light produced by pressure on the eyeball or other non-light stimulus.
– ORIGIN C19: formed irregularly from Gk *phōs* 'light' + *phainein* 'to show'.

**phosphide** /ˈfɒsfʌɪd/ ● **n.** Chemistry a binary compound of phosphorus with another element or group.

**phosphine** /ˈfɒsfiːn/ ● **n.** Chemistry a foul-smelling gaseous compound of phosphorus and hydrogen. [$PH_3$.]
– ORIGIN C19: from **PHOSPHO-** + **-INE**[4], on the pattern of *amine*.

**phospho-** ● **comb. form** representing **PHOSPHORUS**.

**phospholipid** /ˌfɒsfə(ʊ)ˈlɪpɪd/ ● **n.** Biochemistry a lipid containing a phosphate group in its molecule.

**phosphor** /ˈfɒsfə/ ● **n. 1** a synthetic fluorescent or phosphorescent substance, especially one used to coat the screen of a cathode ray tube. **2** old-fashioned term for **PHOSPHORUS**.
– ORIGIN C17: from L. **PHOSPHORUS**.

**phosphor bronze** ● **n.** a tough, hard form of bronze

containing some phosphorus, used especially for bearings.

**phosphorescence** • **n.** light emitted by a substance without combustion or perceptible heat. ➤ Physics the emission of radiation in a similar manner to fluorescence but continuing after excitation ceases.
– DERIVATIVES **phosphoresce** v. **phosphorescent** adj.

**phosphoric** /fɒsˈfɒrɪk/ • **adj.** relating to or containing phosphorus. ➤ Chemistry of phosphorus with a valency of five.

**phosphoric acid** • **n.** Chemistry a crystalline acid obtained by treating phosphates with sulphuric acid, and used in fertilizer and soap manufacture and food processing. [$H_3PO_4$.]

**phosphorite** /ˈfɒsfərʌɪt/ • **n.** a sedimentary rock rich in calcium phosphate.
– ORIGIN C18: from **PHOSPHORUS** + **-ITE**[1].

**phosphorous** /ˈfɒsf(ə)rəs/ • **adj.** **1** relating to or containing phosphorus. ➤ Chemistry of phosphorus with a valency of three. **2** phosphorescent.

**USAGE phosphorous**

The correct spelling for the noun denoting the chemical element is **phosphorus**, while the correct spelling for the adjective is **phosphorous**.

**phosphorus** /ˈfɒsf(ə)rəs/ • **n.** the chemical element of atomic number 15, a poisonous, combustible non-metal which exists as a yellowish waxy solid which ignites spontaneously in air and glows in the dark (**white phosphorus**), and as a less reactive form used in making matches (**red phosphorus**). (Symbol: **P**)
– ORIGIN C17: from L., from Gk *phōsphoros*, from *phōs* 'light' + *-phoros* '-bringing'.

**phosphorylate** /fɒsˈfɒrɪleɪt/ • **v.** chiefly Biochemistry introduce a phosphate group into (a molecule or compound).
– DERIVATIVES **phosphorylation** n.

**phossy jaw** /ˈfɒsi/ • **n.** historical, informal gangrene of the jawbone caused by phosphorus poisoning.
– ORIGIN C19: *phossy* by abbrev. of *phosphorus necrosis*, denoting gangrene of the jaw.

**phot** /fəʊt/ • **n.** a unit of illumination equal to one lumen per square centimetre.
– ORIGIN C20: from Gk *phōs*, *phōt-* 'light'.

**photic** • **adj.** **1** technical of or relating to light. **2** Ecology denoting the layers of the ocean reached by sufficient sunlight to allow plant growth.

**photino** /fə(ʊ)ˈtiːnəʊ/ • **n.** (pl. **-os**) Physics a hypothetical supersymmetric particle corresponding to the photon.
– ORIGIN 1970s: from **PHOTON** + *-ino* from **NEUTRINO**.

**photo** • **n.** (pl. **-os**) a photograph. • **v.** (**-oes**, **-oed**) photograph.

**photo-** /ˈfəʊtəʊ/ • **comb. form** **1** relating to light: *photochemical*. **2** relating to photography: *photofit*.
– ORIGIN sense 1 from Gk *phōs*, *phōt-* 'light'.

**photobiology** • **n.** the study of the effects of light on living organisms.

**photocall** • **n.** Brit. an occasion on which famous people pose for photographers by arrangement.

**photo CD** • **n.** a compact disc from which still photographs can be displayed on a television screen.

**photocell** • **n.** short for **PHOTOELECTRIC CELL**.

**photochemical** • **adj.** of, relating to, or caused by the chemical action of light. ➤ of or relating to photochemistry.
– DERIVATIVES **photochemically** adv.

**photochemistry** • **n.** the branch of chemistry concerned with the chemical effects of light.

**photochromic** • **adj.** undergoing a reversible change in colour when exposed to light of a particular frequency or intensity.
– DERIVATIVES **photochromism** n.
– ORIGIN 1950s: from **PHOTO-** + Gk *khrōma* 'colour' + **-IC**.

**photocomposition** • **n.** another term for **FILMSETTING**.

**photoconductivity** /ˌfəʊtə(ʊ)kɒndʌkˈtɪvɪti/ • **n.** increased electrical conductivity caused by the presence of light.
– DERIVATIVES **photoconductive** adj. **photoconductor** n.

**photocopier** • **n.** a machine for making photocopies.

**photocopy** • **n.** (pl. **-ies**) a photographic copy of something produced by a process involving the action of light on a specially prepared surface. • **v.** (**-ies**, **-ied**) make a photocopy of.
– DERIVATIVES **photocopiable** adj.

**photodegradable** • **adj.** capable of being decomposed by the action of light, especially sunlight.

**photodiode** • **n.** a semiconductor diode which, when exposed to light, generates a potential difference or changes its electrical resistance.

**photodynamic** • **adj.** Medicine denoting treatment for cancer involving the injection of a cytotoxic compound which is activated by a laser beam after collecting in the tumour.

**photoelectric** • **adj.** characterized by or involving the emission of electrons from a surface by the action of light.
– DERIVATIVES **photoelectricity** n.

**photoelectric cell** • **n.** a device using a photoelectric effect to generate current.

**photoelectron** • **n.** an electron emitted from an atom by interaction with a photon.

**photoemission** • **n.** the emission of electrons from a surface caused by the action of light striking it.
– DERIVATIVES **photoemitter** n.

**photo finish** • **n.** a close finish of a race in which the winner is identifiable only from a photograph of competitors crossing the line.

**photofit** • **n.** Brit. a picture of a person, especially one sought by the police, made from composite photographs of facial features.

**photog** /fəˈtɒg/ • **n.** N. Amer. informal a photographer.

**photogenic** /ˌfəʊtə(ʊ)ˈdʒɛnɪk, -ˈdʒiːn-/ • **adj.** **1** looking attractive in photographs. **2** Biology producing or emitting light.
– DERIVATIVES **photogenically** adv.

**photogram** • **n.** a picture produced with photographic materials but without a camera. ➤ archaic a photograph.

**photogrammetry** /ˌfəʊtə(ʊ)ˈgramɪtri/ • **n.** the use of photography in surveying and mapping to ascertain measurements.
– DERIVATIVES **photogrammetric** adj. **photogrammetrist** n.

**photograph** • **n.** a picture made with a camera, in which an image is focused on to film and then made visible and permanent by chemical treatment. • **v.** take a photograph of.
– DERIVATIVES **photographable** adj. **photographer** n. **photographic** adj. **photographically** adv.

**photographic memory** • **n.** an ability to remember information or visual images in great detail.

**photography** • **n.** the taking and processing of photographs.

**photogravure** /ˌfəʊtə(ʊ)grəˈvjʊə/ • **n.** an image produced from a photographic negative transferred to a metal plate and etched in.
– ORIGIN C19: from Fr., from *photo-* 'relating to light' + *gravure* 'engraving'.

**photojournalism** • **n.** the communicating of news by photographs.
– DERIVATIVES **photojournalist** n.

**photolysis** /fə(ʊ)ˈtɒlɪsɪs/ • **n.** Chemistry the decomposition or separation of molecules by the action of light.
– DERIVATIVES **photolyse** v. **photolytic** adj.

**photometer** /fə(ʊ)ˈtɒmɪtə/ • **n.** an instrument measuring the intensity of light.
– DERIVATIVES **photometric** adj. **photometrically** adv. **photometry** n.

**photomicrograph** • **n.** another term for **MICROGRAPH**.
– DERIVATIVES **photomicrography** n.

**photomontage** /ˌfəʊtəʊmɒnˈtɑːʒ/ • **n.** a montage of photographs.

**photomosaic** • **n.** a large-scale picture or map built up from photographs of small areas.

**photomultiplier** • n. an instrument containing a photoelectric cell and a series of electrodes, used to detect and amplify very faint light.

**photon** /ˈfəʊtɒn/ • n. Physics a particle representing a quantum of light or other electromagnetic radiation.
– DERIVATIVES **photonic** adj. **photonics** pl. n.
– ORIGIN C20: from Gk *phōs, phōt-* 'light', on the pattern of *electron*.

**photonegative** • adj. **1** Biology (of an organism) tending to move away from light. **2** Physics (of a substance) exhibiting a decrease in electrical conductivity under illumination.

**photo-offset** • n. offset printing using plates made photographically.

**photo opportunity** • n. a photocall.

**photoperiod** • n. Botany & Zoology the period of daily illumination received by an organism.
– DERIVATIVES **photoperiodic** adj.

**photoperiodism** • n. Botany & Zoology the response of an organism to seasonal changes in day length.

**photophobia** • n. extreme sensitivity to light.
– DERIVATIVES **photophobic** adj.

**photophore** /ˈfəʊtə(ʊ)fɔː/ • n. Zoology a light-producing organ in certain fishes and other animals.
– ORIGIN C19: from Gk *phōtophoros* 'light-bearing'.

**photopic** /fəʊˈtɒpɪk, fəʊˈtəʊpɪk/ • adj. Physiology relating to or denoting vision in bright light. Often contrasted with **SCOTOPIC**.
– ORIGIN C20: from **PHOTO-** + **-OPIA** + **-IC**.

**photopigment** • n. a pigment whose chemical state depends on its degree of illumination, e.g. those in the retina.

**photopolarimeter** /ˌfəʊtəʊpəʊləˈrɪmɪtə/ • n. an apparatus for photographing stars, galaxies, etc. and measuring the polarization of light from them.

**photopositive** • adj. **1** Biology (of an organism) tending to move towards light. **2** Physics (of a substance) increasing in electrical conductivity under illumination.

**photoproduct** • n. a product of a photochemical reaction.

**photorealism** • n. a style of art and sculpture characterized by the highly detailed depiction of ordinary life with the impersonality of a photograph.
– DERIVATIVES **photorealist** n. & adj. **photorealistic** adj.

**photoreceptor** • n. a structure in an organism that responds to light.
– DERIVATIVES **photoreceptive** adj.

**photosensitive** • adj. responding to light.
– DERIVATIVES **photosensitivity** n.

**photo session** • n. a pre-arranged session in which a photographer takes photographs of someone for publication.

**photosetting** (also **phototypesetting**) • n. another term for **FILMSETTING**.
– DERIVATIVES **photoset** v. **photosetter** n.

**photosphere** • n. Astronomy the luminous envelope of a star from which its light and heat radiate.
– DERIVATIVES **photospheric** adj.

**photostat** /ˈfəʊtə(ʊ)stat/ • n. trademark a type of machine for making photocopies on special paper. ➤ a copy made by this means. • v. (**photostatted**, **photostatting**) copy with a photostat.
– DERIVATIVES **photostatic** adj.

**photostory** • n. a strip cartoon with photographs in place of drawings.

**photosynthesis** • n. the process by which green plants use sunlight to synthesize nutrients from carbon dioxide and water.
– DERIVATIVES **photosynthesize** (also **-ise**) v. **photosynthetic** adj. **photosynthetically** adv.

**phototaxis** /ˌfəʊtəʊˈtaksɪs/ • n. (pl. **phototaxes**) Biology the bodily movement of a motile organism in response to light.
– DERIVATIVES **phototactic** adj.

**phototransistor** • n. a transistor that responds to light striking it by generating and amplifying an electric current.

**phototroph** /ˈfəʊtə(ʊ)trəʊf/ • n. Biology an organism using energy from sunlight to synthesize nutriment.

**phototropism** /ˌfəʊtə(ʊ)ˈtrəʊpɪz(ə)m, fəʊˈtɒtrəˌpɪz(ə)m/ • n. Biology the orientation of a plant or other organism in response to light.
– DERIVATIVES **phototropic** adj.

**phototypesetting** • n. variant form of **PHOTOSETTING**.

**photovoltaic** /ˌfəʊtəʊvɒlˈteɪɪk/ • adj. relating to the production of electric current at the junction of two substances exposed to light.

**photovoltaics** • pl. n. [treated as sing.] the branch of technology concerned with the production of electric current at the junction of two substances. ➤ [treated as pl.] devices having such a junction.

**phragmites** /fragˈmʌɪtiːz/ • n. a tall reed of a genus including the common reed. [Genus *Phragmites*.]
– ORIGIN mod. L., from Gk *phragmitēs* 'growing in hedges'.

**phrasal verb** • n. Grammar an idiomatic phrase consisting of a verb and an adverb or preposition, as in *break down* or *see to*.

**phrase** • n. **1** a small group of words standing together as a conceptual unit. ➤ an idiomatic or short pithy expression. **2** Music a group of notes forming a distinct unit within a longer passage. • v. **1** put into a particular form of words. **2** [often as noun **phrasing**] divide (music) into phrases in a particular way.
– DERIVATIVES **phrasal** adj. **phrasally** adv.
– ORIGIN C16: via late L. from Gk *phrasis*, from *phrazein* 'declare, tell'.

**phrase book** • n. a book for people visiting a foreign country, listing useful expressions and their translations.

**phraseology** /ˌfreɪzɪˈɒlədʒi/ • n. (pl. **-ies**) a particular or characteristic mode of expression.
– DERIVATIVES **phraseological** adj.

**phratry** /ˈfreɪtri/ • n. (pl. **-ies**) Anthropology a descent group or kinship group in some tribal societies.
– ORIGIN C19: from Gk *phratria*, from *phratēr* 'clansman'.

**phreaking** • n. informal, chiefly N. Amer. the action of hacking into telecommunications systems, especially to obtain free calls.
– DERIVATIVES **phreak** n. **phreaker** n.
– ORIGIN 1970s: alt. of *freaking* by assoc. with *phone*.

**phreatic** /frɪˈatɪk/ • adj. Geology relating to or denoting underground water in the zone below the water table. Compare with **VADOSE**. ➤ (of a volcanic eruption) caused by the heating and expansion of groundwater.
– ORIGIN C19: from Gk *phrear, phreat-* 'a well' + **-IC**.

**phrenic** /ˈfrɛnɪk/ • adj. Anatomy of or relating to the diaphragm.
– ORIGIN C18: from Fr. *phrénique*, from Gk *phrēn, phren-* 'diaphragm, mind' (because the mind was once thought to lie in the diaphragm).

**phrenology** /frɪˈnɒlədʒi/ • n. chiefly historical the detailed study of the shape and size of the cranium as a supposed indication of character and mental abilities.
– DERIVATIVES **phrenological** adj. **phrenologist** n.
– ORIGIN C19: from Gk *phrēn, phren-* 'mind' + **-LOGY**.

**Phrygian** /ˈfrɪdʒɪən/ • n. **1** a native or inhabitant of Phrygia, an ancient region of west central Asia Minor. **2** the language of the ancient Phrygians, generally classified as Indo-European. • adj. of or relating to Phrygia, its people, or their language.

**Phrygian bonnet** (also **Phrygian cap**) • n. a conical cap with the top bent forwards, worn in ancient times and more recently identified with the cap of liberty.

**Phrygian mode** • n. Music the mode represented by the natural diatonic scale E–E (containing a minor 2nd, 3rd, 6th, and 7th).

**phthalic acid** /ˈ(f)θalɪk/ • n. Chemistry a crystalline acid derived from benzene, with two carboxylic acid groups attached to the benzene ring.
– DERIVATIVES **phthalate** n.
– ORIGIN C19: shortening of *naphthalic* (see **NAPHTHALENE**).

**phthalocyanine** /ˌ(f)θaləʊˈsʌɪəniːn/ • n. Chemistry a

green or blue pigment or dye of the porphyrin class, often one containing copper.
– ORIGIN 1930s: from *phthalic* (see **PHTHALIC ACID**) + Gk *kuan(e)os* 'dark blue' + **-INE**[4].

**phthisis** /ˈ(f)θʌɪsɪs, ˈtʌɪ-/ ● n. archaic pulmonary tuberculosis or a similar progressive wasting disease.
– DERIVATIVES **phthisic** adj. **phthisical** adj.
– ORIGIN C16: via L. from Gk, from *phthinein* 'to decay'.

**phut** ● exclam. used to represent a dull abrupt sound as of a slight impact or explosion.
– ORIGIN C19: perh. from Hindi *phaṭnā* 'to burst'.

**phwoah** /ˈfwɔːə/ (also **phwoar**) ● exclam. Brit. informal used to express sexual desire.

**phyco-** ● comb. form relating to seaweed: *phycology.*
– ORIGIN from Gk *phukos* 'seaweed'.

**phycology** /fʌɪˈkɒlədʒi/ ● n. the branch of botany concerned with seaweeds and other algae.
– DERIVATIVES **phycological** adj. **phycologist** n.

**phyla** plural form of **PHYLUM**.

**phylactery** /fɪˈlakt(ə)ri/ ● n. (pl. **-ies**) a small leather box containing Hebrew texts on vellum, worn by Jewish men at morning prayer.
– ORIGIN ME: via late L. from Gk *phulaktērion* 'amulet', from *phulassein* 'to guard'.

**phyletic** /fʌɪˈlɛtɪk/ ● adj. Biology relating to or denoting the evolutionary development of a species or other group.
– DERIVATIVES **phyletically** adv.
– ORIGIN C19: from Gk *phuletikos*, from *phuletēs* 'tribesman'.

**phyllite** /ˈfɪlʌɪt/ ● n. Geology a fine-grained metamorphic rock with a well-developed laminar structure, intermediate between slate and schist.
– ORIGIN C19: from Gk *phullon* 'leaf' + **-ITE**[1].

**phyllo** ● n. variant spelling of **FILO**.

**phyllo-** ● comb. form of a leaf; relating to leaves: *phyllotaxis.*
– ORIGIN from Gk *phullon* 'leaf'.

**phyllode** /ˈfɪləʊd/ ● n. Botany a winged leaf stalk which functions as a leaf.
– ORIGIN C19: from mod. L. *phyllodium*, from Gk *phullōdēs* 'leaf-like'.

**phylloquinone** /ˌfɪlə(ʊ)ˈkwɪnəʊn/ ● n. Biochemistry vitamin $K_1$, a compound found in cabbage, spinach, and other leafy green vegetables, and essential for the blood-clotting process.

**phyllotaxis** /ˌfɪlə(ʊ)ˈtaksɪs/ (also **phyllotaxy** /-ˈtaksi/) ● n. Botany the arrangement of leaves on an axis or stem.
– DERIVATIVES **phyllotactic** adj.

**phylloxera** /ˌfɪlɒkˈsɪərə, fɪˈlɒksərə/ ● n. a plant louse that is a pest of vines. [*Phylloxera vitifoliae.*]
– ORIGIN C19: mod. L., from Gk *phullon* 'leaf' + *xēros* 'dry'.

**phylogenesis** /ˌfʌɪlə(ʊ)ˈdʒɛnɪsɪs/ ● n. Biology the evolutionary development and diversification of a species or group of organisms.
– DERIVATIVES **phylogenetic** adj. **phylogenetically** adv.
– ORIGIN C19: from Gk *phulon, phulē* 'race, tribe' + **GENESIS**.

**phylogeny** /fʌɪˈlɒdʒ(ə)ni/ ● n. the branch of biology concerned with phylogenesis. Compare with **ONTOGENY**. ➤ another term for **PHYLOGENESIS**.
– DERIVATIVES **phylogenic** adj. **phylogenically** adv.

**phylum** /ˈfʌɪləm/ ● n. (pl. **phyla** /-lə/) **1** Zoology a principal taxonomic category that ranks above class and below kingdom, equivalent to the division in botany. **2** Linguistics a group of languages related to each other less closely than those forming a family.
– ORIGIN C19: mod. L. from Gk *phulon* 'race'.

**physalis** /ˈfʌɪsəlɪs, ˈfɪs-, fʌɪˈseɪlɪs/ ● n. a plant of a genus that includes the Cape gooseberry and Chinese lantern, which has an inflated lantern-like calyx. [Genus *Physalis.*]
– ORIGIN mod. L., from Gk *phusallis* 'bladder'.

**physic** archaic ● n. medicinal drugs or medical treatment. ● v. (**physicked**, **physicking**) treat with a medicine.
– ORIGIN ME: from OFr. *fisique* 'medicine', from L. *physica*, from Gk *phusikē (epistēmē)* '(knowledge) of nature', from *phusis* 'nature'.

**physical** ● adj. **1** of or relating to the body as opposed to the mind. ➤ involving bodily contact or activity: *a physical relationship.* **2** of or relating to things perceived through the senses as opposed to the mind; tangible or concrete. **3** of or relating to physics or the operation of natural forces generally. ● n. **1** a medical examination to determine a person's bodily fitness. **2** (**physicals**) Stock Exchange stocks held in actual commodities for immediate exchange, as opposed, for example, to futures.
– DERIVATIVES **physicality** /-ˈkalɪti/ n. **physicalization** (also **-isation**) n. **physicalize** (also **-ise**) v. **physically** adv. **physicalness** n.

**physical anthropology** ● n. the science of human zoology, evolution, and ecology.

**physical chemistry** ● n. the branch of chemistry concerned with the application of the techniques and theories of physics to the study of chemical systems.

**physical education** ● n. instruction in physical exercise and games, especially in schools.

**physical geography** ● n. the branch of geography concerned with natural features.

**physicalism** ● n. Philosophy the doctrine that the real world consists simply of the physical world.
– DERIVATIVES **physicalist** n. & adj. **physicalistic** adj.

**physical jerks** ● pl. n. Brit. informal energetic exercises done as part of a fitness routine.

**physical sciences** ● pl. n. the sciences concerned with the study of inanimate natural objects, including physics, chemistry, and astronomy.

**physical therapy** ● n. US term for **PHYSIOTHERAPY**.
– DERIVATIVES **physical therapist** n.

**physic garden** ● n. a garden for cultivating medicinal herbs.

**physician** ● n. a person qualified to practise medicine, especially one who specializes in diagnosis and medical treatment as distinct from surgery.

**physico-** ● comb. form physical; physical and ...: *physicomental.*

**physics** ● pl. n. [treated as sing.] the branch of science concerned with the nature and properties of matter and energy. ➤ the physical properties and phenomena of something.
– DERIVATIVES **physicist** n.
– ORIGIN C15 (denoting natural science in general): pl. of obs. *physic* 'physical (thing)', suggested by L. *physica* (see **PHYSIC**).

**physio** ● n. (pl. **-os**) informal physiotherapy or a physiotherapist.

**physio-** ● comb. form **1** relating to nature and natural phenomena: *physiography.* **2** representing **PHYSIOLOGY**.
– ORIGIN from Gk *phusis* 'nature'.

**physiocrat** ● n. a member of an 18th-century group of French economists who believed that agriculture was the source of all wealth and advocated free trade.
– DERIVATIVES **physiocracy** n. **physiocratic** adj.

**physiognomy** /ˌfɪzɪˈɒ(g)nəmi/ ● n. (pl. **-ies**) **1** a person's facial features or expression, especially when regarded as indicative of character or ethnic origin. **2** the supposed art of judging character from facial characteristics.
– DERIVATIVES **physiognomic** adj. **physiognomical** adj. **physiognomically** adv. **physiognomist** n.
– ORIGIN ME: from OFr. *phisonomie*, via med. L. from Gk *phusiognōmonia* 'judging of a man's nature (by his features)', based on *gnōmōn* 'judge or interpreter'.

**physiological saline** ● n. a solution of salts that is isotonic with the body fluids.

**physiology** ● n. the branch of biology concerned with the normal functions of living organisms and their parts. ➤ the way in which a living organism or bodily part functions.
– DERIVATIVES **physiologic** adj. **physiological** adj. **physiologically** adv. **physiologist** n.

**physiotherapy** (US **physical therapy**) ● n. the treatment of disease, injury, or deformity by physical methods

such as massage and exercise rather than by drugs or surgery.
– DERIVATIVES **physiotherapist** n.

**physique** /fɪˈziːk/ ● **n.** the form, size, and development of a person's body.
– ORIGIN C19: from Fr., lit. 'physical' (used as a noun).

**physostigmine** /ˌfʌɪsəʊˈstɪgmiːn/ ● **n.** Chemistry a compound which is the active ingredient of the Calabar bean and is used medicinally in eye drops.
– ORIGIN C19: from the mod. L. genus name *Physostigma* + **-INE**[4].

**-phyte** ● **comb. form** denoting a plant or plant-like organism: *epiphyte.*
– DERIVATIVES **-phytic** comb. form in corresponding adjectives.
– ORIGIN from Gk *phuton* 'a plant'.

**phyto-** ● **comb. form** of a plant; relating to plants: *phytogeography.*

**phytoalexin** /ˌfʌɪtəʊəˈlɛksɪn/ ● **n.** Botany a substance that is produced by plant tissues in response to contact with a parasite and specifically inhibits the growth of that parasite.
– ORIGIN 1940s: from **PHYTO-** + *alexin*, a name for a class of substances found in blood serum, able to destroy bacteria.

**phytochemistry** ● **n.** the branch of chemistry concerned with plants and plant products.
– DERIVATIVES **phytochemical** adj. **phytochemist** n.

**phytochrome** ● **n.** Biochemistry a blue-green pigment found in many plants, in which it regulates various developmental processes.
– ORIGIN C19: from **PHYTO-** + Gk *khrōma* 'colour'.

**phytogeography** ● **n.** the branch of botany concerned with the geographical distribution of plants.
– DERIVATIVES **phytogeographer** n. **phytogeographic** adj. **phytogeographical** adj. **phytogeographically** adv.

**phytolith** /ˈfʌɪtə(ʊ)lɪθ/ ● **n. 1** Botany a minute mineral particle formed inside a plant. **2** Palaeontology a fossilized particle of plant tissue.

**phytophagous** /fʌɪˈtɒfəgəs/ ● **adj.** Zoology (especially of an insect or other invertebrate) feeding on plants.
– DERIVATIVES **phytophagy** n.

**phytoplankton** /ˈfʌɪtəʊˌplaŋktən/ ● **n.** Biology plankton consisting of microscopic plants.

**phytotoxic** ● **adj.** Botany poisonous to plants.
– DERIVATIVES **phytotoxicity** n.

**phytotoxin** ● **n.** Botany **1** a poisonous substance derived from a plant. **2** a substance, especially one produced by a parasite, that is phytotoxic.

**pi**[1] /pʌɪ/ ● **n. 1** the sixteenth letter of the Greek alphabet (Π, π), transliterated as 'p'. **2** the numerical value of the ratio of the circumference of a circle to its diameter (approximately 3.14159). **3** [as modifier] Chemistry & Physics (of an electron or orbital) with one unit of angular momentum about an internuclear axis. ● **symb.** (Π) mathematical product.
– ORIGIN from Gk: the numerical use comes from the initial letter of Gk *periphereia* 'circumference'.

**pi**[2] /pʌɪ/ ● **adj.** Brit. informal short for **PIOUS**.

**pia** /ˈpʌɪə, ˈpiːə/ (in full **pia mater**) ● **n.** Anatomy the delicate innermost membrane enveloping the brain and spinal cord.
– DERIVATIVES **pial** adj.
– ORIGIN C19: from med. L., in full lit. 'tender mother', translating Arab. *al-'umm ar-rakīka.*

**piacular** /pʌɪˈakjʊlə/ ● **adj.** rare making or requiring atonement.
– ORIGIN C17: from L. *piacularis*, from *piaculum* 'expiation'.

**piaffe** /pɪˈaf/ Riding ● **n.** (also **piaffer** /pɪˈafə/) a movement in which the horse executes a slow elevated trot without moving forward. ● **v.** perform such a movement.
– ORIGIN C18: from Fr. *piaffer* 'to strut'.

**pianism** /ˈpɪənɪz(ə)m/ ● **n.** skill or artistry in playing the piano or composing piano music.
– DERIVATIVES **pianistic** adj. **pianistically** adv.

**pianissimo** /ˌpɪəˈnɪsɪməʊ/ ● **adv. & adj.** Music very soft or softly.
– ORIGIN Ital., superlative of *piano* (see **PIANO**[2]).

**piano**[1] /pɪˈanəʊ/ ● **n.** (pl. **-os**) a large keyboard musical instrument with a wooden case enclosing a soundboard and metal strings, which are struck by hammers when the keys are depressed.
– DERIVATIVES **pianist** n.
– ORIGIN C19: from Ital., abbrev. of **PIANOFORTE**.

**piano**[2] /ˈpjɑːnəʊ/ ● **adv. & adj.** Music soft or softly.
– ORIGIN Ital., lit. 'soft'.

**piano accordion** ● **n.** an accordion with the melody played on a small vertical keyboard like that of a piano.

**pianoforte** /pɪˌanəʊˈfɔːteɪ, -ˈfɔːti/ ● **n.** formal term for **PIANO**[1].
– ORIGIN C18: from Ital., earlier *piano e forte* 'soft and loud', expressing the gradation in tone.

**pianola** /ˌpɪəˈnəʊlə/ ● **n.** trademark a piano equipped to be played automatically using a piano roll.
– ORIGIN C19: appar. a dimin. of **PIANO**[1].

**piano nobile** /ˌpjɑːnəʊ ˈnəʊbɪleɪ/ ● **n.** Architecture the main storey of a large house, usually the first floor.
– ORIGIN Ital., lit. 'noble floor'.

**piano organ** ● **n.** a mechanical piano constructed like a barrel organ.

**piano roll** ● **n.** a roll of perforated paper which controls the movement of the keys in a pianola.

**piassava** /ˌpiːəˈsɑːvə/ ● **n.** a stout fibre obtained from the leaf stalks of a number of South American and African palm trees.
– ORIGIN C19: via Port. from Tupi *piaçába.*

**piastre** /pɪˈastə/ (US also **piaster**) ● **n.** a monetary unit of several Middle Eastern countries, equal to one hundredth of a pound.
– ORIGIN from Fr., from Ital. *piastra* (*d'argento*) 'plate (of silver)'.

**piazza** /pɪˈatsə/ ● **n. 1** a public square or marketplace, especially in an Italian town. **2** US archaic the veranda of a house.
– ORIGIN C16: Ital.

**pibroch** /ˈpiːbrɒk, -brɒx/ ● **n.** a form of music for the Scottish bagpipes involving elaborate variations on a theme, typically of a martial or funerary character.
– ORIGIN C18: from Sc. Gaelic *piobaireachd* 'art of piping', from *piobair* 'piper', based on Engl. **PIPE**.

**pic** ● **n.** informal a picture, photograph, or film.

**pica**[1] /ˈpʌɪkə/ ● **n.** Printing **1** a unit of type size and line length equal to 12 points (about ⅙ inch or 4.2 mm). **2** a size of letter in typewriting, with 10 characters to the inch (about 3.9 to the centimetre).
– ORIGIN C16: from Anglo-Latin *pica* (lit. 'magpie'), commonly identified with a C15 book of rules about Church feasts.

**pica**[2] /ˈpʌɪkə/ ● **n.** Medicine a tendency or craving to eat substances other than normal food, occurring during childhood or pregnancy or as a symptom of disease.
– ORIGIN C16: mod. L., from L., lit. 'magpie', prob. translating Gk *kissa* 'magpie', also 'false appetite'.

**picador** /ˈpɪkədɔː/ ● **n.** (in bullfighting) a person on horseback who goads the bull with a lance.
– ORIGIN Sp., from *picar* 'to prick'.

**picante** /pɪˈkanteɪ/ ● **adj.** (of food) spicy.
– ORIGIN Sp., lit. 'pricking, biting'.

**picaresque** /ˌpɪkəˈrɛsk/ ● **adj.** of or relating to an episodic style of fiction dealing with the adventures of a rough and dishonest but appealing hero.
– ORIGIN C19: from Fr., from Sp. *picaresco*, from *pícaro* 'rogue'.

**picaroon** /ˌpɪkəˈruːn/ ● **n.** archaic a rogue or scoundrel.
– ORIGIN C17: from Sp. *picarón*, augmentative of *picaro* 'rogue'.

**picayune** /ˌpɪkəˈjuːn/ N. Amer. ● **adj.** informal petty; worthless. ● **n. 1** informal an insignificant person or thing. **2** dated a small coin of little value, especially a 5-cent piece.
– ORIGIN C19: from Fr. *picaillon*, denoting a Piedmontese copper coin, also used to mean 'cash'.

**piccalilli** /ˌpɪkəˈlɪli/ ● **n.** (pl. **piccalillies** or **piccalillis**) a pickle of chopped vegetables, mustard, and hot spices.

– ORIGIN C18: prob. from a blend of **PICKLE** and **CHILLI**.

**piccaninny** /ˈpɪkənɪni/ (US **pickaninny**) • **n.** (pl. **-ies**) offensive a small black child. • **adj.** archaic very small.
– ORIGIN C17: from W. Ind. creole, from Sp. *pequeño* or Port. *pequeno* 'little', *pequenino* 'tiny'.

**piccolo** • **n.** (pl. **-os**) a small flute sounding an octave higher than the ordinary one.
– ORIGIN C19: from Ital., 'small (flute)'.

**piccy** • **n.** (pl. **-ies**) informal a picture.

**pick**[1] • **v. 1** take hold of and remove (a flower or fruit) from where it is growing. ➤(often **pick someone/thing up**) take hold of and lift or move. ➤(**pick up**) Golf take hold of and lift up one's ball, especially when conceding a hole. **2** choose from a number of alternatives. ➤(**pick one's way**) walk slowly and carefully. **3** (often **pick at**) repeatedly pull at something with one's fingers. ➤eat in small amounts or without much appetite. ➤criticize someone in a niggling way. **4** remove unwanted matter from (one's nose or teeth) with a finger or a pointed instrument. **5** pluck the strings of (a guitar or banjo). • **n. 1** an act or the right of selecting something. ➤(**the pick of**) informal the best person or thing in a particular group. **2** Basketball an act of blocking or screening a defensive player from the ball handler.
– PHRASES **pick and choose** select only the best from among a number of alternatives. **pick someone's brains** informal obtain information by questioning someone well informed. **pick a fight** provoke an argument or fight. **pick holes in** find fault with. **pick a lock** open a lock with an instrument other than the proper key. **pick someone's pockets** steal something surreptitiously from another person's pocket.
– PHRASAL VERBS **pick someone/thing off** shoot a member of a group from a distance. **pick on** repeatedly single out for unfair criticism or unkind treatment. **pick someone/thing out** distinguish or select from among a group. ➤highlight or accentuate by painting or fashioning in a contrasting colour or medium. **pick something over** (or **pick through**) sort through a number of items carefully. **pick up** improve or increase. **pick someone up 1** go somewhere to collect someone. **2** informal casually strike up a relationship with someone as a sexual overture. **3** return to a point or remark made by someone in order to criticize it. **pick something up 1** collect something that has been left elsewhere. **2** obtain, acquire, or learn something. ➤catch an illness or infection. **3** detect or receive a signal or sound. **4** resume something. **5** (also **pick up on**) refer to or develop a point or topic mentioned earlier. ➤become aware of or sensitive to something. **6** N. Amer. tidy a room or building.
– DERIVATIVES **pickable** adj. **picker** n.
– ORIGIN ME (earlier as *pike*): of unknown origin.

**pick**[2] • **n. 1** a tool headed by a curved bar with a point at one end and a chisel edge or point at the other, used for breaking up hard ground or rock. **2** an instrument for picking. ➤informal a plectrum.
– ORIGIN ME: var. of **PIKE**[2].

**pickaback** • **n.**, **adv.**, & **v.** old-fashioned term for **PIGGYBACK**.

**pickaninny** • **n.** US spelling of **PICCANINNY**.

**pickaxe** (US also **pickax**) • **n.** another term for **PICK**[2] (in sense 1).
– ORIGIN ME *pikoys*, from OFr. *picois*, assimilated to **AXE**; rel. to **PIKE**[2].

**pickelhaube** /ˈpɪk(ə)lˌ(h)aʊbə/ • **n.** historical a spiked helmet worn by German soldiers.
– ORIGIN from Ger.

**pickerel** /ˈpɪk(ə)r(ə)l/ • **n.** (pl. same or **pickerels**) **1** a small pike occurring in North America. [Genus *Esox*: several species.] **2** a young pike.
– ORIGIN ME: dimin. of **PIKE**[1].

**picket** • **n. 1** a person or group of people standing outside a workplace trying to persuade others not to enter during a strike. **2** (also **picquet**) a soldier or small body of troops sent out to watch for the enemy. **3** [usu. as modifier] a pointed wooden stake driven into the ground to form a fence or palisade or to tether a horse: *a picket fence*. • **v.** (**picketed**, **picketing**) act as a picket outside (a workplace).
– DERIVATIVES **picketer** n.
– ORIGIN C17 (denoting a pointed stake, on which a soldier was required to stand on one foot as a military punishment): from Fr. *piquet* 'pointed stake'.

**pickings** • **pl. n. 1** profits or gains, especially those made effortlessly or dishonestly. **2** remaining scraps or leftovers.

**pickle** • **n. 1** a relish consisting of vegetables or fruit preserved in vinegar, brine, or mustard. ➤N. Amer. a cucumber preserved in this way. ➤liquid used to preserve food or other perishable items. **2** (**a pickle**) informal a difficult situation. **3** an acid solution for cleaning metal objects. • **v. 1** preserve (food) in pickle. **2** immerse (a metal object) in an acid solution for cleaning. **3** [as adj. **pickled**] informal drunk.
– DERIVATIVES **pickler** n.
– ORIGIN ME: from MDu., Mid. Low Ger. *pekel*, of unknown ultimate origin.

**pick-me-up** • **n.** informal a thing that makes one feel more energetic or cheerful.

**pickney** /ˈpɪkni/ • **n.** black English a child.
– ORIGIN contr. of **PICCANINNY**.

**pickpocket** • **n.** a person who steals from people's pockets.
– DERIVATIVES **pickpocketing** n.

**pickup** • **n. 1** (also **pickup truck**) a small van or truck with low sides. **2** an act of picking up or collecting a person or goods. **3** an improvement, especially in an economy. **4** a device on an electric guitar which converts sound vibrations into electrical signals for amplification. **5** the cartridge of a record player, carrying the stylus. **6** Music a series of introductory notes leading into the opening part of a tune. **7** Fishing a semicircular loop of metal for guiding the line back on to the spool as it is reeled in.

**Pickwickian** /pɪkˈwɪkɪən/ • **adj.** of or like Mr Pickwick in Dickens's *Pickwick Papers*, especially in being jovial, plump, or generous. ➤(of words) misunderstood or misused, especially to avoid offence.

**picky** • **adj.** (**-ier**, **-iest**) informal fastidious, especially excessively so.
– DERIVATIVES **pickiness** n.

**picnic** • **n.** a packed meal eaten outdoors, or an occasion when such a meal is eaten. • **v.** (**picnicked**, **picnicking**) have or take part in a picnic.
– PHRASES **be no picnic** informal be difficult or unpleasant.
– DERIVATIVES **picnicker** n.
– ORIGIN C18: from Fr. *pique-nique*, of unknown origin.

**pico-** /ˈpiːkəʊ, ˈpʌɪkəʊ/ • **comb. form** denoting a factor of $10^{-12}$: *picosecond*. ➤very small: *picornavirus*.
– ORIGIN from Sp. *pico*, lit. 'beak, peak, little bit'.

**picornavirus** /prˈkɔːnəˌvʌɪrəs/ • **n.** any of a group of very small RNA viruses which includes enteroviruses, rhinoviruses, and the virus of foot-and-mouth disease.
– ORIGIN 1960s: from **PICO-** + **RNA** + **VIRUS**.

**picot** /ˈpiːkəʊ/ • **n.** a small decorative loop or series of loops in lace or embroidery.
– ORIGIN C17: from Fr., lit. 'small peak or point'.

**picotee** /ˌpɪkəˈtiː/ • **n.** a type of carnation of which the flowers have a light ground and dark-edged petals.
– ORIGIN C18: from Fr. *picoté(e)* 'marked with points', past part. of *picoter* 'to prick'.

**picquet** • **n.** variant spelling of **PICKET** (in sense 2).

**picric acid** /ˈpɪkrɪk/ • **n.** Chemistry a bitter yellow compound obtained by nitrating phenol, used as a dye and in the manufacture of explosives.
– DERIVATIVES **picrate** /-reɪt/ n.
– ORIGIN C19: *picric* from Gk *pikros* 'bitter' + **-IC**.

**Pict** • **n.** a member of an ancient people inhabiting northern Scotland in Roman times.
– DERIVATIVES **Pictish** adj. & n.
– ORIGIN from late L. *Picti*, perh. from L. *pict-*, *pingere* 'to paint or tattoo', or perh. influenced by a local name.

**pictograph** (also **pictogram**) • **n. 1** a pictorial symbol for a word or phrase. **2** a pictorial representation of statistics on a chart, graph, or computer screen.
– DERIVATIVES **pictographic** adj. **pictography** n.

– ORIGIN C19: from L. *pict-*, *pingere* 'to paint' + **-GRAPH**.

**pictorial** • adj. of or expressed in pictures; illustrated. • n. a newspaper or periodical with pictures as a main feature.
– DERIVATIVES **pictorially** adv.
– ORIGIN C17: from late L. *pictorius* (from L. *pictor* 'painter', from *pingere* 'to paint') + **-AL**.

**picture** • n. **1** a painting, drawing, or photograph. ➤ a portrait. ➤ an image on a television screen. **2** an impression formed from an account or description: *a full picture of the disaster had not yet emerged.* ➤ (often in phr. **in** (or **out of**) **the picture**) informal a state of being fully informed about or involved in something. **3** a cinema film. ➤ (**the pictures**) the cinema. **4** archaic a person or thing resembling another closely. • v. **1** represent in a picture. **2** form a mental image of.
– PHRASES **be** (or **look**) **a picture 1** be beautiful. **2** look amusingly startled. **a** (or **the**) **picture of** —— the embodiment of a specified state or emotion: *she looked a picture of health.* (**as**) **pretty as a picture** very pretty.
– ORIGIN ME: from L. *pictura*, from *pict-*, *pingere* 'to paint'.

**picture book** • n. a book containing many illustrations, especially one for children.

**picture hat** • n. a woman's highly decorated hat with a wide brim, as worn in 18th-century England.

**picture palace** • n. Brit. dated a cinema.

**picture postcard** • n. **1** a postcard with a picture on one side. **2** [as modifier] (of a view) prettily picturesque.

**picture rail** • n. a horizontal strip of wood on a wall from which pictures can be hung.

**picturesque** • adj. visually attractive in a quaint or charming manner. ➤ (of language) unusual and vivid.
– DERIVATIVES **picturesquely** adv. **picturesqueness** n.
– ORIGIN C18: from Fr. *pittoresque*, from Ital. *pittoresco*, from *pittore* 'painter' (from L. *pictor*).

**picture theatre** • n. dated, chiefly N. Amer. a cinema.

**picture tube** • n. Electronics the cathode ray tube of a television set designed for the reproduction of television pictures.

**picture window** • n. a large window consisting of one pane of glass, typically facing an attractive view.

**picture writing** • n. a mode of recording events by pictorial symbols; pictography.

**piculet** /ˈpɪkjʊlɪt/ • n. a tiny woodpecker with a short unstiffened tail. [*Picumnus* (Central and S. America) and other genera.]
– ORIGIN C19: appar. a double dimin. of L. *picus* 'woodpecker'.

**PID** • abbrev. pelvic inflammatory disease.

**piddle** informal • v. **1** urinate. **2** (**piddle about/around**) spend time in trifling activities. **3** [as adj. **piddling**] pathetically trivial; trifling. • n. an act of urinating. ➤ urine.
– DERIVATIVES **piddler** n.
– ORIGIN C16: prob. from a blend of **PISS** and **PUDDLE**.

**piddock** /ˈpɪdək/ • n. a bivalve mollusc which bores into soft rock or other firm surfaces. [*Pholas* and other genera.]
– ORIGIN C19: of unknown origin.

**pidgin** /ˈpɪdʒɪn/ • n. a grammatically simplified form of a language with elements taken from local languages, used for communication between people not sharing a common language. ➤ (**Pidgin**) another term for **TOK PISIN**.
– ORIGIN C19: Chin. alt. of Engl. *business*.

**pi-dog** • n. variant spelling of **PYE-DOG**.

**pie**[1] • n. a baked dish of savoury or sweet ingredients encased in or topped with pastry.
– PHRASES (**as**) —— **as pie** informal very ——. **pie in the sky** informal something pleasant to contemplate but very unlikely to be realized.
– ORIGIN ME: prob. the same word as **PIE**[2], the various combinations of ingredients being compared to objects randomly collected by a magpie.

**pie**[2] • n. used in names of birds resembling a magpie, e.g. **tree pie**.
– ORIGIN ME: from OFr., from L. *pica* 'magpie'.

**pie**[3] • n. a former monetary unit of the Indian subcontinent, equal to one twelfth of an anna.
– ORIGIN from Hindi *pā'ī*, from Sanskrit *pada*, *padī* 'quarter'.

**piebald** • adj. (of a horse) having irregular patches of two colours, typically black and white. • n. a piebald horse.
– ORIGIN C16: from **PIE**[2] (because of the magpie's black-and-white plumage) + **BALD** (in the obs. sense 'streaked with white').

**piece** • n. **1** a portion of an object or of material produced by cutting, tearing, or breaking the whole. **2** an item used in constructing something or forming part of a set; a component. ➤ an instance or example: *a crucial piece of evidence.* **3** a musical or written work: *a piece of music.* **4** a figure or token used to make moves in a board game. ➤ Chess a king, queen, bishop, knight, or rook, as opposed to a pawn. **5** a coin of specified value: *a 10p piece.* **6** informal, chiefly N. Amer. a firearm. **7** Scottish a sandwich or other item of food taken as a snack. **8** informal a woman. • v. **1** (**piece something together**) assemble something from individual parts. **2** (**piece something out**) archaic extend something. **3** archaic patch.
– PHRASES **go to pieces** become so nervous or upset that one is unable to function normally. **in one piece** unharmed or undamaged. (**all**) **of a piece** entirely consistent. **piece by piece** in slow and small stages. **piece of water** a small lake or pond. **piece of work** informal a person of a specified kind, especially an unpleasant one. **say one's piece** give one's opinion or make a prepared statement. **tear** (or **pull**) **someone/thing to pieces** criticize someone or something harshly.
– DERIVATIVES **piecer** n.
– ORIGIN ME: from OFr. *piece* (cf. med. L. *pecia*, *petium*), of obscure ultimate origin.

**pièce de résistance** /ˌpjɛs də reɪˈzɪstɒ̃s, French pjɛs də ʀezistɑ̃s/ • n. the most important or remarkable feature of a creative work, meal, etc.
– ORIGIN Fr., lit. 'piece (i.e. means) of resistance'.

**piece goods** • pl. n. fabrics woven in standard lengths for sale.

**piecemeal** • adj. & adv. characterized by unsystematic partial measures taken over a period of time.
– ORIGIN ME: from **PIECE** + *-meal* from OE *mǣlum*, in the sense 'measure, quantity taken at one time'.

**piece of eight** • n. historical a Spanish dollar, equivalent to eight reals.

**piecework** • n. work paid for according to the amount produced.
– DERIVATIVES **pieceworker** n.

**pie chart** • n. a type of graph in which a circle is divided into sectors that each represent a proportion of the whole.

**piecrust table** • n. a table with an indented edge like a piecrust.

**pied** /pʌɪd/ • adj. having two or more different colours.
– ORIGIN ME (orig. in the sense 'black and white like a magpie'): from **PIE**[2] + **-ED**[1].

**pied-à-terre** /ˌpjeɪdɑːˈtɛː, French pjetatɛʀ/ • n. (pl. **pieds-à-terre** pronunc. same) a small flat, house, or room kept for occasional use.
– ORIGIN C19: Fr., lit. 'foot to earth'.

**piedmont** /ˈpiːdmɒnt/ • n. a gentle slope leading from the foot of mountains to a region of flat land.
– ORIGIN C19: from Ital. *piemonte*, lit. 'mountain foot'.

**Piedmontese** • n. (pl. same) a native or inhabitant of Piedmont, a region of NW Italy. • adj. of or relating to Piedmont.

**pied noir** /pjeɪ ˈnwɑː, French pje nwaʀ/ • n. (pl. **pieds noirs** pronunc. same) a person of European origin who lived in Algeria during French rule, especially one who returned to Europe after Algerian independence.
– ORIGIN Fr., lit. 'black foot', so named because of the western-style black leather shoes worn by the first colonists.

**Pied Piper** • n. a person who entices people to follow them, especially to their doom.
– ORIGIN from the legendary German figure, subject of Robert Browning's poem *The Pied Piper of Hamelin* (1842), who rid the town of Hamelin of rats by enticing

them away with his music, and when refused the promised payment lured away the town's children.

**pie-eyed** • **adj.** informal very drunk.

**pie-faced** • **adj.** informal having a roundish face and typically a blank or stupid expression.

**Piegan** • **n.** (pl. same or **Piegans**) & **adj.** variant spelling of **PEIGAN**.

**pier** • **n.** **1** a structure leading out to sea and used as a landing stage for boats or as a place of entertainment. ➤ a breakwater or mole. **2** Brit. a long narrow structure projecting from an airport terminal and giving access to an aircraft. **3** the pillar of an arch or supporting a bridge. ➤ a wall between windows or other adjacent openings.
– ORIGIN ME: from med. L. *pera*, of unknown origin.

**pierce** • **v.** **1** make a hole in or through with a sharp pointed object. **2** force or cut a way through: *a shrill voice pierced the air.* **3** [as adj. **piercing**] very sharp, cold, or high-pitched. ➤ very astute or intelligent.
– DERIVATIVES **piercer** n. **piercingly** adv.
– ORIGIN ME: from OFr. *percer*, based on L. *pertus-*, *pertundere* 'bore through'.

**pier glass** • **n.** a large mirror, used originally to fill wall space between windows.

**pierid** /ˈpʌɪərɪd/ • **n.** Entomology a butterfly of a family (Pieridae) which includes the whites, brimstones, and sulphurs.
– ORIGIN C19: from mod. L. *Pieridae*, from L. *pieris* 'Muse'.

**pieris** /ˈpɪərɪs, ˈpʌɪ-/ • **n.** an evergreen shrub of the heather family with pink or red young leaves and loose clusters of waxy white bell-shaped flowers. [Genus *Pieris*.]
– ORIGIN mod. L., from L., lit. 'Muse', from *Pieria*, the name of a district in Thessaly said to be the home of the Muses.

**Pierrot** /ˈpɪərəʊ, ˈpjɛrəʊ/ • **n.** a stock male character in French pantomime, with a sad white-painted face, a loose white costume, and a pointed hat.
– ORIGIN Fr., dimin. of the male given name *Pierre* 'Peter'.

**pier table** • **n.** a low table or bracket in the space between two windows, typically placed under a pier glass.

**Piesporter** /ˈpiːzˌpɔːtə/ • **n.** a white Moselle wine produced in the Piesport region of Germany.

**pietà** /pjeɪˈtɑː/ • **n.** a picture or sculpture of the Virgin Mary holding the dead body of Christ on her lap or in her arms.
– ORIGIN Ital., from L. *pietas* 'dutifulness'.

**pietas** /ˈpʌɪətɑːs, piːˈeɪtɑːs/ • **n.** respect due to an ancestor, country, or institution.
– ORIGIN L., lit. 'dutifulness'.

**pietism** /ˈpʌɪətɪz(ə)m/ • **n.** pious sentiment, especially of an exaggerated or affected nature. ➤ (usu. **Pietism**) a 17th-century movement for the revival of piety in the Lutheran Church.
– DERIVATIVES **pietist** n. **pietistic** adj. **pietistical** adj. **pietistically** adv.

**pietra dura** /ˌpjɛtrə ˈduːrə/ • **n.** pictorial mosaic work using semi-precious stones.
– ORIGIN C19: from Ital. (pl. *pietre dure*), lit. 'hard stone'.

**piety** /ˈpʌɪəti/ • **n.** (pl. **-ies**) the quality of being pious or reverent. ➤ a belief accepted with unthinking conventional reverence.
– ORIGIN C16: from OFr. *piete*, from L. *pietas* 'dutifulness', from *pius* (see **PIOUS**).

**piezo** /pʌɪˈiːzəʊ, ˈpiːzəʊ/ • **adj.** piezoelectric.

**piezoelectricity** • **n.** electric polarization produced in certain crystals by the application of mechanical stress.
– DERIVATIVES **piezoelectric** adj. **piezoelectrically** adv.
– ORIGIN C19: from Gk *piezein* 'press, squeeze' + **ELECTRICITY**.

**piezometer** /ˌpʌɪɪˈzɒmɪtə/ • **n.** an instrument for measuring or monitoring pressure in a fluid, especially by determining compressibility.

**piffle** • **n.** informal nonsense.
– ORIGIN C19: dimin. of imitative *piff-*.

**piffling** • **adj.** informal trivial; unimportant.

**pig** • **n.** **1** an omnivorous domesticated hoofed mammal with sparse bristly hair and a flat snout, kept for its meat. [*Sus domesticus*.] ➤ a wild animal related to this; a hog. [Family Suidae.] ➤ N. Amer. a young pig; a piglet. **2** informal a greedy, dirty, or unpleasant person. ➤ Brit. informal an unpleasant or difficult task. **3** informal, derogatory a police officer. **4** an oblong mass of iron or lead from a smelting furnace. **5** a device which fits snugly inside an oil or gas pipeline and is sent through it to clean or test the inside, or to act as a barrier. • **v.** (**pigged**, **pigging**) **1** (often **pig out**) informal gorge oneself with food. **2** (often in phr. **pig it**) informal crowd together with others in disorderly or dirty conditions. **3** (of a sow) give birth to piglets; farrow. **4** operate a pig within an oil or gas pipeline.
– PHRASES **bleed like a (stuck) pig** bleed copiously. **in a pig's eye** informal, chiefly N. Amer. expressing scornful disbelief. **make a pig of oneself** informal overeat. **make a pig's ear of** Brit. informal handle ineptly. **a pig in a poke** something that is bought or accepted without first being seen or assessed.
– DERIVATIVES **piglet** n. **piglike** adj. **pigling** n.
– ORIGIN ME: prob. from the first element of OE *picbrēd* 'acorn', lit. 'pig bread' (i.e. food for pigs).

**pigeon**[1] • **n.** **1** a stout seed- or fruit-eating bird with a small head, short legs, and a cooing voice, similar to but generally larger than a dove. [Family Columbidae: many species.] **2** informal, chiefly N. Amer. a gullible person, especially the victim of a confidence trick.
– ORIGIN ME: from OFr. *pijon*, 'young bird', from an alt. of late L. *pipio(n-)*, 'young cheeping bird' of imitative origin.

**pigeon**[2] • **n.** **1** archaic spelling of **PIDGIN**. **2** (**one's pigeon**) informal, chiefly Brit. a person's particular responsibility or business.

**pigeon-chested** (also **pigeon-breasted**) • **n.** having a narrow, projecting chest.

**pigeon-hearted** • **adj.** timid; cowardly.

**pigeonhole** • **n.** **1** a small recess for a domestic pigeon to nest in. **2** each of a set of small compartments where letters or messages may be left for individuals. **3** a category, especially an overly restrictive one, to which someone or something is assigned. • **v.** **1** assign to a particular category, especially an overly restrictive one. **2** deposit (a document) in a pigeonhole.

**pigeon pair** • **n.** dialect a boy and girl as twins, or as the only children in a family.

**pigeon pea** • **n.** **1** a dark red tropical pealike seed. **2** the woody plant which yields these seeds, with pods and foliage that are used as fodder. [*Cajanus cajan*.]

**pigeon's milk** • **n.** a curd-like secretion from a pigeon's crop, which it regurgitates and feeds to its young.

**pigeon-toed** • **adj.** having the toes or feet turned inwards.

**piggery** • **n.** (pl. **-ies**) **1** a farm or enclosure where pigs are kept. **2** behaviour regarded as characteristic of pigs, especially greed or unpleasantness.

**piggish** • **adj.** resembling or likened to a pig, especially in being unpleasant.
– DERIVATIVES **piggishly** adv. **piggishness** n.

**piggy** • **n.** (pl. **-ies**) a child's word for a pig or piglet. • **adj.** resembling or likened to a pig, especially in features or appetite.
– PHRASES **piggy in the middle** chiefly Brit. **1** a game in which two people attempt to throw a ball to each other without a third person in the middle catching it. **2** a person who is placed in an awkward situation between two others.

**piggyback** • **n.** a ride on someone's back and shoulders. • **adv.** on the back and shoulders of another person. • **v.** **1** carry by or as if by means of a piggyback. **2** mount on or attach to (an existing object or system).

**piggy bank** • **n.** a money box, especially one shaped like a pig.

**pig-headed** • **adj.** stupidly obstinate.
– DERIVATIVES **pig-headedly** adv. **pig-headedness** n.

**pightle** /ˈpʌɪt(ə)l/ • **n.** dialect a small field or enclosure.
– ORIGIN ME: origin obscure, appar. dimin.

**pig-ignorant** • **adj.** informal extremely stupid or crude.

**pig iron** • **n.** crude iron as first obtained from a smelting furnace, in the form of oblong blocks.

**pig Latin** ● n. a secret language formed from English by transferring the initial consonant or consonant cluster of each word to the end of the word and adding a vocalic syllable (usually /eɪ/): so *igpay atinlay.*

**pigment** ● n. **1** the natural colouring matter of animal or plant tissue. **2** a substance used for colouring or painting, especially a dry powder which constitutes a paint or ink when mixed with oil or water. ● v. [usu. as adj. **pigmented**] colour with or as if with pigment.
– DERIVATIVES **pigmentary** adj. **pigmentation** n.
– ORIGIN ME: from L. *pigmentum*, from *pingere* 'to paint'.

**pigmy** ● n. variant spelling of PYGMY.

**pignut** ● n. another term for EARTHNUT.

**pigpen** ● n. N. Amer. a pigsty.

**pigskin** ● n. **1** leather made from the hide of a domestic pig. **2** N. Amer. informal a football.

**pig-sticking** ● n. the sport of hunting wild boar with a spear, carried out on horseback.
– DERIVATIVES **pig-sticker** n.

**pigsty** ● n. (pl. **-ies**) **1** a pen or enclosure for a pig or pigs. **2** a very dirty or untidy house or room.

**pigswill** ● n. kitchen refuse and scraps fed to pigs.

**pigtail** ● n. **1** a plaited lock of hair worn singly at the back or on each side of the head. **2** a short length of braided wire connecting a stationary part to a moving part in an electrical device. **3** a twist of tobacco.
– DERIVATIVES **pigtailed** adj.

**pigweed** ● n. a North American plant used for fodder, naturalized as a weed in other countries. [*Amaranthus retroflexus* and other species.]

**pi-jaw** ● n. informal, dated tediously moralizing talk.

**pika** /ˈpʌɪkə, ˈpiːkə/ ● n. a small mammal related to the rabbits, found mainly in mountains and deserts. [Genus *Ochotona*: many species.]
– ORIGIN C19: from Tungus *piika*.

**pike**[1] ● n. (pl. same) a long-bodied predatory freshwater fish with long teeth. [*Esox lucius* and related species.] ➤used in names of similar predatory fish, e.g. **garpike**.
– ORIGIN ME: from PIKE[2] (because of the fish's pointed jaw).

**pike**[2] ● n. **1** historical an infantry weapon with a pointed steel or iron head on a long wooden shaft. **2** N. English (in the Lake District) a hill with a peaked top: *Scafell Pike.* ● v. historical thrust through or kill with a pike.
– ORIGIN C16: from Fr. *pique*, from *piquer* 'pierce', from *pic* 'pick, pike'; sense 2 is appar. of Scand. origin.

**pike**[3] ● n. short for TURNPIKE.
– PHRASES **come down the pike** N. Amer. appear on the scene; come to notice.

**pike**[4] ● n. a jackknife position in diving or gymnastics.
– ORIGIN 1920s: of unknown origin.

**pike**[5] ● v. informal **1** (often **pike it**) depart or proceed. **2** (**pike on/out**) N. Amer. & Austral./NZ withdraw from (a plan or agreement) because of over-cautiousness.
– ORIGIN ME (as *pike oneself* 'take up a pilgrim's staff'): cf. Dan. *pigge af* 'hasten off'.

**pikelet** ● n. a thin kind of crumpet.
– ORIGIN C18: from Welsh (*bara*) *pyglyd* 'pitchy (bread)'.

**pikeperch** ● n. (pl. same) a zander or related fish. [Genus *Stizostedion*.]

**piker** ● n. N. Amer. & Austral./NZ informal a gambler who makes only small bets. ➤a mean or cautious person.
– ORIGIN C19: from PIKE[5].

**pikestaff** ● n. historical the wooden shaft of a pike.
– PHRASES (**as**) **plain as a pikestaff 1** very obvious. **2** ordinary or unattractive in appearance. [alt. of *as plain as a packstaff*, the staff being that of a pedlar, on which he rested his pack of wares.]

**pilaf** /pɪˈlaf/ (also **pilaff**, **pilau** /pɪˈlaʊ/, **pulao** /pəˈlaʊ/) ● n. a Middle Eastern or Indian dish of spiced rice or wheat and often meat and vegetables.
– ORIGIN from Turk. *pilâv.*

**pilaster** /pɪˈlastə/ ● n. a rectangular column, especially one projecting from a wall.
– DERIVATIVES **pilastered** adj.
– ORIGIN C16: from Fr. *pilastre*, from Ital. *pilastro* or med. L. *pilastrum*, from L. *pila* 'pillar'.

**Pilates** /pɪˈlɑːtiːz/ ● n. a system of exercises using special apparatus, designed to improve physical strength, flexibility, and posture, and enhance mental awareness.
– ORIGIN C20: named after the Ger. physical fitness specialist Joseph *Pilates* (1880–1967).

**pilchard** ● n. a small marine food fish of the herring family. [*Sardina pilchardus* (Europe) and other species.]
– ORIGIN C16: of unknown origin.

**pile**[1] ● n. **1** a heap of things laid or lying one on top of another. ➤informal a large amount: *the growing pile of work.* **2** a large imposing building: *a Gothic pile.* **3** a series of plates of dissimilar metals laid one on another alternately to produce an electric current. ● v. **1** place (things) one on top of the other. ➤(**be piled with**) be stacked or loaded with. ➤(**pile up**) form a pile or large quantity. ➤(**pile something on**) informal intensify or exaggerate something for effect. **2** (**pile into/out of**) get into or out of (a vehicle) in a disorganized manner. ➤(**pile into**) (of a vehicle) crash into.
– PHRASES **make a pile** informal make a lot of money. **pile arms** Military place a number of rifles with their butts on the ground and the muzzles together.
– ORIGIN ME: from OFr., from L. *pila* 'pillar, pier'.

**pile**[2] ● n. **1** a heavy stake or post driven into the ground to support the foundations of a superstructure. **2** Heraldry a triangular charge or ordinary formed by two lines meeting at an acute angle, usually pointing down from the top of the shield. ● v. strengthen or support with piles.
– ORIGIN OE *pīl* 'dart, arrow', also 'stake', of Gmc origin.

**pile**[3] ● n. the soft projecting surface of a carpet or a fabric such as velvet, consisting of many small threads.
– ORIGIN ME: from L. *pilus* 'hair'.

**pilea** /ˈpʌɪlɪə/ ● n. a plant of the nettle family which lacks stinging hairs, grown as an indoor plant. [Genus *Pilea.*]
– ORIGIN mod. L., from L. *pileus* 'felt cap'.

**pileated woodpecker** /ˈpʌɪlɪeɪtɪd/ ● n. a large black and white North American woodpecker with a red cap and crest. [*Dryocopus pileatus.*]
– ORIGIN C18: *pileated* from L. *pileatus* 'capped', from *pileus* 'felt cap'.

**piledriver** ● n. **1** a machine for driving piles into the ground. **2** Brit. informal a forceful act, blow, or shot.
– DERIVATIVES **piledriving** n. & adj.

**piles** ● pl. n. haemorrhoids.
– ORIGIN ME: prob. from L. *pila* 'ball' (because of the globular form of external haemorrhoids).

**pile-up** ● n. informal **1** a crash involving several vehicles. **2** an accumulation of a specified thing.

**pileus** /ˈpʌɪlɪəs/ ● n. (pl. **pilei** /-lɪʌɪ/) Botany the cap of a mushroom or toadstool.
– ORIGIN C18: from L., lit. 'felt cap'.

**pilewort** ● n. the lesser celandine (the bulbils of which are said to resemble, and have efficacy against, piles).

**pilfer** ● v. steal (things of little value).
– DERIVATIVES **pilferage** n. **pilferer** n.
– ORIGIN ME: from OFr. *pelfrer* 'to pillage'; cf. PELF.

**pilgrim** ● n. a person who journeys to a sacred place for religious reasons. ● v. (**pilgrimed**, **pilgriming**) archaic travel or wander like a pilgrim.
– DERIVATIVES **pilgrimize** (also **-ise**) v. (archaic).
– ORIGIN ME: from Provençal *pelegrin*, from L. *peregrinus* (see PEREGRINE).

**pilgrimage** ● n. a pilgrim's journey. ● v. go on a pilgrimage.

**Pilipino** /ˌpɪlɪˈpiːnəʊ/ ● n. & adj. variant of FILIPINO.

**pill** ● n. **1** a small round mass of solid medicine for swallowing whole. ➤(**the Pill**) a contraceptive pill. **2** informal, dated a ball. **3** informal a tedious person. ● v. (of knitted fabric) form small balls of fluff on its surface.
– PHRASES **a bitter pill** an unpleasant or painful necessity. **sugar** (or **sweeten**) **the pill** make an unpleasant or painful necessity more palatable.
– DERIVATIVES **pilular** adj.
– ORIGIN ME: ult. from L. *pilula* 'little ball', dimin. of *pila*.

**pillage** ● v. rob or steal with violence, especially in wartime. ● n. the action of pillaging.

– DERIVATIVES **pillager** n.
– ORIGIN ME: from OFr., from *piller* 'to plunder'.

**pillar** ● n. **1** a tall vertical structure, usually of stone, used as a support for a building or as an ornament or monument. **2** a person or thing providing reliable support: *he was a pillar of his local community.*
– PHRASES **from pillar to post** from one place to another in an unceremonious or fruitless manner.
– DERIVATIVES **pillared** adj. **pillaret** n.
– ORIGIN ME: from Anglo-Norman Fr. *piler*, based on L. *pila* 'pillar'.

**pillar box** ● n. (in the UK) a large red cylindrical public postbox.

**pillbox** ● n. **1** a small shallow cylindrical box for holding pills. **2** a hat of a similar shape. **3** a small enclosed, partly underground, concrete fort used as an outpost.

**pillion** ● n. **1** a seat for a passenger behind a motorcyclist. **2** historical a woman's light saddle. ➤ a cushion attached to the back of a saddle for an additional passenger.
– ORIGIN C15: from Sc. Gaelic *pillean*, Ir. *pillín* 'small cushion', dimin. of *pell*, from L. *pellis* 'skin'.

**pilliwinks** /ˈpɪlɪwɪŋks/ ● pl. n. historical an instrument of torture used for squeezing the fingers.
– ORIGIN ME *pyrwykes, pyrewinkes*, of unknown origin.

**pillock** ● n. Brit. informal a stupid person.
– ORIGIN C16: var. of archaic *pillicock* 'penis'.

**pillory** ● n. (pl. **-ies**) a wooden framework with holes for the head and hands, in which offenders were formerly imprisoned and exposed to public abuse. ● v. (**-ies, -ied**) **1** put in a pillory. **2** attack or ridicule publicly.
– ORIGIN ME: from OFr. *pilori*, prob. from Provençal *espilori* (perh. rel. to a Catalan word meaning 'peephole').

**pillow** ● n. **1** a rectangular cloth bag stuffed with feathers, wadding, or other soft materials, used to support the head when lying or sleeping. **2** short for LACE PILLOW. ● v. rest (one's head) as if on a pillow. ➤ poetic/literary serve as a pillow for.
– DERIVATIVES **pillowy** adj.
– ORIGIN OE *pyle, pylu*, of W. Gmc origin, based on L. *pulvinus* 'cushion'.

**pillow book** ● n. (in Japanese classical literature) a type of private journal or diary.

**pillowcase** ● n. a removable cloth cover for a pillow.

**pillow fight** ● n. a mock fight using pillows.

**pillow lace** ● n. lace made by hand using a lace pillow.

**pillow lava** ● n. lava which has solidified as rounded masses, characteristic of eruption under water.

**pillowslip** ● n. a pillowcase.

**pillow talk** ● n. intimate conversation in bed.

**pill-popper** ● n. informal a person who takes pills freely.
– DERIVATIVES **pill-popping** n.

**pillwort** ● n. a creeping grass-like aquatic fern. [*Pilularia globulifera*.]

**pilocarpine** /ˌpʌɪlə(ʊ)ˈkɑːpiːn/ ● n. Chemistry a volatile alkaloid obtained from jaborandi leaves, used to contract the pupils and to relieve pressure in the eye in glaucoma patients.
– ORIGIN C19: from mod. L. *Pilocarpus* (genus name) + -INE[4].

**pilose** /ˈpʌɪləʊz/ (also **pilous**) ● adj. Botany & Zoology covered with long soft hairs.
– DERIVATIVES **pilosity** n.
– ORIGIN C18: from L. *pilosus*, from *pilus* 'hair'.

**pilot** ● n. **1** a person who operates the flying controls of an aircraft. **2** a person with expert local knowledge qualified to take charge of a ship entering or leaving a harbour. ➤ a navigational handbook for use at sea. ➤ archaic a guide or leader. **3** [often as modifier] something done or produced as an experiment or test before wider introduction: *a pilot scheme.* **4** Telecommunications an unmodulated reference signal transmitted with another signal for the purposes of control or synchronization. ● v. (**piloted, piloting**) **1** act as a pilot of (an aircraft or ship). ➤ guide; steer. **2** test (a scheme, project, etc.) before introducing it more widely.
– DERIVATIVES **pilotage** n. **pilotless** adj.
– ORIGIN C16: from Fr. *pilote*, from med. L. *pilotus*, based on Gk *pēdon* 'oar', (pl.) 'rudder'.

**pilot balloon** ● n. a small meteorological balloon used to track air currents.

**pilot bird** ● n. a brown ground-dwelling Australian songbird, noted for its habit of accompanying superb lyrebirds to feed on disturbed insects. [*Pycnoptilus floccosus*.]

**pilot chute** ● n. a small parachute used to bring the main one into operation.

**pilot cloth** ● n. thick blue woollen cloth, used to make seamen's coats.

**pilotfish** ● n. (pl. same or **-fishes**) a fish of warm seas that often swims close to large fish such as sharks. [*Naucrates ductor*.]

**pilot house** ● n. another term for WHEELHOUSE.

**pilot jacket** ● n. another term for PEA JACKET.

**pilot light** ● n. **1** a small gas burner kept alight permanently to light a larger burner when needed, especially on a gas cooker or boiler. **2** an electric indicator light or control light.

**pilot officer** ● n. the lowest rank of officer in the RAF, above warrant officer and below flying officer.

**pilot whale** ● n. a black toothed whale with a square bulbous head. [Genus *Globicephala*: two species.]

**pilous** /ˈpʌɪləs/ ● adj. another term for PILOSE.

**Pils** /pɪlz, -s/ ● n. short for PILSNER.

**Pilsner** /ˈpɪlznə, ˈpɪls-/ (also **Pilsener**) ● n. a lager beer with a strong hop flavour, originally brewed at Pilsen (Plzeň) in the Czech Republic.

**PIM** ● abbrev. personal information manager.

**Pima** /ˈpiːmə/ ● n. (pl. same or **Pimas**) **1** a member of an American Indian people of Arizona and northern Mexico. **2** the Uto-Aztecan language of this people and the Papago.
– ORIGIN Sp., shortening of *Pimahito*, from Pima *pimahaitu* 'nothing'.

**pimento** /pɪˈmɛntəʊ/ ● n. (pl. **-os**) **1** variant spelling of PIMIENTO. **2** chiefly W. Indian another term for ALLSPICE (in sense 2).

**pi-meson** ● n. another term for PION.

**pimiento** /ˌpɪmɪˈɛntəʊ, pɪmˈjɛn-/ (also **pimento**) ● n. (pl. **-os**) a red sweet pepper.
– ORIGIN C17: from Sp., from med. L. *pigmentum* 'spice'.

**pimp** ● n. **1** a man who controls prostitutes and arranges clients for them, taking a percentage of their earnings in return. **2** Austral. informal a telltale or informer. ● v. **1** [often as noun **pimping**] act as a pimp. **2** (**pimp on**) Austral. informal inform on.
– ORIGIN C16: of unknown origin.

**pimpernel** /ˈpɪmpənɛl/ ● n. a low-growing plant with bright five-petalled flowers. [*Anagallis arvensis* (**scarlet pimpernel**) and other species.]
– ORIGIN ME: from OFr. *pimpernelle*, based on L. *piper* 'pepper'.

**pimping** ● adj. archaic small or insignificant.
– ORIGIN C17: of unknown origin.

**pimple** ● n. a small, hard inflamed spot on the skin.
– DERIVATIVES **pimpled** adj. **pimply** adj.
– ORIGIN ME: rel. to OE *piplian* 'break out in pustules'.

**pimpmobile** /ˈpɪmpməbiːl/ ● n. US informal a large ostentatious car, of a style associated with pimps.

**PIN** (also **PIN number**) ● abbrev. personal identification number.

**pin** ● n. **1** a thin piece of metal with a sharp point at one end and a round head at the other, used for fastening pieces of cloth, paper, etc. ➤ a small brooch or badge. ➤ Medicine a steel rod used to join the ends of fractured bones while they heal. **2** a metal peg that holds down the activating lever of a hand grenade, preventing its explosion. **3** a metal projection from a plug or an integrated circuit which makes an electrical connection with a socket or another part of a circuit. **4** Golf a stick with a flag placed in a hole to mark its position. **5** a skittle in bowling. **6** (**pins**) informal legs. **7** Chess an attack on a piece or pawn which is thereby pinned. **8** Brit. historical a half-firkin cask for beer. ● v. (**pinned, pinning**) **1** attach or fasten with a pin or pins. ➤ (**pin something on**) fix

blame or responsibility on. **2** hold someone firmly so they are unable to move. ➤(**pin someone down**) restrict the actions of an enemy by firing at them. ➤(**pin someone down**) force someone to be specific about their intentions. **3** Chess hinder or prevent (a piece or pawn) from moving because of the danger to a more valuable piece standing behind it along the line of an attack.
– PHRASES **pin one's ears back** listen carefully. **pin one's hopes** (or **faith**) **on** rely heavily on.
– ORIGIN OE *pinn*, of W. Gmc origin, from L. *pinna* 'point, tip, edge'.

**pina colada** /ˌpiːnə kəˈlɑːdə/ ● **n.** a cocktail made with rum, pineapple juice, and coconut.
– ORIGIN from Sp. *piña colada*, lit. 'strained pineapple'.

**pinafore** ● **n. 1** (also **pinafore dress**) a collarless, sleeveless dress worn over a blouse or jumper. **2** Brit. a woman's loose sleeveless garment worn over clothes to keep them clean.
– ORIGIN C18: from **PIN** + **AFORE** (because the term orig. denoted an apron with a bib pinned on the front of a dress).

**pinball** ● **n.** a game in which small metal balls are shot across a sloping board and score points by striking various targets.

**pinboard** ● **n.** a cork-covered board to which messages and pictures may be pinned for display.

**pince-nez** /pɑ̃sˈneɪ/ ● **n.** [treated as sing. or pl.] a pair of eyeglasses with a nose clip instead of earpieces.
– ORIGIN C19: from Fr., lit. '(that) pinches (the) nose'.

**pincer** ● **n. 1** (**pincers**) a tool made of two pieces of metal bearing blunt concave jaws arranged like the blades of scissors, used for gripping and pulling things. **2** a front claw of a lobster, crab, or similar crustacean.
– ORIGIN ME: from Anglo-Norman Fr., from OFr. *pincier* 'to pinch'.

**pincer movement** ● **n.** a movement by two separate bodies of troops converging on the enemy.

**pincette** /pɪnˈsɛt, pɑ̃ˈsɛt/ ● **n.** a small pair of pincers; tweezers.
– ORIGIN C16: from Fr., dimin. of *pince* 'pair of pincers'.

**pinch** ● **v. 1** grip (the flesh) tightly and sharply between finger and thumb. ➤(of a shoe) hurt (a foot) by being too tight. ➤[often as adj. **pinched**] tighten (the lips or a part of the face), especially with worry or tension. **2** live in a frugal way. **3** informal, chiefly Brit. steal. **4** informal arrest (someone). **5** remove (buds or leaves) to encourage bushy growth. **6** Sailing sail (a boat) so close to the wind that the sails begin to lose power. ● **n. 1** an act of pinching. ➤an amount of an ingredient that can be held between fingers and thumb. **2** Baseball a critical point in the game.
– PHRASES **at** (or N. Amer. **in**) **a pinch** if absolutely necessary. **feel the pinch** experience hardship, especially financial.
– ORIGIN ME: from an ONorth. Fr. var. of OFr. *pincier* 'to pinch'.

**pinchbeck** ● **n.** an alloy of copper and zinc resembling gold, used in watchmaking and cheap jewellery. ● **adj.** appearing valuable, but actually cheap or tawdry.
– ORIGIN C18: named after the Engl. watchmaker Christopher *Pinchbeck*.

**pinch-hit** ● **v. 1** Baseball bat instead of another, typically at a critical point in the game. **2** N. Amer. informal act as a substitute for someone in an emergency.
– DERIVATIVES **pinch-hitter** n.

**pinchpenny** ● **n.** (pl. **-ies**) a miserly person.

**pinch-run** ● **v.** Baseball substitute for another as a base runner, typically at a critical point in the game.
– DERIVATIVES **pinch-runner** n.

**pincushion** ● **n. 1** a small pad for holding pins. **2** optical distortion in which straight lines along the edge of a screen or lens bulge towards the centre.

**pine**[1] ● **n. 1** (also **pine tree**) an evergreen coniferous tree having clusters of long needle-shaped leaves, grown for its soft wood or for tar and turpentine. [Genus *Pinus*: many species.] ➤used in names of coniferous trees of other families, e.g. **Chile pine**. **2** used in names of unrelated plants that resemble the pines in some way, e.g. **screw pine**.
– DERIVATIVES **pinery** n. **piny** (also **piney**) adj.
– ORIGIN OE, from L. *pinus*, reinforced in ME by OFr. *pin*.

**pine**[2] ● **v.** suffer a mental and physical decline, especially because of a broken heart. ➤(**pine for**) miss and long for the return of.
– ORIGIN OE *pīnian* '(cause to) suffer', of Gmc origin; ult. based on L. *poena* 'punishment'.

**pineal eye** ● **n.** Zoology (in some reptiles and lower vertebrates) an eye-like structure on the top of the head, covered by almost transparent skin and derived from or linked to the pineal gland.

**pineal gland** /ˈpɪnɪəl, ˈpʌɪ-/ (also **pineal body**) ● **n.** a pea-sized conical mass of tissue behind the third ventricle of the brain, secreting a hormone-like substance in some mammals.
– ORIGIN C17: from Fr. *pinéal*, from L. *pinea* 'pine cone' (with ref. to the shape of the gland).

**pineapple** ● **n. 1** a large juicy tropical fruit consisting of aromatic edible yellow flesh surrounded by a tough segmented skin and topped with a tuft of stiff leaves. **2** the tropical American plant that bears this fruit, with a spiral of spiny sword-shaped leaves on a thick stem. [*Ananas comosus*.]
– ORIGIN ME (denoting a pine cone): from **PINE**[1] + **APPLE**.

**pineapple weed** ● **n.** a pineapple-scented mayweed with flowers that lack rays. [*Matricaria matricarioides*.]

**pine beauty** ● **n.** a brown moth whose caterpillars feed on pine needles and are a serious pest of plantations. [*Panolis flammea*.]

**pine cone** ● **n.** the conical or rounded woody fruit of a pine tree, with scales which open to release the seeds.

**pine marten** ● **n.** an arboreal weasel-like mammal with a dark brown coat. [*Martes martes*.]

**pinene** /ˈpʌɪniːn/ ● **n.** Chemistry a flammable liquid terpene present in turpentine, juniper oil, and other natural extracts.
– ORIGIN C19: from L. *pinus* 'pine' + **-ENE**.

**pine nut** ● **n.** the edible seed of various pine trees.

**pinetum** /pʌɪˈniːtəm/ ● **n.** (pl. **pineta** /-tə/) a plantation of pine trees or other conifers for scientific or ornamental purposes.
– ORIGIN C19: from L., from *pinus* 'pine'.

**pin feather** ● **n.** Ornithology an immature feather, before the veins have expanded and while the shaft is full of fluid.

**pinfold** historical ● **n.** a pound for stray animals. ● **v.** confine (a stray animal) in such a pound.
– ORIGIN OE *pundfald*, from a base shared by **POND** and **POUND**[3] + **FOLD**[2].

**ping** ● **n.** an abrupt high-pitched ringing sound. ● **v. 1** make or cause to make such a sound. **2** US another term for **PINK**[3].
– DERIVATIVES **pinger** n.
– ORIGIN C19: imitative.

**pingo** /ˈpɪŋɡəʊ/ ● **n.** (pl. **-os**) Geology a dome-shaped mound consisting of a layer of soil over a large core of ice, occurring in permafrost areas.
– ORIGIN 1920s: from Inuit *pinguq* 'nunatak'.

**ping-pong** ● **n.** informal term for **TABLE TENNIS**.
– ORIGIN C20: imitative of the sound of a bat striking a ball.

**pinguid** /ˈpɪŋɡwɪd/ ● **adj.** formal of the nature of or resembling fat; oily or greasy.
– DERIVATIVES **pinguidity** n.
– ORIGIN C17: from L. *pinguis* 'fat' + **-ID**[1].

**pinhead** ● **n. 1** the flattened head of a pin. **2** informal a stupid person.
– DERIVATIVES **pinheaded** adj. **pinheadedness** n.

**pinhole** ● **n.** a very small hole.

**pinhole camera** ● **n.** a camera with a pinhole aperture and no lens.

**pinion**[1] /ˈpɪnjən/ ● **n.** the outer part of a bird's wing including the flight feathers. ● **v. 1** tie or hold the arms or legs of. **2** cut off the pinion of (a bird) to prevent flight.
– ORIGIN ME: from OFr. *pignon*, based on L. *pinna*, *penna* 'feather'.

**pinion**[2] /ˈpɪnjən/ ● **n.** a small cogwheel or spindle engaging with a large cogwheel.
– ORIGIN C17: from Fr. *pignon*, alt. of obs. *pignol*, from L. *pinea* 'pine cone'.

**pink**[1] ● **adj. 1** of a colour intermediate between red and white, as of coral or salmon. **2** informal, often derogatory left-wing. **3** of or associated with homosexuals: *the pink economy.* ● **n. 1** pink colour, pigment, or material. ➤(also **hunting pink**) the red clothing or material worn by fox-hunters. **2** (**the pink**) informal the best condition or degree. **3** informal, often derogatory a left-wing person.
– DERIVATIVES **pinkish** adj. **pinkly** adv. **pinkness** n. **pinky** adj.
– ORIGIN C17: from PINK[2].

**pink**[2] ● **n.** a plant with sweet-smelling pink or white flowers and slender grey-green leaves. [Genus *Dianthus.*]
– ORIGIN C16: perh. short for *pink eye*, lit. 'small or half-shut eye'.

**pink**[3] ● **v. 1** cut a scalloped or zigzag edge on. **2** archaic decorate.
– ORIGIN C16 (in the sense 'pierce or nick slightly'): cf. Low Ger. *pinken* 'strike, peck'.

**pink**[4] ● **v.** Brit. (of a vehicle engine) make rattling sounds as a result of over-rapid combustion of the fuel–air mixture in the cylinders.
– ORIGIN C20: imitative.

**pink**[5] ● **n.** historical a small square-rigged sailing ship with a narrow, overhanging stern.
– ORIGIN C15: from MDu. *pin(c)ke*, of unknown ultimate origin.

**pink**[6] ● **n.** dated a yellowish lake pigment made by combining vegetable colouring matter with a white base.
– ORIGIN C17: of unknown origin.

**pink-collar** ● **adj.** relating to or denoting work traditionally associated with women.

**pink elephants** ● **pl. n.** informal hallucinations supposedly typical of those experienced by a person who is drunk.

**pink-eye** ● **n. 1** a viral disease of horses, symptoms of which include fever, abortion, and redness of the eyes. **2** conjunctivitis in humans and some livestock.

**pink gin** ● **n.** Brit. gin flavoured with angostura bitters.

**pinkie** ● **n.** informal the little finger.
– ORIGIN C19: partly from Du. *pink* 'the little finger', reinforced by PINK[1].

**pinking shears** ● **pl. n.** shears with a serrated blade, used to cut a zigzag edge in fabric to prevent it fraying.

**pink noise** ● **n.** Physics random noise having equal energy per octave, and so having more low-frequency components than white noise.

**pinko** ● **n.** (pl. **-os** or **-oes**) informal, derogatory, chiefly N. Amer. a person with left-wing or liberal views.

**pink slip** ● **n.** N. Amer. informal a notice of dismissal from employment.

**pin money** ● **n.** a small sum of money for spending on inessentials.
– ORIGIN C17: orig. denoting an allowance to a woman from her husband for dress and other personal expenses.

**pinna** /ˈpɪnə/ ● **n.** (pl. **pinnae** /-niː/) **1** Anatomy & Zoology the external part of the ear in humans and other mammals; the auricle. **2** Botany a primary division of a pinnate leaf, especially of a fern. **3** Zoology any of a number of animal structures resembling fins or wings.
– ORIGIN C18: mod. L., from a var. of L. *penna* 'feather, wing, fin'.

**pinnace** /ˈpɪnɪs/ ● **n.** chiefly historical a small boat forming part of the equipment of a warship or other large vessel.
– ORIGIN C16: from Fr. *pinace*, prob. based on L. *pinus* (see PINE[1]).

**pinnacle** ● **n. 1** a high pointed piece of rock. **2** a small pointed turret built as an ornament on a roof. **3** the most successful point: *the pinnacle of his career.*
– DERIVATIVES **pinnacled** adj.
– ORIGIN ME: from OFr., from late L. *pinnaculum*, dimin. of *pinna* 'wing, point'.

**pinnae** plural form of PINNA.

**pinnate** ● **adj.** Botany & Zoology having leaflets or other parts arranged on either side of a stem or axis like the vanes of a feather.
– DERIVATIVES **pinnated** adj. **pinnately** adv. **pinnation** /-ˈneɪʃ(ə)n/ n.
– ORIGIN C18: from L. *pinnatus* 'feathered', from *pinna*, *penna* (see PINNA).

**pinni-** /ˈpɪni/ ● **comb. form** relating to wings or fins: *pinniped.*
– ORIGIN from L. *pinna*, *penna* 'wing, fin'.

**pinniped** /ˈpɪnɪpɛd/ ● **n.** Zoology a carnivorous aquatic mammal of an order (Pinnipedia) which comprises the seals, sea lions, and walrus.
– ORIGIN from mod. L. *Pinnipedia*, from L. *pinna* 'wing, fin' + *pes, ped-* foot.

**pinnule** /ˈpɪnjuːl/ ● **n. 1** Botany a secondary division of a pinnate leaf. **2** Zoology a part or organ like a small wing or fin.
– ORIGIN C16 (denoting one of the sights of an astrolabe): from L. *pinnula* 'small wing', dimin. of *pinna*.

**PIN number** ● **n.** see **PIN**.

**pinny** ● **n.** (pl. **-ies**) informal a pinafore.

**pinochle** /ˈpiːnɒk(ə)l/ ● **n.** a North American card game for two or more players using a 48-card pack consisting of two of each card from nine to ace, the object being to score points for various combinations and to win tricks. ➤the combination of queen of spades and jack of diamonds in this game.
– ORIGIN C19: of unknown origin.

**pinocytosis** /ˌpiːnəʊsʌɪˈtəʊsɪs, ˌpɪnəʊ-, ˌpʌɪnəʊ-/ ● **n.** Biology the ingestion of liquid into a cell by the budding of small vesicles from the cell membrane.
– ORIGIN C19: from Gk *pino* 'drink' + *-cytosis* on the pattern of *phagocytosis.*

**pinole** /piːˈnəʊleɪ, -li/ ● **n.** US flour made from parched cornflour mixed with sweet flour made of mesquite beans, sugar, and spice.
– ORIGIN C19: from Latin Amer. Sp., from Nahuatl *pinolli.*

**piñon** /pɪˈnjɒn, ˈpɪnjəʊn/ (also **pinyon**) ● **n.** a small pine tree with edible seeds, native to Mexico and the south-western US. [*Pinus cemebroides.*]
– ORIGIN C19: from Sp., from L. *pinea* 'pine cone'.

**Pinot** /ˈpiːnəʊ/ ● **n.** any of several varieties of wine grape, especially **Pinot Noir** (black) and **Pinot Blanc** (white).
– ORIGIN Fr., var. of earlier *Pineau*, dimin. of *pin* 'pine' (because of the shape of the grape cluster).

**pinotage** /ˈpɪnə(ʊ)tɑːʒ/ ● **n.** a variety of red wine grape grown in South Africa, produced by crossing Pinot Noir and other varieties.
– ORIGIN blend of *Pinot* (*Noir*) and *Hermitage*, names of types of grape.

**pinout** ● **n.** Electronics a diagram showing the arrangement of pins on an integrated circuit and their functions.

**pinpoint** ● **n.** a tiny dot or point. ● **adj.** absolutely precise: *pinpoint accuracy.* ● **v.** find or locate exactly.

**pinprick** ● **n. 1** a prick caused by a pin. **2** a very small dot or amount.

**pins and needles** ● **pl. n.** [treated as sing.] a tingling sensation in a limb recovering from numbness.

**pinspot** ● **n.** a small powerful spotlight.

**pinstripe** ● **n.** a very narrow stripe in cloth, especially of the type used for formal suits.
– DERIVATIVES **pinstriped** adj.

**pint** ● **n.** a unit of liquid or dry capacity equal to one eighth of a gallon, in Britain equal to 0.568 litre and in the US equal to 0.473 litre (for liquid measure) or 0.551 litre (for dry measure). ➤Brit. informal a pint of beer.
– ORIGIN ME: from OFr. *pinte*, of unknown origin.

**pintail** ● **n.** a duck with a long pointed tail. [*Anas acuta* and related species.]

**pintle** /ˈpɪnt(ə)l/ ● **n.** a pin or bolt on which a rudder turns.
– ORIGIN OE *pintel* 'penis', perh. a dimin., of unknown ultimate origin.

**pinto** /ˈpɪntəʊ/ ● **n.** N. Amer. (pl. **-os**) a piebald horse.
– ORIGIN C19: from Sp., lit. 'mottled'.

**pinto bean** ● **n.** a speckled variety of kidney bean.
– ORIGIN C20: from **PINTO**, because of the mottled appearance of the bean.

**pint-sized** ● **adj.** informal very small.

**pin-tuck** ● **n.** a very narrow ornamental tuck.

**pin-up** ● **n.** a poster featuring a sexually attractive person, especially a famous one. ➤a famous person regarded as sexually attractive.

**pinwheel** ● **n. 1** a small Catherine-wheel firework. **2** something shaped or rotating like a pinwheel. ● **v.** spin or rotate like a pinwheel.

**pinworm** ● **n.** a small nematode worm which is an internal parasite of vertebrates. [Family Oxyuridae.]

**Pinyin** /pɪn'jɪn/ ● **n.** the standard system of romanized spelling for transliterating Chinese.
– ORIGIN 1960s: from Chin. *pīn-yīn*, lit. 'spell-sound'.

**pinyon** ● **n.** variant spelling of **PIÑON**.

**piolet** /pjəʊ'leɪ/ ● **n.** Climbing an ice pick.
– ORIGIN C19: from Fr. dial., lit. 'little pick'.

**pion** /'pʌɪɒn/ ● **n.** Physics a meson having a mass approximately 270 times that of an electron.
– DERIVATIVES **pionic** adj.
– ORIGIN 1950s: from **PI**[1] (the letter used as a symbol for the particle) + **-ON**.

**pioneer** ● **n. 1** a person who is the first to explore or settle a new country or area. **2** an innovator or developer of new ideas or techniques. **3** a member of an infantry group preparing roads or terrain for the main body of troops. ● **v. 1** be a pioneer of. **2** open up (a road or terrain) as a pioneer.
– DERIVATIVES **pioneering** adj.
– ORIGIN C16: from Fr. *pionnier* 'foot soldier, pioneer'.

**pious** ● **adj. 1** devoutly religious. **2** making a hypocritical display of virtue. **3** (of a hope) sincere but unlikely to be fulfilled.
– DERIVATIVES **piously** adv. **piousness** n.
– ORIGIN ME: from L. *pius* 'dutiful, pious' + **-OUS**.

**pip**[1] ● **n.** a small hard seed in a fruit.
– PHRASES **squeeze someone until the pips squeak** Brit. informal extract the maximum amount of money from someone.
– DERIVATIVES **pipless** adj.
– ORIGIN C18: abbrev. of **PIPPIN**.

**pip**[2] ● **n.** (**the pips**) Brit. a series of short high-pitched sounds used as a time signal on the radio or to instruct a caller using a pay telephone to insert more money.
– ORIGIN C20: imitative.

**pip**[3] ● **n. 1** Brit. a star (1–3 according to rank) on the shoulder of an army officer's uniform. **2** any of the spots on a playing card, dice, or domino. **3** an image of an object on a radar screen.
– ORIGIN C16 (orig. *peep*, in the sense 'spot'): of unknown origin.

**pip**[4] ● **n.** a disease of poultry or other birds causing thick mucus in the throat and white scale on the tongue.
– PHRASES **give someone the pip** informal, dated make someone angry or depressed.
– ORIGIN ME: from MDu. *pippe*, prob. from an alt. of L. *pituita* 'slime'.

**pip**[5] ● **v.** (**pipped**, **pipping**) Brit. informal **1** (usu. **be pipped**) defeat by a small margin or at the last moment. **2** dated hit or wound with a gun.
– PHRASES **pip someone at** (or **to**) **the post** defeat someone at the last moment.
– ORIGIN C19: from **PIP**[1] or **PIP**[3].

**pip**[6] ● **v.** (**pipped**, **pipping**) (of a young bird) crack (the shell of the egg) when hatching.
– ORIGIN C19: perh. of imitative origin.

**pipal** /'pi:p(ə)l/ ● **n.** variant spelling of **PEEPUL**.

**pipe** ● **n. 1** a tube used to convey water, gas, oil, or other fluids. ➤a cavity in cast metal. **2** a device used for smoking tobacco, consisting of a narrow tube with a bowl at one end in which the tobacco is burned, the smoke from which is then drawn into the mouth. **3** a wind instrument consisting of a single tube with holes along its length that are covered by the fingers to produce different notes. ➤(**pipes**) bagpipes. ➤(**pipes**) a set of musical pipes joined together, as in pan pipes. ➤any of the cylindrical tubes by which notes are produced in an organ. ➤a boatswain's whistle. **4** a high-pitched cry or song, especially of a bird. **5** a cylindrical vein of ore or rock, especially one in which diamonds are found. **6** Computing a command which causes the output from one routine to be the input for another. [short for **PIPELINE**.] **7** a large cask for wine, especially as a measure equal to two hogsheads. ● **v. 1** convey through a pipe or pipes. **2** transmit (music, a programme, a signal, etc.) by wire or cable. **3** play (a tune) on a pipe. ➤signal the arrival or departure of (someone) by playing a pipe or pipes: *the Duke was piped on board.* ➤use a boatswain's pipe to summon (the crew) to work or a meal. **4** sing or say in a high, shrill voice. **5** decorate with piping. **6** propagate (a pink or similar plant) by taking a cutting at the joint of a stem.
– PHRASES **put that in one's pipe and smoke it** informal one will have to accept a particular fact, even if it is unwelcome.
– PHRASAL VERBS **pipe someone away** (or **down**) Nautical dismiss someone from duty. **pipe something away** Nautical give a signal for a boat to start. **pipe down** informal stop talking; be less noisy. **pipe up** say something suddenly.
– DERIVATIVES **pipeful** n. (pl. **-fuls**). **pipeless** adj. **pipy** adj.
– ORIGIN OE *pīpe* 'musical tube', *pīpian* 'play a pipe', of Gmc origin, based on L. *pipare* 'to peep, chirp'.

**pipe berth** (Brit. also **pipe cot**) ● **n.** a collapsible bed with a frame of metal pipes, used on a boat.

**pipeclay** ● **n.** a fine white clay, used especially for making tobacco pipes or for whitening leather. ● **v.** whiten with pipeclay.

**pipe cleaner** ● **n.** a piece of wire covered with fibre, used to clean a tobacco pipe.

**piped music** ● **n.** pre-recorded background music played through loudspeakers.

**pipe dream** ● **n.** an unattainable or fanciful hope or scheme.
– ORIGIN C19: referring to a dream experienced when smoking an opium pipe.

**pipefish** ● **n.** (pl. same or **-fishes**) a narrow, elongated, marine fish with segmented bony armour beneath the skin and a long tubular snout. [*Syngnathus* and other genera: numerous species.]

**pipeline** ● **n. 1** a long pipe for conveying oil, gas, etc. over long distances. **2** (in surfing) the hollow formed by the breaking of a large wave. **3** Computing a linear sequence of specialized modules used for pipelining. ● **v. 1** convey by a pipeline. **2** Computing design or execute using the technique of pipelining.
– PHRASES **in the pipeline** in the process of being developed.

**pipelining** ● **n. 1** the laying of pipelines. ➤transportation by pipeline. **2** Computing a form of computer organization in which successive steps of an instruction sequence are executed in turn, so that another instruction can be begun before the previous one is finished.

**pip emma** ● **adv. & n.** Brit. dated informal term for **P.M.**
– ORIGIN First World War: signallers' name for these letters.

**pipe organ** ● **n.** an organ using pipes instead of or as well as reeds.

**piper** ● **n.** a person who plays a pipe or bagpipes.

**piperazine** /pɪ'pɛrəzi:n, pʌɪ-/ ● **n.** Chemistry a synthetic crystalline compound with basic properties, sometimes used as an anthelmintic and insecticide.
– ORIGIN C19: from **PIPERIDINE** + **AZINE**.

**piperidine** /pɪ'pɛrɪdi:n, pʌɪ-/ ● **n.** Chemistry a peppery-smelling liquid formed by the reduction of pyridine.
– ORIGIN C19: from L. *piper* 'pepper' + **-IDE** + **-INE**[4].

**pipestone** ● **n.** hard red clay used by North American Indians for tobacco pipes.

**pipette** /pɪ'pɛt/ ● **n.** a slender tube with a bulb at one end, filled by sucking liquid into the tube, used for transferring or measuring out quantities of the liquid. ● **v.** pour or draw off using a pipette.
– ORIGIN C19: from Fr., lit. 'little pipe'.

**piping** ● **n. 1** lengths of pipe. **2** thin lines of icing or cream, used to decorate cakes and desserts. **3** thin cord covered in fabric, used for decoration and to reinforce

seams. **4** the action or art of playing a pipe or pipes.
– PHRASES **piping hot** (of food or water) very hot. [so called because of the whistling sound made by very hot liquid or food.]

**pipistrelle** /ˌpɪpɪˈstrɛl, ˈpɪp-/ ● **n.** a small insect-eating bat. [*Pipistrellus pipistrellus* (Eurasia) and related species.]
– ORIGIN C18: from Fr., from Ital. *pipistrello*, from L. *vespertilio(n-)* 'bat', from *vesper* 'evening'.

**pipit** /ˈpɪpɪt/ ● **n.** a mainly ground-dwelling songbird of open country, typically having brown streaky plumage. [*Anthus pratensis* (**meadow pipit**) and other species.]
– ORIGIN C18: prob. imitative.

**pipkin** ● **n.** a small earthenware pot.
– ORIGIN C16: of unknown origin.

**pippin** ● **n. 1** a red and yellow dessert apple. **2** informal, chiefly N. Amer. an excellent person or thing.
– ORIGIN ME: from OFr. *pepin*, of unknown ultimate origin.

**pipsqueak** ● **n.** informal an insignificant or contemptible person.

**piquant** /ˈpiːk(ə)nt, -kɒnt/ ● **adj. 1** having a pleasantly sharp taste or appetizing flavour. **2** pleasantly stimulating or exciting to the mind.
– DERIVATIVES **piquancy** n. **piquantly** adv.
– ORIGIN C16: from Fr., lit. 'stinging, pricking', pres. part. of *piquer*.

**pique**[1] /piːk/ ● **n.** a feeling of irritation or resentment resulting from a slight, especially to one's pride: *he left in a fit of pique.* ● **v.** (**piques**, **piqued**, **piquing**) **1** stimulate (interest or curiosity). **2** (**be piqued**) feel irritated or resentful. **3** (**pique oneself**) archaic pride oneself.
– ORIGIN C16: from Fr. *piquer* 'prick, irritate'.

**pique**[2] /piːk/ ● **n.** (in piquet) the scoring of 30 points on declarations and play before one's opponent scores anything. Compare with **REPIQUE**. ● **v.** (**piques**, **piqued**, **piquing**) score a pique against.
– ORIGIN C17: from Fr. *pic*, from the OFr. sense 'stabbing blow'.

**piqué** /ˈpiːkeɪ/ ● **n.** firm fabric woven in a ribbed or raised pattern.
– ORIGIN C19: from Fr., lit. 'backstitched', past part. of *piquer*.

**piquet**[1] /pɪˈkɛt/ ● **n.** a trick-taking card game for two players, using a 32-card pack consisting of the seven to the ace only.
– ORIGIN C17: from Fr., of unknown origin.

**piquet**[2] ● **n.** variant spelling of **PICKET** (in sense 2).

**PIR** ● **abbrev.** passive infrared.

**piracy** ● **n. 1** the practice of attacking and robbing ships at sea. ➤a similar practice in other contexts, especially hijacking. **2** the unauthorized use or reproduction of another's work: *software piracy.*

**piranha** /pɪˈrɑːnə, -njə/ ● **n.** a deep-bodied South American freshwater fish having very sharp teeth that it uses to tear flesh from prey. [*Serrosalmus* and other genera: several species.]
– ORIGIN C18: via Port. from Tupi *pirá* 'fish' + *sainha* 'tooth'.

**pirate** ● **n. 1** a person who attacks and robs ships at sea. **2** [often as modifier] a person who appropriates or reproduces the work of another for profit without permission: *pirate recordings.* ➤[often as modifier] a person or organization broadcasting without official authorization: *a pirate radio station.* ● **v. 1** dated rob or plunder (a ship). **2** [often as adj. **pirated**] use or reproduce (another's work) for profit without permission.
– DERIVATIVES **piratic** adj. **piratical** adj. **piratically** adv.
– ORIGIN ME: from L. *pirata*, from Gk *peiratēs*, from *peirein* 'to attempt, attack'.

**piriform** ● **adj.** variant spelling of **PYRIFORM**.

**piripiri**[1] /ˈpɪrɪˌpɪri/ ● **n.** (pl. **piripiris**) a New Zealand plant of the rose family, with prickly burrs. [Genus *Acaena*: several species.]
– ORIGIN C19: from Maori.

**piripiri**[2] /ˈpɪrɪˌpɪri/ ● **n.** a very hot sauce made with red chilli peppers.
– ORIGIN Ronga (a Bantu lang. of southern Mozambique), lit. 'pepper'.

**pirogi** /pəˈrəʊgi/ ● **n.** (pl. **pirogies**) N. Amer. a dough dumpling stuffed with a filling such as potato or cheese.
– ORIGIN from Polish *pieróg* or Ukrainian *pyrih*.

**pirogue** /pɪˈrəʊg/ ● **n.** a long narrow canoe made from a single tree trunk, especially in Central America and the Caribbean.
– ORIGIN C17: from Fr., prob. from Galibi.

**piroshki** /pɪˈrɒʃki/ (also **pirozhki** /-ʒki/) ● **pl. n.** small Russian savoury pastries filled with meat or vegetables.
– ORIGIN from Russ. *pirozhki*, pl. of *pirozhok*, dimin. of *pirog*.

**pirouette** /ˌpɪrʊˈɛt/ ● **n.** (in ballet) an act of spinning on one foot, typically with the raised foot touching the knee of the supporting leg. ● **v.** perform a pirouette.
– ORIGIN C17: from Fr., lit. 'spinning top'.

**pis aller** /piːz ˈaleɪ, French piz ale/ ● **n.** a last resort.
– ORIGIN Fr., from *pis* 'worse' + *aller* 'go'.

**piscary** /ˈpɪskəri/ ● **n.** (in phr. **common of piscary**) Brit., chiefly historical the right of fishing in another's water.
– ORIGIN C15: from med. L. *piscaria* 'fishing rights'.

**piscatorial** /ˌpɪskəˈtɔːrɪəl/ (also **piscatory**) ● **adj.** of or concerning fishing.
– ORIGIN C19: from L. *piscatorius* (from *piscator* 'fisherman', from *piscis* 'fish').

**Pisces** /ˈpʌɪsiːz, ˈpɪskiːz/ ● **n. 1** Astronomy a large constellation (the Fish or Fishes), said to represent a pair of fishes tied together by their tails. **2** Astrology the twelfth sign of the zodiac, which the sun enters about 20 February.
– DERIVATIVES **Piscean** /ˈpʌɪsɪən/ n. & adj.
– ORIGIN L., pl. of *piscis* 'fish'.

**pisciculture** /ˈpɪsɪˌkʌltʃə/ ● **n.** the controlled breeding and rearing of fish.
– DERIVATIVES **piscicultural** adj. **pisciculturist** n.
– ORIGIN C19: from L. *piscis* 'fish' + **CULTURE**.

**piscina** /pɪˈsiːnə, pɪˈsʌɪnə/ ● **n.** (pl. **piscinas** or **piscinae** /-niː/) **1** a stone basin near the altar in Catholic and pre-Reformation churches for draining water used in the Mass. **2** (in ancient Roman architecture) a bathing pool.
– ORIGIN C16: from L., lit. 'fish pond', from *piscis* 'fish'.

**piscine** /ˈpɪsʌɪn/ ● **adj.** of or relating to fish.
– ORIGIN C18: from L. *piscis* 'fish' + **-INE**[1].

**piscivorous** /pɪˈsɪv(ə)rəs/ ● **adj.** Zoology feeding on fish.
– DERIVATIVES **piscivore** n.
– ORIGIN C17: from L. *piscis* 'fish' + **-VOROUS**.

**pisco** /ˈpɪskəʊ/ ● **n.** a white brandy made in Peru from muscat grapes.
– ORIGIN named after a port in Peru.

**pish** ● **exclam.** used to express annoyance, impatience, or disgust.
– ORIGIN natural utterance: first recorded in Engl. in the C16.

**pisiform** /ˈpʌɪsɪfɔːm, ˈpɪzɪ-/ ● **n.** a small rounded carpal bone situated where the palm of the hand meets the outer edge of the wrist and articulating with the triquetral.
– ORIGIN C18: from mod. L. *pisiformis* 'pea-shaped'.

**pismire** /ˈpɪsmʌɪə/ ● **n.** archaic an ant.
– ORIGIN ME: from **PISS** (alluding to the smell of an anthill) + obs. *mire* 'ant'.

**piss** vulgar slang ● **v.** urinate. ➤discharge (something, especially blood) when urinating. ● **n.** urine. ➤an act of urinating.
– PHRASES **be** (or **go**) **on the piss** Brit. be engaged in (or go on) a heavy drinking session. **not have a pot to piss in** N. Amer. be very poor. **a piece of piss** Brit. a very easy thing to do. **piss in the wind** do something that is ineffective. **take the piss** Brit. tease or mock someone or something.
– DERIVATIVES **pisser** n.
– PHRASAL VERBS **piss about/around** Brit. mess around. **piss off** go away. **piss someone off** annoy someone.
– ORIGIN ME: from OFr. *pisser*, prob. of imitative origin.

**pissaladière** /ˌpɪsalaˈdjɛː/ ● **n.** a Provençal open tart made with onions, anchovies, and black olives.
– ORIGIN Fr., from Provençal *pissaladiero*, from *pissala* 'salt fish'.

**pissant** /ˈpɪsant/ US vulgar slang ● **n.** an insignificant or con-

temptible person or thing. ● **adj.** worthless; contemptible.
– ORIGIN C17: from **PISS** + **-ANT**.

**piss artist** ● **n.** Brit. vulgar slang **1** a drunkard. **2** an incompetent or useless person.

**pissed** ● **adj.** vulgar slang **1** Brit. drunk. **2** (**pissed off** or N. Amer. **pissed**) very annoyed.

**pissoir** /piːˈswɑː, ˈpɪswɑː, French piswaʀ/ ● **n.** a public urinal.
– ORIGIN from Fr.

**piss-up** ● **n.** Brit. vulgar slang a heavy drinking session.

**pissy** ● **adj.** vulgar slang **1** of or relating to urine. **2** contemptible or inferior.

**pistachio** /pɪˈstɑːʃɪəʊ, pɪˈstatʃəʊ/ ● **n.** (pl. **-os**) **1** the edible pale green seed of an Asian tree. **2** the evergreen tree which produces this nut, with small brownish-green flowers and oval reddish fruit. [*Pistacia vera*.]
– ORIGIN ME *pistace*, from OFr., later influenced by Ital. *pistaccio*, via L. from Gk *pistakion*, from Old Pers.

**piste** /piːst/ ● **n.** a course or run for skiing.
– ORIGIN Fr., lit. 'racetrack'.

**pisteur** /piːˈstəː/ ● **n.** a person employed to prepare the snow on a piste.
– ORIGIN from Fr.

**pistil** /ˈpɪstɪl/ ● **n.** Botany the female organs of a flower, comprising the stigma, style, and ovary.
– ORIGIN C18: from Fr. *pistile* or L. *pistillum* 'pestle'.

**pistillate** /ˈpɪstɪlət/ ● **adj.** Botany having pistils but no stamens. Compare with **STAMINATE**.

**pistol** ● **n.** a small firearm designed to be held in one hand.
– ORIGIN C16: from obs. Fr. *pistole*, from Ger. *Pistole*, from Czech *pišťala*, orig. in sense 'whistle', hence 'a firearm' by the resemblance in shape.

**pistole** /pɪˈstəʊl/ ● **n.** any of various gold coins used in Europe or Scotland in the 17th and 18th centuries.
– ORIGIN C16: from Fr., abbrev. of *pistolet*, of uncertain ultimate origin.

**pistoleer** /ˌpɪstəˈlɪə/ ● **n.** archaic a soldier armed with a pistol.

**pistol grip** ● **n.** a handle shaped like the butt of a pistol.

**pistol-whip** ● **v.** hit or beat with the butt of a pistol.

**piston** /ˈpɪst(ə)n/ ● **n.** **1** a disc or short cylinder fitting closely within a tube in which it moves up and down against a liquid or gas, used in an internal-combustion engine to derive motion, or in a pump to impart motion. **2** a valve in a brass instrument, depressed to alter the pitch of a note.
– ORIGIN C18: from Fr., from Ital. *pistone*, var. of *pestone* 'large pestle'.

**piston ring** ● **n.** a ring on a piston sealing the gap between the piston and the cylinder wall.

**piston rod** ● **n.** a rod or crankshaft attached to a piston to drive a wheel or to impart motion.

**pistou** /ˈpiːstuː/ ● **n.** a paste made from crushed basil, garlic, and cheese, used in Provençal dishes.
– ORIGIN from Provençal; cf. **PESTO**.

**pit**[1] ● **n.** **1** a large hole in the ground. ➤ a mine or excavation for coal or minerals. **2** an area at the side of a track where racing cars are serviced and refuelled. ➤ a sunken area in a workshop floor allowing access to a car's underside. **3** a hollow or indentation in a surface. **4** short for ***orchestra pit*** (see **ORCHESTRA**). **5** (**the pit**) Brit. dated the seating at the back of the stalls of a theatre. **6** a part of the floor of an exchange in which a particular stock or commodity is traded. **7** chiefly historical an enclosure in which animals are made to fight: *a bear pit.* **8** (**the pit**) poetic/literary hell. ➤ (**the pits**) informal a very bad place or situation: *this really is the pits!* **9** Brit. informal a person's bed. ● **v.** (**pitted**, **pitting**) **1** (**pit someone/thing against**) set someone or something in conflict or competition with. **2** make a hollow or indentation in the surface of. ➤ sink in or contract so as to form a hollow. **3** drive a racing car into the pit.
– PHRASES **the pit of the stomach** the region of the lower abdomen.
– DERIVATIVES **pitted** adj.
– ORIGIN OE *pytt*, of W. Gmc origin, based on L. *puteus* 'well, shaft'; sense 1 of the verb derives from the former practice of setting animals to fight each other in a pit.

**pit**[2] chiefly N. Amer. ● **n.** the stone of a fruit. ● **v.** (**pitted**, **pitting**) remove the pit from (fruit).
– DERIVATIVES **pitted** adj.
– ORIGIN C19: appar. from Du.; rel. to **PITH**.

**pita** ● **n.** chiefly N. Amer. variant spelling of **PITTA**[1].

**pitahaya** /ˌpɪtəˈhʌɪə/ ● **n.** a saguaro or other tall cactus of Mexico and the south-western US. ➤ the edible fruit of such a cactus.
– ORIGIN C18: from Sp., from Haitian Creole.

**pit-a-pat** (also **pitapat**) ● **adv.** with a sound like quick light taps. ● **n.** a sound of this kind.
– ORIGIN C16: imitative of alternating sounds.

**pit bull terrier** ● **n.** a dog of an American variety of bull terrier, noted for its ferocity.

**pitch**[1] ● **n.** **1** the quality of a sound governed by the rate of vibrations producing it; the degree of highness or lowness of a tone. ➤ a standard degree of highness or lowness used in performance: *the guitars were strung and tuned to pitch.* **2** the steepness of a slope, especially of a roof. ➤ Climbing a section of a climb. **3** a level of intensity, especially a high level: *he brought the machine to a high pitch of development.* **4** Brit. an area of ground marked out or used for play in an outdoor team game. ➤ Cricket the strip of ground between the two sets of stumps. **5** Baseball a delivery of the ball by the pitcher. ➤ Cricket the spot where the ball bounces when bowled. ➤ (also **pitch shot**) Golf a high approach shot on to the green. **6** a form of words used to persuade or influence: *they were impressed by his sales pitch.* **7** Brit. a place where a street vendor or performer stations themselves or sets up a stall. **8** a swaying or oscillation of a ship, aircraft, or vehicle around a horizontal axis perpendicular to the direction of motion. **9** technical the distance between successive corresponding points or lines, for example between the teeth of a cogwheel. ● **v.** **1** set at a particular musical pitch. **2** throw or fall heavily or roughly: *she pitched forward into blackness.* **3** Baseball throw (the ball) for the batter. ➤ (**pitch something up**) Cricket bowl a ball so that it bounces near the batsman. ➤ Golf hit (the ball) on to the green with a pitch shot. ➤ Cricket & Golf (of the ball) strike the ground in a particular spot. **4** set or aim at a particular level, target, or audience: *he should pitch his talk at a suitable level.* **5** set up and fix in position. **6** (**pitch in**) informal join in enthusiastically with a task or activity. **7** (**pitch up**) informal arrive. **8** (of a moving ship, aircraft, or vehicle) rock or oscillate around a lateral axis, so that the front moves up and down. **9** [often as adj. **pitched**] (chiefly with reference to a roof) slope or cause to slope downwards: *a pitched roof.* **10** pave (a road) with stones.
– PHRASES **make a pitch** make an attempt at or bid for something.
– ORIGIN ME: perh. rel. to OE *picung* 'stigmata', of unknown ultimate origin.

**pitch**[2] ● **n.** a sticky resinous black or dark brown substance which hardens on cooling, obtained by distilling tar or turpentine and used for waterproofing. ● **v.** chiefly archaic cover or coat with pitch.
– ORIGIN OE *pic* (n.), *pician* (v.), of Gmc origin.

**pitch and putt** ● **n.** a form of golf played on a miniature course.

**pitch-black** (also **pitch-dark**) ● **adj.** completely dark.
– DERIVATIVES **pitch-blackness** n.

**pitchblende** /ˈpɪtʃblɛnd/ ● **n.** a form of the mineral uraninite occurring in brown or black pitch-like masses and containing radium.
– ORIGIN C18: from Ger. *Pechblende*, from *Pech* 'pitch' + *Blende* (see **BLENDE**).

**pitch circle** ● **n.** Mechanics an imaginary circle concentric to a toothed wheel, along which the pitch of the teeth is measured.

**pitched battle** ● **n.** a battle in which the time and place are determined beforehand, rather than a casual or chance skirmish.

**pitcher**[1] ● **n.** a large jug.

– DERIVATIVES **pitcherful** n. (pl. **-fuls**).
– ORIGIN ME: from OFr. *pichier* 'pot', based on late L. *picarium*.

**pitcher**[2] /ˈpɪtʃə/ ● n. **1** Baseball the player who pitches the ball. **2** a stone used for paving.

**pitcher plant** ● n. a plant with a deep pitcher-shaped fluid-filled pouch in which insects are trapped and absorbed. [Many species, chiefly in the families Sarraceniaceae (New World) and Nepenthaceae (Old World).]

**pitchfork** ● n. a farm tool with a long handle and two sharp metal prongs, used for lifting hay. ● v. **1** lift with a pitchfork. **2** thrust suddenly into an unexpected and difficult situation: *an ordinary intellect pitchforked into power.*
– ORIGIN ME: from earlier *pickfork*, influenced by **PITCH**[1] in the sense 'throw'.

**pitchman** ● n. (pl. **-men** /-mɛn/) N. Amer. informal a person delivering a sales pitch.

**pitchout** ● n. **1** Baseball a pitch thrown intentionally beyond the reach of the batter to allow the catcher a clear throw at an advancing base runner. **2** American Football a lateral pass.

**pitch pine** ● n. a pine tree with hard, heavy, resinous wood.

**pitch pipe** ● n. Music a small pipe used to set the correct pitch for the voice or another instrument.

**pitchpole** ● v. Nautical (of a boat) overturn so that the stern pitches forward over the bows.
– ORIGIN C17: from **PITCH**[1] + **POLL**.

**pitchstone** ● n. Geology a dull vitreous rock resembling hardened pitch, formed by weathering of obsidian.

**pitchy** ● adj. (**-ier**, **-iest**) of, like, or as dark as pitch.

**piteous** ● adj. deserving or arousing pity.
– DERIVATIVES **piteously** adv. **piteousness** n.
– ORIGIN ME: from OFr. *piteus*, from L. *pietas* (see **PIETY**).

**pitfall** ● n. **1** a hidden or unsuspected danger or difficulty. **2** a covered pit for use as a trap.

**pith** ● n. **1** spongy white tissue lining the rind of citrus fruits. ➤ Botany the spongy cellular tissue in the stems and branches of many higher plants. ➤ archaic spinal marrow. **2** the true nature or essence: *the pith and core of socialism.* **3** vigorous and concise expression. ● v. **1** remove the pith from. **2** kill or immobilize (an animal) by piercing or severing the spinal cord.
– DERIVATIVES **pithless** adj.
– ORIGIN OE *pitha*, of W. Gmc origin.

**pithead** ● n. the top of a mineshaft and the area around it.

**pith helmet** ● n. a head covering made from the dried pith of the sola or a similar plant, used for protection from the sun.

**pithos** /ˈpɪθɒs/ ● n. (pl. **pithoi** /-θɔɪ/) Archaeology a large earthenware storage jar.
– ORIGIN from Gk.

**pithy** ● adj. (**-ier**, **-iest**) **1** (of a fruit or plant) containing much pith. **2** (of language or style) terse and vigorously expressive.
– DERIVATIVES **pithily** adv. **pithiness** n.

**pitiable** ● adj. **1** deserving or arousing pity. **2** contemptibly poor or small.
– DERIVATIVES **pitiableness** n. **pitiably** adv.

**pitiful** ● adj. **1** deserving or arousing pity. ➤ archaic compassionate. **2** very small or poor; inadequate: *a pitiful attempt.*
– DERIVATIVES **pitifully** adv. **pitifulness** n.

**pitiless** ● adj. showing no pity; harsh or cruel.
– DERIVATIVES **pitilessly** adv. **pitilessness** n.

**pitman** ● n. **1** (pl. **-men**) a coal miner. **2** N. Amer. (pl. **-mans**) a connecting rod in machinery.

**piton** /ˈpiːtɒn/ ● n. a peg or spike driven into a crack to support a climber or a rope.
– ORIGIN C19: from Fr., lit. 'eye bolt'.

**pitot** /ˈpiːtəʊ/ (also **pitot tube**) ● n. a device for measuring the speed of flow of a fluid, consisting of or containing an open-ended right-angled tube pointing in opposition to the flow.
– ORIGIN C19: named after the C18 Fr. physicist Henri *Pitot*.

**pit pony** ● n. Brit. historical a pony used to haul loads in a coal mine.

**pit saw** ● n. historical a large saw with handles at the top and bottom, used in a vertical position by two men, one standing above the timber to be cut, the other in a pit below it.

**pit stop** ● n. Motor Racing a brief stop at a pit for servicing and refuelling. ➤ informal a brief rest during a journey.

**pitta**[1] /ˈpɪtə/ (also chiefly N. Amer. **pita**) ● n. flat, slightly leavened bread which can be split open to hold a filling.
– ORIGIN mod. Gk, lit. 'cake or pie'.

**pitta**[2] /ˈpɪtə/ ● n. a small ground-dwelling thrush-like bird with brightly coloured plumage and a very short tail, found in the Old World tropics. [Genus *Pitta*: many species.]
– ORIGIN C19: from Telugu *piṭṭa* '(young) bird'.

**pittance** ● n. **1** a very small or inadequate amount of money. **2** historical a pious bequest to a religious house to provide extra food and wine at particular festivals or other occasions.
– ORIGIN ME: from OFr. *pitance*, from med. L. *pitantia*, from L. *pietas* 'pity'.

**pitter-patter** ● n. a sound as of quick light steps or taps. ● adv. with this sound.
– ORIGIN ME: reduplication of **PATTER**[1].

**pittosporum** /pɪˈtɒsp(ə)rəm/ ● n. an evergreen shrub native to Australasia, typically with small fragrant flowers. [Genus *Pittosporum*.]
– ORIGIN mod. L., from Gk *pitta* 'pitch' (because of the resinous pulp around the seeds) + *sporos* 'seed'.

**pituitary** /pɪˈtjuːɪt(ə)ri/ ● n. (pl. **-ies**) (in full **pituitary gland** or **pituitary body**) the major endocrine gland, a pea-sized body attached to the base of the brain that is important in controlling growth and the functioning of the other endocrine glands.
– ORIGIN C17: from L. *pituitarius* 'secreting phlegm'.

**pit viper** ● n. a venomous snake of a group found in both America and Asia, distinguished by visible sensory pits on the head which can detect prey by heat. [Numerous genera and species, including the rattlesnakes.]

**pity** ● n. (pl. **-ies**) **1** the feeling of sorrow and compassion caused by the sufferings of others. **2** a cause for regret or disappointment: *what a pity.* ● v. (**-ies**, **-ied**) feel pity for.
– PHRASES **for pity's sake** informal used to express impatience or make an urgent appeal. **more's the pity** informal used to express regret.
– DERIVATIVES **pitying** adj. **pityingly** adv.
– ORIGIN ME: from OFr. *pite* 'compassion', from L. *pietas* 'piety'.

**pityriasis** /ˌpɪtɪˈrʌɪəsɪs/ ● n. Medicine a skin disease characterized by the shedding of fine flaky scales.
– ORIGIN C17: mod. L., from Gk *pituriasis* 'scurf'.

**più mosso** /pjuː ˈmɒsəʊ/ ● adv. & adj. Music more quickly.
– ORIGIN from Ital.

**pivot** ● n. **1** the central point, pin, or shaft on which a mechanism turns or oscillates. **2** a person or thing playing a central part in an activity or organization. ➤ (also **pivotman**) chiefly N. Amer. a player in a central position in a team sport. **3** the person or position from which a body of troops takes its reference point when moving or changing course. ● v. (**pivoted**, **pivoting**) **1** turn on or as if on a pivot. ➤ provide with or fix on a pivot. **2** (**pivot on**) depend on.
– DERIVATIVES **pivotability** n. **pivotable** adj.
– ORIGIN ME: from Fr., prob. from dial. *pue* 'tooth of a comb' and Sp. *pu(y)a* 'point'.

**pivotal** ● adj. **1** fixed on or as if on a pivot. **2** of crucial or central importance.

**pix** ● n. variant spelling of **PYX**.

**pixel** /ˈpɪks(ə)l, -sɛl/ ● n. Electronics a minute area of illumination on a display screen, one of many from which an image is composed.
– ORIGIN 1960s: abbrev. of *picture element*.

**pixelate** /ˈpɪksəleɪt/ (also **pixellate** or **pixilate**) ● v. div-

ide (an image) into pixels, typically for display or storage in a digital format. ➤display (a person's image) as a small number of large pixels, typically in order to disguise someone's identity.
– DERIVATIVES **pixelation** n.

**pixie** (also **pixy**) ● **n.** (pl. **-ies**) a supernatural being in folklore, typically portrayed as small and human-like in form, with pointed ears and a pointed hat.
– DERIVATIVES **pixieish** adj.
– ORIGIN C17: of unknown origin.

**pixilate** ● **v.** variant spelling of **PIXELATE**.

**pixilated** (also **pixillated**) ● **adj.** crazy; confused. ➤informal, dated drunk.
– DERIVATIVES **pixilation** n.
– ORIGIN C19: var. of *pixie-led*, lit. 'led astray by pixies', or from **PIXIE**, on the pattern of words such as *elated*.

**pizza** /'piːtsə, 'pɪtsə/ ● **n.** a dish of Italian origin, consisting of a flat, round base of dough baked with a topping of tomatoes, cheese, and other ingredients.
– ORIGIN Ital., lit. 'pie'.

**pizzazz** (also **pizazz** or **pzazz**) ● **n.** informal an attractive combination of vitality and style.
– ORIGIN said to have been invented by Diana Vreeland, fashion editor of *Harper's Bazaar* in the 1930s.

**pizzeria** /,piːtsə'riːə, 'pɪtsə-/ ● **n.** a place where pizzas are made, sold, or eaten.
– ORIGIN from Ital.

**pizzicato** /,pɪtsɪ'kɑːtəʊ/ Music ● **adv. & adj.** plucking the strings of a violin or other stringed instrument with one's finger. ● **n.** (pl. **pizzicatos** or **pizzicati** /-ti/) this technique of playing. ➤a note or passage played in this way.
– ORIGIN Ital., lit. 'pinched, twitched', past part. of *pizzicare*, based on *pizza* 'point, edge'.

**pizzle** ● **n.** dialect or archaic the penis of an animal, especially a bull.
– ORIGIN C15: from Low Ger. *pēsel* or Flemish *pezel*.

**PK** ● **abbrev.** **1** Pakistan (international vehicle registration). **2** psychokinesis.

**pk** ● **abbrev.** **1** (also **Pk**) park. **2** peak. **3** peck(s). **4** pack.

**PKU** ● **abbrev.** phenylketonuria.

**PL** ● **abbrev.** Poland (international vehicle registration).

**pl.** ● **abbrev.** **1** (also **Pl.**) place. **2** plate (referring to illustrations in a book). **3** chiefly Military platoon. **4** plural.

**PLA** ● **abbrev.** **1** People's Liberation Army. **2** (in the UK) Port of London Authority.

**placable** /'plakəb(ə)l/ ● **adj.** archaic easily calmed or placated.
– DERIVATIVES **placability** n. **placably** adv.

**placard** /'plakɑːd/ ● **n.** a sign for public display, either posted on a wall or carried during a demonstration. ● **v.** /also plə'kɑːd/ cover with placards.
– ORIGIN C15 (denoting a warrant or licence): from OFr. *placquart*, from *plaquier* 'to plaster, lay flat'.

**placate** /plə'keɪt, 'plakeɪt, 'pleɪ-/ ● **v.** calm, pacify, or appease.
– DERIVATIVES **placating** adj. **placatingly** adv. **placation** n. **placatory** adj.
– ORIGIN C17: from L. *placat-*, *placare* 'appease'.

**place** ● **n.** **1** a particular position or point in space; a location. ➤informal a person's home. ➤a point in a book reached by a reader at a particular time. **2** a portion of space available or designated for someone. ➤a vacancy or available position: *a place at university.* ➤the regular or proper position of something: *lay each slab in place.* **3** a position in a sequence or hierarchy. ➤a person's rank or status. ➤a specific role or position: *it's not my place to ask.* ➤Brit. any of the first three or sometimes four positions in a race. ➤N. Amer. the second position, especially in a horse race. **4** the position of a figure in a series indicated in decimal notation: *calculate the ratios to one decimal place.* **5** [in place names] a square or short street. ● **v.** **1** put in a particular position. **2** find an appropriate place or role for. ➤arrange for the implementation of (an order, bet, etc.). ➤order or obtain a connection for (a telephone call). ➤dispose of (something, especially shares) by selling. **3** allocate or award a specified position in a sequence or hierarchy. ➤(**be placed**) Brit. achieve a specified position in a race. ➤be among the first three or four in a race (or the first three in the US). **4** remember the relevant background of: *she eventually said she couldn't place him.* **5** Rugby & American Football score (a goal) by a place kick.
– PHRASES **give place to** be succeeded or replaced by. **go places** informal **1** travel. **2** be increasingly successful. **in one's place** in one's appropriate (but inferior) position or status. **in place 1** working or ready to work; established. **2** N. Amer. on the spot; not travelling any distance. **in place of** instead of. **out of place** not in the proper position. ➤in a setting where one is or feels inappropriate or incongruous. **put oneself in another's place** consider a situation from another's point of view. **put someone in his** (or **her**) **place** deflate or humiliate someone regarded as being presumptuous. **take place** occur. **take one's place** take up one's usual or recognized position. **take the place of** replace.
– DERIVATIVES **placeless** adj.
– ORIGIN ME: from OFr., from an alt. of L. *platea* 'open space', from Gk *plateia* (*hodos*) 'broad (way)'.

**placebo** /plə'siːbəʊ/ ● **n.** (pl. **-os**) **1** a medicine or regime prescribed for the psychological benefit to the patient rather than for any physiological effect. ➤a substance that has no therapeutic effect, used as a control in testing new drugs. **2** a measure designed merely to calm or humour another.
– ORIGIN C18: from L., lit. 'I shall be acceptable or pleasing', from *placere* 'to please'.

**placebo effect** ● **n.** a beneficial effect produced by a placebo drug or treatment, due to the patient's belief in that treatment.

**place card** ● **n.** a card bearing a person's name and used to mark their place at a table.

**place kick** American Football, Rugby, & Soccer ● **n.** a kick made after the ball is first placed on the ground. ● **v.** (**place-kick**) take a place kick.
– DERIVATIVES **place-kicker** n.

**placeman** ● **n.** (pl. **-men**) Brit. derogatory a person appointed to a position chiefly for personal profit and as a reward for political support.

**place mat** ● **n.** a small protective mat placed underneath a person's dining plate.

**placement** ● **n.** **1** the action or fact of placing or being placed. **2** the temporary posting of someone in a workplace, especially to gain work experience.

**place name** ● **n.** the name of a geographical location, such as a town, lake, or mountain.

**placenta** /plə'sɛntə/ ● **n.** (pl. **placentae** /-tiː/ or **placentas**) **1** a flattened circular organ in the uterus of pregnant eutherian mammals, nourishing and maintaining the fetus through the umbilical cord. **2** Botany (in flowers) part of the ovary wall to which the ovules are attached.
– ORIGIN C17: from L., from Gk *plakous*, *plakount-* 'flat cake'.

**placental** ● **adj.** of or relating to a placenta. ➤Zoology relating to or denoting mammals that possess a placenta; eutherian. ● **n.** Zoology a placental mammal.

**placenta praevia** /'priːvɪə/ (US **placenta previa**) ● **n.** Medicine a condition in which the placenta partially or wholly blocks the neck of the uterus, so interfering with normal delivery of a baby.
– ORIGIN C19: from L. *praevia* 'going before', fem. of *praevius*.

**placentation** /,plas(ə)n'teɪʃ(ə)n/ ● **n.** Anatomy, Zoology, & Botany the formation or arrangement of a placenta or placentae.

**placer**[1] ● **n.** [often as modifier] a deposit of sand or gravel in the bed of a river or lake, containing particles of valuable minerals: *placer gold deposits.*
– ORIGIN C19: from Latin Amer. Sp., lit. 'deposit, shoal'.

**placer**[2] ● **n.** **1** a person or animal gaining a specified place. **2** a person who places something. **3** Brit. informal a dealer in stolen goods.

**placet** /'pleɪsɛt/ ● **n.** Brit. an affirmative vote in a Church or university assembly.
– ORIGIN L., lit. 'it pleases'.

**placid** ● **adj.** not easily upset or excited; calm.

– DERIVATIVES **placidity** n. **placidly** adv.
– ORIGIN C17: from Fr. *placide*, from L. *placidus*, from *placere* 'to please'.

**placing** • n. **1** the action or fact of placing or being placed. **2** a ranking given to a competitor in relation to a race or other competition. **3** a post that is found for a job-seeker. **4** a sale or new issue of a large quantity of shares.

**placket** • n. an opening or slit in a garment, covering fastenings or for access to a pocket, or the flap of fabric under such an opening.
– ORIGIN C17: var. of **PLACARD** in an obs. sense 'garment worn under an open coat'.

**placoderm** /ˈplakə(ʊ)dəːm/ • n. a fossil fish of the Devonian period, having the front part of the body encased in broad flat bony plates.
– ORIGIN C19: from Gk *plax, plak-* 'flat plate' + *derma* 'skin'.

**placoid** /ˈplakɔɪd/ • adj. Zoology (of fish scales) tooth-like, being made of dentine with enamel, as in sharks and rays. Compare with **CTENOID** and **GANOID**.
– ORIGIN C19: from Gk *plax, plak-* 'flat plate' + **-OID**.

**plafond** /plaˈfɔ̃(d)/ • n. an ornately decorated ceiling.
– ORIGIN Fr., from *plat* 'flat' + *fond* 'bottom, base'.

**plagal** /ˈpleɪg(ə)l/ • adj. Music (of a church mode) containing notes between the dominant and the note an octave higher. Compare with **AUTHENTIC**.
– ORIGIN C16: from med. L. *plagalis*, from *plaga* 'plagal mode', from L. *plagius*, from Gk *plagos* 'side'.

**plagal cadence** • n. Music a cadence in which the chord of the subdominant immediately precedes that of the tonic.

**plage** /pleɪdʒ/ • n. Astronomy an unusually bright region on the sun.
– ORIGIN C19: from Fr., lit. 'beach'.

**plagiarize** /ˈpleɪdʒərʌɪz/ (also **-ise**) • v. take (the work or an idea of someone else) and pass it off as one's own.
– DERIVATIVES **plagiarism** n. **plagiarist** n. **plagiaristic** adj. **plagiarizer** n.
– ORIGIN C18 (earlier (C17) as *plagiarism*): from L. *plagiarius* 'kidnapper'.

**plagio-** /ˈpleɪdʒɪəʊ, ˈplagɪəʊ/ • comb. form oblique: *plagioclase.*
– ORIGIN from Gk *plagios* 'slanting', from *plagos* 'side'.

**plagioclase** /ˈpleɪdʒɪə(ʊ)kleɪz, ˈplagɪəʊ-/ (also **plagioclase feldspar**) • n. a form of feldspar consisting of aluminosilicates of sodium and/or calcium, common in igneous rocks and typically white.
– ORIGIN C19: from **PLAGIO-** + Gk *klasis* 'cleavage' (because orig. characterized as having two cleavages at an oblique angle).

**plague** • n. **1** a contagious bacterial disease characterized by fever and delirium, typically with the formation of buboes (see **BUBONIC PLAGUE**) and sometimes infection of the lungs (**pneumonic plague**). **2** an unusually large number of insects or animals infesting and causing damage to a place: *a plague of locusts.* • v. (**plagues**, **plagued**, **plaguing**) cause continual trouble or distress to. ➤ pester or harass continually.
– ORIGIN ME: L. *plaga* 'stroke, wound', prob. from Gk (Doric dial.) *plaga*, from a base meaning 'strike'.

**plaice** • n. (pl. same) a North Atlantic flatfish, brown with orange spots, which is a commercially important food fish. [*Pleuronectes platessa* (Europe) and *Hippoglossoides platessoides* (America).]
– ORIGIN ME: from OFr. *plaiz*, from late L. *platessa*, from Gk *platus* 'broad'.

**plaid** /plad/ • n. chequered or tartan twilled cloth. ➤ a long piece of plaid worn over the shoulder as part of Scottish Highland dress.
– DERIVATIVES **plaided** adj.
– ORIGIN C16: from Sc. Gaelic *plaide* 'blanket', of unknown ultimate origin.

**plain**[1] • adj. **1** not decorated or elaborate; simple or ordinary. ➤ without a pattern; in only one colour. ➤ unmarked; without identification: *a plain envelope.* **2** easy to perceive or understand; clear. ➤ not using concealment or deception; frank: *he recalled her plain speaking.* **3** (of a person) having no pretensions; not remarkable or special. ➤ (of a woman or girl) not marked by any particular beauty; ordinary looking. **4** sheer; simple (used for emphasis). **5** (of a knitting stitch) made by putting the needle through the front of the stitch from left to right. Compare with **PURL**[1]. • adv. informal **1** used for emphasis: *that's just plain stupid.* **2** clearly; unequivocally. • n. a large area of flat land with few trees.
– DERIVATIVES **plainly** adv. **plainness** n.
– ORIGIN ME: from OFr. *plain*, from L. *planus*, from a base meaning 'flat'.

**plain**[2] • v. archaic **1** mourn; lament. **2** complain.
– ORIGIN ME: from OFr. *plaindre*, from L. *plangere* 'to lament'.

**plainchant** • n. another term for **PLAINSONG**.

**plain chocolate** • n. Brit. dark, slightly bitter, chocolate without added milk.

**plain clothes** • pl. n. ordinary clothes rather than uniform, especially when worn by police officers.

**plain flour** • n. Brit. flour that does not contain a raising agent.

**plain sailing** • n. smooth and easy progress: *teambuilding was not all plain sailing.*
– ORIGIN C18: prob. a popular use of *plane sailing*, the practice of determining a ship's position on the theory that it is moving on a plane.

**plain service** • n. a church service without music.

**Plains Indian** • n. a member of any of various North American Indian peoples who formerly inhabited the Great Plains, a vast plains area east of the Rocky Mountains in North America.

**plainsman** • n. (pl. **-men**) a person who lives on a plain, especially a frontiersman who lived on the Great Plains of North America.

**plainsong** • n. unaccompanied church music sung in unison in medieval modes and in free rhythm corresponding to the accentuation of the words, which are taken from the liturgy.
– ORIGIN ME: translating L. *cantus planus*.

**plain suit** • n. (in bridge and whist) a suit that is not trumps.

**plaint** • n. **1** Law, Brit. an accusation; a charge. **2** chiefly poetic/literary a complaint or lamentation.
– ORIGIN ME: from OFr. *plainte*, fem. past part. of *plaindre* 'complain'.

**plaintiff** • n. Law a person who brings a case against another in a court of law. Compare with **DEFENDANT**.
– ORIGIN ME: from OFr. *plaintif* 'plaintive'.

**plaintive** • adj. sounding sad and mournful.
– DERIVATIVES **plaintively** adv. **plaintiveness** n.

**plain weave** • n. a style of weave in which the weft alternates over and under the warp.

**plait** /plat/ • n. Brit. **1** a single length of hair, rope, or other material made up of three or more interlaced strands. **2** archaic term for **PLEAT**. • v. form into a plait or plaits.
– ORIGIN ME: from OFr. *pleit* 'a fold', based on L. *plicare* 'to fold'.

**plan** • n. **1** a detailed proposal for doing or achieving something. ➤ a scheme for the regular payment of contributions towards a pension, insurance policy, etc.: *a personal pension plan.* **2** an intention or decision about what one is going to do. **3** a map or diagram: *a street plan.* ➤ a scale drawing of a horizontal section showing the layout of a given level of a building. • v. (**planned**, **planning**) **1** decide on and arrange in advance. ➤ make preparations for an anticipated event or time. **2** make a plan of.
– DERIVATIVES **planner** n. **planning** n.
– ORIGIN C17: from Fr., from earlier *plant* 'ground plan, plane surface'; cf. **PLANT**.

**planar** /ˈpleɪnə/ • adj. Mathematics of, relating to, or in the form of a plane.

**planarian** /pləˈnɛːrɪən/ • n. Zoology a free-living aquatic flatworm. [Order Tricladida.]
– ORIGIN C19: from mod. L. *Planaria* (genus name), fem. of L. *planarius* 'lying flat'.

**planche** /plɑːntʃ, plɑːnʃ/ • n. a gymnastic position in which the body is held parallel with the ground by the

arms (as on the parallel bars).
– ORIGIN C20: Fr., lit. 'plank'.

**planchet** /'plan(t)ʃɪt/ ● **n.** a plain metal disc from which a coin is made.
– ORIGIN C17: dimin. of earlier *planch* 'slab of metal', from OFr. *planche* 'plank, slab'.

**planchette** /plɑːn'ʃɛt/ ● **n.** a small board supported on castors, typically heart-shaped and fitted with a vertical pencil, used for automatic writing and in seances.
– ORIGIN C19: from Fr., lit. 'small plank'.

**Planck's constant** ● **n.** Physics a fundamental constant relating the energy of a quantum of electromagnetic radiation to its frequency, equal to $6.626 \times 10^{-34}$ joules.
– ORIGIN C20: named after the Ger. physicist Max *Planck*.

**plane**[1] ● **n. 1** a flat surface on which a straight line joining any two points would wholly lie. ➤an imaginary flat surface through or joining material objects. ➤a flat surface producing lift by the action of air or water over and under it. **2** a level of existence or thought: *the spiritual plane.* ● **adj. 1** completely level or flat. **2** of or relating to only two-dimensional surfaces or magnitudes: *plane and solid geometry.* ● **v. 1** (of a bird or an airborne object) soar without moving the wings; glide. **2** (of a boat, surfboard, etc.) skim over the surface of water as a result of lift produced hydrodynamically.
– ORIGIN C17: from L. *planum* 'flat surface', neut. of *planus* 'plain' (adj.).

**plane**[2] ● **n.** short for **AEROPLANE**.

**plane**[3] ● **n.** a tool consisting of a block with a projecting steel blade, used to smooth a wooden surface by paring shavings from it. ● **v.** smooth with a plane.
– ORIGIN ME: from a var. of obs. Fr. *plaine* 'planing instrument', from late L. *plana*, from L. *planare* 'make level'.

**plane**[4] (also **plane tree**) ● **n.** a tall spreading tree of the northern hemisphere, with maple-like leaves and bark which peels in uneven patches. [Genus *Platanus*.]
– ORIGIN ME: from OFr., from L. *platanus*, from Gk *platanos*, from *platus* 'broad'.

**plane polarization** ● **n.** a process restricting the vibrations of electromagnetic radiation, especially light, to one direction.
– DERIVATIVES **plane-polarized** adj.

**planer** ● **n.** another term for **PLANE**[3].

**planet** ● **n.** a celestial body moving in an elliptical orbit round a star. ➤(**the planet**) the earth. ➤chiefly Astrology & historical a celestial body distinguished from the fixed stars by having an apparent motion of its own (including the moon and sun).
– PHRASES **what planet are you on?** Brit. informal used to indicate that someone is out of touch with reality.
– DERIVATIVES **planetary** adj. **planetologist** n. **planetology** n.
– ORIGIN ME: from OFr. *planete*, from late L. *planeta*, *planetes*, from Gk *planētēs* 'wanderer, planet', from *planan* 'wander'.

**plane table** ● **n.** a surveying instrument used for direct plotting in the field, with a circular drawing board and pivoted alidade.

**planetarium** /ˌplanɪ'tɛːrɪəm/ ● **n.** (pl. **planetariums** or **planetaria** /-rɪə/) **1** a domed building in which images of stars, planets, and constellations are projected for public entertainment or education. **2** another term for **ORRERY**.
– ORIGIN C18: mod. L., from L. *planetarius* 'relating to the planets'.

**planetary gear** ● **n.** another term for **PLANET GEAR**.

**planetary nebula** ● **n.** Astronomy a ring-shaped nebula formed by an expanding shell of gas round an ageing star.

**planetesimal** /ˌplanɪ'tɛsɪm(ə)l/ Astronomy ● **n.** a minute planet; a body which could come together with many others under gravitation to form a planet. ● **adj.** denoting or relating to such bodies.
– ORIGIN C20: from **PLANET**, on the pattern of *infinitesimal*.

**planet gear** (also **planet wheel**) ● **n.** a gearwheel forming part of a sun-and-planet gear system.

**planetoid** ● **n.** another term for **ASTEROID**.

**planform** ● **n.** the shape or outline of an aircraft wing as projected upon a horizontal plane.

**plangent** /'plan(d)ʒ(ə)nt/ ● **adj.** chiefly poetic/literary (of a sound) loud and resonant, with a mournful tone.
– DERIVATIVES **plangency** n. **plangently** adv.
– ORIGIN C19: from L. *plangent-*, *plangere* 'to lament'.

**planigale** /'planɪgeɪl, ˌplanɪ'geɪli/ ● **n.** a very small mouse-like carnivorous marsupial with a long tail, native to Australia and New Guinea. [Genus *Planigale*: several species.]
– ORIGIN 1940s: mod. L., from L. *planus* 'flat' (referring to the flat skull) + Gk *galē* 'weasel'.

**planigraphy** /plə'nɪgrəfi/ ● **n.** Medicine the process of obtaining a visual representation of a plane section through living tissue, by such techniques as tomography and ultrasonography.
– ORIGIN 1930s: from Du. *planigraphie*, from L. *planus* 'flat, level' + **-GRAPHY**.

**planimeter** /plə'nɪmɪtə/ ● **n.** an instrument for measuring the area of a plane figure.
– DERIVATIVES **planimetric** adj. **planimetrically** adv. **planimetry** n.

**planish** /'planɪʃ/ ● **v.** flatten (sheet metal) by hammering or rolling.
– DERIVATIVES **planisher** n.
– ORIGIN ME: from obs. Fr. *planiss-*, lengthened stem of *planir* 'to smooth'.

**planisphere** /'planɪsfɪə/ ● **n.** a map formed by the projection of a sphere, especially a star map that can be adjusted to show the constellations at a specific time and place.
– DERIVATIVES **planispheric** /-'sfɛrɪk/ adj.
– ORIGIN ME *planisperie*, from med. L. *planisphaerium*, from L. *planus* 'level' + *sphaera* 'sphere'.

**plank** ● **n. 1** a long, thin, flat piece of timber, used in building and flooring. **2** a fundamental part of a political or other programme. ● **v. 1** make, provide, or cover with planks. **2** informal, chiefly N. Amer. & Irish set down forcefully or abruptly.
– PHRASES **walk the plank** (formerly) be forced by pirates to walk blindfold along a plank over the side of a ship to one's death in the sea.
– DERIVATIVES **planking** n.
– ORIGIN ME: from ONorth. Fr. *planke*, from late L. *planca* 'board', fem. of *plancus* 'flat-footed'.

**plankton** /'plaŋ(k)t(ə)n, -tɒn/ ● **n.** the small and microscopic organisms drifting or floating in the sea or fresh water, consisting chiefly of diatoms, protozoans, small crustaceans, and the eggs and larval stages of larger animals.
– DERIVATIVES **planktic** adj. **planktonic** adj.
– ORIGIN C19: from Ger., from Gk *planktos* 'wandering', from the base of *plazein* 'wander'.

**planned economy** ● **n.** an economy in which production, investment, prices, and incomes are determined centrally by the government.

**planned obsolescence** ● **n.** a policy of producing consumer goods that rapidly become obsolete and so require replacing.

**planning permission** ● **n.** Brit. formal permission from a local authority for the erection or alteration of buildings or similar development.

**plano-** /'pleɪnəʊ/ ● **comb. form** level; flat: *planoconvex.*
– ORIGIN from L. *planus* 'flat'.

**planoconcave** ● **adj.** (of a lens) with one side plane and the opposite one concave.

**planoconvex** ● **adj.** (of a lens) with one side plane and the opposite one convex.

**plant** ● **n. 1** a living organism of the kind exemplified by trees, shrubs, grasses, ferns, and mosses, typically growing in a permanent site, absorbing water and inorganic substances through the roots, and synthesizing nutrients in the leaves by photosynthesis using the green pigment chlorophyll. ➤a small plant, as distinct from a shrub or tree. **2** a place where an industrial or manufacturing process takes place. ➤machinery used in an industrial or manufacturing process. **3** a person placed in a group as a

spy or informer. ➤a thing put among someone's belongings to incriminate or discredit them. **4** Snooker a shot in which the cue ball is made to strike one of two touching or nearly touching balls with the result that the second is potted. ● **v. 1** place (a seed, bulb, or plant) in the ground so that it can grow. ➤(**plant something out**) place a plant in the ground out of doors. **2** place or fix in a specified position. ➤stock a river or lake with (young fish, spawn, oysters, etc.) ➤secretly place (a bomb). **3** establish (an idea) in someone's mind. **4** found or establish (a colony or community). **5** put or hide (something) among someone's belongings as a plant. ➤send (someone) to join a group to act as a spy or informer.
– PHRASES **have** (or **keep**) **one's feet firmly planted on the ground** be (or remain) level-headed and sensible.
– DERIVATIVES **plantable** adj. **plantlet** n. **plant-like** adj.
– ORIGIN OE *plante* 'seedling', *plantian* (v.), from L. *planta* 'sprout, cutting' (later influenced by Fr. *plante*) and *plantare* 'plant, fix in place'.

**Plantagenet** /plan'tadʒɪnɪt/ ● **n.** a member of the English royal dynasty which held the throne from 1154 until 1485.
– ORIGIN from L. *planta genista* 'sprig of broom', said to be worn as a crest by and given as a nickname to Geoffrey, count of Anjou, the father of Henry II.

**plantain**[1] /'plantɪn, -teɪn/ ● **n.** a low-growing plant, typically with a rosette of leaves and a slender green flower spike. [Genus *Plantago*: many species.]
– ORIGIN ME: from OFr., from L. *plantago, plantagin-*, from *planta* 'sole of the foot' (because of its broad prostrate leaves).

**plantain**[2] /'plantɪn, -teɪn/ ● **n. 1** a type of banana containing high levels of starch and little sugar, which is harvested green and widely used as a cooked vegetable in the tropics. **2** the plant which bears this fruit. [*Musa* × *paradisiaca*.]
– ORIGIN C16: from Sp. *plá(n)tano*, prob. by assimilation of a S. Amer. word to the Sp. *plá(n)tano* 'plane tree'.

**plantain lily** ● **n.** another term for **HOSTA**.

**plantar** /'plantə/ ● **adj.** Anatomy of or relating to the sole of the foot.
– ORIGIN C18: from L. *plantaris*, from *planta* 'sole'.

**plantation** ● **n. 1** a large estate on which crops such as coffee, sugar, and tobacco are grown. **2** an area in which trees have been planted, especially for commercial purposes. **3** historical a colony.

**planter** ● **n. 1** a manager or owner of a plantation. **2** a decorative container in which plants are grown. **3** a machine or person that plants seeds, bulbs, etc.

**planter's punch** ● **n.** a cocktail containing rum, lemon or lime juice, and sugar.
– ORIGIN prob. so called because drunk by plantation owners.

**plantigrade** /'plantɪgreɪd/ ● **adj.** (of a mammal) walking on the soles of the feet, like a human or a bear. Compare with **DIGITIGRADE**.
– ORIGIN C19: from Fr., from mod. L. *plantigradus*, from L. *planta* 'sole' + *-gradus* '-walking'.

**plant louse** ● **n.** an aphid or other small bug that infests plants.

**plantocracy** /plɑːn'tɒkrəsi/ ● **n.** (pl. **-ies**) a group of planters regarded as the dominant class, especially in the West Indies.

**plantsman** ● **n.** (pl. **-men**) an expert in garden plants and gardening.

**planula** /'planjʊlə/ ● **n.** (pl. **planulae** /-liː/) Zoology a free-swimming coelenterate larva with a flattened, ciliated, solid body.
– ORIGIN C19: mod. L., dimin. of L. *planus* 'plane, flat'.

**plaque** /plak, plɑːk/ ● **n. 1** an ornamental tablet fixed to a wall in commemoration of a person or event. **2** a sticky deposit on teeth in which bacteria proliferate. **3** Medicine a small, distinct, typically raised patch on or within the body, caused by local damage or deposition of material. ➤Microbiology a clear area in a cell culture caused by the inhibition of growth or destruction of cells. **4** a flat counter used in gambling.
– ORIGIN C19: from Fr., from Du. *plak* 'tablet', from *plakken* 'to stick'.

**plash** poetic/literary ● **n. 1** a splashing sound. **2** a pool or puddle. ● **v.** make or hit with a splash.
– DERIVATIVES **plashy** adj.
– ORIGIN C16: prob. imitative.

**plasma** /'plazmə/ ● **n. 1** the colourless fluid part of blood, lymph, or milk, in which corpuscles or fat globules are suspended. **2** Physics a gas of positive ions and free electrons with little or no overall electric charge. **3** a bright green translucent ornamental variety of quartz. **4** (also **plasm** /'plaz(ə)m/) cytoplasm or protoplasm.
– DERIVATIVES **plasmatic** adj. **plasmic** adj.
– ORIGIN C18 (in the sense 'mould, shape'): from late L., from Gk *plasma*, from *plassein* 'to shape'.

**plasmapheresis** /ˌplazmə'fɛrɪsɪs, -fə'riːsɪs/ ● **n.** Medicine a method of removing blood plasma from the body, performed especially to remove antibodies in treating autoimmune conditions.
– ORIGIN 1920s: from **PLASMA** + Gk *aphairesis* 'taking away'.

**plasmid** /'plazmɪd/ ● **n.** Biology a genetic structure in a cell that can replicate independently of the chromosomes, especially a small circular DNA strand in a bacterium or protozoan.
– ORIGIN 1950s: from **PLASMA** + **-ID**[2].

**plasmin** /'plazmɪn/ ● **n.** Biochemistry an enzyme formed in the blood which destroys blood clots by attacking fibrin.
– ORIGIN C19: from Fr. *plasmine*, from late L. *plasma* 'mould, image'.

**plasminogen** /plaz'mɪnədʒ(ə)n/ ● **n.** Biochemistry the inactive precursor of the enzyme plasmin, present in blood.

**plasmodium** /plaz'məʊdɪəm/ ● **n.** (pl. **plasmodia** /-dɪə/) **1** a parasitic protozoan of a genus including that causing malaria. [Genus *Plasmodium*.] **2** Biology a form within the life cycle of some simple organisms such as slime moulds, consisting of a mass of protoplasm containing many nuclei.
– DERIVATIVES **plasmodial** adj.
– ORIGIN C19: mod. L., based on late L. *plasma* 'mould, formation'.

**plasmolysis** /plaz'mɒlɪsɪs/ ● **n.** Botany contraction of the protoplast of a plant cell as a result of loss of water.
– DERIVATIVES **plasmolyse** v.
– ORIGIN C19: mod. L., from *plasmo-* **PLASMA** + **-LYSIS**.

**plasteel** /'plastiːl/ ● **n.** (in science fiction) an ultra-strong non-metallic material.
– ORIGIN 1970s: blend of **PLASTIC** and **STEEL**.

**plaster** ● **n. 1** a soft mixture of lime with sand or cement and water for spreading on walls and ceilings to form a smooth hard surface when dried. **2** (also **plaster of Paris**) a hard white substance made by the addition of water to powdered gypsum, used for holding broken bones in place and making sculptures and casts. [so called because the gypsum orig. came from Paris.] **3** (also **sticking plaster**) an adhesive strip of material for covering cuts and wounds. ➤dated a bandage on which a poultice is spread for application. ● **v. 1** cover with plaster; apply plaster to. **2** coat or cover all over with something, especially to an extent considered excessive: *a face plastered in heavy make-up*. ➤display widely and conspicuously: *her story was plastered all over the papers*. **3** apply a plaster cast to. **4** informal, dated bomb or shell (a target) heavily.
– DERIVATIVES **plasterer** n. **plastery** adj.
– ORIGIN OE, denoting a bandage spread with a curative substance, from med. L. *plastrum*, from Gk *emplastron* 'daub, salve'.

**plasterboard** ● **n.** board made of plaster set between two sheets of paper, used especially to line inner walls.

**plastered** ● **adj.** informal very drunk.

**plasterwork** ● **n.** plaster as part of the interior of a building, especially when formed into decorative shapes.

**plastic** ● **n. 1** a synthetic material made from a wide range of organic polymers such as polyethylene, PVC, nylon, etc., that can be moulded into shape while soft, and then set into a rigid or slightly elastic form. **2** informal

credit cards or other plastic cards that can be used as money. ● **adj. 1** made of plastic. **2** easily shaped or moulded. ➤(in science and technology) of or relating to the permanent deformation of a solid without fracture by the temporary application of force. **3** Biology exhibiting adaptability to change in the environment. **4** (in art) of or relating to moulding or modelling in three dimensions, or to produce three-dimensional effects. **5** offering scope for creativity: *words as a plastic medium.* **6** artificial; unnatural: *long-distance flights with their plastic food.*
– DERIVATIVES **plastically** adv. **plasticity** n.
– ORIGIN C17: from Fr. *plastique* or L. *plasticus*, from Gk *plastikos*, from *plassein* 'to mould'.

**plastic arts** ● **pl. n.** visual art forms that involve modelling or moulding, or the creation of three-dimensional effects.

**plastic bullet** ● **n.** a bullet made of PVC or another plastic, used for riot control.

**plastic explosive** ● **n.** a putty-like explosive capable of being moulded by hand.

**plasticine** (also **Plasticine**) ● **n.** trademark a soft modelling material, used especially by children.

**plasticize** ● **v.** [often as adj. **plasticized**] **1** make plastic or mouldable, especially by the addition of a plasticizer. **2** treat or make with plastic.
– DERIVATIVES **plasticization** n.

**plasticizer** ● **n.** a substance (typically a solvent) added to a synthetic resin to promote plasticity and to reduce brittleness.

**plasticky** ● **adj. 1** resembling plastic. **2** artificial or of inferior quality.

**plastic surgery** ● **n.** the process of reconstructing or repairing parts of the body by the transfer of tissue, either in the treatment of injury or for cosmetic reasons.
– DERIVATIVES **plastic surgeon** n.

**plastid** /ˈplastɪd/ ● **n.** Botany any of a class of small organelles in the cytoplasm of plant cells, containing pigment or food.
– ORIGIN C19: from Ger., based on Gk *plastos* 'shaped'.

**plastique** /plaˈstiːk/ ● **n.** plastic explosive.
– ORIGIN C20: Fr., lit. 'plastic'.

**plastron** /ˈplastrən/ ● **n. 1** a large pad worn by a fencer to protect the chest. **2** an ornamental front of a women's bodice, fashionable in the late 19th century. ➤a man's starched shirt front. **3** Zoology the part of a tortoise's or turtle's shell forming the underside. ➤a similar ventral plate in some invertebrate animals.
– DERIVATIVES **plastral** adj.
– ORIGIN C16: from Fr., from Ital. *piastrone*, augmentative of *piastra* 'breastplate'.

**-plasty** ● **comb. form** moulding or formation of a specified part, especially a part of the body: *rhinoplasty.*
– ORIGIN based on Gk *plastos* 'formed, moulded'.

**plat**[1] N. Amer. ● **n. 1** a plot of land. **2** a plan of an area of land showing actual or proposed features. ● **v.** plan out or make a map of.
– ORIGIN ME: var. of the noun PLOT.

**plat**[2] ● **n. & v.** variant spelling of PLAIT.

**plat du jour** /ˌplɑ d(j)uː ˈʒʊə, French pla dy ʒuʀ/ ● **n.** (pl. **plats du jour** pronunc. same) a dish specially prepared by a restaurant on a particular day, in addition to the usual menu.
– ORIGIN Fr., lit. 'dish of the day'.

**plate** ● **n. 1** a flat dish, typically circular, from which food is eaten or served. ➤N. Amer. a main course of a meal. ➤Austral./NZ a plate of food contributed by a guest to a social gathering. **2** any shallow dish, especially one used for collecting donations in a church. ➤Biology a shallow glass dish on which a culture may be grown. **3** bowls, cups, and other utensils made of gold or silver. [from OFr. *vaisselle en plate* 'dishes and plates made of a single piece of metal'.] ➤a silver or gold dish or trophy awarded as a prize. **4** a thin, flat sheet or strip of metal or other material, typically one used to join or strengthen or forming part of a machine. ➤a small, flat piece of metal bearing a name or inscription, designed to be fixed to a wall or door. ➤short for NUMBER PLATE. ➤Baseball short for HOME PLATE. ➤a horizontal timber laid along the top of a wall to support the ends of joists or rafters. ➤a light horseshoe for a racehorse. **5** Botany & Zoology a thin, flat organic structure or formation: *fused bony plates.* ➤Geology each of the several rigid pieces of the earth's lithosphere which together make up the earth's surface. **6** a sheet of metal or other material bearing an image of type or illustrations from which multiple copies are printed. ➤a printed photograph or illustration in a book. ➤a thin sheet of metal or glass coated with a light-sensitive film on which an image is formed, used in larger or older types of camera. **7** a thin piece of metal that acts as an electrode in a capacitor, battery, or cell. ➤N. Amer. the anode of a thermionic valve. ● **v. 1** cover (a metal object) with a thin coating of a different metal. ➤cover with plates of metal for decoration or protection. **2** serve or arrange on a plate. **3** Baseball score or cause to score (a run or runs). **4** Biology inoculate (cells or infective material) on to a culture plate, especially with the object of isolating a particular strain of micro-organisms or estimating viable cell numbers.
– PHRASES **on a plate** informal indicating that something has been achieved with little or no effort. **on one's plate** chiefly Brit. occupying one's time or energy.
– DERIVATIVES **plateful** n. (pl. **-fuls**). **plater** n. **plating** n.
– ORIGIN ME: from OFr., from med. L. *plata* 'plate armour', based on Gk *platus* 'flat'; sense 1 represents OFr. *plat* 'platter'.

**plate armour** ● **n.** protective armour of metal plates, as worn by knights in the Middle Ages.

**plateau** /ˈplatəʊ/ ● **n.** (pl. **plateaux** /-təʊz/ or **plateaus**) **1** an area of fairly level high ground. **2** a state or period of little or no change following a period of activity or progress. ● **v.** (**plateaus**, **plateaued**, **plateauing**) reach a plateau.
– ORIGIN C18: from Fr., from OFr. *platel*, dimin. of *plat* 'level'.

**plate glass** ● **n.** thick fine-quality glass, used for shop windows and doors and originally cast in plates.

**platelet** ● **n.** Physiology a small colourless disc-shaped cell fragment without a nucleus, found in large numbers in blood and involved in clotting.

**platen** /ˈplat(ə)n/ ● **n. 1** the plate in a small letterpress printing press which presses the paper against the type. **2** the cylindrical roller in a typewriter against which the paper is held.
– ORIGIN C16: from Fr. *platine* 'flat piece' from *plat* 'flat'.

**plateresque** /ˌplatəˈrɛsk/ ● **adj.** (especially of Spanish architecture) richly ornamented in a style suggesting silverware.
– ORIGIN C19: from Sp. *plateresco*, from *platero* 'silversmith', from *plata* 'silver'.

**plate tectonics** ● **pl. n.** [treated as sing.] a theory explaining the structure of the earth's crust and many associated phenomena as resulting from the interaction of rigid lithospheric plates which move slowly over the underlying mantle.

**platform** ● **n. 1** a raised level surface on which people or things can stand. **2** a raised structure along the side of a railway track where passengers get on and off trains. **3** a raised structure standing in the sea from which oil or gas wells can be drilled. **4** Computing a standard for the hardware of a computer system, which determines the kinds of software it can run. **5** the declared policy of a political party or group. ➤an opportunity to voice one's views: *a platform for discussion.* **6** [usu. as modifier] a very thick sole on a shoe: *platform shoes.*
– ORIGIN C16: from Fr. *plateforme* 'ground plan', lit. 'flat shape'.

**platinize** /ˈplatɪnʌɪz/ (also **-ise**) ● **v.** [usu. as adj. **platinized**] coat with platinum.
– DERIVATIVES **platinization** n.

**platinoid** /ˈplatɪnɔɪd/ ● **n.** an alloy of copper with zinc, nickel, and sometimes tungsten, used for its high electrical resistance.

**platinum** /ˈplatɪnəm/ ● **n. 1** a precious silvery-white metal, the chemical element of atomic number 78, used in jewellery, electrical contacts, laboratory equipment,

and industrial catalysts. (Symbol: **Pt**) **2** [as modifier] greyish-white or silvery like platinum.
– ORIGIN C19: alt. of earlier *platina*, from Sp., dimin. of *plata* 'silver'.

**platinum black** • n. platinum in the form of a finely divided black powder, used as a catalyst and absorbent for gases.

**platinum blonde** • adj. (of a woman's hair) silvery-blonde. • n. a woman with silvery-blonde hair.

**platinum disc** • n. a framed platinum disc awarded to a recording artist for sales of a record exceeding a specified high figure.

**platinum metals** • pl. n. Chemistry the six metals platinum, palladium, ruthenium, osmium, rhodium, and iridium, which have similar properties and tend to occur together in nature.

**platitude** /'platɪtju:d/ • n. a trite, obvious, or insincere remark or statement.
– DERIVATIVES **platitudinize** (also **-ise**) v. **platitudinous** adj.
– ORIGIN C19: from Fr., from *plat* 'flat'.

**Platonic** /plə'tɒnɪk/ • adj. **1** of or associated with the Greek philosopher Plato or his ideas. **2** (**platonic**) (of love or friendship) intimate and affectionate but not sexual.
– DERIVATIVES **platonically** adv.
– ORIGIN C16: via L. from Gk *Platōnikos*, from *Platōn* 'Plato'.

**Platonic solid** (also **Platonic body**) • n. one of five regular solids (a tetrahedron, cube, octahedron, dodecahedron, or icosahedron).

**Platonism** /'pleɪt(ə)nɪz(ə)m/ • n. the philosophy of Plato or his followers, especially that relating to Plato's theory of 'ideas' or 'forms', in which abstract entities ('universals') are contrasted with their objects ('particulars') in the material world. ➤ the theory that numbers or other abstract objects are objective, timeless entities, independent of the physical world and of the symbols used to represent them.
– DERIVATIVES **Platonist** n. & adj.

**platoon** • n. **1** a subdivision of a company of soldiers, usually commanded by a subaltern or lieutenant and divided into three sections. **2** [as modifier] Baseball engaged in platooning: *a platoon player.* • v. Baseball use the strategy of alternating (a pair of players or one player with another) in a specified field position in successive games.
– DERIVATIVES **platooning** n.
– ORIGIN C17: from Fr. *peloton* 'platoon', lit. 'small ball', dimin. of *pelote.*

**Plattdeutsch** /'platdɔɪtʃ/ • n. & adj. another term for **Low German**.
– ORIGIN Ger., from Du. *Platduits*, from *plat* 'flat, low' + *Duits* 'German'.

**platteland** /'platəland/ S. African • n. remote country districts. • adj. characteristic of country districts; rustic.
– DERIVATIVES **plattelander** n.
– ORIGIN Afrik., lit. 'flat land'.

**platter** • n. **1** a large flat serving dish. ➤ a meal or selection of food placed on a platter. **2** the rotating metal disc forming the turntable of a record player. ➤ Computing a rigid rotating disk on which data is stored in a disk drive; a hard disk. ➤ informal, dated a gramophone record.
– PHRASES **on a** (**silver**) **platter** informal indicating that something is achieved with little or no effort.
– ORIGIN ME: from Anglo-Norman Fr. *plater*, from *plat* (see **PLATE**).

**platy-** • comb. form broad; flat: *platypus.*
– ORIGIN from Gk *platus* 'broad, flat'.

**Platyhelminthes** /,platɪhɛl'mɪnθi:z/ • pl. n. Zoology a phylum of invertebrates that comprises the flatworms.
– DERIVATIVES **platyhelminth** /,platɪ'hɛlmɪnθ/ n.
– ORIGIN mod. L., from **PLATY-** + Gk *helminth* 'worm'.

**platypus** /'platɪpəs/ (also **duck-billed platypus**) • n. (pl. **platypuses**) a semiaquatic egg-laying Australian mammal with a sensitive pliable bill like that of a duck and webbed feet with venomous spurs. [*Ornithorhynchus anatinus.*]
– ORIGIN C18: mod. L., from Gk *platupous* 'flat-footed'.

**platyrrhine** /'platɪrʌɪn/ • adj. Zoology relating to or denoting primates of a group distinguished by having nostrils that are far apart and directed forwards or sideways and typically a prehensile tail, comprising the New World monkeys, marmosets, and tamarins. Compare with **CATARRHINE**.
– ORIGIN C19: from **PLATY-** + Gk *rhis, rhin-* 'nose'.

**platysma** /plə'tɪzmə/ • n. (pl. **platysmas** or **platysmata** /-mətə/) Anatomy a broad sheet of muscle fibres extending from the collar bone to the angle of the jaw.
– ORIGIN C17: mod. L., from Gk *platusma* 'flat piece, plate'.

**plaudits** /'plɔ:dɪts/ • pl. n. praise; enthusiastic approval.
– ORIGIN C17: *plaudit* shortened from L. *plaudite* 'applaud!' (said by Roman actors at the end of a play), imper. pl. of *plaudere.*

**plausible** • adj. apparently reasonable or probable, without necessarily being so.
– DERIVATIVES **plausibility** n. **plausibly** adv.
– ORIGIN C16 (also in the sense 'deserving applause'): from L. *plausibilis*, from *plaus-*, *plaudere* 'applaud'.

**play** • v. **1** engage in games or other activities for enjoyment rather than for a serious or practical purpose. ➤ amuse oneself by engaging in imaginative pretence. ➤ treat inconsiderately for one's own amusement: *she likes to play with people's emotions.* ➤ tamper with something so as to damage it: *has somebody been playing with these taps?* **2** take part in (a sport or contest). ➤ compete against. ➤ take a specified position in a sports team: *he played in goal.* ➤ strike (a ball) or execute (a stroke). ➤ move (a piece) or display (a playing card) in one's turn in a game. ➤ bet or gamble at or on. **3** be cooperative. **4** represent (a character) in a play or film. ➤ give a performance at (a particular venue). ➤ pretend to be: *the skipper played the innocent.* ➤ (**play someone for**) treat someone as being of (a specified type): *don't imagine you can play me for a fool.* **5** perform on or have the skill to perform on (a musical instrument). ➤ produce (notes) from a musical instrument; perform (a piece of music). ➤ make (a record player, radio, etc.) produce sounds. ➤ accompany (someone) with music in a ceremony or procession. **6** move lightly and quickly; flicker: *a smile played about her lips.* **7** allow (a fish) to exhaust itself on a line before reeling it in. • n. **1** games and other activities engaged in for enjoyment, especially by children. ➤ behaviour or speech that is not intended seriously. **2** the progress of a sporting match. ➤ the status of the ball in a game as being available to be played according to the rules: *the ball was put in play.* ➤ a move or manoeuvre in a sport or game. **3** the state of being active, operative, or effective: *luck comes into play.* **4** a dramatic work for the stage or to be broadcast. **5** the ability or freedom of movement in a mechanism. **6** light and constantly changing movement. **7** archaic gambling.
– PHRASES **make a play for** informal attempt to attract or attain. **make** (**great**) **play of** (or **with**) ostentatiously draw attention to. **make play with** treat frivolously. **play both ends against the middle** keep one's options open by supporting opposing sides. **play something by ear 1** perform music without having to read from a score. **2** (**play it by ear**) informal proceed instinctively according to circumstances rather than according to rules or a plan. **play someone false** prove treacherous or deceitful towards someone. **play fast and loose** behave irresponsibly or immorally. **play for time** use specious excuses or unnecessary manoeuvres to gain time. **play a** (or **one's**) **hunch** make an instinctive choice. **play oneself in** Brit. become accustomed to the circumstances and conditions of a game or activity. **play into someone's hands** act in such a way as unintentionally to give someone an advantage. **play it cool** informal make an effort to be or appear to be unconcerned. **a play on words** a pun. **play** (or **play it**) **safe** avoid taking risks. **play with oneself** informal masturbate. **play with fire** take foolish risks.
– PHRASAL VERBS **play about** (or **around**) behave in a casual or irresponsible way. ➤ informal (of a married person) have an affair. **play along** perform a piece of music at

the same time as it is playing on a tape or record. ➤ pretend to cooperate. **play someone along** informal deceive or mislead someone. **play something down** pretend that something is less important than it in fact is. **play someone off** bring other people into conflict for one's own advantage. **play off** (of two competitors) play an extra match to decide a draw or tie. **play on** exploit (someone's weak or vulnerable point). **play up 1** Brit. informal fail to function properly; cause problems. **2** Brit. put all one's energy into a game. **play something up** emphasize the extent or importance of something. **play up to** humour or flatter.
– DERIVATIVES **playability** n. **playable** adj.
– ORIGIN OE *pleg(i)an* 'to exercise', *plega* 'brisk movement'.

**playa** /ˈplʌɪə/ ● n. an area of flat, dried-up land.
– ORIGIN C19: from Sp., lit. 'beach', from late L. *plagia*.

**play-act** ● v. **1** act in a play. **2** engage in histrionic pretence.
– DERIVATIVES **play-acting** n. **play-actor** n.

**playback** ● n. the action or process of reproducing previously recorded sound or moving images.

**playbill** ● n. **1** a poster announcing a theatrical performance. **2** N. Amer. a theatre programme.

**playbook** ● n. N. Amer. a book containing a sports team's strategies and plays, especially in American football.

**playboy** ● n. a wealthy man who spends his time seeking pleasure, especially sexual pleasure.

**play-by-play** ● n. N. Amer. a detailed running commentary on a sporting contest.

**player** ● n. **1** a person taking part in a sport or game. **2** a person that is involved and influential in an activity. **3** a person who plays a musical instrument. ➤ a device for playing compact discs, cassettes, etc. **4** an actor.

**player-manager** ● n. a person who both plays in a sports team and manages it.

**player-piano** ● n. a piano fitted with a pneumatic apparatus enabling it to be played automatically by means of a rotating perforated roll signalling the notes to be played.

**playful** ● adj. **1** fond of games and amusement. **2** intended for amusement; light-hearted.
– DERIVATIVES **playfully** adv. **playfulness** n.

**playground** ● n. an outdoor area provided for children to play on.

**playgroup** ● n. Brit. a regular meeting of a group of preschool children, organized by parents.

**playhouse** ● n. **1** [usu. in names] a theatre. **2** a toy house for children to play in.

**playing card** ● n. each of a set of rectangular pieces of card with numbers and symbols on one side (usually 52 cards divided into four suits), used to play various games.

**playing field** ● n. a field used for outdoor team games.

**playlet** ● n. a short play or dramatic piece.

**playlist** ● n. a list of recorded songs or pieces of music chosen to be broadcast on a radio station. ● v. place (a song or piece of music) on such a list.

**playmaker** ● n. a player in a team game who leads attacks or brings teammates into attacking positions.
– DERIVATIVES **playmaking** n.

**playmate** ● n. **1** a friend with whom a child plays. **2** euphemistic a person's lover.

**play-off** ● n. an additional match played to decide the outcome of a contest.

**playpen** ● n. a small portable enclosure in which a baby or small child can play safely.

**playroom** ● n. a room in a house that is set aside for children to play in.

**playscheme** ● n. a local project providing recreational facilities and activities for children.

**playschool** ● n. a playgroup.

**playsuit** ● n. an all-in-one stretchy garment for a baby or very young child, covering the body, arms, and legs. ➤ a women's all-in-one garment or matching set of garments.

**plaything** ● n. **1** a toy. **2** a person treated as amusing but unimportant.

**playwright** ● n. a person who writes plays.

**plaza** ● n. **1** a public square, marketplace, or similar open space in a built-up area. **2** N. Amer. a shopping centre.
– ORIGIN C17: from Sp., lit. 'place'.

**plc** (also **PLC**) ● abbrev. Brit. public limited company.

**plea** ● n. **1** a request made in an urgent and emotional manner. **2** Law a formal statement by or on behalf of a defendant or prisoner, stating guilt or innocence in response to a charge, offering an allegation of fact, or claiming that a point of law should apply. ➤ an excuse or claim of mitigating circumstances.
– PHRASES **plea of tender** Law a plea that the defendant has always been ready to satisfy the plaintiff's claim and now brings the sum into court.
– ORIGIN ME: from OFr. *plait*, *plaid* 'agreement, discussion', from L. *placitum* 'a decree', neut. past part. of *placere* 'to please'.

**plea-bargaining** ● n. Law an arrangement between prosecutor and defendant whereby the defendant pleads guilty to a lesser charge in the expectation of leniency.
– DERIVATIVES **plea-bargain** v. **plea bargain** n.

**pleach** /pliːtʃ/ ● v. [usu. as adj. **pleached**] entwine or interlace (tree branches) to form a hedge or provide cover for an outdoor walkway.
– ORIGIN ME: from an OFr. var. of *plaissier* (see **PLASH**[2]).

**plead** ● v. (past and past part. **pleaded** or N. Amer., Scottish, or dialect **pled**) **1** make an emotional appeal. **2** present and argue for (a position), especially in court or in another public context. ➤ Law address a court as an advocate on behalf of a party. ➤ Law state formally in court whether one is guilty or not guilty of the offence with which one is charged. ➤ Law invoke (a reason or a point of law) as an accusation or defence: *she pleaded self-defence.* ➤ offer or present as an excuse for doing or not doing something.
– DERIVATIVES **pleadable** adj. (Law). **pleader** n.
– ORIGIN ME (in the sense 'to wrangle'): from OFr. *plaidier* 'go to law', from *plaid* (see **PLEA**).

**pleading** ● n. **1** the action of making an emotional or earnest appeal. **2** Law a formal statement of the cause of an action or defence. ● adj. earnestly appealing: *a pleading look.*
– DERIVATIVES **pleadingly** adv.

**pleasance** ● n. a secluded enclosure or part of a garden, especially one attached to a large house.
– ORIGIN ME (in the sense 'pleasure'): from OFr. *plaisance*, from *plaisant* (see **PLEASANT**).

**pleasant** ● adj. (**-er, -est**) giving a sense of happy satisfaction or enjoyment. ➤ (of a person) friendly and considerate; likeable.
– DERIVATIVES **pleasantly** adv. **pleasantness** n.
– ORIGIN ME: from OFr. *plaisant* 'pleasing', from *plaisir* (see **PLEASE**).

**pleasantry** ● n. (pl. **-ies**) an inconsequential remark made as part of a polite conversation. ➤ a mild joke.

**please** ● v. **1** cause to feel happy and satisfied. **2** (**please oneself**) take only one's own wishes into consideration in deciding how to act or proceed. ➤ wish or desire to do something: *feel free to wander around as you please.* ➤ (**it pleases someone to do something**) formal or dated it is someone's choice to do something. ➤ (**if you please**) used in polite requests or to express indignation. ● adv. used in polite requests or questions, or to agree to a request or accept an offer. ➤ used to add urgency and emotion to a request.
– DERIVATIVES **pleasing** adj. **pleasingly** adv.
– ORIGIN ME: from OFr. *plaisir* 'to please', from L. *placere*.

**pleased** ● adj. feeling or showing pleasure and satisfaction. ➤ (**pleased to do something**) willing or glad to do something. ➤ (**pleased with oneself**) excessively proud of one's achievements; self-satisfied.
– DERIVATIVES **pleasedly** adv.

**pleasurable** ● adj. pleasing; enjoyable.
– DERIVATIVES **pleasurableness** n. **pleasurably** adv.

**pleasure** ● n. **1** a feeling of happy satisfaction and enjoyment. ➤ enjoyment and entertainment, as opposed to necessity. ➤ an event or activity from which one derives

enjoyment. ➤[as modifier] intended for entertainment rather than business: *pleasure boats.* ➤sensual gratification. **2** (**one's pleasure**) formal one's wish or desire: *the landlord could terminate the agreement at his pleasure.* ● **v. 1** give sexual enjoyment or satisfaction to. **2** (**pleasure in**) archaic derive enjoyment from.
– ORIGIN ME: from OFr. *plaisir* 'to please'.

**pleasure principle** ● **n.** Psychoanalysis the instinctive drive to seek pleasure and avoid pain, expressed by the id as a basic motivating force which reduces psychic tension.

**pleat** ● **n. 1** a double or multiple fold in a garment or other item made of cloth, held by stitching the top or side. **2** a plait. ● **v.** [often as adj. **pleated**] fold or form into pleats.
– ORIGIN ME: var. of **PLAIT**.

**pleb** ● **n.** informal, derogatory a member of the lower social classes.
– DERIVATIVES **plebby** adj.

**plebe** /pliːb/ ● **n.** US informal a newly entered cadet or freshman, especially at a military or naval academy.
– ORIGIN C17: perh. an abbrev. of **PLEBEIAN**.

**plebeian** /plɪˈbiːən/ ● **n. 1** (in ancient Rome) a commoner. **2** a member of the lower social classes. ● **adj. 1** of or relating to the plebeians of ancient Rome. **2** lower-class or lacking in refinement.
– ORIGIN C16: from L. *plebeius* (from *plebs, pleb-* 'the common people') + **-AN**.

**plebiscite** /ˈplɛbɪsʌɪt, -sɪt/ ● **n. 1** the direct vote of all the members of an electorate on an important public question. **2** (in ancient Rome) a law enacted by the plebeians' assembly.
– DERIVATIVES **plebiscitary** /-ˈbɪsɪt(ə)ri/ adj.
– ORIGIN C16: from Fr. *plébiscite*, from L. *plebiscitum*, from *plebs, pleb-* 'the common people' + *scitum* 'decree'.

**plectrum** /ˈplɛktrəm/ ● **n.** (pl. **plectrums** or **plectra** /-trə/) a thin flat piece of plastic or tortoiseshell used to pluck the strings of a guitar or similar musical instrument. ➤the corresponding mechanical part which plucks the strings of an instrument such as a harpsichord.
– ORIGIN ME: via L. from Gk *plēktron* 'something with which to strike', from *plēssein* 'to strike'.

**pled** North American, Scottish, or dialect past participle of **PLEAD**.

**pledge** ● **n. 1** a solemn promise or undertaking. ➤a promise of a donation to charity. ➤(**the pledge**) a solemn undertaking to abstain from alcohol. **2** Law a thing that is given as security for the fulfilment of a contract or the payment of a debt and is liable to forfeiture in the event of failure. ➤a thing given as a token of love, favour, or loyalty. **3** archaic the drinking of a person's health; a toast. ● **v. 1** solemnly undertake to do or give something. **2** Law give as security on a loan. **3** archaic drink to the health of.
– DERIVATIVES **pledgee** n. (Law) **pledger** n. **pledgor** n. (Law).
– ORIGIN ME (denoting a person acting as surety for another): from OFr. *plege*, from med. L. *plebium*, perh. rel. to the Gmc base of **PLIGHT**[2].

**pledget** /ˈplɛdʒɪt/ ● **n.** a small wad of soft material used to stop up a wound.
– ORIGIN C16: of unknown origin.

**-plegia** /pliːdʒə/ ● **suffix** Medicine forming nouns denoting a kind of paralysis, as *hemiplegia, paraplegia*.
– DERIVATIVES **-plegic** suffix forming corresponding adjectives.
– ORIGIN from Gk *plēgē* 'blow, stroke' (from *plēssein* 'to strike') + **-IA**[1].

**plein-air** /plɛn ˈɛː, French plɛn ɛʀ/ ● **adj.** denoting or relating to a 19th-century style of painting outdoors which became a central feature of French Impressionism.
– ORIGIN from Fr. *en plein air* 'in the open air'.

**pleiotropy** /plʌɪˈɒtrəpi/ ● **n.** Genetics the production by a single gene of two or more apparently unrelated effects.
– DERIVATIVES **pleiotropic** /-ˈtrəʊpɪk, -ˈtrɒpɪk/ adj. **pleiotropism** n.
– ORIGIN 1930s: from Gk *pleiōn* 'more' + *tropē* 'turning'.

**Pleistocene** /ˈplʌɪstəsiːn/ ● **adj.** Geology relating to or denoting the first epoch of the Quaternary period (between the Pliocene and Holocene epochs, from 1.64 million to about 10,000 years ago), a time which included the ice ages and the appearance of humans.
– ORIGIN C19: from Gk *pleistos* 'most' + *kainos* 'new'.

**plenary** /ˈpliːnəri/ ● **adj. 1** unqualified; absolute. **2** (of a meeting) to be attended by all participants at a conference or assembly. ● **n.** a plenary meeting.
– ORIGIN ME: from late L. *plenarius* 'complete', from *plenus* 'full'.

**plenipotentiary** /ˌplɛnɪpəˈtɛnʃ(ə)ri/ ● **n.** (pl. **-ies**) a person, especially a diplomat, invested with the full power of independent action on behalf of their government. ● **adj.** having full power to take independent action. ➤(of power) absolute.
– ORIGIN C17: from med. L. *plenipotentiarius*, from *plenus* 'full' + *potentia* 'power'.

**plenitude** ● **n.** formal an abundance. ➤the condition of being full or complete.
– ORIGIN ME: from OFr., from late L. *plenitudo*, from *plenus* 'full'.

**plenteous** ● **adj.** poetic/literary plentiful.
– DERIVATIVES **plenteously** adv. **plenteousness** n.
– ORIGIN ME: from OFr. *plentivous*, from *plentif, -ive*, from *plente* 'plenty'.

**plentiful** ● **adj.** existing in or yielding great quantities; abundant.
– DERIVATIVES **plentifully** adv. **plentifulness** n.

**plentitude** ● **n.** another term for **PLENITUDE**.

**plenty** ● **pron.** a large or sufficient amount or quantity; more than enough. ● **n.** a situation in which food and other necessities are available in sufficiently large quantities. ● **adv.** informal fully; sufficiently.
– ORIGIN ME: from OFr. *plente*, from L. *plenitas*, from *plenus* 'full'.

**plenum** /ˈpliːnəm/ ● **n. 1** an assembly of all the members of a group or committee. **2** Physics a space completely filled with matter, or the whole of space so regarded.
– ORIGIN C17: from L., lit. 'full space', neut. of *plenus* 'full'.

**pleo-** ● **comb. form** having more than the usual or expected number: *pleomorphism*.
– ORIGIN from Gk *pleōn* 'more'.

**pleochroic** /ˌpliːə(ʊ)ˈkrəʊɪk/ ● **adj.** Crystallography displaying variable colours owing to differential absorption of light according to wavelength, direction, and/or polarization.
– DERIVATIVES **pleochroism** n.
– ORIGIN C19: from **PLEO-** + *khrōs* 'colour' + **-IC**.

**pleomorphism** /ˌpliːə(ʊ)ˈmɔːfɪz(ə)m/ ● **n.** the occurrence of more than one distinct form of a bacterium or other natural object.
– DERIVATIVES **pleomorphic** adj.

**pleonasm** /ˈpliːə(ʊ)ˌnaz(ə)m/ ● **n.** the use of more words than are necessary to convey meaning (e.g. *see with one's eyes*).
– DERIVATIVES **pleonastic** adj. **pleonastically** adv.
– ORIGIN C16: via late L. from Gk *pleonasmos*, from *pleonazein* 'be superfluous'.

**pleroma** /pləˈrəʊmə/ ● **n. 1** (in Gnosticism) the spiritual universe as the abode of God and of the totality of the divine powers and emanations. **2** (in Christian theology) the totality or fullness of the Godhead which dwells in Christ.
– DERIVATIVES **pleromatic** adj.
– ORIGIN C18: from Gk *plērōma* 'that which fills', based on *plere* 'to fill'.

**plesiosaur** /ˈpliːsɪəsɔː, ˈpliːz-/ ● **n.** a large fossil marine reptile of the Mesozoic era, with large paddle-like limbs and a long flexible neck.
– ORIGIN C19: from mod. L. *Plesiosaurus*, from Gk *plēsios* 'near' (because closely related to the lizards) + *sauros* 'lizard'.

**plessor** /ˈplɛsə/ ● **n.** variant spelling of **PLEXOR**.

**plethora** /ˈplɛθ(ə)rə/ ● **n. 1** (**a plethora of**) an excess of. **2** Medicine an excess of a bodily fluid, particularly blood.
– DERIVATIVES **plethoric** /ˈplɛθ(ə)rɪk, plɪˈθɒrɪk/ adj. (archaic

or Medicine).
– ORIGIN C16: via late L. from Gk *plēthōrē*, from *plēthein* 'be full'.

**plethysmograph** /plɪ'θɪzməgrɑːf/ ● **n.** Medicine an instrument for measuring variation in the volume of a part of the body caused by changes in blood pressure.
– DERIVATIVES **plethysmographic** adj.
– ORIGIN C19: from Gk *plēthusmos* 'enlargement' (based on *plēthus* 'fullness') + **-GRAPH**.

**pleura**[1] /'plʊərə/ ● **n.** (pl. **pleurae** /-riː/) **1** each of a pair of serous membranes lining the thorax and enveloping the lungs in humans and other mammals. **2** Zoology a lateral part in an animal body or structure.
– DERIVATIVES **pleural** adj.
– ORIGIN ME: via med. L. from Gk, lit. 'side of the body, rib'.

**pleura**[2] plural form of **PLEURON**.

**pleurisy** /'plʊərɪsi/ ● **n.** inflammation of the pleurae, causing pain when breathing.
– DERIVATIVES **pleuritic** adj.
– ORIGIN ME: from OFr. *pleurisie*, from late L. *pleurisis*, alt. of earlier L. *pleuritis*, from Gk (see **PLEURA**[1]).

**pleuro-** ● **comb. form** of or relating to the pleura or pleurae: *pleuropneumonia.*

**pleuron** /'plʊərɒn/ ● **n.** (pl. **pleura** /-rə/) Zoology the side wall of each segment of the body of an arthropod.
– ORIGIN C18: from Gk, lit. 'side of the body, rib'.

**pleuropneumonia** ● **n.** pneumonia complicated with pleurisy.

**plew** /pluː/ ● **n.** N. Amer. historical a beaver skin.
– ORIGIN C19: from Canad. Fr. *pélu* 'hairy', from Fr. *poil* 'hair, bristle'.

**plexiglas** /'plɛksɪglɑːs/ ● **n.** trademark, chiefly N. Amer. a tough transparent plastic made of an acrylic resin, used as a substitute for glass.
– ORIGIN 1930s: from Gk *plēxis* 'percussion' + **GLASS**.

**plexor** /'plɛksə/ (also **plessor**) ● **n.** a small hammer with a rubber head used to test reflexes and in medical percussion.
– ORIGIN C19: formed irregularly from Gk *plēxis* 'percussion' + **-OR**[1].

**plexus** ● **n.** (pl. same or **plexuses**) **1** Anatomy a network of nerves or vessels in the body. **2** an intricate network or web-like formation.
– DERIVATIVES **plexiform** adj.
– ORIGIN C17: from L., lit. 'plaited formation', past part. of *plectere* 'to plait'.

**pliable** ● **adj. 1** easily bent; flexible. **2** easily influenced or swayed.
– DERIVATIVES **pliability** n. **pliably** adv.
– ORIGIN ME: from Fr., from *plier* (see **PLY**[1]).

**pliant** ● **adj.** pliable.
– DERIVATIVES **pliancy** n. **pliantly** adv.

**plica** /'plɪkə, 'plʌɪkə/ ● **n.** (pl. **plicae** /-kiː/ or **plicas**) Anatomy & Botany a fold, ridge, or lobe of tissue.
– ORIGIN C17: mod. L., from med. L., from *plicare* 'to fold'.

**plicate** /'plʌɪkət, 'plʌɪkeɪt/ ● **adj.** Biology & Geology folded, crumpled, or corrugated.
– DERIVATIVES **plicated** /plɪ'keɪtɪd/ adj. **plication** n.
– ORIGIN C18 (earlier (ME) as *plication*): from L. *plicat-*, *plicare* 'to fold'.

**plié** /'pliːeɪ/ Ballet ● **n.** a movement in which a dancer bends the knees and straightens them again, usually with the feet turned right out and heels firmly on the ground. ● **v.** perform a plié.
– ORIGIN Fr., lit. 'bent', past part. of *plier* (see also **PLY**[1]).

**pliers** ● **pl. n.** pincers with parallel, flat, serrated jaws, used for gripping small objects or bending wire.
– ORIGIN C16: from dial. *ply* 'bend', from Fr. *plier* 'to bend'.

**plight**[1] ● **n.** a dangerous, difficult, or otherwise unfortunate situation.
– ORIGIN ME: from Anglo-Norman Fr. *plit* 'fold'.

**plight**[2] ● **v.** archaic **1** solemnly pledge or promise (faith or loyalty). **2** (**be plighted to**) be engaged to be married to.
– ORIGIN OE *plihtan* 'endanger', of Gmc origin.

**plimsoll** (also **plimsole**) ● **n.** Brit. a light rubber-soled canvas sports shoe.
– ORIGIN C19: prob. from the resemblance of the side of the sole to a **PLIMSOLL LINE**.

**Plimsoll line** (also **Plimsoll mark**) ● **n.** a marking on a ship's side showing the limit of legal submersion when loaded with cargo under various sea conditions.
– ORIGIN named after the Engl. politician Samuel *Plimsoll*, responsible for the Merchant Shipping Act of 1876.

**Plinian** /'plɪnɪən/ ● **adj.** Geology relating to or denoting a type of volcanic eruption in which a narrow stream of gas and ash is violently ejected from a vent to a height of several miles.
– ORIGIN C17: from Ital. *pliniano*, with ref. to the eruption of Vesuvius in AD 79, in which Pliny the Elder died.

**plink** ● **v. 1** emit a short, sharp, metallic ringing sound. **2** chiefly N. Amer. shoot at (a target) casually. ● **n.** a plinking sound.
– DERIVATIVES **plinky** adj.
– ORIGIN 1940s: imitative.

**plinth** ● **n. 1** a heavy base supporting a statue or vase. **2** Architecture the lower square slab at the base of a column.
– ORIGIN C16: from L. *plinthus*, from Gk *plinthos* 'tile, brick, squared stone'.

**Pliocene** /'plʌɪə(ʊ)siːn/ ● **adj.** Geology relating to or denoting the last epoch of the Tertiary period (between the Miocene and Pleistocene epochs, 5.2 to 1.64 million years ago), a time when the first hominids appeared.
– ORIGIN C19: from Gk *pleiōn* 'more' + *kainos* 'new'.

**pliosaur** /'plʌɪəsɔː/ ● **n.** a plesiosaur with a short neck, large head, and massive toothed jaws.
– ORIGIN C19: from mod. L. *Pliosaurus* (genus name), from Gk *pleiōn* 'more' + *sauros* 'lizard' (because of its greater similarity to a lizard than the ichthyosaur).

**plissé** /'pliːseɪ/ ● **adj.** (of fabric) treated to give a permanent puckered or crinkled effect. ● **n.** material treated in this way.
– ORIGIN C19: Fr., lit. 'pleated', past part. of *plisser.*

**PLO** ● **abbrev.** Palestine Liberation Organization.

**plock** ● **v.** make a short, low clicking sound. ● **n.** a sound of this kind.
– ORIGIN 1930s: imitative.

**plod** ● **v.** (**plodded**, **plodding**) walk doggedly and slowly with heavy steps. ➤ work slowly and perseveringly at a dull task. ● **n. 1** a slow, heavy walk. **2** (also **PC Plod**) Brit. informal a police officer.
– DERIVATIVES **plodder** n. **plodding** adj. **ploddingly** adv.
– ORIGIN C16: prob. symbolic of a heavy gait.

**-ploid** ● **comb. form** Biology denoting the number of sets of chromosomes in a cell: *triploid.*
– ORIGIN based on *(ha)ploid* and *(di)ploid.*

**ploidy** /'plɔɪdi/ ● **n.** Genetics the number of sets of chromosomes in a cell, or in the cells of an organism.
– ORIGIN 1940s: from words such as *diploidy* and *polyploidy.*

**plongeur** /plɔ̃'ʒəː/ ● **n.** a person employed to wash dishes and carry out other menial tasks in a restaurant or hotel.
– ORIGIN Fr., lit. 'person who plunges'.

**plonk**[1] informal ● **v. 1** set down heavily or carelessly. **2** play unskilfully on a musical instrument. ● **n.** a sound as of something being set down heavily.
– ORIGIN C19 (orig. dial.): imitative; cf. **PLUNK**.

**plonk**[2] ● **n.** Brit. informal cheap wine of inferior quality.
– ORIGIN 1930s (orig. Austral.): prob. an alt. of *blanc* in Fr. *vin blanc* 'white wine'.

**plonker** ● **n.** Brit. **1** informal a foolish or inept person. **2** vulgar slang a man's penis.
– ORIGIN C19 (as a dial. word meaning 'something large of its kind'): from **PLONK**[1] + **-ER**[1].

**plook** /pluːk/ (also **pluke**) ● **n.** Scottish a spot or pimple.
– ORIGIN ME: of unknown origin.

**plop** ● **n.** a short sound as of a small, solid object dropping into water without a splash. ● **v.** (**plopped**, **plopping**) fall or drop with such a sound.
– ORIGIN C19: imitative.

**plosion** /'pləʊʒ(ə)n/ ● **n.** Phonetics the sudden release of air in the pronunciation of a plosive consonant.

**plosive** /ˈpləʊsɪv, -z-/ Phonetics ● **adj.** denoting a consonant that is produced by stopping the airflow using the lips, teeth, or palate, followed by a sudden release of air. ● **n.** a plosive speech sound.
– ORIGIN C19: shortening of **EXPLOSIVE**.

**plot** ● **n. 1** a plan made in secret by a group of people to do something illegal or harmful. **2** the main sequence of events in a play, novel, or film. **3** a small piece of ground marked out for building, gardening, etc. **4** a graph showing the relation between two variables. ➤ chiefly US a diagram, chart, or map. ● **v.** (**plotted**, **plotting**) **1** secretly make plans to carry out (something illegal or harmful). **2** devise the plot of (a play, novel, or film). **3** mark (a route or position) on a chart. ➤ mark out or allocate (points) on a graph. ➤ make (a curve) by marking out a number of such points. ➤ illustrate by use of a graph.
– DERIVATIVES **plotless** adj. **plotter** n. **plotty** adj. (informal).
– ORIGIN OE (in sense 3 of the noun), of unknown origin; the sense 'secret plan' is assoc. with OFr. *complot* 'dense crowd, secret project'.

**plotz** ● **v.** N. Amer. informal be greatly affected with frustration, or other strong emotion.
– ORIGIN 1960s: from Yiddish *platsen*, lit. 'to burst'.

**plough** (US **plow**) ● **n. 1** a large farming implement with one or more blades fixed in a frame, drawn over soil to turn it over and cut furrows in preparation for the planting of seeds. ➤ land that has been ploughed. **2** (**the Plough**) a prominent formation of seven stars in the constellation Ursa Major (the Great Bear). ● **v. 1** turn up (earth) with a plough. ➤ chiefly N. Amer. clear snow from (a road) using a snowplough. **2** (often **plough into**) (of a vehicle) move in a fast and uncontrolled manner. **3** (of a ship or boat) travel through (an area of water). **4** (often **plough on**) advance or progress laboriously or forcibly. **5** (**plough something in**) invest or reinvest money in a business. **6** Brit. informal, dated fail (an examination).
– DERIVATIVES **ploughable** adj. **plougher** n.
– ORIGIN OE *plōh*, of Gmc origin.

**ploughman's lunch** ● **n.** Brit. a meal of bread and cheese with pickle and salad.

**ploughshare** ● **n.** the main cutting blade of a plough, behind the coulter.
– ORIGIN ME: from **PLOUGH** + OE *scær*, *scear* 'ploughshare' (rel. to **SHEAR**).

**plover** /ˈplʌvə/ ● **n.** a short-billed gregarious wading bird, typically found by water but sometimes frequenting grassland, tundra, or mountains. [Family Charadriidae: many species.]
– ORIGIN ME: from Anglo-Norman Fr., based on L. *pluvia* 'rain'.

**plow** ● **n. & v.** US spelling of **PLOUGH**.

**ploy** ● **n.** a cunning plan or action designed to turn a situation to one's own advantage.
– ORIGIN C17 (orig. Scots and north. Engl. in the sense 'pastime'): of unknown origin.

**PLP** ● **abbrev.** (in the UK) Parliamentary Labour Party.

**PLR** ● **abbrev.** (in the UK) Public Lending Right.

**pluck** ● **v. 1** take hold of (something) and quickly remove it from its place. ➤ catch hold of and pull quickly. **2** pull the feathers from (a bird's carcass) to prepare it for cooking. ➤ pull some of the hairs from (one's eyebrows) to make them look neater. **3** sound (a stringed musical instrument) with one's finger or a plectrum. **4** (**pluck up**) summon up (enough courage, nerve, etc.) to do something frightening. ● **n. 1** spirited and determined courage. **2** the heart, liver, and lungs of an animal as food.
– DERIVATIVES **-plucker** n.
– ORIGIN OE *ploccian*, *pluccian*, of Gmc origin.

**plucky** ● **adj.** (**-ier**, **-iest**) determined and courageous in the face of difficulties.
– DERIVATIVES **pluckily** adv. **pluckiness** n.

**plug** ● **n. 1** a piece of solid material fitting tightly into a hole and blocking it up. ➤ a mass of solidified lava filling the neck of a volcano. **2** a device consisting of an insulated casing with metal pins that fit into holes in a socket to make an electrical connection. ➤ informal an electrical socket. **3** informal a piece of publicity promoting a product or event. **4** a piece of tobacco cut from a larger cake for chewing. ➤ (also **plug tobacco**) tobacco in large cakes designed to be cut for chewing. **5** Fishing a lure with one or more hooks attached. **6** N. Amer. informal a tired or old horse. **7** N. Amer. informal a baby's dummy. ● **v.** (**plugged**, **plugging**) **1** block or fill in (a hole or cavity). **2** (**plug something in**) connect an electrical appliance to the mains by means of a socket. ➤ (**plug into**) have or gain access to an information system or area of activity. **3** informal promote (a product or event) by mentioning it publicly. **4** informal shoot or hit. **5** (usu. **plug away**) informal proceed steadily and laboriously with a task.
– DERIVATIVES **plugger** n.
– ORIGIN C17: from MDu. and Mid. Low Ger. *plugge*, of unknown ultimate origin.

**plughole** ● **n.** Brit. a hole at the lowest point of a bath or sink, down which waste water drains away.
– PHRASES **go down the plughole** informal be unsuccessful, lost, or wasted.

**plug-in** ● **n.** Computing a module or piece of software which can be added to an existing system to give extra features.

**plug-ugly** informal, chiefly N. Amer. ● **n.** (pl. **-ies**) a thug or villain. ● **adj.** (of a person) very ugly.
– ORIGIN by assoc. with **PLUG** in the sense 'hit with the fist'.

**pluke** ● **n.** variant spelling of **PLOOK**.

**plum** ● **n. 1** an oval fleshy fruit which is purple, reddish, or yellow when ripe, containing a flattish pointed stone. **2** the tree bearing this fruit. [*Prunus domestica* and related species.] **3** a reddish-purple colour. **4** [usu. as modifier] informal something highly desirable: *a plum job.*
– PHRASES **have a plum in one's mouth** Brit. have an upper-class accent.
– ORIGIN OE *plūme*, from med. L. *pruna*, from L. *prunum* (see **PRUNE**[1]).

**plumage** /ˈpluːmɪdʒ/ ● **n.** a bird's feathers collectively.
– DERIVATIVES **-plumaged** adj.
– ORIGIN ME: from OFr., from *plume* 'feather'.

**plumb**[1] ● **v. 1** measure (the depth of a body of water). **2** explore or experience fully or to extremes: *she had plumbed the depths of depravity.* **3** test (an upright surface) to determine the vertical. ● **n.** a lead ball or other heavy object attached to a line for finding the depth of water or determining the vertical on an upright surface. ● **adv. 1** informal exactly: *plumb in the centre.* **2** N. Amer. extremely or completely: *they must be plumb crazy.* **3** archaic vertically. ● **adj. 1** vertical. **2** Cricket (of the wicket) level; true.
– ORIGIN ME: via OFr. from L. *plumbum* 'lead'.

**plumb**[2] ● **v.** (**plumb something in**) install a bath, washing machine, etc. and connect it to water and drainage pipes. ➤ install and connect pipes in (a building or room).
– ORIGIN C19: back-form. from **PLUMBER**.

**plumbago** /plʌmˈbeɪgəʊ/ ● **n.** (pl. **-os**) **1** old-fashioned term for **GRAPHITE**. **2** an evergreen shrub or climber with grey or blue flowers. [Genus *Plumbago*.]
– ORIGIN C17: from L., from *plumbum* 'lead'.

**plumbate** /ˈplʌmbeɪt/ ● **n.** Chemistry a salt in which the anion contains both lead and oxygen.
– ORIGIN C19: from L. *plumbum* 'lead' + **-ATE**[1].

**plumb bob** ● **n.** a bob of lead or other heavy material forming the weight of a plumb line.

**plumbeous** /ˈplʌmbɪəs/ ● **adj.** chiefly Ornithology of the dull grey colour of lead.
– ORIGIN C16: from L. *plumbeus* 'leaden' (from *plumbum* 'lead') + **-OUS**.

**plumber** ● **n.** a person who fits and repairs the pipes and fittings of water supply, sanitation, or heating systems.
– ORIGIN ME (orig. denoting a person dealing in and working with lead): from OFr. *plommier*, from L. *plumbarius*, from *plumbum* 'lead'.

**plumbic** /ˈplʌmbɪk/ ● **adj. 1** Chemistry of lead with a valency of four; of lead(IV). Compare with **PLUMBOUS**. **2** Medicine caused by the presence of lead.
– ORIGIN C18: from L. *plumbum* 'lead' + **-IC**.

**plumbing** ● **n. 1** the system of pipes, tanks, and fittings required for the water supply, heating, and sanitation in a building. ➤ the work of installing and maintaining such a system. **2** euphemistic a person's excretory tracts and urinary system.

**plumbism** /ˈplʌmbɪz(ə)m/ ● **n.** technical acute or chronic poisoning due to the absorption of lead into the body.

**plumbless** /ˈplʌmlɪs/ ● **adj.** poetic/literary (of water) extremely deep.

**plumb line** ● **n.** a line with a plumb attached to it.

**plumbous** /ˈplʌmbəs/ ● **adj.** Chemistry of lead with a valency of two; of lead(II). Compare with **PLUMBIC**.
– ORIGIN C17: from L. *plumbosus* 'full of lead'.

**plumb rule** ● **n.** a plumb line attached to a board, used by builders and surveyors.

**plum duff** ● **n.** a rich, spiced suet pudding made with raisins or currants.

**plume** ● **n. 1** a long, soft feather or arrangement of feathers used by a bird for display or worn on a hat or helmet as decoration. **2** a long spreading cloud of smoke or vapour. **3** Geology a column of magma rising by convection in the earth's mantle. ● **v. 1** [often as adj. **plumed**] decorate with or as if with feathers. ➤ spread out in a shape resembling a feather. **2** (**plume oneself**) chiefly archaic (of a bird) preen itself. **3** chiefly archaic feel a great sense of self-satisfaction.
– DERIVATIVES **plumeless** adj. **plumery** n.
– ORIGIN ME: from OFr., from L. *pluma* 'down'.

**plume moth** ● **n.** a small, slender, long-legged moth with narrow wings divided into feathery plumes. [Family Pterophoridae.]

**plummet** ● **v.** (**plummeted**, **plummeting**) fall or drop straight down at high speed. ➤ decrease rapidly in value or amount. ● **n. 1** a steep and rapid fall or drop. **2** a plumb or plumb line.
– ORIGIN ME: from OFr. *plommet* 'small sounding lead', dimin. of *plomb* 'lead'.

**plummy** ● **adj.** (**-ier**, **-iest**) **1** resembling a plum. **2** Brit. informal (of a person's voice) typical of the English upper classes. **3** Brit. informal choice; highly desirable.

**plumose** /pluːˈməʊs, ˈpluːməʊs, -z/ ● **adj.** chiefly Biology having many fine filaments or branches which give a feathery appearance.
– ORIGIN C18: from L. *plumosus* 'full of down or feathers', from *pluma* 'down'.

**plump**[1] ● **adj.** full and rounded in shape. ➤ rather fat. ● **v.** (often **plump something up**) make or become full and round.
– DERIVATIVES **plumpish** adj. **plumply** adv. **plumpness** n. **plumpy** adj.
– ORIGIN C15 (in the sense 'blunt, forthright'): rel. to MDu. *plomp*, Mid. Low Ger. *plump* 'blunt, obtuse'.

**plump**[2] ● **v. 1** (often **plump something down**) set or sit down heavily or unceremoniously. **2** (**plump for**) decide definitely in favour of (one of two or more possibilities). ● **n.** archaic an abrupt plunge or heavy fall. ● **adv.** informal **1** with a sudden or heavy fall. **2** dated directly and bluntly.
– ORIGIN ME: rel. to Mid. Low Ger. *plumpen*, MDu. *plompen* 'fall into water', prob. of imitative origin.

**plum pudding** ● **n.** a rich boiled suet pudding containing raisins, currants, and spices.

**plum tomato** ● **n.** a plum-shaped variety of tomato.

**plumule** /ˈpluːmjuːl/ ● **n. 1** Botany the rudimentary shoot or stem of an embryo plant. **2** Ornithology a bird's down feather, numbers of which form an insulating layer under the contour feathers.
– ORIGIN C18: from Fr. *plumule* or L. *plumula* 'small feather', dimin. of *pluma* 'down'.

**plumy** ● **adj.** (**-ier**, **-iest**) resembling or decorated with feathers.

**plunder** ● **v.** forcibly steal goods from, especially in time of war or civil disorder. ● **n.** the action of plundering. ➤ property acquired in this way.
– DERIVATIVES **plunderer** n.
– ORIGIN C17: from Ger. *plündern*, lit. 'rob of household goods', from Mid. High Ger. *plunder* 'household effects'.

**plunge** ● **v. 1** fall or move suddenly and uncontrollably. ➤ jump or dive quickly and energetically. **2** (often **plunge in**) embark impetuously on a speech or course of action. **3** push or thrust quickly. **4** (**plunge someone/thing into**) suddenly bring someone or something into a specified condition or state. ● **n.** an act of plunging.
– PHRASES **take the plunge** informal commit oneself to a bold course of action after consideration.
– ORIGIN ME: from OFr. *plungier* 'thrust down', based on L. *plumbum* 'lead, plummet'.

**plunge pool** ● **n. 1** a deep basin at the foot of a waterfall formed by the action of the falling water. **2** a small, deep swimming pool, especially one used to refresh the body after a sauna.

**plunger** ● **n. 1** a part of a device or mechanism that works with a plunging or thrusting movement. **2** a device consisting of a rubber cup on a long handle, used to clear blocked pipes by means of suction. **3** informal a person who gambles or spends money recklessly.

**plunk** informal ● **v. 1** play a keyboard or plucked stringed instrument in an unexpressive way. **2** US hit (someone) abruptly. **3** chiefly N. Amer. set down heavily or abruptly. ● **n. 1** a plunking sound. **2** US a heavy blow. **3** N. Amer. an act of setting something down heavily.
– ORIGIN C19: prob. imitative.

**pluperfect** Grammar ● **adj.** (of a tense) denoting an action completed prior to some past point of time specified or implied, formed in English by *had* and the past participle. ● **n.** a verb in the pluperfect tense.
– ORIGIN C15: from mod. L. *plusperfectum*, from L. (*tempus praeteritum*) *plus quam perfectum* '(past tense) more than perfect'.

**plural** ● **adj.** more than one in number. ➤ Grammar (of a word or form) denoting more than one, or (in languages with dual number) more than two. ● **n.** Grammar a plural word or form. ➤ the plural number.
– DERIVATIVES **plurally** adv.
– ORIGIN ME: from OFr. *plurel* or L. *pluralis*, from *plus*, *plur-* 'more'.

**pluralism** ● **n. 1** a condition or system in which two or more states, groups, principles, etc., coexist. ➤ a political theory or system of power-sharing among a number of political parties. **2** Philosophy a theory or system that recognizes more than one ultimate principle. Compare with **MONISM**. **3** the practice of holding more than one office or Church benefice at a time.
– DERIVATIVES **pluralist** n. & adj. **pluralistic** adj. **pluralistically** adv.

**plurality** ● **n.** (pl. **-ies**) **1** the fact or state of being plural. **2** a large number of people or things. **3** US the number of votes cast for a candidate who receives more than any other but does not receive an absolute majority. ➤ the number by which this exceeds the number of votes cast for the candidate placed second. **4** chiefly historical another term for **PLURALISM** (in sense 3).

**pluralize** (also **-ise**) ● **v. 1** cause to become more numerous. ➤ cause to be made up of several different elements. **2** give a plural form to (a word).
– DERIVATIVES **pluralization** n.

**plural society** ● **n.** a society composed of different ethnic groups or cultural traditions.

**plural voting** ● **n.** the system or practice of casting more than one vote, or of voting in more than one constituency.

**pluri-** ● **comb. form** several: *pluripotent*.
– ORIGIN from L. *plus*, *plur-* 'more', *plures* 'several'.

**pluripotent** /ˌplʊərɪˈpəʊt(ə)nt/ ● **adj.** Biology (of an immature or stem cell) capable of giving rise to several different cell types.

**plus** ● **prep.** with the addition of. ➤ informal together with. ● **adj. 1** [postpos.] (after a number or amount) at least: *$500,000 plus*. ➤ (after a grade) rather better than: *B plus*. **2** (before a number) above zero; positive. **3** having a positive electric charge. ● **n. 1** short for **PLUS SIGN**. ➤ a mathematical operation of addition. **2** informal an advantage. ● **conj.** informal furthermore; also.
– ORIGIN C16: from L., lit. 'more'.

**plus ça change** /ˌpluː sa ˈʃɒ̃ʒ, French ply sa ʃɑ̃ʒ/ ● **exclam.** used to express resigned acknowledgement of the fundamental immutability of things.
– ORIGIN Fr., from *plus ça change, plus c'est la même chose* 'the more it changes, the more it stays the same'.

**plus fours** • pl. n. baggy knickerbockers reaching below the knee, formerly worn by men for hunting and golf.
– ORIGIN 1920s: so named because the overhang at the knee required an extra four inches of material.

**plush** • n. a rich fabric of silk, cotton, or wool, with a long, soft nap. • adj. informal richly luxurious and expensive.
– DERIVATIVES **plushly** adv. **plushness** n. **plushy** adj. (**-ier**, **-iest**).
– ORIGIN C16: from obs. Fr. *pluche*, contr. of *peluche*, from OFr. *peluchier* 'to pluck', based on L. *pilus* 'hair'.

**plush velvet** • n. a kind of plush with a short, soft, dense nap, resembling velvet.

**plus sign** • n. the symbol +, indicating addition or a positive value.

**plus-size** • adj. N. Amer. (of a woman or women's clothing) of a larger size than normal; outsize.

**plus twos** • pl. n. dated a shorter version of plus fours.

**Pluto** • n. the most remote known planet of the solar system, ninth in order from the sun.

**plutocracy** /plu:'tɒkrəsi/ • n. (pl. **-ies**) government by the wealthy. ➤a state or society governed in this way. ➤an elite or ruling class whose power derives from their wealth.
– DERIVATIVES **plutocratic** adj. **plutocratically** adv.
– ORIGIN C17: from Gk *ploutokratia*, from *ploutos* 'wealth' + *kratos* 'strength, authority'.

**plutocrat** • n. often derogatory a person whose power derives from their wealth.

**pluton** /'plu:t(ə)n/ • n. Geology a body of intrusive igneous rock.
– ORIGIN 1930s: back-form. from **PLUTONIC**.

**Plutonian** • adj. **1** relating to the underworld or the Greek god Pluto. **2** relating to the planet Pluto.

**plutonic** • adj. **1** Geology relating to or denoting igneous rock formed by solidification at considerable depth beneath the earth's surface. **2** (**Plutonic**) relating to the underworld or the Greek god Pluto.
– DERIVATIVES **plutonism** n. (Geology).

**plutonium** • n. the chemical element of atomic number 94, a dense silvery radioactive metal of the actinide series, used as a fuel in nuclear reactors and as an explosive in nuclear fission weapons. (Symbol: **Pu**)
– ORIGIN 1940s: from **PLUTO**, on the pattern of *neptunium* (Pluto being the next planet beyond Neptune).

**pluvial** chiefly Geology • adj. relating to or characterized by rainfall. • n. a period marked by increased rainfall.
– ORIGIN C17: from L. *pluvialis*, from *pluvia* 'rain'.

**ply**[1] • n. (pl. **-ies**) **1** a thickness or layer of a folded or laminated material. **2** each of a number of multiple layers or strands of which something is made: [in combination] *four-ply*.
– ORIGIN ME (in the sense 'fold'): from Fr. *pli*, *plier* 'to fold', from L. *plicare* 'to fold'.

**ply**[2] • v. (**-ies**, **-ied**) **1** work steadily with (a tool). ➤work steadily at (one's business or trade). **2** (of a vessel or vehicle) travel regularly over a route, typically for commercial purposes. **3** (**ply someone with**) provide someone with (food or drink) in a continuous or insistent way. ➤direct (numerous questions) at someone.
– ORIGIN ME: shortening of **APPLY**.

**Plymouth Brethren** • pl. n. a strict Calvinistic religious body formed at Plymouth in Devon, having no formal creed or ministry and emphasizing an expected millennium.

**plywood** • n. a type of thin, strong wooden board consisting of two or more layers glued and pressed together.

**PM** • abbrev. **1** post-mortem. **2** Prime Minister. **3** Provost Marshal.

**Pm** • symb. the chemical element promethium.

**p.m.** • abbrev. after noon.
– ORIGIN from L. *post meridiem*.

**PMG** • abbrev. **1** Paymaster General. **2** Postmaster General.

**PMS** • abbrev. premenstrual syndrome.

**PMT** • abbrev. chiefly Brit. premenstrual tension.

**PNdB** • abbrev. perceived noise decibel(s).

**pneumatic** • adj. containing or operated by air or gas under pressure.
– DERIVATIVES **pneumatically** adv. **pneumaticity** n.
– ORIGIN C17: from Fr. *pneumatique* or L. *pneumaticus*, from Gk *pneumatikos*, from *pneuma* 'wind'.

**pneumatic drill** • n. a large, heavy mechanical drill driven by compressed air, used for breaking up a hard surface such as a road.

**pneumatics** • pl. n. [treated as sing.] the branch of physics or technology concerned with the mechanical properties of gases.

**pneumatic trough** • n. Chemistry a shallow liquid-filled container with which gases can be collected by displacing liquid from a jar inverted in the trough.

**pneumatique** /ˌnju:mə'ti:k, French pnømatik/ • n. (pl. same or **pneumatiques**) (in Paris) a system of conveying mail along tubes by air pressure. ➤a message conveyed in this way.
– ORIGIN from Fr.

**pneumato-** /'nju:mətəʊ/ • comb. form **1** of or containing air: *pneumatophore*. **2** relating to the spirit: *pneumatology*.
– ORIGIN from Gk *pneuma*, *pneumat-* 'wind, breath, spirit'.

**pneumatology** • n. the branch of Christian theology concerned with the Holy Ghost and other spiritual concepts.
– DERIVATIVES **pneumatological** adj.

**pneumatophore** /'nju:mətəfɔ:/ • n. **1** Zoology the gas-filled float of some colonial coelenterates, such as the Portuguese man-of-war. **2** Botany (in mangroves) an aerial root specialized for the exchange of gases.

**pneumo-** • comb. form **1** of or relating to the lungs: *pneumogastric*. **2** of or relating to the presence of air or gas: *pneumothorax*.
– ORIGIN sense 1 from Gk *pneumōn* 'lung'; sense 2 from Gk *pneuma* 'air'.

**pneumococcus** /ˌnju:mə(ʊ)'kɒkəs/ • n. (pl. **pneumococci** /-'kɒk(s)ʌɪ, -'kɒk(s)i:/) a bacterium associated with pneumonia and some forms of meningitis. [*Streptococcus pneumoniae*.]
– DERIVATIVES **pneumococcal** adj.

**pneumoconiosis** /ˌnju:mə(ʊ)kəʊnɪ'əʊsɪs/ • n. Medicine a disease of the lungs due to inhalation of dust, characterized by inflammation, coughing, and fibrosis.
– ORIGIN C19: from **PNEUMO-** + Gk *konis* 'dust' + **-OSIS**.

**pneumocystis** /ˌnju:mə(ʊ)'sɪstɪs/ • n. Medicine a parasitic protozoan that can cause fatal pneumonia in people affected with immunodeficiency disease. [*Pneumocystis carinii*.]

**pneumogastric** • adj. of or relating to the lungs and stomach.

**pneumonectomy** /ˌnju:mə(ʊ)'nɛktəmi/ • n. (pl. **-ies**) surgical removal of a lung or part of a lung.

**pneumonia** /nju:'məʊnɪə/ • n. a lung infection in which the air sacs fill with pus.
– DERIVATIVES **pneumonic** adj.
– ORIGIN C17: via L. from Gk, from *pneumōn* 'lung'.

**pneumonitis** /ˌnju:mə(ʊ)'nʌɪtɪs/ • n. Medicine inflammation of the walls of the alveoli (air sacs) in the lungs, usually caused by a virus.

**pneumothorax** • n. Medicine the presence of air or gas in the cavity between the lungs and the chest wall, causing collapse of the lung.

**PNG** • abbrev. Papua New Guinea.

**p-n junction** • n. Electronics a boundary between p-type and n-type material in a semiconductor device, functioning as a rectifier.

**PNP** • adj. Electronics denoting a semiconductor device in which an *n*-type region is sandwiched between two *p*-type regions.

**PO** • abbrev. **1** Petty Officer. **2** Pilot Officer. **3** postal order. **4** Post Office.

**Po** • symb. the chemical element polonium.

**POA** • abbrev. (in the UK) Prison Officers' Association.

**poach**[1] • v. cook by simmering in a small amount of liquid. ➤cook (an egg) without its shell in or over boiling water.
– DERIVATIVES **poacher** n.

– ORIGIN ME: from OFr. *pochier*, earlier in the sense 'enclose in a bag', from *poche* 'bag, pocket'.

**poach²** ● v. **1** illegally hunt or catch (game or fish) on land that is not one's own or in contravention of official protection. **2** take or acquire in an unfair or clandestine way. **3** (of an animal) trample or cut up (turf) with its hoofs.
– DERIVATIVES **poacher** n.
– ORIGIN C16 (in the sense 'push roughly together'): appar. rel. to **POKE¹**; sense 1 is perh. partly from Fr. *pocher* (see **POACH¹**).

**poblano** /pɒ'blɑːnəʊ/ ● n. (pl. **-os**) a large dark green chilli pepper of a mild-flavoured variety.
– ORIGIN from Sp.

**pochard** /'pəʊtʃəd, 'pɒ-/ ● n. (pl. same or **pochards**) a diving duck, the male of which typically has a reddish-brown head. [*Aythya ferina* and other species.]
– ORIGIN C16: of unknown origin.

**pochette** /pɒ'ʃɛt/ ● n. a woman's small handbag shaped like an envelope.
– ORIGIN C19: from Fr., lit. 'small pocket', dimin. of *poche*.

**pock** ● n. a pockmark.
– DERIVATIVES **pocked** adj. **pocky** adj. (archaic).
– ORIGIN OE *poc* 'pustule', of Gmc origin; cf. **POX**.

**pocket** ● n. **1** a small bag sewn into or on clothing so as to form part of it, used for carrying small articles. ➤a pouch-like compartment providing separate storage space. ➤(**one's pocket**) informal one's financial resources. **2** a small, isolated patch, group, or area. **3** an opening at the corner or on the side of a billiard table into which balls are struck. **4** American Football a protected area behind the line of scrimmage, from which the quarterback throws a pass. **5** Baseball a hollow in a baseball mitt in which the ball is caught and held. ● adj. of a suitable size for carrying in a pocket: *a pocket dictionary*. ● v. (**pocketed**, **pocketing**) **1** put into one's pocket. **2** take for oneself, especially dishonestly. **3** Billiards & Snooker drive (a ball) into a pocket.
– PHRASES **in pocket** having enough money or money to spare. ➤having gained in a transaction. **in someone's pocket 1** dependent on someone financially and therefore under their influence. **2** closely involved with someone. **line one's pocket** make money, especially dishonestly. **out of pocket** having lost money in a transaction. **put one's hand in one's pocket** spend or provide one's own money.
– DERIVATIVES **pocketable** adj. **pocketful** n. (pl. **-fuls**). **pocketless** adj.
– ORIGIN ME (in the sense 'bag, sack', also used as a measure of quantity): from Anglo-Norman Fr. *poket(e)*, dimin. of *poke* 'pouch'.

**pocket battleship** ● n. any of a class of cruisers with large-calibre guns, operated by the German navy in the Second World War.

**pocketbook** ● n. **1** Brit. a notebook. **2** US a wallet, purse, or handbag.

**pocket borough** ● n. historical (in the UK) a borough in which the election of political representatives was controlled by one person or family.

**pocket knife** ● n. a penknife.

**pocket money** ● n. Brit. a small amount of money given to a child by their parents, typically on a regular basis. ➤a small amount of money suitable for minor expenses.

**pocket watch** ● n. a watch on a chain, intended to be carried in the pocket of a jacket or waistcoat.

**pockmark** ● n. a pitted scar or mark on the skin left by a pustule or spot. ➤a mark or pitted area disfiguring a surface. ● v. cover or disfigure with pockmarks.

**poco** /'pəʊkəʊ/ ● adv. Music a little; rather.
– ORIGIN from Ital.

**Pocomania** /ˌpəʊkə(ʊ)'meɪnɪə/ ● n. a Jamaican folk religion combining revivalism with ancestor worship and spirit possession.
– ORIGIN 1930s: prob. a Hispanicized form of a local word, the second element being interpreted as **-MANIA**.

**pod¹** ● n. **1** an elongated seed vessel of a leguminous plant such as the pea, splitting open on both sides when ripe. **2** a self-contained or detachable unit on an aircraft or spacecraft. **3** the egg case of a locust. **4** Geology a body of rock or sediment whose length greatly exceeds its other dimensions. **5** a narrow-necked purse net for catching eels. ● v. (**podded**, **podding**) **1** (of a plant) bear or form pods. **2** remove (peas or beans) from their pods prior to cooking.
– PHRASES **in pod** informal, dated pregnant.
– ORIGIN C17: back-form. from dial. *podware*, *podder* 'field crops', of unknown origin.

**pod²** ● n. a small herd or school of marine animals, especially whales.
– ORIGIN C19 (orig. US): of unknown origin.

**podagra** /pə'dagrə, 'pɒdəgrə/ ● n. Medicine gout of the foot, especially the big toe.
– DERIVATIVES **podagral** adj. **podagric** adj. **podagrous** adj.
– ORIGIN ME: from L., from Gk *pous*, *pod-* 'foot' + *agra* 'seizure'.

**podge** ● n. Brit. informal a short, fat person. ➤excess weight; fat.
– ORIGIN C19: of unknown origin.

**podger** ● n. a short metal bar used as a lever, especially for tightening a box spanner.

**podgy** ● adj. (**-ier**, **-iest**) Brit. informal rather fat; chubby.
– DERIVATIVES **podginess** n.

**podiatry** /pə(ʊ)'dʌɪətri/ ● n. another term for **CHIROPODY**.
– DERIVATIVES **podiatrist** n.
– ORIGIN C20: from Gk *pous*, *pod-* 'foot' + *iatros* 'physician'.

**podium** /'pəʊdɪəm/ ● n. (pl. **podiums** or **podia** /-dɪə/) **1** a small platform on which a person may stand to be seen by an audience. ➤N. Amer. a lectern. **2** a continuous projecting base or pedestal under a building. ➤a raised platform surrounding the arena in an ancient amphitheatre.
– ORIGIN C18: via L. from Gk *podion*, dimin. of *pous*, *pod-* 'foot'.

**podzol** /'pɒdzɒl/ (also **podsol** /-sɒl/) ● n. Soil Science an infertile acidic soil with a grey subsurface layer, typical of coniferous woodland.
– DERIVATIVES **podzolic** adj. **podzolization** (also **-isation**) n. **podzolize** (also **-ise**) v.
– ORIGIN C20: from Russ., from *pod* 'under' + *zola* 'ashes'.

**poem** ● n. a literary composition that is given intensity by particular attention to diction (sometimes involving rhyme), rhythm, and imagery.
– ORIGIN C15: from Fr. *poème* or L. *poema*, from Gk *poēma*, early var. of *poiēma* 'fiction, poem', from *poiein* 'create'.

**poesy** /'pəʊɪzi, -si/ ● n. archaic or poetic/literary poetry. ➤the art or composition of poetry.
– ORIGIN ME: from OFr. *poesie*, via L. from Gk *poēsis*, var. of *poiēsis* 'making, poetry'.

**poet** ● n. a person who writes poems. ➤a person possessing special powers of imagination or expression.
– ORIGIN ME: from OFr. *poete*, via L. from Gk *poētēs*, var. of *poiētēs* 'maker, poet'.

**poetaster** /ˌpəʊɪ'tastə/ ● n. a person who writes inferior poetry.
– ORIGIN C16: mod. L., from L. *poeta* 'poet' + **-ASTER**.

**poète maudit** /pəʊˌɛt məʊ'di/ ● n. (pl. **poètes maudits**) a poet who is insufficiently appreciated by their contemporaries.
– ORIGIN Fr., lit. 'cursed poet'.

**poetess** ● n. a female poet.

**poetic** ● adj. relating to or of the nature of poetry.
– DERIVATIVES **poetical** adj. **poetically** adv. **poeticism** n. **poeticize** (also **-ise**) v.

**poetic justice** ● n. fitting or deserved retribution for a person's actions, as encountered in poetry or literature.

**poetic licence** ● n. departure from convention or factual accuracy in order to create an artistic effect.

**poetics** ● pl. n. [treated as sing.] the art of writing poetry. ➤the study of linguistic techniques in poetry and literature.

**poetize** (also **-ise**) ● v. represent in poetic form.

**Poet Laureate** ● n. (pl. **Poets Laureate**) an eminent

poet appointed by the British royal household to write poems for royal and official occasions.

**poetry** ● **n.** poems collectively or as a genre of literature. ➤a quality of beauty and intensity of emotion regarded as characteristic of poetry.

**po-faced** ● **adj.** Brit. humourless and disapproving.
– ORIGIN 1930s: perh. from *po* 'chamber pot', influenced by *poker-faced*.

**pogey** /ˈpəʊgi/ ● **n.** Canadian informal unemployment or welfare benefit.
– ORIGIN C19: of unknown origin.

**pogo** ● **v.** (**-oes, -oed**) informal jump up and down as if on a pogo stick as a form of dancing to rock music, especially punk.

**pogo stick** ● **n.** a toy for jumping about on, consisting of a spring-loaded pole with a handle at the top and rests for the feet near the bottom.
– ORIGIN 1920s: of unknown origin.

**pogrom** /ˈpɒgrəm, -grɒm, pəˈgrɒm/ ● **n.** an organized massacre of a particular ethnic group, originally that of Jews in Russia or eastern Europe.
– ORIGIN C20: from Russ., lit. 'devastation'.

**poi**[1] /pɔɪ/ ● **n.** a Hawaiian dish made from the fermented root of the taro.
– ORIGIN of Polynesian origin.

**poi**[2] /pɔɪ/ ● **n.** (pl. same or **pois**) a small light ball of woven flax, swung rhythmically on the end of a string in Maori action songs and dances.
– ORIGIN from Maori.

**poignant** /ˈpɔɪnjənt/ ● **adj. 1** evoking a keen sense of sadness or regret. **2** archaic sharp or pungent in taste or smell.
– DERIVATIVES **poignance** n. **poignancy** n. **poignantly** adv.
– ORIGIN ME: from OFr., lit. 'pricking', pres. part. of *poindre*, from L. *pungere* 'to prick'.

**poikilo-** ● **comb. form** varied; variable: *poikilotherm*.
– ORIGIN from Gk *poikilos* 'variegated, varied'.

**poikilotherm** /ˈpɔɪkɪlə(ʊ),θəːm/ ● **n.** Zoology an organism that cannot regulate its body temperature except by behavioural means such as basking or burrowing. Often contrasted with HOMEOTHERM.
– DERIVATIVES **poikilothermal** adj. **poikilothermic** adj. **poikilothermy** n.

**poilu** /pwʌˈluː, French pwaly/ ● **n.** historical, informal an infantry soldier in the French army, especially one who fought in the First World War.
– ORIGIN Fr., lit. 'hairy', by extension 'brave'.

**poinciana** /ˌpɔɪnsɪˈɑːnə/ ● **n.** a tropical tree with showy red or red and yellow flowers. [Genera *Caesalpinia* and *Delonix* (formerly *Poinciana*).]
– ORIGIN C18: mod. L., named after M. de *Poinci*, a C17 governor of the Antilles.

**poind** /pɔɪnd, pɪnd/ ● **v.** Scots Law distrain or impound (a person's goods).
– ORIGIN ME: var. of dial. *pind* 'impound'.

**Poindexter** /ˈpɔɪndɛkstə/ ● **n.** US informal a boringly studious or socially inept person.
– ORIGIN appar. from the name of one of the main characters in the comedy film *Revenge of the Nerds* (1984).

**poinsettia** /ˌpɔɪnˈsɛtɪə/ ● **n.** a small shrub with large showy scarlet bracts surrounding the small yellow flowers. [*Euphorbia* (formerly *Poinsettia*) *pulcherrima*.]
– ORIGIN C19: mod. L., named after the Amer. diplomat and botanist Joel R. *Poinsett*.

**point** /pɔɪnt/ ● **n. 1** the tapered, sharp end of a tool, weapon, or other object. ➤Archaeology a pointed flake or blade. ➤Ballet another term for POINTE. ➤Boxing the tip of a person's chin as a spot for a blow. ➤the prong of a deer's antler. **2** a dot or other punctuation mark, in particular a full stop. ➤a decimal point. ➤a dot or small stroke used in Semitic languages to indicate vowels or distinguish particular consonants. ➤a very small dot or mark on a surface. **3** a particular spot, place, or moment. ➤(**the point of**) the verge or brink of. ➤(in geometry) something having position but not spatial extent, magnitude, dimension, or direction. **4** a single item or detail in an extended discussion, list, or text. ➤an argument or idea. ➤the significant or essential element: *come to the point.* ➤[usu. with neg. or in questions] advantage or purpose. ➤(often in phrs **beside/off/to the point**) relevance. ➤a distinctive feature or characteristic, typically a good one. **5** (in sports and games) a mark or unit of scoring awarded for success or performance. ➤a unit used in measuring value, achievement, or extent. ➤(in piquet) the longest suit in a player's hand, containing a specified number of up to eight cards. ➤a unit of weight (2 mg) for diamonds. **6** each of thirty-two directions marked at equal distances round a compass. ➤the angular interval between two successive points of a compass, i.e. one eighth of a right angle (11° 15'). **7** a narrow piece of land jutting out into the sea. **8** Brit. a junction of two railway lines, with a pair of linked tapering rails that can be moved laterally to allow a train to pass from one line to the other. **9** Printing a unit of measurement for type sizes and spacing (in the UK and US 0.351 mm, in Europe 0.376 mm). **10** Brit. a socket in a wall for connecting a device to an electrical supply or communications network: *a power point.* **11** each of a set of electrical contacts in the distributor of a motor vehicle. **12** Cricket a fielding position on the off side near the batsman. ➤Ice Hockey either of two areas to the left and right of the net. **13** a small leading party of an advanced guard of troops. ➤chiefly N. Amer. the position at the head of a column or wedge of troops. **14** the extremities of a horse or cat, such as the face, paws, and tail of a Siamese cat. **15** Hunting a spot to which a straight run is made. ➤a run of this type. ➤the action or position of a dog in pointing. **16** historical a tagged piece of ribbon or cord used for lacing a garment or attaching a hose to a doublet. **17** a short piece of cord at the lower edge of a sail for tying up a reef. **18** Music an important phrase or subject, especially in a contrapuntal composition. ● **v. 1** (often **point at/to**) direct someone's attention in a particular direction by extending one's finger. ➤(**point something out**) make someone aware of a fact or circumstance. ➤face in or indicate a particular direction. ➤(often **point to**) cite or function as evidence. **2** direct or aim (something). **3** (**point something up**) reveal the true nature or importance of something. **4** chiefly Ballet extend (the toes or feet) by tensing the foot and ankle so as to form a point. **5** fill in or repair the joints of (brickwork or tiling) with smoothly finished mortar or cement. ➤[as noun **pointing**] mortar or cement used in pointing. **6** give a sharp, tapered point to. **7** (of a dog) indicate the presence of (game) by acting as pointer. **8** insert points in (written Hebrew). ➤mark (Psalms) with signs for chanting.
– PHRASES **a case in point** an instance or example that illustrates what is being discussed. **make a point of** make a special and noticeable effort to do something. **point the finger** openly accuse someone or apportion blame. **the point of no return** the point in a journey or enterprise at which it becomes essential to continue to the end. **point of sailing** a sailing boat's heading in relation to the wind. **score points** deliberately make oneself appear superior to someone else by making clever remarks. **take someone's point** chiefly Brit. accept the validity of someone's idea or argument. **up to a point** to some extent but not completely.
– ORIGIN ME: the noun partly from OFr. *point*, from L. *punctum* 'something that is pricked'; partly from OFr. *pointe*, from L. *puncta* 'pricking'; the verb is from OFr. *pointer*.

**point-blank** ● **adj. & adv. 1** (of a shot or missile) fired from very close to its target. **2** without explanation or qualification: *he refuses point-blank to give interviews.*
– ORIGIN C16: prob. from POINT + BLANK in the sense 'white spot in the centre of a target'.

**point break** ● **n.** (in surfing) a type of wave characteristic of a coast with a headland.

**point d'appui** /ˌpwã daˈpwiː, French pwɛ̃ dapɥi/ ● **n.** (pl. **points d'appui**) a support or prop.
– ORIGIN Fr., lit. 'point of support'.

**point duty** ● **n.** Brit. the duties of a police officer or other official stationed at a junction to control traffic.

**pointe** /pwãt/ ● **n.** (pl. pronounced same) Ballet the tips of the toes. ➤(also **pointe work**) dancing performed on the

tips of the toes.
– ORIGIN Fr., lit. 'tip'.

**pointed** ● adj. **1** having a sharpened or tapered tip or end. **2** (of a remark or look) clearly directed and unambiguous in intent.
– DERIVATIVES **pointedly** adv. **pointedness** n.

**pointelle** /ˌpɔɪnˈtɛl/ (also trademark **Pointelle**) ● n. a type of knitwear with small eyelet holes that create a lacy effect.
– ORIGIN 1950s: prob. from *point* in the sense 'lace made entirely with a needle' + the Fr. dimin. suffix *-elle*.

**pointer** ● n. **1** a long, thin piece of metal on a scale or dial which moves to give a reading. ➤a rod used for pointing to features on a map or chart. ➤Computing a cursor. ➤Computing a link. **2** a hint as to what might happen in the future. ➤a small piece of advice; a tip. **3** a dog of a breed that on scenting game stands rigid looking towards it.

**point guard** ● n. Basketball the player who directs the team's offence.

**pointillism** /ˈpwantɪlɪz(ə)m/ ● n. a technique of neo-Impressionist painting using tiny dots of various pure colours, which become blended in the viewer's eye.
– DERIVATIVES **pointillist** n. & adj. **pointillistic** adj.
– ORIGIN C20: from Fr. *pointillisme*, from *pointiller* 'mark with dots'.

**point lace** ● n. lace made with a needle on a parchment pattern.

**pointless** ● adj. **1** having little or no sense or purpose. **2** having scored no points.
– DERIVATIVES **pointlessly** adv. **pointlessness** n.

**point man** ● n. **1** the soldier at the head of a patrol. **2** chiefly N. Amer. a person at the forefront of an activity.

**point mutation** ● n. Genetics a mutation affecting only one or very few nucleotides in a gene sequence.

**point of departure** ● n. the starting point of a line of thought or course of action.

**point of honour** ● n. a circumstance that affects one's reputation or conscience.

**point of order** ● n. a query in a formal debate or meeting as to whether correct procedure is being followed.

**point of view** ● n. **1** a particular attitude or way of considering a matter. **2** the position from which something or someone is observed.

**point source** ● n. Physics a source of energy, such as light or sound, which can be regarded as having negligible dimensions.

**point spread** ● n. **1** N. Amer. the margin by which a stronger team is forecast to defeat a weaker one. **2** Physics & Physiology the spread of energy from a point source.

**point-to-point** ● n. (pl. **point-to-points**) an amateur cross-country steeplechase for horses used in hunting.
– DERIVATIVES **point-to-pointer** n. **point-to-pointing** n.

**pointy** ● adj. (**-ier**, **-iest**) informal having a pointed tip.

**pointy-headed** ● adj. N. Amer. informal, chiefly derogatory expert or intellectual.
– DERIVATIVES **pointy head** n.

**poise**[1] ● n. **1** graceful and elegant bearing. ➤composure and dignity of manner. **2** archaic balance; equilibrium. ● v. **1** be or cause to be balanced or suspended. **2** [as adj. **poised**] composed and elegant or self-assured. **3** (**be poised to do something**) be ready and prepared to do something.
– ORIGIN ME (in the sense 'weight'): from OFr. *pois*, *peis* (n.), *peser* (v.), from an alt. of L. *pensum* 'weight'.

**poise**[2] (abbrev.: **P**) ● n. Physics a unit of dynamic viscosity, such that a tangential force of one dyne per square centimetre causes a velocity change of one centimetre per second between two parallel planes separated by one centimetre in a liquid.
– ORIGIN C20: from the name of Jean L. M. *Poiseuille* (1799–1869), Fr. physician.

**poisha** /ˈpɔɪʃə/ ● n. (pl. same) a monetary unit of Bangladesh, equal to one hundredth of a taka.
– ORIGIN Bengali, alt. of **PAISA**.

**poison** ● n. **1** a substance that causes death or harm when introduced into or absorbed by a living organism. **2** something that has a destructive or corrupting influence. **3** Chemistry a substance that reduces the activity of a catalyst. **4** Physics an impurity that retards nuclear fission by absorbing neutrons. ● v. **1** administer poison to or contaminate with poison. **2** corrupt or harm.
– DERIVATIVES **poisoner** n.
– ORIGIN ME: from OFr. *poison* 'magic potion', from L. *potio(n-)* 'potion', rel. to *potare* 'to drink'.

**poisoned chalice** ● n. an assignment or award which is likely to prove a source of problems to the recipient.

**poison ivy** ● n. a North American climbing plant which secretes an irritant oil from its leaves that can cause dermatitis. [*Rhus radicans*.]

**poison oak** ● n. a North American climbing shrub related to poison ivy and having similar properties. [*Rhus toxicodendron*.]

**poisonous** ● adj. **1** producing or of the nature of poison. **2** extremely unpleasant or malicious.
– DERIVATIVES **poisonously** adv.

**poison pen letter** ● n. an anonymous letter that is libellous, abusive, or malicious.

**poison pill** ● n. Finance a tactic used by a company threatened with an unwelcome takeover bid to make itself unattractive to the bidder.

**Poisson distribution** /ˈpwʌsɒ̃/ ● n. Statistics a discrete frequency distribution which gives the probability of a number of independent events occurring in a fixed time.
– ORIGIN named after the Fr. mathematical physicist Siméon-Denis *Poisson* (1781–1840).

**poke**[1] ● v. **1** jab or prod with a finger or a sharp object. ➤prod and stir (a fire) with a poker to make it burn more fiercely. **2** (**poke about/around**) look or search around a place. **3** (often **poke out**) thrust out or protrude in a particular direction. ● n. **1** an act of poking. **2** informal power or acceleration in a car. **3** (also **poke bonnet**) a woman's bonnet with a projecting brim or front, popular in the early 19th century.
– PHRASES **poke fun at** tease or make fun of. **poke one's nose into** informal take an intrusive interest in. **take a poke at someone** informal hit, punch, or criticize someone.
– ORIGIN ME: origin uncertain.

**poke**[2] ● n. chiefly Scottish a bag or small sack. ➤N. Amer. informal a purse or wallet.
– ORIGIN ME: from ONorth. Fr. *poke*, var. of OFr. *poche* 'pocket'; cf. **POUCH**.

**poker**[1] ● n. a metal rod with a handle, used for prodding and stirring an open fire.

**poker**[2] ● n. a card game played by two or more people who bet on the value of the hands dealt to them, sometimes using bluff.
– ORIGIN C19: of US origin; perh. rel. to Ger. *pochen* 'to brag', *Pochspiel* 'bragging game'.

**poker dice** ● pl. n. dice with card designs (from nine to ace) on the faces instead of spots. ➤ [treated as sing.] a dice game in which the thrower aims for combinations of several dice.

**poker face** ● n. an impassive expression that hides one's true feelings.
– DERIVATIVES **poker-faced** adj.

**pokerwork** ● n. British term for **PYROGRAPHY**.

**pokeweed** ● n. a North American plant with red stems, spikes of cream flowers, and purple berries. [*Phytolacca americana*.]
– ORIGIN C18: from Algonquian *poughkone* (see **PUCCOON**) + **WEED**.

**pokie** ● n. (pl. **-ies**) Austral. informal a fruit machine.
– ORIGIN from *poker machine*, a type of fruit machine that pays out according to the combination of playing-card symbols that appear when the lever is pulled.

**pokey** ● n. informal, chiefly N. Amer. prison.
– ORIGIN C20: alt. of **POGEY** (an early sense being 'hostel for the needy'), perh. influenced by **POKY**.

**poky** (also **pokey**) ● adj. (**-ier**, **-iest**) **1** (of a room or building) uncomfortably small and cramped. **2** informal (especially of a car) having considerable power or acceleration. **3** N. Amer. annoyingly slow.
– DERIVATIVES **pokily** adv. **pokiness** n.
– ORIGIN C19: from **POKE**[1] (in the sense 'confine') + **-Y**[1].

**pol** • **n.** informal, chiefly N. Amer. a politician.

**Polack** /ˈpəʊlak/ • **n.** derogatory, chiefly N. Amer. a person from Poland or of Polish descent.
– ORIGIN C16: from Polish *Polak*.

**polar** • **adj. 1** of or relating to a pole or poles, in particular, of the North or South Pole or their adjacent area. **2** Physics & Chemistry having an electrical or magnetic field. **3** directly opposite in character or tendency. • **n.** Geometry the straight line joining the two points at which tangents from a fixed point touch a conic section.
– ORIGIN C16: from med. L. *polaris* 'heavenly', from L. *polus* (see POLE[2]).

**polar bear** • **n.** a large white arctic bear which lives mainly on the pack ice. [*Thalarctos maritimus.*]

**polar body** • **n.** Biology each of the small cells which bud off from an oocyte at the two meiotic divisions and do not develop into ova.

**polar cap** • **n.** Astronomy a region of ice or other frozen matter surrounding a pole of a planet.

**polar coordinates** • **pl. n.** Geometry a pair of positional coordinates representing respectively the length of the straight line connecting a given point to the origin and the angle made by this line with a fixed line.

**polar curve** • **n.** Geometry a curve drawn on polar coordinates around a fixed point.

**polar distance** • **n.** Geometry the angular distance of a point on a sphere from the nearest pole.

**polarimeter** /ˌpəʊləˈrɪmɪtə/ • **n.** an instrument for measuring the polarization of light, especially to determine the optical activity of a substance.
– DERIVATIVES **polarimetric** adj. **polarimetry** n.

**polariscope** /pəˈlarɪskəʊp/ • **n.** another term for POLARIMETER.
– DERIVATIVES **polariscopic** adj.

**polarity** • **n.** (pl. **-ies**) **1** the property of having poles or being polar. **2** the direction of a magnetic or electric field.

**polarize** (also **-ise**) • **v. 1** Physics restrict the vibrations of (a transverse wave, especially light) wholly or partially to one direction. **2** Physics cause to acquire polarity. **3** [usu. as adj. **polarized**] divide into two sharply contrasting groups or sets of beliefs.
– DERIVATIVES **polarizable** adj. **polarization** n. **polarizer** n.

**polarography** /ˌpəʊləˈrɒgrəfi/ • **n.** Chemistry a method of analysis in which a sample is electrolysed using a range of voltages and a plot of current against voltage drawn (showing steps corresponding to particular chemical species).
– DERIVATIVES **polarographic** adj.

**Polaroid** • **n. 1** trademark a composite material with the property of polarizing light, produced in thin plastic sheets. ➤ **(Polaroids)** sunglasses with lenses of polaroid. **2** a type of camera that produces a finished print rapidly after each exposure. ➤ a photograph taken with such a camera.

**polder** /ˈpəʊldə/ • **n.** a piece of low-lying land reclaimed from the sea or a river and protected by dykes, especially in the Netherlands.
– ORIGIN C17: from Du.

**Pole** • **n.** a native or national of Poland, or a person of Polish descent.

**pole[1]** • **n. 1** a long, slender piece of wood or metal, typically used as a support. ➤ a wooden shaft fitted to the front of a cart or carriage drawn by animals and attached to their yokes or collars. ➤ a simple fishing rod. **2** a young tree with a straight slender trunk and no lower branches. **3** historical, chiefly Brit. another term for PERCH[3] (in sense 1). ➤ (also **square pole**) another term for PERCH[3] (in sense 2). • **v.** propel (a boat) with a pole.
– PHRASES **under bare poles** Sailing with no sail set. **up the pole** informal **1** Brit. mad. **2** chiefly Irish pregnant.
– ORIGIN OE *pāl*, of Gmc origin, based on L. *palus* 'stake'.

**pole[2]** • **n. 1** either of the two locations (**North Pole** or **South Pole**) on the earth which are the ends of the axis of rotation. ➤ Geometry each of the two points at which the axis of a circle cuts the surface of a sphere. ➤ Geometry a fixed point to which other points or lines are referred, e.g. the origin of polar coordinates. ➤ Biology an extremity of the main axis of a cell, organ, or part. ➤ each of the two opposite points of a magnet at which magnetic forces are strongest. **2** each of two opposed or contradictory principles or ideas.
– PHRASES **be poles apart** have nothing in common.
– DERIVATIVES **poleward** adj. **polewards** adj. & adv.
– ORIGIN ME: from L. *polus*, from Gk *polos* 'pivot, axis, sky'.

**poleaxe** (US also **poleax**) • **n.** a battleaxe. ➤ a short-handled axe with a spike at the back, formerly used in naval warfare. ➤ a butcher's axe with a hammer head at the back, used to slaughter animals. • **v. 1** hit, kill, or knock down with or as if with a poleaxe. **2** shock greatly.
– ORIGIN ME: rel. to MDu. *pol(l)aex*, Mid. Low Ger. *pol(l)exe* (see POLL, AXE).

**polecat** • **n. 1** a weasel-like mammal with mainly dark brown fur, noted for its fetid smell. [*Mustela putorius* and related species.] **2** North American term for SKUNK.
– ORIGIN ME: perh. from OFr. *pole* 'chicken' + CAT[1].

**pole lathe** • **n.** an ancient form of lathe operated by a treadle, in which the work is turned by a cord passing round it and rotated back by the action of a springy pole attached to its top.

**polemic** /pəˈlɛmɪk/ • **n.** a strong verbal or written attack. ➤ (also **polemics**) the art or practice of engaging in controversial debate or dispute. • **adj.** (also **polemical**) of or involving strong or controversial debate.
– DERIVATIVES **polemically** adv. **polemicist** n. **polemicize** (also **-ise**) v.
– ORIGIN C17: via med. L. from Gk *polemikos*, from *polemos* 'war'.

**polenta** /pəˈlɛntə/ • **n.** maize flour as used in Italian cookery. ➤ a paste or dough made from this flour, which is boiled and then fried or baked.
– ORIGIN C16: Ital., from L., 'pearl barley'.

**pole piece** • **n.** Physics a mass of iron forming the end of an electromagnet, through which the lines of magnetic force are concentrated and directed.

**pole position** • **n.** the most favourable position at the start of a motor race.
– ORIGIN 1950s: from a C19 use of *pole* in horse racing, denoting the starting position next to the inside boundary fence.

**pole vault** • **n.** an athletic event in which competitors attempt to vault over a high bar with the aid of an extremely long flexible pole. • **v.** (**pole-vault**) perform a pole vault.
– DERIVATIVES **pole-vaulter** n.

**police** • **n.** [treated as pl.] a civil force responsible for the prevention and detection of crime and the maintenance of public order. ➤ members of such a force. • **v.** [often as noun **policing**] control and maintain law and order in (an area), with or as with a police force.
– ORIGIN C15 (in the sense 'public order'): from Fr., from med. L. *politia* (see POLICY[1]).

**policeman** (or **policewoman**) • **n.** (pl. **-men** or **-women**) a member of a police force.

**police officer** • **n.** a policeman or policewoman.

**police record** • **n.** a dossier kept by the police on people convicted of crime.

**police state** • **n.** a totalitarian state controlled by a political police force that secretly supervises the citizens' activities.

**police station** • **n.** the office or headquarters of a local police force.

**policier** /ˌpɒlɪˈsjeɪ, French pɔlisje/ • **n.** a film or novel portraying crime and its detection by police.
– ORIGIN Fr., from *roman policier* 'detective novel'.

**policy[1]** • **n.** (pl. **-ies**) **1** a course or principle of action adopted or proposed by an organization or individual. **2** archaic prudent or expedient conduct or action.
– ORIGIN ME: from OFr. *policie* 'civil administration', via L. from Gk *politeia* 'citizenship'.

**policy[2]** • **n.** (pl. **-ies**) a contract of insurance.
– ORIGIN C16: from Fr. *police* 'bill of lading, contract of insurance'.

**polio** ● n. short for **POLIOMYELITIS**.

**poliomyelitis** /ˌpəʊlɪəʊmʌɪəˈlʌɪtɪs, ˌpɒlɪəʊ-/ ● n. Medicine an infectious viral disease that affects the central nervous system and can cause temporary or permanent paralysis.
– ORIGIN C19: mod. L., from Gk *polios* 'grey' + *muelos* 'marrow'.

**poliovirus** ● n. Medicine any of a group of enteroviruses including those that cause poliomyelitis.

**polis**[1] /ˈpɒlɪs/ ● n. (pl. **poleis**) a city state in ancient Greece.
– ORIGIN from Gk.

**polis**[2] /ˈpəʊlɪs, ˈpɒlɪs/ ● n. Scottish and Irish form of **POLICE**.

**Polish** /ˈpəʊlɪʃ/ ● n. the Western Slavic language of Poland. ● adj. of or relating to Poland, its inhabitants, or their language.

**polish** /ˈpɒlɪʃ/ ● v. **1** make smooth and shiny by rubbing. **2** [often as adj. **polished**] improve, refine, or add the finishing touches to. **3** (**polish something off**) finish or consume something quickly. **4** [as adj. **polished**] (of rice) having had the outer husk removed during milling. ● n. **1** a substance used to make something smooth and shiny when rubbed in. ➤an act of polishing. ➤smoothness or glossiness produced by polishing. **2** refinement or elegance.
– DERIVATIVES **polishable** adj. **polisher** n.
– ORIGIN ME: from OFr. *poliss-*, lengthened stem of *polir* 'to polish', from L. *polire*.

**Polish notation** ● n. Logic & Computing a system of formula notation without brackets or special punctuation, used to represent arithmetical operations.

**politburo** /ˈpɒlɪtˌbjʊərəʊ/ ● n. (pl. **-os**) the principal policy-making committee of a communist party, in particular that of the former USSR.
– ORIGIN from Russ. *politbyuro*, from *polit(icheskoe) byuro* 'political bureau'.

**polite** ● adj. (**-er**, **-est**) respectful and considerate of other people. ➤cultured and refined: *polite society*.
– DERIVATIVES **politely** adv. **politeness** n.
– ORIGIN ME: from L. *politus* 'polished, made smooth', past part. of *polire*.

**politesse** /ˌpɒlɪˈtɛs/ ● n. formal politeness or etiquette.
– ORIGIN C18: Fr., from Ital. *politezza*, *pulitezza*, from *pulito* 'polite'.

**politic** ● adj. (of an action) seeming sensible and judicious in the circumstances. ➤(also **politick**) archaic (of a person) prudent and sagacious. ● v. (**politicked**, **politicking**) [often as noun **politicking**] often derogatory engage in political activity.
– ORIGIN ME: from OFr. *politique* 'political', via L. from Gk *politikos*, from *politēs* 'citizen', from *polis* 'city'.

**political** ● adj. **1** of or relating to the government or public affairs of a country. ➤interested in or active in politics. **2** chiefly derogatory done or acting in the interests of status within an organization rather than on principle.
– DERIVATIVES **politically** adv.

**political correctness** ● n. the avoidance of forms of expression or action that are perceived to exclude, marginalize, or insult groups of people who are socially disadvantaged or discriminated against.

**political economy** ● n. dated economics as a branch of knowledge or academic discipline.
– DERIVATIVES **political economist** n.

**politically correct** (or **incorrect**) ● adj. exhibiting (or failing to exhibit) political correctness.

**political prisoner** ● n. a person imprisoned for their political beliefs or actions.

**political science** ● n. the branch of knowledge concerned with political activity and behaviour.
– DERIVATIVES **political scientist** n.

**politician** ● n. **1** a person who is professionally involved in politics, especially as a holder of an elected office. **2** chiefly US a person who acts in a manipulative and devious way, typically to gain advancement.

**politicize** (also **-ise**) ● v. [often as adj. **politicized**] cause to become politically aware or political in character. ➤engage in or talk about politics.
– DERIVATIVES **politicization** n.

**politick** ● adj. archaic spelling of **POLITIC**.

**politico** ● n. (pl. **-os**) informal, chiefly derogatory a politician or person with strong political views.
– ORIGIN Sp. and Ital., 'politic' or 'political person'.

**politico-** ● comb. form politically: *politico-ethical*. ➤political and ...: *politico-economic*.
– ORIGIN from Gk *politikos* 'civic, political'.

**politics** ● pl. n. [usu. treated as sing.] **1** the activities associated with the governance of a country or area. ➤a particular set of political beliefs or principles. **2** activities aimed at improving someone's status within an organization: *office politics*. **3** the principles relating to or inherent in a sphere or activity, especially when concerned with power and status: *the politics of gender*.

**polity** /ˈpɒlɪti/ ● n. (pl. **-ies**) a form or process of civil government or constitution. ➤an organized society; a state as a political entity.
– ORIGIN C16: from obs. Fr. *politie*, via L. from Gk *politeia* 'citizenship, government'.

**polje** /ˈpɒljə/ ● n. Geology a flat-floored depression in a karst landscape, with steep enclosing walls.
– ORIGIN C19: from Serbo-Croat.

**polka** /ˈpɒlkə, ˈpəʊlkə/ ● n. a lively dance of Bohemian origin in duple time. ● v. (**polkas**, **polkaed** or **polka'd**, **polkaing**) dance the polka.
– ORIGIN C19: via Fr. and Ger. from Czech *půlka* 'half-step'.

**polka dot** ● n. each of a number of round dots repeated to form a regular pattern.
– DERIVATIVES **polka-dotted** adj.

**poll** /pəʊl/ ● n. **1** the process of voting in an election. ➤a record of the number of votes cast in an election. ➤an opinion poll. **2** dialect a person's head or scalp. **3** a hornless animal, especially one of a breed of hornless cattle. ● v. **1** record the opinion or vote of. ➤(of a candidate in an election) receive a specified number of votes. **2** cut the horns off (an animal, especially a young cow). ➤[as adj. **polled**] (of a domestic animal) lacking horns. ➤archaic cut off the top of (a tree or plant); pollard. **3** Telecommunications & Computing check the status of (a device), especially as part of a repeated cycle.
– DERIVATIVES **pollee** /pəʊˈliː/ n.
– ORIGIN ME (in the sense 'head', later 'number of people ascertained by counting of heads'): perh. of Low Ger. origin.

**pollack** /ˈpɒlək/ (also **pollock**) ● n. (pl. same or **pollacks**) an edible greenish-brown fish of the cod family, with a protruding lower jaw. [*Pollachius pollachius*.]
– ORIGIN ME: perh. of Celtic origin.

**pollan** /ˈpɒlən/ ● n. an Arctic cisco (fish) of a variety which occurs in Irish lakes.
– ORIGIN C18: from Ir. *pollán*, perh. based on *poll* 'pool'.

**pollard** /ˈpɒləd/ ● v. [often as adj. **pollarded**] cut off the top and branches of (a tree) to encourage new growth at the top. ● n. **1** a tree whose top and branches have been pollarded. **2** archaic an animal that has lost its horns or cast its antlers.
– ORIGIN C17: from **POLL** + **-ARD**.

**pollen** ● n. a powdery substance discharged from the male part of a flower, each microscopic grain containing a male gamete that can fertilize the female ovule.
– ORIGIN C18: from L., lit. 'fine powder'.

**pollen basket** ● n. Entomology a flattened area fringed with hairs on the hind leg of a social bee, used for carrying pollen.

**pollen count** ● n. an index of the amount of pollen in the air.

**pollen tube** ● n. Botany a hollow tube which grows out from a pollen grain into the stigma of a flower on which it is deposited.

**pollex** /ˈpɒlɛks/ ● n. (pl. **pollices** /-lɪsiːz/) Anatomy & Zoology the innermost digit of a forelimb, especially the thumb in primates.
– ORIGIN C19: from L., lit. 'thumb or big toe'.

**pollie** ● n. variant spelling of **POLLY**.

**pollinate** ● v. deposit pollen in (a flower or plant) and so allow fertilization.

– DERIVATIVES **pollination** n. **pollinator** n.

**pollinium** /pəˈlɪnɪəm/ ● n. (pl. **pollinia** /pəˈlɪnɪə/) Botany a coherent mass of pollen grains produced by some flowers, especially orchids.
– ORIGIN C19: mod. L., from L. *pollen, pollin-* 'pollen'.

**polliwog** (also **pollywog**) ● n. dialect & N. Amer. a tadpole.
– ORIGIN ME (earlier as *pollywiggle*): from **POLL** in the sense 'head' + **WIGGLE**.

**pollock** ● n. **1** North American term for **SAITHE**. **2** variant spelling of **POLLACK**.

**pollster** /ˈpəʊlstə/ ● n. a person who conducts or analyses opinion polls.

**poll tax** ● n. **1** a tax levied on every adult, without reference to their income or resources. **2** informal term for **COMMUNITY CHARGE**.

**pollute** ● v. **1** contaminate (water, the air, etc.) with harmful or poisonous substances. **2** corrupt.
– DERIVATIVES **pollutant** adj. & n. **polluter** n. **pollution** n.
– ORIGIN ME: from L. *pollut-, polluere* 'pollute, defile', based on the root of *lutum* 'mud'.

**polly** (also **pollie**) ● n. (pl. **-ies**) Austral./NZ informal a politician.

**Pollyanna** ● n. an excessively cheerful or optimistic person.
– DERIVATIVES **Pollyannaish** adj. **Pollyannaism** n.
– ORIGIN C20: the name of the optimistic heroine created by the Amer. author Eleanor H. Porter (1868–1920).

**pollywog** ● n. variant spelling of **POLLIWOG**.

**polo** ● n. a game of Eastern origin with rules similar to hockey, played on horseback with a long-handled mallet.
– ORIGIN C19: from Balti, 'ball'.

**polonaise** /ˌpɒləˈneɪz/ ● n. **1** a slow dance of Polish origin in triple time, stately and processional in character. ➤ a piece of music for this dance or in its rhythm. **2** historical a woman's dress with a tight bodice and a skirt open from the waist downwards, looped up to show a decorative underskirt. ● adj. (of a dish, especially a vegetable dish) garnished with chopped hard-boiled egg yolk, breadcrumbs, and parsley.
– ORIGIN C18: from Fr., fem. of *polonais* 'Polish'.

**polo neck** ● n. Brit. a high, close-fitting, turned-over collar on a sweater.
– DERIVATIVES **polo-necked** adj.

**polonium** /pəˈləʊnɪəm/ ● n. the chemical element of atomic number 84, a rare radioactive metal. (Symbol: **Po**)
– ORIGIN C19: mod. L., from med. L. *Polonia* 'Poland' (the native country of Marie Curie, the element's co-discoverer).

**polony** /pəˈləʊni/ ● n. (pl. **-ies**) Brit. another term for **BOLOGNA**.
– ORIGIN C18: appar. an alt. of *Bologna*.

**polo shirt** ● n. a casual short-sleeved cotton shirt with a collar and several buttons at the neck.

**poltergeist** /ˈpɒltəɡʌɪst/ ● n. a ghost or other supernatural being supposedly responsible for physical disturbances such as throwing objects about.
– ORIGIN C19: from Ger. *Poltergeist*, from *poltern* 'create a disturbance' + *Geist* 'ghost'.

**poltroon** /pɒlˈtruːn/ ● n. archaic or poetic/literary an utter coward.
– DERIVATIVES **poltroonery** n.
– ORIGIN C16: from Fr. *poltron*, from Ital. *poltrone*, perh. from *poltro* 'sluggard'.

**poly** ● n. (pl. **polys**) informal **1** polyester. **2** polythene. **3** Brit. a polytechnic.

**poly-** ● comb. form many; much: *polychrome*. ➤ Chemistry having many atoms or groups of a particular kind in a molecule (especially a polymer): *polycarbonate*.
– ORIGIN from Gk *polus* 'much', *polloi* 'many'.

**polyadic** /ˌpɒlɪˈadɪk/ ● adj. involving three or more elements or parts.
– ORIGIN C20: from **POLY-**, on the pattern of words such as *dyadic*.

**polyamide** /ˌpɒlɪˈeɪmʌɪd, -ˈam-/ ● n. a synthetic polymer, e.g. nylon, made by linking an amino group of one molecule and a carboxylic acid group of another.

**polyandry** /ˈpɒlɪandri/ ● n. polygamy in which a woman has more than one husband. Compare with **POLYGYNY**.
– DERIVATIVES **polyandrous** adj.
– ORIGIN C17: from **POLY-** + Gk *anēr, andr-* 'male'.

**polyanthus** /ˌpɒlɪˈanθəs/ ● n. (pl. same) a cultivated hybrid of the wild primrose and primulas. [*Primula* × *polyantha*.]
– ORIGIN C18: mod. L., from **POLY-** + Gk *anthos* 'flower'.

**polyatomic** ● adj. consisting of many atoms.

**polycarbonate** ● n. a synthetic resin in which the polymer units are linked through carbonate groups.

**Polychaeta** /ˌpɒlɪˈkiːtə/ ● pl. n. Zoology a class of marine annelid worms which comprises the bristle worms.
– DERIVATIVES **polychaete** /ˈpɒlɪkiːt/ n.
– ORIGIN mod. L., from Gk *polu-* 'many' + *khaitē* 'mane'.

**polychlorinated biphenyl** ● n. Chemistry any of a class of toxic chlorinated aromatic compounds, formed as waste in some industrial processes.

**polychromatic** ● adj. multicoloured.
– DERIVATIVES **polychromatism** n.

**polychrome** ● adj. painted, printed, or decorated in several colours. ● n. **1** varied colouring. **2** a polychrome work of art.
– DERIVATIVES **polychromed** adj. **polychromy** n.
– ORIGIN C19: from Fr., from Gk *polukhrōmos*, from *polu-* 'many' + *khrōma* 'colour'.

**polyclinic** ● n. a clinic where both general and specialist medical care is available.

**polyclonal** /ˌpɒlɪˈkləʊn(ə)l/ ● adj. Medicine & Biology consisting of or derived from many clones.

**polycrystalline** ● adj. consisting of many randomly oriented crystalline parts.

**polyculture** ● n. the simultaneous cultivation or exploitation of several crops or kinds of animals.

**polycyclic** /ˌpɒlɪˈsʌɪklɪk, -ˈsɪk-/ ● adj. **1** of, relating to, or resulting from many cycles. **2** Chemistry having several rings of atoms in the molecule.

**polycystic** ● adj. Medicine characterized by multiple cysts.

**polycythaemia** /ˌpɒlɪsʌɪˈθiːmɪə/ (US **polycythemia**) ● n. Medicine a condition in which there is an abnormally increased concentration of haemoglobin in the blood.
– ORIGIN C19: mod. L., from **POLY-** + **-CYTE** + **HAEMO-** + **-IA**[1].

**polydactyl** /ˌpɒlɪˈdaktɪl/ ● adj. having more than five fingers or toes on a hand or foot.
– DERIVATIVES **polydactyly** n.

**polydipsia** /ˌpɒlɪˈdɪpsɪə/ ● n. Medicine abnormally great thirst.
– ORIGIN C17: from Gk *poludipsios* 'very thirsty', based on *dipsa* 'thirst'.

**polyelectrolyte** /ˌpɒlɪɪˈlɛktrəlʌɪt/ ● n. Chemistry a polymer with several ionizable groups along the molecule.

**polyembryony** /ˌpɒlɪˈɛmbrɪəni/ ● n. Biology the formation of more than one embryo from a single ovum or seed.
– DERIVATIVES **polyembryonic** adj.

**polyester** ● n. a synthetic resin in which the polymer units are linked by ester groups, used chiefly to make textile fibres.

**polyethylene** /ˌpɒlɪˈɛθɪliːn/ ● n. another term for **POLYTHENE**.

**polyethylene terephthalate** /ˌtɛrəfˈθaleɪt/ ● n. a synthetic resin made from ethylene glycol and terephthalic acid, used to make polyester fibre.

**polygamy** ● n. **1** the practice or custom of having more than one wife or husband at the same time. **2** Zoology a pattern of mating in which an animal has more than one mate. **3** Botany the condition of bearing some flowers with stamens only, some with pistils only, and some with both, on the same or different plants.
– DERIVATIVES **polygamist** n. **polygamous** adj. **polygamously** adv.
– ORIGIN C16: from Fr. *polygamie*, via late L. from Gk *polugamia*, from *polugamos* 'often marrying'.

**polygenesis** /ˌpɒlɪˈdʒɛnɪsɪs/ (also **polygeny** /pəˈlɪdʒ(ə)ni/) ● n. origination from a number of inde-

pendent sources or places.
– DERIVATIVES **polygenetic** adj. **polygenetically** adv. **polygenism** n. **polygenist** n. & adj.

**polygenic** /ˌpɒlɪˈdʒɛnɪk/ ● **adj.** Genetics relating to or determined by a group of genes which act together to produce observable variation.
– DERIVATIVES **polygene** n. **polygenically** adv.

**polyglot** /ˈpɒlɪglɒt/ ● **adj. 1** knowing or using several languages. **2** (of a book) having the text translated into several languages. ● **n.** a polyglot person.
– ORIGIN C17: from Fr. *polyglotte*, from Gk *poluglōttos*, from *polu-* 'many' + *glōtta* 'tongue'.

**polygon** /ˈpɒlɪg(ə)n/ ● **n.** Geometry a plane figure with at least three straight sides and angles, and typically five or more.
– DERIVATIVES **polygonal** adj.
– ORIGIN C16: via late L. from Gk *polugōnon*, neut. of *polugōnos* 'many-angled'.

**polygon of forces** ● **n.** Physics a polygon that represents by the length and direction of its sides all the forces acting on a body or point.

**polygonum** /pəˈlɪg(ə)nəm/ ● **n.** a plant of a genus that includes knotgrass and bistort. [Genus *Polygonum*.]
– ORIGIN mod. L., from Gk *polu-* 'many' + *gonu* 'knee, joint' (because of the plant's swollen joints).

**polygraph** ● **n.** a machine designed to record changes in a person's physiological characteristics, such as pulse and breathing rates, used especially as a lie detector.
– DERIVATIVES **polygraphic** adj.

**polygyny** /pəˈlɪdʒɪni/ ● **n.** polygamy in which a man has more than one wife. Compare with **POLYANDRY**.
– DERIVATIVES **polygynous** /pəˈlɪdʒɪnəs/ adj.
– ORIGIN C18: from **POLY-** + Gk *gunē* 'woman'.

**polyhedron** /ˌpɒlɪˈhiːdrən, -ˈhɛd-/ ● **n.** (pl. **polyhedra** /-drə/ or **polyhedrons**) Geometry a solid figure with many plane faces, typically more than six.
– DERIVATIVES **polyhedral** adj. **polyhedric** adj.
– ORIGIN C16: from Gk *poluedron*, neut. of *poluedros* 'many-sided'.

**polyhistor** /ˌpɒlɪˈhɪstə/ ● **n.** another term for **POLYMATH**.
– ORIGIN C16: from Gk *poluistōr* 'very learned'.

**polymath** /ˈpɒlɪmaθ/ ● **n.** a person of wide-ranging knowledge or learning.
– DERIVATIVES **polymathic** adj. **polymathy** /pəˈlɪməθi/ n.
– ORIGIN C17: from Gk *polumathēs* 'having learned much'.

**polymer** /ˈpɒlɪmə/ ● **n.** Chemistry a substance with a molecular structure formed from many identical small molecules or other units bonded together.
– DERIVATIVES **polymeric** adj. **polymerizable** (also **-isable**) adj. **polymerization** (also **-isation**) n. **polymerize** (also **-ise**) v.
– ORIGIN C19: from Ger., from Gk *polumeros* 'having many parts', from *polu-* 'many' + *meros* 'a share'.

**polymerase** /ˈpɒlɪməreɪz, pəˈlɪməreɪz/ ● **n.** Biochemistry an enzyme which brings about the formation of a particular polymer, especially DNA or RNA.

**polymerous** /pəˈlɪm(ə)rəs/ ● **adj.** Biology having or consisting of many parts.

**polymorph** ● **n. 1** an organism, object, or material which takes various forms. **2** Physiology a polymorphonuclear leucocyte.
– ORIGIN C19: from Gk *polumorphos*, from *polu-* 'many' + *morphē* 'form'.

**polymorphism** ● **n.** the occurrence of something in several different forms.
– DERIVATIVES **polymorphic** adj. **polymorphous** adj.

**polymorphonuclear** /ˌpɒlɪˌmɔːfə(ʊ)ˈnjuːklɪə/ ● **adj.** Physiology (of a leucocyte) having a nucleus with several lobes and cytoplasm that contains granules.

**polymorphous perversity** ● **n.** Psychology a generalized sexual desire that can be excited and gratified in many ways.
– DERIVATIVES **polymorphously perverse** adj.

**polymyositis** /ˌpɒlɪmʌɪə(ʊ)ˈsʌɪtɪs/ ● **n.** Medicine a condition marked by inflammation and degeneration of skeletal muscle throughout the body.

**Polynesian** ● **n. 1** a native or inhabitant of Polynesia. **2** a group of Austronesian languages spoken in Polynesia, including Maori, Hawaiian, and Samoan. ● **adj.** of or relating to Polynesia, its people, or their languages.

**polynomial** /ˌpɒlɪˈnəʊmɪəl/ ● **adj.** consisting of several terms. ● **n. 1** Mathematics a polynomial expression, especially the sum of several terms containing different powers of the same variable(s). **2** Biology a Latin name with more than two parts.
– ORIGIN C17: from **POLY-**, on the pattern of *multinomial*.

**polynuclear** ● **adj.** Chemistry another term for **POLYCYCLIC**.

**polynucleotide** ● **n.** Biochemistry a linear polymer composed of many nucleotide units, constituting a section of a nucleic acid molecule.

**polynya** /pə(ʊ)ˈlɪnjə/ ● **n.** a stretch of open water surrounded by ice.
– ORIGIN C19: from Russ., from the base of *pole* 'field'.

**polyp** /ˈpɒlɪp/ ● **n. 1** Zoology the sedentary form of a coelenterate such as a sea anemone, typically columnar with the mouth uppermost and surrounded by a ring of tentacles. Compare with **MEDUSA**. **2** Medicine a small growth, usually benign and with a stalk, protruding from a mucous membrane.
– DERIVATIVES **polypoid** adj. & n. **polypous** adj.
– ORIGIN ME: from OFr. *polipe*, from L. *polypus* (see **POLYPUS**).

**polypary** /ˈpɒlɪp(ə)ri/ ● **n.** (pl. **-ies**) Zoology the common stem or skeletal support of a colony of polyps.
– ORIGIN C18: from mod. L. *polyparium*, from L. **POLYPUS**.

**polypeptide** ● **n.** Biochemistry a linear organic polymer consisting of a large number of amino-acid residues, forming all or part of a protein molecule.

**polyphagia** /ˌpɒlɪˈfeɪdʒə/ ● **n.** Zoology the eating of various or all kinds of food.
– DERIVATIVES **polyphagous** adj.

**polyphase** ● **adj.** (of an electrical device) simultaneously using several alternating currents with different phases.

**polyphonic** ● **adj. 1** having many sounds or voices. **2** Music (especially of vocal music) in two or more parts each having a melody of its own; contrapuntal. ➤ Music (of an instrument) capable of producing more than one note at a time.
– DERIVATIVES **polyphonically** adv. **polyphonous** adj. **polyphony** n. (pl. **-ies**).
– ORIGIN C18: from Gk *poluphōnos* (from *polu-* 'many' + *phōnē* 'voice, sound') + **-IC**.

**polyphyletic** /ˌpɒlɪfʌɪˈlɛtɪk/ ● **adj.** Biology (of a group of organisms) derived from more than one common evolutionary ancestor or ancestral group.

**polypi** plural form of **POLYPUS**.

**polyploid** /ˈpɒlɪplɔɪd/ ● **adj.** Genetics of or denoting cells or nuclei containing more than two homologous sets of chromosomes.
– DERIVATIVES **polyploidy** n.

**polypod** ● **adj.** Zoology having many feet or foot-like appendages.
– ORIGIN C18: from Fr. *polypode* 'many-footed'.

**polypody** /ˈpɒlɪpəʊdi/ ● **n.** (pl. **-ies**) a fern with creeping rhizomes which typically grows on trees, walls, and stones. [*Polypodium vulgare* and related species.]
– ORIGIN ME: via L. from Gk *polupodion*, from *polu-* 'many' + *pous, pod-* 'foot'.

**polypore** /ˈpɒlɪpɔː/ ● **n.** a bracket fungus which expels its spores through fine pores on the underside. [Several species, chiefly in the family Polyporaceae.]

**polyposis** /ˌpɒlɪˈpəʊsɪs/ ● **n.** Medicine the presence of numerous internal polyps, especially in the colon.

**polypropylene** /ˌpɒlɪˈprəʊpɪliːn/ ● **n.** a synthetic resin which is a polymer of propylene.

**polyptych** /ˈpɒlɪptɪk/ ● **n.** a painting, especially an altarpiece, consisting of more than three leaves or panels joined by hinges or folds.
– ORIGIN C19: from late L. *polyptycha* (neut. pl.) 'registers', from Gk *poluptukhos* 'having many folds'.

**polypus** /ˈpɒlɪpəs/ ● **n.** (pl. **polypi** /-pʌɪ/) archaic or technical term for **POLYP**.

– ORIGIN ME: via L. from a var. of Gk *polupous* 'cuttlefish, polyp', from *polu-* 'many' + *pous, pod-* 'foot'.

**polyrhythm** • n. Music the use of two or more different rhythms simultaneously.
– DERIVATIVES **polyrhythmic** adj.

**polysaccharide** • n. Biochemistry a carbohydrate (e.g. starch or cellulose) whose molecules consist of chains of sugar molecules.

**polysemy** /ˈpɒlɪsiːmi, pəˈlɪsɪmi/ • n. Linguistics the coexistence of many possible meanings for a word or phrase.
– DERIVATIVES **polysemic** adj. **polysemous** adj.
– ORIGIN C20: from **POLY-** + Gk *sēma* 'sign'.

**polystyrene** /ˌpɒlɪˈstʌɪriːn/ • n. a synthetic resin which is a polymer of styrene.

**polysulphide** (US **polysulfide**) • n. Chemistry a compound containing two or more sulphur atoms bonded together as an anion or group.

**polysyllabic** • adj. having more than one syllable. ➤ using words of many syllables.
– DERIVATIVES **polysyllabically** adv. **polysyllable** n.

**polytechnic** • n. an institution of higher education offering courses at degree level or below, especially in vocational subjects (little used after 1992, when British polytechnics became able to call themselves 'universities').
– ORIGIN C19: from Fr. *polytechnique*, from Gk *polutekhnos*, from *polu-* 'many' + *tekhnē* 'art'.

**polytene** /ˈpɒlɪtiːn/ • adj. Genetics relating to or denoting a giant chromosome composed of many parallel copies of the genetic material.
– ORIGIN 1930s: from **POLY-** + Gk *tainia* 'band'.

**polytetrafluoroethylene** /ˌpɒlɪˌtɛtrəˌflʊərəʊˈɛθɪliːn, -ˌflɔː-/ • n. a tough synthetic resin used to make seals and bearings and to coat non-stick cooking utensils.

**polytheism** /ˈpɒlɪˌθiːɪz(ə)m/ • n. the belief in or worship of more than one god.
– DERIVATIVES **polytheist** n. **polytheistic** adj.
– ORIGIN C17: from Fr. *polythéisme*, from Gk *polutheos* 'of many gods'.

**polythene** • n. chiefly Brit. a tough, light, flexible synthetic resin made by polymerizing ethylene, chiefly used for packaging.
– ORIGIN 1930s: contr. of **POLYETHYLENE**.

**polythetic** /ˌpɒlɪˈθɛtɪk/ • adj. of or denoting a classification based on a number of shared characteristics, none of which is essential for membership of the class.
– ORIGIN 1960s: from **POLY-** + Gk *thetos* 'placed, arranged' + **-IC**.

**polytonality** • n. the simultaneous use of two or more keys in a musical composition.
– DERIVATIVES **polytonal** adj.

**polytunnel** • n. an elongated polythene-covered frame under which plants are grown outdoors.

**polyunsaturated** • adj. Chemistry (of an organic compound, especially a fat or oil molecule) containing several double or triple bonds between carbon atoms.
– DERIVATIVES **polyunsaturates** pl. n.

**polyurethane** /ˌpɒlɪˈjʊərɪθeɪn/ • n. a synthetic resin in which the polymer units are linked by urethane groups.

**polyuria** /ˌpɒlɪˈjʊərɪə/ • n. Medicine production of abnormally large volumes of dilute urine.
– DERIVATIVES **polyuric** adj.

**polyvalent** /ˌpɒlɪˈveɪl(ə)nt/ • adj. **1** Chemistry having a valency of three or more. **2** Medicine active against several toxins or strains of pathogen. **3** having many different functions, forms, or facets.

**polyvinyl** /ˌpɒlɪˈvʌɪn(ə)l/ • adj. of or denoting synthetic resins which are polymers of vinyl compounds: *polyvinyl chloride*.

**polyvinyl acetate** • n. a synthetic resin made by polymerizing vinyl acetate, used chiefly in paints and adhesives.

**polyvinyl chloride** • n. a tough chemically resistant synthetic resin made by polymerizing vinyl chloride.

**Pom** • n. **1** short for **POMERANIAN**. **2** short for **POMMY**.

**pomace** /ˈpʌmɪs/ • n. (especially in cider-making) the pulpy residue remaining after fruit has been crushed in order to extract its juice. ➤ the pulpy matter remaining after some other substance has been pressed.
– ORIGIN C16: appar. from med. L. *pomacium* 'cider'.

**pomade** /pəˈmeɪd, -ˈmɑːd/ • n. a scented preparation for dressing the hair. • v. [often as adj. **pomaded**] apply pomade to.
– ORIGIN C16: from Fr. *pommade*, based on L. *pomum* 'apple' (from which it was orig. made).

**pomander** /pəˈmandə, ˈpɒməndə/ • n. a ball or perforated container of mixed aromatic substances used to perfume a room or cupboard or (formerly) carried as a supposed protection against infection. ➤ an orange studded with cloves and hung in a wardrobe for a similar purpose.
– ORIGIN C15: from OFr. *pome d'embre*, from med. L. *pomum de ambra* 'apple of ambergris'.

**pomarine skua** /ˈpɒmərʌɪn/ (N. Amer. **pomarine jaeger**) • n. a large Arctic-breeding skua. [*Stercorarius pomarinus*.]
– ORIGIN C19: *pomarine* from Fr. *pomarin*, from Gk *pōma* 'cover, lid' + *rhis, rhin-* 'nose' (because the bird's nostrils are partly covered by a cere).

**pomatum** /pə(ʊ)ˈmeɪtəm/ • n. & v. old-fashioned term for **POMADE**.
– ORIGIN C16: mod. L., from L. *pomum* 'apple'.

**pome** /pəʊm/ • n. Botany a fruit consisting of a fleshy enlarged receptacle and a tough central core containing the seeds, e.g. an apple.
– ORIGIN ME: from OFr., based on L. *poma*, pl. of *pomum* 'apple'.

**pomegranate** /ˈpɒmɪgranɪt/ • n. **1** a spherical fruit with a tough golden-orange outer skin containing many individual segments of sweet red gelatinous flesh. **2** the tree that bears this fruit, native to North Africa and western Asia. [*Punica granatum*.]
– ORIGIN ME: from OFr. *pome grenate*, from *pome* 'apple' + *grenate* 'pomegranate' (from L. (*malum*) *granatum* '(apple) having many seeds').

**pomelo** /ˈpɒmələʊ, ˈpʌm-/ (also **pummelo**) • n. (pl. **-os**) **1** the largest of the citrus fruits, with a thick yellow skin and bitter pulp which resembles grapefruit in flavour. **2** the tree which bears this fruit. [*Citrus maxima*.]
– ORIGIN C19: of unknown origin.

**Pomeranian** • n. a small dog of a breed with long silky hair, a pointed muzzle, and pricked ears.
– ORIGIN from *Pomerania*, a region of central Europe.

**pomfret** /ˈpɒmfrɪt/ • n. an edible deep-bodied sea fish. [*Brama brama* and other species, family Bramidae.]
– ORIGIN C18: appar. from Port. *pampo*.

**pomfret cake** /ˈpɒmfrɪt, ˈpʌm-/ • n. archaic variant of **PONTEFRACT CAKE**.

**pomiculture** /ˈpəʊmɪˌkʌltʃə/ • n. fruit-growing.
– ORIGIN C19: from L. *pomum* 'fruit' + **CULTURE**.

**pommel** /ˈpʌm(ə)l/ • n. **1** the upward curving or projecting part of a saddle in front of the rider. **2** a rounded knob on the end of the handle of a sword, dagger, or old-fashioned gun. • v. (**pommelled**, **pommelling**; US **pommeled**, **pommeling**) another term for **PUMMEL**.
– ORIGIN ME (denoting a finial): from OFr. *pomel*, from a dimin. of L. *pomum* 'fruit, apple'.

**pommel horse** • n. a vaulting horse fitted with a pair of curved handgrips.

**Pommy** (also **Pommie**) • n. (pl. **-ies**) Austral./NZ informal, derogatory a British person.
– ORIGIN C20: of unknown origin; said by some to be short for *pomegranate*, as a near rhyme to *immigrant*.

**po-mo** • adj. informal postmodern.

**pomology** /pə(ʊ)ˈmɒlədʒi/ • n. the science of fruit-growing.
– DERIVATIVES **pomological** adj. **pomologist** n.
– ORIGIN C19: from L. *pomum* 'fruit' + **-LOGY**.

**pomp** • n. **1** ceremony and splendid display. **2** archaic vain and boastful display.
– ORIGIN ME: from OFr. *pompe*, via L. from Gk *pompē* 'procession, pomp', from *pempein* 'send'.

**pompadour** /ˈpɒmpədʊə/ • n. a woman's hairstyle in which the hair is turned back off the forehead in a roll. ➤ N. Amer. a men's hairstyle in which the hair is combed

back from the forehead without a parting. ● **v.** [usu. as adj. **pompadoured**] N. Amer. arrange (hair) in a pompadour.
– ORIGIN C19: named after Madame de *Pompadour*, the mistress of Louis XV.

**pompano** /ˈpɒmpənəʊ/ ● **n.** (pl. **-os**) **1** an edible butterfish of the west coast of North America. [*Peprillus simillimus*.] **2** another term for **JACK**[1] (in sense 10).
– ORIGIN C18: from Sp. *pámpano*, perh. from *pámpana* 'vine leaf', because of its shape.

**pompom** (also **pompon**) ● **n. 1** a small woollen ball attached to a garment for decoration. **2** a dahlia, chrysanthemum, or aster with small tightly clustered petals.
– ORIGIN C18: Fr. *pompon*, of unknown origin.

**pom-pom** ● **n.** Brit. an automatic quick-firing two-pounder cannon of the Second World War period, typically mounted on a ship and used against aircraft.
– ORIGIN C19: imitative of the sound of the discharge.

**pompous** ● **adj. 1** affectedly grand, solemn, or self-important. **2** archaic characterized by pomp or splendour.
– DERIVATIVES **pomposity** n. **pompously** adv. **pompousness** n.
– ORIGIN ME: from OFr. *pompeux* 'full of grandeur', from late L. *pomposus*, from *pompa* 'pomp'.

**ponce** Brit. informal ● **n. 1** a man who lives off a prostitute's earnings. **2** derogatory an effeminate man. ● **v. 1** live off a prostitute's earnings. **2** (**ponce about/around**) behave in an affected or ineffectual way. **3** (**ponce something up**) attempt to improve something by making flashy changes.
– DERIVATIVES **poncey** (also **poncy**) adj.
– ORIGIN C19: perh. from **POUNCE**[1].

**poncho** ● **n.** (pl. **-os**) a garment of a type originally worn in South America, made of a thick piece of woollen cloth with a slit in the middle for the head.
– ORIGIN C18: from Latin Amer. Sp., from Araucanian.

**pond** ● **n. 1** a fairly small body of still water. **2** (**the pond**) humorous the Atlantic ocean. ● **v.** hold back or dam up (flowing water) to form a pond.
– ORIGIN ME: alt. of **POUND**[3], commonly used in dial. in the same sense.

**ponder** ● **v.** consider carefully.
– ORIGIN ME: from OFr. *ponderer* 'consider', from L. *ponderare* 'weigh', from *pondus, ponder-* 'weight'.

**ponderable** ● **adj.** poetic/literary having appreciable weight or significance.
– DERIVATIVES **ponderability** n.
– ORIGIN C17: from late L. *ponderabilis*, from *ponderare* (see **PONDER**).

**ponderosa** /ˌpɒndəˈrəʊzə, -sə/ (also **ponderosa pine**) ● **n.** a tall slender North American pine tree, planted for wood and as an ornamental. [*Pinus ponderosa*.]
– ORIGIN C19: fem. of L. *ponderosus* 'massive', used as a specific epithet in *Pinus ponderosa*.

**ponderous** ● **adj. 1** slow and clumsy because of great weight. **2** dull or laborious.
– DERIVATIVES **ponderosity** n. **ponderously** adv. **ponderousness** n.
– ORIGIN ME: via Fr. from L. *ponderosus*, from *pondus, ponder-* 'weight'.

**pond skater** ● **n.** a slender predatory bug which moves quickly across the surface film of water. [*Gerris lacustris* (Europe) and many other species.]

**pondweed** ● **n.** a submerged aquatic plant of still or running water. [Many species, especially in the genus *Potamogeton*.]

**pone** /pəʊn/ (also **corn pone**) ● **n.** US unleavened maize bread in the form of flat oval cakes or loaves, originally as prepared by North American Indians.
– ORIGIN Algonquian, 'bread'.

**pong** Brit. informal ● **n.** a strong, unpleasant smell. ● **v.** smell strongly and unpleasantly.
– DERIVATIVES **pongy** adj.
– ORIGIN C20: of unknown origin.

**ponga** /ˈpʌŋə/ (also **punga**) ● **n.** NZ a tree fern found in forests throughout New Zealand. [*Cyathea dealbata*.]
– ORIGIN C19: from Maori.

**pongal** /ˈpɒŋg(ə)l/ ● **n. 1** the Tamil New Year festival, celebrated by the cooking of new rice. **2** a southern Indian dish of rice cooked with various herbs and spices.
– ORIGIN from Tamil *poṅkal*, lit. 'swelling' (with ref. to the cooking process of rice).

**pongee** /pʌnˈdʒiː, pɒn-/ ● **n.** a soft, unbleached type of Chinese fabric, originally made from threads of raw silk and now also other fibres such as cotton.
– ORIGIN C18: from Chin. (Mandarin dial.) *běnjī* lit. 'own loom' or *běnzhì* lit. 'home-woven'.

**pongid** /ˈpɒn(d)ʒɪd/ ● **n.** Zoology a primate of a family (Pongidae) which comprises the great apes.
– ORIGIN 1950s: from mod. L. *Pongidae* (pl.), from the genus name *Pongo* (see **PONGO**).

**pongo** ● **n.** (pl. **-os**) Brit. military slang a soldier (used especially by members of the Royal Navy or RAF).
– ORIGIN C20: orig. from Congolese *mpongo*, used as a term in zoology to refer to the great apes.

**poniard** /ˈpɒnjəd/ ● **n.** historical a small, slim dagger.
– ORIGIN C16: from Fr. *poignard*, based on L. *pugnus* 'fist'.

**pons** /pɒnz/ ● **n.** (pl. **pontes** /ˈpɒntiːz/) Anatomy the part of the brainstem that links the medulla oblongata and the thalamus.
– ORIGIN C17: from L., lit.'bridge'.

**pons asinorum** /ˌasɪˈnɔːrəm/ ● **n.** a theory or formula that is difficult for learners to grasp.
– ORIGIN C18: L., lit. 'bridge of asses', term taken from the fifth proposition of the first book of Euclid.

**pont** /pɒnt/ ● **n.** S. African a flat-bottomed ferry worked on cables or ropes.
– ORIGIN from Du.

**Pontefract cake** /ˈpɒntɪfrakt/ ● **n.** Brit. a flat, round liquorice sweet.
– ORIGIN C19: named after *Pontefract* (earlier *Pomfret*), a town in Yorkshire where the sweets were first made.

**pontes** plural form of **PONS**.

**pontifex** /ˈpɒntɪfɛks/ ● **n.** (pl. **pontifices** /-ˈtɪfɪsiːz/) (in ancient Rome) a member of the principal college of priests.
– ORIGIN L., from *pons, pont-* 'bridge' + *-fex* from *facere* 'make'.

**Pontifex Maximus** /ˈmaksɪməs/ ● **n. 1** (in ancient Rome) the head of the principal college of priests. **2** (in the Roman Catholic Church) a title of the Pope.
– ORIGIN *Maximus*, superlative of L. *magnus* 'great'.

**pontiff** (also **sovereign** or **supreme pontiff**) ● **n.** the Pope.
– ORIGIN C17 (earlier (ME) as *pontifical*): from Fr. *pontife*, from L. *pontifex* (see **PONTIFEX**).

**pontifical** /pɒnˈtɪfɪk(ə)l/ ● **adj. 1** papal. **2** characterized by a pompous air of infallibility. ● **n. 1** (in the Roman Catholic Church) an office book of the Western Church containing rites to be performed by the Pope or bishops. **2** (**pontificals**) the vestments and insignia of a bishop, cardinal, or abbot.
– DERIVATIVES **pontifically** adv.

**pontifical Mass** ● **n.** (in the Roman Catholic Church) a High Mass celebrated by a cardinal or bishop.

**pontificate** ● **v.** /pɒnˈtɪfɪkeɪt/ **1** (in the Roman Catholic Church) officiate as bishop, especially at Mass. **2** express one's opinions in a pompous and dogmatic way. ● **n.** /pɒnˈtɪfɪkət/ (also **Pontificate**) (in the Roman Catholic Church) the office or term of office of pope or bishop.
– DERIVATIVES **pontificator** n.
– ORIGIN ME: from L. *pontificatus*, from *pontifex* (see **PONTIFEX**).

**pontifices** plural form of **PONTIFEX**.

**pontil** /ˈpɒntɪl/ ● **n.** (in glass-making) an iron rod used to hold or shape soft glass.
– ORIGIN C19: from Fr., appar. from Ital. *pontello* 'small point'.

**pontine** /ˈpɒntʌɪn/ ● **adj.** Anatomy of, relating to, or affecting the pons.
– ORIGIN C19: from L. *pons, pont-* 'bridge' + **-INE**[1].

**pontoon**[1] /pɒnˈtuːn/ ● **n.** Brit. the card game blackjack or vingt-et-un. ➤ a hand of two cards totalling 21 in this game.
– ORIGIN C20: prob. an alt. of *vingt-et-un* 'twenty-one'.

**pontoon**[2] /pɒnˈtuːn/ ● **n. 1** a flat-bottomed boat or hollow

metal cylinder used with others to support a temporary bridge or floating landing stage. ➤a bridge or landing stage supported by pontoons. **2** a large flat-bottomed barge or lighter equipped with cranes and tackle for careening ships and salvage work. **3** either of two floats fitted to an aircraft to enable it to land on water.
– ORIGIN C17: from Fr. *ponton*, from L. *ponto*, *ponton-*, from *pons*, *pont-* 'bridge'.

**pony** ● n. (pl. **-ies**) **1** a horse of a small breed, especially one below 15 hands (or 14 hands 2 inches). ➤(**the ponies**) informal, chiefly N. Amer. racehorses. **2** informal a small glass or measure of liquor. **3** Brit. informal twenty-five pounds sterling. ● v. (**pony something up**) N. Amer. informal hand over a sum of money, especially to settle an account.
– ORIGIN C17: prob. from Fr. *poulenet* 'small foal'.

**ponytail** ● n. a hairstyle in which the hair is drawn back and tied at the back of the head.
– DERIVATIVES **ponytailed** adj.

**pony-trekking** ● n. Brit. the leisure activity of riding across country on a pony or horse.
– DERIVATIVES **pony-trekker** n.

**Ponzi scheme** /'pɒnzi/ ● n. a form of fraud in which belief in the success of a non-existent enterprise is fostered by the payment of quick returns to the first investors from money invested by later investors.
– ORIGIN named after Charles *Ponzi*, who carried out such a fraud (1919–20).

**poo** ● exclam., n., & v. variant spelling of **POOH**.

**pooch**[1] ● n. informal a dog.
– ORIGIN 1920s: of unknown origin.

**pooch**[2] ● v. US informal protrude or cause to protrude.
– ORIGIN C17: from **POUCH**.

**poodle** ● n. **1** a dog of a breed with a curly coat that is usually clipped. **2** Brit. a servile or obsequious person. ● v. Brit. informal move or travel in a leisurely manner.
– ORIGIN C19: from Ger. *Pudel(hund)*, from Low Ger. *pud(d)eln* 'splash in water' (the poodle being a water-dog).

**poodlefaker** ● n. Brit. informal, dated a man who cultivates women's company.

**poof**[1] /pʊf, pu:f/ (also **pouf**) ● n. Brit. informal, derogatory an effeminate or homosexual man.
– DERIVATIVES **poofy** adj.
– ORIGIN C19: perh. an alt. of the archaic noun *puff* in the sense 'braggart'.

**poof**[2] /pʊf/ (also **pouf**) ● exclam. describing a sudden disappearance or expressing contemptuous dismissal.
– ORIGIN C19: symbolic.

**poofter** /'pʊftə, 'pu:-/ ● n. another term for **POOF**[1].
– ORIGIN C20: extended form.

**pooh** (also **poo**) informal ● exclam. **1** expressing disgust at an unpleasant smell. **2** expressing impatience or contempt. ● n. excrement. ➤an act of defecating. ● v. defecate.
– ORIGIN C16: natural exclam.

**pooh-bah** /pu:'bɑ:/ ● n. a pompous person having much influence or holding many offices simultaneously.
– ORIGIN from the name of a character in W. S. Gilbert's *The Mikado* (1885).

**pooh-pooh** ● v. informal dismiss as being foolish or impractical.

**pooja** ● n. variant spelling of **PUJA**.

**pooka** /'pu:kə/ ● n. (in Irish mythology) a hobgoblin.
– ORIGIN from Ir. *púca*.

**pool**[1] ● n. **1** a small area of still water, typically one formed naturally. ➤a deep place in a river. ➤(also **swimming pool**) an artificial pool for swimming in. **2** a small, shallow patch of liquid lying on a surface. ● v. **1** form a pool. **2** (of blood) accumulate in parts of the venous system.
– ORIGIN OE *pōl*, of W. Gmc origin.

**pool**[2] ● n. **1** a shared supply of vehicles, people, or resources to be drawn on when needed. ➤a common fund into which all contributors pay and from which financial backing is provided. ➤the collective amount of players' stakes in gambling or sweepstakes. ➤(**the pools** or **football pools**) a form of gambling on the results of football matches, the winners receiving large sums accumulated from entry money. **2** an arrangement between competing parties to fix prices and share business in order to eliminate competition. **3** a group of contestants who compete against each other in a tournament for the right to advance to the next round. **4** a game played on a billiard table using two sets of seven balls together with one black ball and a white cue ball. ● v. **1** put (money or other assets) into a common fund. ➤share for the benefit of all. **2** Austral. informal implicate or inform on.
– ORIGIN C17: from Fr. *poule* in the sense 'stake, kitty', assoc. with **POOL**[1].

**poolroom** ● n. N. Amer. **1** (also **pool hall**) a place for playing pool. **2** a betting shop.

**poon**[1] ● n. Austral. informal a simple or foolish person.
– ORIGIN 1940s: from Sinhalese *pūna*.

**poon**[2] ● v. (**poon up**) Austral. informal dress so as to impress the opposite sex.
– ORIGIN 1940s: of unknown origin.

**poon**[3] ● n. short for **POONTANG**.

**poontang** /'pu:ntaŋ/ ● n. N. Amer. vulgar slang **1** sexual activity. **2** a woman or women regarded in terms of potential sexual gratification.
– ORIGIN 1920s: alt. of Fr. *putain* 'prostitute'.

**poop**[1] ● n. (also **poop deck**) the aftermost and highest deck of a ship, especially a sailing ship. ● v. (of a wave) break over the stern of (a ship).
– ORIGIN ME: from OFr. *pupe*, from a var. of L. *puppis* 'stern'.

**poop**[2] ● v. N. Amer. informal **1** [as adj. **pooped**] exhausted. **2** (**poop out**) stop functioning.
– ORIGIN 1930s: of unknown origin.

**poop**[3] N. Amer. informal ● n. excrement. ● v. defecate.
– ORIGIN C18: imitative.

**poop**[4] ● n. informal, chiefly N. Amer. up-to-date or inside information.
– ORIGIN 1940s: of unknown origin.

**poop**[5] ● n. informal, chiefly N. Amer. a stupid or ineffectual person.
– DERIVATIVES **poopy** adj.
– ORIGIN C20: perh. a shortening of **NINCOMPOOP**.

**pooper scooper** (also **poop scoop**) ● n. an implement for clearing up dog excrement.

**poor** ● adj. **1** lacking sufficient money to live at a standard considered comfortable or normal. **2** of a low or inferior standard or quality. ➤(**poor in**) lacking in. **3** deserving of pity or sympathy.
– PHRASES **the poor man's** —— an inferior or cheaper substitute for the thing specified. **poor relation** a person or thing that is considered inferior to others of the same type or group. **take a poor view of** regard with disapproval.
– DERIVATIVES **poorness** n.
– ORIGIN ME: from OFr. *poure*, from L. *pauper*.

**poor box** ● n. historical a collection box, especially one in a church, for gifts of money to aid the poor.

**poor boy** (also **poor-boy sandwich**) ● n. US a large oval sandwich filled with a range of simple but substantial ingredients.

**poorhouse** ● n. Brit. another term for **WORKHOUSE**.

**poorly** ● adv. in a poor manner. ● adj. chiefly Brit. unwell.

**poor man's orchid** ● n. another term for **SCHIZANTHUS**.

**poor man's weather glass** ● n. the scarlet pimpernel.
– ORIGIN C19: so named because its flowers close before rain.

**poor-mouth** ● v. informal **1** N. Amer. & Irish talk disparagingly about. **2** N. Amer. claim to be poor.

**poor rate** ● n. historical a local tax levied by a parish to finance the relief or support of the poor.

**poor relief** ● n. historical financial assistance given to the poor from state or local community funds.

**poort** /'pʊət/ ● n. S. African a narrow mountain pass.
– ORIGIN S. Afr. Du., 'passage'.

**poor white** ● n. derogatory a member of an impoverished white underclass, especially one living in the southern

US.

**poorwill** ● n. a small nightjar found mainly in central and western North America. [*Phalaenoptilus nuttallii* and other species.]
– ORIGIN C19: imitative of its call.

**pootle** ● v. Brit. informal move or travel in a leisurely manner.
– ORIGIN 1970s: blend of the verbs **POODLE** and **TOOTLE**.

**POP** ● abbrev. **1** (also **PoP**) (in computing) point of presence, denoting equipment that acts as access to the Internet. **2** (in the UK) Post Office Preferred, used to specify the size of envelopes and other items.

**pop**[1] ● v. (**popped**, **popping**) **1** make or cause to make a sudden, sharp, explosive sound. **2** (usu. **pop in/out**) go or come for a short time, often without notice. ➤(**pop off**) informal die. **3** put or place quickly in a particular position. **4** (of a person's eyes) open wide and appear to bulge, especially with surprise. **5** informal take or inject (a drug). **6** Brit. informal pawn. ● n. **1** a sudden sharp explosive sound. **2** informal, dated or N. Amer. fizzy soft drink. **3** (also **pop fly** or **pop-up**) Baseball a ball hit high in the air but not far from the home plate.
– PHRASES —— **a pop** N. Amer. informal costing a specified amount per item. **have** (or **take**) **a pop at** informal attack. **pop one's clogs** Brit. informal die. **pop the question** informal propose marriage.
– ORIGIN ME (in the senses 'a blow' and 'to strike'): imitative.

**pop**[2] ● n. (also **pop music**) commercial popular music, in particular accessible, tuneful music of a kind popular since the 1950s. ● adj. **1** of or relating to pop music. **2** often derogatory (especially of a scientific or academic subject) made accessible to the general public.

**pop**[3] ● n. chiefly US informal term for **FATHER**.
– ORIGIN C19: abbrev. of **POPPA**.

**pop.** ● abbrev. population.

**popadom** (also **popadum**) ● n. variant spelling of **POPPADOM**.

**pop art** ● n. art based on modern popular culture and the mass media, especially as a critical or ironic comment on traditional fine art values.

**popcorn** ● n. maize of a variety with hard kernels that swell up and burst open when heated and are then eaten as a snack.

**pop culture** ● n. commercial culture based on popular taste.

**pope**[1] ● n. **1** (**the Pope**) the Bishop of Rome as head of the Roman Catholic Church. **2** the head of the Coptic Church, the Patriarch of Alexandria. **3** another term for **RUFFE**.
– PHRASES **is the Pope** (**a**) **Catholic?** informal used to indicate that something is blatantly obvious.
– DERIVATIVES **popedom** n.
– ORIGIN OE, via eccles. L. from eccles. Gk *papas* 'bishop, patriarch', var. of Gk *pappas* 'father'.

**pope**[2] ● n. a parish priest of the Orthodox Church in Russia and the Balkans.
– ORIGIN C17: from Russ. *pop*, from Old Church Slavonic *popŭ*.

**Popemobile** /ˈpəʊpməbiːl/ ● n. informal a bulletproof vehicle with a raised viewing area, used by the Pope on official visits.

**popery** ● n. derogatory, chiefly archaic Roman Catholicism.

**pope's eye** ● n. Scottish an edible lymph gland surrounded with fat in a sheep's leg.

**pop-eyed** ● adj. informal having bulging or staring eyes.

**pop fly** ● n. Baseball see **POP**[1].

**popgun** ● n. **1** a child's toy gun which shoots a harmless pellet or cork. **2** a small, inefficient, or antiquated gun.

**pop-hole** ● n. a hole in a fence or divider through which animals can pass.

**popinjay** /ˈpɒpɪndʒeɪ/ ● n. **1** dated a vain, foppish, or conceited person. **2** archaic a parrot.
– ORIGIN ME: from OFr. *papingay*, via Sp. from Arab. *babbaġā*.

**popish** ● adj. derogatory Roman Catholic.
– DERIVATIVES **popishly** adv.

**poplar** ● n. a tall, fast-growing tree, often grown in shelter belts or for wood and pulp. [Genus *Populus*: many species.]
– ORIGIN ME: from OFr. *poplier*, from L. *populus*.

**poplin** ● n. a plain-woven fabric, typically a very lightweight cotton, with a corded surface.
– ORIGIN C18: from obs. Fr. *papeline*, perh. from Ital. *papalina* (fem.) 'papal', referring to the town of Avignon (residence of popes in exile), where it was first made.

**popliteal** /pɒˈplɪtɪəl, ˌpɒplɪˈtiːəl/ ● adj. Anatomy relating to or situated in the hollow at the back of the knee.
– ORIGIN C18: from mod. L. *popliteus* (from L. *poples, poplit-* 'ham, hough') + **-AL**.

**pop-out** ● n. Baseball an act of being put out by a caught fly ball. ● adj. N. Amer. designed to be easily removable.

**popover** ● n. N. Amer. a type of very light muffin made from a thin batter, which rises to form a hollow shell when baked.

**poppa** ● n. N. Amer. informal term for **FATHER**.
– ORIGIN C19: alt. of **PAPA**.

**poppadom** /ˈpɒpədəm/ (also **poppadum** or **popadom**) ● n. (in Indian cookery) a large disc of unleavened spiced bread made from ground lentils fried in oil.
– ORIGIN from Tamil *pappaḍam*.

**popper** ● n. **1** Brit. informal a press stud. **2** informal a small vial of amyl nitrite used for inhalation, which makes a popping sound when opened. **3** N. Amer. a utensil for making popcorn.

**poppet** ● n. **1** Brit. informal an endearingly sweet or pretty child. **2** (also **poppet valve**) Engineering a mushroom-shaped valve with a flat end piece that is lifted in and out of an opening by an axial rod.
– ORIGIN ME: based on L. *pup(p)a* 'girl, doll'; cf. **PUPPET**.

**poppet-head** ● n. Brit. the frame at the top of a mineshaft, supporting pulleys for the ropes used in hoisting.

**popping crease** ● n. Cricket a line across the pitch in front of the stumps, behind which the batsman must keep the bat or one foot grounded to avoid the risk of being stumped or run out.
– ORIGIN C18: from **POP**[1], perh. in the obs. sense 'strike'.

**popple** chiefly archaic ● v. (of water) flow in a tumbling or rippling way. ● n. a rolling or rippling of water.
– DERIVATIVES **popply** adj.
– ORIGIN ME: prob. from MDu. *popelen* 'to murmur', of imitative origin.

**poppy**[1] ● n. a plant having showy flowers, typically red or yellow, and rounded seed capsules. [*Papaver rhoeas* (**corn poppy**) and other species.]
– DERIVATIVES **poppied** adj.
– ORIGIN OE *popig*, *papæg*, from a med. L. alt. of L. *papaver*.

**poppy**[2] ● adj. (of popular music) tuneful and immediately appealing.

**poppycock** ● n. informal nonsense.
– ORIGIN C19: from Du. dial. *pappekak*, from *pap* 'soft' + *kak* 'dung'.

**Poppy Day** ● n. Brit. another name for **REMEMBRANCE SUNDAY**.

**poppy head** ● n. an ornamental top on the end of a church pew.

**pop rivet** ● n. a tubular rivet that is inserted into a hole and clinched by the withdrawing of a central rod. ● v. (**pop-rivet**) (**-riveted**, **-riveting**) secure or fasten with pop rivets.

**Popsicle** ● n. N. Amer. trademark an ice lolly.
– ORIGIN 1920s: fanciful formation.

**popsock** ● n. a type of nylon stocking with an elasticated top, reaching to the wearer's knee.

**popster** ● n. informal a pop musician.

**popsy** (also **popsie**) ● n. (pl. **-ies**) informal, chiefly Brit. an attractive young woman.
– ORIGIN C19: alt. of **POPPET**.

**pop-top** ● n. North American term for **RING PULL**.

**populace** /ˈpɒpjʊləs/ ● n. [treated as sing. or pl.] the general public.
– ORIGIN C16: from Fr., from Ital. *popolaccio* 'common

people'.

**popular** • adj. **1** liked or admired by many or by a particular person or group. **2** intended for or suited to the taste or means of the general public. ➤ (of a belief or attitude) widely held among the general public. **3** (of political activity) of or carried on by the people as a whole.
– DERIVATIVES **popularism** n. **popularity** n. **popularly** adv.
– ORIGIN ME: from L. *popularis*, from *populus* 'people'.

**popular etymology** • n. another term for **FOLK ETYMOLOGY**.

**popular front** • n. a political party or coalition representing left-wing elements.

**popularize** (also **-ise**) • v. make popular. ➤ make (something scientific or academic) accessible or interesting to the general public.
– DERIVATIVES **popularization** n. **popularizer** n.

**popular music** • n. music appealing to the popular taste, including rock, pop, reggae, dance music, etc.

**populate** • v. form the population of (a place). ➤ cause people to settle in (a place).
– ORIGIN C16: from med. L. *populat-*, *populare* 'supply with people'.

**population** • n. **1** all the inhabitants of a particular place. ➤ a particular group within this. ➤ the action of populating an area. **2** Biology a community of interbreeding organisms. **3** Statistics a finite or infinite collection of items under consideration.

**populist** • n. **1** a member or adherent of a political party seeking to represent the interests of ordinary people. **2** a person who supports or seeks to appeal to the interests of ordinary people. • adj. of or relating to a populist.
– DERIVATIVES **populism** n. **populistic** adj.
– ORIGIN C19: from L. *populus* 'people' + **-IST**.

**populous** • adj. having a large population.
– DERIVATIVES **populously** adv. **populousness** n.
– ORIGIN ME: from late L. *populosus*, from *populus* 'people'.

**pop-up** • adj. **1** (of a book or greetings card) containing folded pictures that rise up to form a three-dimensional scene or figure when opened. **2** (of an electric toaster) operating so as to push up a piece of toast when it is ready. **3** Computing (of a menu or other utility) able to be superimposed on the screen being worked on and suppressed rapidly. • n. Baseball see **POP**[1] (sense 3).

**porbeagle** /'pɔːbiːg(ə)l/ • n. a large active shark found chiefly in the open seas of the North Atlantic and in the Mediterranean. [*Lamna nasus*.]
– ORIGIN C18: from Cornish dial., perh. from Cornish *porth* 'harbour' + *bugel* 'shepherd'.

**porcelain** /'pɔːs(ə)lɪn/ • n. a white vitrified translucent ceramic; china. See also **HARD-PASTE**, **SOFT-PASTE**. ➤ articles made of this.
– DERIVATIVES **porcellanous** /pɔː'sɛlənəs/ adj.
– ORIGIN C16: from Fr. *porcelaine*, from Ital. *porcellana* 'cowrie shell', hence 'chinaware'.

**porcelain clay** • n. another term for **KAOLIN**.

**porch** • n. **1** a covered shelter projecting in front of the entrance of a building. **2** N. Amer. a veranda.
– DERIVATIVES **porched** adj. **porchless** adj.
– ORIGIN ME: from OFr. *porche*, from L. *porticus* 'colonnade', from *porta* 'passage'.

**porcine** /'pɔːsʌɪn/ • adj. of or resembling a pig or pigs.
– ORIGIN C17: from Fr. *porcin* or L. *porcinus*, from *porcus* 'pig'.

**porcini** /pɔː'tʃiːni/ • pl. n. chiefly N. Amer. ceps.
– ORIGIN Ital., lit. 'little pigs'.

**porcupine** • n. a large rodent with defensive spines or quills on the body and tail. [Families Hystricidae (Old World) and Erethizontidae (New World).]
– ORIGIN ME: from OFr. *porc espin*, from Provençal *porc espi(n)*, from L. *porcus* 'pig' + *spina* 'thorn'.

**porcupine fish** • n. a spiny tropical marine fish which inflates itself when threatened. [*Diodon hystrix* and other species.]

**pore**[1] • n. a minute opening in the skin or other surface through which gases, liquids, or microscopic particles may pass.
– ORIGIN ME: from OFr., via L. from Gk *poros* 'passage, pore'.

**pore**[2] • v. **1** (**pore over/through**) be absorbed in the reading or study of. **2** (**pore on/over**) archaic ponder.
– ORIGIN ME: perh. rel. to **PEER**[1].

**porgy** /'pɔːgi/ • n. (pl. **-ies**) a sea bream chiefly found in North American Atlantic coastal waters. [*Calamus* and other genera: many species.]
– ORIGIN C17: alt. of Sp. and Port. *pargo*.

**Porifera** /pə'rɪf(ə)rə/ • pl. n. Zoology a phylum of aquatic invertebrates that comprises the sponges.
– DERIVATIVES **poriferan** adj. & n.
– ORIGIN mod. L., from L. *porus* 'pore' + *-fer* 'bearing'.

**pork** • n. **1** the flesh of a pig used as food, especially when uncured. **2** short for **PORK BARREL**.
– ORIGIN ME: from OFr. *porc*, from L. *porcus* 'pig'.

**pork barrel** • n. N. Amer. informal the use of government funds for projects designed to win votes.
– DERIVATIVES **pork-barrelling** n.
– ORIGIN from the use of such a barrel by farmers, to keep a reserve supply of meat.

**porker** • n. **1** a young pig raised and fattened for food. **2** informal, derogatory a fat person.

**porkling** • n. a young or small pig.

**pork pie** • n. a raised pie made with minced, cooked pork, eaten cold.

**pork-pie hat** • n. a hat with a flat crown and a brim turned up all round.

**pork scratchings** • pl. n. Brit. crisp pieces of pork fat left after rendering lard, eaten as a snack.

**porky**[1] • adj. (**-ier**, **-iest**) **1** informal fleshy or fat. **2** of or resembling pork. • n. (pl. **-ies**) (also **porky-pie**) Brit. rhyming slang a lie.

**porky**[2] • n. (pl. **-ies**) US informal a porcupine.

**porn** (also **porno**) informal • n. pornography. • adj. pornographic.

**pornography** • n. printed or visual material intended to stimulate sexual excitement.
– DERIVATIVES **pornographer** n. **pornographic** adj. **pornographically** adv.
– ORIGIN C19: from Gk *pornographos* 'writing about prostitutes'.

**porous** • adj. (of a rock or other material) having minute interstices through which liquid or air may pass.
– DERIVATIVES **porosity** n. **porousness** n.
– ORIGIN ME: from OFr. *poreux*, based on L. *porus* 'pore'.

**porphyria** /pɔː'fɪrɪə/ • n. Medicine a rare hereditary disorder of haemoglobin metabolism causing mental disturbance, extreme sensitivity to light, and excretion of dark pigments in the urine.
– ORIGIN 1920s: mod. L., from **PORPHYRIN**.

**porphyrin** /'pɔːfɪrɪn/ • n. Biochemistry a pigment (e.g. haem or chlorophyll) whose molecule contains a flat ring of four linked heterocyclic groups.
– ORIGIN C20: from Gk *porphura* 'purple' + **-IN**[1].

**porphyritic** /ˌpɔːfɪ'rɪtɪk/ • adj. Geology relating to or denoting a rock texture containing distinct crystals or crystalline particles embedded in a compact groundmass.

**porphyry** /'pɔːfɪri/ • n. (pl. **-ies**) a hard igneous rock containing crystals of feldspar in a fine-grained, typically reddish groundmass.
– ORIGIN ME: via med. L. from Gk *porphuritēs*, from *porphura* 'purple'.

**porpoise** /'pɔːpəs, -pɔɪs/ • n. a small toothed whale with a low triangular dorsal fin and a blunt rounded snout. [*Phocoena phocoena* (**harbour porpoise**) and other species, family Phocoenidae.]
– ORIGIN ME: from OFr. *porpois*, based on L. *porcus* 'pig' + *piscis* 'fish'.

**porridge** • n. **1** a dish consisting of oatmeal or another cereal boiled with water or milk. **2** Brit. informal time spent in prison.
– DERIVATIVES **porridgy** adj.
– ORIGIN C16 (denoting soup thickened with barley): alt. of **POTTAGE**.

**porringer** /'pɒrɪn(d)ʒə/ • n. historical a small bowl, often with a handle, used for soup or similar dishes.

– ORIGIN ME (earlier as *potager* and *pottinger*): from OFr. *potager*, from *potage* 'contents of a pot'.

**Porro prism** /ˈpɒrəʊ/ ● **n.** a prism in which the light is reflected on two 45° surfaces and returned parallel to the incoming beam, especially as used in a conventional pair of binoculars.
– ORIGIN named after the C19 Ital. scientist Ignazio *Porro*.

**port**[1] ● **n.** a town or city with a harbour or access to navigable water where ships load or unload.
– PHRASES **port of call** a place where a ship or person stops on a journey. **port of entry** a harbour or airport where customs officers are stationed to oversee passengers and goods entering or leaving a country.
– ORIGIN OE, from L. *portus* 'harbour'.

**port**[2] (also **port wine**) ● **n.** a sweet dark red (occasionally brown or white) fortified wine, originally from Portugal.
– ORIGIN shortened form of *Oporto*, a port in Portugal from which the wine is shipped.

**port**[3] ● **n.** the side of a ship or aircraft that is on the left when one is facing forward. The opposite of **STARBOARD**. ● **v.** turn (a ship or its helm) to port.
– ORIGIN C16: prob. orig. the side turned towards the port.

**port**[4] ● **n. 1** an opening in the side of a ship for boarding or loading. ➤ a porthole. **2** an opening for the passage of steam, liquid, or gas. **3** (also **gun port**) an opening in the body of an aircraft or in a wall or armoured vehicle through which a gun may be fired. **4** Electronics a socket in a computer network into which a device can be plugged. **5** chiefly Scottish a gate or gateway, especially into a walled city.
– ORIGIN OE, from L. *porta* 'gate'.

**port**[5] ● **v. 1** Computing transfer (software) from one system or machine to another. **2** Military carry (a rifle or other weapon) diagonally across and close to the body with the barrel or blade near the left shoulder. ● **n. 1** Military the position required by an order to port a weapon. **2** poetic/literary a person's carriage or bearing. **3** Computing an instance of porting software.
– ORIGIN ME: from OFr. *port* 'bearing, gait', from *porter*, from L. *portare* 'carry'.

**port**[6] ● **n.** Austral. informal a suitcase or travelling bag.
– ORIGIN C20: abbrev. of **PORTMANTEAU**.

**porta-** ● **comb. form** denoting something that is movable or portable (often used as part of a proprietary name): *Portakabin*.

**portable** ● **adj. 1** able to be easily carried or moved. **2** (of a loan or pension) capable of being transferred or adapted in altered circumstances. **3** Computing (of software) able to be ported. ● **n.** a portable object.
– DERIVATIVES **portability** n. **portably** adv.

**portage** /ˈpɔːtɪdʒ/ ● **n. 1** the carrying of a boat or its cargo between two navigable waters. ➤ a place at which this is necessary. **2** archaic the action of carrying or transporting. ● **v.** carry (a boat or its cargo) between navigable waters.
– ORIGIN ME: from Fr., from *porter* 'carry'.

**Portakabin** ● **n.** Brit. trademark a portable building used as a temporary office, classroom, etc.
– ORIGIN 1960s: from **PORTA-** and an alt. of **CABIN**.

**portal**[1] ● **n. 1** a doorway, gate, or gateway, especially a large and imposing one. **2** Computing an Internet site providing a directory of links to other sites.
– ORIGIN ME: from OFr., from med. L. *portale*, neut. of *portalis* 'like a gate', from L. *porta* 'door, gate'.

**portal**[2] ● **adj.** Anatomy of or relating to the transverse fissure of the liver, through which major blood vessels pass.
– ORIGIN C19: from mod. L. *portalis*, from L. *porta* 'gate'.

**portal frame** ● **n.** Engineering a rigid structural frame consisting essentially of two uprights connected at the top by a third member.

**portal vein** (in full **hepatic portal vein**) ● **n.** Anatomy a vein conveying blood to the liver from the spleen, stomach, pancreas, and intestines.

**portamento** /ˌpɔːtəˈmɛntəʊ/ ● **n.** (pl. **portamentos** or **portamenti** /-ti/) Music **1** a slide from one note to another, especially in singing or playing the violin. **2** piano playing in a style between legato and staccato.
– ORIGIN Ital., lit. 'carrying'.

**portative organ** ● **n.** chiefly historical a small portable pipe organ.
– ORIGIN C16: *portative* from OFr. *portatif*, *-ive*, appar. an alt. of *portatil*, based on L. *portare* 'carry'.

**portcullis** ● **n.** a strong, heavy grating that can be lowered down grooves on each side of a gateway to block it.
– DERIVATIVES **portcullised** adj.
– ORIGIN ME: from OFr. *porte coleice* 'sliding door'.

**port de bras** /ˌpɔː də ˈbrɑː/ ● **n.** (pl. **ports de bras** pronunc. same) chiefly Ballet an act or manner of moving and posing the arms. ➤ an exercise designed to develop graceful movement and disposition of the arms.
– ORIGIN Fr., lit. 'bearing of (the) arms'.

**Porte** /pɔːt/ (in full **the Sublime** or **Ottoman Porte**) ● **n.** the Ottoman court at Constantinople.
– ORIGIN C17: from Fr. *la Sublime Porte* 'the exalted gate', translation of the Turk. title of the central office of the Ottoman government.

**porte cochère** /ˌpɔːt kɒˈʃɛː/ ● **n. 1** a covered entrance for vehicles to pass through, leading into a courtyard. **2** N. Amer. a porch where vehicles stop to set down passengers.
– ORIGIN C17: Fr., lit. 'coach gateway'.

**portend** ● **v.** be a sign or warning that (something momentous or calamitous) is likely to happen.
– ORIGIN ME: from L. *portendere*, based on *pro-* 'forth' + *tendere* 'stretch'.

**portent** /ˈpɔːtɛnt, -t(ə)nt/ ● **n. 1** a sign or warning that a momentous or calamitous event is likely to happen. ➤ future significance. **2** archaic an exceptional or wonderful person or thing.
– ORIGIN C16: from L. *portentum* 'omen, token'.

**portentous** ● **adj. 1** of or like a portent. **2** overly solemn.
– DERIVATIVES **portentously** adv. **portentousness** n.

**porter**[1] ● **n. 1** a person employed to carry luggage and other loads. ➤ (also **hospital porter**) a hospital employee who moves equipment or patients. **2** dark brown bitter beer brewed from malt partly charred or browned by drying at a high temperature. **3** N. Amer. a sleeping-car attendant.
– DERIVATIVES **porterage** n.
– ORIGIN ME: from OFr. *porteour*, from med. L. *portator*, from L. *portare* 'carry'; sense 2 derives from the beer orig. being made for porters.

**porter**[2] ● **n.** Brit. an employee in charge of the entrance of a hotel, block of flats, or other large building.
– ORIGIN ME: from OFr. *portier*, from late L. *portarius*, from *porta* 'gate, door'.

**porterhouse** ● **n.** historical, chiefly N. Amer. an establishment at which porter and sometimes steaks were served.

**porterhouse steak** ● **n.** a thick steak cut from the thick end of a sirloin.

**porter's knot** ● **n.** historical a double shoulder pad and forehead loop used for carrying loads.

**portfire** ● **n.** historical a hand-held fuse used for firing cannons, igniting explosives in mining, etc.
– ORIGIN C17: partial Anglicization of Fr. *porte-feu*, from *porter* 'carry' + *feu* 'fire'.

**portfolio** ● **n.** (pl. **-os**) **1** a large, thin, flat case for carrying drawings, maps, etc. **2** a set of pieces of creative work intended to demonstrate a person's ability to a potential employer. **3** a range of investments held by a person or organization. **4** the position and duties of a Minister or Secretary of State.
– ORIGIN C18: from Ital. *portafogli*, from *portare* 'carry' + *foglio* 'leaf'.

**portfolio career** ● **n.** a pattern of employment involving a succession of short-term contracts and part-time work, rather than the more traditional model of a single job for life.

**porthole** ● **n. 1** a small window on the outside of a ship or aircraft. **2** historical an opening for firing a cannon through.

**portico** /ˈpɔːtɪkəʊ/ ● **n.** (pl. **-oes** or **-os**) a structure consisting of a roof supported by columns at regular intervals, typically attached as a porch to a building.
– ORIGIN C17: from Ital., from L. *porticus* 'porch'.

**portière** /ˌpɔːtɪˈɛː/ ● **n.** a curtain hung over a door or doorway.
– ORIGIN C19: Fr., from *porte* 'door'.

**portion** ● **n.** **1** a part or a share. ➤an amount of food suitable for or served to one person. ➤Law the part or share of an estate given or descending by law to an heir. **2** archaic a person's destiny or lot. **3** (also **marriage portion**) archaic a dowry. ● **v.** **1** divide into portions and share out. **2** archaic give a dowry to.
– DERIVATIVES **portionless** adj. (archaic).
– ORIGIN ME: from OFr. *porcion*, from L. *portio(n-)*, from the phr. *pro portione* 'in proportion'.

**Portland cement** ● **n.** cement manufactured from chalk and clay which resembles Portland stone in colour when hard.

**Portland stone** ● **n.** limestone from the Isle of Portland in Dorset, valued as a building material.

**portly** ● **adj.** (**-ier**, **-iest**) **1** (especially of a man) rather fat. **2** archaic stately or dignified.
– DERIVATIVES **portliness** n.
– ORIGIN C15: from PORT[5] in the sense 'bearing' + -LY[1].

**portmanteau** /pɔːtˈmantəʊ/ ● **n.** (pl. **portmanteaus** or **portmanteaux** /-əʊz/) **1** a large travelling bag made of stiff leather and opening into two equal parts. **2** [as modifier] consisting of two or more aspects or qualities.
– ORIGIN C16: from Fr. *portemanteau*, from *porter* 'carry' + *manteau* 'mantle'.

**portmanteau word** ● **n.** a word blending the sounds and combining the meanings of two others, e.g. *brunch* from *lunch* and *breakfast*.

**portolan** /ˈpɔːtəlan/ (also **portolano** /ˌpɔːtəˈlɑːnəʊ/) ● **n.** (pl. **portolans** or **portolanos**) historical a book of sailing directions with charts and descriptions of harbours and coasts.
– ORIGIN C19: from Ital. *portolano*, from *porto* 'harbour'.

**portrait** ● **n.** **1** an artistic representation of a person, especially one depicting only the face or head and shoulders. **2** a description in language or on film or television. **3** [as modifier] denoting a format of printed matter which is higher than it is wide. Compare with LANDSCAPE.
– DERIVATIVES **portraitist** n. **portraiture** n.
– ORIGIN C16: from Fr., past part. of OFr. *portraire* 'portray'.

**portray** ● **v.** **1** depict in a work of art or literature. **2** describe in a particular way. **3** (of an actor) play the part of.
– DERIVATIVES **portrayable** adj. **portrayal** n. **portrayer** n.
– ORIGIN ME: from OFr. *portraire*, based on *traire* 'to draw', from an alt. of L. *trahere*.

**Port Salut** /ˌpɔː saˈluː/ ● **n.** a pale, mild type of cheese.
– ORIGIN named after *Port du Salut*, the Trappist monastery in France where it was first produced.

**Portuguese** /ˌpɔːtjʊˈgiːz, -tʃʊ-/ ● **n.** (pl. same) **1** a native or national of Portugal, or a person of Portuguese descent. **2** the Romance language of Portugal and Brazil. ● **adj.** of or relating to Portugal or its people or their language.
– ORIGIN from Port. *portuguez*, from med. L. *portugalensis*.

**Portuguese man-of-war** ● **n.** a floating jellyfish-like marine coelenterate with a number of polyps, a conspicuous, often blue float, and long stinging tentacles. [*Physalia physalis*.]

**port watch** ● **n.** see WATCH (sense 3).

**port wine stain** ● **n.** a deep red naevus, typically on the face.

**POS** ● **abbrev.** point of sale.

**posada** /pəˈsɑːdə/ ● **n.** (in Spanish-speaking countries) a hotel or inn.
– ORIGIN Sp., from *posar* 'to lodge'.

**pose[1]** ● **v.** **1** present or constitute (a problem, danger, question, etc.). **2** assume a particular position in order to be photographed, painted, or drawn. **3** (**pose as**) pretend to be. **4** behave affectedly in order to impress. ● **n.** **1** a position assumed in order to be painted, drawn, or photographed. **2** a way of behaving adopted in order to impress or give a false impression.
– ORIGIN ME: from OFr. *poser* (v.), from late L. *pausare* 'to pause', which replaced L. *ponere* 'to place'.

**pose[2]** ● **v.** archaic perplex with a question or problem.
– ORIGIN C16: shortening of obs. *appose*, from OFr. *aposer*, var. of *oposer* 'oppose'.

**poser[1]** ● **n.** a person who poses; a poseur.

**poser[2]** ● **n.** a puzzling question or problem.

**poseur** /pəʊˈzəː/ ● **n.** (fem. **poseuse** /pəʊˈzəːz/) a person who behaves affectedly in order to impress.
– ORIGIN Fr., from *poser* 'to place'.

**posey** (also **posy**) ● **adj.** informal pretentious.

**posh** informal ● **adj.** **1** elegant or stylishly luxurious. **2** chiefly Brit. upper-class. ● **adv.** Brit. in an upper-class way. ● **v.** (**posh something up**) Brit. smarten something up.
– DERIVATIVES **poshly** adv. **poshness** n.
– ORIGIN C20: perh. from sl. *posh*, denoting a dandy; there is no evidence for the folk etymology that *posh* is formed from the initials of *port out starboard home* (referring to the more comfortable accommodation, out of the heat of the sun, on ships between England and India).

**posit** /ˈpɒzɪt/ ● **v.** (**posited**, **positing**) **1** put forward as fact or as a basis for argument. ➤(**posit something on**) base something on the truth of (a particular assumption). **2** place. ● **n.** Philosophy a statement which is made on the assumption that it will prove to be true.
– ORIGIN C17: from L. *posit-*, *ponere* 'place'.

**position** ● **n.** **1** a place where someone or something is located or has been put. ➤the correct place. ➤a place where part of a military force is posted for strategic purposes. **2** a way in which someone or something is placed or arranged. ➤the configuration of the pieces and pawns on the board at any point in a game of chess. **3** a situation or set of circumstances. ➤the state of being advantageously placed in a competitive situation. ➤a person's place or rank in relation to others. ➤high rank or social standing. **4** a job. **5** a point of view or attitude. **6** the extent to which an investor, dealer, or speculator has made a commitment in the market by buying or selling securities etc.: *traders were covering short positions.* **7** Logic a proposition laid down or asserted. ● **v.** **1** put or arrange in a particular position. **2** promote (a product, service, or business) within a particular sector of a market.
– DERIVATIVES **positional** adj. **positionally** adv.
– ORIGIN ME: from OFr., from L. *positio(n-)*, from *ponere* 'to place'.

**positioner** ● **n.** a device for moving an object into position and automatically keeping it there.

**position paper** ● **n.** (in business and politics) a written report of attitude or intentions regarding a particular matter.

**positive** ● **adj.** **1** consisting in or characterized by the presence rather than the absence of distinguishing features. ➤expressing or implying affirmation, agreement, or permission. **2** constructive, optimistic, or confident. **3** with no possibility of doubt; certain. **4** (of a quantity) greater than zero. **5** of, containing, producing, or denoting the kind of electric charge opposite to that carried by electrons. **6** (of a photographic image) showing light and shade or colours true to the original. **7** Grammar (of an adjective or adverb) expressing a quality in its basic, primary degree. Contrasted with COMPARATIVE and SUPERLATIVE. **8** chiefly Philosophy dealing only with matters of fact and experience. See also POSITIVISM (sense 1). ● **n.** **1** a positive quality or attribute. **2** a positive photographic image, especially one printed from a negative.
– DERIVATIVES **positively** adv. **positiveness** n. **positivity** n.
– ORIGIN ME (orig. referring to laws as being formally 'laid down'): from OFr. *positif*, *-ive* or L. *positivus*, from *posit-*, *ponere* 'place'.

**positive discrimination** ● **n.** Brit. the practice or policy of favouring individuals belonging to groups which suffer discrimination.

**positive feedback** ● **n.** feedback that tends to enhance the effect by which it is produced.

**positive geotropism** ● n. Botany the tendency of roots to grow downwards.

**positive pole** ● n. the north-seeking pole of a magnet.

**positive sign** ● n. another term for PLUS SIGN.

**positive vetting** ● n. Brit. the investigation of the background and character of a candidate for a Civil Service post that involves access to secret material.

**positivism** ● n. Philosophy **1** a philosophical system (especially as postulated by the French philosopher Auguste Comte (1798–1857)) recognizing only that which can be scientifically verified or which is capable of logical or mathematical proof, and therefore rejecting metaphysics and theism. ➤another term for LOGICAL POSITIVISM. **2** the theory that laws derive validity from the fact of having been enacted by authority or of deriving logically from existing decisions, rather than from any moral considerations.
– DERIVATIVES **positivist** n. & adj. **positivistic** adj. **positivistically** adv.

**positron** /ˈpɒzɪtrɒn/ ● n. Physics a subatomic particle with the same mass as an electron and a numerically equal but positive charge.
– ORIGIN 1930s: from POSITIVE + -TRON.

**posology** /pəˈsɒlədʒi/ ● n. rare the part of medicine concerned with dosage.
– DERIVATIVES **posological** adj.
– ORIGIN C19: from Fr. *posologie*, from Gk *posos* 'how much' + *-logia* (see -LOGY).

**posse** /ˈpɒsi/ ● n. **1** N. Amer. historical a body of men summoned by a sheriff to enforce the law. **2** (also **posse comitatus** /ˌkɒmɪˈteɪtəs/) Brit. historical the body of men above the age of fifteen in a county, whom the sheriff could summon to repress a riot or for other purposes. [*comitatus* from med. L., 'of the county'.] **3** informal a group of people with a common characteristic, interest, or purpose.
– ORIGIN C17: from med. L., lit. 'power', from L. *posse* 'be able'.

**possess** ● v. **1** have as belonging to one. ➤Law have possession of as distinct from ownership. **2** have as an ability, quality, or characteristic. ➤(**possessed of**) in possession of. **3** [usu. as adj. **possessed**] (of a demon or spirit, especially an evil one) have complete power over. **4** (of an emotion, idea, etc.) dominate the mind of. **5** poetic/literary have sexual intercourse with (a woman).
– PHRASES **what possessed you?** used to express surprise at an action regarded as extremely unwise.
– DERIVATIVES **possessor** n. **possessory** adj.
– ORIGIN ME: from OFr. *possesser*, from L. *possess-*, *possidere* 'occupy, hold'.

**possession** ● n. **1** the state of possessing something. ➤Law visible power or control, as distinct from lawful ownership. ➤(in soccer, rugby, and other ball games) temporary control of the ball by a player or team. **2** a thing owned or possessed. ➤a territory or country controlled or governed by another. **3** the state of being possessed by a demon, emotion, etc.
– DERIVATIVES **possessionless** adj.

**possession order** ● n. chiefly Brit. an order made by a court directing that possession of a property be given to the owner or other claimant.

**possessive** ● adj. **1** demanding someone's total attention and love. **2** showing an unwillingness to share one's possessions. **3** Grammar relating to or denoting the case of nouns and pronouns expressing possession.
– DERIVATIVES **possessively** adv. **possessiveness** n.

**possessive determiner** ● n. Grammar a determiner indicating possession, for example *my*.

**possessive pronoun** ● n. Grammar a pronoun indicating possession, for example *mine*.

**posset** /ˈpɒsɪt/ ● n. a drink made of hot milk curdled with ale, wine, etc. and typically flavoured with spices, formerly drunk as a delicacy or as a remedy for colds. ● v. (**possetted**, **possetting**) (of a baby) regurgitate curdled milk.
– ORIGIN ME: of unknown origin.

**possibility** ● n. (pl. **-ies**) **1** a thing that is possible. **2** the state or fact of being possible. **3** (**possibilities**) unspecified qualities of a promising nature.

**possible** ● adj. capable of existing, happening, or being achieved. ➤that may be so, but that is not certain or probable. ● n. **1** a possible candidate for a job or member of a team. **2** (**the possible**) that which is likely or achievable. **3** the highest possible score, especially in a shooting competition.
– ORIGIN ME: from OFr., or from L. *possibilis*, from *posse* 'be able'.

**possibly** ● adv. **1** perhaps. **2** in accordance with what is possible.

**possum** ● n. **1** a tree-dwelling Australasian marsupial, typically with a prehensile tail. [Many species, especially in the family Petauridae.] **2** N. Amer. informal an opossum.
– PHRASES **play possum 1** feign unconsciousness or death (as an opossum does when threatened). **2** feign ignorance.
– ORIGIN C17: shortening of OPOSSUM.

**post**[1] ● n. a long, sturdy piece of timber or metal set upright in the ground and used as a support or a marker. ➤(**the post**) a starting post or winning post. ● v. **1** display (a notice) in a public place. **2** announce or publish. ➤publish the name of (a member of the armed forces) as missing or dead. **3** achieve or record (a particular score or result). **4** (**post up**) Basketball play in a position near the basket, along the side of the key.
– ORIGIN OE, from L. *postis* 'doorpost', later 'rod, beam'.

**post**[2] ● n. **1** chiefly Brit. the official service or system that delivers letters and parcels. ➤letters and parcels delivered. ➤a single collection or delivery of post. **2** historical one of a series of couriers who carried mail on horseback between fixed stages. ● v. **1** chiefly Brit. send via the postal system. **2** (in bookkeeping) enter (an item) in a ledger. **3** historical travel with relays of horses. ➤archaic travel with haste; hurry.
– PHRASES **keep someone posted** keep someone informed of the latest developments or news.
– ORIGIN C16: from Fr. *poste*, from Ital. *posta*, from a contr. of L. *posita*, fem. past part. of *ponere* 'to place'.

**post**[3] ● n. **1** a job. **2** a place where someone is on duty or where an activity is carried out. ➤N. Amer. a force stationed at a permanent position or camp. **3** historical the status or rank of full-grade captain in the Royal Navy. ● v. send to a place to take up an appointment. ➤station in a particular place.
– ORIGIN C16: from Fr. *poste*, from Ital. *posto*, from a contr. of pop. L. *positum*, neut. past part. of *ponere* 'to place'.

**post-** ● prefix after in time or order: *post-date*.
– ORIGIN from L. *post* 'after, behind'.

**postage** ● n. the sending of letters and parcels by post. ➤the amount required to send something by post.

**postage stamp** ● n. an adhesive or printed stamp applied to a letter or parcel to indicate the amount of postage paid.

**postal** ● adj. **1** of or relating to the post. **2** chiefly Brit. carried out by post: *a postal vote*. ● n. US informal a postcard.
– PHRASES **go postal** US informal go mad, especially from stress. [with ref. to cases in which postal employees have run amok and shot colleagues.]
– DERIVATIVES **postally** adv.

**postal card** ● n. US term for POSTCARD.

**postal code** ● n. another term for POSTCODE.

**postal order** ● n. Brit. an order for payment of a specified sum to a named payee, issued by the Post Office.

**post-and-beam** ● adj. (of a building or a method of construction) having or using a framework of upright and horizontal beams.

**postbag** ● n. British term for MAILBAG.

**post-bellum** /ˈbɛləm/ ● adj. occurring or existing after a war, in particular the American Civil War.
– ORIGIN C19: from L. *post* 'after' + *bellum* 'war'.

**postbox** ● n. **1** a large public box having a slot into which letters are posted, for collection by the post office. **2** British term for MAILBOX.

**postcard** ● n. a card for sending a message by post without an envelope.

**post-chaise** /(t)ʃeɪz/ ● n. (pl. **post-chaises** pronunc.

same) historical a horse-drawn carriage used for transporting passengers or mail.
– ORIGIN C17: from **POST²** + **CHAISE**.

**postcode** • n. Brit. a group of letters and numbers which are added to a postal address to assist the sorting of mail.
– DERIVATIVES **postcoded** adj.

**post-coital** • adj. occurring or done after sexual intercourse.
– DERIVATIVES **post-coitally** adv.

**post-date** • v. **1** [usu. as adj. **post-dated**] affix or assign a date later than the actual one to (a document or event). **2** occur or come at a later date than.

**postdoc** • n. informal a person engaged in postdoctoral research.

**postdoctoral** • adj. relating to or denoting research undertaken after the completion of a doctorate.

**poster** • n. **1** a large printed picture or notice used for decoration or advertisement. **2** Computing someone who sends a message to a newsgroup.

**poster boy** (or **poster girl**) • n. N. Amer. **1** a male (or female) poster child. **2** a male (or female) model who appears in a print advertisement.

**poster child** • n. N. Amer. a child who appears on a poster in an advertisement for a charitable organization. ➤ a person who epitomizes or represents a specified quality, cause, etc.

**poste restante** /pəʊst ˈrɛst(ə)nt/ • n. Brit. a department in a post office that keeps letters for an agreed period until collected by the addressee.
– ORIGIN C18: from Fr., lit. 'mail remaining'.

**posterior** • adj. **1** chiefly Anatomy further back in position; of or nearer the rear or hind end. The opposite of **ANTERIOR**. **2** Medicine relating to or denoting presentation of a fetus in which the rear or caudal end is nearest the cervix and emerges first at birth. **3** formal coming after in time or order; later. • n. humorous a person's buttocks.
– DERIVATIVES **posteriority** n. **posteriorly** adv. (Anatomy).
– ORIGIN C16 (as pl. n. 'descendants'): from L., compar. of *posterus* 'following', from *post* 'after'.

**posterity** • n. all future generations.
– ORIGIN ME: from OFr. *posterite*, from L. *posteritas*, from *posterus* 'following'.

**posterize** /ˈpəʊstərʌɪz/ (also **-ise**) • v. print or display (an image) using only a small number of different tones.
– DERIVATIVES **posterization** n.

**postern** /ˈpɒst(ə)n, ˈpəʊst-/ • n. a back or side entrance.
– ORIGIN ME: from OFr. *posterne*, alt. of *posterle*, from late L. *posterula*, dimin. of *posterus* 'following'.

**poster paint** • n. an opaque paint with a water-soluble binder.

**post-feminist** • adj. coming after the feminism of the 1960s and subsequent decades, in particular moving beyond or rejecting some of the ideas of feminism as out of date. • n. a person holding post-feminist views.
– DERIVATIVES **post-feminism** n.

**postfix** • v. Biology treat (a biological substance or specimen) with a second fixative.

**postfrontal** • n. Zoology a bone behind the orbit of the eye in some vertebrates.

**postglacial** • adj. Geology relating to or denoting the period since the last glaciation, about 10,000 years ago.

**postgraduate** • adj. relating to or denoting a course of study undertaken after completing a first degree. • n. a person engaged in postgraduate study.

**post-haste** • adv. with great speed or immediacy.
– ORIGIN C16: from the direction 'haste, post, haste', formerly given on letters.

**post hoc** /ˈhɒk/ • adj. & adv. after the event.
– ORIGIN L., lit. 'after this'.

**post horn** • n. historical a valveless horn used to signal the arrival or departure of a mounted courier or mail coach.

**posthumous** /ˈpɒstjʊməs/ • adj. occurring, awarded, or appearing after the death of the originator.
– DERIVATIVES **posthumously** adv.
– ORIGIN C17: from L. *postumus* 'last' (superlative from *post* 'after'), assoc. in late L. with *humus* 'ground', *humare* 'bury'.

**postie** • n. Brit. informal a postman or postwoman.

**postil** /ˈpɒstɪl/ • n. archaic a marginal note or a commentary, especially on a biblical text.
– ORIGIN ME: from OFr. *postille*, from med. L. *postilla*, perh. from L. *post illa* (*verba*) 'after those words', written as a direction to a scribe.

**postilion** /pɒˈstɪlɪən/ (also **postillion**) • n. a person who rides the leading nearside horse of a team or pair drawing a coach or carriage, when there is no coachman.
– ORIGIN C16 (in the sense 'forerunner acting as guide to the post-horse rider'): from Fr. *postillon*, from Ital. *postiglione* 'post-boy', from *posta* (see **POST²**).

**post-Impressionism** • n. the work or style of a group of late 19th-century and early 20th-century artists who reacted against the naturalism of the Impressionists, using colour, line, and form to express the emotional response of the artist.
– DERIVATIVES **post-Impressionist** n. & adj. **post-Impressionistic** adj.

**post-industrial** • adj. of or relating to an economy which no longer relies on heavy industry.
– DERIVATIVES **post-industrialism** n.

**posting** • n. chiefly Brit. an appointment to a job, especially one abroad or in the armed forces.

**Post-it** • n. trademark a piece of paper with an adhesive strip on one side, designed to be stuck prominently to an object or surface and easily removed when necessary.

**postlude** • n. **1** Music a concluding piece of music. **2** an afterword.
– ORIGIN C19: from **POST-**, on the pattern of *prelude*.

**postman** (or **postwoman**) • n. (pl. **-men** or **-women**) Brit. a person who is employed to deliver or collect post.

**postman's knock** • n. Brit. a children's game in which imaginary letters are delivered in exchange for kisses.

**postmark** • n. an official mark stamped on a letter or other postal package, giving the place, date, and time of posting, and serving to cancel the postage stamp. • v. stamp with a postmark.

**postmaster** (or **postmistress**) • n. a person in charge of a post office.

**postmaster general** • n. the head of a country's postal service.

**postmillennial** /ˌpəʊs(t)mɪˈlɛnɪəl/ • adj. following the millennium.

**postmillennialism** • n. (among fundamentalist Christians) the doctrine that the Second Coming of Christ will be the culmination of the prophesied millennium of blessedness.
– DERIVATIVES **postmillennialist** n.

**postmodernism** • n. a late 20th-century style and concept in the arts and architecture, which represents a departure from modernism and has at its heart a general distrust of theories and ideologies as well as a problematical relationship with the notion of 'art'.
– DERIVATIVES **postmodern** adj. **postmodernist** n. & adj. **postmodernity** n.

**post-mortem** • n. **1** an examination of a dead body to determine the cause of death. **2** an analysis of an event made after it has occurred. • adj. **1** of or relating to a post-mortem. **2** happening after death.
– ORIGIN C18: from L., lit. 'after death'.

**post-natal** • adj. occurring in or relating to the period after childbirth.
– DERIVATIVES **post-natally** adv.

**postnuptial** • adj. **1** occurring in or relating to the period after marriage. **2** Zoology occurring in or relating to the period after mating.

**post-obit** • adj. archaic taking effect after death.
– ORIGIN C18: from L. *post obitum*, from *post* 'after' + *obitus* 'decease' (from *obire* 'to die').

**post office** • n. **1** the public department or corporation responsible for postal services and (in some countries) telecommunications. ➤ a building where postal business is transacted. **2** US term for **POSTMAN'S KNOCK**.

**post office box** (also **PO box**) ● **n.** a numbered box in a post office assigned to a person or organization, where letters for them are kept until called for.

**post-op** ● **abbrev.** post-operative.

**post-operative** ● **adj.** relating to or denoting the period following a surgical operation.

**post-partum** /'pɑːtəm/ ● **adj.** Medicine & Veterinary Medicine relating to or characteristic of the period following childbirth or the birth of young.
– ORIGIN C19: from L. *post partum* 'after childbirth'.

**postpone** ● **v.** arrange for (something) to take place at a time later than that first scheduled.
– DERIVATIVES **postponable** adj. **postponement** n. **postponer** n.
– ORIGIN C15: from L. *postponere*, from *post* 'after' + *ponere* 'to place'.

**postposition** ● **n.** Grammar a word or morpheme placed after the word it governs, for example *-ward* in *homeward*.
– DERIVATIVES **postpositional** adj.
– ORIGIN C19: from **PREPOSITION**, by substitution of the prefix **POST-** for *pre-*.

**postpositive** ● **adj.** (of a word) placed after or as a suffix on the word that it relates to. ● **n.** a postpositive word.
– DERIVATIVES **postpositively** adv.

**postprandial** ● **adj. 1** formal or humorous during or relating to the period after a meal. **2** Medicine occurring after a meal.
– ORIGIN C19: from **POST-** + L. *prandium* 'a meal' + **-AL**.

**postscript** ● **n. 1** an additional remark at the end of a letter, following the signature. **2** a sequel.
– ORIGIN C16: from L. *postscriptum*, neut. past part. of *postscribere* 'write under, add'.

**post-structuralism** ● **n.** an extension and critique of structuralism, especially as used in critical textual analysis, which emphasizes plurality and deferral of meaning and rejects the binary oppositions of structuralism.
– DERIVATIVES **post-structural** adj. **post-structuralist** n. & adj.

**post-synch** ● **v.** add a sound recording to (film or video footage) at a later time.

**post-traumatic stress disorder** ● **n.** Medicine a condition of persistent mental and emotional stress occurring as a result of injury or severe psychological shock.

**postulant** /'pɒstjʊl(ə)nt/ ● **n.** a candidate seeking admission into a religious order.
– ORIGIN C18: from Fr. *postulant* or L. *postulant-* 'asking', from *postulare* (see **POSTULATE**).

**postulate** ● **v.** /'pɒstjʊleɪt/ **1** suggest or assume the existence, fact, or truth of (something) as a basis for reasoning, discussion, or belief. **2** (in ecclesiastical law) nominate or elect to an ecclesiastical office subject to the sanction of a higher authority. ● **n.** /'pɒstjʊlət/ a thing postulated.
– DERIVATIVES **postulation** n. **postulator** n.
– ORIGIN ME: from L. *postulat-*, *postulare* 'ask'.

**posture** ● **n. 1** a particular position of the body. ➤ the way in which a person holds their body. **2** Zoology a particular pose adopted by a bird or other animal, signalling a specific pattern of behaviour. **3** an approach or attitude towards something. ● **v.** [often as noun **posturing**] behave in a way that is intended to impress or mislead others.
– DERIVATIVES **postural** adj. **posturer** n.
– ORIGIN C16: from Fr., from Ital. *postura*, from L. *positura* 'position'.

**postviral syndrome** (also **postviral fatigue syndrome**) ● **n.** myalgic encephalomyelitis following a viral infection.

**postvocalic** ● **adj.** (of a speech sound) occurring immediately after a vowel.

**posy**[1] ● **n.** (pl. **-ies**) **1** a small bunch of flowers. **2** archaic a short motto or line of verse inscribed inside a ring.
– ORIGIN ME (in sense 2): contr. of **POESY**.

**posy**[2] ● **adj.** variant spelling of **POSEY**.

**pot**[1] ● **n. 1** a rounded or cylindrical container, especially one of ceramic, used for storage or cooking. **2** a container used for growing plants; a flowerpot. **3** a receptacle used by young children for urinating or defecating into. **4** (**the pot**) the total sum of the bets made on a round in poker, brag, etc. **5** informal a pot belly. **6** informal an engine cylinder. **7** Billiards & Snooker a shot in which a player strikes a ball into a pocket. ● **v.** (**potted**, **potting**) **1** plant in a pot. ➤ (**pot on**) transplant from a smaller pot to a larger one. ➤ (**pot up**) transplant from a seed tray to a pot. **2** preserve (food) in a sealed pot or jar. **3** Brit. sit (a young child) on a pot. **4** make pottery. **5** Billiards & Snooker strike (a ball) into a pocket. **6** informal hit or kill by shooting. **7** encapsulate (an electrical component or circuit) in a liquid insulating material which sets solid.
– PHRASES **go to pot** informal deteriorate through neglect.
– DERIVATIVES **potful** n. (pl. **-fuls**).
– ORIGIN OE *pott*, prob. reinforced in ME by OFr. *pot*; of unknown ultimate origin.

**pot**[2] ● **n.** informal cannabis.
– ORIGIN 1930s: prob. from Mex. Sp. *potiguaya* 'cannabis leaves'.

**pot**[3] ● **n.** (chiefly in rugby) an attempt to score a goal with a kick. ● **v.** (**potted**, **potting**) score (a goal).
– ORIGIN 1950s: abbrev. of **POTSHOT**.

**pot**[4] ● **n.** short for **POTENTIOMETER**.

**potable** /'pəʊtəb(ə)l/ ● **adj.** drinkable.
– DERIVATIVES **potability** n.
– ORIGIN ME: from Fr. *potable*, from late L. *potabilis*, from L. *potare* 'to drink'.

**potage** /pɒ'tɑːʒ/ ● **n.** thick soup.
– ORIGIN C16: from Fr.; cf. **POTTAGE**.

**potager** /'pɒtədʒə/ ● **n.** a kitchen garden.
– ORIGIN C17: from Fr. *jardin potager* 'garden providing vegetables for the pot'.

**potamology** /,pɒtə'mɒlədʒi/ ● **n.** Geography the study of rivers.
– ORIGIN C19: from Gk *potamos* 'river' + **-LOGY**.

**potash** ● **n.** an alkaline potassium compound, especially potassium carbonate or hydroxide.
– ORIGIN C17: from *pot-ashes*, from obs. Du. *potasschen*, orig. obtained by leaching vegetable ashes and evaporating the solution in iron pots.

**potassium** /pə'tasɪəm/ ● **n.** the chemical element of atomic number 19, a soft silvery-white reactive metal of the alkali-metal group. (Symbol: **K**)
– DERIVATIVES **potassic** adj.
– ORIGIN C19: from **POTASH** + **-IUM**.

**potassium hydroxide** ● **n.** a strongly alkaline white deliquescent compound used in many industrial processes, e.g. soap manufacture. [KOH.]

**potation** /pə(ʊ)'teɪʃ(ə)n/ ● **n.** archaic or humorous **1** the action of drinking alcohol. **2** an alcoholic drink.
– ORIGIN ME: from OFr., from L. *potatio(n-)*, from *potare* 'to drink'.

**potato** ● **n.** (pl. **-oes**) **1** a starchy plant tuber which is one of the most important food crops, cooked and eaten as a vegetable. **2** the plant of the nightshade family which produces these tubers on underground runners. [*Solanum tuberosum*.]
– ORIGIN C16 (orig. denoting the sweet potato): from Sp. *patata*, var. of Taino *batata* 'sweet potato'.

**potato vine** ● **n.** a semi-evergreen climbing plant with pale blue or white flowers, related to the potato and native to South and Central America. [*Solanum jasminoides*.]

**pot-au-feu** /,pɒtəʊ'fəː/ ● **n.** a French soup of meat and vegetables cooked in a large pot.
– ORIGIN Fr., lit. 'pot on the fire'.

**Potawatomi** /,pɒtə'wɒtəmi/ ● **n.** (pl. same or **Potawatomis**) **1** a member of an American Indian people inhabiting the Great Lakes region, principally in Michigan and Wisconsin. **2** the Algonquian language of this people.
– ORIGIN the name in Ojibwa.

**pot-bellied stove** ● **n.** a small bulbous-sided wood-burning stove.

**pot belly** ● **n.** a protruding, rotund stomach.
– DERIVATIVES **pot-bellied** adj.

**potboiler** ● **n.** informal a book, film, etc. produced to make the writer or artist a living by deliberately catering to popular taste.

**pot-bound** ● adj. (of a plant) having roots which fill the pot, leaving no room for them to expand.

**pot cheese** ● n. US a coarse type of cottage cheese.

**poteen** /pɒ'ti:n/ (also **potheen**) ● n. chiefly Irish illicitly made whiskey.
– ORIGIN C19: from Ir. (*fuisce*) *poitín* 'little pot (of whiskey)', dimin. of *pota* 'pot'.

**potent**[1] ● adj. **1** having great power, influence, or effect. **2** (of a male) able to achieve an erection or to reach an orgasm.
– DERIVATIVES **potence** n. **potency** n. **potently** adv.
– ORIGIN ME: from L. *potent-*, *posse* 'be powerful, be able'.

**potent**[2] Heraldry ● adj. [postpos.] **1** formed of crutch-shaped pieces; (especially of a cross) having a straight bar across the end of each extremity. **2** of the fur called potent (as a tincture). ● n. fur resembling vair, but with the alternating pieces T-shaped.
– ORIGIN ME: alt. of OFr. *potence* 'crutch', from L. *potentia* 'power' (in med. L. 'crutch'), from *potent-* (see **POTENT**[1]).

**potentate** ● n. a monarch or ruler.
– ORIGIN ME: from L. *potentatus* 'dominion', from *potent-* (see **POTENT**[1]).

**potential** ● adj. having the capacity to develop into something in the future. ● n. **1** latent qualities or abilities that may be developed and lead to future success or usefulness. **2** (often **potential for/to do something**) the possibility of something happening or of someone doing something in the future. **3** Physics the quantity determining the energy of mass in a gravitational field or of charge in an electric field.
– DERIVATIVES **potentiality** n. **potentialize** (also **-ise**) v. **potentially** adv.
– ORIGIN ME: from late L. *potentialis*, from *potentia* 'power'.

**potential barrier** ● n. Physics a region within a force field in which the potential is significantly higher than at points either side of it, so that a particle requires energy to pass through it.

**potential difference** ● n. Physics the difference of electrical potential between two points.

**potential energy** ● n. Physics energy possessed by a body by virtue of its position or state. Compare with **KINETIC ENERGY**.

**potentiate** /pə(ʊ)'tɛnʃɪeɪt/ ● v. increase the power or effect of (something such as a drug or physiological reaction).
– ORIGIN C19: from **POTENT**[1], on the pattern of *substantiate*.

**potentiation** ● n. Physiology the increase in strength of nerve impulses along pathways which have been used previously, either short-term or long-term.

**potentilla** /ˌpəʊt(ə)n'tɪlə/ ● n. a plant of a genus that includes the cinquefoils, especially a small shrub with yellow or red flowers. [Genus *Potentilla*: many species.]
– ORIGIN mod. L., based on L. *potent-* 'being powerful' (with ref. to its herbal qualities) + the dimin. suffix *-illa*.

**potentiometer** /pə(ʊ)ˌtɛnʃɪ'ɒmɪtə/ ● n. an instrument for measuring or adjusting an electromotive force by balancing it against a known potential difference.

**potentiometry** ● n. Chemistry the measurement of electrical potential as a technique in chemical analysis.
– DERIVATIVES **potentiometric** adj.

**potentize** (also **-ise**) ● v. (especially with reference to a homeopathic medicine) make stronger or more potent.
– DERIVATIVES **potentization** n.

**pothead** ● n. informal a habitual cannabis smoker.

**potheen** /pɒ'tʃi:n/ ● n. variant spelling of **POTEEN**.

**pother** /'pɒðə/ ● n. a commotion or fuss.
– ORIGIN C16: of unknown origin.

**pothole** ● n. **1** a deep natural underground cave formed by the eroding action of water. ➤ a deep circular hole in a river bed formed by the eroding action of stones in an eddy. **2** a depression or hollow in a road surface caused by wear or subsidence. **3** N. Amer. a lake formed by a natural hollow in the ground in which water has collected. ● v. Brit. explore underground potholes as a pastime.
– DERIVATIVES **potholed** adj. **potholer** n. **potholing** n.
– ORIGIN C19: from ME *pot* 'pit' (perh. of Scand. origin) + **HOLE**.

**potion** ● n. a liquid with healing, magical, or poisonous properties.
– ORIGIN ME: from OFr., from L. *potio(n-)* 'drink, poisonous draught', rel. to *potare* 'to drink'.

**potlatch** ● n. (among some North American Indian peoples) a ceremonial feast at which possessions are given away or destroyed to display wealth or enhance prestige. ● v. hold a potlatch.
– ORIGIN Chinook Jargon, from Nootka *p'ačitl* 'make a gift at a potlatch'.

**pot liquor** ● n. chiefly US meat, fish, or vegetable stock.

**pot luck** ● n. **1** the chance that whatever is available will prove to be good or acceptable. **2** (**potluck**) [as modifier] denoting a meal in which all the guests bring a different dish to share.

**potoo** /pə'tu:/ ● n. a nocturnal insectivorous bird resembling a large nightjar, found in tropical America. [*Nyctibius griseus* and related species.]
– ORIGIN C19: from Jamaican creole, from Twi, of imitative origin.

**potoroo** /ˌpɒtə'ru:/ ● n. a small nocturnal rat-kangaroo with long hindlimbs and typically a hopping gait, native to mainland Australia and Tasmania. [Genus *Potorous*: three species.]
– ORIGIN C18: prob. from Dharuk *badaru*.

**pot-pourri** /pəʊ'pʊəri, -'ri:, pɒt'pʊəri/ ● n. (pl. **pot-pourris**) **1** a mixture of dried petals and spices placed in a bowl to perfume a room. **2** a mixture of things; a medley.
– ORIGIN C17 (denoting a stew made of different kinds of meat): from Fr., lit. 'rotten pot'.

**pot roast** ● n. a piece of meat cooked slowly in a covered pot. ● v. (**pot-roast**) cook (meat) in such a way.

**potsherd** /'pɒtʃə:d/ ● n. a piece of broken pottery.

**potshot** ● n. **1** a shot aimed unexpectedly or at random. ➤ a shot at a game bird or other animal made without regard to hunting rules. **2** a random attack or criticism.
– ORIGIN C19: orig. a *shot* at an animal intended for the *pot*, i.e. for food, rather than for display (which would require skilled shooting).

**pot still** ● n. a still to which heat is applied directly and not by means of a steam jacket.

**pottage** ● n. soup or stew.
– ORIGIN ME (as *potage*): from OFr. *potage* 'that which is put into a pot'; cf. **POTAGE** and **PORRIDGE**.

**potted** ● adj. **1** grown or preserved in a pot. **2** (of a biographical or historical account) put into a short and easily assimilable form. **3** (of an electrical component or circuit) encapsulated in insulating material.

**potter**[1] (N. Amer. **putter**) ● v. **1** occupy oneself in a desultory but pleasant manner. **2** move or go in a casual, unhurried way. ● n. a spell of pottering.
– DERIVATIVES **potterer** n.
– ORIGIN C16 (in the sense 'poke repeatedly'): frequentative of dial. *pote* 'to push, kick, or poke' of unknown origin.

**potter**[2] ● n. a person who makes ceramic ware.

**potter's field** ● n. historical a burial place for paupers and strangers.
– ORIGIN with biblical allusion to Matt. 27:7.

**potter's wheel** ● n. a horizontal revolving disc on which wet clay is shaped into pots, bowls, etc.

**pottery** ● n. (pl. **-ies**) pots, dishes, and other articles made of fired clay. ➤ the craft or profession of making such ware. ➤ a factory or workshop where such ware is made.
– ORIGIN ME: from OFr. *poterie*, from *potier* 'a potter'.

**potting compost** ● n. a mixture of loam, peat, sand, and nutrients, used as a growing medium for plants in containers.

**potting shed** ● n. a shed used for potting plants and storing garden tools and supplies.

**pottle** ● n. **1** a former measure for liquids equal to a half gallon. ➤ a pot or container of this capacity. **2** archaic a small punnet.
– ORIGIN ME: from OFr. *potel* 'little pot', dimin. of *pot*.

**potto** /'pɒtəʊ/ (also **potto gibbon**) ● n. (pl. **-os**) a small

nocturnal slow-moving primate with a short tail, living in dense vegetation in the tropical forests of Africa. [*Perodicticus potto.*]
– ORIGIN C18: perh. from Guinea dial.

**Pott's fracture** • n. a fracture of the lower end of the fibula, usually involving a dislocation of the ankle.
– ORIGIN C19: named after the Engl. surgeon Sir Percivall *Pott*.

**potty**[1] • adj. (**-ier, -iest**) informal, chiefly Brit. **1** foolish; crazy. **2** extremely enthusiastic about someone or something.
– DERIVATIVES **pottiness** n.
– ORIGIN C19: of unknown origin.

**potty**[2] • n. (pl. **-ies**) informal a child's pot for urinating or defecating into.

**potty-train** • v. train (a young child) to use a pot.

**pouch** • n. **1** a small flexible bag. ➤a lockable bag for mail or dispatches. **2** a pocket-like abdominal receptacle in which marsupials carry their young during lactation. **3** any of a number of similar animal structures, such as those in the cheeks of rodents. ➤(often **pouches**) a baggy area of skin underneath a person's eyes. • v. **1** put into a pouch. **2** informal take possession of. **3** Cricket catch (the ball). **4** make or form into a pouch.
– DERIVATIVES **pouched** adj. **pouchy** adj.
– ORIGIN ME: from ONorth. Fr. *pouche*, var. of OFr. *poche* 'bag'.

**pouchong** /puː'(t)ʃɒŋ/ • n. a kind of China tea made by fermenting the withered leaves only briefly, typically scented with rose petals.
– ORIGIN from Chin.

**pouf**[1] • n. variant spelling of **POOF**[1] or **POUFFE**. • exclam. variant spelling of **POOF**[2].

**pouf**[2] /puːf/ • n. **1** a part of a dress in which a large mass of material has been gathered so that it stands away from the body. **2** a bouffant hairstyle.
– ORIGIN C19 (denoting an elaborate female headdress): from Fr., of imitative origin.

**pouffe** /puːf/ (also **pouf**) • n. a cushioned footstool or low seat with no back.
– ORIGIN C19: from Fr. *pouf*, of imitative origin.

**poui** /'puːi/ • n. (pl. same or **pouis**) a Caribbean and tropical American tree with trumpet-shaped flowers, valued for its wood. [Genus *Tabebuia*.]
– ORIGIN C19: a local word in Trinidad.

**poult**[1] /pəʊlt/ • n. Farming a young domestic fowl being raised for food.
– ORIGIN ME: contr. of **PULLET**.

**poult**[2] /puːlt, pʊlt/ (also **poult-de-soie** /ˌpuːdə'swɑː/) • n. a fine corded silk or taffeta, used as a dress fabric.
– ORIGIN 1930s: from Fr. *poult-de-soie*, from *poult* (of unknown origin) + *de soie* 'of silk'.

**poulterer** • n. Brit. a dealer in poultry.
– ORIGIN C16: from archaic *poulter*, from OFr. *pouletier*.

**poultice** /'pəʊltɪs/ • n. a soft moist mass of material, typically consisting of bran, flour, herbs, etc., applied with a cloth to the body to relieve inflammation. • v. apply a poultice to.
– ORIGIN ME: from L. *pultes* (pl.), from *puls, pult-* 'pottage, pap'.

**poultry** /'pəʊltri/ • n. chickens, turkeys, ducks, and geese; domestic fowl.
– ORIGIN ME: from OFr. *pouletrie*, from *poulet* 'pullet'.

**pounce**[1] • v. **1** spring or swoop suddenly to catch or as if to catch prey. **2** notice and take swift advantage of a mistake or sign of weakness. • n. an act of pouncing.
– DERIVATIVES **pouncer** n.
– ORIGIN ME (denoting a tool for punching, later 'claw, talon'): origin obscure, perh. from **PUNCHEON**[1].

**pounce**[2] • n. **1** a fine resinous powder formerly used to prevent ink from spreading on unglazed paper or to prepare parchment to receive writing. **2** powdered charcoal or other fine powder dusted over a perforated pattern to transfer the design to the surface beneath. • v. **1** smooth down by rubbing with pounce or pumice. **2** transfer (a design) by the use of pounce.
– DERIVATIVES **pouncer** n.
– ORIGIN C16: from Fr. *poncer*, based on L. *pumex* 'pumice'.

**pouncet-box** /'paʊnsɪt/ • n. archaic a small box with a perforated lid used for holding a substance impregnated with perfume.
– ORIGIN C16: perh. orig. erroneously from *pounced* (= perforated) *box*.

**pound**[1] • n. **1** (abbrev.: **lb**) a unit of weight equal to 16 oz avoirdupois (0.4536 kg), or 12 oz troy (0.3732 kg). **2** (also **pound sterling**) (pl. **pounds sterling**) the basic monetary unit of the UK, equal to 100 pence. **3** another term for **PUNT**[4]. **4** the basic monetary unit of several Middle Eastern countries, equal to 100 piastres. **5** the basic monetary unit of Cyprus, equal to 100 cents. **6** a monetary unit of the Sudan, equal to one tenth of a dinar.
– PHRASES **one's pound of flesh** something to which one is strictly entitled, but which it is ruthless to demand. [with allusion to Shakespeare's *Merchant of Venice*.]
– ORIGIN OE *pund*, of Gmc origin, from L. (*libra*) *pondo*, denoting a Roman 'pound weight' of 12 ounces.

**pound**[2] • v. **1** strike or hit heavily and repeatedly. ➤(**pound something out**) produce a document or piece of music with heavy strokes on a keyboard or instrument. ➤beat or throb with a strong regular rhythm. ➤walk or run with heavy steps. **2** crush or grind into a powder or paste. **3** informal defeat resoundingly.
– DERIVATIVES **pounding** n.
– ORIGIN OE *pūnian*.

**pound**[3] • n. **1** a place where stray dogs may officially be taken and kept until claimed. ➤a place where illegally parked motor vehicles removed by the police are kept until the owner pays a fine. **2** archaic a trap or prison. • v. archaic shut in a pound.
– ORIGIN ME: of uncertain origin.

**poundage** • n. Brit. **1** a commission of a particular amount per pound sterling of the sum involved in a transaction. **2** a percentage of the total earnings of a business, paid as wages. **3** weight.

**poundal** /'paʊnd(ə)l/ • n. Physics a unit of force equal to that required to give a mass of one pound an acceleration of one foot per second per second.
– ORIGIN C19: from **POUND**[1] + the suffix *-al*, perh. suggested by **QUINTAL**.

**pound cake** • n. a rich cake originally made with a pound of each chief ingredient.

**pounder** • n. **1** a person or thing that pounds. **2** [in combination] a person or thing weighing or costing a specified number of pounds: *a three-pounder*.

**pour** • v. **1** flow or cause to flow in a steady stream. ➤(often **pour down**) (of rain) fall heavily. ➤prepare and serve (a drink). **2** (of people or things) come or go in a steady stream. **3** (**pour something out**) express one's feelings in an unrestrained way.
– PHRASES **pour oil on troubled waters** try to calm a dispute with placatory words.
– DERIVATIVES **pourable** adj. **pourer** n.
– ORIGIN ME: of unknown origin.

**pourboire** /pʊə'bwɑː/ • n. a gratuity; a tip.
– ORIGIN Fr., from *pour boire* lit. '(money) for drinking'.

**pousada** /pəʊ'sɑːdə/ • n. an inn or hotel in Portugal.
– ORIGIN Port., lit. 'resting place'.

**poussin** /'puːsã/ • n. a chicken killed young for eating.
– ORIGIN from Fr.

**pout**[1] • v. push one's lips or bottom lip forward as an expression of petulant annoyance or in order to make oneself look sexually attractive. • n. a pouting expression.
– DERIVATIVES **pouting** adj. **poutingly** adv. **pouty** adj.
– ORIGIN ME: perh. from the base of Swed. dial. *puta* 'be inflated'.

**pout**[2] • n. **1** (also **pouting**) another term for **BIB**[1] (in sense 2). **2** North American term for **EELPOUT**.
– ORIGIN OE *-pūta* in *ǣlepūta* 'eelpout', perh. rel. to **POUT**[1].

**pouter** • n. a kind of pigeon that is able to inflate its crop to a considerable extent.

**POV** • abbrev. point of view.

**poverty** • n. **1** the state of being extremely poor. ➤the renunciation of the right to individual ownership of property as part of a religious vow. **2** the state of being insufficient in amount.

– ORIGIN ME: from OFr. *poverte*, from L. *paupertas*, from *pauper* 'poor'.

**poverty line** • n. the estimated minimum level of income needed to secure the necessities of life.

**poverty trap** • n. Brit. a situation in which an increase in someone's income is offset by a consequent loss of state benefits.

**POW** • abbrev. prisoner of war.

**pow** • exclam. expressing the sound of a blow or explosion.

– ORIGIN C19 (orig. US): imitative.

**powder** • n. **1** fine dry particles produced by the grinding, crushing, or disintegration of a solid substance. **2** a cosmetic in this form applied to a person's face. **3** dated a medicine in this form. **4** loose, dry, newly fallen snow. **5** short for **GUNPOWDER** (in sense 1). • v. **1** apply powder to; sprinkle or cover with powder. **2** [usu. as adj. **powdered**] reduce to a powder.

– PHRASES **keep one's powder dry** remain cautious and alert. **take a powder** N. Amer. informal depart quickly.

– DERIVATIVES **powdery** adj.

– ORIGIN ME: from OFr. *poudre*, from L. *pulvis*, *pulver-* 'dust'.

**powder blue** • n. a soft, pale blue.

**powder-coat** • v. cover (an object) with a polyester or epoxy powder, which is then heated to fuse into a protective layer.

**powdered sugar** • n. North American term for **ICING SUGAR**.

**powder keg** • n. **1** a barrel of gunpowder. **2** a potentially explosive situation.

**powder metallurgy** • n. the production and working of metals as fine powders which can be pressed and sintered to form objects.

**powder monkey** • n. **1** historical a boy employed on a sailing warship to carry powder to the guns. **2** N. Amer. a person who works with explosives.

**powder-post beetle** • n. a small brown beetle whose wood-boring larvae reduce wood to a very fine powder. [Family Lyctidae.]

**powder puff** • n. a soft pad for applying powder to the face.

**powder room** • n. euphemistic a women's toilet in a public building.

**power** • n. **1** the ability to do something or act in a particular way. **2** the capacity to influence the behaviour of others, the emotions, or the course of events. **3** a right or authority given or delegated to a person or body. ➤political authority or control. **4** a country viewed in terms of its international influence and military strength: *a world power.* **5** physical strength or force. ➤capacity or performance of an engine or other device. ➤the magnifying capacity of a lens. **6** energy that is produced by mechanical, electrical, or other means. ➤[as modifier] driven by such energy: *a power drill.* **7** Physics the rate of doing work, measured in watts or horse power. **8** Mathematics the product obtained when a number is multiplied by itself a certain number of times. • v. **1** supply with power. ➤(**power something up/down**) switch an electrically powered device on or off. **2** move or cause to move with speed or force: *he powered round a bend.*

– PHRASES **do someone a power of good** informal be very beneficial to someone. **the powers that be** the authorities. [with biblical allusion to Rom. 13:1.]

– DERIVATIVES **-powered** adj. **powerless** adj. **powerlessly** adv. **powerlessness** n.

– ORIGIN ME: from Anglo-Norman Fr. *poeir*, from an alt. of L. *posse* 'be able'.

**power-assisted** • adj. (especially of steering or brakes) using an inanimate source of power to assist manual operation.

**powerboat** • n. a fast motor boat.

**power broker** • n. a person who sets out to affect the distribution of political or economic power by exerting influence or by intrigue.

– DERIVATIVES **power-broking** n. & adj.

**power cut** • n. a temporary withdrawal or failure of an electrical power supply.

**power dive** • n. a steep dive of an aircraft with the engines providing thrust. • v. (**power-dive**) perform a power dive.

**power factor** • n. the ratio of the actual power dissipated by a circuit to the product of the rms values of current and voltage.

**power forward** • n. Basketball a large forward who plays in the low post and typically has good shot-blocking and rebounding skills.

**powerful** • adj. having power. • adv. chiefly dialect very.

– DERIVATIVES **powerfully** adv. **powerfulness** n.

**powerhouse** • n. a person or thing having great energy or power.

**powerlifting** • n. a form of competitive weightlifting in which contestants attempt three types of lift in a set sequence.

– DERIVATIVES **powerlifter** n.

**power of attorney** • n. Law the authority to act for another person in specified legal or financial matters.

**power pack** • n. **1** a self-contained and typically transportable unit which stores and supplies electrical power. **2** a transformer for converting an alternating current (from the mains) to a direct current at a different (usually lower) voltage.

**power plant** • n. **1** another term for **POWER STATION**. **2** an engine or other apparatus which provides power for a machine, building, etc.

**power play** • n. **1** tactics exhibiting or intended to increase a person's power. **2** offensive tactics in a team sport involving the concentration of players in a particular area. **3** Ice Hockey a temporary situation in which one team has a numerical advantage because one or more players is serving a penalty.

**power shower** • n. a shower using an electric pump to produce a high-pressure spray.

**power station** • n. an installation where electrical power is generated.

**power steering** • n. power-assisted steering.

**power stroke** • n. the stage of the cycle of an internal-combustion engine in which the piston is driven outward by the expansion of gases.

**power train** • n. the mechanism that transmits the drive from the engine of a vehicle to its axle.

**Powhatan** /ˈpaʊətan/ • n. (pl. same or **Powhatans**) **1** a member of an American Indian people of eastern Virginia. **2** the extinct Algonquian language of this people.

– ORIGIN from Virginia Algonquian.

**powwow** • n. **1** a North American Indian ceremony involving feasting and dancing. **2** informal a meeting for discussion among friends or colleagues. • v. informal hold a powwow.

– ORIGIN C17: from Narragansett *powah*, *powwaw* 'magician' (lit. 'he dreams').

**pox** • n. **1** any of several viral diseases producing a rash of pimples that become pus-filled and leave pockmarks on healing. ➤(**the pox**) historical smallpox. **2** (**the pox**) informal syphilis.

– PHRASES **a pox on someone** archaic expressing anger with someone.

– ORIGIN ME: alt. of *pocks*, pl. of **POCK**.

**poxvirus** • n. Medicine any of a group of large DNA viruses that cause smallpox and similar infectious diseases.

**poxy** • adj. (**-ier**, **-iest**) informal, chiefly Brit. of poor quality; worthless.

**Pozidriv** /ˈpɒzɪdrʌɪv/ (US **Poz-i-Driv**) • n. trademark a type of cross-head screwdriver with a smaller ridge bisecting each quarter of the cross.

**pozzolana** /ˌpɒtsəˈlɑːnə/ • n. a type of volcanic ash used for mortar or for cement that sets under water.

– ORIGIN C18: from Ital., from *pozz(u)olana* '(earth) of *Pozzuoli*', a town near Naples.

**pp** • abbrev. **1** (**pp.**) pages. **2** (also **p.p.**) per procurationem (used when signing a letter on someone else's behalf). [L. 'through the agency of'.] **3** Music pianissimo.

**PPARC** • abbrev. (in the UK) Particle Physics and Astronomy Research Council.

**PPE** • abbrev. philosophy, politics, and economics.

**ppi** ● **abbrev.** Computing pixels per inch.

**ppm** ● **abbrev.** **1** part(s) per million. **2** Computing page(s) per minute.

**PPP** ● **abbrev.** **1** Pakistan People's Party. **2** (in computing) point to point protocol. **3** purchasing power parity.

**PPS** ● **abbrev.** **1** post (additional) postscript. **2** Brit. Parliamentary Private Secretary.

**PPU** ● **abbrev.** Peace Pledge Union.

**PPV** ● **abbrev.** pay-per-view.

**PQ** ● **abbrev.** **1** Parti Québécois. **2** Province of Quebec.

**PR** ● **abbrev.** **1** proportional representation. **2** public relations. **3** N. Amer. Puerto Rico.

**Pr** ● **symb.** the chemical element praseodymium.

**pr** ● **abbrev.** **1** pair. **2** archaic per.

**PRA** ● **abbrev.** progressive retinal atrophy.

**practicable** ● **adj.** **1** able to be done or put into practice successfully. **2** useful.
– DERIVATIVES **practicability** n. **practicably** adv.

**practical** ● **adj.** **1** of or concerned with practice. **2** likely to be effective in real circumstances; feasible. ➤ suitable for a particular purpose. **3** (of a person) realistic in approach. ➤ (of a person) skilled at manual tasks. **4** so nearly the case that it can be regarded as so; virtual. ● **n.** Brit. an examination or lesson involving the practical application of theories and procedures.
– DERIVATIVES **practicality** n.
– ORIGIN C16: from archaic *practic* 'practical' (from OFr. *practique*, via late L. from Gk *praktikos* 'concerned with action') + **-AL**.

**practicality** ● **n.** (pl. **-ies**) **1** the quality or state of being practical. **2** (**practicalities**) the aspects of a situation that involve the actual doing or experience of something rather than theories or ideas.

**practical joke** ● **n.** a trick played on someone in order to make them look foolish and to amuse others.
– DERIVATIVES **practical joker** n.

**practically** ● **adv.** **1** in a practical manner. ➤ in practical terms. **2** virtually; almost.

**practical nurse** ● **n.** (in North America) a nurse who has completed a training course of a lower standard than that of a registered nurse.

**practice** ● **n.** **1** the actual application or use of a plan or method, as opposed to the theories relating to it. **2** the customary or expected procedure or way of doing something. **3** the practising of a profession. ➤ the business or premises of a doctor or lawyer. **4** the action or process of practising. ● **v.** US spelling of **PRACTISE**.
– PHRASES **in** (or **out of**) **practice** having (or not having) practised an activity or skill on a regular basis.
– ORIGIN ME: from **PRACTISE**, on the pattern of pairs such as *advise, advice*.

**practician** ● **n.** archaic a practitioner.

**practicum** /ˈpraktɪkəm/ ● **n.** (pl. **practicums**) chiefly N. Amer. a practical section of a course of study.
– ORIGIN C20: from late L., neut. of *practicus* 'practical'.

**practise** (US **practice**) ● **v.** **1** perform (an activity) or exercise (a skill) repeatedly or regularly in order to acquire, maintain, or improve proficiency in it. **2** carry out or perform (an activity or custom) habitually or regularly. **3** be engaged in (a particular profession). **4** observe the teaching and rules of (a particular religion). **5** archaic scheme or plot for an evil purpose.
– DERIVATIVES **practised** adj. **practiser** n.
– ORIGIN ME: from OFr. *practiser* or med. L. *practizare*, alt. of *practicare* 'perform, carry out', from *practica* 'practice', from Gk *praktikē*, from *praktikos* (see **PRACTICAL**).

**practitioner** ● **n.** a person actively engaged in an art, discipline, or profession, especially medicine.
– ORIGIN C16: extension of obs. *practitian*, var. of **PRACTICIAN**.

**Prader–Willi syndrome** /ˌprɑːdəˈvɪli/ ● **n.** a rare congenital disorder characterized by mental handicap, growth abnormalities, and obsessive eating.
– ORIGIN 1960s: named after the Swiss paediatricians Andrea *Prader* and Heinrich *Willi*.

**prae-** ● **prefix** (especially in words regarded as Latin or relating to Roman antiquity) equivalent to **PRE-**.
– ORIGIN from L.

**praecipe** /ˈpriːsɪpi/ ● **n.** Law an order requesting a writ or other legal document.
– ORIGIN L. (the first word of the writ), imper. of *praecipere* 'enjoin, command'.

**praemunire** /ˌpriːmjuːˈnɪəri/ ● **n.** historical a writ charging a sheriff to summon a person accused of asserting or maintaining papal jurisdiction in England.
– ORIGIN ME: from med. L., 'forewarn', from L. *praemonere*, from *prae* 'beforehand' + *monere* 'warn'.

**praenomen** /priːˈnəʊmɛn/ ● **n.** the first or personal name given to a citizen of ancient Rome.
– ORIGIN L., from *prae* 'before' + *nomen* 'name'.

**praepostor** /prɪˈpɒstə/ (also **prepostor**) ● **n.** Brit. (at some public schools) a prefect or monitor.
– ORIGIN C18: from *praepositor*, alt. of L. *praepositus* 'head, chief'.

**praesidium** ● **n.** variant spelling of **PRESIDIUM**.

**praetor** /ˈpriːtə, -tɔː/ (US also **pretor**) ● **n.** each of two ancient Roman magistrates ranking below consul.
– DERIVATIVES **praetorial** adj. **praetorian** adj. & n. **praetorship** n.
– ORIGIN from L. *praetor*, perh. from *prae* 'before' + *it-*, *ire* 'go'.

**praetorian guard** ● **n.** (in ancient Rome) the bodyguard of the emperor.

**pragmatic** ● **adj.** **1** dealing with things in a way that is based on practical rather than theoretical considerations. **2** relating to philosophical or political pragmatism. **3** Linguistics of or relating to pragmatics.
– DERIVATIVES **pragmatically** adv.
– ORIGIN C16 (in the senses 'busy, interfering, conceited'): via L. from Gk *pragmatikos* 'relating to fact'.

**pragmatics** ● **pl. n.** [usu. treated as sing.] the branch of linguistics concerned with language in use and the contexts in which it is used.

**pragmatic sanction** ● **n.** historical an imperial or royal ordinance that has the force of law.
– ORIGIN translating Law L. *pragmatica sanctio*.

**pragmatism** ● **n.** **1** a pragmatic attitude or policy. **2** Philosophy an approach that evaluates theories or beliefs in terms of the success of their practical application.
– DERIVATIVES **pragmatist** n. **pragmatistic** adj.

**prahu** /ˈprɑːuː/ ● **n.** variant spelling of **PROA**.

**prairie** ● **n.** (in North America) a large open area of grassland.
– ORIGIN C18: from Fr., from OFr. *praerie*, from L. *pratum* 'meadow'.

**prairie chicken** (also **prairie hen**) ● **n.** a large North American grouse found on the prairies. [Genus *Tympanuchus*: two species.]

**prairie dog** ● **n.** a gregarious ground squirrel that lives in interconnected burrows, native to the grasslands of North America. [Genus *Cynomys*: several species.]

**prairie oyster** ● **n.** **1** a drink made with a raw egg and seasoning, drunk as a cure for a hangover. **2** (**prairie oysters**) chiefly N. Amer. the testicles of a calf cooked and served as food.

**prairie schooner** ● **n.** N. Amer. a covered wagon used by the 19th-century pioneers in crossing the prairies.

**praise** ● **v.** **1** express warm approval of or admiration for. **2** express respect and gratitude towards (a deity). ● **n.** **1** the expression of approval or admiration. **2** the expression of respect and gratitude as an act of worship.
– PHRASES **praise be** expressing relief, joy, or gratitude.
– DERIVATIVES **praiseful** adj.
– ORIGIN ME (also in the sense 'attach value to'): from OFr. *preisier* 'to prize, praise', from late L. *pretiare*, from L. *pretium* 'price'; cf. **PRIZE**[1].

**praiseworthy** ● **adj.** deserving of praise.
– DERIVATIVES **praiseworthily** adv. **praiseworthiness** n.

**prajna** /ˈpraʒnə/ ● **n.** Buddhism direct insight into the truth taught by the Buddha, as a faculty required to attain enlightenment.
– ORIGIN from Sanskrit *prajñā*.

**Prakrit** /ˈprɑːkrɪt/ ● **n.** any of the ancient or medieval vernacular dialects of north and central India which existed

alongside or were derived from Sanskrit.
– ORIGIN from Sanskrit *prākṛta* 'unrefined, natural'.

**praline** /'prɑːliːn/ ● **n.** a sweet substance made by boiling nuts in sugar and grinding the mixture, used especially as a filling for chocolates.
– ORIGIN C18: from Fr., named after Marshal de Plessis-*Praslin*, the Fr. soldier whose cook invented it.

**pralltriller** /'pral,trɪlə/ ● **n.** Music an ornament consisting of one rapid alternation of the written note with the note immediately above it.
– ORIGIN C19: from Ger., from *prallen* 'rebound' + *Triller* 'a trill'.

**pram**[1] /pram/ ● **n.** Brit. a four-wheeled carriage for a baby, pushed by a person on foot.
– ORIGIN C19: contr. of **PERAMBULATOR**.

**pram**[2] /prɑːm, pram/ ● **n.** a flat-bottomed boat.
– ORIGIN ME: from MDu. *prame*, Mid. Low Ger. *prāme*, perh. from Czech *prám* 'raft'.

**prana** /'prɑːnə/ ● **n.** Hinduism breath, considered as a life-giving force.
– ORIGIN from Sanskrit.

**pranayama** /,prɑːnʌ'jɑːmɑː/ ● **n.** (in yoga) the regulation of the breath through certain techniques and exercises.
– ORIGIN Sanskrit, from *prāṇa* 'breath' + *āyāma* 'restraint'.

**prance** ● **v. 1** (of a horse) move with high springy steps. **2** (of a person) walk or move around with ostentatious, exaggerated movements. ● **n.** an act of prancing.
– DERIVATIVES **prancer** n.
– ORIGIN ME: of unknown origin.

**prandial** /'prandɪəl/ ● **adj.** during or relating to a meal.
– ORIGIN C19: from L. *prandium* 'meal' + **-AL**.

**prang** Brit. informal ● **v.** crash (a motor vehicle or aircraft). ➤ strike against. ● **n.** an act of pranging something; a collision or crash.
– ORIGIN 1940s: imitative.

**prank** ● **n.** a practical joke or mischievous act.
– DERIVATIVES **prankish** adj. **prankishness** n.
– ORIGIN C16: of unknown origin.

**prankster** ● **n.** a person fond of playing pranks.

**prase** /preɪz/ ● **n.** a translucent greenish variety of quartz.
– ORIGIN C18: from Fr., via L. from Gk *prasios* 'leek-green', from *prason* 'leek'.

**praseodymium** /,preɪzɪə(ʊ)'dɪmɪəm/ ● **n.** the chemical element of atomic number 59, a soft silvery-white metal of the lanthanide series. (Symbol: **Pr**)
– ORIGIN C19: mod. L., from Ger. *Praseodym*, from Gk *prasios* 'leek-green' (because of its green salts) + Ger. *Didym* 'didymium'.

**prat** ● **n.** informal **1** Brit. an incompetent or stupid person. **2** a person's buttocks.
– ORIGIN C16: of unknown origin.

**prate** ● **v.** talk foolishly or at tedious length.
– ORIGIN ME: from MDu., Mid. Low Ger. *praten*, prob. of imitative origin.

**pratfall** ● **n.** informal a fall on to one's buttocks.

**pratie** /'preɪti/ ● **n.** chiefly Irish a potato.
– ORIGIN C18: from Ir. *prátaí*, pl. of *práta*.

**pratincole** /'pratɪŋkəʊl/ ● **n.** a long-winged fork-tailed insectivorous bird related to the plovers. [*Glareola pratincola* (Africa and the Mediterranean) and other species.]
– ORIGIN C18: from mod. L. *pratincola*, from L. *pratum* 'meadow' + *incola* 'inhabitant'.

**pratique** /'pratiːk/ ● **n.** historical permission granted to a ship to have dealings at a port.
– ORIGIN C17: from Fr., lit. 'practice', via Ital. from med. L. *practica*, fem. of *practicus* 'practical'.

**prattle** ● **v.** talk at length in a foolish or inconsequential way. ● **n.** foolish or inconsequential talk.
– DERIVATIVES **prattler** n.
– ORIGIN C16: from Mid. Low Ger. *pratelen*, from *praten* (see **PRATE**).

**prau** ● **n.** variant spelling of **PROA**.

**prawn** ● **n.** a marine crustacean which resembles a large shrimp. [*Leander* and other genera.]
– ORIGIN ME: of unknown origin.

**prawn cracker** ● **n.** (in Chinese cooking) a light prawn-flavoured crisp made from rice or tapioca flour, which puffs up when deep-fried.

**praxis** /'praksɪs/ ● **n. 1** practice, as distinguished from theory. **2** custom.
– ORIGIN C16: via med. L. from Gk, lit. 'doing', from *prattein* 'do'.

**pray** ● **v. 1** address a prayer to God or another deity. **2** wish or hope earnestly for a particular outcome. ● **adv.** formal or archaic used in polite requests or questions: *pray continue*.
– ORIGIN ME: from OFr. *preier*, from late L. *precare*, alt. of L. *precari* 'entreat'.

**prayer** /prɛː/ ● **n. 1** a solemn request for help or expression of thanks addressed to God or another deity. **2** (**prayers**) a religious service at which people gather to pray together. **3** an earnest hope or wish.
– PHRASES **not have a prayer** informal have no chance.
– ORIGIN ME: from OFr. *preiere*, based on L. *precarius* 'obtained by entreaty', from *prex*, *prec-* 'prayer'.

**prayerful** ● **adj. 1** characterized by the use of prayer. **2** given to praying; devout.
– DERIVATIVES **prayerfully** adv. **prayerfulness** n.

**prayer plant** ● **n.** a Brazilian plant with variegated leaves which are erect at night but lie flat during the day, grown as a house plant. [*Maranta leuconeura*.]

**prayer shawl** ● **n.** Judaism another term for **TALLITH**.

**prayer wheel** ● **n.** a small revolving cylinder inscribed with or containing prayers, a revolution of which symbolizes the repetition of a prayer, used by Tibetan Buddhists.

**praying mantis** ● **n.** see **MANTIS**.

**pre-** ● **prefix** before (in time, place, order, degree, or importance): *pre-adolescent*.
– ORIGIN from L. *prae-*.

**preach** ● **v. 1** deliver a religious address to an assembled group of people. ➤ publicly proclaim (a religious message). **2** earnestly advocate (a principle): *my parents always preached tolerance*. ➤ (**preach at**) give moral advice to (someone) in a self-righteous way.
– DERIVATIVES **preacher** n. **preachiness** n. **preachy** adj. (**-ier**, **-iest**).
– ORIGIN ME: from OFr. *prechier*, from L. *praedicare* 'proclaim', in eccles. L. 'preach'.

**preachify** ● **v.** (**-ies**, **-ied**) informal preach or moralize tediously.

**preachment** ● **n.** dogmatic instruction and exhortation.

**preamble** /priː'amb(ə)l, 'priː-/ ● **n.** a preliminary statement; an introduction.
– DERIVATIVES **preambular** adj.
– ORIGIN ME: from OFr. *preambule*, from med. L. *praeambulum*, from late L. *praeambulus* 'going before'.

**preamp** ● **n.** short for **PREAMPLIFIER**.

**preamplifier** ● **n.** an electronic device that amplifies a very weak signal and transmits it to a main amplifier.

**pre-arrange** ● **v.** arrange or agree in advance.
– DERIVATIVES **pre-arrangement** n.

**Preb.** ● **abbrev.** Prebendary.

**prebend** /'prɛb(ə)nd/ ● **n.** historical **1** the portion of the revenues of a cathedral or collegiate church formerly granted to a canon or member of the chapter as his stipend. ➤ the property from which such a stipend was derived. **2** another term for **PREBENDARY**.
– DERIVATIVES **prebendal** adj.
– ORIGIN ME: from OFr. *prebende*, from late L. *praebenda* 'things to be supplied, pension', neut. pl. gerundive of L. *praebere* 'to grant'.

**prebendary** /'prɛb(ə)nd(ə)ri/ ● **n.** (pl. **-ies**) **1** an honorary canon. **2** historical a canon whose income came from a prebend.
– DERIVATIVES **prebendaryship** n.

**prebiotic** ● **adj.** existing or occurring before the emergence of life.

**Preboreal** /priː'bɔːrɪəl/ ● **adj.** Geology relating to or denoting the first climatic stage of the postglacial period in northern Europe (about 10,000 to 9,000 years ago).

**prebuttal** ● **n.** (in politics) a response formulated in anticipation of a criticism; a pre-emptive rebuttal.

**Precambrian** /priːˈkambrɪən/ ● **adj.** Geology relating to or denoting the earliest aeon of the earth's history, preceding the Cambrian period and ending about 570 million years ago (comprising the Archaean and Proterozoic aeons).

**precancerous** ● **adj.** Medicine (of a cell or medical condition) likely to develop into cancer if untreated.

**precarious** ● **adj.** **1** not securely held or in position; likely to fall. **2** dependent on chance; uncertain.
– DERIVATIVES **precariously** adv. **precariousness** n.
– ORIGIN C17: from L. *precarius* 'obtained by entreaty' (from *prex*, *prec-* 'prayer') + **-ous**.

**precast** ● **v.** (past and past part. **precast**) [usu. as adj. **precast**] cast (an object or material, typically concrete) in its final shape before positioning.

**precatory** /ˈprɛkət(ə)ri/ ● **adj.** formal of, relating to, or expressing a wish or request. ➤ Law (in a will) expressing a wish or intention of the testator.
– ORIGIN C17: from late L. *precatorius*, from *precat-*, *precari* 'pray'.

**precaution** ● **n.** **1** a measure taken in advance to prevent something undesirable from happening. **2** (**precautions**) informal contraception.
– DERIVATIVES **precautionary** adj.
– ORIGIN C16: from Fr. *précaution*, from late L. *praecautio(n-)*, from L. *praecavere*, from *prae* 'before' + *cavere* 'take heed, beware of'.

**precede** ● **v.** come or go before in time, order, or position. ➤ (**precede something with**) preface something with.
– DERIVATIVES **preceding** adj.
– ORIGIN ME: from OFr. *preceder*, from L. *praecedere*, from *prae* 'before' + *cedere* 'go'.

**precedence** /ˈprɛsɪd(ə)ns, ˈpriː-, prɪˈsiːd(ə)ns/ ● **n.** the condition of preceding others in importance, order, or rank. ➤ an acknowledged or legally determined right to such precedence.

**precedent** ● **n.** /ˈprɛsɪd(ə)nt/ an earlier event or action serving as an example or guide. ➤ Law a previous case or legal decision that may be or (**binding precedent**) must be followed in subsequent similar cases. ● **adj.** /prɪˈsiːd(ə)nt, ˈprɛsɪ-/ preceding in time, order, or importance.

**precentor** /prɪˈsɛntə/ ● **n.** **1** a person who leads a congregation in its singing or (in a synagogue) prayers. **2** a canon responsible for choral services in a cathedral.
– DERIVATIVES **precent** v. **precentorship** n.
– ORIGIN C17: from Fr. *précenteur* or L. *praecentor*, from *praecent-*, *praecinere* 'sing before'.

**precept** /ˈpriːsɛpt/ ● **n.** **1** a general rule regulating behaviour or thought. **2** a writ or warrant. **3** Brit. an order issued by one local authority to another specifying the rate of tax to be charged on its behalf. ➤ Brit. this rate, or the tax itself.
– DERIVATIVES **preceptive** adj.
– ORIGIN ME: from L. *praeceptum*, neut. past part. of *praecipere* 'warn, instruct'.

**preceptor** /prɪˈsɛptə/ ● **n.** a teacher or instructor.
– DERIVATIVES **preceptorial** /ˌpriːsɛpˈtɔːrɪəl/ adj. **preceptorship** n.

**precession** ● **n.** **1** Physics the slow movement of the axis of a spinning body around another axis. **2** Astronomy the slow retrograde motion of the equinoctial points along the ecliptic, resulting in the earlier occurrence of equinoxes each year.
– DERIVATIVES **precess** v. **precessional** adj.
– ORIGIN C16: from late L. *praecessio(n-)*, from *praecedere* (see **PRECEDE**).

**precinct** /ˈpriːsɪŋ(k)t/ ● **n.** **1** the area within the walls or perceived boundaries of a particular place. ➤ an enclosed or clearly defined area of ground around a cathedral, church, or college. ➤ Brit. an area in a town designated for specific or restricted use, especially one closed to traffic. **2** N. Amer. a district of a city or town as defined for policing or electoral purposes.
– ORIGIN ME: from med. L. *praecinctum*, neut. past part. of *praecingere* 'encircle'.

**preciosity** /ˌprɛʃɪˈɒsɪti/ ● **n.** over-refinement in language or art.

**precious** ● **adj.** **1** having great value. **2** greatly loved or treasured by someone. **3** informal, chiefly ironic considerable: *a precious lot you know!* **4** derogatory affectedly concerned with elegant or refined language or manners. ● **n.** a term of address to a beloved person.
– PHRASES **precious little** (or **few**) informal extremely little (or few).
– DERIVATIVES **preciously** adv. **preciousness** n.
– ORIGIN ME: from OFr. *precios*, from L. *pretiosus* 'of great value', from *pretium* 'price'.

**precious metals** ● **pl. n.** gold, silver, and platinum.

**precious stone** ● **n.** a highly attractive and valuable piece of mineral, used especially in jewellery.

**precipice** ● **n.** a tall and very steep rock face or cliff.
– ORIGIN C16 (denoting a headlong fall): from Fr. *précipice* or L. *praecipitium* 'abrupt descent', from *praeceps*, *praecip(it)-* 'steep, headlong'.

**precipitancy** ● **n.** rashness or suddenness of action.

**precipitant** ● **n.** **1** a cause of a particular action or event. ➤ chiefly Psychology a cause or stimulus which precipitates a particular condition. **2** Chemistry a substance that causes precipitation.
– DERIVATIVES **precipitance** n.

**precipitate** ● **v.** /prɪˈsɪpɪteɪt/ **1** cause (an undesirable event) to happen unexpectedly or prematurely. **2** cause to move suddenly and with force. ➤ (**precipitate someone/thing into**) send someone or something without warning into a particular state or condition. **3** Chemistry cause (a substance) to be deposited in solid form from a solution. ➤ cause (drops of moisture or particles of dust) to be deposited from the atmosphere or from a vapour or suspension. ● **adj.** /prɪˈsɪpɪtət/ done, acting, or occurring suddenly or without careful consideration. ● **n.** /prɪˈsɪpɪtət, -teɪt/ Chemistry a substance precipitated from a solution.
– DERIVATIVES **precipitable** adj. **precipitately** adv. **precipitateness** n.
– ORIGIN C16 (orig. 'hurl down, send violently', later 'cause to move rapidly': from L. *praecipitat-*, *praecipitare* 'throw headlong', from *praeceps*, *praecip(it)-* 'headlong', from *prae* 'before' + *caput* 'head'.

**precipitation** ● **n.** **1** Chemistry the action or process of precipitating a substance from a solution. **2** rain, snow, sleet, or hail that falls to or condenses on the ground. **3** archaic the fact or quality of acting precipitately.

**precipitator** ● **n.** an apparatus for causing precipitation, especially a device for removing dust from a gas.

**precipitin** /prɪˈsɪpɪtɪn/ ● **n.** Biochemistry an antibody that produces a visible precipitate when it reacts with its antigen.
– ORIGIN C20: from **PRECIPITATE** + **-IN**[1].

**precipitous** /prɪˈsɪpɪtəs/ ● **adj.** **1** dangerously high or steep. **2** (of a change) sudden and dramatic.
– DERIVATIVES **precipitously** adv. **precipitousness** n.
– ORIGIN C17: from obs. Fr. *précipiteux*, from L. *praeceps*, *praecip(it)-* (see **PRECIPITATE**).

**precis** /ˈpreɪsi/ ● **n.** (pl. same /-siːz/) a summary of a text or speech. ● **v.** (**precises** /-siːz/, **precised** /-siːd/, **precising** /-siːɪŋ/) make a precis of.
– ORIGIN C18: from Fr. *précis*, lit. 'precise'.

**precise** ● **adj.** marked by exactness and accuracy of expression or detail. ➤ (of a person) very attentive to detail; careful in the expression of detail. ➤ exact; particular (used for emphasis).
– DERIVATIVES **precisely** adv. **preciseness** n.
– ORIGIN ME: from OFr. *prescis*, from L. *praecis-*, *praecidere* 'cut short'.

**precisian** /prɪˈsɪʒ(ə)n/ ● **n.** chiefly archaic a person who is rigidly precise or punctilious.
– DERIVATIVES **precisianism** n.

**precision** ● **n.** **1** the quality, condition, or fact of being precise. **2** [as modifier] marked by or designed for accuracy and exactness: *a precision instrument.* **3** refinement in a measurement or specification, especially as represented by the number of digits given.

**preclinical** ● **adj.** Medicine relating to or denoting a stage preceding a clinical stage.

**preclude** ● **v.** prevent (something) from happening or (someone) from doing something.
– DERIVATIVES **preclusion** n. **preclusive** adj.
– ORIGIN C15: from L. *praecludere*, from *prae* 'before' + *claudere* 'to shut'.

**precocial** /prɪˈkəʊʃ(ə)l/ ● **adj.** Zoology relating to or denoting a bird or other animal species whose young are hatched or born in an advanced state and are able to feed themselves almost immediately. Often contrasted with **ALTRICIAL**.
– ORIGIN C19: from mod. L. *Praecoces* (the name of a former division of birds, pl. of L. *praecox* 'mature before its time') + **-IAL**.

**precocious** ● **adj.** **1** having developed certain abilities or inclinations at an earlier age than usual. **2** (of a plant) flowering or fruiting earlier than usual.
– DERIVATIVES **precociously** adv. **precociousness** n. **precocity** n.
– ORIGIN C17: from L. *praecox*, *praecoc-* (from *praecoquere* 'ripen fully', from *prae* 'before' + *coquere* 'to cook') + **-IOUS**.

**precognition** /ˌpriːkɒgˈnɪʃ(ə)n/ ● **n.** **1** foreknowledge. **2** Law, chiefly Scottish the preliminary examination of witnesses, especially to decide whether there is ground for a trial.
– DERIVATIVES **precognitive** adj.

**precoital** ● **adj.** occurring before sexual intercourse.
– DERIVATIVES **precoitally** adv.

**pre-Columbian** ● **adj.** of or relating to the history and cultures of the Americas before the arrival of Christopher Columbus in 1492.

**preconceived** ● **adj.** (of an idea or opinion) formed prior to having evidence for its truth or usefulness.
– DERIVATIVES **preconception** n.

**precondition** ● **n.** a condition that must be fulfilled before other things can happen or be done. ● **v.** **1** [often as noun **preconditioning**] prepare or condition (someone or something) to behave or react in a certain way under certain conditions. **2** bring into the desired state for use.

**preconscious** Psychology ● **adj.** of or associated with a part of the mind below the level of conscious awareness, from which memories and emotions that have not been repressed can be recalled. ● **n.** (**one's/the preconscious**) this part of the mind.
– DERIVATIVES **preconsciousness** n.

**precordium** /priːˈkɔːdɪəm/ ● **n.** Anatomy the region of the thorax immediately in front of or over the heart.
– DERIVATIVES **precordial** adj.
– ORIGIN C19: sing. of L. *praecordia* 'diaphragm, entrails'.

**precursor** ● **n.** **1** a person or thing that comes before another of the same kind. **2** a substance from which another is formed, especially by metabolic reaction.
– DERIVATIVES **precursory** adj.
– ORIGIN ME: from L. *praecursor*, from *praecurs-* 'preceded', from *praecurrere*, from *prae* 'beforehand' + *currere* 'to run'.

**predacious** /prɪˈdeɪʃəs/ (also **predaceous**) ● **adj.** (of an animal) predatory.
– DERIVATIVES **predaciousness** n. **predacity** n.
– ORIGIN C18: from L. *praeda* 'booty' + **-ACIOUS**.

**pre-date** ● **v.** exist or occur at a date earlier than.

**predation** /prɪˈdeɪʃ(ə)n/ ● **n.** Zoology the preying of one animal on others.
– DERIVATIVES **predate** v.
– ORIGIN C15 (in the L. sense): from L. *praedatio(n-)* 'taking of booty', from *praedari* 'seize as plunder', from *praeda* 'booty'.

**predator** ● **n.** **1** an animal that preys on others. **2** a person who exploits others. ➤a company that tries to take over another.
– DERIVATIVES **predatorily** adv. **predatoriness** n. **predatory** adj.

**predatory pricing** ● **n.** the pricing of goods or services at such a low level that other firms cannot compete and are forced to leave the market.

**predecease** formal ● **v.** die before (another person). ● **n.** a death preceding that of another person.

**predecessor** ● **n.** **1** a person who held a job or office before the current holder. **2** a thing that has been followed or replaced by another.
– ORIGIN ME: from late L. *praedecessor*, from L. *prae* 'beforehand' + *decessor* 'retiring officer'.

**predella** /prɪˈdɛlə/ ● **n.** a step or platform on which an altar is placed. ➤a raised shelf above an altar. ➤a painting or sculpture on this, typically forming an appendage to an altarpiece.
– ORIGIN C19: from Ital., lit. 'stool'.

**predestinarian** /prɪˌdɛstɪˈnɛːrɪən/ ● **n.** a person who believes in the doctrine of predestination. ● **adj.** upholding or relating to the doctrine of predestination.

**predestinate** ● **v.** /priːˈdɛstɪneɪt/ predestine. ● **adj.** /priːˈdɛstɪnət/ predestined.
– ORIGIN ME: from eccles. L. *praedestinat-*, *praedestinare* 'make firm beforehand', from *prae* 'in advance' + *destinare* 'establish'.

**predestination** ● **n.** (as a doctrine in Christian theology) the divine foreordaining of all that will happen, especially with regard to the salvation of some and not others, as in Calvinism.

**predestine** ● **v.** **1** (of God) destine (someone) for a particular fate or purpose. **2** determine (an outcome) in advance by divine will or fate.
– DERIVATIVES **predestined** adj.

**predetermine** ● **v.** establish or decide in advance. ➤predestine.
– DERIVATIVES **predeterminable** adj. **predeterminate** adj. **predetermination** n. **predetermined** adj.

**predeterminer** ● **n.** Grammar a word or phrase that occurs before a determiner, typically quantifying the noun phrase, for example *both* or *a lot of*.

**predial** /ˈpriːdɪəl/ ● **adj.** **1** archaic agrarian. ➤historical (of a tithe) consisting of agricultural produce. **2** historical relating to or denoting a slave or tenant attached to farms or the land. ● **n.** historical a predial slave.
– ORIGIN ME: from med. L. *praedialis*, from L. *praedium* 'farm'.

**predicable** /ˈprɛdɪkəb(ə)l/ ● **adj.** that may be predicated or affirmed. ● **n.** **1** a thing that is predicable. **2** (in Aristotelian logic) each of the classes to which predicates belong: genus, species, difference, property, and accident.
– DERIVATIVES **predicability** n.

**predicament** ● **n.** **1** a difficult situation. **2** Philosophy each of the ten categories in Aristotelian logic.
– ORIGIN ME (orig. in sense 'category', later 'state of being', hence 'difficult situation'): from late L. *praedicamentum* 'something predicated' (rendering Gk *katēgoria* 'category'), from L. *praedicare* (see **PREDICATE**).

**predicant** /ˈprɛdɪk(ə)nt/ ● **adj.** archaic (especially of the religious order of the Dominicans) characterized by preaching. ● **n.** **1** archaic a preacher, especially a Dominican friar. **2** S. African variant spelling of **PREDIKANT**.
– ORIGIN C16: from L. *praedicant-* 'declaring', from *praedicare*, in eccles. L. meaning 'preach'.

**predicate** ● **n.** /ˈprɛdɪkət/ **1** Grammar the part of a sentence or clause containing a verb and stating something about the subject (e.g. *went home* in *John went home*). **2** Logic something which is affirmed or denied concerning an argument of a proposition. ● **v.** /ˈprɛdɪkeɪt/ **1** Grammar & Logic state, affirm, or assert (something) about the subject of a sentence or an argument of proposition. **2** (**predicate something on/upon**) found or base something on.
– DERIVATIVES **predication** n.
– ORIGIN ME: from L. *praedicatum* 'something declared', neut. of *praedicatus*, from *praedicare*, from *prae* 'beforehand' + *dicare* 'make known'.

**predicate calculus** ● **n.** the branch of symbolic logic concerned with propositions containing predicates, names, and quantifiers.

**predicative** /prɪˈdɪkətɪv/ ● **adj.** **1** Grammar (of an adjective or other modifier) forming or contained in the predicate, as *old* in *the dog is old* (but not in *the old dog*). Contrasted with **ATTRIBUTIVE**. ➤denoting a use of the verb *to be* to

assert something about the subject. **2** Logic acting as a predicate.
– DERIVATIVES **predicatively** adv.

**predict** ● v. state that (a specified event) will happen in the future.
– DERIVATIVES **prediction** n. **predictive** adj. **predictively** adv. **predictor** n.
– ORIGIN C17: from L. *praedict-*, *praedicere* 'make known beforehand, declare', from *prae-* 'beforehand' + *dicere* 'say'.

**predictable** ● adj. able to be predicted. ➤ derogatory always behaving or occurring in the way expected.
– DERIVATIVES **predictability** n. **predictably** adv.

**predigest** ● v. **1** treat (food) so as to make it more easily digestible when eaten. **2** simplify (information) so that it is easier to absorb.
– DERIVATIVES **predigestion** n.

**predikant** /ˌprɛdɪˈkant, ˌprɪədə-/ (also **predicant**) ● n. S. African a minister of the Dutch Reformed Church.
– ORIGIN Du., from eccles. L. *praedicare* 'preach'.

**predilection** /ˌpriːdɪˈlɛkʃ(ə)n/ ● n. a preference or special liking for something.
– ORIGIN C18: from Fr. *prédilection*, from L. *praedilect-*, *praediligere* 'prefer', from *prae* 'in advance' + *diligere* 'to select'.

**predispose** ● v. make liable or inclined to a specified attitude, action, or condition.
– DERIVATIVES **predisposition** n.

**prednisolone** /prɛdˈnɪsələʊn/ ● n. Medicine a synthetic steroid resembling prednisone, of which it is a reduced derivative.
– ORIGIN 1950s: from PREDNISONE, with the insertion of -OL.

**prednisone** /ˈprɛdnɪzəʊn/ ● n. Medicine a synthetic drug similar to cortisone, used to relieve rheumatic and allergic conditions and to treat leukaemia.
– ORIGIN 1950s: perh. from *pre(gnane)* (a synthetic hydrocarbon) + *d(ie)n(e)* + *(cort)isone*.

**predominant** ● adj. present as the strongest or main element. ➤ having or exerting the greatest control or power.
– DERIVATIVES **predominance** n. **predominantly** adv.

**predominate** ● v. be the strongest or main element. ➤ have or exert control or power.

**predominately** ● adv. mainly; for the most part.

**predynastic** /ˌpriːdɪˈnastɪk, -dʌɪ-/ ● adj. relating to or denoting a period before the normally recognized dynasties, especially in ancient Egypt before about 3000 BC.

**pre-echo** ● n. (pl. **-oes**) **1** a faint copy heard just before an actual sound in a recording, caused by the accidental transfer of signals. **2** a foreshadowing. ● v. foreshadow.

**pre-eclampsia** ● n. a condition in pregnancy characterized by high blood pressure, sometimes with fluid retention and proteinuria.
– DERIVATIVES **pre-eclamptic** adj. & n.

**pre-embryo** ● n. a fertilized ovum in the first fourteen days after fertilization, before implantation in the womb.
– DERIVATIVES **pre-embryonic** adj.

**preemie** /ˈpriːmi/ ● n. (pl. **-ies**) N. Amer. informal a baby born prematurely.

**pre-eminent** ● adj. surpassing all others.
– DERIVATIVES **pre-eminence** n. **pre-eminently** adv.

**pre-empt** ● v. **1** take action in order to prevent (an attack or other anticipated event) happening; forestall. **2** acquire or appropriate in advance. ➤ N. Amer. acquire by pre-emption. **3** Bridge make a high opening bid in order to prevent the opponents from bidding effectively.
– DERIVATIVES **pre-emptive** adj. **pre-emptor** n.

**pre-emption** ● n. **1** the purchase of goods or shares by one person or party before the opportunity is offered to others. ➤ historical, chiefly N. Amer. & Austral./NZ the right to purchase public land in this way. **2** the action of pre-empting or forestalling.
– ORIGIN C17: from med. L. *praeemptio(n-)*, from *praeemere* (v.), from *prae* 'in advance' + *emere* 'buy'.

**preen** ● v. **1** (of a bird) tidy and clean its feathers with its beak. **2** (of a person) devote effort to making oneself look attractive. **3** (**preen oneself**) congratulate or pride oneself.
– DERIVATIVES **preener** n.
– ORIGIN ME: appar. a var. of obs. *prune* (based on L. *ungere* 'anoint'), in the same sense, assoc. with Scots and north. Engl. dial. *preen* 'pierce, pin' (because of the 'pricking' action of the bird's beak).

**preen gland** ● n. Ornithology a gland at the base of a bird's tail which produces the oil used in preening.

**pre-establish** ● v. establish in advance.

**pre-exist** ● v. [usu. as adj. **pre-existing**] exist at or from an earlier time. ➤ exist before.
– DERIVATIVES **pre-existence** n. **pre-existent** adj.

**pref.** ● abbrev. **1** preface. **2** (with reference to shares) preference or preferred.

**prefab** ● n. informal a prefabricated building.

**prefabricate** ● v. [usu. as adj. **prefabricated**] manufacture sections of (a building, piece of furniture, etc.) to enable easy assembly on site.
– DERIVATIVES **prefabrication** n.

**preface** /ˈprɛfəs/ ● n. **1** an introduction to a book, typically stating its subject, scope, or aims. **2** Christian Church the introduction to the central part of the Eucharist. ● v. **1** provide with a preface. **2** (**preface something with/by**) introduce or begin a speech or event with or by doing something.
– DERIVATIVES **prefatory** /ˈprɛfət(ə)ri/ adj.
– ORIGIN ME: via OFr. from med. L. *praefatia*, alt. of L. *praefatio(n-)* 'words spoken beforehand', from *praefari* (v.), from *prae* 'before' + *fari* 'speak'.

**prefect** ● n. **1** chiefly Brit. a senior pupil authorized to enforce discipline in a school. **2** a chief officer, magistrate, or regional governor in certain countries. ➤ a senior magistrate or governor in the ancient Roman world.
– DERIVATIVES **prefectoral** adj. **prefectorial** adj.
– ORIGIN ME: from OFr., from L. *praefectus*, *praeficere* 'set in authority over', from *prae* 'before' + *facere* 'make'.

**prefecture** ● n. a district under the government of a prefect. ➤ a prefect's office or tenure. ➤ a prefect's official residence.
– DERIVATIVES **prefectural** adj.

**prefer** ● v. (**preferred**, **preferring**) **1** like (someone or something) better than another or others; tend to choose. **2** formal submit (a charge or information) for consideration. **3** archaic promote to a prestigious position.
– ORIGIN ME: from OFr. *preferer*, from L. *praeferre*, from *prae* 'before' + *ferre* 'to bear, carry'.

**preferable** ● adj. more desirable or suitable.
– DERIVATIVES **preferability** n. **preferably** adv.

**preference** ● n. **1** a greater liking for one alternative over another or others. ➤ a thing preferred. ➤ favour shown to one person over another or others. **2** Law a prior right, especially in connection with the payment of debts.

**preference share** (or **stock**) (N. Amer. **preferred share** or **stock**) ● n. a share which entitles the holder to a fixed dividend whose payment takes priority over that of ordinary share dividends.

**preferential** ● adj. **1** of or involving preference or partiality. **2** (of a creditor) having a claim for repayment which will be met before those of other creditors.
– DERIVATIVES **preferentially** adv.

**preferment** ● n. promotion or appointment to a position or office.

**preferred share** ● n. US term for PREFERENCE SHARE.

**prefetch** /priːˈfɛtʃ/ ● v. Computing transfer (data) from main memory to temporary storage in readiness for later use.

**prefigure** ● v. **1** be an early indication or version of. **2** archaic imagine beforehand.
– DERIVATIVES **prefiguration** n. **prefigurative** adj. **prefigurement** n.
– ORIGIN ME: from eccles. L. *praefigurare* 'represent beforehand', from *prae* 'before' + *figurare* 'to form, fashion'.

**prefix** ● n. a word, letter, or number placed before another. ➤ an element placed at the beginning of a word to

adjust or qualify its meaning (e.g. *ex-*, *non-*, *re-*) or (in some languages) as an inflection. ➤ a title placed before a name (e.g. *Mr*). ● v. add as a prefix or introduction. ➤ add a prefix or introduction to.
– DERIVATIVES **prefixation** n.
– ORIGIN C16 (as v.): from OFr. *prefixer*, from L. *praefixus*, *praefigere* 'fix in front', from *prae* 'before' + *figere* 'to fix'; the noun is from mod. L. *praefixum*, neut. of *praefixus*.

**preform** ● v. [usu. as adj. **preformed**] form beforehand.
– DERIVATIVES **preformation** n.

**prefrontal** ● adj. **1** Anatomy in or relating to the foremost part of the frontal lobe of the brain. **2** Zoology relating to or denoting a bone in front of the eye socket in some lower vertebrates.

**pregenital** ● adj. **1** Psychoanalysis relating to psychosexual development before the genital phase. **2** Zoology situated in front of the genital region.

**preggers** ● adj. informal pregnant.

**preglacial** ● adj. before a glacial period.

**pregnable** ● adj. vulnerable to attack.
– ORIGIN ME: from OFr. *prenable*, from L. *prehendere* 'seize'.

**pregnancy** ● n. (pl. **-ies**) the condition or period of being pregnant.

**pregnant** ● adj. **1** (of a woman or female animal) having a child or young developing in the uterus. **2** full of meaning or significance.
– DERIVATIVES **pregnantly** adv.
– ORIGIN ME: from L. *praegnant-*, prob. from *prae* 'before' + the base of *gnasci* 'be born'.

**preheat** ● v. heat beforehand.

**prehensile** /prɪˈhɛnsʌɪl/ ● adj. (chiefly of an animal's limb or tail) capable of grasping.
– DERIVATIVES **prehensility** n.
– ORIGIN C18: from Fr. *préhensile*, from L. *prehens-*, *prehendere* 'grasp', from *prae* 'before' + *hendere* 'to grasp'.

**prehension** ● n. **1** Zoology & Psychology the action of grasping or seizing. **2** Philosophy an interaction of a subject with an event or entity which involves perception but not necessarily cognition.
– ORIGIN C19: from L. *prehensio(n-)*, from *prehendere* 'to grasp'.

**prehistoric** ● adj. of or relating to prehistory. ➤ informal very old or out of date.
– DERIVATIVES **prehistorically** adv.

**prehistory** ● n. **1** the period of time before written records. **2** the events or conditions leading up to a particular phenomenon.
– DERIVATIVES **prehistorian** n.

**prehuman** ● adj. relating to or denoting the time before the appearance of human beings. ● n. a precursor of the human species.

**pre-ignition** ● n. premature combustion of the fuel–air mixture in an internal-combustion engine.

**pre-industrial** ● adj. before industrialization.

**prejudge** ● v. form a judgement on (an issue or person) prematurely and without having adequate information.
– DERIVATIVES **prejudgement** (also **prejudgment**) n.

**prejudice** ● n. **1** preconceived opinion that is not based on reason or actual experience. ➤ unjust behaviour formed on such a basis. **2** chiefly Law harm or injury that results or may result from some action or judgement. ● v. **1** give rise to prejudice in (someone); make biased. **2** chiefly Law cause harm to (a state of affairs).
– PHRASES **without prejudice** Law without detriment to any existing right or claim.
– DERIVATIVES **prejudiced** adj.
– ORIGIN ME: from OFr., from L. *praejudicium*, from *prae* 'in advance' + *judicium* 'judgement'.

**prejudicial** ● adj. harmful to someone or something; detrimental.
– DERIVATIVES **prejudicially** adv.

**prelacy** /ˈprɛləsi/ ● n. (pl. **-ies**) the government of the Christian Church by prelates. ➤ the office or rank of a prelate.
– ORIGIN ME: from Anglo-Norman Fr. *prelacie*, from med. L. *prelatia*, from *praelatus* (see **PRELATE**).

**prelapsarian** /ˌpriːlapˈsɛːrɪən/ ● adj. Theology or poetic/literary before the Fall of Man; innocent and unspoilt.
– ORIGIN C19: from **PRE-** + L. *lapsus*, from *labi* 'to fall'.

**prelate** /ˈprɛlət/ ● n. formal or historical a bishop or other high ecclesiastical dignitary.
– DERIVATIVES **prelatic** /prɪˈlatɪk/ adj. **prelatical** /prɪˈlatɪk(ə)l/ adj.
– ORIGIN ME: from OFr. *prelat*, from med. L. *praelatus* 'civil dignitary', past part. (used as n.) of L. *praeferre* 'carry before', also 'place before in esteem'.

**prelature** ● n. **1** the office, rank, or sphere of authority of a prelate. **2** prelates collectively.
– ORIGIN C17: from Fr. *prélature*, from med. L. *praelatura*, from *praelatus* (see **PRELATE**).

**prelim** /ˈpriːlɪm, prɪˈlɪm/ ● n. informal **1** a preliminary examination. **2** a preliminary round in a sporting competition. **3** (**prelims**) the pages preceding the main text of a book, including the title, contents, and preface.
– ORIGIN C19: abbrev.

**preliminary** ● adj. preceding or done in preparation for something fuller or more important. ● n. (pl. **-ies**) **1** a preliminary action or event. **2** a preliminary round in a sporting competition. **3** (**preliminaries**) fuller form of *prelims* (see **PRELIM** (sense 3)).
– PHRASES **preliminary to** preparatory to; in advance of.
– DERIVATIVES **preliminarily** adv.
– ORIGIN C17: from mod. L. *praeliminaris* or Fr. *préliminaire*, from L. *prae* 'before' + *limen*, *limin-* 'threshold'.

**prelinguistic** ● adj. of or at a stage before the development of language or the acquisition of speech.

**preliterate** ● adj. relating to or denoting a society or culture that has not developed the use of writing.

**pre-loved** ● adj. informal second-hand.

**prelude** /ˈprɛljuːd/ ● n. **1** an action or event serving as an introduction to something more important. **2** a piece of music serving as an introduction, e.g. to an act of an opera or to a suite or a fugue. **3** the introductory part of a poem or other literary work. ● v. serve as a prelude or introduction to.
– DERIVATIVES **preludial** adj.
– ORIGIN C16: from Fr. *prélude*, from med. L. *praeludium*, from L. *praeludere* 'play beforehand'.

**premarital** ● adj. occurring or existing before marriage.
– DERIVATIVES **premaritally** adv.

**premature** ● adj. **1** occurring or done before the proper time. **2** (of a baby) born before the end of the full term of gestation, especially three or more weeks before.
– DERIVATIVES **prematurely** adv. **prematurity** n.
– ORIGIN ME: from L. *praematurus* 'very early', from *prae* 'before' + *maturus* 'ripe'.

**premaxillary** ● adj. Anatomy situated in front of the maxilla.

**pre-med** ● n. **1** chiefly N. Amer. a premedical student or course of study. **2** short for **PRE-MEDICATION**.

**premedical** ● adj. of, relating to, or engaged in study in preparation for medical school.

**pre-medication** ● n. medication given in preparation for an operation or other treatment.

**premeditate** ● v. [usu. as adj. **premeditated**] think out or plan (an action, especially a crime) beforehand.
– DERIVATIVES **premeditation** n.
– ORIGIN C16 (earlier (ME) as *premeditation*): from L. *praemeditat-*, *praemeditari*, from *prae* 'before' + *meditari* 'meditate'.

**premenopausal** /priːˌmɛnəˈpɔːz(ə)l/ ● adj. closely preceding the menopause.

**premenstrual** /priːˈmɛnstrʊəl/ ● adj. of, occurring, or experienced before menstruation.
– DERIVATIVES **premenstrually** adv.

**premenstrual syndrome** ● n. a complex of symptoms (including emotional tension and fluid retention) experienced by some women prior to menstruation.

**premier** /ˈprɛmɪə, ˈpriː-/ ● adj. first in importance, order, or position. ➤ of earliest creation. ● n. a Prime Minister or other head of government. ➤ (in Australia and Can-

ada) the chief minister of a government of a state or province.
– DERIVATIVES **premiership** n.
– ORIGIN C15: from OFr., 'first', from L. *primarius* 'principal'.

**premier cru** /ˌprɛmɪə 'kruː, French prəmje kry/ ● n. (pl. **premiers crus** pronunc. same) (chiefly in France) a wine of a superior grade. Compare with **GRAND CRU**.
– ORIGIN Fr., lit. 'first growth'.

**premiere** /'prɛmɪɛː/ ● n. the first performance of a musical or theatrical work or the first showing of a film. ● v. give the premiere of.
– ORIGIN C19: Fr. *première*, fem. of *premier* (see **PREMIER**).

**premillennial** ● adj. **1** existing or occurring before a new millennium. **2** Christian Theology relating to or believing in a prophesied millennium of blessedness beginning with the imminent Second Coming of Christ.
– DERIVATIVES **premillennialism** n. **premillennialist** n.

**premise** ● n. /'prɛmɪs/ (Brit. also **premiss**) Logic a previous statement from which another is inferred. ➤ an underlying assumption. ● v. /prɪ'mʌɪz/ **1** (**premise on/upon**) base (an argument, theory, etc.) on. **2** state or presuppose as a premise.
– ORIGIN ME: from OFr. *premisse*, from med. L. *praemissa* (*propositio*) '(proposition) set in front', from L. *praemittere*, from *prae* 'before' + *mittere* 'send'.

**premises** ● pl. n. a house or building, together with its land and outbuildings, occupied by a business or considered in an official context.

**premium** ● n. (pl. **premiums**) **1** an amount paid for a contract of insurance. **2** a sum added to an ordinary price, charge, or other payment. ➤ [as modifier] (of a commodity) superior and more expensive. **3** something given as a reward or incentive.
– PHRASES **at a premium 1** scarce and in demand. **2** above the usual price. **put** (or **place**) **a premium on** regard as particularly valuable.
– ORIGIN C17: from L. *praemium* 'booty, reward', from *prae* 'before' + *emere* 'buy, take'.

**Premium Bond** (also **Premium Savings Bond**) ● n. (in the UK) a government security offering no interest or capital gain but entered in regular draws for cash prizes.

**premix** ● v. mix in advance. ● n. a premixed material.

**premodify** ● v. (**-modifies**, **-modified**) Grammar modify the sense of (a word) by being placed before it.
– DERIVATIVES **premodification** n. **premodifier** n.

**premolar** (also **premolar tooth**) ● n. a tooth situated between the canines and molar teeth.

**premonition** /ˌprɛmə'nɪʃ(ə)n, ˌpriː-/ ● n. a strong feeling that something is about to happen.
– DERIVATIVES **premonitory** adj.
– ORIGIN C16: from Fr. *prémonition*, from late L. *praemonitio(n-)*, from L. *praemonere*, from *prae* 'before' + *monere* 'warn'.

**Premonstratensian** /ˌpriːmɒnstrə'tɛnsɪən/ ● n. a monk or nun of an order founded at Prémontré in France in 1120. ● adj. of or relating to this order.
– ORIGIN from med. L. *Praemonstratensis*, from *Praemonstratus* (lit. 'foreshown'), the L. name of the abbey of Prémontré, so named because the site was prophetically pointed out by the order's founder, St Norbert.

**prenatal** ● adj. before birth.
– DERIVATIVES **prenatally** adv.

**prenominal** ● adj. Grammar preceding a noun.
– DERIVATIVES **prenominally** adv.

**prentice** ● n. & v. archaic term for **APPRENTICE**.
– DERIVATIVES **prenticeship** n.

**prenup** ● n. N. Amer. informal a prenuptial agreement.

**prenuptial** ● adj. before marriage.

**prenuptial agreement** ● n. an agreement made by a couple before they marry concerning ownership of assets in the event of a divorce.

**preoccupation** ● n. the state of being preoccupied. ➤ a matter that preoccupies someone.

**preoccupy** ● v. (**-ies**, **-ied**) dominate or engross the mind of (someone) to the exclusion of other thoughts.
– ORIGIN C16: from **PRE-** + **OCCUPY**, suggested by L. *praeoccupare* 'seize beforehand'.

**preocular** ● adj. in front of the eye.

**pre-op** ● adj. informal short for **PREOPERATIVE**.

**preoperative** ● adj. before a surgical operation.
– DERIVATIVES **preoperatively** adv.

**preordain** ● v. (usu. **be preordained**) decide or determine beforehand.

**pre-owned** ● adj. chiefly N. Amer. second-hand.

**prep**[1] ● n. informal **1** Brit. (especially in a private school) school work done outside lessons. ➤ a period set aside for this. **2** N. Amer. a student in a preparatory school. **3** [as modifier] relating to preparatory education.
– ORIGIN C19: abbrev. of **PREPARATION** or **PREPARATORY**.

**prep**[2] N. Amer. informal ● v. (**prepped**, **prepping**) prepare; make ready. ● n. preparation.
– ORIGIN 1920s: abbrev.

**prep.** ● abbrev. preposition.

**pre-pack** (also **pre-package**) ● v. [usu. as adj. **pre-packed**] pack or wrap (goods) on the site of production or before sale.

**prepaid** past and past participle of **PREPAY**.

**preparation** ● n. **1** the action or process of preparing or being prepared. ➤ (usu. **preparations**) something done to get ready for an event or undertaking. **2** a specially made up substance, especially a medicine or food. **3** Music the sounding of the discordant note in a chord in the preceding chord where it is not discordant, lessening the effect of the discord.
– ORIGIN ME: via OFr. from L. *praeparatio(n-)*, from *praeparare* (see **PREPARE**).

**preparative** ● adj. preparatory. ● n. a thing which acts as a preparation.
– DERIVATIVES **preparatively** adv.

**preparatory** ● adj. serving as or carrying out preparation. ➤ Brit. relating to education in a preparatory school.
– PHRASES **preparatory to** as a preparation for.
– ORIGIN ME: from late L. *praeparatorius*, from *praeparat-*, *praeparare* (see **PREPARE**).

**preparatory school** ● n. **1** Brit. a private school for pupils between the ages of seven and thirteen. **2** N. Amer. a private school that prepares pupils for college or university.

**prepare** ● v. **1** make ready for use or consideration. ➤ make (food) ready for cooking or eating. **2** make or get ready to do or deal with something. ➤ (**be prepared to do something**) be willing to do something. **3** make (a substance) by chemical reaction. **4** Music lead up to (a discord) by means of preparation.
– DERIVATIVES **preparer** n.
– ORIGIN ME: from Fr. *préparer* or L. *praeparare*, from *prae* 'before' + *parare* 'make ready'.

**preparedness** ● n. a state of readiness, especially for war.

**prepay** ● v. (past and past part. **prepaid**) [usu. as adj. **prepaid**] pay for in advance.
– DERIVATIVES **prepayable** adj. **prepayment** n.

**prepense** /prɪ'pɛns/ ● adj. [usu. postpos.] chiefly Law, dated deliberate; intentional.
– DERIVATIVES **prepensely** adv.
– ORIGIN C18: alt. of *prepensed*, past part. of obs. *prepense*, from OFr. *purpenser*, from *por-* 'beforehand' + *penser* 'think'.

**pre-plan** ● v. [usu. as adj. **pre-planned**] plan in advance.

**preponderant** ● adj. predominant in influence, number, or importance.
– DERIVATIVES **preponderance** n. **preponderantly** adv.
– ORIGIN ME: from L. *preponderant-* 'weighing more', from *praeponderare* (see **PREPONDERATE**).

**preponderate** ● v. be preponderant.
– ORIGIN C17 (in the sense 'weigh more, have greater intellectual weight'): from L. *praeponderat-*, *praeponderare*, from *prae* 'before' + *ponderare* 'weigh, consider'.

**prepone** /priː'pəʊn/ ● v. Indian bring forward to an earlier date or time.

– ORIGIN 1970s: from **PRE-** + **POSTPONE**.

**prepose** • v. Linguistics place (an element or word) in front of another.

– ORIGIN C15 (in the sense 'place in authority'): from Fr. *préposer*.

**preposition** /ˌprɛpəˈzɪʃ(ə)n/ • n. Grammar a word governing, and usually preceding, a noun or pronoun and expressing a relation to another word or element, as in 'she arrived *after* dinner' and 'what did you do it *for*?'.

– DERIVATIVES **prepositional** adj. **prepositionally** adv.

– ORIGIN ME: from L. *praepositio(n-)*, from *praeponere* (v.), from *prae* 'before' + *ponere* 'to place'.

**prepositional object** • n. Grammar a noun phrase governed by a preposition.

**prepositive** /priːˈpɒzɪtɪv/ • adj. Grammar (of a word, particle, etc.) placed in front of the word that it governs or modifies.

– ORIGIN C16: from late L. *praepositivus* (see **PRE-**, **POSITIVE**).

**prepossessing** • adj. [often with neg.] attractive or appealing in appearance.

– DERIVATIVES **prepossession** n.

**preposterous** • adj. utterly absurd or ridiculous.

– DERIVATIVES **preposterously** adv. **preposterousness** n.

– ORIGIN C16: from L. *praeposterus* 'reversed, absurd' (from *prae* 'before' + *posterus* 'coming after') + **-OUS**.

**prepostor** • n. variant spelling of **PRAEPOSTOR**.

**prepotent** • adj. **1** greater than others in power or influence. **2** (of an animal) effective in transmitting hereditary characteristics to its offspring.

– DERIVATIVES **prepotence** n. **prepotency** n.

– ORIGIN ME: from L. *praepotent-*, from *prae* 'before, ahead' + *posse* 'be able'.

**preppy** (also **preppie**) N. Amer. informal • n. (pl. **-ies**) a pupil of an expensive preparatory school. • adj. (**-ier**, **-iest**) of or typical of such a person, especially with reference to their neat style of dress.

– ORIGIN C20: from **PREP SCHOOL** + **-Y**[2].

**preprandial** • adj. formal or humorous done or taken before dinner.

– ORIGIN C19: from **PRE-** + L. *prandium* 'a meal' + **-AL**.

**prepreg** • n. a fibrous material pre-impregnated with a particular synthetic resin, used in making reinforced plastics.

– ORIGIN 1950s: from **PRE-** + *(im)preg(nated)*.

**pre-print** • v. [usu. as adj. **pre-printed**] print in advance. • n. a printed document issued before full publication.

**pre-process** • v. subject to preliminary processing.

– DERIVATIVES **preprocessor** n.

**pre-production** • n. work done on a film, broadcast programme, etc. before full-scale production begins.

**pre-program** • v. [usu. as adj. **pre-programmed**] program in advance for ease of use.

**prep school** • n. short for **PREPARATORY SCHOOL**.

**pre-pubertal** • adj. another term for **PRE-PUBESCENT**.

– DERIVATIVES **pre-puberty** n.

**pre-pubescent** • adj. relating to or in the period preceding puberty. • n. a pre-pubescent boy or girl.

– DERIVATIVES **pre-pubescence** n.

**prepuce** /ˈpriːpjuːs/ • n. Anatomy **1** technical term for **FORESKIN**. **2** the fold of skin surrounding the clitoris.

– DERIVATIVES **preputial** adj.

– ORIGIN ME: from Fr. *prépuce*, from L. *praeputium*.

**pre-qualify** • v. qualify in advance to take part in a sporting event.

**prequel** /ˈpriːkw(ə)l/ • n. a story or film containing events which precede those of an existing work.

– ORIGIN 1970s: from **PRE-** + **SEQUEL**.

**Pre-Raphaelite** /priːˈrafəlʌɪt/ • n. a member of a group of English 19th-century artists who sought to emulate the simplicity and sincerity of Italian artists from before the time of Raphael. • adj. of or relating to the Pre-Raphaelites. ➤(especially of women) suggesting Pre-Raphaelite painting in appearance, typically with long, thick, wavy auburn hair and pale skin.

– DERIVATIVES **Pre-Raphaelitism** n.

**pre-record** • v. [often as adj. **pre-recorded**] record (sound or film) in advance.

**prerequisite** /priːˈrɛkwɪzɪt/ • adj. required as a prior condition. • n. a prerequisite thing.

**prerogative** /prɪˈrɒgətɪv/ • n. **1** a right or privilege exclusive to a particular individual or class. **2** (in UK law) the right of the sovereign, theoretically unrestricted but usually delegated to government or the judiciary. • adj. arising from or relating to the royal prerogative.

– ORIGIN ME: via OFr. from L. *praerogativa* '(the verdict of) the political division which was chosen to vote first in the assembly', fem. of *praerogativus* 'asked first', from *prae* 'before' + *rogare* 'ask'.

**Pres.** • abbrev. President.

**presage** /ˈprɛsɪdʒ/ • v. /also prɪˈseɪdʒ/ be a sign or warning of (an imminent event). ➤archaic predict. • n. an omen or portent. ➤archaic a foreboding.

– DERIVATIVES **presager** n. (archaic).

– ORIGIN ME (as n.): via Fr. from L. *praesagium*, from *praesagire* 'forebode', from *prae* 'before' + *sagire* 'perceive keenly'.

**presbyopia** /ˌprɛzbɪˈəʊpɪə/ • n. long-sightedness caused by loss of elasticity of the lens of the eye.

– DERIVATIVES **presbyopic** adj.

– ORIGIN C18: mod. L., from Gk *presbus* 'old man' + *ōps, ōp-* 'eye'.

**presbyter** /ˈprɛzbɪtə/ • n. historical an elder or minister of the Christian Church. ➤formal (in presbyterian Churches) an elder. ➤formal (in episcopal Churches) a minister of the second order, under the authority of a bishop.

– DERIVATIVES **presbyteral** /-ˈbɪt(ə)r(ə)l/ adj. **presbyterate** n. **presbyterial** adj. **presbytership** n.

– ORIGIN C16: via eccles. L. from Gk *presbuteros* 'elder', compar. of *presbus* 'old (man)'.

**Presbyterian** /ˌprɛzbɪˈtɪərɪən/ • adj. relating to or denoting a Protestant Church or denomination governed by elders all of equal rank. • n. a member of a Presbyterian Church. ➤an advocate of the Presbyterian system.

– DERIVATIVES **Presbyterianism** n.

– ORIGIN C17: from eccles. L. *presbyterium* (see **PRESBYTERY**) + **-AN**.

**presbytery** /ˈprɛzbɪt(ə)ri/ • n. (pl. **-ies**) **1** [treated as sing. or pl.] a body of Church elders, especially (in Presbyterian Churches) an administrative court representing the congregations of a district. ➤a district represented by such a body. **2** the house of a Roman Catholic parish priest. **3** chiefly Architecture the eastern part of a church chancel beyond the choir.

– ORIGIN ME: from OFr. *presbiterie*, via eccles. L. from Gk *presbuterion*, from *presbuteros* (see **PRESBYTER**).

**pre-school** • adj. of or relating to the time before a child is old enough to go to school. • n. a nursery school.

– DERIVATIVES **pre-schooler** n.

**prescient** /ˈprɛsɪənt/ • adj. having knowledge of events before they take place.

– DERIVATIVES **prescience** n. **presciently** adv.

– ORIGIN C17: from L. *praescient-*, *praescire* 'know beforehand', from *prae* 'before' + *scire* 'know'.

**prescind** /prɪˈsɪnd/ • v. (**prescind from**) formal leave out of consideration. ➤cut off or separate from something.

– ORIGIN C17: from L. *praescindere*, from *prae* 'before' + *scindere* 'to cut'.

**prescribe** • v. **1** advise and authorize the use of (a medicine or treatment), especially in writing. **2** recommend as something beneficial. ➤state authoritatively that (an action or procedure) should be carried out.

– DERIVATIVES **prescriber** n.

– ORIGIN ME (in the senses 'confine within bounds', 'claim by prescription'): from L. *praescribere* 'direct in writing', from *prae* 'before' + *scribere* 'write'.

**prescript** /ˈpriːskrɪpt/ • n. formal or dated an ordinance, law, or command.

– ORIGIN C16: from L. *praescriptum* 'something directed in writing', neut. past part. of *praescribere* (see **PRESCRIBE**).

**prescription** • n. **1** an instruction written by a medical practitioner that authorizes a patient to be issued with a

medicine or treatment. **2** the action of prescribing. **3** an authoritative recommendation or ruling. **4** (also **positive prescription**) Law the establishment of a claim founded on the basis of long usage or custom.
– ORIGIN ME: via OFr. from L. *praescriptio(n-)*, from *praescribere* (see **PRESCRIBE**).

**prescriptive** ● adj. **1** of or relating to the imposition of a rule or method. **2** (of a right, title, etc.) legally established by long usage or the passage of time.
– DERIVATIVES **prescriptively** adv. **prescriptiveness** n. **prescriptivism** n. **prescriptivist** n. & adj.
– ORIGIN C18: from late L. *praescriptivus* 'relating to a legal exception', from *praescript-* 'directed in writing', from *praescribere* (see **PRESCRIBE**).

**preseason** ● adj. before the start of the season for a particular sport. ● n. the preseason period.

**pre-select** ● v. select in advance.
– DERIVATIVES **pre-selection** n. **pre-selective** adj.

**pre-selector** ● n. a device for selecting a mechanical or electrical operation in advance of its execution.

**presence** ● n. **1** the state or fact of being present. ➤a person or thing that is present but not seen. **2** the impressive manner or appearance of a person.
– PHRASES **make one's presence felt** have a strong influence on a situation. **presence of mind** the ability to remain calm and take quick, sensible action in the face of sudden difficulty.
– ORIGIN ME: via OFr. from L. *praesentia* 'being at hand', from *praeesse* (see **PRESENT**[1]).

**presence chamber** ● n. a room in which a monarch or other distinguished person receives visitors.

**presenile** /priːˈsiːnʌɪl/ ● adj. in or of the period of life preceding old age.

**present**[1] /ˈprɛz(ə)nt/ ● adj. **1** being or occurring in a particular place. **2** existing or occurring now. **3** Grammar (of a tense) expressing an action now going on or habitually performed, or a condition now existing. ● n. **1** (usu. **the present**) the period of time now occurring. **2** Grammar a present tense or form of a verb.
– PHRASES **at present** now. **for the present** for now; temporarily. **these presents** Law, formal this document.
– ORIGIN ME: via OFr. from L. *praesent-* 'being at hand', pres. part. of *praeesse*, from *prae* 'before' + *esse* 'be'.

**present**[2] /prɪˈzɛnt/ ● v. **1** give formally or ceremonially. ➤(**present someone with**) give (something) to someone in such a way. ➤offer for acceptance or consideration. **2** formally introduce to someone. ➤(**present oneself**) appear formally before others. ➤(**present to**) (in church use) recommend (an ordained minister) to a bishop for institution to (a benefice). **3** put (a show or exhibition) before the public. ➤introduce and appear in (a television or radio show). **4** be the cause of (a problem or difficulty). ➤exhibit (a particular appearance) to others. ➤represent to others in a particular way. ➤(**present itself**) (of an opportunity or idea) occur and be available for use or exploitation. ➤(**present with**) Medicine come forward for medical examination for a particular condition or symptom. ➤Medicine (of an illness) manifest itself. **5** Medicine (of a part of a fetus) be directed towards the cervix during labour. **6** aim (a firearm) at something so as to be ready to fire. ● n. (**the present**) the position of a firearm when aimed or held ready to be aimed.
– PHRASES **present arms** hold a rifle vertically in front of the body as a salute.
– ORIGIN ME: from OFr. *presenter*, from L. *praesentare* 'place before', from *praesent-* (see **PRESENT**[1]).

**present**[3] /ˈprɛz(ə)nt/ ● n. a thing given to someone as a gift.
– ORIGIN ME: from OFr., orig. in the phr. *mettre une chose en present à quelqu'un* 'put a thing into the presence of a person'.

**presentable** ● adj. clean, smart, or decent enough to be seen in public.
– DERIVATIVES **presentability** n. **presentably** adv.

**presentation** ● n. **1** the action or an instance of presenting or being presented. ➤the manner or style in which something is presented. ➤a formal introduction. **2** Medicine the position of a fetus at the time of delivery. **3** (**Presentation of Christ**) another term for **CANDLEMAS**.
– DERIVATIVES **presentational** adj. **presentationally** adv.
– ORIGIN ME: via OFr. from late L. *praesentatio(n-)*, from L. *praesentare* (see **PRESENT**[2]).

**presentative** ● adj. historical (of a benefice) to which a patron has the right of presentation.

**presentee** ● n. a person recommended for a position, especially a Church living.

**presenteeism** ● n. the practice of being present at work for longer than required, especially as a manifestation of insecurity.

**presenter** ● n. a person who introduces and appears in a television or radio programme.

**presentiment** /prɪˈzɛntɪm(ə)nt, -ˈsɛn-/ ● n. an intuitive feeling or foreboding about the future.
– ORIGIN C18: from obs. Fr. *présentiment*.

**presentism** ● n. the tendency to interpret past events in terms of modern values and concepts.
– DERIVATIVES **presentist** adj.

**presently** ● adv. **1** after a short time; soon. **2** at the present time; now.

**presentment** /prɪˈzɛntm(ə)nt/ ● n. Law, chiefly historical a formal presentation of information to a court, especially a statement on oath by a jury regarding a matter.

**preservationist** ● n. a supporter of the preservation of something, especially of historic buildings or artefacts.

**preservation order** ● n. chiefly Brit. a legal obligation laid on an owner to preserve a historic building, valuable natural habitat, etc.

**preservative** ● n. a substance used to preserve foodstuffs, wood, or other materials against decay. ● adj. acting to preserve something.

**preserve** ● v. **1** maintain in its original or existing state. ➤keep alive (a memory or quality). **2** keep safe from harm or injury. **3** treat (food) to prevent its decomposition. ➤prepare (fruit) for long-term storage by boiling it with sugar. ● n. **1** a foodstuff made with fruit preserved in sugar. **2** something regarded as reserved for a particular person or group. **3** a place where game is protected and kept for private hunting or shooting.
– DERIVATIVES **preservable** adj. **preservation** n. **preserver** n.
– ORIGIN ME: from OFr. *preserver*, from late L. *praeservare*, from *prae-* 'before, in advance' + *servare* 'to keep'.

**preset** ● v. (**presetting**; past and past part. **preset**) set or adjust (a value that controls the operation of a device) in advance of its use. ● n. a preset value or control.

**pre-shrunk** ● adj. (of a fabric or garment) shrunk during manufacture to prevent further shrinking in use.
– DERIVATIVES **pre-shrink** v.

**preside** ● v. be in a position of authority in a meeting, court, etc. ➤(**preside over**) be in charge of (a situation).
– ORIGIN C17: from Fr. *présider*, from L. *praesidere*, from *prae* 'before' + *sedere* 'sit'.

**presidency** ● n. (pl. **-ies**) the office or status of president. ➤the period of this.
– ORIGIN C16: from med. L. *praesidentia*, from *praesidere* (see **PRESIDE**).

**president** ● n. **1** the elected head of a republican state. ➤the head of a society, council, college, or other organization. **2** Christian Church the celebrant at a Eucharist.
– DERIVATIVES **presidential** adj. **presidentially** adv. **presidentship** n. (archaic).
– ORIGIN ME: via OFr. from L. *praesident-* (see **PRESIDE**).

**presidium** /prɪˈsɪdɪʌm, -ˈzɪ-/ (also **praesidium**) ● n. a standing executive committee in a communist country.
– ORIGIN 1920s: from Russ. *prezidium*, from L. *praesidium* (see **PRESIDE**).

**Presocratic** /ˌpriːsəˈkratɪk/ ● adj. of the time before Socrates.

**press**[1] ● v. **1** move or cause to move into a position of contact with something by exerting continuous physical force. ➤exert continuous physical force on, especially in order to operate a device. ➤squeeze (someone's arm or hand) as a sign of affection. ➤move in a specified direction by pushing. ➤(**press on/ahead**) continue in one's action. **2** apply pressure to (something) to flatten, shape, or smooth it, especially by ironing. ➤extract (juice or oil) by crushing or squeezing fruit, vegetables, etc. ➤manufacture by moulding under pressure. **3** Weightlifting raise (a weight) by lifting it to shoulder height and then gradually pushing it upwards. **4** forcefully put forward (an opinion, claim, etc.). ➤make strong efforts to persuade or force to do something. ➤Golf try too hard to achieve distance. ➤(**press something on/upon**) insist that (someone) accepts an offer or gift. ➤(of time) be short. ➤(**be pressed**) have barely enough of something, especially time. ➤(**be pressed to do something**) have difficulty doing something. ● **n. 1** a device for applying pressure in order to flatten or shape something or to extract juice or oil. **2** a printing press. ➤a printing or publishing business. **3** (**the press**) [treated as sing. or pl.] newspapers or journalists viewed collectively. ➤coverage in newspapers and magazines. **4** an act of pressing something. ➤a closely packed mass of people or things. ➤dated pressure of business. ➤Basketball a form of close guarding by the defending team. **5** a large cupboard for storing linen or clothes.

– PHRASES **go to press** go to be printed. **press (the) flesh** informal, chiefly N. Amer. greet people by shaking hands.

– ORIGIN ME: from OFr. *presse* (n.), *presser* (v.), from L. *pressare* 'keep pressing', frequentative of *premere*.

**press²** ● **v. 1** (**press into**) put to a specified use, especially as a temporary or makeshift measure. **2** historical force to enlist in the army or navy. ● **n.** historical a forcible enlistment of men, especially for the navy.

– ORIGIN C16: alt. (by assoc. with **PRESS¹**) of obs. *prest* 'pay given on enlistment, enlistment by such payment', from OFr. *prest* 'loan, advance pay', based on L. *praestare* 'provide'.

**pressboard** ● **n.** chiefly N. Amer. a smooth, hard, dense board typically made from wood or textile pulp or laminated waste paper.

**press conference** ● **n.** a meeting held with journalists in order to make an announcement or answer questions.

**press fit** ● **n.** an interference fit in which one part is forced into a slightly smaller hole in the other.

– DERIVATIVES **press-fitted** adj.

**press gang** ● **n.** historical a body of men employed to enlist men forcibly into service in the army or navy. ● **v.** (**press-gang**) force into service.

**pressie** ● **n.** variant spelling of **PREZZIE**.

**pressing** ● **adj.** requiring quick or immediate action or attention. ➤expressing something strongly or persistently. ● **n.** a gramophone record or other object made by moulding under pressure.

– DERIVATIVES **pressingly** adv.

**pressman** ● **n.** (pl. **-men**) **1** chiefly Brit. a journalist. **2** a person who operates a printing press.

**pressor** ● **adj.** Physiology producing an increase in blood pressure by stimulating constriction of the blood vessels.

**press release** ● **n.** an official statement issued to journalists on a particular matter.

**press stud** ● **n.** Brit. a small fastener engaged by pressing its two halves together.

**press-up** ● **n.** Brit. an exercise in which a person lies facing the floor and, keeping their back straight, raises their body by pressing down on their hands.

**pressure** ● **n. 1** the continuous physical force exerted on or against an object by something in contact with it. ➤the force per unit area exerted by a fluid against a surface. **2** the use of persuasion, intimidation, etc. to make someone do something. ➤a feeling of stressful urgency. ● **v.** attempt to persuade or coerce into doing something.

– ORIGIN ME: from OFr., from L. *pressura*, from *press-* 'pressed', from *premere* (see **PRESS¹**).

**pressure cooker** ● **n.** an airtight pot in which food can be cooked quickly under steam pressure.

– DERIVATIVES **pressure-cook** v.

**pressure group** ● **n.** a group that tries to influence public policy in the interest of a particular cause.

**pressure hull** ● **n.** the inner hull of a submarine, in which normal pressure is maintained.

**pressure point** ● **n. 1** a point on the surface of the body sensitive to pressure. **2** a point where an artery can be pressed against a bone to inhibit bleeding.

**pressure suit** ● **n.** an inflatable suit that protects the wearer against low pressure.

**pressurize** (also **-ise**) ● **v. 1** produce or maintain raised pressure artificially in. **2** attempt to persuade or coerce into doing something.

– DERIVATIVES **pressurization** n.

**pressurized-water reactor** ● **n.** a nuclear reactor in which the coolant and moderator is water under high pressure.

**presswork** ● **n. 1** the shaping of metal by pressing or drawing it into a shaped hollow die. **2** the process of using a printing press.

**prestidigitation** /ˌprɛstɪˌdɪdʒɪˈteɪʃ(ə)n/ ● **n.** formal magic tricks performed as entertainment.

– DERIVATIVES **prestidigitator** n.

– ORIGIN C19: from Fr., from *preste* 'nimble' + L. *digitus* 'finger' + **-ATION**.

**prestige** ● **n.** widespread respect and admiration attracted through a perception of high achievements or quality.

– DERIVATIVES **prestigeful** adj. **prestigious** adj. **prestigiously** adv. **prestigiousness** n.

– ORIGIN C17 (in the sense 'illusion, conjuring trick'): from Fr., lit. 'illusion, glamour'.

**prestissimo** /prɛˈstɪsɪməʊ/ ● **adv. & adj.** Music in a very quick tempo.

– ORIGIN Ital., superlative of *presto* (see **PRESTO**).

**presto** ● **adv. & adj.** Music in a quick tempo. ● **exclam.** (Brit. also **hey presto**) announcing the successful completion of a conjuring trick or other surprising achievement.

– ORIGIN Ital., 'quick, quickly', from late L. *praestus* 'ready', from L. *praesto* 'at hand'.

**prestressed** ● **adj.** strengthened by the application of stress during manufacture, especially (of concrete) by means of tensioned rods or wires inserted before setting.

– DERIVATIVES **prestressing** n.

**presumably** ● **adv.** as may reasonably be presumed.

**presume** ● **v. 1** suppose that something is the case on the basis of probability. ➤take for granted. **2** be arrogant or impertinent enough to do something. ➤(**presume on/upon**) unjustifiably regard (something) as entitling one to privileges.

– DERIVATIVES **presumable** adj.

– ORIGIN ME: from OFr. *presumer*, from L. *praesumere* 'anticipate' (in late L. 'take for granted'), from *prae* 'before' + *sumere* 'take'.

**presuming** ● **adj.** archaic presumptuous.

– DERIVATIVES **presumingly** adv.

**presumption** ● **n. 1** an act or instance of presuming something to be the case. ➤an idea that is presumed to be true. ➤chiefly Law an attitude adopted towards something in the absence of contrary factors. **2** presumptuous behaviour.

– ORIGIN ME: from OFr. *presumpcion*, from L. *praesumptio(n)* 'anticipation', from *praesumere* (see **PRESUME**).

**presumptive** ● **adj. 1** presumed in the absence of further information. ➤Law giving grounds for a particular inference or interpretation. **2** another term for **PRESUMPTUOUS**.

– DERIVATIVES **presumptively** adv.

– ORIGIN ME: from Fr. *présomptif, -ive*, from late L. *praesumptivus*, from *praesumpt-*, *praesumere* (see **PRESUME**).

**presumptuous** ● **adj.** failing to observe the limits of what is permitted or appropriate.

– DERIVATIVES **presumptuously** adv. **presumptuousness** n.

– ORIGIN ME: from OFr. *presumptueux*, from late L. *praesumptuosus*, *-tiosus*, from *praesumptio* (see **PRESUMPTION**).

**presuppose** ● v. require as a precondition of possibility or coherence. ➤ tacitly assume to be the case.
– DERIVATIVES **presupposition** n.
– ORIGIN ME: from OFr. *presupposer*, suggested by med. L. *praesupponere*, from *prae* 'before' + *supponere* (see **SUPPOSE**).

**prêt-à-porter** /ˌprɛtəˈpɔːteɪ/ ● n. designer clothing sold ready-to-wear.
– ORIGIN Fr., lit. 'ready to wear'.

**pretence** (US **pretense**) ● n. **1** an act of pretending. **2** pretentious behaviour. **3** (**pretence to**) a claim, especially a false or ambitious one.

**pretend** ● v. **1** act so as to make it appear that something is the case when in fact it is not. ➤ engage in an imaginative game or fantasy. ➤ simulate (an emotion or quality). **2** (**pretend to**) lay claim to (a quality or title). ● adj. informal imaginary; make-believe.
– ORIGIN ME: from L. *praetendere* 'stretch forth, claim', from *prae* 'before' + *tendere* 'stretch'.

**pretender** ● n. a person who claims or aspires to a title or position.

**pretense** ● n. US spelling of **PRETENCE**.

**pretension** ● n. **1** (**pretension to**) a claim or aspiration to something. **2** pretentiousness.
– ORIGIN ME: from med. L. *praetensio(n-)*, from *praetens-* 'alleged', from *praetendere* (see **PRETEND**).

**pre-tension** ● v. apply tension to before manufacture or use.
– DERIVATIVES **pre-tensioner** n.

**pretentious** ● adj. attempting to impress by affecting greater importance or merit than is actually possessed.
– DERIVATIVES **pretentiously** adv. **pretentiousness** n.
– ORIGIN C19: from Fr. *prétentieux*, from *prétention* (see **PRETENSION**).

**preter-** /ˈpriːtə/ ● comb. form more than: *preternatural*.
– ORIGIN from L. *praeter* 'past, beyond'.

**preterite** /ˈprɛt(ə)rɪt/ (US also **preterit**) Grammar ● adj. expressing a past action or state. ● n. a simple past tense or form.
– ORIGIN ME (in the sense 'bygone, former'): from L. *praeteritus*, past part. of *praeterire* 'pass, go by', from *praeter* 'past, beyond' + *ire* 'go'.

**preterition** /ˌpriːtəˈrɪʃ(ə)n/ ● n. the rhetorical technique of referring to something by professing to omit it.
– ORIGIN C16: from late L. *praeteritio(n-)*, from *praeterire* (see **PRETERITE**).

**preterm** ● adj. & adv. Medicine born or occurring after a pregnancy significantly shorter than normal.

**pretermit** /ˌpriːtəˈmɪt/ ● v. (**pretermitted**, **pretermitting**) archaic **1** omit to do or mention. **2** abandon for a time.
– DERIVATIVES **pretermission** /-ˈmɪʃ(ə)n/ n.
– ORIGIN C15: from L. *praetermittere*, from *praeter* 'past, beyond' + *mittere* 'let go'.

**preternatural** /ˌpriːtəˈnatʃ(ə)r(ə)l/ (also **praeternatural**) ● adj. beyond what is normal or natural: *preternatural speed*.
– DERIVATIVES **preternaturalism** n. **preternaturally** adv.

**pretext** ● n. an ostensible or false reason used to justify an action.
– ORIGIN C16: from L. *praetextus* 'outward display', from *praetexere* 'to disguise', from *prae* 'before' + *texere* 'weave'.

**pretreat** ● v. treat with a chemical before use.
– DERIVATIVES **pretreatment** n.

**prettify** ● v. (**-ies**, **-ied**) make superficially pretty.
– DERIVATIVES **prettification** n. **prettifier** n.

**pretty** ● adj. (**-ier**, **-iest**) **1** attractive in a delicate way without being truly beautiful. **2** informal used ironically to express displeasure: *he led me a pretty dance*. ● adv. informal to a moderately high degree; fairly. ● n. (pl. **-ies**) informal a pretty thing; a trinket. ➤ (used condescendingly) an attractive person. ● v. (**-ies**, **-ied**) make pretty or attractive.
– PHRASES **pretty much** (or **nearly** or **well**) informal very nearly. **a pretty penny** informal a large sum of money. **be sitting pretty** informal be in an advantageous position or situation.
– DERIVATIVES **prettily** adv. **prettiness** n. **prettyish** adj.
– ORIGIN OE *prættig* (in sense 'cunning, crafty', later 'clever, skilful'), from a W. Gmc base meaning 'trick'.

**pretty boy** ● n. informal, often derogatory a foppish or effeminate man.

**pretzel** /ˈprɛts(ə)l/ chiefly N. Amer. ● n. a crisp biscuit baked as a knot or stick and flavoured with salt. ● v. (**pretzeled**, **pretzeling**) twist, bend, or contort.
– ORIGIN C19: from Ger. *Pretzel*.

**prevail** ● v. **1** prove more powerful; be victorious. ➤ be widespread or current. **2** (**prevail on/upon**) persuade to do something.
– DERIVATIVES **prevailing** adj. **prevailingly** adv.
– ORIGIN ME: from L. *praevalere*, from *prae* 'before' + *valere* 'have power'.

**prevailing wind** ● n. a wind from the predominant or most usual direction.

**prevalent** /ˈprɛv(ə)l(ə)nt/ ● adj. widespread in a particular area at a particular time. ➤ archaic predominant; powerful.
– DERIVATIVES **prevalence** n. **prevalently** adv.
– ORIGIN C16: from L. *praevalent-*, from *praevalere* (see **PREVAIL**).

**prevaricate** /prɪˈvarɪkeɪt/ ● v. speak or act evasively.
– DERIVATIVES **prevarication** n. **prevaricator** n.
– ORIGIN C16 (earlier (ME) as *prevarication* and *prevaricator*), in the sense 'go astray, transgress': from L. *praevaricat-*, *praevaricari* 'walk crookedly, deviate'.

**prevenient** /prɪˈviːnɪənt/ ● adj. formal preceding; antecedent.
– ORIGIN C17: from L. *praevenient-*, *praevenire* 'come before', from *prae* 'before' + *venire* 'come'.

**prevent** ● v. **1** keep from happening or arising. ➤ make unable to do something. **2** archaic (of God) go before (someone) with spiritual guidance and help.
– DERIVATIVES **preventability** n. **preventable** (also **preventible**) adj. **prevention** n.
– ORIGIN ME: from L. *praevent-*, *praevenire* 'precede, hinder', from *prae* 'before' + *venire* 'come'.

**preventative** ● adj. & n. another term for **PREVENTIVE**.
– DERIVATIVES **preventatively** adv.

**preventer** ● n. **1** a person or thing that prevents something. **2** Sailing an extra line rigged to support a piece of rigging or to prevent the boom from gybing.

**preventive** ● adj. designed to prevent something from occurring. ● n. a preventive medicine or other treatment.
– DERIVATIVES **preventively** adv.

**preverbal** ● adj. **1** preceding the development of speech. **2** Grammar occurring before a verb.

**preview** ● n. a viewing or display of something before it is acquired or becomes generally available. ➤ a publicity article, review, or trailer of a forthcoming film, book, etc. ● v. provide or have a preview of (a product, film, etc.).

**previous** ● adj. **1** existing or occurring before in time or order. **2** informal over-hasty.
– PHRASES **previous to** before.
– DERIVATIVES **previously** adv.
– ORIGIN C17: from L. *praevius* 'going before' (from *prae* 'before' + *via* 'way') + **-ous**.

**previse** /prɪˈvʌɪz/ ● v. poetic/literary foresee; predict.
– DERIVATIVES **prevision** n. **provisional** adj.
– ORIGIN C16: from L. *praevis-*, *praevidere*, from *prae* 'before' + *videre* 'to see'.

**prevocalic** /ˌpriːvəˈkalɪk/ ● adj. immediately before a vowel.
– DERIVATIVES **prevocalically** adv.

**pre-wash** ● n. **1** a preliminary wash, especially in an automatic washing machine. **2** a substance applied as a treatment before washing. ● v. give a pre-wash to.

**prexy** (also **prex**) ● n. (pl. **-ies**) US informal a president, especially of a college or society.
– ORIGIN C19: college sl.

**prey** ● n. an animal hunted and killed by another for food. ➤ a victim or quarry. ➤ archaic plunder or (in biblical use) a prize. ● v. (**prey on/upon**) **1** hunt and kill for food. **2** exploit or injure; cause trouble to: *the problem had begun to prey on my mind*.

– DERIVATIVES **preyer** n.
– ORIGIN ME: the noun from OFr. *preie*, from L. *praeda* 'booty', the verb from OFr. *preier*, based on L. *praedari* 'seize as plunder', from *praeda*.

**prezzie** (also **pressie**) • **n.** Brit. informal a present.
– ORIGIN 1930s: abbrev.

**prial** /ˈprʌɪəl/ • **n.** (in card games) a set of three cards of the same denomination.
– ORIGIN C19: alt. of *pair royal*.

**priapic** /prʌɪˈapɪk/ • **adj. 1** phallic. **2** Medicine having a persistently (and painfully) erect penis.
– DERIVATIVES **priapism** n.
– ORIGIN C18: from Gk *Priapos*, name of a god of fertility, + **-IC**.

**Priapulida** /ˌprʌɪəˈpjʊlɪdə/ • **pl. n.** Zoology a phylum of worm-like marine invertebrates which have a large eversible proboscis.
– DERIVATIVES **priapulid** /prʌɪˈapjʊlɪd/ n. & adj.
– ORIGIN mod. L., from *Priapulus* (genus name), dimin. of *Priapus*, Gk *Priapos* (see **PRIAPIC**).

**price** • **n.** the amount of money expected, required, or given in payment for something. ➤something expended or endured in order to achieve an objective. ➤the odds in betting. ➤archaic value; worth. • **v.** decide the price of.
– PHRASES **at any price** no matter what is involved. **at a price** requiring great expense or involving unwelcome consequences. **beyond** (or **without**) **price** priceless. **a price on someone's head** a reward offered for someone's capture or death. **what price ——? 1** what has or would become of ——? **2** what is the chance of ——?
– ORIGIN ME: the noun from OFr. *pris*, from L. *pretium* 'value, reward'; the verb a var. of earlier *prise* 'estimate the value of' (see **PRIZE**[1]); cf. **PRAISE**.

**priceless** • **adj. 1** so precious that its value cannot be determined. **2** informal very amusing or absurd.
– DERIVATIVES **pricelessly** adv. **pricelessness** n.

**price tag** • **n.** a label showing the price of an item. ➤the cost of something.

**price-taker** • **n.** Economics a company that is obliged to accept the market prices of its products.

**pricey** (also **pricy**) • **adj.** (**-ier**, **-iest**) informal expensive.
– DERIVATIVES **priciness** n.

**prick** • **v. 1** press briefly or puncture with a sharp point. ➤(**prick out**) draw or decorate by making small holes in a surface. **2** feel a sensation as though a sharp point were sticking into one. ➤cause mental or emotional discomfort to. **3** (often **prick up**) (chiefly of a horse or dog) make (the ears) stand erect when on the alert. **4** (**prick out**) plant (seedlings) in small holes made in the earth. • **n. 1** an act of pricking something. ➤a small hole or mark made by pricking. **2** a sharp pain caused by being pierced with a fine point. ➤a sudden feeling of distress, anxiety, etc. ➤archaic a goad for oxen. **3** vulgar slang a man's penis. ➤a man regarded as stupid, unpleasant, or contemptible.
– PHRASES **kick against the pricks** hurt oneself by persisting in useless resistance or protest. [with biblical allusion to Acts 9:5.]
– DERIVATIVES **pricker** n.
– ORIGIN OE *pricca* (n.), *prician* (v.), prob. of W. Gmc origin.

**pricket** • **n. 1** a male fallow deer in its second year, with straight, unbranched horns. **2** historical a spike for holding a candle.
– ORIGIN ME: from **PRICK** + **-ET**[1].

**prickle** • **n. 1** a short spine or pointed outgrowth on the surface of a plant or on the skin of an animal. **2** a tingling or mildly painful sensation on the skin. • **v. 1** experience or produce a prickle. ➤cause such a sensation in. **2** react defensively or angrily.
– ORIGIN OE *pricel* 'instrument for pricking, sensation of being pricked'; from the Gmc base of **PRICK**; the verb is partly a dimin. of **PRICK**.

**prickly** • **adj.** (**-ier**, **-iest**) **1** covered in or resembling prickles. ➤having or causing a prickling sensation. **2** ready to take offence. ➤liable to cause someone to take offence: *a prickly subject*.
– DERIVATIVES **prickliness** n.

**prickly heat** • **n.** an itchy skin rash experienced in hot moist weather.

**prickly pear** • **n. 1** a cactus with flattened, jointed stems which produces prickly, pear-shaped fruits. [*Opuntia ficus-indica* and related species.] **2** the edible orange or red fruit of this plant.

**pricy** • **adj.** variant spelling of **PRICEY**.

**pride** • **n. 1** a feeling of deep pleasure or satisfaction derived from achievements, qualities, or possessions that do one credit. ➤something which causes this. **2** consciousness of one's own dignity. ➤the quality of having an excessively high opinion of oneself. ➤poetic/literary the prime of something. **3** a group of lions forming a social unit. • **v.** (**pride oneself on/upon**) be especially proud of (a quality or skill).
– PHRASES **one's pride and joy** a person or thing of which one is very proud. **pride of place** the most prominent or important position.
– DERIVATIVES **prideful** adj. **pridefully** adv.
– ORIGIN OE *prȳde*, var. of *prȳtu*, *prȳte*, from *prūd* (see **PROUD**).

**prie-dieu** /priːˈdjəː/ • **n.** (pl. **prie-dieux** pronunc. same) a narrow desk on which to kneel for prayer.
– ORIGIN C18: Fr., lit. 'pray God'.

**priest** • **n. 1** an ordained minister of the Catholic, Orthodox, or Anglican Church, authorized to perform certain rites and administer certain sacraments. ➤a person who performs ceremonies in a non-Christian religion. **2** a mallet used to kill fish caught when angling. • **v.** (usu. **be priested**) formal ordain to the priesthood.
– DERIVATIVES **priesthood** n. **priestliness** n. **priestly** adj.
– ORIGIN OE *prēost*, of Gmc origin, based on eccles. L. **PRESBYTER**; sense 2 of the noun alludes to the priest's function in performing the last rites.

**priestcraft** • **n.** often derogatory the knowledge and work of a priest.

**priestess** • **n.** a female priest of a non-Christian religion.

**priest-in-charge** • **n.** (pl. **priests-in-charge**) an Anglican minister who has charge of a parish but has not been formally appointed as its incumbent.

**priest's hole** • **n.** historical a hiding place for a Roman Catholic priest during times of religious persecution.

**prig** • **n.** a self-righteously moralistic person.
– DERIVATIVES **priggery** n. **priggish** adj. **priggishly** adv. **priggishness** n.
– ORIGIN C16 (in sense 'tinker, petty thief', later 'disliked person'): of unknown origin.

**prill** • **n.** a congealed pellet of a manufactured substance.
– DERIVATIVES **prilled** adj.
– ORIGIN C18 (denoting rich copper ore remaining after removal of low-grade material): of unknown origin.

**prim** • **adj.** (**-er**, **-est**) feeling or showing disapproval of anything improper; stiffly correct. • **v.** (**primmed**, **primming**) purse (the mouth or lips) into a prim expression.
– DERIVATIVES **primly** adv. **primness** n.
– ORIGIN C17 (as v.): prob. ult. from OFr. *prin*, Provençal *prim* 'excellent, delicate', from L. *primus* 'first'.

**prima ballerina** /ˈpriːmə/ • **n.** the chief female dancer in a ballet or ballet company.
– ORIGIN C19: Ital.

**primacy** /ˈprʌɪməsi/ • **n. 1** pre-eminence. **2** the office of a primate of the Church.
– ORIGIN ME: from OFr. *primatie*, from med. L. *primatia*, from L. *primas*, *primat-* (see **PRIMATE**[1]).

**prima donna** • **n. 1** the chief female singer in an opera or opera company. **2** a very temperamental and self-important person.
– DERIVATIVES **prima donna-ish** adj.
– ORIGIN C18: Ital., lit. 'first lady'.

**primaeval** • **adj.** variant spelling of **PRIMEVAL**.

**prima facie** /ˌprʌɪmə ˈfeɪʃiː/ • **adj. & adv.** Law at first sight; accepted as so until proved otherwise.
– ORIGIN L., from *primus* 'first' + *facies* 'face'.

**primal** /ˈprʌɪm(ə)l/ • **adj. 1** basic; primitive; primeval. **2** Psychology relating to or denoting feelings or behaviour postulated to form the origins of emotional life.

– DERIVATIVES **primally** adv.
– ORIGIN C17: from med. L. *primalis*, from L. *primus* 'first'.

**primarily** /ˈprʌɪm(ə)rɪli, prʌɪˈmɛr-/ ● **adv.** for the most part; mainly.

**primary** ● **adj. 1** of chief importance; principal. **2** earliest in time or order. ➤not caused by or based on anything else. **3** relating to or denoting education for children between the ages of about five and eleven. **4** of or denoting the input side of a transformer or other inductive device. **5** Chemistry (of an organic compound) having its functional group on a carbon atom bonded to no more than one other carbon atom. ➤derived from ammonia by replacement of one hydrogen atom by an organic group. **6** (of a cell or battery) producing current by an irreversible chemical reaction. **7** (**Primary**) Geology former term for **PALAEOZOIC**. ● **n.** (pl. **-ies**) **1** (in the US) a preliminary election to appoint delegates to a party conference or to select the candidates for a principal, especially presidential, election. **2** Astronomy the body orbited by a smaller body.
– ORIGIN ME: from L. *primarius*, from *primus* 'first'.

**primary care** ● **n.** health care provided in the community by medical practitioners and specialist clinics.

**primary colour** ● **n.** any of a group of colours from which all others can be obtained by mixing.

**primary feather** ● **n.** any of the largest flight feathers in a bird's wing, growing from the manus.

**primary industry** ● **n.** Economics an industry concerned with obtaining or providing raw materials, such as mining or agriculture.

**primary planet** ● **n.** a planet that directly orbits the sun.

**primary process** ● **n.** Psychoanalysis an unconscious thought process arising from the pleasure principle, which is irrational and not subject to compulsion.

**primate**[1] /ˈprʌɪmeɪt, -mət/ ● **n.** Christian Church the chief bishop or archbishop of a province.
– DERIVATIVES **primatial** /-ˈmeɪʃ(ə)l/ adj.
– ORIGIN ME: from OFr. *primat*, from L. *primas, primat-* 'of the first rank', from *primus* 'first'.

**primate**[2] /ˈprʌɪmeɪt/ ● **n.** Zoology a mammal of an order (Primates) including the lemurs, bushbabies, tarsiers, marmosets, monkeys, apes, and humans.
– DERIVATIVES **primatological** adj. **primatologist** n. **primatology** n.
– ORIGIN C19: from L. *primas, primat-* (see **PRIMATE**[1]).

**Primate of All England** ● **n.** a title of the Archbishop of Canterbury.

**Primate of England** ● **n.** a title of the Archbishop of York.

**primavera** /ˌpriːməˈvɛrə/ ● **n.** the hard, light-coloured wood of a Central American tree (*Cybistax donnellsmithii*). ● **adj.** [postpos.] (of a pasta dish) made with lightly sautéed spring vegetables.
– ORIGIN C19: from Sp. or Ital., denoting the season of spring.

**prime**[1] ● **adj. 1** of first importance; main; primary. **2** of the best possible quality; excellent. ➤having all the expected characteristics. ➤most suitable or likely. **3** (of a number) divisible only by itself and one (e.g. 2, 3, 5, 7, 11). ● **n. 1** a state or time of greatest vigour or success in a person's life. ➤archaic the beginning or earliest period. **2** a prime number. **3** Printing a symbol (′) written as a distinguishing mark or to denote minutes or feet. **4** Fencing the first of the eight parrying positions. [Fr.] **5** a special section in a cycle race. **6** Christian Church a service traditionally said at the first hour of the day (i.e. 6 a.m.), but now little used.
– DERIVATIVES **primeness** n.
– ORIGIN OE *prīm* (n.), from L. *prima* (*hora*) 'first (hour)', reinforced in ME by OFr. *prime*, from L. *primus* 'first'.

**prime**[2] ● **v. 1** make (something, especially a firearm or bomb) ready for use or action. **2** pour or spray liquid into (a pump) to facilitate its working. ➤inject extra fuel into (an engine) to facilitate starting. ➤(of a boiler) produce steam mixed with water. **3** prepare (someone) for a situation, especially by giving instructions or information. **4** Biology & Medicine induce a susceptibility in. **5** cover (a surface) with primer.
– PHRASES **prime the pump** stimulate growth or success by supplying money.
– ORIGIN C16 (in the sense 'fill, load'): prob. based on L. *primus* 'first'.

**prime cost** ● **n.** the direct cost of a commodity in terms of the materials and labour involved.

**prime lens** ● **n.** Photography a lens of fixed focal length.

**prime minister** ● **n.** the head of an elected government; the principal minister of a sovereign or state.

**prime mover** ● **n. 1** the originator of a plan or project. **2** an initial source of motive power.

**primer**[1] ● **n. 1** a substance painted on wood, metal, etc. as a preparatory coat. **2** a cap or cylinder containing a compound which ignites the charge in a cartridge or explosive. **3** a small pump for priming an engine.

**primer**[2] ● **n.** a book providing a basic introduction to a subject or used for teaching reading.
– ORIGIN ME: from med. L. *primarius* (*liber*) 'primary (book)' and *primarium* (*manuale*) 'primary (manual)'.

**prime rate** ● **n.** the lowest rate of interest for commercial borrowing.

**prime time** ● **n.** the time at which a radio or television audience is expected to be greatest.

**primeur** /priːˈməː/ ● **n. 1** (**primeurs**) fruit or vegetables grown to be available very early in the season. **2** a newly produced wine recently made available.
– ORIGIN Fr., lit. 'newness'.

**primeval** /prʌɪˈmiːv(ə)l/ (also **primaeval**) ● **adj. 1** of the earliest time in history. **2** (of behaviour or emotion) instinctive and unreasoning.
– DERIVATIVES **primevally** adv.
– ORIGIN C17: from L. *primaevus* (from *primus* 'first' + *aevum* 'age') + **-AL**.

**primeval soup** ● **n.** another term for **PRIMORDIAL SOUP**.

**prime vertical** ● **n.** Astronomy a great circle in the celestial sphere passing through the zenith and the east and west points of the horizon.

**primigravida** /ˌpriːmɪˈgravɪdə, ˌprʌɪm-/ ● **n.** (pl. **primigravidae** /-diː/) Medicine a woman pregnant for the first time.
– ORIGIN C19: mod. L., from L. *primus* 'first' + *gravidus* (see **GRAVID**).

**priming** ● **n.** a substance used for priming something; a primer.

**primipara** /prʌɪˈmɪp(ə)rə/ ● **n.** (pl. **primiparae** /-riː/) Medicine a woman giving birth for the first time.
– DERIVATIVES **primiparous** adj.
– ORIGIN C19: mod. L., from *primus* 'first' + *-parus* 'bringing forth' (from *parere*).

**primitive** ● **adj. 1** of, relating to, or denoting the earliest times in history or stages in evolution or development. ➤of or denoting a preliterate, non-industrial society of simple organization. ➤Biology undeveloped; rudimentary. **2** offering an extremely basic level of comfort, convenience, or efficiency. **3** (of behaviour or emotion) instinctive and unreasoning. **4** of or denoting a deliberately simple and direct artistic style. ● **n. 1** a person belonging to a primitive society. **2** a pre-Renaissance painter, or one employing a primitive style. **3** technical a word, expression, etc. from which others are derived. ➤Computing any of a set of basic geometric shapes generated in computer graphics.
– DERIVATIVES **primitively** adv. **primitiveness** n.
– ORIGIN ME: from OFr. *primitif, -ive*, from L. *primitivus* 'first of its kind', from *primus* 'first'.

**primitive cell** ● **n.** Crystallography the smallest possible unit cell of a lattice, with lattice points only at the vertices.

**primitive streak** ● **n.** Biology the earliest trace of the embryo in a fertilized ovum.

**primitivism** ● **n. 1** adoption of a primitive lifestyle or technique. **2** instinctive and unreasoning behaviour.
– DERIVATIVES **primitivist** n. & adj.

**primo** /ˈpriːməʊ/ ● **n.** (pl. **-os**) Music the leading or upper

part in a duet. ● **adj.** N. Amer. informal of top quality or importance.
– ORIGIN C18: Ital., lit. 'first'.

**primogenitor** /ˌprʌɪmə(ʊ)ˈdʒɛnɪtə/ ● **n.** the earliest ancestor of a people; a progenitor.
– ORIGIN C17: var. of **PROGENITOR**, on the pattern of *primogeniture*.

**primogeniture** /ˌprʌɪmə(ʊ)ˈdʒɛnɪtʃə/ ● **n.** the state of being the firstborn child. ➤ a rule or tradition of inheritance by the firstborn child.
– DERIVATIVES **primogenital** adj. **primogenitary** adj.
– ORIGIN C17: from med. L. *primogenitura*, from L. *primo* 'first' + *genitura* 'geniture'.

**primordial** /prʌɪˈmɔːdɪəl/ ● **adj.** existing at or from the beginning of time; primitive.
– DERIVATIVES **primordiality** n. **primordially** adv.
– ORIGIN ME: from late L. *primordialis* 'first of all', from *primordius*, from *primus* 'first' + *ordiri* 'begin'.

**primordial soup** ● **n.** a solution rich in organic compounds in which life on earth is supposed to have originated.

**primordium** /prʌɪˈmɔːdɪəm/ ● **n.** (pl. **primordia** /-dɪə/) Biology an organ, structure, or tissue in the earliest stage of development.
– ORIGIN C19: from L., neut. of *primordius*.

**primp** ● **v.** spend time making minor adjustments to.
– ORIGIN C16: rel. to **PRIM**.

**primrose** ● **n. 1** a woodland and hedgerow plant which produces pale yellow flowers in early spring. [*Primula vulgaris*.] **2** a pale yellow colour.
– PHRASES **primrose path** the pursuit of pleasure, especially when bringing disastrous consequences. [with allusion to Shakespeare's *Hamlet* I. iii. 50.]
– ORIGIN ME: cf. OFr. *primerose* and med. L. *prima rosa*, lit. 'first rose'.

**primula** /ˈprɪmjʊlə/ ● **n.** a plant of a genus that includes primroses, cowslips, and polyanthuses. [Genus *Primula*.]
– DERIVATIVES **primulaceous** adj.
– ORIGIN mod. L., from med. L., fem. of *primulus*, dimin. of *primus* 'first'.

**primum mobile** /ˌprʌɪməm ˈməʊbɪleɪ, ˌpriːməm ˈməʊbɪli/ ● **n. 1** a prime mover. **2** Astronomy, historical the outer sphere of the Ptolemaic universe, supposed to carry the inner spheres with it.
– ORIGIN from med. L., lit. 'first moving thing'.

**Primus** /ˈprʌɪməs/ ● **n.** trademark a portable cooking stove that burns vaporized oil.

**primus** /ˈprʌɪməs/ ● **n.** the elected presiding bishop of the Scottish Episcopal Church.
– ORIGIN C16: from L., lit. 'first'.

**primus inter pares** /ˌpriːməs ɪntə ˈpɑːriːz, ˌprʌɪməs/ ● **n.** a first among equals; the senior or representative member of a group.
– ORIGIN from L.

**prince** ● **n. 1** a son, grandson, or other close male relative of a monarch. ➤ a male monarch of a small state, actually or nominally subject to a king or emperor. ➤ (in some European countries) a nobleman, usually ranking next below a duke. **2** (**prince of/among**) a man or thing preeminent in a particular sphere or group.
– PHRASES **prince of the blood** a prince by right of royal descent.
– DERIVATIVES **princedom** n.
– ORIGIN ME: via OFr. from L. *princeps*, *princip-* 'first, chief, sovereign', from *primus* 'first' + *capere* 'take'.

**Prince Charming** ● **n.** a handsome and honourable young male lover.
– ORIGIN partial translation of Fr. *Roi Charmant*, lit. 'King Charming', the title of a C18 fairy-tale romance.

**prince consort** ● **n.** the husband of a reigning female sovereign who is himself a prince.

**princeling** ● **n. 1** chiefly derogatory the ruler of a small principality or domain. **2** a young prince.

**princely** ● **adj. 1** of, relating to, or suitable for a prince. **2** (of a sum of money) generous.
– DERIVATIVES **princeliness** n.

**Prince of Darkness** ● **n.** the Devil.

**Prince of Peace** ● **n.** a title of Jesus Christ.

**prince royal** (or **princess royal**) ● **n.** the eldest son (or daughter) of a reigning monarch.

**prince's feather** ● **n.** a tall South American plant with upright brush-like spikes of small red flowers. [*Amaranthus hypochondriacus*.]

**princess** ● **n. 1** a daughter, granddaughter, or other close female relative of a monarch. ➤ the wife or widow of a prince. ➤ a female monarch of a small state, actually or nominally subject to a king or emperor. **2** (**princess of/among**) a woman or thing pre-eminent in a particular sphere or group. **3** N. Amer. a spoilt or arrogant young woman.
– PHRASES **princess of the blood** a princess by right of royal descent.
– ORIGIN ME: from OFr. *princesse*.

**principal** ● **adj. 1** first in order of importance; main. **2** denoting an original sum of money invested or lent. ● **n. 1** the most important or senior person in an organization or group. ➤ the head of a school or college. ➤ (in certain professions) a fully qualified practitioner. **2** a sum of money lent or invested, on which interest is paid. **3** a person for whom another acts as an agent or representative. ➤ Law a person directly responsible for a crime. **4** a main rafter supporting purlins. **5** an organ stop sounding a set of pipes typically an octave above the diapason.
– DERIVATIVES **principalship** n.
– ORIGIN ME: via OFr. from L. *principalis* 'first, original', from *princeps*, *princip-* 'first, chief'.

**principal boy** (or **principal girl**) ● **n.** Brit. a woman who takes the leading male (or female) role in a pantomime.

**principality** ● **n.** (pl. **-ies**) a state ruled by a prince. ➤ (**the Principality**) Brit. Wales.
– ORIGIN ME: from OFr. *principalite*, from late L. *principalitas*, from L. *principalis* (see **PRINCIPAL**).

**principally** ● **adv.** for the most part; chiefly.

**principate** /ˈprɪnsɪpət/ ● **n.** the rule of the early Roman emperors, during which some republican features were retained.
– ORIGIN ME (denoting a principality): from L. *principatus* 'first place', from *princeps*, *princip-* (see **PRINCE**).

**principle** ● **n. 1** a fundamental truth or proposition serving as the foundation for belief or action. ➤ a rule or belief governing one's personal behaviour. ➤ morally correct behaviour and attitudes: *a man of principle.* **2** a general scientific theorem or natural law. **3** a fundamental source or basis of something. ➤ a fundamental quality or attribute. **4** Chemistry an active or characteristic constituent of a substance.
– PHRASES **in principle** in theory. **on principle** because of one's adherence to a particular belief.
– ORIGIN ME: from OFr., from L. *principium* 'source', *principia* (pl.) 'foundations', from *princeps*, *princip-* 'first, chief'.

**principled** ● **adj. 1** acting in accordance with morality. **2** (of a system or method) based on a given set of rules.

**prink** ● **v.** (**prink oneself**) make minor adjustments to one's appearance.
– ORIGIN C16: prob. rel. to archaic *prank* 'dress or adorn in a showy manner'.

**print** ● **v. 1** produce (books, newspapers, etc.) by a mechanical process involving the transfer of text or designs to paper. ➤ produce (text or a picture) in such a way. ➤ publish. ➤ produce a paper copy of (information stored on a computer). **2** produce (a photographic print) from a negative. **3** write clearly without joining the letters. **4** mark with a coloured design or pattern. ➤ make (a mark or indentation) by pressing something on a surface or soft substance. **5** fix firmly or indelibly in someone's mind. ● **n. 1** the text appearing in a book, newspaper, etc. ➤ the state of being available in published form. ➤ [as modifier] of or relating to the printing industry or the printed media. ➤ informal a newspaper. **2** an indentation or mark left on a surface or soft substance by pressure. ➤ (**prints**) fingerprints. **3** a printed picture or design. ➤ a photograph printed on paper from a negative or transparency. ➤ a copy of a motion picture on film. **4** a piece of fabric or

clothing with a coloured pattern or design. ➤ a pattern or design of this type.
– PHRASES **appear in print** (of an author) have one's work published. **in print 1** (of a book) available from the publisher. **2** in published form. **out of print** (of a book) no longer available from the publisher.
– DERIVATIVES **printability** n. **printable** adj.
– ORIGIN ME: from OFr. *preinte* 'pressed', fem. past part. of *preindre*, from L. *premere* 'to press'.

**printed circuit** ● n. an electronic circuit based on thin strips of a conductor on an insulating board, made by etching.

**printer** ● n. **1** a person whose job is commercial printing. **2** a machine for printing text or pictures.

**printer's devil** ● n. historical an errand boy in a printing office.

**printer's mark** ● n. a logo serving as a printer's trademark.

**printery** ● n. (pl. **-ies**) a printing works.

**printhead** ● n. Computing a component in a printer that assembles and prints the characters on the paper.

**printing** ● n. **1** the production of books, newspapers, etc. **2** a single impression of a book. **3** handwriting in which the letters are written separately.

**printing press** ● n. a machine for printing from type or plates.

**printing works** ● n. [treated as sing. or pl.] a factory for the printing of newspapers, books, etc.

**printmaker** ● n. a person who prints pictures or designs from plates or blocks.
– DERIVATIVES **printmaking** n.

**printout** ● n. Computing a page of printed material from a computer's printer.

**print run** ● n. the number of copies of a book, magazine, etc. printed at one time.

**printworks** ● n. [treated as sing. or pl.] a factory for the printing of textiles.

**prion**[1] /'prʌɪən/ ● n. a small petrel of southern seas, having a wide bill fringed with comb-like plates for feeding on planktonic crustaceans. [Genus *Pachyptila*: six species.]
– ORIGIN C19: mod. L. (former genus name), from Gk *priōn* 'a saw' (referring to its bill).

**prion**[2] /'priːɒn/ ● n. Microbiology a submicroscopic protein particle believed to be the cause of certain brain diseases such as BSE.
– ORIGIN 1980s: by rearrangement of elements from *pro(teinaceous) in(fectious particle)*.

**prior**[1] ● adj. existing or coming before in time, order, or importance. ● n. N. Amer. informal a previous criminal conviction.
– PHRASES **prior to** before.
– ORIGIN C18: from L., lit. 'former, elder', rel. to *prae* 'before'.

**prior**[2] ● n. (fem. **prioress**) **1** (in an abbey) the person next in rank below an abbot (or abbess). **2** the head of a house of friars (or nuns).
– DERIVATIVES **priorate** n. **priorship** n.
– ORIGIN OE, from a med. L. noun use of L. *prior* (see **PRIOR**[1]).

**prioritize** (also **-ise**) ● v. designate or treat as most important. ➤ determine the relative importance of (items or tasks).
– DERIVATIVES **prioritization** n.

**priority** ● n. (pl. **-ies**) **1** the fact or condition of being regarded as more important. ➤ a thing regarded as more important than others. **2** the right to proceed before other traffic.
– ORIGIN ME: from OFr. *priorite*, from med. L. *prioritas*, from L. *prior* (see **PRIOR**[1]).

**priory** ● n. (pl. **-ies**) a monastery or nunnery governed by a prior or prioress.
– ORIGIN ME: from Anglo-Norman Fr. *priorie*, med. L. *prioria*, from L. *prior* (see **PRIOR**[2]).

**prise** (US **prize**) ● v. **1** use force in order to open or move apart. **2** (**prise something out of/from**) obtain something from (someone) with effort or difficulty.
– ORIGIN C17: from dial. *prise* 'lever', from OFr. *prise* 'grasp, taking hold'; cf. **PRY**[2].

**prism** /'prɪz(ə)m/ ● n. **1** Geometry a solid geometric figure whose two ends are similar, equal, and parallel rectilinear figures, and whose sides are parallelograms. **2** Optics a transparent object in this form, especially one with triangular ends used to separate white light into a spectrum of colours.
– ORIGIN C16: via late L. from Gk *prisma* 'thing sawn', from *prizein* 'to saw'.

**prismatic** /prɪz'matɪk/ ● adj. **1** of, relating to, or having the form of a prism. ➤ incorporating a prism or prisms. **2** (of colours) formed, separated, or distributed by or as by a prism.
– DERIVATIVES **prismatically** adv.

**prismoid** /'prɪzmɔɪd/ ● n. Geometry a body like a prism, in which the end faces have the same number of sides but are not equal.

**prison** ● n. a building for the confinement of criminals or those awaiting trial. ● v. (**prisoned**, **prisoning**) poetic/literary imprison.
– ORIGIN OE, from OFr. *prisun*, from L. *prensio(n-)*, var. of *prehensio(n-)* 'laying hold of', from *prehendere*.

**prison camp** ● n. a camp where prisoners of war or political prisoners are kept.

**prisoner** ● n. a person legally committed to prison. ➤ a person captured and kept confined. ➤ a person trapped by a situation or circumstances.
– PHRASES **take no prisoners** be ruthlessly aggressive or uncompromising in the pursuit of one's objectives.
– ORIGIN ME: from OFr. *prisonier*, from *prison* (see **PRISON**).

**prisoner of conscience** ● n. a person imprisoned for their political or religious views.

**prisoner of state** (also **state prisoner**) ● n. a person confined for political reasons.

**prisoner of war** ● n. a person captured and imprisoned by the enemy in war.

**prisoner's base** ● n. a chasing game played by two groups of children each with a distinct base or home.

**prisoner's dilemma** ● n. (in game theory) a situation in which two players each have two options whose outcome depends crucially on the other's simultaneous choice, exemplified by two prisoners separately deciding whether to confess to a crime.

**prissy** ● adj. (**-ier**, **-iest**) fussily respectable; prim.
– DERIVATIVES **prissily** adv. **prissiness** n.
– ORIGIN C19: perh. a blend of **PRIM** and **SISSY**.

**pristine** /'prɪstiːn, -stʌɪn/ ● adj. in its original condition. ➤ spotless.
– ORIGIN C16 (in the sense 'original, former, primitive and undeveloped'): from L. *pristinus* 'former'.

**prithee** /'prɪðiː/ ● exclam. archaic please.
– ORIGIN C16: abbrev. of *I pray thee*.

**privacy** /'prɪvəsi, 'prʌɪ-/ ● n. a state in which one is not observed or disturbed by others. ➤ freedom from public attention.

**private** ● adj. **1** for or belonging to one particular person or group only. ➤ (of thoughts, feelings, etc.) not to be shared or revealed. ➤ (of a person) not choosing to share their thoughts and feelings. ➤ (of a place) secluded. ➤ alone and undisturbed by others. **2** (of a person) having no official or public position. ➤ not connected with one's work or official position. **3** (of a service or industry) provided or owned by an individual or commercial company rather than the state. ➤ of or relating to a system of education or medical treatment conducted outside the state system and charging fees. **4** relating to or denoting a transaction between individuals. ● n. **1** the lowest rank in the army, below lance corporal or private first class. **2** (**privates**) informal short for **PRIVATE PARTS**.
– PHRASES **in private** with no one else present.
– DERIVATIVES **privately** adv.
– ORIGIN ME: from L. *privatus* 'withdrawn from public life', a use of the past part. of *privare* 'bereave, deprive', from *privus* 'single, individual'.

**private bill** ● n. a legislative bill affecting a particular body or individual only.

**private company** • n. Brit. a company whose shares may not be offered to the public for sale.

**private detective** (also **private investigator**) • n. a freelance detective carrying out investigations for private clients.

**private enterprise** • n. business or industry managed by independent companies rather than the state.

**privateer** /ˌprʌɪvəˈtɪə/ • n. **1** chiefly historical an armed ship owned by private individuals, holding a government commission and authorized for use in war. ➤(also **privateersman**) a commander or crew member of a privateer. **2** an advocate of private enterprise.
– DERIVATIVES **privateering** n.
– ORIGIN C17: from **PRIVATE**, on the pattern of *volunteer*.

**private eye** • n. informal a private detective.

**private first class** • n. a rank in the US army, above private and below corporal.

**private income** • n. income derived from private means.

**private law** • n. a branch of law concerned with the relations between individuals.

**private life** • n. one's personal relationships, interests, etc., as distinct from one's professional or public life.

**private means** • pl. n. Brit. a source of income derived from investments, property, etc. rather than from employment.

**private member** • n. (in the UK, Canada, Australia, and New Zealand) a member of a parliament who is not a minister or does not hold government office.

**private nuisance** • n. Law an unlawful interference with the use and enjoyment of land.

**private parts** • pl. n. euphemistic a person's genitals.

**private practice** • n. the work of a doctor, lawyer, etc. who is self-employed. ➤Brit. medical practice that is not part of the National Health Service.

**private school** • n. **1** Brit. an independent school supported wholly by the payment of fees. **2** N. Amer. a school supported mainly by private individuals.

**private secretary** • n. **1** a secretary who deals with the personal and confidential concerns of their employer. **2** a civil servant acting as an aide to a senior government official.

**private sector** • n. the part of the national economy not under direct state control.

**private soldier** • n. a soldier of the lowest rank. ➤US a soldier of this type who is not a recruit.

**private view** • n. a chance for invited guests to see an art exhibition before it is opened to the public.

**private war** • n. **1** a feud conducted without regard to the law. **2** hostilities against members of another state without government sanction.

**privation** /prʌɪˈveɪʃ(ə)n/ • n. **1** a state in which essentials such as food and warmth are lacking. **2** formal the loss or absence of a quality that is normally present.
– ORIGIN ME: from L. *privatio(n-)*, from *privat-*, *privare* (see **PRIVATE**).

**privatism** /ˈprʌɪvətɪz(ə)m/ • n. a tendency to be concerned with issues only in so far as they affect oneself.

**privative** /ˈprɪvətɪv/ • adj. **1** lacking some quality or attribute that is normally present. ➤(of a statement or term) denoting the absence or loss of an attribute or quality. **2** Grammar (of a particle or affix) expressing absence or negation.
– ORIGIN C16: from L. *privativus* 'denoting privation', from *privat-* (see **PRIVATION**).

**privatize** (also **-ise**) • v. transfer (a business, industry, etc.) from public to private ownership.
– DERIVATIVES **privatization** n. **privatizer** n.

**privet** /ˈprɪvɪt/ • n. a shrub of the olive family, with small white scented flowers and poisonous black berries. [*Ligustrum ovalifolium* and other species.]
– ORIGIN C16: of unknown origin.

**privilege** • n. **1** a special right, advantage, or immunity for a particular person. ➤a special benefit or honour. **2** (also **absolute privilege**) (especially in a parliamentary context) the right to say or write something without the risk of punishment. **3** the right of a lawyer or official to refuse to divulge confidential information. **4** chiefly historical a grant of special rights or immunities, especially in the form of a franchise or monopoly. • v. formal grant a privilege or privileges to. ➤(usu. **be privileged from**) exempt from a liability or obligation.
– DERIVATIVES **privileged** adj.
– ORIGIN ME: via OFr. from L. *privilegium* 'bill or law affecting an individual', from *privus* 'private' + *lex*, *leg-* 'law'.

**privity** /ˈprɪvɪti/ • n. (pl. **-ies**) Law a relation between two parties that is recognized by law, e.g. that of blood, lease, or service.
– ORIGIN ME: from OFr. *privete*, from med. L. *privitas*, from L. *privus* 'private'.

**privy** • adj. **1** (**privy to**) sharing in the knowledge of (something secret). **2** archaic hidden; secret. • n. (pl. **-ies**) **1** a toilet in a small shed outside a house. **2** Law a person having a part or interest in any action or matter.
– DERIVATIVES **privily** adv.
– ORIGIN ME: from OFr. *prive* 'private' (also as n. meaning 'private place' and 'familiar friend'), from L. *privatus* (see **PRIVATE**).

**Privy Council** • n. a body of advisers appointed by a sovereign or a Governor General (now chiefly on an honorary basis and including government ministers). ➤chiefly historical a sovereign's or Governor General's private counsellors.
– DERIVATIVES **privy counsellor** (also **privy councillor**) n.

**privy purse** • n. (in the UK) an allowance from the public revenue for the monarch's private expenses.

**privy seal** • n. (in the UK) a seal affixed to state documents.

**prix fixe** /priː ˈfɪks, French pʀi fiks/ • n. a meal of several courses costing a fixed price.
– ORIGIN Fr., lit. 'fixed price'.

**prize**[1] • n. **1** a thing given as a reward to a winner or in recognition of an outstanding achievement. ➤something won in a game of chance. ➤something of great value that is worth struggling to achieve. **2** chiefly historical an enemy ship captured during warfare. • adj. **1** having been or likely to be awarded a prize. **2** outstanding of its kind. • v. value highly.
– ORIGIN ME: sense 1 of n. is var. of **PRICE**, sense 2 is from OFr. *prise* 'taking, booty'; v. is from OFr. *pris-*, stem of *preisier* (see **PRAISE**).

**prize**[2] • v. US spelling of **PRISE**.

**prize court** • n. a court adjudicating on the distribution of ships and property captured in naval warfare.

**prizefight** • n. a boxing match, typically an unlicensed one, for prize money.
– DERIVATIVES **prizefighter** n. **prizefighting** n.

**prizeman** • n. (pl. **-men**) a winner of a prize, especially an academic one.

**prize ring** • n. **1** a ring used for prizefighting. **2** the practice of prizefighting.

**PRO** • abbrev. **1** Public Record Office. **2** public relations officer.

**pro**[1] • n. (pl. **-os**) informal **1** a professional. **2** a prostitute. • adj. professional.

**pro**[2] • n. (pl. **-os**) (usu. in phr. **pros and cons**) an advantage or argument in favour of something. • prep. & adv. in favour of.
– ORIGIN ME (as n.): from L., lit. 'for, on behalf of'.

**pro-**[1] • prefix **1** favouring; supporting: *pro-choice*. **2** acting as a substitute for: *proconsul*. **3** denoting motion forwards, out, or away: *propel*.
– ORIGIN from L. *pro* 'in front of, on behalf of, instead of, on account of'.

**pro-**[2] • prefix before in time, place, or order: *proactive*.
– ORIGIN from Gk *pro* 'before'.

**proa** /ˈprəʊə/ (also **prahu** or **prau**) • n. a Malaysian or Indonesian sailing boat, typically having a large triangular sail and an outrigger.
– ORIGIN C16: from Malay *perahu*.

**proactive** • adj. creating or controlling a situation rather than just responding to it.
– DERIVATIVES **proaction** n. **proactively** adv. **proactivity** n.
– ORIGIN 1930s: from **PRO-**[2] (denoting earlier occurrence),

on the pattern of *reactive*.

**pro-am** • adj. involving professionals and amateurs. • n. a pro-am event.

**prob** • n. informal a problem.

**probabilistic** • adj. based on or adapted to a theory of probability; involving chance variation.

**probability** • n. (pl. **-ies**) the extent to which something is probable. ➤ a probable or most probable event.
– PHRASES **in all probability** most probably.

**probable** • adj. likely to happen or be the case. • n. a person likely to become or do something.
– ORIGIN ME (in the sense 'worthy of belief'): via OFr. from L. *probabilis*, from *probare* 'to test, demonstrate'.

**probable cause** • n. Law, chiefly N. Amer. reasonable grounds.

**probably** • adv. almost certainly; as far as one knows or can tell.

**proband** /'prəʊbənd/ • n. a person serving as the starting point for the genetic study of a family.
– ORIGIN 1920s: from L. *probandus* 'to be proved', gerundive of *probare* 'to test'.

**probang** /'prəʊbaŋ/ • n. Medicine a flexible strip with a sponge or tuft at the end, used to remove an object from the throat or apply medication to it.
– ORIGIN C17 (named *provang* by its inventor): perh. an alt. suggested by **PROBE**.

**probate** • n. the official proving of a will. ➤ a verified copy of a will with a certificate as handed to the executors. • v. N. Amer. establish the validity of (a will).
– ORIGIN ME: from L. *probatum* 'something proved', neut. past part. of *probare* 'to test, prove'.

**probation** • n. **1** Law the release of an offender from detention, subject to a period of good behaviour under supervision. **2** the process of testing the character or abilities of a person in a certain role.
– DERIVATIVES **probationary** adj.
– ORIGIN ME: from OFr. *probacion*, from L. *probatio(n-)*, from *probare* (see **PROVE**).

**probationer** • n. **1** a person serving a probationary period in a job or position. **2** an offender on probation.

**probation officer** • n. a person who supervises offenders on probation.

**probative** /'prəʊbətɪv/ • adj. chiefly Law affording proof or evidence.
– ORIGIN ME: from L. *probativus*, from *probat-*, *probare* (see **PROVE**).

**probe** • n. **1** a blunt-ended surgical instrument for exploring a wound or part of the body. **2** a small measuring or testing device, especially an electrode. **3** a projecting device on an aircraft for in-flight refuelling or on a spacecraft for docking with another craft. **4** (also **space probe**) an unmanned exploratory spacecraft. **5** an investigation. • v. physically explore or examine. ➤ enquire into closely.
– DERIVATIVES **prober** n. **probing** adj. **probingly** adv.
– ORIGIN ME (as n.): from late L. *proba* 'proof' (in med. L. 'examination'), from L. *probare* 'to test'.

**probit** /'prɒbɪt/ • n. Statistics a unit of probability based on deviation from the mean of a standard distribution.
– ORIGIN 1930s: from *prob(ability un)it*.

**probity** /'prəʊbɪti, 'prɒb-/ • n. honesty and decency.
– ORIGIN ME: from L. *probitas*, from *probus* 'good'.

**problem** • n. **1** an unwelcome or harmful matter needing to be dealt with and overcome. ➤ a thing that is difficult to achieve. **2** Physics & Mathematics an inquiry starting from given conditions to investigate or demonstrate something. **3** (in chess) an arrangement of pieces in which the solver has to achieve a specified result.
– ORIGIN ME: from OFr. *probleme*, via L. from Gk *problēma*, from *proballein* 'put forth', from *pro* 'before' + *ballein* 'to throw'.

**problematic** • adj. constituting or presenting a problem. • n. a problematic thing.
– DERIVATIVES **problematical** adj. **problematically** adv.
– ORIGIN C17: via Fr. from late L. *problematicus*, from Gk *problēmatikos*, from *problēma* (see **PROBLEM**).

**problematize** (also **-ise**) • v. make into or regard as a problem.
– DERIVATIVES **problematization** n.

**pro bono publico** /prəʊ ˌbɒnəʊ 'pʊblɪkəʊ, ˌbəʊnəʊ 'pʌblɪkəʊ/ • adv. & adj. **1** for the public good. **2** (usu. **pro bono**) chiefly N. Amer. denoting legal work undertaken without charge, especially for a client on low income.
– ORIGIN from L.

**proboscidean** /ˌprɒbə'sɪdɪən/ (also **proboscidian**) • n. Zoology a mammal of an order (Proboscidea) comprising the elephants and their extinct relatives.
– ORIGIN from mod. L. *Proboscidea*, from **PROBOSCIS**.

**proboscis** /prə'bɒsɪs/ • n. (pl. **probosces** /-siːz/, **proboscides** /-sɪdiːz/, or **proboscises**) **1** the nose of a mammal, especially when long and mobile like the trunk of an elephant. **2** Zoology an elongated sucking organ or mouthpart.
– ORIGIN C17: via L. from Gk *proboskis* 'means of obtaining food', from *pro* 'before' + *boskein* '(cause to) feed'.

**proboscis monkey** • n. a monkey native to the forests of Borneo, the male of which has a large pendulous nose. [*Nasalis larvatus*.]

**procaine** /'prəʊkeɪn/ • n. a synthetic compound used as a local anaesthetic.
– ORIGIN C20: from **PRO-**[1] (denoting substitution) + *-caine* (from **COCAINE**).

**procaryote** • n. variant spelling of **PROKARYOTE**.

**procedure** • n. **1** an established or official way of doing something. ➤ a series of actions conducted in a certain order or manner. **2** Computing a subroutine.
– DERIVATIVES **procedural** adj. **procedurally** adv.
– ORIGIN C16: from Fr. *procédure*, from *procéder* (see **PROCEED**).

**proceed** • v. **1** begin a course of action. ➤ go on to do something. ➤ (of an action) carry on or continue. **2** move forward. **3** Law start a lawsuit against someone. **4** (**proceed from**) originate from.
– ORIGIN ME: from OFr. *proceder*, from L. *procedere*, from *pro-* 'forward' + *cedere* 'go'.

**proceedings** • pl. n. **1** an event or a series of activities with a set procedure. **2** Law action taken in a court to settle a dispute. **3** a report of a set of meetings or a conference.

**proceeds** • pl. n. money obtained from an event or activity.
– ORIGIN C17: pl. of the obs. noun *proceed*, in the same sense, earlier meaning 'procedure'.

**process**[1] /'prəʊsɛs/ • n. **1** a series of actions or steps towards achieving a particular end. ➤ a natural series of changes. **2** [as modifier] Printing relating to or denoting printing using ink in three colours (cyan, magenta, and yellow) and black. **3** Law a summons to appear in court. **4** Biology & Anatomy a natural appendage or outgrowth on or in an organism. • v. perform a series of operations to change or preserve. ➤ Computing operate on (data) by means of a program. ➤ deal with, using an established procedure.
– DERIVATIVES **processable** adj.
– ORIGIN ME: from OFr. *proces*, from L. *processus* 'progression, course', from *procedere* (see **PROCEED**).

**process**[2] /prə'sɛs/ • v. walk in procession.
– ORIGIN C19: back-form. from **PROCESSION**.

**procession** • n. **1** a number of people or vehicles moving forward in an orderly fashion, especially as part of a ceremony. ➤ the action of moving in such a way. ➤ a relentless succession of people or things. **2** Theology the emanation of the Holy Spirit.
– ORIGIN OE, via OFr. from L. *processio(n-)*, from *procedere* (see **PROCEED**).

**processional** • adj. of, for, or used in a religious or ceremonial procession. • n. a book of litanies and hymns used in religious processions.

**processor** • n. a machine that processes something. ➤ Computing a central processing unit.

**process server** • n. a bailiff.

**processual** /prə'sɛsjʊəl/ • adj. relating to or involving the study of processes.

**procès-verbal** /ˌprɒseɪvəː'bɑːl/ • n. (pl. **procès-verbaux** /-'bəʊ/) a written report of proceedings.

– ORIGIN C17: Fr.

**pro-choice** • adj. advocating the right of a woman to choose to have an abortion.
– DERIVATIVES **pro-choicer** n.

**proclaim** • v. announce officially or publicly. ➤ declare (someone) to be. ➤ indicate clearly.
– DERIVATIVES **proclaimer** n. **proclamation** n. **proclamatory** adj.
– ORIGIN ME *proclame*, from L. *proclamare* 'cry out', from *pro-* 'forth' + *clamare* 'to shout'; the change being due to assoc. with **CLAIM**.

**proclitic** /prə(ʊ)'klɪtɪk/ Linguistics • n. a word pronounced with so little emphasis that it forms part of the following word, e.g. *at* in *at home*. Compare with **ENCLITIC**. • adj. denoting or relating to such a word.
– DERIVATIVES **proclitically** adv.
– ORIGIN C19: from mod. L. *procliticus* (from Gk *proklinein* 'lean forward'), on the pattern of late L. *encliticus* (see **ENCLITIC**).

**proclivity** /prə'klɪvɪti/ • n. (pl. **-ies**) an inclination or predisposition.
– ORIGIN C16: from L. *proclivitas*, from *proclivis* 'inclined', from *pro-* 'forward, down' + *clivus* 'slope'.

**proconsul** /prəʊ'kɒns(ə)l/ • n. **1** a governor of a province in ancient Rome. **2** a governor or deputy consul of a modern colony.
– DERIVATIVES **proconsular** adj. **proconsulate** n. **proconsulship** n.
– ORIGIN from L. *pro consule* '(one acting) for the consul'.

**procrastinate** /prə(ʊ)'krastɪneɪt/ • v. delay or postpone action.
– DERIVATIVES **procrastination** n. **procrastinator** n. **procrastinatory** adj.
– ORIGIN C16: from L. *procrastinat-*, *procrastinare* 'defer till the morning', from *pro-* 'forward' + *crastinus* 'belonging to tomorrow' (from *cras* 'tomorrow').

**procreate** • v. produce young.
– DERIVATIVES **procreant** adj. (archaic). **procreation** n. **procreative** adj. **procreator** n.
– ORIGIN ME: from L. *procreat-*, *procreare* 'generate, bring forth', from *pro-* 'forth' + *creare* 'create'.

**Procrustean** /prə(ʊ)'krʌstɪən/ • adj. enforcing conformity without regard to natural variation or individuality.
– ORIGIN C19: from the name *Procrustes*, a robber in Greek mythology who fitted victims to a bed by stretching or cutting off parts of them + **-AN**.

**proctitis** /prɒk'tʌɪtɪs/ • n. Medicine inflammation of the rectum and anus.
– ORIGIN C19: from Gk *prōktos* 'anus' + **-ITIS**.

**proctology** /prɒk'tɒlədʒi/ • n. the branch of medicine concerned with the anus and rectum.
– DERIVATIVES **proctological** adj. **proctologist** n.
– ORIGIN C19: from Gk *prōktos* 'anus' + **-LOGY**.

**proctor** • n. **1** Brit. an officer at certain universities having mainly disciplinary functions. **2** N. Amer. an invigilator at an examination. **3** (in the Church of England) an elected representative of the clergy in the convocation of Canterbury or York. **4** historical a practitioner of law in ecclesiastical and certain other courts.
– DERIVATIVES **proctorial** adj. **proctorship** n.
– ORIGIN ME: contr. of **PROCURATOR**.

**proctoscope** /'prɒktəskəʊp/ • n. a medical instrument for examining the anus and lower rectum.
– DERIVATIVES **proctoscopy** n.
– ORIGIN C19: from Gk *prōktos* 'anus' + **-SCOPE**.

**procumbent** /prə(ʊ)'kʌmb(ə)nt/ • adj. Botany (of a plant or stem) growing along the ground without throwing out roots.,
– ORIGIN C17: from L. *procumbent-*, *procumbere* 'fall forwards', from *pro-* 'forwards, down' + a verb rel. to *cubare* 'to lie'.

**procuracy** /prə'kjʊərəsi/ • n. (pl. **-ies**) the position or office of a procurator.

**procuration** • n. **1** Law, dated the appointment, authority, or action of an attorney. **2** archaic the action of procuring something.
– ORIGIN ME: via OFr. from L. *procuratio(n-)*, from *procurare* (see **PROCURE**).

**procurator** /'prɒkjʊreɪtə/ • n. **1** Law an agent representing others in a court in countries retaining Roman civil law. **2** (in Scotland) a lawyer practising before the lower courts. **3** historical a treasury officer in a province of the Roman Empire.
– DERIVATIVES **procuratorial** adj. **procuratorship** n.
– ORIGIN ME: from OFr. *procuratour* or L. *procurator* 'administrator, finance agent', from *procurat-*, *procurare* (see **PROCURE**).

**procurator fiscal** • n. (in Scotland) a local coroner and public prosecutor.

**procure** • v. **1** obtain. ➤ obtain as a prostitute for someone else. **2** Law persuade or cause to do something. ➤ archaic or Law cause to happen.
– DERIVATIVES **procurable** adj. **procurement** n. **procurer** n. **procuress** n.
– ORIGIN ME: from OFr. *procurer*, from L. *procurare* 'take care of, manage', from *pro-* 'on behalf of' + *curare* 'see to'.

**Prod** (also **Proddie**, **Proddy**) • n. informal, offensive (especially in Ireland) a Protestant.
– ORIGIN 1940s: abbrev. representing a pronunc.

**prod** • v. (**prodded**, **prodding**) **1** poke with a finger, pointed object, etc. **2** stimulate or persuade to do something. • n. **1** a poke. **2** a stimulus or reminder. **3** a pointed implement, typically discharging an electric current and used as a goad.
– PHRASES **on the prod** N. Amer. informal on the offensive.
– DERIVATIVES **prodder** n.
– ORIGIN C16 (as v.): perh. symbolic of a short poke, or a blend of **POKE**[1] and dial. *brod* 'to goad, prod'.

**prodigal** • adj. **1** wastefully extravagant. **2** lavish. • n. a prodigal person. ➤ (also **prodigal son** or **daughter**) a person who leaves home to lead a prodigal life but returns repentant. [with allusion to the parable in Luke 15:11–32.]
– DERIVATIVES **prodigality** n. **prodigally** adv.
– ORIGIN ME: from late L. *prodigalis*, from L. *prodigus* 'lavish'.

**prodigious** /prə'dɪdʒəs/ • adj. **1** remarkably or impressively large. **2** archaic unnatural; abnormal.
– DERIVATIVES **prodigiously** adv. **prodigiousness** n.
– ORIGIN C15: from L. *prodigiosus*, from *prodigium* (see **PRODIGY**).

**prodigy** • n. (pl. **-ies**) a person, especially a young one, with exceptional abilities. ➤ an outstanding example of a quality. ➤ an amazing or unusual thing.
– ORIGIN C15: from L. *prodigium* 'portent'.

**prodrome** /'prəʊdrəʊm, 'prɒdrəʊm/ • n. Medicine an early symptom indicating the onset of illness.
– DERIVATIVES **prodromal** adj. **prodromic** /prə(ʊ)'drɒmɪk/ adj.
– ORIGIN C17: from Fr., from mod. L. *prodromus*, from Gk *prodromos* 'precursor', from *pro* 'before' + *dromos* 'running'.

**prodrug** • n. a biologically inactive compound which can be metabolized in the body to produce a drug.

**produce** • v. **1** make, manufacture, or create. ➤ create or form as part of a physical, biological, or chemical process. **2** cause to happen or exist. **3** provide for consideration, inspection, or use. **4** administer the financial and managerial aspects of (a film or broadcast) or the staging of (a play). ➤ supervise the making of (a musical recording). **5** Geometry, dated extend or continue (a line). • n. things that have been produced or grown. ➤ the result of work or efforts.
– DERIVATIVES **producer** n. **producibility** n. **producible** adj.
– ORIGIN ME: from L. *producere*, from *pro-* 'forward' + *ducere* 'to lead'.

**producer gas** • n. a low-grade fuel gas containing carbon monoxide, formed by passing air, or air and steam, through red-hot carbon.

**product** • n. **1** an article or substance manufactured or refined for sale. ➤ a substance produced during a natural, chemical, or manufacturing process. ➤ a result of an action or process. **2** a person whose character has been

formed by a particular period or situation. **3** Mathematics a quantity obtained by multiplying quantities together, or from an analogous algebraic operation.
– ORIGIN ME: from L. *productum* 'something produced', neut. past part. (used as n.) of *producere* (see **PRODUCE**).

**production** • **n. 1** the action or process of producing or being produced. ➤the amount of something produced. ➤[as modifier] denoting a vehicle manufactured in large numbers, as opposed to a prototype or other special version. **2** a film, record, or play, viewed in terms of its making or staging.
– ORIGIN ME: via OFr. from L. *productio(n-)*, from *producere* (see **PRODUCE**).

**production line** • **n.** another term for **ASSEMBLY LINE**.

**productive** • **adj. 1** producing or able to produce large amounts of goods, crops, etc. ➤relating to or engaged in the production of goods, crops, etc. **2** achieving or producing a significant amount or result. **3** (**productive of**) producing. **4** Linguistics (of a prefix, suffix, etc.) currently used in forming new words or expressions. **5** Medicine (of a cough) raising mucus from the respiratory tract.
– DERIVATIVES **productively** adv. **productiveness** n.
– ORIGIN C17: from Fr. *productif, -ive* or late L. *productivus*, from *product-, producere* (see **PRODUCE**).

**productivity** • **n. 1** the state or quality of producing something. **2** the effectiveness of productive effort. **3** Ecology the fertility or capacity of a given habitat or area.

**product placement** • **n.** a practice in which companies pay for their products or services to be featured in films and television programmes.

**proem** /ˈprəʊɪm/ • **n.** formal a preface or preamble to a book or speech.
– DERIVATIVES **proemial** /-ˈiːmɪəl/ adj.
– ORIGIN ME: from OFr. *proeme*, via L. from Gk *prooimion* 'prelude', from *pro* 'before' + *oimē* 'song'.

**Prof.** • **abbrev.** professor.

**prof** • **n.** informal a professor.

**profane** /prəˈfeɪn/ • **adj. 1** secular rather than religious. ➤not initiated into religious rites. **2** not respectful of religious practice. ➤(of language) blasphemous or obscene. • **v.** treat with irreverence.
– DERIVATIVES **profanation** n. **profanely** adv. **profaneness** n. **profaner** n.
– ORIGIN ME: from OFr. *prophane*, from L. *profanus* 'outside the temple, not sacred', from *pro-* (from L. *pro* 'before') + *fanum* 'temple'.

**profanity** /prəˈfanɪti/ • **n.** (pl. **-ies**) profane language or behaviour. ➤a swear word.

**profess** • **v. 1** claim that one has (a quality or feeling). **2** affirm one's faith in or allegiance to (a religion). ➤(**be professed**) be received into a religious order under vows. **3** dated or humorous teach (a subject) as a professor. **4** archaic have or claim knowledge or skill in.
– ORIGIN ME: from L. *profess-, profiteri* 'declare publicly', from *pro-* 'before' + *fateri* 'confess'.

**professed** • **adj. 1** (of a quality, feeling, etc.) claimed openly but typically falsely. **2** self-acknowledged: *a professed commitment to human rights.* **3** having taken the vows of a religious order. **4** archaic professional.

**professedly** • **adv.** ostensibly.

**profession** • **n. 1** a paid occupation, especially one involving training and a formal qualification. ➤[treated as sing. or pl.] a body of people engaged in a profession. **2** an open but typically false claim: *a profession of allegiance.* **3** a declaration of belief in a religion. ➤the vows made on entering a religious order. ➤the fact of being professed in a religious order.
– PHRASES **the oldest profession** humorous prostitution.
– ORIGIN ME: via OFr. from L. *professio(n-)*, from *profiteri* (see **PROFESS**).

**professional** • **adj. 1** of, relating to, or belonging to a profession. ➤worthy of or appropriate to a professional person. **2** engaged in an activity as a paid occupation rather than as an amateur. **3** informal, derogatory habitually engaged in a particular activity: *a professional time-waster.* • **n.** a professional person. ➤a person having impressive competence in a particular activity.
– DERIVATIVES **professionalization** (also **-isation**) n. **professionalize** (also **-ise**) v. **professionally** adv.

**professional foul** • **n.** (especially in soccer) a deliberate foul to prevent an opponent from scoring.

**professionalism** • **n. 1** the competence or skill expected of a professional. **2** the practising of an activity by professionals rather than amateurs.

**professor** • **n. 1** a university academic of the highest rank; the holder of a university chair. ➤N. Amer. a university teacher. **2** a person who affirms a faith in or allegiance to something.
– DERIVATIVES **professorate** n. **professorial** adj. **professorially** adv. **professoriate** n. **professorship** n.
– ORIGIN ME: from L. *professor*, from *profess-, profiteri* (see **PROFESS**).

**proffer** • **v.** offer. • **n.** poetic/literary an offer or proposal.
– ORIGIN ME: from Anglo-Norman Fr. *proffrir*, from L. *pro-* 'before' + *offerre* 'to offer'.

**proficient** • **adj.** competent; skilled.
– DERIVATIVES **proficiency** n. **proficiently** adv.
– ORIGIN C16: from L. *proficient-, proficere* 'to advance', from *pro-* 'on behalf of' + *facere* 'do, make'.

**profile** • **n. 1** an outline of something, especially a face, as seen from one side. **2** a vertical cross section of something. ➤a flat outline piece of scenery on stage. **3** a graphical or other representation of information recorded in quantified form. **4** a short descriptive article about someone. **5** the extent to which a person or organization attracts public notice. • **v. 1** describe in a short article. **2** (**be profiled**) appear in outline. **3** shape by means of a tool guided by a template.
– PHRASES **in profile** as seen from one side. **keep a low profile** remain inconspicuous.
– DERIVATIVES **profiler** n.
– ORIGIN C17: from obs. Ital. *profilo*, from *profilare*, from *pro-* 'forth' + *filare* 'to spin', formerly 'draw a line' (from L. *filare*, from *filum* 'thread').

**profiling** • **n.** the analysis of a person's psychological and behavioural characteristics, so as to assess or predict their capabilities or to identify a subgroup of people.

**profit** • **n. 1** a financial gain, especially the difference between an initial outlay and the subsequent amount earned. **2** advantage; benefit. • **v.** (**profited**, **profiting**) benefit, especially financially. ➤be beneficial to.
– DERIVATIVES **profitability** n. **profitable** adj. **profitably** adv. **profitless** adj.
– ORIGIN ME: from OFr., from L. *profectus* 'progress, profit', from *proficere* 'to advance', from *pro-* 'on behalf of' + *facere* 'do'.

**profit and loss account** • **n.** an account to which incomes and gains are credited and expenses and losses debited, so as to show the net profit or loss over a period.

**profiteer** • **v.** [often as noun **profiteering**] make an excessive or unfair profit. • **n.** a person who profiteers.

**profiterole** • **n.** a small ball of soft, sweet choux pastry filled with cream and covered with chocolate sauce.
– ORIGIN Fr., dimin. of *profit* 'profit'.

**profit margin** • **n.** the amount by which revenue from sales exceeds costs in a business.

**profit-sharing** • **n.** a system in which the people who work for a company receive a direct share of the profits.

**profit-taking** • **n.** the sale of securities that have risen in price.

**profligate** /ˈprɒflɪgət/ • **adj.** recklessly extravagant or wasteful. ➤licentious; dissolute. • **n.** a profligate person.
– DERIVATIVES **profligacy** n. **profligately** adv.
– ORIGIN C16: from L. *profligatus* 'dissolute', past part. of *profligare* 'overthrow, ruin', from *pro-* 'forward, down' + *fligere* 'strike down'.

**pro-form** • **n.** Linguistics a word or lexical unit dependent for its meaning on reference to the context, e.g. a pronoun or the verb *do*.

**pro forma** /prəʊ ˈfɔːmə/ • **adv.** as a matter of form or politeness. • **adj. 1** done or produced as a matter of form. ➤denoting a standard document or form. **2** (of a financial statement) showing potential or expected income, costs, assets, or liabilities. • **n.** a standard document or

form.
– ORIGIN C16: from L.

**profound** ● **adj.** (**-er**, **-est**) **1** very great or intense: *profound social changes.* ➤(of a disease or disability) severe. **2** showing great knowledge or insight. ➤demanding deep study or thought. **3** archaic very deep. ● **n.** (**the profound**) poetic/literary profound things; great depths.
– DERIVATIVES **profoundly** adv. **profoundness** n. **profundity** n.
– ORIGIN ME: from OFr. *profund*, from L. *profundus* 'deep', from L. *pro* 'before' + *fundus* 'bottom'.

**profuse** ● **adj. 1** plentiful; abundant. **2** archaic (of a person) extravagant.
– DERIVATIVES **profusely** adv. **profuseness** n. **profusion** n.
– ORIGIN ME: from L. *profusus* 'lavish, spread out', past part. of *profundere*, from *pro-* 'forth' + *fundere* 'pour'.

**prog** informal ● **n.** a television or radio programme. ● **adj.** (of rock music) progressive.

**progenitive** ● **adj.** formal having reproductive power.

**progenitor** /prə(ʊ)'dʒɛnɪtə/ ● **n. 1** an ancestor or parent. **2** the originator of an artistic, political, or intellectual movement.
– DERIVATIVES **progenitorial** adj.
– ORIGIN ME: from OFr. *progeniteur*, from L. *progenitor*, from *progenit-*, *progignere* 'beget', from *pro-* 'forward' + *gignere* 'beget'.

**progeniture** /prə(ʊ)'dʒɛnɪtʃə/ ● **n.** formal **1** procreation. **2** offspring.
– ORIGIN C15: from *progenit-*, *progignere* 'beget' + **-URE**.

**progeny** /'prɒdʒ(ə)ni/ ● **n.** [treated as sing. or pl.] offspring.
– ORIGIN ME: from OFr. *progenie*, from L. *progenies*, from *progignere* (see **PROGENITOR**).

**progeria** /prə(ʊ)'dʒɪərɪə/ ● **n.** Medicine a rare syndrome in children characterized by physical symptoms suggestive of premature old age.
– ORIGIN C20: mod. L., from Gk *progērōs* 'prematurely old'.

**progesterone** /prə'dʒɛstərəʊn/ ● **n.** Biochemistry a steroid hormone released by the corpus luteum that stimulates the uterus to prepare for pregnancy.
– ORIGIN 1930s: blend of **PROGESTIN** and the Ger. synonym *Luteosteron* (from **CORPUS LUTEUM** + **STEROL**).

**progestin** /prə(ʊ)'dʒɛstɪn/ ● **n.** Biochemistry another term for **PROGESTOGEN**.
– ORIGIN 1930s: from **PRO-**[1] + **GESTATION** + **-IN**[1].

**progestogen** /prə(ʊ)'dʒɛstədʒ(ə)n/ ● **n.** Biochemistry a steroid hormone that maintains pregnancy and prevents further ovulation.

**proglottid** /prəʊ'glɒtɪd/ ● **n.** Zoology each segment of a tapeworm, containing a complete sexually mature reproductive system.
– ORIGIN C19: from Gk *proglōssis*, *proglōssid-* 'point of the tongue', based on *glōssa*, *glōtta* 'tongue' (because of its shape).

**prognathous** /prɒg'neɪθəs, 'prɒgnəθəs/ ● **adj.** having a projecting lower jaw or chin. ➤(of a jaw or chin) projecting.
– DERIVATIVES **prognathic** /prɒg'naθɪk/ adj. **prognathism** n.
– ORIGIN C19: from **PRO-**[2] + Gk *gnathos* 'jaw' + **-OUS**.

**prognosis** /prɒg'nəʊsɪs/ ● **n.** (pl. **prognoses** /-siːz/) a forecast, especially of the likely course of a disease or ailment.
– ORIGIN C17: via late L. from Gk *prognōsis*, from *pro-* 'before' + *gignōskein* 'know'.

**prognostic** /prɒg'nɒstɪk/ ● **adj.** predicting the likely course of a disease or ailment. ● **n.** archaic an omen.
– DERIVATIVES **prognostically** adv.
– ORIGIN ME: from L. *prognosticus* from Gk *prognōstikos*, from *prognōsis* (see **PROGNOSIS**).

**prognosticate** ● **v.** foretell; prophesy.
– DERIVATIVES **prognostication** n. **prognosticator** n. **prognosticatory** adj.

**prograde** /'prəʊgreɪd/ ● **adj. 1** Astronomy proceeding from west to east; direct. The opposite of **RETROGRADE**. **2** Geology (of metamorphism) resulting from an increase in temperature or pressure. ● **v.** Geology (of a coastline) advance towards the sea as a result of accumulation of sediment.
– DERIVATIVES **progradation** n.
– ORIGIN C20: from **PRO-**[1] + **RETROGRADE**.

**programme** (US **program**) ● **n. 1** a planned series of events. ➤a set of related measures or activities with a long-term aim. **2** a sheet or booklet detailing items or performers at an event. **3** a radio or television broadcast. **4** (**program**) a series of coded software instructions to control the operation of a computer or other machine. ● **v.** (**programmed**, **programming**; US **programed**, **programing**) **1** (**program**) provide (a computer or other machine) with a program. ➤input (instructions) into a computer or other machine. **2** cause to behave in a predetermined way. **3** arrange according to a plan or schedule. ➤plan; schedule.
– DERIVATIVES **programmability** n. **programmable** adj. **programmatic** adj. **programmatically** adv. **programming** n.
– ORIGIN C17: via late L. from Gk *programma*, from *prographein* 'write publicly', from *pro* 'before' + *graphein* 'write'.

**programme music** ● **n.** music intended to evoke images or tell a story. Compare with **ABSOLUTE MUSIC**.

**programmer** ● **n. 1** a person who writes computer programs. **2** a device controlling the operation of something according to a prescribed programme.

**progress** ● **n. 1** forward or onward movement towards a destination. **2** development towards a better, more complete, or more modern condition. **3** Brit. archaic a state journey or official tour. ● **v. 1** move or develop towards a destination or an improved or advanced condition. ➤cause to make regular progress. **2** [usu. as adj. **progressed**] Astrology calculate the position of (a planet) or of all the planets and coordinates of (a chart).
– ORIGIN ME (as n.): from L. *progressus* 'an advance', from *progredi*, from *pro-* 'forward' + *gradi* 'to walk'.

**progression** ● **n. 1** a gradual movement or development towards a destination or a more advanced state. ➤a succession. ➤Music a passage or movement from one note or chord to another. **2** a sequence of numbers following a mathematical rule. **3** Astrology a predictive technique in which the daily movement of the planets represents a year in the subject's life.
– DERIVATIVES **progressional** adj.

**progressionist** chiefly historical ● **n. 1** Biology a supporter of the theory that all life forms gradually evolve to a higher form. **2** an advocate of political or social progress. ● **adj.** Biology of or being a progressionist.

**progressive** ● **adj. 1** proceeding gradually or in stages: *a progressive decline in popularity.* ➤(of a disease or ailment) increasing in severity. ➤(of tax) increasing as a proportion of the sum taxed as that sum increases. **2** (of a card game or dance) involving a series of sections for which participants successively change place. ➤archaic engaging in or constituting forward motion. **3** favouring social reform. ➤favouring change or innovation. **4** Grammar denoting an aspect or tense of a verb expressing an action in progress, e.g. *am writing*. ● **n.** a person advocating social reform.
– DERIVATIVES **progressively** adv. **progressiveness** n. **progressivism** n. **progressivist** n. & adj.

**proguanil** /prəʊ'gwɑːnɪl/ ● **n.** Medicine a bitter-tasting synthetic compound used in the prevention and treatment of malaria.
– ORIGIN 1940s: from *pro(pyl)* + *bi)guan(ide* + **-IL**.

**pro hac vice** /ˌprəʊ hɑːk 'vʌɪsi/ ● **adv.** for this occasion only.
– ORIGIN from L.

**prohibit** ● **v.** (**prohibited**, **prohibiting**) **1** formally forbid by law, rule, etc. **2** prevent.
– DERIVATIVES **prohibiter** n. **prohibitor** n. **prohibitory** adj.
– ORIGIN ME: from L. *prohibit-*, *prohibere* 'keep in check', from *pro-* 'in front' + *habere* 'to hold'.

**prohibited degrees** ● **pl. n.** another term for ***the forbidden degrees*** (see **FORBID**).

**prohibition** /ˌprəʊhɪ'bɪʃ(ə)n, prəʊɪ-/ ● **n. 1** the action of prohibiting. **2** English Law a writ from a superior court for-

bidding an inferior court from proceeding in a suit deemed to be beyond its cognizance. **3** (**Prohibition**) the prevention by law of the manufacture and sale of alcohol, especially in the US from 1920–1933.
– DERIVATIVES **prohibitionary** adj. **Prohibitionist** n.
– ORIGIN ME: from OFr., from L. *prohibitio(n-)*, from *prohibere* (see **PROHIBIT**).

**prohibitive** • **adj. 1** serving to forbid, restrict, or prevent. **2** (of a price or charge) excessively high.
– DERIVATIVES **prohibitively** adv. **prohibitiveness** n.
– ORIGIN ME: from Fr. *prohibitif, -ive* or L. *prohibitivus*, from *prohibit-*, *prohibere* (see **PROHIBIT**).

**project** • **n. 1** an enterprise carefully planned to achieve a particular aim. ➤ a proposed or planned undertaking. **2** a piece of research work by a school or college student. **3** (also **housing project**) N. Amer. a government-subsidized estate or block of homes. • **v. 1** estimate or forecast on the basis of present trends. ➤ [often as adj. **projected**] plan. **2** protrude. **3** throw or cause to move forward or outward. ➤ cause (light, shadow, or an image) to fall on a surface. ➤ cause (a sound) to be heard at a distance. ➤ imagine as having moved to a different place or time. **4** present or promote. ➤ display (an emotion or quality) in one's behaviour. **5** (**project something on to**) attribute an emotion to (another person), especially unconsciously. **6** Geometry draw straight lines through (a given figure) to produce a corresponding figure on a surface or line. **7** represent (the earth's surface, the heavens, etc.) on a plane surface.
– ORIGIN ME (in the sense 'preliminary design, tabulated statement'): from L. *projectum* 'something prominent', neut. past part. of *proicere* 'throw forth', from *pro-* 'forth' + *jacere* 'to throw'.

**projectile** • **n.** a missile fired or thrown at a target. • **adj. 1** of or relating to a projectile. **2** propelled with great force.
– ORIGIN C17: mod. L., from *project-*, from *proicere* (see **PROJECT**).

**projection** • **n. 1** an estimate or forecast based on present trends. **2** the projecting of an image, sound, etc. **3** the presentation or promotion of someone or something in a particular way. ➤ a mental image viewed as reality. **4** the unconscious transfer of one's own desires or emotions to another person. **5** a protruding thing. **6** a map or diagram made by projecting a given figure, area, etc.
– DERIVATIVES **projectionist** n.

**projective** • **adj. 1** Geometry relating to or derived by projection. ➤ (of a property) unchanged by projection. **2** Psychology relating to the projection of desires or emotions.
– DERIVATIVES **projectively** adv.

**projective geometry** • **n.** the study of the projective properties of geometric figures.

**projector** • **n. 1** a device used to project rays of light, especially an apparatus for projecting slides or film on to a screen. **2** archaic a person who plans and sets up a project. ➤ a promoter of a dubious enterprise.

**prokaryote** /prəʊˈkarɪəʊt, -ɒt/ (also **procaryote**) • **n.** Biology a single-celled organism with neither a distinct nucleus with a membrane nor other specialized structures (i.e. a bacterium or archaean). Compare with **EUKARYOTE**.
– DERIVATIVES **prokaryotic** adj.
– ORIGIN 1960s: from **PRO-**[2] + Gk *karuon* 'nut, kernel' + *-ote* as in **ZYGOTE**.

**prolactin** /prəʊˈlaktɪn/ • **n.** Biochemistry a hormone from the anterior pituitary gland stimulating milk production after childbirth.
– ORIGIN 1930s: from **PRO-**[2] + **LACTATION**.

**prolapse** • **n.** /ˈprəʊlaps, prəˈlaps/ a slipping forward or down of a part or organ of the body. ➤ a prolapsed part or organ. • **v.** /prəʊˈlaps/ [usu. as adj. **prolapsed**] slip forward or down: *a prolapsed uterus.*
– ORIGIN C18: from L. *prolaps-*, *prolabi* 'slip forward', from *pro-* 'forward, down' + *labi* 'to slip'.

**prolapsus** /prəʊˈlapsəs/ • **n.** technical term for **PROLAPSE**.
– ORIGIN C18: mod. L.

**prolate** /ˈprəʊleɪt/ • **adj.** Geometry (of a spheroid) lengthened in the direction of a polar diameter. Often contrasted with **OBLATE**[2].
– ORIGIN C17: from L. *prolatus* 'carried forward', past part. of *proferre* 'prolong', from *pro-* 'forward' + *ferre* 'carry'.

**prole** informal, derogatory • **n.** a member of the working class. • **adj.** working class.
– ORIGIN C19: abbrev. of **PROLETARIAT**.

**proleg** • **n.** Entomology a fleshy abdominal limb of a caterpillar or similar insect larva.

**prolegomenon** /ˌprəʊlɪˈgɒmɪnən/ • **n.** (pl. **prolegomena**) a critical or discursive introduction to a book.
– DERIVATIVES **prolegomenous** adj.
– ORIGIN C17: via L. from Gk, passive pres. part. (neut.) of *prolegein* 'say beforehand', from *pro* 'before' + *legein* 'say'.

**prolepsis** /prəʊˈlɛpsɪs, -ˈliːpsɪs/ • **n.** (pl. **prolepses** /-siːz/) **1** Rhetoric the anticipation and answering of possible objections. ➤ poetic/literary anticipation. **2** the representation of a thing as existing before it actually does or did so, as in *he was a dead man when he entered.*
– DERIVATIVES **proleptic** adj.
– ORIGIN ME: via late L. from Gk *prolēpsis*, from *prolambanein* 'anticipate', from *pro* 'before' + *lambanein* 'take'.

**proletarian** /ˌprəʊlɪˈtɛːrɪən/ • **adj.** of or relating to the proletariat. • **n.** a member of the proletariat.
– DERIVATIVES **proletarianism** n. **proletarianization** (also **-isation**) n. **proletarianize** (also **-ise**) v.
– ORIGIN C17: from L. *proletarius* (from *proles* 'offspring'), denoting a person without wealth, serving the state only by producing offspring, + **-AN**.

**proletariat** (also archaic **proletariate**) • **n.** [treated as sing. or pl.] **1** workers or working-class people (often used with reference to Marxism). **2** the lowest class of citizens in ancient Rome.
– ORIGIN C19: from Fr. *prolétariat*, from L. *proletarius* (see **PROLETARIAN**).

**pro-life** • **adj.** seeking to ban abortion and euthanasia.
– DERIVATIVES **pro-lifer** n.

**proliferate** /prəˈlɪfəreɪt/ • **v.** reproduce rapidly; increase rapidly in number.
– DERIVATIVES **proliferative** adj. **proliferator** n.
– ORIGIN C19: back-form. from **PROLIFERATION**.

**proliferation** • **n.** rapid reproduction or increase in numbers. ➤ a large number of something.
– ORIGIN C19: from Fr. *prolifération*, from *prolifère* 'proliferous'.

**proliferous** • **adj.** Biology (of a plant) producing buds or side shoots from a flower or other terminal part. ➤ (of a plant or invertebrate) propagating or multiplying by means of buds or offsets.
– ORIGIN C17: from L. *proles* 'offspring' + **-FEROUS**.

**prolific** • **adj. 1** producing much fruit or foliage or many offspring. **2** (of an artist, author, etc.) producing many works. **3** plentiful.
– DERIVATIVES **prolificacy** n. **prolifically** adv. **prolificness** n.
– ORIGIN C17: from med. L. *prolificus*, from L. *proles* (see **PROLIFEROUS**).

**proline** /ˈprəʊliːn/ • **n.** Biochemistry an amino acid which is a constituent of most proteins, especially collagen.
– ORIGIN C20: contr. of the chemical name *p(yr)rol(id)ine*-2-carboxylic acid.

**prolix** /ˈprəʊlɪks, prəˈlɪks/ • **adj.** (of speech or writing) tediously lengthy.
– DERIVATIVES **prolixity** n. **prolixly** adv.
– ORIGIN ME: from OFr. *prolixe* or L. *prolixus* 'poured forth, extended', from *pro-* 'outward' + *liquere* 'be liquid'.

**prolocutor** /ˈprəʊləˌkjuːtə, ˈprɒl-, prə(ʊ)ˈlɒkjʊtə/ • **n. 1** a chairperson of the lower house of convocation in a province of the Church of England. **2** archaic or formal a spokesman.
– ORIGIN ME: from L., from *prolocut-*, *proloqui* 'speak out', from *pro-* 'before' + *loqui* 'speak'.

**Prolog** /ˈprəʊlɒg/ ● **n.** Computing a high-level computer programming language first devised for artificial intelligence applications.
– ORIGIN 1970s: from the first elements of *programming* and **LOGIC**.

**prologue** (US **prolog**) ● **n.** **1** a separate introductory section of a literary or musical work. ➤an introductory scene in a play. **2** an event or action leading to another.
– ORIGIN ME: from OFr., via L. from Gk *prologos*, from *pro-* 'before' + *logos* 'saying'.

**prolong** ● **v.** **1** extend the duration of. **2** technical extend in spatial length.
– DERIVATIVES **prolongation** n. **prolonger** n.
– ORIGIN ME: from OFr. *prolonguer*, from late L. *prolongare*, from *pro-* 'forward, onward' + *longus* 'long'.

**prolonged** ● **adj.** lengthy.
– DERIVATIVES **prolongedly** adv.

**prolusion** /prəˈl(j)uːʒ(ə)n/ ● **n.** archaic or formal **1** a prelude. **2** a preliminary essay or article.
– ORIGIN C17: from L. *prolusio(n-)*, from *prolus-*, *proludere* 'practise beforehand', from *pro* 'before' + *ludere* 'to play'.

**prom** ● **n.** informal **1** Brit. short for **PROMENADE** (in sense 1). **2** (also **Prom**) Brit. a promenade concert. **3** N. Amer. a formal dance, especially one at a high school or college.

**promenade** /ˌprɒməˈnɑːd, -ˈneɪd, ˈprɒm-/ ● **n.** **1** a paved public walk, especially one along a seafront. **2** a leisurely walk, ride, or drive, typically in a public place so as to meet or be seen by others. **3** (in country dancing) a movement resembling a march made by couples in formation. **4** N. Amer. archaic term for **PROM** (in sense 3). ● **v.** take a promenade. ➤dated escort (someone) about a place, especially for display.
– ORIGIN C16: from Fr., from *se promener* 'to walk', reflexive of *promener* 'take for a walk'.

**promenade concert** ● **n.** Brit. a concert of classical music at which part of the audience stands in an area without seating, for which tickets are sold at a reduced price.

**promenade deck** ● **n.** an upper, open-air deck on a passenger ship.

**promenader** ● **n.** **1** a person who takes a promenade. **2** Brit. a person standing at a promenade concert.

**promethazine** /prə(ʊ)ˈmɛθəziːn/ ● **n.** Medicine a synthetic antihistamine drug taken chiefly for allergies and motion sickness.
– ORIGIN 1950s: from *pro(pyl)* + *meth(yl)* + *(phenothi)azine*.

**Promethean** /prəˈmiːθɪən/ ● **adj.** daring or skilful like Prometheus, a demigod in Greek mythology who stole fire from the gods and gave it to the human race.

**promethium** /prəˈmiːθɪəm/ ● **n.** the chemical element of atomic number 61, an unstable radioactive metal of the lanthanide series. (Symbol: **Pm**)
– ORIGIN 1940s: mod. L., from the name of *Prometheus* (see **PROMETHEAN**).

**prominence** ● **n.** **1** the state of being prominent. **2** a thing that projects from something. ➤Astronomy a stream of incandescent gas projecting above the sun's chromosphere.

**prominent** ● **adj.** **1** important; famous. **2** protuberant. **3** particularly noticeable. ● **n.** (also **prominent moth**) a drab-coloured moth with tufts on the forewings which stick up while it is at rest. [Family Notodontidae: many species.]
– DERIVATIVES **prominency** n. **prominently** adv.
– ORIGIN ME: from L. *prominent-*, *prominere* 'jut out'; cf. **EMINENT**.

**prominenti** /ˌprɒmɪˈnɛnti/ ● **pl. n.** eminent people.
– ORIGIN Ital., from *prominente* 'prominent'.

**promiscuous** /prəˈmɪskjʊəs/ ● **adj.** **1** having or characterized by many transient sexual relationships. **2** indiscriminate or casual. ➤wide-ranging; unselective.
– DERIVATIVES **promiscuity** n. **promiscuously** adv. **promiscuousness** n.
– ORIGIN C17: from L. *promiscuus* 'indiscriminate' (based on *miscere* 'to mix') + **-OUS**.

**promise** ● **n.** **1** an assurance that one will do something or that something will happen. ➤an indication that something is likely to occur: *the promise of spring.* **2** potential excellence. ● **v.** **1** make a promise. ➤(**be promised**) archaic be pledged to marry. **2** give good grounds for expecting. **3** (**promise oneself**) firmly intend.
– PHRASES **on a promise** informal confidently assured of something.
– DERIVATIVES **promiser** n.
– ORIGIN ME: from L. *promissum* 'something promised', neut. past part. of *promittere* 'put forth, promise' (from *pro-* 'forward' + *mittere* 'send').

**promised land** ● **n.** **1** (**the Promised Land**) (in the Bible) the land of Canaan, promised to Abraham and his descendants (Gen. 12:7). **2** a place or situation where great happiness is expected.

**promisee** ● **n.** Law a person to whom a promise is made.

**promising** ● **adj.** showing great potential.
– DERIVATIVES **promisingly** adv.

**promisor** ● **n.** Law a person who makes a promise.

**promissory** /ˈprɒmɪs(ə)ri/ ● **adj.** **1** chiefly Law conveying or implying a promise. **2** archaic full of promise.
– ORIGIN ME: from med. L. *promissorius*, from *promiss-*, *promittere* (see **PROMISE**).

**promissory note** ● **n.** a signed document containing a written promise to pay a stated sum to a specified person or the bearer at a specified date or on demand.

**prommer** ● **n.** Brit. informal a promenader.

**promo** /ˈprəʊməʊ/ ● **n.** (pl. **-os**) informal a promotional film, video, etc.

**promontory** /ˈprɒm(ə)nt(ə)ri/ ● **n.** (pl. **-ies**) **1** a point of high land jutting out into the sea or a lake. **2** Anatomy a protuberance on an organ or other bodily structure.
– ORIGIN C16: from L. *promontorium*, var. (influenced by *mons*, *mont-* 'mountain') of *promunturium*.

**promote** ● **v.** **1** further the progress of; support or encourage. ➤publicize. ➤attempt to ensure the passing of (a private Act of Parliament). **2** raise to a higher position or rank. **3** Chemistry (of an additive) increase the activity of (a catalyst). **4** Chess exchange (a pawn) for a more powerful piece when it reaches the opponent's end of the board.
– DERIVATIVES **promotability** n. **promotable** adj. **promoter** n. **promotive** adj.
– ORIGIN ME: from L. *promot-*, *promovere* 'move forward', from *pro-* 'forward, onward' + *movere* 'to move'.

**promotion** ● **n.** **1** activity that supports or encourages. **2** the publicizing of a product or venture so as to increase sales or public awareness; a publicity campaign. ➤(**promotions**) the activity or business of organizing such publicity. **3** the action of raising someone to a higher position or rank or the fact of being so raised. ➤the transfer of a sports team to a higher division of a league.
– DERIVATIVES **promotional** adj.

**prompt** ● **v.** **1** cause or bring about. ➤(**prompt someone to/to do something**) cause someone to take a course of action. **2** assist or encourage (a hesitating speaker). ➤supply a forgotten word or line to (an actor). ● **n.** **1** an act of prompting a hesitating speaker. ➤a word or phrase used in prompting an actor. ➤a prompter. **2** Computing a word or symbol on a VDU screen to show that input is required. **3** the time limit for the payment of an account, stated on a prompt note. ● **adj.** done or acting without delay. ➤arriving precisely at a pre-arranged time. ➤(of goods) for immediate delivery and payment. ● **adv.** Brit. exactly (with reference to a specified time).
– DERIVATIVES **prompting** n. **promptitude** n. **promptly** adv. **promptness** n.
– ORIGIN ME (as v.): based on OFr. *prompt* or L. *promptus* 'brought to light', also 'prepared, ready', past part. of *promere* 'to produce', from *pro-* 'out, forth' + *emere* 'take'.

**prompt book** ● **n.** an annotated copy of a play used by a prompter.

**prompter** ● **n.** a person who prompts the actors during the performance of a play.

**prompt note** ● **n.** a note sent as a reminder of payment due.

**prompt side** ● **n.** the side of the stage where the

prompter sits (stage left in the UK and stage right in the US).

**promulgate** /ˈprɒm(ə)lgeɪt/ ● v. promote or make widely known. ➤ put (a law or decree) into effect by official proclamation.
– DERIVATIVES **promulgation** n. **promulgator** n.
– ORIGIN C16 (earlier (C15) as *promulgation*): from L. *promulgat-*, *promulgare*, from *pro-* 'out, publicly' + *mulgere* 'cause to come forth' (lit. 'to milk').

**promulge** /prəˈmʌldʒ/ ● v. archaic variant of **PROMULGATE**.
– ORIGIN C15: from L. *promulgare*.

**pronaos** /prəʊˈneɪɒs/ ● n. (pl. **pronaoi** /-ˈneɪɔɪ/) a vestibule at the front of a classical temple, enclosed by a portico and projecting side walls.
– ORIGIN via L. from Gk *pronaos* 'hall of a temple', from *pro* 'before' + *naos* 'temple'.

**pronate** /ˈprəʊneɪt/ ● v. technical put or hold (a hand, foot, or limb) with the palm or sole turned downwards. Compare with **SUPINATE**.
– DERIVATIVES **pronation** n.
– ORIGIN C19: back-form. from *pronation*, based on L. *pronus* 'leaning forward'.

**pronator** ● n. Anatomy a muscle involved in pronation.

**prone** ● adj. **1** (**prone to**) likely or liable to suffer from, do, or experience (something unfortunate). **2** lying flat, especially face downwards. ➤ with the palm of the hand facing downwards. **3** archaic with a downward slope or direction.
– DERIVATIVES **proneness** n.
– ORIGIN ME: from L. *pronus* 'leaning forward', from *pro* 'forwards'.

**prong** ● n. **1** each of two or more projecting pointed parts on a fork or other device. **2** each of the separate parts of an attack or operation. ● v. pierce or stab with a fork.
– DERIVATIVES **-pronged** adj.
– ORIGIN C15: perh. rel. to Mid. Low Ger. *prange* 'pinching instrument'.

**pronghorn** (also **pronghorn antelope**) ● n. a deer-like North American mammal with a stocky body, long slim legs, and black horns that are shed and regrown annually. [*Antilocapra americana*.]

**pronk** ● v. (of an antelope) leap in the air with an arched back and stiff legs.
– ORIGIN C19: from Afrik., lit. 'show off', from Du. *pronken* 'to strut'.

**pronominal** /prəʊˈnɒmɪn(ə)l/ ● adj. of, relating to, or serving as a pronoun.
– DERIVATIVES **pronominalization** (also **-isation**) n. **pronominalize** (also **-ise**) v. **pronominally** adv.
– ORIGIN C17: from late L. *pronominalis* 'belonging to a pronoun', from L. *pronomen* (see **PRONOUN**).

**pronoun** ● n. a word used instead of a noun to indicate someone or something already mentioned or known, e.g. *I*, *she*, *this*.
– ORIGIN ME: from **PRO-**[1] + **NOUN**, suggested by Fr. *pronom*, L. *pronomen* (from *pro-* 'for, in place of' + *nomen* 'name').

**pronounce** /prəˈnaʊns/ ● v. **1** make the sound of (a word or part of a word). **2** declare or announce. ➤ (**pronounce on**) pass judgement or make a decision on.
– DERIVATIVES **pronounceability** n. **pronounceable** adj. **pronouncement** n. **pronouncer** n.
– ORIGIN ME: from OFr. *pronuncier*, from L. *pronuntiare*, from *pro-* 'out, forth' + *nuntiare* 'announce' (from *nuntius* 'messenger').

**pronounced** ● adj. very noticeable.
– DERIVATIVES **pronouncedly** adv.

**pronto** ● adv. informal promptly.
– ORIGIN C20: from Sp.

**pronunciamento** /prəˌnʌnsɪəˈmɛntəʊ/ ● n. (pl. **-os**) (especially in Spanish-speaking countries) a political manifesto or proclamation.
– ORIGIN Sp. *pronunciamiento*, from *pronunciar* 'pronounce'.

**pronunciation** /prənʌnsɪˈeɪʃ(ə)n/ ● n. the way in which a word is pronounced.

**USAGE pronunciation**

The word **pronunciation** is often pronounced, by analogy with **pronounce**, as if the second syllable rhymed with **bounce**. This is not correct in standard English: the standard pronunciation has the second syllable rhyming with **dunce**.

**pro-nuncio** /prəʊˈnʌnsɪəʊ, -ʃɪəʊ/ ● n. (pl. **-os**) a papal ambassador to a country that does not accord the Pope's ambassador automatic precedence.
– ORIGIN 1960s: from Ital. *pro-nunzio*, from *pro-* 'before' + *nunzio* 'nuncio'.

**proof** ● n. **1** evidence establishing a fact or the truth of a statement. ➤ Law the evidence in a trial. ➤ the proving of the truth of a statement. ➤ archaic a test or trial. ➤ Scots Law a trial or a civil case before a judge without a jury. **2** a series of stages in the resolution of a mathematical or philosophical problem. **3** Printing a trial impression of a page used for making corrections before final printing. ➤ a trial photographic print. ➤ each of a limited number of impressions from an engraved plate, especially before the ordinary issue is printed. ➤ a specially struck specimen coin with a polished or frosted finish. **3** the strength of distilled alcoholic liquor, relative to proof spirit taken as a standard of 100. ● adj. [often in combination] resistant: *bulletproof*. ● v. **1** make waterproof. **2** make a proof of (a printed work, engraving, etc.). ➤ proofread (a text). **3** N. Amer. activate (yeast). ➤ knead (dough) until light and smooth. ➤ (of dough) prove.
– ORIGIN ME *preve*, from OFr. *proeve*, from late L. *proba*, from L. *probare* 'to test, prove'; vowel change due to the influence of **PROVE**.

**proof positive** ● n. final or absolute proof of something.

**proofread** ● v. read (printer's proofs or other material) and mark any errors.
– DERIVATIVES **proofreader** n.

**proof sheet** ● n. Printing a proof.

**proof spirit** ● n. a mixture of alcohol and water containing (in the UK) 57.1 per cent alcohol by volume or (in the US) 50 per cent alcohol by volume, used as a standard of strength of distilled alcoholic liquor.

**prop**[1] ● n. **1** a pole or beam used as a temporary support. **2** a major source of support or assistance. **3** (also **prop forward**) Rugby a forward at either end of the front row of a scrum. **4** chiefly Austral. a sudden stop made by a horse moving at speed. ● v. (**propped**, **propping**) **1** support with or as with a prop. ➤ lean against something else. **2** (**prop someone/thing up**) support or assist someone or something that would otherwise fail or decline. **3** chiefly Austral. (of a horse) come to a dead stop with the forelegs rigid.
– ORIGIN ME: prob. from MDu. *proppe* 'support (for vines)'.

**prop**[2] ● n. **1** a portable object used on the set of a play or film. **2** (**props**) [treated as sing.] informal, dated a property man or mistress.
– ORIGIN C19: abbrev. of **PROPERTY**.

**prop**[3] ● n. informal an aircraft propeller.

**prop.** ● abbrev. **1** proposition. **2** proprietor.

**propaedeutic** /ˌprəʊpɪˈdjuːtɪk/ ● adj. formal serving as an introduction to further study.
– DERIVATIVES **propaedeutical** adj.
– ORIGIN C18: from **PRO-**[2] + Gk *paideutikos* 'of or for teaching', suggested by Gk *propaideuein* 'teach beforehand'.

**propaganda** ● n. **1** information, especially of a biased or misleading nature, used to promote a political cause or point of view. ➤ the dissemination of such information. **2** (**Propaganda**) a committee of Roman Catholic cardinals responsible for foreign missions.
– ORIGIN Ital., from mod. L. *congregatio de propaganda fide* 'congregation for propagation of the faith'.

**propagandist** chiefly derogatory ● n. a person who disseminates propaganda. ● adj. consisting of or spreading propaganda.
– DERIVATIVES **propagandism** n. **propagandistic** adj. **propagandistically** adv. **propagandize** (also **-ise**) v.

**propagate** ● v. **1** breed by natural processes from the

parent stock. ➤ cause to increase in number or amount. **2** promote (an idea, knowledge, etc.) widely. **3** transmit or be transmitted in a particular direction.
– DERIVATIVES **propagation** n. **propagative** adj.
– ORIGIN ME: from L. *propagat-*, *propagare* 'multiply from layers or shoots'; rel. to *propago* 'young shoot' (from a base meaning 'fix').

**propagator** ● n. **1** a covered, heated container of earth or compost, used for germinating seedlings. **2** a person who propagates an idea, knowledge, etc.

**propagule** /ˈprɒpəgjuːl/ ● n. Botany a detachable structure that can give rise to a new plant, e.g. a bud, sucker, or spore.
– ORIGIN C19: from mod. L. *propagulum* 'small shoot', dimin. of *propago* 'shoot, runner'.

**propane** /ˈprəʊpeɪn/ ● n. Chemistry a flammable hydrocarbon gas of the alkane series, present in natural gas and used as bottled fuel. [$C_3H_8$.]
– ORIGIN C19: from **PROPIONIC ACID** + **-ANE**[2].

**propanoic acid** /ˌprəʊpəˈnəʊɪk/ ● n. Chemistry another term for **PROPIONIC ACID**.
– DERIVATIVES **propanoate** /prəˈpanəʊeɪt/ n.

**propanol** /ˈprəʊpənɒl/ ● n. Chemistry a liquid alcohol used as a solvent; propyl alcohol.

**propel** ● v. (**propelled**, **propelling**) drive or push forwards. ➤ drive into a particular situation.
– ORIGIN ME: from L. *propellere*, from *pro-* 'forward' + *pellere* 'to drive'.

**propellant** ● n. **1** an inert fluid, liquefied under pressure, in which the active contents of an aerosol are dispersed. **2** an explosive that fires bullets from a firearm. **3** a substance used as a reagent in a rocket engine to provide thrust. ● adj. variant of **PROPELLENT**.
– ORIGIN C17: orig. from L. *propellent-*, *propellere* 'drive ahead (of oneself)', later from **PROPEL**.

**propellent** ● adj. capable of propelling something.

**propeller** ● n. a revolving shaft with two or more broad, angled blades, for propelling a ship or aircraft.

**propeller-head** ● n. informal a person obsessed with computers or technology.
– ORIGIN 1980s: prob. with ref. to a beanie hat with a propeller on top, popularized by science-fiction enthusiasts.

**propeller shaft** ● n. a shaft transmitting power from an engine to a propeller or to the wheels of a vehicle.

**propeller turbine** ● n. a turboprop.

**propelling pencil** ● n. a pencil with a thin replaceable lead that may be extended as the point is worn away.

**propene** /ˈprəʊpiːn/ ● n. Chemistry another term for **PROPYLENE**.

**propensity** ● n. (pl. **-ies**) an inclination or tendency.
– ORIGIN C16: from archaic *propense* (from L. *propensus* 'inclined', past part. of *propendere*, from *pro-* 'forward, down' + *pendere* 'hang') + **-ITY**.

**proper** ● adj. **1** truly what something is said or regarded to be; genuine: *she's never had a proper job.* ➤ [postpos.] strictly so called: *the World Cup proper.* **2** suitable or appropriate; correct. ➤ respectable. **3** (**proper to**) belonging or relating exclusively to. ➤ (of a psalm, prayer, etc.) appointed for a particular day or occasion. ➤ archaic belonging to oneself. **4** [usu. postpos.] Heraldry in the natural colours. **5** archaic or dialect good-looking. ● adv. Brit. informal or dialect correctly. ➤ thoroughly. ● n. the part of a church service that varies with the season or feast.
– DERIVATIVES **properness** n.
– ORIGIN ME: from OFr. *propre*, from L. *proprius* 'one's own, special'.

**proper fraction** ● n. a fraction that is less than one, with the numerator less than the denominator.

**properly** ● adv. **1** correctly. ➤ suitably; respectably. **2** in the strict sense. **3** informal, chiefly Brit. completely.

**proper motion** ● n. Astronomy the part of the apparent motion of a star due to its actual movement in space relative to the sun.

**proper noun** (also **proper name**) ● n. a name for an individual person, place, or organization, having an initial capital letter. Often contrasted with **COMMON NOUN**.

**propertied** ● adj. owning property and land.

**property** ● n. (pl. **-ies**) **1** a thing or things belonging to someone. **2** a building and the land belonging to it. ➤ (**properties**) shares or investments in property. **3** Law ownership. **4** a characteristic of something. **5** old-fashioned term for **PROP**[2].
– ORIGIN ME: from an Anglo-Norman Fr. var. of OFr. *propriete*, from L. *proprietas*, from *proprius* (see **PROPER**).

**property man** (or **mistress**) ● n. dated a man (or woman) in charge of theatrical props.

**property qualification** ● n. chiefly historical a qualification for office or for the exercise of a right, based on the ownership of property.

**prop forward** ● n. see **PROP**[1] (sense 3).

**prophase** ● n. Biology the first stage of cell division, before metaphase, during which the chromosomes become visible as paired chromatids.
– ORIGIN C19: from **PRO-**[2] + **PHASE**.

**prophecy** /ˈprɒfɪsi/ ● n. (pl. **-ies**) a prediction. ➤ the faculty or practice of prophesying.
– ORIGIN ME: from OFr. *profecie*, via late L. from Gk *prophēteia*, from *prophētēs* (see **PROPHET**).

**prophesy** /ˈprɒfɪsʌɪ/ ● v. (**-ies**, **-ied**) **1** predict. **2** speak or write by divine inspiration.
– DERIVATIVES **prophesier** n.
– ORIGIN ME: from OFr. *profecier*, from *profecie* (see **PROPHECY**); the different spellings of *prophesy* and *prophecy* were established after 1700.

**prophet** (or **prophetess**) ● n. **1** an inspired teacher or proclaimer of the will of God. ➤ (**the Prophet**) (among Muslims) Muhammad. ➤ (**the Prophet**) (among Mormons) Joseph Smith or one of his successors. **2** a person who predicts the future. ➤ a person who advocates a new belief or theory. **3** (**the Prophets**) (in Christian use) the prophetic writings of the Old Testament. ➤ (in Jewish use) one of the three canonical divisions of the Hebrew Bible.
– DERIVATIVES **prophethood** n.
– ORIGIN ME: from OFr. *prophete*, via L. from Gk *prophētēs* 'spokesman', from *pro* 'before' + *phētēs* 'speaker' (from *phēnai* 'speak').

**prophetic** /prəˈfɛtɪk/ ● adj. **1** accurately predicting the future. **2** of, relating to, or characteristic of a prophet or prophecy.
– DERIVATIVES **prophetical** adj. **prophetically** adv.

**prophylactic** /ˌprɒfɪˈlaktɪk/ ● adj. intended to prevent disease. ● n. **1** a preventative medicine or course of action. **2** chiefly N. Amer. a condom.
– DERIVATIVES **prophylactically** adv.
– ORIGIN C16: from Fr. *prophylactique*, from Gk *prophulaktikos*, from *pro* 'before' + *phulassein* 'to guard'.

**prophylaxis** /ˌprɒfɪˈlaksɪs/ ● n. action taken to prevent disease.
– ORIGIN C19: mod. L., from **PRO-**[2] + Gk *phulaxis* 'act of guarding'.

**propinquity** /prəˈpɪŋkwɪti/ ● n. **1** proximity. **2** technical close kinship.
– ORIGIN ME: from OFr. *propinquité*, from L. *propinquitas*, from *propinquus* 'near', from *prope* 'near to'.

**propionic acid** /ˌprəʊpɪˈɒnɪk/ ● n. Chemistry a pungent liquid organic acid produced in some forms of fermentation.
– DERIVATIVES **propionate** /ˈprəʊpɪəneɪt/ n.
– ORIGIN C19: from Fr. *propionique*, from Gk *pro* 'before' + *piōn* 'fat', it being the first member of the fatty acid series to form fats.

**propitiate** /prəˈpɪʃɪeɪt/ ● v. appease.
– DERIVATIVES **propitiator** n. **propitiatory** adj.
– ORIGIN C16: from L. *propitiat-*, *propitiare* 'make favourable', from *propitius* (see **PROPITIOUS**).

**propitiation** ● n. **1** appeasement. **2** atonement, especially that of Christ.
– ORIGIN ME: from late L. *propitiatio(n-)*, from *propitiare* (see **PROPITIATE**).

**propitious** /prəˈpɪʃəs/ ● adj. **1** favourable. **2** archaic favourably disposed towards someone.
– DERIVATIVES **propitiously** adv. **propitiousness** n.

– ORIGIN ME: from OFr. *propicieus* or L. *propitius* 'favourable, gracious'.

**prop jet** • n. a turboprop aircraft or engine.

**propolis** /ˈprɒp(ə)lɪs/ • n. a red or brown resinous substance collected by honeybees from tree buds for constructing and varnishing honeycombs.
– ORIGIN C17: via L. from Gk *propolis* 'suburb', also 'bee glue', from *pro* 'before' + *polis* 'city'.

**proponent** /prəˈpəʊnənt/ • n. a person who advocates a theory, proposal, or project.
– ORIGIN C16: from L. *proponent-*, *proponere* (see PROPOUND).

**proportion** • n. **1** a part, share, or number considered in relation to a whole. ➤the ratio of one thing to another. ➤the correct or pleasing relation of things or between the parts of a whole. **2** (**proportions**) dimensions; size. • v. formal adjust so as to have a particular or suitable relationship to something else.
– PHRASES **in** (or **out of**) **proportion** according (or not according) to a particular relationship in size, amount, or degree. ➤regarded without (or with) exaggeration. **sense of proportion** the ability to judge the relative importance of things.
– DERIVATIVES **proportioned** adj. **proportionless** adj.
– ORIGIN ME: from OFr., from L. *proportio(n-)*, from *pro portione* 'in respect of (its or a person's) share'.

**proportionable** • adj. archaic term for PROPORTIONAL.
– DERIVATIVES **proportionably** adv.

**proportional** • adj. **1** corresponding in size or amount to something else. **2** Mathematics (of a variable quantity) having a constant ratio to another quantity.
– DERIVATIVES **proportionality** n. **proportionally** adv.

**proportional representation** • n. an electoral system in which parties gain seats in proportion to the number of votes cast for them.

**proportionate** • adj. another term for PROPORTIONAL.
– DERIVATIVES **proportionately** adv.

**proposal** • n. **1** a plan or suggestion. ➤the action of proposing something. **2** an offer of marriage.

**propose** • v. **1** put forward (an idea or plan) for consideration by others. ➤nominate for an office or position. ➤put forward (a motion) to a legislature or committee. **2** make an offer of marriage to someone.
– DERIVATIVES **proposer** n.
– ORIGIN ME: from OFr. *proposer*, from L. *proponere* (see PROPONENT); influenced by L. *propositus* 'put or set forth' and OFr. *poser* 'to place'.

**proposition** • n. **1** a statement expressing a judgement or opinion. ➤Logic a statement expressing a concept that can be true or false. ➤Mathematics a formal statement of a theorem or problem. **2** a proposed scheme or plan. ➤US a constitutional proposal. **3** informal an offer of sexual intercourse. **4** a matter or person to be dealt with, with reference to the likelihood of a successful outcome. • v. informal make an offer, especially of sexual intercourse, to.
– DERIVATIVES **propositional** adj.
– ORIGIN ME: from OFr., from L. *propositio(n-)*, from *proponere* (see PROPOUND).

**propound** /prəˈpaʊnd/ • v. put forward (an idea, theory, etc.) for consideration.
– DERIVATIVES **propounder** n.
– ORIGIN C16: alt. of archaic *propone*, from L. *proponere* 'set forth', from *pro-* 'forward' + *ponere* 'put'.

**propranolol** /prəʊˈpranəlɒl/ • n. Medicine a synthetic beta blocker used mainly to treat cardiac arrhythmia.
– ORIGIN 1960s: from *pro(pyl)* + *pr(op)anol*, with the reduplication of *-ol*.

**proprietary** • adj. **1** of, relating to, or characteristic of an owner or ownership. **2** (of a product) marketed under a registered trade name.
– ORIGIN ME: from late L. *proprietarius* 'proprietor', from *proprietas* (see PROPERTY).

**proprietary name** (also **proprietary term**) • n. a name of a product or service registered as a trademark.

**proprietor** • n. (fem. **proprietress**) **1** the owner of a business. **2** a holder of property.
– DERIVATIVES **proprietorial** adj. **proprietorially** adv. **proprietorship** n.

**propriety** • n. (pl. **-ies**) correctness concerning standards of behaviour or morals. ➤(**proprieties**) the details or rules of conventionally accepted behaviour. ➤appropriateness; rightness.
– ORIGIN ME: from OFr. *propriete*, from L. *proprietas* (see PROPERTY).

**proprioceptive** /ˌprəʊprɪə(ʊ)ˈsɛptɪv/ • adj. Physiology of or denoting stimuli produced and perceived within an organism, especially those relating to position and movement of the body.
– DERIVATIVES **proprioception** n. **proprioceptively** adv. **proprioceptor** n.
– ORIGIN C20: from L. *proprius* 'own' + RECEPTIVE.

**propshaft** • n. a propeller shaft.

**proptosis** /prɒpˈtəʊsɪs/ • n. Medicine protrusion or displacement of an eye or other body part.
– ORIGIN C17: via late L. from Gk *proptōsis*, from *pro* 'before' + *piptein* 'to fall'.

**propulsion** • n. the action of driving or pushing forward.
– DERIVATIVES **propulsive** adj.
– ORIGIN C17: from med. L. *propulsio(n-)*, from L. *propellere* 'drive before (oneself)'.

**propulsor** • n. a ducted propeller swivelled to give forward, upward, or downward flight to an airship.

**propyl** /ˈprəʊpʌɪl, -pɪl/ • n. [as modifier] Chemistry of or denoting the alkyl radical $-C_3H_7$, derived from propane: *propyl alcohol*.

**propyla** plural form of PROPYLON.

**propylaeum** /ˌprɒpɪˈliːəm/ • n. (pl. **propylaea** /-ˈliːə/) the entrance to a temple. ➤(**the Propylaeum**) the entrance to the Acropolis at Athens.
– ORIGIN via L. from Gk *propulaion*, neut. (used as n.) of *propulaios* 'before the gate', from *pro* 'before' + *pulē* 'gate'.

**propylene** /ˈprəʊpɪliːn/ • n. Chemistry a gaseous hydrocarbon of the alkene series, made by cracking alkanes. [$C_3H_6$.]

**propylon** /ˈprɒpɪlɒn/ • n. (pl. **propylons** or **propyla** /-lə/) another term for PROPYLAEUM.
– ORIGIN C19: via L. from Gk *propulon*, from *pro* 'before' + *pulē* 'gate'.

**pro rata** /prəʊ ˈrɑːtə, ˈreɪtə/ • adj. proportional. • adv. proportionally.
– ORIGIN C16: L., lit. 'according to the rate'.

**prorate** /prəʊˈreɪt, ˈprəʊ-/ • v. chiefly N. Amer. allocate or assess pro rata.
– DERIVATIVES **proration** n.

**prorogue** /prəˈrəʊg/ • v. (**prorogues**, **prorogued**, **proroguing**) discontinue a session of (a parliament or assembly) without dissolving it.
– DERIVATIVES **prorogation** /-rəˈgeɪʃ(ə)n/ n.
– ORIGIN ME: from OFr. *proroger*, from L. *prorogare* 'prolong, extend', from *pro-* 'in front of, publicly' + *rogare* 'ask'.

**prosaic** /prə(ʊ)ˈzeɪɪk/ • adj. **1** having the style or diction of prose. **2** commonplace; unromantic.
– DERIVATIVES **prosaically** adv. **prosaicness** n.
– ORIGIN C16 (as a noun denoting a prose writer): from late L. *prosaicus*, from L. *prosa* (see PROSE).

**prosaist** /ˈprəʊzeɪɪst/ • n. **1** a person who writes in prose. **2** a prosaic person.
– DERIVATIVES **prosaism** n.
– ORIGIN C19: from Fr. *prosaïste*, from L. *prosa* (see PROSE).

**proscenium** /prə(ʊ)ˈsiːnɪəm/ • n. (pl. **prosceniums** or **proscenia** /-nɪə/) the part of a stage in front of the curtain. ➤(also **proscenium arch**) an arch framing the opening between the stage and the auditorium. ➤the stage of an ancient theatre.
– ORIGIN C17: via L. from Gk *proskēnion*, from *pro* 'before' + *skēnē* 'stage'.

**prosciutto** /prəˈʃuːtəʊ/ • n. raw cured Italian ham.
– ORIGIN from Ital.

**proscribe** • v. forbid, especially by law. ➤denounce or condemn. ➤historical outlaw (someone).
– DERIVATIVES **proscription** n. **proscriptive** adj.

– ORIGIN ME: from L. *proscribere*, from *pro-* 'in front of' + *scribere* 'write'.

**prose** ● n. **1** ordinary written or spoken language, without metrical structure. **2** another term for SEQUENCE (in sense 4). ● v. **1** talk tediously. **2** dated compose in or convert into prose.
– DERIVATIVES **proser** n.
– ORIGIN ME: via OFr. from L. *prosa (oratio)* 'straightforward (discourse)', fem. of *prosus*, earlier *prorsus* 'direct'.

**prosector** /prə(ʊ)'sɛktə/ ● n. chiefly N. Amer. a person who dissects corpses for examination or anatomical demonstration.
– ORIGIN C19: from late L., lit. 'anatomist', based on L. *secare* 'to cut', perh. via Fr. *prosecteur*.

**prosecute** ● v. **1** institute legal proceedings against. ➤ institute legal proceedings in respect of (a claim or offence). ➤ conduct the case against the party being accused or sued in a lawsuit. **2** continue with a view to completion. ➤ archaic carry on (a trade or pursuit).
– DERIVATIVES **prosecutable** adj.
– ORIGIN ME: from L. *prosecut-*, *prosequi* 'pursue, accompany', from *pro-* 'onward' + *sequi* 'follow'.

**prosecution** ● n. **1** the prosecuting of someone in respect of a criminal charge. ➤ (**the prosecution**) [treated as sing. or pl.] the party prosecuting someone in a lawsuit. **2** the continuation of a course of action with a view to its completion.

**prosecutor** ● n. a person, especially a public official, who prosecutes someone. ➤ a barrister or other lawyer who conducts the case against a defendant.
– DERIVATIVES **prosecutorial** adj.

**proselyte** /'prɒsɪlʌɪt/ ● n. a convert from one opinion, religion, or party to another. ➤ a Gentile who has converted to Judaism. ● v. US term for PROSELYTIZE.
– DERIVATIVES **proselytism** /-lɪtɪz(ə)m/ n.
– ORIGIN ME: via late L. from Gk *prosēluthos* 'stranger, convert', from *prosēluth-*, *proserkhesthai* 'approach'.

**proselytize** /'prɒsɪlɪtʌɪz/ (also **-ise**) ● v. convert from one religion, belief, or opinion to another.
– DERIVATIVES **proselytizer** n.

**prosencephalon** /,prɒsɛn'sɛfəlɒn, -'kɛf-/ ● n. another term for FOREBRAIN.
– ORIGIN C19: from Gk *prosō* 'forwards' + ENCEPHALON.

**prosenchyma** /prɒ'sɛŋkɪmə/ ● n. Biology plant tissue consisting of elongated cells with interpenetrating tapering ends, occurring chiefly in vascular tissue.
– DERIVATIVES **prosenchymatous** /,prɒsɛŋ'kɪmətəs/ adj.
– ORIGIN C19: from Gk *pros* 'toward' + *enkhuma* 'infusion', on the pattern of *parenchyma*.

**prosimian** /prəʊ'sɪmɪən/ ● n. Zoology a primate of a suborder (Prosimii) that includes the lemurs, lorises, bushbabies, and tarsiers.
– ORIGIN C19: from PRO-[2] + SIMIAN.

**prosit** /'prəʊzɪt/ ● exclam. used in drinking a person's health.
– ORIGIN Ger., from L., lit. 'may it benefit'.

**Prosobranchia** /,prɒsə(ʊ)'braŋkɪə/ ● pl. n. Zoology a subclass of molluscs including the limpets, abalones, and many snails.
– DERIVATIVES **prosobranch** /'prɒsəbraŋk/ n.
– ORIGIN mod. L., from Gk *prosō* 'forwards' + *brankhia* 'gills'.

**prosody** /'prɒsədi/ ● n. **1** the patterns of rhythm and sound used in poetry. ➤ the study of these patterns. **2** the patterns of stress and intonation in a language.
– DERIVATIVES **prosodic** adj. **prosodist** n.
– ORIGIN C15: from L. *prosodia* 'accent of a syllable', from Gk *prosōidia* 'song sung to music, tone of a syllable', from *pros* 'towards' + *ōidē* 'song'.

**prosoma** /prə(ʊ)'səʊmə/ ● n. another term for CEPHALOTHORAX.
– ORIGIN C19: from PRO-[2] + Gk *sōma* 'body'.

**prosopography** /,prɒsə(ʊ)'pɒgrəfi/ ● n. (pl. **-ies**) a description of a person's appearance, personality, career, etc., or a collection of such descriptions. ➤ the study of such descriptions, especially in Roman history.
– DERIVATIVES **prosopographer** n. **prosopographical** /-pə'grafɪk(ə)l/ adj.
– ORIGIN 1920s: from mod. L. *prosopographia*, from Gk *prosōpon* 'face, person' + *-graphia* 'writing'.

**prosopopoeia** /,prɒsəpə'piːə/ ● n. a figure of speech in which an abstract thing is personified or an imagined or absent person is represented as speaking.
– ORIGIN C16: via L. from Gk *prosōpopoiia*, from *prosōpon* 'person' + *poiein* 'to make'.

**prospect** ● n. **1** the possibility or likelihood of some future event occurring. ➤ a mental picture of a future or anticipated event. ➤ (**prospects**) chances or opportunities for success. **2** a person regarded as a potential customer or as likely to be successful. **3** an extensive view of landscape. **4** a place likely to yield mineral deposits. ● v. search for mineral deposits, especially by means of drilling and excavation.
– DERIVATIVES **prospectless** adj. **prospector** n.
– ORIGIN ME: from L. *prospectus* 'view', from *prospicere* 'look forward'.

**prospective** ● adj. expected or likely to happen or be in the future.
– DERIVATIVES **prospectively** adv. **prospectiveness** n.

**prospectus** ● n. (pl. **prospectuses**) a printed booklet advertising a school or university or giving details of a share offer.
– ORIGIN C18: from L., lit. 'view, prospect', from *prospicere* 'look forward'.

**prosper** ● v. succeed or flourish, especially financially; thrive. ➤ poetic/literary make successful.
– ORIGIN ME: from OFr. *prosperer*, from L. *prosperare*, from *prosperus* 'doing well'.

**prosperous** ● adj. successful or flourishing, especially financially.
– DERIVATIVES **prosperity** n. **prosperously** adv. **prosperousness** n.

**prostacyclin** /,prɒstə'sʌɪklɪn/ ● n. Biochemistry a compound of the prostaglandin type produced in arterial walls, which functions as an anticoagulant and vasodilator.
– ORIGIN 1970s: from PROSTAGLANDIN + CYCLIC + -IN[1].

**prostaglandin** /,prɒstə'glandɪn/ ● n. Biochemistry any of a group of compounds with varying hormone-like effects, notably the promotion of uterine contractions.
– ORIGIN 1930s: from PROSTATE + GLAND[1] + -IN[1].

**prostate** ● n. a gland surrounding the neck of the bladder in male mammals and releasing a fluid component of semen.
– DERIVATIVES **prostatic** adj.
– ORIGIN C17: via Fr. from mod. L. *prostata*, from Gk *prostatēs* 'one that stands before'.

**prosthesis** /prɒs'θiːsɪs, 'prɒsθɪ,sɪs/ ● n. (pl. **prostheses** /-siːz/) **1** an artificial body part. **2** the addition of a letter or syllable at the beginning of a word, as in Spanish *escuela* derived from Latin *scola*.
– DERIVATIVES **prosthetic** /-'θɛtɪk/ adj. **prosthetically** adv.
– ORIGIN C16: via late L. from Gk *prosthesis*, from *prostithenai* 'add'.

**prosthetic group** ● n. Biochemistry a non-protein group forming part of or combined with a protein.

**prosthetics** /prɒs'θɛtɪks/ ● pl. n. **1** artificial body parts; prostheses. ➤ pieces of flexible material applied to actors' faces to transform their appearance. **2** [treated as sing.] the branch of surgery concerned with the making and fitting of artificial body parts.
– DERIVATIVES **prosthetist** /'prɒsθɪtɪst/ n.

**prostitute** ● n. a person, typically a woman, who engages in sexual activity for payment. ● v. (often **prostitute oneself**) **1** offer (someone) as a prostitute. **2** put to an unworthy or corrupt use for the sake of gain.
– DERIVATIVES **prostitution** n. **prostitutor** n.
– ORIGIN C16 (as v.): from L. *prostitut-*, *prostituere* 'expose publicly, offer for sale'.

**prostrate** ● adj. /'prɒstreɪt/ **1** lying stretched out on the ground with one's face downwards. **2** completely overcome with distress or exhaustion. **3** Botany growing along the ground. ● v. /prɒ'streɪt/ **1** (**prostrate oneself**) throw oneself flat on the ground in reverence or submission. **2** (of distress, exhaustion, or illness) completely

overcome (someone).
– DERIVATIVES **prostration** n.
– ORIGIN ME: from L. *prostrat-*, *prosternere* 'throw down'.

**prostyle** /'prəʊstʌɪl/ ● n. Architecture a portico with a maximum of four columns.
– ORIGIN C17: from L. *prostylos* '(building) having pillars in front', from Gk *pro* 'before' + *stulos* 'column'.

**prosy** /'prəʊzi/ ● adj. (-ier, -iest) (of speech or writing) showing no imagination; commonplace or dull.
– DERIVATIVES **prosily** adv. **prosiness** n.

**prot-** ● comb. form variant spelling of **PROTO-** before a vowel (as in *protanopia*).

**protactinium** /,prəʊtak'tɪnɪəm/ ● n. the chemical element of atomic number 91, a radioactive metal of the actinide series, occurring in small amounts as a product of the natural decay of uranium. (Symbol: **Pa**)
– ORIGIN C20: from **PROTO-** + **ACTINIUM**, so named because one of its isotopes decays to form actinium.

**protagonist** ● n. **1** the leading character in a drama, film, or novel. ➤a prominent figure in a real situation. **2** an advocate or champion of a cause or idea.
– ORIGIN C17: from Gk *prōtagōnistēs*, from *prōtos* 'first in importance' + *agōnistēs* 'actor'.

**protandrous** /prəʊ'tandrəs/ ● adj. Botany & Zoology (of a hermaphrodite flower or animal) having the male reproductive organs come to maturity before the female. The opposite of **PROTOGYNOUS**.
– DERIVATIVES **protandry** n.

**protanope** /'prəʊt(ə)nəʊp/ ● n. a person suffering from protanopia.

**protanopia** /,prəʊtə'nəʊpɪə/ ● n. colour blindness resulting from insensitivity to red light, causing confusion of greens, reds, and yellows. Compare with **DEUTERANOPIA**, **TRITANOPIA**.
– ORIGIN C20: from **PROTO-** 'original' (red being regarded as the first component of colour vision) + **AN-**[1] + **-OPIA**.

**pro tanto** /prəʊ 'tantəʊ/ ● adj. & adv. to such an extent.
– ORIGIN L., lit. 'for so much'.

**protasis** /'prɒtəsɪs/ ● n. (pl. **protases** /-siːz/) Grammar the clause expressing the condition in a conditional sentence (e.g. *if you asked me* in *if you asked me I would agree*). Contrasted with **APODOSIS**.
– ORIGIN C16: via L. from Gk *protasis* 'proposition'.

**protea** /'prəʊtɪə/ ● n. a chiefly South African evergreen shrub with large cone-like flower heads surrounded by brightly coloured bracts. [Genus *Protea*: many species.]
– ORIGIN mod. L., from *Proteus* (see **PROTEAN**), with ref. to the many species of the genus.

**protean** /'prəʊtɪən, prəʊ'tiːən/ ● adj. tending or able to change or adapt; variable or versatile.
– ORIGIN C16: from the minor Greek sea god *Proteus* (who was able to change shape at will) + **-AN**.

**protease** /'prəʊtɪeɪz/ ● n. Biochemistry an enzyme which breaks down proteins and peptides.
– ORIGIN C20: from **PROTEIN** + **-ASE**.

**protect** ● v. **1** keep safe from harm or injury. ➤[often as adj. **protected**] aim to preserve (a threatened plant or animal species) by legislating against collecting or hunting. **2** Economics shield (a domestic industry) from competition by imposing import duties on foreign goods. **3** provide funds to meet (a bill of exchange or commercial draft).
– DERIVATIVES **protectable** adj.
– ORIGIN ME: from L. *protect-*, *protegere* 'cover in front'.

**protectant** ● n. a substance that provides protection, e.g. against disease or ultraviolet radiation.

**protection** ● n. **1** the action or state of protecting or being protected. ➤a person or thing that protects. ➤a document guaranteeing safety to the person specified in it. **2** the payment of money to criminals to prevent them from attacking oneself or one's property.

**protectionism** ● n. Economics the theory or practice of shielding a country's domestic industries from foreign competition by taxing imports.
– DERIVATIVES **protectionist** n. & adj.

**protective** ● adj. **1** serving, intended, or wishing to protect. **2** Economics relating to protectionism. ● n. Brit. a thing that protects. ➤dated a condom.
– DERIVATIVES **protectively** adv. **protectiveness** n.

**protective custody** ● n. the detention of a person for their own protection.

**protector** ● n. **1** a person or thing that protects. **2** (**Protector**) historical a regent in charge of a kingdom during the minority, absence, or incapacity of the sovereign. ➤(also **Lord Protector of the Commonwealth**) the title of Oliver Cromwell and his son Richard as heads of state in England 1653–9.
– DERIVATIVES **protectoral** adj. **protectorship** n. **protectress** n.

**protectorate** ● n. **1** a state that is controlled and protected by another. ➤the relationship between a state of this kind and the one that controls it. **2** (**Protectorate**) historical the position or period of office of a Protector.

**protégé** /'prɒtɪʒeɪ, -tɛʒeɪ, 'prəʊ-/ ● n. (fem. **protégée**) a person who is guided and supported by an older and more experienced or influential person.
– ORIGIN C18: Fr., lit. 'protected', past part. of *protéger*.

**protein** ● n. any of a class of nitrogenous organic compounds forming structural components of body tissues and constituting an important part of the diet.
– DERIVATIVES **proteinaceous** adj.
– ORIGIN C19: from Fr. *protéine*, Ger. *Protein*, from Gk *prōteios* 'primary'.

**proteinuria** /,prəʊtiː'njʊərɪə/ ● n. Medicine the presence of abnormal quantities of protein in the urine, possibly indicating damage to the kidneys.

**pro tem** /prəʊ 'tɛm/ ● adv. & adj. for the time being.
– ORIGIN abbrev. of L. *pro tempore*.

**proteoglycan** /,prəʊtɪəʊ'glʌɪkan/ ● n. Biochemistry a compound consisting of a protein bonded to mucopolysaccharide groups, present especially in connective tissue.

**proteolysis** /,prəʊtɪ'ɒlɪsɪs/ ● n. Biochemistry the breakdown of proteins or peptides into amino acids by the action of enzymes.
– DERIVATIVES **proteolytic** adj. **proteolytically** adv.

**proteomics** ● pl. n. [treated as sing.] the branch of molecular biology concerned with the behaviour and interaction of proteins within cells.

**Proterozoic** /,prəʊt(ə)rə'zəʊɪk/ ● adj. Geology relating to or denoting the later part of the Precambrian aeon (between the Archaean aeon and the Cambrian period, about 2,500 to 570 million years ago), in which the earliest forms of life evolved.
– ORIGIN C20: from Gk *proteros* 'former' + *zōē* 'life', *zōos* 'living' + **-IC**.

**protest** ● n. **1** a statement or action expressing disapproval of or objection to something. ➤an organized public demonstration objecting to an official policy or course of action. **2** Law a written declaration, typically by a notary public, that a bill has been presented and payment or acceptance refused. ● v. **1** express an objection to what someone has said or done. ➤engage in public protest. ➤N. Amer. publicly protest against (a policy or course of action). **2** make an emphatic declaration or denial in response to an accusation or criticism. **3** Law write or obtain a protest in regard to (a bill).
– DERIVATIVES **protester** n. **protesting** adj. **protestingly** adv. **protestor** n.
– ORIGIN ME (in the sense 'make a solemn declaration'): from OFr. *protester*, from L. *protestari* 'assert formally', based on *testis* 'a witness'.

**Protestant** /'prɒtɪst(ə)nt/ ● n. a member or follower of any of the Western Christian Churches that are separate from the Roman Catholic Church in accordance with the principles of the Reformation. ● adj. of, relating to, or belonging to any of the Protestant Churches.
– DERIVATIVES **Protestantism** n. **Protestantization** (also **-isation**) n. **Protestantize** (also **-ise**) v.
– ORIGIN C16: via Ger. or Fr. from L. *protestant-* 'protesting', from L. *protestari* (see **PROTEST**).

**Protestant ethic** (also **Protestant work ethic**) ● n. the view that a person's duty and responsibility is to achieve success through hard work and thrift.

**protestation** /,prɒtɪ'steɪʃ(ə)n/ ● n. an emphatic declaration that something is or is not the case. ➤an objection or protest.

**proteus** /ˈprəʊtɪəs/ ● **n. 1** a bacterium found in the intestines of animals and in the soil. [Genus *Proteus*.] **2** another term for **OLM**.
– ORIGIN C19: from *Proteus* (see **PROTEAN**).

**prothalamium** /ˌprəʊθəˈleɪmɪəm/ ● **n.** (pl. **prothalamia** /-mɪə/) poetic/literary a song or poem celebrating a forthcoming wedding.
– ORIGIN C16: from *Prothalamion*, the title of a poem by Spenser, on the pattern of *epithalamium*.

**prothallus** /prəʊˈθaləs/ ● **n.** (pl. **prothalli** /-lʌɪ, -liː/) Botany the gametophyte of ferns and related plants.
– DERIVATIVES **prothallial** adj.
– ORIGIN C19: mod. L., from **PRO-**[2] + Gk *thallos* 'green shoot'.

**prothesis** /ˈprɒθɪsɪs/ ● **n.** (pl. **protheses** /-siːz/) **1** (especially in the Orthodox Church) the action of placing the Eucharistic elements on the credence table. ➤ a credence table, or the part of a church where it stands. **2** another term for **PROSTHESIS** (in sense 2).
– DERIVATIVES **prothetic** adj.
– ORIGIN C16: from Gk, 'placing before or in public view'.

**prothonotary** /ˌprəʊθəˈnəʊt(ə)ri, prəˈθɒnə-/ ● **n.** variant spelling of **PROTONOTARY**.

**prothrombin** /prəʊˈθrɒmbɪn/ ● **n.** Biochemistry a protein present in blood plasma which is converted into active thrombin during coagulation.

**Protista** /prəʊˈtɪstə/ ● **pl. n.** Biology a kingdom or large grouping of typically single-celled organisms including the protozoans, slime moulds, and simple algae and fungi.
– DERIVATIVES **protist** /ˈprəʊtɪst/ n. **protistan** adj. & n. **protistology** n.
– ORIGIN mod. L., from Gk *prōtista*, neut. pl. of *prōtistos* 'very first'.

**protium** /ˈprəʊtɪəm/ ● **n.** Chemistry the common, stable isotope of hydrogen, as distinct from deuterium and tritium.
– ORIGIN 1930s: mod. L., from Gk *prōtos* 'first'.

**proto-** (usu. **prot-** before a vowel) ● **comb. form** original; primitive: *prototype*. ➤ first; anterior; relating to a precursor: *protozoon*.
– ORIGIN from Gk *prōtos* 'first'.

**protoceratops** /ˌprəʊtə(ʊ)ˈsɛrətɒps/ ● **n.** a small quadrupedal dinosaur of the late Cretaceous period, having a bony frill above the neck and probably ancestral to triceratops.

**protocol** ● **n. 1** the official procedure or system of rules governing affairs of state or diplomatic occasions. ➤ the accepted code of procedure or behaviour in a particular situation. **2** the original draft of a diplomatic document, especially of the terms of a treaty agreed to in conference and signed by the parties. ➤ an amendment to a treaty or convention. **3** a formal record of scientific experimental observations. ➤ a procedure for carrying out a scientific experiment or a course of medical treatment. **4** Computing a set of rules governing the exchange or transmission of data between devices.
– ORIGIN ME (denoting the original note of an agreement): from OFr. *prothocole*, via med. L. from Gk *prōtokollon* 'first page, flyleaf'.

**protogynous** /prəʊˈtɒdʒɪnəs/ ● **adj.** Botany & Zoology (of a hermaphrodite flower or animal) having the female reproductive organs come to maturity before the male. The opposite of **PROTANDROUS**.
– DERIVATIVES **protogyny** n.

**Proto-Indo-European** ● **n.** the lost language from which all Indo-European languages derive.

**protomartyr** ● **n.** the first martyr for a cause, especially the first Christian martyr, St Stephen.

**proton** /ˈprəʊtɒn/ ● **n.** Physics a stable subatomic particle occurring in all atomic nuclei, with a positive electric charge equal in magnitude to that of an electron.
– DERIVATIVES **protonic** adj.
– ORIGIN 1920s: from Gk, neut. of *prōtos* 'first'.

**protonate** /ˈprəʊt(ə)neɪt/ ● **v.** Chemistry transfer a proton to (a molecule, group, or atom) which forms a coordinate bond to the proton.
– DERIVATIVES **protonation** n.

**protonotary** /ˌprəʊtəˈnəʊt(ə)ri, prəˈtɒnət(ə)ri/ (also **prothonotary**) ● **n.** (pl. **-ies**) chiefly historical a chief clerk in some law courts, originally in the Byzantine court.
– ORIGIN ME: via med. L. from late Gk *prōtonotarios*, from *prōtos* 'first' + *notarios* 'notary'.

**Protonotary Apostolic** (also **Protonotary Apostolical**) ● **n.** a member of the Roman Catholic college of prelates who register papal acts and direct the canonization of saints.

**protopathic** /ˌprəʊtə(ʊ)ˈpaθɪk/ ● **adj.** Physiology relating to or denoting those sensory nerve fibres of the skin which are capable of discriminating only between relatively coarse stimuli, chiefly heat, cold, and pain.
– ORIGIN C19: from **PROTO-** + Gk *pathos* 'suffering, feeling' + **-IC**.

**protoplasm** /ˈprəʊtə(ʊ)ˌplaz(ə)m/ ● **n.** Biology the colourless material comprising the living part of a cell, including the cytoplasm, nucleus, and other organelles.
– DERIVATIVES **protoplasmic** adj.
– ORIGIN C19: from Gk *prōtoplasma* (see **PROTO-**, **PLASMA**).

**protoplast** /ˈprəʊtə(ʊ)plast, -plɑːst/ ● **n.** chiefly Botany the protoplasm of a living plant or bacterial cell whose cell wall has been removed.
– ORIGIN C19: from Gk *prōtoplastos* 'first formed'.

**protostome** /ˈprəʊtə(ʊ)stəʊm/ ● **n.** Zoology a multicellular organism whose mouth develops from a primary embryonic opening, such as an annelid, mollusc, or arthropod.
– ORIGIN 1950s: from **PROTO-** + Gk *stoma* 'mouth'.

**Prototheria** /ˌprəʊtə(ʊ)ˈθɪərɪə/ ● **pl. n.** Zoology a group of mammals that comprises the monotremes and their extinct relatives.
– DERIVATIVES **prototherian** n. & adj.
– ORIGIN mod. L., from **PROTO-** + Gk *thēr* 'wild beast'.

**prototype** ● **n. 1** a first or preliminary form from which other forms are developed or copied. **2** a typical example of something. ● **v.** make a prototype of.
– DERIVATIVES **prototypal** adj. **prototypic** adj. **prototypical** adj. **prototypically** adv.
– ORIGIN C16: via Fr. or late L. from Gk *prōtotupos* (see **PROTO-**, **TYPE**).

**Protozoa** /ˌprəʊtəˈzəʊə/ ● **pl. n.** Zoology a phylum or group of phyla comprising the single-celled microscopic animals such as amoebas, flagellates, ciliates, and sporozoans.
– DERIVATIVES **protozoal** adj. **protozoan** n. & adj. **protozoic** adj. **protozoon** n.
– ORIGIN mod. L., from **PROTO-** + Gk *zōion* 'animal'.

**protract** ● **v.** prolong; draw out.
– DERIVATIVES **protracted** adj. **protractedly** adv. **protractedness** n.
– ORIGIN C16: from L. *protract-*, *protrahere* 'prolong', from *pro-* 'out' + *trahere* 'to draw'.

**protractile** /prəˈtraktʌɪl, -tɪl/ ● **adj.** another term for ***protrusible*** (see **PROTRUDE**).

**protraction** ● **n. 1** the action or state of prolonging or being prolonged. **2** the action of extending a part of the body.

**protractor** ● **n. 1** an instrument for measuring angles, typically in the form of a flat semicircle marked with degrees along the curved edge. **2** chiefly Zoology a muscle serving to extend a part of the body. Compare with **RETRACTOR**.

**protrude** ● **v.** extend beyond or above a surface. ➤ (of an animal) cause (a body part) to do this.
– DERIVATIVES **protrusible** adj. **protrusion** n. **protrusive** adj.
– ORIGIN C17: from L. *protrudere*, from *pro-* 'forward, out' + *trudere* 'to thrust'.

**protuberance** /prəˈtjuːb(ə)r(ə)ns/ ● **n.** a thing that protrudes. ➤ the fact or state of protruding.

**protuberant** ● **adj.** protruding; bulging.
– ORIGIN C17: from late L. *protuberant-*, *protuberare* 'swell out'.

**proud** ● **adj. 1** feeling pride or satisfaction in one's own or another's achievements. ➤ poetic/literary imposing; splendid. **2** having or showing a high opinion of oneself. ➤ con-

scious of one's own dignity. **3** slightly projecting from a surface. ➤(of flesh) overgrown round a healing wound.
– PHRASES **do someone proud** informal act in a way that gives someone cause to feel pleased or satisfied. ➤treat or entertain someone very well.
– DERIVATIVES **proudly** adv. **proudness** n.
– ORIGIN OE *prūt, prūd*, from OFr. *prud* 'valiant', based on L. *prodesse* 'be of value'.

**Prov.** ● **abbrev. 1** Proverbs (in biblical references). **2** chiefly Canadian Province or Provincial.

**prove** /pruːv/ ● **v.** (past part. **proved** or **proven** /ˈpruːv(ə)n, ˈprəʊ-/) **1** demonstrate by evidence or argument the truth or existence of. ➤Law establish the genuineness and validity of (a will). **2** be seen or found to be: *the scheme has proved a great success.* ➤demonstrate to be. ➤(**prove oneself**) demonstrate one's abilities or courage. **3** subject (a gun) to a testing process. **4** (of bread dough) become aerated by the action of yeast; rise.
– PHRASES **not proven** Scots Law a verdict that there is insufficient evidence to establish guilt or innocence.
– DERIVATIVES **provability** n. **provable** adj. **provably** adv.
– ORIGIN ME: from OFr. *prover*, from L. *probare* 'test, approve, demonstrate'.

**provenance** /ˈprɒv(ə)nəns/ ● **n. 1** the place of origin or earliest known history of something. **2** a record of ownership of a work of art or an antique.
– ORIGIN C18: from Fr., from *provenir* 'come or stem from'.

**Provençal** /ˌprɒvɒ̃ˈsɑːl, French prɔvɑ̃sal/ ● **n. 1** a native or inhabitant of Provence. **2** the language of Provence. ● **adj.** relating to or denoting Provence or its people or language.

**provençale** /ˌprɒvɒ̃ˈsɑːl/ ● **adj.** [postpos.] denoting a dish cooked in a sauce made with tomatoes, garlic, and olive oil, as characteristic of Provençal cuisine.
– ORIGIN from Fr. *à la provençale* 'in the Provençal style'.

**provender** /ˈprɒvɪndə/ ● **n. 1** animal fodder. **2** often humorous food.
– ORIGIN ME: from OFr. *provendre*, based on an alt. of L. *praebenda* (see **PREBEND**).

**provenience** /prəˈviːnɪəns/ ● **n.** US term for **PROVENANCE**.

**proverb** ● **n.** a short pithy saying in general use, stating a general truth or piece of advice.
– ORIGIN ME: from OFr. *proverbe*, from L. *proverbium*, from *pro-* '(put) forth' + *verbum* 'word'.

**proverbial** ● **adj. 1** referred to in a proverb or idiom. **2** well known, especially so as to be stereotypical.
– DERIVATIVES **proverbiality** n. **proverbially** adv.

**pro-vice-chancellor** ● **n.** an assistant or deputy vice chancellor of a university.

**provide** ● **v. 1** make available for use; supply. ➤(**provide someone with**) equip or supply someone with. **2** (**provide for**) make adequate preparation or arrangements for. ➤(of a law) enable or allow (something to be done). **3** stipulate in a will or other legal document. **4** (**provide someone to**) Christian Church, historical appoint an incumbent to (a benefice).
– DERIVATIVES **provider** n.
– ORIGIN ME: from L. *providere* 'foresee, attend to'.

**provided** ● **conj.** on the condition or understanding that.

**providence** ● **n. 1** the protective care of God or of nature as a spiritual power. ➤(**Providence**) God or nature as providing such care. **2** timely preparation for future eventualities.

**provident** ● **adj.** making or indicative of timely preparation for the future.
– DERIVATIVES **providently** adv.

**providential** ● **adj. 1** occurring at a favourable time; opportune. **2** involving divine foresight or interference.
– DERIVATIVES **providentially** adv.

**Provident Society** ● **n.** Brit. another term for **FRIENDLY SOCIETY**.

**providing** ● **conj.** on the condition or understanding that.

**province** ● **n. 1** a principal administrative division of a country or empire. ➤(**the Province**) Brit. Northern Ireland. ➤Christian Church a district under an archbishop or a metropolitan. ➤Roman History a territory outside Italy under a Roman governor. **2** (**one's province**) an area in which one has special knowledge, interest, or responsibility. **3** (**the provinces**) the whole of a country outside the capital, especially when regarded as lacking in sophistication or culture.
– ORIGIN ME: from OFr., from L. *provincia* 'charge, province', of uncertain ultimate origin.

**provincial** ● **adj. 1** of or concerning a province of a country or empire. **2** of or concerning the regions outside the capital city of a country, especially when regarded as unsophisticated or narrow-minded. ● **n. 1** an inhabitant of a province of a country or empire. **2** an inhabitant of the regions outside the capital city of a country. **3** Christian Church the head or chief of a province or of a religious order in a province.
– DERIVATIVES **provinciality** n. **provincialization** (also **-isation**) n. **provincially** adv.

**provincialism** ● **n. 1** the way of life or mode of thought characteristic of the regions outside the capital city of a country, especially when regarded as unsophisticated or narrow-minded. ➤narrow-mindedness, insularity, or lack of sophistication. **2** concern for one's own area or region at the expense of national or supranational unity. **3** a word or phrase peculiar to a local area. **4** the degree to which plant or animal communities are restricted to particular areas.
– DERIVATIVES **provincialist** n. & adj.

**proving ground** ● **n.** an area or situation in which a person or thing is tested or proved.

**provirus** /prəʊˈvʌɪrəs/ ● **n.** Microbiology the genetic material of a virus as incorporated into, and able to replicate with, the genome of a host cell.
– DERIVATIVES **proviral** adj.

**provision** ● **n. 1** the action of providing or supplying. ➤something supplied or provided. ➤(**provision for/against**) arrangements for future eventualities or requirements. **2** (**provisions**) supplies of food, drink, or equipment, especially for a journey. **3** a condition or requirement in a legal document. **4** an amount set aside out of profits in the accounts of an organization for a known liability. **5** Christian Church, historical an appointment to a benefice. ● **v. 1** supply with provisions. **2** set aside a provision for a known liability.
– DERIVATIVES **provisioner** n.

**provisional** ● **adj. 1** arranged or existing for the present, possibly to be changed later. **2** (**Provisional**) denoting or relating to the unofficial wings of the IRA and Sinn Fein. ● **n.** (**Provisional**) a member of the Provisional wings of the IRA or Sinn Fein.
– DERIVATIVES **provisionality** n. **provisionally** adv.

**proviso** /prəˈvʌɪzəʊ/ ● **n.** (pl. **-os**) a condition attached to an agreement.
– ORIGIN ME: from the med. L. phr. *proviso* (*quod*) 'it being provided (that)'.

**provisor** ● **n. 1** (in the Roman Catholic Church) a deputy of a bishop or archbishop. **2** Christian Church, historical the holder of a provision.
– ORIGIN ME: from Anglo-Norman Fr. *provisour*, from L. *provisor*, from *provis-* (see **PROVISION**).

**provisory** ● **adj. 1** subject to a proviso; conditional. **2** provisional.

**provitamin** ● **n.** Biochemistry a substance which is converted into a vitamin within an organism.

**Provo** /ˈprəʊvəʊ/ ● **n.** (pl. **-os**) informal a member of the Provisional IRA or Sinn Fein.

**provocation** ● **n. 1** the action of provoking. ➤action or speech that provokes. ➤Law action or speech held to be likely to prompt physical retaliation. **2** Medicine testing to elicit a particular response or reflex.

**provocative** ● **adj. 1** causing annoyance, anger, or another strong reaction, especially deliberately. **2** arousing sexual desire or interest, especially deliberately.
– DERIVATIVES **provocatively** adv. **provocativeness** n.

**provoke** ● **v. 1** stimulate (a reaction or emotion, typically a strong or unwelcome one) in someone. **2** deliberately

annoy or anger. ➤ incite to do or feel something, especially by arousing anger.
– DERIVATIVES **provokable** adj. **provoker** n. **provoking** adj. **provokingly** adv.
– ORIGIN ME: from OFr. *provoquer*, from L. *provocare* 'challenge', from *pro-* 'forth' + *vocare* 'to call'.

**provolone** /ˌprɒvəˈləʊneɪ, -ˈləʊni/ ● **n.** an Italian soft smoked cheese made from cow's milk.
– ORIGIN Ital., from *provola* 'buffalo's milk cheese'.

**provost** /ˈprɒvəst/ ● **n. 1** Brit. the position of head in certain university colleges and public schools. ➤ N. Amer. a senior administrative officer in certain universities. **2** Scottish term for **MAYOR**. **3** the head of a chapter in a cathedral. ➤ the Protestant minister of the principal church of a town or district, especially in Germany. ➤ historical the head of a Christian community. **4** short for **PROVOST MARSHAL**. **5** historical the chief magistrate of a European town.
– DERIVATIVES **provostship** n.
– ORIGIN OE *profost* 'head of a chapter, prior', reinforced in ME by Anglo-Norman Fr. *provost*, from med. L. *propositus*, synonym of L. *praepositus* (see **PRAEPOSTOR**).

**provost guard** ● **n.** US a detachment of soldiers acting as military police under the command of a provost marshal.

**provost marshal** ● **n. 1** the head of military police in camp or on active service. **2** (in the Royal Navy) a senior commissioned officer in the Regulatory Branch or Naval Dockyard Port.

**prow** /praʊ/ ● **n.** the pointed front part of a ship; the bow.
– ORIGIN C16: from OFr. *proue*, from Provençal *proa*, prob. via L. from Gk *prōira*, from a base represented by L. *pro* 'in front'.

**prowess** ● **n. 1** skill or expertise in a particular activity or field. **2** bravery in battle.
– ORIGIN ME: from OFr. *proesce*, from *prou* 'valiant'.

**prowl** ● **v.** move about stealthily or restlessly in search of or as if in search of prey. ● **n.** an act of prowling.
– DERIVATIVES **prowler** n.
– ORIGIN ME: of unknown origin.

**prowl car** ● **n.** US a police squad car.

**prox.** ● **abbrev.** proximo.

**prox. acc.** ● **abbrev.** proxime accessit.

**proxemics** /prɒkˈsiːmɪks/ ● **pl. n.** [treated as sing.] the branch of study concerned with the amount of space that people set between themselves and others.
– ORIGIN 1960s: from **PROXIMITY**, on the pattern of words such as *phonemics*.

**proximal** ● **adj.** chiefly Anatomy situated nearer to the centre of the body or an area or the point of attachment. The opposite of **DISTAL**.
– DERIVATIVES **proximally** adv.

**proximate** ● **adj. 1** closest in space, time, or relationship: *the proximate cause of the symptoms*. **2** nearly accurate; approximate.
– DERIVATIVES **proximately** adv. **proximation** n.
– ORIGIN C16: from L. *proximat-*, *proximare* 'draw near', from *proximus* 'nearest'.

**proxime accessit** /ˌprɒksɪmeɪ akˈsɛsɪt, -mi/ ● **n.** the person who comes second in an examination or is runner-up for an award.
– ORIGIN L., lit. 'came very near'.

**proximity** ● **n.** nearness in space, time, or relationship.
– ORIGIN C15: from Fr. *proximité*, from L. *proximitas*, from *proximus* 'nearest'.

**proximity fuse** ● **n.** an electronic detonator that causes a projectile to explode when it comes within a preset distance of its target.

**proximo** /ˈprɒksɪməʊ/ ● **adj.** [postpos.] dated of next month.
– ORIGIN from L. *proximo mense* 'in the next month'.

**proxy** ● **n.** (pl. **-ies**) **1** the authority to represent someone else, especially in voting. ➤ a person authorized to act on behalf of another. **2** a figure used to represent the value of something in a calculation.
– ORIGIN ME: contr. of **PROCURACY**.

**Prozac** /ˈprəʊzak/ ● **n.** trademark for **FLUOXETINE**.
– ORIGIN 1980s: an invented name.

**prude** ● **n.** a person who is easily shocked by matters relating to sex or nudity.
– DERIVATIVES **prudery** n. **prudish** adj. **prudishly** adv. **prudishness** n.
– ORIGIN C18: from Fr., back-form. from *prudefemme*, fem. of *prud'homme* 'good man and true'.

**prudent** ● **adj.** acting with or showing care and thought for the future.
– DERIVATIVES **prudence** n. **prudently** adv.
– ORIGIN ME: from OFr., or from L. *prudent-*, contr. of *provident-* (see **PROVIDENT**).

**prudential** ● **adj.** involving or showing care and forethought, typically in business.
– DERIVATIVES **prudentially** adv.
– ORIGIN ME: from **PRUDENT**, on the pattern of words such as *evidential*.

**pruinose** /ˈpruːɪnəʊs, -z/ ● **adj.** chiefly Botany covered with white powdery granules; frosted in appearance.
– ORIGIN C19: from L. *pruinosus*, from *pruina* 'hoar frost'.

**prune**[1] ● **n. 1** a plum preserved by drying and having a black, wrinkled appearance. **2** informal a disagreeable person.
– ORIGIN ME: from OFr., via L. from Gk *prou(m)non* 'plum'.

**prune**[2] ● **v. 1** trim (a tree, shrub, or bush) by cutting away dead or overgrown branches or stems. **2** remove superfluous or unwanted parts from. ● **n.** an instance of pruning.
– DERIVATIVES **pruner** n.
– ORIGIN C15 (in the sense 'abbreviate'): from OFr. *pro(o)ignier*, possibly based on L. *rotundus* 'round'.

**prunella** /prʊˈnɛlə/ ● **n.** a strong silk or worsted fabric used formerly for barristers' gowns and the uppers of women's shoes.
– ORIGIN C17: perh. from Fr. *prunelle* 'sloe' (because of its dark colour).

**prunus** /ˈpruːnəs/ ● **n.** a tree or shrub of a large genus that includes cherry, almond, plum, peach, and apricot trees. [Genus *Prunus*.]
– ORIGIN mod. L., from L., lit. 'plum tree'.

**prurient** /ˈprʊərɪənt/ ● **adj.** having or encouraging an excessive interest in sexual matters.
– DERIVATIVES **prurience** n. **pruriency** n. **pruriently** adv.
– ORIGIN C16 (in the sense 'having a craving'): from L. *prurient-*, *prurire* 'itch, long, be wanton'.

**prurigo** /prʊəˈrʌɪgəʊ/ ● **n.** Medicine a chronic skin disease causing severe itching.
– DERIVATIVES **pruriginous** /prʊəˈrɪdʒɪnəs/ adj.
– ORIGIN C17: from L., from *prurire* 'to itch'.

**pruritus** /prʊˈrʌɪtəs/ ● **n.** Medicine severe itching of the skin, as a symptom of various ailments.
– DERIVATIVES **pruritic** adj.
– ORIGIN C17: from L., 'itching' (see **PRURIGO**).

**prusik** /ˈprʌsɪk/ ● **adj.** Climbing relating to or denoting a method of ascending or descending a rope by means of two movable loops attached by a special knot which tightens under pressure.
– DERIVATIVES **prusiking** n.
– ORIGIN 1930s: from the name of Austrian mountaineer Karl *Prusik*.

**Prussian** ● **n.** a native or inhabitant of the former German kingdom of Prussia. ● **adj.** of or relating to Prussia.

**Prussian blue** ● **n.** a deep blue pigment used in painting and dyeing, made from or in imitation of ferric ferrocyanide.

**prussic acid** /ˈprʌsɪk/ ● **n.** old-fashioned term for **HYDROCYANIC ACID**.
– DERIVATIVES **prussiate** n.
– ORIGIN C18: *prussic* from Fr. *prussique* 'relating to Prussian blue'.

**pry**[1] ● **v.** (**-ies, -ied**) enquire too intrusively into a person's private affairs.
– DERIVATIVES **prying** adj. **pryingly** adv.
– ORIGIN ME (in the sense 'peer inquisitively'): of unknown origin.

**pry**[2] ● **v.** (**-ies, -ied**) chiefly N. Amer. another term for **PRISE**.

– ORIGIN C19: from **PRISE**, interpreted as *pries*, third person sing. of the pres. tense.

**prytany** /'prɪtəni/ ● **n.** (pl. **-ies**) (in ancient Greece) each of the ten divisions of the Athenian Council of Five Hundred. ➤a period of five weeks for which each division presided in turn.
– ORIGIN from Gk *prutaneia*, from *prutanis* 'prince, ruler'.

**PS** ● **abbrev. 1** Police Sergeant. **2** postscript. **3** private secretary. **4** (in the theatre) prompt side.

**Ps.** (pl. **Pss.**) ● **abbrev.** Psalm or Psalms.

**psalm** /sɑːm/ ● **n.** a sacred song or hymn, in particular any of those contained in the biblical Book of Psalms. ➤(**the Psalms** or **the Book of Psalms**) a book of the Bible comprising a collection of religious verses, sung or recited in both Jewish and Christian worship.
– DERIVATIVES **psalmic** adj. **psalmist** n.
– ORIGIN OE (*p*)*sealm*, via eccles. L. from Gk *psalmos* 'song sung to harp music'.

**psalmody** /'sɑːmədi, 'salm-/ ● **n.** the singing of psalms or similar sacred canticles. ➤psalms arranged for singing.
– DERIVATIVES **psalmodic** adj. **psalmodist** n.
– ORIGIN ME: via late L. from Gk *psalmōidia* 'singing to a harp'.

**psalter** /'sɔːltə, 'sɒl-/ ● **n.** a copy of the biblical Psalms, especially for liturgical use. ➤(**the psalter**) the Book of Psalms.
– ORIGIN OE (*p*)*saltere*, via L. *psalterium* from Gk *psaltērion* 'stringed instrument'.

**psalterium** /sɔːl'tɪərɪəm, sɒl-/ ● **n.** another term for **OMASUM**.
– ORIGIN C19: from L., lit. 'psalter' (see **PSALTER**), because of its many folds of tissue, resembling pages of a book.

**psaltery** /'sɔːlt(ə)ri, 'sɒl-/ ● **n.** (pl. **-ies**) an ancient and medieval musical instrument like a dulcimer but played by plucking the strings with the fingers or a plectrum.
– ORIGIN ME *sautrie*, from OFr. *sauterie*, from L. *psalterium* (see **PSALTER**).

**PSBR** ● **abbrev.** Brit. public-sector borrowing requirement.

**psephology** /sɛ'fɒlədʒi, sɪ-/ ● **n.** the statistical study of elections and trends in voting.
– DERIVATIVES **psephological** adj. **psephologically** adv. **psephologist** n.
– ORIGIN 1950s: from Gk *psēphos* 'pebble, vote' + **-LOGY**.

**pseud** /sjuːd/ ● **n.** informal a pretentious person; a poseur.

**pseud-** ● **comb. form** variant spelling of **PSEUDO-** reduced before a vowel (as in *pseudepigrapha*).

**pseudepigrapha** /ˌsjuːdɪ'pɪɡrəfə/ ● **pl. n.** spurious or pseudonymous writings, especially Jewish writings ascribed to various biblical patriarchs and prophets but composed *c.*200 BC–AD 200.
– DERIVATIVES **pseudepigraphal** adj. **pseudepigraphic** adj.
– ORIGIN C17: neut. pl. of Gk *pseudepigraphos* (see **PSEUDO-**, **EPIGRAPH**).

**pseudo** /'sjuːdəʊ/ ● **adj.** not genuine; fake, pretentious, or insincere. ● **n.** (pl. **-os**) a pretentious or insincere person.

**pseudo-** (also **pseud-** before a vowel) ● **comb. form 1** false; not genuine: *pseudonym*. **2** resembling or imitating: *pseudo-hallucination*.
– ORIGIN from Gk *pseudēs* 'false', *pseudos* 'falsehood'.

**pseudocarp** ● **n.** technical term for **FALSE FRUIT**.
– ORIGIN C19: from **PSEUDO-** + Gk *karpos* 'fruit'.

**pseudocyesis** /ˌsjuːdəʊsʌɪ'iːsɪs/ ● **n.** technical term for **PHANTOM PREGNANCY**.
– ORIGIN C19: from **PSEUDO-** + Gk *kuēsis* 'conception'.

**pseudomonas** /ˌsjuːdə(ʊ)'məʊnəs, sjuː'dɒmənas/ ● **n.** Microbiology a bacterium of a genus occurring typically in soil and detritus. [Genus *Pseudomonas*.]
– ORIGIN mod. L., from **PSEUDO-** + *monas* 'monad'.

**pseudomorph** /'sjuːdə(ʊ)mɔːf/ Crystallography ● **n.** a crystal consisting of one mineral but having the form of another. ● **v.** replace to form a pseudomorph.
– DERIVATIVES **pseudomorphic** adj. **pseudomorphism** n. **pseudomorphous** adj.
– ORIGIN C19: from **PSEUDO-** + Gk *morphē* 'form'.

**pseudonym** /'sjuːdənɪm/ ● **n.** a fictitious name, especially one used by an author.
– ORIGIN C19: from Fr. *pseudonyme*, from Gk *pseudōnymos*, from *pseudēs* 'false' + *onoma* 'name'.

**pseudonymous** /sjuː'dɒnɪməs/ ● **adj.** writing or written under a false name.
– DERIVATIVES **pseudonymity** /-'nɪmɪti/ n. **pseudonymously** adv.

**pseudopod** /'sjuːdə(ʊ)pɒd/ ● **n.** another term for **PSEUDOPODIUM**.

**pseudopodium** /ˌsjuːdə(ʊ)'pəʊdɪəm/ ● **n.** (pl. **pseudopodia** /-dɪə/) Biology a temporary protrusion of the surface of an amoeboid cell for movement and feeding.

**pseudopregnancy** ● **n.** (pl. **-ies**) another term for **PHANTOM PREGNANCY**.

**pseudoscience** ● **n.** a collection of beliefs or practices mistakenly regarded as being based on scientific method.
– DERIVATIVES **pseudoscientific** adj. **pseudoscientist** n.

**pseudoscorpion** ● **n.** another term for **FALSE SCORPION**.

**pshaw** /pʃɔː, ʃɔː/ ● **exclam.** dated or humorous an expression of contempt or impatience.

**psi** /psʌɪ, sʌɪ/ ● **n. 1** the twenty-third letter of the Greek alphabet (Ψ, ψ), transliterated as 'ps'. **2** supposed parapsychological or psychic faculties or phenomena.
– ORIGIN from Gk.

**p.s.i.** ● **abbrev.** pounds per square inch.

**psilocybin** /ˌsʌɪlə(ʊ)'sʌɪbɪn/ ● **n.** Chemistry a hallucinogenic compound of the alkaloid class, found in the liberty cap and related toadstools.
– ORIGIN 1950s: from mod. L. *Psilocybe* (genus name), from Gk *psilos* 'bald' + *kubē* 'head'.

**psionic** /sʌɪ'ɒnɪk/ ● **adj.** relating to or denoting the practical use of psychic powers or paranormal phenomena.
– DERIVATIVES **psionically** adv.
– ORIGIN 1950s: from **PSI**, on the pattern of *electronic*.

**psittacine** /'sɪtəkʌɪn, -sʌɪn/ Ornithology ● **adj.** of, relating to, or denoting birds of the parrot family. ● **n.** a bird of the parrot family.
– ORIGIN C19: from L. *psittacinus* 'of a parrot', from *psittacus*, from Gk *psittakos* 'parrot'.

**psittacosis** /ˌsɪtə'kəʊsɪs/ ● **n.** a contagious disease of birds, caused by chlamydiae and transmissible (especially from parrots) to human beings as a form of pneumonia.
– ORIGIN C19: from L. *psittacus* 'parrot' + **-OSIS**.

**psoas** /'səʊas/ ● **n.** Anatomy each of a pair of large muscles used in flexing the hip.
– ORIGIN C17: from Gk, accusative pl. of *psoa*, interpreted as sing.

**psoralen** /'sɔːrəlɛn/ ● **n.** Chemistry any of a group of cyclic compounds present in certain plants, used to treat psoriasis and other skin disorders.
– ORIGIN 1930s: from mod. L. *Psoralea* (former plant genus name), from Gk *psōraleos* 'itchy' (from *psōra* 'itch') + the suffix *-en* (cf. **-ENE**).

**psoriasis** /sɒ'rʌɪəsɪs/ ● **n.** Medicine a skin disease marked by red, itchy, scaly patches.
– DERIVATIVES **psoriatic** /ˌsɔːrɪ'atɪk/ adj.
– ORIGIN C17: mod. L., from Gk *psōriasis*, from *psōrian* 'to itch'.

**psst** ● **exclam.** used to attract someone's attention surreptitiously.

**PST** ● **abbrev.** Pacific Standard Time.

**PSV** ● **abbrev.** Brit. public service vehicle.

**psych** /sʌɪk/ (also **psyche**) ● **v. 1** (often **psych someone up**) informal mentally prepare (someone) for a testing task or occasion. ➤(**psych someone out**) intimidate an opponent or rival by appearing very confident or aggressive. **2** informal subject (someone) to psychological investigation or psychotherapy. **3** (usu. **psyche**) Bridge make a psychic bid. ● **n. 1** informal a psychiatrist or psychologist. ➤ psychiatry or psychology. **2** (usu. **psyche**) Bridge a psychic bid.

**psyche** /'sʌɪki/ ● **n.** the human soul, mind, or spirit.
– ORIGIN C17: via L. from Gk *psukhē* 'breath, life, soul'.

**psychedelia** /ˌsʌɪkə'diːlɪə/ ● **n.** music, culture, or art based on the experiences produced by psychedelic drugs.

**psychedelic** /ˌsʌɪkəˈdɛlɪk, -ˈdiːlɪk/ ● **adj.** **1** relating to or denoting drugs (especially LSD) that produce hallucinations and apparent expansion of consciousness. **2** relating to or denoting a style of rock music characterized by musical experimentation and drug-related lyrics. **3** having an intense, vivid colour or a swirling abstract pattern. ● **n.** a psychedelic drug.
– DERIVATIVES **psychedelically** adv.
– ORIGIN 1950s: formed irregularly from PSYCHE + Gk *dēlos* 'clear, manifest' + -IC.

**psychiatrist** ● **n.** a medical practitioner specializing in the diagnosis and treatment of mental illness.

**psychiatry** /sʌɪˈkʌɪətri/ ● **n.** the branch of medicine concerned with the study and treatment of mental illness, emotional disturbance, and abnormal behaviour.
– DERIVATIVES **psychiatric** /ˌsʌɪkɪˈatrɪk/ adj. **psychiatrically** adv.
– ORIGIN C19: from Gk *psukhē* 'soul, mind' + *iatreia* 'healing' (from *iatros* 'healer').

**psychic** /ˈsʌɪkɪk/ ● **adj.** **1** relating to or denoting faculties or phenomena that are apparently inexplicable by natural laws, especially involving telepathy or clairvoyance. ➤(of a person) appearing or considered to be telepathic or clairvoyant. **2** of or relating to the soul or mind. **3** Bridge denoting a bid that deliberately misrepresents the bidder's hand, in order to mislead the opponents. ● **n.** **1** a person considered or claiming to have psychic powers; a medium. **2** (**psychics**) [treated as sing. or pl.] the study of psychic phenomena.
– DERIVATIVES **psychical** adj. **psychically** adv. **psychism** n.

**psycho** ● **n.** (pl. **-os**) informal a psychopath.

**psycho-** ● **comb. form** relating to the mind or psychology: *psychometrics*.
– ORIGIN from Gk *psukhē* 'breath, soul, mind'.

**psychoactive** ● **adj.** (chiefly of a drug) affecting the mind.

**psychoanalysis** ● **n.** a system of psychological theory and therapy which aims to treat mental disorders by investigating the interaction of conscious and unconscious elements in the mind and bringing repressed fears and conflicts into the conscious mind.
– DERIVATIVES **psychoanalyse** (US **psychoanalyze**) v. **psychoanalyst** n. **psychoanalytic** adj. **psychoanalytical** adj. **psychoanalytically** adv.

**psychobabble** ● **n.** informal, derogatory jargon used in popular psychology.

**psychobiology** ● **n.** the branch of science concerned with the biological basis of behaviour and mental phenomena.
– DERIVATIVES **psychobiological** adj. **psychobiologist** n.

**psychodrama** ● **n.** **1** a form of psychotherapy in which patients act out events from their past. **2** a play, film, or novel in which psychological elements are the main interest.

**psychodynamics** ● **pl. n.** [treated as sing.] the interrelation of the unconscious and conscious mental and emotional forces that determine personality and motivation. ➤the branch of psychology concerned with this.
– DERIVATIVES **psychodynamic** adj. **psychodynamically** adv.

**psychogenesis** /ˌsʌɪkə(ʊ)ˈdʒɛnɪsɪs/ ● **n.** the psychological cause to which a mental illness or behavioural disturbance may be attributed.

**psychogenic** /ˌsʌɪkə(ʊ)ˈdʒɛnɪk/ ● **adj.** having a psychological origin or cause rather than a physical one.

**psychographics** ● **pl. n.** [treated as sing.] the study and classification of people according to their attitudes, aspirations, etc., especially in market research.
– DERIVATIVES **psychographic** adj.

**psychokinesis** /ˌsʌɪkəʊkɪˈniːsɪs, -kʌɪ-/ ● **n.** the supposed ability to move objects by mental effort alone.
– DERIVATIVES **psychokinetic** adj.

**psycholinguistics** ● **pl. n.** [treated as sing.] the study of the relationships between linguistic behaviour and psychological processes, including the process of language acquisition.
– DERIVATIVES **psycholinguist** n. **psycholinguistic** adj.

**psychological** ● **adj.** **1** of, affecting, or arising in the mind; related to the mental and emotional state of a person. **2** of or relating to psychology.
– DERIVATIVES **psychologically** adv.

**psychological warfare** ● **n.** actions intended to reduce an opponent's morale.

**psychologism** ● **n.** Philosophy a tendency to interpret events or arguments in subjective terms, or to exaggerate the relevance of psychological factors.

**psychology** ● **n.** **1** the scientific study of the human mind and its functions, especially those affecting behaviour in a given context. **2** the mental characteristics or attitude of a person. ➤the mental factors governing a situation or activity.
– DERIVATIVES **psychologist** n. **psychologize** (also **-ise**) v.

**psychometrics** ● **pl. n.** [treated as sing.] the science of measuring mental capacities and processes.

**psychometry** /sʌɪˈkɒmɪtri/ ● **n.** **1** the supposed ability to discover facts about an event or person by touching inanimate objects associated with them. **2** another term for PSYCHOMETRICS.
– DERIVATIVES **psychometric** /ˌsʌɪkə(ʊ)ˈmɛtrɪk/ adj. **psychometrically** adv. **psychometrist** n.

**psychomotor** ● **adj.** of or relating to the origination of movement in conscious mental activity.

**psychoneurosis** ● **n.** another term for NEUROSIS.

**psychopath** ● **n.** a person suffering from chronic mental disorder with abnormal or violent social behaviour.
– DERIVATIVES **psychopathic** adj. **psychopathically** adv.

**psychopathology** ● **n.** the scientific study of mental disorders. ➤features of people's mental health considered collectively. ➤mental or behavioural disorder.
– DERIVATIVES **psychopathological** adj. **psychopathologist** n.

**psychopathy** /sʌɪˈkɒpəθi/ ● **n.** mental illness or disorder.

**psychopharmacology** ● **n.** the branch of psychiatry concerned with the effects of drugs on the mind and behaviour.
– DERIVATIVES **psychopharmacological** adj. **psychopharmacologist** n.

**psychophysics** ● **pl. n.** [treated as sing.] the branch of psychology concerned with the relations between physical stimuli and mental phenomena.
– DERIVATIVES **psychophysical** adj.

**psychophysiology** ● **n.** Psychology the study of the relationship between physiological and psychological phenomena.
– DERIVATIVES **psychophysiological** adj. **psychophysiologist** n.

**psychopomp** /ˈsʌɪkə(ʊ)pɒmp/ (also **psychopompos**) ● **n.** (in Greek mythology) a guide of souls to the place of the dead. ➤the spiritual guide of a living person's soul.
– ORIGIN from Gk *psukhopompos*, from *psukhē* 'soul' + *pompos* 'conductor'.

**psychosexual** ● **adj.** of or involving the psychological aspects of the sexual impulse.
– DERIVATIVES **psychosexually** adv.

**psychosis** /sʌɪˈkəʊsɪs/ ● **n.** (pl. **psychoses** /-siːz/) a severe mental disorder in which thought and emotions are so impaired that contact is lost with external reality.

**psychosocial** ● **adj.** of or relating to the interrelation of social factors and individual thought and behaviour.
– DERIVATIVES **psychosocially** adv.

**psychosomatic** /ˌsʌɪkə(ʊ)səˈmatɪk/ ● **adj.** **1** (of a physical illness) caused or aggravated by a mental factor such as internal conflict or stress. **2** of or relating to the interaction of mind and body.
– DERIVATIVES **psychosomatically** adv.

**psychosurgery** ● **n.** brain surgery, such as leucotomy, used to treat mental disorder.
– DERIVATIVES **psychosurgical** adj.

**psychosynthesis** ● **n.** Psychoanalysis the integration of separated elements of the psyche or personality.

**psychotherapy** ● **n.** the treatment of mental disorder by psychological rather than medical means.
– DERIVATIVES **psychotherapeutic** adj. **psychotherapist** n.

**psychotic** /sʌɪˈkɒtɪk/ ● **adj.** of, denoting, or suffering from a psychosis. ● **n.** a psychotic person.
– DERIVATIVES **psychotically** adv.

**psychotronic** /ˌsʌɪkə(ʊ)ˈtrɒnɪk/ ● **adj.** **1** referring to a genre of low-budget films with a science fiction, horror, or fantasy theme. **2** relating to psychotronics.

**psychotronics** ● **pl. n.** [treated as sing.] a particular branch of parapsychology which supposes an energy or force to emanate from living organisms and affect matter.
– ORIGIN 1970s: from **PSYCHO-**, on the pattern of *electronics*.

**psychotropic** /ˌsʌɪkə(ʊ)ˈtrəʊpɪk, ˌsʌɪkə(ʊ)ˈtrɒpɪk/ ● **adj.** referring to drugs that affect a person's mental state.

**psychrometer** /sʌɪˈkrɒmɪtə/ ● **n.** a hygrometer consisting of wet and dry-bulb thermometers, the difference in the two thermometer readings being used to determine atmospheric humidity.
– ORIGIN C18: from Gk *psukhros* 'cold' + **-METER**.

**psyllid** /ˈsɪlɪd/ ● **n.** Entomology a minute insect of a family (Psyllidae) that comprises the jumping plant lice.
– ORIGIN C19: from mod. L. *Psyllidae*, from Gk *psulla* 'flea'.

**psyllium** /ˈsɪlɪəm/ ● **n.** a leafy-stemmed plantain, the seeds of which are used as a laxative and as a bulking agent in the treatment of obesity. [*Plantago psafra.*]
– ORIGIN C16: via L. from Gk *psullion*, from *psulla* 'flea' (because the seeds resemble fleas).

**PT** ● **abbrev.** physical training.

**Pt** ● **abbrev.** **1** Part. **2** (**pt**) pint. **3** (in scoring) point. **4** Printing point (as a unit of measurement). **5** (**Pt.**) Point (on maps). **6** (**pt**) port (a side of a ship or aircraft). ● **symb.** the chemical element platinum.

**PTA** ● **abbrev.** **1** parent–teacher association. **2** (in the UK) Passenger Transport Authority.

**ptarmigan** /ˈtɑːmɪg(ə)n/ ● **n.** a grouse of northern mountains and the Arctic, whose plumage is white in winter. [*Lagopus mutus.*]
– ORIGIN C16: from Sc. Gaelic *tàrmachan*; spelling influenced by Gk words starting with *pt-*.

**PTE** ● **abbrev.** (in the UK) Passenger Transport Executive.

**Pte** ● **abbrev.** Private (in the army).

**pteranodon** /tɛˈranədɒn/ ● **n.** a large tailless pterosaur of the Cretaceous period, with a long toothless beak and a long bony crest.
– ORIGIN mod. L., from Gk *pteron* 'wing' + *an-* 'without' + *odous, odont-* 'tooth'.

**pteridology** /ˌtɛrɪˈdɒlədʒi/ ● **n.** the study of ferns and related plants.
– DERIVATIVES **pteridological** adj. **pteridologist** n.
– ORIGIN C19: from Gk *pteris, pterid-* 'fern' + **-LOGY**.

**Pteridophyta** /ˌtɛrɪdə(ʊ)ˈfʌɪtə/ ● **pl. n.** Botany a division of flowerless plants which comprises the ferns, horsetails, and clubmosses.
– DERIVATIVES **pteridophyte** /ˈtɛrɪdə(ʊ)fʌɪt/ n.
– ORIGIN mod. L., from Gk *pteris, pterid-* 'fern' + *phuton* 'plant'.

**pteridosperm** /ˈtɛrɪdəʊspəːm/ ● **n.** a fossil plant intermediate between the ferns and seed-bearing plants, dying out in the Triassic period.
– ORIGIN C20: from mod. L. *pteridospermeae*, from Gk *pteris, pterid-* 'fern'.

**ptero-** /ˈtɛrəʊ/ ● **comb. form** relating to wings; having wings: *pterosaur.* See word-formation panel.
– ORIGIN from Gk *pteron* 'feather, wing'.

**pterobranch** /ˈtɛrə(ʊ)braŋk/ ● **n.** Zoology a minute tube-dwelling colonial acorn worm of a class (Pterobranchia) found chiefly in deep water.

**pterodactyl** /ˌtɛrəˈdaktɪl/ ● **n.** a pterosaur of the late Jurassic period, with a long slender head and neck and a very short tail. ➤(in general use) any pterosaur.
– ORIGIN C19: from mod. L. *Pterodactylus* (genus name), from Gk *pteron* 'wing' + *daktulos* 'finger'.

**pteropod** /ˈtɛrəpɒd/ ● **n.** Zoology a sea butterfly.
– ORIGIN C19: from mod. L. *Pteropoda*, from Gk *pteron* 'wing' + Gk *pous, pod-* 'foot'.

**pterosaur** /ˈtɛrəsɔː/ ● **n.** a fossil warm-blooded flying reptile of the Jurassic and Cretaceous periods, with membranous wings supported by a greatly lengthened fourth finger.
– ORIGIN C19: from mod. L. *Pterosauria*, from Gk *pteron* 'wing' + *sauros* 'lizard'.

**pterygoid process** /ˈtɛrɪgɔɪd/ ● **n.** Anatomy each of a pair of projections from the sphenoid bone in the skull.
– ORIGIN C18: from mod. L. *pterygoides*, from Gk *pterux, pterug-* 'wing'.

**Pterygota** /ˈtɛrɪgəʊtə/ ● **pl. n.** Entomology a large group of insects that comprises those that have wings or winged ancestors, including the majority of modern species.
– DERIVATIVES **pterygote** n.
– ORIGIN mod. L., from Gk *pterugōtos* 'winged', from *pteron, pterug-* 'wing'.

**PTFE** ● **abbrev.** polytetrafluoroethylene.

**PTO** ● **abbrev.** **1** please turn over. **2** (also **pto**) power take-off.

**Ptolemaic** /ˌtɒləˈmeɪɪk/ ● **adj.** **1** of or relating to the 2nd-century Greek astronomer Ptolemy. **2** of or relating to the Ptolemies, rulers of Egypt 304–30 BC.

**Ptolemaic system** (also **Ptolemaic theory**) ● **n.** Astronomy, historical the theory that the earth is the stationary centre of the universe, with the planets moving in epicyclic orbits within surrounding concentric spheres. Compare with **COPERNICAN SYSTEM**.

**ptomaine** /ˈtəʊmeɪn/ ● **n.** Chemistry, dated any of a group of amine compounds of unpleasant taste and odour formed in putrefying animal and vegetable matter and formerly thought to cause food poisoning.
– ORIGIN C19: from Fr. *ptomaïne*, from Ital. *ptomaina*, formed irregularly from Gk *ptōma* 'corpse'.

**P2P** ● **abbrev.** Computing peer-to-peer, an Internet network that enables a group of users to access and copy files from each other's hard drives.

**ptosis** /ˈtəʊsɪs/ ● **n.** Medicine drooping of the upper eyelid due to paralysis or disease, or as a congenital condition.
– DERIVATIVES **ptotic** /ˈtəʊtɪk/ adj.
– ORIGIN C18: from Gk *ptōsis*, from *piptein* 'to fall'.

**PTSD** ● **abbrev.** post-traumatic stress disorder.

**Pty** ● **abbrev.** Austral./NZ & S. African proprietary.

**ptyalin** /ˈtʌɪəlɪn/ ● **n.** Biochemistry a form of amylase found in the saliva of humans and some other animals.
– ORIGIN C19: from Gk *ptualon* 'spittle' + **-IN**[1].

**p-type** ● **adj.** Electronics denoting a region in a semiconductor in which electrical conduction is due chiefly to the movement of positive holes. Compare with **N-TYPE**.

**Pu** ● **symb.** the chemical element plutonium.

**pub** Brit. ● **n.** **1** an establishment for the sale and consumption of beer and other drinks, often also serving food. **2** Austral. a hotel. ● **v.** [usu. as noun **pubbing**] informal frequent pubs.
– ORIGIN C19: abbrev. of **PUBLIC HOUSE**.

**pub.** ● **abbrev.** **1** publication(s). **2** published. **3** publisher.

**pub crawl** informal, chiefly Brit. ● **n.** a tour taking in several pubs, with one or more drinks at each. ● **v.** (**pub-crawl**) go on a pub crawl.

**pube** /pjuːb/ ● **n.** informal a pubic hair.

**puberty** ● **n.** the period during which adolescents reach sexual maturity and become capable of reproduction.
– DERIVATIVES **pubertal** adj.
– ORIGIN ME: from L. *pubertas*, from *puber* 'adult', rel. to *pubes* (see **PUBES**).

**pubes** ● **n.** **1** /ˈpjuːbiːz/ (pl. same) the lower part of the abdomen at the front of the pelvis, covered with hair from puberty. **2** /ˈpjuːbiːz/ plural form of **PUBIS**. **3** /pjuːbz/ informal plural form of **PUBE**.
– ORIGIN C16: from L., 'pubic hair, groin, genitals'.

**pubescence** /pjʊˈbɛs(ə)ns/ ● **n.** **1** the time when puberty begins. **2** Botany & Zoology soft down on the leaves and stems of plants or on animals, especially insects.
– DERIVATIVES **pubescent** adj. & n.
– ORIGIN ME: from Fr., or from med. L. *pubescentia*, from L.

## Word *Formation*

**ptero-** from Greek *pteron* 'feather, wing'

➤ **1.** Used as the suffix **-ptera** in orders and groups of biological taxonomy, particularly of insects:

| | | |
|---|---|---|
| Anisoptera | a suborder of insects comprising the dragonflies | Gk *anisos* 'unequal' |
| Chiroptera | an order of mammals comprising the bats | Gk *kheir* 'hand' |
| Coleoptera | an order of insects comprising the beetles | Gk *koleos* 'sheath' |
| Diptera | an order of insects comprising the two-winged or true flies | Gk *dipteros* 'two-winged' |
| Hymenoptera | an order of insects including bees, wasps, and ants, having four transparent wings | Gk *humenopteros* 'membrane-winged' (from *humēn* 'membrane') |
| Lepidoptera | an order of insects comprising butterflies and moths | Gk *lepis, lepid-,* 'scale' |
| Orthoptera | an order of insects including grasshoppers and crickets | Gk *orthos* 'straight, right' |
| Siphonaptera | an order of insects comprising the fleas | Gk *siphōn* 'tube' + *apteros* 'wingless' |
| Trichoptera | an order of insects comprising the caddis flies | Gk *thrix, trikhos* 'hair' |
| Zygoptera | a suborder of insects comprising the damselflies | Gk *zugon* 'yoke' |

➤ Related words:

| | |
|---|---|
| -pterous | forming adjectives, e.g. ***coleopterous*** 'of or relating to the order Coleoptera' |
| -pteran | forming nouns, e.g. ***lepidopteran*** 'an insect belonging to the order Lepidoptera' |

Also in more generalized applications:

| | | |
|---|---|---|
| apterous | having no wings | Gk *an* 'without' |
| micropterous | having small or reduced wings | Gk *mikros* 'small' |
| tetrapterous | having two pairs of wings | Gk *tetra-* 'four' |

➤ **2. -pter** words in non-zoological contexts:

| | | |
|---|---|---|
| gyrocopter | a small single-seater autogiro | based on GYRO- + (HELI)COPTER |
| helicopter | a type of aircraft with horizontally revolving rotors | Gk *helix* 'spiral' |
| ornithopter | a machine designed to achieve flight by means of flapping wings | Gk *ornis, ornith-* 'bird' |

*pubescent-, pubescere* 'reach puberty'.

**pubic** ● adj. of or relating to the pubes or pubis.

**pubis** /ˈpjuːbɪs/ ● n. (pl. **pubes** /-biːz/) either of a pair of bones forming the two sides of the pelvis.
– ORIGIN C16: from L. *os pubis* 'bone of the pubes'.

**public** ● adj. **1** of, concerning, or open to the people as a whole. ➤involved in the affairs of the community, especially in government or entertainment: *a public figure.* **2** done, perceived, or existing in open view. **3** of or provided by the state rather than an independent, commercial company. ● n. (**the public**) [treated as sing. or pl.] ordinary people in general; the community.
– PHRASES **go public 1** become a public company. **2** reveal details about a previously private concern. **in public** in view of other people; when others are present.
– DERIVATIVES **publicly** adv.
– ORIGIN ME: from OFr., from L. *publicus*, blend of *poplicus* 'of the people' and *pubes* 'adult'.

**public act** ● n. an act of legislation affecting the public as a whole.

**public address system** ● n. a system of microphones, amplifiers, and loudspeakers used to amplify speech or music.

**publican** ● n. **1** Brit. a person who owns or manages a pub. ➤Austral. a person who owns or manages a hotel. **2** (in ancient Roman and biblical times) a collector or farmer of taxes.
– ORIGIN ME: from OFr. *publicain*, from L. *publicanus*, from *publicum* 'public revenue'.

**public analyst** ● n. Brit. a health official who analyses food.

**publication** ● n. **1** the action or process of publishing something. **2** a book or journal that is published.

**public bar** ● n. Brit. the more plainly furnished bar in a pub.

**public bill** ● n. a bill of legislation affecting the public as a whole.

**public company** ● n. a company whose shares are traded freely on a stock exchange.

**public defender** ● n. US Law a lawyer employed by the state in a criminal trial to represent a defendant who is unable to afford legal assistance.

**public enemy** ● n. a notorious wanted criminal.

**public house** ● n. formal term for PUB.

**publicist** ● n. **1** a person responsible for publicizing a product, person, or company. **2** dated a journalist, especially one concerned with current affairs. **3** archaic a writer or other person skilled in international law.
– DERIVATIVES **publicistic** adj.

**publicity** ● n. notice or attention given to someone or something by the media. ➤the giving out of information for advertising or promotional purposes. ➤material or information used for such a purpose.

**publicize** (also **-ise**) ● v. **1** make widely known. **2** give out publicity about; advertise or promote.

**public law** ● n. the law of relations between individuals and the state.

**public lending right** ● n. (in the UK) the right of authors to receive payment when their books are lent out by public libraries.

**public limited company** ● n. (in the UK) a company with statutory minimum capital requirements and shares offered to the public subject to conditions of limited liability.

**public nuisance** ● n. Brit. **1** an act that is illegal because it interferes with the rights of the public generally. **2** informal an obnoxious or dangerous person or group.

**public prosecutor** ● n. a law officer who conducts criminal proceedings on behalf of the state or in the public interest.

**public purse** ● n. the funds raised by a government by taxation or other means.

**Public Record Office** ● n. (in the UK) an institution where official archives are kept for public inspection.

**public relations** ● pl. n. the professional maintenance of a favourable public image by an organization or famous person. ➤ the relationship between an organization or famous person and the public.

**public school** ● n. 1 (in the UK) a private fee-paying secondary school. 2 (chiefly in North America) a school supported by public funds.

**public sector** ● n. the part of an economy that is controlled by the state.

**public servant** ● n. a person who works for the state or for local government.

**public spirit** ● n. willingness to do things that help the public.
– DERIVATIVES **public-spirited** adj. **public-spiritedly** adv. **public-spiritedness** n.

**public transport** (N. Amer. **public transportation**) ● n. buses, trains, and other forms of transport that are available to the public, charge set fares, and run on fixed routes.

**public utility** ● n. an organization supplying the community with electricity, gas, water, or sewerage.

**public works** ● pl. n. the work of building roads, schools, hospitals, etc., carried out by the state for the community.

**publish** ● v. 1 prepare and issue (a book, journal, or piece of music) for public sale. ➤ print in a book or journal so as to make generally known. 2 formally announce or read (an edict or marriage banns). 3 Law communicate (a libel) to a third party.
– DERIVATIVES **publishable** adj. **publishing** n.
– ORIGIN ME: from the stem of OFr. *puplier*, from L. *publicare* 'make public', from *publicus* (see PUBLIC).

**publisher** ● n. 1 a company or person that prepares and issues books, journals, or music for sale. 2 chiefly N. Amer. a newspaper proprietor.

**puccoon** /pʌˈkuːn/ ● n. a white or yellow-flowered North American plant yielding a dye. [Several species, mainly in the genus *Lithospermum*.]
– ORIGIN C17: from Algonquian *poughkone*.

**puce** /pjuːs/ ● n. a dark red or purple-brown colour.
– ORIGIN C18: from Fr., lit. 'flea(-colour)'.

**Puck** ● n. another name for ROBIN GOODFELLOW. ➤ (**puck**) a mischievous or evil sprite.

**puck** ● n. 1 a black disc made of hard rubber, used in ice hockey. 2 Computing an input device similar to a mouse.
– ORIGIN C19: of unknown origin.

**pucker** ● v. tightly gather or contract into wrinkles or small folds. ● n. a wrinkle or small fold.
– DERIVATIVES **puckery** adj.
– ORIGIN C16: prob. frequentative, from the base of POKE[2] and POCKET (suggesting the formation of small purse-like gatherings).

**puckish** ● adj. playful, especially in a mischievous way.
– DERIVATIVES **puckishly** adv. **puckishness** n.

**pud** ● n. Brit. informal short for PUDDING.

**pudding** ● n. 1 a cooked sweet dish served after the main course of a meal. ➤ chiefly Brit. the dessert course of a meal. ➤ N. Amer. a dessert with a soft or creamy consistency. 2 a sweet or savoury steamed dish made with suet and flour. 3 the intestines of a pig or sheep stuffed with oatmeal, spices, and meat and boiled. 4 informal a fat, dumpy, or stupid person.
– PHRASES **in the pudding club** Brit. informal pregnant.
– DERIVATIVES **puddingy** adj.
– ORIGIN ME: appar. from OFr. *boudin* 'black pudding', from L. *botellus* 'sausage, small intestine'.

**pudding basin** ● n. 1 a deep round bowl used for cooking steamed puddings. 2 [as modifier] denoting a hairstyle produced or seemingly produced by inverting a pudding basin on a person's head and cutting away all the hair that sticks out under it.

**pudding face** ● n. informal a large fat face.
– DERIVATIVES **pudding-faced** adj.

**pudding-head** ● n. informal a stupid person.

**puddingstone** ● n. a conglomerate rock in which dark-coloured round pebbles contrast with a paler fine-grained matrix.

**puddle** ● n. 1 a small pool of liquid, especially of rainwater on the ground. 2 clay and sand mixed with water and used as a watertight covering for embankments. 3 Rowing a circular patch of disturbed water made by the blade of an oar at each stroke. ● v. 1 cover with or form puddles. 2 (**puddle about/around**) dabble or wallow in mud or shallow water. ➤ informal occupy oneself in a disorganized or unproductive way. 3 line (a hole) with puddle. ➤ knead (clay and sand) into puddle. ➤ work (mixed water and clay) to separate gold or opal. 4 [usu. as noun **puddling**] chiefly historical stir (molten iron) with iron oxide in a furnace, to produce wrought iron by oxidizing carbon.
– DERIVATIVES **puddler** n. **puddly** adj.
– ORIGIN ME: dimin. of OE *pudd* 'ditch, furrow'; cf. Ger. dial. *Pfudel* 'pool'.

**puddle jumper** ● n. informal, chiefly N. Amer. a small light aircraft used for short trips.

**pudendum** /pjʊˈdɛndəm/ ● n. (pl. **pudenda** /-də/) a person's external genitals, especially a woman's.
– DERIVATIVES **pudendal** adj. **pudic** /ˈpjuːdɪk/ adj.
– ORIGIN C17: from L. *pudenda* (*membra*) '(parts) to be ashamed of', neut. pl. of the gerundive of *pudere* 'be ashamed'.

**pudeur** /pjuːˈdəː, French pydœʀ/ ● n. a sense of shame or embarrassment, especially with regard to matters of a sexual or personal nature.
– ORIGIN C20: Fr., lit. 'modesty'.

**pudge** ● n. N. Amer. informal fat on a person's body.
– ORIGIN C19 (denoting a fat person): of unknown origin.

**pudgy** ● adj. (**-ier**, **-iest**) informal rather fat.
– DERIVATIVES **pudgily** adv. **pudginess** n.

**pueblo** /ˈpwɛbləʊ/ ● n. (pl. **-os**) 1 a town or village in Spain, Latin America, or the south-western US, especially an American Indian settlement. 2 (**Pueblo**) (pl. same or **-os**) a member of any of various American Indian peoples, including the Hopi, occupying pueblo settlements chiefly in New Mexico and Arizona.
– ORIGIN Sp., lit. 'people'.

**puerile** /ˈpjʊərʌɪl/ ● adj. childishly silly and trivial.
– DERIVATIVES **puerilely** adv. **puerility** /pjʊəˈrɪlɪti/ n. (pl. **-ies**).
– ORIGIN C16 (in the sense 'like a boy'): from Fr. *puéril* or L. *puerilis*, from *puer* 'boy'.

**puerperal fever** ● n. fever caused by uterine infection following childbirth.

**puerperium** /ˌpjuːəˈpɛrɪəm, ˌpjuːəˈpɪːrɪəm/ ● n. Medicine the period of about six weeks after childbirth during which the mother's reproductive organs return to their original non-pregnant condition.
– DERIVATIVES **puerperal** adj.
– ORIGIN C17: from L., from *puerperus* 'parturient' (from *puer* 'child' + *-parus* 'bearing').

**Puerto Rican** /ˌpwɛːtəʊ ˈriːkən/ ● n. a native or inhabitant of Puerto Rico. ● adj. of or relating to Puerto Rico.

**puff** ● n. 1 a short burst of breath or wind. ➤ a small quantity of vapour or smoke emitted in one blast. ➤ an act of drawing quickly on a pipe, cigarette, or cigar. ➤ informal breath. 2 a light pastry case containing a sweet or savoury filling. 3 informal a complimentary review of a book, play, etc. ➤ Brit. an advertisement. 4 a gathered mass of material in a dress or other garment. 5 a rolled protuberant mass of hair. 6 N. Amer. an eiderdown. ● v. 1 breathe in repeated short gasps. ➤ move with short, noisy breaths or bursts of air or steam. ➤ blow (dust, smoke, etc.) with quick breaths or blasts. ➤ smoke a pipe, cigarette, or cigar. ➤ (**be puffed/puffed out**) be out of breath. 2 (**puff out/up** or **puff something out/up**) become swollen or cause something to swell. ➤ cause to become conceited. 3 informal advertise with exaggerated or false praise.

– PHRASES **in all one's puff** informal, chiefly Brit. in one's whole life. **puff and blow** breathe in gasps during or after exertion.
– DERIVATIVES **puffer** n.
– ORIGIN ME: imitative of the sound of a breath, perh. from OE *pyf* (n.), *pyffan* (v.).

**puff adder** • n. **1** a large, sluggish African viper which inflates the upper part of its body and hisses loudly when under threat. [*Bitis arietans.*] **2** North American term for **HOGNOSE SNAKE**.

**puffa jacket** • n. Brit. a type of thick padded jacket.

**puffball** • n. **1** a fungus that produces a large round fruiting body which ruptures when ripe to release a cloud of spores. [*Lycoperdon* and other genera.] **2** a short full skirt gathered around the hemline to produce a soft puffy shape.

**pufferfish** • n. (pl. same or **-fishes**) a stout-bodied fish which inflates itself like a balloon when threatened. [*Tetraodon cutcutia* and other species, family Tetraodontidae.]

**puffery** • n. chiefly N. Amer. exaggerated or false praise.

**puffin** • n. a hole-nesting northern auk with a large head and a massive brightly coloured triangular bill. [*Fratercula arctica* and other species.]
– ORIGIN ME (denoting the Manx shearwater): appar. from **PUFF** + **-ING**[3], with ref. to the Manx shearwater's fat nestlings.

**puffin crossing** • n. (in the UK) a pedestrian crossing with traffic lights which go green again only when no more pedestrians are detected on the crossing by infrared detectors and mats.
– ORIGIN 1990s: *puffin* from *p(edestrian) u(ser) f(riendly) in(telligent)*, respelled by analogy with *pelican crossing*.

**puff pastry** • n. light flaky pastry.

**puff sleeve** (also **puffed sleeve**) • n. a short sleeve gathered at the top and cuff and full in the middle.

**puffy** • adj. (**-ier**, **-iest**) **1** softly inflated. **2** (of a part of the body) swollen and soft.
– DERIVATIVES **puffily** adv. **puffiness** n.

**pug**[1] • n. **1** a dog of a dwarf breed like a bulldog with a broad flat nose and deeply wrinkled face. **2** a small slender moth which rests with its wings stretched out to the sides. [*Eupithecia* and other genera.]
– DERIVATIVES **puggish** adj. **puggy** adj.
– ORIGIN C18: perh. of Low Ger. origin.

**pug**[2] • n. loam or clay mixed and worked into a soft, plastic condition without air pockets for making bricks or pottery. • v. (**pugged**, **pugging**) **1** [usu. as adj. **pugged**] prepare (clay) in this way. **2** [usu. as noun **pugging**] pack (a space) with pug, sawdust, or other material in order to deaden sound.
– ORIGIN C19: of unknown origin.

**pug**[3] • n. the footprint of an animal. • v. (**pugged**, **pugging**) track (an animal) by its footprints.
– ORIGIN C19: from Hindi *pag* 'footprint'.

**pug**[4] • n. informal a boxer.
– ORIGIN C19: abbrev. of **PUGILIST**.

**puggaree** /'pʌg(ə)riː/ (also **pagri**) • n. **1** an Indian turban. **2** a thin muslin scarf tied round a sun helmet so as to hang down over the wearer's neck and shield it from the sun.
– ORIGIN from Hindi *pagṛī* 'turban'.

**pugilist** /'pjuːdʒɪlɪst/ • n. dated or humorous a boxer.
– DERIVATIVES **pugilism** n. **pugilistic** adj.
– ORIGIN C18: from L. *pugil* 'boxer' + **-IST**.

**pugnacious** /pʌg'neɪʃəs/ • adj. eager or quick to argue, quarrel, or fight.
– DERIVATIVES **pugnaciously** adv. **pugnacity** n.
– ORIGIN C17: from L. *pugnax*, *pugnac-* (from *pugnare* 'to fight') + **-IOUS**.

**pug nose** • n. a short nose with an upturned tip.
– DERIVATIVES **pug-nosed** adj.

**puisne** /'pjuːni/ • adj. Law (in the UK and some other countries) denoting a judge of a superior court inferior in rank to chief justices.
– ORIGIN C16 (as n., denoting a junior or inferior person): from OFr., from *puis* 'afterwards' + *ne* 'born'; cf. **PUNY**.

**puisne mortgage** • n. Law, chiefly Brit. a second or subsequent mortgage of unregistered land of which the title deeds are retained by a first mortgagee.

**puissance** /'pjuːɪs(ə)ns, 'pwiː-, 'pwɪ-/ • n. **1** /also 'pwiːsɒ̃s/ a competitive test of a horse's ability to jump large obstacles in showjumping. **2** archaic or poetic/literary great power, influence, or prowess.

**puissant** /'pjuːɪs(ə)nt, 'pwiː-, 'pwɪ-/ • adj. archaic or poetic/literary having great power or influence.
– DERIVATIVES **puissantly** adv.
– ORIGIN ME: via OFr. from L. *posse* 'be able'.

**puja** /'puːdʒɑː/ (also **pooja**) • n. a Hindu ceremonial offering.
– ORIGIN from Sanskrit *pūjā* 'worship'.

**pujari** /pʊ'dʒɑːri/ • n. (pl. **pujaris**) a Hindu priest.
– ORIGIN via Hindi from Sanskrit *pūjā* 'worship'.

**puke** • v. & n. informal vomit.
– DERIVATIVES **pukey** adj.
– ORIGIN C16: prob. imitative.

**pukka** /'pʌkə/ (also **pukkah**) • adj. informal **1** proper or genuine. ➤ of or appropriate to high or respectable society. **2** excellent.
– ORIGIN C17: from Hindi *pakkā* 'cooked, ripe, substantial'.

**puku** /'puːkuː/ • n. (pl. **pukus**) a southern African antelope with a shaggy golden-yellow coat and short thick horns. [*Kobus vardonii.*]
– ORIGIN C19: from Zulu *mpuku*.

**pul** /puːl/ • n. (pl. **puls** or **puli**) a monetary unit of Afghanistan, equal to one hundredth of an afghani.
– ORIGIN Pashto, from Pers. *pūl* 'copper coin'.

**pula** /'pʊlə/ • n. (pl. same) the basic monetary unit of Botswana, equal to 100 thebe.
– ORIGIN Setswana, lit. 'rain'.

**pulao** /pə'laʊ/ • n. variant spelling of **PILAF**.

**pulchritude** /'pʌlkrɪtjuːd/ • n. poetic/literary beauty.
– DERIVATIVES **pulchritudinous** adj.
– ORIGIN ME: from L. *pulchritudo*, from *pulcher*, *pulchr-* 'beautiful'.

**pule** /pjuːl/ • v. [often as adj. **puling**] poetic/literary cry querulously or weakly.
– ORIGIN ME: prob. imitative; cf. Fr. *piauler*, in the same sense.

**puli** /'puːli/ • n. (pl. **pulik** /'puːlɪk/) a sheepdog of a black, grey, or white breed with a long thick coat.
– ORIGIN C20: from Hungarian.

**Pulitzer Prize** • n. an award for an achievement in American journalism, literature, or music.
– ORIGIN named after the C19 Hungarian-born Amer. newspaper proprietor Joseph *Pulitzer*.

**pull** • v. **1** exert force on so as to cause movement towards oneself or the origin of the force. ➤ be attached to the front and be the source of forward movement of (a vehicle). ➤ remove by pulling. ➤ informal bring out (a weapon) for use. ➤ Brit. draw (beer) from a barrel to serve. ➤ (**pull at/on**) inhale deeply while drawing on (a cigarette). ➤ damage (a muscle, ligament, etc.) by abnormal strain. **2** move steadily: *the bus pulled away.* ➤ move one's body against resistance. **3** attract as a customer; cause to show interest. ➤ informal succeed in attracting sexually. **4** informal cancel or withdraw (an entertainment or advertisement). ➤ arrest. ➤ check the speed of (a horse), especially so as to make it lose a race. **5** Cricket play (the ball) round to the leg side from the off. ➤ Golf & Baseball strike (the ball) so that it travels to the left (or, with a left-handed player, the right). **6** print (a proof). **7** Computing retrieve (an item of data) from the top of a stack. • n. **1** an act of pulling something. ➤ a handle to hold while pulling. ➤ a deep draught of a drink. ➤ an injury to a muscle or ligament caused by abnormal strain. **2** a force, influence, or compulsion. **3** (usu. in phr. **on the pull**) informal an attempt to attract someone sexually. **4** (in cricket, golf, baseball, etc.) a pulling stroke. **5** a printer's proof.
– PHRASES **pull someone's leg** deceive someone playfully; tease someone. **pull the plug** informal prevent something from happening or continuing. **pull (one's) punches** [usu. with neg.] be less forceful, severe, or violent than one could be. **pull strings** (or chiefly US **pull wires**) make use

of one's influence and contacts to gain an advantage. **pull the strings** be in control of events or of other people's actions. **pull together** cooperate in a task or undertaking. **pull oneself together** recover control of one's emotions. **pull one's weight** do one's fair share of work.
– PHRASAL VERBS **pull back** (or **pull someone/thing back**) **1** withdraw from an undertaking. **2** improve or restore a team's position in a sporting contest. **pull something down 1** demolish a building. **2** informal earn a sum of money. **pull someone/thing in 1** succeed in securing or obtaining something. ➤informal earn a sum of money. **2** informal arrest someone. **3** use reins to check a horse. **pull something off** informal succeed in achieving or winning something difficult. **pull out** withdraw from an undertaking. ➤retreat from an area. **pull round** chiefly Brit. recover from an illness. **pull through** get through an illness or other dangerous or difficult situation. **pull up** (of a vehicle) come to a halt. **pull someone up** cause someone to stop or pause; check someone. ➤reprimand someone.
– DERIVATIVES **puller** n.
– ORIGIN OE *pullian* 'pluck, snatch'; origin uncertain.

**pullet** ● n. a young hen, especially one less than one year old.
– ORIGIN ME: from OFr. *poulet*, dimin. of *poule*, from the fem. of L. *pullus* 'chicken, young animal'.

**pulley** ● n. (pl. **-eys**) a wheel with a grooved rim around which a cord passes, used to raise heavy weights. ➤a wheel or drum fixed on a shaft and turned by a belt, used to increase speed or power. ● v. (**-eys**, **-eyed**) hoist with a pulley.
– ORIGIN ME: from OFr. *polie*, prob. from a med. Gk dimin. of *polos* 'pivot, axis'.

**Pullman** ● n. (pl. **Pullmans**) **1** a railway carriage or train affording special comfort. **2** (also **Pullman case**) N. Amer. a large suitcase designed to fit under the seat in a Pullman carriage.
– ORIGIN C19: named after its Amer. designer George M. *Pullman*.

**pull-out** ● n. a section of a magazine or newspaper that is designed to be detached and kept for rereading. ● adj. designed to be pulled out or detached.

**pullover** ● n. a knitted garment put on over the head and covering the top half of the body.

**pullulate** /ˈpʌljʊleɪt/ ● v. [often as adj. **pullulating**] breed or spread so as to become extremely common. ➤be very crowded; be full of life and activity.
– DERIVATIVES **pullulation** n.
– ORIGIN C17: from L. *pullulat-*, *pullulare* 'sprout', from *pullulus*, dimin. of *pullus* 'young animal'.

**pull-up** ● n. an exercise involving raising oneself with one's arms by pulling up against a horizontal bar fixed above one's head.

**pulmonaria** /ˌpʌlməˈnɛːrɪə/ ● n. a plant of a genus that includes lungwort. [Genus *Pulmonaria*.]
– ORIGIN mod. L., from med. L. *pulmonaria* (*herba*), fem. (used as n.) of L. *pulmonarius* 'relating to the lungs' (from the belief in its efficacy in curing lung diseases).

**pulmonary** /ˈpʌlmən(ə)ri/ ● adj. of or relating to the lungs.
– ORIGIN C17: from L. *pulmonarius*, from *pulmo*, *pulmon-* 'lung'.

**pulmonary artery** ● n. the artery carrying blood from the right ventricle of the heart to the lungs for oxygenation.

**pulmonary vein** ● n. a vein carrying oxygenated blood from the lungs to the left atrium of the heart.

**Pulmonata** /ˌpʌlməˈneɪtə/ ● pl. n. Zoology a group of molluscs which includes the land snails and slugs and many freshwater snails.
– DERIVATIVES **pulmonate** n. & adj.
– ORIGIN mod. L., from L. *pulmo*, *pulmon-* 'lung'.

**pulmonic** /pʌlˈmɒnɪk/ ● adj. another term for **PULMONARY**.

**pulp** ● n. **1** a soft, wet, shapeless mass of material. ➤the soft fleshy part of a fruit. ➤a soft wet mass of fibres derived from rags or wood, used in papermaking. **2** vascular tissue filling the interior cavity and root canals of a tooth. **3** Mining pulverized ore mixed with water. **4** [as modifier] denoting popular or sensational writing, generally regarded as being of poor quality. ● v. **1** crush into a pulp. **2** withdraw (a publication) from the market and recycle the paper.
– DERIVATIVES **pulper** n. **pulpiness** n. **pulpy** adj.
– ORIGIN ME: from L. *pulpa*; sense 4 is from the printing of such material on cheap paper.

**pulpit** ● n. **1** a raised enclosed platform in a church or chapel from which the preacher delivers a sermon. **2** a raised platform in the bows of a fishing boat or whaler. ➤a guard rail enclosing a small area at the bow of a yacht.
– ORIGIN ME: from L. *pulpitum* 'scaffold, platform'.

**pulque** /ˈpʊlkeɪ, ˈpʊlki/ ● n. a Mexican alcoholic drink made by fermenting sap from the maguey.
– ORIGIN via Amer. Sp. from Nahuatl *puliúhki* 'decomposed'.

**pulsar** /ˈpʌlsɑː/ ● n. Astronomy a celestial object, thought to be a rapidly rotating neutron star, that emits regular rapid pulses of radio waves.
– ORIGIN 1960s: from *puls(ating st)ar*, on the pattern of *quasar*.

**pulsate** /pʌlˈseɪt, ˈpʌlseɪt/ ● v. **1** expand and contract with strong regular movements. **2** [often as adj. **pulsating**] produce a regular throbbing sensation or sound.
– DERIVATIVES **pulsation** n. **pulsator** n. **pulsatory** /ˈpʌlsət(ə)ri/ adj.
– ORIGIN C18 (earlier (ME) as *pulsation*): from L. *pulsat-*, *pulsare* 'throb, pulse'.

**pulsatile** /ˈpʌlsətʌɪl/ ● adj. chiefly Physiology pulsating; relating to pulsation.
– ORIGIN ME: from med. L. *pulsatilis* (in *vena pulsatilis* 'artery'), from *pulsare* (see **PULSATE**).

**pulsatilla** /ˌpʌlsəˈtɪlə/ ● n. a plant of a genus that includes the pasque flower. [Genus *Pulsatilla*.]
– ORIGIN mod. L., dimin. of *pulsatus* 'beaten about', expressing the notion 'small flower beaten by the wind'.

**pulse**[1] ● n. **1** the rhythmical throbbing of the arteries as blood is propelled through them. ➤each successive throb of the arteries or heart. **2** a single vibration or short burst of sound, electric current, light, or other wave. **3** a musical beat or other regular rhythm. **4** the centre of activity in an area or field: *those close to the financial and economic pulse*. **5** Biochemistry a measured amount of an isotopic label given to a culture of cells. ● v. **1** pulsate. **2** modulate (a wave or beam) so that it becomes a series of pulses. **3** apply a pulsed signal to (a device).
– PHRASES **feel** (or **take**) **the pulse of** ascertain the mood or opinion of.
– DERIVATIVES **pulseless** adj.
– ORIGIN ME: from L. *pulsus* 'beating', from *pellere* 'to drive, beat'.

**pulse**[2] ● n. the edible seeds of various leguminous plants, e.g. lentils. ➤the plant or plants producing such seeds.
– ORIGIN ME: from OFr. *pols*, from L. *puls* 'porridge of meal or pulse'; rel. to **POLLEN**.

**pulse code modulation** ● n. Electronics a technique of modulating the amplitude of an analogue signal to represent digital information as a series of pulses.

**pultrude** /pʊlˈtruːd, pʌl-/ ● v. [usu. as adj. **pultruded**] make (a reinforced plastic article) by drawing resin-coated glass fibres through a heated die.
– DERIVATIVES **pultrusion** n.
– ORIGIN 1960s: from *pul(ling)* + **EXTRUDE**.

**pulverize** (also **-ise**) ● v. **1** reduce to fine particles. **2** informal defeat utterly.
– DERIVATIVES **pulverizable** adj. **pulverization** n. **pulverizer** n.
– ORIGIN ME: from late L. *pulverizare*, from *pulvis*, *pulver-* 'dust'.

**pulverulent** /pʌlˈvɛrʊl(ə)nt/ ● adj. archaic consisting of fine particles; powdery or crumbly.
– ORIGIN C17: from L. *pulverulentus*, from *pulvis*, *pulver-* 'dust'.

**puma** ● n. a large American wild cat with a plain tawny to greyish coat, found from Canada to Patagonia. [*Felis concolor*.]

– ORIGIN C18: via Sp. from Quechua.

**pumice** /ˈpʌmɪs/ ● **n.** a light and porous form of solidified lava, used as a skin abrasive. ● **v.** rub with pumice.
– DERIVATIVES **pumiceous** /pjuːˈmɪʃəs/ adj.
– ORIGIN ME: from OFr. *pomis*, from a L. dial. var. of *pumex*, *pumic-*; cf. **POUNCE**[2].

**pummel** ● **v.** (**pummelled**, **pummelling**; US **pummeled**, **pummeling**) strike repeatedly, especially with the fists.
– ORIGIN C16: var. of **POMMEL**.

**pummelo** ● **n.** variant spelling of **POMELO**.

**pump**[1] ● **n. 1** a mechanical device using suction or pressure to raise or move liquids, compress gases, or force air into inflatable objects. **2** Physiology a mechanism in living cells by which specific ions are moved through a cell membrane against a concentration gradient. ● **v. 1** force (liquid, gas, etc.) to move by or as if by means of a pump. ➤move in spurts as though driven by a pump. **2** (often **pump something up**) fill (something) with liquid, gas, etc. **3** move or cause to move vigorously up and down. **4** informal try to elicit information from (someone) by persistent questioning.
– PHRASES **pump iron** informal exercise with weights.
– ORIGIN ME: rel. to Du. *pomp* 'ship's pump', prob. partly of imitative origin.

**pump**[2] ● **n. 1** chiefly N. English a plimsoll. **2** a light shoe for dancing. **3** N. Amer. a court shoe.
– ORIGIN C16: of unknown origin.

**pump-action** ● **adj. 1** denoting a repeating firearm in which a new round is brought into the breech by a slide action in line with the barrel. **2** denoting an unpressurized spray dispenser for a liquid that is worked by finger action.

**pumped** (also **pumped up**) ● **adj.** informal, chiefly N. Amer. filled with enthusiasm or excitement.

**pumpernickel** /ˈpʊmpəˌnɪk(ə)l, ˈpʌm-/ ● **n.** dark, dense German bread made from coarsely ground wholemeal rye.
– ORIGIN C18: transferred use of Ger. *Pumpernickel* 'lout, bumpkin'.

**pumpkin** ● **n. 1** a large rounded orange-yellow fruit with a thick rind and edible flesh. **2** a plant of the gourd family bearing this fruit, native to warm regions of America. [*Cucurbita pepo* and related species.] **3** Brit. another term for **SQUASH**[2].
– ORIGIN C17: alt. of earlier *pumpion*, from obs. Fr. *pompon*, via L. from Gk *pepōn* (see **PEPO**).

**pumpkinseed** ● **n.** (pl. same or **pumpkinseeds**) a small brightly coloured freshwater fish native to North America, popular in aquaria. [*Lepomis gibbosus*.]

**pump-priming** ● **n. 1** the introduction of fluid into a pump to prepare it for working. **2** the stimulation of economic activity by investment.
– DERIVATIVES **pump-prime** v. **pump-primer** n.

**pun**[1] ● **n.** a joke exploiting the different meanings of a word or the fact that there are words of the same sound and different meanings. ● **v.** (**punned**, **punning**) [often as adj. **punning**] make a pun.
– DERIVATIVES **punningly** adv. **punster** n.
– ORIGIN C17: perh. an abbrev. of obs. *pundigrion*, as a fanciful alt. of **PUNCTILIO**.

**pun**[2] ● **v.** (**punned**, **punning**) Brit. consolidate (earth or rubble) by pounding it.
– DERIVATIVES **punner** n.
– ORIGIN C16: dial. var. of **POUND**[2].

**puna** /ˈpuːnə/ ● **n. 1** a high treeless plateau in the Peruvian Andes. **2** another term for **ALTITUDE SICKNESS**.
– ORIGIN via Amer. Sp. from Quechua.

**punch**[1] ● **v. 1** strike with the fist. **2** press (a button or key on a machine). ➤(**punch in** or **out**) N. Amer. (of an employee) clock in (or out). **3** N. Amer. drive (cattle) by prodding them with a stick. ● **n. 1** a blow with the fist. **2** informal effectiveness; impact.
– PHRASES **punch above one's weight** informal engage in an activity perceived as beyond one's abilities. **punch the clock** N. Amer. (of an employee) clock in or out.
– DERIVATIVES **puncher** n.
– ORIGIN ME (in the sense 'puncture, prod'): var. of **POUNCE**[1].

**punch**[2] ● **n. 1** a device or machine for making holes in materials such as paper and metal. **2** a tool or machine for impressing a design or stamping a die on a material. ● **v.** pierce a hole in (a material) with or as if with a punch. ➤pierce (a hole) with or as if with a punch.
– ORIGIN C16: perh. an abbrev. of **PUNCHEON**[1], or from **PUNCH**[1].

**punch**[3] ● **n.** a drink made from wine or spirits mixed with water, fruit juices, spices, etc.
– ORIGIN C17: appar. from Sanskrit *pañca* 'five, five kinds of' (because the drink had five ingredients).

**punch**[4] ● **n. 1** (**Punch**) a grotesque, hook-nosed humpbacked buffoon, the chief male character of the Punch and Judy puppet show. **2** (also **Suffolk punch**) a draught horse of a short-legged thickset breed.
– PHRASES **as pleased** (or **proud**) **as Punch** feeling great delight or pride.
– ORIGIN C17: abbrev. of **PUNCHINELLO**; sense 2 derives from a dial. term denoting a short, fat person.

**punchbag** ● **n.** Brit. a suspended stuffed cylindrical bag, used for punching as exercise or training, especially by boxers.

**punchball** ● **n. 1** Brit. a suspended or mounted stuffed or inflated ball, used for punching as exercise or training, especially by boxers. **2** US a team ball game in which a rubber ball is punched or headed.

**punchboard** ● **n.** N. Amer. a board with holes containing slips of paper which are punched out as a form of gambling, with the object of locating a winning slip.

**punchbowl** ● **n. 1** a deep bowl for mixing and serving punch. **2** chiefly Brit. a deep round hollow in a hilly area.

**punch-drunk** ● **adj.** stupefied by or as if by a series of heavy blows.

**punched card** (also **punchcard**) ● **n.** a card perforated according to a code, for controlling the operation of a machine, formerly used to program computers.

**punched tape** ● **n.** a paper tape perforated according to a code, formerly used for conveying instructions or data to a data processor.

**puncheon**[1] /ˈpʌn(t)ʃ(ə)n/ ● **n. 1** a short post, especially one used for supporting the roof in a coal mine. **2** another term for **PUNCH**[2].
– ORIGIN ME: from OFr. *poinchon*, prob. based on L. *punct-*, *pungere* 'puncture'; cf. **POUNCE**[1].

**puncheon**[2] /ˈpʌn(t)ʃ(ə)n/ ● **n.** historical a large cask for liquids or other commodities, holding from 72 to 120 gallons.
– ORIGIN ME: from OFr. *poinchon*, of uncertain origin.

**Punchinello** /ˌpʌn(t)ʃɪˈnɛləʊ/ ● **n.** (pl. **-os**) **1** another name for **PUNCH**[4] (in sense 1). **2** archaic a short, stout, comical-looking person.
– ORIGIN C17: alt. of Neapolitan dial. *Polecenella*, perh. a dimin. of *pollecena* 'young turkey cock with a hooked beak'.

**punchline** ● **n.** the culmination of a joke or story, providing the humour or climax.

**punch-up** ● **n.** informal, chiefly Brit. a brawl.

**punchy** ● **adj.** (**-ier**, **-iest**) effective; forceful.
– DERIVATIVES **punchily** adv. **punchiness** n.

**puncta** plural form of **PUNCTUM**.

**punctate** /ˈpʌŋ(k)teɪt/ ● **adj.** Biology studded with or denoting dots or tiny holes.
– DERIVATIVES **punctation** n.
– ORIGIN C18: from L. *punctum* 'point' + **-ATE**[2].

**punctilio** /pʌŋ(k)ˈtɪlɪəʊ/ ● **n.** (pl. **-os**) a fine or petty point of conduct or procedure.
– ORIGIN C16: from Ital. *puntiglio(n-)* and Sp. *puntillo*, dimin. of *punto* 'a point'.

**punctilious** /pʌŋ(k)ˈtɪlɪəs/ ● **adj.** showing great attention to detail or correct behaviour.
– DERIVATIVES **punctiliously** adv. **punctiliousness** n.
– ORIGIN C17: from Fr. *pointilleux*, from *pointille*, from Ital. *puntiglio* (see **PUNCTILIO**).

**punctual** /ˈpʌŋ(k)tʃʊəl, -tjʊəl/ ● **adj. 1** happening or doing something at the appointed time. **2** Grammar of or denoting action that takes place at a particular point in time. Contrasted with **DURATIVE**.

– DERIVATIVES **punctuality** n. **punctually** adv.
– ORIGIN C17: from med. L. *punctualis*, from L. *punctum* 'a point'.

**punctuate** /ˈpʌŋ(k)tʃʊeɪt, -tjʊ-/ ● v. **1** occur at intervals throughout. ➤ (**punctuate something with**) interrupt an activity with. **2** insert punctuation marks in.
– ORIGIN C17 (in the sense 'point out'): from med. L. *punctuat-*, *punctuare* 'bring to a point'.

**punctuated equilibrium** ● n. Biology the hypothesis that evolutionary development is marked by isolated episodes of rapid speciation between long periods of little or no change.

**punctuation** ● n. the marks, such as full stop, comma, and brackets, used in writing to separate sentences and their elements and to clarify meaning. ➤ the use of such marks.
– DERIVATIVES **punctuational** adj.

**punctum** /ˈpʌŋ(k)təm/ ● n. (pl. **puncta** /-tə/) technical a small, distinct point.
– ORIGIN C16: from L., lit. 'a point'.

**puncture** ● n. a small hole caused by a sharp object, especially one in a tyre. ● v. **1** make a puncture in. **2** cause a sudden collapse of (a mood, feeling, etc.).
– ORIGIN ME: from L. *punctura*, from *punct-*, *pungere* 'prick'.

**pundit** /ˈpʌndɪt/ ● n. **1** an expert who frequently expresses opinion in public. **2** variant spelling of **PANDIT**.
– DERIVATIVES **punditry** n.
– ORIGIN from Sanskrit *paṇḍita* 'learned'.

**punga** /ˈpʌŋə/ ● n. variant spelling of **PONGA**.

**pungent** ● adj. **1** having a sharply strong taste or smell. **2** (of remarks or humour) sharp and caustic.
– DERIVATIVES **pungency** n. **pungently** adv.
– ORIGIN C16 (in the sense 'very painful'): from L. *pungent-*, *pungere* 'prick'.

**Punic** /ˈpjuːnɪk/ ● adj. Carthaginian. ● n. the language of ancient Carthage, related to Phoenician.
– ORIGIN from L. *Punicus* (earlier *Poenicus*), from *Poenus*, from Gk *Phoinix* 'Phoenician'.

**punish** ● v. **1** inflict a penalty on as retribution for an offence. ➤ inflict a penalty on someone for (an offence). **2** treat harshly.
– DERIVATIVES **punishable** adj. **punisher** n. **punishing** adj. **punishingly** adv.
– ORIGIN ME: from OFr. *puniss-*, lengthened stem of *punir* 'punish', from L. *punire*, from *poena* 'penalty'.

**punishment** ● n. **1** the action of punishing or the state of being punished. ➤ the penalty inflicted. **2** informal rough treatment.

**punitive** /ˈpjuːnɪtɪv/ ● adj. inflicting or intended as punishment.
– DERIVATIVES **punitively** adv. **punitiveness** n.
– ORIGIN C17: from Fr. *punitif*, *-ive* or med. L. *punitivus*, from L. *punit-*, *punire* (see **PUNISH**).

**punitive damages** ● pl. n. Law damages exceeding simple compensation and awarded to punish the defendant.

**Punjabi** /pʌnˈdʒɑːbi, pʊn-/ (also **Panjabi**) ● n. (pl. **Punjabis**) **1** a native or inhabitant of Punjab. **2** the Indic language of Punjab. ● adj. of or relating to Punjab or its people or language.

**punji stick** /ˈpʌndʒi/ ● n. (especially in SE Asia) a sharpened bamboo stake, typically one tipped with poison, set in a camouflaged hole in the ground as a means of defence.
– ORIGIN C19: *punji* prob. of Tibeto-Burman origin.

**punk** ● n. **1** (also **punk rock**) a loud, fast-moving, and aggressive form of rock music, popular in the late 1970s. ➤ (also **punk rocker**) an admirer or player of such music. **2** informal, chiefly N. Amer. a worthless person; a thug or criminal. **3** US informal (in prison slang) a passive male homosexual. **4** chiefly N. Amer. soft, crumbly wood that has been attacked by fungus, used as tinder. ● adj. **1** N. Amer. informal bad; worthless. **2** of or relating to punk rock and its associated subculture.
– DERIVATIVES **punkish** adj. **punky** adj.
– ORIGIN C17: perh., in some senses, rel. to archaic *punk* 'prostitute', also to **SPUNK**.

**punkah** /ˈpʌŋkə, -kɑː/ ● n. chiefly historical (in India) a large cloth fan on a frame suspended from the ceiling, worked by a cord.
– ORIGIN via Hindi from Sanskrit *pakṣaka*, from *pakṣa* 'wing'.

**punker** ● n. chiefly N. Amer. a punk rocker.

**punnet** ● n. Brit. a small light basket or other container for fruit or vegetables.
– ORIGIN C19: perh. a dimin. of dial. *pun* 'a pound'.

**punt**[1] /pʌnt/ ● n. a long, narrow, flat-bottomed boat, square at both ends and propelled with a long pole. ● v. travel or convey in a punt.
– ORIGIN OE, from L. *ponto*, denoting a flat-bottomed ferry boat.

**punt**[2] /pʌnt/ ● v. **1** American Football & Rugby kick the ball after it has dropped from the hands and before it reaches the ground. **2** Soccer kick (the ball) a long distance upfield. ● n. a kick of this kind.
– ORIGIN C19: prob. from dial. *punt* 'push forcibly'; cf. **BUNT**[3].

**punt**[3] /pʌnt/ ● v. (in some gambling card games) lay a stake against the bank. ➤ Brit. informal bet or speculate. ● n. informal, chiefly Brit. a bet.
– ORIGIN C18: from Fr. *ponte* 'player against the bank'.

**punt**[4] /pʊnt/ ● n. the basic monetary unit of the Republic of Ireland, equal to 100 pence.
– ORIGIN Ir., lit. 'pound'.

**punter** ● n. **1** informal a person who gambles, places a bet, or makes a risky investment. **2** Brit. informal a customer or client. ➤ a prostitute's client. **3** American Football & Rugby a player who punts.

**punty** /ˈpʌnti/ ● n. (pl. **-ies**) another term for **PONTIL**.

**puny** /ˈpjuːni/ ● adj. (**-ier**, **-iest**) **1** small and weak. **2** meagre.
– DERIVATIVES **punily** adv. **puniness** n.
– ORIGIN C16 (as n. denoting a younger or more junior person): phonetic spelling of **PUISNE**.

**pup** ● n. **1** a young dog. **2** a young wolf, seal, rat, or other mammal. **3** dated, chiefly Brit. a cheeky or arrogant boy or young man. ● v. (**pupped**, **pupping**) give birth to a pup or pups.
– PHRASES **sell someone** (or **buy**) **a pup** Brit. informal swindle someone (or be swindled), especially by selling (or buying) something worthless.
– ORIGIN C16: back-form. from **PUPPY**, interpreted as a dimin.

**pupa** /ˈpjuːpə/ ● n. (pl. **pupae** /-piː/) an insect in its inactive immature form between larva and adult, e.g. a chrysalis.
– DERIVATIVES **pupal** adj.
– ORIGIN C18: mod. L., from L. *pupa* 'girl, doll'.

**pupate** ● v. become a pupa.
– DERIVATIVES **pupation** n.

**pupil**[1] ● n. **1** a person who is taught by another, especially a schoolchild. **2** Brit. a trainee barrister.
– ORIGIN ME (in the sense 'orphan, ward'): from OFr. *pupille*, from L. *pupillus* (dimin. of *pupus* 'boy') and *pupilla* (dimin. of *pupa* 'girl').

**pupil**[2] ● n. the dark circular opening in the centre of the iris of the eye, which varies in size to regulate the amount of light reaching the retina.
– DERIVATIVES **pupillary** adj.
– ORIGIN ME: from OFr. *pupille* or L. *pupilla*, dimin. of *pupa* 'doll' (from the tiny reflected images visible in the eye).

**pupillage** ● n. **1** the state of being a pupil. **2** Law (in the UK) apprenticeship to a member of the Bar, which qualifies a barrister to practise independently.

**pupiparous** /pjuːˈpɪp(ə)rəs/ ● adj. Entomology (of certain flies, e.g. the tsetse) producing young which are already ready to pupate.
– ORIGIN C19: from mod. L. *pupipara* (neut. pl. of *pupiparus* 'bringing forth young') + **-OUS**.

**puppet** ● n. **1** a movable model of a person or animal, typically moved either by strings or by a hand inside it, used to entertain. **2** a person under the control of another.
– DERIVATIVES **puppeteer** n. **puppeteering** n. **puppetry** n.

– ORIGIN C16: later form of **POPPET**.

**puppy** ● n. (pl. **-ies**) **1** a young dog. **2** informal, dated a conceited or arrogant young man.
– DERIVATIVES **puppyhood** n. **puppyish** adj.
– ORIGIN C15: perh. from OFr. *poupee* 'doll, toy'; cf. **PUPPET**, synonymous with dial. *puppy* (as in *puppy-show* 'puppet show').

**puppy fat** ● n. fat on the body of a child which disappears around adolescence.

**puppy love** ● n. intense but relatively short-lived love, typically associated with adolescents.

**pup tent** ● n. N. Amer. a small triangular tent, especially one for two people and without side walls.

**pur-** ● prefix equivalent to **PRO-**[1] (as in *pursue*).
– ORIGIN from Anglo-Norman Fr., from L. *por-*, *pro-*.

**Purana** /pʊˈrɑːnə/ ● n. any of a class of Sanskrit sacred writings on Hindu mythology and folklore of varying date and origin.
– DERIVATIVES **Puranic** adj.
– ORIGIN from Sanskrit *purāṇa* 'ancient (legend)'.

**Purbeck marble** /ˈpəːbɛk/ (also **Purbeck stone**) ● n. a hard limestone from Purbeck in Dorset, which is polished and used for decorative architectural features.

**purblind** /ˈpəːblʌɪnd/ ● adj. **1** having impaired or defective vision. **2** dim-witted.
– DERIVATIVES **purblindness** n.
– ORIGIN ME (in the sense 'completely blind'): from **PURE** 'utterly' (later assimilated to **PUR-**) + **BLIND**.

**purchase** ● v. **1** buy. **2** Nautical haul up (a rope, cable, or anchor) by means of a pulley or lever. ● n. **1** the action of buying. ➤ a thing bought. ➤ Law the acquisition of property by one's personal action and not by inheritance. **2** firm contact or grip. **3** a pulley or similar device for moving heavy objects. **4** archaic the annual rent or return from land.
– DERIVATIVES **purchasable** adj. **purchaser** n.
– ORIGIN ME: from OFr. *pourchacier* 'seek to obtain or bring about'.

**purchase tax** ● n. a tax added to the price of goods sold to consumers.

**purdah** /ˈpəːdə/ ● n. **1** the practice in certain Muslim and Hindu societies of screening women from men or strangers by means of a curtain or all-enveloping clothes. **2** a curtain used in this way.
– ORIGIN C19: from Urdu and Pers. *parda* 'veil, curtain'.

**pure** ● adj. **1** not mixed or adulterated with any other substance or material. ➤ (of an animal or plant) of unmixed origin or descent. **2** innocent or morally good. **3** (of a sound) perfectly in tune and with a clear tone. **4** (of a subject) theoretical rather than practical. Compare with **APPLIED**. **5** complete; nothing but. **6** Phonetics (of a vowel) not joined with another to form a diphthong.
– DERIVATIVES **purely** adv. **pureness** n.
– ORIGIN ME: from OFr. *pur* 'pure', from L. *purus*.

**pure-bred** ● adj. (of an animal) bred from parents of the same breed or variety.

**purée** /ˈpjʊəreɪ/ ● n. a smooth pulp of liquidized or crushed fruit or vegetables. ● v. (**purées**, **puréed**, **puréeing**) make a purée of.
– ORIGIN C18: Fr., lit. 'purified', fem. past part. of *purer*.

**pure mathematics** ● pl. n. see **MATHEMATICS**.

**purfle** /ˈpəːf(ə)l/ ● n. **1** an ornamental border, typically one inlaid on the back or belly of a violin. **2** archaic an ornamental or embroidered edge of a garment. ● v. [often as noun **purfling**] decorate with a purfle.
– ORIGIN ME: from OFr. *porfil* (n.), *porfiler* (v.), based on L. *pro* 'forward' + *filum* 'thread'.

**purgation** /pəːˈgeɪʃ(ə)n/ ● n. **1** purification. ➤ (in Catholic doctrine) the spiritual cleansing of a soul in purgatory. **2** historical the action of clearing oneself of accusation or suspicion by an oath or ordeal. **3** evacuation of the bowels brought about by laxatives.
– ORIGIN ME: from OFr. *purgacion*, from L. *purgatio(n-)*, from *purgare* (see **PURGE**).

**purgative** /ˈpəːgətɪv/ ● adj. strongly laxative in effect. ● n. a laxative.

**purgatory** /ˈpəːgət(ə)ri/ ● n. (pl. **-ies**) **1** (in Catholic doctrine) a place or state of suffering inhabited by the souls of sinners who are expiating their sins before going to heaven. **2** mental anguish.
– DERIVATIVES **purgatorial** adj.
– ORIGIN ME: from Anglo-Norman Fr. *purgatorie* or med. L. *purgatorium*, neut. of late L. *purgatorius*, from *purgare* (see **PURGE**).

**purge** ● v. **1** rid of an unwanted feeling or condition. **2** remove (a group of people considered undesirable) from an organization or place. **3** remove by a cleansing process. **4** [often as noun **purging**] evacuate one's bowels, especially as a result of taking a laxative. **5** Law atone for or wipe out (contempt of court). ● n. an act of purging people from an organization or place.
– DERIVATIVES **purger** n.
– ORIGIN ME: from OFr. *purgier*, from L. *purgare* 'purify', from *purus* 'pure'.

**puri** /ˈpuːri/ ● n. (pl. **puris**) (in Indian cookery) a small, round, flat piece of unleavened bread, deep-fried and served with meat or vegetables.
– ORIGIN via Hindi from Sanskrit *pūrikā*.

**purify** ● v. (**-ies**, **-ied**) remove contaminants from; make pure.
– DERIVATIVES **purification** n. **purificatory** adj. **purifier** n.
– ORIGIN ME: from OFr. *purifier*, from L. *purificare*, from *purus* 'pure'.

**Purim** /ˈpʊərɪm, pʊˈriːm/ ● n. a lesser Jewish festival held in spring to commemorate the defeat of Haman's plot to massacre the Jews as recorded in the book of Esther.
– ORIGIN Heb., pl. of *pūr*, explained in the book of Esther (3:7, 9:24) as meaning 'lot', with allusion to the casting of lots by Haman.

**purine** /ˈpjʊəriːn/ ● n. Chemistry a colourless crystalline bicyclic compound with basic properties. ➤ (also **purine base**) a substituted derivative of this, especially adenine or guanine present in DNA.
– ORIGIN C19: from Ger. *Purin*, from L. *purus* 'pure' + *uricum* 'uric acid' (which it forms on oxidation) + **-INE**[4].

**purism** ● n. **1** scrupulous observance of traditional rules or structures, especially in language or style. **2** (**Purism**) an early 20th-century artistic style and movement rejecting cubism and emphasizing purity of geometric form and the representation of recognizable objects.
– DERIVATIVES **purist** n. **puristic** adj.

**puritan** ● n. **1** (**Puritan**) a member of a group of English Protestants who regarded the Reformation of the Church under Elizabeth I as incomplete and sought to simplify and regulate forms of worship. **2** a person with censorious moral beliefs, especially about self-indulgence and sex. ● adj. **1** (**Puritan**) of or relating to the Puritans. **2** characteristic of a puritan.
– DERIVATIVES **puritanical** adj. **puritanically** adv. **puritanism** (also **Puritanism**) n.
– ORIGIN C16: from late L. *puritas* 'purity' + **-AN**.

**purity** ● n. the state of being pure.

**Purkinje cell** /pəːˈkɪndʒi/ ● n. Anatomy a nerve cell of a large, branched type found in the cortex of the cerebellum.
– ORIGIN C19: named after the Bohemian physiologist Jan E. *Purkinje*.

**purl**[1] ● adj. (of a knitting stitch) made by putting the needle through the front of the stitch from right to left. Compare with **PLAIN**[1] (in sense 5). ● v. knit with a purl stitch.
– ORIGIN C17: of uncertain origin.

**purl**[2] poetic/literary ● v. (of a stream or river) flow with a swirling motion and babbling sound. ● n. a motion or sound of this kind.
– ORIGIN C16 (denoting a small swirling stream): prob. imitative.

**purler** ● n. Brit. informal a headlong fall.
– ORIGIN C19: from dial. *purl* 'upset, overturn'.

**purlieu** /ˈpəːljuː/ ● n. (pl. **purlieus** or **purlieux**) **1** (**purlieus**) the area near or surrounding a place. **2** Brit. historical a tract on the border of a forest, especially one earlier included in it and still partly subject to forest laws.
– ORIGIN C15: prob. an alt. (suggested by Fr. *lieu* 'place') of Anglo-Norman Fr. *puralee* 'a going round to settle the boundaries'.

**purlin** /ˈpəːlɪn/ ● **n.** a horizontal beam along the length of a roof, resting on principals and supporting the common rafters or boards.
– ORIGIN ME: perh. of Fr. origin.

**purloin** /pəːˈlɔɪn/ ● **v.** formal or humorous steal.
– DERIVATIVES **purloiner** n.
– ORIGIN ME (in the sense 'put at a distance'): from Anglo-Norman Fr. *purloigner* 'put away'.

**purple** ● **n. 1** a colour intermediate between red and blue. **2** (also **Tyrian purple**) a crimson dye obtained from some molluscs, formerly used for fabric worn by an emperor or senior magistrate in ancient Rome or Byzantium. ➤**(the purple)** (in ancient Rome) a position of rank, authority, or privilege. **3** the scarlet official dress of a cardinal. ● **adj.** of a colour intermediate between red and blue. ● **v.** become or make purple in colour.
– PHRASES **born in** (or **to**) **the purple** born into a reigning family or privileged class.
– DERIVATIVES **purpleness** n. **purplish** adj. **purply** adj.
– ORIGIN OE, alt. of *purpre*, from L. *purpura* 'purple', from Gk *porphura*, denoting molluscs that yielded a crimson dye, also cloth dyed with this.

**purple emperor** ● **n.** a large woodland butterfly that has iridescent purplish-black wings with white markings. [*Apatura iris*.]

**purple heart** ● **n. 1** (**Purple Heart**) (in the US) a decoration for those wounded or killed in action. **2** the hard, dark purplish-brown wood of a large American rainforest tree (genus *Peltogyne*).

**purple passage** ● **n.** an excessively ornate passage in a literary composition.

**purple patch** ● **n. 1** informal a run of success or good luck. **2** another term for **PURPLE PASSAGE**.

**purple prose** ● **n.** prose that is too ornate.

**purport** ● **v.** /pəˈpɔːt/ appear to be or do, especially falsely. ● **n.** /ˈpəːpɔːt/ **1** the meaning or substance of a document or speech. **2** the purpose of a person or thing.
– DERIVATIVES **purported** adj. **purportedly** adv.
– ORIGIN ME (in the sense 'signify'): from OFr. *purporter*, from med. L. *proportare*, from L. *pro-* 'forth' + *portare* 'carry, bear'.

**purpose** ● **n. 1** the reason for which something is done or for which something exists. **2** resolve or determination. ● **v.** formal have as one's objective.
– PHRASES **on purpose** intentionally. **to the purpose** relevant or useful.
– DERIVATIVES **purposeless** adj. **purposelessly** adv. **purposelessness** n.
– ORIGIN ME: from OFr. *porpos*, from *porposer*, var. of *proposer* (see **PROPOSE**).

**purposeful** ● **adj. 1** resolute. **2** having a purpose.
– DERIVATIVES **purposefully** adv. **purposefulness** n.

**purposely** ● **adv.** deliberately; on purpose.

**purposive** ● **adj.** having or done with a purpose.
– DERIVATIVES **purposively** adv. **purposiveness** n.

**purpura** /ˈpəːpjʊrə/ ● **n.** Medicine a rash of purple spots on the skin caused by internal bleeding from small blood vessels.
– DERIVATIVES **purpuric** /-ˈpjʊərɪk/ adj.
– ORIGIN C18: from L., from Gk *porphura* 'purple'.

**purpure** /ˈpəːpjʊə/ ● **n.** purple, as a heraldic tincture.
– ORIGIN OE, from L. *purpura* (see **PURPURA**), reinforced by OFr. *purpre*.

**purpurin** /ˈpəːpjʊrɪn/ ● **n.** Chemistry a red dye extracted from madder, also made by oxidizing alizarin.
– ORIGIN C19: from L. *purpura* 'purple' + **-IN**[1].

**purr** ● **v. 1** (of a cat) make a low continuous vibratory sound expressing contentment. **2** (of a vehicle or engine) move or run smoothly while making a similar sound. ● **n.** a purring sound.
– ORIGIN C17: imitative.

**purse** ● **n. 1** a small pouch of leather or plastic used for carrying money. **2** N. Amer. a handbag. **3** an amount of money available; funds. ➤a sum of money given as a prize in a sporting contest. ● **v.** (with reference to the lips) pucker or contract.
– PHRASES **hold the purse strings** have control of expenditure.
– ORIGIN OE, alt. of late L. *bursa*, from Gk *bursa* 'hide, leather'.

**purser** ● **n.** an officer on a ship who keeps the accounts, especially the head steward on a passenger vessel.

**purse seine** /seɪn/ ● **n.** a seine net which may be drawn into the shape of a bag, used for catching shoal fish.
– DERIVATIVES **purse-seiner** n.

**purslane** /ˈpəːslən/ ● **n.** a small fleshy-leaved plant of damp or marshy habitats, some kinds of which are edible. [*Atriplex portulacoides* (**sea purslane**) and other species.]
– ORIGIN ME: from OFr. *porcelaine*, prob. from L. *porcil(l)aca*, var. of *portulaca*, influenced by Fr. *porcelaine* 'porcelain'.

**pursuance** ● **n.** formal the carrying out or pursuing of something.

**pursuant** /pəˈsjuːənt/ ● **adv.** (**pursuant to**) formal in accordance with (a law, resolution, etc.).
– DERIVATIVES **pursuantly** adv.
– ORIGIN ME *poursuiant* (in the sense 'a prosecutor'): from OFr., 'pursuing', from *poursuir*; later influenced in spelling by **PURSUE**.

**pursue** ● **v.** (**pursues**, **pursued**, **pursuing**) **1** follow in order to catch or attack. **2** seek to attain (a goal). **3** proceed along (a path or route). **4** follow or continue with (a course of action). ➤continue to investigate or discuss.
– DERIVATIVES **pursuable** adj. **pursuer** n.
– ORIGIN ME: from Anglo-Norman Fr. *pursuer*, from an alt. of L. *prosequi* 'prosecute'.

**pursuit** ● **n. 1** the action of pursuing. **2** a recreational or sporting activity. **3** a cycling race in which competitors set off from different parts of a track and attempt to overtake one another.
– ORIGIN ME: from Anglo-Norman Fr. *purseute* 'following after', from *pursuer* (see **PURSUE**).

**pursuivant** /ˈpəːsɪv(ə)nt/ ● **n. 1** Brit. an officer of the College of Arms ranking below a herald. **2** archaic a follower or attendant.
– ORIGIN ME: from OFr. *pursivant*, pres. part. of *pursivre* 'follow after'.

**pursy** ● **adj.** archaic **1** (especially of a horse) short of breath; asthmatic. **2** fat.
– DERIVATIVES **pursiness** n.
– ORIGIN ME: reduction of Anglo-Norman Fr. *porsif*, alt. of OFr. *polsif*, from *polser* 'breathe with difficulty', from L. *pulsare* 'set in violent motion'.

**purulent** /ˈpjʊərʊl(ə)nt/ ● **adj.** Medicine consisting of, containing, or discharging pus.
– ORIGIN ME: from L. *purulentus*, from *pus*, *pur-* 'pus'.

**purvey** ● **v.** provide or supply (food, drink, or other goods) as one's business.
– DERIVATIVES **purveyor** n.
– ORIGIN ME (also in the senses 'foresee', 'attend to in advance'): from Anglo-Norman Fr. *purveier*, from L. *providere* (see **PROVIDE**).

**purveyance** ● **n. 1** the action of purveying. **2** Brit. historical the right of the sovereign to buy provisions and use horses and vehicles for a fixed price lower than the market value.

**purview** ● **n. 1** the scope of the influence or concerns of something. **2** a range of experience or thought.
– ORIGIN ME: from Anglo-Norman Fr. *purveu*, *purveier* (see **PURVEY**).

**pus** ● **n.** a thick yellowish or greenish opaque liquid produced in infected tissue, consisting of dead white blood cells and bacteria with tissue debris and serum.
– ORIGIN ME: from L.

**push** ● **v. 1** exert force on (someone or something) in order to move them away from oneself. ➤hold and exert force on (something) so as to cause it to move in front of one. ➤move one's body or a part of it forcefully into a specified position. ➤(**push off**) exert pressure with an oar etc. so as to move a boat out from a bank. **2** move forward by using force. ➤(**push in**) go in front of people who are already queuing. ➤(**push ahead**) proceed with or continue a course of action. ➤(**push along/off**) Brit. informal go away; depart. **3** urge (someone) to greater effort. ➤(**push for**) demand persistently. **4** informal promote

the use, sale, or acceptance of. ➤sell (a narcotic drug) illegally. **5** (**be pushed**) informal have very little of something, especially time. **6** (**be pushing**) informal be nearly (a particular age). ● **n. 1** an act of pushing. **2** a vigorous effort. ➤forcefulness and enterprise. **3** (**a push**) informal something that is hard to achieve.
– PHRASES **at a push** Brit. informal only if necessary or with a certain degree of difficulty. **get** (or **give someone**) **the push** (or **shove**) Brit. informal **1** be dismissed (or dismiss someone) from a job. **2** be rejected in (or end) a relationship. **push one's luck** informal take a risk on the assumption that one will continue to be successful or in favour. **when push comes to shove** informal when one must commit oneself to an action or decision.
– DERIVATIVES **pusher** n.
– ORIGIN ME: from OFr. *pousser*, from L. *pulsare* (see **PULSE**[1]).

**pushbike** ● **n.** Brit. informal a bicycle.

**pushcart** ● **n.** a small handcart or barrow.

**pushchair** ● **n.** Brit. a folding chair on wheels, in which a baby or young child can be pushed along.

**pushful** ● **adj.** dated arrogantly self-assertive.
– DERIVATIVES **pushfully** adv. **pushfulness** n.

**pushover** ● **n. 1** informal a person who is easy to overcome or influence. ➤a thing that is very easily done. **2** Rugby a try in which one side in a scrum pushes the ball over the opponents' goal line.

**pushpin** ● **n.** chiefly N. Amer. a drawing pin with a spherical or cylindrical plastic head.

**pushpit** ● **n.** a raised safety rail in the stern of a yacht.
– ORIGIN 1960s: humorous formation, suggested by **PULPIT**.

**push poll** ● **n.** an ostensible opinion poll in which the true objective is to sway voters using loaded questions.
– DERIVATIVES **push-polling** n.

**push-pull** ● **adj. 1** operated by pushing and pulling. **2** Electronics denoting an arrangement of two matched transistors or valves conducting alternately.

**pushrod** ● **n.** a rod operated by cams that opens and closes the valves in an internal-combustion engine.

**push-start** ● **v.** start (a motor vehicle) by pushing it in order to make the engine turn. ● **n.** an act of push-starting.

**push technology** ● **n.** Computing a service in which the user downloads software from a provider which then continually supplies information from the Internet in categories selected by the user.

**Pushtu** /ˈpʌʃtuː/ ● **n.** variant of **PASHTO**.

**push-up** ● **n.** chiefly N. Amer. another term for **PRESS-UP**.

**pushy** ● **adj.** (**-ier**, **-iest**) excessively self-assertive or ambitious.
– DERIVATIVES **pushily** adv. **pushiness** n.

**pusillanimous** /ˌpjuːsɪˈlanɪməs/ ● **adj.** timid.
– DERIVATIVES **pusillanimity** /-ləˈnɪmɪti/ n. **pusillanimously** adv.
– ORIGIN ME: from eccles. L. *pusillanimis*, from *pusillus* 'very small' + *animus* 'mind', + **-OUS**.

**puss**[1] ● **n.** informal **1** a cat (especially as a form of address). **2** a coquettish girl or young woman: *a glamour puss*.
– ORIGIN C16: prob. from Mid. Low Ger. *pūs* or Du. *poes*.

**puss**[2] ● **n.** N. Amer. informal or Irish & Scottish a person's face or mouth.
– ORIGIN C19: from Ir. *pus* 'lip, mouth'.

**puss moth** ● **n.** a large furry greyish-white moth with darker markings. [*Cerura vinula*.]

**pussy** ● **n.** (pl. **-ies**) **1** (also **pussy cat**) informal a cat. **2** vulgar slang a woman's genitals. ➤women collectively, considered sexually.

**pussyfoot** ● **v. 1** act in an excessively cautious or non-committal way. **2** move stealthily.
– DERIVATIVES **pussyfooter** n.

**pussy willow** ● **n.** a willow with soft fluffy catkins that appear before the leaves, e.g. a sallow.

**pustulate** ● **v.** /ˈpʌstjʊleɪt/ form into pustules. ● **adj.** /ˈpʌstjʊlət/ chiefly Biology having or covered with pustules.
– DERIVATIVES **pustulation** n.
– ORIGIN ME: from late L. *pustulat-*, *pustulare* 'to blister', from *pustula* 'pustule'.

**pustule** /ˈpʌstjuːl/ ● **n.** a small blister or pimple containing pus.
– DERIVATIVES **pustular** adj.
– ORIGIN ME: from L. *pustula*.

**put** ● **v.** (**putting**; past and past part. **put**) **1** move to or place in a particular position. ➤(of a ship) proceed in a particular direction: *the boat put out to sea*. **2** bring into a particular state or condition: *they tried to put me at ease*. ➤express in a particular way: *to put it bluntly, he was not really divorced*. **3** (**put something on/on to**) cause to carry or be subject to something: *commentators put the blame on Congress*. ➤assign a particular value, figure, or limit to. **4** throw (a shot or weight) as an athletic sport. ● **n.** a throw of the shot or weight.
– PHRASES **put someone's eyes out** blind someone, especially in a violent way. **put one's hands together** applaud. **put one's hands up** raise one's hands in surrender. **put it to** make a statement or allegation to (someone) and challenge them to deny it. **put one over on** informal deceive (someone) into accepting something false. **put up or shut up** informal justify oneself or remain silent.
– PHRASAL VERBS **put about** Nautical (of a ship) turn on the opposite tack. **put someone about** chiefly Scottish & N. English upset or trouble someone. **put something about** spread information or rumours. **put something aside** (or **by**) save money for future use. **put someone away** informal confine someone in a prison or psychiatric hospital. **put something away 1** save money for future use. **2** informal consume food or drink in large quantities. **put someone down** informal lower someone's self-esteem by publicly criticizing them. **put something down 1** suppress a rebellion, coup, or riot by force. **2** kill an animal because it is sick, injured, or old. **3** pay a specified sum as a deposit. **4** preserve or store food or wine for future use. **put something down to** attribute something to. **put someone off 1** cancel or postpone an appointment with someone. **2** cause someone to feel dislike or lose enthusiasm. **3** distract someone. **put something off** postpone something. **put something on 1** present or provide a play, service, etc. **2** become heavier by a specified amount. **3** assume a particular expression, accent, etc. **put someone on to** draw someone's attention to. **put out for** informal, chiefly N. Amer. agree to have sexual intercourse with. **put someone out** inconvenience, upset, or annoy someone. **put something out 1** dislocate a joint. **2** (of an engine or motor) produce a particular amount of power. **put something over** N. Amer. postpone something. **put someone through 1** subject someone to a gruelling or unpleasant experience. **2** connect someone by telephone to another person or place. **3** pay for one's child to attend school or college. **put something to 1** submit something to (someone) for consideration. **2** couple an animal with (another of the opposite sex) for breeding. **put up** offer or show (a particular degree of resistance or skill) in a fight, contest, etc. **put someone up 1** accommodate someone temporarily. **2** propose someone for election or adoption. **put something up 1** present something for discussion or consideration. **2** publish banns. **3** provide money as backing for an enterprise. **4** offer something for sale or auction. **5** cause game to rise from cover. **6** archaic return a sword to its sheath. **put upon** [often as adj. **put-upon**] informal take advantage of (someone) by exploiting their good nature. **put someone up to** informal encourage someone to do (something wrong or unwise). **put up with** tolerate; endure.
– ORIGIN OE, of unknown origin; cf. dial. *pote* 'to push, thrust' (an early sense of *put*).

**putative** /ˈpjuːtətɪv/ ● **adj.** generally considered or reputed to be.
– DERIVATIVES **putatively** adv.
– ORIGIN ME: from OFr. *putatif*, *-ive* or late L. *putativus*, from L. *putat-*, *putare* 'think'.

**put-down** ● **n.** informal a remark intended to humiliate or criticize someone.

**put-in** ● **n.** Rugby the act of putting the ball into a scrum.

**putlog** /ˈpʌtlɒg/ (also **putlock** /-lɒk/) ● **n.** a short horizontal pole projecting from a wall, on which scaffold

floorboards rest.
– ORIGIN C17: of unknown origin.

**putonghua** /puːˈtʊŋhwɑː/ ● **n.** the standard spoken form of modern Chinese, based on the dialect of Beijing.
– ORIGIN Chin., lit. 'common spoken language'.

**put option** ● **n.** Stock Exchange an option to sell assets at an agreed price on or before a particular date.

**put-put** /ˈpʌtpʌt/ ● **n. & v.** another term for **PUTTER**[2].

**putrefy** /ˈpjuːtrɪfʌɪ/ ● **v.** (**-ies**, **-ied**) decay or rot and produce a fetid smell.
– DERIVATIVES **putrefaction** n. **putrefactive** adj.
– ORIGIN ME: via Fr. from L. *putrefacere*, from *puter, putr-* 'rotten'.

**putrescent** /pjuːˈtrɛs(ə)nt/ ● **adj.** decaying; rotting.
– DERIVATIVES **putrescence** n.
– ORIGIN C18: from L. *putrescent-*, inceptive of *putrere* (see **PUTRID**).

**putrescible** ● **adj.** liable to decay.

**putrid** ● **adj. 1** decaying or rotting and emitting a fetid smell. **2** informal very unpleasant.
– DERIVATIVES **putridity** n. **putridly** adv. **putridness** n.
– ORIGIN ME: from L. *putridus*, from *putrere* 'to rot', from *puter, putr-* 'rotten'.

**putsch** /pʊtʃ/ ● **n.** a violent attempt to overthrow a government.
– ORIGIN 1920s: from Swiss Ger., lit. 'thrust, blow'.

**putt** /pʌt/ ● **v.** (**putted**, **putting**) strike a golf ball gently so that it rolls into or near the hole. ● **n.** a stroke of this kind.
– ORIGIN C17 (orig. Scots): differentiated from **PUT**.

**puttanesca** /pʊtəˈnɛskə/ ● **adj.** denoting a pasta sauce of tomatoes, garlic, olives, anchovies, etc.
– ORIGIN Ital., from *puttana* 'prostitute' (the sauce is said to have been devised by prostitutes as one which could be cooked quickly between clients' visits).

**puttee** /ˈpʌti/ ● **n.** a strip of cloth wound round the leg from ankle to knee for protection and support.
– ORIGIN C19: from Hindi *paṭṭī* 'band, bandage'.

**putter**[1] /ˈpʌtə/ ● **n.** a golf club designed for putting, typically with a flat-faced mallet-like head.

**putter**[2] /ˈpʌtə/ ● **n.** the rapid intermittent sound of a small petrol engine. ● **v.** move with or make such a sound.
– ORIGIN 1940s: imitative.

**putter**[3] /ˈpʌtə/ ● **v.** North American term for **POTTER**[1].

**putting green** ● **n.** (in golf) a smooth area of short grass surrounding a hole.

**putto** /ˈpʊtəʊ/ ● **n.** (pl. **putti** /-ti/) a representation of a naked child, especially a cherub or a cupid in Renaissance art.
– ORIGIN Ital., lit. 'boy'.

**putty** ● **n. 1** a malleable paste, made from whiting and raw linseed oil, that gradually hardens and is used chiefly for sealing glass in window frames. ➤a malleable substance used as a filler, modelling material, etc. **2** a polishing powder, usually made from tin oxide, used in jewellery work. ● **v.** (**-ies**, **-ied**) seal or cover with putty.
– PHRASES **be (like) putty in someone's hands** be easily manipulated by someone.
– ORIGIN C17: from Fr. *potée*, lit. 'potful'.

**put-up job** ● **n.** informal something intended to deceive.

**put-you-up** ● **n.** Brit. a sofa or settee that can be converted into a bed.

**putz** /pʊts, pʌts/ N. Amer. informal ● **n. 1** a stupid or worthless person. **2** vulgar slang a man's penis. ● **v.** engage in inconsequential or unproductive activity.
– ORIGIN 1960s: Yiddish, lit. 'penis'.

**puzzle** ● **v. 1** confuse because difficult to understand. **2** think hard about something difficult to understand. ● **n. 1** a game, toy, or problem designed to test ingenuity or knowledge. **2** a puzzling person or thing.
– DERIVATIVES **puzzlement** n. **puzzler** n. **puzzling** adj. **puzzlingly** adv.
– ORIGIN C16: of unknown origin.

**PVA** ● **abbrev.** polyvinyl acetate.

**PVC** ● **abbrev.** polyvinyl chloride.

**PVS** ● **abbrev.** Medicine **1** persistent vegetative state. **2** postviral syndrome.

**Pvt.** ● **abbrev. 1** (in the US army) private. **2** private (in company names).

**PW** ● **abbrev.** policewoman.

**p.w.** ● **abbrev.** per week.

**PWA** ● **abbrev.** person with Aids.

**PWR** ● **abbrev.** pressurized-water reactor.

**PY** ● **abbrev.** Paraguay (international vehicle registration).

**pya** /pjɑː/ ● **n.** a monetary unit of Burma (Myanmar), equal to one hundredth of a kyat.
– ORIGIN from Burmese.

**pyaemia** /pʌɪˈiːmɪə/ (US **pyemia**) ● **n.** blood poisoning caused by the release of pus-forming bacteria from an abscess.
– DERIVATIVES **pyaemic** adj.
– ORIGIN C19: mod. L., from Gk *puon* 'pus' + *haima* 'blood'.

**pye-dog** /ˈpʌɪdɒg/ (also **pi-dog**) ● **n.** (in Asia) a half-wild stray mongrel.
– ORIGIN C19: from Anglo-Ind. *pye*, Hindi *pāhī* 'outsider' + **DOG**.

**pyelitis** /ˌpʌɪəˈlʌɪtɪs/ ● **n.** Medicine inflammation of the renal pelvis.
– ORIGIN C19: from Gk *puelos* 'trough, basin' + **-ITIS**.

**pyemia** ● **n.** US spelling of **PYAEMIA**.

**pygidium** /pʌɪˈdʒɪdɪəm, -ˈgɪdɪəm/ ● **n.** (pl. **pygidia** /-ɪə/) Zoology the terminal part or hind segment of the body in certain invertebrates.
– ORIGIN C19: mod. L., from Gk *pugē* 'rump'.

**pygmy** (also **pigmy**) ● **n.** (pl. **-ies**) **1** a member of certain peoples of very short stature in equatorial Africa or parts of SE Asia. **2** chiefly derogatory a very small person or thing. **3** a person who is deficient in a particular respect: *an intellectual pygmy.* ● **adj.** very small; dwarf.
– DERIVATIVES **pygmean** adj. (archaic).
– ORIGIN ME (orig. denoting a mythological race of small people): via L. from Gk *pugmaios* 'dwarf', from *pugmē* 'the length measured from elbow to knuckles'.

**pygmy chimpanzee** ● **n.** another term for **BONOBO**.

**pyjamas** (US **pajamas**) ● **pl. n. 1** a jacket and loose trousers for sleeping in. **2** loose trousers with a drawstring waist, worn by both sexes in some Asian countries.
– ORIGIN C19: from Urdu and Pers., from *pāy* 'leg' + *jāma* 'clothing'.

**pyknic** /ˈpɪknɪk/ ● **adj.** Anthropology relating to or denoting a stocky physique with a rounded body and head, thickset trunk, and a tendency to fat.
– ORIGIN 1920s: from Gk *puknos* 'thick' + **-IC**.

**pylon** ● **n. 1** (also **electricity pylon**) a tall tower-like structure for carrying electricity cables. **2** a pillar-like structure on the wing of an aircraft used for carrying an engine or other load. **3** a tower or post marking a path for light aircraft, cars, or other vehicles, especially in racing. **4** a monumental gateway to an ancient Egyptian temple, formed by two truncated pyramidal towers.
– ORIGIN C19: from Gk *pulōn*, from *pulē* 'gate'.

**pylorus** /pʌɪˈlɔːrəs/ ● **n.** (pl. **pylori** /-rʌɪ/) Anatomy the opening from the stomach into the duodenum.
– DERIVATIVES **pyloric** adj.
– ORIGIN C17: via late L. from Gk *pulouros* 'gatekeeper'.

**pyoderma** /ˌpʌɪə(ʊ)ˈdəːmə/ ● **n.** Medicine a skin infection with formation of pus.
– ORIGIN 1930s: from Gk *puo-* (from *puon* 'pus') + *derma* 'skin'.

**pyogenic** /ˌpʌɪə(ʊ)ˈdʒɛnɪk/ ● **adj.** Medicine involving or relating to the production of pus.
– ORIGIN C19: from Gk *puo-* (from *puon* 'pus') + **-GENIC**.

**pyorrhoea** /ˌpʌɪəˈriːə/ (US **pyorrhea**) ● **n.** another term for **PERIODONTITIS**.
– ORIGIN C19: from Gk *puo-* (from *puon* 'pus') + *rhoia* 'flux'.

**pyracantha** /ˌpʌɪrəˈkanθə/ ● **n.** a thorny evergreen shrub with white flowers and bright red or yellow berries. [Genus *Pyracantha*.]
– ORIGIN mod. L., via L. from Gk *purakantha*, the name of

an unidentified plant, from *pur* 'fire' + *akantha* 'thorn'.

**pyramid** /ˈpɪrəmɪd/ ● **n. 1** a monumental stone structure with a square or triangular base and sloping sides that meet in a point at the top, especially one built as a royal tomb in ancient Egypt. **2** Geometry a polyhedron of which one face is a polygon and the other faces are triangles with a common vertex. **3** Anatomy a pyramid-shaped structure, especially in the brain. **4** a system of financial growth achieved by a small initial investment. **5** (**pyramids**) a game played on a billiard table with fifteen coloured balls arranged in a triangle and a cue ball. ● **v.** chiefly N. Amer. heap or stack in a pyramidal shape.
– DERIVATIVES **pyramidical** /-ˈmɪdɪk(ə)l/ adj. **pyramidically** adv.
– ORIGIN ME: via L. from Gk *puramis, puramid-*.

**pyramidal** /pɪˈramɪd(ə)l/ ● **adj. 1** resembling a pyramid in shape. **2** Anatomy & Medicine relating to or denoting a tract of motor nerves within the pyramid of the medulla oblongata.
– DERIVATIVES **pyramidally** adv.

**pyramid selling** ● **n.** a system of selling goods in which agency rights are sold to an increasing number of distributors at successively lower levels.

**pyrargyrite** /pʌɪˈrɑːdʒɪrʌɪt/ ● **n.** a dark reddish-grey mineral consisting of a sulphide of silver and antimony.
– ORIGIN C19: from Gk *puro-* (from *pur* 'fire') + *arguros* 'silver' + **-ITE**[1].

**pyre** ● **n.** a heap of combustible material, especially one for burning a corpse as part of a funeral ceremony.
– ORIGIN C17: via L. from Gk *pura*, from *pur* 'fire'.

**pyrene** /ˈpʌɪriːn/ ● **n.** Chemistry a crystalline aromatic hydrocarbon present in coal tar.
– ORIGIN C19: from Gk *pur* 'fire' + **-ENE**.

**Pyrenean** /ˌpɪrəˈniːən/ ● **adj.** of or relating to the Pyrenees.

**pyrethrin** /pʌɪˈriːθrɪn/ ● **n.** Chemistry any of a group of insecticidal compounds present in pyrethrum flowers.
– DERIVATIVES **pyrethroid** n.

**pyrethrum** /pʌɪˈriːθrəm/ ● **n. 1** an aromatic plant of the daisy family, typically with feathery foliage and brightly coloured flowers. [Genus *Tanacetum* (formerly *Pyrethrum*): several species.] **2** an insecticide made from the dried flowers of these plants.
– ORIGIN ME (denoting pellitory): from L., from Gk *purethron* 'feverfew'.

**pyretic** /pʌɪˈrɛtɪk, pɪ-/ ● **adj.** feverish or inducing fever.
– ORIGIN C18 (denoting an antipyretic drug): from mod. L. *pyreticus*, from Gk *puretos* 'fever'.

**Pyrex** ● **n.** trademark a hard heat-resistant type of glass.
– ORIGIN C20: an invented word.

**pyrexia** /pʌɪˈrɛksɪə, pɪ-/ ● **n.** Medicine fever.
– DERIVATIVES **pyrexial** adj. **pyrexic** adj.
– ORIGIN C18: mod. L., from Gk *purexis*, from *puressein* 'be feverish'.

**pyridine** /ˈpɪrɪdiːn/ ● **n.** Chemistry a colourless volatile heterocyclic liquid with an unpleasant odour, present in coal tar and used as a solvent.
– ORIGIN C19: from Gk *pur* 'fire' + **-IDE** + **-INE**[4].

**pyridostigmine** /ˌpɪrɪdə(ʊ)ˈstɪgmiːn/ ● **n.** Medicine a synthetic compound related to neostigmine, with similar but weaker and longer-acting effects.
– ORIGIN 1950s: blend of **PYRIDINE** and **NEOSTIGMINE**.

**pyridoxal** /ˌpɪrɪˈdɒksəl/ ● **n.** Biochemistry an oxidized derivative of pyridoxine which acts as a coenzyme in some metabolic processes.

**pyridoxine** /ˌpɪrɪˈdɒksɪn, -iːn/ ● **n.** Biochemistry vitamin $B_6$, a compound present chiefly in cereals, liver oils, and yeast, and important in the metabolism of fats.
– ORIGIN 1930s: from *pyrid(ine)* + **OX-** + **-INE**[4].

**pyriform** /ˈpɪrɪfɔːm/ (also **piriform**) ● **adj.** Anatomy & Biology pear-shaped.
– ORIGIN C18: from mod. L. *pyriformis*, from *pyrum* (misspelling of *pirum* 'pear') + **-IFORM**.

**pyrimidine** /pɪˈrɪmɪdiːn/ ● **n.** Chemistry a colourless crystalline heterocyclic compound with basic properties. ➤(also **pyrimidine base**) a substituted derivative of this, especially thymine or cytosine present in DNA.
– ORIGIN C19: from Ger. *Pyrimidin*, from **PYRIDINE**, with the insertion of *-im-* from **IMIDE**.

**pyrites** /pʌɪˈrʌɪtiːz/ (also **iron pyrites**; Mineralogy **pyrite**) ● **n.** a shiny yellow mineral consisting of iron disulphide, occurring as intersecting cubic crystals. See also **COPPER PYRITES**.
– DERIVATIVES **pyritic** adj. **pyritization** (also **-isation**) n. **pyritize** (also **-ise**) v.
– ORIGIN ME (denoting a mineral used for kindling fire): via L. from Gk *puritēs* 'of fire', from *pur* 'fire'.

**pyro-** ● **comb. form 1** of or relating to fire: *pyromania*. **2** Chemistry & Mineralogy formed or affected by heat: *pyroxene*.
– ORIGIN from Gk *pur* 'fire'.

**pyroclastic** /ˌpʌɪrə(ʊ)ˈklastɪk/ Geology ● **adj.** of or denoting rock fragments or ash erupted by a volcano, especially as a hot, dense, destructive flow. ● **n.** (**pyroclastics**) pyroclastic material.
– DERIVATIVES **pyroclast** n.

**pyroelectric** ● **adj.** having the property of becoming electrically charged when heated.
– DERIVATIVES **pyroelectricity** n.

**pyrogallol** /ˌpʌɪrə(ʊ)ˈgalɒl/ ● **n.** Chemistry a weakly acid crystalline organic compound chiefly used as a photographic developer.

**pyrogenic** ● **adj. 1** Medicine inducing fever. **2** resulting from combustion or heating.
– DERIVATIVES **pyrogenicity** n.

**pyrography** /pʌɪˈrɒgrəfi/ ● **n.** the art or technique of decorating wood or leather by burning a design on the surface with a heated metallic point.

**pyrolysis** /pʌɪˈrɒlɪsɪs/ ● **n.** Chemistry decomposition brought about by high temperatures.
– DERIVATIVES **pyrolyse** (US **pyrolyze**) v. **pyrolytic** adj.

**pyromania** ● **n.** an obsessive desire to set fire to things.
– DERIVATIVES **pyromaniac** n. **pyromaniacal** adj. **pyromanic** adj.

**pyrometer** /pʌɪˈrɒmɪtə/ ● **n.** an instrument for measuring high temperatures, especially in furnaces and kilns.
– DERIVATIVES **pyrometric** adj. **pyrometrically** adv. **pyrometry** n.

**pyrope** /ˈpʌɪrəʊp/ ● **n.** a deep red variety of garnet.
– ORIGIN C19: from Ger. *Pyrop*, via L. from Gk *purōpos* 'gold-bronze', lit. 'fiery-eyed'.

**pyrophoric** /ˌpʌɪrə(ʊ)ˈfɒrɪk/ ● **adj. 1** liable to ignite spontaneously in air. **2** (of an alloy) emitting sparks when scratched or struck.
– ORIGIN C19: from mod. L. *pyrophorus*, from Gk *purophoros* 'fire-bearing'.

**pyrophosphoric acid** /ˌpʌɪrə(ʊ)fɒsˈfɒrɪk/ ● **n.** Chemistry a glassy solid obtained by heating phosphoric acid. [$H_4P_2O_7$.]
– DERIVATIVES **pyrophosphate** n.

**pyrosis** /pʌɪˈrəʊsɪs/ ● **n.** technical term for **HEARTBURN**.
– ORIGIN C18: mod. L., from Gk *purōsis*, from *puroun* 'set on fire'.

**pyrotechnic** /ˌpʌɪrə(ʊ)ˈtɛknɪk/ ● **adj. 1** of or relating to fireworks. **2** brilliant or spectacular.
– DERIVATIVES **pyrotechnical** adj. **pyrotechnist** n.
– ORIGIN C19: from **PYRO-** + Gk *tekhnē* 'art' + **-IC**.

**pyrotechnics** ● **pl. n. 1** a firework display. ➤[treated as sing.] the art of making fireworks or staging firework displays. **2** a spectacular performance or display: *vocal pyrotechnics*.

**pyrotechny** ● **n. 1** historical the use of fire in alchemy. **2** another term for **PYROTECHNICS**.
– ORIGIN C16: from Fr. *pyrotechnie* or mod. L. *pyrotechnia*, from Gk *pur* + *tekhnē* 'art'.

**pyroxene** /pʌɪˈrɒksiːn/ ● **n.** any of a large class of rock-forming silicate minerals typically occurring as prismatic crystals.
– ORIGIN C19: from **PYRO-** + Gk *xenos* 'stranger' (because supposedly alien to igneous rocks).

**pyrrhic**[1] /ˈpɪrɪk/ ● **adj.** (of a victory) won at too great a cost to have been worthwhile for the victor.
– ORIGIN C19: from the name of *Pyrrhus*, a king of Epirus who defeated the Romans at Asculum in 279 BC but sustained heavy losses, + **-IC**.

**pyrrhic**[2] /ˈpɪrɪk/ ● **n.** a metrical foot of two short or un-

accented syllables. • **adj.** written in or based on pyrrhics.
– ORIGIN C17: via L. from Gk *purrhikhios* (*pous*) 'pyrrhic (foot)', the metre of a song accompanying a war dance, named after *Purrhikhos*, inventor of the dance.

**Pyrrhonism** /ˈpɪrənɪz(ə)m/ • **n.** the doctrine of the Greek sceptic philosopher Pyrrho (*c.*365–*c.*270 BC).
– DERIVATIVES **Pyrrhonist** n. & adj.

**pyrrole** /ˈpɪrəʊl/ • **n.** Chemistry a sweet-smelling heterocyclic liquid compound present in bone oil and coal tar.
– ORIGIN C19: from Gk *purrhos* 'reddish' + L. *oleum* 'oil'.

**pyruvic acid** /pʌɪˈruːvɪk/ • **n.** Biochemistry a yellowish organic acid which is an intermediate in many metabolic processes.
– DERIVATIVES **pyruvate** n.
– ORIGIN C19: from mod. L. *acidum pyruvicum*, from *acidum* 'acid' + *pyruvicum* based on **PYRO-** (denoting an acid) + L. *uva* 'grape'.

**Pythagoras' theorem** • **n.** the theorem that the square on the hypotenuse of a right-angled triangle is equal in area to the sum of the squares on the other two sides.

**Pythagorean** /pʌɪˌθagəˈriːən/ • **adj.** of or relating to the Greek philosopher and mathematician Pythagoras (*c.*580–500 BC) or his philosophy. • **n.** a follower of Pythagoras.

**Pythian** /ˈpɪθɪən/ • **adj.** of or relating to Delphi in Greece, or to its ancient oracle of Apollo.
– ORIGIN from *Puthō*, a former name of Delphi.

**python** • **n.** a large non-venomous snake which kills prey by constriction. [*Python* (tropical Asia and Africa) and other genera in Australasia: many species.]
– DERIVATIVES **pythonic** adj.
– ORIGIN C16: via L. from Gk *Puthōn*, the name of a huge serpent killed by Apollo.

**Pythonesque** • **adj.** resembling the absurdist or surrealist humour of *Monty Python's Flying Circus*, a British television comedy series (1969–74).

**pythoness** • **n.** archaic a woman believed to be possessed by a familiar spirit and to be able to foresee the future.
– ORIGIN ME: from OFr. *phitonise*, from an alt. of late L. *pythonissa*, based on Gk *puthōn* 'soothsaying demon'; cf. **PYTHIAN**.

**pyuria** /pʌɪˈjʊərɪə/ • **n.** Medicine the presence of pus in the urine, typically from bacterial infection.
– ORIGIN C19: from Gk *puon* 'pus' + **-URIA**.

**pyx** /pɪks/ (also **pix**) • **n.** **1** Christian Church the container in which the consecrated bread of the Eucharist is kept. **2** (in the UK) a box at the Royal Mint in which specimen gold and silver coins are deposited to be tested annually.
– ORIGIN ME: from L. *pyxis*, from Gk *puxis* 'box'.

**pyxidium** /pɪkˈsɪdɪəm/ • **n.** (pl. **pyxidia** /-dɪə/) Botany a seed capsule that splits open so that the top comes off like the lid of a box.
– ORIGIN C19: mod. L., from Gk *puxidion*, dimin. of *puxis* 'box'.

**pzazz** • **n.** variant spelling of **PIZZAZZ**.

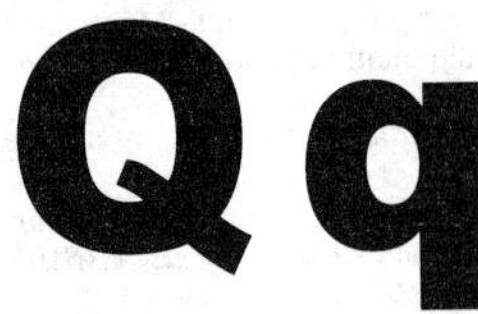

**Q**[1] (also **q**) ● n. (pl. **Qs** or **Q's**) **1** the seventeenth letter of the alphabet. **2** denoting the next after P in a set of items, categories, etc.

**Q**[2] ● abbrev. **1** quarter (used to refer to a specified quarter of the financial year): *Q4*. **2** queen (used especially in card games and chess). **3** question. **4** Theology denoting the hypothetical source of the passages shared by the gospels of Matthew and Luke, but not found in Mark. [prob. from Ger. *Quelle* 'source'.]

**q** ● symb. Physics electric charge.
– ORIGIN C19: initial letter of *quantity*.

**QA** ● abbrev. quality assurance.

**Qabalah** ● n. variant spelling of **KABBALAH**.

**Qatari** /ka'tɑːri/ ● n. a native or inhabitant of Qatar, a country in the Persian Gulf. ● adj. of or relating to Qatar.

**qawwali** /kə'vɑːli/ ● n. a style of Muslim devotional music associated particularly with Sufis in Pakistan.
– ORIGIN from Arab. *qawwālī*, from *Qawwāl* 'loquacious', also 'singer'.

**QB** ● abbrev. **1** American Football quarterback. **2** Law Queen's Bench.

**QC** ● abbrev. **1** quality control. **2** Quebec (in official postal use). **3** Law Queen's Counsel.

**QCD** ● abbrev. quantum chromodynamics.

**Q-Celtic** ● n. & adj. another term for **GOIDELIC**.
– ORIGIN *Q*, from the retention of the Indo-Eur. *kw* sound as *q* or *c* in this group of langs.

**QED** ● abbrev. **1** quantum electrodynamics. **2** quod erat demonstrandum.

**Q fever** ● n. an infectious fever caused by rickettsiae.
– ORIGIN 1930s: from *Q* for *query* + **FEVER**.

**qi** /kiː/ ● n. variant spelling of **CHI**[2].

**qibla** ● n. variant spelling of **KIBLAH**.

**qigong** /tʃiː'gɒŋ/ ● n. a Chinese system of physical exercises and breathing control related to tai chi.
– ORIGIN from Chin.

**qintar** /'kɪntɑː/ ● n. (pl. same, **qintars**, or **qindarka**) a monetary unit of Albania, equal to one hundredth of a lek.
– ORIGIN from Albanian *qindar*, from *qind* 'hundred'.

**Qld** ● abbrev. Queensland.

**QM** ● abbrev. Quartermaster.

**QMG** ● abbrev. Quartermaster General.

**QMS** ● abbrev. Quartermaster Sergeant.

**QPM** ● abbrev. (in the UK) Queen's Police Medal.

**qr** ● abbrev. quarter(s).

**Q-ship** ● n. a merchant ship with concealed weapons, used in an attempt to destroy submarines.
– ORIGIN First World War: from *Q* as a non-explicit symbol of the type of vessel + **SHIP**.

**QSO** ● abbrev. quasi-stellar object, a quasar.

**qt** ● abbrev. quart(s).

**q.t.** ● n. (in phr. **on the q.t.**) informal secretly.
– ORIGIN C19: abbrev. of *quiet*.

**qua** /kweɪ, kwɑː/ ● conj. formal in the capacity of.
– ORIGIN L., ablative fem. sing. of *qui* 'who'.

**quack**[1] ● n. the characteristic harsh sound made by a duck. ● v. make this sound.
– ORIGIN C16: imitative.

**quack**[2] ● n. **1** an unqualified person who dishonestly claims to have medical knowledge. **2** Brit. informal a doctor.
– DERIVATIVES **quackery** n. **quackish** adj.
– ORIGIN C17: abbrev. of earlier *quacksalver*, from Du., prob. from obs. *quacken* 'prattle' + *salf, zalf* (see **SALVE**[1]).

**quack grass** ● n. North American term for **COUCH**[2].
– ORIGIN C19: var. of *quick*, northern form of **QUITCH**.

**quad** ● n. **1** a quadrangle. **2** a quadruplet. **3** quadraphony. **4** (in telephony) a group of four insulated conductors twisted together. **5** Printing a small metal block lower than type height, used in letterpress printing for filling up short lines. [abbrev. of the earlier printing term *quadrat*.]

**quad bike** ● n. a motorcycle with four large tyres, for off-road use.

**quadragenarian** /ˌkwɒdrədʒɪ'nɛːrɪən/ ● n. a person who is between 40 and 49 years old.
– ORIGIN C19: from late L. *quadragenarius* (based on L. *quadraginta* 'forty') + **-AN**.

**Quadragesima** /ˌkwɒdrə'dʒɛsɪmə/ ● n. the first Sunday in Lent.
– ORIGIN from eccles. L., fem. of L. *quadragesimus* 'fortieth', from *quadraginta* 'forty' (Lent lasting forty days).

**quadragesimal** ● adj. archaic belonging or appropriate to the period of Lent.

**quadrangle** ● n. **1** a four-sided geometrical figure, especially a square or rectangle. **2** a square or rectangular courtyard enclosed by buildings.
– ORIGIN ME: from OFr., or from late L. *quadrangulum* 'square', neut. of *quadrangulus*, from L. *quadri-* 'four' + *angulus* 'corner, angle'.

**quadrangular** ● adj. **1** having four sides. **2** Brit. involving four teams competing against each other.

**quadrant** ● n. technical **1** each of four parts of a circle, plane, body, etc. divided by two lines or planes at right angles. **2** historical an instrument for taking angular measurements, consisting of a graduated quarter circle and a sighting mechanism. **3** a frame, typically in the form of a quarter circle, enclosing a steering mechanism or control lever.
– DERIVATIVES **quadrantal** adj.
– ORIGIN ME: from L. *quadrans, quadrant-* 'quarter', from *quattuor* 'four'.

**quadraphonic** (also **quadrophonic**) ● adj. (of sound reproduction) transmitted through four channels.
– DERIVATIVES **quadraphonically** adv. **quadraphonics** pl. n. **quadraphony** /-'drɒf(ə)ni/ n.
– ORIGIN 1960s: from **QUADRI-** + a shortened form of **STEREOPHONIC**.

**quadrat** /'kwɒdrət/ ● n. Ecology a randomly selected small area used in assessing the local distribution of plants or animals.
– ORIGIN C20: var. of **QUADRATE**.

**quadrate** ● n. /'kwɒdrət/ (also **quadrate bone**) Zoology a squarish bone in the skull of a bird or reptile, with which the jaw articulates. ● adj. /'kwɒdrət/ roughly square or rectangular. ● v. /kwɒ'dreɪt, 'kwɒdreɪt/ (usu. **quadrate with**) archaic conform.
– ORIGIN ME: from L. *quadrat-*, *quadrare* 'make square', from *quattuor* 'four'.

**quadratic** /kwɒ'dratɪk/ ● adj. Mathematics involving the second and no higher power of an unknown quantity or variable.
– ORIGIN C17: from Fr. *quadratique* or mod. L. *quadraticus*, from *quadratus*, *quadrare* (see **QUADRATE**).

**quadrature** /'kwɒdrətʃə/ ● n. **1** Mathematics the process of constructing a square with an area equal to that of a circle or other curved figure. **2** Astronomy the position of the moon or a planet when 90° from the sun in the sky. **3** Electronics a phase difference of 90° between two waves of

the same frequency.
– ORIGIN C16: from L. *quadratura* 'a square', from *quadrare* (see **QUADRATE**).

**quadrennial** /kwɒˈdrɛnɪəl/ ● **adj.** lasting for or recurring every four years.
– DERIVATIVES **quadrennially** adv.
– ORIGIN C17: from L. *quadrennium* (from *quadri-* 'four' + *annus* 'year') + **-AL**.

**quadrennium** /kwɒˈdrɛnɪəm/ ● **n.** (pl. **quadrennia** /-nɪə/ or **quadrenniums**) a period of four years.

**quadri-** ● **comb. form** four; having four: *quadriplegia*.
– ORIGIN from L., from *quattuor* 'four'.

**quadric** /ˈkwɒdrɪk/ ● **adj.** Geometry denoting a surface or curve described by an equation of the second degree.
– ORIGIN C19: from L. *quadra* 'square' + **-IC**.

**quadriceps** /ˈkwɒdrɪsɛps/ ● **n.** (pl. same) a large muscle at the front of the thigh which acts to extend the leg.
– ORIGIN C16: from L., 'four-headed', from *quadri-* 'four' + *-ceps* (from *caput* 'head').

**quadrilateral** ● **n.** a four-sided figure. ● **adj.** having four straight sides.
– ORIGIN C17: from late L. *quadrilaterus* + **-AL**.

**quadrille**[1] /kwɒˈdrɪl/ ● **n.** a square dance performed typically by four couples and containing five figures, each of which is a complete dance in itself. ➤ a piece of music for such a dance.
– ORIGIN C18: from Fr., from Sp. *cuadrilla* or Ital. *quadriglia* 'troop, company'.

**quadrille**[2] /kwɒˈdrɪl/ ● **n.** a trick-taking card game for four players using a pack lacking eights, nines, and tens, fashionable in the 18th century.
– ORIGIN C18: from Fr., perh. from Sp. *cuartillo* (from *cuarto* 'fourth').

**quadrille**[3] /kwɒˈdrɪl/ ● **n.** paper printed with a ruled grid of small squares.
– ORIGIN C19: from Fr. *quadrillé*, from *quadrille* 'small square'.

**quadrillion** /kwɒˈdrɪljən/ ● **cardinal number** (pl. **quadrillions** or (with numeral) same) **1** a thousand raised to the power of five ($10^{15}$). **2** dated, chiefly Brit. a thousand raised to the power of eight ($10^{24}$).
– DERIVATIVES **quadrillionth** ordinal number.
– ORIGIN C17: from Fr., from *million*, by substitution of **QUADRI-** for the initial letters.

**quadripartite** /ˌkwɒdrɪˈpɑːtʌɪt/ ● **adj. 1** consisting of four parts. **2** shared by or involving four parties.

**quadriplegia** /ˌkwɒdrɪˈpliːdʒə/ ● **n.** Medicine paralysis of all four limbs.
– DERIVATIVES **quadriplegic** adj. & n.

**quadrivalent** /ˌkwɒdrɪˈveɪl(ə)nt/ ● **adj.** Chemistry another term for **TETRAVALENT**.

**quadrivium** /kwɒˈdrɪvɪəm/ ● **n.** a medieval university course comprising arithmetic, geometry, astronomy, and music. Compare with **TRIVIUM**.
– ORIGIN L., lit. 'the place where four roads meet'.

**quadroon** /kwɒˈdruːn/ ● **n.** a person whose parents are a mulatto and a white person and who is therefore one-quarter black by descent.
– ORIGIN C18: via Fr. from Sp. *cuarterón*, from *cuarto* 'quarter'; later assimilated to words beginning with **QUADRI-**.

**quadrophonic** ● **adj.** variant spelling of **QUADRAPHONIC**.

**quadrumanous** /kwɒˈdruːmənəs, ˌkwɒdrʊˈmɑːnəs/ ● **adj.** Zoology, dated (of primates) having all four feet modified as hands, i.e. having opposable digits.
– ORIGIN C17: from mod. L. *Quadrumana* (former order name, neut. pl. of *quadrumanus*, from *quadru-* 'four' + L. *manus* 'hand') + **-OUS**.

**quadruped** /ˈkwɒdrʊpɛd/ ● **n.** an animal which has four feet, especially an ungulate mammal.
– DERIVATIVES **quadrupedal** /-ˈpiːd(ə)l, -ˈruːpɪd(ə)l/ adj. **quadrupedalism** n.
– ORIGIN C17: from Fr. *quadrupède* or L. *quadrupes, quadruped-*, from *quadru-* 'four' + *pes, ped-* 'foot'.

**quadruple** /ˈkwɒdrʊp(ə)l, kwɒˈdruːp(ə)l/ ● **adj. 1** consisting of four parts or elements. **2** consisting of four times as much or as many. **3** (of time in music) having four beats in a bar. ● **v.** increase or be increased fourfold. ● **n.** a quadruple thing, number, or amount.
– DERIVATIVES **quadruply** adv.
– ORIGIN ME: via Fr. from L. *quadruplus*, from *quadru-* 'four' + *-plus* as in *duplus* (see **DUPLE**).

**quadruplet** /ˈkwɒdrʊplɪt, kwɒˈdruːplɪt/ ● **n. 1** each of four children born at one birth. **2** Music a group of four notes to be performed in the time of three.
– ORIGIN C18: from **QUADRUPLE**, on the pattern of *triplet*.

**quadruplicate** ● **adj.** /kwɒˈdruːplɪkət/ **1** consisting of four parts or elements. **2** of which four copies are made. ● **v.** /kwɒˈdruːplɪkeɪt/ **1** multiply by four. **2** [usu. as adj. **quadruplicated**] make or provide four copies of.
– DERIVATIVES **quadruplication** n. **quadruplicity** n.
– ORIGIN C17: from L. *quadruplicat-, quadruplicare* 'quadruple'.

**quadrupole** /ˈkwɒdrʊpəʊl/ ● **n.** Physics a unit or arrangement of four equal monopoles or two equal dipoles with alternating polarity.

**quaestor** /ˈkwiːstə/ ● **n.** (in ancient Rome) any of a number of officials in charge of public revenue and expenditure.
– DERIVATIVES **quaestorial** adj. **quaestorship** n.
– ORIGIN L., from an old form of *quaesit-, quaerere* 'seek'.

**quaff** /kwɒf/ ● **v.** drink (something) heartily.
– DERIVATIVES **quaffable** adj. **quaffer** n.
– ORIGIN C16: prob. imitative of the sound of drinking.

**quag** /kwag, kwɒg/ ● **n.** archaic a marshy or boggy place.
– DERIVATIVES **quaggy** adj.
– ORIGIN C16: rel. to dial. *quag* 'shake'; prob. symbolic, the *qu-* suggesting movement (as in *quake*).

**quagga** /ˈkwagə/ ● **n.** an extinct South African zebra with a yellowish-brown coat with darker stripes. [*Equus quagga*.]
– ORIGIN S. Afr. Du., prob. from Khoikhoi, imitative of its braying.

**quagmire** /ˈkwagmʌɪə, ˈkwɒg-/ ● **n. 1** a soft boggy area of land that gives way underfoot. **2** a complex or difficult situation.

**quahog** /ˈkwɔːhɒg, ˈkwɑː-/ (also **quahaug** /-hɔːg/) ● **n.** N. Amer. a large, rounded edible clam of the Atlantic coast of North America. [*Venus mercenaria*.]
– ORIGIN C18: from Narragansett *poquaûhock*.

**quaich** /kweɪk, -x/ (also **quaigh**) ● **n.** Scottish a shallow drinking cup, typically with two handles.
– ORIGIN C16: from Sc. Gaelic *cuach* 'cup'.

**quail**[1] ● **n.** (pl. same or **quails**) a small short-tailed game bird. [*Coturnix coturnix* and other species.]
– ORIGIN ME: from OFr. *quaille*, from med. L. *coacula* (prob. imitative of its call).

**quail**[2] ● **v.** feel or show fear or apprehension.
– ORIGIN ME (in the sense 'waste away'): of unknown origin.

**quaint** ● **adj.** attractively unusual or old-fashioned.
– DERIVATIVES **quaintly** adv. **quaintness** n.
– ORIGIN ME (orig. in the sense 'clever', 'ingenious'): from OFr. *cointe*, from L. *cognit-, cognoscere* 'ascertain'.

**quake** ● **v. 1** (especially of the earth) shake or tremble. **2** shudder with fear. ● **n.** informal an earthquake.
– DERIVATIVES **quaky** adj. (**-ier, -iest**).
– ORIGIN OE *cwacian*.

**Quaker** ● **n.** a member of the Religious Society of Friends, a Christian movement devoted to peaceful principles and rejecting both formal ministry and all set forms of worship.
– DERIVATIVES **Quakerish** adj. **Quakerism** n.
– ORIGIN from **QUAKE** + **-ER**[1], perh. alluding to the founder's direction to his followers to 'tremble at the name of the Lord'.

**quaking grass** ● **n.** a grass with oval or heart-shaped flower heads which tremble in the wind. [Genus *Briza*.]

**quale** /ˈkweɪli/ ● **n.** (pl. **qualia** /ˈkweɪlɪə/) Philosophy a quality or property as perceived or experienced by a person.
– ORIGIN C17: from L., neut. of *qualis* 'of what kind'.

**qualification** ● **n. 1** the action of qualifying or the fact of becoming qualified. **2** a pass of an examination or an official completion of a course. **3** a quality that qualifies someone for a job or activity. **4** a condition that must be fulfilled before a right can be acquired. **5** a statement or

assertion that qualifies another.
– DERIVATIVES **qualificatory** adj.

**qualify** ● v. (-ies, -ied) **1** (often **qualify for**) be entitled to a benefit or privilege by fulfilling a necessary condition. ➤ fulfil the necessary conditions to be eligible for a competition. ➤ be or make properly entitled to be classed in a particular way. **2** become officially recognized as a practitioner of a profession or activity, typically by undertaking a course and passing examinations. ➤ make competent or knowledgeable enough to do something. **3** make (a statement or assertion) less absolute. ➤ archaic make less severe or extreme. **4** Grammar (of a word or phrase) attribute a quality to (another word, especially a preceding noun).
– DERIVATIVES **qualifiable** adj. **qualifier** n.
– ORIGIN ME (in the sense 'describe in a particular way'): from Fr. *qualifier*, from med. L. *qualificare*, from L. *qualis* (see QUALITY).

**qualitative** /'kwɒlɪtətɪv/ ● adj. **1** of, concerned with, or measured by quality. Often contrasted with QUANTITATIVE. **2** Grammar (of an adjective) describing the quality of something in size, appearance, etc.
– DERIVATIVES **qualitatively** adv.
– ORIGIN ME: from late L. *qualitativus*, from L. *qualitas* (see QUALITY).

**qualitative analysis** ● n. Chemistry identification of the constituents present in a substance.

**quality** ● n. (pl. -ies) **1** the standard of something as measured against other things of a similar kind. ➤ general excellence. ➤ archaic high social standing. **2** a distinctive attribute or characteristic. ➤ Phonetics the distinguishing characteristic or characteristics of a speech sound.
– ORIGIN ME: from OFr. *qualite*, from L. *qualitas*, from *qualis* 'of what kind, of such a kind'.

**quality control** ● n. a system of maintaining standards in manufactured products by testing a sample of the output against the specification.
– DERIVATIVES **quality controller** n.

**quality time** ● n. time devoted exclusively to another person in order to strengthen a relationship.

**qualm** /kwɑːm, kwɔːm/ ● n. **1** a feeling of doubt or unease, especially about one's conduct. **2** archaic a momentary faint or sick feeling.
– DERIVATIVES **qualmish** adj.
– ORIGIN C16: perh. rel. to OE *cw(e)alm* 'pain', of Gmc origin.

**quamash** /kwə'maʃ, 'kwɒmaʃ/ ● n. variant spelling of CAMAS.

**quandary** /'kwɒnd(ə)ri/ ● n. (pl. -ies) a state of uncertainty over what to do in a difficult situation: *Kate was in a quandary.*
– ORIGIN C16: perh. partly from L. *quando* 'when'.

**quango** /'kwaŋgəʊ/ ● n. (pl. -os) Brit., chiefly derogatory a semi-public administrative body with financial support from and senior appointments made by the government.
– ORIGIN 1970s (orig. US): acronym from *quasi* (or *quasi-autonomous*) *non-government(al) organization*.

**quant** /kwɒnt, kwant/ ● n. Brit. a pole for propelling a barge or punt, with a prong at the bottom to prevent it sinking into the mud.
– ORIGIN ME: perh. from L. *contus*, from Gk *kontos* 'boat pole'.

**quanta** plural form of QUANTUM.

**quantal** /'kwɒnt(ə)l/ ● adj. technical composed of discrete units or quanta; varying in steps rather than continuously.
– DERIVATIVES **quantally** adv.

**quantic** ● n. Mathematics a homogeneous function of two or more variables having rational or integral coefficients.
– ORIGIN C19: from L. *quantus* 'how great, how much' + -IC.

**quantifier** ● n. **1** Logic an expression (e.g. *some*) that indicates the scope of a term to which it is attached. **2** Grammar a determiner or pronoun indicative of quantity (e.g. *all*).

**quantify** ● v. (-ies, -ied) **1** express or measure the quantity of. **2** Logic define the application of (a term or proposition) by the use of a quantifier.
– DERIVATIVES **quantifiability** n. **quantifiable** adj. **quantification** n.
– ORIGIN C16: from med. L. *quantificare*, from L. *quantus* 'how much'.

**quantitate** /'kwɒntɪteɪt/ ● v. Medicine & Biology determine the quantity or extent of.
– DERIVATIVES **quantitation** n.
– ORIGIN 1960s: from QUANTITY + -ATE[3].

**quantitative** /'kwɒntɪˌtətɪv, -ˌteɪtɪv/ ● adj. **1** of, concerned with, or measured by quantity. Often contrasted with QUALITATIVE. **2** denoting or relating to verse whose metre is based on the length of syllables, as in Latin, as opposed to the stress, as in English.
– DERIVATIVES **quantitatively** adv.
– ORIGIN C16 (in the sense 'having spatial extent'): from med. L. *quantitativus*, from L. *quantitas* (see QUANTITY).

**quantitative analysis** ● n. Chemistry measurement of the quantities of particular constituents present in a substance.

**quantitive** ● adj. another term for QUANTITATIVE.
– DERIVATIVES **quantitively** adv.

**quantity** ● n. (pl. -ies) **1** a certain amount or number. ➤ a considerable number or amount. **2** the property of something that is measurable: *wages depended on quantity of output, regardless of quality.* **3** Phonetics the perceived length of a vowel sound or syllable.
– ORIGIN ME: from OFr. *quantite*, from L. *quantitas*, from *quantus* 'how great, how much'.

**quantity surveyor** ● n. Brit. a person who calculates the amount and cost of materials needed for building work.

**quantize** (also -ise) ● v. **1** Physics form into quanta; make subject to quantum theory. **2** Electronics approximate (a continuously varying signal) by one whose amplitude is restricted to prescribed values.
– DERIVATIVES **quantization** n. **quantizer** n.

**quantum** /'kwɒntəm/ ● n. (pl. **quanta** /-tə/) **1** Physics a discrete quantity of energy proportional in magnitude to a particular frequency of radiation and corresponding e.g. to a single photon or to a transition of an atom between energy states. ➤ an analogous unit amount of something. **2** a total amount, especially an amount of money legally payable in damages. ➤ a share.
– ORIGIN C16: from L., neut. of *quantus* (see QUANTITY).

**quantum chromodynamics** ● pl. n. [treated as sing.] Physics a theory in which the strong interaction is described in terms of an interaction between quarks transmitted by gluons.
– ORIGIN *chromodynamics* from CHROMO-[2] 'colour' (property of quarks) + DYNAMICS.

**quantum computer** ● n. a computer which makes use of the quantum states of subatomic particles to store information.
– DERIVATIVES **quantum computing** n.

**quantum electrodynamics** ● pl. n. [treated as sing.] a theory concerned with the electromagnetic field and its interaction with electrically charged particles.

**quantum jump** ● n. **1** Physics an abrupt transition of an electron, atom, etc. from one state to another, with the absorption or emission of a quantum. **2** (also **quantum leap**) a sudden large increase or advance.

**quantum mechanics** ● pl. n. [treated as sing.] the mathematical description of the motion and interaction of subatomic particles in terms of quanta, incorporating the idea that particles can also be regarded as waves.
– DERIVATIVES **quantum-mechanical** adj.

**quantum number** ● n. Physics a number expressing the value of some property of a particle which occurs in quanta.

**quantum theory** ● n. Physics a theory of matter and energy based on the concept of quanta.

**quarantine** ● n. a state, period, or place of isolation for people or animals that have arrived from elsewhere or been exposed to contagious disease. ● v. put in quarantine.
– ORIGIN C17: from Ital. *quarantina* 'forty days', from *quaranta* 'forty'.

**quark**[1] /kwɑːk, kwɔːk/ ● n. Physics any of a group of subatomic particles carrying a fractional electric charge,

postulated as building blocks of the hadrons.
– ORIGIN 1960s: invented by the Amer. physicist Murray Gell-Mann and assoc. with the line 'Three quarks for Muster Mark' in Joyce's *Finnegans Wake* (1939).

**quark**[2] /kwɑːk/ ● **n.** a type of low-fat curd cheese.
– ORIGIN 1930s: from Ger. *Quark* 'curd, curds'.

**quarrel**[1] ● **n. 1** an angry argument or disagreement. **2** a reason for disagreement. ● **v.** (**quarrelled**, **quarrelling**; US **quarreled**, **quarreling**) **1** have a quarrel. ➤(**quarrel with**) disagree with. **2** W. Indian complain; scold.
– DERIVATIVES **quarreller** n.
– ORIGIN ME: from OFr. *querele*, from L. *querel(l)a* 'complaint', from *queri* 'complain'.

**quarrel**[2] ● **n.** historical a short heavy square-headed arrow or bolt for a crossbow or arbalest.
– ORIGIN ME: from OFr., based on late L. *quadrus* 'square'; cf. QUARRY[3].

**quarrelsome** ● **adj.** given to or characterized by quarrelling.
– DERIVATIVES **quarrelsomely** adv. **quarrelsomeness** n.

**quarrion** /ˈkwɒrɪən/ (also **quarrien**) ● **n.** Austral. a cockatiel.
– ORIGIN C20: from Wiradhuri *guwarraying*.

**quarry**[1] ● **n.** (pl. **-ies**) a place, typically a large pit, from which stone or other materials may be extracted. ● **v.** (**-ies**, **-ied**) extract from a quarry. ➤cut into (rock or ground) to obtain stone or other materials.
– DERIVATIVES **quarrier** n. **quarryman** n. (pl. **-men**).
– ORIGIN ME: from a var. of med. L. *quareria*, from OFr. *quarriere*, based on L. *quadrum* 'a square'.

**quarry**[2] ● **n.** (pl. **-ies**) an animal being hunted. ➤a person or thing being chased or sought.
– ORIGIN ME (orig. denoting the parts of a deer placed on a hide for the hounds): from OFr. *cuiree*, alt. of *couree*, based on L. *cor* 'heart'.

**quarry**[3] ● **n.** (pl. **-ies**) **1** a diamond-shaped pane in a lattice window. **2** (also **quarry tile**) an unglazed floor tile.
– ORIGIN C16: alt. of QUARREL[2], which in ME denoted a lattice windowpane.

**quart** ● **n. 1** a unit of liquid capacity equal to a quarter of a gallon or two pints, equivalent in Britain to approximately 1.13 litres and in US to approximately 0.94 litre. ➤N. Amer. a unit of dry capacity equivalent to approximately 1.10 litres. **2** /kɑːt/ (also **quarte** or **carte**) Fencing the fourth of eight parrying positions. **3** (in piquet) a sequence of four cards of the same suit.
– ORIGIN ME: from OFr. *quarte*, from L. *quarta* (*pars*) 'fourth (part)', from *quartus* 'fourth'.

**quartan** /ˈkwɔːt(ə)n/ ● **adj.** Medicine denoting a mild form of malaria causing a fever that recurs every third day.
– ORIGIN ME: from L. (*febris*) *quartana*, based on L. *quartus* 'fourth' (because, by inclusive reckoning, the fever recurs every fourth day).

**quarter** ● **n. 1** each of four equal or corresponding parts into which something is or can be divided. **2** a period of three months, used especially in reference to financial transactions. ➤chiefly US each of four terms into which a school or university year may be divided. **3** a quarter-hour. **4** (**quarters**) the haunches or hindquarters of a horse. **5** a US or Canadian coin worth 25 cents. **6** one fourth of a pound weight (avoirdupois, equal to 4 ounces). ➤one fourth of a hundredweight (Brit. 28 lb or US 25 lb). ➤Brit. a grain measure equivalent to 8 bushels. **7** a part of a town or city with a specific character or use. **8** the direction of one of the points of the compass. **9** either side of a ship aft of the beam. **10** a person, group, area, etc. regarded as the source of something: *help from an unexpected quarter.* **11** (**quarters**) rooms or lodgings. **12** (in combat) pity or mercy. **13** Heraldry each of four or more roughly equal divisions of a shield. ➤a square charge covering the top left quarter of the field. ● **v. 1** divide into quarters. ➤historical cut the body of (an executed person) into four parts. **2** (**be quartered**) be stationed or lodged. **3** range over (an area) in all directions. **4** Heraldry display (different coats of arms) in quarters of a shield.
– ORIGIN ME: from OFr. *quartier*, from L. *quartarius* 'fourth part of a measure', from *quartus* 'fourth', from *quattuor* 'four'.

**quarterage** ● **n.** archaic a sum paid or received quarterly.

**quarterback** American Football ● **n.** a player stationed behind the centre who directs a team's offensive play. ● **v.** play as a quarterback for.

**quarter binding** ● **n.** a type of bookbinding in which the spine is bound in one material and the rest of the cover in another.
– DERIVATIVES **quarter-bound** adj.

**quarter day** ● **n.** Brit. each of four days on which some tenancies begin and end and quarterly payments fall due.

**quarterdeck** ● **n. 1** the part of a ship's upper deck near the stern, traditionally reserved for officers or for ceremonial use. **2** the officers of a ship or the navy.

**quarter-final** ● **n.** a match of a knockout competition preceding the semi-final.

**Quarter Horse** ● **n.** a horse of a small stocky agile breed, reputed to be the fastest breed over a quarter of a mile.

**quarter-hour** ● **n. 1** (also **quarter of an hour**) a period of fifteen minutes. **2** a point of time fifteen minutes before or after a full hour of the clock.

**quartering** ● **n. 1** (**quarterings**) Heraldry the coats of arms on a shield denoting the marriages into a family of the heiresses of others. **2** the provision of lodgings, especially for troops. **3** division into quarters.

**quarter-light** ● **n.** Brit. a window in the side of a motor vehicle other than a main door window.

**quarterly** ● **adj. 1** produced or occurring once every quarter of a year. **2** Heraldry divided into quarters. ● **adv. 1** once every quarter of a year. **2** Heraldry in the four, or in two diagonally opposite, quarters of a shield. ● **n.** (pl. **-ies**) a publication produced four times a year.

**quartermaster** ● **n. 1** a regimental officer in charge of quartering and supplies. **2** a naval petty officer responsible for steering and signals.

**Quartermaster General** ● **n.** the head of the army department in charge of the quartering and equipment of troops.

**quartermaster sergeant** ● **n.** a senior rank of non-commissioned officer in the army, above sergeant, having administrative duties.

**quartern** /ˈkwɔːt(ə)n/ ● **n.** Brit. archaic a quarter of a pint.
– ORIGIN ME: from OFr. *quart(e)ron*, from *quart(e)* (see QUART).

**quartern loaf** ● **n.** archaic a four-pound loaf.

**quarter note** ● **n.** Music, chiefly N. Amer. a crotchet.

**quarter plate** ● **n. 1** Brit. a photographic plate measuring $3\frac{1}{4} \times 4\frac{1}{4}$ inches (c.8.3 × 10.8 cm). **2** a photograph reproduced from this.

**quarter-pounder** ● **n.** a hamburger weighing a quarter of a pound.

**quarter section** ● **n.** N. Amer. a quarter of a square mile.

**quarter sessions** ● **pl. n.** historical (in England, Wales, and Northern Ireland) a court of limited criminal and civil jurisdiction and of appeal, usually held quarterly.

**quarterstaff** ● **n.** a stout pole 6–8 feet long, formerly used as a weapon.

**quarter tone** ● **n.** Music half a semitone.

**quartet** (also **quartette**) ● **n. 1** a group of four people playing music or singing together. ➤a composition for such a group. **2** a set of four people or things.
– ORIGIN C17: from Fr. *quartette*, from Ital. *quartetto*, from *quarto* 'fourth', from L. *quartus*.

**quartic** /ˈkwɔːtɪk/ ● **adj.** Mathematics denoting an equation, curve, etc. involving the fourth and no higher power of an unknown quantity or variable.
– ORIGIN C19: from L. *quartus* 'fourth' + -IC.

**quartile** /ˈkwɔːtʌɪl/ ● **n.** Statistics each of four equal groups into which a population can be divided according to the distribution of values of a particular variable.
– ORIGIN C19: from med. L. *quartilis*, from L. *quartus* 'fourth'.

**quarto** /ˈkwɔːtəʊ/ (abbrev.: **4to**) ● **n.** (pl. **-os**) a page or paper size resulting from folding a sheet into four leaves, typically 10 inches × 8 inches (254 × 203 mm). ➤a book of

this size.
– ORIGIN C16: from L. (*in*) *quarto* '(in) the fourth (of a sheet)', ablative of *quartus* 'fourth'.

**quartz** • n. a hard mineral consisting of silica, typically occurring as colourless or white hexagonal prisms.
– ORIGIN C18: from Ger. *Quarz*, from Polish dial. *kwardy*, corresp. to Czech *tvrdý* 'hard'.

**quartz clock** (or **watch**) • n. a clock (or watch) regulated by vibrations of an electrically driven quartz crystal.

**quartzite** • n. Geology compact, hard, granular rock consisting essentially of quartz.

**quasar** /ˈkweɪzɑː, -sɑː/ • n. Astronomy a massive and extremely remote celestial object which emits large amounts of energy and typically shows a starlike image.
– ORIGIN 1960s: contr. of *quasi-stellar.*

**quash** • v. **1** reject as invalid, especially by legal procedure. **2** suppress: *rumours of job losses were quashed.*
– ORIGIN ME: from OFr. *quasser* 'annul', from late L. *cassare* (med. L. also *quassare*), from *cassus* 'null, void'; cf. SQUASH[1].

**quasi-** /ˈkweɪzʌɪ, -sʌɪ, ˈkwɑːzi/ • comb. form **1** seemingly: *quasi-scientific.* **2** being partly or almost: *quasi-crystalline.*
– ORIGIN from L. *quasi* 'as if, almost'.

**quassia** /ˈkwɒʃə, ˈkwɒʃɪə, ˈkwasɪə/ • n. a South American shrub or small tree whose wood, bark, or root yields a medicinal tonic, insecticide, and vermifuge. [*Quassia amara* and other species.]
– ORIGIN named after Graman *Quassi*, the C18 Surinamese slave who discovered its medicinal properties.

**quatercentenary** /ˌkwatəsɛnˈtiːn(ə)ri, -ˈtɛn-, ˌkweɪtə-/ • n. (pl. **-ies**) a four-hundredth anniversary.
– ORIGIN C19: from L. *quater* 'four times' + CENTENARY.

**quaternary** /kwəˈtəːn(ə)ri/ • adj. **1** fourth in order or rank. **2** (**Quaternary**) Geology relating to or denoting the most recent period in the Cenozoic era, following the Tertiary period (comprising the Pleistocene and Holocene epochs and beginning 1.64 million years ago). **3** Chemistry denoting an ammonium compound containing a cation of the form $NR_4^+$, where R represents organic groups.
– ORIGIN ME: from L. *quaternarius*, from *quaterni* 'four at once', from *quater* 'four times', from *quattuor* 'four'.

**quaternion** /kwəˈtəːnɪən/ • n. **1** Mathematics a complex number of the form $w + xi + yj + zk$, where $w, x, y, z$ are real numbers and $i, j, k$ are imaginary units that satisfy certain conditions. **2** rare a set of four people or things.
– ORIGIN C19: from late L. *quaternio(n-)*, from L. *quarterni* (see QUATERNARY).

**quatorze** /kəˈtɔːz/ • n. (in piquet) a set of four aces, kings, queens, jacks, or tens in one hand.
– ORIGIN C18: Fr., lit. 'fourteen'.

**quatrain** /ˈkwɒtreɪn/ • n. a stanza of four lines, typically with alternate rhymes.
– ORIGIN C16: from Fr., from *quatre* 'four'.

**quatrefoil** /ˈkatrəfɔɪl/ • n. an ornamental design of four lobes or leaves, resembling a flower or clover leaf.
– ORIGIN C15: from Anglo-Norman Fr., from OFr. *quatre* 'four' + *foil* 'leaf'.

**quattrocento** /ˌkwatrə(ʊ)ˈtʃɛntəʊ/ • n. the 15th century as a period of Italian art or architecture.
– ORIGIN Ital., lit. '400' (shortened from *milquattrocento* '1400').

**quaver** • v. (of a voice) tremble. • n. **1** a tremble in a voice. **2** Music, chiefly Brit. a note having the value of an eighth of a semibreve or half a crotchet, represented by a large dot with a hooked stem.
– DERIVATIVES **quavering** adj. **quaveringly** adv. **quavery** adj.
– ORIGIN ME: from dial. *quave* 'quake, tremble', prob. from an OE word rel. to QUAKE.

**quay** • n. a platform lying alongside or projecting into water for loading and unloading ships.
– DERIVATIVES **quayage** n.
– ORIGIN ME *key*, from OFr. *kay*, of Celtic origin; spelling influenced by mod. Fr. *quai*.

**quayside** • n. a quay and the area around it.

**Que.** • abbrev. Quebec.

**quean** /kwiːn/ • n. archaic **1** an impudent girl or woman. **2** a prostitute.
– ORIGIN OE *cwene* 'woman', of Gmc origin.

**queasy** • adj. (-ier, -iest) **1** nauseous. ➤ inducing nausea. **2** slightly nervous or worried.
– DERIVATIVES **queasily** adv. **queasiness** n.
– ORIGIN ME *queisy, coisy*, of uncertain origin; perh. rel. to OFr. *coisier* 'to hurt'.

**Quebecker** /kwɪˈbɛkə/ (also **Quebecer**) • n. a native or inhabitant of the Canadian province or city of Quebec.

**Quechua** /ˈkɛtʃwə/ (also **Quecha** /ˈkɛtʃə/, **Quichua**) • n. (pl. same or **Quechuas**) **1** a member of an American Indian people of Peru and neighbouring countries. **2** the language or group of languages of this people.
– DERIVATIVES **Quechuan** adj. & n.
– ORIGIN Sp., from Quechua *ghechwa* 'temperate valleys'.

**queen** • n. **1** the female ruler of an independent state, especially one who inherits the position by right of birth. ➤ (also **queen consort**) a king's wife. ➤ a woman or girl holding the most important position in a festival or event. **2** a woman or thing regarded as the finest or most important in its sphere or group. **3** informal a man's wife or girlfriend. **4** the most powerful chess piece, able to move in any direction. **5** a playing card bearing a representation of a queen, ranking next below a king. **6** Entomology a reproductive female in a colony of ants, bees, wasps, or termites. **7** an adult female cat that has not been spayed. **8** informal a flamboyantly effeminate male homosexual. • v. **1** (**queen it**) (of a woman) act in an unpleasantly superior way. **2** Chess convert (a pawn) into a queen when it reaches the opponent's end of the board.
– DERIVATIVES **queendom** n. **queen-like** adj. **queenliness** n. **queenly** adj. (**-ier, -iest**). **queenship** n.
– ORIGIN OE *cwēn*, of Gmc origin; rel. to QUEAN.

**Queen Anne** • adj. denoting a style of English furniture or architecture characteristic of the early 18th century.

**Queen Anne's lace** • n. cow parsley.

**queen bee** • n. **1** the single reproductive female in a colony of honeybees. **2** informal a woman with a dominant or controlling position.

**queen cake** • n. a small, typically heart-shaped currant cake.

**queen dowager** • n. the widow of a king.

**queenie** • n. old-fashioned term for QUEEN (in sense 8).

**Queen in Council** • n. (in the UK) the Privy Council as issuing Orders in Council or receiving petitions when the reigning monarch is a queen.

**queen mother** • n. the widow of a king and mother of the sovereign.

**queen of puddings** • n. a pudding made with bread, jam, and meringue.

**Queen of the May** • n. a May queen.

**queen post** • n. either of two upright timbers between the tie beam and principal rafters of a roof truss.

**Queen's Bench** • n. (in the UK) a division of the High Court of Justice.

**Queensberry Rules** /ˈkwiːnzb(ə)ri/ • pl. n. the standard rules of boxing.
– ORIGIN C19: named after the 9th Marquess of *Queensberry*, who supervised the preparation of the rules in 1867.

**queen's bishop** • n. Chess each player's bishop on the queenside at the start of a game.

**Queen's bounty** • n. in the reign of a queen, the term for KING'S BOUNTY.

**Queen's Champion** • n. another term for CHAMPION OF ENGLAND.

**Queen's colour** • n. (in the UK) a union flag carried by a regiment along with its regimental colour.

**Queen's Counsel** • n. a senior barrister appointed on the recommendation of the Lord Chancellor.

**Queen's English** • n. the English language as correctly written and spoken in Britain.

**Queen's evidence** • n. English Law evidence for the prosecution given by a participant in the crime being tried.

**Queen's Guide** • n. (in the UK) a Guide who has

reached the highest rank of proficiency.

**Queen's highway** • **n.** Brit. the public road network.

**queenside** • **n.** Chess the half of the board on which each queen stands at the start of a game (the left-hand side for White, right for Black).

**queen-sized** (also **queen-size**) • **adj.** of a larger size than the standard but smaller than king-sized.

**queen's knight** • **n.** Chess each player's knight on the queenside at the start of a game.

**Queenslander** • **n.** a native or inhabitant of the Australian state of Queensland.

**Queen's Messenger** • **n.** (in the UK) a courier in the diplomatic service.

**queen's pawn** • **n.** Chess the pawn immediately in front of each player's queen at the start of a game.

**Queen's Proctor** • **n.** Law (in the UK) an official who has the right to intervene in probate, divorce, and nullity cases when collusion or the suppression of facts is alleged.

**queen's rook** • **n.** Chess each player's rook on the queenside at the start of a game.

**Queen's Scout** • **n.** (in the UK) a Scout who has reached the highest standard of proficiency.

**Queen's Speech** • **n.** (in the UK) a statement read by the sovereign at the opening of parliament, detailing the government's proposed legislative programme.

**queensware** • **n.** fine, cream-coloured Wedgwood pottery.
– ORIGIN C18 (as *Queen's ware*): named in honour of Queen Charlotte (wife of George III).

**queer** • **adj.** **1** strange; odd. ➤ Brit. informal, dated slightly ill. **2** informal, derogatory (of a man) homosexual. • **n.** informal, derogatory a homosexual man. • **v.** informal spoil or ruin.
– PHRASES **in Queer Street** Brit. informal, dated in difficulty or debt. **queer someone's pitch** Brit. spoil someone's plans or chances of doing something.
– DERIVATIVES **queerish** adj. **queerly** adv. **queerness** n.
– ORIGIN C16: considered to be from Ger. *quer* 'oblique, perverse', but the origin is doubtful.

**USAGE** queer

The word **queer** was first used to mean 'homosexual' in the early 20th century: it was originally, and usually still is, a deliberately derogatory term when used by heterosexual people. In recent years, however, gay people have taken the word **queer** and deliberately used it in place of **gay** or **homosexual**, in an attempt, by using the word positively, to deprive it of its negative power.

**quelea** /ˈkwiːlɪə/ • **n.** a brownish African weaver bird. [Genus *Quelea*: three species.]
– ORIGIN mod. L., perh. from med. L. *qualea* 'quail'.

**quell** • **v.** **1** put an end to, typically by force. **2** subdue or suppress.
– DERIVATIVES **queller** n.
– ORIGIN OE *cwellan* 'kill', of Gmc origin.

**quench** • **v.** **1** satisfy (thirst) by drinking. **2** satisfy (a desire). **3** extinguish (a fire). ➤ rapidly cool (hot metal). **4** stifle (a feeling). ➤ dated reduce to silence. **5** Physics & Electronics suppress or damp (luminescence, an oscillation, etc.). • **n.** an act of quenching something very hot.
– DERIVATIVES **quenchable** adj. **quencher** n. **quenchless** adj. (poetic/literary).
– ORIGIN OE *-cwencan* (in *acwencan* 'put out, extinguish'), of Gmc origin.

**quenelle** /kəˈnɛl/ • **n.** a small seasoned ball of fish or meat.
– ORIGIN Fr., prob. from Alsatian Ger. *knödel*.

**quercetin** /ˈkwəːsɪtɪn/ • **n.** Chemistry a yellow crystalline pigment present in plants, used as a food supplement to reduce allergic responses or boost immunity.
– ORIGIN C19: prob. from L. *quercetum* 'oak grove' (from *quercus* 'oak') + **-IN**[1].

**querist** /ˈkwɪərɪst/ • **n.** chiefly archaic a questioner.
– ORIGIN C17: from L. *quaerere* 'ask' + **-IST**.

**quern** /kwəːn/ • **n.** a simple hand mill for grinding grain, typically consisting of two circular stones (**quernstones**).
– ORIGIN OE *cweorn(e)*, of Gmc origin.

**querulous** /ˈkwɛrʊləs, ˈkwɛrjʊləs/ • **adj.** complaining in a petulant or whining manner.
– DERIVATIVES **querulously** adv. **querulousness** n.
– ORIGIN C15: from late L. *querulosus*, from L. *querulus*, from *queri* 'complain'.

**query** • **n.** (pl. **-ies**) **1** a question, especially one expressing doubt. **2** chiefly Printing a question mark. • **v.** (**-ies**, **-ied**) ask a query about something. ➤ N. Amer. put a query or queries to.
– ORIGIN C17: anglicized form of the L. imper. *quaere!*, from L. *quaerere* 'ask, seek'.

**quesadilla** /ˌkeɪsəˈdiːljə, -ˈdiːjə/ • **n.** a hot tortilla with a spicy cheese filling.
– ORIGIN from Sp.

**quest** • **n.** **1** a long or arduous search. **2** (in medieval romance) an expedition by a knight to accomplish a prescribed task. • **v.** search for something.
– DERIVATIVES **quester** (also **questor**) n. **questing** adj. **questingly** adv.
– ORIGIN ME: from OFr. *queste* (n.), *quester* (v.), based on L. *quaerere* 'ask, seek'.

**question** • **n.** **1** a sentence worded or expressed so as to elicit information. **2** a doubt. ➤ the raising of a doubt or objection. **3** a problem requiring resolution. **4** a matter or concern depending on conditions: *a question of age.* • **v.** **1** ask questions of. **2** express doubt about; object to.
– PHRASES **come** (or **bring**) **into question** become (or raise) an issue for further consideration or discussion. **in question** **1** being considered or discussed. **2** in doubt. **no question of** no possibility of. **out of the question** not possible. **put the question** require supporters and opponents of a debated proposal to record their votes.
– DERIVATIVES **questioner** n. **questioning** adj. **questioningly** adv.
– ORIGIN ME: from OFr. *question* (n.), *questionner* (v.), from L. *quaestio(n-)*, from *quaerere* 'ask, seek'.

**questionable** • **adj.** **1** open to doubt. **2** of suspect morality, honesty, value, etc.
– DERIVATIVES **questionability** n. **questionableness** n. **questionably** adv.

**questionary** • **n.** (pl. **-ies**) chiefly Medicine a questionnaire.

**question mark** • **n.** a punctuation mark (?) indicating a question.

**question master** • **n.** Brit. the questioner in a quiz or panel game.

**questionnaire** /ˌkwɛstʃəˈnɛː, ˌkɛstjə-/ • **n.** a set of printed questions, usually with a choice of answers, devised for a survey or statistical study.
– ORIGIN C19: from Fr., from *questionner* 'to question'.

**question time** • **n.** (in the UK) a period during proceedings in the House of Commons when MPs may question ministers.

**quetzal** /ˈkɛts(ə)l, ˈkwɛt-/ • **n.** **1** a long-tailed tropical American bird with iridescent green plumage and typically red underparts. [*Pharomachrus mocinno* and other species.] **2** the basic monetary unit of Guatemala, equal to 100 centavos.
– ORIGIN C19: from Sp., from Aztec *quetzalli* 'brightly coloured tail feather'.

**queue** • **n.** **1** a line or sequence of people or vehicles awaiting their turn to be attended to or to proceed. ➤ Computing a list of data items, commands, etc., stored so as to be retrievable in a definite order. **2** archaic a plait of hair worn at the back. • **v.** (**queues**, **queued**, **queuing** or **queueing**) wait in a queue. ➤ Computing arrange in a queue.
– ORIGIN C16 (as a heraldic term denoting an animal's tail): from Fr., based on L. *cauda* 'tail'; cf. **CUE**[2].

**queue-jump** • **v.** Brit. move forward out of turn in a queue.
– DERIVATIVES **queue-jumper** n.

**quibble** • **n.** **1** a slight objection or criticism. **2** archaic a pun. • **v.** argue about a trivial matter.
– DERIVATIVES **quibbler** n. **quibbling** adj. **quibblingly** adv.
– ORIGIN C17: dimin. of obs. *quib* 'a petty objection', prob. from L. *quibus*, dative and ablative pl. of *qui, quae, quod* 'who, what, which', freq. used in legal documents.

**quiche** /kiːʃ/ ● **n.** a baked flan with a savoury filling thickened with eggs.
– ORIGIN Fr., from Alsatian dial. *Küchen*.

**Quichua** /ˈkɪtʃwə/ ● **n.** variant of **QUECHUA**.

**quick** ● **adj.** **1** moving fast or doing something in a short time. ➤ lasting a short time. ➤ prompt. **2** intelligent. ➤ (of one's eye or ear) alert. **3** (of a person's temper) easily roused. ● **n.** **1** (**the quick**) the tender flesh below the growing part of a fingernail or toenail. ➤ the central or most sensitive part of someone or something. **2** [as pl. n. **the quick**] archaic those who are living.
– PHRASES **cut someone to the quick** cause someone deep distress. **quick and dirty** informal, chiefly US done or produced hastily. **a quick one** informal a rapidly consumed alcoholic drink. **quick with child** archaic at a stage of pregnancy when the fetus can be felt to move.
– DERIVATIVES **quickly** adv. **quickness** n.
– ORIGIN OE *cwic*, *cwicu* 'alive, animated, alert', of Gmc origin.

**quicken** ● **v.** **1** make or become quicker. **2** stimulate or be stimulated. ➤ give or restore life to. ➤ archaic make (a fire) burn brighter. **3** archaic (of a woman) reach a stage in pregnancy when the fetus can be felt to move. ➤ (of a fetus) begin to show signs of life.

**quick-fire** ● **adj.** **1** unhesitating and rapid. **2** (of a gun) firing shots in rapid succession.

**quick fix** ● **n.** a speedy but inadequate solution.

**quickie** informal ● **n.** **1** a rapidly consumed alcoholic drink. **2** a brief act of sexual intercourse. ● **adj.** done or made quickly.

**quicklime** ● **n.** a white caustic alkaline substance consisting of calcium oxide, obtained by heating limestone.

**quick march** ● **n.** a brisk military march.

**quicksand** ● **n.** (also **quicksands**) loose wet sand that sucks in anything resting on it.

**quickset** ● **n.** Brit. hedging, especially of hawthorn, grown from slips or cuttings.

**quicksilver** ● **n.** **1** liquid mercury. **2** [as modifier] moving or changing rapidly.

**quickstep** ● **n.** a fast foxtrot in 4/4 time. ● **v.** (**-stepped, -stepping**) dance the quickstep.

**quick-tempered** ● **adj.** easily angered.

**quickthorn** ● **n.** another term for **HAWTHORN**.

**quick time** ● **n.** Military marching at about 120 paces per minute.

**quick trick** ● **n.** Bridge a card such as an ace that can normally be relied on to win a trick.

**quick-witted** ● **adj.** showing an ability to think or respond quickly.
– DERIVATIVES **quick-wittedness** n.

**quid**[1] ● **n.** (pl. same) Brit. informal one pound sterling.
– PHRASES **not the full quid** Austral./NZ informal not intelligent. **quids in** Brit. informal profiting or likely to profit from something.
– ORIGIN C17 (denoting a sovereign): of obscure origin.

**quid**[2] ● **n.** a lump of chewing tobacco.
– ORIGIN C18: var. of **CUD**.

**quiddity** /ˈkwɪdɪti/ ● **n.** (pl. **-ies**) chiefly Philosophy the inherent nature or essence of a person or thing.
– ORIGIN ME: from med. L. *quidditas*, from L. *quid* 'what'.

**quidnunc** /ˈkwɪdnʌŋk/ ● **n.** archaic an inquisitive, gossipy person.
– ORIGIN C18: from L. *quid nunc?* 'what now?'

**quid pro quo** /ˌkwɪd prəʊ ˈkwəʊ/ ● **n.** (pl. **-os**) a favour or advantage given in return for something.
– ORIGIN L., 'something for something'.

**quiescent** /kwɪˈɛs(ə)nt, kwʌɪ-/ ● **adj.** in a state or period of inactivity.
– DERIVATIVES **quiescence** n. **quiescently** adv.
– ORIGIN C17: from L. *quiescent-*, *quiescere* 'be still', from *quies* 'quiet'.

**quiet** ● **adj.** (**-er, -est**) **1** making little or no noise. ➤ free from activity, disturbance, or excitement. ➤ undisturbed; uninterrupted. **2** discreet, moderate, or restrained. ➤ (of a person) tranquil and reserved. ➤ (of a colour or garment) unobtrusive. ● **n.** silence; calm. ● **v.** chiefly N. Amer. make or become quiet.
– PHRASES **keep quiet** refrain from speaking or revealing a secret. **keep something quiet** keep something secret. **on the quiet** informal secretly or unobtrusively.
– DERIVATIVES **quieten** v. **quietly** adv. **quietness** n.
– ORIGIN ME (as n. denoting peace as opposed to war): via OFr., based on L. *quies*, *quiet-* 'repose, quiet'.

**quietism** ● **n.** **1** (in the Christian faith) devotional contemplation and abandonment of the will as a form of religious mysticism. **2** calm acceptance of things, without resistance.
– DERIVATIVES **quietist** n. & adj. **quietistic** adj.
– ORIGIN C17: from Ital. *quietismo*, based on L. *quies*, *quiet-* 'quiet'.

**quietude** ● **n.** a state of calmness and quiet.
– ORIGIN C16: from Fr. *quiétude* or med. L. *quietudo*, from L. *quietus* 'quiet'.

**quietus** /kwʌɪˈiːtəs/ ● **n.** (pl. **quietuses**) **1** death or a cause of death, regarded as a release from life. **2** archaic something calming or soothing.
– ORIGIN ME: abbrev. of med. L. *quietus est* (see **QUIT**), orig. used as a form of receipt on payment of a debt.

**quiff** ● **n.** chiefly Brit. a man's tuft of hair, brushed upwards and backwards from the forehead.
– ORIGIN C19 (orig. denoting a lock of hair plastered to the forehead): of unknown origin.

**quill** ● **n.** **1** a main wing or tail feather of a bird. ➤ the hollow shaft of a feather, especially the lower part that lacks barbs. **2** a pen made from a quill. **3** a hollow sharp spine of a porcupine, hedgehog, etc. **4** (**quills**) another term for **PENNE**. ● **v.** form (fabric) into small cylindrical folds.
– ORIGIN ME: prob. from Mid. Low Ger. *quiele*.

**quilling** ● **n.** **1** a piece of quilled lace or other fabric. **2** a type of ornamental craftwork involving the shaping of paper, fabric, or glass into delicate pleats or folds.

**quillwort** ● **n.** an aquatic plant related to the clubmosses, with a dense rosette of long slender leaves. [Genus *Isoetes*.]

**quilt**[1] ● **n.** a warm bed covering made of padding enclosed between layers of fabric and kept in place by lines of decorative stitching. ➤ a bedspread of similar design. ● **v.** [often as adj. **quilted**] join (layers of fabric or padding) with stitching to form a bed covering, a warm garment, or for decorative effect.
– DERIVATIVES **quilter** n. **quilting** n.
– ORIGIN ME: from OFr. *cuilte*, from L. *culcita* 'mattress, cushion'.

**quilt**[2] ● **v.** Austral. informal punch.
– ORIGIN C19: perh. a transferred use of the verb **QUILT**[1] (with the assoc. of quilting for protection).

**quim** ● **n.** Brit. vulgar slang a woman's genitals.
– ORIGIN C18: of unknown origin.

**quin** ● **n.** informal, chiefly Brit. a quintuplet.

**quinacrine** /ˈkwɪnəkriːn, -krɪn/ ● **n.** Medicine a synthetic compound used as an anthelmintic and antimalarial drug.
– ORIGIN 1930s: blend of **QUININE** and **ACRIDINE**.

**quinary** /ˈkwʌɪnəri/ ● **adj.** of or relating to the number five; fifth.
– ORIGIN C17: from L. *quinarius*, from *quini* 'five at once, a set of five', from *quinque* 'five'.

**quince** ● **n.** **1** a hard, acid, pear-shaped fruit used in preserves or as flavouring. **2** the Asian shrub or small tree which bears this fruit. [*Cydonia oblonga*.] **3** (**Japanese quince**) another term for **JAPONICA**.
– ORIGIN ME (orig. a collective pl.): from OFr. *cooin*, from L. *(malum) cotoneum*, var. of *(malum) cydonium* 'apple of *Cydonia* (= Chania, in Crete)'.

**quincentenary** /ˌkwɪnsɛnˈtiːn(ə)ri, -ˈtɛn-/ ● **n.** (pl. **-ies**) a five-hundredth anniversary.
– DERIVATIVES **quincentennial** n. & adj.
– ORIGIN C19: from L. *quinque* 'five' + **CENTENARY**.

**quincunx** /ˈkwɪnkʌŋks/ ● **n.** (pl. **quincunxes**) **1** an arrangement of five objects with four at the corners of a square or rectangle and the fifth at its centre. **2** Astrology an aspect of 150°, equivalent to five zodiacal signs.
– DERIVATIVES **quincuncial** adj. **quincuncially** adv.
– ORIGIN C17: from L., lit. 'five twelfths', from *quinque* 'five'

+ *uncia* 'twelfth'.

**quinella** /kwɪˈnɛlə/ ● **n.** a bet predicting the first two places in a race, but not necessarily in the correct order.
– ORIGIN 1940s (orig. US): from Latin Amer. Sp. *quiniela*.

**quinine** /ˈkwɪniːn, kwɪˈniːn/ ● **n.** a bitter crystalline compound present in cinchona bark, used as a tonic and formerly as an antimalarial drug.
– ORIGIN C19: from Sp. *quina* 'cinchona bark' (from Quechua *kina* 'bark') + **-INE**[4].

**quinoa** /ˈkiːnəʊə, kwɪˈnəʊə/ ● **n. 1** a goosefoot found in the Andes, cultivated for its edible starchy seeds. [*Chenopodium quinoa*.] **2** the seeds of this plant, used as food and to make alcoholic drinks.
– ORIGIN C17: Sp. spelling of Quechua *kinua, kinoa*.

**quinoline** /ˈkwɪnəliːn/ ● **n.** Chemistry a pungent oily liquid present in coal tar and bone oil.
– ORIGIN C19: from Sp. *quina* (see **QUININE**) + **-OL** + **-INE**[4].

**quinone** /ˈkwɪnəʊn, kwɪˈnəʊn/ ● **n.** Chemistry benzoquinone or one of its derivatives, with two oxygen atoms attached to opposite points of a benzene ring.
– ORIGIN C19: from Sp. *quina* (see **QUININE**) + **-ONE**.

**quinquagenarian** /ˌkwɪŋkwədʒɪˈnɛːrɪən/ ● **n.** a person between 50 and 59 years old.
– ORIGIN C19: from L. *quinquagenarius* (based on *quinquaginti* 'fifty') + **-AN**.

**Quinquagesima** /ˌkwɪŋkwəˈdʒɛsɪmə/ ● **n.** the Sunday before the beginning of Lent.
– ORIGIN from med. L., fem. of L. *quinquagesimus* 'fiftieth', on the pattern of *Quadragesima* (because it is ten days before the forty days of Lent).

**quinque-** ● **comb. form** five; having five: *quinquevalent*.
– ORIGIN from L. *quinque* 'five'.

**quinquennial** /kwɪŋˈkwɛnɪəl/ ● **adj.** lasting for or recurring every five years.
– DERIVATIVES **quinquennially** adv.
– ORIGIN C15: from L. *quinquennis* (from *quinque* 'five' + *annus* 'year') + **-AL**.

**quinquennium** /kwɪŋˈkwɛnɪəm/ ● **n.** (pl. **quinquennia** /-nɪə/ or **quinquenniums**) a period of five years.
– ORIGIN C17: from L., from *quinque* 'five' + *annus* 'year'.

**quinquereme** /ˈkwɪŋkwɪˌriːm/ ● **n.** an ancient Roman or Greek galley of a kind believed to have had five oarsmen to a bank of oars.
– ORIGIN C16: from L. *quinqueremis*, from *quinque* 'five' + *remus* 'oar'.

**quinquevalent** /ˌkwɪnkwɪˈveɪl(ə)nt/ ● **adj.** Chemistry pentavalent.

**quinsy** /ˈkwɪnzi/ ● **n.** inflammation of the throat, especially an abscess near the tonsils.
– ORIGIN ME: from OFr. *quinencie*, from med. L. *quinancia*, from Gk *kunankhē* 'canine quinsy', from *kun-* 'dog' + *ankhein* 'throttle'.

**quint** /kɪnt, kwɪnt/ ● **n. 1** (in piquet) a sequence of five cards of the same suit. [C17: from Fr., from L. *quintus* 'fifth', from *quinque* 'five'.] **2** N. Amer. a quintuplet.

**quinta** /ˈkwɪntə, ˈkɪnta/ ● **n.** (in Spain, Portugal, and Latin America) a large country house. ➤a wine-growing estate, especially in Portugal.
– ORIGIN Sp. and Port., from *quinta parte* 'fifth part' (with ref. to the amount of a farm's produce paid in rent).

**quintain** /ˈkwɪntɪn/ ● **n.** historical a post set up as a mark in tilting with a lance, typically with a pivoted sandbag attached to strike an inexpert tilter.
– ORIGIN ME: from OFr. *quintaine*, perh. based on L. *quintana*, a street in a Roman camp separating the fifth and sixth maniples, where military exercises were performed (from *quintus* 'fifth').

**quintal** /ˈkwɪnt(ə)l/ ● **n. 1** a unit of weight equal to a hundredweight (112 lb) or, formerly, 100 lb. **2** a unit of weight equal to 100 kg.
– ORIGIN ME: via OFr. from med. L. *quintale*, from Arab. *ḳinṭār*, based on L. *centenarius* 'containing a hundred'.

**quinte** /kãt/ ● **n.** Fencing the fifth of eight parrying positions.
– ORIGIN C18: Fr., from L. *quintus* 'fifth', from *quinque* 'five'.

**quintessence** /kwɪnˈtɛs(ə)ns/ ● **n. 1** the most perfect or typical example. ➤a central intrinsic aspect of something. **2** a refined essence or extract of a substance. **3** (in ancient philosophy) a fifth substance in addition to the four elements, thought to compose the heavenly bodies and pervade all things.
– ORIGIN ME: via Fr. from med. L. *quinta essentia* 'fifth essence'.

**quintessential** /ˌkwɪntɪˈsɛnʃ(ə)l/ ● **adj.** representing the most perfect or typical example.
– DERIVATIVES **quintessentially** adv.

**quintet** ● **n. 1** a group of five people playing music or singing together. ➤a composition for such a group. **2** a set of five people or things.
– ORIGIN C18: from Fr. *quintette* or Ital. *quintetto*, from *quinto* 'fifth', from L. *quintus*.

**quintile** /ˈkwɪntɪl, -ʌɪl/ ● **n. 1** Statistics each of five equal groups into which a population can be divided according to the distribution of values of a variable. **2** Astrology an aspect of 72° (one fifth of a circle).
– ORIGIN C17: from L. *quintilis*, from *quintus* 'fifth'.

**quintillion** /kwɪnˈtɪljən/ ● **cardinal number** (pl. **quintillions** or (with numeral) same) **1** a thousand raised to the power of six ($10^{18}$). **2** dated, chiefly Brit. a million raised to the power of five ($10^{30}$).
– DERIVATIVES **quintillionth** ordinal number.
– ORIGIN C17: from Fr., from *million*, by substitution of the prefix *quinti-* 'five' for the initial letters.

**quintuple** /ˈkwɪntjʊp(ə)l, kwɪnˈtjuːp(ə)l/ ● **adj. 1** consisting of five parts or elements. **2** five times as much or as many. **3** (of time in music) having five beats in a bar. ● **v.** increase or be increased fivefold. ● **n.** a quintuple thing, number, or amount.
– DERIVATIVES **quintuply** adv.
– ORIGIN C16: via Fr. from med. L. *quintuplus*, from L. *quintus* 'fifth' + *-plus* as in *duplus* (see **DUPLE**).

**quintuplet** /ˈkwɪntjʊˌplɪt, kwɪnˈtjuːplɪt/ ● **n. 1** each of five children born at one birth. **2** Music a group of five notes to be performed in the time of three or four.
– ORIGIN C19: from **QUINTUPLE**, on the pattern of *triplet*.

**quintuplicate** ● **adj. 1** fivefold. **2** of which five copies are made. ● **v.** multiply by five.

**quip** ● **n. 1** a witty remark. **2** archaic a verbal equivocation. ● **v.** (**quipped**, **quipping**) make a quip.
– DERIVATIVES **quipster** n.
– ORIGIN C16: perh. from L. *quippe* 'indeed, forsooth'.

**quipu** /ˈkiːpuː, ˈkwɪ-/ ● **n.** an ancient Inca device for recording information, consisting of coloured threads knotted in different ways.
– ORIGIN from Quechua *khipu* 'knot'.

**quire** /kwʌɪə/ ● **n. 1** four sheets of paper or parchment folded to form eight leaves, as in medieval manuscripts. **2** any collection of leaves one within another in a manuscript or book. **3** 25 (formerly 24) sheets of paper; one twentieth of a ream.
– ORIGIN ME: from OFr. *quaier*, from L. *quaterni* 'set of four'.

**quirk** ● **n. 1** a peculiar behavioural habit. **2** a strange chance occurrence. **3** a sudden twist, turn, or curve. **4** Architecture an acute hollow between convex or other mouldings. ● **v.** move or be moved suddenly or jerkily.
– DERIVATIVES **quirkily** adv. **quirkiness** n. **quirkish** adj. **quirky** adj. (**-ier**, **-iest**).
– ORIGIN C16 (as v.): of unknown origin.

**quirt** /kwəːt/ ● **n.** a short-handled riding whip with a braided leather lash. ● **v.** hit with a quirt.
– ORIGIN C19 (orig. US): from Sp. *cuerda* 'cord' (from L. *chorda* 'cord') or from Mex. Sp. *cuarta* 'whip'.

**quisling** /ˈkwɪzlɪŋ/ ● **n.** a traitor collaborating with an occupying enemy force.
– ORIGIN Second World War: from the name of Major Vidkun *Quisling*, who ruled Norway on behalf of the Ger. occupying forces.

**quit** ● **v.** (**quitting**; past and past part. **quitted** or **quit**) **1** leave, especially permanently. **2** informal resign from (a job). **3** informal, chiefly N. Amer. stop or discontinue. **4** (**quit oneself**) archaic behave in a specified way. ● **adj.** (**quit of**) rid of.
– PHRASES **quit hold of** archaic let go of.

– ORIGIN ME: from OFr. *quiter* (v.), *quite* (adj.), from L. *quietus*, past part. of *quiescere* 'be still', from *quies* 'quiet'.

**quitch** • n. another term for COUCH².
– ORIGIN OE *cwice*, of uncertain origin; perh. rel. to QUICK (with ref. to its vigorous growth).

**quitclaim** • n. Law, historical & US a formal renunciation or relinquishing of a claim.

**quite** • adv. **1** absolutely; completely. ➤US very; really. **2** fairly; moderately. **3** W. Indian all the way. • exclam. (also **quite so**) expressing agreement.
– PHRASES **quite a ——** a remarkable or impressive (person or thing). **quite a lot** (or **a bit**) a considerable number or amount. **quite some** a considerable amount of.
– ORIGIN ME: from the obs. adj. *quite*, var. of QUIT.

**quit-rent** • n. historical a small rent paid by a freeholder or copyholder in lieu of services which might be required of them.

**quits** • adj. on equal terms by retaliation or repayment.
– PHRASES **call it quits 1** agree that terms are now equal. **2** decide to abandon an activity.
– ORIGIN C15 (in the sense 'freed from a liability or debt'): perh. a colloq. abbrev. of med. L. *quittus*, from L. *quietus*, used as a receipt (see QUIETUS).

**quittance** • n. archaic or poetic/literary a release from a debt or obligation. ➤a document certifying this; a receipt.
– ORIGIN ME: from OFr. *quitance*, from *quiter* (see QUIT).

**quitter** • n. informal a person who gives up easily.

**quiver¹** • v. shake or tremble with a slight rapid motion. ➤cause to make a slight rapid motion. • n. a slight trembling movement or sound.
– DERIVATIVES **quivering** adj. **quiveringly** adv. **quivery** adj.
– ORIGIN ME: from OE *cwifer* 'nimble, quick'; the initial *qu-* is prob. symbolic of quick movement (as in *quaver* and *quick*).

**quiver²** • n. an archer's portable case for arrows.
– PHRASES **an arrow in the quiver** one of a number of resources that can be drawn on.
– ORIGIN ME: from Anglo-Norman Fr. *quiveir*, of W. Gmc origin.

**quiverful** • n. (pl. **-fuls**) **1** as much as a quiver can hold. **2** Brit. humorous a large number of offspring. [with biblical allusion to Ps. 127:5.]

**qui vive** /kiː 'viːv/ • n. (in phr. **on the qui vive**) on the alert or lookout.
– ORIGIN C16: from Fr., lit. '(long) live who?', i.e. 'on whose side are you?', used as a sentry's challenge.

**quixotic** /kwɪk'sɒtɪk/ • adj. impractically idealistic or fanciful.
– DERIVATIVES **quixotically** adv. **quixotism** /'kwɪksətɪz(ə)m/ n. **quixotry** /'kwɪksətri/ n.
– ORIGIN C18: from the name of Don *Quixote*, hero of Cervantes' romance, + -IC.

**quiz¹** • n. (pl. **quizzes**) **1** a test of knowledge, especially as a competition for entertainment. **2** informal, chiefly Brit. a period of questioning. **3** N. Amer. an informal written test. • v. (**quizzes**, **quizzed**, **quizzing**) **1** question (someone). **2** N. Amer. give an informal written test to.
– ORIGIN C19 (as v.; orig. US): possibly from QUIZ², influenced by INQUISITIVE.

**quiz²** archaic • v. (**quizzes**, **quizzed**, **quizzing**) **1** look intently at through or as if through an eyeglass. **2** make fun of. • n. (pl. **quizzes**) **1** a hoax. ➤a person who ridicules or hoaxes another. **2** an odd or eccentric person.
– DERIVATIVES **quizzer** n.
– ORIGIN C18: origin uncertain; possibly a deliberately coined nonsense word.

**quizmaster** • n. Brit. a question master.

**quizzical** • adj. **1** indicating mild or amused puzzlement. **2** rare causing mild amusement because of its oddness.
– DERIVATIVES **quizzicality** n. **quizzically** adv. **quizzicalness** n.

**quod** /kwɒd/ • n. Brit. informal, dated prison.
– ORIGIN C17: of unknown origin.

**quod erat demonstrandum** /kwɒd ˌɛrat dɛmən'strandʊm/ • used, especially at the conclusion of a formal proof, to convey that something demonstrates the truth of one's claim.
– ORIGIN L., lit. 'which was to be demonstrated'.

**quodlibet** /'kwɒdlɪbɛt/ • n. **1** archaic a topic for or exercise in philosophical or theological discussion. **2** poetic/literary a light-hearted medley of well-known tunes.
– DERIVATIVES **quodlibetarian** /-bɪ'tɛːrɪən/ n.
– ORIGIN ME: from L., from *quod* 'what' + *libet* 'it pleases'.

**quoin** /kɔɪn, kwɔɪn/ • n. **1** an external angle of a wall or building. **2** Printing a wedge or mechanical device for locking a letterpress forme into a chase. **3** a wedge for raising the level of a gun barrel or to keep it from rolling. • v. **1** provide with quoins. **2** Printing lock with a quoin.
– DERIVATIVES **quoining** n.
– ORIGIN ME: var. of COIN, used earlier in the sense 'cornerstone' and 'wedge'.

**quoit** /kɔɪt, kwɔɪt/ • n. **1** a ring of iron, rope, or rubber thrown in a game to encircle or land as near as possible to an upright peg. ➤(**quoits**) [treated as sing.] a game of aiming and throwing quoits. **2** the flat covering stone of a dolmen. ➤a dolmen. • v. archaic throw like a quoit.
– ORIGIN ME: prob. of Fr. origin.

**quokka** /'kwɒkə/ • n. a small short-tailed wallaby native to Western Australia. [*Setonix brachyurus*.]
– ORIGIN C19: from Nyungar *kwaka*.

**quoll** /kwɒl/ • n. a catlike carnivorous marsupial with a white-spotted coat, native to Australia and New Guinea. [Genus *Dasyurus*: several species.]
– ORIGIN C18: from Guugu Yimidhirr (an Aborig. lang.) *dhigul*.

**quondam** /'kwɒndəm, -dam/ • adj. formal former.
– ORIGIN C16: from L., 'formerly'.

**Quonset** /'kwɒnsɪt/ (also **Quonset hut**) • n. N. Amer. trademark a prefabricated building with a semicylindrical corrugated roof.
– ORIGIN Second World War: named after *Quonset* Point, Rhode Island, where such huts were first made.

**quorate** /'kwɔːrət, -reɪt/ • adj. Brit. (of a meeting) attended by a quorum.

**Quorn** /kwɔːn/ • n. Brit. trademark a form of mycoprotein used as a meat substitute.
– ORIGIN 1980s: the name of a former company in the Leicestershire village of Quorndon.

**quorum** /'kwɔːrəm/ • n. (pl. **quorums**) the minimum number of members of an assembly or society that must be present at a meeting to make the proceedings valid.
– ORIGIN ME: used in commissions for committee members designated by the L. *quorum vos ... unum* (*duos*, etc.) *esse volumus* 'of whom we wish that you ... be one (two, etc.)'.

**quota** • n. **1** a limited quantity of a product which may be produced, exported, or imported. **2** a share of something that one is entitled to receive or bound to contribute. **3** a fixed number of a group allowed to do something, e.g. immigrants entering a country. **4** (in a system of proportional representation) the minimum number of votes required to elect a candidate.
– ORIGIN C17: from med. L. *quota* (*pars*) 'how great (a part)', fem. of *quotus*, from *quot* 'how many'.

**quotable** • adj. suitable for or worth quoting.
– DERIVATIVES **quotability** n.

**quotation** • n. **1** a group of words from a text or speech repeated by someone other than the originator. ➤a short musical passage or visual image taken from one piece of music or work of art and used in another. ➤the action of quoting from a text, work of art, etc. **2** a formal statement of the estimated cost of a job or service. ➤Stock Exchange a price offered by a market-maker for the sale or purchase of a stock. **3** Stock Exchange a registration granted to a company enabling their shares to be officially listed and traded.
– ORIGIN C16: from med. L. *quotatio(n-)*, from *quotare* (see QUOTE).

**quotation mark** • n. each of a set of punctuation marks, single (' ') or double (" "), used either to mark the beginning and end of a title or quotation, or to indicate slang or jargon words.

**quote** • v. **1** repeat or copy out (a passage from a text or speech by another). ➤repeat a passage or statement from. **2** (**quote someone/thing as**) put forward or de-

scribe someone or something as being. **3** give someone (an estimated price). ➤(**quote someone/thing at/as**) name someone or something at (specified odds). **4** Stock Exchange give (a company) a listing on a stock exchange. ● **n. 1** a quotation. **2** (**quotes**) quotation marks.
– PHRASES **quote —— unquote** informal used parenthetically to indicate the beginning and end of a quotation.
– ORIGIN ME (orig. 'mark a book with numbers or marginal references'): from med. L. *quotare*, from *quot* 'how many', or from med. L. *quota* (see **QUOTA**).

**quoth** /kwəʊθ/ ● **v.** archaic or humorous said (used only in first and third person singular before the subject).
– ORIGIN ME: past tense of obs. *quethe* 'say, declare', of Gmc origin.

**quotidian** /kwɒˈtɪdɪən, kwəʊ-/ ● **adj. 1** daily. **2** ordinary or everyday. **3** Medicine denoting the malignant form of malaria.
– ORIGIN ME: via OFr. from L. *quotidianus*, earlier *cotidianus*, from *cotidie* 'daily'.

**quotient** /ˈkwəʊʃ(ə)nt/ ● **n. 1** Mathematics a result obtained by dividing one quantity by another. **2** a degree or amount of a specified quality.
– ORIGIN ME: from L. *quotiens* 'how many times' (from *quot* 'how many'), by confusion with participial forms ending in *-ens*, *-ent-*.

**Qur'an** /kəˈrɑːn/ (also **Quran**) ● **n.** Arabic spelling of **KORAN**.

**qursh** /kʊəʃ/ ● **n.** (pl. same) a monetary unit of Saudi Arabia, equal to one twentieth of a rial.
– ORIGIN from Arab. *ḳirsh*, from Slavic *grossus*.

**q.v.** ● **abbrev.** used to direct a reader to another part of a text for further information.
– ORIGIN from L. *quod vide*, lit. 'which see'.

**qwerty** /ˈkwəːti/ ● **adj.** denoting the standard layout on English-language typewriters and keyboards, having *q*, *w*, *e*, *r*, *t*, and *y* as the first keys on the top row of letters.

# R r

**R**[1] (also **r**) ● **n.** (pl. **Rs** or **R's**) **1** the eighteenth letter of the alphabet. **2** denoting the next after Q in a set of items, categories, etc.
– PHRASES **the R months** the months September to April, considered to be the season for eating oysters. **the three Rs** reading, writing, and arithmetic, regarded as the fundamentals of learning.

**R**[2] ● **abbrev.** **1** rand. **2** (in names of sports clubs) Rangers or Rovers. **3** Réaumur (a temperature scale, now obsolete). **4** Regina or Rex. **5** (®) registered as a trademark. **6** (in the US) Republican. **7** N. Amer. (in film classification) restricted (to viewers over a certain age). **8** (on a gear shift) reverse. **9** (**R.**) River. **10** roentgen(s). **11** Romania (international vehicle registration). **12** rook (in chess). **13** Cricket (on scorecards) run(s). ● **symb.** **1** Chemistry an unspecified organic radical. **2** electrical resistance.

**r** ● **abbrev.** **1** recto. **2** right. **3** Law rule. ● **symb.** **1** radius. **2** Statistics correlation coefficient.

**RA** ● **abbrev.** **1** Argentina (international vehicle registration). [from Sp. *República Argentina* 'Argentine Republic'.] **2** Astronomy right ascension. **3** (in the UK) Royal Academician or Royal Academy. **4** (in the UK) Royal Artillery.

**Ra** ● **symb.** the chemical element radium.

**RAAF** ● **abbrev.** Royal Australian Air Force.

**rabbet** /'rabɪt/ ● **n.** & **v.** chiefly N. Amer. another term for **REBATE**[2].
– ORIGIN ME: from OFr. *rabbat* 'abatement, recess'.

**rabbi** /'rabʌɪ/ ● **n.** (pl. **rabbis**) **1** a Jewish scholar or teacher, especially of Jewish law. **2** a Jewish religious leader.
– DERIVATIVES **rabbinate** /'rabɪnət/ n.
– ORIGIN OE, via eccles. L. and Gk from Heb. *rabbī* 'my master', from *raḇ* 'master'.

**rabbinic** /rə'bɪnɪk/ ● **adj.** of or relating to rabbis or to Jewish law or teachings.
– DERIVATIVES **rabbinical** adj. **rabbinically** adv.

**rabbit** ● **n.** **1** a burrowing gregarious plant-eating mammal, with long ears, long hind legs, and a short tail. [*Oryctolagus cuniculus* and other species.] ➤ the fur of the rabbit. ➤ N. Amer. a hare. **2** informal a poor performer in a sport or game. **3** US a runner acting as pacesetter. **4** Brit. informal a conversation. [from *rabbit and pork*, rhyming sl. for 'talk'.] ● **v.** (**rabbited**, **rabbiting**) **1** [usu. as noun **rabbiting**] hunt rabbits. **2** Brit. informal chatter.
– DERIVATIVES **rabbity** adj.
– ORIGIN ME: appar. from OFr. (cf. Fr. dial. *rabotte* 'young rabbit'), perh. of Du. origin (cf. Flemish *robbe*).

**rabbit fever** ● **n.** informal term for **TULARAEMIA**.

**rabbitfish** ● **n.** (pl. same or **-fishes**) a blunt-nosed fish with rabbit-like teeth or jaws. [*Chimaera monstrosa* (Atlantic), *Siganus oramin* (Indo-Pacific), and other species.]

**rabbit punch** ● **n.** a sharp chop with the edge of the hand to the back of the neck.

**rabble** ● **n.** **1** a disorderly crowd. **2** (**the rabble**) ordinary people regarded as socially inferior or uncouth.
– ORIGIN ME: perh. rel. to dial. *rabble* 'to gabble'.

**rabble-rouser** ● **n.** a person who stirs up a crowd, especially for political reasons.
– DERIVATIVES **rabble-rousing** adj. & n.

**Rabelaisian** /,rabə'leɪzɪən/ ● **n.** an admirer of the French satirist François Rabelais (*c.*1494–1553). ● **adj.** of or like Rabelais or his writings; marked by exuberant imagination and earthy humour.

**rabid** /'rabɪd, 'reɪ-/ ● **adj.** **1** extreme; fanatical. **2** of, relating to, or affected with rabies.
– DERIVATIVES **rabidity** /rə'bɪdɪti/ n. **rabidly** adv. **rabidness** n.
– ORIGIN C17: from L. *rabidus*, from *rabere* 'to rave'.

**rabies** /'reɪbi:z, -ɪz/ ● **n.** a dangerous viral disease of dogs and other mammals, transmissible through the saliva to humans and causing madness and convulsions.
– ORIGIN C16: from L., from *rabere* 'rave'.

**RAC** ● **abbrev.** **1** (in the UK) Royal Armoured Corps. **2** (in the UK) Royal Automobile Club.

**raccoon** /rə'ku:n/ (also **racoon**) ● **n.** a greyish-brown omnivorous American mammal with a black facial mask and a ringed tail. [Genus *Procyon*: two species.]
– ORIGIN C17: from Virginia Algonquian *aroughcun*.

**race**[1] ● **n.** **1** a competition between runners, horses, vehicles, etc. to see which is fastest over a set course. ➤ (**the races**) a series of races for horses or dogs, held at a fixed time on a set course. ➤ a situation in which people compete to be first to achieve something. **2** archaic the course of the sun or moon through the heavens. **3** a strong or rapid current flowing through a narrow channel. **4** a water channel, especially one in a mill or mine. **5** a smooth ring-shaped groove or guide for a ball bearing or roller bearing. **6** a fenced passageway in a stockyard through which animals pass singly for branding, loading, etc. **7** (in weaving) the channel along which the shuttle moves. ● **v.** **1** compete in a race. ➤ compete regularly in races as a sport. ➤ have a race with. ➤ prepare and enter (an animal or vehicle) for races. **2** move or progress swiftly. ➤ operate or cause to operate at excessive speed.
– PHRASES **be in the race** [usu. with neg.] Austral./NZ informal have a chance of success.
– ORIGIN OE (orig. a north. Engl. word meaning 'rapid forward movement'), from ON *rás* 'current'.

**race**[2] ● **n.** **1** each of the major divisions of humankind, having distinct physical characteristics. ➤ racial origin or distinction. ➤ an ethnic group. ➤ a group descended from a common ancestor. **2** a group of people or things with a common feature. **3** Biology a distinct population within a species; a subspecies.
– ORIGIN C16: via Fr. from Ital. *razza*, of unknown ultimate origin.

**USAGE** race

In recent years, the associations of **race** with the ideologies and theories that grew out of the work of 19th-century anthropologists and physiologists has led to the use of the word **race** itself becoming problematic. Although still used in general contexts, it is now often replaced by other words which are less emotionally charged, such as **people(s)** or **community**.

**race**[3] ● **n.** dated a ginger root.
– ORIGIN ME: from OFr. *rais*, from L. *radix*, *radic-* 'root'.

**racecard** ● **n.** a programme giving information about the races at a race meeting.

**racecourse** ● **n.** a ground or track for horse or dog racing.

**racehorse** ● **n.** a horse bred and trained for racing.

**racemate** /'rasɪmeɪt/ ● **n.** Chemistry a racemic mixture.

**raceme** /'rasi:m, rə'si:m/ ● **n.** Botany a flower cluster with the separate flowers attached by short stalks along a central stem, the flowers at the base developing first. Compare with **CYME**.
– ORIGIN C18: from L. *racemus* 'bunch of grapes'.

**race meeting** ● **n.** Brit. a sporting event consisting of a series of horse races held at one course.

**race memory** ● **n.** a supposedly inherited subconscious memory of events in human history or prehistory.

**racemic** /rəˈsiːmɪk, rəˈsɛmɪk/ ● **adj.** Chemistry composed of dextrorotatory and laevorotatory forms in equal proportion.
– DERIVATIVES **racemize** /ˈrasɪmʌɪz/ (also **-ise**) v.
– ORIGIN C19: from Fr. *racémique* 'derived from grape juice' (orig. referring to tartaric acid) + **-IC**.

**racemose** /ˈrasɪməʊs, -z/ ● **adj. 1** Botany of the form of a raceme. **2** Anatomy of the form of a cluster.
– ORIGIN C17: from L. *racemosus*, from *racemus* (see **RACEME**).

**racer** ● **n. 1** an animal or vehicle used for racing. ➤a person who competes in races. **2** a harmless fast-moving slender snake. [*Coluber constrictor* (N. America) and other species.] **3** a circular horizontal rail along which the carriage or traversing platform of a heavy gun moves.

**race relations** ● **pl. n.** relations between members of different races within a country.

**racetrack** ● **n. 1** a racecourse. **2** a track for motor racing.

**raceway** ● **n.** chiefly N. Amer. **1** a water channel, especially an artificial one for rearing fish. **2** a groove or race for bearings. **3** a pipe or tubing enclosing electric wires. **4** a track for trotting, pacing, or harness racing. ➤a racetrack.

**rachis** /ˈreɪkɪs/ ● **n.** (pl. **rachides** /-kɪdiːz/) **1** Botany a stem of a grass or other plant bearing flower stalks at short intervals. ➤the midrib of a compound leaf or frond. **2** Anatomy the vertebral column, or the cord from which it develops. **3** Ornithology the shaft of a feather.
– ORIGIN C18: mod. L., from Gk *rhakhis* 'spine'; the Engl. pl. *-ides* is by false analogy.

**rachitic** /rəˈkɪtɪk/ ● **adj.** Medicine of, relating to, or suffering from rickets.
– ORIGIN C18: from mod. L. *rachitis* 'rickets', from Gk *rhakhitis*, from *rhakhis* 'spine'.

**Rachmanism** /ˈrakmənɪz(ə)m/ ● **n.** Brit. the exploitation and intimidation of tenants by unscrupulous landlords.
– ORIGIN 1960s: named after the notorious London landlord Peter *Rachman*.

**racial** ● **adj. 1** of or relating to a race. **2** relating to relations or differences between races.
– DERIVATIVES **racially** adv.

**racialism** ● **n.** racism.
– DERIVATIVES **racialist** n. & adj. **racialize** (also **-ise**) v.

**racing** ● **n.** a sport involving races. ● **adj. 1** moving swiftly. **2** (of a person) following horse racing.

**racing car** ● **n.** a car built for racing.

**racing demon** ● **n.** a competitive version of the card game patience for a number of players.

**racing driver** ● **n.** a driver of racing cars.

**racism** ● **n. 1** the belief that there are characteristics, abilities, or qualities specific to each race. **2** discrimination against or antagonism towards other races.
– DERIVATIVES **racist** n. & adj.

**rack**[1] ● **n. 1** a framework for holding or storing things. ➤a vertically barred holder for animal fodder. **2** a cogged or toothed bar or rail engaging with a wheel or pinion, or using pegs to adjust the position of something. **3** (**the rack**) historical an instrument of torture consisting of a frame on which the victim was tied by the wrists and ankles and stretched. **4** N. Amer. informal a bed. **5** a triangular frame for positioning pool balls. ➤a single game of pool. **6** N. Amer. a set of antlers. **7** a digital effects unit for a guitar or other instrument. ● **v. 1** (also **wrack**) cause extreme physical or mental pain to. ➤historical torture on the rack. **2** place in or on a rack. **3** (**rack something up**) accumulate or achieve something. **4** chiefly archaic oppress (a tenant) by exacting excessive rent.
– PHRASES **rack** (or **wrack**) **one's brains** make a great mental effort.
– ORIGIN ME: from MDu. *rec*, Mid. Low Ger. *rek* 'horizontal bar or shelf', prob. from *recken* 'to stretch, reach'.

**rack**[2] ● **n.** a horse's gait between a trot and a canter. ● **v.** move with such a gait.
– PHRASAL VERBS **rack off** Austral. informal go away.
– ORIGIN C16: of unknown origin.

**rack**[3] ● **n.** a joint of meat, especially lamb, including the front ribs.
– ORIGIN C16: of unknown origin.

**rack**[4] (also **wrack**) ● **n.** (in phr. **go to rack and ruin**) gradually deteriorate due to neglect.
– ORIGIN OE *wrǣc* 'vengeance, destruction', rel. to **WREAK**; cf. **WRACK**[4].

**rack**[5] ● **v.** draw off (wine, beer, etc.) from the sediment in the barrel.
– ORIGIN C15: from Provençal *arracar*, from *raca* 'stems and husks of grapes, dregs'.

**rack**[6] ● **n.** variant spelling of **WRACK**[3]. ● **v.** archaic (of a cloud) be driven before the wind.
– ORIGIN ME (denoting a rush or collision): prob. of Scand. origin.

**rack-and-pinion** ● **adj.** denoting a mechanism using a fixed cogged or toothed bar or rail engaging with a smaller cog.

**racket**[1] (also **racquet**) ● **n. 1** a bat with a round or oval frame strung with catgut, nylon, etc., used especially in tennis, badminton, and squash. **2** chiefly N. Amer. a snowshoe resembling this.
– ORIGIN C16: from Fr. *raquette* (see **RACKETS**).

**racket**[2] ● **n. 1** a loud unpleasant noise. ➤archaic the liveliness of fashionable society. **2** informal a fraudulent scheme for obtaining money. ➤a person's line of business. ● **v.** (**racketed**, **racketing**) **1** make a racket. **2** (**racket about/around**) enjoy oneself socially.
– DERIVATIVES **rackety** adj.
– ORIGIN C16: perh. imitative of clattering.

**racketeer** ● **n.** a person engaging in fraudulent business dealings.
– DERIVATIVES **racketeering** n.

**rackets** ● **pl. n.** [treated as sing.] a ball game for two or four people played with rackets in a four-walled court, using a harder ball than squash.
– ORIGIN ME (also in the sing.): from Fr. *raquette*, via Ital. from Arab. *rāḥa*, *rāḥat-* 'palm of the hand'.

**rack railway** ● **n.** a railway for steep slopes, having a toothed rail between the bearing rails which engages with a cogwheel under the locomotive.

**rack rent** ● **n.** a very high rent. ● **v.** (**rack-rent**) dated exact excessive rent from (a tenant) or for (a property).
– DERIVATIVES **rack-renter** n.
– ORIGIN C16 (as *rack-rented*): from **RACK**[1] (in the sense 'cause stress') + **RENT**[1].

**raclette** /raˈklɛt/ ● **n.** a Swiss dish of melted cheese, typically with potatoes.
– ORIGIN Fr., lit. 'small scraper', referring to the practice of scraping the cheese on to a plate as it melts.

**racon** /ˈreɪkɒn/ ● **n.** chiefly US a radar beacon that can be identified by its response to a specific radar signal.
– ORIGIN 1940s: blend of **RADAR** and **BEACON**.

**raconteur** /ˌrakɒnˈtəː/ ● **n.** (fem. **raconteuse** /ˌrakɒnˈtəːz/) a skilful teller of anecdotes.
– ORIGIN C19: Fr., from *raconter* 'relate, recount'.

**racoon** ● **n.** variant spelling of **RACCOON**.

**racquet** ● **n.** variant spelling of **RACKET**[1].

**racy** ● **adj.** (**-ier**, **-iest**) **1** suggestive; risqué. ➤showing vigour or spirit. **2** (of a wine, flavour, etc.) having a characteristic quality in a high degree. **3** (of a vehicle or animal) suitable for racing.
– DERIVATIVES **racily** adv. **raciness** n.

**RAD** ● **abbrev.** (in the UK) Royal Academy of Dance.

**rad**[1] ● **abbrev.** radian(s).

**rad**[2] ● **n.** informal a political radical.

**rad**[3] ● **n.** Physics a unit of absorbed dose of ionizing radiation, corresponding to the absorption of 0.01 joule per kilogram of absorbing material.
– ORIGIN C20: acronym from *radiation absorbed dose*.

**rad**[4] ● **adj.** informal, chiefly N. Amer. excellent.
– ORIGIN 1980s: prob. an abbrev. of **RADICAL**.

**rad**[5] ● **n.** a radiator.

**RADA** /ˈrɑːdə/ ● **abbrev.** (in the UK) Royal Academy of Dramatic Art.

**radar** ● **n.** a system for detecting the presence, direction,

and speed of aircraft, ships, etc., by sending out pulses of radio waves which are reflected back off the object.
– ORIGIN 1940s: from *ra(dio) d(etection) a(nd) r(anging)*.

**radar gun** ● n. a hand-held radar device used by traffic police to estimate a vehicle's speed.

**radar trap** ● n. an area of road in which radar is used by the police to detect speeding vehicles.

**RADC** ● abbrev. (in the UK) Royal Army Dental Corps.

**raddle** ● n. variant of **REDDLE**. ● v. colour with reddle.
– ORIGIN C16: rel. to **RED**; cf. **RUDDLE**.

**raddled** ● adj. **1** (of a person) showing signs of age or fatigue. **2** coloured with or as if with raddle.

**radial** ● adj. **1** of or arranged like rays or the radii of a circle; diverging in lines from a common centre. ➤(of a road) running from a town centre to an outlying district. **2** (also **radial-ply**) denoting a tyre in which the layers of fabric have their cords running at right angles to the circumference of the tyre. **3** denoting an internal-combustion engine with its cylinders fixed like the spokes of a wheel around a rotating crankshaft. **4** Anatomy & Zoology of or relating to the radius. ● n. **1** a radial tyre. **2** Zoology a supporting ray in a fish's fin.
– DERIVATIVES **radially** adv.
– ORIGIN C16: from med. L. *radialis*, from L. *radius* (see **RADIUS**).

**radial symmetry** ● n. chiefly Biology symmetry about a central axis, as in a starfish.

**radial velocity** ● n. chiefly Astronomy the velocity of a star or other body along the line of sight of an observer.

**radian** /'reɪdɪən/ ● n. a unit of measurement of angles equal to about 57.3°, equivalent to the angle subtended at the centre of a circle by an arc equal in length to the radius.

**radiant** ● adj. **1** shining or glowing brightly. ➤emanating great joy, love, or health. ➤(of an emotion or quality) emanating powerfully. **2** transmitted by electromagnetic radiation, rather than conduction or convection. ➤(of an appliance) emitting radiant energy for cooking or heating. ● n. **1** a point or object from which light or heat radiates. **2** Astronomy the apparent focal point of a meteor shower.
– DERIVATIVES **radiance** n. **radiancy** n. **radiantly** adv.
– ORIGIN ME: from L. *radiant-*, *radiare* (see **RADIATE**).

**radiate** ● v. **1** emit (light, heat, or other energy) in the form of rays or waves. ➤be emitted in such a way. ➤emanate (a strong feeling or quality). **2** diverge from or as if from a central point. ➤[as adj. **radiated**] used in names of animals with markings arranged like rays. **3** Biology (of an animal or plant group) evolve into a variety of forms. ● adj. rare radial.
– DERIVATIVES **radiative** adj.
– ORIGIN C17: from L. *radiat-*, *radiare* 'emit in rays', from *radius* 'ray, spoke'.

**radiation** ● n. **1** the action or process of radiating. **2** Physics energy emitted as electromagnetic waves or subatomic particles.
– DERIVATIVES **radiational** adj. **radiationally** adv.

**radiation sickness** ● n. illness caused by exposure to X-rays, gamma rays, or other radiation.

**radiation therapy** (also **radiation treatment**) ● n. radiotherapy.

**radiator** ● n. **1** a thing that emits light, heat, or sound. **2** a heating device consisting of a metal case through which hot water is pumped by a central heating system. ➤a portable oil or electric heater resembling this. **3** a cooling device in a vehicle or aircraft engine consisting of a bank of thin tubes in which circulating water is cooled by the surrounding air.

**radical** ● adj. **1** of, relating to, or affecting the fundamental nature of something. ➤innovative or progressive. **2** (of surgery) thorough and intended to be completely curative. **3** advocating thorough political or social reform; politically extreme. ➤Brit. historical belonging to an extreme section of the Liberal party in the 19th century. **4** Mathematics of the root of a number or quantity. **5** denoting or relating to the roots of a word. **6** Music belonging to the root of a chord. **7** Botany of or coming from the root or stem base of a plant. **8** informal, chiefly N. Amer. excellent. ● n. **1** an advocate of radical political or social reform. **2** Chemistry a group of atoms behaving as a unit in a number of compounds. See also **FREE RADICAL**. **3** the root or base form of a word. ➤any of the basic set of Chinese characters constituting semantically or functionally significant elements in the composition of other characters. **4** Mathematics a quantity forming or expressed as the root of another.
– DERIVATIVES **radicalism** n. **radicalization** (also **-isation**) n. **radicalize** (also **-ise**) v. **radically** adv. **radicalness** n.
– ORIGIN ME: from late L. *radicalis*, from L. *radix*, *radic-* 'root'.

**radical chic** ● n. the fashionable affectation of radical left-wing views. ➤the dress, lifestyle, etc. associated with this.
– ORIGIN 1970: coined by the Amer. writer Tom Wolfe.

**radical sign** ● n. Mathematics the sign √ which indicates the square root of the number following (or a higher root indicated by a preceding superscript numeral).

**radicchio** /ra'diːkɪəʊ/ ● n. (pl. **-os**) chicory of a variety with dark red leaves.
– ORIGIN from Ital.

**radices** plural form of **RADIX**.

**radicle** /'radɪk(ə)l/ ● n. **1** Botany the part of a plant embryo that develops into the primary root. **2** Anatomy a root-like subdivision of a nerve or vein.
– DERIVATIVES **radicular** adj. (Anatomy).
– ORIGIN C17: from L. *radicula*, dimin. of *radix*, *radic-* 'root'.

**radii** plural form of **RADIUS**.

**radio** ● n. (pl. **-os**) **1** the transmission and reception of radio waves, especially those carrying audio messages. **2** broadcasting sound. ➤a broadcasting station or channel. **3** an apparatus for receiving radio programmes. ➤an apparatus capable of receiving and transmitting radio messages. ● v. (**-oes**, **-oed**) send a message by radio. ➤communicate with by radio.
– ORIGIN C20: abbrev. of **RADIOTELEPHONE**.

**radio-** ● comb. form **1** denoting radio waves or broadcasting: *radiogram*. **2** Physics connected with rays, radiation, or radioactivity: *radiograph*. ➤denoting artificially prepared radioisotopes: *radio-cobalt*. **3** Anatomy relating to the radius: *radio-carpal*.

**radioactive** ● adj. emitting or relating to the emission of ionizing radiation or particles.
– DERIVATIVES **radioactively** adv.

**radioactivity** ● n. the emission of ionizing radiation or particles caused by the spontaneous disintegration of atomic nuclei. ➤radioactive particles.

**radio astronomy** ● n. the branch of astronomy concerned with radio emissions from celestial objects.

**radiobiology** ● n. the branch of biology concerned with the effects of ionizing radiation and the use of radiological techniques.
– DERIVATIVES **radiobiological** adj. **radiobiologically** adv. **radiobiologist** n.

**radio car** ● n. a car with a two-way radio.

**radiocarbon** ● n. Chemistry a radioactive isotope of carbon, especially carbon-14 used in carbon dating.

**radiochemistry** ● n. the branch of chemistry concerned with radioactive substances.
– DERIVATIVES **radiochemical** adj. **radiochemist** n.

**radio-controlled** ● adj. controllable from a distance by radio.

**radio-element** ● n. a radioactive element or isotope.

**radio frequency** ● n. a frequency or band of frequencies in the range $10^4$ to $10^{11}$ or $10^{12}$ hertz, suitable for use in telecommunications.

**radiogenic** /ˌreɪdɪə(ʊ)'dʒɛnɪk, -'dʒiːn-/ ● adj. **1** produced by radioactivity. **2** suitable for broadcasting by radio.
– DERIVATIVES **radiogenically** adv.

**radiogram** ● n. **1** Brit. a combined radio and record player. [from **RADIO-** + **GRAMOPHONE**.] **2** a radiograph. **3** dated a telegram sent by radio.

**radiograph** ● n. an image produced on a sensitive plate or film by X-rays or other radiation. ● v. produce a radio-

graph of.
– DERIVATIVES **radiographer** n. **radiographic** adj. **radiographically** adv. **radiography** n.

**radioimmunoassay** ● n. Medicine a technique for measuring antibody levels using radioactively labelled antigens.

**radioimmunology** ● n. the use of radiological techniques in immunology.
– DERIVATIVES **radioimmunological** adj. **radioimmunologically** adv.

**radioisotope** ● n. Chemistry a radioactive isotope.
– DERIVATIVES **radioisotopic** adj.

**radiolaria** /ˌreɪdɪə(ʊ)ˈlɛːrɪə/ ● pl. n. Zoology single-celled aquatic animals having a spherical amoebalike body with a spiny skeleton of silica. [Many species in the phylum Actinopoda.]
– DERIVATIVES **radiolarian** n. & adj.
– ORIGIN C19: mod. L. (former order name), from late L. *radiolus* 'faint ray', dimin. of *radius* 'ray'.

**radiology** ● n. the science of X-rays and other high-energy radiation, especially as used in medicine.
– DERIVATIVES **radiologic** adj. **radiological** adj. **radiologically** adv. **radiologist** n.

**radiometer** /ˌreɪdɪˈɒmɪtə/ ● n. an instrument for detecting or measuring radiation.
– DERIVATIVES **radiometry** n.

**radiometric** ● adj. Physics of or relating to the measurement of radioactivity.
– DERIVATIVES **radiometrically** adv.

**radionics** /ˌreɪdɪˈɒnɪks/ ● pl. n. [treated as sing.] a system of alternative medicine based on the study of radiation supposedly emitted by living matter.
– ORIGIN 1940s: from **RADIO-**, on the pattern of *electronics*.

**radionuclide** ● n. a radioactive nuclide.

**radiopaque** /ˌreɪdɪəʊˈpeɪk/ (also **radio-opaque**) ● adj. opaque to X-rays.
– DERIVATIVES **radiopacity** n.

**radiophonic** ● adj. relating to or denoting sound produced electronically.

**radioscopy** /ˌreɪdɪˈɒskəpi/ ● n. Physics the examination by X-rays of objects opaque to light.
– DERIVATIVES **radioscopic** adj.

**radiotelephone** ● n. a telephone using radio transmission.
– DERIVATIVES **radiotelephonic** adj. **radiotelephony** n.

**radio telescope** ● n. Astronomy an instrument used to detect radio emissions from the sky.

**radiotherapy** ● n. the treatment of cancer or other disease using X-rays or similar radiation.
– DERIVATIVES **radiotherapeutic** adj. **radiotherapist** n.

**radio wave** ● n. an electromagnetic wave of radio frequency.

**radish** ● n. **1** a pungent-tasting edible root, typically small, spherical, and red, and eaten raw. **2** the plant of the cabbage family which yields this root. [*Raphanus sativus*.]
– ORIGIN OE *rædic*, from L. *radix*, *radic-* 'root'.

**radium** /ˈreɪdɪəm/ ● n. the chemical element of atomic number 88, a radioactive metal of the alkaline earth series. (Symbol: **Ra**)
– ORIGIN C19: from L. *radius* 'ray' + **-IUM**.

**radium emanation** ● n. archaic term for **RADON**.

**radius** /ˈreɪdɪəs/ ● n. (pl. **radii** /-dɪʌɪ/ or **radiuses**) **1** a straight line from the centre to the circumference of a circle or sphere. ➤a radial line from the focus to any point of a curve. **2** a specified distance from a centre in all directions. **3** Anatomy & Zoology a bone of the forearm or forelimb, in humans the thicker and shorter of two. **4** Zoology a radially symmetric feature in an echinoderm or coelenterate, e.g. an arm of a starfish. **5** Entomology a main vein in an insect's wing. ● v. (**radiused**, **radiusing**) [often as adj. **radiused**] make (a corner or edge) rounded.
– ORIGIN C16: from L., lit. 'staff, spoke, ray'.

**radius vector** ● n. Mathematics a line of variable length extending from a centre to an orbit or other curve.

**radix** /ˈradɪks, ˈreɪ-/ ● n. (pl. **radices** /-dɪsiːz/) **1** Mathematics the base of a system of numeration. **2** formal a source or origin.
– ORIGIN C17: from L., lit. 'root'.

**radome** /ˈreɪdəʊm/ ● n. a dome or other structure protecting radar equipment and made from material transparent to radio waves.
– ORIGIN 1940s: blend of **RADAR** and **DOME**.

**radon** /ˈreɪdɒn/ ● n. the chemical element of atomic number 86, a rare radioactive noble gas. (Symbol: **Rn**)
– ORIGIN C20: from **RADIUM** (from which it is formed by radioactive decay), on the pattern of *argon*.

**radula** /ˈradjʊlə/ ● n. (pl. **radulae** /-liː/) Zoology (in a mollusc) a rasp-like structure for scraping off food particles and drawing them into the mouth.
– DERIVATIVES **radular** adj.
– ORIGIN C19: from L., lit. 'scraper', from *radere* 'to scrape'.

**radwaste** ● n. informal radioactive waste.

**RAF** ● abbrev. (in the UK) Royal Air Force.

**Rafferty's rules** /ˈrafətɪz/ ● pl. n. Austral./NZ informal no rules at all.
– ORIGIN 1920s: *Rafferty*, prob. an Engl. dial. alt. of **REFRACTORY**.

**raffia** ● n. **1** a palm tree of tropical Africa and Madagascar, with a short trunk and extremely long leaves. [*Raphia ruffia*.] **2** the fibre from these leaves, used for making hats, baskets, etc.
– ORIGIN C18: from Malagasy.

**raffinate** /ˈrafɪneɪt/ ● n. Chemistry a liquid which has been purified by extraction with a solvent.
– ORIGIN 1920s: from Fr. *raffiner* or Ger. *raffinieren* 'refine' + **-ATE**[1].

**raffish** ● adj. slightly disreputable, especially in an attractive manner.
– DERIVATIVES **raffishly** adv. **raffishness** n.
– ORIGIN C19: from **RIFF-RAFF** + **-ISH**[1].

**raffle**[1] ● n. a lottery with goods as prizes. ● v. offer as a prize in a raffle.
– ORIGIN ME (denoting a dice game): from OFr., of unknown origin.

**raffle**[2] ● n. dialect rubbish; refuse.
– ORIGIN ME: perh. from OFr. *ne rifle ne rafle* 'nothing at all'.

**rafflesia** /rəˈfliːʒɪə, -ˈzɪə/ ● n. a Malaysian and Indonesian parasitic plant with a single very large flower which smells of carrion. [Genus *Rafflesia*.]
– ORIGIN mod. L., named after the Brit. colonial administrator Sir T. Stamford *Raffles*.

**raft**[1] ● n. **1** a flat buoyant structure of timber or other materials fastened together, used as a boat or floating platform. ➤a small inflatable boat. **2** a floating mass of fallen trees, ice, etc. **3** a foundation of reinforced concrete for a building. ● v. **1** travel or transport on or as if on a raft. **2** make into or transport as a raft.
– DERIVATIVES **rafting** n.
– ORIGIN ME: from ON *raptr* 'rafter'.

**raft**[2] ● n. a large amount of something.
– ORIGIN C19: alt. of dial. *raff* 'abundance' (perh. of Scand. origin), by assoc. with **RAFT**[1] in sense 2.

**rafter**[1] ● n. a beam forming part of the internal framework of a roof.
– DERIVATIVES **raftered** adj.
– ORIGIN OE *ræfter*, of Gmc origin; rel. to **RAFT**[1].

**rafter**[2] ● n. **1** a traveller on a raft. **2** a person who rafts tree trunks.

**raftsman** ● n. (pl. **-men**) a man who works on a raft.

**raft spider** ● n. a large aquatic spider which reaches through the surface to capture prey. [Genus *Dolomedes*.]

**rag**[1] /rag/ ● n. **1** a piece of old cloth, especially one torn from a larger piece. ➤(**rags**) old or tattered clothes. **2** (**rags**) the remnants of something. **3** informal a low-quality newspaper. ● v. give a decorative effect to by applying paint with a rag.
– PHRASES **on the rag** informal, chiefly N. Amer. menstruating. **lose one's rag** informal lose one's temper.
– ORIGIN ME: prob. a back-form. from **RAGGED** or **RAGGY**.

**rag**[2] /rag/ ● n. Brit. **1** a programme of entertainments organized by students to raise money for charity. **2** informal,

dated a prank. ● v. (**ragged**, **ragging**) **1** make fun of loudly and boisterously. **2** rebuke severely.
– PHRASAL VERBS **rag on** N. Amer. informal **1** complain or criticize continually. **2** tease constantly.
– ORIGIN C18: of unknown origin.

**rag**[3] /rag/ ● n. **1** a large coarse roofing slate. **2** (also **ragstone**) Brit. a hard coarse sedimentary rock that can be broken into thick slabs.
– ORIGIN ME: of unknown origin; later assoc. with RAG[1].

**rag**[4] /rag/ ● n. a ragtime composition or tune.
– ORIGIN C19: perh. from RAGGED; cf. RAGTIME.

**rag**[5] /rɑːg/ ● n. variant of RAGA.

**raga** /ˈrɑːgə, ˈrɑːgɑː/ ● n. (in Indian music) a characteristic pattern of notes used as a basis for improvisation.
– ORIGIN C18: from Sanskrit, lit. 'colour, musical tone'.

**ragamuffin** (also **raggamuffin**) ● n. **1** a person in ragged, dirty clothes. **2** an exponent or follower of ragga, typically wearing ragged clothes. ➤another term for RAGGA.
– ORIGIN ME: prob. based on RAG[1], with a fanciful suffix.

**rag-and-bone man** ● n. Brit. an itinerant dealer in old clothes and other second-hand items.

**ragbag** ● n. **1** a bag for storing rags and old clothes. **2** a miscellaneous collection. **3** informal an untidily dressed woman.

**rag bolt** ● n. a bolt with barbs to keep it tight when it has been driven in.

**rag book** ● n. Brit. a cloth book for very small children.

**rag doll** ● n. a doll made from cloth.

**rage** ● n. **1** violent uncontrollable anger. ➤[in combination] violent anger associated with conflict arising from a particular context: *air rage*. ➤the violent action of a natural agency. **2** a vehement desire or passion. ➤poetic/literary prophetic, poetic, or martial enthusiasm or ardour. **3** Austral./NZ informal a lively party. ● v. **1** feel or express rage. ➤continue violently or with great force. **2** Austral./NZ informal enjoy oneself socially.
– PHRASES **all the rage** temporarily very popular or fashionable.
– DERIVATIVES **rager** n. **raging** adj.
– ORIGIN ME: from OFr. *rage* (n.), *rager* (v.), from a var. of L. *rabies* (see RABIES).

**ragga** /ˈragə/ ● n. chiefly Brit. a style of dance music in which a DJ improvises lyrics over a backing track.
– ORIGIN 1990s: from RAGAMUFFIN, because of the clothing worn by its followers.

**raggamuffin** ● n. variant spelling of RAGAMUFFIN.

**ragged** /ˈragɪd/ ● adj. **1** (of cloth or clothes) old and torn. ➤wearing such clothes. **2** rough or irregular. ➤(of an animal) having a rough, shaggy coat. ➤lacking finish, smoothness, or uniformity. ➤Printing (especially of a right margin) uneven. **3** suffering from exhaustion or stress.
– PHRASES **run someone ragged** exhaust someone.
– DERIVATIVES **raggedly** adv. **raggedness** n. **raggedy** adj. (informal, chiefly N. Amer.).
– ORIGIN ME: of Scand. origin.

**ragged robin** ● n. a pink-flowered campion with divided petals that give it a tattered appearance. [*Lychnis flos-cuculi*.]

**raggle-taggle** ● adj. untidy and scruffy.
– ORIGIN C20: appar. a fanciful var. of RAGTAG.

**raggy** ● adj. (**-ier**, **-iest**) informal ragged.
– ORIGIN OE, of Scand. origin.

**raglan** ● adj. having or denoting sleeves continuing in one piece up to the neck of a garment. ● n. an overcoat with raglan sleeves.
– ORIGIN C19: named after Lord *Raglan*, a Brit. commander in the Crimean War.

**ragman** ● n. (pl. **-men**) a rag-and-bone man.

**ragout** /raˈguː/ ● n. a highly seasoned dish of chopped meat stewed with vegetables.
– ORIGIN from Fr. *ragoût*, from *ragoûter* 'revive the taste of'.

**rag paper** ● n. paper made from cotton.

**ragpicker** ● n. historical a person who collected and sold rags.

**rag-roll** ● v. create a striped or marbled effect on (a surface) by painting it with a rag crumpled up into a roll.
– DERIVATIVES **rag-rolled** adj. **rag-rolling** n.

**rag rug** ● n. a rug made from small strips of fabric hooked into or pushed through a material such as hessian.

**ragstone** ● n. see RAG[3] (sense 2).

**ragtag** ● adj. untidy, disorganized, or incongruously varied in character.
– ORIGIN C19: superseding earlier *tag-rag* and *tag and rag* (see RAG[1], TAG[1]).

**ragtime** ● n. music characterized by a syncopated melodic line and regularly accented accompaniment, evolved by black American musicians in the 1890s and played especially on the piano.

**ragtop** ● n. informal a car with a convertible roof.

**rag trade** ● n. informal the clothing or fashion industry.

**raguly** /ˈragjʊli/ ● adj. Heraldry having an edge with oblique notches like a row of sawn-off branches.
– ORIGIN C17: perh. from RAGGED, on the pattern of *nebuly*.

**ragweed** ● n. a North American plant of the daisy family, with tiny green flowers. [*Ambrosia artemisia*.]

**ragworm** ● n. a predatory marine bristle worm, often used as bait by fishermen. [*Nereis diversicolor* and other species, family Nereidae.]

**ragwort** ● n. a yellow-flowered ragged-leaved plant of the daisy family, toxic to livestock. [*Senecio jacobaea* and related species.]

**rah** ● exclam. informal, chiefly N. Amer. a cheer of encouragement or approval.
– ORIGIN C19: shortening of HURRAH.

**rah-rah** ● adj. N. Amer. informal marked by great or uncritical enthusiasm or excitement.

**rah-rah skirt** ● n. a short flounced skirt of a kind typically worn by cheerleaders.

**rai** /rʌɪ/ ● n. a style of music fusing Arabic and Algerian folk elements with Western rock.
– ORIGIN 1980s: perh. from Arab. *ha er-ray*, lit. 'that's the thinking, here is the view', a phr. freq. found in the songs.

**RAID** ● abbrev. Computing redundant array of independent (or inexpensive) disks, a system for providing greater capacity, security, etc. by using several disk drives.

**raid** ● n. **1** a rapid surprise attack on people or premises. **2** a surprise visit by police to arrest suspects or seize illicit goods. **3** Stock Exchange a hostile attempt to buy a controlling interest in the shares of a company. ● v. **1** conduct a raid on. **2** quickly and illicitly take something from (a place).
– DERIVATIVES **raider** n.
– ORIGIN ME: Scots var. of ROAD in the early senses 'journey on horseback', 'foray'.

**rail**[1] /reɪl/ ● n. **1** a bar or series of bars fixed on upright supports or attached to a wall or ceiling, serving as part of a fence or barrier or used to hang things on. **2** a steel bar or continuous line of bars laid on the ground as one of a pair forming a railway track. **3** railways as a means of transport. **4** a horizontal piece in the frame of a panelled door or sash window. Compare with STILE[2]. **5** the edge of a surfboard or sailboard. **6** Electronics a conductor which is maintained at a fixed potential and to which other parts of a circuit are connected. ● v. **1** provide or enclose with a rail or rails. **2** convey (goods) by rail. **3** (in windsurfing) sail the board on its edge.
– PHRASES **go off the rails** informal begin behaving in an uncontrolled way. **on the rails 1** informal functioning in a normal or regulated way. **2** (of a racehorse or jockey) in a position on the racetrack nearest the inside fence.
– DERIVATIVES **railage** n. **railless** adj.
– ORIGIN ME: from OFr. *reille* 'iron rod', from L. *regula* 'straight stick, rule'.

**rail**[2] ● v. (**rail against/at**) complain or protest strongly about or to.
– DERIVATIVES **railer** n.
– ORIGIN ME: from Fr. *railler*, from Provençal *ralhar* 'to jest', based on an alt. of L. *rugire* 'to bellow'.

**rail**[3] ● n. a secretive waterside bird with typically drab grey and brown plumage. [*Rallus* and other genera, fam-

ily Rallidae.]
– ORIGIN ME: from ONorth. Fr. *raille*, perh. imitative.

**railcar** • n. Brit. a powered railway passenger vehicle designed to operate singly or as part of a multiple unit. ➤(**rail car**) N. Amer. any railway carriage or wagon.

**railcard** • n. Brit. a pass entitling the holder to reduced rail fares.

**railhead** • n. **1** a point on a railway from which roads and other transport routes begin. **2** the furthest point reached in constructing a railway.

**railing** • n. (usu. **railings**) a fence or barrier made of rails.

**raillery** /ˈreɪləri/ • n. good-humoured teasing.
– ORIGIN C17: from Fr. *raillerie*, from *railler* (see RAIL²).

**railman** • n. (pl. **-men**) another term for RAILWAYMAN.

**railroad** • n. North American term for RAILWAY. • v. informal **1** rush or coerce (someone) into doing something. ➤cause (a measure) to be passed or approved quickly by applying pressure. **2** N. Amer. send (someone) to prison unjustly. **3** [usu. as noun **railroading**] N. Amer. travel or work on the railways.

**railway** • n. chiefly Brit. **1** a track made of rails along which trains run. **2** a system of such tracks with the trains, organization, and personnel required for its working.

**railwayman** • n. (pl. **-men**) chiefly Brit. a man who works on a railway.

**raiment** /ˈreɪm(ə)nt/ • n. archaic or poetic/literary clothing.
– ORIGIN ME: shortening of obs. *arrayment* 'dress, outfit'.

**rain** • n. **1** the condensed moisture of the atmosphere falling visibly in separate drops. ➤(**rains**) falls of rain. **2** a large quantity of things falling or descending: *a rain of blows.* • v. **1** (**it rains**, **it is raining**, etc.) rain falls. ➤poetic/literary send down rain. **2** (**be rained off**) (of an event) be terminated or cancelled because of rain. **3** fall or cause to fall in large quantities: *it was just raining glass.*
– PHRASES **be as right as rain** be perfectly fit and well. **rain cats and dogs** rain heavily.
– DERIVATIVES **rainless** adj.
– ORIGIN OE *regn* (n.), *regnian* (v.), of Gmc origin.

**rainbird** • n. a bird that is said to foretell rain by its call, especially (in Britain) the green woodpecker.

**rainbow** • n. **1** an arch of colours visible in the sky, caused by the refraction and dispersion of the sun's light by water droplets in the atmosphere. **2** a wide range of things of different colours or kinds.
– ORIGIN OE *regnboga* (see RAIN, BOW¹).

**rainbow coalition** • n. a political alliance of differing groups, especially one comprising minorities and other disadvantaged groups.

**rainbow lorikeet** • n. a small vividly coloured Australasian parrot. [*Trichoglossus haematodus.*]

**rainbow runner** • n. a colourfully striped fish of the jack family, of warm seas worldwide. [*Elagatis bipinnulata.*]

**rainbow trout** • n. a large trout with reddish sides, native to western North America and introduced widely elsewhere for food or sport. [*Onchorhynchus mykiss.*]

**rain check** • n. N. Amer. **1** a ticket given for later use when an outdoor event is interrupted or postponed by rain. **2** a coupon issued by a shop, guaranteeing that a sale item which is out of stock may be purchased at a later date at the same reduced price.
– PHRASES **take a rain check** politely refuse an offer, with the implication that one may take it up at a later date.

**raincoat** • n. a long coat made from waterproofed or water-resistant fabric.

**raindrop** • n. a single drop of rain.

**rainfall** • n. **1** the fall of rain. **2** the quantity of rain falling within a given area in a given time.

**rainfly** • n. (pl. **-flies**) **1** N. Amer. the flysheet of a tent. **2** W. Indian a winged ant or termite, seen in numbers after rain.

**rainforest** • n. a luxuriant, dense forest found in tropical areas with consistently heavy rainfall.

**rainmaker** • n. **1** a person who attempts to cause rain to fall. **2** N. Amer. informal a person who is highly successful, especially in business.
– DERIVATIVES **rainmaking** n.

**rainout** • n. N. Amer. a cancellation or premature ending of an event because of rain.

**rain shadow** • n. a relatively dry region sheltered from prevailing rain-bearing winds by a range of hills.

**rainstorm** • n. a storm with heavy rain.

**rainswept** • adj. frequently or recently exposed to rain and wind.

**rain tree** • n. a large tropical American tree with grooved bark, widely planted as a street tree. [*Albizia saman.*]

**rainwater** • n. water that has fallen as rain.

**rainworm** • n. **1** the earthworm, which often comes to the surface after rain. **2** a soil-dwelling nematode worm which parasitizes grasshoppers. [*Mermis nigrescens.*]

**rainy** • adj. (**-ier**, **-iest**) having or characterized by considerable rainfall.
– PHRASES **a rainy day** a time in the future when money may be needed.
– DERIVATIVES **raininess** n.

**raise** • v. **1** lift or move to a higher position or level. ➤set upright. **2** construct or build (a structure). **3** increase the amount, level, or strength of. ➤promote to a higher rank. **4** (**raise something to**) Mathematics multiply a quantity to (a specified power). **5** (in poker or brag) bet (a specified amount) more than (another player). ➤Bridge make a higher bid in the same suit as that bid by (one's partner). **6** cause to be heard, felt, or considered: *doubts have been raised.* **7** generate (an invoice or other document). **8** collect or levy (money or resources). **9** bring up (a child). **10** breed or grow (animals or plants). **11** wake from sleep or bring back from death. **12** abandon or force to abandon (a blockade, embargo, etc.). **13** drive (an animal) from its lair. **14** (of someone at sea) come in sight of (land or another ship). ➤Brit. informal establish contact with (someone), especially by telephone or radio. **15** Physiology stimulate production of (an antiserum, antibody, etc.) against the appropriate target cell or substance. • n. **1** chiefly N. Amer. an increase in salary. **2** an act of raising a stake or bid. **3** Weightlifting an act of lifting or raising a part of the body while holding a weight.
– PHRASES **raise hell** informal make a noisy disturbance. ➤complain vociferously. **raise the roof** make or cause people to make a great deal of noise, especially cheering. **raise one's voice** speak more loudly.
– DERIVATIVES **raisable** adj. **raiser** n.
– ORIGIN ME: from ON *reisa*; rel. to the verb REAR².

**raised beach** • n. Geology a former beach now above water level owing to changes since its formation.

**raised bog** • n. a peat bog in which growth is most rapid at the centre, giving it a domed shape.

**raisin** • n. a partially dried grape.
– DERIVATIVES **raisiny** adj.
– ORIGIN ME: from OFr., 'grape', from an alt. of L. *racemus* 'grape bunch'.

**raison d'être** /ˌreɪzɒ̃ ˈdɛtrə, French rɛzɔ̃ dɛtʀ/ • n. (pl. **raisons d'être** pronunc. same) the most important reason or purpose for someone or something's existence.
– ORIGIN Fr., lit. 'reason for being'.

**raita** /ˈrʌɪtə/ • n. an Indian side dish of yogurt containing chopped cucumber or other vegetables, and spices.
– ORIGIN from Hindi *rāytā*.

**Raj** /rɑː(d)ʒ/ • n. (**the Raj**) historical British sovereignty in India.
– ORIGIN from Hindi *rāj* 'reign'.

**raja** /ˈrɑːdʒɑː/ (also **rajah**) • n. historical an Indian king or prince.
– ORIGIN from Hindi *rājā*, Sanskrit *rājan* 'king'.

**Rajasthani** /ˌrɑːdʒəˈstɑːni/ • n. a native or inhabitant of the Indian state of Rajasthan. • adj. of or relating to Rajasthan.

**raja yoga** • n. a form of yoga intended to achieve control over the mind and emotions.
– ORIGIN from Sanskrit, from *rājan* 'king' + YOGA.

**Rajput** /ˈrɑːdʒpʊt/ • n. a member of a Hindu military caste claiming Kshatriya descent.
– ORIGIN from Hindi *rājpūt*, from Sanskrit *rājan* 'king' +

*putra* 'son'.

**rake**[1] • n. **1** an implement consisting of a pole having at its end a toothed crossbar or fine tines, used for drawing together leaves, cut grass, etc. or smoothing loose soil or gravel. **2** an act of raking. • v. **1** draw together with a rake. **2** make smooth with a rake. **3** scratch or scrape with a long sweeping movement. **4** draw or drag (something) through something with a long sweeping movement. **5** sweep with gunfire, a look, or a beam of light. **6** (**rake through**) search or rummage through.
– PHRASES **rake and scrape** black English be extremely thrifty; scrimp and save. **rake over** (**old**) **coals** (or **rake over the ashes**) chiefly Brit. revive the memory of a past event.
– PHRASAL VERBS **rake it in** informal make a lot of money. **rake something up/over** revive the memory of an incident or period of time that is best forgotten.
– DERIVATIVES **raker** n.
– ORIGIN OE *raca*, *racu*, of Gmc origin, from a base meaning 'heap up'; the verb is partly from ON *raka* 'to scrape, shave'.

**rake**[2] • n. a fashionable or wealthy man of dissolute habits.
– PHRASES **a rake's progress** a progressive deterioration through self-indulgence. [from the title of a series of engravings by Hogarth (1735).]
– ORIGIN C17: abbrev. of archaic *rakehell* in the same sense.

**rake**[3] • v. **1** set at a sloping angle. **2** (of a ship's mast or funnel) incline from the perpendicular towards the stern. **3** (of a ship's bow or stern) project at its upper part beyond the keel. • n. **1** the angle at which a thing slopes. **2** the angle of the edge or face of a cutting tool.
– DERIVATIVES **raking** adj.
– ORIGIN C17: prob. rel. to Ger. *ragen* 'to project', of unknown ult. origin; cf. Swed. *raka*.

**rake**[4] • n. Brit. a number of railway carriages or wagons coupled together.
– ORIGIN C20 (orig. Scots and north. Engl.): from ON *rák* 'stripe, streak', from an alt. of *rek-* 'to drive'.

**rake-off** • n. informal a commission or share of the profits from a deal, especially one that is disreputable.

**raki** /rəˈkiː, ˈraki/ • n. a strong alcoholic spirit made in eastern Europe or the Middle East.
– ORIGIN from Turk. *rakı*.

**rakish** • adj. **1** having a dashing, jaunty, or slightly disreputable quality or appearance. **2** (of a boat or car) smart and fast-looking, with streamlined angles and curves.
– DERIVATIVES **rakishly** adv. **rakishness** n.
– ORIGIN C18: from RAKE[2] + -ISH[1]; sense 2 influenced by RAKE[3].

**raku** /ˈrɑːkuː/ • n. a kind of lead-glazed Japanese earthenware, used especially for the tea ceremony.
– ORIGIN Japanese, lit. 'enjoyment'.

**rale** /rɑːl/ • n. (usu. **rales**) Medicine an abnormal rattling sound heard when examining unhealthy lungs with a stethoscope.
– ORIGIN C19: from Fr. *râle*, from *râler* 'to rattle'.

**rall.** • abbrev. Music rallentando.

**rallentando** /ˌralənˈtandəʊ/ • adv. & adj. Music with a gradual decrease of speed.
– ORIGIN Ital., lit. 'slowing down', from the verb *rallentare*.

**rally**[1] • v. (-ies, -ied) **1** (with reference to troops) bring or come together again in order to continue fighting. **2** bring or come together for concerted action. **3** assemble in a mass meeting. **4** recover or cause to recover in health, spirits, or poise. **5** (of share, currency, or commodity prices) increase after a fall. **6** drive in a rally. • n. (pl. **-ies**) **1** a mass meeting held as a protest or in support of a cause. **2** an open-air event for people who own a particular kind of vehicle. **3** a competition for motor vehicles in which they are driven a long distance over public roads or rough terrain. **4** a quick or marked recovery. **5** (in tennis and other racket sports) an extended exchange of strokes between players.
– DERIVATIVES **rallier** n. **rallyist** n.
– ORIGIN C17: from Fr. *rallier*, from *re-* 'again' + *allier* 'to ally'.

**rally**[2] • v. (**-ies, -ied**) archaic tease.
– ORIGIN C17: from Fr. *railler* (see RAIL[2]).

**rallycross** • n. Brit. a form of motor racing in which cars are driven in heats over a course including rough terrain and tarmac roads, but not public roads.

**rallying** • n. **1** the action or process of bringing or coming together. ➤[as modifier] having the effect of calling people to action: *a rallying cry*. **2** the action or sport of participating in a motor rally.

**RAM** • abbrev. **1** Computing random-access memory. **2** (in the UK) Royal Academy of Music.

**ram** • n. **1** an uncastrated male sheep. **2** short for BATTERING RAM. **3** the falling weight of a piledriving machine. **4** a hydraulic water-raising or lifting machine. ➤the piston of a hydrostatic press. ➤the plunger of a force pump. **5** historical a projecting part of the bow of a warship, for piercing the sides of other ships. ➤a warship with such a bow. • v. (**rammed, ramming**) **1** roughly force (something) into place. **2** (of a vehicle or vessel) be driven violently into. **3** (**ram into**) crash violently against. **4** [often as adj. **rammed**] beat (earth or the ground) with a heavy implement to make it hard and firm.
– DERIVATIVES **rammer** n.
– ORIGIN OE *ram(m)*, of Gmc origin.

**Ramadan** /ˈramədan, ˌraməˈdan/ (also **Ramadhan** /-zan/) • n. the ninth month of the Muslim year, during which strict fasting is observed from sunrise to sunset.
– ORIGIN from Arab. *ramaḍān*, from *ramaḍa* 'be hot'; supposedly because the fasting period was orig. in one of the hot months.

**ram air** • n. air which is forced to enter a moving aperture, such as the air intake of an aircraft.

**Raman effect** • n. Physics a change of wavelength exhibited by some of the radiation scattered by molecules and ions, used in spectroscopic analysis.
– ORIGIN 1920s: named after the Indian physicist C. V. *Raman*.

**Ramapithecus** /ˌrɑːməˈpɪθɪkəs/ • n. a genus of fossil anthropoid apes known from remains found in Miocene deposits in SW Asia and East Africa.
– ORIGIN mod. L., from the name of the Hindu god *Rama* + Gk *pithēkos* 'ape'.

**ramble** • v. **1** walk for pleasure in the countryside. **2** (of a plant) grow over walls, fences, etc. **3** (often **ramble on**) talk or write at length in a confused or inconsequential way. • n. a walk taken for pleasure in the countryside.
– DERIVATIVES **rambler** n. **rambling** adj. & n. **ramblingly** adv.
– ORIGIN ME: prob. rel. to MDu. *rammelen* (used of animals in the sense 'wander about on heat'), also to RAM.

**Rambo** /ˈrambəʊ/ • n. an extremely tough and aggressive man.
– ORIGIN the name of the hero of David Morrell's novel *First Blood* (1972), popularized in the films *First Blood* (1982) and *Rambo: First Blood Part II* (1985).

**rambunctious** /ramˈbʌŋ(k)ʃəs/ • adj. informal, chiefly N. Amer. uncontrollably exuberant.
– DERIVATIVES **rambunctiously** adv. **rambunctiousness** n.
– ORIGIN C19: of unknown origin.

**rambutan** /ramˈb(j)uːt(ə)n/ • n. **1** a red, plum-sized tropical fruit with soft spines and a slightly acidic taste. **2** the Malaysian tree that bears this fruit. [*Nephelium lappaceum*.]
– ORIGIN C18: from Malay *rambūtan*, from *rambut* 'hair', with allusion to the fruit's spines.

**RAMC** • abbrev. (in the UK) Royal Army Medical Corps.

**ramekin** /ˈramɪkɪn, ˈramkɪn/ • n. a small dish for baking and serving an individual portion of food.
– ORIGIN C17: from Fr. *ramequin*, of Low Ger. or Du. origin.

**ramen** /ˈrɑːmɛn/ • pl. n. (in oriental cuisine) quick-cooking noodles.
– ORIGIN Japanese, from Chin. *lā* 'to pull' + *miàn* 'noodles'.

**ramie** /ˈrami/ • n. **1** a vegetable fibre noted for its length

and toughness, used in the manufacture of textiles. **2** the plant of the nettle family which yields this fibre, native to tropical Asia. [*Boehmeria nivea*.]
– ORIGIN C19: from Malay *rami*.

**ramification** ● **n. 1** the action or state of ramifying or being ramified. **2** (usu. **ramifications**) a complex consequence of an action or event. **3** a subdivision of a complex structure or process.

**ramify** /ˈramɪfʌɪ/ ● **v.** (**-ies**, **-ied**) form or cause to form branches; spread or cause to spread and branch out.
– DERIVATIVES **ramified** adj.
– ORIGIN ME: from OFr. *ramifier*, from med. L. *ramificare*, from L. *ramus* 'branch'.

**ramin** /raˈmiːn/ ● **n.** a hardwood tree of Malaysian swamp forests, yielding pale lightweight wood. [*Gonystylus bancanus*.]
– ORIGIN C20: from Malay.

**ramjet** ● **n.** a type of jet engine in which the air drawn in for combustion is compressed solely by the forward motion of the aircraft.

**rammy** ● **n.** (pl. **-ies**) Scottish a quarrel or brawl.
– ORIGIN 1930s: perh. from Scots *rammle* 'row, uproar', var. of RAMBLE.

**ramp** ● **n. 1** a sloping surface joining two different levels. **2** a movable set of steps for entering or leaving an aircraft. **3** Brit. a transverse ridge in a road to control the speed of vehicles. **4** N. Amer. an inclined slip road leading to or from a main road or motorway. **5** an upward bend in a stair rail. **6** an electrical waveform in which the voltage increases or decreases linearly with time. **7** Brit. informal a swindle involving a fraudulent increase of the price of a share. ● **v. 1** provide with a ramp. **2** (of an electrical waveform) increase or decrease in voltage linearly with time. **3** [usu. as noun **ramping**] Brit. purchase shares or other securities in order to raise their price fraudulently. **4** (**ramp up** or **ramp something up**) (especially in reference to the production of goods) increase or cause something to increase in amount. **5** chiefly dialect (of a plant) grow or climb luxuriantly. **6** archaic (of an animal) rear up on its hind legs. **7** archaic rush about violently.
– ORIGIN ME (as v. in the sense 'rear up', also used as a heraldic term): from OFr. *ramper* 'creep, crawl', of unknown origin.

**rampage** ● **v.** /ramˈpeɪdʒ/ rush around in a violent and uncontrollable manner. ● **n.** /ramˈpeɪdʒ, ˈrampeɪdʒ/ an instance of rampaging.
– DERIVATIVES **rampageous** adj. (archaic). **rampager** n.
– ORIGIN C17: perh. based on RAMP and RAGE.

**rampant** ● **adj. 1** flourishing or spreading unchecked. **2** unrestrained in action or performance. **3** (of a plant) lush in growth. **4** [usu. postpos.] Heraldry (of an animal) represented standing on its left hind foot with its forefeet in the air.
– DERIVATIVES **rampancy** n. **rampantly** adv.
– ORIGIN ME: from OFr., lit. 'crawling', pres. part. of *ramper* (see RAMP).

**rampart** ● **n.** a defensive wall of a castle or walled city, having a broad top with a walkway.
– ORIGIN C16: from Fr. *rempart*, from *remparer* 'fortify, take possession of again', based on L. *ante* 'before' + *parare* 'prepare'.

**rampion** /ˈrampɪən/ ● **n.** a blue-flowered bellflower, some kinds of which have a root that can be eaten in salads. [*Campanula rapunculus* (Mediterranean) and genus *Phyteuma*.]
– ORIGIN C16: from a var. of med. L. *rapuncium*; cf. Ger. *Rapunzel* 'lamb's lettuce'.

**ram raid** ● **n.** a robbery in which a shop window is rammed with a vehicle and looted.
– DERIVATIVES **ram-raider** n. **ram-raiding** n.

**ramrod** ● **n. 1** a rod for ramming down the charge of a muzzle-loading firearm. **2** N. Amer. a rigidly strict foreman or manager. ● **v.** (**ramrodded**, **ramrodding**) (**ramrod something through**) chiefly N. Amer. force a proposed measure to be accepted or completed quickly.

**ramshackle** ● **adj.** in a state of severe disrepair.
– ORIGIN C19 (orig. dial. in the sense 'irregular, disorderly'): alt. of earlier *ramshackled*, alt. form of obs. *ransackled* 'ransacked'.

**ramshorn snail** /ˈramzhɔːn/ ● **n.** a freshwater snail with a flat spiral shell. [Family Planorbidae: many species.]

**ramsons** /ˈrams(ə)nz/ ● **pl. n.** [usu. treated as sing.] a woodland plant with broad shiny leaves and round heads of white flowers, producing a strong aroma of garlic. [*Allium ursinum*.]
– ORIGIN OE *hramsan*, pl. of *hramsa* 'wild garlic', later interpreted as sing.

**ramus** /ˈreɪməs/ ● **n.** (pl. **rami** /ˈreɪmʌɪ, ˈreɪmiː/) **1** Anatomy & Zoology a projecting structure, especially a branch of a bone or nerve. **2** Ornithology a barb of a feather.
– ORIGIN C17: from L., lit. 'branch'.

**RAN** ● **abbrev.** Royal Australian Navy.

**ran** past of RUN.

**ranch** ● **n. 1** a large farm, especially in the western US and Canada, where cattle or other animals are bred. **2** (also **ranch house**) N. Amer. a single-storey house. **3** (also **ranch dressing**) N. Amer. a type of thick white salad dressing made with sour cream. ● **v.** run a ranch. ➤ breed (animals) on a ranch. ➤ use (land) as a ranch.
– DERIVATIVES **rancher** n. **ranching** n.
– ORIGIN C19: from Sp. *rancho* 'group of persons eating together'.

**rancheria** /ˌrɑːn(t)ʃəˈriːə/ ● **n.** (in Spanish America and the western US) a small Indian settlement.
– ORIGIN Sp., from *rancho* (see RANCH).

**ranchero** /rɑːnˈtʃɛːrəʊ/ ● **n.** (pl. **-os**) chiefly N. Amer. a person who farms or works on a ranch, especially in the southwestern US and Mexico.
– ORIGIN Sp., from *rancho* (see RANCH).

**rancid** ● **adj.** (of foods containing fat or oil) smelling or tasting unpleasant as a result of being stale.
– DERIVATIVES **rancidity** n.
– ORIGIN C17: from L. *rancidus* 'stinking'.

**rancour** (US **rancor**) ● **n.** bitterness; resentment.
– DERIVATIVES **rancorous** adj. **rancorously** adv.
– ORIGIN ME: via OFr. from late L. *rancor* 'rankness' (in the Vulgate 'bitter grudge'), rel. to L. *rancidus* 'stinking'.

**rand**[1] /rand, rant/ ● **n. 1** the basic monetary unit of South Africa, equal to 100 cents. [from *the Rand*, the name of a goldfield district near Johannesburg.] **2** S. African an area of high, sloping ground; a long rocky hillock. [Afrik., lit. 'edge'; rel. to RAND[2].]

**rand**[2] /rand/ ● **n.** a strip of leather placed under the back part of a shoe or boot to make it level before the lifts of the heel are attached.
– ORIGIN OE (denoting a border): of Gmc origin.

**R & B** ● **abbrev. 1** rhythm and blues. **2** a kind of melodic pop music with soulful vocals.

**R & D** ● **abbrev.** research and development.

**random** ● **adj. 1** made, done, or happening without method or conscious decision. **2** Statistics governed by or involving equal chances for each item. **3** (of masonry or something similarly constructed) with stones or components of irregular size and shape.
– DERIVATIVES **randomization** (also **-isation**) n. **randomize** (also **-ise**) v. **randomly** adv. **randomness** n.
– ORIGIN ME (in the sense 'impetuous headlong rush'): from OFr. *randon* 'great speed', from *randir* 'gallop', from a Gmc root shared by RAND[2].

**random access** ● **n.** Computing the process of transferring information to or from memory in which every memory location can be accessed directly rather than being accessed in a fixed sequence.

**random error** ● **n.** Statistics an error in measurement caused by factors which vary from one measurement to another.

**random walk** ● **n.** Physics a series of movements of an object or changes in a variable that follow no discernible pattern or trend.

**R & R** ● **abbrev. 1** informal rest and recreation. **2** Medicine rescue and resuscitation. **3** (also **R'n'R**) rock and roll.

**randy** ● **adj.** (**-ier**, **-iest**) **1** informal, chiefly Brit. sexually aroused or excited. **2** Scottish archaic (of a person) having a

rude, aggressive manner.
– DERIVATIVES **randily** adv. **randiness** n.
– ORIGIN C17: perh. from obs. *rand* 'rant, rave', from obs. Du. *randen* 'to rant'.

**ranee** /'rɑːniː/ ● n. archaic spelling of **RANI**.

**rang** past of **RING**[2].

**rangatira** /ˌraŋgə'tɪərə/ ● n. NZ a Maori chief or noble.
– ORIGIN from Maori.

**range** ● n. **1** the area of variation between limits on a particular scale. **2** a set of different things of the same general type. **3** the scope or extent of a person's or thing's abilities or capacity. **4** the distance within which a sense, detector, transmitter, etc. is effective. ➤ the distance that can be covered by a vehicle or aircraft without refuelling. ➤ the distance attained or attainable by a gun, projectile, etc. ➤ the distance between a camera and the subject to be photographed. **5** a line or series of mountains or hills. **6** a large area of open land for grazing or hunting. **7** an area used as a testing ground for military equipment. ➤ (also **shooting range**) an area with targets for shooting practice. **8** the area over which a plant or animal is distributed. **9** a large cooking stove with several burners or hotplates. ● v. **1** vary or extend between specified limits. **2** run or extend in a line in a particular direction. **3** place or arrange in a row or rows or in a specified order or manner. **4** (**range someone against** or **be ranged against**) place oneself or be placed in opposition to. **5** Brit. Printing (with reference to type) align or be aligned at the ends of successive lines. **6** travel or wander over a wide area. **7** embrace a wide number of different topics. **8** find the range of a target. **9** (with reference to a projectile) send or be sent a specified distance.
– ORIGIN ME (in the sense 'line of people or animals'): from OFr. *range* 'row, rank', from *rangier* 'put in order', from *rang* 'rank'.

**rangefinder** ● n. an instrument for estimating the distance of an object, especially for use with a camera or gun.

**ranger** ● n. **1** a keeper of a park, forest, or area of countryside. **2** a member of a body of armed men. **3** (**Ranger** or **Ranger Guide**) Brit. a member of the senior branch of the Guides.

**ranging pole** (also **ranging rod**) ● n. Surveying a pole or rod used for setting a straight line.

**rangy** /'reɪn(d)ʒi/ ● adj. (**-ier**, **-iest**) (of a person) tall and slim; long-limbed.
– DERIVATIVES **ranginess** n.

**rani** /'rɑːniː/ (also **ranee**) ● n. (pl. **ranis**) historical a Hindu queen.
– ORIGIN from Hindi *rānī*, Sanskrit *rājñī*, fem. of *rājan* 'king'.

**ranitidine** /ra'nɪtɪdiːn, -'nʌɪt-/ ● n. Medicine a synthetic compound with antihistamine properties, used to treat ulcers and related conditions.
– ORIGIN 1970s: blend of **FURAN** and **NITRO-**, + **-IDE** + **-INE**[4].

**rank**[1] ● n. **1** a position within a fixed hierarchy, especially that of the armed forces. **2** high social standing. **3** a single line of soldiers or police officers drawn up abreast. ➤ a regular row or line of things or people. **4** (**the ranks**) (in the armed forces) those who are not commissioned officers. **5** (**ranks**) the people belonging to or constituting a group or class: *the ranks of the unemployed*. **6** Chess each of the eight rows of eight squares running from side to side across a chessboard. Compare with **FILE**[2]. **7** Brit. short for **TAXI RANK**. **8** Mathematics the value or the order of the largest non-zero determinant of a given matrix. ● v. **1** give (someone or something) a rank within a grading system. **2** hold a specified rank. **3** US take precedence over (someone) in respect to rank. **4** arrange in a row or rows.
– PHRASES **break rank** (or **ranks**) **1** (of soldiers or police officers) fail to remain in line. **2** fail to maintain solidarity. **close ranks 1** (of soldiers or police officers) come closer together in a line. **2** unite in order to defend common interests. **keep rank** (of soldiers or police officers) remain in line. **pull rank** take unfair advantage of one's seniority.
– ORIGIN ME: from OFr. *ranc*, of Gmc origin; rel. to **RING**[1].

**rank**[2] ● adj. **1** (of vegetation) growing too thickly. **2** having a foul smell. **3** conspicuously undesirable; flagrant.
– DERIVATIVES **rankly** adv. **rankness** n.
– ORIGIN OE *ranc* 'proud, rebellious, sturdy', also 'fully grown', of Gmc origin.

**rank and file** ● n. [treated as pl.] the ordinary members of an organization as opposed to its leaders.
– ORIGIN referring to the 'ranks' and 'files' into which privates and non-commissioned officers form on parade.

**rank correlation** ● n. Statistics an assessment of the degree of correlation between two ways of ranking the members of a set.

**ranker** ● n. **1** chiefly Brit. a soldier in the ranks; a private. ➤ a commissioned officer who has been in the ranks. **2** [in combination] a person or animal of a specified rank: *a top-ranker.*

**ranking** ● n. **1** a position in a hierarchy or scale. **2** the action of giving a rank or status to someone or something. ● adj. [in combination] having a specified rank: *high ranking officers.* ➤ N. Amer. having a high rank.

**rankle** ● v. **1** (of a comment or fact) cause annoyance or resentment. ➤ chiefly N. Amer. annoy or irritate (someone). **2** archaic (of a wound or sore) continue to be painful; fester.
– ORIGIN ME: from OFr. *rancler*, from *rancle*, *draoncle* 'festering sore', from an alt. of med. L. *dracunculus*, dimin. of *draco* 'serpent'.

**ransack** ● v. **1** go hurriedly through (a place) stealing things and causing damage. **2** thoroughly search.
– DERIVATIVES **ransacker** n.
– ORIGIN ME: from ON *rannsaka*, from *rann* 'house' + a second element rel. to *sœkja* 'seek'.

**ransom** ● n. a sum of money demanded or paid for the release of a captive. ● v. obtain the release of (someone) by paying a ransom. ➤ detain (someone) and demand a ransom for their release. ➤ release after receiving a ransom.
– PHRASES **hold someone to ransom 1** hold someone captive and demand payment for their release. **2** demand concessions from a person or organization by threatening damaging action. **a king's ransom** a huge amount of money.
– ORIGIN ME: from OFr. *ransoun* (n.), *ransouner* (v.), from L. *redemptio(n-)* (see **REDEMPTION**).

**rant** ● v. speak or shout at length in a wild, impassioned way. ● n. a spell of ranting.
– DERIVATIVES **ranter** n.
– ORIGIN C16 (in the sense 'behave in a boisterous way'): from Du. *ranten* 'talk nonsense, rave'.

**ranunculaceous** /rəˌnʌŋkjʊ'leɪʃəs/ ● adj. Botany relating to or denoting plants of the buttercup family (Ranunculaceae).

**ranunculus** /rə'nʌŋkjʊləs/ ● n. (pl. **ranunculuses** or **ranunculi** /-lʌɪ, -liː/) a plant of a genus that includes the buttercups and water crowfoots, typically having yellow or white bowl-shaped flowers and lobed or toothed leaves. [Genus *Ranunculus*: many species.]
– ORIGIN mod. L., from L., lit. 'little frog', dimin. of *rana*.

**RAOC** ● abbrev. (in the UK) Royal Army Ordnance Corps.

**rap**[1] ● v. (**rapped**, **rapping**) **1** strike (a hard surface) with a series of rapid audible blows. ➤ strike (something) against a hard surface in such a way. ➤ strike (someone or something) sharply. **2** (usu. **rap something out**) say something sharply or suddenly. **3** informal, chiefly N. Amer. talk or chat in an easy and familiar manner. **4** perform rap music. ● n. **1** a quick, sharp knock or blow. **2** informal a rebuke or criticism. **3** a type of popular music of US black origin in which words are recited rapidly and rhythmically over an instrumental backing. **4** informal, chiefly N. Amer. an impromptu talk or discussion. **5** informal, chiefly N. Amer. a criminal charge: *a murder rap.*
– PHRASES **beat the rap** N. Amer. informal escape punishment for or be acquitted of a crime. **take the rap** informal be punished or blamed for something.
– DERIVATIVES **rapper** n.
– ORIGIN ME: prob. imitative and of Scand. origin.

**rap**[2] ● n. the smallest amount: *he doesn't care a rap.*
– ORIGIN C19: from Ir. *ropaire* 'robber'; used as the name of

a counterfeit coin in C18 Ireland.

**rapacious** /rəˈpeɪʃəs/ • **adj.** aggressively greedy.
– DERIVATIVES **rapaciously** adv. **rapaciousness** n. **rapacity** n.
– ORIGIN C17: from L. *rapac-*, *rapax* (from *rapere* 'to snatch') + **-IOUS**.

**RAPC** • **abbrev.** (in the UK) Royal Army Pay Corps.

**rape**[1] • **v. 1** (of a man) force (another person) to have sexual intercourse with him against their will. **2** spoil or destroy (a place). • **n. 1** an act or the crime of raping someone. **2** the act of raping a place or area.
– DERIVATIVES **raper** n. (chiefly US).
– ORIGIN ME (orig. denoting violent seizure of property): from Anglo-Norman Fr. *rap* (n.), *raper* (v.), from L. *rapere* 'seize'.

**rape**[2] • **n.** a plant of the cabbage family with bright yellow flowers, especially a variety (**oilseed rape**) grown for its oil-rich seed and as stockfeed. [*Brassica napus.*]
– ORIGIN ME (orig. denoting the turnip plant): from L. *rapum*, *rapa* 'turnip'.

**rape**[3] • **n.** historical (in the UK) any of the six ancient divisions of Sussex.
– ORIGIN OE, var. of **ROPE**, with ref. to the fencing-off of land.

**rape**[4] • **n.** (often **rapes**) the stalks and skins of grapes left after winemaking, used in making vinegar.
– ORIGIN C17 (as *rape wine*): from Fr. *râpe*, med. L. *raspa* 'bunch of grapes'.

**rapeseed** • **n.** seeds of the rape plant, used for oil.

**raphe** /ˈreɪfi/ • **n.** (pl. **raphae** /ˈreɪfiː/) Anatomy & Biology a groove, ridge, or seam in an organ or tissue, typically marking the line where two halves fused in the embryo.
– ORIGIN C18: mod. L., from Gk *rhaphē* 'seam'.

**raphide** /ˈreɪfʌɪd/ • **n.** Botany a needle-shaped crystal of calcium oxalate occurring in clusters within the tissues of certain plants.
– ORIGIN C19: via Fr. from Gk *rhaphis*, *rhaphid-* 'needle'.

**rapid** • **adj.** happening in a short time or at great speed. • **n.** (usu. **rapids**) a fast-flowing and turbulent part of the course of a river.
– DERIVATIVES **rapidity** n. **rapidly** adv. **rapidness** n.
– ORIGIN C17: from L. *rapidus*, from *rapere* 'take by force'.

**rapid eye movement** • **n.** the jerky movement of a person's eyes that occurs in REM sleep.

**rapier** • **n.** a thin, light sharp-pointed sword used for thrusting.
– ORIGIN C16: from Fr. *rapière*, from *râpe* 'rasp, grater' (because the perforated hilt resembles a rasp or grater).

**rapine** /ˈrapʌɪn, -pɪn/ • **n.** poetic/literary the violent seizure of property.
– ORIGIN ME: from OFr., or from L. *rapina*, from *rapere* 'seize'.

**rapist** • **n.** a man who commits rape.

**rapparee** /ˌrapəˈriː/ • **n.** archaic an Irish bandit or irregular soldier.
– ORIGIN C17: from Ir. *rapaire* 'short pike'.

**rappee** /raˈpiː/ • **n.** a type of coarse snuff.
– ORIGIN C18: from Fr. (*tabac*) *râpé* 'rasped (tobacco)'.

**rappel** /raˈpɛl/ • **n.** & **v.** (**rappelled**, **rappelling**) another term for **ABSEIL**.
– ORIGIN 1930s: from Fr., lit. 'a recalling', from *rappeler* in the sense 'bring back to oneself' (with ref. to the rope manoeuvre).

**rappen** /ˈrap(ə)n/ • **n.** (pl. same) a monetary unit of the German-speaking cantons of Switzerland and of Liechtenstein, equal to one hundredth of the Swiss franc.
– ORIGIN from Ger. *Rappe* 'raven', with ref. to the depiction of a raven's head on a medieval coin.

**rapport** /raˈpɔː/ • **n.** a close and harmonious relationship in which there is common understanding.
– ORIGIN C17: Fr., from *rapporter* 'bring back'.

**rapporteur** /ˌrapɔːˈtəː/ • **n.** a person appointed by an organization to report on its meetings.
– ORIGIN C18: Fr., from *rapporter* 'bring back'.

**rapprochement** /raˈprɒʃmɒ̃/ • **n.** the establishment or resumption of harmonious relations.
– ORIGIN Fr., from *rapprocher*, from *re-* (expressing intensive force) + *approcher* 'to approach'.

**rapscallion** /rapˈskalɪən/ • **n.** archaic or humorous a mischievous person.
– ORIGIN C17: alt. of earlier *rascallion*, perh. from **RASCAL**.

**rapt** • **adj. 1** fully absorbed and intent; fascinated. **2** enraptured. **3** Austral. informal another term for **WRAPPED**. **4** archaic or poetic/literary transported bodily.
– DERIVATIVES **raptly** adv. **raptness** n.
– ORIGIN ME: from L. *raptus* 'seized', past part. of *rapere*.

**raptor** • **n. 1** a bird of prey. **2** informal a dromaeosaurid dinosaur, such as a velociraptor.
– ORIGIN ME: from L., lit. 'plunderer', from *rapt-*, *rapere* 'seize'.

**raptorial** • **adj.** chiefly Zoology **1** predatory. **2** adapted for seizing prey.
– DERIVATIVES **raptorially** adv.

**rapture** • **n. 1** a feeling of intense pleasure or joy. **2** (**raptures**) the expression of intense pleasure or enthusiasm. **3** (**the Rapture**) N. Amer. (according to some millenarian teaching) the transporting of believers to heaven at the second coming of Christ.
– PHRASES **rapture of the deep** informal nitrogen narcosis.
– DERIVATIVES **rapturous** adj. **rapturously** adv. **rapturousness** n.
– ORIGIN C16 (in the sense 'seizing and carrying off'): from obs. Fr., or from med. L. *raptura* 'seizing', partly influenced by **RAPT**.

**rara avis** /ˌrɛːrə ˈeɪvɪs, ˌrɑːrə ˈavɪs/ • **n.** (pl. **rarae aves** /-riː, -viːz/) another term for **RARE BIRD**.
– ORIGIN from L.

**rare**[1] • **adj.** (**rarer**, **rarest**) **1** occurring very infrequently. **2** remarkable: *a player of rare skill.*
– DERIVATIVES **rareness** n.
– ORIGIN ME: from L. *rarus*.

**rare**[2] • **adj.** (**rarer**, **rarest**) (of red meat) lightly cooked, so that the inside is still red.
– ORIGIN C18: var. of obs. *rear* 'half-cooked'.

**rare bird** • **n.** an exceptional person or thing.
– ORIGIN translating L. *rara avis* (Juvenal's *Satires*, vi.165).

**rarebit** (also **Welsh rarebit** or **Welsh rabbit**) • **n.** a dish of melted and seasoned cheese on toast.
– ORIGIN C18 (as *Welsh rabbit*): the reason for the use of the term *rabbit* is unknown.

**rare earth** (also **rare-earth element** or **metal**) • **n.** Chemistry any of a group of chemically similar metallic elements comprising the lanthanide series and (usually) scandium and yttrium.

**raree show** /ˈrɛːriː/ • **n.** archaic a form of street entertainment, especially one carried in a box, such as a peep show.
– ORIGIN C17: appar. representing *rare show*, as pronounced by Savoyard showmen.

**rarefaction** /ˌrɛːrɪˈfakʃ(ə)n/ • **n.** reduction of the density of something, especially air or a gas.
– ORIGIN C17: from med. L. *rarefactio(n-)*, from *rarefacere* 'grow thin, become rare'.

**rarefied** /ˈrɛːrɪfʌɪd/ • **adj. 1** (of air) of lower pressure than usual; thin. **2** very esoteric or refined.

**rare gas** • **n.** another term for **NOBLE GAS**.

**rarely** • **adv. 1** not often; seldom. **2** archaic remarkably well. ➤ to an unusual degree.

**raring** • **adj.** informal very eager to do something: *she was raring to go.*
– ORIGIN 1920s: pres. part. of *rare*, dial. var. of **ROAR** or **REAR**[2].

**rarity** • **n.** (pl. **-ies**) **1** the state or quality of being rare. **2** a rare thing.

**rascal** • **n.** a mischievous or cheeky person, especially a child.
– DERIVATIVES **rascality** n. **rascally** adj.
– ORIGIN ME (in the senses 'a mob' and 'member of the rabble'): from OFr. *rascaille* 'rabble', of uncertain origin.

**rase** • **v.** variant spelling of **RAZE**.

**rash**[1] • **adj.** acting or done impetuously, without careful

consideration.
– DERIVATIVES **rashly** adv. **rashness** n.
– ORIGIN ME: of Gmc origin.

**rash**[2] ● n. **1** an area of reddening of a person's skin, sometimes with raised spots. **2** an unwelcome series of things happening within a short space of time: *a rash of strikes.*
– ORIGIN C18: prob. rel. to OFr. *rasche* 'eruptive sores, scurf'.

**rasher** ● n. a thin slice of bacon.
– ORIGIN C16: of unknown origin.

**ras malai** /ˈrʌs mʌˌlʌɪ/ ● n. an Indian sweet dish consisting of small cakes of paneer in sweetened milk.
– ORIGIN from Hindi *ras* 'juice' and *malāī* 'cream'.

**rasp** ● n. **1** a coarse file for use on metal, wood, or other hard material. **2** a harsh, grating noise. ● v. **1** file with a rasp. **2** (of a rough surface or object) scrape in a painful or unpleasant way. **3** make a harsh, grating noise.
– DERIVATIVES **rasper** n. **rasping** adj. **raspingly** adv. **raspy** adj.
– ORIGIN ME (as v.): from OFr. *rasper*, perh. of Gmc origin.

**raspberry** ● n. **1** an edible soft fruit related to the blackberry, consisting of a cluster of reddish-pink drupels. **2** the prickly shrub which yields this fruit. [*Rubus idaeus.*] **3** informal a sound made with the tongue and lips, expressing derision or contempt. [from *raspberry tart*, rhyming sl. for 'fart'.]
– ORIGIN C17: from dial. *rasp*, abbrev. of obs. *raspis* 'raspberry', of unknown origin, + BERRY.

**rass** /rɑːs/ ● n. black slang **1** a person's buttocks. **2** a contemptible person.
– ORIGIN C18: alt. of ARSE, perh. partly from *your arse.*

**Rasta** /ˈrastə/ ● n. & adj. informal short for RASTAFARIAN.

**Rastafarian** /ˌrastəˈfɑːrɪən, -ˈfɛːrɪən/ ● adj. of or relating to a religious movement of Jamaican origin holding that Emperor Haile Selassie of Ethiopia was the Messiah and that blacks are the chosen people. ● n. a member of this movement.
– DERIVATIVES **Rastafarianism** n.
– ORIGIN from *Ras Tafari*, the name by which Haile Selassie was known (1916–30) + -AN.

**Rastaman** /ˈrastəman/ ● n. (pl. **-men**) informal a male Rastafarian.

**raster** /ˈrastə/ ● n. a rectangular pattern of parallel scanning lines followed by the electron beam on a television screen or computer monitor.
– ORIGIN C20: from Ger. *Raster*, lit. 'screen', from L. *rastrum* 'rake'.

**rasterize** (also **-ise**) ● v. Computing convert (an image stored as an outline) into pixels that can be displayed on a screen or printed.
– DERIVATIVES **rasterization** n. **rasterizer** n.

**rat** ● n. **1** a rodent resembling a large, long-tailed mouse, typically considered a serious pest. [*Rattus norvegicus* (**brown rat**), *R. rattus* (**black** or **ship rat**), and many other species.] **2** informal a despicable person. **3** informal an informer. **4** N. Amer. informal a person who is associated with or frequents a specified place: *a wharf rat.* ● exclam. (**rats**) informal expressing mild annoyance. ● v. (**ratted, ratting**) **1** hunt or kill rats. **2** informal desert one's party, side, or cause. **3** (**rat on someone** or US also **rat someone out**) informal inform on someone. **4** (**rat on**) informal break (an agreement or promise).
– DERIVATIVES **ratting** n.
– ORIGIN OE *ræt*, prob. of Romance origin; reinforced in ME by OFr. *rat*.

**rata** /ˈrɑːtə/ ● n. a large New Zealand tree with crimson flowers and hard red wood. [*Metrosideros robusta* and related species.]
– ORIGIN C18: from Maori.

**ratable** ● adj. variant spelling of RATEABLE.

**ratafia** /ˌratəˈfɪə/ ● n. **1** a liqueur flavoured with almonds or the kernels of peaches, apricots, or cherries. **2** an almond-flavoured biscuit like a small macaroon.
– ORIGIN C17: from Fr.; perh. rel. to TAFIA.

**ratamacue** /ˈratəməˌkjuː/ ● n. Music a drum rhythm comprising a two-beat figure, the first beat of which is played as a triplet and preceded by two grace notes.
– ORIGIN 1940s: imitative.

**rataplan** /ˌratəˈplan/ ● n. a drumming or beating sound.
– ORIGIN C19: from Fr., of imitative origin.

**rat-arsed** ● adj. Brit. vulgar slang very drunk.

**ratatouille** /ˌratəˈtuːi, -ˈtwiː/ ● n. a vegetable dish consisting of onions, courgettes, tomatoes, aubergines, and peppers, stewed in oil.
– ORIGIN a Fr. dial. word.

**ratbag** ● n. Brit. informal an unpleasant or disliked person.

**ratchet** ● n. a device consisting of a bar or wheel with a set of angled teeth in which a pawl, cog, or tooth engages, allowing motion in one direction only. ● v. (**ratcheted, ratcheting**) **1** operate by means of a ratchet. **2** (**ratchet something up/down**) cause something to rise (or fall) as a step in an irreversible process.
– ORIGIN C17: from Fr. *rochet*, orig. denoting a blunt lance head, later in the sense 'bobbin, ratchet'.

**rate**[1] ● n. **1** a measure, quantity, or frequency. **2** the speed with which something moves, happens, or changes. **3** a fixed price paid or charged for something. **4** the amount of a charge or payment expressed as a percentage of some other amount, or as a basis of calculation. **5** (**rates**) (in the UK) a tax on commercial land and buildings paid to a local authority (formerly levied also on private property). ● v. **1** assign a standard or value to (something) according to a particular scale. **2** assign a standard, optimal, or limiting rating to (a piece of equipment). **3** consider to be of a certain quality or standard. ➤ informal have a high opinion of. ➤ be worthy of; merit. **3** (in the UK) assess the value of (a property) for the purpose of levying rates.
– PHRASES **at any rate** whatever happens or may have happened. **at this** (or **that**) **rate** if things continue in this or that way; should a certain assumption be true.
– ORIGIN ME: from OFr., from med. L. *rata* (from L. *pro rata parte* (or *portione*) 'according to the proportional share'), from *ratus* 'reckoned', past part. of *reri*.

**rate**[2] ● v. archaic scold angrily.
– ORIGIN ME: of unknown origin.

**rate**[3] ● v. variant spelling of RET.

**rateable** (also **ratable**) ● adj. able to be rated or estimated.
– DERIVATIVES **rateability** n. **rateably** adv.

**rateable value** ● n. (in the UK) a value ascribed to a commercial property based on its size, location, etc., used to determine the rates payable by its owner.

**ratel** /ˈreɪt(ə)l, ˈrɑː-/ ● n. a badger-like mammal with a white or grey back and black underparts, native to Africa and Asia. [*Mellivora capensis.*]
– ORIGIN C18: from Afrik., of unknown ultimate origin.

**rate of exchange** ● n. another term for EXCHANGE RATE.

**ratepayer** ● n. **1** (in the UK) a person liable to pay rates. **2** N. Amer. a customer of a public utility.

**rathe** /reɪð/ ● adj. archaic or poetic/literary **1** prompt and eager. **2** blooming or ripening early in the year.
– ORIGIN OE *hræth, hræd*, of Gmc origin.

**rather** ● adv. **1** (**would rather**) indicating one's preference in a particular matter. **2** to a certain or significant extent or degree. **3** on the contrary. **4** more precisely. **5** instead of; as opposed to. ● exclam. Brit. dated expressing emphatic affirmation, agreement, or acceptance.
– PHRASES **had rather** poetic/literary or archaic would rather.
– ORIGIN OE *hrathor* 'earlier, sooner', compar. of *hræthe* 'without delay', from *hræth* 'prompt' (see RATHE).

**rathskeller** /ˈrɑːtsˌkɛlə/ ● n. US a beer hall or restaurant in a basement.
– ORIGIN C20: from obs. Ger. (now *Ratskeller*), from *Rathaus* 'town hall' + *Keller* 'cellar'.

**ratify** ● v. (**-ies, -ied**) give formal consent to; make officially valid.
– DERIVATIVES **ratifiable** adj. **ratification** n. **ratifier** n.
– ORIGIN ME: from OFr. *ratifier*, from med. L. *ratificare*, from L. *ratus* (see RATE[1]).

**rating** ● n. **1** a classification or ranking based on quality, standard, or performance. **2** the value of a property or condition which is claimed to be standard, optimal, or

commissioned sailor in the navy.

limiting for a material, device, etc. **3** (**ratings**) the estimated audience size of a particular television or radio programme. **4** any of the classes into which racing yachts are assigned according to dimensions. **5** Brit. a non-commissioned sailor in the navy.

**ratio** ● n. (pl. **-os**) the quantitative relation between two amounts showing the number of times one value contains or is contained within the other.
– ORIGIN C17: from L., lit. 'reckoning', from *rat-*, *reri* 'reckon'.

**ratiocinate** /ˌratɪˈɒsɪneɪt, ˌraʃɪ-/ ● v. formal form judgements by a process of logic; reason.
– DERIVATIVES **ratiocination** n. **ratiocinative** adj. **ratiocinator** n.
– ORIGIN C17: from L. *ratiocinat-*, *ratiocinari* 'deliberate, calculate', from *ratio* (see **RATIO**).

**ration** ● n. **1** a fixed amount of a commodity officially allowed to each person during a time of shortage, as in wartime. **2** (**rations**) an amount of food supplied on a regular basis to members of the armed forces during a war. **3** (**rations**) food; provisions. ● v. **1** limit the supply of (a commodity) to fixed rations. **2** limit the amount of a commodity available to (someone).
– ORIGIN C18: from Fr., from L. *ratio(n-)* 'reckoning, ratio'.

**rational** ● adj. **1** based on or in accordance with reason or logic. **2** (of a person) able to think sensibly or logically. **3** endowed with the capacity to reason. **4** Mathematics (of a number, quantity, or expression) expressible, or containing quantities which are expressible, as a ratio of whole numbers.
– DERIVATIVES **rationality** n. **rationally** adv.
– ORIGIN ME: from L. *rationalis*, from *ratio(n-)* (see **RATIO**).

**rationale** /ˌraʃəˈnɑːl/ ● n. a set of reasons or a logical basis for a course of action or a particular belief.
– ORIGIN C17: mod. L., neut. (used as n.) of L. *rationalis* (see **RATIONAL**).

**rationalism** ● n. **1** the practice or principle of basing opinions and actions on reason and knowledge rather than on religious belief or emotional response. **2** Philosophy the theory that reason rather than experience is the foundation of certainty in knowledge.
– DERIVATIVES **rationalist** n. **rationalistic** adj. **rationalistically** adv.

**rationalize** (also **-ise**) ● v. **1** attempt to justify (an action or attitude) with logical reasoning. **2** reorganize (a process or system) in such a way as to make it more logical and consistent. **3** make (a company or industry) more efficient by dispensing with superfluous personnel or equipment. **4** Mathematics convert to a rational form.
– DERIVATIVES **rationalization** n. **rationalizer** n.

**ratite** /ˈratʌɪt/ Ornithology ● adj. denoting a bird having a flat breastbone without a keel and so unable to fly, such as an ostrich, emu, etc. Contrasted with **CARINATE**. ● n. a ratite bird.
– ORIGIN C19: from L. *ratis* 'raft' + **-ITE**[1].

**rat-kangaroo** ● n. a small rat-like Australian marsupial with long hindlimbs used for hopping. [Family Potoroidae: several species.]

**ratlines** /ˈratlɪnz/ ● pl. n. a series of small rope lines fastened across a sailing ship's shrouds like the rungs of a ladder, used for climbing the rigging.
– ORIGIN ME: of unknown origin.

**ratoon** /rəˈtuːn/ ● n. a new shoot springing from the base of a crop plant, especially sugar cane, after cropping. ● v. produce or cause to produce ratoons.
– ORIGIN C17: from Sp. *retoño* 'a sprout'.

**rat pack** ● n. informal a group of journalists and photographers perceived as aggressive or relentless in their pursuit of stories.

**rat race** ● n. informal a way of life in which people are caught up in a fiercely competitive struggle for wealth or power.

**rat run** ● n. Brit. informal a minor street used by drivers during peak periods to avoid congestion on main roads.

**ratsbane** ● n. poetic/literary rat poison.

**rat snake** ● n. a harmless constricting snake that feeds on rats and other small mammals. [*Elaphe obsoleta* (N. America), *Ptyas mucosus* (Asia), and other species.]

**rat-tail** ● n. **1** (also **rat's tail**) a narrow hairless tail like that of a rat, or something that resembles one. **2** (**rat's tails**) Brit. informal hair hanging in lank, damp, or greasy strands. **3** another term for **GRENADIER** (in sense 2). **4** another term for **RABBITFISH**.

**rat-tailed maggot** ● n. the aquatic larva of the drone fly, with a tail-like telescopic breathing tube.

**rattan** /rəˈtan/ ● n. **1** the thin, jointed stems of a palm, used to make furniture. **2** a length of such a stem used as a walking stick. **3** the tropical climbing palm which yields these stems. [Genus *Calamus*.]
– ORIGIN C17: from Malay *rotan*, prob. from *raut* 'pare, trim'.

**rat-tat** (also **rat-tat-tat**) ● n. a rapping sound.
– ORIGIN C17: imitative.

**ratted** ● adj. Brit. informal very drunk.

**ratter** ● n. a dog or other animal used for hunting rats.

**rattle** ● v. **1** make or cause to make a rapid succession of short, sharp knocking or clinking sounds. **2** move or travel somewhere while making such sounds: *trains rattled past.* **3** (**rattle about/around in**) be in or occupy (an unnecessarily or undesirably large space). **4** informal cause to feel nervous, worried, or irritated. **5** (**rattle something off**) say, perform, or produce something quickly and effortlessly. **6** (**rattle on/away**) talk rapidly and at length. ● n. **1** a rattling sound. **2** a thing that makes a rattling sound, in particular a baby's toy consisting of a container filled with small pellets. **3** a gurgling sound in the throat. **4** archaic a person who talks incessantly in a lively or inane way. **5** the set of horny rings at the end of a rattlesnake's tail.
– PHRASES **rattle sabres** threaten to take aggressive action.
– DERIVATIVES **rattly** adj.
– ORIGIN ME: rel. to MDu. and Low Ger. *ratelen*, of imitative origin.

**rattler** ● n. **1** a thing that rattles, especially an old or rickety vehicle. **2** N. Amer. informal a rattlesnake.

**rattlesnake** ● n. a heavy-bodied American pit viper with a series of horny rings on the tail that produce a characteristic rattling sound when vibrated as a warning. [Genera *Crotalus* and *Sistrurus*: several species.]

**rattletrap** ● n. informal an old or rickety vehicle.

**rattling** ● adj. **1** making a rattle. **2** informal, dated very good of its kind: *a rattling good story.*

**ratty** ● adj. (**-ier**, **-iest**) **1** resembling or characteristic of a rat. **2** infested with rats. **3** informal shabby, untidy, or in bad condition. **4** Brit. informal bad-tempered and irritable.
– DERIVATIVES **rattily** adv. **rattiness** n.

**raucous** /ˈrɔːkəs/ ● adj. making or constituting a harsh, loud noise.
– DERIVATIVES **raucously** adv. **raucousness** n.
– ORIGIN C18: from L. *raucus* 'hoarse' + **-OUS**.

**raunch** ● n. informal energetic earthiness or vulgarity.
– ORIGIN 1960s: back-form. from **RAUNCHY**.

**raunchy** ● adj. (**-ier**, **-iest**) informal **1** energetically earthy and sexually explicit. **2** chiefly US slovenly or grubby.
– DERIVATIVES **raunchily** adv. **raunchiness** n.
– ORIGIN 1930s: of unknown origin.

**ravage** ● v. cause extensive damage to; devastate. ● n. (**ravages**) the destructive effects of something.
– DERIVATIVES **ravager** n.
– ORIGIN C17: from Fr. *ravager*, from earlier *ravage*, alt. of *ravine* 'rush of water'.

**rave**[1] ● v. **1** talk wildly or incoherently. **2** speak or write about someone or something with great enthusiasm or admiration. **3** informal, chiefly Brit. attend or take part in a rave party. ● n. **1** informal, chiefly N. Amer. an extremely enthusiastic appraisal of someone or something. **2** a person or thing that inspires intense and widely shared enthusiasm. **3** informal a lively party involving dancing and drinking. **4** informal, chiefly Brit. a very large party or event with dancing to loud, fast electronic music. ➤ electronic dance music of the kind played at a rave.
– ORIGIN ME (in the sense 'show signs of madness'): prob. from ONorth. Fr. *raver*.

**rave**[2] ● n. a rail of a cart. ➤ (**raves**) a framework added to

the sides of a cart to increase its capacity.
– ORIGIN C16: var. of the synonymous dial. word *rathe*, of unknown origin.

**ravel** ● v. (**ravelled**, **ravelling**; US **raveled**, **raveling**) **1** (**ravel something out**) untangle something. **2** confuse or complicate (a question or situation). ● n. a tangle or cluster.
– ORIGIN ME: prob. from Du. *ravelen* 'fray out, tangle'.

**ravelin** /ˈravlɪn/ ● n. historical an outwork of fortifications, with two faces forming a salient angle, constructed beyond the main ditch and in front of the curtain.
– ORIGIN C16: from Fr., from obs. Ital. *ravellino*, of unknown origin.

**ravelling** ● n. a thread from a woven or knitted fabric that has frayed or started to unravel.

**raven**[1] /ˈreɪv(ə)n/ ● n. a large heavily built black crow. [*Corvus corax* and related species.] ● adj. (especially of hair) of a glossy black colour.
– ORIGIN OE *hræfn*, of Gmc origin.

**raven**[2] /ˈrav(ə)n/ ● v. archaic **1** (of a wild animal) hunt voraciously for prey. **2** devour voraciously.
– ORIGIN C15: from OFr. *raviner*, orig. 'to ravage', based on L. *rapina* 'pillage'.

**ravening** ● adj. voracious; rapacious.

**ravenous** ● adj. voraciously hungry.
– DERIVATIVES **ravenously** adv. **ravenousness** n.
– ORIGIN ME: from OFr. *ravineus*, from *raviner* (see RAVEN[2]).

**raver** ● n. **1** informal a person who has an exciting and uninhibited social life. **2** informal, chiefly Brit. a person who regularly goes to raves. **3** a person who talks wildly or incoherently.

**rave-up** ● n. **1** Brit. informal a lively, noisy party. **2** N. Amer. informal a fast, loud, or danceable piece of pop music.

**ravin** /ˈravɪn/ ● n. archaic or poetic/literary violent seizure of prey or property; plunder.
– ORIGIN ME: from OFr. *ravine*, from L. *rapina* (see RAPINE).

**ravine** /rəˈviːn/ ● n. a deep, narrow gorge with steep sides.
– DERIVATIVES **ravined** adj.
– ORIGIN C18: from Fr., 'violent rush' (see RAVIN).

**raving** ● n. (usu. **ravings**) wild or incoherent talk. ● adj. & adv. informal extremely or conspicuously the thing mentioned: *raving mad.*

**ravioli** /ˌraviˈəʊli/ ● pl. n. small pasta envelopes containing minced meat, cheese, or vegetables.
– ORIGIN from Ital.

**ravish** ● v. archaic or poetic/literary **1** fill with intense delight; enrapture. **2** seize and carry off by force. **3** rape.
– DERIVATIVES **ravisher** n. **ravishment** n.
– ORIGIN ME: from OFr. *raviss-*, *ravir*, from an alt. of L. *rapere* 'seize'.

**ravishing** ● adj. causing intense delight; entrancing.
– DERIVATIVES **ravishingly** adv.

**raw** ● adj. **1** (of food) uncooked. **2** (of a material or substance) in its natural state; not processed. **3** (of data) not organized, analysed, or evaluated. **4** (of the edge of a piece of cloth) not having a hem or selvedge. **5** new and lacking in experience in an activity or job. **6** (of the skin) red and painful, especially as the result of abrasion. ➤(of the nerves) very sensitive. **7** (of an emotion or quality) strong and undisguised. **8** US informal (of language) coarse or crude. **9** (of the weather) bleak, cold, and damp.
– PHRASES **in the raw 1** in its true state. **2** informal naked. **touch someone on the raw** upset someone by referring to a subject about which they are very sensitive.
– DERIVATIVES **rawish** adj. **rawly** adv. **rawness** n.
– ORIGIN OE *hrēaw*, of Gmc origin.

**raw-boned** ● adj. having a bony or gaunt physique.

**rawhide** ● n. **1** stiff untanned leather. **2** N. Amer. a whip or rope made of rawhide.

**Rawlplug** /ˈrɔːlplʌg/ ● n. Brit. trademark a thin plastic or fibre sheath that is inserted into a hole in masonry in order to hold a screw.
– ORIGIN C20: from *Rawlings* (the name of the engineers who introduced it) + PLUG.

**raw material** ● n. a basic material from which a product is made.

**ray**[1] ● n. **1** each of the lines in which light seems to stream from the sun or any luminous body, or pass through a small opening. **2** the straight line in which light or other electromagnetic radiation travels to a given point. **3** (**rays**) a specified form of non-luminous radiation: *ultraviolet rays.* **4** Mathematics any of a set of straight lines passing through one point. **5** (**rays**) informal, chiefly N. Amer. sunlight considered in the context of sunbathing. **6** an initial or slight indication of a positive or welcome quality: *a ray of hope.* **7** Botany any of the individual strap-shaped florets around the edge of the flower of a daisy or related plant. **8** Zoology each of the long slender bony supports in the fins of most bony fishes. **9** Zoology each radial arm of a starfish. ● v. **1** spread from or as if from a central point. **2** poetic/literary radiate (light).
– PHRASES **ray of sunshine** informal a person who brings happiness into the lives of others.
– DERIVATIVES **-rayed** adj. **rayless** adj.
– ORIGIN ME: from OFr. *rai*, based on L. *radius* 'spoke, ray'.

**ray**[2] ● n. a broad flat cartilaginous fish with wing-like pectoral fins and a long slender tail. [Order Batiformes: many species.]
– ORIGIN ME: from OFr. *raie*, from L. *raia*.

**ray**[3] (also **re**) ● n. Music (in tonic sol-fa) the second note of a major scale. ➤the note D in the fixed-doh system.
– ORIGIN ME *re*, representing (as an arbitrary name for the note) the first syllable of *resonare*, taken from a Latin hymn.

**ray gun** ● n. (in science fiction) a gun causing injury or damage by the emission of rays.

**Rayleigh scattering** ● n. Physics the scattering of light by molecules or other small particles, without change in wavelength.
– ORIGIN C20: named after the C19 British physicist Lord *Rayleigh*.

**Raynaud's disease** /ˈreɪnəʊ/ (also **Raynaud's syndrome**) ● n. a disease characterized by whiteness, numbness, or pain in the fingers, typically brought on by constant cold or vibration.
– ORIGIN C19: named after the Fr. physician Maurice *Raynaud*.

**rayon** ● n. a textile fibre or fabric made from regenerated cellulose (viscose).
– ORIGIN 1920s: an arbitrary formation.

**raze** (also **rase**) ● v. tear down and destroy (a building, town, etc.): *villages were razed to the ground.*
– ORIGIN ME (in the sense 'scratch, incise'): from OFr. *raser* 'shave closely', from L. *ras-*, *radere* 'scrape'.

**razor** ● n. an instrument with a sharp blade, used to shave unwanted hair from the face or body. ● v. cut with a razor.
– ORIGIN ME: from OFr. *rasor*, from *raser* (see RAZE).

**razorback** ● n. **1** a pig of a half-wild breed common in the southern US, with the back formed into a high narrow ridge. **2** a steep-sided narrow ridge of land.

**razorbill** ● n. a black-and-white auk with a deep bill, found in the North Atlantic and Baltic Sea. [*Alca torda*.]

**razor blade** ● n. a blade used in a razor, typically a thin flat piece of metal with a sharp edge or edges used in a safety razor.

**razor clam** ● n. North American term for RAZOR SHELL.

**razor cut** ● n. a short, tapered haircut, effected with a razor. ● v. (**razor-cut**) cut (hair) in this style.

**razorfish** ● n. (pl. same or **-fishes**) **1** a small fish of the Indo-Pacific with a narrow body encased in thin bony shields that meet to form a sharp ridge on the belly. [Family Centriscidae: many species.] **2** a small brightly coloured wrasse of the western Atlantic. [Genus *Hemipteronotus*.] **3** another term for RAZOR SHELL.

**razor shell** ● n. a burrowing bivalve mollusc with a long straight shell. [Family Solenidae.]

**razor wire** ● n. a metal wire or ribbon with sharp edges or studded with small sharp blades, used as a defensive barrier.

**razz** informal, chiefly N. Amer. ● **v.** tease playfully. ● **n.** another term for **RASPBERRY** (in sense 3).
– ORIGIN C20: from informal *razzberry*, alt. of **RASPBERRY**.

**razzle** ● **n.** (in phr. **on the razzle**) informal out celebrating or enjoying oneself.
– ORIGIN C20: abbrev. of **RAZZLE-DAZZLE**.

**razzle-dazzle** ● **n.** another term for **RAZZMATAZZ**.
– ORIGIN C19: reduplication of **DAZZLE**.

**razzmatazz** (also **razzamatazz**) ● **n.** informal noisy, showy, and exciting activity and display.
– ORIGIN C19: prob. an alt. of **RAZZLE-DAZZLE**.

**RB** ● **abbrev.** Botswana (international vehicle registration).
– ORIGIN from *Republic of Botswana*.

**Rb** ● **symb.** the chemical element rubidium.

**RBI** ● **abbrev.** Baseball run(s) batted in.

**RC** ● **abbrev.** **1** (in cycling) racing club. **2** Red Cross. **3** reinforced concrete. **4** Electronics resistance/capacitance (or resistor/capacitor). **5** Roman Catholic.

**RCA** ● **abbrev.** **1** Central African Republic (international vehicle registration). [from Fr. *République Centrafricaine*.] **2** (in the US) Radio Corporation of America. **3** (in the UK) Royal College of Art.

**RCH** ● **abbrev.** Chile (international vehicle registration).
– ORIGIN from Sp. *República de Chile*.

**RCM** ● **abbrev.** (in the UK) Royal College of Music.

**RCMP** ● **abbrev.** Royal Canadian Mounted Police.

**RCN** ● **abbrev.** (in the UK) Royal College of Nursing.

**RCP** ● **abbrev.** (in the UK) Royal College of Physicians.

**RCS** ● **abbrev.** **1** (in the UK) Royal College of Scientists. **2** (in the UK) Royal College of Surgeons. **3** (in the UK) Royal Corps of Signals.

**RCVS** ● **abbrev.** (in the UK) Royal College of Veterinary Surgeons.

**RD** ● **abbrev.** **1** Brit. (in banking) refer to drawer. **2** (in the UK) Royal Naval Reserve Decoration.

**Rd** ● **abbrev.** Road (used in street names).

**RDA** ● **abbrev.** **1** recommended daily (or dietary) allowance. **2** (in the UK) Regional Development Agency.

**RDBMS** ● **abbrev.** Computing relational database management system.

**RDC** ● **abbrev.** historical (in the UK) Rural District Council.

**RDF** ● **abbrev.** **1** radio direction-finder (or -finding). **2** (in the US) rapid deployment force.

**RDI** ● **abbrev.** recommended (or reference) daily intake.

**RDS** ● **abbrev.** **1** radio data system. **2** respiratory distress syndrome.

**RDX** ● **n.** a type of high explosive.
– ORIGIN from *R(esearch) D(epartment) (E)x(plosive)*.

**RE** ● **abbrev.** **1** religious education (as a school subject). **2** (in the UK) Royal Engineers.

**Re** ● **symb.** the chemical element rhenium.

**re**[1] /riː, reɪ/ ● **prep.** **1** in the matter of (used in headings or to introduce a reference). **2** about; concerning.
– ORIGIN L., ablative of *res* 'thing'.

**re**[2] ● **n.** variant spelling of **RAY**[3].

**re-** ● **prefix** **1** once more; afresh; anew: *reactivate*. ➤ with return to a previous state: *restore*. **2** (also **red-**) in return; mutually: *resemble*. ➤ in opposition: *repel*. **3** behind or after: *relic*. ➤ in a withdrawn state: *reticent*. ➤ back and away; down: *recede*. **4** with frequentative or intensive force: *resound*. **5** with negative force: *recant*.
– ORIGIN from L. *re-*, *red-* 'again, back'.

**'re** ● **abbrev.** informal are (usually after the pronouns you, we, and they).

**reabsorb** ● **v.** absorb again.
– DERIVATIVES **reabsorption** n.

**reach** ● **v.** **1** stretch out an arm in a specified direction in order to touch or grasp something. ➤ (**reach something out**) stretch out one's hand or arm. ➤ (**reach something down**) stretch upwards to pick something up and bring it down to a lower level. ➤ hand (something) to. **2** be able to touch (something) with an outstretched arm or leg. **3** arrive at or attain; extend to. **4** succeed in achieving. **5** make contact with. **6** (of a broadcast or other communication) be received by. **7** succeed in influencing or having an effect on. **8** Sailing sail with the wind blowing from the side. ● **n.** **1** an act of reaching. **2** the distance to which someone can stretch out their hand (used especially of a boxer). **3** the extent or range of something's application, effect, or influence. **4** (often **reaches**) a continuous extent of land or water, especially a stretch of river between two bends. **5** Sailing a distance traversed in reaching.
– DERIVATIVES **reachable** adj.
– ORIGIN OE *rǣcan*, of W. Gmc origin.

**reach-me-down** Brit. informal, dated ● **adj.** **1** second-hand. **2** ready-made. ● **n.** a second-hand or ready-made garment.

**reacquaint** ● **v.** (**reacquaint with**) make familiar or acquainted with again.

**react** ● **v.** **1** respond to something in a particular way or with particular behaviour. **2** (**react against**) respond with hostility or a contrary course of action to. **3** suffer from adverse physiological effects after ingesting, breathing, or touching a substance. **4** Chemistry & Physics interact and undergo a chemical or physical change. **5** Stock Exchange (of share prices) fall after rising.
– ORIGIN C17: from **RE-** + **ACT**, orig. suggested by med. L. *react-*, *reagere* 'do again'.

**reactance** ● **n.** Physics the non-resistive component of impedance in an AC circuit, arising from inductance and/or capacitance.

**reactant** ● **n.** Chemistry a substance that takes part in and undergoes change during a reaction.

**reaction** ● **n.** **1** an instance of reacting to or against something. **2** (**reactions**) a person's ability to respond physically and mentally to external stimuli. **3** opposition to political or social progress or reform. **4** a process in which substances interact causing chemical or physical change. **5** Physics a force exerted in opposition to an applied force.
– DERIVATIVES **reactionist** n. & adj.

**reactionary** ● **adj.** opposing political or social progress or reform. ● **n.** (pl. **-ies**) a reactionary person.

**reaction formation** ● **n.** Psychoanalysis the tendency of a repressed wish or feeling to be expressed at a conscious level in a contrasting form.

**reactivate** ● **v.** restore to a state of activity.
– DERIVATIVES **reactivation** n.

**reactive** ● **adj.** **1** showing a response to a stimulus. **2** acting in response to a situation rather than creating or controlling it. **3** having a tendency to react chemically. **4** Physiology showing an immune response to a specific antigen. **5** (of an illness) caused by a reaction to something. **6** Physics of or relating to reactance.
– DERIVATIVES **reactivity** n.

**reactor** ● **n.** **1** (also **nuclear reactor**) an apparatus or structure in which fissile material can be made to undergo a controlled, self-sustaining nuclear reaction releasing energy. **2** a container or apparatus in which substances are made to react chemically. **3** Medicine a person who reacts to a drug, antigen, etc. **4** Physics a coil or other component which provides reactance in a circuit.

**read** ● **v.** (past and past part. **read**) **1** look at and comprehend the meaning of (written or printed matter) by interpreting the characters or symbols of which it is composed. ➤ speak (written or printed words) aloud. ➤ (of a passage, text, or sign) contain or consist of specified words; have a certain wording. **2** habitually read (a particular newspaper or journal). **3** discover (information) by reading it in a written or printed source. ➤ [as adj. **read**] having a specified level of knowledge as a result of reading: *she was well read*. **4** understand or interpret the nature or significance of. ➤ (of a piece of writing) convey a specified impression to the reader. **5** proofread. **6** present (a bill or other measure) before a legislative assembly. **7** inspect and record the figure indicated on (a measuring instrument). ➤ indicate a specified measurement or figure. **8** chiefly Brit. study (an academic subject) at a university. **9** (of a computer) copy or transfer (data). ➤ enter or extract (data) in an electronic storage device. **10** hear and understand the words of (someone speaking on a radio transmitter). ● **n.** **1** chiefly Brit. a period or act of reading. **2** informal a book considered in terms of its readability.
– PHRASES **read between the lines** look for or discover a

meaning that is hidden or implied rather than explicitly stated. **read someone's mind** (or **thoughts**) discern what someone is thinking. **read my lips** N. Amer. informal listen carefully. **take something as read** assume something without the need for further discussion.
– PHRASAL VERBS **read something into** attribute a meaning or significance to (something) that it may not in fact possess. **read someone out of** chiefly US formally expel someone from. **read up on something** acquire information about a particular subject by reading.
– DERIVATIVES **readable** adj. **readability** n. **readably** adv.
– ORIGIN OE *rǣdan*, of Gmc origin; early senses included 'advise' and 'interpret (a riddle or dream)'.

**reader** • n. **1** a person who reads. **2** a person who reports to a publisher on the merits of manuscripts submitted for publication. **3** (**Reader**) Brit. a university lecturer of the highest grade below professor. **4** short for LAY READER. **5** a book containing extracts of a text or texts for teaching purposes. **6** a device that produces on a screen a readable image from a microfiche or microfilm.
– DERIVATIVES **readerly** adj.

**readership** • n. **1** [treated as sing. or pl.] the readers of a newspaper or magazine regarded collectively. **2** (**Readership**) Brit. the position of Reader at a university.

**readily** • adv. **1** willingly. **2** without difficulty.

**readiness** • n. the state or quality of being ready.

**reading** • n. **1** the action or skill of reading. **2** an instance of something being read to an audience. **3** an interpretation of a text. **4** a figure recorded on a measuring instrument. **5** a stage of debate in parliament through which a bill must pass before it can become law.

**reading age** • n. a child's reading ability expressed with reference to an average age at which a comparable ability is found.

**readjust** • v. set or adjust again. ➤ adjust or adapt to a changed situation or environment.
– DERIVATIVES **readjustment** n.

**read-only memory** • n. Computing memory read at high speed but not capable of being changed by program instructions.

**read-write** • adj. Computing capable of reading existing data and accepting alterations or further input.

**ready** • adj. (**-ier**, **-iest**) **1** in a suitable state for an activity or situation; fully prepared. **2** made suitable and available for immediate use. **3** easily available or obtained; within reach. **4** willing to do something. **5** immediate, quick, or prompt. **6** in such a condition as to be likely to do something. • n. (pl. **-ies**) (**readies** or **the ready**) Brit. informal available money; cash. • v. (**-ies**, **-ied**) make (something) ready.
– PHRASES **at the ready** prepared or available for immediate use. **make ready** prepare.
– ORIGIN ME: from OE *rǣde* (from a Gmc base meaning 'arrange, prepare') + -Y¹.

**ready-made** • adj. **1** made to a standard size or specification rather than to order. **2** readily available: *ready-made answers*. **3** (of food) sold ready or almost ready to be served. • n. a ready-made article.

**ready-mixed** • adj. (of concrete, paint, food, etc.) having some or all of the constituents already mixed together.
– DERIVATIVES **ready-mix** n.

**ready money** (also **ready cash**) • n. money in the form of cash that is immediately available.

**ready-to-wear** • adj. (of clothes) sold through shops rather than made to order for an individual customer.

**reaffirm** • v. state again strongly. ➤ confirm the validity of (something previously established).
– DERIVATIVES **reaffirmation** n.

**reafforest** • v. chiefly Brit. another term for REFOREST.
– DERIVATIVES **reafforestation** n.

**reagent** /rɪˈeɪdʒ(ə)nt/ • n. a substance or mixture for use in chemical analysis or other reactions.

**real¹** /riːl/ • adj. **1** actually existing or occurring in fact; not imagined or supposed. **2** significant; serious: *a real danger*. **3** Philosophy relating to something as it is, not merely as it may be described or distinguished. **4** not artificial or made in imitation of something; genuine. **5** rightly so called; proper: *he's my idea of a real man*. **6** adjusted for changes in the value of money; assessed by purchasing power. **7** Mathematics (of a number or quantity) having no imaginary part. **8** Optics (of an image) such that the light that forms it actually passes through it; not virtual. • adv. informal, chiefly N. Amer. really; very.
– PHRASES **for real** informal as a serious or actual concern.
– DERIVATIVES **realness** n.
– ORIGIN ME (as a legal term meaning 'relating to things, especially real property'): from Anglo-Norman Fr., from late L. *realis*, from L. *res* 'thing'.

**real²** /reɪˈɑːl/ • n. **1** the basic monetary unit of Brazil since 1994, equal to 100 centavos. **2** a former coin and monetary unit of various Spanish-speaking countries.
– ORIGIN Sp. and Port., lit. 'royal' (adj. used as n.).

**real account** • n. Finance an account dealing with the material assets of a business, such as its property.

**real ale** • n. chiefly Brit. cask-conditioned beer that is served traditionally, without additional gas pressure.

**real estate** • n. chiefly N. Amer. real property; land.

**real estate agent** • n. N. Amer. an estate agent.
– DERIVATIVES **real estate agency** n.

**realgar** /rɪˈalgə/ • n. a soft reddish mineral consisting of arsenic sulphide, formerly used as a pigment and in fireworks.
– ORIGIN ME: via med. L. from Arab. *rahj al-ġār* 'arsenic', lit. 'dust of the cave'.

**realia** /reɪˈɑːlɪə, rɪˈeɪlɪə/ • n. objects and material from everyday life used as teaching aids.
– ORIGIN 1950s: from late L., neut. pl. (used as n.) of *realis* (see REAL¹).

**realign** • v. **1** change or restore to a different or former position or state. **2** (**realign oneself with**) change one's position or attitude with regard to.
– DERIVATIVES **realignment** n.

**realism** • n. **1** the practice of accepting a situation as it is and dealing with it accordingly. **2** (in art or literature) the representation of things in a way that is accurate and true to life. **3** Philosophy the doctrine that universals or abstract concepts have an objective or absolute existence. Often contrasted with NOMINALISM. ➤ the doctrine that matter as the object of perception has real existence.
– DERIVATIVES **realist** n.

**realistic** • adj. **1** having a sensible and practical idea of what can be achieved or expected. **2** representing things in a way that is accurate and true to life.
– DERIVATIVES **realistically** adv.

**reality** • n. (pl. **-ies**) **1** the state of things as they actually exist, as opposed to an idealistic or notional idea of them. **2** a thing that is actually experienced or seen. **3** the quality of being lifelike. **4** the state or quality of having existence or substance. **5** Philosophy existence that is absolute, self-sufficient, or objective, and not subject to human decisions or conventions.

**reality principle** • n. Psychoanalysis (in Freudian theory) the control by the ego of the pleasure-seeking activity of the id in order to meet the demands of the external world.

**reality testing** • n. Psychology the objective evaluation of an emotion or thought against real life, as a faculty present in normal individuals but defective in psychotics.

**realize** (also **-ise**) • v. **1** become fully aware of as a fact; understand clearly. **2** cause to happen. **3** achieve (something desired or anticipated); fulfil. **4** give actual or physical form to (a concept or work). **5** Music add to or complete (a piece of music left sparsely notated by the composer). **6** sell for or make a profit of. **7** convert (an asset) into cash.
– DERIVATIVES **realizability** n. **realizable** adj. **realization** n. **realizer** n.
– ORIGIN C17: from REAL¹, on the pattern of Fr. *réaliser*.

**really** • adv. **1** in reality; in actual fact. **2** very; thoroughly. • exclam. **1** expressing interest, surprise, doubt, or protest. **2** chiefly US expressing agreement.

**realm** • n. **1** archaic, poetic/literary, or Law a kingdom. **2** a field or domain of activity or interest.
– ORIGIN ME *rewme*, from OFr. *reaume*, from L. *regimen* (see REGIMEN); the spelling with *-l-* was influenced by OFr. *reiel* 'royal'.

**realpolitik** /reɪˈɑːlpɒlɪˌtiːk/ ● **n.** politics based on practical rather than moral or ideological considerations.
– ORIGIN C20: from Ger. *Realpolitik* 'practical politics'.

**real property** ● **n.** Law property consisting of land or buildings. Compare with **PERSONAL PROPERTY**.

**real tennis** ● **n.** the original form of tennis, played with a solid ball on an enclosed court.

**real time** ● **n. 1** the actual time during which something occurs. **2** [as modifier] Computing relating to or denoting a system in which input data is available virtually immediately as feedback to the process from which it is coming, e.g. in a missile guidance system.

**realtor** /ˈrɪəltə/ ● **n.** N. Amer. an estate agent.
– ORIGIN C20: from **REALTY** + **-OR**[1].

**realty** /ˈrɪəlti/ ● **n.** Law a person's real property. Compare with **PERSONALTY**.

**ream**[1] ● **n. 1** 500 (formerly 480) sheets of paper. **2** a large quantity of something, especially paper.
– ORIGIN ME: from OFr. *raime*, based on Arab. *rizma* 'bundle'.

**ream**[2] ● **v. 1** widen (a bore or hole) with a special tool. ➤ N. Amer. clear out or remove (material) from something. **2** N. Amer. vulgar slang have anal intercourse with. **3** N. Amer. informal rebuke angrily.
– ORIGIN C19: of unknown origin.

**reamer** ● **n. 1** a tool for widening or shaping holes. **2** N. Amer. a device for extracting the juice from citrus fruit.

**reanimate** ● **v.** revive.
– DERIVATIVES **reanimation** n.

**reap** ● **v. 1** cut or gather (a crop or harvest). ➤ harvest the crop from (land). **2** receive as a consequence of one's own or others' actions.
– ORIGIN OE *ripan, reopan*, of unknown origin.

**reaper** ● **n. 1** a person or machine that harvests a crop. **2** (**the Reaper** or **the Grim Reaper**) a personification of death as a cloaked skeleton wielding a large scythe.

**reappear** ● **v.** appear again.
– DERIVATIVES **reappearance** n.

**reappoint** ● **v.** appoint again to a position previously held.
– DERIVATIVES **reappointment** n.

**reappraise** ● **v.** appraise again or differently.
– DERIVATIVES **reappraisal** n.

**rear**[1] ● **n. 1** the back or hindmost part of something. **2** (also **rear end**) informal a person's buttocks. ● **adj.** at the back.
– PHRASES **bring up the rear 1** be at the very end of a queue. **2** come last in a race. **take someone in rear** attack an army from behind.
– ORIGIN ME from OFr. *rere*, based on L. *retro* 'back'.

**rear**[2] ● **v. 1** bring up and care for (a child). ➤ (of an animal) care for (young) until fully grown. ➤ breed and raise (animals). ➤ grow or cultivate (plants). **2** (of an animal) raise itself upright on its hind legs. ➤ set or lift upright. **3** (of a building, mountain, etc.) extend or appear to extend to a great height. **4** (**rear up**) show anger or irritation.
– DERIVATIVES **rearer** n.
– ORIGIN OE *rǣran* 'set upright, construct, elevate', of Gmc origin; rel. to **RAISE** and **RISE**.

**rear admiral** ● **n.** a rank of naval officer, above commodore and below vice admiral.

**rear commodore** ● **n.** an officer in a yacht club ranking below vice commodore.

**rearguard** ● **n. 1** the soldiers at the rear of a body of troops, especially those protecting a retreating army. **2** a reactionary or conservative faction.
– ORIGIN ME: from OFr. *rereguarde*.

**rearguard action** ● **n.** a defensive action carried out by a retreating army.

**rear light** (also **rear lamp**) ● **n.** chiefly Brit. a tail light.

**rearm** ● **v.** provide with or acquire a new supply of weapons.
– DERIVATIVES **rearmament** n.

**rearmost** ● **adj.** furthest back.

**rearrange** ● **v.** arrange again in a different way.
– DERIVATIVES **rearrangement** n.

**rearrest** ● **v.** arrest again. ● **n.** an act of rearresting someone.

**rear-view mirror** ● **n.** a mirror fixed inside the windscreen of a motor vehicle enabling the driver to see the vehicle or road behind.

**rearward** ● **adj.** directed towards the back. ● **adv.** (also **rearwards**) towards the back. ● **n.** (usu. **in/at/on the rearward**) archaic or poetic/literary the rear.

**rear-wheel drive** ● **n.** a transmission system that provides power to the rear wheels of a motor vehicle.

**reason** ● **n. 1** a cause, explanation, or justification. ➤ good or obvious cause to do something. ➤ Logic a premise of an argument in support of a belief, especially a minor premise given after the conclusion. **2** the power of the mind to think, understand, and form judgements logically. ➤ (**one's reason**) one's sanity. **3** what is right, practical, or possible. ● **v. 1** think, understand, and form judgements logically. ➤ (**reason something out**) find a solution to a problem by considering possible options. **2** (**reason with**) persuade with rational argument.
– PHRASES **by reason of** formal because of. **listen to reason** be persuaded to act sensibly. **it stands to reason** it is obvious or logical.
– DERIVATIVES **reasoned** adj. **reasoner** n. **reasonless** adj. (archaic).
– ORIGIN ME: from OFr. *reisun* (n.), *raisoner* (v.), from a var. of L. *ratio(n-)*, from *reri* 'consider'.

**reasonable** ● **adj. 1** fair and sensible. **2** archaic able to reason logically. **3** as much as is appropriate or fair; moderate. ➤ fairly good. ➤ relatively inexpensive.
– DERIVATIVES **reasonableness** n. **reasonably** adv.
– ORIGIN ME: from OFr. *raisonable*, suggested by L. *rationabilis* 'rational', from *ratio* (see **REASON**).

**reassemble** ● **v.** assemble again; put back together.
– DERIVATIVES **reassembly** n.

**reassert** ● **v.** assert again.
– DERIVATIVES **reassertion** n.

**reassess** ● **v.** assess again, especially differently.
– DERIVATIVES **reassessment** n.

**reassign** ● **v.** assign again or differently.
– DERIVATIVES **reassignment** n.

**reassure** ● **v.** allay the doubts and fears of.
– DERIVATIVES **reassurance** n. **reassuring** adj. **reassuringly** adv.

**reattach** ● **v.** attach again.
– DERIVATIVES **reattachment** n.

**reattempt** ● **v.** attempt again.

**reave** /riːv/ ● **v.** (past and past part. **reft** /rɛft/) archaic carry out raids; plunder. ➤ rob of something by force. ➤ steal.
– DERIVATIVES **reaver** n.
– ORIGIN OE *rēafian*, of Gmc origin, rel. to **ROB**.

**reawaken** ● **v.** awaken again.

**Reb**[1] /rɛb/ ● **n.** a traditional Jewish title (preceding the forename or surname) for a man who is not a rabbi.
– ORIGIN from Yiddish.

**Reb**[2] /rɛb/ ● **n.** US informal a Confederate soldier in the American Civil War.
– ORIGIN abbrev. of **REBEL**.

**rebadge** ● **v.** relaunch (a product) under a new name or logo.

**rebar** /ˈriːbɑː/ ● **n.** reinforcing steel, especially as rods in concrete.

**rebarbative** /rɪˈbɑːbətɪv/ ● **adj.** formal unattractive and objectionable.
– ORIGIN C19: from Fr. *rébarbatif, -ive*, from OFr. *se rebarber* 'face each other "beard to beard" aggressively', from *barbe* 'beard'.

**rebase** ● **v.** establish a new base level for (a tax level, price index, etc.).

**rebate**[1] /ˈriːbeɪt/ ● **n. 1** a partial refund to someone who has paid too much for tax, rent, or a utility. **2** a deduction or discount on a sum due. ● **v.** pay back as a rebate.
– DERIVATIVES **rebatable** adj.
– ORIGIN ME: from Anglo-Norman Fr. *rebatre* 'beat back', also 'deduct'.

**rebate**[2] /ˈriːbeɪt/ ● **n.** a step-shaped recess cut in a piece of wood, typically forming a match to the edge or tongue

of another piece. ● **v.** (**rebated**, **rebating**) **1** make a rebate in. **2** join or fix with a rebate.
– ORIGIN C17: alt. of **RABBET**.

**rebbe** /ˈrɛbə/ ● **n.** Judaism a rabbi, especially a Hasidic religious leader.
– ORIGIN Yiddish, from Heb. *rabbī* 'rabbi'.

**rebbetzin** /ˈrɛbɪtsɪn/ (also **rebbitzin**) ● **n.** Judaism **1** the wife of a rabbi. **2** a female religious teacher.
– ORIGIN Yiddish, fem. of *rebbe* (see **REBBE**).

**rebec** /ˈriːbɛk/ (also **rebeck**) ● **n.** a medieval three-stringed instrument played with a bow.
– ORIGIN ME: from Fr., based on Arab. *rabāb*.

**rebel** ● **n.** /ˈrɛb(ə)l/ a person who rebels. ● **v.** /rɪˈbɛl/ (**rebelled**, **rebelling**) rise in opposition or armed resistance to an established government or ruler. ➤resist authority, control, or convention. ➤show or feel repugnance.
– ORIGIN ME (orig. referring to a fresh declaration of war by the defeated): from OFr. *rebelle* (n.), *rebeller* (v.), from L. *rebellis*, based on *bellum* 'war'.

**rebellion** ● **n.** **1** armed resistance to an established government or ruler. **2** defiance of authority or control.
– ORIGIN ME: from OFr., from L. *rebellio(n-)*, from *rebellis* (see **REBEL**).

**rebellious** ● **adj.** **1** showing a desire to rebel. ➤engaged in rebellion. **2** unmanageable.
– DERIVATIVES **rebelliously** adv. **rebelliousness** n.

**rebid** ● **v.** (**rebidding**; past and past part. **rebid**) bid again. ● **n.** a further bid.

**rebind** ● **v.** (past and past part. **rebound**) give a new binding to (a book).

**rebirth** ● **n.** **1** reincarnation. **2** a revival.

**rebirthing** ● **n.** a form of therapy involving controlled breathing intended to simulate the trauma of being born.
– DERIVATIVES **rebirther** n.

**reboot** ● **v.** boot (a computer system) again. ● **n.** an act or instance of rebooting.

**rebore** ● **v.** make a new or wider boring in (the cylinders of an internal-combustion engine). ● **n.** an act of reboring. ➤an engine with rebored cylinders.

**reborn** ● **adj.** **1** brought back to life or activity. **2** born-again.

**rebound**[1] ● **v.** /rɪˈbaʊnd/ **1** bounce back after hitting a hard surface. **2** recover in value, amount, or strength. **3** (**rebound on/upon**) have an unexpected adverse consequence for. **4** Basketball gain possession of a missed shot after it bounces off the backboard or basket rim. ● **n.** /ˈriːbaʊnd/ **1** a ball or shot that rebounds. ➤Basketball a recovery of possession of a missed shot. **2** an instance of recovering in value, amount, or strength. **3** [usu. as modifier] Medicine recurrence of a condition after withdrawal of treatment: *rebound hypertension*.
– PHRASES **on the rebound** while still distressed after the ending of a romantic relationship.
– ORIGIN ME: from OFr. *rebondir*, from *re-* 'back' + *bondir* 'bounce up'.

**rebound**[2] past and past participle of **REBIND**.

**rebounder** ● **n.** **1** a small circular trampoline for exercising. **2** Basketball a player who rebounds the ball.

**rebozo** /rɪˈbəʊzəʊ/ ● **n.** (pl. **-os**) a long scarf covering the head and shoulders, traditionally worn by Spanish-American women.
– ORIGIN from Sp.

**rebrand** ● **v.** [usu. as noun **rebranding**] change the corporate image of.

**rebreather** ● **n.** an aqualung in which the diver's exhaled breath is partially purified of carbon dioxide, mixed with more oxygen, and then breathed again.

**rebroadcast** ● **v.** (past **rebroadcast** or **rebroadcasted**; past part. **rebroadcast**) broadcast again. ● **n.** a repeated broadcast.

**rebuff** ● **v.** reject in an abrupt or ungracious manner. ● **n.** an abrupt rejection.
– ORIGIN C16: from obs. Fr. *rebuffer* (v.), *rebuffe* (n.), from Ital. *ri-* (expressing opposition) + *buffo* 'a gust, puff', of imitative origin.

**rebuild** ● **v.** (past and past part. **rebuilt**) build again. ● **n.** **1** an instance of rebuilding. **2** a thing that has been rebuilt.
– DERIVATIVES **rebuilder** n.

**rebuke** ● **v.** criticize or reprimand sharply. ● **n.** a sharp criticism.
– DERIVATIVES **rebuker** n.
– ORIGIN ME: from Anglo-Norman Fr. and ONorth. Fr. *rebuker*, from *re-* 'back, down' + *bukier* 'to beat'.

**rebus** /ˈriːbəs/ ● **n.** (pl. **rebuses**) **1** a puzzle in which words are represented by combinations of pictures and letters. **2** historical an ornamental device suggesting the name of its bearer.
– ORIGIN C17: from Fr. *rébus*, from L. *rebus*, ablative pl. of *res* 'thing'.

**rebut** /rɪˈbʌt/ ● **v.** (**rebutted**, **rebutting**) **1** claim or prove to be false. **2** archaic drive back or repel.
– DERIVATIVES **rebuttable** adj.
– ORIGIN ME: from Anglo-Norman Fr. *rebuter*, from OFr. *re-* (expressing opposition) + *boter* 'to butt'.

**rebuttal** ● **n.** **1** a refutation or contradiction. **2** a rebutter.

**rebutter** ● **n.** Law, archaic a defendant's reply to the plaintiff's surrejoinder.
– ORIGIN C16: from Anglo-Norman Fr. *rebuter* (from OFr. *rebut* 'a reproach, rebuke').

**rec** ● **n.** informal **1** Brit. a recreation ground. **2** N. Amer. recreation.

**recalcitrant** /rɪˈkalsɪtr(ə)nt/ ● **adj.** obstinately uncooperative. ● **n.** a recalcitrant person.
– DERIVATIVES **recalcitrance** n. **recalcitrantly** adv.
– ORIGIN C19: from L. *recalcitrant-*, *recalcitrare* 'kick out with the heels', based on *calx*, *calc-* 'heel'.

**recalculate** ● **v.** calculate again.
– DERIVATIVES **recalculation** n.

**recalescence** /ˌriːkəˈlɛs(ə)ns/ ● **n.** Metallurgy a temporary rise in temperature during cooling of a metal, caused by a change in crystal structure.
– DERIVATIVES **recalescent** adj.
– ORIGIN C19: from **RE-** + L. *calescere* 'grow hot' + **-ENCE**.

**recall** /rɪˈkɔːl/ ● **v.** **1** remember. ➤cause one to remember or think of. ➤(**recall someone/thing to**) bring back the memory of someone or something to. **2** call up (stored computer data). **3** officially order to return. ➤(of a manufacturer) request the return of (faulty products). **4** reselect (a sports player) as a member of a team. **5** bring out of a state of inattention. **6** archaic revoke or annul (an action or decision). ● **n.** /also ˈriːkɔːl/ **1** the action or faculty of remembering. **2** an act of officially recalling someone or something. **3** N. Amer. the removal of an elected government official from office by voting.
– PHRASES **beyond recall** in such a way that restoration is impossible.
– DERIVATIVES **recallable** adj.
– ORIGIN C16: from **RE-** + **CALL**, suggested by L. *revocare* or Fr. *rappeler* 'call back'.

**recant** /rɪˈkant/ ● **v.** renounce a former opinion or belief, especially one considered heretical.
– DERIVATIVES **recantation** /ˌriːkanˈteɪʃ(ə)n/ n. **recanter** n.
– ORIGIN C16: from L. *recantare* 'revoke', from *re-* (expressing reversal) + *cantare* 'sing, chant'.

**recap** informal ● **v.** (**recapped**, **recapping**) recapitulate. ● **n.** a recapitulation.

**recapitalize** (also **-ise**) ● **v.** provide (a business) with more capital.
– DERIVATIVES **recapitalization** n.

**recapitulate** /ˌriːkəˈpɪtjʊleɪt/ ● **v.** **1** summarize and state again the main points of. **2** Biology repeat (an evolutionary or other process) during development and growth.
– DERIVATIVES **recapitulatory** adj.
– ORIGIN C16: from late L. *recapitulat-* 'gone through heading by heading', from *re-* 'again' + *capitulum* 'chapter' (dimin. of *caput* 'head').

**recapitulation** /ˌriːkəpɪtjʊˈleɪʃ(ə)n/ ● **n.** **1** an act or instance of recapitulating something. **2** Music a part of a movement (especially one in sonata form) in which themes from the exposition are restated.

**recapture** • v. **1** capture (an escapee). **2** recover (something taken or lost). **3** recreate (a past time, event, or feeling). • n. an act of recapturing.

**recast** • v. (past and past part. **recast**) **1** cast (metal) again or differently. **2** present in a different form or style. **3** allocate roles in (a play or film) to different actors.

**recce** /ˈrɛki/ chiefly Brit. • n. informal reconnaissance. • v. (**recced**, **recceing**) informal reconnoitre.

**recd** • abbrev. received.

**recede** • v. **1** move back or further away. **2** gradually diminish. **3** (of a man's hair) cease to grow at the temples and above the forehead. **4** [usu. as adj. **receding**] (of a facial feature) slope backwards. **5** (**recede from**) archaic withdraw from (an undertaking, agreement, etc.).
– ORIGIN C15: from L. *recedere*, from *re-* 'back' + *cedere* 'go'.

**receipt** • n. **1** the action of receiving something or the fact of its being received. ➤ a written acknowledgement of this. ➤ (**receipts**) an amount of money received over a period by an organization. **2** archaic a recipe. • v. [usu. as adj. **receipted**] mark (a bill) as paid.
– ORIGIN ME: from Anglo-Norman Fr. *receite*, from med. L. *recepta* 'received', fem. past part. of L. *recipere*.

**receivable** • adj. able to be received. • n. (**receivables**) amounts owed to a business, regarded as assets.

**receive** • v. **1** be given, presented with, or paid. ➤ take delivery of. ➤ buy or accept (goods known to be stolen). **2** detect or pick up (broadcast signals). **3** form (an idea or impression) from an experience. **4** (in tennis and similar games) be the player to whom the server serves (the ball). **5** consent to hear (an oath or confession). **6** serve as a receptacle for. **7** suffer, experience, or be subject to. ➤ respond to in a specified way. ➤ meet with (a specified reaction). ➤ [as adj. **received**] widely accepted as authoritative or true. **8** greet or welcome formally. ➤ be visited by. ➤ admit as a member. **9** accommodate.
– PHRASES **be at** (or **on**) **the receiving end** informal be subjected to something unpleasant.
– ORIGIN ME: from Anglo-Norman Fr. *receivre*, based on L. *recipere*, from *re-* 'back' + *capere* 'take'.

**received pronunciation** (also **received standard**) • n. the standard form of British English pronunciation, based on educated speech in southern England.

**receiver** • n. **1** a person or thing that receives something. **2** a piece of radio or television apparatus converting broadcast signals into sound or images. ➤ a telephone handset, in particular the part that converts electrical signals into sounds. **3** (Brit. also **official receiver**) a person appointed to manage the financial affairs of a bankrupt business. **4** American Football a player who specializes in catching passes.

**receivership** • n. the state of being managed by an official receiver.

**receiving order** • n. Brit. a court order authorizing a receiver to act in a case of bankruptcy.

**recension** /rɪˈsɛnʃ(ə)n/ • n. **1** a revised edition of a text. **2** the revision of a text.
– ORIGIN C17: from L. *recensio(n-)*, from *recensere* 'revise', from *re-* 'again' + *censere* 'to review'.

**recent** • adj. **1** having happened or been done lately; belonging to a period of time not long ago. **2** (**Recent**) Geology another term for **HOLOCENE**.
– DERIVATIVES **recency** n. **recently** adv. **recentness** n.
– ORIGIN ME: from L. *recens*, *recent-* or Fr. *récent*.

**receptacle** /rɪˈsɛptək(ə)l/ • n. **1** an object or space used to contain something. **2** chiefly Zoology an organ or structure which receives a secretion, eggs, etc. **3** Botany the base of a flower, flower head, or other sexual organ.
– ORIGIN ME: from L. *receptaculum*, from *receptare*, frequentative of *recipere* (see **RECEIVE**).

**reception** • n. **1** the action or process of receiving someone or something. ➤ the way in which something is received. **2** a formal social occasion held to welcome someone or celebrate an event. **3** the area in a hotel, office, etc. where visitors are greeted. **4** Brit. the first class in an infant school. **5** the quality with which broadcast signals are received.
– ORIGIN ME: from OFr., or from L. *receptio(n-)*, from *recipere* (see **RECEIVE**).

**receptionist** • n. a person who greets and deals with clients and visitors to a surgery, office, hotel, etc.

**reception order** • n. Brit. an order authorizing the detention of a patient in a psychiatric hospital.

**reception room** • n. a function room in a hotel or other building. ➤ Brit. a room in a private house suitable for entertaining visitors.

**receptive** • adj. **1** able or willing to receive something. ➤ willing to consider new suggestions and ideas. **2** (of a female animal) ready to mate.
– DERIVATIVES **receptively** adv. **receptiveness** n. **receptivity** n.

**receptor** /rɪˈsɛptə/ • n. Physiology **1** an organ or cell that responds to external stimuli and transmits signals to a sensory nerve. **2** a tissue or substance which responds to a particular neurotransmitter, hormone, etc.
– ORIGIN C20: coined in Ger. from L. *receptor*, from *recept-*, *recipere* (see **RECEIVE**).

**recess** /rɪˈsɛs, ˈriːsɛs/ • n. **1** a small space set back in a wall. ➤ a hollow in something. ➤ (**recesses**) remote, secluded, or secret places. **2** a period when the proceedings of a parliament, law court, etc. are temporarily suspended. ➤ chiefly N. Amer. a break between school classes. • v. **1** [usu. as adj. **recessed**] set (a fitment) back into a wall or surface. **2** chiefly N. Amer. (of proceedings) be temporarily suspended. ➤ (of an official body) suspend its proceedings temporarily.
– ORIGIN C16: from L. *recessus*, from *recedere* (see **RECEDE**).

**recession** • n. **1** a temporary economic decline during which trade and industrial activity are reduced. **2** chiefly Astronomy the action of receding.
– DERIVATIVES **recessionary** adj.
– ORIGIN C17: from L. *recessio(n-)*, from *recess-*, *recedere* (see **RECEDE**).

**recessional** • adj. of or relating to recession. • n. a hymn sung while the clergy and choir withdraw after a service.

**recessive** • adj. **1** Genetics relating to or denoting heritable characteristics controlled by genes which are expressed in offspring only when inherited from both parents. Often contrasted with **DOMINANT**. **2** undergoing an economic recession. **3** Phonetics (of stress) tending to fall on the first syllable. • n. Genetics a recessive trait or gene.
– DERIVATIVES **recessively** adv. **recessiveness** n. **recessivity** n.
– ORIGIN C17: from **RECESS**, on the pattern of *excessive*.

**recharge** • v. **1** charge or be charged again. **2** return to a normal state of mind or strength after exertion. • n. the replenishment of an aquifer with water.
– DERIVATIVES **rechargeable** adj. **recharger** n.

**réchauffé** /reɪˈʃəʊfeɪ/ • n. a dish of warmed-up food.
– ORIGIN Fr., lit. 'reheated', past part. of *réchauffer*.

**recheck** • v. check again. • n. an act of rechecking.

**recherché** /rəˈʃɛːʃeɪ/ • adj. rare, exotic, or obscure.
– ORIGIN Fr., lit. 'carefully sought out', past part. of *rechercher*.

**rechristen** • v. give a new name to.

**recidivist** /rɪˈsɪdɪvɪst/ • n. a convicted criminal who reoffends.
– DERIVATIVES **recidivism** n. **recidivistic** adj.
– ORIGIN C19: from Fr. *récidiviste*, from *récidiver* 'fall back', based on L. *recidivus*, *recidere* 'fall back', from *re-* 'back' + *cadere* 'to fall'.

**recipe** /ˈrɛsɪpi/ • n. **1** a set of instructions for preparing a dish. **2** something likely to lead to a particular outcome: *a recipe for disaster*. **3** archaic a medical prescription.
– ORIGIN ME: from L., lit. 'receive!', imper. of *recipere*.

**recipient** • n. a receiver of something.
– DERIVATIVES **recipiency** n.
– ORIGIN C16: from L. *recipient-*, *recipere* 'receive'.

**reciprocal** /rɪˈsɪprək(ə)l/ • adj. **1** given, felt, or done in return. **2** (of an agreement or arrangement) bearing on or binding two parties equally. **3** Grammar (of a pronoun or verb) expressing mutual action or relationship. **4** (of a

course or bearing) opposite in direction. • **n. 1** Mathematics the quantity obtained by dividing the number one by a given quantity. **2** Grammar a reciprocal pronoun or verb.
– DERIVATIVES **reciprocality** n. **reciprocally** adv.
– ORIGIN C16: from L. *reciprocus* (based on *re-* 'back' + *pro-* 'forward') + **-AL**.

**reciprocate** /rɪˈsɪprəkeɪt/ • **v. 1** respond to (a gesture or action) with a corresponding one. ➤return (love, affection, etc.) to someone who gives it. **2** [usu. as adj. **reciprocating**] (of a machine part) move backwards and forwards in a straight line.
– DERIVATIVES **reciprocation** n. **reciprocator** n.
– ORIGIN C16: from L. *reciprocat-*, *reciprocare*, from *reciprocus* (see **RECIPROCAL**).

**reciprocating engine** • **n.** a piston engine.

**reciprocity** /ˌrɛsɪˈprɒsɪti/ • **n.** the practice of exchanging things with others for mutual benefit.
– ORIGIN C18: from Fr. *réciprocité*, from *réciproque*, from L. *reciprocus* (see **RECIPROCATE**).

**recirculate** • **v.** circulate again.
– DERIVATIVES **recirculation** n.

**recital** • **n. 1** the performance of a programme of music by a soloist or small group. **2** the enumeration of connected names, facts, or elements. **3** Law the part of a legal document giving factual information.
– DERIVATIVES **recitalist** n.

**recitative** /ˌrɛsɪtəˈtiːv/ • **n.** musical declamation of the kind usual in the narrative and dialogue parts of opera and oratorio.

**recite** • **v. 1** repeat aloud or declaim from memory before an audience. **2** state (names, facts, etc.) in order.
– DERIVATIVES **recitation** n. **reciter** n.
– ORIGIN ME: from OFr. *reciter* or L. *recitare* 'read out', from *re-* (expressing intensive force) + *citare* 'cite'.

**reck** • **v.** [with neg. or in questions] archaic **1** pay heed to something. **2** (**it recks**) it is important.
– ORIGIN OE, of Gmc origin; cf. **RECKLESS**.

**reckless** • **adj.** without thought or care for the consequences of an action.
– DERIVATIVES **recklessly** adv. **recklessness** n.
– ORIGIN OE *recceléas*, from the Gmc base (meaning 'care') of **RECK**.

**reckon** • **v. 1** calculate. **2** informal be of the opinion. **3** regard in a specified way. ➤(**reckon someone/thing among**) include someone or something in (a group). ➤(**reckon on/to**) informal have a specified view or opinion of. **4** (**reckon on**) rely on or be sure of. ➤informal expect. **5** (**reckon with** (or **without**)) take (or fail to take) into account. **6** (**reckon with**) archaic settle accounts with.
– PHRASES **a —— to be reckoned with** (or **to reckon with**) a thing or person not to be ignored or underestimated.
– ORIGIN OE (orig. 'give an account of items received', hence the notion of 'calculation') (*ge*)*recenian* 'recount, relate', of W. Gmc origin.

**reckoner** (also **ready reckoner**) • **n.** a book, table, etc. listing standard numerical calculations or other kinds of information.

**reckoning** • **n. 1** the action of calculating or estimating something. **2** an opinion or judgement. **3** archaic a bill or account, or its settlement. **4** the working out of consequences or retribution for one's actions: *a terrible reckoning.*
– PHRASES **into** (or **out of**) **the reckoning** into or out of contention for selection, victory, etc.

**reclaim** • **v. 1** retrieve or recover. **2** redeem from a state of vice. ➤archaic tame or civilize (an animal or person). **3** bring (waste land or land formerly under water) under cultivation. ➤recycle. • **n.** the action of reclaiming or being reclaimed.
– DERIVATIVES **reclaimable** adj. **reclaimer** n. **reclamation** n.
– ORIGIN ME: from OFr. *reclamer*, from L. *reclamare* 'cry out against', from *re-* 'back' + *clamare* 'to shout'.

**reclassify** • **v.** (**-ies, -ied**) classify differently.
– DERIVATIVES **reclassification** n.

**recline** • **v. 1** lean or lie back in a relaxed position. **2** (of a seat) have a back able to move into a sloping position.
– DERIVATIVES **reclinable** adj.
– ORIGIN ME: from OFr. *recliner* or L. *reclinare* 'bend back, recline', from *re-* 'back' + *clinare* 'to bend'.

**recliner** • **n. 1** a person who reclines. **2** an armchair with a reclining back, especially one with an integral footrest.

**reclothe** • **v.** clothe again or differently.

**recluse** /rɪˈkluːs/ • **n.** a person who avoids others and lives a solitary life. • **adj.** archaic favouring a solitary life.
– DERIVATIVES **reclusion** n. **reclusive** adj. **reclusiveness** n.
– ORIGIN ME: from OFr. *reclus*, past part. of *reclure*, from L. *recludere* 'enclose', from *re-* 'again' + *claudere* 'to shut'.

**recode** • **v.** code differently.

**recognition** • **n.** the action or process of recognizing or being recognized.
– ORIGIN C15: from L. *recognitio(n-)*, from *recognoscere* (see **RECOGNIZE**).

**recognizance** /rɪˈkɒ(g)nɪz(ə)ns/ (also **recognisance**) • **n.** Law a bond by which a person undertakes before a court or magistrate to observe some condition, e.g. to appear when summoned.
– ORIGIN ME: from OFr. *reconnissance*, from *reconnaistre* 'recognize'.

**recognizant** /rɪˈkɒgnɪz(ə)nt/ (also **recognisant**) • **adj.** (**recognizant of**) formal showing recognition or consciousness of.

**recognize** (also **-ise**) • **v. 1** identify as already known; know again. ➤(of a computer or other device) identify and respond correctly to (a sound, character, etc.). **2** acknowledge the existence, validity, or legality of. ➤formally acknowledge that (a country or government) is eligible to be dealt with as a member of the international community. **3** reward formally. **4** (of a person chairing a meeting or debate) call on (someone) to speak.
– DERIVATIVES **recognizability** n. **recognizable** adj. **recognizably** adv. **recognizer** n.
– ORIGIN ME: from OFr. *reconniss-*, *reconnaistre*, from L. *recognoscere* 'know again, recall to mind', from *re-* 'again' + *cognoscere* 'learn'.

**recoil** • **v. 1** suddenly spring back or flinch in fear, horror, or disgust. ➤feel such emotions at the thought of something. **2** (of a gun) move abruptly backwards as a reaction on firing. ➤spring back through force of impact or elasticity. **3** (**recoil on/upon**) (of an action) have an adverse consequence for (the originator). • **n.** the action of recoiling.
– DERIVATIVES **recoilless** adj.
– ORIGIN ME: from OFr. *reculer* 'move back', based on L. *culus* 'buttocks'.

**recollect**[1] /ˌrɛkəˈlɛkt/ • **v.** remember.
– ORIGIN C16: from L. *recollect-*, *recolligere* 'gather back', from *re-* 'back' + *colligere* 'collect'.

**recollect**[2] /ˌriːkəˈlɛkt/ • **v.** rare **1** collect again. **2** (**recollect oneself**) compose oneself.
– ORIGIN C17: later form of **RECOLLECT**[1], from **RE-** + **COLLECT**[1].

**recollection** /ˌrɛkəˈlɛkʃ(ə)n/ • **n. 1** the action or faculty of remembering. **2** a memory.
– DERIVATIVES **recollective** adj.

**recombinant** /rɪˈkɒmbɪnənt/ Genetics • **adj.** relating to or denoting genetic material, cells, etc. formed by recombination. • **n.** a recombinant gene, cell, etc.

**recombination** • **n. 1** the process of recombining things. **2** Genetics the rearrangement of genetic material, especially by crossing over in chromosomes or by the artificial joining of DNA segments.

**recombine** • **v.** combine or cause to combine again or differently.

**recommence** • **v.** begin or cause to begin again.
– DERIVATIVES **recommencement** n.

**recommend** • **v. 1** put forward with approval as being suitable for a purpose or role. ➤advise as a course of action. ➤advise to do something. **2** make appealing or desirable. **3** (**recommend someone/thing to**) archaic commend or entrust someone or something to.
– DERIVATIVES **recommendable** adj. **recommendation** n. **recommendatory** adj. **recommender** n.

– ORIGIN ME: from med. L. *recommendare*, from L. *re-* (expressing intensive force) + *commendare* 'commit to the care of'.

**recommission** • v. commission again.

**recompense** /ˈrɛkəmpɛns/ • v. **1** compensate. ➤ pay or reward for effort or work. ➤ make amends to or reward someone for (loss, harm, or effort). **2** archaic punish or reward appropriately. • n. **1** compensation or reward. **2** archaic restitution made or punishment inflicted for a wrong or injury.
– ORIGIN ME: from OFr., from *recompenser*, from late L. *recompensare*, from L. *re-* 'again' + *compensare* 'weigh one thing against another'.

**recompose** • v. compose again or differently.
– DERIVATIVES **recomposition** n.

**recon** /rɪˈkɒn/ informal, chiefly N. Amer. • n. short for **RECONNAISSANCE**. • v. (**reconned**, **reconning**) short for **RECONNOITRE**.

**reconcile** /ˈrɛk(ə)nsʌɪl/ • v. **1** restore friendly relations between. ➤ settle (a quarrel). **2** make or show to be compatible. **3** (**reconcile someone to**) make someone accept (a disagreeable thing).
– DERIVATIVES **reconcilability** n. **reconcilable** adj. **reconcilement** n. **reconciler** n. **reconciliation** n. **reconciliatory** adj.
– ORIGIN ME: from OFr. *reconcilier* or L. *reconciliare*, from L. *re-* 'back' (also expressing intensive force) + *conciliare* 'bring together'.

**recondite** /ˈrɛk(ə)ndʌɪt, rɪˈkɒn-/ • adj. (of a subject or knowledge) obscure.
– ORIGIN C17: from L. *reconditus* 'hidden, put away', past part. of *recondere*, from *re-* 'back' + *condere* 'put together, secrete'.

**recondition** • v. **1** condition again. **2** Brit. overhaul or renovate.

**reconfigure** • v. configure differently.
– DERIVATIVES **reconfiguration** n.

**reconfirm** • v. confirm again.

**reconnaissance** /rɪˈkɒnɪs(ə)ns/ • n. military observation of a region to locate an enemy or ascertain strategic features. ➤ preliminary surveying or research.
– ORIGIN C19: from Fr., from *reconnaître* (see **RECONNOITRE**).

**reconnect** • v. connect again.
– DERIVATIVES **reconnection** n.

**reconnoitre** /ˌrɛkəˈnɔɪtə/ (US **reconnoiter**) • v. make a military observation of (a region). • n. informal an act of reconnoitring.
– ORIGIN C18: from obs. Fr. *reconnoître*, from L. *recognoscere* (see **RECOGNIZE**).

**reconsecrate** • v. consecrate again.
– DERIVATIVES **reconsecration** n.

**reconsider** • v. consider again.
– DERIVATIVES **reconsideration** n.

**reconsolidate** • v. consolidate again or anew.
– DERIVATIVES **reconsolidation** n.

**reconstitute** • v. **1** reconstruct. ➤ change the form and organization of (an institution). **2** restore (something dried) to its original state by adding water.
– DERIVATIVES **reconstitution** n.

**reconstruct** • v. **1** construct again. **2** form an impression, model, or re-enactment of (something) from evidence.
– DERIVATIVES **reconstructable** (also **reconstructible**) adj. **reconstruction** n. **reconstructive** adj. **reconstructor** n.

**reconvene** • v. convene or cause to convene again.

**reconvert** • v. convert back to a former state.
– DERIVATIVES **reconversion** n.

**record** • n. **1** a piece of evidence about the past, especially a written or other permanent account of something. ➤ Law an official report of the proceedings and judgement in a court. **2** a person or thing's previous conduct or performance. ➤ a criminal record. **3** the best performance or most remarkable event of its kind on record. **4** a thin plastic disc carrying recorded sound in grooves on each surface, for reproduction by a record player. ➤ a piece or collection of music reproduced on such a disc or on another medium. **5** Computing a number of related items of information handled as a unit. • v. **1** make a record of. ➤ state or express officially. **2** convert (sound, a broadcast, etc.) into permanent form for later reproduction. ➤ produce (music or a programme) by such means.
– PHRASES **for the record** so that the true facts are recorded or known. **on record** officially measured and noted. **on** (or **off**) **the record** made (or not made) as an official or attributable statement. **put** (or **set**) **the record straight** correct a misapprehension.
– DERIVATIVES **recordable** adj. **recording** n.
– ORIGIN ME: from OFr. *record* 'remembrance', from *recorder* 'bring to remembrance', from L. *recordari* 'remember', based on *cor*, *cord-* 'heart'.

**record-breaking** • adj. surpassing a record.
– DERIVATIVES **record-breaker** n.

**recorded delivery** • n. Brit. a service in which the Post Office obtains a signature from the recipient as a record that an item of post has been delivered.

**recorder** • n. **1** an apparatus for recording sound, pictures, or data. **2** a person who keeps records. **3** (**Recorder**) (in England and Wales) a barrister appointed to serve as a part-time judge. ➤ Brit. historical a judge in certain courts. **4** a simple woodwind instrument without keys, played by blowing air through a shaped mouthpiece.
– DERIVATIVES **recordership** n.
– ORIGIN ME: from Anglo-Norman Fr. *recordour*, from OFr. *recorder* 'bring to remembrance'; partly reinforced by the verb **RECORD** (also used in the obs. sense 'practise a tune').

**recording angel** • n. an angel believed to register each person's good and bad actions.

**recordist** • n. a person who makes recordings.

**record player** • n. an apparatus for reproducing sound from gramophone records, with a turntable that spins the record at a constant speed and a stylus that picks up sound from the groove.

**recount**[1] /rɪˈkaʊnt/ • v. give an account of something.
– ORIGIN ME: from ONorth. Fr. *reconter* 'tell again', based on OFr. *counter* (see **COUNT**[1]).

**recount**[2] • v. /riːˈkaʊnt/ count again. • n. /ˈriːkaʊnt/ an act of counting something again.

**recoup** • v. **1** regain (something lost). ➤ reimburse or compensate for money spent or lost. ➤ regain (lost physical or mental resources); recover. **2** Law deduct or keep back (part of a sum due).
– DERIVATIVES **recoupable** adj. **recoupment** n.
– ORIGIN C17: from Fr. *recouper* 'retrench, cut back', from *re-* 'back' + *couper* 'to cut'.

**recourse** • n. **1** a source of help in a difficult situation. ➤ (**recourse to**) use of as a recourse. **2** the legal right to demand compensation or payment.
– PHRASES **without recourse** Finance a formula used to disclaim responsibility for future non-payment.
– ORIGIN ME: from OFr. *recours*, from L. *recursus*, from *re-* 'back, again' + *cursus* 'course, running'.

**recover** • v. **1** return to a normal state of health, mind, or strength. **2** find or regain possession of. ➤ regain control of (oneself or a physical or mental state). ➤ regain or secure (compensation). **3** remove or extract (an energy source, chemical, etc.) for use, reuse, or waste treatment. • n. (**the recover**) a position of a firearm forming part of a military drill.
– DERIVATIVES **recoverability** n. **recoverable** adj. **recoverer** n.
– ORIGIN ME: from Anglo-Norman Fr. *recoverer*, from L. *recuperare* 'get again'.

**re-cover** • v. put a new cover or covering on.

**recovery** • n. (pl. **-ies**) **1** an act or the process of recovering. ➤ the action of taking a vehicle that has broken down or crashed for repair. **2** (also **recovery shot**) Golf a stroke bringing the ball out of the rough or a bunker. **3** (in rowing, swimming, etc.) the action of returning the paddle, leg, or arm to its initial position for a new stroke.

**recovery position** • n. Brit. a position used to prevent an unconscious person from choking, the body being placed face downwards and slightly to the side, supported by bent limbs.

**recreant** /ˈrɛkrɪənt/ archaic ● **adj. 1** cowardly. **2** apostate. ● **n.** a recreant person.
– DERIVATIVES **recreancy** n. **recreantly** adv.
– ORIGIN ME: from OFr., lit. 'surrendering', pres. part. of *recroire*, from med. L. (*se*) *recredere* 'surrender (oneself)'.

**recreate** ● **v.** create again. ➤reproduce.

**recreation**[1] /ˌrɛkrɪˈeɪʃ(ə)n/ ● **n.** enjoyable leisure activity.
– ORIGIN ME: via OFr. from L. *recreatio(n-)*, from *recreare* 'create again, renew'.

**recreation**[2] /ˌriːkrɪˈeɪʃ(ə)n/ ● **n.** the action of recreating something.

**recreational** ● **adj.** of or relating to recreation. ➤relating to or denoting drugs taken occasionally for enjoyment.
– DERIVATIVES **recreationally** adv.

**recreation ground** ● **n.** Brit. a piece of public land used for sports and games.

**recreative** /ˈrɛkrɪˌeɪtɪv, ˌriːkrɪˈeɪtɪv/ ● **adj.** recreational.

**recriminate** /rɪˈkrɪmɪneɪt/ ● **v.** make recriminations.
– DERIVATIVES **recriminative** adj. (archaic). **recriminatory** adj.
– ORIGIN C17: from med. L. *recriminat-*, *recriminari* 'accuse in return', from *re-* (expressing opposition) + *criminare* 'accuse'.

**recrimination** ● **n.** (usu. **recriminations**) an accusation in response to one from someone else.

**rec room** ● **n.** N. Amer. a room in a house used for recreation.

**recross** ● **v.** cross again.

**recrudesce** /ˌriːkruːˈdɛs, ˌrɛk-/ ● **v.** formal break out again; recur.
– DERIVATIVES **recrudescence** n. **recrudescent** adj.
– ORIGIN C19 (earlier (C18) as *recrudescence*): from L. *recrudescere* 'become raw again', from *re-* 'again' + *crudus* 'raw'.

**recruit** ● **v.** enlist (someone) in the armed forces. ➤enrol (someone) as a member or worker in an organization. ➤informal persuade to do or help with something. ● **n.** a newly recruited person.
– DERIVATIVES **recruitable** adj. **recruiter** n.
– ORIGIN C17: from obs. Fr. dial. *recrute*, based on L. *recrescere* 'grow again'.

**recruitment** ● **n. 1** the action of recruiting people. **2** Ecology the increase in a natural population as progeny grow and immigrants arrive.

**recta** plural form of RECTUM.

**rectal** ● **adj.** of, relating to, or affecting the rectum.
– DERIVATIVES **rectally** adv.

**rectangle** ● **n.** a plane figure with four straight sides and four right angles, especially one with unequal adjacent sides.
– ORIGIN C16: from med. L. *rectangulum*, based on L. *rectus* 'straight' + *angulus* 'an angle'.

**rectangular** ● **adj. 1** denoting or shaped like a rectangle. ➤(of a solid) having a rectangular base, section, or side. **2** placed or having parts placed at right angles.
– DERIVATIVES **rectangularity** n. **rectangularly** adv.

**rectangular coordinates** ● **pl. n.** a pair of coordinates measured along axes at right angles to one another.

**rectangular hyperbola** ● **n.** a hyperbola with rectangular asymptotes.

**recti** plural form of RECTUS.

**rectified spirit** ● **n.** a mixture of ethanol (95.6 per cent) and water produced as an azeotrope by distillation.

**rectifier** ● **n.** an electrical device converting an alternating current into a direct one by allowing it to flow in one direction only.

**rectify** ● **v.** (**-ies**, **-ied**) **1** put right; correct. **2** convert (alternating current) to direct current. **3** find a straight line equal in length to (a curve).
– DERIVATIVES **rectifiable** adj. **rectification** n.
– ORIGIN ME: from OFr. *rectifier*, from med. L. *rectificare*, from L. *rectus* 'right'.

**rectilinear** /ˌrɛktɪˈlɪnɪə/ (also **rectilineal** /-nɪəl/) ● **adj. 1** contained by, consisting of, or moving in a straight line or lines. **2** Photography (of a wide-angle lens) corrected so that straight lines in the subject appear straight in the image.
– DERIVATIVES **rectilinearity** n. **rectilinearly** adv.
– ORIGIN C17: from late L. *rectilineus* (from L. *rectus* 'straight' + *linea* 'line') + -AR[1].

**rectitude** ● **n.** formal morally correct behaviour.
– ORIGIN ME: from OFr., from late L. *rectitudo*, from L. *rectus* 'right, straight'.

**recto** ● **n.** (pl. **-os**) a right-hand page of an open book, or the front of a loose document. Contrasted with VERSO.
– ORIGIN C19: from L. *recto (folio)* 'on the right (leaf)'.

**rector** ● **n. 1** (in the Church of England) the incumbent of a parish where all tithes formerly passed to the incumbent. ➤(in other Anglican Churches) a member of the clergy in charge of a parish. ➤(in the Roman Catholic Church) a priest in charge of a church or a religious institution. **2** the head of certain universities, colleges, and schools. ➤(in Scotland) an elected student representative on a university's governing body.
– DERIVATIVES **rectorate** n. **rectorial** adj. **rectorship** n.
– ORIGIN ME: from L. *rector* 'ruler', from *rect-*, *regere* 'rule'.

**rectory** ● **n.** (pl. **-ies**) **1** a rector's house. **2** a Church of England benefice held by a rector.

**rectrices** /ˈrɛktrɪsiːz/ ● **pl. n.** (sing. **rectrix** /-trɪx/) Ornithology the larger feathers in a bird's tail, used for steering in flight.
– ORIGIN C18: from L., fem. pl. of *rector* (see RECTOR).

**rectum** ● **n.** (pl. **rectums** or **recta** /-tə/) the final section of the large intestine, terminating at the anus.
– ORIGIN C16: from L. *rectum (intestinum)* 'straight (intestine)'.

**rectus** /ˈrɛktəs/ ● **n.** (pl. **recti** /-tʌɪ/) Anatomy a straight muscle.
– ORIGIN C18: from L., lit. 'straight'.

**recumbent** /rɪˈkʌmb(ə)nt/ ● **adj. 1** lying down. **2** (of a plant) growing close to the ground. ● **n.** a bicycle ridden in a reclining position.
– DERIVATIVES **recumbency** n. **recumbently** adv.
– ORIGIN C17: from L. *recumbent-*, *recumbere* 'recline', from *re-* 'back' + a verb rel. to *cubare* 'to lie'.

**recuperate** /rɪˈkuːpəreɪt/ ● **v. 1** recover from illness or exertion. **2** regain (something lost).
– DERIVATIVES **recuperable** adj. **recuperation** n. **recuperative** adj.
– ORIGIN C16 (earlier (C15) as *recuperation*): from L. *recuperat-*, *recuperare* 'regain', from *re-* 'back' + *capere* 'take'.

**recuperator** ● **n.** a heat exchanger in which hot waste gases from a furnace are used to heat incoming air or fuel.

**recur** ● **v.** (**recurred**, **recurring**) occur again. ➤(of a thought, image, etc.) come back to one's mind. ➤(**recur to**) go back to in thought or speech.
– DERIVATIVES **recurrence** n. **recurring** adj.
– ORIGIN ME: from L. *recurrere*, from *re-* 'again, back' + *currere* 'run'.

**recurrent** ● **adj. 1** occurring often or repeatedly. **2** Anatomy (of a nerve or blood vessel) turning back so as to reverse direction.
– DERIVATIVES **recurrently** adv.

**recurring decimal** ● **n.** a decimal fraction in which a figure or group of figures is repeated indefinitely, as in *0.666 …*

**recursion** /rɪˈkəːʃ(ə)n/ ● **n.** chiefly Mathematics & Linguistics the repeated application of a procedure or rule to successive results of the process. ➤a recursive procedure or formula.

**recursive** ● **adj. 1** chiefly Mathematics & Linguistics relating to or characterized by recursion. **2** Computing relating to or denoting a program or routine a part of which requires the application of the whole.
– DERIVATIVES **recursively** adv.

**recurve** ● **v.** chiefly Biology bend backwards. ● **n.** Archery a bow that curves forward at the ends, straightening out

when the bow is drawn.
– DERIVATIVES **recurvature** n.

**recusant** /ˈrɛkjʊz(ə)nt/ ● n. a person who refuses to submit to authority or comply with a regulation. ➤chiefly historical a person who refused to attend services of the Church of England. ● adj. of or denoting a recusant.
– DERIVATIVES **recusance** n. **recusancy** n.
– ORIGIN C16: from L. *recusant-*, *recusare* (see **RECUSE**).

**recuse** /rɪˈkjuːz/ ● v. (**recuse oneself**) chiefly N. Amer. & S. African (of a judge) excuse oneself from a case because of a possible lack of impartiality.
– DERIVATIVES **recusal** n.
– ORIGIN ME: from L. *recusare* 'to refuse', from *re-* (expressing opposition) + *causa* 'a cause'.

**recycle** ● v. **1** convert (waste) into reusable material. ➤use again. **2** return (material) to a previous stage in a cyclic process.
– DERIVATIVES **recyclability** n. **recyclable** adj. **recycler** n.

**red** ● adj. (**redder, reddest**) **1** of a colour at the end of the spectrum next to orange and opposite violet, as of blood, fire, or rubies. ➤(of hair or fur) of a reddish-brown colour. ➤(of a person's face) red due to embarrassment, anger, or heat. ➤dated or offensive (of a people) having reddish skin. **2** (of wine) made from dark grapes and coloured by their skins. **3** of or denoting the suits hearts and diamonds in a pack of cards. **4** denoting a red light or flag used as a signal to stop. ➤denoting something forbidden, dangerous, or urgent. **5** (of a ski run) of the second-highest level of difficulty. **6** informal, chiefly derogatory communist or socialist. **7** archaic or poetic/literary involving bloodshed or violence. ● n. **1** red colour or pigment. **2** informal, chiefly derogatory a communist or socialist. **3** (**the red**) the situation of having spent more than is in one's bank account.
– PHRASES **the red planet** Mars. **see red** informal become very angry suddenly.
– DERIVATIVES **reddish** adj. **reddy** adj. **redly** adv. **redness** n.
– ORIGIN OE *rēad*, of Gmc origin.

**red-** ● prefix variant of **RE-** before a vowel (as in *redolent*).

**redact** /rɪˈdakt/ ● v. rare edit for publication.
– DERIVATIVES **redactor** n.
– ORIGIN C19: back-form. from **REDACTION**.

**redaction** ● n. **1** the process of editing text for publication. **2** a version of a text.
– DERIVATIVES **redactional** adj.
– ORIGIN C18: from Fr. *rédaction*, from late L. *redactio(n-)*, from *redigere* 'bring back'.

**red admiral** ● n. a migratory butterfly having dark wings with red bands and white spots. [*Vanessa atalanta*.]

**red algae** ● pl. n. a large group of algae that includes many red seaweeds. [Division Rhodophyta.]

**redan** /rɪˈdan/ ● n. an arrow-shaped embankment as part of a fortification.
– ORIGIN C17: from Fr., from *redent* 'notching (of a saw)', from *re-* 'again' (expressing repetition) + *dent* 'tooth'.

**redback** ● n. a highly venomous Australasian spider with a bright red stripe down the back. [*Latrodectus mactans hasseltii*.]

**red biddy** ● n. Brit. informal, dated a mixture of cheap red wine and methylated spirits.

**red blood cell** ● n. less technical term for **ERYTHROCYTE**.

**red-blooded** ● adj. (of a man) vigorous or virile.
– DERIVATIVES **red-bloodedness** n.

**redbreast** ● n. informal, chiefly Brit. a robin.

**red-brick** ● adj. **1** built with red bricks. **2** (of a British university) founded in the late 19th or early 20th century.

**redbud** ● n. a North American tree of the pea family, with pink flowers growing from the trunk, branches, and twigs. [Genus *Cercis*.]

**redcap** ● n. **1** Brit. informal a member of the military police. **2** N. Amer. a railway porter.

**red card** ● n. (especially in soccer) a red card shown by the referee to a player being sent off the field. ● v. (**red-card**) (of a referee) show a red card to.

**red carpet** ● n. a long, narrow red carpet for a distinguished visitor to walk along.

**red cedar** ● n. a North American cedar with reddish-brown bark. [*Thuja plicata* (western) and *Juniperus virginiana* (eastern).]

**red cell** ● n. less technical term for **ERYTHROCYTE**.

**red cent** ● n. N. Amer. **1** a one-cent coin, formerly made of copper. **2** [usu. with neg.] the smallest amount of money.

**redcoat** ● n. **1** historical a British soldier. **2** (in the UK) an organizer and entertainer at a Butlin's holiday camp.

**red coral** ● n. a branching pinkish-red horny coral used in jewellery. [Genus *Corallium*.]

**Red Crescent** ● n. a national branch in Muslim countries of the International Movement of the Red Cross and the Red Crescent.

**Red Cross** ● n. the International Movement of the Red Cross and the Red Crescent, an organization bringing relief to victims of war or natural disaster.

**redcurrant** ● n. **1** a small edible red berry. **2** the shrub which produces this fruit, related to the blackcurrant. [*Ribes rubrum*.]

**redd**[1] ● v. (past and past part. **redd**) (**redd something up**) Scottish & Irish tidy something up.
– ORIGIN ME: perh. rel. to **RID**.

**redd**[2] ● n. a hollow in a river bed made by a trout or salmon to spawn in.
– ORIGIN C17: of unknown origin.

**red deer** ● n. a deer with a rich red-brown summer coat that turns brownish-grey in winter, the male having large antlers. [*Cervus elaphus*.]

**Red Delicious** ● n. a dessert apple of a soft-fleshed red-skinned variety.

**redden** ● v. **1** make or become red. **2** blush.

**reddle** ● n. red ochre, used especially to mark sheep.
– ORIGIN C18: var. of **RUDDLE**.

**red duster** ● n. Brit. informal the red ensign.

**red dwarf** ● n. Astronomy a small, old, relatively cool star.

**rede** /riːd/ archaic ● n. advice or counsel. ● v. **1** advise. **2** interpret (a riddle or dream).
– ORIGIN OE *rǣd*, of Gmc origin; the verb is a var. of **READ**.

**redecorate** ● v. decorate again or differently.
– DERIVATIVES **redecoration** n.

**rededicate** ● v. dedicate again.
– DERIVATIVES **rededication** n.

**redeem** ● v. **1** compensate for the faults or bad aspects of. ➤(**redeem oneself**) make up for one's poor past performance or behaviour. ➤save from sin, error, or evil. **2** gain or regain possession of in exchange for payment. ➤Finance repay (a stock, bond, etc.) at the maturity date. ➤exchange (a coupon) for goods or money. ➤clear (a debt). **3** fulfil (a pledge or promise). **4** archaic buy the freedom of.
– DERIVATIVES **redeemable** adj. **redeeming** adj.
– ORIGIN ME: from OFr. *redimer* or L. *redimere*, from *re-* 'back' + *emere* 'buy'.

**redeemer** ● n. **1** a person who redeems someone or something. **2** (**the Redeemer**) Christ.

**redefine** ● v. define again or differently.
– DERIVATIVES **redefinition** n.

**redemption** ● n. **1** the action of redeeming someone or something, or of being redeemed. **2** a thing that saves someone from error or evil.
– DERIVATIVES **redemptive** adj.
– ORIGIN ME: from OFr., from L. *redemptio(n-)*, from *redimere* (see **REDEEM**).

**red ensign** ● n. a red flag with the Union Jack in the top corner next to the flagstaff, flown by British-registered ships.

**redeploy** ● v. deploy again or differently.
– DERIVATIVES **redeployment** n.

**redesign** ● v. design again or differently. ● n. the action or process of redesigning something.

**redetermine** ● v. determine again or differently.
– DERIVATIVES **redetermination** n.

**redevelop** ● v. develop again or differently.

– DERIVATIVES **redeveloper** n. **redevelopment** n.

**red-eye** • n. **1** the effect in photography of people appearing to have red eyes, caused by a reflection from the retina when the flashgun is too near the camera lens. **2** (also **red-eye flight**) informal, chiefly N. Amer. a flight on which one cannot expect much sleep. **3** a fish with red eyes, especially (Brit.) a rudd or (N. Amer.) a rock bass. **4** US informal cheap whisky. **5** Canadian a drink made from tomato juice and beer.

**red-faced** • adj. embarrassed; ashamed.

**red-figure** • n. a type of ancient Greek pottery in which the background is painted black, leaving figures in the red colour of the clay. Compare with BLACK-FIGURE.

**redfish** • n. (pl. same or **-fishes**) **1** a bright red edible marine fish. [*Sebastes marinus* (N. Atlantic), *Sciaenops ocellatus* (W. Atlantic), and other species.] **2** Brit. a male salmon in the spawning season.

**red fish** • n. fish with dark flesh, such as herring, mackerel, and sardine. Compare with WHITE FISH.

**red flag** • n. **1** a warning of danger. **2** the symbol of socialist revolution.

**red giant** • n. Astronomy a very large luminous star of low surface temperature.

**red gold** • n. an alloy of gold and copper.

**red grouse** • n. a British moorland grouse with reddish-brown plumage. [*Lagopus lagopus scoticus*.]

**red gum** • n. an Australian gum tree with smooth bark and hard dark red wood. [*Eucalyptus camaldulensis* and other species.] ➤astringent reddish kino gum from such a tree.

**red-handed** • adj. in or just after the act of doing something wrong.

**red hat** • n. a cardinal's hat, especially as the symbol of a cardinal's office.

**redhead** • n. **1** a person, especially a woman, with red hair. **2** a North American diving duck resembling the pochard. [*Aythya americana*.]

**red heat** • n. the temperature or state of something so hot that it emits red light.

**red herring** • n. **1** a dried smoked herring. **2** a misleading clue or distraction. [so named from the practice of using the scent of red herring in training hounds.]

**red-hot** • adj. **1** so hot as to glow red. **2** extremely exciting or popular. **3** very passionate.

**red-hot poker** • n. a South African plant with tall erect spikes of tubular flowers, the upper ones of which are red and the lower ones yellow. [*Kniphofia uvaria*.]

**redial** • v. (**redialled**, **redialling**; US **redialed**, **redialing**) dial (a telephone number) again. • n. the facility on a telephone by which the number just dialled may be redialled by pressing a single button.

**redid** past of REDO.

**rediffusion** • n. Brit. the relaying of broadcast programmes, especially by cable from a central receiver.

**Red Indian** • n. old-fashioned term for AMERICAN INDIAN.

**redingote** /ˈrɛdɪŋgəʊt/ • n. a woman's long coat with a cutaway or contrasting front.
– ORIGIN C18: Fr., from Engl. *riding coat*.

**redintegrate** /rɛˈdɪntɪgreɪt/ • v. archaic restore to a state of wholeness, unity, or perfection.
– DERIVATIVES **redintegration** n. **redintegrative** adj.
– ORIGIN ME: from L. *redintegrat-*, *redintegrare* 'make whole', from *re(d)-* 'again' + *integrare* 'restore'.

**redirect** • v. direct differently.
– DERIVATIVES **redirection** n.

**rediscount** Finance • v. (of a central bank) discount (a bill of exchange) that has already been discounted by a commercial bank. • n. the action of rediscounting.

**rediscover** • v. discover again.
– DERIVATIVES **rediscovery** n. (pl. **-ies**).

**redissolve** • v. dissolve or cause to dissolve again.
– DERIVATIVES **redissolution** n.

**redistribute** • v. distribute again or differently.
– DERIVATIVES **redistribution** n. **redistributive** adj.

**redistributionist** • n. a person who advocates the redistribution of wealth.
– DERIVATIVES **redistributionism** n.

**redivide** • v. divide again or differently.
– DERIVATIVES **redivision** n.

**redivivus** /ˌrɛdɪˈviːvəs/ • adj. [postpos.] poetic/literary come back to life; reborn.
– ORIGIN C16: from L., from *re(d)-* 'again' + *vivus* 'living'.

**red lead** • n. red lead oxide used as a pigment.

**Red Leicester** • n. see LEICESTER (sense 1).

**red-letter day** • n. a noteworthy or memorable day.
– ORIGIN C18: from the practice of highlighting a festival in red on a calendar.

**red light** • n. a red light instructing moving vehicles to stop.

**red-light district** • n. an area with many brothels, strip clubs, etc.
– ORIGIN from the use of a red light as the sign of a brothel.

**redline** N. Amer. informal • v. **1** drive with (the car engine) at its maximum rpm. **2** refuse (a loan or insurance) to someone due to their area of residence. ➤cancel (a project). • n. the maximum number of revolutions per minute for a car engine.
– ORIGIN from the use of *red* as a limit marker, in sense 2 a ring marking part of a map.

**red man** • n. offensive an American Indian.

**red meat** • n. meat that is red when raw, e.g. beef or lamb.

**red mullet** • n. an elongated food fish with long barbels on the chin, living in warmer seas. [*Muletus surmuletus* and other species.]

**redneck** • n. N. Amer. informal, derogatory a working-class white person from the southern US, especially a politically conservative one.
– DERIVATIVES **rednecked** adj.

**redo** • v. (**redoes**; past **redid**; past part. **redone**) do again or differently. ➤informal redecorate.

**redolent** /ˈrɛd(ə)l(ə)nt/ • adj. **1** (**redolent of/with**) strongly reminiscent or suggestive of. ➤poetic/literary strongly smelling of. **2** archaic or poetic/literary fragrant.
– DERIVATIVES **redolence** n. **redolently** adv.
– ORIGIN ME: from OFr., or from L. *redolent-* 'giving out a strong smell', from *re(d)-* 'back, again' + *olere* 'to smell'.

**redouble** • v. **1** make or become much greater, more intense, or more numerous. **2** Bridge double a bid already doubled by an opponent. • n. Bridge a call that redoubles a bid.
– ORIGIN ME: from Fr. *redoubler*, from *re-* 'again' + *doubler* 'to double'.

**redoubt** • n. Military a temporary or supplementary fortification, typically square or polygonal and without flanking defences.
– ORIGIN C17: from Fr. *redoute*, from obs. Ital. *ridotta* and med. L. *reductus* 'refuge', from L. *reducere* 'withdraw'; the *-b-* was added by assoc. with DOUBT.

**redoubtable** • adj. often humorous (of a person) formidable, especially as an opponent.
– DERIVATIVES **redoubtably** adv.
– ORIGIN ME: from OFr. *redoutable*, from *redouter* 'to fear', from *re-* (expressing intensive force) + *douter* 'to doubt'.

**redound** /rɪˈdaʊnd/ • v. **1** (**redound to**) formal contribute greatly to (a person's credit or honour). **2** (**redound upon**) archaic rebound on.
– ORIGIN ME: from OFr. *redonder*, from L. *redundare* 'surge', from *re(d)-* 'again' + *unda* 'a wave'.

**redox** /ˈriːdɒks, ˈrɛdɒks/ • n. [usu. as modifier] Chemistry oxidation and reduction considered together: *redox reactions*.
– ORIGIN 1920s: blend.

**red pepper** • n. the ripe red fruit of a sweet pepper.

**redpoll** /ˈrɛdpəʊl/ • n. **1** a mainly brown finch with a red forehead, related to the linnet. [*Acanthis flammea*.] **2** (**red poll**) an animal of a breed of red-haired polled cattle.

**Red Queen hypothesis** • n. Biology the hypothesis that organisms are constantly struggling to keep up in an evolutionary race between predator and prey species.

– ORIGIN C20: named from a passage in Lewis Carroll's *Through the Looking Glass*, in which the Red Queen tells Alice that 'it takes all the running you can do to stay in the same place'.

**redraft** • v. draft differently. • n. a redrafted document.

**red rattle** • n. a pink-flowered lousewort of marshy places, the seeds of which produce a rattling sound in their capsule when ripe. [*Pedicularis palustris*.]

**redraw** • v. (past **redrew**; past part. **redrawn**) draw or draw up again or differently.

**redress** • v. **1** remedy or set right. **2** archaic set upright again. • n. remedy or compensation for a wrong or grievance.

– PHRASES **redress the balance** restore equality in a situation.

– DERIVATIVES **redressable** adj. **redressal** n. **redresser** n.

– ORIGIN ME: the verb from OFr. *redresser*; the noun via Anglo-Norman Fr. *redresse*.

**re-dress** • v. dress again or differently.

**red ribbon** • n. US an award for coming second in a competition.

**red roan** • adj. (of an animal's coat) bay or chestnut mixed with white or grey. • n. a red roan animal.

**red rose** • n. **1** the emblem of Lancashire or the Lancastrians. **2** the symbol of the British Labour Party.

**red salmon** • n. the sockeye salmon.

**red sandalwood** • n. either of two SE Asian trees of the pea family which yield red wood. [*Pterocarpus santalinus* and *Adenanthera pavonina*.]

**red setter** • n. less formal term for **IRISH SETTER**.

**redshank** • n. a large sandpiper with long red legs. [*Tringa totanus* and *T. erythropus*.]

**red shift** • n. Astronomy the displacement of the spectrum to longer wavelengths in the light from distant celestial objects moving away from the observer. Compare with **BLUE SHIFT**.

**redshirt** informal • n. US a college athlete withdrawn from sporting events for a year to develop their skills and extend their period of eligibility at this level of competition. • v. (usu. **be redshirted**) US keep (an athlete) out of university competition for a year.

– ORIGIN from the red shirts worn by such athletes.

**redskin** • n. dated or offensive an American Indian.

**red snapper** • n. an edible reddish marine fish. [*Sebastes ruberrimus* (N. Pacific) and genus *Lutjanus* (tropics).]

**red squirrel** • n. a small squirrel with a reddish coat. [*Sciurus vulgaris* (Eurasia) and *Tamiasciurus hudsonicus* (N. America).]

**redstart** • n. **1** a small songbird of the thrush family with a reddish tail. [*Phoenicurus phoenicurus* and other species.] **2** an American warbler with red or orange markings. [*Setophaga ruticilla* and other species.]

**red tape** • n. excessive bureaucracy or adherence to rules, especially in public business.

– ORIGIN C18: so named because of the red or pink tape used to bind official documents.

**red tide** • n. a discoloration of seawater caused by a bloom of toxic red dinoflagellates.

**red top** • n. Brit. a tabloid newspaper.

– ORIGIN from the red background on which the titles of certain British tabloid newspapers are printed.

**reduce** • v. **1** make or become smaller or less in amount, degree, or size. ➤ boil (a sauce or other liquid) so that it becomes thicker and more concentrated. ➤ chiefly N. Amer. (of a person) lose weight. ➤ Photography make (a negative or print) less dense. **2** (**reduce someone/thing to**) bring someone or something by force or necessity to (an undesirable state or action). **3** (**reduce something to**) change something to (a simpler or more basic form). ➤ convert a fraction to (the form with the lowest terms). **4** archaic conquer (a place). **5** Chemistry cause to combine chemically with hydrogen. ➤ undergo or cause to undergo a reaction in which electrons are gained from another substance or molecule. The opposite of **OXIDIZE**. **6** restore (a dislocated body part) to its proper position.

– PHRASES **reduced circumstances** poverty after relative prosperity. **reduce someone to the ranks** demote a non-commissioned officer to an ordinary soldier.

– DERIVATIVES **reducer** n. **reducibility** n. **reducible** adj.

– ORIGIN ME (orig. 'restore', hence 'bring to a different state' and 'bring to a simpler or lower state'): from L. *reducere*, from *re-* 'back, again' + *ducere* 'bring, lead'.

**reducing agent** • n. Chemistry a substance that tends to bring about reduction by being oxidized and losing electrons.

**reductant** • n. Chemistry a reducing agent.

**reductase** /rɪˈdʌkteɪz/ • n. Biochemistry an enzyme which promotes chemical reduction.

**reductio ad absurdum** /rɪˌdʌktɪəʊ ad abˈsəːdəm/ • n. Philosophy a method of proving the falsity of a premise by showing that its logical consequence is absurd or contradictory.

– ORIGIN L., lit. 'reduction to the absurd'.

**reduction** • n. **1** the action of reducing something. ➤ the amount by which something is reduced. **2** an arrangement of an orchestral score for piano or a smaller group of performers. **3** a smaller copy of a picture or photograph. **4** a thick and concentrated liquid or sauce.

**reduction gear** • n. a system of gearwheels in which the driven shaft rotates more slowly than the driving shaft.

**reductionism** • n. often derogatory the practice of analysing and describing a complex phenomenon in terms of its simple or fundamental constituents, especially when this is said to provide a sufficient explanation.

– DERIVATIVES **reductionist** n. & adj. **reductionistic** adj.

**reductive** • adj. **1** tending to present a subject or problem in a simplified form, especially one viewed as crude. ➤ (with reference to art) minimal. **2** of or relating to chemical reduction.

– DERIVATIVES **reductively** adv. **reductiveness** n.

**reductivism** • n. **1** minimalism. **2** reductionism.

**redundant** • adj. **1** no longer needed or useful; superfluous. ➤ (of words) able to be omitted without loss of meaning or function. ➤ Engineering (of a component) not strictly necessary but included in case another component fails. **2** chiefly Brit. unemployed.

– DERIVATIVES **redundancy** n. (pl. **-ies**). **redundantly** adv.

– ORIGIN C16 (in the sense 'abundant'): from L. *redundant-*, *redundare* (see **REDOUND**).

**reduplicate** • v. **1** repeat or copy so as to form another of the same kind. **2** repeat (a linguistic element) exactly or with a slight change (e.g. *hurly-burly*).

– DERIVATIVES **reduplication** n. **reduplicative** adj.

– ORIGIN C16 (earlier (ME) as *reduplication*): from late L. *reduplicat-*, *reduplicare* 'double again', from *re-* 'again' + *duplicare* (see **DUPLICATE**).

**redux** /ˈriːdʌks/ • adj. [postpos.] revived; restored.

– ORIGIN C19: from L., from *reducere* 'bring back'.

**redwater** (also **redwater fever**) • n. babesiosis.

**redwing** • n. **1** a small migratory thrush of northern Europe, with red underwings. [*Turdus iliacus*.] **2** any of various other red-winged birds, especially the American red-winged blackbird. See **BLACKBIRD**.

**redwood** • n. a giant coniferous tree with reddish wood, native to California and Oregon. [*Sequoia sempervirens* (**California** or **coast redwood**) and *Sequoiadendron giganteum* (**giant redwood**).] ➤ used in names of other trees with reddish wood, e.g. **dawn redwood**.

**redworm** • n. **1** a red earthworm used to make compost and as fishing bait. [*Lumbricus rubellus*.] **2** a parasitic nematode worm affecting horses. [Genus *Strongylus*.]

**red zone** • n. **1** a dangerous or forbidden region, or one in which an activity is prohibited. **2** American Football the region between the opposing team's 20-yard line and goal line.

**reebok** • n. variant spelling of **RHEBOK**.

**re-echo** • v. (**-oes**, **-oed**) echo again or repeatedly.

**reed** • n. **1** a tall, slender-leaved plant of the grass family, growing in water or on marshy ground. [Genera *Phragmites* and *Arundo*: several species.] ➤ used in names of similar plants growing in wet habitats, e.g. **bur-**

**reed**. **2** a tall, thin, straight stalk of a reed, used especially for thatching. ➤Brit. straw for thatching. **3** poetic/literary a rustic musical pipe made from reeds or straw. **4** a piece of thin cane or metal which vibrates in a current of air to produce the sound of various musical instruments, as in the mouthpiece of a clarinet or at the base of some organ pipes. ➤a wind instrument played with a reed. **5** (also **broken reed**) a weak or impressionable person. **6** poetic/literary an arrow. **7** a weaver's comb-like implement for separating the warp and positioning the weft. **8** (**reeds**) a set of semi-cylindrical adjacent mouldings like reeds laid together. **9** an electrical contact in a magnetically operated switch or relay.
– DERIVATIVES **reeded** adj.
– ORIGIN OE *hrēod*, of W. Gmc origin.

**reed bed** ● n. an area of water or marshland dominated by reeds.

**reedbuck** ● n. an African antelope with a distinctive whistling call and high bouncing jumps. [Genus *Redunca*: three species.]

**reed bunting** ● n. a bunting that frequents reed beds and hedgerows, the male having a black head and white collar. [*Emberiza schoeniclus*.]

**reeding** ● n. a small semi-cylindrical moulding.

**re-edit** ● v. (**re-edited**, **re-editing**) edit again.
– DERIVATIVES **re-edition** n.

**reedling** (also **bearded reedling**) ● n. another term for **BEARDED TIT**.

**reed mace** ● n. a tall reed-like water plant with a dark brown velvety cylindrical flower head. [*Typha latifolia* and related species.]

**reed organ** ● n. a keyboard instrument similar to a harmonium, in which air is drawn upwards past metal reeds.

**reed pipe** ● n. a simple wind instrument having or made from a reed. ➤an organ pipe with a reed.

**reed stop** ● n. an organ stop controlling reed pipes.

**re-educate** ● v. educate or train to behave or think differently.
– DERIVATIVES **re-education** n.

**reed warbler** ● n. a songbird with plain plumage, frequenting reed beds. [*Acrocephalus scirpaceus* and other species.]

**reedy** ● adj. (**-ier**, **-iest**) **1** (of a sound or voice) high and thin in tone. **2** full of or edged with reeds. **3** (of a person) tall and thin.
– DERIVATIVES **reediness** n.

**reef**[1] ● n. **1** a ridge of jagged rock, coral, or sand just above or below the surface of the sea. **2** a vein of gold or other ore.
– ORIGIN C16 (earlier as *riff*): from Mid. Low Ger. and MDu. *rif*, *ref*, from ON *rif*, lit. 'rib'; cf. **REEF**[2].

**reef**[2] Sailing ● n. each of several strips across a sail which can be taken in or rolled up to reduce the area exposed to the wind. ● v. take in one or more reefs of (a sail). ➤shorten (a topmast or a bowsprit).
– ORIGIN ME: from MDu. *reef*, *rif*, from ON *rif*, lit. 'rib'; cf. **REEF**[1].

**reefer**[1] ● n. informal a cannabis cigarette. ➤cannabis.
– ORIGIN 1930s: perh. rel. to Mex. Sp. *grifo* '(smoker of) cannabis'.

**reefer**[2] ● n. a person who reefs a sail. ➤nautical slang, archaic a midshipman.

**reefer**[3] ● n. informal a refrigerated truck, railway wagon, or ship.
– ORIGIN C20: abbrev.

**reefer jacket** ● n. a thick close-fitting double-breasted jacket.

**reef knot** ● n. a double knot made symmetrically to hold securely and cast off easily.

**reefpoint** ● n. Sailing each of several short pieces of rope attached to a sail to secure it when reefed.

**reek** ● v. **1** have a foul smell. ➤archaic give off smoke, steam, or fumes. **2** (**reek of**) be suggestive of (something unpleasant). ● n. **1** a foul smell. **2** chiefly Scottish smoke.
– DERIVATIVES **reeky** adj.
– ORIGIN OE *rēocan* 'give out smoke or vapour', *rēc* (n.) 'smoke', of Gmc origin.

**reel** ● n. **1** a cylinder on which film, wire, thread, etc. can be wound. ➤a length of something wound on a reel. **2** a part of a film. **3** a lively Scottish or Irish folk dance. ➤a piece of music for a reel, typically in simple or duple time. ● v. **1** (**reel something in**) wind a line on to a reel by turning the reel. ➤bring something attached to a line, especially a fish, towards one by turning a reel. **2** (**reel something off**) say or recite something rapidly and effortlessly. **3** stagger or lurch violently. ➤feel giddy or bewildered. **4** dance a reel.
– DERIVATIVES **reeler** n.
– ORIGIN OE *hrēol*, of unknown origin.

**re-elect** ● v. (usu. **be re-elected**) elect again.
– DERIVATIVES **re-election** n.

**re-eligible** ● adj. eligible for re-election.

**reel-to-reel** ● adj. denoting a tape recorder in which the tape passes between two reels mounted separately rather than within a cassette.

**re-emerge** ● v. emerge again.
– DERIVATIVES **re-emergence** n. **re-emergent** adj.

**re-emphasize** (also **-ise**) ● v. emphasize again.
– DERIVATIVES **re-emphasis** n.

**re-enact** ● v. **1** act out (a past event). **2** enact (a repealed law) once more.
– DERIVATIVES **re-enactment** n.

**re-engineer** ● v. **1** redesign (a machine). **2** [often as noun **re-engineering**] restructure (a company or its operations).

**re-enter** ● v. enter again.
– DERIVATIVES **re-entrance** n.

**re-entrant** ● adj. (of an angle) pointing inwards. The opposite of **SALIENT**. ● n. **1** a re-entrant angle; an indentation. **2** a person who has re-entered something.

**re-entry** ● n. (pl. **-ies**) **1** the action or process of re-entering something. ➤the return of a spacecraft or missile into the earth's atmosphere. **2** Law the action of retaking or repossession. **3** a visible duplication of part of the design for a postage stamp. ➤a stamp displaying this.

**reeve**[1] ● n. **1** historical a local official, in particular the chief magistrate of a town or district in Anglo-Saxon England. **2** Canadian the president of a village or town council.
– ORIGIN OE *rēfa*; rel. to **GRIEVE**[2].

**reeve**[2] ● v. (past and past part. **rove** or **reeved**) Nautical thread (a rope or rod) through a ring or other aperture.
– ORIGIN C17: prob. from Du. *reven* (see **REEF**[2]).

**reeve**[3] ● n. a female ruff (bird).
– ORIGIN C17: var. of dial. *ree*, of unknown origin.

**re-examine** ● v. examine again or further. ➤Law examine (a witness) again, after cross-examination by the opposing counsel.
– DERIVATIVES **re-examination** n.

**re-export** ● v. /ˌriːɪkˈspɔːt, -ɛk-/ export (imported goods), typically after further processing or manufacture. ● n. /riːˈɛkspɔːt/ the action of re-exporting. ➤a thing that has or will be re-exported.
– DERIVATIVES **re-exportation** n. **re-exporter** n.

**ref** ● n. informal (in sports) a referee.

**ref.** ● abbrev. **1** reference. **2** refer to.

**reface** ● v. put a new facing on (a building).

**refection** ● n. poetic/literary refreshment by food or drink. ➤a meal or snack.
– ORIGIN ME: from OFr., from L. *refectio(n-)*, from *reficere* (see **REFECTORY**).

**refectory** ● n. (pl. **-ies**) a room used for communal meals, especially in an educational or religious institution.
– ORIGIN ME: from late L. *refectorium*, from L. *reficere* 'refresh, renew'.

**refectory table** ● n. a long, narrow table.

**refer** /rɪˈfəː/ ● v. (**referred**, **referring**) **1** (**refer to**) mention or allude to. ➤(**refer someone to**) direct the attention of someone to. ➤(**refer to**) (of a word or phrase) describe or denote. **2** (**refer something to**) pass a matter to (a higher body) for a decision. ➤send to a medical specialist. ➤(**refer to**) consult (a source of information). **3** (**refer something to**) archaic trace or attribute some-

thing to (someone or something) as a cause or source. **4** fail (a candidate in an examination).
– PHRASES **refer to drawer** Brit. a phrase used by banks when suspending payment of a cheque.
– DERIVATIVES **referable** /rɪˈfəːrəb(ə)l, ˈrɛf(ə)r-/ adj. **referrer** n.
– ORIGIN ME: from OFr. *referer* or L. *referre* 'carry back'.

**referee** • n. **1** an official who watches a game or match closely to ensure that the rules are adhered to. **2** a person willing to testify in writing about the character or ability of a job applicant. **3** a person appointed to examine and assess an academic work for publication. • v. (**referees, refereed, refereeing**) officiate as referee at or over.

**reference** • n. **1** the action of mentioning something. ➤a mention or citation of a source of information in a book or article. **2** the action of referring to a source of information or higher authority. **3** a letter from a previous employer testifying to someone's ability or reliability. • v. provide (a book or article) with references.
– PHRASES **terms of reference** the scope and limitations of an activity or area of knowledge. **with** (or **in**) **reference to** in relation to; as regards.

**reference group** • n. a social group which a person takes as a standard in forming attitudes and behaviour.

**reference library** • n. a library in which the books are for consultation rather than for loan.

**reference point** • n. a basis or standard for evaluation or comparison.

**referendum** /ˌrɛfəˈrɛndəm/ • n. (pl. **referendums** or **referenda** /-də/) a general vote by the electorate on a single political question which has been referred to them for a direct decision.
– ORIGIN C19: from L., gerund ('referring'), or neut. gerundive ('something to be referred') of *referre* (see **REFER**).

**referent** • n. Linguistics the thing in the world that a word or phrase denotes or stands for.

**referential** • adj. **1** containing or of the nature of a reference or references. **2** Linguistics of or relating to a referent, in particular having the external world rather than a text or language as a referent.
– DERIVATIVES **referentiality** n. **referentially** adv.

**referral** • n. the action of referring someone or something for consultation or review, especially the directing of a patient by a GP to a specialist.

**referred pain** • n. Medicine pain felt in a part of the body other than its actual source.

**refill** • v. /riːˈfɪl/ fill or become full again. • n. /ˈriːfɪl/ an act of refilling or a glass that is refilled.
– DERIVATIVES **refillable** adj.

**refinance** • v. finance again, typically with new loans at a lower rate of interest.

**refine** • v. **1** remove impurities or unwanted elements from. **2** make minor changes so as to improve (a theory or method). **3** [as adj. **refined**] elegant and cultured.
– DERIVATIVES **refinement** n. **refiner** n.
– ORIGIN C16: from **RE-** + the verb **FINE**[1], influenced by Fr. *raffiner*.

**refinery** • n. (pl. **-ies**) an industrial installation where a substance is refined.

**refinish** • v. apply a new finish to (a surface or object). • n. an act of refinishing a surface or object.

**refit** • v. (**refitted, refitting**) replace or repair machinery, equipment, and fittings in (a ship, building, etc.). • n. an act of refitting.

**reflag** • v. (**reflagged, reflagging**) change the national registration of (a ship).

**reflate** • v. (of a government) expand the level of output of (an economy) by either fiscal or monetary policy.
– DERIVATIVES **reflation** n. **reflationary** n.
– ORIGIN 1930s: from **RE-**, on the pattern of *inflate, deflate*.

**reflect** • v. **1** (of a surface or body) throw back (heat, light, or sound) without absorbing it. ➤(of a mirror or shiny surface) show an image of. **2** embody or represent in a faithful or appropriate way: *the letters reflect all aspects of his life*. ➤(**reflect well/badly on**) bring about a good or bad impression of. **2** (**reflect on/upon**) think deeply or carefully about.
– ORIGIN ME: from OFr. *reflecter* or L. *reflectere*, from *re-* 'back' + *flectere* 'to bend'.

**reflectance** • n. Physics a property of a surface equal to the proportion of incident light which it reflects or scatters.

**reflecting telescope** • n. a telescope in which a mirror is used to collect and focus light.

**reflection** • n. **1** the fact or phenomenon of light, heat, sound, etc. being reflected. ➤something reflected or an image so formed. **2** a thing bringing discredit. **3** serious thought or consideration. ➤a considered idea, expressed in writing or speech. **4** Mathematics the symmetry operation of inverting something with respect to a plane.

**reflective** • adj. **1** providing or capable of providing a reflection. ➤produced by reflection. **2** thoughtful.
– DERIVATIVES **reflectively** adv. **reflectiveness** n. **reflectivity** n.

**reflector** • n. **1** a piece of reflective material, e.g. a red one on the back of a motor vehicle or bicycle. **2** an object or device which reflects radio waves, seismic vibrations, sound, or other waves. **3** a reflecting telescope.

**reflet** /rəˈfleɪ/ • n. lustre or iridescence, especially on ceramics.
– ORIGIN Fr., lit. 'reflection'.

**reflex** • n. **1** an action performed without conscious thought as a response to a stimulus. ➤(in reflexology) a response in a part of the body to stimulation of a corresponding point on the feet, hands, or head. **2** a thing that reproduces the essential features or qualities of something else. **3** a word formed by development from an earlier stage of a language. **4** archaic a reflected source of light. • adj. **1** (of an action) performed as a reflex. **2** (of an angle) exceeding 180°. **3** archaic (of light) reflected. **4** archaic bent or turned backwards.
– DERIVATIVES **reflexly** adv.
– ORIGIN C16: from L. *reflexus* 'a bending back', from *reflectere* (see **REFLECT**).

**reflex arc** • n. Physiology the nerve pathway involved in a reflex action.

**reflex camera** • n. a camera with a ground-glass focusing screen on which the image is formed by a combination of lens and mirror, enabling a scene to be correctly composed and focused.

**reflexible** • adj. chiefly technical capable of being reflected.
– DERIVATIVES **reflexibility** n.

**reflexion** • n. archaic spelling of **REFLECTION**.

**reflexive** • adj. **1** Grammar denoting a pronoun that refers back to the subject of the clause in which it is used, e.g. *myself*. ➤(of a verb or clause) having a reflexive pronoun as its object (e.g. *wash oneself*). **2** Logic (of a relation) always holding between a term and itself. **3** (of a method or theory in the social sciences) taking account of itself or of the effect of the researcher on what is being investigated. **4** (of an action) performed without conscious thought.
– DERIVATIVES **reflexively** adv. **reflexiveness** n. **reflexivity** n.

**reflexology** • n. **1** a system of massage used to relieve tension and treat illness, based on the theory that there are reflex points on the feet, hands, and head linked to every part of the body. **2** Psychology the scientific study of reflex action as it affects behaviour.
– DERIVATIVES **reflexologist** n.

**refloat** • v. set afloat again.

**reflow** • n. **1** Electronics a soldering technique in which components are held on a circuit board using a paste which melts to leave soldered joints when the board is heated. **2** (in word processing) the action of rearranging text on a page after altering such features as type size and spacing.

**refluent** /ˈrɛflʊənt/ • adj. poetic/literary flowing back; ebbing.
– DERIVATIVES **refluence** n.
– ORIGIN ME: from L. *refluent-*, *refluere* 'flow back'.

**reflux** /ˈriːflʌks/ • n. **1** Chemistry the process of boiling a liquid so that any vapour is liquefied and returned to the stock. **2** technical the flowing back of a bodily fluid. • v. **1** Chemistry boil or cause to boil under reflux. **2** technical (of a bodily fluid) flow back.

**refocus** ● v. (**refocused**, **refocusing** or **refocussed**, **refocussing**) **1** adjust the focus of (a lens or one's eyes). **2** focus (attention or resources) on something new or different.

**reforest** ● v. replant with trees; cover again with forest.
– DERIVATIVES **reforestation** n.

**reform** ● v. **1** make changes in (something, especially an institution or practice) in order to improve it. ➤cause (someone) to relinquish an immoral or criminal lifestyle. **2** Chemistry subject (hydrocarbons) to a catalytic process in which straight-chain molecules are converted to branched forms. ● n. the action or process of reforming.
– DERIVATIVES **reformable** adj. **reformative** adj. **reformed** adj. **reformer** n.
– ORIGIN ME (in the senses 'restore (peace)' and 'restore to the original condition'): from OFr. *reformer* or L. *reformare*, from *re-* 'back' + *formare* 'to form'.

**re-form** ● v. form or cause to form again.
– DERIVATIVES **re-formation** n.

**reformat** ● v. (**reformatted**, **reformatting**) chiefly Computing give a new format to.

**reformation** ● n. **1** the action or process of reforming. **2** (**the Reformation**) a 16th-century movement for the reform of abuses in the Roman Church, ending in the establishment of the Reformed and Protestant Churches.
– DERIVATIVES **reformational** adj.

**reformatory** /rɪˈfɔːmət(ə)ri/ ● n. (pl. **-ies**) N. Amer. dated an institution to which young offenders are sent as an alternative to prison. ● adj. intended to produce reform.

**Reformed Church** ● n. a Church that has accepted the principles of the Reformation, especially a Calvinist Church (as distinct from Lutheran).

**reformist** ● adj. supporting or advocating gradual reform rather than abolition or revolution. ● n. a supporter or advocate of such a policy.
– DERIVATIVES **reformism** n.

**Reform Judaism** ● n. a form of Judaism which has reformed or abandoned aspects of Orthodox Jewish worship and ritual in an attempt to adapt to modern life.
– DERIVATIVES **Reform Jew** n.

**reform school** ● n. historical an institution to which young offenders were sent as an alternative to prison.

**reformulate** ● v. formulate again or differently.
– DERIVATIVES **reformulation** n.

**refract** ● v. **1** (of water, air, or glass) make (a ray of light) change direction when it enters at an angle. ➤change the direction of propagation of (radio, sound, or other waves) by causing them to travel at different speeds at different points along the wave front. **2** measure the focusing characteristics of (an eye).
– ORIGIN C17: from L. *refract-*, *refringere* 'break up'.

**refracting telescope** ● n. a telescope which uses a converging lens to collect the light.

**refraction** ● n. the fact or phenomenon of light, radio waves, etc., being refracted.
– DERIVATIVES **refractive** adj. **refractively** adv.

**refractive index** ● n. the ratio of the velocity of light in a vacuum to its velocity in a specified medium.

**refractometer** /ˌriːfrakˈtɒmɪtə/ ● n. an instrument for measuring a refractive index.
– DERIVATIVES **refractometric** adj. **refractometry** n.

**refractor** ● n. **1** a lens or other object which causes refraction. **2** a refracting telescope.

**refractory** ● adj. formal **1** stubborn or unmanageable. **2** resistant to a process or stimulus. ➤Medicine not yielding to treatment. ➤technical heat-resistant; hard to melt or fuse. ● n. (pl. **-ies**) technical a heat-resistant substance.
– DERIVATIVES **refractoriness** n.
– ORIGIN C17: alt. of obs. *refractary*, from L. *refractarius* 'stubborn' (see also **REFRACT**).

**refrain**[1] ● v. (usu. **refrain from**) stop oneself from doing something.
– ORIGIN ME: from OFr. *refrener*, from L. *refrenare*, from *re-* (expressing intensive force) + *frenum* 'bridle'.

**refrain**[2] ● n. a repeated line or number of lines in a poem or song, typically at the end of each verse. ➤the musical accompaniment for a refrain.
– ORIGIN ME: from OFr., from *refraindre* 'break', based on L. *refringere* 'break up' (because the refrain 'broke' the sequence).

**refrangible** ● adj. able to be refracted.
– DERIVATIVES **refrangibility** n.
– ORIGIN C17: from mod. L. *refrangibilis*, from *refrangere* (see **REFRACT**).

**refreeze** ● v. (past **refroze**; past part. **refrozen**) make or become frozen again.

**refresh** ● v. give new strength or energy to. ➤jog (someone's memory) by going over previous information. ➤revise or update (skills, knowledge, etc.).
– ORIGIN ME: from OFr. *refreschier*, from *re-* 'back' + *fres(che)* 'fresh'.

**refresher** ● n. **1** an activity that refreshes one's skills or knowledge. **2** Law, Brit. an extra fee payable to counsel in a prolonged case.

**refreshing** ● adj. **1** serving to refresh. **2** welcome or stimulating because new or different.
– DERIVATIVES **refreshingly** adv.

**refreshment** ● n. **1** a light snack or drink. **2** the giving of fresh strength or energy.

**Refreshment Sunday** ● n. the fourth Sunday in Lent, when certain Lenten restrictions are lifted.

**refried beans** ● pl. n. (in Mexican cooking) pinto beans boiled and fried in advance and reheated when required.

**refrigerant** ● n. a substance used for refrigeration. ● adj. causing cooling or refrigeration.

**refrigerate** ● v. subject (food or drink) to cold in order to chill or preserve it.
– DERIVATIVES **refrigeration** n. **refrigeratory** adj.
– ORIGIN ME: from L. *refrigerat-*, *refrigerare* 'make cool', from *re-* 'back' + *frigus, frigor-* 'cold'.

**refrigerator** ● n. an appliance or compartment which is artificially kept cool and used to store food and drink.

**refringent** /rɪˈfrɪn(d)ʒ(ə)nt/ ● adj. Physics refractive.
– DERIVATIVES **refringence** n.
– ORIGIN C18: from L. *refringent-*, *refringere*, lit. 'break again'.

**reft** past and past participle of **REAVE**.

**refuel** ● v. (**refuelled**, **refuelling**; US **refueled**, **refueling**) (with reference to a vehicle) supply or be supplied with more fuel.

**refuge** ● n. a place or state of safety from danger or trouble. ➤Brit. a traffic island.
– ORIGIN ME: from OFr., from L. *refugium*, from L. *re-* 'back' + *fugere* 'flee'.

**refugee** ● n. a person who has been forced to leave their country in order to escape war, persecution, or natural disaster.
– ORIGIN C17: from Fr. *réfugié* 'gone in search of refuge', past part. of *(se) réfugier*, from *refuge* (see **REFUGE**).

**refugium** /rɪˈfjuːdʒɪəm/ ● n. (pl. **refugia** /-dʒɪə/) Biology an area in which a population of organisms can survive a period of unfavourable conditions, especially glaciation.
– ORIGIN 1950s: from L., lit. 'place of refuge'.

**refulgent** /rɪˈfʌldʒ(ə)nt/ ● adj. poetic/literary shining very brightly.
– DERIVATIVES **refulgence** n. **refulgently** adv.
– ORIGIN C15: from L. *refulgent-*, *refulgere* 'shine out'.

**refund** ● v. /rɪˈfʌnd/ pay back (money). ➤pay back money to. ● n. /ˈriːfʌnd/ a refunded sum of money.
– DERIVATIVES **refundable** adj.
– ORIGIN ME (also in the sense 'pour back'): from OFr. *refonder* or L. *refundere*, from *re-* 'back' + *fundere* 'pour', later assoc. with **FUND**.

**refurbish** ● v. renovate and redecorate.
– DERIVATIVES **refurbishment** n.

**refuse**[1] /rɪˈfjuːz/ ● v. indicate unwillingness. ➤indicate unwillingness to accept or grant (something offered or requested). ➤(of a horse) decline to jump (a fence or other obstacle).
– DERIVATIVES **refusal** n. **refuser** n.
– ORIGIN ME: from OFr. *refuser*, prob. an alt. of L. *recusare* 'to refuse', influenced by *refutare* 'refute'.

**refuse**[2] /ˈrɛfjuːs/ • **n.** matter thrown away as worthless.
– ORIGIN ME: perh. from OFr. *refusé* 'refused', past part. of *refuser* (see **REFUSE**[1]).

**refusenik** /rɪˈfjuːznɪk/ • **n. 1** a Jew in the former Soviet Union who was refused permission to emigrate to Israel. **2** a person who refuses to comply with orders or the law, especially as a protest.
– ORIGIN 1970s: from **REFUSE**[1] + **-NIK**.

**refute** /rɪˈfjuːt/ • **v. 1** prove (a statement or the person advancing it) to be wrong. **2** deny (a statement or accusation).
– DERIVATIVES **refutable** adj. **refutal** n. (rare). **refutation** n. **refuter** n.
– ORIGIN C16: from L. *refutare* 'repel, rebut'.

**regain** • **v. 1** obtain possession or use of (something) again after losing it. **2** get back to.

**regal** • **adj.** of, resembling, or fit for a monarch, especially in being magnificent or dignified.
– DERIVATIVES **regally** adv.
– ORIGIN ME: from OFr., or from L. *regalis*, from *rex*, *reg-* 'king'.

**regale** • **v. 1** entertain with conversation. **2** lavishly supply with food or drink.
– ORIGIN C17: from Fr. *régaler*, from *re-* (expressing intensive force) + OFr. *gale* 'pleasure'.

**regalia** /rɪˈɡeɪlɪə/ • **pl. n.** [treated as sing. or pl.] **1** the insignia of royalty, especially the crown and other ornaments used at a coronation. **2** the distinctive clothing and trappings of high office, worn at formal occasions.
– ORIGIN C16 (in the sense 'royal powers'): from med. L., lit. 'royal privileges', neut. pl. of *regalis* 'regal'.

**USAGE** regalia

The word **regalia** comes from Latin and is, technically speaking, the plural of *regalis*. However, in modern English use it behaves as a collective noun, similar to words like **staff** or **government**, which means that it can be used with either a singular or plural verb.

**regalism** • **n.** the doctrine of a sovereign's supremacy in ecclesiastical matters.
– DERIVATIVES **regalist** n. & adj.

**regality** • **n.** (pl. **-ies**) **1** the state of being a monarch. **2** historical (in Scotland) territorial jurisdiction granted by the king to a powerful subject. **3** archaic a royal privilege.

**regard** • **v. 1** consider in a particular way. **2** gaze at in a specified fashion. **3** archaic pay attention to. • **n. 1** heed or concern: *she rescued him without regard for herself.* **2** high opinion; esteem. ➤(**regards**) best wishes (used especially at the end of letters). **3** a steady look.
– PHRASES **as regards** concerning. **in this** (or **that**) **regard** in connection with the point previously mentioned. **with** (or **in** or **having**) **regard to** as concerns.
– ORIGIN ME: from OFr. *regarder* 'to watch', from *re-* (expressing intensive force) + *garder* (see **GUARD**).

**regardant** /rɪˈɡɑːd(ə)nt/ • **adj.** Heraldry looking backwards.
– ORIGIN ME: from Anglo-Norman Fr. and OFr., pres. part. of *regarder* 'look (again)'.

**regardful** • **adj.** (**regardful of**) formal mindful of.

**regarding** • **prep.** about; concerning.

**regardless** • **adv.** despite the prevailing circumstances.
– PHRASES **regardless of** without regard for.
– DERIVATIVES **regardlessly** adv. **regardlessness** n.

**regatta** • **n.** a sporting event consisting of a series of boat or yacht races.
– ORIGIN C17: from Ital. (Venetian dial.), lit. 'a fight or contest'.

**regd** • **abbrev.** registered.

**regelation** /ˌriːdʒɪˈleɪʃ(ə)n/ • **n.** technical the fusion of two pieces of ice with moist surfaces, at a temperature above freezing point.

**regency** /ˈriːdʒ(ə)nsi/ • **n.** (pl. **-ies**) the office or period of government by a regent. ➤a commission acting as regent. ➤(**the Regency**) the period of a particular regency, especially (in Britain) from 1811 to 1820 and (in France) from 1715 to 1723. • **adj.** (**Regency**) relating to or denoting a broadly neoclassical style of British architecture, clothing, and furniture of the late 18th and early 19th centuries.
– ORIGIN ME: from med. L. *regentia*, from L. *regent-* (see **REGENT**).

**regenerate** • **v.** /rɪˈdʒɛnəreɪt/ **1** (of a living organism) regrow (new tissue). ➤(of an organ or tissue) regrow. **2** bring new and more vigorous life to (an area or institution). **3** (especially in Christian use) give a new and higher spiritual nature to. **4** [usu. as adj. **regenerated**] Chemistry precipitate (cellulose) as fibres following chemical processing. • **adj.** /rɪˈdʒɛn(ə)rət/ reborn, especially in a spiritual or moral sense.
– DERIVATIVES **regeneration** n. **regenerative** adj. **regeneratively** adv. **regenerator** n.
– ORIGIN ME: from L. *regeneratus*, *regenerare* 'create again'.

**regenerative braking** • **n.** a method of braking in which energy is extracted from the parts braked, to be stored and reused.

**regent** • **n. 1** a person appointed to administer a state because the monarch is a minor or is absent or incapacitated. **2** N. Amer. a member of the governing body of a university or other academic institution. • **adj.** [postpos.] acting as regent: *Prince Regent.*
– ORIGIN ME: from OFr., or from L. *regent-*, *regere* 'to rule'.

**regent bowerbird** • **n.** an Australian bowerbird, the male of which has conspicuous black and gold plumage. [*Sericulus chrysocephalus.*]

**reggae** /ˈrɛɡeɪ/ • **n.** a style of popular music with a strongly accented subsidiary beat, originating in Jamaica.
– ORIGIN perh. rel. to Jamaican Engl. *rege-rege* 'quarrel, row'.

**regicide** /ˈrɛdʒɪsʌɪd/ • **n.** the killing of a king. ➤a person who does this.
– DERIVATIVES **regicidal** adj.
– ORIGIN C16: from L. *rex*, *reg-* 'king' + **-CIDE**.

**regime** /reɪˈʒiːm/ • **n. 1** a government, especially an authoritarian one. **2** a systematic or ordered way of doing something. **3** the conditions under which a scientific or industrial process occurs.
– ORIGIN C15 (in the sense 'regimen'): Fr. *régime*, from L. *regimen* (see **REGIMEN**).

**regimen** /ˈrɛdʒɪmən/ • **n. 1** a therapeutic course of medical treatment, often including recommendations as to diet and exercise. **2** archaic a system of government.
– ORIGIN ME (denoting the action of governing): from L., from *regere* 'to rule'.

**regiment** • **n.** /ˈrɛdʒɪm(ə)nt/ **1** a permanent unit of an army, typically divided into several smaller units and often into two battalions. **2** a large number of people or things. **3** archaic rule or government. • **v.** /ˈrɛdʒɪmɛnt/ (usu. **be regimented**) **1** organize according to a strict system. **2** rare form (troops) into a regiment or regiments.
– DERIVATIVES **regimental** adj. **regimentally** adv. **regimentation** n.
– ORIGIN ME: via OFr. from late L. *regimentum* 'rule', from *regere* 'to rule'.

**regimental colour** • **n.** (in the UK) a regimental standard in the form of a silk flag, carried by a particular regiment along with its Queen's colour.

**regimentals** • **pl. n.** military uniform, especially that of a particular regiment.

**Regina** /rɪˈdʒʌɪnə/ • **n.** the reigning queen (used following a name or in the titles of lawsuits, e.g. *Regina v. Jones*, the Crown versus Jones).
– ORIGIN L., lit. 'queen'.

**region** • **n. 1** an area of a country or the world having definable characteristics but not always fixed boundaries. ➤an administrative district of a city or country. **2** a part of the body, especially around or near an organ.
– PHRASES **in the region of** approximately.
– DERIVATIVES **regional** adj. & n. **regionalization** (also **-isation**) n. **regionalize** (also **-ise**) v. **regionally** adv.
– ORIGIN ME: from OFr., from L. *regio(n-)* 'direction, district', from *regere* 'to rule, direct'.

**regionalism** • **n. 1** the theory or practice of regional

rather than central systems of administration or economic, cultural, or political affiliation. **2** a linguistic feature peculiar to a particular region.
– DERIVATIVES **regionalist** n. & adj.

**regisseur** /ˌreʒɪˈsəː/ ● n. a person who stages a theatrical production, especially a ballet.
– ORIGIN from Fr. *régisseur*.

**register** ● n. **1** an official list or record. ➤a record of attendance, for example of pupils in a class. **2** a particular part of the range of a voice or instrument. **3** Linguistics a variety of a language determined by degree of formality and choice of vocabulary, pronunciation, and syntax. **4** Printing & Photography the exact correspondence of the position of colour components in a printed positive. ➤Printing the exact correspondence of the position of printed matter on the two sides of a leaf. **5** (in electronic devices) a location in a store of data, used for a specific purpose and with quick access time. **6** a sliding device controlling a set of organ pipes which share a tonal quality. ➤a set of organ pipes so controlled. **7** an adjustable plate for widening or narrowing an opening and regulating a draught, especially in a fire grate. ● v. **1** enter in or place on a register. ➤put one's name on a register, especially as an eligible voter or as a guest in a hotel. **2** express (an opinion or emotion). ➤(of an emotion) show in a person's face or gestures. ➤[usu. with neg.] become aware of. **3** (of an instrument) detect and show (a reading) automatically. ➤(of an event) give rise to a specified reading on an instrument. **4** entrust (a letter or parcel) to a post office for transmission by registered post. **5** Printing & Photography correspond or cause to correspond exactly in position.
– DERIVATIVES **registrable** adj.
– ORIGIN ME: from OFr. *regestre* or med. L. *regestrum, registrum*, alt. of *regestum*, sing. of late L. *regesta* 'things recorded', from *regerere* 'enter, record'.

**registered post** ● n. Brit. a postal procedure with special precautions for safety and for compensation in case of loss.

**register office** ● n. (in the UK) a local government building where civil marriages are conducted and births, marriages, and deaths are recorded with the issue of certificates.

**registrant** ● n. a person who registers.

**registrar** /ˈredʒɪstrɑː, ˌredʒɪˈstrɑː/ ● n. **1** an official responsible for keeping a register or official records. **2** the chief administrative officer in a university. **3** (in the UK) the judicial and administrative officer of the High Court. **4** Brit. a middle-ranking hospital doctor undergoing training as a specialist.
– DERIVATIVES **registrarship** n.
– ORIGIN C17: from med. L. *registrarius*, from *registrum* (see REGISTER).

**Registrar General** ● n. a government official responsible for holding a population census.

**registrary** /ˈredʒɪˌstr(ə)ri/ ● n. (pl. **-ies**) the chief administrative officer of Cambridge University.

**registration** ● n. **1** the action or process of registering or of being registered. **2** (also **registration mark** or **registration number**) Brit. the series of letters and figures identifying a motor vehicle, displayed on a number plate. **3** the action or process of acquiring full British citizenship by a Commonwealth resident or a person of British descent.

**registration document** (also **vehicle registration document**) ● n. (in the UK) a document giving registered information about a vehicle, such as the owner's name and the date of its manufacture.

**registration plate** ● n. Brit. another term for NUMBER PLATE.

**registry** ● n. (pl. **-ies**) **1** a place where registers are kept. **2** registration.

**registry office** ● n. another term for REGISTER OFFICE (in informal and non-official use).

**Regius professor** /ˈriːdʒɪəs/ ● n. (in the UK) the holder of a university chair founded by a sovereign or filled by Crown appointment.
– ORIGIN L. *regius* 'royal', from *rex, reg-* 'king'.

**reglet** /ˈreglɪt/ ● n. **1** Printing a thin strip of wood or metal used to separate type. **2** Architecture a narrow strip used to separate mouldings or panels from one another.
– ORIGIN C17: from Fr. *réglet*, dimin. of *règle* 'rule'.

**regnal** /ˈregn(ə)l/ ● adj. of a reign or monarch.
– ORIGIN C17: from Anglo-Latin *regnalis*, from L. *regnum* 'kingdom'.

**regnal year** ● n. a year reckoned from the date or anniversary of a sovereign's accession.

**regnant** /ˈregnənt/ ● adj. **1** reigning. **2** formal dominant.
– ORIGIN C17: from L. *regnant-*, *regnare* 'to reign'.

**regolith** /ˈreg(ə)lɪθ/ ● n. Geology the layer of unconsolidated solid material covering the bedrock of a planet.
– ORIGIN C19: from Gk *rhēgos* 'rug, blanket' + -LITH.

**regrade** ● v. grade again or differently.

**regress** ● v. /rɪˈgres/ **1** return to a former state. ➤return mentally to a former stage of life or a supposed previous life. **2** Statistics calculate the regression of. **3** Astronomy move in a retrograde direction. ● n. /ˈriːgres/ **1** the action of regressing. **2** Philosophy a series of statements in which a logical procedure is continually reapplied to its own result without approaching a useful conclusion.
– ORIGIN ME: from L. *regressus*, from *regredi* 'go back, return'.

**regression** ● n. **1** a return to a former state. ➤a return to an earlier stage of life or a supposed previous life. **2** Statistics a measure of the relation between the mean value of one variable and corresponding values of other variables.

**regressive** ● adj. **1** tending to regress or characterized by regression. **2** (of a tax) taking a proportionally greater amount from those on lower incomes.
– DERIVATIVES **regressively** adv. **regressiveness** n.

**regret** ● v. (**regretted**, **regretting**) feel or express sorrow, repentance, or disappointment over. ● n. a feeling of sorrow, repentance, or disappointment. ➤used in polite formulas to express apology or sadness.
– DERIVATIVES **regretful** adj. **regretfulness** n.
– ORIGIN ME: from OFr. *regreter* 'bewail (the dead)', perh. from the Gmc base of GREET[2].

**regretfully** ● adv. **1** in a regretful manner. **2** it is regrettable that.

**regrettable** ● adj. giving rise to regret; undesirable.
– DERIVATIVES **regrettably** adv.

**regroup** ● v. reassemble into organized groups, typically after being attacked or defeated.
– DERIVATIVES **regroupment** n.

**regrow** ● v. (past **regrew**; past part. **regrown**) grow or cause to grow again.
– DERIVATIVES **regrowth** n.

**Regt** ● abbrev. Regiment.

**regular** ● adj. **1** arranged in a constant or definite pattern, especially with the same space between individual instances. ➤recurring at short uniform intervals. **2** doing the same thing often or at uniform intervals: *regular worshippers*. ➤done or happening frequently. **3** conforming to or governed by an accepted standard of procedure or convention. ➤of or belonging to the permanent professional armed forces of a country. ➤properly trained or qualified and pursuing a full-time occupation. ➤Christian Church subject to or bound by religious rule. Contrasted with SECULAR. **4** usual or customary. ➤chiefly N. Amer. of an ordinary kind. ➤(chiefly in commercial use) denoting merchandise of average size. **5** Grammar (of a word) following the normal pattern of inflection. **6** Geometry (of a figure) having all sides and all angles equal. ➤(of a solid) bounded by a number of equal figures. **7** Botany (of a flower) having radial symmetry. ● n. a regular customer, member of a team, etc. ➤a regular member of the armed forces. ➤Christian Church one of the regular clergy.
– DERIVATIVES **regularity** n. (pl. **-ies**). **regularization** (also **-isation**). n. **regularize** (also **-ise**). v. **regularly** adv.
– ORIGIN ME: from OFr. *reguler*, from L. *regularis*, from *regula* 'rule'.

**regular canon** ● n. see CANON[2].

**regulate** ● v. **1** control or maintain the rate or speed of (a machine or process). **2** control or supervise by means of rules and regulations.

– DERIVATIVES **regulable** adj. **regulative** adj. **regulator** n. **regulatory** adj.
– ORIGIN ME: from late L. *regulat-*, *regulare* 'direct, regulate', from L. *regula* 'rule'.

**regulation** • n. **1** a rule or directive made and maintained by an authority. ➤[as modifier] in accordance with regulations. ➤[as modifier] informal of a familiar or predictable type. **2** the action or process of regulating or being regulated.

**regulo** /ˈrɛgjʊləʊ/ • n. Brit. trademark used before a numeral to denote a setting on a temperature scale in a gas oven.

**regulus** /ˈrɛgjʊləs/ • n. (pl. **reguluses** or **reguli** /-lʌɪ, -liː/) Chemistry, archaic a metallic form of a substance, obtained by smelting or reduction.
– ORIGIN C16: from L., dimin. of *rex*, *reg-* 'king'; orig. as *regulus of antimony*, appar. so named because of its readiness to combine with gold.

**regurgitate** /rɪˈgəːdʒɪteɪt/ • v. **1** bring (swallowed food) up again to the mouth. **2** repeat (information) without analysing or comprehending it.
– DERIVATIVES **regurgitation** n.
– ORIGIN C16: from med. L. *regurgitat-*, *regurgitare*, from L. *re-* 'again' + *gurges*, *gurgit-* 'whirlpool'.

**rehab** /ˈriːhab/ informal • n. **1** rehabilitation. **2** US a building that has been rehabilitated. • v. (**rehabbed**, **rehabbing**) N. Amer. rehabilitate.

**rehabilitate** • v. **1** restore to health or normal life by training and therapy after imprisonment, addiction, or illness. **2** restore the standing or reputation of. **3** restore to a former condition.
– DERIVATIVES **rehabilitation** n. **rehabilitative** adj.
– ORIGIN C16 (earlier (C15) as *rehabilitation*): from med. L. *rehabilitat-*, *rehabilitare* (see **RE-**, **HABILITATE**).

**rehash** • v. reuse (old ideas or material) without significant change or improvement. • n. an instance of rehashing.

**rehearsal** • n. a trial performance of a play or other work for later public performance. ➤the action or process of rehearsing.

**rehearse** • v. **1** practise (a play, piece of music, or other work) for later public performance. **2** state (a list of points that have been made many times before).
– DERIVATIVES **rehearser** n.
– ORIGIN ME (in the sense 'repeat aloud'): from OFr. *rehercier*, perh. from *re-* 'again' + *hercer* 'to harrow', from *herse* (see **HEARSE**).

**reheat** • v. heat again. • n. the process of using the hot exhaust to burn extra fuel in a jet engine and produce extra power. ➤an afterburner.
– DERIVATIVES **reheater** n.

**rehoboam** • n. a wine bottle of about six times the standard size.
– ORIGIN C19: from the name *Rehoboam*, a king of ancient Israel.

**rehome** • v. find a new home for (a pet).

**rehouse** • v. provide with new housing.

**rehydrate** • v. absorb or cause to absorb moisture after dehydration.
– DERIVATIVES **rehydratable** adj. **rehydration** n.

**Reich** /rʌɪk, -x, German raɪç/ • n. the former German state, most often used to refer to the **Third Reich** (the Nazi regime, 1933–45).
– ORIGIN Ger., lit. 'empire'.

**Reichstag** /ˈrʌɪxsˌtɑːg, ˈrʌɪks-/ • n. the main legislature of the German state under the Second and Third Reichs.
– ORIGIN Ger., from *Reichs* 'of the empire' + *Tag* 'assembly'.

**reify** /ˈriːɪfʌɪ, ˈreɪɪ-/ • v. (**-ies**, **-ied**) formal make (something abstract) more concrete or real.
– DERIVATIVES **reification** n. **reificatory** adj.
– ORIGIN C19: from L. *res*, *re-* 'thing' + **-FY**.

**reign** • v. **1** rule as monarch. **2** [as adj. **reigning**] (of a sports player or team) currently holding a particular title. **3** prevail: *confusion reigned.* • n. **1** the period of rule of a monarch. **2** the period during which someone or something is predominant or pre-eminent.
– ORIGIN ME: from OFr. *reignier* 'to reign', *reigne* 'kingdom', from L. *regnum*.

**reign of terror** • n. a period of remorseless repression or bloodshed, in particular (**Reign of Terror**) the period of the Terror during the French Revolution.

**reiki** /ˈreɪki/ • n. a healing technique based on the principle that the therapist can channel energy into the patient by means of touch, to activate the natural healing processes of the patient's body.
– ORIGIN Japanese, lit. 'universal life energy'.

**reimburse** /ˌriːɪmˈbəːs/ • v. repay (a person who has spent or lost money). ➤repay (a sum of money that has been spent or lost).
– DERIVATIVES **reimbursable** adj. **reimbursement** n.
– ORIGIN C17: from **RE-** + obs. *imburse* 'put in a purse', from med. L. *imbursare*, based on late L. *bursa* 'purse'.

**reimport** • v. import (goods processed or made from exported materials). • n. the action of reimporting. ➤a reimported item.
– DERIVATIVES **reimportation** n.

**rein** • n. **1** a long, narrow strap attached at one end to a horse's bit, typically used in pairs to guide or check a horse in riding or driving. ➤a similar device used to restrain a young child. **2** (**reins**) the power to direct and control: *a new chairperson will soon take over the reins.* • v. **1** check or guide (a horse) by pulling on its reins. **2** (often **rein someone/thing in/back**) restrain.
– PHRASES **draw rein** Brit. stop one's horse. (**a**) **free rein** freedom of action or expression. **keep a tight rein on** exercise strict control over.
– ORIGIN ME: from OFr. *rene*, based on L. *retinere* 'retain'.

**reincarnate** • v. /ˌriːɪnˈkɑːneɪt/ cause (someone) to undergo rebirth in another body. • adj. /ˌriːɪnˈkɑːnət/ [usu. postpos.] reborn in another body.

**reincarnation** • n. the rebirth of a soul in a new body. ➤a person or animal in whom a soul is believed to have been reborn.

**reindeer** • n. (pl. same or **reindeers**) a deer with large branching antlers, native to the northern tundra and subarctic and domesticated in parts of Eurasia. [*Rangifer tarandus*.]
– ORIGIN ME: from ON *hreindýri*, from *hreinn* 'reindeer' + *dýr* 'deer'.

**reindeer moss** • n. a bluish-grey arctic lichen, eaten by reindeer in winter. [*Cladonia rangiferina*.]

**reinfect** • v. cause to become infected again.
– DERIVATIVES **reinfection** n.

**reinforce** • v. **1** strengthen (a military force) with additional personnel or material. **2** give added strength to.
– DERIVATIVES **reinforcement** n. **reinforcer** n.
– ORIGIN ME: from Fr. *renforcer*, influenced by *inforce*, an obs. spelling of **ENFORCE**.

**reinforced concrete** • n. concrete in which metal bars or wire are embedded to increase its tensile strength.

**reinstate** • v. restore to a former position or state.
– DERIVATIVES **reinstatement** n.

**reinsure** • v. (of an insurer) transfer (all or part of a risk) to another insurer to provide protection against the risk of the first insurance.
– DERIVATIVES **reinsurance** n. **reinsurer** n.

**reintegrate** • v. **1** restore (elements regarded as disparate) to unity. **2** integrate back into society.
– DERIVATIVES **reintegration** n.

**reinterpret** • v. (**reinterpreted**, **reinterpreting**) interpret in a new or different light.
– DERIVATIVES **reinterpretation** n.

**reintroduce** • v. **1** bring (something, especially a law or system) into effect again. **2** put (a species of animal or plant) back into a former habitat.
– DERIVATIVES **reintroduction** n.

**reinvent** • v. change so much so as to appear entirely new.
– PHRASES **reinvent the wheel** waste a great deal of time or effort in creating something that already exists.
– DERIVATIVES **reinvention** n.

**reinvest** • v. put (the profit on a previous investment) back into the same scheme.

– DERIVATIVES **reinvestment** n.

**reinvigorate** • v. give new energy or strength to.
– DERIVATIVES **reinvigoration** n.

**reissue** • v. (**reissues**, **reissued**, **reissuing**) make a new supply or different form of (a book, record, or other product) available for sale. • n. a new issue of such a product.

**reiterate** • v. say something again or repeatedly.
– DERIVATIVES **reiteration** n. **reiterative** adj.
– ORIGIN ME: from L. *reiterat-*, *reiterare* 'go over again'.

**reive** /riːv/ • v. [usu. as noun **reiving**] chiefly Scottish another term for **REAVE**.
– DERIVATIVES **reiver** n.
– ORIGIN ME: var. of **REAVE**; the usual spelling when referring to the former practice of cattle-raiding on the Scottish Borders.

**reject** • v. /rɪˈdʒɛkt/ **1** dismiss as inadequate or faulty. ➤refuse to consider or agree to. **2** fail to show due affection or concern for. **3** Medicine show a damaging immune response to (a transplanted organ or tissue). • n. /ˈriːdʒɛkt/ a rejected person or thing.
– DERIVATIVES **rejection** n. **rejective** adj. (rare). **rejector** n.
– ORIGIN ME: from L. *reject-*, *reicere* 'throw back'.

**rejectionist** • n. an Arab who refuses to accept a negotiated peace with Israel.

**rejig** • v. (**rejigged**, **rejigging**) chiefly Brit. **1** rearrange. **2** dated refit.

**rejigger** • v. US term for **REJIG** (in sense 1).

**rejoice** • v. feel or show great joy. ➤archaic cause joy to.
– DERIVATIVES **rejoicer** n. **rejoicing** n. & adj. **rejoicingly** adv.
– ORIGIN ME: from OFr. *rejoiss-*, lengthened stem of *rejoir*, from *re-* + *joir* 'experience joy'.

**rejoin**[1] • v. **1** join together again. **2** return to.

**rejoin**[2] • v. say in reply; retort.
– ORIGIN ME (in the sense 'reply to a charge or pleading in a lawsuit'): from OFr. *rejoindre*, from *re-* 'again' + *joindre* 'to join'.

**rejoinder** • n. **1** a sharp or witty reply. **2** Law, dated a defendant's answer to the plaintiff's reply or replication.
– ORIGIN ME: from Anglo-Norman Fr. *rejoindre* (see **REJOIN**[2]).

**rejuvenate** /rɪˈdʒuːvəneɪt/ • v. **1** make or cause to appear younger or more vital. **2** [often as adj. **rejuvenated**] restore (a river or stream) to a condition characteristic of a younger landscape.
– DERIVATIVES **rejuvenation** n. **rejuvenator** n.
– ORIGIN C19: from **RE-** + L. *juvenis* 'young' + **-ATE**[3].

**rejuvenescence** /rɪˌdʒuːvəˈnɛsəns/ • n. **1** the renewal of youth or vitality. **2** Biology the reactivation of vegetative cells, resulting in regrowth from old or injured parts.
– DERIVATIVES **rejuvenescent** adj.
– ORIGIN C17: from late L. *rejuvenescere* (from L. *re-* 'again' + *juvenis* 'young') + **-ENCE**.

**rekey** • v. chiefly Computing key (text or other data) again.

**rekindle** • v. **1** relight (a fire). **2** revive (something lapsed or lost).

**-rel** • suffix forming nouns with diminutive or derogatory force such as *cockerel*.
– ORIGIN from OFr. *-erel(le)*.

**relabel** • v. (**relabelled**, **relabelling**; US **relabeled**, **relabeling**) label again or differently.

**relaid** past and past participle of **RELAY**[2].

**relapse** /rɪˈlaps/ • v. **1** (of a sick or injured person) deteriorate after a period of improvement. **2** (**relapse into**) return to (a worse or less active state). • n. /also ˈriː-/ a deterioration in health after a temporary improvement.
– DERIVATIVES **relapser** n.
– ORIGIN ME: from L. *relaps-*, *relabi* 'slip back'.

**relapsing fever** • n. an infectious bacterial disease marked by recurrent fever.

**relate** • v. **1** give an account of. **2** (**be related**) be connected by blood or marriage. **3** establish a causal connection between. ➤(**relate to**) concern. **4** (**relate to**) feel sympathy with.
– DERIVATIVES **relatable** adj. **related** adj. **relatedness** n. **relater** (also **relator**) n.
– ORIGIN C16 (earlier (ME) as *relation*): from L. *relat-*, *referre* 'bring back' (see **REFER**).

**relation** • n. **1** the way in which two or more people or things are connected or related. ➤(**relations**) the way in which two or more people or groups feel about and behave towards each other. **2** a relative. **3** the action of telling a story. **4** (**relations**) formal sexual intercourse.
– PHRASES **in relation to** in connection with.
– DERIVATIVES **relational** adj. **relationally** adv.

**relational database** • n. Computing a database structured to recognize relations between stored items.

**relationship** • n. **1** the way in which two or more people or things are connected, or the state of being connected. ➤the way in which two or more people or groups regard and behave towards each other. **2** an emotional and sexual association between two people.

**relative** /ˈrɛlətɪv/ • adj. **1** considered in relation or in proportion to something else. ➤existing or possessing a characteristic only in comparison to something else. **2** Grammar denoting a pronoun, determiner, or adverb that refers to an expressed or implied antecedent and attaches a subordinate clause to it, e.g. *which*. ➤(of a clause) attached to an antecedent by a relative word. **3** Music (of major and minor keys) having the same key signature. **4** (of a service rank) corresponding in grade to another in a different service. • n. **1** a person connected by blood or marriage. ➤a species related to another by common origin. **2** Philosophy a term or concept which is dependent on something else.
– PHRASES **relative to 1** compared with or in relation to. **2** concerning.
– DERIVATIVES **relatival** /-ˈtʌɪv(ə)l/ adj. **relatively** adv.

**relative atomic mass** • n. Chemistry the ratio of the average mass of one atom of an element to one twelfth of the mass of an atom of carbon-12.

**relative density** • n. the ratio of the density of a substance to a standard density, usually that of water or air.

**relative humidity** • n. the amount of water vapour present in air, expressed as a percentage of the amount needed for saturation at the same temperature.

**relative molecular mass** • n. Chemistry the ratio of the average mass of one molecule of an element or compound to one twelfth of the mass of an atom of carbon-12.

**relativism** /ˈrɛlətɪvɪz(ə)m/ • n. the doctrine that knowledge, truth, and morality exist in relation to culture, society, or historical context, and are not absolute.
– DERIVATIVES **relativist** n.

**relativistic** • adj. Physics accurately described only by the theory of relativity.
– DERIVATIVES **relativistically** adv.

**relativity** • n. **1** the absence of standards of absolute and universal application. **2** Physics a description of matter, energy, space, and time according to Einstein's theories based on the importance of relative motion and the principle that the speed of light is constant for all observers.

**relativize** (also **-ise**) • v. **1** chiefly Linguistics & Philosophy make or treat as relative. **2** Physics treat according to the principles of relativity.
– DERIVATIVES **relativization** n.

**relator** • n. **1** Law a person who brings a public lawsuit, typically in the name of the Attorney General, regarding the abuse of an office or franchise. **2** variant spelling of ***relater*** (see **RELATE**).

**relaunch** • v. launch again or in a different form. • n. an instance of relaunching.

**relax** • v. **1** make or become less tense or anxious. ➤cause (a limb or muscle) to become less rigid. **2** rest from work or engage in a recreational activity. **3** make (a rule or restriction) less strict.
– DERIVATIVES **relaxed** adj. **relaxedly** adv. **relaxedness** n. **relaxer** n.
– ORIGIN ME: from L. *relaxare*, from *re-* (expressing intensive force) + *laxus* 'lax, loose'.

**relaxant** • n. a drug used to promote relaxation or reduce tension. ➤a thing having a relaxing effect. • adj. causing relaxation.

**relaxation** • n. **1** the action of relaxing or the state of being relaxed. **2** Physics the return of a system to equilibrium following disturbance.

**relay**[1] /ˈriːleɪ/ • n. **1** a group of people or animals engaged in a task for a period of time and then replaced by a similar group. ➤a race between teams of runners, each team member in turn covering part of the total distance. **2** an electrical device which is activated by a current in one circuit to open or close another circuit. **3** a device to receive, reinforce, and retransmit a signal. ➤a message, programme, etc. transmitted by such a device. • v. /also rɪˈleɪ/ **1** receive and pass on (information or a message). **2** broadcast by means of a relay.
– ORIGIN ME: from OFr. *relai* (n.), *relayer* (v.), based on L. *laxare* 'slacken'.

**relay**[2] /riːˈleɪ/ • v. (past and past part. **relaid**) lay again or differently.

**release** • v. **1** set free. **2** allow (information) to be generally available. ➤make (a film or recording) available to the public. **3** allow to move or flow freely. ➤remove (part of a machine or appliance) from a fixed position, allowing something else to move or function. **4** Law remit or discharge (a debt). ➤surrender (a right). ➤make over (property or money) to another. • n. **1** the action or process of releasing or being released. ➤a film or other product released to the public. **2** a handle or catch that releases part of a mechanism. **3** Law the action of releasing property, money, or a right to another. ➤a document effecting this.
– DERIVATIVES **releasable** adj. **releasee** n. (Law). **releaser** n. **releasor** n. (Law).
– ORIGIN ME: from OFr. *reles* (n.), *relesser* (v.), from L. *relaxare* (see **RELAX**).

**relegate** • v. **1** assign an inferior rank or position to. **2** (usu. **be relegated**) Brit. transfer (a sports team) to a lower division of a league.
– DERIVATIVES **relegation** n.
– ORIGIN ME (in the sense 'send into exile'): from L. *relegat-*, *relegare* 'send away'.

**relent** • v. **1** abandon or mitigate a harsh intention or cruel treatment. **2** become less intense.
– ORIGIN ME (in the sense 'dissolve'): based on L. *re-* 'back' + *lentare* 'to bend'.

**relentless** • adj. **1** oppressively constant. **2** harsh or inflexible.
– DERIVATIVES **relentlessly** adv. **relentlessness** n.

**relevant** • adj. closely connected or appropriate to the matter in hand.
– DERIVATIVES **relevance** n. **relevancy** n. **relevantly** adv.
– ORIGIN C16 (as a Scots legal term meaning 'legally pertinent'): from med. L. *relevant-* 'raising up', from L. *relevare*.

**relevé** /ˌrɛləˈveɪ/ • n. **1** Ballet a movement in which the dancer rises on the tips of the toes. **2** Ecology each of a number of small plots of vegetation, analysed as a sample of a wider area.
– ORIGIN Fr., lit. 'raised up'.

**reliable** • adj. able to be relied on.
– DERIVATIVES **reliability** n. **reliableness** n. **reliably** adv.

**reliance** • n. dependence on or trust in someone or something.
– DERIVATIVES **reliant** adj.

**relic** • n. **1** an object of interest surviving from an earlier time. ➤a surviving but outdated object, custom, or belief. **2** a part of a deceased holy person's body or belongings kept as an object of reverence.
– ORIGIN ME: from OFr. *relique* (orig. pl.), from L. *reliquiae* (see **RELIQUIAE**).

**relict** /ˈrɛlɪkt/ • n. **1** an organism or other thing which has survived from an earlier period. ➤Ecology a population, formerly more widespread, that survives in only a few localities. **2** archaic a widow.
– ORIGIN ME: sense 2 from OFr. *relicte* '(woman) left behind', from late L. *relicta*, from L. *relinquere*; sense 1 from L. *relictus*, *relinquere* 'leave behind'.

**relief** • n. **1** the alleviation or removal of pain, anxiety, or distress. ➤a feeling or cause of relief. ➤(usu. **light relief**) a temporary break in a generally tense or tedious situation. **2** financial or practical assistance given to those in special need or difficulty. **3** a person or group of people replacing others who have been on duty. ➤Brit. an extra vehicle providing supplementary public transport at peak times or in emergencies. **4** the raising of a siege on a town. **5** distinctness due to being accentuated. **6** a method of moulding, carving, or stamping in which the design stands out from the surface, to a greater (**high relief**) or lesser (**low relief**) extent. ➤a representation of relief given by an arrangement of line, colour, etc.
– PHRASES **in relief** Baseball acting as a substitute pitcher. **on relief** chiefly N. Amer. receiving state assistance because of need.
– ORIGIN ME: from OFr., from *relever* 'raise up, relieve', from L. *relevare* 'raise again, alleviate'; sense 6 via Fr. from Ital. *rilievo*, from *rilevare* 'raise'.

**relief map** • n. **1** a map indicating hills and valleys by shading rather than by contour lines alone. **2** a map model with elevations and depressions representing hills and valleys, typically on an exaggerated relative scale.

**relief printing** • n. printing from raised images, as in letterpress and flexography.

**relief road** • n. Brit. a road taking traffic around, rather than through, a congested urban area.

**relieve** • v. **1** alleviate or remove (pain, distress, or difficulty). ➤(usu. **be relieved**) cause (someone) to stop feeling distressed or anxious. **2** release (someone) from duty by taking their place. **3** (**relieve someone of**) take (a burden or responsibility) from someone. **4** bring military support for (a besieged place). **5** make less tedious or monotonous. **6** (**relieve oneself**) formal or euphemistic urinate or defecate. **7** archaic make (something) stand out.
– DERIVATIVES **relievable** adj. **relieved** adj. **relievedly** adv. **reliever** n.
– ORIGIN ME: from OFr. *relever*, from L. *relevare*, from *re-* (expressing intensive force) + *levare* 'raise'.

**relievo** /rɪˈliːvəʊ/ • n. (pl. **-os**) chiefly Art another term for **RELIEF** (in sense 6).
– ORIGIN Ital. *rilievo*.

**relight** • v. (past and past part. **relighted** or **relit**) light again.

**religio-** /rɪˈlɪdʒɪəʊ/ • comb. form religious and ...: *religio-political*.

**religion** • n. **1** the belief in and worship of a superhuman controlling power, especially a personal God or gods. ➤a particular system of faith and worship. **2** a pursuit or interest followed with devotion.
– DERIVATIVES **religionless** adj.
– ORIGIN ME (orig. in the sense 'life under monastic vows'): from OFr., or from L. *religio(n-)* 'obligation, reverence'.

**religionism** • n. excessive religious zeal.
– DERIVATIVES **religionist** n.

**religiose** /rɪˈlɪdʒɪəʊs/ • adj. excessively religious.
– DERIVATIVES **religiosity** n.

**religious** • adj. **1** of, concerned with, or believing in a religion. ➤belonging or relating to a monastic order or other group united by their practice of religion. **2** treated or regarded with a devotion and scrupulousness appropriate to worship. • n. (pl. same) a person bound by monastic vows.
– DERIVATIVES **religiously** adv. **religiousness** n.

**relinquish** • v. voluntarily cease to keep or claim; give up.
– DERIVATIVES **relinquishment** n.
– ORIGIN ME: from OFr. *relinquiss-*, lengthened stem of *relinquir*, from L. *relinquere*, from *re-* (expressing intensive force) + *linquere* 'to leave'.

**reliquary** /ˈrɛlɪkwəri/ • n. (pl. **-ies**) a container for holy relics.
– ORIGIN C16: from Fr. *reliquaire*, from OFr. *relique* (see **RELIC**).

**reliquiae** /rɪˈlɪkwiːː/ • pl. n. formal remains. ➤Geology fossil remains of animals or plants.
– ORIGIN C17: L., fem. pl. (used as n.) of *reliquus* 'remaining'.

**relish** • n. **1** great enjoyment. ➤pleasurable anticipation. **2** a piquant sauce or pickle eaten with plain food to add

flavour. **3** archaic an appetizing flavour. ➤ a distinctive taste or tinge. ● **v. 1** enjoy greatly. ➤ anticipate with pleasure. **2** archaic make pleasant to the taste.
– DERIVATIVES **relishable** adj.
– ORIGIN ME (orig. in the sense 'odour, taste'): alt. of obs. *reles*, from OFr. *reles* 'remainder', from *relaisser* 'to release'.

**relive** ● **v.** live through (an experience or feeling) again in one's imagination.

**reload** ● **v.** load (something, especially a gun) again.

**relocate** ● **v.** move to a new place and establish one's home or business there.
– DERIVATIVES **relocation** n.

**reluctance** ● **n. 1** unwillingness. **2** Physics the property of a magnetic circuit of opposing the passage of magnetic flux lines, equal to the ratio of the magnetomotive force to the magnetic flux.

**reluctant** ● **adj.** unwilling and hesitant.
– DERIVATIVES **reluctantly** adv.
– ORIGIN C17 (in the sense 'offering opposition'): from L. *reluctant-*, *reluctari* 'struggle against'.

**rely** ● **v.** (**-ies**, **-ied**) (**rely on/upon**) **1** depend on with full trust. **2** be dependent on.
– ORIGIN ME (orig. in the sense 'gather together', later 'turn to'): from OFr. *relier* 'bind together', from L. *religare*, from *re-* (expressing intensive force) + *ligare* 'bind'.

**rem** ● **n.** (pl. same) a unit of effective absorbed dose of ionizing radiation in human tissue, loosely equivalent to one roentgen of X-rays.
– ORIGIN 1940s: acronym from *roentgen equivalent man*.

**remade** past and past participle of **REMAKE**.

**remain** ● **v. 1** be in the same place or condition during further time. ➤ continue to be: *he remained alert*. **2** be left over after others or other parts have been completed, used, or dealt with.
– ORIGIN ME: from OFr. *remain-*, stressed stem of *remanoir*, from L. *remanere*, from *re-* (expressing intensive force) + *manere* 'to stay'.

**remainder** ● **n. 1** a part, number, or quantity that is left over. ➤ the number which is left over in a division in which one quantity does not exactly divide another. **2** a part that is still to come. **3** a copy of a book left unsold when demand has fallen. **4** Law an interest in an estate that becomes effective in possession only when a prior interest (devised at the same time) ends. ● **v.** (often **be remaindered**) dispose of (a book left unsold) at a reduced price.
– ORIGIN ME: from Anglo-Norman Fr., from L. *remanere* (see **REMAIN**).

**remains** ● **pl. n. 1** things remaining. **2** historical or archaeological relics. **3** a person's body after death.

**remake** ● **v.** (past and past part. **remade**) make again or differently. ● **n.** a film or piece of music that has been filmed or recorded again and re-released.

**remand** Law ● **v.** place (a defendant) on bail or in custody, especially when a trial is adjourned. ● **n.** a committal to custody.
– PHRASES **on remand** in custody pending trial.
– ORIGIN ME (in the sense 'send back again'): from late L. *remandare*, from *re-* 'back' + *mandare* 'commit'.

**remanent** /ˈrɛmənənt/ ● **adj.** (of magnetism) remaining after the magnetizing field has been removed.
– DERIVATIVES **remanence** n.
– ORIGIN ME: from L. *remanent-*, *remanere* 'remain'.

**remark** ● **v. 1** say as a comment; mention. **2** regard with attention; notice. ● **n.** a comment. ➤ notice or comment.
– ORIGIN C16: from Fr. *remarquer* 'note again'.

**re-mark** ● **v.** mark (an examination paper or piece of academic work) again.

**remarkable** ● **adj.** extraordinary or striking.
– DERIVATIVES **remarkableness** n. **remarkably** adv.

**remarry** ● **v.** (**-ies**, **-ied**) marry again.
– DERIVATIVES **remarriage** n.

**remaster** ● **v.** make a new master of (a recording), typically in order to improve the sound quality.

**rematch** ● **n.** a second match or game between two sports teams or players.

**REME** ● **abbrev.** (in the British army) Royal Electrical and Mechanical Engineers.

**remedial** ● **adj. 1** giving or intended as a remedy. **2** provided or intended for children with learning difficulties.
– DERIVATIVES **remedially** adv.

**remediation** /rɪˌmiːdɪˈeɪʃ(ə)n/ ● **n. 1** the action of remedying something, in particular environmental damage. **2** the giving of remedial teaching or therapy.
– DERIVATIVES **remediate** v.
– ORIGIN C19: from L. *remediatio(n-)*, from *remediare* (see **REMEDY**).

**remedy** ● **n.** (pl. **-ies**) **1** a medicine or treatment for a disease or injury. **2** a means of counteracting or eliminating something undesirable. **3** a means of legal reparation. **4** the margin within which coins as minted may differ from the standard fineness and weight. ● **v.** (**-ies**, **-ied**) rectify (an undesirable situation).
– DERIVATIVES **remediable** adj.
– ORIGIN ME: from Anglo-Norman Fr. *remedie*, from L. *remedium*, from *re-* 'back' + *mederi* 'heal'.

**remember** ● **v. 1** have in or be able to bring to one's mind (someone or something from the past). ➤ bear (someone) in mind by making them a gift, making provision for them, or mentioning them in prayer. ➤ (**remember oneself**) recover one's manners after a lapse. **2** keep (something necessary or advisable) in mind. **3** (**remember someone to**) convey greetings from one person to (another).
– DERIVATIVES **rememberer** n.
– ORIGIN ME: from OFr. *remembrer*, from late L. *rememorari* 'call to mind'.

**remembrance** ● **n.** the action of remembering. ➤ a memory. ➤ a thing kept or given as a reminder or in commemoration of someone.

**Remembrance Day** ● **n. 1** another term for **REMEMBRANCE SUNDAY**. **2** historical another term for **ARMISTICE DAY**.

**remembrancer** ● **n.** a chronicler.

**Remembrance Sunday** ● **n.** (in the UK) the Sunday nearest 11 November, when those who were killed in the First and Second World Wars and later conflicts are commemorated.

**remiges** /ˈrɛmɪdʒiːz/ ● **pl. n.** (sing. **remex** /ˈriːmɛks/) Ornithology flight feathers.
– ORIGIN C18: from L., lit. 'rowers'.

**remind** ● **v.** cause (someone) to remember something or to do something. ➤ (**remind someone of**) cause someone to think of (something) because of a resemblance.
– ORIGIN C17: from **RE-** + the verb **MIND**.

**reminder** ● **n.** a thing that causes someone to remember something. ➤ a letter sent to remind someone to pay a bill.

**remindful** ● **adj.** (usu. **remindful of**) acting as a reminder.

**remineralize** (also **-ise**) ● **v.** restore the depleted mineral content of (teeth or other body tissue).
– DERIVATIVES **remineralization** n.

**reminisce** /ˌrɛmɪˈnɪs/ ● **v.** indulge in reminiscence.
– DERIVATIVES **reminiscer** n.

**reminiscence** ● **n. 1** a story told about a past event remembered by the narrator. ➤ the enjoyable recollection of past events. **2** a characteristic of one thing suggestive of another.
– DERIVATIVES **reminiscential** adj. (archaic).
– ORIGIN C16 (denoting the action of remembering): from late L. *reminiscentia*, from L. *reminisci* 'remember'.

**reminiscent** ● **adj. 1** (usu. **reminiscent of**) tending to remind one of something. **2** absorbed in memories.
– DERIVATIVES **reminiscently** adv.

**remise** /rɪˈmiːz/ Fencing ● **v.** make a second thrust after the first has failed. ● **n.** an act of remising.
– ORIGIN Fr., past part. of *remettre* 'put back'.

**remiss** /rɪˈmɪs/ ● **adj.** lacking care or attention to duty.
– DERIVATIVES **remissly** adv. **remissness** n.
– ORIGIN ME (orig. in the senses 'weakened in colour or consistency' and (in describing sound) 'faint'): from L.

*remissus, remittere* 'slacken'.

**remissible** ● adj. (especially of sins) able to be remitted.

**remission** ● n. **1** the cancellation of a debt, charge, or penalty. ➤ Brit. the reduction of a prison sentence, especially as a reward for good behaviour. **2** a temporary diminution of the severity of disease or pain. **3** formal forgiveness of sins.
– ORIGIN ME: from OFr., or from L. *remissio(n-)*, from *remittere* (see **REMIT**).

**remit** ● v. /rɪˈmɪt/ (**remitted**, **remitting**) **1** refrain from exacting or inflicting (a debt or punishment). ➤ Theology pardon (a sin). **2** send (money) in payment, especially by post. **3** refer (a matter for decision) to an authority. ➤ Law send back (a case) to a lower court. ➤ Law send (someone) from one tribunal to another for a trial or hearing. **4** archaic diminish. ● n. /ˈriːmɪt, rɪˈmɪt/ **1** the task or area of activity officially assigned to an individual or organization. **2** an item referred for consideration.
– DERIVATIVES **remittable** adj. **remittal** n. **remitter** n.
– ORIGIN ME: from L. *remiss-*, *remittere* 'send back, restore'.

**remittance** ● n. a sum of money remitted. ➤ the action of remitting money.

**remittance man** ● n. chiefly historical an emigrant supported or assisted by payments of money from home.

**remittent** ● adj. (of a fever) characterized by fluctuating body temperatures.

**remix** ● v. mix again. ➤ produce a different version of (a musical recording) by altering the balance of the separate tracks. ● n. a remixed musical recording.
– DERIVATIVES **remixer** n.

**remnant** ● n. **1** a small remaining quantity. ➤ a piece of cloth left when the greater part has been used or sold. **2** a surviving trace. **3** Christian Theology a small minority of people who will remain faithful to God and so be saved. ● adj. remaining.
– ORIGIN ME: contr. of obs. *remenant* from OFr. *remenant*, from *remenoir, remanoir* 'remain'.

**remodel** ● v. (**remodelled**, **remodelling**; US **remodeled**, **remodeling**) **1** change the structure or form of. **2** shape (a figure or object) again or differently.

**remodeler** ● n. N. Amer. a person who carries out structural alterations to an existing building.

**remold** ● v. US spelling of **REMOULD**.

**remonetize** (also **-ise**) ● v. rare restore (a metal) to its former position as legal tender.
– DERIVATIVES **remonetization** n.

**remonstrance** /rɪˈmɒnstr(ə)ns/ ● n. a forcefully reproachful protest.

**remonstrate** /ˈrɛmənstreɪt/ ● v. make a forcefully reproachful protest.
– DERIVATIVES **remonstration** n. **remonstrative** adj. **remonstrator** n.
– ORIGIN C16 (in the sense 'make plain'): from med. L. *remonstrat-*, *remonstrare* 'demonstrate', from L. *re-* (expressing intensive force) + *monstrare* 'to show'.

**remontant** /rɪˈmɒnt(ə)nt/ ● adj. (of a plant) blooming or producing a crop more than once a season. ● n. a remontant plant.
– ORIGIN C19: from Fr., lit. 'coming up again'.

**remora** /ˈrɛmərə/ ● n. a slender sea fish which attaches itself to large fish by means of a sucker on top of the head. [*Remora remora* and other species, family Echeneidae.]
– ORIGIN C16: from L., lit. 'hindrance' (because of the former belief that the fish slowed down ships).

**remorse** ● n. deep regret or guilt for a wrong committed.
– DERIVATIVES **remorseful** adj. **remorsefully** adv.
– ORIGIN ME: from OFr. *remors*, from med. L. *remorsus*, from L. *remordere* 'vex', from *re-* (expressing intensive force) + *mordere* 'to bite'.

**remorseless** ● adj. **1** without remorse. **2** (of something unpleasant) relentless.
– DERIVATIVES **remorselessly** adv. **remorselessness** n.

**remortgage** ● v. take out another or a different mortgage on. ● n. a different or additional mortgage.

**remote** ● adj. (**-er**, **-est**) **1** far away in space or time. ➤ situated far from the main centres of population. **2** distantly related. ➤ having very little connection with. **3** (of a chance or possibility) unlikely to occur. **4** aloof and unfriendly in manner. **5** (of an electronic device) operating or operated by means of radio or infrared signals.
– DERIVATIVES **remotely** adv. **remoteness** n.
– ORIGIN ME: from L. *remotus, removere* (see **REMOVE**).

**remote control** ● n. control of a machine or apparatus from a distance by means of signals transmitted from a radio or electronic device. ➤ (also **remote controller**) a device that controls an apparatus in this way.
– DERIVATIVES **remote-controlled** adj.

**remote sensing** ● n. the scanning of the earth by satellite or high-flying aircraft in order to obtain information about it.

**remoulade** /ˈrɛmʊlɑːd/ ● n. salad or seafood dressing made with hard-boiled egg yolks, oil, and vinegar, and flavoured with mustard, capers, and herbs.
– ORIGIN Fr. *rémoulade*.

**remould** (US **remold**) ● v. /riːˈməʊld/ **1** mould again or differently. **2** Brit. put a new tread on (a worn tyre). ● n. /ˈriːməʊld/ a remoulded tyre.

**remount** ● v. /riːˈmaʊnt/ **1** get on (a horse or vehicle) again. **2** attach to a new frame or setting. **3** mount (a course of action) again. ● n. /ˈriːmaʊnt/ a fresh horse for a rider. ➤ historical a supply of fresh horses for a regiment.

**removal** ● n. **1** the action of removing. **2** chiefly Brit. the transfer of furniture and other contents when moving house. **3** (also **removal of remains**) Irish the formal procedure of taking a body from the house to the church for the funeral service.

**removalist** ● n. Austral. a person or firm engaged in household or business removals.

**remove** ● v. **1** take off or away from the position occupied. ➤ abolish or get rid of. ➤ dismiss from a post. ➤ (**remove to**) dated relocate to (another place). **2** (**be removed**) be very different from. **3** [as adj. **removed**] separated by a particular number of steps of descent: *his second cousin once removed.* ● n. **1** a degree of remoteness or separation. **2** a form or division in some British schools.
– DERIVATIVES **removability** n. **removable** adj. **remover** n.
– ORIGIN ME: from the OFr. stem *remov-*, from L. *removere*, from *re-* 'back' + *movere* 'to move'.

**REM sleep** ● n. a kind of sleep that occurs at intervals during the night and is characterized by rapid eye movement, more dreaming and bodily movement, and faster pulse and breathing.

**remuage** /ˌrɛmjʊˈɑːʒ, French rəmɥaʒ/ ● n. the periodic turning or shaking of bottled wine, especially champagne, to move sediment towards the cork.
– ORIGIN Fr., lit. 'moving about'.

**remunerate** /rɪˈmjuːnəreɪt/ ● v. pay for services rendered or work done.
– DERIVATIVES **remuneration** n. **remunerative** adj.
– ORIGIN C16 (earlier (ME) as *remuneration*): from L. *remunerat-*, *remunerari* 'reward, recompense'.

**Renaissance** /rɪˈneɪs(ə)ns, -ɒs/ ● n. **1** the revival of art and literature under the influence of classical models in the 14th–16th centuries. **2** (**renaissance**) a revival of or renewed interest in something.
– ORIGIN from Fr. *renaissance*, from *re-* 'back, again' + *naissance* 'birth'.

**Renaissance man** ● n. a person with many talents or interests, especially in the humanities.

**renal** /ˈriːn(ə)l/ ● adj. technical of or relating to the kidneys.
– ORIGIN C17: from Fr. *rénal*, from late L. *renalis*, from L. *renes* 'kidneys'.

**renal calculus** ● n. another term for **KIDNEY STONE**.

**renal pelvis** ● n. see **PELVIS** (sense 2).

**rename** ● v. give a new name to.

**renascence** /rɪˈnas(ə)ns, -ˈneɪ-/ ● n. **1** the revival of something that has been dormant. **2** another term for **RENAISSANCE**.

**renascent** ● adj. becoming active again.
– ORIGIN C18: from L. *renascent-*, *renasci* 'to be born again'.

**rencontre** /rɛnˈkɒntə/ ● n. archaic variant spelling of **RENCOUNTER**.
– ORIGIN C17: Fr.

**rencounter** /rɛnˈkaʊntə/ archaic ● n. **1** a chance meeting. **2** a battle, skirmish, or duel. ● v. meet by chance.
– ORIGIN C16: from Fr. *rencontre* (n.), *rencontrer* 'meet face to face'.

**rend** ● v. (past and past part. **rent**) poetic/literary **1** tear to pieces. ➤ archaic wrench violently. **2** cause great emotional pain to.
– PHRASES **rend the air** sound piercingly. **rend one's garments** (or **hair**) tear one's clothes (or pull one's hair out) as a sign of extreme grief of distress.
– ORIGIN OE *rendan*, rel. to Mid. Low Ger. *rende*.

**render** ● v. **1** provide or give (a service, help, etc.). ➤ submit for inspection, consideration, or payment. ➤ poetic/literary hand over; surrender. **2** cause to be or become. **3** represent or depict artistically. ➤ Music perform (a piece). **4** translate. **5** melt down (fat), typically in order to clarify it. ➤ process (the carcass of an animal) in order to extract proteins, fats, and other usable parts. **6** cover (stone or brick) with a coat of plaster. ● n. a first coat of plaster applied to a brick or stone surface.
– DERIVATIVES **renderer** n.
– ORIGIN ME: from OFr. *rendre*, from an alt. of L. *reddere* 'give back'.

**rendering** ● n. **1** a performance of a piece of music or drama. **2** a translation. **3** the action of rendering a wall. ➤ the plaster so applied. **4** the action of giving or surrendering something.

**render-set** ● v. plaster (a wall) with two coats. ● n. plastering consisting of two coats.

**rendezvous** /ˈrɒndɪvuː, -deɪvuː/ ● n. (pl. same /-vuːz/) a meeting at an agreed time and place. ➤ a meeting place. ● v. (**rendezvouses** /-vuːz/, **rendezvoused** /-vuːd/, **rendezvousing** /-vuːɪŋ/) meet at an agreed time and place.
– ORIGIN C16: from Fr. *rendez-vous!* 'present yourselves!', imper. of *se rendre*.

**rendition** ● n. **1** a rendering of a dramatic, musical, or artistic work. **2** a translation.
– ORIGIN C17: from obs. Fr., from *rendre* 'give back, render'.

**rendzina** /rɛn(d)ˈziːnə/ ● n. Soil Science a fertile lime-rich soil with dark humus above a pale soft calcareous layer, typical of grassland.
– ORIGIN 1920s: via Russ. from Polish *rędzina*.

**renegade** /ˈrɛnɪgeɪd/ ● n. a person who deserts and betrays an organization, country, or set of principles. ➤ archaic a person who abandons religion. ● adj. having treacherously changed allegiance. ● v. archaic become a renegade.
– ORIGIN C15: from Sp. *renegado*, from med. L. *renegatus*, *renegare* 'renounce'.

**renegado** /ˌrɛnɪˈgeɪdəʊ/ ● n. (pl. **-oes**) archaic term for **RENEGADE**.
– ORIGIN from Sp.

**renege** /rɪˈneɪg, rɪˈniːg/ (also **renegue**) ● v. **1** go back on a promise, undertaking, or contract. ➤ archaic renounce or abandon. **2** another term for **REVOKE** (in sense 2).
– DERIVATIVES **reneger** n.
– ORIGIN C16: from med. L. *renegare*, from L. *re-* (expressing intensive force) + *negare* 'deny'.

**renegotiate** ● v. negotiate again in order to change the original agreed terms.
– DERIVATIVES **renegotiable** adj. **renegotiation** n.

**renew** ● v. **1** resume or re-establish after an interruption. **2** give fresh life or strength to. **3** extend the period of validity of (a licence, subscription, or contract). **4** replace or restore (something broken or worn out).
– DERIVATIVES **renewal** n. **renewer** n.

**renewable** ● adj. **1** capable of being renewed. **2** (of energy or its source) not depleted when used.
– DERIVATIVES **renewability** n.

**reniform** /ˈriːnɪfɔːm/ ● adj. chiefly Mineralogy & Botany kidney-shaped.
– ORIGIN C18: from L. *ren* 'kidney' + **-IFORM**.

**renin** /ˈriːnɪn/ ● n. Biochemistry an enzyme secreted by and stored in the kidneys which promotes the production of the protein angiotensin.
– ORIGIN C19: from L. *ren* 'kidney' + **-IN**[1].

**renminbi** /ˈrɛnmɪnbi/ ● n. (pl. same) the national currency of the People's Republic of China.
– ORIGIN from Chin. *rénmínbì*, from *rénmín* 'people' + *bì* 'currency'.

**rennet** /ˈrɛnɪt/ ● n. curdled milk from the stomach of an unweaned calf, containing rennin and used in curdling milk for cheese. ➤ any preparation containing rennin.
– ORIGIN C15: prob. rel. to **RUN**.

**rennin** /ˈrɛnɪn/ ● n. an enzyme secreted into the stomach of unweaned mammals causing the curdling of milk.
– ORIGIN C19: from **RENNET** + **-IN**[1].

**renounce** ● v. **1** formally declare one's abandonment of (a claim, right, or possession). ➤ Law refuse or resign a right or position, especially one as an heir or trustee. **2** refuse to recognize any longer. **3** abandon (a cause, bad habit, or way of life).
– DERIVATIVES **renounceable** adj. **renouncement** n. **renouncer** n.
– ORIGIN ME: from OFr. *renoncer*, from L. *renuntiare* 'protest against'.

**renovate** /ˈrɛnəveɪt/ ● v. **1** restore (something old) to a good state of repair. **2** archaic reinvigorate.
– DERIVATIVES **renovation** n. **renovator** n.
– ORIGIN C16 (earlier (ME) as *renovation*): from L. *renovat-*, *renovare* 'make new again'.

**renown** ● n. the state of being famous.
– DERIVATIVES **renowned** adj.
– ORIGIN ME: from Anglo-Norman Fr. *renoun*, from OFr. *renomer* 'make famous', from *re-* (expressing intensive force) + *nomer* 'to name'.

**rent**[1] ● n. **1** a tenant's regular payment to a landlord for the use of property or land. **2** a sum paid for the hire of equipment. ● v. pay someone for the use of. ➤ let someone use (something) in return for payment. ➤ chiefly N. Amer. be let or hired out at a specified rate.
– DERIVATIVES **rentability** n. **rentable** adj.
– ORIGIN ME: from OFr. *rente*, from a root shared by **RENDER**.

**rent**[2] ● n. a large tear in a piece of fabric.
– ORIGIN C16: from obs. *rent* 'pull to pieces', var. of **REND**.

**rent**[3] past and past participle of **REND**.

**rent-a-** ● comb. form often humorous denoting availability for hire of a specified thing: *rent-a-crowd*.

**rental** ● n. an amount paid or received as rent. ➤ the action of renting. ➤ N. Amer. a rented house or car. ● adj. of, relating to, or available for rent.

**rent boy** ● n. Brit. informal a young male prostitute.

**renter** ● n. **1** a person who rents a flat, car, etc. **2** (in the UK) a person who distributes cinema films. **3** US a rented car or video cassette. **4** Brit. informal a male prostitute.

**rentier** /ˈrɒntɪeɪ, French rɑ̃tje/ ● n. a person living on income from property or investments.
– ORIGIN Fr., from *rente* 'dividend'.

**rent roll** ● n. a register of a landlord's lands and buildings with the rents due from them. ➤ a landlord's total income from rent.

**renumber** ● v. change the number or numbers assigned to.

**renunciation** ● n. **1** the action of renouncing. **2** Law a document expressing renunciation.
– DERIVATIVES **renunciant** n. & adj.
– ORIGIN ME: from late L. *renuntiatio(n-)*, from L. *renuntiare* (see **RENOUNCE**).

**renvoi** /ˈrɒ̃vwʌ/ ● n. Law the action or process of referring a case or dispute to the jurisdiction of another country.
– ORIGIN C19: Fr., from *renvoyer* 'send back'.

**reoccupy** ● v. (**-ies**, **-ied**) occupy again.
– DERIVATIVES **reoccupation** n.

**reoccur** ● v. (**reoccurred**, **reoccurring**) occur again or repeatedly.
– DERIVATIVES **reoccurrence** n.

**reoffend** ● v. commit a further offence.

– DERIVATIVES **reoffender** n.

**reopen** • v. open again.

**reorder** • v. **1** order again. **2** arrange again. • n. a renewed or repeated order for goods.

**reorganize** (also **-ise**) • v. change the way in which (something) is organized.

– DERIVATIVES **reorganization** n. **reorganizer** n.

**reorient** /riːˈɔːrɪɛnt, -ˈɒr-/ • v. **1** change the focus or direction of. **2** (**reorient oneself**) find one's bearings again.

– DERIVATIVES **reorientate** v. **reorientation** n.

**Rep.** • abbrev. **1** (in the US Congress) Representative. **2** Republic. **3** US a Republican.

**rep**[1] informal • n. a representative. • v. (**repped**, **repping**) act as a sales representative.

**rep**[2] • n. informal repertory. ➤a repertory theatre or company.

**rep**[3] (also **repp**) • n. a fabric with a ribbed surface, used in curtains and upholstery.

– ORIGIN C19: from Fr. *reps*, of unknown ultimate origin.

**rep**[4] • n. N. Amer. informal short for **REPUTATION**.

**rep**[5] • n. (in bodybuilding) a repetition of a set of exercises. • v. (as an instruction in knitting patterns) repeat.

**repack** • v. pack (a suitcase or bag) again.

**repackage** • v. package again or differently.

**repaginate** • v. renumber the pages of.

– DERIVATIVES **repagination** n.

**repaid** past and past participle of **REPAY**.

**repaint** • v. cover with a new coat of paint. • n. an act of repainting.

**repair**[1] • v. **1** restore (something damaged, worn, or faulty) to a good condition. **2** set right (a rift in relations). • n. **1** the action of repairing. ➤a result of this. **2** the relative physical condition of an object.

– DERIVATIVES **repairable** adj. **repairer** n.

– ORIGIN ME: from OFr. *reparer*, from L. *reparare*, from *re-* 'back' + *parare* 'make ready'.

**repair**[2] • v. (**repair to**) formal or humorous go to (a place). • n. archaic an abode or haunt. ➤frequent or habitual visiting of a place.

– ORIGIN ME: from OFr. *repairer*, from late L. *repatriare* (see **REPATRIATE**).

**reparable** /ˈrɛp(ə)rəb(ə)l/ • adj. able to be repaired or rectified.

– ORIGIN C16: from Fr. *réparable*, from L. *reparabilis*, from *reparare* (see **REPAIR**[1]).

**reparation** /ˌrɛpəˈreɪʃ(ə)n/ • n. **1** the making of amends for a wrong. ➤(**reparations**) the compensation for war damage paid by a defeated state. **2** the action of repairing something.

– DERIVATIVES **reparative** /ˈrɛp(ə)rətɪv, rɪˈparətɪv/ adj.

– ORIGIN ME: from OFr., from late L. *reparatio(n-)*, from *reparare* (see **REPAIR**[1]).

**repartee** /ˌrɛpɑːˈtiː/ • n. conversation or speech characterized by quick, witty comments or replies.

– ORIGIN C17: from Fr. *repartie* 'replied promptly', fem. past part. of *repartir*, from *re-* 'again' + *partir* 'set off'.

**repast** /rɪˈpɑːst/ • n. formal a meal.

– ORIGIN ME: from OFr., based on late L. *repascere*, from *re-* (expressing intensive force) + *pascere* 'to feed'.

**repatriate** /riːˈpatrɪeɪt, -ˈpeɪ-/ • v. send (someone) back to their own country. • n. a person who has been repatriated.

– DERIVATIVES **repatriation** n.

– ORIGIN C17 (earlier (C16) as *repatriation*): from late L. *repatriat-*, *repatriare* 'return to one's country'.

**repay** • v. (past and past part. **repaid**) **1** pay back (a loan). ➤pay back money owed to (someone). **2** do or give something as recompense for (a favour or kindness received). **3** be worth subjecting to (a specified action).

– DERIVATIVES **repayable** adj. **repayment** n.

**repayment mortgage** • n. a mortgage in which the borrower repays the capital and interest together in fixed instalments over a fixed period.

**repeal** • v. revoke or annul (a law or act of parliament). • n. the action of repealing.

– DERIVATIVES **repealable** adj.

– ORIGIN ME: from Anglo-Norman Fr. *repeler*, from OFr. *re-* (expressing reversal) + *apeler* 'to call, appeal'.

**repeat** • v. **1** say or do again. ➤(**repeat oneself**) say or do the same thing again. **2** (of food) be tasted after being swallowed, as a result of indigestion. • n. **1** an instance of repeating or being repeated. ➤[as modifier] occurring, done, or used more than once: *a repeat prescription*. **2** a repeated broadcast of a television or radio programme. **3** a consignment of goods similar to one already received. **4** a decorative pattern which is repeated uniformly over a surface. **5** Music a passage intended to be repeated. ➤a mark indicating this.

– DERIVATIVES **repeatability** n. **repeatable** adj. **repeated** adj. **repeatedly** adv. **repeater** n. **repeating** adj.

– ORIGIN ME: from OFr. *repeter*, from L. *repetere*, from *re-* 'back' + *petere* 'seek'.

**repeating decimal** • n. a recurring decimal.

**repêchage** /ˈrɛpəʃɑːʒ/ • n. (in rowing and other sports) a contest in which the runners-up in the eliminating heats compete for a place in the final.

– ORIGIN C20: Fr., from *repêcher* 'fish out, rescue'.

**repel** • v. (**repelled**, **repelling**) **1** drive or force back or away. **2** be repulsive or distasteful to. **3** formal refuse to accept; reject. **4** (of a magnetic pole or electric field) force (something similarly magnetized or charged) away. **5** (of a substance) resist mixing with or be impervious to.

– DERIVATIVES **repeller** n.

– ORIGIN ME: from L. *repellere*, from *re-* 'back' + *pellere* 'to drive'.

**repellent** (also **repellant**) • adj. **1** able to repel a particular thing; impervious to: *water-repellent nylon*. **2** causing disgust or distaste. • n. **1** a substance that dissuades insects or other pests from approaching or settling. **2** a substance used to treat something to make it impervious to water.

– DERIVATIVES **repellence** n. **repellency** n. **repellently** adv.

**repent** • v. feel or express sincere regret or remorse. ➤(**repent oneself of**) archaic feel regret or penitence about.

– DERIVATIVES **repentance** n. **repentant** adj. **repenter** n.

– ORIGIN ME: from OFr. *repentir*, based on L. *paenitere* 'cause to repent'.

**repercussion** • n. **1** (usu. **repercussions**) a consequence of an event or action. **2** archaic the recoil of something after impact. **3** archaic an echo or reverberation.

– DERIVATIVES **repercussive** adj.

– ORIGIN ME (as a medical term meaning 'repressing of infection'): from OFr., or from L. *repercussio(n-)*, from *repercutere* 'cause to rebound, push back'.

**repertoire** /ˈrɛpətwɑː/ • n. the body of pieces known or regularly performed by a performer or company.

– ORIGIN C19: from Fr. *répertoire*, from late L. *repertorium* (see **REPERTORY**).

**repertory** /ˈrɛpət(ə)ri/ • n. (pl. **-ies**) **1** the performance by a company of the plays, operas, or ballets in its repertoire at regular short intervals. **2** another term for **REPERTOIRE**. **3** a repository or collection.

– ORIGIN C16 (denoting an index or catalogue): from late L. *repertorium*, from L. *repert-*, *reperire* 'find, discover'.

**repertory company** • n. a theatrical company that performs plays from its repertoire for regular, short periods of time, moving on from one play to another.

**repetend** /ˈrɛpɪtɛnd, ˌrɛpɪˈtɛnd/ • n. **1** Mathematics the repeating figure or figures of a recurring decimal fraction. **2** formal a recurring word or phrase.

– ORIGIN C18: from L. *repetendum* 'something to be repeated', neut. gerundive of *repetere* (see **REPEAT**).

**répétiteur** /rɛˌpɛtɪˈtəː/ • n. a tutor or coach of ballet dancers or musicians, especially opera singers.

– ORIGIN from Fr.

**repetition** • n. the act or an instance of repeating or being repeated. ➤a thing that repeats another.

– DERIVATIVES **repetitional** adj. **repetitious** adj. **repetitiously** adv. **repetitiousness** n.

– ORIGIN ME: from OFr. *repeticion* or L. *repetitio(n-)*, from *repetere* (see **REPEAT**).

**repetitive** ● adj. containing or characterized by repetition.
– DERIVATIVES **repetitively** adv. **repetitiveness** n.

**repetitive strain injury** ● n. a condition in which the prolonged performance of repetitive actions, typically with the hands, causes pain or impairment of function in the tendons and muscles involved.

**rephrase** ● v. express in an alternative way.

**repine** ● v. poetic/literary be discontented; fret.
– ORIGIN C16: from **RE-** + **PINE**[2], on the pattern of *repent*.

**repique** /rɪˈpiːk/ ● n. (in piquet) the scoring of 30 points on declarations alone before beginning to play. Compare with **PIQUE**[2]. ● v. (**repiques**, **repiqued**, **repiquing**) score a repique against (one's opponent).
– ORIGIN C17: from Fr. *repic*; cf. Ital. *ripicco*.

**replace** ● v. **1** take the place of. **2** provide a substitute for. **3** put back in a previous place or position.
– DERIVATIVES **replaceable** adj. **replacement** n. **replacer** n.

**replan** ● v. (**replanned**, **replanning**) plan (something) differently or again.

**replant** ● v. plant again, especially in a new pot or site. ➤provide (an area) with new plants or trees.

**replay** ● v. **1** play back (a recording). **2** play (a match) again. ● n. **1** the act or an instance of replaying. **2** a replayed match.

**replenish** ● v. **1** fill up again. **2** restore to a former level or condition.
– DERIVATIVES **replenisher** n. **replenishment** n.
– ORIGIN ME: from OFr. *repleniss-*, lengthened stem of *replenir*, from *re-* 'again' + *plenir* 'fill'.

**replete** /rɪˈpliːt/ ● adj. **1** filled or well-supplied with something. **2** very full with food; sated.
– DERIVATIVES **repletion** n.
– ORIGIN ME: from OFr. *replet(e)* or L. *repletus* 'filled up', past part. of *replere*, from *re-* 'back, again' + *plere* 'fill'.

**replevin** /rɪˈplɛvɪn/ ● n. Law a procedure whereby seized goods may be provisionally restored to their owner pending the outcome of an action to determine the rights of the parties concerned.
– ORIGIN ME: from Anglo-Norman Fr., from OFr. *replevir* (see **REPLEVY**).

**replevy** /rɪˈplɛvi/ ● v. (**-ies**, **-ied**) Law recover (seized goods) by replevin.
– ORIGIN C16: from OFr. *replevir* 'recover'; appar. rel. to **PLEDGE**.

**replica** ● n. an exact copy or model of something, especially one on a smaller scale.
– ORIGIN C18 (as a musical term in the sense 'a repeat'): from Ital., from *replicare* 'to reply'.

**replicase** /ˈrɛplɪkeɪz/ ● n. Biochemistry an enzyme which catalyses the synthesis of a complementary RNA molecule using an RNA template.
– ORIGIN 1960s: from **REPLICATE** + **-ASE**.

**replicate** ● v. /ˈrɛplɪkeɪt/ make an exact copy of; reproduce. ➤(**replicate itself**) (of genetic material or a living organism) reproduce or give rise to a copy of itself. ➤repeat (a scientific experiment or trial) to obtain a consistent result. ● adj. /ˈrɛplɪkət/ of the nature of a copy. ➤of or relating to a replicated experiment or trial. ● n. /ˈrɛplɪkət/ **1** a close or exact copy; a replica. ➤a replicated experiment or trial. **2** Music a tone one or more octaves above or below the given tone.
– DERIVATIVES **replicability** /ˌrɛplɪkəˈbɪlɪti/ n. **replicable** /ˈrɛplɪkəb(ə)l/ adj. **replication** n. **replicative** adj.
– ORIGIN ME: from L. *replicat-*, *replicare*, from *re-* 'back, again' + *plicare* 'to fold'.

**replicator** ● n. **1** a thing which replicates another. **2** Biology a structural gene at which replication of a specific replicon is believed to be initiated.

**replicon** /ˈrɛplɪkɒn/ ● n. Biology a nucleic acid molecule, or part of one, which replicates as a unit, beginning at a specific site within it.
– ORIGIN 1960s: from *replication* (see **REPLICATE**) + **-ON**.

**reply** ● v. (**-ies**, **-ied**) say or write something in response to something said or written. ● n. (pl. **-ies**) **1** the action of replying. **2** a spoken or written response. ➤Law a plaintiff's response to the defendant's plea.
– DERIVATIVES **replier** n.
– ORIGIN ME: from OFr. *replier*, from L. *replicare* 'repeat', later 'make a reply' (see **REPLICATE**).

**reply coupon** ● n. a coupon used for prepaying the postage for the reply to a letter sent to another country.

**repo** /ˈriːpəʊ/ N. Amer. informal ● n. (pl. **-os**) a car or other item which has been repossessed. ● v. (**repo's**, **repo'd**) repossess.

**repoint** ● v. fill in or repair the joints of (brickwork) again.

**repopulate** ● v. introduce a population into (a previously occupied area or country).
– DERIVATIVES **repopulation** n.

**report** ● v. **1** give a spoken or written account of something. ➤convey information about an event or situation. **2** make a formal complaint about. **3** present oneself as having arrived at a particular place or as ready to do something. **4** (**report to**) be responsible to (a supervisor or manager). **5** Brit. formally announce that a parliamentary committee has dealt with (a bill). ➤(**report a bill out**) US return a bill to the legislative body for action. ● n. **1** an account given of a matter after investigation or consideration. **2** a piece of information about an event or situation. ➤talk; rumour. **3** Brit. a teacher's written assessment of a pupil's work and progress. **4** Law a detailed formal account of a case heard in a court. **5** a sudden loud noise of or like an explosion or gunfire. **6** an employee who reports to another employee.
– DERIVATIVES **reportable** adj. **reported** adj. **reportedly** adv.
– ORIGIN ME: from OFr. *reporter* (v.), *report* (n.), from L. *reportare* 'bring back'.

**reportage** /ˌrɛpɔːˈtɑːʒ, rɪˈpɔːtɪdʒ/ ● n. the reporting of news by the press and the broadcasting media. ➤factual, journalistic presentation in a book or other text.
– ORIGIN C17: Fr., from OFr. *reporter* (see **REPORT**).

**report card** ● n. chiefly N. Amer. **1** a teacher's written assessment of a pupil's work and progress. **2** an evaluation of performance.

**reported speech** ● n. a speaker's words reported in subordinate clauses governed by a reporting verb, with the required changes of person and tense (e.g. *he said that he would go*, based on *I will go*). Contrasted with **DIRECT SPEECH**.

**reporter** ● n. a person who reports news for a newspaper or broadcasting company.

**reporting verb** ● n. a verb belonging to a class of verbs conveying the action of speaking.

**reportorial** /ˌrɛpɔːˈtɔːrɪəl/ ● adj. N. Amer. of or characteristic of newspaper reporters.
– DERIVATIVES **reportorially** adv.

**report stage** ● n. (in the UK and Canada) the stage in the process of a bill becoming law at which it is debated after being reported.

**repose**[1] /rɪˈpəʊz/ ● n. **1** a state of restfulness or tranquillity. **2** composure. ● v. rest. ➤be situated or kept in a particular place.
– DERIVATIVES **reposeful** adj. **reposefully** adv.
– ORIGIN ME: from OFr. *repos* (n.), *reposer* (v.), from late L. *repausare*, from *re-* (expressing intensive force) + *pausare* 'to pause'.

**repose**[2] /rɪˈpəʊz/ ● v. (**repose something in**) place something, especially one's confidence or trust, in.
– ORIGIN ME (in the sense 'put back in the same position'): from **RE-** + **POSE**[1], suggested by L. *reponere* 'replace'.

**reposition** ● v. adjust or alter the position of.

**repository** /rɪˈpɒzɪt(ə)ri/ ● n. (pl. **-ies**) **1** a place where or receptacle in which things are stored. **2** a place where something is found in significant quantities.
– ORIGIN C15: from OFr. *repositoire* or L. *repositorium*, from *reposit-*, *reponere* (see **REPOSE**[2]).

**repossess** ● v. retake possession of (something) when a buyer defaults on payments.
– DERIVATIVES **repossession** n. **repossessor** n.

**repot** ● v. (**repotted**, **repotting**) put (a plant) in another pot.

**repoussé** /rəˈpuːseɪ/ ● adj. (of metalwork) hammered into relief from the reverse side. ● n. ornamental metal-

work fashioned in this way.
– ORIGIN C19: Fr., lit. 'pushed back'.

**repp** ● n. variant spelling of REP[3].

**repr.** ● abbrev. reprint or reprinted.

**reprehend** /ˌrɛprɪˈhɛnd/ ● v. reprimand.
– DERIVATIVES **reprehension** n.
– ORIGIN ME: from L. *reprehendere* 'seize, check, rebuke'.

**reprehensible** ● adj. deserving censure or condemnation.
– DERIVATIVES **reprehensibility** n. **reprehensibly** adv.
– ORIGIN ME: from late L. *reprehensibilis*, from *reprehens-*, *reprehendere* (see REPREHEND).

**represent** ● v. **1** be entitled or appointed to act or speak for. ➤be an elected Member of Parliament or member of a legislature for. ➤act as a substitute for. **2** constitute; amount to. ➤be a specimen or example of; typify. ➤(**be represented**) be present to a particular degree: *abstraction is well represented in this exhibition.* **3** depict in a work of art. ➤portray in a particular way: *they were represented as being in need of protection.* ➤signify, symbolize, or embody. **4** formal state or point out.
– DERIVATIVES **representability** n. **representable** adj.
– ORIGIN ME: from OFr. *representer* or L. *repraesentare*, from *re-* (expressing intensive force) + *praesentare* 'to present'.

**re-present** ● v. present again.
– DERIVATIVES **re-presentation** n.

**representation** ● n. **1** the action or an instance of representing or being represented. **2** an image, model, or other depiction of something. **3** (**representations**) statements made to an authority to communicate an opinion or register a protest.

**representational** ● adj. **1** of, relating to, or characterized by representation. **2** relating to or denoting art which depicts the physical appearance of things.

**representationalism** /ˌrɛprɪzɛnˈteɪʃ(ə)n(ə)lɪz(ə)m/ ● n. **1** the practice or advocacy of representational art. **2** Philosophy another term for REPRESENTATIONISM.
– DERIVATIVES **representationalist** adj. & n.

**representationism** ● n. Philosophy the doctrine that thought is the manipulation of mental representations which correspond to external states or objects.
– DERIVATIVES **representationist** n.

**representative** ● adj. **1** typical of a class or group. ➤containing typical examples of many or all types. **2** (of a legislative or deliberative assembly) consisting of people chosen to act and speak on behalf of a wider group. ➤(of a government or political system) based on such representation of the people. **3** serving as a portrayal of something. ● n. **1** a person chosen or appointed to act or speak for another or others. **2** an agent of a firm who travels to potential clients to sell its products. **3** an example of a class or group.
– DERIVATIVES **representatively** adv. **representativeness** n.

**repress** ● v. **1** subdue by force. **2** restrain, prevent, or inhibit. ➤suppress (a thought, feeling, or desire) in oneself so that it becomes or remains unconscious. **3** Biology prevent the transcription of (a gene).
– DERIVATIVES **represser** n. **repressible** adj. **repression** n.
– ORIGIN ME: from L. *repress-*, *reprimere* 'press back, check'.

**repressed** ● adj. **1** oppressed. **2** (of a thought, feeling, or desire) kept suppressed and unconscious in one's mind. ➤suppressing one's feelings and desires.

**repressive** ● adj. inhibiting or restraining personal freedom; oppressive.
– DERIVATIVES **repressively** adv. **repressiveness** n.

**repressor** ● n. Biochemistry a substance which acts on an operon to inhibit enzyme synthesis.

**reprieve** ● v. cancel or postpone the punishment or demise of. ● n. such a cancellation or postponement.
– ORIGIN C15 (as the past part. *repryed*): from Anglo-Norman Fr. *repris*, past part. of *reprendre*, from L. *re-* 'back' + *prehendere* 'seize'.

**reprimand** /ˈrɛprɪmɑːnd/ ● n. a formal expression of disapproval. ● v. address a reprimand to.
– ORIGIN C17: from Fr. *réprimande*, via Sp. from L. *reprimenda*, 'things to be held in check', neut. pl. gerundive of *reprimere* (see REPRESS).

**reprint** ● v. print again or in a different form. ● n. **1** an act of reprinting. **2** a copy of a book or other material that has been reprinted. ➤an offprint.
– DERIVATIVES **reprinter** n.

**reprisal** ● n. **1** an act of retaliation. **2** historical the forcible seizure of a foreign subject or their goods as an act of retaliation.
– ORIGIN ME: from Anglo-Norman Fr. *reprisaille*, from med. L. *reprisalia* (neut. pl.), based on L. *repraehens-*, *repraehendere* (see REPREHEND).

**reprise** /rɪˈpriːz/ ● n. **1** a repeated passage in music. **2** a further performance of something. ● v. repeat (a piece of music or a performance).
– ORIGIN C18: Fr., lit. 'taken up again', fem. past part. of *reprendre* (see REPRIEVE).

**repro** ● n. (pl. **-os**) informal a reproduction or copy. ➤the reproduction or copying of a document or image.

**reproach** ● v. **1** express to (someone) one's disapproval of or disappointment in their actions. **2** (**reproach someone with**) accuse someone of. ● n. **1** an expression of disapproval or disappointment. **2** (**Reproaches**) (in the Roman Catholic Church) a set of antiphons and responses for Good Friday representing the reproaches of Christ to his people.
– PHRASES **above** (or **beyond**) **reproach** such that no criticism can be made; perfect.
– DERIVATIVES **reproachable** adj. **reproacher** n. **reproachful** adj. **reproachfully** adv. **reproachfulness** n. **reproaching** adj. **reproachingly** adv.
– ORIGIN ME: from OFr. *reprochier* (v.), from a base meaning 'bring back close', based on L. *prope* 'near'.

**reprobate** /ˈrɛprəbeɪt/ ● n. **1** an unprincipled person. **2** Christian Theology, archaic (in Calvinism) a sinner who is not of the elect and is predestined to damnation. ● adj. **1** unprincipled. **2** Christian Theology, archaic (in Calvinism) predestined to damnation. ● v. archaic express or feel disapproval of.
– DERIVATIVES **reprobation** n.
– ORIGIN ME: from L. *reprobat-*, *reprobare* 'disapprove'.

**reprocess** ● v. process (something, especially spent nuclear fuel) again or differently, in order to reuse it.

**reproduce** ● v. **1** produce a copy or representation of. ➤create something in a different medium or context that is very similar to. **2** (of an organism) produce offspring.
– DERIVATIVES **reproducer** n. **reproducibility** n. **reproducible** adj. **reproducibly** adv.

**reproduction** ● n. **1** the action or process of reproducing. ➤the quality of reproduced sound. **2** a copy of a work of art, especially a print made of a painting. ➤[as modifier] made to imitate the style of an earlier period or particular craftsman.
– DERIVATIVES **reproductive** adj. **reproductively** adv. **reproductiveness** n.

**reprogram** (also **reprogramme**) ● v. (**reprogrammed**, **reprogramming**; US also **reprogramed**, **reprograming**) program (a computer) again.
– DERIVATIVES **reprogrammable** adj.

**reprographics** ● pl. n. [treated as sing.] reprography.

**reprography** /rɪˈprɒɡrəfi/ ● n. the science and practice of reproducing documents and graphic material.
– DERIVATIVES **reprographer** n. **reprographic** adj.
– ORIGIN 1960s: from REPRODUCE + -GRAPHY.

**reproof**[1] /rɪˈpruːf/ ● n. a rebuke or reprimand.
– ORIGIN ME: from OFr. *reprove*, from *reprover* 'reprove'.

**reproof**[2] /riːˈpruːf/ ● v. **1** Brit. render waterproof again. **2** make a fresh proof of (printed matter).

**reprove** ● v. rebuke or reprimand.
– DERIVATIVES **reprovable** adj. **reprover** n. **reproving** adj. **reprovingly** adv.
– ORIGIN ME: from OFr. *reprover*, from late L. *reprobare* (see REPROBATE).

**reptile** ● n. **1** a cold-blooded vertebrate animal of a class (Reptilia) that includes snakes, lizards, crocodiles, turtles, and tortoises, typically having a dry scaly skin and laying soft-shelled eggs on land. **2** informal a person

regarded with loathing and contempt.
– DERIVATIVES **reptilian** adj. & n.
– ORIGIN ME: from late L., neut. of *reptilis*, from L. *rept-*, *repere* 'crawl'.

**republic** • n. a state in which supreme power is held by the people and their elected representatives, and which has an elected or nominated president rather than a monarch.
– ORIGIN C16: from Fr. *république*, from L. *respublica*, from *res* 'concern' + *publicus* 'of the people, public'.

**republican** • adj. **1** belonging to or characteristic of a republic. **2** advocating republican government. **3** (**Republican**) (in the US) supporting the Republican Party. • n. **1** a person advocating republican government. **2** (**Republican**) (in the US) a member or supporter of the Republican Party. **3** (**Republican**) an advocate of a united Ireland.
– DERIVATIVES **republicanism** n.

**repudiate** /rɪˈpjuːdɪeɪt/ • v. **1** refuse to accept or be associated with. **2** deny the truth or validity of. **3** chiefly Law refuse to fulfil or discharge (an agreement, obligation, or debt). **4** archaic disown or divorce (one's wife).
– DERIVATIVES **repudiation** n. **repudiator** n. **repudiatory** /rɪˈpjuːdɪəˌt(ə)ri/ adj. (Law).
– ORIGIN ME (orig. an adj. in the sense 'divorced'): from L. *repudiatus* 'divorced, cast off', from *repudium* 'divorce'.

**repugnance** /rɪˈpʌɡnəns/ • n. intense disgust.
– DERIVATIVES **repugnancy** n.
– ORIGIN ME (in the sense 'opposition'): from OFr. *repugnance* or L. *repugnantia*, from *repugnare* 'oppose'.

**repugnant** • adj. **1** extremely distasteful; unacceptable. **2** (**repugnant to**) in conflict with; incompatible with. **3** archaic or poetic/literary given to stubborn resistance.
– DERIVATIVES **repugnantly** adv.

**repulse** • v. **1** drive back (an attacking enemy) by force. ➤ rebuff or refuse to accept. **2** cause to feel intense distaste or disgust. • n. the action or an instant of repulsing or being repulsed.
– ORIGIN ME: from L. *repuls-*, *repellere* (see **REPEL**).

**repulsion** • n. **1** a feeling of intense distaste or disgust. **2** Physics a force under the influence of which objects tend to move away from each other, e.g. through having the same magnetic polarity or electric charge.

**repulsive** • adj. **1** arousing intense distaste or disgust. **2** archaic lacking friendliness or sympathy. **3** of or relating to repulsion between physical objects.
– DERIVATIVES **repulsively** adv. **repulsiveness** n.

**repurchase** • v. buy (something) back. • n. the action of buying something back.

**reputable** • adj. having a good reputation.
– DERIVATIVES **reputably** adv.
– ORIGIN C17: from obs. Fr., or from med. L. *reputabilis*, from L. *reputare* (see **REPUTE**).

**reputation** • n. the beliefs or opinions that are generally held about someone or something. ➤ a widespread belief that someone or something has a particular characteristic.
– ORIGIN ME: from L. *reputatio(n-)*, from *reputare* (see **REPUTE**).

**repute** • n. **1** the opinion generally held of someone or something. **2** the state of being highly regarded: *chefs of international repute.* • v. (**be reputed**) be generally regarded as having done something or as having particular characteristics. ➤ [as adj. **reputed**] being generally believed to exist.
– DERIVATIVES **reputedly** adv.
– ORIGIN ME: from OFr. *reputer* or L. *reputare* 'think over'.

**request** • n. an act of asking politely or formally for something. ➤ a thing that is asked for in such a way. • v. politely or formally ask for. ➤ politely or formally ask (someone) to do something.
– DERIVATIVES **requester** n.
– ORIGIN ME: from OFr. *requeste* (n.), based on L. *requirere* (see **REQUIRE**).

**request stop** • n. Brit. a bus stop at which the bus halts only if requested by a passenger or if hailed.

**requiem** /ˈrɛkwɪəm, -ɪɛm/ • n. **1** (especially in the Roman Catholic Church) a Mass for the repose of the souls of the dead. **2** a musical composition setting parts of such a Mass. **3** an act or token of remembrance.
– ORIGIN ME: from L. (first word of the Mass), accusative of *requies* 'rest'.

**requiescat** /ˌrɛkwɪˈɛskat/ • n. a wish or prayer for the repose of a dead person.
– ORIGIN L., from *requiescat in pace* (see **RIP**).

**require** • v. **1** need or depend on. ➤ wish to have. **2** instruct or expect (someone) to do something. ➤ (**require something of**) regard an action or quality as due from. ➤ specify as compulsory: *required by law.*
– DERIVATIVES **requirement** n. **requirer** n.
– ORIGIN ME: from OFr. *requere*, from L. *requirere*, from *re-* (expressing intensive force) + *quaerere* 'seek'.

**requisite** /ˈrɛkwɪzɪt/ • adj. made necessary by particular circumstances or regulations. • n. a thing that is necessary for the achievement of a specified end.
– DERIVATIVES **requisitely** adv.
– ORIGIN ME: from L. *requisitus* 'searched for, deemed necessary', past part. of *requirere* (see **REQUIRE**).

**requisition** /ˌrɛkwɪˈzɪʃ(ə)n/ • n. **1** an official order laying claim to the use of property or materials. **2** the appropriation of goods for military or public use. **3** a formal written demand that something should be performed or put into operation. • v. demand the use, supply, or performance of through the issue of a requisition.
– DERIVATIVES **requisitioner** n.
– ORIGIN ME: from OFr., or from L. *requisitio(n-)*, from *requirere* (see **REQUIRE**).

**requite** /rɪˈkwʌɪt/ • v. formal **1** make appropriate return for (a favour or demonstration of affection, or a wrongdoing). **2** return a favour to (someone).
– DERIVATIVES **requital** n.
– ORIGIN C16: from **RE-** + obs. *quite*, var. of **QUIT**.

**reran** past of **RERUN**.

**reread** • v. (past and past part. **reread**) read (a text) again. • n. an act of rereading.

**reredos** /ˈrɪədɒs/ • n. (pl. same) an ornamental screen at the back of an altar in a church.
– ORIGIN ME: from Anglo-Norman Fr., from OFr. *areredos*, from *arere* 'behind' + *dos* 'back'.

**re-release** • v. release (a recording or film) again. • n. a re-released recording or film.

**re-route** • v. send by or along a different route.

**rerun** • v. (**rerunning**; past **reran**; past part. **rerun**) show, stage, or perform again. • n. a rerun event, competition, or programme.

**res** • abbrev. informal resolution: *high-res images.*

**resale** • n. the sale of a thing previously bought.
– DERIVATIVES **resaleable** (also **resalable**) adj.

**resat** past and past participle of **RESIT**.

**reschedule** • v. **1** change the time of (a planned event). **2** arrange a new scheme of repayments of (a debt).

**rescind** /rɪˈsɪnd/ • v. revoke, cancel, or repeal (a law, order, or agreement).
– DERIVATIVES **rescindable** adj.
– ORIGIN C16: from L. *rescindere*, from *re-* (expressing intensive force) + *scindere* 'to divide, split'.

**rescission** /rɪˈsɪʒ(ə)n/ • n. formal the rescinding of a law, order, or agreement.
– ORIGIN C17: from late L. *rescissio(n-)*, from *resciss-*, *rescindere* (see **RESCIND**).

**rescript** /ˈriːskrɪpt/ • n. **1** an official edict or announcement. **2** (in ancient Rome) an emperor's written reply to an appeal for guidance, especially on a legal point. **3** the Pope's decision on a question of Roman Catholic doctrine or papal law.
– ORIGIN ME: from L. *rescriptum*, neut. past part. of *rescribere* 'write back'.

**rescue** • v. (**rescues**, **rescued**, **rescuing**) save from a dangerous or distressing situation. • n. an act of rescuing or being rescued.
– DERIVATIVES **rescuable** adj. **rescuer** n.
– ORIGIN ME: from OFr. *rescoure* from L. *re-* (expressing intensive force) + *excutere* 'shake out, discard'.

**reseal** • v. seal (something) again.

– DERIVATIVES **resealable** adj.

**research** /rɪˈsəːtʃ, ˈriːsəːtʃ/ ● n. the systematic investigation into and study of materials and sources in order to establish facts and reach new conclusions. ● v. carry out research into. ➤ use research to discover or verify information presented in (a book, programme, etc.).
– DERIVATIVES **researchable** adj. **researcher** n.
– ORIGIN C16: from obs. Fr. *recerche* (n.), *recercher* (v.), from OFr. *re-* (expressing intensive force) + *cerchier* 'to search'.

**USAGE** research

The traditional pronunciation in British English puts the stress on the second syllable, **-search**. In US English the stress comes on the **re-**. The US pronunciation is becoming more common in British English and, while some traditionalists view it as incorrect, it is now generally accepted as a standard variant in British English.

**research and development** ● n. (in industry) work directed towards innovation in and improvement of products and processes.

**reseat** ● v. **1** seat again. **2** realign or repair (something) to fit it into its correct position. **3** equip with new seats.

**resect** /rɪˈsɛkt/ ● v. [often as adj. **resected**] Surgery cut out (tissue or part of an organ).
– DERIVATIVES **resectable** adj. **resection** n. **resectional** adj. **resectionist** n.
– ORIGIN C17: from L. *resect-*, *resecare* 'to cut off', from *re-* 'back' + *secare* 'to cut'.

**reseed** ● v. sow (land) with seed again.

**reselect** ● v. select again or differently.
– DERIVATIVES **reselection** n.

**resell** ● v. (past and past part. **resold**) sell (something one has bought) to someone else.
– DERIVATIVES **reseller** n.

**resemblance** ● n. the state of resembling. ➤ a way in which two or more things resemble each other.
– DERIVATIVES **resemblant** adj.

**resemble** ● v. have a similar appearance to or features in common with.
– ORIGIN ME: from OFr. *resembler*, based on L. *similare* (from *similis* 'like').

**resent** ● v. feel bitterness or indignation at.
– ORIGIN C16: from obs. Fr. *resentir*, from *re-* (expressing intensive force) + *sentir* 'feel' (from L. *sentire*).

**resentful** ● adj. feeling or expressing bitterness or indignation.
– DERIVATIVES **resentfully** adv. **resentfulness** n.

**resentment** ● n. bitterness; indignation.

**reserpine** /rɪˈsəːpiːn/ ● n. Medicine a compound of the alkaloid class obtained from a snakeroot plant, used in the treatment of hypertension.
– ORIGIN 1950s: from the mod. L. species name *R(auwolfia) serp(entina)*, named after the Ger. botanist Leonhard *Rauwolf*, + **-INE**[4].

**reservation** ● n. **1** the action of reserving. ➤ an arrangement whereby something has been reserved. **2** an area of land set aside for occupation by North American Indians or Australian Aboriginals. **3** Law a right or interest retained in an estate being conveyed. **4** a qualification or expression of doubt attached to a statement or claim. **5** (in the Roman Catholic Church) the action of a superior of reserving the power of absolution. ➤ a right reserved to the Pope of nomination to a vacant benefice.

**reserve** ● v. **1** retain for future use. **2** arrange for (a seat, ticket, etc.) to be kept for the use of a particular person. **3** retain or hold (a right or entitlement). **4** refrain from delivering (a judgement or decision) without due consideration or evidence. ● n. **1** (often **reserves**) a reserved supply of a commodity. ➤ funds kept available by a bank, company, or government. ➤ a part of a company's profits added to capital rather than paid as a dividend. **2** a force or body of troops withheld from action to reinforce or protect others, or additional to the regular forces and available in an emergency. **3** an extra player in a team, serving as a possible substitute. ➤ (**the reserves**) the second-choice team. **4** an area designated as a habitat for a native people. **5** a protected area for wildlife. **6** a lack of warmth or openness. **7** qualification or doubt attached to a statement or claim. **8** (in ceramics or textiles) an area in which the original material or background colour remains visible.
– DERIVATIVES **reservable** adj. **reserver** n.
– ORIGIN ME: from OFr. *reserver*, from L. *reservare* 'keep back'.

**re-serve** ● v. serve again.

**reserve bank** ● n. **1** (in the US) a regional bank operating under and implementing the policies of the Federal Reserve. **2** Austral./NZ a central bank.

**reserve currency** ● n. a strong currency widely used in international trade that a central bank is prepared to hold as part of its foreign exchange reserves.

**reserved** ● adj. slow to reveal emotion or opinions.
– DERIVATIVES **reservedly** adv. **reservedness** n.

**reserved occupation** ● n. Brit. an occupation from which a person will not be taken for military service.

**reserved word** ● n. Computing a word in a programming language which has a fixed meaning and cannot be redefined by the programmer.

**reserve price** ● n. the price stipulated as the lowest acceptable by the seller for an item sold at auction.

**reservist** ● n. a member of a military reserve force.

**reservoir** ● n. **1** a large natural or artificial lake used as a source of water supply. ➤ a supply or source of something. **2** a place where fluid collects, especially in rock strata or in the body. **3** a receptacle or part of a machine designed to hold fluid.
– ORIGIN C17: from Fr. *réservoir*, from *réserver* 'to reserve, keep'.

**reset** ● v. (**resetting**; past and past part. **reset**) **1** set again or differently. **2** Electronics cause (a binary device) to enter the state representing the numeral 0.
– DERIVATIVES **resettability** n. **resettable** adj.

**resettle** ● v. settle or cause to settle in a different place.
– DERIVATIVES **resettlement** n.

**res gestae** /reɪz ˈgɛstʌɪ, riːz ˈdʒɛstiː/ ● pl. n. Law the events, circumstances, or remarks which relate to a particular case, especially as constituting admissible evidence in a court of law.
– ORIGIN L., lit. 'things done'.

**reshape** ● v. shape or form (something) differently or again.

**reshuffle** ● v. **1** interchange the positions of (members of a team, especially government ministers). **2** rearrange. ● n. an act of reshuffling.

**reside** ● v. **1** have one's permanent home in a particular place. **2** (of a right or legal power) belong to a person or body. **3** (of a quality) be present or inherent in something.
– ORIGIN ME: prob. a back-form. from **RESIDENT**, influenced by Fr. *résider* or L. *residere* 'remain'.

**residence** ● n. **1** the fact of residing somewhere. **2** a person's home. **3** the official house of a government minister or other official figure.
– PHRASES **artist** (or **writer**) **in residence** an artist or writer who is based for a set period within a college or other institution and is available for teaching purposes.

**residence time** ● n. technical the average length of time during which a substance, object, etc. is in a given location or condition.

**residency** ● n. (pl. **-ies**) **1** the fact of living in a place. **2** a residential post held by an artist or writer. **3** Brit. a musician's regular engagement at a club or other venue. **4** N. Amer. a period of specialized medical training in a hospital; the position of a resident. **5** a group or organization of intelligence agents in a foreign country. **6** historical the official residence of a British government agent in a semi-independent state.

**resident** ● n. **1** a person who lives somewhere on a long-term basis. ➤ a bird, butterfly, or other animal of a species that does not migrate. ➤ Brit. a guest in a hotel who stays for one or more nights. ➤ US a pupil who boards at a boarding school. **2** N. Amer. a medical graduate engaged in specialized practice under supervision in a hospital. **3** an intelligence agent in a foreign country. **4** historical a British

government agent in any semi-independent state, especially the Governor General's representative at the court of an Indian state. ● **adj. 1** living somewhere on a long-term basis. ➤ having quarters on the premises of one's work. ➤ attached to and working regularly for a particular institution. ➤ (of a bird, butterfly or other animal) non-migratory. **2** (of a computer program, file, etc.) immediately available in computer memory, rather than having to be loaded from elsewhere.
– DERIVATIVES **residentship** n. (historical).
– ORIGIN ME: from L. *resident-*, *residere* 'remain'.

**residential** ● **adj. 1** designed for people to live in. ➤ providing accommodation in addition to other services. ➤ occupied by private houses. **2** concerning or relating to residence.
– DERIVATIVES **residentially** adv.

**residentiary** ● **adj. 1** relating to or involving residence. **2** (of a canon) required to live officially in a cathedral or collegiate church. ● **n.** (pl. **-ies**) a residentiary canon.

**residua** plural form of **RESIDUUM**.

**residual** ● **adj. 1** remaining after the greater part or quantity has gone or been subtracted. ➤ (of a physical state or property) remaining after the removal of or present in the absence of a causative agent. **2** (of an experimental or arithmetical error) not accounted for or eliminated. **3** (of a soil or other deposit) formed in situ by weathering. ● **n. 1** a residual quantity. **2** a difference between a value measured in a scientific experiment and the theoretical or true value. **3** a royalty paid to a performer or writer for a repeat of a play, television show, or advertisement. **4** Geology a portion of rocky or high ground remaining after erosion. **5** the resale value of a new car or other item at a specified time after purchase.
– DERIVATIVES **residually** adv.

**residual current** ● **n.** an electric current which flows briefly in a circuit after the voltage is reduced to zero.

**residual current device** ● **n.** a current-activated circuit-breaker used as a safety device for mains-operated electrical tools and appliances.

**residual stress** ● **n.** Physics the stress present in an object in the absence of any external load or force.

**residuary** ● **adj. 1** technical residual. **2** Law of or relating to the residue of an estate.

**residue** /ˈrɛzɪdjuː/ ● **n. 1** a small amount of something that remains after the main part has gone or been taken or used. ➤ a substance that remains after a process such as combustion or evaporation. **2** Law the part of an estate that is left after the payment of charges, debts, and bequests.
– ORIGIN ME: from OFr. *residu*, from L. *residuum* (see **RESIDUUM**).

**residuum** /rɪˈzɪdjʊəm/ ● **n.** (pl. **residua** /-djʊə/) **1** technical a chemical residue. **2** Sociology a class of society that is unemployed and without privileges or opportunities.
– ORIGIN C17: from L., neut. of *residuus*, *residere* 'to remain'.

**resign** ● **v. 1** voluntarily leave a job or position of office. **2** (**be resigned**) accept that something undesirable cannot be avoided. **3** archaic surrender oneself to another's guidance.
– DERIVATIVES **resigned** adj. **resignedly** adv. **resignedness** n. **resigner** n.
– ORIGIN ME: from OFr. *resigner*, from L. *resignare* 'unseal, cancel'.

**re-sign** ● **v.** sign (a document or contract) again.

**resignal** ● **v.** (**resignalled**, **resignalling**; US **resignaled**, **resignaling**) [often as noun **resignalling**] equip (a railway line) with new signal equipment.

**resignation** ● **n. 1** an act of resigning. ➤ a document conveying an intention to resign. **2** acceptance of something undesirable but inevitable.

**resile** /rɪˈzʌɪl/ ● **v.** formal abandon a position or a course of action.
– ORIGIN C16: from obs. Fr. *resilir* or L. *resilire* 'to recoil'.

**resilient** ● **adj. 1** (of a substance or object) able to recoil or spring back into shape after bending, stretching, or being compressed. **2** (of a person or animal) able to withstand or recover quickly from difficult conditions.
– DERIVATIVES **resilience** n. **resiliency** n. **resiliently** adv.
– ORIGIN C17: from L. *resilient-* 'leaping back', pres. part. of *resilire* (see **RESILE**).

**resin** /ˈrɛzɪn/ ● **n. 1** a sticky flammable organic substance exuded by some trees and other plants (notably fir and pine). **2** a solid or liquid synthetic organic polymer used as the basis of plastics, adhesives, varnishes, etc. ● **v.** (**resined**, **resining**) rub or treat with resin.
– DERIVATIVES **resined** adj. **resinous** adj.
– ORIGIN ME: from L. *resina*; rel. to Gk *rhētinē* 'pine resin'.

**resinate** ● **v.** /ˈrɛzɪneɪt/ impregnate or flavour with resin. ● **n.** /ˈrɛzɪnət/ Chemistry a salt of an acid derived from resin.
– DERIVATIVES **resinated** adj.

**res ipsa loquitur** /ˌreɪz ˌɪpsə ˈlɒkwɪtə/ ● **n.** Law the principle that the occurrence of an accident implies negligence.
– ORIGIN L., lit. 'the matter speaks for itself'.

**resist** ● **v. 1** withstand the action or effect of. **2** try to prevent by action or argument. **3** refrain from (something tempting). **4** struggle against. ● **n.** a resistant substance applied as a coating to protect a surface during some process, for example to prevent dye or glaze adhering.
– DERIVATIVES **resister** n. **resistibility** n. **resistible** adj.
– ORIGIN ME: from OFr. *resister* or L. *resistere*, from *re-* (expressing opposition) + *sistere* 'stop'.

**resistance** ● **n. 1** the action of resisting. **2** armed or violent opposition. **3** (also **resistance movement**) a secret organization resisting political authority. ➤ (**the Resistance**) the underground movement formed in France during the Second World War to fight the German occupying forces and the Vichy government. **4** the impeding effect exerted by one material thing on another. **5** the ability not to be affected by something. ➤ Medicine & Biology lack of sensitivity to a drug, insecticide, etc., especially as a result of continued exposure or genetic change. **6** the degree to which a material or device opposes the passage of an electric current, causing energy dissipation. ➤ a resistor.
– PHRASES **the line** (or **path**) **of least resistance** the easiest course of action.
– DERIVATIVES **resistant** adj.

**resistance thermometer** ● **n.** Physics an instrument used to measure a change in temperature by its effect on the electrical resistance of a platinum or other metal wire.

**resistive** /rɪˈzɪstɪv/ ● **adj. 1** technical able to resist something. **2** Physics of or concerning electrical resistance.

**resistivity** /ˌrɪzɪˈstɪvɪti/ ● **n.** Physics a measure of the resisting power of a specified material to the flow of an electric current.

**resistivity surveying** ● **n.** the measurement of the current passing between electrodes embedded in the ground over a given area, in order to locate buried structural features by their differing resistivity.

**resistless** ● **adj.** archaic **1** powerful; irresistible. **2** powerless to resist.
– DERIVATIVES **resistlessly** adv.

**resistor** ● **n.** Physics a device having resistance to the passage of an electric current.

**resit** Brit. ● **v.** (**resitting**; past and past part. **resat**) take (an examination) again after failing. ● **n.** an examination held for this purpose.

**resite** ● **v.** place or situate in a different place.

**resize** ● **v.** alter the size of (something, especially a computer window or image).

**res judicata** /reɪz ˌdʒuːdɪˈkɑːtə/ ● **n.** (pl. **res judicatae** /ˌdʒuːdɪˈkɑːtʌɪ, ˌdʒuːdɪˈkɑːtiː/) Law a matter that has been adjudicated by a competent court and may not be pursued further by the same parties.
– ORIGIN L., lit. 'judged matter'.

**reskill** ● **v.** teach (a person, especially one who is unemployed) new skills.

**resold** past and past participle of **RESELL**.

**resoluble** /rɪˈzɒljʊb(ə)l/ ● **adj.** archaic able to be resolved.

– ORIGIN C17: from Fr. *résoluble* or late L. *resolubilis*, based on L. *solvere* 'release, loosen'.

**re-soluble** • adj. able to dissolve or be dissolved again.

**resolute** /ˈrɛzəluːt/ • adj. determined; unwavering.
– DERIVATIVES **resolutely** adv. **resoluteness** n.
– ORIGIN ME (in the sense 'paid', describing a rent): from L. *resolutus* 'loosened, released, paid', past part. of *resolvere* (see **RESOLVE**).

**resolution** • n. **1** the quality of being resolute. **2** a firm decision. ➤a formal expression of opinion or intention agreed on by a legislative body. **3** the action of solving a problem or dispute. **4** Music the passing of a discord into a concord during the course of changing harmony. **5** Medicine the disappearance of a symptom or condition. **6** the process of reducing or separating something into components. **7** the smallest interval measurable by a telescope or other scientific instrument. **8** the degree of detail visible in a photographic or television image.

**resolutive** /ˈrɛzəluːtɪv/ • adj. formal or archaic having the power or ability to dissolve or dispel something.

**resolve** • v. **1** settle or find a solution to. ➤Medicine cause (a symptom or condition) to heal or disappear. **2** decide firmly on a course of action. ➤(of a legislative body) take a decision by a formal vote. **3** Music cause (a discord) to pass into a concord during the course of harmonic change. **4** (**resolve something into**) reduce a subject or statement by mental analysis into (separate elements or a more elementary form). ➤chiefly Chemistry separate into constituent parts or components. **5** (of something seen at a distance) turn into a different form when seen more clearly. ➤(of optical or photographic equipment) separate or distinguish between (closely adjacent objects). ➤technical separately distinguish (peaks in a graph or spectrum). **6** Physics analyse (a force or velocity) into components acting in particular directions. • n. **1** firm determination. **2** US a formal resolution by a legislative body or public meeting.
– DERIVATIVES **resolvability** n. **resolvable** adj. **resolved** adj. **resolvedly** adv. **resolver** n.
– ORIGIN ME (in the senses 'dissolve, disintegrate' and 'solve (a problem)'): from L. *resolvere*, from *re-* (expressing intensive force) + *solvere* 'loosen'.

**resolving power** • n. the ability of an optical instrument or type of film to separate or distinguish small or closely adjacent images.

**resonance** • n. **1** the quality of being resonant. **2** Physics the reinforcement or prolongation of sound by reflection or synchronous vibration. **3** Mechanics enhanced vibration of an object subjected to an oscillating force close to a natural frequency of the object. **4** the condition in which an electric circuit produces the largest possible response to an applied oscillating signal. **5** Physics a short-lived subatomic particle that is an excited state of a more stable particle. **6** Astronomy the occurrence of a simple ratio between the periods of revolution of two orbiting bodies. **7** Chemistry the state of having a molecular structure which cannot adequately be represented by a single structural formula but is a composite of two or more structures of higher energy.

**resonant** • adj. **1** (of sound) deep, clear, and continuing to sound or ring. ➤(of a room, musical instrument, or hollow body) tending to reinforce or prolong sounds, especially by synchronous vibration. ➤(**resonant with**) filled or resounding with (a sound). **2** having the ability to evoke or suggest enduring images, memories, or emotions. **3** (of a colour) enhancing another or others by contrast. **4** technical relating to or bringing about resonance in a circuit, atom, or other object.
– DERIVATIVES **resonantly** adv.
– ORIGIN C16 (earlier (ME) as *resonance*): from Fr. *résonnant* or L. *resonant-*, *resonare*, from *re-* (expressing intensive force) + *sonare* 'to sound'.

**resonate** • v. **1** be resonant. **2** chiefly US (of an idea or action) meet with someone's agreement. **3** technical produce electrical or mechanical resonance.
– ORIGIN C19: from L. *resonat-*, *resonare* (see **RESOUND**).

**resonator** • n. a device for producing resonance, or for using resonance to detect or amplify something.

**resorb** /rɪˈsɔːb/ • v. **1** absorb again. **2** Physiology remove (cells, tissue, etc.) by gradual breakdown into component materials and dispersal in the circulation.
– ORIGIN C17: from L. *resorbere*, from *re-* (expressing intensive force) + *sorbere* 'absorb'.

**resorcinol** /rɪˈzɔːsɪnɒl/ • n. Chemistry a crystalline organic compound originally obtained from galbanum resin, used in the production of dyes, resins, and cosmetics.
– ORIGIN C19: from **RESIN** + **ORCIN** + **-OL**.

**resorption** /rɪˈzɔːpʃ(ə)n, -ˈsɔːp-/ • n. the process or action of resorbing or being resorbed.
– DERIVATIVES **resorptive** adj.

**resort** • v. (**resort to**) **1** turn to and adopt (a strategy or course of action) so as to resolve a difficult situation. **2** formal go often or in large numbers to. • n. **1** a place frequented for holidays or recreation or for a particular purpose. **2** the action of resorting to something. ➤a strategy or course of action resorted to.
– PHRASES **as a first** (or **last** or **final**) **resort** before anything else is attempted (or when all else has failed).
– DERIVATIVES **resorter** n.
– ORIGIN ME: from OFr. *resortir*, from *re-* 'again' + *sortir* 'come or go out'.

**resound** /rɪˈzaʊnd/ • v. **1** fill or be filled with a ringing, booming, or echoing sound. **2** (of fame, success, etc.) be much talked of. ➤[as adj. **resounding**] emphatic; unmistakable: *a resounding success*.
– DERIVATIVES **resoundingly** adv.
– ORIGIN ME: from **RE-** + **SOUND**[1], suggested by OFr. *resoner* or L. *resonare* 'sound again'.

**resource** /rɪˈsɔːs, rɪˈzɔːs/ • n. **1** (usu. **resources**) a stock or supply of materials or assets. **2** an action or strategy adopted in adverse circumstances. ➤(**resources**) personal attributes and capabilities that sustain one in adverse circumstances. ➤a teaching aid. • v. provide with resources.
– DERIVATIVES **resourceless** adj. **resourcelessness** n.
– ORIGIN C17: from obs. Fr. *ressourse*, fem. past part. (used as n.) of OFr. dial. *resourdre* 'rise again, recover' (based on L. *surgere* 'to rise').

**resourceful** • adj. having the ability to find quick and clever ways to overcome difficulties.
– DERIVATIVES **resourcefully** adv. **resourcefulness** n.

**respect** • n. **1** a feeling of deep admiration for someone elicited by their qualities or achievements. ➤(**respects**) polite greetings. **2** due regard for the feelings or rights of others. **3** a particular aspect, point, or detail. • v. **1** feel or have respect for. **2** avoid harming or interfering with. ➤agree to recognize and abide by.
– PHRASES **in respect of** (or **with respect to**) as regards; with reference to.
– DERIVATIVES **respecter** n. **respectful** adj. **respectfully** adv. **respectfulness** n.
– ORIGIN ME: from L. *respectus*, from *respicere* 'look back at, regard'.

**respectable** • adj. **1** regarded by society as being proper, correct, and good. **2** of some merit or importance. ➤adequate or acceptable in number, size, or amount.
– DERIVATIVES **respectability** n. **respectably** adv.

**respecting** • prep. with reference or regard to.

**respective** • adj. belonging or relating separately to each of two or more people or things.

**respectively** • adv. separately or individually and in the order already mentioned.

**respell** • v. (past and past part. **respelled** or chiefly Brit. **respelt**) spell (a word) again or differently, especially in order to indicate its pronunciation.

**respirate** /ˈrɛspɪreɪt/ • v. Medicine & Biology assist to breathe by means of artificial respiration.
– ORIGIN C17: back-form. from **RESPIRATION**.

**respiration** • n. **1** the action of breathing. ➤a single breath. **2** Biology a process in living organisms involving the production of energy, typically with the intake of oxygen and the release of carbon dioxide from the oxidation of complex organic substances.
– ORIGIN ME: from L. *respiratio(n-)*, from *respirare* (see **RESPIRE**).

**respirator** • n. **1** an apparatus worn over the mouth and nose or the entire face to prevent the inhalation of dust, smoke, or other noxious substances. **2** an apparatus used to induce artificial respiration.

**respiratory** /rɪ'spɪrət(ə)ri, 'rɛsp(ə)rət(ə)ri, rɪ'spʌɪ-/ ● **adj.** of, relating to, or affecting respiration or the organs of respiration.

**respiratory tract** ● **n.** the passage formed by the mouth, nose, throat, and lungs, through which air passes during breathing.

**respire** ● **v.** breathe. ➤(of a plant) carry out respiration.
– DERIVATIVES **respirable** adj.
– ORIGIN ME: from OFr. *respirer* or L. *respirare* 'breathe out'.

**respirometer** ● **n.** **1** Biology a device for measuring the rate of respiration. **2** Medicine an instrument for measuring the air capacity of the lungs.

**respite** /'rɛspʌɪt, -spɪt/ ● **n.** a short period of rest or relief from something difficult or unpleasant. ● **v.** **1** postpone (a sentence, obligation, etc.). **2** archaic grant respite to.
– ORIGIN ME: from OFr. *respit*, from L. *respectus* 'refuge, consideration'.

**respite care** ● **n.** temporary care of a sick, elderly, or disabled person, providing relief for their usual carer.

**resplendent** /rɪ'splɛnd(ə)nt/ ● **adj.** attractive and impressive through being richly colourful or sumptuous.
– DERIVATIVES **resplendence** n. **resplendency** n. **resplendently** adv.
– ORIGIN ME: from L. *resplendent-*, *resplendere* 'shine out'.

**respond** ● **v.** say or do something in reply or as a reaction. ● **n.** **1** Architecture a half-pillar or half-pier attached to a wall to support an arch. **2** (in church use) a responsory; a response to a versicle.
– DERIVATIVES **responder** n.
– ORIGIN ME: from OFr., from *respondre* 'to answer', from L. *respondere*, from *re-* 'again' + *spondere* 'to pledge'.

**respondent** ● **n.** **1** a defendant in a lawsuit, especially one in an appeal or divorce case. **2** a person who responds to a questionnaire or an advertisement. ● **adj.** **1** in the position of defendant in a lawsuit. **2** responding to something. **3** Psychology involving or denoting a response to a specific stimulus.

**response** ● **n.** **1** an instance of responding; an answer or reaction. **2** Psychology & Physiology an excitation of a nerve impulse.
– ORIGIN ME: from OFr. *respons* or L. *responsum*, neut. past part. of *respondere* (see **RESPOND**).

**responsibility** ● **n.** (pl. **-ies**) **1** the state or fact of being responsible. **2** the opportunity or ability to act independently and take decisions without authorization. ➤(often **responsibilities**) a thing which one is required to do as part of a job, role, or legal obligation.

**responsible** ● **adj.** **1** having an obligation to do something, or having control over or care for someone. **2** being the primary cause of something and so able to be blamed or credited for it. ➤(**responsible to**) reporting to; answerable to. ➤morally accountable for one's behaviour. **3** (of a job or position) involving important duties or decisions or control over others. **4** capable of being trusted.
– DERIVATIVES **responsibleness** n. **responsibly** adv.
– ORIGIN C16: from obs. Fr. *responsible*, from L. *respons-*, *respondere* (see **RESPOND**).

**responsive** ● **adj.** **1** responding readily and positively. **2** in response; answering.
– DERIVATIVES **responsively** adv. **responsiveness** n.

**responsorial** /,rɪspɒn'sɔːrɪəl/ ● **adj.** (of a psalm or liturgical chant) recited in parts with a congregational response between each part.

**responsory** /rɪ'spɒns(ə)ri/ ● **n.** (pl. **-ies**) (in the Christian Church) an anthem said or sung by a soloist and choir after a lesson.

**respray** ● **v.** /riː'spreɪ/ spray with a new coat of paint. ● **n.** /'riːspreɪ/ an instance of respraying.

**res publica** /reɪz 'pʊblɪkə, 'pʌblɪkə/ ● **n.** the state, republic, or commonwealth.
– ORIGIN L., lit. 'public matter'.

**rest**[1] ● **v.** **1** cease work or movement in order to relax or recover strength. ➤allow to be inactive in order to regain or save strength or energy. ➤lie buried. ➤(of a problem or subject) be left without further investigation or discussion. **2** place or be placed so as to stay in a specified position. ➤(**rest on**) (of a look) alight or be steadily directed on. ➤(**rest on**) be based on or grounded in; depend on. ➤(**rest something in/on**) place hope, trust, or confidence on or in. ➤(often **rest with**) (of power, responsibility, etc.) belong to a specified person or group. **3** N. Amer. conclude the case for the prosecution or defence in a court of law. ● **n.** **1** the action or a period of resting. ➤a motionless state. **2** Music an interval of silence of a specified duration. ➤the sign denoting this. ➤a pause in elocution, verse, etc. **3** an object that is used to hold or support something.
– PHRASES **rest one's case** conclude one's presentation of evidence and arguments in a lawsuit.
– DERIVATIVES **restful** adj. **restfully** adv. **restfulness** n. **restless** adj. **restlessly** adv. **restlessness** n.
– ORIGIN OE *ræst*, *rest* (n.), *ræstan*, *restan* (v.), of Gmc origin, from a root meaning 'league' or 'mile' (referring to a distance after which one rests).

**rest**[2] ● **n.** **1** the remaining part of something. ➤[treated as pl.] the remaining people or things; the others. **2** Anatomy a small, detached portion of an organ or tissue. **3** a rally in real tennis. ● **v.** remain or be left in a specified condition: *rest assured we will do everything we can.*
– ORIGIN ME: from OFr. *reste* (n.), *rester* (v.), from L. *restare* 'remain'.

**restart** ● **v.** start again.

**restate** ● **v.** state (something) again or differently.

**restaurant** /'rɛst(ə)rɒnt, -r(ə)nt, -rɒ̃/ ● **n.** a place where people pay to sit and eat meals that are cooked and served on the premises.
– ORIGIN C19: from Fr., from *restaurer* 'provide food for' (lit. 'restore to a former state').

**restaurateur** /,rɛst(ə)rə'təː, ,rɛstɒr-/ ● **n.** a person who owns and manages a restaurant.
– ORIGIN C18: Fr., from *restaurer* (see **RESTAURANT**).

**restharrow** ● **n.** a sticky leguminous plant which has pink flowers and creeping woody stems with spines. [Genus *Ononis*.]
– ORIGIN C16: from obs. *rest* 'stop, arrest' + **HARROW** (because the tough stems impeded the progress of a harrow).

**rest home** ● **n.** a residential institution where old or frail people are cared for.

**restitutio in integrum** /rɛstɪ,tjuːtɪəʊ ɪn ɪn'tɛgrəm/ ● **n.** Law restoration of an injured party to the situation which would have prevailed had no injury been sustained.
– ORIGIN L., lit. 'restoration to the whole (i.e. uninjured) state'.

**restitution** ● **n.** **1** the restoration of something lost or stolen to its proper owner. **2** recompense for injury or loss. **3** the restoration of something to its original state. ➤Physics the resumption of an object's original shape or position through elastic recoil.
– DERIVATIVES **restitutive** adj.
– ORIGIN ME: from OFr., or from L. *restitutio(n-)*, from *restituere* 'restore'.

**restive** ● **adj.** **1** unable to keep still or silent; restless. **2** (of a horse) refusing to advance; stubbornly standing still or moving backwards or sideways.
– DERIVATIVES **restively** adv. **restiveness** n.
– ORIGIN C16: from OFr. *restif*, *-ive*, from L. *restare* 'remain'.

**restock** ● **v.** replenish with fresh stock or supplies.

**restoration** ● **n.** **1** the action or process of restoring. ➤a model or drawing representing the supposed original form of an extinct animal, ruined building, etc. **2** the return of a monarch to a throne, a head of state to government, or a regime to power. ➤(**the Restoration**) the re-establishment of Charles II as King of England in 1660, or the period following this.

**restorationism** ● **n.** a charismatic Christian movement seeking to restore the beliefs and practices of the early Church.
– DERIVATIVES **restorationist** n. & adj.

**restorative** • adj. **1** having the ability to restore health, strength, or a feeling of well-being. **2** Surgery & Dentistry relating to or concerned with the restoration of a damaged tooth or other part of the body. • n. a medicine or drink that restores health, strength, or well-being.
– DERIVATIVES **restoratively** adv.

**restore** • v. **1** bring back (a previous right, practice, or situation); reinstate. ➤return to a former condition or position. **2** repair or renovate. **3** give (something stolen or removed) back to the original owner.
– DERIVATIVES **restorable** adj. **restorer** n.
– ORIGIN ME: from OFr. *restorer*, from L. *restaurare* 'rebuild, restore'.

**restrain** • v. **1** prevent from doing something; keep within limits. ➤deprive of freedom of movement or personal liberty. **2** repress (a strong emotion).
– DERIVATIVES **restrainable** adj. **restrainer** n. **restraining** adj.
– ORIGIN ME: from OFr. *restreign-*, stem of *restreindre*, from L. *restringere*, from *re-* 'back' + *stringere* 'to tie'.

**restrained** • adj. **1** reserved, unemotional, or dispassionate. **2** understated and subtle; not ornate.
– DERIVATIVES **restrainedly** adv.

**restraint** • n. **1** the action of restraining. ➤a measure or condition that restrains. ➤a device which limits or prevents freedom of movement. **2** dispassionate or moderate behaviour; self-control.
– ORIGIN ME: from OFr. *restreinte*, fem. past part. of *restreindre* (see **RESTRAIN**).

**restraint of trade** • n. Law **1** action that interferes with free competition in a market. **2** a clause in a contract that restricts a person's right to carry on their trade or profession.

**restrict** • v. **1** put a limit on; keep under control. **2** deprive of freedom of movement or action.
– ORIGIN C16 (earlier (ME) as *restriction*): from L. *restrict-*, *restringere* (see **RESTRAIN**).

**restricted** • adj. **1** limited in extent, number, or scope. **2** not to be revealed or open to the public for reasons of national security.
– DERIVATIVES **restrictedly** adv. **restrictedness** n.

**restriction** • n. **1** a limiting condition or measure. **2** the action or state of restricting or being restricted.
– DERIVATIVES **restrictionism** n. **restrictionist** adj. & n.

**restriction enzyme** (also **restriction endonuclease**) • n. Biochemistry an enzyme with the property of cleaving DNA molecules at or near a specific sequence of bases.

**restriction fragment** • n. Biochemistry a fragment of a DNA molecule that has been cleaved by a restriction enzyme.

**restrictive** • adj. **1** imposing restrictions. **2** Grammar (of a relative clause or descriptive phrase) serving to specify the particular instance or instances being mentioned.
– DERIVATIVES **restrictively** adv. **restrictiveness** n.

**restrictive covenant** • n. Law a covenant imposing a restriction on the use of land so that the value and enjoyment of adjoining land will be preserved.

**restrictive practice** • n. Brit. **1** an arrangement by a group of workers to limit output or restrict the entry of new workers in order to protect their own interests. **2** an arrangement in industry or trade that restricts or controls competition between firms.

**restring** • v. (past and past part. **restrung**) **1** fit new strings to. **2** string (beads) again.

**restroom** • n. chiefly N. Amer. a toilet in a public building.

**restructure** • v. **1** organize differently. **2** Finance convert (a debt) into debt that is repayable at a later time.

**restyle** • v. **1** rearrange or remake in a new shape or layout. **2** give a new designation to. • n. an instance of restyling.

**resubmit** • v. submit (a plan, application, etc.) again.

**result** • n. **1** a consequence, effect, or outcome. ➤(also **results**) a satisfactory outcome: *persistence guarantees results.* **2** an item of information or a quantity or formula obtained by experiment or calculation. **3** a final score, mark, or placing in a sporting event or examination. **4** (usu. **results**) the outcome of a business's trading over a given period, expressed as a statement of profit or loss. • v. occur or follow as a result. ➤(**result in**) have (a specified end or outcome).
– ORIGIN ME: from med. L. *resultare* 'to result', earlier in the sense 'spring back', from *re-* (expressing intensive force) + *saltare* (frequentative of *salire* 'to jump').

**resultant** • adj. occurring or produced as a result. • n. technical a force or other vector quantity which is equivalent to two or more component vectors acting at the same point.

**resume** • v. begin again or continue after a pause or interruption. ➤take or put on again.
– DERIVATIVES **resumable** adj. **resumption** n.
– ORIGIN ME: from OFr. *resumer* or L. *resumere*, from *re-* 'back' + *sumere* 'take'.

**résumé** /ˈrɛzjʊmeɪ/ • n. **1** a summary. **2** N. Amer. a curriculum vitae.
– ORIGIN C19: Fr., lit. 'resumed', past part. (used as n.) of *résumer.*

**resupinate** /rɪˈsuːpɪneɪt, -ˈsjuː-/ • adj. Botany (of a leaf, flower, fruiting body, etc.) upside down.
– DERIVATIVES **resupination** n.
– ORIGIN C18: from L. *resupinatus* 'bent back'.

**resupply** • v. (**-ies**, **-ied**) provide with or acquire a fresh supply.

**resurface** • v. **1** put a new coating on or re-form (a surface). **2** come back up to the surface of deep water. **3** arise or become evident again.

**resurgent** • adj. increasing or reviving after a period of little activity, popularity, or occurrence.
– DERIVATIVES **resurgence** n.
– ORIGIN C18 (as n.): from L. *resurgent-*, *resurgere* 'rise again'.

**resurrect** • v. **1** restore to life. **2** revive the practice, use, or memory of.
– ORIGIN C18: back-form. from **RESURRECTION**.

**resurrection** • n. the action of resurrecting. ➤(**the Resurrection**) (in Christian belief) Christ's rising from the dead. ➤(**the Resurrection**) (in Christian belief) the rising of the dead at the Last Judgement.
– ORIGIN ME: from OFr., from late L. *resurrectio(n-)*, from *resurgere* (see **RESURGENT**).

**resurrection plant** • n. the rose of Jericho or other plant which is able to survive drought, typically folding up when dry and unfolding when moistened.

**resuscitate** /rɪˈsʌsɪteɪt/ • v. **1** revive from unconsciousness. **2** make active or vigorous again.
– DERIVATIVES **resuscitation** n. **resuscitative** adj. **resuscitator** n.
– ORIGIN C16 (earlier (C15) as *resuscitation*): from L. *resuscitat-*, *resuscitare* 'raise again'.

**ret** /rɛt/ (also **rate**) • v. (**retted**, **retting**) soak (flax or hemp) in water to soften it.
– ORIGIN ME: rel. to **ROT**.

**ret.** • abbrev. retired.

**retable** /rɪˈteɪb(ə)l/ (also **retablo** /rɪˈtɑːbləʊ/) • n. (pl. **retables** or **retablos**) a frame enclosing decorated panels or a ledge for ornaments, above and behind an altar.
– ORIGIN C19: from Fr. *rétable*, from Sp. *retablo*, from med. L. *retrotabulum* 'rear table'.

**retail** /ˈriːteɪl/ • n. the sale of goods to the public for use or consumption rather than for resale. • adv. being sold in such a way. • v. /also rɪˈteɪl/ **1** sell (goods) in such a way. ➤(**retail at/for**) be sold in this way for (a specified price). **2** recount or relate details of.
– DERIVATIVES **retailer** n.
– ORIGIN ME: from an Anglo-Norman Fr. use of OFr. *retaille* 'a piece cut off', from *retaillier*, from *re-* (expressing intensive force) + *tailler* 'to cut'.

**retail price index** • n. (in the UK) an index of the variation in the prices of retail goods and other items.

**retail therapy** • n. humorous the practice of shopping in order to make oneself feel more cheerful.

**retain** • v. **1** continue to have; keep possession of. ➤not abolish, discard, or alter. ➤keep in one's memory. **2** absorb and continue to hold (a substance). **3** keep in place;

hold fixed. **4** keep engaged in one's service. ➤ secure the services of (a barrister) with a preliminary payment.
– DERIVATIVES **retainability** n. **retainable** adj. **retaining** adj. **retainment** n.
– ORIGIN ME: via Anglo-Norman Fr. from OFr. *retenir*, from L. *retinere*, from *re-* 'back' + *tenere* 'hold'.

**retainer** ● n. **1** a thing that holds something in place. **2** a fee paid in advance to a barrister, in order to secure their services for use when required. **3** Brit. a reduced rent paid to retain accommodation during a period of non-occupancy. **4** a servant who has worked for a person or family for a long time.

**retaining wall** ● n. a wall that holds back earth or water on one side of it.

**retake** ● v. (past **retook**; past part. **retaken**) **1** take (a test or examination) again. **2** regain possession of. ● n. **1** a test or examination that is retaken. **2** an instance of filming a scene or recording a piece of music again.

**retaliate** /rɪ'talɪeɪt/ ● v. make an attack or assault in return for a similar attack.
– DERIVATIVES **retaliation** n. **retaliative** adj. **retaliator** n. **retaliatory** adj.
– ORIGIN C17 (earlier (C16) as *retaliation*): from L. *retaliat-*, *retaliare* 'return in kind'.

**retard** ● v. /rɪ'tɑːd/ delay or hold back in terms of development or progress. ● n. /'riːtɑːd/ derogatory a mentally handicapped person.
– DERIVATIVES **retardation** n. **retarder** n.
– ORIGIN C15 (earlier (ME) as *retardation*): from Fr. *retarder*, from L. *retardare*, from *re-* 'back' + *tardus* 'slow'.

**retardant** ● adj. [in combination] preventing or inhibiting: *fire-retardant polymers*. ● n. a fabric or substance that prevents or inhibits the outbreak of fire.
– DERIVATIVES **retardancy** n.

**retardataire** /rɪˌtɑːdə'tɛː/ ● adj. (of a work of art or architecture) executed in an earlier style.
– ORIGIN from Fr.

**retardate** /rɪ'tɑːdeɪt/ ● n. N. Amer., dated or derogatory a mentally handicapped person.

**retarded** ● adj. less advanced in mental, physical, or social development than is usual for one's age.

**retch** ● v. make the sound and movement of vomiting. ● n. an instance of retching.
– ORIGIN C19: var. of dial. *reach*, from a Gmc base meaning 'spittle'.

**retd** (also **ret.**) ● abbrev. retired.

**rete** /'riːti/ ● n. (pl. **retia** /-tɪə, -ʃɪə/) Anatomy an elaborate network of blood vessels or nerve cells.
– ORIGIN C16: from L. *rete* 'net'.

**retell** ● v. (past and past part. **retold**) tell (a story) again or differently.

**retention** ● n. **1** the act of retaining or state of being retained. **2** failure to eliminate a substance from the body.
– ORIGIN ME: from OFr., from L. *retentio(n-)*, from *retinere* (see **RETAIN**).

**retentive** ● adj. **1** (of a person's memory) effective in retaining facts and impressions. **2** able to retain or hold in place.
– DERIVATIVES **retentively** adv. **retentiveness** n.

**retentivity** ● n. (pl. **-ies**) Physics the ability of a substance to retain or resist magnetization.

**rethink** ● v. (past and past part. **rethought**) assess or consider (a policy or course of action) again. ● n. an instance of rethinking.

**retia** plural form of **RETE**.

**retiarius** /ˌrɛtɪ'ɑːrɪəs, -'ɛːrɪəs/ ● n. (pl. **retiarii** /-rɪʌɪ, -rɪiː/) an ancient Roman gladiator who used a net to trap his opponent.
– ORIGIN L., from *rete* 'net'.

**reticent** /'rɛtɪs(ə)nt/ ● adj. not revealing one's thoughts or feelings readily.
– DERIVATIVES **reticence** n. **reticently** adv.
– ORIGIN C19 (earlier (C17) as *reticence*): from L. *reticent-*, *reticere* 'remain silent'.

**reticle** /'rɛtɪk(ə)l/ (also **reticule**) ● n. North American term for **GRATICULE**.
– ORIGIN C18: from L. *reticulum* 'net'.

**reticula** plural form of **RETICULUM**.

**reticular formation** (also **reticular activating system**) ● n. Anatomy a diffuse network of nerve pathways in the brainstem connecting the spinal cord, cerebrum, and cerebellum.

**reticulate** ● v. /rɪ'tɪkjʊleɪt/ divide or mark in such a way as to resemble a net or network. ● adj. /rɪ'tɪkjʊlət/ chiefly Botany & Zoology reticulated.
– DERIVATIVES **reticulation** n.
– ORIGIN C17: from L. *reticulatus* 'reticulated', from *reticulum* (see **RETICULUM**).

**reticulated** ● adj. **1** constructed, arranged, or marked like a net or network. **2** (of porcelain) having a pattern of interlacing lines, especially of pierced work, forming a net or web. **3** Architecture relating to or denoting a style of decorated tracery characterized by circular shapes drawn at top and bottom into ogees, resulting in a net-like framework.

**reticulated python** ● n. a very large Asian python patterned with dark patches outlined in black. [*Python reticulatus*.]

**reticule** /'rɛtɪkjuːl/ ● n. **1** chiefly historical a woman's small handbag, typically having a drawstring and decorated with embroidery or beading. **2** variant spelling of **RETICLE**.
– ORIGIN C18: from Fr. *réticule*, from L. *reticulum* (see **RETICULUM**).

**reticulin** /rɪ'tɪkjʊlɪn/ ● n. Biochemistry a structural protein resembling collagen, present in connective tissue as a network of fine fibres.
– ORIGIN C19: from *reticular* (see **RETICULUM**) + **-IN**[1].

**reticulocyte** /rɪ'tɪkjʊlə(ʊ)sʌɪt/ ● n. Physiology an immature red blood cell without a nucleus, having a granular or reticulated appearance when suitably stained.

**reticuloendothelial** /rɪˌtɪkjʊləʊɛndə(ʊ)'θiːlɪəl/ ● adj. Physiology relating to or denoting a system of fixed and circulating phagocytic cells involved in the immune response.
– ORIGIN 1920s: from **RETICULUM** + ***endothelial*** (see **ENDOTHELIUM**).

**reticulum** /rɪ'tɪkjʊləm/ ● n. (pl. **reticula** /-lə/) **1** a fine network or net-like structure. **2** Zoology the second stomach of a ruminant, having a honeycomb-like structure, receiving food from the rumen and passing it to the omasum.
– DERIVATIVES **reticular** adj.
– ORIGIN C17 (earlier (C16) as *reticular*): from L., dimin. of *rete* 'net'.

**retiform** /'riːtɪfɔːm, 'rɛtɪ-/ ● adj. net-like.
– ORIGIN C17: from L. *rete* 'net' + **-IFORM**.

**retina** /'rɛtɪnə/ ● n. (pl. **retinas** or **retinae** /-niː/) a layer at the back of the eyeball that contains cells sensitive to light, which trigger nerve impulses that pass via the optic nerve to the brain, where a visual image is formed.
– DERIVATIVES **retinal** adj. **retinitis** n.
– ORIGIN ME: from med. L., from L. *rete* 'net'.

**retinitis pigmentosa** /ˌpɪgmɛn'təʊsə/ ● n. Medicine a hereditary eye disease characterized by black pigmentation and gradual degeneration of the retina.
– ORIGIN C19: *pigmentosa*, fem. of L. *pigmentosus*, from *pigmentum* 'pigment'.

**retinoid** /'rɛtɪnɔɪd/ ● n. Biochemistry any of a group of compounds having effects like those of vitamin A.

**retinol** /'rɛtɪnɒl/ ● n. Biochemistry vitamin A, a yellow compound which is essential for growth and vision in dim light and is found in vegetables, egg yolk, and fish-liver oil.

**retinopathy** /ˌrɛtɪ'nɒpəθi/ ● n. Medicine disease of the retina which results in impairment or loss of vision.

**retinue** /'rɛtɪnjuː/ ● n. a group of advisers or assistants accompanying an important person.
– ORIGIN ME: from OFr. *retenue*, fem. past part. (used as n.) of *retenir* 'keep back, retain'.

**retiral** /rɪ'tʌɪr(ə)l/ ● n. Scottish a person's retirement from a job or office.

**retire** ● v. **1** leave one's job and cease to work, especially because one has reached a particular age. ➤(of a sports player) cease to play competitively. **2** withdraw from a race or match because of accident or injury. ➤Baseball put out (a batter); cause (a side) to end a turn at bat. **3** withdraw to or from a particular place. ➤(of a jury) leave the courtroom to decide the verdict of a trial. ➤(of a military force) retreat. **4** go to bed. **5** Economics withdraw (a bill or note) from circulation or currency. **6** Finance pay off or cancel (a debt).

– DERIVATIVES **retired** adj. **retiredness** n. **retirer** n.

– ORIGIN C16: from Fr. *retirer*, from *re-* 'back' + *tirer* 'draw'.

**retiré** /rə'tɪəreɪ/ ● **n.** (pl. pronounced same) Ballet a movement in which one leg is raised at right angles to the body until the toe is in line with the knee of the supporting leg.

– ORIGIN Fr., lit. 'drawn back'.

**retirement** ● **n. 1** the action or fact of retiring. **2** the period of one's life after retiring from work. **3** seclusion. ➤archaic a secluded or private place.

**retirement pension** ● **n.** Brit. a pension paid by the state to retired people above a certain age.

**retiring** ● **adj.** tending to avoid company; shy.

– DERIVATIVES **retiringly** adv.

**retold** past and past participle of **RETELL**.

**retook** past of **RETAKE**.

**retool** ● **v. 1** equip (a factory) with new or adapted tools. **2** chiefly N. Amer. adapt, alter, or prepare for a new purpose or challenge.

**retort**[1] ● **v. 1** say something sharp, angry, or witty in answer to a remark or accusation. **2** archaic return or repay (an insult or injury). ● **n.** a sharp, angry, or witty reply.

– ORIGIN C15: from L. *retort-*, *retorquere* 'twist back'.

**retort**[2] ● **n. 1** a container or furnace for carrying out a chemical process on a large or industrial scale. **2** historical a glass container with a long neck, used in distilling liquids and other chemical operations. ● **v.** heat in a retort.

– ORIGIN C17: from Fr. *retorte*, from med. L. *retorta*, fem. past part. of *retorquere* 'twist back' (with ref. to the long recurved neck of the laboratory container).

**retouch** ● **v.** improve or repair (a painting, photograph, etc.) by making slight additions or alterations.

– DERIVATIVES **retoucher** n.

**retrace** ● **v. 1** go back over (the same route that one has just taken). ➤discover and follow (a route or course taken by someone else). **2** trace (something) back to its source or beginning.

**retract** ● **v. 1** draw or be drawn back or back in. **2** withdraw (a statement or accusation) as untrue or unjustified. ➤withdraw or go back on (an undertaking or promise).

– DERIVATIVES **retractable** adj. **retraction** n. **retractive** adj.

– ORIGIN ME: from L. *retract-*, *retrahere* 'draw back'; the senses 'withdraw (a statement)' and 'go back on' via OFr. from *retractare* 'reconsider'.

**retractile** /rɪ'traktʌɪl/ ● **adj.** Zoology capable of being retracted.

– DERIVATIVES **retractility** n.

**retractor** ● **n. 1** a device for retracting something. **2** (also **retractor muscle**) chiefly Zoology a muscle serving to retract a part of the body. Compare with **PROTRACTOR**.

**retrain** ● **v.** teach or learn new skills, especially for a different job.

**retread** ● **v. 1** (past **retrod**; past part. **retrodden**) go back over (a path or one's steps). **2** (past and past part. **retreaded**) put a new tread on (a worn tyre). ● **n. 1** a tyre that has been given a new tread; a remould. **2** informal an altered or rearranged version of something.

**retreat** ● **v.** (of an army) withdraw from confrontation with enemy forces. ➤move back from a difficult or uncomfortable situation. ➤withdraw to a quiet or secluded place. ● **n. 1** an act of retreating. ➤a signal for a military force to withdraw. **2** a quiet or secluded place. ➤a period or place of seclusion for the purposes of prayer and meditation. **3** a military musical ceremony carried out at sunset.

– ORIGIN ME: from OFr. *retret* (n.), *retraiter* (v.), from L. *retrahere* (see **RETRACT**).

**retrench** ● **v. 1** reduce costs or spending in response to economic difficulty. ➤chiefly Austral. make (an employee) redundant in order to reduce costs. **2** formal reduce or diminish.

– DERIVATIVES **retrenchment** n.

– ORIGIN C16: from obs. Fr. *retrencher*, var. of *retrancher*, from *re-* (expressing reversal) + *trancher* 'to cut, slice'.

**retrial** ● **n.** Law a second or further trial.

**retribution** ● **n.** punishment inflicted in the spirit of moral outrage or personal vengeance.

– DERIVATIVES **retributive** /rɪ'trɪbjʊtɪv/ adj. **retributory** /rɪ'trɪbjʊt(ə)ri/ adj.

– ORIGIN ME: from late L. *retributio(n-)*, from *retribut-*, *retribuere* 'assign again'.

**retrieve** ● **v. 1** get or bring back. **2** (of a dog) find and bring back (game that has been shot). **3** find or extract (information stored in a computer). **4** rescue from a state of difficulty or collapse. ● **n.** an act of retrieving.

– DERIVATIVES **retrievability** n. **retrievable** adj. **retrieval** n.

– ORIGIN ME: from OFr. *retroeve-*, stressed stem of *retrover* 'find again'.

**retriever** ● **n.** a dog of a breed used for retrieving game.

**retro** ● **adj.** imitative of a style from the recent past. ● **n.** retro clothes, music, or style.

– ORIGIN 1960s: from Fr. *rétro*, abbrev. of *rétrograde* 'retrograde'.

**retro-** ● **comb. form 1** denoting action that is directed backwards or is reciprocal: *retroject*. **2** denoting location behind: *retrochoir*.

– ORIGIN from L. *retro* 'backwards'.

**retroactive** ● **adj.** (especially of legislation) taking effect from a date in the past.

– DERIVATIVES **retroaction** n. **retroactively** adv. **retroactivity** n.

**retrocede** /ˌrɛtrə(ʊ)'siːd/ ● **v.** cede (territory) back again.

– DERIVATIVES **retrocession** n.

**retrochoir** /'rɛtrəʊˌkwʌɪə/ ● **n.** the part of a cathedral or large church behind the high altar.

– ORIGIN C19: from med. L. *retrochorus* (see **RETRO-**, **CHOIR**).

**retrod** past of **RETREAD** (in sense 1).

**retrodden** past participle of **RETREAD** (in sense 1).

**retrofit** /'rɛtrəʊfɪt/ ● **v.** (**retrofitted**, **retrofitting**) fit with a component or accessory not fitted during manufacture. ● **n.** an act of retrofitting.

– ORIGIN 1950s: blend of **RETROACTIVE** and **REFIT**.

**retroflex** /'rɛtrə(ʊ)flɛks/ (also **retroflexed**) ● **adj. 1** Anatomy & Medicine turned backwards. **2** Phonetics pronounced with the tip of the tongue curled up towards the hard palate.

– DERIVATIVES **retroflexion** n.

– ORIGIN C18: from L. *retroflex-*, *retroflectere* 'bend backwards'.

**retrograde** ● **adj. 1** directed or moving backwards. ➤(of the order of something) reversed; inverse. **2** reverting to an earlier and inferior condition. **3** Geology (of a metamorphic change) resulting from a decrease in temperature or pressure. **4** Astronomy & Astrology (of the apparent motion of a planet) in a reverse direction from normal (so from east to west), resulting from the relative orbital progress of the earth and the planet. The opposite of **PROGRADE**. **5** Astronomy (of the orbit or rotation of a planet or planetary satellite) in a reverse direction from that normal in the solar system. ● **v. 1** go back in position or time. **2** revert to an earlier and inferior condition. **3** Astronomy show retrograde motion.

– DERIVATIVES **retrogradation** n. **retrogradely** adv.

– ORIGIN ME: from L. *retrogradus*, from *retro* 'backwards' + *gradus* 'step'.

**retrogress** /ˌrɛtrə(ʊ)'grɛs/ ● **v.** go back to an earlier and typically inferior state; engage in retrogression.

**retrogression** ● **n. 1** the process of retrogressing. **2** Astronomy retrogradation.

– DERIVATIVES **retrogressive** adj.

– ORIGIN C17: from **RETRO-**, on the pattern of *progression*.

**retrorocket** • n. a small auxiliary rocket on a spacecraft or missile, fired in the direction of travel to slow it down.

**retrorse** /rɪˈtrɔːs/ • adj. Biology turned or pointing backwards.
– ORIGIN C19: from L. *retrorsus*, contr. of *retroversus*, from *retro* 'backwards' + *vers-*, *vertere* 'turn'.

**retrospect** • n. a survey or review of a past course of events or period of time.
– PHRASES **in retrospect** when looking back on a past event or situation; with hindsight.
– DERIVATIVES **retrospection** n.
– ORIGIN C17: from **RETRO-**, on the pattern of *prospect*.

**retrospective** • adj. **1** looking back on or dealing with past events or situations. ➤(of an exhibition or compilation) showing the development of an artist's work over a period of time. **2** (of a statute or legal decision) taking effect from a date in the past. • n. a retrospective exhibition or compilation.
– DERIVATIVES **retrospectively** adv.

**retrotransposon** /ˌrɛtrəʊtransˈpəʊzɒn, -trɑːns-, -tranz-/ • n. Genetics a transposon whose sequence shows homology with that of a retrovirus.

**retroussé** /rəˈtruːseɪ/ • adj. (of a person's nose) turned up at the tip.
– ORIGIN C19: Fr., lit. 'tucked up', past part. of *retrousser*.

**retroverted** /ˈrɛtrəvəːt/ • adj. Anatomy (of the uterus) tilted abnormally backwards.
– DERIVATIVES **retroversion** n.
– ORIGIN C18: from L. *retrovertere* 'turn backwards' + **-ED**[2].

**retrovirus** /ˈrɛtrəʊˌvʌɪrəs/ • n. Biology any of a group of RNA viruses which insert a DNA copy of their genome into the host cell in order to replicate, e.g. HIV.
– ORIGIN 1970s: mod. L., from the initial letters of *reverse transcriptase* + **VIRUS**.

**retry** • v. (**-ies**, **-ied**) Law try (a defendant or case) again.

**retsina** /rɛtˈsiːnə/ • n. a Greek white wine flavoured with resin.
– ORIGIN from mod. Gk.

**retune** • v. tune again or differently.

**return** • v. **1** come or go back to a place. ➤(**return to**) go back to (a particular state or activity). ➤(of a sensation) come back after a period of absence. ➤Golf play the last nine holes in a round of eighteen holes. ➤give or send back or put back in place. **2** feel, say, or do (the same feeling, action, etc.) in response. ➤(in tennis and other sports) hit or send (the ball) back to an opponent. ➤American Football intercept (a pass, kick, or fumble by the opposing team) and run upfield with the ball. **3** (of a judge or jury) state or present (a verdict). **4** yield or make (a profit). **5** (of an electorate) elect (someone) to office. **6** Bridge lead (a card) after taking a trick. **7** Architecture continue (a wall) in a changed direction, especially at right angles. • n. **1** an act of returning. **2** a thing which has been returned, especially an unwanted ticket for an event. **3** (also **return ticket**) chiefly Brit. a ticket allowing travel to a place and back again. **4** an electrical conductor bringing a current back to its source. **5** (also **return match** or **game**) a second contest between the same opponents. **6** (also **returns**) a profit from an investment. **7** an official report or statement submitted in response to a formal demand. ➤Law an endorsement or report by a court officer or sheriff on a writ. **8** (also **carriage return**) a mechanism or key on a typewriter that returns the carriage to a fixed position at the start of a new line. ➤(also **return key**) a key pressed on a computer keyboard to simulate a carriage return. **9** Architecture a part receding from the line of the front, for example the side of a house or of a window opening.
– PHRASES **by return** (**of post**) Brit. in the next available mail delivery to the sender. **many happy returns** (**of the day**) a greeting to someone on their birthday.
– DERIVATIVES **returnable** adj. **returner** n.
– ORIGIN ME: the verb from OFr. *returner*, from L. *re-* 'back' + *tornare* 'to turn'; the noun via Anglo-Norman Fr.

**return crease** • n. Cricket each of two lines on either side of the wicket between which the bowler must deliver the ball.

**returnee** • n. **1** a refugee returning from abroad. **2** a person returning to work after an extended absence.

**returning officer** • n. Brit. the official in each constituency or electorate who conducts an election and announces the result.

**retype** • v. type (text) again.

**reunify** • v. (**-ies**, **-ied**) restore political unity to.
– DERIVATIVES **reunification** n.

**reunion** • n. **1** the process or an instance of reuniting. **2** a social gathering attended by members of a group of people who have not seen each other for some time.

**reunite** • v. come together or cause to come together again after a period of separation or disunity.

**reuse** • v. /riːˈjuːz/ use again or more than once. • n. /riːˈjuːs/ the action of using something again.
– DERIVATIVES **reusable** adj.

**Rev.** • abbrev. **1** Revelation (in biblical references). **2** Reverend.

**rev** informal • n. (**revs**) the number of revolutions of an engine per minute. • v. (**revved**, **revving**) increase the running speed of (an engine) by pressing the accelerator, especially while the clutch is disengaged.

**revalue** • v. (**revalues**, **revalued**, **revaluing**) **1** value again. **2** Economics adjust the value of (a currency) in relation to other currencies.
– DERIVATIVES **revaluation** n.

**revamp** • v. give new and improved form, structure, or appearance to. • n. a new and improved version.

**revanchism** /rɪˈvan(t)ʃɪz(ə)m/ • n. a policy of seeking to retaliate, especially to recover lost territory.
– DERIVATIVES **revanchist** adj. & n.
– ORIGIN C20: from Fr. *revanche*, lit. 'revenge' + **-ISM**.

**rev counter** • n. an instrument that measures the rate of revolutions of an engine.

**Revd** • abbrev. Reverend.

**reveal**[1] • v. **1** disclose (previously unknown or secret information). ➤make known to humans by divine or supernatural means. **2** cause or allow to be seen.
– DERIVATIVES **revealable** adj. **revealer** n.
– ORIGIN ME: from OFr. *reveler* or L. *revelare*, from *re-* 'again' (expressing reversal) + *velum* 'veil'.

**reveal**[2] • n. either side surface of an aperture in a wall for a door or window.
– ORIGIN C17: from obs. *revale* 'to lower', from OFr. *revaler*, from *re-* 'back' + *avaler* 'go down, sink'.

**revealed religion** • n. religion based on divine revelation.

**revealing** • adj. **1** divulging interesting or significant information. **2** (of a garment) allowing much of the wearer's body to be seen.
– DERIVATIVES **revealingly** adv.

**revegetate** • v. produce new vegetation on (disturbed or barren ground).
– DERIVATIVES **revegetation** n.

**reveille** /rɪˈvali/ • n. a military waking signal sounded especially on a bugle or drum.
– ORIGIN C17: from Fr. *réveillez!* 'wake up!', imper. pl. of *réveiller*, based on L. *vigilare* 'keep watch'.

**revel** • v. (**revelled**, **revelling**; US **reveled**, **reveling**) **1** engage in lively and noisy festivities. **2** (**revel in**) gain great pleasure from. • n. (**revels**) lively and noisy festivities.
– DERIVATIVES **reveller** n. **revelry** n. (pl. **-ies**).
– ORIGIN ME: from OFr. *reveler* 'rise up in rebellion', from L. *rebellare* 'to rebel'.

**revelation** • n. **1** a surprising disclosure. ➤the revealing of something previously unknown. ➤a surprising or remarkable thing. **2** a divine or supernatural disclosure to humans. ➤(**Revelation** or informal **Revelations**) (in full **the Revelation of St John the Divine**) the last book of the New Testament, recounting a divine revelation of the future to St John.
– DERIVATIVES **revelational** adj.
– ORIGIN ME: from OFr., or from late L. *revelatio(n-)*, from *revelare* (see **REVEAL**[1]).

**revelationist** • n. a believer in divine revelation.

**revelatory** /ˌrɛvəˈleɪt(ə)ri, ˈrɛv(ə)lət(ə)ri/ ● **adj.** revealing.

**revenant** /ˈrɛv(ə)nənt/ ● **n.** a person who has returned, especially supposedly from the dead.
– ORIGIN C19: Fr., lit. 'coming back', pres. part. (used as n.) of *revenir*.

**revenge** ● **n.** retaliation for an injury or wrong. ➤the desire to inflict this. ● **v.** (**revenge oneself** or **be revenged**) chiefly poetic/literary inflict revenge for an injury or wrong done to oneself. ➤inflict revenge on behalf of (someone else). ➤inflict revenge for (a wrong or injury).
– DERIVATIVES **revenger** n. (poetic/literary).
– ORIGIN ME: from OFr. *revencher*, from late L. *revindicare*, from *re-* (expressing intensive force) + *vindicare* 'claim, avenge'.

**revengeful** ● **adj.** eager for revenge.
– DERIVATIVES **revengefully** adv. **revengefulness** n.

**revenue** ● **n.** income, especially when of a company and of a substantial nature. ➤a state's annual income from which public expenses are met. ➤(**revenues**) items or amounts constituting revenue. ➤(**the revenue**) the department of the civil service collecting revenue.
– ORIGIN ME: from OFr. *revenu(e)* 'returned', past part. (used as n.) of *revenir*, from L. *revenire* 'return'.

**revenue tariff** ● **n.** a tariff imposed to raise government revenue rather than protect domestic industries.

**reverb** /ˈriːvəːb, rɪˈvəːb/ ● **n.** an effect whereby the sound from an amplifier or amplified musical instrument is made to reverberate. ➤a device producing this effect.

**reverberate** ● **v.** **1** (of a loud noise) be repeated as an echo. ➤archaic return or re-echo (a sound). **2** have continuing serious effects.
– DERIVATIVES **reverberant** adj. **reverberantly** adv. **reverberation** n. **reverberative** adj. **reverberator** n. **reverberatory** adj.
– ORIGIN C15 (earlier (ME) as *reverberation*): from L. *reverberat-*, *reverberare* 'strike again', from *re-* 'back' + *verberare* 'to lash'.

**reverberatory furnace** ● **n.** a furnace in which the roof and walls are heated by flames and radiate heat on to material in the centre.

**revere** /rɪˈvɪə/ ● **v.** respect or admire deeply.
– ORIGIN C17: from Fr. *révérer* or L. *revereri*, from *re-* (expressing intensive force) + *vereri* 'to fear'.

**reverence** ● **n. 1** deep respect. **2** archaic a bow or curtsy. **3** (**His/Your Reverence**) a title given to a member of the clergy, especially a priest in Ireland. ● **v.** regard or treat with reverence.
– ORIGIN ME: from OFr., from L. *reverentia*, from *revereri* (see **REVERE**).

**reverend** ● **adj.** a title or form of address to members of the clergy. ● **n.** informal a clergyman.
– ORIGIN ME: from OFr., or from L. *reverendus* 'person to be revered', gerundive of *revereri* (see **REVERE**).

**Reverend Mother** ● **n.** the title of the Mother Superior of a convent.

**reverent** ● **adj.** showing reverence.
– DERIVATIVES **reverential** adj. **reverentially** adv. **reverently** adv.

**reverie** /ˈrɛv(ə)ri/ ● **n. 1** a daydream. ➤archaic a fanciful idea or theory. **2** Music an instrumental piece suggesting a dreamy or musing state.
– ORIGIN C17: from obs. Fr. *resverie*, from OFr. *reverie* 'rejoicing, revelry', from *rever* 'be delirious'.

**revers** /rɪˈvɪə/ ● **n.** (pl. same /-ˈvɪəz/) the turned-back edge of a garment revealing the underside, especially at the lapel.
– ORIGIN C19: from Fr., lit. 'reverse'.

**reversal** ● **n. 1** a change to an opposite direction, position, or course of action. ➤Law an annulment of a judgement made by a lower court or authority. ➤an adverse change of fortune. **2** Photography direct production of a positive image from an exposed film or plate.

**reverse** /rɪˈvəːs/ ● **v. 1** move or cause to move backwards. ➤(of an engine) work in a contrary direction. **2** turn the other way round or up or inside out. **3** make the opposite of what it was. ➤swap (positions or functions). **4** Law revoke or annul (a judgement by a lower court or authority). ● **adj. 1** going in or turned towards the opposite direction. ➤operating or behaving in a way contrary to that which is usual or expected. **2** Geology denoting a fault in which a relative downward movement occurred in the strata on the underside of the fault plane. ● **n. 1** a complete change of direction or action. **2** reverse gear. **3** (**the reverse**) the opposite or contrary. **4** a setback or defeat. **5** American Football a play in which the direction of attack is reversed. **6** the opposite side or face to the observer. ➤a left-hand page of an open book, or the back of a loose document. ➤the side of a coin or medal bearing the value or secondary design.
– PHRASES **reverse arms** hold a rifle with the butt upwards. **reverse the charges** make the recipient of a telephone call responsible for payment.
– DERIVATIVES **reversely** adv. **reverser** n. **reversibility** n. **reversible** adj. **reversibly** adv.
– ORIGIN ME: from OFr. *revers*, *reverse* (n.), *reverser* (v.), from L. *revers-*, *revertere* 'turn back'.

**reverse engineering** ● **n.** the reproduction of another manufacturer's product after detailed examination of its construction or composition.

**reverse gear** ● **n.** a gear making a vehicle or piece of machinery move or work backwards.

**reverse takeover** ● **n.** a takeover of a public company by a smaller company.

**reversing light** ● **n.** Brit. a white light at the rear of a vehicle that shines when the vehicle is reversing.

**reversion** /rɪˈvəːʃ(ə)n/ ● **n. 1** a return to a previous state, practice, or belief. ➤Biology the action of reverting to a former or ancestral type. **2** Law the right to possess or succeed to property on the death of the present possessor or at the end of a lease. ➤a property to which someone has such a right. **3** a sum payable on a person's death, especially by way of life insurance. **4** (also **reversion disease**) an incurable disease of the blackcurrant transmitted by a mite.
– DERIVATIVES **reversionary** adj.

**reversioner** ● **n.** Law a person with the reversion to a property or privilege.

**revert** ● **v.** (**revert to**) **1** return to (a previous state, condition, etc.). ➤Biology return to (a former or ancestral type). **2** Law (of property) return or pass to by reversion. **3** archaic turn (one's eyes or steps) back.
– DERIVATIVES **reverter** n. (Law).
– ORIGIN ME: from OFr. *revertir* or L. *revertere* 'turn back'.

**revertant** Biology ● **adj.** that has reverted to the normal type from a mutant or abnormal form. ● **n.** a revertant cell, organism, or strain.

**revet** /rɪˈvɛt/ ● **v.** (**revetted**, **revetting**) [usu. as adj. **revetted**] face (a rampart, wall, etc.) with masonry, especially in fortification.
– ORIGIN C19: from Fr. *revêtir*, from late L. *revestire*, from *re-* 'again' + *vestire* 'clothe'.

**revetment** /rɪˈvɛtm(ə)nt/ ● **n. 1** a retaining wall or facing of masonry, supporting or protecting a rampart, wall, etc. **2** a barricade of earth or sandbags providing protection from blast or to prevent aircraft from overrunning when landing.
– ORIGIN C18: from Fr. *revêtement*, from *revêtir* (see **REVET**).

**review** ● **n. 1** a formal assessment of something with the intention of instituting change if necessary. ➤Law a reconsideration of a judgement or sentence by a higher court or authority. **2** a critical appraisal of a book, play, or other work. ➤a periodical with critical articles on current events and the arts. ➤a retrospective survey or report. **3** a ceremonial display and formal inspection of military or naval forces. **4** a facility for playing a tape recording during a fast wind. ● **v. 1** carry out or write a review of. **2** view or inspect again.
– DERIVATIVES **reviewable** adj. **reviewal** n. **reviewer** n.
– ORIGIN ME (as n.): from obs. Fr. *reveue*, from *revoir* 'see again'.

**revile** ● **v.** (usu. **be reviled**) criticize abusively.
– DERIVATIVES **revilement** n. **reviler** n.
– ORIGIN ME: from OFr. *reviler*, based on *vil* 'vile'.

**revise** ● v. **1** examine and improve or amend (something, especially written matter). ➤reconsider and alter (an opinion or judgement). **2** Brit. reread work done previously to improve one's knowledge, typically for an examination. ● n. Printing a proof including corrections made in an earlier proof.
– DERIVATIVES **revisable** adj. **revisal** n. **reviser** n. **revisory** adj.
– ORIGIN C16: from Fr. *réviser* 'look at', or L. *revisere* 'look at again'.

**revision** ● n. the action of revising. ➤a revised edition or form.
– DERIVATIVES **revisionary** adj.

**revisionism** ● n. often derogatory **1** a policy of revision or modification, especially of Marxism on evolutionary socialist or pluralist principles. **2** the theory or practice of revising one's attitude to something.
– DERIVATIVES **revisionist** n. & adj.

**revisit** ● v. (**revisited**, **revisiting**) come back to or visit again.

**revitalize** (also **-ise**) ● v. imbue with new life and vitality.
– DERIVATIVES **revitalization** n.

**revival** ● n. **1** an improvement in the condition or strength of something. **2** an instance of something becoming popular, active, or important again. ➤a reawakening of religious fervour, especially by means of evangelistic meetings. **3** a new production of an old play.

**revivalism** ● n. **1** belief in or the promotion of a revival of religious fervour. **2** a tendency or desire to revive a former custom or practice.
– DERIVATIVES **revivalist** n. & adj. **revivalistic** adj.

**revive** ● v. restore to or regain life, consciousness, or strength. ➤restore interest in or the popularity of. ➤restore or improve the position or condition of.
– DERIVATIVES **revivable** adj. **reviver** n.
– ORIGIN ME: from OFr. *revivre* or late L. *revivere*, from L. *re-* 'back' + *vivere* 'live'.

**revivify** /rɪˈvɪvɪfʌɪ/ ● v. (**-ies**, **-ied**) give new life or vigour to.
– DERIVATIVES **revivification** n.

**revoke** ● v. **1** end the validity or operation of (a decree, decision, or promise). **2** (in card games) fail to follow suit despite being able to do so.
– DERIVATIVES **revocability** n. **revocable** adj. **revocation** n. **revocatory** adj. **revoker** n.
– ORIGIN ME: from OFr. *revoquer* or L. *revocare*, from *re-* 'back' + *vocare* 'to call'.

**revolt** ● v. **1** rise in rebellion. ➤refuse to acknowledge someone or something as having authority. ➤[as adj. **revolted**] archaic having rebelled. **2** (often **be revolted**) cause to feel disgust. ● n. an attempt to end the authority of a person or body by rebelling. ➤a refusal to obey or conform.
– DERIVATIVES **revolting** adj. **revoltingly** adv.
– ORIGIN C16: from Fr. *révolte* (n.), *révolter* (v.), from Ital. *rivoltare*, based on L. *revolvere* (see **REVOLVE**).

**revolute** /ˈrɛvəl(j)uːt/ ● adj. Botany (especially of the edge of a leaf) curved or curled back.
– ORIGIN C18: from L. *revolutus* 'unrolled', past part. of *revolvere* (see **REVOLVE**).

**revolution** ● n. **1** a forcible overthrow of a government or social order, in favour of a new system. ➤(in Marxism) the class struggle expected to lead to political change and the triumph of communism. **2** a dramatic and wide-reaching change. **3** an instance of revolving. ➤motion in orbit or in a circular course or round an axis or centre. ➤the single completion of an orbit or rotation.
– DERIVATIVES **revolutionism** n. **revolutionist** n.
– ORIGIN ME: from OFr., or from late L. *revolutio(n-)*, from *revolvere* (see **REVOLVE**).

**revolutionary** ● adj. **1** involving or causing dramatic change or innovation. **2** engaged in, promoting, or relating to political revolution. ● n. (pl. **-ies**) a person who revolts or advocates revolution.

**revolutionize** (also **-ise**) ● v. change radically or fundamentally.

**revolve** ● v. **1** move in a circle on a central axis. ➤(**revolve about/around**) move in a circular orbit around. **2** (**revolve around**) treat as the most important point or element. **3** consider repeatedly and from different angles.
– ORIGIN ME: from L. *revolvere*, from *re-* 'back' (also expressing intensive force) + *volvere* 'roll'.

**revolver** ● n. **1** a pistol with revolving chambers enabling several shots to be fired without reloading. **2** an agreement to provide revolving credit.

**revolving credit** ● n. credit that is automatically renewed as debts are paid off.

**revolving door** ● n. **1** an entrance to a large building in which four partitions turn about a central axis. **2** a situation or place in which the same events or problems recur in a continuous cycle.

**revue** /rɪˈvjuː/ ● n. a light theatrical entertainment of short sketches, songs, and dances, typically dealing satirically with topical issues.
– ORIGIN Fr., lit. 'review'.

**revulsion** ● n. **1** a sense of disgust and loathing. **2** Medicine, chiefly historical the drawing of disease or blood congestion from one part of the body to another, e.g. by counterirritation.
– ORIGIN C16: from Fr., or from L. *revulsio(n-)*, from *revuls-*, *revellere* 'tear out'.

**reward** ● n. a thing given in recognition of service, effort, or achievement. ➤a fair return for good or bad behaviour. ➤a sum offered for the detection of a criminal, the restoration of lost property, etc. ● v. give a reward to. ➤show one's appreciation of (an action or quality) by making a gift. ➤(**be rewarded**) receive what one deserves.
– PHRASES **go to one's reward** euphemistic die.
– DERIVATIVES **rewardless** adj.
– ORIGIN ME: from Anglo-Norman Fr., var. of OFr. *reguard* 'regard, heed', also an early sense of the Engl. word.

**rewarding** ● adj. providing satisfaction.
– DERIVATIVES **rewardingly** adv.

**rewarewa** /ˈreɪwəˌreɪwə/ ● n. a tall red-flowered New Zealand tree producing decorative wood. [*Knightia excelsa*.]
– ORIGIN C19: from Maori.

**rewind** ● v. (past and past part. **rewound**) wind (a film or tape) back to the beginning. ● n. a mechanism for rewinding a film or tape.
– DERIVATIVES **rewinder** n.

**rewire** ● v. provide with new electric wiring.
– DERIVATIVES **rewirable** adj.

**reword** ● v. put into different words.

**rework** ● v. alter, revise, or reshape.

**rewound** past and past participle of **REWIND**.

**rewritable** ● adj. Computing (of a storage device) supporting overwriting of previously recorded data.

**rewrite** ● v. (past **rewrote**; past part. **rewritten**) write again in an altered or improved form. ● n. an instance of rewriting something. ➤a text that has been rewritten.

**Rex**[1] ● n. the reigning king (following a name or in the titles of lawsuits, e.g. *Rex v. Jones*: the Crown versus Jones).
– ORIGIN L., lit. 'king'.

**Rex**[2] ● n. a cat of a breed with curly fur, which lacks guard hairs.

**Rexine** /ˈrɛksiːn/ ● n. Brit. trademark an artificial leather, used in upholstery and bookbinding.
– ORIGIN C20: of unknown origin.

**Reye's syndrome** /ˈreɪz, ˈrʌɪz/ ● n. a life-threatening metabolic disorder in young children, of uncertain cause.
– ORIGIN 1960s: named after the Austral. paediatrician Ralph D. K. *Reye*.

**Reynard** /ˈrɛnɑːd, ˈreɪ-/ ● n. poetic/literary a fox.
– ORIGIN from OFr. *renart*; influenced by MDu. *Reynaerd*.

**Reynolds number** ● n. Physics a dimensionless number used in fluid mechanics to indicate whether fluid flow is steady or turbulent.
– ORIGIN C20: named after the Engl. physicist Osborne

*Reynolds*.

**Rf** ● **symb.** the chemical element rutherfordium.

**r.f.** ● **abbrev.** radio frequency.

**RFA** ● **abbrev.** (in the UK) Royal Fleet Auxiliary.

**RFC** ● **abbrev.** **1** Computing request for comment. **2** historical Royal Flying Corps. **3** Rugby Football Club.

**RGS** ● **abbrev.** Royal Geographical Society.

**Rh** ● **abbrev.** rhesus (factor). ● **symb.** the chemical element rhodium.

**r.h.** ● **abbrev.** right hand.

**RHA** ● **abbrev.** **1** (in the UK) regional health authority. **2** (in the UK) Royal Horse Artillery.

**rhabdom** /ˈrabdəʊm/ ● **n.** Zoology a translucent cylinder forming part of the light-sensitive receptor in an arthropod's eye.
– ORIGIN C19: from late Gk *rhabdōma*, from *rhabdos* 'rod'.

**rhabdomancy** /ˈrabdəˌmansi/ ● **n.** formal dowsing with a rod or stick.
– ORIGIN C17: from Gk *rhabdomanteia*, from *rhabdos* 'rod'.

**rhabdomyolysis** /ˌrabdə(ʊ)mʌɪˈɒlɪsɪs/ ● **n.** Medicine the destruction of striated muscle cells.
– ORIGIN 1950s: from Gk *rhabdos* 'rod' + **MYO-** + **-LYSIS**.

**Rhadamanthine** /ˌradəˈmanθʌɪn/ ● **adj.** poetic/literary stern and incorruptible in judgement.
– ORIGIN C17: from *Rhadamanthus*, ruler and judge of the underworld in Gk mythology, + **-INE**[1].

**Rhaeto-Romance** /ˌriːtə(ʊ)rəʊˈmans/ (also **Rhaeto-Romanic** /-ˈmanɪk/) ● **adj.** relating to or denoting the Romance dialects spoken in parts of SE Switzerland, NE Italy, and Tyrol. ● **n.** any of these dialects.
– ORIGIN from L. *Rhaetus* 'of *Rhaetia*' (a Roman province in the Alps) + **ROMANCE**.

**rhapsode** /ˈrapsəʊd/ ● **n.** a reciter of epic poems, especially one in ancient Greece who recited the Homeric poems.
– ORIGIN from Gk *rhapsōidos*, from *rhapsōidia* (see **RHAPSODY**).

**rhapsodist** ● **n.** **1** a person who rhapsodizes. **2** a rhapsode.

**rhapsodize** (also **-ise**) ● **v.** enthuse about someone or something.

**rhapsody** ● **n.** (pl. **-ies**) **1** an enthusiastic or ecstatic expression of feeling. **2** Music a piece of music in one extended movement, typically emotional in character. **3** (in ancient Greece) an epic poem of a suitable length for recitation at one time.
– DERIVATIVES **rhapsodic** adj.
– ORIGIN C16: via L. from Gk *rhapsōidia*, from *rhaptein* 'to stitch' + *ōidē* 'song, ode'.

**rhatany** /ˈratəni/ ● **n.** a South American shrub whose roots yield an astringent extract used in medicine. [Genus *Krameria*.]
– ORIGIN C19: from mod. L. *rhatania*, via Port. and Sp. from Quechua *ratánya*.

**RHD** ● **abbrev.** right-hand drive.

**rhea** /ˈriːə/ ● **n.** a large flightless bird of South American grasslands, resembling a small ostrich with greyish-brown plumage. [*Rhea americana* and *Pterocnemia pennata*.]
– ORIGIN C19: mod. L. (genus name), from the name of *Rhea*, a Titan in Gk mythology.

**rhebok** /ˈriːbɒk/ (also **reebok** or **rhebuck**) ● **n.** a small South African antelope with a woolly brownish-grey coat, a long slender neck, and short straight horns. [*Pelea capreolus*.]
– ORIGIN C18: from Du. *reebok* 'roebuck'.

**rheme** /riːm/ ● **n.** Linguistics the part of a clause giving information about the theme.
– ORIGIN C19: from Gk *rhēma* 'that which is said'.

**Rhenish** /ˈrɛnɪʃ/ ● **adj.** of the Rhine and adjacent regions.
– ORIGIN ME: from Anglo-Norman Fr. *reneis*, from a med. L. alt. of L. *Rhenanus*, from *Rhenus* 'Rhine'.

**rhenium** /ˈriːnɪəm/ ● **n.** the chemical element of atomic number 75, a rare silvery-white metal. (Symbol: **Re**)
– ORIGIN 1920s: mod. L., from *Rhenus* (see **RHENISH**).

**rheology** /rɪˈɒlədʒi/ ● **n.** the branch of physics concerned with the deformation and flow of matter.
– DERIVATIVES **rheological** adj. **rheologist** n.
– ORIGIN 1920s: from Gk *rheos* 'stream' + **-LOGY**.

**rheostat** /ˈriːəstat/ ● **n.** an electrical instrument used to control a current by varying the resistance.
– DERIVATIVES **rheostatic** adj.
– ORIGIN C19: from Gk *rheos* 'stream' + **-STAT**.

**rhesus baby** /ˈriːsəs/ ● **n.** a baby suffering from haemolytic disease of the newborn.
– ORIGIN 1960s: see **RHESUS FACTOR**.

**rhesus factor** ● **n.** an antigen occurring on red blood cells which is a cause of haemolytic disease of the newborn and of incompatibility in blood transfusions.
– ORIGIN 1940s: from **RHESUS MONKEY**, in which the antigen was first observed.

**rhesus monkey** ● **n.** a small brown macaque with red skin on the face and rump, native to southern Asia. [*Macaca mulatta*.]
– ORIGIN C19: mod. L. *rhesus*, arbitrary use of L. *Rhesus* (from Gk *Rhēsos*, a mythical king of Thrace).

**rhesus negative** ● **adj.** lacking the rhesus factor.

**rhesus positive** ● **adj.** having the rhesus factor.

**rhetor** /ˈriːtə/ ● **n.** **1** (in ancient Greece and Rome) a teacher of rhetoric. **2** an orator.
– ORIGIN via L. from Gk *rhētōr*.

**rhetoric** /ˈrɛtərɪk/ ● **n.** the art of effective or persuasive speaking or writing. ➤ language with a persuasive or impressive effect, but often lacking sincerity or meaningful content.
– ORIGIN ME: from OFr. *rethorique*, via L. from Gk *rhētorikē* (*tekhnē*) '(art) of rhetoric', from *rhētōr* 'rhetor'.

**rhetorical** /rɪˈtɒrɪk(ə)l/ ● **adj.** **1** of, relating to, or concerned with rhetoric. ➤ expressed in terms intended to persuade or impress. **2** (of a question) asked for effect or to make a statement rather than to elicit information.
– DERIVATIVES **rhetorically** adv.

**rhetorician** ● **n.** **1** an expert in formal rhetoric. **2** a speaker whose words are intended to impress or persuade.

**rheum** /ruːm/ ● **n.** chiefly poetic/literary a watery fluid that collects in or drips from the nose or eyes.
– DERIVATIVES **rheumy** adj.
– ORIGIN ME: from OFr. *reume*, via L. from Gk *rheuma* 'stream' (from *rhein* 'to flow').

**rheumatic** /rʊˈmatɪk/ ● **adj.** of, relating to, caused by, or suffering from rheumatism. ● **n.** a rheumatic person.
– DERIVATIVES **rheumatically** adv. **rheumaticky** adj. (informal).
– ORIGIN ME (orig. referring to infection characterized by rheum): from OFr. *reumatique*, or via L. from Gk *rheumatikos*, from *rheuma* (see **RHEUM**).

**rheumatic fever** ● **n.** an acute fever marked by inflammation and pain in the joints, caused by a streptococcal infection.

**rheumatics** ● **pl. n.** [usu. treated as sing.] informal rheumatism.

**rheumatism** ● **n.** any disease marked by inflammation and pain in the joints, muscles, or fibrous tissue, especially rheumatoid arthritis.
– ORIGIN C17: from Fr. *rhumatisme*, or via L. from Gk *rheumatismos*, from *rheumatizein* 'to snuffle', from *rheuma* 'stream' (because it was believed to be caused by the internal flow of 'watery' humours).

**rheumatoid** /ˈruːmətɔɪd/ ● **adj.** Medicine relating to, affected by, or resembling rheumatism.

**rheumatoid arthritis** ● **n.** a chronic progressive disease causing inflammation in the joints and resulting in painful deformity and immobility.

**rheumatology** /ˌruːməˈtɒlədʒi/ ● **n.** Medicine the study of rheumatism, arthritis, and other disorders of the joints, muscles, and ligaments.
– DERIVATIVES **rheumatological** adj. **rheumatologist** n.

**rhinal** /ˈrʌɪn(ə)l/ ● **adj.** Anatomy of or relating to the nose or the olfactory part of the brain.
– ORIGIN C19: from Gk *rhis, rhin-* 'nose' + **-AL**.

**rhinestone** ● **n.** an imitation diamond.

– ORIGIN C19: translating Fr. *caillou du Rhin*, lit. 'pebble of the Rhine'.

**rhinitis** /rʌɪˈnʌɪtɪs, rɪ-/ • **n.** Medicine inflammation of the mucous membrane of the nose, caused by a viral infection or an allergic reaction.

**rhino** • **n.** (pl. same or **-os**) informal a rhinoceros.

**rhino-** • **comb. form** of or relating to the nose: *rhinoplasty.*
– ORIGIN from Gk *rhis, rhin-* 'nose'.

**rhinoceros** /rʌɪˈnɒs(ə)rəs/ • **n.** (pl. same or **rhinoceroses**) a large, heavily built plant-eating mammal with one or two horns on the nose and thick folded skin, native to Africa and South Asia. [Family Rhinocerotidae: five species.]
– DERIVATIVES **rhinocerotic** /rʌɪˌnɒsəˈrɒtɪk/ adj.
– ORIGIN ME: via L. from Gk *rhinokerōs*, from *rhis, rhin-* 'nose' + *keras* 'horn'.

**rhinoceros beetle** • **n.** a very large mainly tropical beetle, the male of which has a curved horn on the head and typically another on the thorax. [*Oryctes rhinoceros* and other species.]

**rhinoceros bird** • **n.** another term for **OXPECKER**.

**rhinoplasty** /ˈrʌɪnə(ʊ)ˌplasti/ • **n.** (pl. **-ies**) Medicine plastic surgery performed on the nose.
– DERIVATIVES **rhinoplastic** adj.

**rhinovirus** /ˈrʌɪnəʊˌvʌɪrəs/ • **n.** Medicine any of a group of viruses including those which cause some forms of the common cold.

**rhizo-** • **comb. form** Botany relating to a root or roots: *rhizomorph.*
– ORIGIN from Gk *rhiza* 'root'.

**rhizobium** /rʌɪˈzəʊbɪəm/ • **n.** a nitrogen-fixing bacterium that is common in the soil, especially in the root nodules of leguminous plants.
– ORIGIN 1920s: mod. L., from **RHIZO-** + Gk *bios* 'life'.

**rhizoid** /ˈrʌɪzɔɪd/ • **n.** Botany a filamentous root-like outgrowth on the underside of the thallus in mosses and other lower plants.
– DERIVATIVES **rhizoidal** adj.

**rhizome** /ˈrʌɪzəʊm/ • **n.** Botany a continuously growing horizontal underground stem with lateral shoots and adventitious roots at intervals.
– ORIGIN C19: from Gk *rhizōma*, from *rhizousthai* 'take root', based on *rhiza* 'root'.

**rhizomorph** /ˈrʌɪzə(ʊ)mɔːf/ • **n.** Botany a root-like aggregation of hyphae in certain fungi.

**Rhizopoda** /ˌrʌɪzəˈpəʊdə, rʌɪˈzɒpədə/ • **pl. n.** Zoology a phylum of single-celled animals including the amoebas.
– DERIVATIVES **rhizopod** n.
– ORIGIN mod. L., from **RHIZO-** + Gk *pous, pod-* 'foot'.

**rhizosphere** /ˈrʌɪzə(ʊ)ˌsfɪːə/ • **n.** Ecology the region of soil in the vicinity of plant roots.

**rho** /rəʊ/ • **n.** the seventeenth letter of the Greek alphabet (**Ρ**, **ρ**), transliterated as 'r' or 'rh'. • **symb.** (ρ) density.
– ORIGIN from Gk.

**rhodamine** /ˈrəʊdəmiːn/ • **n.** Chemistry any of a group of synthetic textile dyes.
– ORIGIN C19: from **RHODO-** + **AMINE**.

**Rhode Islander** /rəʊd/ • **n.** a native or inhabitant of the US state of Rhode Island.

**Rhode Island Red** • **n.** a bird of a breed of reddish-black domestic chicken, originally from Rhode Island.

**Rhodesian** /rəʊˈdiːʃ(ə)n, -ˈdiːʒ(ə)n/ • **n.** a native or inhabitant of Rhodesia (now Zimbabwe). • **adj.** of or relating to Rhodesia.

**Rhodesian ridgeback** • **n.** a large dog of a breed having a short coat and a ridge of hair growing along the back in the opposite direction to the rest of the coat.

**Rhodes Scholarship** • **n.** any of several scholarships awarded annually and tenable at Oxford University by students from certain Commonwealth countries, the US, and Germany.
– DERIVATIVES **Rhodes Scholar** n.
– ORIGIN named after the South African statesman Cecil *Rhodes*, who founded the scholarships in 1902.

**rhodium** /ˈrəʊdɪəm/ • **n.** the chemical element of atomic number 45, a hard, dense silvery-white metal. (Symbol: **Rh**)
– ORIGIN C19: mod. L., from Gk *rhodon* 'rose' (from the colour of its salts).

**rhodo-** • **comb. form** chiefly Mineralogy & Chemistry rose-coloured: *rhodochrosite.*
– ORIGIN from Gk *rhodon* 'rose'.

**rhodochrosite** /ˌrəʊdə(ʊ)ˈkrəʊsʌɪt/ • **n.** a mineral consisting of manganese carbonate, typically pink, brown, or grey.
– ORIGIN C19: from Gk *rhodokhrōs* 'rose-coloured' + **-ITE**[1].

**rhododendron** /ˌrəʊdəˈdɛndr(ə)n/ • **n.** a shrub or small tree of the heather family, with large clusters of bell-shaped flowers and typically with large evergreen leaves. [Genus *Rhododendron*.]
– ORIGIN via L. from Gk, from *rhodon* 'rose' + *dendron* 'tree'.

**Rhodophyta** /ˌrəʊdə(ʊ)ˈfʌɪtə/ • **pl. n.** Botany a division of lower plants comprising the red algae.
– DERIVATIVES **rhodophyte** n.
– ORIGIN mod. L., from **RHODO-** + Gk *phuta* 'plants'.

**rhodopsin** /rə(ʊ)ˈdɒpsɪn/ • **n.** another term for **VISUAL PURPLE**.
– ORIGIN C19: from Gk *rhodon* 'rose' + *opsis* 'sight' + **-IN**[1].

**rhodora** /rə(ʊ)ˈdɔːrə/ • **n.** a pink-flowered North American shrub of the heather family. [*Rhododendron canadense*.]
– ORIGIN C18: mod. L. (former genus name), based on Gk *rhodon* 'rose'.

**rhomb** /rɒm(b)/ • **n. 1** a rhombohedral crystal. **2** a rhombus.
– DERIVATIVES **rhombic** adj.

**rhombencephalon** /ˌrɒmbɛnˈsɛf(ə)lɒn, -ˈkɛf-/ • **n.** Anatomy another term for **HINDBRAIN**.
– ORIGIN C19: from **RHOMB** + **ENCEPHALON**.

**rhombi** plural form of **RHOMBUS**.

**rhombohedron** /ˌrɒmbə(ʊ)ˈhiːdr(ə)n, -ˈhɛd-/ • **n.** (pl. **rhombohedra** /-drə/ or **rhombohedrons**) a solid figure whose faces are six equal rhombuses.
– DERIVATIVES **rhombohedral** adj.
– ORIGIN C19: from **RHOMBUS** + **-HEDRON**.

**rhomboid** /ˈrɒmbɔɪd/ • **adj.** having or resembling the shape of a rhombus. • **n.** a quadrilateral of which only the opposite sides and angles are equal.
– DERIVATIVES **rhomboidal** adj.

**rhomboideus** /rɒmˈbɔɪdɪəs/ • **n.** (pl. **rhomboidei** /-dɪʌɪ/) Anatomy a muscle connecting the shoulder blade to the vertebrae.
– ORIGIN C19: mod. L., from *rhomboideus* (*musculus*) (see **RHOMBOID**).

**rhombus** /ˈrɒmbəs/ • **n.** (pl. **rhombuses** or **rhombi** /-bʌɪ/) Geometry a parallelogram with oblique angles and equal sides.
– ORIGIN C16: via L. from Gk *rhombos*.

**rhotic** /ˈrəʊtɪk/ • **adj.** Phonetics relating to or denoting a variety of English (e.g. in America and SW England) in which *r* is pronounced before a consonant (as in *hard*) and at the ends of words (as in *far*).
– ORIGIN 1960s: from Gk *rhot-*, stem of *rho* (see **RHO**) + **-IC**.

**RHS** • **abbrev. 1** Royal Historical Society. **2** Royal Horticultural Society. **3** Royal Humane Society.

**rhubarb** • **n. 1** a large-leaved plant of the dock family which produces thick reddish or green leaf stalks. [*Rheum rhaponticum* and related species.] ➤the cooked leaf stalks of this plant, eaten as a dessert. **2** Brit. informal noise made by a group of actors to give the impression of indistinct background conversation. ➤nonsense. **3** N. Amer. informal a heated dispute.
– ORIGIN ME: from OFr. *reubarbe*, from a shortening of med. L. *rheubarbarum*, alt. (by assoc. with *rheum* 'rhubarb') of *rhabarbarum* 'foreign rhubarb', from Gk *rha* (also meaning 'rhubarb') + *barbaros* 'foreign'.

**rhumb** /rʌm/ • **n.** Nautical **1** (also **rhumb line**) an imaginary line on the earth's surface cutting all meridians at the same angle, used to plot a ship's course on a chart. **2** any of the thirty-two points of the compass.
– ORIGIN C16: from Fr. *rumb* (earlier *ryn* (*de vent*) 'point of the compass'); assoc. with L. *rhombus* (see **RHOMBUS**).

**rhumba** • **n.** variant spelling of **RUMBA**.

**rhyme** • **n. 1** correspondence of sound between words or

the endings of words, especially when used in poetry. ➤a word with the same sound as another. **2** a short poem with rhyming lines. ➤rhyming poetry or verse. ● **v. 1** (of a word, syllable, or line) have or end with a sound that corresponds to another. ➤(**rhyme something with**) treat a word as rhyming with (another). ➤(of a poem or song) be composed in rhyme. **2** poetic/literary compose verse or poetry.
– PHRASES **rhyme or reason** [with neg.] logical explanation.
– DERIVATIVES **rhymer** n. **rhymist** n. (archaic).
– ORIGIN ME *rime*, from OFr., from med. L. *rithmus*, via L. from Gk *rhuthmos* (see **RHYTHM**).

**rhyme scheme** ● **n.** the pattern of rhymes in a poem or verse.

**rhymester** ● **n.** a composer of rhymes.

**rhyming slang** ● **n.** a type of slang that replaces words with rhyming words or phrases, typically with the rhyming element omitted (e.g. *butcher's*, short for *butcher's hook*, meaning 'look').

**rhyolite** /ˈrʌɪəlʌɪt/ ● **n.** Geology a pale fine-grained volcanic rock of granitic composition.
– ORIGIN C19: from Ger. *Rhyolit*, from Gk *rhuax* 'lava stream' + *lithos* 'stone'.

**rhythm** /ˈrɪð(ə)m/ ● **n. 1** a strong, regular repeated pattern of movement or sound. ➤the systematic arrangement of musical sounds, according to duration and periodical stress. ➤a type of pattern formed by this. **2** a person's natural feeling for rhythm. **3** the measured flow of words and phrases in verse or prose as determined by the length of and stress on syllables. **4** a regularly recurring sequence of events or actions. **5** Art a harmonious sequence or correlation of colours or elements.
– DERIVATIVES **rhythmless** adj.
– ORIGIN C16 (also orig. in the sense 'rhyme'): from Fr. *rhythme*, or via L. from Gk *rhuthmos* (rel. to *rhein* 'to flow').

**rhythm and blues** ● **n.** popular music of US black origin, arising from a combination of blues with jazz rhythms.

**rhythmic** ● **adj. 1** having or relating to rhythm. **2** occurring regularly.
– DERIVATIVES **rhythmical** adj. **rhythmically** adv.

**rhythmic gymnastics** ● **pl. n.** [usu. treated as sing.] a form of gymnastics with dance-like routines, typically involving the use of ribbons or hoops.

**rhythmicity** ● **n.** rhythmical quality or character.

**rhythm method** ● **n.** a method of birth control involving the avoidance of sexual intercourse when ovulation is likely to occur.

**rhythm section** ● **n.** the part of a pop or jazz group supplying the rhythm, in particular the bass and drums.

**rhyton** /ˈrʌɪtɒn, ˈrɪtɒn/ ● **n.** (pl. **rhytons** or **rhyta** /ˈrʌɪtə, ˈrɪtə/) an ancient Greek drinking container in the form of an animal's head or a horn, with the drinking hole at the lower or pointed end.
– ORIGIN from Gk *rhuton*, neut. of *rhutos* 'flowing'; rel. to *rhein* 'to flow'.

**RI** ● **abbrev. 1** Indonesia (international vehicle registration). [from *Républik Indonésia*.] **2** Rex et Imperator (King and Emperor) or Regina et Imperatrix (Queen and Empress). [Latin.] **3** Rhode Island (in official postal use). **4** Royal Institute or Institution.

**RIA** ● **abbrev. 1** radioimmunoassay. **2** Royal Irish Academy.

**ria** /ˈriːə/ ● **n.** Geography a long narrow inlet formed by the partial submergence of a river valley.
– ORIGIN C19: from Sp. *ría* 'estuary'.

**rial** /ˈriːɑːl/ (also **riyal**) ● **n. 1** the basic monetary unit of Iran and Oman, equal to 100 dinars in Iran and 100 baiza in Oman. **2** (usu. **riyal**) the basic monetary unit of Saudi Arabia, Qatar, and Yemen, equal to 100 halala in Saudi Arabia, 100 dirhams in Qatar, and 100 fils in Yemen.
– ORIGIN via Pers. from Arab. *riyāl*, from Sp. *real* 'royal'.

**rib** ● **n. 1** each of a series of slender curved bones articulated in pairs to the spine, protecting the thoracic cavity and its organs. ➤an animal rib with meat adhering to it used as food. **2** Architecture a curved member supporting a vault or defining its form. **3** a curved transverse strut of metal or timber in a ship, forming part of the framework of the hull. **4** each of the curved pieces of wood forming the body of a lute or violin. **5** each of the hinged rods supporting the fabric of an umbrella. **6** Aeronautics a structural member in an aerofoil. **7** a vein of a leaf or an insect's wing. **8** Knitting alternate plain and purl stitches producing a ridged, slightly elastic fabric. ● **v.** (**ribbed**, **ribbing**) **1** (usu. **be ribbed**) mark with or form into raised bands or ridges. **2** informal tease good-naturedly.
– DERIVATIVES **ribber** n. **ribless** adj.
– ORIGIN OE *rib*, *ribb*, of Gmc origin.

**RIBA** ● **abbrev.** Royal Institute of British Architects.

**ribald** /ˈrɪb(ə)ld, ˈrʌɪbɔːld/ ● **adj.** coarsely or irreverently humorous.
– ORIGIN ME (as a noun denoting a licentious or irreverent person): from OFr. *ribauld*, from *riber* 'indulge in licentious pleasures', from a Gmc base meaning 'prostitute'.

**ribaldry** ● **n.** ribald talk or behaviour.

**riband** /ˈrɪb(ə)nd/ ● **n.** archaic a ribbon.
– ORIGIN ME: from OFr. *riban*, prob. from a Gmc compound of **BAND**[1].

**ribbed** ● **adj.** having a pattern of raised bands. ➤Architecture strengthened with ribs.

**ribbing** ● **n. 1** a rib-like structure or pattern. **2** informal good-natured teasing.

**ribbon** ● **n. 1** a long, narrow strip of fabric, used for tying something or for decoration. ➤a ribbon of a special colour or design awarded as a prize or worn to indicate the holding of an honour. **2** a long, narrow strip of something. **3** a narrow band of impregnated material wound on a spool and forming the inking agent in some typewriters and computer printers. ● **v.** extend or move in a long narrow strip.
– PHRASES **cut** (or **tear**) **something to ribbons** cut (or tear) something into ragged strips. ➤damage something severely.
– DERIVATIVES **ribboned** adj.
– ORIGIN C16: var. of **RIBAND**.

**ribbon development** ● **n.** Brit. the building of houses along a main road.

**ribbonfish** ● **n.** (pl. same or **-fishes**) a dealfish, oarfish, or similar long slender fish with a flattened body.

**ribbon worm** ● **n.** a chiefly aquatic worm with a long flattened body that is typically brightly coloured. [Phylum Nemertea.]

**ribby** ● **adj.** having prominent ribs.

**ribcage** ● **n.** the bony frame formed by the ribs.

**rib-eye** ● **n.** a cut of beef from the outer side of the ribs.

**riboflavin** /ˌrʌɪbə(ʊ)ˈfleɪvɪn/ ● **n.** Biochemistry vitamin $B_2$, a yellow compound essential for energy production and present especially in milk, liver, and green vegetables.
– ORIGIN 1930s: from **RIBOSE** + L. *flavus* 'yellow' + **-IN**[1].

**ribonucleic acid** /ˌrʌɪbə(ʊ)njuːˈkleɪɪk, -ˈkliːɪk/ ● **n.** see **RNA**.
– ORIGIN 1930s: *ribonucleic* from **RIBOSE** + **NUCLEIC ACID**.

**ribose** /ˈrʌɪbəʊz, -s/ ● **n.** Chemistry a sugar which is a constituent of nucleosides and several vitamins and enzymes.
– ORIGIN C19: arbitrary alt. of **ARABINOSE**, a related sugar.

**ribosome** /ˈrʌɪbə(ʊ)səʊm/ ● **n.** Biochemistry a minute particle of RNA and protein found in cells, involved in the synthesis of polypeptides and proteins.
– DERIVATIVES **ribosomal** adj.
– ORIGIN 1950s: from **RIBONUCLEIC ACID** + **-SOME**[3].

**ribozyme** /ˈrʌɪbə(ʊ)zʌɪm/ ● **n.** Biochemistry an RNA molecule capable of acting as an enzyme.
– ORIGIN 1980s: blend of **RIBONUCLEIC ACID** and **ENZYME**.

**rib-tickler** ● **n.** informal a very amusing joke or story.
– DERIVATIVES **rib-tickling** adj. **rib-ticklingly** adv.

**ribulose** /ˈrʌɪbjʊləʊz, -s/ ● **n.** Chemistry a sugar of the pentose class which is an important intermediate in carbohydrate metabolism and photosynthesis.
– ORIGIN 1930s: from **RIBOSE** + *-ulose*.

**ribwort** ● **n.** a plantain with erect ribbed leaves and a rounded flower spike. [*Plantago lanceolata*.]

R

**Ricardian** /rɪ'kɑːdiən/ ● **adj.** **1** of or relating to the time of any of three kings of England, Richard I, II, and III. **2** of or holding the view that Richard III was misrepresented by Shakespeare and other writers. ● **n.** a contemporary or supporter of Richard III.
– DERIVATIVES **Ricardianism** n.
– ORIGIN from med. L. *Ricardus* 'Richard' + **-IAN**.

**rice** ● **n.** a swamp grass which is cultivated as a source of food, especially in Asia. [*Oryza sativa* and other species.] ➤ the grains of this cereal used as food. ● **v.** N. Amer. force (cooked potatoes or other vegetables) through a sieve or ricer.
– ORIGIN ME: from OFr. *ris*, from Ital. *riso*, from Gk *oruza*.

**rice bowl** ● **n.** an area in which rice is grown in abundance.

**ricepaper** ● **n.** thin translucent edible paper made from the flattened and dried pith of a shrub, used in oriental painting and in baking biscuits and cakes.

**ricer** ● **n.** N. Amer. a utensil with small holes through which soft food is pushed to form particles resembling rice grains.

**ricercar** /ˌriːtʃə'kɑː, 'riːtʃəˌkɑː/ (also **ricercare** /ˌriːtʃə'kɑːreɪ, -ri/) ● **n.** (pl. **ricercars** or **ricercari**) Music an elaborate contrapuntal instrumental composition in fugal or canonic style, typically of the 16th to 18th centuries.
– ORIGIN from Ital. *ricercare* 'search out'.

**rich** ● **adj.** **1** having a great deal of money or assets. ➤ (of a country or region) having valuable natural resources or a successful economy. ➤ of expensive materials or workmanship. **2** plentiful; abundant. ➤ (**rich in**) having (something) in large amounts. ➤ (of food) containing much fat, spice, etc. ➤ (of the mixture in an internal-combustion engine) containing a high proportion of fuel. **3** (of a colour, sound, or smell) pleasantly deep and strong. **4** full of interesting diversity or complexity. **5** producing or yielding a large quantity of something. ➤ (of soil or land) fertile. **6** informal (of a remark) causing ironic amusement or indignation.
– DERIVATIVES **richen** v. **richness** n.
– ORIGIN OE *rīce* 'powerful, wealthy', of Gmc origin; ult. from Celtic; reinforced in ME by OFr. *riche* 'rich, powerful'.

**-rich** ● **comb. form** containing a large amount of something specified: *protein-rich*.

**riches** ● **pl. n.** material wealth. ➤ valuable natural resources.
– ORIGIN ME: var. (later interpreted as a pl. form) of archaic *richesse*, from OFr. *richeise* (from *riche* 'rich').

**richly** ● **adv.** **1** in an elaborate, generous, or plentiful way. **2** fully: *a richly deserved holiday*.

**Richter scale** /'rɪktə/ ● **n.** Geology a logarithmic scale for expressing the magnitude of an earthquake on the basis of seismograph oscillations.
– ORIGIN 1930s: named after the Amer. geologist Charles F. *Richter*.

**ricin** /'rʌɪsɪn, 'rɪsɪn/ ● **n.** Chemistry a highly toxic protein obtained from the pressed seeds of the castor oil plant.
– ORIGIN C19: from mod. L. *Ricinus communis* (denoting the castor oil plant) + **-IN**[1].

**rick**[1] ● **n.** **1** a stack of hay, corn, or straw, especially one built into a regular shape and thatched. **2** N. Amer. a pile of firewood smaller than a cord. **3** N. Amer. a set of shelving for barrels. ● **v.** form into a rick or ricks.
– ORIGIN OE *hrēac*, of Gmc origin.

**rick**[2] ● **n.** a slight sprain or strain, especially in the neck or back. ● **v.** strain (one's neck or back) slightly.
– ORIGIN C18 (as v.): of dial. origin.

**rickets** /'rɪkɪts/ ● **n.** [treated as sing. or pl.] Medicine a disease of children caused by vitamin D deficiency, characterized by softening and distortion of the bones typically resulting in bow legs.
– ORIGIN C17: perh. an alt. of Gk *rhakhitis* (see **RACHITIC**).

**rickettsia** /rɪ'kɛtsɪə/ ● **n.** (pl. **rickettsiae** /-iiː/ or **rickettsias**) any of a group of very small bacteria that cause typhus and other febrile diseases. [Genus *Rickettsia*.]
– DERIVATIVES **rickettsial** adj.
– ORIGIN mod. L., named after the Amer. pathologist Howard Taylor *Ricketts*.

**rickety** ● **adj.** **1** poorly made and likely to collapse. **2** suffering from rickets.
– DERIVATIVES **ricketiness** n.
– ORIGIN C17: from **RICKETS** + **-Y**[1].

**rickey** ● **n.** (pl. **-eys**) N. Amer. a drink consisting of a spirit, typically gin, with lime or lemon juice, carbonated water, and ice.
– ORIGIN C19: prob. from the surname *Rickey*.

**rickle** ● **n.** Scottish, Irish, & N. English a loosely piled heap.
– ORIGIN C15: perh. from Norw. dial. *rikl*, or from **RICK**[1].

**rickrack** ● **n.** braided trimming in a zigzag pattern, used on clothes.
– ORIGIN C19: of unknown origin.

**rickshaw** ● **n.** a light two-wheeled hooded vehicle drawn by one or more people, chiefly used in Asian countries.
– ORIGIN C19: abbrev. of Japanese *jinricksha*, from *jin* 'man' + *riki* 'strength' + *sha* 'vehicle'.

**ricochet** /'rɪkəʃeɪ, -ʃɛt/ ● **v.** (**ricocheted** /-ʃeɪd/, **ricocheting** /-ʃeɪɪŋ/ or **ricochetted** /-ʃɛtɪd/, **ricochetting** /-ʃɛtɪŋ/) (of a bullet or other projectile) rebound off a surface. ➤ move or appear to move in such a way. ● **n.** a shot or hit that ricochets. ➤ the ricocheting action of a bullet or other projectile.
– ORIGIN C18: from Fr., of unknown origin.

**ricotta** /rɪ'kɒtə/ ● **n.** a soft white unsalted Italian cheese.
– ORIGIN Ital., lit. 'recooked, cooked twice'.

**RICS** ● **abbrev.** (in the UK) Royal Institution of Chartered Surveyors.

**rictus** /'rɪktəs/ ● **n.** a fixed grimace or grin.
– DERIVATIVES **rictal** adj.
– ORIGIN C19: from L., lit. 'open mouth', from *rict-*, *ringi* 'to gape'.

**rid** ● **v.** (**ridding**; past and past part. **rid** or archaic **ridded**) (**rid someone/thing of**) make someone or something free of (an unwanted person or thing). ➤ (**be** (or **get**) **rid of**) be freed or relieved of.
– ORIGIN ME (orig. 'clear (land)'): from ON *rythja*.

**riddance** ● **n.** the action of getting rid of someone or something.
– PHRASES **good riddance** expressing relief at being rid of someone or something.

**ridden** past participle of **RIDE**.

**riddle**[1] ● **n.** a question or statement phrased so as to require ingenuity in ascertaining its answer or meaning. ➤ a person or thing that is difficult to understand. ● **v.** archaic speak in or pose riddles. ➤ explain (a riddle) to.
– DERIVATIVES **riddler** n.
– ORIGIN OE *rǣdels*, *rǣdelse* 'opinion, conjecture, riddle'; rel. to **READ**.

**riddle**[2] ● **v.** **1** (usu. **be riddled**) make many holes in, especially with gunshot. ➤ fill or permeate with something undesirable. **2** pass through a riddle. ➤ remove ashes or other unwanted material from (a fire, stove, etc.) in such a way. ● **n.** a large coarse sieve, especially one for separating ashes from cinders or sand from gravel.
– ORIGIN OE *hriddel*, of Gmc origin.

**riddling** ● **adj.** expressed in riddles; enigmatic.
– DERIVATIVES **riddlingly** adv.

**ride** ● **v.** (past **rode**; past part. **ridden**) **1** sit on and control the movement of (a horse, bicycle, or motorcycle). ➤ (usu. **ride in/on**) travel in or on (a vehicle or horse). ➤ compete in (a race) on a horse, bicycle, or motorcycle. ➤ N. Amer. travel in (a lift or vehicle). **2** be carried or supported by (something with great momentum). ➤ (of a vessel) sail or float. ➤ (**ride something out**) come safely through something. ➤ yield to (a blow) so as to reduce its impact. **3** project or overlap. ➤ (**ride up**) (of a garment) gradually move upwards out of its proper position. **4** (**ride on**) depend on. **5** [often in comb.] (**be ridden**) be full of or dominated by: *crime-ridden streets*. **6** vulgar slang have sexual intercourse with. **7** N. Amer. annoy or tease. ● **n.** **1** an act of riding. **2** N. Amer. a person giving a lift in a vehicle. **3** US informal a motor vehicle. **4** a path for horse riding. **5** a roller coaster, roundabout, etc. ridden at a fair or amusement park. **6** (also **ride cymbal**) a cymbal keeping up a continuous rhythm. **7** vulgar slang an act of sexual intercourse.

– PHRASES **be riding for a fall** informal be acting in a reckless way that invites failure. **let something ride** take no immediate action over something. **ride herd on** N. Amer. keep watch over. **ride high** be successful. **ride shotgun** chiefly N. Amer. travel as a guard next to the driver of a vehicle. ➤ride in the passenger seat of a vehicle. **ride to hounds** chiefly Brit. go fox-hunting on horseback. **a rough** (or **easy**) **ride** a difficult (or easy) time. **take someone for a ride** informal deceive someone.

– DERIVATIVES **rideable** (also **ridable**) adj.

– ORIGIN OE *rīdan*, of Gmc origin.

**rider** ● n. **1** a person who rides a horse, bicycle, motorcycle, etc. **2** an added condition or proviso. ➤Brit. an addition or amendment to a bill at its third reading. ➤Brit. a recommendation or comment added by the jury to a judicial verdict. ➤a supplementary clause in a performer's contract specifying food, drink, etc. **3** a small weight on the beam of a balance for fine adjustment.

– DERIVATIVES **riderless** adj.

**ridership** ● n. chiefly N. Amer. the number of passengers using a particular form of public transport.

**ridge** ● n. **1** a long narrow hilltop, mountain range, or watershed. **2** the edge formed where the two sloping sides of a roof meet at the top. **3** Meteorology an elongated region of high barometric pressure. **4** a narrow raised band on a surface. **5** a raised strip of arable land, especially one of a set separated by furrows. ● v. [often as adj. **ridged**] mark with or form into ridges.

– DERIVATIVES **ridgy** adj.

– ORIGIN OE *hrycg* 'spine, crest', of Gmc origin.

**ridgeback** ● n. short for **RHODESIAN RIDGEBACK**.

**ridge piece** (also **ridge tree**) ● n. a horizontal beam along the ridge of a roof, into which the rafters are fixed.

**ridge pole** ● n. **1** the horizontal pole of a long tent. **2** a ridge piece.

**ridge tent** ● n. a tent with a central ridge supported by a pole or frame at each end.

**ridge tile** ● n. a curved tile used in making a roof ridge.

**ridgeway** ● n. a road or track along a ridge.

**ridicule** ● n. mockery or derision. ● v. subject to ridicule.

– ORIGIN C17: from Fr., or from L. *ridiculum*, neut. (used as n.) of *ridiculus* 'laughable', from *ridere* 'to laugh'.

**ridiculous** ● adj. inviting ridicule; absurd.

– DERIVATIVES **ridiculously** adv. **ridiculousness** n.

– ORIGIN C16: from L. *ridiculosus*, from *ridiculus* (see **RIDICULE**).

**riding**[1] ● n. **1** the sport or activity of riding horses. **2** a path for horse riding.

**riding**[2] ● n. **1** (usu. **the East/North/West Riding**) one of three former administrative divisions of Yorkshire. **2** an electoral district of Canada.

– ORIGIN OE *trithing*, from ON *thrithjungr* 'third part', from *thrithi* 'third'; the initial *th-* was lost due to assimilation with the preceding *-t* of *East*, *West*, or the *-th* of *North*.

**riding crop** ● n. a short flexible whip with a loop for the hand, used when riding horses.

**riding habit** ● n. a woman's riding dress, consisting of a skirt and a double-breasted jacket.

**riding light** ● n. a light shown by a ship at anchor.

**ridley** ● n. (pl. **-eys**) a small turtle of tropical seas. [*Lepidochelys kempi* and *L. olivacea*.]

– ORIGIN 1940s: of unknown origin.

**riel** /ˈriːəl/ ● n. the basic monetary unit of Cambodia, equal to 100 sen.

– ORIGIN from Khmer.

**Riesling** /ˈriːzlɪŋ, ˈriːs-/ ● n. a variety of wine grape grown especially in Germany and Austria. ➤a dry white wine made from this grape.

– ORIGIN from Ger.

**rifampicin** /rɪˈfampɪsɪn/ (also **rifampin**) ● n. Medicine a bacterial antibiotic used chiefly to treat tuberculosis and leprosy.

– ORIGIN 1960s: from *rifamycin* (a related antibiotic) + the insertion of *pi-* from **PIPERAZINE**.

**rife** ● adj. (especially of something undesirable) widespread. ➤(**rife with**) full of.

– DERIVATIVES **rifeness** n.

– ORIGIN OE *rȳfe*, prob. from ON *rīfr* 'acceptable'.

**riff** ● n. a short repeated phrase in popular music or jazz. ● v. [usu. as noun **riffing**] play riffs.

– ORIGIN 1930s: abbrev. of **RIFFLE**.

**riffle** ● v. **1** turn over something, especially pages, quickly and casually. ➤(**riffle through**) search quickly through. ➤ruffle. **2** shuffle (playing cards) by flicking up and releasing the corners of two piles of cards so that they intermingle. ● n. **1** an act of riffling. **2** chiefly N. Amer. a shallow part of a stream or river. ➤a patch of waves or ripples.

– ORIGIN C18: perh. from a var. of **RUFFLE**, influenced by **RIPPLE**.

**riffler** ● n. an elongated tool for filing concave surfaces.

– ORIGIN C18: from Fr. *rifloir*, from OFr. *rifler* 'to scrape'.

**riff-raff** ● n. disreputable or undesirable people.

– ORIGIN C15 (as *riff and raff*): from OFr. *rif et raf* 'one and all, every bit', of Gmc origin.

**rifle**[1] ● n. **1** a gun, especially one fired from shoulder level, having a long spirally grooved barrel to make a bullet spin and thereby increase accuracy over a long distance. **2** (**rifles**) troops armed with rifles. ● v. **1** [usu. as adj. **rifled**] make spiral grooves in (a gun or its barrel or bore). **2** hit or kick (a ball) hard and straight.

– ORIGIN C17: from Fr. *rifler* 'graze, scratch', of Gmc origin.

**rifle**[2] ● v. search through something hurriedly in order to find or steal something. ➤steal.

– ORIGIN ME: from OFr. *rifler* 'graze, plunder', of Gmc origin.

**rifleman** ● n. (pl. **-men**) **1** a soldier armed with a rifle. **2** a very small greenish-yellow songbird, native to New Zealand. [*Acanthisitta chloris*.]

**rifle range** ● n. a place for practising rifle shooting.

**rifling** ● n. spiral grooves on the inside of a rifle barrel.

**rift** ● n. **1** a crack, split, or break in something. **2** a serious break in friendly relations. **3** Geology a rift valley. ● v. [often as adj. **rifted**] chiefly Geology move or force to move apart.

– ORIGIN ME: of Scand. origin.

**rift valley** ● n. a steep-sided valley formed by subsidence of the earth's surface between nearly parallel faults.

**rig**[1] ● v. (**rigged**, **rigging**) **1** provide (a boat) with sails and rigging. ➤assemble and adjust (the equipment of a sailing boat, aircraft, etc.) in readiness for operation. ➤(often **rig something up**) set up (a device or structure), typically in a makeshift way. **2** (often **rig someone up**) provide with clothes of a particular type. ● n. **1** the arrangement of a boat's sails and rigging. ➤the sail, mast, and boom of a windsurfer. **2** an apparatus or device for a particular purpose. ➤an oil rig or drilling rig. ➤(in CB and short-wave radio) a transmitter and receiver. ➤a type of construction for fishing tackle that bears the bait and hook. **3** a person's costume or outfit. **4** chiefly N. Amer. & Austral./NZ a truck.

– PHRASES **full rig** informal smart or ceremonial clothes.

– DERIVATIVES **-rigged** adj.

– ORIGIN C15: perh. of Scand. origin.

**rig**[2] ● v. (**rigged**, **rigging**) manage or conduct fraudulently so as to gain an advantage. ● n. archaic a trick or swindle.

– ORIGIN C18 (as n.): of unknown origin.

**rigadoon** /ˌrɪɡəˈduːn/ ● n. a lively dance for couples, in duple or quadruple time, of Provençal origin.

– ORIGIN C17: from Fr. *rigaudon*, perh. named after its inventor, said to be called *Rigaud*.

**rigatoni** /ˌrɪɡəˈtəʊni/ ● pl. n. pasta in the form of short hollow fluted tubes.

– ORIGIN from Ital.

**rigger**[1] ● n. **1** [in combination] a ship rigged in a particular way. **2** a person who attends to the rigging of a sailing ship, aircraft, or parachute. **3** a person who erects and maintains scaffolding, cranes, etc. **4** a person who works on an oil rig. **5** an outrigger carrying a rowlock on a racing rowing boat.

**rigger**[2] ● **n.** a person who rigs something to their advantage.

**rigging** ● **n. 1** the system of ropes or chains supporting a ship's masts and controlling or setting the yards and sails. **2** the ropes and wires supporting the structure of an airship, biplane, hang-glider, or parachute. ➤the cables and fittings controlling the flight surfaces and engines of an aircraft.

**right** ● **adj. 1** morally good, justified, or acceptable. **2** factually correct. ➤most appropriate. ➤socially fashionable or important. **3** in a satisfactory, sound, or normal state or condition. **4** on, towards, or relating to the side of a human body or of a thing which is to the east when the person or thing is facing north. **5** informal, chiefly Brit. complete; absolute. **6** of or relating to a right-wing person or group. ● **adv. 1** to the furthest or most complete extent or degree. ➤exactly; directly. ➤informal immediately. ➤dialect or archaic very. **2** correctly. ➤satisfactorily. **3** on or to the right side. ● **n. 1** that which is morally right. **2** a moral or legal entitlement to have or do something. ➤(**rights**) the authority to perform, publish, or film a particular work or event. **3** (**the right**) the right-hand part, side, or direction. ➤a right turn. ➤a person's right fist, or a blow given with it. **4** (often **the Right**) [treated as sing. or pl.] a group or political party favouring conservative views. ● **v. 1** restore to a normal or upright position. ➤restore to a normal or correct condition. **2** rectify. ➤archaic compensate. ● **exclam.** informal indicating agreement or acknowledging a statement or order.

– PHRASES **bang** (or N. Amer. **dead**) **to rights** informal (of a criminal) with positive proof of guilt. **be in the right** be justified in one's views or actions. **by rights** if things were fair or correct. **do right by** treat fairly. **in one's own right** as a result of one's own claims, qualifications, or efforts. (**as**) **of right** (or **by right**) due to a moral or legal claim or entitlement. **put** (or **set**) **someone right** tell someone the true facts of a situation. **put** (or **set**) **something to rights** restore something to its correct or normal state. (**as**) **right as rain** informal completely well or healthy. **right** (or **straight**) **away** (or informal **off**) immediately. **right on** informal expressing support, approval, or encouragement. **a right one** Brit. informal a silly or foolish person. **she's** (or **she'll be**) **right** Austral./NZ informal don't worry.

– DERIVATIVES **rightable** adj. **righter** n. **rightish** adj. **rightmost** adj. **rightness** n. **rightward** adj. & adv. **rightwards** adv.

– ORIGIN OE *riht* (adj. and n.), *rihtan* (v.), *rihte* (adv.), of Gmc origin; rel. to L. *rectus* 'ruled'.

**right about** (also **right about-face**) ● **n.** Military a right turn through 180° so as to face in the opposite direction.

**right angle** ● **n.** an angle of 90°, as in a corner of a square.

– DERIVATIVES **right-angled** adj.

– PHRASES **at right angles to** forming an angle of 90° with.

**right ascension** ● **n.** Astronomy position measured along the celestial equator, expressed in hours, minutes, and seconds.

**right back** ● **n.** a defender in soccer or field hockey who plays primarily on the right of the field.

**right bank** ● **n.** the bank of a river on the right as one faces downstream.

**right brain** ● **n.** the right-hand side of the human brain, believed to be associated with creative thought and the emotions.

**righten** ● **v.** archaic make right, correct, or straight.

**righteous** /ˈrʌɪtʃəs/ ● **adj.** morally right or justifiable.

– DERIVATIVES **righteously** adv. **righteousness** n.

– ORIGIN OE *rihtwīs*, from *riht* 'right' + *wīs* 'manner, state, condition'; the change in the ending was by assoc. with words such as *bounteous*.

**right field** ● **n.** Baseball the part of the outfield to the right of the batter when facing the pitcher.

– DERIVATIVES **right fielder** n.

**rightful** ● **adj.** having a legitimate right to something. ➤legitimately claimed; fitting.

– DERIVATIVES **rightfully** adv. **rightfulness** n.

**right hand** ● **n. 1** the hand of a person's right side. ➤the region or direction on the right side. **2** the most important position next to someone. ➤an indispensable assistant. ● **adj.** on or towards the right side. ➤done with or using the right hand.

**right-hand drive** ● **n.** a motor-vehicle steering system with the steering wheel and other controls fitted on the right side, for use in countries where vehicles drive on the left side of the road.

**right-handed** ● **adj. 1** using or done with the right hand. **2** going towards or turning to the right. ➤(of a screw) advanced by turning clockwise. ➤Biology dextral.

– DERIVATIVES **right-handedly** adv. **right-handedness** n.

**right-hander** ● **n. 1** a right-handed person. **2** a blow struck with the right hand.

**right-hand man** ● **n.** an indispensable helper or chief assistant.

**Right Honourable** ● **adj.** Brit. a title given to certain high officials such as Privy Counsellors and government ministers.

**rightism** ● **n.** the political views or policies of the right.

– DERIVATIVES **rightist** n. & adj.

**rightly** ● **adv.** correctly. ➤with good reason. ➤in accordance with justice or what is morally right.

**right-minded** ● **adj.** having sound views and principles.

**righto** (also **righty-ho**) ● **exclam.** Brit. informal expressing agreement or assent.

**right of abode** ● **n.** chiefly Brit. a person's right to live in a country.

**right of search** ● **n.** the right of a ship of a belligerent state to search a neutral vessel for prohibited goods.

**right of way** ● **n. 1** the legal right to pass along a specific route through property belonging to another. ➤a thoroughfare subject to such a right. **2** the right of a pedestrian, vehicle, or ship to proceed with precedence over others in a situation or place.

**right-on** ● **adj.** informal, often derogatory in keeping with fashionable liberal or left-wing opinions and values.

**Right Reverend** ● **adj.** a title given to a bishop.

**right side** ● **n.** the side of something intended to be uppermost or foremost.

– PHRASES **on the right side of 1** on the safe, appropriate, or desirable side of. **2** somewhat less than (a specified age). **right side out** not inside out.

**rights issue** ● **n.** an issue of shares offered at a special price by a company to its existing shareholders.

**rightsize** ● **v.** chiefly US convert to an appropriate or optimum size, in particular shed staff from (an organization).

**right-thinking** ● **adj.** right-minded.

**right-to-life** ● **adj.** another term for **PRO-LIFE**.

– DERIVATIVES **right-to-lifer** n.

**right triangle** ● **n.** N. Amer. a right-angled triangle.

**right whale** ● **n.** a baleen whale with a large head and a deeply curved jaw, of Arctic and temperate waters. [*Balaena glacialis* and other species.]

– ORIGIN C18: so named because it was regarded as the 'right' whale to hunt.

**right wing** ● **n. 1** the conservative or reactionary section of a political party or system. [see **LEFT WING**.] **2** the right side of a sports team on the field or of an army.

– DERIVATIVES **right-winger** n.

**righty** ● **n.** (pl. **-ies**) N. Amer. informal **1** a right-handed person. **2** a right-wing person.

**righty-ho** ● **exclam.** variant of **RIGHTO**.

**rigid** ● **adj. 1** unable to bend or be forced out of shape. ➤(of a person) stiff and unmoving. **2** not able to be changed or adapted. ● **n.** a truck which is not articulated.

– DERIVATIVES **rigidify** v. **rigidity** n. **rigidly** adv. **rigidness** n.

– ORIGIN ME: from L. *rigidus*, from *rigere* 'be stiff'.

**rigid designator** ● **n.** Philosophy a term that identifies the same object or individual in every possible world.

**rigmarole** /ˈrɪgmərəʊl/ ● **n.** a lengthy and complicated procedure. ➤a long, rambling story.
– ORIGIN C18: appar. an alt. of *ragman roll*, orig. denoting a legal document recording a list of offences.

**rigor¹** /ˈrɪgɔː, ˈrʌɪgɔː, -gə/ ● **n.** Medicine **1** a sudden feeling of cold accompanied by shivering and a rise in temperature, especially at the onset or height of a fever. **2** short for **RIGOR MORTIS**.
– ORIGIN ME: from L., lit. 'stiffness', from *rigere* 'be stiff'.

**rigor²** ● **n.** US spelling of **RIGOUR**.

**rigorism** ● **n.** extreme strictness in interpreting a law or principle. ➤the Roman Catholic doctrine that in doubtful cases of conscience the strict course is always to be followed.
– DERIVATIVES **rigorist** n. & adj.

**rigor mortis** /ˈmɔːtɪs/ ● **n.** Medicine stiffening of the joints and muscles a few hours after death, lasting from one to four days.
– ORIGIN C19: from L., lit. 'stiffness of death'.

**rigorous** ● **adj. 1** extremely thorough, exhaustive, or accurate. **2** (of a rule, system, etc.) strictly applied or adhered to. ➤adhering strictly to a belief, opinion, or system. **3** (of weather) harsh.
– DERIVATIVES **rigorously** adv. **rigorousness** n.
– ORIGIN ME: from OFr. *rigorous* or late L. *rigorosus*, from *rigor* (see **RIGOR¹**).

**rigour** (US **rigor**) ● **n. 1** the quality of being rigorous. **2** (**rigours**) demanding, difficult, or extreme conditions.
– ORIGIN ME: from OFr. *rigour* from L. *rigor* 'stiffness'.

**rig-out** ● **n.** informal, chiefly Brit. an outfit of clothes.

**Rig Veda** /rɪg ˈveɪdə, ˈviːdə/ ● **n.** the oldest and principal of the Vedas.
– ORIGIN from Sanskrit *ṛgveda*, from *ṛc* '(sacred) stanza' + **VEDA**.

**rijsttafel** /ˈrʌɪstˌtɑːf(ə)l/ ● **n.** a meal of SE Asian food consisting of a selection of spiced rice dishes.
– ORIGIN Du., from *rijst* 'rice' + *tafel* 'table'.

**Riksmål** /ˈriːksmɔːl/ ● **n.** another term for **BOKMÅL**.
– ORIGIN Norw., from *rike* 'state, nation' + *mål* 'language'.

**rile** ● **v. 1** informal annoy or irritate. **2** N. Amer. make (water) turbulent or muddy.
– ORIGIN C19: var. of **ROIL**.

**Riley** ● **n.** (in phr. **the life of Riley**) informal a luxurious or carefree existence.
– ORIGIN C20: of unknown origin.

**rill** /rɪl/ ● **n. 1** a small stream. **2** a shallow channel cut in soil or rocks by running water. ➤variant spelling of **RILLE**.
– ORIGIN C16: prob. of Low Ger. origin.

**rille** /rɪl/ (also **rill**) ● **n.** Astronomy a fissure or narrow channel on the moon's surface.
– ORIGIN C19: from Ger. (see **RILL**).

**rillettes** /ˈriːjɛt/ ● **pl. n.** [treated as sing. or pl.] pâté of minced pork or other light meat, seasoned and combined with fat.
– ORIGIN Fr., dimin. (pl.) of OFr. *rille* 'strip of pork'.

**RIM** ● **abbrev.** Mauritania (international vehicle registration).
– ORIGIN from Fr. *République Islamique de Mauritanie*.

**rim¹** ● **n. 1** the upper or outer edge of something, typically something circular. ➤(also **wheel rim**) the outer edge of a wheel, on which the tyre is fitted. ➤the part of a spectacle frame surrounding the lenses. **2** the limit or boundary of something. ➤an encircling stain or deposit. ● **v.** (**rimmed**, **rimming**) (usu. **be rimmed**) provide with a rim.
– DERIVATIVES **rimless** adj. **-rimmed** adj.
– ORIGIN OE *rima* 'a border, coast', rel. to ON *rimi* 'ridge, strip of land'.

**rim²** ● **v.** (**rimmed**, **rimming**) vulgar slang lick or suck the anus of (a partner) for sexual stimulation.
– ORIGIN C20: perh. var. of **REAM²**.

**rime¹** /rʌɪm/ ● **n.** (also **rime ice**) frost formed on cold objects by the rapid freezing of water vapour in cloud or fog. ➤poetic/literary hoar frost. ● **v.** poetic/literary cover with hoar frost.
– ORIGIN OE *hrīm*, of Gmc origin.

**rime²** ● **n. & v.** archaic spelling of **RHYME**.

**rimfire** ● **adj.** (of a cartridge) having the primer around the edge of the base. ➤(of a rifle) adapted for such cartridges.

**rimshot** ● **n.** a drum stroke in which the stick strikes the rim and the head of the drum simultaneously.

**rimu** /ˈriːmuː/ ● **n.** a tall conifer which is the chief native softwood tree of New Zealand. [*Dacrydium cupressinum*.]
– ORIGIN C19: from Maori.

**rimy** /ˈrʌɪmi/ ● **adj.** (**-ier**, **-iest**) poetic/literary frosty.

**rind** ● **n.** a tough outer layer or covering, especially of fruit, cheese, or bacon. ➤the bark of a tree. ● **v.** strip the bark from (a tree).
– DERIVATIVES **-rinded** adj. **rindless** adj.
– ORIGIN OE *rind(e)*, of unknown origin.

**rinderpest** /ˈrɪndəpɛst/ ● **n.** an infectious viral disease of ruminants, especially cattle, characterized by fever and dysentery.
– ORIGIN C19: from Ger., from *Rinder* 'cattle' + *Pest* 'plague'.

**ring¹** ● **n. 1** a small circular band, typically of precious metal, worn on a finger as an ornament or as a token of marriage or engagement. **2** a circular band, article, or mark. ➤a thin band of rock and ice particles round a planet. ➤a flat circular heating device forming part of a gas or electric hob. ➤Archaeology a circular prehistoric earthwork, typically consisting of a bank and ditch. **3** an enclosed space in which a sport, performance, or show takes place. **4** a circle of people or things. ➤a group of people with a shared interest or goal, especially one involving illegal activity. **5** Chemistry a number of atoms bonded together to form a closed loop in a molecule. **6** Mathematics a set of elements with two binary operations, addition and multiplication, the second being distributive over the first and associative. ● **v. 1** surround. ➤draw a circle round. **2** Brit. Ornithology put an identifying strip around the leg of (a bird). **3** put a circular band through the nose of (a bull, pig, etc.) to lead or control it. **4** informal fraudulently change the identity of (a motor vehicle).
– PHRASES **hold the ring** monitor a dispute or conflict without becoming involved. **run** (or **make**) **rings round** (or **around**) informal outclass or outwit (someone) easily.
– DERIVATIVES **ringed** adj. **ringless** adj.
– ORIGIN OE *hring*, of Gmc origin; rel. to **RANK¹**.

**ring²** ● **v.** (past **rang**; past part. **rung**) **1** make or cause to make a clear resonant or vibrating sound. ➤(of a telephone) ring repeatedly to signal an incoming call. ➤call for attention by sounding a bell. ➤(often **ring with**) reverberate with a sound. ➤(of the ears) be filled with a buzzing or humming sound due to a blow or loud noise. ➤(**ring something up**) record an amount on a cash register. **2** chiefly Brit. call by telephone. ➤(**ring off**) Brit. end a telephone call by replacing the receiver. **3** sound (the hour, a peal, etc.) on a bell or bells. ➤(**ring someone/thing in** or **out**) usher someone or something in (or out) by or as if by ringing a bell. **4** convey a specified impression or quality: *the author's honesty rings true*. ➤(**ring with**) be filled with (a quality). ● **n. 1** an act or instance of ringing. ➤a loud clear sound or tone. **2** Brit. informal a telephone call. **3** a quality conveyed by something heard: *the tale had a ring of truth*. **4** a set of bells, especially church bells.
– PHRASES **ring down** (or **up**) **the curtain 1** lower (or raise) a theatre curtain. **2** mark the end (or beginning) of something.
– ORIGIN OE *hringan*, of Gmc origin, perh. imitative.

**ring-a-ring o' roses** ● **n.** a children's singing game in which players hold hands and dance in a circle, falling down at the end of the song.
– ORIGIN said to refer to the inflamed ('rose-coloured') ring of buboes, symptomatic of the plague.

**ringbark** ● **v.** remove a ring of bark from (a tree) to kill it or to check rapid growth and improve fruit production.

**ring binder** ● **n.** a loose-leaf binder with ring-shaped clasps that can be opened to pass through holes in the

paper.
– DERIVATIVES **ring-bound** adj.

**ringbolt** • n. a bolt with a ring attached for fitting a rope to.

**ringbone** • n. osteoarthritis of the pastern joint of a horse.

**ringdove** • n. **1** Brit. another term for **WOOD PIGEON**. **2** N. Amer. a captive or feral African collared dove. [*Streptopelia roseogrisea*.]

**ringer** • n. **1** informal a person's or thing's double. ➤an athlete or horse fraudulently substituted for another in a competition. ➤a motor vehicle whose identity has been fraudulently changed. **2** a person or device that rings something. **3** Austral./NZ a shearer with the highest tally of sheep shorn. ➤a person who looks after livestock.

**Ringer's solution** • n. Biology a physiological saline solution containing sodium chloride and salts of potassium and calcium.
– ORIGIN C19: named after the Engl. physician Sydney *Ringer*.

**ringette** • n. Canadian a game resembling ice hockey, played (especially by women and girls) with a straight stick and a rubber ring.

**ring fence** • n. **1** a fence completely enclosing a piece of land. **2** an effective barrier. • v. (**ring-fence**) **1** enclose with a ring fence. **2** guard securely. **3** guarantee that (funds for a particular purpose) will not be spent on anything else.

**ring finger** • n. the finger next to the little finger, especially of the left hand, on which the wedding ring is worn.

**ringgit** /ˈrɪŋɡɪt/ • n. (pl. same or **ringgits**) the basic monetary unit of Malaysia, equal to 100 sen.
– ORIGIN from Malay.

**ringing** • adj. **1** having a clear resonant sound. **2** (of a statement) forceful and unequivocal.
– DERIVATIVES **ringingly** adv.

**ringleader** • n. a person who leads an illicit activity.

**ringlet** • n. **1** a corkscrew-shaped curl of hair. **2** a brown butterfly with wings bearing eyespots. [*Aphantopus hyperantus* and other species.]
– DERIVATIVES **ringletted** (also **ringleted**) adj. **ringlety** adj.

**ring main** • n. Brit. **1** an electrical supply serving a series of consumers and returning to the original source. **2** an electric circuit serving a number of power points, with one fuse in the supply.

**ringmaster** • n. the person directing a circus performance.

**ringneck** • n. a bird with a ring of colour round the neck, especially a common pheasant with a white neck ring.
– DERIVATIVES **ring-necked** adj.

**ring ouzel** • n. an upland bird resembling a blackbird, with a white crescent across the breast. [*Turdus torquatus*.]

**ring pull** • n. a ring on a can that is pulled to open it.

**ring road** • n. a bypass encircling a town.

**ringside** • n. the area beside a boxing ring or circus ring.
– DERIVATIVES **ringsider** n.

**ringside seat** • n. an advantageous position from which to observe something.

**ring spanner** • n. a spanner in which the jaws form a ring which fits completely around a nut.

**ringtail** • n. **1** a mammal or bird having a tail marked with a ring or rings, e.g. a ring-tailed cat or lemur. **2** an Australian possum that habitually curls its tail into a ring. [*Pseudocheirus peregrinus* and other species.]
– DERIVATIVES **ring-tailed** adj.

**ring-tailed cat** • n. a raccoon-like mammal with a dark-ringed tail, found in North America. [*Bassariscus astutus*.]

**ring-tailed lemur** • n. a grey lemur with black rings around the eyes and a distinctive black-and-white banded tail. [*Lemur catta*.]

**ringwork** • n. Archaeology the circular entrenchment of a minor medieval castle.

**ringworm** • n. a contagious itching skin disease occurring in small circular patches, caused by any of a number of fungi and affecting chiefly the scalp or feet.

**rink** • n. **1** (also **ice rink**) an enclosed area of ice for skating, ice hockey, or curling. ➤(also **roller rink**) a smooth enclosed floor for roller skating. ➤(also **bowling rink**) the strip of a bowling green used for a match. **2** a team in curling or bowls.
– ORIGIN ME (orig. Scots in the sense 'jousting ground'): perh. orig. from OFr. *renc* 'rank'.

**rinkhals** /ˈrɪŋkhals/ • n. a large spitting cobra of southern Africa, with one or two white rings across the throat. [*Hemachatus haemachatus*.]
– ORIGIN C18: from Afrik. *rinkhals*, from *ring* 'ring' + *hals* 'neck'.

**rink rat** • n. N. Amer. informal **1** a young person who spends time around an ice-hockey rink. **2** a synthetic broom used in curling.

**rinky-dink** • adj. informal, chiefly N. Amer. old-fashioned, amateurish, or shoddy.
– ORIGIN C19: of unknown origin.

**Rinpoche** /ˈrɪnpɒtʃeɪ/ • n. a religious teacher held in high regard among Tibetan Buddhists.
– ORIGIN Tibetan, lit. 'precious jewel'.

**rinse** • v. wash with clean water to remove soap or dirt. ➤(often **rinse something off/out**) remove (soap or dirt) by rinsing. • n. **1** an act of rinsing. **2** an antiseptic solution for cleansing the mouth. **3** a preparation for conditioning or tinting the hair.
– DERIVATIVES **rinser** n.
– ORIGIN ME (as v.): from OFr. *rincer*, of unknown origin.

**Rioja** /rɪˈɒhə, rɪˈɒkə/ • n. a wine produced in La Rioja, Spain.

**riot** • n. **1** a violent disturbance of the peace by a crowd. ➤archaic rowdy behaviour. **2** a confused or lavish combination or display: *a riot of colour*. **3** (**a riot**) informal a highly amusing or entertaining person or thing. • v. **1** take part in a riot. **2** behave in an unrestrained way. **3** archaic act in a dissipated way.
– PHRASES **read the Riot Act** give a severe warning or reprimand. [from the name of a former act partly read out to disperse rioters.] **run riot 1** behave or be displayed in a violent and unrestrained way. **2** proliferate or spread uncontrollably.
– DERIVATIVES **rioter** n.
– ORIGIN ME: from OFr. *riote* 'debate', from *rioter* 'to quarrel', of unknown ultimate origin.

**riot girl** (also **riot grrrl**) • n. a member of a movement of young feminists favouring aggressive punk-style rock music.

**riotous** • adj. **1** marked by or involving public disorder. ➤involving wild and uncontrolled behaviour. **2** having a vivid, varied appearance.
– DERIVATIVES **riotously** adv. **riotousness** n.

**RIP** • abbrev. rest in peace (used on graves).
– ORIGIN from L. *requiescat* (or (pl.) *requiescant*) *in pace*.

**rip**[1] • v. (**ripped**, **ripping**) **1** tear or pull forcibly away from something or someone. ➤tear. ➤(**rip something up**) tear something into small pieces. **2** move forcefully and rapidly. **3** (**rip into**) informal make a vehement verbal attack on. **4** (**rip someone off**) informal cheat someone, especially financially. ➤(**rip something off**) informal steal or plagiarize something. **5** Computing use a program to copy (a sound sequence on a compact disc) on to a computer's hard drive. • n. **1** a long tear or cut. **2** N. Amer. a fraud or swindle.
– PHRASES **let rip** informal proceed vigorously or without restraint. ➤express oneself vehemently.
– ORIGIN ME (as v.): of unknown origin; cf. **REAP**.

**rip**[2] • n. a stretch of fast-flowing and rough water caused by the meeting of currents.
– ORIGIN C18: perh. rel. to **RIP**[1].

**rip**[3] • n. informal, dated **1** a dissolute immoral man. ➤a mischievous child. **2** a worthless horse.
– ORIGIN C18: perh. from *rep*, abbrev. of **REPROBATE**.

**riparian** /rʌɪˈpɛːrɪən/ • adj. of, relating to, or situated on the banks of a river.
– ORIGIN C19: from L. *riparius* (from *ripa* 'bank') + **-AN**.

**ripcord** • n. a cord that is pulled to open a parachute.

**rip current** • n. an intermittent strong surface current flowing seaward from the shore.

**ripe** • adj. **1** (of fruit or grain) ready for harvesting and eating. ➤ (of a cheese or wine) fully matured. **2** (**ripe for**) arrived at a fitting time for. **3** (of a person's age) advanced. **4** (**ripe with**) full of. **5** (of a female fish or insect) ready to lay eggs or spawn.
– DERIVATIVES **ripely** adv. **ripeness** n.
– ORIGIN OE *rīpe*, of W. Gmc origin.

**ripen** • v. become or make ripe.

**ripieno** /ˌrɪpɪˈeɪnəʊ/ • n. (pl. **ripienos** or **ripieni** /-ni/) Music the body of instruments accompanying the concertino in baroque concerto music.
– ORIGIN C18 (in the sense 'supplementary'): from Ital., from *ri-* 'again' + *pieno* 'full'.

**rip-off** • n. informal **1** an article that is greatly overpriced. **2** an inferior imitation.

**riposte** /rɪˈpɒst/ • n. **1** a quick clever reply. **2** a quick return thrust in fencing. • v. make a riposte.
– ORIGIN C18: from Fr. *risposte* (n.), *risposter* (v.), from Ital. *risposta* 'response'.

**ripper** • n. **1** a person or thing that rips. **2** informal a thing that is particularly admirable or excellent.

**ripping** • adj. Brit. informal, dated excellent.
– DERIVATIVES **rippingly** adv.

**ripple** • n. **1** a small wave or series of waves. ➤ Physics a small wave in which the dominant force is surface tension rather than gravity. **2** a gentle rising and falling sound that spreads through a group of people. ➤ a feeling that spreads through someone or something. **3** a small periodic voltage variation superposed on a direct voltage or low-frequency alternating voltage. **4** a type of ice cream with wavy lines of coloured flavoured syrup running through it. • v. **1** form or cause to form ripples. **2** (of a sound or feeling) spread through a person or place.
– DERIVATIVES **ripplet** n. **ripply** adj.
– ORIGIN C17: of unknown origin.

**ripple marks** • pl. n. a system of parallel wavy ridges and furrows left on sand, mud, or rock by the action of water or wind.

**riprap** N. Amer. • n. loose stone used to form a foundation for a breakwater or other structure. • v. (**riprapped**, **riprapping**) strengthen with riprap.
– ORIGIN C19: reduplication of RAP[1].

**rip-roaring** • adj. full of energy and vigour.
– DERIVATIVES **rip-roaringly** adv.

**ripsaw** • n. a coarse saw for cutting wood along the grain.

**ripsnorting** • adj. informal showing great vigour or intensity.
– DERIVATIVES **ripsnorter** n. **ripsnortingly** adv.

**ripstop** • n. nylon fabric that is woven so that a tear will not spread.

**rip tide** • n. another term for RIP[2].

**RISC** • n. [usu. as modifier] computers or computing based on a form of microprocessor designed to perform a limited set of operations extremely quickly.
– ORIGIN 1980s: acronym from *reduced instruction set computer* (or *computing*).

**rise** • v. (past **rose**; past part. **risen**) **1** come or go up. ➤ reach a higher social or professional position. ➤ (**rise above**) succeed in not being constrained by. **2** get up from lying, sitting, or kneeling. ➤ chiefly Brit. (of a meeting or a session of a court) adjourn. **3** (of land) incline upwards. ➤ (of a structure or natural feature) be much taller than the surrounding landscape. **4** (of the sun, moon, or stars) appear above the horizon. **5** increase in number, size, intensity, or quality. **6** (**rise to**) respond adequately to (a challenging situation). **7** (often **rise up**) cease to be submissive or peaceful. **8** (of a river) have its source: *the Euphrates rises in Turkey.* **9** be restored to life. • n. **1** an act or instance of rising. **2** an upward slope or hill. **3** Brit. an increase in salary or wages. **4** the source of a river. **5** the vertical height of a step, arch, or incline. ➤ another term for RISER (in sense 2).
– PHRASES **get** (or **take**) **a rise out of** informal provoke an angry or irritated response from. **on the rise 1** increasing. **2** becoming more successful. **rise and shine** informal wake up and get out of bed promptly.
– ORIGIN OE *rīsan* 'make an attack', 'get out of bed', of Gmc origin.

**riser** • n. **1** a person who habitually gets out of bed at a particular time of the morning: *an early riser.* **2** a vertical section between the treads of a staircase. **3** a vertical pipe for the upward flow of liquid or gas. **4** a low platform on a stage or in an auditorium. **5** a strip of webbing joining the harness and the rigging lines of a parachute or paraglider.

**rishi** /ˈrɪʃi/ • n. (pl. **rishis**) a Hindu sage or saint.
– ORIGIN from Sanskrit *ṛṣi*.

**risible** /ˈrɪzɪb(ə)l/ • adj. such as to provoke laughter.
– DERIVATIVES **risibility** n. **risibly** adv.
– ORIGIN C16 (in the sense 'inclined to laughter'): from late L. *risibilis*, from L. *ris-*, *ridere* 'to laugh'.

**rising** • adj. **1** approaching a specified age. **2** [postpos.] Heraldry (of a bird) depicted with the wings open but not fully displayed, as if preparing for flight. • n. a revolt.

**rising damp** • n. Brit. moisture absorbed from the ground into a wall.

**rising sign** • n. Astrology an ascendant sign.

**risk** • n. **1** a situation involving exposure to danger. ➤ the possibility that something unpleasant will happen. **2** a person or thing causing a risk or regarded in relation to risk: *a fire risk.* • v. expose to danger or loss. ➤ act in such a way as to incur the risk of. ➤ incur risk by engaging in (an action).
– PHRASES **at one's** (**own**) **risk** taking responsibility for one's own safety or possessions. **run** (or **take**) **a risk** (or **risks**) act in such a way as to expose oneself to danger.
– ORIGIN C17: from Fr. *risque* (n.), *risquer* (v.), from Ital. *risco* 'danger' and *rischiare* 'run into danger'.

**risk capital** • n. another term for VENTURE CAPITAL.

**risky** • adj. (**-ier**, **-iest**) **1** involving risk. **2** risqué.
– DERIVATIVES **riskily** adv. **riskiness** n.

**risotto** /rɪˈzɒtəʊ/ • n. (pl. **-os**) an Italian dish of rice cooked in stock with ingredients such as meat or seafood.
– ORIGIN Ital., from *riso* 'rice'.

**risqué** /rɪˈskeɪ, ˈrɪskeɪ, ˈriːskeɪ/ • adj. slightly indecent and liable to shock.
– ORIGIN C19: Fr., past part. of *risquer* 'to risk'.

**rissole** • n. a compressed mixture of meat and spices, coated in breadcrumbs and fried.
– ORIGIN C18: from Fr., from OFr. dial. *ruissole*, from a fem. form of late L. *russeolus* 'reddish'.

**rit.** • abbrev. Music **1** ritardando. **2** ritenuto.

**Ritalin** /ˈrɪtəlɪn/ • n. trademark for METHYLPHENIDATE.
– ORIGIN 1940s: invented word.

**ritardando** /ˌrɪtɑːˈdandəʊ/ • adv. & adj. Music another term for RALLENTANDO.
– ORIGIN from Ital.

**rite** • n. **1** a religious or other solemn ceremony or act. **2** a body of customary observances characteristic of a Church or a part of it.
– PHRASES **rite of passage** a ceremony or event, e.g. marriage, marking an important stage in someone's life.
– ORIGIN ME: from L. *ritus* '(religious) usage'.

**ritenuto** /ˌrɪtɛˈn(j)uːtəʊ/ • adv. & adj. Music with an immediate reduction of speed.
– ORIGIN Ital., lit. 'restrained'.

**ritornello** /ˌrɪtɔːˈnɛləʊ/ • n. (pl. **ritornellos** or **ritornelli** /-li/) Music a short instrumental refrain or interlude in a vocal work.
– ORIGIN Ital., dimin. of *ritorno* 'return'.

**ritual** • n. **1** a religious or solemn ceremony involving a series of actions performed according to a prescribed order. ➤ a prescribed order of performing such a ceremony. **2** a series of actions habitually and invariably followed by someone. • adj. of, relating to, or done as a ritual.
– DERIVATIVES **ritually** adv.
– ORIGIN C16: from L. *ritualis*, from *ritus* (see RITE).

**ritual abuse** (also **satanic abuse**) ● n. the alleged sexual abuse or murder of people, especially children, supposedly committed as part of satanic rituals.

**ritualism** ● n. the regular observance or practice of ritual, especially when excessive or without regard to its function.
– DERIVATIVES **ritualist** n. **ritualistic** adj. **ritualistically** adv.

**ritualize** (also **-ise**) ● v. [usu. as adj. **ritualized**] **1** make into a ritual by following a pattern of actions or behaviour. **2** Zoology retain (a behaviour pattern) as a form of display or interaction, without its original function.
– DERIVATIVES **ritualization** n.

**ritz** ● n. informal ostentatious luxury and glamour.
– ORIGIN C20: from *Ritz*, a name assoc. with luxury hotels, from the Swiss hotel owner César *Ritz*.

**ritzy** ● adj. (**-ier**, **-iest**) informal expensively stylish.
– DERIVATIVES **ritzily** adv. **ritziness** n.

**rival** ● n. a person or thing competing with another for superiority or the same objective. ➤ [with neg.] a person or thing equal to another in quality. ● v. (**rivalled**, **rivalling**; US **rivaled**, **rivaling**) be comparable to.
– DERIVATIVES **rivalrous** adj. **rivalry** n. (pl. **-ies**).
– ORIGIN C16: from L. *rivalis*, orig. in the sense 'person using the same stream as another', from *rivus* 'stream'.

**rive** /rʌɪv/ ● v. (past **rived**; past part. **riven** /'rɪv(ə)n/) (usu. **be riven**) tear apart. ➤ archaic (with reference to wood or stone) split.
– ORIGIN ME: from ON *rífa*.

**river** ● n. **1** a large natural flow of water travelling along a channel to the sea, a lake, or another river. ➤ used in names of animals and plants living in or associated with rivers, e.g. **river dolphin**. **2** a large quantity of a flowing substance.
– PHRASES **sell someone down the river** informal betray someone. [orig. with ref. to the sale of a troublesome slave to a plantation owner on the lower Mississippi, where conditions were relatively harsher.] **up the river** informal, chiefly N. Amer. to or in prison. [with allusion to Sing Sing prison, situated up the Hudson River from the city of New York.]
– DERIVATIVES **rivered** adj. **riverless** adj.
– ORIGIN ME: from Anglo-Norman Fr., based on L. *riparius*, from *ripa* 'bank of a river'.

**river blindness** ● n. a tropical skin disease, sometimes also causing blindness, caused by a parasitic filarial worm and transmitted by blackflies which breed in rivers.

**river capture** ● n. Geology the natural diversion of the headwaters of one stream into the channel of another, due to erosion.

**riverine** /'rɪvərʌɪn/ ● adj. technical or poetic/literary of, relating to, or situated on a river or riverbank.

**riverside** ● n. the ground along a riverbank.

**rivet** /'rɪvɪt/ ● n. a short metal pin or bolt for holding together two metal plates, its headless end being beaten out or pressed down when in place. ● v. (**riveted**, **riveting**) **1** join or fasten with a rivet or rivets. **2** (usu. **be riveted**) completely engross. ➤ direct (one's eyes or attention) intently.
– DERIVATIVES **riveter** n. **riveting** adj. **rivetingly** adv.
– ORIGIN ME: from OFr., from *river* 'fix, clinch'.

**riviera** /ˌrɪvɪ'ɛːrə/ ● n. a coastal region with a subtropical climate and vegetation. ➤ (**the Riviera**) part of the Mediterranean coastal region of southern France and northern Italy.
– ORIGIN C18: from Ital., lit. 'seashore'.

**rivière** /ˌrɪvɪ'ɛː/ ● n. a necklace of gems that increase in size towards a large central stone, typically consisting of more than one string.
– ORIGIN C19: Fr., lit. 'river'.

**rivulet** /'rɪvjʊlɪt/ ● n. a very small stream.
– ORIGIN C16: alt. of obs. *riveret* (from Fr., lit. 'small river').

**riyal** ● n. variant spelling of **RIAL**.

**RL** ● abbrev. **1** rugby league. **2** Lebanon (international vehicle registration). [from *Republic of Lebanon*.]

**rly** ● abbrev. railway.

**RM** ● abbrev. **1** Madagascar (international vehicle registration). [from Fr. *République de Madagascar*.] **2** (in the UK) Royal Mail. **3** (in the UK) Royal Marines.

**rm** ● abbrev. room.

**RMA** ● abbrev. Royal Military Academy.

**RMM** ● abbrev. Mali (international vehicle registration).

**RMP** ● abbrev. Royal Military Police.

**rms** ● abbrev. root mean square.

**RMT** ● abbrev. (in the UK) National Union of Rail, Maritime, and Transport Workers.

**RN** ● abbrev. **1** (in the UK) Royal Navy. **2** Niger (international vehicle registration). [from Fr. *République du Niger*.] **3** (chiefly in North America) Registered Nurse.

**Rn** ● symb. the chemical element radon.

**RNA** ● n. Biochemistry ribonucleic acid, a substance in living cells which carries instructions from DNA for controlling the synthesis of proteins and in some viruses carries genetic information instead of DNA.

**RNAS** ● abbrev. (in the UK) Royal Naval Air Station.

**RNase** ● n. Biochemistry an enzyme which breaks down RNA into smaller molecules.
– ORIGIN 1950s: from **RNA** + **-ASE**.

**RNA virus** ● n. a virus in which the genetic information is stored in the form of RNA (as opposed to DNA).

**RNLI** ● abbrev. (in the UK) Royal National Lifeboat Institution.

**RNZAF** ● abbrev. Royal New Zealand Air Force.

**RNZN** ● abbrev. Royal New Zealand Navy.

**roach**[1] ● n. (pl. same) a common freshwater fish of the carp family. [*Rutilus rutilus*.]
– ORIGIN ME: from OFr. *roche*.

**roach**[2] ● n. informal **1** chiefly N. Amer. a cockroach. **2** a roll of card or paper that forms the butt of a cannabis cigarette. [1930s: of unknown origin.]

**roach**[3] ● n. Sailing a curved part of a fore-and-aft sail extending beyond a straight line between its corners, especially on the leech side. ● v. [as adj. **roached**] chiefly US (especially of an animal's back) having an upward curve.
– ORIGIN C18: of unknown origin.

**road** ● n. **1** a wide way between places, especially one surfaced for use by vehicles. **2** a way to achieving a particular outcome. **3** a partly sheltered stretch of water near the shore in which ships can ride at anchor: *Boston Roads*. **4** N. Amer. a railroad. ➤ Brit. a railway track, especially as clear (or otherwise) for a train to proceed. **5** an underground passage or gallery in a mine.
– PHRASES **down the road** informal, chiefly N. Amer. in the future. **in** (or **out of**) **the** (or **one's**) **road** informal in (or out of) someone's way. **one for the road** informal a final alcoholic drink before leaving. **on the road 1** on a long journey or series of journeys. ➤ without a permanent home and moving from place to place. **2** (of a car) able to be driven.
– DERIVATIVES **roadless** adj.
– ORIGIN OE *rād* 'journey on horseback', 'foray', of Gmc origin; rel. to **RIDE**.

**roadbed** ● n. **1** the material laid down to form a road. **2** another term for **TRACKBED**.

**roadblock** ● n. a barrier put across a road by the police or army to stop and examine traffic.

**road fund** ● n. Brit. historical a fund for the construction and maintenance of roads and bridges.

**road fund licence** ● n. Brit. a disc displayed on a vehicle certifying payment of road tax.

**road hog** ● n. informal a motorist who drives recklessly or inconsiderately.

**roadholding** ● n. the ability of a moving vehicle to remain stable, especially when cornering.

**roadhouse** ● n. a pub, club, or restaurant on a country road.

**road hump** ● n. another term for **SLEEPING POLICEMAN**.

**roadie** ● n. informal a person employed by a touring band of musicians to set up and maintain equipment.

**road kill** ● n. chiefly N. Amer. a killing of an animal on the road by a vehicle. ➤ animals so killed.

**road manager** • n. the organizer and supervisor of a musicians' tour.

**road movie** • n. a film of a genre in which the main character spends most of the time travelling.

**road pricing** • n. the practice of charging motorists to use busy roads at certain times, especially to relieve congestion in urban areas.

**road rage** • n. violent anger arising from conflict with the driver of another motor vehicle.

**roadroller** • n. a motor vehicle with a heavy roller, used in road-making.

**roadrunner** • n. a fast-running long-tailed bird of the cuckoo family, found chiefly in arid country from the southern US to Central America. [Genus *Geococcyx*: two species.]

**roadshow** • n. each of a series of radio or television programmes broadcast on location from different venues. ➤a touring political or promotional campaign. ➤a touring show of pop musicians.

**roadside** • n. the strip of land beside a road.

**roadstead** • n. another term for **ROAD** (in sense 3).
– ORIGIN C16: from **ROAD** + **STEAD** in the sense 'a place'.

**roadster** • n. **1** an open-top motor car with two seats. **2** a bicycle designed for use on the road. **3** a horse for use on the road.

**road tax** • n. Brit. a periodic tax payable on motor vehicles using public roads.

**road test** • n. **1** a test of the performance of a vehicle or engine on the road. **2** a test of equipment carried out in working conditions. • v. (**road-test**) subject to a road test.

**road train** • n. chiefly Austral. a large truck pulling one or more trailers.

**roadway** • n. a road. ➤the part of a road intended for vehicles, in contrast to the pavement or verge.

**roadwork** • n. **1** (**roadworks**) Brit. repairs to roads or to utilities under roads. **2** athletic exercise or training involving running on roads.

**roadworthy** • adj. (of a vehicle) fit to be used on the road.
– DERIVATIVES **roadworthiness** n.

**roam** • v. travel aimlessly over a wide area. ➤wander over, through, or about (a place). ➤(of a person's eyes or hands) pass lightly over. • n. an aimless walk.
– DERIVATIVES **roamer** n.
– ORIGIN ME: of unknown origin.

**roan**[1] • adj. denoting an animal, especially a horse or cow, having a coat of a main colour thickly interspersed with hairs of another colour, typically bay, chestnut, or black mixed with white. • n. a roan animal.
– ORIGIN C16: from OFr.

**roan**[2] • n. soft flexible leather made from sheepskin, used in bookbinding as a substitute for morocco.
– ORIGIN C19: perh. from *Roan*, the old name of the Fr. town of *Rouen*.

**roar** • n. a full, deep, prolonged sound as made by a lion, natural force, or engine. ➤a loud, deep sound uttered by a person, especially as an expression of pain, anger, or great amusement. • v. **1** make or utter a roar. ➤express in a roar. ➤laugh loudly. ➤(of a horse) make a loud noise in breathing as a symptom of disease of the larynx. **2** (especially of a vehicle) move at high speed making a roar. ➤act or happen fast and decisively.
– DERIVATIVES **roarer** n.
– ORIGIN OE *rārian* (v.), imitative of a deep prolonged cry, of W. Gmc origin.

**roaring** • adj. informal unmistakable; emphatic: *a roaring success*.
– PHRASES **do a roaring trade** (or **business**) informal do very good business. **the roaring forties** stormy ocean tracts between latitudes 40° and 50° south. **the roaring twenties** the prosperous years of the 1920s.
– DERIVATIVES **roaringly** adv.

**roast** • v. **1** (with reference to food, especially meat) cook or be cooked by prolonged exposure to heat in an oven or over a fire. ➤process (a foodstuff, metal ore, etc.) by subjecting it to intense heat. **2** make or become very warm. **3** criticize or reprimand severely. • adj. (of food) having been roasted. • n. **1** a joint of meat that has been roasted or that is intended for roasting. ➤a dish or meal of roasted food. **2** the process of roasting something, especially coffee. ➤a particular type of roasted coffee. **3** an outdoor party at which meat is roasted.
– DERIVATIVES **roaster** n.
– ORIGIN ME: from OFr. *rostir*, of W. Gmc origin.

**roasting** informal • adj. very hot and dry. • n. a severe criticism or reprimand.

**rob** • v. (**robbed**, **robbing**) **1** take property unlawfully from (a person or place) by force or threat of force. ➤informal or dialect steal. ➤informal overcharge. **2** deprive of something needed, deserved, or significant.
– PHRASES **rob Peter to pay Paul** deprive one person of something in order to pay another. [prob. with ref. to the saints and apostles *Peter* and *Paul*.]
– DERIVATIVES **robber** n.
– ORIGIN ME: from OFr. *rober*, of Gmc origin; rel. to **REAVE**.

**robber baron** • n. a ruthless plutocrat.

**robber fly** • n. a large powerful predatory fly which darts out and grabs insect prey on the wing. [Family Asilidae.]

**robbery** • n. (pl. **-ies**) the action of robbing a person or place. ➤informal unashamed swindling or overcharging.

**robe** • n. **1** a long, loose outer garment reaching to the ankles. ➤such a garment worn, especially on formal or ceremonial occasions, as an indication of the wearer's rank, office, or profession. **2** N. Amer. a lap robe. • v. [usu. as adj. **robed**] clothe in or put on a robe or robes.
– ORIGIN ME: from OFr., from the Gmc base (in the sense 'booty') of **ROB** (because clothing was an important component of booty).

**robin** • n. **1** a small European songbird of the thrush family with a red breast and brown back and wings. [*Erithacus rubecula*.] **2** (also **American robin**) a large North American thrush with an orange-red breast. [*Turdus migratorius*.] **3** used in names of numerous similar or related birds, e.g. **Pekin robin**.
– ORIGIN C16: from OFr., familiar form of the given name *Robert*.

**Robin Goodfellow** • n. a mischievous sprite or goblin formerly believed to haunt the English countryside.

**robinia** /rəˈbɪnɪə/ • n. a North American tree or shrub of a genus that includes the false acacia. [Genus *Robinia*.]
– ORIGIN mod. L., named after Jean and Vespasien *Robin*, C17 Fr. gardeners.

**robin's-egg blue** • n. N. Amer. a greenish-blue colour.

**robin's pincushion** • n. another term for **BEDEGUAR**.

**robot** /ˈrəʊbɒt/ • n. **1** a machine capable of carrying out a complex series of actions automatically, especially one programmable by a computer. **2** S. African a set of automatic traffic lights.
– DERIVATIVES **robotization** (also **-isation**) n. **robotize** (also **-ise**) v.
– ORIGIN from Czech, from *robota* 'forced labour'; the term was coined in K. Čapek's play *R.U.R.* 'Rossum's Universal Robots' (1920).

**robotic** /rə(ʊ)ˈbɒtɪk/ • adj. **1** of or relating to robots. **2** mechanical, stiff, or unemotional.
– DERIVATIVES **robotically** adv.

**robotics** • pl. n. [treated as sing.] the branch of technology concerned with the design, construction, operation, and application of robots.

**robust** • adj. (**-er**, **-est**) **1** sturdy or resilient. ➤strong and healthy. **2** not perturbed by or attending to subtleties. **3** (of wine or food) strong and rich in flavour or smell.
– DERIVATIVES **robustly** adv. **robustness** n.
– ORIGIN C16: from L. *robustus* 'firm and hard'.

**robusta** • n. coffee beans from a West African species of coffee plant (*Coffea canephora*, formerly *robusta*).
– ORIGIN C20: mod. L., fem. of L. *robustus* 'robust'.

**ROC** • abbrev. historical (in the UK) Royal Observer Corps.

**roc** • n. a gigantic mythological bird described in the Arabian Nights.
– ORIGIN C16: ult. from Pers. *ruk*.

**rocaille** /rə(ʊ)ˈkʌɪ/ ● **n.** an 18th-century artistic or architectural style of decoration characterized by elaborate ornamentation with pebbles and shells.
– ORIGIN Fr., from *roc* 'rock'.

**rocambole** /ˈrɒk(ə)mbəʊl/ ● **n.** a plant that is closely related to garlic and is sometimes used as a flavouring. [*Allium scorodoprasum*.]
– ORIGIN C17: from Fr., from Ger. *Rockenbolle*.

**ROCE** ● **abbrev.** Finance return on capital employed.

**Roche limit** /rəʊʃ/ ● **n.** Astronomy the distance within which the gravitational field of a large body is strong enough to prevent any smaller body from being held together by gravity.
– ORIGIN C19: named after the Fr. mathematician Edouard Albert *Roche*.

**roche moutonnée** /ˌrɒʃ muːˈtɒneɪ/ ● **n.** (pl. **roches moutonnées** pronunc. same) Geology a small bare outcrop of rock shaped by glacial erosion, with one side smooth and gently sloping and the other steep, rough, and irregular.
– ORIGIN C19: Fr., lit. 'fleecy rock'.

**rochet** /ˈrɒtʃɪt/ ● **n.** Christian Church a vestment resembling a surplice, worn chiefly by bishops and abbots.
– ORIGIN ME: from OFr., a dimin. from a Gmc base shared by Ger. *Rock* 'coat'.

**rock**[1] ● **n. 1** the hard mineral material of the earth's crust, exposed on the surface or underlying the soil. ➤a mass of this projecting out of the ground or water. ➤(**the Rock**) Gibraltar. ➤a boulder. ➤N. Amer. a stone of any size. **2** Geology any natural material with a distinctive mineral composition. **3** Brit. a kind of hard confectionery in the form of cylindrical peppermint-flavoured sticks. **4** informal a diamond or other precious stone. **5** informal a small piece of crack cocaine. **6** (**rocks**) vulgar slang a man's testicles.
– PHRASES **between a rock and a hard place** informal faced with two equally difficult alternatives. **get one's rocks off** vulgar slang have an orgasm. **on the rocks** informal **1** experiencing difficulties and likely to fail. **2** (of a drink) served undiluted and with ice cubes.
– DERIVATIVES **rockless** adj. **rock-like** adj.
– ORIGIN ME: from OFr. *rocque*, from med. L. *rocca*.

**rock**[2] ● **v. 1** move gently to and fro or from side to side. ➤shake, especially because of an earthquake or explosion. **2** cause great shock or distress to. **3** informal dance to or play rock music. **4** informal have an atmosphere of excitement or much social activity. ● **n. 1** (also **rock music**) a form of popular music derived from rock and roll and pop music but characterized by a more serious approach. ➤rock and roll. **2** a rocking movement.
– ORIGIN OE *roccian*, prob. from a Gmc base meaning 'remove, move'.

**rockabilly** ● **n.** a type of popular music, originating in the south-eastern US, combining elements of rock and roll and country music.
– ORIGIN 1950s: blend of **ROCK AND ROLL** and **HILLBILLY**.

**rock and roll** (also **rock 'n' roll**) ● **n.** a type of popular dance music originating in the 1950s from an amalgamation of rhythm and blues and country music and characterized by a heavy beat and simple melodies.
– DERIVATIVES **rock and roller** n.

**rock bass** ● **n.** a red-eyed North American sunfish of rocky streams. [*Ambloplites rupestris*.]

**rock-bottom** ● **adj.** at the lowest possible level. ● **n.** (**rock bottom**) the lowest possible level.

**rock-bound** ● **adj.** (of a coast or shore) rocky and inaccessible.

**rockburst** ● **n.** a sudden, violent rupture or collapse of highly stressed rock in a mine.

**rock cake** ● **n.** chiefly Brit. a small currant cake with a hard rough surface.

**rock candy** ● **n.** N. Amer. a kind of hard confectionery typically made of masses of crystallized sugar.

**rock climbing** ● **n.** the sport or pastime of climbing rock faces, especially with the aid of ropes and special equipment.
– DERIVATIVES **rock climb** n. **rock climber** n.

**rock cress** ● **n.** another term for **ARABIS**.

**rock crystal** ● **n.** transparent quartz, typically in the form of colourless hexagonal crystals.

**rock dove** ● **n.** a mainly blue-grey pigeon of coastal and inland cliffs, the ancestor of domestic and feral pigeons. [*Columba livia*.]

**rocker** ● **n. 1** a person who performs, dances to, or enjoys rock music. ➤a rock song. ➤Brit. a young person, especially in the 1960s, belonging to a subculture characterized by leather clothing, riding motorcycles, and a liking for rock music. **2** a rocking chair. **3** a curved bar or similar support on which something such as a chair can rock. ➤a rocking device forming part of a mechanism. **4** the amount of curvature in the longitudinal contour of a boat or surfboard.
– PHRASES **off one's rocker** informal mad.

**rocker switch** ● **n.** an electrical on/off switch incorporating a spring-loaded rocker.

**rockery** ● **n.** (pl. **-ies**) a heaped arrangement of rocks with soil between them, planted with rock plants.

**rocket**[1] ● **n. 1** a cylindrical projectile that can be propelled to a great height or distance by the combustion of its contents. ➤a missile or spacecraft propelled by an engine providing thrust on the same principle. **2** Brit. informal a severe reprimand. ● **v.** (**rocketed**, **rocketing**) **1** (of an amount, price, etc.) increase very rapidly and suddenly. **2** move or progress very rapidly. **3** attack with rocket-propelled missiles.
– ORIGIN C17: from Fr. *roquette*, from Ital. *rocchetto*, dimin. of *rocca* 'distaff (for spinning)', with ref. to its cylindrical shape.

**rocket**[2] ● **n.** an edible Mediterranean plant of the cabbage family, eaten in salads. [*Eruca vesicaria* subsp. *sativa*.] ➤used in names of other fast-growing plants of this family, e.g. **sweet rocket**.
– ORIGIN C15: from Fr. *roquette*, from Ital. *ruchetta*, dimin. of *ruca*, from L. *eruca* 'downy-stemmed plant'.

**rocketeer** ● **n.** a person who designs or operates space rockets.

**rocketry** ● **n.** the branch of science and technology concerned with rockets.

**rocket scientist** ● **n.** [usu. with neg.] informal, chiefly N. Amer. a very intelligent person.

**rock face** ● **n.** a bare vertical surface of natural rock.

**rockfall** ● **n.** a descent of loose rocks. ➤a mass of fallen rock.

**rockfish** ● **n.** (pl. same or **-fishes**) a marine fish of the scorpionfish family with a laterally compressed body. [Genus *Sebastes*: numerous species.]

**rock flour** ● **n.** finely powdered rock formed by glacial or other erosion.

**rock garden** ● **n.** a rockery. ➤a garden in which rockeries are the chief feature.

**rockhopper** ● **n.** a small penguin with a yellowish crest, breeding on subantarctic coastal cliffs. [*Eudyptes chrysocome*.]

**rockhound** ● **n.** informal, chiefly N. Amer. a geologist or amateur collector of mineral specimens.
– DERIVATIVES **rockhounding** n.

**rocking chair** ● **n.** a chair mounted on rockers or springs.

**rocking horse** ● **n.** a model of a horse mounted on rockers or springs for a child to ride on.

**rocking stone** ● **n.** a boulder poised in such a way that it can be easily rocked.

**rockling** ● **n.** a slender marine fish of the cod family, typically occurring in shallow water or tidal pools. [Genera *Ciliata* and *Rhinomenus*: several species.]

**rock 'n' roll** ● **n.** variant spelling of **ROCK AND ROLL**.

**rock pigeon** ● **n.** another term for **ROCK DOVE**.

**rock pipit** ● **n.** a dark-coloured pipit frequenting rocky shores in NW Europe. [*Anthus petrosus*.]

**rock plant** ● **n.** a plant that grows on or among rocks.

**rock pool** ● **n.** a pool of water among rocks, typically along a shoreline.

**rock rabbit** ● **n.** another term for **PIKA**.

**rock-ribbed** ● **adj.** N. Amer. uncompromising, especially with respect to political allegiance.

**rock rose** ● **n.** a herbaceous or shrubby plant with rose-like flowers, native to temperate and warm regions. [Genera *Cistus* and *Helianthemum*.]

**rock salmon** ● n. **1** a tropical snapper found both in the sea and in rivers, valued for food and sport. [*Lutjanus argentimaculatus*.] **2** Brit. dogfish or wolf fish as food.

**rock salt** ● n. common salt occurring naturally as a mineral.

**rockslide** ● n. a rockfall.

**rock solid** ● adj. completely firm or stable.

**rocksteady** ● n. an early form of reggae music originating in Jamaica in the 1960s, characterized by a slow tempo.

**rockumentary** ● n. informal a documentary about rock music and musicians.
– ORIGIN 1970s: from ROCK[2] + DOCUMENTARY.

**rock wool** ● n. inorganic material made into matted fibre, used especially for insulation or soundproofing.

**rocky[1]** ● adj. (**-ier**, **-iest**) consisting or formed of rock. ➤ full of rocks.
– DERIVATIVES **rockiness** n.

**rocky[2]** ● adj. (**-ier**, **-iest**) unsteady or unstable.
– DERIVATIVES **rockily** adv. **rockiness** n.

**Rocky Mountain goat** ● n. see MOUNTAIN GOAT (sense 1).

**Rocky Mountain spotted fever** ● n. see SPOTTED FEVER.

**rococo** /rəˈkəʊkəʊ/ ● adj. **1** relating to or denoting an elaborately ornate late baroque style of European furniture or architecture of the 18th century, characterized by asymmetrical patterns involving motifs and scrollwork. **2** (of music or literature) highly ornamented and florid. ● n. the rococo style.
– ORIGIN C19: from Fr., humorous alt. of ROCAILLE.

**rod** ● n. **1** a thin straight bar, especially of wood or metal. **2** a fishing rod. **3** a slender straight stick or shoot growing on or cut from a tree or bush. ➤ (**the rod**) the use of a stick for caning or flogging. **4** historical, chiefly Brit. another term for PERCH[3] (in sense 1). ➤ (also **square rod**) another term for PERCH[3] (in sense 2). **5** US informal a pistol or revolver. **6** Anatomy one of two types of light-sensitive cell present in the retina of the eye, responsible mainly for monochrome vision in poor light. Compare with CONE (in sense 3).
– PHRASES **make a rod for one's own back** do something likely to cause difficulties for oneself later. **rule someone/thing with a rod of iron** control or govern someone or something very harshly.
– DERIVATIVES **rodless** adj. **rodlet** n. **rod-like** adj.
– ORIGIN OE *rodd*; prob. rel. to ON *rudda* 'club'.

**rode[1]** past of RIDE.

**rode[2]** ● v. (of a woodcock) fly on a regular circuit in the evening as a territorial display, making sharp calls and grunts.
– ORIGIN C18: of unknown origin.

**rode[3]** ● n. N. Amer. Nautical a rope securing an anchor or trawl.
– ORIGIN C17: of unknown origin.

**rodent** ● n. a mammal of an order (Rodentia) that includes rats, mice, squirrels, and porcupines, distinguished by strong constantly growing incisors and no canine teeth.
– ORIGIN C19: from L. *rodent-*, *rodere* 'gnaw'.

**rodenticide** /rəˈdɛntɪsʌɪd/ ● n. a poison used to kill rodents.

**rodent ulcer** ● n. Medicine a slow-growing malignant tumour of the face (basal cell carcinoma).

**rodeo** /ˈrəʊdɪəʊ, rəˈdeɪəʊ/ ● n. (pl. **-os**) **1** an exhibition or contest in which cowboys show their skill at riding broncos, roping calves, etc. ➤ a similar exhibition or contest demonstrating other skills, such as motorcycle riding. **2** a round-up of cattle on a ranch for branding and counting. ● v. (**rodeoed**, **rodeoing**) compete in a rodeo.
– ORIGIN C19: from Sp., from *rodear* 'go round'.

**rodham** /ˈrɒdəm/ ● n. a raised bank in the Fen district of East Anglia, formed from silt deposits on the bed of a dry river course.
– ORIGIN C19: of unknown origin.

**rodomontade** /ˌrɒdə(ʊ)mɒnˈteɪd/ ● n. boastful or inflated talk or behaviour.
– ORIGIN C17: from Fr., from obs. Ital. *rodomontada*, from Ital. *rodomonte*, from the name of a boastful character in the medieval *Orlando* epics.

**roe[1]** ● n. **1** (also **hard roe**) the mass of eggs contained in the ovaries of a female fish or shellfish, especially when ripe and used as food. **2** (**soft roe**) the ripe testes of a male fish, especially when used as food.
– ORIGIN ME: rel. to Mid. Low Ger., MDu. *roge*.

**roe[2]** (also **roe deer**) ● n. (pl. same or **roes**) a small deer with a reddish summer coat that turns greyish in winter. [*Capreolus capreolus*.]
– ORIGIN OE *rā(ha)*, of Gmc origin.

**roebuck** ● n. a male roe deer.

**roentgen** /ˈrʌntjən, ˈrəːnt-, ˈrɒnt-/ (abbrev.: **R**) ● n. a unit of ionizing radiation, the amount producing one electrostatic unit of positive or negative ionic charge in one cubic centimetre of air under standard conditions.
– ORIGIN 1920s: named after the Ger. physicist and discoverer of X-rays Wilhelm Conrad *Röntgen*.

**roentgenogram** /ˈrʌntjənə(ʊ)gram, ˈrəːnt-, ˈrɒnt-; -gənəʊ, -ʒənəʊ/ ● n. chiefly Medicine an X-ray photograph.

**roentgenography** /ˌrʌntjəˈnɒgrəfi, ˌrəːnt-, ˌrɒnt-/ ● n. chiefly Medicine X-ray photography.
– DERIVATIVES **roentgenographic** adj. **roentgenographically** adv.

**roentgenology** /ˌrʌntjəˈnɒlədʒi, ˌrəːnt-, ˌrɒnt-/ ● n. chiefly Medicine another term for RADIOLOGY.

**roentgen rays** ● pl. n. dated X-rays.

**rogan josh** /ˌrəʊg(ə)n ˈdʒəʊʃ/ ● n. an Indian dish of curried meat, typically lamb, in a rich tomato-based sauce.
– ORIGIN from Urdu *roġan još*.

**rogation** /rə(ʊ)ˈgeɪʃ(ə)n/ ● n. (in the Christian Church) a solemn supplication consisting of the litany of the saints chanted on the three days before Ascension Day.
– ORIGIN ME: from L. *rogatio(n-)*, from *rogare* 'ask'.

**Rogation Days** ● pl. n. (in the Western Christian Church) the three days before Ascension Day, traditionally marked by fasting and prayer.

**Rogation Sunday** ● n. the Sunday preceding the Rogation Days.

**roger** ● exclam. your message has been received and understood (used in radio communication). ● v. Brit. vulgar slang (of a man) have sexual intercourse with.
– ORIGIN C16: from the given name *Roger*; the verb is from an obs. sense ('penis') of the noun.

**rogue** ● n. **1** a dishonest or unprincipled man. ➤ a mischievous but likeable person. **2** [usu. as modifier] an elephant or other large wild animal with destructive tendencies driven away or living apart from the herd: *a rogue elephant*. ➤ a person or thing that is defective, aberrant, or unpredictable. ➤ a seedling or plant deviating from the standard variety. ● v. remove rogue plants or seedlings from (a crop).
– DERIVATIVES **roguery** n. (pl. **-ies**).
– ORIGIN C16 (denoting an idle vagrant): prob. from L. *rogare* 'beg, ask', and rel. to obs. sl. *roger* 'vagrant beggar'.

**rogues' gallery** ● n. informal a collection of photographs of known criminals, used by police to identify suspects.

**roguish** ● adj. **1** characteristic of a rogue. **2** playfully mischievous: *a roguish smile*.
– DERIVATIVES **roguishly** adv. **roguishness** n.

**Rohypnol** /rəʊˈhɪpnɒl/ ● n. trademark a powerful sedative drug of the benzodiazepine class.
– ORIGIN 1980s: invented name.

**ROI** ● abbrev. Finance return on investment.

**roil** /rɔɪl/ ● v. make (a liquid) turbid by disturbing the sediment. ➤ (of a liquid) move in a turbulent manner. ➤ US word for RILE (in sense 1).
– DERIVATIVES **roily** adj. (N. Amer.).
– ORIGIN C16: perh. from OFr. *ruiler* 'mix mortar'.

**roister** /ˈrɔɪstə/ ● v. enjoy oneself or celebrate in a noisy or boisterous way.
– DERIVATIVES **roisterer** n. **roisterous** adj.
– ORIGIN C16: from obs. *roister* 'roisterer', from Fr. *rustre* 'ruffian'.

**ROK** • abbrev. South Korea (international vehicle registration).
– ORIGIN from *Republic of Korea*.

**Roland** /ˈrəʊlənd/ • n. (in phr. **a Roland for an Oliver**) archaic an effective retort or response.
– ORIGIN from the name of the most famous of Charlemagne's paladins, said (in medieval romances) to have become the friend of another paladin, Oliver, after engaging him in single combat which neither won.

**role** • n. **1** an actor's part in a play, film, etc. **2** a person's or thing's function in a particular situation.
– ORIGIN C17: from obs. Fr. *roule* 'roll', referring orig. to the roll of paper on which the actor's part was written.

**role model** • n. a person looked to by others as an example to be imitated.

**role playing** (also **role play**) • n. **1** chiefly Psychology the acting out of a particular role, either consciously (as a technique in psychotherapy or training) or unconsciously (in accordance with the perceived expectations of society). **2** participation in a role-playing game.
– DERIVATIVES **role-play** v. **role player** n.

**role-playing game** • n. a game in which players take on the roles of imaginary characters who engage in adventures, typically in a fantasy setting.

**Rolfing** • n. a deep massage technique aimed at releasing muscular tension at skeletal level.
– DERIVATIVES **Rolf** v.
– ORIGIN 1970s: from the name of the Amer. physiotherapist Ida P. *Rolf* + **-ING**[1].

**roll** • v. **1** move by turning over and over on an axis. ➤turn over to face a different direction. ➤(of a moving ship, aircraft, or vehicle) sway on an axis parallel to the direction of motion. ➤N. Amer. informal overturn (a vehicle). ➤throw (a die or dice). **2** (with reference to a vehicle or other wheeled object) move or cause to move along. ➤(of waves, smoke, cloud, or fog) move or flow forward with an undulating motion. ➤(of a drop of liquid) flow. ➤(of time) elapse steadily: *the years rolled by.* ➤[as adj. **rolling**] steady and continuous: *a rolling programme of reforms.* ➤[usu. as adj. **rolling**] (of land) extend in gentle undulations. ➤(of credits for a film or television programme) be displayed as if moving on a roller up the screen. ➤(with reference to a machine, device, or system) begin or cause to begin operating. **3** (often **roll something up**) turn (something flexible) over and over on itself to form a cylindrical or spherical shape. ➤curl up tightly. **4** flatten (something) by passing a roller over it or by passing it between rollers. **5** (of a loud, deep sound such as that of thunder) reverberate. ➤pronounce (a consonant, typically an *r*) with a trill. ➤(of words) flow mellifluously: *the names rolled off his lips.* **6** informal rob (a drunk or sleeping person). • n. **1** a cylinder formed by rolling flexible material. ➤a cylindrical mass or a number of items arranged in a cylindrical shape. ➤an item of food made by wrapping a flat sheet of pastry, cake, meat, or fish round a filling. ➤N. Amer. & Austral. a quantity of banknotes rolled together. **2** a rolling movement. ➤a gymnastic exercise in which the body is rolled into a tucked position and turned in a forward or backward circle. **3** a prolonged, deep, reverberating sound. ➤Music one of the basic patterns of drumming, consisting of a sustained, rapid alternation of single or double strokes of each stick. **4** a very small loaf of bread. **5** a roller used to shape metal in a rolling mill. **6** an official list or register of names. ➤the total numbers on such a list. ➤a document, typically an official record, in scroll form.
– PHRASES **a roll in the hay** (or **the sack**) informal an act of sexual intercourse. **be rolling in it** (or **money**) informal be very rich. **on a roll** informal experiencing a prolonged spell of success or good luck. **roll of honour** a list of people whose deeds are honoured, especially a list of those who have died in battle. **roll up one's sleeves** prepare to fight or work. **roll with the punches 1** (of a boxer) move one's body away from an opponent's blows so as to lessen the impact. **2** adapt oneself to adverse circumstances. **strike someone off the roll** Brit. debar a solicitor from practising as a penalty for dishonesty or other misconduct.
– PHRASAL VERBS **roll something back** reverse the progress or reduce the importance of something. **roll in** informal **1** be received in large amounts. **2** arrive in a casual way in spite of being late. **roll on ——** informal used to indicate that one wants a particular time or event to come quickly. **roll something out** officially launch a new product. **roll something over** Finance contrive or extend a particular financial arrangement. **roll up** informal arrive. **roll something up** Military drive the flank of an enemy line back and round so that the line is shortened or surrounded.
– DERIVATIVES **rollable** adj.
– ORIGIN ME: from OFr. *rolle* (n.), *roller* (v.), from L. *rotulus* 'a roll', var. of *rotula* 'little wheel', dimin. of *rota*.

**rollaway** • n. N. Amer. a bed fitted with wheels or castors.

**rollback** • n. **1** chiefly N. Amer. a reduction. **2** Computing the process of restoring a database or program to a previous defined state.

**roll bar** • n. a metal bar running up the sides and across the top of a sports car, strengthening its frame and protecting the occupants if the vehicle overturns.

**roll cage** • n. a framework of reinforcements protecting a car's passenger cabin in the event that it should roll on to its roof.

**roll-call** • n. the process of calling out a list of names to establish who is present.

**roll cast** • n. Fishing a cast in which the angler does not first throw the line backwards.

**rolled gold** • n. gold in the form of a thin coating applied to a baser metal by rolling.

**rolled oats** • pl. n. oats that have been husked and crushed.

**roller** • n. **1** a cylinder that rotates about a central axis and is used in various machines and devices to move, flatten, or spread something. **2** a small cylinder on which hair is rolled in order to produce curls. **3** (also **roller bandage**) a long surgical bandage rolled up for convenient application. **4** a long swelling wave that appears to roll steadily towards the shore. **5** a brightly coloured crow-sized bird, predominantly blue and having a characteristic tumbling display flight. [*Coracias garrulus* and other species.] **6** a breed of tumbler pigeon. **7** a breed of canary with a trilling song.

**rollerball** • n. **1** a ballpoint pen using relatively thin ink. **2** Computing an input device containing a ball which is moved with the fingers to control the cursor.

**roller bearing** • n. a bearing similar to a ball bearing but using small cylindrical rollers instead of balls. ➤a roller used in such a bearing.

**Rollerblade** • n. trademark an in-line skate. • v. skate using Rollerblades.
– DERIVATIVES **rollerblader** n.

**roller blind** • n. a window blind fitted on a roller.

**roller coaster** • n. a fairground attraction consisting of a light railway track with many tight turns and steep slopes, on which people ride in small fast open carriages. • v. (**roller-coaster** or **roller-coast**) move or occur in the dramatically changeable manner of a roller coaster.

**roller skate** • n. each of a pair of boots or metal frames fitted to shoes with four or more small wheels, for gliding across a hard surface.
– DERIVATIVES **roller skater** n. **roller skating** n.

**roller towel** • n. a long towel with the ends joined and hung on a roller.

**roll film** • n. photographic film with a protective light-proof backing paper wound on to a spool.

**rollicking**[1] • adj. exuberantly lively and amusing.
– DERIVATIVES **rollick** v.
– ORIGIN C19: prob. dial., perh. a blend of **ROMP** and **FROLIC**.

**rollicking**[2] (also **rollocking**) • n. Brit. informal a severe reprimand.
– ORIGIN C20: euphemistic alt. of **BOLLOCKING**.

**rolling hitch** • n. a kind of hitch used to attach a rope to a spar or larger rope.

**rolling mill** • n. a factory or machine for rolling steel or other metal into sheets.

**rolling pin** • n. a cylinder for rolling out dough.

**rolling stock** • n. **1** locomotives, carriages, or other vehicles used on a railway. **2** US the road vehicles of a trucking company.

**rolling stone** • n. a person who is unwilling to settle for long in one place.
– ORIGIN from the proverb 'a rolling stone gathers no moss'.

**rolling strike** • n. a strike consisting of a coordinated series of consecutive limited strikes by small groups of workers.

**rollmop** • n. a rolled uncooked pickled herring fillet.
– ORIGIN C20: from Ger. *Rollmops.*

**roll neck** • n. a high loosely turned-over collar.
– DERIVATIVES **roll-necked** adj.

**rollocking** • n. variant spelling of ROLLICKING[2].

**roll-on** • adj. (of a deodorant or cosmetic) applied by means of a rotating ball in the neck of the container. • n. **1** a roll-on deodorant or cosmetic. **2** Brit. a light elastic corset.

**roll-on roll-off** • adj. denoting a ferry or other vessel in which vehicles are driven directly on at the start of the voyage and driven off at the end of it.

**roll-out** • n. **1** the unveiling or launch of a new aircraft, spacecraft, or product. **2** Aeronautics the stage of an aircraft's landing during which it travels along the runway while losing speed. **3** American Football a play in which a quarterback moves out toward the sideline before attempting to pass.

**rollover** • n. **1** Finance the extension or transfer of a debt or other financial arrangement. **2** (in a lottery) the accumulative carry-over of prize money to the following draw.

**roll-top desk** • n. a writing desk with a semicircular flexible cover sliding in curved grooves.

**roll-up** • n. **1** (chiefly N. Amer. also **roll-your-own**) Brit. informal a hand-rolled cigarette. **2** Austral. informal an assembly. • adj. Finance denoting an investment fund in which returns are reinvested and tax liabilities can be reduced.

**Rolodex** /'rəʊlə(ʊ)dɛks/ • n. N. Amer. trademark a type of desktop card index.

**roly-poly** • n. **1** (also **roly-poly pudding**) Brit. a pudding made of a sheet of suet pastry covered with jam or fruit, formed into a roll, and steamed or baked. **2** Austral. a bushy tumbleweed. [*Salsola kali* and other species.] • adj. informal round and plump.
– ORIGIN C17: fanciful formation from ROLL.

**ROM** • abbrev. Computing read-only memory.

**Rom** • n. (pl. **Roma** /'rɒmə/) **1** a gypsy, especially a man. **2** (**Roma**) gypsy people collectively.
– ORIGIN C19: Romany, 'man, husband'.

**Rom.** • abbrev. Epistle to the Romans (in biblical references).

**rom.** • abbrev. roman (used as an instruction for a typesetter).

**Romaic** /rə(ʊ)'meɪɪk/ dated • n. the vernacular language of modern Greece. • adj. of or relating to this language.
– ORIGIN from mod. Gk *romaiikos* 'Roman', used specifically of the eastern Roman Empire.

**romaine** /rə(ʊ)'meɪn/ • n. a cos lettuce.
– ORIGIN C20: from Fr., fem. of *romain* 'Roman'.

**romaji** /'rəʊmədʒi/ • n. a system of romanized spelling used to transliterate Japanese.
– ORIGIN C20: Japanese, from *rōma* 'Roman' + *ji* 'letter(s)'.

**Roman** • adj. **1** of or relating to ancient Rome, its empire, or people. **2** of or relating to medieval or modern Rome. **3** denoting the alphabet used for writing Latin, English, and most European languages, developed in ancient Rome. **4** (**roman**) (of type) of a plain upright kind used in ordinary print, especially as distinguished from italic and Gothic. • n. **1** an inhabitant of ancient or modern Rome. **2** (**roman**) roman type.

**roman-à-clef** /ˌrəʊmɒ̃ɑː'kleɪ, French rɔmɑ̃akle/ • n. (pl. **romans-à-clef** pronunc. same) a novel in which real people or events appear with invented names.
– ORIGIN Fr., lit. 'novel with a key'.

**Roman blind** • n. a window blind made of fabric that draws up into pleats.

**Roman candle** • n. a firework giving off a series of flaming coloured balls and sparks.

**Roman Catholic** • adj. of or relating to the Roman Catholic Church. • n. a member of this Church.
– DERIVATIVES **Roman Catholicism** n.
– ORIGIN C16: translation of L. (*Ecclesia*) *Romana Catholica* (*et Apostolica*) 'Roman Catholic (and Apostolic Church)', appar. first used as a conciliatory term in place of the earlier *Roman, Romanist,* or *Romish,* considered derogatory.

**Roman Catholic Church** • n. the part of the Christian Church which acknowledges the Pope as its head, especially as it has developed since the Reformation.

**Romance** /rə(ʊ)'mans, 'rəʊmans/ • n. the group of Indo-European languages descended from Latin, principally French, Spanish, Portuguese, Italian, Catalan, Occitan, and Romanian. • adj. relating to or denoting this group of languages.
– ORIGIN ME (orig. denoting the vernacular lang. of France as opposed to Latin): from OFr. *romanz,* based on L. *Romanicus* 'Roman'.

**romance** /rə(ʊ)'mans, 'rəʊmans/ • n. **1** a pleasurable feeling of excitement and wonder associated with love. ➤a love affair, especially a relatively brief and light-hearted one. ➤a book or film dealing with love in a sentimental or idealized way. **2** a quality or feeling of mystery, excitement, and remoteness from everyday life. **3** a medieval tale dealing with a hero of chivalry, of the kind common in the Romance languages. **4** Music a short informal piece. • v. **1** dated be involved in an amorous relationship with (someone). ➤informal seek the attention or custom of, especially by use of flattery. **2** romanticize.
– ORIGIN ME (orig. denoting a composition in the vernacular as opposed to works in Latin): from ROMANCE.

**romancer** /rəʊ'mansə/ • n. **1** a person prone to wild exaggeration or falsehood. **2** a writer of medieval romances.

**Roman Empire** • n. the empire under Roman rule established in 27 BC and divided in AD 395 into the Western or Latin and Eastern or Greek Empire.

**Romanesque** /ˌrəʊmə'nɛsk/ • adj. of or relating to a style of architecture which prevailed in Europe *c.*900–1200, with massive vaulting and round arches. • n. Romanesque architecture.
– ORIGIN Fr., from *roman* 'romance'.

**roman-fleuve** /ˌrəʊmɒ̃'fləːv, French rɔmɑ̃flœv/ • n. (pl. **romans-fleuves** pronunc. same) a novel or sequence of novels dealing with the lives of a family or other group of people over a prolonged period of time.
– ORIGIN Fr., lit. 'river novel'.

**Roman holiday** • n. an occasion on which enjoyment or profit is derived from others' suffering.
– ORIGIN C19: from Byron's *Childe Harold,* orig. with ref. to a holiday given for a gladiatorial combat.

**Romanian** (also **Rumanian**) • n. **1** a native or national of Romania, or a person of Romanian descent. **2** the Romance language of Romania. • adj. of or relating to Romania or its people or language.

**Romanic** /rə(ʊ)'manɪk/ • n. & adj. less common term for ROMANCE.

**Romanism** • n. dated Roman Catholicism.

**Romanist** • n. **1** an expert in or student of Roman antiquities or law, or of the Romance languages. **2** chiefly derogatory a member or supporter of the Roman Catholic Church.

**romanize** /'rəʊmənʌɪz/ (also **-ise**) • v. **1** historical bring under Roman influence or authority. **2** make Roman Catholic in character. **3** put (text) into the Roman alphabet or into roman type.
– DERIVATIVES **romanization** n.

**Roman law** • n. the law code of the ancient Romans forming the basis of civil law in many countries today.

**Roman nose** • n. a nose with a high bridge.

**Roman numeral** • n. any of the letters representing numbers in the Roman numerical system: I = 1, V = 5, X = 10, L = 50, C = 100, D = 500, M = 1,000.

**Romano** /rə(ʊ)'mɑːnəʊ/ • n. a strong-tasting hard cheese, originally made in Italy.
– ORIGIN Ital., lit. 'Roman'.

**Romano-** /rə(ʊ)'mɑːnəʊ/ • **comb. form** Roman; Roman and ...: *Romano-British.*

**Romansh** /rə(ʊ)'manʃ, -'mɑːnʃ/ (also **Rumansh**) • **n.** the Rhaeto-Romance language spoken in the Swiss canton of Grisons, an official language of Switzerland.
– ORIGIN from Romansh *Roman(t)sch,* from med. L. *romanice* 'in the Romanic manner'.

**romantic** • **adj. 1** inclined towards or suggestive of romance. ➤ relating to love, especially in a sentimental or idealized way. **2** characterized by an idealized view of reality. **3** (**Romantic**) relating to romanticism. • **n. 1** a person with romantic beliefs or attitudes. **2** (**Romantic**) a writer or artist of the Romantic movement.
– DERIVATIVES **romantically** adv.
– ORIGIN C17: from archaic *romaunt* 'tale of chivalry', from an OFr. var. of *romanz* (see **ROMANCE**).

**romanticism** • **n.** a movement in the arts and literature which originated in the late 18th century, emphasizing inspiration, subjectivity, and the primacy of the individual.
– DERIVATIVES **romanticist** n.

**romanticize** (also **-ise**) • **v.** deal with or describe in an idealized or unrealistic fashion.
– DERIVATIVES **romanticization** n.

**Romany** /'rɒməni, 'rəʊ-/ • **n.** (pl. **-ies**) **1** the Indo-European language of the gypsies. **2** a gypsy.
– ORIGIN C19: from Romany *Romani,* fem. and pl. of the adj. *Romano,* from *Rom* (see **ROM**).

**Romeo** /'rəʊmɪəʊ/ • **n. 1** (pl. **-os**) an attractive, passionate male seducer or lover. **2** a code word representing the letter R, used in radio communication.
– ORIGIN from the name of the hero of Shakespeare's romantic tragedy *Romeo and Juliet.*

**romer** /'rəʊmə/ • **n.** a small piece of plastic or card bearing perpendicularly aligned scales or (if transparent) a grid, used to determine the precise reference of a point within the grid printed on a map.
– ORIGIN 1930s: named after its Brit. inventor Carrol *Romer.*

**Romish** /'rəʊmɪʃ/ • **adj.** chiefly derogatory Roman Catholic.

**romp** • **v. 1** play about roughly and energetically. **2** informal achieve something easily. ➤ (**romp home/in**) finish as the easy winner of a race or other contest. **3** informal engage in sexual activity, especially illicitly. • **n. 1** a spell of romping. **2** a light-hearted film or other work. **3** informal an easy victory.
– ORIGIN C18: perh. an alt. of **RAMP**.

**rompers** (also **romper suit**) • **pl. n. 1** a young child's one-piece outer garment. **2** a similar garment for adults, worn as overalls or sportswear.

**rondavel** /rɒn'dɑːv(ə)l/ • **n.** S. African a traditional circular African dwelling with a conical thatched roof.
– ORIGIN from Afrik. *rondawel.*

**rond de jambe** /ˌrɒ̃ də 'ʒɒmb/ • **n.** (pl. **ronds de jambes** or **ronds de jambe**) Ballet a circular movement of the leg performed on the ground or during a jump.
– ORIGIN from Fr.

**ronde** /rɒnd/ • **n.** a dance in which the dancers move in a circle.
– ORIGIN 1930s: Fr., fem. of *rond* 'round'.

**rondeau** /'rɒndəʊ/ • **n.** (pl. **rondeaux** pronunc. same or /-əʊz/) a poem of ten or thirteen lines with only two rhymes throughout and with the opening words used twice as a refrain.
– ORIGIN C16: Fr., later form of *rondel* (see **RONDEL**).

**rondel** /'rɒnd(ə)l/ • **n.** a rondeau, especially one of three stanzas of thirteen or fourteen lines with a two-line refrain.
– ORIGIN ME: from OFr., from *rond* 'round'; cf. **ROUNDEL**.

**rondo** /'rɒndəʊ/ • **n.** (pl. **-os**) a musical form with a recurring leading theme, often found in the final movement of a sonata or concerto.
– ORIGIN C18: Ital., from Fr. *rondeau* (see **RONDEAU**).

**rone** /rəʊn/ • **n.** Scottish a gutter for carrying off rain from a roof.
– ORIGIN C18: of unknown origin.

**rongo-rongo** /ˌrɒŋgəʊ'rɒŋgəʊ/ • **n.** Archaeology an ancient script of hieroglyphic signs found on wooden tablets on Easter Island.
– ORIGIN C20: a local word.

**ronin** /'rəʊnɪn/ • **n.** (pl. same or **ronins**) (in feudal Japan) a wandering samurai who had no lord or master.
– ORIGIN from Japanese.

**röntgen** etc. • **n.** variant spelling of **ROENTGEN** etc.

**roo** • **n.** Austral. informal a kangaroo.

**roo bar** • **n.** Australian term for **BULL BAR**.

**rood** /ruːd/ • **n. 1** a crucifix, especially one positioned above the rood screen of a church or on a beam over the entrance to the chancel. **2** chiefly Brit. a former measure of land area equal to a quarter of an acre (40 square perches, approximately 0.1012 hectare).
– ORIGIN OE *rōd.*

**rood loft** • **n.** a gallery on top of a rood screen.

**rood screen** • **n.** a screen of wood or stone separating the nave from the chancel of a church.

**roof** • **n.** (pl. **roofs**) **1** the structure forming the upper covering of a building or vehicle. ➤ the top inner surface of a covered area or space. **2** the upper limit or level of prices or wages. • **v.** (usu. **be roofed**) cover with a roof. ➤ function as the roof of.
– PHRASES **go through the roof** informal (of prices or figures) reach extreme levels. **hit** (or **go through**) **the roof** informal suddenly become very angry.
– DERIVATIVES **roofer** n. **roofing** n. **roofless** adj.
– ORIGIN OE *hrōf,* of Gmc origin.

**roof bolt** • **n.** Mining a tensioned rod anchoring the roof of a working to the strata above.
– DERIVATIVES **roof-bolting** n.

**roof light** • **n. 1** a window panel built into a roof. **2** a small interior light on the ceiling of a motor vehicle. **3** a flashing warning light on the top of a police car or other emergency vehicle.

**roof of the mouth** • **n.** the palate.

**roof prism** • **n.** a reflecting prism in which the reflecting surface is in two parts that are angled like the two sides of a pitched roof.

**roof rack** • **n.** a framework for carrying luggage on the roof of a vehicle.

**rooftop** • **n.** the outer surface of a building's roof.

**roof-tree** • **n.** the ridge piece of a roof.

**rooibos** /'rɔɪbɒs/ • **n.** S. African **1** an evergreen shrub whose leaves can be used to make tea. [Genus *Aspalathus.*] **2** a shrub or small tree with spikes of scented yellow flowers. [Genus *Combretum.*]
– ORIGIN C20: from Afrik., lit. 'red bush'.

**rooinek** /'rɔɪnɛk/ • **n.** S. African informal, offensive an English person or an English-speaking South African.
– ORIGIN Afrik., lit. 'red-neck'.

**rook**[1] • **n.** a gregarious crow with black plumage and a bare face, nesting in colonies in treetops. [*Corvus frugilegus.*] • **v.** informal defraud, swindle, or overcharge.
– ORIGIN OE *hrōc,* prob. imitative and of Gmc origin.

**rook**[2] • **n.** a chess piece, typically with its top in the shape of a battlement, that can move in any direction along a rank or file on which it stands.
– ORIGIN ME: from OFr. *rock,* based on Arab. *rukk* (of which the sense remains uncertain).

**rookery** • **n.** (pl. **-ies**) **1** a breeding colony of rooks, typically seen as a collection of nests high in a clump of trees. **2** a breeding colony of seabirds (especially penguins), seals, or turtles. **3** North American term for **HERONRY**. **4** a dense collection of slum housing.

**rookie** • **n.** informal a new recruit, especially in the army or police. ➤ an inexperienced member of a sports team; a novice.
– ORIGIN C19: perh. an alt. of **RECRUIT**, influenced by **ROOK**[1].

**room** /ruːm, rʊm/ • **n. 1** space viewed in terms of its capacity to accommodate contents or allow action: *she was trapped without room to move.* **2** a part of a building enclosed by walls, floor, and ceiling. ➤ (**rooms**) a set of rooms rented out to lodgers. **3** opportunity or scope: *room for improvement.* • **v.** chiefly N. Amer. share lodgings, especially at a college or similar institution.
– PHRASES **no** (or **not**) **room to swing a cat** humorous a

very confined space. [*cat* in the sense 'cat-o'-nine-tails'.]
– DERIVATIVES **-roomed** adj. **roomful** n. (pl. **-fuls**).
– ORIGIN OE *rūm*, of Gmc origin.

**roomer** • n. N. Amer. a lodger occupying a room without board.

**roomette** • n. N. Amer. **1** a private single compartment in a railway sleeping car. **2** a small bedroom for letting.

**roomie** • n. N. Amer. informal a room-mate.

**rooming house** • n. chiefly N. Amer. a lodging house.

**room-mate** • n. a person occupying the same room as another. ➤ N. Amer. a person occupying the same room, flat, or house as another.

**room service** • n. provision of food and drink to hotel guests in their rooms.

**room temperature** • n. a comfortable ambient temperature, generally taken as about 20°C.

**roomy** • adj. (**-ier**, **-iest**) having plenty of room; spacious.
– DERIVATIVES **roomily** adv. **roominess** n.

**roost**[1] • n. a place where birds regularly settle to rest at night, or where bats congregate to rest in the day. • v. (of a bird or bat) settle or congregate for rest.
– ORIGIN OE *hrōst*; of unknown ultimate origin.

**roost**[2] • n. (in the Orkneys and Shetlands) a tidal race.
– ORIGIN C17: from ON *rǫst*.

**rooster** • n. chiefly N. Amer. a male domestic fowl.

**rooster tail** • n. N. Amer. informal the spray of water thrown up behind a speedboat or surfboard.

**root**[1] • n. **1** a part of a plant normally below ground, which acts as a support and collects water and nourishment. ➤ a turnip, carrot, or other vegetable which grows as such a part of a plant. **2** the embedded part of a bodily organ or structure such as a hair. **3** the basic cause, source, or origin: *money is the root of all evil.* ➤ (**roots**) family, ethnic, or cultural origins as the reasons for one's emotional attachment to a place or community. ➤ [as modifier] (**roots**) denoting something, especially music, from a non-Western ethnic or cultural origin: *roots music.* **4** Linguistics a morpheme, not necessarily surviving as a word in itself, from which words have been made by the addition of prefixes or suffixes or by other modification. **5** (also **root note**) Music the fundamental note of a chord. **6** (in biblical use) a descendant. **7** Mathematics a number or quantity that when multiplied by itself one or more times gives a specified number or quantity. ➤ a value of an unknown quantity satisfying a given equation. **8** Austral./NZ & Irish vulgar slang an act of sexual intercourse. • v. **1** (with reference to a plant or cutting) establish or cause to establish roots. **2** (usu. **be rooted**) establish deeply and firmly. ➤ (**be rooted in**) have as a source or origin. **3** [often as adj. **rooted**] cause to stand immobile through fear or amazement. **4** (**root someone/thing out/up**) find and get rid of someone or something. **5** Austral./NZ & Irish vulgar slang have sexual intercourse with. ➤ exhaust or frustrate.
– PHRASES **at root** fundamentally. **put down roots** begin to have a settled life in a place. **root and branch** (of a process or operation) thorough or radical. **take root** become fixed or established.
– DERIVATIVES **rootedness** n. **rootless** adj. **rootlessness** n. **rootlet** n. **root-like** adj. **rooty** adj.
– ORIGIN OE *rōt*, from ON *rót*; rel. to WORT.

**root**[2] • v. **1** (of an animal) turn up the ground with its snout in search of food. ➤ rummage. **2** (**root for**) informal support enthusiastically. ➤ (**root someone on**) N. Amer. informal cheer or urge someone on. • n. an act of rooting.
– ORIGIN OE *wrōtan*, of Gmc origin; rel. to OE *wrōt* 'snout'.

**root beer** • n. N. Amer. an effervescent drink made from an extract of the roots and bark of certain plants.

**root canal** • n. **1** the pulp-filled cavity in the root of a tooth. **2** N. Amer. a procedure to replace infected pulp in a root canal with an inert material.

**rooter** • n. N. Amer. informal a supporter or fan of a sports team or player.

**rootin'-tootin'** • adj. N. Amer. informal boisterous, noisy, or lively.
– ORIGIN C19: reduplication of *rooting* in the sense 'inquisitive', an early dial. sense of the compound.

**rootle** • v. Brit. informal term for ROOT[2].
– ORIGIN C19: frequentative of ROOT[2].

**root mean square** • n. Mathematics the square root of the arithmetic mean of the squares of a set of values.

**root nodule** • n. see NODULE (sense 2).

**root note** • n. see ROOT[1] (sense 5).

**root sign** • n. Mathematics another term for RADICAL SIGN.

**rootstock** • n. **1** a rhizome. **2** a plant on to which another variety is grafted. **3** a primary form or source from which offshoots have arisen.

**rootsy** • adj. informal (of music) unpolished and emphasizing its traditional or ethnic origins.

**root vegetable** • n. the fleshy enlarged root of a plant used as a vegetable, e.g. a carrot.

**rope** • n. **1** a length of stout cord made by twisting together strands of hemp, sisal, nylon, etc. ➤ (**the ropes**) the ropes enclosing a boxing or wrestling ring. ➤ (**the rope**) execution by hanging. **2** a quantity of roughly spherical objects strung together. **3** (**the ropes**) informal the established procedures in an organization or area of activity: *I showed her the ropes.* • v. **1** catch, fasten, or secure with rope. ➤ Climbing (of a party of climbers) connect each other together with a rope. **2** (**rope someone in/into**) persuade someone, despite reluctance, to take part in.
– PHRASES **on the rope** Climbing roped together. **on the ropes 1** Boxing forced against the ropes by the opponent's attack. **2** in state of near collapse. **a rope of sand** poetic/literary illusory security.
– DERIVATIVES **roping** n.
– ORIGIN OE *rāp*, of Gmc origin.

**ropeable** /ˈrəʊpəb(ə)l/ (also **ropable**) • adj. Austral./NZ informal very angry; furious.
– ORIGIN C19: from the notion that the person requires to be restrained.

**rope ladder** • n. two long ropes connected by short crosspieces, used as a ladder.

**rope-moulding** • n. a moulding cut in an interweaving spiral in imitation of rope strands.

**rope's end** • n. historical a short piece of rope used for flogging, especially on ships.

**ropesight** • n. Bell-ringing skill in judging when to pull on a bell rope in change-ringing.

**rope-walk** • n. historical a long piece of ground where ropes are made.

**rope-walker** • n. dated a performer on a tightrope.
– DERIVATIVES **rope-walking** n.

**ropeway** • n. a transport system, used especially in mines or mountainous areas, in which carriers are suspended from moving cables powered by a motor.

**ropy** (also **ropey**) • adj. (**-ier**, **-iest**) **1** resembling a rope. **2** Brit. informal poor in quality or health.
– DERIVATIVES **ropily** adv. **ropiness** n.

**roque** /rəʊk/ • n. US a form of croquet played on a hard court surrounded by a bank.
– ORIGIN C19: alt. of ROQUET.

**Roquefort** /ˈrɒkfɔː/ • n. trademark a soft blue cheese made from ewes' milk.
– ORIGIN from the name of a village in southern France.

**roquet** /ˈrəʊkeɪ, -ki/ Croquet • v. (**roqueted**, **roqueting**) strike (another ball) with one's own. • n. an act of roqueting.
– ORIGIN C19: appar. an arbitrary alt. of the verb CROQUET, orig. used in the same sense.

**roquette** /rɒˈkɛt/ • n. another term for ROCKET[2].
– ORIGIN from Fr.

**ro-ro** • abbrev. Brit. roll-on roll-off.

**rorqual** /ˈrɔːkw(ə)l/ • n. a baleen whale of a small group with pleated skin on the underside, e.g. the blue, fin, and humpback whales. [Family Balaenopteridae.]
– ORIGIN C19: via Fr. from Norw. *røyrkval* 'fin whale', from ON *reythr*, the specific name, + *hvalr* 'whale'.

**Rorschach test** /ˈrɔːʃɑːk/ • n. Psychology a test used in psychoanalysis, in which a standard set of symmetrical ink blots of different shapes and colours is presented one by one to the subject, who is asked to describe what they

suggest or resemble.
– ORIGIN 1920s: named after the Swiss psychiatrist Hermann *Rorschach*.

**rort** /rɔːt/ ● **n.** Austral. informal **1** a fraudulent or dishonest act or practice. **2** a wild party.
– ORIGIN 1930s: back-form. from **RORTY**.

**rorty** ● **adj.** (**-ier**, **-iest**) Brit. informal boisterous and high-spirited.
– ORIGIN C19: of unknown origin.

**rosace** /ˈrəʊzeɪs/ ● **n.** an ornamentation resembling a rose, in particular a rose window.
– ORIGIN C19: from Fr., from L. *rosaceus*, from *rosa* 'rose'.

**rosacea** /rəʊˈzeɪʃɪə/ (also **acne rosacea**) ● **n.** Medicine a condition in which certain facial blood vessels enlarge, giving the cheeks and nose a flushed appearance.
– ORIGIN C19: from L., fem. of *rosaceus* in the sense 'rose-coloured'.

**rosaceous** /rəʊˈzeɪʃəs/ ● **adj.** Botany relating to or denoting plants of the rose family (Rosaceae).
– ORIGIN C18: from mod. L. *Rosaceae* (based on L. *rosa* 'rose') + **-OUS**.

**rosaline** /ˈrəʊzəliːn/ ● **n.** a variety of fine needlepoint or pillow lace.
– ORIGIN C20: prob. from Fr.

**rosaniline** /rə(ʊ)ˈzanɪliːn, -lɪn, -lʌɪn/ ● **n.** Chemistry a reddish-brown synthetic compound from which fuchsin and some other dyes are made.
– ORIGIN C19: from **ROSE**[1] + **ANILINE**.

**rosarian** /rəʊˈzɛːrɪən/ ● **n.** a person who cultivates roses, especially as an occupation.
– ORIGIN C19: from L. *rosarium* 'rose garden, rosary' + **-AN**.

**rosarium** /rəʊˈzɛːrɪəm/ ● **n.** (pl. **rosariums** or **rosaria**) formal a rose garden.
– ORIGIN C19: from L. (see **ROSARY**).

**rosary** /ˈrəʊz(ə)ri/ ● **n.** (pl. **-ies**) **1** (in the Roman Catholic Church) a form of devotion in which five (or fifteen) decades of Hail Marys are repeated, each decade preceded by an Our Father and followed by a Glory Be. **2** a string of beads for keeping count in such a devotion or in the devotions of some other religions.
– ORIGIN ME (in the sense 'rose garden'): from L. *rosarium* 'rose garden', based on *rosa* 'rose'.

**roscoe** /ˈrɒskəʊ/ ● **n.** US informal, dated a pistol or revolver.
– ORIGIN C20: from the surname *Roscoe*.

**rose**[1] ● **n.** **1** a prickly bush or shrub that typically bears red, pink, yellow, or white fragrant flowers, native to north temperate regions and widely grown as an ornamental. [Genus *Rosa*: many species and varieties.] ➤used in names of other plants with similar flowers, e.g. **Christmas rose**. ➤a stylized representation of a rose in heraldry or decoration. **2** a perforated cap attached to a shower, the spout of a watering can, or the end of a hose to produce a spray. **3** a warm pink or light crimson colour. ➤(**roses**) a rosy complexion. **4** (**roses**) favourable circumstances or ease of success: *everything was coming up roses.* ● **v.** poetic/literary make rosy.
– PHRASES **come up** (or **out**) **smelling of roses** emerge from a difficult situation with reputation intact. **under the rose** archaic another way of saying **SUB ROSA**.
– DERIVATIVES **rose-like** adj.
– ORIGIN OE *rōse*, of Gmc origin, from L. *rosa*; reinforced in ME by OFr. *rose*.

**rose**[2] past of **RISE**.

**rosé** /ˈrəʊzeɪ/ ● **n.** any light pink wine, coloured by only brief contact with red grape skins.
– ORIGIN Fr., lit. 'pink'.

**roseapple** ● **n.** a tropical evergreen tree cultivated for its foliage and fragrant fruit. [*Syzygium jambos* (SE Asia) and related species.]

**roseate** /ˈrəʊzɪət/ ● **adj.** rose-coloured.

**rosebay** ● **n.** **1** (also **rosebay willowherb**) a tall willowherb with pink flowers, native to north temperate regions. [*Epilobium angustifolium*.] **2** N. Amer. an azalea. [*Rhododendron lapponicum* (**Lapland rosebay**) and other species.]

**rosebud** ● **n.** **1** the bud of a rose. **2** Brit. dated a pretty young woman.

**rose-coloured** ● **adj.** **1** of a warm pink colour. **2** referring to a naively optimistic or unfoundedly favourable viewpoint: *you are still seeing the profession through rose-coloured spectacles.*

**rose-cut** ● **adj.** (of a gem) cut in tiny triangular facets.

**rosefish** ● **n.** (pl. same or **-fishes**) N. Amer. the redfish of the North Atlantic. [*Sebastes marinus*]

**rose hip** ● **n.** see **HIP**[2].

**rosella** /rə(ʊ)ˈzɛlə/ ● **n.** an Australian parakeet with vivid green, red, yellow, or blue plumage. [Genus *Platycercus*: several species.]
– ORIGIN C19: alt. of *Rosehill*, New South Wales, where the bird was first found.

**rose madder** ● **n.** a pale shade of pink.

**rosemaling** /ˈrəʊsəˌmɑːlɪŋ, -ˌmɔːlɪŋ, -zə-/ ● **n.** chiefly N. Amer. the art of painting wooden furniture and objects with flower motifs.
– DERIVATIVES **rosemaled** adj.
– ORIGIN 1940s: from Norw., lit. 'rose painting'.

**rose mallow** ● **n.** an ornamental hibiscus. [Genus *Hibiscus*, in particular *H. rosa-sinensis*.]

**rosemary** ● **n.** an evergreen aromatic shrub of the mint family, native to southern Europe, the leaves of which are used as a culinary herb, in perfumery, and formerly as an emblem of remembrance. [*Rosmarinus officinalis*.]
– ORIGIN ME *rosmarine*, based on L. *ros marinus*, from *ros* 'dew' + *marinus* 'of the sea'; also influenced by **ROSE**[1] and Mary, mother of Jesus.

**rose of Jericho** ● **n.** a desert plant whose dead branches fold inwards to form a ball, native to North Africa and the Middle East. [*Anastatica hierochuntica*.]

**rose of Sharon** ● **n.** **1** a low shrub with dense foliage and large golden-yellow flowers, native to SE Europe and Asia Minor. [*Hypericum calycinum*.] **2** (in biblical use) a flowering plant whose identity is unknown.
– ORIGIN from *Sharon*, a region of fertile coastal plain in present-day Israel.

**roseola** /rə(ʊ)ˈziːələ/ ● **n.** Medicine a rose-coloured rash occurring in measles, typhoid fever, syphilis, and some other diseases.
– ORIGIN C19: mod. var. of **RUBEOLA**, from L. *roseus* 'rose-coloured'.

**rose quartz** ● **n.** a translucent pink variety of quartz.

**roseroot** ● **n.** a yellow-flowered stonecrop whose roots smell of roses when dried or bruised. [*Rhodiola rosea*.]

**rose-tinted** ● **adj.** another term for **ROSE-COLOURED**.

**rosette** ● **n.** **1** a rose-shaped decoration, typically made of ribbon, worn by supporters of a team or political party or awarded as a prize. **2** a design or growth resembling a rose. ➤Architecture a carved or moulded ornament resembling or representing a rose. **3** a radiating arrangement of horizontally spreading leaves at the base of a low-growing plant. **4** a rose diamond.
– DERIVATIVES **rosetted** adj.
– ORIGIN C18: from Fr., dimin. of *rose* (see **ROSE**[1]).

**rose water** ● **n.** scented water made with rose petals.

**rose window** ● **n.** a circular window with mullions or tracery radiating in a form suggestive of a rose.

**rosewood** ● **n.** **1** a close-grained tropical timber with a distinctive fragrance, used for making furniture and musical instruments. **2** the tree which produces this wood. [Genus *Dalbergia*: several species, in particular *D. nigra* of Brazil.] ➤used in names of other trees which yield similar wood, e.g. **African rosewood**.

**Rosh Hashana** /ˌrɒʃ həˈʃɑːnə/ (also **Rosh Hashanah**) ● **n.** the Jewish New Year festival, held on the first (sometimes the second) day of Tishri (in September).
– ORIGIN Heb., lit. 'head of the year'.

**Roshi** /ˈrəʊʃi/ ● **n.** (pl. **Roshis**) the spiritual leader of a community of Zen Buddhist monks.
– ORIGIN from Japanese.

**Rosicrucian** /ˌrəʊzɪˈkruːʃ(ə)n/ ● **n.** a member of a secretive society devoted to the study of metaphysical, mystical, and alchemical lore. ● **adj.** of or relating to the Rosicrucians.
– DERIVATIVES **Rosicrucianism** n.
– ORIGIN from mod. L. *rosa crucis* (or *crux*), Latinization of

the name of Christian *Rosenkreuz*, legendary C15 founder of the movement.

**rosin** /ˈrɒzɪn/ ● **n.** resin, especially the solid amber residue obtained after the distillation of crude turpentine oleoresin, used in adhesives, varnishes, and inks and for treating the bows of stringed instruments. ● **v.** (**rosined, rosining**) rub or treat with rosin.
– DERIVATIVES **rosiny** adj.
– ORIGIN ME: from med. L. *rosina*, from L. *resina* (see **RESIN**).

**rosolio** /rə(ʊ)ˈzəʊlɪəʊ/ ● **n.** (pl. **-os**) a sweet cordial made in Italy from alcohol, raisins, sugar, rose petals, cloves, and cinnamon.
– ORIGIN Ital., from mod. L. *ros solis* 'dew of the sun'.

**RoSPA** /ˈrɒspə/ ● **abbrev.** (in the UK) Royal Society for the Prevention of Accidents.

**roster** /ˈrɒstə, ˈrəʊst-/ ● **n.** a list or plan showing turns of duty or leave for individuals or groups in an organization. ➤a list of names, in particular of sports players available for team selection. ● **v.** (usu. **be rostered**) assign according to a duty roster.
– ORIGIN C18: from Du. *rooster* 'list', earlier 'gridiron', with ref. to its parallel lines.

**rösti** /ˈrəːsti/ ● **n.** a Swiss dish of grated potatoes formed into a small flat cake and fried.
– ORIGIN Swiss Ger.

**rostral** /ˈrɒstr(ə)l/ ● **adj.** **1** Anatomy at or near the front end of the body. **2** Zoology of or on the rostrum.
– DERIVATIVES **rostrally** adv.

**rostrum** /ˈrɒstrəm/ ● **n.** (pl. **rostra** /-trə/ or **rostrums**) **1** a raised platform on which a person stands to make a public speech, play music, or conduct an orchestra. ➤a similar platform for supporting a film or television camera. **2** chiefly Zoology a beak-like projection.
– DERIVATIVES **rostrate** /-strət/ adj. (chiefly Zoology).
– ORIGIN C16: from L., lit. 'beak'; orig. used to denote an orator's platform in the Forum in Rome, which was decorated with the beaks of captured galleys.

**rosy** ● **adj.** (**-ier, -iest**) **1** (especially of a person's skin) rose-red or pink, typically as an indication of health or youthfulness: *rosy cheeks*. **2** promising or suggesting good fortune; hopeful.
– DERIVATIVES **rosily** adv. **rosiness** n.

**rosy finch** ● **n.** a finch found in Asia and western North America, the male of which has pinkish underparts and rump. [Genus *Leucosticte*: three species, in particular *L. arctoa*.]

**rot** ● **v.** (**rotted, rotting**) **1** decompose by the action of bacteria and fungi; decay. **2** gradually deteriorate or decline. ● **n.** **1** the process of decaying. ➤rotten or decayed matter. **2** (**the rot**) Brit. a process of deterioration; a decline in standards: *there is enough talent to stop the rot.* **3** any of a number of fungal or bacterial diseases that cause tissue deterioration, especially in plants. ➤liver rot in sheep. **4** informal rubbish: *don't talk rot.*
– ORIGIN OE *rotian* (v.), of Gmc origin.

**rota** ● **n.** **1** chiefly Brit. a list showing times and names for people to take their turn to undertake certain duties. **2** (**the Rota**) the supreme ecclesiastical and secular court of the Roman Catholic Church.
– ORIGIN C17: from L., lit. 'wheel'.

**Rotarian** ● **n.** a member of Rotary, a worldwide charitable society of business and professional people organized into local Rotary clubs. ● **adj.** of or relating to Rotary.

**rotary** ● **adj.** revolving around a centre or axis; rotational. ➤acting by means of rotation; having a rotating part or parts: *a rotary mower.* ● **n.** (pl. **-ies**) **1** a rotary machine or device. **2** N. Amer. a traffic roundabout.
– ORIGIN C18: from med. L. *rotarius*, from *rota* 'wheel'.

**rotary press** ● **n.** a printing press that prints from a rotating cylindrical surface on to paper forced against it by another cylinder.

**rotary wing** ● **n.** an aerofoil that rotates in an approximately horizontal plane, providing all or most of the lift in a helicopter or autogiro.

**rotate** /rə(ʊ)ˈteɪt/ ● **v.** **1** move or cause to move in a circle round an axis. **2** pass to each member of a group in a regularly recurring order. **3** grow (different crops) in succession on a particular piece of land.
– DERIVATIVES **rotatable** adj. **rotating** adj. **rotative** /ˈrəʊtətɪv/ adj. **rotatory** /ˈrəʊtət(ə)ri, -ˈteɪt(ə)ri/ adj.
– ORIGIN C17 (earlier (C16) as *rotation*): from L. *rotat-*, *rotare* 'turn in a circle', from *rota* 'wheel'.

**rotation** ● **n.** the action or process of rotating.
– DERIVATIVES **rotational** adj. **rotationally** adv.

**rotator** ● **n.** **1** a thing which rotates or which causes something to rotate. **2** Anatomy a muscle whose contraction causes or assists in the rotation of a part of the body.

**rotator cuff** ● **n.** Anatomy, chiefly N. Amer. a capsule with fused tendons that supports the arm at the shoulder joint.

**rotavator** /ˈrəʊtəveɪtə/ (also **rotovator**) ● **n.** trademark a machine with rotating blades for breaking up the soil.
– DERIVATIVES **rotavate** v.
– ORIGIN 1930s: blend of **ROTARY** + **CULTIVATOR**.

**rotavirus** /ˈrəʊtəˌvʌɪrəs/ ● **n.** Medicine any of a group of wheel-shaped RNA viruses, some of which cause acute enteritis in humans.
– ORIGIN 1970s: mod. L., from L. *rota* 'wheel' + **VIRUS**.

**ROTC** ● **abbrev.** (in the US) Reserve Officers' Training Corps.

**rote** ● **n.** mechanical or habitual repetition: *a poem learnt by rote.*
– ORIGIN ME: of unknown origin.

**rotenone** /ˈrəʊtənəʊn/ ● **n.** Chemistry a toxic crystalline substance obtained from the roots of derris and related plants, widely used as an insecticide.
– ORIGIN 1920s: from Japanese *rotenon* (from *roten* 'derris') + **-ONE**.

**rotgut** ● **n.** informal poor-quality and potentially harmful alcoholic liquor.

**roti** /ˈrəʊti/ ● **n.** (pl. **rotis**) (in Indian cooking) bread, especially a flat round bread cooked on a griddle.
– ORIGIN from Hindi *roṭī*.

**Rotifera** /rəʊˈtɪf(ə)rə/ ● **pl. n.** Zoology a small phylum of minute multicellular aquatic animals which have a characteristic wheel-like ciliated organ used in swimming and feeding.
– DERIVATIVES **rotifer** /ˈrəʊtɪfə/ n.
– ORIGIN mod. L., from L. *rota* 'wheel' + *ferre* 'to bear'.

**rotisserie** /rə(ʊ)ˈtɪs(ə)ri/ ● **n.** **1** a restaurant specializing in roasted or barbecued meat. **2** a rotating spit for roasting and barbecuing meat.
– ORIGIN C19: from Fr. *rôtisserie*, from *rôtir* 'to roast'.

**rotogravure** /ˌrəʊtə(ʊ)grəˈvjʊə/ ● **n.** a printing system using a rotary press with intaglio cylinders. ➤chiefly N. Amer. a sheet or magazine printed with this system.
– ORIGIN C20: from Ger. *Rotogravur*, part of the name of a printing company.

**rotor** ● **n.** **1** the rotating part of a turbine, electric motor, or other device. **2** a hub with a number of radiating blades that is rotated to provide the lift for a helicopter. **3** Meteorology a large eddy in which the air circulates about a horizontal axis.
– ORIGIN C20: formed irregularly from **ROTATOR**.

**rotorcraft** ● **n.** (pl. same) a rotary wing aircraft such as a helicopter or autogiro.

**rotoscope** ● **n.** a device which projects and enlarges individual frames of filmed live action to permit them to be used to create composite film sequences. ● **v.** transfer into another film sequence using a rotoscope.
– ORIGIN 1950s: origin obscure.

**rototiller** /ˈrəʊtə(ʊ)ˌtɪlə/ ● **n.** trademark North American term for **ROTAVATOR**.
– DERIVATIVES **rototill** v.

**rotovator** ● **n.** variant spelling of **ROTAVATOR**.

**rotten** ● **adj.** (**-er, -est**) **1** suffering from decay. **2** corrupt. **3** informal very bad or unpleasant. ● **adv.** informal very much: *your mother spoiled you rotten.*
– DERIVATIVES **rottenly** adv. **rottenness** n.
– ORIGIN ME: from ON *rotinn*.

**rotten borough** ● **n.** Brit. historical (before the Reform Act of 1832) a borough that was able to elect an MP though having very few voters.

**rottenstone** • **n.** decomposed siliceous limestone used as a powder or paste for polishing metals.

**rotter** • **n.** informal, dated a cruel, mean, or unkind person.

**Rottweiler** /ˈrɒtvʌɪlə, -wʌɪlə/ • **n.** a large powerful dog of a tall black-and-tan breed.
– ORIGIN C20: Ger., from *Rottweil*, the name of a town in SW Germany.

**rotund** /rə(ʊ)ˈtʌnd/ • **adj.** large and plump. ➤round; spherical.
– DERIVATIVES **rotundity** n. **rotundly** adv.
– ORIGIN C15: from L. *rotundus*, from *rotare* 'rotate'.

**rotunda** • **n.** a round building or room, especially one with a dome.
– ORIGIN C17: alt. of Ital. *rotonda* (*camera*) 'round (chamber)', fem. of *rotondo*.

**rouble** /ˈruːb(ə)l/ (also **ruble**) • **n.** the basic monetary unit of Russia and some other former republics of the USSR, equal to 100 kopeks.
– ORIGIN via Fr. from Russ. *rubl'*.

**roué** /ˈruːeɪ/ • **n.** a debauched man, especially an elderly one.
– ORIGIN C19: Fr., lit. 'broken on a wheel', referring to the instrument of torture thought to be deserved by such a person.

**rouge** /ruːʒ/ • **n.** a red powder or cream used as a cosmetic for colouring the cheeks or lips. • **v.** colour with rouge.
– ORIGIN ME (denoting the colour red): from Fr., 'red', from L. *rubeus*.

**rough** • **adj. 1** having an uneven or irregular surface; not smooth or level. ➤(of terrain) having many obstacles; difficult to cross. **2** (of a voice) harsh and rasping. ➤(of wine or another alcoholic drink) sharp or harsh in taste. **3** not gentle; violent or boisterous: *rough treatment.* ➤(of weather or the sea) wild and stormy. **4** informal difficult and unpleasant. **5** not finished tidily; plain and basic. ➤not worked out or correct in every detail; approximate: *a rough draft* | *a rough guess.* ➤lacking sophistication or refinement. • **n. 1** chiefly Brit. a disreputable and violent person. **2** (on a golf course) the area of longer grass around the fairway and the green. **3** a preliminary sketch. **4** an uncut precious stone. • **v. 1** work or shape in a rough, preliminary fashion. **2** make uneven. **3** (**rough it**) informal live in discomfort with only basic necessities. **4** (**rough someone up**) informal beat someone up.
– PHRASES **bit of rough** informal a male sexual partner whose toughness or lack of sophistication is a source of attraction. **in the rough 1** in a natural state; without decoration or other treatment. **2** in difficulties. **rough and ready** crude but effective. ➤unsophisticated or unrefined. **the rough edge** (or **side**) **of one's tongue** a scolding. **rough edges** small imperfections in something that is otherwise satisfactory. **rough justice** treatment that is not scrupulously fair or in accordance with the law. **sleep rough** Brit. sleep in uncomfortable conditions, typically out of doors. **take the rough with the smooth** accept the difficult or unpleasant aspects of life as well as the good.
– DERIVATIVES **roughish** adj. **roughness** n.
– ORIGIN OE *rūh*, of W. Gmc origin.

**roughage** • **n.** fibrous indigestible material in vegetable foodstuffs which aids the passage of food and waste products through the gut. ➤Farming coarse, fibrous fodder.

**rough and tumble** • **n.** a situation without rules or organization.
– ORIGIN C19: orig. boxing sl.

**roughcast** • **n.** plaster of lime, cement, and gravel, used on outside walls. • **adj. 1** coated with roughcast. **2** (of a person) lacking refinement. • **v.** coat with roughcast.

**rough cut** • **n.** the first version of a film after preliminary editing. • **v.** (**rough-cut**) make a rough cut or rough copy of.

**rough diamond** • **n. 1** an uncut diamond. **2** a person who is of good character but lacks manners or education.

**roughen** • **v.** make or become rough.

**rough grazing** • **n.** uncultivated land used for grazing livestock.

**rough-hew** • **v. 1** shape (wood or stone) roughly or without smoothing off. **2** [as adj. **rough-hewn**] (of a person) uncultivated or uncouth.

**rough house** informal, chiefly N. Amer. • **n.** a violent disturbance. • **v.** (**rough-house**) act or treat in a rough, violent manner.

**roughie** • **n. 1** dialect & Austral. a hooligan. **2** Austral./NZ an outsider in a horse race. **3** variant spelling of ROUGHY.

**roughly** • **adv. 1** in a rough or harsh manner. **2** approximately.

**roughneck** • **n. 1** informal a rough, uncouth person. **2** an oil rig worker. • **v.** work on an oil rig.
– DERIVATIVES **roughnecking** n.

**rough-rider** • **n.** N. Amer. a person who breaks in or can ride unbroken horses.

**roughshod** • **adj.** archaic (of a horse) having shoes with nail heads projecting to prevent slipping.
– PHRASES **ride roughshod over** arrogantly or inconsiderately disregard.

**rough trade** • **n.** informal male homosexual prostitution, especially when involving brutality or sadism. ➤homosexuals of this kind.

**roughy** /ˈrʌfi/ (also **roughie**) • **n.** (pl. **-ies**) Austral./NZ **1** a marine fish with a deep laterally compressed body and large rough-edged scales which become spiny on the belly. [Several genera and species, including *Trachichthys australis.*] **2** another term for RUFF[2] (in sense 1).

**rouille** /ˈruːi/ • **n.** a Provençal sauce made from pounded red chillies, garlic, breadcrumbs, and stock.
– ORIGIN Fr., lit. 'rust', with ref. to the colour.

**roulade** /ruːˈlɑːd/ • **n. 1** a piece of meat, sponge, or other food, spread with a filling and rolled up. **2** a florid passage of runs in classical music for a solo virtuoso.
– ORIGIN Fr., from *rouler* 'to roll'.

**rouleau** /ˈruːləʊ, ruːˈləʊ/ • **n.** (pl. **rouleaux** or **rouleaus** /-əʊz/) **1** a cylindrical packet of coins. **2** a coil or roll, especially of ribbon or knitted wool, used as trimming.
– ORIGIN C17: Fr., from obs. Fr. *roule* 'a roll'.

**roulement** /ˈruːlmɒ̃/ • **n.** Military movement of troops or equipment, especially to relieve another force.
– ORIGIN C20: Fr., lit. 'rolling'.

**roulette** • **n. 1** a gambling game in which a ball is dropped on to a revolving wheel with numbered compartments, the players betting on the number at which the ball comes to rest. **2** a tool or machine with a revolving toothed wheel, used in engraving or for making perforations between postage stamps. • **v.** use a roulette to make perforations in.
– ORIGIN C18: from Fr., dimin. of *rouelle* 'wheel'.

**Roumanian** /ruːˈmeɪnɪən/ • **adj. & n.** old-fashioned variant of ROMANIAN.

**round** • **adj. 1** shaped like a circle or cylinder. **2** shaped like a sphere. ➤having a curved surface with no sharp projections. **3** (of a person's shoulders) bent forward. **4** (of a voice) rich and mellow. **5** (of a number) expressed in convenient units rather than exactly, for example to the nearest whole number. ➤used to show that a figure has been completely and exactly reached: *the batsman made a round 100.* ➤archaic (of a sum of money) considerable. **6** frank and truthful: *she berated him in good round terms.* • **n. 1** a circular piece or section. **2** an act of visiting a number of people or places in turn, especially in a fixed order as part of one's duties: *a newspaper round.* ➤a regularly recurring sequence of activities. **3** each of a sequence of sessions in a process, especially in a sports contest. ➤a single division of a game or contest, especially in a boxing or wrestling match. ➤an act of playing all the holes in a golf course once. **4** Music a song for three or more unaccompanied voices or parts, each singing the same theme but starting one after another. **5** a set of drinks bought for all the members of a group, typically as part of a sequence in which each member in turn buys such a set. **6** Brit. a slice of bread. ➤the quantity of sandwiches made from two slices of bread. **7** the amount of ammunition needed to fire one shot. ➤Archery a fixed number of arrows shot from a fixed distance. • **adv.** chiefly Brit. **1** so as to rotate or cause rotation. ➤so as to cover the whole area surrounding a particular centre. **2** so as to rotate and face in the opposite direction. ➤used in describing the relative position of something: *it's the wrong way round.* **3** so as to surround. ➤so as to give support. **4** so as to reach a new place or position. **5** used to suggest idle and purposeless motion or activity. ● **prep.** chiefly Brit. **1** on every side of (a focal point). **2** so as to encircle. **3** from or on the other side of. **4** so as to cover the whole of. ● **v.** **1** pass and go round. **2** make (a figure) less exact but more convenient for calculations: *we'll round the weight up to the nearest kilo.* **3** become or cause to become round in shape. **4** Phonetics pronounce (a vowel) with the lips narrowed and protruded.

– PHRASES **go the round** (or **rounds**) be passed on from person to person. **in the round 1** (of sculpture) standing free, rather than carved in relief. **2** (of theatre) with the audience placed on at least three sides of the stage. **3** fully and thoroughly; with all aspects shown.

– PHRASAL VERBS **round something off 1** make the edges of something smooth. **2** complete something in a satisfying or suitable way. **round on** make a sudden attack on. **round someone/thing up** drive or collect a number of people or animals together.

– DERIVATIVES **roundish** adj. **roundness** n.

– ORIGIN ME: from the OFr. stem *round-*, from a var. of L. *rotundus* 'rotund'.

**roundabout** ● **n.** Brit. **1** a road junction at which traffic moves in one direction round a central island to reach one of the roads converging on it. **2** a large revolving device in a playground, for children to ride on. ➤a merry-go-round. ● **adj.** **1** not following a short direct route; circuitous. **2** not clear and direct; circumlocutory.

**round-arm** ● **adj.** Cricket (of bowling) performed with an outward horizontal swing of the arm.

**roundball** ● **n.** US informal term for **BASKETBALL**.

– DERIVATIVES **roundballer** n.

**round dance** ● **n.** **1** a folk dance in which the dancers form one large circle. **2** a ballroom dance such as a waltz or polka in which couples move in circles round the ballroom.

**rounded** ● **adj.** **1** round or curved. **2** well developed in all aspects; complete and balanced: *a rounded human being.*

**roundel** /ˈraʊnd(ə)l/ ● **n.** **1** a small disc, especially a decorative medallion. ➤a circular identifying mark painted on military aircraft. **2** a variation of the rondeau, consisting of three stanzas of three lines each, rhyming alternately, with the opening words repeated as a refrain after the first and third stanzas.

– ORIGIN ME: from OFr. *rondel*, from *ro(u)nd-* (see **ROUND**).

**roundelay** /ˈraʊndəleɪ/ ● **n.** poetic/literary **1** a short simple song with a refrain. **2** a circle dance.

– ORIGIN ME: from OFr. *rondelet*, from *rondel* (see **RONDEL**).

**rounders** ● **pl. n.** [treated as sing.] (in the UK) a ball game similar to baseball, in which players run round a circuit of bases after hitting the ball with a cylindrical wooden bat, scoring a **rounder** if all four bases are reached before the ball is fielded.

**round hand** ● **n.** a style of handwriting in which the letters have clear rounded shapes.

**Roundhead** ● **n.** historical a member or supporter of the Parliamentary party in the English Civil War.

– ORIGIN with ref. to their short-cropped hair.

**roundheel** ● **n.** N. Amer. informal a promiscuous woman.

– DERIVATIVES **roundheeled** adj.

– ORIGIN 1950s: with ref. to worn-down heels.

**roundhouse** ● **n.** **1** a railway locomotive maintenance shed built around a turntable. **2** informal a blow given with a wide sweep of the arm. ➤Baseball a slow, widely curving pitch. ➤a wide turn on a surfboard. **3** chiefly historical a cabin or set of cabins on the quarterdeck of a sailing ship.

**roundly** ● **adv.** **1** in a vehement or emphatic manner. ➤thoroughly. **2** in a circular or roughly circular shape.

**round robin** ● **n.** **1** a tournament in which each competitor plays in turn against every other. **2** a petition, especially one with signatures written in a circle to conceal the order of writing.

**roundsman** ● **n.** (pl. **-men**) **1** Brit. a trader's employee who goes round delivering and taking orders. **2** US a police officer in charge of a patrol. **3** Austral. a journalist covering a specified subject.

**round table** ● **n.** [usu. as modifier] an assembly where parties meet on equal terms for discussion: *round-table talks.*

**round trip** ● **n.** a journey to a place and back again.

**round turn** ● **n.** a complete turn of a rope around another rope or an anchoring point.

**round-up** ● **n.** **1** a systematic gathering together of people or things. **2** a summary of facts or events.

**roundwood** ● **n.** timber which is left as small logs, typically taken from near the tops of trees and used for furniture.

**roundworm** ● **n.** a nematode worm, especially a parasitic one found in the intestines of mammals. [Many species, including the large *Ascaris lumbricoides* in humans.]

**roup**[1] /raʊp/ chiefly Scottish & N. English ● **n.** an auction. ● **v.** (often **be rouped**) sell by auction.

– ORIGIN ME (in the sense 'roar, croak'): of Scand. origin.

**roup**[2] /ruːp/ ● **n.** an infectious disease of poultry affecting the respiratory tract.

– DERIVATIVES **roupy** adj.

– ORIGIN C16: of unknown origin.

**rouse** /raʊz/ ● **v.** **1** bring out of sleep; awaken. ➤cease to sleep; wake up. **2** bring out of inactivity. **3** excite; provoke: *his evasiveness roused my curiosity.* **4** stir (a liquid, especially beer while brewing).

– DERIVATIVES **rousable** adj. **rouser** n.

– ORIGIN ME (orig. as a hawking and hunting term): prob. from Anglo-Norman Fr., of unknown ultimate origin.

**rouseabout** ● **n.** Austral./NZ an unskilled labourer on a farm.

– ORIGIN C19: orig. dial. in the sense 'rough bustling person', from **ROUSE**.

**rousing** ● **adj.** **1** stirring: *a rousing speech.* **2** archaic (of a fire) blazing strongly.

– DERIVATIVES **rousingly** adv.

**Rous sarcoma** /raʊs/ ● **n.** a form of tumour caused by an RNA virus, which affects birds, particularly poultry.

– ORIGIN C20: named after the Amer. physician Francis P. *Rous.*

**roust** /raʊst/ ● **v.** **1** cause to get up or start moving; rouse. **2** N. Amer. informal treat roughly; harass.

– ORIGIN C17: perh. an alt. of **ROUSE**.

**roustabout** /ˈraʊstəbaʊt/ ● **n.** an unskilled or casual labourer, especially a labourer on an oil rig.

– ORIGIN C19: from **ROUST**.

**rout**[1] /raʊt/ ● **n.** **1** a disorderly retreat of defeated troops. ➤a decisive defeat. **2** Law, dated an assembly of people who have made a move towards committing an illegal act which would constitute an offence of riot. **3** archaic a disorderly or tumultuous crowd of people. ● **v.** defeat utterly and force to retreat.

– PHRASES **put to rout** put to flight; defeat utterly.

– ORIGIN ME: ult. based on L. *rupt-*, *rumpere* 'break', via obs. Fr. *route* and Anglo-Norman Fr. *rute.*

**rout**[2] /raʊt/ ● **v.** **1** cut a groove in (a surface). **2** another term for **ROOT**[2]. ➤force to leave a place.

– ORIGIN C16: alt. of the verb **ROOT**[2].

**route** /ruːt/ ● **n.** **1** a way or course taken in getting from a starting point to a destination. ➤the line of a road, path, railway, etc. **2** N. Amer. a round travelled in delivering, selling, or collecting goods. ● **v.** (**routeing** or **routing**) send or direct along a specified course.

– ORIGIN ME: from OFr. *rute* 'road', from L. *rupta (via)* 'broken (way)', fem. past part. of *rumpere.*

**route man** ● **n.** North American term for **ROUNDSMAN** (in sense 1).

**router**[1] /ˈraʊtə/ ● **n.** a power tool with a shaped cutter, used in carpentry.

**router**[2] /ˈruːtə/ ● **n.** Computing a device which forwards data packets to the appropriate parts of a network.

**routine** • n. **1** a sequence of actions regularly followed; a fixed unvarying programme. **2** a set sequence in a theatrical or comic performance. • adj. **1** performed as part of a regular procedure: *a routine inspection.* **2** characteristic of routine; without variety.
– DERIVATIVES **routinely** adv. **routinization** (also **-isation**) n. **routinize** (also **ise**) v.
– ORIGIN C17: from Fr., from *route* (see **ROUTE**).

**roux** /ruː/ • n. (pl. same) Cookery a mixture of fat (especially butter) and flour used in making sauces.
– ORIGIN from Fr. (*beurre*) *roux* 'browned (butter)'.

**ROV** • abbrev. remotely operated vehicle.

**rove**[1] • v. **1** travel constantly without a fixed destination; wander. ➤[usu. as adj. **roving**] travel for one's work, having no fixed base: *a roving reporter.* **2** (of eyes) look around in all directions. • n. chiefly N. Amer. an act of roving.
– ORIGIN C15 (orig. a term in archery): perh. from dial. *rave* 'to stray', prob. of Scand. origin.

**rove**[2] past of **REEVE**[2].

**rove**[3] • n. a piece of fibre drawn out and twisted, especially preparatory to spinning. • v. form into roves.
– ORIGIN C18: of unknown origin.

**rove**[4] • n. a small metal plate or ring for a rivet to pass through, especially in boatbuilding.
– ORIGIN ME: from ON *ró*, with the addition of *-v-*.

**rove beetle** • n. a long-bodied beetle with very short wing cases, typically found among decaying matter.

**rover**[1] • n. **1** a person who spends their time wandering. **2** (in various sports) a player not restricted to a particular position on the field. ➤Australian Rules one of the three players making up a ruck. **3** a vehicle for driving over rough terrain. **4** Archery a mark for long-distance shooting. ➤a mark chosen at random and not at a determined range.

**rover**[2] • n. archaic a pirate.
– ORIGIN ME: from Mid. Low Ger., MDu. *rōver*, from *rōven* 'rob'; rel. to **REAVE**.

**roving** • n. another term for **ROVE**[3]. ➤roves collectively.

**roving commission** • n. Brit. an authorization given to someone conducting an inquiry to travel as is necessary.

**row**[1] /rəʊ/ • n. a number of people or things in a more or less straight line.
– PHRASES **a hard** (or **tough**) **row to hoe** a difficult task. **in a row 1** forming a line. **2** informal in succession.
– ORIGIN OE *rāw*, of Gmc origin.

**row**[2] /rəʊ/ • v. **1** propel (a boat) with oars. ➤travel by propelling a boat in this way. **2** engage in the sport of rowing. ➤(**row someone down**) overtake a team in a rowing race. ➤(**row over**) complete the course of a boat race with little effort. • n. a spell of rowing.
– DERIVATIVES **rower** n. **rowing** n.
– ORIGIN OE *rōwan*, of Gmc origin; rel. to **RUDDER**.

**row**[3] /raʊ/ informal, chiefly Brit. • n. **1** an acrimonious quarrel. **2** a loud noise or uproar. **3** Brit. a severe reprimand. • v. **1** have a row. **2** Brit. rebuke severely.
– ORIGIN C18: of unknown origin.

**rowan** /'rəʊən, 'raʊən/ • n. a small tree with compound leaves, white flowers, and red berries. [*Sorbus aucuparia* and related species.]
– ORIGIN C15 (orig. Scots and north. Engl.): of Scand. origin.

**rowdy** • adj. (**-ier**, **-iest**) noisy and disorderly. • n. (pl. **-ies**) a rowdy person.
– DERIVATIVES **rowdily** adv. **rowdiness** n. **rowdyism** n.
– ORIGIN C19 (orig. US in the sense 'lawless backwoodsman'): of unknown origin.

**rowel** /'raʊ(ə)l/ • n. a spiked revolving disc at the end of a spur. • v. (**rowelled**, **rowelling**; US **roweled**, **roweling**) use a rowel to urge on (a horse).
– ORIGIN ME: from OFr. *roel(e)*, from late L. *rotella*, dimin. of L. *rota* 'wheel'.

**rowen** /'raʊən/ • n. US a second growth of grass or hay in one season.
– ORIGIN ME: from an ONorth. Fr. var. of OFr. *regain* 'an increase'.

**row house** • n. N. Amer. a terrace house.

**rowing machine** • n. an exercise machine with oars and a sliding seat.

**rowlock** /'rɒlək, 'rʌlək/ • n. a fitting on the gunwale of a boat which serves as a fulcrum for an oar and keeps it in place.
– ORIGIN C18: alt. of **OARLOCK**, influenced by **ROW**[2].

**royal** • adj. **1** of, relating to, or having the status of a king or queen or a member of their family. **2** of a quality or size suitable for a king or queen; splendid. • n. **1** informal a member of the royal family. **2** (in full **metric royal**) a paper size, 636 × 480 mm. ➤(in full **royal octavo**) a book size, 234 × 156 mm. ➤(in full **royal quarto**) a book size, 312 × 237 mm. **3** Bell-ringing a system of change-ringing using ten bells.
– DERIVATIVES **royally** adv.
– ORIGIN ME: from OFr. *roial*, from L. *regalis* 'regal'.

**royal antelope** • n. a West African antelope with an arched back, short neck, and a red and brown coat with white underparts. [*Neotragus pygmaeus*, family Bovidae.]

**royal assent** • n. assent of the sovereign to a bill which has been passed by Parliament, and which thus becomes an Act of Parliament.

**royal blue** • n. a deep, vivid blue.

**Royal Commission** • n. (in the UK) a commission of inquiry appointed by the Crown on the recommendation of the government.

**royal fern** • n. a large pale green fern which has very long spreading fronds, occurring worldwide in wet habitats. [*Osmunda regalis.*]

**royal flush** • n. Poker the highest straight flush, including ace, king, queen, jack, and ten all in the same suit.

**Royal Gala** • n. a New Zealand dessert apple of a variety with red and yellow skin.
– ORIGIN 1960s: orig. *Gala*, but renamed following a royal visit.

**royal icing** • n. chiefly Brit. hard white icing, typically used to decorate fruit cakes.

**royalist** • n. **1** a person who supports the principle of monarchy. **2** a supporter of the King against Parliament in the English Civil War. **3** US a supporter of the British during the War of American Independence; a Tory. • adj. giving support to the monarchy.
– DERIVATIVES **royalism** n.

**royal jelly** • n. a substance secreted by honeybee workers and fed by them to larvae which are being raised as potential queen bees.

**royal mast** • n. a section of a sailing ship's mast above the topgallant.

**royal palm** • n. a New World palm which is widely cultivated as an avenue tree. [Genus *Roystonea*: several species, in particular *R. regia*.]

**royal stag** • n. Brit. a red deer stag with a head of twelve or more points.

**royal standard** • n. a banner bearing the royal coat of arms, flown in the presence of royalty.

**royal tennis** • n. another term for **REAL TENNIS**.

**royalty** • n. (pl. **-ies**) **1** people of royal blood or status. ➤an individual member of a royal family. ➤the status or power of a king or queen. **2** a sum paid for the use of a patent or to an author or composer for each copy of a book sold or for each public performance of a work. **3** a royal right (now especially over minerals) granted by the sovereign. ➤a payment made by a producer of minerals, oil, or natural gas to the owner of the site.

**royal warrant** • n. a warrant issued by the sovereign, in particular one authorizing a company to display the royal arms, indicating that goods or services are supplied to the royal family.

**rozzer** • n. Brit. informal a police officer.
– ORIGIN C19: of unknown origin.

**RP** • abbrev. received pronunciation.

**RPG** • abbrev. **1** report program generator (a high-level commercial programming language). **2** rocket-propelled grenade. **3** role-playing game.

**RPI** • abbrev. retail price index.

**rpm** • abbrev. **1** resale price maintenance. **2** revolutions per minute.

**rpt** ● **abbrev.** report.

**RPV** ● **abbrev.** remotely piloted vehicle.

**RR** ● **abbrev.** N. Amer. **1** railroad. **2** rural route.

**-rrhoea** ● **comb. form** discharge; flow: *diarrhoea.*
– ORIGIN from Gk *rhoia* 'flow, flux'.

**RRP** ● **abbrev.** Brit. recommended retail price.

**Rs** ● **abbrev.** rupee(s).

**RSA** ● **abbrev. 1** Republic of South Africa. **2** Royal Scottish Academy; Royal Scottish Academician. **3** Royal Society of Arts.

**RSC** ● **abbrev. 1** Royal Shakespeare Company. **2** (in the UK) Royal Society of Chemistry.

**RSFSR** ● **abbrev.** historical Russian Soviet Federative Socialist Republic.

**RSI** ● **abbrev.** repetitive strain injury.

**RSJ** ● **abbrev.** rolled steel joist.

**RSM** ● **abbrev. 1** (in the British army) Regimental Sergeant Major. **2** San Marino (international vehicle registration). [from Ital. *Repubblica di San Marino.*]

**RSPB** ● **abbrev.** (in the UK) Royal Society for the Protection of Birds.

**RSPCA** ● **abbrev.** (in the UK) Royal Society for the Prevention of Cruelty to Animals.

**RSV** ● **abbrev.** Revised Standard Version (of the Bible).

**RSVP** ● **abbrev.** répondez s'il vous plaît; please reply (used at the end of invitations).
– ORIGIN from Fr.

**RT** ● **abbrev. 1** radio-telegraphy. **2** radiotelephony.

**rt** ● **abbrev.** right.

**RTA** ● **abbrev.** Brit. road traffic accident.

**RTE** ● **abbrev.** Radio Telefis Éireann (the broadcasting authority of the Republic of Ireland).

**rte** ● **abbrev.** route.

**RTF** ● **abbrev.** Computing rich text format.

**Rt Hon.** ● **abbrev.** Brit. Right Honourable.

**Rt Revd** (also **Rt Rev.**) ● **abbrev.** Right Reverend.

**RU** ● **abbrev. 1** Burundi (international vehicle registration). [from *Ruanda-Urundi* (now Rwanda and Burundi).] **2** rugby union.

**Ru** ● **symb.** the chemical element ruthenium.

**RU486** ● **n.** trademark for **MIFEPRISTONE.**

**rub** ● **v.** (**rubbed, rubbing**) **1** apply firm pressure against the surface of, using a repeated back and forth motion. ➤move to and fro against a surface. ➤apply with a rubbing action: *she rubbed some cream on her nose.* ➤(**rub something in/into/through**) blend or mix ingredients together using a rubbing action: *rub in the fat.* ➤(**rub something down**) dry, smooth, or clean something by rubbing. ➤(**rub something out**) erase pencil marks with a rubber. ➤(**rub off**) be transferred by contact or association. **2** (**rub along**) Brit. informal cope or get along without undue difficulty. **3** reproduce the design of (a sepulchral brass or a stone) by rubbing paper laid on it with pencil or chalk. **4** Bowls (of a bowl) be slowed or diverted by the unevenness of the ground. ● **n. 1** an act of rubbing. **2** an ointment designed to be rubbed on the skin. **3** (usu. **the rub**) the central or most important difficulty. [from Shakespeare's *Hamlet* (III. i. 65).] **4** Bowls an inequality of the ground impeding or diverting a bowl; the diversion or hindering of a bowl by this.
– PHRASES **the rub of the green 1** Golf an accidental or unpredictable influence on the course or position of the ball. **2** good fortune. **rub one's hands** rub one's hands together to show keen satisfaction. **rub it in** (or **rub someone's nose in something**) informal emphatically draw someone's attention to an embarrassing or painful fact. **rub noses** rub one's nose against someone else's in greeting (especially as traditional among Maoris and some other peoples). **rub shoulders** (or N. Amer. **elbows**) associate or come into contact. **rub someone** (or Brit. **rub someone up**) **the wrong way** anger or irritate someone.
– ORIGIN ME: perh. from Low Ger. *rubben*, of unknown ultimate origin.

**rubato** /rʊˈbɑːtəʊ/ (also **tempo rubato**) ● **n.** (pl. **rubatos** or **rubati** /-ti/) Music the temporary disregard for strict tempo to allow an expressive quickening or slackening.
– ORIGIN Ital., lit. 'robbed'.

**rubber**[1] ● **n. 1** a tough elastic polymeric substance made from the latex of a tropical plant or synthetically. **2** Brit. a piece of such material used for erasing pencil marks. **3** N. Amer. informal a condom. **4** (**rubbers**) N. Amer. rubber boots; galoshes.
– DERIVATIVES **rubberiness** n. **rubberize** (also **-ise**) v. **rubberoid** adj. **rubbery** adj.
– ORIGIN C16: from **RUB** + **-ER**[1]; an early use of the substance rubber was to rub out pencil marks.

**rubber**[2] ● **n. 1** a contest consisting of a series of matches between the same sides in cricket, tennis, and other games. **2** Bridge a unit of play in which one side scores bonus points for winning the best of three games.
– ORIGIN C16: of unknown origin; early use was as a term in bowls.

**rubber band** ● **n.** a loop of rubber for holding things together.

**rubber bullet** ● **n.** a bullet made of rubber, used especially in riot control.

**rubber cement** ● **n.** a cement or adhesive containing rubber in a solvent.

**rubberneck** informal ● **n.** a person who turns their head to stare at something in a foolish manner. ● **v.** stare in such a way.
– DERIVATIVES **rubbernecker** n.

**rubber plant** ● **n.** an evergreen tree of the fig family, which has large dark green shiny leaves and was formerly grown as a source of rubber. [*Ficus elastica.*]

**rubber stamp** ● **n. 1** a hand-held device for imprinting dates, addresses, etc. **2** a person acting to give automatic authorization, without having the authority or ability to question or reject. ● **v.** (**rubber-stamp**) **1** apply a rubber stamp to. **2** approve automatically without proper consideration.

**rubber tree** ● **n.** a tree that produces the latex from which rubber is manufactured, native to the Amazonian rainforest. [*Hevea brasiliensis.*]

**rubbing** ● **n. 1** the action of rubbing. **2** an impression of a design on brass or stone, made by rubbing.

**rubbing alcohol** ● **n.** denatured alcohol used as an antiseptic or in massage.

**rubbish** ● **n. 1** chiefly Brit. waste material; refuse or litter. **2** material that is considered unimportant or valueless. ➤nonsense; worthless talk or ideas. ● **v.** Brit. informal criticize and reject as worthless. ● **adj.** Brit. informal very bad.
– DERIVATIVES **rubbishy** adj.
– ORIGIN ME: from Anglo-Norman Fr. *rubbous*; perh. rel. to OFr. *robe* 'spoils'; cf. **RUBBLE.**

**rubble** ● **n.** waste or rough fragments of stone, brick, concrete, etc., especially as the debris from the demolition of buildings.
– DERIVATIVES **rubbled** adj. **rubbly** adj.
– ORIGIN ME: perh. from an Anglo-Norman Fr. alt. of OFr. *robe* 'spoils'; cf. **RUBBISH.**

**rubby** ● **n.** (pl. **-ies**) Canadian informal an alcoholic who drinks rubbing alcohol.

**rube** /ruːb/ ● **n.** N. Amer. informal a country bumpkin.
– ORIGIN C19: abbrev. of the given name *Reuben.*

**rubella** /rʊˈbɛlə/ ● **n.** a contagious viral disease, with symptoms like mild measles; German measles.
– ORIGIN C19: mod. L., neut. pl. of L. *rubellus* 'reddish'.

**rubellite** /ˈruːbəlʌɪt/ ● **n.** a red variety of tourmaline.
– ORIGIN C18: from L. *rubellus* 'reddish' + **-ITE**[1].

**rubeola** /rʊˈbiːələ/ ● **n.** medical term for **MEASLES.**
– ORIGIN C17: from med. L., dimin. of L. *rubeus* 'red'.

**rubescent** /rʊˈbɛs(ə)nt/ ● **adj.** chiefly poetic/literary reddening; blushing.
– ORIGIN C18: from L. *rubescent-*, *rubescere* 'redden', from *ruber* 'red'.

**Rubicon** /ˈruːbɪk(ə)n, -kɒn/ ● **n. 1** a point of no return. **2** (in piquet) an act of winning a game against an opponent whose total score is less than 100.
– ORIGIN the name of a stream in NE Italy marking the ancient boundary between Italy and Cisalpine Gaul,

which Julius Caesar crossed in 49 BC, breaking the law and so committing himself to war.

**rubicund** /ˈruːbɪk(ə)nd/ • **adj.** having a ruddy complexion.
– DERIVATIVES **rubicundity** /-ˈkʌndɪti/ n.
– ORIGIN ME: from L. *rubicundus*, from *rubere* 'be red'.

**rubidium** /rʊˈbɪdɪəm/ • **n.** the chemical element of atomic number 37, a rare soft silvery reactive metal of the alkali metal group. (Symbol: **Rb**)
– ORIGIN C19: mod. L., from L. *rubidus* 'red' (with ref. to lines in its spectrum).

**rubiginous** /rʊˈbɪdʒɪnəs/ • **adj.** technical or poetic/literary rust-coloured.
– ORIGIN C17: from L. *rubigo*, *rubigin-* 'rust' + **-OUS**.

**Rubik's cube** /ˈruːbɪks/ • **n.** trademark a puzzle in the form of a plastic cube covered with multicoloured squares, which the player attempts to turn so that all the squares on each face are of the same colour.
– ORIGIN 1980s: named after its Hungarian inventor Erno *Rubik*.

**ruble** • **n.** variant spelling of **ROUBLE**.

**rubric** /ˈruːbrɪk/ • **n.** **1** a heading on a document. **2** a set of instructions or rules. ➤a direction in a liturgical book as to how a church service should be conducted.
– DERIVATIVES **rubrical** adj.
– ORIGIN ME *rubrish* (orig. referring to text written in red for emphasis), from OFr. *rubriche*, from L. *rubrica* (*terra*) 'red (earth or ochre as writing material)'.

**rubricate** /ˈruːbrɪkeɪt/ • **v.** chiefly historical add elaborate, typically red, capital letters or other decorations to (a manuscript).
– DERIVATIVES **rubrication** n. **rubricator** n.
– ORIGIN C16: from L. *rubricat-*, *rubricare* 'mark in red', from *rubrica* (see **RUBRIC**).

**ruby** • **n.** (pl. **-ies**) **1** a precious stone consisting of corundum in colour varieties varying from deep crimson or purple to pale rose. **2** an intense deep red colour. **3** Printing an old type size equal to 5½ points.
– ORIGIN ME: from OFr. *rubi*, from med. L. *rubinus*, from the base of L. *rubeus* 'red'.

**ruby-tail** • **n.** a shiny greenish-blue parasitic wasp with an orange-red tip to the abdomen, which lays its eggs in bees' nests. [*Chrysis ignita* and other species.]

**rubythroat** • **n.** a small thrush, the male having a red throat and striped head, found from Siberia to China. [Genus *Erithacus*: three species.]

**ruby wedding** • **n.** the fortieth anniversary of a wedding.

**RUC** • **abbrev.** Royal Ulster Constabulary.

**ruche** /ruːʃ/ • **n.** a frill or pleat of fabric.
– DERIVATIVES **ruched** adj. **ruching** n.
– ORIGIN C19: from Fr., from med. L. *rusca* 'tree bark', of Celtic origin.

**ruck**[1] • **n.** **1** Rugby a loose scrum formed around a player with the ball on the ground. Compare with **MAUL**. ➤Australian Rules a group of three players who follow the play without fixed positions. **2** a tightly packed crowd of people. • **v.** Rugby & Australian Rules take part in a ruck.
– ORIGIN ME (in the sense 'stack of fuel, heap'): appar. of Scand. origin.

**ruck**[2] • **v.** make or form wrinkles, creases, or folds. • **n.** a crease or wrinkle.
– ORIGIN C18: from ON *hrukka*.

**ruck**[3] • **n.** Brit. informal a brawl.
– ORIGIN 1950s: perh. a shortened form of **RUCTION** or **RUCKUS**.

**ruckle** • **v. & n.** Brit. another term for **RUCK**[2].

**rucksack** /ˈrʌksak, ˈrʊk-/ • **n.** a bag with two shoulder straps which allow it to be carried on the back, used by hikers.
– ORIGIN C19: from Ger., from *rucken* (dial. var. of *Rücken* 'back') + *Sack* 'bag, sack'.

**ruckus** /ˈrʌkəs/ • **n.** a row or commotion.
– ORIGIN C19: perh. rel. to **RUCTION** and **RUMPUS**.

**rucola** /ˈruːkələ/ • **n.** another term for **ARUGULA**.

**ruction** • **n.** informal a disturbance or quarrel. ➤(**ructions**) trouble.
– ORIGIN C19: of unknown origin; perh. assoc. with **INSURRECTION**.

**rudaceous** /rʊˈdeɪʃəs/ • **adj.** Geology (of rock) composed of fragments of relatively large size (larger than sand grains).
– ORIGIN C20: from L. *rudus* 'rubble' + **-ACEOUS**.

**rudbeckia** /ruːdˈbɛkɪə, rʌd-/ • **n.** a North American plant of the daisy family, with yellow or orange flowers and a dark cone-like centre. [Genus *Rudbeckia*.]
– ORIGIN mod. L., named after the Swed. botanist Olaf *Rudbeck* (1660–1740).

**rudd** • **n.** (pl. same) a European freshwater fish of the carp family with a silvery body and red fins. [*Rutilus erythrophthalmus*.]
– ORIGIN C16: appar. rel. to archaic *rud* 'red colour'.

**rudder** • **n.** a flat piece hinged vertically near the stern of a boat for steering. ➤a vertical aerofoil pivoted from the tailplane of an aircraft, for controlling movement about the vertical axis. ➤application of the rudder in steering a boat or aircraft.
– ORIGIN OE *rōther* 'paddle, oar', of W. Gmc origin.

**rudderless** • **adj.** **1** lacking a rudder. **2** lacking direction.

**ruddle** • **n.** another term for **REDDLE**.
– ORIGIN ME: rel. to obs. *rud* 'red colour' and **RED**.

**ruddy** • **adj.** (**-ier**, **-iest**) **1** (especially of a person's face) having a healthy red colour. **2** Brit. informal, dated used as a euphemism for 'bloody'. • **v.** (**-ies**, **-ied**) make ruddy in colour.
– DERIVATIVES **ruddily** adv. (rare). **ruddiness** n.
– ORIGIN OE *rudig*, from the base of archaic *rud* 'red colour'; rel. to **RED**.

**ruddy duck** • **n.** a New World duck with a broad bill, naturalized in Britain, the male having mainly deep red-brown plumage and white cheeks. [*Oxyura jamaicensis*.]

**rude** • **adj.** **1** offensively impolite or ill-mannered. ➤referring to sex in a way considered improper and offensive. **2** very abrupt: *a rude awakening*. **3** chiefly Brit. vigorous or hearty. **4** dated roughly made or done; lacking sophistication. ➤archaic ignorant and uneducated.
– DERIVATIVES **rudely** adv. **rudeness** n. **rudery** n.
– ORIGIN ME: from OFr., from L. *rudis* 'unwrought', figuratively 'uncultivated'; rel. to *rudus* 'broken stone'.

**rude boy** • **n.** (in Jamaica) a lawless urban youth who likes ska or reggae music.

**ruderal** /ˈruːd(ə)r(ə)l/ Botany • **adj.** (of a plant) growing on waste ground or among rubbish. • **n.** a ruderal plant.
– ORIGIN C19: from mod. L. *ruderalis*, from L. *rudera*, pl. of *rudus* 'rubble'.

**rudiment** /ˈruːdɪm(ə)nt/ • **n.** **1** (**rudiments**) the first principles of a subject. ➤an elementary or primitive form of something. **2** Biology an undeveloped or immature part or organ. **3** Music a basic pattern used by drummers, such as the roll, the flam, and the paradiddle.
– ORIGIN C16: from Fr., or from L. *rudimentum*, from *rudis* 'unwrought'.

**rudimentary** /ˌruːdɪˈmɛnt(ə)ri/ • **adj.** **1** involving or limited to basic principles. **2** of or relating to an immature, undeveloped, or basic form.
– DERIVATIVES **rudimentarily** adv.

**rudist** /ˈruːdɪst/ • **n.** a cone-shaped fossil bivalve mollusc which formed colonies resembling reefs in the Cretaceous period.
– ORIGIN C19: from mod. L. *Rudista* (former group name), from L. *rudis* 'unwrought'.

**rue**[1] • **v.** (**rues**, **rued**, **rueing** or **ruing**) bitterly regret (a past event or action) and wish it undone. • **n.** archaic **1** repentance; regret. **2** compassion; pity.
– ORIGIN OE *hrēow* 'repentance', *hrēowan* 'affect with contrition', of Gmc origin.

**rue**[2] • **n.** a perennial evergreen shrub with bitter strong-scented lobed leaves which are used in herbal medicine. [*Ruta graveolens*.] ➤used in names of plants that resemble rue, e.g. **meadow rue**.
– ORIGIN ME: from OFr., via L. from Gk *rhutē*.

**rueful** • **adj.** expressing regret, especially in a wry or humorous way.
– DERIVATIVES **ruefully** adv. **ruefulness** n.

**ruff**[1] • n. **1** a projecting starched frill worn round the neck, characteristic of Elizabethan and Jacobean costume. **2** a projecting or conspicuously coloured ring of feathers or hair round the neck of a bird or mammal. **3** a pigeon of a domestic breed with a ruff of feathers. **4** (pl. same or **ruffs**) a North Eurasian wading bird, the male of which has a large ruff and ear tufts in the breeding season. [*Philomachus pugnax*; the female is called a **reeve**.]
– ORIGIN C16: prob. from a var. of ROUGH.

**ruff**[2] • n. **1** (also **tommy ruff**) an edible marine fish of Australian inshore waters. [*Arripis georgianus*.] **2** variant spelling of RUFFE.
– ORIGIN C19: from RUFFE.

**ruff**[3] • v. (in bridge and whist) play a trump in a trick which was led in a different suit. ➤ play a trump on (a card). • n. an act of ruffing or opportunity to ruff.
– ORIGIN C16 (orig. the name of a card game): from OFr. *rouffle* (perh. an alt. of Ital. *trionfo* 'a trump').

**ruff**[4] • n. Music one of the basic patterns (rudiments) of drumming, consisting of a single note preceded by either two grace notes played with the other stick or three grace notes played with alternating sticks.
– ORIGIN C17: prob. imitative.

**ruffe** /rʌf/ (also **ruff**) • n. a European freshwater fish, with a greenish-brown back and yellow sides and underparts. [*Gymnocephalus cernua*.]
– ORIGIN ME: prob. from a var. of ROUGH.

**ruffed grouse** • n. a North American grouse with a black ruff on the sides of the neck. [*Bonasa umbellus*.]

**ruffian** • n. a violent or lawless person.
– DERIVATIVES **ruffianism** n. **ruffianly** adj.
– ORIGIN C15: from OFr. *ruffian*, from Ital. *ruffiano*, perh. from dial. *rofia* 'scab, scurf', of Gmc origin.

**ruffle** • v. **1** make or become disarranged; disrupt the smooth surface of. ➤ (of a bird) erect (its feathers) in anger or display. **2** disconcert or upset the composure of. **3** [usu. as adj. **ruffled**] ornament with or gather into a frill. • n. **1** an ornamental gathered frill on a garment. **2** a low continuous drum beat.
– ORIGIN ME: of unknown origin.

**rufiyaa** /'ru:fi:jɑ:/ • n. (pl. same) the basic monetary unit of the Maldives, equal to 100 laris.
– ORIGIN from Maldivian.

**rufous** /'ru:fəs/ • adj. reddish brown in colour. • n. a reddish-brown colour.
– ORIGIN C18: from L. *rufus* 'red, reddish'.

**rug** • n. **1** a small carpet. ➤ chiefly Brit. a thick woollen blanket. **2** informal, chiefly N. Amer. a toupee or wig.
– PHRASES **pull the rug out from under** abruptly expose or withdraw support from.
– ORIGIN C16 (denoting a type of coarse woollen cloth): prob. of Scand. origin; rel. to RAG[1].

**rugby** (also **rugby football**) • n. a team game played with an oval ball that may be kicked, carried, and passed by hand, in which points are won by scoring a try or by kicking the ball over the crossbar of the opponents' goal.
– ORIGIN C19: named after *Rugby* School, where the game was first played.

**rugby league** • n. a form of rugby played in teams of thirteen, in which professionalism has always been allowed.

**rugby union** • n. a form of rugby played in teams of fifteen, traditionally strictly amateur but opened to professionalism in 1995.

**rugged** /'rʌgɪd/ • adj. **1** having a rocky and uneven surface. **2** having or requiring toughness and determination. ➤ (of a man) having attractively masculine, rough-hewn features.
– DERIVATIVES **ruggedly** adv. **ruggedness** n.
– ORIGIN ME (in the sense 'shaggy'): prob. of Scand. origin; cf. RUG.

**ruggedized** (also **-ised**) • adj. chiefly N. Amer. designed or improved to be hard-wearing: *ruggedized computers*.
– DERIVATIVES **ruggedization** n.

**rugger** • n. Brit. informal rugby.

**rugola** /'ru:gələ/ • n. another term for ARUGULA.

**rugosa** /ru:'gəʊzə/ • n. a SE Asian rose with dark green wrinkled leaves and deep pink flowers. [*Rosa rugosa*.]
– ORIGIN C19: fem. of L. *rugosus* (see RUGOSE).

**rugose** /'ru:gəʊs, rʊ'gəʊs/ • adj. chiefly Biology wrinkled; corrugated.
– DERIVATIVES **rugosity** n.
– ORIGIN ME: from L. *rugosus*, from *ruga* 'wrinkle'.

**rug rat** • n. N. Amer. informal a small child.

**ruin** • n. **1** physical destruction or collapse. **2** a building (or the remains of a building) that has suffered much damage. **3** a dramatic decline; a downfall. • v. **1** damage irreparably; reduce to a state of ruin. ➤ reduce to poverty or bankruptcy. **2** poetic/literary fall headlong.
– PHRASES **in ruins** in a state of complete collapse.
– ORIGIN ME: from OFr. *ruine*, from L. *ruina*, from *ruere* 'to fall'.

**ruination** • n. the action or fact of ruining or the state of being ruined.

**ruinous** • adj. **1** disastrous or destructive. **2** in ruins; dilapidated.
– DERIVATIVES **ruinously** adv. **ruinousness** n.

**rukh** /ru:k/ • n. another term for ROC.
– ORIGIN from Hindi *rūkh*.

**rule** • n. **1** a regulation or principle governing conduct or procedure within a particular sphere. **2** control or government: *an end to British rule*. **3** a code of practice and discipline for a religious community: *the Rule of St Benedict*. **4** (**the rule**) the normal or customary state of things. **5** a straight strip of rigid material used for measuring; a ruler. **6** a thin printed line or dash. • v. **1** exercise ultimate power over (a people or nation). ➤ exert a powerful and restricting influence on. ➤ be prevalent; be the norm. **2** pronounce authoritatively and legally to be the case. **3** [often as adj. **ruled**] make parallel lines on (paper). ➤ make (a straight line) with a ruler. **4** (**rule something out/in**) exclude (or include) something as a possibility.
– PHRASES **as a rule** usually, but not always. **rule of law** the restriction of power by well-defined and established laws. **rule of thumb** a broadly accurate guide or principle, based on practice rather than theory. **rule the roost** be in complete control. **run the rule over** Brit. examine cursorily.
– DERIVATIVES **ruleless** adj.
– ORIGIN ME: from OFr. *reule* (n.), *reuler* (v.), from late L. *regulare*, from L. *regula* 'straight stick'.

**rule of the road** • n. a custom or law regulating the direction in which two cars, ships, etc. should move to pass one another to avoid collision.

**ruler** • n. **1** a person or agent exercising government or dominion. **2** a straight-edged strip of rigid material, marked at regular intervals and used to draw straight lines or measure distances.
– DERIVATIVES **rulership** n.

**ruling** • n. an authoritative decision or pronouncement. • adj. exercising rule.

**rum**[1] • n. an alcoholic spirit distilled from sugar-cane residues or molasses. ➤ N. Amer. any intoxicating liquor.
– ORIGIN C17: perh. an abbrev. of obs. *rumbullion*, in the same sense.

**rum**[2] • adj. (**rummer**, **rummest**) Brit. informal, dated odd; peculiar.
– DERIVATIVES **rumly** adv. **rumness** n.
– ORIGIN C18: of unknown origin.

**Rumanian** /ru:'meɪnɪən/ • adj. & n. variant spelling of ROMANIAN.

**Rumansh** /rʊ'manʃ, -'mɑ:nʃ/ • n. variant of ROMANSH.

**rumba** /'rʌmbə/ (also **rhumba**) • n. a rhythmic dance with Spanish and African elements, originating in Cuba. ➤ a ballroom dance based on this. • v. (**rumbas**, **rumbaed** /-bəd/ or **rumba'd**, **rumbaing** /-bə(r)ɪŋ/) dance the rumba.
– ORIGIN 1920s: from Latin Amer. Sp.

**rum baba** • n. see BABA[1].

**rumble** • v. **1** make a continuous deep, resonant sound. ➤ move with such a sound. **2** (**rumble on**) (of a dispute) continue in a persistent but low-key way. **3** Brit. informal discover (an illicit activity or its perpetrator): *it wouldn't*

*need a genius to rumble his little game.* **4** US informal take part in a street fight. ● **n. 1** a continuous deep, resonant sound like distant thunder. **2** US informal a street fight between rival gangs.
– DERIVATIVES **rumbler** n. **rumbling** adj.
– ORIGIN ME: prob. from MDu. *rommelen, rummelen*, of imitative origin.

**rumble seat** ● **n.** N. Amer. an uncovered folding seat in the rear of a motor car.

**rumble strip** ● **n.** a series of raised strips set in a road, changing the noise a vehicle's tyres make on the surface and so warning drivers of speed restrictions or an approaching hazard.

**rumbustious** /rʌmˈbʌstʃəs, -tɪəs/ ● **adj.** informal, chiefly Brit. boisterous or unruly.
– DERIVATIVES **rumbustiously** adv. **rumbustiousness** n.
– ORIGIN C18: prob. an alt. of archaic *robustious* 'boisterous, robust'.

**rum butter** ● **n.** a rich, sweet, rum-flavoured sauce made with butter and sugar.

**rumen** /ˈruːmɛn/ ● **n.** (pl. **rumens** or **rumina** /-mɪnə/) Zoology the first stomach of a ruminant, which receives food or cud, partly digests it, and passes it to the reticulum.
– ORIGIN C18: from L., lit. 'throat'.

**ruminant** ● **n. 1** an even-toed ungulate mammal of a type that chews the cud, comprising cattle, sheep, antelopes, deer, giraffes, and their relatives. **2** a person given to meditation. ● **adj.** of or relating to ruminants.
– ORIGIN C17: from L. *ruminant-, ruminari* 'chew over again', from *rumen* (see RUMEN).

**ruminate** /ˈruːmɪneɪt/ ● **v. 1** think deeply about something. **2** (of a ruminant) chew the cud.
– DERIVATIVES **rumination** n. **ruminative** adj. **ruminatively** adv. **ruminator** n.
– ORIGIN C16: from L. *ruminat-, ruminari* 'chew over'.

**rummage** ● **v.** search unsystematically and untidily for something. ➤make a thorough search of (a vessel). ● **n.** an act of rummaging.
– DERIVATIVES **rummager** n.
– ORIGIN C15: from OFr. *arrumage*, from *arrumer* 'stow (in a hold)', from MDu. *ruim* 'room'; in early use the word referred to the arranging of items in the hold of a ship.

**rummage sale** ● **n.** chiefly N. Amer. a jumble sale.

**rummer** ● **n.** a large stemmed drinking glass.
– ORIGIN C17: of Low Du. origin; rel. to Du. *roemer*.

**rummy**[1] ● **n.** a card game in which the players try to form sets and sequences of cards.
– ORIGIN C20: of unknown origin.

**rummy**[2] ● **adj.** (**-ier, -iest**) another term for RUM[2].

**rumour** (US **rumor**) ● **n.** a currently circulating story or report of unverified or doubtful truth. ● **v.** (**be rumoured**) be circulated as a rumour.
– ORIGIN ME: from OFr. *rumur*, from L. *rumor* 'noise'.

**rump** ● **n. 1** the hind part of the body of a mammal or the lower back of a bird. ➤chiefly humorous a person's buttocks. **2** a small or unimportant remnant.
– DERIVATIVES **rumpless** adj.
– ORIGIN ME: prob. of Scand. origin; cf. Dan. and Norw. *rumpe* 'backside'.

**rumple** ● **v.** [usu. as adj. **rumpled**] give a ruffled or dishevelled appearance to. ● **n.** an untidy state.
– DERIVATIVES **rumply** adj.
– ORIGIN C16 (in the sense 'wrinkle'): from MDu. *rompel*.

**rumpsprung** ● **adj.** informal (of furniture) worn and in poor condition.

**rumpus** ● **n.** (pl. **rumpuses**) a noisy disturbance.
– ORIGIN C18: prob. fanciful.

**rumpus room** ● **n.** N. Amer. & Austral./NZ a room for playing games or other noisy activities.

**rumpy pumpy** ● **n.** informal, humorous sexual relations, especially when of a casual nature.
– ORIGIN 1960s: reduplication of RUMP.

**run** ● **v.** (**running**; past **ran** /ran/; past part. **run**) **1** move at a speed faster than a walk, never having both or all feet on the ground at the same time. ➤enter or be entered in a race. ➤(of hounds) chase or hunt their quarry. ➤(of a boat) sail straight and fast directly before the wind. ➤(of a migratory fish) go upriver from the sea in order to spawn. **2** move about in a hurried and hectic way. **3** pass or cause to pass: *Helen ran her fingers through her hair.* ➤move or cause to move forcefully: *the tanker ran aground.* ➤informal fail to stop at (a red traffic light). ➤chiefly N. Amer. navigate (rapids or a waterfall) in a boat. **4** flow or cause to flow. ➤cause water to flow over. ➤emit or exude a liquid: *her nose was running.* ➤(of dye or colour) dissolve and spread when wet. **5** (of a bus, train, etc.) make a regular journey on a particular route. ➤transport in a car: *I'll run you home.* **6** be in charge of; manage or organize. ➤continue, operate, or proceed: *everything's running according to plan.* ➤own, maintain, and use (a vehicle). **7** be in or cause to be in operation; function or cause to function. **8** (**run in**) (of a quality or trait) be common or inherent in. **9** stand as a candidate. **10** pass into or reach a specified state or level. **11** chiefly N. Amer. (of a stocking or pair of tights) develop a ladder. **12** publish or be published in a newspaper or magazine. **13** smuggle (goods). **14** N. Amer. informal cost (someone) (a specified amount). ● **n. 1** an act or spell of running. ➤a running pace. **2** a journey or route. ➤a short excursion made in a car. **3** Cricket a unit of scoring achieved by hitting the ball so that both batsmen are able to run between the wickets. ➤Baseball a point scored by the batter returning to the home plate after touching the bases. **4** a spell of producing, proceeding, or operating: *a run of bad luck.* ➤a continuous stretch or length of something. ➤a rapid series of musical notes. ➤a sequence of cards of the same suit. **5** a widespread and sudden demand: *a big run on nostalgia toys.* **6** a course or track made or regularly used: *a ski run.* **7** (**the run**) the average or usual type: *she stood out from the general run of Tory women.* **8** an enclosed area in which animals or birds may run freely in the open. ➤(**the run of**) free and unrestricted use of or access to somewhere. ➤Austral./NZ a large open stretch of land used for pasture or livestock. **9** a ladder in stockings or tights. **10** a downward trickle of liquid. **11** a small stream or brook. **12** (**the runs**) informal diarrhoea. **13** Nautical the after part of a ship's bottom where it rises and narrows towards the stern. **14** an annual mass migration of fish up or down a river.
– PHRASES **be run off one's feet** be extremely busy. **a** (**good**) **run for one's money 1** challenging competition or opposition. **2** reward or enjoyment in return for one's efforts. **on the run 1** escaping from arrest. **2** while running or moving. **run before one can walk** attempt something difficult before one has grasped the basic skills. **run dry 1** (of a well or river) cease to flow or have any water. **2** (of a supply) be completely used up. (**make a**) **run for it** attempt to escape by running away. **run foul** (or chiefly N. Amer. **afoul**) **of 1** Nautical collide or become entangled with. **2** come into conflict with. **run into the sand** come to nothing. **run low** (or **short**) (of a supply) become depleted. **run off at the mouth** N. Amer. informal talk excessively or indiscreetly. **run a temperature** be suffering from a high temperature. **run someone/thing to earth** (or **ground**) Hunting chase a quarry to its lair. **run to ruin** archaic fall into disrepair.
– PHRASAL VERBS **run across** meet or find by chance. **run after** informal pursue persistently. **run along** informal go away. **run away 1** take flight; escape. **2** try to avoid facing up to danger or difficulty. **run away with 1** escape the control of: *Susan's imagination was running away with her.* **2** win (a competition or prize) easily. **run something by** (or **past**) tell (someone) about something, in order to ascertain an opinion or reaction. **run someone/thing down 1** (of a vehicle) hit and knock over a person or animal. **2** criticize someone or something unfairly or unkindly. **3** discover someone or something after a search. **4** (also **run down**) reduce or become reduced in size or resources. **5** lose or cause to lose power; stop or cause to stop functioning. **6** gradually deteriorate or cause to deteriorate. **run someone in** informal arrest someone. **run something in** Brit. use something new in such a way as not to make maximum demands upon it. **run into 1** collide with. ➤meet by chance. **2** experience (a problem or difficult situation). **run off** informal escape; abscond. **run something off 1** produce a copy on a machine. **2** write or recite something quickly and with little

effort. **3** drain liquid from a container. **run on** continue without stopping; go on longer than is expected. **run out 1** use up or be used up. **2** become no longer valid. **3** (of rope) be paid out. **4** extend; project. **run someone out** Cricket dismiss a batsman by dislodging the bails with the ball while the batsman is still running. **run over 1** overflow. **2** exceed (a limit). **run someone/thing over** knock down a person or animal in a vehicle. **run someone/thing through** stab a person or animal so as to kill them. **run through** (or **over**) go over quickly or briefly as a rehearsal or reminder. **run to 1** extend to or reach. **2** show a tendency towards. **run something up 1** allow a bill, score, etc. to accumulate. **2** make something quickly or hurriedly. **3** raise a flag. **run up against** experience or meet (a difficulty or problem). **run with** proceed with; accept.
– DERIVATIVES **runnable** adj.
– ORIGIN OE *rinnan, irnan* (v.), of Gmc origin; the current form with *-u-* is first recorded in the 16th cent.

**runabout** • n. a small car or light aircraft, especially one used for short journeys.

**runaround** • n. informal **1** (**the runaround**) deceitful or evasive treatment. **2** a runabout.

**runaway** • n. **1** a person who has run away from their home or an institution. **2** [as modifier] (of an animal or vehicle) running out of control. ➤happening or done quickly or uncontrollably: *runaway success.*

**runcible spoon** /ˈrʌnsɪb(ə)l/ • n. a fork curved like a spoon, with three broad prongs, one of which has a sharpened outer edge for cutting.
– ORIGIN C19: used by Edward Lear, perh. suggested by late C16 *rouncival*, denoting a large variety of pea.

**rundown** • n. a brief analysis or summary. • adj. (**run-down**) **1** in a poor or neglected state. **2** tired and rather unwell, especially through overwork.

**rune** /ruːn/ • n. **1** a letter of an ancient Germanic alphabet, related to the Roman alphabet, used especially in Scandinavia. ➤a mysterious symbol, especially in a spell or incantation. **2** an ancient Scandinavian poem or part of one.
– DERIVATIVES **runic** adj.
– ORIGIN OE *rūn* 'a secret, mystery'; reintroduced in the late 17th cent. under the influence of ON *rúnir, rúnar* 'magic signs, hidden lore'.

**rung**[1] • n. **1** a horizontal support on a ladder for a person's foot. ➤a strengthening crosspiece in the structure of a chair. **2** a level in a hierarchical structure.
– DERIVATIVES **runged** adj. **rungless** adj.
– ORIGIN OE *hrung.*

**rung**[2] past participle of **RING**[2].

**run-in** • n. **1** the approach to an action or event. **2** informal a disagreement or fight.

**runlet** • n. a small stream.

**runnel** • n. **1** a gutter. **2** a brook or stream.
– ORIGIN C16: var. of dial. *rindle.*

**runner** • n. **1** a person or animal that runs. ➤a horse that runs in a particular race. ➤a messenger, collector, or agent for a bank, bookmaker, or similar. ➤an orderly in the army. **2** a vehicle or machine that runs in a satisfactory or specified way. **3** Brit. informal an idea that has a chance of being accepted. **4** a rod, groove, or blade on which something slides. ➤a roller for moving a heavy article. ➤a ring capable of sliding or being drawn along a strap or rod. ➤Nautical a rope in a single block with one end round a tackle block and the other having a hook. **5** a shoot which grows along the ground and can take root at points along its length. ➤a climbing plant, or one that spreads by means of runners. **6** a long, narrow rug or strip of carpet. **7** used in names of fast-swimming fish of the jack family, e.g. **rainbow runner**.
– PHRASES **do a runner** Brit. informal leave hastily, in order to escape or avoid something.

**runner bean** • n. chiefly Brit. a Central American climbing bean plant with scarlet flowers, widely cultivated for its long green edible pods. [*Phaseolus coccineus.*]

**runner-up** • n. (pl. **runners-up**) a competitor or team taking second place in a contest.

**running** • n. **1** the activity or movement of a runner. **2** the action or business of managing or operating. • adj. **1** (of water) flowing naturally or supplied through pipes and taps. ➤exuding liquid or pus: *a running sore.* **2** continuous or recurring: *a running joke.* **3** done while running. **4** [postpos.] consecutive; in succession: *he failed to turn up for the third week running.*
– PHRASES **in** (or **out of**) **the running** in (or no longer in) contention. **make the running** set the pace. **take up the running** take over as pacesetter.

**running back** • n. American Football an offensive player who specializes in carrying the ball.

**running battle** • n. a military engagement which does not occur at a fixed location.

**running belay** • n. Climbing a device attached to a rock face through which a climbing rope runs freely, acting as a pulley if the climber falls.

**running board** • n. a footboard extending along the side of a vehicle.

**running commentary** • n. a verbal description of events, given as they occur.

**running dog** • n. informal a servile follower.
– ORIGIN translating Chin. *zǒugǒu.*

**running head** • n. a heading printed at the top of each page of a book or chapter.

**running knot** • n. a knot that slips along the rope and changes the size of a noose.

**running lights** • pl. n. **1** another term for **NAVIGATION LIGHTS**. **2** small lights on a motor vehicle that remain illuminated while the vehicle is running.

**running mate** • n. **1** chiefly US an election candidate for the lesser of two closely associated political offices. **2** chiefly N. Amer. a horse entered in a race in order to set the pace for another horse which is intended to win.

**running repairs** • pl. n. minor or temporary repairs carried out on machinery while it is in use.

**running stitch** • n. a simple needlework stitch consisting of a line of small even stitches which run back and forth through the cloth.

**runny** • adj. (**-ier, -iest**) **1** more liquid in consistency than is usual or expected. **2** (of a person's nose) producing or discharging mucus.

**run-off** • n. **1** a further contest after a tie or inconclusive result. **2** the draining away of rainfall or other liquid from the surface of an area. ➤the liquid that drains in this way. **3** NZ a separate area of land where young animals are kept.

**run-of-the-mill** • adj. lacking unusual or special aspects; ordinary.

**run-out** • n. **1** Cricket the dismissal of a batsman by being run out. **2** informal a short session of play or practice in a sport. **3** a slight error in a rotating tool or machine component, such as being off-centre or not exactly round. **4** a length of time or space over which something gradually lessens or ceases.

**runt** • n. **1** a small pig or other animal, especially the smallest in a litter. **2** a pigeon of a large domestic breed.
– DERIVATIVES **runty** adj.
– ORIGIN C16 (in the sense 'old or decayed tree stump'): of unknown origin.

**run-through** • n. **1** a rehearsal. **2** a brief outline or summary.

**run-time** • n. Computing **1** the length of time a program takes to run. **2** a cut-down version of a program that can be run but not changed.

**run-up** • n. **1** the preparatory period before a notable event. **2** an act of running briefly to gain momentum before bowling, performing a jump, etc. **3** Golf a low approach shot that bounces and runs forward.

**runway** • n. **1** a strip of hard ground along which aircraft take off and land. **2** a raised gangway extending into an auditorium, especially as used for fashion shows. **3** an animal run. **4** a chute down which logs are slid.

**rupee** /ruːˈpiː, rʊˈpiː/ • n. the basic monetary unit of India, Pakistan, Sri Lanka, Nepal, Mauritius, and the Seychelles, equal to 100 paisa in India, Pakistan, and Nepal, and 100 cents in Sri Lanka, Mauritius, and the

Seychelles.
– ORIGIN via Hindi from Sanskrit *rūpya* 'wrought silver'.

**rupiah** /ruːˈpiːə/ ● **n.** the basic monetary unit of Indonesia, equal to 100 sen.
– ORIGIN Indonesian, from Hindi *rūpyah* (see **RUPEE**).

**rupture** ● **v. 1** break or burst suddenly. ➤ cause to break or burst suddenly. ➤ (**be ruptured** or **rupture oneself**) suffer an abdominal hernia. **2** breach or disturb (a harmonious situation). ● **n. 1** an instance of rupturing. **2** an abdominal hernia.
– ORIGIN ME: from OFr. *rupture* or L. *ruptura*, from *rumpere* 'to break'.

**rupturewort** ● **n.** a small Old World plant of the pink family, which was formerly believed to cure hernia. [*Herniaria glabra*.]

**rural** ● **adj.** in, relating to, or characteristic of the countryside rather than the town.
– DERIVATIVES **ruralism** n. **ruralist** n. **rurality** n. **ruralization** (also **-isation**) n. **ruralize** (also **-ise**) v. **rurally** adv.
– ORIGIN ME: from OFr., or from late L. *ruralis*, from *rus, rur-* 'country'.

**Rurik** /ˈrʊərɪk/ (also **Ryurik**) ● **n.** a member of a dynasty that ruled Muscovy and much of Russia from the 9th to the 16th century, reputedly founded by the Varangian chief Rurik.

**Ruritanian** /ˌrʊərɪˈteɪnɪən/ ● **adj.** relating to or characteristic of romantic adventure or its setting.
– ORIGIN C19: from *Ruritania*, an imaginary kingdom in SE Europe used as the setting for the novels of courtly intrigue and romance written by the Engl. novelist Anthony Hope.

**rusa** /ˈruːsə/ ● **n.** an Indonesian deer with a brown coat and branched antlers. [*Cervus timorensis*.]
– ORIGIN C18: mod. L. (former genus name), from Malay.

**ruse** /ruːz/ ● **n.** a stratagem or trick.
– ORIGIN ME (as a hunting term): from OFr., from *ruser* 'use trickery', earlier 'drive back', perh. based on L. *rursus* 'backwards'.

**rush**[1] ● **v. 1** move or act or cause to move or act with urgent haste. ➤ take somewhere with urgent haste. ➤ (**rush something out**) produce and distribute something very quickly. ➤ deal with (something) hurriedly. **2** (of air or a liquid) flow strongly. **3** dash towards (someone or something) in an attempt to attack or capture them or it. ➤ American Football advance towards (an opposing player, especially the quarterback). ➤ American Football gain a specified amount of ground by running forward with the ball. **4** US entertain (a new student) in order to assess suitability for membership of a college fraternity or sorority. **5** Brit. informal, dated overcharge (a customer). ● **n. 1** the action or an instance of rushing. **2** a flurry of hasty activity. **3** a sudden strong demand for a commodity. **4** a sudden intensity of feeling. **5** a sudden thrill experienced after taking certain drugs. **6** (**rushes**) the first prints made of a film after a period of shooting.
– PHRASES **rush one's fences** Brit. act with undue haste. **a rush of blood** (**to the head**) a sudden attack of wild irrationality.
– DERIVATIVES **rusher** n. **rushing** adj. **rushingly** adv.
– ORIGIN ME: from an Anglo-Norman Fr. var. of OFr. *ruser* 'drive back', an early sense of the word in Engl. (see **RUSE**).

**rush**[2] ● **n. 1** a marsh or waterside plant with slender stem-like pith-filled leaves, some kinds of which are used for matting, baskets, etc. [Genus *Juncus*.] **2** used in names of similar plants, e.g. **flowering rush**.
– DERIVATIVES **rushy** adj.
– ORIGIN OE *risc, rysc*, of Gmc origin.

**rush hour** ● **n.** a time at the start and end of the working day when traffic is at its heaviest.

**rushlight** ● **n.** historical a candle made by dipping the pith of a rush in tallow.

**rusk** ● **n.** a dry biscuit or piece of rebaked bread.
– ORIGIN C16: from Sp. or Port. *rosca* 'twist, coil, roll of bread', of unknown ultimate origin.

**Russell's viper** ● **n.** a large venomous Asian snake which has a yellow-brown body with black markings. [*Daboia russelli*.]
– ORIGIN C20: named after the Sc. physician and naturalist Patrick *Russell*.

**russet** ● **adj. 1** reddish brown. **2** archaic rustic; homely. ● **n. 1** a reddish-brown colour. **2** a dessert apple of a variety with a slightly rough greenish-brown skin. **3** historical a coarse homespun reddish-brown or grey cloth.
– DERIVATIVES **russety** adj.
– ORIGIN ME: from an Anglo-Norman Fr. var. of OFr. *rousset*, dimin. of *rous* 'red', from Provençal *ros*, from L. *russus* 'red'.

**Russia leather** ● **n.** a durable leather made from calfskins and impregnated with birchbark oil, used for bookbinding.

**Russian** ● **n. 1** a native or national of Russia, or a person of Russian descent. **2** the language of Russia, an Eastern Slavic language written in the Cyrillic alphabet. ● **adj.** of or relating to Russia, its people, or their language.
– DERIVATIVES **Russianization** (also **-isation**) n. **Russianize** (also **-ise**) v. **Russianness** n.

**Russian boot** ● **n.** a boot that loosely encloses the wearer's calf.

**Russian doll** ● **n.** each of a set of brightly painted hollow wooden dolls of varying sizes, designed to fit inside each other.

**Russian olive** ● **n.** North American term for **OLEASTER**.

**Russian Orthodox Church** ● **n.** the national Church of Russia.

**Russian roulette** ● **n.** a dangerous game of chance in which a single bullet is loaded into the chamber of a revolver, the cylinder is spun, and people take it in turns to hold the gun to their own head and fire it.

**Russian salad** ● **n.** Brit. a salad of mixed diced vegetables with mayonnaise.

**Russian tea** ● **n.** tea laced with rum and typically served with lemon.

**Russian thistle** ● **n.** N. Amer. a prickly tumbleweed which is an inland form of saltwort. [*Salsola pestifera*.]

**Russian vine** ● **n.** a fast-growing Asian climbing plant of the dock family, with long clusters of white or pink flowers. [*Fallopia baldschuanica*.]

**Russify** /ˈrʌsɪfʌɪ/ ● **v.** (**-ies**, **-ied**) make Russian in character.
– DERIVATIVES **Russification** n.

**Russki** /ˈrʌski/ (also **Russky**) ● **n.** (pl. **Russkis** or **Russkies**) informal, often offensive a Russian.
– ORIGIN C19: from Russ. *russkiĭ* 'Russian', or from **RUSSIAN**, on the pattern of Russ. surnames ending in *-skiĭ*.

**Russo-** ● **comb. form** Russian; Russian and ...: *Russo-Japanese*. ➤ relating to Russia.

**Russophile** /ˈrʌsə(ʊ)fʌɪl/ ● **n.** a person who admires or is fond of Russia and things Russian.
– DERIVATIVES **Russophilia** n.

**Russophobe** /ˈrʌsə(ʊ)fəʊb/ ● **n.** a person who dislikes Russia and things Russian.
– DERIVATIVES **Russophobia** n.

**russula** /ˈrʌsələ/ ● **n.** a woodland toadstool that typically has a brightly coloured flattened cap and a white stem and gills. [Genus *Russula*: numerous species.]
– ORIGIN mod. L., from L. *russus* 'red' (because many have a red cap).

**rust** ● **n. 1** a reddish- or yellowish-brown flaking coating of iron oxide that is formed on iron or steel by oxidation, especially in the presence of moisture. **2** a fungal disease of plants which results in reddish or brownish patches. **3** a reddish-brown colour. ● **v.** be affected with rust.
– DERIVATIVES **rustless** adj.
– ORIGIN OE *rūst*, of Gmc origin; rel. to **RED**.

**rust belt** ● **n.** informal a region characterized by declining industry and a falling population, especially in the American Midwest and NE states.

**rust bucket** ● **n.** informal, often humorous a vehicle or ship which is old and badly rusted.

**rustic** ● **adj. 1** of or characteristic of life in the country. ➤ having a simplicity and charm that is considered typical of the countryside. **2** made of rough branches or timber. **3** (of masonry) having a rough-hewn or roughened

surface or sunken joints. **4** denoting freely formed lettering. ● **n.** **1** often derogatory an unsophisticated country person. **2** a small brownish European moth. [Several genera and species in the family Noctuidae.]
– DERIVATIVES **rustically** adv. **rusticity** n.
– ORIGIN ME (in the sense 'rural'): from L. *rusticus*, from *rus* 'the country'.

**rusticate** /ˈrʌstɪkeɪt/ ● **v.** **1** Brit. suspend (a student) from a university as a punishment (used chiefly at Oxford and Cambridge). **2** dated go to, live in, or spend time in the country. **3** fashion (masonry) in large blocks with sunken joints and a roughened surface.
– DERIVATIVES **rustication** n.
– ORIGIN C15 (in the sense 'make countrified'): from L. *rusticat-*, *rusticari* 'live in the country', from *rusticus* (see **RUSTIC**).

**rustle** ● **v.** **1** make a soft, muffled crackling sound like that caused by the movement of dry leaves or paper. ➤ move with such a sound. **2** round up and steal (cattle, horses, or sheep). **3** (**rustle something up**) informal produce something quickly. **4** N. Amer. informal move or act quickly or energetically. ● **n.** a rustling sound.
– DERIVATIVES **rustler** n.
– ORIGIN ME: imitative.

**rustproof** ● **adj.** not susceptible to corrosion by rust. ● **v.** make rustproof.

**rusty** ● **adj.** (**-ier**, **-iest**) **1** affected by rust. **2** rust-coloured. **3** (of knowledge or a skill) impaired by lack of recent practice.
– DERIVATIVES **rustily** adv. **rustiness** n.

**rusty dusty** ● **n.** black English a person's buttocks.
– ORIGIN C16 (in the sense 'dusty, fusty'): reduplication of **RUSTY**; the current use dates from the 1950s.

**rut**[1] ● **n.** **1** a long deep track made by the repeated passage of the wheels of vehicles. **2** a routine or pattern of behaviour that has become dull and unproductive but is hard to change.
– DERIVATIVES **rutted** adj. **rutty** adj.
– ORIGIN C16: prob. from OFr. *rute* (see **ROUTE**).

**rut**[2] ● **n.** an annual period of sexual activity in deer and some other mammals, during which the males fight each other for access to the females. ● **v.** (**rutted**, **rutting**) engage in such activity.
– DERIVATIVES **ruttish** adj.
– ORIGIN ME: from OFr., from L. *rugitus*, from *rugire* 'to roar'.

**rutabaga** /ˌruːtəˈbeɪgə/ ● **n.** chiefly N. Amer. a swede.
– ORIGIN C18: from Swed. dial. *rotabagge*.

**ruth** ● **n.** archaic a feeling of pity, distress, or grief.
– ORIGIN ME: from **RUE**[1], prob. influenced by ON *hrygth*.

**Ruthenian** /ruːˈθiːnɪən/ ● **n.** a native or inhabitant of Ruthenia, a region of central Europe. ● **adj.** of or relating to Ruthenia.

**ruthenium** /rʊˈθiːnɪəm/ ● **n.** the chemical element of atomic number 44, a hard silvery-white metal. (Symbol: **Ru**)
– ORIGIN C19: mod. L., from *Ruthenia* (see **RUTHENIAN**), because it was discovered in ores from the Urals.

**rutherfordium** /ˌrʌðəˈfɔːdɪəm/ ● **n.** the chemical element of atomic number 104, a very unstable element made by high-energy atomic collisions. (Symbol: **Rf**)
– ORIGIN 1960s: mod. L., named after the New Zealand physicist Ernest *Rutherford*.

**ruthless** ● **adj.** having or showing no compassion.
– DERIVATIVES **ruthlessly** adv. **ruthlessness** n.
– ORIGIN ME: from **RUTH** + **-LESS**.

**rutilant** /ˈruːtɪl(ə)nt/ ● **adj.** poetic/literary glowing or glittering with red or golden light.
– ORIGIN ME: from L. *rutilant-*, *rutilare* 'glow red'.

**rutile** /ˈruːtɪl, ˈruːtʌɪl/ ● **n.** a black or reddish-brown mineral consisting of titanium dioxide, typically occurring as needle-like crystals.
– ORIGIN C19: from Fr., or from Ger. *Rutil*, from L. *rutilus* 'reddish'.

**rutin** /ˈruːtɪn/ ● **n.** Chemistry a compound of the flavonoid class found in common rue, buckwheat, capers, and other plants, and sometimes taken as a dietary supplement.
– ORIGIN C19: from L. *ruta* 'rue' + **-IN**[1].

**RV** ● **abbrev.** **1** N. Amer. recreational vehicle (especially a motorized caravan). **2** a rendezvous point. **3** Revised Version (of the Bible).

**RWA** ● **abbrev.** Rwanda (international vehicle registration).

**Rwandan** /ruːˈandən/ (also **Rwandese** /ruːˈandiːz/) ● **n.** a native or inhabitant of Rwanda, a country in central Africa. ● **adj.** of or relating to Rwanda or Rwandans.

**Ry** ● **abbrev.** Railway.

**-ry** ● **suffix** a shortened form of **-ERY** (as in *devilry*).

**rye** ● **n.** **1** a wheat-like cereal plant which tolerates poor soils and low temperatures. [*Secale cereale*.] **2** (also **rye whisky**) whisky in which a significant amount of the grain used in distillation is fermented rye. **3** short for **RYE BREAD**.
– ORIGIN OE *ryge*, of Gmc origin.

**rye bread** ● **n.** a dense, chewy bread made with rye flour.

**ryegrass** ● **n.** a grass used for fodder and lawns. [Genus *Lolium*: several species, in particular *L. perenne*.]
– ORIGIN C18: alt. of obs. *ray-grass*, of unknown origin.

**ryokan** /rɪˈəʊkan/ ● **n.** a traditional Japanese inn.
– ORIGIN from Japanese.

**ryot** /ˈrʌɪət/ ● **n.** an Indian peasant or tenant farmer.
– ORIGIN from Urdu *raiyat*, from Arab. *raʿīyya* 'flock, subjects', from *raʿā* 'to pasture'.

**ryu** /rɪˈuː/ ● **n.** (pl. same or **ryus**) a school or style in Japanese arts, especially in the martial arts.
– ORIGIN from Japanese.

# Ss

**S**[1] (also **s**) ● **n.** (pl. **Ss** or **S's**) **1** the nineteenth letter of the alphabet. **2** denoting the next after R in a set of items, categories, etc.

**S**[2] ● **abbrev. 1** (chiefly in Catholic use) Saint. **2** siemens. **3** small (as a clothes size). **4** South or Southern. **5** Sweden (international vehicle registration). ● **symb. 1** the chemical element sulphur. **2** Chemistry entropy.

**s** ● **abbrev. 1** second(s). **2** Law section (of an act). **3** shilling(s). **4** Grammar singular. **5** Chemistry solid. **6** (in genealogies) son(s). **7** succeeded. **8** Chemistry denoting electrons and orbitals possessing zero angular momentum and total symmetry. [*s* from *sharp*, orig. applied to lines in atomic spectra.] ● **symb.** (in mathematical formulae) distance.

**'s** /s, z after a vowel sound or voiced consonant/ ● **contr.** informal **1** is. **2** has. **3** us. **4** does.

**'s-** /s, z before a voiced consonant/ ● **prefix** archaic (used chiefly in oaths) God's.
– ORIGIN shortened form.

**-s**[1] /s, z after a vowel sound or voiced consonant/ ● **suffix** denoting the plurals of nouns (as in *wagons*). Compare with **-ES**[1].
– ORIGIN OE pl. ending *-as*.

**-s**[2] /s, z after a vowel sound or voiced consonant/ ● **suffix** forming the third person singular of the present of verbs (as in *sews*). Compare with **-ES**[2].
– ORIGIN OE dial.

**-s**[3] /s, z after a vowel sound or voiced consonant/ ● **suffix 1** forming adverbs such as *besides*. **2** forming possessive pronouns such as *hers*.
– ORIGIN OE *-es*, masc. and neut. genitive sing. ending.

**-s**[4] /s, z after a vowel sound or voiced consonant/ ● **suffix** forming nicknames or pet names: *ducks*.
– ORIGIN suggested by **-S**[1].

**-'s**[1] /s, z after a vowel sound or voiced consonant, ɪz after a sibilant/ ● **suffix** denoting possession in singular nouns, also in plural nouns not having a final *-s*: *John's book*.
– ORIGIN OE, masc. and neut. genitive sing. ending.

**-'s**[2] /s, z after a vowel sound or voiced consonant, ɪz after a sibilant/ ● **suffix** denoting the plural of a letter or symbol: *9's*.

**SA** ● **abbrev. 1** Salvation Army. **2** South Africa. **3** South America. **4** South Australia.

**saag** /sɑːg/ (also **sag**) ● **n.** Indian term for **SPINACH**.
– ORIGIN from Hindi *sāg*.

**Saanen** /ˈsɑːnən/ ● **n.** a dairy goat of a white hornless breed, first developed in the region of Saanen in Switzerland.

**sabadilla** /ˌsabəˈdɪlə/ ● **n.** a Mexican plant of the lily family, whose seeds contain veratrine. [*Schoenocaulon officinale.*] ➤ a preparation of these seeds, used as an agricultural insecticide and in medicines.
– ORIGIN C19: from Sp. *cebadilla*, dimin. of *cebada* 'barley'.

**Sabaean** /səˈbiːən/ ● **n.** a member of an ancient Semitic people who ruled Saba in SW Arabia. ● **adj.** of or relating to this people.

**sabayon** /ˈsabʌɪjɒ̃/ ● **n.** French term for **ZABAGLIONE**.

**sabbatarian** /ˌsabəˈtɛːrɪən/ ● **n.** a strict observer of the sabbath. ● **adj.** relating to or upholding the observance of the sabbath.
– DERIVATIVES **sabbatarianism** n.
– ORIGIN C17: from late L. *sabbatarius* (from L. *sabbatum* 'sabbath') + **-AN**.

**sabbath** ● **n. 1** (often **the Sabbath**) a day of religious observance and abstinence from work, kept by Jews from Friday evening to Saturday evening, and by most Christians on Sunday. **2** (also **witches' sabbath**) a supposed annual midnight meeting of witches with the Devil.
– ORIGIN OE, from L. *sabbatum*, via Gk from Heb. *šabbāṯ*, from *šāḇaṯ* 'to rest'.

**sabbatical** /səˈbatɪk(ə)l/ ● **n.** a period of paid leave granted to a university teacher for study or travel (traditionally one year for every seven years worked). ● **adj. 1** of or relating to a sabbatical. **2** archaic of or appropriate to the sabbath.
– ORIGIN C16: via late L. from Gk *sabbatikos* 'of the sabbath' + **-AL**.

**sabbatical year** ● **n. 1** a year's sabbatical leave. **2** (in biblical times) a year observed every seventh year under the Law of Moses as a 'sabbath' during which the land was allowed to rest.

**saber** ● **n. & v.** US spelling of **SABRE**.

**Sabian** /ˈseɪbɪən/ ● **n.** a member of a non-Muslim sect classed in the Koran with Jews, Christians, and Zoroastrians as having a faith revealed by the true God. ● **adj.** of or relating to this sect.
– ORIGIN C17: from Arab. *ṣābi'* + **-AN**.

**sabicu** /ˌsabɪˈkuː/ ● **n.** a Caribbean leguminous tree, with wood that resembles mahogany and is used chiefly in boatbuilding. [*Lysiloma sabicu.*]
– ORIGIN C19: from Cuban Sp. *sabicú*.

**Sabine** /ˈsabʌɪn/ ● **n.** a member of an ancient Oscan-speaking people of the central Apennines in Italy.
– ORIGIN from L. *Sabinus*.

**sabkha** /ˈsabkə, -xə/ ● **n.** Geography an area of coastal flats subject to periodic flooding and evaporation which result in the accumulation of aeolian clays, evaporites, and salts, typically found in North Africa and Arabia.
– ORIGIN C19: from Arab. *sabḵa* 'salt flat'.

**sable**[1] /ˈseɪb(ə)l/ ● **n.** a marten with a short tail and dark brown fur, native to Japan and Siberia. [*Martes zibellina.*] ➤ the fur of the sable.
– ORIGIN ME: from OFr., in the sense 'sable fur', from med. L. *sabelum*, of Slavic origin.

**sable**[2] /ˈseɪb(ə)l/ ● **adj.** poetic/literary or Heraldry black. ● **n. 1** poetic/literary or Heraldry black. ➤ (**sables**) archaic mourning garments. **2** (also **sable antelope**) a large African antelope with long curved horns, the male of which has a black coat and the female a russet coat. [*Hippotragus niger.*]
– ORIGIN ME: from OFr. (as a heraldic term), generally taken to be identical with **SABLE**[1], although sable fur is dark brown.

**sablefish** ● **n.** (pl. same or **-fishes**) a large commercially important fish with a slaty-blue to black back, occurring throughout the North Pacific. [*Anoplopoma fimbria.*]

**sabot** /ˈsabəʊ/ ● **n. 1** a kind of simple shoe, shaped and hollowed out from a single block of wood. **2** a device which ensures the correct positioning of a bullet or shell in the barrel of a gun. **3** a box from which cards are dealt at casinos in certain gambling games.
– DERIVATIVES **saboted** /ˈsabəʊd/ adj.
– ORIGIN C17: Fr., blend of *savate* 'shoe' and *botte* 'boot'.

**sabotage** /ˈsabətɑːʒ/ ● **v.** deliberately destroy or obstruct, especially for political or military advantage. ● **n.** the action of sabotaging.
– ORIGIN C20: from Fr., from *saboter* 'kick with sabots, wilfully destroy'.

**saboteur** /ˌsabəˈtəː/ ● **n.** a person who engages in sabotage.

– ORIGIN C20: from Fr.

**sabra** /'sabrə/ • **n.** a Jew born in Israel (or before 1948 in Palestine).
– ORIGIN from mod. Heb. *ṣabbār* 'opuntia fruit' (opuntias being common in coastal regions of Israel).

**sabre** /'seɪbə/ (US **saber**) • **n.** **1** a heavy cavalry sword with a curved blade and a single cutting edge. ➤ historical a cavalry soldier and horse. **2** a light fencing sword with a tapering, typically curved blade. • **v.** archaic cut down or wound with a sabre.
– ORIGIN C17: from Fr., alt. of obs. *sable*, from Ger. *Sabel* (local var. of *Säbel*), from Hungarian *szablya*.

**sabre-rattling** • **n.** the display or threat of military force.

**sabre saw** • **n.** a portable electric jigsaw.

**sabretache** /'sabətaʃ/ • **n.** historical a flat satchel on long straps worn by some cavalry officers from the left of the waist belt.
– ORIGIN C19: from Fr., from Ger. *Säbeltasche*, from *Säbel* 'sabre' + *Tasche* 'pocket'.

**sabretooth** • **n.** a large extinct carnivore of the cat family with massive curved upper canine teeth. [*Smilodon* (Pleistocene) and other genera.]
– DERIVATIVES **sabre-toothed** adj.

**sabreur** /sa'brəː/ • **n.** a cavalryman or fencer using a sabre.
– ORIGIN Fr., from *sabrer* 'strike with a sabre'.

**sabrewing** • **n.** a large tropical American hummingbird with a green back and long curved wings. [Genus *Campylopterus*: several species.]

**SAC** • **abbrev.** Senior Aircraftman.

**sac** /sak/ • **n.** a hollow, flexible structure resembling a bag or pouch. ➤ a cavity enclosed by a membrane within a living organism. ➤ the distended membrane surrounding a hernia, cyst, or tumour.
– ORIGIN C18: from Fr. *sac* or L. *saccus* 'sack, bag'.

**saccade** /sa'kɑːd/ • **n.** (usu. **saccades**) a rapid movement of the eye between fixation points.
– DERIVATIVES **saccadic** /sa'kadɪk/ adj.
– ORIGIN C18: from Fr., lit. 'violent pull'.

**saccate** /'sakeɪt/ • **adj.** Botany dilated to form a sac.

**saccharide** /'sakərʌɪd/ • **n.** Biochemistry another term for **SUGAR** (in sense 2).
– ORIGIN C19: from mod. L. *saccharum* 'sugar' + **-IDE**.

**saccharin** /'sakərɪn/ • **n.** a sweet-tasting synthetic compound used as a substitute for sugar.
– ORIGIN C19: from mod. L. *saccharum* 'sugar'+ **-IN**[1].

**saccharine** /'sakərʌɪn, -ɪn, -iːn/ • **adj.** **1** excessively sweet or sentimental. **2** relating to or containing sugar. • **n.** another term for **SACCHARIN**.
– ORIGIN C17: from mod. L. *saccharum* + **-INE**[1].

**saccharo-** • **comb. form** of or relating to sugar: *saccharometer*.
– ORIGIN via L. from Gk *sakkharon* 'sugar'.

**saccharometer** /ˌsakə'rɒmɪtə/ • **n.** a hydrometer for estimating the sugar content of a solution.

**saccharose** /'sakərəʊz, -s/ • **n.** Chemistry another term for **SUCROSE**.

**saccule** /'sakjuːl/ (also **sacculus** /'sakjʊləs/) • **n.** Biology & Anatomy **1** a small sac, pouch, or cyst. **2** the smaller of the two fluid-filled sacs forming part of the labyrinth of the inner ear. Compare with **UTRICLE**.
– DERIVATIVES **saccular** adj. **sacculated** adj. **sacculation** n.
– ORIGIN C18: from L., dimin. of *saccus* 'sack'.

**sacerdotal** /ˌsasə'dəʊt(ə)l, ˌsakə-/ • **adj.** **1** relating to priests or the priesthood. **2** Theology relating to or denoting a doctrine which ascribes sacrificial functions and spiritual or supernatural powers to ordained priests.
– DERIVATIVES **sacerdotalism** n.
– ORIGIN ME: from OFr., or from L. *sacerdotalis*, from *sacerdos, sacerdot-* 'priest'.

**sachem** /'seɪtʃəm, 'satʃəm/ • **n.** **1** (among some American Indian peoples) a chief. **2** N. Amer. informal a boss or leader.
– ORIGIN from Narragansett, 'chief, sagamore'.

**Sachertorte** /'zaxəˌtɔːtə, German 'zaxɐˌtɔrtə/ • **n.** (pl. **Sachertorten** /-ˌtɔːt(ə)n, German -ˌtɔrtn/) a chocolate gateau with apricot jam filling.
– ORIGIN Ger., from the name of the pastry chef Franz *Sacher* + *Torte* 'tart, pastry'.

**sachet** /'saʃeɪ/ • **n.** chiefly Brit. a small sealed bag or packet containing a small quantity of something.
– ORIGIN C19: from Fr., 'little bag', dimin. of *sac*, from L. *saccus* 'sack, bag'.

**sack**[1] • **n.** **1** a large bag made of a material such as hessian or thick paper, used for storing and carrying goods. **2** (**the sack**) informal dismissal from employment. **3** (**the sack**) informal, chiefly N. Amer. bed. **4** Baseball, informal a base. **5** American Football a tackle of a quarterback behind the line of scrimmage. • **v.** **1** informal dismiss from employment. **2** (**sack out**) informal, chiefly N. Amer. go to sleep or bed. **3** American Football tackle with a sack. **4** put into a sack or sacks.
– PHRASES **hit the sack** informal go to bed.
– DERIVATIVES **sackable** adj. **sackful** n. (pl. **-fuls**).
– ORIGIN OE *sacc*, from L. *saccus* 'sack, sackcloth', from Gk *sakkos*, of Semitic origin.

**sack**[2] • **v.** plunder and destroy (used chiefly in historical contexts). • **n.** an instance of sacking.
– ORIGIN C16: from Fr. *sac*, in the phr. *mettre à sac* 'put to sack', on the model of Ital. *fare il sacco, mettere a sacco*, which perh. orig. referred to filling a sack with plunder.

**sack**[3] • **n.** historical a dry white wine formerly imported into Britain from Spain and the Canaries.
– ORIGIN C16: from the phr. *wyne seck*, from Fr. *vin sec* 'dry wine'.

**sackbut** /'sakbʌt/ • **n.** an early form of trombone used in Renaissance music.
– ORIGIN C15: from Fr. *saquebute*, from obs. *saqueboute* 'hook for pulling a man off a horse'.

**sackcloth** • **n.** a coarse fabric woven from flax or hemp.
– PHRASES **sackcloth and ashes** used with allusion to the wearing of sackcloth and having ashes sprinkled on the head as a sign of penitence or mourning.

**sack coat** • **n.** historical a loose-fitting coat hanging straight down from the shoulders, as worn by men in the 19th and early 20th centuries.

**sack dress** • **n.** a woman's short loose unwaisted dress, originally fashionable in the 1950s.

**sacking** • **n.** **1** an act of sacking someone or something. **2** coarse material for making sacks; sackcloth.

**sack race** • **n.** a children's race in which each competitor is confined within a sack and moves forward by jumping.

**sack suit** • **n.** chiefly N. Amer. a suit with a straight loose-fitting jacket.

**sacra** plural form of **SACRUM**.

**sacral** /'seɪkr(ə)l, 'sak-/ • **adj.** **1** Anatomy of or relating to the sacrum. **2** Anthropology & Religion of, for, or relating to sacred rites or symbols.
– DERIVATIVES **sacrality** n.

**sacralize** /'seɪkrəlʌɪz/ (also **-ise**) • **v.** chiefly N. Amer. imbue with or treat as having a sacred character or quality.
– DERIVATIVES **sacralization** n.

**sacrament** /'sakrəm(ə)nt/ • **n.** **1** (in the Christian Church) a religious ceremony or ritual regarded as imparting divine grace, such as baptism, the Eucharist, and (in the Catholic and many Orthodox Churches) penance and the anointing of the sick. **2** (also **the Blessed Sacrament** or **the Holy Sacrament**) (in Catholic use) the consecrated elements of the Eucharist, especially the bread or Host. **3** a thing of mysterious or sacred significance; a religious symbol.
– ORIGIN ME: from OFr. *sacrement*, from L. *sacramentum* 'solemn oath', used in Christian L. as a translation of Gk *mustērion* 'mystery'.

**sacramental** • **adj.** relating to or constituting a sacrament or the sacraments. • **n.** an observance analogous to but not reckoned among the sacraments, such as the use of holy water or the sign of the cross.
– DERIVATIVES **sacramentalism** n. **sacramentality** n. **sacramentalize** (also **-ise**) v. **sacramentally** adv.

**sacrarium** /sə'krɛːrɪəm/ • **n.** (pl. **sacraria** /-rɪə/) **1** the sanctuary of a church. **2** (in the Roman Catholic Church)

a piscina. **3** (in the ancient Roman world) a shrine.
– ORIGIN L., from *sacer, sacr-* 'holy'.

**sacré bleu** /ˌsakreɪ ˈbləː, French sakʀe blø/ ● **exclam.** a French expression of surprise, exasperation, or dismay.
– ORIGIN alt. of Fr. *sacré Dieu* 'holy God'.

**sacred** /ˈseɪkrɪd/ ● **adj. 1** connected with a deity and so deserving veneration; holy. ➤(of writing or text) embodying the doctrines of a religion. ➤sacrosanct. **2** religious rather than secular.
– DERIVATIVES **sacredly** adv. **sacredness** n.
– ORIGIN ME: past part. of archaic *sacre* 'consecrate', from OFr. *sacrer*, from L. *sacrare*, from *sacer, sacr-* 'holy'.

**sacred cow** ● **n.** an idea, custom, or institution held, especially unreasonably, to be above criticism (with reference to the respect of Hindus for the cow as a sacred animal).

**sacred ibis** ● **n.** a mainly white ibis with a bare black head and neck, venerated by the ancient Egyptians. [*Threskiornis aethiopicus*.]

**sacrifice** ● **n. 1** the practice or an act of killing an animal or person or surrendering a possession as an offering to a deity. ➤an animal, person, or object offered in this way. **2** an act of giving up something of value for the sake of something that is of greater value or importance. **3** (also **sacrifice bunt** or **sacrifice fly**) Baseball a bunted or fly ball which puts the batter out but allows a base-runner to advance. ● **v.** offer or give up as a sacrifice.
– DERIVATIVES **sacrificial** adj. **sacrificially** adv.
– ORIGIN ME: from OFr., from L. *sacrificium*; rel. to *sacrificus* 'sacrificial', from *sacer* 'holy'.

**sacrilege** /ˈsakrɪlɪdʒ/ ● **n.** violation or misuse of something regarded as sacred or as having great value.
– DERIVATIVES **sacrilegious** adj. **sacrilegiously** adv.
– ORIGIN ME: via OFr. from L. *sacrilegium*, from *sacrilegus* 'stealer of sacred things', from *sacer, sacr-* 'sacred' + *legere* 'take possession of'.

**sacring** /ˈseɪkrɪŋ/ ● **n.** archaic or historical the consecration of a bishop, sovereign, or the Eucharistic elements.
– ORIGIN ME: from the obs. verb *sacre* 'consecrate'.

**sacring bell** ● **n.** a bell rung in some Christian churches at certain points during the Mass or Eucharist, especially at the elevation of the consecrated elements.

**sacrist** /ˈsakrɪst, ˈseɪ-/ ● **n.** another term for SACRISTAN.

**sacristan** /ˈsakrɪstən/ ● **n. 1** a person in charge of a sacristy. **2** archaic the sexton of a parish church.
– ORIGIN ME: from med. L. *sacristanus*, based on L. *sacer, sacr-* 'sacred'.

**sacristy** /ˈsakrɪsti/ ● **n.** (pl. **-ies**) a room in a church where a priest prepares for a service, and where vestments and other things used in worship are kept.
– ORIGIN ME: from Fr. *sacristie*, from med. L. *sacristia*, based on L. *sacer, sacr-* 'sacred'.

**sacro-** /ˈseɪkrəʊ, ˈsakrəʊ-/ ● **comb. form** of or relating to the sacrum: *sacroiliac*.
– ORIGIN from L. *(os) sacrum* 'sacrum'.

**sacroiliac** /ˌseɪkrəʊˈɪlɪak, ˌsak-/ ● **adj.** Anatomy relating to the sacrum and the ilium. ➤denoting the rigid joint at the back of the pelvis between the sacrum and the ilium.

**sacrosanct** /ˈsakrə(ʊ)saŋ(k)t, ˈseɪk-/ ● **adj.** regarded as too important or valuable to be interfered with.
– DERIVATIVES **sacrosanctity** n.
– ORIGIN C15: from L. *sacrosanctus*, from *sacro* 'by a sacred rite' (ablative of *sacrum*) + *sanctus* 'holy'.

**sacrum** /ˈseɪkrəm, ˈsak-/ ● **n.** (pl. **sacra** /-krə/ or **sacrums**) Anatomy a triangular bone in the lower back formed from fused vertebrae and situated between the two hip bones of the pelvis.
– ORIGIN C18: from L. *os sacrum*, translation of Gk *hieron osteon* 'sacred bone' (from the belief that the soul resides in it).

**SACW** ● **abbrev.** Senior Aircraftwoman.

**SAD** ● **abbrev.** seasonal affective disorder.

**sad** ● **adj.** (**sadder, saddest**) **1** feeling sorrow; unhappy. ➤causing or characterized by sorrow or regret. **2** informal pathetically inadequate or unfashionable.
– DERIVATIVES **saddish** adj. **sadness** n.
– ORIGIN OE *sæd* 'sated, weary', also 'weighty, dense', of Gmc origin.

**sadden** ● **v.** (often **be saddened**) cause to feel sad.

**saddle** ● **n. 1** a seat with a raised ridge at the front and back, fastened on the back of a horse for riding. **2** a seat on a bicycle or motorcycle. **3** a low part of a ridge between two higher points or peaks. **4** a shaped support for a cable, pipe, or other object. **5** Mathematics a low region of a curve between two high points. **6** the lower part of the back in a mammal or fowl, especially when distinct in shape or marking. **7** a joint of meat consisting of the two loins. ● **v. 1** put a saddle on (a horse). **2** (usu. **be saddled with**) burden with an onerous responsibility or task. **3** (of a trainer) enter (a horse) for a race.
– PHRASES **in the saddle 1** on horseback. **2** in a position of control or responsibility.
– ORIGIN OE *sadol, sadul*, of Gmc origin.

**saddleback** ● **n. 1** Architecture a tower roof which has two opposite gables connected by a pitched section. **2** a hill with a ridge along the top that dips in the middle. **3** a pig of a black breed with a white stripe across the back. **4** a New Zealand wattlebird, mainly black with a reddish-brown back. [*Creadion carunculatus*.]
– DERIVATIVES **saddlebacked** adj.

**saddlebag** ● **n.** a bag attached to a saddle.

**saddle-bow** ● **n.** chiefly archaic the pommel of a saddle, or a similar curved part behind the rider.

**saddlecloth** ● **n.** a cloth laid on a horse's back under the saddle.

**saddle horse** ● **n. 1** a wooden frame or stand on which saddles are cleaned or stored. **2** chiefly N. Amer. a horse kept for riding only.

**saddler** ● **n.** someone who makes, repairs, or deals in saddlery.

**saddlery** ● **n.** (pl. **-ies**) saddles, bridles, and other equipment for horses. ➤the making or repairing of such equipment. ➤a saddler's business or premises.

**saddle shoe** ● **n.** a shoe with a piece of leather in a contrasting colour stitched across the instep.

**saddle soap** ● **n.** soft soap containing neat's-foot oil, used for cleaning leather.

**saddle-sore** ● **n.** a bruise or sore on a horse's back, caused by an ill-fitting saddle. ● **adj.** chafed by a saddle.

**saddle stitch** ● **n. 1** a stitch of thread or a wire staple passed through the fold of a magazine or booklet. **2** (in needlework) a decorative stitch made with long stitches on the upper side of the cloth alternated with short stitches on the underside. ● **v.** (**saddle-stitch**) sew with such a stitch.

**saddle tank** ● **n.** a small steam locomotive with a water tank that fits over the top and sides of the boiler like a saddle.

**saddo** ● **n.** (pl. **-os**) Brit. informal a person perceived as pathetically inadequate.
– ORIGIN 1990s: extension of SAD.

**Sadducee** /ˈsadjʊsiː/ ● **n.** a member of an ancient Jewish sect that denied the resurrection of the dead, the existence of spirits, and the obligation of oral tradition, emphasizing acceptance of the written Law alone.
– DERIVATIVES **Sadducean** /-ˈsiːən/ adj.
– ORIGIN OE *sadducēas* (pl.), via late L. from Gk *Saddoukaios*, from Heb. *ṣĕḏōqī* in the sense 'descendant of Zadok' (2 Sam. 8:17).

**sadhu** /ˈsɑːduː/ ● **n.** Indian a holy man, sage, or ascetic.
– ORIGIN from Sanskrit.

**sad iron** ● **n.** historical a flat iron.
– ORIGIN from SAD, in the obs. sense 'weighty'.

**sadism** ● **n.** the tendency to derive sexual gratification or general pleasure from inflicting pain, suffering, or humiliation on others.
– DERIVATIVES **sadist** n. **sadistic** adj. **sadistically** adv.
– ORIGIN C19: from Fr. *sadisme*, from the name of the C18 Fr. writer the Marquis de *Sade*.

**sadly** ● **adv. 1** in a sad manner. **2** it is sad or regrettable that; regrettably.

**sadomasochism** /ˌseɪdəʊˈmasəkɪz(ə)m/ ● **n.** the psychological tendency or sexual practice characterized by a combination of sadism and masochism.

– DERIVATIVES **sadomasochist** n. **sadomasochistic** adj.

**sad sack** • n. informal, chiefly US an inept blundering person.

**sae** • abbrev. Brit. stamped addressed envelope.

**safari** • n. (pl. **safaris**) an expedition to observe or hunt animals in their natural habitat, especially in East Africa.
– ORIGIN C19: from Kiswahili, from Arab. *safara* 'to travel'.

**safari jacket** • n. a belted lightweight jacket, typically having short sleeves and four patch pockets.

**safari park** • n. an area of parkland where wild animals are kept in the open and may be observed by visitors driving through.

**safari suit** • n. a lightweight suit consisting of a safari jacket with matching trousers, shorts, or skirt.

**Safavid** /'safəvɪd/ • n. a member of a dynasty which ruled Persia 1502–1736.
– ORIGIN from Arab. *ṣafawī* 'descended from the ruler Sophy'.

**safe** • adj. **1** protected from or not exposed to danger or risk; not likely to be harmed or lost. ➤ not causing or leading to harm or injury. ➤ (of a place) affording security or protection. **2** often derogatory cautious and unenterprising. **3** Law (of an assertion, verdict, bet, etc.) based on good reasons or evidence and not likely to be proved wrong. **4** uninjured; with no harm done. **5** informal excellent. • n. **1** a strong fireproof cabinet with a complex lock, used for the storage of valuables. **2** N. Amer. informal a condom.
– PHRASES **to be on the safe side** in order to have a margin of security against risks.
– DERIVATIVES **safely** adv. **safeness** n.
– ORIGIN ME: from OFr. *sauf*, from L. *salvus* 'uninjured'.

**safe bet** • n. **1** a bet that is certain to succeed. **2** something that can be confidently predicted.

**safe-breaker** (also **safe-blower** or **safe-cracker**) • n. a person who breaks open and robs safes.

**safe conduct** • n. immunity from arrest or harm when passing through an area.

**safe deposit** (also **safety deposit**) • n. a strongroom or safe within a bank or hotel.

**safeguard** • n. a measure taken to protect or prevent something. • v. protect with a safeguard.
– ORIGIN ME: from OFr. *sauve garde*, from *sauve* 'safe' + *garde* 'guard'.

**safe house** • n. a house in a secret location, used by spies or criminals in hiding.

**safe keeping** • n. preservation in a safe place.

**safelight** • n. a light with a coloured filter that can be used in a darkroom without affecting photosensitive film or paper.

**safe period** • n. the time during and near a woman's menstrual period when conception is least likely.

**safe seat** • n. a parliamentary seat that is likely to be retained with a large majority in an election.

**safe sex** • n. sexual activity in which people take precautions to protect themselves against sexually transmitted diseases such as Aids.

**safety** • n. (pl. **-ies**) **1** the condition of being safe. ➤ [as modifier] denoting something designed to prevent injury or damage: *a safety barrier.* **2** US informal a condom. **3** American Football a defensive back who plays in a deep position. **4** American Football a play in which the ball is downed by the offence in their own end zone, scoring two points to the defence.

**safety belt** • n. a belt or strap securing a person to their seat in a vehicle or aircraft.

**safety cage** • n. a framework of reinforced struts protecting a car's passenger cabin against crash damage.

**safety catch** • n. a device that prevents a gun being fired or a machine being operated accidentally.

**safety curtain** • n. a fireproof curtain that can be lowered between the stage and the main part of a theatre to prevent the spread of fire.

**safety deposit** • n. another term for **SAFE DEPOSIT**.

**safety factor** • n. **1** a margin of security against risks. **2** the ratio of a material's strength to an expected strain.

**safety film** • n. fire-resistant cinema film.

**safety fuse** • n. **1** a protective electric fuse. **2** a fuse that burns at a constant slow rate, used for the controlled firing of a detonator.

**safety glass** • n. glass that has been toughened or laminated so that it is less likely to splinter when broken.

**safety lamp** • n. historical a miner's portable lamp with a flame protected by wire gauze to reduce the risk of explosion from ignited methane (firedamp).

**safety match** • n. a match that ignites only when struck on a specially prepared surface, especially the side of a matchbox.

**safety net** • n. **1** a net placed to catch an acrobat in case of a fall. **2** a safeguard against adversity.

**safety pin** • n. a pin with a point that is bent back to the head and is held in a guard when closed.

**safety razor** • n. a razor with a guard to reduce the risk of cutting the skin.

**safety valve** • n. **1** a valve that opens automatically to relieve excessive pressure. **2** a means of giving harmless vent to feelings of tension or stress.

**safflower** • n. an orange-flowered thistle-like plant with seeds that yield an edible oil and petals that were formerly used to produce a red or yellow dye. [*Carthamus tinctorius.*]
– ORIGIN ME: from Du. *saffloer* or Ger. *Saflor*, via OFr. and Ital. from Arab. *aṣfar* 'yellow'.

**saffron** • n. **1** an orange-yellow spice used for flavouring and colouring food, made from the dried stigmas of a crocus. **2** (also **saffron crocus**) an autumn-flowering crocus with reddish-purple flowers that yields this spice. [*Crocus sativus.*]
– DERIVATIVES **saffrony** adj.
– ORIGIN ME: from OFr. *safran*, based on Arab. *za'farān*.

**safranine** /'safrəni:n/ (also **safranin** /-nɪn/) • n. Chemistry any of a large group of synthetic azo dyes, mainly red, used as biological stains.
– ORIGIN C19 (denoting the yellow colouring matter in saffron): from Fr.

**sag**[1] • v. (**sagged**, **sagging**) sink, subside, or bulge downwards gradually under weight or pressure or through lack of strength. ➤ hang down loosely or unevenly. • n. **1** an instance of sagging. **2** Geometry the amount of a downward curve, measured as the perpendicular distance from the middle of the curve to the straight line between the two supporting points.
– DERIVATIVES **saggy** adj.
– ORIGIN ME: appar. rel. to Mid. Low Ger. *sacken*, Du. *zakken* 'subside'.

**sag**[2] • n. variant spelling of **SAAG**.

**saga** /'sɑ:gə/ • n. **1** a long story of heroic achievement, especially a medieval prose narrative in Old Norse or Old Icelandic. **2** a long, involved account or series of incidents.
– ORIGIN C18: from ON, lit. 'narrative'.

**saga boy** • n. W. Indian a playboy.

**sagacious** /sə'geɪʃəs/ • adj. having or showing good judgement.
– DERIVATIVES **sagaciously** adv. **sagacity** n.
– ORIGIN C17 (earlier (C15) as *sagacity*): from L. *sagax*, *sagac-* 'wise' + **-IOUS**.

**sagamore** /'sagəmɔ:/ • n. (among some American Indian peoples) a chief; a sachem.
– ORIGIN from Eastern Abnaki.

**saganaki** /ˌsagə'nɑ:ki/ • n. a Greek appetizer consisting of breaded or floured cheese fried in butter.
– ORIGIN mod. Gk, denoting a small two-handled frying pan, in which the dish is traditionally made.

**sagbag** • n. a large beanbag used as a seat.

**sage**[1] • n. an aromatic plant with greyish-green leaves used as a culinary herb, native to southern Europe and the Mediterranean. [*Salvia officinalis.*] ➤ used in names of similar aromatic plants, e.g. **wood sage**.
– ORIGIN ME: from OFr. *sauge*, from L. *salvia* 'healing

plant', from *salvus* 'safe'.

**sage**[2] ● **n.** (especially in ancient history or legend) a man recognized for his wisdom. ● **adj.** wise; judicious.
– DERIVATIVES **sagely** adv. **sageness** n.
– ORIGIN ME: from OFr., from L. *sapere* 'be wise'.

**sagebrush** ● **n.** a shrubby aromatic North American plant of the daisy family. [*Artemisia tridentata* and related species.] ➤ semi-arid country dominated by this plant.

**sage Derby** ● **n.** a firm cheese made with an infusion of sage.

**sage green** ● **n.** a greyish-green colour like that of sage leaves.

**sage grouse** ● **n.** a large grouse of western North America with long pointed tail feathers, noted for the male's courtship display in which air sacs are inflated to make a popping sound. [*Centrocercus urophasianus*).]

**saggar** /'sagə/ (also **sagger**) ● **n.** a protective fireclay box enclosing ceramic ware while it is being fired.
– ORIGIN C18: prob. a contr. of **SAFEGUARD**.

**sagittal** /'sadʒɪt(ə)l, sə'dʒɪ-/ ● **adj.** Anatomy **1** relating to or denoting the suture on top of the skull which runs between the parietal bones in a front to back direction. **2** of or in a plane parallel to this suture, especially that dividing the body into left and right halves.
– DERIVATIVES **sagitally** adv.
– ORIGIN ME: from med. L. *sagittalis*, from L. *sagitta* 'arrow'.

**sagittal crest** ● **n.** Zoology (in many mammals) a bony ridge on the top of the skull to which the jaw muscles are attached.

**Sagittarius** /ˌsadʒɪ'tɛːriəs/ ● **n. 1** Astronomy a large constellation (the Archer), said to represent a centaur carrying a bow and arrow. **2** Astrology the ninth sign of the zodiac, which the sun enters about 22 November.
– DERIVATIVES **Sagittarian** n. & adj.
– ORIGIN from L.

**sagittate** /'sadʒɪteɪt/ ● **adj.** Botany & Zoology shaped like an arrowhead.
– ORIGIN C18: from L. *sagitta* 'arrow' + **-ATE**[2].

**sago** /'seɪgəʊ/ ● **n.** (pl. **-os**) **1** edible starch obtained from a palm, dried to produce a flour or processed into a granular form. **2** a sweet dish made from sago and milk. **3** (**sago palm**) the palm from which most sago is obtained, growing in freshwater swamps in SE Asia. [*Metroxylon sagu*.] ➤ any of a number of other palms or cycads which yield a similar starch.
– ORIGIN C16: from Malay *sagu* (orig. via Port.).

**saguaro** /sə'gwɑːrəʊ, -'wɑː-/ (also **saguaro cactus**) ● **n.** (pl. **-os**) a giant cactus whose branches are shaped like candelabra, native to the SW United States and Mexico. [*Carnegiea gigantea*.]
– ORIGIN C19: from Mex. Sp.

**Saharan** /sə'hɑːrən/ ● **adj.** of or relating to the Sahara Desert.

**Sahelian** /sə'hiːlɪən/ ● **adj.** of or relating to the Sahel, a semi-arid region of North Africa.

**sahib** /'sɑː(h)ɪb, sɑːb/ ● **n.** Indian a polite title or form of address for a man.
– ORIGIN Urdu, via Pers. from Arab. *ṣāḥib* 'friend, lord'.

**Sahiwal** /'sɑːhɪvɑːl, -wɑːl/ ● **n.** an animal of a breed of cattle with small horns and a hump on the back of the neck, used in tropical regions.
– ORIGIN C20: from the name of a town in the central Punjab, Pakistan.

**said** past and past participle of **SAY**. ● **adj.** denoting someone or something already mentioned or named: *the said agreement.*

**saiga** /'seɪgə, 'sʌɪgə/ ● **n.** an Asian antelope which has a distinctive convex snout with the nostrils opening downwards, living on the cold steppes. [*Saiga tartarica*.]
– ORIGIN C19: from Russ.

**sail** ● **n. 1** a piece of material extended on a mast to catch the wind and propel a boat or ship. ➤ a wind-catching apparatus attached to the arm of a windmill. ➤ the broad fin on the back of a sailfish or of some prehistoric reptiles. ➤ a structure by which an animal is propelled across the surface of water by the wind, e.g. the float of a Portuguese man-of-war. **2** a voyage or excursion in a sailing boat or ship. ● **v. 1** travel in a sailing boat as a sport or for recreation. ➤ travel in a ship or boat using sails or engine power. ➤ begin a voyage; leave a harbour. ➤ travel by ship on or across (a sea) or on (a route). ➤ navigate or control (a boat or ship). **2** move smoothly and rapidly or in a stately or confident manner. ➤ (**sail through**) informal succeed easily at (something, especially a test or examination). ➤ (**sail into**) informal attack physically or verbally with force.
– PHRASES **in** (or **under**) **full sail** with all the sails in position or fully spread. **sail close to** (or **near**) **the wind 1** sail as nearly against the wind as possible. **2** behave or operate in a risky way. **under sail** with the sails hoisted.
– DERIVATIVES **sailable** adj. **-sailed** adj. **sailing** n.
– ORIGIN OE *segel* (n.), *seglian* (v.), of Gmc origin.

**sailboard** ● **n.** a board with a mast and a sail, used in windsurfing.
– DERIVATIVES **sailboarder** n. **sailboarding** n.

**sailboat** ● **n.** North American term for **SAILING BOAT**.

**sailcloth** ● **n.** a canvas or other strong fabric used for making sails. ➤ a similar fabric used for making durable clothes.

**sailer** ● **n.** a sailing boat or ship of specified power or manner of sailing.

**sailfin molly** ● **n.** a small brightly coloured freshwater fish native to North and Central America, the male of which has a long, high dorsal fin. [*Poecilia latipinna* and *Poecilia velifera*.]
– ORIGIN *sailfin* with ref. to the dorsal fin + **MOLLY**.

**sailfish** ● **n.** (pl. same or **-fishes**) an edible migratory billfish with a high sail-like dorsal fin. [*Istiophorus platypterus* and related species.]

**sail-fluke** ● **n.** another term for **MEGRIM**[2].

**sailing boat** ● **n.** chiefly Brit. a boat propelled by sails.

**sailing ship** ● **n.** a ship propelled by sails.

**sailor** ● **n.** a person who works as a member of the crew of a commercial or naval ship or boat, especially one who is below the rank of officer. ➤ a person who sails as a sport or recreation. ➤ (**a good/bad sailor**) a person who rarely (or often) becomes sick at sea in rough weather.
– DERIVATIVES **sailorly** adj.
– ORIGIN C17: var. of obs. *sailer*.

**sailor collar** ● **n.** a collar cut deep and square at the back, tapering to a V-neck at the front.

**sailor hat** ● **n.** another term for **BOATER** (in sense 1).

**sailor suit** ● **n.** a suit of blue and white material resembling the dress uniform of an ordinary seaman, especially as fashionable dress for young boys during the 19th century.

**sailplane** ● **n.** a glider designed for sustained flight.

**sainfoin** /'seɪnfɔɪn, 'san-/ ● **n.** a pink-flowered leguminous plant native to Asia, grown widely for fodder. [*Onobrychis viciifolia*.]
– ORIGIN C17: from obs. Fr. *saintfoin*, from mod. L. *sanum foenum* 'wholesome hay' (with ref. to its medicinal properties).

**saint** /seɪnt, before a name usually s(ə)nt/ ● **n. 1** a person who is acknowledged as holy or virtuous and regarded in Christian faith as being in heaven after death. ➤ a person of exalted virtue who is canonized by the Church after death and who may be the object of veneration and prayers for intercession. ➤ informal a very virtuous person. **2** (**Saint**) a member of the Church of Jesus Christ of Latter-Day Saints; a Mormon. ● **v. 1** formally recognize as a saint; canonize. **2** [as adj. **sainted**] worthy of being a saint; very virtuous: *his sainted sister.*
– DERIVATIVES **saintdom** n. **sainthood** n. **saintliness** n. **saintly** adj. **saintship** n.
– ORIGIN ME, from OFr. *seint*, from L. *sanctus* 'holy', past part. of *sancire* 'consecrate'.

**St Andrew's cross** ● **n.** a diagonal or X-shaped cross, especially white on a blue background (as a national emblem of Scotland).

**St Anthony cross** (also **St Anthony's cross**) ● **n.** a T-shaped cross.

**St Anthony's fire** ● **n. 1** another term for **ERYSIPELAS**.

2 another term for **ERGOTISM**.

**St Bernard** • **n.** a very large dog of a breed originally kept to rescue travellers by the monks of the hospice on the Great St Bernard, a pass across the Alps.

**St Elmo's fire** /ˈɛlməʊz/ • **n.** a phenomenon in which a luminous electrical discharge appears on a ship or aircraft during a storm.
– ORIGIN regarded as a sign of protection given by *St Elmo*, the patron saint of sailors.

**St George's cross** • **n.** a +-shaped cross, red on a white background (especially as a national emblem of England).

**St Helenian** /hɛˈliːnɪən/ • **n.** a native or inhabitant of the South Atlantic island of St Helena. • **adj.** of or relating to St Helena.

**St John's wort** • **n.** a herbaceous plant or shrub with distinctive yellow five-petalled flowers and paired oval leaves. [Genus *Hypericum*: many species.]
– ORIGIN so named because some species come into flower near the feast day of St John the Baptist (24 June).

**St Louis encephalitis** • **n.** a form of viral encephalitis which can be fatal and is transmitted by mosquitoes.
– ORIGIN from the name of *St Louis* in Missouri, US.

**St Lucian** /ˈluːʃ(ə)n/ • **n.** a native or inhabitant of the Caribbean island of St Lucia. • **adj.** of or relating to St Lucia.

**St Mark's fly** • **n.** a fly that drifts slowly over low vegetation with the legs hanging down, first appearing around St Mark's Day (April 25). [*Bibio marci*.]

**St Patrick's cabbage** • **n.** a saxifrage with a rosette of long-stalked leaves and branching clusters of small white flowers. [*Saxifraga spathularis*.]

**saintpaulia** /s(ə)ntˈpɔːlɪə/ • **n.** an African violet. [Genus *Saintpaulia*.]
– ORIGIN mod. L., from the name of the Ger. explorer Baron W. von *Saint Paul* (1860–1910).

**St Peter's fish** • **n.** a tilapia with a dark mark near each pectoral fin, native to North Africa and the Middle East. [*Sarotherodon galileus*.]
– ORIGIN with biblical allusion to Matt. 17:27.

**saint's day** • **n.** (in the Christian Church) a day on which a saint is particularly commemorated.

**St Swithin's day** • **n.** 15 July, a Church festival commemorating St Swithin and popularly believed to be a day on which, if it rains, it will continue raining for the next forty days.

**St Vitus's dance** /ˈvʌɪtəsɪz/ • **n.** old-fashioned term for **SYDENHAM'S CHOREA**.
– ORIGIN so named because a visit to *St Vitus*'s shrine was believed to alleviate the disease.

**saith** /sɛθ/ archaic third person singular present of **SAY**.

**saithe** /seɪθ/ • **n.** a North Atlantic food fish of the cod family. [*Pollachius virens*.]
– ORIGIN C16: from ON *seithr*.

**sake**[1] /seɪk/ • **n.** **1** (**for the sake of something**) for the purpose of or in the interest of something; in order to achieve or preserve something. ➤(**for its own sake** or **something for something's sake** or **for the sake of it**) indicating something that is done as an end in itself rather than to achieve some other purpose. ➤(**for old times' sake**) in memory of former times; in acknowledgement of a shared past. **2** (**for the sake of someone**) out of consideration for or in order to help someone. **3** (**for God's** or **goodness** etc. **sake**) expressing impatience, annoyance, urgency, or desperation.
– ORIGIN OE *sacu* 'contention, crime', of Gmc origin, from a base meaning 'affair, legal action, thing'.

**sake**[2] /ˈsɑːki, ˈsakeɪ/ • **n.** a Japanese alcoholic drink made from fermented rice.
– ORIGIN from Japanese.

**saker** /ˈseɪkə/ • **n.** **1** a large falcon with a brown back and whitish head, used in falconry. [*Falco cherrug*.] **2** an early form of cannon.
– ORIGIN ME: from OFr. *sacre*, from Arab. *ṣaḳr* 'falcon'.

**saki** /ˈsɑːki/ • **n.** (pl. **sakis**) a tropical American monkey with coarse fur and a long bushy non-prehensile tail. [Genera *Pithecia* and *Chiropotes*: several species.]
– ORIGIN C18: via Fr. from Tupi *saui*.

**Sakti** • **n.** variant spelling of **SHAKTI**.

**sal** /sɑːl/ • **n.** a North Indian tree which yields teak-like wood and dammar resin. [*Shorea robusta*.]
– ORIGIN C18: from Hindi *sāl*.

**salaam** /səˈlɑːm/ • **n.** a gesture of greeting or respect in Arabic-speaking and Muslim countries, consisting of a low bow of the head and body with the hand or fingers touching the forehead. • **v.** make a salaam.
– ORIGIN C17: from Arab. (*al-*)*salām* (*'alaikum*) 'peace (be upon you)'.

**salable** • **adj.** variant spelling of **SALEABLE**.

**salacious** /səˈleɪʃəs/ • **adj.** having or conveying undue or indecent interest in sexual matters.
– DERIVATIVES **salaciously** adv. **salaciousness** n.
– ORIGIN C17: from L. *salax, salac-* (from *salire* 'to leap') + **-IOUS**.

**salad** • **n.** a dish consisting of a mixture of raw vegetables or other cold ingredients, typically served with a dressing.
– ORIGIN ME: from OFr. *salade*, from Provençal *salada*, based on L. *sal* 'salt'.

**salad cream** • **n.** Brit. a creamy salad dressing resembling mayonnaise.

**salad days** • **pl. n.** (**one's salad days**) **1** the period when one is young and inexperienced. **2** the peak or heyday of something.
– ORIGIN from Shakespeare's *Antony and Cleopatra* (I. v. 72).

**salade** /səˈlɑːd/ • **n.** another term for **SALLET**.

**salal** /səˈlal/ • **n.** a North American plant of the heather family, with clusters of pink or white flowers and edible purple-black berries. [*Gaultheria shallon*.]
– ORIGIN C19: from Chinook Jargon *sallal*.

**salamander** /ˈsaləˌmandə/ • **n.** **1** a long-tailed amphibian resembling a newt and typically with bright markings. [Order Urodela: many species.] **2** a mythical lizard-like creature said to live in fire or to be able to withstand its effects. ➤an elemental spirit living in fire. **3** a metal plate heated and placed over food to brown it. **4** archaic a red-hot iron or poker.
– DERIVATIVES **salamandrine** /-ˈmandrɪn/ adj.
– ORIGIN ME (in sense 2): from OFr. *salamandre*, via L. from Gk *salamandra*.

**salami** /səˈlɑːmi/ • **n.** (pl. same or **salamis**) a type of highly seasoned preserved sausage, originally from Italy.
– ORIGIN Ital., pl. of *salame*, from a late L. word meaning 'to salt'.

**sal ammoniac** /ˌsal əˈməʊnɪak/ • **n.** dated ammonium chloride, a white crystalline salt.
– ORIGIN ME: from L. *sal ammoniacus* 'salt of Ammon', from Gk *ammōniakos* 'of Ammon', used as a name for the salt and gum obtained near the temple of Jupiter *Ammon* at Siwa in Egypt.

**salariat** /səˈlɛːrɪət/ • **n.** (**the salariat**) salaried white-collar workers.
– ORIGIN C20: from Fr., from *salaire* 'salary', on the pattern of *prolétariat* 'proletariat'.

**salary** • **n.** (pl. **-ies**) a fixed regular payment made usually on a monthly basis by an employer to an employee, especially a professional or white-collar worker. • **v.** (**-ies, -ied**) pay a salary to.
– DERIVATIVES **salaried** adj.
– ORIGIN ME: from Anglo-Norman Fr. *salarie*, from L. *salarium*, orig. denoting a Roman soldier's allowance to buy salt, from *sal* 'salt'.

**salaryman** • **n.** (pl. **-men**) (in Japan) a white-collar worker.

**salat** /saˈlɑːt/ • **n.** the ritual prayer of Muslims, performed five times daily in a set form.
– ORIGIN Arab., pl. of *salāh* 'prayer, worship'.

**salbutamol** /salˈbjuːtəmɒl/ • **n.** Medicine a synthetic compound related to aspirin, used as a bronchodilator in the treatment of asthma and other conditions involving constriction of the airways.
– ORIGIN 1960s: from *sal*(*icylic acid*) + *but*(*yl*) + *am*(*ine*)

+ **-OL**.

**salchow** /ˈsalkəʊ/ ● **n.** a jump in figure skating from the backward inside edge of one skate to the backward outside edge of the other, with one or more full turns in the air.
– ORIGIN 1920s: named after the Swed. skater Ulrich *Salchow.*

**sale** ● **n. 1** the exchange of a commodity for money; the process of selling something. ➤ **(sales)** a quantity or amount sold. **2** **(sales)** the activity or profession of selling. **3** a period in which goods are disposed of at reduced prices. **4** a public or charitable event at which goods are sold. ➤ a public auction.
– PHRASES **for** (or **on**) **sale** offered for purchase. **sale or return** Brit. an arrangement by which a purchaser takes a quantity of goods with the right to return any surplus without payment.
– ORIGIN OE *sala*, from ON *sala*, of Gmc origin.

**saleable** (US also **salable**) ● **adj.** fit or able to be sold.
– DERIVATIVES **saleability** n.

**saleratus** /ˌsaləˈreɪtəs/ ● **n.** US sodium bicarbonate (or sometimes potassium bicarbonate) as the main ingredient of baking powder.
– ORIGIN C19: from mod. L. *sal aeratus* 'aerated salt'.

**saleroom** (also **salesroom**) ● **n.** chiefly Brit. a room in which auctions are held.

**sales clerk** ● **n.** N. Amer. a shop assistant.

**salesgirl** ● **n.** a female shop assistant.

**Salesian** /səˈliːzɪən, -ʒ(ə)n/ ● **adj.** of or relating to a Roman Catholic educational religious order named after St Francis de Sales. ● **n.** a member of this order.

**salesman** (or **saleswoman**) ● **n.** (pl. **-men** or **-women**) a person whose job involves selling or promoting commercial products.
– DERIVATIVES **salesmanship** n.

**salesperson** ● **n.** (pl. **-persons** or **-people**) a salesman or saleswoman.

**Salian** /ˈseɪlɪən/ ● **adj.** of or relating to the Salii, a 4th-century Frankish people from whom the Merovingians were descended. ● **n.** a member of this people.

**Salic** /ˈsalɪk, ˈseɪ-/ ● **adj.** another term for **SALIAN**.

**salicin** /ˈsalɪsɪn/ ● **n.** Chemistry a bitter compound present in willow bark, a glucoside related to aspirin.
– ORIGIN C19: from Fr. *salicine*, from L. *salix*, *salic-* 'willow'.

**salicional** /səˈlɪʃ(ə)n(ə)l/ ● **n.** an organ stop with a soft reedy tone.
– ORIGIN C19: from Ger. *Salicional*, from L. *salix*, *salic-* 'willow' + the obscurely derived suffix *-ional*.

**Salic law** ● **n.** historical **1** a law excluding females from dynastic succession, especially as the alleged fundamental law of the French monarchy. **2** a Frankish law book extant in Merovingian and Carolingian times.

**salicylic acid** /ˌsalɪˈsɪlɪk/ ● **n.** Chemistry a bitter compound present in certain plants, used as a fungicide and in the manufacture of aspirin and dyestuffs.
– DERIVATIVES **salicylate** /səˈlɪsɪleɪt/ n.
– ORIGIN C19: from Fr. *salicyle*, the radical of the acid, from L. *salix*, *salic-* 'willow', + **-IC**.

**salient** /ˈseɪlɪənt/ ● **adj. 1** most noticeable or important. **2** (of an angle) pointing outwards. The opposite of **RE-ENTRANT**. **3** [postpos.] Heraldry (of an animal) standing on its hind legs with the forepaws raised, as if leaping. ● **n. 1** a piece of land or section of fortification that juts out to form an angle. **2** an outward bulge in a military line.
– DERIVATIVES **salience** n. **saliency** n. **saliently** adv.
– ORIGIN C16: from L. *salient-*, *salire* 'to leap'.

**Salientia** /ˌseɪlɪˈɛnʃɪə, -ˈɛnt-/ ● **pl. n.** Zoology another term for **ANURA**.
– DERIVATIVES **salientian** n. & adj.
– ORIGIN mod. L. (pl.), from L. *salire* 'to leap'.

**salina** /səˈlʌɪnə/ ● **n.** (chiefly in the Caribbean or South America) a salt pan, salt lake, or salt marsh.
– ORIGIN C16: from Sp., from med. L., 'salt pit', in L. *salinae* (pl.) 'salt pans'.

**saline** /ˈseɪlʌɪn/ ● **adj. 1** containing or impregnated with salt. **2** chiefly Medicine (of a solution) containing sodium chloride and/or a salt or salts of magnesium or another alkali metal. ● **n.** a saline solution.
– DERIVATIVES **salinity** n. **salinization** (also **-isation**) n.
– ORIGIN C15: from L. *sal* 'salt' + **-INE**[1].

**salinometer** /ˌsalɪˈnɒmɪtə/ ● **n.** an instrument for measuring the salinity of water.

**Salish** /ˈseɪlɪʃ/ ● **n.** (pl. same) **1** a member of a group of American Indian peoples inhabiting areas of the northwestern US and the west coast of Canada. **2** the group of related languages spoken by the Salish.
– DERIVATIVES **Salishan** adj.
– ORIGIN a local name, lit. 'Flatheads'.

**saliva** /səˈlʌɪvə/ ● **n.** a watery liquid secreted into the mouth by glands, providing lubrication for chewing and swallowing, and aiding digestion.
– DERIVATIVES **salivary** /səˈlʌɪ-, ˈsalɪ-/ adj.
– ORIGIN ME: from L.

**salivate** /ˈsalɪveɪt/ ● **v. 1** secrete saliva, especially in anticipation of food. ➤ cause to produce a copious secretion of saliva. **2** display great relish at the sight or prospect of something.
– DERIVATIVES **salivation** n.
– ORIGIN C17: from L. *salivat-*, *salivare* 'produce saliva', from *saliva* (see **SALIVA**).

**sallee** ● **n.** variant spelling of **SALLY**[3].

**sallet** /ˈsalɪt/ ● **n.** historical a light helmet with an outward curve extending over the back of the neck, worn as part of medieval armour.
– ORIGIN ME: from Fr. *salade*, based on L. *caelare* 'engrave'.

**sallow**[1] ● **adj.** (**-er**, **-est**) (of a person's face or complexion) of a yellowish or pale brown colour. ● **v.** make sallow.
– DERIVATIVES **sallowish** adj. **sallowness** n.
– ORIGIN OE *salo* 'dusky', of Gmc origin.

**sallow**[2] ● **n. 1** chiefly Brit. a willow tree of a typically low-growing or shrubby kind. [*Salix cinerea* and related species.] **2** a moth whose larvae feed on willows. [*Xanthia icteritia* and related species.]
– DERIVATIVES **sallowy** adj.
– ORIGIN OE *salh*, of Gmc origin; rel. to L. *salix* 'willow'.

**sally**[1] ● **n.** (pl. **-ies**) **1** a sortie. **2** a witty or lively retort. ● **v.** (**-ies**, **-ied**) make a sortie; set forth.
– ORIGIN ME: from Fr. *saillie*, fem. past part. (used as n.) of *saillir* 'come or jut out', from OFr. *salir* 'to leap', from L. *salire*.

**sally**[2] ● **n.** (pl. **-ies**) the part of a bell rope that has coloured wool woven into it to provide a grip for the bell-ringer's hands.
– ORIGIN C17 (denoting the first movement of a bell when set for ringing): perh. from **SALLY**[1] in the sense 'leaping motion'.

**sally**[3] (also **sallee**) ● **n.** (pl. **sallies** or **sallees**) Austral. an acacia or eucalyptus that resembles a willow.
– ORIGIN C19: dial. var. of **SALLOW**[2].

**Sally Lunn** ● **n.** a sweet, light teacake.
– ORIGIN said to be from the name of a woman selling such cakes in Bath *c.*1800.

**sally port** ● **n.** a small exit point in a fortification for the passage of troops when making a sortie.

**salmagundi** /ˌsalməˈɡʌndi/ ● **n.** (pl. **salmagundis**) **1** a dish of chopped meat, anchovies, eggs, onions, and seasoning. **2** a general mixture; a miscellaneous collection.
– ORIGIN from Fr. *salmigondis*, of unknown origin.

**salmanazar** /ˌsalməˈneɪzə/ ● **n.** a wine bottle of approximately twelve times the standard size.
– ORIGIN 1930s: named after *Shalmaneser*, an ancient king of Assyria.

**salmi** /ˈsalmi/ ● **n.** (pl. **salmis**) a ragout of game stewed in a rich sauce.
– ORIGIN Fr., abbrev. of *salmigondis* (see **SALMAGUNDI**).

**salmon** /ˈsamən/ ● **n.** (pl. same or (especially of types) **salmons**) **1** a large edible fish that matures in the sea and migrates to freshwater streams to spawn. [*Salmo salar* (Atlantic) and genus *Oncorhynchus* (Pacific).] ➤ any of various unrelated marine fish resembling this. [*Arripis trutta* (Australasia) and other species.] ➤ the flesh of such a fish as food. **2** a pale pink colour like that of the flesh of a salmon.

– DERIVATIVES **salmony** adj.
– ORIGIN ME *samoun*, from Anglo-Norman Fr. *saumoun*, from L. *salmo, salmon-*.

**salmonberry** • n. (pl. **-ies**) a North American bramble which bears pink raspberry-like edible fruit. [Genus *Rubus*: several species, in particular *R. spectabilis*.]

**salmonella** /ˌsalmə'nɛlə/ • n. (pl. **salmonellae** /-liː/) a bacterium that occurs mainly in the gut and can cause food poisoning. [Genus *Salmonella*.] ➤ food poisoning caused by this.
– DERIVATIVES **salmonellosis** /-'ləʊsɪs/ n.
– ORIGIN mod. L., named after the Amer. veterinary surgeon Daniel E. *Salmon*.

**salmonid** /'salmənɪd, sal'mɒnɪd/ • n. Zoology a fish of a family (Salmonidae) including salmon, trout, charr, and whitefish.

**salmon ladder** (also **salmon leap**) • n. a series of natural steps in a cascade or steeply sloping river bed, or a similar arrangement incorporated into a dam, allowing salmon to pass upstream.

**salmon trout** • n. a large trout or trout-like fish, especially (Brit.) a sea trout.

**salon** • n. **1** an establishment where a hairdresser, beautician, or couturier conducts their trade. **2** a reception room in a large house. **3** chiefly historical a regular gathering of writers, artists, etc., held in a fashionable household. **4** (**Salon**) an annual exhibition of the work of living artists held by the Royal Academy of Painting and Sculpture in Paris (originally in the Salon d'Apollon in the Louvre).
– ORIGIN C17: from Fr. (see **SALOON**).

**saloon** • n. **1** a public room or building used for a specified purpose. ➤ (also **saloon bar**) Brit. another term for **LOUNGE BAR**. ➤ a large public room for use as a lounge on a ship. **2** N. Amer. historical or humorous a place where alcoholic drinks may be bought and drunk. **3** (also **saloon car**) Brit. a car having a closed body and separate boot. **4** (also **saloon car**) Brit. a luxurious railway carriage used as a lounge or restaurant or as private accommodation.
– ORIGIN C18 (in the sense 'drawing room'): from Fr. *salon*, from Ital. *salone* 'large hall', augmentative of *sala* 'hall'.

**saloon deck** • n. a deck on the same level as a ship's saloon, for the use of passengers.

**saloon keeper** • n. N. Amer. a person who runs a bar; a bartender.

**saloon pistol** (also **saloon rifle**) • n. a gun adapted for firing at short range.

**salopettes** /ˌsalə'pɛts/ • pl. n. trousers with a high waist and shoulder straps, made from a padded or other warm fabric, worn for skiing.
– ORIGIN 1970s: from Fr. *salopette* in the same sense + *-s* by analogy with such words as *trousers*.

**salp** /salp/ • n. a free-swimming marine invertebrate related to the sea squirts, with a transparent barrel-shaped body. [Many species in the class Thaliacea.]
– ORIGIN C19: from Fr. *salpe*, based on Gk *salpē* 'fish'.

**salpiglossis** /ˌsalpɪ'glɒsɪs/ • n. a South American plant of the nightshade family, with brightly patterned funnel-shaped flowers. [Genus *Salpiglossis*.]
– ORIGIN mod. L., formed irregularly from Gk *salpinx* 'trumpet' + *glōssa* 'tongue'.

**salpingectomy** /ˌsalpɪŋ'dʒɛktəmi/ • n. (pl. **-ies**) surgical removal of the Fallopian tubes.
– ORIGIN from **SALPINGO-** + **-ECTOMY**.

**salpingitis** /ˌsalpɪŋ'dʒʌɪtɪs/ • n. Medicine inflammation of the Fallopian tubes.

**salpingo-** /'salpɪŋgəʊ/ (also **salping-** before a vowel) • comb. form relating to the Fallopian tubes: *salpingostomy*.
– ORIGIN from Gk *salpinx, salping-* 'trumpet'.

**salpingostomy** /ˌsalpɪŋ'gɒstəmi/ • n. surgical unblocking of a blocked Fallopian tube.

**salsa** /'salsə/ • n. **1** a type of Latin American dance music incorporating elements of jazz and rock. ➤ a dance performed to this music. **2** (especially in Latin American cookery) a spicy tomato sauce.
– ORIGIN Sp., lit. 'sauce', extended in Amer. Sp. to denote the dance.

**salsa verde** /ˌsalsə 'vəːdeɪ, 'vəːdi/ • n. **1** an Italian sauce made with olive oil, garlic, capers, anchovies, vinegar or lemon juice, and parsley. **2** a Mexican sauce of chopped onion, garlic, coriander, parsley, and hot peppers.
– ORIGIN Sp., lit. 'green sauce'.

**salsify** /'salsɪfi/ • n. **1** an edible plant of the daisy family, with a long root like that of a parsnip. [*Tragopogon porrifolius*.] **2** the root of this plant used as a vegetable.
– ORIGIN C17: from Fr. *salsifis*, from obs. Ital. *salsefica*, of unknown ultimate origin.

**SALT** /sɔːlt, sɒlt/ • abbrev. Strategic Arms Limitation Talks.

**salt** /sɔːlt, sɒlt/ • n. **1** (also **common salt**) sodium chloride, a white crystalline substance which gives seawater its characteristic taste and is used for seasoning or preserving food. ➤ poetic/literary something which adds freshness or piquancy. **2** Chemistry any chemical compound formed by the reaction of an acid with a base, with the hydrogen of the acid replaced by a metal or other cation. **3** (usu. **old salt**) informal an experienced sailor. • adj. **1** impregnated with salt. **2** (of a plant) growing on the coast or in salt marshes. • v. **1** [often as adj. **salted**] season or preserve with salt. ➤ make piquant or more interesting. ➤ sprinkle (a road or path) with salt in order to melt snow or ice. **2** informal fraudulently make (a mine) appear to be a paying one by placing rich ore into it. **3** (**salt something away**) informal secretly store or put by something, especially money. **4** [as adj. **salted**] (of a horse) having developed a resistance to disease by surviving it. **5** (**salt something out**) cause soap to separate from lye by adding salt. ➤ Chemistry cause an organic compound to separate from an aqueous solution by adding an electrolyte.
– PHRASES **rub salt into the wound** make a painful experience even more painful. **the salt of the earth** a person of great goodness and strength of character. [with biblical allusion to Matt 5:13.] **sit below the salt** be of lower social standing. [from the former custom of placing a salt cellar in the middle of a dining table with the host at one end.] **take something with a pinch** (or **grain**) **of salt** regard something as exaggerated; believe only part of something. **worth one's salt** good or competent at one's job or allotted task.
– DERIVATIVES **saltish** adj. **saltless** adj. **saltness** n.
– ORIGIN OE *sealt* (n.), *sealtan* (v.), of Gmc origin.

**salt-and-pepper** • adj. another way of saying **PEPPER-AND-SALT**.

**saltarello** /ˌsaltə'rɛləʊ/ • n. (pl. **saltarellos** or **saltarelli** /-li/) an energetic Italian or Spanish dance for one couple, characterized by leaps and skips.
– ORIGIN C18: Ital. *salterello*, Sp. *saltarelo*, based on L. *saltare* 'to dance'.

**saltation** /sal'teɪʃ(ə)n, sɔː-, sɒ-/ • n. **1** Biology abrupt evolutionary change; sudden large-scale mutation. **2** Geology the transport of hard particles over an uneven surface in a turbulent flow of air or water. **3** archaic the action of leaping or dancing.
– DERIVATIVES **saltatory** /'saltət(ə)ri, 'sɔː-, 'sɒ-/ adj.
– ORIGIN C17 (in sense 3): from L. *saltatio(n-)*, from *saltare* 'to dance', frequentative of *salire* 'to leap'.

**saltatorial** /ˌsaltə'tɔːrɪəl, sɔː-, sɒ-/ • adj. chiefly Entomology (especially of grasshoppers or their limbs) adapted for leaping.

**saltbox** • n. N. Amer. a frame house having up to three storeys at the front and one fewer at the back with a steeply pitched roof.

**salt bridge** • n. Chemistry **1** a tube containing an electrolyte (typically in the form of a gel), providing electrical contact between two solutions. **2** a link between electrically charged acidic and basic groups, especially on different parts of a large molecule such as a protein.

**saltbush** • n. a salt-tolerant orache plant, sometimes planted on saline soils. [*Atriplex vesicaria* (Australia) and related species.]

**salt cedar** • n. N. Amer. a European tamarisk with reddish-brown branches and feathery grey foliage. [*Tamarix gallica*.]

**salt cellar** • n. a dish or container for storing salt, typically a closed container with perforations in the lid for

sprinkling.
– ORIGIN ME: from SALT + obs. *saler*, from OFr. *salier* 'salt-box', from L. *salarium* (see SALARY); the change in spelling of the second word was due to assoc. with CELLAR.

**salt dome** ● n. a dome-shaped structure in sedimentary rocks, formed where a large mass of salt has been forced upwards.

**salter** ● n. historical **1** a person dealing in or employed in the production of salt, or who used salt to preserve meat or fish. **2** another term for DRY-SALTER.

**saltern** /'sɔːltən, 'sɒ-/ ● n. a set of pools in which seawater is left to evaporate to make salt.
– ORIGIN OE *sealtærn* 'salt building' (the original use denoting a salt works).

**salt finger** ● n. Oceanography one of several alternating columns of rising and descending water produced when a layer of water is overlain by a denser, saltier layer.
– DERIVATIVES **salt fingering** n.

**salt fish** ● n. fish, especially cod, that has been preserved in salt.

**salt flats** ● pl. n. areas of flat land covered with a layer of salt.

**salt glaze** ● n. a hard glaze with a pitted surface, produced on stoneware by adding salt to the kiln during firing.
– DERIVATIVES **salt-glazed** adj. **salt glazing** n.

**saltimbocca** /ˌsaltɪm'bɒkə/ ● n. a dish consisting of rolled pieces of veal or poultry cooked with herbs, bacon, and other flavourings.
– ORIGIN Ital., lit. 'leap into the mouth'.

**saltine** /sɔːl'tiːn, sɒ-/ ● n. N. Amer. a thin crisp savoury biscuit baked with salt sprinkled on its surface.
– ORIGIN from SALT + -INE[4].

**salting** ● n. (usu. **saltings**) Brit. an area of coastal land that is regularly covered by the tide.

**saltire** /'saltʌɪə, 'sɔː-/ ● n. Heraldry a diagonal cross as a heraldic ordinary.
– DERIVATIVES **saltirewise** adv.
– ORIGIN ME: from OFr. *saultoir* 'stirrup cord, stile, saltire', based on L. *saltare* 'to dance'.

**salt lick** ● n. a place where animals go to lick salt from the ground. ➤a block of salt provided for animals to lick.

**salt marsh** ● n. an area of coastal grassland that is regularly flooded by seawater.

**salt pan** ● n. a shallow container or depression in the ground in which salt water evaporates to leave a deposit of salt.

**saltpetre** /sɔːlt'piːtə, sɒ-/ (US **saltpeter**) ● n. potassium nitrate or (**Chile saltpetre**) sodium nitrate.
– ORIGIN ME: from OFr. *salpetre*, from med. L. *salpetra*, prob. representing *sal petrae* 'salt of rock' (i.e. found as an encrustation); the change in the first element was due to assoc. with SALT.

**salt spoon** ● n. a tiny spoon with a roundish deep bowl, used for serving oneself with salt.

**saltus** /'saltəs/ ● n. poetic/literary a sudden transition; a breach of continuity.
– ORIGIN C17: from L., lit. 'leap'.

**saltwater** ● adj. of or found in salt water; living in the sea.

**saltwort** ● n. a plant of the goosefoot family, typically growing in salt marshes, which is rich in alkali. [Genus *Salsola*.]

**salty** ● adj. (**-ier**, **-iest**) **1** tasting of, containing, or preserved with salt. **2** (of language or humour) down-to-earth; coarse.
– DERIVATIVES **saltily** adv. **saltiness** n.

**salubrious** /sə'luːbrɪəs/ ● adj. **1** health-giving; healthy. **2** (of a place) pleasant; not run-down.
– DERIVATIVES **salubriously** adv. **salubriousness** n. **salubrity** n.
– ORIGIN C16: from L. *salubris* (from *salus* 'health') + -OUS.

**saluki** /sə'luːki/ ● n. (pl. **salukis**) a tall, swift, slender dog of a silky-coated breed with large drooping ears and fringed feet.
– ORIGIN C19: from Arab. *salūḳī*.

**salut** /sa'luː/ ● exclam. used as a toast.
– ORIGIN from Fr.

**salutary** /'saljʊt(ə)ri/ ● adj. **1** (of something disadvantageous) beneficial in providing an opportunity for learning from experience. **2** archaic health-giving.
– ORIGIN ME: from Fr. *salutaire* or L. *salutaris*, from *salus*, *salut-* 'health'.

**salutation** ● n. a greeting.
– DERIVATIVES **salutational** adj.
– ORIGIN ME: from OFr., or from L. *salutatio(n-)*, from *salutare* (see SALUTE).

**salutatorian** /səˌljuːtə'tɔːrɪən/ ● n. N. Amer. the student ranking second highest in a graduating class who delivers the salutatory.

**salutatory** /sə'ljuːtət(ə)ri/ ● adj. relating to or of the nature of a salutation. ● n. (pl. **-ies**) N. Amer. an address of welcome, especially one given as an oration by the student ranking second highest in a graduating class at a university or college.

**salute** ● n. **1** a gesture of respect and recognition. **2** a prescribed or specified movement, typically a raising of a hand to the head, made as a salute by a member of a military or similar force. **3** the discharge of a gun or guns as a formal or ceremonial sign of respect or celebration. **4** Fencing the formal performance of certain guards or other movements by fencers before engaging. ● v. **1** make a formal salute to. **2** greet. **3** show or express admiration and respect for.
– DERIVATIVES **saluter** n.
– ORIGIN ME: from L. *salutare* 'greet, pay one's respects to', from *salus*, *salut-* 'health, welfare, greeting'; the noun partly from OFr. *salut*.

**Salvadorean** /ˌsalvə'dɔːrɪən/ ● n. a native or inhabitant of El Salvador. ● adj. of or relating to El Salvador.

**salvage** ● v. **1** rescue (a ship or its cargo) from loss at sea. **2** retrieve or preserve from loss or destruction. ● n. **1** the process or an instance of salvaging. **2** the cargo saved from a wrecked or sunken ship. ➤Law payment made or due to a person who has saved a ship or its cargo.
– DERIVATIVES **salvageable** adj. **salvager** n.
– ORIGIN C17 (as a noun denoting payment for saving a ship or its cargo): from Fr., from med. L. *salvagium*, from L. *salvare* 'to save'.

**salvage yard** ● n. a place where disused machinery, vehicles, etc. are broken up and parts salvaged.

**Salvarsan** /'salvəsan/ ● n. Medicine, historical another term for ARSPHENAMINE.
– ORIGIN C20: from Ger., from L. *salvare* 'save' + Ger. *Arsenik* 'arsenic' + -AN.

**salvation** ● n. **1** Theology deliverance from sin and its consequences, believed by Christians to be brought about by faith in Christ. **2** preservation or deliverance from harm, ruin, or loss. ➤(**one's salvation**) a source or means of being saved in this way.
– ORIGIN ME: from OFr. *salvacion*, from eccles. L. *salvation-* (from *salvare* 'to save'), translating Gk *sōtēria*.

**salvationist** ● n. (**Salvationist**) a member of the Salvation Army, a Christian evangelical organization. ● adj. **1** of or relating to salvation. **2** (**Salvationist**) of or relating to the Salvation Army.
– DERIVATIVES **salvationism** n.

**salve**[1] ● n. **1** an ointment used to soothe or promote healing of the skin. **2** something that soothes wounded feelings or an uneasy conscience. ● v. apply a salve to; soothe.
– ORIGIN OE *sealfe* (n.), *sealfian* (v.), of Gmc origin.

**salve**[2] ● v. archaic term for SALVAGE.
– DERIVATIVES **salvable** adj.
– ORIGIN C18: back-form. from SALVAGE.

**salver** ● n. a tray, typically one made of silver and used in formal circumstances.
– ORIGIN C17: from Fr. *salve* 'tray for presenting food to the king', from Sp. *salva* 'sampling of food', from *salvar* 'make safe'.

**Salve Regina** /ˌsalveɪ rə'dʒiːnə/ ● n. a Roman Catholic

hymn or prayer said or sung after compline, and after the Divine Office from Trinity Sunday to Advent.
– ORIGIN the opening words in L., 'hail (holy) queen'.

**salvia** • n. a plant of a genus including sage, especially one cultivated for its spikes of bright flowers. [Genus *Salvia*.]
– ORIGIN mod. L., from L. *salvia* 'sage'.

**salvo** • n. (pl. **-os** or **-oes**) **1** a simultaneous discharge of artillery or other guns in a battle. **2** a sudden vigorous series of aggressive statements or acts.
– ORIGIN C16: from Fr. *salve*, Ital. *salva* 'salutation'.

**sal volatile** /ˌsal vəˈlatɪli/ • n. a scented solution of ammonium carbonate in alcohol, used as smelling salts.
– ORIGIN C17: mod. L., lit. 'volatile salt'.

**salvor** /ˈsalvə, ˈsalvɔː/ • n. a person engaged in salvage of a ship or items lost at sea.

**salwar** /sʌlˈwɑː/ (also **shalwar**) • n. a pair of light, loose, pleated trousers tapering to a tight fit around the ankles, worn by women from the Indian subcontinent, typically with a kameez.
– ORIGIN from Pers. and Urdu *šalwār*.

**SAM** • abbrev. surface-to-air missile.

**Sam.** • abbrev. Samuel (in biblical references).

**samadhi** /sʌˈmɑːdi/ • n. (pl. **samadhis**) Hinduism & Buddhism a state of intense concentration achieved through meditation.
– ORIGIN from Sanskrit *samādhi* 'contemplation'.

**samara** /ˈsamərə, səˈmɑːrə/ • n. Botany a winged nut or achene containing one seed, as in ash and maple.
– ORIGIN C16: mod. L., from L., denoting an elm seed.

**Samaritan** • n. **1** (usu. **good Samaritan**) a charitable or helpful person (with reference to Luke 10:33). **2** a member of a people inhabiting Samaria in biblical times, or of the modern community claiming descent from them. **3** the dialect of Aramaic formerly spoken in Samaria. **4** (**the Samaritans**) (in the UK) an organization which counsels those in distress, mainly through a telephone service. • adj. of or relating to Samaria or the Samaritans.
– DERIVATIVES **Samaritanism** n.
– ORIGIN from late L. *Samaritanus*, from Gk *Samareitēs*, from *Samareia* 'Samaria'.

**samarium** /səˈmɛːrɪəm/ • n. the chemical element of atomic number 62, a hard silvery-white metal of the lanthanide series. (Symbol: **Sm**)
– ORIGIN C19: from *samar(skite)*, a mineral in which its spectrum was first observed (named after *Samarsky*, a C19 Russ. official) + **-IUM**.

**Sama Veda** /ˈsɑːmə/ • n. one of the four Vedas, a collection of liturgical chants.
– ORIGIN from Sanskrit *sāmaveda*, from *sāman* 'chant' and **VEDA**.

**samba** /ˈsambə/ • n. a Brazilian dance of African origin. ➤ a ballroom dance based on this. • v. (**sambas**, **sambaed** /-bəd/ or **samba'd**, **sambaing** /-bə(r)ɪŋ/) dance the samba.
– ORIGIN C19: from Port., of Afr. origin.

**sambal** /ˈsambal/ • n. (in oriental cookery) relish made with vegetables or fruit and spices.
– ORIGIN from Malay.

**sambar** /ˈsambə/ • n. a dark brown southern Asian woodland deer with branched antlers. [*Cervus unicolor*.]
– ORIGIN C17: from Hindi *sābar*, from Sanskrit *śambara*.

**Sambo** • n. (pl. **-os** or **-oes**) **1** offensive a black person. [C18: perh. from Fula *sambo* 'uncle'.] **2** (**sambo**) historical a person of mixed race. [C18: from Amer. Sp. *zambo*, denoting a kind of yellow monkey.]

**Sam Browne** • n. a leather belt with a supporting strap that passes over the right shoulder, worn by army and police officers.
– ORIGIN C20: named after the Brit. military commander Sir *Samuel* J. *Brown(e)*.

**sambuca** /samˈbuːkə/ • n. an Italian aniseed-flavoured liqueur.
– ORIGIN Ital., from L. *sambucus* 'elder tree'.

**Samburu** /samˈbʊruː/ • n. (pl. same) **1** a member of a mainly pastoral people of northern Kenya. **2** the Nilotic language of this people.
– ORIGIN a local name.

**same** • adj. (**the same**) **1** identical; unchanged. **2** (**this/that same**) referring to a person or thing just mentioned. • pron. **1** (**the same**) the same thing as previously mentioned. ➤ identical people or things. **2** the person or thing just mentioned. • adv. in the same way.
– PHRASES **all** (or **just**) **the same** nevertheless. ➤ anyway. **at the same time 1** simultaneously. **2** on the other hand. **same difference** informal no difference. **same here** informal the same applies to me. (**the**) **same to you!** may you do or have the same thing.
– DERIVATIVES **sameness** n.
– ORIGIN ME: from ON *sami*.

**samey** • adj. (**-ier**, **-iest**) Brit. informal monotonous.
– DERIVATIVES **sameyness** n.

**samfu** /ˈsamfuː/ • n. a suit consisting of a high-necked jacket and loose trousers, worn by Chinese women.
– ORIGIN 1950s: from Chin. (Cantonese dial.) *shaam foò*, from *shaam* 'coat' + *foò* 'trousers'.

**Samhain** /saʊn, ˈsaʊɪn, ˈsawɪn, Irish ˈsəʊnʲ/ • n. 1 November, celebrated by the ancient Celts as a festival marking the beginning of winter and their new year.
– ORIGIN Ir., from Old Ir. *samain*.

**Sam Hill** • n. N. Amer. informal, euphemistic hell.
– ORIGIN C19: of unknown origin.

**Sami** /ˈsɑːmi, sɑːm/ • pl. n. the Lapps of northern Scandinavia.
– ORIGIN Lappish, of unknown origin.

**USAGE** Sami

Sami is the term by which the Lapps themselves prefer to be known. See **LAPP**.

**Samian** /ˈseɪmɪən/ • n. a native or inhabitant of Samos, a Greek island in the Aegean. • adj. of or relating to Samos.

**Samian ware** • n. a type of fine, glossy, reddish-brown pottery widely made in the Roman Empire.

**samisen** /ˈsamɪsɛn/ (also **shamisen** /ˈʃamɪsɛn/) • n. a Japanese three-stringed lute with a square body, played with a large plectrum.
– ORIGIN C17: Japanese, from Chin. *san-hsien*, from *san* 'three' + *hsien* 'string'.

**samite** /ˈsamʌɪt, ˈseɪ-/ • n. a rich silk fabric interwoven with gold and silver threads, made in the Middle Ages.
– ORIGIN ME: from OFr. *samit*, via med. L. from med. Gk *hexamiton*, from Gk *hexa-* 'six' + *mitos* 'thread'.

**samizdat** /ˈsamɪzdat, ˌsamɪzˈdat/ • n. the clandestine copying and distribution of literature banned by the state, especially formerly in the communist countries of eastern Europe.
– ORIGIN 1960s: Russ., lit. 'self-publishing house'.

**Samnite** /ˈsamnʌɪt/ • n. a member of an ancient Oscan-speaking people of southern Italy.
– ORIGIN from L. *Samnites* (pl.); rel. to *Sabinus* (see **SABINE**).

**Samoan** • n. **1** a native or inhabitant of Samoa. **2** the Polynesian language of Samoa. • adj. of or relating to Samoa, its people, or their language.

**samosa** /səˈməʊsə/ • n. a triangular fried pastry containing spiced vegetables or meat.
– ORIGIN from Pers. and Urdu.

**samovar** /ˈsaməvɑː, ˌsaməˈvɑː/ • n. a highly decorated Russian tea urn.
– ORIGIN Russ., lit. 'self-boiler'.

**Samoyed** /ˈsaməjɛd, ˌsamɔɪˈjɛd/ • n. **1** a member of a group of mainly nomadic peoples of northern Siberia. **2** any of several Samoyedic languages of these peoples. **3** a dog of a white Arctic breed.
– ORIGIN from Russ. *samoed*.

**Samoyedic** • n. a group of Uralic languages of northern Siberia. • adj. of or relating to the Samoyeds or their languages.

**samp** • n. US & S. African coarsely ground maize, or porridge made from this.
– ORIGIN C17: from Algonquian *nasamp* 'softened by water'.

**sampan** /ˈsampan/ • n. a small boat used in the Far East,

typically with an oar or oars at the stern.
– ORIGIN C17: from Chin. *san-ban*, from *san* 'three' + *ban* 'board'.

**samphire** /'samfʌɪə/ ● n. a fleshy-leaved plant which grows near the sea. [*Crithmum maritimum* (**rock samphire**) and other species.]
– ORIGIN C16 (earlier as *sampiere*): from Fr. (*herbe de*) *Saint Pierre* 'St Peter('s herb)'.

**sample** ● n. **1** a small part or quantity intended to show what the whole is like. ➤ Statistics a portion of a population, serving as a basis for estimates of the attributes of the whole population. **2** a specimen taken for scientific testing or analysis. **3** a sound created by sampling. ● v. **1** take a sample or samples of. **2** get a representative experience of. **3** Electronics ascertain the momentary value of (an analogue signal) many times a second so as to convert the signal to digital form.
– ORIGIN ME (as n.): from an Anglo-Norman Fr. var. of OFr. *essample* 'example'.

**sampler** ● n. **1** a piece of embroidery worked in various stitches as a specimen of skill. **2** a representative collection or example of something. **3** a person or device that takes samples. ➤ a device for sampling music and sound.
– ORIGIN ME: from OFr. *essamplaire* 'exemplar'.

**sampling** ● n. **1** the taking of a sample or samples. ➤ Statistics a sample. **2** the technique of digitally encoding music or sound and reusing it as part of a composition or recording.

**sampling frame** ● n. Statistics a list of the items or people forming a population from which a sample is taken.

**samsara** /sʌm'sɑːrə/ ● n. Hinduism & Buddhism the cycle of death and rebirth to which life in the material world is bound.
– DERIVATIVES **samsaric** adj.
– ORIGIN from Sanskrit *saṃsāra*.

**samskara** /sʌm'skɑːrə/ ● n. Hinduism a purificatory ceremony or rite marking a major event in one's life.
– ORIGIN from Sanskrit *saṃskāra* 'a making perfect, preparation'.

**Samson post** ● n. a strong pillar fixed to a ship's deck to act as a support for a tackle or other equipment.
– ORIGIN C16 (denoting a mousetrap): prob. with biblical allusion to *Samson*, an Israelite leader famous for his strength.

**samurai** /'sam(j)ʊrʌɪ/ ● n. (pl. same) historical a member of a powerful military caste in feudal Japan.
– ORIGIN from Japanese.

**San** /sɑːn/ ● n. (pl. same) **1** a member of the Bushmen of southern Africa. See **BUSHMAN**. **2** the group of Khoisan languages spoken by these peoples.
– ORIGIN from Nama *sān* 'aboriginals, settlers'.

**san** ● n. informal a sanatorium.

**sanative** /'sanətɪv/ ● adj. archaic healing.
– ORIGIN ME: from OFr. *sanatif* or late L. *sanativus*, from L. *sanare* 'to cure'.

**sanatorium** /ˌsanə'tɔːrɪəm/ ● n. (pl. **sanatoriums** or **sanatoria** /-rɪə/) an establishment for the treatment of people who are convalescing or have a chronic illness. ➤ Brit. a place in a boarding school for children who are unwell.
– ORIGIN C19: mod. L., based on L. *sanare* 'heal'.

**Sancerre** /sɒ̃'sɛː, French sɑ̃sɛʀ/ ● n. a light white wine produced in the part of France around Sancerre.

**sanctify** /'saŋ(k)tɪfʌɪ/ ● v. (**-ies**, **-ied**) **1** consecrate. **2** make legitimate or binding by religious sanction. **3** free from sin. **4** give the appearance of being right or good.
– DERIVATIVES **sanctification** n. **sanctifier** n.
– ORIGIN ME: from OFr. *saintifier* (influenced later by *sanctifier*), from eccles. L. *sanctificare*, from L. *sanctus* 'holy'.

**sanctimonious** /ˌsaŋ(k)tɪ'məʊnɪəs/ ● adj. derogatory making a show of being morally superior.
– DERIVATIVES **sanctimoniously** adv. **sanctimoniousness** n. **sanctimony** /'saŋ(k)tɪməni/ n.
– ORIGIN C17: from L. *sanctimonia* 'sanctity' (from *sanctus* 'holy') + **-OUS**.

**sanction** ● n. **1** a threatened penalty for disobeying a law or rule. ➤ (**sanctions**) measures taken by a state to coerce another to conform to an international agreement or norms of conduct. ➤ Ethics a consideration operating to enforce obedience to any rule of conduct. **2** official permission or approval for an action. ➤ official confirmation or ratification of a law. ➤ Law, historical a law or decree, especially an ecclesiastical one. ● v. **1** give official sanction for. **2** impose a sanction or penalty on.
– DERIVATIVES **sanctionable** adj.
– ORIGIN ME: from Fr., from L. *sanctio(n-)*, from *sancire* 'ratify'.

**sanctitude** ● n. formal holiness; saintliness.
– ORIGIN ME: from L. *sanctitudo*, from *sanctus* 'holy'.

**sanctity** ● n. (pl. **-ies**) **1** holiness; saintliness. **2** ultimate importance and inviolability.
– ORIGIN ME: from OFr. *saintite*, reinforced by L. *sanctitas*, from *sanctus* 'holy'.

**sanctuary** ● n. (pl. **-ies**) **1** a place of refuge or safety. ➤ immunity from arrest. **2** a nature reserve. ➤ a place where injured or unwanted animals are cared for. **3** a holy place. ➤ the innermost recess or holiest part of a temple. ➤ the part of the chancel of a church containing the high altar.
– ORIGIN ME (orig. 'a sacred place where a fugitive was immune from arrest'): from OFr. *sanctuaire*, from L. *sanctuarium*, from *sanctus* 'holy'.

**sanctum** /'saŋ(k)təm/ ● n. (pl. **sanctums**) **1** a sacred place, especially a shrine in a temple or church. **2** a private place.
– ORIGIN C16: from L., neut. of *sanctus* 'holy', from *sancire* 'consecrate'.

**sanctum sanctorum** /saŋ(k)'tɔːrəm/ ● n. (pl. **sancta sanctorum** or **sanctum sanctorums**) the holy of holies in the Jewish temple.
– ORIGIN ME: L. *sanctum* (see **SANCTUM**) + *sanctorum* 'of holy places', translating Heb. *qōḏeš haqqŏḏāšîm* 'holy of holies'.

**Sanctus** /'saŋ(k)təs/ ● n. Christian Church a hymn beginning *Sanctus, sanctus, sanctus* (Holy, holy, holy) forming a set part of the Mass.
– ORIGIN ME: from L., lit. 'holy'.

**sanctus bell** ● n. a sacring bell.

**sand** ● n. **1** a loose granular substance, typically pale yellowish brown, resulting from the erosion of siliceous and other rocks and forming a major constituent of beaches, river beds, the seabed, and deserts. ➤ (**sands**) an expanse of sand. ➤ technical sediment whose particles are larger than silt. **2** N. Amer. informal firmness of purpose. **3** a pale yellow-brown colour. ● v. **1** smooth with sandpaper or a sander. **2** sprinkle or overlay with sand.
– PHRASES **drive** (or **run**) (**something**) **into the sand** come (or bring something) to a halt. **the sands** (**of time**) **are running out** the allotted time is nearly at an end. [with ref. to the sand of an hourglass.]
– ORIGIN OE, of Gmc origin.

**sandal**[1] ● n. a light shoe with an openwork upper or straps attaching the sole to the foot.
– DERIVATIVES **sandalled** (US **sandaled**) adj.
– ORIGIN ME: via L. from Gk *sandalion*, dimin. of *sandalon* 'wooden shoe', prob. of Asiatic origin.

**sandal**[2] ● n. short for **SANDALWOOD**.

**sandalwood** ● n. **1** the fragrant wood of an Indian or SE Asian tree. ➤ perfume or incense derived from this wood. **2** the tree yielding this wood. [*Santalum album* (**white sandalwood**) and other species.]
– ORIGIN C16: *sandal* from med. L. *sandalum* (based on Sanskrit *candana*) + **WOOD**.

**sandarac** /'sandərak/ ● n. a gum resin obtained from the alerce (cypress), used in making varnish.
– ORIGIN ME (denoting realgar): from L. *sandaraca*, from Gk *sandarakē*, of Asiatic origin.

**sandbag** ● n. a bag of sand, used for defensive purposes or as ballast in a boat. ● v. (**-bagged**, **-bagging**) **1** [usu. as adj. **sandbagged**] barricade with sandbags. **2** hit or fell with or as if with a blow from a sandbag. **3** N. Amer. bully. **4** deliberately underperform in a contest to gain an unfair advantage.
– DERIVATIVES **sandbagger** n.

**sandbank** ● n. a deposit of sand forming a shallow area

in the sea or a river.

**sandbar** • n. a long, narrow sandbank.

**sand bath** • n. a container of heated sand, used in a laboratory to supply uniform heating.

**sandblast** • v. roughen or clean with a jet of sand driven by compressed air or steam. • n. such a jet of sand.
– DERIVATIVES **sandblaster** n.

**sandbox** • n. **1** a box containing sand, especially one on a train to hold sand for sprinkling on to slippery rails. **2** historical a perforated container for sprinkling sand on to wet ink to dry it. **3** N. Amer. a sandpit.

**sandboy** • n. (in phr. (**as**) **happy as a sandboy**) extremely happy or carefree.
– ORIGIN prob. orig. denoting a boy hawking sand.

**sandcastle** • n. a model of a castle built out of sand.

**sand crack** • n. a vertical fissure in the wall of a horse's hoof.

**sand dab** • n. a flatfish of sandy coastal waters. [*Scophthalmus aquosus* (W. Atlantic) and other species.]

**sand dollar** • n. a flattened sea urchin which lives partly buried in sand, feeding on detritus. [Order Clypeasteroida: many species.]

**sand eel** • n. a small elongated marine fish living in shallow waters, often found burrowing in the sand. [*Ammodytes tobianus* and other species.]

**sander** • n. a power tool used for smoothing a surface with sandpaper or other abrasive material.

**sanderling** /ˈsandəlɪŋ/ • n. a small migratory sandpiper, typically seen running after receding waves on the beach. [*Calidris alba*.]
– ORIGIN C17: of unknown origin.

**sanders** /ˈsɑːndəz, ˈsan-/ (also **sanderswood**) • n. the timber of the red sandalwood, from which a red dye is obtained.
– ORIGIN ME: from OFr. *sandre*, var. of *sandle* 'sandalwood'.

**sand flea** • n. **1** another term for **CHIGGER** (in sense 1). **2** another term for **SANDHOPPER**.

**sandfly** • n. (pl. **-flies**) **1** a small hairy biting fly of tropical and subtropical regions, which transmits a number of diseases. [*Phlebotomus* and other genera.] **2** Austral./NZ another term for **BLACKFLY** (in sense 2).

**sandglass** • n. an hourglass.

**Sandgroper** • n. Austral. informal a non-Aboriginal Western Australian.
– ORIGIN C19: so named because of the large amount of sand in Western Australia.

**sandgrouse** • n. (pl. same) a seed-eating ground-dwelling bird with brownish plumage, found in arid regions. [Genera *Pterocles* and *Syrrhaptes*: several species.]

**sandhi** /ˈsʌndi/ • n. Grammar the process whereby the form of a word changes as a result of its position in an utterance (e.g. the change from *a* to *an* before a vowel).
– ORIGIN from Sanskrit *saṃdhi* 'putting together'.

**sandhog** • n. N. Amer. a person doing construction work underground or under water.

**sandhopper** • n. a small seashore crustacean which typically lives among seaweed and leaps when disturbed. [*Orchestia* and other genera.]

**Sandinista** /ˌsandɪˈniːstə/ • n. a member of a left-wing Nicaraguan political organization, in power from 1979 until 1990.
– ORIGIN named after a similar organization founded by the nationalist leader Augusto César *Sandino*.

**sand iron** • n. Golf a sand wedge.

**sandiver** /ˈsandɪvə/ • n. scum on molten glass.
– ORIGIN ME: appar. from OFr. *suin de verre* 'exudation from glass', from *suer* 'to sweat' + *verre* 'glass'.

**S & L** • abbrev. savings and loan.

**sandlot** • n. N. Amer. **1** a piece of unoccupied land used by children for games. **2** [as modifier] denoting or relating to sport played by amateurs.

**sandman** • n. (**the sandman**) a fictional man supposed to make children sleep by sprinkling sand in their eyes.

**sand martin** • n. a small gregarious swallow with dark brown and white plumage, excavating nest holes in sandy banks near water. [*Riparia riparia* and other species.]

**sandpaper** • n. paper with sand or another abrasive stuck to it, used for smoothing wooden or other surfaces. • v. smooth with sandpaper.
– DERIVATIVES **sandpapery** adj.

**sandpiper** • n. a wading bird, typically long-billed and long-legged and frequenting coastal areas. [*Calidris*, *Tringa*, and other genera; family Scolopacidae: numerous species.]

**sandpit** • n. **1** Brit. a shallow box or hollow, partly filled with sand for children to play in. **2** a quarry from which sand is excavated.

**sand shark** • n. **1** a voracious brown-spotted tropical Atlantic shark. [*Odontaspis taurus*.] **2** a ray, dogfish, or small shark of shallow coastal waters.

**sandshoe** • n. chiefly Scottish & Austral./NZ a plimsoll.

**sandstone** • n. sedimentary rock consisting of sand or quartz grains cemented together, typically red, yellow, or brown in colour.

**sandstorm** • n. a strong wind in a desert carrying clouds of sand.

**sand wedge** • n. Golf a heavy, lofted iron used for hitting the ball out of sand.

**sandwich** /ˈsan(d)wɪdʒ, -wɪtʃ/ • n. **1** an item of food consisting of two pieces of bread with a filling between them. **2** Brit. a sponge cake of two or more layers with jam or cream between them. **3** [as modifier] of or relating to a sandwich course. • v. (**sandwich something between**) insert something between (two people or things). ➤(**sandwich things together**) squeeze two things together.
– ORIGIN C18: named after the 4th Earl of *Sandwich*, an Engl. nobleman said to have eaten food in this form.

**sandwich board** • n. a pair of advertisement boards connected by straps by which they are hung over a person's shoulders.

**sandwich course** • n. Brit. a training course with alternate periods of formal instruction and practical experience.

**sandwich tern** • n. a large crested tern found in Europe and the Americas. [*Thalassius sandvicensis*.]
– ORIGIN C18: named after *Sandwich*, a town in Kent.

**sandwort** • n. a low-growing plant of the pink family, typically having small white flowers and growing in dry sandy ground. [*Arenaria* and other genera.]

**sandy** • adj. (**-ier**, **-iest**) **1** covered in or consisting of sand. **2** (especially of hair) light yellowish brown.
– DERIVATIVES **sandiness** n. **sandyish** adj.
– ORIGIN OE *sandig* (see **SAND**, **-Y**[1]).

**sand yacht** • n. a wind-driven three-wheeled vehicle with a sail, used for racing on beaches.

**sandy blight** • n. Austral. conjunctivitis or trachoma with granular inflammation of the eyelids.

**sane** • adj. **1** of sound mind; not mad. **2** reasonable; sensible.
– DERIVATIVES **sanely** adv. **saneness** n.
– ORIGIN C17: from L. *sanus* 'healthy'.

**Sanforized** /ˈsanfərʌɪzd/ (also **-ised**) • adj. trademark (of cotton or other fabrics) pre-shrunk by a controlled compressive process.
– ORIGIN 1930s: from the name of the Amer. inventor *Sanford* L. Cluett.

**San Franciscan** /ˌsan franˈsɪskən/ • n. a native or inhabitant of San Francisco. • adj. of or relating to San Francisco.

**sang** past of **SING**.

**sangar** /ˈsaŋgə/ (also **sanga**) • n. a small protected structure built up from the ground, used for observing or firing from.
– ORIGIN C19: from Pashto, prob. from Pers. *sang* 'stone'.

**sangaree** /ˌsaŋgəˈriː/ • n. a cold drink of wine, water, and spices.
– ORIGIN from Sp. *sangría* (see **SANGRIA**).

**sangfroid** /sɒ̃ˈfrwɑː/ • n. composure or coolness under trying circumstances.
– ORIGIN C18: from Fr. *sang-froid*, lit. 'cold blood'.

**sangha** /ˈsʌŋɡə/ ● **n.** the Buddhist monastic order.
– ORIGIN from Sanskrit *saṃgha* 'community'.

**Sangiovese** /ˌsandʒɪə(ʊ)ˈveɪzi/ ● **n.** a variety of black wine grape used to make Chianti and other Italian red wines.
– ORIGIN from Ital.

**sangoma** /saŋˈɡɔːma/ ● **n.** (in southern Africa) a witch doctor.
– ORIGIN from Zulu *isangoma*.

**sangrail** /saŋˈɡreɪl/ (also **sangreal**) ● **n.** another term for **GRAIL**.
– ORIGIN ME: from OFr. *saint graal* 'Holy Grail'.

**sangria** /saŋˈɡriːə/ ● **n.** a Spanish drink of red wine, lemonade, fruit, and spices.
– ORIGIN Sp., lit. 'bleeding'; cf. **SANGAREE**.

**sanguinary** /ˈsaŋɡwɪn(ə)ri/ ● **adj.** chiefly archaic involving or causing much bloodshed.
– ORIGIN ME: from L. *sanguinarius*, from *sanguis, sanguin-* 'blood'.

**sanguine** /ˈsaŋɡwɪn/ ● **adj.** **1** cheerfully optimistic. **2** (in medieval medicine) having a predominance of blood among the bodily humours, supposedly marked by a ruddy complexion and an optimistic disposition. ➤ archaic (of the complexion) ruddy. **3** archaic bloody or bloodthirsty. **4** poetic/literary & Heraldry blood-red. ● **n.** a blood-red colour.
– DERIVATIVES **sanguinely** adv. **sanguineness** n.
– ORIGIN ME: from OFr. *sanguin(e)* 'blood red', from L. *sanguineus* 'of blood', from *sanguis, sanguin-* 'blood'.

**Sanhedrin** /ˈsanɪdrɪn, sanˈhiːdrɪn, sanˈhɛdrɪn/ (also **Sanhedrim** /-rɪm/) ● **n.** the highest court of justice and the supreme council in ancient Jerusalem.
– ORIGIN from late Heb. *sanhedrīn*, from Gk *sunedrion* 'council', from *sun-* 'with'+ *hedra* 'seat'.

**sanicle** /ˈsanɪk(ə)l/ ● **n.** a plant of the parsley family with burr-like fruit. [*Sanicula europaea* and other species.]
– ORIGIN ME: via OFr. from med. L. *sanicula*.

**sanidine** /ˈsanɪdiːn/ ● **n.** a glassy mineral of the alkali feldspar group.
– ORIGIN C19: from Gk *sanis, sanid-* 'board' + **-INE**[4].

**sanitarian** ● **n.** chiefly archaic a person responsible for public health or in favour of public health reform.
– ORIGIN C19: from **SANITARY** + **-IAN**.

**sanitarium** /ˌsanɪˈtɛːrɪəm/ ● **n.** (pl. **sanitariums** or **sanitaria** /-rɪə/) North American term for **SANATORIUM**.
– ORIGIN C19: pseudo-Latin, from L. *sanitas* 'health'.

**sanitary** ● **adj.** **1** of or relating to conditions affecting hygiene and health. **2** hygienic.
– DERIVATIVES **sanitarily** adv. **sanitariness** n.
– ORIGIN C19: from Fr. *sanitaire*, from L. *sanitas* 'health', from *sanus* 'healthy'.

**sanitary protection** ● **n.** sanitary towels and tampons collectively.

**sanitary towel** (N. Amer. **sanitary napkin**) ● **n.** an absorbent pad worn by women to absorb menstrual blood.

**sanitaryware** ● **n.** toilet bowls, cisterns, and other fittings.

**sanitation** ● **n.** conditions relating to public health.
– ORIGIN C19: formed irregularly from **SANITARY**.

**sanitize** (also **-ise**) ● **v.** **1** make hygienic. **2** derogatory make more acceptable.
– DERIVATIVES **sanitization** n. **sanitizer** n.

**sanity** ● **n.** the condition of being sane. ➤ reasonable and rational behaviour.
– ORIGIN ME: from L. *sanitas* 'health', from *sanus* 'healthy'.

**sank** past of **SINK**[1].

**sannyasi** /sənˈjɑːsi/ (also **sanyasi** or **sannyasin**) ● **n.** (pl. same) a Hindu religious mendicant.
– ORIGIN based on Sanskrit *saṃnyāsin* 'laying aside, ascetic', from *saṃ* 'together' + *ni* 'down' + *as* 'throw'.

**sans** /sanz/ ● **prep.** poetic/literary or humorous without.
– ORIGIN ME: from OFr. *sanz*, from L. *sine* 'without'.

**sans-culotte** /ˌsan(z)kjʊˈlɒt, French sɑ̃kylɔt/ ● **n.** **1** a lower-class Parisian republican in the French Revolution. **2** an extreme republican or revolutionary.
– DERIVATIVES **sans-culottism** n.
– ORIGIN Fr., lit. 'without knee breeches'.

**sansei** /ˈsanseɪ/ ● **n.** (pl. same) N. Amer. an American or Canadian whose grandparents immigrated from Japan. Compare with **NISEI** and **ISSEI**.
– ORIGIN 1940s: Japanese, from *san* 'third' + *sei* 'generation'.

**Sanskrit** /ˈsanskrɪt/ ● **n.** an ancient Indo-European language of India, still used as a language of religion and scholarship.
– DERIVATIVES **Sanskritic** adj. **Sanskritist** n.
– ORIGIN from Sanskrit *saṃskṛta* 'composed, elaborated', from *saṃ* 'together' + *kṛ* 'make' + the past part. ending *-ta*.

**sans serif** /san ˈsɛrɪf/ (also **sanserif**) Printing ● **n.** a style of type without serifs. ● **adj.** without serifs.
– ORIGIN C19: appar. from Fr. *sans* 'without' + **SERIF**.

**Santa Claus** (also informal **Santa**) ● **n.** Father Christmas.
– ORIGIN orig. a US usage, alt. of Du. dial. *Sante Klaas* 'St Nicholas'.

**santeria** /ˌsantɛˈriːə/ ● **n.** a pantheistic Afro-Cuban religious cult developed from the beliefs of the Yoruba people and having some elements of Catholicism.
– ORIGIN Sp., lit. 'holiness'.

**santero** /sanˈtɛːrəʊ/ ● **n.** (pl. **-os**) **1** (in Mexico and Spanish-speaking areas of the south-western US) a person who makes religious images. **2** a priest of the santeria cult.
– ORIGIN from Sp.

**santim** /ˈsantiːm/ ● **n.** a monetary unit of Latvia, equal to one hundredth of a lat.
– ORIGIN from Latvian *santims*, from Fr. *centime* + the Latvian masc. ending *-s*.

**santo** /ˈsantəʊ/ ● **n.** (pl. **-os**) (in Mexico and Spanish-speaking areas of the south-western US) a religious symbol, especially an image of a saint.
– ORIGIN from Sp. or Ital.

**santolina** /ˌsantəˈliːnə/ ● **n.** a plant of a genus including cotton lavender. [Genus *Santolina*.]
– ORIGIN mod. L., perh. an alt. of **SANTONICA**.

**santonica** /sanˈtɒnɪkə/ ● **n.** the dried flower heads of a wormwood plant, containing santonin.
– ORIGIN C17: from L. *Santonica* (*herba*) '(plant) of the Santoni', referring to a tribe of Aquitaine, France.

**santonin** /ˈsantənɪn/ ● **n.** Chemistry a toxic crystalline compound present in santonica and related plants, used as an anthelmintic.

**santoor** /sʌnˈtʊə/ ● **n.** an Indian musical instrument resembling a dulcimer.
– ORIGIN from Arab. *santīr*, alt. of Gk *psaltērion* 'psaltery'.

**sanyasi** ● **n.** variant spelling of **SANNYASI**.

**saola** /ˈʃaʊlɑː/ ● **n.** a small two-horned mammal discovered in Vietnam in 1992, with similarities to both antelopes and oxen. [*Pseudoryx nghetinhensis*.]
– ORIGIN local name, lit. 'spindle horn'.

**sap**[1] ● **n.** **1** the fluid, chiefly water with dissolved sugars and mineral salts, circulating in the vascular system of a plant. **2** vigour or energy. ● **v.** (**sapped**, **sapping**) gradually weaken (a person's strength or power). ➤ (**sap someone of**) drain someone of (strength or power).
– DERIVATIVES **sapless** adj.
– ORIGIN OE *sæp*, prob. of Gmc origin; the verb is derived orig. from the verb **SAP**[2], in the sense 'undermine'.

**sap**[2] ● **n.** historical a tunnel or trench to conceal an assailant's approach to a fortified place. ● **v.** (**sapped**, **sapping**) **1** historical dig a sap. **2** archaic make insecure by removing the foundations. **3** [often as noun **sapping**] Geography undercut by water or glacial action.
– ORIGIN C16: from Fr. *saper*, from Ital. *zappare*, from *zappa* 'spade, spadework', prob. from Arab. *sarab* 'underground passage', or *sabora* 'probe a wound, explore'.

**sap**[3] ● **n.** informal, chiefly N. Amer. a foolish person.
– ORIGIN C19: abbrev. of dial. *sapskull* 'person with a head like sapwood'.

**sap**[4] N. Amer. informal ● **n.** a bludgeon or club. ● **v.** (**sapped**, **sapping**) hit with a sap.
– ORIGIN C19: abbrev. of **SAPLING**.

**sapele** /səˈpiːli/ ● **n.** a large tropical African hardwood

tree, with reddish-brown wood resembling mahogany. [Genus *Entandrophragma*.]
– ORIGIN C20: from the name of a port on the Benin River, Nigeria.

**sap green** ● n. a vivid yellowish-green pigment made from buckthorn berries.

**saphenous** /sə'fi:nəs/ ● adj. Anatomy relating to or denoting either of the two large superficial veins in the leg.
– ORIGIN C19: from med. L. *saphena* 'vein' + **-OUS**.

**sapid** /'sapɪd/ ● adj. chiefly N. Amer. **1** flavoursome. **2** pleasant or interesting.
– DERIVATIVES **sapidity** /sə'pɪdɪti/ n.
– ORIGIN C17: from L. *sapidus*, from *sapere* 'to taste'.

**sapient** /'seɪpɪənt/ ● adj. **1** formal wise, or attempting to appear wise. **2** of or relating to the human species (*Homo sapiens*).
– DERIVATIVES **sapience** n. **sapiently** adv.
– ORIGIN ME: from OFr., or from L. *sapient-*, *sapere* 'to be wise'.

**sapiential** ● adj. poetic/literary of or relating to wisdom.
– ORIGIN C15: from OFr., or from eccles. L. *sapientialis*, from L. *sapientia* 'wisdom'.

**sapling** ● n. **1** a young, slender tree. **2** poetic/literary a young and slender or inexperienced person. **3** a greyhound in its first year.
– ORIGIN ME: from **SAP**[1] + **-LING**.

**sapodilla** /ˌsapə'dɪlə/ ● n. **1** a large evergreen tropical American tree which has hard durable wood and yields chicle. [*Manilkara zapota*.] **2** (also **sapodilla plum**) the sweet brownish bristly fruit of this tree.
– ORIGIN C17: from Sp. *zapotillo*, dimin. of *zapote*, from Nahuatl *tzápotl*.

**saponaceous** /ˌsapə'neɪʃəs/ ● adj. soapy.
– ORIGIN C18: from mod. L. *saponaceus* (from L. *sapo*, *sapon-* 'soap') + **-OUS**.

**saponify** /sə'pɒnɪfʌɪ/ ● v. (**-ies**, **-ied**) Chemistry turn (fat or oil) into soap by reaction with an alkali. ➤ convert (any ester) into an alcohol and a salt by alkaline hydrolysis.
– DERIVATIVES **saponifiable** adj. **saponification** n.
– ORIGIN C19: from Fr. *saponifier*, from L. *sapo*, *sapon-* 'soap'.

**saponin** /'sapənɪn/ ● n. Chemistry any of a class of toxic compounds which foam when shaken with water, found in soapwort and other plants.
– ORIGIN C19: from Fr. *saponine*, from L. *sapo*, *sapon-* 'soap'.

**sapper** ● n. **1** a military engineer who lays or detects and disarms mines. **2** Brit. a soldier in the Corps of Royal Engineers.
– ORIGIN C17: from **SAP**[2] + **-ER**[1].

**sapphic** /'safɪk/ ● adj. **1** (**Sapphic**) of or relating to the Greek lyric poet Sappho, or her poetry expressing love and affection for women. **2** formal or humorous of or relating to lesbians or lesbianism. ● n. (**sapphics**) verse in a metre associated with Sappho.
– ORIGIN C16: from Fr. *saphique*, via L. from Gk *Sapphikos*, from *Sapphō*.

**sapphire** /'safʌɪə/ ● n. **1** a transparent precious stone, typically blue, which is a form of corundum. **2** a bright blue colour. **3** a hummingbird with shining blue or violet plumage. [*Hylocharis* and other genera.]
– DERIVATIVES **sapphirine** /'safɪrʌɪn/ adj.
– ORIGIN ME: from OFr. *safir*, via L. from Gk *sappheiros*, prob. denoting lapis lazuli.

**sapphism** /'safɪz(ə)m/ ● n. formal or humorous lesbianism.

**sappy** ● adj. (**-ier**, **-iest**) **1** informal, chiefly N. Amer. oversentimental. **2** (of a plant) containing a lot of sap.
– DERIVATIVES **sappily** adv. **sappiness** n.

**sapro-** ● comb. form Biology relating to putrefaction or decay: *saprogenic*.
– ORIGIN from Gk *sapros* 'putrid'.

**saprogenic** /ˌsaprə(ʊ)'dʒɛnɪk/ ● adj. Biology causing or produced by putrefaction or decay.

**saprophagous** /sa'prɒfəgəs/ ● adj. Biology feeding on decaying matter.
– DERIVATIVES **saprophage** n.

**saprophyte** /'saprə(ʊ)fʌɪt/ ● n. Biology a plant, fungus, or micro-organism that lives on decaying matter.
– DERIVATIVES **saprophytic** adj. **saprophytically** adv.

**saprotrophic** ● adj. Biology feeding on decaying organic matter.

**sapsucker** ● n. an American woodpecker that pecks rows of small holes in trees and visits them for sap and insects. [*Sphyrapicus*: four species.]

**sapwood** ● n. the soft outer layers of new wood between the heartwood and the bark.

**SAR** ● abbrev. search and rescue (an emergency service).

**saraband** /'sarəband/ (also **sarabande**) ● n. a slow, stately Spanish dance in triple time. ➤ a piece of music for this.
– ORIGIN C17: from Fr. *sarabande*, from Sp. and Ital. *zarabanda*.

**Saracen** /'sarəs(ə)n/ ● n. **1** an Arab or Muslim, especially at the time of the Crusades. **2** a nomad of the Syrian and Arabian desert at the time of the Roman Empire.
– DERIVATIVES **Saracenic** adj.
– ORIGIN ME, from OFr. *sarrazin*, via late L. from late Gk *Sarakēnos*, perh. from Arab. *šarḳī* 'eastern'.

**Saracen's head** ● n. a conventionalized depiction of the head of a Saracen as a heraldic charge or inn sign.

**Saran** /sə'ran/ (also **Saran Wrap**) ● n. N. Amer. trademark cling film.
– ORIGIN 1940s: of unknown origin.

**sarangi** /sə'raŋgi, sɑː'rʌŋgi/ ● n. (pl. **sarangis**) an Indian stringed instrument played with a bow.
– ORIGIN from Hindi *sāraṅgī*.

**sarape** /sɛ'rɑːpeɪ/ ● n. variant of **SERAPE**.

**sarcasm** ● n. the use of irony to mock or convey contempt.
– DERIVATIVES **sarcastic** adj. **sarcastically** adv.
– ORIGIN C16: from Fr. *sarcasme*, or via late L. from late Gk *sarkasmos*, from Gk *sarkazein* 'tear flesh', in late Gk 'gnash the teeth, speak bitterly' (from *sarx*, *sark-* 'flesh').

**sarcenet** ● n. variant spelling of **SARSENET**.

**sarcoid** /'sɑːkɔɪd/ ● n. Medicine a disease in which the lymph nodes become enlarged and granulomas appear in reticuloendothelial tissue. ➤ a granuloma of this type.
– DERIVATIVES **sarcoidosis** n.
– ORIGIN C19 (in the sense 'resembling flesh'): from Gk *sarx*, *sark-* 'flesh' + **-OID**.

**sarcolemma** /'sɑːkəʊˌlɛmə/ ● n. Physiology the fine transparent tubular sheath enveloping the fibres of skeletal muscles.
– DERIVATIVES **sarcolemmal** adj.
– ORIGIN C19: from Gk *sarx*, *sark-* 'flesh' + *lemma* 'husk'.

**sarcoma** /sɑː'kəʊmə/ ● n. (pl. **sarcomas** or **sarcomata** /-mətə/) Medicine a malignant tumour of connective or other non-epithelial tissue.
– DERIVATIVES **sarcomatosis** n. **sarcomatous** adj.
– ORIGIN C19: mod. L., from Gk *sarkōma*, from *sarkoun* 'become fleshy', from *sarx*, *sark-* 'flesh'.

**sarcomere** /'sɑːkə(ʊ)mɪə/ ● n. Anatomy a structural unit of a myofibril in striated muscle.
– ORIGIN C19: from Gk *sarx*, *sark-* 'flesh' + *meros* 'part'.

**sarcophagus** /sɑː'kɒfəgəs/ ● n. (pl. **sarcophagi** /-gʌɪ, -dʒʌɪ/) a stone coffin, typically associated with ancient Egypt, Rome, and Greece.
– ORIGIN ME: via L. from Gk *sarkophagos* 'flesh-consuming', from *sarx*, *sark-* 'flesh' + *-phagos* '-eating'.

**sarcoplasm** /'sɑːkə(ʊ)plaz(ə)m/ ● n. Physiology the cytoplasm of striated muscle cells.
– DERIVATIVES **sarcoplasmic** adj.
– ORIGIN C19: from Gk *sarx*, *sark-* 'flesh' + **PLASMA**.

**sarcoptic mange** /sɑː'kɒptɪk/ ● n. a form of mange chiefly affecting the abdomen and hindquarters.
– ORIGIN C19: from mod. L. *Sarcoptes* (genus name of the itch mite, from Gk *sarx*, *sark-* 'flesh') + **-IC**.

**Sard** /sɑːd/ ● adj. & n. another term for **SARDINIAN**.

**sard** /sɑːd/ ● n. a yellow or brownish-red variety of chalcedony.
– ORIGIN ME: from Fr. *sarde* or L. *sarda*, from Gk *sardios*, prob. from *Sardō* 'Sardinia'.

**sardar** /'sədɑː/ (also **sirdar**) ● n. chiefly Indian **1** a leader. **2** a

Sikh.
– ORIGIN from Pers. and Urdu *sar-dār*.

**sardelle** /sɑːˈdɛl/ ● **n.** a sardine, anchovy, or other small fish similarly prepared for eating.
– ORIGIN C16: from Ital. *sardella*, dimin. of *sarda* (see **SARDINE**[1]).

**sardine**[1] /sɑːˈdiːn/ ● **n. 1** a young pilchard or other young or small herring-like fish. **2** (**sardines**) [treated as sing.] Brit. a children's game in which one child hides and the other children, as they find the hider, join him or her in the hiding place. ● **v.** informal pack closely together.
– PHRASES **packed like sardines** crowded close together, as sardines in tins.
– ORIGIN ME: from Fr., or from L. *sardina*, from *sarda*, from Gk, prob. from *Sardō* 'Sardinia'.

**sardine**[2] /ˈsɑːdʌɪn/ ● **n.** another term for **SARDIUS**.
– ORIGIN ME: via late L. from Gk *sardinos*, var. of *sardios* (see **SARDIUS**).

**Sardinian** ● **adj.** of or relating to Sardinia, its people, or their language. ● **n. 1** a native or inhabitant of Sardinia. **2** the Romance language of Sardinia, which has several distinct dialects.

**sardius** /ˈsɑːdɪəs/ ● **n.** a red precious stone mentioned in the Bible (e.g. Exod. 28:17) and in classical writings, probably ruby or carnelian.
– ORIGIN ME: via late L. from Gk *sardios*.

**sardonic** /sɑːˈdɒnɪk/ ● **adj.** grimly mocking or cynical.
– DERIVATIVES **sardonically** adv. **sardonicism** n.
– ORIGIN C17: from Fr. *sardonique*, earlier *sardonien*, via L. from Gk *sardonios* 'of Sardinia', alt. of *sardanios*, used by Homer to describe bitter or scornful laughter.

**sardonyx** /ˈsɑːdənɪks/ ● **n.** onyx in which white layers alternate with sard.
– ORIGIN ME: via L. from Gk *sardonux*, prob. from *sardios* 'sardius' + *onux* 'onyx'.

**saree** ● **n.** variant spelling of **SARI**.

**sargassum** /sɑːˈgasəm/ (also **sargasso**) ● **n.** a brown seaweed with berry-like air bladders, typically floating in large masses. [Genus *Sargassum*.]
– ORIGIN C16 (as *sargasso*): mod. L., from Port. *sargaço*, of unknown origin.

**sarge** ● **n.** informal sergeant.

**sari** /ˈsɑːri/ (also **saree**) ● **n.** (pl. **saris** or **sarees**) a garment consisting of a length of cotton or silk elaborately draped around the body, traditionally worn by women from the Indian subcontinent.
– ORIGIN C18: from Hindi *sāṛī*.

**sarin** /ˈsɑːrɪn/ ● **n.** an organophosphorus nerve gas, developed during the Second World War.
– ORIGIN from Ger. *Sarin*, of unknown origin.

**sark** ● **n.** Scottish & N. English a shirt or chemise.
– ORIGIN OE *serc*, of Gmc origin.

**sarkar** /səˈkɑː/ ● **n.** Indian a man in a position of authority, especially a landowner.
– ORIGIN from Pers. and Urdu *sarkār*, from *sar* 'chief' + *kār* 'agent, doer'.

**sarking** ● **n.** boarding or building felt between the rafters of a roof and the tiles.
– ORIGIN ME: from **SARK** + **-ING**[1].

**sarky** ● **adj.** (**-ier**, **-iest**) Brit. informal sarcastic.
– DERIVATIVES **sarkily** adv. **sarkiness** n.

**sarnie** ● **n.** Brit. informal a sandwich.

**sarod** /səˈrəʊd/ ● **n.** a lute used in classical North Indian music.
– ORIGIN Urdu, from Pers. *surod* 'song, melody'.

**sarong** /səˈrɒŋ/ ● **n.** a garment consisting of a long piece of cloth wrapped round the body and tucked at the waist or under the armpits, traditionally worn in SE Asia and now also by Western women.
– ORIGIN C19: Malay, lit. 'sheath'.

**saros** /ˈsɛːrɒs/ ● **n.** Astronomy a period of about 18 years between repetitions of solar and lunar eclipses.
– ORIGIN C19: from Gk, from Babylonian *šār(u)* '3,600 (years)', the sense appar. based on a misinterpretation of the number.

**sarrusophone** /səˈrʌsəfəʊn/ ● **n.** a member of a family of wind instruments similar to saxophones but with a double reed.
– ORIGIN C19: from the name of a Fr. bandmaster W. *Sarrus* + **-PHONE**.

**sarsaparilla** /ˌsɑːs(ə)pəˈrɪlə/ ● **n. 1** a preparation of the dried rhizomes of various plants, especially smilax, used to flavour some drinks and medicines and formerly as a tonic. ➤a sweet drink flavoured with this. **2** the tropical American climbing plant from which these rhizomes are obtained. [*Smilax regelii* and other species.]
– ORIGIN C16: from Sp. *zarzaparilla*, from *zarza* 'bramble' + a dimin. of *parra* 'vine'.

**sarsen** /ˈsɑːs(ə)n/ ● **n.** a silicified sandstone boulder of a kind used at Stonehenge and in other prehistoric monuments in southern England.
– ORIGIN C17: prob. a var. of **SARACEN**.

**sarsenet** /ˈsɑːsnɪt/ (also **sarcenet**) ● **n.** a fine soft silk fabric.
– ORIGIN ME: from Anglo-Norman Fr. *sarzinett*, perh. a dimin. of *sarzin* 'Saracen', suggested by OFr. *drap sarrasinois* 'Saracen cloth'.

**sartorial** /sɑːˈtɔːrɪəl/ ● **adj.** of or relating to tailoring, clothes, or style of dress.
– DERIVATIVES **sartorially** adv.
– ORIGIN C19: from L. *sartor* 'tailor' (from *sarcire* 'to patch') + **-IAL**.

**sartorius** /sɑːˈtɔːrɪəs/ ● **n.** Anatomy a long, narrow muscle running obliquely across the front of each thigh.
– ORIGIN C18: mod. L., from L. *sartor* 'tailor' (because the muscle is used when sitting cross-legged, a position assoc. with tailors).

**SAS** ● **abbrev.** Special Air Service.

**SASE** ● **abbrev.** N. Amer. self-addressed stamped envelope.

**sash**[1] ● **n.** a long strip or loop of cloth worn over one shoulder or round the waist.
– DERIVATIVES **sashed** adj. **sashless** adj.
– ORIGIN C16 (earlier as *shash*, denoting fabric worn as a turban): from Arab. *šāš* 'muslin, turban'.

**sash**[2] ● **n.** a frame holding the glass in a window, typically one of two sliding frames in a sash window.
– DERIVATIVES **sashed** adj.
– ORIGIN C17: alt. of **CHASSIS**, interpreted as pl.

**sashay** /saˈʃeɪ/ ● **v.** informal, chiefly N. Amer. **1** walk ostentatiously, with exaggerated hip and shoulder movements. **2** perform the sashay. ● **n.** (in American square dancing) a figure in which partners circle each other by taking sideways steps.
– ORIGIN C19 (as v.): alt. of **CHASSÉ**.

**sash cord** ● **n.** a strong cord attaching either of the weights of a sash window to a sash.

**sashimi** /ˈsaʃɪmi/ ● **n.** a Japanese dish of bite-sized pieces of raw fish eaten with soy sauce and horseradish paste.
– ORIGIN from Japanese.

**sash weight** ● **n.** a weight attached by a cord to each side of the sash of a sash window to balance it at any height.

**sash window** ● **n.** a window with one or two sashes which can be slid vertically to open it.

**sasine** /ˈseɪsɪn/ ● **n. 1** Scots Law investment by registration of a deed transferring ownership of property. ➤an act or record of this. **2** historical the conferring of possession of feudal property.
– ORIGIN C17: var. of **SEISIN**.

**Sask.** ● **abbrev.** Saskatchewan.

**Sasquatch** /ˈsaskwatʃ, -wɒtʃ/ ● **n.** another name for **BIGFOOT**.
– ORIGIN C20: Salish.

**sass** N. Amer. informal ● **n.** cheek. ● **v.** be cheeky to.
– ORIGIN C19: var. of **SAUCE**.

**sassafras** /ˈsasəfras/ ● **n. 1** a deciduous North American tree with aromatic leaves and bark. [*Sassafras albidum*.] **2** an extract of the leaves or bark of this tree, used medicinally or in perfumery.
– ORIGIN C16: from Sp. *sasafrás*, based on L. *saxifraga* 'saxifrage'.

**Sassanian** /saˈseɪnɪən/ (also **Sassanid** /ˈsasənɪd/) ● **adj.** of or relating to a dynasty that ruled Persia from the

early 3rd century AD until 651. ● **n.** a member of this dynasty.
– ORIGIN from *Sasan* (the name of the grandfather or father of Ardashir, the first Sassanian) + **-IAN**.

**Sassenach** /ˈsasənax, -nak/ Scottish & Irish derogatory ● **n.** an English person. ● **adj.** English.
– ORIGIN C18 (as n.): from Sc. Gaelic *Sasunnoch*, Ir. *Sasanach*, from L. *Saxones* 'Saxons'.

**sassy** ● **adj.** (**-ier**, **-iest**) informal, chiefly N. Amer. bold and spirited; cheeky.
– DERIVATIVES **sassily** adv. **sassiness** n.
– ORIGIN C19: var. of **SAUCY**.

**sastrugi** /saˈstruːgi/ ● **pl. n.** parallel wave-like ridges caused by winds on the surface of hard snow.
– ORIGIN C19: from Russ. *zastrugi* 'small ridges'.

**SAT** ● **abbrev. 1** trademark (in the US) Scholastic Aptitude Test. **2** standard assessment task.

**Sat.** ● **abbrev.** Saturday.

**sat** past and past participle of **SIT**.

**Satan** ● **n.** the Devil; Lucifer.
– ORIGIN OE, via late L. and Gk from Heb. *śāṭān*, lit. 'adversary', from *śāṭan* 'plot against'.

**satang** /ˈsataŋ/ ● **n.** (pl. same or **satangs**) a monetary unit of Thailand, equal to one hundredth of a baht.
– ORIGIN Thai, from Pali *sata* 'hundred'.

**satanic** ● **adj. 1** of or characteristic of Satan. **2** connected with satanism.
– DERIVATIVES **satanically** adv.

**satanic abuse** ● **n.** another term for **RITUAL ABUSE**.

**satanism** ● **n.** the worship of Satan, typically involving a travesty of Christian symbols and practices.
– DERIVATIVES **satanist** n. & adj.

**satanize** (also **-ise**) ● **v.** rare portray as satanic or evil.

**satay** /ˈsateɪ/ (also **saté**) ● **n.** an Indonesian and Malaysian dish consisting of small pieces of meat grilled on a skewer and served with spiced sauce.
– ORIGIN from Malay *satai*, Indonesian *sate*.

**SATB** ● **abbrev.** soprano, alto, tenor, and bass (as a combination of singing voices required for a piece of music).

**satchel** ● **n.** a shoulder bag with a long strap, used especially for school books.
– ORIGIN ME: from OFr. *sachel*, from L. *saccellus* 'small bag'.

**satcom** (also **SATCOM**) ● **n.** satellite communications.

**sate**[1] ● **v. 1** satisfy fully. **2** supply with as much as or more than is desired or can be managed.
– DERIVATIVES **sateless** adj. (poetic/literary).
– ORIGIN C17: prob. an alt. of dial. *sade*, from OE *sadian* 'become sated or weary' (rel. to **SAD**); the spelling was influenced by **SATIATE**.

**sate**[2] ● **v.** archaic spelling of **SAT**.

**saté** ● **n.** variant spelling of **SATAY**.

**sateen** /saˈtiːn/ ● **n.** a cotton fabric woven like satin with a glossy surface.
– ORIGIN C19: alt. of **SATIN**, on the pattern of *velveteen*.

**satellite** ● **n. 1** an artificial body placed in orbit round the earth or another planet to collect information or for communication. ➤ [as modifier] using or relating to satellite technology. ➤ satellite television. **2** Astronomy a celestial body orbiting a planet. **3** a thing separate from something else but dependent on or controlled by it. ➤ a small town, country, etc. dependent on another. **4** Biology a portion of DNA with repeating base sequences and of different density from the main sequence.
– ORIGIN C16 (in the sense 'follower, obsequious underling'): from Fr. *satellite* or L. *satelles*, *satellit-* 'attendant'.

**satellite dish** ● **n.** a bowl-shaped aerial with which signals are transmitted to or received from a communications satellite.

**satellite television** ● **n.** television in which the signals are broadcast via satellite.

**sati** ● **n.** (pl. **satis**) variant spelling of **SUTTEE**.

**satiate** /ˈseɪʃɪeɪt/ ● **v.** another term for **SATE**[1]. ● **adj.** archaic fully satisfied.
– DERIVATIVES **satiable** adj. (archaic). **satiation** n.
– ORIGIN ME: from L. *satiatus*, past part. of *satiare*, from *satis* 'enough'.

**satiety** /səˈtʌɪɪti/ ● **n.** the feeling or state of being sated.
– ORIGIN C16: from OFr. *saciete*, from L. *satietas*, from *satis* 'enough'.

**satin** ● **n. 1** a smooth, glossy fabric, usually of silk, produced by a weave in which the threads of the warp are caught and looped by the weft only at certain intervals. **2** [as modifier] denoting or having a smooth, glossy surface or finish. ● **v.** (**satined**, **satining**) give a satin surface to.
– DERIVATIVES **satinize** (also **-ise**) v. **satiny** adj.
– ORIGIN ME: via OFr. from Arab. *zaytūnī* 'of Tsinkiang', a town in China.

**satinette** /ˌsatɪˈnɛt, ˈsatɪnɪt/ (also **satinet**) ● **n.** a satin-like fabric of cotton or synthetic fibre.

**satin spar** ● **n.** a fibrous variety of gypsum.

**satin stitch** ● **n.** a long straight embroidery stitch, giving the appearance of satin.

**satinwood** ● **n. 1** glossy yellowish wood valued for cabinetwork. **2** the tropical tree that produces this wood. [*Chloroxylon swietenia* (India and Sri Lanka), *Zanthoxylum flava* (Caribbean region), and other species.]

**satire** /ˈsatʌɪə/ ● **n. 1** the use of humour, irony, exaggeration, or ridicule to expose and criticize people's stupidity or vices. **2** a play, novel, etc. using satire. ➤ (in Latin literature) a literary miscellany, especially a poem ridiculing prevalent vices or follies.
– DERIVATIVES **satirist** n.
– ORIGIN C16: from Fr., or from L. *satira*, later form of *satura* 'poetic medley'.

**satiric** /səˈtɪrɪk/ ● **adj.** another term for **SATIRICAL**.

**satirical** ● **adj.** containing or using satire. ➤ sarcastic; humorously critical.
– DERIVATIVES **satirically** adv.
– ORIGIN C16: from late L. *satiricus* (from *satira*: see **SATIRE**) + **-AL**.

**satirize** /ˈsatɪrʌɪz/ (also **-ise**) ● **v.** deride and criticize by means of satire.
– DERIVATIVES **satirization** n.

**satisfaction** ● **n. 1** the state of being satisfied. **2** Law the payment of a debt or fulfilment of an obligation or claim. **3** [with neg.] what is felt to be owed or due to one. **4** Christian Theology Christ's atonement for sin. **5** historical the chance to defend one's honour in a duel.
– ORIGIN ME: from OFr., or from L. *satisfactio(n-)*, from *satisfacere* (see **SATISFY**).

**satisfactory** ● **adj.** fulfilling expectations or needs; acceptable.
– DERIVATIVES **satisfactorily** adv. **satisfactoriness** n.
– ORIGIN ME: from OFr. *satisfactoire* or med. L. *satisfactorius*, from L. *satisfacere* (see **SATISFY**).

**satisfice** /ˈsatɪsfʌɪs/ ● **v.** formal satisfy only the minimum requirements necessary to achieve a particular goal.
– ORIGIN C16: alt. of **SATISFY**, influenced by L. *satisfacere*.

**satisfy** ● **v.** (**-ies**, **-ied**) **1** meet the expectations, needs, or desires of. ➤ fulfil (a desire or need). **2** provide with adequate information about or proof of something. **3** comply with (a condition, obligation, or demand). ➤ pay off (a debt or creditor). **4** Mathematics (of a quantity) make (an equation) true.
– DERIVATIVES **satisfiability** n. **satisfiable** adj. **satisfied** adj. **satisfying** adj. **satisfyingly** adv.
– ORIGIN ME: from OFr. *satisfier*, formed irregularly from L. *satisfacere* 'to content', from *satis* 'enough' + *facere* 'make'.

**satnav** /ˈsatnav/ ● **n.** navigation using information from satellites.

**satori** /səˈtɔːri/ ● **n.** Buddhism sudden enlightenment.
– ORIGIN Japanese, lit. 'awakening'.

**satrap** /ˈsatrap/ ● **n. 1** a provincial governor in the ancient Persian empire. **2** a subordinate or local ruler.
– ORIGIN ME: from OFr. *satrape* or L. *satrapa*, based on Old Pers. *kšathra-pāvan* 'country-protector'.

**satrapy** /ˈsatrəpi/ ● **n.** (pl. **-ies**) a province governed by a satrap.

**satsuma** /satˈsuːmə/ ● **n. 1** a tangerine of a hardy loose-skinned variety, originally grown in Japan. **2** /also ˈsatsʊmə, -sjʊ-/ (**Satsuma** or **Satsuma ware**) Japanese pottery, often elaborately painted, with a crackled cream-

coloured glaze.
– ORIGIN C19: named after the former Japanese province of *Satsuma*.

**saturate** • v. /ˈsatʃəreɪt/ **1** soak thoroughly with water or other liquid. **2** cause to combine with, dissolve, or hold the greatest possible quantity of another substance. ➤(usu. **be saturated with**) fill until no more can be held or absorbed. **3** magnetize or charge (a substance or device) fully. **4** supply (a market) beyond the point at which the demand for a product is satisfied. **5** overwhelm (an enemy target) by concentrated bombing. • n. /ˈsatʃərət/ a saturated fat.
– DERIVATIVES **saturable** adj.
– ORIGIN ME (as adj. meaning 'satisfied'): from L. *saturat-*, *saturare* 'fill, glut', from *satur* 'full'.

**saturated** • adj. **1** Chemistry (of a solution) containing the largest possible amount of solute. **2** Chemistry (of an organic molecule) containing the greatest possible number of hydrogen atoms, without double or triple bonds. **3** (of colour) bright, rich, and free from an admixture of white.

**saturation** • n. **1** the action of saturating or state of being saturated. **2** [as modifier] to the fullest extent.

**saturation diving** • n. diving in which the diver's bloodstream is saturated with helium or other gas at the pressure of the surrounding water, so that decompression time is independent of the duration of the dive.

**saturation point** • n. the stage beyond which no more can be absorbed or accepted.

**Saturday** • n. the day of the week before Sunday and following Friday. • adv. chiefly N. Amer. on Saturday. ➤(**Saturdays**) on Saturdays; each Saturday.
– ORIGIN OE *Sæter(es)dæg*, translation of L. *Saturni dies* 'day of Saturn'.

**Saturday night special** • n. informal, chiefly N. Amer. a cheap low-calibre pistol or revolver.

**Saturn** • n. a planet of the solar system, sixth in order from the sun and circled by broad flat rings.
– DERIVATIVES **Saturnian** adj.

**Saturnalia** /ˌsatəˈneɪlɪə/ • n. [treated as sing. or pl.] the ancient Roman festival of Saturn in December, a period of unrestrained merrymaking. ➤(**saturnalia**) an occasion of wild revelry.
– DERIVATIVES **saturnalian** adj.
– ORIGIN L., lit. 'matters relating to Saturn', neut. pl. of *Saturnalis*.

**saturniid** /səˈtəːnɪɪd/ • n. Entomology a moth of a family (Saturniidae) which includes the emperor moths and the giant Indian silk moths.
– ORIGIN C19: from mod. L. *Saturniidae*, from the genus name *Saturnia*.

**saturnine** /ˈsatənʌɪn/ • adj. **1** gloomy. ➤(of looks, etc.) dark and brooding. **2** archaic of or relating to lead.
– DERIVATIVES **saturninely** adv.
– ORIGIN ME: from OFr. *saturnin*, from med. L. *Saturninus* 'of Saturn' (identified with lead by alchemists and assoc. with slowness and gloom by astrologers).

**saturnism** • n. archaic lead poisoning.
– DERIVATIVES **saturnic** adj.
– ORIGIN C19: from *Saturn* in the obs. alchemical sense 'lead' + **-ISM**.

**satyagraha** /sʌˈtjɑːgrəhɑː/ • n. passive political resistance, especially as advocated by Mahatma Gandhi against British rule in India.
– ORIGIN Sanskrit, from *satya* 'truth' + *āgraha* 'obstinacy'.

**satyr** /ˈsatə/ • n. **1** Greek Mythology one of a class of lustful, drunken woodland gods, represented as a man with a horse's ears and tail or (in Roman representations) with a goat's ears, tail, legs, and horns. **2** a man with strong sexual desires. **3** a butterfly with chiefly dark brown wings. [*Satyrus* and other genera.]
– DERIVATIVES **satyric** adj.
– ORIGIN ME: from OFr. *satyre*, or via L. from Gk *saturos*.

**satyriasis** /ˌsatɪˈrʌɪəsɪs/ • n. excessive sexual desire in a man.
– ORIGIN ME: via late L. from Gk *saturiasis*, from *saturos* (see **SATYR**).

**sauce** • n. **1** thick liquid served with food to add moistness and flavour. **2** N. Amer. stewed fruit, especially apples. **3** (**the sauce**) informal, chiefly N. Amer. alcoholic drink. **4** informal, chiefly Brit. impertinence. • v. **1** (usu. **be sauced**) season with a sauce. **2** make more interesting and exciting. **3** informal be impudent to.
– DERIVATIVES **sauceless** adj.
– ORIGIN ME: from OFr., based on L. *salsus* 'salted', past part. of *salere* 'to salt', from *sal* 'salt'; cf. **SALAD**.

**sauce boat** • n. a long, narrow jug for serving sauce.

**sauced** • adj. informal, chiefly N. Amer. drunk.

**saucepan** • n. a deep cooking pan, typically round, made of metal, and with one long handle and a lid.
– DERIVATIVES **saucepanful** n. (pl. **-fuls**).

**saucer** • n. a shallow dish, typically with a central circular indentation, on which a cup is placed.
– DERIVATIVES **saucerful** n. (pl. **-fuls**). **saucerless** adj.
– ORIGIN ME: from OFr. *saussier(e)* 'sauce boat', prob. suggested by late L. *salsarium*.

**saucier** /ˈsəʊsɪeɪ/ • n. a chef who prepares sauces.
– ORIGIN from Fr.

**saucy** • adj. (**-ier**, **-iest**) informal **1** chiefly Brit. sexually suggestive, typically in a humorous way. **2** chiefly N. Amer. bold, lively, and spirited. **3** chiefly N. Amer. covered with sauce.
– DERIVATIVES **saucily** adv. **sauciness** n.

**saudade** /saʊˈdɑːdə/ • n. a feeling of longing or melancholy supposedly characteristic of the Portuguese or Brazilian temperament.
– ORIGIN from Port.

**Saudi** /ˈsaʊdi, ˈsɔːdi/ • n. (pl. **Saudis**) a citizen of Saudi Arabia, or a member of its ruling dynasty. • adj. of or relating to Saudi Arabia or its ruling dynasty.
– ORIGIN from the name of Abdul-Aziz ibn *Saud*, first king of Saudi Arabia.

**Saudi Arabian** • n. a native or inhabitant of Saudi Arabia. • adj. of or relating to Saudi Arabia.

**sauerkraut** /ˈsaʊəkraʊt/ • n. a German dish of chopped pickled cabbage.
– ORIGIN from Ger., from *sauer* 'sour' + *Kraut* 'vegetable'.

**sauger** /ˈsɔːgə/ • n. a slender North American pikeperch with silver eyes, which is active at twilight and at night. [*Stizostedion canadense*.]
– ORIGIN C19: of unknown origin.

**sauna** /ˈsɔːnə/ • n. **1** a small room used as a hot-air or steam bath for cleaning and refreshing the body. **2** a session in a sauna.
– ORIGIN C19: from Finnish.

**saunter** • v. walk in a slow, relaxed manner. • n. a leisurely stroll.
– DERIVATIVES **saunterer** n.
– ORIGIN ME (in the sense 'to muse'): of unknown origin.

**-saur** • comb. form forming names of reptiles, especially extinct ones: *ichthyosaur*. See word-formation panel.
– ORIGIN mod. L., from Gk *sauros* 'lizard'; cf. **-SAURUS**, a suffix of mod. L. genus names.

**saurian** /ˈsɔːrɪən/ • adj. of or like a lizard. • n. a large reptile, especially a dinosaur.
– ORIGIN C19: from mod. L. *Sauria* (former suborder name, from Gk *sauros* 'lizard') + **-AN**.

**saurischian** /sɔːˈrɪskɪən, -ˈrɪʃɪən/ • n. Palaeontology a dinosaur of a group with a pelvic structure resembling that of lizards. Compare with **ORNITHISCHIAN**.
– ORIGIN C19: from mod. L. *Saurischia* (name of an order), from Gk *sauros* 'lizard' + *iskhion* 'hip joint'.

**sauropod** /ˈsɔːrəpɒd, ˈsaʊr-/ • n. an apatosaurus, brachiosaurus, or similar huge herbivorous dinosaur with a long neck and tail and massive limbs.
– ORIGIN C19: from mod. L. *Sauropoda* (pl.), from Gk *sauros* 'lizard' + *pous*, *pod-* 'foot'.

**-saurus** • comb. form forming genus names of reptiles, especially extinct ones: *stegosaurus*. See word-formation panel.
– ORIGIN from mod. L.; cf. **-SAUR**.

**saury** /ˈsɔːri/ • n. (pl. **-ies**) a long slender-bodied edible marine fish with an elongated snout. [*Scomberesox saurus* (Atlantic), *Cololabis saira* (Pacific), and other species.]
– ORIGIN C18: perh. via late L. from Gk *sauros* 'horse

## Word *Formation*

**-saur**, **-saurus** 'a fossil reptile', from Greek *sauros* 'lizard'

Most **-saur** and **-saurus** words relate to dinosaurs (including the word ***dinosaur*** itself). In each case **-saurus** is used to form the name of the genus in modern Latin and **-saur** for the corresponding shorter Anglicized form. In practice, however, both **-saur** and **-saurus** words are used in English, some of the best known being:

| | | |
|---|---|---|
| ankylosaur | a heavily built herbivorous dinosaur with bony plates | Gk *ankulōsis* (from *ankulos* 'crooked') |
| apatosaurus | a huge herbivorous dinosaur with a long neck and tail (also called ***brontosaurus***) | Gk *apatē* 'deceit' (because of the deceptive similarity between certain bones of apatosaurus and some other fossil reptiles) |
| brachiosaurus | a huge herbivorous dinosaur with forelegs much longer than the hind legs | Gk *brakhiōn* 'arm' |
| brontosaurus | alternative (and less technical) term for ***apatosaurus*** | Gk *brontē* 'thunder' |
| dinosaur | a Mesozoic fossil reptile of a large and diverse group | Gk *deinos* 'terrible' |
| hadrosaur | a large, mainly bipedal, herbivorous dinosaur with flattened jaws | Gk *hadros* 'thick, stout' |
| ichthyosaur | a fossil marine reptile resembling a dolphin | Gk *ikhthus* 'fish' |
| megalosaurus | a large carnivorous bipedal dinosaur | Gk *megas*, *megal-* 'great' |
| plesiosaur | a large fossil marine reptile with paddle-like limbs and a long neck | Gk *plēsios* 'near' (because closely related to the lizards) |
| pterosaur | a fossil warm-blooded flying reptile | Gk *pteron* 'wing' |
| stegosaur | a large herbivorous dinosaur with a double row of bony plates along its back | Gk *stegē* 'covering' |
| tyrannosaur | a very large carnivorous dinosaur with powerful jaws and small claw-like front legs | Gk *turannos* 'tyrant' |

mackerel'.

**sausage** • **n. 1** a short cylindrical tube of minced pork, beef, etc. encased in a skin, typically sold raw and grilled or fried before eating. ➤a cylindrical tube of minced meat seasoned and cooked or preserved, sold mainly to be eaten cold in slices. **2** a sausage-shaped object.
– PHRASES **not a sausage** Brit. informal nothing at all.
– ORIGIN ME: from ONorth. Fr. *saussiche*, from med. L. *salsicia*, from L. *salsus* (see **SAUCE**).

**sausage dog** • **n.** Brit. informal term for **DACHSHUND**.

**sausage meat** • **n.** minced meat with spices and a binder such as cereal, used in sausages or as a stuffing.

**sausage roll** • **n.** a piece of sausage meat baked in a roll of pastry.

**sausage tree** • **n.** a tropical African tree with red bell-shaped flowers and pendulous sausage-shaped fruits. [*Kigelia pinnata*.]

**sauté** /ˈsəʊteɪ/ • **adj.** fried quickly in a little hot fat. • **n. 1** a dish cooked in such a way. **2** Ballet a jump off both feet, landing in the same position. • **v.** (**sautés**, **sautéed** or **sautéd**, **sautéing**) cook in such a way.
– ORIGIN C19: Fr., lit. 'jumped', past part. of *sauter*.

**Sauternes** /sə(ʊ)ˈtəːn, French sotɛʀn/ • **n.** a sweet white wine from Sauternes in the Bordeaux region of France.

**Sauvignon** /ˈsəʊvɪnjɒ̃/ (also **Sauvignon Blanc**) • **n.** a variety of white wine grape. ➤a white wine made from this grape.
– ORIGIN from Fr.

**savage** • **adj. 1** fierce, violent, and uncontrolled. ➤cruel and vicious. **2** primitive; uncivilized. **3** (of a place) wild; uncultivated. • **n. 1** a member of a people regarded as primitive and uncivilized. **2** a brutal or vicious person. **3** Heraldry a representation of a bearded and semi-naked man with a wreath of leaves. • **v. 1** (especially of a dog) attack ferociously. **2** criticize brutally.
– DERIVATIVES **savagely** adv. **savageness** n. **savagery** n.
– ORIGIN ME: from OFr. *sauvage* 'wild', from L. *silvaticus* 'of the woods', from *silva* 'a wood'.

**savannah** (also **savanna**) • **n.** a grassy plain in tropical and subtropical regions, with few trees.
– ORIGIN C16: from Sp. *sabana*, from Taino *zavana*.

**savant** /ˈsav(ə)nt, French savɑ̃/ (or **savante** /ˈsav(ə)nt, French savɑ̃t/) • **n.** a learned person.
– ORIGIN C18: Fr., lit. 'knowing (person)', pres. part. (used as n.) of *savoir*.

**savarin** /ˈsavərɪn/ • **n.** a light ring-shaped cake made with yeast and soaked in liqueur-flavoured syrup.
– ORIGIN named after the Fr. gastronome Anthelme Brillat-*Savarin*.

**savate** /səˈvɑːt/ • **n.** a French method of boxing using feet and fists.
– ORIGIN Fr., orig. denoting an ill-fitting shoe.

**save**[1] • **v. 1** keep safe or rescue from harm or danger. ➤prevent from dying. ➤(in Christian use) preserve (a soul) from damnation. **2** store up for future use. ➤preserve. **3** Computing keep (data) by moving a copy to a storage location. **4** (**save it**) N. Amer. informal be quiet. **5** avoid the need to use up or spend. ➤avoid, lessen, or guard against. **6** prevent an opponent from scoring (a goal or point) or from winning (the game). ➤Soccer prevent (a shot) from entering the goal. ➤Baseball (of a relief pitcher) preserve (a winning position) gained by another pitcher. • **n.** chiefly Soccer an act of preventing an opponent's scoring. ➤Baseball an instance of saving a winning position.
– PHRASES **save one's breath** not bother to say something pointless. **save the day** (or **situation**) provide a solution to a problem. **save someone's skin** (or **neck** or **bacon**) rescue someone from difficulty. **save the tide** Nautical, archaic get in and out of port while the tide lasts.
– DERIVATIVES **savable** (also **saveable**) adj.
– ORIGIN ME: from OFr. *sauver*, from late L. *salvare*, from L. *salvus* 'safe'.

**save**[2] • **prep. & conj.** formal or poetic/literary except; other than.
– ORIGIN ME: from OFr. *sauf*, *sauve*, from L. *salvo*, *salva* (ablative sing. of *salvus* 'safe'), used in phrs such as *salvo jure*, *salva innocentia* 'with no violation of right or innocence'.

**save as you earn** • **n.** (in the UK) a method of saving money that carries tax privileges.

**saveloy** /ˈsavəlɔɪ/ • **n.** Brit. a seasoned red pork sausage, dried and smoked and sold ready to eat.
– ORIGIN C19: alt. of obs. Fr. *cervelat*, from Ital. *cervellata*;

cf. **CERVELAT**.

**saver** ● n. **1** a person who regularly saves money through a bank or recognized scheme. **2** [in combination] something that prevents a particular resource from being used up. **3** a reduced travel fare. **4** Horse Racing, informal a hedging bet.

**savin** /ˈsavɪn/ ● n. **1** a bushy juniper typically having horizontally spreading branches. [*Juniperus sabina*.] **2** an extract obtained from this plant, formerly used as an abortifacient.
– ORIGIN OE, from OFr. *savine*, from L. *sabina* (*herba*) 'Sabine (herb)'.

**saving** ● n. **1** an economy of or reduction in money, time, etc. **2** (**savings**) money saved, especially through a bank or official scheme. **3** Law a reservation; an exception. ● adj. [in combination] preventing waste of a particular resource. ● prep. **1** except. **2** archaic with due respect to.
– ORIGIN ME: from **SAVE**[1]; the preposition prob. from **SAVE**[2], on the pattern of *touching*.

**saving grace** ● n. **1** the redeeming grace of God. **2** a redeeming quality or characteristic.

**savings account** ● n. a deposit account.

**savings and loan** (also **savings and loan association**) ● n. (in the US) an institution which accepts savings at interest and lends money to savers.

**savings bank** ● n. a non-profit-making financial institution receiving small deposits at interest.

**Savings Bond** ● n. **1** a Premium Bond. **2** (in the US) a government bond sold to the general public, yielding variable interest.

**savings certificate** ● n. (in the UK) a document issued to savers by the government guaranteeing fixed interest for five years on a deposit.

**saviour** (US **savior**) ● n. **1** a person who saves someone or something from danger or harm. **2** (**the/our Saviour**) (in Christianity) God or Jesus Christ.
– ORIGIN ME: from OFr. *sauveour*, from eccles. L. *salvator* (translating Gk *sōtēr*), from late L. *salvare* 'to save'.

**savoir faire** /ˌsavwɑː ˈfɛː, French savwar fɛr/ ● n. the ability to act appropriately in social situations.
– ORIGIN C19: Fr., lit. 'know how to do'.

**savor** ● v. & n. US spelling of **SAVOUR**.

**savory**[1] ● n. an aromatic plant of the mint family, used as a culinary herb. [*Satureja hortensis* (**summer savory**) and *S. montana* (**winter savory**).]
– ORIGIN ME: perh. from OE *sætherie*, or via OFr., from L. *satureia*.

**savory**[2] ● adj. & n. US spelling of **SAVOURY**.

**savour** (US **savor**) ● v. **1** appreciate and enjoy the taste of (good food or drink). ➤ enjoy or appreciate to the full. **2** (**savour of**) have a suggestion or trace of. ● n. **1** a characteristic taste, flavour, or smell. **2** a suggestion or trace.
– DERIVATIVES **savourless** adj.
– ORIGIN ME: from OFr., from L. *sapor*, from *sapere* 'to taste'.

**savoury** (US **savory**) ● adj. **1** (of food) salty or spicy rather than sweet. **2** [usu. with neg.] morally wholesome or acceptable. ● n. (pl. **-ies**) chiefly Brit. a savoury snack.
– DERIVATIVES **savourily** adv. **savouriness** n.
– ORIGIN ME: from OFr. *savoure* 'tasty, fragrant', based on L. *sapor* 'taste'.

**savoy** ● n. a cabbage of a hardy variety with densely wrinkled leaves.
– ORIGIN C16: from *Savoy*, an area of SE France.

**Savoyard** ● n. a native or inhabitant of the Savoy area of SE France.

**savvy** informal ● n. shrewdness. ● v. (**-ies**, **-ied**) know or understand. ● adj. (**-ier**, **-iest**) shrewd and knowledgeable.
– ORIGIN C18: orig. black and pidgin Engl. imitating Sp. *sabe usted* 'you know'.

**saw**[1] ● n. **1** a hand tool for cutting wood, etc., typically with a long, thin serrated blade and operated using a backwards and forwards movement. ➤ a mechanical power-driven cutting tool with a toothed rotating disc or moving band. **2** Zoology a serrated organ or part, e.g. the toothed snout of a sawfish. ● v. (past part. chiefly Brit. **sawn** or chiefly N. Amer. **sawed**) **1** cut, make, or form with a saw. ➤ cut as if with a saw, especially roughly. ➤ make rapid sawlike motions. **2** (**saw off**) Canadian compromise by making concessions.
– ORIGIN OE *saga*, of Gmc origin.

**saw**[2] past of **SEE**[1].

**saw**[3] ● n. a proverb or maxim.
– ORIGIN OE *sagu* 'a saying, speech', of Gmc origin; rel. to **SAY** and **SAGA**.

**sawbench** ● n. a circular saw mounted under a bench so that the blade projects up through a slot.

**sawbill** ● n. another term for **MERGANSER**.

**sawbones** ● n. (pl. same) informal, dated a doctor or surgeon.

**sawbuck** ● n. N. Amer. **1** a sawhorse. **2** informal a $10 note. [by assoc. of the X-shaped ends of a sawhorse with the Roman numeral X (= 10).]
– ORIGIN C19: from Du. *zaagbok*, from *zaag* 'saw' + *bok* 'vaulting horse'.

**saw doctor** ● n. a person or device that sharpens saws.

**sawdust** ● n. powdery particles of wood produced by sawing.

**sawed-off** ● adj. & n. North American term for **SAWN-OFF**.

**sawfish** ● n. (pl. same or **-fishes**) a large fish related to the rays, with a long flattened snout bearing large blunt teeth along each side. [Family Pristidae: several species.]

**sawfly** ● n. (pl. **-flies**) an insect related to the wasps, with a saw-like tube used in laying eggs in plant tissues. [Suborder Symphyta: many species.]

**sawgrass** ● n. chiefly N. Amer. a sedge with spiny-edged leaves. [Genus *Cladium*.]

**sawhorse** ● n. N. Amer. a rack supporting wood for sawing.

**sawmill** ● n. a factory in which logs are sawn by machine.

**sawn** past participle of **SAW**[1].

**sawn-off** (N. Amer. **sawed-off**) ● adj. **1** (of a gun) having a shortened barrel for ease of handling and a wider field of fire. **2** informal (of a garment) having been cut short. ➤ US informal (of a person) short.

**saw palmetto** ● n. a small palm with fan-shaped leaves that have sharply toothed stalks, native to the south-eastern US. [*Serenoa repens* and other species.]

**saw set** ● n. a tool for giving the teeth of a saw an alternating sideways inclination.

**sawtooth** (also **sawtoothed**) ● adj. **1** shaped like the teeth of a saw. **2** (of a waveform) showing a slow linear rise and rapid linear fall or vice versa.

**saw-wort** ● n. a plant of the daisy family, with purple flowers and serrated leaves. [*Serratula tinctoria*.]

**sawyer** ● n. **1** a person who saws timber. **2** US an uprooted tree floating in a river but held fast at one end. [with allusion to the log's movement backwards and forwards.] **3** a large insect whose larvae bore tunnels in wood. [Genus *Monochamus* (a longhorn beetle) and other species.]
– ORIGIN ME (earlier as *sawer*): from **SAW**[1] + **-YER**.

**sax**[1] ● n. informal **1** a saxophone. **2** a saxophone player.
– DERIVATIVES **saxist** n.

**sax**[2] (also **zax**) ● n. a small axe for cutting roof slates, with a point for making nail holes.
– ORIGIN OE *seax* 'knife', of Gmc origin.

**saxe** ● n. a light blue colour with a greyish tinge.
– ORIGIN C19: from Fr., lit. 'Saxony', the source of a dye of this colour.

**saxhorn** ● n. a brass instrument with valves and a funnel-shaped mouthpiece, used mainly in military and brass bands.
– ORIGIN from the name of the Belgian instrument-makers Charles J. *Sax* and his son Antoine-Joseph 'Adolphe' *Sax* + **HORN**.

**saxifrage** /ˈsaksɪfreɪdʒ/ ● n. a low-growing plant of poor soils, bearing small white, yellow, or red flowers and forming rosettes of succulent leaves or hummocks of mossy leaves. [Genus *Saxifraga*.]
– ORIGIN ME: from OFr. *saxifrage* or late L. *saxifraga*

(*herba*), from L. *saxum* 'rock' + *frangere* 'break'.

**Saxon** ● n. **1** a member of a Germanic people that conquered and settled in much of southern England in the 5th–6th centuries. **2** a native of modern Saxony in Germany. **3** (**Old Saxon**) the West Germanic language of the ancient Saxons. **4** another term for **OLD ENGLISH**. **5** the Low German dialect of modern Saxony. ● **adj. 1** of or relating to the Anglo-Saxons, their language, or their period of dominance in England (5th–11th centuries). **2** of or relating to Saxony or the continental Saxons.
– DERIVATIVES **Saxonize** (also **-ise**) v.
– ORIGIN ME: from OFr., from late L. and Gk *Saxones* (pl.), of W. Gmc origin; rel. to OE *Seaxan*, *Seaxe* (pl.), perh. from the base of **SAX**[2].

**saxony** /'saks(ə)ni/ ● n. a fine kind of wool. ➤a fine-quality cloth made from this wool.
– ORIGIN C19: from *Saxony*, a large region of Germany.

**saxophone** /'saksəfəʊn/ ● n. a member of a family of metal wind instruments with a reed like a clarinet, used especially in jazz and dance music.
– DERIVATIVES **saxophonic** /-'fɒnɪk/ adj. **saxophonist** /sak'sɒf(ə)nɪst, 'saksə,fəʊnɪst/ n.
– ORIGIN from the name of Adolphe *Sax* (see **SAXHORN**) + **-PHONE**.

**say** ● v. (**says**; past and past part. **said**) **1** utter words so as to convey information, an opinion, an instruction, etc. ➤(of a text or symbol) convey information or instructions. ➤(of a clock or watch) indicate (a time). ➤(**be said**) be asserted or reported. ➤recite (a speech or formula). **2** (**say something for**) present a consideration in favour of or excusing. **3** assume as a hypothesis. ● **exclam.** N. Amer. informal used to express surprise or to draw attention to a remark or question. ● n. an opportunity to state one's opinion or feelings. ➤an opportunity to influence events.
– PHRASES **go without saying** be obvious. **how say you?** Law how do you find? (used to request a jury's verdict). **I say!** Brit. dated used to express surprise or to draw attention to a remark. **say the word** give permission or instructions. **there is no saying** it is impossible to know. **they say** it is rumoured. **when all is said and done** when everything is taken into account.
– DERIVATIVES **sayable** adj. **-sayer** n.
– ORIGIN OE *secgan*, of Gmc origin.

**SAYE** ● **abbrev.** save as you earn.

**saying** ● n. a short, commonly known expression containing advice or wisdom; an adage or maxim.
– PHRASES **as** (or **so**) **the saying goes** (or **is**) used to introduce a proverb, cliché, etc.

**say-so** ● n. informal **1** the power or action of deciding or allowing something. **2** mere assertion.

**Sb** ● **symb.** the chemical element antimony.
– ORIGIN from L. *stibium*.

**SBS** ● **abbrev.** Special Boat Service.

**SC** ● **abbrev. 1** South Carolina (in official postal use). **2** (in the UK) special constable.

**Sc** ● **symb.** the chemical element scandium.

**sc.** ● **abbrev.** scilicet.

**s.c.** ● **abbrev.** small capitals.

**scab** ● n. **1** a dry, rough protective crust that forms over a cut or wound during healing. **2** mange or a similar skin disease in animals. ➤any of a number of fungal diseases of plants in which rough patches develop, especially on apples and potatoes. **3** informal a person or thing regarded with contempt. ➤a person who refuses to strike or who takes the place of a striking worker. ● v. (**scabbed**, **scabbing**) **1** [usu. as adj. **scabbed**] become encrusted with a scab or scabs. **2** act or work as a scab. ➤Brit. informal scrounge.
– DERIVATIVES **scabbiness** n. **scabby** adj.
– ORIGIN ME: from ON *skabb*; rel. to dial. *shab* (cf. **SHABBY**).

**scabbard** /'skabəd/ ● n. a sheath for the blade of a sword or dagger. ➤a sheath for a gun or other weapon or tool.
– ORIGIN ME: from Anglo-Norman Fr. *escalberc*, from a Gmc compound of words meaning 'cut' and 'protect'.

**scabbardfish** ● n. (pl. same or **-fishes**) an elongated marine fish with heavy jaws and large teeth, which occurs mostly in the deeper waters of warm seas. [Several genera and species, including the edible silvery-white *Lepidopus caudatus*.]

**scabies** /'skeɪbiːz/ ● n. a contagious skin disease marked by itching and small raised red spots, caused by the itch mite.
– ORIGIN ME: from L., from *scabere* 'to scratch'.

**scabious** /'skeɪbɪəs/ ● n. a plant of the teasel family, with blue, pink, or white pincushion-shaped flowers. [*Scabiosa*, *Knautia*, and other genera: several species, including the **devil's bit scabious**.] ● **adj.** affected with mange; scabby.
– ORIGIN ME: based on L. *scabiosus* 'rough, scabby' and med. L. *scabiosa* (*herba*) 'rough, scabby (plant)', formerly regarded as a cure for skin disease.

**scabrous** /'skeɪbrəs, 'skabrəs/ ● **adj. 1** rough and covered with, or as if with, scabs. **2** salacious or sordid.
– DERIVATIVES **scabrously** adv. **scabrousness** n.
– ORIGIN C16: from Fr. *scabreux* or late L. *scabrosus*, from L. *scaber* 'rough'.

**scad** ● n. another term for **JACK**[1] (in sense 10) or **HORSE MACKEREL**.
– ORIGIN C17: of unknown origin.

**scads** ● **pl. n.** informal, chiefly N. Amer. a large number or quantity.
– ORIGIN C19: of unknown origin.

**scaffold** /'skafəʊld, -f(ə)ld/ ● n. **1** a raised wooden platform used formerly for public executions. **2** a structure made using scaffolding. ● v. attach scaffolding to.
– DERIVATIVES **scaffolder** n.
– ORIGIN ME: from Anglo-Norman Fr., from OFr. (*e*)*schaffaut*, from the base of **CATAFALQUE**.

**scaffolding** ● n. a temporary structure on the outside of a building, made of wooden planks and metal poles, used while building, repairing, or cleaning. ➤the materials used in such a structure.

**scag** ● n. variant spelling of **SKAG**.

**scagliola** /skal'jəʊlə/ ● n. imitation marble or other stone, made of plaster mixed with glue and dyes which is then painted or polished.
– ORIGIN C18: from Ital. *scagliuola*, dimin. of *scaglia* 'a scale'.

**scalable** ● **adj. 1** able to be scaled or climbed. **2** able to be changed in size or scale. **3** technical able to be graded according to a scale.
– DERIVATIVES **scalability** n.

**scalar** /'skeɪlə/ Mathematics & Physics ● **adj.** (of a quantity) having only magnitude, not direction. ● n. a scalar quantity.
– ORIGIN C17: from L. *scalaris*, from *scala* (see **SCALE**[3]).

**scalar field** ● n. Mathematics a function of a space whose value at each point is a scalar quantity.

**scalariform** /skə'larɪfɔːm/ ● **adj.** Botany (especially of the walls of water-conducting cells) having thickened bands arranged like the rungs of a ladder.
– ORIGIN C19: from L. *scalaris* 'of a ladder' + **-IFORM**.

**scalar product** ● n. Mathematics a quantity (written as **a.b** or **ab**) equal to the product of the magnitudes of two vectors and the cosine of the angle between them.

**scalawag** ● n. variant spelling of **SCALLYWAG**.

**scald**[1] ● v. **1** injure with very hot liquid or steam. **2** heat (milk or other liquid) to near boiling point. ➤immerse briefly in boiling water. ➤archaic clean by rinsing with boiling water. **3** cause to feel a searing sensation like that of boiling water on skin. ● n. **1** a burn or other injury caused by hot liquid or steam. **2** any of a number of plant diseases which produce a similar effect to that of scalding, especially a disease of fruit marked by browning and caused by excessive sunlight, bad storage conditions, or atmospheric pollution.
– PHRASES **like a scalded cat** at a very fast speed.
– DERIVATIVES **scalding** adj.
– ORIGIN ME: from Anglo-Norman Fr. *escalder*, from late L. *excaldare*, from L. *ex-* 'thoroughly' + *calidus* 'hot'.

**scald**[2] ● n. variant spelling of **SKALD**.

**scaldfish** ● n. (pl. same or **-fishes**) a small edible flatfish, the fragile scales of which are easily scraped off, giving the appearance of a scald. [*Arnoglossus laterna*.]

**scale**[1] ● **n. 1** each of the small overlapping horny or bony plates protecting the skin of fish and reptiles. ➤each of numerous microscopic tile-like structures covering the wings of butterflies and moths. ➤a rudimentary leaf, feather, or bract. **2** a thick dry flake of skin. **3** a flaky deposit, in particular: ➤a white deposit formed in a kettle, boiler, etc. by the evaporation of water containing lime. ➤tartar formed on teeth. ➤a coating of oxide formed on heated metal. ● **v. 1** remove scale or scales from. **2** [often as noun **scaling**] (especially of the skin) form scales. ➤come off in scales; flake off.
– PHRASES **the scales fall from someone's eyes** someone is no longer deceived. [with biblical ref. to Acts 9:18.]
– DERIVATIVES **-scaled** adj. **scaleless** adj. **scaler** n.
– ORIGIN ME: shortening of OFr. *escale*, from the Gmc base of **SCALE**[2].

**scale**[2] ● **n.** (usu. **scales**) an instrument for weighing, originally a simple balance but now usually a device with an electronic or other internal weighing mechanism. ➤either of the dishes on a simple balance. ● **v.** have a weight of.
– PHRASES **throw something on** (or **into**) **the scale** contribute something to one side of an argument or debate. **tip** (or **turn**) **the scales** (or **balance**) be the deciding factor; make the critical difference.
– ORIGIN ME (in the sense 'drinking cup', surviving in S. Afr. Engl.): from ON *skál* 'bowl', of Gmc origin.

**scale**[3] ● **n. 1** a graduated range of values forming a standard system for measuring or grading something. ➤a measuring instrument based on such a system. **2** the relative size or extent of something: *no one foresaw the scale of the disaster.* ➤a ratio of size in a map, model, drawing, or plan. **3** Music an arrangement of the notes in any system of music in ascending or descending order of pitch. ● **v. 1** climb up or over (something high and steep). **2** represent or draw according to a common scale. ➤(of a quantity or property) be variable according to a particular scale. **3** (**scale something back/down** or **up**) reduce (or increase) something in size, number, or extent.
– PHRASES **to scale** with a uniform reduction or enlargement: *not drawn to scale.* **in scale** in proportion to the surroundings.
– DERIVATIVES **scaler** n.
– ORIGIN ME: from L. *scala* 'ladder', from the base of L. *scandere* 'to climb'.

**scale armour** ● **n.** historical armour consisting of small overlapping plates of metal, leather, or horn.

**scale board** ● **n.** very thin wood used (especially formerly) in bookbinding, making hatboxes, and backing pictures.

**scale insect** ● **n.** a small bug which secretes a protective shield-like scale and spends its life attached to a single plant. [Family Coccidae: many species.]

**scale leaf** ● **n.** Botany a small modified leaf, as on a rhizome or forming part of a bulb.

**scalene** /ˈskeɪliːn/ ● **adj.** (of a triangle) having sides unequal in length. ● **n.** Anatomy another term for **SCALENUS**.
– ORIGIN C17: via late L. from Gk *skalēnos* 'unequal'.

**scalenus** /skəˈliːnəs/ ● **n.** (pl. **scaleni** /-nʌɪ/) any of several muscles extending from the neck to the first and second ribs.
– ORIGIN C18: mod. L., from late L. *scalenus* (*musculus*) (see **SCALENE**).

**scallion** /ˈskalɪən/ ● **n.** a long-necked onion with a small bulb, in particular a shallot or spring onion.
– ORIGIN ME: from Anglo-Norman Fr. *scaloun*, based on L. *Ascalonia* (*caepa*) '(onion) of *Ascalon*', a port in ancient Palestine.

**scallop** /ˈskɒləp, ˈskaləp/ ● **n. 1** an edible bivalve mollusc with a ribbed fan-shaped shell, which swims by rapidly opening and closing the shell valves. [*Chlamys*, *Pecten*, and other genera.] ➤a scallop shell or similarly shaped dish used for baking or serving food. **2** each of a series of convex rounded projections forming an ornamental edging in material, knitting, etc. **3** another term for **ESCALOPE**. ● **v.** (**scalloped**, **scalloping**) **1** [usu. as adj. **scalloped**] ornament with scallops. ➤shape in the form of a scallop shell. **2** [usu. as noun **scalloping**] N. Amer. gather or dredge for scallops. **3** bake with milk or a sauce.
– DERIVATIVES **scalloper** n.
– ORIGIN ME: shortening of OFr. *escalope*, prob. of Gmc origin.

**scally** ● **n.** (pl. **-ies**) informal (in NW English dialect) a rascal; a rogue.
– ORIGIN 1980s: abbrev. of **SCALLYWAG**.

**scallywag** (US also **scalawag**) ● **n. 1** informal a mischievous person; a rascal. **2** US a white Southerner who collaborated with northern Republicans during the post-Civil War reconstruction period.
– ORIGIN C19: of unknown origin; perh. orig. in the sense 'undersized cattle'.

**scalp** ● **n. 1** the skin covering the top and back of the head. **2** historical the scalp with the hair cut away from an enemy's head as a battle trophy, a former practice among American Indians. **3** Scottish a bare rock projecting above surrounding water or vegetation. ● **v. 1** take the scalp of (an enemy). ➤informal punish severely. **2** informal, chiefly N. Amer. resell (shares or tickets) at a large or quick profit.
– DERIVATIVES **scalper** n.
– ORIGIN ME (denoting the skull): prob. of Scand. origin.

**scalpel** ● **n.** a knife with a small sharp blade, as used by a surgeon.
– ORIGIN C18: from Fr., or from L. *scalpellum*, dimin. of *scalprum* 'chisel', from *scalpere* 'to scratch'.

**scaly** ● **adj.** (**-ier**, **-iest**) **1** covered in scales. **2** (of skin) dry and flaking.
– DERIVATIVES **scaliness** n.

**scaly anteater** ● **n.** another term for **PANGOLIN**.

**scam** ● **n.** informal a dishonest scheme; a fraud. ● **v.** (**scammed**, **scamming**) swindle.
– DERIVATIVES **scammer** n.
– ORIGIN 1960s: of unknown origin.

**scammony** /ˈskaməni/ ● **n.** a plant of the convolvulus family, the dried roots of which yield a powerful purgative. [Two species: *Convolvulus scammonia* of Asia, and *Ipomoea orizabensis* of Mexico.]
– ORIGIN OE, from OFr. *escamonie* or L. *scammonia*, from Gk *skammōnia*.

**scamp**[1] ● **n.** informal a mischievous person, especially a child.
– DERIVATIVES **scampish** adj.
– ORIGIN C18 (denoting a highwayman): from obs. *scamp* 'rob on the highway', prob. from MDu. *schampen* 'slip away'.

**scamp**[2] ● **v.** dated perform in a perfunctory or inadequate way.
– ORIGIN C19: perh. from **SCAMP**[1], but assoc. in sense with **SKIMP**.

**scamper** ● **v.** run with quick light steps, especially through fear or excitement. ● **n.** an act of scampering.
– ORIGIN C17: prob. from **SCAMP**[2].

**scampi** ● **n.** [treated as sing. or pl.] Norway lobsters when prepared or cooked, typically fried in breadcrumbs.
– ORIGIN from Ital.

**scan** ● **v.** (**scanned**, **scanning**) **1** look at quickly in order to identify relevant features or information. **2** traverse with a detector or an electromagnetic beam, especially to obtain an image. ➤cause (a beam) to traverse across a surface or object. ➤resolve (a picture) into its elements of light and shade in a pre-arranged pattern for the purposes of television transmission. ➤convert (a document or picture) into digital form for storage or processing on a computer. **3** analyse the metre of (a line of verse) by reading with appropriate intonation or by examining the pattern of feet or syllables. ➤(of verse) conform to metrical principles. ● **n. 1** an act of scanning. **2** a medical examination using a scanner. ➤an image obtained by scanning or with a scanner.
– DERIVATIVES **scannable** adj.
– ORIGIN ME: from L. *scandere* 'climb' (in late L. 'scan (verses)'), by analogy with the raising and lowering of one's foot when marking rhythm; later arose the senses 'analyse' and 'look at searchingly'.

**scandal** ● **n.** an action or event regarded as morally or legally wrong and causing general public outrage. ➤out-

rage, rumour, or gossip arising from this.
– DERIVATIVES **scandalous** adj. **scandalously** adv. **scandalousness** n.
– ORIGIN ME (in the sense 'discredit to religion'): from OFr. *scandale*, from eccles. L. *scandalum* 'cause of offence', from Gk *skandalon* 'snare, stumbling block'.

**scandalize** (also **-ise**) • v. **1** shock or horrify by a violation of propriety or morality. **2** Sailing reduce the area of (a sail) by lowering the head or raising the boom. [C19: alt. of obs. *scantelize*, from *scantle* 'make small'.]

**scandent** /ˈskandənt/ • adj. chiefly Palaeontology (especially of a graptolite) having a climbing habit.
– ORIGIN C17: from L. *scandent-*, *scandere* 'climb'.

**Scandinavian** • adj. of or relating to Scandinavia, its people, or their languages. • n. **1** a native or inhabitant of Scandinavia, or a person of Scandinavian descent. **2** the northern branch of the Germanic languages, comprising Danish, Norwegian, Swedish, Icelandic, and Faroese, all descended from Old Norse.

**scandium** /ˈskandɪəm/ • n. the chemical element of atomic number 21, a soft silvery-white metal resembling the rare-earth elements. (Symbol: **Sc**)
– ORIGIN C19: mod. L., from *Scandia*, contr. of *Scandinavia* (where minerals are found containing this element).

**scanner** • n. **1** Medicine a machine that examines the body through the use of radiation, ultrasound, or magnetic resonance imaging, as a diagnostic aid. **2** a device that scans documents and converts them into digital data.

**scanning electron microscope** • n. an electron microscope in which the surface of a specimen is scanned by a beam of electrons that are reflected to form an image.

**scanning tunnelling microscope** • n. a high-resolution microscope using neither light nor an electron beam, but with an ultra-fine tip able to reveal atomic and molecular details of surfaces.

**scansion** /ˈskanʃ(ə)n/ • n. the action of scanning a line of verse to determine its rhythm. ➤ the rhythm of a line of verse.
– ORIGIN C17: from L. *scansio(n-)*, from *scandere* 'to climb'; cf. **SCAN**.

**scant** • adj. barely sufficient or adequate. ➤ barely amounting to the amount specified: *a scant two pounds.* • v. chiefly N. Amer. provide grudgingly or in insufficient amounts. ➤ deal with inadequately; neglect.
– DERIVATIVES **scantly** adv. **scantness** n.
– ORIGIN ME: from ON *skamt*, neut. of *skammr* 'short'.

**scantling** • n. **1** a timber beam of small cross section. ➤ the size to which a piece of timber or stone is measured and cut. **2** (often **scantlings**) a set of standard dimensions for parts of a structure, especially in shipbuilding. **3** archaic a specimen, sample, or small amount.
– ORIGIN C16: alt. of obs. *scantillon* (from OFr. *escantillon* 'sample'), by assoc. with the suffix **-LING**.

**scanty** • adj. (**-ier**, **-iest**) small or insufficient in quantity or amount. ➤ (of clothing) revealing; skimpy.
– DERIVATIVES **scantily** adv. **scantiness** n.

**scape** • n. Entomology the basal segment of an insect's antenna, especially when it is enlarged and lengthened (as in a weevil).
– ORIGIN C19: via L. from Gk *skapos* 'rod'; rel. to **SCEPTRE**.

**-scape** • comb. form denoting a specified type of scene: *moonscape.*
– ORIGIN on the pattern of *(land)scape.*

**scapegoat** • n. **1** a person who is blamed for the wrongdoings or mistakes of others. **2** (in the Bible) a goat sent into the wilderness after the Jewish chief priest had symbolically laid the sins of the people upon it (Lev. 16). • v. make a scapegoat of.
– ORIGIN C16: from archaic *scape* 'escape' + **GOAT**.

**scapegrace** • n. archaic a mischievous person; a rascal.
– ORIGIN C19: from archaic *scape* 'escape' + **GRACE**, i.e. a person who lacks the grace of God.

**scaphoid** /ˈskafɔɪd/ • n. Anatomy a large carpal bone articulating with the radius below the thumb.
– ORIGIN C18 (in the sense 'boat-shaped'): from mod. L. *scaphoides*, from Gk *skaphoeidēs*, from *skaphos* 'boat'.

**scapula** /ˈskapjʊlə/ • n. (pl. **scapulae** /-liː/ or **scapulas**) Anatomy technical term for **SHOULDER BLADE**.
– ORIGIN C16: from late L., sing. of L. *scapulae* 'shoulder blades'.

**scapular** • adj. Anatomy & Zoology of or relating to the shoulder or shoulder blade. ➤ Ornithology denoting a feather covering the shoulder, growing above the region where the wing joins the body. • n. **1** a short monastic cloak covering the shoulders. ➤ a symbol of affiliation to an ecclesiastical order, consisting of two strips of cloth hanging down the breast and back and joined across the shoulders. **2** Medicine a bandage passing over and around the shoulders.
– ORIGIN C15: from late L. *scapulare*, from *scapula* 'shoulder'.

**scapulary** • n. (pl. **-ies**) **1** a scapular feather. **2** another term for **SCAPULAR** (in sense 1).

**scar** • n. **1** a mark left on the skin or within body tissue after the healing of a wound or burn. ➤ a mark left at the point of separation of a leaf, frond, or other part from a plant. **2** a lasting effect left following an unpleasant experience. **3** a steep high cliff or rock outcrop. • v. (**scarred**, **scarring**) mark or be marked with a scar or scars.
– DERIVATIVES **scarless** adj.
– ORIGIN ME: from OFr. *escharre*, via late L. from Gk *eskhara* 'scab'; sense 3 is from ON *sker* 'low reef'.

**scarab** /ˈskarəb/ • n. **1** a large dung beetle, regarded as sacred in ancient Egypt. [*Scarabaeus sacer.*] ➤ any scarabaeid. **2** an ancient Egyptian gem in the form of a scarab beetle, engraved with hieroglyphs on the flat underside.
– ORIGIN C16: from L. *scarabaeus*, from Gk *skarabeios*.

**scarabaeid** /ˌskarəˈbiːɪd/ • n. Entomology a beetle of a family (Scarabaeidae) including the scarab, chafers, and many dung beetles.

**scaramouch** /ˈskarəmaʊtʃ, -muːtʃ/ • n. archaic a boastful but cowardly person.
– ORIGIN C17: from Ital. *Scaramuccia*, the name of a stock character in Ital. farce, from *scaramuccia* 'skirmish'.

**scarce** • adj. (of a resource) insufficient for the demand. ➤ rare. • adv. archaic scarcely.
– PHRASES **make oneself scarce** informal leave a place, especially so as to avoid a difficult situation.
– DERIVATIVES **scarcely** adv. **scarceness** n. **scarcity** n.
– ORIGIN ME (in the sense 'restricted in size', also 'parsimonious'): from Anglo-Norman *escars*, from a Romance word meaning 'selected'.

**scare** /skɛː/ • v. **1** cause great fear or nervousness in; frighten. ➤ (**scare someone away/off**) drive or keep someone away by fear. ➤ become scared. **2** (**scare something up**) informal, chiefly N. Amer. find or obtain something. • n. a sudden attack of fright. ➤ a period of general anxiety or alarm about something: *a bomb scare.*
– DERIVATIVES **scared** adj. **scarer** n.
– ORIGIN ME: from ON *skirra* 'frighten', from *skjarr* 'timid'.

**scarecrow** • n. an object made to resemble a human figure, set up to scare birds away from a field where crops are growing.

**scaredy-cat** • n. informal a timid person.

**scarf**[1] • n. (pl. **scarves** or **scarfs**) a length or square of fabric worn around the neck or head.
– DERIVATIVES **scarfed** (also **scarved**) adj.
– ORIGIN C16: prob. based on ONorth. Fr. *escarpe*, prob. identical with OFr. *escharpe* 'pilgrim's scrip'.

**scarf**[2] • v. **1** join the ends of (two pieces of timber or metal) by bevelling or notching them so that they fit together. **2** make an incision in the blubber of (a whale). • n. an instance of scarfing; a joint made by scarfing.
– ORIGIN ME: prob. via OFr. from ON.

**scarf**[3] • v. N. Amer. informal eat or drink hungrily or enthusiastically.
– ORIGIN 1960s: var. of **SCOFF**[2].

**scarf-skin** • n. archaic the thin outer layer of the skin.

**scarify**[1] /ˈskarɪfʌɪ, ˈskɛːrɪ-/ • v. (**-ies**, **-ied**) **1** cut and remove debris from (a lawn). **2** break up the surface of (soil or a road or pavement). **3** make shallow incisions in (the skin), as a medical procedure or traditional cosmetic

practice. **4** criticize severely and hurtfully.
– DERIVATIVES **scarification** n. **scarifier** n.
– ORIGIN ME: from OFr. *scarifier*, via late L. from Gk *skariphasthai* 'scratch an outline', from *skariphos* 'stylus'.

**scarify**[2] /'skɛːrɪfʌɪ/ ● v. (**-ies, -ied**) [usu. as adj. **scarifying**] informal frighten.
– ORIGIN C18: formed irregularly from SCARE.

**scarlatina** /ˌskɑːlə'tiːnə/ (also **scarletina**) ● n. another term for SCARLET FEVER.
– ORIGIN C19: mod. L., from Ital. *scarlattina*, based on *scarlatto* 'scarlet'.

**scarlet** ● n. a brilliant red colour.
– ORIGIN ME (orig. denoting brightly coloured cloth): shortening of OFr. *escarlate*, from med. L. *scarlata*, via Arab. and med. Gk from late L. *sigillatus* 'decorated with small images', from *sigillum* 'small image'.

**scarlet fever** ● n. an infectious bacterial disease affecting especially children, and causing fever and a scarlet rash.

**scarletina** ● n. variant spelling of SCARLATINA.

**scarlet runner** ● n. another term for RUNNER BEAN.

**scarlet woman** ● n. a notoriously promiscuous or immoral woman.
– ORIGIN C19: orig. applied as a derogatory ref. to the Roman Catholic Church.

**scarp** ● n. a very steep bank or slope; an escarpment. ➤ the inner wall of a ditch in a fortification. ● v. cut or erode so as to form a scarp.
– ORIGIN C16 (with ref. to fortification): from Ital. *scarpa*.

**scarper** ● v. Brit. informal run away.
– ORIGIN C19: prob. from Ital. *scappare* 'to escape', influenced by rhyming sl. *Scapa Flow* 'go'.

**scarp slope** ● n. Geology the steeper slope of a cuesta, cutting across the underlying strata. Often contrasted with DIP SLOPE.

**Scart** (also **SCART**) ● n. a 21-pin socket used to connect video equipment.
– ORIGIN 1980s: acronym from Fr. *Syndicat des Constructeurs des Appareils Radiorécepteurs et Téléviseurs*, the committee which designed the connector.

**scarves** plural form of SCARF[1].

**scary** ● adj. (**-ier, -iest**) informal frightening; causing fear.
– DERIVATIVES **scarily** adv. **scariness** n.

**scat**[1] ● v. (**scatted, scatting**) informal go away; leave.
– ORIGIN C19: perh. an abbrev. of SCATTER, or perh. from the sound of a hiss + *-cat*.

**scat**[2] ● n. improvised jazz singing in which the voice is used in imitation of an instrument. ● v. (**scatted, scatting**) sing in such a way.
– ORIGIN 1920s: prob. imitative.

**scat**[3] ● n. droppings, especially those of carnivorous mammals.
– ORIGIN 1950s: from Gk *skōr, skat-* 'dung'.

**scathe** /skeɪð/ archaic ● v. harm; injure. ● n. harm; injury.
– DERIVATIVES **scatheless** adj.
– ORIGIN ME: from ON *skathi* (n.), *skatha* (v.).

**scathing** ● adj. witheringly scornful; severely critical.
– DERIVATIVES **scathingly** adv.

**scatology** /ska'tɒlədʒi/ ● n. a preoccupation with excrement and excretion.
– DERIVATIVES **scatological** adj.
– ORIGIN C19: from Gk *skōr, skat-* 'dung' + -LOGY.

**scatter** ● v. throw in various random directions. ➤ separate or cause to separate and move off in different directions. ➤ (**be scattered**) occur or be found at various places rather than all together. ➤ Physics deflect or diffuse (electromagnetic radiation or particles). ● n. **1** a small, dispersed amount of something. **2** Statistics the degree to which repeated measurements or observations of a quantity differ.
– DERIVATIVES **scatterer** n. **scattering** n.
– ORIGIN ME: prob. a var. of SHATTER.

**scatterbrain** ● n. a person who tends to be disorganized and lacking in concentration.
– DERIVATIVES **scatterbrained** adj.

**scatter cushion** ● n. a small cushion placed randomly so as to create a casual effect.

**scatter diagram** (also **scatter plot** or **scattergram**) ● n. Statistics a graph in which the values of two variables are plotted along two axes, the pattern of the resulting points revealing any correlation present.

**scattergun** ● n. **1** chiefly N. Amer. a shotgun. **2** (also **scattershot**) [as modifier] covering a broad range in a random and unsystematic way: *the scattergun approach.*

**scatter rug** ● n. a small decorative rug designed to be placed with a casual effect.

**scatty** ● adj. (**-ier, -iest**) informal absent-minded and disorganized.
– DERIVATIVES **scattily** adv. **scattiness** n.
– ORIGIN C20: abbrev. of *scatterbrained*.

**scaup** /skɔːp/ ● n. a diving duck, the male of which has a black head with a green or purple gloss. [*Aythya marila* and related species.]
– ORIGIN C17: Scots var. of Scots and north. Engl. *scalp* 'mussel-bed', a feeding ground of the duck.

**scauper** ● n. variant of SCORP.

**scaur** ● n. archaic spelling of SCAR (in sense 3).

**scavenge** /'skavɪn(d)ʒ/ ● v. **1** search for and collect (anything usable) from discarded waste. ➤ search for (carrion) as food. **2** remove (combustion products) from an internal-combustion engine cylinder on the return stroke of the piston. **3** Chemistry combine with and remove (molecules, radicals, etc.) from a particular medium.
– ORIGIN C17 (in the sense 'clean out'): back-form. from SCAVENGER.

**scavenger** ● n. **1** a person or animal that scavenges. **2** Chemistry a substance that reacts with and removes particular molecules, radicals, etc.
– ORIGIN C16: from Anglo-Norman Fr. *scawager*, from ONorth. Fr. *escauwer* 'inspect'; the term orig. denoted an officer who collected *scavage*, a toll on foreign merchants' goods.

**scazon** /'skeɪz(ə)n, 'ska-/ ● n. Prosody a modification of the iambic trimeter, in which a spondee or trochee takes the place of the final iambus.
– ORIGIN C17: via L. from Gk *skazōn*, neut. pres. part. (used as a noun) of *skazein* 'to limp'.

**ScD** ● abbrev. Doctor of Science.
– ORIGIN from L. *scientiae doctor.*

**SCE** ● abbrev. Scottish Certificate of Education.

**scena** /'ʃeɪnə/ ● n. a scene in an opera. ➤ an elaborate dramatic solo usually including recitative.
– ORIGIN Ital., from L., 'scene'.

**scenario** /sɪ'nɑːrɪəʊ/ ● n. (pl. **-os**) **1** a written outline of a film, novel, or stage work giving details of the plot and individual scenes. ➤ a setting, in particular for a work of art or literature. **2** a postulated sequence or development of events.
– ORIGIN C19: from Ital., from L. *scena* 'scene'.

**scenarist** /sɪ'nɑːrɪst/ ● n. a screenwriter.

**scend** /sɛnd/ (also **send**) archaic ● n. the push or surge created by a wave. ➤ a pitching or surging movement in a boat. ● v. (of a vessel) pitch or surge up in a heavy sea.
– ORIGIN C15: alt. of SEND[1] or DESCEND.

**scene** ● n. **1** the place where an incident in real life or fiction occurs or occurred. ➤ a landscape. ➤ a representation of an incident, or the incident itself: *scenes of 1930s America.* **2** a sequence of continuous action in a play, film, opera, etc. ➤ a subdivision of an act in a play, in which the time is continuous and the setting fixed. ➤ the pieces of scenery used in a play or opera. **3** a public display of emotion or anger. **4** a specified area of activity or interest. ➤ (usu. **the scene**) informal a social environment frequented by homosexuals.
– PHRASES **behind the scenes** out of public view. **change of scene** a move to different surroundings. **come** (or **appear** or **arrive**) **on the scene** arrive; appear. **hit** (or **make**) **the scene** US arrive; appear. **not one's scene** informal not something one enjoys or is interested in.
– ORIGIN C16: from L. *scena*, from Gk *skēnē* 'tent, stage'.

**scene dock** ● n. a space in a theatre near the stage, in which scenery is stored.

**scenery** • n. **1** the natural features of a landscape considered in terms of their appearance, especially when picturesque. **2** the painted background used to represent the fictional surroundings on a stage or film set.
– ORIGIN C18: from Ital. *scenario* (see **SCENARIO**).

**scenester** /ˈsiːnstə/ • n. informal, chiefly N. Amer. a person associated with a particular fashionable cultural scene.

**scenic** • adj. **1** of or relating to impressive or beautiful natural scenery: *the scenic route.* **2** of or relating to theatrical scenery. **3** (of a picture) representing an incident.
– DERIVATIVES **scenically** adv.

**scenic railway** • n. an attraction at a fair consisting of a miniature railway that goes past natural features and artificial scenery.

**scenography** • n. **1** the design and painting of theatrical scenery. **2** (in painting and drawing) the representation of objects in perspective.
– DERIVATIVES **scenographic** adj.

**scent** • n. **1** a distinctive smell, especially one that is pleasant. **2** pleasant-smelling liquid worn on the skin; perfume. **3** a trail indicated by the characteristic smell of an animal. ➤a trail of evidence assisting someone in a search or investigation. **4** archaic the faculty or sense of smell. • v. **1** impart a pleasant scent to. **2** discern by the sense of smell. ➤sense the presence or imminence of: *the Premier scented victory last night.*
– DERIVATIVES **scented** adj. **scentless** adj.
– ORIGIN ME: from OFr. *sentir* 'perceive, smell', from L. *sentire.*

**scent gland** • n. an animal gland that secretes an odorous pheromone or defensive substance.

**scent mark** • n. (also **scent marking**) an odoriferous substance containing a pheromone that is deposited by a mammal from a scent gland or in the urine or faeces. • v. (**scent-mark**) (of a mammal) deposit a scent mark.

**scepter** • n. US spelling of **SCEPTRE**.

**sceptic** (US **skeptic**) • n. **1** a person inclined to question or doubt accepted opinions. ➤a person who doubts the truth of Christianity and other religions; an atheist. **2** Philosophy a philosopher who denies the possibility of knowledge, or even rational belief, in certain spheres.
– DERIVATIVES **sceptical** adj. **scepticism** n.
– ORIGIN C16: from Fr. *sceptique*, or via L. from Gk *skeptikos*, from *skepsis* 'inquiry, doubt'.

**sceptre** (US **scepter**) • n. a staff carried by rulers on ceremonial occasions as a symbol of sovereignty.
– DERIVATIVES **sceptred** adj.
– ORIGIN ME: from OFr. *ceptre*, via L. from Gk *skēptron*, from *skēptein* 'lean on'.

**sch.** • abbrev. **1** scholar. **2** school. **3** schooner.

**Schadenfreude** /ˈʃɑːd(ə)nˌfrɔɪdə, German ˈʃaːdnˌfrɔydə/ • n. pleasure derived from another's misfortune.
– ORIGIN Ger., from *Schaden* 'harm' + *Freude* 'joy'.

**schappe** /ʃap, ˈʃapə/ • n. fabric or yarn made from waste silk.
– ORIGIN C19: from Ger. *Schappe* 'waste silk'.

**schedule** /ˈʃɛdjuːl, ˈskɛd-/ • n. **1** a plan for carrying out a process or procedure, giving lists of intended events and times. ➤a timetable. **2** chiefly Law an appendix to a formal document or statute, especially as a list, table, or inventory. **3** (with reference to the British income tax system) any of the forms (named 'A', 'B', etc.) issued relating to various classes of taxable income. • v. **1** arrange or plan to take place at a particular time. **2** include in a schedule. **3** Brit. include (a building) in a list for legal preservation or protection.
– PHRASES **to** (or **on** or **according to**) **schedule** on time; as planned.
– DERIVATIVES **schedular** adj. **scheduler** n.
– ORIGIN ME (in the sense 'scroll, note, appendix'): from OFr. *cedule*, from late L. *schedula* 'slip of paper', dimin. of *scheda*, from Gk *skhedē* 'papyrus leaf'.

**scheduled** • adj. **1** forming part of a schedule. ➤(of an airline or flight) forming part of a regular service rather than specially chartered. **2** Brit. (of a building) included in a list for legal preservation and protection.

**scheduled caste** • n. the official name given in India to the untouchable caste, who are given special concessions in recognition of their disadvantaged status.

**scheduled tribe** • n. (in India) a category of people officially regarded as socially disadvantaged, who are granted special concessions in recognition of this.

**scheelite** /ˈʃiːlʌɪt/ • n. a fluorescent mineral, white when pure, which consists of calcium tungstate and is an important ore of tungsten.
– ORIGIN C19: from the name of the C18 Swed. chemist Karl W. *Scheele* + **-ITE**[1].

**schefflera** /ˈʃɛflərə/ • n. an evergreen tropical or subtropical shrub which is grown as a pot plant for its decorative foliage. [Genus *Schefflera.*]
– ORIGIN mod. L., named after the C18 Ger. botanist J. C. *Scheffler.*

**schema** /ˈskiːmə/ • n. (pl. **schemata** /-mətə/ or **schemas**) **1** technical a representation of a plan or theory in the form of an outline or model. **2** Logic a syllogistic figure. **3** (in Kantian philosophy) a conception of what is common to all members of a class; a general or essential type.
– ORIGIN C18: from Gk *skhēma* 'form, figure'.

**schematic** • adj. **1** (of a diagram or representation) symbolic and simplified. **2** (of thought, ideas, etc.) simplistic or formulaic in character: *a highly schematic reading of the play.* • n. technical a schematic diagram, in particular of an electric or electronic circuit.
– DERIVATIVES **schematically** adv.

**schematism** • n. arrangement or presentation according to a scheme or schema.

**schematize** (also **-ise**) • v. arrange or represent in a schematic form.
– DERIVATIVES **schematization** n.

**scheme** • n. **1** a systematic plan or arrangement for attaining some particular object or putting a particular idea into effect. ➤a particular ordered system or arrangement: *a classical rhyme scheme.* **2** a secret or underhand plan; a plot. • v. **1** form a scheme, especially a devious one or with intent to do something wrong. **2** arrange according to a colour scheme.
– DERIVATIVES **schemer** n. **scheming** adj. & n. **schemingly** adv.
– ORIGIN C16 (denoting a figure of speech, later 'diagram of the position of celestial objects'): from L. *schema*, from Gk (see **SCHEMA**).

**schemozzle** • n. variant spelling of **SHEMOZZLE**.

**scherzando** /skɛːtˈsandəʊ/ • adv. & adj. Music in a playful manner.
– ORIGIN Ital., lit. 'joking'.

**scherzo** /ˈskɛːtsəʊ/ • n. (pl. **scherzos** or **scherzi** /-tsi/) Music a vigorous, light, or playful composition, typically comprising a movement in a symphony or sonata.
– ORIGIN Ital., lit. 'jest'.

**Schick test** /ʃɪk/ • n. Medicine a skin test for previously acquired immunity to diphtheria, using an injection of diphtheria toxin.
– ORIGIN C20: named after the Amer. paediatrician Bela *Schick.*

**Schiff base** • n. Chemistry an organic compound having the structure $R^1R^2C{=}NR^3$ (where $R^{1,2,3}$ are alkyl groups and $R^1$ may be hydrogen).
– ORIGIN C19: named after the Ger. chemist Hugo *Schiff.*

**Schiff's reagent** /ʃɪfs/ • n. Chemistry an acid solution of fuchsin decolorized by sulphur dioxide or potassium metabisulphite, used in testing for aldehydes (which restore the magenta colour).
– ORIGIN C19: see **SCHIFF BASE**.

**schilling** /ˈʃɪlɪŋ/ • n. the basic monetary unit of Austria, equal to 100 groschen.
– ORIGIN from Ger. *Schilling*; cf. **SHILLING**.

**schipperke** /ˈskɪpəki, ˈʃɪp-, -kə/ • n. a small black tailless dog of a breed with a ruff of fur round its neck.
– ORIGIN C19: from Du. dial., lit. 'little boatman', with ref. to its use as a watchdog on barges.

**schism** /ˈsɪz(ə)m, ˈskɪz(ə)m/ • n. **1** a division between strongly opposed parties, caused by differences in opinion or belief. **2** the formal separation of a Church into two Churches or the secession of a group owing to doctrinal and other differences.

– ORIGIN ME: from OFr. *scisme*, via eccles. L. from Gk *skhisma* 'cleft', from *skhizein* 'to split'.

**schismatic** ● adj. of, characterized by, or favouring schism. ● n. chiefly historical (especially in the Christian Church) a person who promotes schism.
– DERIVATIVES **schismatically** adv.

**schist** /ʃɪst/ ● n. Geology a coarse-grained metamorphic rock which consists of layers of different minerals and can be split into thin irregular plates.
– ORIGIN C18: from Fr. *schiste*, via L. from Gk *skhistos* 'split', from the base of *skhizein* 'cleave'.

**schistose** /ˈʃɪstəʊs/ ● adj. Geology having a laminar structure like that of schist.
– DERIVATIVES **schistosity** n.

**schistosome** /ˈʃɪstə(ʊ)ˌsəʊm/ ● n. a parasitic flatworm which causes bilharzia in humans, infesting freshwater snails when immature and the blood vessels of birds and mammals when adult. [Genus *Schistosoma*.]
– ORIGIN C20: from mod. L. *Schistosoma*, from Gk *skhistos* 'divided' + *sōma* 'body'.

**schistosomiasis** /ˌʃɪstə(ʊ)səˈmʌɪəsɪs/ ● n. another term for **BILHARZIA**.

**schizandra** /skɪtˈsandrə/ ● n. a Chinese herb whose berries are credited with various stimulant or medicinal properties. [*Schisandra chinensis*.]
– ORIGIN mod. L.

**schizanthus** /skɪtˈsanθəs/ ● n. a South American plant of the nightshade family, with irregularly lobed flowers having contrasting colours. [Genus *Schizanthus*.]
– ORIGIN mod. L., from Gk *skhizein* 'to split' + *anthos* 'flower'.

**schizo** ● adj. & n. (pl. **-os**) informal schizophrenic.

**schizo-** ● comb. form **1** divided; split: *schizocarp*. **2** relating to schizophrenia: *schizotype*.
– ORIGIN from Gk *skhizein* 'to split'.

**schizocarp** /ˈʃʌɪzə(ʊ)kɑːp, ˈskɪts-/ ● n. Botany a dry fruit that splits into single-seeded parts when ripe.
– ORIGIN C19: from **SCHIZO-** + Gk *karpos* 'fruit'.

**schizogenous** /ʃʌɪˈzɒdʒənəs, skɪts-/ ● adj. Botany (of an intercellular space in a plant) formed by the splitting of the common wall of contiguous cells.
– DERIVATIVES **schizogenic** adj. **schizogeny** n.

**schizogony** /ʃʌɪˈzɒɡəni, skɪts-/ ● n. Biology asexual reproduction by multiple fission, found in some protozoans.
– DERIVATIVES **schizogonous** adj.
– ORIGIN C19: from **SCHIZO-** + Gk *-gonia* 'production'.

**schizoid** /ˈskɪtsɔɪd, ˈskɪdz-/ ● adj. Psychiatry denoting a personality type characterized by emotional aloofness and solitary habits. ➤informal resembling schizophrenia in having contradictory elements; mad or crazy.

**schizont** /ˈʃʌɪzɒnt, ˈskɪ-/ ● n. Biology (in certain sporozoan protozoans) a cell that divides by schizogony to form daughter cells.
– ORIGIN C20: from **SCHIZO-** + **-ONT**.

**schizophrenia** /ˌskɪtsə(ʊ)ˈfriːnɪə/ ● n. a long-term mental disorder of a type involving a breakdown in the relation between thought, emotion, and behaviour, leading to faulty perception, inappropriate actions and feelings, and withdrawal from reality into fantasy and delusion.
– DERIVATIVES **schizophrenic** /-ˈfrɛnɪk/ adj. & n.
– ORIGIN C20: mod. L., from Gk *skhizein* 'to split' + *phrēn* 'mind'.

**schizostylis** /ˌʃʌɪzə(ʊ)ˈstʌɪlɪs, ˌskɪts-/ ● n. (pl. same) a plant of a genus that includes the Kaffir lily. [Genus *Schizostylis*.]
– ORIGIN mod. L., from **SCHIZO-** + L. *stilus* 'style' (because of the split styles of the plant).

**schizotype** /ˈskɪtsəʊtʌɪp/ ● n. a personality type in which mild symptoms of schizophrenia are present.
– DERIVATIVES **schizotypal** adj. **schizotypy** n.

**schlemiel** /ʃləˈmiːl/ ● n. N. Amer. informal a stupid, awkward, or unlucky person.
– ORIGIN C19: from Yiddish *shlemiel*.

**schlep** /ʃlɛp/ (also **schlepp**) informal, chiefly N. Amer. ● v. (**schlepped**, **schlepping**) **1** haul or carry with difficulty. **2** go or move reluctantly or with effort. ● n. **1** a tedious or difficult journey. **2** (also **schlepper**) a stupid person.
– ORIGIN C20: from Yiddish *shlepn* 'drag', from Mid. High Ger. *sleppen*.

**schlieren** /ˈʃlɪərən/ ● pl. n. **1** technical discernible layers in a transparent material that differ from the surrounding material in density or composition. **2** Geology irregular streaks or masses in igneous rock.
– ORIGIN C19: from Ger. *Schlieren*, pl. of *Schliere* 'streak'.

**schlock** /ʃlɒk/ ● n. informal, chiefly N. Amer. cheap or inferior goods; trash.
– DERIVATIVES **schlocky** adj.
– ORIGIN C20: appar. from Yiddish *shlak* 'an apoplectic stroke', *shlog* 'wretch, untidy person'.

**schlockmeister** /ˈʃlɒkˌmʌɪstə/ ● n. informal, chiefly N. Amer. a purveyor of cheap or trashy goods.
– ORIGIN C20: from **SCHLOCK** + Ger. *Meister* 'master'.

**schloss** /ʃlɒs/ ● n. (in Germany, Austria, or their former territories) a castle.
– ORIGIN C19: from Ger. *Schloss*.

**schlub** /ʃlʌb/ (also **shlub**) ● n. N. Amer. informal a talentless, unattractive, or boorish person.
– ORIGIN 1960s: Yiddish *shlub*, perh. from Polish *żłób*.

**schlump** /ʃlʊmp/ ● n. N. Amer. informal a slow, slovenly, or inept person.
– ORIGIN 1940s: appar. rel. to Yiddish *shlumperdik* 'dowdy' and Ger. *Schlumpe* 'slattern'.

**schmaltz** /ʃmɔːlts, ʃmalts/ ● n. informal excessive sentimentality.
– DERIVATIVES **schmaltzy** adj. (**-ier**, **-iest**).
– ORIGIN 1930s: from Yiddish *shmaltz*, from Ger. *Schmalz* 'dripping, lard'.

**schmear** /ʃmɪə/ (also **schmeer**, **shmeer**, or **shmear**) ● n. US informal fat or grease.
– PHRASES **the whole schmear** N. Amer. everything possible or available.
– ORIGIN 1960s: from Yiddish *shmirn* 'flatter, grease'.

**Schmidt telescope** ● n. a type of catadioptric telescope used for wide-angle astronomical photography, with a thin glass plate at the front to correct for spherical aberration.
– ORIGIN 1930s: named after the Ger. inventor Bernhard V. *Schmidt*.

**schmo** /ʃməʊ/ (also **shmo**) ● n. (pl. **-oes**) N. Amer. informal a foolish or inept person.
– ORIGIN 1940s: alt. of **SCHMUCK**.

**schmooze** /ʃmuːz/ chiefly N. Amer. ● v. chat; gossip. ➤chat to (someone) in order to gain an advantage. ● n. an intimate conversation.
– DERIVATIVES **schmoozer** n. **schmoozy** adj.
– ORIGIN C19: from Yiddish *shmuesn* 'converse, chat'.

**schmuck** /ʃmʌk/ ● n. N. Amer. informal a foolish or contemptible person.
– ORIGIN C19: from Yiddish *shmok* 'penis'.

**schnapps** /ʃnaps/ ● n. a strong alcoholic drink resembling gin.
– ORIGIN from Ger. *Schnaps*, lit. 'dram of liquor', from Low Ger. and Du. *snaps* 'mouthful'.

**schnauzer** /ˈʃnaʊzə/ ● n. a dog of a German breed with a close wiry coat and heavy whiskers round the muzzle.
– ORIGIN C20: from Ger., from *Schnauze* 'muzzle, snout'.

**schnitzel** /ˈʃnɪtz(ə)l/ ● n. a thin slice of veal or other pale meat, coated in breadcrumbs and fried.
– ORIGIN from Ger. *Schnitzel*, lit. 'slice'.

**schnook** /ʃnʊk/ ● n. US informal a fool.
– ORIGIN 1940s: perh. from Ger. *Schnucke* 'small sheep' or from Yiddish *shnuk* 'snout'.

**schnorrer** /ˈʃnɒrə, ˈʃnɔːrə/ ● n. informal, chiefly N. Amer. a beggar or scrounger.
– ORIGIN C19: from Yiddish *shnorrer*, var. of Ger. *Schnurrer*.

**schnozz** /ʃnɒz/ (also **schnozzle** or **schnozzola**) ● n. N. Amer. informal a person's nose.
– ORIGIN 1940s: from Yiddish *shnoytz*, from Ger. *Schnauze* 'snout'.

**scholar** ● n. **1** a specialist in a particular branch of study, especially the humanities; a distinguished academic. ➤chiefly archaic a person who is highly educated or has an aptitude for study. **2** a university student holding a scholarship. **3** archaic a student or pupil.
– DERIVATIVES **scholarliness** n. **scholarly** adj.

– ORIGIN OE *scol(i)ere* 'student', from late L. *scholaris*, via L. from Gk *skholē* (see SCHOOL[1]).

**scholarship** • n. 1 academic achievement; learning of a high level. 2 a grant made to support a student's education, awarded on the basis of achievement.

**scholastic** • adj. 1 of or concerning schools and education. 2 relating to medieval scholasticism. ➤ typical of scholasticism in being pedantic or overly subtle. • n. 1 Philosophy & Theology, historical an adherent of scholasticism; a schoolman. 2 (in the Roman Catholic Church) a member of a religious order, especially the Society of Jesus, who is between the novitiate and the priesthood.
– DERIVATIVES **scholastically** adv.
– ORIGIN C16: via L. from Gk *skholastikos* 'studious', from *skholazein*, from *skholē* (see SCHOOL[1]).

**scholasticism** /skəˈlastɪˌsɪz(ə)m/ • n. 1 the system of theology and philosophy taught in medieval European universities, based on Aristotelian logic and the writings of the early Christian Fathers and having a strong emphasis on tradition and dogma. 2 narrow-minded insistence on traditional doctrine.

**scholiast** /ˈskəʊlɪast/ • n. historical a commentator on ancient or classical literature.
– DERIVATIVES **scholiastic** adj.

**scholium** /ˈskəʊlɪəm/ • n. (pl. **scholia** /-lɪə/) historical a marginal note made by a scholiast.
– ORIGIN C16: mod. L., from Gk *skholion*, from *skholē* 'learned discussion'.

**school[1]** • n. 1 an institution for educating children. ➤ a day's work at school; lessons. 2 any institution at which instruction is given in a particular discipline: *a dancing school*. ➤ N. Amer. informal a university. ➤ a department or faculty of a university: *the School of Dental Medicine*. 3 a group of people sharing similar ideas, methods, or style. ➤ a specified style, approach, or method. 4 Brit. a group of people gambling together. ➤ a group of people drinking together and taking turns to buy the drinks. • v. 1 chiefly formal or N. Amer. send to school; educate. 2 train in a particular skill or activity. ➤ Riding train (a horse) on the flat or over fences.
– PHRASES **school of thought** a particular way of thinking.
– ORIGIN OE *scōl, scolu*, via L. from Gk *skholē* 'leisure, philosophy, lecture-place', reinforced in ME by OFr. *escole*.

**school[2]** • n. a large group of fish or sea mammals. • v. (of fish or sea mammals) form a school.
– ORIGIN ME: from Mid. Low Ger., MDu. *schōle*, of W. Gmc origin; cf. SHOAL[1].

**school board** • n. N. Amer. or historical a local board or authority responsible for the provision and maintenance of schools.

**schoolboy** (or **schoolgirl**) • n. a boy (or girl) attending school.

**schooler** • n. [in combination] chiefly N. Amer. a pupil or student of a particular level or status: *a high-schooler*.

**schoolhouse** • n. 1 a building used as a school, especially in a rural community. 2 Brit., chiefly historical a house adjoining a school, lived in by the schoolteacher.

**schoolie** • n. informal, Austral. & dialect a schoolteacher or school student.

**schooling** • n. 1 education received at school. 2 Riding the training of a horse on the flat or over fences.

**schoolman** • n. (pl. **-men**) historical 1 a teacher in a university in medieval Europe. 2 a scholastic theologian.

**schoolmarm** • n. chiefly N. Amer. a schoolmistress, especially one regarded as prim and strict.
– DERIVATIVES **schoolmarmish** adj.

**schoolmaster** • n. 1 a male teacher in a school. 2 an experienced horse that is used to train or give confidence to inexperienced riders or horses.
– DERIVATIVES **schoolmastering** n. **schoolmasterly** adj.

**schoolmate** • n. informal a fellow pupil.

**schoolmistress** • n. a female teacher in a school.

**schoolteacher** • n. a person who teaches in a school.
– DERIVATIVES **schoolteaching** n.

**schooner** /ˈskuːnə/ • n. 1 a sailing ship with two or more masts, typically with the foremast smaller than the mainmast. 2 Brit. a large glass for sherry. ➤ N. Amer. & Austral./NZ a tall beer glass.
– ORIGIN C18: perh. from dial. *scun* 'skim along', influenced by Du. words beginning with *sch-*.

**schorl** /ʃɔːl/ • n. a black iron-rich variety of tourmaline.
– ORIGIN C18: from Ger. *Schörl*, of unknown origin.

**schottische** /ʃɒˈtiːʃ, ˈʃɒtɪʃ/ • n. a dance resembling a slow polka.
– ORIGIN C19: from Ger. *der schottische Tanz* 'the Scottish dance'.

**Schrödinger equation** • n. Physics a differential equation which forms the basis of the quantum-mechanical description of a particle.
– ORIGIN C20: named after the Austrian physicist Erwin *Schrödinger*.

**schtuck** • n. variant spelling of SHTOOK.

**schtum** /ʃtʊm/ • adj. variant spelling of SHTUM.

**schtup** /ʃtʊp/ • v. variant spelling of SHTUP.

**schuss** /ʃʊs/ • n. a straight downhill run on skis. • v. perform a schuss.
– ORIGIN 1930s: from Ger. *Schuss*, lit. 'shot'.

**schwa** /ʃwɑː/ • n. Phonetics the unstressed central vowel (as in *a* moment *ago*), represented by the symbol /ə/ in the International Phonetic Alphabet.
– ORIGIN C19: from Ger., from Heb. *šĕwā'*.

**sciagraphy** /sʌɪˈagrəfi/ (also **skiagraphy**) • n. the use of shading to show perspective in architectural or technical drawing.
– DERIVATIVES **sciagram** n. **sciagraph** n. & v. **sciagraphic** adj.
– ORIGIN C16: from Fr. *sciagraphie*, via L. from Gk *skiagraphia*, from *skia* 'shadow'.

**sciatic** /sʌɪˈatɪk/ • adj. 1 of or relating to the hip. 2 of or affecting the sciatic nerve. ➤ suffering from or liable to sciatica.
– DERIVATIVES **sciatically** adv.
– ORIGIN C16 (as n.): from Fr. *sciatique*, via late L. from Gk *iskhiadikos* 'relating to the hips', from *iskhion* 'hip joint'.

**sciatica** • n. pain affecting the back, hip, and outer side of the leg, caused by compression of a spinal nerve root in the lower back.
– ORIGIN ME: from late L. *sciatica (passio)* '(affliction) of sciatica' (see SCIATIC).

**sciatic nerve** • n. Anatomy a major nerve extending from the lower end of the spinal cord down the back of the thigh.

**SCID** • abbrev. severe combined immune deficiency, a rare genetic disorder in which affected children have no resistance to disease.

**science** • n. 1 the intellectual and practical activity encompassing the systematic study of the structure and behaviour of the physical and natural world through observation and experiment. 2 a systematically organized body of knowledge on any subject. 3 archaic knowledge.
– ORIGIN ME: from OFr., from L. *scientia*, from *scire* 'know'.

**science fiction** • n. fiction based on imagined future worlds portraying scientific or technological changes.

**science park** • n. an area devoted to scientific research or the development of science-based industries.

**scienter** /sʌɪˈɛntə/ • n. Law the fact of an act having been done knowingly, especially as grounds for civil damages.
– ORIGIN L., from *scire* know.

**sciential** /sʌɪˈɛnʃ(ə)l/ • adj. archaic concerning or having knowledge.
– ORIGIN ME: from late L. *scientialis*, from *scientia* (see SCIENCE).

**scientific** • adj. 1 of, relating to, or based on science. 2 systematic; methodical.
– DERIVATIVES **scientifically** adv. **scientificity** n.
– ORIGIN C16: from Fr. *scientifique* or late L. *scientificus* 'producing knowledge', from *scientia* (see SCIENCE).

**scientism** • n. thought or expression regarded as characteristic of scientists. ➤ excessive belief in the power of scientific knowledge and techniques.

– DERIVATIVES **scientistic** adj.

**scientist** • n. a person who is studying or has expert knowledge of one or more of the natural or physical sciences.

**Scientology** • n. trademark a religious system based on the seeking of self-knowledge and spiritual fulfilment through graded courses of study and training.
– DERIVATIVES **Scientologist** n.
– ORIGIN from L. *scientia* 'knowledge' + **-LOGY**.

**sci-fi** • n. informal short for **SCIENCE FICTION**.

**scilicet** /ˈsʌɪlɪsɛt, ˈskiːlɪkɛt/ • adv. that is to say; namely (introducing a missing word or an explanation).
– ORIGIN L., from *scire licet* 'one is permitted to know'.

**scilla** /ˈsɪlə/ • n. a plant of the lily family which typically bears small blue star- or bell-shaped flowers and glossy strap-like leaves. [Genus *Scilla*.]
– ORIGIN mod. L., from L. *scilla* 'sea onion', from Gk *skilla*.

**Scillonian** /sɪˈləʊnɪən/ • n. a native or inhabitant of the Scilly Isles. • adj. of or relating to the Scilly Isles.

**scimitar** /ˈsɪmɪtə/ • n. a short sword with a curved blade that broadens towards the point, used originally in Eastern countries.
– ORIGIN C16: from Fr. *cimeterre* or Ital. *scimitarra*, of unknown origin.

**scintigram** /ˈsɪntɪgram/ • n. Medicine an image of an internal part of the body produced by scintigraphy.

**scintigraphy** /sɪnˈtɪgrəfi/ • n. Medicine a technique in which a scintillation counter or similar detector is used with a radioactive tracer to obtain an image of a bodily organ.
– DERIVATIVES **scintigraphic** adj.
– ORIGIN 1950s: from **SCINTILLATION** + **-GRAPHY**.

**scintilla** /sɪnˈtɪlə/ • n. a tiny trace or amount: *not a scintilla of doubt.*
– ORIGIN C17: L. 'spark'.

**scintillate** /ˈsɪntɪleɪt/ • v. emit flashes of light; sparkle. ➤ Physics fluoresce momentarily when struck by a charged particle or photon.
– DERIVATIVES **scintillant** adj. & n.
– ORIGIN C17: from L. *scintillat-*, *scintillare* 'to sparkle', from *scintilla* 'spark'.

**scintillating** • adj. **1** sparkling or shining brightly. **2** brilliant and exciting: *his scintillating wit.*
– DERIVATIVES **scintillatingly** adv.

**scintillation** • n. **1** a flash of light. ➤ the process or state of emitting flashes. **2** Physics a small flash of visible or ultraviolet light emitted by fluorescence in a phosphor when struck by a charged particle or high-energy photon. **3** Astronomy the twinkling of the stars, caused by the earth's atmosphere diffracting starlight unevenly.

**scintillator** • n. Physics **1** a material that scintillates. **2** a detector for charged particles and gamma rays in which scintillations are amplified by a photomultiplier, giving an electrical output signal.

**scintiscan** • n. Medicine another term for **SCINTIGRAM**.

**sciolist** /ˈsʌɪəlɪst/ • n. archaic a person who purports to be knowledgeable.
– DERIVATIVES **sciolism** n. **sciolistic** adj.
– ORIGIN C17: from late L. *sciolus* (dimin. of L. *scius* 'knowing', from *scire* 'know') + **-IST**.

**scion** /ˈsʌɪən/ • n. **1** (US also **cion**) a young shoot or twig of a plant, especially one cut for grafting or rooting. **2** a descendant of a notable family or one with a long lineage.
– ORIGIN ME: from OFr. *ciun* 'shoot, twig', of unknown origin.

**scire facias** /ˌsʌɪriː ˈfeɪʃɪas/ • n. US Law a writ requiring a person to show why a judgement regarding a record or patent should not be enforced or annulled.
– ORIGIN L., lit. 'let (the person) know'.

**scirocco** • n. variant spelling of **SIROCCO**.

**scirrhus** /ˈsɪrəs, ˈskɪ-/ • n. (pl. **scirrhi** /-rʌɪ/) Medicine a carcinoma that is hard to the touch.
– DERIVATIVES **scirrhous** adj.
– ORIGIN ME: mod. L., from Gk *skirros*, from *skiros* 'hard'.

**scissel** /ˈsɪs(ə)l/ • n. pieces of waste metal produced during the manufacture of coins.
– ORIGIN C17: from Fr. *cisaille*, from *cisailler* 'clip with shears'.

**scissile** /ˈsɪsʌɪl, -sɪl/ • adj. chiefly Biochemistry readily undergoing scission.
– ORIGIN C17: from L. *scissilis*, from *sciss-*, *scindere* 'cut, divide'.

**scission** /ˈsɪʃ(ə)n/ • n. **1** a division or split; a schism. **2** chiefly Biochemistry breakage of a chemical bond.
– ORIGIN ME: from OFr., or from late L. *scissio(n-)*, from *scindere* 'cut, cleave'.

**scissor** • v. **1** cut with scissors. **2** move or cause to move in a way resembling the action of scissors.

**scissorbill** • n. **1** another term for **SKIMMER** (in sense 2). **2** N. Amer. informal an incompetent or objectionable person.

**scissor hold** (also **scissors hold**) • n. Wrestling a hold in which the opponent's body or head is gripped between the legs which are then locked at the feet to apply pressure.

**scissors** • pl. n. **1** (also **a pair of scissors**) an instrument used for cutting cloth and paper, consisting of two crossing blades pivoted in the middle and operated by thumb and fingers inserted in rings at each end. **2** (also **scissor**) [as modifier] denoting an action in which two things cross each other or open and close like a pair of scissors: *a scissor kick.*
– ORIGIN ME: from OFr. *cisoires*, from late L. *cisoria*, pl. of *cisorium* 'cutting instrument'; the *sc-* spelling arose by assoc. with the L. stem *sciss-* 'cut'.

**sclera** /ˈsklɪərə/ • n. Anatomy the white outer layer of the eyeball.
– DERIVATIVES **scleral** adj.
– ORIGIN C19: mod. L., from Gk *sklēros* 'hard'.

**Scleractinia** /ˌsklɛrakˈtɪnɪə/ • pl. n. Zoology an order of coelenterates that comprises the stony corals.
– DERIVATIVES **scleractinian** n. & adj.
– ORIGIN mod. L., from Gk *sklēros* 'hard' + *aktis*, *aktin-* 'ray'.

**sclerenchyma** /sklɪəˈrɛŋkɪmə, sklə-/ • n. Botany strengthening tissue in a plant, formed from cells with thickened walls.
– DERIVATIVES **sclerenchymatous** adj.
– ORIGIN C19: mod. L., from Gk *sklēros* 'hard' + *enkhuma* 'infusion'.

**sclerite** /ˈsklɪərʌɪt, ˈsklɛ-/ • n. Zoology a component section of an exoskeleton, especially each of the plates forming the skeleton of an arthropod.
– ORIGIN C19: from Gk *sklēros* 'hard' + **-ITE**[1].

**scleritis** /sklɪəˈrʌɪtɪs, sklə-/ • n. Medicine inflammation of the sclera of the eye.

**sclero-** /ˈsklɪərəʊ/ • comb. form hard; hardened; hardening: *sclerotherapy.*
– ORIGIN from Gk *sklēros* 'hard'.

**scleroderma** /ˌsklɪərəˈdəːmə/ • n. Medicine a chronic hardening and contraction of the skin and connective tissue, either locally or throughout the body.

**sclerophyll** /ˈsklɪərəfɪl, ˈsklɛ-/ • n. Botany a woody plant with evergreen leaves that are tough and thick in order to reduce water loss.
– DERIVATIVES **sclerophyllous** /-ˈrɒfɪləs/ adj.
– ORIGIN C20: from Gk *sklēros* 'hard' + *phullon* 'leaf'.

**scleroprotein** /ˌsklɪərə(ʊ)ˈprəʊtiːn, ˌsklɛ-/ • n. Biochemistry an insoluble structural protein such as keratin, collagen, or elastin.

**sclerose** /sklɪəˈrəʊs, sklə-, ˈsklɪə-/ • v. Medicine [usu. as adj. **sclerosed** or **sclerosing**] affect with sclerosis.

**sclerosis** /sklɪəˈrəʊsɪs, sklə-/ • n. Medicine **1** abnormal hardening of body tissue. **2** (in full **multiple sclerosis**) a chronic, typically progressive disease involving damage to the sheaths of nerve cells in the brain and spinal cord, whose symptoms may include numbness, impairment of speech and muscular coordination, blurred vision, and severe fatigue.
– ORIGIN ME: via med. L. from Gk *sklērōsis*, from *sklēroun* 'harden'.

**sclerotherapy** /ˌsklɪərə(ʊ)ˈθɛrəpi, ˌsklɛ-/ • n. Medicine the treatment of varicose blood vessels by the injection of an irritant which causes inflammation, coagulation of blood, and narrowing of the blood vessel wall.

**sclerotic** /sklɪə'rɒtɪk, sklə-/ ● **adj.** **1** Medicine of or having sclerosis. **2** Anatomy of or relating to the sclera. **3** rigid; unable to adapt: *sclerotic management.* ● **n.** another term for **SCLERA**.

**sclerotin** /'sklɪərətɪn, 'sklɛ-/ ● **n.** Biochemistry a structural protein which forms the cuticles of insects and is hardened and darkened by a natural tanning process.
– ORIGIN 1940s: from **SCLERO-**, on the pattern of *keratin.*

**sclerotium** /sklɪə'rəʊtɪəm, sklə-/ ● **n.** (pl. **sclerotia** /-tɪə/) Botany the hard dark resting body of certain fungi, consisting of a mass of hyphal threads.
– ORIGIN C19: mod. L., from Gk *sklēros* 'hard'.

**sclerotized** /'sklɪərətʌɪzd, 'sklɛ-/ (also **-ised**) ● **adj.** Entomology hardened by conversion into sclerotin.
– DERIVATIVES **sclerotization** n.

**SCM** ● **abbrev.** (in the UK) **1** State Certified Midwife. **2** Student Christian Movement.

**scoff**[1] ● **v.** speak about something in a scornfully derisive way. ● **n.** an expression of scornful derision. ➤ archaic an object of ridicule.
– DERIVATIVES **scoffer** n. **scoffing** adj. **scoffingly** adv.
– ORIGIN ME: perh. of Scand. origin.

**scoff**[2] informal, chiefly Brit. ● **v.** eat quickly and greedily. ● **n.** food.
– ORIGIN C18: v. orig. a var. of Scots and dial. *scaff*; n. from Afrik. *schoff*, representing Du. *schoft* 'quarter of a day, meal'.

**scofflaw** ● **n.** N. Amer. informal a person who flouts the law.

**scold** ● **v.** angrily remonstrate with or rebuke. ● **n.** archaic a woman who nags or grumbles constantly.
– DERIVATIVES **scolder** n.
– ORIGIN ME: prob. from ON *skáld* 'skald'.

**scold's bridle** ● **n.** another term for **BRANKS**.

**scolex** /'skəʊlɛks/ ● **n.** (pl. **scolices** /-lɪsiːz/) Zoology the anterior end of a tapeworm, bearing suckers and hooks for attachment.
– ORIGIN C19: mod. L., from Gk *skōlēx* 'worm'.

**scoliosis** /ˌskɒlɪ'əʊsɪs, ˌskəʊ-/ ● **n.** Medicine abnormal lateral curvature of the spine.
– DERIVATIVES **scoliotic** adj.
– ORIGIN C18: mod. L., from Gk, from *skolios* 'bent'.

**scollop** ● **n.** & **v.** archaic spelling of **SCALLOP**.

**sconce**[1] ● **n.** a candle holder attached to a wall with an ornamental bracket.
– ORIGIN ME (orig. denoting a portable lantern): from OFr. *esconse* 'lantern' or med. L. *sconsa*, from L. *absconsa* (*laterna*) 'dark (lantern)', from *abscondere* 'to hide'.

**sconce**[2] ● **n.** archaic a small fort or earthwork.
– ORIGIN ME: from Du. *schans* 'brushwood', from Mid. High Ger. *schanze.*

**scone** /skɒn, skəʊn/ ● **n.** a small unsweetened or lightly sweetened cake made from flour, fat, and milk.
– ORIGIN C16 (orig. Scots): perh. from MDu. *schoon(broot)* 'fine (bread)'.

**scoop** ● **n.** **1** a utensil resembling a spoon, having a short handle and a deep bowl, used for extracting liquids or substances from a container. ➤ the bowl-shaped part of a digging machine or dredger. ➤ a long-handled spoon-like surgical instrument. **2** informal a piece of news published or broadcast in advance of being released by other newspapers or broadcast stations. ➤ (**the scoop**) N. Amer. the latest news. **3** an exaggerated upward slide or portamento in singing. ● **v.** **1** pick up with a scoop. ➤ create (a hollow) with or as if with a scoop. ➤ pick or gather up in a swift, fluid movement: *he laughed and scooped her up in his arms.* **2** informal publish a scoop. **3** win.
– DERIVATIVES **scooper** n. **scoopful** n. (pl. **-fuls**).
– ORIGIN ME: from MDu., Mid. Low Ger. *schōpe* 'waterwheel bucket'; rel. to **SHAPE**.

**scoop neck** ● **n.** a deeply curved wide neckline on a woman's garment.
– DERIVATIVES **scoop-necked** adj.

**scoosh** Scottish ● **v.** squirt or splash. ● **n.** a splash or squirt of liquid.
– ORIGIN imitative.

**scoot** ● **v.** informal go or leave somewhere quickly. ➤ move or cause to move with a rapid, darting motion.
– ORIGIN C18: of unknown origin.

**scooter** ● **n.** **1** (also **motor scooter**) a light two-wheeled motorcycle. **2** any small light vehicle able to travel quickly across water or snow. **3** a child's toy consisting of a footboard mounted on two wheels and a long steering handle, propelled by pushing one foot against the ground. ● **v.** travel or ride on a scooter.
– DERIVATIVES **scooterist** n.

**scope**[1] ● **n.** **1** the extent of the area or subject matter that something deals with or to which it is relevant: *these complex matters are beyond the scope of this book.* **2** the opportunity or possibility for doing something. ➤ archaic a purpose or intention. **3** Nautical the length of cable extended when a ship rides at anchor.
– ORIGIN C16 (in the sense 'target for shooting at'): from Ital. *scopo* 'aim', from Gk *skopos* 'target'.

**scope**[2] ● **n.** informal a telescope, microscope, or other device having a name ending in *-scope.* ● **v.** N. Amer. informal look at carefully; scan. ➤ assess; weigh up.

**-scope** ● **comb. form** denoting an instrument for observing or examining: *telescope.* See word-formation panel.
– DERIVATIVES **-scopic** comb. form in corresponding adjectives.
– ORIGIN from mod. L. *-scopium*, from Gk *skopein* 'look at'.

**scopolamine** /skə(ʊ)'pɒləmiːn/ ● **n.** another term for **HYOSCINE**.
– ORIGIN C19: from *Scopolia* (genus name) + **AMINE**.

**scops owl** /skɒps/ ● **n.** a small owl with ear tufts. [*Otus scops* (Eurasia) and related species.]
– ORIGIN C18: from mod. L. *Scops* (former genus name), from Gk *skōps.*

**-scopy** ● **comb. form** indicating observation or examination: *microscopy.*
– ORIGIN from Gk *skopia* 'observation', from *skopein* 'examine, look at'.

**scorbutic** /skɔː'bjuːtɪk/ ● **adj.** relating to or affected with scurvy.
– ORIGIN C17: from mod. L. *scorbuticus*, from med. L. *scorbutus* 'scurvy'.

**scorch** ● **v.** **1** become burnt or cause to become burnt on the surface or edges. ➤ [often as adj. **scorched**] cause to become dried out and withered as a result of extreme heat. **2** informal move very fast. ● **n.** **1** the burning or charring of the surface of something. **2** Botany a form of plant necrosis marked by browning of leaf margins.
– DERIVATIVES **scorching** adj. **scorchingly** adv.
– ORIGIN ME: perh. rel. to ON *skorpna* 'be shrivelled'.

**scorched earth policy** ● **n.** a military strategy of burning or destroying all crops and resources that might be of use to an invading enemy force.

**scorcher** ● **n.** informal **1** a day or period of very hot weather. **2** Brit. a remarkable or powerful example of something: *a scorcher of a story.*

**scordatura** /skɔːdə'tjʊərə/ ● **n.** Music the technique of altering the normal tuning of a stringed instrument to produce particular effects.
– ORIGIN C19: Ital., from *scordare* 'be out of tune'.

**score** ● **n.** **1** the number of points, goals, runs, etc. achieved in a game or by an individual. ➤ a mark or grade. **2** (**the score**) informal the state of affairs; the real facts. **3** (pl. same) a group or set of twenty. ➤ a large amount or number: *he sent scores of letters to friends.* **4** a written representation of a musical composition showing all the vocal and instrumental parts. **5** a notch or line cut or scratched into a surface. ➤ historical a running account kept by marks against a customer's name, typically in a public house. **6** informal an act of buying illegal drugs. ➤ informal the proceeds of a crime. ● **v.** **1** gain (a point, goal, run, etc.) in a competitive game. ➤ be worth (a number of points). ➤ record the score during a game. ➤ Baseball cause (a teammate) to score. **2** orchestrate or arrange (a piece of music). ➤ compose the music for (a film or play). **3** cut or scratch a mark or notch on (a surface). ➤ (**score something out/through**) delete text by drawing a line through it. **4** informal secure (a success or an advantage). ➤ be successful. ➤ succeed in obtaining (illegal drugs).

## Word *Formation*

**-scope** from Greek *skopein* 'look at'

➤ Most **-scope** words have the sense 'an instrument used in observation or examination':

| | | |
|---|---|---|
| arthroscope | an instrument for inspecting the interior of a joint | Gk *arthron* 'joint' |
| bronchoscope | a fibre-optic cable passed down the windpipe to view the bronchi | Gk *bronkhos* 'windpipe' |
| electroscope | an instrument for detecting electric charge | ELECTRO- |
| endoscope | an instrument for viewing internal organs | Gk *endon* 'within' |
| fibrescope | a fibre-optic device for viewing normally inaccessible structures | based on FIBRE OPTICS |
| gyroscope | a device used to provide or maintain stability, consisting of a disc spinning rapidly about an axis | Gk *guros* 'a ring' |
| kaleidoscope | a tube containing mirrors and coloured glass, forming changing patterns when the base is rotated | Gk *kalos* 'beautiful' + *eidos* 'form' |
| microscope | an instrument for viewing tiny objects through magnification | Gk *mikros* 'small' |
| oscilloscope | a device for viewing oscillations on the screen of a cathode ray tube | OSCILLO- |
| periscope | a device having a series of mirrors, for viewing objects normally out of direct line of sight | Gk *peri* 'about, around' |
| statoscope | a type of barometer, used to measure minute pressure variations | Gk *statos* 'standing' |
| stereoscope | a device for creating an image with depth, using two photos from different angles | Gk *stereos* 'solid' |
| stethoscope | an instrument for listening to a person's heartbeat | Gk *stēthos* 'breast' |
| stroboscope | a device producing a bright, rapidly flashing light | Gk *strobos* 'whirling' |
| telescope | an instrument for making distant objects appear nearer | Gk *tēle-* 'far off' |

The majority of the **-scope** words above are of 19th or 20th century origin, including ***stethoscope***, ***periscope***, and ***stroboscope***. A few are earlier: ***microscope*** and ***telescope*** are first recorded in the 17th century, for example. The term *telescopio* is found in the letters of Galileo from 1611, replacing earlier terms for similar devices, such as *perspicillum* (L. *perspicere* 'look through') and *conspicillum* (L. *conspicere* 'look at attentively').

The word ***horoscope*** is of very early origin, being used in astrological senses in Old English. It derives from Greek *hōroskopos* (*hōra* 'hour' + *skopos* 'observer').

➤ succeed in attracting a sexual partner. **5** (**score off** or **score points off**) Brit. informal outdo or humiliate, especially in an argument.
– PHRASES **know the score** informal be aware of the essential facts. **on the score of** Brit. because of. **on that** (or **this**) **score** so far as that (or this) is concerned. **settle** (or **pay**) **a** (or **the**) **score 1** take revenge on someone. **2** dated pay off a debt or other obligation.
– DERIVATIVES **scoreless** adj. **scorer** n.
– ORIGIN OE *scoru* 'set of twenty', from ON *skor* 'notch, tally, twenty', of Gmc origin; rel. to **SHEAR**; the verb is from ON *skora* 'make an incision'.

**scorecard** ● n. **1** (also **scoresheet** or **scorebook**) a card, sheet, or book in which scores are entered. **2** a card listing the names, positions, etc. of players in a team.

**scoreline** ● n. the number of points or goals scored in a match.

**scoria** /ˈskɔːrɪə/ ● n. (pl. **scoriae** /-rɪiː/) **1** basaltic lava ejected as fragments from a volcano, typically with a frothy texture. **2** slag separated from molten metal during smelting.
– DERIVATIVES **scoriaceous** /-ˈeɪʃəs/ adj.
– ORIGIN ME: via L. from Gk *skōria* 'refuse', from *skōr* 'dung'.

**scorn** ● n. **1** contempt or disdain expressed openly. **2** archaic a statement or gesture showing contempt. ● v. **1** express scorn for. **2** reject in a contemptuous way.
– DERIVATIVES **scorner** n. **scornful** adj. **scornfully** adv. **scornfulness** n.
– ORIGIN ME: shortening of OFr. *escarn* (n.), *escharnir* (v.), of Gmc origin.

**scorp** (also **scorper** or **scauper**) ● n. a drawknife with a circular blade and a single handle, used to scoop out wood when carving.
– ORIGIN C19: based on L. *scalper* 'knife'.

**Scorpio** ● n. Astrology the eighth sign of the zodiac (the Scorpion), which the sun enters about 23 October.
– DERIVATIVES **Scorpian** n. & adj.
– ORIGIN from L.

**scorpion** ● n. **1** an arachnid with lobster-like pincers and a poisonous sting at the end of its tail. [Order Scorpiones.] ➤ used in names of similar arachnids and insects, e.g. **false scorpion**. **2** (**scorpions**) poetic/literary a whip with metal points. [with allusion to 1 Kings 12:11.]
– ORIGIN ME: via OFr. from L. *scorpio(n-)*, based on Gk *skorpios* 'scorpion'.

**scorpionfish** ● n. (pl. same or **-fishes**) a marine fish, typically red, with spines on the head that are sometimes venomous. [Family Scorpaenidae: many species.]

**scorpion fly** ● n. a slender predatory insect with membranous wings, the males of which have a swollen abdomen curved up like a scorpion's sting. [Family Panorpidae.]

**scorzonera** /ˌskɔːzə(ʊ)ˈnɪərə/ ● n. a plant of the daisy family with tapering purple-brown edible roots, which can be eaten as a vegetable. [*Scorzonera hispanica*.]
– ORIGIN C17: from Ital., from *scorzone*, from an alt. of med. L. *curtio(n-)* 'venomous snake' (against whose venom the plant may have been regarded as an antidote).

**Scot** ● n. **1** a native of Scotland or a person of Scottish descent. **2** a member of a Gaelic people that migrated from Ireland to Scotland around the late 5th century.
– ORIGIN OE *Scottas* (pl.), from late L. *Scottus*, of unknown ultimate origin.

**Scot.** • **abbrev. 1** Scotland. **2** Scottish.

**scot** • **n.** archaic a payment corresponding to a modern tax or other assessed contribution.
– PHRASES **scot and lot** historical a tax levied by a municipal corporation on its members.
– ORIGIN OE, from ON *skot* 'a shot', of Gmc origin.

**Scotch** • **adj.** old-fashioned term for **SCOTTISH**. • **n. 1** short for **SCOTCH WHISKY**. **2** [as pl. n. **the Scotch**] dated the people of Scotland. **3** dated the form of English spoken in Scotland.
– ORIGIN C16: contr. of **SCOTTISH**.

**scotch[1]** • **v. 1** decisively put an end to. **2** archaic injure and render harmless. **3** wedge or prevent from moving with a wedge. • **n.** archaic a wedge placed under a rolling object to prevent it slipping.
– ORIGIN C17 (as n.): of unknown origin; perh. rel. to **SKATE[1]**.

**scotch[2]** • **v.** archaic cut or score the skin or surface of. • **n.** archaic a cut or score in skin or another surface.
– ORIGIN ME: of unknown origin.

**Scotch argus** • **n.** a brown and orange upland butterfly with a chain of eyespots near the wing margins. [*Erebia aethiops*.]

**Scotch bonnet** • **n.** W. Indian & N. Amer. a small chilli pepper which is the hottest variety available.

**Scotch broth** • **n.** a traditional Scottish soup made from meat stock with pearl barley and vegetables.

**Scotch cap** • **n.** a bonnet of the type worn by men and boys in Scotland.

**Scotch catch** • **n.** another term for **SCOTCH SNAP**.

**Scotch egg** • **n.** a hard-boiled egg enclosed in sausage meat, rolled in breadcrumbs, and fried.

**Scotchgard** • **n.** trademark a preparation for giving a waterproof stain-resistant finish to textiles and other materials.

**Scotchlite** • **n.** trademark a light-reflecting material containing a layer of minute glass lenses.

**Scotchman** (or **Scotchwoman**) • **n.** (pl. **-men** or **-women**) dated a Scotsman (or Scotswoman).

**Scotch mist** • **n. 1** a thick drizzly mist of a kind common in the Scottish Highlands. **2** Brit. used sarcastically to imply that a person has failed to understand or see something obvious: *What's this then? Scotch mist?*

**Scotch pancake** • **n.** another term for **DROP SCONE**.

**Scotch snap** (also **Scotch catch**) • **n.** Music a rhythmic feature in which a dotted note is preceded by a stressed shorter note, characteristic of strathspeys.

**Scotch tape** • **n.** trademark, chiefly N. Amer. transparent adhesive tape.

**Scotch whisky** • **n.** whisky distilled in Scotland.

**scoter** /'skəʊtə/ • **n.** (pl. same or **scoters**) a northern diving duck that winters off the coast, the male of which has mainly black plumage. [Genus *Melanitta*: three species.]
– ORIGIN C17: of unknown origin.

**scot-free** • **adv.** without suffering any punishment or injury.
– ORIGIN from **SCOT**.

**scotia** /'skəʊʃə/ • **n.** Architecture a concave moulding, especially at the base of a column.
– ORIGIN C16: via L. from Gk *skotia*, from *skotos* 'darkness', with ref. to the shadow produced.

**Scoticism** • **n.** variant spelling of **SCOTTICISM**.

**scotoma** /skɒ'təʊmə, skə(ʊ)-/ • **n.** (pl. **scotomas** or **scotomata** /-mətə/) Medicine a partial loss of vision or blind spot in an otherwise normal visual field.
– ORIGIN C16: via late L. from Gk *skotōma*, from *skotoun* 'darken', from *skotos* 'darkness'.

**scotopic** /skə(ʊ)'tɒpɪk/ • **adj.** Physiology relating to or denoting vision in dim light. Often contrasted with **PHOTOPIC**.
– ORIGIN C20: from Gk *skotos* 'darkness' + **-OPIA** + **-IC**.

**Scots** • **adj.** another term for **SCOTTISH**. • **n.** the form of English used in Scotland.

**Scotsman** (or **Scotswoman**) • **n.** (pl. **-men** or **-women**) a native or national of Scotland or a person of Scottish descent.

**Scots pine** • **n.** a pine tree, now widely planted for commercial use, forming the dominant tree of the old Caledonian pine forest of the Scottish Highlands. [*Pinus sylvestris*.]

**Scotticism** /'skɒtɪsɪz(ə)m/ (also **Scoticism**) • **n.** a characteristically Scottish phrase, word, or idiom.

**Scottie** • **n.** informal **1** (also **Scottie dog**) a Scottish terrier. **2** a nickname for a Scotsman.

**Scottish** • **adj.** of or relating to Scotland or its people. • **n.** [as pl. n. **the Scottish**] the people of Scotland.
– DERIVATIVES **Scottishness** n.

**Scottish Blackface** • **n.** a long-coated sheep of a hardy breed developed in upland areas of northern Britain.

**Scottish Nationalist** • **n.** a member or supporter of Scottish nationalism or of the Scottish National Party.

**Scottish terrier** • **n.** a small terrier of a rough-haired short-legged breed.

**scoundrel** • **n.** a dishonest or unscrupulous person; a rogue.
– DERIVATIVES **scoundrelism** n. **scoundrelly** adj.
– ORIGIN C16: of unknown origin.

**scour[1]** • **v. 1** clean or brighten by vigorous rubbing, typically with an abrasive or detergent. ➤remove (dirt or unwanted matter) by rubbing in such a way. **2** (of running water) erode (a channel or pool). **3** (of livestock) suffer from diarrhoea. • **n. 1** the action of scouring or the state of being scoured. **2** (also **scours**) diarrhoea in livestock, especially cattle and pigs.
– DERIVATIVES **scourer** n.
– ORIGIN ME: from MDu., Mid. Low Ger. *schūren*, from OFr. *escurer*, from late L. *excurare* 'clean (off)'.

**scour[2]** • **v. 1** subject to a thorough search. **2** move rapidly.
– ORIGIN ME: rel. to obs. *scour* 'moving hastily', of unknown origin.

**scourge** • **n. 1** historical a whip used as an instrument of punishment. **2** a person or thing causing great trouble or suffering. • **v. 1** historical whip with a scourge. **2** cause great suffering to.
– DERIVATIVES **scourger** n. (historical).
– ORIGIN ME: shortening of OFr. *escorge* (n.), *escorgier* (v.), from L. *ex-* 'thoroughly' + *corrigia* 'thong, whip'.

**scouring rush** • **n.** a horsetail with a very rough ridged stem, formerly used for scouring and polishing. [Genus *Equisetum*, in particular *E. hyemale*.]

**Scouse** /skaʊs/ Brit. informal • **n. 1** the dialect or accent of people from Liverpool. **2** (also **Scouser**) a person from Liverpool. • **adj.** of or relating to Liverpool.
– ORIGIN C19: abbrev. of **LOBSCOUSE**.

**scout[1]** • **n. 1** a soldier or other person sent out ahead of a main force so as to gather information about the enemy's position, strength, or movements. ➤a ship or aircraft employed for reconnaissance. **2** (also **Scout**) a member of the Scout Association. **3** a talent scout. **4** (also **scout bee**) a honeybee that searches for a new site for a swarm to settle or for a new food source. **5** an instance of scouting. **6** informal, dated a man or boy. **7** a domestic worker at a college at Oxford University. • **v. 1** make a detailed search of a place. ➤explore or examine so as to gather information: *they are keen to scout out business opportunities.* **2** act as a scout.
– DERIVATIVES **scouter** n. **scouting** n.
– ORIGIN ME: from OFr. *escouter* 'listen', earlier *ascolter*, from L. *auscultare*.

**scout[2]** • **v.** archaic reject (a proposal or idea) with scorn.
– ORIGIN C17: of Scand. origin.

**scout car** • **n.** chiefly US a fast armoured vehicle used for military reconnaissance and liaison.

**scow** /skaʊ/ • **n. 1** a wide-beamed sailing dinghy. **2** chiefly N. Amer. a flat-bottomed boat used for transporting cargo to and from ships in harbour.
– ORIGIN C17: from Du. *schouw* 'ferry boat'.

**scowl** • **n.** an angry or bad-tempered expression. • **v.** frown in an angry or bad-tempered way.
– DERIVATIVES **scowler** n.
– ORIGIN ME: prob. of Scand. origin.

**SCPO** • **abbrev.** Senior Chief Petty Officer.

**SCPS** • **abbrev.** (in the UK) Society of Civil and Public

Servants.

**SCR** ● abbrev. Brit. Senior Common (or Combination) Room.

**scrabble** ● v. **1** scratch or grope around with one's fingers to find, collect, or hold on to something. **2** move quickly and in a disorderly manner; scramble. ● n. **1** an act of scrabbling. **2** a disorderly struggle or fight. **3** (**Scrabble**) trademark a board game in which players build up words from small lettered squares or tiles.
– ORIGIN C16 (in the sense 'scrawl'): from MDu. *schrabbelen*, from *schrabben* 'to scrape'.

**scrag** ● v. (**scragged**, **scragging**) informal **1** chiefly Brit. handle roughly; beat up. **2** US kill; murder. ● n. **1** an unattractively thin person or animal. **2** archaic, informal the neck.
– ORIGIN C16: perh. an alt. of Scots and north. Engl. *crag* 'neck'; the verb is from the early use 'hang, strangle'.

**scrag-end** ● n. Brit. the inferior end of a neck of mutton.

**scraggy** ● adj. (**-ier**, **-iest**) **1** scrawny. **2** (also chiefly N. Amer. **scraggly**) ragged or untidy in form or appearance.
– DERIVATIVES **scraggily** adv. **scragginess** n.

**scram** ● v. (**scrammed**, **scramming**) informal go away or leave quickly.
– ORIGIN C20: prob. from **SCRAMBLE**.

**scramble** ● v. **1** move or make one's way quickly and awkwardly, typically by using one's hands as well as one's feet. ➤informal act in a hurried, disorderly, or undignified manner: *firms scrambled to win public-sector contracts*. **2** (with reference to fighter aircraft) take off or cause to take off immediately in an emergency or for action. **3** make or become jumbled or muddled. ➤cook (beaten eggs with a little liquid) in a pan. **4** make (a broadcast transmission or telephone conversation) unintelligible unless received by an appropriate decoding device. **5** American Football (of a quarterback) run with the ball behind the line of scrimmage, avoiding tackles. ● n. **1** an act of scrambling. **2** a walk up steep terrain involving the use of one's hands. **3** Brit. a motorcycle race over rough and hilly ground. **4** a disordered mixture.
– DERIVATIVES **scrambling** n.
– ORIGIN C16: imitative; cf. the dial. words *scamble* 'stumble' and *cramble* 'crawl'.

**scrambled egg** ● n. **1** (also **scrambled eggs**) a dish of eggs prepared by beating with a little liquid and then cooking and stirring gently. **2** informal gold braid on a military officer's cap.

**scrambler** ● n. **1** a device for scrambling. **2** a person who walks over steep, mountainous terrain as a pastime. ➤Brit. a motorcycle for racing over rough ground. **3** a plant with long slender stems supported by other plants.

**scramjet** ● n. Aeronautics a ramjet in which combustion takes place in a stream of gas moving at supersonic speed.
– ORIGIN 1960s: from *s(upersonic)* + *c(ombustion)* + **RAMJET**.

**scran** ● n. dialect food.
– ORIGIN C18 (denoting a bill at an inn): of unknown origin.

**scrap**[1] ● n. **1** a small piece or amount of something, especially one that is left over after the greater part has been used. ➤(**scraps**) bits of uneaten food left after a meal. **2** material, especially metal, discarded for reprocessing. ● v. (**scrapped**, **scrapping**) **1** remove (an old or redundant vehicle, vessel, or machine) from use or service, especially so as to convert it to scrap metal. **2** abolish or cancel (a plan, policy, or law).
– ORIGIN ME: from ON *skrap* 'scraps'; rel. to *skrapa* 'to scrape'.

**scrap**[2] informal ● n. a fight or quarrel, especially a minor or spontaneous one. ● v. (**scrapped**, **scrapping**) engage in such a fight or quarrel. ➤compete fiercely.
– DERIVATIVES **scrapper** n.
– ORIGIN C17 (as n. in the sense 'sinister plot, scheme'): perh. from **SCRAPE**.

**scrapbook** ● n. a book of blank pages for sticking cuttings, drawings, or pictures in.

**scrape** ● v. **1** drag or pull a hard or sharp implement across (a surface or object) ➤use a sharp or hard implement to remove (dirt or unwanted matter). **2** rub or cause to rub against a rough or hard surface. ➤humorous play a violin tunelessly. **3** just manage to achieve, succeed, or pass. ➤(**scrape something together/up**) collect or accumulate something with difficulty. ➤try to save as much money as possible; economize. ➤(**scrape by/along**) manage to live with difficulty. ● n. **1** an act or sound of scraping. ➤an injury or mark caused by scraping. ➤Brit. a thinly applied layer of butter or margarine on bread. **2** informal an embarrassing or difficult predicament. **3** archaic an obsequious bow in which one foot is drawn backwards along the ground.
– PHRASES **scrape acquaintance with** dated contrive to get to know. **scrape the barrel** (or **the bottom of the barrel**) informal be reduced to using the last and poorest resources.
– DERIVATIVES **scraper** n. **scraping** adj. & n.
– ORIGIN OE *scrapian* 'scratch with the fingernails', of Gmc origin, reinforced in ME by ON *skrapa* or MDu. *schrapen* 'to scratch'.

**scraperboard** ● n. Brit. cardboard or board with a blackened surface which can be scraped off for making white line drawings.

**scrap heap** ● n. a pile of discarded materials or articles.

**scrapie** ● n. a disease of sheep involving the central nervous system, characterized by a lack of coordination causing affected animals to rub against objects for support.
– ORIGIN C20: from **SCRAPE** + **-IE**.

**scrapple** ● n. US scraps of pork or other meat stewed with maize meal and shaped into large cakes.

**scrappy** ● adj. (**-ier**, **-iest**) **1** consisting of disorganized, untidy, or incomplete parts. **2** N. Amer. informal determined, argumentative, or pugnacious.
– DERIVATIVES **scrappily** adv. **scrappiness** n.

**scrapyard** ● n. Brit. a place where scrap is collected before being discarded, reused, or recycled.

**scratch** ● v. **1** score or mark with a sharp or pointed object. ➤make a long, narrow superficial wound in the skin of. ➤rub (a part of one's body) with one's fingernails to relieve itching. ➤(of a bird or mammal) rake the ground with the beak or claws in search of food. ➤(often **scratch around/along**) make a living or find resources with difficulty. **2** cancel or strike out (writing) with a pen or pencil. ➤withdraw from a competition. ➤cancel or abandon (an undertaking or project). **3** play a record using the scratch technique. ● n. **1** a mark or wound made by scratching. ➤informal a slight or insignificant wound or injury. ➤an act or spell of scratching. **2** the starting point in a handicap for a competitor receiving no odds. ➤Golf a handicap of zero, indicating that a player is good enough to achieve par on a course. **3** a technique, used especially in rap music, of stopping a record by hand and moving it back and forwards to give a rhythmic scratching effect. **4** informal money. ● adj. **1** assembled or made from whatever is available. **2** (of a sports competitor or event) with no handicap given.
– PHRASES **from scratch** from the very beginning, especially without making use of any previous work. **scratch one's head** informal think hard in order to find a solution. **scratch the surface** deal with or investigate a matter only in the most superficial way. **up to scratch** up to the required standard; satisfactory.
– DERIVATIVES **scratcher** n. **scratching** n.
– ORIGIN ME: prob. a blend of the synonymous dial. words *scrat* and *cratch*, both of uncertain origin.

**scratchboard** ● n. another term for **SCRAPERBOARD**.

**scratch card** ● n. a card with a section or sections coated in an opaque waxy substance which may be scraped away to reveal a symbol indicating whether a prize has been won.

**scratch pad** ● n. **1** chiefly N. Amer. a notepad. **2** Computing a small, fast memory for the temporary storage of data.

**scratchplate** ● n. a plate attached to the front of a guitar to protect it from being scratched by the plectrum.

**scratchy** ● adj. (**-ier**, **-iest**) causing or characterized by

scratching. ➤(of a voice or sound) rough; grating. ➤(of a record) making a crackling sound because of scratches on the surface.
– DERIVATIVES **scratchily** adv. **scratchiness** n.

**scrawl** ● v. write in a hurried, careless way. ● n. an example of hurried, careless writing.
– DERIVATIVES **scrawly** adj.
– ORIGIN C17: appar. an alt. of **CRAWL**, perh. influenced by obs. *scrawl* 'sprawl'.

**scrawny** ● adj. (**-ier**, **-iest**) unattractively thin and bony.
– DERIVATIVES **scrawniness** n.
– ORIGIN C19: var. of dial. *scranny*; cf. archaic *scrannel* 'weak, feeble' (referring to sound).

**scream** ● v. **1** make a long, loud, piercing cry or sound, especially expressing extreme emotion or pain. **2** move very rapidly with or as if with such a sound. **3** informal, dated turn informer. ● n. **1** a screaming cry or sound. **2** (**a scream**) informal an irresistibly funny person or thing.
– ORIGIN ME: origin uncertain; perh. from MDu.

**screamer** ● n. **1** a person or thing that makes a screaming sound. **2** informal a thing remarkable for speed or impact. ➤chiefly US a sensational or very large headline. ➤dated a thing that causes screams of laughter. **3** a large goose-like South American waterbird with a harsh honking call. [Family Anhimidae: three species.]

**screamingly** ● adv. to a very great extent; extremely.

**scree** ● n. a mass of small loose stones that form or cover a slope on a mountain.
– ORIGIN C18: prob. a back-form. from the pl. *screes*, from ON *skritha* 'landslip'.

**screech** ● n. a loud, harsh, piercing cry or sound. ● v. **1** make a screech. **2** move rapidly with a screech.
– DERIVATIVES **screecher** n. **screechy** adj. (**-ier**, **-iest**).
– ORIGIN C16 (as v.): alt. of archaic *scritch*, of imitative origin.

**screech owl** ● n. **1** Brit. another term for **BARN OWL**. **2** a small American owl with a screeching call. [*Otus asio* and related species.]

**screed** ● n. **1** a long speech or piece of writing, typically a tedious one. **2** a levelled layer of material (e.g. cement) applied to a floor or other surface. ➤a strip of plaster or other material placed on a surface as a guide to thickness.
– DERIVATIVES **screeding** n.
– ORIGIN ME (in sense 'fragment', then 'torn strip, tatter'): prob. a var. of **SHRED**.

**screel** /skriːl/ ● v. chiefly Scottish & W. Indian emit a high-pitched or a discordant cry or sound; screech.
– ORIGIN C19: of imitative origin, or rel. to **SKIRL**.

**screen** ● n. **1** an upright partition used to divide a room, give shelter, or provide concealment. ➤a windscreen of a motor vehicle. ➤a frame with fine wire netting used to keep out flying insects. **2** the surface of a cathode ray tube or similar electronic device, especially that of a television, VDU, or monitor, on which images and data are displayed. ➤a blank surface on which a photographic image is projected. ➤(**the screen**) films or television. ➤Photography a flat piece of ground glass on which the image formed by a camera lens is focused. **3** Printing a transparent finely ruled plate or film used in half-tone reproduction. **4** a system or act of screening for the presence or absence of something. **5** a large sieve or riddle. **6** Military a detachment of troops or ships detailed to cover the movements of the main body. **7** a part of an electrical or other instrument which protects it from or prevents it causing electromagnetic interference. ➤(also **screen grid**) Electronics a grid placed between the control grid and the anode of a valve to reduce the capacitance between these electrodes. ● v. **1** conceal, protect, or shelter with a screen. ➤protect from something dangerous or unpleasant. **2** show (a film or video) or broadcast (a television programme). **3** test for the presence or absence of a disease. ➤investigate (someone), typically to ascertain suitability for a job. **4** pass (a substance such as grain or coal) through a large sieve or screen, especially so as to sort it into different sizes. **5** Printing project (a photograph or other image) through a screen so as to reproduce it as a half-tone.
– DERIVATIVES **screenable** adj. **screener** n. **screenful** n. (pl. **-fuls**) **screening** n.
– ORIGIN ME: shortening of ONorth. Fr. *escren*, of Gmc origin.

**screenager** ● n. informal a person in their teens or twenties who has an aptitude for computers and the Internet.

**screenplay** ● n. the script of a film, including acting instructions and scene directions.

**screen-print** ● v. [often as adj. **screen-printed**] force ink on to (a surface) through a prepared screen of fine material so as to create a picture or pattern. ● n. (**screen print**) a picture or design produced by screen-printing.

**screen saver** ● n. Computing a program which, after a set time, replaces an unchanging screen display with a moving image to prevent damage to the phosphor.

**screen test** ● n. a filmed test to ascertain whether an actor is suitable for a film role. ● v. (**screen-test**) give such a test to.

**screenwriter** ● n. a person who writes a screenplay.
– DERIVATIVES **screenwriting** n.

**screw** ● n. **1** a short, slender, sharp-pointed metal pin with a raised helical thread running around it and a slotted head, used to join things together by being rotated in under pressure. ➤a cylinder with a helical ridge or thread running round the outside that can be turned to seal an opening, apply pressure, adjust position, etc. ➤(**the screws**) historical an instrument of torture acting in this way. **2** an act of turning a screw. ➤Brit. a small twisted-up piece of paper containing a substance such as salt or tobacco. **3** (also **screw propeller**) a ship's or aircraft's propeller. **4** informal, derogatory a prison warder. **5** vulgar slang an act of sexual intercourse. **6** Brit. informal, dated an amount of salary or wages. **7** Brit. archaic, informal a mean or miserly person. **8** Brit. informal a worn-out horse. ● v. **1** fasten or tighten with a screw or screws. ➤rotate (something) so as to attach or remove it by means of a spiral thread. ➤impart spin or curl to (a ball or shot). ➤(**screw something around/round**) turn one's head or body round sharply. **2** informal cheat or swindle. ➤informal ruin or render ineffective. **3** vulgar slang have sexual intercourse with. ➤informal used to express anger or contempt.
– PHRASES **have one's head screwed on** (**the right way**) informal have common sense. **have a screw loose** informal be slightly eccentric or mentally disturbed. **put** (or **turn** or **tighten**) **the screw** (or **screws**) **on** informal exert strong psychological pressure on.
– PHRASAL VERBS **screw around 1** vulgar slang have many different sexual partners. **2** informal fool about. **screw someone over** informal, chiefly US treat someone unfairly; cheat or swindle someone. **screw up** informal, chiefly N. Amer. completely mismanage or mishandle a situation. **screw someone up** informal cause someone to be emotionally or mentally disturbed. **screw something up 1** crush a piece of paper or fabric into a tight mass. ➤tense the muscles of one's face or around one's eyes. **2** informal cause something to go wrong. **3** summon up one's courage.
– DERIVATIVES **screwable** adj. **screwer** n.
– ORIGIN ME (as n.): from OFr. *escroue* 'female screw, nut', from L. *scrofa*, lit. 'sow', later 'screw'.

**screwball** chiefly N. Amer. ● n. **1** Baseball a ball pitched with reverse spin as compared to a curve ball. **2** informal a crazy or eccentric person. ● adj. informal crazy; absurd. ➤relating to or denoting a style of fast-moving comedy film involving eccentric characters or ridiculous situations.
– DERIVATIVES **screwballer** n.

**screw cap** ● n. a round cap or lid that can be screwed on to a bottle or jar.
– DERIVATIVES **screw-capped** adj.

**screw coupling** ● n. a female screw with threads at both ends for joining lengths of pipes or rods.

**screwdriver** ● n. **1** a tool with a shaped tip that fits into the head of a screw to turn it. **2** a cocktail made from vodka and orange juice.

**screw eye** ● n. a screw with a loop for passing a cord through, instead of a slotted head.

**screw gear** ● n. a gear consisting of an endless screw with a cogwheel or pinion.

**screw hook** ● n. a hook with a point and thread for

fastening it to woodwork.

**screw jack** • n. a vehicle jack worked by a screw device.

**screw pine** • n. another term for PANDANUS.

**screw plate** • n. a steel plate with threaded holes for making male screws.

**screw tap** • n. a tool for making female screws.

**screw top** • n. a round cap or lid that can be screwed on to a bottle or jar.
– DERIVATIVES **screw-topped** adj.

**screw valve** • n. a stopcock worked by a screw.

**screw worm** • n. a large American blowfly larva which enters wounds and develops under the skin. [*Cochliomyia hominivorax*.]

**screwy** • adj. (**-ier, -iest**) informal, chiefly N. Amer. rather odd or eccentric.
– DERIVATIVES **screwiness** n.

**scribble**[1] • v. **1** write or draw carelessly or hurriedly. **2** informal write for a living or as a hobby. • n. a piece of writing or a picture produced carelessly or hurriedly.
– DERIVATIVES **scribbler** n. **scribbly** adj.
– ORIGIN ME: from med. L. *scribillare*, dimin. of L. *scribere* 'write'.

**scribble**[2] • v. [often as noun **scribbling**] card (wool, cotton, etc.) coarsely.
– ORIGIN C17: prob. from Low Ger.; cf. Ger. *schrubbeln* (in the same sense), from Low Ger. *schrubben* 'to scrub'.

**scribe** • n. **1** historical a person who copied out documents. ➤ informal, often humorous a writer, especially a journalist. **2** Jewish History an ancient Jewish record-keeper or, later, a professional theologian and jurist. **3** (also **scriber** or **scribe awl**) a pointed instrument used for making marks to guide a saw or in signwriting. • v. **1** chiefly poetic/literary write. **2** mark with a pointed instrument.
– DERIVATIVES **scribal** adj.
– ORIGIN ME: from L. *scriba*, from *scribere* 'write'; the verb is perh. partly a shortening of DESCRIBE.

**scrim** • n. **1** strong, coarse fabric used for lining or upholstery. **2** Theatre a piece of gauze cloth that appears opaque until lit from behind, used as a screen or backcloth. **3** chiefly N. Amer. something that conceals or obscures.
– ORIGIN C18: of unknown origin.

**scrimmage** • n. **1** a confused struggle or fight. **2** American Football a sequence of play beginning with the placing of the ball on the ground with its longest axis at right angles to the goal line. • v. American Football engage in a scrimmage. ➤ put (the ball) into a scrimmage.
– DERIVATIVES **scrimmager** n.
– ORIGIN ME: alt. of dial. *scrimish*, var. of SKIRMISH.

**scrimp** • v. be thrifty or parsimonious; economize.
– ORIGIN C18 (in the sense 'keep short of (food)'): from Scots *scrimp* 'meagre'; perh. rel. to SHRIMP.

**scrimshander** /ˈskrɪmˌʃandə/ • v. another term for SCRIMSHAW. • n. a person who makes scrimshaw.
– ORIGIN C19: from a var. of SCRIMSHAW + -ER[1].

**scrimshank** /ˈskrɪmʃaŋk/ • v. Brit. informal (especially of a person in the armed services) shirk one's duty.
– DERIVATIVES **scrimshanker** n.
– ORIGIN C19: of unknown origin.

**scrimshaw** • v. adorn (shells, ivory, or other materials) with carved designs. • n. work done in such a way.
– ORIGIN C19: of unknown origin.

**scrip**[1] • n. **1** a provisional certificate of money subscribed to a bank or company, entitling the holder to a formal certificate and dividends. ➤ certificates of this type collectively. ➤ Finance an issue of additional shares to shareholders in proportion to the shares already held. **2** N. Amer. a certificate entitling the holder to acquire possession of certain portions of public land. **3** N. Amer. historical paper money in amounts of less than a dollar.
– ORIGIN C18: abbrev. of *subscription receipt*.

**scrip**[2] • n. historical a small bag or pouch, as carried by a pilgrim, shepherd, or beggar.
– ORIGIN ME: prob. a shortening of OFr. *escrepe* 'purse'.

**scrip**[3] • n. another term for SCRIPT[2].

**scripophily** /skrɪˈpɒfɪli/ • n. the collection of old bond and share certificates as a pursuit or hobby.
– DERIVATIVES **scripophilist** n.

**script**[1] • n. **1** handwriting as distinct from print; written characters. ➤ writing using a particular alphabet: *Russian script*. **2** the written text of a play, film, or broadcast. **3** Brit. a candidate's written answers in an examination. **4** Computing a program or sequence of instructions that is carried out by another program rather than by the computer processor. • v. write a script for.
– ORIGIN ME (in the sense 'something written'): shortening of OFr. *escript*, from L. *scriptum*, neut. past part. (used as n.) of *scribere* 'write'.

**script**[2] • n. informal a doctor's prescription.

**script kiddie** • n. (pl **kiddies** or **kiddiez**) informal, derogatory a person who uses existing computer scripts or codes to hack into computers, lacking the expertise to write their own.

**scriptorial** • adj. rare of or relating to writing.

**scriptorium** /skrɪpˈtɔːrɪəm/ • n. (pl. **scriptoria** /-rɪə/ or **scriptoriums**) chiefly historical a room set apart for writing, especially one in a monastery where manuscripts were copied.
– ORIGIN C18: from med. L., from L. *script-*, *scribere* 'write'.

**scriptural** • adj. of, from, or relating to the Bible.
– DERIVATIVES **scripturally** adv.

**scripture** /ˈskrɪptʃə/ (also **scriptures**) • n. the sacred writings of Christianity contained in the Bible. ➤ the sacred writings of another religion.
– ORIGIN ME: from L. *scriptura* 'writings', from *script-*, *scribere* 'write'.

**scriptwriter** • n. a person who writes a script for a play, film, or broadcast.
– DERIVATIVES **scriptwriting** n.

**scrivener** /ˈskrɪv(ə)nə/ • n. historical **1** a clerk, scribe, or notary. **2** a person who invested money at interest for clients and lent funds to those who wanted to raise money on security.
– ORIGIN ME: shortening of OFr. *escrivein*, from L. *scriba* (see SCRIBE).

**scrod** /skrɒd/ • n. N. Amer. a young cod, haddock, or similar fish.
– ORIGIN C19: of unknown origin.

**scrofula** /ˈskrɒfjʊlə/ • n. chiefly historical a disease with glandular swellings, probably a form of tuberculosis.
– DERIVATIVES **scrofulous** adj.
– ORIGIN ME: from med. L., dimin. of L. *scrofa* 'breeding sow' (said to be subject to the disease).

**scroll** • n. **1** a roll of parchment or paper for writing or painting on. ➤ an ancient book or document on such a roll. **2** an ornamental design or carving resembling a partly unrolled scroll of parchment. • v. **1** move displayed text or graphics on a computer screen in order to view different parts of them. **2** cause to move like paper rolling or unrolling.
– DERIVATIVES **scrollable** adj. **scroller** n. **scrolling** n.
– ORIGIN ME: alt. of obs. *scrow* 'roll', shortening of ESCROW.

**scroll bar** • n. a long thin section at the edge of a computer display by which material can be scrolled using a mouse.

**scrolled** • adj. having an ornamental design or carving resembling a scroll of parchment.

**scroll saw** • n. a narrow-bladed saw for cutting decorative spiral lines or patterns.

**scrollwork** • n. decoration consisting of spiral lines or patterns.

**scrooch** • v. informal, chiefly US crouch; bend.
– ORIGIN C19: dial. var. of US *scrouge* 'squeeze, crowd'.

**Scrooge** • n. a person who is mean with money.
– ORIGIN from the name of Ebenezer *Scrooge*, a miser in Charles Dickens's novel *A Christmas Carol*.

**scrotum** /ˈskrəʊtəm/ • n. (pl. **scrota** /-tə/ or **scrotums**) a pouch of skin containing the testicles.
– DERIVATIVES **scrotal** adj.
– ORIGIN C16: from L.

**scrounge** informal • v. seek to obtain (something) at the expense of others or by stealth. • n. an act or the action of scrounging.

– DERIVATIVES **scrounger** n.
– ORIGIN C20: var. of dial. *scrunge* 'steal'.

**scrub**[1] ● v. (**scrubbed**, **scrubbing**) **1** rub hard so as to clean. ➤(**scrub up**) thoroughly clean one's hands and arms before performing surgery. **2** informal cancel or abandon. **3** use water to remove impurities from (gas or vapour). ● n. **1** an act of scrubbing. **2** a semi-abrasive cosmetic lotion applied to the face or body in order to cleanse the skin. **3** (**scrubs**) special hygienic clothing worn by surgeons during operations.
– ORIGIN C16: prob. from Mid. Low Ger., MDu. *schrobben*, *schrubben*.

**scrub**[2] ● n. **1** vegetation consisting mainly of brushwood or stunted forest growth. ➤(also **scrubs**) land covered with such vegetation. **2** [as modifier] denoting a shrubby or small form of a plant. ➤N. Amer. denoting an animal of inferior breed or physique. **3** informal an insignificant or contemptible person. ➤N. Amer. a mediocre sports team or player.
– DERIVATIVES **scrubby** adj.
– ORIGIN ME (in the sense 'stunted tree'): var. of **SHRUB**[1].

**scrubber** ● n. **1** a person or thing that scrubs. ➤an apparatus using water or a solution for purifying gases or vapours. **2** derogatory, chiefly Brit. a sexually promiscuous woman.

**scrubland** ● n. (also **scrublands**) land consisting of scrub vegetation.

**scrub oak** ● n. N. Amer. a shrubby dwarf oak which forms thickets. [*Quercus ilicifolia* and related species.]

**scrub-turkey** ● n. another term for **BRUSH-TURKEY**.

**scrub typhus** ● n. a rickettsial disease transmitted to humans by mites and found in parts of east Asia.

**scruff**[1] ● n. the back of a person's or animal's neck.
– ORIGIN C18: alt. of dial. *scuff*, of obscure origin.

**scruff**[2] ● n. Brit. informal a scruffy person.
– ORIGIN C16 (in the sense 'scurf'): var. of **SCURF**.

**scruffy** ● adj. (**-ier**, **-iest**) shabby and untidy or dirty.
– DERIVATIVES **scruffily** adv. **scruffiness** n.

**scrum** ● n. **1** Rugby an ordered formation of players in which the forwards of each team push against each other with arms interlocked and heads down and the ball is thrown in to restart play. **2** Brit. informal a disorderly crowd. ● v. (**scrummed**, **scrumming**) **1** Rugby form or take part in a scrum. **2** informal jostle; crowd.
– ORIGIN C19: abbrev. of **SCRUMMAGE**.

**scrum half** ● n. Rugby a halfback who puts the ball into the scrum and stands ready to receive it again.

**scrummage** ● n. & v. fuller form of **SCRUM**.
– DERIVATIVES **scrummager** n.
– ORIGIN C19: var. of **SCRIMMAGE**.

**scrummy** ● adj. (**-ier**, **-iest**) informal delicious.
– ORIGIN C20: from **SCRUMPTIOUS** + **-Y**[1].

**scrump** ● v. Brit. informal steal (fruit) from an orchard or garden.
– ORIGIN C19: from dial. *scrump* 'withered apple'.

**scrumple** ● v. Brit. crumple (paper or cloth).
– ORIGIN C16: alt. of **CRUMPLE**.

**scrumptious** ● adj. informal (of food) extremely appetizing or delicious. ➤(of a person) very attractive.
– DERIVATIVES **scrumptiously** adv. **scrumptiousness** n.
– ORIGIN C19: of unknown origin.

**scrumpy** ● n. Brit. rough strong cider, especially as made in the West Country of England.

**scrunch** ● v. **1** make a loud crunching noise. **2** crush or squeeze into a compact mass. ● n. a loud crunching noise.
– ORIGIN C18 (in the sense 'eat or bite noisily'): prob. imitative; cf. **CRUNCH**.

**scrunch-dry** ● v. dry (hair) while scrunching it to give a tousled look.

**scrunchy** ● adj. making a loud crunching noise when crushed or compressed. ● n. (also **scrunchie**) (pl. **-ies**) chiefly Brit. a circular band of fabric-covered elastic used for fastening the hair.

**scruple** ● n. **1** a feeling of doubt or hesitation with regard to the morality or propriety of an action. **2** historical a unit of weight equal to 20 grains used by apothecaries. ➤archaic a very small amount. ● v. hesitate or be reluctant to do something that one thinks may be wrong.
– ORIGIN ME: from Fr. *scrupule* or L. *scrupulus*, from *scrupus*, lit. 'rough pebble', (figuratively) 'anxiety'.

**scrupulous** ● adj. **1** diligent, thorough, and attentive to details. **2** very concerned to avoid doing wrong.
– DERIVATIVES **scrupulosity** n. **scrupulously** adv. **scrupulousness** n.
– ORIGIN ME (in the sense 'troubled with doubts'): from Fr. *scrupuleux* or L. *scrupulosus*, from *scrupulus* (see **SCRUPLE**).

**scrutator** /skruːˈteɪtə/ ● n. a scrutineer.
– ORIGIN C16: from L., from *scrutari* 'search, examine'.

**scrutineer** ● n. a person who examines something closely and thoroughly. ➤chiefly Brit. a person who supervises the conduct of an election or competition.

**scrutinize** (also **-ise**) ● v. examine or inspect closely and thoroughly.
– DERIVATIVES **scrutinization** n. **scrutinizer** n.

**scrutiny** ● n. (pl. **-ies**) critical observation or examination.
– ORIGIN ME: from L. *scrutinium*, from *scrutari* 'to search' (orig. 'sort rubbish', from *scruta* 'rubbish').

**scry** /skrʌɪ/ ● v. (**-ies**, **-ied**) foretell the future, especially using a crystal ball.
– DERIVATIVES **scryer** n.
– ORIGIN C16: shortening of **DESCRY**.

**SCSI** ● abbrev. Computing small computer system interface.

**scuba** /ˈskuːbə, ˈskjuːbə/ ● n. an aqualung.
– ORIGIN 1950s: acronym from *self-contained underwater breathing apparatus*.

**scuba-diving** ● n. the sport or pastime of swimming underwater using a scuba.
– DERIVATIVES **scuba-dive** v. **scuba-diver** n.

**scud** ● v. (**scudded**, **scudding**) move fast in a straight line because or as if driven by the wind. ● n. **1** chiefly poetic/literary vapoury clouds or spray driven fast by the wind. ➤a driving shower of rain. **2** the action of scudding.
– ORIGIN C16: perh. an alt. of **SCUT**[1], reflecting the sense 'race like a hare'.

**scudo** /ˈskuːdəʊ/ ● n. (pl. **scudi** /-di/) historical a former coin of various Italian states.
– ORIGIN Ital., from L. *scutum* 'shield'.

**scuff** ● v. scrape (a shoe or other object) against something. ➤[often as adj. **scuffed**] mark by scuffing. ➤drag (one's feet) when walking. ● n. a mark made by scuffing.
– ORIGIN C18: perh. of imitative origin.

**scuffle** ● n. **1** a short, confused fight or struggle at close quarters. **2** an act or sound of moving in a scuffling manner. ● v. **1** engage in a scuffle. **2** move in a hurried, confused, or shuffling way.
– ORIGIN C16: prob. of Scand. origin; cf. Swed. *skuffa* 'to push'; rel. to **SHOVE** and **SHUFFLE**.

**scull** ● n. each of a pair of small oars used by a single rower. ➤an oar placed over the stern of a boat to propel it with a side to side motion. ➤a light, narrow boat propelled with a scull or a pair of sculls. ➤(**sculls**) a race between boats in which each participant uses a pair of oars. ● v. propel a boat with sculls.
– DERIVATIVES **sculler** n.
– ORIGIN ME: of unknown origin.

**scullery** /ˈskʌl(ə)ri/ ● n. (pl. **-ies**) a small kitchen or room at the back of a house used for washing dishes and other dirty household work.
– ORIGIN ME: from OFr. *escuelerie*, from *escuele* 'dish', from L. *scutella* 'salver'.

**scullion** ● n. archaic a servant assigned the most menial kitchen tasks.
– ORIGIN C15: of unknown origin but perh. influenced by **SCULLERY**.

**sculpin** /ˈskʌlpɪn/ ● n. a chiefly marine fish with a broad flattened head and spiny scales and fins. [Many species, chiefly in the family Cottidae.]
– ORIGIN C17: perh. from obs. *scorpene*, via L. from Gk *skorpaina*, denoting a kind of fish.

**sculpt** (also **sculp**) ● v. create or represent by sculpture.

**sculptor** ● n. (fem. **sculptress**) an artist who makes sculptures.

**sculpture** ● n. **1** the art of making three-dimensional representative or abstract forms, especially by carving stone or wood or by casting metal or plaster. ➤ a work of such a kind. **2** raised or sunken patterns on a shell, pollen grain, etc. ● v. make or represent by sculpture. ➤ [usu. as adj. **sculptured**] form or shape as if by sculpture, especially with strong, smooth curves.
– DERIVATIVES **sculptural** adj. **sculpturally** adv. **sculpturesque** adj. **sculpturing** n.
– ORIGIN ME: from L. *sculptura*, from *sculpere* 'carve'.

**scum** ● n. **1** a layer of dirt or froth on the surface of a liquid. **2** informal a worthless or contemptible person or group of people. ● v. (**scummed**, **scumming**) cover or become covered with a layer of scum.
– DERIVATIVES **scummy** adj. (**-ier**, **-iest**).
– ORIGIN ME: from Mid. Low Ger., MDu. *schūm*, of Gmc origin.

**scumbag** ● n. informal a contemptible person.

**scumble** /ˈskʌmb(ə)l/ Art ● v. give a softer or duller effect to (a picture or colour) by applying a very thin coat of opaque paint or a layer of light pencil or charcoal shading. ● n. a coat of paint or layer of shading applied in this way, or the effect thus produced.
– ORIGIN C17: perh. a frequentative of the verb **SCUM**.

**scuncheon** /ˈskʌn(t)ʃ(ə)n/ ● n. the inside face of a door jamb or window frame.
– ORIGIN ME: shortening of OFr. *escoinson*, based on *coin* 'corner'.

**scunge** ● n. Austral./NZ informal a disagreeable person.
– DERIVATIVES **scungy** adj. (**-ier**, **-iest**).
– ORIGIN C19 (orig. Scots in the sense 'scrounger'): of unknown origin; cf. **SCROUNGE**.

**scunner** chiefly Scottish ● n. a strong dislike. ➤ a source of irritation or strong dislike. ● v. feel disgust or strong dislike.
– ORIGIN ME (first used in the sense 'shrink back with fear'): of unknown origin.

**scup** ● n. (pl. same) a common porgy (fish) with faint dark vertical bars. [*Stenotomus chrysops*.]
– ORIGIN C19: from Narragansett *mishcup*, from *mishe* 'big' + *cuppi* 'close together' (because of the shape of the scales).

**scupper**[1] ● n. a hole in a ship's side to allow water to run away from the deck.
– ORIGIN ME: perh. via Anglo-Norman Fr. from OFr. *escopir* 'to spit'.

**scupper**[2] ● v. chiefly Brit. **1** sink (a ship) deliberately. **2** informal prevent from working or succeeding; thwart.
– ORIGIN C19 (as military sl. in the sense 'kill, especially in an ambush'): of unknown origin.

**scurf** ● n. flakes on the surface of the skin that form as fresh skin develops below, occurring especially as dandruff. ➤ a similar flaky deposit on a plant resulting from a fungal infection.
– DERIVATIVES **scurfy** adj.
– ORIGIN OE *sceorf*, from the base of *sceorfan* 'gnaw', *sceorfian* 'cut to shreds'.

**scurrilous** /ˈskʌrɪləs/ ● adj. making scandalous claims about someone with the intention of damaging their reputation. ➤ humorously insulting.
– DERIVATIVES **scurrility** n. (pl. **-ies**). **scurrilously** adv. **scurrilousness** n.
– ORIGIN C16: from Fr. *scurrile* or L. *scurrilus* (from *scurra* 'buffoon') + **-OUS**.

**scurry** ● v. (**-ies**, **-ied**) move hurriedly with short quick steps. ● n. **1** a situation of hurried and confused movement. **2** a flurry of rain or snow.
– ORIGIN C19: abbrev. of *hurry-scurry*, reduplication of **HURRY**.

**scurvy** ● n. a disease caused by a deficiency of vitamin C, characterized by swollen bleeding gums and the opening of previously healed wounds. ● adj. (**-ier**, **-iest**) archaic worthless or contemptible.
– DERIVATIVES **scurvily** adv.
– ORIGIN ME (as adj. meaning 'scurfy'): from **SCURF** + **-Y**[1]; n. use is by assoc. with Fr. *scorbut* (see **SCORBUTIC**).

**scurvy grass** ● n. a small cress-like plant, formerly eaten to prevent scurvy. [Genus *Cochlearia*.]

**scut**[1] ● n. the short tail of a hare, rabbit, or deer.
– ORIGIN ME: of unknown origin; cf. obs. *scut* 'short', also 'shorten'.

**scut**[2] ● n. informal, chiefly Irish a foolish, contemptible, or objectionable person.
– ORIGIN C19: of unknown origin.

**scuta** plural form of **SCUTUM**.

**scutage** /ˈskjuːtɪdʒ/ ● n. (in a feudal society) money paid by a vassal to his lord in lieu of military service.
– ORIGIN ME: from med. L. *scutagium*, from L. *scutum* 'shield'.

**scutch** /skʌtʃ/ ● v. dress (fibrous material, especially retted flax) by beating it.
– DERIVATIVES **scutcher** n.
– ORIGIN C18: from obs. Fr. *escoucher*, from L. *excutere* 'shake out'.

**scutcheon** ● n. archaic spelling of **ESCUTCHEON**.

**scute** /skjuːt/ ● n. Zoology a thickened horny or bony plate on a turtle's shell or on the back of a crocodile, stegosaurus, etc.
– ORIGIN ME (denoting a coin): from L. **SCUTUM**.

**scutellum** /skjʊˈtɛləm/ ● n. (pl. **scutella** /-lə/) **1** Botany a modified cotyledon in the embryo of a grass seed. **2** Entomology one of the dorsal sclerites of an insect's thorax.
– DERIVATIVES **scutellar** adj.
– ORIGIN C18: mod. L., dimin. of L. *scutum* 'shield'.

**scutter** chiefly Brit. ● v. move hurriedly with short steps. ● n. an act or sound of scuttering.
– ORIGIN C18: perh. an alt. of **SCUTTLE**[2].

**scuttle**[1] ● n. **1** a metal container with a sloping hinged lid and a handle, used to fetch and store coal for a domestic fire. **2** Brit. the part of a car's bodywork between the windscreen and the bonnet.
– ORIGIN OE *scutel* 'dish, platter', from ON *skutill*, from L. *scutella* 'dish'.

**scuttle**[2] ● v. run hurriedly or furtively with short quick steps. ● n. an act or sound of scuttling.
– ORIGIN C15: cf. dial. *scuddle*, frequentative of **SCUD**.

**scuttle**[3] ● v. **1** sink (one's own ship) deliberately. **2** deliberately cause (a scheme) to fail. ● n. an opening with a lid in a ship's deck or side.
– ORIGIN C15 (as n.): perh. from OFr. *escoutille*, from the Sp. dimin. *escotilla* 'hatchway'.

**scuttlebutt** ● n. informal, chiefly N. Amer. rumour; gossip.
– ORIGIN C19 (denoting a water butt on the deck of a ship, providing drinking water): from *scuttled butt*.

**scutum** /ˈskjuːtəm/ ● n. (pl. **scuta** /-tə/) **1** Zoology another term for **SCUTE**. **2** Entomology the second dorsal sclerite in each thoracic segment of an insect.
– ORIGIN C18: from L., lit. 'oblong shield'.

**scutwork** ● n. informal, chiefly US tedious, menial work.
– ORIGIN 1970s: of unknown origin; cf. **SCUT**[2].

**scuzz** ● n. informal, chiefly N. Amer. something disgusting or disreputable. ➤ a disreputable or unpleasant person.
– DERIVATIVES **scuzzy** adj.
– ORIGIN 1960s: prob. an informal abbrev. of *disgusting*.

**scuzzball** (also **scuzzbag**) ● n. informal, chiefly N. Amer. a despicable or disgusting person.

**Scyphozoa** /ˌsʌɪfəˈzəʊə, ˌskʌɪf-, ˌskɪf-/ ● pl. n. Zoology a class of marine coelenterates which comprises the jellyfishes.
– DERIVATIVES **scyphozoan** n. & adj.
– ORIGIN mod. L., from Gk *skuphos* 'drinking cup' + Gk *zōion* 'animal'.

**scythe** ● n. a tool used for cutting crops such as grass or corn, with a long curved blade at the end of a long pole attached to one or two short handles. ● v. **1** cut with a scythe. **2** move through or penetrate rapidly and forcefully.
– ORIGIN OE *sīthe*, of Gmc origin.

**Scythian** /ˈsɪðɪən/ ● n. a native or inhabitant of Scythia, an ancient region of SE Europe and Asia. ● adj. of or relating to Scythia.

**SD** • abbrev. **1** South Dakota (in official postal use). **2** Swaziland (international vehicle registration).

**S. Dak.** • abbrev. South Dakota.

**SDI** • abbrev. Strategic Defense Initiative.

**SDLP** • abbrev. (in Northern Ireland) Social Democratic and Labour Party.

**SDP** • abbrev. (in the UK) Social Democratic Party.

**SDR** • abbrev. special drawing right (from the International Monetary Fund).

**SE** • abbrev. **1** south-east. **2** south-eastern.

**Se** • symb. the chemical element selenium.

**se-** • prefix in words adopted from Latin originally meaning 'apart' (as in *separate*) or meaning 'without' (as in *secure*).
– ORIGIN from L. *se-*, from the earlier preposition and adverb *se*.

**SEA** • abbrev. Single European Act.

**sea** • n. **1** the expanse of salt water that covers most of the earth's surface and surrounds its land masses. ➤a roughly definable area of this: *the Black Sea*. ➤(also **seas**) waves as opposed to calm sea. **2** a vast expanse or quantity: *a sea of faces*.
– PHRASES **at sea 1** sailing on the sea. **2** (also **all at sea**) confused; uncertain. **put (out) to sea** leave land on a voyage. **one's sea legs** one's ability to keep one's balance and not feel seasick when on board a moving ship.
– DERIVATIVES **seaward** adj. & adv. **seawards** adv.
– ORIGIN OE *sǣ*, of Gmc origin.

**sea anchor** • n. an object dragged in the water behind a boat in order to keep its bows pointing into the waves or to lessen leeway.

**sea anemone** • n. a sedentary marine coelenterate with a columnar body which bears a ring of stinging tentacles around the mouth. [Order Actiniaria.]

**sea-angel** • n. an angel shark.

**seabag** • n. chiefly N. Amer. a sailor's travelling bag or trunk.

**sea bass** • n. a marine fish with a spiny dorsal fin, resembling the freshwater perch. [Many species, mainly in the family Serranidae.]

**seabed** • n. the ground under the sea; the ocean floor.

**seabird** • n. a bird that frequents the sea or coast.

**sea biscuit** • n. **1** another term for **SHIP'S BISCUIT**. **2** another term for **SAND DOLLAR**.

**seaboard** • n. a region bordering the sea; the coastline.

**seaborgium** /siːˈbɔːgɪəm/ • n. the chemical element of atomic number 106, a very unstable element made by high-energy atomic collisions. (Symbol: **Sg**)
– ORIGIN 1990s: mod. L., named after the Amer. nuclear chemist Glenn *Seaborg*.

**sea bream** • n. a deep-bodied marine fish that resembles the freshwater bream. [Several species, mainly in the family Sparidae.]

**sea breeze** • n. a breeze blowing towards the land from the sea.

**sea buckthorn** • n. a bushy shrub or small tree that grows on sandy coasts, bearing orange berries. [*Hippophae rhamnoides*.]

**sea butterfly** • n. a small gastropod mollusc with wing-like extensions to its body which it uses for swimming. [Orders Thecosomata and Gymnosomata.]

**SeaCat** • n. trademark a large, high-speed catamaran used as a passenger and car ferry on short sea crossings.

**sea change** • n. a profound or notable transformation.
– ORIGIN from Shakespeare's *Tempest* (I. ii. 403).

**sea chest** • n. a sailor's storage chest.

**sea coal** • n. archaic mineral coal, as distinct from other types of coal such as charcoal.

**seacock** • n. a valve sealing off a pipe through a ship's hull below or near to the waterline.

**sea cow** • n. a sirenian, especially a manatee.

**sea cucumber** • n. an echinoderm having a thick worm-like body with tentacles around the mouth. [Class Holothuroidea.]

**Sea Dayak** • n. another term for **IBAN** (in sense 1).

**sea dog** • n. **1** informal an old or experienced sailor. **2** Heraldry a mythical beast like a dog with fins, webbed feet, and a scaly tail.

**sea eagle** • n. a large fish-eating eagle that frequents coasts and wetlands. [*Haliaeetus albicilla* and related species.]

**sea elephant** • n. another term for **ELEPHANT SEAL**.

**sea fan** • n. a horny coral with a vertical tree- or fan-like skeleton. [*Gorgonis* and other genera.]

**seafaring** • adj. travelling by sea. • n. travel by sea.
– DERIVATIVES **seafarer** n.

**seafood** • n. shellfish and sea fish served as food.

**seafront** • n. the part of a coastal town next to and directly facing the sea.

**sea-girt** • adj. poetic/literary surrounded by sea.

**seagoing** • adj. **1** (of a ship) suitable for voyages on the sea. **2** characterized by or relating to travelling by sea.

**sea gooseberry** • n. a common comb jelly with a spherical body bearing two long retractile branching tentacles. [*Pleurobrachia pileus*.]

**sea grape** • n. a salt-resistant tree of the dock family, bearing grape-like bunches of edible purple fruit. [*Coccoloba uvifera*.]

**seagrass** • n. eelgrass or a similar grass-like plant that grows near the sea.

**sea green** • n. a pale bluish green colour.

**seagull** • n. a gull.

**sea hare** • n. a large sea slug which has a minute internal shell and lateral extensions to the foot. [*Aplysia* and other genera.]

**sea holly** • n. a spiny-leaved plant of the parsley family, with metallic blue teasel-like flowers, growing in sandy places by the sea. [*Eryngium maritimum*.]

**sea horse** • n. **1** a small marine fish with an upright posture and a head and neck suggestive of a horse. [Genus *Hippocampus*: many species.] **2** a mythical creature with a horse's head and fish's tail.

**sea-island cotton** • n. a fine-quality long-stapled cotton grown on islands off the southern US.

**seakale** • n. a maritime plant of the cabbage family cultivated for its edible young shoots. [*Crambe maritima*.]

**seakeeping** • n. the ability of a vessel to withstand rough conditions at sea.

**seal**[1] • n. **1** a device or substance used to join two things together or render something impervious. ➤the state or fact of being joined or rendered impervious with a seal. **2** a piece of wax, lead, etc. with an individual design stamped into it, attached to a document as a guarantee of authenticity. ➤a design embossed in paper for this purpose. ➤an engraved device used for stamping a seal. ➤a decorative adhesive stamp. **3** a confirmation or guarantee: *a seal of approval*. **4** (**the seal** or **the seal of the confessional**) the obligation on a priest not to divulge anything said during confession. **5** the water standing in the trap of a drain to prevent foul air from rising. • v. **1** fasten or close securely. ➤(**seal something off**) isolate an area by preventing or monitoring entrance to and exit from it. **2** apply a non-porous coating to (a surface) to make it impervious. **3** conclude, establish, or secure definitively: *victory was sealed*. **4** authenticate (a document) with a seal.
– PHRASES **my lips are sealed** I will not discuss or reveal a particular secret. **put** (or **set**) **the seal on** finally confirm or conclude. **set** (or **put**) **one's seal to** (or **on**) mark with one's distinctive character.
– DERIVATIVES **sealable** adj.
– ORIGIN ME: from OFr. *seel* (n.), *seeler* (v.), from L. *sigillum* 'small picture', dimin. of *signum* 'a sign'.

**seal**[2] • n. a fish-eating aquatic mammal with a streamlined body and feet developed as flippers. [Families Phocidae and Otariidae (**eared seals**): many species.] • v. [usu. as noun **sealing**] hunt for seals.
– ORIGIN OE *seolh*, of Gmc origin.

**sealant** • n. material used for sealing something so as to make it airtight or watertight.

**sea lavender** • n. a chiefly maritime plant with small pink or lilac funnel-shaped flowers. [Genus *Limonium*.]

**sea lawyer** • n. informal an eloquently and obstinately argumentative person.

**sealed-beam** • adj. denoting a vehicle headlamp with a sealed unit consisting of the light source, reflector, and lens.

**sealed orders** • pl. n. Military orders which are not to be opened before a specified time.

**sealer**[1] • n. a device or substance used to seal something.

**sealer**[2] • n. a ship or person engaged in hunting seals.

**sea lettuce** • n. an edible seaweed with green fronds that resemble lettuce leaves. [*Ulva lactuca*.]

**sea level** • n. the level of the sea's surface, used in reckoning the height of geographical features and as a barometric standard.

**sea lily** • n. a sedentary marine echinoderm which has a small body on a long jointed stalk, with feather-like arms to trap food. [Class Crinoidea.]

**sealing wax** • n. a mixture of shellac and rosin with turpentine and pigment, softened by heating and used to make seals.

**sea lion** • n. an eared seal occurring mainly on Pacific coasts, the large male of which has a mane on the neck and shoulders. [Five genera and species in the family Otariidae.]

**Sea Lord** • n. either of two senior officers in the Royal Navy (**First Sea Lord**, **Second Sea Lord**) serving originally as members of the Admiralty Board (now of the Ministry of Defence).

**sealpoint** • n. a dark brown marking on the fur of the head, tail, and paws of a Siamese cat. ➤ a cat with such markings.

**sealskin** • n. the skin or prepared fur of a seal, especially when made into a garment.

**seals of office** • pl. n. (in the UK) engraved seals held during tenure of an official position, especially that of Lord Chancellor or Secretary of State.

**sealstone** • n. a gemstone bearing an engraved device for use as a seal.

**Sealyham** /ˈsiːlɪəm/ • n. a terrier of a wire-haired short-legged breed.
– ORIGIN C19: from *Sealyham*, the name of a village in SW Wales, where the dog was first bred.

**seam** • n. **1** a line where two pieces of fabric are sewn together in a garment or other article. ➤ a line where the edges of two pieces of wood or other material touch each other. **2** an underground layer of a mineral such as coal or gold. **3** a long thin indentation or scar. • v. **1** join with a seam. **2** [usu. as adj. **seamed**] make a long narrow indentation in.
– PHRASES **bursting** (or **bulging**) **at the seams** informal full to overflowing. **come** (or **fall**) **apart at the seams** informal be in a very poor condition and near to collapse.
– ORIGIN OE *sēam*, of Gmc origin.

**seaman** • n. (pl. **-men**) a sailor, especially one below the rank of officer. ➤ the lowest rank in the US navy, below petty officer.
– DERIVATIVES **seamanlike** adj. **seamanly** adj. **seamanship** n.

**sea mat** • n. a bryozoan forming mat-like encrustations on underwater objects. [*Membranipora* and other genera.]

**seam bowler** • n. Cricket a bowler who makes the ball deviate by causing it to bounce on its seam.
– DERIVATIVES **seam bowling** n.

**seamer** • n. **1** Cricket another term for **SEAM BOWLER**. ➤ a ball which deviates by bouncing on its seam. **2** a person who seams garments.

**sea mile** • n. a unit of distance equal to a minute of arc of a great circle, varying between approximately 2,014 yards (1,842 metres) at the equator and 2,035 yards (1,861 metres) at the pole.

**seamless** • adj. smooth and without seams or obvious joins.
– DERIVATIVES **seamlessly** adv.

**seamount** • n. a submarine mountain.

**sea mouse** • n. a large marine bristle worm with a stout oval body which bears matted fur-like chaetae. [Genus *Aphrodite*.]

**seamstress** • n. a woman who sews, especially as a job.
– ORIGIN C16: from archaic *seamster*, *sempster* 'tailor, seamstress' + **-ESS**[1].

**seamy** • adj. (**-ier**, **-iest**) sordid and disreputable.
– DERIVATIVES **seaminess** n.

**seance** /ˈseɪɒns, -ɒ̃s, -ɑːns/ • n. a meeting at which people attempt to make contact with the dead.
– ORIGIN C18: Fr. *séance*, from OFr. *seoir*, from L. *sedere* 'sit'.

**sea nettle** • n. a jellyfish with tentacles that can sting bathers. [*Chrysaora* and other genera.]

**sea pen** • n. a marine coelenterate related to the corals, forming a feather-shaped colony with a horny or calcareous skeleton. [Order Pennatulacea.]

**Sea Peoples** • pl. n. invaders of uncertain identity who encroached on Egypt and the eastern Mediterranean by land and sea in the late 13th century BC.

**sea pink** • n. another term for **THRIFT** (in sense 3).

**seaplane** • n. an aircraft with floats or skis instead of wheels, designed to land on and take off from water.

**seaport** • n. a town or city with a harbour for seagoing ships.

**SEAQ** • abbrev. (in the UK) Stock Exchange Automated Quotations.

**seaquake** • n. a sudden disturbance of the sea caused by a submarine eruption or earthquake.

**sear** • v. **1** burn or scorch with a sudden intense heat. ➤ brown (food) quickly at a high temperature. **2** [usu. as adj. **searing**] (of pain) be experienced as a sudden burning sensation. **3** archaic cause to wither or become insensitive. • adj. (also **sere**) poetic/literary withered.
– DERIVATIVES **searingly** adv.
– ORIGIN OE *sēar* (adj.), *sēarian* (v.), of Gmc origin.

**search** • v. **1** try to find something by looking or otherwise seeking carefully and thoroughly. ➤ examine thoroughly in order to find something. **2** [as adj. **searching**] scrutinizing thoroughly, especially in a disconcerting way. • n. (often in phr. **in search of**) an act of searching. ➤ Law an investigation of public records to find if a property is subject to any liabilities or encumbrances.
– PHRASES **search me!** informal I do not know.
– DERIVATIVES **searchable** adj. **searcher** n. **searchingly** adv.
– ORIGIN ME: from OFr. *cerchier* (v.), from late L. *circare* 'go round', from L. *circus* 'circle'.

**search engine** • n. Computing a program for the retrieval of data, files, or documents from a database or network, especially the Internet.

**searchlight** • n. a powerful outdoor electric light with a concentrated beam that can be turned in the required direction.

**search party** • n. a group of people organized to look for someone or something that is lost.

**search warrant** • n. a legal document authorizing a police officer or other official to enter and search premises.

**sea robin** • n. a gurnard (fish), especially one of warm seas, with brightly coloured wing-like pectoral fins.

**sea room** • n. clear space at sea for a ship to turn or manoeuvre in.

**sea salt** • n. salt produced by the evaporation of seawater.

**seascape** • n. a view or picture of an expanse of sea.

**Sea Scout** • n. (especially in the UK) a member of the maritime branch of the Scout Association.

**sea serpent** • n. a legendary serpent-like sea monster.

**seashell** • n. the shell of a marine mollusc.

**seashore** • n. an area of sandy, stony, or rocky land bordering and level with the sea. ➤ Law the land between high- and low-water marks.

**seasick** • adj. suffering from nausea caused by the motion of a ship at sea.
– DERIVATIVES **seasickness** n.

**seaside** • n. a place by the sea, especially a beach area or holiday resort.

**sea slug** • n. a shell-less marine mollusc with external gills and a number of appendages on the upper surface. [Order Nudibranchia.]

**sea snail** • n. **1** a marine mollusc, especially one with a spiral shell. [Subclass Prosobranchia.] **2** another term for **SNAILFISH**.

**sea snake** • n. a venomous marine snake found in warm coastal waters of the Indian and Pacific oceans. [Subfamily Hydrophiinae: several species.]

**season** • n. **1** each of the four divisions of the year (spring, summer, autumn, and winter) marked by particular weather patterns and daylight hours. ➤ the time of year when a particular fruit, vegetable, etc., is plentiful and in good condition. **2** a period of the year characterized by an activity or event, especially a particular sport: *the football season.* ➤ (**the season**) the time of year traditionally marked by fashionable upper-class social events. **3** (usu. in phr. **in season**) a period when a female mammal is ready to mate. **4** archaic a proper or suitable time: *to everything there is a season.* ➤ an indefinite or unspecified period of time; a while. • v. **1** add salt, herbs, or spices to (food). **2** add an enlivening quality or feature to. **3** keep (wood) so as to dry it for use as timber. **4** [as adj. **seasoned**] accustomed to particular conditions; experienced.
– ORIGIN ME: from OFr. *seson*, from L. *satio(n-)* 'sowing', later 'time of sowing'.

**seasonable** • adj. **1** usual for or appropriate to a particular season of the year. **2** archaic opportune or suitable.
– DERIVATIVES **seasonability** n. **seasonableness** n. **seasonably** adv.

**seasonal** • adj. relating to or characteristic of a particular season of the year. ➤ fluctuating according to the season.
– DERIVATIVES **seasonality** n. **seasonally** adv.

**seasonal affective disorder** • n. depression associated with late autumn and winter and thought to be caused by a lack of light.

**seasoning** • n. salt, herbs, or spices added to food to enhance the flavour.

**season ticket** • n. a ticket allowing travel within a particular period or admission to a series of events.

**sea squirt** • n. a marine tunicate which has a bag-like body with orifices through which water flows into and out of a central pharynx. [Class Ascidiacea.]

**sea state** • n. the degree of turbulence at sea, generally measured on a scale of 0 to 9 according to average wave height.

**seat** • n. **1** a thing made or used for sitting on, such as a chair or stool. ➤ the roughly horizontal part of a chair. ➤ a sitting place for a passenger in a vehicle or for a member of an audience. **2** a person's buttocks. ➤ a manner of sitting on a horse. **3** chiefly Brit. a place in an elected parliament or council. ➤ Brit. a parliamentary constituency. **4** a site or location. ➤ a large country house and estate belonging to an aristocratic family: *a country seat.* **5** a part of a machine that supports or guides another part. • v. arrange for (someone) to sit somewhere. ➤ (**seat oneself** or **be seated**) sit down. ➤ (of a place) have sufficient seats for. ➤ fit in position.
– DERIVATIVES **seating** n. **seatless** adj.
– ORIGIN ME (as n.): from ON *sæti*, from the Gmc base of **SIT**.

**seat belt** • n. a belt used to secure someone in the seat of a motor vehicle or aircraft.

**-seater** • comb. form denoting a vehicle, sofa, or building with a specified number of seats: *a six-seater.*

**SEATO** • abbrev. South-East Asia Treaty Organization.

**sea trout** • n. **1** Brit. a brown trout of a salmon-like migratory race. [*Salmo trutta trutta*.] **2** N. Amer. a trout-like marine fish of the drum family occurring in the western Atlantic. [Genus *Cynoscion*: several species, including the weakfish.]

**sea urchin** • n. a marine echinoderm which has a spherical or flattened shell covered in mobile spines, with a mouth on the underside and calcareous jaws. [Class Echinoidea.]

**sea wall** • n. a wall or embankment erected to prevent the sea encroaching on an area of land.

**sea wasp** • n. a box jellyfish which can inflict a dangerous sting.

**seaway** • n. **1** a waterway or channel used by or capable of accommodating ships. **2** a rough sea in which to sail.

**seaweed** • n. large algae growing in the sea or on rocks below the high-water mark.

**sea wolf** • n. another term for **WOLF FISH**.

**seaworthy** • adj. (of a boat) in a good enough condition to sail on the sea.
– DERIVATIVES **seaworthiness** n.

**sebaceous** /sɪ'beɪʃəs/ • adj. technical of or relating to oil or fat. ➤ of or relating to a sebaceous gland or its secretion.
– ORIGIN C18: from L. *sebaceus* (from *sebum* 'tallow') + **-OUS**.

**sebaceous cyst** • n. a swelling in the skin arising in a sebaceous gland, typically filled with yellowish sebum.

**sebaceous gland** • n. a small gland in the skin which secretes a lubricating oily matter (sebum) into the hair follicles to lubricate the skin and hair.

**Sebat** /'si:bat/ (also **Shebat**, **Shevat**) • n. (in the Jewish calendar) the fifth month of the civil and eleventh of the religious year, usually coinciding with parts of January and February.
– ORIGIN from Heb. *šəḇaṭ*.

**seborrhoea** /ˌsɛbə'ri:ə/ (US **seborrhea**) • n. Medicine excessive discharge of sebum from the sebaceous glands.
– DERIVATIVES **seborrhoeic** adj.

**sebum** /'si:bəm/ • n. an oily secretion of the sebaceous glands.
– ORIGIN C19: mod. L., from L. *sebum* 'grease'.

**SEC** • abbrev. (in the US) Securities and Exchange Commission.

**Sec.** • abbrev. secretary.

**sec**[1] • abbrev. secant.

**sec**[2] • n. informal a second or a very short space of time.

**sec**[3] • adj. (of wine) dry.
– ORIGIN Fr., from L. *siccus*.

**sec.** • abbrev. second(s).

**secant** /'si:k(ə)nt, 'sɛk-/ • n. **1** Mathematics the ratio of the hypotenuse (in a right-angled triangle) to the shorter side adjacent to an acute angle. **2** Geometry a straight line that cuts a curve in two or more parts.
– ORIGIN C16; from Fr. *sécante*, based on L. *secare* 'to cut'.

**secateurs** /ˌsɛkə'tə:z, 'sɛkətə:z/ • pl. n. chiefly Brit. a pair of pruning clippers for use with one hand.
– ORIGIN C19: pl. of Fr. *sécateur* 'cutter', formed irregularly from L. *secare* 'to cut'.

**secco** /'sɛkəʊ/ (also **fresco secco**) • n. the technique of painting on dry plaster with pigments mixed in water.
– ORIGIN C19: from Ital., lit. 'dry', from L. *siccus*.

**secede** /sɪ'si:d/ • v. withdraw formally from membership of a federal union or a political or religious organization.
– DERIVATIVES **seceder** n.
– ORIGIN C18: from L. *secedere*, from *se-* 'apart' + *cedere* 'go'.

**secession** /sɪ'sɛʃ(ə)n/ • n. the action of seceding from a federation or organization. ➤ (**the Secession**) historical the withdrawal of eleven Southern states from the US Union in 1860, leading to the Civil War.
– DERIVATIVES **secessional** adj. **secessionism** n. **secessionist** n.

**seclude** • v. keep (someone) away from other people.
– ORIGIN ME (in the sense 'obstruct access to'): from L. *secludere*, from *se-* 'apart' + *claudere* 'to shut'.

**secluded** • adj. (of a place) not seen or visited by many people; sheltered and private.

**seclusion** • n. **1** the state of being private and away from other people. **2** archaic a sheltered or private place.
– DERIVATIVES **seclusive** adj.

**Seconal** /'sɛk(ə)nal, -(ə)l/ • n. trademark a barbiturate drug used as a sedative and hypnotic.
– ORIGIN 1930s: blend of **SECONDARY** and **ALLYL**.

**second**[1] /ˈsɛk(ə)nd/ ● **ordinal number 1** constituting number two in a sequence; coming after the first in time or order; 2nd. ➤secondly. ➤(**seconds**) informal a second course or second helping of food at a meal. ➤denoting someone or something reminiscent of a better-known predecessor: *the conflict could turn into a second Vietnam.* **2** subordinate or inferior in position, rank, or importance. ➤Brit. denoting the second highest division in the results of the examinations for a university degree. ➤Music performing a lower or subordinate of two or more parts for the same instrument or voice. ➤(**seconds**) goods of an inferior quality. ➤coarse flour, or bread made from it. **3** Music an interval spanning two consecutive notes in a diatonic scale. ➤the note which is higher by this interval than the tonic of a diatonic scale or root of a chord. **4** an attendant assisting a combatant in a duel or boxing match. **5** a Cub or Brownie who assists the Sixer. ● **v. 1** formally support or endorse (a nomination or resolution) before adoption or further discussion. ➤express agreement with. **2** archaic support; back up.
– PHRASES **second to none** the best, worst, fastest, etc.
– DERIVATIVES **seconder** n. **secondly** adv.
– ORIGIN ME: via OFr. from L. *secundus* 'following, second', from the base of *sequi* 'follow'.

**second**[2] /ˈsɛk(ə)nd/ ● **n. 1** (abbrev.: **s** or ") a sixtieth of a minute of time, which as the SI unit of time is defined in terms of the natural periodicity of the radiation of a caesium-133 atom. ➤informal a very short time. **2** (also **arc second** or **second of arc**) a sixtieth of a minute of angular distance. (Symbol: ")
– ORIGIN ME: from med. L. *secunda* (*minuta*) 'second (minute)', fem. (used as n.) of *secundus*, referring to the 'second' operation of dividing an hour by sixty.

**second**[3] /sɪˈkɒnd/ ● **v.** Brit. temporarily transfer (a worker) to another position.
– DERIVATIVES **secondee** /-ˈdiː/ n. **secondment** n.
– ORIGIN C19: from Fr. *en second* 'in the second rank (of officers)'.

**Second Advent** ● **n.** another term for **SECOND COMING**.

**secondary** ● **adj. 1** coming after, less important than, or resulting from something primary. **2** of or relating to education for children from the age of eleven to sixteen or eighteen. **3** of or denoting the output side of a transformer or other inductive device. **4** Chemistry (of an organic compound) having its functional group on a carbon atom bonded to two other carbon atoms. ➤derived from ammonia by replacement of two hydrogen atoms by organic groups. **5** (**Secondary**) Geology former term for **MESOZOIC**. **6** (of a cell or battery) having a reversible chemical reaction and therefore able to store energy.
– DERIVATIVES **secondarily** adv. **secondariness** n.

**secondary colour** ● **n.** a colour resulting from the mixing of two primary colours.

**secondary feather** ● **n.** any of the flight feathers growing from the second joint of a bird's wing.

**secondary industry** ● **n.** Economics industry that converts raw materials into commodities and products; manufacturing industry.

**secondary modern school** ● **n.** chiefly historical (in the UK) a secondary school for children not selected for grammar or technical schools.

**secondary picketing** ● **n.** Brit. picketing of a firm not directly involved in a particular dispute.

**secondary planet** ● **n.** a satellite of a planet.

**secondary sexual characteristics** ● **pl. n.** physical characteristics developed at puberty which distinguish between the sexes but are not involved in reproduction.

**second ballot** ● **n.** a further ballot held to confirm the selection of a candidate where a previous ballot did not yield an absolute majority.

**second best** ● **adj.** next after the best. ● **n.** a less adequate or less desirable alternative.

**second cause** ● **n.** Logic a cause that is itself caused.

**second chamber** ● **n.** the upper house of a parliament with two chambers.

**second class** ● **n. 1** a set of people or things grouped together as the second best. **2** the second-best accommodation in an aircraft, train, or ship. **3** Brit. the second-highest division in the results of the examinations for a university degree. ● **adj. & adv.** of the second-best quality or in the second class.

**Second Coming** ● **n.** Christian Theology the prophesied return of Christ to Earth at the Last Judgement.

**second-degree** ● **adj. 1** Medicine denoting burns that cause blistering but not permanent scars. **2** Law, chiefly N. Amer. denoting a category of a crime, especially murder, that is less serious than a first-degree crime.

**seconde** /səˈkɒ̃d/ ● **n.** Fencing the second of eight parrying positions.
– ORIGIN C18: from Fr., fem. of *second* 'second'.

**second-generation** ● **adj. 1** denoting the offspring of parents who have immigrated to a particular country. **2** of a more advanced stage of technology than previous models or systems.

**second-guess** ● **v. 1** anticipate or predict (someone's actions or thoughts) by guesswork. **2** judge or criticize (someone) with hindsight.

**second-hand** ● **adj. & adv. 1** (of goods) having had a previous owner; not new. **2** accepted on another's authority and not from original investigation.
– PHRASES **at second hand** by hearsay rather than direct observation or experience.

**second hand** ● **n.** an extra hand in some watches and clocks which moves round to indicate the seconds.

**second in command** ● **n.** the officer next in authority to the commanding or chief officer.

**second intention** ● **n.** Medicine the healing of a wound in which the edges do not meet and new epithelium must form across granulation tissue.

**second lieutenant** ● **n.** a rank of officer in the army and the US air force, above warrant officer or chief warrant officer and below lieutenant or first lieutenant.

**second line** ● **n. 1** a battle line behind the front line to support it and make good its losses. **2** [as modifier] ranking second in strength, effectiveness, or ability.

**second master** ● **n.** a deputy headmaster.

**second mate** ● **n.** another term for **SECOND OFFICER**.

**second name** ● **n.** Brit. a surname.

**second nature** ● **n.** a tendency or habit that has become instinctive.

**secondo** /sɪˈkɒndəʊ/ ● **n.** (pl. **secondi** /-di/) Music the second or lower part in a duet.
– ORIGIN from Ital.

**second officer** ● **n.** an assistant mate on a merchant ship.

**second person** ● **n.** see **PERSON** (sense 5).

**second position** ● **n. 1** Ballet a posture in which the feet form a straight line, being turned out to either side with the heels separated by the distance of a small step. **2** Music a position of the left hand on the fingerboard of a stringed instrument nearer to the bridge than the first position.

**second-rate** ● **adj.** of mediocre or inferior quality.
– DERIVATIVES **second-rater** n.

**second reading** ● **n.** a second presentation of a bill to a legislative assembly, in the UK to approve its general principles and in the US to debate committee reports.

**second sight** ● **n.** the supposed ability to perceive future or distant events; clairvoyance.
– DERIVATIVES **second-sighted** adj.

**second string** ● **n.** an alternative resource or course of action in case another one fails.

**second thoughts** (US also **second thought**) ● **pl. n.** a change of opinion or resolve reached after reconsidering something.

**second wind** ● **n.** regained ability to breathe freely during exercise, after having been out of breath.

**Second World** ● **n.** the former communist block consisting of the Soviet Union and some countries in eastern Europe.

**secret** ● **adj.** not known or seen or not meant to be known or seen by others. ➤fond of having or keeping secrets; secretive. ● **n. 1** something kept or meant to be kept se-

cret. ➤something not properly understood; a mystery: *the secrets of the universe.* **2** a valid but not commonly known method of achieving something: *the secret of a happy marriage is compromise.* **3** a prayer said quietly by the priest after the offertory in a Roman Catholic Mass.
– DERIVATIVES **secrecy** n. **secretly** adv.
– ORIGIN ME: from OFr., from L. *secretus* 'separate, set apart', from *secernere*, from *se-* 'apart' + *cernere* 'sift'.

**secret agent** ● **n.** a spy acting for a country.

**secretagogue** /sɪ'kriːtəgɒg/ ● **n.** Physiology a substance which promotes secretion.
– ORIGIN C20: from **SECRETE**[1] + Gk *agōgos* 'leading'.

**secretaire** /ˌsɛkrɪ'tɛː/ ● **n.** a small writing desk; an escritoire.
– ORIGIN C18: from Fr. *secrétaire*, lit. 'secretary'.

**secretariat** /ˌsɛkrɪ'tɛːrɪət/ ● **n.** a governmental administrative office or department.
– ORIGIN C19: from Fr. *secrétariat*, from med. L. *secretariatus*, from *secretarius* (see **SECRETARY**).

**secretary** ● **n.** (pl. **-ies**) **1** a person employed to assist with correspondence, keep records, etc. **2** an official of a society or other organization who conducts its correspondence and keeps its records. **3** the principal assistant of a UK government minister or ambassador.
– DERIVATIVES **secretarial** adj. **secretaryship** n.
– ORIGIN ME (orig. in the sense 'person entrusted with a secret'): from late L. *secretarius* 'confidential officer', from L. *secretum* 'a secret', neut. of *secretus* (see **SECRET**).

**secretary bird** ● **n.** a slender long-legged African bird of prey that feeds on snakes, having a crest likened to a quill pen stuck behind the ear. [*Sagittarius serpentarius.*]

**Secretary General** ● **n.** (pl. **Secretaries General**) the title of the principal administrator of some organizations.

**Secretary of State** ● **n. 1** (in the UK) the head of a major government department. **2** (in the US) the head of the State Department, responsible for foreign affairs.

**secrete**[1] /sɪ'kriːt/ ● **v.** (of a cell, gland, or organ) produce by secretion.
– DERIVATIVES **secretor** n. **secretory** adj.

**secrete**[2] /sɪ'kriːt/ ● **v.** conceal; hide.
– ORIGIN C18: alt. of the obs. verb *secret* 'keep secret'.

**secretion** ● **n.** a process by which substances are produced and discharged from a cell, gland, or organ for a particular function in the organism or for excretion. ➤a substance discharged in such a way.
– ORIGIN C17: from Fr. *sécrétion* or L. *secretio(n-)* 'separation', from *secret-*, *secernere* 'move apart'.

**secretive** ● **adj.** inclined to conceal feelings and intentions or not to disclose information.
– DERIVATIVES **secretively** adv. **secretiveness** n.
– ORIGIN C19: back-form. from *secretiveness*, suggested by Fr. *secrétivité*, from *secret* 'secret'.

**secret police** ● **n.** [treated as pl.] a police force working in secret against a government's political opponents.

**secret service** ● **n. 1** a government department concerned with espionage. **2** (**Secret Service**) (in the US) a branch of the Treasury Department dealing with counterfeiting and providing protection for the President.

**secret society** ● **n.** an organization whose members are sworn to secrecy about its activities.

**sect** ● **n. 1** a religious group or faction regarded as heretical or as deviating from orthodox tradition. ➤often derogatory a group that has separated from an established Church; a nonconformist Church. **2** a group with extreme or dangerous philosophical or political ideas.
– ORIGIN ME: from OFr. *secte* or L. *secta*, lit. 'following', hence 'faction, party', from the stem of *sequi* 'follow'.

**sect.** ● **abbrev.** section.

**sectarian** ● **adj.** denoting, concerning, or deriving from a sect or sects. ➤carried out on the grounds of membership of a sect, denomination, or other group: *sectarian killings.* ● **n.** a member or follower of a sect.
– DERIVATIVES **sectarianism** n. **sectarianize** (also **-ise**) v.

**sectary** /'sɛktəri/ ● **n.** (pl. **-ies**) a member of a religious or political sect.

**section** ● **n. 1** any of the more or less distinct parts into which something is or may be divided or from which it is made up. ➤N. Amer. a measure of land, equal to one square mile. ➤chiefly N. Amer. a particular district of a town. ➤NZ a building plot. **2** a distinct group within a larger body of people or things. ➤a subdivision of an army platoon. ➤Biology a secondary taxonomic category, especially a subgenus. **3** the cutting of a solid by or along a plane. ➤the shape resulting from cutting a solid along a plane. ➤a representation of the internal structure of something as if it has been cut through. **4** Surgery a separation by cutting. **5** Biology a thin slice of plant or animal tissue prepared for microscopic examination. ● **v. 1** divide into sections. **2** Surgery divide by cutting. **3** Brit. commit (someone) compulsorily to a psychiatric hospital in accordance with a section of a mental health act.
– DERIVATIVES **sectional** adj. **sectionalize** (also **-ise**) v. **sectionally** adv. **sectioned** adj.
– ORIGIN ME: from Fr. *section* or L. *sectio(n-)*, from *secare* 'to cut'.

**sectionalism** ● **n.** restriction of interest to parochial concerns.
– DERIVATIVES **sectionalist** n. & adj.

**section house** ● **n.** chiefly Brit. a building providing residential accommodation for unmarried police officers.

**section mark** ● **n.** a sign (§) used as a reference mark or to indicate a section of a book.

**sector** ● **n. 1** an area or portion that is distinct from others. ➤a distinct part of an economy, society, or sphere of activity. ➤a subdivision of an area for military operations. **2** the plane figure enclosed by two radii of a circle or ellipse and the arc between them. **3** a mathematical instrument consisting of two arms hinged at one end and marked with sines, tangents, etc. for making diagrams.
– DERIVATIVES **sectoral** adj.
– ORIGIN C16: from late L., a technical use of L. *sector* 'cutter'.

**sectorial** /sɛk'tɔːrɪəl/ ● **adj. 1** of or like a sector. **2** Zoology denoting a carnassial tooth, or a similar cutting tooth in mammals other than carnivores.

**secular** /'sɛkjʊlə/ ● **adj. 1** not religious, sacred, or spiritual. **2** Christian Church not subject to or bound by religious rule. Contrasted with **REGULAR**. **3** Astronomy of or denoting slow changes in the motion of the sun or planets. **4** Economics (of a fluctuation or trend) occurring or persisting over an indefinitely long period. **5** occurring once every century or similarly long period (used especially in reference to celebratory games in ancient Rome). ● **n.** a secular priest.
– DERIVATIVES **secularism** n. **secularist** n. **secularity** n. **secularization** (also **-isation**) n. **secularize** (also **-ise**) v. **secularly** adv.
– ORIGIN ME: senses 1 and 2 from OFr. *seculer*, from L. *saecularis*, from *saeculum* 'generation', used in Christian L. to mean 'the world'; senses 3, 4, and 5 (C19) from L. *saecularis* 'relating to an age or period'.

**secular arm** ● **n.** the legal authority of the civil power as invoked by the Church to punish offenders.

**secund** /sɪ'kʌnd/ ● **adj.** Botany arranged on one side only (such as the flowers of lily of the valley).
– DERIVATIVES **secundly** adv.
– ORIGIN C18: from L. *secundus* (see **SECOND**[1]).

**secure** ● **adj. 1** fixed or fastened so as not to give way, become loose, or be lost. **2** certain to remain safe and unthreatened. ➤protected against attack or other criminal activity. **3** feeling free from fear or anxiety. ➤(**secure of**) dated feeling no doubts about attaining. **4** (of a place of detention) having provisions against the escape of inmates. ● **v. 1** make secure; fix or fasten securely. **2** protect against threats. **3** succeed in obtaining. ➤seek to guarantee repayment of (a loan) by having a right to take possession of an asset in the event of non-payment. **4** Surgery compress (a blood vessel) to prevent bleeding.
– PHRASES **secure arms** Military hold a rifle with the muzzle downward and the lock in the armpit to guard it from rain.
– DERIVATIVES **securable** adj. **securely** adv. **securement**

n. **secureness** n.
– ORIGIN C16 (earlier (ME) as *security*): from L. *securus*, from *se-* 'without' + *cura* 'care'.

**securitize** (also **-ise**) ● v. [often as adj. **securitized**] convert (an asset, especially a loan) into marketable securities, typically for the purpose of raising cash.
– DERIVATIVES **securitization** n.

**security** ● n. (pl. **-ies**) **1** the state of being or feeling secure. **2** the safety of a state or organization against criminal activity such as terrorism. ➤measures taken to ensure such safety. **3** a thing deposited or pledged as a guarantee of the fulfilment of an undertaking or the repayment of a loan, to be forfeited in case of default. **4** a certificate attesting credit, the ownership of stocks or bonds, or the right to ownership connected with tradable derivatives.

**security blanket** ● n. **1** a blanket or other familiar object which is a comfort to a child. **2** Brit. an official sanction imposed on information in order to maintain complete secrecy.

**sedan** /sɪˈdan/ ● n. **1** (also **sedan chair**) an enclosed chair for conveying one person, carried between horizontal poles by two porters, common in the 17th and 18th centuries. **2** chiefly N. Amer. a motor car for four or more people.
– ORIGIN perh. an alt. of an Ital. dial. word, based on L. *sella* 'saddle'.

**sedate**[1] ● adj. **1** calm and unhurried. **2** staid and rather dull.
– DERIVATIVES **sedately** adv. **sedateness** n.
– ORIGIN ME (also as a medical term in the sense 'not sore or painful'): from L. *sedatus*, *sedare* 'settle', from *sedere* 'sit'.

**sedate**[2] ● v. put under sedation.
– ORIGIN 1960s: back-form. from SEDATION.

**sedation** ● n. the administering of a sedative drug to produce a state of calm or sleep.
– ORIGIN C16: from Fr. *sédation* or L. *sedatio(n-)*, from *sedare* (see SEDATE[1]).

**sedative** ● adj. promoting calm or inducing sleep. ● n. a sedative drug.
– ORIGIN ME: from OFr. *sedatif* or med. L. *sedativus*, from L. *sedat-*, *sedare* (see SEDATE[1]).

**sedentary** /ˈsɛd(ə)nt(ə)ri/ ● adj. **1** tending to spend much time seated. ➤(of work or a way of life) characterized by much sitting and little physical exercise. ➤sitting. **2** Zoology & Anthropology inhabiting the same locality throughout life. **3** Zoology sessile.
– DERIVATIVES **sedentarily** adv. **sedentariness** n.
– ORIGIN C16 (in the sense 'not migratory'): from Fr. *sédentaire* or L. *sedentarius*, from *sedere* 'sit'.

**Seder** /ˈseɪdə/ ● n. a Jewish ritual service and ceremonial dinner for the first night or first two nights of Passover.
– ORIGIN from Heb. *sēḏer* 'order, procedure'.

**sederunt** /sɪˈdɪərənt, -ˈdɛː-/ ● n. (in Scotland) a sitting of an ecclesiastical assembly or other body.
– ORIGIN C17: from L., lit. '(the following persons) sat'.

**sedge** ● n. a grass-like plant with triangular stems and inconspicuous flowers, growing typically in wet ground. [*Carex* and other genera.]
– DERIVATIVES **sedgy** adj.
– ORIGIN OE *secg*, of Gmc origin.

**sedge warbler** ● n. a common migratory songbird with streaky brown plumage, frequenting marshes and reed beds. [*Acrocephalus schoenobaenus*]

**sedilia** /sɪˈdɪlɪə/ ● pl. n. (sing. **sedile** /sɪˈdʌɪli/) a group of three stone seats for clergy in the south chancel wall of a church.
– ORIGIN C18: from L., 'seat'.

**sediment** ● n. **1** matter that settles to the bottom of a liquid. **2** Geology particulate matter carried by water or wind and deposited on the land surface or seabed. ● v. settle or deposit as sediment.
– DERIVATIVES **sedimentation** n.
– ORIGIN C16: from Fr. *sédiment* or L. *sedimentum* 'settling'.

**sedimentary** ● adj. of or relating to sediment. ➤Geology (of rock) that has formed from sediment deposited by water or wind.

**sedition** ● n. conduct or speech inciting rebellion against the authority of a state or monarch.
– DERIVATIVES **seditious** adj. **seditiously** adv.
– ORIGIN ME (in the sense 'violent strife'): from OFr., or from L. *seditio(n-)*, from *sed-* 'apart' + *itio(n-)* 'going'.

**seduce** ● v. **1** persuade to do something inadvisable. **2** entice into sexual activity.
– DERIVATIVES **seducer** n. **seducible** adj. **seduction** n. **seductress** n.
– ORIGIN C15 (earlier (ME) as *seduction*): from L. *seducere*, from *se-* 'away' + *ducere* 'to lead'.

**seductive** ● adj. tempting and attractive.
– DERIVATIVES **seductively** adv. **seductiveness** n.

**sedulous** /ˈsɛdjʊləs/ ● adj. showing dedication and diligence.
– DERIVATIVES **sedulity** /sɪˈdjuːlɪti/ n. **sedulously** adv. **sedulousness** n.
– ORIGIN C16: from L. *sedulus* 'zealous' + **-ous**.

**sedum** /ˈsiːdəm/ ● n. a fleshy-leaved plant of a large genus including the stonecrops, with small star-shaped flowers. [Genus *Sedum*.]
– ORIGIN from mod. L., denoting a houseleek.

**see**[1] ● v. (**sees**, **seeing**; past **saw**; past part. **seen**) **1** perceive with the eyes. ➤watch (a game, film, or other entertainment). ➤experience or witness (an event or situation). **2** deduce after reflection or from information. ➤ascertain after inquiry or consideration. **3** regard in a specified way. ➤envisage. **4** meet (someone one knows) socially or by chance. ➤meet regularly as a boyfriend or girlfriend. ➤consult (a specialist or professional). ➤give an interview or consultation to. **5** escort to a specified place. **6** (**see to**) attend to. **7** ensure. **8** (in poker or brag) equal the bet of (an opponent) and require them to reveal their cards to determine who has won the hand.
– PHRASES **let me see** said as an appeal for time to think before speaking. **see here!** said for emphasis or to express a protest. **see one's way clear to do** (or **doing**) **something** find that it is possible or convenient to do something. **see someone coming** recognize a person who can be fooled. **see someone right** Brit. informal make sure that a person is appropriately rewarded or looked after. **see the back of** Brit. informal be rid of.
– PHRASAL VERBS **see about** attend to. **see after** chiefly N. Amer. or archaic look after. **see something of** spend a specified amount of time with (someone) socially. **see someone off 1** accompany a person who is leaving to their point of departure. **2** Brit. repel an intruder or counter someone posing a threat. **see someone out** Brit. (of an article) last longer than the remainder of someone's life. **see something out** Brit. come to the end of a period of time or undertaking. **see over** tour and examine. **see through** detect the true nature of. **see someone through** support a person for the duration of a difficult time. **see something through** persist with an undertaking until it is completed.
– DERIVATIVES **seeable** adj.
– ORIGIN OE *sēon*, of Gmc origin.

**see**[2] ● n. the place in which a cathedral church stands, identified as the seat of authority of a bishop or archbishop.
– ORIGIN ME: from Anglo-Norman Fr. *sed*, from L. *sedes* 'seat', from *sedere* 'sit'.

**seed** ● n. **1** a flowering plant's unit of reproduction, capable of developing into another such plant. ➤a quantity of these. **2** the beginning of a feeling, process, or condition. **3** archaic a man's semen. **4** archaic (chiefly in biblical use) offspring or descendants. **5** a small crystal introduced into a liquid to act as a nucleus for crystallization. **6** a small container of radioactive material placed in body tissue during radiotherapy. **7** any of a number of stronger competitors in a sports tournament who have been assigned a position in an ordered list to ensure they do not play each other in the early rounds. ● v. **1** sow (land) with seeds. ➤sow (seed). **2** produce or drop seeds. **3** remove the seeds from. **4** initiate the development or growth of. **5** place a crystalline substance in (a cloud or solution) in order to cause condensation or crystallization. **6** give (a competitor) the status of seed in a

tournament.
– PHRASES **go** (or **run**) **to seed 1** cease flowering as the seeds develop. **2** deteriorate in condition or strength.
– DERIVATIVES **seeded** adj. **seedless** adj.
– ORIGIN OE *sǣd*, of Gmc origin; rel. to **sow**[1].

**seedbed** • n. a bed of fine soil in which seedlings are germinated.

**seed cake** • n. cake containing caraway seeds.

**seed capital** • n. another term for **SEED MONEY**.

**seedcorn** • n. **1** good-quality corn kept for seed. **2** Brit. assets set aside for the generation of future profit.

**seeder** • n. **1** a machine for sowing seed. **2** a plant that produces seeds in a particular way or under particular conditions.

**seed fern** • n. another term for **PTERIDOSPERM**.

**seed head** • n. a flower head in seed.

**seed leaf** • n. Botany a cotyledon.

**seedling** • n. a young plant, especially one raised from seed and not from a cutting.

**seed-lip** • n. historical a basket for holding seed, used when sowing by hand.

**seed money** • n. money allocated to initiate a project.

**seed pearl** • n. a very small pearl.

**seed potato** • n. a potato intended for replanting to produce a new plant.

**seedsman** • n. (pl. **-men**) a person who deals in seeds as a profession.

**seedy** • adj. (**-ier**, **-iest**) **1** sordid or squalid. **2** dated unwell.
– DERIVATIVES **seedily** adv. **seediness** n.

**seeing** • conj. because; since. • n. Astronomy the quality of observed images as determined by atmospheric conditions.

**Seeing Eye dog** • n. trademark, chiefly N. Amer. a guide dog for the blind.

**seek** • v. (past and past part. **sought**) **1** attempt to find. ➤ (**seek someone/thing out**) search for and find someone or something. **2** attempt to obtain or do. **3** ask for. **4** archaic go to (a place).
– PHRASES **seek dead** Brit. used to instruct a retriever to go and look for game that has been shot. **to seek** archaic not yet found; lacking.
– DERIVATIVES **seeker** n.
– ORIGIN OE *sēcan*, of Gmc origin.

**seel** /siːl/ • v. archaic close (a person's eyes).
– ORIGIN C15 (orig. a term in falconry meaning 'stitch shut the eyelids of (a hawk)'): from Fr. *ciller*, or med. L. *ciliare*, from L. *cilium* 'eyelid'.

**seem** • v. **1** give the impression of being. **2** (**cannot seem to do something**) be unable to do something, despite having tried.
– ORIGIN ME (also in the sense 'be appropriate'): from ON *sœma* 'to honour', from *sœmr* 'fitting'.

**seeming** • adj. apparent. ➤ [in combination] giving the impression of having a specified quality: *an angry-seeming man*. • n. poetic/literary outward appearance, especially when deceptive or different from reality.
– DERIVATIVES **seemingly** adv.

**seemly** • adj. conforming to propriety or good taste.
– DERIVATIVES **seemliness** n.
– ORIGIN ME: from ON *sœmiligr*, from *soemr* (see **SEEM**).

**seen** past participle of **SEE**[1].

**See of Rome** • n. another term for **HOLY SEE**.

**seep** • v. (of a liquid) flow or leak slowly through porous material or small holes. • n. N. Amer. a place where petroleum or water seeps out of the ground.
– DERIVATIVES **seepage** n.
– ORIGIN C18: perh. a dial. form of OE *sīpian* 'to soak'.

**seer**[1] /ˈsiːə, sɪə/ • n. **1** a person of supposed supernatural insight who sees visions of the future. **2** chiefly archaic a person who sees something specified.

**seer**[2] /sɪə/ • n. (in the Indian subcontinent) a varying unit of weight (about one kilogram) or liquid measure (about one litre).
– ORIGIN from Hindi *ser*.

**seersucker** • n. a fabric with a surface consisting of puckered and flat sections.
– ORIGIN C18: from Pers. *šir o šakar*, lit. 'milk and sugar', (by transference) 'striped cotton garment'.

**see-saw** • n. **1** a long plank balanced on a fixed support, on each end of which children sit and move up and down by pushing the ground alternately with their feet. **2** a situation characterized by rapid, repeated changes from one state or position to another. • v. change rapidly and repeatedly from one state or position to another and back again.
– ORIGIN C17 (orig. used by sawyers as a rhythmical refrain): reduplication of the verb **SAW**[1].

**seethe** • v. **1** (of a liquid) boil or be turbulent as if boiling. ➤ archaic cook (food) by boiling. **2** be filled with intense but unexpressed anger. **3** be crowded with people or things moving about in a rapid or hectic way.
– ORIGIN OE *sēothan* 'make or keep boiling'.

**see-through** • adj. (especially of clothing) translucent.

**Sefer** /ˈseɪfə/ • n. (pl. **Sifrei**) Judaism a book of Hebrew religious literature. ➤ (usu. **Sefer Torah** /ˈtɔːrə, ˈtəʊrə/) a scroll containing the Torah or Pentateuch.
– ORIGIN from Heb. *sēper tōrāh* 'book of (the) Law'.

**segment** /ˈsɛgm(ə)nt/ • n. **1** each of the parts into which something is or may be divided. **2** Geometry a part of a circle cut off by a chord, or a part of a sphere cut off by a plane not passing through the centre. **3** Phonetics the smallest distinct part of a spoken utterance, especially with regard to vowel and consonant sounds. **4** Zoology each of a series of similar anatomical units of which the body and appendages of some animals are composed. • v. /usu. sɛgˈmɛnt/ **1** divide into segments. **2** Embryology (of a cell) undergo cleavage.
– DERIVATIVES **segmentary** adj. **segmentation** n.
– ORIGIN C16: from L. *segmentum*, from *secare* 'to cut'.

**segmental** • adj. **1** composed of segments. ➤ Phonetics denoting or relating to the division of speech into segments. **2** Architecture denoting an arch in which the curve forms a shallow arc of a circle, less than a semicircle.
– DERIVATIVES **segmentalization** (also **-isation**) n. **segmentalize** (also **-ise**) v. **segmentally** adv.

**segregate**[1] /ˈsɛgrɪgeɪt/ • v. **1** set apart from the rest or from each other. **2** separate along racial, sexual, or religious lines. **3** Genetics (of pairs of alleles) be separated at meiosis and transmitted independently via separate gametes.
– DERIVATIVES **segregable** adj. **segregation** n. **segregational** adj. **segregationist** adj. & n. **segregative** adj.
– ORIGIN C16: from L. *segregat-*, *segregare* 'separate from the flock'.

**segregate**[2] /ˈsɛgrɪgət/ • n. **1** Genetics an allele that has undergone segregation. **2** Botany a species within an aggregate.
– ORIGIN C19: from L. *segregatus* 'separate', past part. of *segregare* (see **SEGREGATE**[1]).

**segue** /ˈsɛgweɪ/ • v. (**segues**, **segued**, **seguing**) (in music and film) move without interruption from one song, melody, or scene to another. • n. an instance of this.
– ORIGIN Ital., lit. 'follows'.

**seguidilla** /ˌsɛgɪˈdiːljə, -ˈdiːjə/ • n. a Spanish dance in triple time.
– ORIGIN C18: Sp., from *seguida* 'sequence'.

**Sehnsucht** /ˈzeɪnzuːxt, German ˈzeːnzʊxt/ • n. poetic/literary wistful longing.
– ORIGIN from Ger.

**sei** • n. another term for **SEI WHALE**.

**seicento** /seɪˈtʃɛntəʊ/ • n. the style of Italian art and literature of the 17th century.
– DERIVATIVES **seicentist** n.
– ORIGIN Ital., '600', shortened from *mille seicento* '1600', used with ref. to the years 1600–99.

**seiche** /seɪʃ/ • n. a temporary disturbance or oscillation in the water level of a lake or partially enclosed body of water, especially one caused by changes in atmospheric pressure.
– ORIGIN C19: from Swiss Fr., perh. from Ger. *Seiche* 'sinking (of water)'.

**Seidlitz powder** /ˈsɛdlɪts/ • n. a laxative preparation containing tartaric acid, sodium potassium tartrate, and

sodium bicarbonate which effervesces when mixed with water.
– ORIGIN C18: named with ref. to the mineral water of *Seidlitz*, a village in Bohemia.

**seif** /siːf, seɪf/ ● n. a sand dune in the form of a long narrow ridge.
– ORIGIN C20: from Arab. *sayf* 'sword' (because of the shape).

**seigneur** /seɪˈnjəː/ (also **seignior** /ˈseɪnjə/) ● n. a feudal lord; the lord of a manor.
– DERIVATIVES **seigneurial** adj.
– ORIGIN C16: from OFr., from L. *senior* 'older, elder'.

**seigniorage** /ˈseɪnjərɪdʒ/ (also **seignorage**) ● n. **1** profit made by a government by issuing currency, especially the difference between the face value of coins and their production costs. ➤historical the Crown's right to a percentage on bullion brought to a mint for coining. **2** historical a thing claimed by a sovereign or feudal superior as a prerogative.
– ORIGIN ME: from OFr. *seignorage*, from *seigneur* (see **SEIGNEUR**).

**seigniory** /ˈseɪnjəri/ (also **seigneury**) ● n. (pl. **-ies**) the position, authority, or domain of a feudal lord.
– ORIGIN ME: from OFr. *seignorie*, from *seigneur* (see **SEIGNEUR**).

**seine** /seɪn/ ● n. a fishing net which hangs vertically in the water with floats at the top and weights at the bottom edge, the ends being drawn together to encircle the fish. ● v. fish or catch with a seine.
– DERIVATIVES **seiner** n.
– ORIGIN OE *segne*, of W. Gmc origin, via L. from Gk *sagēnē*; reinforced in ME by OFr. *saine*.

**seise** ● v. see **SEIZE** (sense 5).

**seisin** /ˈsiːzɪn/ (also **seizin**) ● n. Law possession of land by freehold. ➤Brit. historical possession, especially of land.
– ORIGIN ME: from OFr. *seisine*, from *saisir* 'seize'.

**seismic** /ˈsʌɪzmɪk/ ● adj. **1** of or relating to earthquakes or other vibrations of the earth and its crust. ➤relating to or denoting geological surveying methods involving vibrations produced artificially by explosions. **2** of enormous proportions or effect.
– DERIVATIVES **seismical** adj. **seismically** adv.
– ORIGIN C19: from Gk *seismos* 'earthquake' + **-IC**.

**seismicity** /sʌɪzˈmɪsɪti/ ● n. Geology the occurrence or frequency of earthquakes in a region.

**seismo-** ● comb. form of an earthquake; relating to earthquakes: *seismograph*.
– ORIGIN from Gk *seismos* 'earthquake'.

**seismogram** /ˈsʌɪzmə(ʊ)gram/ ● n. a record produced by a seismograph.

**seismograph** /ˈsʌɪzmə(ʊ)grɑːf/ ● n. an instrument that measures and records details of earthquakes, such as force and duration.
– DERIVATIVES **seismographic** adj. **seismographical** adj.

**seismology** /sʌɪzˈmɒlədʒi/ ● n. the branch of science concerned with earthquakes and related phenomena.
– DERIVATIVES **seismological** adj. **seismologically** adv. **seismologist** n.

**seismometer** /sʌɪzˈmɒmɪtə/ ● n. another term for **SEISMOGRAPH**.

**seismosaurus** /ˈsʌɪzmə(ʊ)sɔːrəs/ ● n. a huge late Jurassic sauropod dinosaur.
– ORIGIN mod. L., from **SEISMO-** + Gk *sauros* 'lizard'.

**sei whale** /seɪ/ ● n. a small rorqual with dark steely-grey skin and white grooves on the belly. [*Balaenoptera borealis*.]
– ORIGIN C20: from Norw. *sejhval*.

**seize** ● v. **1** take hold of suddenly and forcibly. ➤take forcible possession of. ➤(of the police or another authority) take possession of by warrant or legal right. **2** take (an opportunity) eagerly and decisively. ➤(**seize on/upon**) take eager advantage of. **3** affect suddenly or acutely. **4** (of a machine with moving parts or a moving part in a machine) become jammed. **5** (also **seise**) (**be seized of**) English Law be in legal possession of. ➤historical have or receive freehold possession of (property). ➤be aware or informed of. **6** Nautical, archaic fasten or attach by binding with turns of rope.
– DERIVATIVES **seizable** adj. **seizer** n.
– ORIGIN ME: from OFr. *seizir* 'give seisin', from med. L. *sacire*, in the phr. *ad proprium sacire* 'claim as one's own', from a Gmc base meaning 'procedure'.

**seizin** ● n. variant spelling of **SEISIN**.

**seizing** ● n. Nautical, archaic a length of cord or rope used for fastening or tying.

**seizure** ● n. **1** the action of seizing. **2** a sudden attack of illness, especially a stroke or an epileptic fit.

**sejant** /ˈsiːdʒ(ə)nt/ ● adj. [postpos.] Heraldry (of an animal) sitting upright.
– ORIGIN C15: alt. of an OFr. var. of *seant* 'sitting'.

**Sejm** /seɪm/ ● n. the lower house of parliament in Poland.
– ORIGIN from Polish.

**Sekt** /zɛkt/ ● n. a German sparkling white wine.
– ORIGIN from Ger.

**selachian** /sɪˈleɪkɪən/ ● n. Zoology a cartilaginous fish of a group that comprises the sharks and dogfishes.
– ORIGIN C19: from mod. L. *Selachii* (former class name, from Gk *selakhos* 'shark') + **-AN**.

**seladang** /səˈlɑːdaŋ/ ● n. another term for **GAUR**.
– ORIGIN C19: from Malay.

**selah** /ˈsiːlə, -lɑː/ ● exclam. a word occurring frequently at the end of a verse in Psalms and Habakkuk, probably as a musical direction.
– ORIGIN from Heb. *selāh*.

**seldom** ● adv. not often. ● adj. dated infrequent.
– ORIGIN OE *seldan*, of Gmc origin, from a base meaning 'strange, wonderful'.

**select** ● v. **1** carefully choose as being the best or most suitable. **2** (**select for/against**) Biology (in terms of evolution) determine whether (a characteristic or organism) will survive. ● adj. **1** carefully chosen from a larger number as being the best. **2** used by or consisting of a wealthy or sophisticated elite.
– DERIVATIVES **selectable** adj. **selectness** n.
– ORIGIN C16: from L. *select-*, *seligere* 'choose'.

**select committee** ● n. a small parliamentary committee appointed for a special purpose.

**selectee** ● n. **1** a person who is selected. **2** US a conscript.

**selection** ● n. **1** the action or fact of selecting. ➤a number of selected things. ➤a range of things from which a choice may be made. ➤a horse or horses tipped as worth bets in a race or meeting. **2** Biology the evolutionary process which determines which types of organism thrive; natural selection.

**selectional** ● adj. Linguistics denoting or relating to the process by which only certain words or structures can occur naturally, normally, or correctly in the context of other words.
– DERIVATIVES **selectionally** adv.

**selection rule** ● n. Physics a rule which describes whether particular quantum transitions in an atom or molecule are allowed or forbidden.

**selective** ● adj. **1** relating to or involving selection. ➤tending to choose carefully. **2** (of a process or agent) affecting some things and not others.
– DERIVATIVES **selectively** adv. **selectiveness** n. **selectivity** n.

**selective service** ● n. N. Amer. service in the armed forces under conscription.

**selectman** ● n. (pl. **-men**) a member of the local government board of a New England town.

**selector** ● n. **1** a person appointed to select a team in a sport. **2** a device for selecting a particular gear or other setting of a machine or device.

**selenite** /ˈsɛlɪnʌɪt/ ● n. a form of gypsum occurring as transparent crystals or thin plates.
– ORIGIN C17: via L. from Gk *selēnitēs lithos* 'moonstone'.

**selenium** /sɪˈliːnɪəm/ ● n. the chemical element of atomic number 34, a grey crystalline non-metal with semiconducting properties. (Symbol: **Se**)
– DERIVATIVES **selenide** n.
– ORIGIN C19: mod. L., from Gk *selēnē* 'moon'.

**selenium cell** ● n. a photoelectric device containing a

piece of selenium.

**seleno-** ● comb. form of, relating to, or shaped like the moon: *selenography.*
– ORIGIN from Gk *selēnē* 'moon'.

**selenography** /ˌsɛlɪˈnɒgrəfi, ˌsiː-/ ● n. the scientific mapping of the moon.
– DERIVATIVES **selenographer** n. **selenographic** adj. **selenographical** adj.

**selenology** /ˌsɛlɪˈnɒlədʒi, ˌsiː-/ ● n. the scientific study of the moon.
– DERIVATIVES **selenologist** n.

**Seleucid** /sɪˈluːsɪd/ ● n. a member of a dynasty ruling over Syria and a great part of western Asia from 311 to 65 BC.
– ORIGIN from *Seleucus* Nicator (the name of the founder, one of Alexander the Great's generals) + **-ID**[3].

**self** ● n. (pl. **selves**) a person's essential being that distinguishes them from others, especially considered as the object of introspection or reflexive action. ➤a person's particular nature or personality. ➤one's own interests or pleasure. ● pron. (pl. **selves**) **1** (**one's self**) used ironically to refer in specified favourable terms to oneself or someone else: *a picture of my good self.* **2** used on counterfoils, cheques, and other papers to refer to the holder or person who has signed. ● adj. (of a trimming, woven design, etc.) of the same material or colour as the rest. ● v. chiefly Botany self-pollinate; self-fertilize.
– ORIGIN OE, of Gmc origin.

**self-** /sɛlf/ ● comb. form **1** of or directed towards oneself or itself: *self-hatred.* **2** by one's own efforts; by its own action: *self-adjusting.* **3** on, in, for, or relating to oneself or itself: *self-adhesive.*

**self-abandonment** (also **self-abandon**) ● n. the action of completely surrendering oneself to a desire or impulse.
– DERIVATIVES **self-abandoned** adj.

**self-absorption** ● n. **1** preoccupation with one's own emotions, interests, or situation. **2** Physics the absorption by a body of radiation which it has itself emitted.
– DERIVATIVES **self-absorbed** adj.

**self-abuse** ● n. **1** behaviour which causes damage or harm to oneself. **2** euphemistic masturbation.

**self-addressed** ● adj. (especially of an envelope) bearing one's own address.

**self-adhesive** ● adj. adhering without requiring moistening.

**self-adjusting** ● adj. (chiefly of machinery) adjusting itself to meet varying requirements.
– DERIVATIVES **self-adjustment** n.

**self-advertisement** ● n. the active publicizing of oneself.
– DERIVATIVES **self-advertiser** n. **self-advertising** adj.

**self-affirmation** ● n. the recognition and assertion of the existence and value of one's individual self.

**self-alienation** ● n. the distancing of oneself from one's feelings or activities, such as may occur in mental illness.

**self-appointed** ● adj. having assumed a position or role without the endorsement of others.

**self-assembly** ● n. **1** the construction of a piece of furniture from materials sold in kit form. **2** Biology the spontaneous formation of a ribosome, virus, etc. in a medium containing the appropriate components.
– DERIVATIVES **self-assemble** v.

**self-assertion** ● n. the confident and forceful expression or promotion of oneself or one's views.
– DERIVATIVES **self-assertive** adj. **self-assertiveness** n.

**self-assessment** ● n. **1** assessment of oneself or one's performance in relation to an objective standard. **2** calculation of one's own taxable liability.

**self-assurance** ● n. confidence in one's own abilities or character.
– DERIVATIVES **self-assured** adj. **self-assuredly** adv.

**self-awareness** ● n. conscious knowledge of one's own character, feelings, motives, and desires.
– DERIVATIVES **self-aware** adj.

**self-betrayal** ● n. the intentional or inadvertent revelation of the truth about one's actions or thoughts.

**self-build** ● n. Brit. the building of homes by their owners.
– DERIVATIVES **self-builder** n.

**self-cancelling** ● adj. **1** having elements which contradict or negate one another. **2** (of a mechanical device) designed to stop working automatically when no longer required.

**self-catering** Brit. ● adj. (of a holiday or accommodation) offering facilities for people to cook their own meals. ● n. the action of catering for oneself.

**self-censorship** ● n. the exercising of control over what one says and does, especially to avoid reprisal.

**self-centred** ● adj. preoccupied with oneself and one's affairs.
– DERIVATIVES **self-centredly** adv. **self-centredness** n.

**self-certification** ● n. the practice of attesting something about oneself in a formal statement, rather than asking a disinterested party to do so. ➤the practice, for the purpose of claiming sick pay, by which an employee rather than a doctor declares in writing that an absence was due to illness.
– DERIVATIVES **self-certificate** n.

**self-certify** ● v. Brit. attest (one's financial standing) in a formal statement. ➤[as adj. **self-certified**] (of a loan or mortgage) obtained as a result of such self-certification.

**self-cocking** ● adj. (of a gun) having a hammer that is raised by the trigger, not by hand.

**self-colour** ● n. **1** a single uniform colour. **2** the natural colour of something.
– DERIVATIVES **self-coloured** adj.

**self-conceit** ● n. another term for **SELF-CONGRATULATION**.
– DERIVATIVES **self-conceited** adj.

**self-confessed** ● adj. having openly admitted to being a person with certain characteristics.
– DERIVATIVES **self-confessedly** adv. **self-confession** n. **self-confessional** adj.

**self-confidence** ● n. a feeling of trust in one's abilities, qualities, and judgement.
– DERIVATIVES **self-confident** adj. **self-confidently** adv.

**self-congratulation** ● n. undue pride regarding one's achievements or qualities.
– DERIVATIVES **self-congratulatory** adj.

**self-conscious** ● adj. **1** nervous or awkward because unduly aware of oneself or one's actions. **2** (especially of an action) deliberate and with full awareness. **3** Philosophy & Psychology having knowledge of one's own existence, especially the knowledge of oneself as a conscious being.
– DERIVATIVES **self-consciously** adv. **self-consciousness** n.

**self-consistent** ● adj. not having conflicting parts or aspects; consistent.
– DERIVATIVES **self-consistency** n.

**self-contained** ● adj. **1** complete, or having all that is needed, in itself. ➤chiefly Brit. (of accommodation) having its own kitchen and bathroom, and typically its own private entrance. **2** not depending on or influenced by others.
– DERIVATIVES **self-containment** n.

**self-contradiction** ● n. inconsistency between aspects or parts of a whole.
– DERIVATIVES **self-contradicting** adj. **self-contradictory** adj.

**self-control** ● n. the ability to control one's emotions or behaviour, especially in difficult situations.
– DERIVATIVES **self-controlled** adj.

**self-deception** ● n. the action or practice of deceiving oneself into believing that a false or unvalidated feeling, idea, or situation is true.
– DERIVATIVES **self-deceit** n. **self-deceiver** n. **self-deceiving** adj. **self-deceptive** adj.

**self-defeating** ● adj. (of an action or policy) unable to achieve the end it is designed to bring about.

**self-defence** ● n. the defence of one's person or interests, especially through the use of physical force, which is permitted in certain cases as an answer to a charge of

violent crime.
– DERIVATIVES **self-defensive** adj.

**self-denial** • n. the denial of one's own interests and needs.
– DERIVATIVES **self-denying** adj.

**self-deprecating** • adj. modest about or critical of oneself, especially humorously so.
– DERIVATIVES **self-deprecatingly** adv. **self-deprecation** n. **self-deprecatory** adj.

**self-depreciatory** • adj. another term for SELF-DEPRECATING.
– DERIVATIVES **self-depreciation** n.

**self-destruct** • v. explode or disintegrate automatically, having been preset to do so.

**self-destructive** • adj. destroying or causing harm to oneself.
– DERIVATIVES **self-destruction** n. **self-destructively** adv.

**self-determination** • n. **1** the process by which a country determines its own statehood and forms its own allegiances and government. **2** the process by which a person controls their own life.

**self-directed** • adj. **1** (of an emotion, statement, or activity) directed at one's self. **2** (of an activity) under one's own control.
– DERIVATIVES **self-direction** n.

**self-discipline** • n. the ability to control one's feelings and overcome one's weaknesses.
– DERIVATIVES **self-disciplined** adj.

**self-doubt** • n. lack of confidence in oneself and one's abilities.

**self-drive** • adj. **1** Brit. (of a hired vehicle) driven by the hirer. **2** (of a holiday) involving use of one's own car rather than transport arranged by the operator.

**self-educated** • adj. educated largely through one's own efforts, rather than by formal instruction.
– DERIVATIVES **self-education** n.

**self-effacing** • adj. not claiming attention for oneself.
– DERIVATIVES **self-effacement** n. **self-effacingly** adv.

**self-employed** • adj. working for oneself as a freelance or the owner of a business rather than for an employer.
– DERIVATIVES **self-employment** n.

**self-enclosed** • adj. (of a person, community, or system) not choosing or able to communicate with others or with external systems.

**self-esteem** • n. confidence in one's own worth or abilities.

**self-evaluation** • n. another term for SELF-ASSESSMENT.

**self-evident** • adj. not needing to be demonstrated or explained.
– DERIVATIVES **self-evidence** n. **self-evidently** adv.

**self-examination** • n. **1** the study of one's behaviour and motivations. **2** the examination of one's body for signs of illness.

**self-explanatory** • adj. not needing explanation.

**self-expression** • n. the expression of one's feelings, thoughts, or ideas, especially in writing, art, music, or dance.
– DERIVATIVES **self-expressive** adj.

**self-faced** • adj. (of stone) having an undressed surface.

**self-feeder** • n. **1** a furnace or machine that renews its own fuel or material automatically. **2** a device for supplying food to farm animals automatically.
– DERIVATIVES **self-feeding** adj.

**self-fertile** • adj. Botany (of a plant) capable of self-fertilization.
– DERIVATIVES **self-fertility** n.

**self-fertilization** (also **-isation**) • n. Biology the fertilization of plants and some invertebrate animals by their own pollen or sperm.
– DERIVATIVES **self-fertilize** v.

**self-financing** • adj. (of an organization or enterprise) having or generating enough income to finance itself.
– DERIVATIVES **self-financed** adj.

**self-flagellation** • n. **1** the action of flogging oneself, especially as a form of religious discipline. **2** excessive self-criticism.

**self-fulfilling** • adj. (of an opinion or prediction) bound to be proved correct or to come true as a result of behaviour caused by its being expressed.

**self-governing** • adj. **1** (of a British hospital or school) having opted out of local authority control. **2** (of a former colony or dependency) administering its own affairs.

**self-government** • n. **1** government of a country by its own people, especially after having been a colony. **2** another term for SELF-CONTROL.
– DERIVATIVES **self-governed** adj.

**self-heal** • n. a purple-flowered plant of the mint family, formerly used for healing wounds. [*Prunella vulgaris*.]

**self-help** • n. the use of one's own efforts and resources to achieve things without relying on others.

**selfhood** • n. the quality that constitutes one's individuality.

**self-identification** • n. the attribution of certain characteristics or qualities to oneself.

**self-image** • n. the idea one has of one's abilities, appearance, and personality.

**self-immolation** • n. the offering of oneself as a sacrifice, especially by burning.

**self-importance** • n. an exaggerated sense of one's own value or importance.
– DERIVATIVES **self-important** adj. **self-importantly** adv.

**self-improvement** • n. the improvement of one's knowledge, status, or character by one's own efforts.

**self-induced** • adj. **1** brought about by oneself. **2** produced by electrical self-induction.

**self-induction** • n. Physics the induction of an electromotive force in a circuit when the current in that circuit is varied.
– DERIVATIVES **self-inductance** n. **self-inductive** adj.

**self-indulgent** • adj. indulging or tending to indulge one's desires.
– DERIVATIVES **self-indulgence** n. **self-indulgently** adv.

**self-inflicted** • adj. (of a wound or other harm) inflicted on oneself.

**self-insurance** • n. insurance of oneself or one's interests by maintaining a fund to cover possible losses rather than by purchasing an insurance policy.

**self-interest** • n. one's personal interest or advantage, especially when pursued without regard for others.
– DERIVATIVES **self-interested** adj.

**self-involved** • adj. wrapped up in oneself or one's own thoughts.
– DERIVATIVES **self-involvement** n.

**selfish** • adj. concerned chiefly with one's own personal profit or pleasure at the expense of consideration for others.
– DERIVATIVES **selfishly** adv. **selfishness** n.

**selfism** • n. concentration on one's own interests.
– DERIVATIVES **selfist** n.

**selfless** • adj. concerned more with the needs and wishes of others than with one's own.
– DERIVATIVES **selflessly** adv. **selflessness** n.

**self-limiting** • adj. **1** Medicine (of a condition) ultimately resolving itself without treatment. **2** (in psychology) preventing the development or expression of the self.

**self-liquidating** • adj. denoting an asset, project, etc. that earns sufficiently over a certain period to pay for its cost.

**self-loading** • adj. (especially of a gun) loading automatically.
– DERIVATIVES **self-loader** n.

**self-love** • n. regard for one's own well-being and happiness.

**self-made** • adj. **1** having become successful or rich by one's own efforts. **2** made by oneself.

**self-management** • n. **1** management of or by oneself. **2** the distribution of political control to individual regions of a state, especially as a form of socialism.
– DERIVATIVES **self-managing** adj.

**selfmate** • n. Chess a problem in which the solver's task is to force the opponent to deliver checkmate.

**self-motivated** • adj. motivated to do something because of one's own enthusiasm or interest, without needing pressure from others.
– DERIVATIVES **self-motivating** adj. **self-motivation** n.

**self-mutilation** • n. deliberate injury to one's own body.

**selfness** • n. **1** a person's essential individuality. **2** archaic selfishness.

**self-opinionated** • adj. having an arrogantly high regard for oneself or one's own opinions.
– DERIVATIVES **self-opinion** n.

**self-parody** • n. the intentional or inadvertent parodying of one's own behaviour, style, etc.
– DERIVATIVES **self-parodic** adj. **self-parodying** adj.

**self-perpetuating** • adj. perpetuating itself or oneself without external agency or intervention.
– DERIVATIVES **self-perpetuation** n.

**self-pity** • n. excessive unhappiness over one's own troubles.
– DERIVATIVES **self-pitying** adj. **self-pityingly** adv.

**self-policing** • n. the process of keeping order or maintaining control within a community without accountability or reference to an external authority.

**self-pollination** • n. Botany the pollination of a flower by pollen from the same plant.
– DERIVATIVES **self-pollinate** v. **self-pollinator** n.

**self-portrait** • n. a portrait by an artist of himself or herself.
– DERIVATIVES **self-portraiture** n.

**self-possessed** • adj. calm, confident, and in control of one's feelings.
– DERIVATIVES **self-possession** n.

**self-preservation** • n. the protection of oneself from harm or death, especially regarded as a basic instinct in human beings and animals.

**self-proclaimed** • adj. proclaimed to be such by oneself, without endorsement by others.

**self-propelled** • adj. moving or able to move without external propulsion or agency.
– DERIVATIVES **self-propelling** adj.

**self-raising flour** • n. Brit. flour that has a raising agent already added.

**self-realization** (also **-isation**) • n. fulfilment of one's own potential.

**self-referential** • adj. (especially of a literary or other creative work) making reference to itself, its creator, or their other work.
– DERIVATIVES **self-referentiality** n. **self-referentially** adv.

**self-regard** • n. **1** consideration for oneself. **2** vanity.
– DERIVATIVES **self-regarding** adj.

**self-regulating** • adj. regulating itself without intervention from external bodies.
– DERIVATIVES **self-regulation** n. **self-regulatory** adj.

**self-reliance** • n. reliance on one's own powers and resources rather than those of others.
– DERIVATIVES **self-reliant** adj. **self-reliantly** adv.

**self-respect** • n. pride and confidence in oneself.
– DERIVATIVES **self-respecting** adj.

**self-restraint** • n. self-control.
– DERIVATIVES **self-restrained** adj.

**self-revealing** • adj. revealing one's character or motives, especially inadvertently.
– DERIVATIVES **self-revelation** n. **self-revelatory** adj.

**self-righteous** • adj. certain that one is totally correct or morally superior.
– DERIVATIVES **self-righteously** adv. **self-righteousness** n.

**self-righting** • adj. (of a boat) designed to right itself when capsized.

**self-rising flour** • n. US term for **SELF-RAISING FLOUR**.

**self-rule** • n. another term for **SELF-GOVERNMENT** (in sense 1).

**self-sacrifice** • n. the giving up of one's own interests or wishes in order to help others or advance a cause.
– DERIVATIVES **self-sacrificial** adj. **self-sacrificing** adj.

**selfsame** • adj. exactly the same.

**self-satisfied** • adj. smugly complacent.
– DERIVATIVES **self-satisfaction** n.

**self-sealing** • adj. **1** (of a tyre, fuel tank, etc.) able to seal small punctures automatically. **2** (of an envelope) self-adhesive.

**self-seed** • v. (of a plant) propagate itself by seed.
– DERIVATIVES **self-seeder** n.

**self-seeking** • adj. pursuing one's own welfare and interests before those of others.
– DERIVATIVES **self-seeker** n.

**self-selection** • n. **1** the action of putting oneself forward for something. **2** the action of selecting something for oneself.
– DERIVATIVES **self-selecting** adj.

**self-service** • adj. denoting a shop, restaurant, or other outlet where customers select goods for themselves and pay at a checkout. • n. a self-service system or outlet.

**self-serving** • adj. another term for **SELF-SEEKING**.

**self-sow** • v. (of a plant) propagate itself by seed.

**self-starter** • n. **1** a self-motivated and ambitious person who acts on their own initiative. **2** dated the starter of a motor-vehicle engine.
– DERIVATIVES **self-starting** adj.

**self-sterile** • adj. Biology incapable of self-fertilization.
– DERIVATIVES **self-sterility** n.

**self-styled** • adj. using a description or title that one has given oneself.

**self-sufficient** • adj. **1** able to satisfy one's basic needs without outside help, especially with regard to the production of food. **2** emotionally and intellectually independent.
– DERIVATIVES **self-sufficiency** n. **self-sufficiently** adv.

**self-supporting** • adj. **1** having the resources to be able to survive without outside assistance. **2** staying up or upright without being supported by something else.
– DERIVATIVES **self-support** n.

**self-surrender** • n. the surrender of oneself or one's will to an external influence, an emotion, etc.

**self-sustaining** • adj. able to continue in a healthy state without outside assistance.
– DERIVATIVES **self-sustained** adj.

**self-tailing** • adj. (of a winch) designed to maintain constant tension in the rope so that it does not slip.

**self-tapping** • adj. (of a screw) able to cut a thread in the material into which it is inserted.

**self-taught** • adj. having acquired knowledge or skill on one's own initiative rather than through formal instruction or training.

**self-timer** • n. a mechanism in a camera that introduces a delay between the operation of the shutter release and the opening of the shutter, enabling the photographer to be included in the photograph.

**self-willed** • adj. obstinately pursuing one's own wishes.
– DERIVATIVES **self-will** n.

**self-winding** • adj. (chiefly of a watch) wound by automatic means rather than by hand.

**self-worth** • n. another term for **SELF-ESTEEM**.

**Seljuk** /ˈsɛldʒuːk/ • n. a member of any of the Turkish dynasties which ruled Asia Minor in the 11th to 13th centuries.
– DERIVATIVES **Seljukian** /-ˈdʒuːkɪən/ adj. & n.
– ORIGIN from Turk. *seljūq*, the name of the reputed ancestor of the dynasty.

**selkie** (also **selky** or **silkie**) • n. (pl. **-ies**) Scottish a mythical creature that resembles a seal in the water but assumes human form on land.
– ORIGIN from *selch*, var. of **SEAL**, + **-IE**.

**sell** • v. (past and past part. **sold**) **1** hand over in exchange for money. ➤ deal in. ➤ be subject to a specified demand on the market: *the book didn't sell well.* ➤ (**sell out**) sell all of one's stock of something. ➤ (**sell oneself**) have sex in exchange for money. **2** persuade someone of the merits of. ➤ make enthusiastic about. **3** (**sell someone out**) betray someone for one's own financial or material benefit. ➤ (**sell out**) abandon one's principles for reasons of expedience. **4** archaic trick or deceive. • n. informal **1** an act of

selling or attempting to sell. **2** a disappointment.
– PHRASES **sell someone/thing short** fail to recognize or state the true value of someone or something. **sell one's soul (to the devil)** be willing to do anything, no matter how wrong it is, in order to achieve one's objective.
– DERIVATIVES **sellable** adj.
– ORIGIN OE *sellan* (v.), of Gmc origin.

**sell-by date** • n. **1** chiefly Brit. a date marked on a perishable product indicating the recommended time by which it should be sold. **2** informal a time after which something or someone is no longer considered desirable or effective.

**selldown** • n. Austral./NZ widespread selling of shares, resulting in falling prices.

**seller** • n. **1** a person who sells. **2** a product that sells in a specified way.
– PHRASES **seller's** (or **sellers'**) **market** an economic situation in which goods or shares are scarce and sellers can keep prices high.

**sell-in** • n. the sale of goods to retail traders prior to public retailing.

**selling point** • n. a feature of a product for sale that makes it attractive to customers.

**selling race** • n. a horse race after which the winning horse must be auctioned.

**sell-off** • n. a sale of assets, typically at a low price, carried out in order to dispose of them rather than as normal trade. ➤ chiefly N. Amer. a sale of shares, bonds, or commodities, especially one that causes a fall in price.

**Sellotape** Brit. • n. trademark transparent adhesive tape. • v. fasten or stick with Sellotape.
– ORIGIN 1940s: from an alt. of **CELLULOSE** + **TAPE**.

**sell-out** • n. **1** the selling of an entire stock of something. ➤ an event for which all tickets are sold. **2** a sale of a business or company. **3** a betrayal.

**sell-through** • n. **1** the ratio of the quantity of goods sold by a retail outlet to the quantity distributed to it wholesale. **2** the retail sale of something, especially a prerecorded video cassette, as opposed to its rental.

**seltzer** /ˈsɛltzə/ • n. dated **1** soda water. **2** medicinal mineral water from Niederselters in Germany.
– ORIGIN C18: alt. of Ger. *Selterser*, from *(Nieder)selters* (see above).

**selva** • n. a tract of land covered by dense equatorial forest, especially in the Amazon basin.
– ORIGIN C19: from Sp. or Port., from L. *silva* 'wood'.

**selvedge** /ˈsɛlvɪdʒ/ (chiefly N. Amer. also **selvage**) • n. **1** an edge produced on woven fabric during manufacture that prevents it from unravelling. **2** Geology a zone of altered rock at the edge of a rock mass.
– ORIGIN ME: from an alt. of **SELF** + **EDGE**, on the pattern of early mod. Du. *selfegghe*.

**selves** plural form of **SELF**.

**SEM** • abbrev. scanning electron microscope.

**semanteme** /sɪˈmantiːm/ • n. Linguistics a minimal distinctive unit of meaning. Compare with **SEMEME**.
– ORIGIN C20: from Fr. *sémantème*, from *sémantique* (see **SEMANTIC**), on the pattern of words such as *morphème* 'morpheme'.

**semantic** /sɪˈmantɪk/ • adj. relating to meaning in language or logic.
– DERIVATIVES **semantically** adv. **semanticity** n.
– ORIGIN C17: from Fr. *sémantique*, from Gk *sēmantikos* 'significant'.

**semantic field** • n. Linguistics a lexical set of semantically related items, for example verbs of perception.

**semantics** • pl. n. [usu. treated as sing.] **1** the branch of linguistics and logic concerned with meaning. **2** the meaning of a word, phrase, sentence, or text.
– DERIVATIVES **semantician** n. **semanticist** n.

**semaphore** • n. **1** a system of sending messages by holding the arms or two flags or poles in certain positions according to an alphabetic code. **2** an apparatus for signalling in this way, consisting of an upright with movable parts. • v. send by semaphore or by signals resembling semaphore.
– DERIVATIVES **semaphoric** adj. **semaphorically** adv.
– ORIGIN C19: from Fr. *sémaphore*, formed irregularly from Gk *sēma* 'sign' + *-phoros*.

**semasiology** /sɪˌmeɪzɪˈɒlədʒi/ • n. the branch of knowledge concerned with concepts and the terms that represent them.
– DERIVATIVES **semasiological** adj.
– ORIGIN C19: from Ger. *Semasiologie*, from Gk *sēmasia* 'meaning'.

**semblable** /ˈsɛmbləb(ə)l/ • n. poetic/literary a counterpart or equal.
– ORIGIN ME (as adj. meaning 'similar'): from OFr., from *sembler* 'seem'.

**semblance** • n. **1** the outward appearance or apparent form of something. **2** archaic resemblance.
– ORIGIN ME: from OFr., from *sembler* 'seem', from L. *similare, simulare* 'simulate'.

**seme** /siːm/ • n. another term for **SEMANTEME**.
– ORIGIN C19: from Gk *sēma* 'sign'.

**semé** /ˈsɛmi, ˈsɛmeɪ/ (also **semée**) • adj. Heraldry covered with small bearings of indefinite number (e.g. stars) arranged all over the field.
– ORIGIN ME: Fr., lit. 'sown', past part. of *semer*.

**sememe** /ˈsɛmiːm, ˈsiːm-/ • n. Linguistics the unit of meaning carried by a morpheme. Compare with **SEMANTEME**.
– ORIGIN C20: from **SEME** + **-EME**.

**semen** /ˈsiːmən/ • n. the male reproductive fluid, containing spermatozoa in suspension.
– ORIGIN ME: from L., lit. 'seed', from *serere* 'to sow'.

**semester** /sɪˈmɛstə/ • n. a half-year term in a school or university, especially in North America, typically lasting for fifteen to eighteen weeks.
– ORIGIN C19: from Ger. *Semester*, from L. *semestris* 'six-monthly'.

**semi** • n. (pl. **semis**) informal **1** Brit. a semi-detached house. **2** a semi-final. **3** N. Amer. a semi-trailer.

**semi-** • prefix **1** half: *semicircular*. ➤ occurring or appearing twice in a specified period: *semi-annual*. **2** partly: *semi-conscious*. ➤ almost: *semi-darkness*.
– ORIGIN from L.; rel. to Gk *hemi-*.

**semi-acoustic** • adj. (of a guitar) having both one or more pickups and a hollow body, typically with f-holes.

**semi-annual** • adj. occurring twice a year.
– DERIVATIVES **semi-annually** adv.

**semiaquatic** • adj. **1** (of an animal) living partly on land and partly in water. **2** (of a plant) growing in very wet or waterlogged ground.

**semi-automatic** • adj. partially automatic. ➤ (of a firearm) having a mechanism for self-loading but not for continuous firing.

**semi-autonomous** • adj. **1** having a degree of self-government. **2** acting independently to some degree.

**semi-basement** • n. a storey of a building partly below ground level.

**semibold** • adj. Printing printed in a typeface with thick strokes but not as thick as bold.

**semibreve** /ˈsɛmɪbriːv/ • n. Music, chiefly Brit. a note having the time value of two minims or four crotchets, represented by a ring with no stem.

**semicircle** • n. a half of a circle or of its circumference.
– DERIVATIVES **semicircular** adj.

**semicircular canals** • pl. n. a system of three fluid-filled bony channels in the inner ear, involved in sensing and maintaining balance.

**semicolon** /ˌsɛmɪˈkəʊlən, -ˈkəʊlɒn/ • n. a punctuation mark (;) indicating a more pronounced pause than that indicated by a comma.

**semiconductor** • n. a solid, e.g. silicon, whose conductivity is between that of an insulator and a conductive metal and increases with temperature.
– DERIVATIVES **semi-conducting** adj.

**semi-conscious** • adj. partially conscious.

**semi-cylinder** • n. Geometry half of a cylinder cut longitudinally.
– DERIVATIVES **semi-cylindrical** adj.

**semidemisemiquaver** • n. Music, chiefly Brit. another term for **HEMIDEMISEMIQUAVER**.

**semi-deponent** ● **adj.** (of a Latin verb) having active forms in present tenses, and passive forms with active sense in perfect tenses.

**semi-detached** ● **adj.** (of a house) joined to another house on one side only by a common wall.

**semidiameter** /ˌsɛmɪdʌɪˈamɪtə/ ● **n.** Geometry half of a diameter.

**semi-documentary** ● **adj.** (of a film) having a factual background and a fictitious story.

**semi-dome** ● **n.** Architecture a half-dome formed by vertical section.

**semi-double** ● **adj.** (of a flower) intermediate between single and double in having only the outer stamens converted to petals.

**semi-final** ● **n.** a match or round immediately preceding the final.
– DERIVATIVES **semi-finalist** n.

**semi-finished** ● **adj.** prepared for the final stage of manufacture.

**semi-fitted** ● **adj.** (of a garment) shaped to the body but not closely fitted.

**semi-fluid** ● **adj.** having a thick consistency between solid and liquid. ● **n.** a semi-fluid substance.

**semi-independent** ● **adj. 1** having some degree of independence or autonomy. **2** (of an institution) not wholly supported by public funds.

**semi-infinite** ● **adj.** Mathematics (of a line or solid) limited in one direction and stretching to infinity in the other.

**semi-invalid** ● **n.** a partially disabled or somewhat infirm person.

**semi-liquid** ● **adj. & n.** another term for **SEMI-FLUID**.

**semi-literate** ● **adj. 1** unable to read or write with ease or fluency. **2** (of a text) poorly written. ● **n.** a semi-literate person.
– DERIVATIVES **semi-literacy** n.

**Sémillon** /ˈsɛmɪjɒ̃/ ● **n.** a variety of white wine grape grown in France and elsewhere. ➤a white wine made from this grape.
– ORIGIN Fr. dial., based on L. *semen* 'seed'.

**semilunar** ● **adj.** chiefly Anatomy shaped like a half-moon or crescent.

**semilunar bone** ● **n.** the lunate bone.

**semilunar cartilage** ● **n.** a crescent-shaped cartilage in the knee.

**semilunar valve** ● **n.** Anatomy each of a pair of valves in the heart at the bases of the aorta and the pulmonary artery.

**semimetal** ● **n.** Chemistry an element (e.g. arsenic or tin) whose properties are intermediate between those of metals and solid non-metals or semiconductors.
– DERIVATIVES **semimetallic** adj.

**semi-modal** ● **n.** a verb that functions to some extent like a modal verb, typically in the way it forms negative and interrogative constructions (e.g. *need* and *dare* in English).

**semi-monocoque** ● **adj.** relating to or denoting aircraft or vehicle structures combining a load-bearing shell with integral frames.

**semi-monthly** ● **adj.** chiefly N. Amer. occurring or published twice a month.

**seminal** ● **adj. 1** (of a work, event, or person) strongly influencing later developments. **2** relating to or denoting semen. **3** Botany of, relating to, or derived from the seed of a plant.
– DERIVATIVES **seminally** adv.
– ORIGIN ME: from OFr. *seminal* or L. *seminalis*, from *semen* 'seed'.

**seminar** /ˈsɛmɪnɑː/ ● **n. 1** a conference or other meeting for discussion or training. **2** a small group of students at university, meeting to discuss topics with a teacher.
– ORIGIN C19: from Ger. *Seminar*, from L. *seminarium* (see **SEMINARY**).

**seminary** /ˈsɛmɪn(ə)ri/ ● **n.** (pl. **-ies**) a training college for priests or rabbis.
– DERIVATIVES **seminarian** /-ˈnɛːrɪən/ n. **seminarist** n.
– ORIGIN ME (denoting a seed plot): from L. *seminarium*, neut. of *seminarius* 'of seed', from *semen* 'seed'.

**seminiferous** /ˌsɛmɪˈnɪf(ə)rəs/ ● **adj.** producing or conveying semen.
– ORIGIN C17: from L. *semen, semin-* 'seed' + **-FEROUS**.

**Seminole** /ˈsɛmɪnəʊl/ ● **n.** (pl. same or **Seminoles**) **1** a member of an American Indian people of the Creek confederacy. **2** the Muskogean language of the Seminoles.
– ORIGIN via Creek from Amer. Sp. *cimarrón* 'wild'.

**semi-official** ● **adj.** having some, but not full, official authority or recognition.
– DERIVATIVES **semi-officially** adv.

**semiology** /ˌsiːmɪˈɒlədʒi, ˌsɛmɪ-/ ● **n.** another term for **SEMIOTICS**.
– DERIVATIVES **semiological** adj. **semiologist** n.
– ORIGIN C20: from Gk *sēmeion* 'sign' + **-LOGY**.

**semi-opera** ● **n.** a drama or similar entertainment with a substantial proportion of vocal music in addition to instrumental movements.

**semiosis** /ˌsiːmɪˈəʊsɪs, ˌsɛmɪ-/ ● **n.** Linguistics the process of signification in language or literature.
– ORIGIN C20: from Gk *sēmeiosis* '(inference from) a sign'.

**semiotics** /ˌsiːmɪˈɒtɪks, ˌsɛmɪ-/ ● **pl. n.** [treated as sing.] the study of signs and symbols and their use or interpretation.
– DERIVATIVES **semiotic** adj. **semiotically** adv. **semiotician** /-əˈtɪʃ(ə)n/ n.
– ORIGIN C19: from Gk *sēmeiotikos* 'of signs'.

**semipalmated** /ˌsɛmɪpalˈmeɪtɪd/ ● **adj.** (of a bird) having toes webbed for part of their length.

**semipermeable** ● **adj.** permeable only to certain substances, especially allowing the passage of a solvent but not of the solute.

**semi-precious** ● **adj.** denoting minerals which can be used as gems but are considered to be less valuable than precious stones.

**semi-professional** ● **adj.** receiving payment for an activity but not relying on it for a living. ● **n.** a semi-professional person.

**semi-prone position** ● **n.** another term for **RECOVERY POSITION**.

**semiquaver** /ˈsɛmɪˌkweɪvə/ ● **n.** Music, chiefly Brit. a note having the time value of a sixteenth of a semibreve or half a quaver, represented by a large dot with a two-hooked stem.

**semi-retired** ● **adj.** having retired from employment or an occupation but continuing to work part-time or occasionally.
– DERIVATIVES **semi-retirement** n.

**semi-rigid** ● **adj. 1** (of an airship) having a stiffened keel attached to a flexible gas container. **2** (of an inflatable boat) having a rigid hull and inflatable sponsons.

**semi-skilled** ● **adj.** (of work or a worker) having or needing some, but not extensive, training.

**semi-skimmed** ● **adj.** Brit. (of milk) having had some of the cream removed.

**semi-solid** ● **adj.** highly viscous; slightly thicker than semi-fluid.

**semi-submersible** ● **adj.** denoting an oil or gas drilling platform or barge with submerged hollow pontoons able to be flooded with water when the vessel is anchored on site in order to provide stability.

**semi-sweet** ● **adj. 1** (of food) slightly sweetened, but less so than normal. **2** (of wine) slightly sweeter than medium dry.

**semi-synthetic** ● **adj.** Chemistry made by synthesis from a naturally occurring material.

**Semite** /ˈsiːmʌɪt, ˈsɛm-/ ● **n.** a member of a people speaking a Semitic language, in particular the Jews and Arabs.
– ORIGIN from mod. L. *Semita*, via late L. from Gk *Sēm* 'Shem', son of Noah in the Bible, from whom these people are traditionally descended.

**Semitic** /sɪˈmɪtɪk/ ● **n.** an Afro-Asiatic subfamily of languages that includes Hebrew, Arabic, and Aramaic and certain ancient languages such as Phoenician and Akkadian. ● **adj.** of or relating to these languages or their speakers.

**semitone** • **n.** Music the smallest interval used in classical Western music, equal to a twelfth of an octave or half a tone.

**semi-trailer** • **n.** chiefly N. Amer. a trailer having wheels at the back but supported at the front by a towing vehicle. ➤ an articulated truck.

**semi-tropics** • **pl. n.** another term for SUBTROPICS.
– DERIVATIVES **semi-tropical** adj.

**semivowel** • **n.** a speech sound intermediate between a vowel and a consonant, e.g. *w* or *y*.

**semmit** /'sɛmɪt/ • **n.** Scottish an undershirt; a vest.
– ORIGIN ME: of unknown origin.

**semolina** • **n.** the hard grains left after the milling of flour, used in puddings and in pasta.
– ORIGIN C18: from Ital. *semolino*, dimin. of *semola* 'bran'.

**sempervivum** /ˌsɛmpə'vʌɪvəm/ • **n.** a plant of a genus that includes the houseleek. [Genus *Sempervivum*.]
– ORIGIN mod. L., from L. *semper* 'always' + *vivus* 'living'.

**sempiternal** /ˌsɛmpɪ'təːn(ə)l/ • **adj.** eternal and unchanging; everlasting.
– DERIVATIVES **sempiternally** adv. **sempiternity** n.
– ORIGIN ME: from OFr. *sempiternel* or late L. *sempiternalis*, from L. *sempiternus*, from *semper* 'always' + *aeternus* 'eternal'.

**semplice** /'sɛmplɪtʃeɪ/ • **adv.** Music in a simple style of performance.
– ORIGIN Ital., lit. 'simple'.

**sempre** /'sɛmpreɪ/ • **adv.** Music throughout; always.
– ORIGIN from Ital.

**sempstress** /'sɛm(p)strɪs/ • **n.** another term for SEAMSTRESS.

**Semtex** • **n.** a very pliable, odourless plastic explosive.
– ORIGIN 1980s: prob. a blend of *Semtin* (the name of a village in the Czech Republic near the place of production) and EXPLOSIVE.

**SEN** • **abbrev.** (in the UK) State Enrolled Nurse.

**Sen.** • **abbrev.** **1** N. Amer. Senate. **2** N. Amer. Senator. **3** Senior.

**sen** /sɛn/ • **n.** (pl. same) **1** a monetary unit of Brunei, Cambodia, Indonesia, and Malaysia, equal to one hundredth of the basic unit. **2** a former monetary unit of Japan, equal to one hundredth of a yen.
– ORIGIN sense 1 represents CENT; sense 2 from Japanese.

**senarius** /sɪ'nɛːrɪəs/ • **n.** (pl. **senarii** /-rɪiː, -rɪʌɪ/) Prosody a verse of six feet, especially an iambic trimeter.
– ORIGIN C16: from L. (see SENARY).

**senary** /'siːnəri, 'sɛn-/ • **adj.** rare relating to or based on the number six.
– ORIGIN C16: from L. *senarius* 'containing six', based on *sex* 'six'.

**senate** • **n.** **1** the smaller upper assembly in the US, US states, France, and other countries. ➤ the governing body of a university or college. **2** the state council of the ancient Roman republic and empire.
– ORIGIN ME: from OFr. *senat*, from L. *senatus*, from *senex* 'old man'.

**senator** • **n.** **1** a member of a senate. **2** Scots Law a Lord of Session.
– DERIVATIVES **senatorial** adj. **senatorship** n.

**senatus consultum** /sɛˌnɑːtuːs kɒn'sʊltʊm/ • **n.** (pl. **senatus consulta** /kɒn'sʊltə/) a decree of the ancient Roman senate.
– ORIGIN from L.

**send**[1] • **v.** (past and past part. **sent**) **1** cause to go or be taken or delivered to a particular destination. ➤ (**send someone to**) arrange for someone to attend (an institution). **2** cause to move sharply or quickly; propel. **3** cause to be in a specified state: *it nearly sent me crazy.* **4** informal cause to feel ecstasy or elation.
– PHRASES **send someone to Coventry** chiefly Brit. refuse to associate with or speak to someone. [perh. from the unpopularity of royalist soldiers or prisoners quartered in *Coventry* (sympathetic to parliament) during the Engl. Civil war.] **send word** send a message.
– PHRASAL VERBS **send someone down** Brit. **1** expel a student from a university. **2** informal sentence someone to imprisonment. **send for 1** order or instruct (someone) to come to one; summon. **2** order by post. **send someone off** (of a soccer or rugby referee) order a player to leave the field and take no further part in the game. **send someone up** US sentence someone to imprisonment. **send someone/thing up** informal ridicule someone or something by exaggerated imitation.
– DERIVATIVES **sendable** adj. **sender** n.
– ORIGIN OE *sendan*, of Gmc origin.

**send**[2] • **n. & v.** variant spelling of SCEND.

**sendal** /'sɛnd(ə)l/ • **n.** historical a fine silk material used to make ceremonial robes and banners.
– ORIGIN ME: from OFr. *cendal*, ult. from Gk *sindōn*.

**send-off** • **n.** a celebratory demonstration of goodwill at a person's departure.

**send-up** • **n.** informal a parody or exaggerated imitation of someone or something.

**sene** /'sɛni/ • **n.** (pl. same or **senes**) a monetary unit of Samoa, equal to one hundredth of a tala.
– ORIGIN from Samoan.

**Seneca** /'sɛnɪkə/ • **n.** (pl. same or **Senecas**) **1** a member of an American Indian people forming part of the original Iroquois confederacy. **2** the Iroquoian language of this people.
– ORIGIN via Du. from Algonquian.

**senecio** /sə'niːsɪəʊ, -ʃɪəʊ/ • **n.** (pl. **-os**) a plant of a genus that includes ragwort and groundsel. [Genus *Senecio*.]
– ORIGIN mod. L., from L., lit. 'old man, groundsel', with ref. to the hairy white fruits.

**Senegalese** /ˌsɛnɪgə'liːz/ • **n.** a native or inhabitant of Senegal. • **adj.** of or relating to Senegal.

**senesce** /sɪ'nɛs/ • **v.** Biology (of a living organism) deteriorate with age.
– DERIVATIVES **senescence** n. **senescent** adj.
– ORIGIN C17: from L. *senescere*, from *senex* 'old'.

**seneschal** /'sɛnɪʃ(ə)l/ • **n.** **1** historical the steward or major-domo of a medieval great house. **2** chiefly historical a governor or other administrative or judicial officer.
– ORIGIN ME: from OFr., from med. L. *seniscalus*, from a Gmc compound of words meaning 'old' and 'servant'.

**senhor** /sɛn'jɔː/ • **n.** (in Portuguese-speaking countries) a form of address for a man, corresponding to *Mr* or *sir*.
– ORIGIN Port., from L. *senior* (see SENIOR).

**senhora** /sɛn'jɔːrə/ • **n.** (in Portuguese-speaking countries) a form of address for a woman, corresponding to *Mrs* or *madam*.

**senhorita** /ˌsɛnjə'riːtə/ • **n.** (in Portuguese-speaking countries) a form of address for a young woman, corresponding to *Miss*.

**senile** • **adj.** having the weaknesses or diseases of old age, especially a loss of mental faculties. ➤ characteristic of or caused by old age. • **n.** a senile person.
– DERIVATIVES **senility** n.
– ORIGIN C17: from Fr. *sénile* or L. *senilis*, from *senex* 'old man'.

**senile dementia** • **n.** severe mental deterioration in old age, characterized by loss of memory and lack of control of bodily functions.

**senior** /'siːnɪə, 'siːnjə/ • **adj.** **1** of a more advanced age. ➤ Brit. of, for, or denoting schoolchildren above a certain age, typically eleven. ➤ US of the final year at a university or high school. ➤ [postpos.] denoting the elder of two with the same name in a family. **2** high or higher in rank or status. • **n.** **1** a person who is a specified number of years older than someone else: *she was two years his senior.* **2** a student in one of the higher forms of a senior school. **3** (in sport) a competitor of above a certain age or of the highest status. **4** an elderly person, especially an old-age pensioner.
– DERIVATIVES **seniority** n.
– ORIGIN ME: from L., lit. 'older, older man', compar. of *senex*, *sen-* 'old man, old'.

**senior aircraftman** (or **senior aircraftwoman**) • **n.** a rank in the RAF, above leading aircraftman (or leading aircraftwoman) and below junior technician.

**senior chief petty officer** • **n.** a rank in the US navy, above chief petty officer and below master chief petty officer.

**senior citizen** ● n. an elderly person, especially an old-age pensioner.

**senior common room** ● n. Brit. a room used for social purposes by fellows, lecturers, and other senior members of a college.

**senior high school** ● n. N. Amer. a secondary school typically comprising the three highest grades.

**senior master sergeant** ● n. a rank of non-commissioned officer in the US air force, above master sergeant and below chief master sergeant.

**senior nursing officer** ● n. Brit. the person in charge of nursing services in a hospital.

**senior registrar** ● n. Brit. a hospital doctor undergoing specialist training, one grade below that of consultant.

**Senior Service** ● n. Brit. the Royal Navy.

**seniti** /'sɛnɪti/ ● n. (pl. same) a monetary unit of Tonga, equal to one hundredth of a pa'anga.
– ORIGIN from Tongan.

**senna** ● n. **1** the cassia tree. **2** a laxative prepared from the dried pods of this tree. **3** used in names of similar plants, e.g. **bladder senna**.
– ORIGIN C16: from med. L. *sena*, from Arab. *sanā*.

**sennet** /'sɛnɪt/ ● n. (in the stage directions of Elizabethan plays) a call on a trumpet or cornet to signal the ceremonial entrance or exit of an actor.
– ORIGIN C16: perh. a var. of **SIGNET**.

**sennight** /'sɛnʌɪt/ ● n. archaic a week.
– ORIGIN OE *seofon nihta* 'seven nights'.

**sennit** ● n. **1** plaited straw, hemp, or similar material used to make hats. **2** Nautical variant spelling of **SINNET**.

**señor** /sɛ'njɔː/ ● n. (pl. **señores** /-reɪz/) (in Spanish-speaking countries) a form of address for a man, corresponding to *Mr* or *sir*.
– ORIGIN Sp., from L. *senior* (see **SENIOR**).

**señora** /sɛ'njɔːrə/ ● n. (in Spanish-speaking countries) a form of address for a woman, corresponding to *Mrs* or *madam*.

**señorita** /ˌsɛnjə'riːtə/ ● n. (in Spanish-speaking countries) a form of address for an unmarried woman, corresponding to *Miss*.

**Senr** ● abbrev. Senior (in names).

**sensate** /'sɛnseɪt, -sət/ ● adj. perceiving or perceived with the senses.

**sensation** ● n. **1** a physical feeling or perception resulting from something that happens to or comes into contact with the body. ➤the capacity to have such feelings or perceptions. **2** an inexplicable awareness or impression. **3** a widespread reaction of interest and excitement. ➤a person or thing that arouses such interest and excitement.
– ORIGIN C17: from med. L. *sensatio(n-)*, from L. *sensus* (see **SENSE**).

**sensational** ● adj. **1** causing or seeking to cause great public interest and excitement. **2** informal very impressive or attractive.
– DERIVATIVES **sensationalize** (also **-ise**) v. **sensationally** adv.

**sensationalism** ● n. **1** the deliberate use of sensational stories or language in the media. **2** Philosophy another term for **PHENOMENALISM**.
– DERIVATIVES **sensationalist** n. & adj. **sensationalistic** adj.

**sense** ● n. **1** a faculty by which the body perceives an external stimulus; one of the faculties of sight, smell, hearing, taste, and touch. ➤**(one's senses)** one's sanity. **2** an awareness of something or feeling that something is the case. **3** a sane and realistic attitude to situations and problems. ➤a reasonable or comprehensible rationale. **4** a way in which an expression or situation can be interpreted; a meaning. **5** chiefly Mathematics & Physics the property distinguishing two opposite but otherwise identical things, e.g. motion in opposite directions. **6** [as modifier] Genetics relating to or denoting a coding sequence of nucleotides, complementary to an antisense sequence. ● v. **1** perceive by a sense or senses. ➤be vaguely or indefinably aware of. **2** (of a machine or similar device) detect.
– PHRASES **make sense** be intelligible, justifiable, or practicable. **make sense of** find meaning or coherence in.
– ORIGIN ME: from L. *sensus* 'faculty of feeling, thought, meaning', from *sentire* 'feel'.

**sense datum** ● n. Philosophy an immediate object of perception which is not a material object.

**sensei** /sɛn'seɪ/ ● n. (pl. same) (in martial arts) a teacher.
– ORIGIN Japanese, from *sen* 'previous' + *sei* 'birth'.

**senseless** ● adj. **1** unconscious or incapable of sensation. **2** without discernible meaning or purpose. ➤lacking common sense; wildly foolish.
– DERIVATIVES **senselessly** adv. **senselessness** n.

**sense organ** ● n. an organ of the body which responds to external stimuli by conveying impulses to the sensory nervous system.

**sensibility** ● n. (pl. **-ies**) **1** (also **sensibilities**) the ability to appreciate and respond to complex emotional or aesthetic influences; sensitivity. ➤**(sensibilities)** a person's tendency to be offended or shocked. **2** Zoology, dated sensitivity to sensory stimuli.

**sensible** ● adj. **1** wise and prudent; having or showing common sense. ➤practical and functional rather than decorative. **2** archaic readily perceived; appreciable. ➤**(sensible of/to)** able to notice or appreciate.
– DERIVATIVES **sensibleness** n. **sensibly** adv.
– ORIGIN ME: from OFr., or from L. *sensibilis*, from *sensus* (see **SENSE**).

**sensillum** /sɛn'sɪləm/ ● n. (pl. **sensilla** /sɛn'sɪlə/) Zoology (in some invertebrates) a simple sensory receptor consisting of a modified cell or cells of the cuticle or epidermis.
– ORIGIN C20: mod. L., dimin. of L. *sensus* 'sense'.

**sensitive** ● adj. **1** quick to detect, respond to, or be affected by slight changes, signals, or influences. ➤(of photographic materials) responding rapidly to the action of light. **2** quickly and delicately appreciating the feelings of others. **3** easily offended or upset. **4** kept secret or with restrictions on disclosure. ● n. a person supposedly able to respond to paranormal influences.
– DERIVATIVES **sensitively** adv. **sensitiveness** n.
– ORIGIN ME (in the sense 'sensory'): from OFr. *sensitif, -ive* or med. L. *sensitivus*, formed irregularly from L. *sentire* 'feel'.

**sensitive plant** ● n. a tropical American plant of the pea family, whose leaflets fold together and leaves bend down when touched. [*Mimosa pudica*.]

**sensitivity** ● n. (pl. **-ies**) **1** the quality or condition of being sensitive. **2** **(sensitivities)** a person's feelings which might be easily offended or hurt.

**sensitize** (also **-ise**) ● v. cause to respond to certain stimuli; make sensitive.
– DERIVATIVES **sensitization** n. **sensitizer** n.

**sensitometer** /ˌsɛnsɪ'tɒmɪtə/ ● n. Photography a device for measuring the sensitivity of equipment to light.

**sensor** ● n. a device which detects or measures a physical property.

**sensorimotor** /ˌsɛns(ə)rɪ'məʊtə/ ● adj. Physiology (of nerves or their actions) having or involving both sensory and motor functions or pathways.

**sensorium** /sɛn'sɔːrɪəm/ ● n. (pl. **sensoria** /-rɪə/ or **sensoriums**) the sensory apparatus or faculties considered as a whole.
– DERIVATIVES **sensorial** adj. **sensorially** adv.
– ORIGIN C17: from late L., from L. *sens-*, *sentire* 'perceive'.

**sensory** ● adj. of or relating to sensation or the senses.
– DERIVATIVES **sensorily** adv.

**sensual** /'sɛnsjʊəl, -ʃʊəl/ ● adj. **1** of or relating to the physical senses, especially as a source of pleasure. **2** arousing sexual or other physical gratification.
– DERIVATIVES **sensualism** n. **sensualist** n. **sensuality** n. **sensualize** (also **-ise**) v. **sensually** adv.
– ORIGIN ME: from late L. *sensualis*, from *sensus* (see **SENSE**).

**USAGE sensual**

The words **sensual** and **sensuous** are frequently used interchangeably to mean 'gratifying the senses', especially in a sexual sense. This goes against a traditional distinction, by which **sensuous** is the more neutral term, meaning 'relating to the senses rather than the intellect'. Evidence suggests that the 'neutral' use of **sensuous** is rare in modern English; if a neutral use is intended it is advisable to use alternative wording.

**sensu lato** /ˌsɛnsuː ˈlɑːtəʊ/ ● **adv.** formal in the broad sense.
– ORIGIN from L.

**sensum** /ˈsɛnsəm/ ● **n.** (pl. **sensa** /-sə/) Philosophy a sense datum.
– ORIGIN C19: mod. L., 'something sensed', neut. past part. of L. *sentire* 'feel'.

**sensuous** /ˈsɛnsjʊəs, ˈsɛnʃʊəs/ ● **adj.** **1** relating to or affecting the senses rather than the intellect. **2** attractive or gratifying physically, especially sexually.
– DERIVATIVES **sensuously** adv. **sensuousness** n.
– ORIGIN C17: from L. *sensus* 'sense' + **-OUS**.

**sensu stricto** /ˌsɛnsuː ˈstrɪktəʊ/ ● **adv.** formal strictly speaking; in the narrow sense.
– ORIGIN L., 'in the restricted sense'.

**sent**[1] past and past participle of **SEND**[1].

**sent**[2] /ˈsɛnt/ ● **n.** a monetary unit of Estonia, equal to one hundredth of a kroon.
– ORIGIN respelling of **CENT**.

**sente** /ˈsɛnti/ ● **n.** (pl. **lisente** /lɪˈsɛnti/) a monetary unit of Lesotho, equal to one hundredth of a loti.
– ORIGIN from Sesotho.

**sentence** ● **n.** **1** a set of words that is complete in itself, conveying a statement, question, exclamation, or command and typically containing a subject and predicate. ➤Logic a series of signs or symbols expressing a proposition in an artificial or logical language. **2** the punishment assigned to a defendant found guilty by a court. ● **v.** declare the punishment decided for (an offender).
– ORIGIN ME (also in the sense 'way of thinking, opinion'): via OFr. from L. *sententia* 'opinion'.

**sentence adverb** ● **n.** Grammar an adverb that expresses an attitude to the content of the sentence in which it occurs or places the sentence in a particular context.

**sentential** /sɛnˈtɛnʃ(ə)l/ ● **adj.** Grammar & Logic of or relating to a sentence.

**sententious** /sɛnˈtɛnʃəs/ ● **adj.** given to moralizing in a pompous or affected manner.
– DERIVATIVES **sententiously** adv. **sententiousness** n.
– ORIGIN ME (in sense 'full of meaning or wisdom'): from L. *sententiosus*, from *sententia* (see **SENTENCE**).

**sentient** /ˈsɛnʃ(ə)nt/ ● **adj.** able to perceive or feel things.
– DERIVATIVES **sentience** n. **sentiently** adv.
– ORIGIN C17: from L. *sentient-*, *sentire* 'to feel'.

**sentiment** ● **n.** **1** a view, opinion, or feeling. ➤general feeling or opinion. **2** exaggerated and self-indulgent feelings of tenderness, sadness, or nostalgia.
– ORIGIN ME (in the senses 'personal experience' and 'physical feeling, sensation'): from OFr. *sentement*, from med. L. *sentimentum*, from L. *sentire* 'feel'.

**sentimental** ● **adj.** deriving from feelings of tenderness, sadness, or nostalgia. ➤having or arousing such feelings in an exaggerated and self-indulgent way.
– PHRASES **sentimental value** value of an object deriving from personal or emotional associations rather than material worth.
– DERIVATIVES **sentimentalism** n. **sentimentalist** n. **sentimentality** n. **sentimentalization** (also **-isation**) n. **sentimentalize** (also **-ise**) v. **sentimentally** adv.

**sentinel** /ˈsɛntɪn(ə)l/ ● **n.** **1** a soldier or guard whose job is to stand and keep watch. **2** Medicine a thing that acts as an indicator of the presence of disease. ● **v.** (**sentinelled**, **sentinelling**; US **sentineled**, **sentineling**) station a sentinel to keep watch over.
– ORIGIN C16: from Fr. *sentinelle*, from Ital. *sentinella*, of unknown origin.

**sentry** ● **n.** (pl. **-ies**) a soldier stationed to keep guard or to control access to a place.
– ORIGIN C17: perh. from obs. *centrinel*, var. of **SENTINEL**.

**sentry box** ● **n.** a structure providing shelter for a standing sentry.

**sentry-go** ● **n.** Military the duty of being a sentry.

**sepal** /ˈsɛp(ə)l, ˈsiːp(ə)l/ ● **n.** Botany each of the parts of the calyx of a flower, enclosing the petals and typically green and leaf-like.
– ORIGIN C19: from Fr. *sépale*, mod. L. *sepalum*, from Gk *skepē* 'covering', influenced by Fr. *pétale* 'petal'.

**separable** ● **adj.** **1** able to be separated or treated separately. **2** Grammar (of a verb) having a prefix that is written as a separate word in some circumstances.
– DERIVATIVES **separability** n. **separableness** n. **separably** adv.

**separate** ● **adj.** /ˈsɛp(ə)rət/ forming or viewed as a unit apart or by itself; not joined or united with others. ➤different; distinct. ● **v.** /ˈsɛpəreɪt/ **1** move or come apart; make or become detached or disconnected. ➤stop living together as a couple. ➤US discharge or dismiss from service or employment. **2** divide into constituent or distinct elements. ➤extract or remove for use or rejection. ➤distinguish between or from another; consider individually. **3** form a distinction or boundary between. ● **n.** /ˈsɛp(ə)rət/ (**separates**) things forming units by themselves, in particular individual items of clothing suitable for wearing in different combinations.
– DERIVATIVES **separately** adv. **separateness** n. **separative** adj. **separator** n.
– ORIGIN ME: from L. *separat-*, *separare* 'disjoin, divide', from *se-* 'apart' + *parare* 'prepare'.

**separation** ● **n.** **1** the action or state of separating or being separated. ➤the state in which a husband and wife remain married but live apart: *a trial separation.* **2** distinction between the signals carried by the two channels of a stereophonic system. **3** Physics & Aeronautics the generation of a turbulent boundary layer between a surface and a moving fluid.
– PHRASES **separation of powers** the vesting of the legislative, executive, and judiciary powers of government in separate bodies.

**separatism** ● **n.** the advocacy or practice of separation of a group of people from a larger body on the basis of ethnicity, religion, or gender.
– DERIVATIVES **separatist** n. & adj.

**Sephardi** /sɪˈfɑːdi/ ● **n.** (pl. **Sephardim** /-dɪm/) a Jew of Spanish or Portuguese descent. Compare with **ASHKENAZI**. ➤any Jew of the Middle East or North Africa.
– DERIVATIVES **Sephardic** adj.
– ORIGIN mod. Heb., from *sěp̄āraḏ*, a country mentioned in Obad. 20 and taken to be Spain.

**sepia** /ˈsiːpɪə/ ● **n.** **1** a reddish-brown colour associated particularly with early monochrome photographs. **2** a brown pigment prepared from cuttlefish ink, used in monochrome drawing and in watercolours. **3** cuttlefish ink.
– ORIGIN ME (denoting a cuttlefish): via L. from Gk *sēpia*.

**sepoy** /ˈsiːpɔɪ, sɪˈpɔɪ/ ● **n.** historical an Indian soldier serving under British or other European orders.
– ORIGIN from Urdu and Pers. *sipāhī* 'soldier'.

**seppuku** /sɛˈpuːkuː/ ● **n.** another term for **HARA-KIRI**.
– ORIGIN Japanese, from *setsu* 'to cut' + *fuku* 'abdomen'.

**sepsis** /ˈsɛpsɪs/ ● **n.** Medicine the presence in tissues of harmful bacteria and their toxins, typically through infection of a wound.
– ORIGIN C19: mod. L., from Gk *sēpsis*, from *sēpein* 'make rotten'.

**Sept.** ● **abbrev.** **1** September. **2** Septuagint.

**sept** ● **n.** a subdivision of a clan, originally one in Ireland.
– ORIGIN C16: prob. an alt. of **SECT**.

**sept-** ● **comb. form** variant spelling of **SEPTI-** (as in *septcentenary*).

**septa** plural form of **SEPTUM**.

**septal**[1] ● **adj.** **1** Anatomy & Biology relating to a septum or septa. **2** Archaeology (of a stone or slab) separating compartments in a burial chamber.

**septal**[2] ● **adj.** of or relating to a sept or clan.

**septate** ● **adj.** Anatomy & Biology having or partitioned by a septum or septa.
– DERIVATIVES **septation** n.

**septcentenary** /ˌsɛp(t)sɛnˈtiːn(ə)ri, -ˈtɛn-/ ● **n.** (pl. **-ies**) the seven-hundredth anniversary of a significant event.

**September** ● **n.** the ninth month of the year.
– ORIGIN OE, from L., from *septem* 'seven' (being orig. the seventh month of the Roman year).

**septenarius** /ˌsɛptɪˈnɛːrɪəs/ ● **n.** (pl. **septenarii** /-rɪʌɪ/) Prosody a verse line of seven feet, especially a trochaic or iambic tetrameter catalectic.
– ORIGIN C19: from L., from *septeni* 'in sevens'.

**septenary** /ˈsɛptɪn(ə)ri, -ˈtiːn(ə)ri/ ● **adj.** of, relating to, or divided into seven. ● **n.** (pl. **-ies**) a group or set of seven, in particular a period of seven years.
– ORIGIN ME: from L. *septenarius* (see **SEPTENARIUS**).

**septennial** ● **adj.** lasting for or recurring every seven years.
– ORIGIN C17: from late L. *septennis* (from L. *septem* 'seven' + *annus* 'year') + **-AL**.

**septennium** /sɛpˈtɛnɪəm/ ● **n.** (pl. **septennia** /-nɪə/ or **septenniums**) rare a period of seven years.

**septet** /sɛpˈtɛt/ (also **septette**) ● **n.** a group of seven people playing music or singing together. ➤a composition for such a group.
– ORIGIN C19: from Ger. *Septett*, from L. *septem* 'seven'.

**septi-** (also **sept-**) ● **comb. form** seven; having seven: *septivalent*.
– ORIGIN from L. *septem* 'seven'.

**septic** /ˈsɛptɪk/ ● **adj. 1** (of a wound or a part of the body) infected with bacteria. **2** denoting a drainage system incorporating a septic tank.
– DERIVATIVES **septically** adv. **septicity** /-ˈtɪsɪti/ n.
– ORIGIN C17: via L. from Gk *sēptikos*, from *sēpein* 'make rotten'.

**septicaemia** /ˌsɛptɪˈsiːmɪə/ (US **septicemia**) ● **n.** blood poisoning, especially that caused by bacteria or their toxins.
– DERIVATIVES **septicaemic** adj.

**septic tank** ● **n.** a tank, typically underground, in which sewage is allowed to decompose through bacterial activity before draining by means of a soakaway.

**septillion** /sɛpˈtɪljən/ ● **cardinal number** (pl. **septillions** or (with numeral) same) a thousand raised to the eighth power ($10^{24}$). ➤dated, chiefly Brit. a million raised to the seventh power ($10^{42}$).
– ORIGIN C17: from Fr., from *million*, by substitution of the prefix *septi-* 'seven' (from L. *septimus* 'seventh') for the initial letters.

**septimal** /ˈsɛptɪm(ə)l/ ● **adj.** of or relating to the number seven.
– ORIGIN C19: from L. *septimus* 'seventh' + **-AL**.

**septime** /ˈsɛptɪm, -tiːm/ ● **n.** Fencing the seventh of the eight parrying positions.
– ORIGIN C19: from L. *septimus* 'seventh'.

**septivalent** /ˌsɛptɪˈveɪl(ə)nt/ ● **adj.** Chemistry another term for **HEPTAVALENT**.

**septoria** /sɛpˈtɔːrɪə/ ● **n.** a fungus of a genus that includes many kinds that cause diseases in plants. [Genus *Septoria*.] ➤leaf spot disease caused by such a fungus.
– ORIGIN mod. L., from L. *septum* (see **SEPTUM**).

**septuagenarian** /ˌsɛptjʊədʒɪˈnɛːrɪən/ ● **n.** a person who is between 70 and 79 years old.
– ORIGIN C18: from L. *septuagenarius* (based on *septuaginta* 'seventy') + **-AN**.

**Septuagesima** /ˌsɛptjʊəˈdʒɛsɪmə/ ● **n.** the Sunday before Sexagesima.
– ORIGIN ME: from L., 'seventieth (day)', prob. named by analogy with **QUINQUAGESIMA**.

**Septuagint** /ˈsɛptjʊədʒɪnt/ ● **n.** a Greek version of the Hebrew Bible (or Old Testament), including the Apocrypha, produced in the 3rd and 2nd centuries BC.
– ORIGIN C16: from L. *septuaginta* 'seventy', because of the tradition that it was produced by seventy-two translators working independently.

**septum** /ˈsɛptəm/ ● **n.** (pl. **septa** /-tə/) chiefly Anatomy & Biology a partition separating two chambers, such as that between the nostrils or the chambers of the heart.
– ORIGIN C17: from L. *septum*, from *sepire* 'enclose'.

**septuple** /ˈsɛptjʊp(ə)l, sɛpˈtjuːp(ə)l/ ● **adj. 1** consisting of seven parts or elements. ➤(of time in music) having seven beats in a bar. **2** consisting of seven times as much or as many as usual. ● **v.** multiply by seven; increase sevenfold.
– ORIGIN C17: from late L. *septuplus*, from L. *septem* 'seven'.

**septuplet** /ˈsɛptjʊplɪt, sɛpˈtjuːplɪt/ ● **n. 1** each of seven children born at one birth. **2** Music a group of seven notes to be performed in the time of four or six.
– ORIGIN C19: from **SEPTUPLE**, on the pattern of words such as *triplet*.

**sepulchral** /sɪˈpʌlkr(ə)l/ ● **adj. 1** of or relating to a tomb or interment. **2** gloomy; dismal.
– DERIVATIVES **sepulchrally** adv.

**sepulchre** /ˈsɛp(ə)lkə/ (US **sepulcher**) ● **n.** a small room or monument, cut in rock or built of stone, in which a dead person is laid or buried. ● **v.** chiefly poetic/literary lay or bury in or as if in a sepulchre.
– ORIGIN ME: via OFr. from L. *sepulcrum* 'burial place', from *sepelire* 'bury'.

**sepulture** /ˈsɛp(ə)ltʃə/ ● **n.** archaic burial; interment.
– ORIGIN ME: via OFr. from L. *sepultura*, from *sepelire* 'bury'.

**seq.** (also **seqq.**) ● **adv.** short for **ET SEQ.**

**sequacious** /sɪˈkweɪʃəs/ ● **adj.** formal lacking independence or originality of thought.
– DERIVATIVES **sequaciously** adv. **sequacity** /sɪˈkwasɪti/ n.
– ORIGIN C17: from L. *sequax*, *sequac-* 'following' (from *sequi* 'follow') + **-IOUS**.

**sequel** ● **n. 1** a published, broadcast, or recorded work that continues the story or develops the theme of an earlier one. **2** something that takes place after or as a result of an earlier event.
– PHRASES **in the sequel** Brit. formal as things develop.
– ORIGIN ME: from OFr. *sequelle* or L. *sequella*, from *sequi* 'follow'.

**sequela** /sɪˈkwiːlə/ ● **n.** (pl. **sequelae** /-liː/) Medicine a condition which is the consequence of a previous disease or injury.
– ORIGIN C18: from L., from *sequi* 'follow'.

**sequence** ● **n. 1** a particular order in which related events, movements, etc., follow each other. ➤Music a repetition of a phrase or melody at a higher or lower pitch. ➤Biochemistry the order in which amino-acid or nucleotide residues are arranged in a protein, DNA, etc. **2** a set of related events, movements, etc., that follow each other in a particular order. ➤a set of three or more playing cards of the same suit next to each other in value. **3** a part of a film dealing with one particular event or topic. **4** (in the Eucharist) a hymn said or sung after the Gradual or Alleluia that precedes the Gospel. ● **v. 1** arrange in a sequence. **2** play or record (music) with a sequencer. **3** Biochemistry ascertain the sequence of amino-acid or nucleotide residues in (a protein, DNA, etc.).
– ORIGIN ME: from late L. *sequentia*, from L. *sequent-*, *sequi* 'to follow'.

**sequence dancing** ● **n.** a type of ballroom dancing in which the couples all perform the same steps and movements simultaneously.

**sequence of tenses** ● **n.** Grammar the dependence of the tense of a subordinate verb on the tense of the verb in the main clause (e.g. *I think that you* are *wrong*; *I thought that you* were *wrong*).

**sequencer** ● **n. 1** a programmable electronic device for storing sequences of musical notes, chords, or rhythms and transmitting them to an electronic musical instrument. **2** Biochemistry an apparatus for ascertaining the sequence of amino acids or other monomers in a biological polymer.

**sequent** ● **adj.** archaic following in a sequence or as a logical conclusion.
– DERIVATIVES **sequently** adv.

**sequential** ● **adj.** forming or following in a logical order or sequence.

– DERIVATIVES **sequentiality** n. **sequentially** adv.

**sequester** /sɪˈkwɛstə/ ● v. **1** [often as adj. **sequestered**] isolate or hide away. **2** another term for SEQUESTRATE. **3** Chemistry form a chelate or other stable compound with (an ion, molecule, etc.) so that it cannot react.
– ORIGIN ME: from OFr. *sequestrer* or late L. *sequestrare* 'commit for safe keeping', from L. *sequester* 'trustee'.

**sequestrate** /sɪˈkwɛstreɪt, ˈsiːkwɪs-/ ● v. **1** take legal possession of (assets) until a debt has been paid or other claims have been met. ➤ legally place (the property of a bankrupt) in the hands of a trustee for division among the creditors. ➤ declare bankrupt. **2** take forcible possession of; confiscate.
– DERIVATIVES **sequestrable** adj. **sequestrator** /ˈsiːkwɪˌstreɪtə/ n.

**sequestration** /ˌsiːkwɪˈstreɪʃ(ə)n/ ● n. the action of sequestrating or sequestering.

**sequestrum** /sɪˈkwɛstrəm/ ● n. (pl. **sequestra** /-trə/) Medicine a piece of dead bone tissue formed within a diseased or injured bone, typically in chronic osteomyelitis.
– DERIVATIVES **sequestral** adj. **sequestrectomy** /ˌsiːkwɪˈstrɛktəmi/ n. (pl. **-ies**).
– ORIGIN C19: mod. L., neut. of L. *sequester* 'standing apart'.

**sequin** ● n. **1** a small, shiny disc sewn on to clothing for decoration. **2** historical a Venetian gold coin.
– DERIVATIVES **sequinned** (also **sequined**) adj.
– ORIGIN C16: from Fr., from Ital. *zecchino*, from *zecca* 'a mint', from Arab. *sikka* 'a die for coining'.

**sequoia** /sɪˈkwɔɪə/ ● n. a redwood tree, especially the California redwood.
– ORIGIN from mod. L. *Sequoia* (genus name), from *Sequoya*, the name of the Cherokee Indian who invented the Cherokee syllabary.

**sera** plural form of SERUM.

**serac** /ˈsɛrak, sɛˈrak/ ● n. a pinnacle or ridge of ice on the surface of a glacier.
– ORIGIN C19: from Swiss Fr. *sérac*, orig. the name of a compact white cheese.

**seraglio** /sɛˈrɑːlɪəʊ, sɪ-/ ● n. (pl. **-os**) **1** the women's apartments in a Muslim palace. ➤ a harem. **2** historical a Turkish palace, especially the Sultan's court and government offices at Constantinople.
– ORIGIN C16: from Ital. *serraglio*, via Turk. from Pers. *sarāy* 'palace'.

**serai** /səˈrʌɪ/ ● n. another term for CARAVANSERAI (in sense 1).

**serang** /səˈraŋ/ ● n. Indian an Asian head of a Lascar crew.
– ORIGIN from Pers. and Urdu *sar-hang* 'commander'.

**serape** /sɛˈrɑːpeɪ/ (also **sarape**) ● n. a shawl or blanket worn as a cloak by people from Latin America.
– ORIGIN from Mex. Sp.

**seraph** /ˈsɛrəf/ ● n. (pl. **seraphim** /-fɪm/ or **seraphs**) an angelic being associated with light, ardour, and purity.
– DERIVATIVES **seraphic** adj. **seraphically** adv.
– ORIGIN OE, back-form. from *seraphim* (pl.), via late L. and Gk from Heb. *śĕrāpīm*; cf. CHERUB.

**seraskier** /ˌsɛrəˈskɪə/ ● n. historical the commander-in-chief and minister of war of the Ottoman Empire.
– ORIGIN Turk., from Pers. *sar'askar* 'head (of the) army'.

**Serb** ● n. a native or national of Serbia, or a person of Serbian descent.

**Serbian** ● n. **1** the Southern Slavic language of the Serbs, almost identical to Croatian but written in the Cyrillic alphabet. **2** a Serb. ● adj. of or relating to Serbia, the Serbs, or their language.

**Serbo-** ● comb. form Serbian; Serbian and ...: *Serbo-Croat*.

**Serbo-Croat** /ˌsəːbəʊˈkrəʊat/ (also **Serbo-Croatian** /-krəʊˈeɪʃ(ə)n/) ● n. the Southern Slavic language spoken in Serbia, Croatia, and elsewhere in the former Yugoslavia.

**Sercial** /ˈsəːsɪəl/ ● n. a variety of wine grape grown chiefly in Madeira. ➤ a dry light Madeira made from this grape.
– ORIGIN from Port.

**sere**[1] ● adj. variant spelling of SEAR.

**sere**[2] /sɪə/ ● n. Ecology a series of plant or animal communities formed by succession.
– ORIGIN C20: from L. *serere* 'join in a series'.

**serenade** ● n. **1** a piece of music sung or played in the open air, especially by a man at night under the window of his beloved. **2** another term for SERENATA. ● v. entertain with a serenade.
– DERIVATIVES **serenader** n.
– ORIGIN C17: from Fr. *sérénade*, from Ital. *serenata*, from *sereno* 'serene'.

**serenata** /ˌsɛrəˈnɑːtə/ ● n. Music **1** a cantata with a pastoral subject. **2** a simple form of suite for orchestra or wind band.
– ORIGIN Ital. (see SERENADE).

**serendipity** /ˌsɛr(ə)nˈdɪpɪti/ ● n. the occurrence and development of events by chance in a happy or beneficial way.
– DERIVATIVES **serendipitous** adj. **serendipitously** adv.
– ORIGIN 1754: coined by Horace Walpole, suggested by *The Three Princes of Serendip*, the title of a fairy tale in which the heroes were always making fortunate discoveries.

**serene** ● adj. calm, peaceful, and untroubled; tranquil. ● n. (**the serene**) archaic clear sky or calm sea.
– DERIVATIVES **serenely** adv. **serenity** n.
– ORIGIN ME: from L. *serenus*.

**serf** ● n. (in the feudal system) an agricultural labourer who was tied to working on a particular estate.
– DERIVATIVES **serfage** n. **serfdom** n.
– ORIGIN C15 (in the sense 'slave'): from OFr., from L. *servus* 'slave'.

**serge** /səːdʒ/ ● n. a durable twilled woollen or worsted fabric.
– ORIGIN ME: from OFr. *sarge*, from a var. of L. *serica* (*lana*) 'silken (wool)', from *sericus* (see SILK).

**sergeant** /ˈsɑːdʒ(ə)nt/ ● n. **1** a rank of non-commissioned officer in the army or air force, above corporal and below staff sergeant. **2** Brit. a police officer ranking below an inspector. **3** US a police officer ranking below a lieutenant.
– DERIVATIVES **sergeancy** n. (pl. **-ies**).
– ORIGIN ME (in senses 'attendant, servant' and 'common soldier'): from OFr. *sergent*, from L. *servire* 'serve'.

**sergeant-at-arms** ● n. variant spelling of SERJEANT-AT-ARMS.

**Sergeant Baker** ● n. a brightly coloured edible fish with two elongated dorsal fin rays, occurring in Australian coastal waters. [*Aulopus purpurissatus*.]
– ORIGIN C19: of unknown origin.

**sergeant major** ● n. **1** a warrant officer in the British army whose job is to assist the adjutant of a regiment or battalion or a subunit commander. **2** a high rank of non-commissioned officer in the US army, above master sergeant and below warrant officer.

**Sergt** ● abbrev. Sergeant.

**serial** ● adj. **1** consisting of, forming part of, or taking place in a series. **2** repeatedly committing the same offence or following a characteristic behaviour pattern: *a serial killer*. **3** Music relating to or using serialism. **4** Computing (of a device) involving the transfer of data as a single sequence of bits. ● n. **1** a published or broadcast story or play appearing in regular instalments. **2** (in a library) a periodical.
– DERIVATIVES **seriality** n. **serially** adv.
– ORIGIN C19: from SERIES + -AL, perh. suggested by Fr. *sérial*.

**serialism** ● n. Music a compositional technique using a fixed series of notes which is subject to change only in specific ways.
– DERIVATIVES **serialist** adj. & n.

**serialize** (also **-ise**) ● v. **1** publish or broadcast (a story or play) in regular instalments. **2** arrange in a series. **3** Music compose according to the techniques of serialism.
– DERIVATIVES **serialization** n.

**serial number** ● n. an identification number showing the position of a manufactured or printed item in a series.

**seriate** technical ● adj. /ˈsɪərɪət/ arranged or occurring in

one or more series. ● **v.** /ˈsɪərɪeɪt/ arrange in a sequence according to prescribed criteria.
– DERIVATIVES **seriation** n.

**seriatim** /ˌsɪərɪˈeɪtɪm, ˌsɛrɪ-/ ● **adv.** formal taking one subject after another in regular order; point by point.
– ORIGIN C15: from med. L., from L. *series*, on the pattern of L. *gradatim* and *literatim*.

**sericulture** /ˈsɛrɪˌkʌltʃə/ ● **n.** the production of silk and the rearing of silkworms for this purpose.
– DERIVATIVES **sericultural** adj. **sericulturist** n.
– ORIGIN C19: abbrev. of Fr. *sériciculture*, from late L. *sericum* 'silk' + Fr. *culture* 'cultivation'.

**seriema** /ˌsɛrɪˈiːmə/ ● **n.** a large crested ground-dwelling South American bird with a long neck and legs. [Family Cariamidae: two species.]
– ORIGIN C19: mod. L., from Tupi *siriema* 'crested'.

**series** ● **n.** (pl. same) **1** a number of similar or related things coming one after another. ➤a set of books, periodicals, etc., published in a common format. ➤a set of stamps, banknotes, or coins issued at a particular time. **2** a sequence of related television or radio programmes. **3** Music another term for **TONE ROW**. **4** [as modifier] having or denoting electrical components connected in series. **5** Geology a range of strata corresponding to an epoch in time, being a subdivision of a system and itself subdivided into stages. **6** Mathematics a set of quantities constituting a progression or having values determined by a common relation.
– PHRASES **in series** (of electrical components or circuits) arranged so that the current passes through each successively.
– ORIGIN C17: from L., lit. 'row, chain', from *serere* 'join, connect'.

**serif** /ˈsɛrɪf/ ● **n.** a slight projection finishing off a stroke of a letter, as in T contrasted with T.
– DERIVATIVES **seriffed** adj.
– ORIGIN C19: perh. from Du. *schreef* 'dash, line'.

**serigraph** /ˈsɛrɪgrɑːf/ ● **n.** chiefly N. Amer. a printed design produced by means of a silk screen.
– DERIVATIVES **serigrapher** n. **serigraphy** n.
– ORIGIN C19: formed irregularly from L. *sericum* 'silk' + **-GRAPH**.

**serin** /ˈsɛrɪn/ ● **n.** a small yellow finch related to the canary. [*Serinus serinus* and related species.]
– ORIGIN C16 (denoting a canary): from Fr., of unknown ultimate origin.

**serine** /ˈsɪəriːn, ˈsɛr-/ ● **n.** Biochemistry a hydrophilic amino acid which is a constituent of most proteins.
– ORIGIN C19: from L. *sericum* 'silk' + **-INE**[4].

**serio-comic** /ˈsɪərɪəʊ/ ● **adj.** combining the serious and the comic.
– DERIVATIVES **serio-comically** adv.

**serious** ● **adj. 1** demanding or characterized by careful consideration or application. ➤solemn or thoughtful. **2** sincere and in earnest, rather than joking or half-hearted. **3** significant or worrying in terms of danger or risk: *serious injury*. **4** informal substantial in terms of size, number, or quality: *serious money*.
– DERIVATIVES **seriousness** n.
– ORIGIN ME: from OFr. *serieux* or late L. *seriosus*, from L. *serius* 'earnest, serious'.

**seriously** ● **adv.** in a serious manner or to a serious extent.
– PHRASES **take someone/thing seriously** regard someone or something as important and worthy of attention.

**serjeant** ● **n.** (in official lists) a sergeant in the Foot Guards.
– ORIGIN ME: var. of **SERGEANT**.

**serjeant-at-arms** (also **sergeant-at-arms**) ● **n.** (pl. **serjeants-at-arms**) **1** an official of a legislative assembly whose duties include maintaining order and security. **2** historical a knight or armed officer in the service of the monarch or a lord.

**serjeant-at-law** ● **n.** (pl. **serjeants-at-law**) historical a barrister of the highest rank.

**serjeanty** ● **n.** (pl. **-ies**) historical a form of feudal tenure conditional on rendering some personal service to the monarch.

**sermon** ● **n. 1** a talk on a religious or moral subject, especially one given during a church service and based on a passage from the Bible. **2** informal a long or tedious piece of admonition or reproof.
– DERIVATIVES **sermonic** adj. **sermonize** (also **-ise**) v. **sermonizer** (also **-iser**) n.
– ORIGIN ME: from OFr., from L. *sermo(n-)* 'discourse, talk'.

**sero-** ● **comb. form** relating to serum: *serotype*.

**seroconvert** /ˌsɪərəʊkənˈvəːt/ ● **v.** Medicine undergo a change from a seronegative to a seropositive condition.
– DERIVATIVES **seroconversion** n.

**serology** /sɪəˈrɒlədʒi/ ● **n.** the scientific study or diagnostic examination of blood serum.
– DERIVATIVES **serologic** adj. **serological** adj. **serologically** adv. **serologist** n.

**seropositive** (or **seronegative**) ● **adj.** Medicine giving a positive (or negative) result in a test of blood serum, especially for the presence of a virus.
– DERIVATIVES **seronegativity** n. **seropositivity** n.

**serosa** /sɪˈrəʊsə/ ● **n.** Physiology the tissue of a serous membrane.
– DERIVATIVES **serosal** adj. **serositis** n.
– ORIGIN mod. L., fem. of med. L. *serosus* 'serous'.

**serotine** /ˈsɛrətiːn/ ● **n.** a medium-sized insectivorous bat. [*Eptesicus serotinus* (Eurasia) and other species.]
– ORIGIN C18: from Fr. *sérotine*, from L. *serotinus* 'of the evening, late'.

**serotonin** /ˌsɛrəˈtəʊnɪn/ ● **n.** Biochemistry a compound present in blood platelets and serum, which constricts the blood vessels and acts as a neurotransmitter.
– ORIGIN 1940s: from **SERUM** + **TONIC** + **-IN**[1].

**serotype** /ˈsɪərə(ʊ)tʌɪp/ Microbiology ● **n.** a serologically distinguishable strain of a micro-organism. ● **v.** assign to a particular serotype.
– DERIVATIVES **serotypic** /ˌsɪərə(ʊ)ˈtɪpɪk/ adj.

**serous** /ˈsɪərəs/ ● **adj.** Physiology of, resembling, or producing serum.
– DERIVATIVES **serosity** n.
– ORIGIN ME: from Fr. *séreux* or med. L. *serosus*, from *serum* (see **SERUM**).

**serous membrane** ● **n.** a smooth transparent two-layered membrane lining certain internal cavities of the body and lubricated by a fluid derived from serum.

**serow** /ˈsɛrəʊ/ ● **n.** a goat-antelope with short sharp horns and long coarse hair, native to SE Asia, Taiwan, and Japan. [Genus *Capricornis*: two species.]
– ORIGIN C19: prob. from Lepcha *sā-ro*.

**serpent** ● **n. 1** chiefly poetic/literary a large snake. ➤a dragon or other mythical snake-like reptile. ➤(**the Serpent**) a biblical name for Satan (see Gen. 3, Rev. 20). ➤a sly or treacherous person. **2** historical a bass wind instrument made of leather-covered wood in three U-shaped turns, with a cup-shaped mouthpiece and few keys.
– ORIGIN ME: via OFr. from L. *serpent-*, *serpere* 'to creep'.

**serpentine** /ˈsəːp(ə)ntʌɪn/ ● **adj.** of or like a serpent or snake. ➤winding and twisting. ➤complex, cunning, or treacherous. ● **n. 1** a dark green mineral consisting of hydrated magnesium silicate, sometimes mottled or spotted like a snake's skin. **2** a riding exercise consisting of a series of half-circles made alternately to right and left. **3** historical a kind of cannon. ● **v.** move or lie in a winding path or line.

**serpentine verse** ● **n.** Prosody a metrical line beginning and ending with the same word.

**serpentinite** /ˈsəːp(ə)ntɪˌnʌɪt/ ● **n.** Geology a metamorphic rock consisting largely of serpentine.

**serpiginous** /səːˈpɪdʒɪnəs/ ● **adj.** Medicine (of a skin lesion or ulcerated region) having a wavy margin.
– ORIGIN ME: from med. L. *serpigo*, *serpigin-* 'ringworm' + **-OUS**.

**SERPS** /səːps/ ● **abbrev.** (in the UK) state earnings-related pension scheme.

**serrate** /ˈsɛreɪt/ ● **adj.** chiefly Botany serrated.

**serrated** ● **adj.** having or denoting a jagged edge; saw-like.
– ORIGIN ME (as *serrate* v.): from late L. *serratus*, from L. *serra* 'saw'.

**serration** • n. a tooth or point of a serrated edge or surface.

**serried** • adj. (of rows of people or things) standing close together.
– ORIGIN C17: past part. of *serry* 'press close', prob. from Fr. *serré* 'close together'.

**sertão** /ˈsɛːtɑ̃ːʊ/ • n. (pl. **-os**) (in Brazil) an arid region of scrub.
– ORIGIN C19: Port.

**serum** /ˈsɪərəm/ • n. (pl. **sera** /-rə/ or **serums**) **1** an amber-coloured, protein-rich liquid which separates out when blood coagulates. **2** the blood serum of an animal, used to provide immunity to a pathogen or toxin by inoculation or as a diagnostic agent.
– ORIGIN C17: from L., lit. 'whey'.

**serval** /ˈsəːv(ə)l/ • n. a slender African wild cat with long legs, large ears, and a black-spotted orange-brown coat. [*Felis serval*.]
– ORIGIN C18: from Fr., from Port. *cerval* 'deer-like', from *cervo* 'deer'.

**servant** • n. a person employed to perform duties for others, especially in a house on domestic duties or as a personal attendant. ➤a person employed in the service of a government. ➤a devoted and helpful follower or supporter.
– ORIGIN ME: from OFr., lit. '(person) serving', pres. part. (used as n.) of *servir* 'to serve'.

**serve** • v. **1** perform duties or services for. ➤be employed as a member of the armed forces. ➤spend (a period) in office, in an apprenticeship, or in prison. **2** present food or drink to (someone). ➤(of food or drink) be enough for. ➤attend to (a customer in a shop). ➤Christian Church act as a server at the celebration of the Eucharist. **3** Law formally deliver (a summons or writ) to the person to whom it is addressed. **4** be of use in achieving something or fulfilling a purpose. ➤treat in a specified way. ➤(of a male breeding animal) copulate with (a female). **5** (in tennis and other racket sports) hit the ball or shuttlecock to begin play for each point of a game. ➤(**serve out**) Tennis win the final game of a set or match while serving. **6** Nautical bind (a rope) with thin cord to protect or strengthen it. **7** Military operate (a gun). **8** archaic play (a trick) on. • n. **1** an act of serving in tennis, badminton, etc. **2** Austral. informal a reprimand.
– PHRASES **serve someone right** be someone's deserved punishment or misfortune. **serve one's** (or **its**) **turn** be useful. ➤(**serve someone's turn**) be useful to someone.
– ORIGIN ME: from OFr. *servir*, from L. *servire*, from *servus* 'slave'.

**server** • n. **1** a person or thing that serves. ➤N. Amer. a waiter or waitress. **2** a computer or computer program which manages access to a centralized resource or service in a network.

**servery** • n. (pl. **-ies**) Brit. a counter, hatch, or room from which meals are served.

**Servian** /ˈsəːvɪən/ • n. & adj. archaic variant of **SERBIAN**.

**service** • n. **1** the action or process of serving. ➤an act of assistance. ➤a period of employment with a company or organization: *he retired after 40 years' service.* ➤(often in phrs **in** or **out of service**) use for a particular purpose. ➤(often in phr. **in service**) employment as a servant. **2** a system supplying a public need such as transport, or utilities such as electricity and water. ➤a public department or organization run by the state: *the probation service.* ➤(**the services**) the armed forces. ➤(**services**) chiefly Brit. a motorway service area. **3** a ceremony of religious worship according to a prescribed form. **4** a set of matching crockery used for serving a particular meal. **5** (in tennis, badminton, etc.) a serve. **6** a periodic routine inspection and maintenance of a vehicle or other machine. • v. **1** perform routine maintenance or repair work on (a vehicle or machine). ➤provide a service or services for. **2** pay interest on (a debt). **3** (of a male animal) mate with (a female animal).
– PHRASES **be at someone's service** be ready to assist someone whenever required. **be of service** be available to assist someone.
– ORIGIN OE, from OFr. *servise* or L. *servitium* 'slavery', from *servus* 'slave'.

**serviceable** • adj. **1** fulfilling its function adequately; usable or in working order. **2** functional and durable rather than attractive.
– DERIVATIVES **serviceability** n. **serviceably** adv.

**service area** • n. chiefly Brit. a roadside area where services are available to motorists.

**serviceberry** • n. **1** the fruit of the service tree. **2** another term for **JUNEBERRY**.

**service book** • n. a book of authorized forms of worship used in a church.

**service charge** • n. an extra charge made for serving customers in a restaurant. ➤a charge made for maintenance on a rented property.

**service club** • n. N. Amer. an association of business or professional people with the aims of promoting community welfare and goodwill.

**service dress** • n. Brit. military uniform worn on formal but not ceremonial occasions.

**service flat** • n. Brit. a rented flat in which domestic service and sometimes meals are provided by the management.

**service industry** • n. a business that does work for a customer, and sometimes provides goods, but is not involved in manufacturing.

**service line** • n. (in tennis and other racket sports) a line on a court marking the limit of the area into which the ball must be served.

**serviceman** (or **servicewoman**) • n. (pl. **-men** or **-women**) **1** a person serving in the armed forces. **2** a person providing maintenance for machinery.

**service provider** • n. Computing a company which gives its subscribers access to the Internet.

**service road** • n. a subsidiary road running parallel to a main road and giving access to houses, shops, or businesses.

**service station** • n. a roadside establishment selling petrol and oil and sometimes offering vehicle maintenance.

**service tree** • n. a tree resembling a rowan, with brown berries. [*Sorbus torminalis* (**wild service tree**) and *S. domestica*.]
– ORIGIN C16: from an alt. of the pl. of obs. *serve*, from OE *syrfe*, based on L. *sorbus*.

**serviette** • n. Brit. a table napkin.
– ORIGIN C15: from OFr., from *servir* 'to serve'.

**servile** • adj. **1** excessively willing to serve or please others. **2** of or characteristic of a slave or slaves.
– DERIVATIVES **servilely** adv. **servility** n.
– ORIGIN ME (in the sense 'suitable for a slave or for the working class'): from L. *servilis*, from *servus* 'slave'.

**serving** • n. a quantity of food suitable for or served to one person.

**servingman** (or **servingwoman**) • n. (pl. **-men** or **-women**) archaic a domestic servant or attendant.

**Servite** /ˈsəːvʌɪt/ • n. a friar or nun of the Catholic religious order of the Servants of Blessed Mary.
– ORIGIN from med. L. *Servitae* (pl.), from L., from *Servi Beatae Mariae*, the formal title of the order.

**servitor** /ˈsəːvɪtə/ • n. **1** archaic a person who serves or attends on a social superior. **2** historical an Oxford undergraduate performing menial duties in exchange for assistance from college funds.
– DERIVATIVES **servitorship** n.
– ORIGIN ME: via OFr. from late L., from *servit-*, *servire* (see **SERVE**).

**servitude** /ˈsəːvɪtjuːd/ • n. **1** the state of being a slave or completely subject to someone more powerful. **2** Law, archaic the subjection of property to an easement.
– ORIGIN ME: via OFr. from L. *servitudo*, from *servus* 'slave'.

**servo** • n. (pl. **-os**) short for **SERVOMECHANISM** or **SERVOMOTOR**.
– ORIGIN C19: from L. *servus* 'slave'.

**servomechanism** • n. a powered mechanism producing motion or forces at a higher level of energy than the input level, e.g. in the brakes and steering of large motor vehicles.

**servomotor** • n. the motive element in a servomechanism.

**sesame** /ˈsɛsəmi/ • n. a tall annual herbaceous plant of tropical and subtropical areas of the Old World, cultivated for its oil-rich seeds. [*Sesamum indicum*.]
– PHRASES **open sesame** a free or unrestricted means of admission or access. [from the magic formula in the tale of Ali Baba and the Forty Thieves.]
– ORIGIN ME: via L. from Gk *sēsamon*, *sēsamē*; cf. Arab. *simsim*.

**sesamoid** /ˈsɛsəmɔɪd/ (also **sesamoid bone**) • n. a small bony nodule developed in a tendon passing over an angular structure, especially in the hands and feet.
– ORIGIN C17: from SESAME (with ref. to the similarity in shape of a sesame seed) + -OID.

**sesamum** /ˈsɛsəməm/ • n. another term for SESAME.
– ORIGIN C16: via L. from Gk.

**sesh** • n. informal a drinking session.

**Sesotho** /sɛˈsuːtuː/ • n. the South Sotho language of the Basotho people.
– ORIGIN the name in Sesotho.

**sesqui-** • comb. form denoting one and a half: *sesquicentenary*. ➤ Chemistry (of a compound) in which a particular element or group is present in a ratio of 3:2 compared with another.
– ORIGIN from L. *semi-* (see SEMI-) + *que* 'and'.

**sesquicentenary** /ˌsɛskwɪsɛnˈtiːn(ə)ri, -ˈtɛn-/ • n. (pl. **-ies**) the one-hundred-and-fiftieth anniversary of a significant event.
– DERIVATIVES **sesquicentennial** adj. & n.

**sesquipedalian** /ˌsɛskwɪpɪˈdeɪlɪən/ • adj. formal **1** (of a word) polysyllabic; long. **2** characterized by long words; long-winded.
– ORIGIN C17: from L. *sesquipedalis* 'a foot and a half long', from *sesqui-* (see SESQUI-) + *pes, ped-* 'foot'.

**sess** • n. variant spelling of CESS[1].

**sessile** /ˈsɛsʌɪl, ˈsɛsɪl/ • adj. Biology **1** (of an organism) fixed in one place; immobile. **2** (of a structure) attached directly by its base without a stalk or peduncle.
– ORIGIN C18: from L. *sessilis*, from *sess-*, *sedere* 'sit'.

**sessile oak** • n. an oak tree with stalkless egg-shaped acorns, common in hilly areas. [*Quercus petraea*.]

**session** • n. **1** a period devoted to a particular activity: *a training session*. ➤ informal a period of heavy or sustained drinking. ➤ a period of recording music in a studio. **2** (often in phr. **in session**) a meeting of a deliberative or judicial body to conduct its business. ➤ a period during which such meetings are regularly held. **3** an academic year. ➤ the period during which a school has classes. **4** the governing body of a Presbyterian Church.
– DERIVATIVES **sessional** adj.
– ORIGIN ME: from OFr., or from L. *sessio(n-)*, from *sess-* (see SESSILE).

**session clerk** • n. a chief lay official in the session of a Presbyterian Church.

**session musician** • n. a freelance musician hired to play on recording sessions.

**sesterce** /ˈsɛstəːs/ (also **sestertius** /sɛˈstəːʃəs/) • n. (pl. **sesterces** /-siːz/ or **sestertii** /-ˈstəːʃiː/) an ancient Roman coin and monetary unit equal to one quarter of a denarius.
– ORIGIN from L. *sestertius (nummus)* '(coin) that is two and a half (asses)'.

**sestet** /sɛsˈtɛt/ • n. **1** Prosody the last six lines of a sonnet. **2** Music, rare a sextet.
– ORIGIN C19: from Ital. *sestetto*, from *sesto*, from L. *sextus* 'a sixth'.

**sestina** /sɛˈstiːnə/ • n. Prosody a poem with six stanzas of six lines and a final triplet, all stanzas having the same six words at the line-ends in six different sequences.
– ORIGIN C19: from Ital., from *sesto* (see SESTET).

**set**[1] • v. (**setting**; past and past part. **set**) **1** put, lay, or stand (something) in a specified place or position. ➤ (**be set**) be situated in a specified place or position. ➤ represent (a story) as happening at a specified time or in a specified place. ➤ mount a precious stone in (a piece of jewellery). ➤ Printing arrange (type or text) as required. ➤ prepare (a table) for a meal by placing cutlery, crockery, etc., on it. ➤ (**set something to**) add (music) to a written work. ➤ Sailing put (a sail) up in position to catch the wind. **2** put, bring, or place into a specified state: *the hostages were set free*. ➤ instruct (someone) to do something. ➤ give someone (a task): *the problem we have been set*. ➤ establish as (an example or record). ➤ decide on or fix (a time, value, or limit). **3** adjust (a device) as required. **4** harden into a solid, semi-solid, or fixed state. ➤ arrange (damp hair) into the required style. ➤ put (a broken or dislocated bone or limb) into the correct position for healing. ➤ (of a hunting dog) adopt a rigid attitude indicating the presence of game. **5** (of the sun, moon, etc.) appear to move towards and below the earth's horizon as the earth rotates. **6** (of a tide or current) take or have a specified direction or course. **7** chiefly N. Amer. start (a fire). **8** (of blossom or a tree) form into or produce (fruit). **9** informal or dialect sit. **10** (of a dancer) acknowledge one's partner using the steps prescribed. **11** give the teeth of (a saw) an alternate outward inclination.
– PHRASES **set one's heart** (or **hopes**) **on** have a strong desire for or to do. **set out one's stall** display or show off one's abilities or attributes. **set sail** hoist the sails of a boat. ➤ begin a voyage. **set one's teeth** clench one's teeth together. ➤ become resolute. **set the wheels in motion** begin a process or put a plan into action.
– PHRASAL VERBS **set about 1** start doing something with vigour or determination. **2** Brit. informal attack (someone). **set someone against** cause someone to be in opposition or conflict with. **set something (off) against** offset something against. **set someone apart** give someone an air of unusual superiority. **set something apart** separate something and keep it for a special purpose. **set something aside 1** save or keep something for a particular purpose. ➤ remove land from agricultural production. **2** annul a legal decision or process. **set someone/thing back 1** delay or impede the progress of someone or something. **2** informal cost someone a particular amount of money. **set something by** archaic or US save something for future use. **set someone down** stop and allow someone to alight from a vehicle. **set something down** record something in writing or as an authoritative rule or principle. **set forth** begin a journey or trip. **set something forth** state or describe something in writing or speech. **set forward** archaic start on a journey. **set in** (of something unwelcome) begin and seem likely to continue. **set something in** insert something, especially a sleeve, into a garment. **set off** begin a journey. **set something off 1** cause a bomb or alarm to go off. **2** serve as decorative embellishment to. **set on** (or **upon**) attack (someone) violently. **set someone/thing on** (or **upon**) cause or urge a person or animal to attack. **set out 1** begin a journey. **2** aim or intend to do something. **set something out** arrange or display something in a particular order or position. **set to** begin doing something vigorously. **set someone up 1** establish someone in a particular capacity or role. **2** informal restore or enhance the health of someone. **3** informal make an innocent person appear guilty of something. **set something up 1** place or erect something in position. **2** establish a business, institution, etc. **3** begin making a loud sound.
– ORIGIN OE *settan*, of Gmc origin; rel. to SIT.

**set**[2] • n. **1** a group or collection of things belonging or used together or resembling one another. ➤ a group of people with common interests or occupations: *the literary set*. ➤ a group of pupils or students who are taught together. ➤ (in tennis, darts, and other games) a group of games counting as a unit towards a match. ➤ (in jazz or popular music) a sequence of songs or pieces constituting or forming part of a live show or recording. ➤ a group of people making up the required number for a country dance. ➤ Mathematics & Logic a collection of distinct entities regarded as a unit, being either individually specified or (more usually) satisfying specified conditions. **2** the way in which something is set, disposed, or positioned. ➤ (also **dead set**) a setter's pointing in the presence of game. ➤ a warp or bend in wood, metal, etc., caused by

continued strain or pressure. **3** a radio or television receiver. **4** a collection of scenery, stage furniture, etc., used for a scene in a play or film. **5** a cutting, young plant, or bulb used in the propagation of new plants. ➤a young fruit that has just formed. **6** the last coat of plaster on a wall. **7** Printing the amount of spacing in type controlling the distance between letters. ➤the width of a piece of type. **8** variant spelling of **SETT**. **9** Snooker another term for **PLANT** (in sense 4). **10** Austral./NZ informal a grudge.
– PHRASES **make a dead set at** Brit. make a determined attempt to win the affections of. [by assoc. with hunting (see *dead set* above).]
– ORIGIN ME: partly from OFr. *sette*, from L. *secta* 'sect', partly from **SET**[1].

**set**[3] ● **adj. 1** fixed or arranged in advance. ➤(of a restaurant menu) offered at a fixed price with a limited choice of dishes. ➤(of a book) prescribed for study. ➤having a conventional or predetermined wording; formulaic. **2** firmly fixed and unchanging. **3** ready, prepared, or likely to do something: *we're all set for tonight!* ➤(**set against**) firmly opposed to. ➤(**set on**) determined to do.
– ORIGIN OE, past part. of **SET**[1].

**seta** /ˈsiːtə/ ● **n.** (pl. **setae** /-tiː/) chiefly Zoology a stiff hair-like or bristle-like structure.
– DERIVATIVES **setaceous** /-ˈteɪʃəs/ adj. **setal** adj.
– ORIGIN C18: from L., 'bristle'.

**set-aside** ● **n.** the policy of taking land out of production to reduce crop surpluses. ➤land taken out of production in this way.

**setback** ● **n. 1** a reversal or check in progress. **2** Architecture a plain, flat offset in a wall. **3** N. Amer. the distance by which a building is set back from the property line.

**se-tenant** /siːˈtɛnənt/ ● **adj.** Philately (of stamps of different designs) joined together side by side as when printed.
– ORIGIN C20: from Fr., lit. 'holding together'.

**SETI** ● **abbrev.** search for extraterrestrial intelligence.

**set-off** ● **n. 1** an item or amount set off against another. ➤Law a counterbalancing debt pleaded by the defendant in an action to recover money due. ➤dated a counterbalancing or compensating circumstance or condition. **2** a step or shoulder at which the thickness of part of a building or machine is reduced. **3** Printing the unwanted transference of ink from one printed sheet or page to another.

**seton** /ˈsiːt(ə)n/ ● **n.** Medicine, historical a skein of absorbent material passed below the skin and left with the ends protruding, to promote drainage of fluid or to act as a counterirritant.
– ORIGIN ME: from med. L. *seto(n-)*, appar. from L. *seta* 'bristle'.

**setose** /ˈsiːtəʊs, -z/ ● **adj.** chiefly Zoology bearing bristles or setae; bristly.
– ORIGIN C17: from L. *seta* 'bristle' + **-OSE**[1].

**set phrase** ● **n.** an unvarying phrase having a specific meaning or being the only context in which a word appears.

**set piece** ● **n. 1** a passage or section of a novel, film, etc., arranged for maximum effect. ➤a formal and carefully structured speech. **2** a carefully organized and practised move in a team game. **3** an arrangement of fireworks forming a picture or design.

**set point** ● **n.** (in tennis and other sports) a point which if won by one of the players will also win them a set.

**set screw** ● **n.** a screw for adjusting or clamping parts of a machine.

**set shot** ● **n.** Basketball a shot at the basket made without jumping.

**set square** ● **n.** a right-angled triangular plate for drawing lines, especially at 90°, 45°, 60°, or 30°.

**Setswana** /sɛˈtswɑːnə/ ● **n.** the Bantu language of the Tswana people.
– ORIGIN the name in Setswana.

**sett** (also **set**) ● **n. 1** the earth or burrow of a badger. **2** a granite paving block. **3** the particular pattern of stripes in a tartan.
– ORIGIN ME: var. of **SET**[2], the spelling with *-tt* prevailing in technical senses.

**settee** ● **n.** a long upholstered seat for more than one person, typically with a back and arms.
– ORIGIN C18: perh. a fanciful var. of **SETTLE**[2].

**setter** ● **n. 1** a dog of a large long-haired breed trained to stand rigid when scenting game. **2** a person or thing that sets something.

**set theory** ● **n.** the branch of mathematics concerned with the formal properties and applications of sets.

**setting** /ˈsɛtɪŋ/ ● **n. 1** the surroundings of a place or the location where an event happens. ➤the place and time at which a story is represented as happening. **2** a piece of metal in which a precious stone or gem is fixed to form a piece of jewellery. **3** a piece of vocal or choral music composed for particular words. **4** (also **place setting**) a complete set of crockery and cutlery for one person at a meal. **5** a level at which a machine or device can be adjusted to operate.

**settle**[1] ● **v. 1** reach an agreement or decision about (an argument or problem); resolve. ➤(**settle for**) accept or agree to (something less than satisfactory). **2** pay (a debt or account). ➤(**settle something on**) give money or property to (someone) through a deed of settlement or a will. **3** (often **settle down**) adopt a more steady or secure style of life, especially through establishing a permanent home. ➤begin to feel comfortable or established in a new situation. ➤(**settle down to**) apply oneself to. ➤become or make calmer or quieter. **4** sit or come to rest in a comfortable position. **5** fall or come down on to a surface. ➤(of suspended particles) sink slowly in a liquid to form sediment. ➤(of an object) gradually sink down under its own weight. ➤(of a ship) begin to sink. **6** dated silence (a troublesome person) by some means.
– DERIVATIVES **settleable** adj.
– ORIGIN OE *setlan* 'to seat, place', from **SETTLE**[2].

**settle**[2] ● **n.** a wooden bench with a high back and arms, typically incorporating a box under the seat.
– ORIGIN OE *setl* 'a place to sit', of Gmc origin; rel. to L. *sella* 'seat', also to **SIT**.

**settlement** ● **n. 1** the action or process of settling. **2** an official agreement intended to resolve a dispute or conflict. **3** a place where people establish a community. **4** Law an arrangement whereby property passes to a person or succession of people as dictated by the settlor.

**settler** ● **n.** a person who settles in an area, especially one with no or few previous inhabitants.

**settlor** /ˈsɛtlə/ ● **n.** Law a person who makes a settlement, especially of a property.

**set-to** ● **n.** (pl. **-os**) informal a fight or argument.

**set-up** ● **n.** informal **1** the way in which something is organized or arranged. ➤an organization or arrangement. ➤a set of equipment for a particular activity. **2** a scheme or trick intended to incriminate or deceive someone. ➤chiefly N. Amer. a contest with a pre-arranged outcome.

**seven** ● **cardinal number 1** equivalent to the sum of three and four; one more than six, or three less than ten; 7. (Roman numeral: **vii** or **VII**.) **2** (**sevens**) seven-a-side rugby.
– PHRASES **the seven deadly sins** (in Christian tradition) the sins of pride, covetousness, lust, anger, gluttony, envy, and sloth. **the seven seas** all the oceans of the world (conventionally the Arctic, Antarctic, North Pacific, South Pacific, North Atlantic, South Atlantic, and Indian Oceans). **the Seven Wonders of the World** the seven most spectacular man-made structures of the ancient world. **the seven year itch** a supposed tendency to infidelity after seven years of marriage.
– DERIVATIVES **sevenfold** adj. & adv.
– ORIGIN OE *seofon*, of Gmc origin.

**seventeen** ● **cardinal number** one more than sixteen, or seven more than ten; 17. (Roman numeral: **xvii** or **XVII**.)
– DERIVATIVES **seventeenth** adj. & n.
– ORIGIN OE *seofontīene*, from the Gmc base of **SEVEN**.

**seventh** ● **ordinal number 1** constituting number seven in a sequence; 7th. **2** (**a seventh/one seventh**) each of seven equal parts into which something is or may be divided. **3** Music an interval spanning seven consecutive notes in a diatonic scale. ➤the note which is higher by this interval than the tonic of a diatonic scale or root of a chord. ➤a chord in which the seventh note of the scale

forms an important component.
– DERIVATIVES **seventhly** adv.

**Seventh-Day Adventist** • n. a member of a strict Protestant sect which preaches the imminent return of Christ to Earth and observes Saturday as the sabbath.

**seventy** • cardinal number (pl. **-ies**) the number equivalent to the product of seven and ten; ten less than eighty; 70. (Roman numeral: **lxx** or **LXX**.)
– DERIVATIVES **seventieth** ordinal number. **seventyfold** adj. & adv.
– ORIGIN OE *hundseofontig*, from *hund-* (of uncertain origin) + *seofon* 'seven' + *-tig* (see **-TY**²).

**seventy-eight** • n. an old gramophone record designed to be played at 78 rpm.

**sever** • v. **1** divide by cutting or slicing. **2** put an end to (a connection or relationship).
– DERIVATIVES **severable** adj.
– ORIGIN ME: from Anglo-Norman Fr. *severer*, from L. *separare* 'disjoin, divide'.

**several** • det. & pron. more than two but not many. • adj. **1** separate or respective. **2** Law applied or regarded separately. Contrasted with **JOINT**.
– DERIVATIVES **severally** adv.
– ORIGIN ME: from Anglo-Norman Fr., from med. L. *separalis*, from L. *separ* 'separate, different'.

**severalty** • n. archaic the condition of being separate.

**severance** • n. **1** the action of ending a connection or relationship. **2** the state of being separated or cut off. **3** dismissal or discharge from employment.

**severance pay** • n. money paid to an employee on the early termination of a contract.

**severe** • adj. **1** (of something bad, undesirable, or difficult) very great; intense. **2** strict or harsh. **3** very plain in style or appearance.
– DERIVATIVES **severely** adv. **severity** n.
– ORIGIN C16: from Fr. *sévère* or L. *severus*.

**severy** /'sɛvəri/ • n. (pl. **-ies**) Architecture a bay or compartment in a vaulted ceiling.
– ORIGIN ME: from OFr. *civoire* 'ciborium'.

**seviche** /sɛ'vi:tʃeɪ/ • n. variant spelling of **CEVICHE**.

**Seville orange** /'sɛvɪl/ • n. a bitter orange used for marmalade.
– ORIGIN from *Seville* in Spain.

**Sèvres** /'sɛvr(ə), French sɛvʀ/ • n. a type of fine porcelain characterized by elaborate decoration on backgrounds of intense colour.
– ORIGIN from *Sèvres* in the suburbs of Paris, the place of manufacture.

**sevruga** /sɛv'ru:gə/ • n. a migratory sturgeon found only in the basins of the Caspian and Black Seas, fished for its caviar. [*Acipenser stellatus*.]
– ORIGIN C16: from Russ. *sevryuga*.

**sew** • v. (past part. **sewn** or **sewed**) **1** join, fasten, or repair by making stitches with a needle and thread or a sewing machine. **2** (**sew something up**) informal bring something to a favourable state or conclusion.
– ORIGIN OE *siwan*, of Gmc origin.

**sewage** /'su:ɪdʒ/ • n. waste water and excrement conveyed in sewers.
– ORIGIN C19: from **SEWER**¹, by substitution of the suffix **-AGE**.

**sewage farm** (also **sewage works**) • n. a place where sewage is treated, especially for use as fertilizer.

**sewellel** /sɪ'wɛləl/ • n. another term for **MOUNTAIN BEAVER**.
– ORIGIN C19: from Chinook Jargon *šwalál* 'robe of mountain-beaver skin'.

**sewer**¹ /'su:ə, 'sju:ə/ • n. an underground conduit for carrying off drainage water and waste matter.
– ORIGIN ME: from ONorth. Fr. *seuwiere* 'channel to drain the overflow from a fish pond', based on L. *ex-* 'out of' + *aqua* 'water'.

**sewer**² /'səʊə/ • n. a person that sews.

**sewerage** • n. **1** the provision of drainage by sewers. **2** US term for **SEWAGE**.

**sewing machine** • n. a machine with a mechanically driven needle for sewing or stitching cloth.

**sewn** past participle of **SEW**.

**sex** • n. **1** either of the two main categories (male and female) into which humans and most other living things are divided on the basis of their reproductive functions. ➤ the fact of belonging to one of these categories. ➤ the group of all members of either sex. **2** sexual activity, specifically sexual intercourse. ➤ euphemistic a person's genitals. • v. **1** determine the sex of. **2** (**sex someone up**) informal arouse or attempt to arouse someone sexually.
– DERIVATIVES **sexer** n.
– ORIGIN ME: from OFr. *sexe* or L. *sexus*.

**sex-** • comb. form variant spelling of **SEXI-**, shortened before a vowel (as in *sexennial*) or a consonant (as in *sexfoil*).

**sexagenarian** /ˌsɛksədʒɪ'nɛ:rɪən/ • n. a person who is between 60 and 69 years old.
– ORIGIN C18: from L. *sexagenarius* (based on *sexaginta* 'sixty') + **-AN**.

**Sexagesima** /ˌsɛksə'dʒɛsɪmə/ • n. the Sunday before Quinquagesima.
– ORIGIN ME: from eccles. L., lit. 'sixtieth (day)', prob. named by analogy with **QUINQUAGESIMA**.

**sexagesimal** /ˌsɛksə'dʒɛsɪm(ə)l/ • adj. relating to or based on sixtieths.
– DERIVATIVES **sexagesimally** adv.
– ORIGIN C17: from L. *sexagesimus* 'sixtieth' + **-AL**.

**sex appeal** • n. the quality of being attractive in a sexual way.

**sex bomb** • n. informal a woman who is very sexually attractive.

**sexcentenary** /ˌsɛk(s)sɛn'ti:n(ə)ri, -'tɛn-/ • n. (pl. **-ies**) the six-hundredth anniversary of a significant event.

**sex chromosome** • n. a chromosome concerned in determining the sex of an organism (in mammals the X and Y chromosomes).

**sex drive** • n. the urge to seek satisfaction of sexual needs.

**sexed** • adj. **1** having specified sexual appetites: *highly sexed*. **2** having sexual characteristics.

**sexennial** /sɛk'sɛnɪəl/ • adj. lasting for or recurring every six years.
– ORIGIN C17: from L. **SEXENNIUM** + **-AL**.

**sexennium** /sɛk'sɛnɪəm/ • n. (pl. **sexennia** /-nɪə/ or **sexenniums**) rare a period of six years.
– ORIGIN 1950s: from L., from *sex* 'six' + *annus* 'year'.

**sexfoil** • n. (especially in architecture) an ornamental design having six leaves or petals radiating from a common centre.
– ORIGIN C17: from **SEXI-**, on the pattern of words such as *trefoil*.

**sex hormone** • n. a hormone affecting sexual development or reproduction, such as oestrogen or testosterone.

**sexi-** (also **sex-**) • comb. form six; having six: *sexivalent*.
– ORIGIN from L. *sex* 'six'.

**sexism** • n. prejudice, stereotyping, or discrimination, typically against women, on the basis of sex.
– DERIVATIVES **sexist** adj. & n.

**sexivalent** /ˌsɛksɪ'veɪl(ə)nt/ • adj. Chemistry another term for **HEXAVALENT**.

**sex kitten** • n. informal a young woman who asserts or exploits her sexual attractiveness.

**sexless** • adj. **1** lacking in sexual desire, activity, or attractiveness. **2** neither male nor female.
– DERIVATIVES **sexlessly** adv. **sexlessness** n.

**sex life** • n. a person's sexual activity and relationships considered as a whole.

**sex object** • n. a person regarded chiefly in terms of their sexual attractiveness or availability.

**sexology** • n. the study of human sexual life or relationships.
– DERIVATIVES **sexological** adj. **sexologist** n.

**sexpartite** /sɛks'pɑ:tʌɪt/ • adj. divided or involving division into six parts.

**sexploitation** • n. informal the commercial exploitation of sex or sexually explicit material.

**sexpot** • n. informal a sexy person.

**sex symbol** • **n.** a person widely noted for their sexual attractiveness.

**sext** • **n.** a service forming part of the Divine Office of the Western Christian Church, traditionally said (or chanted) at the sixth hour of the day (i.e. noon).
– ORIGIN ME: from L. *sexta* (*hora*) 'sixth (hour)', from *sextus* 'sixth'.

**sextant** /ˈsɛkst(ə)nt/ • **n.** an instrument with a graduated arc of 60° and a sighting mechanism, used for measuring the angular distances between objects and especially for taking altitudes in navigation and surveying.
– ORIGIN C16 (denoting the sixth part of a circle): from L. *sextans*, *sextant-* 'sixth part', from *sextus* 'sixth'.

**sextet** (also **sextette**) • **n. 1** a group of six people playing music or singing together. ➤ a composition for such a group. **2** a set of six people or things.
– ORIGIN C19: alt. of SESTET, suggested by L. *sex* 'six'.

**sextile** /ˈsɛkstʌɪl, -tɪl/ • **n.** Astrology an aspect of 60° (one sixth of a circle).
– ORIGIN ME: from L. *sextilis*, from *sextus* 'sixth'.

**sextillion** /sɛksˈtɪljən/ • **cardinal number** (pl. **sextillions** or (with numeral) same) a thousand raised to the seventh power ($10^{21}$). ➤ dated, chiefly Brit. a million raised to the sixth power ($10^{36}$).
– DERIVATIVES **sextillionth** ordinal number.
– ORIGIN C17: from Fr., from *million*, by substitution of the prefix *sexti-* 'six' (from L. *sextus* 'sixth') for the initial letters.

**sextodecimo** /ˌsɛkstə(ʊ)ˈdɛsɪməʊ/ (abbrev.: **16mo**) • **n.** (pl. **-os**) a size of book page that results from folding each printed sheet into sixteen leaves (thirty-two pages).
– ORIGIN C17: from L. *sexto decimo*, ablative of *sextus decimus* 'sixteenth'.

**sexton** • **n.** a person who looks after a church and churchyard, typically acting as bell-ringer and gravedigger.
– ORIGIN ME: from Anglo-Norman Fr. *segrestein*, from med. L. *sacristanus* (see SACRISTAN).

**sexton beetle** • **n.** another term for BURYING BEETLE.

**sex tourism** • **n.** travel abroad with the aim of taking advantage of the lack of restrictions on sexual activity and prostitution in some countries.
– DERIVATIVES **sex tourist** n.

**sextuple** /ˈsɛkstjʊp(ə)l, sɛksˈtjuːp(ə)l/ • **adj. 1** consisting of six parts or elements. **2** six times as much or as many. • **v.** increase or be increased sixfold. • **n.** a sixfold number or amount.
– DERIVATIVES **sextuply** adv.
– ORIGIN C17: from med. L. *sextuplus*, formed irregularly from L. *sex* 'six', on the pattern of late L. *quintuplus* 'quintuple'.

**sextuplet** /ˈsɛkstjʊplɪt, sɛksˈtjuːplɪt/ • **n. 1** each of six children born at one birth. **2** Music a group of six notes to be performed in the time of four.
– ORIGIN C19: from SEXTUPLE, on the pattern of words such as *triplet*.

**sexual** • **adj. 1** relating to the instincts, physiological processes, and activities connected with physical attraction or intimate physical contact between individuals. **2** of or relating to the two sexes or to gender. **3** (of reproduction) involving the fusion of gametes. ➤ Biology being of one sex or the other; capable of sexual reproduction.
– DERIVATIVES **sexualization** (also **-isation**) n. **sexualize** (also **-ise**) v. **sexually** adv.

**sexual harassment** • **n.** the repeated making of unwanted sexual advances or obscene remarks to a person, especially in a workplace.

**sexual intercourse** • **n.** sexual contact between individuals involving penetration, especially the insertion of a man's erect penis into a woman's vagina culminating in orgasm and the ejaculation of semen.

**sexuality** • **n.** (pl. **-ies**) capacity for sexual feelings. ➤ a person's sexual orientation or preference. ➤ sexual activity.

**sexual politics** • **pl. n.** [treated as sing.] relations between the sexes regarded in terms of power.

**sexual selection** • **n.** Biology natural selection arising through preference by one sex for certain characteristics in individuals of the other sex.

**sex worker** • **n.** euphemistic a prostitute.

**sexy** • **adj.** (**-ier**, **-iest**) **1** sexually attractive or exciting. ➤ sexually aroused. **2** informal very exciting or appealing.
– DERIVATIVES **sexily** adv. **sexiness** n.

**Seychellois** /seɪʃɛlˈwɑː/ • **n.** a native or inhabitant of the Seychelles. • **adj.** of or relating to the Seychelles.

**Seyfert galaxy** /ˈseɪfəːt/ • **n.** Astronomy a galaxy of a type characterized by a bright compact core showing strong infrared emission.
– ORIGIN C20: named after the Amer. astronomer Carl K. *Seyfert*.

**sez** • **v.** non-standard spelling of 'says'.

**SF** • **abbrev. 1** Finland (international vehicle registration). [from Finnish *Suomi* + Swed. *Finland*.] **2** science fiction. **3** Sinn Fein.

**sf** • **abbrev.** Music sforzando.

**SFA** • **abbrev. 1** Scottish Football Association. **2** (in the UK) Securities and Futures Authority.

**sforzando** /sfɔːˈtsandəʊ/ (also **sforzato** /-ˈtsɑːtəʊ/) • **adv. & adj.** Music with sudden emphasis.
– ORIGIN Ital., lit. 'using force'.

**sfumato** /sfʊˈmɑːtəʊ/ • **n.** Art the technique of allowing tones and colours to shade gradually into one another.
– ORIGIN C19: Ital., lit. 'shaded off', past part. of *sfumare*.

**SFX** • **abbrev.** special effects.
– ORIGIN *FX* representing a pronunc. of *effects*.

**sfz** • **abbrev.** Music sforzando.

**SG** • **abbrev. 1** Law Solicitor General. **2** Physics specific gravity.

**Sg** • **symb.** the chemical element seaborgium.

**sgd** • **abbrev.** signed.

**SGML** • **abbrev.** Computing Standard Generalized Mark-up Language, a system for encoding electronic texts so that they can be displayed in any desired format.

**SGP** • **abbrev.** Singapore (international vehicle registration).

**sgraffito** /sgraˈfiːtəʊ/ • **n.** (pl. **sgraffiti** /-ti/) a form of decoration made by scratching through a surface to reveal a lower layer of a contrasting colour.
– ORIGIN C18: Ital., lit. 'scratched away', past part. of *sgraffiare*.

**Sgt** • **abbrev.** Sergeant.

**sh.** • **abbrev.** Brit. shilling(s).

**Shabbat** /ʃaˈbat/ • **n.** (among Sephardic Jews and in Israel) the Sabbath.
– ORIGIN from Heb. *šabbāṯ*.

**Shabbos** /ˈʃabəs/ (also **Shabbes**) • **n.** (among Ashkenazic Jews) the Sabbath.
– ORIGIN Yiddish, from Heb. *šabbāṯ*.

**shabby** • **adj.** (**-ier**, **-iest**) **1** worn out or dilapidated. ➤ dressed in old or worn clothes. **2** mean and unfair.
– DERIVATIVES **shabbily** adv. **shabbiness** n.
– ORIGIN C17: from dial. *shab* 'scab' (from a Gmc base meaning 'itch') + **-Y**[1].

**shack** • **n.** a roughly built hut or cabin. • **v.** (**shack up**) informal live with someone as a lover.
– ORIGIN C19: perh. from Mexican *jacal*, Nahuatl *xacatli* 'wooden hut'.

**shackle** • **n. 1** (**shackles**) a pair of fetters connected by a chain, used to fasten a prisoner's wrists or ankles together. ➤ restraints or impediments. **2** a metal link, typically U-shaped, closed by a bolt and used to secure a chain or rope to something. • **v. 1** chain with shackles. **2** restrain; limit.
– ORIGIN OE *sc(e)acul* 'fetter', of Gmc origin.

**shacky** • **adj.** N. Amer. informal dilapidated; ramshackle.

**shad** • **n.** (pl. same or **shads**) an edible herring-like marine fish that enters rivers to spawn. [Genera *Alosa* and *Caspialosa*: several species.]
– ORIGIN OE *sceadd*, of unknown origin.

**shadbush** (also **shadblow**) • **n.** North American term for JUNEBERRY.
– ORIGIN C19: so named because it flowers at the same time as shad are found in the rivers.

**shadchan** /ˈʃadxən, ˈʃɒd-/ • **n.** (pl. same /ˈʃadxɛn/,

**shadchanim** /'ʃadxənɪm/, or **shadchans**) a Jewish professional matchmaker.
– ORIGIN from Yiddish *shadkhn*, based on Heb. *šiddēḵ* 'negotiate'.

**shaddock** /'ʃadək/ ● n. another term for **POMELO**.
– ORIGIN C17: named after Captain *Shaddock*, who introduced it to the West Indies.

**shade** ● n. **1** comparative darkness and coolness caused by shelter from direct sunlight. **2** a position of relative inferiority or obscurity. **3** a colour, especially with regard to how light or dark it is. ➤ a slight degree of difference between colours. **4** a slightly differing variety: *all shades of opinion*. **5** a slight amount. **6** a lampshade. **7** N. Amer. a screen or blind on a window. **8** (**shades**) informal sunglasses. **9** poetic/literary a ghost. ➤ (**the Shades**) the underworld. ● v. **1** screen from direct light. ➤ cover, moderate, or exclude the light of. **2** darken or colour with parallel pencil lines or a block of colour. **3** informal narrowly win. **4** reduce or decline in amount, rate, or price.
– PHRASES **shades of** —— suggestive or reminiscent of someone or something.
– DERIVATIVES **shadeless** adj. **shader** n.
– ORIGIN OE *sc(e)adu*, of Gmc origin; cf. **SHADOW**.

**shading** ● n. **1** the representation of light and shade on a drawing or map. **2** a very slight variation. **3** something providing shade.

**shadoof** /ʃə'du:f/ ● n. a pole with a bucket and counterpoise used especially in Egypt for raising water.
– ORIGIN C19: from Egyptian Arab. *šādūf*.

**shadow** ● n. **1** a dark area or shape produced by a body coming between light rays and a surface. ➤ partial or complete darkness. ➤ a dark patch or area. **2** an air or expression of sadness and gloom. **3** a position of relative inferiority or obscurity. **4** [with neg.] the slightest trace. **5** a weak or inferior remnant or version of something. **6** an inseparable attendant or companion. ➤ a person secretly following and observing another. **7** [as modifier] Brit. denoting the opposition counterpart of a government minister. ● v. **1** envelop in shadow; cast a shadow over. **2** follow and observe secretly. ➤ accompany (a worker) in their daily activities for experience of or insight into a job.
– DERIVATIVES **shadower** n. **shadowiness** n. **shadowless** adj. **shadowy** adj. (**-ier**, **-iest**).
– ORIGIN OE *scead(u)we* (n.), oblique case of *sceadu* (see **SHADE**), *sceadwian* 'screen or shield from attack', of Gmc origin.

**shadow-box** ● v. spar with an imaginary opponent as a form of training.

**shadow economy** ● n. Economics illicit economic activity existing alongside a country's official economy, e.g. black market transactions and undeclared work.

**shadowgraph** ● n. **1** an image formed by the shadow of an object on a surface. **2** an image formed when light shone through a fluid is refracted differently by regions of different density. **3** a radiograph.

**shadowland** ● n. poetic/literary **1** a place in shadow. **2** an indeterminate borderland between places or states.

**shadow price** ● n. Economics the estimated price of something for which no market price exists.

**shadow stitch** ● n. an embroidery stitch worked on the reverse side of sheer materials so as to show through in a shadowy way.

**shadow theatre** ● n. a display in which the shadows of flat jointed puppets are cast on a screen which is viewed by the audience from the other side.

**shady** ● adj. (**-ier**, **-iest**) **1** situated in or full of shade. **2** giving shade. **3** informal of doubtful honesty or legality.
– DERIVATIVES **shadily** adv. **shadiness** n.

**shaft** ● n. **1** a long, narrow part or section forming the handle of a tool or club, the body of a spear or arrow, or similar. ➤ an arrow or spear. ➤ a column, especially the part between the base and capital. ➤ a long cylindrical rotating rod for the transmission of motive power in a machine. ➤ each of the pair of poles between which a horse is harnessed to a vehicle. **2** a ray of light or bolt of lightning. **3** a sudden flash of a quality or feeling. ➤ a witty, wounding, or provoking remark. **4** vulgar slang a man's penis. **5** (**the shaft**) N. Amer. informal harsh or unfair treatment. **6** a long, narrow, typically vertical hole giving access to a mine, accommodating a lift, etc. ● v. **1** (of light) shine in beams. **2** vulgar slang (of a man) have sexual intercourse with. **3** informal treat harshly or unfairly.
– DERIVATIVES **shafted** adj.
– ORIGIN OE *scæft*, *sceaft* 'handle, pole', of Gmc origin; perh. rel. to **SCEPTRE**.

**shafting** ● n. a system of shafts for transmitting motive power in a machine.

**shag**[1] ● n. **1** a carpet or rug with a long, rough pile. ➤ [as modifier] (of pile) long and rough. ➤ cloth with a velvet nap on one side. **2** a thick, tangled hairstyle. **3** coarse cut tobacco.
– ORIGIN OE *sceacga* 'rough matted hair', of Gmc origin; rel. to **SHAW**[2].

**shag**[2] ● n. a cormorant with greenish-black plumage and a long curly crest in the breeding season. [*Phalacrocorax aristotelis*.] ➤ chiefly NZ any cormorant.
– ORIGIN C16: perh. a use of **SHAG**[1], with ref. to the bird's 'shaggy' crest.

**shag**[3] Brit. vulgar slang ● v. (**shagged**, **shagging**) have sexual intercourse with. ● n. an act of sexual intercourse.
– DERIVATIVES **shagger** n.
– ORIGIN C18: of unknown origin.

**shag**[4] ● n. a dance originating in the US, characterized by vigorous hopping from one foot to the other.
– ORIGIN 1930s: of obscure derivation; perh. from obs. *shag* 'waggle'.

**shag**[5] ● v. Baseball chase or catch (fly balls) for practice.
– ORIGIN C20: of unknown origin.

**shagged** ● adj. Brit. informal exhausted. ➤ damaged or ruined.

**shaggy** ● adj. (**-ier**, **-iest**) (of hair or fur) long, thick, and unkempt. ➤ having shaggy hair or fur. ➤ of or having a covering resembling shaggy hair.
– PHRASES **shaggy-dog story** a long, rambling joke, amusing only because it is absurdly inconsequential.
– DERIVATIVES **shaggily** adv. **shagginess** n.

**shagreen** /ʃa'gri:n/ ● n. **1** sharkskin used for decoration or as an abrasive. **2** untanned leather with a rough granulated surface.
– ORIGIN C17: var. of **CHAGRIN** in the sense 'rough skin'.

**shah** /ʃɑ:/ ● n. a title of the former monarch of Iran.
– DERIVATIVES **shahdom** n.
– ORIGIN C16: from Pers. *šāh*, from Old Pers. *ḵšāyaṯiya* 'king'.

**shahada** /ʃa'hɑ:da/ ● n. the Muslim profession of faith ('there is no god but Allah, and Muhammad is the messenger of Allah').
– ORIGIN from Arab. *šahāda* 'testimony, evidence'.

**shahtoosh** /ʃɑ:'tu:ʃ/ ● n. high-quality fabric made from the wool of the chiru, an endangered Tibetan antelope. ➤ a shawl made from this fabric.
– ORIGIN C19: via Punjabi from Pers. *šāh* 'king' + Kashmiri *tośa* 'fine shawl material'.

**Shaitan** /ʃeɪ'tɑ:n/ ● n. (in Muslim countries) Satan or an evil spirit.
– ORIGIN from Arab. *šaytān*.

**shake** ● v. (past **shook**; past part. **shaken**) **1** tremble or vibrate or cause to do so. ➤ tremble uncontrollably with strong emotion. **2** move forcefully or quickly up and down or to and fro. ➤ remove from something by shaking. ➤ brandish in anger or as a warning. **3** (often **shake someone/thing off**) informal get rid of or put an end to. **4** shock or astonish. ➤ cause a change of mood by shocking or disturbing. ➤ weaken or impair (confidence, a belief, etc.). ● n. **1** an act of shaking. ➤ an amount sprinkled from a container. **2** informal a milkshake. **3** (**the shakes**) informal a fit of trembling or shivering. **4** Music a trill.
– PHRASES **get** (or **give someone**) **a fair shake** N. Amer. informal get (or give someone) fair treatment. **in two shakes** (**of a lamb's tail**) informal very quickly. **no great shakes** informal not very good or significant. **shake a leg** informal make a start; rouse oneself.
– PHRASAL VERBS **shake down** settle down. **shake someone down** N. Amer. informal extort money from someone. **shake on** informal confirm (an agreement) by shaking

hands. **shake someone up** rouse someone from lethargy or apathy. **shake something up** make radical changes to the structure of an institution or system. **be shook on** Austral./NZ be keen on or enthusiastic about.
– ORIGIN OE *sc(e)acan* (v.), of Gmc origin.

**shakedown** • n. informal, chiefly N. Amer. **1** a radical change or restructuring. **2** a thorough search. **3** a swindle. **4** a test of a new product or model. **5** a makeshift bed.

**shake hole** • n. another term for **SINKHOLE**.

**shaken** past participle of **SHAKE**.

**shaken baby syndrome** • n. a condition characterized by cranial injury, retinal haemorrhage, etc. observed in infants who have been violently jolted.

**shaker** • n. **1** a container used for mixing ingredients by shaking. ➤a container with a pierced top from which a powder is poured by shaking. **2** (**Shaker**) a member of an American Christian sect living simply in celibate mixed communities. [so named from the wild, ecstatic movements engaged in during worship.] ➤[as modifier] denoting a style of elegantly functional furniture traditionally produced by Shakers.
– DERIVATIVES **Shakeress** n. **Shakerism** n.

**Shakespearean** /ʃeɪk'spɪərɪən/ (also **Shakespearian**) • adj. of, relating to, or in the style of William Shakespeare or his works. • n. an expert in or student of Shakespeare's works.

**shake-up** (also **shake-out**) • n. informal a radical reorganization.

**shako** /'ʃeɪkəʊ, 'ʃakəʊ/ • n. (pl. **-os**) a cylindrical or conical military hat with a peak and a plume or pompom.
– ORIGIN C19: via Fr. from Hungarian *csákó (süveg)* 'peaked (cap)', from *csák* 'peak', from Ger. *Zacken* 'spike'.

**Shakti** /ʃʌk'tiː/ (also **Sakti**) • n. Hinduism the female principle of divine energy.
– ORIGIN from Sanskrit *śakti* 'power, divine energy'.

**shakuhachi** /ˌʃakʊ'hatʃi/ • n. (pl. **shakuhachis**) a Japanese bamboo flute, held vertically when played.
– ORIGIN C19: Japanese, from *shaku*, a measure of length (approx. 0.33 metre) + *hachi* 'eight (tenths)'.

**shaky** • adj. (**-ier**, **-iest**) **1** shaking or trembling. **2** unstable. ➤not safe or reliable.
– DERIVATIVES **shakily** adv. **shakiness** n.

**shale** • n. soft finely stratified sedimentary rock formed from consolidated mud or clay.
– DERIVATIVES **shaly** (also **shaley**) adj.
– ORIGIN C18: prob. from Ger. *Schale*; rel. to Engl. dial. *shale* 'dish' (see **SCALE**[2]).

**shale oil** • n. mineral oil distilled from bituminous shale.

**shall** • modal v. (3rd sing. present **shall**) **1** (in the first person) expressing the future tense. **2** expressing a strong assertion or intention. **3** expressing an instruction or command. **4** used in questions indicating offers or suggestions.
– ORIGIN OE *sceal*, of Gmc origin, from a base meaning 'owe'.

**shallop** /'ʃaləp/ • n. chiefly historical a light sailing boat used in shallow waters.
– ORIGIN C16: from Fr. *chaloupe*, from Du. *sloep* 'sloop'.

**shallot** /ʃə'lɒt/ • n. **1** a small onion-like bulb, used in cookery and pickling. **2** the plant which produces these bulbs. [*Allium ascalonicum*.]
– ORIGIN C17: shortening of *eschalot*, from Fr. *eschalotte*, alt. of OFr. *eschaloigne* (in Anglo-Norman Fr. *scaloun*: see **SCALLION**).

**shallow** • adj. **1** of little depth. **2** not showing, requiring, or capable of serious thought. • n. (**shallows**) a shallow area of water. • v. become shallow.
– DERIVATIVES **shallowly** adv. **shallowness** n.
– ORIGIN ME: obscurely rel. to **SHOAL**[2].

**shalom** /ʃə'lɒm/ • exclam. used as salutation by Jews at meeting or parting.
– ORIGIN from Heb. *šālōm* 'peace'.

**shalt** archaic second person singular of **SHALL**.

**shalwar** /ʃʌl'wɑː/ • n. variant spelling of **SALWAR**.

**sham** • n. **1** a person or thing that is not what they are purported to be. **2** pretence. • adj. bogus; false. • v. (**shammed**, **shamming**) **1** falsely present something as the truth. **2** pretend to be or to be experiencing.
– DERIVATIVES **shammer** n.
– ORIGIN C17: perh. a north. Engl. dial. var. of **SHAME**.

**shaman** /'ʃamən, 'ʃeɪm-/ • n. (pl. **shamans**) a person regarded as having access to, and influence in, the world of good and evil spirits, especially among some peoples of northern Asia and North America.
– DERIVATIVES **shamanic** /ʃə'manɪk/ adj. **shamanism** n. **shamanist** n. & adj. **shamanistic** adj. **shamanize** (also **-ise**) v.
– ORIGIN C17: from Ger. *Schamane* and Russ. *shaman*, from Tungus *šaman*.

**shamateur** • n. derogatory a sports player who makes money from sporting activities though classified as amateur.
– DERIVATIVES **shamateurism** n.
– ORIGIN C19: blend of **SHAM** and **AMATEUR**.

**shamba** /'ʃambə/ • n. (in East Africa) a cultivated plot of ground.
– ORIGIN from Kiswahili.

**shamble** • v. move with a slow, shuffling, awkward gait. • n. a shambling gait.
– ORIGIN C16: prob. from dial. *shamble* 'ungainly', perh. from the phr. *shamble legs*, with ref. to the legs of trestle tables (typical of meat markets: see **SHAMBLES**).

**shambles** • n. **1** informal a chaotic state. **2** archaic a butcher's slaughterhouse. **3** a scene of carnage.
– ORIGIN ME (in the sense 'meat market'): pl. of earlier *shamble* 'stool, stall', of W. Gmc origin, from L. *scamellum*, dimin. of *scamnum* 'bench'.

**shambly** • adj. informal **1** ramshackle. **2** awkward; ungainly.

**shambolic** • adj. informal, chiefly Brit. chaotic, disorganized, or mismanaged.
– ORIGIN 1970s: from **SHAMBLES**, prob. on the pattern of *symbolic*.

**shame** • n. **1** a feeling of humiliation or distress caused by the consciousness of wrong or foolish behaviour. **2** dishonour. ➤a person or thing bringing dishonour. **3** a regrettable or unfortunate thing. • v. cause to feel ashamed.
– PHRASES **put someone to shame** shame someone by outdoing or surpassing them. **shame on you!** you should be ashamed.
– ORIGIN OE *sc(e)amu* (n.), *sc(e)amian* 'feel shame', of Gmc origin.

**shamefaced** • adj. showing shame.
– DERIVATIVES **shamefacedly** adv. **shamefacedness** n.
– ORIGIN C16 (in the sense 'modest, shy'): alt. of archaic *shamefast*, by assoc. with **FACE**.

**shameful** • adj. worthy of or causing shame.
– DERIVATIVES **shamefully** adv. **shamefulness** n.

**shameless** • adj. showing a lack of shame.
– DERIVATIVES **shamelessly** adv. **shamelessness** n.

**shamisen** • n. variant spelling of **SAMISEN**.

**shammy** (also **shammy leather**) • n. (pl. **-ies**) informal term for **CHAMOIS** (in sense 2).
– ORIGIN C18: a phonetic spelling.

**shampoo** • n. **1** a liquid preparation for washing the hair. ➤a similar substance for cleaning a carpet, car, etc. **2** an act of washing with shampoo. • v. (**shampoos**, **shampooed**) wash or clean with shampoo.
– ORIGIN C18 (in the sense 'massage'): from Hindi *cāṃpo!* 'press!', imper. of *cāṃpnā*.

**shamrock** • n. a low-growing clover-like plant with three-lobed leaves, the national emblem of Ireland. [*Trifolium minus* and other species.]
– ORIGIN C16: from Ir. *seamróg* 'trefoil' (dimin. of *seamar* 'clover').

**shamus** /'ʃeɪməs/ • n. N. Amer. informal a private detective.
– ORIGIN 1920s: of unknown origin.

**Shan** /ʃɑːn/ • n. (pl. same or **Shans**) **1** a member of a people living mainly in northern Burma (Myanmar) and adjacent parts of China. **2** the language of this people, related to Thai.
– ORIGIN from Burmese.

**shandy** • n. (pl. **-ies**) beer mixed with lemonade or ginger

beer.
– ORIGIN C19: abbrev. of *shandygaff*, in the same sense, of unknown origin.

**Shangaan** /ˈʃaŋgɑːn/ ● **n.** (pl. same or **Shangaans**) **1** a member of the Tsonga people of southern Africa. **2** the Bantu language of this people.
– ORIGIN prob. named after the founding chief *Soshangane*.

**shanghai**[1] /ʃaŋˈhʌɪ/ ● **v.** (**shanghais**, **shanghaied**, **shanghaiing**) **1** historical force to join a ship's crew by underhand means. **2** informal coerce or trick into a place or action.
– ORIGIN C19: from *Shanghai*, a major Chinese seaport.

**shanghai**[2] /ʃaŋˈhʌɪ/ Austral./NZ ● **n.** (pl. **shanghais**) a catapult. ● **v.** (**shanghais**, **shanghaied**, **shanghaiing**) shoot with or as with a catapult.
– ORIGIN C19: prob. an alt. of Scots dial. *shangan* 'a stick cleft at one end'.

**Shangri-La** /ˌʃaŋgrɪˈlɑː/ ● **n.** an imaginary earthly paradise.
– ORIGIN the name of a Tibetan utopia in James Hilton's *Lost Horizon* (1933), from *Shangri* (an invented name) + Tibetan *la* 'mountain pass'.

**shank** ● **n. 1** a person's leg, especially the lower part. ➤the lower part of an animal's foreleg, especially as a cut of meat. **2** a long narrow part of a tool connecting the handle to the operational end. ➤the stem of a key, spoon, anchor, etc. ➤the straight part of a nail or fish hook. **3** a part by which something is attached to something else. **4** the band of a ring. **5** the narrow middle of the sole of a shoe. ● **v.** Golf strike (a ball) with the heel of the club.
– DERIVATIVES **-shanked** adj.
– ORIGIN OE *sceanca*, of W. Gmc origin.

**Shanks's pony** (also **Shanks's mare**) ● **n.** one's own legs as a means of conveyance.
– ORIGIN C18: first recorded as *shanks-nag* in R. Fergusson's *Poems* (1785).

**shanny** ● **n.** (pl. **-ies**) a small greenish-brown blenny. [*Blennius pholis*.]
– ORIGIN C19: rel. to earlier *shan*, of unknown origin.

**shan't** ● **contr.** shall not.

**shantung** /ʃanˈtʌŋ/ ● **n.** a soft dress fabric spun from tussore silk.
– ORIGIN C19: from *Shantung* in China, where it was orig. made.

**shanty**[1] ● **n.** (pl. **-ies**) a small, crudely built shack.
– ORIGIN C19: perh. from Canad. Fr. *chantier* 'lumberjack's cabin, logging camp'.

**shanty**[2] (also **chanty** or **sea shanty**) ● **n.** (pl. **-ies**) a song with alternating solo and chorus, of a kind originally sung by sailors working together.
– ORIGIN C19: prob. from Fr. *chantez!* 'sing!', imper. pl. of *chanter*.

**shantyman** ● **n.** (pl. **-men**) N. Amer. a lumberjack.

**shanty town** ● **n.** a deprived area consisting of large numbers of shanty dwellings.

**SHAPE** ● **abbrev.** Supreme Headquarters Allied Powers Europe.

**shape** ● **n. 1** the external form or appearance of someone or something; the outline of an area or figure. ➤a specific form or guise assumed by someone or something. ➤a piece of material, paper, etc., made or cut in a particular form. **2** the condition or state of someone or something. ➤the distinctive nature or qualities of something. **3** definite or orderly arrangement. ● **v. 1** give a particular shape or form to. ➤make (something) fit the form of something else. **2** determine the nature of. **3** (often **shape up**) develop in a particular way. **4** (**shape up**) become physically fit. ➤(**shape something up**) informal improve something. **5** form or produce (a sound or words).
– PHRASES **in (good) shape** in good physical condition. **in the shape of** by way of. **lick** (or **knock** or **whip**) **someone/thing into shape** act forcefully to bring someone or something into a better state. **out of shape 1** not having its usual or original shape. **2** in poor physical condition. **take shape** assume a distinct form.
– DERIVATIVES **shapable** (also **shapeable**) adj. **shaped** adj. **shaper** n.
– ORIGIN OE *gesceap* 'external form', also 'creation', *sceppan* 'create', of Gmc origin.

**shapeless** ● **adj.** lacking definite or attractive shape.
– DERIVATIVES **shapelessly** adv. **shapelessness** n.

**shapely** ● **adj.** (**-ier**, **-iest**) having an attractive or well-proportioned shape.
– DERIVATIVES **shapeliness** n.

**shape-shifter** ● **n.** an imaginary being who is able to change their physical form at will.
– DERIVATIVES **shape-shifting** n. & adj.

**shard** ● **n.** a sharp piece of broken ceramic, metal, glass, etc.
– ORIGIN OE *sceard* 'gap, notch, potsherd', of Gmc origin; rel. to **SHEAR**.

**share**[1] ● **n. 1** a part or portion of a larger amount which is divided among or contributed by a number of people. ➤any of the equal parts into which a company's capital is divided. ➤part-ownership of property. **2** the allotted or due amount of something expected to be had or done. ➤a contribution to something. ● **v. 1** have a share of with another or others. ➤(often **share something out**) give a share of (something) to another or others. ➤possess in common with others. ➤(**share in**) have a part in (an activity). **2** tell someone about.
– PHRASES **share and share alike** have or receive an equal share.
– DERIVATIVES **shareable** (also **sharable**) adj. **sharer** n.
– ORIGIN OE *scearu*, of Gmc origin; rel. to **SHEAR**.

**share**[2] ● **n.** short for **PLOUGHSHARE**.

**sharecropper** ● **n.** chiefly N. Amer. a tenant farmer who gives a part of each crop as rent.
– DERIVATIVES **sharecrop** v. (**-cropped**, **-cropping**).

**share-farmer** ● **n.** chiefly Austral./NZ a tenant farmer who receives a share of the profits from the owner.

**shareholder** ● **n.** an owner of shares in a company.
– DERIVATIVES **shareholding** n.

**share option** ● **n.** an option for an employee to buy shares in their company at a discount or at a stated fixed price.

**shareware** ● **n.** Computing software that is available free of charge and often distributed informally for evaluation.

**sharia** /ʃəˈriːə/ (also **shariah** or **shariat** /ʃəˈriːət/) ● **n.** Islamic canonical law based on the teachings of the Koran and the traditions of the Prophet.
– ORIGIN from Arab. *šarīʿa*; the var. *shariat* from Urdu and Pers.

**sharif** /ʃəˈriːf/ ● **n. 1** a descendant of Muhammad through his daughter Fatima, entitled to wear a green turban or veil. **2** a Muslim ruler, magistrate, or religious leader.
– ORIGIN from Arab. *šarīf* 'noble', from *šarafa* 'be exalted'.

**shark**[1] ● **n. 1** a long-bodied cartilaginous marine fish, typically predatory and voracious, with a prominent dorsal fin. [Many species in the subclass Elasmobranchii.] **2** a small black SE Asian freshwater fish. [*Labeo bicolor* and *Morulius chrysophekadion*.] **3** a light greyish-brown moth. [*Cucullia umbratica*.]
– ORIGIN ME: of unknown origin.

**shark**[2] ● **n.** informal **1** a person who exploits or swindles others. **2** US an expert in a specified field.
– ORIGIN C16: perh. from Ger. *Schurke* 'worthless rogue', influenced by **SHARK**[1].

**sharkskin** ● **n.** a stiff, slightly lustrous synthetic fabric.

**sharon fruit** /ˈʃɛːr(ə)n, ˈʃar(ə)n/ ● **n.** a persimmon, especially of an orange variety grown in Israel.
– ORIGIN from *Sharon*, a fertile coastal plain in Israel.

**sharp** ● **adj. 1** having an edge or point able to cut or pierce something. ➤tapering to a point or edge. ➤(of sand or gravel) composed of angular grains. **2** producing a sudden, piercing sensation or effect. **3** (of a food, taste, or smell) acidic and intense. **4** (of a sound) sudden and penetrating. **5** (of words or a speaker) critical or hurtful. ➤(of an emotion or experience) painful. **6** clearly defined. **7** informal smart and stylish. **8** sudden and marked. ➤making a sudden change of direction: *a sharp bend*. **9** showing speed of perception, comprehension, or response. ➤quick to take advantage, especially in a dishonest way. **10** (of musical sound) above true or normal

pitch. ➤ [postpos.] (of a note) a semitone higher than a specified note. ➤ [postpos.] (of a key) having a sharp or sharps in the signature. ● **adv.** **1** punctually: *at 7.30 sharp.* **2** suddenly or abruptly. **3** above the true or normal pitch of musical sound. ● **n.** **1** a musical note raised a semitone above natural pitch. ➤ the sign (♯) indicating this. **2** a long, sharply pointed needle used for general sewing. ➤ a thing with a sharp edge or point. ● **v.** **1** [usu. as adj. **sharped**] US Music raise the pitch of (a note). **2** archaic cheat or swindle, especially at cards.
– DERIVATIVES **sharply** adv. **sharpness** n.
– ORIGIN OE *sc(e)arp*, of Gmc origin.

**Shar Pei** /ʃɑː ˈpeɪ/ ● **n.** (pl. **Shar Peis**) a compact squarely built dog of a Chinese breed, with a wrinkly skin and short bristly coat.
– ORIGIN 1970s: from Chin. *shā pí*, lit. 'sand skin'.

**sharpen** ● **v.** make or become sharp.
– DERIVATIVES **sharpener** n.

**sharper** ● **n.** informal a swindler, especially at cards.

**sharp-featured** ● **adj.** having well-defined facial features.

**sharpie** ● **n.** (pl. **-ies**) **1** a sharp-prowed, flat-bottomed New England sailing boat, with one or two masts each with a triangular sail. **2** informal, chiefly N. Amer. a dishonest and cunning person. **3** Austral. informal a young person with close-cropped hair and distinctive dress.

**sharpish** informal ● **adj.** fairly sharp. ● **adv.** chiefly Brit. quickly; soon.

**sharp practice** ● **n.** dishonest or barely honest dealings.

**sharp-set** ● **adj.** dated very hungry.

**sharpshooter** ● **n.** a person skilled in shooting.
– DERIVATIVES **sharpshooting** n. & adj.

**sharp-tongued** ● **adj.** given to using harsh or critical language.

**sharp-witted** ● **adj.** perceptive or intelligent.
– DERIVATIVES **sharp-wittedly** adv. **sharp-wittedness** n.

**shashlik** /ˈʃaʃlɪk/ ● **n.** (pl. same or **shashliks**) (in Asia and eastern Europe) a mutton kebab.
– ORIGIN from Russ. *shashlyk*, based on Turk. *şiş* 'spit, skewer'; cf. **SHISH KEBAB**.

**Shasta daisy** /ˈʃastə/ ● **n.** a tall Pyrenean plant bearing a single large white daisy-like flower. [*Leucanthemum maximum.*]
– ORIGIN C19: named after Mount *Shasta* in California.

**shastra** /ˈʃɑːstrə/ ● **n.** (in Hinduism and some forms of Buddhism) a work of sacred scripture.
– ORIGIN from Sanskrit *śāstra*.

**shat** past and past participle of **SHIT**.

**shatter** ● **v.** **1** break or cause to break suddenly and violently into pieces. ➤ damage or destroy. **2** upset greatly. **3** [usu. as adj. **shattered**] informal exhaust.
– DERIVATIVES **shatterer** n. **shattering** adj. **shatteringly** adv. **shatterproof** adj.
– ORIGIN ME: perh. imitative; cf. **SCATTER**.

**shave** ● **v.** **1** cut the hair off one's face with a razor. ➤ cut the hair off (a person or part of the body) with a razor. **2** cut (a thin slice or slices) off something. **3** reduce by a small amount. **4** pass or send something very close to. ● **n.** **1** an act of shaving. **2** a tool for shaving very thin slices or layers from wood.
– ORIGIN OE *sc(e)afan*, of Gmc origin.

**shaveling** /ˈʃeɪvlɪŋ/ ● **n.** archaic, derogatory a clergyman or priest with a tonsured head.

**shaven** ● **adj.** shaved.

**shaver** ● **n.** **1** an electric razor. **2** informal, dated a young lad.

**shavetail** ● **n.** US military slang, often derogatory a newly commissioned officer. ➤ informal an inexperienced person.
– ORIGIN from the early sense 'untrained pack animal' (identified by a shaven tail).

**Shavian** /ˈʃeɪvɪən/ ● **adj.** of, relating to, or in the manner of the Irish dramatist George Bernard Shaw (1856–1950) or his works or ideas. ● **n.** an admirer of Shaw or his work.
– ORIGIN from *Shavius* (Latinized form of *Shaw*) + **-AN**.

**shaving** ● **n.** **1** a thin strip cut off a surface. **2** [as modifier] used when shaving.

**Shavuoth** /ʃəˈvuːəs, ʃɑːvʊˈɒt/ (also **Shavuot**) ● **n.** a major Jewish festival held fifty days after the second day of Passover, originally a harvest festival but now also commemorating the giving of the Torah.
– ORIGIN from Heb. *šāḇūʿōṯ* 'weeks', with ref. to the weeks between Passover and Pentecost.

**shaw**[1] ● **n.** Farming, chiefly Scottish the parts of a potato plant above the ground.
– ORIGIN C19: perh. a var. of **SHOW**.

**shaw**[2] ● **n.** archaic, chiefly Scottish a thicket.
– ORIGIN OE *sceaga*, of Gmc origin; rel. to **SHAG**[1].

**shawl** ● **n.** a piece of fabric worn by women over the shoulders or head or wrapped round a baby.
– DERIVATIVES **shawled** adj.
– ORIGIN from Urdu and Pers. *šāl*, prob. from *Shāliāt*, the name of a town in India.

**shawl collar** ● **n.** a rounded collar without lapel notches that extends down the front of a garment.

**shawm** /ʃɔːm/ ● **n.** a medieval and Renaissance wind instrument, forerunner of the oboe, with a double reed in a wooden mouthpiece.
– ORIGIN ME: from OFr. *chalemel*, via L. from Gk *kalamos* 'reed'.

**Shawnee** /ʃɔːˈniː/ ● **n.** (pl. same or **Shawnees**) **1** a member of an American Indian people formerly living in the eastern US. **2** the Algonquian language of this people.
– ORIGIN the name in Delaware.

**shay** ● **n.** informal term for **CHAISE** (in sense 1).
– ORIGIN C18: back-form. from **CHAISE**, interpreted as pl.

**shaykh** ● **n.** variant spelling of **SHEIKH**.

**shazam** /ʃəˈzam/ ● **exclam.** used to introduce something extraordinary.
– ORIGIN 1940s: an invented word, used by conjurors.

**shchi** /ʃtʃiː/ ● **n.** a Russian cabbage soup.
– ORIGIN from Russ.

**she** ● **pron.** [third person sing.] **1** used to refer to a woman, girl, or female animal previously mentioned or easily identified. **2** used to refer to a ship, country, or other inanimate thing regarded as female. **3** any female person (in modern use, now largely replaced by 'anyone' or 'the person'). **4** Austral./NZ informal it; the state of affairs. ● **n.** a female; a woman.
– ORIGIN ME: prob. a phonetic development of the OE fem. personal pronoun *hēo, hīe*.

**shea** /ʃiː, ˈʃiːə/ ● **n.** a small tropical African tree bearing oily nuts. [*Vitellaria paradoxa* or *Butyrospermum parkii.*]
– ORIGIN C18: from Mande *sye*.

**shea butter** ● **n.** a fatty substance from the nuts of the shea tree, used in cosmetic skin preparations, food, etc.

**sheading** /ˈʃiːdɪŋ/ ● **n.** each of the six administrative divisions of the Isle of Man.
– ORIGIN C16: var. of *shedding* (from **SHED**[2]).

**sheaf** ● **n.** (pl. **sheaves**) **1** a bundle of grain stalks laid lengthways and tied together after reaping. **2** a bundle of objects, especially papers. ● **v.** bundle into sheaves.
– ORIGIN OE *scēaf*, of Gmc origin; rel. to **SHOVE**.

**shealing** ● **n.** variant spelling of **SHIELING**.

**shear** ● **v.** (past part. **shorn** or **sheared**) **1** cut the wool off (a sheep or other animal). ➤ cut off with scissors or shears. ➤ (**be shorn of**) have something cut off. **2** break off or cause to break off, owing to a structural strain. ● **n.** a strain produced by pressure in the structure of a substance, when its layers are laterally shifted in relation to each other.
– DERIVATIVES **shearer** n.
– ORIGIN OE *sceran*, of Gmc origin, from a base meaning 'divide, shear, shave'.

**shearling** ● **n.** a sheep that has been shorn once. ➤ wool or fleece from such a sheep. ➤ chiefly US a coat made from such wool.

**shears** (also **a pair of shears**) ● **pl. n.** a cutting instrument in which two blades move past each other, like very large scissors.
– ORIGIN OE *scēara* (pl.) 'scissors, cutting instrument', of Gmc origin; rel. to **SHEAR**.

**shearwater** ● **n.** **1** a long-winged seabird related to the petrels, often flying low over the water far from land. [*Puffinus* and other genera: many species.] **2** North American term for **SKIMMER** (in sense 2).

**sheath** ● **n.** (pl. **sheaths** /ʃiːðz, ʃiːθs/) **1** a cover for the blade of a knife or sword. **2** a structure in living tissue which closely envelops another. **3** a protective covering around an electric cable. **4** a condom. **5** (also **sheath dress**) a close-fitting dress.
– DERIVATIVES **sheathless** adj.
– ORIGIN OE *scǣth, scēath*, of Gmc origin; rel. to **SHED²**.

**sheathbill** ● **n.** a mainly white pigeon-like bird of sub-Antarctic islands, with a horny sheath around the base of the bill. [Genus *Chionis*.]

**sheathe** /ʃiːð/ ● **v.** **1** put (a knife or sword) into a sheath. **2** (often **be sheathed in**) encase in a close-fitting or protective covering.
– ORIGIN ME: from **SHEATH**.

**sheathing** /ˈʃiːðɪŋ/ ● **n.** protective casing or covering.

**sheath knife** ● **n.** a short knife similar to a dagger, carried in a sheath.

**sheave¹** ● **v.** a sheaf.
– ORIGIN C16: from **SHEAVES**.

**sheave²** ● **n.** a wheel with a groove for a rope to run on, as in a pulley block.
– ORIGIN ME: from a Gmc base meaning 'wheel, pulley'.

**sheaves** plural form of **SHEAF**.

**shebang** /ʃɪˈbaŋ/ ● **n.** **1** informal a matter, operation, or set of circumstances: *the whole shebang.* **2** N. Amer. archaic a rough hut or shelter.
– ORIGIN C19: of unknown origin.

**Shebat** /ˈʃiːbat/ ● **n.** variant of **SEBAT**.

**shebeen** /ʃɪˈbiːn/ ● **n.** (especially in Ireland, Scotland, and South Africa) an unlicensed establishment or private house selling alcoholic liquor.
– ORIGIN C18: from Anglo-Ir. *síbín*, from *séibe* 'mugful'.

**shed¹** ● **n.** a simple roofed structure, typically of wood and used for storage or to shelter animals. ➤a larger structure, typically with one or more sides open, for storing vehicles or machinery. ➤Austral./NZ an open-sided building for shearing sheep or milking cattle. ● **v.** (**shedded**, **shedding**) park (a vehicle) in a depot.
– ORIGIN C15: appar. a var. of **SHADE**.

**shed²** ● **v.** (**shedding**; past and past part. **shed**) **1** (of a plant) allow (leaves or fruit) to fall to the ground. ➤(of a reptile, insect, etc.) allow (its skin, shell, etc.) to come off, to be replaced by another growing underneath. ➤lose (hair) as a result of moulting, disease, or age. **2** take off (clothes). **3** discard. **4** cast or give off (light). **5** resist the absorption of. **6** accidentally drop or spill. **7** eliminate part of (an electrical power load) by disconnecting circuits.
– PHRASES **shed tears** cry.
– ORIGIN OE *sc(e)ādan* 'separate out (one selected group), divide', also 'scatter', of Gmc origin; cf. **SHEATH**.

**she'd** ● **contr.** she had; she would.

**shedder** ● **n.** **1** a person or thing that sheds something. **2** a female salmon after spawning.

**she-devil** ● **n.** a malicious or spiteful woman.

**shedload** ● **n.** Brit. informal a large amount or number.
– ORIGIN 1990s: from **SHED¹** + **LOAD**; perh. euphem. after **SHITLOAD**.

**sheen** ● **n.** a soft lustre on a surface. ● **v.** poetic/literary shine or cause to shine softly.
– ORIGIN C17: from obs. *sheen* 'beautiful, resplendent'; appar. rel. to **SHINE**.

**sheeny** ● **adj.** lustrous. ● **n.** N. Amer. offensive a Jewish person.

**sheep** ● **n.** (pl. same) **1** a domesticated ruminant mammal with a thick woolly coat, kept in flocks for its wool or meat. [*Ovis aries*.] ➤a wild mammal related to this, e.g. a bighorn. **2** a person who is too easily influenced or led. **3** a member of a minister's congregation.
– PHRASES **make sheep's eyes at** look at (someone) in a foolishly amorous way.
– DERIVATIVES **sheeplike** adj.
– ORIGIN OE *scēp, scǣp, scēap*, of W. Gmc origin; sense 3 with biblical allusion to Luke 15:6.

**sheep dip** ● **n.** **1** a liquid preparation for cleansing sheep of parasites or preserving their wool. **2** a place where sheep are dipped in this.

**sheepdog** ● **n.** **1** a dog trained to guard and herd sheep. **2** a dog of a breed suitable for this.

**sheepdog trials** ● **pl. n.** a public competitive display of the skills of sheepdogs.

**sheepfold** ● **n.** a pen for sheep.

**sheepish** ● **adj.** showing embarrassment from shame or shyness.
– DERIVATIVES **sheepishly** adv. **sheepishness** n.

**sheep run** ● **n.** (especially in Australia) an extensive tract of land for pasturing sheep.

**sheep's-bit** ● **n.** a blue-flowered plant resembling a scabious. [*Jasione montana*.]

**sheepshank** ● **n.** a knot used to shorten a rope, made by taking two bights of rope and securing them to the standing rope with two half hitches.

**sheepshead** ● **n.** (pl. same) a boldly marked edible fish of warm American waters. [*Archosargus probatocephalus* (Atlantic) and *Semicossyphus pulcher* (California).]

**sheepskin** ● **n.** **1** a sheep's skin with the wool on, especially when made into a garment or rug. **2** (in South Africa) a party with country dancing. [orig. held to celebrate sheep shearing.]

**sheep walk** ● **n.** Brit. a tract of land on which sheep are pastured.

**sheer¹** ● **adj.** **1** nothing other than; unmitigated: *sheer hard work.* **2** (of a cliff, wall, etc.) perpendicular or nearly so. **3** (of a fabric) very thin. ● **adv.** **1** perpendicularly. **2** archaic completely; right.
– DERIVATIVES **sheerly** adv. **sheerness** n.
– ORIGIN ME: prob. an alt. of dial. *shire* 'pure, clear', from the Gmc base of **SHINE**.

**sheer²** ● **v.** **1** (especially of a boat) swerve or change course quickly. **2** avoid or move away from an unpleasant topic. ● **n.** a sudden deviation from a course.
– ORIGIN C17: perh. from Mid. Low Ger. *scheren* 'to shear'.

**sheer³** ● **n.** the upward slope of a ship's lines towards the bow and stern.
– ORIGIN C17: prob. from **SHEAR**.

**sheer legs** ● **pl. n.** [treated as sing.] a hoisting apparatus made from poles joined at or near the top and separated at the bottom, used for masting ships and lifting heavy objects.

**sheet¹** ● **n.** **1** a large rectangular piece of cotton or other fabric, used on a bed to cover the mattress or as a layer beneath blankets. **2** a broad flat piece of metal or glass. **3** a rectangular piece of paper. ➤a quantity of text or data on a sheet of paper. ➤Printing a flat piece of paper as opposed to a reel of continuous paper, the pages of a book, or a folded map. ➤a set of unseparated postage stamps. **4** an extensive unbroken surface area of something. ➤a broad moving mass of flames or water. ● **v.** **1** cover with or wrap in a sheet of cloth. **2** (of rain) fall heavily.
– ORIGIN OE *scēte, sciete*, of Gmc origin; rel. to **SHOOT**.

**sheet²** Nautical ● **n.** **1** a rope attached to the lower corner of a sail. **2** (**sheets**) the space at the bow or stern of an open boat. ● **v.** (**sheet something in/out**) make a sail more or less taut. ➤(**sheet something home**) set a sail as flat as possible.
– PHRASES **two** (or **three**) **sheets to the wind** informal drunk.
– ORIGIN OE *scēata* 'lower corner of a sail', of Gmc origin; rel. to **SHEET¹**.

**sheet anchor** ● **n.** **1** an additional anchor for use in emergencies. **2** a dependable person or thing relied upon in the last resort.
– ORIGIN C15: perh. rel. to obs. *shot*, denoting two cables spliced together, later influenced by **SHEET²**.

**sheet bend** ● **n.** a method of temporarily fastening one rope through the loop of another.

**sheeting** ● **n.** material formed into or used as a sheet.

**sheet lightning** • n. lightning with its brightness diffused by reflection within clouds.

**sheet metal** • n. metal formed into thin sheets.

**sheet music** • n. **1** printed music, as opposed to performed or recorded music. **2** music published in single or interleaved sheets.

**Sheetrock** • n. US trademark plasterboard made of gypsum layered between sheets of heavy paper.

**Sheffield plate** • n. copper plated with silver, especially as produced in Sheffield from 1760 to 1840.

**sheikh** /ʃeɪk, ʃiːk/ (also **shaykh** or **sheik**) • n. **1** an Arab leader, especially the chief or head of a tribe, family, or village. **2** a leader in a Muslim community or organization.
– DERIVATIVES **sheikhdom** n.
– ORIGIN C16: based on Arab. *šayḵ* 'old man, sheikh', from *šāḵa* 'be or grow old'.

**sheila** • n. Austral./NZ informal a girl or woman.
– ORIGIN C19 (orig. as *shaler*): of unknown origin, later assimilated to the given name *Sheila*.

**shekel** /ˈʃɛk(ə)l/ • n. **1** the basic monetary unit of modern Israel, equal to 100 agora. **2** historical a silver coin and unit of weight used in ancient Israel and the Middle East. **3** (**shekels**) informal money; wealth.
– ORIGIN from Heb. *šeqel*, from *šāqal* 'weigh'.

**Shekinah** /ʃɪˈkʌɪnə/ (also **Shekhinah**) • n. Jewish & Christian Theology the glory of the divine presence, represented as light or interpreted (in Kabbalism) as a divine feminine aspect.
– ORIGIN C17: from late Heb., from *šākan* 'dwell, rest'.

**shelduck** /ˈʃɛldʌk/ • n. (pl. same or **shelducks**) a large goose-like duck with boldly marked plumage. [*Tadorna tadorna* and related species.]
– ORIGIN C18: prob. from dial. *sheld* 'pied' (rel. to MDu. *schillede* 'variegated') + **DUCK**[1]; the term *sheldrake* (sometimes used for the male) dates from ME.

**shelf**[1] • n. (pl. **shelves**) **1** a flat length of wood or rigid material attached to a wall or forming part of a piece of furniture, providing a surface for the storage or display of objects. **2** a ledge of rock or protruding strip of land. ➤a submarine bank, or a part of the continental shelf.
– PHRASES **off the shelf** not designed or made to order. **on the shelf 1** no longer useful or desirable. **2** past an age when one might expect to be married.
– DERIVATIVES **shelf-ful** n. (pl. **-fuls**). **shelf-like** adj.
– ORIGIN ME: from Mid. Low Ger. *schelf*; rel. to OE *scylfe* 'partition', *scylf* 'crag'.

**shelf**[2] Austral./NZ informal • n. (pl. **shelfs**) an informer. • v. inform upon.
– ORIGIN C20: prob. from the phr. *on the shelf* 'out of the way'.

**shelf life** • n. the length of time for which an item remains usable, edible, or saleable.

**shelf mark** • n. a notation on a book showing its place in a library.

**shell** • n. **1** the hard protective outer case of a mollusc or crustacean. ➤the thin outer covering of a bird's or reptile's egg. ➤the outer case of a nut kernel or seed. ➤the carapace of a tortoise, turtle, or terrapin. ➤the wing cases of a beetle. ➤the integument of an insect pupa or chrysalis. **2** an explosive artillery projectile or bomb. ➤a hollow metal or paper case used as a container for fireworks, explosives, or cartridges. ➤N. Amer. a cartridge. **3** something resembling or likened to a shell, especially a hollow case. **4** an outer form without substance. **5** the walls of an unfinished or gutted building. **6** a light racing boat. **7** the metal framework of a vehicle body. **8** an inner or roughly made coffin. **9** the handguard of a sword. **10** Physics each of a set of orbitals in an atom, occupied by electrons of similar energies. **11** Computing short for **SHELL PROGRAM**. • v. **1** bombard with shells. **2** remove the shell or pod from. **3** (**shell out**) informal pay a specified amount of money, especially an amount regarded as excessive.
– PHRASES **come out of one's shell** cease to be shy.
– DERIVATIVES **-shelled** adj. **shell-less** adj. **shell-like** adj. **shelly** adj.
– ORIGIN OE *scell* (n.), of Gmc origin; rel. to **SCALE**[1].

**she'll** • contr. she shall; she will.

**shellac** /ʃəˈlak/ • n. lac resin melted into thin flakes, used for making varnish. • v. (**shellacked**, **shellacking**) **1** [often as adj. **shellacked**] varnish with shellac. **2** N. Amer. informal defeat decisively.
– ORIGIN C17: from **SHELL** + **LAC**[1], translating Fr. *laque en écailles* 'lac in thin plates'.

**shellback** • n. N. Amer. informal an experienced sailor, especially one who has crossed the equator.

**shell bit** • n. a gouge-shaped boring bit.

**shell company** • n. a non-trading company used as a vehicle for various financial manoeuvres.

**shell egg** • n. an egg sold in its natural state in the shell.

**shellfire** • n. bombardment by shells.

**shellfish** • n. (pl. same) an aquatic shelled mollusc or crustacean, especially an edible one.

**shell game** • n. N. Amer. **1** another term for **THIMBLERIG**. **2** a deceptive and evasive action or ploy.

**shell heap** (also **shell mound**) • n. Archaeology a kitchen midden consisting mainly of shells.

**shell jacket** • n. an army officer's tight-fitting undress jacket reaching to the waist.

**shell lime** • n. fine-quality lime produced by roasting seashells.

**shell pink** • n. a delicate pale pink.

**shell program** • n. Computing a program providing an interface between the user and the operating system.

**shell shock** • n. psychological disturbance caused by prolonged exposure to active warfare.
– DERIVATIVES **shell-shocked** adj.

**shell suit** • n. a casual outfit consisting of a loose jacket and trousers with a soft lining and a shiny polyester outer shell.

**shell top** • n. a short sleeveless top, typically having a simple shape with a high neckline.

**shell-work** • n. ornamentation consisting of shells cemented on to a surface.

**Shelta** /ˈʃɛltə/ • n. an ancient secret language used by Irish and Welsh tinkers and gypsies, based on altered Irish or Gaelic words.
– ORIGIN C19: of unknown origin.

**shelter** • n. **1** a place giving protection from bad weather or danger. **2** a place providing food and accommodation for the homeless. **3** an animal sanctuary. **4** a shielded condition; protection. • v. **1** provide with shelter. ➤find refuge or take cover. **2** [often as adj. **sheltered**] prevent from having to do or face something difficult. **3** protect (income) from taxation.
– DERIVATIVES **shelterer** n. **shelterless** adj.
– ORIGIN C16: perh. an alt. of obs. *sheltron* 'phalanx', from OE *scieldtruma*, lit. 'shield troop'.

**shelter belt** • n. a line of trees or shrubs planted to protect an area from fierce weather.

**sheltered housing** (also **sheltered accommodation**) • n. Brit. accommodation for the elderly or handicapped consisting of private independent units with some shared facilities and a warden.

**shelterwood** • n. mature trees left standing to shelter saplings.

**sheltie** (also **shelty**) • n. (pl. **-ies**) a Shetland pony or sheepdog.
– ORIGIN C17: prob. representing an Orkney pronunc. of ON *Hjalti* 'Shetlander'.

**shelve**[1] • v. **1** place on a shelf. **2** abandon or defer (a plan or project). **3** fit with shelves.
– DERIVATIVES **shelver** n.
– ORIGIN C16 (in the sense 'project like a shelf'): from *shelves*, pl. of **SHELF**[1].

**shelve**[2] • v. (of ground) slope downwards.
– ORIGIN ME: origin uncertain; perh. from **SHELF**[1].

**shelves** plural form of **SHELF**[1].

**shelving** • n. shelves collectively.

**shemozzle** /ʃɪˈmɒz(ə)l/ (also **schemozzle**) • n. informal a muddle.
– ORIGIN C19: Yiddish, suggested by late Heb. *šel-lō'-mazzāl* 'of no luck'.

**shen** /ʃɛn/ ● **n.** (pl. same) (in Chinese thought) the spiritual element of a person's psyche.
– ORIGIN from Chin. *shén*.

**shenanigans** /ʃɪˈnanɪg(ə)nz/ ● **pl. n.** informal **1** secret or dishonest activity. **2** mischief.
– ORIGIN C19: of unknown origin.

**she-oak** ● **n.** another term for **CASUARINA**.

**Sheol** /ˈʃiːəʊl, ˈʃiːɒl/ ● **n.** the Hebrew underworld, abode of the dead.
– ORIGIN from Heb.

**shepherd** ● **n. 1** a person who tends sheep. **2** a member of the clergy providing spiritual care and guidance for a congregation. ● **v. 1** [usu. as noun **shepherding**] tend (sheep). **2** guide or direct somewhere. **3** give spiritual or other guidance to.
– DERIVATIVES **shepherdess** n.
– ORIGIN OE *scēaphierde*, from **SHEEP** + obs. *herd* 'herdsman'.

**shepherd dog** ● **n.** a sheepdog.

**shepherd's crook** ● **n.** a shepherd's staff with a hook at one end.

**shepherd's needle** ● **n.** a white-flowered plant of the parsley family, with long needle-shaped fruit. [*Scandix pecten-veneris*.]

**shepherd's pie** ● **n.** a dish of minced meat under a layer of mashed potato.

**shepherd's plaid** ● **n.** a small black-and-white check pattern. ➤ woollen cloth with this pattern.

**shepherd's purse** ● **n.** a white-flowered weed of the cabbage family, with triangular or heart-shaped seed pods. [*Capsella bursa-pastoris*.]

**sherardize** /ˈʃɛrədʌɪz/ (also **-ise**) ● **v.** coat (iron or steel) with zinc by heating it in contact with zinc dust.
– ORIGIN C20: from the name of the Engl. inventor *Sherard* Cowper-Coles + **-IZE**.

**Sheraton** /ˈʃɛrət(ə)n/ ● **adj.** (of furniture) designed by or in the simple, graceful style of the English furniture-maker Thomas Sheraton (1751–1806).

**sherbet** ● **n. 1** Brit. a flavoured sweet effervescent powder eaten alone or made into a drink. **2** (especially in Arab countries) a drink of sweet diluted fruit juices. **3** N. Amer. water ice; sorbet. **4** Austral. humorous beer.
– ORIGIN C17: from Turk. *şerbet*, Pers. *šerbet*, from Arab. *šarba* 'drink', from *šariba* 'to drink'; cf. **SYRUP**.

**sherd** /ʃəːd/ ● **n.** another term for **POTSHERD**.

**shereef** (also **sherif**) ● **n.** variant spelling of **SHARIF**.

**sheriff** ● **n. 1** (also **high sheriff**) (in England and Wales) the chief executive officer of the Crown in a county, having administrative and judicial functions. ➤ an honorary officer elected annually in some English towns. **2** (in Scotland) a judge. **3** US an elected officer in a county, responsible for keeping the peace.
– DERIVATIVES **sheriffdom** n. **sheriffhood** n. **sheriffship** n.
– ORIGIN OE *scīrgerēfa* (see **SHIRE**, **REEVE**[1]).

**sheriff court** ● **n.** (in Scotland) a court for civil cases, equivalent to a county court.

**sheriff-depute** ● **n.** (pl. **sheriffs-deputes**) historical (in Scotland) the chief judge of a county or district.

**sheriff principal** ● **n.** (pl. **sheriffs principal**) (in Scotland) a chief judge.

**Sherpa** /ˈʃəːpə/ ● **n.** (pl. same or **Sherpas**) a member of a Himalayan people living on the borders of Nepal and Tibet.
– ORIGIN from Tibetan *sharpa* 'inhabitant of an Eastern country'.

**sherry** ● **n.** (pl. **-ies**) a fortified wine originally and mainly from southern Spain.
– ORIGIN C16: alt. of archaic *sherris*, interpreted as pl., from Sp. (*vino de*) *Xeres* 'Xeres (wine)' (Xeres being the former name of the city of *Jerez de la Frontera*).

**she's** ● **contr.** she is; she has.

**Shetlander** /ˈʃɛtləndə/ ● **n.** a native or inhabitant of the Shetland Islands.

**Shetland lace** ● **n.** a black or white bobbin lace made from Shetland wool.

**Shetland pony** ● **n.** a pony of a small, hardy rough-coated breed.

**Shetland sheepdog** ● **n.** a small dog of a collie-like breed.

**Shevat** /ˈʃiːvat/ ● **n.** variant of **SEBAT**.

**shew** ● **v.** old-fashioned variant of **SHOW**.

**shewbread** /ˈʃəʊbrɛd/ ● **n.** twelve loaves placed every Sabbath in the Jewish Temple and eaten by the priests.
– ORIGIN C16: suggested by Ger. *Schaubrot*, representing Heb. *leḥem pānīm*, lit. 'bread of the face (of God)'.

**shh** (also **sh**) ● **exclam.** used to call for silence.
– ORIGIN C19: var. of **HUSH**.

**Shia** /ˈʃɪə/ (also **Shi'a**) ● **n.** (pl. same or **Shias**) one of the two main branches of Islam, regarding Ali, the fourth caliph, as Muhammad's first true successor. Compare with **SUNNI**. ➤ a Muslim who adheres to this branch of Islam.
– ORIGIN from Arab. *šīʿa* 'party (of Ali)'.

**shiatsu** /ʃɪˈatsuː/ ● **n.** a Japanese therapy based on the same principles as acupuncture, in which pressure is applied with the hands to points on the body.
– ORIGIN 1960s: Japanese, lit. 'finger pressure'.

**shibboleth** /ˈʃɪbəlɛθ/ ● **n.** a custom, principle, or belief distinguishing a particular class or group of people.
– ORIGIN C17: from Heb. *šibbōleṯ* 'ear of corn', used as a test of nationality by its difficult pronunc. (Judg. 12:6).

**shicer** /ˈʃʌɪsə/ ● **n.** Austral./NZ **1** informal a worthless person or thing, especially a swindler. **2** Mining an unproductive claim or mine.
– ORIGIN C19: from Ger. *Scheisser* 'contemptible person'.

**shicker** /ˈʃɪkə/ (also **shikker**) US & Austral./NZ informal ● **adj.** (also **shickered**, **shikkered**) drunk. ● **n.** a drunk.
– ORIGIN C19: from Yiddish *shiker*, from Heb. *šikkōr*, from *šākar* 'be drunk'.

**shied** past and past participle of **SHY**[2].

**shield** ● **n. 1** a broad piece of armour held by straps or a handle on one side, used for protection against blows or missiles. ➤ Heraldry a stylized representation of a shield used for displaying a coat of arms. **2** a sporting trophy consisting of an engraved metal plate mounted on a piece of wood. **3** a US police officer's badge. **4** Geology a large rigid area of Precambrian rock, unaffected by later crustal processes. **5** a person or thing providing protection. ➤ a protective plate, screen, or other structure. ● **v. 1** protect from a danger, risk, etc. ➤ enclose or screen (machinery) to protect the user. **2** prevent from being seen. **3** prevent or reduce the escape of sound, light, or other radiation from.
– DERIVATIVES **shieldless** adj.
– ORIGIN OE *scild* (n.), *scildan* (v.), of Gmc origin, from a base meaning 'divide, separate'.

**shield bug** ● **n.** a heteropterous bug with a flattened, shield-shaped body. [Many species in Pentatomidae and other families.]

**shield fern** ● **n.** a fern with circular shield-like scales protecting the spore cases. [*Polystichum* and other genera.]

**shield volcano** ● **n.** Geology a very broad volcano with gently sloping sides.

**shieling** /ˈʃiːlɪŋ/ (also **shealing**) ● **n.** Scottish **1** a hut used while pasturing animals. **2** an area of pasture.
– ORIGIN C16: from Scots *shiel* 'hut' (of unknown origin) + **-ING**[1].

**shift** /ʃɪft/ ● **v. 1** move or change or cause to move or change from one position to another. ➤ move one's body slightly due to discomfort. **2** Brit. informal move quickly. ➤ (**shift oneself**) Brit. informal move or rouse oneself. **3** Brit. remove (a stain). **4** informal sell (merchandise) quickly or in large quantities. **5** Brit. informal eat or drink hastily or in large amounts. **6** chiefly N. Amer. change gear. **7** archaic be evasive. ● **n. 1** a slight change in position, direction, or tendency. **2** a key used to switch between two sets of characters or functions on a keyboard. **3** N. Amer. a gear lever or gear-changing mechanism. **4** Building the positioning of successive rows of bricks so that their ends do not coincide. **5** each of two or more periods in which different groups of workers do the same jobs in relay. ➤ a group of people who work in this way. **6** a straight unwaisted dress. ➤ historical a long, loose undergarment. **7** archaic an

ingenious or devious device or stratagem.
– PHRASES **make shift** dated manage or contrive to do something. **shift for oneself** manage alone as best one can. **shift one's ground** change one's position in an argument.
– DERIVATIVES **shiftable** adj. **shifter** n.
– ORIGIN OE *sciftan* 'arrange, divide, apportion' (also ME 'change, replace'), of Gmc origin.

**shiftless** • adj. lazy, indolent, and lacking ambition.
– DERIVATIVES **shiftlessly** adv. **shiftlessness** n.

**shifty** • adj. (**-ier**, **-iest**) informal **1** deceitful or evasive. **2** constantly changing.
– DERIVATIVES **shiftily** adv. **shiftiness** n.

**shigella** /ʃɪˈgɛlə/ • n. (pl. same or **shigellae** /-iː/) a bacterium of a genus including some kinds responsible for dysentery. [Genus *Shigella*.]
– ORIGIN mod. L., from the name of the Japanese bacteriologist Kiyoshi *Shiga*, + the dimin. suffix *-ella*.

**shih-tzu** /ʃiːˈtsuː/ • n. a dog of a breed with long silky erect hair and short legs.
– ORIGIN 1920s: from Chin. *shizi* 'lion'.

**shiitake** /ʃɪˈtɑːkeɪ, ʃɪɪ-/ • n. an edible mushroom cultivated in Japan and China. [*Lentinus edodes*.]
– ORIGIN C19: from Japanese, from *shii*, denoting a kind of oak, + *take* 'mushroom'.

**Shiite** /ˈʃiːʌɪt/ (also **Shi'ite**) • n. an adherent of the Shia branch of Islam. • adj. of or relating to Shia.
– DERIVATIVES **Shiism** /ˈʃiːɪz(ə)m/ (also **Shi'ism**) n.

**shikar** /ʃɪˈkɑː/ • n. Indian hunting.
– ORIGIN from Urdu and Pers. *šikār*.

**shikker** • adj. & n. variant spelling of **SHICKER**.

**shiksa** /ˈʃɪksə/ • n. derogatory (used especially by Jews) a gentile girl or woman.
– ORIGIN C19: from Yiddish *shikse*, from Heb. *šiqṣāh* (from *šeqeṣ* 'detested thing' + the fem. suffix *-āh*).

**shill** N. Amer. informal • n. an accomplice of a hawker, gambler, or swindler who acts as an enthusiastic customer to entice others. • v. act as a shill.
– ORIGIN C20: prob. from earlier *shillaber*, of unknown origin.

**shillelagh** /ʃɪˈleɪlə, -li/ • n. (In Ireland) a cudgel of blackthorn or oak.
– ORIGIN C18: from the name of the town *Shillelagh*, in Co. Wicklow, Ireland.

**shilling** • n. **1** a former British coin and monetary unit equal to one twentieth of a pound or twelve pence. **2** the basic monetary unit of Kenya, Tanzania, and Uganda, equal to 100 cents.
– PHRASES **not the full shilling** Brit. informal not very clever. **take the King's** (or **Queen's**) **shilling** Brit. enlist as a soldier. [with ref. to the former practice of paying a shilling to a new recruit.]
– ORIGIN OE *scilling*, of Gmc origin.

**shilly-shally** • v. (**-ies**, **-ied**) be indecisive. • n. indecisive behaviour.
– DERIVATIVES **shilly-shallyer** (also **-shallier**) n.
– ORIGIN C18: orig. as *shill I, shall I*, reduplication of *shall I?*

**shim** • n. a washer or thin strip of material used to align parts, make them fit, or reduce wear. • v. (**shimmed**, **shimming**) wedge or fill up with a shim.
– ORIGIN C18: of unknown origin.

**shimmer** • v. shine with a soft tremulous light. • n. a light with such qualities.
– DERIVATIVES **shimmering** adj. **shimmeringly** adv. **shimmery** adj.
– ORIGIN OE *scymrian*, of Gmc origin; rel. to **SHINE**.

**shimmy** • n. (pl. **-ies**) **1** a kind of ragtime dance in which the whole body shakes or sways. **2** shaking, especially abnormal vibration of the wheels of a motor vehicle. • v. (**-ies**, **-ied**) **1** dance the shimmy. **2** shake or vibrate abnormally. **3** move swiftly and effortlessly.
– ORIGIN C20: of unknown origin.

**shin** • n. the front of the leg below the knee. ➤ a cut of beef from the lower part of a cow's leg. • v. (**shinned**, **shinning**) (**shin up/down**) climb quickly up or down by gripping with one's arms and legs.
– ORIGIN OE *scinu*, prob. from a Gmc base meaning 'narrow or thin piece'.

**shin bone** • n. the tibia.

**shindig** • n. informal **1** a large, lively party. **2** a noisy disturbance or quarrel.
– ORIGIN C19: prob. from **SHIN** and **DIG**, influenced later by **SHINDY**.

**shindy** • n. (pl. **-ies**) informal **1** a noisy disturbance or quarrel. **2** a large, lively party.
– ORIGIN C19: perh. an alt. of **SHINTY**.

**shine** • v. (past and past part. **shone** or **shined**) **1** give out a bright light; glow with reflected light. ➤ direct (a torch or other light) somewhere. ➤ (of a person's eyes) be bright with the expression of emotion. **2** [often as adj. **shining**] excel at something. **3** (**shine through**) (of a quality or skill) be clearly evident. **4** (past and past part. **shined**) polish. • n. **1** a quality of brightness, especially through reflecting light. **2** an act of polishing.
– PHRASES **take the shine off** spoil the brilliance or excitement of. **take a shine to** informal develop a liking for.
– DERIVATIVES **shiningly** adv.
– ORIGIN OE *scīnan*, of Gmc origin.

**shiner** • n. **1** a thing that shines. **2** a person or thing that polishes something. **3** informal a black eye. **4** a small silvery North American freshwater fish with colourful markings. [*Notropis* and other genera: several species.]

**shingle¹** • n. a mass of small rounded pebbles, especially on a seashore.
– DERIVATIVES **shingly** adj.
– ORIGIN ME: of unknown origin.

**shingle²** • n. **1** a rectangular wooden tile used on walls or roofs. **2** dated a woman's short haircut, tapering from the back of the head to the nape of the neck. **3** N. Amer. a small signboard, especially one outside an office. • v. **1** roof or clad with shingles. **2** dated cut (hair) in a shingle.
– PHRASES **hang out one's shingle** N. Amer. begin to practise a profession.
– ORIGIN ME: appar. from L. *scindula*, earlier *scandula* 'a split piece of wood'.

**shingles** • pl. n. [treated as sing.] an acute painful inflammation of nerve endings, with a skin eruption often forming a girdle around the body, caused by the herpes zoster virus.
– ORIGIN ME: representing med. L. *cingulus*, var. of L. *cingulum* 'girdle'.

**Shinkansen** /ˈʃiːnkɑːnˌsɛn/ • n. (pl. same) (in Japan) a railway system carrying high-speed passenger trains. ➤ a train operating on such a system.
– ORIGIN Japanese, from *shin* 'new' + *kansen* 'main line'.

**shinny¹** • v. (**-ies**, **-ied**) North American term for **SHIN**.
– ORIGIN C19: from **SHIN** + **-Y²**.

**shinny²** • n. N. Amer. an informal form of ice hockey played on the street or on ice.
– ORIGIN var. of **SHINTY**.

**Shinola** /ʃʌɪˈnəʊlə/ • n. US trademark a brand of boot polish.
– PHRASES **not know shit from Shinola** vulgar slang be ignorant or innocent.
– ORIGIN C20: from **SHINE** + *-ola* (suffix chiefly in US usage).

**shin pad** • n. a protective pad worn on the shins when playing soccer and other sports.

**shinplaster** • n. historical, informal **1** US & Austral./NZ a banknote or promissory note of little or no value. **2** Canadian a twenty-five cent bill.
– ORIGIN so named because of the resemblance to a square piece of paper used to bandage the shin.

**shin splints** • pl. n. [treated as sing. or pl.] acute pain in the shin and lower leg caused by prolonged running on hard surfaces.

**Shinto** /ˈʃɪntəʊ/ • n. a Japanese religion incorporating the worship of ancestors and nature spirits.
– DERIVATIVES **Shintoism** n. **Shintoist** n.
– ORIGIN Japanese, from Chin. *shen dao* 'way of the gods'.

**shinty** • n. (pl. **-ies**) a Scottish twelve-a-side game resembling hockey, played with curved sticks and taller goalposts and derived from hurling.
– ORIGIN C18 (earlier as *shinny*): appar. from the cry *shin ye, shin you, shin t' ye*, used in the game, of unknown

origin; cf. **SHINNY**[2].

**shiny** • **adj.** (**-ier**, **-iest**) reflecting light because very smooth, clean, or polished.
– DERIVATIVES **shinily** adv. **shininess** n.

**ship** • **n. 1** a large seagoing boat. ➤a sailing vessel with a bowsprit and three or more square-rigged masts. **2** a spaceship. **3** N. Amer. an aircraft. • **v.** (**shipped**, **shipping**) **1** transport on a ship. ➤transport by other means. ➤(of a sailor) take service on a ship. **2** Electronics make (a product) available for purchase. **3** (of a boat) take in (water) over the side. **4** take (oars) from the rowlocks and lay them inside a boat. ➤fix (a rudder, mast, etc.) in place on a ship.
– PHRASES **a sinking ship** a failing organization or endeavour. **take ship** set off on a voyage by ship. **when one's ship comes in** (or **home**) when one's fortune is made.
– DERIVATIVES **shipless** adj. **shipload** n. **shippable** adj. **shipper** n.
– ORIGIN OE *scip* (n.), late OE *scipian* (v.), of Gmc origin.

**-ship** • **suffix** forming nouns: **1** denoting a quality or condition: *companionship*. **2** denoting status, office, or honour: *citizenship*. ➤denoting a tenure of office: *chairmanship*. **3** denoting a skill in a certain capacity: *workmanship*. **4** denoting the collective individuals of a group: *membership*.
– ORIGIN OE *-scipe*, *scype*, of Gmc origin.

**shipboard** • **n.** [as modifier] used or occurring on board a ship.
– PHRASES **on shipboard** on board a ship.

**ship-breaker** • **n.** a contractor who breaks up old ships for scrap.

**shipbroker** • **n.** a broker who arranges charters, cargo space, and passenger bookings on ships.

**shipbuilder** • **n.** a person or company that designs and builds ships.
– DERIVATIVES **shipbuilding** n.

**ship burial** • **n.** Archaeology a burial in a wooden ship under a mound, carried out in Britain in Anglo-Saxon and Viking times.

**ship canal** • **n.** a canal large enough for use by ships.

**shiplap** • **v.** fit (boards) together by halving so that each overlaps the one below. • **n.** shiplapped boards, typically used for cladding. ➤a joint between boards made by halving.

**shipmaster** • **n.** a ship's captain.

**shipmate** • **n.** a fellow member of a ship's crew.

**shipment** • **n. 1** the action of shipping goods. **2** a consignment of goods shipped.

**ship money** • **n.** historical a tax raised in medieval England to provide ships for the navy.

**ship of the desert** • **n.** poetic/literary a camel.

**ship of the line** • **n.** historical a warship of the largest size, used in the line of battle.

**shipowner** • **n.** a person owning a ship or shares in a ship.

**shippen** /ˈʃɪp(ə)n/ • **n.** variant spelling of **SHIPPON**.

**shipping** • **n. 1** ships collectively. **2** the transport of goods by sea or other means.

**shipping agent** • **n.** an agent in a port who transacts a ship's business for the owner.

**shipping bill** • **n.** (in the UK) a form used by Customs and Excise to list goods before they are exported or removed from a bonded warehouse.

**shipping master** • **n.** Brit. an official presiding over the signing-on and discharging of seamen.

**shipping office** • **n.** the office of a shipping agent or shipping master.

**shippon** /ˈʃɪp(ə)n/ (also **shippen**) • **n.** dialect a cattle shed.
– ORIGIN OE *scypen*, of Gmc origin.

**ship-rigged** • **adj.** (of a sailing ship) square-rigged.

**ship's biscuit** • **n.** a hard, coarse kind of biscuit formerly taken on sea voyages.

**ship's company** • **n.** the crew of a ship.

**shipshape** • **adj.** orderly and neat.

**ship's husband** • **n.** an agent providing maintenance and supplies for a ship in port.

**ship-to-shore** • **adj.** from a ship to land. • **n.** a radiotelephone for such use.

**shipway** • **n.** a slope on which a ship is built and down which it slides to be launched.

**shipworm** • **n.** another term for **TEREDO**.

**shipwreck** • **n.** the destruction of a ship at sea by sinking or breaking up. ➤a ship so destroyed. • **v.** (**be shipwrecked**) suffer a shipwreck.

**shipwright** • **n.** a shipbuilder.

**shipyard** • **n.** a place where ships are built and repaired.

**shiralee** /ˈʃɪrəliː/ • **n.** Austral. informal a bundle of belongings carried by a tramp.
– ORIGIN C19: of unknown origin.

**Shiraz** /ˈʃɪəraz, ʃɪˈraz/ • **n.** a variety of black wine grape. ➤a red wine made from this grape.
– ORIGIN from *Shiraz* in Iran, appar. an alt. of Fr. *syrah*, from the belief that the vine was brought from Iran by the Crusades.

**shire** /ˈʃʌɪə/ • **n. 1** Brit. a county, especially in England. ➤(**the Shires**) the parts of England regarded as strongholds of traditional rural culture, especially the rural Midlands. **2** a medieval administrative district ruled jointly by an alderman and a sheriff. **3** Austral. a rural area with its own elected council.
– ORIGIN OE *scīr* 'care, official charge, county', of Gmc origin.

**-shire** /ʃɪə, ʃə/ • **comb. form** forming the names of counties: *Oxfordshire*.

**shire county** • **n.** (in the UK since 1974) a non-metropolitan county.

**shire horse** • **n.** a heavy powerful horse of a draught breed, originally from the English Midlands.

**shirk** • **v.** avoid or neglect (a duty or responsibility). • **n.** archaic a person who shirks.
– DERIVATIVES **shirker** n.
– ORIGIN C17: from obs. *shirk* 'sponger', perh. from Ger. *Schurke* 'scoundrel'.

**shirr** /ʃəː/ • **v. 1** [often as adj. **shirred**] gather (fabric) by means of drawn or elasticized threads in parallel rows. **2** US bake (an egg without its shell).
– ORIGIN C19: of unknown origin.

**shirt** • **n. 1** a garment for the upper body, with a collar and sleeves and buttons down the front. ➤a similar garment of stretchable material without full fastenings, worn for sports. **2** Brit. a place on a particular sports team.
– PHRASES **keep your shirt on** informal stay calm. **lose one's shirt** informal lose all one's possessions. **put one's shirt on** Brit. informal bet all one has on. **the shirt off one's back** informal one's last remaining possessions.
– DERIVATIVES **shirted** adj. **shirtless** adj.
– ORIGIN OE *scyrte*, of Gmc origin; rel. to **SKIRT** and **SHORT**; prob. from a base meaning 'short garment'.

**shirt dress** • **n.** a dress with a collar and button fastening in the style of a shirt, without a seam at the waist.

**shirting** • **n.** fabric for making shirts.

**shirtlifter** • **n.** Brit. informal, derogatory a male homosexual.

**shirtsleeve** • **n.** the sleeve of a shirt.
– PHRASES **in (one's) shirtsleeves** wearing a shirt with nothing over it.
– DERIVATIVES **shirtsleeved** adj.

**shirt tail** • **n.** the curved part of a shirt which comes below the waist.

**shirtwaist** • **n.** N. Amer. a woman's blouse resembling a shirt. ➤a shirtwaister.

**shirtwaister** • **n.** a shirt dress with a seam at the waist.

**shirty** • **adj.** (**-ier**, **-iest**) Brit. informal ill-tempered or annoyed.
– DERIVATIVES **shirtily** adv. **shirtiness** n.

**shish kebab** /ˌʃɪʃ kɪˈbab/ • **n.** a dish of pieces of marinated meat and vegetables cooked and served on skewers.
– ORIGIN from Turk. *şiş kebap*, from *şiş* 'skewer' + *kebap* 'roast meat'.

**shit** vulgar slang ● v. (**shitting**; past and past part. **shitted** or **shit** or **shat**) **1** defecate. **2** (**shit oneself**) be very frightened. ● n. **1** faeces. ➤an act of defecating. **2** a contemptible person. ➤something worthless; rubbish. **3** an intoxicating drug, especially cannabis. ● exclam. expressing disgust or annoyance.
– PHRASES **be shitting bricks** be extremely nervous or frightened. **in the shit** in trouble. **not give a shit** not care at all. **be up shit creek (without a paddle)** be in an awkward predicament. **when the shit hits the fan** when the disastrous consequences of something become known.
– ORIGIN OE *scitte* 'diarrhoea', of Gmc origin.

**shite** ● n. & exclam. vulgar slang another term for **SHIT**.

**shit-eating** ● adj. vulgar slang, chiefly US smug.

**shit-faced** ● adj. vulgar slang drunk or stoned.

**shit-hot** ● adj. vulgar slang excellent.

**shitkicker** ● n. N. Amer. vulgar slang an unsophisticated or oafish person.

**shitless** ● adj. (in phr. **be scared shitless**) vulgar slang be extremely frightened.

**shitlist** ● n. N. Amer. vulgar slang a list of those whom one dislikes or plans to harm.

**shitload** ● n. vulgar slang a large amount or number.

**shit-scared** ● adj. vulgar slang terrified.

**shit-stirrer** ● n. vulgar slang a person who takes pleasure in causing trouble or discord.
– DERIVATIVES **shit-stirring** n.

**shitty** ● adj. (**-ier, -iest**) vulgar slang **1** contemptible. ➤awful. **2** covered with excrement.

**shitwork** ● n. vulgar slang work considered to be menial or routine.

**shiur** /'ʃiːʊə/ ● n. (pl. **shiurim** /-rɪm/) Judaism a Talmudic study session, usually led by a rabbi.
– ORIGIN from Heb. *šiʻūr* 'measure, portion'.

**shiv** /ʃɪv/ ● n. N. Amer. informal a knife or razor used as a weapon.
– ORIGIN prob. from Romany *chiv* 'blade'.

**shiva** /'ʃɪvə/ (also **shivah**) ● n. Judaism a period of seven days' formal mourning for the dead, beginning immediately after the funeral.
– ORIGIN from Heb. *šiḇʻāh* 'seven'.

**shivaree** /ˌʃɪvə'riː/ ● n. chiefly US variant spelling of **CHARIVARI**.

**shive** /ʃʌɪv/ ● n. a broad bung hammered into a hole in the top of a cask when the cask has been filled.
– ORIGIN ME (in sense 'slice (of bread)', later 'piece of split wood'): rel. to **SHEAVE**[2].

**shiver**[1] ● v. shake slightly and uncontrollably as a result of being cold, frightened, or excited. ● n. a momentary trembling movement. ➤(**the shivers**) a spell or attack of shivering.
– DERIVATIVES **shiverer** n. **shivering** adj. **shiveringly** adv. **shivery** adj.
– ORIGIN ME *chivere*, perh. an alt. of dial. *chavele* 'to chatter', from OE *ceafl* 'jaw'.

**shiver**[2] ● n. a splinter. ● v. break into shivers.
– PHRASES **shiver my timbers** a mock oath attributed to sailors.
– ORIGIN ME: from a Gmc base meaning 'to split'.

**shlub** /ʃlʌb/ ● n. variant spelling of **SCHLUB**.

**shm** ● abbrev. Physics simple harmonic motion.

**shmear** /ʃmiːə/ (also **shmeer**) ● n. & v. variant spelling of **SCHMEAR**.

**shmo** ● n. (pl. **-oes**) variant spelling of **SCHMO**.

**Shoah** /'ʃəʊə/ ● n. (in Jewish use) the Holocaust.
– ORIGIN mod. Heb., lit. 'catastrophe'.

**shoal**[1] ● n. **1** a large number of fish swimming together. **2** informal, chiefly Brit. a large number of people. ● v. (of fish) form shoals.
– ORIGIN C16: prob. from MDu. *schōle* 'troop'; cf. **SCHOOL**[2].

**shoal**[2] ● n. **1** an area of shallow water. **2** a submerged sandbank visible at low water. ● v. (of water) become shallower. ● adj. dialect or N. Amer. (of water) shallow.
– DERIVATIVES **shoaly** adj.
– ORIGIN OE *sceald* (adj.), of Gmc origin; rel. to **SHALLOW**.

**shoat** /ʃəʊt/ (also **shote**) ● n. N. Amer. a young pig, especially one which is newly weaned.
– ORIGIN ME: of unknown origin; cf. W. Flemish *schote*.

**shochet** /'ʃɒkɛt, -x-/ ● n. (pl. **shochetim** /-ɪm/) a person certified as competent to kill cattle and poultry in the manner prescribed by Jewish law.
– ORIGIN C19: from Heb. *šōḥēṭ* 'slaughtering'.

**shochu** /'ʃəʊtʃuː/ ● n. a rough Japanese spirit distilled from sake dregs or other ingredients.
– ORIGIN from Japanese *shōchū*.

**shock**[1] ● n. **1** a sudden upsetting or surprising event or experience, or the resulting feeling. ➤short for **ELECTRIC SHOCK**. **2** an acute medical condition associated with a fall in blood pressure, caused by loss of blood, severe burns, sudden emotional stress, etc. **3** a violent shaking movement caused by an impact, explosion, or tremor. **4** short for **SHOCK ABSORBER**. ● v. **1** cause (someone) to feel surprised and upset. ➤offend the moral feelings of; outrage. **2** affect with physiological shock, or with an electric shock. **3** archaic collide violently.
– DERIVATIVES **shockability** n. **shockable** adj. **shock-proof** adj.
– ORIGIN C16: from Fr. *choc* (n.), *choquer* (v.), of unknown origin.

**shock**[2] ● n. a group of twelve sheaves of grain placed upright and supporting each other to allow the grain to dry and ripen. ● v. arrange in shocks.
– ORIGIN ME: perh. from MDu., Mid. Low Ger. *schok*, of unknown origin.

**shock**[3] ● n. an unkempt or thick mass of hair.
– ORIGIN C17 (denoting a dog with long shaggy hair): origin uncertain; cf. obs. *shough*, denoting a breed of lapdog.

**shock absorber** ● n. a device for absorbing jolts and vibrations, especially on a vehicle.

**shock cord** ● n. heavy elasticated cord; bungee cord.

**shocker** ● n. informal **1** a person or thing that shocks, especially through being unacceptable or sensational. **2** Brit. a shock absorber.

**shock-headed** ● adj. having thick, shaggy, and unkempt hair.

**shocking** ● adj. **1** causing shock or disgust. **2** Brit. informal very bad.
– DERIVATIVES **shockingly** adv. **shockingness** n.

**shocking pink** ● n. a vibrant shade of pink.

**shock jock** ● n. informal a radio disc jockey who expresses opinions in a deliberately offensive or provocative way.

**shock stall** ● n. a marked increase in drag and a loss of lift and control on an aircraft approaching the speed of sound.

**shock tactics** ● pl. n. the use of sudden violent or extreme action to shock someone into doing something.

**shock therapy** (also **shock treatment**) ● n. treatment of chronic mental conditions by electroconvulsive therapy or by inducing physiological shock.

**shock troops** ● pl. n. troops trained for carrying out sudden assaults.

**shock wave** ● n. an intense travelling pressure wave caused by explosion or by a body moving faster than sound.

**shod** past and past participle of **SHOE**.

**shoddy** ● adj. (**-ier, -iest**) **1** badly made or done. **2** lacking moral principle; sordid. ● n. an inferior yarn or fabric made from shredded woollen waste.
– DERIVATIVES **shoddily** adv. **shoddiness** n.
– ORIGIN C19: of unknown origin.

**shoe** ● n. **1** a covering for the foot having a sturdy sole and not reaching above the ankle. ➤a horseshoe. **2** a drag for a wheel. **3** a socket on a camera for fitting a flash unit. **4** a metal rim or ferrule, especially on the runner of a sledge. **5** a step for a mast. **6** a box from which cards are dealt at baccarat or some other card games. ● v. (**shoes, shoeing**; past and past part. **shod**) **1** fit (a horse) with a shoe or shoes. **2** (**be shod**) be wearing shoes of a specified kind. **3** protect with a metal shoe.
– PHRASES **be** (or **put oneself**) **in another person's shoes** imagine oneself in another's situation or predicament. **dead men's shoes** property or a position coveted

by a prospective successor but available only on a person's death. **wait for the other shoe to drop** N. Amer. informal be prepared for a further event to occur.
– DERIVATIVES **shoeless** adj.
– ORIGIN OE *scōh* (n.), *scōg(e)an* (v.), of Gmc origin.

**shoebill** ● n. an African stork with grey plumage and a very large bill shaped like a clog. [*Balaeniceps rex*.]

**shoeblack** ● n. dated, chiefly Brit. a person who cleans the shoes of passers-by for payment.

**shoebox** ● n. **1** a box in which a pair of shoes is delivered or sold. **2** informal a very cramped room or space.

**shoehorn** ● n. a curved instrument used for easing one's heel into a shoe. ● v. force into an inadequate space.

**shoelace** ● n. a cord or leather strip passed through eyelets or hooks on opposite sides of a shoe and pulled tight and fastened.

**shoemaker** ● n. a person who makes shoes and other footwear as a profession.
– DERIVATIVES **shoemaking** n.

**shoeshine** ● n. chiefly N. Amer. an act of polishing someone's shoes.
– DERIVATIVES **shoeshiner** n.

**shoestring** ● n. **1** N. Amer. a shoelace. **2** informal a small or inadequate budget: *living on a shoestring.*

**shoe tree** ● n. a shaped block inserted into a shoe when it is not being worn to keep it in shape.

**shofar** /ˈʃəʊfə/ ● n. (pl. **shofars** or **shofroth** /ˈʃəʊfrəʊt/) a ram's-horn trumpet used by Jews in religious ceremonies and as an ancient battle signal.
– ORIGIN from Heb. *šōpār*, (pl.) *šōpārōṯ*.

**shogun** /ˈʃəʊgʊn/ ● n. (in feudal Japan) a hereditary commander-in-chief.
– DERIVATIVES **shogunate** /-nət/ n.
– ORIGIN Japanese, from Chin. *jiāng jūn* 'general'.

**shoji** /ˈʃəʊdʒi/ ● n. (pl. same or **shojis**) (in Japan) a sliding door made of a latticed screen covered with white paper.
– ORIGIN from Japanese *shōji*.

**Shona** /ˈʃəʊnə/ ● n. (pl. same or **Shonas**) **1** a member of a group of peoples inhabiting parts of southern Africa, particularly Zimbabwe. **2** any of the closely related Bantu languages spoken by these peoples.
– ORIGIN the name in Shona.

**shone** past and past participle of **SHINE**.

**shonky** Austral./NZ informal ● adj. (**-ier**, **-iest**) dishonest, unreliable, or illegal. ● n. (also **shonk**) a person engaged in suspect business activities.
– ORIGIN 1970s: perh. from Engl. dial. *shonk* 'smart'.

**shoo** ● exclam. used to frighten or drive away a person or animal. ● v. (**shoos**, **shooed**) cause to go away by waving one's arms and saying 'shoo'.

**shoo-fly pie** ● n. N. Amer. a rich tart made of treacle baked in a pastry case with a crumble topping.

**shoogly** /ˈʃuːgli/ ● adj. Scottish unsteady; wobbly.
– ORIGIN ME: prob. of imitative origin.

**shoo-in** ● n. chiefly N. Amer. a person or thing that is certain to succeed or win.

**shook**[1] past of **SHAKE**.

**shook**[2] ● n. N. Amer. a set of components ready for assembly into a box or cask.
– ORIGIN C18: of unknown origin.

**shoot** ● v. (past and past part. **shot**) **1** kill or wound (a person or animal) with a bullet or arrow. ➤ cause (a gun) to fire. ➤ hunt game with a gun. ➤ (**shoot someone/thing down**) bring down an aircraft or person by shooting. **2** move suddenly and rapidly. ➤ [as adj. **shooting**] (of a pain) sudden and piercing. ➤ direct (a glance, question, or remark) at someone. **3** (in football, basketball, etc.) kick, hit, or throw the ball or puck in an attempt to score a goal. ➤ informal make (a specified score) for a round of golf. ➤ N. Amer. informal play a game of (pool, dice, or cards). **4** film or photograph (a scene, film, etc.). **5** send out buds or shoots; germinate. **6** (**shoot up**) informal inject oneself with a narcotic drug. **7** plane (the edge of a board) accurately. **8** (of a boat) sweep swiftly down or under (rapids, a waterfall, or a bridge). ➤ informal drive past (a traffic light at red). ➤ move (a door bolt) to fasten or unfasten a door. ● n. **1** a young branch or sucker springing from the main stock of a tree or other plant. **2** an occasion when a group of people hunt and shoot game for sport. ➤ Brit. land used for shooting game. **3** an occasion of taking photographs professionally or making a film or video: *a fashion shoot.* **4** variant spelling of **CHUTE**[1]. **5** a rapid in a stream. ● exclam. N. Amer. informal used as a euphemism for 'shit'.
– PHRASES **shoot the breeze** (or **the bull**) N. Amer. informal have a casual conversation. **shoot one's cuffs** pull one's shirt cuffs out to project beyond the cuffs of one's jacket or coat. **shoot oneself in the foot** informal inadvertently make a situation worse for oneself. **shoot a line** Brit. informal describe something in an exaggerated, untruthful, or boastful way. **shoot one's mouth off** informal talk boastfully or indiscreetly. **the whole shooting match** informal everything. **shoot through** Austral./NZ informal depart, especially hurriedly.
– DERIVATIVES **shootable** adj.
– ORIGIN OE *scēotan*, of Gmc origin; rel. to **SHEET**[1], **SHOT**[1], and **SHUT**.

**shooter** ● n. **1** a person who uses a gun. ➤ informal a gun. **2** (in netball, basketball, etc.) a player whose role is to attempt to score goals. ➤ a person who throws a dice. **3** Cricket a bowled ball that moves rapidly along the ground after pitching. **4** informal, chiefly N. Amer. a small drink of spirits.

**shooting box** ● n. Brit. a lodge used by hunters in the shooting season.

**shooting brake** ● n. Brit. dated an estate car.

**shooting gallery** ● n. **1** a room or fairground booth for recreational shooting at targets. **2** N. Amer. informal a place used for injecting drugs.

**shooting iron** ● n. informal, chiefly US a firearm.

**shooting jacket** ● n. another term for **SAFARI JACKET**.

**shooting star** ● n. **1** a small, rapidly moving meteor burning up on entering the earth's atmosphere. **2** a North American plant having white, pink, or purple hanging flowers with backward-curving petals. [Genus *Dodecatheon*.]

**shooting stick** ● n. a walking stick with a handle that unfolds to form a seat and a sharpened end which can be stuck firmly in the ground.

**shootist** ● n. N. Amer. informal a person who shoots, especially a marksman.

**shoot-out** ● n. **1** informal a decisive gun battle. **2** (usu. **penalty shoot-out**) Soccer a tiebreaker decided by each side taking a specified number of penalty kicks.

**shop** ● n. **1** a building or part of a building where goods or services are sold. ➤ informal an act of going shopping. **2** a place where things are manufactured or repaired; a workshop. **3** (often in phr. **talk shop**) matters concerning one's work, especially when discussed at an inappropriate time. ● v. (**shopped**, **shopping**) **1** go to a shop or shops to buy goods. ➤ (**shop around**) look for the best available price or rate for something. **2** informal, chiefly Brit. inform on (someone).
– ORIGIN ME: shortening of OFr. *eschoppe* 'lean-to booth'.

**shopaholic** ● n. informal a compulsive shopper.

**shop assistant** ● n. Brit. a person who serves customers in a shop.

**shopfitter** ● n. a person whose job it is to fit the counters, shelves, etc. with which a shop is equipped.
– DERIVATIVES **shopfitting** n.

**shop floor** ● n. Brit. the part of a workshop or factory where production as distinct from administrative work is carried out.

**shopfront** ● n. the facade of a shop.

**shopkeeper** ● n. the owner and manager of a shop.
– DERIVATIVES **shopkeeping** n.

**shoplifting** ● n. the theft of goods from a shop by someone pretending to be a customer.
– DERIVATIVES **shoplift** v. **shoplifter** n.

**shopper** ● n. **1** a person who is shopping. **2** Brit. a bag for holding shopping, attached to wheels and pushed or pulled along. **3** a small-wheeled bicycle with a basket.

**shopping** ● n. **1** the purchasing of goods from shops.

2 goods bought from shops, especially food and household goods.

**shopping centre** ● n. an area or complex of shops.

**shopping list** ● n. a list of purchases to be made. ➤ a list of items to be considered or acted on.

**shop-soiled** ● adj. Brit. (of an article) made dirty or imperfect by being displayed or handled in a shop.

**shop steward** ● n. a person elected by workers in a factory to represent them in dealings with management.

**shopwalker** ● n. Brit. dated a senior employee in a large shop who supervises assistants and directs customers.

**shop window** ● n. **1** a display window of a shop. **2** a position that allows a person or organization to demonstrate their strengths.

**shopworn** ● adj. chiefly N. Amer. another term for **SHOP-SOILED**.

**shore**[1] ● n. **1** the land along the edge of a sea, lake, etc. ➤ Law the land between ordinary high- and low-water marks. **2** (also **shores**) poetic/literary a country or other geographic area bounded by a coast: *distant shores*.
– PHRASES **in shore** on the water near land or nearer to land. **on shore** ashore; on land.
– DERIVATIVES **shoreless** adj. **shoreward** adj. & adv. **shorewards** adv.
– ORIGIN ME: from MDu., Mid. Low Ger. *schōre*; perh. rel. to **SHEAR**.

**shore**[2] ● n. a prop or beam set obliquely against something weak or unstable as a support. ● v. (often **shore something up**) support or hold up with shores.
– DERIVATIVES **shoring** n.
– ORIGIN ME: from MDu., Mid. Low Ger. *schore* 'prop', of unknown origin.

**shore**[3] archaic past of **SHEAR**.

**shore leave** ● n. leisure time spent ashore by a sailor.

**shoreline** ● n. the line along which a large body of water meets the land.

**shoreweed** ● n. a small plant with grass-like leaves, growing at the edge of ponds. [*Littorella uniflora*.]

**shorn** past participle of **SHEAR**.

**short** ● adj. **1** of a small length or duration. ➤ (of a ball in sport) travelling only a small distance before bouncing. **2** relatively small in extent. **3** (of a person) small in height. **4** (**short of/on**) not having enough of (something); lacking or deficient in. ➤ in insufficient supply. **5** (of a person) terse; uncivil. **6** Phonetics (of a vowel) categorized as short with regard to quality and length (e.g. in standard British English the vowel /ʊ/ in *good*). ➤ Prosody (of a vowel or syllable) having the lesser of the two recognized durations. **7** (of odds or a chance) reflecting or representing a high level of probability. **8** Stock Exchange (of shares or other assets) sold in advance of being acquired. ➤ (of a security) maturing at a relatively early date. **9** (of pastry) containing a high proportion of fat to flour and therefore crumbly. ➤ (of clay) having poor plasticity. ● adv. (in sport) at, to, or over a short distance. ➤ not as far as the point aimed at. ● n. **1** Brit. informal a strong alcoholic drink, especially spirits, served in small measures. **2** a short film as opposed to a feature film. ➤ a short sound, vowel, or syllable. ➤ a short circuit. **3** Stock Exchange a person who sells short. ➤ (**shorts**) short-dated stocks. **4** (**shorts**) a mixture of bran and coarse flour. ● v. short-circuit.
– PHRASES **be caught** (or Brit. **taken**) **short 1** be put at a disadvantage. **2** Brit. informal urgently need to urinate or defecate. **a brick short of a load** (or **two sandwiches short of a picnic**, etc.) informal (of a person) stupid or crazy. **bring** (or **pull**) **someone up short** cause someone to stop or pause abruptly. **for short** as an abbreviation or nickname. **get** (or **have**) **someone by the short and curlies** informal have complete control of a person. **go short** not have enough of something, especially food. **in short** to sum up; briefly. **in short order** chiefly N. Amer. immediately; rapidly. **in the short run** (or **term**) in the near future. **in short supply** (of a commodity) scarce. **make short work of** accomplish, consume, or destroy quickly. **short and sweet** brief and pleasant. **short for** an abbreviation or nickname for. **short of 1** less than. **2** not reaching as far as. **3** without going so far as (some extreme action). **short of breath** panting; short-winded. **stop short** stop suddenly or abruptly.
– DERIVATIVES **shortish** adj. **shortness** n.
– ORIGIN OE *sceort*, of Gmc origin; rel. to **SHIRT, SKIRT**.

**short-acting** ● adj. (chiefly of a drug) having effects that last for only a short time.

**shortage** ● n. a state or situation in which something needed cannot be obtained in sufficient amounts.

**short-arm** ● adj. denoting a blow or throw executed with the arm not fully extended or with motion from the elbow only.

**short back and sides** ● n. Brit. a haircut in which the hair is cut short at the back and the sides.

**shortbread** ● n. a crisp, rich, crumbly type of biscuit made with butter, flour, and sugar.

**shortcake** ● n. **1** another term for **SHORTBREAD**. **2** N. Amer. a rich dessert made from short pastry and topped with fruit and whipped cream.

**short change** ● n. insufficient money given as change. ● v. (**short-change**) **1** cheat by giving short change. **2** treat unfairly by withholding something of value.

**short circuit** ● n. an electrical circuit of lower than usual resistance, especially one formed unintentionally. ● v. (**short-circuit**) **1** suffer or cause to suffer a short circuit. **2** shorten (a process or activity) by using a more direct but irregular method.

**shortcoming** ● n. a failure to meet a certain standard; a fault or defect.

**shortcrust pastry** ● n. Brit. crumbly pastry made with flour, fat, and a little water.

**short cut** ● n. **1** an alternative route that is shorter than the one usually taken. **2** an accelerated but somewhat irregular way of doing something.

**short-dated** ● adj. (of a stock or bond) due for early payment or redemption.

**short-day** ● adj. (of a plant) needing a relatively long daily period of darkness to initiate flowering.

**short division** ● n. arithmetical division in which the quotient is written directly without a succession of intermediate workings.

**shorten** ● v. **1** make or become shorter. **2** Sailing reduce the amount of (sail spread).

**shortening** ● n. fat used for making pastry.

**shortfall** ● n. a deficit of something required or expected.

**short field** ● n. Baseball the part of the outfield nearest the infield.

**short fuse** ● n. informal a quick temper.
– DERIVATIVES **short-fused** adj.

**shorthair** ● n. a cat of a short-haired breed.

**shorthand** ● n. **1** a method of rapid writing by means of abbreviations and symbols, used especially for taking dictation. **2** a short and simple way of expressing or referring to something.

**short-handed** ● adj. not having enough or the usual number of staff or crew. ➤ Ice Hockey (of a goal) scored by a team playing with fewer players on the ice than their opponent. ➤ Ice Hockey (of a situation) occurring while or because a team has fewer than six players on the ice. ● adv. with fewer staff, crew, or players than usual.

**shorthand typist** ● n. Brit. a typist qualified to take and transcribe shorthand.

**short haul** ● n. a relatively short distance in terms of travel or the transport of goods.

**short head** ● n. Brit. Horse Racing a distance less than the length of a horse's head.

**shorthold** ● adj. English Law denoting a tenancy whereby the tenant agrees to rent a property for a stated term, at the end of which the landlord may recover it.

**shorthorn** ● n. an animal of a breed of cattle with short horns.

**shortie** ● n. variant spelling of **SHORTY**.

**shortlist** ● n. a list of selected candidates from which a final choice is made. ● v. put on a shortlist.

**short-lived** ● adj. lasting only a short time.

**shortly** ● adv. **1** in a short time; soon. **2** in a few words;

briefly. ➤ abruptly, sharply, or curtly.

**short mark** ● n. another term for **BREVE** (in sense 2).

**short measure** ● n. an amount less than that which is declared or paid for.

**short metre** ● n. a metrical pattern for hymns in which the stanzas have four lines with 6, 6, 8, and 6 syllables.

**short-order** ● adj. N. Amer. of or denoting food dishes which can be quickly prepared and served: *a short-order cook*.

**short-pitched** ● adj. Cricket (of a delivery) bowled so that the ball bounces relatively near the bowler.

**short-range** ● adj. **1** able to be used or be effective only over short distances. **2** of or over a short period of future time.

**short rib** ● n. **1** Brit. another term for **FLOATING RIB**. **2** (**short ribs**) N. Amer. a narrow cut of beef containing the ends of the ribs near to the breastbone.

**shorts** ● pl. n. **1** short trousers that reach only to the knees or thighs. **2** N. Amer. men's underpants.

**short score** ● n. Music a score in which the parts are condensed on to a small number of staves.

**short shrift** ● n. **1** rapid and unsympathetic dismissal; curt treatment. **2** archaic little time between condemnation and execution or punishment.

**short sight** ● n. the inability to see things clearly unless they are relatively close to the eyes; myopia.

**short-sighted** ● adj. **1** having short sight. **2** lacking imagination or foresight.
– DERIVATIVES **short-sightedly** adv. **short-sightedness** n.

**short-staffed** ● adj. not having enough or the usual number of staff.

**shortstop** /ˈʃɔːtstɒp/ ● n. Baseball a fielder positioned between second and third base.

**short story** ● n. a story with a fully developed theme but significantly shorter and less elaborate than a novel.

**short subject** ● n. chiefly US a short film, typically one shown before the screening of a feature film.

**short suit** ● n. (in bridge or whist) a holding of only one or two cards of one suit in a hand.

**short temper** ● n. a tendency to lose one's temper quickly.
– DERIVATIVES **short-tempered** adj.

**short-termism** ● n. concentration on immediate profit or advantage at the expense of long-term security.

**short time** ● n. the condition of working fewer than the regular hours per day or days per week.

**short title** ● n. an abbreviated form of a title of a book or document.

**short waist** ● n. a high waist on a woman's dress or a person's body.
– DERIVATIVES **short-waisted** adj.

**short wave** ● n. a radio wave of a wavelength between about 10 and 100 m (and a frequency of about 3 to 30 MHz). ➤ broadcasting using radio waves of this wavelength.

**short weight** ● n. weight that is less than that declared.

**short-winded** ● adj. out of breath, or tending to run out of breath quickly.

**shorty** (also **shortie**) ● n. (pl. **-ies**) informal **1** a short person. **2** a short dress, nightdress, or raincoat.

**Shoshone** /ʃəˈʃəʊni/ ● n. (pl. same or **Shoshones**) **1** a member of an American Indian people living chiefly in Wyoming, Idaho, and Nevada. **2** the Uto-Aztecan language of this people.
– ORIGIN of unknown origin.

**Shoshonean** ● n. a branch of the Uto-Aztecan language family that includes Comanche and Shoshone. ● adj. relating to or denoting this group of languages.

**shot**[1] ● n. **1** the firing of a gun or cannon. ➤ a person with a specified level of ability in shooting: *he was an excellent shot*. ➤ a critical or aggressive remark. **2** a hit, stroke, or kick of the ball in sports, in particular an attempt to score. ➤ informal an attempt to do something. **3** (pl. same) a ball of stone or metal fired from a large gun or cannon. ➤ (also **lead shot**) tiny lead pellets used in a single charge or cartridge in a shotgun. ➤ a heavy ball thrown by a shot-putter. **4** a photograph. ➤ a film sequence photographed continuously by one camera. ➤ the range of a camera's view: *standing just out of shot*. **5** informal a small drink of spirits. ➤ an injection of a drug or vaccine. **6** the launch of a rocket: *a moon shot*.
– PHRASES **give it one's best shot** informal do the best that one can. **like a shot** informal without hesitation; willingly. **not a shot in one's locker** Brit. no money or chances left. **a shot in the arm** informal an encouraging stimulus.
– ORIGIN OE *sc(e)ot*, *gesc(e)ot*, of Gmc origin; from the base of **SHOOT**.

**shot**[2] past and past participle of **SHOOT**. ● adj. **1** (of coloured cloth) woven with a warp and weft of different colours, giving a contrasting effect when looked at from different angles. ➤ interspersed with a different colour. **2** informal ruined or worn out. ➤ US & Austral./NZ drunk.
– PHRASES **get** (or **be**) **shot of** Brit. informal get (or be) rid of. **shot through with** suffused with. **shot to pieces** (or **to hell**) informal ruined.

**shot**[3] ● n. Brit. informal, dated a bill or one's share of it, especially in a pub.
– ORIGIN ME: from **SHOT**[1]; cf. OE *scēotan* 'shoot, pay, contribute' and **SCOT**.

**shot-blast** ● v. clean or strip (a surface) by directing a high-speed stream of steel particles at it.

**shote** ● n. variant spelling of **SHOAT**.

**shot-firer** ● n. a person who fires a blasting charge, for example in mining.

**shot glass** ● n. N. Amer. a small glass used for serving spirits.

**shotgun** ● n. a smooth-bore gun for firing small shot at short range.

**shotgun marriage** (also **shotgun wedding**) ● n. informal an enforced or hurried wedding, especially because the bride is pregnant.

**shotgun microphone** ● n. another term for **GUN MICROPHONE**.

**shot hole** ● n. **1** a hole made by the passage of a shot. **2** a hole bored in rock for the insertion of a blasting charge. **3** a small round hole made in a leaf by a fungus or bacterium, or in wood by a boring beetle.

**shot-peen** ● v. shape (sheet metal) by bombarding it with a stream of metal shot.

**shot put** ● n. an athletic contest in which a very heavy round ball is thrown as far as possible.
– DERIVATIVES **shot-putter** n. **shot-putting** n.

**shotted** ● adj. filled or weighted with shot.

**shotten** /ˈʃɒt(ə)n/ ● adj. (of a herring) having spawned.
– ORIGIN ME: archaic past part. of **SHOOT**.

**shot tower** ● n. historical a tower in which shot was made from molten lead poured through sieves at the top and falling into water at the bottom.

**should** ● modal v. (3rd sing. **should**) **1** used to indicate obligation, duty, or correctness. ➤ used to give or ask advice or suggestions. **2** used to indicate what is probable. **3** formal expressing the conditional mood. ➤ (in the first person) indicating the consequence of an imagined event. ➤ referring to a possible event or situation. **4** used in a clause with 'that' after a main clause describing feelings. **5** used in a clause with 'that' expressing purpose. **6** (in the first person) expressing a polite request or acceptance. **7** (in the first person) expressing a conjecture or hope.
– ORIGIN OE *sceolde*: past of **SHALL**.

**shoulder** ● n. **1** the joint between the upper arm or forelimb and the main part of the body. ➤ the part of a bird or insect at which the wing is attached. **2** a part of something resembling a shoulder, in particular a point at which a steep slope descends from a plateau or highland area. **3** short for **HARD SHOULDER**. ● v. **1** put (something heavy) over one's shoulder or shoulders to carry. **2** take on (a burden or responsibility). **3** push out of one's way with one's shoulder.
– PHRASES **be looking over one's shoulder** be anxious or insecure about a possible danger. **put one's shoulder to the wheel** set to work vigorously. **shoulder arms** hold a

rifle against the right side of the body, barrel upwards. **shoulder to shoulder** side by side or acting together.
– DERIVATIVES **-shouldered** adj.
– ORIGIN OE *sculdor*, of W. Gmc origin.

**shoulder bag** • n. a bag with a long strap that is hung over the shoulder.

**shoulder belt** • n. a bandolier or other strap passing over one shoulder and under the opposite arm.

**shoulder blade** • n. either of the large, flat, triangular bones which lie against the ribs in the upper back; the scapula.

**shoulder pad** • n. a pad sewn into the shoulder of a garment to provide shape or give protection.

**shoulder season** • n. a travel period between peak and off-peak seasons.

**shoulder strap** • n. **1** a narrow strip of material going over the shoulder from front to back of a garment. **2** a long strap attached to a bag for carrying it over the shoulder. **3** a strip of cloth from shoulder to collar on a military uniform, coat, etc.

**shouldn't** • contr. should not.

**shout** • v. **1** speak or call out very loudly. ➤(**shout at**) reprimand loudly. ➤(**shout someone down**) prevent someone from speaking or being heard by shouting. **2** Austral./NZ informal treat (someone) to (something, especially a drink). • n. **1** a loud cry or call. **2** (**one's shout**) Brit. informal one's turn to buy a round of drinks.
– PHRASES **all over bar the shouting** informal (of a contest) almost finished and therefore virtually decided. **give someone a shout** informal call on or get in touch with someone. **in with a shout** informal having a good chance. **shout the odds** talk loudly and in an opinionated way.
– DERIVATIVES **shouter** n. **shouty** adj. (informal).
– ORIGIN ME: perh. rel. to **SHOOT**; cf. ON *skúta* 'a taunt', also **SCOUT**[2].

**shouting match** • n. informal a loud quarrel.

**shove** • v. **1** push roughly. **2** informal put (something) somewhere carelessly or roughly. ➤(**shove it**) used to express angry dismissal. • n. a strong push.
– PHRASAL VERBS **shove off 1** informal go away. **2** push away from the shore in a boat. **shove up** informal move oneself to make room for someone.
– ORIGIN OE *scūfan* (v.), of Gmc origin; rel. to **SHUFFLE**.

**shove-halfpenny** • n. a game in which coins are struck so that they slide across a marked board on a table.

**shovel** • n. a tool resembling a spade with a broad blade and upturned sides, used for moving coal, earth, snow, etc. • v. (**shovelled**, **shovelling**; US **shoveled**, **shoveling**) **1** move with a shovel. **2** (**shovel something down/in**) informal eat food quickly and in large quantities.
– DERIVATIVES **shovelful** n. (pl. **-fuls**).
– ORIGIN OE *scofl*, of Gmc origin; rel. to **SHOVE**.

**shovelboard** • n. Brit. a game played by pushing discs with the hand or with a long-handled shovel over a marked surface.
– ORIGIN C16: alt. of obs. *shoveboard*, from **SHOVE** + **BOARD**.

**shovel hat** • n. a black felt hat with a low round crown and a broad brim turned up at the sides, formerly worn especially by clergymen.

**shoveller** (US **shoveler**) • n. **1** a person or thing that shovels something. **2** (usu. **shoveler**) a dabbling duck with a long broad bill. [*Anas clypeata* and related species.]

**show** • v. (past part. **shown** or **showed**) **1** be, allow, or cause to be visible. ➤exhibit or produce for inspection. ➤present (a film or television programme) on a screen for viewing. ➤represent or depict in art. ➤(**show oneself** or **one's face**) allow oneself to be seen; appear in public. ➤(also **show up**) informal arrive for an appointment or at a gathering. **2** display or allow to be perceived (a quality, emotion, or characteristic). ➤accord or treat someone with (a specified quality). **3** demonstrate or prove. ➤explain or demonstrate something to. ➤conduct or lead: *show them in, please.* **4** N. Amer. finish third or in the first three in a race. **5** informal (of a woman) be visibly pregnant. • n. **1** a spectacle or display. **2** a play or other stage performance, especially a musical. ➤a light entertainment programme on television or radio. ➤an event or competition involving the public display of animals, plants, or products. ➤informal an undertaking, project, or organization: *I run the show.* **3** an outward appearance or display of a quality or feeling. ➤(often in phr. **for show**) an outward display intended to give a false impression. **4** Medicine a discharge of blood and mucus from the vagina at the onset of labour or menstruation. **5** US & Austral./NZ informal an opportunity or chance.
– PHRASES **all over the show** another way of saying ***all over the place*** (see **ALL**). **get the show on the road** informal begin an undertaking or enterprise. **good** (or **bad** or **poor**) **show!** informal, dated used to express approval (or disapproval or dissatisfaction). **have something** (or **nothing**) **to show for** have a (or no) visible result of (one's work or experience). **on show** being exhibited. **show cause** Law produce satisfactory grounds for application of (or exemption from) a procedure or penalty. **show (someone) a clean pair of heels** informal run away from (someone) extremely fast. **show someone the door** dismiss or eject someone. **show one's hand** (or **cards**) disclose one's plans. **show of force** a demonstration of the forces at one's command and of one's readiness to use them. **show of hands** a vote by the raising of hands. **show one's teeth** Brit. use one's power or authority in an aggressive or intimidating way. **show willing** display a willingness to help.
– PHRASAL VERBS **show something forth** archaic exhibit something. **show off** informal boastfully display one's abilities or accomplishments. **show something off** display something that is a source of pride. **show out** Bridge reveal that one has no cards of a particular suit. **show someone round** (or chiefly N. Amer. **around**) point out interesting features in a place or building to someone. **show someone/thing up 1** expose someone or something as being bad or faulty. **2** (**show someone up**) informal embarrass or humiliate someone.
– ORIGIN OE *scēawian* 'look at, inspect', from a W. Gmc base meaning 'look'.

**show-and-tell** • n. chiefly N. Amer. a teaching method in which pupils bring items to class and describe them to their classmates.

**showband** • n. **1** a band which plays cover versions of popular songs. **2** a jazz band which performs with theatrical extravagance.

**showbiz** • n. informal term for **SHOW BUSINESS**.
– DERIVATIVES **showbizzy** adj.

**showboat** • n. **1** (in the US) a river steamer on which theatrical performances are given. **2** informal, chiefly N. Amer. a show-off; an exhibitionist. • v. informal, chiefly N. Amer. show off.
– DERIVATIVES **showboater** n.

**show business** • n. the theatre, films, television, and pop music as a profession or industry.

**showcard** • n. a large card bearing a conspicuous design, used in advertising, teaching, etc.

**showcase** • n. **1** a glass case used for displaying articles in a shop or museum. **2** a place or occasion for presenting something to general attention. • v. exhibit; display.

**showdown** • n. **1** a final test or confrontation intended to settle a dispute. **2** (in poker or brag) the requirement at the end of a round that the players who remain in should show their cards to determine which is the strongest hand.

**shower** /ˈʃaʊə/ • n. **1** a brief and usually light fall of rain or snow. **2** a mass of small things falling or moving at once. ➤a large number of things happening or given at the same time: *a shower of awards.* ➤a group of particles produced by a cosmic-ray particle in the earth's atmosphere. **3** a cubicle or bath in which a person stands under a spray of water to wash. ➤an act of washing oneself in a shower. **4** N. Amer. a party at which presents are given to a woman who is about to get married or have a baby. **5** Brit. informal an incompetent or worthless group of people. • v. **1** fall, throw, or be thrown in a shower: *broken glass showered down.* **2** (**shower something on/upon** or **shower someone with**) give a great number of things to someone. **3** wash oneself in a shower.
– ORIGIN OE *scūr* 'light fall of rain', of Gmc origin.

**showerproof** ● **adj.** (of a garment) resistant to light rain. ● **v.** make showerproof.

**showery** ● **adj.** characterized by frequent showers of rain.

**showgirl** ● **n.** an actress who sings and dances in musicals, variety acts, etc.

**showground** ● **n.** an area of land on which a show takes place.

**show house** (also **show home**) ● **n.** Brit. a house on a newly built estate which is furnished and decorated to be shown to prospective buyers.

**showing** ● **n.** **1** a presentation of a cinema film or television programme. **2** a performance of a specified quality: *poor opinion poll showings.*

**showjumping** ● **n.** the competitive sport of riding horses over a course of fences and other obstacles in an arena, with penalty points for errors.
– DERIVATIVES **showjump** v. **showjumper** n.

**showman** ● **n.** (pl. **-men**) **1** the manager or presenter of a circus, fair, or other variety show. **2** a person skilled at entertaining, theatrical presentation, or performance.
– DERIVATIVES **showmanship** n.

**shown** past participle of **SHOW**.

**show-off** ● **n.** informal a person who boastfully displays their abilities or accomplishments.

**showpiece** ● **n.** **1** something which attracts admiration as an outstanding example of its type. **2** an item of work presented for exhibition or display.

**showplace** ● **n.** a place of beauty or interest attracting many visitors.

**showreel** ● **n.** a short videotape containing examples of an actor's or director's work for showing to potential employers.

**showroom** ● **n.** a room used to display cars, furniture, or other goods for sale.

**show-stopper** ● **n.** informal a performance or item receiving prolonged applause.
– DERIVATIVES **show-stopping** adj.

**show trial** ● **n.** a judicial trial held in public with the intention of influencing or satisfying public opinion, rather than of ensuring justice.

**showy** ● **adj.** (**-ier**, **-iest**) strikingly bright, colourful, or ostentatious.
– DERIVATIVES **showily** adv. **showiness** n.

**shoyu** /ˈʃəʊjuː/ ● **n.** a type of Japanese soy sauce.
– ORIGIN from Japanese *shōyu*.

**s.h.p.** ● **abbrev.** shaft horsepower.

**shrank** past of **SHRINK**.

**shrapnel** /ˈʃrapn(ə)l/ ● **n.** small metal fragments thrown out by the explosion of a shell, bomb, etc. ➤ shells designed to burst short of the target and shower it with such fragments.
– ORIGIN C19: named after the Brit. soldier General Henry *Shrapnel*, inventor of shrapnel shells.

**shred** ● **n.** **1** a strip of material that has been torn, cut, or scraped from something larger. **2** a very small amount. ● **v.** (**shredded**, **shredding**) tear or cut into shreds.
– ORIGIN OE *scrēad* 'piece cut off', *scrēadian* 'trim, prune', of W. Gmc origin; rel. to **SHROUD**.

**shredder** ● **n.** **1** a device for shredding something, especially documents. **2** informal a snowboarder.

**shrew** ● **n.** **1** a small mouse-like insectivorous mammal with a long pointed snout and tiny eyes. [Family Soricidae: many species.] **2** a bad-tempered or aggressively assertive woman.
– DERIVATIVES **shrewish** adj. **shrewishly** adv. **shrewishness** n.
– ORIGIN OE *scrēawa*, *scrǣwa*, of Gmc origin; cf. **SHREWD**.

**shrewd** ● **adj.** **1** having or showing sharp powers of judgement; astute. **2** archaic (of weather) piercingly cold. ➤ (of a blow) severe. ➤ mischievous; malicious.
– DERIVATIVES **shrewdly** adv. **shrewdness** n.
– ORIGIN ME (in the sense 'evil in nature or character'): from **SHREW** in the sense 'evil person or thing', or as the past part. of obs. *shrew* 'to curse'.

**Shri** /ʃriː/ ● **n.** Indian variant spelling of **SRI**.

**shriek** ● **v.** utter a high-pitched piercing sound, cry, or words. ● **n.** **1** a high-pitched piercing cry or sound. **2** informal an exclamation mark.
– DERIVATIVES **shrieker** n. **shrieking** adj. **shriekingly** adv.
– ORIGIN C15: imitative; cf. **SCREECH**.

**shrieval** /ˈʃriːv(ə)l/ ● **adj.** chiefly historical of or relating to a sheriff.
– ORIGIN C17: from *shrieve*, obs. var. of **SHERIFF**.

**shrievalty** ● **n.** (pl. **-ies**) chiefly historical the office, jurisdiction, or tenure of a sheriff.

**shrift** ● **n.** archaic confession, especially to a priest. ➤ absolution by a priest. See also **SHORT SHRIFT**.
– ORIGIN OE *scrift* 'penance imposed after confession', from **SHRIVE**.

**shrike** ● **n.** a predatory songbird with a hooked bill, often impaling its prey on thorns. [Family Laniidae: many species.]
– ORIGIN C16: perh. rel. to OE *scrīc* 'thrush' and Mid. Low Ger. *schrīk* 'corncrake', of imitative origin.

**shrill** ● **adj.** (of a voice or sound) high-pitched and piercing. ➤ derogatory (of a complaint or demand) loud and forceful. ● **v.** make a shrill noise.
– DERIVATIVES **shrillness** n. **shrilly** adv.
– ORIGIN ME: of Gmc origin.

**shrimp** ● **n.** **1** (pl. same or **shrimps**) a small free-swimming edible crustacean with ten legs, mainly marine. [*Pandalus*, *Crangon*, and other genera.] **2** informal, derogatory a small, physically weak person. ● **v.** fish for shrimps.
– DERIVATIVES **shrimper** n.
– ORIGIN ME: prob. rel. to Mid. Low Ger. *schrempen* 'to wrinkle', Mid. High Ger. *schrimpfen* 'to contract', also to **SCRIMP**.

**shrimp plant** ● **n.** a Mexican shrub with clusters of small flowers in pinkish-brown bracts, said to resemble shrimps. [*Justicia brandegeana*.]

**shrine** ● **n.** **1** a place regarded as holy because of its associations with a divinity or a sacred person. **2** a casket containing sacred relics; a reliquary. ➤ a niche or enclosure containing a religious statue or other object. ● **v.** poetic/literary enshrine.
– ORIGIN OE *scrīn* 'cabinet, chest, reliquary', of Gmc origin.

**shrink** ● **v.** (past **shrank**; past part. **shrunk** or (especially as adj.) **shrunken**) **1** become or make smaller in size or amount; contract. ➤ (of clothes or material) become smaller as a result of being immersed in water. **2** move back or away in fear or disgust. ➤ (**shrink from**) be averse to or unwilling to do (something). ● **n.** informal a psychiatrist.
– DERIVATIVES **shrinkable** adj. **shrinker** n.
– ORIGIN OE *scrincan*, of Gmc origin; the noun is from *headshrinker*.

**shrinkage** ● **n.** **1** the process, fact, or amount of shrinking. **2** an allowance made for reduction in the takings of a business due to wastage or theft.

**shrinking violet** ● **n.** informal an exaggeratedly shy person.

**shrink wrap** ● **n.** clinging transparent plastic film used to enclose an article as packaging. ● **v.** (**shrink-wrap**) enclose in shrink wrap.

**shrive** /ʃrʌɪv/ ● **v.** (past **shrove**; past part. **shriven**) archaic (of a priest) hear the confession of, assign penance to, and absolve. ➤ (**shrive oneself**) present oneself to a priest for confession, penance, and absolution.
– ORIGIN OE *scrīfan* 'impose as a penance', of Gmc origin, from L. *scribere* 'write'.

**shrivel** ● **v.** (**shrivelled**, **shrivelling**; US **shriveled**, **shriveling**) wrinkle and contract, or cause to wrinkle and contract, through loss of moisture.
– ORIGIN C16: perh. of Scand. origin.

**shroud** ● **n.** **1** a length of cloth or an enveloping garment in which a dead person is wrapped for burial. **2** a thing that envelops or obscures: *a shroud of mist.* **3** technical a protective casing or cover. **4** (**shrouds**) a set of ropes forming part of the standing rigging of a sailing boat and supporting the mast or topmast. ➤ (also **shroud line**) each of the lines joining the canopy of a parachute to the harness. ● **v.** **1** wrap or dress in a shroud. **2** cover or

envelop so as to conceal from view.
– ORIGIN OE *scrūd* 'garment, clothing', of Gmc origin, from a base meaning 'cut'; rel. to **SHRED**.

**shroud-laid** • **adj.** (of rope) made of four strands laid right-handed on a core.

**shrove** past of **SHRIVE**.

**Shrovetide** • **n.** Shrove Tuesday and the two days preceding it, when it was formerly customary to attend confession.

**Shrove Tuesday** • **n.** the day before Ash Wednesday, traditionally marked by feasting before the Lenten fast.

**shrub**[1] • **n.** a woody plant which is smaller than a tree and has several main stems arising at or near the ground.
– DERIVATIVES **shrubby** adj.
– ORIGIN OE *scrubb, scrybb* 'shrubbery'; cf. **SCRUB**[2].

**shrub**[2] • **n. 1** a drink made of sweetened fruit juice and rum or brandy. **2** N. Amer. a slightly acid cordial made from fruit juice and water.
– ORIGIN C18: from Arab. *šurb, šarāb*, from *šariba* 'to drink'; cf. **SHERBET** and **SYRUP**.

**shrubbery** • **n.** (pl. **-ies**) an area in a garden planted with shrubs.

**shrug** • **v.** (**shrugged**, **shrugging**) raise (one's shoulders) slightly and momentarily to express doubt, ignorance, or indifference. ➤(**shrug something off**) dismiss something as unimportant. • **n. 1** an act of shrugging one's shoulders. **2** a woman's close-fitting cardigan or jacket cut short at the front and back so that only the arms and shoulders are covered.
– ORIGIN ME (in the sense 'fidget'): of unknown origin.

**shrunk** (also **shrunken**) past participle of **SHRINK**.

**shtetl** /ˈʃtɛt(ə)l/ • **n.** (pl. **shtetlach** /ˈʃtɛtlɑːx/ or **shtetls**) historical a small Jewish town or village in eastern Europe.
– ORIGIN 1940s: Yiddish, 'little town'.

**shtick** /ʃtɪk/ • **n.** informal an attention-getting or theatrical routine, gimmick, or talent.
– ORIGIN 1960s: Yiddish, from Ger. *Stück* 'piece'.

**shtook** /ʃtʊk/ (also **schtuck**) • **n.** informal trouble.
– ORIGIN 1930s: of unknown origin.

**shtum** /ʃtʊm/ (also **schtum**) informal • **adj.** silent; non-communicative. • **v.** (**shtummed**, **shtumming**) be or become quiet and non-communicative.
– ORIGIN 1950s: Yiddish, from Ger. *stumm*.

**shtup** /ʃtʊp/ (also **schtup**) vulgar slang • **v.** (**shtupped**, **shtupping**) have sexual intercourse with. • **n.** an act of sexual intercourse.
– ORIGIN 1960s: Yiddish.

**shubunkin** /ʃʊˈbʌŋkɪn/ • **n.** a goldfish of an ornamental variety with black spots, red patches, and long fins and tail.
– ORIGIN C20: from Japanese.

**shuck** /ʃʌk/ chiefly N. Amer. • **n.** an outer covering such as a husk or pod, especially the husk of an ear of maize. ➤the shell of an oyster or clam. • **v. 1** remove the shucks from. **2** informal abandon; get rid of. ➤take off (a garment). **3** informal fool or tease (someone).
– DERIVATIVES **shucker** n.
– ORIGIN C17: of unknown origin.

**shucks** • **exclam.** informal, chiefly N. Amer. used to express surprise, regret, etc.

**shudder** • **v.** tremble or shake convulsively, especially from fear or repugnance. • **n.** an act of shuddering.
– DERIVATIVES **shuddering** adj. **shudderingly** adv. **shuddery** adj.
– ORIGIN ME: from MDu. *schūderen*, from a Gmc base meaning 'shake'.

**shuffle** /ˈʃʌf(ə)l/ • **v. 1** walk by dragging one's feet along or without lifting them fully from the ground. ➤restlessly shift one's position. ➤(**shuffle something off/shuffle out of something**) get out of or avoid a responsibility or obligation. **2** rearrange (a pack of cards) by sliding them over each other quickly. ➤(**shuffle through**) sort or look through (a number of things) hurriedly. **3** move (people or things) around into different positions or a different order. • **n. 1** a shuffling movement, walk, or sound. ➤a quick dragging or scraping movement of the feet in dancing. ➤a dance performed with such steps. **2** an act of shuffling a pack of cards. **3** a change of order or relative positions; a reshuffle. **4** a facility on a CD player for playing tracks in an arbitrary order. **5** archaic a piece of equivocation or subterfuge.
– DERIVATIVES **shuffler** n.
– ORIGIN C16: perh. from Low Ger. *schuffeln* 'walk clumsily', also 'deal dishonestly, shuffle (cards)', of Gmc origin; rel. to **SHOVE** and **SCUFFLE**.

**shuffleboard** • **n.** North American term for **SHOVELBOARD**.

**shufti** /ˈʃʊfti/ • **n.** (pl. **shuftis**) Brit. informal a quick look or reconnoitre.
– ORIGIN 1940s (orig. military sl.): from Arab. *šāfa* 'try to see'.

**shul** /ʃuːl/ • **n.** a synagogue.
– ORIGIN C19: Yiddish, from Ger. *Schule* 'school'.

**shun** • **v.** (**shunned**, **shunning**) persistently avoid, ignore, or reject.
– ORIGIN OE *scunian* 'abhor, shrink back with fear, seek safety from an enemy', of unknown origin.

**shunt** • **v. 1** slowly push or pull (a railway vehicle or vehicles) so as to make up or remove from a train. ➤push or shove. ➤direct or divert to a less important place or position. **2** provide (an electrical circuit) with a shunt, through which some of the current may be diverted. • **n. 1** an act of shunting. **2** Brit. informal a motor accident, especially a collision of vehicles travelling one close behind the other. **3** an electrical conductor joining two points of a circuit. **4** Surgery an alternative path created for the passage of blood or other fluid.
– ORIGIN ME: perh. from **SHUN**.

**shunter** • **n. 1** a small locomotive used for shunting. **2** a railway worker engaged in such work.

**shuriken** /ˈʃʊərɪkɛn/ • **n.** a weapon in the form of a star with projecting blades or points, used as a missile in some martial arts.
– ORIGIN Japanese, lit. 'dagger in the hand'.

**shush** /ʃʊʃ, ʃʌʃ/ • **exclam.** be quiet. • **n. 1** an utterance of 'shush'. **2** a soft swishing or rustling sound. • **v. 1** tell or signal to be silent. ➤become or remain silent. **2** move with or make a soft swishing or rustling sound.

**shut** • **v.** (**shutting**; past and past part. **shut**) **1** move or cause to move into position to block an opening. ➤(usu. **shut someone/thing in/out**) confine or exclude by closing something such as a door. ➤(**shut someone out**) prevent an opponent from scoring in a game. ➤(**shut up** or **shut someone up**) informal stop or cause someone to stop talking. **2** fold or bring together the sides or parts of. **3** chiefly Brit. make or become unavailable for business or service. ➤(**shut down** or **shut something down**) cease or cause something to cease business or operation. **4** (**shut off** or **shut something off**) stop or cause something to stop flowing or working.
– PHRASES **be** (or **get**) **shut of** informal be (or get) rid of. **shut up shop** cease trading, either temporarily or permanently.
– ORIGIN OE *scyttan* 'put (a bolt) in position to hold fast', of W. Gmc origin; rel. to **SHOOT**.

**shutdown** • **n.** a closure of a factory or instance of turning off a machine or computer.

**shut-eye** • **n.** informal sleep.

**shutout** • **n.** chiefly N. Amer. a play, game, or inning in which the opposition is prevented from scoring.

**shut-out bid** • **n.** Bridge a high bid intended to end the auction; a pre-emptive bid.

**shutter** • **n. 1** each of a pair of hinged panels fixed inside or outside a window that can be closed for security or privacy or to keep out the light. **2** Photography a device that opens and closes to expose the film in a camera. **3** Music the blind enclosing the swell box in an organ, used for controlling the volume of sound. • **v.** close the shutters of (a window or building).
– DERIVATIVES **shuttering** n. **shutterless** adj.

**shutterbug** • **n.** informal, chiefly N. Amer. an enthusiastic photographer.

**shuttle** • **n. 1** a form of transport that travels regularly

between two places. **2** a bobbin with two pointed ends used for carrying the weft thread across between the warp threads in weaving. ➤a bobbin carrying the lower thread in a sewing machine. **3** short for SHUTTLECOCK. ● **v.** travel regularly between two or more places. ➤transport in a shuttle.
– ORIGIN OE *scytel* 'dart, missile', of Gmc origin; rel. to SHOOT.

**shuttlecock** ● **n.** a light cone-shaped object struck with rackets in the games of badminton and battledore, traditionally of cork with feathers attached.

**shuttle diplomacy** ● **n.** negotiations conducted by a mediator who travels between two or more parties that are reluctant to hold direct discussions.

**shy**[1] ● **adj.** (**shyer, shyest**) **1** nervous or timid in the company of other people. ➤(**shy of/about**) slow or reluctant to do. ➤[in combination] having a specified dislike or aversion: *camera-shy.* ➤(of a wild animal) reluctant to remain in sight of humans. **2** (**shy of**) informal less than; short of or before. **3** (of a plant) not bearing flowers or fruit well or prolifically. ● **v.** (**-ies, -ied**) (especially of a horse) start suddenly aside in fright. ➤(**shy from**) avoid through nervousness or lack of confidence. ● **n.** a sudden startled movement, especially of a frightened horse.
– DERIVATIVES **shyer** n. **shyly** adv. **shyness** n.
– ORIGIN OE *scēoh* '(of a horse) easily frightened', of Gmc origin; cf. ESCHEW.

**shy**[2] ● **v.** (**-ies, -ied**) fling or throw at a target. ● **n.** (pl. **-ies**) (often in phr. **have a shy at**) an act of shying.
– ORIGIN C18: of unknown origin.

**shyster** ● **n.** informal a person, especially a lawyer, who uses unscrupulous methods.
– ORIGIN C19: said to be from *Scheuster*, the name of a lawyer, perh. reinforced by Ger. *Scheisser* 'worthless person'.

**SI** ● **abbrev.** **1** Système International, the international system of units of measurement based on the metre, kilogram, second, ampere, kelvin, candela, and mole, together with prefixes indicating multiplication or division by powers of ten. **2** Law statutory instrument.

**Si** ● **symb.** the chemical element silicon.

**si** /siː/ ● **n.** Music another term for TE.
– ORIGIN C18: from the initial letters of *Sancte Iohannes*, the closing words of a Latin hymn.

**sialagogue** /ˈsʌɪələɡɒɡ/ ● **n.** Medicine a drug that promotes the secretion of saliva.
– ORIGIN C18: from Fr., from Gk *sialon* 'saliva' + *agōgos* 'leading'.

**sialic acid** /sʌɪˈalɪk/ ● **n.** Biochemistry a substance present in saliva, consisting of a sugar with amino and ester groups.
– ORIGIN 1950s: from Gk *sialon* 'saliva' + -IC.

**siamang** /ˈsʌɪəmaŋ, ˈsiːə-/ ● **n.** a large black gibbon native to Sumatra and Malaya. [*Hylobates syndactylus.*]
– ORIGIN C19: from Malay.

**Siamese** ● **n.** (pl. same) **1** dated a native of Siam (now Thailand) in SE Asia. **2** old-fashioned term for THAI (the language). **3** (also **Siamese cat**) a cat of a lightly built short-haired breed characterized by slanting blue eyes and pale fur with darker points. ● **adj.** dated of or relating to Siam, its people, or their language.

**Siamese twins** ● **pl. n.** twins that are physically joined at birth, in some cases sharing organs.
– ORIGIN with ref. to the *Siamese* men Chang and Eng (1811–74), who were joined at the waist.

**SIB** ● **abbrev.** Securities and Investment Board.

**sib** ● **n.** **1** chiefly Zoology a brother or sister; a sibling. **2** Anthropology a group of people recognized by an individual as his or her kindred.
– ORIGIN OE 'relative' and 'related by birth or descent', of unknown origin.

**Siberian** /sʌɪˈbɪərɪən/ ● **n.** a native or inhabitant of Siberia. ● **adj.** of or relating to Siberia.

**sibilant** ● **adj.** **1** making or characterized by a hissing sound. **2** Phonetics (of a speech sound) sounded with a hissing effect, for example *s, sh.* ● **n.** Phonetics a sibilant speech sound.
– DERIVATIVES **sibilance** n.
– ORIGIN C17: from L. *sibilant-*, *sibilare* 'hiss'.

**siblicide** /ˈsɪblɪsʌɪd/ ● **n.** Zoology the killing of a sibling or siblings.

**sibling** ● **n.** each of two or more children or offspring having one or both parents in common; a brother or sister.
– ORIGIN OE, in the sense 'relative' (see SIB, -LING).

**sibship** ● **n.** **1** chiefly Zoology a group of offspring having the same two parents. **2** Anthropology the state of belonging to a sib or the same sib.

**sibyl** ● **n.** (in ancient times) a woman supposedly able to utter the oracles and prophecies of a god. ➤poetic/literary a woman able to foretell the future.
– DERIVATIVES **sibylline** adj.
– ORIGIN from OFr. *Sibile* or med. L. *Sibilla*, via L. from Gk *Sibulla*.

**sic** /sɪk/ ● **adv.** (after a copied or quoted word) written exactly as it stands in the original.
– ORIGIN L., lit. 'so, thus'.

**siccative** /ˈsɪkətɪv/ ● **n.** a drying agent used as a component of paint.
– ORIGIN ME: from late L. *siccativus*, from *siccare* 'to dry'.

**sice**[1] /sʌɪs/ ● **n.** (in gambling) the six on a dice.
– ORIGIN ME: from OFr. *sis*, from L. *sex* 'six'.

**sice**[2] ● **n.** variant spelling of SYCE.

**Sicilian** ● **n.** a native or inhabitant of Sicily. ● **adj.** of or relating to Sicily.

**siciliano** /sɪˌtʃɪlɪˈɑːnəʊ, -ˌsɪlɪ-/ (also **siciliana**) ● **n.** (pl. **-os**) a dance, song, or instrumental piece in 6/8 or 12/8 time, typically in a minor key and evoking a pastoral mood.
– ORIGIN Ital., lit. 'Sicilian'.

**sick**[1] ● **adj.** **1** affected by physical or mental illness. **2** feeling nauseous and wanting to vomit. **3** informal disappointed, mortified, or miserable. **4** (**sick of**) bored by or annoyed with through excessive exposure; weary of. **5** informal (of humour) dealing offensively with unpleasant or upsetting subjects. ➤having abnormal or unnatural tendencies; perverted. **6** archaic pining or longing. **7** informal excellent. ● **n.** Brit. informal vomit. ● **v.** (**sick something up**) Brit. informal bring something up by vomiting.
– PHRASES **be sick 1** be ill. **2** Brit. vomit. **get sick 1** be ill. **2** N. Amer. vomit. **sick to one's stomach 1** nauseous. **2** disgusted.
– DERIVATIVES **sickish** adj.
– ORIGIN OE *sēoc*, of Gmc origin.

**sick**[2] ● **v.** **1** (**sick something on**) set a dog on. **2** (**sick someone on**) informal set someone to pursue, keep watch on, or accompany.
– ORIGIN C19: dial. var. of SEEK.

**sickbay** ● **n.** a room or building set aside for sick people, especially on a ship.

**sickbed** ● **n.** an invalid's bed.

**sick building syndrome** ● **n.** a condition marked by headaches, respiratory problems, etc. affecting office workers, attributed to factors such as poor ventilation in the working environment.

**sicken** ● **v.** **1** become disgusted or appalled. ➤[as adj. **sickening**] informal very irritating or annoying. ➤archaic feel disgust or horror. **2** become ill. ➤(**sicken for**) begin to show symptoms of (a particular illness).
– DERIVATIVES **sickeningly** adv.

**sickener** ● **n.** **1** informal something which causes disgust or severe disappointment. **2** a poisonous toadstool with a red cap. [*Russula emetica.*]

**sick headache** ● **n.** a headache accompanied by nausea, particularly a migraine.

**sickie** ● **n.** informal **1** chiefly Brit. a period of sick leave taken when one is not actually ill. **2** another word for SICKO.

**sickle** ● **n.** a short-handled farming tool with a semicircular blade, used for cutting corn, lopping, or trimming.
– ORIGIN OE *sicol, sicel*, of Gmc origin, based on L. *secula*, from *secare* 'to cut'.

**sick leave** ● **n.** leave of absence granted because of illness.

**sickle-cell anaemia** (also **sickle-cell disease**) ● **n.** a severe hereditary form of anaemia in which a mutated form of haemoglobin distorts the red blood cells into a crescent shape at low oxygen levels.

**sickly** ● adj. (**-ier, -iest**) **1** often ill; in poor health. ➤causing, characterized by, or indicative of poor health. **2** inducing discomfort or nausea: *a sickly green.* ➤excessively sentimental or mawkish.
– DERIVATIVES **sickliness** n.

**sick-making** ● adj. informal nauseatingly unpleasant, shocking, or sentimental.

**sickness** ● n. **1** the state of being ill. ➤a particular type of illness or disease. **2** nausea or vomiting.

**sickness benefit** ● n. (in the UK) benefit paid weekly by the state to an individual for sickness which interrupts paid employment.

**sicko** ● n. (pl. **-os**) informal a mentally ill or perverted person, especially a dangerous one.

**sickroom** ● n. a room occupied by or set apart for people who are unwell.

**sidalcea** /sɪ'dalsɪə/ ● n. a herbaceous North American plant of the mallow family. [Genus *Sidalcea*.]
– ORIGIN mod. L., from *Sida* + *Alcea*, names of related genera.

**siddha** /'sɪdʌ/ ● n. Hinduism an ascetic who has achieved enlightenment.
– ORIGIN from Sanskrit.

**siddhi** /'sɪdi/ ● n. (pl. **siddhis**) Hinduism **1** complete understanding; enlightenment. **2** a paranormal power possessed by a siddha.
– ORIGIN from Sanskrit.

**side** ● n. **1** a position to the left or right of an object, place, or central point. **2** either of the two halves of something regarded as divided by an imaginary central line. **3** an upright or sloping surface of a structure or object that is not the top or bottom and generally not the front or back. ➤each of the flat surfaces of a solid object. ➤each of the lines forming the boundary of a plane rectilinear figure. ➤each of the two surfaces of something flat and thin, e.g. paper. ➤each of the two faces of a record or of the two separate tracks on a cassette tape. **4** a part or region near the edge and away from the middle of something. ➤[as modifier] subsidiary or less important: *a side dish.* **5** a person or group opposing another or others in a dispute or contest. ➤the cause, interests, or attitude of one person or group. ➤a particular aspect: *he had a disagreeable side.* ➤a person's kinship or line of descent as traced through either their father or mother: *Richard was of French descent on his mother's side.* **6** Brit. informal a television channel. **7** a sports team. **8** (also **side spin**) horizontal spinning motion given to a ball, especially by hitting it on one side. **9** Brit. informal boastful or pretentious manner or attitude. ● v. (**side with/against**) support or oppose in a conflict or dispute.
– PHRASES **from side to side 1** alternately left and right from a central point. **2** across the entire width; right across. **on the side 1** in addition to one's regular job. **2** secretly, especially as an illicit sexual relationship. **3** N. Amer. served separately from the main dish. **side by side** close together and facing the same way. **take sides** support one person or cause against another or others.
– DERIVATIVES **-sided** adj. **-sidedly** adv. **-sidedness** n. **sideless** adj. **sideward** adj. & adv. **sidewards** adv.
– ORIGIN OE *sīde* 'left or right part of the body', of Gmc origin, prob. from a base meaning 'extending lengthways'.

**sidearm** /'sʌɪdɑːm/ chiefly Baseball ● adj. & adv. performed with a sweeping motion of the arm from the side of the body at or below shoulder level. ● v. throw or pitch in this way.
– DERIVATIVES **sidearmer** n.

**side arms** ● pl. n. weapons worn at a person's side, such as pistols.

**sideband** ● n. Telecommunications each of two frequency bands either side of the carrier wave, which contain the modulated signal.

**sidebar** ● n. chiefly N. Amer. **1** a short note or supplement placed alongside a main article of text. ➤a side issue. **2** (in a court of law) a discussion between the lawyers and the judge held out of earshot of the jury.

**sideboard** ● n. **1** a flat-topped piece of furniture with cupboards and drawers, used for storing crockery, glasses, etc. **2** Brit. a sideburn.

**sideburn** ● n. a strip of hair grown by a man down each side of the face in front of his ears.
– ORIGIN C19: orig. *burnside*, from the name of General *Burnside*, who affected this style.

**sidecar** ● n. **1** a small, low vehicle attached to the side of a motorcycle for carrying passengers. **2** a cocktail of brandy and lemon juice with orange liqueur.

**side chain** ● n. Chemistry a group of atoms attached to the main part of a molecule with a ring or chain structure.

**side chair** ● n. an upright wooden chair without arms.

**side drum** ● n. a small drum in the form of a short cylinder with a membrane at each end, the upper one being struck with hard sticks and the lower one often fitted with rattling cords or wires (snares).

**side effect** ● n. a secondary, typically undesirable effect of a drug or medical treatment.

**side-foot** ● v. kick (a ball) with the inside of the foot.

**side glance** ● n. a sideways or brief glance.

**sidehill** ● n. N. Amer. a hillside.

**side issue** ● n. a subsidiary point or topic connected to or raised by some other issue.

**sidekick** ● n. informal a person's assistant or junior associate.

**sidelight** ● n. **1** Brit. a small supplementary light on either side of a motor vehicle's headlights. ➤(**sidelights**) a ship's navigation lights. **2** a narrow pane of glass set alongside a door or larger window. **3** a piece of incidental information that helps to clarify or enliven a subject.

**sideline** ● n. **1** an activity done in addition to one's main job. **2** either of the two lines bounding the longer sides of a football field, basketball court, or similar. **3** (**the sidelines**) a position of observing a situation rather than being directly involved in it. ● v. remove or bar from a team, game, or active position.

**sidelong** ● adj. & adv. directed to or from one side; sideways.
– ORIGIN ME: alt. of earlier *sideling*, from **SIDE** + the adverbial suffix *-ling*.

**sideman** ● n. (pl. **-men**) a supporting musician in a jazz band or rock group.

**side-on** ● adj. & adv. on, from, or towards a side.

**sidereal** /sʌɪ'dɪərɪəl/ ● adj. relating to the distant stars, especially with reference to their apparent positions and diurnal motion.
– ORIGIN C17: from L. *sidereus* (from *sidus, sider-* 'star') + **-AL**.

**sidereal day** ● n. Astronomy the time between consecutive meridional transits of the First Point of Aries, almost four minutes shorter than the solar day.

**sidereal period** ● n. Astronomy the period of revolution of one body about another, measured with respect to the distant stars.

**sidereal time** ● n. Astronomy time reckoned from the motion of the earth (or a planet) relative to the distant stars (rather than with respect to the sun).

**sidereal year** ● n. Astronomy the sidereal period of the earth about the sun, about twenty minutes longer than the solar year.

**siderite** /'sʌɪdərʌɪt, 'sɪd-/ ● n. **1** a brown mineral consisting of ferrous carbonate. **2** a meteorite consisting mainly of nickel and iron.
– DERIVATIVES **sideritic** adj.
– ORIGIN C16 (denoting lodestone): from Gk *sidēros* 'iron' + **-ITE**[1].

**sidero-**[1] ● comb. form of or relating to the stars.
– ORIGIN from L. *sidus, sider-* 'star'.

**sidero-**[2] ● comb. form of or relating to iron: *siderophore.*
– ORIGIN from Gk *sidēros* 'iron'.

**side road** ● n. a minor or subsidiary road, especially one joining or diverging from a main road.

**siderophore** /'sɪdərə(ʊ),fɔː, 'sʌɪ-/ ● n. Biochemistry a molecule which binds and transports iron in microorganisms.

**side saddle** ● n. a saddle in which the rider has both feet on the same side of the horse, used by women riders wearing skirts. • **adv.** (**side-saddle**) sitting in this position on a horse.

**side salad** • **n.** a salad served as a side dish.

**sideshow** • **n.** **1** a small show or stall at an exhibition, fair, or circus. **2** a minor but diverting incident or issue.

**side-slip** • **n.** **1** a sideways skid or slip. **2** Aeronautics a sideways movement of an aircraft, especially downwards towards the inside of a turn. • **v.** perform a side-slip.

**sidesman** • **n.** (pl. **-men**) Brit. a churchwarden's assistant.

**side-splitting** • **adj.** informal extremely amusing.
– DERIVATIVES **side-splittingly** adv.

**sidestep** • **v.** (**-stepped**, **-stepping**) **1** avoid by stepping sideways. **2** avoid dealing with or discussing. • **n.** an instance of sidestepping.
– DERIVATIVES **sidestepper** n.

**side street** • **n.** a minor or subsidiary street.

**sidestroke** • **n.** a swimming stroke similar to the breaststroke in which the swimmer lies on their side.

**side suit** • **n.** Bridge a suit other than the trump suit.

**sideswipe** • **n.** **1** a passing critical remark. **2** chiefly N. Amer. a glancing blow from or on the side, especially of a motor vehicle. • **v.** chiefly N. Amer. strike with a glancing blow.

**sidetrack** • **v.** **1** distract from an immediate or important issue. **2** chiefly N. Amer. direct (a train) into a branch line or siding. • **n.** chiefly N. Amer. a railway branch line or siding.

**side valve** • **n.** a valve in an internal-combustion engine mounted alongside the cylinder.

**sidewalk** • **n.** N. Amer. a pavement.

**sidewall** • **n.** the side of a tyre.

**sideways** • **adv.** & **adj.** **1** to, towards, or from the side. ➤so as to occupy a job or position at the same level as one previously held. **2** unconventional or unorthodox: *a sideways look at daily life.*

**side-wheeler** • **n.** N. Amer. a steamer with paddle wheels on either side.

**side whiskers** • **pl. n.** whiskers or sideburns on a man's cheeks.

**side wind** • **n.** a wind blowing predominantly from one side.

**sidewinder**[1] /ˈsʌɪdˌwʌɪndə/ • **n.** a nocturnal burrowing rattlesnake that moves sideways over sand by throwing its body into S-shaped curves. [*Crotalus cerastes.*]

**sidewinder**[2] /ˈsʌɪdˌwɪndə/ • **n.** N. Amer. a heavy blow with the fist delivered from or on the side.

**sidewise** • **adv.** & **adj.** another term for **SIDEWAYS**.

**siding** • **n.** **1** a short track at the side of and opening on to a railway line, for shunting or stabling trains. **2** N. Amer. a loop line. **3** N. Amer. cladding material for the outside of a building.

**sidle** • **v.** walk in a furtive or stealthy manner, especially sideways or obliquely. • **n.** an instance of sidling.
– ORIGIN C17: back-form. from *sideling* (see **SIDELONG**).

**SIDS** • **abbrev.** sudden infant death syndrome.

**siege** • **n.** **1** a military operation in which enemy forces surround a town or building, cutting off essential supplies, with the aim of compelling the surrender of those inside. **2** a similar operation by a police team to compel the surrender of an armed person.
– PHRASES **lay siege to** conduct a siege of. **under siege** undergoing a siege.
– ORIGIN ME: from OFr. *sege*, from *asegier* 'besiege'.

**siege mentality** • **n.** a defensive or paranoid attitude based on the belief that others are hostile towards one.

**siemens** /ˈsiːmənz/ (abbrev.: **S**) • **n.** Physics the SI unit of conductance, equal to one reciprocal ohm.
– ORIGIN 1930s: named after the German-born Brit. engineer Sir Charles William *Siemens.*

**sienna** • **n.** a kind of ferruginous earth used as a pigment in painting, normally yellowish-brown in colour (**raw sienna**) or deep reddish-brown when roasted (**burnt sienna**).
– ORIGIN C18: from Ital. (*terra di*) *Sienna* '(earth of) Siena'.

**sierra** /sɪˈɛrə, sɪˈɛːrə/ • **n.** **1** (especially in Spanish-speaking countries or the western US) a long jagged mountain chain. **2** a code word representing the letter S, used in radio communication.
– ORIGIN C16: Sp., from L. *serra* 'saw'.

**Sierra Leonean** /lɪˈəʊnɪən/ • **n.** a native or inhabitant of Sierra Leone, a country in West Africa. • **adj.** of or relating to Sierra Leone.

**siesta** /sɪˈɛstə/ • **n.** an afternoon rest or nap, especially one taken during the hottest hours of the day in a hot climate.
– ORIGIN C17: Sp., from L. *sexta* (*hora*) 'sixth hour'.

**sieve** /sɪv/ • **n.** a utensil consisting of a wire or plastic mesh held in a frame, used for straining solids from liquids, for separating coarser from finer particles, or for reducing soft solids to a pulp. • **v.** **1** put through a sieve. **2** (**sieve through**) examine in detail.
– ORIGIN OE *sife* (n.), of W. Gmc origin.

**sievert** /ˈsiːvət/ (abbrev.: **Sv**) • **n.** Physics the SI unit of dose equivalent, defined as a dose which delivers a joule of energy per kilogram of recipient mass.
– ORIGIN 1940s: named after the Swed. physicist Rolf M. *Sievert.*

**sifaka** /sɪˈfakə/ • **n.** a large gregarious lemur which leaps from tree to tree in an upright position. [Genus *Propithecus*: two species.]
– ORIGIN C19: from Malagasy.

**sift** • **v.** **1** put (a dry substance) through a sieve so as to remove lumps or large particles. **2** cause to flow or pass as through a sieve. **3** (**sift down**) (of snow, ash, light, etc.) descend lightly or sparsely as if having passed through a sieve. **4** examine thoroughly so as to isolate that which is important or useful. • **n.** an act of sifting.
– DERIVATIVES **sifted** adj. **sifter** n. **sifting** n.
– ORIGIN OE *siftan*, of W. Gmc origin; rel. to **SIEVE**.

**SIG** • **abbrev.** Computing special interest group.

**Sig.** • **abbrev.** Signor.

**sig** • **n.** Computing, informal a short personalized message at the end of an email message.
– ORIGIN 1990s: abbrev. of **SIGNATURE**.

**Sigatoka** /ˌsɪgəˈtəʊkə/ • **n.** a fungal disease of banana plants.
– ORIGIN 1920s: named after a district in Fiji.

**sigh** • **n.** **1** a long, deep, audible exhalation expressing sadness, tiredness, relief, etc. **2** a sound resembling this. • **v.** **1** emit a sigh. **2** (**sigh for**) poetic/literary yearn for.
– ORIGIN ME (as v.): prob. a back-form. from *sighte*, past tense of *siche, sike*, from OE *sīcan*.

**sight** • **n.** **1** the faculty or power of seeing. **2** the action or fact of seeing someone or something. **3** the area or distance within which someone can see or something can be seen. **4** a thing that one sees or that can be seen. **5** (**sights**) places of interest to tourists and other visitors. **6** (**a sight**) informal a person or thing having a ridiculous or unattractive appearance. **7** (usu. **sights**) a device on a gun or optical instrument used for assisting in precise aim or observation. • **v.** **1** manage to see or briefly observe. **2** take aim by looking through the sights of a gun. **3** take a detailed visual measurement with or as with a sight. **4** adjust the sight of (a gun or optical instrument).
– PHRASES **at first sight** at the first glimpse; on the first impression. **catch sight of** glimpse for a moment. **in sight 1** visible. **2** near at hand; close to being achieved or realized. **in** (or **within**) **sight of 1** so as to see or be seen from. **2** within reach of; close to attaining. **in** (or **within**) **one's sights 1** visible, especially through the sights of one's gun. **2** within the scope of one's ambitions or expectations. **lose sight of 1** be no longer able to see. **2** fail to consider, be aware of, or remember. **on** (or **at**) **sight** as soon as someone or something has been seen. **out of sight 1** not visible. **2** (also **outasight**) informal extremely good; excellent. **raise** (or **lower**) **one's sights** become more (or less) ambitious; increase (or lower) one's expectations. **set one's sights on** hope strongly to achieve or reach. **a sight ——** informal indicating considerable extent: *she is a sight cleverer than Sarah.* **a sight for sore eyes** informal a person or thing that one is extremely

pleased or relieved to see. **a sight to behold** a person or thing that is particularly impressive or worth seeing.
– DERIVATIVES **sighted** adj. **sighter** n. **sighting** n.
– ORIGIN OE *(ge)sihth* 'something seen', of W. Gmc origin.

**sight deposit** • n. a bank deposit that can be withdrawn immediately without notice or penalty.

**sight glass** • n. a transparent tube or window through which the level of liquid in a reservoir or supply line can be checked visually.

**sighting shot** • n. an experimental shot to guide shooters in adjusting their sights.

**sightless** • adj. **1** unable to see; blind. **2** poetic/literary invisible.
– DERIVATIVES **sightlessly** adv. **sightlessness** n.

**sight line** • n. a hypothetical line from someone's eye to what is seen.

**sightly** • adj. pleasing to the eye.
– DERIVATIVES **sightliness** n.

**sight-read** • v. read and perform (music) at sight, without preparation.
– DERIVATIVES **sight-reader** n.

**sight screen** • n. Cricket a large white screen placed near the boundary in line with the wicket to help the batsman see the ball.

**sightseeing** • n. the activity of visiting places of interest in a particular location.
– DERIVATIVES **sightsee** v. **sightseer** n.

**sight-sing** • v. sing (music) at sight, without preparation.

**sight unseen** • adv. without the opportunity to look at the object in question beforehand.

**sigil** /ˈsɪdʒɪl/ • n. **1** a sign or symbol. **2** archaic a seal.
– ORIGIN ME: from late L. *sigillum* 'sign'.

**SIGINT** /ˈsɪgɪnt/ • abbrev. signals intelligence.

**siglum** /ˈsɪgləm/ • n. (pl. **sigla** /-lə/) a letter or symbol which stands for a word or name, especially to denote a particular manuscript or edition of a text.
– ORIGIN C18: from late L. *sigla* (pl.), perh. from *singula*, neut. pl. of *singulus* 'single'.

**sigma** /ˈsɪgmə/ • n. **1** the eighteenth letter of the Greek alphabet (Σ, σ, or at the end of a word ς), transliterated as 's'. **2** [as modifier] Chemistry & Physics (of an electron or orbital) with zero angular momentum about an internuclear axis. • symb. **1** (Σ) mathematical sum. **2** (σ) standard deviation.
– ORIGIN from Gk.

**sigmate** /ˈsɪgmət/ • adj. having the shape of a Σ or a letter S.

**sigmoid** /ˈsɪgmɔɪd/ • adj. **1** curved like the uncial sigma; crescent-shaped. **2** S-shaped. **3** Anatomy of or denoting the curved part of the colon leading into the rectum.
– DERIVATIVES **sigmoidal** adj.
– ORIGIN C17: from Gk *sigmoeidēs*, from *sigma* (see SIGMA).

**sigmoidoscopy** /ˌsɪgmɔɪˈdɒskəpi/ • n. examination of the sigmoid colon by means of a flexible tube inserted through the anus.
– DERIVATIVES **sigmoidoscope** n. **sigmoidoscopic** adj.

**sign** • n. **1** an object, quality, or event whose presence or occurrence indicates the probable presence, occurrence, or advent of something else. **2** Medicine an indication of a disease detectable by a medical practitioner even if not apparent to the patient. Compare with SYMPTOM. **3** N. Amer. the trail of a wild animal. **4** a signal conveying information or an instruction. **5** a public notice giving information or instructions in a written or symbolic form. **6** a gesture used in sign language. **7** a symbol or word used to represent an operation, instruction, concept, or object in algebra, music, or other subjects. **8** Astrology each of the twelve equal sections into which the zodiac is divided, named from the constellations formerly situated in each, and associated with successive periods of the year according to the position of the sun on the ecliptic. **9** Mathematics the positiveness or negativeness of a quantity. • v. **1** write one's name on (something) for the purposes of identification or authorization. ➤ write (one's name) for such a purpose. **2** (with reference to a sports player, musician, etc.) engage for or commit oneself to work by signing a contract. **3** use gestures to convey information or instructions. **4** communicate in sign language. **5** (usu. **be signed**) indicate with signposts or other markers. **6** mark or consecrate with the sign of the cross.
– PHRASAL VERBS **sign in** sign a register on arrival in a hotel or workplace. **sign someone in** record someone's arrival in a register. **sign off 1** conclude a letter, broadcast, or other message. **2** sign to record that one is leaving work for the day. **3** Brit. register to stop receiving unemployment benefit after finding work. **sign someone off** record that someone is entitled to miss work. **sign off on** US informal assent or give one's approval to. **sign on 1** commit oneself to employment, membership of a society, etc. **2** Brit. register as unemployed. **sign someone on** take someone into one's employment. **sign out** sign a register to record one's departure from a hotel or workplace. **sign someone out** authorize someone's release or record their departure by signing a register. **sign something out** sign to indicate that one has borrowed or hired something. **sign up 1** commit oneself to a period of employment, education, etc. **2** (also **sign something up**) conclude a business deal. **sign someone up** formally engage someone in employment.
– DERIVATIVES **signed** adj. **signer** n.
– ORIGIN ME: from OFr. *signe* (n.), *signer* (v.), from L. *signum* 'mark, token'.

**signage** • n. chiefly N. Amer. signs collectively, especially commercial or public display signs.

**signal**[1] • n. **1** a gesture, action, or sound conveying information or an instruction. **2** an indication of a state of affairs. **3** an event or statement that provides the impulse or occasion for something to happen. **4** a light or semaphore on a railway, giving indications to train drivers of whether or not to proceed. **5** Bridge a pre-arranged convention of bidding or play intended to convey information to one's partner. **6** an electrical impulse or radio wave transmitted or received. • v. (**signalled**, **signalling**; US **signaled**, **signaling**) **1** transmit a signal. **2** instruct or indicate by means of a signal.
– DERIVATIVES **signaller** n.
– ORIGIN ME: from OFr., from med. L. *signale*, neut. of late L. *signalis*, from L. *signum* (see SIGN).

**signal**[2] • adj. striking; outstanding.
– DERIVATIVES **signally** adv.
– ORIGIN C17: from Fr. *signalé*, from the Ital. past part. *segnalato* 'distinguished', from *segnale* 'a signal'.

**signal box** • n. Brit. a building beside a railway track from which signals, points, and other equipment are controlled.

**signalize** (also **-ise**) • v. **1** mark or indicate. **2** archaic make noteworthy or remarkable. **3** US & Austral. provide (an intersection) with traffic signals.

**signalman** • n. (pl. **-men**) **1** a railway worker responsible for operating signals and points. **2** a person responsible for sending and receiving naval or military signals.

**signal-to-noise ratio** • n. the ratio of the strength of an electrical or other signal carrying information to that of unwanted interference, generally expressed in decibels.

**signatory** /ˈsɪgnət(ə)ri/ • n. (pl. **-ies**) a party that has signed an agreement.
– ORIGIN C19: from L. *signatorius* 'of sealing', from *signare* (see SIGNATURE).

**signature** • n. **1** a person's name written in a distinctive way as a form of identification or authorization. **2** the action of applying one's signature. **3** a distinctive product or characteristic by which someone or something can be identified. **4** Music short for KEY SIGNATURE or TIME SIGNATURE. **5** Printing a letter or figure printed at the foot of one or more pages of each sheet of a book as a guide in binding. **6** a printed sheet after being folded to form a group of pages. **7** N. Amer. the part of a medical prescription that gives instructions about the use of the medicine or drug prescribed.
– ORIGIN C16: from med. L. *signatura* 'sign manual', from L. *signare* 'to sign, mark'.

**signature tune** • n. chiefly Brit. a distinctive piece of music associated with a particular programme or performer on television or radio.

**signboard** • n. **1** a board displaying the name or logo of a business or product. **2** chiefly N. Amer. a board displaying a sign to direct traffic or travellers.

**signee** • n. a person who has signed a contract or other official document.

**signet** • n. historical **1** a small seal, especially one set in a ring, used instead of or with a signature to give authentication to an official document. **2** (usu. **the Signet**) the royal seal formerly used for special purposes in England and Scotland, and in Scotland later as the seal of the Court of Session.
– ORIGIN ME: from OFr., or from med. L. *signetum*, dimin. of *signum* 'token, seal'.

**signet ring** • n. a ring with a seal set into it.

**significance** • n. **1** the quality of being significant; importance. **2** the unstated meaning to be found in words or events. **3** (also **statistical significance**) the extent to which a result deviates from that expected to arise simply from random variation or errors in sampling.
– ORIGIN ME: from OFr., or from L. *significantia*, from *significare* 'indicate, portend'.

**significant** • adj. **1** having an unstated meaning; indicative of something. **2** extensive or important enough to merit attention. **3** Statistics of, relating to, or having significance.
– DERIVATIVES **significantly** adv.

**significant figure** • n. Mathematics each of the digits of a number that are used to express it to the required degree of accuracy, starting from the first non-zero digit.

**signified** • n. Linguistics the meaning or idea expressed by a sign, as distinct from the physical form in which it is expressed.

**signifier** • n. Linguistics a sign's physical form (such as a sound, printed word, or image) as distinct from its meaning.

**signify** • v. (**-ies, -ied**) **1** be an indication of. **2** be a symbol of; have as meaning. **3** (of a person) indicate or declare (a feeling or intention). **4** [with neg.] be of importance. **5** US informal (among black Americans) exchange boasts or insults as a game or ritual.
– DERIVATIVES **signification** n.
– ORIGIN ME: from OFr. *signifier*, from L. *significare* 'indicate, portend', from *signum* 'token'.

**signing** • n. **1** Brit. a person who has recently been signed to join a sports team, record company, etc. **2** an event at which an author signs copies of their book to gain publicity and sales. **3** sign language. **4** the provision of signs in a street.

**sign language** • n. a system of communication used among and with deaf people, consisting of facial and manual gestures and signs.

**signor** /'si:njɔ:, si:'njɔ:/ (also **signore**) • n. (pl. **signori** /-'njɔ:ri:/) a title or form of address used of or to an Italian-speaking man, corresponding to *Mr* or *sir*.
– ORIGIN Ital., from L. *senior* (see **SENIOR**).

**signora** /si:'njɔ:rə/ • n. a title or form of address used of or to an Italian-speaking married woman, corresponding to *Mrs* or *madam*.
– ORIGIN Ital., fem. of *signor* (see **SIGNOR**).

**signorina** /ˌsi:njə'ri:nə/ • n. a title or form of address used of or to an Italian-speaking unmarried woman, corresponding to *Miss*.
– ORIGIN Ital., dimin. of *signora* (see **SIGNORA**).

**signory** /'si:njəri/ • n. (pl. **-ies**) **1** another term for **SEIGNIORY**. **2** historical the governing body of a medieval Italian republic. [influenced by Ital. *signoria*.]

**signpost** • n. a sign on a post, giving information such as the direction and distance to a nearby town. • v. **1** provide (an area) with a signpost or signposts. **2** chiefly Brit. indicate (a place or feature) with a signpost.

**signwriter** (also **sign painter**) • n. a person who paints commercial signs and advertisements.
– DERIVATIVES **signwriting** n.

**sika** /'si:kə/ (also **sika deer**) • n. a forest-dwelling deer with a greyish winter coat that turns yellowish-brown with white spots in summer, native to Japan and SE Asia and naturalized in Britain and elsewhere. [*Cervus nippon*.]
– ORIGIN C19: from Japanese *shika*.

**sike** /sʌɪk/ • n. Scottish & N. English a small stream or rill.
– ORIGIN OE *sīc*.

**Sikh** /si:k/ • n. an adherent of Sikhism. • adj. of or relating to Sikhs or Sikhism.
– ORIGIN from Punjabi 'disciple', from Sanskrit *śiṣya*.

**Sikhism** /'si:kɪz(ə)m, 'sɪk-/ • n. a monotheistic religion founded in Punjab in the 15th century by Guru Nanak.

**Sikkimese** /sɪkɪ'mi:z/ • n. a native or inhabitant of the Indian state of Sikkim. • adj. of or relating to Sikkim.

**Siksika** /'sɪksɪkə/ • pl. n. the northernmost of the three peoples forming the Blackfoot confederacy.
– ORIGIN from Blackfoot *siksi-* 'black' + *ka-* 'foot'.

**silage** /'sʌɪlɪdʒ/ • n. grass or other green fodder that is compacted and stored in airtight conditions, without first being dried, and used as animal feed in the winter. • v. **1** make silage. **2** preserve as silage.
– DERIVATIVES **silaging** n.
– ORIGIN C19: alt. of **ENSILAGE**, influenced by **SILO**.

**silane** /'sʌɪleɪn/ • n. Chemistry a spontaneously flammable gaseous compound of silicon and hydrogen. [$SiH_4$.] ➤any of the series of silicon hydrides analogous to the alkanes.
– ORIGIN C20: from **SILICON** + **-ANE**[2].

**sild** • n. (pl. same) a small immature herring.
– ORIGIN 1920s: from Dan. and Norw.

**silence** • n. **1** complete absence of sound. **2** the fact or state of abstaining from speech. **3** the avoidance of mentioning or discussing something. • v. **1** make silent. **2** fit with a silencer.
– DERIVATIVES **silenced** adj.
– ORIGIN ME: from OFr., from L. *silentium*, from *silere* 'be silent'.

**silencer** • n. a device for reducing the noise emitted by a mechanism, especially a gun or exhaust system.

**silent** • adj. **1** not making or accompanied by any sound. ➤(of a film) without an accompanying soundtrack. **2** not speaking or not spoken aloud. ➤not prone to speak much. **3** (of a letter) written but not pronounced, e.g. *b* in *doubt*. **4** saying or recording nothing on a particular subject.
– DERIVATIVES **silently** adv.

**silent partner** • n. North American term for **SLEEPING PARTNER**.

**Silesian** /sʌɪ'li:zɪən, -'li:ʒən/ • n. a native or inhabitant of Silesia, a region of central Europe. • adj. of or relating to Silesia.

**silex** /'sʌɪlɛks/ • n. silica, especially quartz or flint.
– ORIGIN C16: from L., 'flint'.

**silhouette** /ˌsɪlʊ'ɛt/ • n. **1** the dark shape and outline of someone or something visible in restricted light against a brighter background. **2** a representation of someone or something showing the shape and outline only, typically coloured in solid black. • v. cast or show as a silhouette: *the castle was silhouetted against the sky.*
– ORIGIN C18: named (although the reason remains obscure) after the Fr. author and politician Étienne de *Silhouette*.

**silica** /'sɪlɪkə/ • n. silicon dioxide, a hard, unreactive, colourless compound which occurs as quartz and as the principal constituent of sandstone and other rocks. [$SiO_2$.]
– DERIVATIVES **siliceous** /sɪ'lɪʃəs/ (also **silicious**) adj.
– ORIGIN C19: from L. *silex, silic-* 'flint', on the pattern of words such as *alumina*.

**silica gel** • n. hydrated silica in a hard granular hygroscopic form used as a desiccant.

**silicate** /'sɪlɪkeɪt, -kət/ • n. **1** Chemistry a salt in which the anion contains both silicon and oxygen. **2** a mineral consisting of silica combined with metal oxides, as a common constituent of rocks.

**silicic** /sɪ'lɪsɪk/ • adj. Geology (of rocks) rich in silica.

**silicic acid** • n. Chemistry a hydrated form of silica made by acidifying solutions of silicates.

**silicide** /'sɪlɪsʌɪd/ • n. Chemistry a compound of silicon with a metal or other element.

**silicify** /sɪ'lɪsɪfʌɪ/ ● v. (**-ies**, **-ied**) convert into or impregnate with silica.
– DERIVATIVES **silicification** n. **silicified** adj.

**silicon** /'sɪlɪk(ə)n/ ● n. the chemical element of atomic number 14, a shiny grey crystalline non-metal with semiconducting properties, used in making electronic circuits. (Symbol: **Si**)
– ORIGIN C19: alt. of earlier *silicium*, from L. *silex, silic-* 'flint', on the pattern of *carbon* and *boron*.

**silicon carbide** ● n. a hard refractory compound of silicon and carbon; carborundum. [SiC.]

**silicon chip** ● n. a microchip.

**silicone** /'sɪlɪkəʊn/ ● n. a durable synthetic resin with a structure based on chains of silicon and oxygen atoms with organic side chains. ● v. treat with a silicone.
– DERIVATIVES **siliconize** (also **-ise**) v. **siliconized** (also **-ised**) adj.

**silicosis** /ˌsɪlɪ'kəʊsɪs/ ● n. Medicine lung fibrosis caused by the inhalation of dust containing silica.
– DERIVATIVES **silicotic** adj.

**siliqua** /'sɪlɪkwə/ (also **silique** /sɪ'liːk/) ● n. (pl. **siliquae** /-kwiː/ or **siliques** /sɪ'liːks/) **1** Botany the long, narrow seed pod of many plants of the cabbage family. **2** a Roman silver coin of the 4th and 5th centuries AD, worth 1/24 solidus.
– DERIVATIVES **siliquose** /-kwəʊs/ adj.
– ORIGIN L., lit. 'pod'.

**silk** ● n. **1** a fine, strong, soft lustrous fibre produced by silkworms in making cocoons. **2** thread or fabric made from this fibre. **3** (**silks**) garments made from silk, especially as worn by a jockey in the colours of a particular horse owner. **4** Brit. informal a Queen's (or King's) Counsel. [so named because of the right accorded to wear a gown made of silk.] **5** (**silks**) the silky styles of the female maize flower.
– PHRASES **take silk** Brit. become a Queen's (or King's) Counsel.
– DERIVATIVES **silken** adj.
– ORIGIN OE *sioloc, seolec*, from late L. *sericum*, neut. of L. *sericus*, based on Gk *Sēres*, the name given to the inhabitants of the Far Eastern countries from which silk first came overland to Europe.

**silk cotton** ● n. another term for KAPOK.

**silk-cotton tree** ● n. a tree which produces kapok. [*Bombax ceiba* (India) and *Ceiba pentandra* (the ceiba, tropical America).]

**silk gland** ● n. a gland in a silkworm, spider, or other arthropod that secretes the substance which hardens as threads of silk or web.

**silk hat** ● n. a man's tall, cylindrical hat covered with black silk plush.

**silkie** ● n. (pl. **-ies**) **1** a small chicken of a breed characterized by long soft plumage. **2** variant spelling of SELKIE.

**silk moth** ● n. a large moth with a caterpillar that produces silk. [*Bombyx mori* (Asia) and other species.]

**silk screen** ● n. a screen of fine mesh used in screen printing. ● v. (**silk-screen**) print, decorate, or reproduce using a silk screen.

**silk-stocking** ● adj. N. Amer. affluent.

**silkworm** ● n. a caterpillar of a domesticated silk moth, which spins a silk cocoon that is processed to yield silk fibre.

**silky** ● adj. (**-ier**, **-iest**) **1** of or resembling silk. **2** suave and smooth: *a silky, seductive voice.*
– DERIVATIVES **silkily** adv. **silkiness** n.

**sill** (also chiefly Building **cill**) ● n. **1** a shelf or slab of stone, wood, or metal at the foot of a window or doorway. **2** a strong horizontal member at the base of any structure, e.g. in the frame of a motor or rail vehicle. **3** Geology a tabular sheet of igneous rock intruded between and parallel with the existing strata. Compare with DYKE[1]. **4** an underwater ridge or rock ledge extending across the bed of a body of water.
– ORIGIN OE *syll, sylle* 'horizontal beam forming a foundation', of Gmc origin.

**sillabub** ● n. archaic spelling of SYLLABUB.

**sillimanite** /'sɪlɪmənʌɪt/ ● n. an aluminosilicate mineral typically occurring as fibrous masses, commonly in schist or gneiss.
– ORIGIN C19: from the name of the Amer. chemist Benjamin *Silliman* + -ITE[1].

**silly** ● adj. (**-ier**, **-iest**) **1** lacking in common sense or judgement; foolish. **2** trivial or frivolous. **3** archaic weak-minded. **4** archaic helpless; defenceless. **5** Cricket denoting fielding positions very close to the batsman: *silly mid-on.* ● n. (pl. **-ies**) informal a silly person.
– PHRASES **the silly season** chiefly Brit. high summer, regarded as the season when newspapers often publish trivial material because of a lack of important news.
– DERIVATIVES **sillily** adv. **silliness** n.
– ORIGIN ME (in the sense 'deserving of pity or sympathy'): alt. of dial. *seely* 'happy', later 'innocent, feeble', from a W. Gmc base meaning 'luck, happiness'.

**silly billy** ● n. informal, chiefly Brit. a foolish person.

**silo** /'sʌɪləʊ/ ● n. (pl. **-os**) **1** a tall tower or pit on a farm, used to store grain. **2** a pit or other airtight structure in which green crops are compressed and stored as silage. **3** an underground chamber in which a guided missile is kept ready for firing.
– ORIGIN C19: from Sp., via L. from Gk *siros* 'corn pit'.

**silt** ● n. **1** fine sand, clay, or other material carried by running water and deposited as a sediment. **2** technical sediment whose particles are between clay and sand in size (typically 0.002–0.06 mm). ● v. fill or block or become filled or blocked with silt.
– DERIVATIVES **siltation** n. **silting** n. **silty** adj.
– ORIGIN ME: prob. orig. denoting a salty deposit and of Scand. origin, rel. to SALT.

**siltstone** ● n. fine-grained sedimentary rock consisting of consolidated silt.

**Silurian** /sʌɪ'ljʊərɪən, sɪ-/ ● adj. Geology relating to or denoting the third period of the Palaeozoic era (between the Ordovician and Devonian periods, about 439 to 409 million years ago), a time when land plants and the first true fish appeared.
– ORIGIN C18: from *Silures*, the L. name of a people of ancient SE Wales + -IAN.

**silvan** ● adj. variant spelling of SYLVAN.

**silver** ● n. **1** a precious shiny greyish-white metal, the chemical element of atomic number 47. (Symbol: **Ag**) **2** a shiny grey-white colour or appearance like that of silver. **3** silver dishes, containers, or cutlery. ➤household cutlery of any material. **4** coins made from silver or from a metal that resembles silver. ➤chiefly Scottish money. ● v. **1** coat or plate with silver. **2** provide (mirror glass) with a backing of a silver-coloured material in order to make it reflective. **3** poetic/literary (especially of the moon) give a silvery appearance to. **4** (with reference to hair) turn or cause to turn grey or white.
– PHRASES **be born with a silver spoon in one's mouth** be born into a wealthy family of high social standing. **the silver screen** the cinema industry.
– DERIVATIVES **silvered** adj. **silveriness** n. **silvering** n. **silverware** n. **silvery** adj.
– ORIGIN OE *seolfor*, of Gmc origin.

**silver age** ● n. a period regarded as notable but inferior to a golden age.

**silverback** ● n. a mature male mountain gorilla, which is distinguished by an area of white or silvery hair across the back and is the dominant member of its social group.

**silver birch** ● n. a birch with silver-grey bark, common on poorer soils to the northern limit of tree growth. [*Betula pendula*.]

**silver disc** ● n. a framed silver-coloured disc awarded to a recording artist or group for sales of a recording exceeding a specified figure (lower than those required for a gold disc).

**silver fern** ● n. **1** another term for PONGA. **2** a stylized fern leaf in silver, as an emblem of New Zealand.

**silverfish** ● n. (pl. same or **-fishes**) a silvery bristletail that lives in buildings, chiefly nocturnal and feeding on starchy materials. [*Lepisma saccharina*.]

**silver fox** ● n. a red fox of a North American variety which has black fur with white tips.

**silver gilt** ● n. **1** gilded silver. **2** an imitation gilding of yellow lacquer over silver leaf.

**silver jubilee** ● n. the twenty-fifth anniversary of a significant event.

**silver Latin** ● n. literary Latin from the death of Augustus (AD 14) to the mid second century.

**silver medal** ● n. a medal made of or coloured silver, customarily awarded for second place in a race or competition.

**silvern** /ˈsɪlv(ə)n/ ● adj. archaic made of or coloured silver.
– ORIGIN OE *seolfren, silfren* (see **SILVER**, **-N**[1]).

**silver plate** ● n. **1** a thin layer of silver electroplated or otherwise applied as a coating to another metal. **2** plates, dishes, etc. made of or plated with silver. ● v. (**silver-plate**) cover with a thin layer of silver.

**silverpoint** ● n. the art of drawing with a silver-pointed instrument on paper prepared with a coating of powdered bone or zinc white, creating a fine indelible line composed of metal fragments.

**silver sand** ● n. Brit. a fine, white sand used in gardening.

**silver service** ● n. a style of serving food at formal meals in which the server uses a silver spoon and fork in one hand to place food on the diner's plate.

**silverside** ● n. **1** Brit. the upper side of a round of beef from the outside of the leg. **2** (also **silversides**) a small, slender, chiefly marine fish with a bright silver line along its sides. [Family Atherinidae: numerous species.]

**silversmith** ● n. a person who makes silver articles.
– DERIVATIVES **silversmithing** n.

**silver thaw** ● n. a glassy coating of ice formed by freezing rain or the refreezing of thawed ice.

**silver tongue** ● n. a tendency to be eloquent and persuasive in speaking.
– DERIVATIVES **silver-tongued** adj.

**silver wedding** ● n. the twenty-fifth anniversary of a wedding.

**silverweed** ● n. a yellow-flowered herbaceous potentilla with silvery compound leaves, a common grassland weed of north temperate regions. [*Potentilla anserina*.]

**silviculture** /ˈsɪlvɪˌkʌltʃə/ ● n. the growing and cultivation of trees.
– DERIVATIVES **silvicultural** adj. **silviculturist** n.
– ORIGIN C19: from Fr. *sylviculture*, from L. *silva* 'wood' + Fr. *culture* 'cultivation'.

**sim** ● n. informal a video game that simulates an activity such as flying an aircraft or playing a sport.
– ORIGIN C20: abbrev. of *simulation* (see **SIMULATE**).

**simazine** /ˈsɪməziːn, ˈsʌɪ-/ ● n. a synthetic herbicide derived from triazine.
– ORIGIN 1950s: blend of **SYMMETRICAL** and **TRIAZINE**.

**simcha** /ˈsɪmtʃə, -xa/ ● n. a Jewish private party or celebration.
– ORIGIN from Heb. *śimḥāh* 'rejoicing'.

**simian** /ˈsɪmɪən/ ● adj. of, relating to, or resembling apes or monkeys. ● n. an ape or monkey.
– ORIGIN C17: from L. *simia* 'ape', perh. via L. from Gk *simos* 'flat-nosed'.

**similar** ● adj. **1** of the same kind in appearance, character, or quantity, without being identical. **2** Geometry (of geometrical figures) having the same angles and proportions, though of different sizes. ● n. **1** chiefly archaic a person or thing similar to another. **2** a substance that produces effects resembling the symptoms of a disease (the basis of homeopathic treatment).
– DERIVATIVES **similarity** n. **similarly** adv.
– ORIGIN C16: from Fr. *similaire* or med. L. *similaris*, from L. *similis* 'like'.

**simile** /ˈsɪmɪli/ ● n. a figure of speech involving the comparison of one thing with another thing of a different kind (e.g. *as solid as a rock*).
– ORIGIN ME: from L., neut. of *similis* 'like'.

**similitude** /sɪˈmɪlɪtjuːd/ ● n. **1** the quality or state of being similar. **2** archaic a comparison between two things. **3** archaic a person or thing resembling another.
– ORIGIN ME: from OFr., from L. *similitudo*, from *similis* 'like'.

**SIMM** ● abbrev. Computing single in-line memory module.

**Simmental** /ˈsɪm(ə)ntɑːl/ ● n. an animal of a red and white breed of cattle farmed for both meat and milk.
– ORIGIN 1950s: named after a valley in central Switzerland.

**simmer** ● v. **1** stay or cause to stay just below boiling point while bubbling gently. **2** be in a state of suppressed anger or excitement. ➤(**simmer down**) become calmer and quieter. ● n. a state or temperature just below boiling point.
– ORIGIN C17: alt. of dial. *simper* (in the same sense), perh. imitative.

**simnel cake** /ˈsɪmn(ə)l/ ● n. chiefly Brit. a rich fruit cake with a layer of marzipan on top and sometimes also inside, eaten especially at Easter or during Lent.
– ORIGIN C17: *simnel* from OFr. *simenel*, based on L. *simila* or Gk *semidalis* 'fine flour'.

**simoleon** /sɪˈməʊlɪɒn/ ● n. US informal a dollar.
– ORIGIN C19: perh. on the pattern of *napoleon*.

**simonize** /ˈsʌɪmənʌɪz/ ● v. US polish (a motor vehicle).
– ORIGIN 1930s: from the proprietary name *Simoniz* + **-IZE**.

**simon-pure** ● adj. completely genuine or honest.
– ORIGIN C18: from (*the real*) *Simon Pure*, a character in Centlivre's *Bold Stroke for a Wife* (1717), who for part of the play is impersonated by another character.

**simony** /ˈsʌɪməni, ˈsɪm-/ ● n. chiefly historical the buying or selling of pardons, benefices, and other ecclesiastical privileges.
– DERIVATIVES **simoniac** /-ˈməʊnɪak/ adj. & n. **simoniacal** /-ˈnʌɪək(ə)l/ adj.
– ORIGIN ME: from OFr. *simonie*, from late L. *simonia*, from *Simon* Magus (Acts 8:18).

**simoom** /sɪˈmuːm/ (also **simoon** /-ˈmuːn/) ● n. a hot, dry, dust-laden wind blowing in the desert, especially in Arabia.
– ORIGIN C18: from Arab. *samūm*, from *samma* 'to poison'.

**simp** ● n. N. Amer. informal a silly or foolish person.
– ORIGIN C20: abbrev. of **SIMPLETON**.

**simpatico** /sɪmˈpatɪkəʊ/ ● adj. **1** likeable and easy to get on with. **2** similar in attributes or interests; compatible.
– ORIGIN from Ital. and Sp.

**simper** ● v. smile in an affectedly coquettish, coy, or ingratiating manner. ● n. such a smile.
– DERIVATIVES **simpering** adj. **simperingly** adv.
– ORIGIN C16: of unknown origin; cf. Ger. *zimpfer* 'elegant, delicate'.

**simple** ● adj. (**-er**, **-est**) **1** easily understood or done. **2** plain and uncomplicated in form, nature, or design. ➤humble and unpretentious. **3** composed of a single element; not compound. ➤Botany (of a leaf or stem) not divided or branched. ➤(of a lens, microscope, etc.) consisting of a single lens or component. **4** of very low intelligence. **5** (in English grammar) denoting a tense formed without an auxiliary. **6** (of interest) payable on the sum loaned only. Compare with **COMPOUND**[1]. ● n. chiefly historical a medicinal herb, or a medicine made from one.
– DERIVATIVES **simpleness** n.
– ORIGIN ME: from OFr., from L. *simplus*.

**simple eye** ● n. a small eye of an insect or other arthropod which has only one lens, typically present in one or more pairs. Contrasted with **COMPOUND EYE**.

**simple fracture** ● n. a fracture of the bone only, without damage to the surrounding tissues or breaking of the skin.

**simple harmonic motion** ● n. Physics oscillatory motion under a retarding force proportional to the amount of displacement from an equilibrium position.

**simple interval** ● n. Music an interval of one octave or less.

**simple machine** ● n. Mechanics any of the basic mechanical devices for applying a force, such as an inclined plane, wedge, or lever.

**simple-minded** ● adj. having or showing very little intelligence or judgement.
– DERIVATIVES **simple-mindedly** adv. **simple-mindedness** n.

**simple sentence** ● n. a sentence consisting of only one

clause, with a single subject and predicate.

**Simple Simon** ● **n.** a foolish or gullible person.
– ORIGIN prob. from the name of a character in various nursery rhymes.

**simple time** ● **n.** musical rhythm or metre in which each beat in a bar may be subdivided simply into halves or quarters. Compare with **COMPOUND TIME**.

**simpleton** ● **n.** a foolish or gullible person.
– ORIGIN C17: from **SIMPLE**, on the pattern of surnames derived from place names ending in *-ton*.

**simplex** ● **adj.** technical **1** composed of or characterized by a single part or structure. **2** (of a communication system, computer circuit, etc.) only allowing transmission of signals in one direction at a time. ● **n.** a simple or uncompounded word.
– ORIGIN C16: from L., lit. 'single', var. of *simplus* 'simple'.

**simpliciter** /sɪm'plɪsɪtə/ ● **adv.** chiefly Law simply; unconditionally.
– ORIGIN L., lit. 'simply'.

**simplicity** ● **n. 1** the quality or condition of being simple. **2** a thing that is simple.
– ORIGIN ME: from OFr. *simplicite* or L. *simplicitas*, from *simplex* (see **SIMPLEX**).

**simplify** ● **v.** (**-ies**, **-ied**) make more simple.
– DERIVATIVES **simplification** n.

**simplistic** ● **adj.** treating complex issues and problems as simpler they really are.
– DERIVATIVES **simplistically** adv.

**simply** ● **adv. 1** in a simple manner. **2** merely; just. **3** absolutely; completely (used for emphasis).

**simul** /'sɪm(ə)l/ ● **n.** Chess a display in which a player plays a number of games simultaneously against different opponents.
– ORIGIN 1960s: abbrev. of **SIMULTANEOUS**.

**simulacrum** /ˌsɪmjʊ'leɪkrəm/ ● **n.** (pl. **simulacra** /-krə/ or **simulacrums**) **1** an image or representation of someone or something. **2** an unsatisfactory imitation or substitute.
– ORIGIN C16: from L., from *simulare* (see **SIMULATE**).

**simulate** /'sɪmjʊleɪt/ ● **v.** imitate or reproduce the appearance, character, or conditions of.
– DERIVATIVES **simulant** n. **simulation** n. **simulative** adj.
– ORIGIN C17 (earlier (ME) as *simulation*): from L. *simulat-*, *simulare* 'copy, represent'.

**simulator** ● **n.** a machine that simulates the controls and conditions of a real vehicle, process, etc., used for training or testing.

**simulcast** /'sɪm(ə)lkɑːst/ ● **n. 1** a simultaneous transmission of the same programme on radio and television, or on two or more channels. **2** N. Amer. a live transmission of a public celebration or sports event. ● **v.** broadcast (such a transmission).
– ORIGIN 1940s: blend of **SIMULTANEOUS** and **BROADCAST**.

**simultaneous** /ˌsɪm(ə)l'teɪnɪəs/ ● **adj.** occurring, operating, or done at the same time.
– DERIVATIVES **simultaneity** /-tə'niːɪti, -tə'neɪɪti/ n. **simultaneously** adv. **simultaneousness** n.
– ORIGIN C17: based on L. *simul* 'at the same time', prob. influenced by late L. *momentaneus*.

**simultaneous equations** ● **pl. n.** equations involving two or more unknowns that are to have the same values in each equation.

**sin**[1] /sɪn/ ● **n. 1** an immoral act considered to be a transgression against divine law. **2** an act regarded as a serious offence. ● **v.** (**sinned**, **sinning**) commit a sin. ➤(**sin against**) cause offence or harm to.
– PHRASES **for one's sins** humorous, chiefly Brit. as a punishment. **live in sin** informal, dated (of an unmarried couple) live together.
– DERIVATIVES **sinful** adj. **sinfully** adv. **sinfulness** n. **sinless** adj. **sinlessly** adv. **sinlessness** n.
– ORIGIN OE *synn* (n.), *syngian* (v.); prob. rel. to L. *sons*, *sont-* 'guilty'.

**sin**[2] /sʌɪn/ ● **abbrev.** sine.

**sin bin** informal ● **n. 1** (in sport, especially ice hockey) a box or bench to which offending players can be sent as a penalty during a game. **2** Brit. a detention centre for offenders. ● **v.** (**sin-bin**) send (a player) to a sin bin.

**since** ● **prep.** in the intervening period between (the time mentioned) and the time under consideration. ● **conj. 1** during or in the time after. **2** for the reason that; because. ● **adv. 1** from the time mentioned until the present or the time under consideration. **2** ago.
– ORIGIN ME: contr. of obs. *sithence*, or from dial. *sin* (both from dial. *sithen* 'thereupon, afterwards, ever since').

**sincere** ● **adj.** (**-er**, **-est**) proceeding from or characterized by genuine feelings; free from pretence or deceit.
– DERIVATIVES **sincerely** adv. **sincereness** n. **sincerity** n.
– ORIGIN C16: from L. *sincerus* 'clean, pure'.

**sinciput** /'sɪnsɪpʌt/ ● **n.** Anatomy the front of the skull from the forehead to the crown.
– DERIVATIVES **sincipital** /-'sɪpɪt(ə)l/ adj.
– ORIGIN C16: from L., from *semi-* 'half' + *caput* 'head'.

**Sindebele** /sɪn'deɪbəli, ˌsɪndɛ'beɪli/ ● **n.** another term for **NDEBELE** (the language).

**Sindhi** /'sɪndi/ ● **n.** (pl. **Sindhis**) **1** a native or inhabitant of Sind, a province of SE Pakistan. **2** the Indic language of Sind. ● **adj.** of or relating to Sind, the Sindhi, or their language.

**sine** /sʌɪn/ ● **n.** Mathematics the trigonometric function that is equal to the ratio of the side opposite a given angle (in a right-angled triangle) to the hypotenuse.
– ORIGIN C16: from L. *sinus* 'curve', used in med. L. as a translation of Arab. *jayb* 'pocket, sine'.

**sinecure** /'sʌɪnɪkjʊə, 'sɪn-/ ● **n.** a position requiring little or no work but giving the holder status or financial benefit.
– DERIVATIVES **sinecurism** n. **sinecurist** n.
– ORIGIN C17: from L. *sine cura* 'without care'.

**sine curve** (also **sine wave**) ● **n.** a curve representing periodic oscillations of constant amplitude as given by a sine function.

**sine die** /ˌsiːneɪ 'diːeɪ, ˌsʌɪnɪ 'dʌɪiː/ ● **adv.** (with reference to an adjournment) with no appointed date for resumption.
– ORIGIN L., lit. 'without a day'.

**sine qua non** /kweɪ 'nɒn, kwɑː 'nəʊn/ ● **n.** a thing that is absolutely essential.
– ORIGIN L., lit. '(cause) without which not'.

**sinew** ● **n. 1** a piece of tough fibrous tissue uniting muscle to bone; a tendon or ligament. **2** (**sinews**) the parts of a structure or system that give it strength or bind it together.
– DERIVATIVES **sinewed** adj. **sinewless** adj. **sinewy** adj.
– ORIGIN OE *sin(e)we* 'tendon', of Gmc origin.

**sinfonia** /sɪn'fəʊnɪə, ˌsɪnfə'niːə/ ● **n.** Music **1** a symphony. ➤(in baroque music) an orchestral piece used as an introduction to an opera, cantata, or suite. **2** a small symphony orchestra.
– ORIGIN from Ital.

**sinfonia concertante** ● **n.** a piece of music for orchestra with one or (usually) more soloists, typically from the 18th century.
– ORIGIN Ital., lit. 'harmonizing symphony'.

**sinfonietta** /ˌsɪnfəʊnɪ'ɛtə/ ● **n.** Music **1** a short or simple symphony. **2** a small symphony orchestra.
– ORIGIN Ital., dimin. of *sinfonia* (see **SINFONIA**).

**sing** ● **v.** (past **sang**; past part. **sung**) **1** make musical sounds with the voice, especially words with a set tune. ➤perform (a song) in this way. ➤(**sing along**) sing in accompaniment to a song or piece of music. **2** (of a bird) make characteristic melodious whistling and twittering sounds. **3** make a high-pitched sound. **4** informal act as an informer to the police. **5** recount or celebrate, especially in poetry: *sing someone's praises*. ➤archaic compose poetry. ● **n.** informal an act or spell of singing.
– DERIVATIVES **singable** adj. **singer** n. **singing** n. & adj. **singingly** adv.
– ORIGIN OE *singan* (v.), of Gmc origin.

**sing.** ● **abbrev.** singular.

**singalong** ● **n.** an informal occasion when people sing together in a group.

**Singaporean** /ˌsɪŋə'pɔːrɪən/ ● **n.** a native or inhabitant of Singapore. ● **adj.** of or relating to Singapore.

**singe** ● **v.** (**singeing**) **1** burn or be burnt lightly or superficially. **2** burn the bristles or down off (the carcass of a

pig or fowl) to prepare it for cooking. ● **n.** a light or superficial burn.
– ORIGIN OE *sencgan*, of W. Gmc origin.

**Singh** /sɪŋ/ ● **n.** a title or surname adopted by certain warrior castes of northern India, especially by male members of the Sikh Khalsa.
– ORIGIN from Punjabi *siṅgh* 'lion', from Sanskrit *siṃha* 'lion'.

**Singhalese** /ˌsɪŋgəˈliːz/ ● **n. & adj.** variant spelling of **SINHALESE**.

**singing hinny** ● **n.** a kind of currant cake baked on a griddle, originating in northern England.
– ORIGIN C19: from **HINNY**[2] in sense 'honey'.

**single** ● **adj. 1** only one; not one of several. ➤regarded as distinct from others in a group. ➤[with neg.] even one (used for emphasis): *they didn't receive a single reply.* ➤designed or suitable for one person. **2** not involved in a stable romantic or sexual relationship. **3** consisting of one part. ➤(of a flower) having only one whorl of petals. **4** Brit. (of a ticket) valid for an outward journey only. **5** archaic free from duplicity or deceit: *a pure and single heart.* ● **n. 1** a single person or thing. **2** a short record with one song on each side. **3** US informal a one-dollar note. **4** Cricket a hit for one run. ➤Baseball a hit which allows the batter to proceed safely to first base. **5** (**singles**) (especially in tennis and badminton) a game or competition for individual players. **6** Bell-ringing a system of change-ringing in which one pair of bells changes places at each round. ● **v. 1** (**single someone/thing out**) choose someone or something from a group for special treatment. **2** thin out (seedlings or saplings). **3** reduce (a railway track) to a single line. **4** Baseball hit a single. ➤cause (a run) to be scored by hitting a single. ➤advance (a runner) by hitting a single.
– DERIVATIVES **singleness** n. **singly** adv.
– ORIGIN ME: via OFr. from L. *singulus*, rel. to *simplus* 'simple'.

**single acrostic** ● **n.** an acrostic using the first letter only of each line.

**single-action** ● **adj.** (of a gun) needing to be cocked by hand before it can be fired.

**single-blind** ● **adj.** denoting a test or experiment in which information that may bias the results is concealed from either tester or subject.

**single bond** ● **n.** a chemical bond in which one pair of electrons is shared between two atoms.

**single-breasted** ● **adj.** (of a jacket or coat) fastened by one row of buttons at the centre of the front.

**single-cell protein** ● **n.** protein derived from a culture of single-celled organisms, used especially as a food supplement.

**single combat** ● **n.** fighting between two people.

**single cream** ● **n.** Brit. thin cream with a relatively low fat content.

**single-decker** ● **n.** chiefly Brit. a bus having only one floor or level.

**single-ended** ● **adj.** (of an electronic device) designed for use with unbalanced signals and therefore having one input and one output terminal connected to earth.

**single-entry** ● **adj.** denoting a system of bookkeeping in which each transaction is entered in one account only.

**single file** ● **n.** a line of people or things arranged one behind another. ● **adv.** one behind another.

**single-foot** ● **v.** N. Amer. (of a horse) walk by moving both legs on each side in alternation, each foot falling separately.

**single-handed** ● **adv. & adj. 1** done without help from others. **2** done or designed to be used with one hand.
– DERIVATIVES **single-handedly** adv. **single-hander** n.

**single-lens reflex** ● **adj.** denoting a reflex camera in which the lens that forms the image on the film also provides the image in the viewfinder.

**single malt** ● **n.** whisky that has not been blended with any other malt.

**single market** ● **n.** an association of countries trading with each other without restrictions or tariffs.

**single-minded** ● **adj.** concentrating purposefully on one particular thing.
– DERIVATIVES **single-mindedly** adv. **single-mindedness** n.

**single parent** ● **n.** a person bringing up a child or children without a partner.

**single-source** ● **v.** give a franchise to a single supplier for (a particular product).

**single stick** ● **n.** Fencing a stick of about a sword's length.

**singlet** ● **n. 1** chiefly Brit. a vest or similar sleeveless garment. **2** Physics a single line in a spectrum, not part of a multiplet. **3** Physics a state or energy level with zero spin, giving a single value for a particular quantum number.
– ORIGIN C18 (orig. denoting a man's short jacket): from **SINGLE** (because the garment was unlined) + **-ET**[1], on the pattern of *doublet*.

**singleton** ● **n. 1** a single person or thing of the kind under consideration. ➤a child or animal born singly, rather than one of a multiple birth. ➤(in card games, especially bridge) a card that is the only one of its suit in a hand. **2** informal a person who is not in a long-term relationship. **3** Mathematics & Logic a set which contains exactly one element.
– ORIGIN C19: from **SINGLE**, on the pattern of *simpleton*.

**single transferable vote** ● **n.** an electoral system of proportional representation in which a person's vote can be transferred to a second or further choice of candidate.

**singletree** ● **n.** North American term for **SWINGLETREE**.

**single-vision** ● **adj.** denoting glasses of which each lens is a single optical element; not bifocal.

**sing-song** ● **adj.** (of a person's voice) having a repeated rising and falling rhythm. ● **n.** Brit. informal an informal gathering for singing.

**singular** ● **adj. 1** exceptionally good or great; remarkable. ➤strange or eccentric in some respect. **2** single; unique. ➤Grammar (of a word or form) denoting or referring to just one person or thing. **3** Mathematics (of a square matrix) having a zero determinant. **4** Physics & Mathematics relating to or of the nature of a singularity. ● **n.** Grammar the singular form of a word.
– DERIVATIVES **singularly** adv.
– ORIGIN ME: from OFr. *singuler*, from L. *singularis*, from *singulus* (see **SINGLE**).

**singularity** ● **n.** (pl. **-ies**) **1** the state, fact, or quality of being singular. **2** Physics & Mathematics a point at which a function takes an infinite value, especially a point of infinite density at the centre of a black hole.

**singularize** (also **-ise**) ● **v. 1** make distinct or conspicuous. **2** give a singular form to (a word).
– DERIVATIVES **singularization** n.

**sinh** /ʃʌɪn, sɪntʃ, sʌɪˈneɪtʃ/ ● **abbrev.** Mathematics hyperbolic sine.
– ORIGIN C19: from *sin(e)* + *h(yperbolic)*.

**Sinhalese** /ˌsɪnhəˈliːz, ˌsɪnə-/ (also **Singhalese**, **Sinhala** /sɪnˈhɑːlə/) ● **n.** (pl. same) **1** a member of an Indian people now forming the majority of the population of Sri Lanka. **2** an Indic language spoken by this people, descended from Sanskrit. ● **adj.** of or relating to the Sinhalese or their language.
– ORIGIN from Sanskrit *Siṅhala* 'Sri Lanka' + **-ESE**.

**sinister** ● **adj. 1** suggestive of evil or harm. **2** archaic & Heraldry on or towards the left-hand side (in a coat of arms, from the bearer's point of view, i.e. the right as it is depicted). The opposite of **DEXTER**[1].
– DERIVATIVES **sinisterly** adv. **sinisterness** n.
– ORIGIN ME: from OFr. *sinistre* or L. *sinister* 'left'.

**sinistral** /ˈsɪnɪstr(ə)l/ ● **adj. 1** of or on the left side or the left hand. The opposite of **DEXTRAL**. ➤left-handed. **2** Geology relating to or denoting a strike-slip fault in which the motion of the block on the further side of the fault is towards the left. **3** Zoology (of a spiral mollusc shell) with whorls rising to the left and coiling clockwise. ● **n.** a left-handed person.
– DERIVATIVES **sinistrality** n. **sinistrally** adv.

**Sinitic** /sɪˈnɪtɪk/ ● **adj.** relating to or denoting the division of the Sino-Tibetan language family that includes the

many forms of Chinese.
– ORIGIN via late L. *Sinae* from Gk *Sinai* 'the Chinese', from Arab. *ṣīn*, denoting the Chinese empire.

**sink**[1] ● v. (past **sank**; past part. **sunk**) **1** go down below the surface of liquid; become submerged. ➤(with reference to a ship) go or cause to go to the bottom of the sea. **2** disappear and not be seen or heard of again. ➤conceal or ignore: *they agreed to sink their differences.* ➤cause to fail. **3** drop downwards. ➤lower oneself or drop down gently. ➤pocket (a ball) in snooker or billiards. ➤Golf hit the ball into the hole with (a putt or other shot). **4** (**sink in**) (of words or facts) become fully understood. **5** insert beneath a surface. ➤(**sink something into**) cause something sharp to penetrate (a surface). ➤excavate (a well) or bore (a shaft) vertically downwards. **6** gradually decrease or decline in amount or intensity. **7** lapse or fall into a particular state or condition. **8** informal rapidly consume (an alcoholic drink). **9** (**sink something in/into**) put money or energy into.
– PHRASES **a** (or **that**) **sinking feeling** an unpleasant bodily sensation caused by apprehension or dismay. **sink or swim** fail or succeed by one's own efforts.
– DERIVATIVES **sinkable** adj. **sinkage** n.
– ORIGIN OE *sincan*, of Gmc origin.

**sink**[2] ● n. **1** a fixed basin with a water supply and outflow pipe. **2** short for SINKHOLE. **3** a pool or marsh in which a river's water disappears by evaporation or percolation. **4** technical a body or process which absorbs or removes energy or a particular component from a system. The opposite of SOURCE. **5** [as modifier] denoting a school or estate situated in a socially deprived area: *a sink school.*
– ORIGIN ME: from SINK[1].

**sinker** ● n. **1** a weight used to sink a fishing line or sounding line. **2** (also **sinker ball**) Baseball a pitch which drops markedly as it nears home plate. **3** a type of windsurfing board of insufficient buoyancy to support its crew unless moving fast. **4** US a doughnut.

**sinkhole** ● n. a cavity in the ground, especially in a limestone formation, caused by water erosion and providing a route for surface water to disappear underground.

**sinking fund** ● n. a fund formed by periodically setting aside money for the gradual repayment of a debt or replacement of a wasting asset.

**sinner** ● n. a person who sins.

**sinnet** /'sɪnɪt/ (also **sennit**) ● n. Nautical braided cordage in flat, round, or square form.
– ORIGIN C17: of unknown origin.

**Sino-** /'sʌɪnəʊ/ ● comb. form Chinese; Chinese and ...: *Sino-American.* ➤relating to China.
– ORIGIN from late L. *Sinae* (see SINITIC).

**sino-atrial node** /ˌsʌɪnəʊ'eɪtrɪəl/ ● n. Anatomy a small body of specialized muscle tissue in the wall of the heart that acts as a pacemaker.
– ORIGIN C20: from SINUS + *atrial* (see ATRIUM).

**sinology** /sʌɪ'nɒlədʒi, sɪ-/ ● n. the study of Chinese language, history, and culture.
– DERIVATIVES **sinological** adj. **sinologist** n.

**Sino-Tibetan** ● adj. relating to or denoting a large language family of eastern Asia which includes Chinese, Burmese, Tibetan, and (in some classifications) Thai. ● n. this language family.

**sinsemilla** /ˌsɪnsə'mɪlə/ ● n. cannabis of a variety which has a particularly high concentration of narcotic agents.
– ORIGIN 1970s: from Amer. Sp., lit. 'without seed'.

**sinter** /'sɪntə/ ● n. **1** Geology a hard siliceous or calcareous deposit precipitated from mineral springs. **2** solid material which has been sintered. ● v. coalesce or cause to coalesce from powder into solid by heating (and usually also by compression).
– ORIGIN C18: from Ger. *Sinter*; cf. CINDER.

**Sintu** /'sɪntu:/ ● adj. & n. South African term for BANTU (the language family), used to avoid offensive connotations.
– ORIGIN 1970s: from the Bantu elements (*i*)*si-* denoting language or culture, and *-ntu* '(African) person'.

**sinuate** /'sɪnjʊət/ ● adj. Botany & Zoology having a wavy or sinuous margin; with alternate rounded notches and lobes.
– ORIGIN C17: from L. *sinuatus*, past part. of *sinuare* 'to bend'.

**sinuous** /'sɪnjʊəs/ ● adj. **1** having many curves and turns. **2** lithe and supple.
– DERIVATIVES **sinuosity** n. **sinuously** adv. **sinuousness** n.
– ORIGIN C16: from Fr. *sinueux* or L. *sinuosus*, from *sinus* 'a bend'.

**sinus** /'sʌɪnəs/ ● n. **1** Anatomy & Zoology a cavity within a bone or other tissue, especially one in the bones of the face or skull connecting with the nasal cavities. **2** Anatomy & Zoology an irregular venous or lymphatic cavity, reservoir, or dilated vessel. **3** Medicine an infected tract leading from a deep-seated infection and discharging pus to the surface. **4** Botany a rounded notch between two lobes on the margin of a leaf or petal. **5** [as modifier] Physiology relating to the sino-atrial node of the heart: *sinus rhythm.*
– DERIVATIVES **sinusitis** n.
– ORIGIN ME: from L., lit. 'a recess, bend'.

**sinusoid** /'sʌɪnəsɔɪd/ ● n. **1** another term for SINE CURVE. **2** Anatomy a small irregularly shaped blood vessel found in certain organs, especially the liver.
– DERIVATIVES **sinusoidal** adj. **sinusoidally** adv.

**Sion** /'sʌɪən/ ● n. variant spelling of ZION.

**-sion** ● suffix forming nouns such as *mansion.*
– ORIGIN from L. participial stems ending in *-s* + -ION.

**Siouan** /'su:ən/ ● n. a family of North American Indian languages spoken by the Sioux and related people, including Dakota, Hidatsa, and Crow. ● adj. relating to or denoting this language family.

**Sioux** /su:/ ● n. (pl. same) another term for the Dakota people of North America or their language.
– ORIGIN N. Amer. Fr., from *Nadouessioux* from Ojibwa (Ottawa dial.) *nātowēssiwak*, by substitution of the Fr. pl. ending *-x* for the Ojibwa pl. *-ak*.

**sip** ● v. (**sipped**, **sipping**) drink (something) by taking small mouthfuls. ● n. a small mouthful of liquid.
– DERIVATIVES **sipper** n.
– ORIGIN ME: perh. a modification of SUP[1], as symbolic of a less vigorous action.

**sipe** /sʌɪp/ ● n. a groove or channel in the tread of a tyre.
– ORIGIN 1950s: from dial. *sipe* 'oozing, trickling', of unknown origin.

**siphon** /'sʌɪf(ə)n/ (also **syphon**) ● n. **1** a tube used to convey liquid upwards from a container and then down to a lower level, the flow being forced initially by suction and maintained by atmospheric pressure. **2** Zoology a tubular organ in an aquatic animal through which water is drawn in or expelled. ● v. **1** draw off or convey (liquid) by means of a siphon. **2** draw off (small amounts of money) over a period of time, especially illicitly: *he's been siphoning money off the firm.*
– DERIVATIVES **siphonage** n. **siphonal** adj. (Zoology) **siphonic** /-'fɒnɪk/ adj.
– ORIGIN ME: from Fr., or via L. from Gk *siphōn* 'pipe'.

**Siphonaptera** /ˌsʌɪfə'napt(ə)rə/ ● pl. n. Entomology an order of insects that comprises the fleas.
– DERIVATIVES **siphonapteran** n. & adj.
– ORIGIN mod. L., from Gk *siphōn* 'tube' + *apteros* 'wingless'.

**Siphonophora** /ˌsʌɪfə'nɒf(ə)rə/ ● pl. n. Zoology an order of colonial marine coelenterates that includes the Portuguese man-of-war, having a float or swimming bell for drifting or swimming on the open sea.
– DERIVATIVES **siphonophore** /sʌɪ'fɒnəfɔ:/ n.
– ORIGIN mod. L., from Gk *siphōn* 'tube' + *pherein* 'to bear'.

**sippet** ● n. archaic a small piece of bread or toast, used to dip into soup or sauce.
– ORIGIN C16: appar. a dimin. of SOP.

**Sir.** ● abbrev. (in biblical references) Sirach (Apocrypha).

**sir** (also **Sir**) ● n. **1** a polite or respectful form of address to a man. **2** used to address a man at the beginning of a formal or business letter. **3** used as a title before the forename of a knight or baronet.
– ORIGIN ME: reduced form of SIRE.

**sirdar** ● n. variant spelling of **SARDAR**.

**sire** /sʌɪə/ ● n. **1** the male parent of an animal, especially a stallion or bull kept for breeding. **2** a father or other male forebear. **3** archaic a respectful form of address to someone of high social status, especially a king. ● v. be the sire of.
– ORIGIN ME: from OFr., from an alt. of L. *senior* (see **SENIOR**).

**siree** /sɪˈriː/ (also **sirree**) ● exclam. N. Amer. informal sir (used for emphasis, especially after *yes* and *no*).
– ORIGIN C19: from **SIR** + the emphatic suffix *-ee*.

**siren** ● n. **1** a device that makes a loud prolonged signal or warning sound. **2** Greek Mythology each of a number of women or winged creatures whose singing lured unwary sailors on to rocks. **3** a woman who is considered to be alluring but also dangerous in some way. **4** an eel-like American amphibian, typically living in muddy pools. [Family Sirenidae.]
– PHRASES **siren song** (or **call**) the appeal of something that is alluring but also potentially dangerous.
– ORIGIN ME (denoting an imaginary type of snake): from OFr. *sirene*, from late L. *Sirena*, fem. of L. *Siren*, from Gk *Seirēn*.

**Sirenia** /sʌɪˈriːnɪə/ ● pl. n. Zoology an order of large aquatic plant-eating mammals which includes the manatees and dugong.
– DERIVATIVES **sirenian** n. & adj.
– ORIGIN mod. L. (see **SIREN**).

**Sir Galahad** ● n. see **GALAHAD**.

**sirloin** ● n. the choicer part of a loin of beef.
– ORIGIN ME: from OFr. (see **SUR-**[1], **LOIN**).

**sirocco** /sɪˈrɒkəʊ/ (also **scirocco**) ● n. (pl. **-os**) a hot wind blowing from North Africa across the Mediterranean to southern Europe.
– ORIGIN C17: via Fr. from Ital. *scirocco*, based on Sp. Arab. *Šalūḳ* 'east wind'.

**sirrah** /ˈsɪrə/ ● n. archaic a term of address to a man or boy, especially one younger or of lower status than the speaker.
– ORIGIN C16: prob. from **SIRE**, when still two syllables in ME, with the second syllable assimilated to **AH**.

**sirup** ● n. US spelling of **SYRUP**.

**SIS** ● abbrev. (in the UK) Secret Intelligence Service.

**sis** /sɪs/ ● n. informal sister.

**sisal** /ˈsʌɪs(ə)l/ ● n. **1** a Mexican agave with large fleshy leaves, cultivated for the fibre it yields. [*Agave sisalana*.] **2** the fibre made from this plant, used especially for ropes or matting.
– ORIGIN C19: from *Sisal*, the name of a port in Yucatán, Mexico.

**siskin** ● n. a small yellowish-green finch associated with conifers. [*Carduelis spinus* (northern Eurasia) and related species.]
– ORIGIN C16: from MDu. *siseken*, of Slavic origin.

**sissy** (also **cissy**) informal ● n. (pl. **-ies**) a person regarded as feeble or effeminate. ● adj. (**-ier**, **-iest**) feeble or effeminate.
– DERIVATIVES **sissified** adj. **sissiness** n. **sissyish** adj.
– ORIGIN C19 (in the sense 'sister'): from **SIS** + **-Y**[2].

**sister** ● n. **1** a woman or girl in relation to other daughters and sons of her parents. **2** a female friend or associate. ➤ N. Amer. a fellow black woman. **3** [as modifier] denoting an organization or a place which bears a relationship to another of common origin or allegiance. **4** (often **Sister**) a member of a religious order of women. **5** (often **Sister**) Brit. a senior female nurse.
– DERIVATIVES **sisterliness** n. **sisterly** adj.
– ORIGIN OE, of Gmc origin.

**sister-german** ● n. (pl. **sisters-german**) archaic a sister sharing both parents, as opposed to a half-sister or step-sister.

**sisterhood** ● n. **1** the relationship between sisters. **2** a feeling of kinship with and closeness to a group of women or all women. **3** (often **Sisterhood**) an association or community of women linked by a common interest, religion, or trade.

**sister-in-law** ● n. (pl. **sisters-in-law**) **1** the sister of one's wife or husband. **2** the wife of one's brother or brother-in-law.

**Sistine** /ˈsɪstiːn, -tʌɪn/ ● adj. of or relating to any of the popes called Sixtus, especially Sixtus IV.
– ORIGIN from Ital. *Sistino*, from *Sisto* 'Sixtus'.

**sistrum** /ˈsɪstrəm/ ● n. (pl. **sistra** /-trə/) a musical instrument of ancient Egypt consisting of a metal frame with transverse metal rods which rattled when the instrument was shaken.
– ORIGIN ME: via L. from Gk *seistron*, from *seiein* 'to shake'.

**Siswati** /sɪˈswɑːti/ ● n. another term for **SWAZI** (the language).

**Sisyphean** /ˌsɪsɪˈfiːən/ ● adj. (of a task) such that it can never be completed.
– ORIGIN C16: from *Sisyphus* in Gk mythology, who was condemned to the eternal task of rolling a large stone to the top of a hill, from which it always rolled down again.

**sit** ● v. (**sitting**; past and past part. **sat** /sat/) **1** be or cause to be in a position in which one's weight is supported by one's buttocks rather than one's feet and one's back is upright. ➤ (of an animal) rest with the hind legs bent and the body close to the ground. ➤ (of a bird) remain on its nest to incubate its egg. ➤ (**sit for**) pose for (an artist or photographer). **2** be or remain in a particular position or state. ➤ (**sit with**) be harmonious with. **3** (of a parliament, committee, court of law, etc.) be engaged in its business. ➤ serve as a member of a council, jury, or other official body. ➤ Brit. take (an examination). **4** (of a table or room) have enough seats for. **5** [usu. in combination] look after children, pets, or a house while the parents or owners are away: *they want me to house-sit for them.* **6** N. Amer. not use (a player) in a game. ● n. a period of sitting.
– PHRASES **sit tight** informal **1** remain firmly in one's place. **2** refrain from taking action or changing one's mind.
– PHRASAL VERBS **sit in 1** (of demonstrators) occupy a place as a form of protest. **2** attend a meeting without taking an active part. **sit in for** temporarily carry out the duties of. **sit on** informal **1** fail to deal with. **2** subdue or suppress. **sit something out** not take part in an event or activity. ➤ wait without taking action until an unwelcome situation or process is over. **sit up 1** move from a lying or slouching to a sitting position. **2** refrain from going to bed until later than usual.
– ORIGIN OE *sittan*, of Gmc origin.

**sitar** /ˈsɪtɑː, sɪˈtɑː/ ● n. a large, long-necked Indian lute with movable frets, played with a wire pick.
– DERIVATIVES **sitarist** /sɪˈtɑːrɪst/ n.
– ORIGIN via Urdu from Pers. *sitār*, from *sih* 'three' + *tār* 'string'.

**sitatunga** /ˌsɪtəˈtʌŋgə/ ● n. a brown or greyish antelope with splayed hoofs and, in the male, spiral horns, inhabiting swampy areas in central and East Africa. [*Tragelaphus spekii*.]
– ORIGIN C19: from Kiswahili.

**sitcom** ● n. informal a situation comedy.
– ORIGIN 1960s: abbrev.

**sit-down** ● adj. **1** denoting a meal eaten sitting at a table. **2** denoting a protest in which demonstrators occupy their workplace or sit down on the ground in a public place, refusing to leave until their demands are met. ● n. **1** a period of sitting down. **2** a sit-down protest.

**site** ● n. **1** an area of ground on which something is located. **2** a place where a particular event or activity is occurring or has occurred. ● v. fix or build in a particular place.
– ORIGIN ME: from Anglo-Norman Fr., or from L. *situs* 'local position'.

**Sitka** /ˈsɪtkə/ ● n. a fast-growing North American spruce tree, widely cultivated for its strong lightweight wood. [*Picea sitchensis*.]
– ORIGIN C19: named after *Sitka*, a town in Alaska.

**sitrep** ● n. informal a report on the current military situation in a particular area.
– ORIGIN 1940s: from *sit(uation) rep(ort)*.

**sits vac** ● pl. n. Brit. informal situations vacant. See **SITUATION**.

**sitter** ● n. **1** a person who sits, especially for a portrait or examination. **2** a sitting hen. **3** [usu. in combination] a person who looks after children, pets, or a house while the parents or owners are away: *a house-sitter.* **4** a person who provides care and companionship for people who are ill. **5** informal (in sport) an easy catch or shot.

**sitting** ● n. **1** a period or spell of sitting. **2** a period of time when a group of people are served a meal. ● adj. **1** in a seated position. **2** currently present or in office.

**sitting duck** (also **sitting target**) ● n. informal a person or thing with no protection against attack.

**sitting room** ● n. chiefly Brit. a room that is furnished for sitting and relaxing in.

**sitting tenant** ● n. Brit. a tenant already in occupation of premises, especially when there is a change of owner.

**situate** ● v. /ˈsɪtʃʊeɪt, -tjʊ-/ **1** (usu. **be situated**) place in a particular location or context. **2** (**be situated**) be in a specified financial or marital position. ● adj. /ˈsɪtʃʊət, -tjʊət/ Law or archaic situated.
– ORIGIN ME: from med. L. *situat-*, *situare* 'place', from L. *situs* 'site'.

**situation** ● n. **1** a set of circumstances in which one finds oneself. **2** the location and surroundings of a place. **3** a job.
– PHRASES **situations vacant** (or **wanted**) chiefly Brit. jobs currently available (or sought).
– DERIVATIVES **situational** adj. **situationally** adv.

**situation comedy** ● n. a television or radio series in which the same set of characters are involved in various amusing situations.

**situationism** ● n. **1** the theory that human behaviour is determined by surrounding circumstances rather than by personal qualities. **2** a revolutionary political theory which regards modern industrial society as being inevitably oppressive and exploitative.
– DERIVATIVES **situationist** n. & adj.

**sit-up** ● n. a physical exercise designed to strengthen the abdominal muscles, in which a person sits up from a supine position without using the arms for leverage.

**situs** /ˈsʌɪtəs/ ● n. Law, chiefly US the place to which for purposes of legal jurisdiction or taxation a property belongs.

**situs inversus** /ˌsʌɪtəs ɪnˈvəːsəs, ˌsiːtəs/ ● n. Medicine an uncommon condition in which the heart and other organs of the body are transposed through the sagittal plane to lie on the opposite (left or right) side from the usual.
– ORIGIN C19: from L. *situs inversus viscerum* 'inverted placing of the internal organs'.

**sitz bath** /ˈsɪts/ ● n. a bath in which only the buttocks and hips are immersed in water.
– ORIGIN C19: partial translation of Ger. *Sitzbad*, from *sitzen* 'sit' + *Bad* 'bath'.

**Sivan** /ˈsiːvɑːn/ ● n. (in the Jewish calendar) the ninth month of the civil and third of the religious year, usually coinciding with parts of May and June.
– ORIGIN from Heb. *sīwān*.

**Siwash** /ˈsʌɪwɒʃ/ ● n. derogatory **1** an American Indian of the northern Pacific coast. **2** another term for **CHINOOK JARGON**.
– ORIGIN Chinook Jargon, from Canad. Fr. *sauvage* 'wild'.

**six** ● cardinal number **1** equivalent to the product of two and three; one more than five, or four less than ten; 6. (Roman numeral: **vi** or **VI**.) **2** Cricket a hit that reaches the boundary without first striking the ground, scoring six runs. **3** a group of six Brownies or Cubs.
– PHRASES **at sixes and sevens** in a state of confusion or disarray. **knock** (or **hit**) **someone for six** Brit. informal utterly surprise or overcome someone. **six feet under** informal dead and buried. **six of one and half a dozen of the other** a situation in which there is little difference between two alternatives.
– DERIVATIVES **sixfold** adj. & adv.
– ORIGIN OE *siex*, *six*, *syx*, of Gmc origin.

**sixain** /ˈsɪkseɪn/ ● n. a six-line stanza.
– ORIGIN C16: from Fr., from *six* 'six'.

**sixer** ● n. **1** the leader of a group of six Brownies or Cubs. **2** Cricket, chiefly Indian a hit for six runs. **3** US a six-pack.

**six-gun** ● n. another term for **SIX-SHOOTER**.

**six-pack** ● n. **1** a pack of six cans of beer. **2** informal a set of well-developed abdominal muscles.

**sixpence** ● n. Brit. **1** a small coin worth six old pence (2½ p), withdrawn in 1980. **2** the sum of six pence, especially before decimalization (1971).

**sixpenny** ● adj. Brit. costing or worth six pence, especially before decimalization (1971).

**six-shooter** ● n. a revolver with six chambers.

**sixte** /sɪkst/ ● n. Fencing the sixth of the eight parrying positions.
– ORIGIN C19: Fr., from L. *sextus* 'sixth'.

**sixteen** ● cardinal number equivalent to the product of four and four; one more than fifteen, or six more than ten; 16. (Roman numeral: **xvi** or **XVI**.)
– DERIVATIVES **sixteenth** ordinal number.
– ORIGIN OE *siextīene* (see **SIX**, **-TEEN**).

**sixteenmo** ● n. (pl. **-os**) another term for **SEXTODECIMO**.

**sixteenth note** ● n. Music, chiefly N. Amer. a semiquaver.

**sixth** ● ordinal number **1** constituting number six in a sequence; 6th. **2** (**a sixth/one sixth**) each of six equal parts into which something is or may be divided. **3** chiefly Brit. the sixth form of a school. **4** Music an interval spanning six consecutive notes in a diatonic major or minor scale, e.g. C to A (**major sixth**) or A to F (**minor sixth**). ➤the note which is higher by this interval than the tonic of a scale or root of a chord.
– DERIVATIVES **sixthly** adv.

**sixth-form college** ● n. Brit. a college for pupils in their final years of secondary education, starting at the age of 16.

**sixth sense** ● n. a supposed intuitive faculty giving awareness not explicable in terms of normal perception.

**sixty** ● cardinal number (pl. **-ies**) the number equivalent to the product of six and ten; ten more than fifty; 60. (Roman numeral: **lx** or **LX**.)
– DERIVATIVES **sixtieth** ordinal number. **sixtyfold** adj. & adv.
– ORIGIN OE *siextig* (see **SIX**, **-TY²**).

**sixty-fourmo** ● n. (pl. **-os**) **1** a size of book in which each leaf is one sixty-fourth the size of a printing sheet. **2** a book of this size.

**sixty-fourth note** ● n. Music, chiefly N. Amer. a hemidemisemiquaver.

**sixty-four thousand dollar question** ● n. informal something that is not known and on which a great deal depends.
– ORIGIN 1940s: orig. *sixty-four dollar question*, from a question posed for the top prize in a broadcast quiz show.

**sixty-nine** ● n. another term for **SOIXANTE-NEUF**.

**sizable** ● adj. variant spelling of **SIZEABLE**.

**sizar** /ˈsʌɪzə/ ● n. an undergraduate at Cambridge University or at Trinity College, Dublin, receiving financial help from the college and formerly having certain menial duties.
– DERIVATIVES **sizarship** n.
– ORIGIN C16: from obs. *size* 'ration of bread, beer, etc.' + **-AR³**.

**size¹** ● n. **1** a thing's overall dimensions or magnitude. **2** each of the classes into which garments or other articles are divided according to how large they are. ● v. **1** alter or sort in terms of size or according to size. **2** (**size something up**) estimate or measure something's dimensions. **3** (**size someone/thing up**) informal form an estimate or rough judgement of someone or something.
– PHRASES **of a size** (of two or more people or things) having the same dimensions. **that's the size of it** informal that is the truth about a situation, however unpalatable. **to size** to the dimensions wanted.
– DERIVATIVES **-sized** (also **-size**) adj. **sizer** n.
– ORIGIN ME (also in the sense 'assize, ordinance fixing a rate of payment'): from OFr. *sise*, from *assise* 'ordinance', or a shortening of **ASSIZE**.

**size²** ● n. a gelatinous solution used in glazing paper, stiffening textiles, and preparing plastered walls for decoration. ● v. treat with size.
– ORIGIN ME: perh. the same word as **SIZE¹**.

**sizeable** (also **sizable**) ● **adj.** fairly large.
– DERIVATIVES **sizeably** adv.

**sizeism** (also **sizism**) ● **n.** prejudice or discrimination on the grounds of a person's size.
– DERIVATIVES **sizeist** adj.

**sizzle** ● **v. 1** (of food) make a hissing sound when frying or roasting. **2** informal be very hot. **3** informal be very exciting or passionate, especially sexually. ● **n.** an instance or the sound of sizzling.
– DERIVATIVES **sizzler** n. **sizzling** adj.
– ORIGIN C17: imitative.

**SJ** ● **abbrev.** Society of Jesus.

**sjambok** /ˈʃambɒk/ ● **n.** (in South Africa) a long, stiff whip, originally made of rhinoceros hide. ● **v.** flog with a sjambok.
– ORIGIN from S. Afr. Du. *tjambok*, via Malay from Urdu *chābuk*.

**SJC** ● **abbrev.** (in the US) Supreme Judicial Court.

**SK** ● **abbrev.** Saskatchewan (in official postal use).

**ska** /skɑː/ ● **n.** a style of fast popular music having a strong offbeat and originating in Jamaica in the 1960s, a forerunner of reggae.
– ORIGIN 1960s: of unknown origin.

**skag** (also **scag**) ● **n.** informal, chiefly N. Amer. heroin.
– ORIGIN C20: of unknown origin.

**skald** /skɔːld, skald/ (also **scald**) ● **n.** (in ancient Scandinavia) a composer and reciter of poems honouring heroes and their deeds.
– DERIVATIVES **skaldic** adj.
– ORIGIN from ON *skáld*, of unknown origin.

**skank** /skaŋk/ ● **n. 1** a dance performed to reggae music, characterized by rhythmically bending forward, raising the knees, and extending the hands palms-downwards. ➤ reggae music suitable for such dancing. **2** informal, chiefly N. Amer. a sleazy or unpleasant person. ● **v. 1** play reggae music or dance in this style. **2** informal walk or move in a sexually suggestive way.
– DERIVATIVES **skanking** adj.
– ORIGIN 1970s: of unknown origin.

**skanky** ● **adj.** informal, chiefly N. Amer. very unpleasant.

**skarn** /skɑːn/ ● **n.** Geology lime-bearing siliceous rock produced by the metamorphic alteration of limestone or dolomite.
– ORIGIN C20: from Swed., lit. 'dung, filth'.

**skat** ● **n.** a three-handed trick-taking card game with bidding, played chiefly in Germany.
– ORIGIN C19: from Ger., from Ital. *scarto* 'a discard'.

**skate**[1] ● **n. 1** an ice skate or roller skate. **2** a wheeled device used to move a heavy or unwieldy object. ● **v. 1** move on ice skates or roller skates. ➤ ride on a skateboard. **2** (**skate over/round/around**) pass over or refer only fleetingly to (a subject or problem). ➤ (**skate through**) make quick and easy progress through.
– PHRASES **get one's skates on** Brit. informal hurry up.
– DERIVATIVES **skater** n. **skating** n.
– ORIGIN C17 (orig. as the pl. *scates*): from Du. *schaats* (sing. but interpreted as pl.), from OFr. *eschasse* 'stilt'.

**skate**[2] ● **n.** (pl. same or **skates**) an edible marine fish of the ray family with a diamond-shaped body. [*Raja batis* and other species.]
– ORIGIN ME: from ON *skata*.

**skate**[3] ● **n.** informal, dated or S. African a disreputable or contemptible person, especially a man.
– ORIGIN C19: origin uncertain; S. Afr. use perh. influenced by Afrik. *skuit*.

**skateboard** ● **n.** a short narrow board with two small wheels fixed to the bottom of either end, on which a person can ride in a standing or crouching position. ● **v.** [often as noun **skateboarding**] ride on a skateboard.
– DERIVATIVES **skateboarder** n.

**skatepark** ● **n.** an area equipped for skateboarding.

**skean** /skiːn, ˈskiːən/ ● **n.** a dagger formerly used in Ireland and Scotland.
– ORIGIN ME: from Ir. and Sc. Gaelic *sgian* 'knife'.

**skean-dhu** /ˈduː/ ● **n.** a dagger worn in the stocking as part of Highland dress.
– ORIGIN C19: from SKEAN + Sc. Gaelic *dubh* 'black'.

**sked** ● **n. & v.** (**skedded, skedding**) informal, chiefly N. Amer. short for SCHEDULE.

**skedaddle** /skɪˈdad(ə)l/ ● **v.** informal depart quickly.
– ORIGIN C19: of unknown origin.

**skeet** (also **skeet shooting**) ● **n.** a shooting sport in which a clay target is thrown from a trap to simulate the flight of a bird.
– ORIGIN 1920s: appar. a pseudo-archaic alt. of the verb SHOOT.

**skeeter**[1] ● **n.** informal, chiefly N. Amer. & Austral. a mosquito.
– ORIGIN C19: shortened form, representing a casual pronunc.

**skeeter**[2] ● **v.** another term for SKITTER.

**skeg** ● **n.** a tapering or projecting after section of a vessel's keel. ➤ a fin underneath the rear of a surfboard.
– ORIGIN C17: from ON *skegg* 'beard', perh. from Du. *scheg*.

**skein** /skeɪn/ ● **n. 1** a length of thread or yarn, loosely coiled and knotted. **2** a flock of wild geese or swans in flight, typically in a V-shaped formation.
– ORIGIN ME: shortening of OFr. *escaigne*, of unknown origin.

**skeletal** /ˈskɛlɪt(ə)l, skəˈliːt(ə)l/ ● **adj. 1** relating to or functioning as a skeleton. ➤ very thin; emaciated. **2** existing only in outline or as a framework.
– DERIVATIVES **skeletally** adv.

**skeletal muscle** ● **n.** another term for STRIATED MUSCLE.

**skeleton** ● **n. 1** an internal or external framework of bone, cartilage, or other rigid material supporting or containing the body of an animal or plant. ➤ a very thin or emaciated person or animal. **2** a supporting framework, basic structure, or essential part. ➤ [as modifier] denoting an essential or minimum number of people or things: *a skeleton staff.*
– PHRASES **skeleton in the cupboard** (N. Amer. **skeleton in the closet**) a discreditable or embarrassing fact that someone wishes to keep secret.
– DERIVATIVES **skeletonize** (also **-ise**) v.
– ORIGIN C16: mod. L., from Gk, neut. of *skeletos* 'dried up'.

**skeleton key** ● **n.** a key designed to fit many locks by having the interior of the bit hollowed.

**skelf** /skɛlf/ ● **n.** Scottish **1** a splinter or sliver. **2** informal an annoying person.
– ORIGIN ME (in the sense 'shelf'): prob. from Mid. Low Ger. *schelf*; cf. SHELF[1].

**skell** ● **n.** US informal (in New York) a tramp or homeless person.
– ORIGIN C20: perh. a shortening of SKELETON.

**skelly** /ˈskɛli/ ● **adj.** Scottish cross-eyed.
– ORIGIN C18: based on ON *skjálgr* 'wry, oblique'.

**skelp** /skɛlp/ ● **v.** Scottish & N. English strike, slap, or smack.
– ORIGIN ME: prob. imitative.

**skene** /ˈskiːni/ ● **n.** (in ancient Greek theatre) a three-dimensional structure which formed part of the stage or set.
– ORIGIN from Gk *skēnē* 'hut, tent'.

**skep** (also **skip**) ● **n. 1** a straw or wicker beehive. **2** archaic a wooden or wicker basket.
– ORIGIN OE *sceppe* 'basket', from ON *skeppa* 'basket, bushel'.

**skeptic** ● **n.** US spelling of SCEPTIC.

**skerrick** /ˈskɛrɪk/ ● **n.** [usu. with neg.] Austral./NZ informal the smallest bit.
– ORIGIN C19 (also as Engl. sl. term meaning 'halfpenny'): of unknown origin.

**skerry** /ˈskɛri/ ● **n.** (pl. **-ies**) Scottish a reef or rocky island.
– ORIGIN C17: Orkney dial., from ON *sker*.

**sketch** ● **n. 1** a rough or unfinished drawing or painting. ➤ a brief written or spoken account or description. **2** a short humorous play, scene, or performance. **3** informal, dated a comical or amusing person or thing. ● **v.** make a sketch of. ➤ give a brief account or general outline of.
– DERIVATIVES **sketcher** n.
– ORIGIN C17: from Du. *schets* or Ger. *Skizze*, from Ital.

*schizzo*, based on Gk *skhedios* 'done extempore'.

**sketchbook** (also **sketch pad**) • **n.** a pad of drawing paper for sketching on.

**sketch map** • **n.** a roughly drawn map that shows only basic details.

**sketchy** • **adj.** (**-ier**, **-iest**) not thorough or detailed.
– DERIVATIVES **sketchily** adv. **sketchiness** n.

**skeuomorph** /ˈskjuːə(ʊ)mɔːf/ • **n.** an object or feature which imitates the design of a similar artefact in another material.
– DERIVATIVES **skeuomorphic** adj.
– ORIGIN C19: from Gk *skeuos* 'container, implement' + *morphē* 'form'.

**skew** • **adj.** **1** neither parallel nor at right angles to a specified or implied line; askew. **2** Statistics (of a statistical distribution) not symmetrical. **3** Mathematics (of a pair of lines) neither parallel nor intersecting. ➤(of a curve) not lying in a plane. • **n.** **1** an oblique angle; a slant. **2** a bias towards one particular group or subject. **3** Statistics the state of not being symmetrical. • **v.** **1** suddenly change direction or move at an angle. **2** make biased or distorted. **3** Statistics cause (a distribution) to be asymmetrical.
– DERIVATIVES **skewness** n.
– ORIGIN ME: shortening of ONorth. Fr. *eskiuwer*, var. of OFr. *eschiver* 'eschew'.

**skew arch** (also **skew bridge**) • **n.** an arch (or bridge) with the line of the arch not at right angles to the abutment.

**skewback** • **n.** the sloping face of the abutment on which an extremity of an arch rests.

**skewbald** • **adj.** (of a horse) with irregular patches of white and another colour (properly not black). • **n.** a skewbald horse.
– ORIGIN C17: from obs. *skewed* 'skewbald' (of uncertain origin ), on the pattern of *piebald*.

**skewer** • **n.** a long piece of wood or metal used for holding pieces of food together during cooking. • **v.** fasten together or pierce with a pin or skewer.
– ORIGIN ME: of unknown origin.

**skew gear** • **n.** a gear consisting of two cogwheels having non-parallel, non-intersecting axes.

**skew-whiff** • **adv. & adj.** informal, chiefly Brit. not straight; askew.

**ski** • **n.** (pl. **skis**) each of a pair of long, narrow pieces of hard flexible material fastened under the feet for travelling over snow. ➤a similar device attached beneath a vehicle or aircraft. • **v.** (**skis**, **skied**, **skiing** or **ski-ing**) travel over snow on skis.
– DERIVATIVES **skiable** adj. **skiing** n.
– ORIGIN C18: from Norw., from ON *skíth* 'billet, snow-shoe'.

**ski-bob** • **n.** a device resembling a bicycle with skis instead of wheels, used for sliding down snow-covered slopes. • **v.** ride a ski-bob.
– DERIVATIVES **ski-bobber** n.

**skid** • **v.** (**skidded**, **skidding**) **1** (of a vehicle) slide, typically sideways, on slippery ground or as a result of stopping or turning too quickly. ➤slip; slide. **2** fasten a skid to (a wheel) as a brake. • **n.** **1** an act of skidding. **2** a runner attached to the underside of an aircraft for use when landing on snow or grass. ➤N. Amer. each of a set of wooden rollers for moving a log or other heavy object. **3** a braking device consisting of a wooden or metal shoe that prevents a wheel from revolving. **4** a beam or plank of wood used to support a ship under construction or repair.
– PHRASES **hit the skids** informal begin a rapid decline. **on the skids** informal in a bad state; failing. **put the skids under** informal hasten the decline or failure of.
– ORIGIN C17: perh. rel. to ON *skíth* (see **SKI**).

**skid lid** • **n.** Brit. informal a crash helmet.

**skidoo**[1] /skɪˈduː/ trademark, chiefly N. Amer. • **n.** a motorized toboggan. • **v.** (**skidoos**, **skidooed**) ride on a skidoo.
– ORIGIN C20: an arbitrary formation from **SKI**.

**skidoo**[2] /skɪˈduː/ (also **skiddoo**) • **v.** (**skidoos**, **skidooed**) N. Amer. informal, dated leave quickly.
– PHRASES **twenty-three skidoo** a hasty departure.
– ORIGIN C20: perh. from **SKEDADDLE**.

**skidpan** (N. Amer. **skidpad**) • **n.** a slippery road surface prepared for drivers to practise control of skidding.

**skid road** • **n.** N. Amer. **1** a road formed of skids along which logs are hauled. **2** historical a part of a town frequented by loggers. **3** another term for **SKID ROW**.

**skid row** • **n.** informal, chiefly N. Amer. a run-down part of a town frequented by vagrants and alcoholics.
– ORIGIN 1930s: alt. of **SKID ROAD**.

**skier**[1] • **n.** a person who skis.

**skier**[2] • **n.** variant spelling of **SKYER**.

**skiff** • **n.** a light rowing boat or sculling boat, typically for one person.
– ORIGIN C15: from Fr. *esquif*, from Ital. *schifo*, of Gmc origin; rel. to **SHIP**.

**skiffle** • **n.** **1** Brit. a kind of folk music popular in the 1950s, often incorporating improvised instruments such as washboards. **2** US a style of 1920s and 1930s jazz using both improvised and conventional instruments.
– ORIGIN 1920s: perh. imitative.

**skijoring** /ˈskiːdʒɔːrɪŋ, -ˈdʒɔː-/ • **n.** the sport or recreation of being pulled over snow or ice on skis by a horse or dog.
– DERIVATIVES **skijorer** n.
– ORIGIN 1920s: from Norw. *skikjøring*, from *ski* 'ski' + *kjøre* 'drive'.

**ski jump** • **n.** a steep slope levelling off before a sharp drop to allow a skier to leap through the air. ➤a leap made from such a slope.
– DERIVATIVES **ski jumper** n. **ski jumping** n.

**skilful** (also chiefly N. Amer. **skillful**) • **adj.** having or showing skill.
– DERIVATIVES **skilfully** adv. **skilfulness** n.

**ski lift** • **n.** a system used to transport skiers up a slope to the top of a run, typically consisting of moving seats attached to an overhead cable.

**skill** • **n.** the ability to do something well; expertise or dexterity. • **v.** [usu. as noun **skilling**] train (a worker) to do a particular task.
– DERIVATIVES **skilless** adj. (archaic).
– ORIGIN OE *scele* 'knowledge', from ON *skil* 'discernment, knowledge'.

**skilled** • **adj.** having or showing skill. ➤(of work) requiring special abilities or training.

**skillet** • **n.** **1** a frying pan. **2** Brit. historical a small metal cooking pot with a long handle, typically with legs.
– ORIGIN ME: perh. from OFr. *escuelete*, dimin. of *escuele* 'platter', from late L. *scutella*.

**skilly** • **n.** Brit., chiefly historical thin broth, typically made from oatmeal and water and flavoured with meat.
– ORIGIN C19: abbrev. of archaic *skilligalee*, a fanciful formation.

**skim** • **v.** (**skimmed**, **skimming**) **1** remove (a substance) from the surface of a liquid. **2** move quickly and lightly over or on a surface or through the air. ➤throw (a flat stone) so that it bounces several times on the surface of water. **3** read (something) quickly, noting only the important points. ➤(**skim over**) deal with or treat briefly or superficially. **4** informal steal or embezzle (money) in small amounts over a period of time. • **n.** **1** a thin layer of a substance on the surface of a liquid. **2** an act of reading something quickly or superficially.
– ORIGIN ME: back-form. from **SKIMMER**, or from OFr. *escumer*, from *escume* 'scum, foam'.

**ski mask** • **n.** a protective covering for the head and face, with holes for the eyes, nose, and mouth.

**skimmed milk** (N. Amer. also **skim milk**) • **n.** milk from which the cream has been removed.

**skimmer** • **n.** **1** a person or thing that skims. **2** a long-winged seabird which feeds by skimming over the water surface with its knife-like lower mandible immersed. [Genus *Rynchops*: three species.] **3** chiefly N. Amer. a flat, broad-brimmed straw hat. ➤informal a close-fitting dress. **4** North American term for **DARTER** (in sense 3).
– ORIGIN ME: from OFr. *escumoir*, from *escumer* 'skim', from *escume* 'scum'.

**skimmia** /ˈskɪmɪə/ • **n.** an evergreen East Asian shrub

with creamy-white flowers and red berries. [Genus *Skimmia*.]
– ORIGIN from mod. L., from Japanese.

**skimming** • n. the fraudulent copying of credit or debit card details with a card swipe or other device.

**skimmington** • n. historical a procession intended to ridicule and make an example of a nagging wife or an unfaithful husband.
– ORIGIN C17: perh. from *skimming-ladle*, used as a thrashing instrument during the procession.

**skimobile** /'ski:məbi:l/ • n. N. Amer. a motor vehicle for travelling over snow, with caterpillar tracks at the back and steerable skis in front.

**skimp** • v. (often **skimp on**) expend fewer resources on something than are necessary in an attempt to economize.
– ORIGIN C18: of unknown origin; cf. **SCAMP**[2] and **SCRIMP**.

**skimpy** • adj. (**-ier**, **-iest**) providing or consisting of less than is necessary; meagre. ➤(of clothes) short and revealing.
– DERIVATIVES **skimpily** adv. **skimpiness** n.

**skin** • n. **1** the thin layer of tissue forming the natural outer covering of the body of a person or animal. ➤the skin of a dead animal used as material for clothing or other items. ➤a container made from the skin of an animal, used for holding liquids. **2** the peel or outer layer of a fruit or vegetable. ➤the outermost layer of a structure such as an aircraft. ➤the thin outer covering of a sausage. ➤a thin layer forming on the surface of a hot liquid as it cools. **3** Brit. informal a skinhead. **4** informal a drum or drum head. **5** [as modifier] informal relating to or denoting pornography: *the skin trade*. **6** US a card game in which each player has one card which they bet will not be the first to be matched by a card dealt from the pack. **7** informal a cigarette paper. • v. (**skinned**, **skinning**) **1** remove the skin from. ➤graze (a part of one's body). **2** archaic cover with or form skin. **3** informal take money from or swindle. **4** Soccer, informal take the ball past (a defender) with ease. **5** (**skin up**) Brit. informal make a cannabis cigarette.
– PHRASES **be skin and bone** be very thin. **by the skin of one's teeth** by a very narrow margin. **get under someone's skin** informal **1** annoy or irritate someone intensely. **2** fill someone's mind in a compelling and persistent way. **3** reach or display a deep understanding of someone. **give someone (some) skin** US black slang shake or slap hands together as a gesture or friendship or solidarity. **have a thick** (or **thin**) **skin** be insensitive (or oversensitive) to criticism or insults. **it's no skin off my nose** (or US **off my back**) informal one is not offended or adversely affected. **keep** (or **sleep in**) **a whole skin** archaic escape being wounded or injured. **skin and blister** Brit. rhyming slang a person's sister. **under the skin** in reality, as opposed to superficial appearances.
– DERIVATIVES **skinless** adj. **skinned** adj. **skinner** n.
– ORIGIN OE *scinn*, from ON *skinn*.

**skincare** • n. the use of cosmetics to care for the skin.

**skin-deep** • adj. not deep or lasting; superficial.

**skin diving** • n. the action or sport of swimming under water without a diving suit, typically using an aqualung and flippers.
– DERIVATIVES **skin-dive** v. **skin-diver** n.

**skinflint** • n. informal a miser.

**skinful** • n. Brit. informal enough alcoholic drink to make one drunk.

**skin game** • n. N. Amer. informal a rigged gambling game; a swindle.

**skinhead** • n. a young person of a subculture characterized by close-cropped hair and heavy boots, often perceived as aggressive, violent, and racist.

**skink** • n. a smooth-bodied lizard with short or absent limbs. [Family Scincidae: numerous species.]
– ORIGIN C16: from Fr. *scinc* or L. *scincus*, from Gk *skinkos*.

**skinny** • adj. (**-ier**, **-iest**) **1** (of a person) unattractively thin. **2** (of an article of clothing) tight-fitting. • n. (**the skinny**) US informal confidential information or gossip.
– DERIVATIVES **skinniness** n.

**skinny-dip** informal • v. swim naked. • n. a naked swim.
– DERIVATIVES **skinny-dipper** n.

**skinnymalinks** /'skɪnɪməlɪŋks/ (also **skinnymalink**) • n. Scottish a very thin person.
– ORIGIN C19: origin uncertain; a Sc. children's song related the adventures of a thin man known as 'Skinamalinky Long Leg'.

**skinny-rib** • n. a tightly fitting sweater or cardigan.

**skint** • adj. Brit. informal having little or no money available.
– ORIGIN 1920s: var. of colloq. *skinned*, in the same sense, past part. of **SKIN**.

**skin test** • n. a test to determine whether an immune reaction is elicited when a substance is applied to or injected into the skin.

**skintight** • adj. (of a garment) very close-fitting.

**skip**[1] • v. (**skipped**, **skipping**) **1** move along lightly, stepping from one foot to the other with a hop or bounce. ➤throw (a stone) so that it skims the surface of water. **2** jump repeatedly over a rope which is held at both ends and turned over the head and under the feet. ➤N. Amer. jump over (a rope) in such a way. **3** jump lightly over. ➤omit or move quickly and unmethodically over (a stage or point). ➤fail to attend or deal with; miss. ➤informal leave quickly and secretly. • n. **1** a skipping movement. **2** N. Amer. informal a person who defaults or absconds.
– ORIGIN ME: prob. of Scand. origin.

**skip**[2] • n. **1** Brit. a large transportable open-topped container for bulky refuse. **2** a cage or bucket in which workers or materials are lowered and raised in mines and quarries. **3** variant spelling of **SKEP**.

**skip**[3] • n. the captain or director of a side at bowls or curling. • v. (**skipped**, **skipping**) act as skip of (a side).
– ORIGIN C19 (orig. Scots): abbrev. of **SKIPPER**[1].

**ski pants** • pl. n. women's trousers made of stretchy fabric with tapering legs and an elastic stirrup under each foot.

**skipjack** • n. **1** (also **skipjack tuna**) a small tuna with dark horizontal stripes. [*Katsuwonus pelamis*.] **2** another term for **CLICK BEETLE**. **3** a sloop-rigged sailing boat of a kind used off the east coast of the US.
– ORIGIN C18: from **SKIP**[1] + **JACK**[1] (with ref. to the fish's habit of jumping out of the water).

**ski-plane** • n. an aircraft having its undercarriage fitted with skis for landing on snow or ice.

**skipper**[1] informal • n. the captain of a ship, boat, or aircraft. ➤the captain of a side in a game or sport. • v. act as captain of.
– ORIGIN ME: from MDu., Mid. Low Ger. *schipper*, from *schip* 'ship'.

**skipper**[2] • n. **1** a person or thing that skips. **2** a small brownish moth-like butterfly with rapid darting flight. [Family Hesperiidae: many species.]

**skippet** • n. chiefly historical a small round wooden box used to preserve documents and seals.
– ORIGIN ME: of unknown origin.

**skirl** /skə:l/ • n. a shrill sound, especially that of bagpipes. • v. (of bagpipes) make such a sound.
– ORIGIN ME: prob. of Scand. origin; ult. imitative.

**skirmish** • n. an episode of irregular or unpremeditated fighting, especially between small or outlying parts of armies. • v. engage in a skirmish.
– DERIVATIVES **skirmisher** n.
– ORIGIN ME: from OFr. *eskirmiss-*, lengthened stem of *eskirmir*, from a Gmc verb meaning 'defend'.

**skirr** /skə:/ • v. rare move rapidly, especially with a whirring sound.
– ORIGIN C16: perh. rel. to **SCOUR**[1] or **SCOUR**[2].

**skirret** /'skɪrɪt/ • n. a plant of the parsley family with an edible carrot-like root. [*Sium sisarum*.]
– ORIGIN ME *skirwhit(e)*, perh. from Scots *skire* 'bright, clear' + **WHITE**.

**skirt** • n. **1** a woman's outer garment fastened around the waist and hanging down around the legs. ➤the part of a coat or dress that hangs below the waist. ➤informal women regarded as objects of sexual desire. **2** a surface that conceals or protects the wheels or underside of a vehicle or aircraft. ➤the curtain that hangs round the base of a

hovercraft to contain the air cushion. **3** an animal's diaphragm and other membranes as food. ➤ Brit. a cut of meat from the lower flank. **4** a small flap on a saddle covering the bar from which the stirrup hangs. **5** archaic an edge, border, or extreme part. ● **v.** (also **skirt along/around**) go round or past the edge of. ➤ avoid dealing with.
– DERIVATIVES **-skirted** adj.
– ORIGIN ME: from ON *skyrta* 'shirt'; cf. synonymous OE *scyrte*, also **SHORT**.

**skirting** (also **skirting board**) ● **n.** Brit. a wooden board running along the base of an interior wall.

**skit** ● **n.** a short comedy sketch or piece of humorous writing, especially a parody.
– ORIGIN C18 (in the sense 'satirical comment or attack'): rel. to the rare verb *skit* 'move lightly and rapidly', perh. from ON (cf. *skjóta* 'shoot').

**skite** /skʌɪt/ informal ● **v. 1** Austral./NZ boast. **2** move or glance off quickly and forcefully. ● **n. 1** Austral./NZ a boaster. ➤ boasting or boastfulness. **2** Scottish a drinking bout.
– ORIGIN C18 (in sense 2 of the verb): perh. of ON origin; cf. **SKIT** and **BLATHERSKITE**.

**skitter** ● **v. 1** move lightly and quickly or hurriedly. **2** draw (bait) jerkily across the surface of the water as a technique in fishing.
– ORIGIN C19: appar. a frequentative of **SKITE**.

**skittery** ● **adj.** restless; skittish.

**skittish** ● **adj.** (of a horse) nervous; inclined to shy. ➤ lively and unpredictable; playful.
– DERIVATIVES **skittishly** adv. **skittishness** n.
– ORIGIN ME: perh. from the rare verb *skit* (see **SKIT**).

**skittle** ● **n. 1** (**skittles**) [treated as sing.] a game played with wooden pins, typically nine in number, set up at the end of an alley to be bowled down with a wooden ball or disc. ➤ (also **table skittles**) a game played with similar pins set up on a board to be knocked down by swinging a suspended ball. **2** a pin used in the game of skittles. **3** (**skittles**) [treated as sing.] Brit. informal chess that is not played seriously. ● **v.** knock over as if in a game of skittles. ➤ Cricket get (batsmen) out in rapid succession.
– ORIGIN C17: of unknown origin.

**skive¹** /skʌɪv/ Brit. informal ● **v.** avoid work or a duty; shirk. ● **n.** an instance of shirking. ➤ an easy option.
– DERIVATIVES **skiver** n.
– ORIGIN C20: perh. from Fr. *esquiver* 'slink away'.

**skive²** /skʌɪv/ ● **v.** technical pare (the edge of a piece of leather or other material) to reduce its thickness.
– ORIGIN C19: from ON *skífa*; rel. to **SHIVE**.

**skivvy** ● **n.** (pl. **-ies**) **1** Brit. informal a low-ranking female domestic servant. ➤ a person doing menial work. **2** US a lightweight high-necked long-sleeved garment. ➤ a T-shirt or short-sleeved vest. ➤ (**skivvies**) N. Amer. trademark underwear of vest and underpants. ● **v.** (**-ies**, **-ied**) informal do menial household tasks.
– ORIGIN C20: of unknown origin.

**skol** /skɒl, skəʊl/ (also **skoal**) ● **exclam.** used as a toast before drinking.
– ORIGIN C17: from Dan. and Norw. *skaal*, Swed. *skål*, from ON *skál* 'bowl'.

**skookum** /ˈskuːkəm/ N. Amer. ● **adj.** informal strong, vigorous, or impressive. ● **n.** archaic a street party or trade fair.
– ORIGIN C19: from Chinook Jargon.

**skookum house** ● **n.** N. Amer. informal a jail.

**skosh** /skəʊʃ/ ● **n.** US informal a small amount; a little.
– ORIGIN 1950s: from Japanese *sukoshi*.

**Skraeling** /ˈskreɪlɪŋ/ ● **n.** an indigenous inhabitant of Greenland or NE North America at the time of early Norse settlement.
– ORIGIN from ON *Skrœling(j)ar* (pl.).

**skua** /ˈskjuːə/ ● **n.** a large predatory seabird, chiefly brown, which pursues other birds to make them disgorge fish. [*Catharacta skua* (**great skua**), *Stercorarius parasiticus* (**Arctic skua**), and related species.]
– ORIGIN C17: mod. L., from Faroese *skúvur*, from ON *skúfr* (appar. imitative).

**skulduggery** /skʌlˈdʌg(ə)ri/ (also **skullduggery**) ● **n.** underhand or unscrupulous behaviour; trickery.
– ORIGIN C19: alt. of Scots *sculduddery*, of unknown origin.

**skulk** ● **v.** hide or move around secretly, typically with a sinister or cowardly motive. ● **n.** a group of foxes.
– DERIVATIVES **skulker** n.
– ORIGIN ME: of Scand. origin.

**skull** ● **n.** a bone framework enclosing the brain of a vertebrate. ➤ informal a person's head or brain. ● **v.** informal hit on the head.
– PHRASES **out of one's skull** informal **1** out of one's mind; crazy. **2** very drunk. **skull and crossbones** a representation of a skull with two thigh bones crossed below it as an emblem of piracy or death.
– DERIVATIVES **-skulled** adj.
– ORIGIN ME *scolle*; of unknown origin; cf. ON *skoltr*.

**skullcap** ● **n. 1** a small close-fitting peakless cap or protective helmet. **2** the top part of the skull. **3** a plant of the mint family, whose tubular flowers have a helmet-shaped cup at the base. [Genus *Scutellaria*.]

**skunk** ● **n. 1** a black-and-white striped American mammal of the weasel family, able to spray foul-smelling irritant liquid from its anal glands at attackers. [*Mephitis mephitis* and other species.] **2** informal a contemptible person. **3** informal short for **SKUNKWEED**. ● **v.** N. Amer. informal **1** defeat (an opponent) overwhelmingly, especially by preventing them from scoring at all. **2** dated fail to pay (a bill or creditor).
– ORIGIN C17: from Abnaki *segankw*.

**skunk cabbage** ● **n.** a North American arum, the flower of which has a distinctive unpleasant smell. [*Lysichiton americanum* and *Symplocarpus foetidus*.]

**skunkweed** ● **n.** cannabis of a variety which has a high concentration of narcotic agents.

**skunkworks** ● **pl. n.** [usu. treated as sing.] US informal a small experimental laboratory or department of a company or institution.
– ORIGIN 1970s: allegedly from an association with the *Skonk Works*, an illegal still in the Li'l Abner comic strip.

**sky** ● **n.** (pl. **-ies**) **1** the region of the atmosphere and outer space seen from the earth. **2** poetic/literary heaven; heavenly power. ● **v.** (**-ies**, **-ied**) informal hit (a ball) high into the air.
– PHRASES **the sky is the limit** there is practically no limit. **to the skies** very highly; enthusiastically. **under the open sky** out of doors.
– DERIVATIVES **skyey** adj. **skyless** adj. **skyward** adj. & adv. **skywards** adv.
– ORIGIN ME, from ON *ský* 'cloud'.

**sky blue** ● **n.** a bright clear blue.

**sky-blue pink** ● **n.** humorous a non-existent colour.

**skybox** ● **n.** N. Amer. a luxurious enclosed seating area high up in a sports arena.

**sky burial** ● **n.** a Tibetan funeral ritual involving the exposure of a dismembered corpse to sacred vultures.

**skycap** ● **n.** N. Amer. a porter at an airport.

**sky-clad** ● **adj.** (in the context of modern pagan ritual) naked.
– ORIGIN C20: prob. a translation of Sanskrit *Digāmbara* (see **DIGAMBARA**).

**sky cloth** ● **n.** a backdrop painted or coloured to represent the sky.

**skydiving** ● **n.** the sport of jumping from an aircraft and performing acrobatic manoeuvres in the air under free fall before landing by parachute.
– DERIVATIVES **skydive** v. **skydiver** n.

**skyer** (also **skier**) ● **n.** Cricket a hit which goes very high.

**Skye terrier** ● **n.** a small long-haired terrier of a slate-coloured or fawn-coloured Scottish breed.

**skyglow** ● **n.** brightness of the night sky in a built-up area as a result of light pollution.

**sky-high** ● **adv. & adj. 1** as if reaching the sky; very high. **2** at or to a very high level; very great.

**skyhook** ● **n. 1** Climbing a small flattened hook, with an eye for attaching a rope, fixed temporarily into a rock face. **2** Basketball a lob.

**skyjack** ● **v.** hijack (an aircraft). ● **n.** an act of skyjacking.

– DERIVATIVES **skyjacker** n.

**skylark** • n. a common lark of open country, noted for its prolonged song given in hovering flight. [*Alauda arvensis*.] • v. play practical jokes or indulge in horseplay.

**skylight** • n. a window set in a roof or ceiling at the same angle.

**skyline** • n. an outline of land and buildings defined against the sky.

**skylit** (also **skylighted**) • adj. fitted with or lit by a skylight or skylights.

**sky pilot** • n. informal a clergyman.

**skyr** /skɪə/ • n. an Icelandic dish consisting of curdled milk.

– ORIGIN from Icelandic.

**skyrocket** • n. a rocket designed to explode high in the air as a signal or firework. • v. (**-rocketed**, **-rocketing**) informal (of a price or amount) increase very rapidly.

**skysail** /ˈskʌɪseɪl, -s(ə)l/ • n. a light sail above the royal in a square-rigged ship.

**skyscape** • n. a view or picture of an expanse of sky.

**skyscraper** • n. a very tall building of many storeys.

**sky surfing** • n. the sport of jumping from an aircraft and surfing through the air on a board before landing by parachute.

**skywatch** • v. informal observe or monitor the sky, especially for heavenly bodies or aircraft.

– DERIVATIVES **skywatcher** n.

**sky wave** • n. a radio wave reflected from the ionosphere.

**skyway** • n. chiefly N. Amer. **1** a recognized route followed by aircraft. **2** (also **skywalk**) a covered overhead walkway between buildings. **3** a raised motorway.

**skywriting** • n. words in the form of smoke trails made by an aircraft, especially for advertising.

– DERIVATIVES **skywriter** n.

**slab** • n. **1** a large, thick, flat piece of solid material, in particular stone, concrete, or heavy food. **2** a flat, heavy table top or counter used for food preparation. ➤ Brit. a table used for laying a body on in a mortuary. **3** an outer piece of timber sawn from a log. **4** Climbing a large, smooth body of rock lying at a sharp angle to the horizontal. • v. (**slabbed**, **slabbing**) remove slabs from (a log or tree) to prepare it for sawing into planks.

– DERIVATIVES **slabbed** adj. **slabby** adj.

– ORIGIN ME: of unknown origin.

**slabber** chiefly Scottish & Irish • v. **1** dribble at the mouth; slaver. **2** splatter or splash. **3** chatter trivially. • n. a dribble of saliva.

– ORIGIN C16: rel. to dial. *slab* 'muddy place, puddle'.

**slack**[1] • adj. **1** not taut or held tightly in position; loose. **2** (of business or trade) not busy; quiet. **3** careless, lazy, or negligent. **4** W. Indian lewd or promiscuous. **5** (of a tide) neither ebbing nor flowing. • n. **1** the part of a rope or line which is not held taut. **2** (**slacks**) casual trousers. **3** informal a spell of inactivity or laziness. • v. **1** loosen or reduce the intensity or speed of; slacken. ➤ (**slack off/up**) decrease in intensity or speed. **2** Brit. informal work slowly or lazily. **3** slake (lime).

– PHRASES **cut someone some slack** N. Amer. informal allow someone some leeway in their conduct. **take** (or **pick**) **up the slack 1** improve the use of resources to avoid an undesirable lull in business. **2** pull on the loose part of a rope to make it taut.

– DERIVATIVES **slacken** v. **slackly** adv. **slackness** n.

– ORIGIN OE *slæc* 'inclined to be lazy, unhurried', of Gmc origin.

**slack**[2] • n. coal dust or small pieces of coal.

– ORIGIN ME: prob. from Low Ger. or Du.

**slacker** • n. informal **1** a person who avoids work or effort. ➤ US a person who evades military service. **2** chiefly N. Amer. a young person of a subculture characterized by apathy and aimlessness.

**slack water** • n. the state of the tide when it is turning, especially at low tide.

**slag** • n. **1** stony waste matter separated from metals during the smelting or refining of ore. ➤ similar material produced by a volcano; scoria. **2** Brit. informal, derogatory a promiscuous woman. ➤ a contemptible or insignificant person. • v. (**slagged**, **slagging**) **1** [usu. as noun **slagging**] produce deposits of slag. **2** (often **slag someone off**) Brit. informal criticize abusively.

– DERIVATIVES **slaggy** adj. (**-ier**, **-iest**).

– ORIGIN C16: from Mid. Low Ger. *slagge*, perh. from *slagen* 'strike', with ref. to fragments formed by hammering.

**slag heap** • n. a hill or area of refuse from a mine or industrial site.

**slag wool** • n. mineral wool made from blast-furnace slag.

**slain** past participle of SLAY[1].

**slainte** /ˈslɑːntʃə/ • exclam. used as a toast before drinking.

– ORIGIN from Sc. Gaelic *slàinte*, lit. 'health'.

**slake** • v. **1** quench (one's thirst). ➤ satisfy (a desire). **2** combine (quicklime) with water to produce calcium hydroxide.

– ORIGIN OE *slacian* 'become less eager', also 'slacken', from *slæc* (see SLACK[1]).

**slaked lime** • n. calcium hydroxide, made by adding water to quicklime.

**slalom** /ˈslɑːləm/ • n. a ski race down a winding course marked out by poles. ➤ a canoeing or sailing race over a similar course. • v. move or race in a winding path, avoiding obstacles.

– DERIVATIVES **slalomer** n.

– ORIGIN 1920s: from Norw., lit. 'sloping track'.

**slam**[1] • v. (**slammed**, **slamming**) **1** shut or be shut forcefully and loudly. ➤ push or put somewhere with great force. ➤ (often **slam into**) crash or strike heavily into. ➤ put into action suddenly or forcefully: *I slammed on the brakes.* **2** informal criticize severely. **3** informal, chiefly N. Amer. easily score points against or defeat. **4** [usu. as noun **slamming**] US (of a telephone company) take over the account of (a telephone customer) without their permission. • n. **1** a loud bang caused by the forceful shutting of something. **2** N. Amer. informal prison. [abbrev. of SLAMMER.] **3** chiefly US a poetry contest in which competitors recite their entries and are judged by members of the audience.

– ORIGIN C17: prob. of Scand. origin.

**slam**[2] • n. Bridge a grand slam (all thirteen tricks) or small slam (twelve tricks), for which bonus points are scored if bid and made.

– ORIGIN C17 (orig. the name of a card game): perh. from obs. *slampant* 'trickery'.

**slam-bang** • adj. informal, chiefly N. Amer. exciting and energetic. ➤ direct and forceful.

**slam-dancing** • n. chiefly N. Amer. a form of dancing to rock music in which the dancers deliberately collide with one another.

– DERIVATIVES **slam-dance** v. **slam dancer** n.

**slam dunk** • n. **1** Basketball a shot thrust down through the basket. **2** N. Amer. informal a foregone conclusion or certainty. • v. (**slam-dunk**) **1** Basketball thrust (the ball) down through the basket. **2** N. Amer. informal defeat or dismiss decisively.

**slammer** • n. **1** informal prison. **2** chiefly N. Amer. a person who slam-dances. **3** (also **tequila slammer**) a cocktail made with tequila and champagne or another fizzy drink, which is covered, slammed on the table, and then drunk in one.

**slander** • n. Law the action or crime of making a false spoken statement damaging to a person's reputation. Compare with LIBEL. ➤ a false and malicious spoken statement. • v. make such statements about.

– DERIVATIVES **slanderer** n. **slanderous** adj. **slanderously** adv.

– ORIGIN ME: from OFr. *esclandre*, alt. of *escandle*, from late L. *scandalum* (see SCANDAL).

**slang** • n. informal language that is more common in speech than in writing and is typically restricted to a particular context or group. • v. informal attack (someone) using abusive language.

– DERIVATIVES **slangily** adv. **slanginess** n. **slangy** adj. (**-ier**, **-iest**).

– ORIGIN C18: of unknown origin.

**slanging match** ● n. chiefly Brit. a prolonged exchange of insults.

**slant** ● v. **1** diverge from the vertical or horizontal; slope or lean. **2** [often as adj. **slanted**] present or view (information) from a particular angle, especially in a biased or unfair way. ● n. **1** a sloping position. **2** a point of view. ● adj. sloping.
– DERIVATIVES **slantwise** adj. & adv.
– ORIGIN ME: var. of dial. *slent*, of Scand. origin, prob. influenced by **ASLANT**.

**slant height** ● n. the height of a cone from the vertex to the periphery of the base.

**slap** ● v. (**slapped**, **slapping**) **1** hit or strike with the palm of one's hand or a flat object. ➤hit against with the sound of such an action. ➤(**slap someone down**) informal reprimand someone forcefully. **2** (**slap something on**) apply something quickly, carelessly, or forcefully. ➤informal impose a fine or other penalty on. ● n. **1** an act or sound of slapping. **2** informal make-up. ● adv. (also **slap bang**) informal suddenly and directly, especially with great force. ➤exactly; right.
– PHRASES **slap in the face** an unexpected rejection or affront. **slap on the back** a congratulation or commendation. **slap on the wrist** a mild reprimand or punishment.
– ORIGIN ME: prob. imitative.

**slap and tickle** ● n. Brit. informal physical amorous play.

**slap bass** ● n. a style of playing double bass or bass guitar by pulling and releasing the strings sharply against the fingerboard.

**slapdash** ● adj. & adv. done too hurriedly and carelessly.

**slap-happy** ● adj. informal **1** cheerfully casual or flippant. **2** dazed or stupefied from happiness or relief.

**slaphead** ● n. Brit. informal, derogatory a bald or balding man.

**slapjack** ● n. N. Amer. a kind of pancake cooked on a griddle.

**slapper** ● n. Brit. informal, derogatory a promiscuous or vulgar woman.

**slap shot** ● n. Ice Hockey a hard shot struck with a sharp slapping motion.

**slapstick** ● n. **1** comedy based on deliberately clumsy actions and humorously embarrassing events. **2** a device consisting of two flexible pieces of wood joined together at one end, used by clowns and in pantomime to produce a loud slapping noise.

**slap-up** ● adj. informal, chiefly Brit. (of a meal) large and sumptuous.

**slash** ● v. **1** cut with a violent sweeping movement. **2** informal reduce (a price, quantity, etc.) greatly. ➤[as adj. **slashing**] vigorously incisive or effective. **3** archaic lash, whip, or thrash severely. ➤criticize severely. ● n. **1** a cut made with a wide, sweeping stroke. **2** a bright patch or flash of colour or light. **3** an oblique stroke (/) used between alternatives, in fractions and ratios, or between separate elements of a text. **4** Brit. informal an act of urinating. **5** N. Amer. debris resulting from the felling or destruction of trees.
– ORIGIN ME: perh. imitative, or from OFr. *esclachier* 'break in pieces'.

**slash-and-burn** ● adj. relating to or denoting a method of agriculture in which vegetation is cut down and burned off before new seeds are sown.

**slashed** ● adj. (of a garment) having slits to show the lining material or skin beneath.

**slasher** ● n. **1** a person or thing that slashes. **2** (also **slasher film**) informal a horror film, especially one in which victims are slashed with knives.

**slat** ● n. a thin, narrow piece of wood or other material, especially one of a series which overlap or fit into each other, as in a Venetian blind.
– DERIVATIVES **slatted** adj.
– ORIGIN ME (in the sense 'roofing slate'): shortening of OFr. *esclat* 'splinter'.

**slate** ● n. **1** a fine-grained grey, green, or bluish-purple metamorphic rock easily split into smooth, flat plates. ➤a flat plate of such rock used as roofing material. **2** a plate of slate formerly used in schools for writing on. **3** a bluish-grey colour. **4** a list of candidates for election to a post or office. ➤Brit. a record of a person's debt or credit: *put it on the slate.* ➤chiefly N. Amer. a range of something on offer. **5** a board showing the identifying details of a take of a film, held in front of the camera at the beginning and end of the take. ● v. **1** cover (a roof) with slates. **2** Brit. informal criticize severely. **3** chiefly N. Amer. schedule; plan. ➤nominate as a candidate for an office or post.
– DERIVATIVES **slaty** adj.
– ORIGIN ME *sclate*, *sklate*, shortening of OFr. *esclate*, fem. synonymous with *esclat* (see **SLAT**).

**slater** ● n. **1** a person who slates roofs for a living. **2** a woodlouse or similar isopod crustacean.

**slather** /ˈslaðə/ informal ● v. spread or smear thickly or liberally. ● n. (also **slathers**) N. Amer. a large amount.
– PHRASES **open slather** Austral./NZ freedom to act without restriction; free rein.
– ORIGIN C19: of unknown origin.

**slattern** /ˈslat(ə)n/ ● n. dated a dirty, untidy woman.
– DERIVATIVES **slatternliness** n. **slatternly** adj.
– ORIGIN C17: rel. to *slattering* 'slovenly', from dial. *slatter* 'to spill or slop'.

**slaughter** /ˈslɔːtə/ ● n. **1** the killing of farm animals for food. **2** the killing of a large number of people in a cruel or violent way. **3** informal a thorough defeat. ● v. **1** kill (animals) for food. **2** kill (people) in a cruel or violent way. **3** informal defeat (an opponent) thoroughly.
– DERIVATIVES **slaughterer** n. **slaughterous** adj.
– ORIGIN ME (as n.): from ON *slátr* 'butcher's meat'; rel. to **SLAY**[1].

**slaughterhouse** ● n. a place where animals are slaughtered for food.

**Slav** /slɑːv/ ● n. a member of a group of peoples in central and eastern Europe speaking Slavic languages.
– ORIGIN from med. L. *Sclavus*, late Gk *Sklabos*, later also from med. L. *Slavus*.

**slave** ● n. **1** historical a person who is the legal property of another and is forced to obey them. ➤a person who is excessively dependent upon or controlled by something: *a slave to fashion.* **2** a device, or part of one, directly controlled by another. Compare with **MASTER**[1]. ● v. **1** work excessively hard. **2** [as noun **slaving**] historical the action or process of enslaving people. **3** subject (a device) to control by another.
– ORIGIN ME: shortening of OFr. *esclave*, equivalent of med. L. *sclava* (fem.) 'Slavonic (captive)'.

**slave bangle** (also **slave bracelet**) ● n. a bangle or bracelet worn above the elbow.

**slave-driver** ● n. informal a person who works others very hard.
– DERIVATIVES **slave-drive** v.

**slave labour** ● n. labour which is coerced and inadequately rewarded.

**slaver**[1] /ˈsleɪvə/ ● n. historical a person dealing in or owning slaves. ➤a ship used for transporting slaves.

**slaver**[2] /ˈslavə, ˈsleɪvə/ ● n. **1** saliva running from the mouth. **2** archaic excessive or obsequious flattery. ● v. **1** let saliva run from the mouth. **2** (usu. **slaver over**) show excessive desire.
– ORIGIN ME: prob. from Low Ger.; cf. **SLOBBER**.

**slavery** ● n. the state of being a slave. ➤the practice or system of owning slaves.

**slave state** ● n. historical any of the Southern states of the US in which slavery was legal before the Civil War.

**slave trade** ● n. historical the procuring, transporting, and selling of human beings, especially African blacks, as slaves.
– DERIVATIVES **slave trader** n.

**Slavey** /ˈsleɪvi/ ● n. **1** a member of a Dene people of NW Canada. **2** either of the two languages (**North** and **South Slavey**) spoken by this people.
– ORIGIN translating Cree *awahkān* 'captive, slave'.

**slavey** ● n. (pl. **-eys**) Brit. informal, dated a maidservant, especially a hard-worked one.

**Slavic** /ˈslɑːvɪk, ˈslavɪk/ ● n. the branch of the Indo-European language family that includes Russian, Polish,

Czech, Bulgarian, and Serbo-Croat. ● **adj.** relating to or denoting this branch of languages or their speakers.

**slavish** ● **adj. 1** showing no attempt at originality. **2** servile or submissive.
– DERIVATIVES **slavishly** adv. **slavishness** n.

**Slavonian grebe** /slə'vəʊnɪən/ ● **n.** a northern grebe with reddish underparts and a black and gold crest in the breeding season. [*Podiceps auritus.*]
– ORIGIN *Slavonian* from med. L. *S(c)lavonia* 'country of the Slavs'.

**Slavonic** /slə'vɒnɪk/ ● **n. & adj.** another term for **Slavic**.

**slaw** ● **n.** N. Amer. coleslaw.
– ORIGIN C18: from Du. *sla*, shortened from *salade* 'salad'.

**slay**[1] ● **v.** (past **slew**; past part. **slain**) **1** archaic or poetic/literary kill in a violent way. ➤ N. Amer. murder (someone). **2** informal greatly impress or amuse.
– DERIVATIVES **slayer** n.
– ORIGIN OE *slēan* 'strike, kill', of Gmc origin.

**slay**[2] ● **n.** variant spelling of **sley**.

**SLBM** ● **abbrev.** submarine-launched ballistic missile.

**SLD** ● **abbrev.** Social and Liberal Democrats.

**SLE** ● **abbrev.** systemic lupus erythematosus.

**sleaze** informal ● **n.** immoral, sordid, and corrupt behaviour or material. ➤ (also **sleazebag** or **sleazeball**) informal, chiefly N. Amer. a sordid, corrupt, or immoral person. ● **v.** behave in an immoral, corrupt, or sordid way.
– ORIGIN 1960s: back-form. from **sleazy**.

**sleazy** ● **adj.** (**-ier**, **-iest**) **1** sordid, corrupt, or immoral. ➤ (of a place) squalid and seedy. **2** dated (of textiles and clothing) flimsy.
– DERIVATIVES **sleazily** adv. **sleaziness** n.
– ORIGIN C17: of unknown origin.

**sled** ● **n. & v.** (**sledded**, **sledding**) North American term for **sledge**[1].
– ORIGIN ME: from Mid. Low Ger. *sledde*; rel. to **slide**.

**sledge**[1] ● **n.** a vehicle on runners for travelling over snow or ice, either pushed, pulled, or allowed to slide downhill. ➤ Brit. a toboggan. ● **v.** ride or carry on a sledge.
– DERIVATIVES **sledging** n.
– ORIGIN C16: from MDu. *sleedse*; rel. to **sled**.

**sledge**[2] ● **n.** a sledgehammer. ● **v.** [usu. as noun **sledging**] Cricket (of a fielder) make offensive remarks to (an opposing batsman) in order to break their concentration.
– ORIGIN OE *slecg* (n.), from a Gmc base meaning 'to strike', rel. to **slay**[1].

**sledgehammer** ● **n. 1** a large, heavy hammer used for breaking rocks, driving in posts, etc. **2** [as modifier] very powerful, forceful, or unsubtle: *sledgehammer blows.*

**sleek** ● **adj. 1** (especially of hair or fur) smooth, glossy, and healthy-looking. **2** wealthy and well-groomed in appearance. ➤ elegant and streamlined: *a sleek car.* ● **v.** make (the hair) sleek by applying pressure or moisture.
– DERIVATIVES **sleekly** adv. **sleekness** n. **sleeky** adj.
– ORIGIN ME: a later var. of **slick**.

**sleep** ● **n. 1** a regularly recurring condition of body and mind in which the nervous system is inactive, the eyes closed, the postural muscles relaxed, and consciousness practically suspended. **2** a gummy secretion found in the corners of the eyes after sleep. ● **v.** (past and past part. **slept** /slɛpt/) **1** rest in such a condition. ➤ (**sleep something off**) recover from something by going to sleep. ➤ (**sleep in**) remain asleep or in bed later than usual in the morning. **2** provide (a specified number of people) with beds or bedrooms. **3** (**sleep together/with**) have sexual intercourse or be involved in a sexual relationship. ➤ (**sleep around**) have many casual sexual partners.
– PHRASES **put someone to sleep** make someone unconscious with drugs or anaesthetic. **put something to sleep** kill an animal painlessly. **sleep like a log** (or **top**) sleep very soundly.
– DERIVATIVES **sleepless** adj. **sleeplessly** adv. **sleeplessness** n.
– ORIGIN OE *slēp*, *slǣp* (n.), *slēpan*, *slǣpan* (v.), of Gmc origin.

**sleeper** ● **n. 1** a sleeping car or a train carrying sleeping cars. **2** chiefly N. Amer. a sleepsuit for a baby or small child. **3** N. Amer. a sofa or chair that converts into a bed. **4** a film, book, play, etc. that suddenly achieves success after initially attracting little attention. **5** a secret agent who remains inactive for a long period while establishing a secure position. **6** Brit. a ring or bar worn in a pierced ear to keep the hole from closing. **7** chiefly Brit. a wooden or concrete beam laid transversely under railway track to support it. **8** a stocky fish with mottled coloration. [*Dormitator* and other genera.]

**sleeping bag** ● **n.** a warm lined padded bag to sleep in, especially when camping.

**sleeping car** (Brit. also **sleeping carriage**) ● **n.** a railway carriage provided with beds or berths.

**sleeping draught** ● **n.** Brit. dated a drink or drug intended to induce sleep.

**sleeping partner** ● **n.** Brit. a partner not sharing in the actual work of a firm.

**sleeping pill** ● **n.** a tablet of a sleep-inducing drug.

**sleeping policeman** ● **n.** Brit. a hump in the road intended to cause traffic to reduce speed.

**sleeping sickness** ● **n. 1** a tropical disease caused by a parasitic protozoan (trypanosome) transmitted by the bite of the tsetse fly, marked by extreme lethargy. **2** US term for **sleepy sickness**.

**sleepover** ● **n.** chiefly N. Amer. an occasion of spending the night away from home.

**sleepsuit** ● **n.** Brit. a young child's one-piece garment, typically worn as nightwear.

**sleepwalk** ● **v.** walk around and sometimes perform other actions while asleep.
– DERIVATIVES **sleepwalker** n.

**sleepy** ● **adj.** (**-ier**, **-iest**) **1** needing or ready for sleep. **2** (of a place) without much activity. ➤ not dynamic or able to respond to change.
– DERIVATIVES **sleepily** adv. **sleepiness** n.

**sleepyhead** ● **n.** informal a sleepy or inattentive person.

**sleepy sickness** ● **n.** Brit. encephalitis lethargica, a brain infection causing drowsiness and sometimes coma.

**sleet** ● **n.** rain containing some ice, or snow melting as it falls. ➤ US a thin coating of ice formed by sleet or rain freezing on coming into contact with a cold surface. ● **v.** (**it sleets**, **it is sleeting**, etc.) sleet falls.
– DERIVATIVES **sleety** adj.
– ORIGIN ME: of Gmc origin.

**sleeve** ● **n. 1** the part of a garment that wholly or partly covers a person's arm. **2** a protective paper or cardboard cover for a record. ➤ a protective or connecting tube fitting over a rod, spindle, or smaller tube. **3** a windsock. ➤ a drogue towed by an aircraft.
– PHRASES **up one's sleeve** kept secret and in reserve for use when needed.
– DERIVATIVES **sleeved** adj. **sleeveless** adj.
– ORIGIN OE *slēfe*, *slīef(e)*, *slȳf*.

**sleeveen** /'sliːviːn, sliː'viːn/ ● **n.** Irish informal an untrustworthy or cunning person.
– ORIGIN C19: from Ir. *slibhin* 'trickster'.

**sleeve note** ● **n.** Brit. an article printed on a record sleeve giving information about the music or musician.

**sleeve nut** ● **n.** a long nut with right-hand and left-hand screw threads for drawing together conversely threaded pipes or shafts.

**sleeve valve** ● **n.** a valve in the form of a cylinder which slides to cover and uncover an inlet or outlet.

**sleeving** ● **n.** Brit. tubular covering for electrical or other cables.

**sleigh** ● **n.** a sledge drawn by horses or reindeer. ● **v.** ride on a sleigh.
– ORIGIN C17: from Du. *slee*; rel. to **sled**.

**sleigh bell** ● **n.** a tinkling bell attached to the harness of a sleigh horse.

**sleight** /slʌɪt/ ● **n.** poetic/literary the use of dexterity or cunning, especially so as to deceive.
– PHRASES **sleight of hand** manual dexterity, typically in performing conjuring tricks. ➤ skilful deception.
– ORIGIN ME *sleghth* 'cunning, skill', from ON *slœgth*, from *slœgr* 'sly'.

**slender** • adj. (**-er, -est**) **1** gracefully thin. **2** barely sufficient: *people of slender means.*
– DERIVATIVES **slenderize** (also **-ise**) v. (chiefly N. Amer.). **slenderly** adv. **slenderness** n.
– ORIGIN ME: of unknown origin.

**slept** past and past participle of SLEEP.

**sleuth** /sluːθ/ informal • n. a detective. • v. [often as noun **sleuthing**] carry out a search or investigation in the manner of a detective.
– ORIGIN ME (orig. in the sense 'track', in SLEUTH-HOUND): from ON *slóth*; cf. SLOT².

**sleuth-hound** • n. **1** dated a bloodhound. **2** informal an investigator or detective.

**S level** • n. (in the UK except Scotland) an examination taken together with an A level in the same subject but having a more advanced syllabus.
– ORIGIN abbrev. of *Special level* or (formerly) *Scholarship level.*

**slew¹** (also **slue**) • v. **1** turn or slide violently or uncontrollably. **2** [usu. as noun **slewing**] (of an electronic device) give a maximum response to a sudden large increase in input. • n. a slewing movement.
– ORIGIN C18 (orig. in naut. use): of unknown origin.

**slew²** past of SLAY¹.

**slew³** • n. informal, chiefly N. Amer. a large number or quantity.
– ORIGIN C19: from Ir. *sluagh.*

**sley** /sleɪ/ (also **slay**) • n. a tool used in weaving to force the weft into place.
– ORIGIN OE *slege*; rel. to SLAY¹.

**slice** • n. **1** a thin, broad piece of food cut from a larger portion. ➤a portion or share. **2** a utensil with a broad, flat blade for lifting foods such as cake and fish. **3** (in sports) a sliced stroke or shot. • v. **1** cut into slices. ➤(often **slice something off/from**) cut with or as if with a sharp implement. **2** move easily and quickly. **3** Golf strike (the ball) so that it curves away to the right (for a left-handed player, the left). ➤(in other sports) propel (the ball) with a glancing contact so that it travels forward spinning.
– DERIVATIVES **sliceable** adj. **slicer** n.
– ORIGIN ME (in the sense 'fragment, splinter'): shortening of OFr. *esclice* 'splinter', from the verb *esclicier*, of Gmc origin; rel. to SLIT.

**slick** • adj. **1** done or operating in an impressively smooth and efficient way. ➤glibly assured. **2** (of skin or hair) smooth and glossy. ➤(of a surface) smooth, wet, and slippery. • n. **1** an oil slick. **2** a racing-car or bicycle tyre without a tread, for use in dry weather conditions. **3** N. Amer. informal a glossy magazine. **4** N. Amer. informal a glibly assured person. • v. **1** make (hair) flat and slick with water, oil, or cream. ➤cover with a film of liquid. **2** (**slick someone/thing up**) N. Amer. make someone or something smart, tidy, or stylish.
– DERIVATIVES **slickly** adv. **slickness** n.
– ORIGIN ME: prob. from OE and rel. to ON *slíkr* 'smooth'; cf. SLEEK.

**slickenside** • n. Geology a polished and striated rock surface that results from friction along a fault or bedding plane.
– ORIGIN C18: from a dial. var. of SLICK + SIDE.

**slicker** • n. chiefly N. Amer. **1** informal a convincing rogue. **2** short for CITY SLICKER. **3** a raincoat made of smooth material.

**slide** • v. (past and past part. **slid**) **1** move along a smooth surface, especially downwards, while maintaining continuous contact with it. **2** change gradually to a worse condition or lower level. • n. **1** a structure with a smooth sloping surface for children to slide down. ➤a smooth stretch of ice or packed snow for sliding or tobogganing on. **2** an act of sliding. ➤a part of a machine or instrument that slides. **3** a rectangular piece of glass on which an object is mounted or placed for examination under a microscope. **4** a mounted transparency, especially one placed in a projector for viewing on a screen. **5** Brit. a hairslide.
– DERIVATIVES **slidable** adj. **slidably** adv.
– ORIGIN OE *slīdan* (v.); rel. to SLED and SLEDGE¹.

**slide fastener** • n. N. Amer. a zip fastener or similar fastening device.

**slide guitar** • n. a style of guitar playing in which a glissando effect is produced by moving a bottleneck or similar device over the strings.

**slider** • n. **1** a North American freshwater turtle with a red or yellow patch on the side of the head. [*Trachemys scripta* (**pond slider**) and related species.] **2** a knob or lever which is moved horizontally or vertically to control a variable. **3** Baseball a pitch that moves laterally as it nears home plate.

**slide rule** • n. a ruler with a sliding central strip, marked with logarithmic scales and used for making rapid calculations.

**slide valve** • n. a piece that opens and closes an aperture by sliding across it.

**sliding scale** • n. a scale of fees, wages, etc., that varies in accordance with variation of some standard.

**slight** • adj. **1** small in degree; inconsiderable. ➤not profound or substantial. **2** not sturdy and strongly built. • v. **1** insult (someone) by treating them without proper respect or attention. **2** archaic raze or destroy (a fortification). • n. an insult caused by a failure to show someone proper respect or attention.
– DERIVATIVES **slighting** adj. **slightingly** adv. **slightish** adj. **slightly** adv. **slightness** n.
– ORIGIN ME: from ON *sléttr* (adj.) 'smooth' (an early sense in Engl.), *slétta* (v.), of Gmc origin.

**slily** • adv. variant spelling of ***slyly*** (see SLY).

**slim** • adj. (**-er, -est**) **1** gracefully thin; slenderly built. ➤small in width and long and narrow in shape. **2** very small: *a slim chance.* **3** S. African crafty or unscrupulous. • v. (**slimmed, slimming**) make or become thinner, especially by dieting and sometimes exercising. ➤reduce (an organization) to a smaller size to make it more efficient. • n. **1** a course or period of slimming. **2** (also **slim disease**) African term for AIDS.
– DERIVATIVES **slimly** adv. **slimmer** n. **slimness** n.
– ORIGIN C17: from Low Ger. or Du. (from a base meaning 'slanting, cross, bad'), of Gmc origin.

**slime** • n. an unpleasantly moist, soft, and slippery substance. • v. cover with slime.
– ORIGIN OE *slīm*, of Gmc origin.

**slimeball** • n. informal a repulsive or despicable person.

**slime mould** • n. a simple organism that consists of creeping jelly-like protoplasm containing nuclei, or a mass of amoeboid cells. [Division Myxomycota or (regarded as a protist) phylum Gymnomyxa.]

**slimline** • adj. **1** slender in design or build. **2** (of food or drink) low in calories.

**slimy** • adj. (**-ier, -iest**) **1** covered by or having the feel or consistency of slime. **2** informal repulsively obsequious.
– DERIVATIVES **slimily** adv. **sliminess** n.

**sling¹** • n. **1** a flexible strap or belt used in the form of a loop to support or raise a hanging weight. ➤a bandage or soft strap looped round the neck to support an injured arm. ➤a pouch or frame for carrying a baby, supported by a strap round the neck or shoulders. **2** a simple weapon in the form of a strap or loop, used to hurl stones or other small missiles. **3** Austral./NZ informal a bribe or gratuity. • v. (past and past part. **slung**) **1** suspend or carry loosely with or as with a sling or strap. **2** informal throw; fling. **3** hurl from a sling or similar weapon. **4** Austral./NZ informal pay a bribe or gratuity. **5** (**sling off**) Austral./NZ informal mock; make fun.
– PHRASES **put someone's** (or **have one's**) **ass in a sling** N. Amer. vulgar slang cause someone to be (or be) in trouble.
– DERIVATIVES **slinger** n.
– ORIGIN ME: prob. from Low Ger., of symbolic origin.

**sling²** • n. a sweetened drink of spirits, especially gin, and water.
– ORIGIN C18: of unknown origin.

**slingback** • n. a shoe held in place by a strap around the ankle above the heel.

**slingshot** • n. **1** a hand-held catapult. ➤a shot from a slingshot. **2** the effect of the gravitational pull of a celestial body in accelerating and changing the course of another body or a spacecraft. • v. (**-shotting**; past and past part. **-shot** or **-shotted**) forcefully accelerate through use of gravity.

**slink** ● v. (past and past part. **slunk**) move quietly with gliding steps, in a stealthy or sensuous manner. ➤ come or go unobtrusively or furtively. ● n. an act of slinking.
– ORIGIN OE *slincan* 'crawl, creep'.

**slinky** ● adj. (**-ier**, **-iest**) informal graceful and sinuous in movement or form: *a slinky black evening dress.*
– DERIVATIVES **slinkily** adv. **slinkiness** n.

**slip**[1] ● v. (**slipped**, **slipping**) **1** lose one's balance or footing and slide unintentionally for a short distance. ➤ accidentally slide or move out of position or from someone's grasp. ➤ fail to grip or make proper contact with a surface. **2** pass gradually to a worse condition. ➤ (usu. **slip up**) make a careless error. **3** move or place quietly, quickly, or stealthily. **4** escape or get loose from (a means of restraint). ➤ fail to be remembered by (one's mind or memory). ➤ release (a hunting dog) from restraint. ➤ release (the clutch of a motor vehicle) slightly or for a moment. **5** Knitting move (a stitch) to the other needle without knitting it. **6** (of an animal) produce (dead young) prematurely; abort. ● n. **1** an act of slipping. ➤ a sideways movement of an aircraft in flight. ➤ Geology the relative horizontal displacement of corresponding points on either side of a fault plane. **2** a minor or careless mistake. **3** a loose-fitting garment, especially a short petticoat. **4** Cricket a fielding position close behind the batsman on the off side. **5** short for SLIPWAY. **6** a leash which enables a dog to be released quickly.
– PHRASES **give someone the slip** informal evade or escape from someone. **let something slip 1** reveal something inadvertently in conversation. **2** archaic release a hound from the leash to begin the chase. **slip of the pen** (or **the tongue**) a minor mistake in writing (or speech).
– DERIVATIVES **slippage** n.
– ORIGIN ME: prob. from Mid. Low Ger. *slippen* (v.); cf. SLIPPERY.

**slip**[2] ● n. **1** a small piece of paper for writing on or that gives printed information. **2** a long, thin, narrow strip of wood or other material. **3** (**a slip of a** ——) a small, slim young person: *a slip of a girl.* **4** Printing a printer's proof on a long piece of paper; a galley proof. **5** a cutting taken from a plant for grafting or planting; a scion.
– ORIGIN ME: prob. from MDu., Mid. Low Ger. *slippe* 'cut, strip'.

**slip**[3] ● n. a creamy mixture of clay, water, and typically a pigment of some kind, used for decorating earthenware.
– ORIGIN C17: of obscure origin; cf. Norw. *slip(a)* 'slime'.

**slip carriage** (also **slip coach**) ● n. Brit. historical a railway carriage on an express which could be detached so as to come to rest at a station where the main part of the train did not stop.

**slip case** ● n. a close-fitting case open at one side or end for an object such as a book.

**slip casting** ● n. the manufacture of ceramic ware by allowing slip to solidify in a mould.
– DERIVATIVES **slip-cast** adj.

**slip cover** ● n. **1** a detachable cover for a chair or sofa. **2** a jacket or slip case for a book.

**slip form** ● n. a mould in which a concrete structure is cast by filling the mould with liquid concrete and then continuously moving and refilling it at a sufficiently slow rate for the emerging part to have partially set.

**slip knot** ● n. **1** a knot that can be undone by a pull. **2** a running knot.

**slip-on** ● adj. (of shoes or clothes) having no fastenings and therefore able to be put on and taken off quickly. ● n. a slip-on shoe or garment.

**slipover** ● n. a pullover, typically one without sleeves.

**slipped** ● adj. Heraldry (of a flower or leaf) depicted with a stalk.

**slipped disc** ● n. a cartilaginous disc between vertebrae in the spine that is displaced or partly protruding, pressing on nearby nerves and causing back pain or sciatica.

**slipper** ● n. a comfortable slip-on shoe that is worn indoors. ➤ a light slip-on shoe, especially one used for dancing. ● v. beat with a slipper.
– DERIVATIVES **slippered** adj.

**slipper bath** ● n. Brit., chiefly historical a bath with one high end to lean against and the other end covered in.

**slipper flower** ● n. another term for CALCEOLARIA.

**slipper orchid** ● n. another term for LADY'S SLIPPER.

**slippery** ● adj. **1** difficult to hold firmly or stand on through being smooth, wet, or slimy. **2** (of a person) evasive and unpredictable. ➤ (of a word or concept) changing in meaning according to context or point of view.
– PHRASES **slippery slope** a course of action likely to lead to something bad.
– DERIVATIVES **slipperily** adv. **slipperiness** n.
– ORIGIN C15: from dial. *slipper* 'slippery', prob. suggested by Luther's *schlipfferig*.

**slippery elm** ● n. a North American elm with slimy inner bark, used medicinally. [*Ulmus fulva*.]

**slippy** ● adj. (**-ier**, **-iest**) informal slippery.
– PHRASES **look** (or **be**) **slippy** Brit. dated be quick.
– DERIVATIVES **slippiness** n.

**slip ring** ● n. a ring for sliding electrical contact in a dynamo or electric motor.

**slip road** ● n. Brit. a road entering or leaving a motorway or dual carriageway.

**slip rope** ● n. a mooring rope with both ends on board ship, enabling the crew to cast off without disembarking.

**slip sheet** ● n. Printing a sheet of paper placed between newly printed sheets to prevent set-off or smudging.

**slipshod** ● adj. **1** lacking in care, thought, or organization. **2** archaic (of shoes) worn down at the heel.
– ORIGIN C16 (orig. in the sense 'wearing slippers or loose shoes'): from SLIP[1] + SHOD.

**slip stitch** ● n. **1** (in sewing) a loose stitch joining layers of fabric and not visible externally. **2** Knitting a type of stitch in which the stitches are moved from one needle to the other without being knitted. ● v. (**slip-stitch**) sew or knit with slip stitches.

**slipstone** ● n. a shaped oilstone used to sharpen gouges.

**slipstream** ● n. **1** a current of air or water driven back by a revolving propeller or jet engine. ➤ the partial vacuum created in the wake of a moving vehicle. **2** an assisting force regarded as drawing something along in its wake. ● v. follow in the slipstream of a vehicle, especially when awaiting an opportunity to overtake in motor racing.

**slip-up** ● n. informal a mistake or blunder.

**slipware** ● n. pottery decorated with slip (see SLIP[3]).

**slipway** ● n. a slope leading into water, used for launching and landing boats and ships or for building and repairing them.

**slit** ● n. a long, narrow cut or opening. ● v. (**slitting**; past and past part. **slit**) **1** make a slit in. ➤ cut into strips. **2** (past and past part. **slitted**) form (one's eyes) into slits.
– DERIVATIVES **slitter** n.
– ORIGIN OE *slite* (n.); rel. to OE *slītan* 'split, rend' (of Gmc origin).

**slither** ● v. move smoothly over a surface with a twisting or oscillating motion. ➤ slide or slip unsteadily on a loose or slippery surface. ● n. **1** a slithering movement. **2** a sliver.
– DERIVATIVES **slithery** adj.
– ORIGIN ME: alt. of the dial. verb *slidder*, frequentative from the base of SLIDE.

**slit trench** ● n. a narrow trench for a soldier or a small group of soldiers and their equipment.

**slitty** ● adj. (**-ier**, **-iest**) chiefly derogatory (of the eyes) long and narrow.

**sliver** /ˈslɪvə, ˈslʌɪ-/ ● n. **1** a small, narrow, sharp piece cut or split off a larger piece. **2** a strip of loose untwisted textile fibres produced by carding. ● v. **1** cut or break into slivers. **2** convert (textile fibres) into slivers.
– ORIGIN ME: from dial. *slive* 'cleave'.

**slivovitz** /ˈslɪvəvɪts/ ● n. a type of plum brandy made chiefly in the former Yugoslavia and in Romania.
– ORIGIN from Serbo-Croat *šljivovica*, from *šljiva* 'plum'.

**Sloane** (also **Sloane Ranger**) ● n. Brit. informal a fashionable upper-class young woman.

– DERIVATIVES **Sloaney** adj.
– ORIGIN 1970s: from *Sloane* Square, London + Lone *Ranger*, the name of a fictitious cowboy hero.

**slob** • **n. 1** informal a lazy and slovenly person. **2** Irish muddy land. • **v.** informal behave in a lazy and slovenly manner.
– DERIVATIVES **slobbish** adj. **slobbishness** n. **slobby** adj.
– ORIGIN C18: from Ir. *slab* 'mud', from Anglo-Ir. *slab* 'ooze, sludge', prob. of Scand. origin.

**slobber** • **v. 1** have saliva dripping copiously from the mouth. **2** (**slobber over**) show excessive enthusiasm for. • **n.** saliva dripping copiously from the mouth.
– DERIVATIVES **slobbery** adj.
– ORIGIN ME: prob. from MDu. *slobberen* 'walk through mud', also 'feed noisily', of imitative origin.

**sloe** • **n.** another term for **BLACKTHORN**. ➤ the small bluish-black fruit of the blackthorn, with a sharp sour taste.
– ORIGIN OE *slā(h)*, of Gmc origin.

**sloe-eyed** • **adj.** having attractive dark almond-shaped eyes.

**sloe gin** • **n.** a liqueur made by steeping sloes in gin.

**slog** • **v.** (**slogged**, **slogging**) **1** work hard over a period of time. ➤ walk or move with difficulty or effort. **2** hit or strike forcefully. ➤ (**slog it out**) fight or compete fiercely. • **n. 1** a spell of difficult, tiring work or travelling. **2** a forceful hit or strike.
– DERIVATIVES **slogger** n.
– ORIGIN C19: of unknown origin; cf. **SLUG**[2].

**slogan** • **n. 1** a short, memorable phrase used in advertising or associated with a political party or group. **2** historical a Scottish Highland war cry.
– ORIGIN C16: from Sc. Gaelic *sluagh-ghairm*, from *sluagh* 'army' + *gairm* 'shout'.

**sloganeer** chiefly N. Amer. • **v.** [usu. as noun **sloganeering**] employ or invent slogans, especially in a political context. • **n.** a person who does this.

**sloka** /ˈʃləʊkə/ • **n.** a couplet of Sanskrit verse, especially one in which each line contains sixteen syllables.
– ORIGIN from Sanskrit *śloka* 'noise, praise'.

**slo-mo** • **n.** short for **SLOW MOTION**.

**sloop** • **n. 1** a one-masted sailing boat with a mainsail and jib rigged fore and aft. **2** (also **sloop of war**) historical a small square-rigged sailing warship with two or three masts. **3** a small anti-submarine warship used for convoy escort in the Second World War.
– ORIGIN C17: from Du. *sloep(e)*, of unknown origin.

**sloosh** Brit. informal • **n.** a rushing of water or energetic rinsing. • **v.** flow, pour, or rinse with a rush.
– ORIGIN C20: imitative.

**sloot** /sluːt/ (also **sluit**) • **n.** S. African a deep gully eroded by rainfall. ➤ historical a narrow water channel constructed for irrigation.
– ORIGIN Afrik., from Du. *sloot* 'ditch'.

**slop**[1] • **v.** (**slopped**, **slopping**) **1** (of a liquid) spill or flow over the edge of a container. ➤ apply casually or carelessly. ➤ (**slop out**) (especially in prison) empty the contents of a chamber pot. **2** (**slop through**) wade through (a wet or muddy area). **3** (**slop about/around**) chiefly Brit. dress in an untidy or casual manner. **4** feed slops to (an animal). **5** chiefly N. Amer. speak or write in a sentimentally effusive manner; gush. • **n. 1** (**slops**) waste water or liquid that has to be emptied by hand. ➤ semi-liquid kitchen refuse. ➤ unappetizing weak, semi-liquid food. **2** chiefly N. Amer. sentimental language or material. **3** Nautical a choppy sea.
– ORIGIN C16: prob. rel. to **SLIP**[3].

**slop**[2] • **n.** archaic **1** a workman's loose outer garment. **2** (**slops**) wide, baggy trousers, especially as worn by sailors. ➤ clothes and bedding supplied to sailors by the navy. ➤ ready-made or cheap clothing.
– ORIGIN ME: from the second element of OE *oferslop* 'surplice', of Gmc origin.

**slope** • **n. 1** a surface of which one end or side is at a higher level than another. ➤ a difference in level or sideways position between two ends or sides. ➤ a part of the side of a hill or mountain, especially as a place for skiing. **2** US informal, offensive an oriental person, especially a Vietnamese. • **v. 1** be inclined from a horizontal or vertical line; slant up or down. **2** informal move in an idle or aimless manner. ➤ (**slope off**) leave unobtrusively, typically in order to evade work or duty.
– PHRASES **at the slope** Military (of a rifle) held with the barrel on the left shoulder and the butt in the left hand. **slope arms** Military hold a rifle at the slope.
– ORIGIN C16: from the obs. adverb *slope*, a shortening of **ASLOPE**.

**sloppy** • **adj.** (**-ier**, **-iest**) **1** (of semi-fluid matter) containing too much liquid; watery. **2** careless and unsystematic; excessively casual. **3** (of a garment) casual and loose-fitting. **4** weakly or foolishly sentimental.
– DERIVATIVES **sloppily** adv. **sloppiness** n.

**sloppy joe** • **n.** informal **1** a long, loose-fitting sweater. **2** N. Amer. a hamburger in which the minced-beef filling is made into a kind of meat sauce.

**slosh** • **v. 1** (of liquid in a container) move irregularly with a splashing sound. ➤ move through liquid with a splashing sound. ➤ pour (liquid) clumsily. **2** Brit. informal hit hard. • **n. 1** an act or sound of splashing. ➤ a quantity of liquid that is poured out. **2** Brit. informal a heavy blow.
– ORIGIN C19: var. of **SLUSH**.

**sloshed** • **adj.** informal drunk.

**sloshy** • **adj.** (**-ier**, **-iest**) **1** wet and sticky; slushy. **2** excessively sentimental; sloppy.

**slot**[1] • **n. 1** a long, narrow aperture or slit into which something may be fitted or inserted. **2** an allotted place in an arrangement or scheme such as a broadcasting schedule. • **v.** (**slotted**, **slotting**) place or be placed into a slot. ➤ Brit. informal (in soccer) score (a goal) with a precise shot. ➤ (**slot in/into**) fit easily into (a new role or situation).
– DERIVATIVES **slotted** adj.
– ORIGIN ME (in the sense 'slight depression running down the middle of the chest'): from OFr. *esclot*, of obscure origin.

**slot**[2] • **n.** the track of a deer, visible as slotted footprints in soft ground.
– ORIGIN C16: from OFr. *esclot* 'hoofprint of a horse', prob. from ON *slóth* 'trail'; cf. **SLEUTH**.

**slotback** • **n.** American Football a back between the tackle and the split end.

**sloth** /sləʊθ/ • **n. 1** reluctance to work or make an effort; laziness. **2** a slow-moving tropical American mammal that hangs upside down from branches using its long limbs and hooked claws. [Genus *Bradypus* (**three-toed sloths**) and *Choloepus* (**two-toed sloths**).]
– DERIVATIVES **slothful** adj. **slothfully** adv. **slothfulness** n.
– ORIGIN OE: from **SLOW** + **-TH**[2].

**sloth bear** • **n.** a shaggy-coated Indian bear with long curved claws, noted for hanging upside down like a sloth. [*Melursus ursinus*.]

**slot machine** • **n.** a fruit machine or (Brit.) vending machine.

**slouch** • **v. 1** stand, move, or sit in a lazy, drooping way. **2** dated bend one side of the brim of (a hat) downwards. • **n. 1** a lazy, drooping posture or movement. **2** [usu. with neg.] informal an incompetent person: *he was no slouch at making a buck*. **3** a downward bend of a hat brim.
– DERIVATIVES **slouchy** adj.
– ORIGIN C16 (in the sense 'lazy, slovenly person'): of unknown origin.

**slouch hat** • **n.** a hat with a wide flexible brim.

**slough**[1] /slaʊ/ • **n. 1** a swamp. ➤ N. Amer. a muddy side channel or inlet. **2** a situation characterized by lack of progress or activity.
– DERIVATIVES **sloughy** adj.
– ORIGIN OE *slōh*, *slō(g)*, of unknown origin.

**slough**[2] /slʌf/ • **v. 1** (of an animal, especially a snake) cast off or shed (an old skin). **2** (**slough away/down**) (of soil or rock) collapse or slide into a hole or depression. • **n.** the dropping off of dead tissue from living flesh.
– DERIVATIVES **sloughy** adj.
– ORIGIN ME (as n. denoting a skin, especially the outer skin shed by a snake): perh. rel. to Low Ger. *slu(we)* 'husk, peel'.

**Slovak** /ˈsləʊvak/ • **n. 1** a native or national of Slovakia, or a person of Slovak descent. **2** the Western Slavic lan-

guage of Slovakia.
– ORIGIN the name in Slovak, from a Slavic root shared with **SLOVENE** and perh. rel. to *slovo* 'word'.

**Slovakian** /slə'vakɪən, -'vɑːkɪən/ • **n.** a native or inhabitant of Slovakia. • **adj.** of or relating to Slovakia.

**sloven** /'slʌv(ə)n/ • **n.** dated a person who is habitually untidy or careless.
– ORIGIN C15: perh. from Flemish *sloef* 'dirty' or Du. *slof* 'careless, negligent'.

**Slovene** /'sləʊviːn, sləʊ'viːn/ • **n. 1** a native or national of Slovenia, or a person of Slovene descent. **2** the Southern Slavic language of this people.
– DERIVATIVES **Slovenian** n. & adj.

**slovenly** • **adj. 1** untidy and dirty. **2** careless; excessively casual.
– DERIVATIVES **slovenliness** n.

**slow** • **adj. 1** moving or capable of moving only at a low speed. ➤lasting or taking a long time. **2** (of a clock or watch) showing a time earlier than the correct time. **3** not prompt to understand, think, or learn. **4** uneventful and rather dull. ➤(of business) with little activity; slack. **5** Photography (of a film) needing long exposure. **6** (of a fire or oven) burning or giving off heat gently. • **v.** (often **slow down/up**) reduce one's speed or the speed of a vehicle or process. ➤live or work less actively or intensely.
– PHRASES **slow but** (or **and**) **sure** not quick but achieving the required result eventually.
– DERIVATIVES **slowish** adj. **slowly** n. **slowness** n.
– ORIGIN OE *slāw* 'slow-witted, sluggish', of Gmc origin.

**slowcoach** • **n.** Brit. informal a person who acts or moves slowly.

**slow cooker** • **n.** a large electric pot used for cooking food very slowly.

**slow drag** • **n.** a slow blues rhythm or piece of music.

**slow handclap** • **n.** a slow, rhythmic clapping by an audience as a sign of displeasure or impatience.

**slow march** • **n.** a military marching pace approximately half the speed of the quick march.

**slow match** • **n.** historical a slow-burning wick or cord for lighting explosives.

**slow motion** • **n.** the action of showing film or video more slowly than it was made or recorded, so that the action appears much slower than in real life.

**slowpoke** • **n.** informal North American term for **SLOWCOACH**.

**slow puncture** • **n.** chiefly Brit. a puncture causing only gradual deflation of a tyre.

**slow virus** • **n.** a virus or virus-like organism that multiplies slowly in the host organism and has a long incubation period.

**slow-worm** • **n.** a small snake-like legless lizard that gives birth to live young. [*Anguis fragilis*]
– ORIGIN OE *slāwyrm*, from *slā-* (of uncertain origin) + *wyrm* 'snake'.

**SLR** • **abbrev. 1** self-loading rifle. **2** single-lens reflex.

**slub** • **n. 1** a lump or thick place in yarn or thread. ➤fabric woven from yarn with such a texture. **2** wool that has been slightly twisted in preparation for spinning. • **adj.** (of fabric) having an irregular appearance caused by uneven thickness of the warp. • **v.** (**slubbed**, **slubbing**) twist (wool) in preparation for spinning.
– DERIVATIVES **slubbed** adj.
– ORIGIN C18: of unknown origin.

**sludge** • **n. 1** thick, soft, wet mud or a similar viscous mixture. ➤dirty oil or industrial waste. **2** sea ice newly formed in small pieces. **3** an unattractive muddy shade of brown or green.
– DERIVATIVES **sludgy** adj.
– ORIGIN C17: of uncertain origin; cf. **SLUSH**.

**slue** • **v. & n.** variant spelling of **SLEW**[1].

**slug**[1] • **n. 1** a tough-skinned terrestrial mollusc which lacks a shell and secretes a film of mucus for protection. [Order Stylommatophora.] **2** an amount of an alcoholic drink that is gulped or poured. **3** an elongated, typically rounded piece of metal. ➤a bullet. **4** a line of type in Linotype printing. • **v.** (**slugged**, **slugging**) gulp (something, typically alcohol).
– ORIGIN ME (in the sense 'sluggard'): prob. of Scand. origin.

**slug**[2] informal, chiefly N. Amer. • **v.** (**slugged**, **slugging**) strike with a hard blow. ➤(**slug it out**) settle a dispute or contest by fighting or competing fiercely. • **n.** a hard blow.
– DERIVATIVES **slugger** n.
– ORIGIN C19: of unknown origin; cf. **SLOG**.

**slugabed** • **n.** chiefly US or archaic a lazy person who stays in bed late.
– ORIGIN C16: from the rare verb *slug* 'be lazy or slow' + **ABED**.

**sluggard** • **n.** a lazy, sluggish person.
– DERIVATIVES **sluggardliness** n. **sluggardly** adj.
– ORIGIN ME: from the rare verb *slug* 'be lazy or slow' + **-ARD**.

**sluggish** • **adj.** slow-moving or inactive. ➤lacking energy or alertness.
– DERIVATIVES **sluggishly** adv. **sluggishness** n.
– ORIGIN ME: from the noun **SLUG**[1] or the verb *slug* (see **SLUGGARD**) + **-ISH**[1].

**slug pellet** • **n.** a pellet containing a substance poisonous to slugs, placed among growing plants to prevent them being damaged.

**sluice** /sluːs/ • **n. 1** (also **sluice gate**) a sliding gate or other device for controlling the flow of water, especially in a lock gate. **2** (also **sluiceway**) an artificial water channel for carrying off overflow or surplus water. **3** an act of rinsing or showering with water. • **v.** wash or rinse freely with a stream or shower of water.
– ORIGIN ME: from OFr. *escluse* 'sluice gate', based on L. *excludere* 'exclude'.

**sluit** /sluːt, 'sluːɪt/ • **n.** variant spelling of **SLOOT**.

**slum** • **n.** a squalid and overcrowded urban area inhabited by very poor people. ➤a house in such a place. • **v.** (**slummed**, **slumming**) (often **slum it**) informal voluntarily spend time in uncomfortable conditions or at a lower social level than one's own.
– DERIVATIVES **slummer** n. **slumminess** n. **slummy** adj.
– ORIGIN C19 (orig. sl., in the sense 'room'): of unknown origin.

**slumber** poetic/literary • **v.** sleep. • **n.** a sleep.
– DERIVATIVES **slumberer** n. **slumberous** (also **slumbrous**) adj.
– ORIGIN ME: alt. of Scots and north. Engl. *sloom*, in the same sense. The *-b-* was added for ease of pronunc.

**slumgullion** /slʌm'gʌljən/ • **n.** N. Amer. informal cheap or insubstantial stew.

**slumlord** • **n.** N. Amer. informal a landlord of slum property, especially one who profiteers.

**slummock** Brit. informal • **n.** a slovenly person. • **v.** behave in an indolent or careless way.
– ORIGIN C19: of unknown origin.

**slump** • **v. 1** sit, lean, or fall heavily and limply. **2** fail or decline substantially or over a prolonged period. • **n. 1** an instance of slumping. **2** a prolonged period of abnormally low economic activity.
– DERIVATIVES **slumped** adj. **slumpy** adj.
– ORIGIN C17 (in the sense 'fall into a bog'): prob. imitative and rel. to Norw. *slumpe* 'to fall'.

**slung** past and past participle of **SLING**[1].

**slung shot** • **n.** a hard object, such as a metal ball, attached by a strap or thong to the wrist and used as a weapon.

**slunk** past and past participle of **SLINK**.

**slur** • **v.** (**slurred**, **slurring**) **1** (with reference to speech) articulate or be articulated indistinctly. **2** pass over (a fact or aspect) so as to conceal or minimize it. **3** Music perform (a group of two or more notes) legato. ➤mark (notes) with a slur. **4** chiefly US make insinuations or allegations about. • **n. 1** an insinuation or allegation. **2** an indistinct utterance. **3** Music a curved line indicating that notes are to be slurred.
– DERIVATIVES **slurred** adj.
– ORIGIN ME (as n. in sense 'thin mud', later as v. meaning 'smear' and 'disparage'); of unknown origin.

**slurp** • **v.** eat or drink with a loud sucking sound. • **n.** an act or sound of slurping.

– DERIVATIVES **slurpy** adj.
– ORIGIN C17: from Du. *slurpen*.

**slurry** • n. (pl. **-ies**) a semi-liquid mixture, especially of fine particles of manure, cement, or coal and water.
– ORIGIN ME: rel. to dial. *slur* 'thin mud', of unknown origin.

**slush** • n. **1** partially melted snow or ice. **2** watery mud. **3** informal excessive sentiment. • v. make a soft splashing sound.
– DERIVATIVES **slushiness** n. **slushy** adj.
– ORIGIN C17: prob. imitative; cf. SLOSH.

**slush fund** • n. a reserve of money used for illicit purposes, especially political bribery.
– ORIGIN C19: orig. naut. sl. denoting money collected to buy luxuries, from the sale of watery food known as *slush*.

**slut** • n. a slovenly or promiscuous woman.
– DERIVATIVES **sluttish** adj. **sluttishness** n.
– ORIGIN ME: of unknown origin.

**sly** • adj. (**slyer**, **slyest**) **1** having a cunning and deceitful nature. **2** (of a remark, glance, or expression) insinuating. **3** (of an action) surreptitious.
– PHRASES **on the sly** in a surreptitious fashion.
– DERIVATIVES **slyly** (also **slily**) adv. **slyness** n.
– ORIGIN ME (also in the sense 'dexterous'): from ON *slœgr* 'cunning'.

**slyboots** • n. informal a sly person.

**slype** /slʌɪp/ • n. a covered way or passage between a cathedral transept and the chapter house or deanery.
– ORIGIN C19: perh. a var. of dial. *slipe* 'long narrow piece of ground'.

**SM** • abbrev. **1** sadomasochism. **2** Sergeant Major. **3** short metre.

**Sm** • symb. the chemical element samarium.

**smack**[1] • n. **1** a sharp blow or slap, typically one given with the palm of the hand. **2** a loud, sharp sound made by or as by such a blow. **3** a loud kiss. • v. **1** hit with a smack. **2** smash, drive, or put forcefully into or on to something. **3** part (one's lips) noisily. **4** archaic crack (a whip). • adv. (Brit. also **smack bang**) informal **1** in a sudden and violent way. **2** (N. Amer. also **smack dab**) exactly; precisely.
– PHRASES **a smack in the face** (or **eye**) informal a strong rebuff.
– ORIGIN C16: from MDu. *smacken*, of imitative origin.

**smack**[2] • v. (**smack of**) **1** have a flavour or smell of. **2** suggest the presence or effects of. • n. (**a smack of**) a flavour, smell, or suggestion of.
– ORIGIN OE *smæc* 'flavour, smell', of Gmc origin.

**smack**[3] • n. a single-masted sailing boat used for coasting or fishing.
– ORIGIN C17: from Du. *smak*, of unknown ultimate origin.

**smack**[4] • n. informal heroin.
– ORIGIN 1940s: prob. an alt. of Yiddish *shmek* 'a sniff'.

**smacker** (also **smackeroo**) • n. informal **1** a loud kiss. **2** Brit. one pound sterling. **3** N. Amer. one dollar.

**small** • adj. **1** of a size that is less than normal or usual. **2** not great in amount, number, strength, or power. **3** not fully grown or developed; young. **4** insignificant; unimportant. **5** archaic (of a person) low or inferior in rank or position. **6** (of a business or its owner) operating on a modest scale. • n. (**smalls**) Brit. informal underwear. • adv. **1** into small pieces. **2** in a small manner or size.
– PHRASES **feel** (or **look**) **small** feel (or look) contemptibly weak or insignificant. **the small of the back** the part of a person's back where the spine curves in at the level of the waist. **the small screen** television as a medium.
– DERIVATIVES **smallish** adj. **smallness** n.
– ORIGIN OE *smæl*, of Gmc origin.

**small arms** • pl. n. portable firearms.

**small beer** • n. **1** chiefly Brit. a thing that is considered unimportant. **2** archaic weak beer.

**small-bore** • adj. **1** denoting a firearm with a narrow bore, in international and Olympic shooting generally .22 inch calibre (5.6 millimetre bore). **2** N. Amer. informal trivial; unimportant.

**small-cap** • adj. Finance denoting or relating to the stock of a company with a small capitalization.

**small capital** • n. a capital letter which is of the same height as a lower-case x in the same typeface, as THIS.

**small change** • n. **1** money in the form of coins of low value. **2** a thing that is considered trivial.

**small circle** • n. a circle on the surface of a sphere whose plane does not pass through the sphere's centre.

**small claims court** • n. a local court in which claims for small sums of money can be heard and decided quickly and cheaply, without legal representation.

**small coal** • n. another term for SLACK[2].

**small end** • n. (in a piston engine) the end of the connecting rod connected to the piston.

**small forward** • n. Basketball a versatile forward who is effective outside the key as well as near the net.

**small fry** • pl. n. **1** young or small fish. **2** young or insignificant people or things.

**small heath** • n. a small light brown and orange butterfly inhabiting heathland. [*Coenonympha pamphilus*.]

**smallholding** • n. Brit. an agricultural holding that is smaller than a farm.
– DERIVATIVES **smallholder** n.

**small hours** • pl. n. (**the small hours**) the early hours of the morning after midnight.

**small intestine** • n. the part of the intestine that runs between the stomach and the large intestine, consisting of the duodenum, the jejunum, and the ileum.

**small letter** • n. a lower-case letter, as distinct from a capital letter.

**small-minded** • adj. having a narrow outlook; petty.
– DERIVATIVES **small-mindedly** adv. **small-mindedness** n.

**smallpox** • n. an acute contagious viral disease, with fever and pustules usually leaving permanent scars.

**small print** • n. **1** printed matter in small type. **2** inconspicuous but binding details or conditions printed in an agreement or contract.

**small-scale** • adj. of limited size or extent.

**small slam** • n. Bridge the bidding and winning of twelve of the thirteen tricks.

**small-sword** • n. chiefly historical a light tapering thrusting-sword used for duelling.

**small talk** • n. polite conversation about uncontroversial matters.

**small-time** • adj. informal unimportant; minor.
– DERIVATIVES **small-timer** n.

**small-town** • adj. relating to or characteristic of a small town, especially in being unsophisticated or petty.

**smalt** /smɔːlt, smɒlt/ • n. chiefly historical glass coloured blue with cobalt oxide. ➤ a pigment made by pulverizing such glass.
– ORIGIN C16: from Fr., from Ital. *smalto*, of Gmc origin; rel. to SMELT[1].

**smarm** informal • v. **1** chiefly Brit. behave in an ingratiating way. **2** smooth down (one's hair), especially with oil or gel. • n. ingratiating behaviour.
– DERIVATIVES **smarmily** adv. **smarminess** n. **smarmy** adj. (**-ier**, **-iest**).
– ORIGIN C19 (orig. dial. in the sense 'smear, bedaub'): of unknown origin.

**smart** • adj. **1** clean, tidy, and stylish. **2** bright and fresh in appearance. **3** (of a place) fashionable and upmarket. **4** informal having a quick intelligence. ➤ (of a device) capable of independent and seemingly intelligent action. ➤ chiefly N. Amer. impertinently clever or sarcastic. **5** quick; brisk. • v. **1** present a sharp, stinging pain. **2** feel upset and annoyed. • n. **1** (**smarts**) N. Amer. informal intelligence; acumen. **2** a smarting pain. • adv. archaic in a quick or brisk manner.
– PHRASES **look smart** chiefly Brit. be quick.
– DERIVATIVES **smarting** adj. **smartingly** adv. **smartly** adv. **smartness** n.
– ORIGIN OE *smeortan* (v.), of W. Gmc origin.

**smart alec** (also **smart aleck**) • n. informal a person considered irritating in always having a clever answer to a question.

– DERIVATIVES **smart-alecky** adj.
– ORIGIN C19: from **SMART** + *Alec*, dimin. of the given name *Alexander*.

**smart-arse** (US **smart-ass**) • **n.** informal another term for **SMART ALEC.**

**smart card** • **n.** a plastic card with a built-in microprocessor, used for electronic processes such as financial transactions and personal identification.

**smarten** • **v.** (often **smarten up**) make or become smarter.

**smartish** • **adv.** informal, chiefly Brit. quickly; briskly.

**smart-mouth** • **v.** N. Amer. informal make impudent remarks.
– DERIVATIVES **smart-mouthed** adj.

**smash** • **v. 1** break or cause to break violently into pieces. ➤(**smash down**) violently knock down. **2** crash and severely damage (a vehicle). ➤(**smash into**) hit or collide with forcefully. **3** (in sport) strike (the ball) or score (a goal, run, etc.) with great force. ➤(in tennis, badminton, and similar sports) strike (the ball or shuttlecock) downwards with a hard overarm stroke. **4** completely defeat, destroy, or foil. ➤informal, dated (of a business) fail financially. • **n. 1** an act, instance, or sound of smashing. **2** (also **smash hit**) informal a very successful song, film, or show. **3** a mixture of spirits (typically brandy) with flavoured water and ice. • **adv.** with a sudden smash.
– ORIGIN C18 (as n.): prob. imitative, representing a blend of words such as *smack*, *smite* with *bash*, *mash*, etc.

**smash-and-grab** • **adj.** denoting a robbery in which the thief smashes a shop window and seizes goods.

**smashed** • **adj.** informal very drunk.

**smasher** • **n. 1** a person or device that smashes something. **2** Brit. informal a very attractive or impressive person or thing.

**smashing** • **adj.** informal, chiefly Brit. excellent; wonderful.
– DERIVATIVES **smashingly** adv.

**smash-up** • **n.** informal a violent collision between vehicles.

**smattering** (also **smatter**) • **n. 1** a small amount. **2** a slight knowledge of a language or subject.
– ORIGIN C16: from *smatter* 'talk ignorantly, prate', of unknown origin.

**SME** • **abbrev. 1** small to medium-sized enterprise, a company with no more than 500 employees. **2** Suriname (international vehicle registration).

**smear** • **v. 1** coat or mark with a greasy or sticky substance. **2** spread (a greasy or sticky substance) over a surface. **3** blur or smudge. **4** damage the reputation of (someone) by false or unwarranted accusations. • **n. 1** a greasy or sticky mark. **2** a false or unwarranted accusation. **3** a sample thinly spread on a microscopic slide. ➤short for **SMEAR TEST. 4** Climbing an insecure foothold.
– DERIVATIVES **smearer** n. **smeary** adj.
– ORIGIN OE *smierwan* (v.), *smeoru* 'ointment, grease', of Gmc origin.

**smear test** • **n.** a test to detect signs of cervical cancer, conducted by taking a cervical smear.

**smectic** /ˈsmɛktɪk/ • **adj.** denoting or involving a state of a liquid crystal in which the molecules are oriented in parallel and arranged in well-defined planes. Compare with **NEMATIC.**
– ORIGIN C17: via L. from Gk *smēktikos* 'cleansing' (because of the soap-like consistency).

**smegma** /ˈsmɛgmə/ • **n.** a sebaceous secretion in the folds of the skin, especially under a man's foreskin.
– ORIGIN C19: via L. from Gk *smēgma* 'soap'.

**smell** • **n. 1** the faculty of perceiving odours by means of the organs in the nose. **2** a quality in something that is perceived by this faculty; an odour. ➤an unpleasant odour. **3** an act of inhaling in order to ascertain an odour. • **v.** (past and past part. **smelt** or **smelled**) **1** perceive or detect the odour of. ➤sniff at (something) in order to ascertain its odour. **2** (**smell something out**) detect or discover something by the faculty of smell. **3** detect or suspect by means of instinct or intuition. **4** emit an odour of a specified kind. ➤have a strong or unpleasant odour. **5** be suggestive of something.
– PHRASES **smell a rat** informal suspect trickery.
– DERIVATIVES **smellable** adj. **smeller** n. **smelliness** n. **-smelling** adj. **smelly** adj.
– ORIGIN ME: of unknown origin.

**smelling bottle** • **n.** chiefly historical a small bottle containing smelling salts or perfume.

**smelling salts** • **pl. n.** chiefly historical a pungent substance typically consisting of ammonium carbonate mixed with perfume, sniffed as a restorative.

**smelt**[1] • **v.** extract (metal) from its ore by a process involving heating and melting. ➤extract metal from (ore) by this process.
– DERIVATIVES **smelter** n. **smelting** n.
– ORIGIN C16: from MDu., Mid. Low Ger. *smelten*.

**smelt**[2] past and past participle of **SMELL.**

**smelt**[3] • **n.** (pl. same or **smelts**) a small silvery fish of both marine and fresh water. [*Osmerus* and other genera.]
– ORIGIN OE; obscurely rel. to various European names of fish; cf. **SMOLT.**

**smew** /smjuː/ • **n.** a small migratory merganser of northern Eurasia, the male of which has white plumage with a crest and fine black markings. [*Mergus albellus*.]
– ORIGIN C17: obscurely rel. to Du. *smient* 'wigeon' and Ger. *Schmeiente* 'small wild duck'.

**smidge** • **n.** informal another term for **SMIDGEN.**

**smidgen** (also **smidgeon** or **smidgin**) • **n.** informal a tiny amount.
– ORIGIN C19: perh. from Scots *smitch* in the same sense.

**smilax** /ˈsmʌɪlaks/ • **n. 1** a climbing shrub with hooks and tendrils, several South American species of which yield sarsaparilla from their roots. [Genus *Smilax*.] **2** a climbing asparagus with decorative foliage. [*Asparagus asparagoides*.]
– ORIGIN C16: via L. from Gk, lit. 'bindweed'.

**smile** • **v. 1** form one's features into a pleased, friendly, or amused expression, with the corners of the mouth turned up. **2** (**smile at/on/upon**) regard favourably or indulgently. • **n.** an act of smiling; a smiling expression.
– DERIVATIVES **smiler** n. **smiling** adj. **smilingly** adv.
– ORIGIN ME: perh. of Scand. origin; rel. to **SMIRK.**

**smiley** (also **smilie**) • **adj.** informal smiling; cheerful. • **n.** (pl. **-eys** or **-ies**) a symbol representing a smiling face, formed by the characters :-) and used in electronic communications.

**smirch** /sməːtʃ/ • **v. 1** make dirty. **2** discredit; taint. • **n. 1** a dirty mark or stain. **2** a flaw.
– ORIGIN C15: prob. symbolic.

**smirk** • **v.** smile in an irritatingly smug or silly way. • **n.** a smug or silly smile.
– DERIVATIVES **smirker** n. **smirkily** adv. **smirking** adj. **smirkingly** adv. **smirky** adj.
– ORIGIN OE *sme(a)rcian*, from a base shared by **SMILE.**

**smit** /smɪt/ archaic past participle of **SMITE.**

**smite** • **v.** (past **smote**; past part. **smitten**) **1** archaic or poetic/literary strike with a firm blow. **2** archaic or poetic/literary defeat or conquer. **3** (usu. **be smitten**) (especially of a disease) attack or affect severely. **4** (**be smitten**) be strongly attracted to someone or something. • **n.** archaic or poetic/literary a firm blow.
– DERIVATIVES **smiter** n.
– ORIGIN OE *smītan* 'to smear, blemish', of Gmc origin.

**smith** • **n.** a worker in metal. ➤short for **BLACKSMITH.** • **v.** treat (metal) by heating, hammering, and forging it.
– ORIGIN OE, of Gmc origin.

**-smith** • **comb. form** denoting a person skilled in creating something with a specified material: *goldsmith*.

**smithereens** /ˌsmɪðəˈriːnz/ (also **smithers** /ˈsmɪðəz/) • **pl. n.** informal small pieces.
– ORIGIN C19: prob. from Ir. *smidirín*.

**smithery** • **n.** the work of or goods made by a smith.

**smithy** /ˈsmɪði/ • **n.** (pl. **-ies**) a blacksmith's workshop; a forge.
– ORIGIN ME, from ON *smithja*.

**smitten** past participle of **SMITE.**

**smock** • **n. 1** a loose dress or blouse having the upper part closely gathered in smocking. **2** a loose overall worn

to protect one's clothes. ➤(also **smock-frock**) historical a smocked linen overgarment worn by an agricultural worker. ● v. decorate with smocking.
– DERIVATIVES **smocked** adj.
– ORIGIN OE *smoc* 'woman's loose-fitting undergarment'.

**smocking** ● n. decoration on a garment created by gathering a section of the material into tight pleats and holding them together with parallel stitches in an ornamental pattern.

**smog** ● n. fog or haze intensified by smoke or other atmospheric pollutants.
– DERIVATIVES **smoggy** adj.
– ORIGIN C20: blend of **SMOKE** and **FOG**[1].

**smoke** ● n. **1** a visible suspension of carbon or other particles in the air, typically one emitted from a burning substance. **2** an act of smoking tobacco. **3** informal a cigarette or cigar. **4** (**the Smoke** or **the Big Smoke**) Brit. a big city, especially London. ● v. **1** emit smoke. **2** inhale and exhale the smoke of tobacco or a drug. **3** cure or preserve (meat or fish) by exposure to smoke. **4** treat (glass) so as to darken it. **5** fumigate, cleanse, or purify by exposure to smoke. ➤subdue (bees in a hive) by exposing them to smoke. **6** (**smoke someone/thing out**) drive someone or something out of a place by using smoke. **7** N. Amer. informal kill by shooting. **8** archaic make fun of.
– PHRASES **go up in smoke** informal **1** be destroyed by fire. **2** (of a plan) come to nothing. **no smoke without fire** rumours usually have some basis in fact. **smoke and mirrors** N. Amer. the use of misleading or irrelevant information to obscure or embellish the truth. **smoke like a chimney** smoke tobacco incessantly.
– DERIVATIVES **smokable** (also **smokeable**) adj. **smoked** adj. **smokeless** adj. **smoking** adj. & n.
– ORIGIN OE *smoca* (n.), *smocian* (v.), from the Gmc base of *smēocan* 'emit smoke'.

**smoke alarm** ● n. a device that detects and gives a warning of the presence of smoke.

**smoke ball** ● n. a projectile filled with material which emits dense smoke on ignition, used to conceal military operations.

**smoke bomb** ● n. a bomb that emits dense smoke as it explodes.

**smokebox** ● n. **1** a smoke-producing oven for smoking food. **2** the chamber in a steam engine or boiler between the flues and the funnel or chimney stack. **3** another term for **SMOKER** (in sense 4).

**smoke bush** ● n. another term for **SMOKE TREE**.

**smokehouse** ● n. a shed or room for smoking fish or meat.

**smokejumper** ● n. N. Amer. a firefighter who arrives by parachute to extinguish a forest fire.

**smokeless zone** ● n. Brit. a district in which it is illegal to create smoke and where only smokeless fuel may be used.

**smoker** ● n. **1** a person who smokes tobacco regularly. **2** a person or device that smokes fish or meat. **3** chiefly N. Amer. an informal social gathering for men. **4** a device which emits smoke for subduing bees in a hive.

**smokescreen** ● n. **1** a cloud of smoke created to conceal military operations. **2** irrelevant activity designed to disguise someone's real intentions or activities.

**smoke signal** ● n. a column of smoke used to convey a message to a distant person.

**smokestack** ● n. a chimney or funnel for discharging smoke from a locomotive, ship, factory, etc.

**smokestone** ● n. another term for **SMOKY QUARTZ**.

**smoke tree** ● n. a shrub or small tree which bears feathery plumes of purple or reddish flowers and fruit, giving it a smoky appearance. [*Cotinus coggygria* (formerly *Rhus cotinus*).]

**smokie** ● n. Scottish a smoked haddock.

**smoking gun** ● n. a piece of incontrovertible incriminating evidence.

**smoking jacket** ● n. a man's comfortable jacket, typically made of velvet, formerly worn while smoking after dinner.

**smoky** ● adj. (**-ier**, **-iest**) **1** producing, filled with, smelling of, or resembling smoke. **2** having the taste or aroma of smoked food.
– DERIVATIVES **smokily** adv. **smokiness** n.

**smoky quartz** ● n. a semi-precious variety of quartz ranging in colour from light greyish-brown to nearly black.

**smolder** ● v. US spelling of **SMOULDER**.

**smolt** /sməʊlt/ ● n. a young salmon or trout after the parr stage, when it becomes silvery and migrates to the sea for the first time.
– ORIGIN ME (orig. Scots and north. Engl.): of unknown origin; cf. **SMELT**[3].

**smooch** informal ● v. kiss and cuddle amorously. ➤Brit. dance slowly in a close embrace. ● n. a spell of smooching.
– DERIVATIVES **smoocher** n. **smoochy** adj. (**-ier**, **-iest**).
– ORIGIN 1930s: from dial. *smouch*, of imitative origin.

**smoodge** (also **smooge**) Austral./NZ informal ● v. **1** behave amorously. **2** behave in an ingratiating manner. ● n. **1** a display of amorous affection. **2** an act or instance of being ingratiating.
– DERIVATIVES **smoodger** n.
– ORIGIN C20: prob. an alt. of dial. *smouch* 'kiss, sidle up to'.

**smooth** ● adj. **1** having an even and regular surface; free from projections or indentations. ➤(of a liquid) having an even consistency; without lumps. **2** (of movement) without jerks. **3** without problems or difficulties. **4** (of a flavour) without harshness or bitterness. **5** suavely or unctuously charming. ● v. (also **smoothe**) make smooth. ● adv. archaic in a way that is without difficulties.
– DERIVATIVES **smoothable** adj. **smoother** n. **smoothish** adj. **smoothly** adv. **smoothness** n.
– ORIGIN OE *smōth*, prob. of Gmc origin.

**smooth-bore** ● n. a gun with an unrifled barrel.

**smooth-faced** ● adj. clean-shaven.

**smooth hound** ● n. a small shark which typically lives close to the seabed in shallow waters. [Genus *Mustelus*: two species.]

**smoothie** ● n. **1** informal a man with a smooth, suave manner. **2** N. Amer. & Austral./NZ a thick, smooth drink of fresh fruit puréed with milk, yogurt, or ice cream.

**smoothing iron** ● n. historical a flat iron.

**smoothing plane** ● n. a small plane for finishing the surface of wood.

**smooth muscle** ● n. Physiology muscle tissue in which the contractile fibrils are not highly ordered, occurring in the gut and other internal organs and not under voluntary control. Often contrasted with **STRIATED MUSCLE**.

**smooth snake** ● n. a harmless snake which is grey to reddish in colour, typically living in heathy country where it feeds on lizards. [*Coronella austriaca*.]

**smooth talk** ● n. persuasively charming or flattering language. ● v. (**smooth-talk**) informal address or persuade with smooth talk.
– DERIVATIVES **smooth-talker** n. **smooth-talking** adj.

**smooth tongue** ● n. the tendency to use smooth talk.
– DERIVATIVES **smooth-tongued** adj.

**smorgasbord** /ˈsmɔːɡəsbɔːd/ ● n. a range of open sandwiches and savoury delicacies served as hors d'oeuvres or a buffet.
– ORIGIN Swed., from *smörgås* '(slice of) bread and butter' + *bord* 'table'.

**smorzando** /smɔːˈtsandəʊ/ ● adv. & adj. Music dying away.
– ORIGIN Ital., lit. 'extinguishing'.

**smote** past of **SMITE**.

**smother** ● v. **1** suffocate by covering the nose and mouth. **2** extinguish (a fire) by covering it. **3** (**smother someone/thing in/with**) cover someone or something entirely with. **4** cause to feel trapped and oppressed. **5** suppress (a feeling or action). ➤(in sport) stop the motion of (the ball or a shot). ● n. a mass of something that stifles or obscures.
– ORIGIN ME: from the base of OE *smorian* 'suffocate'.

**smothered mate** ● n. Chess checkmate in which the

king has no vacant square to move to and is checkmated by a knight.

**smoulder** (US also **smolder**) • v. **1** burn slowly with smoke but no flame. **2** (with reference to an intense feeling) express or be expressed in a barely suppressed state. • n. an instance of smouldering.
– DERIVATIVES **smouldering** adj. **smoulderingly** adv.
– ORIGIN ME: rel. to Du. *smeulen*.

**smriti** /ˈsmrɪti/ • n. (pl. **smritis**) a Hindu religious text containing traditional teachings.
– ORIGIN from Sanskrit *smṛti* 'remembrance'.

**SMS** • abbrev. Short Message (or Messaging) Service, a system that enables mobile phone users to send and receive text messages.

**SMSgt** • abbrev. Senior Master Sergeant.

**smudge¹** • v. make or become blurred or smeared. • n. a smudged mark or image.
– DERIVATIVES **smudgily** adv. **smudginess** n. **smudgy** adj. (**-ier**, **-iest**).
– ORIGIN ME: of unknown origin.

**smudge²** • n. N. Amer. a smoky outdoor fire lit to keep off insects or protect plants against frost.
– ORIGIN C18 (in the sense 'suffocating smoke'): of unknown origin; rel. to obs. *smudge* 'cure (herring) by smoking', of obscure origin.

**smug** • adj. (**smugger**, **smuggest**) irritatingly pleased with oneself; self-satisfied.
– DERIVATIVES **smugly** adv. **smugness** n.
– ORIGIN C16 (orig. in the sense 'neat, spruce'): from Low Ger. *smuk* 'pretty'.

**smuggle** • v. **1** move (goods) illegally into or out of a country. **2** convey secretly and illicitly.
– DERIVATIVES **smuggler** n. **smuggling** n.
– ORIGIN C17: from Low Ger. *smuggelen*.

**smut** • n. **1** a small flake of soot or dirt. **2** a fungal disease of cereals in which parts of the ear change to black powder. **3** indecent or obscene talk, writing, or pictures. • v. (**smutted**, **smutting**) **1** mark with smuts. **2** infect with smut.
– DERIVATIVES **smuttily** adv. **smuttiness** n. **smutty** adj. (**-ier**, **-iest**).
– ORIGIN ME (in the sense 'defile, make obscene').

**smut ball** • n. a grain of cereal affected by smut.

**smut mill** • n. a machine for removing smut from cereal grain.

**SN** • abbrev. Senegal (international vehicle registration).

**Sn** • symb. the chemical element tin.
– ORIGIN from late L. *stannum* 'tin'.

**snack** • n. **1** a small quantity of food or a light meal, eaten between meals or in place of a meal. **2** Austral. informal a thing that is easy to accomplish. • v. eat a snack.
– ORIGIN ME (orig. in the sense 'snap, bite'): from MDu. *snac(k)*, from *snacken* 'to bite', var. of *snappen*.

**snaffle** • n. a simple bit on a bridle, used with a single set of reins. • v. informal illicitly take for oneself.
– ORIGIN C16 (denoting a bridle bit): prob. from Low Ger. or Du.; the verb (C19) is perh. a different word.

**snafu** /snaˈfuː, ˈsnafuː/ informal, chiefly N. Amer. • n. a confused or chaotic state; a mess. • adj. confused; chaotic. • v. throw into confusion or chaos.
– ORIGIN 1940s: acronym from *situation normal: all fouled (or fucked) up*.

**snag¹** • n. **1** an unexpected or hidden obstacle or drawback. **2** a sharp or jagged projection. **3** a small rent or tear. **4** N. Amer. a dead tree. • v. (**snagged**, **snagging**) **1** catch or tear on a snag. **2** N. Amer. informal catch; obtain.
– DERIVATIVES **snaggy** adj.
– ORIGIN C16: prob. of Scand. origin.

**snag²** • n. Austral./NZ informal a sausage.
– ORIGIN 1940s: of unknown origin.

**snaggle** • n. a tangled or knotted mass. • v. become knotted or tangled.
– ORIGIN C20: from **SNAG¹** + **-LE²**.

**snaggle-toothed** • adj. having irregular or projecting teeth.

**snail** • n. a slow-moving mollusc with a spiral shell into which the whole body can be withdrawn. [Many species in the class Gastropoda.]
– ORIGIN OE *snæg(e)l*, of Gmc origin.

**snailfish** • n. (pl. same or **-fishes**) a small sea fish with loose jelly-like skin and typically a ventral sucker. [*Liparis liparis* (N. Atlantic) and other species.]

**snail mail** • n. informal the ordinary post as opposed to email.

**snake** • n. **1** a predatory reptile with a long slender limbless supple body, many kinds of which have a venomous bite. [Suborder Ophidia: many species.] **2** (also **snake in the grass**) a treacherous or deceitful person. **3** (in full **plumber's snake**) a long flexible wire for clearing obstacles in piping. • v. move or extend with the twisting motion of a snake.
– ORIGIN OE *snaca*, of Gmc origin.

**snakebird** • n. another term for **DARTER** (in sense 1).

**snakebite** • n. Brit. a drink consisting of draught cider and lager in equal proportions.

**snakebitten** • adj. N. Amer. informal unlucky.

**snakeboard** • n. trademark a type of skateboard consisting of two footplates joined by a bar, allowing for greater speed and manoeuvrability than with a standard skateboard.
– DERIVATIVES **snakeboarder** n. **snakeboarding** n.

**snake charmer** • n. an entertainer who appears to make snakes move by playing music.

**snake eyes** • pl. n. [treated as sing.] **1** a throw of two ones with a pair of dice. **2** the worst possible result; a complete lack of success.

**snakehead** • n. a member of a Chinese criminal network chiefly engaged in smuggling illegal immigrants.
– ORIGIN translation of Chin. *shetou*.

**snake mackerel** • n. another term for **ESCOLAR**.

**snake oil** • n. informal, chiefly N. Amer. a substance with no real medicinal value sold as a cure-all.

**snakeroot** • n. **1** a North American plant reputed to contain an antidote to snake poison. [*Aristolochia serpentaria* and other species.] **2** a plant with snake-like roots, yielding medicinal drugs. [*Rauwolfia serpentina* (**Indian snakeroot**, SE Asia) and related species.]

**snakes and ladders** • pl. n. [treated as sing.] a children's board game in which players proceed up ladders or fall back down snakes depicted on the board.

**snake's head** • n. a fritillary with flowers chequered in red and purple, typically growing in damp hay meadows and water meadows. [*Fritillaria meleagris*.]

**snakeskin** • n. the skin of a snake.

**snaky** • adj. (**-ier**, **-iest**) **1** long and sinuous like a snake. **2** cold and cunning. **3** Austral./NZ informal angry; irritable.
– DERIVATIVES **snakily** adv. **snakiness** n.

**snap** • v. (**snapped**, **snapping**) **1** break or cause to break with a sharp cracking sound. **2** (of an animal) make a sudden audible bite. ➤(**snap something up**) quickly secure something that is in short supply. **3** open or close with a brisk movement or sharp sound. **4** suddenly lose one's self-control. ➤say something quickly and irritably. **5** (**snap out of**) informal get out of (a bad mood) by a sudden effort. **6** take a snapshot of. **7** American Football put (the ball) into play by a quick backward movement. • n. **1** an act of snapping; a sudden snapping sound or movement. **2** a brief spell of cold or otherwise distinctive weather. **3** vigour; liveliness. **4** a snapshot. **5** Brit. a card game in which players compete to call 'snap' as soon as two cards of the same type are exposed. **6** a crisp, brittle biscuit. **7** N. Amer. informal an easy task. **8** N. Amer. a press stud. • adj. done on the spur of the moment: *a snap decision*.
– PHRASES **in a snap** informal, chiefly N. Amer. in a moment.
– DERIVATIVES **snapping** adj. **snappingly** adv.
– ORIGIN C15: prob. from MDu. or Mid. Low Ger. *snappen* 'seize'; partly imitative.

**snap bean** • n. N. Amer. a bean of a variety having an edible pod.
– ORIGIN C18: so named because the pods are broken into pieces to be eaten.

**snap-brim** • adj. denoting a hat with a brim that can be turned up and down at opposite sides.

**snapdragon** • n. a plant bearing spikes of brightly coloured two-lobed flowers which gape like a mouth when a bee lands on the curved lip. [*Antirrhinum majus.*]

**snap fastener** ● **n.** another term for **PRESS STUD**.

**snap hook** (also **snap link**) ● **n.** a hook with a spring allowing the entrance but preventing the escape of a cord, link, etc.

**snap-lock** ● **adj.** denoting a device or component which is fastened automatically when pushed into position.

**snap pea** ● **n.** another term for **SUGAR SNAP**.

**snapper** ● **n. 1** a marine fish noted for snapping its toothed jaws. [Many species, chiefly in the family Lutjanidae.] **2** a snapping turtle. **3** American Football a centre player.

**snapping turtle** ● **n.** a large American freshwater turtle with strong hooked jaws. [*Chelydra serpentina* and *Macroclemys temminckii* (the alligator snapper).]

**snappish** ● **adj. 1** (of a dog) irritable and inclined to bite. **2** (of a person) irritable; curt.
– DERIVATIVES **snappishly** adv. **snappishness** n.

**snappy** ● **adj.** (**-ier, -iest**) informal **1** irritable; curt. **2** cleverly concise: *a snappy catchphrase.* **3** neat and stylish: *a snappy dresser.*
– PHRASES **make it snappy** do it quickly.
– DERIVATIVES **snappily** adv. **snappiness** n.

**snap roll** ● **n.** a manoeuvre in which an aircraft makes a single quick revolution about its longitudinal axis while flying horizontally.

**snapshot** ● **n. 1** an informal photograph, taken quickly. **2** (**snap shot**) a shot in soccer or hockey taken quickly with little backlift.

**snare** ● **n. 1** a trap for catching small animals, consisting of a loop of wire or cord that pulls tight. ➤ Surgery a wire loop for severing polyps or other growths. **2** a length of wire, gut, or hide stretched across a drumhead to produce a rattling sound. ➤ (also **snare drum**) another term for **SIDE DRUM**. ● **v.** catch in a snare.
– DERIVATIVES **snarer** n.
– ORIGIN OE *sneare*, from ON *snara*; sense 2 is prob. from Mid. Low Ger., MDu. *snare* 'harp string'.

**snarf** ● **v.** informal, chiefly N. Amer. consume quickly or greedily.
– ORIGIN 1950s: perh. imitative.

**snark** ● **n.** an imaginary elusive animal.
– ORIGIN 1876: nonsense word coined by Lewis Carroll in *The Hunting of the Snark*.

**snarky** ● **adj.** (**-ier, -iest**) N. Amer. informal sharply critical.
– ORIGIN C20: from dial. verb *snark* 'snore, snort', 'find fault'.

**snarl**[1] ● **v. 1** growl with bared teeth. **2** say something aggressively. ● **n.** an act or sound of snarling.
– DERIVATIVES **snarler** n. **snarling** adj. **snarlingly** adv. **snarly** adj.
– ORIGIN C16: extension of obs. *snar*, of Gmc origin.

**snarl**[2] ● **v. 1** (**snarl up**) entangle or become entangled. **2** decorate (metalwork) with raised shapes by hammering the underside. ● **n.** a knot or tangle.
– ORIGIN ME: from **SNARE**.

**snarling iron** ● **n.** a tool struck with a hammer to create decorative raised work on metal.

**snarl-up** ● **n.** informal **1** a traffic jam. **2** a muddle.

**snash** ● **n.** Scottish insolence; abuse.
– ORIGIN C18: prob. imitative.

**snatch** ● **v.** seize quickly and deftly. ➤ informal steal or kidnap by seizing suddenly. ➤ quickly secure or obtain. ● **n. 1** an act of snatching. **2** a fragment of music or talk. **3** Weightlifting the rapid raising of a weight from the floor to above the head in one movement. **4** vulgar slang a woman's genitals.
– DERIVATIVES **snatcher** n. **snatchy** adj.
– ORIGIN ME *sna(c)che* (v.) 'suddenly snap at', (n.) 'a snare'; perh. rel. to **SNACK**.

**snazzy** ● **adj.** (**-ier, -iest**) informal smart; stylish.
– DERIVATIVES **snazzily** adv. **snazziness** n.
– ORIGIN 1960s: of unknown origin.

**sneak** ● **v.** (past and past part. **sneaked** or informal, chiefly N. Amer. **snuck**) **1** move, go, or convey in a furtive or stealthy manner. ➤ stealthily acquire or obtain: *she sneaked a glance at her watch.* **2** Brit. informal inform someone in authority of a person's misdeeds. ● **n.** informal **1** a furtive person. **2** Brit. a telltale. **3** N. Amer. short for **SNEAKER**. ● **adj.** acting or done surreptitiously: *a sneak preview.*
– DERIVATIVES **sneakily** adv. **sneakiness** n. **sneaky** adj. (**-ier, -iest**).
– ORIGIN C16: prob. dial.; perh. rel. to obs. *snike* 'to creep'.

**sneakbox** ● **n.** US a small, flat boat masked with brush or weeds, used in wildfowl shooting.

**sneaker** ● **n.** chiefly N. Amer. a soft shoe worn for sports or casual occasions.

**sneaking** ● **adj.** (of a feeling) persistent in one's mind but reluctantly held; nagging.
– DERIVATIVES **sneakingly** adv.

**sneck** Scottish & N. English ● **n.** a latch on a door or window. ● **v.** close or fasten with a latch.
– ORIGIN ME: obscurely rel. to **SNATCH**.

**sneer** ● **n.** a contemptuous or mocking smile, remark, or tone. ● **v.** smile or speak in a contemptuous or mocking manner.
– DERIVATIVES **sneerer** n. **sneering** adj. **sneeringly** adv.
– ORIGIN ME: prob. of imitative origin.

**sneeze** ● **v.** make a sudden involuntary expulsion of air from the nose and mouth due to irritation of one's nostrils. ● **n.** an act or the sound of sneezing.
– PHRASES **not to be sneezed at** informal not to be rejected without careful consideration.
– DERIVATIVES **sneezer** n. **sneezy** adj.
– ORIGIN ME: appar. an alt. of ME *fnese* due to misreading or misprinting (after initial *fn-* had become unfamiliar), later adopted because it sounded appropriate.

**sneezewort** ● **n.** a plant related to the yarrow, with dried leaves which can induce sneezing. [*Achillea ptarmica.*]

**snell** N. Amer. ● **n.** a short line by which a fish hook is attached to a longer line. ● **v.** tie or fasten (a hook) to a line.
– ORIGIN C19: of unknown origin.

**snib** chiefly Scottish & Irish ● **n.** a lock, latch, or fastening for a door or window. ➤ a small catch on a lock which holds the bolt in or out. ● **v.** (**snibbed, snibbing**) fasten or lock.
– ORIGIN C19: perh. from Low Ger. *snibbe* 'beak-like point'.

**snick** ● **v. 1** cut a small notch or incision in. **2** Cricket deflect (the ball) slightly with the edge of the bat; deflect a ball delivered by (a bowler) in this way. **3** make or cause to make a sharp click. ● **n. 1** a small notch or cut. **2** Cricket a slight deflection of the ball by the bat. **3** a sharp click.
– ORIGIN C17: prob. from obs. *snick or snee* 'fight with knives'.

**snicker** ● **v. 1** snigger. **2** (of a horse) whinny. ● **n.** a snigger or whinny.
– DERIVATIVES **snickering** adj. **snickeringly** adv.
– ORIGIN C17: imitative.

**snicket** ● **n.** chiefly N. English a narrow alley between houses.
– ORIGIN C19: of unknown origin.

**snide** ● **adj. 1** derogatory or mocking in an indirect way. **2** chiefly N. Amer. (of a person) devious and underhand. **3** counterfeit; inferior. ● **n.** a snide person or remark.
– DERIVATIVES **snidely** adv. **snideness** n. **snidey** adj.
– ORIGIN C19: of unknown origin.

**sniff** ● **v. 1** draw air audibly through the nose. **2** (**sniff at**) show contempt or dislike for: *the price is not to be sniffed at.* **3** (**sniff around/round**) informal investigate something covertly. ➤ (**sniff something out**) informal discover something by covert investigation. ● **n. 1** an act or sound of sniffing. **2** informal a hint or sign.
– DERIVATIVES **sniffer** n.
– ORIGIN ME: imitative.

**sniffer dog** ● **n.** informal a dog trained to find drugs or explosives by smell.

**sniffle** ● **v.** sniff slightly or repeatedly, typically because of a cold or fit of crying. ● **n. 1** an act of sniffling. **2** a slight head cold.
– DERIVATIVES **sniffler** n. **sniffly** adj.
– ORIGIN C17: imitative.

**sniffy** ● **adj.** (**-ier, -iest**) informal scornful; contemptuous.
– DERIVATIVES **sniffily** adv. **sniffiness** n.

**snifter** ● n. informal **1** a small quantity of an alcoholic drink. **2** chiefly N. Amer. a balloon glass for brandy.
– ORIGIN C19: imitative; cf. dial. *snift* 'to snort'.

**snifting valve** ● n. a valve on a steam engine that allows air in or out.

**snig** ● v. (**snigged**, **snigging**) Austral./NZ haul with ropes or chains.
– ORIGIN C18: of unknown origin.

**snigger** ● n. a smothered or half-suppressed laugh. ● v. give such a laugh.
– DERIVATIVES **sniggerer** n. **sniggering** adj. **sniggeringly** adv. **sniggery** adj.
– ORIGIN C18: later var. of **SNICKER**.

**sniggle** ● v. fish for eels by pushing a baited hook into holes in which they are hiding.
– ORIGIN C17: frequentative, based on earlier *snig* 'small eel', of unknown origin.

**snip** ● v. (**snipped**, **snipping**) cut with scissors or shears, with small, quick strokes. ● n. **1** an act of snipping. **2** a small piece that has been cut off. **3** Brit. informal a bargain. **4** informal a thing that is easily achieved. **5** (**snips**) hand shears for cutting metal. **6** N. Amer. informal a small or insignificant person.
– ORIGIN C16: from Low Ger. *snip* 'small piece', of imitative origin.

**snipe** /snʌɪp/ ● n. (pl. same or **snipes**) a wading bird with brown camouflaged plumage and a long straight bill. [*Gallinago gallinago* and other species.] ● v. **1** shoot at someone from a hiding place at long range. **2** make a sly or petty verbal attack.
– DERIVATIVES **sniper** n. **sniping** adj. & n.
– ORIGIN ME: prob. of Scand. origin.

**snipe eel** ● n. a slender marine eel with a long, thin beak-like snout. [Family Nemichthyidae.]

**snipefish** ● n. (pl. same or **-fishes**) a marine fish that has a long, slender snout with the mouth at the tip. [Family Macrorhamphosidae.]

**snippet** ● n. a small piece or brief extract.
– DERIVATIVES **snippety** adj.

**snippy** ● adj. (**-ier**, **-iest**) informal curt or sharp.
– DERIVATIVES **snippily** adv. **snippiness** n.

**snit** ● n. N. Amer. informal a fit of irritation or pique.
– ORIGIN 1930s: of unknown origin.

**snitch** informal ● v. **1** steal. **2** inform on someone. ● n. an informer.
– ORIGIN C17: of unknown origin.

**snivel** ● v. (**snivelled**, **snivelling**; US **sniveled**, **sniveling**) **1** cry and sniffle. **2** complain in a whining or tearful way. ● n. a spell of snivelling.
– DERIVATIVES **sniveller** n. **snivelling** adj. **snivellingly** adv.
– ORIGIN OE (recorded only in the verbal noun *snyflung* 'mucus'), from *snofl*, in the same sense.

**snob** ● n. a person who has an exaggerated respect for high social position or wealth and who looks down on those regarded as socially inferior. ➤a person with a similar respect for tastes considered superior in a particular area: *a wine snob.*
– DERIVATIVES **snobbery** n. (pl. **-ies**). **snobbish** adj. **snobbishly** adv. **snobbishness** n. **snobbism** n. **snobby** adj. (**-ier**, **-iest**).
– ORIGIN C18 (orig. dial. in the sense 'cobbler'): of unknown origin.

**SNOBOL** /ˈsnəʊbɒl/ ● n. a high-level computer programming language used especially in manipulating textual data.
– ORIGIN 1960s: formed from letters taken from *string-oriented symbolic language*, on the pattern of *COBOL*.

**snoek** /snuːk/ ● n. South African term for **BARRACOUTA**.
– ORIGIN Afrik. from Du., 'pike'; cf. **SNOOK²**.

**snog** Brit. informal ● v. (**snogged**, **snogging**) kiss and caress amorously. ● n. an act or spell of snogging.
– DERIVATIVES **snogger** n.
– ORIGIN 1940s: of unknown origin.

**snood** /snuːd/ ● n. **1** an ornamental hairnet or pouch worn over the hair at the back of a woman's head. ➤historical (in Scotland) a hair ribbon or band worn by unmarried women. **2** a wide ring of knitted material worn as a hood or scarf. **3** a short line attaching a hook to a main line in sea fishing.
– ORIGIN OE *snōd*, of unknown origin.

**snook¹** /snuːk/ ● n. (in phr. **cock a snook**) informal, chiefly Brit. place one's hand so that the thumb touches one's nose and the fingers are spread out, in order to express contempt. ➤openly show contempt or a lack of respect for someone or something.
– ORIGIN C18: of unknown origin.

**snook²** /snuːk/ ● n. a large edible game fish of the Caribbean. [*Centropomus undecimalis.*]
– ORIGIN C17: from Du. *snoek* (see **SNOEK**).

**snooker** ● n. **1** a game played with cues on a billiard table in which the players use a white cue ball to pocket the other balls in a set order. **2** a position in a game of snooker or pool in which a player cannot make a direct shot at any permitted ball. ● v. subject to a snooker. ➤(**be snookered**) informal be ruined or placed in an impossible position.
– ORIGIN C19: of unknown origin.

**snoop** informal ● v. investigate or look around furtively in an attempt to find out something. ● n. **1** an act of snooping. **2** a person who snoops.
– DERIVATIVES **snooper** n. **snoopy** adj.
– ORIGIN C19: from Du. *snœpen* 'eat on the sly'.

**snoot** ● n. **1** informal a person's nose. **2** informal a snob. **3** an attachment used to produce a narrow beam from a spotlight. ● adj. informal stylish and sophisticated.
– ORIGIN C19: var. of **SNOUT**.

**snooty** ● adj. (**-ier**, **-iest**) informal showing disapproval of or contempt towards others, especially those considered to be socially inferior.
– DERIVATIVES **snootily** adv. **snootiness** n.
– ORIGIN C20: from **SNOOT** + **-Y¹**; cf. **SNOTTY**.

**snooze** informal ● n. a short, light sleep. ● v. have a snooze.
– DERIVATIVES **snoozer** n. **snoozy** adj. (**-ier**, **-iest**).
– ORIGIN C18: of unknown origin.

**snooze button** ● n. a control on a clock which sets an alarm to repeat after a short interval.

**snore** ● n. a snorting or grunting sound in a person's breathing while they are asleep. ● v. make such a sound while asleep.
– DERIVATIVES **snorer** n.
– ORIGIN ME: prob. imitative.

**snorkel** /ˈsnɔːk(ə)l/ ● n. a tube for a swimmer to breathe through while under water. ● v. (**snorkelled**, **snorkelling**; US **snorkeled**, **snorkeling**) swim using a snorkel.
– DERIVATIVES **snorkeller** n. **snorkelling** n.
– ORIGIN 1940s: from Ger. *Schnorchel*.

**snort** ● n. **1** an explosive sound made by the sudden forcing of breath through the nose. **2** informal an inhaled dose of cocaine. **3** informal a measure of an alcoholic drink. ● v. **1** make a snort. ➤express indignation or derision by making a snort. **2** informal inhale (cocaine).
– DERIVATIVES **snorter** n.
– ORIGIN ME: prob. imitative.

**snot** ● n. informal **1** nasal mucus. **2** a contemptible person.
– ORIGIN ME: prob. from MDu., Mid. Low Ger.; rel. to **SNOUT**.

**snot-nosed** ● adj. informal **1** childish and inexperienced. **2** considering oneself superior; snobbish.

**snot rag** ● n. informal a handkerchief.

**snotter¹** ● n. informal, chiefly Scottish a piece or drop of nasal mucus.

**snotter²** ● n. Nautical **1** a fitting which holds the heel of a sprit close to the mast. **2** a length of rope with an eye spliced in each end.
– ORIGIN C18: of unknown origin.

**snotty** ● adj. (**-ier**, **-iest**) informal **1** full of or covered with nasal mucus. **2** having a superior or conceited attitude.
– DERIVATIVES **snottily** adv. **snottiness** n.

**snout** ● n. **1** the projecting nose and mouth of an animal, especially a mammal. ➤the projecting front or end of something such as a pistol. **2** Brit. informal a cigarette. ➤tobacco. **3** Brit. informal a police informer.
– DERIVATIVES **snouted** adj. **snouty** adj.

– ORIGIN ME: from MDu., Mid. Low Ger. *snūt*; rel. to SNOT.

**snout beetle** ● n. North American term for WEEVIL.

**snow** ● n. **1** atmospheric water vapour frozen into ice crystals and falling in light white flakes or lying on the ground as a white layer. ➤**(snows)** falls of snow. **2** a mass of flickering white spots on a television or radar screen, caused by interference or a poor signal. **3** informal cocaine. ● v. **1** **(it snows, it is snowing**, etc.) snow falls. ➤**(be snowed in/up)** be confined or blocked by a large quantity of snow. **2** arrive in overwhelming quantities: *in the last week it had snowed letters.* ➤**(be snowed under)** be overwhelmed with a large quantity of something, especially work. **3** informal, chiefly N. Amer. mislead or charm (someone) with elaborate and insincere words.

– DERIVATIVES **snowily** adv. **snowiness** n. **snowless** adj. **snowy** adj. **(-ier, -iest)**.

– ORIGIN OE *snāw*, of Gmc origin.

**snowball** ● n. **1** a ball of packed snow. **2** a thing that grows rapidly in size, intensity, or importance. **3** a cocktail containing advocaat and lemonade. ● v. **1** throw snowballs at. **2** increase rapidly in size, intensity, or importance.

**snowball bush** ● n. a guelder rose of a sterile variety which produces large globular white flower heads.

**snowberry** ● n. a North American shrub of the honeysuckle family, bearing white berries and often cultivated as an ornamental or for hedging. [*Symphoricarpos albus.*]

**snowbird** ● n. N. Amer. informal a northerner who moves to a warmer Southern state in the winter.

**snow-blind** ● adj. temporarily blinded by the glare of light reflected by a large expanse of snow.

– DERIVATIVES **snow blindness** n.

**snowblink** ● n. a white reflection in the sky of snow or ice on the ground.

**snowboard** ● n. a board resembling a short, broad ski, used for sliding downhill on snow. ● v. slide downhill on a snowboard.

– DERIVATIVES **snowboarder** n. **snowboarding** n.

**snow boot** ● n. a warm padded waterproof boot worn in the snow.

**snowbound** ● adj. prevented from travelling or going out by snow or snowy weather. ➤cut off or inaccessible because of snow.

**snow bunting** ● n. a northern bunting that breeds mainly in the Arctic, the male having white plumage with a black back in the breeding season. [*Plectrophenax nivalis.*]

**snowcap** ● n. **1** a covering of snow on the top of a mountain. **2** a small Central American hummingbird with mainly purple plumage and a white crown. [*Microchera albocoronata.*]

– DERIVATIVES **snow-capped** adj.

**snowcat** (also US trademark **Sno-Cat**) ● n. a tracked vehicle for travelling over snow.

– ORIGIN 1940s: from SNOW + CATERPILLAR.

**snowdrift** ● n. a bank of deep snow heaped up by the wind.

**snowdrop** ● n. a bulbous plant which bears drooping white flowers during the late winter. [*Galanthus nivalis.*]

**snowfall** ● n. **1** a fall of snow. **2** the quantity of snow falling within a given area in a given time.

**snowfield** ● n. a permanent wide expanse of snow in mountainous or polar regions.

**snowflake** ● n. **1** each of the many feathery ice crystals, typically displaying delicate sixfold symmetry, that fall as snow. **2** a white-flowered plant related to and resembling the snowdrop, typically blooming in the summer or autumn. [Genus *Leucojum.*]

**snow goose** ● n. a gregarious goose that breeds in Arctic Canada and Greenland, typically having white plumage with black wing tips. [*Anser caerulescens.*]

**snow-in-summer** ● n. a white-flowered plant with silvery-green leaves. [*Cerastium tomentosum* (a pink, southern Europe) and *Helichrysum rosmarinifolium* (an evergreen shrub, Australia).]

**snow job** ● n. informal a deception or concealment of one's real motive in an attempt to flatter or persuade.

**snow leopard** ● n. a rare large cat which has pale grey fur patterned with dark blotches and rings, living in the Altai mountains, Hindu Kush, and Himalayas. [*Panthera uncia.*]

**snowline** ● n. the altitude in a particular place above which some snow remains on the ground throughout the year.

**snowman** ● n. (pl. **-men**) a representation of a human figure created with compressed snow.

**snowmobile** /'snəʊməbiːl/ ● n. a motor vehicle, especially one with runners or caterpillar tracks, for travelling over snow.

**snowpack** ● n. a mass of lying snow that is compressed and hardened by its own weight.

**snow partridge** ● n. a Himalayan partridge with fine black and white bars on the upper parts and a red bill and legs. [*Lerwa lerwa.*]

**snow pea** ● n. chiefly N. Amer. another term for MANGETOUT.

**snowplough** (US **snowplow**) ● n. **1** an implement or vehicle for clearing roads of snow. **2** Skiing an act of turning the points of one's skis inwards in order to slow down or turn. ● v. Skiing execute a snowplough.

**snowscape** ● n. a landscape covered in snow. ➤a picture of such a landscape.

**snowshoe** ● n. a flat device resembling a racket, which is attached to the sole of a boot and used for walking on snow. ● v. proceed wearing snowshoes.

– DERIVATIVES **snowshoer** n.

**snowshoe hare** (N. Amer. also **snowshoe rabbit**) ● n. a North American hare with large hairy hind feet, fairly small ears, and a white winter coat. [*Lepus americanus.*]

**snowstorm** ● n. a heavy fall of snow accompanied by a high wind.

**snowy mespilus** ● n. a white-flowered shrub or small tree, often grown as an ornamental. [*Amelanchier vulgaris* and related species, formerly in the genus *Mespilus.*]

– ORIGIN mod. L. *Mespilus*, from L. *mespilus* 'medlar tree'.

**snowy owl** ● n. a large northern owl that breeds mainly in the Arctic tundra, the male being entirely white and the female having darker markings. [*Nyctea scandiaca.*]

**SNP** ● abbrev. Scottish National Party.

**Snr** ● abbrev. Senior.

**snub** ● v. **(snubbed, snubbing) 1** ignore or spurn disdainfully. **2** restrict the movement of (a horse or boat) by means of a rope wound round a post. ● n. an act of snubbing. ● adj. (of a person's nose) short and turned up at the end.

– ORIGIN ME: from ON *snubba* 'chide, check the growth of'.

**snubber** ● n. **1** a simple kind of shock absorber. **2** an electric circuit intended to suppress voltage spikes.

**snuck** informal, chiefly N. Amer. past and past participle of SNEAK.

**snuff**[1] ● v. **1** extinguish (a candle). **2** **(snuff out)** abruptly put an end to. ➤**(snuff it)** Brit. informal die. **3** trim the charred wick from (a candle). ● n. the charred part of a candle wick.

– ORIGIN ME: of unknown origin.

**snuff**[2] ● n. powdered tobacco that is sniffed up the nostril. ● v. **1** inhale or sniff at. **2** archaic sniff up snuff.

– PHRASES **up to snuff** informal **1** up to the required standard. ➤in good health. **2** Brit. archaic not easily deceived.

– ORIGIN ME: from MDu. *snuffen* 'to snuffle'.

**snuffer** ● n. a small hollow metal cone on the end of a handle, used to extinguish a candle by smothering the flame.

**snuffle** ● v. **1** breathe noisily through the nose due to a cold or crying. **2** (of an animal) make repeated sniffing sounds. ● n. **1** a snuffling sound. **2** **(the snuffles)** informal a cold.

– DERIVATIVES **snuffler** n. **snuffly** adj.

– ORIGIN C16: prob. from Low Ger. and Du. *snuffelen*.

**snuff movie** • n. informal a pornographic film or video recording of an actual murder.

**snuffy**[1] • adj. (**-ier**, **-iest**) archaic **1** supercilious or contemptuous. **2** easily offended; annoyed.

**snuffy**[2] • adj. archaic resembling snuff in colour or substance.

**snug** • adj. (**snugger**, **snuggest**) **1** warm and cosy. **2** archaic (of an income or employment) allowing one to live in comfort. **3** very tight or close-fitting. • n. Brit. a small, cosy public room in a pub or small hotel. • v. chiefly N. Amer. place or settle safely or cosily.
– DERIVATIVES **snugly** adv. **snugness** n.
– ORIGIN C16 (orig. in naut. use in the sense 'shipshape, compact, prepared for bad weather'): prob. of Low Ger. or Du. origin.

**snuggery** • n. (pl. **-ies**) a cosy place, especially someone's private room. ➤ Brit. archaic another term for **SNUG**.

**snuggle** • v. settle into a warm, comfortable position.
– ORIGIN C17: frequentative of the verb **SNUG**.

**So.** • abbrev. South.

**so**[1] • adv. **1** to such a great extent. ➤ extremely; very much. **2** [with neg.] to the same extent: *he isn't so bad*. **3** referring back to something previously mentioned: *I believe so*. ➤ similarly: *so have I*. **4** in the way described or demonstrated; thus. • conj. **1** and for this reason; therefore. **2** (**so that**) with the result or aim that. **3** and then. **4** introducing a question or concluding statement. **5** in the same way; correspondingly.
– PHRASES **and so on** (or **forth**) and similar things; et cetera. **only so much** only a limited amount. **so be it** an expression of acceptance or resignation. **so long!** informal goodbye. **so much as** [with neg.] even: *without so much as a word*. **so to speak** (or **say**) indicating that one is talking in an unusual or metaphorical way.
– ORIGIN OE *swā*, of Gmc origin.

**so**[2] • n. variant spelling of **SOH**.

**-so** • comb. form equivalent to **-SOEVER**.

**soak** • v. **1** make or become thoroughly wet by immersion in liquid. **2** make extremely wet: *the rain soaked their hair*. **3** (**soak something up**) absorb a liquid. ➤ expose oneself to something beneficial or enjoyable. **4** (**soak oneself in**) immerse oneself in (a particular experience). **5** informal impose heavy charges or taxation on. **6** archaic, informal drink heavily. • n. **1** an act or spell of soaking. **2** informal a heavy drinker. **3** Austral. a hollow where rainwater collects.
– DERIVATIVES **soakage** n. **soaked** adj. **soaking** adj. & n.
– ORIGIN OE *socian*; rel. to *sūcan* 'to suck'.

**soakaway** • n. Brit. a pit through which waste water drains slowly out into the surrounding soil.

**so-and-so** • n. (pl. **-os**) **1** a person or thing whose name the speaker does not know, remember, or need to specify. **2** informal a person who is disliked or considered to have a particular unfavourable characteristic: *a nosy so-and-so*.

**soap** • n. **1** a substance used with water for washing and cleaning, made of a compound of natural oils or fats with sodium hydroxide or another strong alkali, and typically perfumed. **2** informal a soap opera. • v. wash with soap.
– PHRASES **no soap** N. Amer. informal no chance at all.
– DERIVATIVES **soapily** adv. **soapiness** n. **soapless** adj. **soapy** adj. (**-ier**, **-iest**).
– ORIGIN OE *sāpe*, of W. Gmc origin.

**soapberry** • n. **1** a tree or shrub with berries that produce a soapy froth when crushed. [Several species, mainly of the genus *Sapindus*.] **2** the berry of such a plant.

**soapbox** • n. a box or crate used as a makeshift stand for public speaking.

**soap opera** • n. a television or radio drama serial dealing with daily events in the lives of the same group of characters.
– ORIGIN 1930s: so named because such serials were orig. sponsored in the US by soap manufacturers.

**soapstone** • n. a soft rock consisting largely of steatite (talc).

**soapsuds** • pl. n. another term for **SUDS** (in sense 1).

**soapwort** • n. a plant of the pink family, with fragrant pink or white flowers and leaves that were formerly used to make soap. [*Saponaria officinalis*.]

**soar** • v. **1** fly or rise high into the air. ➤ glide high in the air. **2** increase rapidly above the usual level.
– DERIVATIVES **soarer** n. **soaring** adj. **soaringly** adv.
– ORIGIN ME: shortening of OFr. *essorer*, based on L. *ex-* 'out of' + *aura* 'breeze'.

**Soave** /ˈswɑːveɪ, səʊˈɑːveɪ/ • n. a dry white wine produced in the region of northern Italy around Soave.

**Soay sheep** /ˈsəʊeɪ/ • n. a small domesticated sheep of a primitive breed with brown fleece and horns in both sexes, formerly confined to the island of Soay in the St Kilda group.

**sob** • v. (**sobbed**, **sobbing**) cry making loud, convulsive gasps. ➤ say while sobbing. • n. an act or sound of sobbing.
– DERIVATIVES **sobbing** adj. **sobbingly** adv.
– ORIGIN ME: perh. of Du. or Low Ger. origin.

**s.o.b.** • abbrev. N. Amer. informal son of a bitch.

**soba** /ˈsəʊbə/ • n. Japanese noodles made from buckwheat flour.
– ORIGIN from Japanese.

**sober** • adj. (**-er**, **-est**) **1** not affected by alcohol; not drunk. **2** serious; thoughtful. **3** muted in colour. • v. **1** (usu. **sober up**) make or become sober after drinking alcohol. **2** make or become serious.
– DERIVATIVES **sobering** adj. **soberingly** adv. **soberly** adv.
– ORIGIN ME: from OFr. *sobre*, from L. *sobrius*.

**sobersides** • n. informal, chiefly N. Amer. a sedate and serious person.
– DERIVATIVES **sobersided** adj.

**sobriety** /səˈbrʌɪəti/ • n. the state of being sober.
– ORIGIN ME: from OFr. *sobriete* or L. *sobrietas*, from *sobrius* (see **SOBER**).

**sobriquet** /ˈsəʊbrɪkeɪ/ (also **soubriquet**) • n. a person's nickname.
– ORIGIN C17: Fr., orig. in the sense 'tap under the chin', of unknown origin.

**sob story** • n. informal a story or account intended to arouse sympathy.

**Soc.** • abbrev. **1** Socialist. **2** Society.

**soca** /ˈsəʊkə/ • n. calypso music with elements of soul, originally from Trinidad.
– ORIGIN 1970s: blend of **SOUL** and **CALYPSO**.

**socage** /ˈsɒkɪdʒ/ (also **soccage**) • n. historical a feudal tenure of land involving payment of rent or other non-military service to a superior.
– ORIGIN ME: from Anglo-Norman Fr., from *soc*, var. of **SOKE**.

**so-called** • adj. commonly designated by the name or term specified. ➤ expressing one's view that such a name or term is inappropriate: *her so-called friends*.

**soccer** • n. a form of football played by two teams of eleven players with a round ball which may not be handled during play except by the goalkeepers, the object of the game being to score goals by kicking or heading the ball into the opponents' goal.
– ORIGIN C19: shortening of *Assoc* (from **ASSOCIATION FOOTBALL**) + **-ER**[3].

**soccer mom** • n. US a middle-class suburban housewife, typically having children who play soccer rather than a traditional American sport.

**sociable** • adj. engaging readily with other people. ➤ marked by friendliness. • n. **1** historical an open carriage with facing side seats. **2** historical a tricycle with two seats side by side. **3** chiefly Brit. an S-shaped couch for two people who sit partially facing each other. **4** US dated an informal social gathering.
– DERIVATIVES **sociability** n. **sociableness** n. **sociably** adv.
– ORIGIN C16: from Fr., or from L. *sociabilis*, from *sociare* 'unite', from *socius* 'companion'.

**social** • adj. **1** of or relating to society or its organization. ➤ of or relating to rank and status in society: *a woman of high social standing*. **2** needing companionship; suited to living in communities. **3** relating to or designed for activities in which people meet each other for pleasure. **4** Zoology (of birds, insects, or mammals) breeding or living in

colonies or organized communities. ● **n.** an informal social gathering organized by the members of a particular club or group.
– DERIVATIVES **sociality** n. **socially** adv.
– ORIGIN ME: from OFr., or from L. *socialis* 'allied', from *socius* 'friend'.

**social anthropology** (also **cultural anthropology**) ● **n.** the comparative study of human societies and cultures and their development.

**social assistance** ● **n.** Canadian term for SOCIAL SECURITY.

**social climber** ● **n.** derogatory a person who is anxious to gain a higher social status.
– DERIVATIVES **social climbing** n.

**social contract** (also **social compact**) ● **n.** an implicit agreement among the members of a society to cooperate for mutual social benefit, for example by sacrificing some individual freedom for state protection (originally promoted by theorists such as Thomas Hobbes, John Locke, and Jean-Jacques Rousseau).

**social credit** ● **n.** the economic theory that consumer purchasing power should be increased either by subsidizing producers so that they can lower prices or by distributing the profits of industry to consumers.

**social Darwinism** ● **n.** the theory that individuals, groups, and peoples are subject to the same Darwinian laws of natural selection as plants and animals (now largely discredited).

**social democracy** ● **n.** a socialist system of government achieved by democratic means.
– DERIVATIVES **social democrat** n.

**social fund** ● **n.** (in the UK) a social security fund from which loans or grants are made to people in need.

**social geography** ● **n.** the study of people and their environment with particular emphasis on social factors.

**social gospel** ● **n.** Christian faith practised as a call not just to personal conversion but to social reform.
– DERIVATIVES **social gospeller** n.

**social insurance** ● **n.** a system of compulsory contribution to provide state assistance in sickness, unemployment, etc.

**socialism** ● **n.** a political and economic theory of social organization which advocates that the means of production, distribution, and exchange should be owned or regulated by the community as a whole. ➤(in Marxist theory) a transitional social state between the overthrow of capitalism and the realization of Communism.
– DERIVATIVES **socialist** n. & adj. **socialistic** adj. **socialistically** adv.

**socialist realism** ● **n.** the theory that art, literature, and music should reflect and promote the ideals of a socialist society (especially in the Soviet Union under Stalin).

**socialite** ● **n.** a person who is well known in fashionable society and is fond of social activities.

**socialize** (also **-ise**) ● **v.** **1** mix socially with others. **2** make (someone) behave in a way that is acceptable to society. **3** organize according to the principles of socialism.
– DERIVATIVES **socialization** n. **socialized** adj. **socializing** adj.

**socialized medicine** ● **n.** US the provision of medical and hospital care for all by means of public funds.

**social market economy** (also **social market**) ● **n.** an economic system based on a free market operated in conjunction with state provision for those unable to sell their labour, such as the elderly or unemployed.

**social partner** ● **n.** an individual or organization, such as an employer, trade union, or employee, participating in a cooperative relationship for the mutual benefit of all concerned.

**social psychology** ● **n.** the branch of psychology concerned with social interactions.
– DERIVATIVES **social psychologist** n.

**social realism** ● **n.** the realistic depiction in art of contemporary life, as a means of social or political comment.

**social science** ● **n.** the scientific study of human society and social relationships. ➤a subject within this field, such as economics or politics.
– DERIVATIVES **social scientist** n.

**social secretary** ● **n.** a person who arranges the social activities of a person or organization.

**social security** ● **n.** **1** (in the UK) monetary assistance from the state for people with an inadequate or no income. **2** (**Social Security**) (in the US) a federal insurance scheme providing benefits for pensioners, the unemployed, and the disabled.

**social service** ● **n.** **1** (**social services**) government services provided for the benefit of the community, such as education, medical care, and housing. **2** activity aiming to promote the welfare of others.

**social studies** ● **pl. n.** [treated as sing.] the study of human society.

**social wage** ● **n.** the cost per person of the amenities provided within a society from public funds.

**social work** ● **n.** work carried out by trained personnel with the aim of alleviating the conditions of those people in a community suffering from social deprivation.
– DERIVATIVES **social worker** n.

**society** ● **n.** (pl. **-ies**) **1** the aggregate of people living together in a more or less ordered community. ➤a particular community of people. ➤(also **high society**) people who are fashionable, wealthy, and influential, regarded as forming a distinct group. **2** a plant or animal community. **3** an organization or club formed for a particular purpose or activity. **4** the situation of being in the company of other people: *she shunned the society of others.*
– DERIVATIVES **societal** adj. **societally** adv.
– ORIGIN C16: from Fr. *société*, from L. *societas*, from *socius* 'companion'.

**socio-** /ˈsəʊsɪəʊ, ˈsəʊʃɪəʊ/ ● **comb. form** **1** relating to society; society and ...: *socio-economic.* **2** relating to sociology; sociology and ...: *sociolinguistics.*
– ORIGIN from L. *socius* 'companion'.

**sociobiology** ● **n.** the scientific study of the biological (especially ecological and evolutionary) aspects of social behaviour in animals and humans.
– DERIVATIVES **sociobiological** adj. **sociobiologically** adv. **sociobiologist** n.

**socioecology** ● **n.** the branch of science concerned with the interactions among the members of a species, and between them and the environment.
– DERIVATIVES **socioecological** adj. **socioecologist** n.

**socio-economic** ● **adj.** relating to or concerned with the interaction of social and economic factors.
– DERIVATIVES **socio-economically** adv.

**sociolect** /ˈsəʊsɪə(ʊ)lɛkt, ˈsəʊʃɪə(ʊ)-/ ● **n.** the dialect of a particular social class.
– ORIGIN 1970s: from **socio-** + *-lect* as in DIALECT.

**sociolinguistics** ● **pl. n.** [treated as sing.] the study of language in relation to social factors.
– DERIVATIVES **sociolinguist** n. **sociolinguistic** adj. **sociolinguistically** adv.

**sociology** ● **n.** the study of the development, structure, and functioning of human society. ➤the study of social problems.
– DERIVATIVES **sociological** adj. **sociologically** adv. **sociologist** n.

**sociometry** /ˌsəʊsɪˈɒmɪtri, ˌsəʊʃɪ-/ ● **n.** the study of relationships within a group of people.
– DERIVATIVES **sociometric** adj. **sociometrically** adv. **sociometrist** n.

**sociopath** /ˈsəʊsɪə(ʊ)paθ, ˈsəʊʃɪə(ʊ)-/ ● **n.** a person with a personality disorder manifesting itself in extreme antisocial attitudes and behaviour.
– DERIVATIVES **sociopathic** adj. **sociopathy** n.

**sock** ● **n.** **1** a knitted garment for the foot and lower part of the leg. **2** an insole. **3** a white marking on the lower part of a horse's leg. **4** informal a hard blow. ➤US force or emphasis. ● **v.** informal **1** hit forcefully. **2** (**sock something away**) N. Amer. save up money. **3** (usu. **be socked in**) N. Amer. envelop or make impassable by inhospitable weather conditions: *the beach was socked in with fog.*

– PHRASES **knock** (or **blow**) **someone's socks off** informal amaze or impress someone. **knock the socks off** informal surpass or beat. **pull one's socks up** informal make an effort to improve. **put a sock in it** Brit. informal stop talking. **sock it to someone** informal attack or make a forceful impression on someone.
– ORIGIN OE *socc* 'light shoe', of Gmc origin, from L. *soccus* 'comic actor's shoe, light low-heeled slipper', from Gk *sukkhos*.

**socket** ● n. **1** a hollow in which something fits or revolves. ➤ the part of the head of a golf club into which the shaft is fitted. **2** an electrical device receiving a plug or light bulb to make a connection. ● v. (**socketed**, **socketing**) **1** place in or fit with a socket. **2** Golf dated shank (a ball).
– ORIGIN ME: from an Anglo-Norman Fr. dimin. of OFr. *soc* 'ploughshare', prob. of Celtic origin.

**socket wrench** ● n. a ratchet tool with detachable sockets for tightening and untightening nuts of different sizes.

**sockeye** ● n. a commercially valuable salmon of the North Pacific region. [*Oncorhynchus nerka*.]
– ORIGIN C19: from Salish *sukai*, lit. 'fish of fishes'.

**socking** ● adv. Brit. informal used for emphasis: *a socking great diamond*.

**socko** ● adj. informal, chiefly N. Amer. stunningly effective or successful.
– ORIGIN 1920s: from **SOCK** in the sense 'forceful blow' + **-O**.

**socle** /'səʊk(ə)l, 'sɒk-/ ● n. Architecture a plain low block or plinth supporting a column, statue, etc. or as the foundation of a wall.
– ORIGIN C18: from Fr., from Ital. *zoccolo*, lit. 'wooden shoe', from L. *socculus*, from *soccus* (see **SOCK**).

**Socratic** /sə'kratɪk/ ● adj. of or relating to the Athenian philosopher Socrates (469–399 BC) or his philosophy or methods. ● n. a follower of Socrates.
– DERIVATIVES **Socratically** adv.

**Socratic irony** ● n. a pose of ignorance assumed in order to entice others into making statements that can then be challenged.

**Socred** /'səʊkrɛd/ ● n. Canadian a person or political party advocating social credit.

**sod**[1] ● n. turf. ➤ a piece of turf. ● v. (**sodded**, **sodding**) rare cover with sods or turf.
– PHRASES **under the sod** dead and buried.
– ORIGIN ME: from MDu., Mid. Low Ger. *sode*, of unknown ultimate origin.

**sod**[2] vulgar slang, chiefly Brit. ● n. **1** an unpleasant person. ➤ a person of a specified kind. **2** a difficult or problematic thing. ● v. (**sodded**, **sodding**) used to express anger or annoyance. ➤ (**sod off**) go away. ➤ [as adj. **sodding**] used as a general term of contempt.
– PHRASES **sod all** absolutely nothing.
– ORIGIN C19: abbrev. of **SODOMITE**.

**soda** ● n. **1** (also **soda water**) carbonated water (originally made with sodium bicarbonate). ➤ chiefly N. Amer. a sweet carbonated drink. **2** sodium carbonate. ➤ sodium in chemical combination: *nitrate of soda*.
– ORIGIN ME: from med. L., from Arab. *suwwad* 'saltwort'.

**soda ash** ● n. commercially manufactured anhydrous sodium carbonate.

**soda bread** ● n. bread leavened with baking soda.

**soda fountain** ● n. chiefly N. Amer. a device dispensing soda water or soft drinks. ➤ a shop or counter selling drinks from such a device.

**soda lime** ● n. a mixture of calcium oxide and sodium hydroxide.

**sodalite** /'səʊdəlʌɪt/ ● n. a blue mineral consisting of an aluminosilicate and chloride of sodium.
– ORIGIN C19: from **SODA** + **-LITE**.

**sodality** /səʊ'dalɪti/ ● n. (pl. **-ies**) a confraternity or association, especially a Roman Catholic religious guild or brotherhood.
– ORIGIN C17: from Fr. *sodalité* or L. *sodalitas*, from *sodalis* 'comrade'.

**soda pop** ● n. US informal a sweet carbonated drink.

**soda siphon** ● n. a bottle from which carbonated water is dispensed by allowing the gas pressure to force it out.

**soda water** ● n. see **SODA** (sense 1).

**sodbuster** ● n. N. Amer. informal a farmer or farm worker.

**sodden** ● adj. **1** soaked through. **2** [in combination] having drunk an excessive amount of a particular alcoholic drink: *whisky-sodden*. ● v. archaic saturate with water.
– DERIVATIVES **soddenly** adv. **soddenness** n.
– ORIGIN ME (in the sense 'boiled'): archaic past part. of **SEETHE**.

**sodium** ● n. the chemical element of atomic number 11, a soft silver-white reactive metal of the alkali-metal group. (Symbol: **Na**)
– DERIVATIVES **sodic** adj. (Mineralogy).
– ORIGIN C19: from **SODA** + **-IUM**.

**sodium bicarbonate** ● n. a soluble white powder used in fire extinguishers and effervescent drinks and as a raising agent in baking. [$NaHCO_3$.]

**sodium carbonate** ● n. a white alkaline compound used in making soap and glass. [$Na_2CO_3$.]

**sodium chloride** ● n. the chemical name for common salt. [NaCl.]

**sodium hydroxide** ● n. a strongly alkaline white deliquescent compound used in many industrial processes. [NaOH.]

**sodium thiosulphate** ● n. a white soluble compound used in photography as a fixer. [$Na_2S_2O_3$.]

**sodium-vapour lamp** (also **sodium lamp**) ● n. a lamp in which an electrical discharge in sodium vapour gives a yellow light.

**Sodom** /'sɒdəm/ ● n. a wicked or depraved place.
– ORIGIN from *Sodom*, a town in ancient Palestine destroyed for its wickedness (Gen. 19:24).

**sodomite** /'sɒdəmʌɪt/ ● n. a person who engages in sodomy.
– DERIVATIVES **sodomitic** adj. **sodomitical** adj.
– ORIGIN ME: via OFr. from late L. *Sodomita*, from Gk *Sodomitēs* 'inhabitant of Sodom'.

**sodomy** ● n. anal intercourse.
– DERIVATIVES **sodomize** (also **-ise**) v.
– ORIGIN ME: from med. L. *sodomia*, from late L. *peccatum Sodomiticum* 'sin of Sodom' (after Gen. 19:5, which implies that the men of Sodom practised homosexual rape) (see **SODOM**).

**Sod's Law** ● n. another name for **MURPHY'S LAW**.

**soever** ● adv. archaic or poetic/literary of any kind; to any extent.

**-soever** ● comb. form of any kind; to any extent: *whosoever*.
– ORIGIN ME: orig. as the phr. *so ever*.

**sofa** ● n. a long upholstered seat with a back and arms, for two or more people.
– ORIGIN C17: from Fr., based on Arab. *ṣuffa*.

**sofa bed** ● n. a sofa that can be converted into a bed.

**soffit** /'sɒfɪt/ ● n. the underside of an arch, a balcony, overhanging eaves, etc.
– ORIGIN C17: from Fr. *soffite* or Ital. *soffitto*, based on L. *suffixus* 'fastened below'.

**S. of S.** ● abbrev. Song of Songs (in biblical references).

**soft** ● adj. **1** easy to mould, cut, compress, or fold. **2** not rough or coarse. **3** quiet and gentle. ➤ (of a consonant) pronounced as a fricative (as *c* in *ice*). **4** (of light or shadow) pleasingly subtle. **5** sympathetic or lenient, especially excessively so. ➤ denoting a faction within a political party that is willing to compromise: *the soft left*. ➤ informal (of a job or way of life) requiring little effort. **6** informal foolish. ➤ (**soft on**) infatuated with. **7** (of a market, currency, or commodity) falling or likely to fall in value. **8** (of a drink) not alcoholic. ➤ (of a drug) not likely to cause addiction. **9** (of water) free from mineral salts. **10** (of radiation) having little penetrating power. **11** (also **soft-core**) (of pornography) suggestive but not explicit. **12** dialect (of weather) rainy, moist, or thawing. ● adv. softly. ➤ weakly or foolishly.
– PHRASES **have a soft spot for** be fond of. **soft touch** (also **easy touch**) informal a person who is easily persuaded or imposed upon.

– DERIVATIVES **softish** adj. **softly** adv. **softness** n.
– ORIGIN OE *sōfte* 'agreeable, calm, gentle', of W. Gmc origin.

**softa** /ˈsɒftə/ ● n. a Muslim student of sacred law and theology.
– ORIGIN Turk., from Pers. *sūkta* 'burnt, on fire'.

**softback** ● adj. & n. another term for **PAPERBACK**.

**softball** ● n. a modified form of baseball played on a smaller field with a larger, softer ball.

**soft-boiled** ● adj. (of an egg) lightly boiled, leaving the yolk soft or liquid.

**soft-centred** ● adj. **1** (of a sweet) having a soft filling. **2** (of a person) compassionate or sentimental.

**soft coal** ● n. bituminous coal.

**soft copy** ● n. Computing a legible version of a piece of information, stored or displayed on a computer.

**soft-core** ● adj. another term for **SOFT** (in sense 11).

**soften** ● v. **1** make or become soft or softer. **2** (often **soften someone/thing up**) undermine the resistance of.

**softener** ● n. a substance or device that softens something, especially a fabric conditioner.

**soft focus** ● n. deliberate slight blurring or lack of definition in a photograph or film.

**soft fruit** ● n. Brit. a small stoneless fruit, e.g. a strawberry.

**soft furnishings** ● pl. n. Brit. curtains, chair coverings, and other cloth items used to decorate a room.

**soft goods** ● pl. n. Brit. textiles.

**soft-headed** ● adj. not intelligent.
– DERIVATIVES **soft-headedness** n.

**soft-hearted** ● adj. kind and compassionate.
– DERIVATIVES **soft-heartedness** n.

**softie** (also **softy**) ● n. (pl. **-ies**) informal a weak or soft-hearted person.

**soft iron** ● n. easily magnetizable iron with a low carbon content, used to make the cores of solenoids.

**soft loan** ● n. a loan made on terms very favourable to the borrower.

**softly-softly** ● adj. cautious and patient.

**soft-nosed** ● adj. (of a bullet) expanding on impact.

**soft palate** ● n. the fleshy, flexible part towards the back of the roof of the mouth.

**soft-paste** ● adj. denoting artificial porcelain, typically containing ground glass and fired at a comparatively low temperature.

**soft pedal** ● n. a pedal on a piano that can be pressed to soften the tone. ● v. (**soft-pedal**) **1** Music play with the soft pedal down. **2** play down the unpleasant aspects of.

**soft roe** ● n. see **ROE**[1].

**soft sell** ● n. subtly persuasive selling. ● v. (**soft-sell**) sell by such a method.

**softshell clam** ● n. see **CLAM**.

**soft-shoe** ● n. a tap dance performed in soft-soled shoes. ● v. **1** perform such a dance. **2** move quietly and carefully so as not to be noticed.

**soft shoulder** ● n. chiefly N. Amer. an unmetalled strip of land at the side of a road.

**soft soap** ● n. **1** a semi-fluid soap, especially one made with potassium rather than sodium salts. **2** informal persuasive flattery. ● v. (**soft-soap**) informal use flattery to persuade or cajole.

**soft sugar** ● n. Brit. granulated or powdered sugar.

**soft tack** ● n. archaic bread or other nourishing food, especially as rations for sailors or soldiers.

**soft target** ● n. a relatively vulnerable person or thing.

**soft-top** ● n. a motor vehicle with a roof that can be folded back.

**software** ● n. programs and other operating information used by a computer. Compare with **HARDWARE**.

**softwood** ● n. **1** the wood from a conifer as distinguished from that of broadleaved trees. **2** (in gardening) young pliable growth on shrubs or bushes from which cuttings can be taken.

**softy** ● n. variant spelling of **SOFTIE**.

**soggy** ● adj. (**-ier, -iest**) very wet and soft.
– DERIVATIVES **soggily** adv. **sogginess** n.
– ORIGIN C18: from dial. *sog* 'a swamp' + **-Y**[1].

**soh** /səʊ/ (also **so** or **sol**) ● n. Music (in tonic sol-fa) the fifth note of a major scale. ➤ the note G in the fixed-doh system.
– ORIGIN ME *sol*: representing (as an arbitrary name for the note) the first syllable of *solve*, taken from a Latin hymn.

**SOHO** ● abbrev. (with reference to marketing electronic products) small office, home office.

**soi-disant** /ˌswɑːdiːˈzɒ̃/ ● adj. self-styled: *a soi-disant novelist.*
– ORIGIN Fr., from *soi* 'oneself' + *disant* 'saying'.

**soigné** /ˈswʌnjeɪ/ ● adj. (fem. **soignée** pronunc. same) elegant and well groomed.
– ORIGIN past part. of Fr. *soigner* 'take care of'.

**soil**[1] ● n. **1** the upper layer of earth in which plants grow, a black or dark brown material typically consisting of organic remains, clay, and rock particles. **2** the territory of a particular nation.
– DERIVATIVES **soil-less** adj.
– ORIGIN ME: from Anglo-Norman Fr., perh. representing L. *solium* 'seat', by assoc. with *solum* 'ground'.

**soil**[2] ● v. **1** make dirty. ➤ make dirty by defecating in or on. **2** bring discredit to. ● n. **1** waste matter, especially sewage. **2** archaic a stain.
– ORIGIN ME (as v.): from OFr. *soiller*, based on L. *sucula*, dimin. of *sus* 'pig'.

**soil**[3] ● v. rare feed (cattle) on fresh-cut green fodder (originally for purging them).
– ORIGIN C17: perh. from **SOIL**[2].

**soil mechanics** ● pl. n. [usu. treated as sing.] the study of the properties and behaviour of soil as they affect civil engineering.

**soil pipe** ● n. a sewage or waste water pipe.

**soil science** ● n. the branch of science concerned with the formation, nature, ecology, and classification of soil.

**soil stack** ● n. a pipe which takes the waste water from the upstairs plumbing system of a building.

**soirée** /ˈswɑːreɪ/ ● n. an evening party or gathering, typically in a private house, for conversation or music.
– ORIGIN Fr., from *soir* 'evening'.

**soixante-neuf** /ˌswasɒntˈnəːf/ ● n. informal sexual activity between two people involving mutual oral stimulation of the genitals.
– ORIGIN Fr., lit. 'sixty-nine', from the position of the couple.

**sojourn** /ˈsɒdʒ(ə)n, -dʒəːn/ formal ● n. a temporary stay. ● v. stay temporarily.
– DERIVATIVES **sojourner** n.
– ORIGIN ME: from OFr. *sojourner*, based on L. *sub-* 'under' + late L. *diurnum* 'day'.

**sokaiya** /ˈsəʊkʌɪjə/ ● n. (pl. same) a shareholder in a Japanese company who tries to extort money by threatening to cause trouble at a shareholders' meeting.
– ORIGIN Japanese, from *sōkai* 'general meeting' + *-ya* 'dealer'.

**soke** ● n. Brit. historical a right of local jurisdiction. ➤ a minor administrative district.
– ORIGIN OE, back-form. from obs. *soken* 'habitual visiting of a place'.

**sol**[1] /sɒl/ ● n. variant of **SOH**.

**sol**[2] /sɒl/ ● n. Chemistry a fluid suspension of a colloidal solid in a liquid.
– ORIGIN C19: abbrev. of **SOLUTION**.

**sol**[3] /sɒl/ (also **nuevo sol**) ● n. (pl. **soles** /ˈsɒlɛz, ˈsəʊlɛz/) the basic monetary unit of Peru, equal to 100 cents.
– ORIGIN Sp., lit. 'sun'.

**-sol** ● comb. form in nouns denoting different kinds and states of soil: *histosol.*
– ORIGIN from L. *solum* 'soil'.

**sola**[1] /ˈsəʊlə/ ● n. an Indian swamp plant of the pea family, with stems that yield the pith used to make sola topis. [*Aeschynomene indica.*]
– ORIGIN C19: from Bengali *solā*, Hindi *śolā*.

**sola**[2] ● n. feminine form of **SOLUS**.

**solace** /'sɒlɪs/ ● **n.** comfort or consolation in time of distress. ● **v.** give solace to.
– ORIGIN ME: from OFr. *solas* (n.), *solacier* (v.), based on L. *solari* 'to console'.

**solanaceous** /,sɒlə'neɪʃəs/ ● **adj.** Botany relating to or denoting plants of the nightshade family (Solanaceae).
– ORIGIN C19: from mod. L. *Solanaceae* (pl.), based on L. *solanum* 'nightshade', + **-OUS**.

**solanine** /'sɒləni:n/ ● **n.** Chemistry a poisonous compound present in green potatoes and related plants.
– ORIGIN C19: from Fr., from the genus name *Solanum* + **-INE**[4].

**solar**[1] /'səʊlə/ ● **adj.** of, relating to, or determined by the sun or its rays.
– ORIGIN ME: from L. *solaris*, from *sol* 'sun'.

**solar**[2] /'sɒlə, 'səʊlə/ ● **n.** Brit. an upper chamber in a medieval house.
– ORIGIN ME: from Anglo-Norman Fr. *soler*, from L. *solarium* 'gallery, terrace'.

**solar battery** (also **solar cell**) ● **n.** a device converting solar radiation into electricity.

**solar constant** ● **n.** Physics the rate at which energy reaches the earth's surface from the sun (equal to 1,388 watts per square metre).

**solar day** ● **n.** the time between successive meridian transits of the sun at a particular place.

**solar eclipse** ● **n.** an eclipse in which the sun is obscured by the moon.

**solar energy** ● **n.** radiant energy emitted by the sun. ➤ solar power.

**solar flare** ● **n.** Astronomy a brief eruption of intense high-energy radiation from the sun's surface.

**solarium** /sə'lɛ:rɪəm/ ● **n.** (pl. **solariums** or **solaria** /-rɪə/) **1** a room equipped with sunlamps or sunbeds. **2** a room with extensive areas of glass to admit sunlight.
– ORIGIN C19: from L., lit. 'sundial, place for sunning oneself', from L. *sol* 'sun'.

**solarize** (also **-ise**) ● **v.** Photography change the relative darkness of (a part of an image) by overexposure to light.
– DERIVATIVES **solarization** n.

**solar panel** ● **n.** a panel designed to absorb the sun's rays as a source of energy for generating electricity or heating.

**solar plexus** ● **n.** a complex of ganglia and radiating nerves of the sympathetic system at the pit of the stomach.

**solar power** ● **n.** power obtained by harnessing the energy of the sun's rays.

**solar system** ● **n.** the sun together with the planets, asteroids, comets, etc. in orbit around it.

**solar wind** ● **n.** the continuous flow of charged particles from the sun which permeates the solar system.

**solar year** ● **n.** the time between successive spring or autumn equinoxes, or winter or summer solstices (365 days, 5 hours, 48 minutes, and 46 seconds).

**SOLAS** /'səʊləs/ ● **n.** the provisions made during a series of international conventions governing maritime safety.
– ORIGIN 1960s: acronym from *safety of life at sea*.

**solatium** /sə'leɪʃɪəm/ ● **n.** (pl. **solatia** /-ʃɪə/) formal a thing given as a compensation or consolation.
– ORIGIN C19: from L., lit. 'solace'.

**sola topi** ● **n.** an Indian sun hat made from the pith of the sola plant.

**sold** past and past participle of **SELL**.

**soldanella** /,sɒldə'nɛlə/ ● **n.** a dwarf alpine plant with bell-shaped flowers that have fringed petals and often appear in snow. [Genus *Soldanella*.]
– ORIGIN mod. L., from Ital., of unknown ultimate origin.

**solder** /'səʊldə, 'sɒldə/ ● **n.** a low-melting alloy, especially one based on lead and tin, used for joining less fusible metals. ● **v.** join with solder.
– DERIVATIVES **solderable** adj. **solderer** n.
– ORIGIN ME: from OFr. *soudure*, from the verb *souder*, from L. *solidare* 'fasten together', from *solidus* 'solid'.

**soldering iron** ● **n.** an electrical tool for melting and applying solder.

**soldi** plural form of **SOLDO**.

**soldier** ● **n.** **1** a person who serves in an army. ➤ (also **common soldier** or **private soldier**) a private in an army. **2** Entomology a wingless caste of ant or termite with a large modified head and jaws, involved chiefly in defence. **3** Brit. informal a strip of bread or toast, dipped into a soft-boiled egg. **4** an upright brick, timber, or other building element. ● **v.** **1** serve as a soldier. **2** (**soldier on**) informal persevere.
– DERIVATIVES **soldierly** adj. **soldiership** n. (archaic).
– ORIGIN ME: from OFr. *soldier*, from *soulde* '(soldier's) pay', from L. *solidus* (see **SOLIDUS**).

**soldier beetle** ● **n.** an elongated flying beetle with soft downy wing cases. [Family Cantharidae.]

**soldier of Christ** ● **n.** an active or proselytizing Christian.

**soldier of fortune** ● **n.** a mercenary.

**soldiery** ● **n.** (pl. **-ies**) **1** soldiers collectively. **2** military training or knowledge.

**soldo** /'sɒldəʊ/ ● **n.** (pl. **soldi** /'sɒldi/) a former Italian coin and monetary unit worth the twentieth part of a lira.
– ORIGIN Ital., from L. *solidus* (see **SOLIDUS**).

**sole**[1] ● **n.** **1** the underside of a person's foot. ➤ the section forming the underside of a piece of footwear. **2** the underside of a tool or implement, e.g. a plane or the head of a golf club. **3** the floor of a ship's cabin or cockpit. ● **v.** (usu. **be soled**) put a new sole on (a shoe).
– DERIVATIVES **-soled** adj.
– ORIGIN ME: from OFr., from L. *solea* 'sandal, sill', from *solum* 'bottom, pavement, sole'.

**sole**[2] ● **n.** an edible marine flatfish. [Several species in the families Soleidae, Pleuronectidae, and Bothidae.]
– ORIGIN ME: from OFr., from Provençal *sola*, from L. *solea* (see **SOLE**[1]), named from its shape.

**sole**[3] ● **adj.** **1** one and only. ➤ belonging or restricted to one person or group. **2** archaic (especially of a woman) unmarried. ➤ alone.
– DERIVATIVES **solely** adv.
– ORIGIN ME: from OFr. *soule*, from L. *sola*, fem. of *solus* 'alone'.

**solecism** /'sɒlɪsɪz(ə)m/ ● **n.** a grammatical mistake. ➤ a piece of bad manners or incorrect behaviour.
– DERIVATIVES **solecistic** /-'sɪstɪk/ adj.
– ORIGIN C16: from Fr. *solécisme*, or via L. from Gk *soloikismos*, from *soloikos* 'speaking incorrectly'.

**solemn** ● **adj.** **1** formal and dignified: *a solemn procession*. **2** not cheerful; serious. ➤ deeply sincere.
– DERIVATIVES **solemnly** adv. **solemnness** n.
– ORIGIN ME (in the sense 'associated with religious rites'): from OFr. *solemne*, from L. *sollemnis* 'customary, celebrated at a fixed date', from *sollus* 'entire'.

**solemnity** /sə'lɛmnɪti/ ● **n.** (pl. **-ies**) **1** the state or quality of being solemn. **2** a solemn rite or ceremony.

**solemnize** /'sɒləmnʌɪz/ (also **-ise**) ● **v.** duly perform (a ceremony, especially that of marriage). ➤ mark with a formal ceremony.
– DERIVATIVES **solemnization** n.

**Solemn Mass** ● **n.** another term for **HIGH MASS**.

**solenoid** /'sɒlənɔɪd, 'səʊl-/ ● **n.** a cylindrical coil of wire acting as a magnet when carrying electric current.
– DERIVATIVES **solenoidal** adj.
– ORIGIN C19: from Fr. *solénoïde*, from Gk *sōlēn* 'channel, pipe'.

**soleplate** ● **n.** **1** a metal plate forming the base of an electric iron, machine saw, or other machine. **2** a horizontal timber at the base of a wall frame.

**soleus** /sə(ʊ)'li:əs/ ● **n.** Anatomy a broad muscle in the lower calf which flexes the foot to point the toes downwards.
– ORIGIN C17: mod. L., from L. *solea* 'sole'.

**sol-fa** /'sɒlfɑ:/ ● **n.** short for **TONIC SOL-FA**. ● **v.** (**sol-fas**, **sol-faed**, **sol-faing**) sing using the sol-fa syllables.

**solfatara** /,sɒlfə'tɑ:rə/ ● **n.** Geology a volcanic crater containing fumaroles.
– ORIGIN C18: from the name of a volcano near Naples, from Ital. *solfo* 'sulphur'.

**solfeggio** /sɒlˈfɛdʒɪəʊ/ ● **n.** (pl. **solfeggi** /-dʒi/) Music **1** an exercise in singing using sol-fa syllables. **2** solmization.
– ORIGIN from Ital.

**soli** plural form of **SOLO**.

**solicit** ● **v.** (**solicited**, **soliciting**) **1** ask for or try to obtain (something) from someone. ➤ask for something from. **2** accost someone and offer one's or someone else's services as a prostitute.
– DERIVATIVES **solicitation** n.
– ORIGIN ME: from OFr. *solliciter*, from L. *sollicitare* 'agitate', from *sollicitus* 'anxious', from *sollus* 'entire' + *citus* (past part. of *ciere* 'set in motion').

**solicitor** ● **n.** **1** Brit. a member of the legal profession qualified to deal with conveyancing, draw up wills, advise clients and instruct barristers, and represent clients in lower courts. Compare with **BARRISTER**. ➤N. Amer. the chief law officer of a city, town, or government department. **2** N. Amer. a canvasser.

**Solicitor General** ● **n.** (pl. **Solicitors General**) (in the UK) the Crown law officer below the Attorney General or (in Scotland) below the Lord Advocate. ➤(in the US) the law officer below the Attorney General.

**solicitous** ● **adj.** showing interest or concern. ➤archaic eager or anxious to do something.
– DERIVATIVES **solicitously** adv. **solicitousness** n.
– ORIGIN C16: from L. *sollicitus* (see **SOLICIT**) + **-OUS**.

**solicitude** ● **n.** care or concern.
– ORIGIN ME: from OFr. *sollicitude*, from L. *sollicitudo*, from *sollicitus* (see **SOLICIT**).

**solid** ● **adj.** (**-er**, **-est**) **1** firm and stable in shape: *solid fuel*. ➤strongly built or made. **2** Geometry three-dimensional. ➤relating to three-dimensional objects. **3** not hollow or having spaces or gaps. ➤consisting of the same substance throughout. ➤(of time) continuous. **4** dependable; reliable. ➤sound but without special qualities. **5** (**solid with**) US informal on good terms with. **6** Austral. informal severe; unfair. ● **n.** **1** a solid substance or object. ➤(**solids**) food that is not liquid. **2** Geometry a three-dimensional body or geometric figure.
– DERIVATIVES **solidity** n. **solidly** adv. **solidness** n.
– ORIGIN ME: from L. *solidus*; rel. to *salvus* 'safe' and *sollus* 'entire'.

**solid angle** ● **n.** a three-dimensional angle, such as that formed by the apex of a cone.

**solidarity** ● **n.** unity or agreement of feeling or action, especially among individuals with a common interest.
– ORIGIN C19: from Fr. *solidarité*, from *solidaire* 'solidary'.

**solidary** ● **adj.** characterized by solidarity.
– ORIGIN C19: from Fr. *solidaire*, from *solide* 'solid'.

**solid-drawn** ● **adj.** (of a tube) pressed or drawn out from a solid bar of metal.

**solidi** plural form of **SOLIDUS**.

**solidify** ● **v.** (**-ies**, **-ied**) make or become hard or solid.
– DERIVATIVES **solidification** n. **solidifier** n.

**solid solution** ● **n.** Chemistry a solid mixture containing a minor component uniformly distributed within the crystal lattice of the major component.

**solid state** ● **n.** the state of matter in which materials are not fluid but retain their boundaries without support. ● **adj.** (**solid-state**) making use of the electronic properties of solid semiconductors (as opposed to valves).

**solidus** /ˈsɒlɪdəs/ ● **n.** (pl. **solidi** /-dʌɪ/) **1** chiefly Brit. another term for **SLASH** (in sense 3). **2** Chemistry a curve in a graph of the temperature and composition of a mixture, below which the substance is entirely solid. **3** historical a gold coin of the later Roman Empire.
– ORIGIN L., lit. 'solid'; sense 3 is from L. *solidus (nummus)*.

**solifluction** /ˌsɒlɪˈflʌkʃ(ə)n, ˌsəʊlɪ-/ ● **n.** Geology the gradual movement of wet soil down a slope.
– ORIGIN C20: from L. *solum* 'soil' + *fluctio(n-)* 'flowing', from *fluere* 'to flow'.

**soliloquy** /səˈlɪləkwi/ ● **n.** (pl. **-ies**) an act of speaking one's thoughts aloud when alone or regardless of hearers, especially by a character in a play.
– DERIVATIVES **soliloquist** n. **soliloquize** (also **-ise**) v.
– ORIGIN ME: from late L. *soliloquium*, from L. *solus* 'alone' + *loqui* 'speak'.

**solipsism** /ˈsɒlɪpsɪz(ə)m/ ● **n.** the view that the self is all that can be known to exist.
– DERIVATIVES **solipsist** n. **solipsistic** adj. **solipsistically** adv.
– ORIGIN C19: from L. *solus* 'alone' + *ipse* 'self' + **-ISM**.

**solitaire** /ˈsɒlɪtɛː, ˌsɒlɪˈtɛː/ ● **n.** **1** a game for one player played by removing pegs from a board one at a time by jumping others over them from adjacent holes, the object being to be left with only one peg. **2** the card game patience. **3** a single diamond or other gem in a piece of jewellery. ➤a ring with a single gem. **4** an extinct flightless bird related to the dodo, formerly inhabiting two Indian Ocean islands. [*Pezophaps solitaria* and *Ornithaptera solitaria*.] **5** a mainly grey American songbird of the thrush family. [Genus *Myadestes*: several species.]
– ORIGIN C18: from Fr., from L. *solitarius* (see **SOLITARY**).

**solitary** ● **adj.** **1** done or existing alone. ➤(of a bee, wasp, etc.) not social or colonial. **2** secluded or isolated. **3** [often with neg.] single; only. **4** (of a flower or other part) borne singly. ● **n.** (pl. **-ies**) **1** a recluse or hermit. **2** informal solitary confinement.
– DERIVATIVES **solitarily** adv. **solitariness** n.
– ORIGIN ME: from L. *solitarius*, from *solus* 'alone'.

**solitary confinement** ● **n.** the isolation of a prisoner in a separate cell as a punishment.

**solitary wave** ● **n.** Physics a long-lived travelling wave which is neither preceded nor followed by another such disturbance, especially a soliton.

**soliton** /ˈsɒlɪtɒn/ ● **n.** Physics a quantum propagated in the manner of a solitary wave.
– ORIGIN 1960s: from **SOLITARY** + **-ON**.

**solitude** ● **n.** the state of being alone. ➤a lonely or uninhabited place.
– ORIGIN ME: from OFr., or from L. *solitudo*, from *solus* 'alone'.

**solmization** /ˌsɒlmɪˈzeɪʃ(ə)n/ (also **-isation**) ● **n.** Music a system of associating each note of a scale with a particular syllable (typically the sequence doh, ray, me, fah, so, la, te), especially to teach singing.
– DERIVATIVES **solmizate** v.
– ORIGIN C18: from Fr. *solmisation*, based on *sol* 'soh' + *mi* (see **ME**[2]).

**solo** ● **n.** (pl. **-os**) **1** (pl. **solos** or **soli**) a piece of music, song, or dance for one performer. **2** an unaccompanied flight by a pilot. **3** (also **solo whist**) a card game resembling whist in which the players make bids and the highest bidder plays against the others. ➤a bid by which a player undertakes to win five tricks in this game. **4** a motorbike without a sidecar. ● **adj.** & **adv.** for or done by one person. ● **v.** (**-oes**, **-oed**) **1** perform a solo. **2** fly an aircraft unaccompanied.
– ORIGIN C17: from Ital., from L. *solus* 'alone'.

**soloist** ● **n.** a performer of a solo.

**Solomon** /ˈsɒləmən/ ● **n.** a very wise person.
– DERIVATIVES **Solomonic** /sɒləˈmɒnɪk/ adj.
– ORIGIN the name of a king of ancient Israel *c.*970–*c.*930 BC, famed for his wisdom.

**Solomon Gundy** ● **n.** West Indian and Canadian term for **SALMAGUNDI**.

**Solomon Islander** ● **n.** a native or inhabitant of the Solomon Islands in the SW Pacific.

**Solomon's seal** ● **n.** **1** a figure like the Star of David. **2** a plant with arching stems bearing a double row of broad leaves and drooping green and white flowers. [Genus *Polygonatum*: many species.]

**solo stop** ● **n.** an organ stop suitable for imitating a solo performance on another instrument.

**solo whist** ● **n.** see **SOLO** (sense 3).

**solstice** /ˈsɒlstɪs/ ● **n.** each of the two times in the year, respectively at midsummer and midwinter, when the sun reaches its highest or lowest point in the sky at noon, marked by the longest and shortest days.
– DERIVATIVES **solstitial** adj.
– ORIGIN ME: from OFr., from L. *solstitium*, from *sol* 'sun' + *stit-*, *sistere* 'stop, be stationary'.

**solubilize** /ˈsɒljʊbɪlʌɪz/ (also **-ise**) ● **v.** technical make soluble or more soluble.

– DERIVATIVES **solubilization** n.

**soluble** • adj. **1** (of a substance) able to be dissolved, especially in water. **2** able to be solved.

– DERIVATIVES **solubility** n.

– ORIGIN ME: from OFr., from late L. *solubilis*, from *solvere* (see **SOLVE**).

**solunar** /sɒˈluːnə/ • adj. of or relating to the combined influence or conjunction of the sun and moon.

– ORIGIN C18: from L. *sol* 'sun' + **LUNAR**.

**solus** /ˈsəʊləs/ • adj. (fem. **sola** /-lə/) alone (used especially as a stage direction).

– ORIGIN from L.

**solute** /ˈsɒljuːt, sɒˈljuːt/ • n. the minor component in a solution, dissolved in the solvent.

– ORIGIN C19: from L. *solutum*, neut. of *solutus* 'loosened', past part. of *solvere*.

**solution** • n. **1** a means of solving a problem. ➤ the correct answer to a puzzle. **2** a liquid mixture in which the minor component (the solute) is uniformly distributed within the major component (the solvent). ➤ the process or state of being dissolved. **3** archaic dissolution.

– ORIGIN ME: from OFr., from L. *solutio(n-)*, from *solvere* (see **SOLVE**).

**Solutrean** /səˈluːtrɪən/ • adj. Archaeology relating to or denoting an Upper Palaeolithic culture of central and SW France and parts of Iberia, dated to about 21,000–18,000 years ago.

– ORIGIN C19: from *Solutré* in eastern France, where objects from this culture were found, + **-AN**.

**solvate** Chemistry • v. /sɒlˈveɪt/ (of a solvent) enter into reversible chemical combination with (a solute). • n. /ˈsɒlveɪt/ a complex formed by solvation.

– DERIVATIVES **solvation** n.

– ORIGIN C20: formed irregularly from **SOLVE** + **-ATE**[1].

**solve** • v. find an answer to, explanation for, or way of dealing with (a problem or mystery).

– DERIVATIVES **solvable** adj. **solver** n.

– ORIGIN ME: from L. *solvere* 'loosen, unfasten'.

**solvent** • adj. **1** having assets in excess of liabilities. **2** able to dissolve other substances. • n. **1** the liquid in which a solute is dissolved to form a solution. ➤ a liquid used for dissolving other substances. **2** something that weakens or dispels a particular attitude or situation.

– DERIVATIVES **solvency** n.

– ORIGIN C17: from L. *solvent-*, *solvere* 'loose, unfasten'.

**solvent abuse** • n. the use of certain volatile organic solvents as intoxicants by inhalation, e.g. glue-sniffing.

**Som.** • abbrev. Somerset.

**som** /səʊm/ • n. (pl. same) the basic monetary unit of Kyrgyzstan, equal to 100 tiyin.

**soma**[1] /ˈsəʊmə/ • n. **1** Biology the parts of an organism other than the reproductive cells. **2** the body as distinct from the soul, mind, or psyche.

– ORIGIN C19: from Gk *sōma* 'body'.

**soma**[2] /ˈsəʊmə/ • n. Hinduism an intoxicating drink prepared from a plant and used in Vedic ritual.

– ORIGIN from Sanskrit *sōma*.

**somaesthetic** /ˌsəʊmiːsˈθɛtɪk/ (US **somesthetic**) • adj. another term for **SOMATOSENSORY**.

– ORIGIN C19: from Gk *sōma* 'body' + **AESTHETIC**.

**Somali** /səˈmɑːli/ • n. (pl. same or **Somalis**) **1** a member of a mainly Muslim people of Somalia. **2** the Cushitic language of this people, also spoken in Djibouti and parts of Kenya and Ethiopia. **3** a native or national of Somalia. • adj. of or relating to Somalia, the Somalis, or their language.

– DERIVATIVES **Somalian** adj. & n.

– ORIGIN the name in Somali.

**soman** /ˈsəʊmən/ • n. a lethal organophosphorus nerve gas, developed during the Second World War.

– ORIGIN 1950s: from Ger., of unknown origin.

**somatic** /səˈmatɪk/ • adj. of or relating to the body, especially as distinct from the mind.

– DERIVATIVES **somatically** adv.

– ORIGIN C18: from Gk *sōmatikos*, from *sōma* 'body'.

**somatic cell** • n. Biology any cell of an organism other than the reproductive cells.

**somatization** /ˌsəʊmətʌɪˈzeɪʃ(ə)n/ (also **-isation**) • n. Psychiatry the production of recurrent and multiple medical symptoms with no discernible organic cause.

**somato-** • comb. form of or relating to the human or animal body: *somatotype*.

– ORIGIN from Gk *sōma*, *sōmat-* 'body'.

**somatosensory** • adj. Physiology relating to or denoting a sensation which can occur anywhere in the body, in contrast to one localized at a sense organ.

**somatostatin** /ˌsəʊmətə(ʊ)ˈstatɪn/ • n. Biochemistry a hormone which inhibits gastric secretion and somatotrophin release.

**somatotrophin** /ˌsəʊmətə(ʊ)ˈtrəʊfɪn/ • n. Biochemistry a growth hormone secreted by the anterior pituitary gland.

**somatotype** • n. a category to which people are assigned according to their bodily physique (usually endomorphic, mesomorphic, or ectomorphic).

– DERIVATIVES **somatotyping** n.

– ORIGIN 1940s: coined by W. H. Sheldon in *Varieties of Human Physique*.

**sombre** (US also **somber**) • adj. **1** dark or dull. **2** oppressively solemn or sober.

– DERIVATIVES **sombrely** adv. **sombreness** n.

– ORIGIN C18: from Fr., based on L. *sub* 'under' + *umbra* 'shade'.

**sombrero** /sɒmˈbrɛːrəʊ/ • n. (pl. **-os**) a broad-brimmed felt or straw hat, typically worn in Mexico and the southwestern US.

– ORIGIN from Sp.

**some** • det. **1** an unspecified amount or number of. **2** denoting an unknown or unspecified person or thing. **3** (used with a number) approximately. **4** a considerable amount or number of. **5** at least a small amount or number of. **6** expressing admiration: *that was some goal*. ➤ used ironically to express disapproval or disbelief. • pron. **1** an unspecified number or amount of people or things. **2** at least a small number or amount of people or things. • adv. informal, chiefly N. Amer. to some extent.

– PHRASES **and then some** informal and plenty more than that.

– ORIGIN OE *sum*, of Gmc origin.

**-some**[1] • suffix forming adjectives meaning: **1** productive of: *loathsome*. **2** characterized by being: *wholesome*. ➤ apt to: *tiresome*.

– ORIGIN OE *-sum*.

**-some**[2] • suffix (forming nouns) denoting a group of a specified number: *foursome*.

– ORIGIN OE *sum* 'some'.

**-some**[3] • comb. form denoting a portion of a body, especially a particle of a cell: *chromosome*.

– ORIGIN from Gk *sōma* 'body'.

**somebody** • pron. someone.

**some day** (also **someday**) • adv. at some time in the future.

**somehow** • adv. in some way. ➤ for an unknown or unspecified reason.

**someone** • pron. **1** an unknown or unspecified person. **2** a person of importance or authority.

**someplace** • adv. & pron. informal, chiefly N. Amer. somewhere.

**somersault** /ˈsʌməsɒlt, -sɔːlt/ • n. **1** an acrobatic movement in which a person turns head over heels in the air or on the ground and finishes on their feet. **2** a dramatic upset or reversal of policy or opinion. • v. perform a somersault.

– ORIGIN C16 (as n.): from OFr. *sombresault*, from Provençal *sobresaut*, from *sobre* 'above' + *saut* 'leap'.

**somesthetic** • adj. US spelling of **SOMAESTHETIC**.

**something** • pron. **1** an unspecified or unknown thing. **2** an unspecified or unknown amount or degree. • adv. **1** informal used for emphasis with a following adjective: *my back hurts something terrible*. **2** archaic or dialect somewhat.

– PHRASES **quite** (or **really**) **something** informal something impressive or notable. **something else** informal an exceptional person or thing. **something of** to some degree. **thirty-something** (**forty-something**, etc.) informal an unspecified age between thirty and forty (forty and fifty, etc.).

**sometime** ● **adv.** at some unspecified or unknown time. ➤ archaic formerly. ● **adj. 1** former. **2** N. Amer. occasional.

**sometimes** ● **adv.** occasionally.

**someway** (also **someways**) ● **adv.** informal, chiefly N. Amer. by some means.

**somewhat** ● **adv.** to some extent.
– PHRASES **somewhat of** something of.

**somewhen** ● **adv.** informal at some time.

**somewhere** ● **adv. 1** in or to some place. **2** used to indicate an approximate amount. ● **pron.** some unspecified place.
– PHRASES **get somewhere** informal make progress; achieve success.

**somite** /ˈsəʊmʌɪt/ ● **n.** Zoology each of a number of body segments containing the same internal structures, e.g. in an earthworm.
– ORIGIN C19: from Gk *sōma* 'body' + **-ITE**[1].

**sommelier** /ˈsɒm(ə)ljeɪ, səˈmɛljeɪ/ ● **n.** a waiter who serves wine.
– ORIGIN C19: Fr., lit. 'butler'.

**sommer** /ˈsɒmə/ ● **adv.** S. African informal just; simply.
– ORIGIN from Afrik.

**somnambulism** /sɒmˈnambjʊlɪz(ə)m/ ● **n.** sleepwalking.
– DERIVATIVES **somnambulant** adj. **somnambulantly** adv. **somnambulist** n. **somnambulistic** adj. **somnambulistically** adv.
– ORIGIN C18: from Fr. *somnambulisme*, from L. *somnus* 'sleep' + *ambulare* 'to walk'.

**somniferous** /sɒmˈnɪf(ə)rəs/ ● **adj.** inducing sleep.
– ORIGIN C17: from L. *somnifer* (from *somnium* 'dream') + **-OUS**.

**somnolent** /ˈsɒmnəl(ə)nt/ ● **adj.** sleepy; drowsy. ➤ inducing drowsiness.
– DERIVATIVES **somnolence** n. **somnolency** n. **somnolently** adv.
– ORIGIN ME: from OFr. *sompnolent* or L. *somnolentus*, from *somnus* 'sleep'.

**son** ● **n. 1** a boy or man in relation to his parents. ➤ a male descendant. ➤ a man regarded as the product of a particular influence or environment. **2** (**the Son**) (in Christian belief) the second person of the Trinity; Christ. **3** (also **my son**) used as a form of address for a boy or younger man.
– PHRASES **son of a bitch** (pl. **sons of bitches**) informal used as a general term of abuse. **son of a gun** (pl. **sons of guns**) informal a jocular way of addressing or referring to someone. [with ref. to the guns carried on ships: said to have been applied orig. to babies born at sea to women allowed to accompany their husbands.]
– DERIVATIVES **sonship** n.
– ORIGIN OE *sunu*, of Gmc origin.

**sonar** /ˈsəʊnɑː/ ● **n. 1** a system for the detection of objects under water based on the emission and measured reflection of sound pulses. ➤ an apparatus used for this. **2** the method of echolocation used in air or water by animals such as whales and bats.
– ORIGIN 1940s: from *so(und) na(vigation and) r(anging)*, on the pattern of *radar*.

**sonata** /səˈnɑːtə/ ● **n.** a classical composition for an instrumental soloist, often with a piano accompaniment.
– ORIGIN C17: Ital., lit. 'sounded' (orig. as distinct from 'sung'), fem. past part. of *sonare*.

**sonata form** ● **n.** a type of composition in three sections (exposition, development, and recapitulation) in which two themes or subjects are explored according to set key relationships.

**sonatina** /ˌsɒnəˈtiːnə/ ● **n.** a simple or short sonata.
– ORIGIN C18: Ital., dimin. of **SONATA**.

**sonde** /sɒnd/ ● **n.** a probe that transmits information about its surroundings underground or under water.
– ORIGIN C20: from Fr., lit. 'sounding (line)'.

**sone** /səʊn/ ● **n.** a unit of subjective loudness, equal to 40 phons.
– ORIGIN 1930s: from L. *sonus* 'a sound'.

**son et lumière** /ˌsɒn eɪ ˈluːmjɛː, French sɔ̃ e lymjɛʀ/ ● **n.** an entertainment held by night at a historic monument or building, telling its history by the use of lighting effects and recorded sound.
– ORIGIN Fr., lit. 'sound and light'.

**song** ● **n. 1** a short poem or other set of words set to music. ➤ singing or vocal music. ➤ a musical composition suggestive of a song. **2** the musical phrases uttered by some birds, whales, and insects, used chiefly for territorial defence or for attracting mates. **3** a poem, especially one in rhymed stanzas. ➤ archaic poetry.
– PHRASES **for a song** informal very cheaply. **on song** Brit. informal performing well. **a song and dance** informal a fuss. ➤ N. Amer. a long and pointless or evasive explanation.
– ORIGIN OE *sang*, of Gmc origin; rel. to **SING**.

**songbird** ● **n.** a bird with a musical song. ➤ Ornithology any oscine bird.

**songbook** ● **n.** a collection of songs with music.

**song cycle** ● **n.** a set of related songs forming a single musical entity.

**Songhai** /sɒŋˈgʌɪ/ ● **n.** (pl. same or **Songhais**) **1** a member of a people of West Africa living mainly in Niger and Mali. **2** the Nilo-Saharan language of this people.
– ORIGIN the name in Songhai.

**songsmith** ● **n.** informal a writer of popular songs.

**song sparrow** ● **n.** a sparrow-like North American bird related to the buntings, noted for its constant and characteristic song. [*Melospiza melodia*.]

**songster** ● **n.** (fem. **songstress**) **1** a person who sings. **2** a writer of songs or verse. **3** a songbird.

**song thrush** ● **n.** a thrush with a buff spotted breast and a song in which phrases are repeated two or three times. [*Turdus philomelos*.]

**songwriter** ● **n.** a writer of songs or the music for them.
– DERIVATIVES **songwriting** n.

**sonic** ● **adj. 1** relating to or using sound waves. **2** denoting or having a speed equal to that of sound.
– DERIVATIVES **sonically** adv.
– ORIGIN 1920s: from L. *sonus* 'sound' + **-IC**.

**sonicate** /ˈsɒnɪkeɪt/ ● **v.** Biochemistry subject to fragmentation by ultrasonic vibration.
– DERIVATIVES **sonication** n.
– ORIGIN 1950s: from **SONIC** + **-ATE**[2].

**sonic barrier** ● **n.** the sound barrier.

**sonic boom** ● **n.** an explosive noise caused by the shock wave from an aircraft or other object travelling faster than the speed of sound.

**sonics** ● **pl. n.** musical sounds artificially produced or reproduced.

**son-in-law** ● **n.** (pl. **sons-in-law**) the husband of one's daughter.

**sonnet** ● **n.** a poem of fourteen lines using any of a number of formal rhyme schemes, in English typically having ten syllables per line. ● **v.** (**sonneted**, **sonneting**) archaic compose sonnets. ➤ celebrate in a sonnet.
– ORIGIN C16: from Fr., or from Ital. *sonetto*, dimin. of *suono* 'a sound'.

**sonneteer** /ˌsɒnɪˈtɪə/ ● **n.** a writer of sonnets.

**sonny** ● **n.** informal a familiar form of address to a young boy. ➤ (also **Sonny Jim**) a humorous or patronizing way of addressing a man.

**sono-** /ˈsəʊnəʊ, ˈsɒnəʊ/ ● **comb. form** of or relating to sound: *sonometer*.
– ORIGIN from L. *sonus* 'sound'.

**sonobuoy** ● **n.** a buoy detecting underwater sounds and transmitting them by radio.

**Son of Man** ● **n.** Jesus Christ.

**sonogram** ● **n. 1** a graph showing the distribution of energy at different frequencies in a sound. **2** a visual image produced from an ultrasound examination.
– DERIVATIVES **sonograph** n. **sonographic** adj. **sonography** n.

**sonoluminescence** ● **n.** Physics luminescence associated with the passage of sound waves.
– DERIVATIVES **sonoluminescent** adj.

**sonometer** /səˈnɒmɪtə/ ● **n.** another term for **MONOCHORD**.

**sonorant** /ˈsɒn(ə)r(ə)nt, səˈnɔːr(ə)nt/ ● n. Phonetics a sound produced with the vocal cord so positioned that spontaneous voicing is possible.
– ORIGIN 1930s: from **SONOROUS** + **-ANT**.

**sonorous** /ˈsɒn(ə)rəs, səˈnɔːrəs/ ● adj. **1** (of a sound) deep and full. **2** capable of producing a deep or ringing sound. **3** using imposing language.
– DERIVATIVES **sonority** n. **sonorously** adv. **sonorousness** n.
– ORIGIN C17: from L. *sonorus* (from *sonor* 'sound') + **-OUS**.

**sonsy** /ˈsɒnsi/ (also **sonsie**) ● adj. (**-ier**, **-iest**) Scottish poetic/literary attractive and healthy.
– ORIGIN C16 (also in the sense 'lucky'): from Ir. and Sc. Gaelic *sonas* 'good fortune' (from *sona* 'fortunate') + **-Y**[1].

**sook** /suːk, sʊk/ ● n. informal, chiefly Austral./NZ & Canadian **1** a cowardly or ineffectual person. **2** a hand-reared calf.
– ORIGIN C19: dial. var. of **SUCK**.

**sool** /suːl/ ● v. chiefly Austral./NZ **1** (of a dog) attack or worry (an animal). **2** urge or goad into doing something.
– DERIVATIVES **sooler** n.
– ORIGIN C19: var. of dial. *sowl* 'seize by the ears', of unknown origin.

**soon** ● adv. **1** in or after a short time. ➤early. **2** readily (used to indicate a preference).
– PHRASES **no sooner than** as soon as; at the very moment that. **sooner or later** eventually.
– DERIVATIVES **soonish** adv.
– ORIGIN OE *sōna* 'immediately', of W. Gmc origin.

**soot** ● n. a black powdery or flaky substance consisting largely of amorphous carbon, produced by the incomplete burning of organic matter. ● v. cover or clog with soot.
– ORIGIN OE *sōt*, of Gmc origin.

**sooth** /suːθ/ ● n. archaic truth.
– PHRASES **in sooth** truly.
– ORIGIN OE *sōth* (orig. as adj. 'genuine, true'), of Gmc origin.

**soothe** ● v. gently calm. ➤reduce pain or discomfort in. ➤relieve (pain).
– DERIVATIVES **soother** n. **soothing** adj. **soothingly** adv.
– ORIGIN OE *sōthian* 'verify, show to be true', from *sōth* 'true' (see **SOOTH**).

**soothsayer** ● n. a person supposed to be able to foresee the future.
– DERIVATIVES **soothsaying** n.
– ORIGIN ME (in the sense 'person who speaks the truth'): see **SOOTH**.

**sooty** ● adj. (**-ier**, **-iest**) covered with or coloured like soot.
– DERIVATIVES **sootily** adv. **sootiness** n.

**sop** ● n. **1** a thing given or done to appease or bribe someone. **2** a piece of bread dipped in gravy, soup, or sauce. ● v. (**sopped**, **sopping**) (**sop something up**) soak up liquid. ➤archaic soak.
– ORIGIN OE *soppian* 'dip (bread) in liquid', *sopp* (n.), prob. from the base of OE *sūpan* 'sup'.

**sophism** /ˈsɒfɪz(ə)m/ ● n. a fallacious argument, especially one used to deceive.
– ORIGIN ME: from OFr. *sophime*, via L. from Gk *sophisma* 'clever device', from *sophizesthai* (see **SOPHIST**).

**sophist** /ˈsɒfɪst/ ● n. **1** a paid teacher of philosophy and rhetoric in ancient Greece, associated in popular thought with moral scepticism and specious reasoning. **2** a person who uses clever but fallacious arguments.
– DERIVATIVES **sophistic** /səˈfɪstɪk/ adj. **sophistical** /səˈfɪstɪk(ə)l/ adj. **sophistically** adv.
– ORIGIN C16: via L. from Gk *sophistēs*, from *sophizesthai* 'devise, become wise', from *sophos* 'wise'.

**sophisticate** ● v. **1** cause to become discerning and aware of complex issues through education or experience. ➤develop into a more complex form. **2** archaic talk or reason in a complex and educated manner. ➤mislead or corrupt by sophistry. ● adj. archaic sophisticated. ● n. a sophisticated person.
– DERIVATIVES **sophistication** n.
– ORIGIN ME: from med. L. *sophisticatus* 'tampered with', past part. of *sophisticare*, from *sophisticus* 'sophistic'.

**sophisticated** ● adj. **1** (of a machine, system, or technique) highly complex. ➤(of a person) aware of and able to interpret complex issues. **2** showing worldly experience and knowledge of fashion and culture. ➤appealing to sophisticated people.
– DERIVATIVES **sophisticatedly** adv.

**sophistry** /ˈsɒfɪstri/ ● n. (pl. **-ies**) the use of fallacious arguments, especially to deceive. ➤a fallacious argument.

**sophomore** /ˈsɒfəmɔː/ ● n. N. Amer. a second-year university or high-school student.
– DERIVATIVES **sophomoric** adj.
– ORIGIN C17: perh. from earlier *sophumer*, from *sophum*, *sophom* (obs. vars of **SOPHISM**) + **-ER**[1].

**Sophy** /ˈsəʊfi/ ● n. (pl. **-ies**) historical a former title for the ruler of Persia, associated especially with the Safavid dynasty.
– ORIGIN from Arab. *Ṣafī-al-dīn* 'pure of religion'.

**soporific** /ˌsɒpəˈrɪfɪk/ ● adj. inducing drowsiness or sleep. ➤sleepy. ● n. a soporific drug or other agent.
– DERIVATIVES **soporifically** adv.
– ORIGIN C17: from L. *sopor* 'sleep' + **-IFIC**.

**sopping** ● adj. wet through.
– ORIGIN C19: pres. part. of **SOP**.

**soppy** ● adj. (**-ier**, **-iest**) Brit. informal **1** self-indulgently sentimental. **2** feeble.
– DERIVATIVES **soppily** adv. **soppiness** n.
– ORIGIN C19 (in the sense 'soaked with water'): from **SOP** + **-Y**[1].

**sopranino** /ˌsɒprəˈniːnəʊ/ ● n. (pl. **-os**) Music an instrument, especially a recorder or saxophone, higher than soprano.
– ORIGIN C20: Ital., dimin. of **SOPRANO**.

**soprano** /səˈprɑːnəʊ/ ● n. (pl. **-os**) **1** the highest singing voice. ➤a singer with such a voice. **2** an instrument of a high or the highest pitch in its family.
– ORIGIN C18: Ital., from *sopra* 'above', from L. *supra*.

**soprano clef** ● n. Music an obsolete clef placing middle C on the lowest line of the stave.

**soprano recorder** ● n. N. Amer. a descant recorder.

**sora** /ˈsɔːrə, ˈsəʊrə/ ● n. a small brown and grey American crake, frequenting marshes. [*Porzana carolina*.]
– ORIGIN C18: prob. from an Amer. Ind. lang.

**Sorb** /sɔːb/ ● n. a member of a Slavic people living in parts of SE Brandenburg and eastern Saxony.
– DERIVATIVES **Sorbian** n. & adj.
– ORIGIN from Ger. *Sorbe*.

**sorb** /sɔːb/ ● n. the fruit of the true service tree.
– ORIGIN C16: from Fr. *sorbe* or L. *sorbus* 'service tree', *sorbum* 'serviceberry'.

**sorbent** /ˈsɔːb(ə)nt/ ● n. Chemistry a substance which collects molecules of another substance by sorption.

**sorbet** /ˈsɔːbeɪ, -bɪt/ ● n. **1** a water ice. **2** archaic an Arabian sherbet.
– ORIGIN C16: from Fr., from Ital. *sorbetto*, from Turk. *şerbet*, based on Arab. *šariba* 'to drink'; cf. **SHERBET**.

**sorbitol** /ˈsɔːbɪtɒl/ ● n. Chemistry a sweet-tasting crystalline compound found in some fruit.
– ORIGIN C19: from **SORB** + **-ITE**[1] + **-OL**.

**sorcerer** ● n. (fem. **sorceress**) a person believed to have magic powers.
– DERIVATIVES **sorcerous** adj. **sorcery** n.
– ORIGIN ME: from *sorser* (from OFr. *sorcier*, based on L. *sors*, *sort-* 'lot') + **-ER**[1].

**sordid** ● adj. **1** involving ignoble actions and motives. **2** dirty or squalid.
– DERIVATIVES **sordidly** adv. **sordidness** n.
– ORIGIN ME: from Fr. *sordide* or L. *sordidus*, from *sordere* 'be dirty'.

**sordino** /sɔːˈdiːnəʊ/ ● n. (pl. **sordini** /-ni/) Music a mute for a musical instrument. ➤(**sordini**) (on a piano) the dampers.
– ORIGIN C16: from Ital., from *sordo* 'mute', from L. *surdus*.

**sordor** /ˈsɔːdə/ ● n. chiefly poetic/literary sordidness.
– ORIGIN C19: from **SORDID**, on the pattern of the pair *squalid*, *squalor*.

**sore** ● **adj. 1** painful or aching. ➤ suffering pain. **2** informal, chiefly N. Amer. upset and angry. **3** severe; urgent. ● **n. 1** a raw or painful place on the body. **2** a source of distress or annoyance. ● **adv.** archaic extremely; severely.
– PHRASES **sore point** an issue about which someone feels distressed or annoyed. **stand** (or **stick**) **out like a sore thumb** be quite obviously different.
– DERIVATIVES **soreness** n.
– ORIGIN OE *sār* (n. and adj.), *sāre* (adv.), of Gmc origin.

**sorehead** ● **n.** N. Amer. informal a person who is angry or easily irritated.

**sorel** /ˈsɒr(ə)l/ ● **n.** Brit. a male fallow deer in its third year.
– ORIGIN C15: var. of **SORREL**².

**sorely** ● **adv.** extremely; badly.

**sorghum** /ˈsɔːgəm/ ● **n.** a cereal which is a major source of grain and stockfeed, native to warm regions of the Old World. [*Sorghum bicolor* and related species.]
– ORIGIN C16: mod. L., from Ital. *sorgo*, perh. based on a var. of L. *syricum* 'Syrian'.

**sori** plural form of **SORUS**.

**sororal** /səˈrɔːr(ə)l/ ● **adj.** formal of or like a sister or sisters.
– ORIGIN C17: from L. *soror* 'sister' + **-AL**.

**sorority** /səˈrɒrɪti/ ● **n.** (pl. **-ies**) N. Amer. a society for female students in a university or college.
– ORIGIN C16: from med. L. *sororitas*, or from L. *soror* 'sister' (on the pattern of *fraternity*).

**sorosis** /səˈrəʊsɪs/ ● **n.** (pl. **soroses** /-siːz/) Botany a fleshy multiple fruit, e.g. a pineapple, derived from the ovaries of several flowers.
– ORIGIN C19: mod. L., from Gk *sōros* 'heap'.

**sorption** /ˈsɔːpʃ(ə)n/ ● **n.** Chemistry absorption and adsorption considered as a single process.
– ORIGIN C20: back-form. from *absorption* and *adsorption*.

**sorrel**¹ /ˈsɒr(ə)l/ ● **n.** an edible plant of the dock family with arrow-shaped leaves and an acidic flavour. [*Rumex acetosa* and other species.] ➤ used in names of other plants with acid leaves, e.g. **wood sorrel**.
– ORIGIN ME: from OFr. *sorele*, of Gmc origin; rel. to **SOUR**.

**sorrel**² /ˈsɒr(ə)l/ ● **n.** a horse with a light reddish-brown coat. ➤ a light reddish-brown colour.
– ORIGIN ME: from OFr. *sorel*, from *sor* 'yellowish', from a Gmc adj. meaning 'dry'.

**sorrow** ● **n.** a feeling of deep distress caused by loss or disappointment. ➤ a cause of sorrow. ➤ the outward expression of grief. ● **v.** feel sorrow.
– DERIVATIVES **sorrowful** adj. **sorrowfully** adv. **sorrowfulness** n.
– ORIGIN OE *sorh*, *sorg* (n.), *sorgian* (v.), of Gmc origin.

**sorry** ● **adj.** (**-ier**, **-iest**) **1** feeling distress, especially through sympathy with someone else's misfortune. ➤ (**sorry for**) filled with compassion for. **2** feeling regret or penitence. ➤ used to express apology. **3** in a poor or pitiful state. ➤ unpleasant and regrettable.
– DERIVATIVES **sorrily** adv. **sorriness** n.
– ORIGIN OE *sārig* 'pained, distressed', of W. Gmc origin, from the base of **SORE**.

**sort** ● **n. 1** a category of people or things with a common feature. ➤ informal a person with a specified nature. **2** archaic a manner or way. **3** Computing the arrangement of data in a prescribed sequence. ● **v. 1** arrange systematically in groups. ➤ separate from a mixed group. ➤ (**sort through**) look at in succession for classification or to make a selection. **2** (**sort someone/thing out**) resolve a problem or difficulty. ➤ (**sort someone out**) informal deal with a troublesome person.
– PHRASES **in some sort** to some extent. **of a sort** (or **of sorts**) of a somewhat unusual or inferior kind. **out of sorts** slightly unwell or unhappy. **sort of** informal to some extent.
– DERIVATIVES **sortable** adj. **sorter** n.
– ORIGIN ME: from OFr. *sorte*, from an alt. of L. *sors*, *sort-* 'lot, condition'.

**sorted** ● **adj.** Brit. informal **1** organized; arranged. **2** having obtained illegal drugs. **3** emotionally well balanced.

**sortie** ● **n. 1** an attack by troops coming out from a position of defence. ➤ an operational flight by a single military aircraft. **2** a short trip. ● **v.** (**sorties**, **sortied**, **sortieing**) make a sortie.
– ORIGIN C18: from Fr., fem. past part. of *sortir* 'go out'.

**sortilege** /ˈsɔːtɪlɪdʒ/ ● **n.** chiefly historical the practice of foretelling the future from a card or other item drawn at random.
– ORIGIN ME: via OFr. from med. L. *sortilegium* 'sorcery', from L. *sortilegus* 'sorcerer', from L. *sors*, *sort-* 'lot, chance' + *legere* 'choose'.

**sorting office** ● **n.** a place in which mail is sorted according to its destination.

**sorus** /ˈsɔːrəs/ ● **n.** (pl. **sori** /-rʌɪ/) Botany a cluster of spore-producing receptacles on the underside of a fern frond.
– ORIGIN C19: mod. L., from Gk *sōros* 'heap'.

**SOS** ● **n.** an international coded signal of extreme distress, used especially by ships at sea. ➤ an urgent appeal for help. ➤ Brit. a message broadcast to an untraceable person in an emergency.
– ORIGIN C20: letters chosen as being easily transmitted and recognized in Morse code; by folk etymology an abbrev. of *save our souls*.

**so-so** ● **adj.** neither very good nor very bad.

**sostenuto** /ˌsɒstəˈnuːtəʊ/ ● **adj.** Music to be played in a sustained or prolonged manner.
– ORIGIN Ital., 'sustained'.

**sot** ● **n.** a habitual drunkard. ● **v.** (**sotted**, **sotting**) archaic drink habitually.
– DERIVATIVES **sottish** adj.
– ORIGIN OE *sott* 'foolish person', from med. L. *sottus*, reinforced by OFr. *sot* 'foolish'.

**soteriology** /sə(ʊ)ˌtɪərɪˈɒlədʒi, sɒ-/ ● **n.** Theology the doctrine of salvation.
– DERIVATIVES **soteriological** adj.
– ORIGIN C19: from Gk *sōtēria* 'salvation' + **-LOGY**.

**Sothic** /ˈsəʊθɪk, ˈsɒθ-/ ● **adj.** relating to or denoting an ancient Egyptian calendric system based on the heliacal rising of Sirius.
– ORIGIN C19: from Gk *Sōthis* (from an Egyptian name of Sirius) + **-IC**.

**Sotho** /ˈsuːtuː/ ● **n.** (pl. same or **-os**) **1** a member of a group of peoples living chiefly in Botswana, Lesotho, and northern South Africa. **2** the Bantu languages spoken by these peoples.
– ORIGIN the stem of **BASOTHO** and **SESOTHO**.

**sotol** /ˈsəʊtəʊl/ ● **n.** a North American desert agave with small white flowers. [Genus *Dasylirion*: several species.] ➤ an alcoholic drink made from the sap of this plant.
– ORIGIN C19: via Amer. Sp. from Nahuatl *tzotolli*.

**sotto voce** /ˌsɒtəʊ ˈvəʊtʃeɪ/ ● **adv. & adj.** in a quiet voice.
– ORIGIN from Ital. *sotto* 'under' + *voce* 'voice'.

**sou** /suː/ ● **n.** historical a former French coin of low value. ➤ [usu. with neg.] informal a very small amount of money.
– ORIGIN Fr., orig. as *sous* (pl.), from OFr. *sout* from L. *solidus* (see **SOLIDUS**).

**soubresaut** /ˈsuːbrəsəʊ/ ● **n.** (pl. pronounced same) Ballet a straight-legged jump from both feet with the toes pointed and feet together, one behind the other.
– ORIGIN from Fr.

**soubrette** /suːˈbrɛt/ ● **n.** a pert maidservant or similar female role in a comedy.
– ORIGIN C18: Fr., from Provençal *soubreto*, fem. of *soubret* 'coy', from *sobrar*, from L. *superare* 'be above'.

**soubriquet** /ˈsuːbrɪkeɪ/ ● **n.** variant spelling of **SOBRIQUET**.

**souchong** /ˈsuːʃɒŋ/ ● **n.** a fine black variety of China tea.
– ORIGIN C18: from Chin. *siú* 'small' + *chúng* 'sort'.

**souffle** /ˈsuːf(ə)l/ ● **n.** Medicine a low murmur heard through a stethoscope.
– ORIGIN C19: from Fr., from *souffler* 'to blow', from L. *sufflare*.

**soufflé** ● **n.** a light, spongy baked dish made typically by adding flavoured egg yolks to stiffly beaten egg whites.
– ORIGIN Fr., lit. 'blown', past part. of *souffler* (see **SOUFFLE**).

**sough** /saʊ, sʌf/ ● **v.** (of the wind, sea, etc.) make a moaning, whistling, or rushing sound. ● **n.** a sound of this type.
– ORIGIN OE *swōgan*, of Gmc origin.

**sought** past and past participle of **SEEK**.

**sought after** ● **adj.** much in demand.

**souk** /su:k/ (also **suk**, **sukh**, or **suq**) ● **n.** an Arab bazaar.
– ORIGIN from Arab. *sūḳ*.

**soukous** /ˈsu:ku:s/ ● **n.** a style of African popular music with syncopated rhythms and intricate contrasting guitar melodies.
– ORIGIN perh. from Fr. *secouer* 'to shake'.

**soul** ● **n. 1** the spiritual or immaterial part of a human, regarded as immortal. ➤ one's moral or emotional nature or sense of identity. ➤ emotional or intellectual energy or intensity. **2** short for **SOUL MUSIC**. **3** a person regarded as the embodiment of some quality: *he was the soul of discretion*. ➤ an individual. ➤ a person regarded with affection or pity.
– PHRASES **lost soul** a soul that is damned. ➤ chiefly humorous a person who seems unable to cope with everyday life. **upon my soul** dated an exclamation of surprise.
– DERIVATIVES **-souled** adj.
– ORIGIN OE *sāwol, sāw(e)l*, of Gmc origin.

**soul-destroying** ● **adj.** unbearably monotonous.

**soul food** ● **n.** food traditionally associated with black people of the southern US.

**soulful** ● **adj.** expressing deep and typically sorrowful feeling.
– DERIVATIVES **soulfully** adv. **soulfulness** n.

**soulless** ● **adj. 1** lacking character and individuality. ➤ (of an activity) tedious and uninspiring. **2** lacking or suggesting a lack of human feelings.
– DERIVATIVES **soullessly** adv. **soullessness** n.

**soulmate** ● **n.** a person ideally suited to another.

**soul music** ● **n.** a kind of music incorporating elements of rhythm and blues and gospel music, popularized by American blacks.

**soul-searching** ● **n.** close examination of one's emotions and motives. ● **adj.** characterized by such examination.

**soulster** ● **n.** informal a singer of soul music.

**sound**[1] ● **n. 1** vibrations which travel through the air or another medium and are sensed by the ear. ➤ a thing that can be heard. ➤ the area within which something can be heard. **2** (also **musical sound**) sound produced by continuous and regular vibrations, as opposed to noise. **3** music, speech, and sound effects accompanying a film or broadcast. ➤ radio broadcasting as distinct from television. **4** an idea or impression conveyed by words. ● **v. 1** emit or cause to emit sound. ➤ utter. **2** convey a specified impression when heard. **3** (**sound off**) express one's opinions loudly or forcefully. **4** test (the lungs or another body cavity) by noting the sound they produce.
– DERIVATIVES **soundless** adj. **soundlessly** adv. **soundlessness** n.
– ORIGIN ME *soun*, from Anglo-Norman Fr. *soun* (n.), *suner* (v.), from L. *sonus*.

**sound**[2] ● **adj. 1** in good condition. ➤ based on reason or judgement. ➤ competent or reliable. ➤ financially secure. ➤ Brit. informal excellent. **2** (of sleep) deep and unbroken. **3** severe: *a sound thrashing*. ● **adv.** soundly.
– DERIVATIVES **soundly** adv. **soundness** n.
– ORIGIN ME: from OE *gesund*, of W. Gmc origin.

**sound**[3] ● **v. 1** ascertain (the depth of water in the sea, a lake, etc.) by means of a line or pole or using sound echoes. ➤ find the depth of water in (a ship's hold). **2** Medicine examine (the bladder or other internal cavity) with a long surgical probe. **3** (**sound someone out**) question someone discreetly or cautiously. **4** (especially of a whale) dive steeply to a great depth. ● **n.** a long surgical probe, typically with a curved, blunt end.
– DERIVATIVES **sounder** n.
– ORIGIN ME: from OFr. *sonder*, based on L. *sub-* 'below' + *unda* 'wave'.

**sound**[4] ● **n.** a narrow stretch of water forming an inlet or connecting two larger bodies of water.
– ORIGIN ME: from ON *sund* 'swimming, strait'; rel. to **SWIM**.

**soundalike** ● **n.** a person or thing sounding very like another.

**sound barrier** ● **n.** the speed of sound, regarded as presenting problems of drag, controllability, etc. for aircraft.

**sound bite** ● **n.** a short extract from a recorded interview, chosen for its pungency or aptness.

**soundboard** (also **sounding board**) ● **n.** a thin board under the strings of a piano or similar instrument to increase the sound produced.

**soundbox** ● **n.** the hollow chamber forming the body of a stringed instrument and providing resonance.

**sound card** ● **n.** a device which can be slotted into a computer to allow the use of audio components for multimedia applications.

**soundcheck** ● **n.** a test of sound equipment before a musical performance or recording.

**sound effect** ● **n.** a sound other than speech or music made artificially for use in a play, film, etc.

**sound engineer** ● **n.** a technician dealing with acoustics for a broadcast or musical performance.

**soundhole** ● **n.** a hole in the belly of a stringed instrument.

**sounding**[1] ● **n. 1** the action of sounding the depth of water. ➤ a measurement taken by sounding. ➤ the determination of any physical property at a depth in the sea or at a height in the atmosphere. **2** (**soundings**) information or evidence ascertained before taking action. **3** (**soundings**) archaic coastal waters shallow enough for the seabed to be reached with a sounding line.

**sounding**[2] ● **adj.** archaic giving forth sound. ➤ having an imposing sound but little substance.

**sounding board** ● **n. 1** a board over or behind a pulpit or stage to reflect a speaker's voice forward. **2** a soundboard. **3** a person whose reactions to ideas are used as a test of their validity or likely success. ➤ a channel through which ideas are disseminated.

**sounding line** ● **n.** a weighted line used to measure the depth of water under a boat.

**sounding rod** ● **n.** a rod used to measure the depth of water in a ship's hold.

**sound post** ● **n.** a small wooden rod wedged between the front and back surfaces of a violin or similar instrument and modifying its vibrations.

**soundproof** ● **adj.** preventing the passage of sound. ● **v.** make soundproof.

**soundscape** ● **n.** a piece of music considered in terms of its component sounds.

**sound shift** ● **n.** Linguistics a change in the pronunciation of a set of speech sounds as a language evolves.

**sound spectrograph** ● **n.** an instrument for analysing sound into its frequency components.

**sound system** ● **n.** a set of equipment for the reproduction and amplification of sound.

**soundtrack** ● **n. 1** the sound accompaniment to a film. **2** a strip on the edge of a film on which sound is recorded. ● **v.** provide (a film) with a soundtrack.

**sound wave** ● **n.** Physics a wave of compression and rarefaction, by which sound is propagated in an elastic medium such as air.

**soup** ● **n. 1** a savoury liquid dish made by boiling meat, fish, or vegetables in stock or water. **2** US informal nitroglycerine or gelignite, especially as used for safe-breaking. **3** informal the chemicals in which film is developed. ● **v.** (**soup something up**) [often as adj. **souped-up**] informal increase the power and efficiency of an engine. ➤ make something more elaborate or impressive.
– PHRASES **in the soup** informal in trouble.
– ORIGIN ME: from OFr. *soupe* 'sop, broth (poured on slices of bread)', from late L. *suppa*, of Gmc origin; the verb was perh. influenced by **SUPER-**.

**soup and fish** ● **n.** Brit. informal, dated men's evening dress.
– ORIGIN so named from the traditional first two courses of a formal dinner.

**soupçon** /ˈsu:psɒn, -sɔ̃/ ● **n.** a very small quantity.

– ORIGIN C18: Fr., from OFr. *souspeçon*, from med. L. *suspectio* (see **SUSPICION**).

**soup kitchen** • n. a place where free food is served to the homeless or destitute.

**soup plate** • n. a deep, wide-rimmed plate in which soup is served.

**soup spoon** • n. a large spoon with a round bowl, used for eating soup.

**soupy** • adj. (**-ier, -iest**) **1** having the appearance or consistency of soup. **2** informal mawkishly sentimental.
– DERIVATIVES **soupily** adv. **soupiness** n.

**sour** • adj. **1** having an acid taste like lemon or vinegar. **2** (of food, especially milk) having gone bad because of fermentation. ➤ having a rancid smell. **3** showing resentment, disappointment, or anger. **4** (of soil) deficient in lime. **5** (of petroleum or natural gas) containing a high proportion of sulphur. • n. a cocktail made by mixing a spirit with lemon or lime juice. • v. make or become sour.
– PHRASES **go** (or **turn**) **sour** become less pleasant; turn out badly. **sour grapes** an attitude in which someone affects to despise something because they cannot have it themselves. [with allusion to Aesop's fable *The Fox and the Grapes*.]
– DERIVATIVES **sourish** adj. **sourly** adv. **sourness** n.
– ORIGIN OE *sūr*, of Gmc origin.

**source** • n. **1** a place, person, or thing from which something originates. ➤ a spring or fountain head from which a river or stream issues. **2** a person who provides information. ➤ a book or document providing evidence for research. **3** technical a body or process by which energy or a component enters a system. The opposite of **SINK**[2]. • v. obtain from a particular source. ➤ find out where to obtain.
– PHRASES **at source** at the point of origin or issue.
– ORIGIN ME: from OFr. *sours(e)*, past part. of *sourdre* 'to rise', from L. *surgere*.

**sourcebook** • n. a collection of writings for the study of a particular subject.

**source code** • n. Computing a text listing of commands to be compiled into an executable computer program.

**source criticism** • n. the analysis and study of sources used by biblical authors.

**sour cream** • n. cream deliberately fermented by adding certain bacteria.

**sourdough** • n. **1** leaven for making bread, consisting of fermenting dough, originally that left over from a previous baking. ➤ bread made using such leaven. **2** N. Amer. an experienced prospector in the western US or Canada.

**sour grass** • n. grass which is coarse, unpalatable, or of low nutritional value. [Species in several genera, in particular *Elionurus* (in South Africa), and *Andropogon* and *Valota* (in the Caribbean).]

**sour mash** • n. US a mash used in distilling certain malt whiskeys. ➤ whiskey distilled from this.

**sourpuss** • n. informal a bad-tempered or habitually sullen person.
– ORIGIN 1930s: from **SOUR** + **PUSS**[2].

**soursop** • n. **1** a large acidic custard apple with white fibrous flesh. **2** the evergreen tropical American tree which bears this fruit. [*Annona muricata*.]

**sourwood** • n. a North American tree of the heather family, which has acid-tasting leaves. [*Oxydendrum arboreum*.]

**sous-** /su:(z)/ • prefix (in words adopted from French) subordinate: *sous-chef*.
– ORIGIN from Fr. *sous* 'under'.

**sousaphone** /'su:zəfəʊn/ • n. an American form of tuba with a wide bell pointing forward above the player's head.
– DERIVATIVES **sousaphonist** /-'zɒf(ə)nɪst/ n.
– ORIGIN 1920s: named after the Amer. composer J. P. *Sousa*, on the pattern of *saxophone*.

**souse** /saʊs/ • v. **1** soak in or drench with liquid. **2** [often as adj. **soused**] put (gherkins, fish, etc.) in pickle or a marinade: *soused herring*. **3** [as adj. **soused**] informal drunk. • n. **1** liquid used for pickling. ➤ N. Amer. & W. Indian food, especially a pig's head, in pickle. **2** informal a drunkard.
– ORIGIN ME: from OFr. *sous* 'pickle', of Gmc origin; rel. to **SALT**.

**souslik** /'su:slɪk/ • n. a short-tailed Eurasian and Arctic ground squirrel. [*Spermophilus citellus* and related species.]
– ORIGIN C18: from Russ.

**sous vide** /su: 'vi:d/ • n. a method of treating food by partial cooking followed by vacuum-sealing and chilling. • adj. & adv. involving such preparation.
– ORIGIN Fr., lit. 'under vacuum'.

**soutache** /su:'taʃ/ • n. a narrow, flat ornamental braid used to trim garments.
– ORIGIN C19: from Fr., from Hungarian *sujtás*.

**soutane** /su:'tɑ:n/ • n. a type of cassock worn by Roman Catholic priests.
– ORIGIN C19: from Fr., from Ital. *sottana*, from *sotto* 'under', from L. *subtus*.

**souteneur** /ˌsu:tə'nə:/ • n. a pimp.
– ORIGIN Fr., lit. 'protector'.

**souter** /'su:tə/ (also **soutar**) • n. Scottish & N. English a shoemaker.
– ORIGIN OE *sūtere*, from L. *sutor*, from *suere* 'sew'.

**souterrain** /'su:tərem/ • n. chiefly Archaeology an underground chamber or passage.
– ORIGIN C18: from Fr., from *sous* 'under' + *terre* 'earth'.

**south** • n. (usu. **the south**) **1** the direction towards the point of the horizon 90° clockwise from east. **2** the southern part of a country, region, or town. ➤ (**the South**) the Southern states of the United States. • adj. **1** lying towards, near, or facing the south. **2** (of a wind) blowing from the south. • adv. to or towards the south. • v. **1** move towards the south. **2** (of a celestial body) cross the meridian.
– PHRASES **south by east** (or **west**) between south and south-south-east (or south-south-west).
– DERIVATIVES **southbound** adj. & adv.
– ORIGIN OE *sūth*, of Gmc origin.

**South African** • n. a native or inhabitant of South Africa. • adj. of or relating to South Africa.

**South African Dutch** • n. the Afrikaans language from the 17th to the 19th centuries, during its development from Dutch. • adj. dated of or relating to Afrikaans-speaking South Africans.

**South American** • n. a native or inhabitant of South America. • adj. of or relating to South America.

**Southdown** • n. a sheep of a breed raised especially for mutton, originally on the South Downs of Hampshire and Sussex.

**south-east** • n. (usu. **the south-east**) **1** the direction towards the point of the horizon midway between south and east. **2** the south-eastern part of a country, region, or town. • adj. **1** lying towards, near, or facing the south-east. **2** (of a wind) blowing from the south-east. • adv. to or towards the south-east.
– DERIVATIVES **south-eastern** adj.

**southeaster** • n. a wind blowing from the south-east.

**south-easterly** • adj. & adv. in a south-eastward position or direction. • n. another term for **SOUTHEASTER**.

**south-eastward** • adv. (also **south-eastwards**) towards the south-east. • adj. situated in, directed toward, or facing the south-east.

**southerly** • adj. & adv. **1** in a southward position or direction. **2** (of a wind) blowing from the south. • n. (often **southerlies**) a wind blowing from the south.

**southern** • adj. **1** situated, directed towards, or facing the south. **2** (usu. **Southern**) living in, coming from, or characteristic of the south.
– DERIVATIVES **southernmost** adj.

**Southern Baptist** • n. a member of a large convention of Baptist churches in the US, typically having a fundamentalist and evangelistic approach to Christianity.

**Southern blot** • n. Biology a procedure for identifying specific sequences of DNA.
– ORIGIN C20: named after the Brit. biochemist Edwin M. *Southern*.

**Southern Comfort** • n. trademark a whisky-based liqueur of US origin.

**southerner** ● n. a native or inhabitant of the south of a particular region or country.

**southern-fried** ● adj. chiefly N. Amer. (of food, especially chicken) coated in flour, egg, and breadcrumbs and then deep-fried.

**Southern Lights** ● pl. n. the aurora australis (see **AURORA**).

**southernwood** ● n. a bushy artemisia of southern Europe. [*Artemisia abrotanum*.]

**southing** ● n. **1** distance travelled or measured southward, especially at sea. **2** a figure or line representing southward distance on a map. **3** Astronomy the transit of the sun across the meridian due south of the observer.

**South Korean** ● n. a native or inhabitant of South Korea. ● adj. of or relating to South Korea.

**southpaw** ● n. a left-handed boxer who leads with the right hand. ➤ informal, chiefly N. Amer. a left-hander in any sphere.

– ORIGIN C19: from **PAW**.

**south-south-east** ● n. the compass point or direction midway between south and south-east.

**south-south-west** ● n. the compass point or direction midway between south and south-west.

**southward** /ˈsaʊθwəd/ Nautical /ˈsʌðəd/ ● adj. in a southerly direction. ● adv. (also **southwards**) towards the south. ● n. (**the southward**) the direction or region to the south.

– DERIVATIVES **southwardly** adj. & adv.

**south-west** ● n. **1** (usu. **the south-west**) the direction towards the point of the horizon midway between south and west. **2** the south-western part of a country, region, or town. ● adj. **1** lying towards, near, or facing the south-west. **2** (of a wind) blowing from the south-west. ● adv. to or towards the south-west.

– DERIVATIVES **south-western** adj.

**southwester** ● n. a wind blowing from the south-west.

**south-westerly** ● adj. & adv. in a south-westward position or direction. ● n. another term for **SOUTHWESTER**.

**south-westward** ● adv. (also **south-westwards**) towards the south-west. ● adj. situated in, directed toward, or facing the south-west.

**souvenir** /ˌsuːvəˈnɪə/ ● n. a thing that is kept as a reminder of a person, place, or event.

– ORIGIN C18: from Fr., from *souvenir* 'remember', from L. *subvenire* 'occur to the mind'.

**souvlaki** /suːˈvlɑːki/ ● n. (pl. **souvlakia** /-kɪə/ or **souvlakis**) a Greek dish of pieces of meat grilled on a skewer.

– ORIGIN from mod. Gk.

**sou'wester** /saʊˈwɛstə/ ● n. a waterproof hat with a broad flap covering the neck.

**sovereign** ● n. **1** a supreme ruler, especially a monarch. **2** a former British gold coin worth one pound sterling, now only minted for commemorative purposes. ● adj. **1** possessing supreme or ultimate power. ➤ archaic or poetic/literary possessing royal power and status. **2** (of a nation or its affairs) acting or done independently and without outside interference. **3** dated very good or effective.

– DERIVATIVES **sovereignly** adv.

– ORIGIN ME: from OFr. *soverain*, based on L. *super* 'above'.

**sovereignty** ● n. (pl. **-ies**) **1** supreme power or authority. ➤ the authority of a state to govern itself or another state. **2** a self-governing state.

**soviet** /ˈsəʊvɪət, ˈsɒv-/ ● n. **1** an elected local, district, or national council in the former USSR. ➤ a revolutionary council of workers or peasants in Russia before 1917. **2** (**Soviet**) a citizen of the former USSR. ● adj. (**Soviet**) of or concerning the former Soviet Union.

– DERIVATIVES **Sovietism** n. **Sovietization** (also **-isation**) n. **Sovietize** (also **-ise**) v.

– ORIGIN C20: from Russ. *sovet* 'council'.

**Sovietologist** /ˌsəʊvɪəˈtɒlədʒɪst, ˌsɒ-/ ● n. a student of or expert on the former Soviet Union.

– DERIVATIVES **Sovietological** adj. **Sovietology** n.

**sovkhoz** /ˈsɒvkɒz, sʌvˈkɔːz/ ● n. (pl. same, **sovkhozes** /ˈsɒvkɒzɪz, sʌvˈkɔːzɪz/, or **sovkhozy** /ˈsɒvkɒzi, sʌvˈkɔːzi/) a state-owned farm in the former USSR.

– ORIGIN Russ., from *sov(etskoe) khoz(yaĭstvo)* 'Soviet farm'.

**sow¹** /səʊ/ ● v. (past **sowed** /səʊd/; past part. **sown** /səʊn/ or **sowed**) **1** plant (seed) by scattering it on or in the earth. ➤ plant (an area) with seed. **2** disseminate or introduce (something unwelcome): *the new policy has sown confusion and doubt.*

– DERIVATIVES **sower** n.

– ORIGIN OE *sāwan*, of Gmc origin.

**sow²** /saʊ/ ● n. **1** an adult female pig, especially one which has farrowed. ➤ the female of certain other mammals, e.g. the guinea pig. **2** a large block of metal (larger than a 'pig') made by smelting.

– ORIGIN OE *sugu*.

**sowbread** /ˈsaʊbrɛd/ ● n. a cyclamen with pale pink or white flowers and leaves that do not appear until late summer after flowering, native to southern Eurasia. [*Cyclamen hederifolium*.]

– ORIGIN C16: so named because the roots are reputedly eaten by wild boars in Sicily.

**sow bug** /ˈsaʊ/ ● n. chiefly N. Amer. another term for **WOODLOUSE**.

**Sowetan** /səˈwɛtən, -ˈweɪtən/ ● n. a native or inhabitant of Soweto, an urban area of South Africa. ● adj. of or relating to Soweto.

**sown** past participle of **sow¹**.

**sowthistle** /ˈsaʊθɪs(ə)l/ ● n. a plant with yellow flowers, thistle-like leaves, and milky sap. [Genus *Sonchus*.]

**soy** ● n. **1** (also **soy sauce**) a sauce made with fermented soya beans, used in Chinese and Japanese cooking. **2** another term for **SOYA**.

– ORIGIN from Japanese *shō-yu*, from Chin. *shi-yu*, from *shi* 'salted beans' + *yu* 'oil'.

**soya** ● n. **1** protein derived from the beans of an Asian plant, used as a replacement for animal protein in certain foods. ➤ chiefly Brit. soy sauce. **2** the plant of the pea family which produces these beans. [*Glycine max*.]

– ORIGIN C17: from Du. *soja*, from Malay *soi* (see **SOY**).

**soya milk** ● n. the liquid obtained by suspending soya bean flour in water, used as a fat-free substitute for milk, particularly by vegans.

**soybean** (also **soya bean**) ● n. a bean of the soya plant.

**sozzled** ● adj. informal very drunk.

– ORIGIN C19: past part. of dial. *sozzle* 'mix sloppily', prob. of imitative origin.

**SP** ● abbrev. starting price.

**sp.** ● abbrev. species (usually singular).

**spa** ● n. a mineral spring considered to have health-giving properties. ➤ a place or resort with such a spring. ➤ a commercial establishment offering health and beauty treatment.

– ORIGIN C17: from *Spa*, a small town in eastern Belgium noted for its mineral springs.

**space** ● n. **1** a continuous area or expanse which is free or unoccupied. ➤ a gap between printed or written words or characters. ➤ pages in a newspaper, or time between broadcast programmes, available for advertising. ➤ the freedom and scope to live and develop as one wishes. ➤ Telecommunications one of two possible states of a signal in certain systems. The opposite of **MARK¹**. **2** an interval of time (indicating that the time is short): *both cars were stolen in the space of a few hours.* **3** the dimensions of height, depth, and width within which all things exist and move. ➤ (also **outer space**) the physical universe beyond the earth's atmosphere. ➤ the near-vacuum extending between the planets and stars. **4** Mathematics a mathematical concept generally regarded as a set of points having some specified structure. ● v. **1** position (two or more items) at a distance from one another. ➤ (in printing or writing) insert spaces between. **2** (**be spaced out** or chiefly N. Amer. **space out**) informal be or become euphoric or disorientated, especially from taking drugs.

– DERIVATIVES **spacer** n. **spacing** n.

– ORIGIN ME: shortening of OFr. *espace*, from L. *spatium*.

**space age** ● n. (**the space age**) the era starting when the exploration of space became possible. ● adj. (**space-**

**age**) very modern; technologically advanced.

**space bar** • n. a long key on a typewriter or computer keyboard for making a space between words.

**space blanket** • n. a light metal-coated sheet designed to retain heat, originally developed for use during space travel.

**space cadet** • n. **1** a trainee astronaut. **2** informal a person perceived as out of touch with reality.

**space capsule** • n. a small spacecraft or the part of a larger one that contains the instruments or crew, designed to be returned to earth.

**spacecraft** • n. (pl. same or **spacecrafts**) a vehicle used for travelling in space.

**spacefaring** • n. the action or activity of travelling in space.
– DERIVATIVES **spacefarer** n.

**space frame** • n. a three-dimensional structural framework designed to withstand loads applied at any point.

**space heater** • n. a heater used to warm an enclosed space within a building.
– DERIVATIVES **space-heated** adj. **space heating** n.

**spaceman** • n. (pl. **-men**) a male astronaut.

**space opera** • n. informal, chiefly N. Amer. a novel or drama set in outer space.

**spaceplane** • n. an aircraft that takes off and lands conventionally but is capable of entry into orbit or travel through space.

**spaceport** • n. a base from which spacecraft are launched.

**space probe** • n. see **PROBE**.

**spaceship** • n. a manned spacecraft.

**space shuttle** • n. a rocket-launched spacecraft able to land like an unpowered aircraft, used to make journeys between earth and earth orbit.

**space station** • n. a large artificial satellite used as a long-term base for manned operations in space.

**spacesuit** • n. a sealed and pressurized suit designed to allow an astronaut to survive in space.

**space–time** • n. Physics the concepts of time and three-dimensional space regarded as fused in a four-dimensional continuum.

**space walk** • n. an excursion by an astronaut outside a spacecraft.

**space warp** • n. a hypothetical distortion of space–time that enables space travellers to travel faster than light or otherwise make journeys contrary to the laws of physics.

**spacey** (also **spacy**) • adj. (**-ier**, **-iest**) informal out of touch with reality. ➤(of popular music) drifting and ethereal.

**spacial** • adj. variant spelling of **SPATIAL**.

**spacious** • adj. (of a room or building) having plenty of space.
– DERIVATIVES **spaciously** adv. **spaciousness** n.
– ORIGIN ME: from OFr. *spacios* or L. *spatiosus*, from *spatium* (see **SPACE**).

**spackle** /ˈspak(ə)l/ • n. N. Amer. trademark a compound used to fill cracks in plaster before decoration. • v. repair or fill with spackle.
– ORIGIN 1920s: perh. a blend of **SPARKLE** and Ger. *Spachtel* 'putty knife, mastic'.

**spade**[1] • n. **1** a tool with a sharp-edged, rectangular metal blade and a long handle, used for digging. **2** [as modifier] shaped like a spade: *a spade bit.* • v. dig over with a spade. ➤move or lift with a spade.
– PHRASES **call a spade a spade** speak plainly and frankly.
– DERIVATIVES **spadeful** n. (pl. **-fuls**).
– ORIGIN OE *spadu*, *spada*, of Gmc origin.

**spade**[2] • n. **1** (**spades**) one of the four suits in a conventional pack of playing cards, denoted by a black inverted heart-shaped figure with a small stalk. ➤(**a spade**) a card of this suit. **2** informal, offensive a black person.
– PHRASES **in spades** informal in large amounts or to a high degree.
– ORIGIN C16: from Ital. *spade*, pl. of *spada* 'sword', via L. from Gk *spathē*; cf. **SPADE**[1].

**spade beard** • n. an oblong-shaped beard.

**spadefish** • n. (pl. same or **-fishes**) a fish with an almost disc-shaped body, found in tropical inshore waters. [*Chaetodipterus faber* (W. Atlantic) and other species.]

**spadefoot** • n. **1** (usu. **spadefoot toad**) (pl. **spadefoots**) a plump, short-legged burrowing toad with a prominent sharp-edged tubercle on the hind feet. [*Scaphiophus* (America), *Pelobates* (Europe), and other genera.] **2** a square enlargement at the end of a chair leg.

**spadework** • n. hard or routine preparatory work.

**spadille** /spəˈdɪl/ • n. (in ombre and quadrille) the ace of spades.
– ORIGIN C17: from Fr., from Sp. *espadilla*, dimin. of *espada* (see **SPADE**[2]).

**spadix** /ˈspeɪdɪks/ • n. (pl. **spadices** /-siːz/) **1** Botany a spike of minute flowers closely arranged round a fleshy axis and typically enclosed in a spathe, characteristic of the arums. **2** Zoology (in certain invertebrates) a part or organ which is more or less conical in shape.
– ORIGIN C18: via L. from Gk, lit. 'palm branch'.

**spae** /speɪ/ • v. Scottish predict.
– ORIGIN ME: from ON *spá*, of unknown origin.

**spaetzle** /ˈʃpɛtslə, ˈʃpɛts(ə)l/ (also **spätzle**) • pl. n. small dough dumplings of a type made in southern Germany and Alsace.
– ORIGIN from Ger. dial. *Spätzle*, lit. 'little sparrows'.

**spaewife** • n. Scottish a woman who is believed to be able to predict the future.

**spaghetti** /spəˈgɛti/ • pl. n. pasta made in solid strings, between macaroni and vermicelli in thickness.
– ORIGIN Ital., pl. of the dimin. of *spago* 'string'.

**spaghetti Bolognese** /ˌbɒləˈneɪz/ • n. a dish of spaghetti with a sauce of minced beef, tomato, onion, and herbs.
– ORIGIN Ital., lit. 'spaghetti of Bologna'.

**spaghettification** • n. Physics the process by which (in some theories) an object would be stretched and ripped apart by gravitational forces on falling into a black hole.

**spaghettini** /ˌspagɛˈtiːni/ • pl. n. pasta in the form of strings of thin spaghetti.
– ORIGIN Ital., dimin. of *spaghetti*.

**spaghetti strap** • n. a thin rounded shoulder strap on an item of women's clothing.

**spaghetti western** • n. informal a western film made cheaply in Europe by an Italian director.

**spahi** /ˈspɑːhiː/ • n. historical **1** a member of the Turkish irregular cavalry. **2** a member of the Algerian cavalry in French service.
– ORIGIN C16: from Turk. *sipahi*, from Pers. *sipāhī* (see **SEPOY**).

**spake** archaic or poetic/literary past of **SPEAK**.

**spall** /spɔːl/ • n. a splinter or chip of rock. • v. break or cause to break into spalls.
– ORIGIN ME: of unknown origin.

**spallation** /spɔːˈleɪʃ(ə)n/ • n. **1** Physics the breaking up of a bombarded nucleus into several parts. **2** Geology separation of fragments from the surface of a rock.

**spalpeen** /spalˈpiːn/ • n. Irish a rascal.
– ORIGIN C18 (denoting a migratory farm worker): from Ir. *spailpín*, of unknown origin.

**spalted** /ˈspɔːltəd/ • adj. (of wood) containing blackish irregular lines as a result of fungal decay.
– ORIGIN 1970s: from dial. *spalt* 'to splinter'.

**spam** • n. **1** trademark a tinned meat product made mainly from ham. **2** irrelevant or inappropriate messages sent on the Internet to a large number of newsgroups or users. • v. send the same message indiscriminately to (large numbers of users) on the Internet.
– DERIVATIVES **spammer** n. **spamming** n.
– ORIGIN 1930s: appar. from *sp(iced h)am*; the Internet sense appar. derives from a sketch by the Brit. 'Monty Python' comedy group, set in a cafe in which every item on the menu includes spam.

**span**[1] • n. **1** the full extent of something from end to end; the amount of space covered. ➤a wingspan. ➤a part of a

bridge between piers or supports. **2** the length of time for which something lasts. **3** the maximum distance between the tips of the thumb and little finger, taken as the basis of a measurement equal to 9 inches. **4** archaic a short distance or time. ● **v.** (**spanned**, **spanning**) extend across or over.
– ORIGIN OE, 'distance between thumb and little finger', of Gmc origin.

**span**[2] ● **n. 1** Nautical a rope with its ends fastened at different points in order to provide a purchase. **2** a team of people or animals, especially a matched pair of horses or oxen. ● **v.** S. African yoke (an animal).
– ORIGIN C16: from Du. or Low Ger. *spannen*.

**span**[3] ● **adj.** see **SPICK AND SPAN**.

**span**[4] chiefly archaic past of **SPIN**.

**spanakopita** /ˌspanəˈkɒpɪtə/ ● **n.** (in Greek cooking) a filo pastry stuffed with spinach and feta cheese.
– ORIGIN mod. Gk, lit. 'spinach pie'.

**spandex** ● **n.** trademark a type of stretchy polyurethane fabric.
– ORIGIN 1950s: an arbitrary formation from **EXPAND**.

**spandrel** /ˈspandrɪl/ ● **n.** Architecture the almost triangular space between one side of the outer curve of an arch, a wall, and the ceiling or framework. ➤ the space between the shoulders of adjoining arches and the ceiling or moulding above.
– ORIGIN ME: perh. from Anglo-Norman Fr. *spaund(e)re*, or from *espaundre* 'expand'.

**spang** ● **adv.** US informal directly; completely: *looking the General spang in the eye.*
– ORIGIN C19: of unknown origin.

**spangle** ● **n. 1** a small thin piece of glittering material, used to ornament a garment; a sequin. **2** a spot of bright colour or light. ● **v.** cover with spangles or sparkling objects.
– DERIVATIVES **spangly** adj.
– ORIGIN ME: dimin. from obs. *spang* 'glittering ornament', from MDu. *spange* 'buckle'.

**Spanglish** /ˈspaŋglɪʃ/ ● **n.** hybrid language combining words and idioms from both Spanish and English.

**Spaniard** /ˈspanjəd/ ● **n. 1** a native or national of Spain, or a person of Spanish descent. **2** a spiny rock plant of the parsley family, native to New Zealand. [Genus *Aciphylla*.]
– ORIGIN ME: shortening of OFr. *Espaignart*.

**spaniel** ● **n.** a dog of a breed with a long silky coat and drooping ears.
– ORIGIN ME: from OFr. *espaigneul* 'Spanish (dog)', from L. *Hispaniolus* 'Spanish'.

**Spanish** ● **n.** the main language of Spain and of much of Central and South America. ● **adj.** of or relating to Spain, its people, or their language.
– DERIVATIVES **Spanishness** n.

**Spanish-American** ● **n.** a native or inhabitant of the Spanish-speaking countries of Central and South America. ● **adj.** of or relating to the Spanish-speaking countries or peoples of Central and South America.

**Spanish flu** ● **n.** influenza caused by an influenza virus of type A, in particular that of the pandemic which began in 1918.

**Spanish fly** ● **n.** a toxic preparation of the dried bodies of a bright green blister beetle (*Lytta vesicatoria*), formerly used in medicine as a counterirritant and sometimes taken as an aphrodisiac.

**Spanish guitar** ● **n.** the standard six-stringed acoustic guitar, used especially for classical and folk music.

**Spanish mackerel** ● **n.** a large edible game fish related to the mackerel. [*Scomberomorus maculatus* (tropical Atlantic) and related species.]

**Spanish moss** ● **n.** a tropical American plant which grows as silvery-green festoons on trees, obtaining water and nutrients directly through its surface. [*Tillandsia usneoides*.]

**Spanish omelette** ● **n.** an omelette containing chopped vegetables, especially potatoes.

**Spanish onion** ● **n.** a large onion with a mild flavour.

**Spanish rice** ● **n.** a dish of rice cooked with onions, peppers, tomatoes, and spices.

**Spanish windlass** ● **n.** a device for tightening a rope or cable by twisting it using a stick as a lever.

**spank** ● **v.** slap with one's open hand or a flat object, especially on the buttocks as a punishment. ● **n.** a slap or series of slaps of this type.
– ORIGIN C18: perh. imitative.

**spanker** ● **n. 1** a fore-and-aft sail set on the after side of a ship's mast, especially the mizzenmast. **2** informal, dated a very fine person or thing.

**spanking** ● **adj. 1** lively; brisk. **2** informal very good; impressive or pleasing: *it's in spanking condition.* ● **n.** a series of spanks.

**spanner** ● **n.** chiefly Brit. a tool with a shaped opening or jaws for gripping and turning a nut or bolt.
– PHRASES **spanner in the works** a person or thing that prevents the successful implementation of a plan.
– ORIGIN C18: from Ger. *spannen* 'draw tight' + **-ER**[1].

**spanspek** /ˈspanspɛk/ ● **n.** South African term for **CANTALOUPE**.
– ORIGIN from Afrik.

**spanworm** ● **n.** North American term for **LOOPER**.

**spar**[1] ● **n.** a thick, strong pole such as is used for a mast or yard on a ship. ➤ the main longitudinal beam of an aircraft wing.
– ORIGIN ME: shortening of OFr. *esparre*, or from ON *sperra*.

**spar**[2] ● **v.** (**sparred**, **sparring**) **1** make the motions of boxing without landing heavy blows, as a form of training. **2** engage in argument without marked hostility. **3** (of a gamecock) fight with the feet or spurs. ● **n. 1** a period or bout of sparring. **2** informal a close friend.
– ORIGIN OE *sperran*, *spyrran* 'strike out', of unknown origin.

**spar**[3] ● **n.** a crystalline, easily cleavable, translucent or transparent mineral.
– DERIVATIVES **sparry** adj.
– ORIGIN C16: from Middle Low Ger.

**sparable** /ˈsparəb(ə)l/ ● **n.** a headless nail used for the soles and heels of shoes.
– ORIGIN C17: contr. of *sparrow-bill*, with ref. to the nail's shape.

**sparaxis** /spəˈraksɪs/ ● **n.** a South African plant with slender sword-shaped leaves and showy multicoloured flowers. [Genus *Sparaxis*.]
– ORIGIN mod. L., from Gk, lit. 'laceration', from *sparassein* 'to tear'.

**spar buoy** ● **n.** a buoy made of a spar with one end moored so that the other stands up.

**spar deck** ● **n.** the light upper deck of a vessel.

**spare** ● **adj. 1** additional to what is required for ordinary use. ➤ not currently in use or occupied. **2** with no excess fat; thin. **3** elegantly simple. ● **n. 1** an item kept in case another item of the same type is lost, broken, or worn out. **2** (in tenpin bowling) an act of knocking down all the pins with two balls. ● **v. 1** give (something of which one has enough) to. ➤ make free or available. **2** refrain from killing or harming. ➤ refrain from inflicting (harm) on: *they have been spared the violence.* **3** archaic be frugal.
– PHRASES **go spare** Brit. informal become extremely angry or distraught. **spare no expense** (or **no expense spared**) be prepared to pay any amount. **to spare** left over.
– DERIVATIVES **sparely** adv. **spareness** n.
– ORIGIN OE *spær* 'not plentiful, meagre', *sparian* 'refrain from injuring or using', of Gmc origin.

**spare rib** ● **n.** (usu. **spare ribs**) a trimmed rib of pork.
– ORIGIN C16: prob. a transposition of Mid. Low Ger. *ribbesper*; also assoc. with **SPARE**.

**spare tyre** ● **n. 1** an extra tyre carried in a motor vehicle for use in case of puncture. **2** informal a roll of fat round a person's waist.

**sparge** /spɑːdʒ/ chiefly technical ● **v.** (chiefly in brewing) moisten by sprinkling with water. ● **n.** the action of sparging. ➤ a spray of hot water, especially sprinkled over malt during brewing.
– DERIVATIVES **sparger** n.
– ORIGIN C16: appar. from L. *spargere* 'to sprinkle'.

**sparid** /ˈsparɪd, ˈspeɪrɪd/ ● **n.** Zoology a fish of the sea

bream family (Sparidae), whose members have deep bodies with long spiny dorsal fins.
– ORIGIN 1960s: from mod. L. *Sparidae* (pl.), via L. from Gk *sparos* 'sea bream'.

**sparing** • **adj.** moderate; economical.
– DERIVATIVES **sparingly** adv. **sparingness** n.

**spark**[1] • **n.** **1** a small fiery particle thrown off from a fire, alight in ashes, or produced by striking together two surfaces. **2** a light produced by a sudden disruptive electrical discharge through the air. ➤a discharge such as this serving to ignite the explosive mixture in an internal-combustion engine. **3** a small bright object or point. **4** a small but concentrated amount or trace: *a tiny spark of anger.* ➤a sense of liveliness and excitement. • **v.** **1** emit sparks. ➤produce sparks at the point where an electric circuit is interrupted. **2** ignite. **3** (usu. **spark something off**) provide the stimulus for.
– PHRASES **spark out** Brit. informal completely unconscious.
– DERIVATIVES **sparkless** adj. **sparky** adj.
– ORIGIN OE *spærca, spearca*, of unknown origin.

**spark**[2] • **n.** (in phr. **bright spark**) a lively person. • **v.** archaic engage in courtship.
– DERIVATIVES **sparkish** adj.
– ORIGIN C16: prob. from SPARK[1].

**spark chamber** • **n.** Physics an apparatus designed to show ionizing particles.

**spark gap** • **n.** a space between electrical terminals across which a transient discharge passes.

**sparkle** • **v.** **1** shine brightly with flashes of light. **2** be vivacious and witty. **3** [as adj. **sparkling**] (of drink) effervescent. • **n.** **1** a glittering flash of light. **2** vivacity and wit.
– DERIVATIVES **sparklingly** adv. **sparkly** adj.
– ORIGIN ME: frequentative (v.) or dimin. (n.) of SPARK[1].

**sparkler** • **n.** a hand-held firework that emits sparks.

**spark plug** (also **sparking plug**) • **n.** a device for firing the explosive mixture in an internal-combustion engine.

**sparling** • **n.** an edible smelt (fish) which migrates into fresh water to spawn. [*Osmerus eperlanus.*]
– ORIGIN ME: shortening of OFr. *esperlinge*, of Gmc origin.

**sparrow** • **n.** a small, typically brown and grey finch-like bird related to the weaver birds. [*Passer domesticus* (**house sparrow**) and other species.] ➤used in names of many other birds which resemble this, especially American birds of the bunting family (Emberizidae), e.g. **Java sparrow, song sparrow.**
– ORIGIN OE *spearwa*, of Gmc origin.

**sparrow grass** • **n.** dialect term for ASPARAGUS.
– ORIGIN C17: corruption (by folk etymology) of obs. *sparagus* 'asparagus'.

**sparrowhawk** • **n.** a small Old World hawk that preys on small birds. [*Accipiter nisus* and related species.] ➤N. Amer. the American kestrel.

**sparse** • **adj.** thinly dispersed.
– DERIVATIVES **sparsely** adv. **sparseness** n. **sparsity** n.
– ORIGIN C18: from L. *sparsus*, past part. of *spargere* 'scatter'.

**Spartacist** /ˈspɑːtəsɪst, -təkɪst/ • **n.** a member of the Spartacus League, a German revolutionary socialist group founded in 1916.
– ORIGIN from *Spartacus*, the pseudonym of one of its founders (orig. the name of a rebellious Roman slave).

**Spartan**[1] • **adj.** **1** of or relating to Sparta, a city state in ancient Greece. **2** (usu. **spartan**) showing the indifference to comfort or luxury traditionally associated with ancient Sparta. • **n.** a citizen of Sparta.

**Spartan**[2] • **n.** a Canadian dessert apple of a variety with crisp white flesh and maroon-flushed yellow skin.

**spartina** /spɑːˈtʌɪnə, -ˈtiːnə/ • **n.** a plant of a genus that comprises the cordgrasses. [Genus *Spartina*.]
– ORIGIN mod. L., from Gk *spartinē* 'rope'.

**spasm** • **n.** **1** a sudden involuntary muscular contraction or convulsive movement. **2** a sudden brief spell of activity or sensation.
– ORIGIN ME: from OFr. *spasme*, or via L. from Gk *spasmos*, *spasma*, from *span* 'pull'.

**spasmodic** • **adj.** **1** occurring or done in brief, irregular bursts. **2** of or caused by a spasm or spasms.
– DERIVATIVES **spasmodically** adv.
– ORIGIN C17: from mod. L. *spasmodicus*, from Gk *spasmōdēs*, from *spasma* (see SPASM).

**spastic** • **adj.** **1** relating to or affected by muscle spasm. ➤of or having a form of muscular weakness (**spastic paralysis**) typical of cerebral palsy, involving reflex resistance to passive movement of the limbs and difficulty in initiating and controlling muscular movement. **2** informal, offensive incompetent or uncoordinated. • **n.** **1** a person with cerebral palsy. **2** informal, offensive an incompetent or uncoordinated person.
– DERIVATIVES **spastically** adv. **spasticity** n.
– ORIGIN C18: via L. from Gk *spastikos* 'pulling', from *span* 'pull'.

**USAGE** spastic

In modern use the term **spastic** is likely to cause offence. It is preferable to use phrasing such as *people with cerebral palsy* instead.

**spat**[1] past and past participle of SPIT[1].

**spat**[2] • **n.** **1** a short cloth gaiter covering the instep and ankle. **2** a cover for the upper part of an aircraft wheel.
– ORIGIN C19: abbrev. of SPATTERDASH.

**spat**[3] informal • **n.** a petty quarrel. • **v.** (**spatted**, **spatting**) quarrel pettily.
– ORIGIN C19: prob. imitative.

**spat**[4] • **n.** the spawn or larvae of shellfish, especially oysters.
– ORIGIN C17: from Anglo-Norman Fr., of unknown ultimate origin.

**spatchcock** • **n.** a chicken or game bird split open and grilled. • **v.** **1** prepare (a poultry or game bird) in this way. **2** informal, chiefly Brit. add (a phrase, sentence, etc.) in a context where it is inappropriate.
– ORIGIN C18 (orig. an Ir. usage): perh. rel. to DISPATCH + COCK[1], but cf. SPITCHCOCK.

**spate** • **n.** **1** a large number of similar things or events coming in quick succession. **2** chiefly Brit. a sudden flood in a river.
– PHRASES **in (full) spate** (of a river) overflowing.
– ORIGIN ME (orig. dial.): of unknown origin.

**spathe** /speɪð/ • **n.** Botany a large sheathing bract enclosing the flower cluster of certain plants, especially the spadix of arums and palms.
– ORIGIN C18: via L. from Gk *spathē* 'broad blade'.

**spathulate** /ˈspatjʊlət/ • **adj.** Botany & Zoology variant spelling of SPATULATE.

**spatial** /ˈspeɪʃ(ə)l/ (also **spacial**) • **adj.** of or relating to space.
– DERIVATIVES **spatiality** n. **spatialization** (also **-isation**) n. **spatialize** (also **-ise**) v. **spatially** adv.
– ORIGIN C19: from L. *spatium* 'space' + -AL.

**spatio-temporal** /ˌspeɪʃɪəʊˈtɛmp(ə)r(ə)l/ • **adj.** Physics & Philosophy belonging to both space and time or to space–time.
– DERIVATIVES **spatio-temporally** adv.

**Spätlese** /ˈʃpɛtˌleɪzə/ • **n.** (pl. **Spätleses** or **Spätlesen** /-ˌleɪz(ə)n/) a white wine of German origin or style made from grapes harvested late in the season.
– ORIGIN from Ger., from *spät* 'late' + *Lese* 'picking, vintage'.

**spatter** • **v.** cover with drops or spots. ➤splash or be splashed over a surface. • **n.** **1** a spray or splash. **2** a short outburst of sound.
– ORIGIN C16 (in the sense 'splutter'): frequentative, from a base shared by Du., Low Ger. *spatten* 'burst, spout'.

**spatterdash** • **n.** historical a long gaiter or legging, worn especially when riding.

**spatterdock** • **n.** N. Amer. a yellow-flowered water lily. [Genus *Nuphar*: several species, in particular *N. advena*.]

**spatula** • **n.** an implement with a broad, flat, blunt blade, used especially for mixing or spreading.
– ORIGIN C16: from L., var. of *spathula*, dimin. of *spatha* 'spathe'.

**spatulate** /ˈspatjʊlət/ • **adj.** having a broad, rounded end. ➤(also **spathulate**) Botany & Zoology broad at the apex and tapered to the base.

**spätzle** • **pl. n.** variant spelling of **SPAETZLE**.

**spavin** /ˈspavɪn/ • **n.** a disorder of a horse's hock.
– DERIVATIVES **spavined** adj.
– ORIGIN ME: shortening of OFr. *espavin*, var. of *esparvain*, of Gmc origin.

**spawn** • **v. 1** (of a fish, frog, mollusc, etc.) release or deposit eggs. ➤ chiefly derogatory (of a person) produce (offspring). **2** produce or generate; give rise to. • **n. 1** the eggs of fish, frogs, etc. **2** chiefly derogatory offspring. **3** the mycelium of a fungus, especially a cultivated mushroom.
– DERIVATIVES **spawner** n.
– ORIGIN ME: shortening of Anglo-Norman Fr. *espaundre* 'to shed roe', var. of OFr. *espandre* 'pour out'.

**spay** • **v.** sterilize (a female animal) by removing the ovaries.
– ORIGIN ME: shortening of OFr. *espeer* 'cut with a sword', from *espee* 'sword', from L. *spatha* 'spathe'.

**SPCK** • **abbrev.** Society for Promoting Christian Knowledge.

**speak** • **v.** (past **spoke**; past part. **spoken**) **1** say something. ➤ make a speech. ➤ communicate in or be able to communicate in (a specified language). ➤ (**speak for**) express the views or position of. ➤ (**speak out/up**) express one's opinions frankly and publicly. ➤ (**speak up**) speak more loudly. ➤ Nautical, archaic hail and hold communication with (a ship) at sea. **2** (**speak to**) talk to in order to advise, pass on information, etc. ➤ appeal or relate to. **3** (of behaviour, an event, etc.) serve as evidence for something. ➤ archaic show or manifest to be. **4** make a sound. ➤ (of a hound) bark.
– PHRASES **speak in tongues** speak in an unknown language during religious worship, regarded as one of the gifts of the Holy Spirit (Acts 2). **speak one's mind** express one's opinions frankly. **speak volumes** convey a great deal without using words: *a look that spoke volumes.* **speak well** (or **ill**) **of** praise (or criticize). **to speak of** of a substantial or important nature: *I've no capital—well, none to speak of.*
– DERIVATIVES **speakable** adj.
– ORIGIN OE *sprecan*, later *specan*, of W. Gmc origin.

**-speak** • **comb. form** forming nouns denoting a manner of speaking, characteristic of a specified group: *technospeak.*
– ORIGIN on the pattern of (*New*)*speak*.

**speakeasy** • **n.** (pl. **-ies**) informal (in the US during Prohibition) an illicit liquor shop or drinking club.

**speaker** • **n. 1** a person who speaks, especially at a formal occasion. **2** (**Speaker**) the presiding officer in a legislative assembly, especially the House of Commons. **3** short for **LOUDSPEAKER**.
– DERIVATIVES **speakership** n.

**speakerphone** • **n.** chiefly N. Amer. a telephone with a loudspeaker and microphone, which does not need to be held in the hand.

**speaking** • **n.** the action of expressing oneself in speech or giving speeches. • **adj. 1** used for or engaged in speech. ➤ able to communicate in a specified language. **2** conveying meaning as though in words. **3** (of a portrait) strikingly lifelike.
– PHRASES **on speaking terms** slightly acquainted; moderately friendly.

**speaking clock** • **n.** Brit. a telephone service giving the correct time in recorded speech.

**speaking trumpet** • **n.** historical an instrument for making the voice carry, especially at sea.

**speaking tube** • **n.** a pipe for conveying a person's voice from one room or building to another.

**spear** • **n. 1** a metal weapon with a pointed tip and a long shaft, used for thrusting or throwing. **2** a plant shoot, especially a pointed stem of asparagus or broccoli. **3** [as modifier] denoting the male side or members of a family. Compare with **DISTAFF**. • **v.** pierce or strike with a spear or other pointed object.
– ORIGIN OE *spere*, of Gmc origin.

**spearfish** • **n.** (pl. same or **-fishes**) a billfish that resembles the marlin. [Genus *Tetrapturus*: several species.]

**speargrass** • **n. 1** any of a number of grasses with hard pointed seed heads. [*Heteropogon*, *Stipa*, and other genera.] **2** chiefly NZ any spiny or prickly plant.

**speargun** • **n.** a gun used to propel a spear in underwater fishing.

**spearhead** • **n. 1** the point of a spear. **2** an individual or group leading an attack or movement. • **v.** lead (an attack or movement).

**spearmint** • **n.** the common garden mint, which is used as a culinary herb and in flavouring. [*Mentha spicata*.]

**spearwort** • **n.** an aquatic buttercup with long narrow spear-shaped leaves. [*Ranunculus flammula* and *R. lingua*.]

**spec**[1] • **n.** (in phr. **on spec**) informal in the hope of success but without any specific preparation or plan.
– ORIGIN C18: abbrev. of *speculation*.

**spec**[2] • **n.** informal short for **SPECIFICATION**.

**special** • **adj. 1** better, greater, or otherwise different from what is usual. **2** designed for or belonging to a particular person, place, or event. ➤ (of a subject) studied in particular depth. **3** used to denote education for children with particular needs. • **n. 1** something designed or organized for a particular occasion or purpose. ➤ a dish not on the regular menu but served on a particular day. **2** a person assigned to a special duty.
– DERIVATIVES **specialness** n.
– ORIGIN ME: shortening of OFr. *especial* 'especial' or L. *specialis*, from *species* (see **SPECIES**).

**special case** • **n.** Law a written statement of fact presented by litigants to a court.

**special constable** • **n.** (in the UK) a person who is trained to act as a police officer on particular occasions, especially in times of emergency.

**special delivery** • **n.** a service offering delivery of an item of mail within a short time period or outside normal hours.

**special drawing rights** • **pl. n.** a form of international money created by the International Monetary Fund, defined as a weighted average of various convertible currencies.

**special effects** • **pl. n.** illusions created for films and television by props, camerawork, computer graphics, etc.

**specialist** • **n.** a person who concentrates on a particular subject or activity; a person highly skilled in a specific field. • **adj.** of, relating to, or involving detailed knowledge or a specific focus within a field.
– DERIVATIVES **specialism** n.

**speciality** /ˌspɛʃɪˈalɪti/ (chiefly N. Amer. & Medicine also **specialty**) • **n.** (pl. **-ies**) **1** a pursuit, area of study, or skill to which someone has devoted themselves and in which they are expert. ➤ a product for which a person or region is famous. **2** (usu. **specialty**) a branch of medicine or surgery.
– ORIGIN ME: from OFr. *especialite* or late L. *specialitas*, from L. *specialis* (see **SPECIAL**).

**specialize** (also **-ise**) • **v.** concentrate on and become expert in a particular skill or area. ➤ make a habit of engaging in. ➤ (usu. **be specialized**) Biology adapt or set apart (an organ or part) to serve a special function.
– DERIVATIVES **specialization** n. **specialized** adj.

**special jury** • **n.** Brit. historical a jury with members of a particular social standing. Compare with **COMMON JURY**.

**special licence** • **n.** Brit. a licence allowing a marriage to take place at a time or place not normally permitted.

**specially** • **adv.** for a special purpose.

**special needs** • **pl. n.** particular educational requirements resulting from learning difficulties, physical disability, or emotional and behavioural difficulties.

**special pleading** • **n.** argument in which the speaker deliberately ignores aspects that are unfavourable to their point of view.

**special school** • **n.** (in the UK) a school catering for children with special needs.

**special sort** • **n.** Printing a character, such as an accented letter or a symbol, not normally included in a font.

**special team** • **n.** American Football a squad that is used for kick-offs, punts, and other special plays.

**specialty** /ˈspɛʃ(ə)lti/ ● **n.** (pl. **-ies**) **1** chiefly N. Amer. & Medicine another term for **SPECIALITY**. **2** Law a contract under seal.
– ORIGIN ME (denoting special attachment): shortening of OFr. *especialte*, from *especial* (see **SPECIAL**).

**speciation** /ˌspiːʃɪˈeɪʃ(ə)n, ˌspiːs-/ ● **n.** Biology the formation of new and distinct species in the course of evolution.
– DERIVATIVES **speciate** v.

**specie** /ˈspiːʃiː, ˈspiːʃi/ ● **n.** money in the form of coins rather than notes.
– PHRASES **in specie 1** in coin. **2** Law in the real, precise, or actual form specified.
– ORIGIN C16: from L., ablative of *species* 'form, kind'.

**species** /ˈspiːʃiːz, -ʃɪz, ˈspiːs-/ ● **n.** (pl. same) **1** Biology a group of living organisms consisting of similar individuals capable of exchanging genes or interbreeding, considered as the basic unit of taxonomy and denoted by a Latin binomial, e.g. *Homo sapiens*. **2** [as modifier] denoting a plant belonging to a distinct species rather than to one of the many varieties produced by hybridization: *a species rose*. **3** a kind or sort. **4** Christian Church the visible form of each of the elements of consecrated bread and wine in the Eucharist.
– ORIGIN ME: from L., lit. 'appearance, form, beauty', from *specere* 'to look'.

**speciesism** /ˈspiːʃiːˌzɪz(ə)m, ˈspiːs-/ ● **n.** the assumption of human superiority over other creatures, leading to the exploitation of animals.
– DERIVATIVES **speciesist** adj. & n.

**specific** /spəˈsɪfɪk/ ● **adj. 1** clearly defined or identified. ➤precise and clear: *when ordering goods be specific*. ➤of or relating uniquely to a particular subject. **2** Biology of, relating to, or connected with species or a species. **3** (of a duty or a tax) levied at a fixed rate per physical unit of the thing taxed, regardless of its price. **4** Physics of or denoting a physical quantity expressed in terms of a unit mass, volume, or other measure, or calculated as a ratio to the corresponding value for a substance used as a reference. ● **n. 1** chiefly dated a medicine or remedy effective in treating a particular disease or part of the body. **2** (usu. **specifics**) a precise detail.
– DERIVATIVES **specifically** adv. **specificity** /ˌspɛsɪˈfɪsɪti/ n. **specificness** n.
– ORIGIN C17: from late L. *specificus*, from L. *species* (see **SPECIES**).

**specification** /ˌspɛsɪfɪˈkeɪʃ(ə)n/ ● **n. 1** the action of specifying. ➤(usu. **specifications**) a detailed description of the design and materials used to make something. ➤a description of an invention accompanying an application for a patent. **2** a standard of workmanship, materials, etc. required to be met in a piece of work.

**specific charge** ● **n.** Physics the ratio of the charge of an ion or subatomic particle to its mass.

**specific epithet** ● **n.** chiefly Botany & Microbiology the second element in the Latin binomial name of a species, which distinguishes the species from others in the same genus.

**specific gravity** ● **n.** another term for **RELATIVE DENSITY**.

**specific heat capacity** ● **n.** Physics the heat required to raise the temperature of the unit mass of a given substance by a given amount (usually one degree).

**specific performance** ● **n.** Law the performance of a contractual duty, as ordered in cases where damages would not be adequate remedy.

**specify** ● **v.** (**-ies, -ied**) **1** identify clearly and definitely. **2** include in an architect's or engineer's specifications.
– DERIVATIVES **specifiable** adj. **specifier** n.

**specimen** /ˈspɛsɪmɪn/ ● **n. 1** an individual animal, plant, object, etc. used as an example of its species or type for scientific study or display. ➤an example of something regarded as typical of its class or group: [as modifier] *a specimen signature*. ➤informal used to refer humorously to a person or animal. **2** a sample for medical testing, especially of urine.
– ORIGIN C17 (in the sense 'pattern, model'): from L., from *specere* 'to look'.

**specious** /ˈspiːʃəs/ ● **adj.** superficially plausible, but actually wrong. ➤misleadingly attractive in appearance.
– DERIVATIVES **speciously** adv. **speciousness** n.
– ORIGIN ME (in the sense 'beautiful'): from L. *speciosus* 'fair, plausible, specious', from *species* (see **SPECIES**).

**speck** ● **n.** a tiny spot. ➤a small particle. ● **v.** mark with small spots.
– DERIVATIVES **speckless** adj.
– ORIGIN OE *specca*; cf. **SPECKLE**.

**speckle** ● **n.** a small spot or patch of colour. ● **v.** mark with speckles.
– DERIVATIVES **speckled** adj.
– ORIGIN ME: from MDu. *spekkel*.

**speckled wood** ● **n.** a brown butterfly with cream or orange markings, favouring woodland habitats. [*Pararge aegeria*.]

**specs** ● **pl. n.** informal a pair of spectacles.

**spectacle** ● **n.** a visually striking performance or display.
– PHRASES **make a spectacle of oneself** draw attention to oneself by behaving in a ridiculous way in public.
– ORIGIN ME: via OFr. from L. *spectaculum* 'public show', from *spectare*, from *specere* 'to look'.

**spectacled** ● **adj. 1** wearing spectacles. **2** used in names of animals with markings around the eyes that resemble spectacles.

**spectacles** ● **pl. n.** Brit. a pair of glasses.

**spectacular** ● **adj. 1** very impressive, striking, or dramatic. **2** strikingly large; marked. ● **n.** a performance or event produced on a large scale and with striking effects.
– DERIVATIVES **spectacularly** adv.

**spectate** ● **v.** be a spectator.
– ORIGIN C18: back-form. from **SPECTATOR**.

**spectator** ● **n.** a person who watches at a show, game, or other event.
– DERIVATIVES **spectatorial** adj. (rare).
– ORIGIN C16: from Fr. *spectateur* or L. *spectator*, from *spectare* (see **SPECTACLE**).

**specter** ● **n.** US spelling of **SPECTRE**.

**spectinomycin** /ˌspɛktɪnə(ʊ)ˈmʌɪsɪn/ ● **n.** Medicine a bacterial antibiotic used as an alternative to penicillin.
– ORIGIN 1960s: from *spectabilis* (from *Streptomyces spectabilis*, the name of the bacterium), lit. 'visible, remarkable' + **-MYCIN**.

**spectra** plural form of **SPECTRUM**.

**spectral** ● **adj. 1** of or like a spectre. **2** of or concerning spectra or the spectrum.
– DERIVATIVES **spectrally** adv.

**spectre** (US **specter**) ● **n. 1** a ghost. **2** something unpleasant or dangerous imagined or expected: *the spectre of nuclear holocaust*.
– ORIGIN C17: from Fr. *spectre* or L. *spectrum* (see **SPECTRUM**).

**spectro-** ● **comb. form** representing **SPECTRUM**.

**spectrogram** ● **n.** a visual or electronic record of a spectrum.

**spectrograph** ● **n.** an apparatus for photographing or otherwise recording spectra.
– DERIVATIVES **spectrographic** adj. **spectrographically** adv. **spectrography** n.

**spectroheliograph** /ˌspɛktrə(ʊ)ˈhiːlɪəgrɑːf/ ● **n.** an instrument for photographing or recording the sun's image using light of particular wavelengths.

**spectrohelioscope** /ˌspɛktrə(ʊ)ˈhiːlɪəskəʊp/ ● **n.** a device similar to a spectroheliograph for observing the sun directly.

**spectrometer** /spɛkˈtrɒmɪtə/ ● **n.** an apparatus used for recording and measuring spectra, especially as a method of analysis.
– DERIVATIVES **spectrometric** adj. **spectrometry** n.

**spectrophotometer** /ˌspɛktrə(ʊ)fəʊˈtɒmɪtə/ ● **n.** an apparatus for measuring the intensity of light in a part of the spectrum, especially as transmitted or emitted by particular substances.
– DERIVATIVES **spectrophotometric** /-təˈmɛtrɪk/ adj.

**spectrophotometrically** adv. **spectrophotometry** n.

**spectroscope** • n. an apparatus for producing and recording spectra for examination.

**spectroscopy** • n. the branch of science concerned with the investigation and measurement of spectra produced when matter interacts with or emits electromagnetic radiation.
– DERIVATIVES **spectroscopic** adj. **spectroscopically** adv. **spectroscopist** n.

**spectrum** • n. (pl. **spectra** /-trə/) **1** a band of colours produced by separation of the components of light by their different degrees of refraction according to wavelength, e.g. in a rainbow. ➤the entire range of wavelengths of electromagnetic radiation. ➤a characteristic series of frequencies of electromagnetic radiation emitted or absorbed by a substance. ➤the components of a sound or other phenomenon arranged according to frequency, energy, etc. **2** a scale extending between two points; a range: *the political spectrum.*
– ORIGIN C17 (in the sense 'spectre'): from L., lit. 'image, apparition', from *specere* 'to look'.

**specula** plural form of **SPECULUM**.

**specular** /'spɛkjʊlə/ • adj. of, relating to, or having the properties of a mirror.
– ORIGIN C16: from L. *specularis*, from *speculum* (see **SPECULUM**).

**speculate** /'spɛkjʊleɪt/ • v. **1** form a theory or conjecture without firm evidence. **2** invest in stocks, property, or other ventures in the hope of gain but with the risk of loss.
– DERIVATIVES **speculation** n. **speculator** n.
– ORIGIN C16: from L. *speculat-*, *speculari* 'observe', from *specula* 'watchtower', from *specere* 'to look'.

**speculative** • adj. **1** engaged in, expressing, or based on conjecture rather than knowledge. **2** (of an investment) involving a high risk of loss.
– DERIVATIVES **speculatively** adv. **speculativeness** n.

**speculum** /'spɛkjʊləm/ • n. (pl. **specula** /-lə/) **1** Medicine a metal instrument that is used to dilate an orifice or canal in the body to allow inspection. **2** Ornithology a bright patch of plumage on the wings of certain birds, especially ducks. **3** a mirror or reflector, especially (formerly) a metallic mirror in a reflecting telescope. ➤short for **SPECULUM METAL**.
– ORIGIN ME: from L., lit. 'mirror', from *specere* 'to look'.

**speculum metal** • n. an alloy of copper and tin used to make mirrors, especially formerly for telescopes.

**sped** past and past participle of **SPEED**.

**speech** • n. **1** the expression of or the ability to express thoughts and feelings by articulate sounds. **2** a formal address delivered to an audience. ➤a sequence of lines written for one character in a play.
– ORIGIN OE *sprǣc*, *sprēc*, later *spēc*, of W. Gmc origin.

**speech act** • n. Linguistics & Philosophy an utterance considered as an action, particularly with regard to its intention, purpose, or effect.

**speech day** • n. Brit. an annual event held at some schools, especially public schools, at which speeches are made and prizes are presented.

**speechify** • v. (**-ies**, **-ied**) deliver a speech, especially in a tedious or pompous way.
– DERIVATIVES **speechification** n. **speechifier** n.

**speechless** • adj. unable to speak, especially as the temporary result of shock or strong emotion.
– DERIVATIVES **speechlessly** adv. **speechlessness** n.

**speech-reading** • n. lip-reading.

**speech recognition** • n. the process of enabling a computer to identify and respond to the sounds produced in human speech.

**speech therapy** • n. treatment to help people with speech and language problems.
– DERIVATIVES **speech therapist** n.

**speed** • n. **1** the rate at which someone or something moves or operates or is able to move or operate. ➤rapidity of movement or action. **2** each of the possible gear ratios of a bicycle. **3** the light-gathering power or f-number of a camera lens. ➤the duration of a photographic exposure. ➤the sensitivity of photographic film to light. **4** informal an amphetamine drug, especially methamphetamine. **5** archaic success; prosperity. • v. (past and past part. **speeded** or **sped**) **1** move quickly. ➤(**speed up**) move or work more quickly. **2** (of a motorist) travel at a speed greater than the legal limit. **3** informal take or be under the influence of an amphetamine drug. **4** archaic make prosperous or successful: *may God speed you.*
– PHRASES **at speed** quickly. **up to speed 1** operating at full speed or capacity. **2** fully informed or up to date.
– DERIVATIVES **speeder** n.
– ORIGIN OE *spēd* (n.), *spēdan* (v.), from the Gmc base of OE *spōwan* 'prosper, succeed'.

**speed bag** • n. N. Amer. a small punchbag used by boxers for practising quick punches.

**speedball** • n. **1** informal a mixture of cocaine with heroin. **2** a small punchball used by boxers for practising quick punches. **3** US a ball game resembling soccer but in which the ball may be handled.

**speedboat** • n. a motor boat designed for high speed.

**speed bump** (Brit. also **speed hump**) • n. a ridge set in a road to control the speed of vehicles.

**speed camera** • n. a roadside camera designed to catch speeding vehicles by taking video footage or a photograph.

**speed limit** • n. the maximum speed at which a vehicle may legally travel on a particular stretch of road.

**speedo** • n. (pl. **-os**) informal short for **SPEEDOMETER**.

**speedometer** /spiː'dɒmɪtə/ • n. an instrument on a vehicle's dashboard indicating its speed.

**speedster** • n. informal a person or thing that operates well at high speed.

**speedway** • n. **1** a form of motorcycle racing in which the riders race laps around an oval dirt track. ➤a stadium or track used for this sport. **2** N. Amer. a highway for fast motor traffic.

**speedwell** • n. a small creeping plant with blue or pink flowers. [Genus *Veronica*: several species.]

**speedy** • adj. (**-ier**, **-iest**) **1** done or occurring quickly. **2** moving quickly.
– DERIVATIVES **speedily** adv. **speediness** n.

**speiss** /spʌɪs/ • n. a mixture of impure arsenides and antimonides of nickel, cobalt, iron, and other metals, produced in the smelting of cobalt and other ores.
– ORIGIN C18: from Ger. *Speise* 'food, amalgam'.

**spekboom** /'spɛkbʊəm/ • n. S. African a South African shrub with succulent leaves, which is used for fodder during times of drought. [*Portulacaria afra*.]
– ORIGIN C19: from Afrik., from *spek* 'bacon' + *boom* 'tree'.

**speleology** /ˌspiːlɪ'ɒlədʒi, ˌspɛl-/ • n. the study or exploration of caves.
– DERIVATIVES **speleological** adj. **speleologist** n.
– ORIGIN C19: from Fr. *spéléologie*, via L. from Gk *spēlaion* 'cave'.

**speleothem** /'spiːlɪə(ʊ)θɛm/ • n. Geology a structure formed in a cave by the deposition of minerals from water, e.g. a stalactite or stalagmite.
– ORIGIN 1950s: from Gk *spēlaion* 'cave' + *thema* 'deposit'.

**spell**[1] • v. (past and past part. **spelled** or chiefly Brit. **spelt**) **1** write or name the letters that form (a word) in correct sequence. ➤(of letters) make up or form (a word). **2** be a sign of; lead to: *the plans would spell disaster for the economy.* **3** (**spell something out**) explain something simply and in detail.
– DERIVATIVES **spelling** n.
– ORIGIN ME: shortening of OFr. *espeller*, from the Gmc base of **SPELL**[2].

**spell**[2] • n. **1** a form of words used as a magical charm or incantation. **2** a state of enchantment or influence induced by or as if by a spell.
– ORIGIN OE *spel(l)* 'narration', of Gmc origin.

**spell**[3] • n. **1** a short period of time. ➤Austral./NZ a period of rest from work. **2** Cricket a series of overs in which a particular bowler bowls. • v. chiefly N. Amer. take someone's place in order to allow them to rest briefly. ➤Austral./NZ take a brief rest.
– ORIGIN C16: var. of dial. *spele* 'take the place of', of unknown origin.

**spell**[4] ● n. a splinter of wood.
– ORIGIN ME: perh. a var. of obs. *speld* 'chip, splinter'.

**spellbind** ● v. (past and past part. **spellbound**) hold the complete attention of, as if by a spell.
– DERIVATIVES **spellbinder** n. **spellbinding** adj. **spellbindingly** adv.

**spellchecker** (also **spelling checker**) ● n. a computer program which checks the spelling of words in files of text, usually by comparing them with a stored list of words.
– DERIVATIVES **spellcheck** v. & n.

**speller** ● n. **1** a person of a specified spelling ability. **2** chiefly N. Amer. a book for teaching spelling. ➤short for SPELLCHECKER.

**spelling bee** ● n. a spelling competition.

**spelt**[1] past and past participle of SPELL[1].

**spelt**[2] ● n. an old kind of wheat with bearded ears and spikelets that each contain two narrow grains, favoured as a health food. [*Triticum spelta*.]
– ORIGIN OE, from Old Saxon *spelta*.

**spelter** /ˈspɛltə/ ● n. commercial crude smelted zinc. ➤a solder or other alloy in which zinc is the main constituent.
– ORIGIN C17: cf. OFr. *espeautre*, MDu. *speauter*; rel. to PEWTER.

**spelunking** /spɪˈlʌŋkɪŋ/ ● n. N. Amer. the exploration of caves, especially as a hobby.
– DERIVATIVES **spelunker** n.
– ORIGIN 1940s: from obs. *spelunk* 'cave' (from L. *spelunca*).

**spence** ● n. archaic a larder.
– ORIGIN ME: shortening of OFr. *despense*, from L. *dispensa*, fem. past part. of *dispendere* (see DISPENSE).

**spencer**[1] ● n. **1** a short, close-fitting jacket, worn by women and children in the early 19th century. **2** a thin woollen vest.
– ORIGIN prob. named after the second Earl *Spencer* (1758–1834), Engl. politician.

**spencer**[2] ● n. Sailing a trysail.
– ORIGIN C19: of unknown origin.

**spend** ● v. (past and past part. **spent**) **1** pay out (money) in buying or hiring goods or services. **2** use or use up (energy or resources); exhaust. ➤pass (time) in a specified way. ● n. informal an amount of money paid out.
– PHRASES **spend a penny** Brit. informal, euphemistic urinate.
– DERIVATIVES **spendable** adj. **spender** n.
– ORIGIN OE *spendan*, from L. *expendere* 'pay out'; also a shortening of obs. *dispend*, from L. *dispendere* 'pay out'.

**spending money** ● n. an allowance for entertainment and day-to-day expenditure.

**spendthrift** ● n. a person who spends money in an extravagant, irresponsible way.

**Spenserian** /spɛnˈsɪərɪən/ ● adj. of, relating to, or in the style of the English poet Edmund Spenser (*c.*1552–99) or his works. ● n. an expert in or student of Spenser's works.

**Spenserian stanza** ● n. the stanza used by Spenser in the *Faerie Queene*, consisting of eight iambic pentameters and an alexandrine, with the rhyming scheme *ababbcbcc*.

**spent** past and past participle of SPEND. ● adj. used up; exhausted.

**sperm** ● n. (pl. same or **sperms**) **1** semen. ➤a spermatozoon. **2** short for SPERM WHALE, SPERMACETI, or SPERM OIL.
– ORIGIN ME: via late L. from Gk *sperma* 'seed', from *speirein* 'to sow'.

**spermaceti** /ˌspəːməˈsiːti, -ˈsɛti/ ● n. a white waxy substance obtained from an organ in the head of the sperm whale, which focuses acoustic signals and aids in the control of buoyancy, and was formerly used in candles and ointments.
– ORIGIN C15: from med. L., from late L. *sperma* 'sperm' + *ceti* 'of a whale' (from Gk *kētos* 'whale'), from the belief that it was whale spawn.

**spermatheca** /ˌspəːməˈθiːkə/ ● n. (pl. **spermathecae** /-ˈθiːkiː/) Zoology a receptacle in many female or hermaphrodite invertebrates in which sperm is stored after mating.
– ORIGIN C19: from late L. *sperma* 'sperm' + THECA.

**spermatic** ● adj. of or relating to sperm or semen.
– DERIVATIVES **spermatically** adv.
– ORIGIN ME: via late L. from Gk *spermatikos*, from *sperma* (see SPERM).

**spermatic cord** ● n. (in mammals) a bundle of nerves, ducts, and blood vessels connecting the testicles to the abdominal cavity.

**spermatid** /ˈspəːmətɪd/ ● n. Biology an immature male sex cell formed from a spermatocyte, which may develop into a spermatozoon without further division.
– DERIVATIVES **spermatidal** /ˌspəːməˈtʌɪd(ə)l/ adj.

**spermato-** ● comb. form Biology relating to sperm or seeds: *spermatozoid*.
– ORIGIN from Gk *sperma*, *spermat-* 'sperm'.

**spermatocyte** /ˈspəːmətə(ʊ)sʌɪt, spəˈmat-/ ● n. Biology a cell produced at the second stage in the formation of spermatozoa, formed from a spermatogonium and dividing by meiosis into spermatids.

**spermatogenesis** /ˌspəːmətə(ʊ)ˈdʒɛnɪsɪs, spəˌmat-/ ● n. Biology the production or development of mature spermatozoa.

**spermatogonium** /ˌspəːmətə(ʊ)ˈɡəʊnɪəm, spəˌmat-/ ● n. (pl. **spermatogonia** /-nɪə/) Biology a cell produced at an early stage in the formation of spermatozoa, giving rise by mitosis to spermatocytes.
– DERIVATIVES **spermatogonial** adj.
– ORIGIN C19: from SPERM + mod. L. *gonium* (from Gk *gonos* 'offspring, seed').

**spermatophore** /ˈspəːmətə(ʊ)fɔː, spəˈmat-/ ● n. Zoology a protein capsule containing a mass of spermatozoa, transferred during mating in various insects, arthropods, cephalopod molluscs, etc.

**spermatophyte** /ˈspəːmətə(ʊ)ˌfʌɪt, spəˈmat-/ ● n. Botany a plant of a large division that comprises those that bear seeds, including the gymnosperms and angiosperms.

**spermatozoid** /ˌspəːmətə(ʊ)ˈzəʊɪd, spəˌmat-/ ● n. Botany a motile male gamete produced by a lower plant or a gymnosperm.

**spermatozoon** /ˌspəːmətə(ʊ)ˈzəʊɒn, spəˌmat-/ ● n. (pl. **spermatozoa** /-ˈzəʊə/) Biology the mature motile male sex cell of an animal, by which the ovum is fertilized, typically having a compact head and one or more long flagella for swimming.
– DERIVATIVES **spermatozoal** adj. **spermatozoan** adj.
– ORIGIN C19: from Gk *sperma*, *spermat-* 'seed' + *zōion* 'animal'.

**sperm bank** ● n. a place where semen is kept in cold storage for use in artificial insemination.

**sperm count** ● n. a measure of the number of spermatozoa per measured amount of semen, used as an indication of a man's fertility.

**spermicide** ● n. a substance that kills spermatozoa, used as a contraceptive.
– DERIVATIVES **spermicidal** adj.

**spermidine** /ˈspəːmɪdiːn/ ● n. Biochemistry a colourless compound with a similar distribution and effect to spermine.
– ORIGIN 1920s: from SPERM + -IDE + -INE[4].

**spermine** /ˈspəːmiːn/ ● n. Biochemistry a deliquescent compound which acts to stabilize various components of living cells and is widely distributed in living and decaying tissues.

**spermo-** ● comb. form equivalent to SPERMATO-.

**sperm oil** ● n. an oil found with spermaceti in the head of the sperm whale, used formerly as a lubricant.

**sperm whale** ● n. a toothed whale with a massive head, feeding at great depths largely on squid. [*Physeter macrocephalus* and other species.]
– ORIGIN C19: abbrev. of SPERMACETI.

**spessartine** /ˈspɛsətiːn/ ● n. a form of garnet containing manganese and aluminium, occurring as orange-red to dark brown crystals.
– ORIGIN C19: from Fr., from *Spessart*, the name of a district in NW Bavaria, + -INE[4].

**spew** ● v. **1** expel or be expelled in large quantities rapidly and forcibly. **2** informal vomit. ● n. informal vomit.
– DERIVATIVES **spewer** n.
– ORIGIN OE *spīwan*, *spēowan*, of Gmc origin.

**SPF** ● abbrev. sun protection factor.

**sphagnum** /ˈsfagnəm/ ● n. a plant of a genus that comprises the peat mosses. [Genus *Sphagnum*.]
– ORIGIN C18: mod. L., from Gk *sphagnos*, denoting a kind of moss.

**sphalerite** /ˈsfalərʌɪt/ ● n. a shiny mineral, yellow to dark brown or black in colour, consisting of zinc sulphide.
– ORIGIN C19: from Gk *sphaleros* 'deceptive' + **-ITE**[1]; cf. **BLENDE**.

**sphene** /sfiːn/ ● n. a greenish-yellow or brown mineral consisting of a silicate of calcium and titanium, occurring in granitic and metamorphic rocks in wedge-shaped crystals.
– ORIGIN C19: from Fr. *sphène*, from Gk *sphēn* 'wedge'.

**sphenoid** /ˈsfiːnɔɪd/ ● n. Anatomy a large compound bone which forms the base of the cranium.
– DERIVATIVES **sphenoidal** adj.
– ORIGIN C18: from mod. L. *sphenoides*, from Gk *sphēnoeidēs*, from *sphēn* 'wedge'.

**sphere** ● n. **1** a round solid figure, with every point on its surface equidistant from its centre. **2** each of a series of revolving concentrically arranged spherical shells in which celestial bodies were formerly thought to be set in a fixed relationship. ➤ chiefly poetic/literary a celestial body. ➤ poetic/literary the sky perceived as a vault upon or in which celestial bodies are represented as lying. ➤ a globe representing the earth. **3** an area of activity, interest, or expertise; a group or section distinguished and unified by a particular characteristic. ● v. archaic enclose in or form into a sphere.
– PHRASES **music** (or **harmony**) **of the spheres** the natural harmonic tones supposedly produced by the movement of the celestial spheres or the bodies fixed in them.
– DERIVATIVES **spheral** adj. (archaic).
– ORIGIN ME: from OFr. *espere*, from late L. *sphera*, from Gk *sphaira* 'ball'.

**-sphere** ● comb. form denoting a structure or region of spherical form, especially a region round the earth: *ionosphere*.

**spheric** /ˈsfɛrɪk/ ● adj. spherical.
– DERIVATIVES **sphericity** n.

**spherical** ● adj. shaped like a sphere. ➤ of or relating to the properties of spheres. ➤ formed inside or on the surface of a sphere.
– DERIVATIVES **spherically** adv.
– ORIGIN C15: via late L. from Gk *sphairikos*, from *sphaira* (see **SPHERE**).

**spherical aberration** ● n. a loss of definition in the image arising from the surface geometry of a spherical mirror or lens.

**spherical angle** ● n. an angle formed by the intersection of two great circles of a sphere.

**spherical coordinates** ● pl. n. coordinates that locate a point in three dimensions in terms of its distance from the origin and two angles defined with reference to vertical and horizontal planes.

**spherical triangle** ● n. a triangle formed by three arcs of great circles on a sphere.

**spheroid** /ˈsfɪərɔɪd/ ● n. a sphere-like but not perfectly spherical body.
– DERIVATIVES **spheroidal** adj. **spheroidicity** n.

**spherule** /ˈsfɛrjuːl/ ● n. a small sphere.
– DERIVATIVES **spherular** adj.
– ORIGIN C17: from late L. *sphaerula*, dimin. of L. *sphaera* (see **SPHERE**).

**spherulite** /ˈsfɛrjʊlʌɪt/ ● n. chiefly Geology a small spheroidal mass of crystals grouped radially around a point.
– DERIVATIVES **spherulitic** adj.
– ORIGIN C19: from **SPHERULE** + **-ITE**[1].

**sphincter** /ˈsfɪŋktə/ ● n. Anatomy a ring of muscle surrounding and serving to guard or close an opening.
– DERIVATIVES **sphincteral** adj. **sphincteric** adj.
– ORIGIN C16: via L. from Gk *sphinktēr*, from *sphingein* 'bind tight'.

**sphingomyelin** /ˌsfɪŋgə(ʊ)ˈmʌɪəlɪn/ ● n. Biochemistry a substance consisting of phosphates of sphingosine and choline, found in the brain and nervous tissue.

**sphingosine** /ˈsfɪŋgə(ʊ)sʌɪn/ ● n. Biochemistry a basic compound which is a constituent of a number of substances important in the metabolism of nerve cells, especially sphingomyelins.
– ORIGIN C19: from Gk *Sphing-*, *Sphinx* 'sphinx', with ref. to the enigmatic nature of the compound.

**sphinx** ● n. **1** an ancient Egyptian stone figure having a lion's body and a human or animal head. **2** an enigmatic or inscrutable person. **3** North American term for **HAWKMOTH**.
– ORIGIN ME: via L. from Gk *Sphinx* (appar. from *sphingein* 'draw tight'), the name of a winged monster in Greek mythology, having a woman's head and a lion's body, who propounded a riddle and killed those who failed to solve it.

**sphygmo-** /ˈsfɪgməʊ/ ● comb. form Physiology of or relating to the pulse or pulsation: *sphygmograph*.
– ORIGIN from Gk *sphugmos* 'pulse'.

**sphygmograph** ● n. an instrument for recording the strength and rate of the pulse.

**sphygmomanometer** /ˌsfɪgməʊməˈnɒmɪtə/ ● n. an instrument for measuring blood pressure, typically consisting of an inflatable rubber cuff which is applied to the arm and connected to a column of mercury next to a graduated scale.
– DERIVATIVES **sphygmomanometry** n.

**Sphynx** /sfɪŋks/ ● n. a cat of a hairless breed, originally from North America.

**spic** ● n. US informal, offensive a Spanish-speaking person from Central or South America or the Caribbean, especially a Mexican.
– ORIGIN C20: abbrev. of US sl. *spiggoty*, in the same sense, of uncertain origin: perh. an alt. of *speak the* in 'no speak the English'.

**spica** /ˈspʌɪkə/ ● n. Medicine a bandage folded into a spiral arrangement resembling an ear of wheat or barley.
– ORIGIN C17: from L., lit. 'spike, ear of corn'; influenced by Gk *stakhus* 'ear of wheat'.

**spic and span** ● adj. variant spelling of **SPICK AND SPAN**.

**spiccato** /spɪˈkɑːtəʊ/ ● n. Music a style of staccato playing on stringed instruments involving bouncing the bow on the strings.
– ORIGIN Ital., lit. 'detailed, distinct'.

**spice** ● n. **1** an aromatic or pungent vegetable substance used to flavour food, e.g. pepper. **2** an element providing interest and excitement. **3** N. English confectionery. ● v. **1** [often as adj. **spiced**] flavour with spice. **2** (often **spice something up**) make more exciting or interesting.
– ORIGIN ME: shortening of OFr. *espice*, from L. *species* 'sort, kind', in late L. 'wares'.

**spicebush** ● n. a North American aromatic shrub, the fruit of which was used as a substitute for allspice. [*Lindera benzoin*.]

**spick and span** (also **spic and span**) ● adj. neat, clean, and well looked after.
– ORIGIN C16 (in the sense 'brand new'): from *spick and span new*, emphatic extension of dial. *span new*, from ON *spán-nýr*, from *spánn* 'chip' + *nýr* 'new'; *spick* influenced by Du. *spiksplinternieuw*, lit. 'splinter new'.

**spicule** /ˈspɪkjuːl/ ● n. **1** chiefly Zoology a small needle-like structure, in particular any of those making up the skeleton of a sponge. **2** Astronomy a short-lived jet of gas in the sun's corona.
– DERIVATIVES **spicular** adj. **spiculate** /-lət/ adj. **spiculation** n.
– ORIGIN C18: from mod. L. *spicula*, *spiculum*, dimin. of *spica* 'ear of grain'.

**spicy** (also **spicey**) ● adj. (**-ier**, **-iest**) **1** flavoured with spice. **2** mildly indecent.
– DERIVATIVES **spicily** adv. **spiciness** n.

**spider** ● n. **1** an eight-legged predatory arachnid with an unsegmented body consisting of a fused head and thorax

and a rounded abdomen, most kinds of which spin webs in which to capture insects. [Order Araneae.] ➤used in names of other arachnids, e.g. **sea spider**. **2** a long-legged rest for a billiard cue that can be placed over a ball without touching it. **3** Brit. a set of radiating elastic ties used to hold a load in place on a vehicle. **4** Computing another term for CRAWLER (in sense 2). ● v. **1** move in a scuttling manner. **2** form a pattern suggestive of a spider or its web.
– DERIVATIVES **spiderish** adj.
– ORIGIN OE *spīthra*, from *spinnan* (see SPIN).

**spider crab** ● n. a crab with long thin legs and a compact pear-shaped body. [*Macropodia* and other genera.]

**spiderman** ● n. (pl. **-men**) Brit. informal a person who works at great heights in building work.

**spider mite** ● n. an active plant-feeding mite resembling a minute spider. [*Tetranychus urticae* (**red spider mite**) and other species.]

**spider monkey** ● n. a South American monkey with very long limbs and a long prehensile tail. [Genus *Brachyteles*: four species.]

**spider plant** ● n. a plant of the lily family having long narrow leaves with a central yellow stripe, native to southern Africa and popular as a house plant. [*Chlorophytum comosum*.]

**spiderweb** ● n. a type of turquoise criss-crossed with fine dark lines. ● v. (**-webbed**, **-webbing**) cover with a pattern resembling a spider's web.

**spiderwort** ● n. an American plant whose flowers bear long hairy stamens. [*Tradescantia virginiana* (N. America) and related species.]

**spidery** ● adj. resembling a spider, especially having long, thin, angular lines like a spider's legs.

**spiegeleisen** /ˈspiːɡ(ə)lˌʌɪz(ə)n/ ● n. an alloy of iron and manganese, used in steel-making.
– ORIGIN C19: from Ger., from *Spiegel* 'mirror' + *Eisen* 'iron'.

**spiel** /ʃpiːl, spiːl/ informal ● n. an elaborate and glib speech or story, typically one used by a salesperson. ● v. speak or utter at length or glibly.
– ORIGIN C19: from Ger. *Spiel* 'a game'.

**spieler** /ˈʃpiːlə, ˈspiːlə/ ● n. informal **1** a glib or voluble speaker. **2** Austral./NZ a gambler or swindler. **3** a gambling club.

**spiff** ● v. (**spiff someone/thing up**) informal make someone or something smart or stylish.
– ORIGIN C19: perh. from dial. *spiff* 'well dressed'.

**spiffing** ● adj. Brit. informal, dated excellent; splendid.
– ORIGIN C19: of unknown origin.

**spifflicate** /ˈspɪflɪkeɪt/ (also **spiflicate**) ● v. informal, humorous destroy or defeat utterly.
– DERIVATIVES **spifflication** n.
– ORIGIN C18: a fanciful formation.

**spiffy** ● adj. (**-ier**, **-iest**) N. Amer. informal smart or stylish.
– DERIVATIVES **spiffily** adv.
– ORIGIN C19: of unknown origin.

**spignel** /ˈspɪɡn(ə)l/ ● n. an aromatic white-flowered mountain plant of the parsley family. [*Meum athamanticum*.]
– ORIGIN C16: perh. from Anglo-Norman Fr. *spigurnelle*, the name of an unidentified plant.

**spigot** /ˈspɪɡət/ ● n. **1** a small peg or plug, especially for insertion into the vent of a cask. **2** US a tap. ➤a device for controlling the flow of liquid in a tap. **3** the plain end of a section of a pipe fitting into the socket of the next one.
– ORIGIN ME: perh. an alt. of Provençal *espigou(n)*, from L. *spiculum*, dimin. of *spicum*, var. of *spica* (see SPICA).

**spike**[1] ● n. **1** a thin, pointed piece of metal or another rigid material. ➤a large stout nail, especially one used to fasten a rail to a railway sleeper. ➤each of several metal points set into the sole of a sports shoe to prevent slipping. ➤(**spikes**) a pair of sports shoes with spikes. ➤chiefly Brit. a pointed metal rod standing on a base and used for filing bills or journalistic material rejected for publication. **2** a sharp increase in magnitude or intensity. ➤Electronics a pulse of very short duration. **3** Brit. informal the casual ward of a hostel offering temporary accommodation for the homeless. ● v. **1** impale on or pierce with a spike. ➤historical render (a gun) useless by plugging up the vent with a spike. **2** form into or cover with sharp points. **3** (of a newspaper editor) reject (a story) by or as if by filing it on a spike. ➤thwart. **4** informal lace (drink or food) with alcohol or a drug surreptitiously. ➤Physics & Chemistry enrich with a particular isotope. **5** increase and then decrease sharply. **6** (in volleyball) hit (the ball) forcefully from a position near the net so that it moves downward into the opposite court. ➤American Football fling (the ball) forcefully to the ground, typically in celebration of a touchdown or victory.
– PHRASES **spike someone's guns** thwart someone's plans.
– ORIGIN ME: perh. from Mid. Low Ger., MDu. *spiker*, rel. to SPOKE[1].

**spike**[2] ● n. Botany a flower cluster formed of many flower heads attached directly to a long stem.
– ORIGIN ME (denoting an ear of corn): from L. *spica* (see SPICA).

**spikelet** ● n. Botany the basic unit of a grass flower, consisting of two glumes or outer bracts at the base and one or more florets above.

**spikenard** /ˈspʌɪknɑːd/ ● n. **1** a costly perfumed ointment much valued in ancient times. **2** the Himalayan plant of the valerian family that produces the rhizome from which this ointment was prepared. [*Nardostachys grandiflora*.]
– ORIGIN ME: from med. L. *spica nardi* (see SPIKE[2], NARD), translating Gk *nardostakhus*.

**spiky** ● adj. (**-ier**, **-iest**) **1** like a spike or spikes or having many spikes. **2** informal easily offended or annoyed.
– DERIVATIVES **spikily** adv. **spikiness** n.

**spile** /spʌɪl/ ● n. **1** a small wooden peg or spigot. **2** N. Amer. a small spout for tapping the sap from a sugar maple. **3** a large, heavy timber driven into the ground to support a superstructure. ● v. chiefly US or dialect broach (a cask) with a peg to draw off liquid.
– ORIGIN C16: from MDu., Mid. Low Ger., 'wooden peg'; in sense 3 appar. an alt. of PILE[2].

**spill**[1] ● v. (past and past part. **spilt** or **spilled**) **1** (with reference to liquid) flow or cause to flow over the edge of its container. **2** (with reference to contents or occupants) be discharged or cause to be discharged from a container or place. **3** informal reveal (confidential information). **4** Sailing let (wind) out of a sail, typically by slackening the sheets. ● n. **1** a quantity of liquid that has spilled or been spilt. ➤an instance of a liquid spilling or being spilt. **2** a fall from a horse or bicycle. **3** Austral. a vacating of all or several posts in a cabinet or parliamentary party to allow reorganization after one important change of office.
– PHRASES **spill the beans** informal reveal secret information unintentionally or indiscreetly. **spill (someone's) blood** kill or wound people.
– DERIVATIVES **spillage** n. **spiller** n.
– ORIGIN OE *spillan* 'kill, waste, shed (blood)'.

**spill**[2] ● n. a thin strip of wood or paper used for lighting a fire, pipe, etc.
– ORIGIN ME: obscurely rel. to SPILE.

**spillikin** /ˈspɪlɪkɪn/ ● n. **1** (**spillikins**) [treated as sing.] a game played with a heap of small rods of wood, bone, or plastic, in which players try to remove one at a time without disturbing the others. **2** a splinter or fragment.
– ORIGIN C18: from SPILL[2] + -KIN.

**spillover** ● n. **1** an instance of spilling over into another area. ➤a thing that spills or has spilt over. **2** an unexpected consequence or by-product.

**spillway** ● n. a passage for surplus water from a dam.

**spilt** past and past participle of SPILL[1].

**spilth** ● n. archaic the action of spilling or material that is spilt.

**spin** ● v. (**spinning**; past and past part. **spun**) **1** turn or cause to turn round quickly. ➤(of a person's head) give a sensation of dizziness. ➤chiefly Cricket (with reference to a ball) move or cause to move through the air with a revolving motion. ➤shape (sheet metal) by pressure applied during rotation on a lathe. **2** draw out (wool, cotton, or other material) and convert it into threads. ➤make (threads) in this way. **3** (of a spider or a silkworm or other insect) produce (gossamer or silk) or construct (a web or cocoon) by extruding a fine viscous thread from a special gland. **4** (**spin something out**) make something last as long as possible. **5** (**spin out**) N. Amer. (of a driver or car) lose control in a skid. **6** (**spin something off**) (of a parent company) turn a subsidiary into a new and separate company. **7** fish with a spinner. ● **n. 1** a spinning motion. ➤a fast revolving motion of an aircraft as it descends rapidly. ➤Physics the intrinsic angular momentum of a subatomic particle. **2** informal a brief trip in a vehicle for pleasure. **3** a favourable bias or slant given to a news story. **4** Austral./NZ informal a piece of good or bad luck.

– PHRASES **flat spin 1** a spin in which an aircraft descends in tight circles while remaining horizontal. **2** Brit. informal a state of agitation. **spin one's wheels** N. Amer. informal waste one's time or efforts. **spin a yarn** tell a long, far-fetched story.

– DERIVATIVES **spinning** n. & adj.

– ORIGIN OE *spinnan* 'draw out and twist (fibre)'.

**spina bifida** /ˌspʌɪnə ˈbɪfɪdə/ ● **n.** a congenital defect in which part of the spinal cord is exposed through a gap in the backbone, and which can cause paralysis and mental handicap.

– ORIGIN C18: mod. L. (see **SPINE**, **BIFID**).

**spinach** /ˈspɪnɪdʒ, -ɪtʃ/ ● **n.** an edible Asian plant of the goosefoot family, with large dark green leaves which are eaten as a vegetable. [*Spinacia oleracea*.]

– DERIVATIVES **spinachy** adj.

– ORIGIN ME: prob. from OFr. *espinache*, via Arab. from Pers. *aspānāḵ*.

**spinach beet** ● **n.** beet of a variety cultivated for its spinach-like leaves.

**spinal** ● **adj.** of or relating to the spine.

– DERIVATIVES **spinally** adv.

**spinal canal** ● **n.** a cavity which runs successively through each of the vertebrae and encloses the spinal cord.

**spinal column** ● **n.** the spine.

**spinal cord** ● **n.** the cylindrical bundle of nerve fibres which is enclosed in the spine and connected to the brain, with which it forms the central nervous system.

**spinal tap** ● **n.** North American term for **LUMBAR PUNCTURE**.

**spindle** ● **n. 1** a slender rounded rod with tapered ends used in hand spinning to twist and wind thread from a mass of wool or flax held on a distaff. ➤a pin bearing the bobbin of a spinning machine. **2** a rod or pin serving as an axis that revolves or on which something revolves. **3** a turned piece of wood used as a banister or chair leg. **4** Biology a slender mass of microtubules formed when a cell divides. **5** a measure of length for yarn, equal to 15,120 yards (13,826 metres) for cotton or 14,400 yards (13,167 metres) for linen. **6** N. Amer. a spike for filing papers.

– ORIGIN OE *spinel*, from the base of **SPIN**.

**spindle-shanks** ● **pl. n.** informal, dated **1** long thin legs. **2** [treated as sing.] a person with such legs.

– DERIVATIVES **spindle-shanked** adj.

**spindle-shaped** ● **adj.** having a circular cross section and tapering towards each end.

**spindle tree** (also **spindle bush**) ● **n.** a shrub or small tree with slender toothed leaves and hard wood formerly used for spindles. [*Euonymus europaea* and related species.]

**spindly** ● **adj.** long or tall and thin.

**spin doctor** ● **n.** informal a spokesperson for a political party or politician employed to give a favourable interpretation of events to the media.

**spindrift** ● **n. 1** spray blown from the crests of waves by the wind. **2** driving snow.

– ORIGIN C17 (orig. Scots): var. of *spoondrift*, from archaic *spoon* 'run before wind or sea' + **DRIFT**.

**spin dryer** ● **n.** a machine for extracting water from wet clothes by spinning them in a revolving perforated drum.

– DERIVATIVES **spin-dry** v.

**spine** ● **n. 1** a series of vertebrae extending from the skull to the small of the back, enclosing the spinal cord and providing support for the thorax and abdomen; the backbone. **2** a central feature or main source of strength. **3** the part of a book's jacket or cover that encloses the inner edges of the pages. **4** chiefly Zoology & Botany a prickle or other hard pointed projection or structure. **5** (also **pay spine**) a linear pay scale operated by some large organizations that allows flexibility for local and specific conditions.

– DERIVATIVES **-spined** adj.

– ORIGIN ME: shortening of OFr. *espine*, or from L. *spina* 'thorn, backbone'.

**spine-chiller** ● **n.** a story or film that inspires terror and excitement.

– DERIVATIVES **spine-chilling** adj.

**spinel** /spɪˈnɛl, ˈspɪn(ə)l/ ● **n.** a hard glassy mineral consisting chiefly of magnesium and aluminium oxides. ➤Chemistry any of a class of similar crystalline oxides.

– ORIGIN C16: from Fr. *spinelle*, from Ital. *spinella*, dimin. of *spina* 'thorn'.

**spineless** ● **adj. 1** having no spine; invertebrate. **2** (of an animal or plant) lacking spines. **3** weak and purposeless.

– DERIVATIVES **spinelessly** adv. **spinelessness** n.

**spinel ruby** ● **n.** a deep red variety of spinel, often of gem quality.

**spinet** /spɪˈnɛt, ˈspɪnɪt/ ● **n. 1** a small harpsichord with the strings set obliquely to the keyboard, popular in the 18th century. **2** US a type of small upright piano.

– ORIGIN C17: shortening of obs. Fr. *espinette*, from Ital. *spinetta* 'virginal, spinet', dimin. of *spina* (see **SPINE**), the strings being plucked by quills.

**spine-tingling** ● **adj.** informal thrilling or pleasurably frightening.

**spinifex** /ˈspɪnɪfɛks/ ● **n.** a grass with coarse spiny leaves and spiny flower heads which break off and are blown about, occurring from east Asia to Australia. [Genus *Spinifex*.]

– ORIGIN C19: mod. L., from L. *spina* 'thorn' + *-fex* from *facere* 'make'.

**spinnaker** /ˈspɪnəkə/ ● **n.** a large three-cornered sail set forward of the mainsail of a racing yacht when running before the wind.

– ORIGIN C19: appar. a fanciful formation from *Sphinx*, the name of the yacht first using it, perh. influenced by **SPANKER**.

**spinner** ● **n. 1** a person occupied in spinning thread. **2** Cricket a bowler who is expert in spinning the ball. **3** (also **spinnerbait**) Fishing a lure designed to revolve when pulled through the water. ➤a type of fishing fly, used chiefly for trout.

**spinneret** /ˈspɪnərɛt/ ● **n. 1** Zoology any of a number of different organs through which the silk, gossamer, or thread of spiders, silkworms, and certain other insects is produced. **2** (in the production of man-made fibres) a cap or plate with a number of small holes through which a fibre-forming solution is forced.

**spinney** ● **n.** (pl. **-eys**) Brit. a small area of trees and bushes.

– ORIGIN C16: shortening of OFr. *espinei*, from an alt. of L. *spinetum* 'thicket'.

**spinning jenny** ● **n.** historical a machine for spinning with more than one spindle at a time.

**spinning mule** ● **n.** see **MULE**[1] (sense 4).

**spinning top** ● **n.** see **TOP**[2] (sense 1).

**spinning wheel** ● **n.** an apparatus for spinning yarn or thread with a spindle driven by a wheel attached to a crank or treadle.

**spin-off** ● **n. 1** a product or incidental benefit produced during or after the primary activity. **2** a subsidiary of a parent company that has been sold off, creating a new company.

**Spinone** /spɪˈnəʊni/ ● **n.** (pl. **Spinoni**) a wire-haired gun dog of an Italian breed, typically white with brown markings, drooping ears, and a docked tail.

– ORIGIN 1940s: Ital.

**spinose** /ˈspʌɪnəʊs, spʌɪˈnəʊs/ (also **spinous** /ˈspʌɪnəs/) ● **adj.** chiefly Botany & Zoology having spines; spiny.

**spin-out** ● **n.** N. Amer. informal **1** another term for **SPIN-OFF**. **2** a skidding spin by a vehicle out of control.

**Spinozism** /spɪˈnəʊzɪz(ə)m/ ● n. the doctrine of the Dutch philosopher Baruch (or Benedict) de Spinoza (1632–77), regarding 'God or nature' as a single infinite substance, with mind and matter being two incommensurable ways of conceiving the one reality.
– DERIVATIVES **Spinozist** n. & adj. **Spinozistic** adj.

**spinster** ● n. chiefly derogatory an unmarried woman, typically an older woman beyond the usual age for marriage.
– DERIVATIVES **spinsterhood** n. **spinsterish** adj.
– ORIGIN ME (in the sense 'woman who spins'): from **SPIN** + **-STER**.

**spinthariscope** /spɪnˈθarɪskəʊp/ ● n. Physics an instrument that shows the incidence of alpha particles by flashes on a fluorescent screen.
– ORIGIN C20: formed irregularly from Gk *spintharis* 'spark' + **-SCOPE**.

**spinto** /ˈspɪntəʊ/ ● n. (pl. **-os**) a lyric soprano or tenor voice of powerful dramatic quality.
– ORIGIN 1950s: Ital., lit. 'pushed', past part. of *spingere* 'push'.

**spinulose** /ˈspɪnjʊləʊs/ ● adj. Botany & Zoology having small spines.
– ORIGIN C19: from mod. L. *spinulosus*, from *spinula*, dimin. of *spina* 'thorn, spine'.

**spiny** ● adj. (**-ier**, **-iest**) **1** full of or covered with prickles. **2** informal difficult to understand or handle.
– DERIVATIVES **spininess** n.

**spiny anteater** ● n. another term for **ECHIDNA**.

**spiny lobster** ● n. a large edible crustacean with a spiny shell and long heavy antennae, but without large claws. [Family Palinuridae: several species.]

**spiracle** /ˈspʌɪrək(ə)l/ ● n. Zoology an external respiratory opening in insects, cartilaginous fish, and other animals.
– DERIVATIVES **spiracular** adj.
– ORIGIN C18: from L. *spiraculum*, from *spirare* 'breathe'.

**spiraea** /spʌɪˈriːə/ (chiefly US also **spirea**) ● n. a shrub of the rose family with clusters of small white or pink flowers, cultivated as an ornamental. [Genus *Spiraea*.]
– ORIGIN mod. L., from Gk *speiraia*, from *speira* 'a coil'.

**spiral** ● adj. winding in a continuous and gradually widening (or tightening) curve around a central point or axis. ➤ winding in a continuous curve of constant diameter about a central axis, as though along a cylinder; helical. ➤ Astronomy denoting galaxies in which the stars and gas clouds are concentrated mainly in spiral arms. ● n. **1** a spiral curve, shape, or pattern. **2** a progressive rise or fall of prices, wages, etc., each responding to an upward or downward stimulus provided by a previous one. ➤ a process of progressive deterioration. ● v. (**spiralled**, **spiralling**; US **spiraled**, **spiraling**) **1** take or cause to follow a spiral course. **2** show a continuous and dramatic increase. ➤ (**spiral down/downward**) decrease continuously.
– DERIVATIVES **spirally** adv.
– ORIGIN C16: from med. L. *spiralis*, from L. *spira* (see **SPIRE²**).

**spiral-bound** ● adj. (of a book or notepad) bound with a wire or plastic spiral threaded through a row of holes along one edge.

**spirant** /ˈspʌɪr(ə)nt/ Phonetics ● adj. (of a consonant) uttered with a continuous expulsion of breath. ● n. a spirant consonant.
– DERIVATIVES **spirantization** (also **-isation**) n. **spirantize** (also **-ise**) v.
– ORIGIN C19: from L. *spirant-*, *spirare* 'breathe'.

**spire¹** ● n. **1** a tapering conical or pyramidal structure on the top of a building, typically a church tower. **2** the continuation of a tree trunk above the point where branching begins, especially in a tree of a tapering form.
– DERIVATIVES **spired** adj. **spiry** adj.
– ORIGIN OE *spīr* 'tall slender stem of a plant'.

**spire²** ● n. Zoology the upper tapering part of the spiral shell of a gastropod mollusc.
– ORIGIN C16: from Fr., or via L. from Gk *speira* 'a coil'.

**spirea** ● n. US variant spelling of **SPIRAEA**.

**spirillum** /spʌɪˈrɪləm/ ● n. (pl. **spirilla** /-lə/) a bacterium with a rigid spiral structure, found in stagnant water and sometimes causing disease.
– ORIGIN mod. L., irregular dimin. of L. *spira* 'a coil'.

**spirit** ● n. **1** the non-physical part of a person which is the seat of emotions and character. ➤ this regarded as surviving after the death of the body, often manifested as a ghost. ➤ a supernatural being. **2** the prevailing or typical quality or mood: *the nation's egalitarian spirit.* ➤ a person identified with their role or most prominent quality: *he was a leading spirit in the conference.* ➤ (**spirits**) a person's mood. **3** courage, energy, and determination. **4** the real meaning or intention of something as opposed to its strict verbal interpretation. **5** chiefly Brit. strong distilled liquor such as rum. ➤ [with modifier] a volatile liquid, especially a fuel, prepared by distillation: *aviation spirit.* ➤ archaic a solution of volatile components extracted from something: *spirits of turpentine.* **6** archaic a highly refined substance or fluid thought to govern vital phenomena. ● v. (**spirited**, **spiriting**) **1** (usu. **spirit something away**) convey rapidly and secretly. **2** (**spirit someone up**) archaic animate or cheer up someone.
– PHRASES **in** (or **in the**) **spirit** in thought or intention though not physically. **when the spirit moves someone** when someone feels inclined to do something. [a phr. orig. in Quaker use, with ref. to the Holy Spirit.]
– ORIGIN ME: from Anglo-Norman Fr., from L. *spiritus* 'breath, spirit', from *spirare* 'breathe'.

**spirited** ● adj. **1** full of energy, enthusiasm, and determination. **2** [in combination] having a specified character or mood: *a generous-spirited man.*
– DERIVATIVES **spiritedly** adv. **spiritedness** n.

**spirit gum** ● n. a quick-drying solution of gum, chiefly used by actors to attach false hair to their faces.

**spiritism** ● n. another term for **SPIRITUALISM** (in sense 1).
– DERIVATIVES **spiritist** adj. & n. **spiritistic** adj.

**spirit lamp** ● n. a lamp burning methylated or other volatile spirits instead of oil.

**spiritless** ● adj. lacking courage, energy, or determination.
– DERIVATIVES **spiritlessly** adv. **spiritlessness** n.

**spirit level** ● n. a device consisting of a sealed glass tube partially filled with alcohol or other liquid, containing an air bubble whose position reveals whether a surface is perfectly level.

**spirit of wine** (also **spirits of wine**) ● n. archaic purified alcohol.

**spiritous** ● adj. another term for **SPIRITUOUS**.

**spirits of salt** ● n. archaic term for **HYDROCHLORIC ACID**.

**spiritual** /ˈspɪrɪtʃʊəl, -tjʊəl/ ● adj. **1** of, relating to, or affecting the human spirit as opposed to material or physical things. **2** of or relating to religion or religious belief. ● n. (also **negro spiritual**) a religious song of a kind associated with black Christians of the southern US.
– DERIVATIVES **spirituality** n. **spiritualization** (also **-isation**) n. **spiritualize** (also **-ise**) v. **spiritually** adv.

**spiritualism** ● n. **1** a system of belief or religious practice based on supposed communication with the spirits of the dead, especially through mediums. **2** Philosophy the doctrine that the spirit exists as distinct from matter, or that spirit is the only reality.
– DERIVATIVES **spiritualist** n. **spiritualistic** adj.

**spirituous** /ˈspɪrɪtjʊəs/ ● adj. formal or archaic containing much alcohol.
– ORIGIN C16 (in the sense 'lively'): from L. *spiritus* 'spirit' + **-OUS**, or from Fr. *spiritueux*.

**spiro-¹** ● comb. form **1** spiral; in a spiral: *spirochaete.* **2** Chemistry denoting a molecule with two rings with one atom common to both.
– ORIGIN from L. *spira*, Gk *speira* 'a coil'.

**spiro-²** ● comb. form relating to breathing: *spirometer.*
– ORIGIN formed irregularly from L. *spirare* 'breathe'.

**spirochaete** /ˈspʌɪrə(ʊ)kiːt/ (US **spirochete**) ● n. a flexible spirally twisted bacterium of an order (Spirochaetales) including that responsible for syphilis.
– ORIGIN C19: from **SPIRO-¹** + Gk *khaitē* 'long hair'.

**spirograph** ● n. **1** an instrument for recording breathing movements. **2** (**Spirograph**) trademark a toy which is

used to draw intricate curved patterns using interlocking plastic cogs and toothed rings of different sizes.
– DERIVATIVES **spirographic** adj.

**spirogyra** /ˌspʌɪrə(ʊ)ˈdʒʌɪrə/ ● **n.** Botany a filamentous green alga of a genus that includes blanket weed. [Genus *Spirogyra*.]
– ORIGIN mod. L., from **SPIRO-**[1] + Gk *guros*, *gura* 'round'.

**spirometer** /spʌɪˈrɒmɪtə/ ● **n.** an instrument for measuring the air capacity of the lungs.
– DERIVATIVES **spirometry** n.

**spirt** ● **v. & n.** old-fashioned spelling of **SPURT**.

**spirulina** /ˌspɪrʊˈlʌɪnə, ˌspʌɪrʊ-/ ● **n.** a filamentous cyanobacterium of a genus typically forming tangled masses in warm alkaline lakes. [Genus *Spirulina*.]
– ORIGIN mod. L., from *spirula* 'small spiral (shell)'.

**spit**[1] ● **v.** (**spitting**; past and past part. **spat** or **spit**) **1** eject saliva forcibly from one's mouth. ➤forcibly eject (food or liquid) from one's mouth. ➤(**spit up**) N. Amer. (especially of a baby) vomit. **2** utter in a hostile way. **3** (of a fire or something being cooked) emit small bursts of sparks or hot fat with a series of explosive noises. **4** (**it spits**, **it is spitting**, etc.) Brit. light rain falls. ● **n. 1** saliva. **2** an act of spitting.
– PHRASES **be the spit** (or **the dead spit**) **of** informal look exactly like. [see **SPITTING IMAGE**.] **spit blood** (or Austral. **chips**) feel or express vehement anger. **spit in the eye** (or **face**) **of** show contempt or scorn for. **spit it out** [in imper.] informal say something unhesitatingly. **spit-and-sawdust** Brit. informal denoting a pub that appears dirty or run-down.
– ORIGIN OE *spittan*, of imitative origin.

**spit**[2] ● **n. 1** a long, thin metal rod pushed through meat in order to hold and turn it while it is roasted over an open fire. **2** a narrow point of land projecting into the sea. ● **v.** (**spitted**, **spitting**) put a spit through (meat).
– DERIVATIVES **spitty** adj.
– ORIGIN OE *spitu*, of W. Gmc origin.

**spit**[3] ● **n.** (pl. same or **spits**) a layer of earth whose depth is equal to the length of the blade of a spade.
– ORIGIN C16: from MDu. and Mid. Low Ger.; prob. rel. to **SPIT**[2].

**spit and polish** ● **n.** thorough cleaning and polishing, especially by a soldier.

**spitball** N. Amer. ● **n. 1** a ball of chewed paper used as a missile. **2** Baseball an illegal swerving pitch made with a ball moistened with saliva or sweat. ● **v.** informal throw out (a suggestion) for discussion.
– DERIVATIVES **spitballer** n.

**spitchcock** ● **n.** an eel that has been split and grilled or fried. ● **v.** prepare (an eel or other fish) in this way.
– ORIGIN C15: of unknown origin; cf. **SPATCHCOCK**.

**spit curl** ● **n.** North American term for **KISS CURL**.

**spite** ● **n.** a desire to hurt, annoy, or offend. ● **v.** deliberately hurt, annoy, or offend.
– PHRASES **in spite of** without being affected by the particular factor mentioned. **in spite of oneself** although one did not want or expect to do so.
– DERIVATIVES **spiteful** adj. **spitefully** adv. **spitefulness** n.
– ORIGIN ME: shortening of OFr. *despit* 'contempt', *despiter* 'show contempt for'.

**spitfire** ● **n.** a person with a fierce temper.

**spit-roast** ● **v.** [usu. as adj. **spit-roasted**] cook (a piece of meat) on a spit.

**spitter** ● **n. 1** a person who spits. **2** another term for **SPITBALL** (in sense 2).

**spitting cobra** ● **n.** an African cobra that defends itself by spitting venom from the fangs. [*N. nigricollis* and other species.]

**spitting image** ● **n.** (**the spitting image of**) informal the exact double of.
– ORIGIN C19: orig. as *the spit of* or *the spit and image of*; perh. from the idea of a person apparently being formed from the spit of another, so great is the similarity between them.

**spittle** ● **n.** saliva, especially as ejected from the mouth.
– DERIVATIVES **spittly** adj.
– ORIGIN C15: alt. of dial. *spattle*, by assoc. with **SPIT**[1].

**spittlebug** ● **n.** another term for **FROGHOPPER**.

**spittoon** /spɪˈtuːn/ ● **n.** a container for spitting into.

**spitz** ● **n.** a dog of a small breed with a pointed muzzle, especially a Pomeranian.
– ORIGIN C19: from Ger. *Spitz(hund)*, from *spitz* 'pointed' + *Hund* 'dog'.

**spiv** ● **n.** Brit. informal a man, typically a flashy dresser, who makes a living by disreputable dealings.
– DERIVATIVES **spivvish** adj. **spivvy** adj.
– ORIGIN 1930s: perh. rel. to **SPIFFY**.

**splake** /spleɪk/ ● **n.** a hybrid trout of North American lakes.
– ORIGIN 1950s: blend of *sp(eckled trout)* and *lake (trout)* (the species hybridized).

**splanchnic** /ˈsplaŋknɪk/ ● **adj.** of or relating to the viscera or internal organs, especially those of the abdomen.
– ORIGIN C17: from mod. L. *splanchnicus*, from Gk *splankhnikos*, from *splankhna* 'entrails'.

**splash** ● **v. 1** make (liquid) strike or fall on something in drops. ➤(of a liquid) fall or be scattered in drops. ➤strike or move around in water, causing it to fly about. ➤(**splash down**) (of a spacecraft) land on water. **2** display (a story or photograph) in a prominent place in a newspaper or magazine. **3** (**splash out** or **splash money out**) Brit. informal spend money freely. **4** (**be splashed with**) be decorated with scattered patches of. ● **n. 1** an instance of splashing or the sound made by this. ➤a small quantity of liquid that has splashed on to a surface. ➤a small quantity of liquid added to a drink. **2** a bright patch of colour. **3** informal a prominent news feature or story.
– PHRASES **make a splash** informal attract a great deal of attention.
– DERIVATIVES **splashy** adj. (**-ier**, **-iest**).
– ORIGIN C18: alt. of **PLASH**[1].

**splashback** ● **n.** Brit. a panel behind a sink or cooker that protects the wall from splashes.

**splat**[1] ● **n.** a piece of thin wood in the centre of a chair back.
– ORIGIN C19: from obs. *splat* 'split up'; rel. to **SPLIT**.

**splat**[2] informal ● **n.** a sound of something soft and wet or heavy striking a surface. ● **adv.** with a splat. ● **v.** (**splatted**, **splatting**) hit or land with a splat.
– ORIGIN C19: abbrev. of **SPLATTER**.

**splatter** ● **v.** splash with a sticky or viscous liquid. ➤(of such a liquid) splash. ● **n. 1** a splash of a sticky or viscous liquid. **2** [as modifier] informal denoting or referring to films featuring many violent and gruesome deaths.
– ORIGIN C18: imitative.

**splatterpunk** ● **n.** informal a literary genre characterized by the explicit description of horrific, violent, or pornographic scenes.

**splay** ● **v. 1** spread or be spread out or further apart. **2** [usu. as adj. **splayed**] construct (a window, doorway, or other aperture) so that it is wider at one side of the wall than the other. ● **n. 1** a tapered widening of a road at an intersection to increase visibility. **2** a surface making an oblique angle with another, especially a splayed window or other aperture. ● **adj.** [usu. in combination] turned outward or widened: *the girl sat splay-legged*.
– ORIGIN ME (in the sense 'unfold to view'): shortening of **DISPLAY**.

**splay-footed** ● **n.** having a broad flat foot turned outward.
– DERIVATIVES **splay-foot** n.

**spleen** ● **n. 1** Anatomy an abdominal organ involved in the production and removal of blood cells and forming part of the immune system. **2** bad temper; spite.
– DERIVATIVES **spleenful** adj.
– ORIGIN ME: shortening of OFr. *esplen*, via L. from Gk *splēn*; sense 2 derives from the former belief that the spleen was the seat of bad temper.

**spleenwort** ● **n.** a small fern which grows on rocks and walls, formerly used to treat disorders of the spleen. [Genus *Asplenium*.]

**splen-** ● **comb. form** Anatomy of or relating to the spleen: *splenectomy*.
– ORIGIN from Gk *splēn* 'spleen'.

**splendent** • **adj.** archaic shining brightly.
– ORIGIN C15: from L. *splendent-*, *splendere* 'shine'.

**splendid** • **adj. 1** magnificent; very impressive. **2** informal excellent.
– DERIVATIVES **splendidly** adv. **splendidness** n.
– ORIGIN C17: from Fr. *splendide* or L. *splendidus*, from *splendere* 'shine'.

**splendiferous** /splɛnˈdɪf(ə)rəs/ • **adj.** informal, humorous splendid.
– DERIVATIVES **splendiferously** adv. **splendiferousness** n.
– ORIGIN C19: formed irregularly from **SPLENDOUR**.

**splendour** (US **splendor**) • **n.** splendid appearance.
– ORIGIN ME: from Anglo-Norman Fr. *splendur* or L. *splendor*, from *splendere* 'shine'.

**splenectomy** /splɪˈnɛktəmi/ • **n.** (pl. **-ies**) a surgical operation involving removal of the spleen.

**splenetic** /splɪˈnɛtɪk/ • **adj. 1** bad-tempered or spiteful. **2** archaic term for **SPLENIC**.
– DERIVATIVES **splenetically** adv.
– ORIGIN ME (as a noun denoting a person with a diseased spleen): from late L. *spleneticus*, from Gk *splēn* (see **SPLEEN**).

**splenic** /ˈsplɛnɪk, ˈspliːnɪk/ • **adj.** of or relating to the spleen.

**splenitis** /splɪˈnʌɪtɪs/ • **n.** Medicine inflammation of the spleen.

**splenius** /ˈspliːnɪəs/ • **n.** (pl. **splenii** /-nɪʌɪ/) Anatomy either of two muscles attached to the vertebrae in the neck and upper back which draw back the head.
– ORIGIN C18: mod. L., from Gk *splēnion* 'bandage'.

**splenomegaly** /ˌspliːnə(ʊ)ˈmɛg(ə)li/ • **n.** abnormal enlargement of the spleen.
– ORIGIN C20: from **SPLEN-** + Gk *megas*, *megal-* 'great'.

**splice** • **v.** join (a rope or ropes) by interweaving the strands at the ends. ➤join (pieces of timber, film, or tape) at the ends. ➤Genetics join or insert (a gene or gene fragment). • **n.** a spliced join. ➤the wedge-shaped tang of a cricket-bat handle, forming a joint with the blade.
– PHRASES **get** (or **be**) **spliced** informal get married. **splice the main brace** Brit. historical (in the navy) serve out an extra tot of rum.
– DERIVATIVES **splicer** n.
– ORIGIN C16: prob. from MDu. *splissen*, of unknown origin.

**spliff** • **n.** informal a cannabis cigarette.
– ORIGIN 1930s: of unknown origin.

**spline** /splʌɪn/ • **n. 1** a rectangular key fitting into grooves in the hub and shaft of a wheel, especially one formed integrally with the shaft which allows movement of the wheel on the shaft. ➤a corresponding groove in a hub along which the key may slide. **2** a slat. **3** a flexible wood or rubber strip used especially in drawing large curves. **4** Mathematics a continuous curve constructed so as to pass through a given set of points. • **v.** secure by means of a spline. ➤[usu. as adj. **splined**] fit with a spline.
– ORIGIN C18 (orig. East Anglian dial.): perh. rel. to **SPLINTER**.

**splint** • **n. 1** a strip of rigid material for supporting a broken bone when it has been set. **2** a long, thin strip of wood used in basketwork or to light a fire. **3** a bony enlargement on the inside of a horse's leg, on the splint bone. • **v.** secure with a splint or splints.
– ORIGIN ME (also denoting a section of armour): from MDu., Mid. Low Ger. *splinte* 'metal plate or pin'; rel. to **SPLINTER**.

**splint bone** • **n.** either of two small bones in the foreleg of a horse or other large quadruped, lying behind and close to the cannon bone.

**splinter** • **n.** a small, thin, sharp piece of wood, glass, etc. broken off from a larger piece. • **v.** break or cause to break into splinters.
– DERIVATIVES **splintery** adj.
– ORIGIN ME: from MDu. *splinter*, *splenter*; rel. to **SPLINT**.

**splinter bar** • **n.** Brit. another term for **SWINGLETREE**.

**splinter group** (also **splinter party**) • **n.** a small organization that has broken away from a larger one.

**splinter-proof** • **adj. 1** capable of withstanding splinters from bursting shells or bombs. **2** not producing splinters when broken.

**split** • **v.** (**splitting**; past and past part. **split**) **1** break or cause to break forcibly into parts. ➤cause the fission of (an atom). **2** divide or cause to divide into parts or groups. ➤(often **split up**) end a marriage or other relationship. **3** informal (of one's head) suffer great pain from a headache. **4** (usu. **split on**) Brit. informal betray the secrets of or inform on someone. **5** informal leave, especially suddenly. • **n. 1** a tear, crack, or fissure. **2** an instance of splitting or being split. **3** (**the splits**) Brit. (in gymnastics and dance) an act of leaping in the air or sitting down with the legs straight and at right angles to the body, one in front and the other behind, or one at each side. **4** a split osier used in basketwork. **5** a single thickness of split hide. **6** N. Amer. a drawn match or series. **7** each strip of steel or cane that makes up the reed in a loom. **8** half a bottle or glass of champagne or other liquor. **9** the time taken to complete a recognized part of a race, or the point in the race where such a time is measured.
– PHRASES **split the difference** take the average of two proposed amounts. **split one's sides** (N. Amer. also **split a gut**) informal be convulsed with laughter. **split the ticket** (or **one's vote**) US vote for candidates of more than one party. **split the vote** (of a candidate or minority party) attract votes from another candidate or party with the result that both are defeated by a third.
– DERIVATIVES **splitter** n.
– ORIGIN C16 (orig. in the sense '(of a storm or rock) break up (a ship)'): from MDu. *splitten*, of unknown ultimate origin.

**split end** • **n. 1** a tip of a person's hair which has split from dryness or ill-treatment. **2** American Football an offensive end positioned on the line of scrimmage but some distance away from the other linemen.

**split infinitive** • **n.** a construction (regarded as an error by some traditionalists) consisting of an infinitive with an adverb or other word inserted between *to* and the verb, e.g. *she seems to really like it*.

**split-level** • **adj. 1** (of a room or building) having the floor level of one part about half a storey above or below the floor level of an adjacent part. **2** (of a cooker) having the oven and hob in separately installed units.

**split pea** • **n.** a pea dried and split in half for cooking.

**split pin** • **n.** a metal cotter pin with two arms passed through a hole, held in place by the springing apart of the arms.

**split ring** • **n.** a small steel ring with two spiral turns, such as a key ring.

**split screen** • **n.** a cinema, television, or computer screen on which two or more separate images are displayed.

**split second** • **n.** a very brief moment of time. • **adj.** (**split-second**) very rapid or accurate.

**split shift** • **n.** a working shift comprising two or more separate periods of duty in a day.

**split shot** • **n. 1** small pellets used to weight a fishing line. **2** Croquet a stroke driving two touching balls in different directions.

**splittism** • **n.** (among communists, or in communist countries) the pursuance of factional interests in opposition to official Communist Party policy.
– DERIVATIVES **splittist** n.

**splodge** • **n.** & **v.** Brit. another term for **SPLOTCH**.
– DERIVATIVES **splodgy** adj.

**splosh** informal • **v.** move with a soft splashing sound. • **n. 1** a splash or splashing sound. **2** dated money.
– ORIGIN C19: imitative.

**splotch** informal • **n.** a spot, splash, or smear. • **v.** make a splotch on.
– DERIVATIVES **splotchy** adj.
– ORIGIN C17: perh. a blend of **SPOT** and obs. *plotch* 'blotch'.

**splurge** informal • **n. 1** a sudden burst of extravagance. **2** a large or excessive amount. • **v.** spend extravagantly.
– ORIGIN C19 (orig. US): prob. imitative.

**splurt** informal • **n.** a sudden gush of liquid. • **v.** push out with force.

– ORIGIN C18: imitative.

**splutter** ● v. **1** make a series of short explosive spitting or choking sounds. **2** say in a rapid indistinct way. ● n. a spluttering sound.
– DERIVATIVES **splutterer** n. **spluttering** adj. & n. **splutteringly** adv.
– ORIGIN C17: imitative; cf. **SPUTTER**.

**spod** ● n. Brit. informal a dull or socially inept person.
– DERIVATIVES **spoddy** adj.
– ORIGIN 1980s: origin unknown.

**Spode** /spəʊd/ ● n. trademark fine ornately decorated pottery or porcelain made at the factories of the English potter Josiah Spode (1755–1827) or his successors.

**spodosol** /ˈspɒdə(ʊ)sɒl/ ● n. Soil Science a soil with a horizon rich in aluminium and iron oxides and organic matter, e.g. a podzol.
– ORIGIN 1960s: from Gk *spodos* 'ashes, embers' + **-SOL** + L. *solum* 'soil'.

**spodumene** /ˈspɒdjʊmiːn/ ● n. a translucent, typically greyish-white aluminosilicate mineral which is an important source of lithium.
– ORIGIN C19: from Fr. *spodumène*, from Gk *spodoumenos*, *spodousthai* 'burn to ashes'.

**spoil** ● v. (past and past part. **spoilt** (chiefly Brit.) or **spoiled**) **1** diminish or destroy the value or quality of. ➤(of food) become unfit for eating. ➤mark (a ballot paper) incorrectly so as to invalidate one's vote. **2** harm the character of (a child) by being too indulgent. ➤treat with great or excessive kindness or generosity. **3** (**be spoiling for**) be extremely or aggressively eager for. **4** archaic rob by force or violence. ● n. **1** (**spoils**) stolen goods. **2** waste material brought up during the course of an excavation or a dredging or mining operation.
– PHRASES **be spoilt for choice** Brit. have so many options that it is difficult to make a choice.
– DERIVATIVES **spoilage** n.
– ORIGIN ME: shortening of OFr. *espoille* (n.), *espoillier* (v.), from L. *spoliare*, from *spolium* 'plunder, skin stripped from an animal', or a shortening of **DESPOIL**.

**spoiler** ● n. **1** a person or thing that spoils. ➤a news story published to divert attention from and spoil the impact of a similar story published elsewhere. **2** a flap on an aircraft wing which can be projected to create drag and so reduce speed. ➤a similar device on a motor vehicle intended to improve road-holding at high speeds.

**spoilsman** ● n. (pl. **-men**) US a person who seeks to profit by or who supports the spoils system.

**spoilsport** ● n. a person who spoils others' pleasure.

**spoils system** ● n. chiefly US the practice of a successful political party of giving public office to its supporters.

**spoilt** chiefly Brit. past and past participle of **SPOIL**.

**spoke**[1] ● n. **1** each of the bars or wire rods connecting the centre of a wheel to its rim. **2** each of a set of radial handles projecting from a ship's wheel. **3** each of the metal rods in an umbrella to which the material is attached.
– PHRASES **put a spoke in someone's wheel** Brit. prevent someone from carrying out a plan.
– DERIVATIVES **-spoked** adj.
– ORIGIN OE *spāca*, of W. Gmc origin, from the base of **SPIKE**[1].

**spoke**[2] past of **SPEAK**.

**spoken** past participle of **SPEAK**. ● adj. [in combination] speaking in a specified way: *a soft-spoken man.*
– PHRASES **be spoken for 1** be already claimed or reserved. **2** already have a romantic commitment.

**spokeshave** /ˈspəʊkʃeɪv/ ● n. a small plane with a handle on each side of its blade, used for shaping curved surfaces (originally wheel spokes).

**spokesman** (or **spokeswoman**) ● n. (pl. **-men** or **-women**) a person who makes statements on behalf of a group.
– ORIGIN C16: formed irregularly from **SPOKE**[2], on the pattern of words such as *craftsman*.

**spokesperson** ● n. (pl. **-persons** or **-people**) a spokesman or spokeswoman (used as a neutral alternative).

**spoliation** /ˌspəʊlɪˈeɪʃ(ə)n/ ● n. **1** the action of spoiling. **2** the action of plundering.
– DERIVATIVES **spoliator** n.
– ORIGIN ME: from L. *spoliatio(n-)*, from *spoliare* (see **SPOIL**).

**spondaic** /spɒnˈdeɪɪk/ ● adj. Prosody of or concerning spondees. ➤(of a hexameter) having a spondee as its fifth foot.

**spondee** /ˈspɒndiː/ ● n. Prosody a foot consisting of two long (or stressed) syllables.
– ORIGIN ME: from OFr., or via L. from Gk *spondeios (pous)* '(foot) of a libation', from *spondē* 'libation' (being characteristic of music accompanying libations).

**spondulicks** /spɒnˈd(j)uːlɪks/ ● pl. n. Brit. informal money.
– ORIGIN C19: of unknown origin.

**spondylitis** /ˌspɒndɪˈlʌɪtɪs/ ● n. Medicine inflammation of the joints of the backbone. See also **ANKYLOSING SPONDYLITIS**.
– ORIGIN C19: from L. *spondylus* 'vertebra' + **-ITIS**.

**sponge** ● n. **1** a sedentary aquatic invertebrate with a soft porous body supported by a framework of fibres or spicules. [Phylum Porifera.] **2** a piece of a soft, light, porous, absorbent substance originally consisting of the fibrous skeleton of a sponge but now usually made of synthetic material, used for washing, as padding, etc. ➤a piece of sponge impregnated with spermicide and inserted into a woman's vagina as a form of barrier contraceptive. **3** a very light cake made with eggs, sugar, and flour but little or no fat. **4** informal a person who lives at someone else's expense. **5** informal a heavy drinker. **6** metal in a porous form. ● v. (**sponging** or **spongeing**) **1** wipe or clean with a wet sponge or cloth. **2** (often **sponge off**) informal obtain money or food from others without giving anything in return. **3** give a decorative effect to (a wall or surface) by applying paint with a sponge. ➤decorate (pottery) using a sponge.
– DERIVATIVES **spongeable** adj. **sponge-like** adj.
– ORIGIN OE, via L. from Gk *spongia*, later form of *spongos*, reinforced in ME by OFr. *esponge*.

**sponge bag** ● n. Brit. a toilet bag.

**sponge bath** ● n. North American term for **BLANKET BATH**.

**sponge cloth** ● n. soft, lightly woven cloth with a slightly wrinkled surface.

**sponge pudding** ● n. Brit. a steamed or baked pudding of fat, flour, and eggs.

**sponger** ● n. **1** informal a person who lives at others' expense. **2** a person who applies decoration to pottery using a sponge.

**sponge rubber** ● n. rubber latex processed into a sponge-like substance.

**sponge tree** ● n. another term for **OPOPANAX** (in sense 1).

**spongiform** /ˈspʌndʒɪfɔːm/ ● adj. chiefly Veterinary Medicine having, relating to, or denoting a porous structure or consistency resembling that of a sponge.

**spongy** /ˈspʌn(d)ʒi/ ● adj. (**-ier**, **-iest**) **1** like a sponge, especially in being porous, compressible, or absorbent. **2** (of metal) having an open, porous structure. **3** (of a motor vehicle's braking system) lacking firmness.
– DERIVATIVES **spongily** adv. **sponginess** n.

**sponson** /ˈspɒns(ə)n/ ● n. **1** a gun platform standing out from a warship's side. **2** a short subsidiary wing that serves to stabilize a seaplane. **3** a buoyancy chamber fitted to the hull of a canoe. **4** a triangular platform supporting the wheel on a paddle steamer.
– ORIGIN C19: of unknown origin.

**sponsor** ● n. **1** a person or organization that pays for or contributes to the costs of a sporting or artistic event or a radio or television programme in return for advertising. **2** a person who pledges a certain amount of money to a charity after another person has participated in a fund-raising event. **3** a person who introduces and supports a proposal for legislation. **4** a person taking official responsibility for the actions of another. ➤a godparent at a child's baptism. ➤(especially in the Roman Catholic Church) a person presenting a candidate for confirmation. ● v. be a sponsor for.
– DERIVATIVES **sponsorship** n.
– ORIGIN C17: from L., from *spondere* 'promise solemnly'.

**spontaneous** /spɒn'teɪnɪəs/ ● **adj. 1** performed or occurring as a result of an unpremeditated inner impulse and without external stimulus. ➤(of a process or event) occurring without apparent external cause. ➤Biology (of movement or activity) instinctive or involuntary. **2** open, natural, and uninhibited. **3** archaic (of a plant) growing naturally and without being tended or cultivated.
– DERIVATIVES **spontaneity** n. **spontaneously** adv.
– ORIGIN C17: from late L. *spontaneus* (from *(sua) sponte* 'of (one's) own accord') + **-ous**.

**spontaneous combustion** ● **n.** the ignition of organic matter without apparent cause, especially through heat generated internally by rapid oxidation.

**spontaneous generation** ● **n.** historical the supposed production of living organisms from non-living matter.

**spoof** informal ● **n. 1** a parody, typically of a film or a genre of film. **2** a hoax. ● **v. 1** parody. **2** hoax. **3** interfere with (radio or radar signals) so as to make them useless.
– DERIVATIVES **spoofer** n. **spoofery** n.
– ORIGIN C19: coined by the Engl. comedian Arthur Roberts.

**spook** informal ● **n. 1** a ghost. **2** chiefly N. Amer. a spy. ● **v.** frighten or become frightened.
– ORIGIN C19: from Du., of unknown origin.

**spooky** ● **adj.** (**-ier**, **-iest**) informal **1** sinister or ghostly. **2** chiefly N. Amer. easily frightened.
– DERIVATIVES **spookily** adv. **spookiness** n.

**spool** ● **n.** a cylindrical device on which thread, film, magnetic tape, fishing line, etc. can be wound. ● **v. 1** wind or be wound on to a spool. **2** Computing send (data for printing or peripheral processing) to an intermediate store. **3** (**spool up**) increase the speed of rotation of a device to the working speed.
– ORIGIN ME: shortening of OFr. *espole* or from Mid. Low Ger. *spōle*, of W. Gmc origin; sense 2 of the verb is an acronym from *simultaneous peripheral operation online*.

**spoon** ● **n. 1** an implement consisting of a small, shallow oval or round bowl on a long handle, used for eating, stirring, and serving food. ➤(**spoons**) a pair of spoons held in the hand and beaten together rhythmically as a percussion instrument. **2** (also **spoon bait**) a fishing lure designed to wobble when pulled through the water. **3** an oar with a broad curved blade. ● **v. 1** transfer with a spoon. **2** informal, dated (of a couple) behave in an amorous way. **3** hit (a ball) up into the air with a soft or weak stroke.
– DERIVATIVES **spooner** n. **spoonful** n. (pl. **-fuls**).
– ORIGIN OE *spōn* 'chip of wood', of Gmc origin: rel. to Ger. *Span* 'shaving'.

**spoonbill** ● **n.** a tall mainly white or pinkish wading bird related to ibises, having a long bill with a very broad flat tip. [Genera *Platalea* and *Ajaia*: several species.]

**spoon bread** ● **n.** US soft maize bread.

**spoonerism** ● **n.** an error in speech in which the initial sounds or letters of two or more words are accidentally transposed, often to humorous effect, as in *you have hissed the mystery lectures*.
– ORIGIN C20: named after the Engl. scholar Revd W. A. *Spooner*, who reputedly made such errors in speaking.

**spoon-feed** ● **v. 1** feed (a baby or infirm adult) using a spoon. **2** provide (someone) with so much help or information that they do not need to think for themselves.

**spoony** informal ● **adj.** (**-ier**, **-iest**) **1** dated sentimentally or foolishly amorous. **2** archaic foolish; silly. ● **n.** (pl. **-ies**) archaic a simple or foolish person.
– DERIVATIVES **spoonily** adv. **spooniness** n.

**spoor** /spʊə, spɔː/ ● **n.** the track or scent of an animal. ● **v.** follow the spoor of.
– DERIVATIVES **spoorer** n.
– ORIGIN C19: from Afrik., from MDu. *spor*.

**sporadic** /spə'radɪk/ ● **adj.** occurring at irregular intervals or only in a few places.
– DERIVATIVES **sporadically** adv.
– ORIGIN C17: via med. L. from Gk *sporadikos*, from *sporas*, *sporad-* 'scattered'; rel. to *speirein* 'to sow'.

**sporangium** /spə'ran(d)ʒɪəm/ ● **n.** (pl. **sporangia** /-dʒɪə/) Botany (in ferns and lower plants) a receptacle in which asexual spores are formed.
– DERIVATIVES **sporangial** adj.
– ORIGIN C19: mod. L., from Gk *spora* 'spore' + *angeion* 'vessel'.

**spore** ● **n. 1** Biology a minute, typically single-celled, reproductive unit characteristic of lower plants, fungi, and protozoans, capable of giving rise to a new individual without sexual fusion. **2** Microbiology (in bacteria) a rounded resistant form adopted by a bacterial cell in adverse conditions.
– ORIGIN C19: from mod. L. *spora*, from Gk *spora* 'sowing, seed'.

**sporo-** ● **comb. form** Biology of or relating to spores: *sporogenesis*.
– ORIGIN from Gk *spora* 'spore'.

**sporocyst** ● **n.** Zoology **1** a larva of a parasitic fluke in a sac-like form after infection of the host's tissues. **2** (in parasitic sporozoans) an encysted zygote in an invertebrate host.

**sporogenesis** /ˌspɒrə(ʊ)'dʒɛnɪsɪs, ˌspɔːrə(ʊ)-/ ● **n.** chiefly Botany the process of spore formation.

**sporogenous** /spə'rɒdʒɪnəs/ ● **adj.** chiefly Botany (of an organism or tissue) producing spores.

**sporogony** /spə'rɒgəni/ ● **n.** Zoology the asexual process of spore formation in parasitic sporozoans.

**sporophore** /'spɒrəfɔː, 'spɔː-/ ● **n.** Botany the spore-bearing structure of a fungus.

**sporophyte** /'spɒrəfʌɪt, 'spɔː-/ ● **n.** Botany (in the life cycle of plants with alternating generations, e.g. ferns) the asexual phase (typically diploid), which produces spores from which the gametophyte arises.
– DERIVATIVES **sporophytic** adj.

**Sporozoa** /ˌspɒrə'zəʊə/ ● **pl. n.** Zoology a phylum of mainly parasitic protozoans with complex life cycles, including the organisms responsible for malaria, toxoplasmosis, etc.
– DERIVATIVES **sporozoan** n. & adj.
– ORIGIN mod. L., from **spore** + Gk *zōia* 'animals'.

**sporozoite** /ˌspɒrə(ʊ)'zəʊʌɪt, ˌspɔː-/ ● **n.** Zoology & Medicine a motile spore-like stage in the life cycle of some sporozoans.
– ORIGIN C19: from **sporo-** + Gk *zoion* 'animal' + **-ite**[1].

**sporran** /'spɒr(ə)n/ ● **n.** a small pouch worn around the waist so as to hang in front of the kilt as part of men's Scottish Highland dress.
– ORIGIN C18: from Sc. Gaelic *sporan*.

**sport** ● **n. 1** an activity involving physical exertion and skill in which an individual or team competes against another or others for entertainment. ➤success or pleasure derived from an activity such as hunting. **2** informal a person who behaves in a good or specified way in response to teasing, defeat, etc. **3** chiefly Austral./NZ a friendly form of address, especially between unacquainted men. **4** Biology a spontaneously mutated animal or plant showing abnormal or striking variation from the parent type. **5** dated entertainment; fun. ● **v. 1** wear or display (a distinctive or noticeable item). **2** amuse oneself or play in a lively, energetic way.
– PHRASES **the sport of kings** horse racing.
– DERIVATIVES **sporter** n.
– ORIGIN ME: shortening of **disport**.

**sportif** /spɔː'tiːf/ ● **adj. 1** interested in athletic sports. **2** (of a garment) suitable for sport or casual wear.
– ORIGIN from Fr.

**sporting** ● **adj. 1** connected with or interested in sport. **2** fair and generous in one's behaviour or dealing with others.
– DERIVATIVES **sportingly** adv.

**sporting chance** ● **n.** a reasonable chance of winning or succeeding.

**sportive** ● **adj.** playful; light-hearted.
– DERIVATIVES **sportively** adv. **sportiveness** n.

**sports bar** ● **n.** a bar where televised sport is shown continuously.

**sports car** ● **n.** a low-built, often convertible, car designed for performance at high speeds.

**sportscast** ● **n.** chiefly N. Amer. a broadcast of sports news or a sports event.
– DERIVATIVES **sportscaster** n.

**sports jacket** (US also **sport jacket** or **sports coat**) ● n. a man's jacket resembling a suit jacket, for informal wear.

**sportsman** (or **sportswoman**) ● n. (pl. **-men** or **-women**) **1** a person who takes part in a sport, especially as a professional. **2** a person who behaves sportingly.
– DERIVATIVES **sportsmanlike** adj. **sportsmanship** n.

**sportsperson** ● n. (pl. **-persons** or **-people**) a sportsman or sportswoman (used as a neutral alternative).

**sportster** ● n. a sports car.

**sportswear** ● n. clothes worn for sport or for casual outdoor use.

**sport utility** ● n. N. Amer. a high-performance four-wheel-drive vehicle.

**sporty** ● adj. (**-ier**, **-iest**) informal **1** fond of or good at sport. **2** (of clothing) suitable for wearing for sport or for casual use. **3** (of a car) compact and with fast acceleration.
– DERIVATIVES **sportily** adv. **sportiness** n.

**sporulate** /ˈspɒrjʊleɪt/ ● v. Biology produce or form a spore or spores.
– DERIVATIVES **sporulation** n.

**spot** ● n. **1** a small round or roundish mark, differing in colour or texture from the surface around it. ➤chiefly N. Amer. a pip on a domino, playing card, or dice. **2** a pimple. **3** a particular place, point, or position. ➤a small feature or part with a particular quality: *his bald spot.* ➤a place for an individual item within a show. **4** informal, chiefly Brit. a small amount of something: *a spot of lunch.* **5** [as modifier] denoting a system of trading in which commodities or currencies are delivered and paid for immediately after a sale. **6** (also **spot board**) a board for working plaster before application. **7** [in combination] informal, chiefly N. Amer. a banknote of a specified value. ● v. (**spotted**, **spotting**) **1** see, notice, or recognize (someone or something) that is difficult to detect or sought-after. ➤Military locate an enemy's position, typically from the air. **2** mark or become marked with spots. **3** (**it spots**, **it is spotting**, etc.) rain slightly. **4** place (a ball) on its designated starting point on a billiard table. **5** N. Amer. informal give or lend (money) to. ➤allow (an advantage) to (someone) in a game or sport.
– PHRASES **hit the spot** informal be exactly what is required. **in a spot** informal in a difficult situation. **on the spot 1** immediately. **2** at the scene of an action or event. **3** chiefly Brit. (of an action) performed without moving from one's original position. **put someone on the spot** informal force someone into a situation in which they must respond or act.
– DERIVATIVES **spotted** adj. **spottedness** n.
– ORIGIN ME: perh. from MDu. *spotte.*

**spot ball** ● n. Billiards one of two white cue balls, distinguished from the other by two black spots.

**spot check** ● n. a test made without warning on a randomly selected subject. ● v. (**spot-check**) subject to a spot check.

**spot height** ● n. the altitude of a point, especially as shown on a map.

**spot kick** ● n. another term for **PENALTY KICK**.

**spotlamp** ● n. another term for **SPOTLIGHT**.

**spotless** ● adj. absolutely clean or pure.
– DERIVATIVES **spotlessly** adv. **spotlessness** n.

**spotlight** ● n. **1** a lamp projecting a narrow, intense beam of light directly on to a place or person. **2** (**the spotlight**) intense public attention. ● v. (past and past part. **-lighted** or **-lit**) **1** illuminate with a spotlight. **2** direct attention to.

**spot on** ● adj. & adv. Brit. informal completely accurate or accurately.

**spotted dick** ● n. Brit. a suet pudding containing currants.

**spotted dog** ● n. **1** a Dalmatian dog. **2** Brit. another term for **SPOTTED DICK**.

**spotted fever** ● n. a disease characterized by fever and skin spots, especially (also **Rocky Mountain spotted fever**) a rickettsial disease transmitted by ticks.

**spotter** ● n. **1** [usu. in combination] a person who observes or looks for a particular thing as a hobby or job: *bus-spotters.* **2** an aviator or aircraft employed in spotting enemy positions.

**spotty** ● adj. (**-ier**, **-iest**) **1** marked with or having spots. **2** chiefly N. Amer. of uneven quality.
– DERIVATIVES **spottily** adv. **spottiness** n.

**spot-weld** ● v. join by welding at a number of separate points. ● n. (**spot weld**) a weld so made.
– DERIVATIVES **spot-welder** n.

**spousal** /ˈspaʊz(ə)l/ ● adj. Law, chiefly N. Amer. of or relating to marriage or to a husband or wife.

**spouse** /spaʊz, -s/ ● n. a husband or wife.
– ORIGIN ME: from OFr. *spous(e)*, var. of *espous(e)*, from L. *sponsus* (masc.), *sponsa* (fem.), past participles of *spondere* 'betroth'.

**spout** ● n. **1** a projecting tube or lip through or over which liquid can be poured from a container. **2** a stream of liquid issuing with great force. **3** a pipe, trough, or chute for conveying liquid, grain, etc. ➤historical a lift in a pawnshop used to convey pawned items up for storage. ● v. **1** send out or issue forcibly in a stream. **2** express (one's views) in a lengthy or declamatory way.
– PHRASES **up the spout** Brit. informal **1** useless, ruined, or wasted. **2** (of a woman) pregnant. **3** (of a bullet or cartridge) in the barrel of a gun and ready to be fired.
– DERIVATIVES **spouted** adj. **spouter** n. **spoutless** adj.
– ORIGIN ME: from MDu. *spouten*, from an imitative base shared by ON *spýta* 'to spit'.

**spp.** ● abbrev. species (plural).

**SPQR** ● abbrev. **1** historical the Senate and people of Rome. **2** small profits and quick returns.
– ORIGIN sense 1 from L. *Senatus Populusque Romanus.*

**Spr** ● abbrev. (in the UK) Sapper.

**Sprachgefühl** /ˈʃprɑːxgəˌfuːl, German ˈʃpraːxgəˌfyːl/ ● n. intuitive feeling for the natural idiom of a language.
– ORIGIN Ger., from *Sprache* 'speech, a language' + *Gefühl* 'feeling'.

**spraddle** ● v. [usu. as adj. **spraddled**] W. Indian & N. Amer. spread (one's legs) far apart.
– ORIGIN C17 (in the sense 'sprawl'): prob. from *sprad*, dial. past part. of **SPREAD**.

**sprag** ● n. **1** a stout stick or bar inserted between the spokes of a wheel to act as a brake. **2** a prop in a coal mine.
– ORIGIN C19: of unknown origin.

**sprain** ● v. wrench the ligaments of (an ankle, wrist, or other joint) violently so as to cause pain and swelling but not dislocation. ● n. the result of such a wrench.
– ORIGIN C17: of unknown origin.

**spraing** /spreɪŋ/ ● n. a viral disease of potatoes characterized by curved lesions inside the tubers and rings or lesions on the leaves.
– ORIGIN C16 (orig. Scots, denoting a brightly coloured stripe): appar. of Scand. origin.

**spraint** /spreɪnt/ (also **spraints**) ● n. otter droppings.
– ORIGIN ME: from OFr. *espreintes*, from *espraindre* 'squeeze out', based on L. *exprimere* 'to express'.

**sprang** past of **SPRING**.

**sprat** ● n. a small marine fish of the herring family, caught for food and fish products. [*Sprattus sprattus* (Europe) and other species.] ➤informal any small sea fish. ● v. (**spratted**, **spratting**) fish for sprats.
– PHRASES **a sprat to catch a mackerel** Brit. a small outlay or risk ventured in the hope of a significant return.
– ORIGIN C16: var. of OE *sprot*, of unknown origin.

**sprauncy** /ˈsprɔːnsi/ ● adj. (**-ier**, **-iest**) Brit. informal smart or showy.
– ORIGIN 1950s: perh. rel. to dial. *sprouncey* 'cheerful'.

**sprawl** ● v. **1** sit, lie, or fall with one's limbs spread out in an ungainly way. **2** spread out irregularly over a large area. ● n. **1** a sprawling position or movement. **2** a sprawling group or mass. ➤the disorganized expansion of an urban or industrial area into the adjoining countryside.
– DERIVATIVES **sprawling** n. & adj. **sprawlingly** adv.
– ORIGIN OE *spreawlian* 'move the limbs convulsively'.

**spray**[1] ● n. liquid sent through the air in tiny drops. ➤a liquid preparation which can be forced out of an aerosol

or other container in a spray. ● v. **1** apply (liquid) in a spray. ➤ cover or treat with a spray. ➤ (of liquid) be sent through the air in a spray. ➤ (of a male cat) direct a stream of urine over (an object or area) to mark a territory. **2** scatter over an area with force.
– DERIVATIVES **sprayable** adj. **sprayer** n.
– ORIGIN C17 (orig. as *spry*): rel. to MDu. *spra(e)yen* 'sprinkle'.

**spray²** ● n. **1** a stem or small branch of a tree or plant, bearing flowers and foliage. **2** a bunch of cut flowers arranged in an attractive way. ➤ a brooch in the form of a bouquet.
– ORIGIN ME: representing OE *(e)sprei*, recorded in personal and place names, of unknown origin.

**spraydeck** ● n. a flexible cover fitted to the opening in the top of a kayak to form a waterproof seal around the canoeist's body.

**spray-dry** ● v. dry (a foodstuff or a ceramic material) by spraying particles of it into a current of hot air.
– DERIVATIVES **spray-dryer** n.

**spray gun** ● n. a device resembling a gun which is used to spray a liquid such as paint under pressure.

**sprayskirt** ● n. another term for **SPRAYDECK**.

**spread** ● v. (past and past part. **spread**) **1** open out so as to increase in surface area, width, or length. ➤ stretch out (limbs, hands, fingers, or wings) so that they are far apart. **2** extend or distribute over a wide area or a specified period of time. ➤ (**spread out**) (of a group of people) move apart so as to cover a wider area. ➤ gradually reach or cause to reach a wider area or more people. **3** apply (a substance) in an even layer. ➤ cover (a surface) with a substance in such a way. ➤ be able to be applied in such a way. ● n. **1** the fact or action of spreading. **2** the extent, width, or area covered by something. ➤ an expanse. **3** the range of something. ➤ the difference between two rates or prices. **4** a soft paste that can be spread on bread. **5** an article or advertisement covering several columns or pages of a newspaper or magazine. **6** N. Amer. a large farm or ranch. **7** informal a large and elaborate meal.
– PHRASES **spread oneself too thin** be involved in so many different activities that one's time and energy are not used to good effect.
– DERIVATIVES **spreadable** adj.
– ORIGIN OE *-sprǣdan* (used in combinations), of W. Gmc origin.

**spread betting** ● n. a form of betting in which the bettor wins or loses money according to the margin by which the value of a particular outcome varies from the spread of expected values quoted by the bookmaker.

**spreadeagle** ● v. **1** (usu. **be spreadeagled**) stretch (someone) out with their arms and legs extended. **2** informal utterly defeat (an opponent in a sporting contest). ● n. (**spread eagle**) a representation of an eagle with its legs and wings extended, used especially as an emblem of the United States. ● adj. US spreadeagled.

**spreader** ● n. **1** a device for spreading. ➤ a bar attached to a yacht's mast so as to spread the angle of the upper shrouds. **2** a person who disseminates something.

**spreadsheet** ● n. a computer program used chiefly for accounting, in which figures arranged in a grid can be manipulated and used in calculations.

**Sprechgesang** /ˈʃprɛxgəˌzaŋ, German ˈʃprɛçgəˌzaŋ/ ● n. Music a style of dramatic vocalization intermediate between speech and song.
– ORIGIN Ger., lit. 'speech song'.

**Sprechstimme** /ˈʃprɛxˌʃtɪmə, German ˈʃprɛçˌʃtɪmə/ ● n. Music another term for **SPRECHGESANG**. ➤ the kind of voice used in Sprechgesang.
– ORIGIN Ger., lit. 'speech voice'.

**spree** ● n. a spell of unrestrained activity of a particular kind. ● v. (**sprees**, **spreed**, **spreeing**) dated take part in a spree.
– ORIGIN C18: of unknown origin.

**sprezzatura** /ˌsprɛtsəˈt(j)ʊərə/ ● n. studied carelessness, especially in art or literature.
– ORIGIN from Ital.

**sprig¹** ● n. **1** a small stem bearing leaves or flowers, taken from a bush or plant. **2** a descendant or younger member of a family or social class. **3** a small moulded decoration applied to a piece of pottery before firing. ● v. decorate (pottery) with sprigs. ➤ [as adj. **sprigged**] (of fabric or wallpaper) decorated with a design of sprigs.
– DERIVATIVES **spriggy** adj.
– ORIGIN ME: from or rel. to Low Ger. *sprick*.

**sprig²** ● n. a small tapering tack with no head, used chiefly to hold glass in a window frame until the putty dries.
– ORIGIN ME: of unknown origin.

**sprightly** (also **spritely**) ● adj. (**-ier**, **-iest**) (especially of an old person) lively; energetic.
– DERIVATIVES **sprightliness** n.
– ORIGIN C16: from *spright* (rare var. of **SPRITE**) + **-LY¹**.

**spring** ● v. (past **sprang** or chiefly N. Amer. **sprung**; past part. **sprung**) **1** move suddenly or rapidly upwards or forwards. ➤ cause (a game bird) to rise from cover. **2** move suddenly by or as if by the action of a spring. **3** operate or cause to operate by means of a spring mechanism. **4** (**spring from**) originate or appear from. ➤ (**spring up**) suddenly develop or appear. ➤ (**spring something on**) present something suddenly or unexpectedly to. **5** informal bring about the escape or release of (a prisoner). **6** [usu. as adj. **sprung**] provide (a vehicle or item of furniture) with springs. **7** (of wood) become warped or split. **8** (**spring for**) N. Amer. & Austral. informal pay for. ● n. **1** the season after winter and before summer, in which vegetation begins to appear. ➤ Astronomy the period from the vernal equinox to the summer solstice. **2** an elastic device, typically a helical metal coil, that can be pressed or pulled but returns to its former shape when released. ➤ elastic quality. **3** a sudden jump upwards or forwards. **4** a place where water wells up from an underground source. **5** an upward curvature of a ship's deck planking from the horizontal. ➤ a split in a wooden plank or spar under strain. **6** Nautical a hawser laid out from a ship's bow or stern and secured to a fixed point in order to prevent movement or assist manoeuvring.
– PHRASES **spring a leak** (of a boat or container) develop a leak. [orig. in naut. use, referring to timbers springing out of position.]
– DERIVATIVES **springless** adj. **springlet** n. (poetic/literary). **springlike** adj.
– ORIGIN OE *spring* (n.), *springan* (v.), of Gmc origin.

**spring balance** ● n. a balance that measures weight by the tension of a spring.

**springboard** ● n. **1** a strong, flexible board from which a diver or gymnast may jump in order to gain added impetus. **2** a thing providing impetus to an action or enterprise. **3** Canadian & Austral. a platform fixed to the side of a tree and used by a lumberjack when working at some height from the ground.

**springbok** /ˈsprɪŋbɒk/ ● n. **1** a southern African gazelle with a characteristic habit of leaping when disturbed. [*Antidorcas marsupialis*.] **2** (**Springbok**) a member of a sports team selected to represent South Africa, especially in rugby union.
– ORIGIN C18: from Afrik., from Du. *springen* 'to spring' + *bok* 'antelope'.

**spring chicken** ● n. **1** [usu. with neg.] informal a young person. **2** a young chicken for eating (originally available only in spring).

**spring clean** ● n. Brit. a thorough cleaning of a house or room, typically undertaken in spring. ● v. (**spring-clean**) clean thoroughly.

**springe** /sprɪn(d)ʒ/ ● n. a noose or snare for catching small game.
– ORIGIN ME: from the base of **SPRING**.

**springer** ● n. **1** (also **springer spaniel**) a small spaniel of a breed originally used to spring game. **2** Architecture the lowest stone in an arch, where the curve begins. **3** a cow near to calving.

**spring fever** ● n. a feeling of restlessness and excitement felt at the beginning of spring.

**spring greens** ● pl. n. the leaves of young cabbage plants of a variety that does not develop a heart.

**spring-loaded** ● adj. containing a compressed or stretched spring pressing one part against another.

**spring lock** ● n. a type of lock with a spring-loaded bolt which requires a key only to open it, as distinct from a deadlock.

**spring onion** ● n. chiefly Brit. an onion taken from the ground before the bulb has formed, typically eaten raw in salad.

**spring peeper** ● n. see **PEEPER**[2].

**spring roll** ● n. a Chinese snack consisting of a pancake filled with vegetables and sometimes meat, rolled into a cylinder and fried.

**springtail** ● n. a minute wingless insect which has a spring-like organ under the abdomen that enables it to leap when disturbed. [Order Collembola.]

**springtide** ● n. poetic/literary springtime.

**spring tide** ● n. a tide just after a new or full moon, when there is the greatest difference between high and low water.

**springy** ● adj. (**-ier**, **-iest**) **1** springing back quickly when squeezed or stretched. **2** (of movements) light and confident.
– DERIVATIVES **springily** adv. **springiness** n.

**sprinkle** ● v. **1** scatter or pour small drops or particles over. ➤ scatter or pour (small drops or particles) over an object or surface. **2** distribute something randomly throughout. **3** (**it sprinkles**, **it is sprinkling**, etc.) N. Amer. rain very lightly. ● n. **1** a small quantity or amount that is sprinkled. **2** N. Amer. a light rain. **3** (**sprinkles**) N. Amer. tiny sugar strands and balls used for decorating cakes and desserts.
– ORIGIN ME: perh. from MDu. *sprenkelen*.

**sprinkler** ● n. **1** a device for watering lawns. **2** an automatic fire extinguisher installed in a ceiling.

**sprinkling** ● n. a small, thinly distributed amount.

**sprint** ● v. run at full speed over a short distance. ● n. an act or spell of sprinting. ➤ a short, fast race run over a distance of 400 metres or less. ➤ a short, fast race in cycling, horse racing, etc.
– DERIVATIVES **sprinter** n. **sprinting** n.
– ORIGIN C18 (as a dial. term meaning 'a bound or spring'): rel. to Swed. *spritta*.

**sprit** ● n. Sailing a small spar reaching diagonally from a mast to the upper outer corner of a sail.
– ORIGIN OE *sprēot* '(punting) pole'; rel. to **SPROUT**.

**sprite** ● n. **1** an elf or fairy. **2** Computing a graphical figure which can be moved and manipulated as a single entity. **3** a faint flash emitted in the upper atmosphere over a thunderstorm.
– ORIGIN ME: alt. of *sprit*, a contr. of **SPIRIT**.

**spritely** ● adj. variant spelling of **SPRIGHTLY**.

**spritsail** /ˈsprɪts(ə)l, -seɪl/ ● n. **1** a sail extended by a sprit. **2** a sail extended by a yard set under a ship's bowsprit.

**spritz** chiefly N. Amer. ● v. squirt or spray in quick short bursts at or on to. ● n. an act or instance of spritzing.
– ORIGIN C20: from Ger. *spritzen* 'to squirt'.

**spritzer** ● n. a mixture of wine and soda water.
– ORIGIN 1960s: from Ger. *Spritzer* 'a splash'.

**sprocket** ● n. **1** each of several projections on the rim of a wheel that engage with the links of a chain or with holes in film, tape, or paper. **2** (also **sprocket wheel**) a wheel with projections of this kind.
– ORIGIN C16 (denoting a triangular piece of timber used in a roof): of unknown origin.

**sprog** Brit. informal, chiefly derogatory ● n. **1** a child. **2** military slang a recruit or trainee. ● v. (**sprogged**, **sprogging**) have a baby.
– ORIGIN 1940s: perh. from obs. *sprag* 'lively young man', of unknown origin.

**sprout** ● v. produce shoots. ➤ grow (plant shoots or hair). ➤ start to grow or develop. ● n. **1** a shoot of a plant. **2** short for **BRUSSELS SPROUT**.
– ORIGIN ME: of W. Gmc origin.

**spruce**[1] ● adj. neat and smart. ● v. (**spruce someone/thing up**) make a person or place smarter.
– DERIVATIVES **sprucely** adv. **spruceness** n.
– ORIGIN C16: perh. from **SPRUCE**[2] in the obs. sense 'Prussian', in the phr. *spruce (leather) jerkin*.

**spruce**[2] ● n. a widespread coniferous tree which has a distinctive conical shape and hanging cones, grown for wood, pulp, and Christmas trees. [Genus *Picea*: many species.]
– ORIGIN ME (denoting Prussia or something originating in Prussia): alt. of obs. *Pruce* 'Prussia'.

**spruce**[3] ● v. Brit. informal, dated engage in pretence, especially by feigning illness.
– DERIVATIVES **sprucer** n.
– ORIGIN C20: of unknown origin.

**spruce beer** ● n. a fermented drink using spruce twigs and needles as flavouring.

**sprue**[1] /spruː/ ● n. **1** a channel through which metal or plastic is poured into a mould. **2** a piece of metal or plastic which has solidified in a sprue.
– ORIGIN C19: of unknown origin.

**sprue**[2] /spruː/ ● n. a disease characterized by ulceration of the mouth and chronic enteritis, suffered by visitors to tropical regions.
– ORIGIN C19: from Du. *spruw* 'thrush'.

**spruik** /spruːk/ ● v. Austral. informal speak in public, especially to advertise a show.
– DERIVATIVES **spruiker** n.
– ORIGIN C20: of unknown origin.

**spruit** /spreɪt/ ● n. S. African a small watercourse, typically dry except during the rainy season.
– ORIGIN Du.; rel. to **SPROUT**.

**sprung** past participle and (especially in North America) past of **SPRING**.

**sprung rhythm** ● n. a poetic metre approximating to speech, each foot having one stressed syllable followed by a varying number of unstressed ones.
– ORIGIN C19: coined by the Engl. poet G. M. Hopkins.

**spry** ● adj. (**-er**, **-est**) (especially of an old person) lively.
– DERIVATIVES **spryly** adv. **spryness** n.
– ORIGIN C18: of unknown origin.

**spud** ● n. **1** informal a potato. **2** a small, narrow spade for cutting the roots of weeds. **3** a short length of pipe used to connect two plumbing fixtures. **4** informal, chiefly N. Amer. a foolish or incompetent person. ● v. (**spudded**, **spudding**) **1** dig up or cut (weeds) with a spud. **2** make the initial drilling for (an oil well).
– ORIGIN ME (denoting a short knife): of unknown origin.

**spud-bashing** ● n. Brit. informal the chore of peeling potatoes, especially as a punishment in the army.

**spud wrench** ● n. a long bar with a socket on the end for tightening bolts.

**spue** ● v. archaic spelling of **SPEW**.

**spumante** /spuːˈmanteɪ, -ˈmanti/ ● n. an Italian sparkling white wine.
– ORIGIN Ital., lit. 'sparkling'.

**spume** /spjuːm/ poetic/literary ● n. froth or foam, especially that found on waves. ● v. froth or foam.
– DERIVATIVES **spumous** adj. **spumy** adj.
– ORIGIN ME: from OFr. *(e)spume* or L. *spuma*.

**spumoni** /spuːˈməʊni/ (also **spumone**) ● n. N. Amer. a kind of ice-cream dessert with different colours and flavours in layers.
– ORIGIN from Ital. *spumone*, from *spuma* 'foam'.

**spun** past and past participle of **SPIN**.

**spunk** ● n. **1** informal courage and determination. **2** Brit. vulgar slang semen. **3** Austral. informal a sexually attractive person.
– DERIVATIVES **spunkily** adv. **spunky** adj. (**-ier**, **-iest**).
– ORIGIN C16 (in the sense 'a spark, vestige'): of unknown origin; perh. a blend of **SPARK**[1] and obs. *funk* 'spark'.

**spun silk** ● n. a cheap material made of short-fibred and waste silk.

**spun sugar** ● n. stiff sugar syrup drawn out into long filaments and used to make candyfloss or as a decoration for sweet dishes.

**spun yarn** ● n. Nautical cord made by twisting loose strands of rope together.

**spur** ● n. **1** a device with a small spike or a spiked wheel, worn on a rider's heel for urging a horse forward. **2** an incentive. **3** a projection from a mountain or mountain range. ➤ Botany a slender tubular projection from the base

of a flower, e.g. an orchid, typically containing nectar. ➤a short fruit-bearing side shoot. ➤a horny spike on the back of the leg of a cock or male game bird. **4** a short branch road or railway line. **5** a small support for ceramic ware in a kiln. ● v. (**spurred, spurring**) **1** urge (a horse) forward with spurs. **2** (often **spur someone on**) encourage; give an incentive to. **3** prune in (a side shoot) so as to form a spur close to the stem.
– PHRASES **on the spur of the moment** on a momentary impulse.
– DERIVATIVES **spurless** adj. **spurred** adj.
– ORIGIN OE *spora, spura*, of Gmc origin; rel. to SPURN.

**spurdog** ● n. a large white-spotted grey dogfish of the North Atlantic with venomous spines in front of the dorsal fins. [*Squalus acanthias*.]

**spurge** /spəːdʒ/ ● n. a plant or shrub with milky latex and small, typically greenish flowers. [Genus *Euphorbia*: numerous species.]
– ORIGIN ME: shortening of OFr. *espurge*, from *espurgier*, from L. *expurgare* 'cleanse' (because of the purgative properties of the milky latex).

**spur gear** ● n. another term for SPUR WHEEL.

**spurge laurel** ● n. a low-growing evergreen shrub with leathery leaves, small green flowers, and black poisonous berries. [*Daphne laureola*.]

**spurious** /ˈspjʊərɪəs/ ● adj. **1** false or fake. **2** (of a line of reasoning) apparently but not actually valid. **3** archaic (of offspring) illegitimate.
– DERIVATIVES **spuriously** adv. **spuriousness** n.
– ORIGIN C16: from L. *spurius* 'false' + **-OUS**.

**spurn** ● v. **1** reject with disdain or contempt. **2** archaic strike or push away with the foot.
– DERIVATIVES **spurner** n.
– ORIGIN OE *spurnan, spornan*; rel. to L. *spernere* 'to scorn'; cf. SPUR.

**spurrey** /ˈspʌri/ (also **spurry**) ● n. (pl. **-eys** or **-ies**) a small plant of the pink family with pink or white flowers. [Genera *Spergula* and *Spergularia*: several species.]
– ORIGIN C16: from Du. *spurrie*; prob. rel. to med. L. *spergula*.

**spurrier** /ˈspʌrɪə, ˈspəː-/ ● n. rare a person who makes spurs.

**spur royal** ● n. a gold coin worth fifteen shillings, made chiefly in the reign of James I and bearing a representation of a sun with rays.

**spurt** ● v. **1** gush or cause to gush out in a sudden stream. **2** move with a sudden burst of speed. ● n. **1** a sudden gushing stream. **2** a sudden burst of activity or speed.
– ORIGIN C16: of unknown origin.

**spur wheel** ● n. a gearwheel with teeth projecting parallel to the wheel's axis.

**sputnik** /ˈspʊtnɪk, ˈspʌt-/ ● n. each of a series of Soviet satellites, the first of which (launched in October 1957) was the first artificial satellite to be placed in orbit.
– ORIGIN Russ., lit. 'fellow-traveller'.

**sputter** ● v. **1** make a series of soft explosive sounds. **2** speak in a series of incoherent bursts. **3** Physics deposit (metal) on a surface by using fast ions to eject particles of it from a target. ● n. a sputtering sound.
– DERIVATIVES **sputterer** n.
– ORIGIN C16: from Du. *sputteren*, of imitative origin.

**sputum** /ˈspjuːtəm/ ● n. a mixture of saliva and mucus coughed up from the respiratory tract, typically as a result of infection or other disease.
– ORIGIN C17: from L., neut. past part. of *spuere* 'to spit'.

**spy** ● n. (pl. **-ies**) **1** a person employed by a government or other organization to collect and report secret information on an enemy or competitor. **2** a person who observes others secretly. ● v. (**-ies, -ied**) **1** be a spy. ➤(**spy on**) observe furtively. **2** observe or notice.
– PHRASES **spy out the land** collect information about a situation before deciding how to act.
– ORIGIN ME: shortening of OFr. *espie* 'espying', *espier* 'espy', of Gmc origin.

**spyglass** ● n. a small telescope.

**spyhole** ● n. Brit. a peephole.

**sq** ● abbrev. square.

**SQL** ● abbrev. Computing Structured Query Language, an international standard for database manipulation.

**Sqn Ldr** ● abbrev. Squadron Leader.

**squab** /skwɒb/ ● n. **1** a young unfledged pigeon. **2** Brit. the padded back or side of a vehicle seat. ➤a thick cushion, especially one covering the seat of a chair or sofa. ● adj. archaic short and fat.
– ORIGIN C17 (in the sense 'inexperienced person'): of unknown origin; cf. obs. *quab* 'shapeless thing' and Swed. dial. *skvabba* 'fat woman'.

**squabble** ● n. a trivial noisy quarrel. ● v. engage in a squabble.
– DERIVATIVES **squabbler** n.
– ORIGIN C17: prob. imitative; cf. Swed. dial. *skvabbel* 'a dispute'.

**squab pie** ● n. Brit. **1** pigeon pie. **2** archaic a pie with a thick crust containing mutton, pork, onions, and apples.

**squacco heron** /ˈskwakəʊ/ ● n. a small crested buff and white heron found in southern Europe, the Middle East, and Africa. [*Ardeola ralloides*.]
– ORIGIN C18: *squacco* from Ital. dial. *sguacco*.

**squad** ● n. [treated as sing. or pl.] **1** a small number of soldiers assembled for drill or assigned to a particular task. **2** a group of sports players from which a team is chosen. **3** a division of a police force dealing with a particular type of crime.
– ORIGIN C17: shortening of Fr. *escouade*, var. of *escadre*, from Ital. *squadra* 'square'.

**squad car** ● n. a police patrol car.

**squaddie** (also **squaddy**) ● n. (pl. **-ies**) Brit. informal a private soldier.

**squadron** ● n. **1** an operational unit in an air force consisting of two or more flights of aircraft. **2** a principal division of an armoured or cavalry regiment, consisting of two or more troops. **3** a group of warships detached on a particular duty or under the command of a flag officer.
– ORIGIN C16 (orig. denoting a group of soldiers in square formation): from Ital. *squadrone*, from *squadra* 'square'.

**squadron leader** ● n. a rank of officer in the RAF, above flight lieutenant and below wing commander.

**squalid** ● adj. **1** extremely dirty and unpleasant. **2** showing a contemptible lack of moral standards: *a squalid attempt to buy votes.*
– DERIVATIVES **squalidly** adv. **squalidness** n.
– ORIGIN C16: from L. *squalidus*, from *squalere* 'be rough or dirty'.

**squall** /skwɔːl/ ● n. **1** a sudden violent gust of wind or localized storm, especially one bringing rain, snow, or sleet. **2** a loud cry. ● v. (of a baby or small child) cry noisily and continuously.
– DERIVATIVES **squally** adj.
– ORIGIN C17: prob. an alt. of SQUEAL, influenced by BAWL.

**squall line** ● n. Meteorology a narrow band of high winds and storms associated with a cold front.

**squalor** /ˈskwɒlə/ ● n. the state of being squalid.
– ORIGIN C17: from L., from *squalere* 'be dirty'.

**Squamata** /skwəˈmɑːtə/ ● pl. n. Zoology a large order of reptiles comprising the snakes, lizards, and worm lizards.
– DERIVATIVES **squamate** adj. & n.
– ORIGIN mod. L., from L. *squama* 'scale'.

**squamous** /ˈskweɪməs/ ● adj. **1** covered with or characterized by scales. **2** Anatomy of or denoting a layer of epithelium consisting of very thin flattened cells. **3** Anatomy denoting the flat portion of the temporal bone which forms part of the side of the skull.
– ORIGIN ME: from L. *squamosus*, from *squama* 'scale'.

**squamule** /ˈskweɪmjuːl/ ● n. Botany & Zoology a small scale.
– DERIVATIVES **squamulose** adj.
– ORIGIN C18: from L. *squamula*, dimin. of *squama* 'scale'.

**squander** ● v. waste in a reckless or foolish manner.
– DERIVATIVES **squanderer** n.
– ORIGIN C16: of unknown origin.

**square** ● n. **1** a plane figure with four equal straight sides and four right angles. **2** an open, typically four-sided, area surrounded by buildings. **3** an area within a military barracks or camp used for drill. **4** Cricket a closer-cut area at the centre of a ground, any strip of which may be prepared as a wicket. **5** historical a body of infantry drawn up in rectangular form. **6** US a block of buildings bounded by four streets. **7** the product of a number multiplied by itself. **8** a unit of 100 square ft used as a measure of flooring, roofing, etc. **9** an L-shaped or T-shaped instrument used for obtaining or testing right angles. **10** informal a person considered to be old-fashioned or boringly conventional. **11** Astrology an aspect of 90° (one quarter of a circle). ● **adj. 1** having the shape or approximate shape of a square. ➤ having or forming a right angle, exactly or approximately. **2** denoting a unit of measurement equal to the area of a square whose side is of the unit specified. ➤ [postpos.] denoting the length of each side of a square shape or object. **3** at right angles. ➤ Cricket & Soccer in a direction transversely across the field or pitch. **4** broad and solid in shape. **5** level or parallel. ➤ properly arranged. ➤ on even terms. **6** fair and honest. **7** informal old-fashioned or boringly conventional. **8** (of rhythm) simple and straightforward. ● **adv. 1** directly; straight. **2** Cricket & Soccer in a direction transversely across the field or pitch. ● **v. 1** make square or rectangular. ➤ [usu. as adj. **squared**] mark out in squares. **2** multiply (a number) by itself. **3** make or be compatible. **4** balance (an account) or settle (a bill or debt). ➤ make the score of (a match or game) even. **5** informal secure the help or acquiescence of (someone), especially by offering an inducement. **6** bring (one's shoulders) into a position in which they appear square and broad. **7** Sailing set (a yard or other part of a ship) at right angles to the keel or other point of reference. **8** Astrology (of a planet) have a square aspect with (another planet or position).

– PHRASES **back to** (or **at**) **square one** informal back to where one started, with no progress having been made. **on the square 1** informal honest; straightforward. **2** having membership of the Freemasons. **out of square** not at right angles. **square the circle 1** construct a square equal in area to a given circle (a problem incapable of a purely geometrical solution). **2** do something considered to be impossible. **a square deal** see **DEAL**[1]. **a square peg in a round hole** see **PEG**.

– PHRASAL VERBS **square something away** N. Amer. deal with something in a satisfactory way. **square off 1** N. Amer. another way of saying ***square up*** below. **2** Austral./NZ settle a difference. **square someone off** Austral./NZ conciliate or placate someone. **square up 1** assume the attitude of a person about to fight. **2** (**square up to**) face and tackle (a difficulty or problem) resolutely.

– DERIVATIVES **squareness** n. **squarer** n. **squarish** adj.

– ORIGIN ME: shortening of OFr. *esquare* (n.), *esquarre* (past part.), *esquarrer* (v.), based on L. *quadra* 'square'.

**square-bashing** ● **n.** Brit. informal military drill performed repeatedly on a barrack square.

**square dance** ● **n.** a country dance that starts with four couples facing one another in a square, with the steps and movements shouted out by a caller.

– DERIVATIVES **square dancer** n.

**square eyes** ● **pl. n.** Brit. humorous eyes supposedly affected by excessive television viewing.

– DERIVATIVES **square-eyed** adj.

**square go** ● **n.** Scottish an unarmed brawl.

**square knot** ● **n.** another term for **REEF KNOT**.

**square leg** ● **n.** Cricket a fielding position level with the batsman approximately halfway towards the boundary on the leg side.

**squarely** ● **adv.** without deviation or equivocation; directly.

**square meal** ● **n.** a substantial and balanced meal.

– ORIGIN said to derive from naut. use, with ref. to the square platters on which meals were served.

**square measure** ● **n.** a unit of measurement relating to area.

**square number** ● **n.** the product of a number multiplied by itself, e.g. 1, 4, 9, 16.

**square piano** ● **n.** an early type of piano, small and oblong in shape.

**square-rigged** ● **adj.** (of a sailing ship) having the principal sails at right angles to the length of the ship, supported by horizontal yards attached to the mast or masts.

**square-rigger** ● **n.** a square-rigged sailing ship.

**square root** ● **n.** a number which produces a specified quantity when multiplied by itself.

**square-toed** ● **adj. 1** (of shoes) having broad, square toes. **2** archaic old-fashioned or formal.

**square wave** ● **n.** Electronics a periodic wave that varies abruptly in amplitude between two fixed values.

**squark** /skwɑːk/ ● **n.** Physics the supersymmetric counterpart of a quark.

– ORIGIN 1980s: from *s*(*uper*) + **QUARK**[1].

**squash**[1] ● **v. 1** crush or squeeze (something) so that it becomes flat, soft, or out of shape. ➤ squeeze or force into a restricted space. **2** suppress or subdue. ➤ firmly reject (an idea or suggestion). ➤ silence (someone), typically with a humiliating remark. ● **n. 1** a state of being squashed. **2** dated a social gathering or informal meeting. **3** Brit. a concentrated liquid made from fruit juice and sugar, diluted to make a drink. **4** (also **squash rackets**) a game in which two players use rackets to hit a small, soft rubber ball against the walls of a closed court.

– DERIVATIVES **squashily** adv. **squashiness** n. **squashy** adj. (**-ier, -iest**).

– ORIGIN C16 (as v.): alt. of **QUASH**.

**squash**[2] ● **n.** (pl. same or **squashes**) **1** a gourd with flesh that can be cooked and eaten as a vegetable. **2** the plant which produces such gourds. [Several species and varieties of the genus *Cucurbita*.]

– ORIGIN C17: abbrev. of Narragansett *asquutasquash*.

**squat** ● **v.** (**squatted, squatting**) **1** crouch or sit with the knees bent and the heels close to or touching the buttocks or thighs. **2** unlawfully occupy an uninhabited building or area of land. ● **adj.** (**squatter, squattest**) short or low, and disproportionately broad or wide. ● **n. 1** a squatting position or movement. ➤ Weightlifting an exercise in which a person squats down and rises again with a barbell behind their neck. **2** a building occupied by squatters. ➤ an act of squatting in an uninhabited building. **3** N. Amer. informal short for **DIDDLY-SQUAT**.

– DERIVATIVES **squatly** adv. **squatness** n.

– ORIGIN ME: from OFr. *esquatir* 'flatten', based on L. *coactus*, past part. of *cogere* 'compel'.

**squatt** ● **n.** the larva of the common housefly, used by anglers as bait.

– ORIGIN 1930s: perh. from the adj. **SQUAT**.

**squatter** ● **n. 1** a person who squats in a building or on unused land. ➤ N. Amer. & Austral./NZ historical a settler with no legal title to the land occupied. **2** Austral./NZ a large-scale sheep or cattle farmer. ➤ Austral./NZ historical a person occupying a tract of pastoral land as a tenant of the Crown.

**squat thrust** ● **n.** an exercise in which the legs are thrust backwards to their full extent from a squatting position with the hands on the floor.

**squaw** /skwɔː/ ● **n.** offensive an American Indian woman or wife.

– ORIGIN C17: from Narragansett *squaws* 'woman', with rel. forms in many Algonquin dials.

**squawfish** ● **n.** (pl. same or **-fishes**) a large predatory freshwater fish of the carp family, found in western North America. [*Ptychocheilus oregonensis* and other species.]

– ORIGIN C19: referring to the former importance to Amer. Indians of such fish.

**squawk** ● **v. 1** (of a bird) make a loud, harsh noise. **2** say something in a loud, discordant tone. ➤ complain about something. ● **n.** an act of squawking.

– DERIVATIVES **squawker** n.

– ORIGIN C19: imitative.

**squawk box** ● **n.** informal, chiefly N. Amer. a loudspeaker.

**squaw man** ● **n.** N. Amer. offensive a white or black man married to an American Indian woman.

**squeak** ● **n.** a short, high-pitched sound or cry. ➤ [with neg.] a single remark or communication. ● **v. 1** make a squeak. ➤ say something in a high-pitched tone. **2** informal inform on someone. **3** informal achieve something by a narrow margin: *the bill squeaked through*.

– DERIVATIVES **squeakily** adv. **squeakiness** n. **squeaky**

adj. (**-ier**, **-iest**).
– ORIGIN ME (as v.): imitative; cf. **SQUEAL** and **SHRIEK**.

**squeaker** • n. **1** a person or thing that squeaks. **2** informal, chiefly N. Amer. a contest won by a narrow margin. **3** chiefly Brit. a young pigeon.

**squeaky clean** • adj. informal **1** completely clean. **2** beyond reproach.

**squeal** • n. a long, high-pitched cry or noise. • v. **1** make a squeal. ➤ say something in a high-pitched, excited tone. **2** complain. **3** informal inform on someone.
– DERIVATIVES **squealer** n.
– ORIGIN ME (as v.): imitative.

**squeamish** • adj. **1** easily nauseated or disgusted. **2** having fastidious moral views.
– DERIVATIVES **squeamishly** adv. **squeamishness** n.
– ORIGIN ME: alt. of dial. *squeamous*, from Anglo-Norman Fr. *escoymos*, of unknown origin.

**squeegee** /ˈskwiːdʒiː/ • n. a scraping implement with a rubber-edged blade, typically used for cleaning windows. ➤ a similar small instrument or roller used especially in developing photographs. • v. (**squeegees**, **squeegeed**, **squeegeeing**) clean or scrape with a squeegee.
– ORIGIN C19: from archaic *squeege* 'to press', strengthened form of **SQUEEZE**.

**squeeze** • v. **1** firmly press from opposite or all sides, typically with the fingers. ➤ extract (liquid or a soft substance) from something by squeezing. **2** (usu. **squeeze something out of/from**) obtain from someone with difficulty. ➤ informal put pressure on (someone) to supply information, authorization, etc. ➤ have a damaging or restricting effect on: *the economy is being squeezed by foreign debt repayments.* ➤ Bridge force (an opponent) to discard a guarding or potentially winning card. **3** (**squeeze something off**) informal shoot a round or shot from a gun. ➤ take a photograph. **4** (**squeeze in/into/through**) manage to get into or through (a restricted space). ➤ (**squeeze up**) move closer to and press tightly against someone or something. ➤ (**squeeze someone/thing in**) manage to find time for someone or something. ➤ (**squeeze someone/thing out**) force someone or something out of a domain or activity. • n. **1** an act of squeezing or state of being squeezed. **2** a hug. **3** a small amount of liquid extracted by squeezing. **4** dated a crowded social gathering. **5** a strong financial demand or pressure. ➤ informal money illegally extorted or exacted from someone. **6** a moulding or cast of an object, or a copy of a design, obtained by pressing a pliable substance round or over it. **7** Bridge a tactic that forces an opponent to discard an important card. **8** (also **squeeze play**) Baseball an act of hitting a ball short to the infield to enable a runner on third base to start for home as soon as the ball is pitched. **9** (often **main squeeze**) N. Amer. informal a person's girlfriend or boyfriend.
– PHRASES **put the squeeze on** informal coerce or pressurize.
– DERIVATIVES **squeezable** adj. **squeezer** n.
– ORIGIN C16: from earlier *squise*, from obs. *queise*, of unknown origin.

**squeeze box** • n. informal an accordion or concertina.

**squeezy** • adj. **1** (especially of a container) flexible and able to be squeezed to force out the contents. **2** archaic restricted or confined.

**squelch** • v. **1** make a soft sucking sound as that of treading in thick mud. **2** informal forcefully silence or suppress. • n. **1** a squelching sound. **2** Electronics a circuit that suppresses the output of a radio receiver if the signal strength falls below a certain level.
– DERIVATIVES **squelcher** n. **squelchy** adj.
– ORIGIN C17: imitative.

**squib** • n. **1** a small firework that hisses before exploding. **2** a short piece of satirical writing. ➤ N. Amer. a short news item. **3** informal a small or weak person. **4** American Football a short kick on a kick-off. • v. (**squibbed**, **squibbing**) **1** American Football kick (the ball) a short distance on a kick-off. **2** archaic utter, write, or publish a satirical or sarcastic attack. ➤ lampoon.
– ORIGIN C16: of unknown origin; perh. imitative of a small explosion.

**SQUID** • abbrev. Physics superconducting quantum interference device (used in very sensitive magnetometers).

**squid** • n. (pl. same or **squids**) an elongated, fast-swimming cephalopod mollusc with eight arms and two long tentacles. [*Loligo* and other genera: many species.] ➤ the flesh of this animal as food. ➤ an artificial fishing bait resembling a squid. • v. (**squidded**, **squidding**) fish using squid as bait.
– ORIGIN C16: of unknown origin.

**squidge** • v. informal squash or crush. ➤ squelch.
– ORIGIN C19: perh. imitative.

**squidgy** • adj. (**-ier**, **-iest**) informal, chiefly Brit. soft and moist.

**squiffed** • adj. N. Amer. informal slightly drunk.
– ORIGIN C19: var. of **SQUIFFY**.

**squiffy** • adj. (**-ier**, **-iest**) informal **1** chiefly Brit. slightly drunk. **2** askew; awry.
– ORIGIN C19: of unknown origin.

**squiggle** • n. a short line that curls and loops irregularly. • v. chiefly N. Amer. wriggle; squirm. ➤ squeeze from a tube so as to make squiggles on a surface.
– DERIVATIVES **squiggly** adj.
– ORIGIN C19: perh. a blend of **SQUIRM** and **WIGGLE** or **WRIGGLE**.

**squill** • n. **1** (also **sea squill**) a coastal Mediterranean bulbous plant with broad leaves and white flowers. [*Drimia maritima*.] ➤ (also **squills**) an extract of the squill bulb, which is poisonous and has medicinal uses. **2** a small plant resembling a hyacinth, with clusters of violet-blue or blue-striped flowers. [*Scilla verna*, *Puschkinia scilloides*, and other species.]
– ORIGIN ME: via L. from Gk *skilla*.

**squillion** /ˈskwɪljən/ • cardinal number (pl. **squillions** or (with numeral) same) informal an indefinite very large number.
– ORIGIN 1940s: fanciful formation on the pattern of *billion* and *trillion*.

**squinancywort** /ˈskwɪnənsɪˌwəːt/ • n. a small plant with narrow leaves and scented white or lilac flowers, formerly used to treat quinsy. [*Asperula cynanchica*.]
– ORIGIN C18: from med. L. *squinantia* (appar. formed by confusion of Gk *sunankhē* with *kunankhē*, both denoting throat diseases) + **WORT**.

**squinch**[1] • n. a straight or arched structure across an interior angle of a square tower, bearing a superstructure such as a dome.
– ORIGIN C15: alt. of obs. *scunch*, abbrev. of **SCUNCHEON**.

**squinch**[2] • v. chiefly N. Amer. **1** tense up the muscles of (one's eyes or face). **2** crouch down.
– ORIGIN C19: perh. a blend of **SQUEEZE** and **PINCH**.

**squint** • v. **1** look at someone or something with partly closed eyes. ➤ partly close (one's eyes). **2** have a squint affecting one eye. • n. **1** a permanent deviation in the direction of the gaze of one eye. **2** informal a quick or casual look. **3** an oblique opening through a wall in a church permitting a view of the altar. • adj. chiefly Scottish not straight or level.
– DERIVATIVES **squinter** n. **squinty** adj.
– ORIGIN C16: shortening of **ASQUINT**.

**squint-eyed** • adj. **1** derogatory having a squint. **2** archaic spiteful.

**squire** • n. **1** a country gentleman, especially the chief landowner in an area. ➤ US archaic a title given to a magistrate, lawyer, or judge in some rural districts. **2** Brit. informal used as a friendly form of address by one man to another. **3** historical a young nobleman acting as an attendant to a knight before becoming a knight himself. • v. (of a man) accompany or escort (a woman). ➤ dated (of a man) have a romantic relationship with (a woman).
– DERIVATIVES **squiredom** n. **squireship** n.
– ORIGIN ME: shortening of OFr. *esquier* 'esquire'.

**squirearchy** /ˈskwʌɪərɑːki/ • n. (pl. **-ies**) landowners collectively.
– DERIVATIVES **squirearch** n. **squirearchical** adj.
– ORIGIN C18: from **SQUIRE**, on the pattern of words such as *hierarchy*.

**squireen** /ˌskwʌɪəˈriːn/ • n. Brit. a minor landowner, especially in Ireland.

– ORIGIN C19: from **SQUIRE** + *-een* (representing the Ir. dimin. suffix *-ín*).

**squirl** ● n. informal an ornamental flourish or curve, especially in handwriting.
– ORIGIN C19: perh. a blend of **SQUIGGLE** and **TWIRL**.

**squirm** ● v. wriggle or twist the body from side to side, especially due to nervousness or discomfort. ➤ be embarrassed or ashamed. ● n. a wriggling movement.
– DERIVATIVES **squirmer** n. **squirmy** adj.
– ORIGIN C17: symbolic of writhing movement; prob. assoc. with **WORM**.

**squirrel** ● n. an agile tree-dwelling rodent with a bushy tail, typically feeding on nuts and seeds. [*Sciurus* and other genera: numerous species.] ➤ used in names of other rodents of the same family (Sciuridae), e.g. **ground squirrel**. ● v. (**squirrelled**, **squirrelling**; US also **squirreled**, **squirreling**) **1** (**squirrel something away**) hide money or valuables in a safe place. **2** move about inquisitively or busily.
– ORIGIN ME: shortening of OFr. *esquireul*, from a dimin. of L. *sciurus*, from Gk *skiouros*, from *skia* 'shade' + *oura* 'tail'.

**squirrel cage** ● n. **1** a rotating cylindrical cage in which a small captive animal can exercise as on a treadmill. **2** a form of rotor in small electric motors, resembling a squirrel cage.

**squirrelfish** ● n. (pl. same or **-fishes**) a large-eyed marine fish, typically brightly coloured, that lives around reefs in warm seas. [Family Holocentridae: several species.]

**squirrelly** ● adj. **1** relating to or resembling a squirrel. **2** informal, chiefly N. Amer. restless or nervous. ➤ eccentric.

**squirrel monkey** ● n. a small South American monkey with a non-prehensile tail, typically moving through trees by leaping. [*Saimiri sciureus* and other species.]

**squirt** ● v. **1** (with reference to a liquid) be or cause to be ejected in a thin jet from a small opening. ➤ wet with a jet of liquid. **2** transmit (information) in highly compressed or speeded-up form. ● n. **1** a thin jet of liquid. ➤ a device from which liquid may be squirted. **2** informal a puny or insignificant person. **3** a compressed radio signal transmitted at high speed.
– DERIVATIVES **squirter** n.
– ORIGIN ME: imitative.

**squirt gun** ● n. N. Amer. a water pistol.

**squirting cucumber** ● n. a Mediterranean plant bearing a small cucumber-like fruit which falls when ripe and squirts out an irritant pulp containing its seeds. [*Ecballium elaterium*.]

**squish** ● v. make a soft squelching sound. ➤ informal squash. ➤ (**squish in/into**) informal squeeze oneself into. ● n. a soft squelching sound.
– DERIVATIVES **squishy** adj. (**-ier**, **-iest**).
– ORIGIN C17: imitative.

**squit** ● n. Brit. informal **1** a small or insignificant person. **2** (**the squits**) diarrhoea.
– ORIGIN C19: perh. rel. to dial. *squit* 'to squirt'.

**squitters** ● pl. n. informal diarrhoea.
– ORIGIN C17: perh. from dial. *squit* 'to squirt'.

**squiz** ● n. Austral./NZ informal a look or glance.
– ORIGIN C20: prob. a blend of **QUIZ**² and **SQUINT**.

**Sr** ● abbrev. **1** senior (in names). **2** Señor. **3** Signor. **4** Sister (in a religious order). ● symb. the chemical element strontium.

**sr** ● abbrev. steradian(s).

**SRAM** ● abbrev. Electronics static random-access memory.

**Sranan** /'srɑːnən/ ● n. another term for **TAKI-TAKI**.
– ORIGIN from Taki-Taki *Sranan tongo*, lit. 'Suriname tongue'.

**Sri** /sri/ (also **Shri**) ● n. Indian a title of respect used before the name of a man, god, or sacred book.
– ORIGIN from Sanskrit *Śrī* 'beauty, fortune', used as an honorific title.

**Sri Lankan** /srɪ 'laŋkən, ʃrɪ/ ● n. a native or inhabitant of Sri Lanka. ● adj. of or relating to Sri Lanka.

**SRN** ● abbrev. State Registered Nurse.

**SRO** ● abbrev. **1** (in the UK) self-regulatory organization, a body that regulates the activities of investment businesses. **2** standing room only.

**SS**¹ ● abbrev. **1** Saints. **2** Baseball shortstop. **3** social security. **4** steamship.

**SS**² ● n. the Nazi special police force.
– ORIGIN abbrev. of Ger. *Schutzstaffel* 'defence squadron'.

**SSAFA** ● abbrev. (in the UK) Soldiers', Sailors', and Airmen's Families Association.

**SSC** ● abbrev. **1** (in Scotland) Solicitor in the Supreme Court. **2** Physics superconducting super collider.

**SSE** ● abbrev. south-south-east.

**SSL** ● abbrev. Secure Sockets Layer, a computing protocol that ensures the security of data sent via the Internet by using encryption.

**SSP** ● abbrev. (in the UK) statutory sick pay.

**ssp.** ● abbrev. subspecies.

**SSRC** ● abbrev. (in the UK) Social Science Research Council.

**SSSI** ● abbrev. (in the UK) Site of Special Scientific Interest.

**SST** ● abbrev. supersonic transport.

**SSW** ● abbrev. south-south-west.

**St** ● abbrev. **1** Saint. **2** Physics stokes. **3** Street.

**st** ● abbrev. **1** stone (in weight). **2** Cricket (on scorecards) stumped by.

**-st** ● suffix variant of **-EST**².

**Sta.** ● abbrev. railway station.

**stab** ● v. (**stabbed**, **stabbing**) **1** thrust a knife or other pointed weapon into. **2** thrust a pointed object at. **3** (usu. **stab at**) (of a pain or painful thing) cause a sudden sharp sensation. ● n. **1** an act of stabbing. ➤ a wound made by stabbing. **2** a sudden sharp feeling or pain. **3** (**a stab at**) informal an attempt to do.
– PHRASES **stab someone in the back** betray someone.
– DERIVATIVES **stabber** n. **stabbing** n. & adj.
– ORIGIN ME: of unknown origin.

**Stabat Mater** /ˌstɑːbat 'mɑːtə, 'meɪtə/ ● n. a medieval Latin hymn on the suffering of the Virgin Mary at the Crucifixion.
– ORIGIN from the opening words *Stabat mater dolorosa* 'Stood the mother, full of grief'.

**stabilator** /'steɪbɪleɪtə/ ● n. a combined stabilizer and elevator at the tail of an aircraft.

**stabile** /'steɪbʌɪl/ ● n. Art a free-standing abstract structure, in the style of a mobile but rigid and stationary.
– ORIGIN 1940s: from L. *stabilis* 'stable', influenced by **MOBILE**.

**stability** ● n. the state of being stable.

**stabilize** (also **-ise**) ● v. make or become stable.
– DERIVATIVES **stabilization** n.

**stabilizer** (also **-iser**) ● n. **1** the horizontal tailplane of an aircraft. **2** a gyroscopic device used to reduce the rolling of a ship. **3** (**stabilizers**) Brit. a pair of small supporting wheels fitted on a child's bicycle. **4** a substance preventing the breakdown of emulsions, especially in food or paint.

**stable**¹ ● adj. (**-er**, **-est**) **1** not likely to give way or overturn; firmly fixed. **2** not deteriorating in health after an injury or operation. **3** emotionally well-balanced. **4** not likely to change or fail. **5** not liable to undergo chemical decomposition or radioactive decay.
– DERIVATIVES **stably** adv.
– ORIGIN ME: from Anglo-Norman Fr., from L. *stabilis*, from the base of *stare* 'to stand'.

**stable**² ● n. **1** a building for housing horses. **2** an establishment where racehorses are kept and trained. **3** an establishment producing particular types of people or things. ● v. **1** put or keep (a horse) in a stable. **2** put or base (a train) in a depot.
– DERIVATIVES **stableful** n. (pl. **-fuls**).
– ORIGIN ME: shortening of OFr. *estable* 'stable, pigsty', from L. *stabulum*, from the base of *stare* 'to stand'.

**stable boy** (or **stable girl**, also Brit. **stable lad**) ● n. a boy or man (or girl or woman) employed in a stable.

**stable companion** ● n. a stablemate.

**stable door** ● n. a door of a kind found in a stable, divided into two parts horizontally so that one half may be shut and the other left open.

**stable fly** ● n. a bloodsucking fly related to the housefly, biting large mammals including humans. [*Stomoxis calcitrans.*]

**Stableford** /ˈsteɪb(ə)lfəd/ ● n. a form of stroke-play golf in which points are awarded according to the number of strokes taken to complete each hole.
– ORIGIN named after its Engl. inventor Frank B. *Stableford*.

**stablemate** ● n. **1** a horse, especially a racehorse, from the same stable as another. **2** a person or product from the same organization or background as another.

**stabling** ● n. accommodation for horses.

**stablish** ● v. archaic form of **ESTABLISH**.

**staccato** /stəˈkɑːtəʊ/ ● adv. & adj. Music with each sound or note sharply detached or separated from the others. ● n. (pl. **-os**) **1** Music a staccato passage or performance. **2** a series of short, detached sounds or words.
– ORIGIN Ital., lit. 'detached'.

**staccato mark** ● n. a dot or stroke above or below a note indicating that it is to be played staccato.

**stack** ● n. **1** a pile, especially a neat one. **2** a rectangular or cylindrical pile of hay, straw, etc. **3** informal a large quantity of something. **4** a vertical arrangement of hi-fi or guitar amplification equipment. **5** a number of aircraft flying in circles at different altitudes around the same point while waiting to land at an airport. **6** a pyramidal group of rifles. **7** (**the stacks**) compact units of shelving in part of a library normally closed to the public. **8** Computing a set of storage locations from which the most recently stored item is the first to be retrieved. **9** a chimney or vertical exhaust pipe. **10** (also **sea stack**) Brit. a column of rock standing in the sea. **11** Brit. a measure for a pile of wood of 108 cu. ft (3.06 cubic metres). ● v. **1** arrange in a stack. ➤ fill or cover with stacks of things. **2** cause (aircraft) to fly in stacks. **3** shuffle or arrange (a pack of cards) dishonestly. **4** (**be stacked against/in favour of**) (of a situation) be overwhelmingly likely to produce an unfavourable or favourable outcome for. **5** (**stack up**) N. Amer. informal measure up; compare. **6** (in snowboarding) fall over.
– DERIVATIVES **stackable** adj. **stacker** n.
– ORIGIN ME: from ON *stakkr* 'haystack', of Gmc origin.

**stacked** ● adj. **1** arranged in a stack or stacks. **2** filled or covered with goods. **3** (of a heel) made from thin layers of wood or leather glued one on top of the other. **4** (of a pack of cards) shuffled or arranged dishonestly. **5** informal (of a woman) having large breasts. **6** Computing placed in a queue for subsequent processing.

**staddle** ● n. a platform or framework supporting a stack or rick.
– ORIGIN OE *stathol* 'base, support', of Gmc origin; rel. to the verb **STAND**.

**stadium** ● n. (pl. **stadiums** or **stadia** /ˈsteɪdɪə/) **1** an athletic or sports ground with tiers of seats for spectators. **2** (in ancient Rome or Greece) a racing track. **2** (pl. **stadia**) an ancient Roman or Greek measure of length, about 185 metres.
– ORIGIN ME: via L. from Gk *stadion*.

**stadtholder** /ˈstadˌhəʊldə, ˈstat-/ (also **stadholder**) ● n. historical the chief magistrate of the United Provinces of the Netherlands.
– DERIVATIVES **stadtholdership** n.
– ORIGIN C16: from Du. *stadhouder* 'deputy', from *stad* 'place' + *houder* 'holder'.

**staff**[1] ● n. **1** [treated as sing. or pl.] the employees of a particular organization. **2** [treated as sing. or pl.] a group of officers assisting an officer in command of an army formation or administration headquarters. ➤ (usu. **Staff**) short for **STAFF SERGEANT**. **3** a long stick used as a support or weapon. ➤ a rod or sceptre held as a sign of office or authority. ➤ Surveying a rod for measuring distances or heights. **4** Brit. a spindle in a watch. **5** Music another term for **STAVE** (in sense 2). **6** Brit. a token in the form of a rod given to a train driver as authority to proceed over a single-track line. ● v. (usu. **be staffed**) provide with staff.
– PHRASES **the staff of life** bread or another staple food.
– ORIGIN OE *stæf* (in sense 3), of Gmc origin.

**staff**[2] ● n. a mixture of plaster of Paris, cement, etc. used for temporary building work.
– ORIGIN C19: of unknown origin.

**staffage** /stəˈfɑːʒ/ ● n. accessory items in a painting, especially figures in a landscape.
– ORIGIN C19: from Ger., from *staffieren* 'decorate', perh. from OFr. *estoffer*, from *estoffe* 'stuff'.

**staff college** ● n. a college at which military officers are trained for staff duties.

**staffer** ● n. chiefly N. Amer. a member of a staff, especially of a newspaper.

**staff notation** ● n. Music notation by means of a stave, especially as distinct from the tonic sol-fa.

**staff nurse** ● n. Brit. an experienced nurse less senior than a sister or charge nurse.

**staff officer** ● n. a military officer serving on the staff of a headquarters or government department.

**Staffordshire bull terrier** ● n. a terrier of a small, stocky breed, with a short, broad head and dropped ears.

**staffroom** ● n. chiefly Brit. a common room for teachers in a school or college.

**Staffs.** ● abbrev. Staffordshire.

**staff sergeant** ● n. a rank of non-commissioned officer in the army, above sergeant and below warrant officer. ➤ a rank of non-commissioned officer in the US air force, above airman and below technical sergeant.

**stag** ● n. **1** a fully adult male deer. **2** an adult male turkey. **3** [as modifier] denoting a social gathering attended by men only. ➤ chiefly N. Amer. a man who attends a social gathering unaccompanied by a female partner. **4** Brit. Stock Exchange a person who applies for shares in a new issue with a view to selling at once for a profit. ● adv. chiefly N. Amer. without a female partner at a social gathering. ● v. (**stagged**, **stagging**) **1** Brit. Stock Exchange buy (shares in a new issue) and sell them at once for a profit. **2** N. Amer. informal roughly cut (trousers) off short.
– ORIGIN ME: rel. to ON *steggr* 'male bird'.

**stag beetle** ● n. a large dark beetle, the male of which has large branched jaws resembling antlers. [*Lucanus cervus* and other species.]

**stage** ● n. **1** a point, period, or step in a process or development. ➤ a section of a journey or race. **2** each of two or more sections of a rocket or spacecraft that are jettisoned in turn when their propellant is exhausted. **3** Electronics a part of a circuit containing a single amplifying transistor or valve. **4** a raised floor or platform on which actors, entertainers, or speakers perform. ➤ (**the stage**) the acting or theatrical profession. **5** a scene of action or forum of debate. **6** a floor of a building. **7** (on a microscope) a raised plate on which a slide or specimen is placed for examination. **8** Geology a range of strata corresponding to an age in time, forming a subdivision of a series. **9** archaic term for **STAGECOACH**. ● v. **1** present a performance of (a play or other show). ➤ organize and participate in (a public event). ➤ cause (something dramatic or unexpected) to happen. **2** chiefly Medicine assign to a particular stage in a process.
– PHRASES **hold the stage** dominate a scene of action or forum of debate. **set the stage for** prepare the conditions for. **stage left** (or **right**) on the left (or right) side of a stage from the point of view of a performer facing the audience.
– DERIVATIVES **stageability** n. **stageable** adj.
– ORIGIN ME: shortening of OFr. *estage* 'dwelling', based on L. *stare* 'to stand'.

**stagecoach** ● n. a large closed horse-drawn vehicle formerly used to carry passengers and often mail along a regular route.

**stagecraft** ● n. skill in writing or staging plays.

**stage direction** ● n. an instruction in a play script indicating the position or tone of an actor, or specifying sound effects, lighting, etc.

**stage door** ● n. an actors' and workmen's entrance from the street to the backstage area of a theatre.

**stage fright** ● n. nervousness before or during a performance.

**stagehand** • n. a person dealing with scenery or props during a play.

**stage-manage** • v. **1** be the stage manager of. **2** arrange carefully to create a certain effect.
– DERIVATIVES **stage management** n.

**stage manager** • n. the person responsible for lighting and other technical arrangements for a stage play.

**stage name** • n. a name assumed for professional purposes by an actor.

**stager** • n. archaic an actor.

**stage-struck** • adj. having a passionate love of the theatre and wishing to become an actor.

**stage whisper** • n. a loud whisper by an actor on stage, intended to be heard by the audience.

**stagey** • adj. variant spelling of **STAGY**.

**stagflation** • n. Economics persistent high inflation combined with high unemployment and stagnant demand in a country's economy.
– ORIGIN 1960s: blend of *stagnation* and **INFLATION**.

**stagger** • v. **1** walk or move unsteadily, as if about to fall. ➤ archaic (of a blow) cause (someone) to stagger. **2** astonish. **3** spread over a period of time. **4** arrange (objects or parts) so that they are not in line. **5** archaic hesitate. • n. **1** an act of staggering. **2** (**the stagger**) the staggered arrangement of the runners on a track at the start of a race. **3** an arrangement of the wings of a biplane so that their front edges are not in line.
– DERIVATIVES **staggerer** n. **staggering** n. & adj. **staggeringly** adv.
– ORIGIN ME: alt. of dial. *stacker*, from ON *stakra*, frequentative of *staka* 'push, stagger'.

**staggers** • pl. n. [usu. treated as sing.] **1** a diseased condition of farm animals manifested by staggering or loss of balance. **2** (**the staggers**) the inability to stand or walk steadily.

**staghorn** (also **stag's horn**) • n. the material of a stag's antler, used chiefly to make handles for cutlery.

**staghorn fern** (also **stag's-horn fern**) • n. a fern with fronds that resemble antlers, occurring in tropical rainforests and typically epiphytic. [Genus *Platycerium*.]

**staghound** • n. a large dog of a breed used for hunting deer.

**staging** • n. **1** an instance or method of staging something. **2** a stage or set of stages or platforms for performers or between levels of scaffolding. ➤ Brit. shelving for plants in a greenhouse.

**staging area** • n. a stopping place or assembly point en route to a destination.

**staging post** • n. a place at which people or vehicles regularly stop during a journey.

**stagnant** /ˈstagnənt/ • adj. (of water or air) motionless and often having an unpleasant smell as a consequence. ➤ showing little activity.
– DERIVATIVES **stagnancy** n. **stagnantly** adv.
– ORIGIN C17: from L. *stagnant-*, *stagnare* 'form a pool of standing water', from *stagnum* 'pool'.

**stagnate** /stagˈneɪt, ˈstagneɪt/ • v. become stagnant.
– DERIVATIVES **stagnation** n.
– ORIGIN C17: from L. *stagnat-*, *stagnare* 'settle as a still pool', from *stagnum* 'pool'.

**stag night** (also **stag party**) • n. an all-male celebration, especially one held for a man about to be married.

**stagy** /ˈsteɪdʒi/ (also **stagey**) • adj. (**-ier**, **-iest**) excessively theatrical or exaggerated.
– DERIVATIVES **stagily** adv. **staginess** n.

**staid** • adj. respectable and unadventurous.
– DERIVATIVES **staidly** adv. **staidness** n.
– ORIGIN C16: archaic past part. of **STAY**[1].

**stain** • v. **1** mark or discolour with something that is not easily removed. **2** damage (someone's or something's reputation). **3** colour with a penetrative dye or chemical. • n. **1** a stubborn discoloured patch or dirty mark. **2** a thing that damages a reputation. **3** a dye or chemical used to colour materials. ➤ Biology a dye used to colour organic tissue so as to make the structure visible for microscopic examination. **4** Heraldry any of the minor colours used in blazoning and liveries.
– DERIVATIVES **stainable** adj. **stainer** n.
– ORIGIN ME: shortening of archaic *distain*, from OFr. *desteindre* 'tinge with a different colour'.

**stained glass** • n. coloured glass used to form decorative or pictorial designs, typically set in a lead framework and used for church windows.

**stainless** • adj. unmarked by or resistant to stains.

**stainless steel** • n. a form of steel containing chromium, resistant to tarnishing and rust.

**stair** • n. each of a set of fixed steps. ➤ (**stairs**) a set of such steps leading from one floor of a building to another.
– ORIGIN OE *stǣger*, of Gmc origin, from a base meaning 'climb'.

**staircase** • n. a set of stairs and its surrounding structure. ➤ Brit. a part of a large building containing a staircase.

**stairhead** • n. chiefly Brit. a landing at the top of a set of stairs.

**stairlift** • n. a lift in the form of a chair that can be raised or lowered at the edge of a domestic staircase.

**stair rod** • n. a rod securing a carpet in the angle between two steps.

**stairway** • n. a staircase.

**stairwell** • n. a shaft in which a staircase is built.

**staithe** /steɪð/ • n. (in the north and east of England) a landing stage for loading or unloading cargo boats.
– ORIGIN ME: from ON *stǫth* 'landing stage'.

**stake**[1] • n. **1** a strong post with a point at one end, driven into the ground to support a tree, form part of a fence, etc. **2** historical a wooden post to which a person was tied before being burned alive as a punishment. **3** a small anvil, typically with a projection for fitting into a socket on a bench. **4** a long vertical rod used in basket-making. **5** a territorial division of the Mormon Church. • v. **1** support (a plant) with a stake. **2** (**stake something out**) mark an area with stakes so as to claim ownership. **3** (**stake someone/thing out**) informal keep a place or person under surveillance.
– PHRASES **pull up stakes** N. Amer. move or go to live elsewhere. **stake a claim** assert one's right to something.
– ORIGIN OE *staca*, of W. Gmc origin; rel. to **STICK**[2].

**stake**[2] • n. **1** a sum of money gambled on a risky game or venture. **2** a share or interest in a business or situation. **3** (**stakes**) prize money. ➤ [in names] a horse race in which the owners of the horses running contribute to the prize money. **4** (**stakes**) a competitive situation: *one step ahead in the fashion stakes*. • v. **1** gamble (money or something of value). **2** N. Amer. informal give financial or other support to.
– PHRASES **at stake 1** at risk. **2** at issue or in question.
– ORIGIN ME: perh. a specialized usage of **STAKE**[1], from the notion of an object being placed as a wager on a post or stake.

**stake boat** • n. an anchored boat used to mark the course for a boat race.

**stake body** • n. US a body of a truck having a flat open platform with removable posts along the sides.

**stakebuilding** • n. Finance the building up of a holding of shares in a company.

**stakeholder** • n. **1** an independent party with whom money or counters wagered are deposited. **2** a person with an interest or concern in something.

**stake net** • n. a fishing net hung on stakes.

**stake-out** • n. informal a period of secret surveillance.

**staker** • n. a person who stakes money on something.

**Stakhanovite** /stəˈkɑːnəvʌɪt, -ˈkanə-/ • n. a worker, especially in the former USSR, who is exceptionally productive or zealous.
– DERIVATIVES **Stakhanovism** n. **Stakhanovist** n. & adj.
– ORIGIN 1930s: from the name of the Russ. coal miner Aleksei Grigorevich *Stakhanov*.

**stalactite** /ˈstaləktʌɪt/ • n. a tapering structure hanging from the roof of a cave, formed of calcium salts deposited by dripping water.
– DERIVATIVES **stalactitic** adj.
– ORIGIN C17: from mod. L. *stalactites*, from Gk *stalaktos*

'dripping', based on *stalassein* 'to drip'.

**Stalag** /ˈstalag, ˈʃtalag/ ● n. (in the Second World War) a German prison camp, especially for non-commissioned officers and privates.
– ORIGIN Ger., contr. of *Stammlager*, from *Stamm* 'base, main stock' + *Lager* 'camp'.

**stalagmite** /ˈstaləgmʌɪt/ ● n. a mound or tapering column rising from the floor of a cave, formed of calcium salts deposited by dripping water.
– DERIVATIVES **stalagmitic** adj.
– ORIGIN C17: from mod. L. *stalagmites*, from Gk *stalagma* 'a drop', based on *stalassein* (see **STALACTITE**).

**stale**[1] ● adj. (**staler**, **stalest**) **1** (of food) no longer fresh or pleasant to eat. **2** no longer new and interesting. **3** (of a person) no longer performing well because of having done something for too long. **4** (of a cheque or legal claim) invalid because out of date. ● v. make or become stale.
– DERIVATIVES **stalely** adv. **staleness** n.
– ORIGIN ME (describing beer in the sense 'clear from long standing'): prob. from Anglo-Norman Fr. and OFr., from *estaler* 'to halt'; cf. **STALL**.

**stale**[2] ● v. (of a horse or cow) urinate.
– ORIGIN ME: perh. from OFr. *estaler* 'come to a stand, halt' (cf. **STALE**[1]).

**stalemate** ● n. **1** Chess a position counting as a draw, in which a player is not in check but can only move into check. **2** a situation in which further progress by opposing parties seems impossible. ● v. bring to or cause to reach stalemate.
– ORIGIN C18: from obs. *stale* (from Anglo-Norman Fr. *estale* 'position', from *estaler* 'be placed') + **MATE**[2].

**Stalinism** ● n. the ideology and policies adopted by the Soviet Communist Party leader and head of state Joseph Stalin (1879–1953), based on centralization, totalitarianism, and the pursuit of communism.
– DERIVATIVES **Stalinist** n. & adj.

**stalk**[1] ● n. **1** the main stem of a herbaceous plant. ➤ the attachment or support of a leaf, flower, or fruit. **2** a similar support for a sessile animal, or for an organ in an animal. **3** a slender support or stem. **4** (in a vehicle) a lever on the steering column controlling the indicators, lights, etc.
– DERIVATIVES **-stalked** adj. **stalkless** adj. **stalk-like** adj. **stalky** adj.
– ORIGIN ME: prob. a dimin. of dial. *stale* 'rung of a ladder, long handle'.

**stalk**[2] ● v. **1** pursue or approach stealthily. ➤ harass or persecute with unwanted and obsessive attention. ➤ chiefly poetic/literary move silently or threateningly through. **2** stride in a proud, stiff, or angry manner. ● n. **1** a stealthy pursuit. **2** a stiff, striding gait.
– DERIVATIVES **stalker** n.
– ORIGIN OE *-stealcian* (in *bistealcian* 'walk cautiously or stealthily'), of Gmc origin; rel. to **STEAL**.

**stalking horse** ● n. **1** a screen in the shape of a horse behind which a hunter hides when stalking prey. **2** a false pretext concealing someone's real intentions. **3** a candidate for the leadership of a political party who stands only in order to provoke the election and thus allow a stronger candidate to come forward.
– ORIGIN C16: from the former practice of using a horse trained to allow a fowler to hide behind it.

**stall** ● n. **1** a stand, booth, or compartment for the sale of goods in a market. **2** an individual compartment for an animal in a stable or cowshed, enclosed on three sides. ➤ a stable or cowshed. ➤ (also **starting stall**) a cage-like compartment in which a horse is held prior to the start of a race. **3** a compartment for one person in a set of toilets, shower cubicles, etc. **4** N. Amer. a marked-out parking space. **5** a seat in the choir or chancel of a church, enclosed at the back and sides and often canopied, typically reserved for a member of the clergy. **6** (**stalls**) Brit. the ground-floor seats in a theatre. **7** an instance of an engine or vehicle stalling. ● v. **1** (with reference to a motor vehicle or its engine) stop or cause to stop running. ➤ (of an aircraft) be moving at a speed too low to allow effective operation of the controls. ➤ Sailing have insufficient wind power to give controlled motion. **2** stop or cause to stop making progress. **3** prevaricate. ➤ delay or divert by prevarication. **4** keep (an animal) in a stall, especially in order to fatten it.
– ORIGIN OE *steall* 'stable or cattle shed', of Gmc origin; rel. to **STAND**.

**stallage** /ˈstɔːlɪdʒ/ ● n. Brit., chiefly historical rental, taxation, or fees charged for the holding of a market stall. ➤ the right to hold a market stall.
– ORIGIN ME: shortening of OFr. *estalage*, from *estal* 'stall'.

**stall-feed** ● v. feed and keep (an animal) in a stall, especially in order to fatten it.

**stallholder** ● n. Brit. a person in charge of a market stall.

**stallion** ● n. an uncastrated adult male horse.
– ORIGIN ME: from an Anglo-Norman Fr. var. of OFr. *estalon*, from a derivative of a Gmc base shared by **STALL**.

**stalwart** /ˈstɔːlwət, ˈstal-/ ● adj. **1** loyal, reliable, and hard-working. **2** dated sturdy. ● n. a stalwart supporter or participant in an organization.
– DERIVATIVES **stalwartly** adv. **stalwartness** n.
– ORIGIN ME: Scots var. of obs. *stalworth*, from OE *stǣl* 'place' + *weorth* 'worth'.

**stamen** /ˈsteɪmən/ ● n. Botany a male fertilizing organ of a flower, typically consisting of a pollen-containing anther and a filament.
– ORIGIN C17: from L., lit. 'warp in an upright loom, thread'.

**stamina** ● n. the ability to sustain prolonged physical or mental effort.
– ORIGIN C17 (in the sense 'rudiments, essential elements of something'): from L., pl. of **STAMEN** in the sense 'threads spun by the Fates'.

**staminate** /ˈstamɪnət/ ● adj. Botany having stamens but no pistils. Compare with **PISTILLATE**.

**staminode** /ˈstamɪnəʊd/ ● n. Botany a sterile or abortive stamen.

**stammer** ● v. speak with sudden involuntary pauses and a tendency to repeat the initial letters of words. ➤ utter (words) in such a way. ● n. a tendency to stammer.
– DERIVATIVES **stammerer** n. **stammering** n. & adj. **stammeringly** adv.
– ORIGIN OE *stamerian*, of W. Gmc origin; rel. to **STUMBLE**.

**stamp** ● v. **1** bring down (one's foot) heavily on the ground or an object. ➤ crush, flatten, or remove with a heavy blow from one's foot. ➤ crush or pulverize (ore). **2** walk with heavy, forceful steps. **3** (**stamp something out**) suppress or put an end to something. **4** impress a pattern or mark on with a stamp. ➤ impress (a pattern or mark). ➤ cut out using a die or mould. **5** fix a postage stamp to. ● n. **1** an instrument for stamping a pattern or mark, especially an engraved or inked block or die. ➤ a mark or pattern made by a stamp. **2** a characteristic or distinctive impression or quality. ➤ a particular type of person or thing. **3** a small adhesive piece of paper recording payment of postage. **4** an act or sound of stamping the foot. **5** a block for crushing ore in a stamp mill.
– DERIVATIVES **stamper** n.
– ORIGIN ME: of Gmc origin; reinforced by OFr. *estamper* 'to stamp'; cf. **STOMP**.

**stamp duty** ● n. a duty levied on the legal recognition of certain documents.

**stampede** ● n. a sudden panicked rush of a number of horses, cattle, etc. ➤ a sudden rapid movement or reaction of a mass of people due to interest or panic. ● v. take part or cause to take part in a stampede.
– DERIVATIVES **stampeder** n.
– ORIGIN C19: Mex. Sp. use of Sp. *estampida* 'crash, uproar', of Gmc origin; rel. to **STAMP**.

**stamp hinge** ● n. a small piece of gummed transparent paper for fixing postage stamps in an album.

**stamping ground** (N. Amer. also **stomping ground**) ● n. a place one regularly frequents.

**stamp mill** ● n. a mill for crushing ore.

**stamp office** ● n. Brit. an office issuing government

stamps and receiving stamp duty.

**stance** /stɑːns, stans/ ● **n.** **1** the way in which someone stands, especially when deliberately adopted. **2** a standpoint. **3** Scottish a street site for a market, stall, or taxi rank. **4** Climbing a ledge or foothold.
– ORIGIN ME: from Fr., from Ital. *stanza*.

**stanch**[1] /stɔːn(t)ʃ, stɑːn(t)ʃ/ ● **v.** chiefly US variant spelling of **STAUNCH**[2].

**stanch**[2] /stɔːn(t)ʃ/ ● **adj.** variant spelling of **STAUNCH**[1] (in sense 2).

**stanchion** /ˈstanʃ(ə)n/ ● **n.** an upright bar, post, or frame forming a support or barrier.
– DERIVATIVES **stanchioned** adj.
– ORIGIN ME: from Anglo-Norman Fr. *stanchon*, from OFr. *estanchon*, from *estance* 'a support', prob. based on L. *stant-*, *stare* 'stand'.

**stand** ● **v.** (past and past part. **stood**) **1** be in or rise to an upright position, supported by one's feet. ➤move in this position to a specified place. **2** place or be situated in a particular position. ➤(especially of a vehicle) remain stationary. ➤(of a ship) remain on a specified course. **3** (of food, liquid, etc.) rest without disturbance. **4** be in a specified state or condition. ➤(of a building) remain upright and entire. ➤remain valid or unaltered. ➤be of a specified height. **5** adopt a particular attitude towards an issue. **6** be likely to do something: *investors stood to lose heavily.* **7** act in a specified capacity: *he stood security for the government's borrowings.* **8** (also **stand at stud**) (of a stallion) be available for breeding. **9** [usu. with neg.] tolerate or like. ➤withstand without being damaged. **10** Brit. be a candidate in an election. **11** umpire a cricket match. **12** provide (food or drink) for (someone) at one's expense. ● **n.** **1** an attitude towards a particular issue. ➤a determined effort to hold one's ground or resist something. ➤Cricket a partnership. **2** a large raised tiered structure for spectators. ➤a raised platform for a band, orchestra, or speaker. ➤a rack, base, or item of furniture for holding or displaying something. ➤a small temporary stall or booth from which promotional goods are sold or displayed. ➤(**the stand**) a witness box. **3** the place where someone usually stands or sits. ➤a place where vehicles wait for passengers. **4** a cessation from motion or progress. **5** a group of trees or other plants.
– PHRASES **stand and deliver!** a highwayman's order to hand over money and valuables. **stand on one's own (two) feet** be or become self-reliant or independent. **stand trial** be tried in a court of law. **stand up and be counted** state publicly one's support for someone or something.
– PHRASAL VERBS **stand alone** be unequalled. **stand by 1** look on without intervening. **2** support or remain loyal to. ➤adhere to or abide by. **3** be ready to take action if required. **stand down 1** (also **stand aside**) resign from a position or office. **2** (**stand down** or **stand someone down**) relax or cause someone to relax after a state of readiness. **3** (of a witness) leave the witness box after giving evidence. **stand for 1** be an abbreviation of or symbol for. **2** [with neg.] endure or tolerate. **stand in 1** deputize. **2** Nautical sail closer to the shore. **stand off** move or keep away. ➤Nautical sail further away from the shore. **stand on 1** be scrupulous in the observance of. **2** Nautical continue on the same course. **stand out 1** project. ➤be easily noticeable. ➤be clearly better. **2** persist in opposition to or support of something. **stand over** (or **stand something over**) be postponed or cause something to be postponed. **stand to** Military stand ready for an attack. **stand someone up** informal fail to keep a date. **stand up for** speak or act in support of. **stand up to 1** make a spirited defence against. **2** be resistant to the harmful effects of.
– DERIVATIVES **stander** n.
– ORIGIN OE *standan* (v.), *stand* (n.), of Gmc origin; rel. to **STEAD**.

**standard** ● **n.** **1** a level of quality or attainment. ➤a required or agreed level of quality or attainment. ➤Brit. historical (in elementary schools) a grade of proficiency tested by examination. ➤S. African a class or year in a high school. **2** something used as a measure, norm, or model in comparative evaluations. ➤(**standards**) principles of honourable, decent behaviour. ➤the prescribed weight of fine metal in gold or silver coins. ➤a system by which the value of a currency is defined in terms of gold or silver. ➤a measure for timber, equivalent to 165 cu. ft (4.67 cubic metres). **3** a military or ceremonial flag. **4** a tree that grows on an erect stem of full height. ➤a shrub grafted on an erect stem and trained in tree form. **5** an upright water or gas pipe. ● **adj.** used or accepted as normal or average. ➤(of a size, measure, etc.) such as is regularly used or produced. ➤(of a work, writer, etc.) viewed as authoritative and so widely read.
– PHRASES **raise one's** (or **the**) **standard** take up arms.
– DERIVATIVES **standardly** adv.
– ORIGIN ME: shortening of OFr. *estendart*, from *estendre* 'extend'; in sense 3, influenced by **STAND**.

**standard assessment task** ● **n.** (in the UK) a standard test given to schoolchildren to assess their progress in a core subject of the national curriculum.

**standard-bearer** ● **n.** **1** a soldier carrying the standard of a unit, regiment, or army. **2** a leading figure in a cause or movement.

**Standardbred** ● **n.** N. Amer. a horse of a breed able to attain a specified speed, developed especially for trotting.

**standard deviation** ● **n.** Statistics a quantity calculated to indicate the extent of deviation for a group as a whole.

**Standard Grade** ● **n.** (in Scotland) an examination equivalent to the GCSE.

**standardize** (also **-ise**) ● **v.** cause to conform to a standard. ➤(**standardize on**) adopt as one's standard. ➤determine the properties of by comparison with a standard.
– DERIVATIVES **standardizable** adj. **standardization** n. **standardizer** n.

**standard lamp** ● **n.** chiefly Brit. a lamp with a tall stem whose base stands on the floor.

**standard of living** ● **n.** the degree of material comfort available to a person or community.

**standard time** ● **n.** a uniform time for places in approximately the same longitude.

**standby** ● **n.** (pl. **standbys**) **1** readiness for duty or immediate deployment. ➤a person or thing ready to be deployed in an emergency. **2** the state of waiting to secure an unreserved place for a journey or performance.

**standee** /stanˈdiː/ ● **n.** chiefly N. Amer. a person who is standing.

**stand-in** ● **n.** a substitute.

**standing** ● **n.** **1** position, status, or reputation. **2** duration: *a squabble of long standing.* **3** a stall for cattle or horses. ● **adj.** **1** (of a jump or start of a race) performed from rest or an upright position. **2** long-term or regularly repeated: *a standing invitation.* **3** (of water) stagnant or still. **4** (of corn) not yet reaped. **5** Printing (of metal type) kept set up after use.
– PHRASES **all standing** Sailing without time to lower the sails. **in good standing** on good terms. **leave someone/thing standing** informal be much better or faster than someone or something else.

**standing committee** ● **n.** a permanent committee meeting regularly.

**standing joke** ● **n.** something regularly causing amusement or provoking ridicule.

**standing order** ● **n.** **1** Brit. an instruction to a bank by an account holder to make regular fixed payments to someone. **2** Brit. an order placed on a regular basis with a retailer. **3** (**standing orders**) rulings governing the procedures of a parliament, council, etc.

**standing ovation** ● **n.** a period of prolonged applause during which the audience rise to their feet.

**standing stone** ● **n.** another term for **MENHIR**.

**standing wave** ● **n.** Physics a vibration of a system in which some particular points remain fixed while others between them vibrate with the maximum amplitude.

**standish** ● **n.** chiefly historical a stand holding pens and ink.
– ORIGIN ME: commonly held to be from **STAND** + **DISH**.

**stand of arms** • n. Brit. archaic a complete set of weapons for one man.

**stand of colours** • n. Brit. a battalion's flags.

**stand-off** • n. **1** a deadlock between two equally matched opponents. **2** Rugby short for **STAND-OFF HALF**.

**stand-off half** • n. Rugby a halfback who forms a link between the scrum half and the three-quarters.

**stand-offish** • adj. informal distant and cold in manner.
– DERIVATIVES **stand-offishly** adv. **stand-offishness** n.

**standout** • n. informal an outstanding person or thing.

**standpipe** • n. a vertical pipe extending from a water supply, especially one connecting a temporary tap to the mains.

**standpoint** • n. **1** an attitude towards a particular issue. **2** the position from which a scene or an object is viewed.

**standstill** /'stan(d)stɪl/ • n. a situation or condition without movement or activity.

**stand-to** • n. Military the action or state of standing to. ➤ the beginning of a spell of duty.

**stand-up** • adj. **1** involving or used by people standing up. **2** (of a comedian) performing by standing in front of an audience and telling jokes. ➤ (of comedy) performed in such a way. **3** (of a fight or argument) involving direct confrontation; loud or violent. **4** designed to stay upright or erect. • n. **1** a stand-up comedian. ➤ stand-up comedy. **2** a brief monologue by a television news reporter.

**stanhope** /'stanəp, -həʊp/ • n. historical a light open horse-drawn carriage for one person, with two or four wheels.
– ORIGIN C19: named after the Engl. clergyman Fitzroy *Stanhope*, for whom the first one was made.

**stank** past of **STINK**.

**Stanley knife** • n. Brit. trademark a sharp knife with a short, strong replaceable blade, for cutting various materials.

**stannary** /'stan(ə)ri/ • n. (pl. **-ies**) Brit., chiefly historical a tin-mining district in Cornwall or Devon.
– ORIGIN ME: from med. L. *stannaria* (pl.), from late L. *stannum* 'tin'.

**stannary court** • n. Brit. historical a legal body for the regulation of tin miners.

**stannic** /'stanɪk/ • adj. Chemistry of tin with a valency of four; of tin(IV).
– ORIGIN C18: from late L. *stannum* 'tin' + **-IC**.

**stannous** /'stanəs/ • adj. Chemistry of tin with a valency of two; of tin(II).
– ORIGIN C19: from late L. *stannum* 'tin' + **-OUS**.

**stanza** /'stanzə/ • n. a group of lines forming the basic recurring metrical unit in a poem. ➤ a group of four lines in some ancient Greek and Latin metres.
– DERIVATIVES **stanza'd** (also **stanzaed**) adj. **stanzaic** /-'zeɪɪk/ adj.
– ORIGIN C16: from Ital., lit. 'standing place', also 'stanza'.

**stapes** /'steɪpiːz/ • n. (pl. same) Anatomy a small stirrup-shaped bone in the middle ear, transmitting vibrations from the incus to the inner ear.
– ORIGIN C17: from mod. L., lit. 'stirrup'.

**staph** /staf/ • n. informal short for **STAPHYLOCOCCUS**.

**staphylococcus** /ˌstafɪlə(ʊ)'kɒkəs/ • n. (pl. **staphylococci** /-'kɒk(s)ʌɪ, -'kɒk(s)iː/) a bacterium of a genus including many pathogenic kinds that cause pus formation. [Genus *Staphylococcus*.]
– DERIVATIVES **staphylococcal** adj.
– ORIGIN mod. L., from Gk *staphulē* 'bunch of grapes' + *kokkos* 'berry'.

**staple**[1] • n. **1** a small flattened U-shaped piece of wire used to fasten papers together. **2** a small U-shaped metal bar with pointed ends for driving into wood to hold electric wires, battens, etc. in place. • v. secure with a staple or staples.
– ORIGIN OE *stapol*, of Gmc origin.

**staple**[2] • n. **1** a main or important element of something. **2** the fibre of cotton or wool considered with regard to its length and fineness. **3** historical a centre of trade in a specified commodity. • adj. main or important.
– ORIGIN ME: from OFr. *estaple* 'market', from Mid. Low Ger., MDu. *stapel* 'pillar, emporium'; rel. to **STAPLE**[1].

**staple gun** • n. a hand-held mechanical tool for driving staples into a hard surface.

**stapler** • n. a device for fastening papers together with staples.

**star** • n. **1** a fixed luminous point in the night sky which is a large, remote incandescent body like the sun. **2** a stylized representation of a star, typically with five or more points. ➤ a star-shaped symbol indicating a category of excellence. ➤ used in names of starfishes and similar echinoderms, e.g. **cushion star**. **3** a famous or talented entertainer or sports player. ➤ an outstanding person or thing. **4** Astrology a planet, constellation, or configuration regarded as influencing one's fortunes or personality. ➤ (**stars**) a horoscope. **5** a white patch on the forehead of a horse or other animal. • v. (**starred**, **starring**) **1** (of a film, play, etc.) have (someone) as a principal performer. ➤ (of a performer) have a principal role in a film, play, etc. **2** decorate or cover with star-shaped marks or objects. ➤ mark for special notice or recommendation with a star.
– PHRASES **my stars!** informal, dated an expression of surprise. **see stars** seem to see flashes of light, especially as a result of a blow on the head.
– DERIVATIVES **stardom** n. **starless** adj. **starlike** adj.
– ORIGIN OE *steorra*, of Gmc origin.

**star anise** • n. **1** a small star-shaped fruit with an aniseed flavour, used in Asian cookery. **2** a Chinese tree from which this fruit is obtained. [*Illicium verum*.]

**star apple** • n. an edible purple fruit of a tropical American tree (*Chrysophyllum cainito*), having a star-shaped cross section.

**starboard** /'stɑːbɔːd, -bəd/ • n. the side of a ship or aircraft on the right when one is facing forward. The opposite of **PORT**[3]. • v. turn (a ship or its helm) to starboard.
– ORIGIN OE *stēorbord* 'rudder side' (see **STEER**[1], **BOARD**), because early Teutonic sailing vessels were steered with a paddle on the right side.

**starboard watch** • n. see **WATCH** (sense 3).

**starburst** • n. **1** a pattern of lines or rays radiating from a central point. ➤ an explosion producing such an effect. ➤ a camera lens attachment that produces such a pattern. **2** Astronomy an intense episode of star formation.

**starch** • n. **1** an odourless, tasteless carbohydrate which is obtained chiefly from cereals and potatoes and is an important constituent of the human diet. **2** powder or spray made from this substance, used to stiffen fabric. **3** stiffness of manner. • v. **1** stiffen with starch. **2** N. Amer. informal (of a boxer) defeat by a knockout.
– DERIVATIVES **starcher** n. **starchily** adv. **starchiness** n. **starchy** adj. (**-ier**, **-iest**).
– ORIGIN OE (recorded only in the past part. *sterced* 'stiffened'), of Gmc origin; rel. to **STARK**.

**star connection** • n. a Y-shaped arrangement of three-phase electrical windings.
– DERIVATIVES **star-connected** adj.

**star-crossed** • adj. poetic/literary ill-fated.

**stardust** • n. magical or charismatic quality or feeling.

**stare** • v. **1** look fixedly at someone or something with the eyes wide open. ➤ (**stare someone out/down**) look fixedly at someone until they feel forced to look away. **2** be unpleasantly prominent or striking. • n. an act of staring.
– PHRASES **be staring someone in the face** be glaringly obvious.
– DERIVATIVES **starer** n.
– ORIGIN OE *starian*, of Gmc origin, from a base meaning 'be rigid'.

**stare decisis** /ˌstɛːrɪ dɪ'sʌɪzɪs, ˌstɑːreɪ dɪ'siːsɪs/ • n. Law the legal principle of determining points in litigation according to precedent.
– ORIGIN L., lit. 'stand by things decided'.

**starfish** • n. (pl. same or **-fishes**) a marine echinoderm with five or more radiating arms bearing tube feet underneath. [Class Asteroidea: many species.]

**starfruit** • n. **1** another term for **CARAMBOLA**. **2** a small aquatic plant with tiny white flowers and six-pointed star-shaped fruit. [*Damasonium alisma*.]

**stargazer** • n. **1** informal an astronomer or astrologer. **2** Austral. informal a horse that turns its head when galloping. **3** a fish with electric organs that normally lies buried in the sand with only its eyes protruding. [Families Uranoscopidae and Dactyloscopidae.]
– DERIVATIVES **stargaze** v.

**stark** • adj. **1** severe or bare in appearance. **2** unpleasantly or sharply clear. **3** complete; sheer: *stark terror.* **4** rare naked. **5** archaic or poetic/literary rigid or incapable of movement. ➤ physically strong.
– PHRASES **stark naked** completely naked. **stark raving** (or **staring**) **mad** informal completely mad.
– DERIVATIVES **starkly** adv. **starkness** n.
– ORIGIN OE *stearc* 'unyielding, severe', of Gmc origin.

**Stark effect** • n. Physics the splitting of a spectrum line into several components by an electric field.
– ORIGIN C20: named after the Ger. physicist Johannes *Stark.*

**starkers** • adj. informal, chiefly Brit. completely naked.

**starlet** • n. informal a promising young actress or sportswoman.

**starlight** • n. light coming from the stars.

**starling**[1] • n. a gregarious songbird typically with dark lustrous or iridescent plumage. [*Sturnus vulgaris* and other species, family Sturnidae.]
– ORIGIN OE *stærlinc*, from *stær* 'starling' (of Gmc origin) + **-LING**.

**starling**[2] • n. a wooden pile erected with others near a bridge or pier to protect it from the current or floating objects.
– ORIGIN C17: perh. a corruption of dial. *staddling* 'staddle'.

**starlit** • adj. lit by stars.

**star network** • n. a data or communication network in which all nodes are independently connected to one central unit.

**star of Bethlehem** • n. a plant of the lily family with white or yellow star-shaped flowers typically striped with green on the outside. [*Ornithogalum umbellatum* and other species.]

**Star of David** • n. a six-pointed figure consisting of two interlaced equilateral triangles, used as a Jewish and Israeli symbol.

**star route** • n. US a postal delivery route served by a private contractor.

**starry** • adj. (**-ier, -iest**) **1** full of or lit by stars. ➤ resembling a star. **2** informal of or relating to stars in entertainment.
– DERIVATIVES **starrily** adv. **starriness** n.

**starry-eyed** • adj. naively enthusiastic or idealistic.

**Stars and Bars** • pl. n. [treated as sing.] historical the flag of the Confederate States of America.

**Stars and Stripes** • pl. n. [treated as sing.] the national flag of the US.

**star sapphire** • n. a cabochon sapphire that reflects a starlike image resulting from its regular internal structure.

**star shell** • n. an explosive projectile which bursts in the air to light up an enemy's position.

**starship** • n. (in science fiction) a large manned spaceship for interstellar travel.

**star sign** • n. a sign of the zodiac.

**star-spangled** • adj. **1** poetic/literary covered or decorated with stars. **2** informal glitteringly successful.

**star-struck** • adj. fascinated and greatly impressed by famous people.

**star-studded** • adj. **1** (of the sky) filled with stars. **2** informal featuring a number of famous people.

**START** • abbrev. Strategic Arms Reduction Talks.

**start** • v. **1** come or bring into being. ➤ begin to do. ➤ begin to attend (a school, college, etc.) or engage in (an occupation). **2** cause to happen. ➤ begin to operate. ➤ cause or enable to begin doing something. ➤ signal (competitors) to begin a race. **3** (**start at**) cost at least (a specified amount). **4** begin to move or travel. **5** give a small jump or jerking movement from surprise. ➤ poetic/literary move or appear suddenly. ➤ rouse (game) from its lair. ➤ (of eyes) bulge. **6** displace or be displaced by pressure or shrinkage. • n. **1** the beginning. ➤ an act of beginning. **2** an advantage given at the beginning of a race. **3** a sudden movement of surprise. ➤ dated a surprising occurrence.
– PHRASES **for a start** in the first place. **start something** informal cause trouble. **to start with** as the first thing to be taken into account.
– PHRASAL VERBS **start in** informal begin doing something. ➤ (**start in on**) N. Amer. begin to do or deal with. ➤ (**start in on**) N. Amer. attack verbally. **start off** (or **start someone/thing off**) begin (or cause someone or something to begin) working, operating, etc. **start on 1** begin to work on or deal with. **2** informal begin to talk in a critical or hostile way to. **start over** N. Amer. make a new beginning. **start out** (or **up**) embark on a venture or undertaking.
– ORIGIN OE *styrtan* 'to caper, leap', of Gmc origin.

**starter** • n. **1** chiefly Brit. the first course of a meal. **2** an automatic device for starting a machine. ➤ a railway signal controlling the starting of trains. **3** a person who signals the start of a race. **4** a competitor taking part in a race or game at the start. ➤ Baseball the pitcher who starts the game. **5** a person or thing starting in a specified way: *a slow starter.* **6** a topic or question with which to start a discussion or course of study. **7** a preparation used to initiate souring, fermentation, etc.
– PHRASES **for starters** informal first of all. **under starter's orders** (of horses, runners, etc.) waiting for the signal to start a race.

**starter home** • n. a small house or flat designed for people buying their first home.

**starting block** • n. a shaped rigid block for bracing the feet of a runner at the start of a race.

**starting gate** • n. a barrier raised at the start of a race, especially in horse racing, to ensure a simultaneous start.

**starting pistol** • n. a pistol used to signal the start of a race.

**starting post** • n. a marker indicating the starting place for a race.

**starting price** • n. the final odds at the start of a horse race.

**startle** • v. cause to feel sudden shock or alarm.
– DERIVATIVES **startler** n.
– ORIGIN OE *steartlian* 'kick, struggle', from the base of **START**.

**startling** • adj. **1** alarming. **2** very surprising or remarkable.
– DERIVATIVES **startlingly** adv.

**star turn** • n. the act giving the most heralded or impressive performance in a programme.

**starve** • v. **1** suffer or die or cause to suffer or die from hunger. ➤ (**starve someone out** or **into**) force someone out of (a place) or into (a specified state) by starving them. ➤ (usu. **be starved of** or US **for**) deprive of. ➤ (**be starving** or **starved**) informal feel very hungry. **2** archaic be freezing cold.
– DERIVATIVES **starvation** n.
– ORIGIN OE *steorfan* 'to die', of Gmc origin, prob. from a base meaning 'be rigid' (cf. **STARE**).

**starveling** /'stɑːvlɪŋ/ archaic • adj. starving or emaciated. • n. a starveling person or animal.

**starwort** • n. a plant with starlike flowers or leaves. [*Stellaria, Callitriche* (**water starwort**), and other genera: several species.]

**stash** informal • v. store safely in a secret place. • n. **1** a secret store of something. **2** dated a hiding place.
– ORIGIN C18: of unknown origin.

**stasis** /'steɪsɪs, 'sta-/ • n. **1** formal or technical a period or state of inactivity or equilibrium. **2** Medicine a stoppage of flow of a body fluid.
– ORIGIN C18: mod. L., from Gk, lit. 'standing, stoppage', from *sta-*, base of *histanai* 'to stand'.

**-stasis** • comb. form (pl. **-stases**) Physiology slowing down; stopping: *haemostasis.*
– DERIVATIVES **-static** comb. form in corresponding adjectives.

– ORIGIN from Gk *stasis* 'standing, stoppage'.

**stat**[1] /stat/ ● abbrev. informal **1** photostat. **2** statistic(s). **3** thermostat.

**stat**[2] /stat/ ● adv. (in a medical direction or prescription) immediately.
– ORIGIN C19: abbrev. of L. *statim*.

**-stat** ● comb. form denoting instruments, substances, etc. maintaining a controlled state: *thermostat*.
– ORIGIN partly from (*helio*)*stat*, partly a back-form. from **STATIC**.

**statant** /ˈsteɪtənt/ ● adj. Heraldry (of an animal) standing with all four paws on the ground.
– ORIGIN C15: formed irregularly from L. *stat-* 'fixed, stationary' (from *stare* 'to stand') + **-ANT**.

**state** ● n. **1** the condition of someone or something. ➤ a physical condition as regards internal or molecular form or structure. ➤ (**a state**) informal an agitated, disorderly, or dirty condition. **2** a nation or territory considered as an organized political community under one government. ➤ an organized political community or area forming part of a federal republic. ➤ (**the States**) the US. **3** the civil government of a country. ➤ (**the States**) the legislative body in Jersey, Guernsey, and Alderney. **4** pomp and ceremony associated with monarchy or government. **5** an impression taken from an etched or engraved plate at a particular stage. ➤ a particular printed version of the first edition of a book. ● v. **1** express definitely or clearly in speech or writing. ➤ chiefly Law specify the facts of (a case) for consideration. **2** Music present or introduce (a theme or melody) in a composition.
– PHRASES **state of affairs** (or **things**) a situation. **state-of-the-art** incorporating the newest ideas and most up-to-date features. **state of emergency** a situation of national danger or disaster in which a government suspends normal constitutional procedures. **state of grace** a state of being free from sin. **state of life** (in religious contexts) a person's occupation or status. **the state of play** Brit. the score at a particular time in a cricket or football match. ➤ the current situation.
– DERIVATIVES **statable** (also **stateable**) adj. **statehood** n.
– ORIGIN ME: partly a shortening of **ESTATE**, partly from L. *status* (see **STATUS**).

**state capitalism** ● n. a political system in which the state has control of production and the use of capital.

**statecraft** ● n. the skilful management of state affairs.

**State Department** ● n. (in the US) the department of foreign affairs.

**state house** ● n. **1** (in the US) the building where the legislature of a state meets. **2** NZ a private house owned and let by the government.

**stateless** ● adj. not recognized as a citizen of any country.
– DERIVATIVES **statelessness** n.

**statelet** ● n. a small state.

**stately** ● adj. (**-ier**, **-iest**) dignified, imposing, or grand.
– DERIVATIVES **stateliness** n.

**stately home** ● n. Brit. a large and fine house occupied or formerly occupied by an aristocratic family.

**statement** ● n. **1** a definite or clear expression of something in speech or writing. ➤ a formal account of facts or events, especially one given to the police or in court. **2** a document setting out items of debit and credit between a bank or other organization and a customer. **3** (in the UK) an official assessment of a child's special educational needs. ● v. officially assess as having special educational needs.

**state prisoner** ● n. another term for **PRISONER OF STATE**.

**stater** /ˈsteɪtə/ ● n. an ancient Greek gold or silver coin.
– ORIGIN via late L. from Gk *statēr*, from a base meaning 'weigh'.

**stateroom** /ˈsteɪtruːm, -rʊm/ ● n. **1** a large room in a palace or public building, for use on formal occasions. **2** a captain's or superior officer's room on a ship. ➤ a private compartment on a ship. ➤ N. Amer. a private compartment on a train.

**state school** ● n. Brit. a school funded and controlled by the state.

**state's evidence** ● n. US Law evidence for the prosecution given by a participant in or accomplice to the crime being tried.

**States General** (also **Estates General**) ● n. the legislative body in the Netherlands from the 15th to the 18th century, and in France until 1789.

**stateside** /ˈsteɪtsʌɪd/ ● adj. & adv. informal, chiefly US of, in, or towards the US.

**statesman** /ˈsteɪtsmən/ (or **stateswoman**) ● n. (pl. **-men** or **-women**) a skilled, experienced, and respected political leader or figure.
– DERIVATIVES **statesmanlike** adj. **statesmanship** n.
– ORIGIN C16: from *state's man*, translating Fr. *homme d'état*.

**state socialism** ● n. a political system in which the state has control of industries and services.

**states' rights** ● pl. n. (in the US) the rights and powers held by individual states.

**state trial** ● n. prosecution by the state.

**statewide** ● adj. & adv. extending throughout a state in the US.

**static** /ˈstatɪk/ ● adj. **1** lacking movement, action, or change. **2** Physics concerned with bodies at rest or forces in equilibrium. Often contrasted with **DYNAMIC**. **3** relating to or denoting electric charges acquired by objects that cannot conduct a current. ● n. **1** static electricity. **2** crackling or hissing on a telephone, radio, etc. **3** informal, chiefly N. Amer. angry or critical talk or behaviour.
– DERIVATIVES **statically** adv.
– ORIGIN C16: via mod. L. from Gk *statikē* (*tekhnē*) 'science of weighing'; the adjective from mod. L. *staticus*, from Gk *statikos* 'causing to stand', from the verb *histanai*.

**statice** /ˈstatɪsi/ ● n. another term for **SEA LAVENDER**.
– ORIGIN C18: from mod. L. *Statice* (former genus name), based on Gk, fem. of *statikos* 'causing to stand still' (because the plant was used to staunch blood).

**static line** ● n. a cord used instead of a rip cord for opening a parachute, attached at one end to the aircraft and temporarily snapped to the parachute at the other.

**statics** ● pl. n. **1** [usu. treated as sing.] the branch of mechanics concerned with bodies at rest and forces in equilibrium. Compare with **DYNAMICS**. **2** another term for **STATIC** (in sense 2).

**statin** /ˈstatɪn/ ● n. Medicine any of a group of drugs which act to reduce levels of cholesterol in the blood.

**station** ● n. **1** a place where passenger trains stop on a railway line, typically with platforms and buildings. **2** a place where a specified activity or service is based: *a radar station*. ➤ a small military base. ➤ N. Amer. a subsidiary post office. **3** a broadcasting company of a specified kind. **4** the place where someone or something stands or is placed for a particular purpose or duty. ➤ dated one's social rank or position. **5** Austral./NZ a large sheep or cattle farm. **6** Botany a site at which an interesting or rare plant grows. ● v. assign to a station.
– ORIGIN ME: via OFr. from L. *statio(n-)*, from *stare* 'to stand'.

**stationary** ● adj. **1** not moving. **2** not changing in quantity or condition.
– ORIGIN ME: from L. *stationarius*, from *statio(n-)* (see **STATION**).

**stationary bicycle** ● n. an exercise bike.

**stationary point** ● n. Mathematics a point on a curve where the gradient is zero.

**stationary wave** ● n. Physics another term for **STANDING WAVE**.

**station bill** ● n. a list showing the prescribed stations of a ship's crew.

**station break** ● n. N. Amer. a pause between broadcast programmes for an announcement of the identity of the station transmitting them.

**stationer** ● n. a seller of stationery.
– ORIGIN ME: from med. L. *stationarius* 'tradesman (at a fixed location)'; cf. **STATIONARY**.

**stationery** ● n. paper and other materials needed for writing.

**station hand** ● **n.** Austral./NZ a worker on a large sheep or cattle farm.

**station house** ● **n.** N. Amer. a police or fire station.

**station-keeping** ● **n.** the maintenance of a ship's proper position in a fleet.

**stationmaster** ● **n.** an official in charge of a railway station.

**Station of the Cross** ● **n.** each of a series of fourteen pictures representing incidents during Jesus' progress from Pilate's house to his crucifixion at Calvary.

**station pointer** ● **n.** a navigational instrument that fixes a ship's position by determining its place relative to two landmarks or conspicuous objects at sea.

**station wagon** ● **n.** N. Amer. & Austral./NZ an estate car.

**statism** /ˈsteɪtɪz(ə)m/ ● **n.** a political system in which the state has substantial central control over social and economic affairs.
– DERIVATIVES **statist** n. & adj.

**statistic** ● **n.** a fact or piece of data obtained from a study of a large quantity of numerical data. ● **adj.** statistical.
– ORIGIN C18: from Ger. *statistisch* (adj.), *Statistik* (n.).

**statistical** ● **adj.** of or relating to statistics.
– DERIVATIVES **statistically** adv.

**statistical mechanics** ● **pl. n.** [treated as sing.] the description of physical phenomena in terms of a statistical treatment of the behaviour of large numbers of atoms or molecules, especially as regards the distribution of energy among them.

**statistical significance** ● **n.** see **SIGNIFICANCE**.

**statistics** ● **pl. n.** [treated as sing.] the practice or science of collecting and analysing numerical data in large quantities, especially for the purpose of inferring proportions in a whole from those in a representative sample.
– DERIVATIVES **statistician** n.

**stative** /ˈsteɪtɪv/ ● **adj.** Linguistics (of a verb) expressing a state or condition. Contrasted with **DYNAMIC**.
– ORIGIN C17: from L. *stativus*, from *stat-*, *stare* 'stop, stand'.

**stato-** ● **comb. form** relating to statics: *statocyst*.
– ORIGIN from Gk *statos* 'standing'.

**statocyst** ● **n.** Zoology an organ of balance and orientation in some aquatic invertebrates.

**statolith** ● **n.** Zoology a calcareous particle in a statocyst, which stimulates sensory receptors in response to gravity.

**stator** /ˈsteɪtə/ ● **n.** the stationary part of an electric generator or motor. ➤a row of stationary aerofoils positioned between the rotors of an axial-flow turbine.
– ORIGIN C19: from **STATIONARY**, on the pattern of *rotor*.

**statoscope** ● **n.** an aneroid barometer measuring minute variations of pressure, used especially to indicate aircraft altitude.
– ORIGIN C20: from Gk *statos* 'standing' + **-SCOPE**.

**stats** ● **pl. n.** informal statistics.

**statuary** /ˈstatjʊəri, -tʃʊə-/ ● **n.** **1** statues collectively. ➤archaic the making of statues. **2** archaic a sculptor.
– ORIGIN C16: from L. *statuarius*, from *statua* (see **STATUE**).

**statue** /ˈstatjuː, -tʃuː/ ● **n.** a carved or cast figure of a person or animal, especially one that is life-size or larger.
– DERIVATIVES **statued** adj.
– ORIGIN ME: from OFr., from L. *statua*, from *stare* 'to stand'.

**statuesque** /ˌstatjʊˈɛsk, -tʃʊ-/ ● **adj.** attractively tall, graceful, and dignified.
– DERIVATIVES **statuesquely** adv. **statuesqueness** n.
– ORIGIN C18: from **STATUE**, on the pattern of *picturesque*.

**statuette** ● **n.** a small statue.
– ORIGIN C19: from Fr., dimin. of *statue*.

**stature** ● **n.** **1** a person's natural height when standing. **2** importance or reputation gained by ability or achievement.
– ORIGIN ME: via OFr. from L. *statura*, from *stare* 'to stand'.

**status** ● **n.** **1** relative social or professional standing. ➤high rank or social standing. ➤the official classification given to a person, country, etc., determining their rights or responsibilities. **2** the position of affairs at a particular time.
– ORIGIN C18: from L., lit. 'standing', from *stare* 'to stand'.

**status epilepticus** /ˌɛpɪˈlɛptɪkəs/ ● **n.** Medicine a condition in which epileptic fits follow one another without recovery of consciousness between them.
– ORIGIN from mod. L.

**status quo** /ˈkwəʊ/ ● **n.** the existing state of affairs.
– ORIGIN L., lit. 'the state in which'.

**status quo ante** /kwəʊ ˈanti/ ● **n.** the previous state of affairs.
– ORIGIN L., lit. 'the state in which before'.

**status symbol** ● **n.** a possession taken to indicate a person's wealth or high status.

**statute** /ˈstatjuːt, -tʃuːt/ ● **n.** a written law passed by a legislative body. ➤a rule of an organization or institution. ➤(in biblical use) a law or decree made by a sovereign or by God.
– ORIGIN ME: from OFr. *statut*, from late L. *statutum*, neut. past part. of L. *statuere* 'set up' from *status* (see **STATUS**).

**statute-barred** ● **adj.** English Law (especially of a debt claim) no longer legally enforceable due to the lapse of time.

**statute book** ● **n.** a book in which laws are written. ➤(**the statute book**) a nation's laws collectively.

**statute law** ● **n.** the body of principles and rules of law laid down in statutes.

**statute of limitations** ● **n.** Law a statute limiting the period for the bringing of certain kinds of actions.

**statutes at large** ● **pl. n.** chiefly N. Amer. a country's original statutes, regardless of later modifications.

**statutory** /ˈstatjʊt(ə)ri, -tʃʊ-/ ● **adj.** **1** required, permitted, or enacted by statute. **2** having come to be required or expected due to being done regularly: *the statutory Christmas phone call to his mother.*
– DERIVATIVES **statutorily** adv.

**statutory instrument** ● **n.** Law a government or executive order of subordinate legislation.

**statutory order** ● **n.** Law former term for **STATUTORY INSTRUMENT**.

**statutory rape** ● **n.** US Law the offence of having sexual intercourse with a minor.

**statutory tenant** ● **n.** Law a person who is legally entitled to remain in a property although their original tenancy has expired.

**staunch**[1] /stɔːn(t)ʃ/ ● **adj.** **1** very loyal and committed. **2** (of a wall) of sturdy construction. ➤(also **stanch**) archaic (of a ship) watertight.
– DERIVATIVES **staunchly** adv. **staunchness** n.
– ORIGIN ME (in the sense 'watertight'): from OFr. *estanche*, fem. of *estanc*, from a base meaning 'dried up, weary'.

**staunch**[2] /stɔːn(t)ʃ, stɑːn(t)ʃ/ (US also **stanch**) ● **v.** stop or restrict (a flow of blood from a wound); stop from bleeding.
– ORIGIN ME: from OFr. *estanchier*, from the base of **STAUNCH**[1].

**staurolite** /ˈstɔːrəlʌɪt/ ● **n.** a brown glassy mineral consisting of a silicate of aluminium and iron.
– ORIGIN C19: from Gk *stauros* 'cross' (the mineral is often twinned in the shape of a cross) + **-LITE**.

**stave** ● **n.** **1** a vertical wooden post or plank in a building or other structure. ➤any of the lengths of wood fixed side by side to make a barrel, bucket, etc. ➤a strong wooden stick or iron pole used as a weapon. **2** (also **staff**) Music a set of five parallel lines on or between any of which a note is written to indicate its pitch. **3** a verse or stanza of a poem. ● **v.** **1** (past and past part. **staved** or **stove**) (**stave something in**) break something by forcing it inwards or piercing it roughly with a hole. **2** (past and past part. **staved**) (**stave something off**) avert or delay something bad or dangerous.
– ORIGIN ME: back-form. from *staves*, var. pl. form of **STAFF**[1].

**stavesacre** /ˈsteɪvˌzeɪkə/ ● **n.** a southern European larkspur whose seeds were formerly used as an insecticide.

[*Delphinium staphisagria.*]
– ORIGIN ME: via L. from Gk *staphis agria* 'wild raisin'.

**stay**[1] • v. **1** remain in the same place. ➤(**stay on**) continue to study, work, or be somewhere after others have left. ➤(**stay over**) stay for the night at someone's home or a hotel. ➤(**stay up**) not go to bed. **2** remain in a specified state or position. ➤continue, persevere, or keep up with (an activity or person). **3** live somewhere temporarily as a visitor or guest. ➤Scottish & S. African live permanently. **4** stop, delay, or prevent, in particular suspend or postpone (judicial proceedings) or refrain from pressing (charges). ➤assuage (hunger) for a short time. **5** poetic/literary support or prop up. • n. **1** a period of staying somewhere. **2** a curb or check, especially a suspension or postponement of judicial proceedings. **3** a device used as a brace or support. **4** (**stays**) historical a corset made of two pieces laced together and stiffened by strips of whalebone.
– PHRASES **stay the course** (or **distance**) keep going to the end of a race or contest. ➤pursue a difficult task or activity to the end. **a stay of execution** a delay in carrying out a court order. **stay put** remain somewhere without moving.
– DERIVATIVES **stayer** n.
– ORIGIN ME: from Anglo-Norman Fr. *estai-*, stem of OFr. *ester*, from L. *stare* 'to stand'; in the sense 'support', partly from OFr. *estaye* (n.), *estayer* (v.), of Gmc origin.

**stay**[2] • n. **1** a large rope, wire, or rod used to support a ship's mast. **2** a guy or rope supporting a flagstaff or other upright pole. **3** a supporting wire or cable on an aircraft. • v. secure or steady by means of a stay.
– PHRASES **be in stays** (of a sailing ship) be head to the wind while tacking. **miss stays** (of a sailing ship) fail in an attempt to go about from one tack to another.
– ORIGIN OE *stæg*, of Gmc origin, from a base meaning 'be firm'.

**stay bar** (or **stay rod**) • n. a support used in building or in machinery.

**staying power** • n. informal endurance or stamina.

**staysail** /ˈsteɪseɪl, -s(ə)l/ • n. a triangular fore-and-aft sail extended on a stay.

**stay stitching** • n. stitching placed along a bias or curved seam to prevent the fabric of a garment from stretching while the garment is being made.

**stay-up** • n. a stocking that has an elasticated top and stays in position without a need for suspenders.

**STD** • abbrev. **1** Doctor of Sacred Theology. [from L. *Sanctae Theologiae Doctor.*] **2** sexually transmitted disease. **3** Brit. subscriber trunk dialling.

**stead** • n. the place or role that someone or something should have or fill: *appointed in his stead.*
– PHRASES **stand someone in good stead** be advantageous to someone over time or in the future.
– ORIGIN OE *stede* 'place', of Gmc origin.

**steadfast** /ˈstɛdfɑːst, -fəst/ • adj. resolutely or dutifully firm and unwavering.
– DERIVATIVES **steadfastly** adv. **steadfastness** n.
– ORIGIN OE *stedefæst* 'standing firm' (see **STEAD**, **FAST**[1]).

**Steadicam** • n. trademark a lightweight mounting for a film camera which keeps it steady for filming when hand-held or moving.

**steading** • n. Scottish & N. English a farmstead.

**steady** • adj. (**-ier**, **-iest**) **1** firmly fixed, supported, or balanced. **2** not faltering or wavering; controlled. **3** sensible and reliable. **4** regular, even, and continuous in development, frequency, or intensity. • v. (**-ies**, **-ied**) make or become steady. • exclam. a warning to keep calm or take care. • n. (pl. **-ies**) **1** informal a person's regular boyfriend or girlfriend. **2** a strut for stabilizing a caravan or other vehicle when stationary.
– PHRASES **go steady** informal have a regular romantic or sexual relationship with someone. **steady on!** Brit. calm down; be more reasonable.
– DERIVATIVES **steadier** n. **steadily** adv. **steadiness** n. **steadying** adj. & n.
– ORIGIN ME: from **STEAD** + **-Y**[1].

**steady-going** • adj. moderate and sensible.

**steady-state theory** • n. a cosmological theory which holds that the universe is eternal and maintained by constant creation of matter.

**steak** • n. **1** high-quality beef taken from the hindquarters of the animal, typically cut into thick slices for grilling or frying. ➤a thick slice of other meat or fish. **2** poorer-quality beef that is cubed or minced and cooked by braising or stewing.
– ORIGIN ME: from ON *steik*; rel. to *steikja* 'roast on a spit' and *stikna* 'be roasted'.

**steak tartare** • n. a dish consisting of raw minced steak mixed with raw egg.

**steal** • v. (past **stole**; past part. **stolen**) **1** take (something) without permission or legal right and without intending to return it. ➤dishonestly pass off (another person's ideas) as one's own. **2** give or take surreptitiously or without permission: *I stole a look at my watch.* ➤move somewhere quietly or surreptitiously. **3** (in various sports) gain (an advantage, a run, or possession of the ball) unexpectedly or by exploiting the temporary distraction of an opponent. ➤Baseball run to (a base) while the pitcher is in the act of delivery. • n. **1** informal a bargain. **2** chiefly N. Amer. an act of stealing. ➤an idea taken from another work. ➤Baseball an act of stealing a base.
– PHRASES **steal a march on** gain an advantage over by taking early action. **steal someone's heart** win someone's love. **steal the show** attract the most attention and praise. **steal someone's thunder** win praise or attention for oneself by pre-empting someone else's attempt to impress.
– DERIVATIVES **stealer** n.
– ORIGIN OE *stelan* (v.), of Gmc origin.

**stealth** • n. **1** cautious and surreptitious action or movement. **2** [as modifier] (chiefly of aircraft) designed in accordance with technology which makes detection by radar or sonar difficult: *a stealth bomber.*
– ORIGIN ME (in the sense 'theft'): prob. representing an OE word rel. to **STEAL**, + **-TH**[2].

**stealthy** • adj. (**-ier**, **-iest**) characterized by stealth.
– DERIVATIVES **stealthily** adv. **stealthiness** n.

**steam** • n. **1** the hot vapour into which water is converted when heated, which condenses in the air into a mist of minute water droplets. **2** the expansive force of this vapour used as a source of power for machines. **3** momentum; impetus: *the dispute gathered steam.* • v. **1** give off or produce steam. ➤(**steam up** or **steam something up**) become or cause something to become misted over with steam. **2** cook (food) by heating it in steam from boiling water. **3** clean or otherwise treat with steam. ➤apply steam to (something fixed with adhesive) so as to open or loosen it. **4** (of a ship or train) travel somewhere under steam power. ➤generate steam in and operate (a steam locomotive). **5** (**be/get steamed up**) be or become extremely agitated or angry. **6** informal come, go, or move somewhere rapidly or in a forceful way.
– PHRASES **get up** (or **pick up**) **steam** **1** generate enough pressure to drive a steam engine. **2** (of an activity, project, etc.) gradually gain impetus. **have steam coming out of one's ears** informal be extremely angry. **let** (or **blow**) **off steam** informal get rid of pent-up energy or strong emotion. **run out of** (or **lose**) **steam** informal lose impetus or enthusiasm. **under one's own steam** without assistance from others.
– ORIGIN OE *stēam* 'vapour', *stēman* 'emit a scent, be exhaled', of Gmc origin.

**steam age** • n. the time when trains were drawn by steam locomotives.

**steam bath** • n. a room that is filled with hot steam for the purpose of cleaning and refreshing the body and for relaxation. ➤a session in such a bath.

**steamboat** • n. a boat that is propelled by a steam engine, especially (in the US) a paddle-wheel craft of a type used widely on rivers in the 19th century.

**steam distillation** • n. Chemistry distillation of a liquid in a current of steam.

**steamed** • adj. **1** Brit. informal very drunk. **2** informal, chiefly N. Amer. angry; upset. **3** (of food) cooked by steaming.

**steam engine** • n. an engine that uses the expansion or rapid condensation of steam to generate power. ➤a steam locomotive.

**steamer** ● n. 1 a ship or boat powered by steam. 2 a type of saucepan in which food can be steamed. 3 a device used to direct a jet of hot steam on to a garment in order to remove creases. 4 informal a wetsuit.

**steamer clam** ● n. another term for SOFTSHELL CLAM.

**steamer duck** ● n. a greyish South American duck which churns the water with its wings when fleeing danger. [*Tachyeres brachypterus* (Falkland Islands, flightless) and related species.]

**steamer rug** ● n. US dated a travelling rug, especially for use on the deck of a passenger ship.

**steamer trunk** ● n. a sturdy trunk designed or intended for use on board a steamboat.

**steaming** ● adj. 1 giving off steam. 2 Brit. informal extremely drunk. 3 Brit. informal very angry.

**steam iron** ● n. an electric iron that emits steam from holes in its flat surface.

**steam jacket** ● n. a steam-filled casing that is fitted around a cylinder in order to heat its contents.

**steamroller** ● n. a heavy, slow-moving vehicle with a roller, used to flatten the surfaces of roads during construction. ● v. (also **steamroll**) (of a government or other authority) forcibly pass (a measure) by restricting debate or otherwise overriding opposition. ➤force (someone) into doing or accepting something.

**steam turbine** ● n. a turbine in which a high-velocity jet of steam rotates a bladed disc or drum.

**steamy** ● adj. (**-ier**, **-iest**) 1 producing, filled with, or clouded with steam. 2 hot and humid. 3 informal of or involving erotic sexual activity.
– DERIVATIVES **steamily** adv. **steaminess** n.

**stearic acid** /ˈstɪərɪk, stɪˈarɪk/ ● n. Chemistry a solid saturated fatty acid obtained from animal or vegetable fats.
– DERIVATIVES **stearate** /ˈstɪəreɪt/ n.
– ORIGIN C19: *stearic* from Fr. *stéarique*, from Gk *stear* 'tallow'.

**stearin** /ˈstɪərɪn/ ● n. a white crystalline substance which is the main constituent of tallow and suet.
– ORIGIN C19: from Fr. *stéarine*, from Gk *stear* 'tallow'.

**steatite** /ˈstɪətʌɪt/ ● n. the mineral talc occurring in consolidated form, especially as soapstone.
– DERIVATIVES **steatitic** adj.
– ORIGIN C18: via L. from Gk *steatītēs*, from *stear, steat-* 'tallow'.

**steato-** ● comb. form relating to fatty matter or tissue: *steatosis*.
– ORIGIN from Gk *stear, steat-* 'tallow, fat'.

**steatopygia** /ˌstɪətə(ʊ)ˈpɪdʒɪə/ ● n. accumulation of large amounts of fat on the buttocks, especially as a normal condition in the Khoikhoi and other peoples of arid parts of southern Africa.
– DERIVATIVES **steatopygous** /ˌstɪətə(ʊ)ˈpʌɪgəs, ˌstɪəˈtɒpɪgəs/ adj.
– ORIGIN C19: mod. L., from Gk *stear, steat-* 'tallow' + *pugē* 'rump'.

**steatorrhoea** /ˌstɪətə(ʊ)ˈriːə/ ● n. Medicine the excretion of abnormal quantities of fat in the faeces owing to reduced absorption of fat by the intestine.

**steatosis** /ˌstɪəˈtəʊsɪs/ ● n. Medicine infiltration of liver cells with fat, associated with disturbance of the metabolism.

**steed** ● n. archaic or poetic/literary a horse.
– ORIGIN OE *stēda* 'stallion'; rel. to STUD².

**steel** ● n. 1 a hard, strong grey or bluish-grey alloy of iron with carbon and usually other elements, used extensively as a structural and fabricating material. 2 a rod of roughened steel on which knives are sharpened. 3 strength and determination: *nerves of steel*. ● v. mentally prepare (oneself) to do or face something difficult.
– ORIGIN OE *stȳle, stēli*, of Gmc origin.

**steel band** ● n. a band that plays music on steel drums.

**steel drum** (also **steel pan**) ● n. a percussion instrument originating in Trinidad, made out of an oil drum with one end beaten down and divided by grooves into sections to give different notes.

**steel engraving** ● n. the process of engraving a design into a steel plate. ➤a print made using this process.

**steelhead** ● n. a large, migratory form of rainbow trout found in the sea.

**steel wool** ● n. fine strands of steel matted together into a mass, used as an abrasive.

**steelwork** ● n. articles made of steel.

**steelworks** ● pl. n. [usu. treated as sing.] a factory where steel is manufactured.
– DERIVATIVES **steelworker** n.

**steely** ● adj. (**-ier**, **-iest**) 1 resembling steel in colour, brightness, or strength. 2 coldly determined; severe.
– DERIVATIVES **steeliness** n.

**steelyard** /ˈstiːljɑːd, ˈstɪljəd/ ● n. an apparatus for weighing that has a short arm taking the item to be weighed and a long graduated arm along which a weight is moved until it balances.
– ORIGIN C17: from STEEL + YARD¹ in obs. sense 'rod, measuring stick'.

**steenbok** /ˈstiːnbɒk, ˈsteɪn-/ (also **steinbok** or **steenbuck**) ● n. a small African antelope with large ears, a small tail, and smooth upright horns. [*Raphiceros campestris*.]
– ORIGIN C18: from Du., from *steen* 'stone' + *bok* 'buck'.

**steep¹** ● adj. 1 rising or falling sharply; almost perpendicular. 2 (of a rise or fall in an amount) very large or rapid. 3 informal (of a price or demand) not reasonable; excessive. ➤(of a claim or account) exaggerated. ● n. chiefly Skiing or poetic/literary a steep mountain slope.
– DERIVATIVES **steepish** adj. **steeply** adv. **steepness** n.
– ORIGIN OE *stēap* 'extending to a great height', of W. Gmc origin; rel. to STEEPLE and STOOP¹.

**steep²** ● v. 1 soak or be soaked in water or other liquid. 2 (usu. **be steeped in**) fill or imbue with a particular quality or influence.
– ORIGIN ME: of Gmc origin; rel. to STOUP.

**steepen** ● v. become or cause to become steeper.

**steeple** ● n. a church tower and spire. ➤a spire on the top of a church tower or roof.
– DERIVATIVES **steepled** adj.
– ORIGIN OE *stēpel*, of Gmc origin; rel. to STEEP¹.

**steeplechase** ● n. a horse race run on a racecourse having ditches and hedges as jumps. ➤a running race in which runners must clear hurdles and water jumps.
– DERIVATIVES **steeplechaser** n. **steeplechasing** n.
– ORIGIN C18: from STEEPLE (because orig. a steeple marked the finishing point across country) + CHASE¹.

**steeple-crowned** ● adj. (of a hat) having a tall, pointed crown.

**steeplejack** ● n. a person who climbs tall structures such as chimneys and steeples in order to carry out repairs.

**steer¹** ● v. 1 guide or control the movement of (a vehicle, ship, etc.). ➤follow (a course) in a specified direction. 2 direct or guide in a particular direction. ● n. 1 the type of steering of a vehicle. 2 informal a piece of advice or information.
– PHRASES **steer clear of** take care to avoid.
– DERIVATIVES **steerable** adj. **steerer** n. **steering** n.
– ORIGIN OE *stīeran*, of Gmc origin.

**steer²** ● n. another term for BULLOCK.
– ORIGIN OE *stēor*, of Gmc origin.

**steerage** ● n. 1 historical the part of a ship providing accommodation for passengers with the cheapest tickets. 2 archaic or poetic/literary the action of steering a boat.

**steerage way** ● n. the rate of headway required if a ship is to be controlled by the helm.

**steer-by-wire** ● n. a semi-automatic and typically computer-regulated system for controlling the engine, handling, and other functions of a motor vehicle.

**steering column** ● n. a shaft that connects the steering wheel of a vehicle to the rest of the steering mechanism.

**steering committee** (also **steering group**) ● n. a committee that decides on the priorities or order of business of an organization.

**steering wheel** ● n. a wheel that a driver rotates in

order to steer a vehicle.

**steersman** • n. (pl. **-men**) a person who steers a boat or ship.

**steeve**[1] • n. (in a sailing ship) the angle of the bowsprit in relation to the horizontal. • v. give (the bowsprit) a specified inclination.
– ORIGIN C17: of unknown origin.

**steeve**[2] • n. a derrick consisting of a long pole with a block at the end.
– ORIGIN C15: from OFr. *estiver* or Sp. *estibar*, from L. *stipare* 'pack tight'.

**stegosaur** /ˈstɛɡəsɔː/ (also **stegosaurus** /ˌstɛɡəˈsɔːrəs/) • n. a quadrupedal herbivorous dinosaur with a double row of large bony plates along the back.
– ORIGIN mod. L. *Stegosaurus*, from Gk *stegē* 'covering' + *sauros* 'lizard'.

**stein** /stʌɪn/ • n. a large earthenware beer mug.
– ORIGIN C19: from Ger. *Stein*, lit. 'stone'.

**steinbock** /ˈstʌɪnbɒk/ • n. (pl. same or **-bocks**) an ibex, especially one living in the Alps.
– ORIGIN C17: from Ger., from *Stein* 'stone' + *Bock* 'buck'.

**steinbok** /ˈstʌɪnbɒk/ • n. variant spelling of **STEENBOK**.

**stela** /ˈstiːlə/ • n. (pl. **stelae** /-liː/) Archaeology an upright stone slab or column typically bearing a commemorative inscription or relief design.
– ORIGIN C18: via L. from Gk (see **STELE**).

**stele** /stiːl, ˈstiːli/ • n. **1** Botany the central core of the stem and root of a vascular plant, consisting of the vascular tissue (xylem and phloem) and associated supporting tissue. **2** Archaeology another term for **STELA**.
– DERIVATIVES **stelar** adj.
– ORIGIN C19: from Gk *stēlē* 'standing block'.

**stellar** /ˈstɛlə/ • adj. **1** of or relating to a star or stars. **2** informal, chiefly N. Amer. of or having the quality of a star performer; excellent.
– DERIVATIVES **stelliform** adj.
– ORIGIN C17: from late L. *stellaris*, from L. *stella* 'star'.

**stellar wind** • n. Astronomy a continuous flow of charged particles from a star.

**stellate** /ˈstɛleɪt, -lət/ • adj. arranged in a radiating pattern like that of a star.
– DERIVATIVES **stellated** adj.
– ORIGIN C17: from L. *stellatus*, from *stella* 'star'.

**stem**[1] • n. **1** the main body or stalk of a plant or shrub. ➤ the stalk supporting a fruit, flower, or leaf, and attaching it to a larger branch, twig, or stalk. **2** a long, thin supportive or main section of something, such as that of a wine glass or tobacco pipe. **3** a rod or cylinder in a mechanism. **4** a vertical stroke in a letter or musical note. **5** Grammar the root or main part of a word, to which inflections or formative elements are added. **6** the main upright timber or metal piece at the bow of a ship. **7** archaic or poetic/literary the main line of descent of a family or nation. • v. (**stemmed**, **stemming**) **1** (**stem from**) originate in or be caused by. **2** remove the stems from (fruit or tobacco leaves). **3** (of a boat) make headway against (the tide or current).
– PHRASES **from stem to stern** from one end to the other, especially of a ship.
– DERIVATIVES **stemmed** adj. **stemless** adj.
– ORIGIN OE *stemn*, *stefn*, of Gmc origin.

**stem**[2] • v. (**stemmed**, **stemming**) **1** stop or restrict (the flow of something). **2** Skiing slide the tail of one ski or both skis outwards in order to turn or slow down.
– ORIGIN ME: from ON *stemma*, of Gmc origin; the skiing term (early C20) is from the Ger. verb *stemmen*.

**stem cell** • n. Biology an undifferentiated cell of a multicellular organism which is capable of giving rise to indefinitely more cells of the same type, and from which certain other kinds of cell arise by differentiation.

**stem ginger** • n. pieces of crystallized or preserved ginger.

**stemma** /ˈstɛmə/ • n. (pl. **stemmata** /-mətə/) **1** a recorded genealogy of a family; a family tree. **2** a diagram showing the relationship between a text and its various manuscript versions.
– ORIGIN C17: via L. from Gk *stemma* 'wreath', from *stephein* 'wreathe, crown'.

**stemmatics** /stɛˈmatɪks/ • pl. n. [treated as sing.] the branch of study concerned with analysing the relationship between surviving variant versions of a text, especially so as to reconstruct a lost original.

**stemple** • n. archaic each of a number of crossbars in a mineshaft, serving as supports or steps.
– ORIGIN C17: perh. rel. to Ger. *Stempel*.

**stem stitch** • n. an embroidery stitch forming a continuous line of long, overlapped stitches.

**stem turn** • n. Skiing a turn made by stemming with the upper ski and lifting the lower one parallel to it towards the end.

**stemware** • n. N. Amer. goblets and stemmed glasses regarded collectively.

**stem-winder** • n. US **1** informal a rousing speech. **2** a watch wound by turning a knob on the end of a stem.

**stench** • n. a strong and very unpleasant smell.
– ORIGIN OE *stenc* 'smell', of Gmc origin; rel. to **STINK**.

**stencil** • n. a thin sheet of card, plastic, or metal with a pattern or letters cut out of it, used to produce the cut design on the surface below by the application of ink or paint through the holes. • v. (**stencilled**, **stencilling**; US **stenciled**, **stenciling**) decorate using a stencil. ➤ produce (a design) with a stencil.
– DERIVATIVES **stencilled** adj. **stencilling** n.
– ORIGIN C18: from earlier *stansel* 'ornament with various colours' (based on L. *scintilla* 'spark').

**Sten gun** • n. a type of lightweight British sub-machine gun.
– ORIGIN 1940s: from the initials of the inventors' surnames, *S*hepherd and *T*urpin, suggested by **BREN GUN**.

**steno** /ˈstɛnəʊ/ • n. (pl. **-os**) N. Amer. informal **1** a shorthand typist. **2** short for **STENOGRAPHY**.

**stenography** /stɪˈnɒɡrəfi/ • n. N. Amer. the action or process of writing in shorthand and transcribing the shorthand on a typewriter.
– DERIVATIVES **stenographer** n. **stenographic** adj.
– ORIGIN C17: from Gk *stenos* 'narrow' + **-GRAPHY**.

**stenohaline** /ˌstɛnəʊˈheɪlʌɪn, -liːn/ • adj. Ecology able to tolerate only a narrow range of salinity. Often contrasted with **EURYHALINE**.
– ORIGIN 1930s: from Gk *stenos* 'narrow' + *halinos* 'of salt'.

**stenosis** /stɪˈnəʊsɪs/ • n. (pl. **stenoses**) Medicine the abnormal narrowing of a passage in the body.
– DERIVATIVES **stenosed** adj. **stenosing** adj. **stenotic** adj.
– ORIGIN C19: mod. L., from Gk *stenōsis* 'narrowing', from *stenoun* 'make narrow'.

**stenothermal** /ˌstɛnə(ʊ)ˈθəːm(ə)l/ • adj. Ecology able to tolerate only a small range of temperature. Often contrasted with **EURYTHERMAL**.
– ORIGIN C19: from Gk *stenos* 'narrow' + **THERMAL**.

**stenotype** • n. a machine resembling a typewriter that is used for recording speech in syllables or phonemes.
– DERIVATIVES **stenotypist** n.
– ORIGIN C19: from **STENOGRAPHY** + **TYPE**.

**stent**[1] • n. Medicine **1** a splint placed inside a duct, canal, or blood vessel to aid healing or relieve an obstruction. **2** an impression or cast of a part or body cavity, used to maintain pressure so as to promote healing, especially of a skin graft.
– ORIGIN C19: from the name of the Engl. dentist Charles T. Stent.

**stent**[2] historical, chiefly Scottish • n. an assessment of property made for purposes of taxation. • v. assess and charge for purposes of taxation.
– ORIGIN ME: from OFr. *estente* 'valuation', rel. to Anglo-Norman Fr. *extente* (see **EXTENT**).

**stenter** • n. another term for **TENTER**[1].
– ORIGIN from Scots *stent* 'set up (a tent)' (perh. a shortening of **EXTEND**) + **-ER**[1].

**stentor** /ˈstɛntə/ • n. **1** poetic/literary a person with a powerful voice. **2** Zoology a sedentary trumpet-shaped single-celled animal that is widespread in fresh water. [Genus *Stentor*.]
– ORIGIN C17: from Gk *Stentōr*, the name of a herald in the Trojan War.

**stentorian** /stɛnˈtɔːrɪən/ • adj. (of a person's voice) loud and powerful.

**step** ● n. **1** an act or movement of putting one leg in front of the other in walking or running. ➤the distance covered by such a movement. ➤a short and easily walked distance. **2** one of the sequences of movement of the feet which make up a dance. **3** a flat surface, especially one in a series, on which to place one's foot when moving from one level to another. ➤a doorstep. ➤a rung of a ladder. ➤(**steps** or **a pair of steps**) Brit. a stepladder. ➤Climbing a foothold cut in a slope of ice. **4** a block fixed to a boat's keel in order to take the base of a mast or other fitting. **5** Physics an abrupt change in the value of a quantity, especially voltage. **6** a position or grade in a scale or hierarchy. **7** a measure or action, especially one of a series taken in order to deal with or achieve a particular thing. **8** Music, chiefly US an interval in a scale; a tone (whole step) or semitone (half step). **9** step aerobics. ● v. (**stepped, stepping**) **1** lift and set down one's foot or one foot after the other in order to walk somewhere or move to a new position. **2** Nautical set up (a mast) in its step.
– PHRASES **in** (or **out of**) **step 1** walking, marching, or dancing in the same (or a different) rhythm and pace as others. **2** conforming (or not conforming) to what others are doing or thinking. **3** Physics (of two or more oscillations or other cyclic phenomena) having (or not having) the same frequency and always in the same phase. **follow** (or **tread**) **in someone's steps** do as someone else did, especially in making a journey or following a career. **mind** (or **watch**) **one's step** walk or act carefully. **step into someone's shoes** take control of a task or job from another person. **step on it** informal go faster. **step out of line** behave inappropriately or disobediently.
– PHRASAL VERBS **step aside** another way of saying ***step down***. **step back** mentally withdraw from a situation in order to consider it objectively. **step down** withdraw or resign from a position or office. **step something down** decrease voltage by using a transformer. **step forward** offer one's help or services. **step in 1** become involved in a difficult situation, especially in order to help. **2** act as a substitute for someone. **step out 1** leave a room or building, typically for a short time. **2** N. Amer. informal have a romantic or sexual relationship with someone. **3** walk with long or vigorous steps. **step something up** increase the amount, speed, or intensity of something. ➤increase voltage using a transformer.
– DERIVATIVES **stepped** adj. **stepwise** adj.
– ORIGIN OE *stæpe*, *stepe* (n.), *stæppan*, *steppan* (v.), of Gmc origin.

**step-** ● comb. form denoting a relationship resulting from a remarriage: *stepmother*.
– ORIGIN OE *stēop-*, from a Gmc base meaning 'bereaved, orphaned'.

**step aerobics** ● pl. n. [treated as sing. or pl.] a type of aerobics that involves stepping up on to and down from a portable block.

**stepbrother** ● n. a son of one's step-parent, by a marriage other than that with one's own father or mother.

**stepchild** ● n. (pl. **-children**) a child of one's husband or wife by a previous marriage.

**stepdaughter** ● n. a daughter of one's husband or wife by a previous marriage.

**stepfather** ● n. a man who is married to one's mother after the divorce of one's parents or the death of one's father.

**stephanotis** /ˌstɛfəˈnəʊtɪs/ ● n. a Madagascan climbing plant cultivated for its fragrant waxy white flowers. [Genus *Stephanotis*.]
– ORIGIN mod. L., from Gk, lit. 'fit for a wreath', from *stephanos* 'wreath'.

**step-in** ● adj. denoting a garment or pair of shoes that is put on by being stepped into and has no need for fastenings. ● n. (**step-ins**) **1** a pair of such shoes; slip-ons. **2** dated, chiefly N. Amer. a pair of women's briefs.

**stepladder** ● n. a short folding ladder with flat steps and a small platform.

**stepmother** ● n. a woman who is married to one's father after the divorce of one's parents or the death of one's mother.

**steppe** /stɛp/ ● n. a large area of flat unforested grassland in SE Europe or Siberia.
– ORIGIN C17: from Russ. *step'*.

**steppe lemming** ● n. a burrowing vole-like central Asian rodent with a black dorsal stripe, sometimes a serious pest of crops and pasture. [*Lagurus lagurus*.]

**stepper** ● n. **1** an electric motor or other device which moves or rotates in a series of small discrete steps. **2** a portable block used in step aerobics.

**stepping stone** ● n. **1** a raised stone on which to step when crossing a stream or muddy area. **2** an action that helps one to make progress towards a specified goal.

**stepsister** ● n. a daughter of one's step-parent by a marriage other than with one's own father or mother.

**stepson** ● n. a son of one's husband or wife by a previous marriage.

**-ster** ● suffix **1** denoting a person engaged in or associated with a particular activity or thing: *songster*. **2** denoting a person having a particular quality: *youngster*.
– ORIGIN OE *-estre*, *-istre*, etc., of Gmc origin.

**steradian** /stəˈreɪdɪən/ (abbrev.: **sr**) ● n. the SI unit of solid angle, equal to the angle at the centre of a sphere subtended by a part of the surface equal in area to the square of the radius.
– ORIGIN C19: from Gk *stereos* 'solid' + **RADIAN**.

**stere** /stɪə/ ● n. a unit of volume equal to one cubic metre.
– ORIGIN C18: from Fr. *stère*, from Gk *stereos* 'solid'.

**stereo** /ˈstɛrɪəʊ, ˈstɪərɪəʊ/ ● n. (pl. **-os**) **1** stereophonic sound. **2** a stereophonic CD player, record player, etc. **3** Printing short for **STEREOTYPE**. ● adj. **1** stereophonic. **2** stereoscopic.

**stereo-** ● comb. form having or relating to three dimensions: *stereography* | *stereophonic*.
– ORIGIN from Gk *stereos* 'solid'.

**stereobate** /ˈstɛrɪə(ʊ)beɪt, ˈstɪə-/ ● n. Architecture a solid mass of masonry serving as a foundation for a wall or row of columns.
– ORIGIN C19: from Fr. *stéréobate*, via L. from Gk *stereobatēs*, from Gk *stereos* 'solid' + *batēs* 'base'.

**stereochemistry** ● n. the branch of chemistry concerned with the three-dimensional arrangement of atoms in molecules and the effect of this on reactions.
– DERIVATIVES **stereochemical** adj. **stereochemically** adv.

**stereogram** ● n. a diagram or computer-generated image giving a three-dimensional representation of a solid object or surface.

**stereography** ● n. the representation of three-dimensional things on a two-dimensional surface, as in cartography.
– DERIVATIVES **stereograph** n. **stereographic** adj.

**stereoisomer** /ˌstɛrɪəʊˈʌɪsəmə, ˌstɪə-/ ● n. Chemistry each of two or more molecules differing only in the spatial arrangement of their atoms.
– DERIVATIVES **stereoisomeric** adj. **stereoisomerism** n.

**stereolithography** ● n. the creation layer by layer of a three-dimensional object from a computer-generated design, using a liquid polymer which hardens on contact with a moving laser beam.
– DERIVATIVES **stereolithographic** adj.

**stereophonic** /ˌstɛrɪə(ʊ)ˈfɒnɪk, ˌstɪərɪə(ʊ)-/ ● adj. of or denoting sound recording and reproduction using two or more channels so that the reproduced sound seems to surround the listener and to come from more than one source. Compare with **MONOPHONIC**.
– DERIVATIVES **stereophonically** adv. **stereophony** /-ˈɒf(ə)ni/ n.

**stereopsis** /ˌstɛrɪˈɒpsɪs, ˌstɪərɪ-/ ● n. the perception of depth produced by the reception in the brain of visual stimuli from both eyes in combination; binocular vision.
– DERIVATIVES **stereoptic** adj.
– ORIGIN C20: from **STEREO-** + Gk *opsis* 'sight'.

**stereopticon** /ˌstɛrɪˈɒptɪk(ə)n, ˌstɪərɪ-/ ● n. a slide projector that combines two images to create a three-dimensional effect.
– ORIGIN C19: from **STEREO-** + Gk *optikon*, neut. of *optikos* 'relating to vision'.

S

**stereoscope** /ˈstɛrɪə(ʊ)skəʊp, ˈstɪə-/ ● **n.** a device by which two photographs of the same object taken at slightly different angles are viewed together, creating an impression of depth and solidity.
– DERIVATIVES **stereoscopic** adj. **stereoscopically** adv. **stereoscopy** n.

**stereoselective** /ˌstɛrɪəʊsɪˈlɛktɪv, ˌstɪə-/ ● **adj.** Chemistry (of a reaction) preferentially producing a particular stereoisomeric form of the product.
– DERIVATIVES **stereoselectivity** n.

**stereospecific** ● **adj.** Chemistry another term for STEREOSELECTIVE.
– DERIVATIVES **stereospecifically** adv. **stereospecificity** n.

**stereotactic** /ˌstɛrɪə(ʊ)ˈtaktɪk, ˌstɪərɪə(ʊ)-/ (also **stereotaxic** /-ˈtaksɪk/) ● **adj.** relating to or denoting techniques for surgical treatment or scientific investigation that permit the accurate positioning of probes inside the brain or other parts of the body.
– DERIVATIVES **stereotactically** adv. **stereotaxis** n.

**stereotype** ● **n. 1** an image or idea of a particular type of person or thing that has become fixed through being widely held. **2** a relief printing plate cast in a mould made from composed type or an original plate. ● **v.** view or represent as a stereotype.
– DERIVATIVES **stereotypic** adj. **stereotypical** adj. **stereotypically** adv. **stereotypy** n.
– ORIGIN C18: from Fr. *stéréotype* (adj.).

**steric** /ˈstɛrɪk, ˈstɪərɪk/ ● **adj.** Chemistry of or relating to the spatial arrangement of atoms in a molecule, especially as it affects reactions.
– DERIVATIVES **sterically** adv.
– ORIGIN C19: formed irregularly from Gk *stereos* 'solid' + -IC.

**sterilant** /ˈstɛrɪl(ə)nt/ ● **n.** an agent used to destroy micro-organisms, or pests and diseases in soil.

**sterile** ● **adj. 1** not able to produce children or young. ➤ (of a plant) not able to produce fruit or seeds. ➤ (of land or soil) too poor in quality to produce crops. **2** lacking in imagination, creativity, or excitement. **3** free from bacteria or other living micro-organisms.
– DERIVATIVES **sterilely** adv. **sterility** n.
– ORIGIN ME: from OFr., or from L. *sterilis*; rel. to Gk *steira* 'barren cow'.

**sterilize** (also **-ise**) ● **v. 1** make sterile. **2** deprive of the ability to produce offspring by removing or blocking the sex organs.
– DERIVATIVES **sterilizable** adj. **sterilization** n. **sterilized** adj. **sterilizer** n.

**sterlet** /ˈstəːlɪt/ ● **n.** a small sturgeon of the Danube basin and Caspian Sea area, farmed and fished for its flesh and caviar. [*Acipenser ruthenus*.]
– ORIGIN C16: from Russ. *sterlyad'*.

**sterling** ● **n.** British money. ● **adj.** chiefly Brit. (of a person or their work) excellent; of great value.
– ORIGIN ME: prob. from *steorra* 'star' + -LING (because some early Norman pennies bore a small star).

**sterling silver** ● **n.** silver of at least 92¼ per cent purity.

**stern**[1] ● **adj. 1** grimly serious or strict, especially in the exercise of discipline. **2** severe; demanding.
– DERIVATIVES **sternly** adv. **sternness** n.
– ORIGIN OE *styrne*, prob. from the W. Gmc base of STARE.

**stern**[2] ● **n.** the rearmost part of a ship or boat.
– DERIVATIVES **sterned** adj. **sternmost** adj. **sternwards** adv.
– ORIGIN ME: prob. from ON *stjórn* 'steering', from *stýra* 'to steer'.

**sternal** ● **adj.** of or relating to the sternum.

**sternal rib** ● **n.** another term for TRUE RIB.

**sternocleidomastoid** /ˌstəːnə(ʊ)ˌklʌɪdə(ʊ)ˈmastɔɪd/ ● **n.** Anatomy each of a pair of long muscles which connect the sternum, clavicle, and mastoid process and serve to turn and nod the neck.

**sternpost** ● **n.** the central upright support at the stern of a boat, traditionally bearing the rudder.

**sternsheets** ● **pl. n.** the flooring planks in a boat's after section, or the seating in this section of an open boat.

**sternum** /ˈstəːnəm/ ● **n.** (pl. **sternums** or **sterna** /-nə/) **1** the breastbone. **2** Zoology a thickened ventral plate on each segment of the body of an arthropod.
– ORIGIN C17: mod. L., from Gk *sternon* 'chest'.

**sternutation** /ˌstəːnjʊˈteɪʃ(ə)n/ ● **n.** formal the action of sneezing.
– DERIVATIVES **sternutatory** adj.
– ORIGIN ME: from L. *sternutatio(n-)*, from *sternutare*, frequentative of *sternuere* 'to sneeze'.

**sternutator** /ˈstəːnjʊˌteɪtə/ ● **n.** a chemical warfare agent that causes irritation to the nose and eyes, pain in the chest, and nausea.

**sternway** ● **n.** backward movement of a ship.

**sternwheeler** ● **n.** a steamer propelled by a paddle wheel positioned at the stern.

**steroid** /ˈstɪərɔɪd, ˈstɛrɔɪd/ ● **n.** Biochemistry any of a large class of organic compounds (including many hormones, alkaloids, and vitamins) with a molecule containing four rings of carbon atoms. ➤ short for ANABOLIC STEROID.
– DERIVATIVES **steroidal** adj.
– ORIGIN 1930s: from STEROL + -OID.

**sterol** /ˈstɪərɒl, ˈstɛrɒl/ ● **n.** Biochemistry any of a group of naturally occurring unsaturated steroid alcohols, typically waxy solids.
– ORIGIN C20: independent usage of the ending of words such as CHOLESTEROL.

**stertorous** /ˈstəːt(ə)rəs/ ● **adj.** (of breathing) noisy and laboured.
– DERIVATIVES **stertorously** adv.
– ORIGIN C19: from mod. L. *stertor* 'snoring sound' (from L. *stertere* 'to snore') + -OUS.

**stet** ● **v.** (**stetted**, **stetting**) let it stand (used as an instruction on a printed proof to ignore a correction). ➤ write such an instruction against.
– ORIGIN L., 'let it stand', from *stare* 'to stand'.

**stethoscope** /ˈstɛθəskəʊp/ ● **n.** a medical instrument for listening to the action of someone's heart or breathing, having a small disc-shaped resonator that is placed against the chest and two tubes connected to earpieces.
– DERIVATIVES **stethoscopic** adj.
– ORIGIN C19: from Fr. *stéthoscope*, from Gk *stēthos* 'breast' + *skopein* 'look at'.

**Stetson** /ˈstɛts(ə)n/ ● **n.** (trademark in the US) a hat with a high crown and a very wide brim, traditionally worn by cowboys and ranchers in the US.
– ORIGIN C19: named after the Amer. hat manufacturer John B. *Stetson*.

**stevedore** /ˈstiːvədɔː/ ● **n.** a person employed at a dock to load and unload ships.
– ORIGIN C18: from Sp. *estivador*, from *estivar* 'stow a cargo', from L. *stipare* (see STEEVE[2]).

**Stevengraph** /ˈstiːv(ə)ngrɑːf/ ● **n.** a type of small picture made from brightly coloured woven silk, produced during the late 19th century.
– ORIGIN named after the Engl. weaver Thomas *Stevens*.

**stew**[1] ● **n. 1** a dish of meat and vegetables cooked slowly in liquid in a closed dish or pan. **2** informal a state of anxiety or agitation. **3** archaic a public room used for hot steam baths. ➤ a brothel. ● **v. 1** cook or be cooked slowly in liquid in a closed dish or pan. ➤ Brit. (of tea) become strong and bitter with prolonged brewing. **2** informal remain in a heated or stifling atmosphere. **3** informal remain in an anxious or agitated state.
– PHRASES **stew in one's own juice** informal be left to suffer the consequences of one's own actions.
– ORIGIN ME: from OFr. *estuve* (rel. to *estuver* 'heat in steam'), prob. based on Gk *tuphos* 'smoke, steam'.

**stew**[2] ● **n.** Brit. **1** a pond or large tank for keeping fish for eating. **2** an artificial oyster bed.
– ORIGIN ME: from OFr. *estui*, from *estoier* 'confine'.

**stew**[3] ● **n.** N. Amer. informal an air steward or stewardess.
– ORIGIN 1970s: abbrev.

**steward** ● **n. 1** a person who looks after the passengers on a ship or aircraft. **2** a person responsible for supplies of food to a college, club, etc. **3** an official appointed to supervise arrangements at a large public event. **4** short for SHOP STEWARD. **5** a person employed to manage another's property, especially a large house or estate.

➤ chiefly historical an officer of the British royal household, especially an administrator of Crown estates. ● **v.** act as a steward of.
– DERIVATIVES **stewardship** n.
– ORIGIN OE *stīweard*, from *stig* (prob. in the sense 'house, hall') + *weard* 'ward'.

**stewardess** /ˈstjuːədɪs, ˌstjuːəˈdɛs/ ● **n.** a woman who looks after the passengers on a ship or aircraft.

**stewed** ● **adj.** informal drunk.

**stewpot** ● **n.** a large pot in which stews are cooked.

**stg** ● **abbrev.** sterling.

**Sth** ● **abbrev.** south.

**sthenic** /ˈsθɛnɪk/ ● **adj.** having a high or excessive level of strength and energy.
– ORIGIN C18: from Gk *sthenos* 'strength', on the pattern of *asthenic*.

**stibnite** /ˈstɪbnʌɪt/ ● **n.** a lead-grey mineral consisting of antimony sulphide.
– ORIGIN C19: from L. *stibium* 'black antimony' + **-INE**[4] + **-ITE**[1].

**stichomythia** /ˌstɪkə(ʊ)ˈmɪθɪə/ ● **n.** dialogue in which two characters speak alternate lines of verse, used as a stylistic device in ancient Greek drama.
– ORIGIN C19: mod. L., from Gk *stikhomuthia*, from *stikhos* 'row, line of verse' + *muthos* 'speech, talk'.

**stick**[1] ● **n. 1** a thin piece of wood that has fallen or been cut off a tree. ➤ a stick used for support in walking or as a weapon. **2** (in hockey, polo, etc.) a long, thin implement with a curved head or angled blade, used to hit or direct the ball or puck. ➤ **(sticks)** (in field hockey) the foul play of raising the stick above the shoulder. **3 (the sticks)** informal goalposts or cricket stumps. **4** a long, thin object or piece of something: *a stick of dynamite*. **5** a conductor's baton. **6** a gear or control lever. **7** Nautical, archaic a mast or spar. **8** a group of bombs or paratroopers dropped from an aircraft. **9** a small group of soldiers assigned to a particular duty. **10** the threat of punishment as a means of persuasion (as contrasted with the 'carrot' or enticement). ➤ Brit. informal severe criticism or treatment. **11 (the sticks)** informal, derogatory rural areas. **12** informal, dated a person of a specified kind: *Janet's not a bad old stick*. **13** Stock Exchange a large quantity of unsold stock, especially the proportion of shares which must be taken up by underwriters after an unsuccessful issue.
– PHRASES **up sticks** Brit. informal go to live elsewhere. [from naut. sl. *to up sticks* 'set up a boat's mast' (ready for departure).]
– ORIGIN OE *sticca* 'peg, stick, spoon', of W. Gmc origin.

**stick**[2] ● **v.** (past and past part. **stuck**) **1** insert, thrust, or push (an object or its point) into or through something. ➤ **(stick in/into/through)** be or remain fixed with its point embedded in. ➤ stab or pierce with a sharp object. **2** put somewhere in a quick or careless way. ➤ informal used to express angry dismissal of a particular thing: *they can stick the job*. **3** protrude or extend in a certain direction. **4** adhere or cause to adhere. **5 (be stuck)** be fixed in a particular position or unable to move or be moved. ➤ be unable to progress with a task or find the answer or solution. ➤ **(be stuck for)** be at a loss for or in need of. ➤ **(be stuck with)** informal be unable to get rid of or escape from. ➤ **(be stuck on)** informal be infatuated with. **6** Brit. informal accept; tolerate; endure: *I can't stick Geoffrey*. ➤ **(stick at)** informal persevere with (a task or endeavour). ➤ **(stick it out)** informal put up with or persevere with something difficult or disagreeable.
– PHRASES **get stuck in** (or **into**) Brit. informal start doing something with determination. **stick in one's throat** (or **craw**) be difficult or impossible to accept. **stick it to** informal, chiefly N. Amer. treat harshly. **stick one's neck out** informal risk incurring criticism or anger by acting or speaking boldly.
– PHRASAL VERBS **stick around** informal remain in or near a place. **stick by** continue to support or be loyal to. **stick something on** informal place the blame for a mistake or wrongdoing on. **stick out** be extremely noticeable. **stick out for** refuse to accept less than. **stick to** continue or confine oneself to doing, using, or practising. **stick together** informal remain united or mutually loyal. **stick someone/thing up** informal, chiefly N. Amer. rob someone or something at gunpoint. **stick up for** support or defend. **stick with** informal persevere or continue with.
– DERIVATIVES **stickability** n.
– ORIGIN OE *stician*, of Gmc origin.

**stickball** ● **n.** N. Amer. an informal game played with a stick and a ball, resembling baseball or lacrosse.

**sticker** ● **n. 1** an adhesive label or notice. **2** informal a determined or persistent person.

**stick insect** ● **n.** a long, slender, slow-moving insect that resembles a twig. [Family Phasmatidae: many species.]

**stick-in-the-mud** ● **n.** informal a person who resists change.

**stickleback** ● **n.** a small freshwater or coastal fish with sharp spines along its back. [*Gasterosteus aculeatus* (**three-spined stickleback**) and other species.]
– ORIGIN ME: from OE *sticel* 'thorn, sting' + *bæc* 'back'.

**stickler** ● **n.** a person who insists on a certain quality or type of behaviour.
– ORIGIN C16 (in the sense 'umpire'): from obs. *stickle* 'be umpire', alt. of obs. *stightle* 'to control', frequentative of OE *stiht(i)an* 'set in order'.

**stickpin** ● **n.** N. Amer. a straight pin with an ornamental head, worn to keep a tie in place or as a brooch.

**stick shift** ● **n.** N. Amer. a gear lever or manual transmission.

**stickum** /ˈstɪkəm/ ● **n.** informal, chiefly N. Amer. sticky gum or paste.
– ORIGIN C20: from the verb **STICK**[2] + *-um* (representing the pronoun *them*).

**stick-up** ● **n.** informal, chiefly US an armed robbery in which a gun is used to threaten people.

**sticky** ● **adj.** (**-ier**, **-iest**) **1** tending or designed to stick; adhesive. ➤ glutinous; viscous. **2** (of the weather) hot and humid; muggy. **3** damp with sweat. **4** informal difficult; awkward. **5** informal (of a website) attracting a long visit or repeat visits from users.
– PHRASES **come to a sticky end** be led by one's own actions to ruin or an unpleasant death. **sticky fingers** informal a propensity to steal.
– DERIVATIVES **stickily** adv. **stickiness** n.

**stickybeak** Austral./NZ informal ● **n.** an inquisitive person. ● **v.** pry.

**sticky-fingered** ● **adj.** informal given to stealing.

**stiction** /ˈstɪkʃ(ə)n/ ● **n.** Physics the friction which tends to prevent stationary surfaces from being set in motion.

**stifado** /stɪˈfɑːdəʊ/ ● **n.** a Greek dish of meat stewed with onions and sometimes tomatoes.
– ORIGIN from mod. Gk *stiphado*.

**stiff** ● **adj. 1** not easily bent; rigid. ➤ not moving freely; difficult to turn or operate. ➤ unable to move easily and without pain. **2** not relaxed or friendly; constrained. **3** severe or strong: *they face stiff fines*. ➤ (of a wind) blowing strongly. ➤ (of an alcoholic drink) strong. **4 (stiff with)** informal full of. **5** (—— **stiff**) informal having a specified unpleasant feeling to an extreme extent: *scared stiff*. ● **n.** informal **1** a dead body. **2** chiefly N. Amer. a boring, conventional person. ● **v.** informal **1** N. Amer. cheat (someone). ➤ fail to leave (someone) a tip. **2** N. Amer. ignore deliberately; snub. **3** kill.
– PHRASES **a stiff upper lip** a quality of uncomplaining stoicism.
– DERIVATIVES **stiffish** adj. **stiffly** adv. **stiffness** n.
– ORIGIN OE *stīf*, of Gmc origin.

**stiff-arm** ● **v.** tackle or fend off by extending an arm rigidly.

**stiffen** ● **v. 1** make or become stiff. **2** make or become stronger or more steadfast.
– DERIVATIVES **stiffener** n. **stiffening** n.

**stiff-necked** ● **adj.** haughty and stubborn.

**stifftail** ● **n.** a duck with a tail of pointed feathers often held up at an angle, e.g. the ruddy duck.

**stiffy** ● **n.** (pl. **-ies**) vulgar slang an erection of a man's penis.

**stifle**[1] ● **v. 1** prevent from breathing freely; suffocate.

**2** smother or suppress: *she stifled a giggle.* ➤prevent or constrain (an activity or idea).
– DERIVATIVES **stifler** n. **stifling** adj. **stiflingly** adv.
– ORIGIN ME: perh. from a frequentative of OFr. *estouffer* 'smother, stifle'.

**stifle²** ● n. a joint in the legs of horses, dogs, and other animals, equivalent to the knee in humans.
– ORIGIN ME: of unknown origin.

**stifle bone** ● n. the bone in front of a stifle joint.

**stigma** /'stɪgmə/ ● n. (pl. **stigmas** or especially in sense 2 **stigmata** /-mətə, -'mɑːtə/) **1** a mark of disgrace associated with a particular circumstance, quality, or person. **2** (**stigmata**) (in Christian tradition) marks corresponding to those left on Christ's body by the Crucifixion, said to have been impressed by divine favour on the bodies of St Francis of Assisi and others. **3** Medicine a visible sign or characteristic of a disease. ➤a mark or spot on the skin. **4** Botany the part of a pistil that receives the pollen during pollination.
– ORIGIN C16: via L. from Gk *stigma* 'a mark made by a pointed instrument, a dot'; rel. to **STICK¹**.

**stigmatic** ● adj. **1** of or relating to a stigma or stigmas. **2** another term for **ANASTIGMATIC**. ● n. a person bearing stigmata.
– DERIVATIVES **stigmatically** adv.
– ORIGIN C16: from L. *stigma, stigmat-* + **-IC**.

**stigmatist** ● n. another term for **STIGMATIC**.

**stigmatize** (also **-ise**) ● v. **1** (usu. **be stigmatized**) regard as worthy of disgrace. **2** mark with stigmata.
– DERIVATIVES **stigmatization** n.

**stilb** ● n. a unit of luminance equal to one candela per square centimetre.
– ORIGIN 1940s: from Fr., from Gk *stilbein* 'to glitter'.

**stilbene** /'stɪlbiːn/ ● n. Chemistry a synthetic aromatic hydrocarbon which forms phosphorescent crystals.
– ORIGIN C19: from Gk *stilbein* 'to glitter' + **-ENE**.

**stilboestrol** /stɪl'biːstrɒl/ (US **stilbestrol**) ● n. Biochemistry a powerful synthetic oestrogen used in hormone therapy, as a post-coital contraceptive, and as a growth-promoting agent for livestock.
– ORIGIN 1930s: from **STILBENE** + **OESTRUS** + **-OL**.

**stile¹** ● n. an arrangement of steps set into a fence or wall that allows people to climb over.
– ORIGIN OE *stigel*, from a Gmc root meaning 'to climb'.

**stile²** ● n. a vertical piece in the frame of a panelled door or sash window. Compare with **RAIL¹**.
– ORIGIN C17: prob. from Du. *stijl* 'pillar, doorpost'.

**stiletto** ● n. (pl. **-os**) **1** chiefly Brit. a thin, high tapering heel on a woman's shoe. **2** a short dagger with a tapering blade. **3** a sharp-pointed tool for making eyelet holes.
– ORIGIN C17: from Ital., dimin. of *stilo* 'dagger'.

**still¹** ● adj. **1** not moving. **2** (of air or water) undisturbed by wind, sound, or current. **3** (of a drink) not effervescent. ● n. **1** a state of deep and quiet calm: *the still of the night.* **2** a photograph or a single shot from a cinema film. ● adv. **1** even now or at a particular time: *it was still raining.* **2** nevertheless. **3** even (used with comparatives for emphasis): *better still.* ● v. make or become still.
– DERIVATIVES **stillness** n.
– ORIGIN OE *stille* (adj. and adv.), *stillan* (v.), of W. Gmc origin, from a base meaning 'be fixed, stand'.

**still²** ● n. an apparatus for distilling alcoholic drinks such as whisky.
– ORIGIN C16: from the rare verb *still* 'extract by distillation', shortening of **DISTIL**.

**stillage** ● n. a wooden rack or pallet for holding stored goods off the floor or separating goods in transit.
– ORIGIN C16: appar. from Du. *stellagie* 'scaffold', from *stellen* 'to place'.

**stillbirth** ● n. the birth of an infant that has died in the womb.
– DERIVATIVES **stillborn** adj.

**still-hunt** chiefly N. Amer. ● v. hunt game stealthily; stalk. ● n. a stealthy hunt for game.
– DERIVATIVES **still-hunting** n.

**still life** ● n. (pl. **still lifes**) a painting or drawing of a static arrangement of objects, typically flowers and/or fruit.

**still room** ● n. Brit. historical a room in a large house used to store preserves and to prepare tea and coffee.
– ORIGIN C18: orig. denoting a room with a still.

**Stillson** /'stɪls(ə)n/ ● n. a large wrench with jaws that tighten as pressure is increased.
– ORIGIN C20: named after its Amer. inventor Daniel C. *Stillson.*

**stilly** poetic/literary ● adv. /'stɪlli/ quietly and with little movement. ● adj. /'stɪli/ still and quiet.

**stilt** ● n. **1** either of a pair of upright poles with supports for the feet enabling the user to walk raised above the ground. **2** each of a set of posts or piles supporting a building. **3** a small support for ceramic ware in a kiln. **4** a long-billed wading bird, predominantly black and white, with very long slender legs. [Genera *Himantopus* and *Cladorhynchus*: several species.]
– ORIGIN ME: of Gmc origin.

**stilted** ● adj. **1** (of speech or writing) stiff and self-conscious or unnatural. **2** standing on stilts. **3** Architecture (of an arch) with pieces of upright masonry between the imposts and the springers.
– DERIVATIVES **stiltedly** adv. **stiltedness** n.

**Stilton** ● n. trademark a kind of strong, rich blue cheese, originally made in Leicestershire.
– ORIGIN so named because it was formerly sold at a coaching inn in *Stilton*, Cambridgeshire.

**stimulant** ● n. **1** a substance that acts to increase physiological or nervous activity in the body. **2** something that promotes activity, interest, or enthusiasm. ● adj. acting as a stimulant.

**stimulate** ● v. **1** apply or act as a stimulus to. **2** animate or excite.
– DERIVATIVES **stimulating** adj. **stimulatingly** adv. **stimulation** n. **stimulative** adj. **stimulator** n. **stimulatory** adj.
– ORIGIN C16 (in the sense 'sting, afflict'): from L. *stimulat-*, *stimulare* 'urge, goad'.

**stimulus** /'stɪmjʊləs/ ● n. (pl. **stimuli** /-lʌɪ, -liː/) **1** a thing that evokes a specific functional reaction in an organ or tissue. **2** something that promotes activity, interest, or enthusiasm.
– ORIGIN C17: from L., 'goad, spur, incentive'.

**sting** ● n. **1** a small sharp-pointed organ of an insect, plant, etc. capable of inflicting a painful wound by injecting poison. **2** a wound from such an organ. **3** a sharp tingling sensation or hurtful effect. **4** informal a carefully planned undercover operation. ● v. (past and past part. **stung**) **1** wound with a sting. **2** produce a stinging sensation. ➤hurt; upset. ➤(**sting someone into**) goad someone into. **3** informal swindle or exorbitantly overcharge.
– PHRASES **sting in the tail** an unexpected and unpleasant end to something.
– DERIVATIVES **stinger** n. **stinging** adj. **stingingly** adv. **stingless** adj.
– ORIGIN OE *sting* (n.), *stingan* (v.), of Gmc origin.

**stingaree** /ˌstɪŋgə'riː, 'stɪŋgəriː/ ● n. a cinnamon-brown stingray occurring in shallow Australian waters. [*Urolophus testaceus.*] ➤US & Austral./NZ informal any stingray.
– ORIGIN C19: alt. of **STINGRAY**.

**stinging nettle** ● n. a nettle covered in stinging hairs. [*Urtica dioica* and related species.]

**stingray** ● n. a marine ray with a long poisonous serrated spine at the base of the tail. [Families Dasyatidae and Urolophidae: several species.]

**stingy** /'stɪn(d)ʒi/ ● adj. (**-ier**, **-iest**) informal mean; ungenerous.
– DERIVATIVES **stingily** adv. **stinginess** n.
– ORIGIN C17: perh. a dial. var. of **STING** + **-Y¹**.

**stink** ● v. (past **stank** or **stunk**; past part. **stunk**) **1** have a strong unpleasant smell. ➤(**stink a place out**) fill a place with such a smell. **2** informal be contemptible or scandalous. ➤(**stink of**) be highly suggestive of (something disapproved of). ● n. **1** a strong, unpleasant smell. **2** informal a row or fuss.
– PHRASES **like stink** informal extremely hard or intensely.
– DERIVATIVES **stinky** adj. (informal).
– ORIGIN OE *stincan*, of W. Gmc origin; rel. to **STENCH**.

**stink bomb** ● n. a small container holding a sulphurous

compound that is released when the container is broken, emitting a very unpleasant smell.

**stink bug** • **n.** a shield bug which emits a foul smell when handled or molested.

**stinker** • **n.** informal **1** a person or thing that stinks. **2** a contemptible or very unpleasant person or thing. **3** a difficult task.

**stinkhorn** • **n.** a fungus with a rounded greenish-brown gelatinous head that turns into a foul-smelling slime containing the spores. [Family Phallaceae: many species.]

**stinking** • **adj. 1** foul-smelling. **2** informal contemptible or very unpleasant. • **adv.** informal extremely: *stinking rich.*
– DERIVATIVES **stinkingly** adv.

**stinko** • **adj.** informal extremely drunk.

**stinkpot** • **n. 1** informal, chiefly US a contemptible or foul-smelling person or thing. **2** an American freshwater turtle with a domed shell, producing a strong unpleasant smell when disturbed. [*Kinosternon odoratum*.]

**stinkweed** • **n.** a foul-smelling plant, e.g. jimson weed.

**stinkwood** • **n.** a tree that yields wood with an unpleasant odour. [*Ocotea bullata* (S. Africa) and other species.]

**stint**[1] • **v.** [often with neg.] be restrictive or ungenerous towards or in the supply of. ➤(**stint on**) be restrictive or frugal in acquiring or providing: *he doesn't stint on wining and dining.* • **n. 1** an allotted period of work. **2** limitation of supply or effort.
– ORIGIN OE *styntan* 'make blunt', of Gmc origin; rel. to **STUNT**[1].

**stint**[2] • **n.** a very small short-legged northern sandpiper. [*Calidris minuta* (**little stint**) and related species.]
– ORIGIN ME: of unknown origin.

**stipe** /stʌɪp/ • **n.** Botany a stalk or stem, especially of a seaweed, fungus, or fern frond.
– ORIGIN C18: from Fr., from L. *stipes* (see **STIPES**).

**stipend** /ˈstʌɪpɛnd/ • **n.** a fixed regular sum paid as a salary or as expenses to a clergyman, teacher, or public official.
– ORIGIN ME: from OFr. *stipendie* or L. *stipendium*, from *stips* 'wages' + *pendere* 'to pay'.

**stipendiary** /stʌɪˈpɛndɪəri, stɪ-/ • **adj. 1** receiving a stipend; working for pay rather than voluntarily. **2** of, relating to, or of the nature of a stipend. • **n.** (pl. **-ies**) a person receiving a stipend.

**stipes** /ˈstʌɪpiːz/ • **n.** (pl. **stipites** /ˈstɪpɪtiːz/) **1** Zoology a part or organ resembling a stalk, especially the second joint of the maxilla of an insect. **2** Botany more technical term for **STIPE**.
– DERIVATIVES **stipitate** adj. (Botany).
– ORIGIN C18: from L., lit. 'log, tree trunk'.

**stipple** • **v. 1** (in drawing, painting, or engraving) mark (a surface) with numerous small dots or specks. **2** produce a decorative effect on (paint or other material) by roughening its surface when wet. • **n.** the process, technique, or effect of stippling.
– DERIVATIVES **stippler** n. **stippling** n.
– ORIGIN C17: from Du. *stippelen*, frequentative of *stippen* 'to prick', from *stip* 'a point'.

**stipulate**[1] /ˈstɪpjʊleɪt/ • **v.** demand or specify as part of a bargain or agreement.
– DERIVATIVES **stipulation** n. **stipulator** n.
– ORIGIN C17: from L. *stipulat-*, *stipulari* 'demand as a formal promise'.

**stipulate**[2] /ˈstɪpjʊlət/ • **adj.** Botany having stipules.
– ORIGIN C18: from L. *stipula* (see **STIPULE**) + **-ATE**[2].

**stipule** /ˈstɪpjuːl/ • **n.** Botany a small leaf-like appendage to a leaf, typically borne in pairs at the base of the leaf stalk.
– DERIVATIVES **stipular** adj.
– ORIGIN C18: from Fr. *stipule* or L. *stipula* 'straw'.

**stir**[1] • **v.** (**stirred**, **stirring**) **1** move an implement round and round in (a liquid or other substance) in order to mix it thoroughly. **2** move or cause to move slightly. ➤wake or rise from sleep. ➤begin or cause to begin to be active. **3** arouse strong feeling in. ➤arouse or prompt (a feeling or memory). **4** Brit. informal deliberately cause trouble by spreading rumours or gossip. • **n. 1** an act or an instance of stirring or being stirred. **2** a disturbance or commotion.
– DERIVATIVES **stirrer** n. **stirring** adj. & n. **stirringly** adv.
– ORIGIN OE *styrian*, of Gmc origin.

**stir**[2] • **n.** informal prison.
– ORIGIN C19: perh. from Romany *sturbin* 'jail'.

**stirabout** • **n.** chiefly Irish porridge made by stirring oatmeal in boiling water or milk.

**stir-crazy** • **adj.** informal, chiefly N. Amer. psychologically disturbed as a result of being confined or imprisoned.

**stir-fry** • **v.** fry rapidly over a high heat while stirring briskly. • **n.** a stir-fried dish.
– DERIVATIVES **stir-fried** adj.

**stirk** /stəːk/ • **n.** dialect a yearling bullock or heifer.
– ORIGIN OE *stirc*, perh. from *stēor* 'steer' + *-oc* (see **-OCK**).

**Stirling engine** • **n.** a machine used to provide power or refrigeration which operates on a closed cycle in which a working fluid is cyclically compressed and expanded at different temperatures.
– ORIGIN named after the C19 Sc. engineer Robert *Stirling*.

**stirrup** • **n. 1** each of a pair of devices attached at either side of a horse's saddle, in the form of a loop with a flat base to support the rider's foot. **2** (**lithotomy stirrups**) a pair of metal supports for the ankles used during gynaecological examinations and childbirth (originally used in lithotomy). **3** another term for **STAPES**.
– ORIGIN OE *stigrāp*, from the Gmc base of obs. *sty* 'climb' + **ROPE**.

**stirrup cup** • **n.** an alcoholic drink offered to a person on horseback who is about to depart.

**stirrup pants** • **pl. n.** a pair of stretch trousers having a band of elastic at the bottom of each leg which passes under the arch of the foot.

**stirrup pump** • **n.** chiefly historical a portable hand-operated water pump with a footrest resembling a stirrup, used to extinguish small fires.

**stishovite** /ˈstɪʃəvʌɪt/ • **n.** a dense form of silica produced by very high pressures, e.g. in meteorite craters.
– ORIGIN 1960s: from the name of the Russ. chemist Sergei M. *Stishov* + **-ITE**[1].

**stitch** • **n. 1** a loop of thread or yarn resulting from a single pass or movement of the needle in sewing, knitting, or crocheting. ➤a method of sewing, knitting, or crocheting producing a particular pattern: *an embroidery stitch.* **2** [usu. with neg.] informal the smallest item of clothing: *swimming around with not a stitch on.* **3** a sudden sharp pain in the side of the body, caused by strenuous exercise. • **v. 1** make or mend with stitches; apply a stitch or stitches to. **2** (**stitch someone up**) Brit. informal manipulate a situation to someone's disadvantage. ➤(**stitch something up**) manipulate a situation or secure a deal to one's own advantage.
– PHRASES **in stitches** informal laughing uncontrollably.
– DERIVATIVES **stitcher** n. **stitchery** n. **stitching** n.
– ORIGIN OE *stice*, of Gmc origin; rel. to **STICK**[2].

**stitchwort** • **n.** a plant with a slender stem and white starry flowers, formerly thought to cure a stitch in the side. [Genus *Stellaria*: several species.]

**stiver** /ˈstʌɪvə/ • **n. 1** a small coin formerly used in the Netherlands, equal to one twentieth of a guilder. **2** [with neg.] archaic a very small sum or insignificant amount.
– ORIGIN from Du. *stuiver*; prob. rel. to **STUB**.

**STM** • **abbrev.** scanning tunnelling microscope.

**stoa** /ˈstəʊə/ • **n.** (in ancient Greek architecture) a portico or roofed colonnade.
– ORIGIN from Gk.

**stoat** • **n.** a small carnivorous mammal of the weasel family with chestnut fur (which in northern areas turns white in winter), white underparts, and a black-tipped tail. [*Mustela erminea*.]
– ORIGIN ME: of unknown origin.

**stob** /stɒb/ • **n.** dialect, chiefly Scottish & US **1** a broken branch or a stump. **2** a stake used for fencing.
– ORIGIN ME: var. of **STUB**.

**stochastic** /stəˈkastɪk/ • **adj.** having a random probability distribution or pattern that can be analysed statistically but not predicted precisely.
– DERIVATIVES **stochastically** adv.
– ORIGIN C17: from Gk *stokhastikos*, from *stokhazesthai*

'aim at, guess', from *stokhos* 'aim'.

**stock** • **n.** **1** a supply of goods or materials available for sale or use. **2** farm animals bred and kept for their meat or milk; livestock. **3** the capital raised by a company through the issue and subscription of shares. ➤(usu. **stocks**) a portion of this as held by an individual or group as an investment. ➤securities issued by the government in fixed units with a fixed rate of interest. **4** water in which bones, meat, fish, or vegetables have been slowly simmered. ➤the raw material from which a specified commodity can be manufactured. **5** a person's ancestry or line of descent. ➤a breed, variety, or population of an animal or plant. **6** the trunk or woody stem of a tree or shrub, especially one into which a graft (scion) is inserted. ➤the perennial part of a herbaceous plant, especially a rhizome. **7** a plant cultivated for its fragrant flowers, typically lilac, pink, or white. [Genus *Matthiola*: several species.] **8** (**the stocks**) [treated as sing. or pl.] historical an instrument of punishment consisting of a wooden structure with holes for securing a person's feet and hands, in which criminals were locked and exposed to public ridicule or assault. **9** the part of a rifle or other firearm to which the barrel and firing mechanism are attached. ➤the crossbar of an anchor. ➤the handle of a whip, fishing rod, etc. **10** a band of white material tied like a cravat and worn as a part of formal horse-riding dress. ➤a piece of black material worn under a clerical collar. **11** (**stocks**) a frame used to support a ship or boat when out of water. • **adj.** **1** usually kept in stock and thus regularly available for sale. **2** constantly recurring; common or conventional: *the stock characters in every cowboy film.* • **v.** **1** have or keep a stock of. ➤provide or fill with a stock of something. ➤(**stock up**) amass stocks of something. **2** fit (a rifle or other firearm) with a stock.
– PHRASES **in** (or **out of**) **stock** available (or unavailable) for immediate sale or use. **on the stocks** in construction or preparation. **put stock in** have a specified amount of belief or faith in. **take stock** make an overall assessment of a particular situation.
– DERIVATIVES **stockless** adj.
– ORIGIN OE *stoc(c)* 'trunk, block of wood, post', of Gmc origin.

**stockade** • **n.** **1** a barrier or enclosure formed from upright wooden posts or stakes. **2** chiefly N. Amer. a military prison. • **v.** enclose with a stockade.
– DERIVATIVES **stockaded** adj.
– ORIGIN C17: shortening of obs. Fr. *estocade*, alt. of *estacade*, from Sp. *estacada*, from the Gmc base of **STAKE**[1].

**stockbreeder** • **n.** a farmer who breeds livestock.
– DERIVATIVES **stockbreeding** n.

**stockbroker** • **n.** a broker who buys and sells securities on a stock exchange on behalf of clients.
– DERIVATIVES **stockbrokerage** n. **stockbroking** n.

**stockbroker belt** • **n.** Brit. an affluent residential area outside a large city.

**stock car** • **n.** **1** an ordinary car that has been strengthened for use in a type of race in which competing cars collide with each other. **2** N. Amer. a railway wagon for transporting livestock.

**stock company** • **n.** N. Amer. a repertory company that is largely based in one theatre.

**stock cube** • **n.** a cube of concentrated dehydrated meat, vegetable, or fish stock for use in cooking.

**stock dove** • **n.** a small grey pigeon nesting in holes in trees, resembling a wood pigeon. [*Columba oenas*.]

**stocker** • **n.** **1** N. Amer. a farm animal destined for slaughter but kept until matured or fattened. **2** a person who stocks the shelves of a shop or supermarket. **3** N. Amer. informal a stock car.

**stock exchange** • **n.** a market in which securities are bought and sold.

**stockfeed** • **n.** food for livestock.

**stockfish** • **n.** (pl. same or **-fishes**) **1** a commercially valuable hake of coastal waters of southern Africa. [*Merluccius capensis*.] **2** cod or a similar fish split and dried in the open air without salt.
– ORIGIN ME: from Mid. Low Ger., MDu. *stokvisch*, of unknown origin.

**stockholder** • **n.** **1** chiefly N. Amer. a shareholder. **2** a holder of supplies for manufacturers.
– DERIVATIVES **stockholding** n.

**stockinet** (also **stockinette**) • **n.** a soft, loosely knitted stretch fabric, formerly used for making underwear and now used for cleaning, wrapping, or bandaging.
– ORIGIN C18: prob. an alt. of *stocking-net*.

**stocking** • **n.** **1** a woman's garment that fits closely over the foot and leg, typically made of fine knitted nylon yarn, held up by suspenders or an elasticated strip at the upper thigh. ➤a cylindrical bandage or other medical covering for the leg resembling a stocking. **2** US or archaic a long sock worn by men. **3** a real or ornamental stocking hung up by children on Christmas Eve for Father Christmas to fill with presents. **4** a white marking of the lower part of a horse's leg.
– DERIVATIVES **stockinged** adj. **stockingless** adj.
– ORIGIN C16: from **STOCK** in the dial. sense 'stocking' + **-ING**[1].

**stocking cap** • **n.** a knitted conical hat with a long tapered end that hangs down.

**stocking filler** (N. Amer. **stocking stuffer**) • **n.** Brit. a small present for putting in a Christmas stocking.

**stocking mask** • **n.** a nylon stocking pulled over the face to disguise the features, used by criminals.

**stocking stitch** • **n.** a knitting stitch consisting of alternate rows of plain and purl stitch.

**stock-in-trade** • **n.** **1** the typical subject or commodity a person, company, or profession uses or deals in. **2** the type of stock kept regularly by a shop.

**stockist** • **n.** Brit. a retailer that stocks goods of a particular type for sale.

**stockjobber** • **n.** **1** Brit. another term for **JOBBER** (in sense 1). **2** N. Amer. derogatory a stockbroker.
– DERIVATIVES **stockjobbing** n.

**stockman** • **n.** (pl. **-men**) **1** a person who looks after livestock. **2** US an owner of livestock.

**stock market** • **n.** a stock exchange.

**stock option** • **n.** another term for **SHARE OPTION**.

**stockpile** • **n.** a large accumulated stock of goods or materials. • **v.** accumulate a large stock of.
– DERIVATIVES **stockpiler** n.

**stockpot** • **n.** a pot in which stock is prepared by long, slow cooking.

**stockroom** • **n.** a room in which stocks of goods or materials are stored.

**stock split** • **n.** N. Amer. an issue of new shares in a company to existing shareholders in proportion to their current holdings.

**stock-still** • **adv.** without any movement.

**stocktaking** • **n.** the action or process of recording the amount of stock held by a business.
– DERIVATIVES **stocktake** n. **stocktaker** n.

**stocky** • **adj.** (**-ier**, **-iest**) (especially of a person) short and sturdy.
– DERIVATIVES **stockily** adv. **stockiness** n.

**stockyard** • **n.** N. Amer. a large yard containing pens and sheds in which livestock is kept and sorted.

**stodge** • **n.** informal, chiefly Brit. **1** food that is heavy, filling, and high in carbohydrates. **2** dull and uninspired material or work.
– DERIVATIVES **stodgily** adv. **stodginess** n. **stodgy** adj.
– ORIGIN C17 (as v. in the sense 'stuff to stretching point'): suggested by **STUFF** and **PODGE**.

**stoep** /stu:p/ • **n.** S. African a terraced veranda in front of a house.
– ORIGIN Afrik., from Du.; rel. to **STEP**.

**stogy** /'stəʊgi/ (also **stogie**) • **n.** (pl. **-ies**) N. Amer. a long, thin, cheap cigar.
– ORIGIN C19 (orig. as *stoga*): short for *Conestoga* in Pennsylvania.

**stoic** /'stəʊɪk/ • **n.** **1** a stoical person. **2** (**Stoic**) a member of the ancient philosophical school of Stoicism. • **adj.** **1** stoical. **2** (**Stoic**) of or belonging to the Stoics or Stoicism.

– ORIGIN ME: via L. from Gk *stōïkos*, from **STOA** (with ref. to the teaching of the ancient Gk philosopher Zeno, in the *Stoa Poikilē* or Painted Porch, at Athens).

**stoical** /ˈstəʊɪk(ə)l/ ● **adj.** enduring pain and hardship without showing one's feelings or complaining.
– DERIVATIVES **stoically** adv.

**stoichiometry** /ˌstɔɪkɪˈɒmɪtri/ ● **n.** Chemistry the relationship between the relative quantities of substances taking part in a reaction or forming a compound, typically a ratio of whole integers.
– DERIVATIVES **stoichiometric** adj. **stoichiometrically** adv.
– ORIGIN C19: from Gk *stoikheion* 'element' + **-METRY**.

**stoicism** /ˈstəʊɪsɪz(ə)m/ ● **n. 1** stoical behaviour. **2** (**Stoicism**) an ancient Greek school of philosophy which taught that it is wise to remain indifferent to the vicissitudes of fortune and to pleasure and pain.

**stoke** ● **v. 1** add coal to (a fire, furnace, etc.). **2** encourage or incite (a strong emotion). **3** (**stoke up**) informal consume a large quantity of food to give one energy.
– ORIGIN C17: back-form. from **STOKER**.

**stokehold** ● **n.** a compartment in a steamship in which the boilers and furnace are housed.

**stokehole** ● **n.** a space in front of a furnace in which a stoker works.

**stoker** ● **n. 1** a person who tends the furnace on a steamship or steam train. **2** a mechanical device for supplying fuel to a furnace.
– ORIGIN C17: from Du., from *stoken* 'stoke (a furnace)', from MDu. *stoken* 'push, poke'; rel. to **STICK**[1].

**stokes** (abbrev.: **St**) ● **n.** (pl. same) Physics the cgs unit of kinematic viscosity, corresponding to a dynamic viscosity of 1 poise and a density of 1 gram per cubic centimetre and equivalent to $10^{-4}$ square metres per second.
– ORIGIN C20: from the name of the Brit. physicist Sir George *Stokes*.

**STOL** ● **abbrev.** Aeronautics short take-off and landing.

**stole**[1] ● **n. 1** a woman's long scarf or shawl, worn loosely over the shoulders. **2** a priest's vestment worn over the shoulders and hanging down to the knee or below.
– ORIGIN OE, via L. from Gk *stolē* 'clothing', from *stellein* 'array'.

**stole**[2] past of **STEAL**.

**stolen** past participle of **STEAL**.

**stolen generation** ● **n.** Austral. the Aboriginal people forcibly removed from their families as children between the 1900s and the 1960s, to be brought up by white foster families or in institutions.

**stolid** ● **adj.** calm, dependable, and showing little emotion or animation.
– DERIVATIVES **stolidity** n. **stolidly** adv. **stolidness** n.
– ORIGIN C16: from obs. Fr. *stolide* or L. *stolidus* (perh. rel. to *stultus* 'foolish').

**stollen** /ˈstɒlən, ˈʃtɒ-/ ● **n.** a rich German fruit and nut loaf.
– ORIGIN from Ger. *Stollen*.

**stolon** /ˈstəʊlɒn/ ● **n. 1** Botany a creeping horizontal stem or runner that takes root at several points to form new plants. **2** Zoology a branched stem-like structure attaching a colony of hydroids to the substrate.
– DERIVATIVES **stolonate** adj. **stoloniferous** adj.
– ORIGIN C17: from L. *stolo*, *stolon-* 'shoot, scion'.

**stoma** /ˈstəʊmə/ ● **n.** (pl. **stomas** or **stomata** /-mətə/) **1** Botany any of the minute pores in the epidermis of the leaf or stem of a plant, allowing movement of gases in and out of the intercellular spaces. **2** Zoology a small mouth-like opening in some lower animals. **3** Medicine an artificial opening made into a hollow organ, especially one on the surface of the body leading to the gut or trachea.
– DERIVATIVES **stomal** adj.
– ORIGIN C17: mod. L., from Gk *stoma* 'mouth'.

**stomach** ● **n. 1** an internal organ in which the first part of digestion occurs, being (in humans and many mammals) a pear-shaped enlargement of the alimentary canal linking the oesophagus to the small intestine. ➤ each of four such organs in a ruminant. **2** the abdominal area of the body; the belly. **3** [usu. with neg.] an appetite or desire for something. ● **v. 1** [usu. with neg.] consume (food or drink) without feeling sick. **2** endure or accept.
– PHRASES **a strong stomach** an ability to see or do unpleasant things without feeling sick or squeamish.
– DERIVATIVES **stomachful** n. (pl. **-fuls**).
– ORIGIN ME: from OFr. *estomac*, *stomaque*, via L. from Gk *stomakhos* 'gullet'.

**stomacher** ● **n.** historical a V-shaped ornamental panel worn over the chest and stomach by men and women in the 16th century, later only by women.
– ORIGIN ME: prob. a shortening of OFr. *estomachier*, from *estomac* (see **STOMACH**).

**stomachic** /stəˈmakɪk/ dated ● **adj.** promoting the appetite or assisting digestion. ● **n.** a stomachic medicine.

**stomata** plural form of **STOMA**.

**stomate** /ˈstəʊmeɪt/ ● **n.** Botany another term for **STOMA**.
– DERIVATIVES **stomatal** adj.
– ORIGIN C19: appar. an Engl. sing. of **STOMATA**.

**stomatitis** /ˌstəʊməˈtʌɪtɪs, ˌstɒ-/ ● **n.** Medicine inflammation of the mucous membrane of the mouth.
– ORIGIN C19: from Gk *stoma* 'mouth' + **-ITIS**.

**stomp** ● **v. 1** tread heavily and noisily, typically in order to show anger. **2** dance with heavy stamping steps. ● **n.** a tune or dance with a fast tempo and a heavy beat.
– DERIVATIVES **stomper** n. **stomping** adj. **stompy** adj.
– ORIGIN C19 (orig. US dial.): var. of **STAMP**.

**stomping ground** ● **n.** N. Amer. another term for **STAMPING GROUND**.

**stone** ● **n. 1** hard, solid non-metallic mineral matter of which rock is made. ➤ a small piece of stone found on the ground. ➤ a piece of stone shaped for a purpose, especially one of commemoration or demarcation. ➤ Astronomy a meteorite made of rock, as opposed to metal. **2** a gem. **3** Medicine a gallstone or kidney stone; a calculus. **4** a hard seed in a cherry, plum, peach, etc. **5** (pl. same) Brit. a unit of weight equal to 14 lb (6.35 kg). **6** a whitish or brownish-grey colour. ● **v. 1** throw stones at in order to injure or kill. **2** remove the stone from (a fruit). **3** build, face, or pave with stone. ● **adv.** extremely or totally: *stone cold.*
– PHRASES **leave no stone unturned** try every possible course of action in order to achieve something. **a stone's throw** a short distance.
– DERIVATIVES **stoneless** adj.
– ORIGIN OE *stān* (n.), of Gmc origin.

**Stone Age** ● **n.** a prehistoric period when weapons and tools were made of stone, preceding the Bronze Age.

**stonechat** ● **n.** a small heathland bird of the thrush family, with a call like two stones being knocked together. [*Saxicola torquata* and related species.]

**stone circle** ● **n.** a megalithic monument consisting of stones or menhirs arranged more or less in a circle.

**stonecrop** ● **n.** a small fleshy-leaved plant which typically has star-shaped yellow or white flowers and grows among rocks or on walls. [Genus *Sedum*: many species.]

**stone curlew** ● **n.** a large-eyed plover-like bird with mottled brownish plumage, inhabiting open stony or sandy country. [*Burhinus oedicnemus* and other species.]

**stoned** ● **adj.** informal under the influence of drugs, especially cannabis, or alcohol.

**stone face** ● **n.** informal an emotionless expression.
– DERIVATIVES **stone-faced** adj.

**stonefish** ● **n.** (pl. same or **-fishes**) a tropical Indo-Pacific fish of bizarre appearance which rests motionless in the sand with its venomous dorsal spines projecting. [*Synanceia verrucosa* and other species.]

**stonefly** ● **n.** (pl. **-flies**) a slender insect with transparent membranous wings, the larvae of which live in clean running water. [Order Plecoptera: many families.]

**stone fruit** ● **n.** a fruit with flesh or pulp enclosing a stone, such as a peach, plum, or cherry.

**stoneground** ● **adj.** (of flour) ground with millstones.

**stonemason** ● **n.** a person who cuts, prepares, and builds with stone.
– DERIVATIVES **stonemasonry** n.

**stone pine** ● **n.** an umbrella-shaped southern European pine tree with seeds that are eaten as pine nuts. [*Pinus pinea*.]

**stonewall** ● **v. 1** delay or block by refusing to answer

questions or by giving evasive replies, especially in politics. **2** Cricket bat extremely defensively.
– DERIVATIVES **stonewaller** n.

**stoneware** ● n. a type of pottery which is impermeable and partly vitrified but opaque.

**stonewashed** (also **stonewash**) ● adj. (of a garment or fabric, especially denim) washed with abrasives to produce a worn or faded appearance.

**stonework** ● n. **1** the parts of a building that are made of stone. **2** the work of a mason.
– DERIVATIVES **stoneworker** n.

**stonewort** ● n. a freshwater plant related to green algae, with whorls of slender leaves sometimes encrusted with chalky deposits. [*Chara* and other genera.]

**stonk** military slang ● n. a concentrated artillery bombardment. ● v. bombard with concentrated artillery fire.
– ORIGIN 1940s: said to be formed from elements of the artillery term *Standard Regimental Concentration*.

**stonker** ● n. Brit. informal something very large or impressive of its kind.
– DERIVATIVES **stonking** adj.

**stonkered** ● adj. Austral./NZ informal utterly exhausted or defeated. ➤ drunk.
– ORIGIN 1920s: from Scots and north. Engl. *stonk* 'game of marbles', perh. of imitative origin.

**stony** ● adj. (**-ier**, **-iest**) **1** full of stones. **2** of or resembling stone. **3** cold and unfeeling.
– PHRASES **fall on stony ground** (of words or a suggestion) be ignored or badly received. [with biblical ref. to the parable of the sower (Matt. 13:5).]
– DERIVATIVES **stonily** adv. **stoniness** n.

**stony broke** ● adj. Brit. informal entirely without money.

**stood** past and past participle of STAND.

**stooge** ● n. **1** derogatory a subordinate used by another to do routine or unpleasant work. **2** a performer whose act involves being the butt of a comedian's jokes. ● v. **1** informal move about aimlessly. **2** be a comedian's stooge.
– ORIGIN C20: of unknown origin.

**stook** /stʊk, stuːk/ Brit. ● n. a group of sheaves of grain stood on end in a field. ● v. arrange in stooks.
– ORIGIN ME: from or rel. to Middle Low Ger. *stūke*.

**stool** ● n. **1** a seat without a back or arms, typically resting on three or four legs or on a single pedestal. **2** chiefly Medicine a piece of faeces. **3** a root or stump of a tree or plant from which shoots spring. **4** US a decoy bird in hunting. ● v. throw up shoots from the root. ➤ cut back (a plant) to or near ground level to induce new growth.
– PHRASES **fall between two stools** Brit. fail to be or take either of two satisfactory alternatives.
– ORIGIN OE, of Gmc origin; rel. to STAND.

**stoolball** ● n. a team game resembling cricket, with a board (originally a stool) as a wicket.

**stoolie** ● n. N. Amer. informal short for STOOL PIGEON.

**stool pigeon** ● n. **1** a police informer. **2** a person acting as a decoy.
– ORIGIN C19: so named from the original use of a pigeon fixed to a stool as a decoy.

**stoop**[1] ● v. **1** bend one's head or body forwards and downwards. ➤ have the head and shoulders habitually bent forwards. **2** lower one's moral standards so far as to do something reprehensible. **3** (of a bird of prey) swoop down on a quarry. ● n. **1** a stooping posture. **2** the downward swoop of a bird of prey.
– ORIGIN OE *stūpian* (v.), of Gmc origin; rel. to STEEP[1].

**stoop**[2] ● n. N. Amer. a porch with steps in front of a house or other building.
– ORIGIN C18: from Du. *stoep* (see STOEP).

**stoor** ● n. variant of STOUR.

**stooshie** /ˈstʊʃi/ (also **stushie**) ● n. Scottish informal a row or fracas.
– ORIGIN C19: of unknown origin.

**stop** ● v. (**stopped**, **stopping**) **1** come or cause to come to an end. ➤ discontinue an action, practice, or habit. **2** prevent from happening or from doing something. ➤ instruct a bank to withhold payment on (a cheque). ➤ refuse to supply as usual. ➤ Boxing defeat (an opponent) by a knockout. **3** cease or cause to cease moving or operating. ➤ (of a bus or train) call at a designated place to pick up or set down passengers. ➤ Brit. informal stay somewhere for a short time. **4** block or close up (a hole or leak). ➤ plug the upper end of (an organ pipe), giving a note an octave lower. **5** obtain the required pitch from (the string of a violin or similar instrument) by pressing at the appropriate point with the finger. ● n. **1** an act of stopping. ➤ a place designated for a bus or train to stop. **2** an object or part of a mechanism which prevents movement. ➤ Bridge a high card that prevents the opponents from establishing a particular suit. ➤ Nautical a stopper. **3** Phonetics a consonant produced with complete closure of the vocal tract. **4** a set of organ pipes of a particular tone and range of pitch. ➤ (also **stop knob**) a knob, lever, etc. in an organ or harpsichord which brings into play a set of pipes or strings of a particular tone and range of pitch. **5** Photography the effective diameter of a lens. ➤ a device for reducing this. ➤ a unit of change of relative aperture or exposure.
– PHRASES **pull out all the stops** make a very great effort to achieve something. [with ref. to the stops of an organ.] **put a stop to** cause to end. **stop dead** (or **short**) suddenly cease moving, speaking, or acting. **stop payment** instruct a bank to withhold payment on a cheque.
– PHRASAL VERBS **stop by** (or **in**) call briefly as a visitor. **stop something down** Photography reduce the aperture of a lens with a diaphragm. **stop off** (or **over**) pay a short visit en route to one's destination. **stop out** Brit. informal stay out later than expected. **stop something out** cover an area that is not to be printed or etched. **stop up** Brit. informal refrain from going to bed.
– DERIVATIVES **stoppable** adj.
– ORIGIN OE (*for*)*stoppian* 'block up (an aperture)', of W. Gmc origin, from late L. *stuppare* 'to stuff'.

**stopbank** ● n. Austral./NZ an embankment built to prevent a river flooding.

**stopcock** ● n. an externally operated valve regulating the flow of a liquid or gas through a pipe.

**stope** /stəʊp/ ● n. a step-like working in a mine. ● v. [usu. as noun **stoping**] cut a series of stopes in.
– ORIGIN C18: appar. rel. to STEP.

**stopgap** ● n. a temporary solution or substitute.

**stop-go** ● n. Brit. the alternate restriction and stimulation of economic demand by a government.

**stop knob** ● n. see STOP sense 4.

**stop light** ● n. a red traffic signal.

**stop list** ● n. **1** a list of people with whom members of an association are forbidden to do business. **2** a list of words automatically omitted from a computer-generated concordance or index.

**stop-motion** ● n. a technique of cinematographic animation whereby the camera is repeatedly stopped and started to give the impression of movement.

**stopover** ● n. a break in a journey.

**stoppage** ● n. **1** an instance of stopping or being stopped. ➤ an instance of industrial action. **2** a blockage. **3** (**stoppages**) Brit. deductions from wages by an employer for the payment of tax, National Insurance, etc.

**stoppage time** ● n. another term for INJURY TIME.

**stopper** ● n. **1** a plug for sealing a hole, especially in the neck of a bottle. **2** (in soccer or American football) a player whose function is to block attacks on goal from the middle of the field. **3** Baseball a pitcher who prevents opponents from scoring highly. **4** (in sailing or climbing) a rope or clamp for preventing a rope or cable from being run out. ● v. [usu. as adj. **stoppered**] seal with a stopper.
– PHRASES **put a** (or **the**) **stopper on** informal prevent.

**stopple** N. Amer. ● n. a stopper or plug. ● v. seal with a stopper.
– ORIGIN ME: partly a shortening of OFr. *estouppail* 'bung', reinforced by STOP.

**stop press** ● n. Brit. late news inserted in a newspaper or periodical either just before printing or after printing has begun.

**stop volley** ● n. Tennis a checked volley played close to the net, dropping the ball dead on the other side.

**stopwatch** ● n. a special watch with buttons that start, stop, and then zero the display, used to time races.

**storage** ● **n. 1** the action of storing. **2** space available for storing. **3** a charge for warehouse storage.

**storage battery** (also **storage cell**) ● **n.** a battery (or cell) used for storing electrical energy.

**storage heater** ● **n.** Brit. an electric heater that accumulates heat during the night (when electricity is cheaper) and releases it during the day.

**storax** /'stɔːraks/ (also **styrax**) ● **n. 1** a fragrant gum resin obtained from a tree, used in medicine, perfumery, and incense. ➤ (**Levant** or **liquid storax**) liquidambar. **2** the tree yielding storax, or one of its relatives, with clusters of white flowers. [*Styrax officinalis* (E. Mediterranean region) and related species.]
– ORIGIN ME: from L., from a var. of Gk *sturax*.

**store** ● **n. 1** a quantity or supply kept for use as needed. ➤ (**stores**) supplies of equipment and food kept for use by members of an army, navy, or other institution. **2** a place where things are kept for future use or sale. ➤ chiefly N. Amer. a shop. ➤ Brit. a large shop selling different types of goods. **3** Brit. a computer memory. **4** a sheep, steer, cow, or pig acquired or kept for fattening. ● **v. 1** keep or accumulate for future use. **2** retain or enter (information) for future electronic retrieval. **3** (**be stored with**) have a useful supply of.
– PHRASES **in store** about to happen. **set** (or **lay** or **put**) **store by** (or **on**) consider to be of a particular degree of importance: *she set much store by privacy.*
– DERIVATIVES **storable** adj. **storer** n.
– ORIGIN ME: shortening of OFr. *estore* (n.), *estorer* (v.), from L. *instaurare* 'renew'; cf. **RESTORE**.

**store card** ● **n.** a credit card that can be used only in one store or chain of stores.

**storefront** ● **n.** chiefly N. Amer. **1** another term for **SHOPFRONT**. **2** a room or rooms facing the street on the ground floor of a commercial building, typically used as a shop.

**storehouse** ● **n. 1** a building used for storing goods. **2** a repository: *an enormous storehouse of facts.*

**storekeeper** ● **n. 1** a person responsible for stored goods. **2** N. Amer. a shopkeeper.

**storeman** ● **n.** (pl. **-men**) Brit. a man responsible for stored goods.

**storeroom** ● **n.** a room in which items are stored.

**storey** (N. Amer. also **story**) ● **n.** (pl. **-eys** or **-ies**) a part of a building comprising all the rooms that are on the same level.
– DERIVATIVES **-storeyed** (N. Amer. also **-storied**) adj.
– ORIGIN ME: shortening of L. *historia* 'history', a special use in Anglo-Latin, perh. orig. denoting a tier of painted windows or sculptures representing a historical subject.

**storiated** /'stɔːrɪeɪtɪd/ ● **adj.** rare decorated with historical, legendary, or emblematic designs.
– DERIVATIVES **storiation** n.
– ORIGIN C19: cf. **HISTORIATED**.

**storied** ● **adj.** poetic/literary celebrated in or associated with stories or legends.

**stork** ● **n.** a very tall long-legged bird with a long heavy bill and typically white and black plumage. [*Ciconia ciconia* (**white stork**, Europe, nesting on buildings) and other species.]
– ORIGIN OE *storc*, of Gmc origin; prob. rel. to **STARK** (because of its rigid stance).

**storksbill** ● **n.** a plant related to the cranesbill, with small pink flowers and fruits that have long twisted beaks. [Genus *Erodium*.]

**storm** ● **n. 1** a violent disturbance of the atmosphere with strong winds and usually rain, thunder, lightning, or snow. **2** a sudden violent display of strong feeling. **3** a direct assault by troops. ● **v. 1** move angrily or forcefully in a specified direction. **2** (of troops) suddenly attack and capture (a place). **3** shout angrily. **4** (**it storms, it is storming**, etc.) be stormy.
– PHRASES **go down a storm** be enthusiastically received. **storm and stress** another term for **STURM UND DRANG**. **a storm in a teacup** Brit. great anger or excitement about a trivial matter. **take something by storm 1** capture a place by a sudden and violent attack. **2** have great and rapid success. —— **up a storm** chiefly N. Amer. perform the specified action with great enthusiasm and energy.
– DERIVATIVES **stormproof** adj.
– ORIGIN OE, of Gmc origin; prob. rel. to **STIR**[1].

**stormbound** ● **adj.** prevented by storms from starting or continuing a journey.

**storm cloud** ● **n. 1** a heavy, dark rain cloud. **2** (**storm clouds**) an ominous state of affairs.

**stormcock** ● **n.** dialect the mistle thrush.

**storm cone** ● **n.** (in the UK) a black conical object hoisted by coastguards as a gale warning.

**storm cuff** ● **n.** a tight-fitting inner cuff which excludes rain or wind from a coat.

**storm door** ● **n.** chiefly N. Amer. an additional outer door for protection in bad weather or winter.

**storm drain** (US **storm sewer**) ● **n.** a drain built to carry away excess water in times of heavy rain.

**stormer** ● **n.** Brit. informal a thing which is particularly impressive of its kind.
– DERIVATIVES **storming** adj.

**storm flap** ● **n.** a flap intended to protect an opening or fastening on a tent or coat from the effects of rain.

**storm glass** ● **n.** historical a sealed tube containing a liquid, the clarity of which was thought to change when storms approached.

**storm lantern** ● **n.** chiefly Brit. a hurricane lamp.

**storm petrel** ● **n.** a small petrel with blackish plumage, formerly believed to be a harbinger of bad weather. [*Hydrobates pelagicus* (NE Atlantic and Mediterranean) and other species.]

**storm sail** ● **n.** a sail of smaller size and stronger material than the corresponding one used ordinarily.

**storm sewer** ● **n.** US variant of **STORM DRAIN**.

**storm troops** ● **pl. n.** another term for **SHOCK TROOPS**.
– DERIVATIVES **storm trooper** n.

**storm window** ● **n.** chiefly N. Amer. an additional outer window for protection in bad weather or winter.

**stormy** ● **adj.** (**-ier, -iest**) **1** affected or disturbed by a storm. **2** full of angry or violent outbursts of feeling.
– DERIVATIVES **stormily** adv. **storminess** n.

**stormy petrel** ● **n. 1** dated term for **STORM PETREL**. **2** a person who delights in conflict or attracts controversy.

**story**[1] ● **n.** (pl. **-ies**) **1** an account of imaginary or real people and events told for entertainment. ➤ a storyline. **2** an account of past events, experiences, etc. ➤ an item of news. **3** informal a lie. **4** the commercial prospects or circumstances of a particular company: *profitable businesses with solid stories.*
– PHRASES **the same old story** a bad situation that is tediously familiar. **the story goes** it is said. **the story of one's life** informal a misfortune that one has experienced too often. **to cut** (or N. Amer. **make**) **a long story short** used to end an account of events quickly.
– ORIGIN ME: shortening of Anglo-Norman Fr. *estorie*, from L. *historia* (see **HISTORY**).

**story**[2] ● **n.** N. Amer. variant spelling of **STOREY**.

**storyboard** ● **n.** a sequence of drawings representing the shots planned for a film or television production.

**storybook** ● **n. 1** a book containing a story or stories for children. **2** [as modifier] idyllically perfect.

**story editor** ● **n.** an editor who advises on the content and form of film or television scripts.

**storyline** ● **n.** the plot of a novel, play, film, etc.

**stot** /staʊt, stɒt/ ● **v.** (**stotted, stotting**) Scottish **1** bounce or cause to bounce. **2** stagger or lurch.
– ORIGIN C16: of unknown origin.

**stotin** /stɒ'tiːn/ ● **n.** a monetary unit of Slovenia, equal to one hundredth of a tolar.
– ORIGIN from Slovene.

**stotinka** /stɒ'tɪŋkə/ ● **n.** (pl. **stotinki** /stɒ'tɪŋki/) a monetary unit of Bulgaria, equal to one hundredth of a lev.
– ORIGIN Bulgarian, lit. 'one hundredth'.

**stoup** /stuːp/ ● **n. 1** a basin for holy water in a church. **2** archaic a flagon or beaker.
– ORIGIN ME (in the sense 'pail, small cask'): from ON *staup*, of Gmc origin; rel. to **STEEP**[2].

**stour** /stʊə/ (also **stoor**) ● **n.** Scottish & N. English dust forming a cloud or deposited in a mass.

– DERIVATIVES **stoury** adj.
– ORIGIN ME: of uncertain origin.

**stoush** /staʊʃ/ Austral./NZ informal • **v.** hit; fight with. • **n.** a brawl or other fight.
– ORIGIN C19: of unknown origin.

**stout** • **adj. 1** rather fat or heavily built. **2** (of an object) sturdy and thick. **3** brave and determined. • **n.** a kind of strong, dark beer brewed with roasted malt or barley.
– DERIVATIVES **stoutish** adj. **stoutly** adv. **stoutness** n.
– ORIGIN ME: from Anglo-Norman Fr. and OFr. dial., of W. Gmc origin.

**stout-hearted** • **adj.** courageous or determined.
– DERIVATIVES **stout-heartedly** adv. **stout-heartedness** n.

**stove**[1] • **n. 1** an apparatus for cooking or heating that operates by burning fuel or using electricity. **2** Brit. a hothouse for plants. • **v. 1** heat (an object) in a stove so as to apply a desired coating. **2** Brit. force or raise (plants) in a hothouse.
– ORIGIN ME (in the sense 'sweating-room'): from MDu. or Middle Low Ger. *stove*; perh. rel. to **STEW**[1].

**stove**[2] past and past participle of **STAVE**.

**stove enamel** • **n.** Brit. a heatproof enamel produced by heat treatment in a stove.

**stovepipe** • **n.** a pipe taking the smoke and gases from a stove up through a roof or to a chimney.

**stovepipe hat** • **n.** a type of tall top hat.

**stovies** /ˈstəʊvɪz/ • **pl. n.** Scottish a dish of stewed potatoes.
– ORIGIN C19: from Scots *stove* 'stew (meat or vegetables)', perh. partly from Du. *stoven*.

**stow** • **v. 1** pack or store (an object) tidily in an appropriate place. **2** (**stow away**) conceal oneself on a ship, aircraft, etc. so as to travel without paying or surreptitiously.
– PHRASES **stow it!** informal be quiet!
– DERIVATIVES **stowage** n.
– ORIGIN ME: shortening of **BESTOW**.

**stowaway** • **n.** a person who stows away.

**STP** • **abbrev. 1** Physiology short-term potentiation. **2** Chemistry standard temperature and pressure. **3** Professor of Sacred Theology. [from L. *Sanctae Theologiae Professor*.]

**str.** • **abbrev. 1** strait. **2** Rowing stroke.

**strabismus** /strəˈbɪzməs/ • **n.** the condition of having a squint.
– DERIVATIVES **strabismic** adj.
– ORIGIN C17: mod. L., from Gk *strabismos*, from *strabizein* 'to squint'.

**stracciatella** /ˌstratʃəˈtɛlə/ • **n.** an Italian soup containing eggs and cheese.
– ORIGIN from Ital.

**Strad** • **n.** informal a Stradivarius.

**straddle** • **v. 1** sit or stand with one leg on either side of. ➤ archaic stand, walk, or sit with one's legs wide apart. **2** extend across both sides of. **3** N. Amer. maintain an equivocal position regarding (a political issue). **4** fire shots or bombs at (a target) so that they fall short of and beyond it. • **n. 1** an act of straddling. **2** Stock Exchange a simultaneous purchase of options to buy and to sell a security or commodity at a fixed price.
– DERIVATIVES **straddler** n.
– ORIGIN C16: alt. of dial. *striddle*, back-form. from dial. *striddling* 'astride'.

**Stradivarius** /ˌstradɪˈvɛːrɪəs/ • **n.** a violin or other stringed instrument made by the Italian violin-maker Antonio Stradivari (*c.*1644–1737) or his followers.
– ORIGIN C19: Latinized form of *Stradivari*.

**strafe** /strɑːf, streɪf/ • **v.** attack with machine-gun fire or bombs from low-flying aircraft. • **n.** an act of strafing.
– ORIGIN C20: humorous adaptation of the Ger. First World War catchphrase *Gott strafe England* 'may God punish England'.

**straggle** • **v. 1** move along slowly so as to trail behind the person or people in front. **2** grow or spread out in an irregular, untidy way. • **n.** an irregular and untidy group.
– DERIVATIVES **straggler** n. **straggly** adj.
– ORIGIN ME: perh. from dial. *strake* 'go'.

**straight** • **adj. 1** extending uniformly in one direction only; without a curve or bend. ➤ (of an arch) flat-topped. **2** properly positioned so as to be level, upright, or symmetrical. ➤ in proper order or condition. **3** not evasive; honest. ➤ (of a choice) simple. ➤ (of thinking) clear and logical. **4** in continuous succession. **5** (of an alcoholic drink) undiluted. **6** (of drama) serious as opposed to comic or musical. **7** informal conventional or respectable. **8** informal heterosexual. • **adv. 1** in a straight line or in a straight manner. **2** archaic at once. • **n. 1** the straight part of something, especially the concluding stretch of a racecourse. ➤ archaic a straight form or position. **2** Poker a continuous sequence of five cards. **3** informal a conventional person. **4** informal a heterosexual.
– PHRASES **go straight** live an honest life after being a criminal. **a straight face** a blank or serious facial expression, especially when trying not to laugh. **the straight and narrow** the honest and morally acceptable way of living. **straight away** immediately. **a straight fight** Brit. a contest between just two opponents. **straight from the shoulder 1** dated (of a blow) swift and well delivered. **2** (of words) frank or direct. **straight off** (or **out**) informal without hesitation or deliberation. **straight up** informal **1** Brit. honestly. **2** chiefly N. Amer. undiluted or unadulterated.
– DERIVATIVES **straightish** adj. **straightly** adv. **straightness** n.
– ORIGIN ME: archaic past part. of **STRETCH**.

**straight angle** • **n.** Mathematics an angle of 180°.

**straight-arm** • **v.** N. Amer. informal push away (an opponent or obstacle) with the arm outstretched.

**straightaway** • **adv.** variant spelling of ***straight away*** at **STRAIGHT**. • **adj.** N. Amer. extending or moving in a straight line. • **n.** N. Amer. a straight section of a road or racetrack.

**straight chain** • **n.** Chemistry a chain of atoms in a molecule that is neither branched nor formed into a ring.

**straight-cut** • **adj.** (of tobacco) cut lengthwise into long silky fibres.

**straight edge** • **n.** a bar with one edge accurately straight, used for testing straightness.

**straight-eight** (or **straight-six**) • **n.** an internal-combustion engine with eight (or six) cylinders in line.

**straighten** • **v. 1** make or become straight. ➤ stand or sit erect after bending. **2** (**straighten up**) (of a vehicle, ship, or aircraft) stop turning and move in a straight line.
– DERIVATIVES **straightener** n.

**straight flush** • **n.** (in poker or brag) a hand of cards all of one suit and in a continuous sequence.

**straightforward** • **adj. 1** easy to do or understand. **2** honest and open.
– DERIVATIVES **straightforwardly** adv. **straightforwardness** n.

**straightjacket** • **n.** & **v.** variant spelling of **STRAITJACKET**.

**straight-laced** • **adj.** variant spelling of **STRAIT-LACED**.

**straight-line** • **adj.** Finance (of depreciation) allocating a given percentage of the cost of an asset each year for a fixed period.

**straight man** • **n.** a comedian's stooge.

**straight razor** • **n.** North American term for **CUT-THROAT RAZOR**.

**straight shooter** • **n.** informal, chiefly N. Amer. an honest and forthright person.
– DERIVATIVES **straight-shooting** adj.

**straight time** • **n.** chiefly US normal working hours, paid at a regular rate.

**straight-up** • **adj.** N. Amer. informal honest; trustworthy.

**straightway** • **adv.** archaic form of ***straight away*** (see **STRAIGHT**).

**strain**[1] • **v. 1** force (a part of one's body or oneself) to make an unusually great effort. ➤ injure (a limb, muscle, or organ) by overexertion. ➤ make a strenuous and continuous effort. **2** make severe or excessive demands on. **3** pull or push forcibly at something. **4** pour (a mainly li-

quid substance) through a sieve or similar device to separate out any solid matter. ➤ drain off (liquid) in this way. ● **n. 1** a force tending to strain something to an extreme degree. ➤ Physics the magnitude of a deformation, equal to the change in the dimension of a deformed object divided by its original dimension. **2** an injury caused by straining a muscle, limb, etc. **3** a severe demand on strength or resources. ➤ a state of tension or exhaustion resulting from this. **4** the sound of a piece of music as it is played or performed.
– DERIVATIVES **strainable** adj.
– ORIGIN ME: from OFr. *estreindre*, from L. *stringere* 'draw tight'.

**strain**[2] ● **n. 1** a distinct breed, stock, or variety of an animal, plant, or other organism. **2** a tendency in a person's character.
– ORIGIN OE *strīon* 'acquisition, gain', of Gmc origin.

**strained** ● **adj. 1** not relaxed or comfortable; showing signs of strain. **2** produced by deliberate effort; artificial or laboured.

**strainer** ● **n.** a device for straining liquids, having holes punched in it or made of crossed wire.

**strain gauge** ● **n.** a device for indicating the strain of a material or structure at the point of attachment.

**strait** ● **n. 1** (also **straits**) a narrow passage of water connecting two seas or other large areas of water. **2** (**straits**) a situation characterized by a specified degree of trouble or difficulty: *in dire straits.* ● **adj.** archaic **1** narrow or cramped. **2** strict or rigorous.
– DERIVATIVES **straitly** adv. **straitness** n.
– ORIGIN ME: shortening of OFr. *estreit* 'tight, narrow', from L. *strictus* (see **STRICT**).

**straiten** ● **v. 1** [as adj. **straitened**] restricted in range. ➤ restricted because of poverty: *they lived in straitened circumstances.* **2** archaic make or become narrow.

**straitjacket** (also **straightjacket**) ● **n. 1** a strong garment with long sleeves which can be tied together to confine the arms of a violent prisoner or mental patient. **2** a severe restriction. ● **v.** (**-jacketed**, **-jacketing**) restrain with or as if with a straitjacket.

**strait-laced** (also **straight-laced**) ● **adj.** having or showing very strict moral attitudes.

**strake** ● **n. 1** a continuous line of planking or plates from the stem to the stern of a ship or boat. **2** a protruding ridge fitted to an aircraft or other structure to improve aerodynamic stability.
– ORIGIN ME: from Anglo-Latin *stracus, straca*; prob. from the Gmc base of **STRETCH**.

**stramash** /strə'maʃ/ ● **n.** Scottish & N. English an uproar; a row.
– ORIGIN C18: appar. imitative.

**strand**[1] ● **v.** [often as adj. **stranded**] **1** drive or leave aground on a shore. **2** leave without the means to move from a place. ● **n.** poetic/literary the shore of a sea, lake, or large river.
– ORIGIN OE, of unknown origin.

**strand**[2] ● **n. 1** a single thin length of thread, wire, etc., especially as twisted together with others. **2** an element that forms part of a complex whole.
– DERIVATIVES **stranded** adj.
– ORIGIN C15: of unknown origin.

**strange** ● **adj. 1** unusual or surprising. **2** not previously visited, seen, or encountered. ➤ (**strange to/at/in**) archaic unaccustomed to or unfamiliar with. **3** Physics having a non-zero value for strangeness.
– PHRASES **feel strange 1** feel indefinably unwell. **2** be uncomfortable in a situation. **strange to say** (or poetic/literary **tell**) it is surprising or unusual that.
– DERIVATIVES **strangely** adv.
– ORIGIN ME: shortening of OFr. *estrange*, from L. *extraneus* 'external, strange'.

**strange attractor** ● **n.** Mathematics a complex pattern of behaviour displayed by a chaotic system.

**strangeness** ● **n. 1** the state or fact of being strange. **2** Physics one of the six flavours of quark.

**stranger** ● **n. 1** a person whom one does not know. **2** a person who does not know, or is not known in, a particular place. **3** (**stranger to**) a person entirely unaccustomed to (a feeling, experience, or situation). **4** a person who is not a member or official of the House of Commons.
– ORIGIN ME: shortening of OFr. *estrangier*, from L. *extraneus* (see **STRANGE**).

**strangle** ● **v. 1** squeeze or constrict the neck of, especially so as to cause death. **2** suppress or hinder (an impulse, action, or sound).
– DERIVATIVES **strangler** n.
– ORIGIN ME: shortening of OFr. *estrangler*, from L. *strangulare*, from Gk *strangalan*, from *strangalē* 'halter'.

**stranglehold** ● **n. 1** a grip around the neck of a person that can kill by asphyxiation if held for long enough. **2** complete or overwhelming control.

**strangles** ● **pl. n.** [usu. treated as sing.] bacterial infection of the upper respiratory tract of horses, causing enlarged lymph nodes in the throat.

**strangulate** /'straŋgjʊleɪt/ ● **v.** [often as adj. **strangulated**] **1** Medicine prevent blood circulation through (a part, especially a hernia) by constriction. **2** informal strangle. ➤ [as adj. **strangulated**] sounding as though the speaker's throat is constricted.
– DERIVATIVES **strangulation** n.
– ORIGIN C17 (in the sense 'suffocate'): from L. *strangulat-*, *strangulare* 'choke' (see **STRANGLE**).

**strangury** /'straŋgjʊri/ ● **n.** Medicine a painful condition of blockage or irritation at the base of the bladder, with a strong desire to urinate.
– DERIVATIVES **strangurious** /-'gjʊərɪəs/ adj.
– ORIGIN ME: via L. from Gk *strangouria*, from *stranx*, *strang-* 'drop squeezed out' + *ouron* 'urine'.

**strap** ● **n. 1** a strip of leather, cloth, or other flexible material, used for fastening, securing, carrying, or holding on to. **2** a strip of metal, often hinged, used for fastening or securing. **3** (**the strap**) punishment by beating with a leather strap. ● **v.** (**strapped**, **strapping**) **1** fasten or secure with a strap. **2** Brit. bind (an injured part of the body) with adhesive plaster. **3** beat with a leather strap. **4** [as adj. **strapped**] informal short of money: *I'm constantly strapped for cash.*
– DERIVATIVES **strapless** adj. **strappy** adj.
– ORIGIN C16 (denoting a trap for birds, also a piece of wood fastening two objects together): dial. form of **STROP**[1].

**straphanger** ● **n.** informal a standing passenger in a bus or train.
– DERIVATIVES **strap-hang** v.

**strap hinge** ● **n.** a hinge with long leaves or flaps for screwing on to the surface of a door or gate.

**strapline** ● **n.** a subsidiary heading or caption in a newspaper or magazine.

**strappado** /strə'pɑːdəʊ, -eɪdəʊ/ ● **n.** (pl. **-os**) historical a form of punishment or torture in which the victim was secured to a rope and made to fall from a height almost to the ground before being stopped with an abrupt jerk. ➤ the instrument used for this.
– ORIGIN C16: from Fr. *(e)strapade*, from Ital. *strappata*, from *strappare* 'to snatch'.

**strapper** ● **n.** chiefly Austral. a person who grooms racehorses.

**strapping**[1] ● **adj.** (especially of a young person) big and strong.

**strapping**[2] ● **n. 1** adhesive plaster for strapping injuries. **2** leather or metal straps.

**strapwork** ● **n.** ornamentation imitating pierced and interlaced straps.

**strata** plural form of **STRATUM**.

**stratagem** /'stratədʒəm/ ● **n. 1** a plan or scheme intended to outwit an opponent. **2** archaic cunning.
– ORIGIN C15 (orig. denoting a military ploy): from Fr. *stratagème*, via L. from Gk *stratēgēma*, from *stratēgein* 'be a general'.

**stratal** ● **adj.** of or relating to strata or a stratum.

**strategic** /strə'tiːdʒɪk/ ● **adj. 1** forming part of a long-term plan or aim to achieve a specific purpose. **2** relating to the gaining of overall or long-term military advantage. ➤ (of bombing or weapons) done or for use against an enemy's territory or infrastructure. Often contrasted with **TACTICAL**.

– DERIVATIVES **strategical** adj. **strategically** adv.

**strategy** /ˈstratɪdʒi/ ● n. (pl. **-ies**) **1** a plan designed to achieve a particular long-term aim. **2** the art of planning and directing military activity in a war or battle. Often contrasted with ***tactics*** (see **TACTIC**). ➤ a plan so devised.

– DERIVATIVES **strategist** n. **strategize** (also **-ise**) v. (N. Amer.).

– ORIGIN C19: from Fr. *stratégie*, from Gk *stratēgia* 'generalship', from *stratēgos* (see **STRATAGEM**).

**strath** /straθ/ ● n. Scottish a broad river valley.

– ORIGIN C16: from Sc. Gaelic *srath*.

**strathspey** /straθˈspeɪ/ ● n. a slow Scottish dance. ➤ a piece of music for such a dance, typically in 4/4 time.

– ORIGIN C18: named after *Strathspey* in Scotland.

**stratify** /ˈstratɪfʌɪ/ ● v. (**-ies**, **-ied**) **1** [usu. as adj. **stratified**] form or arrange into strata. **2** arrange or classify. **3** place (seeds) close together in layers in moist sand or peat to preserve them or to help them germinate.

– DERIVATIVES **stratification** n. **stratiform** adj.

**stratigraphy** /strəˈtɪgrəfi/ ● n. **1** the branch of geology concerned with the order and relative dating of strata. **2** the analysis of the order and position of layers of archaeological remains. **3** the structure of a particular set of strata.

– DERIVATIVES **stratigrapher** n. **stratigraphic** adj. **stratigraphical** adj.

– ORIGIN C19: from **STRATUM** + **-GRAPHY**.

**stratocracy** /strəˈtɒkrəsi/ ● n. (pl. **-ies**) archaic government by military forces. ➤ a military government.

– ORIGIN C17: from Gk *stratos* 'army' + **-CRACY**.

**stratocumulus** /ˌstratə(ʊ)ˈkjuːmjʊləs, ˌstreɪ-, ˌstrɑː-/ ● n. cloud forming a low layer of clumped or broken grey masses.

**stratopause** /ˈstratə(ʊ)pɔːz, ˌstreɪ-, ˌstrɑː-/ ● n. the interface between the stratosphere and the ionosphere.

**stratosphere** /ˈstratəˌsfɪə/ ● n. **1** the layer of the earth's atmosphere above the troposphere, extending to about 50 km above the earth's surface (the lower boundary of the mesosphere). **2** informal the very highest levels of something: *the fashion stratosphere*.

– DERIVATIVES **stratospheric** /-ˈsfɛrɪk/ adj. **stratospherically** adv.

**stratovolcano** /ˌstratəʊvɒlˈkeɪnəʊ/ ● n. (pl. **-oes**) a volcano built up of alternate layers of lava and ash.

**stratum** /ˈstrɑːtəm, ˈstreɪtəm/ ● n. (pl. **strata** /-tə/) **1** a layer or a series of layers of rock. **2** a thin layer within any structure. **3** a level or class of society.

– ORIGIN C16: mod. L., from L., lit. 'something spread or laid down', neut. past part. of *sternere* 'strew'.

**stratum corneum** /ˌstrɑːtəm ˈkɔːnɪəm/ ● n. Anatomy the relatively tough outer layer of the skin.

– ORIGIN L., lit. 'horny layer'.

**stratus** /ˈstrɑːtəs, ˈstreɪtəs/ ● n. cloud forming a continuous horizontal grey sheet, often with rain or snow.

– ORIGIN C19: mod. L., from L., lit. 'strewn', past part. of *sternere*.

**stravaig** /strəˈveɪg/ (also **stravage**) ● v. chiefly Scottish & Irish wander about aimlessly.

– ORIGIN C18: prob. a shortening of obs. *extravage* 'digress, ramble'.

**straw** ● n. **1** dried stalks of grain, used especially as fodder or for thatching, packing, or weaving. **2** a single dried stalk of grain. **3** a thin hollow tube of paper or plastic for sucking drink from a glass or bottle. **4** a pale yellow colour like that of straw. **5** [with neg.] anything or at all: *he didn't care a straw if they disliked him*.

– PHRASES **clutch** (or **grasp** or **catch**) **at straws** resort in desperation to unlikely or inadequate means of salvation. [from the proverb *a drowning man will clutch at a straw*.] **draw the short straw** be chosen to perform an unpleasant task. **the last** (or **final**) **straw** a further minor difficulty that comes after a series of difficulties and makes a situation unbearable. [from the proverb *the last straw breaks the* (*laden*) *camel's back*.] **a straw in the wind** a slight hint of future developments.

– DERIVATIVES **strawy** adj.

– ORIGIN OE *strēaw*, of Gmc origin; rel. to **STREW**.

**strawberry** ● n. **1** a sweet soft red fruit with a seed-studded surface. **2** the low-growing plant which produces this fruit, with white flowers, lobed leaves, and runners. [Genus *Fragaria*.] **3** a deep pinkish-red colour.

– ORIGIN OE *strēa(w)berige*, *strēowberige* (see **STRAW**, **BERRY**).

**strawberry blonde** ● adj. denoting hair that is a light reddish-blonde colour. ● n. a woman with such hair.

**strawberry mark** ● n. a soft red birthmark.

**strawberry roan** ● adj. denoting an animal's coat which is chestnut mixed with white or grey.

**strawberry tree** ● n. a small tree bearing clusters of whitish flowers and strawberry-like fruit. [*Arbutus unedo*.]

**strawboard** ● n. board made of straw pulp, used in building (faced with paper) and in book covers.

**straw boss** ● n. N. Amer. informal a junior supervisor with some responsibility but little authority.

**strawflower** ● n. an everlasting flower of the daisy family. [*Helichrysum bracteatum* (Australia) and genus *Helipterum*.]

**straw man** ● n. another term for ***man of straw*** at **MAN**.

**straw poll** (N. Amer. also **straw vote**) ● n. an unofficial ballot conducted as a test of opinion.

**stray** ● v. **1** move away aimlessly from a group or from the right course or place. ➤ (of the eyes or a hand) move idly in a specified direction. **2** be unfaithful to a spouse or partner. ● adj. **1** not in the right place; separated from a group. **2** (of a domestic animal) having no home or having wandered away from home. **3** Physics arising naturally but unwanted and usually detrimental: *stray voltages*. ● n. **1** a stray person or thing, especially a domestic animal. **2** (**strays**) electrical phenomena interfering with radio reception.

– DERIVATIVES **strayer** n.

– ORIGIN ME: shortening of Anglo-Norman Fr. and OFr. *estrayer* (v.), Anglo-Norman Fr. *strey* (n.), partly from **ASTRAY**.

**streak** ● n. **1** a long, thin mark of a different substance or colour from its surroundings. **2** an element of a specified kind in someone's character: *a ruthless streak*. **3** a spell of specified success or luck. ● v. **1** mark with streaks. **2** move very fast in a specified direction. **3** informal run naked in a public place so as to shock or amuse.

– PHRASES **like a streak** informal very fast. **streak of lightning** a flash of lightning.

– DERIVATIVES **streaker** n. **streaking** n.

– ORIGIN OE *strica*, of Gmc origin; rel. to **STRIKE**.

**streaky** ● adj. (**-ier**, **-iest**) **1** having streaks. ➤ Brit. (of bacon) from the belly, thus having alternate strips of fat and lean. **2** informal, chiefly N. Amer. unpredictable; variable.

– DERIVATIVES **streakily** adv. **streakiness** n.

**stream** ● n. **1** a small, narrow river. **2** a continuous flow of liquid, air, gas, people, or things. **3** Brit. a group in which schoolchildren of the same age and ability are taught. ● v. **1** (of liquid) run in a continuous flow. ➤ (of a mass of people or things) move in a continuous flow. **2** (usu. **be streaming**) run with tears, sweat, or other liquid. **3** float at full extent in the wind. **4** Brit. put (schoolchildren) in streams.

– PHRASES **against** (or **with**) **the stream** against (or with) the prevailing view or tendency. **on stream** in or into operation or existence.

– DERIVATIVES **streamlet** n.

– ORIGIN OE *strēam* (n.), of Gmc origin.

**streamer** ● n. **1** a long, narrow strip of material used as a decoration or flag. **2** a banner headline in a newspaper. **3** Fishing a fly with feathers attached. **4** Astronomy an elongated mass of luminous matter, e.g. in an aurora. **5** (also **tape streamer**) Computing a device for writing data very quickly on to magnetic tape.

**streamer weed** ● n. a freshwater plant with long fronds that stream and wave in the current, especially water crowfoot.

**streaming** ● adj. (of a cold) accompanied by copious running of the nose and eyes. ● n. a method of relaying data (especially video and audio material) over a computer network as a steady continuous stream.

**streamline** ● **v. 1** [usu. as adj. **streamlined**] design or provide with a form that presents very little resistance to a flow of air or water. **2** make (an organization or system) more efficient by employing faster or simpler working methods. ● **n.** a line along which the flow of a moving fluid is least turbulent. ● **adj.** (of fluid flow) free from turbulence.

**stream of consciousness** ● **n. 1** Psychology a person's thoughts and reactions to events, perceived as a continuous flow. **2** a literary style in which such ideas are recorded without interruption by objective description or conventional dialogue.

**streel** /stri:l/ Irish ● **n.** a disreputable, untidy person, especially a woman. ● **v.** wander aimlessly.
– DERIVATIVES **streelish** adj.
– ORIGIN C19: from Ir. *s(t)raoill(e)*.

**street** ● **n. 1** a public road in a city, town, or village, typically with buildings on one or both sides. **2** [as modifier] of or relating to the subculture of fashionable urban youth. **3** [as modifier] homeless: *street children*.
– PHRASES **not in the same street** Brit. informal far inferior in terms of ability. **on the streets 1** homeless. **2** working as a prostitute. **streets ahead** Brit. informal greatly superior. **up** (or **right up**) **one's street** (or N. Amer. **alley**) informal well suited to one's tastes, interests, or abilities.
– DERIVATIVES **-streeted** adj. **streetward** adj. & adv.
– ORIGIN OE *strǣt*, of W. Gmc origin, from late L. *strāta (via)* 'paved (way)', fem. past part. of *sternere* 'lay down'.

**street Arab** ● **n.** archaic a raggedly dressed homeless child wandering the streets.

**streetcar** ● **n.** N. Amer. a tram.

**street door** ● **n.** the main door of a house opening on the street.

**street furniture** ● **n.** objects placed or fixed in the street for public use, such as postboxes or road signs.

**street-legal** ● **adj.** (of a vehicle) meeting all legal requirements for use on ordinary roads.

**street light** (also **street lamp**) ● **n.** a light illuminating a road, typically mounted on a tall post.
– DERIVATIVES **street lighting** n.

**street name** ● **n.** N. Amer. the name of a stockbroking firm, bank, or dealer in which stock is held on behalf of a purchaser.

**street-smart** ● **adj.** chiefly N. Amer. another term for **STREETWISE**.

**street value** ● **n.** the price a commodity, especially an amount of drugs, would fetch if sold illicitly.

**streetwalker** ● **n.** a prostitute who seeks clients in the street.
– DERIVATIVES **streetwalking** n. & adj.

**streetwise** ● **adj.** informal having the skills and knowledge necessary for dealing with modern urban life.

**Strega** /ˈstreɪgə/ ● **n.** trademark a kind of orange-flavoured Italian liqueur.
– ORIGIN Ital., lit. 'witch'.

**strelitzia** /strəˈlɪtsɪə/ ● **n.** a southern African plant of a genus including the bird of paradise flower. [Genus *Strelitzia*.]
– ORIGIN mod. L, named after Charlotte of Mecklenburg-*Strelitz* (1744–1818), queen of George III.

**strength** /strɛŋθ, strɛŋkθ/ ● **n. 1** the quality or state of being strong. **2** a good or beneficial quality or attribute. ➤ poetic/literary a source of mental or emotional support. **3** the number of people comprising a group. ➤ a full complement of people: *below strength*.
– PHRASES **from strength** from a secure or advantageous position. **go from strength to strength** progress with increasing success. **in strength** in large numbers. **on the strength of** on the basis or with the justification of. **the strength of** chiefly Austral./NZ the meaning of; the truth about. **tower** (or **pillar**) **of strength** a person who can be relied upon to support and comfort others.
– DERIVATIVES **strengthless** adj.
– ORIGIN OE *strengthu*, from the Gmc base of **STRONG**.

**strengthen** /ˈstrɛŋθ(ə)n, -ŋkθ(ə)n/ ● **v.** make or become stronger.
– PHRASES **strengthen someone's hand** (or **hands**) enable a person to act more effectively.
– DERIVATIVES **strengthener** n.

**strenuous** /ˈstrɛnjʊəs/ ● **adj.** requiring or using great exertion.
– DERIVATIVES **strenuously** adv. **strenuousness** n.
– ORIGIN C17: from L. *strenuus* 'brisk' + **-OUS**.

**strep** ● **n.** Medicine, informal short for **STREPTOCOCCUS**.

**strepto-** ● **comb. form** twisted; in the form of a twisted chain: *streptomycete*. ➤ associated with streptococci or streptomycetes: *streptokinase*.
– ORIGIN from Gk *streptos* 'twisted'.

**streptocarpus** /ˌstrɛptə(ʊ)ˈkɑːpəs/ ● **n.** an African plant with funnel-shaped pink, white, or violet flowers, cultivated as indoor or greenhouse plants. [Genus *Streptocarpus*.]
– ORIGIN mod. L., from **STREPTO-** + Gk *karpos* 'fruit'.

**streptococcus** /ˌstrɛptə(ʊ)ˈkɒkəs/ ● **n.** (pl. **streptococci** /-ˈkɒk(s)ʌɪ, -ˈkɒk(s)iː/) a bacterium of a genus including the agents of souring of milk and dental decay and the pathogens causing scarlet fever and pneumonia. [Genus *Streptococcus*.]
– DERIVATIVES **streptococcal** adj.

**streptokinase** /ˌstrɛptə(ʊ)ˈkʌɪneɪz/ ● **n.** Biochemistry an enzyme produced by some streptococci which is able to break down red blood cells.

**streptomycete** /ˌstrɛptə(ʊ)ˈmʌɪsiːt/ ● **n.** (pl. **streptomycetes** /-ˈmʌɪsiːts, -mʌɪˈsiːtiːz/) a bacterium which occurs chiefly in soil and of which some kinds yield antibiotics. [*Streptomyces* and related genera.]
– ORIGIN 1950s: anglicized sing. of mod. L. *Streptomyces*, from **STREPTO-** + Gk *mukēs*, *mukēt-* 'fungus'.

**streptomycin** /ˌstrɛptə(ʊ)ˈmʌɪsɪn/ ● **n.** Medicine a bacterial antibiotic used against tuberculosis.

**stress** ● **n. 1** pressure or tension exerted on a material object. ➤ Physics the magnitude of this measured in units of force per unit area. **2** a state of mental, emotional, or other strain. **3** particular emphasis. ➤ emphasis given to a syllable or word in speech. ● **v. 1** emphasize. ➤ give emphasis to (a syllable or word) when pronouncing it. **2** subject to stress.
– DERIVATIVES **stressful** adj. **stressfully** adv. **stressfulness** n. **stressless** adj. **stressor** n.
– ORIGIN ME (denoting pressure exerted on a person for the purpose of compulsion): shortening of **DISTRESS**, or partly from OFr. *estresse* 'narrowness, oppression', based on L. *strictus* (see **STRICT**).

**stretch** ● **v. 1** (of something soft or elastic) be made or be able to be made longer or wider without tearing or breaking. ➤ pull (something) tightly from one point to another or across a space. **2** straighten or extend one's body or a part of one's body to its full length. **3** last or cause to last longer than expected. ➤ (of finances or resources) be sufficient for a particular purpose. **4** extend over an area or period of time. **5** make demands on. ● **n. 1** an act of stretching. ➤ the fact or condition of being stretched. ➤ the capacity to stretch or be stretched; elasticity. **2** a continuous expanse or period. ➤ informal a period of time spent in prison. ➤ chiefly N. Amer. a straight part of a racetrack, typically the home straight. ➤ Sailing the distance covered on one tack. **3** [usu. as modifier] informal a motor vehicle or aircraft modified so as to have extended seating or storage capacity. **4** a difficult or demanding task.
– PHRASES **at full stretch** using the maximum amount of one's resources or energy. **at a stretch 1** in one continuous period. **2** just possible but with difficulty. **stretch one's legs** go for a short walk, typically after sitting for some time. **stretch a point** allow or do something not usually acceptable.
– DERIVATIVES **stretchability** n. **stretchable** adj. **stretchiness** n. **stretchy** adj. (**-ier**, **-iest**).
– ORIGIN OE *streccan*, of W. Gmc origin.

**stretcher** ● **n. 1** a framework of two poles with a long piece of canvas slung between them, used for carrying sick, injured, or dead people. **2** a wooden frame over which a canvas is stretched ready for painting. **3** a rod or bar joining and supporting chair legs. **4** a board in a boat against which a rower presses their feet for support. **5** a brick or stone laid with its long side along the face of a wall. Compare with **HEADER** (in sense 3). **6** archaic, informal an exaggeration or lie. ● **v.** carry on a stretcher.

**stretch marks** ● **pl. n.** marks on the skin, especially on the abdomen, caused by distention of the skin from obesity or during pregnancy.

**stretto** /ˈstrɛtəʊ/ ● **adv.** Music in quicker time.
– ORIGIN Ital., lit. 'narrow'.

**streusel** /ˈstrɔɪz(ə)l, ˈstruːz(ə)l/ ● **n.** a crumbly topping or filling for a cake or pastry, made from fat, flour, sugar, and often cinnamon.
– ORIGIN from Ger. *Streusel*, from *streuen* 'sprinkle'.

**strew** ● **v.** (past part. **strewn** or **strewed**) (usu. **be strewn**) scatter untidily over a surface or area. ➤(usu. **be strewn with**) cover (a surface or area) with untidily scattered things.
– DERIVATIVES **strewer** n.
– ORIGIN OE *stre(o)wian*, of Gmc origin.

**strewth** (also **struth**) ● **exclam.** informal used to express surprise or dismay.
– ORIGIN C19: contr. of *God's truth*.

**stria** /ˈstrʌɪə/ ● **n.** (pl. **striae** /-iː/) **1** technical a linear mark, ridge, or groove, especially one of a number of similar parallel features. **2** Anatomy a longitudinal collection of nerve fibres in the brain.
– ORIGIN C17: from L., lit. 'furrow'.

**striate** technical ● **adj.** /ˈstrʌɪət, ˈstrʌɪeɪt/ marked with striae. ● **v.** /strʌɪˈeɪt/ [usu. as adj. **striated**] mark with striae.
– DERIVATIVES **striation** n.

**striated muscle** ● **n.** Physiology muscle tissue in which the contractile fibrils are aligned in parallel bundles, occurring in the muscles attached to bones and under voluntary control. Often contrasted with **SMOOTH MUSCLE**.

**striatum** /strʌɪˈeɪtəm/ ● **n.** (pl. **striata** /strʌɪˈeɪtə/) Anatomy short for **CORPUS STRIATUM**.
– DERIVATIVES **striatal** adj.

**stricken** North American or archaic past participle of **STRIKE**. ● **adj.** seriously affected by an undesirable condition or unpleasant feeling. ➤(of a face or look) showing great distress.
– PHRASES **stricken in years** archaic or poetic/literary enfeebled by age.

**strickle** ● **n.** **1** a rod used to level off a heaped measure. **2** a whetting tool.
– ORIGIN OE *stricel*; rel. to **STRIKE**.

**strict** ● **adj.** **1** demanding that rules concerning behaviour are obeyed. ➤(of a rule) demanding total compliance; rigidly enforced. **2** following rules or beliefs exactly. **3** not allowing deviation or relaxation.
– DERIVATIVES **strictly** adv. **strictness** n.
– ORIGIN ME (in the sense 'restricted in space or extent'): from L. *strictus*, *stringere* 'tighten'.

**strict construction** ● **n.** Law a literal interpretation of a statute or document by a court.

**strict liability** ● **n.** Law liability which does not depend on actual negligence or intent to harm.

**stricture** /ˈstrɪktʃə/ ● **n.** **1** a rule restricting behaviour or action. **2** a sternly critical remark. **3** Medicine abnormal narrowing of a canal or duct in the body.
– DERIVATIVES **strictured** adj.
– ORIGIN ME: from L. *strictura*, from *stringere* (see **STRICT**).

**stride** ● **v.** (past **strode**; past part. **stridden**) **1** walk with long, decisive steps. **2** (**stride across/over**) cross (an obstacle) with one long step. **3** poetic/literary bestride. ● **n.** **1** a long, decisive step. ➤the length of a step or manner of taking steps. **2** a step in progress towards an aim. ➤(**one's stride**) a good or regular rate of progress, especially after a slow start. **3** (**strides**) Brit. informal trousers. **4** [as modifier] denoting or relating to a rhythmic style of jazz piano playing in which the left hand alternately plays single bass notes on the downbeat and chords an octave higher on the upbeat.
– PHRASES **take something in one's stride** deal with something difficult in a calm way.
– DERIVATIVES **strider** n.
– ORIGIN OE *stride* (n.) 'single long step', *strīdan* (v.) 'stand or walk with the legs wide apart', prob. from a Gmc base meaning 'strive, quarrel'.

**strident** ● **adj.** **1** loud and harsh. **2** presenting a point of view in an excessively forceful way. **3** Phonetics sibilant.
– DERIVATIVES **stridency** n. **stridently** adv.
– ORIGIN C17: from L. *strident-*, *stridere* 'creak'.

**stridor** /ˈstrʌɪdə/ ● **n.** a strident sound. ➤Medicine a harsh vibrating noise when breathing, caused by obstruction of the windpipe or larynx.
– ORIGIN C17: from L., from *stridere* 'to creak'.

**stridulate** /ˈstrɪdjʊleɪt/ ● **v.** (of an insect, especially a male cricket or grasshopper) make a shrill sound by rubbing the legs, wings, or other parts of the body together.
– DERIVATIVES **stridulant** adj. **stridulation** n. **stridulatory** adj.
– ORIGIN C19: from Fr. *striduler*, from L. *stridulus* 'creaking'.

**strife** ● **n.** **1** angry or bitter disagreement; conflict. **2** Austral./NZ trouble or difficulty of any kind.
– ORIGIN ME: shortening of OFr. *estrif* (rel. to OFr. *estriver* 'strive').

**strigil** /ˈstrɪdʒɪl/ ● **n.** **1** a scraper with a curved blade used by ancient Greeks and Romans to remove sweat and dirt from the skin after bathing or exercise. **2** Entomology a comb-like structure on the forelegs of some insects, used chiefly for grooming.
– ORIGIN from L. *strigilis*, from *stringere* 'touch lightly'.

**strigose** /ˈstrʌɪgəʊs/ ● **adj.** **1** Botany covered with short stiff adpressed hairs. **2** Entomology finely grooved or furrowed.
– ORIGIN C18: from L. *striga* 'swathe, furrow' + **-OSE**[1].

**strike** ● **v.** (past and past part. **struck** /strʌk/) **1** deliver a blow to. ➤accidentally hit (a part of one's body) against something. ➤come into forcible contact with. ➤(in sporting contexts) hit or kick (a ball) so as to score a run, point, or goal. ➤ignite (a match) by rubbing it briskly against an abrasive surface. ➤bring (an electric arc) into being. **2** (of a disaster, disease, etc.) occur suddenly and have harmful effects on. ➤attack suddenly. ➤(**strike something into**) cause a strong emotion in. ➤cause to become suddenly: *he was struck dumb.* **3** suddenly come into the mind of. ➤cause to have a particular impression. ➤(**be struck by/with**) find particularly interesting or impressive. ➤(**be struck on**) informal be deeply fond of. **4** (of employees) refuse to work as a form of organized protest. ➤N. Amer. undertake such action against (an employer). **5** cancel or remove by or as if by crossing out with a pen. ➤(**strike someone off**) officially remove someone from membership of a professional group. **6** move or proceed vigorously or purposefully. ➤(**strike out**) start out on a new or independent course. **7** reach (an agreement, balance, or compromise). ➤(in financial contexts) reach (a figure) by balancing an account. **8** (of a clock) indicate the time by sounding a chime or stroke. **9** make (a coin or medal) by stamping metal. **10** discover (gold, minerals, or oil) by drilling or mining. ➤(**strike on/upon**) discover or think of, especially unexpectedly. **11** take down or dismantle (a tent, camp, or theatrical scenery). ➤lower or take down (a flag or sail). **12** insert (a cutting of a plant) in soil to take root. ➤develop roots. ➤(of a young oyster) attach itself to a bed. **13** Fishing secure a hook in the mouth of a fish by jerking or tightening the line after it has taken the bait or fly. ● **n.** **1** an act of striking by employees. ➤a refusal to do something as an organized protest: *a rent strike.* **2** a sudden attack, typically a military one. **3** (in sporting contexts) an act of striking a ball. ➤(in tenpin bowling) an act of knocking down all the pins with one's first ball. ➤Baseball a batter's unsuccessful attempt to hit a pitched ball. ➤Baseball a pitch that passes through the strike zone. **4** N. Amer. something to one's discredit. **5** an act of striking gold, minerals, or oil. **6** the horizontal or compass direction of a stratum, fault, or other geological feature.
– PHRASES **strike an attitude** (or **pose**) hold one's body in a particular position to create an impression. **strike a blow for** (or **at** or **against**) do something to help (or hinder) a cause, belief, or principle. **strike a light** Brit. informal, dated used to express surprise, dismay, or alarm. **strike while the iron is hot** make use of an opportunity immediately. [with ref. to smithing.]

– PHRASAL VERBS **strike back 1** retaliate. **2** (of a gas burner) burn from an internal point before the gas has become mixed with air. **strike someone out** (or **strike out**) **1** Baseball dismiss someone (or be dismissed) by means of three strikes. **2** (**strike out**) N. Amer. informal be unsuccessful. **strike up** (or **strike something up**) **1** begin to play a piece of music. **2** (**strike something up**) begin a friendship or conversation with someone.
– ORIGIN OE *strīcan* 'go, flow' and 'rub lightly', of W. Gmc origin; rel. to **STROKE**.

**strike-breaker** • **n.** a person who works or is employed in place of others who are on strike.
– DERIVATIVES **strike-break** v.

**strike force** • **n.** [treated as sing. or pl.] a military force equipped and organized for sudden attack.

**strikeout** • **n.** Baseball an out called when a batter has made three strikes.

**strike pay** • **n.** money paid to strikers by their trade union.

**strike price** • **n.** Finance **1** the price fixed by the seller of a security after receiving bids in a tender offer. **2** the price at which a put or call option can be exercised.

**striker** • **n. 1** an employee on strike. **2** the player who is to strike the ball in a game; a player considered in terms of ability to strike the ball. ➤ (chiefly in soccer) a forward or attacker. **3** Brit. a device striking the primer in a gun.

**strike rate** • **n.** the success rate of a sports team, typically in scoring goals or runs.

**strike-slip fault** • **n.** Geology a fault in which rock strata are displaced mainly in a horizontal direction, parallel to the line of the fault.

**strike zone** • **n.** Baseball an imaginary area over home plate extending from the armpits to the knees of a batter in the batting position.

**striking** • **adj. 1** noticeable. **2** dramatically good-looking or beautiful.
– DERIVATIVES **strikingly** adv.

**striking circle** • **n.** an elongated semicircle on a hockey field in front of the goal, from within which the ball must be hit in order to score.

**striking price** • **n.** another term for **STRIKE PRICE**.

**strimmer** • **n.** trademark an electrically powered grass trimmer with a nylon cutting cord which rotates rapidly on a spindle.
– ORIGIN 1970s: prob. a blend of **STRING** and **TRIMMER**.

**Strine** /strʌɪn/ • **n.** informal Australian English or the Australian accent.
– ORIGIN 1960s: representing *Australian* in Strine.

**string** • **n. 1** material consisting of threads of cotton, hemp, etc. twisted together to form a thin length. ➤ a piece of such material. **2** a length of catgut or wire on a musical instrument, producing a note by vibration. ➤ (**strings**) the stringed instruments in an orchestra. **3** a piece of catgut, nylon, etc., interwoven with others to form the head of a sports racket. **4** a set of things tied or threaded together on a thin cord. **5** a sequence of similar items or events. ➤ Computing a linear sequence of characters, words, or other data. ➤ a group of racehorses trained at one stable. ➤ a reserve team or player holding a specified position in an order of preference. ➤ a player assigned a specified rank in a team in an individual sport. **6** a tough piece of fibre in vegetables, meat, or other food. **7** Physics a hypothetical one-dimensional subatomic particle having the dynamical properties of a flexible loop. ➤ (also **cosmic string**) a hypothetical thread-like concentration of energy within the structure of space-time. • **v.** (past and past part. **strung**) **1** arrange on or as on a string. ➤ (**be strung** or **be strung out**) be arranged in a long line. **2** fit a string or strings to (a musical instrument, a racket, or a bow). **3** remove the strings from (a bean). **4** informal, chiefly N. Amer. hoax. **5** work as a stringer in journalism. **6** Billiards determine the order of play by striking the cue ball from baulk to rebound as far as possible from the top cushion.
– PHRASES **no strings attached** informal there are no special conditions or restrictions. **on a string** under one's control or influence.
– PHRASAL VERBS **string along** informal stay with a person or group as long as it is convenient. **string someone along** informal mislead someone deliberately over a length of time. **string something out 1** prolong something. **2** (**be strung out**) be nervous or tense. **3** (**be strung out**) N. Amer. be under the influence of alcohol or drugs. **string someone up 1** kill someone by hanging. **2** (**be strung up**) Brit. be tense or nervous.
– DERIVATIVES **stringed** adj. **stringless** adj. **string-like** adj.
– ORIGIN OE *streng* (n.), of Gmc origin; rel. to **STRONG**.

**string bass** • **n.** (especially among jazz musicians) a double bass.

**string bean** • **n.** any of various beans eaten in their fibrous pods, especially runner beans or French beans.

**stringboard** • **n.** a supporting timber or skirting in which the ends of the steps in a staircase are set.

**string course** • **n.** a raised horizontal band or course of bricks on a building.

**stringendo** /strɪnˈdʒɛndəʊ/ • **adv. & adj.** Music with increasing speed.
– ORIGIN Ital., lit. 'squeezing, binding together'.

**stringent** /ˈstrɪn(d)ʒ(ə)nt/ • **adj.** (of regulations or requirements) strict, precise, and exacting.
– DERIVATIVES **stringency** n. **stringently** adv.
– ORIGIN C17: from L. *stringent-*, *stringere* 'draw tight'.

**stringer** • **n. 1** a longitudinal structural piece in a framework, especially that of a ship or aircraft. **2** informal a journalist who is not on the regular staff of a newspaper, but who is retained on a part-time basis to report on a particular place. **3** a stringboard.

**stringhalt** /ˈstrɪŋhɔːlt/ • **n.** a condition affecting one or both of a horse's hind legs, causing exaggerated bending of the hock.

**string line** • **n.** Billiards another term for **BAULK LINE**.

**stringpiece** • **n.** a long piece supporting and connecting the parts of a wooden framework.

**string quartet** • **n.** a chamber music ensemble consisting of first and second violins, viola, and cello. ➤ a piece of music for such an ensemble.

**string tie** • **n.** a very narrow necktie.

**string vest** • **n.** a man's undergarment made of a meshed fabric.

**stringy** • **adj.** (**-ier**, **-iest**) **1** resembling string in being long and thin. **2** tall, wiry, and thin. **3** (of food) tough and fibrous. **4** (of a liquid) viscous; forming strings.
– DERIVATIVES **stringily** adv. **stringiness** n.

**stringy-bark** • **n.** Austral. a eucalyptus with tough fibrous bark.

**strip**[1] • **v.** (**stripped**, **stripping**) **1** remove all coverings or clothes from. ➤ take off one's clothes. **2** leave bare of accessories or fittings. ➤ remove the accessory fittings of or take apart (a machine, motor vehicle, etc.) for inspection or adjustment. **3** remove (paint) from a surface with solvent. **4** (**strip someone of**) deprive someone of (rank, power, or property). **5** sell off (the assets of a company) for profit. **6** tear the thread or teeth from (a screw, gearwheel, etc.). **7** (of a bullet) be fired from a rifled gun without spin owing to a loss of surface. • **n. 1** an act of undressing, especially in a striptease. ➤ [as modifier] used for or involving the performance of stripteases. **2** Brit. the identifying outfit worn by the members of a sports team while playing.
– ORIGIN ME: of Gmc origin; sense 2 of the noun is perh. from the notion of clothing to which a player 'strips' down.

**strip**[2] • **n. 1** a long, narrow piece of cloth, paper, etc. ➤ steel or other metal in the form of narrow flat bars. **2** a long, narrow area of land. ➤ chiefly N. Amer. a main road lined with shops and other facilities.
– ORIGIN ME: from or rel. to Middle Low Ger. *strippe* 'strap, thong', prob. also to **STRIPE**.

**stripe** • **n. 1** a long narrow band or strip of a different colour or texture from the surface on either side of it. **2** a chevron sewn on to a uniform to denote military rank. **3** chiefly N. Amer. a type or category. **4** archaic a blow with a lash. • **v.** (usu. **be striped**) mark with stripes.
– DERIVATIVES **striped** adj. **stripy** (also **stripey**) adj.
– ORIGIN ME: perh. a back-form. from *striped*, of Du. or Low Ger. origin.

**striped muscle** ● n. another term for **STRIATED MUSCLE**.

**strip light** ● n. Brit. a tubular fluorescent lamp.

**stripling** ● n. archaic or humorous a young man.
– ORIGIN ME: prob. from **STRIP**[2] (from the notion of 'narrowness', i.e. slimness) + **-LING**.

**strip mill** ● n. a mill in which steel slabs are rolled into strips.

**strip-mine** chiefly N. Amer. ● v. obtain (ore or coal) by opencast mining. ● n. (**strip mine**) an opencast mine.

**stripper** ● n. **1** a device or substance for stripping. **2** a striptease performer.

**strippergram** ● n. a novelty greetings message delivered by a man or woman who accompanies it with a striptease act.

**strip poker** ● n. a form of poker in which a player with a losing hand takes off an item of clothing as a forfeit.

**strip-search** ● v. search (someone) for concealed drugs, weapons, or other items, by stripping off their clothes. ● n. an act of strip-searching.

**striptease** ● n. a form of entertainment in which a performer gradually undresses to music in a sexually exciting way.
– DERIVATIVES **stripteaser** n.

**strive** ● v. (past **strove** or **strived**; past part. **striven** or **strived**) make great efforts. ➤(**strive against**) fight vigorously against.
– DERIVATIVES **striver** n.
– ORIGIN ME: shortening of OFr. *estriver*; rel. to *estrif* 'strife'.

**strobe** informal ● n. **1** a stroboscope. ➤a stroboscopic lamp. **2** N. Amer. an electronic flash for a camera. ● v. **1** flash intermittently. **2** exhibit or give rise to strobing.

**strobilus** /'strəʊbɪləs/ ● n. (pl. **strobili** /-lʌɪ, -liː/) Botany **1** the cone of a pine, fir, or other conifer. **2** a cone-like structure.
– ORIGIN C18: from late L., from Gk *strobilos*, from *strephein* 'to twist'.

**strobing** /'strəʊbɪŋ/ ● n. **1** irregular movement and loss of continuity of lines and stripes in a television picture. **2** jerkiness in what should be a smooth movement of a cinematographic image.

**stroboscope** /'strəʊbəskəʊp/ ● n. Physics an instrument which shines a bright light at rapid intervals so that a moving or rotating object appears stationary.
– DERIVATIVES **stroboscopic** adj. **stroboscopically** adv.
– ORIGIN C19: from Gk *strobos* 'whirling' + **-SCOPE**.

**strode** past of **STRIDE**.

**stroganoff** /'strɒɡənɒf/ ● n. a dish in which the central ingredient, typically strips of beef, is cooked in a sauce containing sour cream.
– ORIGIN named after the Russ. diplomat Count Pavel *Stroganov* (1772–1817).

**stroke** ● n. **1** an act of hitting: *he received three strokes of the cane.* ➤Golf an act of hitting the ball with a club, as a unit of scoring. ➤a sound made by a striking clock. **2** a mark made by drawing a pen, pencil, or paintbrush once across paper or canvas. ➤a line forming part of a written or printed character. ➤a short diagonal line separating characters or figures. **3** an act of stroking. **4** one of a series of repeated movements. ➤the whole motion of a piston in either direction. ➤a style of moving the arms and legs in swimming. ➤the mode or action of moving the oar in rowing. ➤(also **stroke oar**) the oarsman nearest the stern, setting the timing for the other rowers. **5** a sudden disabling attack or loss of consciousness caused by an interruption in the flow of blood to the brain. ● v. **1** move one's hand with gentle pressure over (a surface). **2** N. Amer. informal manipulate by means of flattery or persuasion. **3** act as the stroke of (a boat or crew).
– PHRASES **at a** (or **one**) **stroke** by a single action having immediate effect. **not** (or **never**) **do a stroke of work** do no work at all. **on the stroke of ——** precisely at the specified time. **put someone off their stroke** disconcert someone so that they make a mistake or hesitate. **stroke of genius** an outstandingly original idea. **stroke of luck** (or **good luck**) a fortunate unexpected occurrence.
– ORIGIN OE *strācian* 'caress lightly', of Gmc origin; rel. to **STRIKE**.

**stroke play** ● n. play in golf in which the score is reckoned by counting the number of strokes taken overall. Compare with **MATCH PLAY**.
– DERIVATIVES **stroke player** n.

**stroll** ● v. **1** walk in a leisurely way. **2** achieve a sporting victory easily. ● n. **1** a short leisurely walk. **2** a victory easily achieved.
– ORIGIN C17 (in the sense 'roam as a vagrant'): prob. from Ger. *strollen*, *strolchen*, from *Strolch* 'vagabond'.

**stroller** ● n. **1** N. Amer. a pushchair. **2** S. African a young urban vagrant.

**strolling players** ● pl. n. historical a troupe of itinerant actors.

**stroma** /'strəʊmə/ ● n. (pl. **stromata** /-mətə/) Biology **1** the supportive tissue or matrix of an organ, tumour, cell, etc. **2** a cushion-like mass of fungal tissue containing spore-bearing structures.
– DERIVATIVES **stromal** adj. (chiefly Anatomy). **stromatic** adj. (chiefly Botany).
– ORIGIN C19: mod. L., via late L. from Gk *strōma* 'coverlet'.

**stromatolite** /strə(ʊ)'matəlʌɪt/ ● n. Biology a calcareous mound built up of layers of blue-green algae and trapped sediment, especially as fossilized in Precambrian rocks.
– ORIGIN 1930s: from mod. L. *stroma*, *stromat-* 'layer, covering' + **-LITE**.

**strong** ● adj. (**-er**, **-est**) **1** physically powerful. **2** done with or exerting great force. ➤(of language or actions) forceful and extreme. **3** able to withstand great force or pressure. ➤secure, stable, or firmly established. ➤(of a market) having steadily high or rising prices. **4** great in intensity or degree: *strong competition for land.* ➤(of something seen or heard) not soft or muted. ➤pungent and full-flavoured. ➤(of a solution or drink) containing a large proportion of a substance. **5** great in power, influence, or ability. **6** used after a number to indicate the size of a group. **7** Grammar denoting a class of verbs in Germanic languages that form the past tense and past participle by a change of vowel within the stem rather than by addition of a suffix (e.g. *swim, swam, swum*).
– PHRASES **come on strong** informal behave aggressively or assertively. **going strong** informal continuing to be healthy, vigorous, or successful. **strong on 1** good at. **2** possessing large quantities of. **strong meat** Brit. ideas or language likely to be found unacceptably forceful or extreme.
– DERIVATIVES **strongish** adj. **strongly** adv.
– ORIGIN OE, of Gmc origin; rel. to **STRING**.

**strong-arm** ● adj. using or characterized by force or violence.

**strongbox** ● n. a small lockable metal box in which valuables may be kept.

**strong drink** ● n. alcohol, especially spirits.

**stronghold** ● n. **1** a place that has been fortified against attack. **2** a place of strong support for a cause or political party.

**strong interaction** (also **strong force**) ● n. Physics the powerful short-range interaction between hadrons which binds protons and neutrons together in atomic nuclei.

**strongman** ● n. (pl. **-men**) **1** a man of great physical strength, especially one who performs feats of strength for entertainment. **2** a leader who rules by the exercise of threats, force, or violence.

**strongpoint** ● n. a specially fortified defensive position.

**strongroom** ● n. a room, typically one in a bank, designed to protect valuable items against fire and theft.

**strong suit** ● n. **1** (in bridge or whist) a holding of a number of high cards of one suit in a hand. **2** a thing at which a person excels.

**strongyle** /'strɒndʒɪl/ ● n. a nematode worm of a group that includes several common disease-causing parasites of mammals and birds. [Genus *Strongylus*. See also **REDWORM** (sense 2).]
– ORIGIN C19: from mod. L. *Strongylus*, from Gk *strongulos* 'round'.

**strontia** /ˈstrɒnʃ(ɪ)ə/ ● **n.** Chemistry strontium oxide, a white solid resembling quicklime. [SrO.]
– ORIGIN C19: from earlier *strontian*, denoting native strontium carbonate from *Strontian*, a parish in Scotland, where it was discovered.

**strontium** /ˈstrɒntɪəm, ˈstrɒnʃ(ɪ)əm/ ● **n.** the chemical element of atomic number 38, a soft silver-white metal of the alkaline earth series. (Symbol: **Sr**)
– ORIGIN C19: from **STRONTIA** + **-IUM**.

**strop**[1] ● **n.** **1** a device, typically a strip of leather, for sharpening razors. **2** Nautical a collar of leather, spliced rope, or iron, used for handling cargo. ● **v.** (**stropped**, **stropping**) sharpen on or with a strop.
– ORIGIN ME (in the sense 'thong', also as a naut. term): prob. a W. Gmc adoption of L. *stroppus* 'thong'.

**strop**[2] ● **n.** Brit. informal a temper.
– ORIGIN C20: prob. a back-form. from **STROPPY**.

**strophanthin** /strə(ʊ)ˈfanθɪn/ ● **n.** Medicine a poisonous substance obtained from certain African trees and used as a heart stimulant.
– ORIGIN C19: from mod. L. *Strophanthus* (genus name), (from Gk *strophos* 'twisted cord' + *anthos* 'flower', referring to the long segments of the corolla) + **-IN**[1].

**strophe** /ˈstrəʊfi/ ● **n.** **1** the first section of an ancient Greek choral ode or of one division of it. Compare with **ANTISTROPHE**. **2** a group of lines forming a section of a lyric poem.
– DERIVATIVES **strophic** adj.
– ORIGIN C17 (orig. denoting a movement from right to left made by a Greek chorus, or lines of song recited during this): from Gk *strophē*, lit. 'turning'.

**stroppy** ● **adj.** (**-ier**, **-iest**) Brit. informal bad-tempered; argumentative.
– DERIVATIVES **stroppily** adv. **stroppiness** n.
– ORIGIN 1950s: perh. an abbrev. of **OBSTREPEROUS**.

**strove** past of **STRIVE**.

**strow** /strəʊ/ ● **v.** (past part. **strown** /strəʊn/ or **strowed**) archaic variant of **STREW**.

**struck** past and past participle of **STRIKE**.

**structural** ● **adj.** of, relating to, or forming part of a structure.
– DERIVATIVES **structurally** adv.

**structural engineering** ● **n.** the branch of civil engineering concerned with large modern buildings and similar structures.
– DERIVATIVES **structural engineer** n.

**structural formula** ● **n.** Chemistry a formula which shows the arrangement of atoms in a molecule.

**structuralism** ● **n.** a method of interpretation and analysis of human cognition, behaviour, culture, and experience, which focuses on relationships of contrast between elements in a conceptual system.
– DERIVATIVES **structuralist** n. & adj.

**structural linguistics** ● **pl. n.** [treated as sing.] the branch of linguistics concerned with language as a system of interrelated structures.

**structural steel** ● **n.** strong mild steel in shapes suited to construction work.

**structural unemployment** ● **n.** unemployment resulting from industrial reorganization due to technological change, rather than fluctuations in supply or demand.

**structuration** ● **n.** the state or process of organization in a structured form.

**structure** ● **n.** **1** the arrangement of and relations between the parts of something complex. **2** a building or other object constructed from several parts. **3** the quality of being well organized. ● **v.** give structure to.
– DERIVATIVES **structureless** adj.
– ORIGIN ME: from OFr., or from L. *structura*, from *struere* 'to build'.

**structure plan** ● **n.** a plan drawn up by a local planning authority for the use of a prescribed area of land.

**strudel** /ˈstruːd(ə)l, ˈʃtruː-/ ● **n.** a confection of thin pastry rolled up round a fruit filling and baked.
– ORIGIN from Ger. *Strudel*, lit. 'whirlpool'.

**struggle** ● **v.** **1** make forceful efforts to get free. **2** strive under difficult circumstances to do something. ➤ have difficulty in gaining recognition or a living. **3** contend or compete. **4** make one's way with difficulty. ● **n.** **1** an act of struggling. **2** a very difficult task.
– DERIVATIVES **struggler** n.
– ORIGIN ME: frequentative, perh. of imitative origin.

**strum** ● **v.** (**strummed**, **strumming**) play (a guitar or similar instrument) by sweeping the thumb or a plectrum up or down the strings. ➤ play casually or unskilfully on a stringed instrument. ● **n.** an instance or the sound of strumming.
– DERIVATIVES **strummer** n.
– ORIGIN C18: imitative; cf. **THRUM**[1].

**struma** /ˈstruːmə/ ● **n.** (pl. **strumae** /-miː/) Medicine a goitre.
– ORIGIN C16: mod. L., from L., 'scrofulous tumour'.

**strumous** /ˈstruːməs/ ● **adj.** archaic scrofulous.
– ORIGIN C16: from L. *strumosus*, from *struma* (see **STRUMA**).

**strumpet** ● **n.** archaic or humorous a female prostitute or a promiscuous woman.
– ORIGIN ME: of unknown origin.

**strung** past and past participle of **STRING**.

**strut** ● **n.** **1** a bar forming part of a framework and designed to resist compression. **2** a strutting gait. ● **v.** (**strutted**, **strutting**) **1** walk with a stiff, erect, and conceited gait. **2** brace with a strut or struts.
– PHRASES **strut one's stuff** informal dance or behave in a confident and expressive way.
– DERIVATIVES **strutter** n. **strutting** adj. **struttingly** adv.
– ORIGIN OE *strūtian* 'protrude stiffly', of Gmc origin.

**struth** ● **exclam.** variant spelling of **STREWTH**.

**strychnine** /ˈstrɪkniːn, -ɪn/ ● **n.** a bitter and highly poisonous alkaloid obtained from nux vomica and related plants.
– ORIGIN C19: from Fr., via L. from Gk *strukhnos*, denoting a kind of nightshade.

**Sts** ● **abbrev.** Saints.

**Stuart** (also **Stewart**) ● **adj.** of or relating to the royal family ruling Scotland 1371–1714 and Britain 1603–1714 (interrupted by the Commonwealth 1649–60). ● **n.** a member of this family.

**stub** ● **n.** **1** the truncated remnant of a pencil, cigarette, or similar-shaped object after use. **2** a truncated or unusually short thing: *he wagged his little stub of tail.* **3** the counterfoil of a cheque, ticket, or other document. **4** [as modifier] denoting a projection or hole that goes only part of the way through a surface. ● **v.** (**stubbed**, **stubbing**) **1** accidentally strike (one's toe) against something. **2** extinguish (a cigarette) by pressing the lighted end against something. **3** grub up (a plant) by the roots.
– ORIGIN OE *stub(b)* 'stump of a tree', of Gmc origin.

**stub axle** ● **n.** an axle supporting only one wheel of a pair on opposite sides of a vehicle.

**stubble** ● **n.** **1** the cut stalks of cereal plants left in the ground after harvesting. **2** short, stiff hairs growing on a man's face when he has not shaved for a while.
– DERIVATIVES **stubbled** adj. **stubbly** adj.
– ORIGIN ME: from Anglo-Norman Fr. *stuble*, from L. *stupla*, *stupula*, vars of *stipula* 'straw'.

**stubborn** ● **adj.** **1** determined not to change one's attitude or position. **2** difficult to move, remove, or cure.
– DERIVATIVES **stubbornly** adv. **stubbornness** n.
– ORIGIN ME: of unknown origin.

**stubby** ● **adj.** (**-ier**, **-iest**) short and thick. ● **n.** (pl. **-ies**) Austral./NZ informal a small squat bottle of beer.
– DERIVATIVES **stubbily** adv. **stubbiness** n.

**stucco** ● **n.** fine plaster used for coating wall surfaces or moulding into architectural decorations. ● **v.** (**-oes**, **-oed**) [usu. as adj. **stuccoed**] coat or decorate with stucco.
– ORIGIN C16: from Ital.

**stuck** past participle of **STICK**[2].

**stuck-up** ● **adj.** informal snobbishly aloof.

**stud**[1] ● **n.** **1** a large-headed piece of metal that pierces and projects from a surface, especially for decoration. ➤ a small projection fixed to the base of a shoe or boot to provide better grip. ➤ a small object projecting slightly

from a road surface as a marker. **2** a small piece of jewellery which is pushed through a pierced ear or nostril. **3** a fastener consisting of two buttons joined with a bar, used in formal wear to fasten a shirt front or to fasten a collar to a shirt. **4** an upright timber in a wall to which laths and plasterboard are nailed. ➤ US the height of a room as indicated by the length of this. **5** a rivet or crosspiece in each link of a chain cable. ● **v.** (**studded**, **studding**) (usu. **be studded**) **1** decorate with studs or similar small objects. **2** strew or scatter: *the sky was studded with stars.*
– DERIVATIVES **studding** n.
– ORIGIN OE *studu, stuthu* 'post, upright prop'.

**stud²** ● **n.** **1** an establishment where horses or other domesticated animals are kept for breeding. **2** (also **stud horse**) a stallion. **3** informal a sexually active or virile young man. **4** (also **stud poker**) a form of poker in which the first card of a player's hand is dealt face down and the others face up, with betting after each round of the deal.
– ORIGIN OE *stōd*, of Gmc origin; rel. to STAND.

**stud book** ● **n.** a book containing the pedigrees of horses.

**studdingsail** /ˈstʌns(ə)l/ ● **n.** an additional sail on a square-rigged sailing ship, set at the end of a yard in light winds.
– ORIGIN C16: *studding* perh. from Mid. Low Ger., MDu. *stōtinge* 'a thrusting'.

**student** ● **n.** **1** a person studying at a university or other place of higher education. ➤ chiefly N. Amer. a school pupil. ➤ [as modifier] denoting someone who is studying to enter a particular profession: *a student nurse.* **2** a person who takes a particular interest in a subject.
– DERIVATIVES **studentship** n. (Brit.). **studenty** adj. (Brit. informal).
– ORIGIN ME: from L. *student-*, *studere* 'apply oneself to', rel. to *studium* 'painstaking application'.

**Student's t-test** ● **n.** a test for statistical significance based on a fraction (*t*) whose numerator is drawn from a normal distribution with a mean of zero, and whose denominator is the root mean square of a number of terms drawn from the same normal distribution.
– ORIGIN C20: *Student*, the pseudonym of William Sealy Gosset, Engl. brewery employee.

**stud horse** ● **n.** see STUD² (sense 2).

**studio** ● **n.** (pl. **-os**) **1** a room where an artist works or where dancers practise. **2** a room from which television or radio programmes are broadcast, or in which they are recorded. **3** a place where films or musical or sound recordings are made. **4** a film production company. **5** a studio flat.
– ORIGIN C19: from Ital., from L. *studium* (see STUDY).

**studio couch** ● **n.** chiefly N. Amer. a sofa bed.

**studio flat** ● **n.** Brit. a flat containing one main room.

**studio theatre** ● **n.** a small theatre where experimental and innovative productions are staged.

**studious** ● **adj.** **1** spending a lot of time studying or reading. **2** done deliberately or with great care.
– DERIVATIVES **studiously** adv. **studiousness** n.
– ORIGIN ME: from L. *studiosus*, from *studium* 'painstaking application'.

**studmuffin** ● **n.** N. Amer. informal a man perceived as sexually attractive.

**stud poker** ● **n.** see STUD² (sense 4).

**study** ● **n.** (pl. **-ies**) **1** the devotion of time and attention to acquiring knowledge, especially from books. **2** a detailed investigation and analysis of a subject or situation. ➤ archaic a thing that is or deserves to be investigated. **3** a room for reading, writing, or academic work. **4** a piece of work, especially a drawing, done for practice or as an experiment. ➤ a musical composition designed to develop a player's technical skill. **5** (**a study in**) a good example of (a quality or emotion): *he perched on the bed, a study in misery.* **6** theatrical slang a person who memorizes a role at a specified speed. ● **v.** (**-ies, -ied**) **1** acquire knowledge on. ➤ make a study of. ➤ apply oneself to study. ➤ (**study up**) US learn intensively about something, especially in preparation for a test. ➤ (of an actor) try to learn (the words of one's role). **2** look at closely in order to observe or read. **3** [as adj. **studied**] done with deliberate and careful effort.
– PHRASES **in a brown study** absorbed in one's thoughts. [appar. orig. from *brown* in the sense 'gloomy'.]
– DERIVATIVES **studiedly** adv. **studiedness** n.
– ORIGIN ME: shortening of OFr. *estudie* (n.), *estudier* (v.), both based on L. *studium* 'zeal, painstaking application'.

**study hall** ● **n.** N. Amer. the period of time in a school curriculum designated for study and the preparation of homework.

**stuff** ● **n.** **1** matter, material, articles, or activities of a specified or indeterminate kind. ➤ informal drink or drugs. ➤ (**the stuff**) informal money. ➤ (**one's stuff**) one's area of expertise. **2** basic characteristics; substance: *Healey was made of sterner stuff.* **3** Brit. dated woollen fabric, especially as distinct from silk, cotton, and linen. **4** N. Amer. (in sport) spin given to a ball. **5** Brit. informal, dated nonsense; rubbish. ● **v.** **1** fill tightly with something. ➤ force tightly into a receptacle or space. ➤ fill out the skin of (a dead animal or bird) with material to restore the original shape and appearance. ➤ push hastily into a space. ➤ (**be stuffed up**) have one's nose blocked up with catarrh. ➤ informal eat greedily. **2** [usu. in imper.] Brit. informal used to express indifference or rejection. **3** Brit. informal defeat heavily in sport. **4** Brit. vulgar slang (of a man) have sexual intercourse with. **5** N. Amer. place bogus votes in (a ballot box).
– PHRASES **get stuffed** [usu. in imper.] Brit. informal said to express dismissal or contempt. **that's the stuff** Brit. informal that is good or what is needed.
– DERIVATIVES **-stuffer** n.
– ORIGIN ME: shortening of OFr. *estoffe* 'material, furniture', *estoffer* 'equip, furnish', from Gk *stuphein* 'draw together'.

**stuffed shirt** ● **n.** informal a conservative, pompous person.

**stuff gown** ● **n.** Brit. a gown worn by a barrister who is not a Queen's (or King's) Counsel.

**stuffing** ● **n.** **1** a mixture used to stuff poultry or meat before cooking. **2** padding used to stuff cushions, furniture, or soft toys.
– PHRASES **knock** (or **take**) **the stuffing out of** informal severely impair the confidence or strength of.

**stuffing box** ● **n.** a casing in which material such as greased wool is compressed around a shaft or axle to form a seal against gas or liquid.

**stuff sack** ● **n.** a bag into which a sleeping bag, clothing, etc. can be stuffed for storage or ease of carrying.

**stuffy** ● **adj.** (**-ier, -iest**) **1** lacking fresh air or ventilation. **2** conventional and narrow-minded. **3** (of a person's nose) blocked up.
– DERIVATIVES **stuffily** adv. **stuffiness** n.

**stultify** /ˈstʌltɪfʌɪ/ ● **v.** (**-ies, -ied**) **1** [usu. as adj. **stultifying**] cause to feel bored or enervated. **2** cause to appear foolish or absurd.
– DERIVATIVES **stultification** n. **stultifier** n.
– ORIGIN C18: from late L. *stultificare*, from L. *stultus* 'foolish'.

**stum** /stʌm/ ● **n.** unfermented grape juice. ● **v.** (**stummed**, **stumming**) **1** prevent or stop the fermentation of (wine) by fumigating a cask with burning sulphur. **2** renew the fermentation of (wine) by adding stum.
– ORIGIN C17: from Du. *stom* (n.), *stommen* (v.), from *stom* 'dumb'.

**stumble** ● **v.** **1** trip or momentarily lose one's balance. ➤ walk unsteadily. **2** make a mistake or repeated mistakes in speaking. **3** (**stumble across/on/upon**) find by chance. ● **n.** an act of stumbling.
– DERIVATIVES **stumbler** n. **stumbling** adj. **stumblingly** adv.
– ORIGIN ME: from ON, from the Gmc base of STAMMER.

**stumblebum** ● **n.** N. Amer. informal a clumsy or inept person.

**stumbling block** ● **n.** an obstacle.

**stumer** /ˈstjuːmə/ ● **n.** Brit. informal **1** a worthless cheque or a counterfeit coin or note. **2** a failure.
– ORIGIN C19: of unknown origin.

**stump** ● n. **1** the part of a tree trunk left projecting from the ground after the rest has fallen or been felled. **2** a projecting remnant of something worn away or cut or broken off. **3** Cricket each of the three upright pieces of wood which form a wicket. ➤(**stumps**) informal close of play. **4** a cylinder with conical ends made of rolled paper or other soft material, used in art for softening or blending pencil or crayon marks. **5** [as modifier] engaged in or involving political campaigning. ● v. **1** (usu. **be stumped**) baffle. **2** Cricket (of a wicketkeeper) dismiss (a batsman) by dislodging the bails with the ball while the batsman is out of the crease but not running. **3** walk stiffly and noisily. **4** (**stump something up**) Brit. informal pay a sum of money. **5** chiefly N. Amer. travel around (a district) making political speeches. **6** use a stump on (a drawing, line, etc.).
– PHRASES **on the stump** informal engaged in political campaigning. **up a stump** N. Amer. informal in difficulties.
– ORIGIN ME: from Middle Low Ger. *stump(e)* or MDu. *stomp*; sense 5 of the noun refers to the use of a tree stump as a platform for a speaker.

**stumper** ● n. informal **1** a puzzling question. **2** Cricket a wicketkeeper.

**stump work** ● n. a type of raised embroidery popular between the 15th and 17th centuries and characterized by elaborate designs padded with wool or hair.

**stumpy** ● adj. (**-ier**, **-iest**) short and thick; squat.
– DERIVATIVES **stumpily** adv. **stumpiness** n.

**stun** ● v. (**stunned**, **stunning**) **1** knock unconscious or into a dazed or semi-conscious state. **2** astonish or shock (someone) so that they are temporarily unable to react.
– ORIGIN ME: shortening of OFr. *estoner* 'astonish'.

**stung** past and past participle of **STING**.

**stun gun** ● n. a device used to immobilize an attacker without causing serious injury.

**stunk** past and past participle of **STINK**.

**stunner** ● n. informal a strikingly beautiful or impressive person or thing. ➤an amazing turn of events.

**stunning** ● adj. extremely impressive or attractive.
– DERIVATIVES **stunningly** adv.

**stunsail** /ˈstʌns(ə)l/ (also **stuns'l**) ● n. another term for **STUDDINGSAIL**.
– ORIGIN C18: contr.

**stunt**[1] ● v. [often as adj. **stunted**] retard the growth or development of. ➤frustrate and spoil.
– DERIVATIVES **stuntedness** n.
– ORIGIN C16 (in the sense 'bring to an abrupt halt'): from dial. *stunt* 'foolish, stubborn', of Gmc origin; perh. rel. to **STUMP**.

**stunt**[2] ● n. an action displaying spectacular skill and daring. ➤something unusual done to attract attention. ● v. perform stunts, especially aerobatics.
– ORIGIN C19 (orig. US college sl.): of unknown origin.

**stuntman** (or **stuntwoman**) ● n. (pl. **-men** or **-women**) a person taking an actor's place in performing dangerous stunts.

**stupa** /ˈstuːpə/ ● n. a dome-shaped building erected as a Buddhist shrine.
– ORIGIN from Sanskrit *stūpa*.

**stupe**[1] /stjuːp/ archaic ● n. a piece of soft cloth or cotton wool dipped in hot water and used to make a poultice. ● v. treat with such a poultice.
– ORIGIN ME: via L. from Gk *stupē*.

**stupe**[2] /stjuːp/ ● n. informal a stupid person.

**stupefacient** /ˌstjuːpɪˈfeɪs(ə)nt/ Medicine ● adj. (chiefly of a drug) causing semi-consciousness. ● n. a stupefacient drug.

**stupefy** /ˈstjuːpɪfʌɪ/ ● v. (**-ies**, **-ied**) **1** make (someone) unable to think or feel properly. **2** astonish and shock.
– DERIVATIVES **stupefaction** n. **stupefier** n. **stupefying** adj. **stupefyingly** adv.
– ORIGIN ME: from Fr. *stupéfier*, from L. *stupefacere*, from *stupere* 'be struck senseless'.

**stupendous** /stjuːˈpɛndəs/ ● adj. extremely impressive.
– DERIVATIVES **stupendously** adv. **stupendousness** n.
– ORIGIN C16: from L. *stupendus* 'to be wondered at' (gerundive of *stupere*) + **-OUS**.

**stupid** ● adj. (**-er**, **-est**) **1** lacking intelligence or common sense. ➤informal used to express exasperation or boredom: *stop messing about with your stupid paintings!* **2** dazed and unable to think clearly.
– DERIVATIVES **stupidity** n. **stupidly** adv. **stupidness** n. (chiefly W. Indian).
– ORIGIN C16: from Fr. *stupide* or L. *stupidus*, from *stupere* 'be amazed or stunned'.

**stupor** /ˈstjuːpə/ ● n. a state of near-unconsciousness or insensibility.
– DERIVATIVES **stuporous** adj.
– ORIGIN ME: from L., from *stupere* 'be amazed or stunned'.

**sturdy** ● adj. (**-ier**, **-iest**) strongly and solidly built or made. ➤confident and determined: *a sturdy independence*. ● n. vertigo in sheep caused by a tapeworm larva encysted in the brain.
– DERIVATIVES **sturdied** adj. **sturdily** adv. **sturdiness** n.
– ORIGIN ME (in the senses 'reckless, violent' and 'intractable, obstinate'): shortening of OFr. *esturdi* 'stunned, dazed'; perh. based on L. *turdus* 'a thrush' (cf. the Fr. phr. *soûl comme une grive* 'drunk as a thrush').

**sturgeon** /ˈstəːdʒ(ə)n/ ● n. a very large primitive fish with bony plates on the body, commercially important for its caviar and flesh. [Family Acipenseridae: several species.]
– ORIGIN ME: from Anglo-Norman Fr., of Gmc origin.

**Sturm und Drang** /ˌʃtʊəm ʊnt ˈdraŋ, German ˌʃtʊrm ʊnt ˈdraŋ/ ● n. an 18th-century German literary and artistic movement characterized by the expression of emotional unrest and a rejection of neoclassical literary norms.
– ORIGIN Ger., lit. 'storm and stress'.

**stutter** ● v. talk with continued involuntary repetition of sounds, especially initial consonants. ➤(of a machine or gun) produce a series of short, sharp sounds. ● n. a tendency to stutter while speaking.
– DERIVATIVES **stutterer** n. **stuttering** adj. **stutteringly** adv.
– ORIGIN C16: frequentative of dial. *stut*, of Gmc origin.

**sty**[1] ● n. (pl. **-ies**) a pigsty. ● v. (**-ies**, **-ied**) archaic keep (a pig) in a sty.
– ORIGIN OE *stī-* (in *stīfearh* 'sty pig'), prob. identical with *stig* 'hall' (see **STEWARD**), of Gmc origin.

**sty**[2] (also **stye**) ● n. (pl. **sties** or **styes**) an inflamed swelling on the edge of an eyelid.
– ORIGIN C17: from dial. *styany*, from *styan* (from OE *stīgend* 'riser') + **EYE**.

**Stygian** /ˈstɪdʒɪən/ ● adj. poetic/literary very dark.
– ORIGIN from the River *Styx*, an underworld river in Gk mythology.

**stylar** /ˈstʌɪlə/ ● adj. Botany of or relating to the style or styles of a flower.

**style** ● n. **1** a manner of doing something. ➤a way of painting, writing, etc., characteristic of a particular period, person, etc. **2** a distinctive appearance, design, or arrangement. **3** elegance and sophistication. **4** an official or legal title. **5** Botany a narrow, typically elongated extension of the ovary, bearing the stigma. **6** Zoology (in an invertebrate) a small, slender pointed appendage; a stylet. **7** archaic term for **STYLUS** (in sense 2). ● v. **1** design, make, or arrange in a particular form. **2** designate with a particular name, description, or title.
– DERIVATIVES **styleless** adj. **stylelessness** n. **styler** n.
– ORIGIN ME: from OFr. *stile*, from L. *stilus*.

**-style** ● suffix (forming adjectives and adverbs) in a manner characteristic of: *family-style*.

**stylet** /ˈstʌɪlɪt/ ● n. **1** Medicine a slender probe. ➤a wire or piece of plastic run through a catheter or cannula to stiffen or clear it. **2** Zoology (in an invertebrate) a small style, especially a piercing mouthpart of an insect.
– ORIGIN C17: from Fr. *stilet*, from Ital. *stiletto* (see **STILETTO**).

**styli** plural form of **STYLUS**.

**stylish** ● adj. having or displaying a good sense of style. ➤fashionably elegant.
– DERIVATIVES **stylishly** adv. **stylishness** n.

**stylist** ● n. **1** a person who designs fashionable clothes or cuts hair. **2** a writer noted for their literary style. ➤(in sport or music) a person who performs with style.

**stylistic** ● **adj.** of or concerning style, especially literary style.
– DERIVATIVES **stylistically** adv.

**stylistics** ● **pl. n.** [treated as sing.] the study of the literary styles of particular genres or writers.

**stylite** /ˈstʌɪlʌɪt/ ● **n.** historical an ancient or medieval ascetic living on top of a pillar.
– ORIGIN C17: from eccles. Gk *stulitēs*, from *stulos* 'pillar'.

**stylize** (also **-ise**) ● **v.** [usu. as adj. **stylized**] depict or treat in a mannered and non-realistic style.
– DERIVATIVES **stylization** n.

**stylobate** /ˈstʌɪlə(ʊ)beɪt/ ● **n.** a continuous base supporting a row of columns in classical Greek architecture.
– ORIGIN C17: via L. from Gk *stulobatēs*, from *stulos* 'pillar' + *batēs* 'base'.

**stylograph** ● **n.** a kind of fountain pen having a fine perforated tube instead of a split nib.
– DERIVATIVES **stylographic** adj.
– ORIGIN C19: from **STYLUS** + **-GRAPH**.

**styloid** ● **adj.** technical resembling a stylus or pen. ➤Anatomy denoting a slender projection of bone, such as those at the lower ends of the ulna and radius.

**stylometry** /stʌɪˈlɒmɪtri/ ● **n.** the statistical analysis of variations in literary style between writers or genres.
– DERIVATIVES **stylometric** /ˌstʌɪləˈmɛtrɪk/ adj.

**stylophone** ● **n.** a miniature electronic musical instrument producing a distinctive buzzing sound when a stylus is drawn along its metal keyboard.

**stylops** /ˈstʌɪlɒps/ ● **n.** (pl. same) a minute insect that is an internal parasite of bees, wasps, or other insects. [Order Strepsiptera.]
– DERIVATIVES **stylopid** /stʌɪˈlɒpɪd/ n. & adj.
– ORIGIN C19: mod. L. *Stylops* (genus name), from Gk *stulos* 'column' + *ōps* 'eye, face'.

**stylus** /ˈstʌɪləs/ ● **n.** (pl. **styli** /-lʌɪ, -liː/ or **styluses**) **1** a hard point, typically of diamond or sapphire, following a groove in a gramophone record and transmitting the recorded sound for reproduction. **2** an ancient writing implement for scratching letters on wax-covered tablets. ➤a similar implement for engraving and tracing. ➤Computing a pen-like device used to input handwritten text or drawings directly into a computer.
– ORIGIN C18 (as a mod. L. term in botany: see **STYLE**): erroneous spelling of L. *stilus*.

**stymie** /ˈstʌɪmi/ ● **v.** (**stymies**, **stymied**, **stymying** or **stymieing**) informal prevent or hinder the progress of.
– ORIGIN C19 (orig. a golfing term, denoting a situation on the green where a ball obstructs the shot of another player): of unknown origin.

**styptic** /ˈstɪptɪk/ Medicine ● **adj.** capable of causing bleeding to stop. ● **n.** a styptic substance.
– ORIGIN ME: via L. from Gk *stuptikos*, from *stuphein* 'to contract'.

**styrax** /ˈstʌɪraks/ ● **n.** variant of **STORAX**.

**styrene** /ˈstʌɪriːn/ ● **n.** Chemistry an unsaturated liquid hydrocarbon obtained as a petroleum by-product and used to make plastics and resins.
– ORIGIN C19: from **STYRAX** + **-ENE**.

**styrofoam** ● **n.** (trademark in the US) a kind of expanded polystyrene, used especially for making food containers.
– ORIGIN 1950s: from **POLYSTYRENE** + **FOAM**.

**suasion** /ˈsweɪʒ(ə)n/ ● **n.** formal persuasion as opposed to force or compulsion.
– DERIVATIVES **suasive** adj.
– ORIGIN ME: from OFr., or from L. *suasio(n-)*, from *suadere* 'to urge'.

**suave** /swɑːv/ ● **adj.** (**suaver**, **suavest**) (of a man) charming, confident, and elegant.
– DERIVATIVES **suavely** adv. **suaveness** n. **suavity** /-vɪti/ n. (pl. **-ies**).
– ORIGIN ME: from OFr., or from L. *suavis* 'agreeable'.

**sub** informal ● **n. 1** a submarine. **2** a subscription. **3** a substitute, especially in a sporting team. **4** a subeditor. **5** Brit. an advance or loan against expected income. ● **v.** (**subbed**, **subbing**) **1** act as a substitute. **2** Brit. lend or advance a sum to. **3** subedit.

**sub-** (also **suc-** before *c*; **suf-** before *f*; **sug-** before *g*; **sup-** before *p*; **sur-** before *r*; **sus-** before *c, p, t*) ● **prefix 1** at, to, or from a lower level or position: *subalpine*. ➤lower in rank or importance: *subdeacon*. **2** somewhat; nearly; more or less: *subantarctic*. **3** denoting subsequent or secondary action of the same kind: *subdivision*. **4** denoting support: *subvention*. **5** Chemistry in names of compounds containing a relatively small proportion of a component: *suboxide*.
– ORIGIN from L. *sub* 'under, close to'.

**subacid** ● **adj.** (of a fruit) moderately sharp to the taste.

**subacute** ● **adj. 1** Medicine (of a condition) between acute and chronic. **2** moderately acute in shape or angle.

**subadult** ● **n.** Zoology an animal that is not fully adult.

**subaerial** ● **adj.** Geology existing, occurring, or formed in the open air or on the earth's surface, not under water or underground.
– DERIVATIVES **subaerially** adv.

**subalpine** ● **adj.** of or situated on the higher slopes of mountains just below the treeline.

**subaltern** /ˈsʌb(ə)lt(ə)n/ ● **n.** an officer in the British army below the rank of captain, especially a second lieutenant. ● **adj. 1** of lower status. **2** Logic, dated (of a proposition) implied by another proposition but not implying it in return.
– ORIGIN C16 (as adj.): from late L. *subalternus*, from L. *sub-* 'next below' + *alternus* 'every other'.

**subantarctic** ● **adj.** of or relating to the region immediately north of the Antarctic Circle.

**sub-aqua** ● **adj.** of or relating to swimming or exploring under water, especially with an aqualung.

**sub-aquatic** ● **adj.** underwater.

**subaqueous** ● **adj.** existing, formed, or taking place under water.

**subarctic** ● **adj.** of or relating to the region immediately south of the Arctic Circle.

**sub-assembly** ● **n.** (pl. **-ies**) a unit assembled separately but designed to be incorporated with other units into a larger manufactured product.

**Sub-Atlantic** ● **adj.** Geology relating to or denoting the fifth climatic stage of the postglacial period in northern Europe (from about 2,800 years ago to the present).

**subatomic** ● **adj.** smaller than or occurring within an atom.

**Sub-Boreal** /ˈbɔːrɪəl/ ● **adj.** Geology relating to or denoting the fourth climatic stage of the postglacial period in northern Europe (about 5,000 to 2,800 years ago).

**subcategory** ● **n.** (pl. **-ies**) a secondary or subordinate category.
– DERIVATIVES **subcategorization** (also **-isation**) n. **subcategorize** (also **-ise**) v.

**subclass** ● **n.** a secondary or subordinate class. ➤Biology a taxonomic category that ranks below class and above order.

**sub-clause** ● **n. 1** chiefly Law a subsidiary section of a clause of a bill, contract, or treaty. **2** Grammar a subordinate clause.

**subclavian** /sʌbˈkleɪvɪən/ ● **adj.** Anatomy relating to or denoting an artery or vein which serves the neck and arm on the left or right side of the body.
– ORIGIN C17: from mod. L. *subclavius*, from *sub* 'under' + *clavis* (see **CLAVICLE**), + **-IAN**.

**subclinical** ● **adj.** Medicine relating to or denoting a disease which is not severe enough to present readily observable symptoms.

**subconscious** ● **adj.** of or concerning the part of the mind of which one is not fully aware but which influences one's actions and feelings. ● **n.** (**one's/the subconscious**) this part of the mind.
– DERIVATIVES **subconsciously** adv. **subconsciousness** n.

**subcontinent** ● **n.** a large distinguishable part of a continent, such as North America or southern Africa.
– DERIVATIVES **subcontinental** adj.

**subcontract** ● **v.** /sʌbkənˈtrakt/ employ a firm or person outside one's company to do (work). ➤carry out work for a company as part of a larger project. ● **n.**

/sʌbˈkɒntrakt/ a contract to do work for another company as part of a larger project.

**subcontractor** ● **n.** a firm or person that carries out work for a company as part of a larger project.

**subcontrary** /sʌbˈkɒntrəri/ ● **adj.** Logic, dated denoting propositions which can both be true, but cannot both be false.

**subcortical** ● **adj.** Anatomy below the cortex.

**subcostal** ● **adj.** Anatomy beneath a rib; below the ribs.

**subcritical** ● **adj.** Physics **1** (in nuclear physics) containing or involving less than the critical mass. **2** (of a flow of fluid) slower than the speed at which waves travel in the fluid.

**subculture** ● **n.** a cultural group within a larger culture, often having beliefs or interests at variance with those of the larger culture.
– DERIVATIVES **subcultural** adj.

**subcutaneous** ● **adj.** Anatomy & Medicine situated or applied under the skin.
– DERIVATIVES **subcutaneously** adv.

**subdeacon** ● **n.** (in some Christian Churches) a minister of an order ranking below deacon.
– DERIVATIVES **subdeaconate** n.

**subdivide** ● **v.** divide (something that has already been divided or that is a separate unit).

**subdivision** ● **n. 1** the action of subdividing or being subdivided. ➤a secondary or subordinate division. **2** N. Amer. & Austral./NZ an area of land divided into plots for sale.

**subdominant** ● **n.** Music the fourth note of the diatonic scale of any key.

**subduction** /səbˈdʌkʃ(ə)n/ ● **n.** Geology the sideways and downward movement of the edge of a plate of the earth's crust into the mantle beneath another plate.
– DERIVATIVES **subduct** v.
– ORIGIN 1970s: via Fr. from L. *subductio(n-)*, from *subduct-*, *subducere* 'draw from below'.

**subdue** ● **v.** (**subdues**, **subdued**, **subduing**) overcome, quieten, or bring under control. ➤bring (a country) under control by force.
– DERIVATIVES **subduable** adj.
– ORIGIN ME: from Anglo-Norman Fr. *suduire*, from L. *subducere*, lit. 'draw from below'.

**subdued** ● **adj. 1** (of a person) quiet and rather reflective or depressed. **2** (of colour or lighting) soft; muted.

**subdural** /sʌbˈdjʊər(ə)l/ ● **adj.** Anatomy situated or occurring between the dura mater and the arachnoid membrane of the brain and spinal cord.

**subedit** ● **v.** (**subedited**, **subediting**) chiefly Brit. check and correct (newspaper or magazine text) before printing, typically also writing headlines and captions.
– DERIVATIVES **subeditor** n.

**subfamily** ● **n.** (pl. **-ies**) a subdivision of a group. ➤Biology a taxonomic category that ranks below family and above tribe or genus.

**subfloor** ● **n.** the foundation for a floor in a building.

**subframe** ● **n.** a supporting frame.

**subfusc** /ˈsʌbfʌsk, sʌbˈfʌsk/ ● **adj.** poetic/literary dull or gloomy. ● **n.** Brit. the formal clothing worn for examinations and formal occasions at some universities.
– ORIGIN C18: from L. *subfuscus*, from *sub-* 'somewhat' + *fuscus* 'dark brown'.

**subgenus** ● **n.** (pl. **subgenera**) Biology a taxonomic category that ranks below genus and above species.
– DERIVATIVES **subgeneric** adj.

**subglacial** ● **adj.** Geology situated or occurring underneath a glacier or ice sheet.

**subgroup** ● **n.** a subdivision of a group. ➤Mathematics a group whose members are all members of another group subject to the same operations.

**subharmonic** ● **n.** an oscillation with a frequency equal to an integral submultiple of another frequency. ● **adj.** denoting or involving a subharmonic.

**sub-heading** (also **sub-head**) ● **n.** a heading given to a subsection of a piece of writing.

**subhuman** ● **adj. 1** of a lower order of being than the human. ➤Zoology (of a primate) closely related to humans. **2** derogatory not worthy of a human being; debased or depraved. ● **n.** a subhuman creature or person.

**subjacent** /səbˈdʒeɪs(ə)nt/ ● **adj.** technical situated below something else.
– DERIVATIVES **subjacency** n.
– ORIGIN C16: from L. *subjacent-* 'lying underneath', from *sub-* 'under' + *jacere* 'to lie'.

**subject** ● **n.** /ˈsʌbdʒɪkt/ **1** a person or thing that is being discussed or dealt with or that gives rise to something. ➤Logic the part of a proposition about which a statement is made. ➤a person who is the focus of scientific or medical attention or experiment. **2** a branch of knowledge studied or taught in a school, college, or university. **3** Grammar a noun phrase about which the rest of the clause is predicated. **4** a member of a state owing allegiance to its monarch or supreme ruler. **5** Music a theme of a fugue or of a piece in sonata form; a leading phrase or motif. **6** Philosophy a thinking or feeling entity; the conscious mind or ego. ➤the central substance or core of a thing as opposed to its attributes. ● **adj.** /ˈsʌbdʒɪkt/ (**subject to**) **1** likely or prone to be affected by (something bad). **2** dependent or conditional upon. **3** under the control or authority of. ● **adv.** /ˈsʌbdʒɪkt/ (**subject to**) conditionally upon. ● **v.** /səbˈdʒɛkt/ (usu. **subject someone/thing to**) **1** cause or force to undergo. **2** bring under one's control or jurisdiction, typically by force.
– DERIVATIVES **subjection** n. **subjectless** adj.
– ORIGIN ME: from OFr. *suget*, from L. *subject-*, *subicere* 'bring under'.

**subjective** ● **adj. 1** based on or influenced by personal feelings, tastes, or opinions. **2** dependent on the mind for existence. **3** Grammar relating to or denoting a case of nouns and pronouns used for the subject of a sentence.
– DERIVATIVES **subjectively** adv. **subjectiveness** n. **subjectivity** n.

**subjective case** ● **n.** Grammar the nominative.

**subjectivism** ● **n.** Philosophy the doctrine that knowledge is merely subjective and that there is no external or objective truth.
– DERIVATIVES **subjectivist** n. & adj.

**subject matter** ● **n.** the topic dealt with or the subject represented in a debate, exposition, or work of art.

**subjoin** ● **v.** formal add (comments or supplementary information) at the end of a speech or text.
– ORIGIN C16: from obs. Fr. *subjoindre*, from L. *subjungere*, from *sub-* 'in addition' + *jungere* 'to join'.

**sub judice** /sʌb ˈdʒuːdɪsi, sʊb ˈjuːdɪkeɪ/ ● **adj.** Law under judicial consideration and therefore prohibited from public discussion elsewhere.
– ORIGIN L., lit. 'under a judge'.

**subjugate** /ˈsʌbdʒʊgeɪt/ ● **v.** (often **subjugate someone/thing to**) bring under domination or control, especially by conquest.
– DERIVATIVES **subjugation** n. **subjugator** n.
– ORIGIN ME: from late L. *subjugat-*, *subjugare* 'bring under a yoke', based on *jugum* 'yoke'.

**subjunctive** /səbˈdʒʌŋ(k)tɪv/ Grammar ● **adj.** denoting a mood of verbs expressing what is imagined or wished or possible. Compare with INDICATIVE. ● **n.** a verb in the subjunctive mood.
– DERIVATIVES **subjunctively** adv.
– ORIGIN C16: from Fr. *subjonctif*, *-ive* or late L. *subjunctivus*, from *subjungere* (see SUBJOIN), rendering Gk *hupotaktikos* 'subjoined'.

**sublate** /səˈbleɪt/ ● **v.** Philosophy assimilate (a smaller entity) into a larger one.
– DERIVATIVES **sublation** n.
– ORIGIN C19 (earlier (C16) as *sublation*): from L. *sublat-* 'taken away', from *sub-* 'from below' + *lat-* (from the stem of *tollere* 'take away').

**sublease** ● **n. & v.** another term for SUBLET.

**sub-lessee** ● **n.** a person who holds a sublease.

**sub-lessor** ● **n.** a person who grants a sublease.

**sublet** ● **v.** /sʌbˈlɛt/ (**subletting**; past and past part. **sublet**) lease (a property) to a subtenant. ● **n.** /ˈsʌblɛt/ a lease of a property by a tenant to a subtenant.

**sub lieutenant** ● **n.** a rank of officer in the Royal Navy, above midshipman and below lieutenant.

**sublimate** /ˈsʌblɪmeɪt/ ● v. **1** (in psychoanalytic theory) divert or modify (an instinctual impulse) into a culturally higher or socially more acceptable activity. **2** transform into a purer or idealized form. **3** Chemistry another term for **SUBLIME**. ● n. /also ˈsʌblɪmət/ Chemistry a solid deposit of a substance which has sublimed.
– DERIVATIVES **sublimation** n.
– ORIGIN ME: from L. *sublimat-*, *sublimare* 'raise up'.

**sublime** ● adj. (**-er**, **-est**) **1** of such excellence, grandeur, or beauty as to inspire great admiration or awe. **2** extreme or unparalleled: *the sublime confidence of youth.* ● v. **1** Chemistry (with reference to a solid substance) change directly into vapour when heated, typically forming a solid deposit again on cooling. **2** archaic elevate to a high degree of purity or excellence.
– DERIVATIVES **sublimely** adv. **sublimity** n.
– ORIGIN C16 (in the sense 'dignified, aloof'): from L. *sublimis*, from *sub-* 'up to' + a second element perh. rel. to *limen* 'threshold', *limus* 'oblique'.

**subliminal** /səˈblɪmɪn(ə)l/ ● adj. Psychology (of a stimulus or mental process) perceived by or affecting someone's mind without their being aware of it.
– DERIVATIVES **subliminally** adv.
– ORIGIN C19: from **SUB-** + L. *limen*, *limin-* 'threshold' + **-AL**.

**subliminal advertising** ● n. advertising that uses images and sounds to influence consumers subliminally.

**sublingual** ● adj. Anatomy & Medicine situated or applied under the tongue. ➤ denoting a pair of small salivary glands beneath the tongue.
– DERIVATIVES **sublingually** adv.

**sublittoral** /sʌbˈlɪt(ə)r(ə)l/ ● adj. chiefly Ecology living, growing, or situated near to or just below the shore.

**Sub-Lt.** ● abbrev. Sub Lieutenant.

**sublunar** ● adj. Astronomy within the moon's orbit and subject to its influence.

**sublunary** /sʌbˈluːn(ə)ri/ ● adj. poetic/literary belonging to this world rather than a better or more spiritual one.

**subluxation** /ˌsʌblʌkˈseɪʃ(ə)n/ ● n. Medicine a partial dislocation.

**sub-machine gun** ● n. a hand-held lightweight machine gun.

**submandibular** /ˌsʌbmanˈdɪbjʊlə/ ● adj. Anatomy situated beneath the jaw or mandible.

**submandibular gland** (also **submaxillary gland**) ● n. Anatomy either of a pair of salivary glands situated below the parotid glands.

**submarginal** ● adj. (of land) not allowing profitable farming or cultivation.

**submarine** ● n. **1** a streamlined warship designed to operate completely submerged in the sea for long periods. **2** (also **submarine sandwich**) N. Amer. another term for **HOAGIE**. ● adj. existing, occurring, done, or used under the surface of the sea.
– DERIVATIVES **submariner** n.

**submediant** ● n. Music the sixth note of the diatonic scale of any key.

**submerge** ● v. **1** cause to be under water. ➤ descend below the surface of water. **2** completely cover or obscure.
– DERIVATIVES **submergence** n. **submergible** adj.
– ORIGIN C17: from L. *submergere*, from *sub-* 'under' + *mergere* 'to dip'.

**submerse** /səbˈməːs/ ● v. technical submerge.
– ORIGIN ME: from L. *submers-* 'plunged below', from *submergere* (see **SUBMERGE**).

**submersible** ● adj. designed to operate while submerged. ● n. a small boat or craft that is submersible.

**submersion** ● n. the action or state of submerging or being submerged.

**submicroscopic** ● adj. too small to be seen by an ordinary light microscope.

**submission** ● n. **1** the action or fact of submitting. ➤ Wrestling an act of surrendering to a hold by one's opponent. **2** a proposal or application submitted for consideration. ➤ Law a proposition or argument presented by counsel to a judge or jury. **3** archaic humility; meekness.

**submissive** ● adj. meekly obedient or passive.
– DERIVATIVES **submissively** adv. **submissiveness** n.

**submit** ● v. (**submitted**, **submitting**) **1** accept or yield to a superior force or stronger person. **2** (usu. **submit something to**) subject to a particular process, treatment, or condition. ➤ (**submit oneself to**) consent to undergo. ➤ agree to refer a matter to a third party for decision or adjudication. **3** present (a proposal or application) for consideration or judgement. ➤ (especially in judicial contexts) suggest; argue.
– DERIVATIVES **submitter** n.
– ORIGIN ME: from L. *submittere*, from *sub-* 'under' + *mittere* 'send, put'.

**submodifier** ● n. Grammar an adverb used in front of an adjective or another adverb to modify its meaning, e.g. *very* in *very cold.*
– DERIVATIVES **submodification** n. **submodify** v.

**submucosa** /ˌsʌbmjuːˈkəʊsə/ ● n. (pl. **submucosae**) Physiology the layer of areolar connective tissue lying beneath a mucous membrane.
– DERIVATIVES **submucosal** adj.
– ORIGIN C19: from mod. L. *submucosa* (*membrana*), fem. of *submucosus* 'submucous'.

**submultiple** ● n. a number that can be divided exactly into a specified number. ● adj. being such a number.

**subnormal** ● adj. not reaching a level regarded as usual, especially with respect to intelligence or development.
– DERIVATIVES **subnormality** n.

**sub-nuclear** ● adj. Physics occurring in or smaller than an atomic nucleus.

**suboptimal** ● adj. technical of less than the highest standard or quality.

**sub-orbital** ● adj. **1** situated below or behind the orbit of the eye. **2** relating to or denoting a trajectory that does not complete a full orbit of the earth or other celestial body.

**suborder** ● n. Biology a taxonomic category that ranks below order and above family.

**subordinary** ● n. (pl. **-ies**) Heraldry a simple device or bearing that is less common than the ordinaries.

**subordinate** ● adj. /səˈbɔːdɪnət/ lower in rank or position. ➤ of less or secondary importance. ● n. /səˈbɔːdɪnət/ a person under the authority or control of another. ● v. /səˈbɔːdɪneɪt/ treat or regard as subordinate. ➤ make subservient or dependent.
– DERIVATIVES **subordinately** adv. **subordination** n. **subordinative** adj.
– ORIGIN ME: from med. L. *subordinatus* 'placed in an inferior rank', from L. *sub-* 'below' + *ordinare* 'ordain'.

**subordinate clause** ● n. a clause that forms part of and is dependent on a main clause (e.g. 'when it rang' in 'she answered the phone when it rang').

**subordinate legislation** ● n. Law law which is enacted under delegated powers.

**subordinating conjunction** ● n. a conjunction that introduces a subordinating clause, e.g. *although*, *because.* Contrasted with **COORDINATING CONJUNCTION**.

**suborn** /səˈbɔːn/ ● v. bribe or otherwise induce (someone) to commit an unlawful act such as perjury.
– DERIVATIVES **subornation** n. **suborner** n.
– ORIGIN C16: from L. *subornare* 'incite secretly', from *sub-* 'secretly' + *ornare* 'equip'.

**suboxide** ● n. Chemistry an oxide containing the lowest or an unusually small proportion of oxygen.

**subphylum** ● n. (pl. **subphyla**) Zoology a taxonomic category that ranks below phylum and above class.

**sub-plot** ● n. a subordinate plot in a play, novel, etc.

**subpoena** /səˈpiːnə/ Law ● n. a writ ordering a person to attend a court. ● v. (**subpoenas**, **subpoenaed** or **subpoena'd**, **subpoenaing**) summon with a subpoena. ➤ require (a document or other evidence) to be submitted to a court.
– ORIGIN ME: from L. *sub poena* 'under penalty' (the first words of the writ).

**sub-postmaster** ● n. (fem. **sub-postmistress**) a person in charge of a sub-post office.

**sub-post office** • **n.** (in the UK) a small local post office offering fewer services than a main post office.

**subprogram** • **n.** Computing a subroutine.

**subrogation** /ˌsʌbrəˈgeɪʃ(ə)n/ • **n.** Law the substitution of one person or group by another in respect of a debt or insurance claim, accompanied by the transfer of any associated rights and duties.
– DERIVATIVES **subrogate** /ˈsʌbrəgeɪt/ v.
– ORIGIN ME (in the general sense 'substitution'): from late L. *subrogatio(n-)*, from *subrogare* 'choose as substitute'.

**sub rosa** /sʌb ˈrəʊzə/ • **adj. & adv.** formal happening or done in secret.
– ORIGIN L., lit. 'under the rose', as an emblem of secrecy.

**subroutine** • **n.** Computing a set of instructions designed to perform a frequently used operation within a program.

**sub-Saharan** • **adj.** from or forming part of the African regions south of the Sahara desert.

**subsample** • **n.** a sample drawn from a larger sample. • **v.** take a subsample from.

**subscribe** • **v. 1** (usu. **subscribe to**) arrange to receive something, especially a periodical, regularly by paying in advance. ➤ contribute or undertake to contribute a sum of money to a project or cause. ➤ apply to participate in. ➤ apply for an issue of shares. ➤ (of a bookseller) agree before publication to take (a certain number of copies of a book). **2** formal sign (a will, contract, etc.). ➤ (**subscribe oneself**) archaic sign oneself as. **3** (**subscribe to**) feel agreement with (an idea or proposal).
– DERIVATIVES **subscriber** n.
– ORIGIN ME (in the sense 'sign at the bottom of a document'): from L. *subscript-*, *subscribere*, from *sub-* 'under' + *scribere* 'write'.

**subscriber trunk dialling** • **n.** Brit. the automatic connection of trunk calls by dialling without the assistance of an operator.

**subscript** • **adj.** (of a letter, figure, or symbol) written or printed below the line. • **n.** a subscript letter, figure, or symbol.

**subscription** • **n. 1** the action or fact of subscribing. ➤ a payment to subscribe to something. **2** formal a signature or short piece of writing at the end of a document. ➤ archaic a signed declaration or agreement.

**subscription concert** • **n.** one of a series of concerts for which tickets are sold mainly in advance.

**subsection** • **n.** a division of a section.

**subsellium** /səbˈsɛlɪəm/ • **n.** (pl. **subsellia** /-lɪə/) another term for **MISERICORD** (in sense 1).
– ORIGIN L., from *sub-* 'secondary' + *sella* 'seat'.

**subsequence**[1] /ˈsʌbsɪkw(ə)ns/ • **n.** formal the state of following or being a consequence of something.

**subsequence**[2] /ˈsʌbˌsiːkw(ə)ns/ • **n.** a sequence contained in or derived from another sequence.

**subsequent** • **adj.** coming after something in time.
– DERIVATIVES **subsequently** adv.
– ORIGIN ME: from OFr., or from L. *subsequent-*, *subsequi* 'follow after'.

**subserve** • **v.** formal help to further or promote.
– ORIGIN C17: from L. *subservient-*, *subservire* (see **SUB-**, **SERVE**).

**subservient** • **adj.** (often **subservient to**) **1** prepared to obey others unquestioningly; obsequious. **2** less important; subordinate.
– DERIVATIVES **subservience** n. **subserviency** n. **subserviently** adv.

**subset** • **n.** a part of a larger group of related things. ➤ Mathematics a set of which all the elements are contained in another set.

**subshrub** • **n.** Botany a dwarf shrub, especially one that is woody only at the base.
– DERIVATIVES **subshrubby** adj.

**subside** • **v. 1** become less intense, violent, or severe. ➤ (**subside into**) give way to (an overwhelming feeling). **2** (of water) go down to a lower or the normal level. ➤ (of a swelling) reduce until gone. **3** (of a building) sink lower into the ground. ➤ (of the ground) cave in; sink. ➤ informal sink into a sitting, kneeling, or lying position.
– ORIGIN C17: from L. *subsidere*, from *sub-* 'below' + *sidere* 'settle'.

**subsidence** /səbˈsʌɪd(ə)ns, ˈsʌbsɪd(ə)ns/ • **n.** the gradual caving in or sinking of an area of land.

**subsidiarity** /səbˌsɪdɪˈarɪti/ • **n.** (in politics) the principle that a central authority should have a subsidiary function, performing only those tasks which cannot be performed at a more local level.

**subsidiary** • **adj.** less important than but related or supplementary to. ➤ (of a company) controlled by a holding or parent company. • **n.** (pl. **-ies**) a subsidiary company.
– DERIVATIVES **subsidiarily** adv. (rare).
– ORIGIN C16 (in the sense 'serving to help or supplement'): from L. *subsidiarius*, from *subsidium* (see **SUBSIDY**).

**subsidize** (also **-ise**) • **v.** support (an organization or activity) financially. ➤ pay part of the cost of producing (something) to reduce its price.
– DERIVATIVES **subsidization** n. **subsidizer** n.

**subsidy** • **n.** (pl. **-ies**) **1** a sum of money granted from public funds to help an industry or business keep the price of a commodity or service low. ➤ a sum of money granted to support an undertaking held to be in the public interest. ➤ a grant or contribution of money. **2** historical a parliamentary grant to the sovereign for state needs. ➤ a tax levied on a particular occasion.
– ORIGIN ME: from Anglo-Norman Fr. *subsidie*, from L. *subsidium* 'assistance'.

**subsist** • **v. 1** maintain or support oneself, especially at a minimal level. ➤ archaic provide sustenance for. **2** chiefly Law remain in being, force, or effect. ➤ (**subsist in**) be attributable to.
– DERIVATIVES **subsistent** adj.
– ORIGIN C16 (in the sense 'continue to exist'): from L. *subsistere* 'stand firm'.

**subsistence** • **n. 1** the action or fact of subsisting. ➤ the means of doing this. ➤ [as modifier] denoting or relating to production at a level sufficient only for one's own use or consumption, without any surplus for trade: *subsistence agriculture*. **2** chiefly Law the state of remaining in force or effect.

**subsistence allowance** (also **subsistence money**) • **n.** chiefly Brit. an allowance or advance on wages, especially when granted as travelling expenses.

**subsistence level** (also **subsistence wage**) • **n.** a standard of living (or wage) that provides only the bare necessities of life.

**subsoil** • **n.** the soil lying immediately under the surface soil. • **v.** [usu. as noun **subsoiling**] plough (land) so as to cut into the subsoil.
– DERIVATIVES **subsoiler** n.

**subsonic** • **adj.** relating to or flying at a speed or speeds less than that of sound.
– DERIVATIVES **subsonically** adv.

**subspace** • **n. 1** Mathematics a space that is wholly contained in another space. **2** (in science fiction) a hypothetical space–time continuum used for communication at a speed faster than that of light.

**sub specie aeternitatis** /sʌb ˈspiːʃiː ɪˌtəːnɪˈtɑːtɪs/ • **adv.** viewed in relation to the eternal; in a universal perspective.
– ORIGIN L., lit. 'under the aspect of eternity'.

**subspecies** • **n.** (pl. same) Biology a taxonomic category that ranks below species, typically a fairly permanent geographically isolated race.
– DERIVATIVES **subspecific** adj.

**substance** • **n. 1** a particular kind of matter with uniform properties. ➤ an intoxicating or narcotic drug. **2** the real physical matter of which a person or thing consists. ➤ solid basis in reality or fact: *the claim has no substance*. ➤ dependability or stability. **3** the quality of being important, valid, or significant. ➤ the most important or essential part or meaning. ➤ the subject matter of a text or work of art, especially as contrasted with its form or style. ➤ wealth and possessions: *a woman of substance*. **4** Philosophy the essential nature underlying phenomena, which is subject to changes and accidents.
– PHRASES **in substance** essentially.
– ORIGIN ME: from OFr., from L. *substantia* 'being, essence', from *substant-*, *substare* 'stand firm'.

**substandard** ● **adj. 1** below the usual or required standard. **2** another term for **NON-STANDARD**.

**substantial** ● **adj. 1** of considerable importance, size, or worth. ➤strongly built or made. ➤important in material or social terms; wealthy. **2** concerning the essentials of something. **3** real and tangible rather than imaginary.
– DERIVATIVES **substantiality** n. **substantialize** (also **-ise**) v.

**substantialism** ● **n.** Philosophy the doctrine that behind phenomena there are substantial realities.
– DERIVATIVES **substantialist** n. & adj.

**substantially** ● **adv. 1** to a great or significant extent. **2** for the most part; essentially.

**substantiate** /səbˈstanʃɪeɪt/ ● **v.** provide evidence to support or prove the truth of.
– DERIVATIVES **substantiation** n.
– ORIGIN C17: from med. L. *substantiat-*, *substantiare* 'give substance'.

**substantive** /ˈsʌbst(ə)ntɪv/ ● **adj.** /also səbˈstantɪv/ **1** having a firm basis in reality and so important or meaningful. **2** having a separate and independent existence. ➤(of a rank or appointment) permanent. ➤(of a dye) not needing a mordant. ➤(of an enactment, motion, or resolution) made in due form as such; not amended. **3** (of law) defining rights and duties as opposed to giving the rules by which such things are established. ● **n.** Grammar, dated a noun.
– DERIVATIVES **substantival** /-ˈtʌɪv(ə)l/ adj. **substantively** adv.

**substation** ● **n. 1** a set of equipment reducing the high voltage of electrical power transmission to that suitable for supply to consumers. **2** a subordinate police station or fire station. **3** N. Amer. a small local post office.

**substituent** /səbˈstɪtjʊənt/ ● **n.** Chemistry an atom or group of atoms taking the place of another or occupying a specified position in a molecule.

**substitute** ● **n. 1** a person or thing acting or serving in place of another. **2** a sports player nominated as eligible to replace another after a match has begun. **3** Scots Law a deputy. ● **v. 1** (usu. **substitute something for**) use, add, or serve in place of. ➤(usu. **substitute something with**) replace with another. ➤Chemistry replace (an atom or group in a molecule) with another. **2** replace (a sports player) with a substitute during a match.
– DERIVATIVES **substitutability** n. **substitutable** adj. **substitution** n. **substitutional** adj. **substitutionary** adj. **substitutive** adj.
– ORIGIN ME (denoting a deputy or delegate): from L. *substitut-*, *substituere* 'put in place of'.

**substrate** /ˈsʌbstreɪt/ ● **n. 1** the surface or material on which an organism lives, grows, or feeds. **2** the substance on which an enzyme acts. **3** a surface on which something is deposited or inscribed.
– ORIGIN C19: anglicized form of **SUBSTRATUM**.

**substratum** /sʌbˈstrɑːtəm, -ˈstreɪtəm/ ● **n.** (pl. **substrata**) **1** an underlying layer or substance, in particular a layer of rock or soil beneath the surface of the ground. **2** a foundation or basis.

**substructure** ● **n.** an underlying or supporting structure.
– DERIVATIVES **substructural** adj.

**subsume** /səbˈsjuːm/ ● **v.** include or absorb in something else.
– DERIVATIVES **subsumable** adj. **subsumption** n.
– ORIGIN C16 (in the sense 'subjoin, add'): from med. L. *subsumere*, from *sub-* 'from below' + *sumere* 'take'.

**subtenant** ● **n.** a person who leases property from a tenant.
– DERIVATIVES **subtenancy** n.

**subtend** /sʌbˈtɛnd/ ● **v. 1** (of a line, arc, etc.) form (an angle) at a particular point when straight lines from its extremities meet. ➤(of an angle or chord) have bounding lines or points that meet or coincide with those of (a line or arc). **2** Botany (of a bract) extend under (a flower) so as to support or enfold it.
– ORIGIN C16: from L. *subtendere*, from *sub-* 'under' + *tendere* 'stretch'.

**subterfuge** /ˈsʌbtəfjuːdʒ/ ● **n.** a trick or deception used in order to achieve one's goal.
– ORIGIN C16: from Fr., or from late L. *subterfugium*, from L. *subterfugere* 'escape secretly', from *subter-* 'beneath' + *fugere* 'flee'.

**subterminal** ● **adj.** technical near the end of a chain or other structure.

**subterranean** /ˌsʌbtəˈreɪnɪən/ ● **adj. 1** existing, occurring, or done under the earth's surface. **2** secret.
– DERIVATIVES **subterraneously** adv.
– ORIGIN C17: from L. *subterraneus* (from *sub-* 'below' + *terra* 'earth') + **-AN**.

**subtext** ● **n.** an underlying theme in a piece of writing or speech.

**subtilize** /ˈsʌtɪlʌɪz/ (also **-ise**) ● **v.** archaic make more subtle; refine.
– DERIVATIVES **subtilization** n.

**subtitle** ● **n. 1** (**subtitles**) captions displayed at the bottom of a cinema or television screen that translate or transcribe the dialogue or narrative. **2** a subordinate title of a published work or article. ● **v.** provide with a subtitle or subtitles.

**subtle** ● **adj.** (**-er**, **-est**) **1** so delicate or precise as to be difficult to analyse or describe: *a subtle distinction.* ➤capable of making fine distinctions. ➤delicately complex and understated: *subtle lighting.* **2** making use of clever and indirect methods to achieve something. **3** archaic crafty; cunning.
– DERIVATIVES **subtleness** n. **subtlety** n. **subtly** adv.
– ORIGIN ME: from OFr. *sotil*, from L. *subtilis*.

**subtonic** ● **n.** Music the note below the tonic, the seventh note of the diatonic scale of any key.

**subtopia** ● **n.** Brit. unsightly, sprawling suburban development.
– DERIVATIVES **subtopian** adj.
– ORIGIN 1950s: blend of **SUBURB** and **UTOPIA**.

**subtotal** ● **n.** the total of one set of a larger group of figures to be added. ● **v.** (**subtotalled**, **subtotalling**; US **subtotaled**, **subtotaling**) add (numbers) so as to obtain a subtotal. ● **adj.** Medicine (of an injury or a surgical operation) partial; not total.

**subtract** ● **v.** take away (a number or amount) from another to calculate the difference. ➤remove (a part of something).
– DERIVATIVES **subtracter** n. **subtraction** n. **subtractive** adj.
– ORIGIN C16 (earlier (ME) as *subtraction*): from L. *subtract-*, *subtrahere* 'draw away'.

**subtrahend** /ˈsʌbtrəˌhɛnd/ ● **n.** Mathematics a quantity or number to be subtracted from another.
– ORIGIN C17: from L. *subtrahendus* 'to be taken away', gerundive of *subtrahere* (see **SUBTRACT**).

**subtropics** ● **pl. n.** the regions adjacent to or bordering on the tropics.
– DERIVATIVES **subtropical** adj.

**Subud** /sʊˈbuːd/ ● **n.** a movement based on a system of exercises by which the individual seeks to approach a state of perfection through divine power.
– ORIGIN contr. of Javanese *susila budhi dharma*, from Sanskrit *suśīla* 'good disposition' + *buddhi* 'understanding' + *dharma* 'religious duty'.

**subulate** /ˈsjuːbjʊlət, -leɪt/ ● **adj.** Botany & Zoology slender and tapering to a point; awl-shaped.
– ORIGIN C18: from L. *subula* 'awl' + **-ATE**[2].

**subunit** ● **n.** a distinct component of something.

**suburb** ● **n.** an outlying district of a city, especially a residential one.
– DERIVATIVES **suburban** adj. **suburbanite** n. **suburbanization** (also **-isation**) n. **suburbanize** (also **-ise**) v.
– ORIGIN ME: from OFr. *suburbe* or L. *suburbium*, from *sub-* 'near to' + *urbs*, *urb-* 'city'.

**suburbia** ● **n.** the suburbs viewed collectively.

**subvent** ● **v.** formal support or assist by the payment of a subvention.

**subvention** ● **n.** a grant of money, especially from a government.
– ORIGIN ME (in the sense 'provision of help'): from OFr., from late L. *subventio(n-)*, from L. *subvenire* 'assist'.

**subversive** ● **adj.** seeking or intended to subvert an established system or institution. ● **n.** a subversive person.
– DERIVATIVES **subversively** adv. **subversiveness** n.

**subvert** ● **v.** undermine the power and authority of (an established system or institution).
– DERIVATIVES **subversion** n. **subverter** n.
– ORIGIN ME: from OFr. *subvertir* or L. *subvers-*, *subvertere*, from *sub-* 'from below' + *vertere* 'to turn'.

**subway** ● **n. 1** Brit. a tunnel under a road for use by pedestrians. **2** chiefly N. Amer. an underground railway.

**subwoofer** ● **n.** a loudspeaker component designed to reproduce very low bass frequencies.

**sub-zero** ● **adj.** (of temperature) lower than zero; below freezing.

**suc-** ● **prefix** variant spelling of **SUB-** assimilated before *c* (as in *succeed*, *succussion*).

**succah** /ˈsʊkə/ (also **sukkah**) ● **n.** a booth in which a practising Jew spends part of the Feast of Tabernacles.
– ORIGIN C19: from Heb. *sukkāh* 'hut'.

**succedaneum** /ˌsʌksɪˈdeɪnɪəm/ ● **n.** (pl. **succedanea** /-nɪə/) archaic or poetic/literary a substitute, especially for a medicine or drug.
– DERIVATIVES **succedaneous** adj.
– ORIGIN C17: mod. L., neut. of L. *succedaneus* 'following after', from *succedere* (see **SUCCEED**).

**succeed** ● **v. 1** achieve an aim or purpose. ➤ attain fame, wealth, or social status. **2** take over an office, title, etc. from (someone). ➤ (often **succeed to**) become the new rightful holder of an office, title, etc. **3** come after and take the place of: *her embarrassment was succeeded by fear.*
– DERIVATIVES **succeeder** n. (archaic).
– ORIGIN ME: from OFr. *succeder* or L. *success-*, *succedere* 'come close after'.

**succentor** /səkˈsɛntə/ ● **n.** a precentor's deputy in some cathedrals.
– ORIGIN C17: from late L., from L. *succinere* 'sing to, chime in'.

**succès de scandale** /sʊkˌseɪ də skɒnˈdɑːl, French syksɛ də skɑ̃dal/ ● **n.** a success due to notoriety or a thing's scandalous nature.
– ORIGIN Fr., lit. 'success of scandal'.

**succès d'estime** /sʊkˌseɪ dɛˈstiːm, French syksɛ dɛstim/ ● **n.** (pl. same) a success in terms of critical appreciation, as opposed to popularity or commercial gain.
– ORIGIN Fr., lit. 'success of opinion'.

**success** ● **n. 1** the accomplishment of an aim or purpose. ➤ the attainment of fame, wealth, or social status. ➤ a person or thing that achieves success. **2** archaic the good or bad outcome of an undertaking.
– ORIGIN C16: from L. *successus*, from *succedere* (see **SUCCEED**).

**successful** ● **adj.** accomplishing an aim or purpose. ➤ having achieved fame, wealth, or social status.
– DERIVATIVES **successfully** adv. **successfulness** n.

**succession** ● **n. 1** a number of people or things following one after the other. **2** the action, process, or right of inheriting an office, title, etc. **3** Ecology the process by which a plant or animal community successively gives way to another until a stable climax is reached.
– PHRASES **in quick** (or **rapid**) **succession** following one another at short intervals. **in succession** following one after the other without interruption. **in succession to** inheriting or elected to the place of.
– DERIVATIVES **successional** adj.

**successive** ● **adj.** following one another or following others.
– DERIVATIVES **successively** adv. **successiveness** n.

**successor** ● **n.** a person or thing that succeeds another.

**success story** ● **n.** informal a successful person or thing.

**succinct** /səkˈsɪŋ(k)t/ ● **adj.** briefly and clearly expressed.
– DERIVATIVES **succinctly** adv. **succinctness** n.
– ORIGIN ME (in the sense 'encircled'): from L. *succinct-*, *succingere* 'tuck up', from *sub-* 'from below' + *cingere* 'gird'.

**succinic acid** /sʌkˈsɪnɪk/ ● **n.** Biochemistry a crystalline organic acid which occurs in living tissue as an intermediate in glucose metabolism.
– DERIVATIVES **succinate** /ˈsʌksɪneɪt/ n.
– ORIGIN C18: from Fr. *succinique*, from L. *succinum* 'amber' (from which it was first derived).

**succory** /ˈsʌk(ə)ri/ ● **n.** another term for **CHICORY** (in sense 1).
– ORIGIN C16: alt. of obs. Fr. *cicorée*.

**succotash** /ˈsʌkətaʃ/ ● **n.** US a dish of maize and lima beans boiled together.
– ORIGIN C18: from Narragansett *msiquatash* (pl.).

**Succoth** /sʊˈkəʊt, ˈsʌkəθ/ ● **n.** a major Jewish festival held in the autumn to commemorate the sheltering of the Israelites in the wilderness, marked by the erection of small booths.
– ORIGIN from Heb. *sukkōṯ*, pl. of *sukkāh* 'thicket, hut'.

**succour** /ˈsʌkə/ (US **succor**) ● **n.** assistance and support in times of hardship and distress. ➤ (**succours**) archaic reinforcements of troops. ● **v.** give assistance or aid to.
– DERIVATIVES **succourless** adj.
– ORIGIN ME: via OFr. from med. L. *succursus*, from L. *succurrere* 'run to the help of'.

**succubus** /ˈsʌkjʊbəs/ ● **n.** (pl. **succubi** /-bʌɪ/) a female demon believed to have sexual intercourse with sleeping men.
– ORIGIN ME: from med. L. *succubus* 'prostitute', from *succubare*, from *sub-* 'under' + *cubare* 'to lie'.

**succulent** ● **adj. 1** (of food) tender, juicy, and tasty. **2** Botany (of a plant, especially a xerophyte) having thick fleshy leaves or stems adapted to storing water. ● **n.** Botany a succulent plant.
– DERIVATIVES **succulence** n. **succulently** adv.
– ORIGIN C17: from L. *succulentus*, from *succus* 'juice'.

**succumb** ● **v. 1** (often **succumb to**) fail to resist (pressure, temptation, etc.). **2** die from the effect of a disease or injury.
– ORIGIN C15 (in the sense 'bring low, overwhelm'): from OFr. *succomber* or L. *succumbere*, from *sub-* 'under' + a verb rel. to *cubare* 'to lie'.

**succursal** /səˈkəːs(ə)l/ ● **adj.** (of a religious establishment such as a monastery) subsidiary to a principal establishment.
– ORIGIN C19: from Fr. *succursale*, from med. L. *succursus*, from *succurrere* (see **SUCCOUR**).

**succuss** /səˈkʌs/ ● **v.** (in preparing homeopathic remedies) shake (a solution) vigorously.
– DERIVATIVES **succussion** n.
– ORIGIN C19: from L. *succuss-*, *succutere* 'shake'.

**such** ● **det., predet., & pron. 1** of the type previously mentioned. **2** (**such —— as/that**) of the type about to be mentioned. **3** to so high a degree; so great.
– PHRASES **and such** and similar things. **as such** in the exact sense of the word. **such-and-such** an unspecified person or thing. **such as 1** for example. **2** of a kind that; like. **3** archaic those who. **such as it is** what little there is; for what it's worth. **such a one** such a person or thing. **such that** to the extent that.
– ORIGIN OE *swilc*, *swylc*, from the Gmc bases of **SO**[1] and **ALIKE**.

**suchlike** ● **pron.** things of the type mentioned. ● **det.** of the type mentioned.

**suck** ● **v. 1** draw into the mouth by contracting the muscles of the lip and mouth to make a partial vacuum. ➤ hold (something) in the mouth and draw at it by contracting the lip and cheek muscles. ➤ draw in a specified direction by creating a vacuum. ➤ (of a pump) make a gurgling sound as a result of drawing air instead of water. **2** (usu. **suck someone in/into**) involve (someone) in something without their choosing. **3** (**suck up**) informal attempt to gain advantage by behaving obsequiously. **4** N. Amer. informal be very bad or disagreeable: *the weather here sucks.* ● **n.** an act or sound of sucking. ● **exclam.** (**sucks**) Brit. informal used to express derision and defiance.
– PHRASES **give suck** archaic suckle. **suck someone dry** exhaust someone's physical, material, or emotional resources. **suck it up** US informal accept a hardship.

– ORIGIN OE *sūcan* (v.), from an Indo-Eur. imitative root; rel. to **SOAK**.

**sucker** ● n. **1** a rubber cup that adheres to a surface by suction. ➤ a flat or concave organ enabling an animal to cling to a surface by suction. **2** the piston of a suction pump. ➤ a pipe through which liquid is drawn by suction. **3** informal a gullible or easily deceived person. ➤ (**a sucker for**) a person especially susceptible to or fond of (a specified thing). **4** informal, chiefly N. Amer. an unspecified person or thing. **5** Botany a shoot springing from the base of a tree or other plant, especially one arising from the root at some distance from the trunk. ➤ a side shoot from an axillary bud. **6** a freshwater fish with thick lips that sucks up food from the bottom. [Family Catostomidae: many species.] **7** N. Amer. informal a lollipop. ● v. **1** Botany (of a plant) produce suckers. **2** informal, chiefly N. Amer. fool or trick (someone).

**suckerfish** ● n. (pl. same or **-fishes**) another term for **REMORA**.

**sucker punch** ● n. an unexpected punch or blow. ● v. (**sucker-punch**) hit with a sucker punch.

**suckhole** ● n. **1** US informal a whirlpool. **2** Canadian & Austral. vulgar slang a sycophant. ● v. Canadian & Austral. vulgar slang behave in a sycophantic way towards someone.

**sucking** ● adj. (of a child or animal) not yet weaned.

**suckle** ● v. (with reference to a baby or young animal) feed from the breast or teat.
– DERIVATIVES **suckler** n.
– ORIGIN ME: prob. a back-form. from **SUCKLING**.

**suckling** ● n. an unweaned child or animal.
– ORIGIN ME: from **SUCK** + **-LING**.

**sucky** ● adj. informal **1** ingratiating and obsequious. **2** disagreeable; unpleasant.

**sucrase** /'s(j)u:kreɪz/ ● n. another term for **INVERTASE**.

**sucre** /'su:kreɪ/ ● n. the basic monetary unit of Ecuador, equal to 100 centavos.
– ORIGIN named after the Venezuelan revolutionary Antonio José de *Sucre* (1795–1830).

**sucrier** /'su:krɪeɪ/ ● n. a sugar bowl, typically one made of porcelain and with a cover.
– ORIGIN C19: Fr., from *sucre* 'sugar'.

**sucrose** /'s(j)u:krəʊz, -əʊs/ ● n. Chemistry a compound which is the chief component of cane or beet sugar.
– ORIGIN C19: from Fr. *sucre* 'sugar' + **-OSE**[2].

**suction** ● n. the production of a partial vacuum by the removal of air in order to force fluid into a vacant space or procure adhesion. ● v. remove using suction.
– ORIGIN C17: from late L. *suctio(n-)*. from L. *sugere* 'suck'.

**suction pump** ● n. a pump for drawing liquid through a pipe into a chamber emptied by a piston.

**suctorial** /sʌk'tɔ:rɪəl/ ● adj. chiefly Zoology adapted for sucking. ➤ (of an animal) having a sucker for feeding or adhering to something.
– DERIVATIVES **suctorially** adv.

**Sudanese** /su:də'ni:z/ ● n. a native or inhabitant of the Sudan. ● adj. of or relating to the Sudan.

**sudarium** /s(j)u:'dɛ:rɪəm/ ● n. (pl. **sudaria** /-rɪə/) (in the Roman Catholic Church) another term for **VERONICA** (in sense 2).
– ORIGIN C17: from L., lit. 'napkin', from *sudor* 'sweat'.

**sudatorium** /ˌs(j)u:də'tɔ:rɪəm/ ● n. (pl. **sudatoria** /-rɪə/) a room, especially in ancient Roman times, used for hot-air or steam baths.
– ORIGIN L., neut. of *sudatorius*, from *sudare* 'to sweat'.

**sudd** /sʌd/ ● n. an area of floating vegetation in a stretch of the White Nile, thick enough to impede navigation.
– ORIGIN Arab., lit. 'obstruction'.

**sudden** ● adj. occurring or done quickly and unexpectedly.
– PHRASES (**all**) **of a sudden** (or archaic **on a sudden**) suddenly.
– DERIVATIVES **suddenness** n.
– ORIGIN ME: from Anglo-Norman Fr. *sudein*, from an alt. of L. *subitaneus*, from *subitus* 'sudden'.

**sudden death** ● n. a means of deciding the winner in a tied match, in which play continues and the winner is the first side or player to score.

**sudden infant death syndrome** ● n. technical term for **COT DEATH**.

**suddenly** ● adv. quickly and unexpectedly.

**sudoriferous** /ˌs(j)u:də'rɪf(ə)rəs/ ● adj. (of a gland) secreting sweat.
– ORIGIN C16 (in the sense 'sudorific'): from late L. *sudorifer* (from L. *sudor* 'sweat') + **-OUS**.

**sudorific** /ˌs(j)u:də'rɪfɪk/ Medicine ● adj. relating to or causing sweating. ● n. a sudorific drug.
– ORIGIN C17: from mod. L. *sudorificus*, from L. *sudor* 'sweat'.

**Sudra** /'su:drə, 'ʃu:drə/ ● n. a member of the worker caste, lowest of the four Hindu castes.
– ORIGIN from Sanskrit *śūdra*.

**suds** ● pl. n. **1** froth made from soap and water. **2** N. Amer. informal beer. ● v. chiefly N. Amer. cover or wash in soapy water. ➤ form suds.
– DERIVATIVES **sudsy** adj.
– ORIGIN C19: perh. orig. denoting the flood water of the fens; cf. Mid. Low Ger. *sudde*, MDu. *sudse* 'marsh, bog'; prob. rel. to **SEETHE**.

**sudser** /'sʌdzə/ ● n. N. Amer. informal a soap opera.

**sue** ● v. (**sues**, **sued**, **suing**) **1** institute legal proceedings against (a person or institution), typically for redress. **2** formal appeal formally to a person for something.
– DERIVATIVES **suer** n.
– ORIGIN ME (also in sense 'follow'): from Anglo-Norman Fr. *suer*, based on L. *sequi* 'follow'.

**suede** ● n. leather, especially the skin of a young goat, with the flesh side rubbed to make a velvety nap.
– ORIGIN C17: from Fr. (*gants de*) *Suède* '(gloves of) Sweden'.

**suedehead** ● n. a young person of a subculture characterized by an appearance similar to that of skinheads but with slightly longer hair and smarter clothes.

**suerte** /'swɛ:teɪ/ ● n. each of the three stages of a bullfight.
– ORIGIN Sp., lit. 'chance, fate'.

**suet** /'s(j)u:ɪt/ ● n. the hard white fat on the kidneys and loins of cattle, sheep, and other animals, used in making foods.
– DERIVATIVES **suety** adj.
– ORIGIN ME: from Anglo-Norman Fr., from the synonymous word *su*, from L. *sebum* 'tallow'.

**suet pudding** ● n. a boiled or steamed pudding of suet and flour.

**suf-** ● prefix variant spelling of **SUB-** assimilated before *f* (as in *suffocate*, *suffuse*).

**suffer** ● v. **1** experience or be subjected to (something bad or unpleasant). ➤ (**suffer from**) be affected by or subject to (an illness or ailment). ➤ become or appear worse in quality. ➤ archaic undergo martyrdom or execution. **2** archaic tolerate. ➤ allow (someone) to do something.
– DERIVATIVES **sufferable** adj. **sufferer** n.
– ORIGIN ME: from Anglo-Norman Fr. *suffrir*, from L. *sufferre*, from *sub-* 'from below' + *ferre* 'to bear'.

**sufferance** ● n. **1** absence of objection rather than genuine approval; toleration. **2** archaic patient endurance. **3** archaic the suffering or undergoing of something bad or unpleasant.

**suffice** /sə'fʌɪs/ ● v. be enough or adequate. ➤ meet the needs of.
– PHRASES **suffice** (**it**) **to say** used to indicate that one is withholding something for reasons of discretion or brevity.
– ORIGIN ME: from OFr. *suffis-*, stem of *suffire*, from L. *sufficient-*, *sufficere* 'put under, meet the need of'.

**sufficiency** ● n. (pl. **-ies**) **1** the condition or quality of being sufficient. ➤ an adequate amount, especially of something essential. **2** archaic self-sufficiency or independence of character.

**sufficient** ● adj. & det. enough; adequate.
– DERIVATIVES **sufficiently** adv.
– ORIGIN ME (in the sense 'legally satisfactory'): from OFr., or from L. *sufficient-* (see **SUFFICE**).

**suffix** /'sʌfɪks/ ● n. **1** a morpheme added at the end of a word to form a derivative (e.g. *-ation*). **2** Mathematics another term for **SUBSCRIPT**. ● v. /also sə'fɪks/ append, es-

pecially as a suffix.
– DERIVATIVES **suffixation** n.
– ORIGIN C18: from mod. L. *suffixum*, neut. past part. (used as n.) of L. *suffigere*, from *sub-* 'subordinately' + *figere* 'fasten'.

**suffocate** • v. die or cause to die from lack of air or inability to breathe. ➤ have or cause to have difficulty in breathing.
– DERIVATIVES **suffocating** adj. **suffocatingly** adv. **suffocation** n.
– ORIGIN C15: from L. *suffocat-*, *suffocare* 'stifle', from *sub-* 'below' + *fauces* 'throat'.

**suffragan** /'sʌfrəg(ə)n/ (also **suffragan bishop** or **bishop suffragan**) • n. a bishop appointed to help a diocesan bishop. ➤ a bishop in relation to his archbishop or metropolitan.
– ORIGIN ME: from Anglo-Norman Fr. and OFr., representing med. L. *suffraganeus* 'assistant (bishop)', from L. *suffragium* 'suffrage'.

**suffrage** /'sʌfrɪdʒ/ • n. **1** the right to vote in political elections. ➤ archaic a vote given for a person or in assent to a proposal. **2** (**suffrages**) (in the Book of Common Prayer) the intercessory petitions pronounced by a priest in the Litany. ➤ a series of petitions pronounced by the priest with the responses of the congregation. ➤ archaic intercessory prayers, especially those for the dead.
– ORIGIN ME: from L. *suffragium*, reinforced by Fr. *suffrage*.

**suffragette** /ˌsʌfrə'dʒɛt/ • n. historical a woman seeking the right to vote through organized protest.

**suffragist** • n. chiefly historical a person advocating the extension of suffrage, especially to women.
– DERIVATIVES **suffragism** n.

**suffuse** /sə'fjuːz/ • v. (often **be suffused with**) gradually spread through or over.
– DERIVATIVES **suffusion** n.
– ORIGIN C16: from L. *suffus-*, *suffundere* 'pour into'.

**Sufi** /'suːfi/ • n. (pl. **Sufis**) a Muslim ascetic and mystic.
– DERIVATIVES **Sufic** adj. **Sufism** n.
– ORIGIN C17: from Arab. *ṣūfī*, perh. from *ṣūf* 'wool' (referring to the woollen garment worn).

**sug-** • prefix variant spelling of SUB- assimilated before *g* (as in *suggest*).

**sugar** • n. **1** a sweet crystalline substance obtained especially from sugar cane and sugar beet, consisting essentially of sucrose and used as a sweetener in food and drink. **2** Biochemistry any of the class of soluble, crystalline, typically sweet-tasting carbohydrates found in living tissues and exemplified by glucose and sucrose. **3** informal, chiefly N. Amer. used as a term of endearment. **4** informal a narcotic drug, especially heroin or LSD. • v. **1** sweeten, sprinkle, or coat with sugar. ➤ make more agreeable or palatable. **2** [usu. as noun **sugaring**] Entomology spread a sugar mixture on a tree trunk in order to catch moths. **3** [as noun **sugaring**] N. Amer. the boiling down of maple sap until it thickens into syrup or crystallizes into sugar. **4** [as noun **sugaring**] a method of removing unwanted hair by applying a mixture of lemon juice, sugar, and water to the skin and then peeling it off together with the hair.
– DERIVATIVES **sugarless** adj.
– ORIGIN ME: from OFr. *sukere*, from Ital. *zucchero*, prob. via med. L. from Arab. *sukkar*.

**sugar apple** • n. another term for SWEETSOP.

**sugar beet** • n. beet of a variety from which sugar is extracted.

**sugar candy** • n. fuller term for CANDY.

**sugar cane** • n. a perennial tropical grass with tall stout jointed stems from which sugar is extracted. [*Saccharum officinarum.*]

**sugar-coated** • adj. superficially attractive or excessively sentimental.
– DERIVATIVES **sugar-coat** v.

**sugarcraft** • n. the art of creating confectionery or cake decorations from sugar paste.

**sugar daddy** • n. informal a rich older man who lavishes gifts on a young woman in return for her company or sexual favours.

**sugar glider** • n. a flying phalanger that feeds on wattle gum and eucalyptus sap. [*Petaurus breviceps.*]

**sugar gum** • n. an Australian eucalyptus with sweet foliage. [*Eucalyptus cladocalyx* and other species.]

**sugarloaf** • n. a conical moulded mass of sugar.

**sugar lump** • n. a small cube of compacted sugar used for sweetening hot drinks.

**sugar maple** • n. a North American maple, the sap of which is used to make maple sugar and maple syrup. [*Acer saccharum.*]

**sugar of lead** • n. Chemistry, dated lead acetate, a soluble white crystalline salt.

**sugarplum** • n. archaic a small round boiled sweet.

**sugar snap** (also **sugar snap pea**, **sugar pea**) • n. mangetout, especially of a variety with thicker and more rounded pods.

**sugar soap** • n. Brit. an alkaline preparation containing washing soda and soap, used for cleaning or removing paint.

**sugary** • adj. **1** resembling, or containing much, sugar. **2** excessively sentimental.
– DERIVATIVES **sugariness** n.

**suggest** • v. **1** put forward for consideration. ➤ (**suggest itself**) (of an idea) come into one's mind. **2** cause one to think that (something) exists or is the case; evoke. ➤ state or express indirectly.
– DERIVATIVES **suggester** n.
– ORIGIN C16 (earlier (ME) as *suggestion*): from L. *suggest-*, *suggerere* 'suggest, prompt', from *sub-* 'from below' + *gerere* 'bring'.

**suggestible** • adj. open to suggestion; easily swayed.
– DERIVATIVES **suggestibility** n.

**suggestion** • n. **1** an idea or plan put forward for consideration. ➤ the action of suggesting. **2** something that implies or indicates a certain fact or situation. **3** a slight trace or indication: *a suggestion of a smile.* **4** Psychology the influencing of a person to accept a belief or impulse uncritically.

**suggestive** • adj. **1** (often **suggestive of**) tending to suggest or evoke something. **2** hinting at or bringing to mind sexual matters; mildly indecent.
– DERIVATIVES **suggestively** adv. **suggestiveness** n.

**suicide** /'s(j)uːɪsʌɪd/ • n. **1** the action of killing oneself intentionally. ➤ a person who does this. ➤ [as modifier] relating to or denoting a military operation carried out by people who do not expect to survive it: *a suicide bomber.* **2** a course of action which is disastrously damaging to one's own interests. • v. intentionally kill oneself.
– DERIVATIVES **suicidal** adj. **suicidally** adv.
– ORIGIN C17: from mod. L. *suicida* 'act of suicide', *suicidium* 'person who commits suicide', from L. *sui* 'of oneself' + *caedere* 'kill'.

**suicide pact** • n. an agreement between two or more people to commit suicide together.

**sui generis** /ˌsuːʌɪ 'dʒɛn(ə)rɪs, suːiː, sjuː-, 'gɛn-/ • adj. unique.
– ORIGIN L., lit. 'of its own kind'.

**sui juris** /'dʒʊərɪs, 'jʊə-/ • adj. Law of age; independent.
– ORIGIN L., lit. 'of one's own right'.

**suint** /swɪnt/ • n. the natural grease in sheep's wool, from which lanolin is obtained.
– ORIGIN C18: from Fr., from *suer* 'sweat'.

**suit** • n. **1** a set of outer clothes made of the same fabric and designed to be worn together, typically consisting of a jacket and trousers or a jacket and skirt. ➤ a set of clothes for a particular activity: *a jogging suit.* ➤ informal a high-ranking business executive. **2** any of the sets into which a pack of playing cards is divided (in conventional packs spades, hearts, diamonds, and clubs). **3** short for LAWSUIT. **4** the process of trying to win a woman's affection with a view to marriage. ➤ poetic/literary a petition or entreaty made to a person in authority. **5** a complete set of sails for a ship or for a set of spars. • v. **1** be convenient for or acceptable to. ➤ (**suit oneself**) act entirely according to one's own wishes. ➤ [as adj. **suited**] appropriate or fitting. ➤ (**suit something to**) archaic adapt or make something appropriate for. **2** go well with or enhance the features, figure, or character of (someone). **3** N. Amer. put on clothes.

– PHRASES **suit the action to the word** carry out one's stated intentions. **suit someone's book** Brit. informal be convenient or acceptable to someone. **suit someone down to the ground** Brit. be extremely convenient or appropriate for someone.
– DERIVATIVES **suited** adj. **suiting** n.
– ORIGIN ME: from Anglo-Norman Fr. *siwte*, from a fem. past part. of a Romance verb based on L. *sequi* 'follow'.

**suitable** ● adj. right or appropriate for a particular person, purpose, or situation.
– DERIVATIVES **suitability** n. **suitableness** n. **suitably** adv.

**suitcase** ● n. a case with a handle and a hinged lid, used for carrying clothes and other personal possessions.

**suite** /swi:t/ ● n. **1** a set of rooms for one person's or family's use or for a particular purpose. **2** a set of furniture of the same design. **3** Music a set of instrumental compositions to be played in succession. ➤a set of pieces from an opera or musical arranged as one instrumental work. **4** a group of people in attendance on a monarch or other person of high rank.
– ORIGIN C17: from Fr., from Anglo-Norman Fr. *siwte* (see **SUIT**).

**suitor** /'s(j)u:tə/ ● n. a man who pursues a relationship with a woman with a view to marriage. ➤a prospective buyer of a business or corporation.
– ORIGIN ME: from Anglo-Norman Fr. *seutor*, from L. *secutor*, from *sequi* 'follow'.

**suk** (also **sukh**) ● n. variant spelling of **SOUK**.

**sukiyaki** /ˌsʊkɪ'jaki, -'jɑ:ki/ ● n. a Japanese dish of sliced meat, especially beef, fried rapidly with vegetables and sauce.
– ORIGIN from Japanese.

**sukkah** ● n. variant spelling of **SUCCAH**.

**sulcate** /'sʌlkeɪt/ ● adj. Botany & Zoology marked with parallel grooves.
– ORIGIN C18: from L. *sulcatus* 'furrowed', past part. of *sulcare*.

**sulcus** /'sʌlkəs/ ● n. (pl. **sulci** /-sʌɪ/) Anatomy a groove or furrow, especially one on the surface of the brain.
– ORIGIN C17: from L., 'furrow, wrinkle'.

**sulfur** etc. ● n. US spelling of **SULPHUR** etc.

**sulk** ● v. be silent, morose, and bad-tempered through annoyance or disappointment. ● n. a period of sulking.
– DERIVATIVES **sulker** n.
– ORIGIN C18: perh. a back-form. from **SULKY**.

**sulky** ● adj. (**-ier**, **-iest**) morose, bad-tempered, and resentful. ● n. (pl. **-ies**) a light two-wheeled horse-drawn vehicle for one person, used chiefly in trotting races.
– DERIVATIVES **sulkily** adv. **sulkiness** n.
– ORIGIN C18: perh. from obs. *sulke* 'hard to dispose of', of unknown origin.

**sullage** /'sʌlɪdʒ/ ● n. **1** waste from household sinks, showers, and baths, but not toilets. **2** archaic refuse, especially sewage.
– ORIGIN C16: perh. from Anglo-Norman Fr. *suillage*, from *suiller* 'to soil'.

**sullen** ● adj. bad-tempered and sulky.
– DERIVATIVES **sullenly** adv. **sullenness** n.
– ORIGIN ME (in the senses 'solitary, averse to company', and 'unusual'): from Anglo-Norman Fr. *sulein*, from *sol* 'sole'.

**sully** /'sʌli/ ● v. (**-ies**, **-ied**) poetic/literary or ironic damage the purity or integrity of; defile.
– ORIGIN C16: perh. from Fr. *souiller* 'to soil'.

**sulpha** /'sʌlfə/ (US **sulfa**) ● n. [usu. as modifier] short for **SULPHONAMIDE**: *sulpha drugs*.

**sulphamic acid** /sʌl'famɪk/ (US **sulfamic acid**) ● n. Chemistry a crystalline acid used in cleaning agents.
– DERIVATIVES **sulphamate** /'sʌlfəmeɪt/ n.
– ORIGIN C19: from **SULPHUR** + **AMIDE** + **-IC**.

**sulphanilamide** /ˌsʌlfə'nɪləmʌɪd/ (US **sulfanilamide**) ● n. Medicine a synthetic antibacterial compound which is the basis of the sulphonamide drugs.
– ORIGIN 1930s: from *sulphanilic* (from **SULPHUR** + **ANILINE** + **-IC**) + **AMIDE**.

**sulphate** /'sʌlfeɪt/ (US **sulfate**) ● n. Chemistry a salt or ester of sulphuric acid.

**sulphide** /'sʌlfʌɪd/ (US **sulfide**) ● n. Chemistry a compound of sulphur with another element or group.

**sulphite** /'sʌlfʌɪt/ (US **sulfite**) ● n. Chemistry a salt of sulphurous acid.

**sulphonamide** /sʌl'fɒnəmʌɪd/ (US **sulfonamide**) ● n. Medicine any of a class of drugs, derived from sulphanilamide, which are able to prevent the multiplication of some pathogenic bacteria.
– ORIGIN C19: from **SULPHONE** + **AMIDE**.

**sulphonate** /'sʌlfəneɪt/ (US **sulfonate**) Chemistry ● n. a salt or ester of a sulphonic acid. ● v. convert into a sulphonate.
– DERIVATIVES **sulphonation** n.

**sulphone** /'sʌlfəʊn/ (US **sulfone**) ● n. Chemistry an organic compound containing the group $-SO_2-$ linking two organic groups.

**sulphonic acid** (US **sulfonic**) ● n. Chemistry an organic acid containing the group $-SO_2OH$.

**sulphur** (US & Chemistry **sulfur**) ● n. **1** the chemical element of atomic number 16, a combustible non-metal which typically occurs as yellow crystals. (Symbol: **S**) ➤the material of which hellfire and lightning were formerly believed to consist. **2** a pale greenish-yellow colour. **3** an American butterfly with predominantly yellow wings. [*Colias* and other genera.] ● v. disinfect or fumigate with sulphur.
– DERIVATIVES **sulphureous** adj. **sulphury** adj.
– ORIGIN ME: from Anglo-Norman Fr. *sulfre*, from L. *sulfur*, *sulphur*.

**sulphur dioxide** ● n. Chemistry a colourless pungent toxic gas formed by burning sulphur. [$SO_2$.]

**sulphuretted hydrogen** /ˌsʌlfjʊ'rɛtɪd/ (US **sulfureted**) ● n. Chemistry archaic term for **HYDROGEN SULPHIDE**.

**sulphuric** /sʌl'fjʊərɪk/ (US **sulfuric**) ● adj. containing sulphur or sulphuric acid.

**sulphuric acid** ● n. a strong acid made by oxidizing solutions of sulphur dioxide. [$H_2SO_4$.]

**sulphurous** /'sʌlf(ə)rəs/ (US **sulfurous**) ● adj. **1** containing or derived from sulphur. **2** pale yellow. **3** marked by anger or profanity.

**sulphurous acid** ● n. Chemistry an unstable weak acid formed when sulphur dioxide dissolves in water. [$H_2SO_3$.]

**sulphur spring** ● n. a spring impregnated with sulphur or its compounds.

**Sulpician** /sʌl'pɪʃɪən, sʌl'pɪʃ(ə)n/ ● n. a member of a congregation of secular Roman Catholic priests. ● adj. relating to or denoting this congregation.
– ORIGIN from St *Sulpice*, Paris, where the Sulpicians were founded.

**sultan** ● n. **1** a Muslim sovereign. ➤(**the Sultan**) historical the sultan of Turkey. **2** a bird of a breed of white domestic chicken from Turkey.
– DERIVATIVES **sultanate** n.
– ORIGIN C16: from Fr., or from med. L. *sultanus*, from Arab. *sulṭān* 'power, ruler'.

**sultana** ● n. **1** a small light brown seedless raisin. **2** a wife or concubine of a sultan. ➤any other woman in a sultan's family.
– ORIGIN C16: from Ital., fem. of *sultano* (see **SULTAN**).

**sultry** /'sʌltri/ ● adj. (**-ier**, **-iest**) **1** (of the weather) hot and humid. **2** displaying or suggesting passion; provocative.
– DERIVATIVES **sultrily** adv. **sultriness** n.
– ORIGIN C16: from obs. *sulter* 'swelter'.

**sulu** /'su:lu:/ ● n. (pl. **sulus**) a Melanesian kind of sarong.
– ORIGIN from Fijian.

**sum** ● n. **1** a particular amount of money. **2** (**the sum of**) the total amount resulting from the addition of two or more numbers or amounts. ➤the total amount of something that exists. **3** an arithmetical problem, especially at an elementary level. ● v. (**summed**, **summing**) **1** (**sum someone/thing up**) concisely describe the nature or character of someone or something. ➤(**sum up**) summarize briefly. **2** (**sum up**) Law (of a judge) review the evidence at the end of a case, and direct the jury regard-

ing points of law. **3** technical find the sum of (two or more amounts).
– PHRASES **in sum** to sum up.
– ORIGIN ME: via OFr. from L. *summa* 'main part, sum total', fem. of *summus* 'highest'.

**sumac** /'s(j)u:mak, 'ʃu:-/ (also **sumach**) ● **n.** a shrub or small tree with compound leaves, conical clusters of fruits, and bright autumn colours. [Genera *Rhus* and *Cotinus*: several species.]
– ORIGIN ME: from OFr. *sumac* or med. L. *sumac(h)*, from Arab. *summāķ*.

**Sumatran** /sʊ'mɑ:trən/ ● **n.** a native or inhabitant of the Indonesian island of Sumatra. ● **adj.** of or relating to Sumatra.

**Sumerian** /sʊ'mɪərɪən, sju:-/ ● **n. 1** a member of an indigenous non-Semitic people of ancient Sumer in Babylonia. **2** the language of this people, the oldest known written language. ● **adj.** of or relating to Sumer or the Sumerians or their language.

**sumi-e** /'su:mɪeɪ/ ● **n.** Japanese painting using solid sticks of black ink.
– ORIGIN C20: from Japanese *sumi* 'ink, blacking' + *e* 'painting'.

**summa** /'sʊmə, 'sʌmə/ ● **n.** (pl. **summae** /-mi:/) poetic/literary a summary of what is known of a subject.
– ORIGIN C18: from L., lit. 'sum total' (a sense reflected in ME).

**summa cum laude** /ˌsʌmə kʌm 'lɔ:di:, ˌsʊmə kʊm 'laʊdeɪ/ ● **adv. & adj.** chiefly N. Amer. (of a degree, diploma, etc.) with the highest distinction.
– ORIGIN L., lit. 'with highest praise'.

**summary** ● **n.** (pl. **-ies**) a brief statement of the main points of something. ● **adj. 1** dispensing with needless details or formalities. **2** Law (of a judicial process) conducted without the customary legal formalities. ➤(of a conviction) made by a judge or magistrate without a jury.
– DERIVATIVES **summarily** adv. **summariness** n. **summarization** (also **-isation**) n. **summarize** (also **-ise**) v. **summarizer** (also **-iser**) n.
– ORIGIN ME: from L. *summarius*, from *summa* (see **SUM**).

**summary jurisdiction** ● **n.** Law the authority of a court to use summary proceedings and arrive at a judgement.

**summary offence** ● **n.** Law an offence within the scope of a summary court.

**summation** /sʌ'meɪʃ(ə)n/ ● **n. 1** the process of adding things together. ➤a sum total. **2** the action of summing up. ➤a summary.
– DERIVATIVES **summational** adj. **summative** adj.

**summer**[1] ● **n. 1** the season after spring and before autumn, when the weather is warmest. ➤Astronomy the period from the summer solstice to the autumnal equinox. **2** (**summers**) poetic/literary years, especially of a person's age. ● **v.** spend the summer in a particular place. ➤pasture (cattle) for the summer.
– DERIVATIVES **summery** adj.
– ORIGIN OE *sumor*, of Gmc origin.

**summer**[2] (also **summer tree**) ● **n.** a horizontal bearing beam, especially one supporting joists or rafters.
– ORIGIN ME: from OFr. *somier* 'packhorse', from late L. *sagmarius*, from Gk *sagma* 'packsaddle'.

**summer camp** ● **n.** see **CAMP**[1] (sense 2).

**summer house** ● **n.** a small building in a garden, used for relaxation during fine weather.

**summer lightning** ● **n.** distant sheet lightning without audible thunder, typically occurring on a summer night.

**summer pudding** ● **n.** Brit. a pudding of soft summer fruit encased in bread or sponge.

**summersault** ● **n. & v.** archaic spelling of **SOMERSAULT**.

**summer sausage** ● **n.** N. Amer. a type of hard dried and smoked sausage which is similar to salami and can be made in winter to keep until summer.

**summer school** ● **n.** a course of lectures held during school and university summer vacations.

**summer season** ● **n.** the summer period when most people take holidays.

**summer squash** ● **n.** a squash of a variety eaten before the seeds and rind have hardened, unsuitable for storage.

**summer stock** ● **n.** N. Amer. theatrical productions by a repertory company organized for the summer season, especially at holiday resorts.

**summertime** ● **n.** the season or period of summer.

**summer time** ● **n.** Brit. time as advanced one hour ahead of standard time to achieve longer evening daylight in summer.

**summer tree** ● **n.** see **SUMMER**[2].

**summer-weight** ● **adj.** (of clothes) light and cool.

**summing-up** ● **n.** a summary. ➤Law a judge's review of evidence at the end of a case, with a direction to the jury regarding points of law.

**summit** ● **n. 1** the highest point of a hill or mountain. **2** the highest attainable level of achievement. **3** a meeting between heads of government.
– ORIGIN ME: from OFr. *somete*, from *som* 'top', from L. *summum*, neut. of *summus* 'highest'.

**summiteer** ● **n. 1** a participant in a government summit. **2** a climber who has reached the summit of a mountain.

**summon** ● **v. 1** authoritatively call on (someone) to be present, especially to appear in a law court. **2** call people to attend (a meeting). **3** (usu. **summon something up**) cause (a quality or reaction) to emerge from within oneself: *she managed to summon up a smile.*
– DERIVATIVES **summonable** adj. **summoner** n.
– ORIGIN ME: from OFr. *somondre*, from L. *summonere* 'give a hint', later 'call, summon', from *sub-* 'secretly' + *monere* 'warn'.

**summons** ● **n.** (pl. **summonses**) **1** an order to appear in a law court. **2** an act of summoning. ● **v.** chiefly Law serve with a summons.
– ORIGIN ME: from OFr. *sumunse*, from an alt. of L. *summonita*, fem. past part. of *summonere* (see **SUMMON**).

**summum bonum** /ˌsʊməm 'bɒnəm, ˌsʌməm 'bəʊnəm/ ● **n.** the highest good, especially as the ultimate goal according to which values and priorities are established in an ethical system.
– ORIGIN from L.

**sumo** /'su:məʊ/ ● **n.** (pl. **-os**) a Japanese form of heavyweight wrestling, in which a wrestler wins a bout by forcing his opponent outside a marked circle or by making him touch the ground with any part of his body except the soles of his feet.
– ORIGIN from Japanese *sūmo*.

**sump** ● **n. 1** the base of an internal-combustion engine, which serves as a reservoir of oil for the lubrication system. **2** a depression in the floor of a mine or cave in which water collects. **3** a cesspool.
– ORIGIN ME (in the sense 'marsh'): from MDu. or Low Ger. *sump*, or (in the mining sense) from Ger. *Sumpf*; rel. to **SWAMP**.

**sumph** /sʌmf/ ● **n.** Scottish a stupid or clumsy person.
– ORIGIN C18: of unknown origin.

**sumpter** /'sʌm(p)tə/ ● **n.** archaic a pack animal.
– ORIGIN ME: from OFr. *sommetier*, via late L. from Gk *sagma*, *sagmat-* 'packsaddle'; cf. **SUMMER**[2].

**sumptuary** /'sʌm(p)tjʊəri/ ● **adj.** chiefly historical relating to or denoting laws that limit private expenditure on food and personal items.
– ORIGIN C17: from L. *sumptuarius*, from *sumptus* 'cost'.

**sumptuous** ● **adj.** splendid and expensive-looking.
– DERIVATIVES **sumptuosity** n. **sumptuously** adv. **sumptuousness** n.
– ORIGIN ME: from OFr. *somptueux*, from L. *sumptuosus*, from *sumptus* (see **SUMPTUARY**).

**sum total** ● **n.** another term for **SUM** (in sense 2).

**Sun.** ● **abbrev.** Sunday.

**sun** ● **n. 1** (also **Sun**) the star round which the earth orbits. ➤any similar star, with or without planets. **2** the light or warmth received from the sun. **3** poetic/literary a day or a year. ● **v.** (**sunned**, **sunning**) (**sun oneself**) sit or lie in the sun. ➤expose to the sun.

– PHRASES **against the sun** Nautical against the direction of the sun's apparent movement (in the northern hemisphere); anticlockwise. **shoot the sun** Nautical ascertain the altitude of the sun with a sextant in order to determine one's latitude. **under the sun** in existence. **with the sun** Nautical in the direction of the sun's apparent movement (in the northern hemisphere); clockwise.
– DERIVATIVES **sunless** adj. **sunlessness** n. **sunlike** adj. **sunward** adj. & adv. **sunwards** adv.
– ORIGIN OE *sunne*, of Gmc origin.

**sun-and-planet gear** • n. a system of gearwheels consisting of a central wheel (a **sun gear** or **sun wheel**) around which other wheels (**planet gears**) travel.

**sun-baked** • adj. exposed to the heat of the sun.

**sunbath** • n. a period of sunbathing.

**sunbathe** • v. sit or lie in the sun to get a suntan.
– DERIVATIVES **sunbather** n.

**sunbeam** • n. a ray of sunlight.

**sun bear** (also **Malayan sun bear**) • n. a small mainly nocturnal bear which has a brownish-black coat with a light-coloured mark on the chest, native to SE Asia. [*Helarctos malayanus*.]

**sunbed** • n. Brit. **1** a lounger used for sunbathing. **2** an apparatus for acquiring a tan, consisting of two banks of sunlamps between which one lies or stands.

**sunbelt** • n. a strip of territory receiving a high amount of sunshine, especially the southern US from California to Florida.

**sunbird** • n. a small, brightly coloured bird of warmer parts of the Old World, resembling a hummingbird but not able to hover. [Family Nectariniidae: numerous species.]

**sunbittern** • n. a tropical American wading bird with a long bill, neck, and legs, having mainly greyish plumage but showing chestnut and orange on the wings when they are spread in display. [*Eurypyga helias*.]
– ORIGIN C19: so named because of the pattern on the spread wings.

**sunblind** • n. Brit. a window blind used to exclude the sun.

**sunblock** • n. a cream or lotion for protecting the skin from sunburn.

**sun bonnet** • n. a child's close-fitting peaked cotton hat that protects the head and neck from the sun.

**sunburn** • n. inflammation of the skin caused by overexposure to the ultraviolet rays of the sun. • v. (past and past part. **sunburned** or **sunburnt**) (**be sunburned**) suffer from sunburn.

**sunburst** • n. **1** a sudden brief appearance of the full sun from behind clouds. **2** a design or ornament representing the sun and its rays.

**suncream** • n. a creamy preparation for protecting the skin from sunburn and typically to promote a suntan.

**sundae** • n. a dish of ice cream with added ingredients such as fruit, nuts, and syrup.
– ORIGIN C19 (orig. US): perh. an alt. of **SUNDAY**, either because the dish was made with ice cream left over from Sunday, or because it was sold only on Sundays.

**sun dance** • n. a dance performed by North American Indians in honour of the sun.

**Sundanese** /ˌsʌndəˈniːz/ • n. (pl. same) **1** a member of a mainly Muslim people of western Java. **2** the Indonesian language of this people. • adj. of or relating to the Sundanese or their language.
– ORIGIN from Sundanese *Sunda*, the western part of Java, + **-ESE**.

**Sunday** • n. the day of the week before Monday and following Saturday, observed by Christians as a day of rest and religious worship. • adv. chiefly N. Amer. on Sunday. ➤(**Sundays**) on Sundays; each Sunday.
– ORIGIN OE *Sunnandæg* 'day of the sun', translation of L. *dies solis*.

**Sunday best** • n. a person's best clothes.

**Sunday driver** • n. a person who drives over-cautiously or unskilfully.

**Sunday painter** • n. an amateur painter.

**Sunday school** • n. a class held on Sundays to teach children about Christianity.

**sun deck** • n. **1** the deck of a yacht or cruise ship that is open to the sky. **2** N. Amer. a terrace or balcony positioned to catch the sun.

**sunder** • v. poetic/literary split apart.
– PHRASES **in sunder** apart or into pieces.
– ORIGIN OE *sundrian*.

**sundew** • n. a small carnivorous plant of boggy places, with leaves bearing sticky hairs for trapping insects. [Genus *Drosera*: several species.]

**sundial** • n. an instrument showing the time by the shadow of a pointer cast by the sun on to a plate marked in hours.

**sun disc** • n. (especially in ancient Egypt) a winged disc representing a sun god.

**sun dog** • n. another term for **PARHELION**.

**sundown** • n. chiefly N. Amer. sunset.

**sundowner** • n. Brit. informal an alcoholic drink taken at sunset.

**sundress** • n. a light, loose sleeveless dress, typically having a wide neckline and thin shoulder straps.

**sundry** • adj. of various kinds. • n. (pl. **-ies**) **1** (**sundries**) various items not important enough be mentioned individually. **2** Cricket Australian term for **EXTRA**.
– ORIGIN OE *syndrig* 'distinct, separate'; rel. to **SUNDER**.

**sun-dry** • v. [usu. as adj. **sun-dried**] dry in the sun, as opposed to using artificial heat.

**sunfast** • adj. US (of a dye or fabric) not prone to fade in sunlight.

**sun filter** • n. another term for **SUNSCREEN**.

**sunfish** • n. (pl. same or **-fishes**) **1** a large, short-tailed sea fish with tall dorsal and anal fins near the rear of the body. [*Mola mola* and other species.] **2** a nest-building North American freshwater fish. [Several species in the family Centrarchidae.]

**sunflower** • n. a tall North American plant with very large golden-rayed flowers, grown for its edible seeds which yield oil. [*Helianthus annus*.]

**sung** past participle of **SING**.

**sun gear** • n. see **SUN-AND-PLANET GEAR**.

**sunglasses** • pl. n. glasses tinted to protect the eyes from sunlight or glare.

**sun helmet** • n. chiefly historical a rigid hat made of cork or a similar material, worn in tropical climates.

**sun in splendour** • n. Heraldry the sun as heraldically blazoned, depicted with rays and often a human face.

**sunk** past and past participle of **SINK**[1].

**sunken** archaic past participle of **SINK**[1]. • adj. **1** having sunk. **2** at a lower level than the surrounding area. ➤(of a person's eyes or cheeks) deeply recessed.

**sunk fence** • n. a ha-ha.

**sun-kissed** • adj. made warm or brown by the sun.

**sunlamp** • n. **1** a lamp emitting ultraviolet rays, used chiefly to produce an artificial suntan or in therapy. **2** a large lamp with a parabolic reflector used in film-making.

**sunlight** • n. light from the sun.
– DERIVATIVES **sunlit** adj.

**Sunna** /ˈsʊnə, ˈsʌnə/ • n. the traditional portion of Muslim law based on Muhammad's words or acts, accepted (together with the Koran) as authoritative by Muslims.
– ORIGIN Arab., lit. 'form, way, rule'.

**Sunni** /ˈsʊni, ˈsʌni/ • n. (pl. same or **Sunnis**) one of the two main branches of Islam, differing from Shia in its understanding of the Sunna and in its acceptance of the first three caliphs. Compare with **SHIA**. ➤a Muslim who adheres to this branch of Islam.
– DERIVATIVES **Sunnite** adj. & n.
– ORIGIN Arab., lit. 'custom, normative rule'.

**sunny** • adj. (**-ier**, **sunniest**) **1** bright with or receiving much sunlight. **2** cheerful.
– PHRASES **sunny side up** N. Amer. (of an egg) fried on one side only.
– DERIVATIVES **sunnily** adv. **sunniness** n.

**sunray** • n. a radiating line or broadening stripe resembling a ray of the sun.

**sunray pleats** • pl. n. widening pleats radiating out from a skirt's waistband.

**sunrise** • n. the time in the morning when the sun rises. ➤ the colours and light visible in the sky at sunrise.

**sunrise industry** • n. a new and growing industry.

**sunroof** • n. a panel in the roof of a car that can be opened for extra ventilation.

**sunroom** • n. chiefly N. Amer. a room with large windows, designed to allow in a lot of sunlight.

**sunscreen** • n. a cream or lotion rubbed on to the skin to protect it from the sun.

**sunset** • n. **1** the time in the evening when the sun sets. ➤ the colours and light visible in the sky at sunset. **2** the final declining phase of something. **3** [as modifier] N. Amer. denoting a clause or provision under which an agency or programme is to be disbanded or terminated at the end of a fixed period unless it is formally renewed.

**sunset industry** • n. an old and declining industry.

**sunshade** • n. a parasol, awning, or other device giving protection from the sun.

**sunshine** • n. **1** sunlight unbroken by cloud. **2** cheerfulness. **3** Brit. informal used as a familiar form of address.
– DERIVATIVES **sunshiny** adj.

**sunshine law** • n. US a law requiring certain proceedings of government agencies to be open or available to the public.

**sun sign** • n. Astrology another term for **BIRTH SIGN**.

**sunspace** • n. N. Amer. a room or area in a building having a glass roof and walls and intended to maximize the power of the sun's rays.

**sun spider** • n. a fast-moving predatory arachnid with a pair of massive vertical pincers. [Order Solifugae.]

**sunspot** • n. Astronomy a temporary, relatively darker and cooler patch on the sun's surface, associated with the sun's magnetic field.

**sunstar** • n. a kind of starfish with a central disc and about a dozen arms. [Genus *Solaster*.]

**sunstone** • n. a chatoyant gem consisting of feldspar, with a red or gold lustre.

**sunstroke** • n. heatstroke brought about by excessive exposure to the sun.

**sunsuit** • n. dated a child's suit of clothes, typically consisting of shorts and top, worn in hot weather.

**suntan** • n. a golden-brown colouring of the skin caused by exposure to the sun. • v. [usu. as adj. **suntanned**] expose to the sun to achieve a suntan.

**suntrap** • n. Brit. a place sheltered from the wind and positioned to receive much sunshine.

**sunup** • n. chiefly N. Amer. sunrise.

**sun visor** • n. a small hinged screen above a vehicle's windscreen that can be lowered to protect the occupants' eyes from bright sunlight.

**sun wheel** • n. see **SUN-AND-PLANET GEAR**.

**sunyata** /ˈʃuːnjətɑː, ˈsuː-/ • n. Buddhism the doctrine that phenomena are devoid of an immutable or determinate intrinsic nature, often regarded as a means of gaining an intuition of ultimate reality. Compare with **TATHATA**.
– ORIGIN from Sanskrit *śūnyatā* 'emptiness'.

**sup**[1] • v. (**supped**, **supping**) dated or N. English take (drink or liquid food) by sips or spoonfuls. • n. **1** a sip. **2** N. English & Irish alcoholic drink.
– ORIGIN OE *sūpan* (v.), *sūpa* (n.), of Gmc origin.

**sup**[2] • v. (**supped**, **supping**) dated eat supper.
– ORIGIN ME: from OFr. *super*, of Gmc origin; rel. to **SUP**[1].

**sup-** • prefix variant spelling of **SUB-** assimilated before *p* (as in *suppurate*).

**Supadriv** /ˈsuːpədrʌɪv/ • n. trademark a type of cross-head screwdriver with extra ridges between the arms of the cross.

**super** • adj. **1** informal excellent. **2** (of a manufactured product) of extra fine quality. **3** Building, chiefly Brit. short for **SUPERFICIAL**. • adv. informal especially. • n. informal **1** a superintendent. **2** theatrical slang, dated or N. Amer. an extra. **3** superphosphate. **4** superfine fabric or manufacture.

**super-** • comb. form **1** above; over; beyond: *superstructure*. **2** to a great or extreme degree: *superabundant*. **3** extra large of its kind: *supercontinent*. ➤ having greater influence, capacity, etc. than another of its kind: *superpower*. **4** of a higher kind (especially in names of classificatory divisions): *superfamily*.
– ORIGIN from L. *super-*, from *super* 'above, beyond'.

**superabundant** • adj. formal or literary term for **OVER-ABUNDANT**.
– DERIVATIVES **superabundance** n. **superabundantly** adv.

**superadd** • v. add to what has already been added.
– DERIVATIVES **superaddition** n.

**superaltar** • n. a portable slab of stone consecrated for use where there is no consecrated altar.

**superannuate** /ˌs(j)uːpərˈanjʊeɪt/ • v. **1** retire with a pension. ➤ [as adj. **superannuated**] belonging to a superannuation scheme. **2** [as adj. **superannuated**] too old or outdated to be effective or useful.
– DERIVATIVES **superannuable** adj.
– ORIGIN C17: from med. L. *superannuatus*, from L. *super-* 'over' + *annus* 'year'.

**superannuation** • n. regular payment made into a fund by an employee towards a future pension.

**superb** • adj. **1** excellent. **2** magnificent or splendid. ➤ used in names of birds with attractive or colourful plumage, e.g. **superb lyrebird**.
– DERIVATIVES **superbly** adv. **superbness** n.
– ORIGIN C16: from L. *superbus* 'proud, magnificent'.

**superbike** • n. a high-performance motorcycle.

**superbug** • n. informal a bacterium, insect, etc. regarded as having enhanced qualities, especially of resistance to antibiotics or pesticides.

**supercalender** • v. give a highly glazed finish to (paper) by additional calendering.

**supercar** • n. a high-performance sports car.

**supercargo** • n. (pl. **-oes** or **-os**) a representative of the ship's owner on board a merchant ship, responsible for the supervision and sale of the cargo.
– ORIGIN C17: alt. of earlier *supracargo*, from Sp. *sobrecargo*, from *sobre* 'over' + *cargo* 'cargo'.

**supercede** • v. variant spelling of **SUPERSEDE**.

> **USAGE** supercede
>
> The spelling **supercede** is widely regarded as an error: see **SUPERSEDE**.

**supercharge** • v. **1** provide with a supercharger. **2** [as adj. **supercharged**] having powerful emotional associations.

**supercharger** • n. a device that increases the pressure of the fuel-air mixture in an internal-combustion engine, thereby giving greater efficiency.

**superciliary** /ˌs(j)uːpəˈsɪlɪəri/ • adj. Anatomy of or relating to the eyebrow or the region over the eye.
– ORIGIN C18: from L. *supercilium* 'eyebrow' + **-ARY**[1].

**supercilious** • adj. having an air of contemptuous superiority.
– DERIVATIVES **superciliously** adv. **superciliousness** n.
– ORIGIN C16: from L. *superciliosus* 'haughty', from *supercilium* 'eyebrow'.

**superclass** • n. Biology a taxonomic category that ranks above class and below phylum.

**supercomputer** • n. a particularly powerful mainframe computer.
– DERIVATIVES **supercomputing** n.

**superconductivity** • n. Physics the property of zero electrical resistance in some substances at very low temperatures.
– DERIVATIVES **superconduct** v. **superconducting** adj. **superconductive** adj. **superconductor** n.

**superconscious** • adj. transcending human or normal consciousness.
– DERIVATIVES **superconsciously** adv. **superconsciousness** n.

**supercontinent** • n. a large land mass believed to have divided in the geological past to form some of the present continents.

**supercool** • v. **1** Chemistry cool (a liquid) below its freezing point without solidification or crystallization. **2** Biology (of an organism) survive body temperatures below freezing point.

**supercritical** • adj. Physics greater than or above a critical threshold such as critical mass or temperature.

**super-duper** • adj. informal, humorous excellent; super.

**superego** • n. (pl. **-os**) Psychoanalysis the part of the mind that acts as a self-critical conscience, reflecting social standards learned from parents and teachers. Compare with **EGO** and **ID**.

**superelevation** • n. the amount by which the outer edge of a curve on a road or railway is banked above the inner edge.

**supererogation** /ˌs(j)uːpərɛrəˈgeɪʃ(ə)n/ • n. the performance of more work than duty requires.
– PHRASES **works of supererogation** (in the Roman Catholic Church) actions believed to form a fund of merit that can be drawn on by prayer in favour of sinners.
– DERIVATIVES **supererogatory** /-ɪˈrɒgət(ə)ri/ adj.
– ORIGIN C16: from late L. *supererogatio(n-)*, from *supererogare* 'pay in addition'.

**superette** • n. chiefly US a small supermarket.

**superfamily** • n. (pl. **-ies**) Biology a taxonomic category that ranks above family and below order.

**superfatted** • adj. (of soap) containing excess fats compared with its alkali content.

**superfecundation** /ˌs(j)uːpəfɛk(ə)nˈdeɪʃ(ə)n, -fiːk-/ • n. Medicine & Zoology fertilization of a second ovum during the same oestrus cycle as a result of a second mating, leading to fetuses of the same age but different parentage.

**superfetation** /ˌs(j)uːpəfiːˈteɪʃ(ə)n/ • n. **1** Medicine & Zoology fertilization of a second ovum after the start of a pregnancy, leading to fetuses of different ages. **2** the accretion of one thing on another.
– ORIGIN C17: from Fr. *superfétation* or mod. L. *superfetatio(n-)*, from L. *superfetare*, from *super-* 'above' + *fetus* 'foetus'.

**superficial** • adj. **1** existing or occurring at or on the surface. **2** apparent rather than actual. **3** not thorough or deep; cursory. ➤lacking depth of character or understanding. **4** Building, chiefly Brit. denoting a quantity of a material expressed in terms of area covered.
– DERIVATIVES **superficiality** /-ʃɪˈalɪti/ n. (pl. **-ies**). **superficially** adv. **superficialness** n.
– ORIGIN ME: from late L. *superficialis*, from L. *superficies* (see **SUPERFICIES**).

**superficies** /ˌs(j)uːpəˈfɪʃiiːz/ • n. (pl. same) archaic **1** a surface. **2** an outward part or appearance.
– ORIGIN C16: from L., from *super-* 'above' + *facies* 'face'.

**superfine** • adj. **1** of especially high quality. **2** very fine.

**superfluidity** • n. Physics the property of flowing without friction or viscosity, as shown by liquid helium below about 2.18 kelvins.
– DERIVATIVES **superfluid** n. & adj.

**superfluous** • adj. unnecessary, especially through being more than enough.
– DERIVATIVES **superfluity** n. (pl. **-ies**). **superfluously** adv. **superfluousness** n.
– ORIGIN ME: from L. *superfluus*, from *super-* 'over' + *fluere* 'to flow'.

**superfly** • adj. US informal (of clothing or a person's appearance) self-consciously or ostentatiously fashionable.
– ORIGIN 1970s: from **SUPER-** + **FLY**[3].

**supergiant** • n. Astronomy a star that is greater and more luminous than a giant.

**superglue** • n. a very strong quick-setting adhesive.

**supergrass** • n. Brit. informal a police informer who implicates a large number of people.

**supergroup** • n. a rock group formed by musicians already famous from playing in other groups.

**superheat** • v. Physics **1** heat (a liquid) under pressure above its boiling point without vaporization. **2** heat (steam or other vapour) above the temperature of the liquid from which it was formed.
– DERIVATIVES **superheater** n.

**superheavyweight** • n. a weight above heavyweight in boxing and other sports.

**superhero** • n. (pl. **-oes**) a benevolent fictional character with superhuman powers.

**superheterodyne** /ˌs(j)uːpəˈhɛt(ə)rə(ʊ)dʌɪn/ • adj. relating to or denoting a system of radio and television reception in which the receiver produces a tunable signal which is combined with the incoming signal to produce a predetermined intermediate frequency, on which most of the amplification is formed.
– ORIGIN 1920s: from **SUPERSONIC** + **HETERODYNE**.

**superhighway** • n. N. Amer. a dual carriageway with controlled access.

**superhuman** • adj. having or showing ability or powers above those of a normal human being.
– DERIVATIVES **superhumanly** adv.

**superimpose** • v. place or lay (one thing) over another, typically so that both are evident.
– DERIVATIVES **superimposable** adj. **superimposition** n.

**superincumbent** /ˌs(j)uːp(ə)rɪnˈkʌmb(ə)nt/ • adj. poetic/literary lying on something else.

**superinduce** • v. introduce or induce in addition.

**superintend** • v. act as superintendent of.
– DERIVATIVES **superintendence** n. **superintendency** n.
– ORIGIN C17 (earlier (C16) as *superintendent*): from eccles. L. *superintendere*, translating Gk *episkopein*.

**superintendent** • n. **1** a person who supervises or is in charge of an organization, department, etc. **2** (in the UK) a police officer ranking above chief inspector. **3** (in the US) the chief of a police department. **4** N. Amer. the caretaker of a building.

**superior** • adj. **1** higher in rank, status, or quality. ➤of high standard or quality. ➤greater in size or power. **2** Anatomy further above or out; higher in position. ➤Botany (of the ovary of a flower) situated above the sepals and petals. **3** (of a letter, figure, or symbol) written or printed above the line. **4** (**superior to**) above yielding to or being influenced by. **5** conceited. • n. **1** a person of superior rank. ➤the head of a monastery or other religious institution. **2** Printing a superior letter, figure, or symbol.
– DERIVATIVES **superiority** n. **superiorly** adv.
– ORIGIN ME: from OFr. *superiour*, from L. *superior*, compar. of *superus* 'that is above', from *super* 'above'.

**superior court** • n. Law **1** (in England) a higher court whose decisions have weight as precedents and which is not subject to control by any other court except by way of appeal. **2** (in some US states) a court of appeals or a court of general jurisdiction.

**superiority complex** • n. an attitude of superiority which conceals actual feelings of inferiority and failure.

**superior planet** • n. Astronomy any of the planets Mars, Jupiter, Saturn, Uranus, Neptune, and Pluto, whose orbits are further from the sun than the earth's.

**superius** /s(j)uːˈpɪərɪəs/ • n. another term for **CANTUS**.
– ORIGIN C18: from L., neut. of *superior* (see **SUPERIOR**).

**superjacent** /ˌs(j)uːpəˈdʒeɪs(ə)nt/ • adj. technical overlying.
– ORIGIN C16: from L. *superjacent-*, from *super-* 'over' + *jacere* 'to lie'.

**superlative** /s(j)uːˈpəːlətɪv/ • adj. **1** of the highest quality or degree. **2** Grammar (of an adjective or adverb) expressing the highest or a very high degree of a quality (e.g. *bravest*, *most fiercely*). Contrasted with **POSITIVE** and **COMPARATIVE**. • n. a hyperbolical expression of praise.
– DERIVATIVES **superlatively** adv. **superlativeness** n.
– ORIGIN ME: from OFr. *superlatif*, *-ive*, from late L. *superlativus*, from L. *superlatus*, *superferre* 'carry beyond'.

**superluminal** /ˌs(j)uːpəˈluːmɪn(ə)l/ • adj. Physics denoting or having a speed greater than that of light.
– ORIGIN 1950s: from **SUPER-** + L. *lumen*, *lumin-* 'a light' + **-AL**.

**superlunary** /ˌs(j)uːpəˈluːnəri/ • adj. poetic/literary belonging to a higher world; celestial.
– ORIGIN C17: from med. L. *superlunaris* (see **SUPER-**, **LUNAR**).

**supermajority** • n. (pl. **-ies**) a number that is much

more than a half of a total, especially in a vote.

**superman** • **n.** (pl. **-men**) **1** another term for **ÜBERMENSCH**. **2** informal a man with exceptional physical or mental ability.
– ORIGIN C20: from **SUPER-** + **MAN**, coined by G. B. Shaw in imitation of Ger. *Übermensch* (used by Nietzsche).

**supermarket** • **n.** a large self-service shop selling foods and household goods.

**supermini** • **n.** (pl. **superminis**) a type of small car with a relatively powerful engine.

**supermodel** • **n.** a highly successful fashion model enjoying celebrity status.

**supermundane** /ˌs(j)uːpəˈmʌndeɪn/ • **adj.** rare superior to worldly affairs.

**supernal** /s(j)uːˈpəːn(ə)l/ • **adj.** chiefly poetic/literary **1** of or relating to the sky or the heavens. **2** supremely excellent.
– DERIVATIVES **supernally** adv.
– ORIGIN ME: from OFr., or from med. L. *supernalis*, from L. *supernus*, from *super* 'above'.

**supernatant** /ˌs(j)uːpəˈneɪt(ə)nt/ • **adj.** technical denoting the liquid lying above a solid residue after crystallization, centrifugation, or other process.

**supernatural** • **adj.** **1** (of a manifestation or event) attributed to some force beyond scientific understanding or the laws of nature. **2** exceptionally or extraordinarily great. • **n.** (**the supernatural**) supernatural manifestations or events.
– DERIVATIVES **supernaturalism** n. **supernaturalist** n. **supernaturally** adv.

**supernormal** • **adj.** beyond what is normal.
– DERIVATIVES **supernormality** n.

**supernova** /ˌs(j)uːpəˈnəʊvə/ • **n.** (pl. **supernovae** /-viː/ or **supernovas**) Astronomy a star that undergoes a catastrophic explosion, becoming suddenly very much brighter.

**supernumerary** /ˌs(j)uːpəˈnjuːm(ə)r(ə)ri/ • **adj.** **1** present in excess of the normal or requisite number. **2** not belonging to a regular staff but engaged for extra work. ➤(of an actor) appearing on stage but not speaking. • **n.** (pl. **-ies**) a supernumerary person or thing.
– ORIGIN C17: from late L. *supernumerarius* '(soldier) added to a legion after it is complete'.

**superorder** • **n.** Biology a taxonomic category that ranks above order and below class.

**superordinate** /ˌs(j)uːpərˈɔːdɪnət/ • **n.** **1** a thing that represents a superior order or category within a system of classification. ➤Linguistics a word whose meaning includes the meaning of one or more other words. **2** a person of superior rank or status. • **adj.** superior in status.
– ORIGIN C17: from **SUPER-**, on the pattern of *subordinate*.

**superoxide** • **n.** Chemistry an oxide containing the anion $O_2^-$.

**superphosphate** • **n.** a fertilizer made by treating phosphate rock with sulphuric or phosphoric acid.

**superpose** • **v.** place (something) on or above something else, especially so that they coincide.
– DERIVATIVES **superposed** adj. **superposition** n.
– ORIGIN C19: from Fr. *superposer*.

**superpower** • **n.** any of the top few most powerful and influential nations of the world.

**supersaturate** • **v.** Chemistry increase the concentration of (a solution) beyond saturation point.
– DERIVATIVES **supersaturation** n.

**superscribe** • **v.** **1** write or print (an inscription) at the top of or on the outside of a document. **2** write or print (a character, word, or line) above an existing one.
– DERIVATIVES **superscription** n.
– ORIGIN C15: from L. *superscribere*, from *super-* 'over' + *scribere* 'write'.

**superscript** • **adj.** (of a letter, figure, or symbol) written or printed above the line.
– ORIGIN C19: from L. *superscriptus*, *superscribere* 'write above'.

**supersede** /ˌs(j)uːpəˈsiːd/ • **v.** take the place of; supplant.
– DERIVATIVES **supersession** n.
– ORIGIN C15 (in the sense 'postpone, defer'): from OFr. *superseder*, from L. *supersedere* 'be superior to'.

**USAGE** supersede

The standard spelling is **supersede** rather than **supercede**. The **c** spelling is recorded as early as the 16th century; although still often regarded as incorrect, it is now being entered without comment in some modern dictionaries.

**supersonic** • **adj.** involving or denoting a speed greater than that of sound.
– DERIVATIVES **supersonically** adv.

**supersonics** • **pl. n.** [treated as sing.] another term for **ULTRASONICS**.

**superstar** • **n.** an extremely famous and successful performer or sports player.
– DERIVATIVES **superstardom** n.

**superstate** • **n.** a large and powerful state formed from a federation or union of nations.

**superstation** • **n.** N. Amer. a television station using satellite technology to broadcast over a very large area, especially an entire continent.

**superstition** • **n.** excessively credulous belief in and reverence for the supernatural. ➤a widely held but irrational belief in supernatural influences, especially as bringing good or bad luck.
– DERIVATIVES **superstitious** adj. **superstitiously** adv. **superstitiousness** n.
– ORIGIN ME: from OFr., or from L. *superstitio(n-)*, from *super-* 'over' + *stare* 'to stand'.

**superstore** • **n.** a very large out-of-town supermarket.

**superstratum** /s(j)uːpəˈstrɑːtəm, -ˈstreɪtəm/ • **n.** (pl. **superstrata** /-tə/) an overlying stratum.

**superstring** • **n.** Physics a subatomic particle in a version of string theory that incorporates supersymmetry.

**superstructure** • **n.** **1** a structure built on top of something else. ➤the part of a building above its foundations. **2** a concept or idea based on others. **3** (in Marxist theory) the institutions and culture considered to result from or reflect the economic system underlying a society.
– DERIVATIVES **superstructural** adj.

**supersymmetry** • **n.** Physics a very general type of mathematical symmetry which relates fermions and bosons.
– DERIVATIVES **supersymmetric** adj.

**supertanker** • **n.** a very large oil tanker.

**supertax** • **n.** an additional tax on something already taxed.

**supertitle** • **n.** & **v.** North American term for **SURTITLE**.

**supertonic** • **n.** Music the second note of the diatonic scale of any key; the note above the tonic.

**supervene** /ˌs(j)uːpəˈviːn/ • **v.** **1** occur as an interruption or change to an existing situation. **2** Philosophy (of a fact or property) be entailed by or consequent on the existence or establishment of another.
– DERIVATIVES **supervenient** adj. **supervention** n.
– ORIGIN C17: from L. *supervenire*, from *super-* 'in addition' + *venire* 'come'.

**supervise** • **v.** observe and direct the execution of (a task or activity) or the work of (a person).
– DERIVATIVES **supervision** n. **supervisor** n. **supervisory** adj.
– ORIGIN C15 (in the sense 'survey, peruse'): from med. L. *supervis-*, *supervidere* 'survey, supervise'.

**supervision order** • **n.** English Law a court order placing a child or young person under the supervision of a local authority or a probation officer in a case of delinquency or where care proceedings are appropriate.

**superwoman** • **n.** (pl. **-women**) informal a woman with exceptional physical or mental ability.

**supinate** /ˈs(j)uːpɪneɪt/ • **v.** technical put or hold (a hand, foot, or limb) with the palm or sole turned upwards. Compare with **PRONATE**.
– DERIVATIVES **supination** n.
– ORIGIN C19 (earlier (C17) as *supination*): back-form. from *supination*, from L. *supinatio(n-)*, from *supinare* 'lay backwards'.

**supinator** • **n.** Anatomy a muscle involved in supination.

**supine** /ˈs(j)uːpʌɪn/ • **adj.** **1** lying face upwards. ➤with

the palm of the hand upwards. **2** failing to act as a result of moral weakness or indolence. ● **n.** a Latin verbal noun used only in the accusative and ablative cases, especially to denote purpose (e.g. *mirabile dictu* 'wonderful to relate').
– DERIVATIVES **supinely** adv. **supineness** n.
– ORIGIN ME: from L. *supinus* 'bent backwards'.

**supper** ● **n. 1** a light or informal evening meal. **2** Scottish & N. English a meal consisting of the specified food with chips: *a fish supper.*
– PHRASES **sing for one's supper** provide a service in return for a benefit.
– DERIVATIVES **supperless** adj.
– ORIGIN ME: from OFr. *super* 'to sup' (see **SUP**[2]).

**supplant** ● **v.** supersede and replace.
– DERIVATIVES **supplanter** n.
– ORIGIN ME: from OFr. *supplanter* or L. *supplantare* 'trip up', from *sub-* 'from below' + *planta* 'sole'.

**supple** ● **adj.** (**-er, -est**) flexible or pliant. ● **v.** make more flexible.
– DERIVATIVES **supplely** (also **supply**) adv. **suppleness** n.
– ORIGIN ME: from OFr. *souple*, from L. *supplex, supplic-* 'submissive', from *sub-* 'under' + *placere* 'propitiate'.

**supplejack** ● **n.** a climbing plant with tough, supple stems. [*Berchemia scandens* (N. America), *Paullinia plumieri* (tropical America), and other species.]

**supplement** ● **n. 1** a thing added to something else to enhance or complete it. **2** a separate section, especially a colour magazine, added to a newspaper or periodical. **3** an additional charge payable for an extra service or facility. **4** Geometry the amount by which a given angle is less than 180°. ● **v.** provide a supplement for.
– DERIVATIVES **supplemental** adj. **supplementally** adv. **supplementarily** adv. **supplementary** adj. & n. (pl. **-ies**). **supplementation** n.
– ORIGIN ME: from L. *supplementum*, from *supplere* (see **SUPPLY**[1]).

**supplementary angle** ● **n.** Mathematics either of two angles whose sum is 180°.

**supplementary benefit** ● **n.** (in the UK) payment made by the state to those on a low income, now replaced by income support.

**suppletion** /sə'pli:ʃ(ə)n/ ● **n.** Linguistics the occurrence of an unrelated form to fill a gap in a conjugation (e.g. *went* as the past tense of *go*).
– DERIVATIVES **suppletive** adj.
– ORIGIN ME: from OFr., from med. L. *suppletio(n-)*, from *supplere* (see **SUPPLY**[1]).

**Supplex** /'sʌplɛks/ ● **n.** trademark a synthetic stretchable fabric which is permeable to air and water vapour, used in sports and outdoor clothing.

**suppliant** /'sʌplɪənt/ ● **n.** a person who supplicates. ● **adj.** making or expressing a humble or earnest plea.
– DERIVATIVES **suppliantly** adv.

**supplicate** /'sʌplɪkeɪt/ ● **v.** ask or beg for something earnestly or humbly.
– DERIVATIVES **supplicant** adj. & n. **supplication** n. **supplicatory** adj.
– ORIGIN ME: from L. *supplicat-*, *supplicare* 'implore', from *sub-* 'from below' + *placere* 'propitiate'.

**supply**[1] /sə'plʌɪ/ ● **v.** (**-ies, -ied**) **1** make (something needed) available to someone. ➤provide with something needed. ➤be adequate to satisfy (a requirement or demand). **2** archaic take over (a vacant place or role). ● **n.** (pl. **-ies**) **1** a stock or amount of something supplied or available. ➤the action of supplying. **2** [usu. as modifier] a person, especially a schoolteacher, acting as a temporary substitute for another. **3** (**supplies**) Brit. a grant of money by Parliament for the costs of government.
– PHRASES **on supply** (of a schoolteacher) acting as a temporary substitute. **supply and demand** the amount of a good or service available and the desire of buyers for it, considered as factors regulating its price.
– DERIVATIVES **supplier** n.
– ORIGIN ME: from OFr. *soupleer*, from L. *supplere* 'fill up'.

**supply**[2] /'sʌpli/ ● **adv.** variant spelling of ***supplely*** (see **SUPPLE**).

**supply-side** ● **adj.** Economics denoting a policy designed to increase output and employment by reducing taxation and other forms of restriction.
– DERIVATIVES **supply-sider** n.

**support** ● **v. 1** bear all or part of the weight of. **2** give assistance, encouragement, or approval to. ➤be actively interested in (a sports team). ➤[as adj. **supporting**] (of an actor or a role) of secondary importance to the leading roles in a play or film. ➤(of a pop or rock group or performer) function as a secondary act to (another) at a concert. **3** provide with a home and the necessities of life. ➤be capable of sustaining. **4** corroborate. **5** endure; tolerate. ● **n. 1** a person or thing that supports. ➤the action of supporting or the state of being so supported. **2** assistance, encouragement, or approval.
– DERIVATIVES **supportability** n. **supportable** adj. **supportive** adj. **supportively** adv. **supportiveness** n.
– ORIGIN ME: from OFr. *supporter*, from L. *supportare*, from *sub-* 'from below' + *portare* 'carry'.

**supporter** ● **n. 1** a person who supports a sports team, policy, etc. **2** Heraldry a representation of an animal or other figure, typically one of a pair, holding up or standing beside an escutcheon.

**support price** ● **n.** a minimum price guaranteed to a farmer for agricultural produce and maintained by subsidy or the buying in of surplus stock.

**suppose** ● **v. 1** think or assume that something is true or probable, but without proof. ➤(of a theory or argument) assume or require that something is the case as a precondition. ➤[in imper.] used to introduce a suggestion. **2** (**be supposed to do something**) be required or expected to do something.
– DERIVATIVES **supposable** adj.
– ORIGIN ME: from OFr. *supposer*, from L. *supponere*, from *sub-* 'from below' + *ponere* 'to place'.

**supposedly** ● **adv.** according to what is generally believed or supposed.

**supposition** ● **n.** an assumption or hypothesis.
– DERIVATIVES **suppositional** adj.

**suppositious** ● **adj.** based on assumption rather than fact.
– DERIVATIVES **suppositiously** adv. **suppositiousness** n.

**supposititious** /sə,pɒzɪ'tɪʃəs/ ● **adj.** substituted for the real thing; counterfeit.
– DERIVATIVES **supposititiously** adv. **supposititiousness** n.
– ORIGIN C17: from L. *supposititius* (from *supponere* 'to substitute') + **-ous**.

**suppository** ● **n.** (pl. **-ies**) a solid medical preparation in a roughly conical or cylindrical shape, designed to dissolve after insertion into the rectum or vagina.
– ORIGIN ME: from med. L. *suppositorium*, neut. of late L. *suppositorius* 'placed underneath'.

**suppress** ● **v. 1** forcibly put an end to. **2** prevent from being expressed or published. ➤Psychoanalysis consciously avoid thinking of (an unpleasant idea or memory). **3** prevent or inhibit (a process or phenomenon).
– DERIVATIVES **suppressible** adj. **suppression** n. **suppressive** adj. **suppressor** n.
– ORIGIN ME: from L. *suppress-*, *supprimere* 'press down'.

**suppressant** ● **n.** a drug or other substance which acts to suppress something.

**suppurate** /'sʌpjʊreɪt/ ● **v.** form or discharge pus.
– DERIVATIVES **suppuration** n. **suppurative** /-rətɪv/ adj.
– ORIGIN ME: based on L. *sub-* 'below' + *pus, pur-* 'pus'.

**supra** /'s(j)u:prə/ ● **adv.** formal (in academic or legal texts) someone or something mentioned earlier.
– ORIGIN from L.

**supra-** /'s(j)u:prə/ ● **prefix 1** above: *suprarenal.* **2** beyond; transcending: *supranational.*
– ORIGIN from L. *supra* 'above, beyond, before in time'.

**supranational** ● **adj.** having power or influence that transcends national boundaries or governments.
– DERIVATIVES **supranationalism** n. **supranationality** n.

**suprarenal** ● **adj.** Anatomy another term for **ADRENAL**.

**suprasegmental** ● **adj.** Linguistics denoting a feature of an utterance other than the consonantal and vocalic components, for example (in English) stress and intonation.

**supremacist** ● n. an advocate of the supremacy of a particular group, especially one determined by race or sex. ● adj. relating to or advocating such supremacy.
– DERIVATIVES **supremacism** n.

**suprematism** ● n. a Russian abstract art movement developed *c.*1915, characterized by simple geometrical shapes and associated with ideas of spiritual purity.
– DERIVATIVES **suprematist** n.

**supreme** ● adj. **1** highest in authority or rank. **2** very great or greatest; most important. ➤(of a penalty or sacrifice) involving death. ● n. (also **suprême**) a rich cream sauce or a dish served in this.
– PHRASES **the Supreme Being** a name for God.
– DERIVATIVES **supremacy** n. **supremely** adv.
– ORIGIN C15: from L. *supremus*, superlative of *superus* 'that is above'; the noun is from Fr. *suprême*.

**supreme court** ● n. the highest judicial court in a country or state. ➤(in full **Supreme Court of Judicature**) (in England and Wales) the highest court below the House of Lords.

**supreme pontiff** ● n. see PONTIFF.

**Supreme Soviet** ● n. the governing council of the former USSR or one of its constituent republics.

**supremo** /s(j)uːˈpriːməʊ, -ˈpreɪməʊ/ ● n. (pl. **-os**) Brit. informal **1** a person in overall charge. **2** a person with great authority or skill in a certain area.
– ORIGIN Sp., lit. 'supreme'.

**supremum** /s(j)uːˈpriːməm/ ● n. Mathematics the smallest quantity that is greater than or equal to each of a given set or subset of quantities. The opposite of INFIMUM.
– ORIGIN 1940s: from L. *suppremum* 'highest part'.

**Supt** ● abbrev. Superintendent.

**suq** ● n. variant spelling of SOUK.

**sur-**[1] ● prefix equivalent to SUPER-.
– ORIGIN from Fr.

**sur-**[2] ● prefix variant spelling of SUB- assimilated before *r* (as in *surrogate*).

**sura** /ˈsʊərə/ (also **surah**) ● n. a chapter or section of the Koran.
– ORIGIN from Arab. *sūra*.

**surah** /ˈsʊərə, ˈsjʊərə/ ● n. a soft twilled silk fabric used in dressmaking.
– ORIGIN C19: representing the Fr. pronunc. of *Surat*, a city in India, where it was orig. made.

**surahi** /sʊˈrɑːhi/ ● n. (pl. **surahis**) an Indian clay pot with a long neck, used for storing water.
– ORIGIN via Urdu from Arab. *ṣurāḥiya* 'pure wine'.

**sural** /ˈs(j)ʊər(ə)l/ ● adj. Anatomy of or relating to the calf of the leg.
– ORIGIN C17: from mod. L. *suralis*, from L. *sura* 'calf'.

**surcease** ● n. archaic or N. Amer. **1** cessation. **2** relief. ● v. archaic cease.
– ORIGIN ME: from OFr. *sursis*, *surseoir* 'refrain, delay', from L. *supersedere* (see SUPERSEDE); the change in the ending was due to assoc. with CEASE.

**surcharge** ● n. **1** an additional charge or payment. ➤Brit. an amount in an official account not passed by the auditor and having to be refunded by the person responsible. ➤the showing of an omission in an account for which credit should have been given. **2** a mark printed on a postage stamp changing its value. ● v. **1** exact a surcharge from. **2** mark (a postage stamp) with a surcharge.

**surcingle** /ˈsəːsɪŋg(ə)l/ ● n. a wide strap which runs over the back and under the belly of a horse, used to keep a rug or other equipment in place.
– ORIGIN ME: from OFr. *surcengle*, based on *cengle* 'girth', from L. *cingula*, from *cingere* 'gird'.

**surcoat** /ˈsəːkəʊt/ ● n. **1** historical an outer coat or garment of rich material, typically worn over armour. **2** a short sleeveless garment worn as part of the insignia of an order of knighthood.
– ORIGIN ME: from OFr. *surcot*, from *sur* 'over' + *cot* 'coat'.

**surd** /səːd/ ● n. **1** Mathematics an irrational number. **2** Phonetics a speech sound uttered with the breath and not the voice (e.g. *f*, *k*, *p*).
– ORIGIN C16 (as adj.): from L. *surdus* 'deaf, mute'; as a mathematical term, translating Gk *alogos* 'irrational, speechless'.

**sure** /ʃʊə, ʃɔː/ ● adj. **1** completely confident that one is right. **2** (**sure of/to do something**) certain to receive, get, or do something. **3** undoubtedly true; completely reliable. ● adv. [often as exclam.] informal certainly.
– PHRASES **be sure** [usu. in imper.] do not fail. **for sure** informal without doubt. **make sure** confirm or ensure. **sure enough** informal used to introduce a statement that confirms something previously predicted. **sure thing** informal a certainty. ➤[as exclam.] chiefly N. Amer. certainly. **to be sure** certainly; it must be admitted.
– DERIVATIVES **sureness** n.
– ORIGIN ME: from OFr. *sur*, from L. *securus* 'free from care'.

**sure-fire** ● adj. informal certain to succeed.

**sure-footed** ● adj. **1** unlikely to stumble or slip. **2** confident and competent.
– DERIVATIVES **sure-footedly** adv. **sure-footedness** n.

**surely** ● adv. **1** it must be true that (used for emphasis). ➤certainly. ➤[as exclam.] informal, chiefly N. Amer. of course. **2** with assurance.

**surety** /ˈʃʊərɪti, ˈʃʊəti/ ● n. (pl. **-ies**) **1** a person who takes responsibility for another's undertaking, e.g. the payment of a debt. **2** money given as a guarantee that someone will do something. **3** the state of being sure.
– PHRASES **of** (or **for**) **a surety** archaic for certain. **stand surety** become a surety.
– DERIVATIVES **suretyship** n.
– ORIGIN ME: from OFr. *surte*, from L. *securitas* (see SECURITY).

**surf** ● n. the mass or line of foam formed by waves breaking on a seashore or reef. ● v. **1** stand or lie on a surfboard and ride on the crest of a wave towards the shore. **2** informal ride on the roof or outside of a fast-moving vehicle, typically a train, for excitement. **3** occupy oneself by moving from site to site on (the Internet).
– DERIVATIVES **surfer** n. **surfing** n. **surfy** adj.
– ORIGIN C17: appar. from obs. *suff*, of unknown origin, perh. influenced by the spelling of *surge*.

**surface** ● n. **1** the outside part or uppermost layer of something. ➤(also **surface area**) the area of this. **2** the upper limit of a body of liquid. **3** outward appearance as distinct from less obvious aspects. **4** Geometry a set of points that has length and breadth but no thickness. ● adj. of, relating to, or occurring on the surface. ➤carried by or denoting transportation by sea or overland as contrasted with by air. ● v. **1** rise or come up to the surface. **2** become apparent. **3** provide (something, especially a road) with a particular surface. **4** informal appear after having been asleep.
– DERIVATIVES **surfaced** adj. **surfacer** n.
– ORIGIN C17: from Fr. (see SUR-[1], FACE), suggested by L. *superficies*.

**surface-active** ● adj. (of a substance) tending to reduce the surface tension of a liquid in which it is dissolved.

**surface noise** ● n. extraneous noise in playing a gramophone record, caused by imperfections in the grooves or in the pickup system.

**surface structure** ● n. (in transformational grammar) the structure of a phrase or sentence in a language, as opposed to its underlying logical form. Contrasted with DEEP STRUCTURE.

**surface tension** ● n. the tension of the surface film of a liquid, which tends to minimize surface area.

**surface-to-air** ● adj. (of a missile) designed to be fired from the ground or a vessel at an aircraft.

**surface-to-surface** ● adj. (of a missile) designed to be fired from one point on the ground or a vessel at another such point or vessel.

**surfactant** /səˈfakt(ə)nt/ ● n. a surface-active substance.
– ORIGIN 1950s: from *surf(ace)-act(ive)* + -ANT.

**surfboard** ● n. a long, narrow board used in surfing.

**surfcasting** ● n. fishing by casting a line into the sea from the shore.
– DERIVATIVES **surfcaster** n.

**surfeit** ● n. **1** an excess. **2** archaic an illness caused or regarded as being caused by excessive eating or drinking. ● v. (**surfeited**, **surfeiting**) **1** cause to be wearied of something through excess. **2** archaic overeat.
– ORIGIN ME: from OFr. *surfeit*, based on L. *super-* 'above, in excess' + *facere* 'do'.

**surficial** /sə'fɪʃ(ə)l/ ● adj. Geology of or relating to the earth's surface.
– DERIVATIVES **surficially** adv.
– ORIGIN C19: from SURFACE, on the pattern of *superficial*.

**surfie** ● n. informal, chiefly Austral./NZ a surfing enthusiast.

**surf 'n' turf** (also **surf and turf**) ● n. chiefly N. Amer. a dish containing both seafood and meat, typically shellfish and steak.

**surge** ● n. **1** a sudden powerful forward or upward movement: *tidal surges*. **2** a sudden large temporary increase. **3** a powerful rush of an emotion or feeling. ● v. **1** move in a surge. **2** increase suddenly and powerfully. **3** Nautical (of a rope, chain, or windlass) slip back with a jerk.
– ORIGIN C15 (in the sense 'fountain, stream'): the noun from OFr. *sourgeon*; the verb partly from the OFr. stem *sourge-*, based on L. *surgere* 'to rise'.

**surge chamber** ● n. another term for SURGE TANK.

**surgeon** ● n. **1** a medical practitioner qualified to practise surgery. **2** a doctor in the navy.
– ORIGIN ME: from Anglo-Norman Fr. *surgien*, contr. of OFr. *serurgien*, based on L. *chirurgia*, from Gk *kheirourgia* 'handiwork, surgery'.

**surgeonfish** ● n. (pl. same or **-fishes**) a tropical marine fish with a scalpel-like spine on each side of the tail. [Family Acanthuridae: many species.]

**surgeon general** ● n. (pl. **surgeons general**) (in the US) the head of a public health service or of the medical service of the armed forces.

**surgeon's knot** ● n. a reef knot with one or more extra turns in the first half knot, as used to tie a ligature in surgery.

**surgery** ● n. (pl. **-ies**) **1** the branch of medicine concerned with treatment of bodily injuries or disorders by incision or manipulation, especially with instruments. **2** Brit. a place where a medical practitioner treats or advises patients. **3** Brit. an occasion on which an MP, lawyer, or other professional person gives advice.
– ORIGIN ME: from OFr. *surgerie*, contr. of *serurgerie*, from *serurgien* (see SURGEON).

**surge tank** ● n. a tank designed to neutralize sudden changes of pressure in a flow of liquid.

**surgical** ● adj. **1** of, relating to, or used in surgery. **2** (of a special garment or appliance) worn to correct or relieve an injury, illness, or deformity. **3** denoting something done with great precision, especially a military attack from the air.
– DERIVATIVES **surgically** adv.

**surgical spirit** ● n. Brit. methylated spirit (often with oil of wintergreen) used especially for cleansing the skin before injections or surgery.

**suricate** /'s(j)ʊərɪkeɪt/ ● n. a gregarious burrowing meerkat with dark bands on the back and a black-tipped tail, native to southern Africa. [*Suricata suricatta*.]
– ORIGIN C18: via Fr. from a local Afr. word.

**Surinamer** /,sʊərɪ'namə, -'nɑːmə/ ● n. a native or inhabitant of Surinam, a country on the NE coast of South America.
– DERIVATIVES **Surinamese** /-nə'miːz/ adj. & n.

**surly** ● adj. (**-ier**, **-iest**) bad-tempered and unfriendly.
– DERIVATIVES **surlily** adv. **surliness** n.
– ORIGIN C16 (in the sense 'lordly, haughty'): alt. of obs. *sirly* (see SIR, -LY[1]).

**surmise** /sə'mʌɪz/ ● v. suppose without having evidence. ● n. a supposition or guess.
– ORIGIN ME (in the senses 'formal allegation' and 'allege formally'): from Anglo-Norman Fr. and OFr. *surmise*, fem. past part. of *surmettre* 'accuse', from late L. *supermittere* 'put in afterwards'.

**surmount** ● v. **1** overcome (a difficulty or obstacle). **2** stand or be placed on top of.
– DERIVATIVES **surmountable** adj.
– ORIGIN ME (also in the sense 'surpass'): from OFr. *surmonter* (see SUR-[1], MOUNT[1]).

**surmullet** ● n. a red mullet of the tropical Indo-Pacific. [*Pseudupeneus fraterculus*.]
– ORIGIN C17: from Fr. *surmulet*, from OFr. *sor* 'red' + *mulet* 'mullet'.

**surname** ● n. **1** a hereditary name common to all members of a family, as distinct from a forename. **2** archaic a descriptive or allusive name, title, or epithet added to a person's name. ● v. give a surname to.
– ORIGIN ME: partial translation of Anglo-Norman Fr. *surnoun*, suggested by med. L. *supernomen*.

**surpass** ● v. be greater or better than. ➤[as adj. **surpassing**] archaic or poetic/literary incomparable or outstanding.
– DERIVATIVES **surpassable** adj. **surpassingly** adv.
– ORIGIN C16: from Fr. *surpasser*, from *sur-* 'above' + *passer* 'to pass'.

**surplice** /'səːplɪs/ ● n. a loose white linen vestment worn over a cassock by clergy and choristers at Christian church services.
– DERIVATIVES **surpliced** adj.
– ORIGIN ME: from OFr. *sourpelis*, from med. L. *superpellicium*, from *super-* 'above' + *pellicia* 'fur garment'.

**surplus** ● n. an amount left over when requirements have been met. ➤an excess of income or assets over expenditure or liabilities in a given period. ➤the excess value of a company's assets over the face value of its stock. ● adj. excess; extra.
– ORIGIN ME: from OFr. *sourplus*, from med. L. *superplus*, from *super-* 'in addition' + *plus* 'more'.

**surplus value** ● n. Economics (in Marxist theory) the excess of value produced by the labour of workers over the wages they are paid.

**surprise** ● n. **1** a feeling of mild astonishment or shock caused by something unexpected. **2** an unexpected or astonishing thing. **3** [as modifier] Bell-ringing denoting a complex method of change-ringing: *surprise major*. ● v. **1** cause to feel surprise. **2** capture, attack, or discover suddenly and unexpectedly.
– PHRASES **take someone/thing by surprise** attack or capture someone or something unexpectedly. ➤(**take someone by surprise**) happen unexpectedly to someone.
– DERIVATIVES **surprised** adj. **surprisedly** adv. **surprising** adj. **surprisingly** adv. **surprisingness** n.
– ORIGIN ME (in the sense 'unexpected seizure or attack'): from OFr., fem. past part. of *surprendre*, from med. L. *superprehendere* 'seize'.

**surreal** ● adj. having the qualities of surrealism; bizarre.
– DERIVATIVES **surreality** n. **surreally** adv.

**surrealism** ● n. a 20th-century avant-garde movement in art and literature which sought to release the creative potential of the unconscious mind, for example by the irrational juxtaposition of images.
– DERIVATIVES **surrealist** n. & adj. **surrealistic** adj. **surrealistically** adv.
– ORIGIN C20: from Fr. *surréalisme* (see SUR-[1], *realism*).

**surrebuttal** /,sʌrɪ'bʌtəl/ ● n. another term for SURREBUTTER.

**surrebutter** /,sʌrɪ'bʌtə/ ● n. Law, archaic a plaintiff's reply to the defendant's rebutter.
– ORIGIN C16: from SUR-[1] + REBUTTER.

**surrejoinder** /,sʌrɪ'dʒɔɪndə/ ● n. Law, archaic a plaintiff's reply to the defendant's rejoinder.
– ORIGIN C16: from SUR-[1] + REJOINDER.

**surrender** ● v. **1** cease resistance to an opponent and submit to their authority. **2** give up (a person, right, or possession) on compulsion or demand. ➤give up (a lease) before its expiry. **3** (**surrender to**) abandon oneself entirely to (a powerful emotion or influence). **4** (of a person assured) cancel (a life insurance policy) and receive back a proportion of the premiums paid. ● n. the action of surrendering.
– PHRASES **surrender to bail** Law duly appear in court after release on bail.
– ORIGIN ME: from Anglo-Norman Fr. (see SUR-[1], RENDER).

**surrender value** ● **n.** the amount payable to a person who surrenders a life insurance policy.

**surreptitious** /ˌsʌrəpˈtɪʃəs/ ● **adj.** covert or clandestine.
– DERIVATIVES **surreptitiously** adv. **surreptitiousness** n.
– ORIGIN ME (in the sense 'obtained by suppression of the truth'): from L. *surreptitius* (from *surripere*, from *sub-* 'secretly' + *rapere* 'seize') + **-ous**.

**surrey** ● **n.** (pl. **-eys**) historical (in the US) a light four-wheeled carriage with two seats facing forwards.
– ORIGIN C19: orig. denoting a *Surrey cart*, first made in *Surrey*, England.

**surrogate** /ˈsʌrəgət/ ● **n.** a substitute, especially a person deputizing for another in a specific role or office. ➤(in the Christian Church) a bishop's deputy who grants marriage licences. ➤(in the US) a judge in charge of probate, inheritance, and guardianship.
– DERIVATIVES **surrogacy** n.
– ORIGIN C17: from L. *surrogatus*, *surrogare* 'elect as a substitute'.

**surrogate mother** ● **n.** a woman who bears a child on behalf of another woman, either from her own egg or from the implantation in her womb of a fertilized egg from the other woman.

**surround** ● **v. 1** be all round; encircle. **2** be associated with: *the killings were surrounded by controversy.* ● **n. 1** a border or edging. **2** (**surrounds**) surroundings.
– ORIGIN ME (in the sense 'overflow'): from OFr. *souronder*, from late L. *superundare*, from *super-* 'over' + *undare* 'to flow'; later assoc. with **ROUND**.

**surroundings** ● **pl. n.** the conditions or area around a person or thing.

**surtax** ● **n.** an additional tax on something already taxed, especially a higher rate of tax on incomes above a certain level.

**surtitle** ● **n.** a caption projected on a screen above the stage in an opera, translating the text being sung. ● **v.** provide with surtitles.

**surtout** /ˈsəːtuː, səːˈtuː(t)/ ● **n.** historical a man's greatcoat of a similar style to a frock coat.
– ORIGIN C17: from Fr., from *sur* 'over' + *tout* 'everything'.

**surveillance** /səˈveɪl(ə)ns, -ˈveɪəns/ ● **n.** close observation, especially of a suspected spy or criminal.
– ORIGIN C19: from Fr., from *sur-* 'over' + *veiller* 'watch'.

**survey** ● **v.** /səˈveɪ/ **1** look carefully and thoroughly at. **2** examine and record the area and features of (an area of land) so as to construct a map, plan, or description. **3** Brit. examine and report on the condition of (a building), especially for a prospective buyer. **4** conduct a survey among (a group of people). ● **n.** /ˈsəːveɪ/ **1** a general view, examination, or description. ➤an investigation of the opinions or experience of a group of people, based on a series of questions. **2** an act of surveying. **3** a map, plan, or report obtained by surveying.
– ORIGIN ME: from Anglo-Norman Fr. *surveier*, from med. L. *supervidere*, from *super-* 'over' + *videre* 'to see'.

**surveyor** ● **n. 1** a person who surveys land, buildings, etc. as a profession. **2** Brit. an official inspector, especially for measurement and valuation purposes.
– DERIVATIVES **surveyorship** n.

**survival** ● **n. 1** the state or fact of surviving. **2** an object or practice that has survived from an earlier time.
– PHRASES **survival of the fittest** Biology the continued existence of the organisms best adapted to their environment; natural selection.

**survivalism** ● **n. 1** the policy of trying to ensure one's own survival or that of one's social or national group. **2** the practising of outdoor survival skills as a sport or hobby.
– DERIVATIVES **survivalist** n. & adj.

**survival kit** ● **n.** a pack of emergency equipment, including food, medical supplies, and tools, especially as carried by members of the armed forces.

**survive** ● **v.** continue to live or exist. ➤continue to live or exist in spite of (an accident or ordeal). ➤remain alive after the death of.
– DERIVATIVES **survivable** adj.
– ORIGIN ME: from OFr. *sourvivre*, from L. *supervivere*, from *super-* 'in addition' + *vivere* 'live'.

**survivor** ● **n. 1** a person who has survived. **2** Law a joint tenant who has the right to the whole estate on the other's death.
– DERIVATIVES **survivorship** n.

**Sus.** ● **abbrev.** (in biblical references) Susanna (Apocrypha).

**sus** /sʌs/ Brit. informal ● **n. 1** suspicion of having committed a crime. ➤[as modifier] historical relating to or denoting a law under which a person could be arrested on suspicion of having committed an offence. **2** variant spelling of **suss** (in sense 1). ● **adj.** variant spelling of **suss**.

**sus-** ● **prefix** variant spelling of **SUB-** before *c, p, t* (as in *susceptible, suspend*).

**susceptibility** ● **n.** (pl. **-ies**) **1** the state or fact of being susceptible. **2** (**susceptibilities**) a person's feelings, regarded as being easily hurt. **3** Physics the ratio of the magnetization produced in a material to the magnetizing force.

**susceptible** /səˈsɛptɪb(ə)l/ ● **adj. 1** (often **susceptible to**) likely to be influenced or harmed by a particular thing. ➤easily influenced by feelings or emotions. **2** (**susceptible of**) capable or admitting of.
– DERIVATIVES **susceptibly** adv.
– ORIGIN C17: from late L. *susceptibilis*, from L. *suscipere* 'take up, sustain'.

**susceptive** ● **adj.** archaic susceptible.

**sushi** /ˈsuːʃi, ˈsʊʃi/ ● **n.** a Japanese dish consisting of small balls or rolls of vinegar-flavoured cold rice served with a garnish of vegetables, egg, or raw seafood.
– ORIGIN from Japanese.

**suspect** ● **v.** /səˈspɛkt/ **1** believe (something) to be probable or possible. ➤believe (someone) to be guilty of a crime or offence, without certain proof. **2** doubt the genuineness or truth of. ● **n.** /ˈsʌspɛkt/ a person suspected of a crime or offence. ● **adj.** /ˈsʌspɛkt/ possibly dangerous or false.
– ORIGIN ME: from L. *suspectus*, *suspicere* 'mistrust', from *sub-* 'from below' + *specere* 'to look'.

**suspend** ● **v. 1** halt temporarily. **2** debar temporarily from a post, duties, etc., as a punishment. **3** defer or delay (an action, event, or judgement). ➤Law (of a judge or court) cause (an imposed sentence) to be unenforced as long as no further offence is committed within a specified period. **4** hang from somewhere. **5** (**be suspended**) be dispersed in a suspension.
– PHRASES **suspend payment** (of a company) cease to meet its financial obligations as a result of insolvency or insufficient funds.
– ORIGIN ME: from OFr. *suspendre* or L. *suspendere*, from *sub-* 'from below' + *pendere* 'hang'.

**suspended animation** ● **n.** temporary cessation of most vital functions, without death.

**suspended ceiling** ● **n.** a ceiling with a space between it and the floor above from which it hangs.

**suspender** ● **n. 1** Brit. an elastic strap attached to a belt or garter, fastened to the top of a stocking to hold it up. **2** (**suspenders**) N. Amer. a pair of braces for holding up trousers.

**suspender belt** ● **n.** Brit. a woman's undergarment consisting of a decorative belt and suspenders.

**suspense** ● **n. 1** a state or feeling of excited or anxious uncertainty about what may happen. **2** chiefly Law the temporary cessation or suspension of something.
– DERIVATIVES **suspenseful** adj.
– ORIGIN ME: from OFr. *suspens* 'abeyance', based on L. *suspensus*, *suspendere* (see **SUSPEND**).

**suspense account** ● **n.** an account in which items are entered temporarily before allocation to the correct or final account.

**suspension** ● **n. 1** the action of suspending or the condition of being suspended. **2** the system of springs and shock absorbers by which a vehicle is supported on its wheels. **3** a mixture in which particles are dispersed throughout the bulk of a fluid. **4** Music a discord made by prolonging a note of a chord into the following chord.

**suspension bridge** ● **n.** a bridge in which the deck is suspended from cables running between towers.

**suspensive** • **adj.** **1** of or relating to the suspension of an event, action, or legal obligation. **2** archaic causing suspense.
– DERIVATIVES **suspensively** adv. **suspensiveness** n.

**suspensory** • **adj.** **1** holding and supporting an organ or part. **2** of or relating to the suspension of an event, action, or legal obligation.

**suspicion** • **n.** **1** a feeling that something is possible or probable or that someone is guilty of a crime or offence. **2** cautious distrust. **3** a very slight trace: *a suspicion of a smile.*
– PHRASES **above suspicion** too good or honest to be thought capable of wrongdoing. **under suspicion** suspected of wrongdoing.
– DERIVATIVES **suspicious** adj. **suspiciously** adv. **suspiciousness** n.
– ORIGIN ME: from Anglo-Norman Fr. *suspeciun*, from med. L. *suspectio(n-)*, from *suspicere* 'mistrust'.

**suspire** /sə'spʌɪə/ • **v.** poetic/literary breathe.
– DERIVATIVES **suspiration** n.
– ORIGIN ME (in the sense 'yearn after'): from L. *suspirare*, from *sub-* 'from below' + *spirare* 'breathe'.

**suss** Brit. informal • **v.** (**sussed**, **sussing**) **1** realize. ➤ understand the true character or nature of. **2** [as adj. **sussed**] clever and well informed. • **n.** **1** (also **sus**) a police suspect. **2** knowledge or awareness of a specified kind: *business suss.* • **adj.** (also **sus**) shrewd and wary.
– ORIGIN 1930s: abbrev. of **SUSPECT**, **SUSPICION**.

**Sussex** • **n.** a speckled or red bird of a domestic English breed of chicken.
– ORIGIN *Sussex*, a former county of southern England.

**sustain** • **v.** **1** strengthen or support physically or mentally. ➤ bear (the weight of an object). **2** keep (something) going over time or continuously. **3** suffer (something unpleasant). **4** uphold or confirm the justice or validity of. • **n.** Music an effect or facility on a keyboard or electronic instrument whereby a note can be sustained after the key is released.
– DERIVATIVES **sustained** adj. **sustainedly** adv. **sustainer** n. **sustainment** n.
– ORIGIN ME: from OFr. *soustenir*, from L. *sustinere*, from *sub-* 'from below' + *tenere* 'hold'.

**sustainable** • **adj.** able to be sustained.
– DERIVATIVES **sustainability** n. **sustainably** adv.

**sustained yield** • **n.** a level of exploitation or crop production which is maintained by restricting the quantity harvested to avoid long-term depletion.

**sustenance** • **n.** **1** food and drink regarded as sustaining life. **2** the sustaining of someone or something in life or existence.
– ORIGIN ME: from OFr. *soustenance*, from *soustenir* (see **SUSTAIN**).

**sustentation** /ˌsʌst(ə)n'teɪʃ(ə)n/ • **n.** formal sustenance.
– ORIGIN ME: from OFr., or from L. *sustentatio(n-)*, from *sustentare* 'uphold, sustain', frequentative of *sustinere* (see **SUSTAIN**).

**susurration** /ˌs(j)uːsʌ'reɪʃ(ə)n/ (also **susurrus** /s(j)uː'sʌrəs/) • **n.** poetic/literary whispering or rustling.
– ORIGIN ME: from late L. *susurratio(n-)*, from L. *susurrare* 'to murmur, hum'.

**sutler** /'sʌtlə/ • **n.** historical a person who followed an army and sold provisions to the soldiers.
– ORIGIN C16: from obs. Du. *soeteler*, from *soetelen* 'perform mean duties'.

**sutra** /'suːtrə/ • **n.** **1** a rule or aphorism in Sanskrit literature, or a set of these on grammar or Hindu law or philosophy. See also **KAMA SUTRA**. **2** a Buddhist or Jainist scripture.
– ORIGIN from Sanskrit *sūtra* 'thread, rule', from *siv* 'sew'.

**suttee** /sʌ'tiː, 'sʌti/ (also **sati**) • **n.** (pl. **suttees**) the former Hindu practice of a widow immolating herself on her husband's funeral pyre.
– ORIGIN Hindi, from Sanskrit *satī* 'faithful wife', from *sat* 'good'.

**suture** /'suːtʃə/ • **n.** **1** a stitch or row of stitches holding together the edges of a wound or surgical incision. ➤ a thread or wire used for this. **2** the action of suturing. **3** chiefly Anatomy a seam-like immovable junction between two parts, especially between bones of the skull. • **v.** stitch up with a suture.
– DERIVATIVES **sutural** adj.
– ORIGIN ME: from Fr., or from L. *sutura*, from *suere* 'sew'.

**SUV** • **abbrev.** sport utility vehicle.

**suzerain** /'suːzəreɪn/ • **n.** **1** a sovereign or state having some control over another state that is internally autonomous. **2** a feudal overlord.
– DERIVATIVES **suzerainty** n.
– ORIGIN C19: from Fr., appar. from *sus* 'above', suggested by *souverain* 'sovereign'.

**Sv** • **abbrev.** sievert(s).

**s.v.** • **abbrev.** (in textual references) under the word or heading given.
– ORIGIN from L. *sub voce* or *sub verbo*, lit. 'under the word or voice'.

**svelte** • **adj.** slender and elegant.
– ORIGIN C19: from Fr., from Ital. *svelto*.

**Svengali** /svɛn'gɑːli/ • **n.** a person who exercises a controlling influence on another, especially for a sinister purpose.
– ORIGIN *Svengali*, a musician in George du Maurier's novel *Trilby* (1894) who controls Trilby's stage singing hypnotically.

**Svetambara** /swɛ'tɑːmbərə/ • **n.** a member of one of the two principal sects of Jainism, who practise asceticism and wear white clothing. See also **DIGAMBARA**.
– ORIGIN from Sanskrit *śvetāmbara*, lit. 'white-clad'.

**SVGA** • **abbrev.** super video graphics array, a high-resolution standard for monitors and screens.

**S-VHS** • **abbrev.** super video home system, an improved version of VHS.

**SW** • **abbrev.** **1** south-west. **2** south-western.

**SWA** • **abbrev.** Namibia (international vehicle registration).
– ORIGIN from *South West Africa*.

**swab** • **n.** **1** an absorbent pad used in surgery and medicine for cleaning wounds or applying medication. ➤ a specimen of a secretion taken with a swab. **2** a mop or other absorbent device for cleaning or mopping up. **3** archaic a contemptible person. ➤ US another term for **SWABBIE**. • **v.** (**swabbed**, **swabbing**) clean or absorb with a swab.
– ORIGIN C17: back-form. from *swabber* 'sailor detailed to swab decks', from early mod. Du. *zwabber*.

**swabbie** • **n.** (pl. **-ies**) US nautical slang a member of the navy of low rank.

**swacked** • **adj.** N. Amer. informal drunk.
– ORIGIN 1930s: past part. of Scots *swack* 'strike heavily'.

**swaddle** • **v.** wrap in garments or cloth.
– ORIGIN ME: frequentative of **SWATHE**[2].

**swaddling clothes** • **pl. n.** historical cloth bands wrapped round a newborn child to calm it.

**swag** • **n.** **1** an ornamental festoon of flowers, fruit, and greenery. ➤ a curtain or drape fastened to hang in a drooping curve. **2** informal money or goods taken by a thief or burglar. **3** Austral./NZ a traveller's or miner's bundle of personal belongings. **4** Austral./NZ informal a large number or amount. • **v.** (**swagged**, **swagging**) **1** arrange in or decorate with swags. **2** Austral./NZ travel with a swag of belongings. **3** chiefly poetic/literary hang or sway heavily.
– ORIGIN ME (in the sense 'bulging bag'): prob. of Scand. origin.

**swage** /sweɪdʒ/ • **n.** **1** a tool or die for shaping metal by hammering or pressure. **2** a groove, ridge, or other moulding on an object. • **v.** shape or compress using a swage.
– ORIGIN ME: from OFr. *souage* 'decorative groove', of unknown origin.

**swagger** • **v.** walk or behave arrogantly or self-importantly. • **n.** an arrogant or self-important gait or manner. • **adj.** **1** denoting a coat cut with a loose flare from the shoulders. **2** Brit. informal, dated smart or fashionable.
– DERIVATIVES **swaggerer** n. **swaggering** adj. **swaggeringly** adv.

– ORIGIN C16: appar. a frequentative of the verb **SWAG**.

**swagger stick** • n. a short cane carried by a military officer.

**swagman** • n. (pl. **-men**) Austral./NZ a man carrying a swag; an itinerant worker.

**Swahili** /swəˈhiːli, swɑː-/ • n. (pl. same) **1** a Bantu language widely used as a lingua franca in East Africa. **2** a member of a people of Zanzibar and nearby coastal regions.

– ORIGIN from Arab. *sawāḥil*, pl. of *sāḥil* 'coast'.

**swain** • n. **1** archaic a country youth. **2** poetic/literary a young lover or suitor.

– ORIGIN OE (denoting a young man attendant on a knight), from ON *sveinn* 'lad'.

**swale** • n. chiefly N. Amer. & dialect a low or hollow place, especially a marshy depression between ridges.

– ORIGIN C16: of unknown origin.

**swallow[1]** • v. **1** cause or allow (food, drink, etc.) to pass down the throat. ➤make a similar movement of the throat, especially through fear or nervousness. **2** take in and cause to disappear; engulf. **3** put up with or meekly accept. ➤resist expressing: *he swallowed his pride.* **4** believe (an untrue or unlikely statement) unquestioningly. • n. an act of swallowing something.

– DERIVATIVES **swallowable** adj. **swallower** n.

– ORIGIN OE *swelgan*, of Gmc origin.

**swallow[2]** • n. a migratory swift-flying insectivorous songbird with a forked tail. [*Hirundo rustica* and other species, family Hirundinidae.]

– ORIGIN OE *swealwe*, of Gmc origin.

**swallow dive** • n. Brit. a dive performed with one's arms outspread until close to the water.

**swallow hole** • n. another term for **SINKHOLE**.

**swallowtail** • n. **1** a deeply forked tail. **2** a large brightly coloured butterfly with tail-like projections on the hindwings. [*Papilio machaon* and other species, family Papilionidae.]

– DERIVATIVES **swallow-tailed** adj.

**swam** past of **SWIM**.

**swami** /ˈswɑːmi/ • n. (pl. **swamis**) a male Hindu religious teacher.

– ORIGIN from Hindi *swāmī* 'master, prince', from Sanskrit *svāmin*.

**swamp** • n. an area of waterlogged ground; a bog or marsh. • v. **1** overwhelm or flood with water. **2** overwhelm with too much of something; inundate.

– DERIVATIVES **swampish** adj. **swampy** adj.

– ORIGIN C17: prob. from a Gmc base meaning 'sponge'.

**swamp fever** • n. a contagious and usually fatal viral disease of horses.

**swampland** • n. (also **swamplands**) land consisting of swamps.

**swan** • n. a large waterbird, typically all white, with a long flexible neck, short legs, and webbed feet. [Several species, chiefly in the genus *Cygnus*.] • v. (**swanned**, **swanning**) Brit. informal move or go in a casual, irresponsible, or ostentatious way.

– DERIVATIVES **swanlike** adj.

– ORIGIN OE, of Gmc origin.

**swan dive** • n. N. Amer. a swallow dive.

**swank** informal • v. display one's wealth, knowledge, or achievements so as to impress others. • n. behaviour, talk, or display intended to impress others. • adj. North American term for **SWANKY**.

– ORIGIN C19: of unknown origin.

**swanky** • adj. (**-ier**, **-iest**) informal **1** stylishly luxurious and expensive. **2** inclined to show off.

– DERIVATIVES **swankily** adv. **swankiness** n.

**swan mussel** • n. a large freshwater mussel, the larvae of which parasitize fish. [*Anodonta cygnea*.]

**swan neck** • n. a curved structure shaped like a swan's neck.

– DERIVATIVES **swan-necked** adj.

**swannery** • n. (pl. **-ies**) Brit. a place where swans are kept or bred.

**swansdown** • n. **1** the fine down of a swan, used for trimmings and powder puffs. **2** a thick cotton fabric with a soft nap on one side. ➤a soft, thick woollen fabric containing a little silk or cotton.

**swansong** • n. the final performance or activity of a person's career.

– ORIGIN C19: suggested by Ger. *Schwanengesang*, denoting a song fabled to be sung by a dying swan.

**swan-upping** • n. Brit. the annual practice of catching swans on the River Thames and marking them to indicate ownership by the Crown or a corporation.

**swap** (also **swop**) • v. (**swapped**, **swapping**) exchange or substitute. • n. an act of exchanging one thing for another.

– DERIVATIVES **swappable** adj. **swapper** n.

– ORIGIN ME (in the sense 'throw forcibly'): prob. imitative of a resounding blow.

**swapfile** • n. Computing a file on a hard disk used for programs transferred from the processor's memory.

**SWAPO** • abbrev. South West Africa People's Organization.

**sward** /swɔːd/ • n. an expanse of short grass. ➤the upper layer of soil, especially when covered with grass.

– DERIVATIVES **swarded** adj.

– ORIGIN OE *sweard* 'skin'.

**sware** archaic past of **SWEAR**.

**swarf** /swɑːf/ • n. fine chips or filings produced by machining.

– ORIGIN C16: either from OE *geswearf* 'filings' or from ON *svarf* 'file dust'.

**swarm** • n. **1** a large or dense group of flying insects. ➤a large number of honeybees that leave a hive with a queen in order to establish a new colony. **2** a large group of people or things. • v. **1** move in or form a swarm. **2** move somewhere in large numbers. ➤(**swarm with**) be crowded or overrun with.

– PHRASAL VERBS **swarm up** climb rapidly by gripping with one's hands and feet.

– DERIVATIVES **swarmer** n.

– ORIGIN OE *swearm*, of Gmc origin.

**swart** /swɔːt/ • adj. archaic or poetic/literary swarthy.

– ORIGIN OE *sweart*, of Gmc origin.

**swarthy** • adj. (**-ier**, **-iest**) dark-complexioned.

– DERIVATIVES **swarthily** adv. **swarthiness** n.

– ORIGIN C16: alt. of obs. *swarty* (from **SWART**).

**swash[1]** • v. **1** (of water) move with a splashing sound. **2** archaic flamboyantly swagger about or wield a sword. • n. the rush of seawater up the beach after the breaking of a wave. ➤archaic the motion or sound of water washing against something.

– ORIGIN C16: imitative.

**swash[2]** • adj. Printing denoting an ornamental written or printed character, typically a capital letter.

– ORIGIN C17: of unknown origin.

**swashbuckler** • n. a person who takes a flamboyant part in daring adventures. ➤a film or book portraying such a person.

– DERIVATIVES **swashbuckling** adj.

– ORIGIN C16: from **SWASH[1]** + **BUCKLER**.

**swash plate** • n. an inclined disc revolving on an axle and giving reciprocating motion to a part in contact with it.

**swastika** /ˈswɒstɪkə/ • n. an ancient symbol in the form of an equal-armed cross with each arm continued at a right angle, used (in clockwise form) as the emblem of the German Nazi party.

– ORIGIN C19: from Sanskrit *svastika*, from *svasti* 'well-being', from *su* 'good' + *asti* 'being'.

**swat** • v. (**swatted**, **swatting**) hit or crush with a sharp blow from a flat object. • n. such a sharp blow.

– ORIGIN C17 (in the sense 'sit down'): north. Engl. dial. and US var. of **SQUAT**.

**swatch** • n. **1** a piece of fabric used as a sample. ➤a number of these bound together. **2** a patch or area.

– ORIGIN C16: orig. Scots and north. Engl., of unknown origin.

**swathe[1]** /sweɪð/ (chiefly N. Amer. also **swath** /swɔːθ, swɒθ/) • n. (pl. **swathes** or **swaths** /sweɪðz, swɔːðz, swɒθz/) **1** a row or line of grass, corn, etc. as it falls when mown or reaped. **2** a broad strip or area: *vast swathes of land.*

– PHRASES **cut a swathe through** pass through (an area) causing destruction or upheaval. **cut a wide swathe** N. Amer. attract much attention.
– ORIGIN OE *swæth, swathu* 'track, trace', of W. Gmc origin.

**swathe²** /sweɪð/ • v. wrap in several layers of fabric. • n. a strip of material in which something is wrapped.
– ORIGIN OE *swath-* (n.), *swathian* (v.); cf. SWADDLE.

**swather** /'swɔːθə, 'swɒθə/ • n. a device on a mowing machine for raising uncut fallen corn and marking the limit of cut corn.

**sway** • v. **1** move slowly or rhythmically backwards and forwards or from side to side. **2** cause to change in opinion, action, etc.; influence. **3** poetic/literary rule; govern. • n. **1** a rhythmical movement from side to side. **2** influence; rule.
– PHRASES **hold sway** have great power or influence.
– ORIGIN ME: rel. to Low Ger. *swājen* 'be blown to and fro' and Du. *zwaaien* 'swing, walk totteringly'.

**swayback** • n. an abnormally hollowed back, especially in a horse.
– DERIVATIVES **sway-backed** adj.

**Swazi** /'swɑːzi/ • n. (pl. same or **Swazis**) **1** a member of a people inhabiting Swaziland and parts of eastern Transvaal. ➤a native or national of Swaziland. **2** the Nguni language of this people.
– ORIGIN from the name of *Mswati*, a C19 king of the Swazis.

**swear** • v. (past **swore**; past part. **sworn**) **1** state or promise solemnly or on oath. ➤(**swear someone in**) admit someone to a position or office by directing them to take a formal oath. ➤compel to observe a certain course of action: *I am sworn to secrecy.* ➤(**swear to**) give an assurance that something is the case. ➤(**swear off**) informal promise to abstain from. ➤(**swear by**) informal have or express great confidence in. ➤(**swear something out**) US Law obtain the issue of a warrant for arrest by making a charge on oath. **2** use offensive language, especially to express anger.
– PHRASES **swear blind** (or N. Amer. **swear up and down**) Brit. informal affirm something emphatically.
– DERIVATIVES **swearer** n.
– ORIGIN OE *swerian* of Gmc origin; rel. to ANSWER.

**swear word** • n. an offensive or obscene word.

**sweat** • n. **1** moisture exuded through the pores of the skin, especially as a reaction to heat, physical exertion, or anxiety. **2** informal a state of anxiety or distress. ➤informal hard work; a laborious undertaking. **3** (**sweats**) informal, chiefly N. Amer. a sweatsuit; sweatpants. • v. (past and past part. **sweated** or N. Amer. **sweat**) **1** exude sweat. ➤(**sweat something out/off**) get rid of something by exuding sweat. ➤cause to exude sweat by exercise or exertion. ➤exert a great deal of strenuous effort. ➤be or remain in a state of extreme anxiety. ➤N. Amer. informal worry about. **2** (of a substance) exude moisture. **3** cook (chopped vegetables) slowly in a pan with a small amount of fat. **4** subject (metal) to surface melting, especially to fasten or join by solder without a soldering iron.
– PHRASES **break sweat** (or US **break a sweat**) informal exert oneself physically. **by the sweat of one's brow** by one's own hard labour. **no sweat** informal used to convey that one perceives no difficulty or problem with something. **sweat blood** informal make an extraordinarily strenuous effort. ➤be extremely anxious. **sweat bullets** N. Amer. informal be extremely anxious or nervous. **sweat it out** informal endure prolonged heat, exertion, or anxiety.
– ORIGIN OE *swāt* (n.), *swǣtan* (v.), of Gmc origin.

**sweatband** • n. a band of absorbent material worn to soak up sweat.

**sweated** • adj. of or denoting manual workers employed for long hours and under poor conditions: *sweated labour.*

**sweat equity** • n. N. Amer. informal an interest in a property earned by a tenant in return for labour towards upkeep or restoration.

**sweater** • n. **1** a pullover with long sleeves. **2** dated an employer of sweated labour.

**sweat gland** • n. a coiled tubular gland in the skin, secreting sweat.

**sweating sickness** • n. a fever with intense sweating, epidemic in England in the 15th–16th centuries.

**sweat lodge** • n. a hut used by North American Indians for ritual steam baths.

**sweatpants** • pl. n. loose trousers with an elasticated or drawstring waist, worn for exercise or leisure.

**sweatshirt** • n. a loose sweater, typically of knitted cotton, worn for exercise or leisure.

**sweatshop** • n. a factory or workshop employing sweated labour.

**sweat sock** • n. N. Amer. a thick, absorbent sock.

**sweatsuit** • n. a suit consisting of a sweatshirt and sweatpants.

**sweaty** • adj. (**-ier, -iest**) exuding, soaked in, or inducing sweat.
– DERIVATIVES **sweatily** adv. **sweatiness** n.

**Swede** • n. a native or national of Sweden, or a person of Swedish descent.
– ORIGIN from Mid. Low Ger. and MDu. *Swēde*, prob. from ON *Svíthjóth*, from *Svíar* 'Swedes' + *thjóth* 'people'.

**swede** • n. Brit. a large, round yellow-fleshed root vegetable originally introduced into Scotland from Sweden; rutabaga. ➤the variety of rape which produces this root.

**swedge** /swɛdʒ/ Scottish informal • n. a fight or brawl. • v. fight or brawl.
– ORIGIN perh. rel. to dial. *swag* 'sway heavily'.

**Swedish** • n. the Scandinavian language of Sweden. • adj. of or relating to Sweden, its people, or their language.

**sweep** • v. (past and past part. **swept**) **1** clean (an area) by brushing away dirt or litter. ➤move or remove by brushing. ➤move or push with great force in a particular direction. ➤(**sweep someone/thing away/aside**) remove or abolish someone or something swiftly and suddenly. **2** search or survey (an area) for something. ➤cover (an entire area) with a gun. **3** pass or traverse swiftly and smoothly in a particular direction. ➤affect (an area or place) swiftly and widely: *violence swept the country.* ➤extend continuously, especially in an arc or curve. ➤Cricket hit to the leg side by bringing the bat across the body from a half-kneeling position. **4** N. Amer. be victorious in (a series of games). • n. **1** an act of sweeping. ➤short for CHIMNEY SWEEP. **2** a long, swift, curving movement. ➤Electronics the movement of a beam across the screen of a cathode ray tube. **3** a long, typically curved stretch of road, river, etc. **4** the range or scope of something. **5** informal a sweepstake. **6** N. Amer. an instance of winning every event, award, or place in a contest. **7** a long heavy oar. **8** a sail of a windmill. **9** a long pole mounted as a lever for raising buckets from a well.
– PHRASES **sweep the board** win every event or prize in a contest.
– ORIGIN OE *swāpan*, of Gmc origin.

**sweepback** • n. the angle at which an aircraft's wing is set back from a right angle to the body.

**sweeper** • n. **1** a person or device that cleans by sweeping. **2** Soccer a player stationed behind the other defenders, free to defend at any point across the field.

**sweeping** • adj. **1** extending or performed in a long, continuous curve. **2** wide in range or effect. ➤(of a statement) taking no account of particular cases or exceptions; too general. • n. (**sweepings**) dirt or refuse collected by sweeping.
– DERIVATIVES **sweepingly** adv. **sweepingness** n.

**sweepstake** • n. (also **sweepstakes**) a form of gambling, especially on sporting events, in which all the stakes are divided among the winners.

**sweet** • adj. **1** having the pleasant taste characteristic of sugar or honey; not salt, sour, or bitter. **2** (of air, water, etc.) fresh, pure, and untainted. ➤fragrant. **3** pleasing in general; delightful. ➤working, moving, or done smoothly or easily. ➤melodious or harmonious. ➤chiefly US denoting music, especially jazz, played at a steady tempo without improvisation. **4** (of a person or action) pleasant and kind or thoughtful. ➤charming and endearing. ➤(**sweet**

**on**) informal, dated infatuated or in love with. ➤dear; beloved. ➤archaic used as a respectful form of address. ● **n. 1** Brit. a small shaped piece of confectionery made with sugar. **2** Brit. a sweet dish forming a course of a meal; a pudding or dessert. **3** used as a very affectionate form of address. **4** (**sweets**) the pleasures or delights found in something.
– PHRASES **keep someone sweet** informal keep someone well disposed towards oneself, especially by favours or bribery. **she's sweet** Austral./NZ informal all is well.
– DERIVATIVES **sweetish** adj. **sweetly** adv.
– ORIGIN OE *swēte*, of Gmc origin.

**sweet-and-sour** ● **adj.** cooked with both sugar and a sour substance, such as vinegar or lemon.

**sweetbread** ● **n.** the thymus gland (or, rarely, the pancreas) of an animal, used for food.

**sweetbriar** ● **n.** a wild rose with fragrant leaves and flowers. [*Rosa rubiginosa*.]

**sweet butter** ● **n.** unsalted butter made from fresh pasteurized cream.

**sweet cicely** ● **n.** see **CICELY**.

**sweetcorn** ● **n.** maize of a variety with kernels that have a high sugar content, eaten as a vegetable.

**sweeten** ● **v. 1** make or become sweet or sweeter. **2** make more agreeable or acceptable. ➤informal induce (someone) to be well disposed to oneself.

**sweetener** ● **n. 1** a substance used to sweeten food or drink, especially one other than sugar. **2** informal, chiefly Brit. an inducement, especially in the form of money or a concession.

**sweet Fanny Adams** ● **n.** see **FANNY ADAMS**.

**sweet flag** ● **n.** a waterside plant of the arum family with leaves like an iris and roots used medicinally and as a flavouring. [*Acorus calamus*.]

**sweet gale** ● **n.** another term for **BOG MYRTLE**.
– ORIGIN C17: *gale* from OE *gagel*, *gagelle*, of Gmc origin.

**sweetgrass** ● **n.** any of a number of grasses which are fragrant or attractive to livestock. [*Glyceria*, *Hierochloe*, and other genera.]

**sweet gum** ● **n.** a North American liquidambar tree which yields a balsam and decorative heartwood. [*Liquidambar styraciflua*.]

**sweetheart** ● **n. 1** a person that one is in love with. ➤used as a term of endearment or affectionate form of address. **2** [as modifier] informal denoting an arrangement reached privately by two sides in their own interests: *a sweetheart deal.*

**sweetheart neckline** ● **n.** a low neckline shaped like the top of a heart.

**sweetie** ● **n.** informal **1** Brit. a sweet. **2** (also **sweetie-pie**) used as a term of endearment. **3** a sweet green-skinned grapefruit.

**sweeting** ● **n. 1** an apple of a sweet-flavoured variety. **2** archaic darling.

**sweetlips** ● **n.** (pl. same) a fish of Indo-Pacific seas that changes its colour and markings with age. [*Plectorhynchus* and other genera: several species.]

**sweetmeal** ● **n.** Brit. sweetened wholemeal.

**sweetmeat** ● **n.** archaic an item of confectionery or sweet food.

**sweet milk** ● **n.** fresh whole milk, as opposed to buttermilk.

**sweetness** ● **n.** the quality of being sweet.
– PHRASES **sweetness and light** good-natured benevolence or harmony. [taken from Jonathan Swift, orig. by Matthew Arnold in *Culture and Anarchy* (1869).]

**sweet pea** ● **n.** a climbing plant of the pea family, cultivated for its colourful fragrant flowers. [*Lathyrus odoratus* and related species.]

**sweet pepper** ● **n.** a large green, yellow, orange, or red variety of capsicum with a mild or sweet flavour.

**sweet potato** ● **n. 1** an edible tuber with pinkish-orange slightly sweet flesh. **2** the Central American climbing plant which yields this tuber, widely cultivated in warm countries. [*Ipomoea batatas*.]

**sweet rocket** ● **n.** a plant of the cabbage family, with long spikes of mauve or white flowers which are fragrant in the evening. [*Hesperis matronalis*.]

**sweetsop** ● **n. 1** a round or heart-shaped custard apple with green scaly rind and a sweet pulp. **2** the tropical American shrub which yields this fruit. [*Annona squamosa*.]

**sweet-talk** ● **v.** informal persuade to do something by insincere flattery or kind words.

**sweet tooth** ● **n.** (pl. **sweet tooths**) a great liking for sweet-tasting foods.
– DERIVATIVES **sweet-toothed** adj.

**sweet violet** ● **n.** a sweet-scented violet with heart-shaped leaves, used in perfumery and as a flavouring. [*Viola odorata*.]

**sweet william** ● **n.** a fragrant garden pink with flattened clusters of vivid red, pink, or white flowers. [*Dianthus barbatus*.]

**swell** ● **v.** (past part. **swollen** or **swelled**) **1** become larger or rounder in size, especially as a result of an accumulation of fluid. **2** become or make greater in intensity, amount, or volume. ● **n. 1** a full or gently rounded form. **2** a gradual increase in sound, amount, or intensity. ➤a welling up of a feeling. **3** a slow, regular movement of the sea in rolling waves that do not break. **4** a mechanism for producing a crescendo or diminuendo in an organ or harmonium. **5** informal, dated a fashionable or stylish person of wealth or high social position. ● **adj.** N. Amer. informal, dated **1** excellent; very good. **2** archaic smart; fashionable. ● **adv.** N. Amer. informal, dated excellently; very well.
– PHRASES **someone's head swells** someone becomes conceited.
– ORIGIN OE *swellan*, of Gmc origin.

**swell box** ● **n.** a part of a large organ in which some of the pipes are enclosed, with a movable shutter for controlling the sound level.

**swelling** ● **n.** an abnormal enlargement of a part of the body as a result of an accumulation of fluid. ➤a natural rounded protuberance.

**swell organ** ● **n.** a section of a large organ consisting of pipes enclosed in a swell box, usually played with an upper keyboard.

**swelter** ● **v.** be uncomfortably hot. ● **n.** an uncomfortably hot atmosphere.
– DERIVATIVES **sweltering** adj. **swelteringly** adv.
– ORIGIN ME: from the base of dial. *swelt* 'perish', of Gmc origin.

**swept** past and past participle of **SWEEP**.

**swept-wing** ● **adj.** (of an aircraft) having wings directed backwards from the fuselage.

**swerve** ● **v.** abruptly diverge or cause to diverge from a straight course. ● **n.** such a change of course. ➤a tendency to swerve imparted to a ball.
– DERIVATIVES **swerver** n.
– ORIGIN OE *sweorfan* 'depart, leave, turn aside', of Gmc origin.

**SWG** ● **abbrev.** (in the UK) standard wire gauge.

**swidden** /ˈswɪd(ə)n/ ● **n.** the practice of clearing land for cultivation by slashing and burning vegetation. ➤an area of land cleared in this way.
– ORIGIN C18 (as v.): var. of dial. *swithen* 'to burn'.

**swift** ● **adj. 1** happening quickly or promptly. **2** moving or capable of moving at high speed. ● **adv.** poetic/literary except in combination swiftly: *a swift-acting poison.* ● **n. 1** a fast-flying insectivorous bird with long, slender wings, spending most of its life on the wing. [*Apus apus* (Eurasia) and other species, family Apodidae.] **2** a moth, typically yellow-brown, with fast darting flight. [Family Hepialidae.] **3** a light adjustable reel for holding a skein of silk or wool.
– DERIVATIVES **swiftly** adv. **swiftness** n.
– ORIGIN OE, from the Gmc base of OE *swīfan* 'move in a course, sweep'.

**swiftlet** ● **n.** a small swift found in South Asia and Australasia. [Genera *Aerodramus* and *Collocalia*.]

**swifty** (also **swiftie**) ● **n.** (pl. **-ies**) informal, chiefly Austral./NZ **1** a deceptive trick. **2** a person who acts or thinks quickly.

**swig** ● **v.** (**swigged**, **swigging**) drink in large draughts. ● **n.** a large draught of drink.
– DERIVATIVES **swigger** n.

– ORIGIN C16 (as n. in the obs. sense 'liquor'): of unknown origin.

**swill** • v. **1** Brit. wash or rinse out (an area or container) by pouring large amounts of water over or into it. ➤cause to swirl round in a container or cavity. **2** informal drink greedily or in large quantities. ➤accompany (food) with large quantities of drink. • n. **1** kitchen refuse and waste food mixed with water for feeding to pigs. ➤informal alcohol of inferior quality. **2** informal a large mouthful of a drink.
– DERIVATIVES **swiller** n.
– ORIGIN OE *swillan, swilian* (v.), of unknown origin.

**swim** • v. (**swimming**; past **swam**; past part. **swum**) **1** propel oneself through water by bodily movement. ➤cross (a stretch of water) in this way. ➤float. **2** be immersed in or covered with liquid. **3** appear to whirl before one's eyes. ➤experience a dizzily confusing sensation. • n. **1** an act or period of swimming. **2** a pool in a river which is a particularly good spot for fishing.
– PHRASES **in the swim** involved in or aware of current affairs or events.
– DERIVATIVES **swimmable** adj. **swimmer** n. **swimming** n.
– ORIGIN OE *swimman*, of Gmc origin.

**swim bladder** • n. a gas-filled sac in a fish's body, used to maintain buoyancy.

**swimfeeder** • n. Fishing a small perforated container for bait, used to attract fish.

**swimmeret** /'swɪmərɛt/ • n. Zoology a forked swimming limb attached to a crustacean's abdomen.

**swimming costume** • n. Brit. a garment worn for swimming, especially a woman's one-piece swimsuit.

**swimmingly** • adv. informal smoothly and satisfactorily.

**swimming trunks** (also **swim trunks**) • pl. n. shorts worn by men for swimming.

**swimsuit** • n. a woman's one-piece swimming costume.
– DERIVATIVES **swimsuited** adj.

**swimwear** • n. clothing worn for swimming.

**swindle** • v. use deception to deprive of money or possessions. ➤obtain fraudulently. • n. a fraudulent scheme or action.
– DERIVATIVES **swindler** n.
– ORIGIN C18: back-form. from *swindler*, from Ger. *Schwindler*, from *schwindeln* 'be giddy', also 'tell lies'.

**swine** • n. **1** (pl. same) formal or N. Amer. a pig. **2** (pl. same or **swines**) informal a contemptible or disgusting person.
– DERIVATIVES **swinish** adj. **swinishly** adv. **swinishness** n.
– ORIGIN OE *swīn*, of Gmc origin; rel. to **sow**[2].

**swine fever** • n. an intestinal viral disease of pigs.

**swineherd** • n. chiefly historical a person who tends pigs.

**swine vesicular disease** • n. an infectious viral disease of pigs causing blisters around the mouth and feet.

**swing** • v. (past and past part. **swung**) **1** move or cause to move back and forth or from side to side while or as if suspended. ➤informal be executed by hanging. **2** move by grasping a support and leaping. ➤move quickly round to the opposite direction. **3** move or cause to move in a smooth, curving line. ➤(**swing at**) attempt to hit or punch, especially with a wide curving movement. ➤throw (a punch) with such a movement. **4** shift or cause to shift from one opinion, mood, or state of affairs to another. ➤have a decisive influence on (a vote, judgement, etc.). ➤informal succeed in bringing about. **5** play music with an easy flowing but vigorous rhythm. **6** informal be lively, exciting, or fashionable. **7** informal be promiscuous, especially by swapping sexual partners. • n. **1** a seat suspended by ropes or chains, on which someone can sit and swing back and forth. **2** an act of swinging. ➤the manner in which a golf club or a bat is swung. ➤the motion of swinging. ➤Cricket sideways deviation of the ball. **3** a discernible change in public opinion, especially in an election. **4** a style of jazz or dance music with an easy flowing but vigorous rhythm. **5** N. Amer. a swift tour involving a number of stops.
– PHRASES **get** (**back**) **into the swing of things** informal become accustomed to (or return to) an activity or routine. **go with a swing** informal (of a party or other event) be lively and enjoyable. **in full swing** at the height of activity. **swing the lead** Brit. informal malinger; shirk one's duty. [with naut. allusion to using a lead to ascertain the depth of water.] **swings and roundabouts** Brit. a situation in which different actions result in no eventual gain or loss.
– DERIVATIVES **swinger** n. **swingy** adj.
– ORIGIN OE *swingan* 'to beat, whip', also 'rush', *geswing* 'a stroke with a weapon', of Gmc origin.

**swingbin** • n. Brit. a rubbish bin with a lid that swings shut.

**swing bridge** • n. a bridge that can be swung to one side to allow ships to pass.

**swing coat** • n. a coat cut so as to swing when the wearer moves.

**swing door** • n. a door that can be opened in either direction and swings back when released.

**swinge** • v. (**swingeing**) poetic/literary strike hard; beat.
– ORIGIN OE *swengan* 'shake, shatter, move violently', of Gmc origin.

**swingeing** • adj. chiefly Brit. severe or otherwise extreme.
– DERIVATIVES **swingeingly** adv.

**swinging** • adj. informal lively, exciting, and fashionable. ➤sexually liberated or promiscuous.
– DERIVATIVES **swingingly** adv.

**swingle** • n. **1** a wooden tool for beating flax and removing the woody parts. **2** the swinging part of a flail. • v. beat with a swingle.
– ORIGIN ME: from MDu. *swinghel*, from the base of **swing**.

**swingletree** /'swɪŋg(ə)ltriː/ • n. chiefly Brit. a crossbar pivoted in the middle, to which the traces are attached in a horse-drawn cart or plough.

**swingman** • n. (pl. **-men**) Basketball a player who can play both guard and forward.

**swingometer** /swɪŋ'ɒmɪtə/ • n. informal a device or computerized display used to demonstrate the effect of a political swing in an election.

**swing shift** • n. N. Amer. a work shift from afternoon to late evening.

**swing-wing** • n. an aircraft wing that can move from a right-angled to a swept-back position.

**swipe** informal • v. **1** hit or try to hit with a swinging blow. **2** steal. **3** pass (a swipe card) through an electronic reader. • n. a sweeping blow. ➤an attack or criticism.
– DERIVATIVES **swiper** n.
– ORIGIN C18: perh. a var. of **sweep**.

**swipe card** • n. a plastic card bearing magnetically encoded information which is read when the card is slid through an electronic device.

**swirl** • v. move or cause to move in a twisting or spiralling pattern. • n. a swirling movement or pattern.
– DERIVATIVES **swirly** adj.
– ORIGIN ME (orig. Scots in the sense 'whirlpool'): perh. of Low Ger. or Du. origin.

**swish** • v. **1** move or cause to move with a hissing or rushing sound. **2** Basketball sink (a shot) without the ball touching the backboard or rim. • n. **1** a swishing sound or movement. **2** Basketball a swishing shot. • adj. Brit. informal impressively smart and fashionable.
– ORIGIN C18: imitative.

**swishy** • adj. **1** making a swishing sound or movement. **2** informal effeminate.

**Swiss** • adj. of or relating to Switzerland or its people. • n. (pl. same) a native or national of Switzerland, or a person of Swiss descent.
– ORIGIN C16: from Fr. *Suisse*, from Middle High Ger. *Swīz* 'Switzerland'.

**Swiss cheese plant** • n. a house plant with perforated leaves (supposedly resembling the holes in a Swiss cheese). [*Monstera deliciosa*.]

**Swiss darning** • n. a technique in which coloured stitches are sewn on to knitted garments to make patterns that seem to have been knitted.

**Swiss roll** • n. Brit. a cake made from a sponge cake spread with a filling such as jam and rolled up.

**switch** • n. **1** a device for making and breaking an electrical connection. ➤Computing a program variable which

activates or deactivates a function. **2** a change, especially a radical one. **3** a slender, flexible shoot cut from a tree. **4** N. Amer. a set of points on a railway track. **5** a tress of hair tied at one end, used in hairdressing to supplement natural hair. ● **v. 1** change in position, direction, or focus. ➤exchange. **2** (**switch something off/on**) turn an electrical device off (or on). **3** (**switch off**) informal cease to pay attention. **4** archaic beat with or as if with a switch.
– DERIVATIVES **switchable** adj.
– ORIGIN C16 (denoting a thin tapering riding whip): prob. from Low Ger.

**switchback** ● **n. 1** Brit. a road, railway, etc. with alternate sharp ascents and descents. ➤a roller coaster. **2** N. Amer. a hairpin bend.

**switchblade** ● **n.** chiefly N. Amer. another term for **FLICK KNIFE**.

**switchboard** ● **n. 1** an installation for the manual control of telephone connections. **2** an apparatus for varying connections between electric circuits.

**switched-on** ● **adj.** Brit. informal aware of what is going on or up to date.

**switcher** ● **n. 1** US a shunting engine. **2** a device used to select or combine different video and audio signals.

**switcheroo** /ˌswɪtʃəˈruː/ ● **n.** N. Amer. informal a change or exchange, especially a surprising or deceptive one.
– ORIGIN C20: from **SWITCH** + *-eroo* in the sense 'unexpected'.

**switchgear** ● **n.** electrical switching equipment.

**switchgrass** ● **n.** a tall North American panic grass. [*Panicum virgatum*.]

**switch-hitter** ● **n. 1** Baseball an ambidextrous batter. **2** N. Amer. informal a bisexual.
– DERIVATIVES **switch-hitting** adj.

**swither** /ˈswɪðə/ Scottish ● **v.** be indecisive. ● **n.** a state of indecision.
– ORIGIN C16: of unknown origin.

**swive** /swʌɪv/ ● **v.** archaic or humorous have sexual intercourse with.
– ORIGIN ME: appar. from the OE verb *swīfan* (see **SWIVEL**).

**swivel** ● **n.** a coupling between two parts enabling one to revolve without turning the other. ● **v.** (**swivelled**, **swivelling**; US **swiveled**, **swiveling**) turn on or as if on a swivel.
– ORIGIN ME, from the base of the OE v. *swīfan* 'move (along a course), sweep'.

**swivel chair** ● **n.** a chair able to be turned on its base to face in any direction.

**swivet** /ˈswɪvɪt/ ● **n.** informal, chiefly US a fluster or panic.
– ORIGIN C19: of unknown origin.

**swizz** (also **swiz**) ● **n.** Brit. informal an instance of being mildly cheated or disappointed.
– ORIGIN C20: abbrev. of **SWIZZLE**².

**swizzle**¹ ● **n.** a mixed alcoholic drink, especially a frothy one of rum or gin and bitters. ● **v.** stir with a swizzle stick.
– ORIGIN C19: of unknown origin.

**swizzle**² ● **n.** Brit. informal another term for **SWIZZ**.
– ORIGIN C20: prob. an alt. of **SWINDLE**.

**swizzle stick** ● **n.** a stick used for frothing up or taking the fizz out of drinks.

**swollen** past participle of **SWELL**.

**swoon** ● **v.** faint, especially from extreme emotion. ● **n.** an occurrence of swooning.
– ORIGIN ME: as *swown* 'fainting', *aswoon* 'in a faint', both from OE *geswōgen* 'overcome'.

**swoop** ● **v. 1** (especially of a bird) move rapidly downwards through the air. ➤carry out a sudden raid. **2** informal seize with a sweeping motion. ● **n.** an act of swooping.
– PHRASES **at** (or **in**) **one fell swoop** see **FELL**⁴.
– ORIGIN C16 (in the sense 'sweep along in a stately manner'): perh. a dial. var. of OE *swāpan* (see **SWEEP**).

**swoosh** /swuːʃ, swʊʃ/ ● **n.** the sound produced by a sudden rush of air or liquid. ● **v.** move with such a sound.
– ORIGIN C19: imitative.

**swop** ● **v.** & **n.** variant spelling of **SWAP**.

**sword** ● **n. 1** a weapon with a long metal blade and a hilt with a handguard, used for thrusting or striking and often worn as part of ceremonial dress. ➤(**the sword**) poetic/literary military power; violence. **2** (**swords**) one of the suits in a tarot pack.
– PHRASES **beat** (or **turn**) **swords into ploughshares** devote resources to peaceful rather than warlike ends. [with biblical allusion to Is. 2:4 and Mic. 4:3.] **put to the sword** kill, especially in war.
– ORIGIN OE *sw(e)ord*, of Gmc origin.

**sword-bearer** ● **n.** an official who carries a sword for a dignitary on formal occasions.

**swordfish** ● **n.** (pl. same or **-fishes**) a large edible marine fish with a streamlined body and a long sword-like snout. [*Xiphias gladius*.]

**sword knot** ● **n.** a ribbon or tassel attached to a sword hilt, originally for securing it to the wrist.

**sword of Damocles** /ˈdaməkliːz/ ● **n.** an impending danger.
– ORIGIN with ref. to *Damocles*, who flattered the Gk ruler Dionysius I so much that the king made him feast sitting under a sword suspended by a single hair.

**sword of state** ● **n.** the sword carried in front of a sovereign on state occasions.

**swordplay** ● **n.** the activity or skill of fencing with swords or foils.

**swordsman** ● **n.** (pl. **-men**) a man who fights with a sword.
– DERIVATIVES **swordsmanship** n.

**swordstick** ● **n.** a hollow walking stick containing a blade that can be used as a sword.

**swordtail** ● **n.** a Central American freshwater fish popular in aquaria, the male of which has a tail with an elongated and brightly marked lower edge. [*Xiphophorus helleri*.]

**swore** past of **SWEAR**.

**sworn** past participle of **SWEAR**. ● **adj. 1** given under oath: *a sworn statement*. **2** determined to remain such: *sworn enemies*.

**SWOT** ● **abbrev.** (in business) strengths, weaknesses, opportunities, threats.

**swot** Brit. informal, derogatory ● **v.** (**swotted**, **swotting**) (also **swot up**) study assiduously or intensively. ● **n.** a person who spends a lot of or too much time studying.
– DERIVATIVES **swotty** adj.
– ORIGIN C19: dial. var. of **SWEAT**.

**swum** past participle of **SWIM**.

**swung** past and past participle of **SWING**.

**swung dash** ● **n.** a curving printed dash (~).

**swy** /swʌɪ/ ● **n.** Austral./NZ the game of two-up.
– ORIGIN 1940s: from Ger. *zwei* 'two'.

**SY** ● **abbrev.** steam yacht.

**-sy** ● **suffix** forming diminutive nouns and adjectives such as *folksy*, *mopsy*, also pet names such as *Patsy*.
– ORIGIN var. of **-Y**².

**sybarite** /ˈsɪbərʌɪt/ ● **n.** a person who is self-indulgently fond of sensuous luxury.
– DERIVATIVES **sybaritic** adj. **sybaritism** n.
– ORIGIN C16 (orig. denoting an inhabitant of Sybaris, an ancient Gk city in southern Italy, noted for luxury): via L. from Gk *Subaritēs*.

**sycamore** ● **n. 1** a large maple native to central and southern Europe. [*Acer pseudoplatanus*.] **2** N. Amer. a buttonwood tree. **3** (also **sycomore**) a Middle Eastern fig tree. [*Ficus sycomorus*.]
– ORIGIN ME: from OFr. *sic(h)amor*, via L. from Gk *sukomoros*, from *sukon* 'fig' + *moron* 'mulberry'.

**syce** /sʌɪs/ (also **sice**) ● **n.** (especially in India) a groom.
– ORIGIN from Pers. and Urdu *sā'is*, from Arab.

**syconium** /sʌɪˈkəʊnɪəm/ ● **n.** (pl. **syconia** /-nɪə/) Botany a fleshy hollow receptacle that develops into a multiple fruit, as in the fig.
– ORIGIN C19: mod. L., from Gk *sukon* 'fig'.

**sycophant** /ˈsɪkəfant/ ● **n.** a toady; a servile flatterer.
– DERIVATIVES **sycophancy** n. **sycophantic** adj. **sycophantically** adv.
– ORIGIN C16 (denoting an informer): from Fr. *sycophante*, or via L. from Gk *sukophantēs* 'informer', from *sukon*

'fig' + *phainein* 'to show', perh. with ref. to making the insulting gesture of the 'fig' (sticking the thumb between two fingers) to informers.

**sycosis** /sʌɪˈkəʊsɪs/ ● n. Medicine inflammation of facial hair follicles, caused by bacterial infection.
– ORIGIN C16 (orig. denoting a fig-shaped skin ulcer): mod. L., from Gk *sukōsis*, from *sukon* 'fig'.

**Sydenham's chorea** ● n. a form of chorea chiefly affecting children, associated with rheumatic fever.
– ORIGIN C19: named after the C17 Engl. physician Thomas *Sydenham*.

**syenite** /ˈsʌɪənʌɪt/ ● n. Geology a coarse-grained grey igneous rock composed typically of alkali feldspar and hornblende.
– DERIVATIVES **syenitic** adj.
– ORIGIN C18: from Fr. *syénite*, from L. *Syenites (lapis)* '(stone) of *Syene*', Gk name of Aswan in Egypt.

**syl-** ● prefix variant spelling of **SYN-** assimilated before *l* (as in *syllogism*).

**syllabary** /ˈsɪləb(ə)ri/ ● n. (pl. **-ies**) a set of written characters representing syllables, serving the purpose of an alphabet.
– ORIGIN C19: from mod. L. *syllabarium*, from L. *syllaba* 'syllable'.

**syllabi** plural form of **SYLLABUS**.

**syllabic** /sɪˈlabɪk/ ● adj. of, relating to, or based on syllables. ➤(of a consonant) constituting a whole syllable.
– DERIVATIVES **syllabically** adv. **syllabicity** n.

**syllabification** /sɪˌlabɪfɪˈkeɪʃ(ə)n/ (also **syllabication**) ● n. the division of words into syllables.
– DERIVATIVES **syllabify** v. (**-ies**, **-ied**).

**syllabize** (also **-ise**) ● v. divide into or articulate by syllables.

**syllable** /ˈsɪləb(ə)l/ ● n. a unit of pronunciation having one vowel sound, with or without surrounding consonants, and forming all or part of a word. ● v. pronounce clearly, syllable by syllable.
– DERIVATIVES **syllabled** adj.
– ORIGIN ME: from an alt. of OFr. *sillabe*, via L. from Gk *sullabē*, from *sun-* 'together' + *lambanein* 'take'.

**syllabub** /ˈsɪləbʌb/ ● n. a whipped cream dessert, typically flavoured with white wine or sherry.
– ORIGIN of unknown origin.

**syllabus** /ˈsɪləbəs/ ● n. (pl. **syllabuses** or **syllabi** /-bʌɪ/) **1** the subjects in a course of study or teaching. **2** (in the Roman Catholic Church) a summary of points decided by papal decree regarding heresy.
– ORIGIN C17: mod. L., orig. a misreading of L. *sittybas*, accusative pl. of *sittyba*, from Gk *sittuba* 'title slip, label'.

**syllepsis** /sɪˈlɛpsɪs/ ● n. (pl. **syllepses** /-siːz/) a figure of speech in which a word is applied to two others of which it grammatically suits only one (e.g. *neither they nor it is working*). ➤another term for **ZEUGMA**.
– DERIVATIVES **sylleptic** adj.
– ORIGIN ME: via late L. from Gk *sullēpsis* 'taking together'.

**syllogism** /ˈsɪləˌdʒɪz(ə)m/ ● n. a form of reasoning in which a conclusion is drawn from two given or assumed propositions (premises); a common or middle term is present in the two premises but not in the conclusion, which may be invalid (e.g. *all dogs are animals; all animals have four legs; therefore all dogs have four legs*).
– DERIVATIVES **syllogistic** adj. **syllogistically** adv. **syllogize** (also **-ise**) v.
– ORIGIN ME: via OFr. or L. from Gk *sullogismos*, from *sullogizesthai*, from *sun-* 'with' + *logizesthai* 'to reason' (from *logos* 'reasoning').

**sylph** /sɪlf/ ● n. **1** an imaginary spirit of the air. **2** a slender woman or girl. **3** a mainly dark green and blue hummingbird with a long forked tail. [Genera *Aglaiocercus* and *Neolesbia*.]
– DERIVATIVES **sylphlike** adj.
– ORIGIN C17: from mod. L. *sylphes*, *sylphi* and the Ger. pl. *Sylphen*, perh. based on L. *sylvestris* 'of the woods' + *nympha* 'nymph'.

**sylvan** (also **silvan**) ● adj. chiefly poetic/literary consisting of or associated with woods; wooded. ➤pleasantly rural or pastoral.
– ORIGIN C16 (as noun denoting an inhabitant of the woods): from Fr. *sylvain* or L. *Silvanus* 'woodland deity', from *silva* 'a wood'.

**sylvatic** /sɪlˈvatɪk/ ● adj. Veterinary Medicine relating to or denoting forms of disease contracted by wild animals.
– ORIGIN 1930s: from L. *silvaticus*, from *silva* 'wood'.

**Sylvian fissure** /ˈsɪlvɪən/ ● n. Anatomy a large diagonal fissure which separates off the temporal lobe of the brain.
– ORIGIN C19: named after the C17 Flemish anatomist François de la Boë *Sylvius*.

**sylvine** /ˈsɪlviːn/ ● n. another term for **SYLVITE**.

**sylvite** /ˈsɪlvʌɪt/ ● n. a colourless or white mineral consisting of potassium chloride.
– ORIGIN C19: from mod. L. (*sal digestivus*) *Sylvii*, the old name of this salt, + **-ITE**[1].

**sym-** ● prefix variant spelling of **SYN-** assimilated before *b*, *m*, *p* (as in *symbiosis*, *symmetry*, *symphysis*).

**symbiont** /ˈsɪmbɪɒnt, -bʌɪ-/ ● n. Biology an organism living in symbiosis with another.
– ORIGIN C19: formed irregularly from Gk *sumbiōn* 'living together', pres. part. of *sumbioun* (see **SYMBIOSIS**).

**symbiosis** /ˌsɪmbɪˈəʊsɪs, -bʌɪ-/ ● n. (pl. **symbioses** /-siːz/) Biology an interaction between two different organisms living in close physical association, especially to the advantage of both.
– DERIVATIVES **symbiotic** /-ˈɒtɪk/ adj. **symbiotically** adv.
– ORIGIN C19: mod. L., from Gk *sumbiōsis* 'a living together', from *sumbioun* 'live together', from *sumbios* 'companion'.

**symbol** ● n. **1** a thing that represents or stands for something else, especially a material object representing something abstract. **2** a mark or character used as a conventional representation of something, e.g. a letter standing for a chemical element or a character in musical notation. ● v. (**symbolled**, **symbolling**; US **symboled**, **symboling**) archaic symbolize.
– ORIGIN ME (denoting the Apostles' Creed): from L. *symbolum* 'symbol, Creed (as the mark of a Christian)', from Gk *sumbolon* 'mark, token', from *sun-* 'with' + *ballein* 'to throw'.

**symbolic** ● adj. **1** serving as a symbol. **2** involving the use of symbols or symbolism.
– DERIVATIVES **symbolical** adj. **symbolically** adv.
– ORIGIN C17: from Fr. *symbolique* or late L. *symbolicus*, from Gk *sumbolikos*.

**symbolic logic** ● n. the use of symbols to denote propositions, terms, and relations in order to assist reasoning.

**symbolism** ● n. **1** the use of symbols to represent ideas or qualities. ➤symbolic meaning. **2** (also **Symbolism**) an artistic and poetic movement or style originating in the late 19th century, using symbolic images and indirect suggestion to express mystical ideas, emotions, and states of mind.
– DERIVATIVES **symbolist** n. & adj.

**symbolize** (also **-ise**) ● v. be a symbol of. ➤represent by means of symbols.
– DERIVATIVES **symbolization** n.

**symbology** ● n. the study or use of symbols. ➤symbols collectively.

**symmetrical** ● adj. made up of exactly similar parts facing each other or around an axis; showing symmetry.
– DERIVATIVES **symmetric** adj. **symmetrically** adv.

**symmetry** /ˈsɪmɪtri/ ● n. (pl. **-ies**) the quality of being made up of exactly similar parts facing each other or around an axis. ➤correct or pleasing proportion of parts. ➤similarity or exact correspondence. ➤Physics & Mathematics the property of being unchanged by a given operation or process.
– DERIVATIVES **symmetrize** (also **-ise**) v.
– ORIGIN C16: from Fr. *symétrie* or L. *symmetria*, from Gk, from *sun-* 'with' + *metron* 'measure'.

**sympathectomy** /ˌsɪmpəˈθɛktəmi/ ● n. the surgical cutting or removal of a sympathetic nerve.

**sympathetic** ● adj. **1** feeling, showing, or expressing sympathy. ➤showing approval of an idea or action.

**2** likeable. ➤designed in a sensitive or fitting way. **3** Physiology relating to or denoting the part of the autonomic nervous system supplying the internal organs, blood vessels, and glands, and balancing the action of the parasympathetic nerves. **4** of or denoting an effect which arises in response to a similar action elsewhere.
– DERIVATIVES **sympathetically** adv.

**sympathetic magic** ● **n.** occult rituals using objects or actions to represent the event or person over which influence is sought.

**sympathetic strings** ● **pl. n.** additional strings fitted to certain stringed instruments to give extra resonance.

**sympathize** (also **-ise**) ● **v. 1** feel or express sympathy. **2** agree with a sentiment or opinion.
– DERIVATIVES **sympathizer** n.

**sympathomimetic** /ˌsɪmpəθəʊmɪˈmɛtɪk, -mʌɪ-/ Medicine ● **adj.** promoting the stimulation of sympathetic nerves. ● **n.** a sympathomimetic drug.

**sympathy** ● **n.** (pl. **-ies**) **1** feelings of pity and sorrow for someone else's misfortune. ➤(**one's sympathies**) condolences. **2** understanding between people; common feeling. ➤a favourable attitude. ➤(**in sympathy**) relating harmoniously to something else; in keeping. ➤the state or fact of responding in a way corresponding to an action elsewhere.
– ORIGIN C16: via L. from Gk *sumpatheia*, from *sumpathēs*, from *sun-* 'with' + *pathos* 'feeling'.

**sympatric** /sɪmˈpatrɪk/ ● **adj.** Biology (of animal or plant species or populations) occurring in the same or overlapping geographical areas. Compare with **ALLOPATRIC**.
– DERIVATIVES **sympatry** n.
– ORIGIN C20: from **SYM-** + Gk *patra* 'fatherland' + **-IC**.

**sympetalous** /sɪmˈpɛt(ə)ləs/ ● **adj.** Botany having the petals united along their margins to form a tubular shape.
– DERIVATIVES **sympetaly** n.

**symphonic** ● **adj.** relating to or having the form or character of a symphony.
– DERIVATIVES **symphonically** adv.

**symphonic poem** ● **n.** another term for **TONE POEM**.

**symphonist** ● **n.** a composer of symphonies.

**symphony** ● **n.** (pl. **-ies**) an elaborate musical composition for full orchestra, typically in four movements with at least one in sonata form. ➤chiefly historical an orchestral interlude in a large-scale vocal work. ➤chiefly N. Amer. (especially in names) short for **SYMPHONY ORCHESTRA**.
– ORIGIN ME (denoting any of various instruments such as the dulcimer or the virginal): from OFr. *symphonie*, via L. from Gk *sumphōnia*, from *sumphōnos* 'harmonious', from *sun-* 'together' + *phōnē* 'sound'.

**symphony orchestra** ● **n.** a large classical orchestra, including string, wind, brass, and percussion instruments.

**symphysis** /ˈsɪmfɪsɪs/ ● **n.** (pl. **symphyses** /-siːz/) Anatomy a place where two bones are immovably joined (e.g. the pubic bones in the pelvis) or completely fused (e.g. at the midline of the lower jaw).
– DERIVATIVES **symphyseal** (also **symphysial**) /-ˈfɪzɪəl/ adj.
– ORIGIN C16: mod. L., from Gk *sumphusis*, from *sun-* 'together' + *phusis* 'growth'.

**symplasm** /ˈsɪmplaz(ə)m/ ● **n.** Botany the cytoplasm of a symplast.
– DERIVATIVES **symplasmic** adj.

**symplast** /ˈsɪmplast, -plɑːst/ ● **n.** Botany a continuous network of interconnected plant cell protoplasts.
– DERIVATIVES **symplastic** adj.
– ORIGIN 1930s: from Ger. *Symplast*.

**sympodium** /sɪmˈpəʊdɪəm/ ● **n.** (pl. **sympodia** /-dɪə/) Botany an apparent main axis or stem made up of successive secondary axes.
– DERIVATIVES **sympodial** adj.
– ORIGIN C19: mod. L., from Gk *syn-* 'together' + *pous, pod-* 'foot'.

**symposiast** /sɪmˈpəʊzɪast/ ● **n.** a participant in a symposium.

**symposium** /sɪmˈpəʊzɪəm/ ● **n.** (pl. **symposia** /-zɪə/ or **symposiums**) **1** a conference or meeting to discuss a particular academic or specialist subject. ➤a collection of related papers by a number of contributors. **2** a drinking party or convivial discussion, as held in ancient Greece after a banquet.
– ORIGIN C16: via L. from Gk *sumposion*, from *sumpotēs* 'fellow drinker', from *sun-* 'together' + *potēs* 'drinker'.

**symptom** ● **n.** Medicine a feature which indicates a condition of disease, in particular one apparent to the patient. Compare with **SIGN**. ➤an indication of an undesirable situation.
– DERIVATIVES **symptomless** adj.
– ORIGIN ME *synthoma*, from med. L., based on Gk *sumptōma* 'chance, symptom', from *sumpiptein* 'happen'; later influenced by Fr. *symptome*.

**symptomatic** ● **adj.** acting as a symptom of something. ➤Medicine exhibiting or involving symptoms.
– DERIVATIVES **symptomatically** adv.

**symptomatology** /ˌsɪm(p)tə(ʊ)məˈtɒlədʒi/ ● **n.** Medicine a set of symptoms.

**syn-** ● **prefix** united; acting together: *synchrony.*
– ORIGIN from Gk *sun* 'with'.

**synaesthesia** /ˌsɪnɪsˈθiːzɪə/ (US **synesthesia**) ● **n.** Physiology & Psychology the production of a sense impression relating to one sense or part of the body by stimulation of another sense or part of the body.
– DERIVATIVES **synaesthete** /sɪnˈiːsθiːt, -ˈɛs-/ n. **synaesthetic** adj.
– ORIGIN C19: mod. L., from **SYN-**, on the pattern of *anaesthesia*.

**synagogue** /ˈsɪnəgɒg/ ● **n.** a building where a Jewish assembly or congregation meets for religious observance and instruction. ➤such an assembly or congregation.
– DERIVATIVES **synagogal** adj. **synagogical** adj.
– ORIGIN ME: via OFr. and late L. from Gk *sunagōgē* 'meeting', from *sun-* 'together' + *agein* 'bring'.

**synapomorphy** /sɪˈnapə(ʊ)ˌmɔːfi/ ● **n.** (pl. **-ies**) Biology the possession by two organisms of a characteristic derived from one in an evolutionary ancestor.
– ORIGIN 1960s: from **SYN-** + **APO-** + Gk *morphē* 'form'.

**synapse** /ˈsʌɪnaps, ˈsɪn-/ ● **n.** a gap between two nerve cells, across which impulses pass by diffusion of a neurotransmitter.
– DERIVATIVES **synaptic** adj. **synaptically** adv.
– ORIGIN C19: from Gk *sunapsis*, from *sun-* 'together' + *hapsis* 'joining', from *haptein* 'to join'.

**synapsis** /sɪˈnapsɪs/ ● **n.** Biology the fusion of chromosome pairs at the start of meiosis.

**synarchy** /ˈsɪnɑːki/ ● **n.** joint rule or government by two or more individuals or parties.
– DERIVATIVES **synarchic** adj. **synarchist** n.
– ORIGIN C18: from Gk *sunarkhia*, from *sunarkhein* 'rule jointly'.

**synarthrosis** /ˌsɪnɑːˈθrəʊsɪs/ ● **n.** (pl. **synarthroses** /-siːz/) Anatomy an immovable joint between bones connected by fibrous tissue (e.g. the sutures of the skull).
– ORIGIN C16: from mod. L., from Gk *sunarthrōsis*, from *sun-* 'together' + *arthrōsis* 'jointing' (from *arthron* 'joint').

**sync** (also **synch**) informal ● **n.** synchronization. ● **v.** synchronize.
– PHRASES **in** (or **out of**) **sync** working well (or badly) together.

**syncarpous** /sɪnˈkɑːpəs/ ● **adj.** Botany having the carpels united.
– ORIGIN C19: from **SYN-** + Gk *karpos* 'fruit' + **-OUS**.

**synchondrosis** /ˌsɪŋkɒnˈdrəʊsɪs/ ● **n.** (pl. **synchondroses** /-siːz/) Anatomy an almost immovable joint between bones bound by a layer of cartilage, as in the spinal vertebrae.
– ORIGIN C16: from mod. L., from Gk *sunkhondrōsis*, from *sun-* 'together' + *khondros* 'cartilage'.

**synchro** /ˈsɪŋkrəʊ/ ● **n. 1** short for **SYNCHROMESH**. **2** synchronized or synchronization. **3** short for **SYNCHRONIZED SWIMMING**.

**synchro-** ● **comb. form** synchronous: *synchrotron.*

**synchromesh** ● **n.** a system of gear changing in which the driving and driven gearwheels are made to revolve at the same speed during engagement.

– ORIGIN 1920s: contr. of *synchronized mesh*.

**synchronic** /sɪŋ'krɒnɪk/ ● **adj.** concerned with something (especially a language) as it exists at one point in time. Often contrasted with **DIACHRONIC**.
– DERIVATIVES **synchronically** adv.

**synchronicity** /ˌsɪŋkrə'nɪsɪti/ ● **n. 1** the simultaneous occurrence of events with no discernible causal connection. **2** the state of being synchronous or synchronic.

**synchronism** /'sɪŋkrənɪz(ə)m/ ● **n.** another term for **SYNCHRONY**.
– DERIVATIVES **synchronistic** adj. **synchronistically** adv.

**synchronize** /'sɪŋkrənʌɪz/ (also **-ise**) ● **v.** cause to occur or operate at the same time or rate.
– DERIVATIVES **synchronization** n. **synchronizer** n.

**synchronized swimming** ● **n.** a sport in which teams of swimmers perform coordinated or identical movements in time to music.

**synchronous** /'sɪŋkrənəs/ ● **adj. 1** existing or occurring at the same time. **2** of or denoting a satellite which revolves in its orbit in exactly the same time as the primary body rotates on its axis.
– DERIVATIVES **synchronously** adv.
– ORIGIN C17: from late L. *synchronus* (from Gk *sunkhronos*, from *sun-* 'together' + *khronos* 'time') + **-OUS**.

**synchronous motor** ● **n.** an electric motor having a speed exactly proportional to the current frequency.

**synchrony** /'sɪŋkrəni/ ● **n. 1** simultaneous action, development, or occurrence. **2** synchronic treatment or study.

**synchrotron** /'sɪŋkrə(ʊ)trɒn/ ● **n.** Physics a cyclotron in which the magnetic field strength increases with the energy of the particles to keep their orbital radius constant.

**synchrotron radiation** ● **n.** Physics polarized radiation emitted by a charged particle spinning in a magnetic field.

**syncline** /'sɪŋklʌɪn/ ● **n.** Geology a trough or fold of stratified rock in which the strata slope upwards from the axis. Compare with **ANTICLINE**.
– DERIVATIVES **synclinal** adj.
– ORIGIN C19: from **SYN-** + Gk *klinein* 'to lean', on the pattern of *incline*.

**syncopate** /'sɪŋkəpeɪt/ ● **v. 1** [usu. as adj. **syncopated**] displace the beats or accents in (music or a rhythm) so that strong beats become weak and vice versa. **2** Grammar shorten by syncope.
– DERIVATIVES **syncopation** n. **syncopator** n.

**syncope** /'sɪŋkəpi/ ● **n. 1** Medicine temporary loss of consciousness caused by low blood pressure. **2** Grammar the omission of sounds or letters from within a word, for example when *library* is pronounced /'lʌɪbri/.
– DERIVATIVES **syncopal** adj.
– ORIGIN ME: via late L. from Gk *sunkopē*, from *sun-* 'together' + *koptein* 'strike, cut off'.

**syncretism** /'sɪŋkrɪtɪz(ə)m/ ● **n. 1** the amalgamation of different religions, cultures, or schools of thought. **2** Linguistics the merging of different inflectional varieties of a word during the development of a language.
– DERIVATIVES **syncretic** adj. **syncretist** n. & adj. **syncretistic** adj.
– ORIGIN C17: from mod. L. *syncretismus*, from Gk *sunkrētismos*, from *sunkrētizein* 'unite against a third party', from *sun-* 'together' + *krēs* 'Cretan' (orig. with ref. to ancient Cretan communities).

**syncretize** (also **-ise**) ● **v.** attempt to amalgamate (differing religious beliefs, schools of thought, etc.).
– DERIVATIVES **syncretization** n.

**syncytium** /sɪn'sɪtɪəm/ ● **n.** (pl. **syncytia** /-tɪə/) Biology a single cell or cytoplasmic mass containing several nuclei.
– DERIVATIVES **syncytial** adj.
– ORIGIN C19: from **SYN-** + **-CYTE** + **-IUM**.

**syndactyl** /sɪn'daktɪl/ ● **adj.** Medicine & Zoology having digits wholly or partly united, either naturally (as in web-footed animals) or as a malformation.
– DERIVATIVES **syndactyly** n.

**syndesmosis** /ˌsɪndɛz'məʊsɪs/ ● **n.** (pl. **syndesmoses** /-siːz/) Anatomy an immovable joint in which bones are joined by connective tissue (e.g. between the fibula and tibia at the ankle).
– ORIGIN C16: mod. L., from Gk *sundesmos* 'binding, fastening'.

**syndetic** /sɪn'dɛtɪk/ ● **adj.** Grammar of or using conjunctions.
– ORIGIN C17: from Gk *sundetikos*, from *sundein* 'bind together'.

**syndic** ● **n. 1** a government official in various countries. **2** (in the UK) a business agent of certain universities and corporations.
– DERIVATIVES **syndical** adj.
– ORIGIN C17: from Fr., via late L. from Gk *sundikos*, from *sun-* 'together' + *dikē* 'justice'.

**syndicalism** ● **n.** historical a movement for transferring the ownership and control of the means of production and distribution to workers' unions.
– DERIVATIVES **syndicalist** n. & adj.
– ORIGIN C20: from Fr. *syndicalisme*, from *syndical*, from *syndic* (see **SYNDIC**).

**syndicate** ● **n.** /'sɪndɪkət/ a group of individuals or organizations combined to promote some common interest. ➤an agency supplying material simultaneously to a number of news media. ➤a committee of syndics. ● **v.** /'sɪndɪkeɪt/ control or manage by a syndicate. ➤publish or broadcast simultaneously in a number of media.
– DERIVATIVES **syndication** n.
– ORIGIN C17: from Fr. *syndicat*, from med. L. *syndicatus*, from late L. *syndicus* (see **SYNDIC**).

**syndrome** ● **n. 1** a group of symptoms which consistently occur together. **2** a characteristic combination of opinions, emotions, or behaviour.
– DERIVATIVES **syndromic** adj.
– ORIGIN C16: mod. L., from Gk *sundromē*, from *sun-* 'together' + *dramein* 'to run'.

**syne** /sʌɪn/ ● **adv.** Scottish ago.
– ORIGIN ME: contr. of dial. *sithen* 'ever since'.

**synecdoche** /sɪ'nɛkdəki/ ● **n.** a figure of speech in which a part is made to represent the whole or vice versa, as in *England lost by six wickets* (meaning 'the English cricket team').
– DERIVATIVES **synecdochic** adj. **synecdochical** adj. **synecdochically** adv.
– ORIGIN ME: via L. from Gk *sunekdokhē*, from *sun-* 'together' + *ekdekhesthai* 'take up'.

**synecology** /ˌsɪnɪ'kɒlədʒi/ ● **n.** the ecological study of whole plant or animal communities. Contrasted with **AUTECOLOGY**.
– DERIVATIVES **synecological** /-ˌiːkə'lɒdʒɪk(ə)l, -ˌɛk-/ adj.

**syneresis** /sɪ'nɪərɪsɪs/ ● **n.** (pl. **synereses** /-siːz/) **1** the contraction of two vowels into a diphthong or single vowel. **2** Chemistry the contraction of a gel accompanied by the separating out of liquid.
– ORIGIN C16: via late L. from Gk *sunairesis*, based on *sun-* 'together' + *hairein* 'take'.

**synergist** ● **n.** an agent that participates in synergy.
– DERIVATIVES **synergistic** adj. **synergistically** adv.

**synergy** /'sɪnədʒi/ (also **synergism**) ● **n.** interaction or cooperation of two or more organizations, substances, or other agents to produce a combined effect greater than the sum of their separate effects.
– DERIVATIVES **synergetic** adj. **synergic** adj.
– ORIGIN C19: from Gk *sunergos* 'working together'.

**synesthesia** ● **n.** US spelling of **SYNAESTHESIA**.

**syngamy** /'sɪŋgəmi/ ● **n.** Biology the fusion of two cells in reproduction.
– ORIGIN 1904: from **SYN-** + Gk *gamos* 'marriage'.

**syngas** ● **n.** a mixture of carbon monoxide and hydrogen used as a feedstock in making synthetic chemicals.
– ORIGIN 1970s: abbrev. of *synthesis gas*.

**synod** /'sɪnəd, -ɒd/ ● **n. 1** an assembly of the clergy (and sometimes also the laity) in a division of a Christian Church. **2** a Presbyterian ecclesiastical court above the presbyteries and subject to the General Assembly.
– DERIVATIVES **synodal** adj.
– ORIGIN ME: via late L. from Gk *sunodos* 'meeting', from *sun-* 'together' + *hodos* 'way'.

**synodic** /sɪˈnɒdɪk/ • **adj.** Astronomy relating to or involving a conjunction.
– ORIGIN C17: via late L. from Gk *sunodikos*, from *sunodos* (see **SYNOD**).

**synodical** • **adj. 1** Christian Church of, relating to, or constituted as a synod. **2** Astronomy another term for **SYNODIC**.

**synodic month** • **n.** Astronomy another term for **LUNAR MONTH**.

**synodic period** • **n.** Astronomy the time between successive conjunctions of a planet with the sun.

**synonym** /ˈsɪnənɪm/ • **n.** a word or phrase that means the same as another word or phrase in the same language, e.g. *shut* and *close*.
– DERIVATIVES **synonymic** adj. **synonymity** n. **synonymy** /sɪˈnɒnɪmi/ n.
– ORIGIN ME: via L. from Gk *sunōnumon*, neut. of the adj. *sunōnumos*, from *sun-* 'with' + *onoma* 'name'.

**synonymous** /sɪˈnɒnɪməs/ • **adj.** (of a word or phrase) having the same meaning as another word or phrase in the same language. ➤closely associated with something: *his name was synonymous with victory.*
– DERIVATIVES **synonymously** adv. **synonymousness** n.

**synopsis** /sɪˈnɒpsɪs/ • **n.** (pl. **synopses** /-siːz/) a brief summary of something.
– DERIVATIVES **synopsize** (also **-ise**) v.
– ORIGIN C17: via late L. from Gk, from *sun-* 'together' + *opsis* 'seeing'.

**synoptic** • **adj. 1** of, forming, or involving a synopsis or general view. **2** (**Synoptic**) relating to or denoting the Gospels of Matthew, Mark, and Luke, which describe events from a similar point of view, as contrasted with that of John.
– DERIVATIVES **synoptical** adj. **synoptically** adv.

**synostosis** /ˌsɪnɒˈstəʊsɪs/ • **n.** (pl. **synostoses** /-siːz/) Physiology & Medicine the union of adjacent bones by the growth of bony substance.
– ORIGIN C19: from **SYN-** + Gk *osteon* 'bone' + **-OSIS**.

**synovial** /sʌɪˈnəʊvɪəl, sɪ-/ • **adj.** relating to or denoting a type of joint which is surrounded by a thick flexible membrane containing a viscous fluid that lubricates the joint.
– ORIGIN C18: from mod. L. *synovia*, prob. formed arbitrarily by the C16 Swiss physician Paracelsus.

**synovitis** /ˌsʌɪnə(ʊ)ˈvʌɪtɪs, ˌsɪn-/ • **n.** Medicine inflammation of a synovial membrane.

**syntagm** /ˈsɪntam/ (also **syntagma** /sɪnˈtagmə/) • **n.** (pl. **syntagms**, **syntagmas**, or **syntagmata** /-mətə/) Linguistics a set of forms in a sequential relationship. Often contrasted with **PARADIGM**.
– DERIVATIVES **syntagmatic** /ˌsɪntagˈmatɪk/ adj. **syntagmatically** adv. **syntagmatics** pl. n.
– ORIGIN C17: via late L. from Gk *suntagma*, from *suntassein* 'arrange together'.

**syntax** /ˈsɪntaks/ • **n. 1** the arrangement of words and phrases to create well-formed sentences. ➤a set of rules for or an analysis of this. **2** the structure of statements in a computer language.
– DERIVATIVES **syntactic** adj. **syntactical** adj. **syntactically** adv.
– ORIGIN C16: from Fr. *syntaxe*, or via late L. from Gk *suntaxis*, from *sun-* 'together' + *tassein* 'arrange'.

**synth** • **n.** informal short for **SYNTHESIZER**.
– DERIVATIVES **synthy** adj.

**synthase** /ˈsɪnθeɪz/ • **n.** Biochemistry an enzyme which brings about the linkage of two molecules.

**synthesis** /ˈsɪnθɪsɪs/ • **n.** (pl. **syntheses** /-siːz/) **1** the combination of components to form a connected whole. Often contrasted with **ANALYSIS**. **2** the production of chemical compounds by reaction from simpler materials. **3** (in Hegelian philosophy) the final stage in the process of dialectical reasoning, in which a new idea resolves the conflict between thesis and antithesis. **4** Grammar the process of making compound and derivative words.
– DERIVATIVES **synthesist** n.
– ORIGIN C17: via L. from Gk *sunthesis*, from *suntithenai* 'place together'.

**synthesize** /ˈsɪnθɪsʌɪz/ (also **synthetize**, **-ise**) • **v. 1** make by synthesis. ➤combine into a coherent whole. **2** produce (sound) electronically.

**synthesizer** • **n.** an electronic musical instrument, typically operated by a keyboard, producing sounds by generating and combining signals of different frequencies.

**synthetic** /sɪnˈθɛtɪk/ • **adj. 1** made by chemical synthesis, especially to imitate a natural product. ➤not genuine; unnatural. **2** Logic having truth or falsity determinable by recourse to experience. Compare with **ANALYTIC**. **3** Linguistics (of a language) tending to use inflections rather than word order to express grammatical structure. Contrasted with **ANALYTIC**. • **n.** a synthetic substance, especially a textile fibre.
– DERIVATIVES **synthetical** adj. **synthetically** adv.
– ORIGIN C17: from Fr. *synthétique* or mod. L. *syntheticus*, from Gk *sunthetikos*, based on *suntithenai* 'place together'.

**syntonic** /sɪnˈtɒnɪk/ • **adj.** Psychology responsive to and in harmony with one's situation and personality.
– ORIGIN C19: from Ger. *Syntonie* 'state of being syntonic' + **-IC**.

**syntype** • **n.** Botany & Zoology each of a set of type specimens upon which the description and name of a new species is jointly based.

**syphilis** • **n.** a sexually transmitted bacterial disease, progressing if untreated from infection of the genitals via the skin and mucous membranes to the bones, muscles, and brain.
– DERIVATIVES **syphilitic** adj. & n.
– ORIGIN C18: mod. L., from *Syphilis, sive Morbus Gallicus*, the title of a poem (1530), from the name of the character *Syphilus*, the supposed first sufferer of the disease.

**syphon** • **n. & v.** variant spelling of **SIPHON**.

**SYR** • **abbrev.** Syria (international vehicle registration).

**Syrah** /ˈsiːrə/ • **n.** another term for **SHIRAZ**.

**syrette** /sɪˈrɛt/ • **n.** Medicine, trademark a disposable syringe with a single dose of a drug.
– ORIGIN 1940s: from **SYRINGE** + **-ETTE**.

**Syriac** /ˈsɪrɪak/ • **n.** the language of ancient Syria, a western dialect of Aramaic.

**Syrian** /ˈsɪrɪən/ • **n.** a native or inhabitant of Syria. • **adj.** of or relating to Syria.

**syringe** /sɪˈrɪn(d)ʒ, ˈsɪ-/ • **n.** a tube with a nozzle and piston or bulb for sucking in and ejecting liquid in a thin stream, often one fitted with a hollow needle for injecting or withdrawing fluids into or from the body. • **v.** (**syringing**) spray liquid into or over with a syringe.
– ORIGIN ME: from med. L. *syringa*, from *syrinx* (see **SYRINX**).

**syrinx** /ˈsɪrɪŋks/ • **n.** (pl. **syrinxes**) **1** a set of pan pipes. **2** Ornithology the lower larynx or voice organ, especially in songbirds (in which it is well developed).
– ORIGIN C17: via L. from Gk *surinx* 'pipe, channel'.

**Syro-** /ˈsʌɪrəʊ/ • **comb. form** Syrian; Syrian and ...: *Syro-Palestinian.*

**syrphid** /ˈsəːfɪd/ • **n.** Entomology a fly of the hoverfly family (Syrphidae).
– ORIGIN C19: from mod. L. *Syrphidae*, from the genus name *Syrphus*, from Gk *surphos* 'gnat'.

**syrup** (US also **sirup**) • **n.** a thick sweet liquid made by dissolving sugar in boiling water, used for preserving fruit. ➤a thick sweet liquid containing medicine or used as a drink. ➤a thick, sticky liquid obtained from sugar cane as part of the processing of sugar.
– ORIGIN ME: from OFr. *sirop* or med. L. *siropus*, from Arab. *šarāb* 'beverage'; cf. **SHERBET** and **SHRUB**[2].

**syrupy** (US also **sirupy**) • **adj. 1** having the consistency or sweetness of syrup. **2** excessively sentimental.

**sysop** /ˈsɪsɒp/ • **n.** Computing a system operator.
– ORIGIN 1980s: abbrev.

**system** • **n. 1** a complex whole; a set of things working together as a mechanism or interconnecting network. ➤the human or animal body as a whole. **2** an organized scheme or method. ➤orderliness; method. **3** the prevailing political or social order, especially when regarded as oppressive and intransigent. **4** Geology a major range of strata corresponding to a period in time. **5** Music a set of staves joined by a brace.
– PHRASES **get something out of one's system** informal

get rid of a preoccupation or anxiety.
– DERIVATIVES **systemless** adj.
– ORIGIN C17: from Fr. *système* or late L. *systema*, from Gk *sustēma*, from *sun-* 'with' + *histanai* 'set up'.

**systematic** ● adj. done or acting according to a fixed plan or system; methodical.
– DERIVATIVES **systematically** adv. **systematist** /ˈsɪstəmətɪst/ n.
– ORIGIN C18: from Fr. *systématique*, via late L. from late Gk *sustēmatikos*, from *sustēma* (see **SYSTEM**).

**systematic error** ● n. Statistics an error whose effect is not reduced when observations are averaged.

**systematics** ● pl. n. [treated as sing.] the branch of biology concerned with classification and nomenclature; taxonomy.

**systematic theology** ● n. a form of theology in which the aim is to arrange religious beliefs in a self-consistent whole.

**systematize** /ˈsɪstəmə,tʌɪz/ (also **-ise**) ● v. arrange according to an organized system; make systematic.
– DERIVATIVES **systematization** n. **systematizer** n.

**systemic** /sɪˈstɛmɪk, -ˈstiːm-/ ● adj. **1** of or relating to a system as a whole. **2** Physiology denoting the non-pulmonary part of the circulatory system. **3** (of an insecticide, fungicide, etc.) entering the plant via the roots or shoots and passing through the tissues. **4** Linguistics (of grammar) based on the conception of language as a network of systems determining options from which speakers make choices.
– DERIVATIVES **systemically** adv.

**systemize** (also **-ise**) ● v. another term for **SYSTEMATIZE**.
– DERIVATIVES **systemization** n. **systemizer** n.

**system operator** (also **systems operator**) ● n. Computing a person who manages the operation of an electronic bulletin board or other computer system.

**systems analyst** ● n. a person who analyses a complex process or operation in order to improve its efficiency, especially by applying a computer system.
– DERIVATIVES **systems analysis** n.

**systole** /ˈsɪst(ə)li/ ● n. Physiology the phase of the heartbeat when the heart muscle contracts and pumps blood into the arteries. Often contrasted with **DIASTOLE**.
– DERIVATIVES **systolic** /-ˈstɒlɪk/ adj.
– ORIGIN C16: via late L. from Gk *sustolē*, from *sustellein* 'to contract'.

**syzygy** /ˈsɪzɪdʒi/ ● n. (pl. **-ies**) **1** Astronomy conjunction or opposition, especially of the moon with the sun. **2** a pair of connected or corresponding things.
– ORIGIN C17: via late L. from Gk *suzugia*, from *suzugos* 'yoked, paired', from *sun-* 'with, together' + the stem of *zeugnunai* 'to yoke'.

# T t

**T**[1] (also **t**) ● **n.** (pl. **Ts** or **T's**) **1** the twentieth letter of the alphabet. **2** denoting the next after S in a set of items, categories, etc.
– PHRASES **to a T** informal exactly; to perfection.

**T**[2] ● **abbrev. 1** tera- ($10^{12}$). **2** tesla. **3** Thailand (international vehicle registration). **4** (in names of sports clubs) Town. ● **symb. 1** temperature. **2** Chemistry the hydrogen isotope tritium.

**t** ● **abbrev.** ton(s). ● **symb.** (***t***) Statistics a number characterizing the distribution of a sample taken from a population with a normal distribution (see **STUDENT'S T-TEST**).

**-t**[1] ● **suffix** equivalent to **-ED**[2] (as in *crept*, *sent*, *spoilt*).

**-t**[2] ● **suffix** equivalent to **-EST**[2] (as in *shalt*).

**TA** ● **abbrev.** (in the UK) Territorial Army.

**Ta** ● **symb.** the chemical element tantalum.

**ta** ● **exclam.** Brit. informal thank you.
– ORIGIN C18: a child's word.

**TAB** ● **abbrev. 1** Austral./NZ Totalizator Agency Board. **2** typhoid-paratyphoid A and B vaccine.

**tab**[1] ● **n. 1** a small flap or strip of material attached to something, for holding, manipulation, identification, etc. ➤ Brit. Military a collar marking distinguishing an officer of high rank. ➤ North American term for **RING PULL**. **2** informal, chiefly N. Amer. a restaurant bill. **3** (**tabs**) short for **TABLEAU CURTAINS**. **4** Aeronautics a hinged part of a control surface. **5** N. English & informal a cigarette. ● **v.** (**tabbed**, **tabbing**) mark with a tab.
– PHRASES **keep tabs** (or **a tab**) **on** informal monitor the activities or development of. **pick up the tab** informal, chiefly N. Amer. pay for something.
– DERIVATIVES **tabbed** adj.
– ORIGIN ME: perh. rel. to **TAG**[1].

**tab**[2] ● **n.** short for **TABULATOR**. ● **v.** (**tabbed**, **tabbing**) short for **TABULATE**.

**tab**[3] ● **n.** informal a tablet, especially one containing an illicit drug.
– ORIGIN 1960s: abbrev.

**tab**[4] ● **n.** N. Amer. informal a tabloid newspaper.

**tabard** /ˈtabəd, -ɑːd/ ● **n. 1** a sleeveless jerkin consisting only of front and back pieces with a hole for the head. **2** a herald's official coat emblazoned with the arms of the sovereign.
– ORIGIN ME: from OFr. *tabart*, of unknown origin.

**tabaret** /ˈtabərɪt/ ● **n.** an upholstery fabric of alternate satin and watered silk stripes.
– ORIGIN C18: prob. from **TABBY**.

**Tabasco** /təˈbaskəʊ/ ● **n.** trademark a pungent sauce made from capsicums.
– ORIGIN C19: named after the state of *Tabasco* in Mexico.

**tabbouleh** /təˈbuːleɪ, ˈtabuːleɪ/ ● **n.** a salad of cracked wheat mixed with finely chopped tomatoes, onions, parsley, etc.
– ORIGIN from Arab. *tabbūla*.

**tabby** ● **n.** (pl. **-ies**) **1** a grey or brownish cat mottled or streaked with dark stripes. **2** silk or other fabric with a watered pattern. **3** a plain weave. **4** concrete made of lime, shells, gravel, and stones, which dries very hard.
– ORIGIN C16 (denoting a striped silk taffeta): from Fr. *tabis*, based on Arab. *al-ʿAttābiyya*, the name of a part of Baghdad where it was manufactured.

**tabernacle** /ˈtabəˌnak(ə)l/ ● **n. 1** (in biblical use) a fixed or movable habitation, typically of light construction. ➤ a tent used as a sanctuary for the Ark of the Covenant by the Israelites during the Exodus. **2** a meeting place for Nonconformist or Mormon worship. **3** an ornamented receptacle or cabinet in which a pyx containing the reserved sacrament may be placed in Catholic churches. ➤ archaic a canopied recess in the wall of a church. **4** a partly open socket on a sailing boat's deck into which a mast is fixed, with a pivot so that the mast can be lowered.
– DERIVATIVES **tabernacled** adj.
– ORIGIN ME: via Fr. from L. *tabernaculum* 'tent', dimin. of *taberna* 'hut, tavern'.

**tabernacle clock** ● **n.** a small clock with a metal case in the form of a tower.

**tabes** /ˈteɪbiːz/ ● **n.** Medicine emaciation.
– DERIVATIVES **tabetic** /təˈbɛtɪk/ adj.
– ORIGIN C16: from L., lit. 'wasting away'.

**tabescent** /təˈbɛs(ə)nt/ ● **adj.** wasting away.
– ORIGIN C19: from L. *tabescent-*, *tabescere* 'begin to waste away', from *tabere* 'waste away'.

**tabi** /ˈtɑːbi/ ● **n.** (pl. same) a thick-soled Japanese ankle sock with a separate section for the big toe.
– ORIGIN from Japanese.

**tabla** /ˈtablə, ˈtʌblə/ ● **n.** a pair of small hand drums fixed together, used in Indian music.
– ORIGIN from Pers. and Urdu *tablah*, Hindi *tablā*, from Arab. *ṭabl* 'drum'.

**tablature** /ˈtablətʃə/ ● **n.** a form of musical notation indicating fingering rather than the pitch of notes, written on lines corresponding to e.g. the strings of a guitar.
– ORIGIN C16: from Fr., prob. from Ital. *tavolatura*, from *tavolare* 'set to music'.

**table** ● **n. 1** a piece of furniture with a flat top and one or more legs, providing a level surface for eating, writing, or working at. ➤ food provided in a restaurant or household. **2** a set of facts or figures systematically displayed, especially in columns. ➤ a league table. ➤ (**tables**) multiplication tables. **3** Architecture a flat, typically rectangular, vertical surface. ➤ a horizontal moulding, especially a cornice. ➤ a slab bearing an inscription. **4** a flat surface of a gem. ➤ a cut gem with two flat faces. **5** each half or quarter of a folding board for backgammon. **6** Bridge the dummy hand. ● **v. 1** Brit. present formally for discussion or consideration at a meeting. **2** chiefly US postpone consideration of. **3** Sailing strengthen (a sail) by making a hem at the edge.
– PHRASES **lay something on the table 1** make something known so that it can be discussed. **2** chiefly US postpone something indefinitely. **on the table** offered for discussion. **turn the tables** turn a position of disadvantage relative to someone else into one of advantage. **under the table 1** informal very drunk. **2** another term for ***under the counter*** (see **COUNTER**[1]).
– DERIVATIVES **tableful** n. (pl. **-fuls**).
– ORIGIN OE *tabule* 'flat slab, inscribed tablet', from L. *tabula* 'plank, tablet, list', reinforced in ME by OFr. *table*.

**tableau** /ˈtabləʊ/ ● **n.** (pl. **tableaux** /-ləʊz/) a group of models or motionless figures representing a scene.
– ORIGIN C17 (in the sense 'picture', 'picturesque description'): from Fr., dimin. of *table* (see **TABLE**).

**tableau curtains** ● **pl. n.** (in the theatre) a pair of curtains drawn open by diagonal cords fixed to the lower inner corners.

**tableau vivant** /ˌtabləʊ ˈviːvɒ̃, French tablo vivɑ̃/ ● **n.** (pl. **tableaux vivants** pronunc. same) a silent and motionless group of people arranged to represent a scene.
– ORIGIN Fr., lit. 'living picture'.

**tablecloth** ● **n.** a cloth spread over a table, especially during meals.

**table d'hôte** /ˌtɑːbl(ə) ˈdəʊt, French tabl dot/ ● **n.** a restaurant meal offered at a fixed price and with few if any choices.
– ORIGIN C17: Fr., lit. 'host's table'.

**tableland** ● **n.** a broad, high, level region; a plateau.

**table licence** ● **n.** Brit. a licence permitting alcoholic drinks to be served only with meals.

**table manners** ● **pl. n.** behaviour that is conventionally required while eating at table.

**table mat** ● **n.** a small mat used for protecting the surface of a table from hot dishes.

**tablespoon** ● **n.** a large spoon for serving food. ➤(abbrev.: **tbsp**) the amount held by such a spoon, in the UK considered to be 15 millilitres when used as a measurement in cookery.
– DERIVATIVES **tablespoonful** n. (pl. **-fuls**).

**tablet** ● **n. 1** a flat slab of stone, clay, or wood, used especially for an inscription. ➤Architecture another term for TABLE (in sense 3). **2** a small disc or cylinder of a compressed solid substance, typically a medicine or drug; a pill. **3** Brit. a small flat piece of soap. **4** N. Amer. a writing pad. **5** a token giving authority for a train to proceed over a single-track line.
– ORIGIN ME: from OFr. *tablete*, from a dimin. of L. *tabula* (see TABLE).

**table tennis** ● **n.** an indoor game based on tennis, played with small bats and a small, hollow ball bounced on a table divided by a net.

**tableware** ● **n.** crockery, cutlery, and glassware used for serving and eating meals at a table.

**table wine** ● **n.** wine of moderate quality considered suitable for drinking with a meal.

**tablier** /ˈtablɪeɪ/ ● **n.** historical a part of a woman's dress resembling an apron.
– ORIGIN C19: from Fr., based on L. *tabula* (see TABLE).

**tabloid** ● **n.** a newspaper having pages half the size of those of the average broadsheet, typically popular in style and dominated by sensational stories.
– ORIGIN C19: from TABLET + -OID; orig. a proprietary term for a medicinal tablet; the current sense reflects the notion of 'concentrated, easily assimilable'.

**taboo** (also **tabu**) ● **n.** (pl. **taboos** or **tabus**) a social or religious custom placing prohibition or restriction on a particular thing or person. ● **adj.** prohibited or restricted by social custom. ➤designated as sacred and prohibited. ● **v.** (**taboos, tabooed** or **tabus, tabued**) place under such prohibition.
– ORIGIN C18: from Tongan *tabu* 'set apart, forbidden'.

**tabor** /ˈteɪbə/ ● **n.** historical a small drum, especially one used simultaneously by the player of a simple pipe.
– ORIGIN ME: from OFr. *tabour* 'drum'; perh. rel. to Pers. *tabīra* 'drum'; cf. TAMBOUR.

**tabouret** /ˈtabərɛt, -reɪ/ (US also **taboret**) ● **n.** a low stool or small table.
– ORIGIN C17: from Fr., 'stool', dimin. of *tabour* (see TABOR).

**tabular** /ˈtabjʊlə/ ● **adj. 1** (of data) consisting of or presented in columns or tables. **2** broad and flat like the top of a table. ➤(of a crystal) relatively broad and thin, with two well-developed parallel faces.
– DERIVATIVES **tabularly** adv.
– ORIGIN C17: from L. *tabularis*, from *tabula* (see TABLE).

**tabula rasa** /ˌtabjʊlə ˈrɑːzə/ ● **n.** (pl. **tabulae rasae** /ˌtabjʊliː ˈrɑːziː/) an absence of preconceived ideas or predetermined goals; a clean slate. ➤the human mind, especially at birth, viewed as having no innate ideas.
– ORIGIN L., lit. 'scraped tablet', i.e. a tablet with the writing erased.

**tabulate** /ˈtabjʊleɪt/ ● **v.** arrange (data) in tabular form.
– DERIVATIVES **tabulation** n.

**tabulator** ● **n.** a facility in a word-processing program, or a device on a typewriter, for advancing to a sequence of set positions in tabular work.

**tabun** /ˈtɑːbʊn/ ● **n.** an organophosphorus nerve gas, developed in Germany during the Second World War.
– ORIGIN Ger., of unknown origin.

**tac-au-tac** /ˈtakəʊˌtak/ ● **n.** Fencing a parry combined with a riposte.
– ORIGIN C20: Fr., lit. 'clash for clash', from imitative *tac*.

**tacet** /ˈtasɪt, ˈteɪ-/ ● **v.** Music indicating that a voice or instrument is silent.
– ORIGIN L., lit. 'is silent'.

**tach** /tak/ ● **n.** N. Amer. informal short for TACHOMETER.

**tache** ● **n.** variant spelling of TASH.

**tachi** /ˈtatʃi/ ● **n.** historical a long, single-edged samurai sword with a slightly curved blade.
– ORIGIN from Japanese.

**tachism** /ˈtaʃɪz(ə)m/ (also **tachisme**) ● **n.** a French style of painting originating in the 1940s, involving the use of dabs or splotches of colour.
– ORIGIN 1950s: from Fr. *tachisme*, from *tache* 'a stain'.

**tachistoscope** /taˈkɪstəˌskəʊp/ ● **n.** an instrument used for exposing objects to the eye for a very brief measured period of time.
– DERIVATIVES **tachistoscopic** adj. **tachistoscopically** adv.
– ORIGIN C19: from Gk *takhistos* 'swiftest' + -SCOPE.

**tacho** /ˈtakəʊ/ ● **n.** (pl. **-os**) Brit. short for TACHOGRAPH or TACHOMETER.

**tacho-** ● **comb. form** relating to speed: *tachograph*.
– ORIGIN from Gk *takhos* 'speed'.

**tachograph** ● **n.** a tachometer used in commercial road vehicles to provide a record of engine speed over a period.

**tachometer** /taˈkɒmɪtə/ ● **n.** an instrument which measures the working speed of an engine, typically in revolutions per minute.

**tachy-** ● **comb. form** rapid: *tachycardia*.
– ORIGIN from Gk *takhus* 'swift'.

**tachycardia** /ˌtakɪˈkɑːdɪə/ ● **n.** an abnormally rapid heart rate.
– ORIGIN C19: from TACHY- + Gk *kardia* 'heart'.

**tachygraphy** /taˈkɪgrəfi/ ● **n.** stenography or shorthand, especially that of ancient or medieval scribes.
– DERIVATIVES **tachygraphic** adj.

**tachymeter** /taˈkɪmɪtə/ ● **n. 1** a theodolite for the rapid measurement of distances in surveying. **2** a facility on a watch for measuring speed.
– DERIVATIVES **tachymetric** adj.

**tachyon** /ˈtakɪɒn/ ● **n.** Physics a hypothetical particle that travels faster than light.

**tachyphylaxis** /ˌtakɪfɪˈlaksɪs/ ● **n.** Medicine rapidly diminishing response to successive doses of a drug, rendering it less effective.

**tacit** /ˈtasɪt/ ● **adj.** understood or implied without being stated.
– DERIVATIVES **tacitly** adv.
– ORIGIN C17 (in the sense 'wordless, noiseless'): from L. *tacitus* 'silent', from *tacere* 'be silent'.

**taciturn** /ˈtasɪtəːn/ ● **adj.** reserved or uncommunicative in speech; saying little.
– DERIVATIVES **taciturnity** n. **taciturnly** adv.
– ORIGIN C18: from L. *taciturnus*, from *tacitus* (see TACIT).

**tack¹** ● **n. 1** a small, sharp broad-headed nail. ➤N. Amer. a drawing pin. **2** a long stitch used to fasten fabrics together temporarily, prior to permanent sewing. **3** a method of dealing with a situation; a course of action. **4** Sailing an act of tacking. ➤a boat's course relative to the direction of the wind. **5** Sailing a rope for securing the corner of certain sails. ➤the corner to which such a rope is fastened. **6** the quality of being sticky. ● **v. 1** fasten or fix with tacks or with temporary long stitches. **2** (**tack something on**) add or append something to something already existing. **3** Sailing change course by turning a boat's head into and through the wind. ➤make a series of such changes of course while sailing.
– DERIVATIVES **tacker** n.
– ORIGIN ME: prob. rel. to OFr. *tache* 'clasp, large nail'.

**tack²** ● **n.** equipment used in horse riding, including the saddle and bridle.
– ORIGIN C18 (in the sense 'apparatus, equipment'): contr. of TACKLE.

**tack³** ● **n.** informal cheap, shoddy, or tasteless material.
– ORIGIN 1980s: back-form. from TACKY².

**tackle** • n. **1** the equipment required for a task or sport. **2** a mechanism consisting of ropes, pulley blocks, and hooks for lifting heavy objects. ➤ the running rigging and pulleys used to work a boat's sails. **3** (in sport) an act of tackling an opponent. **4** American Football a player who lines up next to the end along the line of scrimmage. **5** (also **wedding tackle**) Brit. vulgar slang a man's genitals. • v. **1** make determined efforts to deal with (a difficult task). ➤ initiate discussion with (someone) about a sensitive issue. **2** (in soccer, hockey, rugby, etc.) intercept (an opponent in possession of the ball).
– DERIVATIVES **tackler** n.
– ORIGIN ME: prob. from Mid. Low Ger. *takel*, from *taken* 'lay hold of'.

**tackle block** • n. a pulley over which a rope runs.

**tackle fall** • n. a rope for applying force to the blocks of a tackle.

**tacky**[1] • adj. (**-ier**, **-iest**) (of glue, paint, etc.) slightly sticky because not fully dry.
– DERIVATIVES **tackiness** n.

**tacky**[2] • adj. (**-ier**, **-iest**) informal showing poor taste and quality.
– DERIVATIVES **tackily** adv. **tackiness** n.
– ORIGIN C19 (denoting a horse of little value): of unknown origin.

**taco** /ˈtakəʊ, ˈtɑːkəʊ/ • n. (pl. **-os**) a Mexican dish consisting of a folded tortilla filled with spicy meat or beans.
– ORIGIN Mex. Sp., from Sp., lit. 'plug, wad'.

**taco chip** • n. a fried fragment of a taco, spiced and eaten as a snack.

**taconite** /ˈtakənʌɪt/ • n. a low-grade iron ore consisting largely of chert.
– ORIGIN C20: from the name of the *Taconic* Range of mountains, US, + **-ITE**[1].

**tact** • n. adroitness and sensitivity in dealing with others or with difficult issues.
– ORIGIN C17 (denoting the sense of touch): via Fr. from L. *tactus* 'touch, sense of touch', from *tangere* 'to touch'.

**Tactel** • n. trademark a polyamide fabric or fibre with a soft, silky feel.
– ORIGIN an invented word: perh. influenced by **TACTILE**.

**tactful** • adj. having or showing tact.
– DERIVATIVES **tactfully** adv. **tactfulness** n.

**tactic** • n. **1** an action or strategy carefully planned to achieve a specific end. **2** (**tactics**) the art of disposing armed forces in order of battle and of organizing operations, especially during contact with an enemy. Often contrasted with **STRATEGY**.
– DERIVATIVES **tactician** n.
– ORIGIN C18: from mod. L. *tactica*, from Gk *taktikē* (*tekhnē*) '(art) of tactics', fem. of *taktikos*, from *taktos* 'ordered, arranged'.

**tactical** • adj. **1** done or planned to gain a specific military end. ➤ (of bombing or weapons) done or for use in immediate support of military or naval operations. Often contrasted with **STRATEGIC**. **2** planned in order to achieve an end beyond the immediate action. ➤ (of voting) aimed at preventing the strongest candidate from winning by supporting the next strongest, without regard to one's true political allegiance.
– DERIVATIVES **tactically** adv.

**tacticity** • n. Chemistry the stereochemical arrangement of the units in the main chain of a polymer.

**tactile** • adj. **1** relating to the sense of touch. ➤ perceptible or designed to be perceived by touch. **2** given to touching others in a friendly or sympathetic way.
– DERIVATIVES **tactility** n.
– ORIGIN C17: from L. *tactilis*, from *tangere* 'to touch'.

**tactless** • adj. having or showing a lack of tact.
– DERIVATIVES **tactlessly** adv. **tactlessness** n.

**tactual** • adj. formal or technical term for **TACTILE**.

**tad** informal • adv. (**a tad**) to a minor extent; somewhat. • n. a small amount.
– ORIGIN C19 (denoting a small child): origin uncertain, perh. from **TADPOLE**.

**tadger** • n. variant spelling of **TODGER**.

**Tadjik** (also **Tadzhik**) • n. & adj. variant spelling of **TAJIK**.

**tadpole** • n. the tailed aquatic larva of an amphibian, breathing through gills and lacking legs until the later stages of its development.
– ORIGIN C15: from OE *tāda* 'toad' + **POLL** (prob. because the tadpole seems to consist of a large head and a tail in its early development stage).

**taedium vitae** /ˌtiːdiəm ˈviːtʌɪ, ˈvʌɪtiː/ • n. a state of extreme ennui; weariness of life.
– ORIGIN from L.

**tae-bo** /tʌɪˈbəʊ/ • n. trademark an exercise system combining elements of aerobics and kick-boxing.
– ORIGIN from Korean *tae* 'leg' + *bo*, short for ***boxing*** (see **BOX**[2]).

**tae kwon do** /ˌtʌɪ kwɒn ˈdəʊ/ • n. a modern Korean martial art similar to karate.
– ORIGIN Korean, lit. 'art of hand and foot fighting'.

**tael** /teɪl/ • n. **1** a weight used in China and the Far East, about 38 grams (1⅓ oz). **2** a former Chinese monetary unit.
– ORIGIN from Malay *tahil* 'weight'.

**taenia** /ˈtiːnɪə/ (US **tenia**) • n. (pl. **taeniae** /-nɪiː/ or **taenias**) **1** Anatomy a flat ribbon-like structure in the body. ➤ (**taeniae coli** /ˈkəʊlʌɪ/) the smooth longitudinal muscles of the colon. **2** Architecture a fillet between a Doric architrave and frieze. **3** (in ancient Greece) a band or ribbon worn round a person's head.
– DERIVATIVES **taenioid** adj.
– ORIGIN C16: via L. from Gk *tainia* 'band, ribbon'.

**taffeta** /ˈtafɪtə/ • n. a fine lustrous silk or similar synthetic fabric with a crisp texture.
– ORIGIN ME: from OFr. *taffetas* or med. L. *taffata*, based on Pers. *tāftan* 'to shine'.

**taffrail** • n. a rail round a ship's stern.
– ORIGIN C19: alt. (by assoc. with **RAIL**[1]), of obs. *tafferel* 'panel', used to denote the flat part of a ship's stern above the transom, from Du. *tafereel*.

**Taffy** (also **Taff**) • n. (pl. **-ies**) Brit. informal, often offensive a Welshman.
– ORIGIN C17: representing a supposed Welsh pronunc. of the given name *Davy* or *David* (Welsh *Dafydd*).

**taffy** • n. (pl. **-ies**) N. Amer. a sweet similar to toffee.
– ORIGIN C19: earlier form of **TOFFEE**.

**tafia** /ˈtafɪə/ • n. W. Indian a drink similar to rum, distilled from molasses or waste from the production of brown sugar.
– ORIGIN via Fr. from W. Ind. creole, alt. of **RATAFIA**.

**tag**[1] • n. **1** a label providing identification or giving other information. ➤ an electronic device attached to someone or something for monitoring purposes. ➤ a nickname or popular description. ➤ US a vehicle licence plate. **2** a small piece or part that is attached to a main body. ➤ a ragged lock of wool on a sheep. ➤ the tip of an animal's tail when it is distinctively coloured. ➤ a loose or spare end of something; a leftover. ➤ a metal or plastic point at the end of a shoelace. **3** a frequently repeated quotation or stock phrase. ➤ Theatre a closing speech addressed to the audience. ➤ the refrain of a song. ➤ a phrase at the end of a piece of music. **4** Computing a character or set of characters appended to an item of data in order to identify it. • v. (**tagged**, **tagging**) **1** attach a label or tag to. **2** add to something as an afterthought. ➤ (**tag along**) accompany someone without invitation. **3** shear away ragged locks of wool from (sheep).
– ORIGIN ME (denoting a narrow hanging section of a decoratively slashed garment): of unknown origin.

**tag**[2] • n. **1** a children's game in which one chases the rest, and anyone who is caught then becomes the pursuer. **2** Baseball the action of tagging a runner. • v. (**tagged**, **tagging**) **1** touch (someone being chased) in a game of tag. **2** Baseball put (a runner) out by touching with the ball or with the hand holding the ball.
– ORIGIN C18: perh. a var. of **TIG**.

**Tagalog** /təˈɡɑːlɒɡ/ • n. **1** a member of a people originally of central Luzon in the Philippine Islands. **2** the Austronesian language of this people, the basis of the national language of the Philippines (Filipino).

– ORIGIN the name in Tagalog, from *tagá* 'native' + *ilog* 'river'.

**tag day** • n. North American term for FLAG DAY.

**tag end** • n. chiefly N. Amer. the last remaining part of something.

**tagetes** /tə'dʒi:ti:z/ • n. a plant of a genus including some African and American marigolds. [Genus *Tagetes*.]
– ORIGIN mod. L., from L. *Tages*, the name of an Etruscan god.

**tagine** /tə'ʒi:n, tə'dʒi:n/ • n. a North African stew of spiced meat and vegetables prepared by slow cooking in a shallow earthenware cooking dish with a tall, conical lid.
– ORIGIN C20: from Moroccan Arab. *ṭažin* from Arab. *ṭājin* 'frying pan'.

**tagliatelle** /ˌtaljə'tɛleɪ, -li/ • pl. n. pasta in narrow ribbons.
– ORIGIN Ital., from *tagliare* 'to cut'.

**tag line** • n. informal, chiefly N. Amer. a catchphrase, slogan, or punchline.

**tagma** /'tagmə/ • n. (pl. **tagmata** /-mətə/) Zoology a distinct region of a segmented body, e.g. the head, thorax, or abdomen of an insect.
– ORIGIN C20: from Gk, lit. 'something arranged', from *tassein* 'set in order'.

**tagmeme** /'tagmi:m/ • n. Linguistics (in tagmemics) a slot in a syntactic frame which may be filled by any member of a set of appropriate linguistic items.
– ORIGIN 1930s: from Gk *tagma* 'arrangement' + -EME.

**tagmemics** /tag'mi:mɪks/ • pl. n. [treated as sing.] Linguistics a mode of linguistic analysis based on identifying the function of each grammatical position in the sentence or phrase and the class of words by which it can be filled.
– DERIVATIVES **tagmemic** adj.

**tag sale** • n. US a sale of miscellaneous second-hand items.

**tag team** • n. **1** a pair of wrestlers who fight as a team, taking the ring alternately. **2** informal, chiefly N. Amer. a pair of people working together.

**tagua nut** /'tagwə/ • n. another term for IVORY NUT.
– ORIGIN C19: *tagua*, via Sp. from Quechua *tawa*.

**tag wrestling** • n. a form of wrestling involving tag teams.

**tahini** /tɑ:'hi:ni/ (also **tahina** /tɑ:'hi:nə/) • n. a Middle Eastern paste or spread made from ground sesame seeds.
– ORIGIN from mod. Gk *takhini*, based on Arab. *ṭaḥana* 'to crush'.

**Tahitian** /tɑ:'hi:ʃ(ə)n, -'hi:tɪən/ • n. **1** a native or national of Tahiti, or a person of Tahitian descent. **2** the Polynesian language of Tahiti. • adj. of or relating to Tahiti, its people, or their language.

**tahr** /tɑ:/ (also **thar**) • n. a goat-like mammal found in Oman, southern India, and the Himalayas. [Genus *Hemitragus*: three species.]
– ORIGIN C19: a local word in Nepal.

**Tai** /tʌɪ/ • adj. relating to or denoting a family of tonal SE Asian languages, including Thai and Lao.

**t'ai chi ch'uan** /ˌtʌɪ tʃi: 'tʃwɑ:n/ (also **t'ai chi**) • n. **1** a Chinese martial art and system of callisthenics, consisting of sequences of very slow controlled movements. **2** (in Chinese philosophy) the ultimate source and limit of reality, from which spring yin and yang and all of creation.
– ORIGIN Chin., lit. 'great ultimate boxing'.

**Taig** /teɪg/ • n. informal, offensive (in Northern Ireland) a Protestant name for a Catholic.
– ORIGIN 1970s: var. of *Teague*, anglicized spelling of the Ir. name *Tadhg*, a nickname for an Irishman.

**taiga** /'tʌɪgə/ • n. swampy coniferous forest of high northern latitudes, especially that between the tundra and steppes of Siberia.
– ORIGIN C19: from Russ. *taĭga*, from Mongolian.

**tail**[1] • n. **1** the hindmost part of an animal, especially when extended beyond the rest of the body, such as the flexible extension of the backbone in a vertebrate or the feathers at the hind end of a bird. **2** something extending downwards, outwards, or back like an animal's tail. ➤the luminous trail of particles following a comet. ➤the lower end of a pool or stream. ➤the exposed end of a slate or tile in a roof. ➤the final, more distant, or weaker part of something. ➤Cricket the end of the batting order, with the weakest batsmen. **3** the rear part of an aircraft, with the tailplane and rudder. **4** (**tails**) the side of a coin without the image of a head on it (used when tossing a coin to determine a winner). **5** the lower or hanging part at the back of a shirt or coat. ➤(**tails**) informal a tailcoat, or a man's formal evening suit with such a coat. **6** informal, chiefly N. Amer. a person's buttocks. ➤vulgar slang a woman's genitals. ➤informal women collectively regarded as a means of sexual gratification. **7** informal a person secretly following another to observe their movements. • v. **1** informal secretly follow and observe (someone). **2** (**tail off/away**) gradually diminish in amount, strength, or intensity. ➤(**tail back**) Brit. (of traffic) become congested and form a tailback. **3** N. Amer. (of an object in flight) drift or curve in a particular direction. **4** (**tail something in/into**) insert the end of a beam, stone, or brick into (a wall). **5** archaic join (one thing) to another.
– PHRASES **on someone's tail** informal following someone closely. **with one's tail between one's legs** informal in a state of dejection or humiliation. **with one's tail up** informal in a confident or cheerful mood.
– DERIVATIVES **tailed** adj. **tailless** adj.
– ORIGIN OE *tæg(e)l*, from a Gmc base meaning 'hair, hairy tail'.

**tail**[2] • n. Law, chiefly historical limitation of ownership, especially of an estate or title limited to a person and their heirs.
– ORIGIN ME (denoting a tallage): from OFr. *taille* 'notch, tax', from *taillier* 'to cut'.

**tailback** • n. **1** Brit. a long queue of traffic extending back from a junction or obstruction. **2** American Football the offensive back stationed furthest from the line of scrimmage.

**tailboard** • n. Brit. a tailgate.

**tail bone** • n. less technical term for COCCYX.

**tailcoat** • n. Brit. a man's formal morning or evening coat, with a long skirt divided at the back into tails and cut away in front.

**tail end** • n. the last or hindmost part of something, in particular the batting order in cricket.
– DERIVATIVES **tail-ender** n. (Cricket).

**tail-end Charlie** • n. informal a crew member of a bomber aircraft who operates a gun from a compartment at the rear.

**tail fin** • n. **1** Zoology a fin at the posterior extremity of a fish's body, typically continuous with the tail. **2** a projecting vertical surface on the tail of an aircraft, housing the rudder. **3** an upswept projection on each rear corner of a motor car, popular in the 1950s.

**tailgate** • n. a hinged flap giving access to the back of a truck. ➤the door at the back of an estate or hatchback car. • v. informal, chiefly N. Amer. drive too closely behind (another vehicle).
– DERIVATIVES **tailgater** n.

**tailing** • n. **1** (**tailings**) the residue of something, especially ore. ➤grain or flour of inferior quality. **2** the part of a beam or projecting brick or stone embedded in a wall.

**taille** /tɑ:j, French taj/ • n. (pl. pronounced same) **1** (in France before 1789) a tax levied on the common people by the king or an overlord. **2** Music, historical the register of a tenor or similar voice, or an instrument of this register. **3** juice or wine produced from a second pressing of grapes.
– ORIGIN from Fr.

**tail light** (also **tail lamp**) • n. a red light at the rear of a vehicle.

**tailor** • n. a person whose occupation is making clothes, especially men's outer garments for individual customers. • v. **1** (of a tailor) make (clothes) to fit individual

customers. **2** (usu. **tailor something for/to**) make or adapt for a particular purpose or person.
– DERIVATIVES **tailoring** n.
– ORIGIN ME: from Anglo-Norman Fr. *taillour*, lit. 'cutter', based on late L. *taliare* 'to cut'.

**tailorbird** • n. a small South Asian warbler that stitches leaves together with fibres to hold its nest. [Genus *Orthotomus*: several species.]

**tailored** • adj. (of clothes) smart, fitted, and well cut.

**tailor-made** • adj. **1** (of clothes) made by a tailor for a particular customer. **2** made or adapted for a particular purpose or person.

**tailpiece** • n. **1** the final or end part of something. ➤the piece at the base of a stringed instrument to which the strings are attached. **2** a small decorative design at the foot of a page or the end of a chapter or book. ➤a part added to the end of a piece of writing.

**tailpipe** • n. the rear section of the exhaust pipe of a motor vehicle.

**tailplane** • n. Brit. a horizontal aerofoil at the tail of an aircraft.

**tail race** • n. a fast-flowing stretch of a river or stream below a dam or watermill.

**tailspin** • n. **1** a spin by an aircraft. **2** a state of rapidly increasing chaos or panic. • v. (**-spinning**; past and past part. **-spun**) become out of control.

**tailstock** • n. the adjustable part of a lathe holding the fixed spindle.

**tailwind** • n. a wind blowing in the direction of travel of a vehicle or aircraft.

**taimen** /'tʌɪmən/ • n. (pl. same) a large food fish found in Siberia and east Asia. [*Hucho taimen*.]
– ORIGIN 1970s: from Russ.

**Taino** /'tʌɪnəʊ/ • n. an extinct Caribbean language of the Arawakan group.
– ORIGIN from Taino *taino* 'noble, lord'.

**taint** • n. **1** a trace of a bad or undesirable quality or substance. ➤a contaminating influence or effect. **2** an unpleasant smell. • v. **1** contaminate or pollute. ➤affect with a bad or undesirable quality. **2** archaic (of food or water) become contaminated or polluted.
– DERIVATIVES **taintless** adj. (poetic/literary).
– ORIGIN ME (as a verb in the sense 'convict, prove guilty'): partly from OFr. *teint* 'tinged', based on L. *tingere* 'to dye, tinge'; partly a shortening of **ATTAINT**.

**taipan**[1] /'tʌɪpan/ • n. a foreigner who is head of a business in China.
– ORIGIN C19: from Chin. (Cantonese dial.) *daaihbāan*.

**taipan**[2] /'tʌɪpan/ • n. a large, brown, highly venomous Australian snake. [*Oxyuranus scutellatus*.]
– ORIGIN 1930s: from *dhayban*, the name in an extinct Aborig. lang.

**Taiwanese** /tʌɪwə'niːz/ • n. (pl. same) a native or inhabitant of Taiwan. • adj. of or relating to Taiwan.

**taj** /tɑːdʒ/ • n. a tall conical cap worn by a dervish. ➤historical a crown worn by an Indian prince.
– ORIGIN C19: from Pers. *tāj* 'crown'.

**Tajik** /tɑː'dʒiːk/ (also **Tadjik** or **Tadzhik**) • n. **1** a member of a mainly Muslim people inhabiting Tajikistan and parts of neighbouring countries. ➤a native or national of the republic of Tajikistan. **2** (also **Tajiki** /tɑː'dʒiːki/) the Iranian language of the Tajiks.
– ORIGIN from Pers. *tājik* 'a Persian, someone who is neither an Arab nor a Turk'.

**taka** /'tɑːkɑː/ • n. (pl. same) the basic monetary unit of Bangladesh, equal to 100 poisha.
– ORIGIN from Bengali *ṭākā*.

**takahe** /'tɑːkəhi/ • n. a large, rare flightless rail found in New Zealand. [*Porphyrio mantelli*.]
– ORIGIN C19: from Maori.

**take** • v. (past **took**; past part. **taken**) **1** lay hold of with one's hands; reach for and hold. ➤consume as food, drink, medicine, or drugs. ➤occupy (a place or position). ➤buy, rent, or subscribe to. ➤ascertain by measurement or observation. ➤capture or gain possession of by force or military means. ➤(of illness) suddenly strike or afflict. ➤have sexual intercourse with. **2** remove from a place. ➤subtract. **3** carry or bring with one; convey or guide. ➤bring into a specified state. ➤use as a route or a means of transport. **4** accept or receive. ➤understand or accept as valid. ➤acquire or assume (a position, state, or form). ➤act on (an opportunity). ➤experience or be affected by. ➤regard, view, or deal with in a specified way. ➤(**be taken by/with**) be attracted or charmed by. ➤submit to, tolerate, or endure. ➤(**take it**) assume. **5** make, undertake, or perform (an action or task). ➤be taught or examined in (a subject). ➤Brit. obtain (an academic degree) after fulfilling the required conditions. **6** require or use up (a specified amount of time). ➤need or call for. ➤hold; accommodate. ➤wear or require (a particular size of garment). ➤Grammar have or require as part of the appropriate construction. **7** (of a plant or seed) take root or begin to grow; germinate. ➤(of an added substance) become successfully established. • n. **1** a scene or sequence of sound or vision photographed or recorded continuously at one time. ➤a particular version of or approach to something: *his own whimsical take on life*. **2** an amount gained or acquired from one source or in one session. **3** Printing an amount of copy set up at one time or by one compositor.
– PHRASES **be on the take** informal take bribes. **be taken ill** become ill suddenly. **have what it takes** informal have the necessary qualities for success. **take something as read** Brit. assume something. **take five** informal, chiefly N. Amer. have a short break. **take someone in hand** undertake to control or reform someone. **take something in hand** start doing or dealing with a task. **take ill** (US **sick**) informal become ill suddenly. **take something ill** archaic resent something done or said. **take it on one** (or **oneself**) **to do something** decide to do something without asking for permission or advice. **take it out of** exhaust the strength of. **take that!** exclaimed when hitting someone or taking retributive action against them. **take one's time** not hurry.
– PHRASAL VERBS **take after** resemble (a parent or ancestor). **take against** Brit. begin to dislike (someone). **take something apart 1** dismantle something. **2** (**take someone/thing apart**) informal forcefully attack, criticize, or defeat someone or something. **take (away) from** detract from. **take something back 1** retract a statement. **2** return unsatisfactory goods to a shop. ➤(of a shop) accept such goods. **3** Printing transfer text to the previous line. **take someone in** cheat or deceive someone. **take something in 1** make a garment tighter by altering its seams. **2** Sailing furl a sail. **3** encompass, understand, or absorb something. **4** casually visit or attend a place or event. **take off 1** (of an aircraft or bird) become airborne. ➤(of an enterprise) become successful or popular. **2** (also **take oneself off**) depart hastily. **take someone off** informal, chiefly Brit. mimic someone humorously. **take something off 1** remove clothing. **2** deduct part of an amount. **take on** Brit. informal become very upset, especially needlessly. **take someone on 1** engage an employee. **2** be willing or ready to meet an opponent. **take something on 1** undertake a task or responsibility. **2** acquire a particular meaning or quality. **take someone out** Bridge respond to a bid or double by one's partner by bidding a different suit. **take someone/thing out** informal kill, destroy, or disable. **take something out** obtain an official document or service. **take something out on** relieve frustration or anger by attacking or mistreating. **take something over 1** (also **take over**) assume control of or responsibility for something. **2** Printing transfer text to the next line. **take to 1** begin or fall into the habit of. **2** form a liking for. ➤develop an ability for. **3** go to (a place) to escape danger. **take someone up 1** adopt someone as a protégé. **2** (usu. **take someone up on**) accept an offer or challenge from someone. **take something up 1** become interested or engaged in a pursuit. ➤begin to hold or fulfil a position or post. ➤accept an offer or challenge. **2** occupy time, space, or attention. **3** pursue a matter further. **take up with** begin to associate with (someone).
– DERIVATIVES **takable** (also **takeable**) adj. **taker** n.
– ORIGIN OE *tacan* 'get (especially by force), capture', from

ON *taka* 'grasp, lay hold of', of unknown ultimate origin.

**takeaway** ● n. 1 Brit. a restaurant or shop selling cooked food to be eaten elsewhere. ➤ a meal or dish of such food. 2 Golf another term for **BACKSWING**.

**takedown** ● n. chiefly N. Amer. 1 a wrestling manoeuvre in which an opponent is swiftly brought to the mat from a standing position. 2 informal a police raid or arrest. 3 [as modifier] denoting a firearm with a detachable barrel and magazine.

**take-home pay** ● n. the pay received by an employee after the deduction of tax and insurance.

**take-off** ● n. 1 the action of becoming airborne. 2 an act of mimicking.

**takeout** ● n. 1 chiefly N. Amer. a takeaway. 2 Bridge a bid (in a different suit) made in response to a bid or double by one's partner.

**takeover** ● n. an act of assuming control of something, especially the buying-out of one company by another.

**takht** /tɑːkt/ ● n. (in Eastern countries) a sofa or long bench, or a bed.
– ORIGIN from Pers. *takt*.

**takin** /'tɑːkɪn/ ● n. a large goat-antelope found in the eastern Himalayas. [*Budorcas taxicolor*.]
– ORIGIN C19: a local word.

**taking** ● n. 1 the action or process of taking. 2 (**takings**) the amount of money earned by a business from the sale of goods or services. ● adj. dated captivating in manner; charming.
– PHRASES **for the taking** ready or available to take advantage of.
– DERIVATIVES **takingly** adv.

**Taki-Taki** /'tɑːkɪˌtɑːki/ ● n. an English-based creole language of Suriname.
– ORIGIN an alt. of *talkee-talkee* (from **TALK**), an English-based creole of the Caribbean region.

**tala**[1] /'tɑːlə/ ● n. a traditional rhythmic pattern in classical Indian music.
– ORIGIN from Sanskrit *tāla* 'handclapping, musical time'.

**tala**[2] /'tɑːlə/ ● n. (pl. same or **talas**) the basic monetary unit of Samoa, equal to 100 sene.
– ORIGIN from Samoan *tālā*.

**Talaing** /tə'lʌɪŋ/ ● n. (pl. same or **Talaings**) & adj. another term for **MON**.
– ORIGIN the name in Burmese.

**talapoin** /'taləpɔɪn/ ● n. 1 a Buddhist monk or priest. 2 a small West African monkey. [*Miopithecus talapoin*.]
– ORIGIN C16: from Port. *talapão*, from Mon *tala pói*, lit. 'lord of merit'.

**talaria** /tə'lɛːrɪə/ ● pl. n. (in Roman mythology) winged sandals, as worn by the god Mercury.
– ORIGIN L., neut. pl. of *talaris*, from *talus* 'ankle'.

**talc** ● n. 1 talcum powder. 2 a soft mineral with a greasy feel, occurring as translucent masses or laminae and consisting of hydrated magnesium silicate. ● v. (**talced, talcing**) powder or treat with talc.
– DERIVATIVES **talcose** adj. (Geology). **talcy** adj.

**talcum powder** ● n. a preparation for the body and face consisting of the mineral talc in powdered form. ● v. (**talcumed, talcuming**) powder with this substance.
– ORIGIN C16: from med. L. *talcum*, from Arab. *ṭalk*, from Pers.

**tale** ● n. 1 a fictitious or true narrative or story, especially one that is imaginatively recounted. ➤ a lie. 2 archaic a number or total.
– PHRASES **a tale of a tub** archaic an apocryphal story.
– ORIGIN OE *talu* 'telling, something told', of Gmc origin.

**talebearer** ● n. dated a person who maliciously gossips or reveals secrets.
– DERIVATIVES **talebearing** n. & adj.

**taleggio** /ta'lɛdʒɪəʊ/ ● n. a type of soft Italian cheese made from cows' milk.
– ORIGIN named after the *Taleggio* valley in Lombardy.

**talent** ● n. 1 natural aptitude or skill. ➤ people possessing such aptitude or skill. ➤ informal people regarded as sexually attractive or as prospective sexual partners. 2 a former weight and unit of currency used by the ancient Romans and Greeks.
– DERIVATIVES **talentless** adj.
– ORIGIN OE *talente, talentan* (as a unit of weight), from L. *talenta*, pl. of *talentum* 'weight, sum of money', from Gk *talanton*.

**talented** ● adj. having a natural aptitude or skill for something.

**talent scout** ● n. a person whose job is searching for talented performers, especially in sport and entertainment.

**tales** /'teɪliːz/ ● n. Law a writ for summoning substitute jurors when the original jury has become deficient in number.
– ORIGIN from L. *tales* (*de circumstantibus*) 'such (of the bystanders)', the first words of the writ.

**talesman** /'teɪliːzmən, 'teɪlz-/ ● n. (pl. **-men**) Law a person summoned by a tales.

**tali** plural form of **TALUS**[1].

**talipes** /'talɪpiːz/ ● n. Medicine technical term for **CLUB FOOT**.
– ORIGIN C19: mod. L., from L. *talus* 'ankle' + *pes* 'foot'.

**talipot** /'talɪpɒt/ ● n. a tall Indian palm with very large fan-shaped leaves. [*Corypha umbraculifera*.]
– ORIGIN C17: from Malayalam *tālipat*, from Sanskrit *tālīpatra*, from *tālī* 'palm' + *patra* 'leaf'.

**talisman** /'talɪzmən/ ● n. (pl. **talismans**) an object thought to have magic powers and to bring good luck.
– DERIVATIVES **talismanic** /-'manɪk/ adj.
– ORIGIN C17: based on Arab. *ṭilsam*, appar. from an alt. of late Gk *telesma* 'completion, religious rite'.

**talk** ● v. speak in order to give information or express ideas or feelings; converse or communicate by speech. ➤ have the power of speech. ➤ (**talk something over/through**) discuss something thoroughly. ➤ (**talk back**) reply defiantly or insolently. ➤ (**talk down to**) speak patronizingly or condescendingly to. ➤ (**talk someone round**) convince someone that they should adopt a particular point of view. ➤ (**talk someone into/out of**) persuade or dissuade someone to or from. ➤ (**talk something out**) Brit. (in Parliament) block the course of a bill by prolonging discussion to the time of adjournment. ➤ (**be talking**) informal be discussing in specified terms: *we're talking big money*. ➤ gossip. ● n. 1 conversation; discussion. ➤ rumour, gossip, or speculation. ➤ (**the talk of**) a current subject of widespread gossip or speculation in. ➤ (**talks**) formal discussions or negotiations over a period. 2 an address or lecture.
– PHRASES **you can't** (or **can**) (US **shouldn't** or **should**) **talk** informal used to convey that a criticism made applies equally well to the person making it. **look** (or **hark**) **who's talking** another way of saying ***you can't talk***. **now you're talking** informal expressing enthusiastic agreement or approval. **talk big** informal talk boastfully or overconfidently. **talk the hind leg off a donkey** see **DONKEY**. **talk nineteen to the dozen** see **DOZEN**.
– DERIVATIVES **talker** n.
– ORIGIN ME: from the Gmc base of **TALE** or **TELL**[1].

**talkathon** ● n. informal a prolonged discussion or debate.
– ORIGIN 1930s (orig. US, denoting a debate artificially prolonged to prevent the progress of a bill): blend of **TALK** and **MARATHON**.

**talkative** ● adj. fond of or given to talking.
– DERIVATIVES **talkatively** adv. **talkativeness** n.

**talkback** ● n. 1 a system of two-way communication by loudspeaker. 2 another term for **PHONE-IN**.

**talkfest** ● n. informal, chiefly N. Amer. a lengthy discussion or debate, especially as part of a television chat show.

**talkie** ● n. informal a film with a soundtrack, as distinct from a silent film.

**talking blues** ● pl. n. a style of blues music in which the lyrics are more or less spoken rather than sung.

**talking book** ● n. a recorded reading of a book.

**talking drum** ● n. each of a set of West African drums which are beaten to transmit a tonal language.

**talking head** ● n. informal, chiefly derogatory a presenter or reporter on television who addresses the camera and is viewed in close-up.

**talking point** ● n. a topic that invites discussion or

argument.

**talking shop** (also **talk shop**) ● n. Brit. a place or group regarded as a centre for unproductive talk rather than action.

**talking-to** ● n. informal a sharp reprimand.

**talk radio** ● n. chiefly N. Amer. a type of radio broadcast in which topical issues are discussed by the presenter and by listeners who phone in.

**talk show** ● n. a chat show.

**tall** ● adj. **1** of great or more than average height. ➤ measuring a specified distance from top to bottom. **2** fanciful and difficult to believe; unlikely: *a tall story.*
– PHRASES **a tall order** an unreasonable or difficult demand.
– DERIVATIVES **tallish** adj. **tallness** n.
– ORIGIN ME (in senses 'swift, prompt', 'fine, handsome', and 'bold, strong'): prob. from OE *getæl* 'swift, prompt'.

**tallage** /'talɪdʒ/ ● n. historical a form of arbitrary taxation levied by kings on the towns and lands of the Crown. ➤ a tax levied on feudal dependants by their superiors.
– ORIGIN ME: from OFr. *taillage*, from *tailler* (see TAIL[2]).

**tallboy** ● n. Brit. a tall chest of drawers in two sections, one standing on the other.

**tallith** /'talɪθ/ ● n. a fringed shawl traditionally worn by Jewish men at prayer.
– ORIGIN from Rabbinical Heb. *ṭallīt*, from biblical Heb. *ṭillel* 'to cover'.

**tallow** ● n. a hard fatty substance made from rendered animal fat, used in making candles and soap.
– DERIVATIVES **tallowy** adj.
– ORIGIN ME: perh. from Mid. Low Ger.

**tallow tree** ● n. a tree with fatty seeds from which vegetable tallow or other oils are extracted. [*Sapium sebiferum* (E. Asia) and other species.]

**tall ship** ● n. a sailing ship with a high mast or masts.

**tally** ● n. (pl. **-ies**) **1** a current score or amount. ➤ a record of a score or amount. **2** a particular number taken as a group or unit to facilitate counting. ➤ a mark registering such a number. **3** (also **tally stick**) historical a piece of wood scored across with notches for the items of an account and then split into halves, each party keeping one. **4** archaic a counterpart or duplicate. **5** an identifying label for a plant or tree. ● v. (**-ies**, **-ied**) **1** agree or correspond. **2** calculate the total number of.
– DERIVATIVES **tallier** n.
– ORIGIN ME: from Anglo-Norman Fr. *tallie*, from L. *talea* 'twig, cutting'; cf. TAIL[2].

**tally-ho** ● exclam. a huntsman's cry to the hounds on sighting a fox. ● v. (**-oes**, **-oed**) utter such a cry.
– ORIGIN C18: appar. an alt. of Fr. *taïaut*, of unknown origin.

**tallyman** ● n. (pl. **-men**) **1** Brit. a person who sells goods on credit, especially from door to door. **2** a person who keeps a score or record of something.

**tally system** ● n. Brit. a system of selling goods on short-term credit or an instalment plan.

**Talmud** /'talmʊd, -məd/ ● n. the body of Jewish civil and ceremonial law and legend comprising the Mishnah and the Gemara.
– DERIVATIVES **Talmudic** adj. **Talmudical** adj. **Talmudist** n.
– ORIGIN from late Heb. *talmūḏ* 'instruction', from Heb. *lāmaḏ* 'learn'.

**Talmud Torah** ● n. **1** the field of study concerned with the Jewish law. **2** a communal school where children are instructed in Judaism.

**talon** ● n. **1** a claw, especially one belonging to a bird of prey. **2** the shoulder of a bolt against which the key presses to slide it in a lock. **3** (in various card games) the cards remaining undealt. **4** a printed form attached to a bearer bond that enables the holder to apply for a new sheet of coupons when the existing coupons have been used up. **5** Architecture an ogee moulding.
– DERIVATIVES **taloned** adj.
– ORIGIN ME: from OFr., lit. 'heel', from L. *talus* 'ankle bone, heel'.

**talus**[1] /'teɪləs/ ● n. (pl. **tali** /-lʌɪ/) Anatomy the large bone in the ankle, which articulates with the tibia of the leg and the calcaneus and navicular bone of the foot.
– ORIGIN C16: from L., lit. 'ankle, heel'.

**talus**[2] /'teɪləs/ ● n. (pl. **taluses**) **1** a sloping mass of rock fragments at the foot of a cliff. **2** the sloping side of an earthwork, or of a wall that tapers to the top.
– ORIGIN C17: from Fr., of unknown origin.

**TAM** ● abbrev. television audience measurement.

**tam** ● n. a tam-o'-shanter.

**tamagotchi** /ˌtamə'gɒtʃi/ ● n. trademark an electronic toy displaying a digital image of a creature, which has to be looked after by the 'owner' as if it were a pet.
– ORIGIN from Japanese.

**tamale** /tə'mɑːleɪ, -'mɑːli/ ● n. a Mexican dish of seasoned meat and maize flour steamed or baked in maize husks.
– ORIGIN from Mex. Sp. *tamal*, pl. *tamales*, from Nahuatl *tamalli*.

**tamandua** /tə'mand(j)ʊə, ˌtam(ə)n'duːə/ ● n. a small arboreal anteater with a naked prehensile tail, native to tropical America. [Genus *Tamandua*: two species.]
– ORIGIN C17: via Port. from Tupi *tamanduá*, from *taly* 'ant' + *monduar* 'hunter'.

**tamarack** /'tamərak/ ● n. a slender North American larch. [*Larix laricina*.]
– ORIGIN C19: from Canad. Fr. *tamarac*, prob. of Algonquian origin.

**tamari** /tə'mɑːri/ ● n. a variety of rich, naturally fermented soy sauce.
– ORIGIN from Japanese.

**tamarillo** /ˌtamə'rɪləʊ/ ● n. (pl. **-os**) the red egg-shaped fruit of a tropical South American plant (*Cyphomandra betaceae*).
– ORIGIN 1960s: an invented name, perh. suggested by Sp. *tomatillo*, dimin. of *tomate* 'tomato'.

**tamarin** /'tam(ə)rɪn/ ● n. a small forest-dwelling South American monkey of the marmoset family. [Genera *Saguinus* and *Leontopithecus*: several species.]
– ORIGIN C18: from Fr., from Galibi.

**tamarind** /'tam(ə)rɪnd/ ● n. **1** sticky brown acidic pulp from the pod of a tree of the pea family, used as a flavouring in Asian cookery. **2** the tropical African tree which yields these pods. [*Tamarindus indica*.]
– ORIGIN ME: from med. L. *tamarindus*, from Arab. *tamr hindī* 'Indian date'.

**tamarisk** /'tam(ə)rɪsk/ ● n. a shrub or small tree with tiny scale-like leaves borne on slender branches. [Genus *Tamarix*: many species.]
– ORIGIN ME: from late L. *tamariscus*, var. of L. *tamarix*, of unknown origin.

**tambala** /tam'bɑːlə/ ● n. (pl. same or **tambalas**) a monetary unit of Malawi, equal to one hundredth of a kwacha.
– ORIGIN from Nyanja, lit. 'cockerel'.

**tambour** /'tambʊə/ ● n. **1** historical a small drum. **2** a circular frame for holding fabric taut while it is being embroidered. **3** Architecture a wall of circular plan, such as one supporting a dome. ➤ each of the cylindrical stones forming the shaft of a column. **4** a lobby enclosed by a ceiling and folding doors to prevent draughts. ➤ a sliding flexible shutter or door. **5** a sloping buttress or projection in a real tennis or fives court. ● v. [often as adj. **tamboured**] decorate or embroider on a tambour.
– ORIGIN C15: from Fr. *tambour* 'drum'; perh. rel. to Pers. *tabīra* 'drum'; cf. TABOR.

**tamboura** /tam'bʊərə/ (also **tambura**) ● n. **1** (also **tanpura**) a large four-stringed lute used in Indian music as a drone accompaniment. **2** a long-necked lute or mandolin of Balkan countries.
– ORIGIN C16: from Arab. *ṭanbūr* or Pers. *tunbūra*, both from Pers. *dunbara*, lit. 'lamb's tail'.

**tambourin** /'tambərɪn/ ● n. **1** a long narrow drum used in Provence. **2** a dance accompanied by such a drum.
– ORIGIN Fr., dimin. of *tambour* (see TAMBOUR).

**tambourine** /ˌtambə'riːn/ ● n. a percussion instrument resembling a shallow drum with metal discs around the edge, played by being shaken or hit with the hand.
– DERIVATIVES **tambourinist** n.
– ORIGIN C16: from Fr. *tambourin* (see TAMBOURIN).

**tamburitza** /tam'bʊrɪtsə/ ● **n.** a kind of long-necked mandolin played in Croatia and neighbouring countries.
– ORIGIN Serbo-Croat, dimin. of *tambura* (see **TAMBOURA**).

**tame** ● **adj. 1** (of an animal) not dangerous or frightened of people; domesticated. ➤ informal (of a person) willing to cooperate. **2** not exciting, adventurous, or controversial. **3** N. Amer. (of a plant) produced by cultivation. ➤ (of land) cultivated. ● **v. 1** domesticate (an animal). **2** make less powerful and easier to control.
– DERIVATIVES **tameable** (also **tamable**) adj. **tamely** adv. **tameness** n. **tamer** n.
– ORIGIN OE *tam* (adj.), *temmian* (v.), of Gmc origin.

**Tamil** /'tamɪl/ ● **n. 1** a member of a people inhabiting parts of South India and Sri Lanka. **2** the Dravidian language of the Tamils.
– DERIVATIVES **Tamilian** adj. & n.
– ORIGIN the name in Tamil.

**Tammany** /'taməni/ (also **Tammany Hall**) ● **n.** N. Amer. a corrupt political organization or group.
– DERIVATIVES **Tammanyite** n.
– ORIGIN orig. the name of a powerful organization within the US Democratic Party that was widely associated with corruption and had headquarters at *Tammany* Hall, New York.

**tam-o'-shanter** /ˌtamə'ʃantə/ ● **n.** a round Scottish cap with a bobble in the centre.
– ORIGIN C19: named after the hero of Robert Burns's poem *Tam o' Shanter* (1790).

**tamoxifen** /tə'mɒksɪfɛn/ ● **n.** a synthetic drug used to treat breast cancer and infertility in women.
– ORIGIN 1970s: an arbitrary formation based on **TRANS-**, **AMINE**, **OXY-**[2], **PHENOL**, elements of the drug's chemical name.

**tamp** ● **v. 1** pack (a blast hole) full of clay or sand to concentrate the force of the explosion. **2** firmly ram or pack (a substance) down or into something.
– ORIGIN C19: prob. a back-form. from *tampin* (interpreted as 'tamping'), var. of **TAMPION**.

**Tampax** ● **n.** (pl. same) trademark a sanitary tampon.
– ORIGIN 1930s: an arbitrary formation from **TAMPON**.

**tamper** ● **v.** (**tamper with**) interfere with (something) without authority or so as to cause damage. ● **n.** a machine or tool for tamping down earth or ballast.
– DERIVATIVES **tamperer** n.
– ORIGIN C16 (in the sense 'busy oneself to a particular end, machinate'): alt. of the verb **TEMPER**.

**tampion** /'tampɪən/ (also **tompion**) ● **n. 1** a wooden stopper for the muzzle of a gun. **2** a plug for the top of an organ pipe.
– ORIGIN ME: from Fr. *tampon* 'tampon'.

**tampon** ● **n. 1** a plug of soft material inserted into the vagina to absorb menstrual blood. **2** Medicine a plug of material used to stop a wound or block an opening in the body and absorb blood or secretions. ● **v.** (**tamponed**, **tamponing**) plug with a tampon.
– ORIGIN C19: from Fr., nasalized var. of *tapon* 'plug, stopper', ult. of Gmc origin and rel. to **TAP**[1].

**tamponade** /ˌtampə'neɪd/ ● **n.** Medicine **1** (also **cardiac tamponade**) compression of the heart by an accumulation of fluid in the pericardial sac. **2** the surgical use of a plug of absorbent material.

**tam-tam** ● **n.** a large metal gong.
– ORIGIN C19: perh. from Hindi *ṭam-ṭam* (see **TOM-TOM**).

**tan**[1] ● **n. 1** a yellowish-brown colour. **2** a golden-brown shade of skin developed by pale-skinned people after exposure to the sun. **3** (also **tanbark**) bark of oak or other trees, bruised and used as a source of tannin for converting hides into leather. ➤ (also **spent tan**) such bark from which the tannin has been extracted, used for covering paths and in gardening. ● **v.** (**tanned**, **tanning**) **1** [often as adj. **tanned**] give or acquire a tan after exposure to the sun. **2** convert (animal skin) into leather, especially by soaking in a liquid containing tannic acid. **3** informal, dated beat (someone) as a punishment. ● **adj.** N. Amer. having a tan after exposure to the sun.
– DERIVATIVES **tannable** adj. **tannish** adj.
– ORIGIN OE *tannian* 'convert into leather', prob. from med. L. *tannare*, perh. of Celtic origin; reinforced in ME by OFr. *tanner*.

**tan**[2] ● **abbrev.** tangent.

**tanager** /'tanədʒə/ ● **n.** a brightly coloured American songbird of the bunting family. [Subfamily Thraupinae: numerous species.]
– ORIGIN C17 (orig. as *tangara*): from Tupi *tangará*, later refashioned on the mod. L. genus name *Tanagra*.

**Tánaiste** /'tɔːnɪʃtə, Irish 'taːnəsʲtʲə/ ● **n.** the deputy Prime Minister of the Republic of Ireland.
– ORIGIN from Ir. *tánaiste*, lit. 'second in excellence'.

**tanbark** /'tanbɑːk/ ● **n.** see **TAN**[1] (sense 3).

**tandem** ● **n. 1** a bicycle with seats and pedals for two riders, one behind the other. **2** a carriage driven by two animals harnessed one in front of the other. **3** a group of two people or machines working together. ● **adv.** one behind another.
– PHRASES **in tandem 1** alongside each other; together. **2** one behind another.
– ORIGIN C18: humorously from L., lit. 'at length'.

**tandoor** /'tandʊə, tan'dʊə/ ● **n.** a clay oven of a type used originally in northern India and Pakistan.
– ORIGIN from Urdu *tandūr*, from Pers. *tanūr*, based on Arab. *tannūr* 'oven'.

**tandoori** /tan'dʊəri/ ● **adj.** denoting or relating to a style of Indian cooking based on the use of a tandoor.

**tang**[1] ● **n. 1** a strong taste, flavour, or smell. **2** the projection on the blade of a knife or other tool by which the blade is held firmly in the handle.
– ORIGIN ME (denoting a snake's tongue or the sting of an insect): from ON *tangi* 'point, tang of a knife'.

**tang**[2] ● **v.** make a loud ringing or clanging sound.
– ORIGIN C16: imitative.

**tang**[3] ● **n.** a surgeonfish which occurs around reefs and rocks. [Genus *Acanthurus*: several species.]
– ORIGIN C18: from **TANG**[1].

**tanga** /'taŋgə/ ● **n.** Brit. a pair of briefs consisting of small panels connected by strings at the sides.
– ORIGIN C20 (denoting a loincloth worn by indigenous peoples in tropical America): from Port., ult. of Bantu origin.

**tangelo** /'tan(d)ʒələʊ/ ● **n.** (pl. **-os**) a hybrid of the tangerine and grapefruit.
– ORIGIN C20: blend of **TANGERINE** and **POMELO**.

**tangent** /'tan(d)ʒ(ə)nt/ ● **n. 1** a straight line or plane that touches a curve or curved surface at a point, but if extended does not cross it at that point. **2** Mathematics the trigonometric function that is equal to the ratio of the sides (other than the hypotenuse) opposite and adjacent to an angle in a right-angled triangle. **3** a completely different line of thought or action. ● **adj.** (of a line or plane) touching, but not intersecting, a curve or curved surface.
– DERIVATIVES **tangency** n.
– ORIGIN C16: from L. *tangent-*, *tangere* 'touch'.

**tangential** /tan'dʒɛnʃ(ə)l/ ● **adj. 1** of, relating to, or along a tangent. **2** having only a slight connection or relevance; peripheral. **3** diverging from a previous course; erratic.
– DERIVATIVES **tangentially** adv.

**tangerine** ● **n. 1** a small citrus fruit with a loose skin, especially one of a variety with deep orange-red skin. **2** the citrus tree which bears this fruit. [*Citrus reticulata*.] **3** a deep orange-red colour.
– ORIGIN C19: from *Tanger* (former name of *Tangier*, from where the fruit was exported) + **-INE**[1].

**tangible** /'tan(d)ʒɪb(ə)l/ ● **adj. 1** perceptible by touch. **2** clear and definite; real. ● **n.** a thing that is perceptible by touch.
– DERIVATIVES **tangibility** n. **tangibleness** n. **tangibly** adv.
– ORIGIN C16: from Fr., or from late L. *tangibilis*, from L. *tangere* 'to touch'.

**tangle**[1] ● **v. 1** twist (strands) together into a confused mass. **2** (**tangle with**) informal become involved in a conflict with. ● **n. 1** a confused mass of something twisted together. **2** a confused or complicated state; a muddle. ➤ informal a fight, argument, or disagreement.

– DERIVATIVES **tangly** adj.
– ORIGIN ME: prob. of Scand. origin and rel. to Swed. dial. *taggla* 'disarrange'.

**tangle**[2] ● n. any of a number of brown seaweeds, especially oarweed.
– ORIGIN C16: prob. from Norw. *tongul*.

**tango** ● n. (pl. **-os**) **1** a ballroom dance originating in Buenos Aires, characterized by marked rhythms and postures and abrupt pauses. ➤ a piece of music in the style of this dance, typically in a slow, dotted duple rhythm. **2** a code word representing the letter T, used in radio communication. ● v. (**-oes**, **-oed**) dance the tango.
– ORIGIN C19: from Latin Amer. Sp., perh. of Afr. origin.

**tangram** /'tangram/ ● n. a Chinese geometrical puzzle consisting of a square cut into seven pieces which can be arranged to make various other shapes.
– ORIGIN C19: of unknown origin.

**tangy** ● adj. (**-ier**, **-iest**) having a strong, piquant flavour or smell.
– DERIVATIVES **tanginess** n.

**tanh** /tan'eɪtʃ, tanʃ, θan/ ● abbrev. Mathematics hyperbolic tangent.

**tania** ● n. variant spelling of **TANNIA**.

**tanist** /'tanɪst/ ● n. the heir apparent to a Celtic chief.
– DERIVATIVES **tanistry** n.
– ORIGIN C16: from Ir., Sc. Gaelic *tánaiste*, lit. 'second in excellence'.

**tank** ● n. **1** a large receptacle or storage chamber, especially for liquid or gas. ➤ the container holding the fuel supply in a motor vehicle. ➤ Indian & Austral./NZ a reservoir. **2** a receptacle with transparent sides in which to keep fish; an aquarium. **3** a heavy armoured fighting vehicle carrying guns and moving on a continuous articulated metal track. **4** N. Amer. informal a cell in a police station or jail. ● v. **1** (**be/get tanked up**) informal drink heavily or become drunk. **2** (usu. **tank up**) fill the tank of a vehicle with fuel. **3** US informal fail completely or disastrously. ➤ N. Amer. informal (in sport) deliberately lose or fail to finish (a match).
– DERIVATIVES **tankful** n. (pl. **-fuls**). **tankless** adj.
– ORIGIN C17: perh. from Gujarati *tāṅkū* or Marathi *tāṅkē* 'underground cistern', prob. influenced by Port. *tangue* 'pond'.

**tanka**[1] /'taŋkə/ ● n. (pl. same or **tankas**) a Japanese poem in five lines and thirty-one syllables, giving a complete picture of an event or mood.
– ORIGIN Japanese, from *tan* 'short' + *ka* 'song'.

**tanka**[2] /'tɑːŋkə/ ● n. (pl. **tankas**) a Tibetan religious painting on a scroll, hung as a banner in temples and carried in processions.
– ORIGIN from Tibetan *t'án-ka* 'image, painting'.

**tankage** ● n. **1** storage in a tank. **2** a fertilizer or animal feed obtained from the residue from tanks in which animal carcasses have been rendered.

**tankard** ● n. a tall beer mug, typically made of silver or pewter, with a handle and sometimes a hinged lid.
– ORIGIN ME (denoting a large tub for carrying liquid): perh. rel. to Du. *tanckaert*.

**tank engine** ● n. a steam locomotive carrying fuel and water receptacles in its own frame, not in a tender.

**tanker** ● n. a ship, road vehicle, or aircraft for carrying liquids, especially mineral oils, in bulk. ● v. transport (a liquid) in a tanker.

**tank-farming** ● n. the practice of growing plants in tanks of water without soil.

**tank top** ● n. a close-fitting sleeveless top worn over a shirt or blouse.

**tank town** ● n. N. Amer. informal a small unimportant town (originally a town at which trains stopped to take on water).

**tanner**[1] ● n. **1** a person employed to tan animal hides. **2** a lotion or cream designed to promote or simulate the development of a suntan.

**tanner**[2] ● n. Brit. informal, historical a sixpence.
– ORIGIN C19: of unknown origin.

**tannery** ● n. (pl. **-ies**) a place where animal hides are tanned.

**tannia** /'tanɪə/ (also **tania**) ● n. a tall Caribbean plant of the arum family, cultivated for its edible pear-shaped tubers and large arrow-shaped leaves. [*Xanthosoma sagittifolium*.]
– ORIGIN C18: from Carib *taya*, Tupi *taña*.

**tannic acid** ● n. another term for **TANNIN**.
– DERIVATIVES **tannate** n.

**tannin** ● n. a yellowish or brownish bitter-tasting organic substance present in some galls, barks, etc.
– DERIVATIVES **tannic** adj.
– ORIGIN C19: from Fr. *tanin*, from *tan* 'tanbark' (ult. rel. to **TAN**[1]) + **-IN**[1].

**tannoy** Brit. ● n. trademark a type of public address system. ● v. transmit or announce over such a system.
– ORIGIN 1920s: contr. of *tantalum alloy*, which is used as a rectifier in the system.

**Tanoan** /tə'nəʊən/ ● n. a small language family comprising a number of Pueblo Indian languages. ● adj. of or relating to this language family.
– ORIGIN from Sp. *Tano* + **-AN**.

**tanpura** /tʌn'puːrə/ ● n. variant form of **TAMBOURA** (in sense 1).

**tansy** /'tanzi/ ● n. a plant with yellow flat-topped button-like flower heads and aromatic leaves. [*Tanacetum vulgare* and related species.]
– ORIGIN ME: from OFr. *tanesie*, prob. from med. L. *athanasia* 'immortality', from Gk.

**tantalite** /'tantəlʌɪt/ ● n. a rare, dense black mineral consisting of a mixed oxide of iron and tantalum, of which it is the principal source.
– ORIGIN C19: from **TANTALUM** + **-ITE**[1].

**tantalize** (also **-ise**) ● v. torment or tease with the sight or promise of something that is unobtainable or withheld.
– DERIVATIVES **tantalization** n. **tantalizer** n. **tantalizing** adj. **tantalizingly** adv.
– ORIGIN C16: from *Tantalus* in Gk mythology, who was punished for his crimes by being provided with fruit and water which receded when he reached for them, + **-IZE**.

**tantalum** /'tantələm/ ● n. the chemical element of atomic number 73, a hard silver-grey metal. (Symbol: **Ta**)
– DERIVATIVES **tantalic** adj.
– ORIGIN C19: from *Tantalus* (see **TANTALIZE**), with ref. to its frustrating insolubility in acids.

**tantalus** /'tantələs/ ● n. Brit. a stand in which spirit decanters may be locked up though still visible.
– ORIGIN from *Tantalus* (see **TANTALIZE**).

**tantamount** ● adj. (**tantamount to**) equivalent in seriousness to; virtually the same as.
– ORIGIN C17: from the earlier verb *tantamount* 'amount to as much', from Ital. *tanto montare*.

**tante** /tɑ̃ːt, tɑːnt, 'tantə/ ● n. (among those of French, German, or Afrikaans origin) a respectful form of address for an older woman.
– ORIGIN Fr., Du. *tante*, Ger. *Tante* 'aunt'.

**tantivy** /tan'tɪvi/ archaic ● n. (pl. **-ies**) a rapid gallop or ride. ● exclam. used as a hunting cry. ● adj. moving or riding swiftly.
– ORIGIN C17: prob. imitative of the sound of galloping.

**tant mieux** /tɒ̃ 'mjəː, French tɑ̃ mjø/ ● exclam. so much the better.
– ORIGIN from Fr.

**tanto** /'tantəʊ/ ● adv. [usu. with neg.] Music too much.
– ORIGIN from Ital.

**tant pis** /tɒ̃ 'piː, French tɑ̃ pi/ ● exclam. so much the worse; too bad.
– ORIGIN from Fr.

**tantra** /'tantrə, 'tʌntrə/ ● n. **1** a Hindu or Buddhist mystical or magical text. **2** adherence to the doctrines or principles of the tantras, involving mantras, meditation, yoga, and ritual.
– DERIVATIVES **tantric** adj. **tantrism** n. **tantrist** n.
– ORIGIN Sanskrit, lit. 'loom, groundwork, doctrine', from *tan* 'stretch'.

**tantrum** ● n. an uncontrolled outburst of anger and frustration, typically in a young child.
– ORIGIN C18: of unknown origin.

**Tanzanian** /ˌtanzəˈniːən/ • **n.** a native or inhabitant of Tanzania. • **adj.** of or relating to Tanzania.

**Tao** /taʊ, ˈtɑːəʊ/ • **n.** (in Chinese philosophy) the absolute principle underlying the universe, combining within itself the principles of yin and yang and signifying the way, or code of behaviour, that is in harmony with the natural order.
– ORIGIN Chin., lit. '(right) way'.

**Taoiseach** /ˈtiːʃəx, Irish ˈtiːsʲəx/ • **n.** the Prime Minister of the Irish Republic.
– ORIGIN Ir., lit. 'chief, leader'.

**Taoism** /ˈtaʊɪz(ə)m, ˈtɑːəʊ-/ • **n.** a Chinese philosophy based on the writings of Lao-Tzu (including the Tao-te-Ching), advocating humility and religious piety.
– DERIVATIVES **Taoist** n. & adj. **Taoistic** adj.

**Tao-te-Ching** /ˌtaʊtiːˈtʃɪŋ/ • **n.** the central Taoist text.
– ORIGIN Chin., lit. 'the Book of the Way and its Power'.

**tap**[1] • **n. 1** a device by which a flow of liquid or gas from a pipe or container can be controlled. **2** an instrument for cutting a threaded hole in a material. **3** a device connected to a telephone for listening secretly to conversation. **4** (also **tapping**) Brit. an electrical connection made to some point between the end terminals of a transformer coil or other component. **5** Brit. a taproom. • **v.** (**tapped**, **tapping**) **1** draw liquid through the tap or spout of (a cask, barrel, etc.). **2** draw sap from (a tree) by cutting into it. **3** exploit or draw a supply from (a resource). ➤ informal obtain money or information from. **4** connect a device to (a telephone) so that conversation can be listened to secretly. **5** cut a thread in (something) to accept a screw.
– PHRASES **on tap 1** ready to be poured from a tap. ➤ informal freely available whenever needed. **2** N. Amer. informal on schedule to occur.
– DERIVATIVES **tappable** adj.
– ORIGIN OE *tæppa* 'stopper for a cask', *tæppian* 'provide (a cask) with a stopper', of Gmc origin.

**tap**[2] • **v.** (**tapped**, **tapping**) **1** strike or knock with a quick light blow or blows. ➤ strike lightly and repeatedly against something else: *she was tapping her feet.* **2** US informal designate or select for a task or honour. • **n. 1** a quick light blow or the sound of such a blow. **2** tap dancing. ➤ a piece of metal attached to the toe and heel of a tap dancer's shoe to make a tapping sound. **3** (**taps**) [treated as sing. or pl.] US a bugle call for lights to be put out in army quarters. ➤ a similar call sounded at a military funeral. ➤ Brit. (in the Guide movement) a closing song sung at an evening camp fire or at the end of a meeting.
– DERIVATIVES **tapper** n.
– ORIGIN ME: from OFr. *taper*, or of imitative origin; cf. **CLAP**[1] and **RAP**[1].

**tapa** /ˈtɑːpə/ • **n. 1** the bark of the paper mulberry tree. **2** (also **tapa cloth**) cloth made from such bark, used in the Pacific islands.
– ORIGIN C19: of Polynesian origin.

**tapas** /ˈtapəs/ • **pl. n.** small Spanish savoury dishes, typically served with drinks at a bar.
– ORIGIN Sp., lit. 'cover, lid' (because the dishes were given free with the drink, served on a dish balanced on the glass).

**tap dance** • **n.** a dance performed wearing shoes fitted with metal taps, characterized by rhythmical tapping of the toes and heels. • **v.** (**tap-dance**) perform such a dance.
– DERIVATIVES **tap dancer** n. **tap-dancing** n.

**tape** • **n. 1** light, flexible material in a narrow strip, used to hold, fasten, or mark off something. ➤ (also **adhesive tape**) a strip of paper or plastic coated with adhesive, used to stick things together. **2** long, narrow material with magnetic properties, used for recording sound, pictures, or computer data. ➤ a cassette or reel containing such material. **3** a strip of material stretched across the finishing line of a race, to be broken by the winner. **4** a tape measure. • **v. 1** record (sound or pictures) on audio or video tape. **2** fasten, attach, or mark off with tape.
– ORIGIN OE *tæppa*, *tæppe*; perh. rel. to Mid. Low Ger. *teppen* 'pluck, tear'.

**tape deck** • **n.** a piece of equipment for playing audio tapes, especially as part of a stereo system.

**tape measure** • **n.** a length of tape or thin flexible metal, marked at graded intervals for measuring.

**tapenade** /ˈtapənɑːd/ • **n.** a Provençal savoury paste or dip, made from black olives, capers, and anchovies.
– ORIGIN Fr., from Provençal.

**taper** • **v. 1** diminish or reduce in thickness towards one end. **2** (usu. **taper off**) gradually lessen. • **n.** a slender candle. ➤ a wick coated with wax, used for conveying a flame.
– ORIGIN OE, dissimilated form (by alt. of *p-* to *t-*) of L. *papyrus* (see **PAPYRUS**), the pith of which was used for candle wicks.

**tape recorder** • **n.** an apparatus for recording sounds on magnetic tape and afterwards reproducing them.
– DERIVATIVES **tape-record** v. **tape recording** n.

**taperer** • **n.** a person carrying a taper in a religious ceremony.

**tape streamer** • **n.** see **STREAMER** (sense 5).

**tapestry** • **n.** (pl. **-ies**) a piece of thick textile fabric with pictures or designs formed by weaving coloured weft threads or by embroidering on canvas.
– DERIVATIVES **tapestried** adj.
– ORIGIN ME: from OFr. *tapisserie*, from *tapissier* 'tapestry worker' or *tapisser* 'to carpet', from *tapis* 'carpet, tapis'.

**tapetum** /təˈpiːtəm/ • **n.** Zoology a reflective layer of the choroid in the eyes of many animals, causing them to shine in the dark.
– ORIGIN C18: from late L., from L. *tapete* 'carpet'.

**tapeworm** • **n.** a parasitic flatworm with a long ribbon-like body, the adult of which lives in the intestines. [Class Cestoda: many species.]

**taphonomy** /taˈfɒnəmi/ • **n.** the branch of palaeontology concerned with the processes of fossilization.
– DERIVATIVES **taphonomic** adj. **taphonomist** n.
– ORIGIN 1940s: from Gk *taphos* 'grave' + **-NOMY**.

**tapioca** /ˌtapɪˈəʊkə/ • **n.** a starchy substance in the form of hard white grains, obtained from cassava and used for puddings and other dishes.
– ORIGIN C18: from Tupi-Guarani *tipioca*, from *tipi* 'dregs' + *og*, *ok* 'squeeze out'.

**tapir** /ˈteɪpə, -ɪə/ • **n.** a hoofed mammal with a short flexible proboscis, native to tropical America and Malaysia. [Genus *Tapirus*: four species.]
– ORIGIN C18: via Sp. and Port. from Tupi *tapyra*.

**tapis** /ˈtapiː/ • **n.** (pl. same) archaic a tapestry or richly decorated cloth, used as a hanging or a covering.
– ORIGIN Fr., from OFr. *tapiz*, via late L. from Gk *tapētion*, dimin. of *tapēs* 'tapestry'.

**tapotement** /təˈpəʊtm(ə)nt/ • **n.** rapid and repeated striking of the body as a technique in massage.
– ORIGIN C19: Fr., from *tapoter* 'to tap'.

**tap pants** • **pl. n.** N. Amer. brief lingerie shorts, usually worn with a camisole top.

**tappet** /ˈtapɪt/ • **n.** a lever or projecting part on a machine which intermittently makes contact with a cam or other part so as to give or receive motion.
– ORIGIN C18: appar. an irregular dimin. of **TAP**[2].

**taproom** • **n.** a room in which alcoholic drinks, especially beer, are available on tap.

**taproot** • **n.** a straight tapering root growing vertically downwards and forming the centre from which subsidiary rootlets spring.

**tapster** • **n.** archaic a person who draws and serves alcoholic drinks at a bar.

**tapu** /ˈtɑːpuː/ • **adj.** NZ forbidden; taboo.
– ORIGIN from Maori.

**taqueria** /ˌtɑːkəˈriːə/ • **n.** chiefly US a Mexican restaurant specializing in tacos.
– ORIGIN from Mex. Sp.

**tar**[1] • **n.** a dark, thick flammable liquid distilled from wood or coal, used in road-making and for coating and preserving timber. ➤ a similar substance formed by burning tobacco or other material. • **v.** (**tarred**, **tarring**) [usu. as adj. **tarred**] cover with tar.
– PHRASES **beat** (or **whale**) **the tar out of** N. Amer. informal

beat or thrash severely. **tar and feather** smear with tar and then cover with feathers as a punishment. **tar people with the same brush** consider specified people to have the same faults.
– ORIGIN OE *teru*, *teoru*, of Gmc origin.

**tar²** • n. informal, dated a sailor.
– ORIGIN C17: perh. an abbrev. of **TARPAULIN**, used as a nickname for a sailor at this time.

**ta-ra** • exclam. informal, chiefly N. English goodbye.
– ORIGIN 1950s: var. of **TA-TA**.

**taradiddle** /ˈtarəˌdɪd(ə)l/ (also **tarradiddle**) • n. informal, chiefly Brit. **1** a petty lie. **2** pretentious nonsense.
– ORIGIN C18: perh. rel. to **DIDDLE**.

**tarakihi** /ˌtarəˈkiːhi, ˌtarəˈkiː/ • n. a silver marine fish with a black band behind the head, related to the morwong and caught off New Zealand coasts. [*Cheilodactylus macropterus*.]
– ORIGIN C19: from Maori.

**taramasalata** /ˌtarəməsəˈlɑːtə/ (also **tarama** /ˈtarəmə/) • n. a pinkish paste or dip made from the roe of certain fish, mixed with olive oil and seasoning.
– ORIGIN from mod. Gk *taramas* 'roe' + *salata* 'salad'.

**tarantass** /ˌtar(ə)nˈtas/ • n. a four-wheeled, horse-drawn Russian carriage without springs, mounted on a long flexible wooden chassis.
– ORIGIN from Russ. *tarantas*.

**tarantella** /ˌtar(ə)nˈtɛlə/ (also **tarantelle** /-ˈtɛl/) • n. a rapid whirling dance originating in southern Italy. ➤ a piece of music written in fast 6/8 time in the style of this dance.
– ORIGIN C18: Ital., from the name of the seaport *Taranto*; so named because it was thought to be a cure for tarantism.

**tarantism** /ˈtar(ə)nˌtɪz(ə)m/ • n. a psychological illness characterized by an extreme impulse to dance, prevalent in southern Italy from the 15th to the 17th century and formerly believed to be caused by the bite of a tarantula.
– ORIGIN C17: from Ital. *tarantismo*, from the name of the seaport *Taranto*, after which the tarantula is also named.

**tarantula** /təˈrantjʊlə/ • n. **1** a very large hairy spider found chiefly in tropical and subtropical America. [Family Theraphosidae.] **2** a large black wolf spider of southern Europe, whose bite was formerly believed to cause tarantism. [*Lycosa tarentula*.]
– ORIGIN C16: from med. L., from Old Ital. *tarantola*, from the name of the seaport *Taranto* in southern Italy; cf. **TARANTISM**.

**tar baby** • n. informal a difficult problem which is only aggravated by attempts to solve it.
– ORIGIN with allusion to the doll smeared with tar as a trap for Brer Rabbit, in J. C. Harris's *Uncle Remus*.

**tarboosh** /tɑːˈbuːʃ/ • n. a man's cap similar to a fez, typically of red felt with a tassel at the top.
– ORIGIN C18: from Egyptian Arab. *ṭarbūš*, based on Pers. *sarpūš*, from *sar* 'head' + *pūš* 'cover'.

**Tardenoisian** /ˌtɑːdɪˈnɔɪzɪən/ • adj. of or relating to a late Mesolithic culture of west and central Europe, especially France, dated to about 8,000–6,000 years ago.
– ORIGIN 1920s: from Fr. *Tardenoisien*, from the name of *Fère-en-Tardenois* in NE France, where objects from this culture were found.

**Tardigrada** /ˌtɑːdɪˈɡreɪdə/ • pl. n. Zoology a small phylum that comprises the water bears.
– DERIVATIVES **tardigrade** /ˈtɑːdɪɡreɪd/ n.
– ORIGIN mod. L., from L. *tardigradus*, from *tardus* 'slow' + *gradi* 'to walk'.

**tardive dyskinesia** /ˌtɑːdɪv ˌdɪskɪˈniːzɪə/ • n. Medicine a neurological disorder characterized by involuntary movements of the face and jaw.
– ORIGIN 1960s: *tardive* from Fr. *tardif*, *tardive* (see **TARDY**).

**tardy** • adj. (**-ier**, **-iest**) delaying or delayed beyond the right or expected time; late. ➤ slow in action or response; sluggish.
– DERIVATIVES **tardily** adv. **tardiness** n.
– ORIGIN C16: from Fr. *tardif*, *-ive*, from L. *tardus* 'slow'.

**tare¹** /tɛː/ • n. **1** a vetch, especially the common vetch. **2** (**tares**) (in biblical use) a harmful weed resembling corn when young (Matt. 13:24–30).
– ORIGIN ME: of unknown origin.

**tare²** /tɛː/ • n. an allowance made for the weight of the packaging in order to determine the net weight of goods. ➤ the weight of a vehicle without its fuel or load.
– ORIGIN ME: from Fr., lit. 'deficiency, tare', from med. L. *tara*, based on Arab. *ṭaraḥa* 'reject, deduct'.

**tare and tret** • n. historical the arithmetical rule used for calculating the net weight of goods by subtracting the tare and the tret from the gross weight.

**targa** /ˈtɑːɡə/ • n. a type of convertible sports car with a panel that can be removed, leaving a central roll bar.
– ORIGIN Ital., lit. 'shield', given as a name to a model of Porsche with a detachable hood (1965), prob. suggested by the *Targa Florio* ('Florio Shield'), a motor time trial held annually in Sicily.

**targe** /tɑːdʒ/ • n. archaic term for **TARGET** (in sense 3).
– ORIGIN OE *targa*, *targe*, of Gmc origin.

**target** • n. **1** a person, object, or place selected as the aim of an attack. ➤ a round or rectangular board marked with concentric circles, aimed at in archery or shooting. **2** an objective or result towards which efforts are directed: *a sales target*. **3** historical a small round shield or buckler. • v. (**targeted**, **targeting**) select as an object of attention or attack. ➤ aim or direct (something).
– PHRASES **on** (or **off**) **target** succeeding (or not succeeding) in hitting or achieving the thing aimed at.
– DERIVATIVES **targetable** adj.
– ORIGIN ME: dimin. of **TARGE**.

**target language** • n. the language into which a text, document, or speech is translated.

**target man** • n. Soccer & Hockey a forward to whom other players direct long passes.

**Targum** /ˈtɑːɡəm/ • n. an ancient Aramaic paraphrase or interpretation of the Hebrew Bible.
– ORIGIN from Aramaic *targūm* 'interpretation'.

**tariff** • n. **1** a tax or duty to be paid on a particular class of imports or exports. **2** a table of the fixed charges made by a business, especially in a hotel or restaurant. **3** Law a scale of sentences and damages for crimes and injuries of different severities. • v. fix the price of (something) according to a tariff.
– ORIGIN C16: via Fr. from Ital. *tariffa*, based on Arab. *'arrafa* 'notify'.

**tarlatan** /ˈtɑːlət(ə)n/ • n. a thin, open-weave muslin fabric, used for stiffening ball dresses.
– ORIGIN C18: from Fr. *tarlatane*, prob. of Ind. origin.

**tarmac** • n. (trademark in the UK) material used for surfacing roads or other outdoor areas, consisting of broken stone mixed with tar. ➤ a runway or other area surfaced with such material. • v. (**tarmacked**, **tarmacking**) surface with tarmac.
– ORIGIN C20: abbrev. of **TARMACADAM**.

**tarmacadam** /ˌtɑːməˈkadəm/ • n. another term for **TARMAC**.
– ORIGIN C19: from **TAR¹** + **MACADAM**.

**tarn** • n. a small mountain lake.
– ORIGIN ME (orig. north. Engl. dial.): from ON *tjǫrn*.

**tarnation** • n. & exclam. chiefly N. Amer. used as a euphemism for 'damnation'.
– ORIGIN C18: alt.

**tarnish** • v. **1** lose or cause to lose lustre, especially as a result of exposure to air or moisture. **2** make or become less valuable or respected. • n. dullness of colour; loss of brightness. ➤ a film or stain formed on an exposed surface of a mineral or metal.
– DERIVATIVES **tarnishable** adj.
– ORIGIN ME: from Fr. *terniss-*, lengthened stem of *ternir*, from *terne* 'dark, dull'.

**taro** /ˈtɑːrəʊ, ˈtarəʊ/ • n. a tropical Asian plant with edible starchy corms and fleshy leaves, grown as a staple in the Pacific. [*Colocasia esculenta*.]
– ORIGIN C18: of Polynesian origin.

**tarot** /ˈtarəʊ/ • n. playing cards, traditionally a pack of 78 with five suits, used for fortune telling.
– ORIGIN C16: from Fr., from Ital. *tarocchi*, of unknown

origin.

**tarp** • n. informal, chiefly N. Amer. a tarpaulin sheet or cover.

**tarpan** /ˈtɑːpan/ • n. a greyish wild horse that was formerly common in eastern Europe and western Asia, hunted to extinction by 1919. [*Equus caballus gomelini*.]
– ORIGIN from Kyrgyz.

**tarpaulin** /tɑːˈpɔːlɪn/ • n. **1** heavy-duty waterproof cloth, originally of tarred canvas. ➤a sheet or covering of this. **2** historical a sailor's tarred or oilskin hat.
– ORIGIN C17: prob. from TAR[1] + PALL[1] + -ING[1].

**tar pit** • n. a hollow in which natural tar accumulates by seepage.

**tarpon** /ˈtɑːpɒn/ • n. a large tropical marine fish of herring-like appearance. [*Tarpon atlanticus* (Atlantic) and *Megalops cyprinoides* (Indo-Pacific).]
– ORIGIN C17: prob. from Du. *tarpoen*, perh. from a Central Amer. lang.

**tarradiddle** • n. variant spelling of TARADIDDLE.

**tarragon** /ˈtarəg(ə)n/ • n. a perennial plant of the daisy family, with narrow aromatic leaves that are used as a culinary herb. [*Artemisia dracunculus*.]
– ORIGIN C16: representing med. L. *tragonia* and *tarchon*, perh. from an Arab. alt. of Gk *drakōn* 'dragon'.

**Tarragona wine** /ˌtarəˈgəʊnə/ • n. a sweet fortified red or white wine produced in the Tarragona region of Spain.

**tarry**[1] /ˈtɑːri/ • adj. (**-ier**, **-iest**) of, like, or covered with tar.
– DERIVATIVES **tarriness** n.

**tarry**[2] /ˈtari/ • v. (**-ies**, **-ied**) archaic stay longer than intended; delay leaving a place.
– DERIVATIVES **tarrier** n. (rare).
– ORIGIN ME: of unknown origin.

**tarsal** /ˈtɑːs(ə)l/ Anatomy & Zoology • adj. of or relating to the tarsus. • n. a bone of the tarsus.

**tar sand** • n. Geology a deposit of sand impregnated with bitumen.

**tarsi** plural form of TARSUS.

**tarsier** /ˈtɑːsɪə/ • n. a small tree-dwelling insectivorous primate with very large eyes, a long tufted tail, and very long hindlimbs, native to the islands of SE Asia. [Genus *Tarsius*: four species.]
– ORIGIN C18: from Fr., from *tarse* 'tarsus', with ref. to the animal's long tarsal bones.

**tarsus** /ˈtɑːsəs/ • n. (pl. **tarsi** /-sʌɪ, -siː/) **1** Anatomy the group of small bones between the main part of the hindlimb and the metatarsus, forming the ankle and upper foot in humans. ➤Zoology the shank of the leg of a bird or reptile. ➤Zoology the foot or fifth leg joint of an insect or other arthropod, typically ending in a claw. **2** Anatomy a thin sheet of fibrous connective tissue supporting the edge of the eyelid.
– ORIGIN ME: mod. L., from Gk *tarsos* 'flat of the foot, the eyelid'.

**tart**[1] • n. an open pastry case containing a sweet or savoury filling.
– DERIVATIVES **tartlet** n.
– ORIGIN ME: from OFr. *tarte* or med. L. *tarta*, of unknown origin.

**tart**[2] • n. informal, derogatory a prostitute or promiscuous woman. • v. (**tart oneself up**) informal, chiefly Brit. dress or make oneself up in order to look attractive. ➤(**tart something up**) decorate or improve the appearance of something.
– DERIVATIVES **tartily** adv. **tartiness** n. **tarty** adj. (**-ier**, **-iest**).
– ORIGIN C19: prob. an abbrev. of SWEETHEART.

**tart**[3] • adj. **1** sharp or acid in taste. **2** (of a remark or tone of voice) cutting, bitter, or sarcastic.
– DERIVATIVES **tartly** adv. **tartness** n.
– ORIGIN OE *teart* 'harsh, severe', of unknown origin.

**tartan**[1] • n. a woollen cloth woven in one of several patterns of coloured checks and intersecting lines, especially of a design associated with a particular Scottish clan.
– ORIGIN C15: perh. from OFr. *tertaine*, denoting a kind of cloth; cf. *tartarin*, a rich fabric formerly imported from the east through Tartary.

**tartan**[2] • n. historical a lateen-rigged, single-masted ship used in the Mediterranean.
– ORIGIN C17: from Fr. *tartane*, from Ital. *tartana*, perh. from Arab. *ṭarīda*.

**Tartar** /ˈtɑːtə/ • n. **1** historical a member of the combined forces of central Asian peoples, including Mongols and Turks. **2** (**tartar**) a harsh, fierce, or intractable person.
– DERIVATIVES **Tartarian** /-ˈtɛːrɪən/ adj.
– ORIGIN from OFr. *Tartare* or med. L. *Tartarus*, alt. of TATAR.

**tartar** /ˈtɑːtə/ • n. **1** a hard calcified deposit that forms on the teeth and contributes to their decay. **2** a deposit of impure potassium hydrogen tartrate formed during the fermentation of wine.
– PHRASES **cream of tartar** potassium hydrogen tartrate, an acidic crystalline compound used in baking powder.
– ORIGIN ME: via med. L. from med. Gk *tartaron*, of unknown origin.

**tartare** /tɑːˈtɑː/ • adj. [postpos.] (of fish or meat) served raw, typically seasoned and shaped into small cakes.
– ORIGIN Fr., lit. 'Tartar'.

**Tartarean** /tɑːˈtɛːrɪən/ • adj. relating to or reminiscent of Tartarus, a part of the underworld in Greek mythology where the wicked were punished.

**tartar emetic** • n. potassium antimony tartrate, a toxic compound used in dyeing and to treat protozoal disease in animals.

**tartare sauce** (also **tartar sauce**) • n. a cold sauce, typically eaten with fish, consisting of mayonnaise mixed with chopped onions, gherkins, and capers.

**tartaric acid** • n. Chemistry a crystalline organic acid which is present especially in unripe grapes and is used in baking powders and as a food additive.
– ORIGIN C18: from obs. Fr. *tartarique*, from med. L. *tartarum* (see TARTAR).

**tarte Tatin** /ˌtɑːt taˈtã/ • n. a type of upside-down apple tart consisting of pastry baked over slices of fruit in caramelized sugar, served fruit side up after cooking.
– ORIGIN Fr., from *tarte* 'tart' + *Tatin*, the surname of the sisters said to have created the dish.

**tartrate** /ˈtɑːtreɪt/ • n. Chemistry a salt or ester of tartaric acid.
– ORIGIN C18: from Fr., from *tartre* 'tartar' + -ATE[1].

**tartrazine** /ˈtɑːtrəziːn/ • n. Chemistry a brilliant yellow synthetic dye derived from tartaric acid and used to colour food, drugs, and cosmetics.
– ORIGIN C19: from Fr. *tartre* 'tartar' + AZO- + -INE[4].

**tartufo** /tɑːˈtuːfəʊ/ • n. **1** an edible fungus, especially a truffle. **2** an Italian chocolate dessert of a creamy mousse-like consistency.
– ORIGIN Ital., lit. 'truffle'.

**tarwhine** /ˈtɑːwʌɪn/ • n. (pl. same) a yellowish sea bream of warm shallow inshore waters, an important food and game fish in the Indo-Pacific. [*Rhabdosargus globiceps*.]
– ORIGIN C19: from Dharuk *darawayn* 'a fish'.

**Tarzan** • n. a man of great agility and powerful physique.
– ORIGIN from the name of a fictitious character created by the Amer. writer Edgar Rice Burroughs.

**Tas.** • abbrev. chiefly Austral. Tasmania.

**taser** /ˈteɪzə/ • n. US trademark a weapon firing barbs attached by wires to batteries, causing temporary paralysis.
– ORIGIN 1970s: from the initial letters of *Tom Swift's electric rifle* (a fictitious weapon), on the pattern of *laser*.

**tash** (also **tache**) • n. informal a moustache.
– ORIGIN C19: shortened form.

**Tashi Lama** /ˈtaʃɪ ˌlɑːmə/ • n. another name for PANCHEN LAMA.

**task** • n. a piece of work. • v. **1** (usu. **be tasked with**) assign a particular task to. **2** make great demands on.
– PHRASES **take someone to task** reprimand or criticize someone.
– ORIGIN ME: from an ONorth. Fr. var. of OFr. *tasche*, from med. L. *tasca*, alt. of *taxa*, from L. *taxare* (see TAX).

**task force** • n. an armed force organized for a special operation. ➤a unit specially organized for a task.

**taskmaster** • n. a person who imposes an onerous workload on someone.

**Tasmanian** /taz'meɪnɪən/ • n. a native or inhabitant of the Australian state of Tasmania. • adj. of or relating to Tasmania.

**Tasmanian devil** • n. a heavily built aggressive marsupial with a large head, powerful jaws, and mainly black fur, found only in Tasmania. [*Sarcophilus harrisii.*]

**Tasmanian wolf** (also **Tasmanian tiger**) • n. another term for **THYLACINE**.

**tass** • n. Scottish archaic a cup or small goblet. ➤a small draught of an alcoholic drink.
– ORIGIN C15: from OFr. *tasse* 'cup', via Arab. from Pers. *tašt* 'bowl'.

**tassa drum** /'tasə/ • n. W. Indian a large goatskin drum, typically hung from the neck.
– ORIGIN *tassa* from Hindi.

**tassel**[1] • n. **1** a tuft of hanging threads, knotted together at one end and used for decoration in soft furnishing and clothing. **2** the tufted head of some plants, especially a flower head with prominent stamens at the top of a maize stalk. • v. (**tasselled**, **tasselling**; US **tasseled**, **tasseling**) **1** provide with a tassel or tassels. **2** N. Amer. (of maize or other plants) form tassels.
– DERIVATIVES **tasselled** adj.
– ORIGIN ME: from OFr. *tassel* 'clasp', of unknown origin.

**tassel**[2] • n. a small piece of stone or wood supporting the end of a beam or joist.
– ORIGIN C17: from obs. Fr., from L. *taxillus* 'small die'.

**taste** • n. **1** the sensation of flavour perceived in the mouth on contact with a substance. ➤the faculty of perceiving this. **2** a small portion of food or drink taken as a sample. **3** a brief experience of something. **4** a person's liking for something. **5** the ability to discern what is of good quality or of a high aesthetic standard. ➤conformity to a specified degree with generally held views on what is appropriate or offensive: *a joke in bad taste.* • v. **1** perceive or experience the flavour of. ➤have a specified flavour. ➤sample or test the flavour of. ➤eat or drink a small portion of. **2** have a brief experience of.
– PHRASES **to taste** according to personal liking.
– DERIVATIVES **tasting** n.
– ORIGIN ME: from OFr. *tast* (n.), *taster* (v.) 'touch, try, taste', perh. based on a blend of L. *tangere* 'to touch' and *gustare* 'to taste'.

**taste bud** • n. any of the clusters of bulbous nerve endings on the tongue and in the lining of the mouth which provide the sense of taste.

**tasteful** • adj. showing good aesthetic judgement or appropriate behaviour.
– DERIVATIVES **tastefully** adv. **tastefulness** n.

**tasteless** • adj. **1** lacking flavour. **2** lacking in aesthetic judgement or constituting inappropriate behaviour.
– DERIVATIVES **tastelessly** adv. **tastelessness** n.

**tastemaker** • n. a person who decides or influences what is or will become fashionable.

**taster** • n. **1** a person who tests food or drink by tasting it. ➤a small cup for tasting wine. ➤an instrument for extracting a small sample from within a cheese. **2** a sample or brief experience of something.

**tasty** • adj. (**-ier**, **-iest**) **1** (of food) having a pleasant, distinct flavour. **2** informal, chiefly Brit. attractive; appealing.
– DERIVATIVES **tastily** adv. **tastiness** n.

**tat**[1] • n. Brit. informal tasteless or shoddy articles.
– ORIGIN C19: prob. a back-form. from **TATTY**.

**tat**[2] • v. (**tatted**, **tatting**) do tatting; make by tatting.
– ORIGIN C19: back-form. from **TATTING**.

**tat**[3] • n. (in phr. **tit for tat**) see **TIT**[3].

**ta-ta** • exclam. informal, chiefly Brit. goodbye.
– ORIGIN C19: of unknown origin; cf. earlier *da-da*.

**tatami** /tə'tɑːmi/ • n. (pl. same or **tatamis**) a rush-covered straw mat forming a traditional Japanese floor covering.
– ORIGIN from Japanese.

**Tatar** /'tɑːtə/ • n. **1** a member of a Turkic people living in Tatarstan and various other parts of Russia and Ukraine. **2** the Turkic language of this people.
– ORIGIN the Turkic name of a Tartar tribe.

**tater** /'teɪtə/ (Brit. also **tatie** /-ti/) • n. informal a potato.
– ORIGIN C18: alt.

**tathata** /ˌtatə'tɑː, ˌtaθə'tɑː/ • n. Buddhism the ultimate nature of all things, as expressed in phenomena but inexpressible in language. Compare with **SUNYATA**.
– ORIGIN Pali, lit. 'true state of things'.

**tatterdemalion** /ˌtatədɪ'meɪljən/ • adj. tattered or dilapidated. • n. a person in tattered clothing.
– ORIGIN C17: from **TATTERS** or **TATTERED**: ending unexplained.

**tattered** • adj. old and torn; in poor condition.
– ORIGIN ME: appar. orig. from *tatter* 'scrap of cloth' + **-ED**[1]; later treated as a past part.

**tatters** • pl. n. irregularly torn pieces of cloth, paper, etc.
– PHRASES **in tatters** informal **1** torn; in shreds. **2** destroyed; ruined.
– ORIGIN ME: from ON *tǫtrar* 'rags'.

**tattersall** /'tatəs(ə)l, -sɔːl/ • n. a woollen fabric with a pattern of coloured checks and intersecting lines, resembling a tartan.
– ORIGIN C19: named after *Tattersalls*, the firm of horse auctioneers, by assoc. with the traditional design of horse blankets.

**tattie** • n. informal, chiefly Scottish a potato.
– ORIGIN C18: alt.

**tatting** • n. **1** a kind of knotted lace made by hand with a small shuttle. **2** the process of making such lace.
– ORIGIN C19: of unknown origin.

**tattle** • n. gossip; idle talk. • v. engage in tattle.
– DERIVATIVES **tattler** n.
– ORIGIN C15: from Mid. Flemish *tatelen*, *tateren*, of imitative origin.

**tattletale** US • n. a telltale. • v. tell tales.

**tattoo**[1] • n. (pl. **tattoos**) **1** an evening drum or bugle signal recalling soldiers to their quarters. **2** a military display consisting of music, marching, and exercises. **3** a rhythmic tapping or drumming.
– ORIGIN C17 (orig. as *tap-too*) from Du. *taptoe!*, lit. 'close the tap (of the cask)!'.

**tattoo**[2] • v. (**tattoos**, **tattooed**) mark with an indelible design by inserting pigment into punctures in the skin. • n. (pl. **tattoos**) a design made in such a way.
– DERIVATIVES **tattooer** n. **tattooist** n.
– ORIGIN C18: from Tahitian, Tongan, and Samoan *ta-tau* or Marquesan *ta-tu*.

**tatty** • adj. (**-ier**, **-iest**) informal worn and shabby; in poor condition.
– DERIVATIVES **tattily** adv. **tattiness** n.
– ORIGIN C16: appar. ult. rel. to OE *tættec* 'rag', of Gmc origin; cf. **TATTERED**.

**tau** /tɔː, taʊ/ • n. **1** the nineteenth letter of the Greek alphabet (Τ, τ), transliterated as 't'. **2** (also **tau particle**) Physics an unstable lepton with a charge of −1 and a mass roughly 3,500 times that of the electron.
– ORIGIN from Gk.

**tau cross** • n. a T-shaped cross.

**taught** past and past participle of **TEACH**.

**taunt** • n. a jeering or mocking remark made in order to wound or provoke. • v. provoke or wound with taunts.
– DERIVATIVES **taunter** n. **taunting** adj. **tauntingly** adv.
– ORIGIN C16: from Fr. *tant pour tant* 'like for like, tit for tat', from *tant* 'so much', from L. *tantus*.

**taupe** /təʊp/ • n. a grey tinged with brown.
– ORIGIN C20: from Fr., lit. 'mole, moleskin', from L. *talpa*.

**taurine**[1] /'tɔːriːn/ • n. Biochemistry a sulphur-containing amino acid important in the metabolism of fats.
– ORIGIN C19: from Gk *tauros* 'bull' (because it was orig. obtained from ox bile) + **-INE**[4].

**taurine**[2] /'tɔːrʌɪn/ • adj. **1** of or like a bull. **2** of or relating to bullfighting.
– ORIGIN C17: from L. *taurinus*, from *taurus* 'bull'.

**taurocholic acid** /ˌtɔːrə(ʊ)'kɒlɪk/ • n. Biochemistry an acid formed by the combination of taurine with cholic acid, occurring in bile.
– DERIVATIVES **taurocholate** n.

– ORIGIN C19: from Gk *tauros* 'bull' + *kholē* 'bile' + **-IC**.

**tauromachy** /tɔːˈrɒməki/ ● **n.** (pl. **-ies**) bullfighting or a bullfight.
– DERIVATIVES **tauromachian** adj. **tauromachic** adj.
– ORIGIN C19: from Gk *tauromakhia*, from *tauros* 'bull' + *makhē* 'battle'.

**Taurus** /ˈtɔːrəs/ ● **n. 1** Astronomy a constellation (the Bull), said to represent a bull tamed by Jason (a hero of Greek mythology). **2** Astrology the second sign of the zodiac, which the sun enters about 21 April.
– DERIVATIVES **Taurean** /ˈtɔːrɪən, tɔːˈriːən/ n. & adj.
– ORIGIN from L.

**taut** ● **adj. 1** stretched or pulled tight. ➤(of muscles or nerves) tense. **2** (of writing, music, etc.) concise and controlled. **3** (of a ship) having a disciplined crew.
– DERIVATIVES **tauten** v. **tautly** adv. **tautness** n.
– ORIGIN ME *tought* 'distended', perh. from **TOUGH**.

**tauto-** /ˈtɔːtəʊ/ ● **comb. form** same: *tautology.*
– ORIGIN from Gk *tauto*, contr. of *to auto* 'the same'.

**tautog** /tɔːˈtɒg/ ● **n.** a greyish-olive edible wrasse found off the Atlantic coast of North America. [*Tautoga onitis.*]
– ORIGIN C17: from Narragansett *tautauog*, pl. of *taut*.

**tautology** /tɔːˈtɒlədʒi/ ● **n.** (pl. **-ies**) **1** the unnecessary repetition within a statement of the same thing in different words. **2** Logic a statement that is true by necessity or by virtue of its logical form.
– DERIVATIVES **tautological** adj. **tautologically** adv. **tautologist** n. **tautologize** (also **-ise**) v. **tautologous** adj.
– ORIGIN C16: via late L. from Gk, from *tautologos* 'repeating what has been said', from *tauto-* 'same' + *-logos* (see **-LOGY**).

**tautomer** /ˈtɔːtəmə/ ● **n.** Chemistry each of two or more readily interconvertible isomers of a compound which exist together in equilibrium.
– DERIVATIVES **tautomeric** /-ˈmɛrɪk/ adj. **tautomerism** /-ˈtɒmərɪz(ə)m/ n.
– ORIGIN C20: blend of **TAUTO-** and **ISOMER**.

**tavern** ● **n.** chiefly archaic or N. Amer. an inn or public house.
– ORIGIN ME: from OFr. *taverne*, from L. *taberna* 'hut, tavern'.

**taverna** /təˈvəːnə/ ● **n.** a small Greek restaurant.
– ORIGIN mod. Gk, from L. *taberna* (see **TAVERN**).

**taw**[1] /tɔː/ ● **v.** make (hide) into leather by soaking it in a solution of alum and salt (rather than using tannin).
– DERIVATIVES **tawer** n.
– ORIGIN OE *tawian*, of Gmc origin; rel. to **TOOL**.

**taw**[2] /tɔː/ ● **n.** a large marble. ➤a game of marbles. ➤a line from which players throw marbles.
– ORIGIN C18: of unknown origin.

**tawa** /ˈtɑːwə, ˈtaʊə/ ● **n.** a tall New Zealand forest tree of the laurel family, which bears damson-like fruit. [*Beilschmiedia tawa.*]
– ORIGIN C19: from Maori.

**tawdry** ● **adj.** (**-ier**, **-iest**) **1** showy but cheap and of poor quality. **2** sordid; sleazy. ● **n.** archaic cheap and gaudy finery.
– DERIVATIVES **tawdrily** adv. **tawdriness** n.
– ORIGIN C17: short for *tawdry lace*, a fine silk lace or ribbon, contr. of *St Audrey's lace*: *Audrey* was a later form of *Etheldrida*, patron saint of Ely where tawdry laces, along with cheap imitations, were traditionally sold at a fair.

**tawny** ● **adj.** (**-ier**, **-iest**) of an orange-brown or yellowish-brown colour. ● **n.** this colour.
– DERIVATIVES **tawniness** n.
– ORIGIN ME: from OFr. *tane*, from *tan* 'tanbark'; rel. to **TAN**[1].

**tawny owl** ● **n.** a common owl with either reddish-brown or grey plumage, and a familiar quavering hoot. [*Strix aluco.*]

**tawse** /tɔːz/ (also **taws**) ● **n.** Scottish a thong with a slit end, formerly used in schools as a whip.
– ORIGIN C16: appar. the pl. of obs. *taw* 'tawed leather', from **TAW**[1].

**tax** ● **n. 1** a compulsory contribution to state revenue, levied by the government on personal income and business profits or added to the cost of some goods, services, and transactions. **2** a strain or heavy demand. ● **v. 1** impose a tax on. ➤pay tax on (a vehicle). **2** make heavy demands on. **3** charge with a fault or wrongdoing. **4** Law examine and assess (the costs of a case).
– DERIVATIVES **taxable** adj. **taxer** n.
– ORIGIN ME: from OFr. *taxer*, from L. *taxare* 'to censure, charge, compute', perh. from Gk *tassein* 'fix'.

**taxa** plural form of **TAXON**.

**taxation** ● **n.** the levying of tax. ➤money paid as tax.

**tax avoidance** ● **n.** Brit. the arrangement of one's financial affairs to minimize tax liability within the law. Compare with **TAX EVASION**.

**tax break** ● **n.** informal a tax concession or advantage allowed by government.

**tax-deductible** ● **adj.** permitted to be deducted from taxable income.

**tax disc** ● **n.** Brit. a circular label displayed on the windscreen of a vehicle, certifying payment of road tax.

**tax evasion** ● **n.** the illegal non-payment or underpayment of tax. Compare with **TAX AVOIDANCE**.

**tax exile** ● **n.** a person who chooses to live in a country or area with low rates of taxation to avoid paying high taxes.

**tax haven** ● **n.** a country or independent area where taxes are levied at a low rate.

**taxi** ● **n.** (pl. **taxis**) a motor vehicle licensed to transport passengers in return for payment of a fare. ● **v.** (**taxies**, **taxied**, **taxiing** or **taxying**) **1** (with reference to an aircraft) move or cause to move slowly along the ground before take-off or after landing. **2** travel in a taxi.
– ORIGIN C20: abbrev. of *taxicab* or *taximeter cab.*

**taxicab** ● **n.** a taxi.

**taxidermy** /ˈtaksɪˌdəːmi/ ● **n.** the art of preparing, stuffing, and mounting the skins of animals so as to appear lifelike.
– DERIVATIVES **taxidermal** adj. **taxidermic** adj. **taxidermically** adv. **taxidermist** n.
– ORIGIN C19: from Gk *taxis* 'arrangement' + *derma* 'skin'.

**taximeter** ● **n.** a device used in taxis that automatically records the distance travelled and the fare payable.

**taxing** ● **adj.** physically or mentally demanding.

**taxi rank** (N. Amer. **taxi stand**) ● **n.** a place where taxis park while waiting to be hired.

**taxis** /ˈtaksɪs/ ● **n.** (pl. **taxes** /ˈtaksiːz/) **1** Surgery the restoration of displaced bones or organs by manual pressure alone. **2** Biology a motion or orientation of a cell, organism, or part in response to an external stimulus. Compare with **KINESIS**. **3** Linguistics the systematic arrangement of linguistic units in linear sequence.
– ORIGIN C18: from Gk, lit. 'arrangement', from *tassein* 'arrange'.

**taxi squad** ● **n.** American Football a group of reserve players who practise with the team.

**taxiway** ● **n.** a route along which an aircraft taxies when moving to or from a runway.

**taxman** ● **n.** (pl. **-men**) informal an inspector or collector of taxes.

**taxol** /ˈtaksɒl/ ● **n.** Medicine, trademark a compound, originally obtained from the bark of the Pacific yew tree, which inhibits the growth of certain cancers.
– ORIGIN 1970s: from L. *taxus* 'yew' + **-OL**.

**taxon** /ˈtaksɒn/ ● **n.** (pl. **taxa** /ˈtaksə/) Biology a taxonomic group of any rank.
– ORIGIN 1920s: back-form. from **TAXONOMY**.

**taxonomy** /takˈsɒnəmi/ ● **n.** chiefly Biology the branch of science concerned with classification. ➤a scheme of classification.
– DERIVATIVES **taxonomic** adj. **taxonomical** adj. **taxonomically** adv. **taxonomist** n.
– ORIGIN C19: coined in Fr. from Gk *taxis* 'arrangement' + *-nomia* 'distribution'.

**taxpayer** ● **n.** a person who pays taxes.

**tax point** ● **n.** the date on which value added tax becomes chargeable on a transaction.

**tax return** ● **n.** a form on which a taxpayer makes a statement of income and personal circumstances, used to assess liability for tax.

**tax shelter** • n. a financial arrangement made to avoid or minimize taxes.

**tax year** • n. a year as reckoned for taxation (in Britain from 6 April).

**tayberry** • n. (pl. **-ies**) a dark red soft fruit produced by crossing a blackberry and a raspberry.
– ORIGIN named after the River *Tay* in Scotland, near where it was introduced in 1977.

**Tay–Sachs disease** /teɪˈsaks/ • n. an inherited metabolic disorder in which certain lipids accumulate in the brain, causing spasticity and death in childhood.
– ORIGIN C20: from the names of Engl. ophthalmologist Warren *Tay* and Amer. neurologist Bernard *Sachs*.

**tazza** /ˈtɑːtsə/ • n. a saucer-shaped cup mounted on a pedestal.
– ORIGIN C19: from Ital., from Arab. *ṭasa* (see **TASS**).

**TB** • abbrev. **1** (also **Tb**) terabyte(s). **2** tubercle bacillus; tuberculosis.

**Tb** • symb. the chemical element terbium.

**t.b.a.** • abbrev. to be announced.

**T-bar** • n. **1** a beam or bar shaped like the letter T. **2** a type of ski lift in the form of a series of inverted T-shaped bars for towing two skiers at a time uphill.

**T-bone** • n. a large choice piece of loin steak containing a T-shaped bone.

**tbsp** (also **tbs**) (pl. same or **tbsps**) • abbrev. tablespoonful.

**Tc** • symb. the chemical element technetium.

**TCD** • abbrev. Trinity College, Dublin.

**TCDD** • abbrev. tetrachlorodibenzoparadioxin, fuller name of the chemical dioxin.

**T-cell** • n. another term for **T-LYMPHOCYTE**.

**tchagra** /ˈtʃagrə/ • n. an African shrike that feeds mainly on the ground, typically having a brown back and black eyestripe. [Genus *Tchagra*: several species.]
– ORIGIN mod. L., perh. imitative.

**tchotchke** /ˈtʃɒtʃkə/ (also **tsatske**) • n. **1** N. Amer. informal a trinket. **2** US informal a pretty girl or woman.
– ORIGIN 1960s: Yiddish.

**TCP** • n. Brit. trademark a germicidal solution containing various phenols and sodium salicylate.
– ORIGIN 1930s: abbrev. of *trichlorophenyl*, part of the chemical name of one of the ingredients.

**TCP/IP** • abbrev. Computing, trademark transmission control protocol/Internet protocol, used to govern the connection of computer systems to the Internet.

**TD** • abbrev. **1** (in the Republic of Ireland) Teachta Dála, Member of the Dáil. **2** technical drawing. **3** (in the UK) Territorial (Officer's) Decoration. **4** American Football touchdown.

**Te** • symb. the chemical element tellurium.

**te** (N. Amer. **ti**) • n. (in tonic sol-fa) the seventh note of a major scale. ➤ the note B in the fixed-doh system.
– ORIGIN C19: alt. of **SI**, adopted to avoid having two notes (*soh* and *si*) beginning with the same letter.

**tea** • n. **1** a hot drink made by infusing the dried, crushed leaves of the tea plant in boiling water. ➤ the dried leaves used to make tea. ➤ a similar drink made from the leaves, fruits, or flowers of other plants. **2** the evergreen shrub or small tree which produces these leaves, native to south and east Asia. [*Camellia sinensis*.] **3** chiefly Brit. a light afternoon meal consisting of sandwiches, cakes, etc., with tea to drink. ➤ Brit. a cooked evening meal.
– ORIGIN C17: prob. via Malay from Chin. (Min dial.) *te*, rel. to Mandarin *chá*; cf. **CHAR**[3].

**tea bag** • n. a small porous sachet containing tea leaves, on to which boiling water is poured in order to make tea.

**tea ball** • n. a hollow ball of perforated metal to hold tea leaves, over which boiling water is poured to make tea.

**tea bread** • n. a type of cake containing dried fruit that has been soaked in tea before baking.

**tea break** • n. Brit. a short rest period during the working day.

**teacake** • n. Brit. a light yeast-based sweet bun containing dried fruit, typically served toasted and buttered.

**tea ceremony** • n. an elaborate Japanese ritual of serving and drinking tea, as an expression of Zen Buddhist philosophy.

**teach** • v. (past and past part. **taught**) **1** impart knowledge to or instruct (someone) in how to do something, especially in a school or as part of a recognized programme. ➤ give instruction in (a subject or skill). ➤ cause to learn by example or experience. **2** advocate as a practice or principle.
– DERIVATIVES **teachability** n. **teachable** adj. **teachableness** n. **teaching** n.
– ORIGIN OE *tǣcan* 'show, present, point out', of Gmc origin.

**teacher** • n. a person who teaches in a school.
– DERIVATIVES **teacherly** adj.

**teacherage** /ˈtiːtʃərɪdʒ/ • n. N. Amer. a house or lodgings provided for a teacher by a school.

**tea chest** • n. a light metal-lined wooden box in which tea is transported.

**teaching fellow** • n. Brit. a university fellow who carries out teaching duties.

**teaching hospital** • n. a hospital affiliated to a medical school, in which medical students receive training.

**Teachta Dála** /ˌtjɒxtə ˈdɔːlə, Irish ˌtʲaxtə ˈdɑːlə/ (abbrev.: **TD**) • n. (pl. **Teachti** /-ti/) (in the Republic of Ireland) a member of the Dáil or lower House of Parliament.
– ORIGIN from Ir.

**tea cloth** • n. a tea towel.

**tea cosy** • n. a thick or padded cover placed over a teapot to keep the tea hot.

**teacup** • n. a cup from which tea is drunk.
– DERIVATIVES **teacupful** n. (pl. **-fuls**).

**tea dance** • n. a dance held in the afternoon.

**tea garden** • n. **1** a garden in which tea and other refreshments are served to the public. **2** a tea plantation.

**teak** • n. **1** hard durable wood used in shipbuilding and for making furniture. **2** the large deciduous tree native to India and SE Asia which yields this wood. [*Tectona grandis*.]
– ORIGIN C17: from Port. *teca*, from Tamil and Malayalam *tēkku*.

**teal** • n. (pl. same or **teals**) **1** a small freshwater duck, typically with a blue-green speculum. [*Anas crecca* and related species.] **2** (also **teal blue**) a dark greenish-blue colour.
– ORIGIN ME: of unknown origin.

**tea lady** • n. Brit. a woman employed to make and serve tea in a workplace.

**tea leaf** • n. **1** (**tea leaves**) dried leaves of tea. **2** Brit. rhyming slang a thief.

**team** • n. [treated as sing. or pl.] **1** a group of players forming one side in a competitive game or sport. **2** two or more people working together. ➤ two or more horses in harness together to pull a vehicle. • v. **1** (**team up**) come together as a team to achieve a common goal. **2** (usu. **team something with**) match or coordinate one thing with (another). **3** harness (horses) together to pull a vehicle.
– ORIGIN OE *tēam* 'team of draught animals', of Gmc origin; rel. to **TEEM**[1] and **TOW**[1].

**teammate** • n. a fellow member of a team.

**team ministry** • n. a group of clergy of incumbent status who minister jointly to several parishes under the leadership of a rector or vicar.

**team player** • n. a person who plays or works well as a member of a team.

**team spirit** • n. feelings of camaraderie among the members of a team.

**teamster** • n. **1** N. Amer. a truck driver. **2** a driver of a team of animals.

**teamwork** • n. the combined effective action of a group.

**teapot** • n. a pot with a handle, spout, and lid, in which tea is prepared.

**teapoy** /ˈtiːpɔɪ/ • n. a small three-legged table or stand, especially one that holds a tea caddy.
– ORIGIN C19: from Hindi *tī-* 'three' + Urdu and Pers. *pāī* 'foot', the sense and spelling influenced by **TEA**.

**tear**[1] /tɛː/ • **v.** (past **tore**; past part. **torn**) **1** pull or rip apart or to pieces. ➤rip a hole or split in. ➤damage (a muscle or ligament) by overstretching it. ➤(**tear something down**) demolish or destroy something. **2** disrupt and force apart (people). ➤(**be torn**) be in a state of conflict and uncertainty between two opposing options or parties. **3** (**tear oneself away**) leave despite a strong desire to stay. **4** informal move very quickly and in a reckless or excited manner. **5** (**tear into**) attack verbally. • **n.** a hole or split caused by tearing.
– PHRASES **tear one's hair out** informal feel extreme desperation. **tear someone off a strip** (or **tear a strip off someone**) Brit. informal rebuke someone angrily. **that's torn it** Brit. informal expressing dismay when something has happened to disrupt someone's plans.
– DERIVATIVES **tearable** adj. **tearer** n.
– ORIGIN OE *teran*, of Gmc origin.

**tear**[2] /tɪə/ • **n.** a drop of clear salty liquid secreted from glands in a person's eye when they are crying or when the eye is irritated.
– PHRASES **in tears** crying.
– DERIVATIVES **teary** adj.
– ORIGIN OE *tēar*, of Gmc origin.

**tearaway** • **n.** Brit. a person who behaves in a wild or reckless manner.

**teardrop** • **n. 1** a single tear. **2** [as modifier] shaped like a tear: *teardrop handles*.

**tear duct** • **n.** a passage through which tears pass from the lachrymal glands to the eye or from the eye to the nose.

**tearful** • **adj. 1** crying or inclined to cry. **2** sad.
– DERIVATIVES **tearfully** adv. **tearfulness** n.

**tear gas** • **n.** gas that causes severe irritation to the eyes, used in warfare and riot control. • **v.** (**tear-gas**) attack with tear gas.

**tearing** /'tɛːrɪŋ/ • **adj.** violent; extreme: *a tearing hurry*.

**tear jerker** • **n.** informal a story, film, or song that is calculated to evoke sadness or sympathy.
– DERIVATIVES **tear-jerking** adj.

**tearless** • **adj.** not crying.
– DERIVATIVES **tearlessly** adv. **tearlessness** n.

**tea room** • **n. 1** a small restaurant or cafe where tea and other light refreshments are served. **2** N. Amer. informal a public toilet used as a meeting place by homosexuals.

**tea rose** • **n.** a garden rose with flowers that are typically pale yellow with a pink tinge and have a delicate scent resembling that of tea. [Cultivars of the Chinese hybrid *Rosa* × *odorata*.]

**tear sheet** • **n.** a page that can be removed from a magazine, book, etc. for use separately.

**tease** • **v. 1** playfully make fun of or attempt to provoke. ➤tempt sexually. **2** gently pull or comb (tangled wool, hair, etc.) into separate strands. ➤chiefly N. Amer. backcomb (hair) in order to make it appear fuller. ➤archaic comb (the surface of woven cloth) to raise a nap. **3** (**tease something out**) find something out by searching through a mass of information. • **n.** informal **1** an act of teasing. **2** a person who teases. ➤a person who teases someone sexually with no intention of satisfying the desire aroused.
– DERIVATIVES **teasing** adj. & n. **teasingly** adv.
– ORIGIN OE *tǣsan*, of W. Gmc origin; rel. to **TEASEL**.

**teasel** (also **teazle** or **teazel**) • **n. 1** a tall prickly plant with spiny purple flower heads. [Genus *Dipsacus*: several species.] **2** a dried head from a teasel, or a similar man-made device, used to raise a nap on woven cloth. • **v.** chiefly archaic raise a nap on (cloth) with a teasel.
– DERIVATIVES **teaseling** n.
– ORIGIN OE *tǣsl*, *tǣsel*, of W. Gmc origin; rel. to **TEASE**.

**teaser** • **n. 1** a person who teases others. **2** informal a tricky question or task. **3** a short introductory advertisement for a product, that stimulates interest by remaining cryptic. **4** Fishing a lure or bait trailed behind a boat to attract fish. **5** an inferior stallion or ram used to excite mares or ewes before they are served by the stud animal.

**tea set** /'tiːsɛt/ • **n.** a set of crockery for serving tea.

**Teasmade** • **n.** trademark an automatic tea-maker.

**teaspoon** • **n.** a small spoon used for adding sugar to and stirring hot drinks. ➤(abbrev.: **tsp**) the amount held by such a spoon, in the UK considered to be 5 millilitres when used as a measurement in cookery.
– DERIVATIVES **teaspoonful** n. (pl. **-fuls**).

**teat** • **n. 1** a nipple of the mammary gland of a female mammal. **2** Brit. a perforated plastic bulb by which an infant or young animal can suck milk from a bottle.
– ORIGIN ME: from OFr. *tete*, prob. of Gmc origin.

**teatime** • **n.** chiefly Brit. the time in the afternoon when tea is served.

**tea towel** • **n.** chiefly Brit. a cloth for drying washed crockery, cutlery, and glasses.

**tea tree** • **n. 1** (also **ti tree**) an Australasian flowering shrub or small tree with leaves that are sometimes used for tea. [*Leptospermum scoparium* (manuka) and related species.] **2** (also **Duke of Argyll's tea tree**) an ornamental boxthorn native to the Mediterranean. [*Lycium barbarum*.]

**teazle** (also **teazel**) • **n.** variant spelling of **TEASEL**.

**Tebet** /'tɛbɛt/ (also **Tevet**) • **n.** (in the Jewish calendar) the fourth month of the civil and tenth of the religious year, usually coinciding with parts of December and January.
– ORIGIN from Heb. *ṭēḇēṯ*.

**TEC** • **abbrev.** (in the UK) Training and Enterprise Council.

**tech** (also **tec**) • **n.** informal **1** Brit. a technical college. **2** technology. **3** a technician.

**techie** /'tɛki/ (also **techy**) • **n.** (pl. **-ies**) informal a person who is an expert in technology, especially computing.

**technetium** /tɛk'niːʃɪəm/ • **n.** the chemical element of atomic number 43, an artificially made radioactive metal. (Symbol: **Tc**)
– ORIGIN 1940s: mod. L., from Gk *tekhnētos* 'artificial'.

**technic** /'tɛknɪk/ • **n.** chiefly N. Amer. **1** /also tɛk'niːk/ technique. **2** (**technics**) [treated as sing. or pl.] technical terms, details, and methods; technology.
– DERIVATIVES **technicist** n.
– ORIGIN C17 (as adj. in the sense 'to do with art'): from L. *technicus*, from Gk *tekhnikos*, from *tekhnē* 'art'.

**technical** • **adj. 1** of or relating to a particular subject, art, or craft, or its techniques. ➤requiring special knowledge to be understood. **2** of, involving, or concerned with applied and industrial sciences. ➤relating to the operation of machines: *a technical fault*. **3** according to a strict application or interpretation of the law or rules. • **n. 1** chiefly N. Amer. a small truck with a machine gun mounted on the back. ➤a gunman who rides in such a truck. **2** short for **TECHNICAL FOUL**.
– DERIVATIVES **technically** adv.

**technical college** • **n.** a college of further education providing courses in applied sciences and other practical subjects.

**technical foul** • **n.** Basketball a foul which does not involve contact between opponents.

**technicality** • **n.** (pl. **-ies**) **1** a small formal detail specified within a set of rules. **2** (**technicalities**) details of theory or practice within a particular field. **3** the use of technical terms or methods.

**technical knockout** • **n.** Boxing the ending of a fight by the referee on the grounds of a contestant's inability to continue, the opponent being declared the winner.

**technical sergeant** • **n.** a rank of non-commissioned officer in the US air force, above staff sergeant and below master sergeant.

**technician** • **n. 1** a person employed to look after technical equipment or do practical work in a laboratory. **2** an expert in the practical application of a science. ➤a person skilled in the technique of an art or craft.

**Technicolor** • **n.** trademark **1** a process of colour cinematography using synchronized monochrome films, each of a different colour, to produce a colour print. **2** (**technicolor** or Brit. also **technicolour**) informal vivid colour.
– DERIVATIVES **technicolored** (Brit. also **technicoloured**) adj.
– ORIGIN C20: blend of **TECHNICAL** and **COLOR**.

**technique** • **n.** a way of carrying out a particular task, especially the execution of an artistic work or a scientific procedure. ➤a procedure that is effective in achieving an

aim.
– ORIGIN C19: from Fr., from L. *technicus* (see **TECHNIC**).

**techno** • n. a style of fast, heavy electronic dance music, with few or no vocals.
– ORIGIN 1980s: abbrev. of ***technological*** (see **TECHNOLOGY**).

**techno-** • comb. form relating to technology or its use: *technophobe*.
– ORIGIN from Gk *tekhnē* 'art, craft'.

**technobabble** • n. informal incomprehensible technical jargon.

**technocracy** /tɛk'nɒkrəsi/ • n. (pl. **-ies**) government by an elite of technical experts.
– DERIVATIVES **technocrat** n. **technocratic** adj. **technocratically** adv.

**technology** • n. (pl. **-ies**) the application of scientific knowledge for practical purposes. ➤machinery and equipment based on such knowledge. ➤the branch of knowledge concerned with applied sciences.
– DERIVATIVES **technological** adj. **technologically** adv. **technologist** n.
– ORIGIN C17: from Gk *tekhnologia* 'systematic treatment', from *tekhnē* 'art, craft' + *-logia* (see **-LOGY**).

**technology transfer** • n. the transfer of new technology from the originator to a secondary user.

**technophile** • n. a person who is enthusiastic about new technology.
– DERIVATIVES **technophilia** n. **technophilic** adj.

**technophobe** • n. a person who fears or dislikes new technology.
– DERIVATIVES **technophobia** n. **technophobic** adj.

**technospeak** • n. technobabble.

**techy** • n. variant spelling of **TECHIE**.

**tectonic** /tɛk'tɒnɪk/ • adj. **1** Geology of or relating to the structure of the earth's crust and the large-scale processes which take place within it. **2** of or relating to building or construction.
– DERIVATIVES **tectonically** adv.
– ORIGIN C17: via late L. from Gk *tektonikos*, from *tektōn* 'carpenter, builder'.

**tectonics** • pl. n. [treated as sing. or pl.] Geology large-scale processes affecting the structure of the earth's crust.

**tectonophysics** /tɛk,tɒnə(ʊ)'fɪzɪks/ • pl. n. [treated as sing.] the branch of geophysics concerned with the forces that cause movement and deformation in the earth's crust.
– ORIGIN 1950s: from **TECTONICS** + **PHYSICS**.

**tectorial** /tɛk'tɔːrɪəl/ • adj. Anatomy forming a covering. ➤denoting the membrane covering the organ of Corti in the inner ear.
– ORIGIN C19: from L. *tectorium* 'covering, a cover' + **-AL**.

**tectrices** /'tɛktrɪsiːz, tɛk'trʌɪsiːz/ • pl. n. (sing. **tectrix** /-trɪks/) Ornithology the coverts of a bird.
– ORIGIN C19: mod. L., from L. *tect-*, *tegere* 'cover'.

**ted** • v. (**tedded**, **tedding**) turn over and spread out (grass, hay, or straw) to dry or for bedding.
– DERIVATIVES **tedder** n. **tedding** n.
– ORIGIN ME: from ON *tethja* 'spread manure' (past tense *tadda*), rel. to *tad* 'dung'.

**teddy** • n. (pl. **-ies**) **1** (also **teddy bear**) a soft toy bear. **2** a woman's all-in-one undergarment.
– ORIGIN C20: from *Teddy*, familiar form of the given name *Theodore*: in sense 1 alluding to the US President *Theodore* Roosevelt (1858–1919), an enthusiastic bear-hunter.

**Teddy boy** • n. Brit. (in the 1950s) a young man of a subculture characterized by a style of dress based on Edwardian fashion, hair slicked up in a quiff, and a liking for rock-and-roll music.
– ORIGIN from *Teddy*, familiar form of the given name *Edward* (with ref. to the style of dress).

**Te Deum** /tiː 'diːəm, teɪ 'deɪəm/ • n. a hymn beginning *Te Deum laudamus*, 'We praise Thee, O God', sung at matins or on special occasions such as a thanksgiving.
– ORIGIN from L.

**tedious** • adj. too long, slow, or dull.
– DERIVATIVES **tediously** adv. **tediousness** n.
– ORIGIN ME: from OFr. *tedieus* or late L. *taediosus*, from L. *taedium* (see **TEDIUM**).

**tedium** • n. the state of being tedious.
– ORIGIN C17: from L. *taedium*, from *taedere* 'be weary of'.

**tee**[1] • n. **1** a cleared space on a golf course, from which the ball is struck at the beginning of play for each hole. **2** a small peg with a concave head which is placed in the ground to support a golf ball before it is struck from a tee. **3** a mark aimed at in bowls, quoits, curling, and other similar games. • v. (**tees**, **teed**, **teeing**) Golf **1** (usu. **tee up**) place the ball on a tee ready to make the first stroke of the round or hole. **2** (**tee off**) begin a round or hole of golf by playing the ball from a tee.
– ORIGIN C17 (orig. Scots, as *teaz*): of unknown origin.

**tee**[2] • n. informal, chiefly N. Amer. a T-shirt.

**tee-hee** • n. a titter or giggle. • v. (**tee-hees**, **tee-heed**, **tee-heeing**) titter or giggle.
– ORIGIN ME: imitative.

**teem**[1] • v. (**teem with**) be full of or swarming with.
– DERIVATIVES **teeming** adj.
– ORIGIN OE *tēman*, *tīeman*, in senses 'give birth to' and 'be or become pregnant': of Gmc origin.

**teem**[2] • v. (especially of rain) pour down; fall heavily.
– ORIGIN ME: from ON *tœma* 'to empty', from *tómr* 'empty'.

**teen** informal • adj. of or relating to teenagers. • n. a teenager.

**-teen** • suffix forming the names of numerals from 13 to 19: *fourteen*.
– ORIGIN OE, inflected form of **TEN**.

**teenage** • adj. denoting, relating to, or characteristic of a teenager or teenagers.
– DERIVATIVES **teenaged** adj.

**teenager** • n. a person aged between 13 and 19 years.

**teens** • pl. n. the years of a person's age from 13 to 19.
– ORIGIN C17: pl. of *teen*, independent usage of **-TEEN**.

**teensy** /'tiːnzi, -si/ • adj. (**-ier**, **-iest**) informal tiny.
– ORIGIN C19 (orig. US dial.): prob. an extension of **TEENY**.

**teeny** • adj. (**-ier**, **-iest**) informal tiny.
– ORIGIN C19: var. of **TINY**.

**teeny-bopper** • n. informal a young teenager who follows the latest fashions in clothes and pop music.
– DERIVATIVES **teeny-bop** adj.

**teeny-weeny** (also **teensy-weensy**) • adj. informal very tiny.

**teepee** • n. variant spelling of **TEPEE**.

**tee shirt** • n. variant spelling of **T-SHIRT**.

**teeter** • v. **1** move or balance unsteadily. **2** (often **teeter between**) waver between different courses.
– ORIGIN C19: var. of dial. *titter*, from ON *titra* 'shake, shiver'.

**teeter-totter** N. Amer. or dialect • n. a see-saw. • v. teeter; waver.
– ORIGIN C19: reduplication of **TEETER** or **TOTTER**.

**teeth** plural form of **TOOTH**.

**teethe** • v. cut one's milk teeth.
– DERIVATIVES **teething** n.
– ORIGIN ME: from **TEETH**.

**teething ring** • n. a small ring for an infant to bite on while teething.

**teething troubles** (also **teething problems**) • pl. n. short-term problems that occur in the early stages of a new project.

**teetotal** • adj. choosing or characterized by abstinence from alcohol.
– DERIVATIVES **teetotalism** n. **teetotaller** n.
– ORIGIN C19: emphatic extension of **TOTAL**, appar. first used by Richard Turner, a worker from Preston, in a speech (1833) urging total abstinence from all alcohol.

**teetotum** /tiː'təʊtəm/ • n. a small spinning top spun with the fingers, especially one with four sides lettered to determine whether the spinner has won or lost.
– ORIGIN C18 (as *T totum*): from *T* (representing *totum*, inscribed on one side of the toy) + L. *totum* 'the whole' (stake).

**teff** /tɛf/ • n. an African cereal cultivated almost exclusively in Ethiopia, used mainly to make flour. [*Eragrostis tef*.]
– ORIGIN C18: from Amharic *ṭēf*.

**tefillin** /tiːˈfɪliːn/ ● **pl. n.** collective term for Jewish phylacteries.
– ORIGIN from Aramaic *tĕpillīn* 'prayers'.

**TEFL** /ˈtɛf(ə)l/ ● **abbrev.** teaching of English as a foreign language.

**Teflon** /ˈtɛflɒn/ ● **n.** **1** trademark for **POLYTETRAFLUOROETHYLENE.** **2** [as modifier] (especially of a politician) having an undamaged reputation, in spite of scandal or misjudgement.
– ORIGIN 1940s: from **TETRA-** + **FLUORO-** + *-on* on the pattern of words such as *nylon* and *rayon*.

**teg** ● **n.** a sheep in its second year.
– ORIGIN C16 (as a contemptuous term for a woman; later applied specifically to a ewe in her second year): perh. rel. to Swed. *tacka* 'ewe'.

**tegmentum** /tɛgˈmɛntəm/ ● **n.** (pl. **tegmenta** /-ə/) Anatomy a region of grey matter in the midbrain.
– DERIVATIVES **tegmental** adj.
– ORIGIN C19: from L., var. of *tegumentum* 'tegument'.

**tegument** /ˈtɛgjʊm(ə)nt/ ● **n.** chiefly Zoology the integument of an organism, especially a parasitic flatworm.
– DERIVATIVES **tegumental** adj. **tegumentary** adj.
– ORIGIN ME: from L. *tegumentum*, from *tegere* 'to cover'.

**tein** /ˈteɪɪn/ ● **n.** (pl. same or **teins**) a monetary unit of Kazakhstan, equal to one hundredth of a tenge.

**Tejano** /tɛˈhɑːnəʊ/ ● **n.** (pl. **-os**) **1** a Mexican-American inhabitant of southern Texas. **2** a style of folk or popular music originating among the Tejanos, featuring accordion and guitar.
– ORIGIN Amer. Sp., alt. of *Texano* 'Texan'.

**tektite** /ˈtɛktʌɪt/ ● **n.** Geology a small black glassy object found in numbers over certain areas of the earth's surface, believed to have been formed as molten debris in meteorite impacts and scattered widely through the air.
– ORIGIN C20: coined in Ger. from Gk *tēktos* 'molten' + **-ITE**[1].

**tel.** (also **Tel.**) ● **abbrev.** telephone.

**telamon** /ˈtɛləmən, -məʊn/ ● **n.** (pl. **telamones** /-ˈməʊniːz/) Architecture a male figure used as a pillar to support an entablature or other structure.
– ORIGIN C17: via L. from Gk *telamōnes*, pl. of *Telamōn*, the name of a mythical hero.

**telangiectasia** /tɛˌlandʒɪɛkˈteɪzɪə/ (also **telangiectasis** /tɛˌlandʒɪˈɛktəsɪs/) ● **n.** Medicine a condition characterized by dilatation of the capillaries, causing them to appear as small red or purple clusters on the skin or the surface of an organ.
– DERIVATIVES **telangiectatic** adj.
– ORIGIN C19: mod. L., from Gk *telos* 'end' + *angeion* 'vessel' + *ektasis* 'dilatation'.

**telco** ● **n.** (pl. **-os**) a telecommunications company.

**tele-** /ˈtɛli/ ● **comb. form** **1** to or at a distance: *telekinesis*. ➤ used in names of instruments for operating over long distances: *telemeter*. **2** relating to television: *telecine*. **3** done by means of the telephone: *telemarketing*.
– ORIGIN from Gk *tēle-* 'far off'.

**telebanking** ● **n.** a method of banking in which the customer conducts transactions by telephone.

**telecast** ● **n.** a television broadcast. ● **v.** (usu. **be telecast**) transmit by television.
– DERIVATIVES **telecaster** n.

**telecentre** ● **n.** another term for **TELECOTTAGE**.

**telecine** /ˈtɛlɪˌsɪni/ ● **n.** the broadcasting of cinema film on television.

**telecommunication** ● **n.** communication over a distance by cable, telegraph, telephone, or broadcasting. ➤ (**telecommunications**) [treated as sing.] the branch of technology concerned with this.

**telecommute** ● **v.** work from home, communicating with a central workplace using equipment such as telephones, fax machines, and modems.
– DERIVATIVES **telecommuter** n. **telecommuting** n.

**telecomputer** ● **n.** a device which combines the capabilities of a computer with those of a television and a telephone.
– DERIVATIVES **telecomputing** n.

**telecoms** (also **telecomms**) ● **pl. n.** [treated as sing.] telecommunications.

**teleconference** ● **n.** a conference with participants in different locations linked by telecommunication devices.
– DERIVATIVES **teleconferencing** n.

**teleconverter** ● **n.** Photography a lens designed to be fitted in front of a standard lens to increase its effective focal length.

**telecottage** ● **n.** a place, especially in a rural area, where computer equipment is available for communal use.

**tele-evangelist** ● **n.** variant of **TELEVANGELIST**.

**telefilm** ● **n.** a film made for or broadcast on television.

**telegenic** /ˌtɛlɪˈdʒɛnɪk/ ● **adj.** having an appearance or manner that is attractive on television.
– ORIGIN 1930s (orig. US): from **TELE-** + **-GENIC**, on the pattern of *photogenic*.

**telegram** ● **n.** a message sent by telegraph and delivered in written or printed form, used in the UK only for international messages since 1981.

**telegraph** ● **n.** **1** a system or device for transmitting messages from a distance along a wire, especially one creating signals by making and breaking an electrical connection. **2** (also **telegraph board**) a board displaying scores or other information at a sports match or race meeting. ● **v.** send (someone) a message by telegraph. ➤ send (a message) by telegraph.
– DERIVATIVES **telegrapher** /ˈtɛlɪˌgrɑːfə, tɪˈlɛgrəfə/ n. **telegraphist** /tɪˈlɛgrəfɪst/ n. **telegraphy** /tɪˈlɛgrəfi/ n.

**telegraphese** ● **n.** informal the terse, abbreviated style of language used in telegrams.

**telegraphic** ● **adj.** **1** of or by telegraphs or telegrams. **2** (of language) omitting inessential words; concise.
– DERIVATIVES **telegraphically** adv.

**telegraph key** ● **n.** a button which is pressed to produce a signal when transmitting Morse code.

**telegraph plant** ● **n.** a tropical Asian leguminous plant whose leaves have a spontaneous jerking motion. [*Codariocalyx motorius*.]

**telegraph pole** ● **n.** a tall pole used to carry telegraph or telephone wires above the ground.

**Telegu** /ˈtɛlɪguː/ ● **n.** variant spelling of **TELUGU**.

**telekinesis** /ˌtɛlɪkʌɪˈniːsɪs, -kɪˈniːsɪs/ ● **n.** the supposed ability to move objects at a distance by mental power or other non-physical means.
– DERIVATIVES **telekinetic** adj.
– ORIGIN C19: from **TELE-** + Gk *kinēsis* 'motion'.

**telemark** Skiing ● **n.** a turn with the outer ski advanced and the knee bent, performed on skis to which only the toe of each boot is fixed. ● **v.** perform such a turn.
– ORIGIN C20: named after *Telemark*, a district in Norway, where it originated.

**telemarketing** ● **n.** the marketing of goods or services by telephone calls to potential customers.
– DERIVATIVES **telemarketer** n.

**telematics** ● **pl. n.** [treated as sing.] the branch of information technology which deals with the long-distance transmission of computerized information.
– DERIVATIVES **telematic** adj.
– ORIGIN 1970s: blend of **TELECOMMUNICATION** and **INFORMATICS**.

**telemedicine** ● **n.** the remote diagnosis and treatment of patients by means of telecommunications technology.

**telemessage** ● **n.** a message sent by telephone or telex and delivered in written form, which replaced the telegram for inland messages in the UK in 1981.

**telemeter** /ˈtɛlɪmiːtə, tɪˈlɛmɪtə/ ● **n.** an apparatus for recording the readings of an instrument and transmitting them by radio. ● **v.** transmit (readings) to a distant receiving set or station.
– DERIVATIVES **telemetric** adj. **telemetry** n.

**telencephalon** /ˌtɛlɛnˈsɛf(ə)lɒn, -ˈkɛf-, ˌtiːlɛnˈsɛf(ə)lɒn, -ˈkɛf-/ ● **n.** Anatomy the most highly developed and anterior part of the forebrain, consisting chiefly of the cerebral hemispheres. Compare with **DIENCEPHALON**.
– ORIGIN C19: from **TELE-** + **ENCEPHALON**.

**telenovela** /ˈtɛlɪnəʊˌvɛlə/ ● **n.** (in Latin America) a tele-

vision soap opera.
– ORIGIN from Sp.

**teleology** /ˌtɛlɪˈɒlədʒi, ˌtiːl-/ • **n.** (pl. **-ies**) **1** Philosophy the explanation of phenomena by the purpose they serve rather than by postulated causes. **2** Theology the doctrine of design and purpose in the material world.
– DERIVATIVES **teleologic** adj. **teleological** adj. **teleologically** adv. **teleologism** n. **teleologist** n.
– ORIGIN C18: from mod. L. *teleologia*, from Gk *telos* 'end' + *-logia* (see **-LOGY**).

**teleost** /ˈtɛlɪɒst, ˈtiːl-/ • **n.** Zoology a fish of a large group (division Teleostei) that comprises most bony fishes (apart from sturgeons, lungfishes, and some other kinds).
– ORIGIN C19: from Gk *teleos* 'complete' + *osteon* 'bone'.

**telepathy** • **n.** the supposed communication of thoughts or ideas by means other than the known senses.
– DERIVATIVES **telepath** n. **telepathic** adj. **telepathically** adv. **telepathist** n. **telepathize** (also **-ise**) v.

**telephone** • **n. 1** a system for transmitting voices over a distance using wire or radio, by converting acoustic vibrations to electrical signals. **2** an instrument used as part of such a system, typically including a handset with a transmitting microphone and a set of numbered buttons by which a connection can be made to another such instrument. • **v.** ring or speak to (someone) using the telephone. ➤make a telephone call.
– DERIVATIVES **telephoner** n. **telephonic** adj. **telephonically** adv.

**telephone box** • **n.** chiefly Brit. a public booth or enclosure housing a payphone.

**telephone directory** • **n.** a book listing the names, addresses, and telephone numbers of the people in a particular area.

**telephone exchange** • **n.** a set of equipment that connects telephone lines during a call.

**telephone number** • **n. 1** a number assigned to a particular telephone and used in making connections to it. **2** (**telephone numbers**) informal a large sum of money.

**telephonist** • **n.** Brit. an operator of a telephone switchboard.

**telephony** /tɪˈlɛf(ə)ni/ • **n.** the working or use of telephones.

**telephoto lens** • **n.** a lens with a longer focal length than standard, giving a narrow field of view and a magnified image.

**teleport** • **n.** a centre providing interconnections between different forms of telecommunications, especially one which links satellites to ground-based communications. • **v.** (especially in science fiction) transport or be transported across space and distance instantly.
– DERIVATIVES **teleportation** n.
– ORIGIN 1950s: back-form. from *teleportation* (1930s), from **TELE-** + a shortened form of *transportation*.

**telepresence** • **n.** the use of virtual reality technology, especially for remote control of machinery or for apparent participation in distant events.

**teleprinter** • **n.** Brit. a device for transmitting telegraph messages as they are keyed, and for printing messages received.

**teleprompter** • **n.** North American term for **AUTOCUE**.

**telerecord** • **v.** record (a television programme) during transmission.
– DERIVATIVES **telerecording** n.

**telesales** • **pl. n.** the selling of goods or services over the telephone.

**telescope** • **n.** an optical instrument designed to make distant objects appear nearer, containing an arrangement of lenses, or of curved mirrors and lenses, by which rays of light are collected and focused and the resulting image magnified. • **v. 1** (with reference to an object made of concentric tubular parts) slide or cause to slide into itself, so that it becomes smaller. ➤crush (a vehicle) by the force of an impact. **2** condense or conflate so as to occupy less space or time.
– DERIVATIVES **telescopic** adj. **telescopically** adv.

**teleshopping** • **n.** the ordering of goods by customers using a telephone or direct computer link.

**telesoftware** • **n.** Brit. software transmitted or broadcast via a network or television system.

**teletex** • **n.** trademark an enhanced version of telex.
– ORIGIN 1970s: prob. a blend of **TELEX** and **TEXT**.

**teletext** • **n.** a news and information service transmitted to televisions with appropriate receivers.

**telethon** • **n.** a very long television programme, typically one broadcast to raise money for a charity.
– ORIGIN 1940s (orig. US): from **TELE-** + *-thon* on the pattern of *marathon*.

**teletype** • **n.** trademark a kind of teleprinter. ➤a message received and printed by a teleprinter. • **v.** send (a message) by means of a teleprinter.

**teletypewriter** • **n.** chiefly US a teleprinter.

**televangelist** (also **tele-evangelist**) • **n.** chiefly N. Amer. an evangelical preacher who appears regularly on television.
– DERIVATIVES **televangelical** adj. **televangelism** n.

**televise** • **v.** record for or transmit by television.
– DERIVATIVES **televisable** adj. **televised** adj.
– ORIGIN 1920s: back-form. from **TELEVISION**.

**television** • **n. 1** a system for converting visual images (with sound) into electrical signals, transmitting them by radio or other means, and displaying them electronically on a screen. **2** the activity, profession, or medium of broadcasting on television. **3** (also **television set**) a device with a screen for receiving television signals.

**television tube** • **n.** another term for **PICTURE TUBE**.

**televisual** • **adj.** relating to or suitable for television.
– DERIVATIVES **televisually** adv.

**telework** • **v.** another term for **TELECOMMUTE**.
– DERIVATIVES **teleworker** n.

**telex** • **n. 1** an international system of telegraphy with printed messages transmitted and received by teleprinters using the public telecommunications network. **2** a device used for this. **3** a message sent by this system. • **v.** communicate with by telex. ➤send (a message) by telex.
– ORIGIN 1930s: blend of **TELEPRINTER** and **EXCHANGE**.

**telic** /ˈtɛlɪk/ • **adj. 1** (of an action or attitude) directed to a definite end. **2** Linguistics (of a verb, conjunction, or clause) expressing purpose.
– DERIVATIVES **telicity** n.
– ORIGIN C19: from Gk *telikos* 'final', from *telos* 'end'.

**tell**[1] • **v.** (past and past part. **told**) **1** communicate information to. ➤instruct (someone) to do something. ➤relate (a story). ➤reveal (information) in a non-verbal way: *the figures tell a different story.* ➤divulge confidential information. ➤(**tell on**) informal inform on. ➤(**tell someone off**) informal reprimand someone. **2** determine correctly or with certainty. ➤perceive (a distinction). **3** (often **tell on**) (of an experience or period of time) have a noticeable effect on someone. ➤(of a particular factor) play a part in the success or otherwise of someone or something: *lack of fitness told against him.* **4** chiefly archaic count (the members of a group).
– PHRASES **tell tales** gossip about another person's secrets or faults. **tell the time** (or N. Amer. **tell time**) be able to ascertain the time from reading the face of a clock or watch. **tell someone where to get off** (or **where they get off**) informal angrily dismiss or rebuke someone. **there is no telling** conveying the impossibility of knowing what has happened or will happen. **you're telling me** informal emphasizing that one is already well aware of or in complete agreement with something.
– DERIVATIVES **tellable** adj.
– ORIGIN OE *tellan* 'relate, count, estimate', of Gmc origin; rel. to **TALE**.

**tell**[2] • **n.** Archaeology (in the Middle East) a mound formed by the accumulated remains of ancient settlements.
– ORIGIN C19: from Arab. *tall* 'hillock'.

**teller** • **n. 1** a person who deals with customers' transactions in a bank. **2** a person appointed to count votes. **3** a person who tells something.

**telling** • **adj.** having a striking or revealing effect; significant.
– DERIVATIVES **tellingly** adv.

**telling-off** • **n.** (pl. **tellings-off**) informal a reprimand.

**telltale** ● adj. revealing or betraying something. ● n. **1** a person who tells tales. **2** a device or object that automatically gives a visual indication of the state or presence of something.

**tellurian** /tɛˈljʊərɪən/ formal or poetic/literary ● adj. of or inhabiting the earth. ● n. an inhabitant of the earth.
– ORIGIN C19: from L. *tellus, tellur-* 'earth' + **-IAN**.

**telluric** /tɛˈljʊərɪk/ ● adj. **1** of the earth as a planet. **2** of the soil.
– ORIGIN C19: from L. *tellus, tellur-* 'earth' + **-IC**.

**telluric acid** ● n. Chemistry a crystalline acid made by oxidizing tellurium dioxide.
– DERIVATIVES **tellurate** n.

**tellurite** /ˈtɛljʊrʌɪt/ ● n. Chemistry a salt of the anion $TeO_3^{2-}$.

**tellurium** /tɛˈljʊərɪəm/ ● n. the chemical element of atomic number 52, a brittle silvery-white semimetal resembling selenium. (Symbol: **Te**)
– DERIVATIVES **telluride** /ˈtɛljʊrʌɪd/ n.
– ORIGIN C19: mod. L., from L. *tellus, tellur-* 'earth'.

**telly** ● n. (pl. **-ies**) Brit. informal term for **TELEVISION**.

**telnet** Computing ● n. a network protocol or program that allows a user on one computer to log in to another computer that is part of the same network. ● v. (**telnetted, telnetting**) informal log into a remote computer using a telnet program.
– DERIVATIVES **telnettable** adj.
– ORIGIN 1970s: blend of **TELECOMMUNICATION** and **NETWORK**.

**telomere** /ˈtiːlə(ʊ)mɪə, ˈtɛl-/ ● n. Genetics a compound structure at the end of a chromosome.
– DERIVATIVES **telomeric** adj.
– ORIGIN 1940s: from Gk *telos* 'end' + *meros* 'part'.

**telophase** /ˈtiːlə(ʊ)feɪz, ˈtɛl-/ ● n. Biology the final stage of cell division, between anaphase and interphase, in which the two daughter nuclei are formed.
– ORIGIN C19: from Gk *telos* 'end' + **PHASE**.

**telos** /ˈtɛlɒs/ ● n. (pl. **teloi** /-lɔɪ/) chiefly Philosophy or poetic/literary an ultimate object or aim.
– ORIGIN Gk, lit. 'end'.

**telson** /ˈtɛls(ə)n/ ● n. Zoology the last segment in the abdomen in crustaceans, chelicerates, and embryonic insects.
– ORIGIN C19: from Gk, lit. 'limit'.

**Telugu** /ˈtɛləguː/ (also **Telegu**) ● n. (pl. same or **Telugus**) **1** a member of a people of SE India. **2** the Dravidian language of this people.
– ORIGIN from the name in Telugu, *telungu*.

**temazepam** /təˈmeɪzɪpam, -ˈmazɪ-/ ● n. Medicine a tranquillizing drug of the benzodiazepine group.
– ORIGIN 1970s: from *tem-* (of unknown origin), on the pattern of *oxazepam*.

**temblor** /tɛmˈblɔː/ ● n. US an earthquake.
– ORIGIN C19: from Amer. Sp.

**Tembu** /ˈtɛmbuː/ ● n. (pl. same or **Tembus**) a member of a Xhosa-speaking people originating in present-day KwaZulu/Natal and now living in the Transkei.
– ORIGIN from Xhosa *umtembu*.

**temenos** /ˈtɛmənɒs/ ● n. (pl. **temenoi** /-nɔɪ/) Archaeology a sacred enclosure or precinct surrounding or adjacent to a temple.
– ORIGIN C19: from Gk, from the stem of *temnein* 'cut off'.

**temerarious** /ˌtɛməˈrɛːrɪəs/ ● adj. poetic/literary reckless; rash.

**temerity** /tɪˈmɛrɪti/ ● n. excessive confidence or boldness.
– ORIGIN ME: from L. *temeritas*, from *temere* 'rashly'.

**Temne** /ˈtɛmni/ ● n. (pl. same or **Temnes**) **1** a member of a people of Sierra Leone. **2** the Niger–Congo language of this people, the main language of Sierra Leone.
– ORIGIN the name in Temne.

**temp¹** informal ● n. a temporary employee, typically an office worker who finds employment through an agency. ● v. work as a temp.

**temp²** ● abbrev. temperature.

**temp.** ● abbrev. in or from the time of.
– ORIGIN from L. *tempore*, ablative of *tempus* 'time'.

**tempeh** /ˈtɛmpeɪ/ ● n. an Indonesian dish consisting of deep-fried fermented soya beans.
– ORIGIN from Indonesian *tempe*.

**temper** ● n. **1** a person's state of mind in terms of their being angry or calm. **2** a tendency to become angry easily. ➤ an angry state of mind. **3** the degree of hardness and elasticity in steel or other metal. ● v. **1** improve the temper of (a metal) by reheating and then cooling it. ➤ improve the consistency or resiliency of (a substance) by heating it or adding particular substances to it. **2** (often **be tempered with**) serve as a neutralizing or counterbalancing force to. **3** tune (a piano or other instrument) so as to adjust the note intervals correctly.
– PHRASES **keep** (or **lose**) **one's temper** retain (or fail to retain) composure or restraint when angry.
– DERIVATIVES **temperer** n.
– ORIGIN OE *temprian* 'bring into the required condition by mixing', from L. *temperare* 'mingle, restrain'; the noun orig. denoted a proportionate mixture of elements, also the combination of the four bodily humours, formerly believed to be the basis of temperament.

**tempera** /ˈtɛmp(ə)rə/ ● n. a method of painting with pigments dispersed in an emulsion miscible with water, typically egg yolk. ➤ emulsion used in tempera.
– ORIGIN C19: from Ital., in the phr. *pingere a tempera* 'paint in distemper'.

**temperament** ● n. **1** a person's nature with regard to the effect it has on their behaviour. **2** the adjustment of intervals in tuning a piano or other musical instrument so as to fit the scale for use in different keys. ➤ (**equal temperament**) an adjustment in which the twelve semitones are equal intervals.
– ORIGIN ME (in sense 'blending of elements in due proportions', later 'temperature'): from L. *temperamentum* 'correct mixture', from *temperare* 'mingle'; cf. **TEMPER**.

**temperamental** ● adj. **1** relating to or caused by temperament. **2** liable to unreasonable changes of mood.
– DERIVATIVES **temperamentally** adv.

**temperance** ● n. abstinence from alcoholic drink.
– ORIGIN ME: from Anglo-Norman Fr. *temperaunce*, from L. *temperantia* 'moderation', from *temperare* 'restrain'.

**temperate** ● adj. **1** relating to or denoting a region or climate characterized by mild temperatures. **2** showing moderation or self-restraint.
– DERIVATIVES **temperately** adv. **temperateness** n.
– ORIGIN ME: from L. *temperatus*, *temperare* 'mingle, restrain'.

**temperate zone** ● n. each of the two belts of latitude between the torrid zone and the northern and southern frigid zones.

**temperature** ● n. **1** the degree or intensity of heat present in a substance or object. ➤ informal a body temperature above the normal: *he was running a temperature.* **2** the degree of excitement or tension present in a situation or discussion.
– ORIGIN ME (in sense 'the state of being tempered or mixed', later synonymous with **TEMPERAMENT**): from Fr. *température* or L. *temperatura*, from *temperare* 'restrain'.

**-tempered** ● comb. form having a specified temper or disposition: *ill-tempered.*
– DERIVATIVES **-temperedly** comb. form in corresponding adverbs. **-temperedness** comb. form in corresponding nouns.

**tempest** ● n. a violent windy storm.
– PHRASES **a tempest in a teapot** North American term for ***a storm in a teacup*** (see **STORM**).
– ORIGIN ME: from OFr. *tempeste*, from L. *tempestas* 'season, weather, storm', from *tempus* 'time, season'.

**tempestuous** /tɛmˈpɛstjʊəs/ ● adj. **1** very stormy. **2** characterized by strong and turbulent emotion.
– DERIVATIVES **tempestuously** adv. **tempestuousness** n.

**tempi** plural form of **TEMPO¹**.

**Templar** /ˈtɛmplə/ ● n. historical a member of the Knights Templars, a powerful religious and military order.
– ORIGIN ME: from OFr. *templier*, from med. L. *templarius*, from L. *templum* (see **TEMPLE¹**).

**template** /ˈtɛmplɪt, -pleɪt/ (also **templet**) ● n. **1** a shaped

piece of rigid material used as a pattern for processes such as cutting out, shaping, or drilling. **2** something that serves as a model or example. ➤ Biochemistry a nucleic acid molecule that acts as a pattern for the sequence of assembly of a protein, nucleic acid, or other large molecule. **3** a timber or plate used to distribute the weight in a wall or under a support.
– ORIGIN C17 (as *templet*): prob. from **TEMPLE**[3] + **-ET**[1]; influenced by **PLATE**.

**temple**[1] ● n. a building devoted to the worship of a god or gods. ➤ N. Amer. a synagogue.
– ORIGIN OE *templ*, *tempel*, reinforced in ME by OFr. *temple*, both from L. *templum* 'open or consecrated space'.

**temple**[2] ● n. the flat part either side of the head between the forehead and the ear.
– ORIGIN ME: from OFr., from an alt. of L. *tempora*, pl. of *tempus* 'temple of the head'.

**temple**[3] ● n. a device in a loom for keeping the cloth stretched.
– ORIGIN ME: from OFr., perh. ult. the same word as **TEMPLE**[2].

**temple block** ● n. a percussion instrument consisting of a hollow block of wood which is struck with a stick.

**templet** ● n. variant spelling of **TEMPLATE**.

**tempo** ● n. (pl. **tempos** or **tempi** /-piː/) **1** Music the speed at which a passage of music is played. **2** the pace of an activity or process.
– ORIGIN C17: from Ital., from L. *tempus* 'time'.

**temporal**[1] /'tɛmp(ə)r(ə)l/ ● adj. **1** of or relating to time. **2** relating to worldly affairs; secular.
– DERIVATIVES **temporally** adv.
– ORIGIN ME: from OFr. *temporel* or L. *temporalis*, from *tempus*, *tempor-* 'time'.

**temporal**[2] /'tɛmpər(ə)l/ ● adj. Anatomy of or situated in the temples of the head.

**temporal bone** ● n. Anatomy either of a pair of bones which form part of the side of the skull on each side and enclose the middle and inner ear.

**temporalis** /ˌtɛmpə'reɪlɪs/ ● n. Anatomy a fan-shaped muscle which runs from the side of the skull to the back of the lower jaw.
– ORIGIN C17: from late L.

**temporality** ● n. (pl. **-ies**) **1** the state of existing within or having some relationship with time. **2** (**temporalities**) the properties and revenues of a religious body or a member of the clergy.

**temporal lobe** ● n. each of the paired lobes of the brain lying beneath the temples, including areas concerned with the understanding of speech.

**temporal power** ● n. the power of a bishop or cleric, especially the Pope, in secular matters.

**temporary** ● adj. lasting for only a limited period. ● n. (pl. **-ies**) a person employed on a temporary basis.
– DERIVATIVES **temporarily** adv. **temporariness** n.
– ORIGIN C16: from L. *temporarius*, from *tempus*, *tempor-* 'time'.

**temporary hardness** ● n. the presence in water of mineral salts (chiefly calcium bicarbonate) that are removed by boiling.

**temporize** (also **-ise**) ● v. avoid making a decision or committing oneself in order to gain time.
– DERIVATIVES **temporization** n. **temporizer** n.
– ORIGIN C16: from Fr. *temporiser* 'bide one's time'.

**temporomandibular joint** /ˌtɛmpərəʊman'dɪbjʊlə/ ● n. Anatomy the hinge joint between the temporal bone and the lower jaw.

**tempo rubato** ● n. see **RUBATO**.

**Tempranillo** /ˌtɛmprə'niːjəʊ, -'niːljəʊ/ ● n. a variety of wine grape grown in Spain, used to make Rioja wine.
– ORIGIN named after a village in northern Spain.

**tempt** ● v. **1** entice (someone) to do something against their better judgement. **2** attract; charm. **3** archaic risk provoking (a deity or abstract force).
– PHRASES **tempt fate** (or **providence**) do something that is risky or dangerous.
– DERIVATIVES **temptability** n. **temptable** adj. **tempting** adj. **temptingly** adv.
– ORIGIN ME: from OFr. *tempter* 'to test', from L. *temptare* 'handle, test, try'.

**temptation** ● n. the state or quality of being tempted; a desire to do something. ➤ a tempting thing.

**tempter** ● n. a person or thing that tempts. ➤ (**the Tempter**) the Devil.

**temptress** ● n. a woman who tempts, especially one who is sexually alluring.

**tempura** /'tɛmpʊrə/ ● n. a Japanese dish of fish, shellfish, or vegetables, fried in batter.
– ORIGIN Japanese, prob. from Port. *tempêro* 'seasoning'.

**ten** ● cardinal number equivalent to the product of five and two; one more than nine; 10. (Roman numeral: **x** or **X**.)
– PHRASES **ten out of ten** denoting an excellent performance. **ten to one** very probably.
– DERIVATIVES **tenfold** adj. & adv.
– ORIGIN OE *tēn*, *tīen*, of Gmc origin.

**ten.** ● abbrev. Music tenuto.

**tenable** ● adj. **1** able to be maintained or defended against attack or objection. **2** (of an office, position, etc.) able to be held or used: *a scholarship tenable for three years.*
– DERIVATIVES **tenability** n.
– ORIGIN C16: from Fr., from *tenir* 'to hold'.

**tenace** /'tɛnəs/ ● n. (in bridge, whist, etc.) a pair of cards in one hand which rank immediately above and below a card held by an opponent.
– ORIGIN C17: from Fr., from Sp. *tenaza*, lit. 'pincers'.

**tenacious** /tɪ'neɪʃəs/ ● adj. not readily relinquishing something; keeping a firm hold.
– DERIVATIVES **tenaciously** adv. **tenaciousness** n. **tenacity** /tɪ'nasɪti/ n.
– ORIGIN C17: from L. *tenax*, *tenac-* (from *tenere* 'to hold') + **-IOUS**.

**tenaculum** /tɪ'nakjʊləm/ ● n. (pl. **tenacula** /-lə/) a sharp hook used by a surgeon for picking up the ends of arteries and other small pieces of tissue.
– ORIGIN C17: from L., lit. 'holder, holding instrument'.

**tenancy** ● n. (pl. **-ies**) possession of land or property as a tenant.

**tenant** ● n. a person occupying rented land or property. ➤ Law a person holding real property by private ownership. ● v. (usu. **be tenanted**) occupy (property) as a tenant.
– DERIVATIVES **tenantable** adj. (formal). **tenantless** adj.
– ORIGIN ME: from OFr., lit. 'holding', pres. part. of *tenir*, from L. *tenere*.

**tenant at will** ● n. (pl. **tenants at will**) Law a tenant that can be evicted without notice.

**tenant farmer** ● n. a person who farms rented land.

**tenantry** ● n. **1** [treated as sing. or pl.] the tenants of an estate. **2** tenancy.

**tench** ● n. (pl. same) a freshwater fish of the carp family, popular with anglers. [*Tinca tinca.*]
– ORIGIN ME: from OFr. *tenche*, from late L. *tinca*.

**Ten Commandments** ● pl. n. (in the Bible) the divine rules of conduct given by God to Moses on Mount Sinai, according to Exod. 20:1–17.

**tend**[1] ● v. **1** frequently behave in a particular way or have a certain characteristic: *written language tends to be formal.* ➤ (**tend to/towards**) be liable to possess (a particular characteristic). **2** go or move in a particular direction.
– ORIGIN ME: from OFr. *tendre* 'stretch, tend', from L. *tendere*.

**tend**[2] ● v. **1** care for or look after. ➤ archaic wait on as an attendant or servant. **2** US direct or manage.
– DERIVATIVES **tendance** n. (archaic).
– ORIGIN ME: shortening of **ATTEND**.

**tendency** ● n. (pl. **-ies**) **1** an inclination towards a particular characteristic or type of behaviour. **2** a group within a larger political party or movement.

**tendentious** /tɛn'dɛnʃəs/ ● adj. calculated to promote a particular cause or point of view.
– DERIVATIVES **tendentiously** adv. **tendentiousness** n.
– ORIGIN C20: suggested by Ger. *tendenziös*.

**tender**[1] ● adj. (**-er**, **-est**) **1** gentle and sympathetic.

➤ (**tender of**) archaic solicitous of. **2** (of food) easy to cut or chew. **3** (of a part of the body) sensitive. **4** young and vulnerable: *the tender age of five.* **5** requiring tact or careful handling. **6** Nautical (of a ship) leaning or inclined to roll in response to the wind.
– PHRASES **tender mercies** ironic attention or treatment not in the best interests of its recipients.
– DERIVATIVES **tenderly** adv. **tenderness** n.
– ORIGIN ME: from OFr. *tendre*, from L. *tener* 'tender, delicate'.

**tender²** ● v. **1** offer or present formally. ➤ make a formal written offer to carry out work, supply goods, etc. for a stated fixed price. **2** offer as payment. ● n. a tendered offer.
– PHRASES **put something out to tender** seek tenders to carry out work, supply goods, etc.
– DERIVATIVES **tenderer** n.
– ORIGIN C16: from OFr. *tendre*, from L. *tendere* (see **TEND¹**).

**tender³** ● n. **1** a vehicle used by a fire service or the armed forces for carrying supplies or fulfilling a specified role. **2** a boat used to ferry people and supplies to and from a ship. **3** a truck closely coupled to a steam locomotive to carry fuel and water. **4** a person who looks after a machine, place, or other people.
– ORIGIN ME (in the sense 'attendant, nurse'): from **TEND²** or shortening of *attender* (see **ATTEND**).

**tenderfoot** ● n. (pl. **tenderfoots** or **tenderfeet**) **1** chiefly N. Amer. a newcomer or novice. **2** dated a newly enrolled member of the Scout or Guide movement.

**tender-hearted** ● adj. having a kind, gentle, or sentimental nature.
– DERIVATIVES **tender-heartedness** n.

**tenderize** (also **-ise**) ● v. make (meat) more tender by beating or slow cooking.
– DERIVATIVES **tenderizer** n.

**tenderloin** ● n. **1** the tenderest part of a loin of beef, pork, etc., taken from under the short ribs in the hindquarters. ➤ US the undercut of a sirloin. **2** N. Amer. informal a district of a city where vice and corruption are prominent. [C19: orig. a term applied to a district of New York, seen as a 'choice' assignment by police because of the bribes offered to them to turn a blind eye.]

**tender-minded** ● adj. sensitive.
– DERIVATIVES **tender-mindedness** n.

**tendinitis** /ˌtɛndɪˈnʌɪtəs/ (also **tendonitis** /ˌtɛndə-/) ● n. inflammation of a tendon.

**tendon** /ˈtɛndən/ ● n. a flexible but inelastic cord of strong fibrous tissue attaching a muscle to a bone. ➤ the hamstring of a quadruped.
– DERIVATIVES **tendinous** adj.
– ORIGIN ME: from Fr. or med. L. *tendo(n-)*, translating Gk *tenōn* 'sinew', from *teinein* 'to stretch'.

**tendresse** /tɒ̃ˈdrɛs/ (also **tendre** /ˈtɒ̃dr(ə)/) ● n. a feeling of fondness or love.
– ORIGIN from Fr.

**tendril** ● n. **1** a slender thread-like appendage of a climbing plant, which stretches out and twines round any suitable support. **2** a slender ringlet of hair.
– ORIGIN C16: prob. a dimin. of OFr. *tendron* 'young shoot', from L. *tener* 'tender'.

**tendu** /tɒ̃ˈd(j)uː/ ● adj. [postpos.] Ballet (of a position) stretched out or held tautly.
– ORIGIN from Fr.

**tendu leaf** /teɪnˈduː/ ● n. the leaves of an ebony tree, gathered in India as a cheap tobacco substitute.
– ORIGIN Hindi *tendu*.

**Tenebrae** /ˈtɛnɪbriː, -breɪ/ ● pl. n. historical (in the Roman Catholic Church) matins and lauds for the last three days of Holy Week, at which candles were successively extinguished.
– ORIGIN L., lit. 'darkness'.

**tenebrous** /ˈtɛnɪbrəs/ ● adj. poetic/literary dark; shadowy.
– ORIGIN ME: via OFr. from L. *tenebrosus*, from *tenebrae* 'darkness'.

**tenement** /ˈtɛnəm(ə)nt/ ● n. **1** (especially in Scotland or the US) a separate residence within a house or block of flats. ➤ (also **tenement house**) a house divided into several separate residences. **2** a piece of land held by an owner. ➤ Law any permanent property, e.g. lands or rents, held from a superior.
– ORIGIN ME: via OFr. from med. L. *tenementum*, from *tenere* 'to hold'.

**tenesmus** /tɪˈnɛzməs/ ● n. Medicine a continual inclination to evacuate the bowels.
– ORIGIN C16: via med. L. from Gk *teinesmos* 'straining'.

**tenet** /ˈtɛnɪt, ˈtiːnɛt/ ● n. a principle or belief.
– ORIGIN C16 (superseding earlier *tenent*): from L., lit. 'he holds', from *tenere*.

**ten-gallon hat** ● n. a large, broad-brimmed hat, traditionally worn by cowboys.

**tenge** /ˈtɛŋgeɪ/ ● n. (pl. same or **tenges**) **1** the basic monetary unit of Kazakhstan, equal to 100 teins. **2** a monetary unit of Turkmenistan, equal to one hundredth of a manat.

**tenia** ● n. US spelling of **TAENIA**.

**Tenn.** ● abbrev. Tennessee.

**tenné** /ˈtɛni/ ● n. & adj. Heraldry orange-brown.
– ORIGIN C16: obs. Fr., var. of OFr. *tane* (see **TAWNY**).

**tenner** ● n. Brit. informal a ten-pound note.

**Tennesseean** /ˌtɛnəˈsiːən/ ● n. a native or inhabitant of the US state of Tennessee. ● adj. of or relating to Tennessee.

**tennies** ● pl. n. N. Amer. informal tennis shoes.

**tennis** ● n. a game in which two or four players strike a hollow rubber ball with rackets over a net stretched across a grass or clay court. See also **REAL TENNIS**.
– ORIGIN ME *tenetz*, *tenes* 'real tennis', appar. from OFr. *tenez* 'take, receive' (called by the server to an opponent), imper. of *tenir*.

**tennis elbow** ● n. inflammation of the tendons of the elbow (epicondylitis) caused by overuse of the forearm muscles.

**tennis shoe** ● n. a light canvas or leather soft-soled shoe suitable for tennis or casual wear.

**Tenno** /ˈtɛnəʊ/ ● n. (pl. **-os**) the Emperor of Japan.
– ORIGIN from Japanese.

**Tennysonian** /ˌtɛnɪˈsəʊnɪən/ ● adj. of, relating to, or in the style of the English poet Alfred (Lord) Tennyson (1809–92). ● n. an admirer or student of Tennyson or his work.

**tenon** ● n. a projecting piece of wood made for insertion into a mortise in another piece. ● v. (usu. **be tenoned**) join by means of a tenon. ➤ cut as a tenon.
– DERIVATIVES **tenoner** n.
– ORIGIN ME: from Fr., from *tenir* 'to hold', from L. *tenere*.

**tenon saw** ● n. a small saw with a strong brass or steel back for precise work.

**tenor¹** ● n. **1** a singing voice between baritone and alto or countertenor, the highest of the ordinary adult male range. **2** [as modifier] denoting an instrument of the second or third lowest pitch in its family. **3** (in full **tenor bell**) the largest and deepest bell of a ring or set.
– ORIGIN ME: via OFr. from med. L., based on *tenere* 'to hold'; so named because the tenor part 'held' the melody.

**tenor²** ● n. **1** the general meaning, sense, or content of something. **2** a prevailing character or direction: *the even tenor of life in the kitchen.* **3** Law the actual wording of a document. **4** Finance the time that must elapse before a bill of exchange or promissory note becomes due for payment.
– ORIGIN ME: from OFr. *tenour*, from L. *tenor* 'course, substance, import of a law', from *tenere* 'to hold'.

**tenor clef** ● n. Music a clef placing middle C on the second-highest line of the stave, used chiefly for cello and bassoon music.

**tenorino** /ˌtɛnəˈriːnəʊ/ ● n. (pl. **tenorini** /-ˈriːni/) a high tenor.
– ORIGIN Ital., dimin. of *tenore* 'tenor'.

**tenorist** ● n. a player of a tenor instrument.

**tenosynovitis** /ˌtɛnəʊˌsʌɪnə(ʊ)ˈvʌɪtɪs/ ● n. Medicine inflammation and swelling of a tendon, especially in the wrist and typically caused by repetitive movement.
– ORIGIN C19: from Gk *tenōn* 'tendon' + **SYNOVITIS**.

**tenotomy** /tə'nɒtəmi/ ● **n.** the surgical cutting of a tendon, especially as a remedy for club foot.
– ORIGIN C19: coined in Fr. from Gk *tenōn* 'tendon' + *-tomia* (see **-TOMY**).

**tenpin** ● **n.** a skittle used in tenpin bowling. ➤ **(tenpins)** [treated as sing.] N. Amer. tenpin bowling.

**tenpin bowling** ● **n.** a game in which ten skittles are set up at the end of a track and bowled down with hard rubber or plastic balls.

**tenrec** /'tɛnrɛk/ ● **n.** a small insectivorous mammal of Madagascar and the Comoro Islands. [Family Tenrecidae: many species.]
– ORIGIN C18: from Fr. *tanrec*, from Malagasy *tàndraka*.

**TENS** ● **abbrev.** transcutaneous electrical nerve stimulation, a technique designed to provide pain relief by applying electrodes to the skin.

**tense**[1] ● **adj. 1** (especially of a muscle) stretched tight or rigid. **2** (of a person) unable to relax. ➤ causing or showing anxiety and nervousness. **3** Phonetics (of a speech sound, especially a vowel) pronounced with the vocal muscles stretched tight. The opposite of **LAX**. ● **v.** make or become tense.
– DERIVATIVES **tensely** adv. **tenseness** n. **tensity** n.
– ORIGIN C17: from L. *tensus*, *tendere* 'stretch'.

**tense**[2] ● **n.** Grammar a set of forms taken by a verb to indicate the time (and sometimes the continuance or completeness) of the action in relation to the time of the utterance.
– DERIVATIVES **tenseless** adj.
– ORIGIN ME: from OFr. *tens*, from L. *tempus* 'time'.

**tensile** /'tɛnsʌɪl/ ● **adj. 1** of or relating to tension. **2** capable of being drawn out or stretched.
– DERIVATIVES **tensility** n.
– ORIGIN C17: from med. L. *tensilis*, from L. *tendere* 'to stretch'.

**tensile strength** ● **n.** the resistance of a material to breaking under tension. Compare with **COMPRESSIVE STRENGTH**.

**tension** ● **n. 1** the state of being tense. ➤ a strained state or condition resulting from forces acting in opposition to each other. **2** mental or emotional strain. ➤ a strained political or social state. **3** the degree of stitch tightness in knitting and machine sewing. **4** voltage of specified magnitude: *high tension*. ● **v.** subject to tension.
– DERIVATIVES **tensional** adj. **tensionally** adv. **tensioner** n. **tensionless** adj.
– ORIGIN C16: from Fr., or from L. *tensio(n-)*, from *tendere* 'stretch'.

**tensive** ● **adj.** causing or expressing tension.

**tenson** /'tɛns(ə)n/ (also **tenzon**) ● **n.** historical a contest in verse-making between troubadours. ➤ a verse composed for such a contest.
– ORIGIN C19: from Fr. *tenson* (rel. to Provençal *tenso*), based on L. *tendere* 'to stretch'.

**tensor** /'tɛnsə, -sɔː/ ● **n. 1** Mathematics a generalized form of vector represented by an array of components that are functions of spatial coordinates. **2** Anatomy a muscle that tightens or stretches a part of the body.
– DERIVATIVES **tensorial** adj.
– ORIGIN C18: mod. L., from L. *tendere* 'to stretch'.

**tent**[1] ● **n.** a portable shelter made of cloth, supported by one or more poles and stretched tight by cords attached to pegs driven into the ground. ● **v. 1** cover with or as if with a tent. ➤ arrange in a tent-like shape. ➤ [as adj. **tented**] composed of or provided with tents. **2** live in a tent.
– ORIGIN ME: from OFr. *tente*, based on L. *tent-*, *tendere* 'stretch'.

**tent**[2] ● **n.** a deep red sweet wine chiefly from Spain, used especially as sacramental wine.
– ORIGIN ME: from Sp. *tinto* 'deep-coloured', from L. *tinctus* 'dyed, stained', from *tingere*.

**tent**[3] ● **n.** Surgery a piece of absorbent material inserted into an opening to keep it open or widen it gradually.
– ORIGIN ME (also denoting a probe): from OFr. *tente*, from *tenter* 'to probe', from L. *temptare* 'handle, test, try'.

**tentacle** ● **n. 1** a long slender flexible appendage of an animal, used for grasping or moving about, or bearing sense organs. **2** a tendril or sensitive glandular hair on a plant. **3** an insidious spread of influence and control: *the Party's tentacles reached into every part of people's lives.*
– DERIVATIVES **tentacled** adj. **tentacular** adj. **tentaculate** adj.
– ORIGIN C18: anglicized from mod. L. *tentaculum*, from L. *tentare*, *temptare* 'to feel, try'.

**tentage** ● **n.** tents collectively.

**tentative** ● **adj.** provisional. ➤ hesitant.
– DERIVATIVES **tentatively** adv. **tentativeness** n.
– ORIGIN C16: from med. L. *tentativus*, from *tentare*, var. of *temptare* 'handle, try'.

**tent caterpillar** ● **n.** chiefly N. Amer. a moth caterpillar that lives gregariously inside a silken web in a tree.

**tent dress** ● **n.** a full, loose-fitting dress having no waistline or darts.

**tenter**[1] ● **n.** a framework on which fabric can be held taut for drying or other treatment during manufacture.
– ORIGIN ME: from med. L. *tentorium*, from *tent-*, *tendere* 'stretch'.

**tenter**[2] ● **n.** Brit. archaic a person in charge of something, especially of machinery in a factory.
– ORIGIN C19: from Scots and north. Engl. dial. *tent* 'pay attention', appar. from ME *attent* 'heed'.

**tenterhook** ● **n.** historical a hook used to fasten cloth on a tenter.
– PHRASES **on tenterhooks** in a state of agitated suspense.

**tenth** ● **ordinal number 1** constituting number ten in a sequence; 10th. **2** Music an interval or chord spanning an octave and a third in the diatonic scale, or a note separated from another by this interval.
– DERIVATIVES **tenthly** adv.

**tent stitch** ● **n.** a series of parallel diagonal stitches.

**tenuity** /tɪ'njuːɪti/ ● **n.** lack of solidity or substance.
– ORIGIN ME: from L. *tenuitas*, from *tenuis* 'thin'.

**tenuous** ● **adj.** very weak or slight. ➤ very slender or fine.
– DERIVATIVES **tenuously** adv. **tenuousness** n.
– ORIGIN C16: formed irregularly from L. *tenuis* 'thin' + **-OUS**.

**tenure** /'tɛnjə/ ● **n. 1** the conditions under which land or buildings are held or occupied. **2** the holding of an office. ➤ the period of this. ● **v.** give a permanent post to. ➤ [as adj. **tenured**] having or denoting such a post.
– PHRASES **security of tenure 1** the right of a tenant of property to occupy it after the lease expires (unless a court should order otherwise). **2** guaranteed permanent employment after a probationary period.
– ORIGIN ME: from OFr., from *tenir* 'to hold', from L. *tenere*.

**tenure track** ● **n.** chiefly N. Amer. an employment structure whereby the holder of a post is guaranteed consideration for eventual tenure.

**tenurial** ● **adj.** relating to the tenure of land.
– DERIVATIVES **tenurially** adv.

**tenuto** /tə'nuːtəʊ/ ● **adv. & adj.** Music (of a note) held for its full time value or slightly more.
– ORIGIN Ital., lit. 'held', past part. of *tenere*.

**tenzon** /'tiːnz(ə)n/ ● **n.** variant of **TENSON**.

**teocalli** /ˌtiːə'kali/ ● **n.** (pl. **teocallis**) a temple of the Aztecs or other Mexican peoples, typically standing on a truncated pyramid.
– ORIGIN Amer. Sp., from Nahuatl *teo:kalli*, from *teo:tl* 'god' + *kalli* 'house'.

**teosinte** /ˌtiːəʊ'sɪnteɪ/ ● **n.** a Mexican fodder grass believed to be a parent plant of maize. [*Zea mays* subsp. *mexicana*.]
– ORIGIN C19: from Fr. *téosinté*, from Nahuatl *teocintli*, appar. from *teo:tl* 'god' + *cintli* 'dried ear of maize'.

**tepal** /'tɛp(ə)l, 'tiːp(ə)l/ ● **n.** Botany a petal or sepal in a flower in which there is no distinction between them.
– ORIGIN C19: from Fr. *tépale*, blend of *pétale* 'petal' and *sépal* 'sepal'.

**tepary bean** /'tɛpəri/ ● **n.** a bean cultivated in the southwestern US. [*Phaseolus acutifolius*.]
– ORIGIN C20: of unknown origin.

**tepee** /ˈtiːpiː/ (also **teepee** or **tipi**) ● **n.** a conical tent made of skins or cloth on a frame of poles, used by American Indians of the Plains and Great Lakes regions.
– ORIGIN C18: from Sioux *tīpī* 'dwelling'.

**tephra** /ˈtɛfrə/ ● **n.** Geology rock fragments and particles ejected by a volcanic eruption.
– ORIGIN 1940s: from Gk, lit. 'ash, ashes'.

**tephrochronology** /ˌtɛfrə(ʊ)krəˈnɒlədʒi/ ● **n.** Geology the dating of volcanic eruptions and other events by studying layers of tephra.
– DERIVATIVES **tephrochronological** adj.

**tepid** ● **adj. 1** lukewarm. **2** unenthusiastic.
– DERIVATIVES **tepidity** n. **tepidly** adv. **tepidness** n.
– ORIGIN ME: from L. *tepidus*, from *tepere* 'be warm'.

**tepidarium** /ˌtɛpɪˈdɛːrɪəm/ ● **n.** (pl. **tepidaria** /-rɪə/) a warm room in an ancient Roman bath.
– ORIGIN from L.

**tequila** /tɛˈkiːlə/ ● **n.** a Mexican liquor made from an agave.
– ORIGIN Mex. Sp., named after the town of *Tequila* in Mexico.

**tequila slammer** ● **n.** see **SLAMMER** (sense 3).

**tequila sunrise** ● **n.** a cocktail of tequila, orange juice, and grenadine.

**ter-** ● **comb. form** three; having three: *tercentenary*.
– ORIGIN from L. *ter* 'thrice'.

**tera-** /ˈtɛrə/ ● **comb. form 1** denoting a factor of $10^{12}$: *terawatt*. **2** Computing denoting a factor of $2^{40}$: *terabyte*.
– ORIGIN from Gk *teras* 'monster'.

**terabyte** ● **n.** Computing a unit of information equal to one million million ($10^{12}$) or (strictly) $2^{40}$ bytes.

**teraflop** ● **n.** Computing a unit of computing speed equal to one million million floating-point operations per second.

**terai** /təˈrʌɪ/ ● **n.** a wide-brimmed felt hat, typically with a double crown, worn chiefly by travellers in subtropical regions.
– ORIGIN C19: from *Terai*, the name of a belt of marshy jungle near the Himalayan foothills.

**teraphim** /ˈtɛrəfɪm/ ● **pl. n.** small images used as domestic deities or oracles by ancient Semitic peoples.
– ORIGIN ME: via late L. from Gk *theraphin*, from Heb. *tĕrāpīm*.

**terato-** ● **comb. form** relating to monsters or abnormal forms: *teratology*.
– ORIGIN from Gk *teras, terat-* 'monster'.

**teratogen** /tɛˈratədʒ(ə)n, ˈtɛrətədʒ(ə)n/ ● **n.** an agent or factor causing malformation of an embryo.
– DERIVATIVES **teratogenesis** n. **teratogenic** adj. **teratogenicity** n.

**teratology** /ˌtɛrəˈtɒlədʒi/ ● **n. 1** Medicine & Biology the branch of medicine concerned with congenital abnormalities and abnormal formations. **2** mythology relating to fantastic creatures and monsters.
– DERIVATIVES **teratological** /-təˈlɒdʒɪk(ə)l/ adj. **teratologist** n.

**teratoma** /ˌtɛrəˈtəʊmə/ ● **n.** (pl. **teratomas** or **teratomata** /-mətə/) Medicine a tumour composed of tissues not normally present at the site.

**terawatt** /ˈtɛrəwɒt/ ● **n.** a unit of power equal to $10^{12}$ watts or a million megawatts.

**terbium** /ˈtəːbɪəm/ ● **n.** the chemical element of atomic number 65, a silvery-white metal of the lanthanide series. (Symbol **Tb**)
– ORIGIN C19: mod. L., from *Ytterby* (see **YTTERBIUM**).

**terce** /təːs/ ● **n.** a service forming part of the Divine Office of the Western Christian Church, traditionally said at the third hour of the day (9 a.m.).
– ORIGIN ME: from OFr., from L. *tertia*, fem. of *tertius* 'third'; cf. **TIERCE**.

**tercel** /ˈtəːs(ə)l/ (also **tiercel**) ● **n.** Falconry a male hawk, especially a peregrine or a goshawk. Compare with **FALCON**.
– ORIGIN ME: from OFr., based on L. *tertius* 'third', perh. from the belief that the third egg of a clutch produced a male.

**tercentenary** ● **n.** (pl. **-ies**) a three-hundredth anniversary.
– DERIVATIVES **tercentennial** adj. & n.

**tercet** /ˈtəːsɪt/ ● **n.** Prosody a set or group of three lines of verse rhyming together or connected by rhyme with an adjacent triplet.
– ORIGIN C16: from Fr., from Ital. *terzetto*, dimin. of *terzo* 'third', from L. *tertius*.

**terebinth** /ˈtɛrəbɪnθ/ ● **n.** a small tree which was formerly a source of turpentine and galls for tanning. [*Pistacia terebinthus*.]
– ORIGIN ME: from OFr. *therebinte*, or via L. from Gk *terebinthos*.

**teredo** /təˈriːdəʊ/ ● **n.** (pl. **-os**) Zoology a worm-like marine bivalve mollusc which bores into wood and can damage wooden structures. [*Teredo navalis* and related species.]
– ORIGIN ME: via L. from Gk *terēdōn*; rel. to *teirein* 'rub hard, wear away'.

**terephthalic acid** /ˌtɛrəfˈθalɪk/ ● **n.** Chemistry a crystalline organic acid used in making polyester resins and other polymers.
– DERIVATIVES **terephthalate** n.
– ORIGIN C19: blend of *terebic* 'of or from turpentine' (from **TEREBINTH**) and **PHTHALIC ACID**.

**terete** /təˈriːt/ ● **adj.** chiefly Botany smooth and cylindrical or slightly tapering.
– ORIGIN C17: from L. *teres, teret-* 'rounded off'.

**tergal** /ˈtəːg(ə)l/ ● **adj.** Zoology of or relating to a tergum.

**tergiversate** /ˈtəːdʒɪvəˌseɪt, -ˈvəːseɪt/ ● **v. 1** equivocate. **2** change one's loyalties.
– DERIVATIVES **tergiversation** n. **tergiversator** n.
– ORIGIN C17: from L. *tergiversat-, tergiversari* 'turn one's back'.

**tergum** /ˈtəːgəm/ ● **n.** (pl. **terga**) Zoology a thickened dorsal plate on a body segment of an arthropod.
– ORIGIN C19: from L., lit. 'back'.

**-teria** ● **suffix** denoting self-service establishments: *washeteria*.
– ORIGIN on the pattern of *(cafe)teria*.

**teriyaki** /ˌtɛrɪˈjɑːki/ ● **n.** a Japanese dish of fish or meat marinated in soy sauce and grilled. ➤(also **teriyaki sauce**) a mixture of soy sauce, sake, and ginger, used in Japanese cookery as a marinade or glaze.
– ORIGIN from Japanese.

**term** ● **n. 1** a word or phrase used to describe a thing or to express a concept. ➤**(terms)** a way of expressing oneself. ➤Logic a word or words that may be the subject or predicate of a proposition. **2** a fixed or limited period for which something lasts or is intended to last. ➤(also **term day**) (especially in Scotland) a fixed day of the year appointed for the making of payments, the start of tenancies, etc. ➤(also **full term**) the completion of a normal length of pregnancy. ➤(Brit. also **term of years** or US **term for years**) Law a tenancy of a fixed period. ➤archaic a boundary or limit, especially of time. **3** each of the periods in the year during which instruction is given in a school, college, etc., or during which a law court holds sessions. **4 (terms)** stipulated or agreed requirements. ➤conditions with regard to payment. ➤agreed conditions under which a dispute is settled. **5** Mathematics each of the quantities in a ratio, series, or mathematical expression. **6** Architecture a terminus. ● **v.** call by a specified term.
– PHRASES **come to terms with** reconcile oneself to. **in terms of** (or **in —— terms**) with regard to the aspect or subject specified. **the —— term** a period that is a specified way into the future: *investments that pay dividends in the long term*. **on terms** in a state of friendship or equality. ➤(in sport) level in score. **on —— terms** on a specified footing. **terms of reference** Brit. the scope of an inquiry or discussion.
– DERIVATIVES **termly** adj. & adv.
– ORIGIN ME: from OFr. *terme*, from L. *terminus* 'end, boundary, limit'.

**termagant** /ˈtəːməg(ə)nt/ ● **n. 1** a harsh-tempered or overbearing woman. **2 (Termagant)** historical an imaginary deity of violent and turbulent character, often appearing in morality plays.

– ORIGIN ME: via OFr. from Ital. *Trivagante*, taken to be from L. *tri-* 'three' + *vagant-* 'wandering', and to refer to the moon 'wandering' between heaven, earth, and hell.

**term for years** ● n. see **TERM** (sense 2).

**terminable** ● adj. **1** able to be terminated. **2** coming to an end after a certain time.

**terminal** ● adj. **1** of, forming, or situated at the end of something. ➤ of or forming a transport terminal. **2** (of a disease) predicted to lead to death. ➤ having or relating to a terminal disease. **3** informal extreme and irreversible. **4** done or occurring each school, college, etc. term. ● n. **1** the end of a railway or other transport route, or a station at this point. ➤ a departure and arrival building for passengers at an airport. **2** a point of connection for closing an electric circuit. **3** a device at which a user enters data or commands for a computer and which displays the received output. **4** an installation where oil or gas is stored at the end of a pipeline or at a port. **5** (also **terminal figure**) Architecture a terminus. **6** Brit. a patient with a terminal illness.
– DERIVATIVES **terminally** adv.
– ORIGIN C19: from L. *terminalis*, from *terminus* 'end, boundary'.

**terminal velocity** ● n. Physics the constant speed that a freely falling object reaches when the resistance of the medium through which it is falling prevents further acceleration.

**terminate** ● v. **1** bring to an end. ➤ end (a pregnancy) before term by artificial means. ➤ (of a train or bus service) end its journey. **2** (**terminate in**) have an end at (a specified place) or of (a specified form). **3** chiefly N. Amer. end the employment of. **4** euphemistic, chiefly N. Amer. assassinate. **5** archaic form the physical end or extremity of (an area).
– PHRASES **terminate someone with extreme prejudice** euphemistic, chiefly US murder someone.
– DERIVATIVES **termination** n. **terminational** adj.
– ORIGIN C16: from L. *terminat-*, *terminare* 'limit, end', from *terminus* 'end, boundary'.

**terminator** ● n. **1** a person or thing that terminates. **2** Astronomy the dividing line between the light and dark part of a planetary body. **3** Biochemistry the region of a DNA molecule at which transcription ends.

**termini** plural form of **TERMINUS**.

**terminological inexactitude** ● n. humorous a lie.
– ORIGIN first used by Winston Churchill in 1906.

**terminology** ● n. (pl. **-ies**) the body of terms used in a subject of study, profession, etc.
– DERIVATIVES **terminological** adj. **terminologically** adv. **terminologist** n.
– ORIGIN C19: from Ger. *Terminologie*, from med. L. *terminus* 'term'.

**terminus** ● n. (pl. **termini** or **terminuses**) **1** chiefly Brit. a railway or bus terminal. ➤ an oil or gas terminal. **2** an end or extremity. **3** Architecture a figure of a human bust or animal ending in a square pillar from which it appears to spring, originally a boundary marker in ancient Rome.
– ORIGIN C16: from L., 'end, limit, boundary'.

**terminus ad quem** /ˌtəːmɪnəs ad ˈkwɛm/ ● n. an end or finishing point. ➤ an aim or goal.
– ORIGIN L., lit. 'end to which'.

**terminus ante quem** /ˌantɪ ˈkwɛm/ ● n. the latest possible date.
– ORIGIN L., lit. 'end before which'.

**terminus a quo** /ɑː ˈkwəʊ/ ● n. the earliest possible date. ➤ a starting point.
– ORIGIN L., lit. 'end from which'.

**terminus post quem** /pəʊst ˈkwɛm/ ● n. the earliest possible date.
– ORIGIN L., lit. 'end after which'.

**termitarium** /ˌtəːmʌɪˈtɛːrɪəm/ ● n. (pl. **termitaria**) a colony of termites, typically within a mound of cemented earth.
– ORIGIN C19: mod. L., from L. *termes*, *termit-* 'termite'.

**termitary** /ˈtəːmɪtəri/ ● n. (pl. **-ies**) a termitarium.

**termite** /ˈtəːmʌɪt/ ● n. a small, pale soft-bodied social insect, typically making large nests of earth and feeding on wood. [Order Isoptera: many species.]
– ORIGIN C18: from late L. *termes*, *termit-* 'woodworm', alt. of L. *tarmes*, perh. by assoc. with *terere* 'to rub'.

**term of years** ● n. see **TERM** (sense 2).

**term paper** ● n. N. Amer. a long essay on a subject studied during a school or college term.

**terms of trade** ● pl. n. Economics the ratio of an index of a country's export prices to an index of its import prices.

**tern**[1] /təːn/ ● n. a seabird related to the gulls, typically smaller and more slender, with long pointed wings and a forked tail. [*Sterna* and other genera: many species.]
– ORIGIN C17: of Scand. origin.

**tern**[2] /təːn/ ● n. rare a set of three, especially three lottery numbers that when drawn together win a large prize.
– ORIGIN ME: appar. from Fr. *terne*, from L. *terni* 'three at once, three each', from *ter* 'thrice'.

**ternary** /ˈtəːnəri/ ● adj. composed of three parts. ➤ Mathematics using three as a base.
– ORIGIN ME: from L. *ternarius*, from *terni* 'three at once'.

**ternary form** ● n. Music the form of a movement in which the first subject is repeated after an interposed second subject in a related key.

**ternate** /ˈtəːneɪt/ ● adj. Botany (of a compound leaf) having three leaflets.
– ORIGIN C18: from mod. L. *ternatus*, from med. L. *ternare* 'make threefold', from *terni* 'three at once'.

**terne** /təːn/ ● n. a lead alloy containing about 20 per cent tin and often some antimony, used for plating steel.
– ORIGIN C19: prob. from Fr. *terne* 'dull, tarnished'.

**terotechnology** /ˌtɛrə(ʊ)tɛkˈnɒlədʒi, ˌtɪərə(ʊ)-/ ● n. Brit. the branch of technology and engineering concerned with the installation and maintenance of equipment.
– ORIGIN 1970s: from Gk *tērein* 'take care of' + **TECHNOLOGY**.

**terpene** /ˈtəːpiːn/ ● n. Chemistry any of a large group of volatile unsaturated hydrocarbons with cyclic molecules, found in the essential oils of conifers and other plants.
– DERIVATIVES **terpenoid** n. & adj.
– ORIGIN C19: from Ger. *Terpentin* 'turpentine' + **-ENE**.

**terpsichorean** /ˌtəːpsɪkəˈriːən/ formal or humorous ● adj. of or relating to dancing. ● n. a dancer.
– ORIGIN C19: from *Terpsichore*, the ancient Greek and Roman Muse of dance, + **-AN**.

**terra** /ˈtɛrə/ ● n. land or territory.
– ORIGIN L., lit. 'earth'.

**terrace** ● n. **1** a patio. **2** each of a series of flat areas on a slope, used for cultivation. ➤ Brit. a flight of wide, shallow steps providing standing room for spectators in a stadium. ➤ Geology a natural horizontal shelf-like formation, such as a raised beach. **3** chiefly Brit. a row of houses built in one block in a uniform style. ● v. make or form (sloping land) into terraces.
– DERIVATIVES **terracing** n.
– ORIGIN C16: from OFr., lit. 'rubble, platform', based on L. *terra* 'earth'.

**terraced** ● adj. **1** (of a house) forming part of a terrace. **2** (of land) having been formed into terraces.

**terraced roof** ● n. a flat roof.

**terracotta** /ˌtɛrəˈkɒtə/ ● n. **1** unglazed, typically brownish-red earthenware, used chiefly as an ornamental building material and in modelling. **2** a statuette or other object made of terracotta. **3** a strong brownish-red colour.
– ORIGIN C18: from Ital. *terra cotta* 'baked earth'.

**terra firma** /ˈfəːmə/ ● n. dry land; the ground.
– ORIGIN C17: from L., lit. 'firm land'.

**terraform** ● v. (especially in science fiction) transform (a planet) so as to resemble the earth.
– DERIVATIVES **terraformer** n.
– ORIGIN 1940s: from L. *terra* 'earth' + **FORM**.

**terrain** /tɛˈreɪn/ ● n. a stretch of land, especially with regard to its physical features.
– ORIGIN C18: from Fr., from a pop. L. var. of L. *terrenum*, neut. of *terrenus* (see **TERRENE**).

**terra incognita** /ɪnˈkɒgnɪtə, ˌɪnkɒgˈniːtə/ ● n. unknown territory.
– ORIGIN L., 'unknown land'.

**terramare** /ˌtɛrəˈmɑːri, -ˈmɛːri/ ● n. an ammoniacal earthy deposit found in mounds in prehistoric lake

dwellings. ➤a dwelling of this type.
– ORIGIN C19: from Fr., from Ital. dial. *terramara*, from Ital. *terra* 'earth' + *marna* 'marl'.

**terrane** /tɛ'reɪn/ ● **n.** Geology a geologically distinct region bounded by faults.
– ORIGIN C19: var. of **TERRAIN**.

**terrapin** ● **n. 1** a small freshwater turtle. [*Malaclemys terrapin* (**diamondback terrapin**, eastern US) and many other species elsewhere.] **2** (**Terrapin**) Brit. trademark a prefabricated one-storey building for temporary use.
– ORIGIN C17: of Algonquian origin.

**terraqueous** /tɛ'reɪkwɪəs/ ● **adj.** consisting or formed of land and water.
– ORIGIN C17: from L. *terra* 'land' + **AQUEOUS**.

**terrarium** /tɛ'rɛːrɪəm/ ● **n.** (pl. **terrariums** or **terraria** /-rɪə/) **1** a vivarium for smaller land animals, e.g. reptiles or amphibians, typically in the form of a glass-fronted case. **2** a sealed transparent globe or similar container in which plants are grown.
– ORIGIN C19: mod. L., from L. *terra* 'earth', on the pattern of *aquarium*.

**terra sigillata** /ˌsɪdʒɪ'leɪtə/ ● **n. 1** astringent clay from Lemnos or Samos, formerly used as a medicine. **2** Samian ware.
– ORIGIN ME: from med. L., lit. 'sealed earth'.

**terrazzo** /tɛ'ratsəʊ/ ● **n.** flooring material consisting of chips of marble or granite set in concrete and polished smooth.
– ORIGIN C20: Ital., lit. 'terrace'.

**terrene** /tɛ'riːn/ ● **adj.** archaic **1** of or like earth. ➤occurring on or inhabiting dry land. **2** worldly.
– ORIGIN ME: from Anglo-Norman Fr., from L. *terrenus*, from *terra* 'earth'.

**terreplein** /'tɛːpleɪn/ ● **n.** chiefly historical a level space where a battery of guns is mounted.
– ORIGIN C16: from Fr. *terre-plein*, from Ital. *terrapieno*, from *terrapienare* 'fill with earth'.

**terrestrial** /tə'rɛstrɪəl/ ● **adj. 1** of, on, or relating to the earth or dry land. ➤(of an animal or plant) living on or in the ground. ➤Astronomy (of a planet) resembling the earth. **2** denoting television broadcast other than by satellite. ● **n.** an inhabitant of the earth.
– DERIVATIVES **terrestrially** adv.
– ORIGIN ME: from L. *terrestris* (from *terra* 'earth') + **-AL**.

**terrestrial globe** ● **n.** a spherical representation of the earth with a map on the surface.

**terrestrial telescope** ● **n.** a telescope for observing terrestrial objects, giving an uninverted image.

**terret** /'tɛrɪt/ ● **n.** each of the loops or rings on a horse's harness pad for the driving reins to pass through.
– ORIGIN C15: from OFr. *touret*, dimin. of *tour* 'a turn'.

**terre verte** /tɛː 'vɛːt/ ● **n.** a greyish-green pigment made from glauconite, used for watercolours and tempera.
– ORIGIN C17: Fr., lit. 'green earth'.

**terribilità** /ˌtɛrɪbɪlɪ'tɑː/ ● **n.** awesomeness or emotional intensity in an artist or work of art.
– ORIGIN from Ital.

**terrible** ● **adj. 1** extremely bad, serious, or unpleasant. **2** troubled or guilty. **3** causing terror.
– DERIVATIVES **terribleness** n.
– ORIGIN ME: via Fr. from L. *terribilis*, from *terrere* 'frighten'.

**terribly** ● **adv. 1** extremely: *I'm terribly sorry.* **2** very badly.

**terricolous** /tɛ'rɪkələs/ ● **adj.** Biology living on the ground or in the soil.
– ORIGIN C19: from L. *terricola* 'earth-dweller' + **-OUS**.

**terrier**[1] /'tɛrɪə/ ● **n. 1** a small dog of a breed originally used for turning out foxes and other animals from their earths. **2** a tenacious or eager person. **3** (**Terrier**) Brit. informal a member of the Territorial Army.
– ORIGIN ME: from OFr. (*chien*) *terrier* 'earth (dog)', from med. L. *terrarius*, from L. *terra* 'earth'.

**terrier**[2] /'tɛrɪə/ ● **n.** historical a register of the lands belonging to a landowner. ➤an inventory of property or goods.
– ORIGIN C15: from OFr. *terrier*, from med. L. *terrarius* (*liber*) '(book) of land', from L. *terra* 'earth'.

**terrific** ● **adj. 1** of great size, amount, or intensity. ➤informal excellent. **2** archaic causing terror.
– DERIVATIVES **terrifically** adv.
– ORIGIN C17: from L. *terrificus*, from *terrere* 'frighten'.

**terrify** ● **v.** (**-ies**, **-ied**) cause to feel terror.
– DERIVATIVES **terrifier** n. **terrifying** adj. **terrifyingly** adv.
– ORIGIN C16: from L. *terrificare*, from *terrificus* (see **TERRIFIC**).

**terrigenous** /tɛ'rɪdʒɪnəs/ ● **adj.** Geology denoting marine sediment eroded from the land.
– ORIGIN C17: from L. *terrigenus* (from *terra* 'earth' + *-genus* 'born') + **-OUS**.

**terrine** /tə'riːn/ ● **n. 1** a meat, fish, or vegetable mixture cooked or otherwise prepared in advance and allowed to cool or set in its container. **2** an oblong, typically earthenware, container for such a dish.
– ORIGIN C18: from Fr., lit. 'large earthenware pot', from *terrin* 'earthen'; cf. **TUREEN**.

**territorial** ● **adj. 1** of or relating to the ownership of land or sea. ➤Zoology (of an animal) defending a territory. **2** of or relating to a territory or area. ➤(**Territorial**) of or relating to a Territory. ● **n.** (**Territorial**) (in the UK) a member of the Territorial Army.
– DERIVATIVES **territoriality** n. **territorially** adv.

**Territorial Army** ● **n.** (in the UK) a volunteer force locally organized to provide a reserve of trained manpower for use in an emergency.

**territorial waters** ● **pl. n.** the waters under the jurisdiction of a state, traditionally the part of the sea extending three miles from the shore.

**territory** ● **n.** (pl. **-ies**) **1** an area under the jurisdiction of a ruler or state. **2** (**Territory**) (especially in the US, Canada, or Australia) an organized division of a country not having the full rights of a state. **3** Zoology an area defended by an animal against others of the same sex or species. **4** an area defended by a team or player in a game or sport. **5** an area in which one has certain rights or responsibilities. **6** an area of knowledge or experience. **7** land with a specified characteristic: *woodland territory.*
– ORIGIN ME: from L. *territorium*, from *terra* 'land'.

**terror** ● **n. 1** extreme fear. ➤the use of terror to intimidate people. ➤a cause of terror. ➤(**the Terror**) the period of the French Revolution when the ruling Jacobin faction ruthlessly executed anyone considered a threat to their regime. **2** (also **holy terror**) informal a person causing trouble or annoyance.
– ORIGIN ME: from OFr. *terrour*, from L. *terror*, from *terrere* 'frighten'.

**terrorist** ● **n.** a person who uses violence and intimidation in the pursuit of political aims.
– DERIVATIVES **terrorism** n. **terroristic** adj. **terroristically** adv.

**terrorize** (also **-ise**) ● **v.** create and maintain a feeling of terror in.
– DERIVATIVES **terrorization** n. **terrorizer** n.

**terry** ● **n.** (pl. **-ies**) fabric with raised uncut loops of thread on both sides, used especially for towels.
– ORIGIN C18: of unknown origin.

**terse** ● **adj.** (**terser**, **tersest**) sparing in the use of words; abrupt.
– DERIVATIVES **tersely** adv. **terseness** n.
– ORIGIN C17 (orig. 'polished, trim', hence 'concise and to the point'): from L. *tersus* 'wiped, polished'.

**tertian** /'təːʃ(ə)n/ ● **adj.** Medicine denoting a form of malaria causing a fever that recurs every second day.
– ORIGIN ME (*fever*) *terciane*, from L. (*febris*) *tertiana*, from *tertius* 'third' (the fever recurring every third day by inclusive reckoning).

**tertiary** /'təːʃ(ə)ri/ ● **adj. 1** third in order or level. ➤chiefly Brit. relating to or denoting education at a level beyond that provided by schools. **2** relating to or denoting medical treatment provided at a specialist institution. **3** (**Tertiary**) Geology relating to or denoting the first period of the Cenozoic era (between the Cretaceous and Quaternary periods, about 65 to 1.64 million years ago). **4** Chemistry (of an organic compound) having its functional group on a carbon atom bonded to three other carbon atoms. ➤Chemistry derived from ammonia by replacement of three

hydrogen atoms by organic groups. ● **n.** a lay associate of certain Christian monastic organizations.
– ORIGIN C16: from L. *tertiarius* 'of the third part or rank'.

**tertiary industry** ● **n.** Economics the service industry of a country.

**tertium quid** /ˌtəːʃɪəm ˈkwɪd, ˌtəːtɪəm/ ● **n.** an indefinite and undefined third thing related to two definite or known things.
– ORIGIN C18: from late L., translation of Gk *triton ti* 'some third thing'.

**tervalent** /təːˈveɪl(ə)nt/ ● **adj.** Chemistry trivalent.

**terylene** ● **n.** Brit. trademark a polyester fibre used to make light, crease-resistant clothing, bed linen, and sails.
– ORIGIN 1940s: formed by inversion of (*polyeth*)*ylene ter-* (*ephthalate*).

**terza rima** /ˌtɛːtsə ˈriːmə/ ● **n.** Prosody an arrangement of triplets, especially in iambic pentameter, that rhyme *aba bcb cdc* etc.
– ORIGIN Ital., lit. 'third rhyme'.

**terzetto** /tɛːtˈsɛtəʊ, təːt-/ ● **n.** (pl. **terzettos** or **terzetti** /-ti/) Music a vocal or instrumental trio.
– ORIGIN Ital. (see **TERCET**).

**TESL** ● **abbrev.** teaching of English as a second language.

**tesla** /ˈtɛslə, ˈtɛzlə/ (abbrev.: **T**) ● **n.** Physics the SI unit of magnetic flux density.
– ORIGIN 1960s: named after the Amer. electrical engineer Nikola *Tesla*.

**Tesla coil** ● **n.** a form of induction coil producing high-frequency alternating currents.

**TESOL** /ˈtɛsɒl/ ● **abbrev.** teaching of English to speakers of other languages.

**TESSA** ● **n.** (in the UK) a tax-exempt special savings account allowing savers to invest a certain amount without paying tax on the interest, provided that the capital remains in the account for five years.

**tessellate** /ˈtɛsəleɪt/ ● **v.** **1** decorate (a floor) with mosaics. **2** Mathematics cover (a plane surface) by repeated use of a single shape, without gaps or overlapping.
– DERIVATIVES **tesselated** adj. **tesselation** n.
– ORIGIN C18: from late L. *tessellat-*, *tessellare*, from *tessella*, dimin. of *tessera* (see **TESSERA**).

**tessera** /ˈtɛs(ə)rə/ ● **n.** (pl. **tesserae** /-riː/) **1** a small block of stone, tile, etc. used in a mosaic. **2** (in ancient Greece and Rome) a small tablet of wood or bone used as a token.
– DERIVATIVES **tesseral** adj.
– ORIGIN C17: via L. from Gk, neut. of *tesseres*, var. of *tessares* 'four'.

**tessitura** /ˌtɛsɪˈtjʊərə/ ● **n.** Music the range within which most notes of a vocal part fall.
– ORIGIN Ital., lit. 'texture'.

**test**[1] ● **n.** **1** a procedure intended to establish the quality, performance, or reliability of something. ➤a short examination of proficiency or knowledge. ➤a difficult situation revealing the strength or quality of someone or something. ➤an examination of part of the body or a body fluid for medical purposes. ➤Chemistry a procedure employed to identify a substance or to reveal the presence or absence of a constituent within a substance. **2** a means of testing something. **3** short for **TEST MATCH**. **4** Metallurgy a movable hearth in a reverberating furnace, used for separating gold or silver from lead. ● **v.** subject to a test. ➤produce a specified result in a medical test. ➤Chemistry examine by means of a reagent. ➤touch or taste before proceeding further.
– PHRASES **test the water** ascertain feelings or opinions before proceeding further.
– DERIVATIVES **testability** n. **testable** adj. **testee** n.
– ORIGIN ME (denoting a cupel used to treat gold or silver alloys or ore): via OFr. from L. *testu*, *testum* 'earthen pot', var. of *testa* 'jug, shell'; cf. **TEST**[2].

**test**[2] ● **n.** Zoology the shell or integument of some invertebrates and protozoans.
– ORIGIN C19: from L. *testa* 'tile, jug, shell'; cf. **TEST**[1].

**testa** ● **n.** (pl. **testae** /-tiː/) Botany the protective outer covering of a seed.
– ORIGIN C18: from L., lit. 'tile, shell'.

**testaceous** /tɛˈsteɪʃəs/ ● **adj.** chiefly Entomology of a dull brick-red colour.
– ORIGIN C17: from L. *testaceus* (from *testa* 'tile') + **-OUS**.

**Test Act** ● **n.** **1** (in the UK) an act in force between 1673 and 1828 that made an oath of allegiance to the Church of England a condition of eligibility for public office. **2** (in the UK) an act of 1871 relaxing restrictions on university entrance.

**testament** ● **n.** **1** a person's will. **2** evidence or proof of a fact, event, or quality. **3** (in biblical use) a covenant or dispensation. **4** (**Testament**) a division of the Bible. See also **OLD TESTAMENT**, **NEW TESTAMENT**. ➤(**Testament**) a copy of the New Testament.
– ORIGIN ME: from L. *testamentum* 'a will' (from *testari* 'testify'), in Christian L. also translating Gk *diathēkē* 'covenant'.

**testamentary** ● **adj.** of, relating to, or bequeathed or appointed through a will.

**testate** /ˈtɛsteɪt/ ● **adj.** having made a valid will before one dies. ● **n.** a person who dies testate.
– ORIGIN ME: from L. *testatus* 'testified, witnessed', past part. of *testari*, from *testis* 'a witness'.

**testation** ● **n.** Law the disposal of property by will.

**testator** /tɛˈsteɪtə/ ● **n.** Law a person who has made a will or given a legacy.
– ORIGIN ME: from Anglo-Norman Fr. *testatour*, from L. *testator*, from *testari* 'testify'.

**testatrix** /tɛˈsteɪtrɪks/ ● **n.** (pl. **testatrices** /-trɪsiːz/ or **testatrixes**) Law a female testator.
– ORIGIN C16: from late L., fem. of *testator* (see **TESTATOR**).

**test bed** ● **n.** a piece of equipment for testing new machinery, especially aircraft engines.

**test card** ● **n.** Brit. a still television picture transmitted outside normal programme hours and designed for use in judging the quality and position of the image.

**test case** ● **n.** Law a case setting a precedent for other cases.

**test drive** ● **n.** a drive taken in a motor vehicle that one is considering buying, in order to determine its qualities. ● **v.** (**test-drive**) take (a vehicle) for a test drive.

**tester**[1] ● **n.** **1** a person or device that tests. **2** a sample of a product allowing customers to try it before purchase.

**tester**[2] ● **n.** a canopy over a four-poster bed.
– ORIGIN ME: from med. L. *testerium*, *testrum*, from a Romance word meaning 'head', based on L. *testa* 'tile'.

**testes** plural form of **TESTIS**.

**test flight** ● **n.** a flight during which the performance of an aircraft or its equipment is tested.
– DERIVATIVES **test-fly** v.

**testicle** ● **n.** either of the two oval organs that produce sperm in male mammals, enclosed in the scrotum behind the penis. Compare with **TESTIS**.
– DERIVATIVES **testicular** adj.
– ORIGIN ME: from L. *testiculus*, dimin. of *testis*, lit. 'a witness' (i.e. to virility).

**testiculate** /tɛˈstɪkjʊlət/ ● **adj.** Botany (especially of the twin tubers of some orchids) shaped like a pair of testicles.
– ORIGIN C18: from late L. *testiculatus*, from *testiculus* (see **TESTICLE**).

**testify** ● **v.** (**-ies**, **-ied**) **1** give evidence as a witness in a law court. **2** serve as evidence or proof of something.
– DERIVATIVES **testifier** n.
– ORIGIN ME: from L. *testificari*, from *testis* 'a witness'.

**testimonial** /ˌtɛstɪˈməʊnɪəl/ ● **n.** a formal statement testifying to someone's character and qualifications. ➤a public tribute to someone and to their achievements.

**testimony** ● **n.** (pl. **-ies**) **1** a formal statement, especially one given in a court of law. ➤archaic a solemn protest or declaration. **2** evidence or proof of something.
– ORIGIN ME: from L. *testimonium*, from *testis* 'a witness'.

**testing ground** ● **n.** an area or field of activity for the testing of a product or an idea.

**testis** /ˈtɛstɪs/ ● **n.** (pl. **testes** /-tiːz/) Anatomy & Zoology an organ which produces sperm. Compare with **TESTICLE**.
– ORIGIN C18: from L. (see **TESTICLE**).

**test match** • n. an international cricket or rugby match played between teams representing two different countries.

**testosterone** /tɛˈstɒstərəʊn/ • n. a steroid hormone stimulating development of male secondary sexual characteristics.
– ORIGIN 1930s: from **TESTIS** + *sterone* (blend of **STEROL** and **KETONE**).

**test pilot** • n. a pilot who test-flies aircraft.

**test tube** • n. **1** a thin glass tube closed at one end, used to hold material for laboratory testing or experiments. **2** [as modifier] denoting things produced or processes performed in a laboratory.

**test-tube baby** • n. informal a baby conceived by in vitro fertilization.

**testudo** /tɛˈstjuːdəʊ, -ˈstuː-/ • n. (pl. **testudos** or **testudines** /-dɪniːz/) (in ancient Rome) a screen on wheels and with an arched roof, used to protect besieging troops. ➤ a protective screen formed by a body of troops holding their shields above their heads.
– ORIGIN ME: from L., lit. 'tortoise', from *testa* 'tile, shell'.

**testy** • adj. irritable.
– DERIVATIVES **testily** adv. **testiness** n.
– ORIGIN ME (in the sense 'headstrong, impetuous'): from Anglo-Norman Fr. *testif*, from OFr. *teste* 'head', from L. *testa* 'shell'.

**tetanic** /tɪˈtanɪk/ • adj. relating to or characteristic of tetanus.
– DERIVATIVES **tetanically** adv.

**tetanus** • n. **1** a bacterial disease causing rigidity and spasms of the voluntary muscles. **2** Physiology the prolonged contraction of a muscle caused by rapidly repeated stimuli.
– DERIVATIVES **tetanize** (also **-ise**) v. **tetanoid** adj.
– ORIGIN ME: from L., from Gk *tetanos* 'muscular spasm', from *teinein* 'to stretch'.

**tetany** /ˈtɛt(ə)ni/ • n. Medicine a condition of intermittent muscular spasms, caused by parathyroid malfunction and consequent calcium deficiency.
– ORIGIN C19: from Fr. *tétanie*, from L. *tetanus* (see **TETANUS**).

**tetchy** (also **techy**) • adj. irritable.
– DERIVATIVES **tetchily** adv. **tetchiness** n.
– ORIGIN C16: prob. from a var. of Scots *tache* 'blotch, fault', from OFr. *teche*.

**tête-à-tête** /ˌtɛtaˈtɛt, ˌteɪtɑːˈteɪt/ • n. (pl. same or **tête-à-têtes** pronunc. same) **1** a private conversation between two people. **2** an S-shaped sofa on which two people can sit face to face. • adj. & adv. involving or happening privately between two people.
– ORIGIN C17: Fr., lit. 'head-to-head'.

**tête-bêche** /ˌtɛtˈbɛʃ, French tɛtbɛʃ/ • adj. (of a postage stamp) printed upside down or sideways relative to another.
– ORIGIN Fr., from *tête* 'head' and *bêche*, contr. of obs. *béchevet* 'double bedhead'.

**tether** • n. a rope or chain with which an animal is tied to restrict its movement. • v. tie with a tether.
– ORIGIN ME: from ON *tjóthr*, from a Gmc base meaning 'fasten'.

**Teton** /ˈtiːtɒn, -t(ə)n/ (also **Teton Sioux**) • n. another term for **LAKOTA**.
– ORIGIN the name in Dakota, lit. 'dwellers on the prairie'.

**tetra** /ˈtɛtrə/ • n. a small brightly coloured tropical freshwater fish of the characin family, popular in aquaria. [*Paracheirodon innesi* (**neon tetra**, Amazonia), and other species.]
– ORIGIN C20: abbrev. of mod. L. *Tetragonopterus* (former genus name), lit. 'tetragonal-finned'.

**tetra-** (also **tetr-** before a vowel) • comb. form **1** four; having four: *tetragram*. **2** Chemistry (in names of compounds) containing four atoms or groups of a specified kind: *tetracycline*.
– ORIGIN from Gk, from *tettares* 'four'.

**tetrachord** • n. Music **1** a scale of four notes, the interval between the first and last being a perfect fourth. **2** historical an instrument with four strings.

**tetracycline** /ˌtɛtrəˈsʌɪkliːn, -lɪn/ • n. Medicine any of a large group of antibiotics with a molecular structure containing four rings.
– ORIGIN 1950s: from **TETRA-** + **CYCLIC** + **-INE**[4].

**tetrad** /ˈtɛtrad/ • n. technical a group or set of four.
– ORIGIN C17: from Gk *tetras*, *tetrad-* 'four, a group of four'.

**tetradactyl** /ˌtɛtrəˈdaktɪl/ • adj. Zoology having four toes or fingers.
– DERIVATIVES **tetradactyly** n.

**tetraethyl lead** /ˌtɛtrəˈiːθʌɪl/ • n. Chemistry an oily organic compound of lead, used as an anti-knock agent in leaded petrol.

**tetragonal** /tɪˈtrag(ə)n(ə)l/ • adj. denoting a crystal system with three axes at right angles, two of them equal.
– DERIVATIVES **tetragonally** adv.
– ORIGIN C16: via late L. from Gk *tetragōnon* (neut. of *tetragōnos* 'four-angled') + **-AL**.

**tetragram** • n. a word with four letters or characters.

**Tetragrammaton** /ˌtɛtrəˈgramətɒn/ • n. the Hebrew name of God transliterated in four letters as *YHWH* or *JHVH* and articulated as *Yahweh* or *Jehovah*.
– ORIGIN Gk, neut. of *tetragrammatos* 'having four letters'.

**tetrahedrite** /ˌtɛtrəˈhiːdrʌɪt, -ˈhɛdrʌɪt/ • n. a grey mineral consisting of a sulphide of antimony, iron, and copper.

**tetrahedron** /ˌtɛtrəˈhiːdrən, -ˈhɛd-/ • n. (pl. **tetrahedra** /-drə/ or **tetrahedrons**) a solid having four plane triangular faces.
– DERIVATIVES **tetrahedral** adj.
– ORIGIN C16: from late Gk *tetraedron*, neut. (used as n.) of *tetraedros* 'four-sided'.

**tetrahydrocannabinol** /ˌtɛtrəˌhʌɪdrə(ʊ)ˈkanəbɪnɒl, -kəˈnab-/ • n. Chemistry a crystalline compound that is the main active ingredient of cannabis.

**tetralogy** /tɪˈtralədʒi/ • n. (pl. **-ies**) **1** a group of four related literary or operatic works. ➤ a series of four ancient Greek dramas, three tragic and one satyric, originally presented together. **2** Medicine a set of four related symptoms occurring together.

**tetramer** /ˈtɛtrəmə/ • n. Chemistry a polymer comprising four monomer units.
– DERIVATIVES **tetrameric** adj.

**tetramerous** /tɪˈtram(ə)rəs/ • adj. Botany & Zoology having parts arranged in groups of four. ➤ consisting of four joints or parts.

**tetrameter** /tɪˈtramɪtə/ • n. Prosody a verse of four measures.
– ORIGIN C17: from late L. *tetrametrus*, from Gk *tetrametros*, from *tetra-* 'four' + *metron* 'measure'.

**tetraplegia** /ˌtɛtrəˈpliːdʒə/ • n. another term for **QUADRIPLEGIA**.
– DERIVATIVES **tetraplegic** adj. & n.

**tetraploid** /ˈtɛtrəplɔɪd/ Biology • adj. (of a cell or nucleus) containing four homologous sets of chromosomes. ➤ (of an organism) composed of such cells. • n. a tetraploid organism.
– DERIVATIVES **tetraploidy** n.

**tetrapod** • n. **1** Zoology an animal of a group (superclass Tetrapoda) which includes all vertebrates apart from fishes. **2** an object or structure with four feet, legs, or supports.
– ORIGIN C19: from mod. L. *tetrapodus*, from Gk *tetrapous*, *tetrapod-* 'four-footed'.

**tetrapterous** /tɪˈtrapt(ə)rəs/ • adj. Entomology having two pairs of wings.
– ORIGIN C19: from mod. L. *tetrapterus* (from Gk *tetrapteros*, from *tetra-* 'four' + *pteron* 'wing') + **-OUS**.

**tetrarch** /ˈtɛtrɑːk/ • n. (in the Roman Empire) the governor of one of four divisions of a country or province. ➤ one of four joint rulers. ➤ archaic a subordinate ruler.
– DERIVATIVES **tetrarchy** n. (pl. **-ies**).
– ORIGIN OE, from late L. *tetrarcha*, from L. *tetrarches*, from Gk *tetrarkhēs*, from *tetra-* 'four' + *arkhein* 'to rule'.

**tetrastich** /ˈtɛtrəstɪk/ • n. Prosody a group of four lines of verse.
– ORIGIN C16: via L. from Gk *tetrastikhon* 'having four

rows'.

**tetrastyle** Architecture ● **n.** a building or part of a building with four pillars. ● **adj.** having four pillars.
– ORIGIN C18: via L. from Gk *tetrastulos*, from *tetra-* 'four' + *stulos* 'column'.

**tetrasyllable** ● **n.** a word having four syllables.
– DERIVATIVES **tetrasyllabic** adj.

**tetrathlon** /tɛˈtraθlɒn, -lən/ ● **n.** a sporting contest in which participants compete in four events, typically riding, shooting, swimming, and running.
– ORIGIN 1950s: from **TETRA-** + Gk *athlon* 'contest', on the pattern of *pentathlon*.

**tetratomic** ● **adj.** Chemistry consisting of four atoms.

**tetravalent** /ˌtɛtrəˈveɪl(ə)nt/ ● **adj.** Chemistry having a valency of four.

**tetrode** /ˈtɛtrəʊd/ ● **n.** a thermionic valve with four electrodes.
– ORIGIN C20: from **TETRA-** + Gk *hodos* 'way'.

**tetrodotoxin** /ˌtɛtrədə(ʊ)ˈtɒksɪn/ ● **n.** a powerful neurotoxin present in some pufferfish ovaries.
– ORIGIN C20: from mod. L. *Tetrodon* (former genus name, from Gk *tetra-* 'fourfold' + *odous, odont-* 'tooth') + **TOXIN**.

**tetter** ● **n.** chiefly archaic a skin disease causing itchy or pustular patches, e.g. eczema or ringworm.
– ORIGIN OE *teter*, of Gmc origin.

**Teuton** /ˈtjuːt(ə)n/ ● **n.** a member of a Germanic people who lived in Jutland in the 4th century BC.
– ORIGIN from L. *Teutones, Teutoni* (pl.), from an Indo-Eur. root meaning 'people' or 'country'.

**Teutonic** /tjuːˈtɒnɪk/ ● **adj.** **1** of or relating to the Teutons. ➤ informal, often derogatory displaying characteristics popularly attributed to Germans. **2** archaic denoting the Germanic branch of the Indo-European language family. ● **n.** archaic the language of the Teutons.
– DERIVATIVES **Teutonicism** n.

**Tevet** /ˈtɛvɛt/ ● **n.** variant of **TEBET**.

**Tewa** /ˈteɪwə/ ● **n.** (pl. same or **Tewas**) **1** a member of a Pueblo Indian people of the Rio Grande area in the southwestern US. **2** the Tanoan language of this people.
– ORIGIN from Tewa *téwa* 'moccasins'.

**Tex.** ● **abbrev.** Texas.

**Texan** ● **n.** a native or inhabitant of the US state of Texas. ● **adj.** of or relating to Texas.

**Texel** /ˈtɛks(ə)l/ ● **n.** a sheep of a hardy, hornless breed, originally from the West Frisian island of Texel.

**Tex-Mex** ● **adj.** (especially of food and music) having a blend of Mexican and southern American features. ● **n.** **1** Tex-Mex music or food. **2** a variety of Mexican Spanish spoken in Texas.
– ORIGIN 1940s: blend of *Texan* and *Mexican*.

**text** ● **n.** **1** a written or printed work regarded in terms of content rather than form. ➤ the original words of an author or document. ➤ Computing data corresponding to a body of writing. **2** the main body of a book or other piece of writing, as distinct from appendices, illustrations, etc. **3** a written work chosen as a subject of study. ➤ a passage from the Bible or other religious work, especially as the subject of a sermon. **4** (also **text-hand**) archaic fine, large handwriting, used especially for manuscripts. ● **v.** send a text message to.
– DERIVATIVES **textless** adj.
– ORIGIN ME: from ONorth. Fr. *texte*, from L. *textus* 'tissue, literary style' (in med. L., 'Gospel'), from *text-*, *texere* 'weave'.

**textbook** ● **n.** a book used as a standard work for the study of a subject. ● **adj.** conforming to an established standard.
– DERIVATIVES **textbookish** adj.

**text editor** ● **n.** Computing a system or program allowing a user to edit text.

**textile** ● **n.** **1** a type of cloth or woven fabric. **2** informal (among nudists) a person who wears clothes. ● **adj.** of or relating to fabric or weaving.
– ORIGIN C17: from L. *textilis*, from *text-*, *texere* 'weave'.

**text message** ● **n.** an electronic communication sent and received via mobile phone.

**textual** ● **adj.** of or relating to a text or texts.
– DERIVATIVES **textually** adv.

**textual criticism** ● **n.** the process of attempting to ascertain the original wording of a text.

**textualist** ● **n.** a person adhering strictly to a text, especially that of the scriptures.
– DERIVATIVES **textualism** n.

**textuality** ● **n.** **1** the quality or use of language characteristic of written works as opposed to spoken usage. **2** textualism.

**texture** ● **n.** **1** the feel, appearance, or consistency of a surface or a substance. ➤ the character of a textile fabric as determined by its threads. **2** Art the representation of the tactile quality of a surface. **3** the quality created by the combination of elements in a work of music or literature: *a closely knit symphonic texture*. ● **v.** [usu. as adj. **textured**] give a rough or raised texture to.
– DERIVATIVES **textural** adj. **texturally** adv. **textureless** adj.
– ORIGIN ME: from L. *textura* 'weaving', from *text-*, *texere* 'weave'.

**textured vegetable protein** ● **n.** a protein obtained from soya beans and made to resemble minced meat.

**texture mapping** ● **n.** Computing the application of patterns or images to three-dimensional graphics to enhance their realism.

**texturize** (also **-ise**) ● **v.** impart a particular texture to. ➤ cut (hair) in such a way as to create extra fullness.

**text wrap** ● **n.** (in word processing) a facility allowing text to surround embedded features such as pictures.

**TFT** ● **abbrev.** Electronics thin-film transistor, used to make flat colour display screens.

**TG** ● **abbrev.** **1** Togo (international vehicle registration). **2** transformational (or transformational-generative) grammar.

**T-group** ● **n.** Psychology a group of people observing and seeking to improve their own interpersonal behaviour.
– ORIGIN 1950s: *T* for *training*.

**TGV** ● **n.** a French high-speed passenger train.
– ORIGIN abbrev. of Fr. *train à grande vitesse*.

**TGWU** ● **abbrev.** (in the UK) Transport and General Workers' Union.

**Th** ● **symb.** the chemical element thorium.

**Th.** ● **abbrev.** Thursday.

**-th**[1] (also **-eth**) ● **suffix** forming ordinal and fractional numbers from *four* onwards: *sixth*.
– ORIGIN OE *-(o)tha, -(o)the*.

**-th**[2] ● **suffix** forming nouns: **1** (from verbs) denoting an action or process: *growth*. **2** (from adjectives) denoting a state: *filth*.
– ORIGIN OE *-thu, -tho, -th*.

**-th**[3] ● **suffix** variant spelling of **-ETH**[2] (as in *doth*).

**Thai** /tʌɪ/ ● **n.** (pl. same or **Thais**) **1** a native or national of Thailand. ➤ a member of the largest ethnic group in Thailand. **2** the official language of Thailand. ● **adj.** of or relating to Thailand, its people, or their language.
– ORIGIN Thai, lit. 'free'.

**Thai stick** ● **n.** strong cannabis in leaf form, twisted into a tightly packed cylinder ready for smoking.

**thalamus** /ˈθaləməs/ ● **n.** (pl. **thalami** /-mʌɪ, -miː/) Anatomy each of two masses of grey matter in the forebrain, relaying sensory information.
– DERIVATIVES **thalamic** /θəˈlamɪk, ˈθaləmɪk/ adj.
– ORIGIN C17: via L. from Gk *thalamos*.

**thalassaemia** /ˌθaləˈsiːmɪə/ (US **thalassemia**) ● **n.** Medicine a hereditary haemolytic disease caused by faulty haemoglobin synthesis, prevalent in Mediterranean, African, and Asian countries.
– ORIGIN 1930s: from Gk *thalassa* 'sea' (because first known around the Mediterranean) + **-AEMIA**.

**thalassic** /θəˈlasɪk/ ● **adj.** poetic/literary or technical of or relating to the sea.
– ORIGIN C19: from Fr. *thalassique*, from Gk *thalassa* 'sea'.

**thalassotherapy** /θəˌlasəʊˈθɛrəpi/ ● **n.** the use of seawater in cosmetic and health treatment.
– ORIGIN C19: from Gk *thalassa* 'sea' + **THERAPY**.

**thale cress** /θeɪl/ ● **n.** a small white-flowered plant, commonly used in genetics experiments. [*Arabidopsis*

*thaliana.*]
– ORIGIN C18: named after the Ger. physician Johann *Thal.*

**thaler** /ˈtɑːlə/ ● n. historical a German silver coin.
– ORIGIN Ger., earlier form of *Taler* (see **DOLLAR**).

**thali** /ˈtɑːli/ ● n. (pl. **thalis**) **1** a set meal at an Indian restaurant. **2** a metal plate on which Indian food is served.
– ORIGIN from Hindi *thālī*, from Sanskrit *sthālī*.

**thalidomide** /θəˈlɪdəmʌɪd/ ● n. a drug formerly used as a sedative, but found to cause fetal malformation when taken in early pregnancy.
– ORIGIN 1950s: from *(ph)thal(ic acid)* + *(im)ido* + *(i)mide*.

**thalli** plural form of **THALLUS**.

**thallium** /ˈθalɪəm/ ● n. the chemical element of atomic number 81, a soft silvery-white metal whose compounds are very poisonous. (Symbol: **Tl**)
– ORIGIN C19: mod. L., from Gk *thallos* 'green shoot', because of a green line in its spectrum.

**thallophyte** /ˈθalə(ʊ)fʌɪt/ ● n. Botany a plant consisting of a thallus.
– ORIGIN C19: from mod. L. *Thallophyta* (former taxon), from Gk *thallos* (see **THALLUS**) + **-PHYTE**.

**thallus** /ˈθaləs/ ● n. (pl. **thalli** /-lʌɪ, -liː/) Botany a plant body not differentiated into stem, leaves, and roots and without a vascular system, typical of algae, fungi, lichens, and some liverworts.
– DERIVATIVES **thalloid** adj.
– ORIGIN C19: from Gk *thallos* 'green shoot'.

**thalweg** /ˈtɑːlvɛg, ˈθɑːlwɛg/ ● n. Geology a line connecting the lowest points of successive cross-sections of a valley.
– ORIGIN C19: from Ger., from obs. *Thal* 'valley, dale' + *Weg* 'way'.

**Thammuz** /ˈtamʊz/ (also **Tammuz**) ● n. (in the Jewish calendar) the tenth month of the civil and fourth of the religious year, coinciding with parts of June and July.
– ORIGIN from Heb. *tammūz*.

**than** ● conj. & prep. **1** introducing the second element in a comparison. **2** used to introduce an exception or contrast. **3** used in expressions indicating one thing happening immediately after another.
– ORIGIN OE *than(ne)*, *thon(ne)*, *thænne*, orig. the same word as **THEN**.

**thanage** /ˈθeɪnɪdʒ/ ● n. historical the tenure, land, and rank granted to a thane.

**thanatology** /ˌθanəˈtɒlədʒi/ ● n. the scientific study of death and practices associated with it.
– DERIVATIVES **thanatological** adj. **thanatologist** n.
– ORIGIN C19: from Gk *thanatos* 'death' + **-LOGY**.

**Thanatos** /ˈθanətɒs/ ● n. (in Freudian theory) the death instinct. Often contrasted with **EROS**.
– ORIGIN from Gk *thanatos* 'death'.

**thane** /θeɪn/ ● n. (in Anglo-Saxon England) a man granted land by the king or a military nobleman, ranking between a freeman and a hereditary noble. ➤(in Scotland) a man who held land from a Scottish king and ranked with an earl's son.
– DERIVATIVES **thanedom** n.
– ORIGIN OE *theg(e)n* 'servant, soldier', of Gmc origin.

**thank** ● v. **1** express gratitude to. **2** ironic blame: *you have only yourself to thank.*
– PHRASES **I will thank you to do something** used to make a reproachful request. **thank goodness** (or **God** or **heavens**) an expression of relief. **thank one's lucky stars** feel grateful for one's good fortune.
– ORIGIN OE *thancian*, of Gmc origin; cf. **THANKS**.

**thankful** ● adj. **1** pleased and relieved. **2** expressing gratitude.
– DERIVATIVES **thankfulness** n.

**thankfully** ● adv. **1** in a thankful manner. **2** fortunately.

**thankless** ● adj. **1** (of a job or task) unpleasant and unlikely to gain the appreciation of others. **2** (of a person) not showing or feeling gratitude.
– DERIVATIVES **thanklessly** adv. **thanklessness** n.

**thank-offering** ● n. an offering made as an act of thanksgiving.

**thanks** ● pl. n. an expression of gratitude. ➤another way of saying **THANK YOU**.
– PHRASES **no thanks to** despite the unhelpfulness of. **thanks a million** informal thank you very much. **thanks to** due to.
– ORIGIN OE *thancas*, pl. of *thanc* '(kindly) thought, gratitude', of Gmc origin; rel. to **THINK**.

**thanksgiving** ● n. **1** the expression of gratitude, especially to God. **2** (**Thanksgiving** or **Thanksgiving Day**) (in North America) an annual national holiday marked by religious observances and a traditional meal, held in the US on the fourth Thursday in November, and in Canada usually on the second Monday in October.

**thank you** ● exclam. a polite expression of gratitude. ● n. an instance or means of expressing thanks.

**thar** /tɑː/ ● n. variant of **TAHR**.

**that** ● pron. & det. (pl. **those**) **1** used to identify a specific person or thing observed or heard by the speaker. ➤referring to the more distant of two things near to the speaker. **2** referring to a specific thing previously mentioned or known. **3** used in singling out someone or something with a particular feature. **4** informal, chiefly Brit. expressing strong agreement with something just said: *'He's a fussy man.' 'He is that.'* **5** [as pron.] (pl. **that**) used instead of which, who, when etc. to introduce a defining clause, especially one essential to identification. ● adv. to such a degree. ➤[with neg.] informal very: *he wasn't that far away.* ● conj. **1** introducing a subordinate clause. **2** poetic/literary expressing a wish or regret.
– PHRASES **and all that** (or **and that**) informal and so on. **like that** informal instantly or effortlessly. **that is** (or **that is to say**) a formula introducing or following an explanation or further clarification. **that said** even so. **that's that** there is nothing more to do or say about the matter.
– ORIGIN OE *thæt*, nominative and accusative sing. neut. of *se* 'the', of Gmc origin.

**thataway** ● adv. informal, chiefly N. Amer. that way.

**thatch** ● n. **1** a roof covering of straw, reeds, or similar material. ➤material used for such a covering. **2** informal the hair on a person's head. **3** dead stalks, moss, etc. on a lawn. ● v. [often as adj. **thatched**] cover with thatch.
– DERIVATIVES **thatcher** n.
– ORIGIN OE *theccan* 'cover', of Gmc origin.

**Thatcherism** ● n. the political and economic policies advocated by the former UK Conservative Prime Minister Margaret Thatcher (Baroness Thatcher of Kesteven, b. 1925).
– DERIVATIVES **Thatcherite** n. & adj.

**thaumatin** /ˈθɔːmətɪn/ ● n. a sweet-tasting protein isolated from a West African fruit, used as a sweetener in food.
– ORIGIN 1970s: *thaumat-* from mod. L. *Thaumatococcus daniellii* (name of the plant from which the fruit is obtained), + **-IN**[1].

**thaumatrope** /ˈθɔːmətrəʊp/ ● n. **1** a 19th-century scientific toy consisting of a disc with a different picture on each side, these appearing to combine into one when the disc is rapidly rotated. **2** another term for **ZOETROPE**.
– ORIGIN C19: from Gk *thauma* 'marvel' + *-tropos* '-turning'.

**thaumaturge** /ˈθɔːmətəːdʒ/ ● n. a worker of wonders or miracles.
– DERIVATIVES **thaumaturgic** adj. **thaumaturgical** adj. **thaumaturgist** n. **thaumaturgy** n.
– ORIGIN C18 (as *thaumaturg*): via med. L. from Gk *thaumatourgos*, from *thauma* 'marvel' + *-ergos* '-working'.

**thaw** ● v. **1** (of ice, snow, or a frozen thing) become liquid or soft as a result of warming up. ➤(**it thaws**, **it is thawing**, etc.) the weather becomes warmer and causes snow and ice to melt. ➤cause to thaw. **2** (of a part of the body) become warm enough to stop feeling numb. **3** make or become friendlier or more cordial. ● n. **1** a period of warmer weather that thaws ice and snow. **2** an increase in friendliness or cordiality.
– ORIGIN OE *thawian* (v.), of W. Gmc origin.

**THC** ● abbrev. tetrahydrocannabinol.

**the** ● det. **1** denoting one or more people or things already mentioned or assumed to be common knowledge; the def-

inite article. ➤used to refer to a person, place, or thing that is unique. ➤(with a unit of time) the present. ➤informal used instead of a possessive. ➤used with a surname to refer to a family or married couple. **2** used to point forward to a following qualifying or defining clause or phrase. ➤(chiefly with rulers and family members with the same name) used after a name to qualify it. **3** used to make a generalized reference rather than identifying a particular instance. **4** enough of. **5** (pronounced stressing 'the') used to indicate that someone or something is the best known or most important of that name or type. **6** used adverbially with comparatives to indicate how one amount or degree of something varies in relation to another. ➤(usu. **all the** ——) used to emphasize the amount or degree to which something is affected.
– ORIGIN OE *se, sēo, thœt*, ult. superseded by forms from Northumbrian and North Mercian *thē*, of Gmc origin.

**theanthropic** /ˌθiːanˈθrɒpɪk/ ● **adj.** embodying deity in a human form.
– ORIGIN C17: from eccles. Gk *theanthrōpos* 'god-man' (from *theos* 'god' + *anthrōpos* 'human being') + **-IC**.

**thearchy** /ˈθiːɑːki/ ● **n.** (pl. **-ies**) archaic rule by a god or gods.
– ORIGIN C17: from eccles. Gk *thearkhia* 'godhead', from *theos* 'god' + *arkhein* 'to rule'.

**theatre** (US **theater**) ● **n. 1** a building in which plays and other dramatic performances are given. ➤chiefly N. Amer. & W. Indian a cinema. **2** the writing and production of plays. **3** a play or other activity considered in terms of its dramatic quality. **4** (also **lecture theatre**) a room for lectures with seats in tiers. **5** Brit. an operating theatre. **6** the area in which something happens: *a new theatre of war has been opened up*. ➤[as modifier] denoting weapons intermediate between tactical and strategic.
– ORIGIN ME: from OFr., or from L. *theatrum*, from Gk *theatron*, from *theasthai* 'behold'.

**Theatre of the Absurd** ● **n.** drama portraying the futility of human struggle in a senseless world.

**theatric** /θɪˈatrɪk/ ● **adj.** theatrical. ● **n.** (**theatrics**) theatricals.

**theatrical** ● **adj. 1** of, for, or relating to acting, actors, or the theatre. **2** excessively dramatic. ● **n. 1** a professional actor or actress. **2** (**theatricals**) theatrical performances or behaviour.
– DERIVATIVES **theatricalism** n. **theatricality** n. **theatricalization** (also **-isation**) n. **theatricalize** (also **-ise**) v. **theatrically** adv.

**Theban** /ˈθiːbən/ ● **n.** a native or inhabitant of either the ancient Egyptian or the ancient Greek city of Thebes. ● **adj.** of or relating to Thebes.

**thebe** /ˈθeɪbeɪ/ ● **n.** (pl. same) a monetary unit of Botswana, equal to one hundredth of a pula.
– ORIGIN Setswana, lit. 'shield'.

**theca** /ˈθiːkə/ ● **n.** (pl. **thecae** /-siː/) **1** Anatomy the loose sheath enclosing the spinal cord. **2** Anatomy the outer layer of cells of a Graafian follicle. **3** Zoology a cup-like or tubular structure containing a coral polyp. **4** Botany each of the lobes of an anther, containing two pollen sacs.
– DERIVATIVES **thecate** adj.
– ORIGIN C17: via L. from Gk *thēkē* 'case'.

**thecodont** /ˈθiːkə(ʊ)dɒnt/ ● **n.** Palaeontology a Triassic fossil reptile of a group ancestral to dinosaurs and other archosaurs.
– ORIGIN C19: from mod. L. *Thecodontia*, from Gk *thēkē* 'case' + *odous, odont-* 'tooth' (because the teeth were fixed in sockets in the jaw).

**thé dansant** /ˌteɪ dɒ̃ˈsɒ̃, French te dɑ̃sɑ̃/ ● **n.** (pl. **thés dansants** pronunc. same) a tea dance.
– ORIGIN from Fr.

**thee** ● **pron.** [second person sing.] archaic or dialect form of **YOU**, as the singular object of a verb or preposition.
– ORIGIN OE *thē*, accusative and dative case of *thū* 'thou'.

**theft** ● **n.** the action or crime of stealing.
– ORIGIN OE *thīefth, thēofth*, of Gmc origin; rel. to **THIEF**.

**thegn** /θeɪn/ ● **n.** an English thane.
– ORIGIN C19: mod. representation of OE *theg(e)n*, adopted to distinguish the OE use of **THANE** from the Scots use made familiar by Shakespeare.

**theine** /ˈθiːiːn, ˈθiːɪn/ ● **n.** caffeine, especially in tea.
– ORIGIN C19: from mod. L. *Thea* (former genus name of the tea plant) + **-INE**[4].

**their** ● **possess. det. 1** belonging to or associated with the people or things previously mentioned or easily identified. **2** belonging to or associated with a person of unspecified sex (used in place of either 'his' or 'his or her'). **3** (**Their**) used in titles.
– ORIGIN ME: from ON *their(r)a* 'of them', genitive pl. of the demonstrative *sá*; rel. to **THEM** and **THEY**.

**theirs** ● **possess. pron.** used to refer to something belonging to or associated with two or more people or things previously mentioned.
– ORIGIN ME: from **THEIR** + **-'S**.

**theirselves** ● **pron.** [third person pl.] dialect form of **THEMSELVES**.

**theism** /ˈθiːɪz(ə)m/ ● **n.** belief in the existence of a god or gods, specifically of a creator who intervenes in the universe. Compare with **DEISM**.
– DERIVATIVES **theist** n. **theistic** /-ˈɪstɪk/ adj.
– ORIGIN C17: from Gk *theos* 'god' + **-ISM**.

**them** ● **pron.** [third person pl.] **1** used as the object of a verb or preposition to refer to two or more people or things previously mentioned or easily identified. ➤used after the verb 'to be' and after 'than' or 'as'. **2** referring to a person of unspecified sex (used in place of either 'him' or 'him or her'). **3** archaic themselves. ● **det.** informal or dialect those.
– ORIGIN ME: from ON *theim* 'to those, to them', dative pl. of *sá*; rel. to **THEIR** and **THEY**.

**thematic** ● **adj. 1** having or relating to subjects or a particular subject. **2** Music of, relating to, or containing melodic subjects. **3** Linguistics of or relating to the theme of an inflected word. ➤(of a vowel) connecting the theme of a word to its inflections. ➤(of a word) having a thematic vowel. ● **n.** (**thematics**) [treated as sing. or pl.] a body of topics for study or discussion.
– DERIVATIVES **thematically** adv.
– ORIGIN C17: from Gk *thematikos*, from *thema* (see **THEME**).

**thematic apperception test** ● **n.** Psychology a test designed to reveal drives or needs by the interpretation of pictures of emotionally ambiguous situations.

**thematic catalogue** ● **n.** Music a catalogue giving the opening themes of works as well as their names etc.

**thematize** (also **-ise**) ● **v. 1** present or select as a theme. **2** Linguistics place (a word or phrase) at the start of a sentence to focus attention on it.
– DERIVATIVES **thematization** n.

**theme** ● **n. 1** a subject or topic on which a person speaks, writes, or thinks. ➤Linguistics the first major constituent of a clause, indicating the subject matter. Contrasted with **RHEME**. **2** Music a prominent or frequently recurring melody or group of notes in a composition. ➤[as modifier] (of music) frequently recurring in or accompanying the beginning and end of a film, play, etc. **3** [as modifier] denoting a restaurant or pub in which the decor, food, and drink are intended to suggest a particular country, historical period, etc. **4** US an essay written on a set subject. **5** Linguistics the stem of a noun or verb. **6** historical any of the twenty-nine provinces in the Byzantine empire. ● **v.** [often as adj. **themed**] give a particular setting or ambience to.
– ORIGIN ME: via OFr. from L. *thema*, from Gk, lit. 'proposition'; rel. to *tithenai* 'to set or place'.

**theme park** ● **n.** an amusement park with a unifying setting or idea.

**themself** ● **pron.** [third person sing.] informal used instead of 'himself' or 'herself' to refer to a person of unspecified sex.

**themselves** ● **pron.** [third person pl.] **1** used as the object of a verb or preposition to refer to a group of people or things previously mentioned as the subject of the clause. **2** [emphatic] used to emphasize a particular group of people or things mentioned. **3** used instead of 'himself' or 'herself' to refer to a person of unspecified sex.

**then** ● **adv. 1** at that time. **2** after that; next. ➤also. **3** therefore.
– PHRASES **but then** (**again**) on the other hand. **then and there** immediately.

– ORIGIN OE *thœnne, thanne, thonne*, of Gmc origin; rel. to **THAT** and **THE**.

**thence** (also **from thence**) ● **adv.** formal **1** from a place or source previously mentioned. **2** as a consequence.

– ORIGIN ME *thennes*, from earlier *thenne* (from OE *thanon*, of W. Gmc origin) + **-s³** (later respelled *-ce* to denote the unvoiced sound).

**thenceforth** (also **from thenceforth**) ● **adv.** archaic or poetic/literary from that time, place, or point onward.

**thenceforward** ● **adv.** thenceforth.

**theo-** ● **comb. form** relating to God or deities: *theocracy.*

– ORIGIN from Gk *theos* 'god'.

**theobromine** /ˌθɪə(ʊ)ˈbrəʊmɪn, -miːn/ ● **n.** Chemistry a bitter, volatile compound obtained from cacao seeds, resembling caffeine.

– ORIGIN C19: from mod. L. *Theobroma* (genus name, from Gk *theos* 'god' and *brōma* 'food') + **-INE⁴**.

**theocentric** /ˌθɪə(ʊ)ˈsɛntrɪk/ ● **adj.** having God as a central focus.

**theocracy** /θɪˈɒkrəsi/ ● **n.** (pl. **-ies**) a system of government in which priests rule in the name of God or a god. ➤ **(the Theocracy)** the commonwealth of Israel from the time of Moses until Saul became King.

– DERIVATIVES **theocrat** n. **theocratic** adj. **theocratically** adv.

– ORIGIN C17: from Gk *theokratia* (see **THEO-**, **-CRACY**).

**theodicy** /θɪˈɒdɪsi/ ● **n.** (pl. **-ies**) the vindication of divine providence in view of the existence of evil.

– DERIVATIVES **theodicean** /-ˈsiːən/ adj.

– ORIGIN C18: from Fr. *Théodicée*, the title of a work by Leibniz, from Gk *theos* 'god' + *dikē* 'justice'.

**theodolite** /θɪˈɒdəlʌɪt/ ● **n.** a surveying instrument with a rotating telescope for measuring horizontal and vertical angles.

– DERIVATIVES **theodolitic** adj.

– ORIGIN C16: from mod. L. *theodelitus*, of unknown origin.

**theogony** /θɪˈɒgəni/ ● **n.** (pl. **-ies**) the genealogy of a group or system of gods.

– ORIGIN C17: from Gk *theogonia*, from *theos* 'god' + *-gonia* '-begetting'.

**theologian** /θɪəˈləʊdʒɪən, -dʒ(ə)n/ ● **n.** a person expert in or engaged in theology.

**theological virtue** ● **n.** each of the three virtues of faith, hope, and charity. Often contrasted with **NATURAL VIRTUES**.

**theology** ● **n.** (pl. **-ies**) the study of the nature of God and religious belief. ➤ religious beliefs and theory when systematically developed.

– DERIVATIVES **theological** adj. **theologically** adv. **theologist** n. **theologize** (also **-ise**) v.

– ORIGIN ME: from Fr. *théologie*, from L. *theologia*, from Gk, from *theos* 'god' + *-logia* (see **-LOGY**).

**theomachy** /θɪˈɒməki/ ● **n.** (pl. **-ies**) a war or struggle against God or among the gods.

– ORIGIN C16: from Gk *theomakhia*, from *theos* 'god' + *-makhia* 'fighting'.

**theophany** /θɪˈɒf(ə)ni/ ● **n.** (pl. **-ies**) a visible manifestation to humankind of God or a god.

– ORIGIN OE, via eccles. L. from Gk *theophaneia*, from *theos* 'god' + *phainein* 'to show'.

**theophoric** /θɪəˈfɒrɪk/ (also **theophorous**) ● **adj.** bearing the name of a god.

**theophylline** /θɪəˈfɪliːn, -lɪn/ ● **n.** Chemistry a bitter compound present in tea leaves, isomeric with theobromine.

– ORIGIN C19: from mod. L. *Thea* (former genus name of the tea plant) + Gk *phullon* 'leaf' + **-INE⁴**.

**theorbo** /θɪˈɔːbəʊ/ ● **n.** (pl. **-os**) a large lute with the neck extended to carry several long bass strings, used in the 17th and early 18th centuries.

– ORIGIN C17: from Ital. *tiorba*, of unknown origin.

**theorem** /ˈθɪərəm/ ● **n.** Physics & Mathematics a general proposition not self-evident but proved by a chain of reasoning. ➤ a rule in algebra or other branches of mathematics expressed by symbols or formulae.

– DERIVATIVES **theorematic** /-ˈmatɪk/ adj.

– ORIGIN C16: from Fr. *théorème*, or via late L. from Gk *theōrēma* 'speculation, proposition'.

**theoretical** (also **theoretic**) ● **adj.** concerned with or involving theory rather than its practical application. ➤ based on or calculated through theory.

– DERIVATIVES **theoretically** adv.

**theoretician** /ˌθɪərɪˈtɪʃ(ə)n/ ● **n.** a person who develops or studies the theoretical framework of a subject.

**theorist** ● **n.** a theoretician.

**theorize** (also **-ise**) ● **v.** form a theory or theories about something. ➤ create a theoretical premise or framework for.

– DERIVATIVES **theorization** n. **theorizer** n.

**theory** ● **n.** (pl. **-ies**) **1** a supposition or a system of ideas intended to explain something, especially one based on general principles independent of the thing to be explained. ➤ an idea accounting for or justifying something. **2** a set of principles on which an activity is based: *a theory of education.* ➤ Mathematics a collection of propositions illustrating the principles of a subject.

– PHRASES **in theory** in an ideal or hypothetical situation.

– ORIGIN C16: via late L. from Gk *theōria* 'contemplation, speculation'.

**theosophy** /θɪˈɒsəfi/ ● **n.** any of a number of philosophies maintaining that a knowledge of God may be achieved through spiritual ecstasy, direct intuition, or special individual relations.

– DERIVATIVES **theosopher** n. **theosophic** adj. **theosophical** adj. **theosophically** adv. **theosophist** n.

– ORIGIN C17: from med. L. *theosophia*, from late Gk, from *theosophos* 'wise concerning God', from *theos* 'god' + *sophos* 'wise'.

**therapeutic** /ˌθɛrəˈpjuːtɪk/ ● **adj.** of or relating to the healing of disease. ➤ having a good effect on the body or mind.

– DERIVATIVES **therapeutical** adj. **therapeutically** adv. **therapeutist** n. (archaic).

– ORIGIN C17: via mod. L. from Gk *therapeutikos*, from *therapeuein* 'minister to, treat medically'.

**therapeutics** ● **pl. n.** [treated as sing.] the branch of medicine concerned with the treatment of disease and the action of remedial agents.

**therapsid** /θɛˈrapsɪd/ ● **n.** Palaeontology a fossil reptile of a large group including the cynodonts, related to the ancestors of mammals.

– ORIGIN C20: from mod. L. *Therapsida* (name of an order), from Gk *thēr* 'beast' + *hapsis, hapsid-* 'arch' (referring to the structure of the skull).

**therapy** ● **n.** (pl. **-ies**) treatment intended to relieve or heal a disorder. ➤ the treatment of mental or psychological disorders by psychological means: *he is currently in therapy.*

– DERIVATIVES **therapist** n.

– ORIGIN C19: from mod. L. *therapia*, from Gk *therapeia* 'healing', from *therapeuein* 'minister to, treat medically'.

**Theravada** /ˌθɛrəˈvɑːdə/ (also **Theravada Buddhism**) ● **n.** the more conservative of the two major traditions of Buddhism (the other being Mahayana), practised mainly in Sri Lanka, Burma (Myanmar), Thailand, Cambodia, and Laos.

– ORIGIN from Pali *theravāda*, lit. 'doctrine of the elders', from *thera* 'elder, old' + *vāda* 'speech, doctrine'.

**there** ● **adv. 1** in, at, or to that place or position. ➤ in that respect; on that issue. **2** used in attracting attention to someone or something. **3** (usu. **there is/are**) used to indicate the fact or existence of something. ● **exclam. 1** used to focus attention. **2** used to comfort someone.

– PHRASES **be there for** be available to provide support or comfort for. **have been there before** informal know all about a situation from experience. **here and there** in various places. **so there** informal used to express defiance. **there and then** immediately.

– ORIGIN OE *thǣr, thēr* of Gmc origin; rel. to **THAT** and **THE**.

**thereabouts** (also **thereabout**) ● **adv. 1** near that place. **2** used to indicate that a date or figure is approximate.

**thereafter** ● **adv.** formal after that time.

**thereat** ● **adv.** archaic or formal **1** at that place. **2** on account

## Word *Formation*

**-therm**, **-thermal**, etc. from Greek *thermē* 'heat'

| | | |
|---|---|---|
| ectotherm | an animal dependent on external sources of body heat | Gk *ektos* 'outside' |
| endotherm | an animal dependent on internal generation of heat | Gk *endon* 'within' |
| endothermic | (of a reaction) accompanied by the absorption of heat | Gk *endon* 'within' |
| eurythermal | (of an organism) tolerant of a wide temperature range | Gk *eurus* 'wide' |
| exothermic | (of a reaction) accompanied by the release of heat | Gk *exō* 'outside' |
| geothermal | relating to the internal heat of the earth | Gk *gē* 'earth' |
| homeotherm | an organism that maintains constant body heat by metabolic activity | Gk *homoios* 'like' |
| isotherm | a line on a map joining places of equal temperature | Gk *isos* 'equal' |
| poikilotherm | an organism that cannot regulate body temperature internally | Gk *poikilos* 'varied' |
| stenothermal | (of an organism) able to tolerate only small ranges in temperature | Gk *stenos* 'narrow' |

The dish called ***lobster thermidor*** is named after *Thermidor*, a month in the French Republican Calendar of 1793–1805 corresponding to parts of July and August, itself based on Greek *thermē* 'heat' and *dōron* 'gift'.

of or after that.

**thereby** ● **adv.** by that means; as a result of that.

**therefor** ● **adv.** archaic for that object or purpose.

**therefore** ● **adv.** for that reason; consequently.

**therefrom** ● **adv.** archaic or formal from that or that place.

**therein** ● **adv.** archaic or formal in that place, document, or respect.

**thereinafter** ● **adv.** archaic or formal in a later part of that document.

**thereinbefore** ● **adv.** archaic or formal in an earlier part of that document.

**thereinto** ● **adv.** archaic or formal into that place.

**theremin** /ˈθɛrəmɪn/ ● **n.** an electronic musical instrument in which the tone is generated by two high-frequency oscillators and the pitch controlled by the movement of the performer's hand towards and away from the circuit.
– ORIGIN C20: named after its Russ. inventor Lev *Theremin*.

**thereof** ● **adv.** formal of the thing just mentioned; of that.

**thereon** ● **adv.** formal on or following from the thing just mentioned.

**thereout** ● **adv.** archaic out of that; from that source.

**there's** ● **contr.** **1** there is. **2** there has.

**thereto** ● **adv.** archaic or formal to that or that place.

**theretofore** ● **adv.** archaic or formal before that time.

**thereunto** ● **adv.** archaic or formal to that.

**thereupon** ● **adv.** formal immediately or shortly after that.

**therewith** ● **adv.** archaic or formal **1** with or in the thing mentioned. **2** soon or immediately after that; forthwith.

**therewithal** ● **adv.** archaic together with that; besides.

**Theria** /ˈθɪərɪə/ ● **pl. n.** Zoology the marsupials and placental mammals (i.e. all mammals apart from the Prototheria).
– DERIVATIVES **therian** n. & adj.
– ORIGIN mod. L., from Gk *thēria* 'wild animals'.

**theriac** /ˈθɪərɪak/ ● **n.** archaic an ointment or other compound used as an antidote to snake venom or other poison.
– ORIGIN ME: from L. *theriaca* (see **TREACLE**).

**therianthropic** /ˌθɪərɪanˈθrɒpɪk/ ● **adj.** (especially of a deity) combining the form of an animal with that of a man.
– ORIGIN C19: from Gk *thērion* 'wild animal' + *anthrōpos* 'human being' + **-IC**.

**theriomorphic** /ˌθɪərɪə(ʊ)ˈmɔːfɪk/ ● **adj.** (especially of a deity) having an animal form.
– ORIGIN C19: from Gk *thērion* 'wild animal' + **-MORPH** + **-IC**.

**therm** ● **n.** a unit of heat, especially as the former statutory unit of gas supplied in the UK equivalent to 100,000 British thermal units or $1.055 \times 10^8$ joules.
– ORIGIN 1920s: from Gk *thermē* 'heat'.

**thermae** /ˈθəːmiː/ ● **pl. n.** (in ancient Greece and Rome) hot baths used for public bathing.
– ORIGIN L., from Gk *thermai* 'hot baths', from *thermē* 'heat'.

**thermal** ● **adj.** **1** of or relating to heat. ➤ another term for **GEOTHERMAL**. ➤ Physics relating to or denoting particles in thermodynamic equilibrium with their surroundings: *thermal neutrons*. **2** (of a garment) made of a fabric that provides good insulation to keep the body warm. ● **n.** **1** an upward current of warm air, used by birds, gliders, and balloonists to gain height. **2** (**thermals**) thermal garments, especially underwear.
– DERIVATIVES **thermally** adv.
– ORIGIN C18 (in the sense 'relating to hot springs'): from Fr., from Gk *thermē* 'heat'.

**thermal capacity** ● **n.** the quantity of heat needed to raise the temperature of a body by one degree.

**thermal efficiency** ● **n.** the efficiency of a heat engine measured by the ratio of the work done by it to the heat supplied to it.

**thermal imaging** ● **n.** the technique of using the heat given off by an object to produce an image of it or locate it.
– DERIVATIVES **thermal imager** n.

**thermalize** (also **-ise**) ● **v.** attain or cause to attain thermal equilibrium with the environment.
– DERIVATIVES **thermalization** n.

**thermal printer** ● **n.** a printer in which fine heated pins form characters on heat-sensitive paper.

**thermal spring** ● **n.** a spring of naturally hot water.

**thermic** ● **adj.** of or relating to heat.

**thermionic** ● **adj.** relating to or denoting the emission of electrons from substances heated to very high temperatures.
– DERIVATIVES **thermionics** pl. n.

**thermionic valve** (US **thermionic tube**) ● **n.** Electronics a vacuum tube giving a flow of thermionic electrons in one direction, used especially in the rectification of a current and in radio reception.

**thermistor** /θəːˈmɪstə/ ● **n.** an electrical resistor whose resistance is greatly reduced by heating, used for measurement and control.
– ORIGIN 1940s: contr. of *thermal resistor*.

**thermite** /ˈθəːmʌɪt/ (also **thermit** /-mɪt/) ● **n.** a mixture of finely powdered aluminium and iron oxide that produces a very high temperature on combustion, used in welding and for incendiary bombs.
– ORIGIN C20: coined in Ger. from **THERMO-** + **-ITE**[1].

**thermo-** ● **comb. form** relating to heat: *thermodynamics*.

– ORIGIN from Gk *thermos* 'hot', *thermē* 'heat'.

**thermochemistry** ● **n.** the branch of chemistry concerned with the quantities of heat evolved or absorbed during chemical reactions.
– DERIVATIVES **thermochemical** adj.

**thermochromic** /ˌθəːmə(ʊ)ˈkrəʊmɪk/ ● **adj.** undergoing a reversible change of colour when heated or cooled.

**thermocline** /ˈθəːmə(ʊ)klʌɪn/ ● **n.** a temperature gradient in a lake or other body of water, separating layers at different temperatures.

**thermocouple** ● **n.** a device for measuring or sensing a temperature difference, consisting of two wires of different metals connected at two points, between which a voltage is developed in proportion to any temperature difference.

**thermodynamics** ● **pl. n.** [treated as sing.] the branch of science concerned with the relations between heat and other forms of energy involved in physical and chemical processes.
– DERIVATIVES **thermodynamic** adj. **thermodynamical** adj. **thermodynamically** adv. **thermodynamicist** n.

**thermoelectric** ● **adj.** producing electricity by a difference of temperatures.
– DERIVATIVES **thermoelectrically** adv. **thermoelectricity** n.

**thermogenesis** /ˌθəːmə(ʊ)ˈdʒɛnɪsɪs/ ● **n.** Physiology the production of bodily heat.
– DERIVATIVES **thermogenic** adj.

**thermogram** ● **n.** a record made by a thermograph.

**thermograph** ● **n.** an instrument that produces a record of the varying temperature or infrared radiation over an area or during a period of time.

**thermography** ● **n. 1** the production and use of thermograms, especially in medicine. **2** a printing technique in which a wet ink image is fused by heating with a resinous powder to produce a raised impression.
– DERIVATIVES **thermographic** adj.

**thermohaline** /ˌθəːmə(ʊ)ˈheɪlʌɪn, -ˈheɪliːn/ ● **adj.** Oceanography relating to or denoting the circulation of seawater driven by temperature variations which cause changes in salinity and density.

**thermokarst** /ˈθəːmə(ʊ)kɑːst/ ● **n.** Geology a periglacial landscape resembling karst, resulting from the selective melting of permafrost.

**thermolabile** /ˌθəːmə(ʊ)ˈleɪbʌɪl, -bɪl/ ● **adj.** chiefly Biochemistry readily destroyed or deactivated by heat.

**thermoluminescence** ● **n.** the property of some ceramics and other materials of becoming luminescent when pretreated and heated, used as a means of dating ancient artefacts.
– DERIVATIVES **thermoluminescent** adj.

**thermolysis** /θəˈmɒlɪsɪs/ ● **n.** Chemistry the breakdown of molecules by the action of heat.
– DERIVATIVES **thermolytic** adj.

**thermometer** ● **n.** an instrument for measuring and indicating temperature, typically consisting of a graduated glass tube containing mercury or alcohol which expands when heated.
– DERIVATIVES **thermometric** adj. **thermometrical** adj. **thermometry** n.
– ORIGIN C17: from Fr. *thermomètre* or mod. L. *thermometrum*, from **THERMO-** + *-metrum* 'measure'.

**thermonuclear** ● **adj.** (chiefly with reference to weapons) using or denoting nuclear fusion reactions that occur at very high temperatures.

**thermophile** /ˈθəːmə(ʊ)fʌɪl/ ● **n.** Microbiology a bacterium or other micro-organism that grows best at higher than normal temperatures.
– DERIVATIVES **thermophilic** adj.

**thermopile** /ˈθəːmə(ʊ)pʌɪl/ ● **n.** a set of thermocouples arranged for measuring small quantities of radiant heat.

**thermoplastic** ● **adj.** denoting substances (especially synthetic resins) which become plastic when heated. Often contrasted with **THERMOSETTING**.

**thermoregulation** ● **n.** Physiology the regulation of bodily temperature.
– DERIVATIVES **thermoregulate** v. **thermoregulatory** adj.

**Thermos** ● **n.** trademark a vacuum flask.
– ORIGIN C20: from Gk, lit. 'hot'.

**thermosetting** (also **thermoset**) ● **adj.** denoting substances (especially synthetic resins) which set permanently when heated. Often contrasted with **THERMOPLASTIC**.

**thermosphere** ● **n.** the upper region of the atmosphere above the mesosphere.

**thermostable** ● **adj.** chiefly Biochemistry not readily destroyed or deactivated by heat.

**thermostat** /ˈθəːməstat/ ● **n.** a device that automatically regulates temperature or activates a device at a set temperature.
– DERIVATIVES **thermostatic** adj. **thermostatically** adv.

**thermotropism** /ˌθəːmə(ʊ)ˈtrəʊpɪz(ə)m/ ● **n.** Biology the orientation of a plant or other organism in response to a source of heat.
– DERIVATIVES **thermotropic** adj.

**theropod** /ˈθɪərə(ʊ)pɒd/ ● **n.** a dinosaur of a group including bipedal carnivores such as the carnosaurs and dromaeosaurs.
– ORIGIN 1930s: from mod. L. *Theropoda* (pl.), from Gk *thēr* 'beast' + *pous, pod-* 'foot'.

**thesaurus** /θɪˈsɔːrəs/ ● **n.** (pl. **thesauri** /-rʌɪ/ or **thesauruses**) **1** a book that lists words in groups of synonyms and related concepts. **2** archaic a dictionary or encyclopedia.
– ORIGIN C16: via L. from Gk *thēsauros* 'storehouse, treasure'.

**these** plural form of **THIS**.

**thesis** /ˈθiːsɪs/ ● **n.** (pl. **theses** /-siːz/) **1** a statement or theory that is put forward as a premise to be maintained or proved. ➤(in Hegelian philosophy) a proposition forming the first stage in the process of dialectical reasoning. Compare with **ANTITHESIS**, **SYNTHESIS**. **2** a long essay or dissertation involving personal research, written as part of a university degree. **3** /also ˈθɛsɪs/ Prosody an unstressed syllable or part of a metrical foot in Greek or Latin verse. Often contrasted with **ARSIS**.
– ORIGIN ME: via late L. from Gk, lit. 'placing, a proposition', from the root of *tithenai* 'to place'.

**thespian** /ˈθɛspɪən/ ● **adj.** of or relating to drama and the theatre. ● **n.** an actor or actress.
– ORIGIN C17: from the name of the Gk dramatic poet *Thespis* (6th cent. BC).

**Thess.** ● **abbrev.** Epistle to the Thessalonians (in biblical references).

**theta** /ˈθiːtə/ ● **n.** the eighth letter of the Greek alphabet (Θ, θ), transliterated as 'th'. ● **symb. 1** (θ) temperature. **2** (θ) a plane angle. **3** (θ) a polar coordinate. Often coupled with φ.
– ORIGIN from Gk.

**theta rhythm** ● **n.** Physiology electrical activity observed in the brain under certain conditions, consisting of oscillations (**theta waves**) with a frequency of 4 to 7 hertz.

**theurgy** /ˈθiːəːdʒi/ ● **n. 1** the operation or effect of a supernatural or divine agency in human affairs. **2** a system of white magic practised by the early Neoplatonists.
– DERIVATIVES **theurgic** adj. **theurgical** adj. **theurgist** n.
– ORIGIN C16: via late L. from Gk *theourgia* 'sorcery', from *theos* 'god' + *-ergos* 'working'.

**thew** /θjuː/ ● **n.** (also **thews**) poetic/literary muscle or muscular strength.
– DERIVATIVES **thewed** adj. **thewy** adj.
– ORIGIN OE *thēaw* 'usage, custom', later 'a virtue or good quality', (pl.) 'physical endowments, strength', of unknown origin.

**they** ● **pron.** [third person pl.] **1** used to refer to two or more people or things previously mentioned or easily identified. ➤people in general. ➤informal people in authority regarded collectively. **2** used to refer to a person of unspecified sex (in place of either 'he' or 'he or she').
– ORIGIN ME: from ON *their*, nominative pl. masc. of *sá*.

**they'd** ● **contr. 1** they had. **2** they would.

**they'll** ● **contr. 1** they shall. **2** they will.

**they're** • contr. they are.

**they've** • contr. they have.

**THI** • abbrev. temperature–humidity index.

**thiabendazole** /ˌθʌɪəˈbɛndəzəʊl/ • n. Medicine a synthetic compound with anthelmintic properties, derived from thiazole.
– ORIGIN 1960s: from elements of **THIAZOLE** + **BENZENE** + **IMIDAZOLE**.

**thiamine** /ˈθʌɪəmiːn, -mɪn/ (also **thiamin**) • n. Biochemistry vitamin $B_1$, a compound found in unrefined cereals, beans, and liver, a deficiency of which causes beriberi.
– ORIGIN 1930s: from **THIO-** + **AMINE**.

**thiazide** /ˈθʌɪəzʌɪd/ • n. Medicine any of a class of sulphur-containing drugs that increase the excretion of sodium and chloride and are used as diuretics and to lower the blood pressure.
– ORIGIN 1950s: from elements of **THIO-** + **AZINE** + **OXIDE**.

**thiazole** /θʌɪˈeɪzəʊl/ • n. Chemistry a synthetic liquid with an unpleasant smell, whose molecule is a ring of one nitrogen, one sulphur, and three carbon atoms, used in dyes and fungicides.

**thick** • adj. **1** with opposite sides or surfaces relatively far apart. ➤(of a garment or similar item) made of heavy material. **2** made up of a large number of things or people close together. ➤(**thick with**) densely filled or covered with. ➤(of the air or atmosphere) opaque, heavy, or dense: *thick fog.* **3** (of a liquid or a semi-liquid substance) relatively firm in consistency; not flowing freely. **4** informal of low intelligence; stupid. **5** (of a voice) not clear or distinct; hoarse or husky. ➤(of an accent) very marked and difficult to understand. **6** informal having a very close, friendly relationship. • n. (**the thick**) the middle or the busiest part of something: *in the thick of battle.* • adv. in or with deep, dense, or heavy mass.
– PHRASES **be thick on the ground** see **GROUND**[1]. **a bit thick** Brit. informal unfair or unreasonable. **give someone** (or **get**) **a thick ear** Brit. informal punish someone (or be punished) with a blow on the ear. **have a thick skin** see **SKIN**. **thick and fast** rapidly and in great numbers. (**as**) **thick as thieves** informal very close or friendly. (**as**) **thick as two** (**short**) **planks** (or **as a plank**) Brit. informal very stupid. **the thick end of something** Brit. the greater part of something. **through thick and thin** under all circumstances, no matter how difficult.
– DERIVATIVES **thickish** adj. **thickly** adv.
– ORIGIN OE *thicce*, of Gmc origin.

**thicken** • v. make or become thick or thicker.
– PHRASES **the plot thickens** the situation is becoming more complicated and puzzling.
– DERIVATIVES **thickener** n.

**thickening** • n. **1** the process or result of becoming thicker. ➤a thicker area of animal or plant tissue. **2** a substance added to a liquid to make it thicker.

**thicket** • n. a dense group of bushes or trees.
– ORIGIN OE *thiccet* (see **THICK**, **-ET**[1]).

**thickhead** • n. informal a stupid person.
– DERIVATIVES **thickheaded** adj. **thickheadedness** n.

**thick-knee** • n. another term for **STONE CURLEW**.

**thickness** • n. **1** the distance through an object, as distinct from width or height. ➤a layer of material. ➤a thicker part of something. **2** the state or quality of being thick. • v. plane or cut (wood) to a desired thickness.
– DERIVATIVES **thicknesser** n.

**thicko** • n. (pl. **-os**) informal an unintelligent person.

**thickset** • adj. (of a person or animal) heavily or solidly built; stocky.

**thick-skulled** (also **thick-witted**) • adj. dull and stupid.

**thief** • n. (pl. **thieves**) a person who steals another person's property.
– ORIGIN OE *thīof*, *thēof*, of Gmc origin.

**thieve** • v. be a thief; steal things.
– DERIVATIVES **thievery** n. **thieving** n. & adj. **thievish** adj. **thievishly** adv. **thievishness** n.
– ORIGIN OE *thēofian*, from *thēof* 'thief'.

**thigh** • n. the part of the human leg between the hip and the knee. ➤the corresponding part in other animals.
– DERIVATIVES **-thighed** adj.
– ORIGIN OE *thēh*, *thēoh*, *thīoh*, of Gmc origin.

**thigh bone** • n. the femur.

**thigh-slapper** • n. informal a very funny joke or anecdote.
– DERIVATIVES **thigh-slapping** adj.

**thigmotropism** /ˌθɪgmə(ʊ)ˈtrəʊpɪz(ə)m/ • n. Biology the turning or bending of a plant or other organism in response to a touch stimulus.
– DERIVATIVES **thigmotropic** adj.
– ORIGIN C20: from Gk *thigma* 'touch' + **TROPISM**.

**thill** • n. historical a shaft, especially one of a pair, used to attach a cart or carriage to the animal drawing it.
– ORIGIN ME: of unknown origin.

**thiller** • n. historical a horse attached to a thill.

**thimble** • n. **1** a metal or plastic cap with a closed end, worn to protect the finger and push the needle in sewing. ➤any short metal tube or ferrule. **2** Nautical a metal ring, concave on the outside, around which a loop of rope is spliced.
– ORIGIN OE *thȳmel* 'finger-stall' (see **THUMB**, **-LE**[1]).

**thimbleberry** • n. (pl. **-ies**) a North American blackberry or raspberry with thimble-shaped fruit. [*Rubus odoratus* and related species.]

**thimbleful** • n. (pl. **-fuls**) a small quantity of something.

**thimblerig** • n. a game involving sleight of hand, in which three inverted thimbles or cups are moved about, contestants having to spot which is the one with a pea or other object underneath.
– DERIVATIVES **thimblerigger** n.
– ORIGIN C19: from **THIMBLE** + **RIG**[2] in the sense 'trick, dodge'.

**thin** • adj. (**thinner**, **thinnest**) **1** having opposite surfaces or sides close together. ➤(of a garment or fabric) having become less thick as a result of wear. **2** having little flesh or fat on the body. **3** having few parts or members relative to the area covered or filled; sparse. ➤not dense or heavy: *the thin cold air of the mountains.* **4** containing much liquid and not much solid substance. **5** (of a sound) faint and high-pitched. ➤(of a smile) weak and forced. **6** too weak to justify a result or effect; inadequate: *the evidence is rather thin.* • adv. with little thickness or depth. • v. (**thinned**, **thinning**) **1** make or become less thick. **2** remove some plants from (a row or area) to allow the others more room to grow. **3** Golf hit (a ball) above its centre.
– PHRASES **have a thin time** Brit. informal have a miserable or uncomfortable time. **thin air** used to refer to the state of being invisible or non-existent. **the thin blue line** informal the police. **thin on the ground** see **GROUND**[1].
– DERIVATIVES **thinly** adv. **thinness** n. **thinnish** adj.
– ORIGIN OE *thynne*, of Gmc origin.

**-thin** • comb. form denoting a specified degree of thinness: *wafer-thin.*

**thine** • possess. pron. archaic form of **YOURS**; the thing or things belonging to or associated with thee. • possess. det. form of **THY** used before a vowel.
– ORIGIN OE *thīn*, of Gmc origin; rel. to **THOU**[1].

**thing** • n. **1** an object that one need not, cannot, or does not wish to give a specific name to. ➤(**things**) personal belongings or clothing. **2** an inanimate material object, especially as distinct from a living sentient being. ➤a living creature or plant. ➤a person or animal in terms of one's feelings of pity, approval, etc.: *you lucky thing!* **3** an action, activity, concept, or thought. ➤(**things**) unspecified circumstances or matters. **4** (**the thing**) informal what is needed or required. ➤what is socially acceptable or fashionable. **5** (**one's thing**) informal one's special interest or concern.
– PHRASES **be on to a good thing** informal be in a situation that is pleasant, profitable, or easy. **be hearing** (or **seeing**) **things** imagine that one can hear (or see) something that is not in fact there. **a close** (or **near**) **thing** a narrow avoidance of something unpleasant. **do one's own thing** informal follow one's own inclinations regardless of others. **have a thing about** informal have a preoccupation or obsession with. **there is only one thing for it** there is only one possible course of action. (**now**)

**there's a thing** informal used as an expression of surprise.
– ORIGIN OE (also in the senses 'meeting' and 'matter, concern'), of Gmc origin.

**thingamabob** /ˈθɪŋəməbɒb/ (also **thingumabob**, **thingamajig**, or **thingumajig** /ˈθɪŋəmədʒɪɡ/) ● n. another term for **THINGUMMY**.

**thingummy** /ˈθɪŋəmi/ (also **thingamy**) ● n. (pl. **-ies**) informal a person or thing whose name one has forgotten, does not know, or does not wish to mention.
– ORIGIN C18: from **THING** + a meaningless suffix.

**thingy** ● n. (pl. **-ies**) another term for **THINGUMMY**.

**think** ● v. (past and past part. **thought**) **1** have a particular opinion, belief, or idea about someone or something. **2** direct one's mind towards someone or something; use one's mind actively to form connected ideas. ➤(**think of/about**) take into account or consideration. ➤(**think of/about**) consider the possibility or advantages of. ➤have a particular mental attitude or approach. ➤(**think of**) have a particular opinion of. **3** call something to mind; remember. ● n. informal an act of thinking.
– PHRASES **have (got) another think coming** informal used to express disagreement. **think aloud** express one's thoughts as they occur. **think better of** decide not to do (something) after reconsideration. **think big** see **BIG**. **think nothing** (or **little**) **of** consider (an activity others regard as odd, wrong, or difficult) as straightforward or normal. **think twice** consider a course of action carefully before embarking on it.
– PHRASAL VERBS **think back** recall a past event or time. **think on** dialect & N. Amer. think of or about. **think something out** (or **through**) consider something in all its aspects before taking action. **think something over** consider something carefully. **think something up** informal invent or devise something.
– DERIVATIVES **thinkable** adj. **thinker** n.
– ORIGIN OE *thencan*, of Gmc origin.

**thinking** ● adj. using thought or rational judgement; intelligent. ● n. a person's ideas or opinions. ➤(**thinkings**) archaic thoughts; meditations.
– PHRASES **good thinking!** an expression of approval for an ingenious plan or observation. **put on one's thinking cap** informal meditate on a problem.

**think tank** ● n. a body of experts providing advice and ideas on specific political or economic problems.
– DERIVATIVES **think-tanker** n.

**thinner** ● n. a volatile solvent used to make paint or other solutions less viscous.

**thinnings** ● pl. n. seedlings, trees, or fruit which have been thinned out to improve the growth of those remaining.

**thio-** ● comb. form Chemistry denoting replacement of oxygen by sulphur in a compound: *thiosulphate*.
– ORIGIN from Gk *theion* 'sulphur'.

**thiocyanate** /ˌθʌɪə(ʊ)ˈsʌɪəneɪt/ ● n. Chemistry a salt containing the anion $SCN^-$.

**thiol** /ˈθʌɪɒl/ ● n. Chemistry an organic compound containing the group –SH, i.e. a sulphur-containing analogue of an alcohol.

**thionyl** /ˈθʌɪənɪl/ ● n. [as modifier] Chemistry of or denoting the divalent radical =SO.

**thiopental** ● n. North American term for **THIOPENTONE**.

**thiopentone** /ˌθʌɪə(ʊ)ˈpɛntəʊn/ ● n. Medicine a sulphur-containing barbiturate drug used as a general anaesthetic and hypnotic, and (reputedly) as a truth drug.
– ORIGIN 1940s: from **THIO-** + a contr. of **PENTOBARBITONE**.

**thiosulphate** (US **thiosulfate**) ● n. Chemistry a salt containing the anion $S_2O_3^{2-}$, i.e. a sulphate with one oxygen atom replaced by sulphur.

**third** ● ordinal number **1** constituting number three in a sequence; 3rd. **2** (**a third/one third**) each of three equal parts into which something is or may be divided. **3** Music an interval spanning three consecutive notes in a diatonic scale, e.g. C to E (**major third**, equal to two tones) or A to C (**minor third**, equal to a tone and a semitone). ➤Music the note which is higher by this interval than the tonic of a diatonic scale or root of a chord. **4** Brit. a place in the third grade in an examination, especially that for a degree.
– PHRASES **third time lucky** (or US **third time is the charm**) used to express the hope that one may succeed in the third attempt.
– DERIVATIVES **thirdly** adv.
– ORIGIN OE *thridda*, of Gmc origin; rel. to **THREE**.

**third age** ● n. Brit. the period in life of active retirement, following middle age.
– DERIVATIVES **third ager** n.

**third class** ● n. **1** a group of people or things considered together as the third best. **2** Brit. the third-highest division in the results of the examinations for a university degree. **3** US a cheap class of mail for unsealed printed material. **4** chiefly historical the cheapest and least comfortable accommodation in a train or ship. ● adj. & adv. of the third-best quality or in the third class.

**third-degree** ● adj. **1** denoting burns of the most severe kind, affecting tissue below the skin. **2** Law, chiefly N. Amer. denoting the least serious category of a crime, especially murder. ● n. (**the third degree**) long and harsh questioning to obtain information or a confession.

**third estate** ● n. [treated as sing. or pl.] the third order or class in a country or society, comprising the common people. See also **ESTATE** (in sense 5).

**third eye** ● n. **1** Hinduism & Buddhism the 'eye of insight' in the forehead of an image of a deity, especially the god Shiva. ➤the faculty of intuitive insight or prescience. **2** informal term for **PINEAL EYE**.

**third eyelid** ● n. informal term for **NICTITATING MEMBRANE**.

**third force** ● n. a political group or party acting as a check on conflict between two extreme or opposing groups.

**third man** ● n. Cricket a fielding position near the boundary behind the slips.

**third party** ● n. a person or group besides the two primarily involved in a situation, especially in a dispute. ● adj. **1** of or relating to a third party. **2** Brit. (of insurance) covering damage or injury suffered by a person other than the insured.

**third person** ● n. **1** a third party. **2** see **PERSON** (sense 5).

**third position** ● n. **1** Ballet a posture in which the turned-out feet are placed one in front of the other, so that the heel of the front foot fits into the hollow of the instep of the back foot. **2** Music a position of the left hand on the fingerboard of a stringed instrument nearer to the bridge than the second position.

**third rail** ● n. an additional rail supplying electric current, used in some electric railway systems.

**third-rate** ● adj. of inferior or very poor quality.
– DERIVATIVES **third-rater** n.

**third reading** ● n. a third presentation of a bill to a legislative assembly, in the UK to debate committee reports and in the US to consider it for the last time.

**third way** ● n. any option regarded as an alternative to two extremes, especially a political agenda which is centrist and consensus-based rather than left- or right-wing.

**Third World** ● n. the developing countries of Asia, Africa, and Latin America.
– ORIGIN 1950s: translating *tiers monde*, first used to distinguish the developing countries from the capitalist and Communist blocs.

**thirst** ● n. **1** a feeling of needing or wanting to drink. ➤lack of the liquid needed to sustain life. **2** (**thirst for**) a strong desire for. ● v. **1** archaic feel a need to drink. **2** (**thirst for/after**) have a strong desire for.
– ORIGIN OE *thurst* (n.), *thyrstan* (v.), of Gmc origin.

**thirsty** ● adj. (**-ier**, **-iest**) **1** feeling thirst. ➤(of land, plants, etc.) in need of water; dry or parched. ➤(of an engine, plant, or crop) consuming a lot of fuel or water. **2** informal causing thirst: *modelling is thirsty work*.
– DERIVATIVES **thirstily** adv. **thirstiness** n.

**thirteen** ● cardinal number equivalent to the sum of six and seven; one more than twelve, or seven less than twenty; 13. (Roman numeral: **xiii** or **XIII**.)

– DERIVATIVES **thirteenth** ordinal number.
– ORIGIN OE *thrēotīene* (see **THREE**, **-TEEN**).

**thirty** • cardinal number (pl. **-ies**) the number equivalent to the product of three and ten; ten less than forty; 30. (Roman numeral: **xxx** or **XXX**.)
– DERIVATIVES **thirtieth** ordinal number. **thirtyfold** adj. & adv.
– ORIGIN OE *thrītig* (see **THREE**, **-TY**[2]).

**thirty-eight** • n. a revolver of .38 calibre.

**thirty-second note** • n. Music, chiefly N. Amer. a demisemiquaver.

**thirty-two-mo** • n. (pl. **-os**) a size of book that results from folding each printed sheet into thirty-two leaves (sixty-four pages).

**this** • pron. & det. (pl. **these**) **1** used to identify a specific person or thing close at hand or being indicated or experienced. ➤referring to the nearer of two things close to the speaker. **2** referring to a specific thing or situation just mentioned. **3** [as det.] used with periods of time related to the present. • adv. to the degree or extent indicated.
– PHRASES **this and that** (or **this, that, and the other**) informal various unspecified things. **this here** informal used to show emphasis.
– ORIGIN OE, neut. of *thes*, of W. Gmc origin; rel. to **THAT** and **THE**.

**thistle** • n. **1** a widely distributed herbaceous plant of the daisy family, typically with a prickly stem and leaves and rounded heads of purple flowers. [*Carlina*, *Carduus*, and other genera.] **2** a plant of this type as the Scottish national emblem.
– DERIVATIVES **thistly** adj.
– ORIGIN OE *thistel*, of Gmc origin.

**thistledown** • n. the light fluffy down of thistle seeds, enabling them to be blown about in the wind.

**thither** /ˈðɪðə/ • adv. archaic or poetic/literary to or towards that place.
– ORIGIN OE *thider*, alt. (by assoc. with **HITHER**) of *thæder*, of Gmc origin; rel. to **THAT** and **THE**.

**thixotropy** /θɪkˈsɒtrəpi/ • n. Chemistry the property of becoming less viscous when subjected to an applied stress, such as being shaken or stirred.
– DERIVATIVES **thixotropic** adj.
– ORIGIN 1920s: from Gk *thixis* 'touching' + *tropē* 'turning'.

**tho'** (also **tho**) • conj. & adv. informal spelling of **THOUGH**.

**thole**[1] /θəʊl/ (also **thole pin**) • n. a pin, typically one of a pair, fitted to the gunwale of a rowing boat to act as the fulcrum for an oar.
– ORIGIN OE, of Gmc origin.

**thole**[2] /θəʊl/ • v. Scottish or archaic endure without complaint; tolerate.
– ORIGIN OE *tholian*, of Gmc origin.

**tholeiite** /ˈθəʊlɪʌɪt/ • n. Geology a silica-rich basaltic rock containing augite and pyroxene.
– DERIVATIVES **tholeiitic** /ˌθəʊlɪˈɪtɪk/ adj.
– ORIGIN C19: from *Tholei*, the name of a village (now *Tholey*) in the Saarland, Germany, + **-ITE**[1].

**tholos** /ˈθɒlɒs/ • n. (pl. **tholoi** /-lɔɪ/) Archaeology a dome-shaped tomb of ancient Greek origin, especially one dating from the Mycenaean period.
– ORIGIN from Gk.

**Thomism** /ˈtəʊmɪz(ə)m/ • n. the theology and philosophy of St Thomas Aquinas (1225–74), the foremost figure of scholasticism, or of his followers.
– DERIVATIVES **Thomist** n. & adj. **Thomistic** adj.

**Thomson's gazelle** • n. a light brown gazelle with a dark band along the flanks, living in herds on the open plains of East Africa. [*Gazella thomsonii*.]
– ORIGIN C19: named after Joseph *Thomson* (1858–94), Sc. explorer.

**thong** • n. **1** a narrow strip of leather or other material, used especially as a fastening or as the lash of a whip. **2** a skimpy bathing garment or pair of knickers like a G-string. **3** chiefly N. Amer. another term for **FLIP-FLOP** (in sense 1).
– DERIVATIVES **thonged** adj. **thongy** adj.
– ORIGIN OE *thwang*, *thwong*, of Gmc origin.

**thoracic** /θɔːˈrasɪk/ • adj. Anatomy & Zoology of or relating to the thorax.

**thorax** /ˈθɔːraks/ • n. (pl. **thoraces** /ˈθɔːrəsiːz/ or **thoraxes**) Anatomy & Zoology the part of the body of a mammal between the neck and the abdomen, including the cavity enclosed by the ribs, breastbone, and dorsal vertebrae. ➤Zoology the corresponding part of a bird, reptile, amphibian, or fish. ➤Entomology the middle section of the body of an insect, between the head and the abdomen, bearing the legs and wings.
– ORIGIN ME: via L. from Gk *thōrax*.

**Thorazine** /ˈθɔːrəziːn/ • n. trademark for **CHLORPROMAZINE**.
– ORIGIN 1950s: formed from elements of the systematic name.

**thoria** /ˈθɔːrɪə/ • n. Chemistry thorium dioxide, a white refractory solid used in making gas mantles and other materials for high-temperature applications.
– ORIGIN C19: from **THORIUM**.

**thorium** /ˈθɔːrɪəm/ • n. the chemical element of atomic number 90, a white radioactive metal of the actinide series. (Symbol: **Th**)
– ORIGIN C19: named after *Thor*, the Scand. god of thunder.

**thorn** • n. **1** a stiff, sharp-pointed woody projection on the stem or other part of a plant. **2** a thorny bush, shrub, or tree, especially a hawthorn. **3** an Old English and Icelandic runic letter, þ or Þ, representing the dental fricatives /ð/ and /θ/, eventually superseded by the digraph *th*.
– PHRASES **a thorn in someone's side** (or **flesh**) a source of continual annoyance or trouble.
– DERIVATIVES **thornless** adj.
– ORIGIN OE, of Gmc origin; the OE letter was named from the word of which it was the first letter.

**thorn apple** • n. a poisonous shrubby plant with large trumpet-shaped white flowers, toothed leaves, and a prickly fruit resembling that of a horse chestnut. [*Datura stramonium*.]

**thornback ray** • n. a prickly skinned ray which is often eaten as 'skate'. [*Raja clavata*.]

**thorny** • adj. (**-ier**, **-iest**) **1** having many thorns or thorn bushes. **2** causing distress, difficulty, or trouble.
– DERIVATIVES **thornily** adv. **thorniness** n.

**thorough** • adj. **1** complete with regard to every detail. ➤performed with or showing great care and completeness. **2** absolute; utter (used for emphasis).
– DERIVATIVES **thoroughly** adv. **thoroughness** n.
– ORIGIN OE *thuruh*, alt. of *thurh* 'through'; orig. used as adv. and prep. in senses of *through*; this sense survives in *thoroughfare*.

**thorough bass** • n. Music basso continuo (see **CONTINUO**).

**thoroughbred** • adj. **1** of pure breed, especially of a breed of horse originating from English mares and Arab stallions. **2** informal of outstanding quality. • n. **1** a thoroughbred animal. **2** informal an outstanding or first-class person or thing.

**thoroughfare** • n. a road or path forming a route between two places.

**thoroughgoing** • adj. **1** involving or attending to every detail or aspect. **2** complete; absolute.

**thorough-paced** • adj. archaic **1** highly skilled or trained. **2** complete; thoroughgoing.

**thorp** (also **thorpe**) • n. [in place names] a village or hamlet.
– ORIGIN OE *thorp*, *throp*, of Gmc origin.

**Thos** • abbrev. Thomas.

**those** plural form of **THAT**.

**thou**[1] • pron. [second person sing.] archaic or dialect form of **YOU**, as the singular subject of a verb.
– ORIGIN OE *thu*, of Gmc origin.

**thou**[2] • n. (pl. same or **thous**) **1** informal a thousand. **2** one thousandth of an inch.

**though** • conj. **1** despite the fact that; although. **2** however; but: *her name was Rose, though no-one called her that.* • adv. however: *he was able to write, though.*
– ORIGIN OE *thēah*, of Gmc origin; superseded in ME by

forms from ON *thó, thau*.

**thought**[1] • n. **1** an idea or opinion produced by thinking or occurring suddenly in the mind. ➤ **(one's thoughts)** one's mind or attention. ➤ an act of considering or remembering. **2** the action or process of thinking. ➤ careful consideration or attention. **3** the formation of opinions, especially as a philosophy or system of ideas, or the opinions so formed.
– PHRASES **a second thought** [with neg.] more than the slightest consideration. **a thought** dated to a small extent.
– ORIGIN OE *thōht*, of Gmc origin; rel. to **THINK**.

**thought**[2] past and past participle of **THINK**.

**thought experiment** • n. a mental assessment of the implications of a hypothesis.

**thoughtful** • adj. **1** absorbed in or involving thought. ➤ showing careful consideration or attention. **2** showing regard for other people.
– DERIVATIVES **thoughtfully** adv. **thoughtfulness** n.

**thoughtless** • adj. **1** not showing consideration for other people. **2** without consideration of the consequences.
– DERIVATIVES **thoughtlessly** adv. **thoughtlessness** n.

**thought police** • n. [treated as pl.] a group of people who aim to suppress ideas that deviate from the way of thinking that they believe to be correct.

**thought reform** • n. the systematic alteration of a person's mode of thinking, especially a process of political indoctrination.

**thought transference** • n. another term for **TELEPATHY**.

**thousand** • cardinal number (pl. **thousands** or (with numeral or quantifying word) same) **1** **(a/one thousand)** the number equivalent to the product of a hundred and ten; 1,000. (Roman numeral: **m** or **M**.) **2** **(thousands)** informal an unspecified large number.
– DERIVATIVES **thousandfold** adj. & adv. **thousandth** ordinal number.
– ORIGIN OE *thūsend*, of Gmc origin.

**Thousand Island dressing** • n. a dressing for salad or seafood consisting of mayonnaise with ketchup and chopped pickles.
– ORIGIN 1916: from the name of a large group of islands in the St Lawrence River between the US and Canada.

**Thracian** /ˈθreɪʃ(ə)n/ • n. a native or inhabitant of Thrace, an ancient country lying west of the Black Sea and north of the Aegean. • adj. of or relating to Thrace.

**thrall** /θrɔːl/ • n. **1** the state of being in another's power: *she was in thrall to her abusive husband.* **2** historical a slave, servant, or captive.
– DERIVATIVES **thraldom** (also **thralldom**) n.
– ORIGIN OE *thrǣl* 'slave', from ON *thrǽll*.

**thrash** • v. **1** beat repeatedly and violently with or as with a stick or whip. **2** move in a violent or uncontrolled way: *he lay thrashing around in pain.* **3** informal defeat heavily. **4** **(thrash something out)** discuss something frankly and thoroughly, especially to reach a decision. • n. **1** a violent or noisy movement of beating or thrashing. ➤ informal a fast and exciting motor race or other sporting event. **2** Brit. informal a party, especially a loud or lavish one. **3** (also **thrash metal**) a style of fast, loud, harsh-sounding rock music, combining elements of punk and heavy metal.
– ORIGIN OE, var. of **THRESH**.

**thrasher**[1] • n. **1** a person or thing that thrashes. **2** archaic spelling of **THRESHER**.

**thrasher**[2] • n. a thrush-like American songbird of the mockingbird family, with mainly brown or grey plumage, a long tail, and a downcurved bill. [*Toxostoma* and other genera.]
– ORIGIN C19: perh. from Engl. dial. *thrusher, thresher* 'thrush'.

**thrawn** /θrɔːn/ • adj. Scottish **1** perverse; ill-tempered. **2** twisted; crooked.
– ORIGIN ME: Scots form of *thrown*, in the obs. sense 'twisted, wrung'.

**thread** • n. **1** a long, thin strand of cotton, nylon, or other fibres used in sewing or weaving. **2** a long thin line or piece of something. **3** (also **screw thread**) a helical ridge on the outside of a screw, bolt, etc. or on the inside of a cylindrical hole, to allow two parts to be screwed together. **4** a theme or characteristic running throughout a situation or piece of writing. ➤ Computing a group of linked messages posted on the Internet that share a common subject or theme. ➤ Computing a programming structure or process formed by linking a number of separate elements or subroutines. **5** **(threads)** informal, chiefly N. Amer. clothes. • v. **1** pass a thread through (a needle). ➤ pass (a thread) through something and into the required position for use. ➤ put (beads or other objects) on a thread. **2** move or weave in and out of obstacles. **3** [usu. as adj. **threaded**] cut a screw thread in or on (a hole, screw, or other object).
– DERIVATIVES **threader** n. **thread-like** adj.
– ORIGIN OE *thrǣd* (n.), of Gmc origin.

**threadbare** • adj. thin and tattered with age; worn out.

**threadfin** • n. an edible tropical marine fish with long streamers arising from its pectoral fins. [Family Polynemidae: several species.]

**thread mark** • n. a thin line made in banknote paper with highly coloured silk fibres to prevent photographic counterfeiting.

**threadworm** • n. a very slender parasitic nematode worm, especially a pinworm.

**thready** • adj. (**-ier**, **-iest**) **1** of, relating to, or resembling a thread. **2** (of a sound) thin and scarcely audible. ➤ Medicine (of a person's pulse) scarcely perceptible.

**threat** • n. **1** a statement of an intention to inflict injury, damage, or other hostile action as retribution. ➤ Law a menace of bodily harm, such as may restrain a person's freedom of action. **2** a person or thing likely to cause damage or danger. ➤ the possibility of trouble or danger.
– ORIGIN OE *thrēat* 'oppression', of Gmc origin.

**threaten** • v. **1** make or express a threat to (someone) or to do (something). **2** put at risk; endanger. ➤ (of a situation or the weather) seem likely to produce an unwelcome result: *the air was raw and threatened rain.*
– DERIVATIVES **threatener** n. **threatening** adj. **threateningly** adv.

**three** • cardinal number equivalent to the sum of one and two; one more than two; 3. (Roman numeral: **iii** or **III**.)
– PHRASES **three parts** three out of four equal parts; three quarters.
– DERIVATIVES **threefold** adj. & adv.
– ORIGIN OE *thrīe* (masc.), *thrīo, thrēo* (fem.), of Gmc origin.

**three-card trick** • n. a game in which bets are made on which is the queen among three cards lying face downwards.

**three-colour process** • n. Photography a means of reproducing natural colours by combining photographic images in the three primary colours.

**three-dimensional** • adj. **1** having or appearing to have length, breadth, and depth. **2** having depth; lifelike or real: *they have the same three-dimensional quality as the originals.*
– DERIVATIVES **three-dimensionality** n. **three-dimensionally** adv.

**three-legged race** • n. a race run by pairs of people, one member of each pair having their left leg tied to the right leg of the other.

**three-line whip** • n. (in the UK) a written notice, underlined three times to denote urgency, to members of a political party to attend a parliamentary vote.

**three-peat** N. Amer. • v. win a particular sporting championship three times. • n. a third win, especially the third of three consecutive wins.
– ORIGIN 1980s: from **THREE** + a shortened form of **REPEAT**.

**threepence** /ˈθrɛp(ə)ns, ˈθrʊ-, ˈθrʌ-/ • n. Brit. the sum of three pence, especially before decimalization (1971).

**threepenny bit** • n. Brit. historical a coin worth three old pence (1¼ p).

**three-phase** • adj. relating to or denoting an electricity supply using three separate alternating components with phases differing by a third of a period.

**three-piece** • **adj.** consisting of three matching items. ➤(of a set of furniture) consisting of a sofa and two armchairs. ➤(of a set of clothes) consisting of trousers or a skirt with a waistcoat and jacket. • **n. 1** a set of three matching items. **2** a group of three musicians.

**three-point landing** • **n.** a landing of an aircraft on the two main wheels and the tailwheel or skid simultaneously.

**three-point turn** • **n.** a method of turning a vehicle round in a narrow space by moving forwards, backwards, and forwards again in a sequence of arcs.

**three-quarter** • **adj.** consisting of three quarters of something in terms of length, angle, time, etc. • **n. 1** Rugby each of four players in a team positioned across the field behind the halfbacks. **2** (**the three-quarter**) a point in time forty-five minutes after any full hour of the clock. • **adv.** to a size or extent of three quarters.

**three quarters** • **pl. n.** three of the four equal parts into which something may be divided. • **adv.** to the extent of three quarters.

**three-ring circus** • **n.** chiefly US **1** a circus with three rings for simultaneous performances. **2** a confused situation; a shambles.

**threescore** • **cardinal number** poetic/literary sixty.

**threesome** • **n.** a group of three people or things.

**three strikes** • **n.** US legislation which provides that an offender's third felony, however minor, is punishable by life imprisonment or other severe sentence.
– ORIGIN 1990s: from the phr. *three strikes and you're out* (with allusion to baseball).

**three-wheeler** • **n.** a vehicle with three wheels.

**threnody** /ˈθrɛnədi/ • **n.** (pl. **-ies**) a lament.
– DERIVATIVES **threnodial** adj. **threnodic** adj. **threnodist** n.
– ORIGIN C17: from Gk *thrēnōidia*, from *thrēnos* 'wailing' + *ōidē* 'song'.

**threonine** /ˈθriːəniːn/ • **n.** Biochemistry a hydrophilic amino acid which is a constituent of most proteins and is an essential nutrient in the diet of vertebrates.
– ORIGIN 1930s: from *threose* (the name of a sugar) + **-INE**[4].

**thresh** • **v. 1** /θrɛʃ/ separate grain from (corn or other crops), typically with a flail or by the action of a revolving mechanism. **2** /θraʃ/ variant spelling of **THRASH**.
– DERIVATIVES **threshing** n.
– ORIGIN OE *therscan*, later *threscan*, of Gmc origin; cf. **THRASH**.

**thresher** /ˈθrɛʃə/ • **n. 1** a person or machine that threshes. **2** a shark with a long upper lobe to the tail, sometimes used in hunting to lash the water to guide its prey. [*Alopias vulpinus*.]

**threshold** /ˈθrɛʃəʊld, ˈθrɛʃˌhəʊld/ • **n. 1** a strip of wood or stone forming the bottom of a doorway and crossed in entering a house or room. **2** a level or point at which something would start or cease to happen or come into effect. ➤Physiology & Psychology a limit below which a stimulus causes no reaction: *a low pain threshold.*
– ORIGIN OE *therscold*, *threscold*; first element rel. to **THRESH** (in the sense 'tread').

**threw** past of **THROW**.

**thrice** /θrʌɪs/ • **adv.** archaic or poetic/literary **1** three times. **2** extremely; very: *I was thrice blessed.*
– ORIGIN ME *thries*, from earlier *thrie* (from OE *thrīga*, rel. to **THREE**) + **-S**[3]; cf. **ONCE**.

**thrift** • **n. 1** the quality of being careful and not wasteful with money and other resources. **2** US another term for **SAVINGS AND LOAN**. **3** a plant which forms low-growing tufts of slender leaves with rounded pink flower heads, growing chiefly on sea cliffs and mountains. [*Armeria maritima*.]
– ORIGIN ME (in the sense 'prosperity'): from ON, from *thrífa* 'grasp, get hold of'; cf. **THRIVE**.

**thriftless** • **adj.** spending money in an extravagant and wasteful way.
– DERIVATIVES **thriftlessly** adv. **thriftlessness** n.

**thrift shop** (also **thrift store**) • **n.** N. Amer. a shop selling second-hand clothes and other household goods, typically to raise funds for a Church or charity.

**thrifty** • **adj.** (**-ier**, **-iest**) **1** careful and prudent with money. **2** chiefly archaic or dialect (of livestock or plants) strong and healthy.
– DERIVATIVES **thriftily** adv. **thriftiness** n.

**thrill** • **n. 1** a sudden feeling of excitement and pleasure. ➤an experience that produces such a feeling. ➤a wave or nervous tremor of emotion or sensation. **2** Medicine a vibratory movement or resonance heard through a stethoscope. ➤archaic a throb or pulsation. • **v. 1** have or cause to have a thrill. **2** (of an emotion or sensation) pass with a nervous tremor. ➤quiver or tremble.
– PHRASES **thrills and spills** excitement and exhilaration.
– DERIVATIVES **thrilling** adj. **thrillingly** adv.
– ORIGIN ME (in the sense 'pierce or penetrate'): alt. of dial. *thirl* 'pierce, bore'.

**thriller** • **n.** a novel, play, or film with an exciting plot, typically involving crime or espionage.

**thrips** /θrɪps/ (also **thrip**) • **n.** (pl. same) a minute black insect which sucks plant sap, noted for swarming on warm still summer days. [Order Thysanoptera: many species.]
– ORIGIN C18: via L. from Gk, lit. 'woodworm'.

**thrive** • **v.** (past **thrived** or **throve**; past part. **thrived** or **thriven**) (of a child, animal, or plant) grow or develop well or vigorously. ➤prosper; flourish.
– ORIGIN ME: from ON *thrífask*, reflexive of *thrífa* 'grasp, get hold of'; cf. **THRIFT**.

**thro'** • **prep., adv., & adj.** poetic/literary or informal spelling of **THROUGH**.

**throat** • **n. 1** the passage which leads from the back of the mouth of a person or animal. ➤the front part of the neck. **2** poetic/literary a voice of a person or a songbird. **3** Sailing the forward upper corner of a quadrilateral fore-and-aft sail.
– PHRASES **be at each other's throats** quarrel or fight. **force something down someone's throat** force something on a person's attention. **stick in one's throat** be unwelcome or unacceptable.
– DERIVATIVES **-throated** adj.
– ORIGIN OE *throte*, *throtu*, of Gmc origin; cf. **THROTTLE**.

**throatlatch** (also **throatlash**) • **n.** a strap passing under a horse's throat to help keep the bridle in position.

**throat microphone** • **n.** a microphone attached to a speaker's throat and actuated by the larynx.

**throaty** • **adj.** (**-ier**, **-iest**) **1** (of a voice or other sound) deep and husky. **2** (of an animal) having loose, pendulous skin around the throat.
– DERIVATIVES **throatily** adv. **throatiness** n.

**throb** • **v.** (**throbbed**, **throbbing**) **1** beat or sound with a strong, regular rhythm; pulsate. **2** feel pain in a series of pulsations. • **n.** a strong, regular beat or sound.
– ORIGIN ME: prob. imitative.

**throes** /θrəʊz/ • **pl. n.** intense or violent pain and struggle: *he convulsed in his death throes.*
– PHRASES **in the throes of** struggling in the midst of.
– ORIGIN ME *throwe* (sing.); perh. rel. to OE *thrēa*, *thrawu* 'calamity', influenced by *thrōwian* 'suffer'.

**thrombi** plural form of **THROMBUS**.

**thrombin** /ˈθrɒmbɪn/ • **n.** Biochemistry an enzyme in blood plasma which causes the clotting of blood by converting fibrinogen to fibrin.
– ORIGIN C19: from Gk *thrombos* 'blood clot' + **-IN**[1].

**thrombo-** • **comb. form** relating to the clotting of blood: *thromboembolism.*
– ORIGIN from Gk *thrombos* 'blood clot'.

**thrombocyte** /ˈθrɒmbə(ʊ)sʌɪt/ • **n.** another term for **PLATELET**.

**thrombocytopenia** /ˌθrɒmbə(ʊ)ˌsʌɪtə(ʊ)ˈpiːnɪə/ • **n.** Medicine deficiency of platelets in the blood, leading to bleeding into the tissues, bruising, and slow blood clotting after injury.
– ORIGIN 1920s: from **THROMBOCYTE** + Gk *penia* 'poverty'.

**thromboembolism** /ˌθrɒmbəʊˈɛmbəlɪz(ə)m/ • **n.** Medicine obstruction of a blood vessel by a blood clot that has become dislodged from its original site.
– DERIVATIVES **thromboembolic** adj.

**thrombolysis** /θrɒmˈbɒlɪsɪs/ • **n.** Medicine the dissolution

of a blood clot, especially as induced artificially by infusion of an enzyme into the blood.
– DERIVATIVES **thrombolytic** adj.

**thrombose** /θrɒm'bəʊz, -s/ ● v. affect with or be affected by thrombosis.
– ORIGIN C19: back-form. from **THROMBOSIS**.

**thrombosis** /θrɒm'bəʊsɪs/ ● n. (pl. **thromboses** /-siːz/) local coagulation or clotting of the blood in a part of the circulatory system.
– DERIVATIVES **thrombotic** adj.
– ORIGIN C18: mod. L., from Gk *thrombōsis* 'curdling', from *thrombos* 'blood clot'.

**thromboxane** /θrɒm'bɒkseɪn/ ● n. Biochemistry a hormone of the prostacyclin type released from blood platelets, which induces platelet aggregation and arterial constriction.

**thrombus** /'θrɒmbəs/ ● n. (pl. **thrombi** /-bʌɪ/) a blood clot formed in situ within the vascular system of the body and impeding blood flow.
– ORIGIN C19: mod. L., from Gk *thrombos* 'blood clot'.

**throne** ● n. a ceremonial chair for a sovereign, bishop, or similar figure. ➤(**the throne**) the power or rank of a sovereign: *the heir to the throne*. ● v. poetic/literary place on a throne.
– ORIGIN ME: from OFr. *trone*, via L. from Gk *thronos* 'elevated seat'.

**throng** ● n. a large, densely packed crowd. ● v. gather in large numbers in (a place): *a crowd thronged the station*. ➤flock or be present in great numbers.
– ORIGIN OE (*ge*)*thrang* 'crowd, tumult', of Gmc origin.

**throstle** /'θrɒs(ə)l/ ● n. **1** Brit. old-fashioned term for **SONG THRUSH**. **2** (also **throstle frame**) historical a spinning machine having a continuous action for drawing and twisting yarn.
– ORIGIN OE, of Gmc origin; sense 2 was appar. named from the humming sound of the machine.

**throttle** ● n. **1** a device controlling the flow of fuel or power to an engine. **2** archaic a person's throat, gullet, or windpipe. ● v. **1** attack or kill by choking or strangling. **2** control (an engine or vehicle) with a throttle. ➤(**throttle back/down**) reduce power by use of the throttle.
– DERIVATIVES **throttler** n.
– ORIGIN ME: perh. from **THROAT**, but the history of the word is not clear.

**through** ● prep. & adv. **1** moving in one side and out of the other side of (an opening or location). ➤so as to make a hole or passage in. ➤[prep.] expressing the position or location of something beyond (an opening or an obstacle). ➤expressing the extent of changing orientation. **2** continuing in time to or towards completion of. ➤from beginning to end of (an experience or activity). **3** so as to inspect all or part of. **4** [prep.] N. Amer. up to and including (a particular point in a sequence): *from March 24 through May 7*. **5** by means of. **6** [adv.] so as to be connected by telephone. ● adj. **1** (of public transport or a ticket) continuing or valid to the final destination. **2** (of traffic, roads, etc.) passing continuously from one side and out of the other side. **3** having successfully passed to the next stage of a competition. **4** informal, chiefly N. Amer. having finished an activity, relationship, etc.: *you and I are through*.
– PHRASES **through and through** thoroughly or completely.
– ORIGIN OE *thurh*, of Gmc origin.

**through-composed** ● adj. another term for **DURCHKOMPONIERT**.

**throughother** Scottish & Irish ● adv. mingled through one another. ● adj. disordered; confused.

**throughout** ● prep. & adv. all the way through.

**throughput** ● n. the amount of material or items passing through a system or process.

**throughway** (also **thruway**) ● n. N. Amer. a major road or motorway.

**throve** past of **THRIVE**.

**throw** ● v. (past **threw**; past part. **thrown**) **1** propel with force through the air by a rapid movement of the arm and hand. ➤send (one's opponent) to the ground in wrestling, judo, etc. ➤(of a horse) unseat (its rider). ➤Cricket bowl (the ball) with an illegitimate bent arm action. **2** move or put into place quickly, hurriedly, or roughly. **3** send suddenly into a particular position or condition: *he threw all her emotions into turmoil*. ➤disconcert; confuse. **4** project, direct, or cast (light, an expression, etc.) in a particular direction. ➤project (one's voice) so that it appears to come from somewhere else, as in ventriloquism. **5** form (ceramic ware) on a potter's wheel. ➤turn (wood) on a lathe. ➤twist (silk or other material) into yarn. **6** have (a fit or tantrum). **7** informal give or hold (a party). **8** informal lose (a race or contest) intentionally, especially in return for a bribe. **9** (of an animal) give birth to. ● n. **1** an act of throwing. **2** a small rug or light cover for furniture. **3** Geology the extent of vertical displacement in a fault. **4** a machine or device by or on which an object is turned while being shaped. **5** the action or motion of a slide valve or of a crank, eccentric wheel, or cam. ➤the extent of such motion. **6** (**a throw**) informal a single turn, round, or item: *on-the-spot portraits at £25 a throw*.
– PHRASES **be thrown back on** be forced to rely on (something) because there is no alternative. **throw good money after bad** incur further loss in a hopeless attempt to recoup a previous loss. **throw one's hand in** withdraw from a card game because one has a poor hand. ➤withdraw; give up. **throw in the towel** (or **sponge**) (of boxers or their seconds) throw a towel (or sponge) into the ring as a token of defeat. ➤admit defeat. **throw up one's hands** raise both hands in the air as an indication of one's exasperation.
– PHRASAL VERBS **throw something away 1** discard something as useless or unwanted. ➤waste or fail to make use of an opportunity or advantage. **2** (of an actor) deliver a line with deliberate underemphasis. **throw something in 1** include something extra with something that is being sold or offered. **2** make a remark casually as an interjection in a conversation. **throw oneself into** start to do (something) with enthusiasm and vigour. **throw off** (of hounds or a hunt) begin hunting. **throw something off 1** rid oneself of something. **2** write or utter something in an offhand manner. **throw something open** make something generally accessible. **throw someone out 1** expel someone unceremoniously. **2** Cricket & Baseball put out an opponent by throwing the ball to the wicket or a base. **throw something out 1** discard something as unwanted. **2** (of a court, legislature, or other body) dismiss or reject. **3** cause numbers or calculations to become inaccurate. **throw someone over** abandon or reject someone as a lover. **throw people together** bring people into contact, especially by chance. **throw something together** make or produce something hastily or without careful planning. **throw up** vomit. **throw something up 1** abandon something. **2** produce something and bring it to notice.
– DERIVATIVES **throwable** adj. **thrower** n.
– ORIGIN OE *thrāwan* 'to twist, turn', of W. Gmc origin.

**throwaway** ● adj. **1** intended to be discarded after being used once or a few times. **2** (of a remark) expressed in a casual or understated way.

**throwback** ● n. a reversion to an earlier ancestral type or characteristic.

**throw-in** ● n. Soccer & Rugby the act of throwing the ball from the sideline to restart play after the ball has gone into touch.

**throw-over** ● adj. denoting a bedspread or other large piece of cloth used as a loose-fitting decorative cover.

**throwster** ● n. a person who twists silk fibres into thread.

**thru** ● prep., adv., & adj. chiefly US informal spelling of **THROUGH**.

**thrum**[1] ● v. (**thrummed**, **thrumming**) make a continuous rhythmic humming sound. ➤strum (the strings of a musical instrument) in a rhythmic way. ● n. a continuous rhythmic humming sound.
– ORIGIN C16: imitative.

**thrum**[2] ● n. (in weaving) an unwoven end of a warp thread, or a fringe of such ends, left in the loom when the finished cloth is cut away. ● v. (**thrummed**, **thrumming**) adorn with thrums.

– DERIVATIVES **thrummer** n. **thrummy** adj.
– ORIGIN OE *thrum* (only in *tungethrum* 'ligament of the tongue'): of Gmc origin.

**thrush**[1] ● n. a small or medium-sized songbird, typically with a brown back and spotted breast. [*Turdus* and other genera: many species.]
– ORIGIN OE *thrysce*, of Gmc origin; rel. to THROSTLE.

**thrush**[2] ● n. **1** infection of the mouth and throat by a yeast-like fungus (Genus *Candida*), causing whitish patches. ➤ infection of the female genitals with the same fungus. **2** a chronic condition affecting the frog of a horse's foot, causing the accumulation of a dark, foul-smelling substance.
– ORIGIN C17: origin uncertain; sense 2 perh. from dial. *frush*, perh. from OFr. *fourchette* 'frog of a horse's hoof'.

**thrust** ● v. (past and past part. **thrust**) **1** push suddenly or violently in the specified direction. **2** (of a thing) extend so as to project conspicuously. **3** (**thrust something on/upon**) impose something unwelcome on. ● n. **1** a sudden or violent lunge or attack. **2** the principal purpose or theme of a course of action or line of reasoning: *anti-Americanism became the main thrust of their policy.* **3** the propulsive force of a jet or rocket engine. ➤ the lateral pressure exerted by an arch or other support in a building. **4** (also **thrust fault**) Geology a reverse fault of low angle, with older strata displaced horizontally over newer.
– ORIGIN ME: from ON *thrýsta*; perh. rel. to L. *trudere* 'to thrust'.

**thruster** ● n. **1** a person or thing that thrusts. **2** a small rocket engine on a spacecraft, used to make alterations in its flight path or altitude. ➤ a secondary jet or propeller on a ship or offshore rig, used for accurate manoeuvring and maintenance of position. **3** a surfboard or sailboard capable of increased speed and manoeuvrability.

**thrusting** ● adj. **1** aggressively ambitious. **2** projecting in a conspicuous way.

**thrust stage** ● n. a stage that extends into the auditorium so that the audience is seated around three sides.

**thrutch** ● n. N. English a narrow gorge or ravine. ● v. chiefly Climbing push, press, or squeeze into a space.
– ORIGIN OE, of W. Gmc origin.

**thud** ● n. a dull, leaden sound, such as that made by a heavy object falling to the ground. ● v. (**thudded**, **thudding**) move, fall, or strike something with a thud.
– DERIVATIVES **thudding** n. **thuddingly** adv.
– ORIGIN ME (orig. in the sense 'a sudden gust of wind', later 'a thunderclap'): prob. from OE *thyddan* 'to thrust, push'.

**thug** ● n. **1** a violent and uncouth man, especially a criminal. **2** (**Thug**) a member of a religious organization of robbers and assassins in India, suppressed by the British in the 1830s.
– DERIVATIVES **thuggery** n. **thuggish** adj. **thuggishly** adv. **thuggishness** n.
– ORIGIN C19: from Hindi *ṭhag* 'swindler, thief'.

**thuggee** /θʌ'giː/ ● n. historical the robbery and murder practised by the Thugs in accordance with their ritual.
– DERIVATIVES **thuggism** n.
– ORIGIN from Hindi *ṭhagī*, from *ṭhag* (see THUG).

**thuja** /'θ(j)uːjə/ (also **thuya**) ● n. an evergreen coniferous tree of a genus that includes the western red cedar. [Genus *Thuja*.]
– ORIGIN mod. L. (genus name), from Gk *thuia*, denoting an Afr. tree formerly in the genus.

**thulium** /'θ(j)uːlɪəm/ ● n. the chemical element of atomic number 69, a soft silvery-white metal of the lanthanide series. (Symbol: **Tm**)
– ORIGIN C19: mod. L., from *Thule*, the name of a country identified by the ancients as the northernmost part of the world.

**thumb** ● n. the short, thick first digit of the hand, set lower and apart from the other four and opposable to them. ● v. **1** press, touch, or indicate with one's thumb. **2** turn over (pages) with or as if with one's thumb. ➤ [usu. as adj. **thumbed**] wear or soil (a book's pages) by repeated handling. **3** request or obtain (a free ride in a passing vehicle) by signalling with one's thumb.
– PHRASES **thumb one's nose at** informal show disdain or contempt for. [with ref. to the gesture of putting one's thumb on one's nose and spreading the fingers.] **thumbs up** (or **down**) informal an indication of satisfaction or approval (or of rejection or failure). [with ref. to the signal of approval or disapproval used by spectators at a Roman amphitheatre (although the Romans used the symbols in reverse).] **under someone's thumb** completely under someone's influence or control.
– DERIVATIVES **thumbed** adj. **thumbless** adj.
– ORIGIN OE *thūma*, of W. Gmc origin.

**thumb index** ● n. a set of lettered indentations cut down the side of a book for easy reference.
– DERIVATIVES **thumb-indexed** adj.

**thumbnail** ● n. **1** the nail of the thumb. **2** [as modifier] brief or concise in description or representation: *a thumbnail sketch.*

**thumb nut** ● n. another term for WING NUT.

**thumb piano** ● n. any of various musical instruments, mainly of African origin, made from strips of metal fastened to a resonator and played by plucking with the fingers and thumbs.

**thumbscrew** ● n. **1** an instrument of torture that crushes the thumbs. **2** a screw with a protruding winged or flattened head for turning with the thumb and forefinger.

**thumb stick** ● n. **1** a tall walking stick with a forked thumb rest at the top. **2** a control lever for audio and televisual equipment.

**thumbtack** ● n. North American term for DRAWING PIN.

**thumbwheel** ● n. a control device for electrical or mechanical equipment in the form of a wheel operated with the thumb.

**thump** ● v. **1** hit heavily, especially with the fist or a blunt implement. ➤ put down forcefully, noisily, or decisively. ➤ (of a person's heart or pulse) beat or pulsate strongly. **2** (**thump something out**) play a tune enthusiastically but heavy-handedly. **3** informal defeat heavily. ● n. a heavy dull blow or noise.
– DERIVATIVES **thumper** n.
– ORIGIN C16: imitative.

**thumping** ● adj. **1** pounding; throbbing. **2** informal impressively large: *a thumping 64 per cent majority.*

**thunder** ● n. **1** a loud rumbling or crashing noise heard after a lightning flash due to the expansion of rapidly heated air. **2** a resounding loud deep noise. ● v. **1** (**it thunders**, **it is thundering**, etc.) thunder sounds. **2** move or cause to move heavily and forcefully. **3** speak loudly, angrily, and forcefully, especially to protest: *he thundered against the evils of the age.*
– DERIVATIVES **thunderer** n. **thundery** adj.
– ORIGIN OE *thunor* (n.), *thunrian* (v.), of Gmc origin.

**thunderbird** ● n. a mythical bird thought by some North American Indians to bring thunder.

**thunderbolt** ● n. a flash of lightning with a simultaneous crash of thunder. ➤ a supposed bolt or shaft believed to be the destructive agent in a lightning flash, especially as an attribute of a god such as Jupiter or Thor.

**thunderbox** ● n. Brit. informal a primitive or makeshift toilet.

**thunderbug** (also **thunderfly**) ● n. another term for THRIPS.

**thunderclap** ● n. a crash of thunder.

**thundercloud** ● n. a cumulus cloud with a towering or spreading top, charged with electricity and producing thunder and lightning.

**thunderflash** ● n. a noisy but harmless pyrotechnic device used especially in military exercises.

**thunderhead** ● n. a rounded, projecting head of a cumulus cloud, which portends a thunderstorm.

**thundering** ● adj. **1** making a resounding, loud, deep noise. **2** informal extremely great, severe, or impressive: *a thundering bore.*
– DERIVATIVES **thunderingly** adv.

**thunderous** • adj. **1** of, relating to, or resembling thunder. **2** (of a person's expression or behaviour) very angry or menacing.
– DERIVATIVES **thunderously** adv. **thunderousness** n.

**thunderstorm** • n. a storm with thunder and lightning and typically also heavy rain or hail.

**thunderstruck** • adj. extremely surprised or shocked.

**Thur.** (also **Thurs.**) • abbrev. Thursday.

**thurible** /ˈθjʊərɪb(ə)l/ • n. a censer.
– ORIGIN ME: from OFr., or from L. *thuribulum*, from *thus*, *thur-* (see **THURIFER**).

**thurifer** /ˈθjʊərɪfə/ • n. an acolyte carrying a censer.
– ORIGIN C19: from late L., from L. *thus, thur-* 'incense' + *-fer* '-bearing'.

**Thursday** • n. the day of the week before Friday and following Wednesday. • adv. chiefly N. Amer. on Thursday. ➤ **(Thursdays)** on Thursdays; each Thursday.
– ORIGIN OE *Thu(n)resdæg* 'day of thunder' (named after the Germanic thunder god *Thor*), translation of late L. *Jovis dies* 'day of Jupiter'.

**thus** • adv. poetic/literary or formal **1** as a result or consequence of this; therefore. **2** in the manner now being indicated or exemplified; in this way. **3** to this point; so.
– ORIGIN OE, of unknown origin.

**thusly** • adv. informal thus.

**thuya** • n. variant spelling of **THUJA**.

**thwack** • v. strike forcefully with a sharp blow. • n. a sharp blow.
– ORIGIN ME: imitative.

**thwaite** /θweɪt/ • n. [in place names] a piece of wild land cleared or reclaimed for cultivation.
– ORIGIN ME: from ON *thveit, thveiti* 'paddock', lit. 'cut piece'.

**thwart** /θwɔːt/ • v. prevent from succeeding in or accomplishing something. • n. a structural crosspiece forming a seat for a rower in a boat. • prep. & adv. archaic or poetic/literary from one side to another side of; across.
– ORIGIN ME *thwerte*, from *thwert* 'perverse, obstinate, adverse', from ON *thvert*, neut. of *thverr* 'transverse'.

**thy** (also **thine** before a vowel) • possess. det. archaic or dialect form of **YOUR**.
– ORIGIN ME *thi* (orig. before words beginning with any consonant except *h*), reduced from *thin*, from OE *thīn* (see **THINE**).

**thylacine** /ˈθʌɪləsiːn, -sʌɪn, -sɪn/ • n. a doglike carnivorous Tasmanian marsupial with striped hindquarters, probably extinct. [*Thylacinus cynocephalus*.]
– ORIGIN C19: from mod. L. *Thylacinus*, from Gk *thulakos* 'pouch'.

**thyme** /tʌɪm/ • n. a low-growing aromatic plant of the mint family, used as a culinary herb. [*Thymus vulgaris* and related species.]
– DERIVATIVES **thymy** adj.
– ORIGIN ME: from OFr. *thym*, via L. from Gk *thumon*, from *thuein* 'burn, sacrifice'.

**thymi** plural form of **THYMUS**.

**thymic** /ˈθʌɪmɪk/ • adj. Physiology of or relating to the thymus gland or its functions.

**thymidine** /ˈθʌɪmɪdiːn/ • n. Biochemistry a nucleoside consisting of thymine combined with deoxyribose.

**thymine** /ˈθʌɪmiːn/ • n. Biochemistry a compound which is one of the four constituent bases of nucleic acids.
– ORIGIN C19: from **THYMUS** + **-INE**[4].

**thymol** /ˈθʌɪmɒl/ • n. Chemistry a white crystalline compound present in oil of thyme and used as a flavouring and preservative.
– ORIGIN C19: from Gk *thumon* 'thyme' + **-OL**.

**thymus** /ˈθʌɪməs/ • n. (pl. **thymi** /-mʌɪ/) a lymphoid organ situated in the neck of vertebrates which produces T-lymphocytes for the immune system, and which decreases markedly in size at the approach of puberty.
– ORIGIN C16 (denoting a bud-like growth): from Gk *thumos* 'excrescence, thymus gland'.

**thyristor** /θʌɪˈrɪstə/ • n. Electronics a four-layered semiconductor rectifier in which the flow of current between two electrodes is triggered by a signal at a third electrode.
– ORIGIN 1950s: blend of *thyratron*, denoting a kind of thermionic valve (from Gk *thura* 'gate') and **TRANSISTOR**.

**thyro-** • comb. form representing **THYROID**.

**thyroid** /ˈθʌɪrɔɪd/ • n. **1** (also **thyroid gland**) a large ductless gland in the neck which secretes hormones regulating growth and development through the rate of metabolism. ➤ an extract prepared from the thyroid gland of animals and used in treating deficiency of thyroid hormones. **2** (also **thyroid cartilage**) a large cartilage of the larynx, a projection of which forms the Adam's apple in humans.
– ORIGIN C18: from Gk (*khondros*) *thureoeidēs* 'shield-shaped (cartilage)', from *thureos* 'oblong shield'.

**thyroid-stimulating hormone** • n. another term for **THYROTROPIN**.

**thyrotoxicosis** /ˌθʌɪrəʊˌtɒksɪˈkəʊsɪs/ • n. another term for **HYPERTHYROIDISM**.

**thyrotropin** /ˌθʌɪrə(ʊ)ˈtrəʊpɪn/ (also **thyrotrophin** /-ˈtrəʊfɪn/) • n. Biochemistry a hormone secreted by the pituitary gland which regulates the production of thyroid hormones.

**thyroxine** /θʌɪˈrɒksiːn, -sɪn/ • n. Biochemistry the main hormone produced by the thyroid gland, acting to increase metabolic rate and so regulating growth and development.
– ORIGIN C20: from **THYROID** + **OX-** + *in* from **INDOLE** (because of an early misunderstanding of its chemical structure).

**thyrsus** /ˈθəːsəs/ • n. (pl. **thyrsi** /-sʌɪ, -siː/) (in ancient Greece and Rome) a staff or spear tipped with an ornament like a pine cone, carried by Bacchus and his followers.
– ORIGIN L., from Gk *thursos* 'plant stalk, Bacchic staff'.

**thyself** • pron. [second person sing.] archaic or dialect form of **YOURSELF**, corresponding to the subject **THOU**[1].

**Ti** • symb. the chemical element titanium.

**ti** • n. North American form of **TE**.

**TIA** • abbrev. Medicine transient ischaemic attack (a slight and temporary stroke).

**Tia Maria** /ˌtiːə məˈriːə/ • n. trademark a coffee-flavoured liqueur based on rum, made originally in the Caribbean.
– ORIGIN from Sp. *Tía María*, lit. 'Aunt Mary'.

**tian** /tjɑ̃/ • n. (pl. pronounced same) **1** a dish of finely chopped vegetables cooked in olive oil and then baked au gratin. **2** a large oval earthenware cooking pot traditionally used in Provence.
– ORIGIN Provençal, based on Gk *tēganon* 'frying pan'.

**tiara** • n. **1** a jewelled ornamental band worn on the front of a woman's hair. ➤ a high diadem encircled with three crowns and worn by a pope. **2** a turban worn by kings in ancient Persia.
– ORIGIN C16: via L. from Gk, partly via Ital.

**Tibetan** • n. **1** a native of Tibet or a person of Tibetan descent. **2** the Sino-Tibetan language of Tibet. • adj. of or relating to Tibet, its people, or their language.

**Tibeto-Burman** • adj. relating to or denoting a division of the Sino-Tibetan language family that includes Tibetan, Burmese, and a number of other languages spoken in mountainous regions of central southern Asia.

**tibia** /ˈtɪbɪə/ • n. (pl. **tibiae** /-bɪiː/) Anatomy the inner and typically larger of the two bones between the knee and the ankle, parallel with the fibula. ➤ Entomology the fourth segment of the leg of an insect, between the femur and the tarsus.
– DERIVATIVES **tibial** adj.
– ORIGIN ME: from L., 'shin bone'.

**tibiotarsus** /ˌtɪbɪə(ʊ)ˈtɑːsəs/ • n. (pl. **tibiotarsi** /-sʌɪ, -siː/) Zoology the bone in a bird's leg corresponding to the tibia, fused at the lower end with some bones of the tarsus.
– ORIGIN C19: blend of **TIBIA** and **TARSUS**.

**tic** • n. a habitual spasmodic contraction of the muscles, most often in the face.
– ORIGIN C19: from Fr., from Ital. *ticchio*.

**tic douloureux** /tɪk ˌduːləˈruː, -ˈrəː/ • n. another term for **TRIGEMINAL NEURALGIA**.

– ORIGIN C19: Fr., lit. 'painful tic'.

**tich** /tɪtʃ/ ● n. variant spelling of TITCH.

**tick**[1] ● n. 1 a mark (✓) used to indicate that a textual item is correct or has been chosen or checked. 2 a regular short, sharp sound, especially that made every second by a clock or watch. ➤ Brit. informal a moment. 3 Stock Exchange the smallest amount by which the price of a security or future may fluctuate. ● v. 1 mark with a tick. 2 make regular ticking sounds. 3 (**tick away/by/past**) (of time) pass inexorably. ➤ (**tick along**) proceed; progress. 4 (**tick over**) (of an engine) run slowly in neutral. 5 (**tick someone off**) Brit. informal reprimand or rebuke someone.
– PHRASES **make someone tick** informal motivate someone.
– ORIGIN ME: prob. of Gmc origin.

**tick**[2] ● n. 1 a parasitic arachnid which attaches itself to the skin, from which it sucks blood. [Suborder Ixodida: many species.] ➤ informal a parasitic louse fly, especially the sheep ked. 2 Brit. informal a worthless or contemptible person.
– ORIGIN OE *ticia*, of Gmc origin.

**tick**[3] ● n. (in phr. **on tick**) on credit.
– ORIGIN C17: appar. short for TICKET in the phr. *on the ticket*, referring to a promise to pay.

**tick**[4] ● n. a fabric case stuffed with feathers or other material to form a mattress or pillow. ➤ short for TICKING.
– ORIGIN ME: prob. Mid. Low Ger., MDu. *tēke*, or MDu. *tīke*, via W. Gmc from L. *theca* 'case', from Gk *thēkē*.

**ticker** ● n. 1 informal a watch. ➤ a person's heart. 2 N. Amer. a telegraphic or electronic machine that prints out data on a strip of paper.

**ticker tape** ● n. a paper strip on which messages are recorded in a telegraphic tape machine. ➤ [as modifier] denoting a parade or other event in which this or similar material is thrown from windows.

**ticket** ● n. 1 a piece of paper or card giving the holder a right to admission to a place or event or to travel on public transport. 2 a certificate or warrant, especially an official notice of a traffic offence. 3 a label attached to a retail product, giving its price, size, etc. 4 chiefly N. Amer. a list of candidates put forward by a party in an election. ➤ a set of principles or policies supported by a party in an election. 5 (**the ticket**) informal the desirable thing: *a holiday would be just the ticket.* 6 Scottish & US informal a person of a specified kind. ● v. (**ticketed**, **ticketing**) 1 issue with a ticket. 2 (**be ticketed**) US be destined or heading for a specified state or position.
– DERIVATIVES **ticketed** adj. **ticketless** adj.
– ORIGIN C16: shortening of obs. Fr. *étiquet*, from OFr. *estiquet(te)*, from *estiquier* 'to fix'; cf. ETIQUETTE.

**tickety-boo** ● adj. Brit. informal, dated in good order.
– ORIGIN 1930s: perh. from Hindi *ṭhīk hai* 'all right'.

**tick fever** ● n. any bacterial or rickettsial fever transmitted by the bite of a tick.

**ticking** ● n. a strong, durable material, typically striped, used to cover mattresses.
– ORIGIN C17: from TICK[4] + -ING[1].

**tickle** ● v. 1 lightly touch in a way that causes itching or twitching and often laughter. ➤ catch (a trout) by lightly rubbing it so that it moves backwards into the hand. 2 be appealing or amusing to. ● n. an act of tickling or sensation of being tickled.
– PHRASES **be tickled pink** (or **to death**) informal be extremely amused or pleased. **tickle the ivories** informal play the piano.
– DERIVATIVES **tickler** n. **tickly** adj.
– ORIGIN ME: perh. a frequentative of TICK[1], or an alt. of Scots and dial. *kittle* 'to tickle' (cf. KITTLE).

**ticklish** ● adj. 1 sensitive to being tickled. ➤ (of a cough) characterized by persistent irritation in the throat. 2 (of a situation or problem) difficult to deal with; sensitive.
– DERIVATIVES **ticklishly** adv. **ticklishness** n.

**tick-tack-toe** ● n. variant spelling of TIC-TAC-TOE.

**tick-tock** ● n. the sound of a large clock ticking. ● v. make a tick-tock.
– ORIGIN C19: imitative; cf. TICK[1].

**ticky-tacky** ● n. informal, chiefly N. Amer. inferior or cheap material, especially as used in suburban building.
– ORIGIN 1960s: prob. a reduplication of TACKY[2].

**tic-tac** (also **tick-tack**) ● n. (in the UK) a kind of manual semaphore used by racecourse bookmakers to exchange information.
– ORIGIN C16: imitative; cf. TICK-TOCK

**tic-tac-toe** (also **tick-tack-toe**) ● n. North American term for NOUGHTS AND CROSSES.
– ORIGIN 1960s: imitative; from *tick-tack*, used earlier to denote games in which the pieces made clicking sounds.

**tidal basin** ● n. a basin accessible or navigable only at high tide.

**tidal bore** ● n. a large wave or bore caused by the constriction of the spring tide as it enters a long, narrow, shallow inlet.

**tidal wave** ● n. 1 an exceptionally large ocean wave, especially one caused by an underwater earthquake or volcanic eruption. 2 a widespread or overwhelming manifestation of an emotion or phenomenon.

**tidbit** ● n. US spelling of TITBIT.

**tiddledywink** ● n. US spelling of TIDDLYWINK.

**tiddler** ● n. Brit. informal a small fish, especially a stickleback or minnow. ➤ a young or unusually small person or thing.
– ORIGIN C19: perh. rel. to TIDDLY[2] or *tittlebat*, a childish form of *stickleback*.

**tiddly**[1] ● adj. (**-ier**, **-iest**) informal, chiefly Brit. slightly drunk.
– ORIGIN C19 (as n. denoting an alcoholic drink): perh. from sl. *tiddlywink*, denoting an unlicensed public house.

**tiddly**[2] ● adj. (**-ier**, **-iest**) Brit. informal little; tiny.
– ORIGIN C19: var. of colloq. *tiddy*, of unknown origin.

**tiddlywink** (US **tiddledywink**) ● n. 1 (**tiddlywinks**) [treated as sing.] a game in which small plastic counters are flicked into a central receptacle, using a larger counter. 2 a counter used in such a game.
– ORIGIN C19 (orig. denoting an unlicensed public house, also a game of dominoes): of unknown origin; perh. rel. to TIDDLY[1].

**tiddy oggy** /ˈtɪdɪ ˌɒgi/ ● n. Brit. dialect or nautical slang a Cornish pasty.
– ORIGIN prob. from West Country dial. *tiddy* 'potato' and Cornish *hogen* 'pastry'.

**tide** ● n. 1 the alternate rising and falling of the sea due to the attraction of the moon and sun. 2 a powerful surge of feeling or trend of events: *a tide of euphoria.* ● v. 1 (**tide someone over**) help someone through a difficult period, especially with financial assistance. 2 archaic drift with or as if with the tide. ➤ (of a ship) move in or out of harbour with the help of the tide.
– DERIVATIVES **tidal** adj. **tidally** adv. **tideless** adj.
– ORIGIN OE *tīd* 'time, period, era', of Gmc origin; rel. to TIME.

**-tide** ● comb. form poetic/literary denoting a specified time or season: *springtide.* ➤ denoting a festival of the Christian Church: *Shrovetide.*

**tideland** ● n. (also **tidelands**) N. Amer. land that is submerged at high tide.

**tideline** ● n. a line left or reached by the sea on a shore at the highest point of a tide.

**tidemark** ● n. 1 a tideline. 2 Brit. a grimy mark left around the inside of a bath or washbasin at the level reached by the water.

**tide rip** ● n. an area of rough water typically caused by opposing tides or by a rapid current passing over an uneven bottom.

**tidewaiter** ● n. historical a customs officer who boarded ships on their arrival to enforce the customs regulations.

**tidewater** ● n. water brought or affected by tides.

**tideway** ● n. a channel in which a tide runs, especially the tidal part of a river.

**tidings** ● pl. n. poetic/literary news; information.
– ORIGIN OE *tīdung* 'announcement, piece of news', prob. from ON *títhindi* 'news of events', from *títhr* 'occurring'.

**tidy** ● adj. (**-ier**, **-iest**) 1 arranged neatly and in order. ➤ inclined to keep things or one's appearance neat and in

order. ➤not messy; neat and controlled. **2** informal (of an amount, especially of money) considerable. ● **n.** (pl. **-ies**) **1** (also **tidy-up**) an act or spell of tidying. **2** a receptacle for holding small objects. **3** chiefly US a detachable ornamental cover for a chair back. ● **v.** (**-ies**, **-ied**) (often **tidy up**) make tidy. ➤(**tidy something away**) put something away for the sake of tidiness.
– DERIVATIVES **tidily** adv. **tidiness** n.
– ORIGIN ME (orig. in sense 'timely, opportune'): from TIDE + -Y[1].

**tie** ● **v.** (**tying**) **1** attach or fasten with string, cord, etc. ➤form into a knot or bow. ➤(**tie someone up**) restrict someone's movement by binding their arms or legs or binding them to something. ➤(**tie something up**) bring something to a satisfactory conclusion. **2** restrict; limit. ➤(**tie someone down**) restrict someone to a particular situation or place. ➤(usu. **be tied up**) informal occupy someone to the exclusion of other activity. ➤(**tie something up**) invest or reserve capital so that it is not immediately available for use. **3** connect; link. ➤(**tie in**) be or cause to be in harmony with something. ➤hold together by a crosspiece or tie. ➤Music unite (written notes) by a tie. ➤Music perform (two notes) as one unbroken note. **4** achieve the same score or ranking as another competitor. **5** (**tie into**) N. Amer. informal attack or get to work on vigorously. ● **n.** (pl. **-ies**) **1** a thing that ties. **2** a strip of material worn around the neck beneath a collar, tied in a knot at the front. **3** a rod or beam holding parts of a structure together. **4** N. Amer. short for CROSS TIE. **5** Music a curved line above or below two notes of the same pitch indicating that they are to be played for the combined duration of their time values. **6** US a shoe tied with a lace. **7** Brit. a sports match between two or more players or teams in which the winners proceed to the next round of the competition: *a cup tie*. **8** a result in a game or match in which two or more competitors have tied. ➤Cricket a game in which the scores are level and both sides have completed their innings. Compare with DRAW.
– DERIVATIVES **tieless** adj.
– ORIGIN OE *tīgan* (v.), *tēah* (n.), of Gmc origin.

**tie-back** ● **n.** a decorative strip of fabric or cord used for holding an open curtain back from the window.

**tie beam** ● **n.** a horizontal beam connecting two rafters in a roof.

**tie-break** (also **tie-breaker**) ● **n.** a means of deciding a winner from competitors who have tied, in particular (in tennis) a game to decide the winner of a set when the score is six games all.

**tie clip** ● **n.** an ornamental clip for holding a tie in place.

**tied** ● **adj.** **1** Brit. (of a house) occupied subject to the tenant's working for its owner. ➤(of a public house) owned and controlled by a brewery. **2** (of aid or an international loan) given subject to the condition that it should be spent on goods or services from the donor or lender.

**tie-dye** ● **n.** a method of producing textile patterns by tying parts of the fabric to shield it from the dye. ● **v.** dye by such a process.

**tie-in** ● **n.** a connection or association. ➤a book, film, or other product produced to take commercial advantage of a related work in another medium. ➤[as modifier] chiefly N. Amer. denoting sales made conditionally on the purchase of an additional item or items from the same supplier.

**tie line** ● **n.** a transmission line connecting parts of a system, especially a telephone line connecting two private branch exchanges.

**tienda** /tɪ'ɛndə/ ● **n.** (in the south-western US) a shop.
– ORIGIN from Sp., lit. 'tent'.

**tiepin** ● **n.** an ornamental pin for holding a tie in place.

**tier** ● **n.** **1** one of a series of rows or levels stacked one above the other. **2** a level or grade within a hierarchy.
– DERIVATIVES **tiered** adj.
– ORIGIN C15: from Fr. *tire* 'sequence, order'.

**tierce** /tɪəs/ ● **n.** **1** another term for TERCE. **2** Music an organ stop sounding two octaves and a major third above the pitch of the diapason. **3** (in piquet) a sequence of three cards of the same suit. **4** Fencing the third of eight parrying positions. **5** a former measure of wine equal to one third of a pipe, usually equivalent to 35 gallons (about 156 litres).
– ORIGIN ME: var. of TERCE.

**tierced** /tɪəst/ (also **tiercé** /'tjə:seɪ/) ● **adj.** Heraldry divided into three equal parts of different tinctures.
– ORIGIN C18: orig. as *tiercé* 'divided into three parts', Fr. past part. of *tiercer*.

**tiercel** /'tɪəs(ə)l/ ● **n.** variant spelling of TERCEL.

**tie-up** ● **n.** **1** a link or connection, especially one between commercial companies. ➤US a telecommunications link or network. **2** N. Amer. a building where cattle are tied up for the night. ➤a place for mooring a boat. **3** N. Amer. a traffic hold-up.

**TIFF** ● **abbrev.** Computing tagged image file format.

**tiff** ● **n.** informal a quarrel.
– ORIGIN C18 (denoting a slight outburst of temper): prob. of dial. origin.

**tiffany** /'tɪf(ə)ni/ ● **n.** thin gauze muslin.
– ORIGIN C17: from OFr. *tifanie*, via eccles. L. from Gk *theophaneia* 'epiphany'; usu. taken to be short for *Epiphany silk* or *muslin*, i.e., that worn on Twelfth Night, but may be a humorous allusion to *epiphany* in the sense 'manifestation', tiffany being semi-transparent.

**tiffin** ● **n.** (in India) a light midday meal.
– ORIGIN C19: appar. from dial. *tiffing* 'sipping', of unknown origin.

**tig** ● **n. & v.** chiefly Brit. another term for TAG[2].
– ORIGIN C18: perh. a var. of the verb TICK[1].

**tiger** ● **n.** **1** a very large solitary cat with a yellow-brown coat striped with black, native to the forests of Asia. [*Panthera tigris*.] **2** used in names of tiger moths and striped butterflies, e.g. **scarlet tiger**, **plain tiger**. **3** (also **tiger economy**) a dynamic economy of one of the smaller East Asian countries, especially that of Singapore, Taiwan, or South Korea.
– DERIVATIVES **tigerish** adj. **tigerishly** adv.
– ORIGIN ME: from OFr. *tigre*, from L. *tigris*, from Gk.

**Tiger balm** ● **n.** trademark a mentholated ointment widely used in Eastern medicine for a variety of conditions.

**tiger beetle** ● **n.** a fast-running predatory beetle with spotted or striped wing cases. [Family Cicindelidae: many species.]

**tiger lily** ● **n.** a tall Asian lily which has orange flowers spotted with black or purple. [*Lilium lancifolium*.]

**tiger moth** ● **n.** a stout moth which has boldly spotted and streaked wings and a hairy caterpillar (woolly bear). [*Arctia* and other genera: many species.]

**tiger prawn** (also **tiger shrimp**) ● **n.** a large edible prawn marked with dark bands, found in the Indian and Pacific oceans. [*Penaeus monodon* and related species.]

**tiger's eye** (also **tiger eye**) ● **n.** a yellowish-brown semi-precious variety of quartz with a silky or chatoyant lustre, formed by replacement of crocidolite.

**tiger shark** ● **n.** an aggressive shark of warm seas, with dark vertical stripes on the body. [*Galeocerdo cuvieri*.]

**tiger snake** ● **n.** a deadly Australian snake, typically marked with brown and yellow bands. [*Notechis scutatus*.]

**tiger worm** ● **n.** another term for BRANDLING.

**tight** ● **adj.** **1** fixed or fastened firmly; hard to move, undo, or open. ➤(of clothes) close-fitting, especially uncomfortably so. ➤(of a grip) very firm. ➤well sealed against something such as water or air. **2** (of a rope, fabric, or surface) stretched so as to leave no slack. ➤tense: *a tight smile*. **3** (of a form of control) strictly imposed: *security was tight at the ceremony*. **4** (of a written work or form) concise. **5** (of an organization or group) disciplined and well coordinated. **6** (of an area or space) allowing little room for manoeuvre. ➤(of money or time) limited; restricted: *a tight deadline*. **7** secretive. **8** informal miserly. **9** informal drunk. ● **adv.** very firmly, closely, or tensely.
– PHRASES **a tight ship** a strictly controlled and disciplined organization or operation. **a tight corner** (or **spot** or **place**) a difficult situation.
– DERIVATIVES **tighten** v. **tightly** adv. **tightness** n.
– ORIGIN ME (in the sense 'healthy, vigorous', later 'firm, solid'): prob. an alt. of *thight* 'firm, solid', later 'close-

packed, dense', of Gmc origin.

**tight-ass** ● **n.** informal, chiefly N. Amer. an inhibited or repressed person.
– DERIVATIVES **tight-assed** adj.

**tight end** ● **n.** American Football an offensive end who lines up close to the tackle.

**tight-fisted** ● **adj.** informal not willing to spend or give much money; miserly.

**tight head** ● **n.** Rugby the prop forward supporting the hooker on the opposite side of the scrum from the loose head.

**tight-knit** (also **tightly knit**) ● **adj.** (of a group of people) bound together by strong relationships and common interests.

**tight-lipped** ● **adj.** with the lips firmly closed, especially as a sign of suppressed emotion or determined reticence.

**tight money** ● **n.** Finance money or finance that is available only at high rates of interest.

**tightrope** ● **n.** a rope or wire stretched high above the ground, on which acrobats perform balancing feats.

**tights** ● **pl. n.** a close-fitting garment made of a knitted yarn, covering the legs, hips, and bottom.

**tightwad** ● **n.** informal, chiefly N. Amer. a miserly person.

**tigon** /'tʌɪg(ə)n/ (also **tiglon** /'tʌɪglɒn, 'tɪg-/) ● **n.** the hybrid offspring of a male tiger and a lioness.

**Tigre** /'tiːgreɪ/ ● **n.** a Semitic language spoken in Eritrea and adjoining parts of Sudan. Compare with **TIGRINYA**.
– ORIGIN the name in Tigre.

**tigress** ● **n.** a female tiger.

**Tigrinya** /tɪ'griːnjə/ ● **n.** a Semitic language spoken in Tigray. Compare with **TIGRE**.
– ORIGIN the name in Tigrinya.

**Tigua** ● **n. & adj.** variant spelling of **TIWA**.

**tike** ● **n.** variant spelling of **TYKE**.

**tiki** /'tɪki/ ● **n.** (pl. **tikis**) NZ a large wooden or small greenstone image of a human figure.
– ORIGIN Maori, lit. 'image'.

**tikka** /'tɪkə, 'tiːkə/ ● **n.** an Indian dish of small pieces of meat or vegetables marinated in a spice mixture.
– ORIGIN from Punjabi *ṭikkā*.

**tilapia** /tɪ'leɪpɪə, -'lap-/ ● **n.** an African freshwater cichlid fish, introduced to many areas for food. [*Tilapia* and other genera: several species.]
– ORIGIN mod. L., of unknown origin.

**tilbury** /'tɪlb(ə)ri/ ● **n.** (pl. **-ies**) historical a light, open two-wheeled carriage.
– ORIGIN C19: named after its inventor.

**tilde** /'tɪldə/ ● **n.** an accent (˜) placed over Spanish *n* when pronounced *ny* (as in *señor*) or Portuguese *a* or *o* when nasalized (as in *São Paulo*), or over a vowel in phonetic transcription, indicating nasalization. ➤a similar symbol used in mathematics and logic to indicate negation, inversion, etc.
– ORIGIN C19: from Sp., based on L. *titulus* (see **TITLE**).

**tile** /tʌɪl/ ● **n. 1** a thin square or rectangular slab of baked clay, concrete, etc., used in overlapping rows for covering roofs. ➤a similar slab of glazed pottery or other material for covering floors or walls. **2** a thin, flat piece used in Scrabble, mah-jong, and other games. ● **v. 1** cover with tiles. **2** Computing arrange (two or more windows) on a computer screen so that they do not overlap.
– PHRASES **on the tiles** informal, chiefly Brit. having a lively night out.
– ORIGIN OE *tigele*, from L. *tegula*, from an Indo-Eur. root meaning 'cover'.

**tiler** ● **n. 1** a person who lays tiles. **2** the doorkeeper of a Freemasons' lodge.

**tiling** ● **n. 1** the action of laying tiles. ➤a surface covered by tiles. **2** Computing a technique for tiling windows on a computer screen. **3** Mathematics a way of arranging identical plane shapes so that they completely cover an area without overlapping.

**till**[1] ● **prep. & conj.** less formal way of saying **UNTIL**.
– ORIGIN OE *til*, of Gmc origin (not, as is commonly assumed, a shortened form of *until*).

**till**[2] ● **n.** a cash register or drawer for money in a shop, bank, or restaurant.
– ORIGIN ME (in the sense 'drawer or compartment for valuables'): of unknown origin.

**till**[3] ● **v.** prepare and cultivate (land) for crops.
– DERIVATIVES **tillable** adj. **tillage** n.
– ORIGIN OE *tilian* 'strive for, obtain by effort', of Gmc origin; ult. rel. to **TILL**[1].

**till**[4] ● **n.** Geology boulder clay or other unstratified sediment deposited by melting glaciers or ice sheets.
– ORIGIN C17 (orig. Scots, denoting shale): of unknown origin.

**tiller**[1] ● **n.** a horizontal bar fitted to the head of a boat's rudder post and used for steering.
– ORIGIN ME: from Anglo-Norman Fr. *telier* 'weaver's beam, stock of a crossbow', from med. L. *telarium*, from L. *tela* 'web'.

**tiller**[2] ● **n.** a lateral shoot from the base of the stem, especially in a grass or cereal. ● **v.** develop tillers.
– DERIVATIVES **tillering** n.
– ORIGIN C17: appar. based on OE *telga* 'bough', of Gmc origin.

**tiller**[3] ● **n.** an implement or machine for breaking up soil; a plough or cultivator.

**tilleul** /tɪ'jəːl/ ● **n.** a tea made from an infusion of lime flowers.
– ORIGIN C16: from Fr., 'lime or linden tree', from a dimin. form of L. *tilia* 'linden'.

**tilley lamp** /'tɪli/ (also **tilly lamp**) ● **n.** trademark a portable oil or paraffin lamp in which air pressure is used to supply the burner with fuel.
– ORIGIN 1930s: from the name of the manufacturers.

**tillite** /'tɪlʌɪt/ ● **n.** Geology sedimentary rock composed of compacted glacial till.

**tilt** ● **v. 1** move or cause to move into a sloping position. ➤move (a camera) in a vertical plane. **2** (**tilt at**) historical (in jousting) thrust at with a lance or other weapon. ➤(**tilt with**) archaic engage in a contest with. ● **n. 1** a tilting position or movement. ➤an inclination or bias. **2** historical a joust.
– PHRASES (**at**) **full tilt** with maximum speed or force. **tilt at windmills** attack imaginary enemies. [with allusion to the story of Don Quixote tilting at windmills, believing they were giants.]
– DERIVATIVES **tilter** n.
– ORIGIN ME (in the sense 'fall or cause to fall'): perh. rel. to OE *tealt* 'unsteady', or perh. of Scand. origin and rel. to Norw. *tylten* 'unsteady' and Swed. *tulta* 'totter'.

**tilth** ● **n.** cultivation of land; tillage. ➤the condition of tilled soil. ➤prepared surface soil.
– ORIGIN OE *tilth, tilthe*, from *tilian* (see **TILL**[3]).

**tilt hammer** ● **n.** a heavy pivoted hammer used in forging, raised mechanically and allowed to drop on the metal being worked.

**Tim.** ● **abbrev.** Timothy (especially in biblical references).

**timbal** /'tɪmb(ə)l/ ● **n.** archaic a kettledrum.
– ORIGIN C17: from Fr. *timbale*, alt. (influenced by *cymbale* 'cymbal') of obs. *tamballe*, from Sp. *atabal*, from Arab. *aṭ-ṭabl* 'the drum'.

**timbale** /tam'bɑːl/ ● **n. 1** a dish of finely minced meat or fish cooked with other ingredients in a pastry shell or in a mould. **2** (**timbales**) paired cylindrical drums played with sticks in Latin American dance music.
– ORIGIN Fr., 'drum'.

**timber** ● **n. 1** wood prepared for use in building and carpentry. ➤trees grown for such wood. ➤a wooden beam or board used in building and shipbuilding. **2** informal, chiefly US suitable quality or character: *she is hailed as presidential timber.* ● **exclam.** used to warn that a tree is about to fall after being cut.
– DERIVATIVES **timbered** adj. **timbering** n.
– ORIGIN OE in the sense 'a building', also 'building material', of Gmc origin.

**timber-frame** ● **adj.** denoting a house or other structure having a wooden frame, traditionally of oak or elm. ● **n.** pre-prepared sections of wood used for building a house.
– DERIVATIVES **timber-framed** adj. **timber-framing** n.

**timber hitch** ● **n.** a knot used in attaching a rope to a log or spar.

**timberline** • n. chiefly N. Amer. another term for **TREELINE**.

**timberman** • n. (pl. **-men**) **1** a person who works with timber. **2** a greyish-brown longhorn beetle of northern European pine forests. [*Acanthocinus aedilis*.]

**timber wolf** • n. a wolf of a large variety found mainly in northern North America, with grey brindled fur.

**timbre** /'tambə/ • n. the character or quality of a musical sound or voice as distinct from its pitch and intensity.
– ORIGIN C19: from Fr., from med. Gk *timbanon*, from Gk *tumpanon* 'drum'.

**timbrel** /'tɪmbr(ə)l/ • n. archaic a tambourine or similar instrument.
– ORIGIN C16: perh. a dimin. of obs. *timbre*, in the same sense, from OFr. (see **TIMBRE**).

**time** • n. **1** the indefinite continued progress of existence and events in the past, present, and future, regarded as a whole. **2** a point of time as measured in hours and minutes past midnight or noon. ➤ the favourable or appropriate moment to do something: *it was time to go.* ➤ (**a time**) an indefinite period: *he worked for a time as a gardener.* ➤ (also **times**) a more or less definite portion of time characterized by particular events or circumstances: *Victorian times.* ➤ (**one's time**) a period regarded as characteristic of a particular stage of one's life. ➤ the length of time taken to run a race or complete an activity. ➤ informal a prison sentence. ➤ an apprenticeship. **3** Brit. the moment at which the opening hours of a public house end. ➤ Baseball & American Football a moment at which play stops temporarily within a game. **4** time as allotted, available, or used: *a waste of time.* **5** the normal rate of pay for time spent working: *they are paid time and a half.* **6** an instance of something happening or being done: *the nurse came in four times a day.* **7** (**times**) (following a number) expressing multiplication. **8** the rhythmic pattern or tempo of a piece of music. • v. **1** arrange a time for. ➤ perform at a particular time. **2** measure the time taken by. **3** (**time something out**) Computing (of a computer or a program) cancel an operation automatically because a predefined interval of time has passed. **4** (**times**) informal multiply (a number).
– PHRASES **about time** conveying that something should have happened earlier. **all the time** at all times. ➤ very frequently or regularly. **at the same time 1** simultaneously. **2** nevertheless. **at a time** separately in the specified groups or numbers: *he took the stairs two at a time.* **behind the times** not aware of or using the latest ideas or techniques. **for the time being** until some other arrangement is made. **have no time for** be unable or unwilling to spend time on. ➤ dislike or disapprove of. **in time 1** not late. **2** eventually. **3** in accordance with the appropriate musical rhythm or tempo. **keep good** (or **bad**) **time 1** (of a clock or watch) record time accurately (or inaccurately). **2** (of a person) be habitually punctual (or not punctual). **keep time** play or rhythmically accompany music in time. **on time** punctual; punctually. **pass the time of day** exchange greetings or casual remarks. **time immemorial** a point of time in the distant past beyond recall or knowledge. **the time of one's life** a period or occasion of exceptional enjoyment. **time out of mind** another way of saying ***time immemorial***. **time will tell** the truth about something will be established in the future.
– ORIGIN OE *tīma*, of Gmc origin; rel. to **TIDE**, which it superseded in temporal senses.

**time-and-motion study** • n. a procedure in which the efficiency of an industrial or other operation is evaluated.

**time bomb** • n. a bomb designed to explode at a preset time.

**time capsule** • n. a container storing a selection of objects chosen as being typical of the present time, buried for discovery in the future.

**time code** • n. Electronics a coded signal on videotape or film giving information about such things as frame number or time of recording.

**time constant** • n. Physics a quantity (in units of time) expressing the speed of response of a device or system.

**time frame** • n. a specified period of time.

**time-honoured** • adj. (of a custom or tradition) respected or valued because it has existed for a long time.

**timekeeper** • n. **1** a person who records the amount of time taken by a process or activity. **2** a person regarded in terms of their punctuality. ➤ a watch or clock regarded in terms of its accuracy. **3** archaic a clock.
– DERIVATIVES **timekeeping** n.

**time-lapse** • adj. denoting the photographic technique of taking a sequence of frames at set intervals to record changes that take place slowly over time.

**timeless** • adj. not affected by the passage of time or changes in fashion.
– DERIVATIVES **timelessly** adv. **timelessness** n.

**time lock** • n. a lock fitted with a device that prevents it from being unlocked until a set time. ➤ a device built into a computer program to stop it operating after a certain time. • v. (**time-lock**) secure with a time lock.

**timely** • adj. done or occurring at a favourable or appropriate time.
– DERIVATIVES **timeliness** n.

**time machine** • n. (in science fiction) a machine capable of time travel.

**time off** • n. time for rest or recreation away from one's usual work or studies.

**timeous** /'tʌɪməs/ • adj. chiefly Scottish in good time; sufficiently early.
– DERIVATIVES **timeously** adv.

**time out** • n. **1** chiefly N. Amer. time for rest or recreation. ➤ (**timeout**) a brief break from play in a game or sport. ➤ a brief period of time during which a misbehaving child is put on their own so as to regain control. **2** (**timeout**) Computing a cancellation or cessation that automatically occurs when a predefined interval of time has passed.

**timepiece** • n. an instrument for measuring time; a clock or watch.

**timer** • n. **1** an automatic mechanism for activating a device at a preset time. **2** a person or device that records the amount of time taken by a process or activity. **3** [in combination] indicating how many times someone has done something: *a first-timer.*

**time-release** • adj. denoting something that releases an active substance gradually.

**timescale** • n. the time allowed for or taken by a process or sequence of events: *a timescale of thousands of years.*

**time-server** • n. **1** a person who changes their views to suit the prevailing circumstances or fashion. **2** a person who makes very little effort at work because they are waiting to leave or retire.
– DERIVATIVES **time-serving** adj.

**timeshare** • n. an arrangement whereby joint owners use a property as a holiday home at different specified times. ➤ a property owned in such a way.
– DERIVATIVES **time-sharing** n.

**time sheet** • n. a piece of paper for recording the number of hours worked.

**time signature** • n. Music an indication of rhythm following a clef, generally expressed as a fraction with the denominator defining the beat as a division of a semibreve and the numerator giving the number of beats in each bar.

**times table** • n. informal term for **MULTIPLICATION TABLE**.

**time switch** • n. a switch automatically activated at a preset time.

**timetable** • n. a list or plan of times at which events are scheduled to take place. • v. schedule to take place at a particular time.

**time travel** • n. (in science fiction) travel through time into the past or the future.
– DERIVATIVES **time traveller** n.

**time trial** • n. **1** (in various sports) a test of a competitor's individual speed over a set distance. **2** an exercise designed to test the time needed for a task or activity.

**time warp** • n. an imaginary distortion of space in relation to time whereby people or objects of one period can be moved to another.

**time-wasting** • n. the tactic of slowing down play towards the end of a match to prevent the opposition scoring.
– DERIVATIVES **time-waster** n.

**time-worn** • adj. impaired or made less striking as a result of age or long use.

**timid** • adj. (**-er, -est**) lacking in courage or confidence.
– DERIVATIVES **timidity** n. **timidly** adv. **timidness** n.
– ORIGIN C16: from L. *timidus*, from *timere* 'to fear'.

**timing** • n. **1** the choice, judgement, or control of when something should be done. **2** a particular time when something happens. ➤(in an internal-combustion engine) the times when the valves open and close, and the time of the ignition spark, in relation to the movement of the piston in the cylinder.

**timocracy** /tɪˈmɒkrəsi/ • n. (pl. **-ies**) chiefly Philosophy **1** a form of government in which possession of property is required in order to hold office. **2** a form of government in which rulers are motivated by ambition or love of honour.
– DERIVATIVES **timocratic** adj.
– ORIGIN C15: from OFr. *timocracie*, via med. L. from Gk *timokratia*, from *timē* 'honour, worth' + *-kratia* 'power'.

**Timorese** /ˌtiːmɔːˈriːz/ • n. (pl. same) a native or inhabitant of Timor, an island in the southern Malay Archipelago. • adj. of or relating to Timor.

**timorous** • adj. lacking in courage or confidence; nervous.
– DERIVATIVES **timorously** adv. **timorousness** n.
– ORIGIN ME: from OFr. *temoreus*, from med. L. *timorosus*, from L. *timor* 'fear', from *timere* 'to fear'.

**timothy** • n. a grass which is widely grown for grazing and hay. [*Phleum pratense*.]
– ORIGIN C18: named after the Amer. farmer *Timothy* Hanson.

**timpani** /ˈtɪmpəni/ (also **tympani**) • pl. n. kettledrums.
– DERIVATIVES **timpanist** n.
– ORIGIN C19: from Ital., pl. of *timpano* 'kettledrum', from L. *tympanum* (see **TYMPANUM**).

**tin** • n. **1** a silvery-white metal, the chemical element of atomic number 50. (Symbol: **Sn**) **2** a lidded airtight container made of tinplate or aluminium. ➤chiefly Brit. a sealed container for preserving food, made of tinplate or aluminium; a can. ➤an open metal container for baking food. • v. (**tinned**, **tinning**) **1** cover with a thin layer of tin. **2** [usu. as adj. **tinned**] chiefly Brit. preserve in a tin: *tinned fruit*. **3** [as noun **tinning**] tin mining.
– PHRASES **have a tin ear** informal be tone-deaf.
– DERIVATIVES **tinner** n. **tinware** n.
– ORIGIN OE, of Gmc origin.

**tinamou** /ˈtɪnəmuː/ • n. a grouse-like tropical American bird related to the rhea. [Family Tinamidae: many species.]
– ORIGIN C18: via Fr. from Galibi *tinamu*.

**tinctorial** /tɪŋ(k)ˈtɔːrɪəl/ • adj. of or relating to dyeing, colouring, or staining properties.
– ORIGIN C17: from L. *tinctorius* (from *tinctor* 'dyer', from *tingere* 'to dye or colour') + **-AL**.

**tincture** /ˈtɪŋ(k)tʃə/ • n. **1** a medicine made by dissolving a drug in alcohol. **2** a slight trace. **3** Heraldry any of the conventional colours used in coats of arms. • v. (**be tinctured**) be tinged, flavoured, or imbued with a slight trace.
– ORIGIN ME (denoting a dye or pigment): from L. *tinctura* 'dyeing', from *tingere* 'to dye or colour'.

**tinder** • n. dry, flammable material, such as wood or paper, used for lighting a fire.
– DERIVATIVES **tindery** adj.
– ORIGIN OE *tynder*, *tyndre*, of Gmc origin.

**tinderbox** • n. historical a box containing tinder, flint, a steel, and other items for kindling fires.

**tine** /tʌɪn/ • n. a prong or sharp point.
– DERIVATIVES **tined** adj.
– ORIGIN OE *tind*, of Gmc origin.

**tinea** /ˈtɪnɪə/ • n. technical term for **RINGWORM**.
– ORIGIN ME: from L., 'worm'.

**tinfoil** • n. foil made of aluminium or a similar metal, used especially for covering or wrapping food.

**ting** • n. a sharp, clear ringing sound. • v. emit a ting.
– ORIGIN ME: imitative.

**tinge** • v. (**tinging** or **tingeing**) (often **be tinged**) **1** colour slightly. **2** have a slight influence on: *a visit tinged with sadness*. • n. a slight trace.
– ORIGIN C15: from L. *tingere* 'to dip or colour'.

**tin glaze** • n. a glaze made white and opaque by the addition of tin oxide.
– DERIVATIVES **tin-glazed** adj.

**tingle**[1] • n. a slight prickling or stinging sensation. • v. experience or cause to experience a tingle.
– DERIVATIVES **tingly** adj.
– ORIGIN ME: perh. a var. of **TINKLE**.

**tingle**[2] • n. an S-shaped metal clip used to support heavy panes of glass or slates on a roof.
– ORIGIN ME (denoting a small tack): rel. to Mid. High Ger. *zingel* 'small tack or hook'.

**tin god** • n. a person, especially a minor official, who is pompous and self-important. ➤an object of unjustified veneration or respect.

**tin hat** • n. informal, chiefly Brit. a soldier's steel helmet.

**tinhorn** • n. N. Amer. informal a person who pretends to have money, influence, or ability.

**tinker** • n. **1** an itinerant mender of pots, kettles, etc. **2** Brit., chiefly derogatory a gypsy or other person living in an itinerant community. **3** Brit. informal a mischievous child. **4** an act of tinkering with something. • v. (**tinker with**) attempt in a casual manner to repair or improve.
– PHRASES **not give a tinker's curse** (or **cuss** or **damn**) informal not care at all.
– DERIVATIVES **tinkerer** n.
– ORIGIN ME (first recorded in Anglo-Latin as a surname): of unknown origin.

**tinkle** • v. **1** make or cause to make a light, clear ringing sound. **2** informal urinate. • n. **1** a tinkling sound. ➤Brit. informal a telephone call. **2** informal an act of urinating.
– DERIVATIVES **tinkly** adj.
– ORIGIN ME (also in the sense 'tingle'): frequentative of obs. *tink* 'to chink or clink', of imitative origin.

**tin Lizzie** • n. N. Amer. informal, dated a motor car, especially a very early Ford.
– ORIGIN C20: *Lizzie*, a familiar form of the given name *Elizabeth*.

**tinnitus** /tɪˈnʌɪtəs, ˈtɪnɪtəs/ • n. Medicine ringing or buzzing in the ears.
– ORIGIN C19: from L., from *tinnire* 'to ring, tinkle', of imitative origin.

**tinny** • adj. **1** having a thin, metallic sound. **2** made of thin or poor-quality metal. **3** having an unpleasantly metallic taste. **4** Austral./NZ informal lucky. [C20: from *tin* 'luck' (lit. 'money, cash') + **-Y**[1].] • n. (also **tinnie**) (pl. **-ies**) Austral./NZ informal a can of beer.
– DERIVATIVES **tinnily** adv. **tinniness** n.

**tin-opener** • n. chiefly Brit. a tool for opening tins of food.

**tinplate** • n. sheet steel or iron coated with tin. • v. coat with tin.
– DERIVATIVES **tin-plated** adj.

**tinpot** • adj. informal (especially of a country or its leader) having or showing poor leadership or organization.

**tinsel** • n. **1** a form of decoration consisting of thin strips of shiny metal foil attached to a length of thread. **2** superficial attractiveness or glamour.
– DERIVATIVES **tinselled** adj. **tinselly** adj.
– ORIGIN ME (denoting fabric either interwoven with metallic thread or spangled): from OFr. *estincele* 'spark', or *estinceler* 'to sparkle', based on L. *scintilla* 'a spark'.

**Tinseltown** • n. derogatory the superficially glamorous world of Hollywood and its film industry.

**tinsmith** • n. a person who makes or repairs articles of tin or tinplate.

**tinsnips** • pl. n. a pair of clippers for cutting sheet metal.

**tin soldier** • n. a toy soldier made of metal.

**tinstone** • n. another term for **CASSITERITE**.

**tint** • n. **1** a shade or variety of colour. ➤a trace of something. **2** the process or dye used in artificial colouring of

the hair. **3** Printing an area of faint colour printed as a half-tone. ➤a set of parallel engraved lines giving uniform shading. ●**v.** colour slightly; tinge. ➤dye (hair) with a tint.
– DERIVATIVES **tinter** n.
– ORIGIN C18: alt. (perh. influenced by Ital. *tinta*) of obs. *tinct* 'to colour, tint', from L. *tinctus* 'dyeing'.

**tintinnabulation** /ˌtɪntɪnabjʊˈleɪʃ(ə)n/ ●**n.** a ringing or tinkling sound.
– ORIGIN C19: from L. *tintinnabulum* 'tinkling bell' + **-ATION**.

**tintype** ●**n.** historical a photograph taken as a positive on a thin tin plate.

**tin whistle** ●**n.** a small flute-like instrument made from a thin metal tube, with six finger holes of varying size on top and no thumb holes.

**tiny** ●**adj.** (**-ier**, **-iest**) very small. ●**n.** (pl. **-ies**) informal a very young child.
– DERIVATIVES **tinily** adv. **tininess** n.
– ORIGIN C16: extension of obs. *tine*, 'small, diminutive', of unknown origin.

**-tion** ●**suffix** forming nouns of action, condition, etc. such as *completion*.
– ORIGIN from L. participial stems ending in *-t* + **-ION**.

**tip**[1] ●**n.** the pointed or rounded extremity of something slender or tapering. ➤a small part fitted to the end of an object. ●**v.** (**tipped**, **tipping**) **1** attach to or cover the tip of. **2** colour (something) at its tip or edge. **3** (**tip something in**) (in bookbinding) paste a page to a neighbouring page with a fine layer of paste down its inner margin.
– PHRASES **on the tip of one's tongue** almost but not quite spoken or coming to mind.
– DERIVATIVES **tipped** adj.
– ORIGIN ME: from ON *typpi* (n.), *typpa* (v.), *typptr* 'tipped'; rel. to **TOP**[1].

**tip**[2] ●**v.** (**tipped**, **tipping**) **1** overbalance or cause to overbalance so as to fall or turn over. ➤be or cause to be in a sloping position. **2** empty out (the contents of a container) by holding it at an angle. ➤(**it tips down**, **it is tipping down**, etc.) Brit. informal rain heavily. **3** strike or touch lightly. ➤cause to move by a light strike or touch. **4** (**tip off**) Basketball put the ball in play by throwing it up between two opponents. ●**n. 1** Brit. a place where rubbish is left. ➤informal a dirty or untidy place. **2** Baseball a pitched ball that is slightly deflected by the batter.
– PHRASES **tip one's hand** N. Amer. informal reveal one's intentions inadvertently. **tip one's hat** raise or touch one's hat as a greeting or mark of respect.
– ORIGIN ME: perh. of Scand. origin, influenced later by **TIP**[1] in the sense 'touch with a tip or point'.

**tip**[3] ●**n. 1** a small sum of money given as a reward for services rendered. **2** a piece of practical advice. ➤a prediction or piece of expert information about the likely winner of a race or contest. ●**v.** (**tipped**, **tipping**) **1** give a tip to. **2** Brit. predict as likely to win or achieve something. **3** (**tip someone off**) informal give someone confidential information.
– PHRASES **tip someone the wink** Brit. informal secretly give someone confidential information.
– ORIGIN C17 (in the sense 'give, hand'): prob. from **TIP**[1].

**tip-and-run** ●**n. 1** an informal way of playing cricket in which the batsman must run after every hit. **2** [as modifier] (of a military raid) executed swiftly and followed by immediate withdrawal.

**tipcat** ●**n.** chiefly historical a game in which a piece of wood tapered at both ends is struck at one end with a stick so as to spring up and is then knocked away by the same player.

**tipi** ●**n.** variant spelling of **TEPEE**.

**tip-in** ●**n.** Basketball a score made by tipping a rebound into the basket.

**tip-off** ●**n.** informal a piece of confidential information.

**tipper** ●**n. 1** a truck having a rear platform which can be raised at its front end, thus enabling a load to be discharged. **2** a person who regularly leaves a specified size of tip as a reward. **3** a person who dumps waste, especially illegally.

**tippet** ●**n.** a woman's fur cape or woollen shawl. ➤a similar ceremonial garment worn especially by the clergy. ➤historical a long, narrow strip of cloth forming part of or attached to a hood or sleeve.
– ORIGIN ME: prob. from an Anglo-Norman derivative of **TIP**[1].

**Tipp-Ex** (also **Tippex**) ●**n.** Brit. trademark a type of correction fluid. ●**v.** delete with correction fluid.
– ORIGIN 1960s: from Ger., from *tippen* 'to type' and L. *ex* 'out'.

**tipple** ●**v. 1** drink alcohol regularly. **2** (**it tipples down**, **it is tippling down**, etc.) Brit. informal rain heavily. ●**n.** informal an alcoholic drink.
– ORIGIN C15 (in the sense 'sell (alcoholic drink) by retail'): back-form from **TIPPLER**[1].

**tippler**[1] ●**n.** a habitual drinker of alcohol.
– ORIGIN ME (denoting a retailer of alcoholic liquor): of unknown origin.

**tippler**[2] ●**n.** a revolving frame or cage in which a truck is inverted to discharge its load.
– ORIGIN C19: from dial. *tipple* 'tumble over' + **-ER**[1].

**tippy** ●**adj.** N. Amer. inclined to tilt or overturn; unsteady.

**tippy-toe** ●**v.** informal, chiefly N. Amer. tiptoe.
– PHRASES **on tippy-toe** (or **tippy-toes**) on tiptoe.
– ORIGIN C19: alt. of **TIPTOE**.

**tipstaff** ●**n.** a sheriff's officer; a bailiff.
– ORIGIN C16 (first denoting a metal-tipped staff): contr. of *tipped staff* (carried by a bailiff).

**tipster** ●**n.** a person who gives tips, especially about the likely winner of a race or contest.

**tipsy** ●**adj.** (**-ier**, **-iest**) slightly drunk.
– DERIVATIVES **tipsily** adv. **tipsiness** n.
– ORIGIN C16: from the verb **TIP**[2] + **-SY**.

**tipsy cake** ●**n.** Brit. a sponge cake saturated with wine or spirits, typically served with custard.

**tiptoe** ●**v.** (**tiptoes**, **tiptoed**, **tiptoeing**) walk quietly and carefully with one's heels raised and one's weight on the balls of the feet.
– PHRASES **on tiptoe** (or **tiptoes**) with one's heels raised and one's weight on the balls of the feet.

**tip-top** ●**adj.** of the very best; excellent. ●**n. 1** the highest part or point of excellence. **2** N. Amer. a line guide on a fishing rod.

**tip-up** ●**adj. 1** denoting a seat that tips up vertically when unoccupied. **2** denoting the raisable rear platform of a tipper truck. ●**n.** N. Amer. a device used in ice-fishing in which a wire attached to the rod is tripped, raising a signal flag, when a fish takes the bait.

**tirade** /tʌɪˈreɪd, tɪ-/ ●**n.** a long speech of angry criticism or accusation.
– ORIGIN C19: from Fr., lit. 'long speech'.

**tiramisu** /ˌtɪrəmɪˈsuː/ ●**n.** an Italian dessert consisting of layers of sponge cake soaked in coffee and brandy or liqueur, with powdered chocolate and mascarpone cheese.
– ORIGIN Ital., from the phr. *tira mi sù* 'pick me up'.

**tire**[1] ●**v.** become or cause to become in need of rest or sleep. ➤exhaust the patience or interest of. ➤(**tire of**) become impatient or bored with.
– DERIVATIVES **tired** adj. **tiredly** adv. **tiredness** n. **tireless** adj. **tirelessly** adv. **tirelessness** n.
– ORIGIN OE *tēorian* (also in the sense 'fail, come to an end'), of unknown origin.

**tire**[2] ●**n.** US spelling of **TYRE**.

**tiresome** ●**adj.** causing one to feel bored or impatient.
– DERIVATIVES **tiresomely** adv. **tiresomeness** n.

**tiro** ●**n.** variant spelling of **TYRO**.

**'tis** ●**contr.** chiefly poetic/literary it is.

**tisane** /tɪˈzan/ ●**n.** a herb tea.
– ORIGIN 1930s: from Fr.

**Tishri** /ˈtɪʃriː/ (also **Tisri** /ˈtɪzriː/) ●**n.** (in the Jewish calendar) the first month of the civil and seventh of the religious year, usually coinciding with parts of September and October.
– ORIGIN from Heb. *tišrī*.

**tissue** /ˈtɪʃuː, ˈtɪsjuː/ ●**n. 1** any of the distinct types of material of which animals or plants are made, consisting

of specialized cells and their products. **2** tissue paper. ➤a piece of absorbent paper, used especially as a disposable handkerchief. **3** fabric of a delicate gauzy texture. **4** a web-like structure or network: *a tissue of lies.*
– DERIVATIVES **tissuey** adj.
– ORIGIN ME: from OFr. *tissu* 'woven', past part. of *tistre*, from L. *texere* 'to weave'.

**tissue culture** • n. Biology & Medicine the growth in an artificial medium of cells derived from living tissue. ➤a cell culture of this kind.

**tissue paper** • n. very thin, soft paper.

**tissue type** • n. a class of tissues which are immunologically compatible with one another. • v. (**tissue-type**) determine the tissue type of.
– DERIVATIVES **tissue-typing** n.

**Tit.** • abbrev. Titus (in biblical references).

**tit**[1] • n. a titmouse.
– ORIGIN C16: prob. of Scand. origin.

**tit**[2] • n. **1** vulgar slang a woman's breast. **2** Brit. informal a foolish or ineffectual person. **3** military slang a push-button, especially one used to fire a gun or release a bomb.
– PHRASES **get on someone's tits** Brit. vulgar slang irritate someone intensely.
– ORIGIN OE *tit* 'teat, nipple', of Gmc origin.

**tit**[3] • n. (in phr. **tit for tat**) the infliction of an injury or insult in retaliation for one received.
– ORIGIN C16: var. of obs. *tip for tap.*

**Titan** /ˈtʌɪt(ə)n/ • n. **1** any of a family of giant gods in Greek mythology. **2** (**titan**) a person or thing of very great strength, intellect, or importance.

**titanate** /ˈtʌɪtəneɪt/ • n. Chemistry a salt in which the anion contains both titanium and oxygen.

**titanic**[1] • adj. of exceptional strength, size, or power.
– DERIVATIVES **titanically** adv.
– ORIGIN from Gk *titanikos*, from *Titan* (see **TITAN**).

**titanic**[2] • adj. Chemistry of titanium with a valency of four; of titanium(IV). Compare with **TITANOUS**.
– ORIGIN C19: from **TITANIUM** + **-IC**.

**titanium** /tʌɪˈteɪnɪəm, tɪ-/ • n. the chemical element of atomic number 22, a hard silver-grey metal used in strong, light, corrosion-resistant alloys. (Symbol: **Ti**)
– ORIGIN C18: from **TITAN**, on the pattern of *uranium.*

**titanium dioxide** (also **titanium oxide**) • n. a white unreactive solid which occurs naturally as the mineral rutile and is used extensively as a white pigment. [$TiO_2$.]

**titanous** /tʌɪˈtanəs/ • adj. Chemistry of titanium with a lower valency, usually three. Compare with **TITANIC**[2].
– ORIGIN C19: from **TITANIUM**, on the pattern of words such as *ferrous.*

**titbit** (N. Amer. **tidbit**) • n. **1** a small piece of tasty food. **2** a small and particularly interesting item of gossip or information.
– ORIGIN C17 (as *tyd bit, tid-bit*): from dial. *tid* 'tender' (of unknown origin) + **BIT**[1].

**titch** (also **tich**) • n. Brit. informal a small person.
– DERIVATIVES **titchy** adj. (**-ier**, **-iest**).
– ORIGIN 1930s: from *Little Tich*, stage name of Harry Relph, an Engl. music-hall comedian of small stature, given the nickname because he resembled Arthur Orton, the unsuccessful claimant to the valuable Tichborne estate.

**titer** • n. US spelling of **TITRE**.

**titfer** • n. Brit. informal a hat.
– ORIGIN 1930s: abbrev. of rhyming sl. *tit for tat.*

**tithe** /tʌɪð/ • n. **1** one tenth of annual produce or earnings, formerly taken as a tax for the support of the Church and clergy. **2** archaic a tenth of a specified thing. • v. subject to or pay as a tithe.
– DERIVATIVES **tithable** adj.
– ORIGIN OE *tēotha* (adj. in the ordinal sense 'tenth', used in a specialized sense as a noun), *tēothian* (v.).

**tithe barn** • n. a barn built to hold produce made over as tithes.

**tithing** /ˈtʌɪðɪŋ/ • n. **1** the practice of taking or paying a tithe. **2** historical (in England) a group of ten householders who lived close together and were collectively responsible for each other's behaviour. ➤a rural division, originally regarded as a tenth of a hundred.
– ORIGIN OE *tēothung* (see **TITHE**, **-ING**[1]).

**titi**[1] /ˈtiːtiː/ • n. (pl. **titis**) a small forest-dwelling monkey of South America. [Genus *Callicebus*: several species.]
– ORIGIN C18: from Aymara.

**titi**[2] /ˈtʌɪtʌɪ, ˈtiːtiː/ • n. (pl. **titis**) an evergreen American shrub or small tree with tough flexible bark. [*Cyrilla racemiflora.*]
– ORIGIN C19: perh. of Amer. Ind. origin.

**Titian** /ˈtɪʃ(ə)n/ • adj. (of hair) bright golden auburn.
– ORIGIN C19: from *Titian*, C16 Ital. painter, by assoc. with the bright auburn hair portrayed in many of his works.

**titillate** /ˈtɪtɪleɪt/ • v. **1** arouse to mild excitement or interest, especially through images or words. **2** archaic lightly touch; tickle.
– DERIVATIVES **titillating** adj. **titillatingly** adv. **titillation** n.
– ORIGIN C17 (earlier (ME) as *titillation*): from L. *titillat-*, *titillare* 'tickle'.

**titivate** /ˈtɪtɪveɪt/ • v. informal adorn or smarten up. ➤(**titivate oneself**) adjust one's appearance.
– DERIVATIVES **titivation** n.
– ORIGIN C19 (in early use, also as *tidivate*): perh. from **TIDY**, on the pattern of *cultivate.*

**titlark** • n. dialect a pipit, especially the meadow pipit.

**title** • n. **1** the name of a book, musical composition, or other artistic work. ➤a caption or credit in a film or broadcast. **2** a name that describes someone's position or job. **3** a word used before or instead of someone's name, indicating social or official rank, profession, or academic or marital status. **4** a descriptive or distinctive name that is earned or chosen: *the title of Best Restaurant of the Year.* **5** the position of being the champion of a major sports competition: *he won the world title.* **6** Law a right or claim to the ownership of property or to a rank or throne. **7** (in church use) a fixed sphere of work and source of income as a condition for ordination. ➤a parish church in Rome under a cardinal. • v. (usu. **be titled**) give a title to.
– DERIVATIVES **titled** adj.
– ORIGIN OE *titul*, reinforced by OFr. *title*, both from L. *titulus* 'inscription, title'.

**title deed** • n. a legal document constituting evidence of a right, especially to ownership of property.

**title music** • n. music played during the credits at the beginning or end of a television programme or film.

**title role** • n. the part in a play or film from which the work's title is taken.

**titling**[1] /ˈtʌɪtlɪŋ/ • n. Printing type consisting only of capital letters and figures which are the full height of the type size.

**titling**[2] /ˈtɪtlɪŋ/ • n. Scottish & N. English the meadow pipit.
– ORIGIN C16: from **TIT**[1] + **-LING**.

**titmouse** • n. (pl. **titmice**) a small songbird, typically foraging acrobatically among foliage and branches. [Many species, chiefly in the family Paridae.]
– ORIGIN ME: from **TIT**[1] + obs. *mose* 'titmouse' (assimilated to **MOUSE**).

**titrate** /tʌɪˈtreɪt, tɪ-/ • v. **1** Chemistry ascertain the amount of a substance in (a solution) by measuring the volume of a standard reagent required to react with it. **2** Medicine continuously measure and adjust (a physiological function or drug dosage).
– DERIVATIVES **titratable** adj. **titration** n.
– ORIGIN C19: from Fr. *titrer* (from *titre* in the sense 'fineness of alloyed gold or silver') + **-ATE**[3].

**titre** /ˈtʌɪtə, ˈtiːtə/ (US **titer**) • n. **1** Chemistry the concentration of a solution as determined by titration. **2** Medicine the concentration of an antibody, determined by finding the highest dilution at which it is still active.
– ORIGIN C19: from Fr., from *titrer* (see **TITRATE**).

**ti tree** • n. variant spelling of **TEA TREE** (in sense 1).

**titter** • n. a short, half-suppressed laugh. • v. give a titter.
– DERIVATIVES **titterer** n. **tittering** n. & adj. **titteringly** adv.
– ORIGIN C17: imitative.

**tittle** • n. a tiny amount or part of something.
– ORIGIN ME: from L. *titulus* (see **TITLE**), in med. L. 'small stroke, accent'.

**tittle-tattle** • n. gossip. • v. engage in gossip.

– ORIGIN C16: reduplication of **TATTLE**.

**tittup** /ˈtɪtəp/ • **v.** (**tittuped**, **tittuping** or **tittupped**, **tittupping**) chiefly Brit. (in horse riding) proceed with jerky or exaggerated movements.

– ORIGIN C17 (as n.): perh. imitative of hoof-beats.

**titty** (also **tittie**) • **n.** (pl. **-ies**) another term for **TIT**².

**titubation** /ˌtɪtjʊˈbeɪʃ(ə)n/ • **n.** Medicine nodding movement of the head or body, especially as caused by a nervous disorder.

– ORIGIN C17: from L. *titubatio(n-)*, from *titubare* 'totter'.

**titular** /ˈtɪtjʊlə/ • **adj.** **1** of or relating to a title. **2** holding or constituting a formal position or title without any real authority. ➤(of a cleric) nominally appointed to serve a diocese, abbey, etc. no longer in existence (typically having real authority elsewhere). **3** denoting any of the parish churches in Rome to which cardinals are formally appointed.

– DERIVATIVES **titularly** adv.

**Tiwa** /ˈtiːwə/ (also **Tigua**) • **n.** (pl. same or **Tiwas**) **1** a member of a Pueblo Indian people living mainly in the region of Taos, New Mexico. **2** the Tanoan language of this people.

– ORIGIN the name in Tiwa.

**tiyin** /tiːˈjɪn/ • **n.** (pl. same or **tiyins**) a monetary unit of Kyrgyzstan, equal to one hundredth of a som.

**tizzy** (also **tizz**) • **n.** (pl. **-ies**) informal a state of nervous excitement or agitation.

– ORIGIN 1930s (orig. US): of unknown origin.

**T-junction** • **n.** a junction in the shape of a 'T', especially a road junction at which one road joins another at right angles without crossing it.

**TKO** • **abbrev.** Boxing technical knockout.

**Tl** • **symb.** the chemical element thallium.

**TLC** • **abbrev.** informal tender loving care.

**Tlingit** /ˈklɪŋkɪt, ˈklɪŋgɪt, ˈtlɪŋ-/ • **n.** (pl. same or **Tlingits**) **1** a member of an American Indian people of the coasts and islands of SE Alaska. **2** the language of this people.

– ORIGIN the name in Tlingit.

**T-lymphocyte** • **n.** Physiology a lymphocyte of a type produced or processed by the thymus gland and participating in the cell-mediated immune response. Compare with **B-LYMPHOCYTE**.

– ORIGIN 1970s: from *T* for *thymus*.

**TM** • **abbrev.** (trademark in the US) Transcendental Meditation.

**Tm** • **symb.** the chemical element thulium.

**tmesis** /ˈtmiːsɪs/ • **n.** (pl. **tmeses** /-siːz/) the separation of parts of a compound word by an intervening word (used informally for emphasis, e.g. *can't find it any-blooming-where*).

– ORIGIN C16: from Gk *tmēsis* 'cutting'.

**TMV** • **abbrev.** tobacco mosaic virus.

**TN** • **abbrev.** **1** Tennessee (in official postal use). **2** Tunisia (international vehicle registration).

**tn** • **abbrev.** US ton(s).

**TNT** • **abbrev.** trinitrotoluene, a high explosive made by nitrating toluene.

**to** • **prep.** **1** expressing direction or position in relation to a particular location, point, or condition. ➤chiefly Brit. (in telling the time) before (the hour specified). **2** identifying the person or thing affected. **3** identifying a particular relationship between one person or thing and another. ➤indicating a rate of return on something: *ten miles to the gallon.* **4** indicating that two things are attached. **5** governing a phrase expressing someone's reaction to something: *to her astonishment, he smiled.* **6** used to introduce the second element in a comparison. **7** placed before a debit entry in accounting. • **infinitive marker** **1** used with the base form of a verb to indicate that the verb is in the infinitive. ➤(**about to**) forming a future tense with reference to the immediate future. **2** used without a verb following when the missing verb is clearly understood: *she said she didn't want to.* • **adv.** so as to be closed or nearly closed.

– ORIGIN OE *tō* (adv. and prep.), of W. Gmc origin.

**toad** • **n.** **1** a tailless amphibian with a short stout body and short legs, typically having dry warty skin that can exude poison. [Many species, chiefly in the family Bufonidae.] **2** a detestable person.

– DERIVATIVES **toadish** adj. **toadlet** n.

– ORIGIN OE *tādde, tāda*, abbrev. of *tādige*, of unknown origin.

**toadfish** • **n.** (pl. same or **-fishes**) a fish of warm seas with a wide head and large mouth, able to produce loud grunts. [Family Batrachoididae: several species.]

**toadflax** • **n.** a plant with yellow or purplish snapdragon-like flowers and slender leaves. [*Linaria vulgaris* (**yellow toadflax**) and other species.]

**toad-in-the-hole** • **n.** Brit. a dish consisting of sausages baked in batter.

**toadstone** • **n.** a gem, fossil tooth, or other stone formerly supposed to have been formed in the body of a toad, and credited with therapeutic or protective properties.

**toadstool** • **n.** the spore-bearing fruiting body of a fungus, typically in the form of a rounded cap on a stalk, especially one that is inedible or poisonous.

– ORIGIN ME: a fanciful name.

**toady** • **n.** (pl. **-ies**) **1** a person who behaves obsequiously towards others. **2** Australian term for **PUFFERFISH**. • **v.** (**-ies**, **-ied**) act obsequiously.

– DERIVATIVES **toadyish** adj. **toadyism** n.

– ORIGIN C19: said to be a contr. of *toad-eater*, a charlatan's assistant who ate toads (regarded as poisonous) as a demonstration of the efficacy of the charlatan's remedy.

**to and fro** • **adv.** in a constant movement backwards and forwards or from side to side. • **v.** (**be toing and froing**) be moving to and fro. ➤vacillate. • **n.** constant movement backwards and forwards. ➤vacillation.

– DERIVATIVES **toing and froing** n.

**toast**¹ • **n.** **1** sliced bread browned on both sides by exposure to radiant heat. **2** an act or instance of raising glasses at a gathering and drinking together in honour of a person or thing. ➤a person who is toasted or held in high regard: *he was the toast of the baseball world.* • **v.** **1** cook or brown by exposure to radiant heat. ➤warm (oneself or part of one's body) beside a fire or other source or heat. **2** drink a toast to.

– PHRASES **be toast** informal, chiefly N. Amer. be finished, defunct, or dead. **have someone on toast** Brit. informal be in a position to deal with someone as one wishes.

– DERIVATIVES **toasted** adj. **toasty** adj. (**-ier**, **-iest**).

– ORIGIN ME (as v. in the sense 'burn as the sun does, parch'): from OFr. *toster* 'roast', from L. *torrere* 'parch'; sense 2 originated (C17) in the idea that the name of the lady being honoured flavoured the drink like the pieces of spiced toast formerly placed in wine.

**toast**² • **v.** (of a DJ) accompany a reggae backing track or music with improvised rhythmic speech.

– DERIVATIVES **toasting** n.

– ORIGIN C20: perh. the same word as **TOAST**¹.

**toaster** • **n.** **1** an electrical device for making toast. **2** a DJ who toasts.

**toastie** • **n.** Brit. informal a toasted sandwich or snack.

**toasting fork** • **n.** a long-handled fork for making toast in front of a fire.

**toastmaster** (or **toastmistress**) • **n.** an official responsible for proposing toasts, introducing speakers, and making other formal announcements at a large social event.

**Tob.** • **abbrev.** (in biblical references) Tobit (Apocrypha).

**tobacco** • **n.** (pl. **-os**) **1** a preparation of the dried and fermented nicotine-rich leaves of an American plant, used for smoking or chewing. **2** the plant of the nightshade family yielding these leaves. [*Nicotiana tabacum*.]

– ORIGIN C16: from Sp. *tabaco*; perh. from a Carib word denoting a tobacco pipe or from a Taino word for a primitive cigar, or from Arab.

**tobacco mosaic virus** • **n.** a virus that causes mosaic disease in tobacco, much used in biochemical research.

**tobacconist** • **n.** chiefly Brit. a shopkeeper who sells cigarettes and tobacco.

**tobacco plant** • **n.** the plant which yields tobacco. See **TOBACCO** (sense 2). ➤an ornamental plant related to this. [Genus *Nicotiana*.]

**Tobagonian** /təˈbeɪgən/ • **n.** a native or inhabitant of the Caribbean island of Tobago. • **adj.** of or relating to Tobago.

**toboggan** • **n.** a light, narrow vehicle, typically on runners, used for sliding downhill over snow or ice. • **v.** ride on a toboggan.
– DERIVATIVES **tobogganer** n. **tobogganing** n. **tobogganist** n.
– ORIGIN C19: from Canad. Fr. *tabaganne*, from Micmac *topağan* 'sled'.

**toby jug** • **n.** chiefly Brit. a beer jug or mug in the form of a stout old man wearing a three-cornered hat.
– ORIGIN C19: familiar form of the given name *Tobias*, and said to come from a poem (C18) about *Toby Philpot* (with a pun on *fill pot*), a soldier who liked to drink.

**TOC** • **abbrev.** (in the UK) train operating company.

**toccata** /tə'kɑːtə/ • **n.** a musical composition for a keyboard instrument designed to exhibit the performer's touch and technique.
– ORIGIN C18: from Ital., fem. past part. of *toccare* 'to touch'.

**Tocharian** /tə'kɛːrɪən, -'kɑːrɪən/ • **n. 1** a member of an ancient people of central Asia. **2** either of two extinct languages spoken by this people. • **adj.** of or relating to this people or their languages.
– ORIGIN from Fr. *tocharien*, via L. from Gk *Tokharoi*, the name of a Scythian tribe (almost certainly unrelated to the Tocharians).

**toco** /'təʊkə/ • **n.** (pl. **-os**) the largest and most familiar South American toucan, with mainly black plumage, a white throat and breast, and a massive black-tipped orange bill. [*Ramphastos toco*.]
– ORIGIN C18: via Port. from Tupi; cf. **TOUCAN**.

**tocopherol** /tɒ'kɒfərɒl/ • **n.** Biochemistry vitamin E, any of a group of compounds found in wheatgerm oil, egg yolk, and leafy vegetables and important in the stabilization of cell membranes.
– ORIGIN 1930s: from Gk *tokos* 'offspring' + *pherein* 'to bear' + **-OL**.

**tocsin** /'tɒksɪn/ • **n.** archaic an alarm bell or signal.
– ORIGIN C16: from OFr. *toquassen*, from Provençal *tocasenh*, from *tocar* 'to touch' + *senh* 'signal bell'.

**tod** • **n.** (in phr. **on one's tod**) Brit. informal on one's own.
– ORIGIN 1930s: from rhyming sl. *Tod Sloan*, the name of an Amer. jockey.

**today** • **adv.** on or in the course of this present day. ➤ at the present period of time; nowadays. • **n.** this present day. ➤ the present period of time.
– PHRASES **today week** Brit. a week from today.
– ORIGIN OE *tō dæg* 'on (this) day'; cf. **TOMORROW** and **TONIGHT**.

**toddle** • **v.** (of a young child) move with short unsteady steps while learning to walk. ➤ informal walk or go in a casual or leisurely way. • **n.** an act of toddling.
– ORIGIN C16: of unknown origin.

**toddler** • **n.** a young child who is just beginning to walk.
– DERIVATIVES **toddlerhood** n.

**toddy** • **n.** (pl. **-ies**) **1** a drink made of spirits with hot water and sugar. **2** the sap of some kinds of palm, fermented to produce arrack.
– ORIGIN C17: from Marathi *tāḍī*, Hindi *tāṛī*, from Sanskrit *tāḍī* 'palmyra'.

**todger** (also **tadger**) • **n.** Brit. informal a man's penis.
– ORIGIN 1950s: of unknown origin.

**to-do** • **n.** informal a commotion or fuss.
– ORIGIN C16: from *to do* as in *much to do*, orig. meaning 'much needing to be done' but later interpreted as the adjective *much* and a noun; cf. **ADO**.

**tody** /'təʊdi/ • **n.** (pl. **-ies**) a small insectivorous Caribbean bird with a large head, long bill, bright green upper parts, and a red throat. [Genus *Todus*: five species.]
– ORIGIN C18: from Fr. *todier*, from L. *todus*, the name of a small bird.

**toe** • **n. 1** any of the five digits at the end of the human foot. ➤ any of the digits of the foot of a quadruped or bird. ➤ the part of an item of footwear that covers a person's toes. **2** the lower end, tip, or point of something. ➤ the tip of the head of a golf club. • **v.** (**toes**, **toed**, **toeing**) **1** push, touch, or kick with one's toes. ➤ Golf strike (the ball) with the toe of the club. **2** (**toe in/out**) walk with the toes pointed in (or out). ➤ (of a pair of wheels) converge (or diverge) slightly at the front.
– PHRASES **make someone's toes curl** informal bring about an extreme reaction of delight or disgust in someone. **on one's toes** ready and alert. **toe the line** comply with authority, especially unwillingly or under pressure. **turn up one's toes** informal die.
– DERIVATIVES **toed** adj. **toeless** adj.
– ORIGIN OE *tā*, of Gmc origin.

**toea** /'təʊeɪə/ • **n.** (pl. same) a monetary unit of Papua New Guinea, equal to one hundredth of a kina.
– ORIGIN Motu, lit. 'cone-shaped shell'.

**toecap** • **n.** a piece of steel or leather constituting or fitted over the front part of a boot or shoe.

**toe clip** • **n.** a clip on a bicycle pedal to prevent the foot from slipping.

**toehold** • **n. 1** a small foothold. **2** a tentative position from which further progress may be made.

**toe loop** • **n.** Skating a jump in which the skater makes a full turn in the air, taking off from and landing on the outside edge of the same foot.

**toenail** • **n. 1** a nail on the upper surface of the tip of each toe. **2** a nail driven obliquely through a piece of wood to secure it. • **v.** fasten (wood) with a toenail.

**toerag** • **n.** Brit. informal a contemptible person.
– ORIGIN C19: orig. denoting a rag wrapped round the foot as a sock or, by extension, the wearer (such as a vagrant).

**toe-tapping** • **adj.** informal (of music) making one want to tap one's feet; lively.

**toey** • **adj.** Austral./NZ informal nervous; restive.

**toff** • **n.** Brit. informal, derogatory a rich or upper-class person.
– ORIGIN C19: perh. an alt. of **TUFT**, used to denote a gold tassel worn on the cap by titled undergraduates at Oxford and Cambridge.

**toffee** • **n.** a kind of firm or hard sweet which softens when sucked or chewed, made by boiling together sugar and butter.
– PHRASES **not be able to do something for toffee** Brit. informal be totally incompetent at doing something.
– ORIGIN C19: alt. of **TAFFY**.

**toffee apple** • **n.** Brit. an apple coated with a thin layer of toffee and fixed on a stick.

**toffee-nosed** • **adj.** informal, chiefly Brit. pretentiously superior; snobbish.
– DERIVATIVES **toffee nose** n.

**toft** • **n.** archaic a homestead.
– ORIGIN OE, from ON *topt*.

**tofu** /'təʊfuː/ • **n.** curd made from mashed soya beans, used chiefly in Asian and vegetarian cookery.
– ORIGIN from Japanese *tōfu*, from Chin. *dòufu*, from *dòu* 'beans' + *fǔ* 'rot, turn sour'.

**tog**[1] informal • **n.** (**togs**) clothes. • **v.** (**togged**, **togging**) (**be/get togged up/out**) be or get fully dressed for a particular occasion or activity.
– DERIVATIVES **toggery** n.
– ORIGIN C18: appar. an abbrev. of obs. criminals' sl. *togeman(s)* 'a light cloak', from Fr. *toge* or L. *toga* (see **TOGA**).

**tog**[2] • **n.** Brit. a unit of thermal resistance used to express the insulating properties of clothes and quilts.
– ORIGIN 1940s: from **TOG**[1], on the pattern of an earlier unit called the *clo* (first element of *clothes*).

**toga** /'təʊgə/ • **n.** a loose flowing outer garment worn by the citizens of ancient Rome, made of a single piece of cloth and covering the whole body apart from the right arm.
– ORIGIN L.; rel. to *tegere* 'to cover'.

**together** • **adv. 1** with or in proximity to another person or people. ➤ so as to touch or combine. ➤ in combination; collectively. ➤ into companionship or close association. ➤ (of two people) married or in a sexual relationship. ➤ so as to be united or in agreement. **2** at the same time. **3** without interruption. • **adj.** informal level-headed and well organized.
– PHRASES **together with** as well as.

– DERIVATIVES **togetherness** n.
– ORIGIN OE *tōgædere*, based on the prep. **TO** + a W. Gmc word rel. to **GATHER**.

**toggle** • n. **1** a narrow piece of wood or plastic attached to one side of a garment, pushed through a loop on the other side to act as a fastener. ➤ a pin or other crosspiece put through the eye of a rope or a link of a chain to keep it in place. ➤ (also **toggle bolt**) a kind of wall fastener for use on open-backed plasterboard, having a part that springs open or turns through 90° after it is inserted so as to prevent withdrawal. ➤ a movable pivoted crosspiece acting as a barb on a harpoon. **2** Computing a key or command that is operated the same way but with opposite effect on successive occasions. • v. **1** Computing switch from one effect, feature, or state to another by using a toggle. **2** provide or fasten with a toggle or toggles.
– ORIGIN C18 (orig. in naut. use): of unknown origin.

**toggle switch** • n. **1** an electric switch operated by means of a projecting lever that is moved up and down. **2** Computing another term for **TOGGLE**.

**Togolese** /ˌtəʊɡəˈliːz/ • n. (pl. same) a native or inhabitant of Togo, a country in West Africa. • adj. of or relating to Togo.

**toil** • v. work extremely hard or incessantly. ➤ move somewhere slowly and with difficulty. • n. exhausting work.
– DERIVATIVES **toiler** n.
– ORIGIN ME: from Anglo-Norman Fr. *toiler* 'strive, dispute', *toil* 'confusion', from L. *tudiculare* 'stir about', from *tudicula* 'machine for crushing olives', rel. to *tundere* 'crush'.

**toile** /twɑːl/ • n. **1** an early version of a finished garment made up in cheap material so that the design can be tested. **2** a translucent fabric. **3** short for **TOILE DE JOUY**.
– ORIGIN ME: from Fr. *toile* 'cloth, web', from L. *tela* 'web'.

**toile de Jouy** /də ʒwiː/ • n. a type of printed calico with a characteristic blue or red floral, figure, or landscape design on a light background.
– ORIGIN orig. made at *Jouy*-en-Josas, near Paris.

**toilet** • n. **1** a large bowl for urinating or defecating into, typically plumbed into a sewage system. **2** the process of washing oneself, dressing, and attending to one's appearance. ➤ [as modifier] denoting articles used in this process. **3** the cleansing of part of a person's body as a medical procedure. • v. (**toileted**, **toileting**) [usu. as noun **toileting**] assist or supervise (an infant or invalid) in using a toilet.
– ORIGIN C16 (orig. denoting a cloth cover for a dressing table, later a dressing room, and, in the US, one with washing facilities): from Fr. *toilette* 'cloth, wrapper', dimin. of *toile* (see **TOILE**).

**toilet bag** • n. Brit. a waterproof bag for holding toothpaste, soap, etc. when travelling.

**toilet paper** • n. paper for wiping oneself clean after urination or defecation.

**toiletries** • pl. n. articles used in washing and taking care of one's body, such as soap and shampoo.

**toilet set** • n. a set of items used in arranging the hair, typically including a hairbrush, comb, and mirror.

**toilet table** • n. dated a dressing table.

**toilette** /twɑːˈlɛt/ • n. old-fashioned term for **TOILET** (in sense 2).
– ORIGIN C17: Fr. (see **TOILET**).

**toilet tissue** • n. toilet paper.

**toilet-train** • v. teach (a young child) to use the toilet.

**toilet water** • n. a dilute form of perfume.

**toils** • pl. n. poetic/literary a situation regarded as a trap.
– ORIGIN C16 (denoting a net into which a hunted quarry is driven): pl. of *toil*, from OFr. *toile* (see **TOILE**).

**toilsome** • adj. archaic or poetic/literary involving hard work.
– DERIVATIVES **toilsomely** adv. **toilsomeness** n.

**toilworn** • adj. poetic/literary exhausted by toil.

**tokamak** /ˈtəʊkəmak/ • n. Physics a toroidal apparatus for producing controlled fusion reactions in hot plasma.
– ORIGIN 1960s: Russ., from *toroidal'naya kamera s magnitnym polem* 'toroidal chamber with magnetic field'.

**Tokay** /təʊˈkeɪ/ • n. a sweet aromatic wine, originally made near Tokaj in Hungary.

**tokay** /təʊˈkeɪ/ • n. a large grey SE Asian gecko with orange and blue spots. [*Gekko gecko*.]
– ORIGIN C18: from Malay dial. *toke'*, from Javanese *tekèk*, imitative of its call.

**toke** informal • n. a pull on a cigarette or pipe, typically one containing cannabis. • v. smoke cannabis or tobacco.
– DERIVATIVES **toker** n.
– ORIGIN 1950s: of unknown origin.

**token** • n. **1** a thing serving to represent a fact, quality, feeling, etc. ➤ archaic a badge or favour worn to indicate allegiance to a person or party. ➤ archaic a word or object conferring authority on or serving to authenticate the speaker or holder. ➤ a device given to a train driver on a single-track railway as authority to proceed. **2** a voucher that can be exchanged for goods or services. ➤ a metal or plastic disc used to operate a machine or in exchange for particular goods or services. **3** Linguistics an individual occurrence of a linguistic unit in speech or writing. Contrasted with **TYPE**. **4** Computing a sequence of bits passed between nodes in a fixed order and enabling a node to transmit information. • adj. **1** done for the sake of appearances or as a symbolic gesture. **2** chosen by way of tokenism to represent a particular group.
– PHRASES **by the same** (or **that** or **this**) **token** in the same way or for the same reason. **in token of** as a sign or symbol of.
– ORIGIN OE *tāc(e)n*, of Gmc origin; rel. to **TEACH**.

**tokenism** • n. the practice of making only a perfunctory or symbolic effort to do a particular thing, especially by recruiting a small number of people from under-represented groups in order to give the appearance of sexual or racial equality within a workforce.
– DERIVATIVES **tokenistic** adj.

**token money** • n. money where the face value of notes or coins is unrelated to the value of the material of which they are composed.

**token ring** • n. Computing a local area network in which a node can only transmit when in possession of a token, which is passed to each node in turn.

**tokonoma** /ˌtɒkəʊˈnəʊmə/ • n. (in Japan) a recess or alcove for displaying flowers, pictures, and ornaments.
– ORIGIN from Japanese.

**Tok Pisin** /tɒk ˈpɪsɪn/ • n. an English-based creole used as a commercial and administrative language in Papua New Guinea.
– ORIGIN the name in Tok Pisin, lit. 'pidgin talk'.

**tolar** /ˈtɒlɑː/ • n. the basic monetary unit of Slovenia, equal to 100 stotins.
– ORIGIN Slovene; cf. **THALER**.

**tolbooth** • n. variant spelling of **TOLLBOOTH**.

**told** past and past participle of **TELL**[1].

**tole** /təʊl/ (also **tôle** /tɔːl/) • n. painted, enamelled, or lacquered tin plate used to make decorative domestic objects.
– ORIGIN 1940s: Fr. *tôle*, 'sheet iron'.

**tolerable** • adj. **1** able to be tolerated. **2** fairly good.
– DERIVATIVES **tolerability** n. **tolerably** adv.
– ORIGIN ME: via OFr. from L. *tolerabilis*, from *tolerare* (see **TOLERATE**).

**tolerance** • n. **1** the ability, willingness, or capacity to tolerate something. **2** an allowable amount of variation of a specified quantity, especially in the dimensions of a machine or part.
– ORIGIN ME: via OFr. from L. *tolerantia*, from *tolerare* (see **TOLERATE**).

**tolerant** • adj. **1** showing tolerance. **2** (of a plant, animal, or machine) able to endure specified conditions or treatment.
– DERIVATIVES **tolerantly** adv.

**tolerate** • v. **1** allow the existence or occurrence of (something that one dislikes or disagrees with) without interference. **2** endure (someone or something unpleasant) with forbearance. **3** be capable of continued exposure to (a drug, toxin, etc.) without adverse reaction.
– DERIVATIVES **toleration** n. **tolerator** n.
– ORIGIN C16 (earlier (C15) as *toleration*, denoting the

granting of permission by authority): from L. *tolerat-*, *tolerare* 'endure'.

**toll**[1] /təʊl/ ● n. **1** a charge payable to use a bridge or road. ➤ N. Amer. a charge for a long-distance telephone call. **2** the number of deaths or casualties arising from an accident, disaster, etc. **3** the cost or damage resulting from something. ● v. [usu. as noun **tolling**] charge a toll for the use of (a bridge or road).
– PHRASES **take its toll** (or **take a heavy toll**) have an adverse effect.
– ORIGIN OE, from med. L. *toloneum*, alt. of late L. *teloneum*, from Gk *telōnion* 'toll house', from *telos* 'tax'.

**toll**[2] /təʊl/ ● v. (with reference to a bell) sound or cause to sound with a slow, uniform succession of strokes. ➤ (of a bell) announce (the time, a service, or a person's death) in this way. ● n. a single ring of a bell.
– ORIGIN ME: prob. a special use of dial. *toll* 'drag, pull'.

**tollbooth** (also **tolbooth**) ● n. **1** a roadside kiosk where tolls are paid. **2** Scottish archaic a town hall. ➤ a town jail.

**toll gate** ● n. a barrier across a road where a toll must be paid to proceed further.

**toll plaza** ● n. US a row of tollbooths on a toll road.

**Toltec** /'tɒltɛk/ ● n. a member of an American Indian people that flourished in Mexico before the Aztecs.
– DERIVATIVES **Toltecan** adj.
– ORIGIN via Sp. from Nahuatl *toltecatl*, lit. 'a person from *Tula*' (a town and former Toltec site in central Mexico).

**tolu** /tə'luː, 'təʊluː/ ● n. a fragrant brown balsam obtained from a South American tree, used in perfumery and medicine.
– ORIGIN C17: named after *Santiago de Tolú* in Colombia, from where it was exported.

**toluene** /'tɒljʊiːn/ ● n. Chemistry a colourless liquid hydrocarbon resembling benzene, present in coal tar and petroleum.
– ORIGIN C19: from **TOLU** + **-ENE**.

**tom** ● n. **1** the male of various animals, especially a domestic cat. **2** Brit. a female prostitute. ● v. (**tommed**, **tomming**) informal **1** (**be tomming**) Brit. work as a prostitute. **2** US (of a black person) behave in an excessively obedient or servile way.
– ORIGIN ME (denoting an ordinary man): abbrev. of the given name *Thomas*; sense 2 of the noun is from criminals' sl.; sense 2 of the verb is from **UNCLE TOM**.

**tomahawk** /'tɒməhɔːk/ ● n. a light axe formerly used as a tool or weapon by American Indians. ➤ Austral./NZ a hatchet. ● v. strike or cut with or as if with a tomahawk.
– ORIGIN C17: from a Virginia Algonquian lang.

**tomalley** /'tɒmali/ ● n. N. Amer. the digestive gland of a lobster, cooked and eaten as a delicacy.
– ORIGIN C17: from Fr. *taumalin*, from Carib *taumali*.

**tomatillo** /ˌtɒmə'tɪləʊ, -'tiːjəʊ, -'tiːljəʊ/ ● n. (pl. **-os**) **1** an edible purple or yellow fruit used for sauces and preserves. **2** the Mexican plant which bears this fruit. [*Physalis philadelphica*.]
– ORIGIN C20: from Sp., dimin. of *tomate* 'tomato'.

**tomato** ● n. (pl. **-oes**) **1** a glossy red or yellow edible fruit, eaten as a vegetable or in salads. **2** the South American plant of the nightshade family which produces this fruit. [*Lycopersicon esculentum*.]
– DERIVATIVES **tomatoey** adj.
– ORIGIN C17: from Fr., Sp., or Port. *tomate*, from Nahuatl *tomatl*.

**tomb** ● n. **1** a burial place, especially a large underground vault. ➤ a monument to a dead person, erected over their burial place. **2** (**the tomb**) poetic/literary death.
– ORIGIN ME: from OFr. *tombe*, from late L. *tumba*, from Gk *tumbos*.

**tombola** /tɒm'bəʊlə/ ● n. Brit. a game, typically played at a fête or fair, in which tickets are drawn from a revolving drum to win prizes.
– ORIGIN C19: from Fr. or Ital., from Ital. *tombolare* 'turn a somersault'.

**tombolo** /'tɒmbələʊ/ ● n. (pl. **-os**) a bar of sand or shingle joining an island to the mainland.
– ORIGIN C19: from Ital., lit. 'sand dune'.

**tomboy** ● n. a girl who enjoys rough, noisy activities traditionally associated with boys.
– DERIVATIVES **tomboyish** adj. **tomboyishness** n.

**tombstone** ● n. **1** a large, flat inscribed stone standing or laid over a grave. **2** (also **tombstone advertisement**) an advertisement listing the underwriters or firms associated with a new issue of shares, bonds, etc.

**tomcat** ● n. a male domestic cat.

**tomcod** ● n. (pl. same or **tomcods**) a small edible greenish-brown North American cod. [*Microgadus proximus* (Pacific coast) and *M. tomcod* (Atlantic coast).]

**Tom Collins** ● n. a cocktail made from gin mixed with soda, sugar, and lemon or lime juice.
– ORIGIN sometimes said to have been named after a C19 London bartender.

**Tom, Dick, and Harry** (also **Tom, Dick, or Harry**) ● n. ordinary people in general.

**tome** ● n. chiefly humorous a book, especially a large, scholarly one.
– ORIGIN C16: from Fr., via L. from Gk *tomos* 'section, roll of papyrus, volume'.

**-tome** ● comb. form **1** denoting an instrument for cutting: *microtome*. **2** denoting a section or segment.
– ORIGIN sense 1 from Gk *-tomon* (neut.) 'that cuts'; sense 2 from Gk *tomē* 'a cutting'.

**tomentum** /tə'mɛntəm/ ● n. (pl. **tomenta** /-tə/) Botany a layer of matted woolly down on the surface of a plant.
– DERIVATIVES **tomentose** /tə'mɛntəʊs, 'təʊ-/ adj. **tomentous** adj.
– ORIGIN C17: from L., lit. 'cushion stuffing'.

**tomfoolery** ● n. foolish or silly behaviour.
– DERIVATIVES **tomfool** n. (dated).

**Tommy** ● n. (pl. **-ies**) informal a British private soldier.
– ORIGIN C19: familiar form of the given name *Thomas*; from a use of the name *Thomas Atkins* in specimens of completed official forms in the British army.

**tommy bar** ● n. a short bar used to turn a box spanner.

**tommy gun** ● n. informal a type of sub-machine gun.
– ORIGIN 1920s: contr. of *Thompson gun*, named after John T. *Thompson*, the Amer. army officer who conceived it.

**tommyrot** ● n. informal, dated nonsense.

**tommy ruff** (also **tommy rough**) ● n. see **RUFF**[2] (sense 1).

**tomography** /tə'mɒgrəfi/ ● n. a technique for displaying a cross section through a human body or other solid object using X-rays or ultrasound.
– DERIVATIVES **tomogram** n. **tomographic** adj.
– ORIGIN 1930s: from Gk *tomos* 'slice, section' + **-GRAPHY**.

**tomorrow** ● adv. **1** on the day after today. **2** in the near future. ● n. **1** the day after today. **2** the near future.
– PHRASES **like there was no tomorrow** informal completely without restraint. **tomorrow week** Brit. a week from tomorrow.
– ORIGIN ME (as two words): from **TO** + **MORROW**; cf. **TODAY** and **TONIGHT**.

**tompion** /'tɒmpɪən/ ● n. variant spelling of **TAMPION**.

**tom thumb** ● n. a dwarf variety of a cultivated flower or vegetable.
– ORIGIN C19: from the name of the hero of a children's story, who was only as tall as his father's thumb.

**tomtit** ● n. a small, active titmouse or similar bird, especially (Brit.) the blue tit.

**tom-tom** ● n. **1** a medium-sized cylindrical drum, of which one to three may be used in a drum kit. **2** a drum beaten with the hands, associated with North American Indian, African, or Eastern cultures.
– ORIGIN C17: from Hindi *ṭam ṭam*, Telugu *ṭamaṭama*, of imitative origin.

**-tomy** ● comb. form cutting, especially as part of a surgical process: *episiotomy*. See word-formation panel.
– ORIGIN from Gk *-tomia* 'cutting'.

**ton**[1] /tʌn/ (abbrev.: **t**, also US **tn**) ● n. **1** (also **long ton**) a unit of weight equal to 2,240 lb avoirdupois (1016.05 kg). **2** (also **short ton**) chiefly N. Amer. a unit of weight equal to 2,000 lb avoirdupois (907.19 kg). **3** short for **METRIC TON**. **4** (also **displacement ton**) a unit of measurement of a ship's weight representing the weight of water it displaces with the load line just immersed, equal to 2,240 lb

## Word *Formation*

**-tomy** from Greek *-tomia* 'cutting'

➤ Most **-tomy** words relate to specific types of surgical operation:

| | | |
|---|---|---|
| appendectomy | an operation to remove the appendix | APPENDIX + -ECTOMY (from Gk *ek* 'out' + *tomē* 'cutting') |
| clitoridectomy | removal of the clitoris; female circumcision | based on CLITORIS + -ECTOMY |
| episiotomy | a surgical cut made during childbirth to aid delivery | Gk *epision* 'pubic region' |
| hysterectomy | an operation to remove the womb | Gk *hustera* 'womb' + -ECTOMY |
| laparotomy | a surgical incision into the abdomen | Gk *lapara* 'flank' |
| lumpectomy | an operation to remove a lump (tumour) | based on LUMP + -ECTOMY |
| mastectomy | an operation to remove a breast | Gk *mastos* 'breast' + -ECTOMY |
| nephrectomy | an operation to remove a kidney | Gk *nephros* 'kidney' + -ECTOMY |
| penectomy | amputation of the penis | based on PENIS + -ECTOMY |
| tracheotomy | a surgical incision made in the windpipe | based on TRACHEA |
| vasectomy | male sterilization by cutting and sealing each vas deferens | based on VAS + -ECTOMY |

The word ***anatomy***, first recorded in the 1540s, was used earlier in the sense 'dissection of the body' (from Gk *ana-* 'up' + -TOMY), which in modern use has become generalized to 'the science of bodily structure'. Early uses of the word also included the senses 'a skeleton' and 'a corpse'. By the 17th century the word was often shortened to ***atomy*** according to a mistaken assumption that *anatomy* was equivalent to 'an atomy'.

The word ***dichotomy*** 'a division between two opposed things', is also based on **-tomy**, formed on Greek *dikho-* 'in two, apart'.

***Colostomy***, meaning 'a surgical operation to shorten the colon and divert the end through the abdominal wall', is not, despite appearances, based on **-tomy**. It is formed on COLON + Greek *stoma* 'mouth'.

or 35 cu. ft (0.99 cubic metres). **5** (also **freight ton**) a unit of weight or volume of sea cargo, equal to a metric ton (1,000 kg) or 40 cu. ft. **6** (also **gross ton**) a unit of gross internal capacity, equal to 100 cu. ft (2.83 cubic metres). ➤(also **net** or **register ton**) an equivalent unit of net internal capacity. **7** a unit of refrigerating power able to freeze 2,000 lb of water at 0°C in 24 hours. **8** a measure of capacity for various materials, especially 40 cu. ft of wood. **9** informal a large number or amount. **10** informal, chiefly Brit. a hundred, in particular a speed of 100 mph, a score of 100 or more, or a sum of £100. ● **adv.** (**tons**) Brit. informal much; a lot: *I feel tons better.*
– ORIGIN ME: var. of **TUN**, both spellings being used for the container and the weight.

**ton**[2] /tɒ̃/ ● **n. 1** fashionable style or distinction. **2** (**the ton**) [treated as sing. or pl.] fashionable society.
– ORIGIN Fr., from L. *tonus* (see **TONE**).

**tonal** /ˈtəʊn(ə)l/ ● **adj. 1** of or relating to tone. **2** of or relating to music written using conventional keys and harmony.
– DERIVATIVES **tonally** adv.

**tonalite** /ˈtɒn(ə)lʌɪt/ ● **n.** Geology a coarse-grained plutonic rock consisting chiefly of sodic plagioclase, quartz, and hornblende or other mafic minerals.
– ORIGIN C19: from *Tonale* Pass, northern Italy, + **-ITE**[1].

**tonality** ● **n.** (pl. **-ies**) **1** the character of a piece of music as determined by the key in which it is played or the relations between the notes of a scale or key. **2** the use of conventional keys and harmony as the basis of musical composition. **3** the range of tones used in a picture.

**tondo** /ˈtɒndəʊ/ ● **n.** (pl. **tondi** /-di/) a circular painting or relief.
– ORIGIN C19: from Ital., lit. 'round object'.

**tone** ● **n. 1** a musical or vocal sound with reference to its pitch, quality, and strength. **2** a modulation of the voice expressing a feeling or mood. **3** general character: *trust her to lower the tone of the conversation.* **4** (also **whole tone**) a basic interval in classical Western music, equal to two semitones and separating, for example, the first and second notes of an ordinary scale; a major second. **5** the particular quality of brightness, deepness, or hue of a colour. ➤the general effect of colour or of light and shade in a picture. **6** a musical note, warble, or other sound used as a signal on a telephone or answering machine. **7** Phonetics (in some languages, such as Chinese) a particular pitch pattern on a syllable used to make semantic distinctions. ➤(in some languages, such as English) intonation on a word or phrase used to add functional meaning. **8** (also **muscle tone**) the normal level of firmness or slight contraction in a resting muscle. ● **v. 1** (often **tone something up**) give greater strength or firmness to (the body or a muscle). **2** (**tone something down**) make something less harsh in sound or colour. ➤make something less extreme or intense. **3** (**tone with**) harmonize with in terms of colour. **4** Photography give (a monochrome picture) an altered colour in finishing by means of a chemical solution.
– DERIVATIVES **-toned** adj. **toneless** adj. **tonelessly** adv.
– ORIGIN ME: from OFr. *ton*, from L. *tonus*, from Gk *tonos* 'tension, tone', from *teinein* 'to stretch'.

**tone arm** ● **n.** the movable arm supporting the pickup of a record player.

**toneburst** ● **n.** an audio signal used in testing the transient response of audio components.

**tone colour** ● **n.** Music another term for **TIMBRE**.

**tone-deaf** ● **adj.** unable to perceive differences of musical pitch accurately.
– DERIVATIVES **tone-deafness** n.

**tone group** ● **n.** Phonetics a group of words forming a distinctive unit in an utterance, containing a nucleus and optionally one or more other syllables before and after the nucleus.

**toneme** /ˈtəʊniːm/ ● **n.** Phonetics a phoneme distinguished from another only by its tone.
– DERIVATIVES **tonemic** adj.
– ORIGIN 1920s: from **TONE**, on the pattern of *phoneme*.

**tonepad** ● **n.** a device generating specific tones to control another device at the other end of a telephone line.

**tone poem** ● **n.** a piece of orchestral music, typically in one movement, on a descriptive or rhapsodic theme.

**toner** ● **n. 1** an astringent liquid applied to the skin to reduce oiliness and improve its condition. **2** a device or exercise for toning a specified part of the body. **3** a black or coloured powder used in xerographic copying processes. **4** a chemical bath for changing the tone of a photographic print.

**tone row** • **n.** Music a particular sequence of the twelve notes of the chromatic scale used as a basis for twelve-note (serial) music.

**tone unit** • **n.** another term for **TONE GROUP**.

**tong**[1] • **n.** a Chinese association or secret society, frequently associated with organized crime.
– ORIGIN C19: from Chin. (Cantonese dial.) *t'ōng*, lit. 'meeting place'.

**tong**[2] • **v.** **1** curl (hair) using tongs. **2** collect (oysters) using oyster tongs.

**Tonga** /ˈtɒŋgə/ • **n.** (pl. same or **Tongas**) **1** a member of any of three peoples of southern Africa, living mainly in Zambia, Malawi, and Mozambique respectively. **2** any of the three different Bantu languages spoken by these peoples.
– ORIGIN the name in Tonga.

**tonga** /ˈtɒŋgə/ • **n.** a light horse-drawn two-wheeled vehicle used in India.
– ORIGIN from Hindi *tā̃gā*.

**Tongan** /ˈtɒŋən, ˈtɒŋg(ə)n/ • **n.** **1** a native or national of Tonga, an island group in the South Pacific. **2** the Polynesian language spoken in Tonga. • **adj.** of or relating to Tonga, its people, or their language.

**tongs** • **pl. n.** **1** a tool with two movable arms that are joined at one end, used for picking up and holding things. **2** short for **CURLING TONGS**.
– ORIGIN OE *tang(e)* (sing.), of Gmc origin.

**tongue** • **n.** **1** the fleshy muscular organ in the mouth, used for tasting, licking, swallowing, and (in humans) articulating speech. ➤the tongue of an ox or lamb, as food. **2** a person's style or manner of speaking. **3** a particular language. **4** a strip of leather or fabric under the laces in a shoe, attached only at the front end. **5** the free-swinging metal piece inside a bell which strikes the bell to produce the sound. **6** a long, low promontory of land. **7** a projecting strip on a wooden board fitting into a groove on another. **8** the vibrating reed of a musical instrument or organ pipe. • **v.** (**tongues**, **tongued**, **tonguing**) **1** Music sound (a note) distinctly on a wind instrument by interrupting the air flow with the tongue. **2** lick or caress with the tongue.
– PHRASES **find** (or **lose**) **one's tongue** be able (or unable) to express oneself after a shock. **get one's tongue round** pronounce (words). **the gift of tongues** the power of speaking in unknown languages, regarded as one of the gifts of the Holy Spirit (Acts 2). **give tongue 1** (of hounds) bark, especially on finding a scent. **2** express one's feelings or opinions freely. **(with) tongue in cheek** insincerely or ironically. **someone's tongue is hanging out** someone is very eager for something.
– DERIVATIVES **tongued** adj. **tongueless** adj.
– ORIGIN OE *tunge*, of Gmc origin.

**tongue and groove** • **n.** wooden planking in which adjacent boards are joined by means of interlocking ridges and hollows down their sides.
– DERIVATIVES **tongued-and-grooved** adj.

**tongue-in-cheek** • **adj. & adv.** with ironic or flippant intent.

**tongue-lashing** • **n.** a loud or severe scolding.

**tongue tie** • **n.** a malformation which restricts the movement of the tongue.

**tongue-tied** • **adj.** **1** too shy or embarrassed to speak. **2** having a tongue tie.

**tongue-twister** • **n.** a sequence of words, typically of an alliterative kind, that are difficult to pronounce quickly and correctly.
– DERIVATIVES **tongue-twisting** adj.

**tonic** • **n.** **1** a medicinal substance taken to give a feeling of vigour or well-being. **2** something with an invigorating effect. **3** short for **TONIC WATER**. **4** Music the first note in a scale which, in conventional harmony, provides the keynote of a piece of music. • **adj.** **1** Music relating to or denoting the first degree of a scale. **2** Phonetics denoting or relating to the syllable within a tone group that has greatest prominence. **3** Physiology relating to or restoring muscle tone. ➤of or denoting continuous muscular contraction.
– DERIVATIVES **tonically** adv.
– ORIGIN C17: from Fr. *tonique*, from Gk *tonikos* 'of or for stretching', from *tonos* (see **TONE**).

**tonicity** /tə(ʊ)ˈnɪsɪti/ • **n.** **1** muscle tone. **2** Linguistics the pattern of tones or stress in speech. **3** Biology osmotic pressure.

**tonic sol-fa** • **n.** a system of naming the notes of the scale used especially to teach singing, with doh as the keynote of all major keys and lah as the keynote of all minor keys. See **SOLMIZATION**.

**tonic water** • **n.** a carbonated soft drink with a bitter flavour, used as a mixer with gin or other spirits.

**tonify** /ˈtəʊnɪfʌɪ/ • **v.** (**-ies**, **-ied**) (of acupuncture or herbal medicine) increase the available energy of (a bodily part or system).
– DERIVATIVES **tonification** n.

**tonight** • **adv.** on the present or approaching evening or night. • **n.** the evening or night of the present day.
– ORIGIN OE *tō niht*, from the preposition **TO** + **NIGHT**; cf. **TODAY** and **TOMORROW**.

**tonka bean** /ˈtɒŋkə/ • **n.** the black fragrant seed of a South American tree (*Dipteryx odorata*), used in perfumery and as flavouring.
– ORIGIN C18: *tonka*, a local word in Guyana.

**ton-mile** • **n.** one ton of goods carried one mile, as a unit of traffic.

**tonnage** • **n.** **1** weight in tons. **2** the size or carrying capacity of a ship measured in tons. ➤shipping considered in terms of total carrying capacity.

**tonne** /tʌn/ • **n.** another term for **METRIC TON**.
– ORIGIN C19: from Fr.; cf. **TON**[1].

**tonneau** /ˈtɒnəʊ/ • **n.** **1** the part of an open car occupied by the back seats. **2** (also **tonneau cover**) a protective cover for the seats in an open car or cabin cruiser when they are not in use.
– ORIGIN C18 (denoting a unit of capacity for French wine): Fr., lit. 'cask, tun'.

**tonometer** /tə(ʊ)ˈnɒmɪtə/ • **n.** **1** a tuning fork or other instrument for measuring pitch. **2** an instrument for measuring pressure in an eyeball, blood vessel, etc.
– ORIGIN C18: from Gk *tonos* (see **TONE**) + **-METER**.

**tonsil** • **n.** either of two small masses of lymphoid tissue in the throat, one on each side of the root of the tongue.
– DERIVATIVES **tonsillar** adj.
– ORIGIN C16: from Fr. *tonsilles* or L. *tonsillae* (pl.).

**tonsillectomy** /ˌtɒnsɪˈlɛktəmi/ • **n.** (pl. **-ies**) a surgical operation to remove the tonsils.

**tonsillitis** • **n.** inflammation of the tonsils.

**tonsorial** /tɒnˈsɔːrɪəl/ • **adj.** formal or humorous of or relating to hairdressing.
– ORIGIN C19: from L. *tonsorius* (from *tonsor* 'barber', from *tondere* 'shear, clip') + **-AL**.

**tonsure** /ˈtɒnsjə, ˈtɒnʃə/ • **n.** **1** a part of a monk's or priest's head left bare on top by shaving off the hair. **2** an act of shaving a monk's or priest's head in this way as a preparation for entering a religious order. • **v.** [often as adj. **tonsured**] give a tonsure to.
– ORIGIN ME: from OFr., or from L. *tonsura*, from *tondere* 'shear, clip'.

**tontine** /tɒnˈtiːn, ˈtɒn-/ • **n.** an annuity shared by subscribers to a loan or common fund, the shares increasing as subscribers die until the last survivor enjoys the whole income.
– ORIGIN C18: from Fr., named after Lorenzo *Tonti*, a Neapolitan banker who started such a scheme to raise government loans in France.

**ton-up** • **adj.** Brit. informal denoting a person achieving a speed of 100 mph or a score of 100 or more.

**Tony** • **n.** (pl. **Tonys**) (in the US) any of a number of awards given annually for outstanding achievement in the theatre in various categories.
– ORIGIN 1947: from the nickname of the Amer. actress and director Antoinette Perry.



T U

**tony** ● adj. (**-ier**, **-iest**) N. Amer. informal fashionable, stylish, or high-class.
– ORIGIN C19: from **TONE** + **-Y**[1].

**too** ● adv. **1** to a higher degree than is desirable, permissible, or possible. ➤ informal very. **2** in addition. ➤ moreover.
– PHRASES **none too** —— not very.
– ORIGIN OE, stressed form of **TO**.

**toodle-oo** ● exclam. informal, dated goodbye.
– ORIGIN C20: perh. an alt. of Fr. *à tout à l'heure* 'see you soon'.

**took** past of **TAKE**.

**tool** ● n. **1** a device or implement, typically hand-held, used to carry out a particular function. **2** a thing used to help perform a job. **3** a person used by another. **4** a distinct design in the tooling of a book. ➤ a small stamp or roller used to make such a design. **5** vulgar slang a man's penis. ● v. **1** (usu. **be tooled**) impress a design on (a leather book cover) with a heated tool. **2** equip or be equipped with tools for industrial production. **3** (**tool up** or **be tooled up**) Brit. informal be or become armed. **4** informal drive or ride in a casual or leisurely manner. **5** dress (stone) with a chisel.
– DERIVATIVES **tooler** n. **tooling** n.
– ORIGIN OE *tōl*, from a Gmc base meaning 'prepare'.

**toolbar** ● n. Computing a strip of icons used to perform certain functions.

**toolbox** ● n. a box or container for tools. ➤ Computing a set of software tools. ➤ Computing the set of programs or functions accessible from a single menu.

**toolmaker** ● n. a person who makes and maintains tools for use in a manufacturing process.
– DERIVATIVES **toolmaking** n.

**tool pusher** ● n. a person who directs the drilling on an oil rig.

**toon** ● n. informal a cartoon film or character.

**toot** ● n. **1** a short, sharp sound made by a horn, trumpet, or similar instrument. **2** informal, chiefly N. Amer. a snort of a drug, especially cocaine. ➤ cocaine. **3** N. Amer. informal a spree. ● v. **1** make or cause to make a toot. **2** informal, chiefly N. Amer. snort (cocaine).
– DERIVATIVES **tooter** n.
– ORIGIN C16: prob. from Mid. Low Ger. *tūten*, but possibly an independent imitative formation.

**tooth** ● n. (pl. **teeth**) **1** each of a set of hard, bony enamel-coated structures in the jaws, used for biting and chewing. **2** a similar projecting part, especially a cog on a gearwheel or a point on a saw or comb. **3** (**teeth**) genuine force or effectiveness: *the Charter would be fine if it had teeth.* **4** an appetite or liking for a particular thing.
– PHRASES **armed to the teeth** formidably armed. **fight tooth and nail** fight very fiercely. **get** (or **sink**) **one's teeth into** work energetically and productively on. **in the teeth of 1** directly against (the wind). **2** in spite of (opposition or difficulty).
– DERIVATIVES **toothed** adj. **toothless** adj. **toothlessly** adv. **toothlessness** n. **tooth-like** adj.
– ORIGIN OE *tōth* (pl. *tēth*), of Gmc origin.

**toothache** ● n. pain in a tooth or teeth.

**toothbrush** ● n. a small brush with a long handle, used for cleaning the teeth.

**toothcomb** ● n. Brit. used with reference to a very thorough search: *the police went over the area with a fine toothcomb.*
– ORIGIN orig. from a misreading of the compound noun *fine-tooth comb.*

**toothed whale** ● n. any of the large group of predatory whales with teeth, including sperm whales, killer whales, dolphins, porpoises, etc. [Suborder Odontoceti.]

**tooth fairy** ● n. a fairy said to take children's milk teeth after they fall out and leave a coin under their pillow.

**toothglass** ● n. a glass for holding toothbrushes or dentures, or one used as a tumbler for mouthwash.

**toothing** ● n. **1** the teeth on a saw. **2** projecting bricks or stones left at the end of a wall to allow its continuation.

**toothpaste** ● n. a paste used on a brush for cleaning the teeth.

**toothpick** ● n. a short pointed piece of wood or plastic used for removing bits of food lodged between the teeth.

**tooth powder** ● n. powder used for cleaning the teeth.

**tooth shell** ● n. another term for **TUSK SHELL**.

**toothsome** ● adj. **1** (of food) temptingly tasty. **2** informal attractive; alluring.
– DERIVATIVES **toothsomely** adv. **toothsomeness** n.

**toothwort** ● n. a plant with a thick rhizome bearing rows of tooth-like scales, parasitic on hazel and beech roots. [*Lathraea squamaria.*]

**toothy** ● adj. (**-ier**, **-iest**) having or showing numerous or prominent teeth.
– DERIVATIVES **toothily** adv.

**tootin'** ● adj. N. Amer. informal used for emphasis: *'You're angry, aren't you?' 'Darn tootin'.'*

**tootle** ● v. **1** casually make a series of sounds on a horn, trumpet, etc. ➤ make (a sound or tune) in such a way. **2** informal go or travel in a leisurely way. ● n. **1** an act or sound of tootling. **2** informal a leisurely journey.
– ORIGIN C19: frequentative of **TOOT**.

**too-too** ● adv. & adj. informal, dated excessive or excessively.
– ORIGIN C19: reduplication of **TOO**.

**tootsie** (also **tootsy**) ● n. (pl. **-ies**) informal **1** a person's foot. **2** a young woman, especially one perceived as being sexually available.
– ORIGIN C19: humorous dimin. of **FOOT**.

**top**[1] ● n. **1** the highest or uppermost point, part, or surface. ➤ the leaves, stems, and shoots of a plant, especially those of a vegetable grown for its root. **2** a thing or part placed on, fitted to, or covering the upper part of something. ➤ a platform at the head of a ship's mast. **3** (**the top**) the highest or most important rank, level, or position. ➤ the utmost degree: *she shouted at the top of her voice.* ➤ (**tops**) informal a particularly good person or thing. ➤ the high-frequency component of reproduced sound. **4** chiefly Brit. the end that is furthest from the speaker or a point of reference. **5** a bundle of long wool fibres prepared for spinning. **6** Physics one of six flavours of quark. ● adj. **1** highest in position, rank, or degree. **2** chiefly Brit. furthest away from the speaker or a point of reference. ● v. (**topped**, **topping**) **1** be more, better, or taller than. ➤ be at the highest place or rank in. **2** reach the top of (a hill, rise, etc.). **3** (usu. **be topped**) provide with a top or topping. ➤ complete (an outfit) with an upper garment, hat, or item of jewellery. **4** informal kill. **5** Golf mishit (the ball or a stroke) by hitting above the centre of the ball. ● adv. (**tops**) informal at the most.
– PHRASES **from top to bottom** thoroughly. **from top to toe** all over. **get on top of** be more than (someone) can bear or cope with. **on top 1** on the highest point or surface. **2** in a leading or the dominant position. **3** in addition. **on top of 1** so as to cover. **2** in close proximity to. **3** in command or control of. **4** in addition to. **on top of the world** informal happy and elated. **over the top 1** informal, chiefly Brit. to an excessive or exaggerated degree. **2** chiefly historical over the parapet of a trench and into battle. **top and tail** Brit. **1** remove the top and bottom of (a fruit or vegetable) while preparing it as food. **2** wash the face and bottom of (a baby or small child). **top dollar** N. Amer. informal a very high price. **the top of the tree** the highest level of a profession or career. **top ten** (or **twenty** etc.) the first ten (or twenty etc.) records in the pop music charts. **to top it all** as a culminating, typically unpleasant, event or action in a series.
– PHRASAL VERBS **top something off 1** (often **be topped off**) finish something in a memorable way. **2** US informal fill up a partly full tank with fuel. **top out** reach an upper limit. **top something out** put the highest structural feature on a building, typically as a ceremony to mark the building's completion. **top something up 1** add to a number or amount to bring it up to a certain level. **2** fill up a glass or other partly full container.
– DERIVATIVES **topmost** adj. **topped** adj.
– ORIGIN OE *topp* (n.), of Gmc origin.

**top**[2] ● n. **1** (also **spinning top**) a conical, spherical, or pear-shaped toy that may be set to spin. **2** used in names of top shells, e.g. **strawberry top**.
– ORIGIN OE, of unknown origin.

**topaz** ● n. **1** a precious stone, typically colourless, yellow,

or pale blue, consisting of a fluorine-containing aluminium silicate. **2** a dark yellow colour.
– ORIGIN ME (denoting a yellow sapphire): from OFr. *topace*, via L. from Gk *topazos*.

**top boot** ● **n.** chiefly historical a high boot with a broad band of a different material or colour at the top.

**top brass** ● **n.** see **BRASS** (sense 4).

**topcoat** ● **n.** **1** an overcoat. **2** an outer coat of paint.

**top copy** ● **n.** the original copy of a letter or document of which carbon copies have been made.

**top dog** ● **n.** informal a person who is successful or dominant in their field.

**top-down** ● **adj.** **1** controlled from the highest level of government or management; hierarchical. **2** proceeding from the general to the particular.

**top drawer** ● **n.** informal high social position or class. ● **adj.** informal of the highest quality or social class.

**top dressing** ● **n.** an application of manure or fertilizer to the surface layer of soil or a lawn.
– DERIVATIVES **top-dress** v.

**tope**[1] ● **v.** archaic or poetic/literary drink alcohol to excess, especially habitually.
– DERIVATIVES **toper** n.
– ORIGIN C17: perh. an alt. of obs. *top* 'overbalance'.

**tope**[2] ● **n.** (in the Indian subcontinent) a grove or plantation, especially of mango trees.
– ORIGIN from Telugu *tōpu* or Tamil *tōppu*.

**tope**[3] ● **n.** another term for **STUPA**.
– ORIGIN from Punjabi *thūp*, *thop* 'barrow, mound', appar. rel to Sanskrit *stūpa*.

**tope**[4] ● **n.** a small greyish slender-bodied shark of inshore waters. [*Galeorhinus galeus* (E. Atlantic) and *G. australis* (Australia).]
– ORIGIN C17: perh. of Cornish origin.

**topee** ● **n.** variant spelling of **TOPI**[1].

**top fermentation** ● **n.** the process by which ale-type beers are fermented, proceeding for a limited period at high temperature with the yeast rising to the top.

**top flight** ● **n.** the highest rank or level. ● **adj.** of the highest rank or level.

**top fruit** ● **n.** Brit. fruit grown on trees rather than bushes.

**topgallant** /tɒp'gal(ə)nt, tə'gal-/ ● **n.** **1** (also **topgallant mast**) the section of a square-rigged sailing ship's mast immediately above the topmast. **2** (also **topgallant sail**) a sail set on such a mast.

**top hamper** ● **n.** Sailing sails, rigging, or other things above decks creating top-heavy weight or wind-resistant surfaces.

**top hat** ● **n.** a man's formal hat with a high cylindrical crown.

**top-heavy** ● **adj.** **1** disproportionately heavy at the top so as to be unstable. **2** (of an organization) having a disproportionately large number of senior executives.
– DERIVATIVES **top-heavily** adv. **top-heaviness** n.

**Tophet** /'təʊfɪt/ ● **n.** poetic/literary hell.
– ORIGIN ME: from Heb. *tōpeṯ*, the name of a place near Jerusalem used for idolatrous worship, including the sacrifice of children (see Jer. 19:6).

**top-hole** ● **adj.** Brit. informal, dated excellent.

**tophus** /'təʊfəs/ ● **n.** (pl. **tophi** /-fʌɪ/) Medicine a deposit of crystalline uric acid at joints or in skin or cartilage, especially as a feature of gout.
– ORIGIN C17: from L., denoting loose porous stones of various kinds.

**topi**[1] /'təʊpi/ (also **topee**) ● **n.** (pl. **topis** or **topees**) short for **SOLA TOPI**.
– ORIGIN from Hindi *ṭopī* 'hat'.

**topi**[2] /'təʊpi/ ● **n.** (pl. same or **topis**) a large African antelope with a pattern of bold black patches on a reddish coat. [*Damaliscus lunatus*.]
– ORIGIN C19: from Mende.

**topiary** /'təʊpɪəri/ ● **n.** (pl. **-ies**) **1** the art or practice of clipping shrubs or trees into ornamental shapes. **2** shrubs or trees clipped in such a way.
– DERIVATIVES **topiarian** /-pɪ'ɛːrɪən/ adj. **topiarist** n.
– ORIGIN C16: from Fr. *topiaire*, from L. *topiarius* 'ornamental gardener'.

**topic** ● **n.** **1** a subject of a text, speech, conversation, etc. **2** Linguistics that part of a sentence about which something is said, typically the first major constituent.
– ORIGIN C15: from L. *topica*, from Gk *ta topika*, lit. 'matters concerning commonplaces' (the title of a treatise by Aristotle).

**topical** ● **adj.** **1** relating to or dealing with current affairs. **2** relating to a particular subject. **3** chiefly Medicine relating or applied directly to a part of the body.
– DERIVATIVES **topicality** n. **topically** adv.

**topicalize** (also **-ise**) ● **v.** Linguistics make (a word, phrase, etc.) the topic of a sentence or discourse.
– DERIVATIVES **topicalization** n.

**topknot** ● **n.** **1** a knot of hair arranged on the top of the head. **2** a decorative knot or bow of ribbon worn on the top of the head, popular in the 18th century. **3** a tuft or crest of hair or feathers on the head of an animal or bird.

**topless** ● **adj.** having or leaving the breasts uncovered.
– DERIVATIVES **toplessness** n.

**top-line** ● **adj.** of the highest quality or ranking.

**toplofty** ● **adj.** US informal haughty and arrogant.

**topman** ● **n.** (pl. **-men**) chiefly historical **1** a sawyer working the upper handle of a pit saw. **2** a sailor on duty in a sailing ship's tops.

**topmast** /'tɒpmɑːst, -məst/ ● **n.** the second section of a square-rigged sailing ship's mast, immediately above the lower mast.

**top-notch** ● **adj.** informal of the highest quality.
– DERIVATIVES **top-notcher** n.

**topo** /'tɒpəʊ/ ● **n.** (pl. **-os**) informal, chiefly N. Amer. **1** a topographical map. **2** Climbing a diagram of a mountain marked with details of routes to the top.

**topography** /tə'pɒgrəfi/ ● **n.** **1** the arrangement of the natural and artificial physical features of an area. ➤a detailed description or representation on a map of such features. **2** Anatomy & Biology the arrangement of features of an organ or organism.
– DERIVATIVES **topographer** n. **topographic** adj. **topographical** adj. **topographically** adv.
– ORIGIN ME: via late L. from Gk *topographia*, from *topos* 'place' + *-graphia* (see **-GRAPHY**).

**topoi** plural form of **TOPOS**.

**topology** /tə'pɒlədʒi/ ● **n.** **1** Mathematics the study of geometrical properties and spatial relations which remain unaffected by smooth changes in shape or size of figures. **2** the way in which constituent parts are interrelated or arranged.
– DERIVATIVES **topological** adj. **topologically** adv. **topologist** n.
– ORIGIN C19: via Ger. from Gk *topos* 'place' + **-LOGY**.

**toponym** /'tɒpənɪm/ ● **n.** a place name, especially one derived from a topographical feature.
– DERIVATIVES **toponymic** adj. **toponymy** n.
– ORIGIN 1930s: from Gk *topos* 'place' + *onoma* 'a name'.

**topos** /'tɒpɒs/ ● **n.** (pl. **topoi** /'tɒpɔɪ/) a traditional theme or formula in literature.
– ORIGIN 1940s: from Gk, lit. 'place'.

**topper** ● **n.** **1** a person or thing that tops. **2** informal a top hat. **3** Brit. informal, dated an exceptionally good person or thing.

**topping** ● **adj.** Brit. informal, dated excellent. ● **n.** a layer of food poured or spread over another food.

**topple** ● **v.** overbalance or cause to overbalance and fall.
– ORIGIN C16: frequentative of **TOP**[1].

**top rope** Climbing ● **n.** a rope lowered from above to the lead climber in a group, to give assistance at a difficult part of a climb. ● **v.** (**top-rope**) climb (a route) using a top rope.

**topsail** /'tɒpseɪl, -s(ə)l/ ● **n.** **1** a sail set on a ship's topmast. **2** a fore-and-aft sail set above the gaff.

**top-sawyer** ● **n.** **1** chiefly historical a sawyer holding the upper handle of a pit saw and standing above the saw-pit. **2** archaic a distinguished person.

**top secret** ● **adj.** of the highest secrecy.

**top shell** ● **n.** a marine mollusc having a low conical shell with a pearly interior. [Family Trochidae.]

**topside** • n. **1** Brit. the outer side of a round of beef. **2** the upper part of a ship's side, above the waterline. • adv. on or towards the upper decks of a ship.

**Topsider** • n. US trademark a casual shoe, typically made of canvas with a rubber sole, designed to be worn on boats.

**top-slicing** • n. a method of assessing tax chargeable on a lump sum by averaging the sum out over the years it has accrued and charging accordingly.

**topsoil** • n. the top layer of soil.

**topspin** • n. a fast forward spin given to a moving ball, often resulting in a curved path or a strong forward motion on rebounding.
– DERIVATIVES **topspinner** n.

**topstitch** • v. make a row of continuous decorative stitches on the right side of a garment or other article.

**topsy-turvy** • adj. & adv. **1** upside down. **2** in a state of confusion.
– DERIVATIVES **topsy-turvily** adv. **topsy-turviness** n.
– ORIGIN C16: a jingle appar. based on TOP[1] and obs. *terve* 'overturn'.

**toque** /təʊk/ • n. **1** a woman's small hat, typically having a narrow, closely turned-up brim. ➤ historical a small cap or bonnet of such a type worn by a man or woman. **2** a tall white hat with a full pouched crown, worn by chefs.
– ORIGIN C16: from Fr., of unknown origin.

**tor** /tɔː/ • n. a hill or rocky peak.
– ORIGIN OE *torr*, perh. of Celtic origin.

**Torah** /ˈtɔːrɑː, tɔːˈrɑː/ • n. (in Judaism) the law of God as revealed to Moses and recorded in the Pentateuch.
– ORIGIN from Heb. *tōrāh* 'instruction, doctrine, law', from *yārāh* 'show, instruct'.

**torc** /tɔːk/ (also **torque**) • n. a neck ornament consisting of a band of twisted metal, worn especially by the ancient Gauls and Britons.
– ORIGIN C19: from Fr. *torque*, from L. *torques* (see TORCH).

**torch** • n. **1** Brit. a portable battery-powered electric lamp. **2** chiefly historical a portable means of illumination such as a piece of wood soaked in tallow and ignited. **3** a valuable quality, principle, or cause, which needs to be protected and maintained: *Britain could carry the torch of freedom.* **4** chiefly N. Amer. a blowlamp. • v. informal set fire to.
– PHRASES **carry a torch for** suffer from unrequited love for. **put to the torch** (or **put a torch to**) destroy by burning.
– ORIGIN ME: from OFr. *torche*, from L. *torqua*, var. of *torques* 'necklace, wreath', from *torquere* 'to twist'.

**torchère** /tɔːˈʃɛː/ • n. a tall ornamental flat-topped stand for holding a candlestick.
– ORIGIN C20: Fr., from *torche* (see TORCH).

**torchon** /ˈtɔːʃ(ə)n/ (also **torchon lace**) • n. coarse bobbin lace with geometrical designs.
– ORIGIN C19: from Fr., lit. 'duster, dishcloth'.

**torch race** • n. a ritual competition held at festivals in ancient Greece, in which runners carried lighted torches.

**torch song** • n. a sad or sentimental song of unrequited love.
– DERIVATIVES **torch singer** n.

**tore**[1] past of TEAR[1].

**tore**[2] /tɔː/ • n. archaic term for TORUS.
– ORIGIN C17: from Fr.

**toreador** /ˈtɒrɪədɔː, ˌtɒrɪəˈdɔː/ • n. a bullfighter, especially one on horseback.
– ORIGIN Sp., from *torear* 'fight bulls', from *toro* 'bull'.

**toreador pants** • pl. n. chiefly N. Amer. women's tight-fitting calf-length trousers.

**torero** /tɒˈrɛːrəʊ/ • n. (pl. **-os**) a bullfighter, especially one on foot.
– ORIGIN Sp., from *toro* (see TOREADOR).

**toreutics** /təˈruːtɪks/ • pl. n. [treated as sing.] the art of chasing, carving, and embossing in metal to create designs in relief or intaglio.
– DERIVATIVES **toreutic** adj.
– ORIGIN C19: from Gk *toreutikos*, from *toreuein* 'to work in relief'.

**torgoch** /ˈtɔːgɒx/ • n. (in Wales) an Arctic charr.
– ORIGIN C17: Welsh, from *tor* 'belly' + *coch* 'red'.

**tori** plural form of TORUS.

**toric** /ˈtɒrɪk, ˈtɔːrɪk/ • adj. Geometry having the form of a torus or part of a torus.

**torii** /ˈtɔːrɪiː/ • n. (pl. same) the gateway of a Shinto shrine, with two uprights and two crosspieces.
– ORIGIN Japanese, from *tori* 'bird' + *i* 'sit, perch'.

**torment** • n. severe physical or mental suffering. ➤ a cause of torment. • v. **1** subject to torment. **2** annoy or tease unkindly.
– DERIVATIVES **tormented** adj. **tormentedly** adv. **tormenting** adj. **tormentingly** adv. **tormentor** n.
– ORIGIN ME: from OFr. *torment* (n.), *tormenter* (v.), from L. *tormentum* 'instrument of torture', from *torquere* 'to twist'.

**tormentil** /ˈtɔːm(ə)ntɪl/ • n. a low-growing plant with bright yellow flowers, the root of which is used in herbal medicine to treat diarrhoea. [*Potentilla erecta*.]
– ORIGIN ME: from Fr. *tormentille*, from med. L. *tormentilla*, of unknown origin.

**torn** past participle of TEAR[1].

**tornado** /tɔːˈneɪdəʊ/ • n. (pl. **-oes** or **-os**) a mobile, destructive vortex of violently rotating winds having the appearance of a funnel-shaped cloud.
– DERIVATIVES **tornadic** /-ˈnadɪk/ adj.
– ORIGIN C16: perh. an alt. of Sp. *tronada* 'thunderstorm', by assoc. with Sp. *tornar* 'to turn'.

**toroid** /ˈtɒrɔɪd, ˈtɔː-/ • n. Geometry a figure having the shape of a torus.
– DERIVATIVES **toroidal** adj. **toroidally** adv.

**torpedo** • n. (pl. **-oes**) **1** a cigar-shaped self-propelled underwater missile designed to be fired from a ship, submarine, or an aircraft and to explode on reaching a target. **2** US a railway fog signal. **3** US a firework exploding on impact with a hard surface. **4** (also **torpedo ray**) an electric ray. • v. (**-oes**, **-oed**) **1** attack with a torpedo or torpedoes. **2** ruin (a plan or project).
– DERIVATIVES **torpedo-like** adj.
– ORIGIN C16: from L., lit. 'stiffness, numbness', by extension 'electric ray' (which gives a shock causing numbness).

**torpedo boat** • n. a small, fast, light warship armed with torpedoes.

**torpedo net** • n. historical a net made of steel wire, hung in the water round an anchored ship to intercept torpedoes.

**torpedo tube** • n. a tube in a submarine or other ship from which torpedoes are fired by the use of compressed air or an explosive charge.

**torpefy** /ˈtɔːpɪfʌɪ/ • v. (**-ies**, **-ied**) formal make numb, paralysed, or torpid.
– ORIGIN C19: from L. *torpefacere*, from *torpere* 'be numb or sluggish'.

**torpid** • adj. **1** mentally or physically inactive. **2** (of an animal) dormant, especially during hibernation.
– DERIVATIVES **torpidity** n. **torpidly** adv. **torpor** n.
– ORIGIN ME: from L. *torpidus*, from *torpere* 'be numb or sluggish'.

**torque** /tɔːk/ • n. **1** Mechanics a force that tends to cause rotation. **2** variant spelling of TORC. • v. apply torque to.
– DERIVATIVES **torquey** adj.
– ORIGIN C19: from L. *torquere* 'to twist'.

**torque converter** • n. a device that transmits or multiplies torque generated by an engine.

**torque wrench** • n. a tool for setting and adjusting the tightness of nuts and bolts to a desired value.

**torr** /tɔː/ • n. (pl. same) a unit of pressure equivalent to 1 mm of mercury in a barometer and equal to 133.32 pascals.
– ORIGIN 1940s: named after the C17 Ital. mathematician and physicist Evangelista *Torricelli*.

**torrent** • n. **1** a strong and fast-moving stream of water or other liquid. **2** an overwhelmingly copious outpouring: *a torrent of abuse.*
– DERIVATIVES **torrential** adj. **torrentially** adv.

– ORIGIN C16: from Fr., from Ital. *torrente*, from L. *torrent-* 'boiling, roaring', from *torrere* 'scorch'.

**Torricellian vacuum** /ˌtɒrɪˈtʃɛlɪən, -ˈsɛlɪən/ ● n. a vacuum formed above the mercury column in a barometer when the tube is longer than the height of mercury sustainable by atmospheric pressure.
– ORIGIN from the name of the C17 Ital. mathematician and physicist Evangelista *Torricelli*.

**torrid** ● adj. **1** very hot and dry. **2** full of intense emotions arising from sexual love. **3** full of difficulty.
– DERIVATIVES **torridity** n. **torridly** adv.
– ORIGIN C16: from Fr. *torride* or L. *torridus*, from *torrere* 'parch, scorch'.

**Torridonian** /ˌtɒrɪˈdəʊnɪən/ ● adj. Geology of or denoting the later stage of the Proterozoic aeon in NW Scotland, from about 1100 to 600 million years ago.
– ORIGIN C19: from the name of Loch *Torridon*, in NW Scotland, + **-IAN**.

**torrid zone** ● n. the hot central belt of the earth bounded by the tropics of Cancer and Capricorn.

**torsade de pointes** /tɔːˌsɑːd də ˈpwãt/ ● n. Medicine a form of tachycardia in which the heart's electrical activity varies cyclically.
– ORIGIN 1960s: Fr., lit. 'twist of spikes' (with ref. to the characteristic electrocardiogram produced).

**torse** /tɔːs/ ● n. Heraldry a wreath.
– ORIGIN C16: from obs. Fr., from L. *torta*, fem. past part. of *torquere* 'twist'.

**torsion** /ˈtɔːʃ(ə)n/ ● n. **1** the action of twisting or the state of being twisted, especially of one end of an object relative to the other. ➤ the twisting of the cut end of an artery after surgery to impede bleeding. **2** Mathematics the extent to which a curve departs from being planar.
– DERIVATIVES **torsional** adj. **torsionally** adv. **torsionless** adj.
– ORIGIN ME: via OFr. from late L. *torsio(n-)*, var. of *tortio(n-)* 'twisting, torture', from L. *torquere* 'to twist'.

**torsion balance** ● n. an instrument for measuring very weak forces by their effect upon a system of fine twisted wire.

**torsion bar** ● n. a bar forming part of a vehicle suspension, twisting in response to the motion of the wheels and absorbing their vertical movement.

**torsion pendulum** ● n. a pendulum that rotates rather than swings.

**torsk** /tɔːsk/ ● n. a North Atlantic deep-water fish of the cod family. [*Brosme brosme.*]
– ORIGIN C18: from Norw., from ON *thorskr.*

**torso** ● n. (pl. **torsos** or US also **torsi**) **1** the trunk of the human body. **2** the trunk of a statue without, or considered independently of, the head and limbs. **3** an unfinished or mutilated thing, especially a work of art or literature.
– ORIGIN C18: from Ital., lit. 'stalk, stump'.

**tort** ● n. Law a wrongful act or an infringement of a right (other than under contract) leading to legal liability.
– ORIGIN ME: from OFr., from med. L. *tortum* 'wrong, injustice', neut. past part. of L. *torquere* 'to twist'.

**torte** /ˈtɔːtə/ ● n. (pl. **torten** /ˈtɔːt(ə)n/ or **tortes**) a sweet cake or tart.
– ORIGIN from Ger. *Torte*, via Ital. from late L. *torta* 'round loaf, cake'; cf. **TORTILLA**.

**tortelli** /tɔːˈtɛli/ ● pl. n. small pasta parcels stuffed with a cheese or vegetable mixture.
– ORIGIN Ital., pl. of *tortello* 'small cake, fritter'.

**tortellini** /ˌtɔːtəˈliːni/ ● n. tortelli which have been rolled and formed into small rings.
– ORIGIN Ital., pl. of *tortellino*, dimin. of *tortello* 'small cake, fritter'.

**tortfeasor** /ˈtɔːtfiːzə/ ● n. Law a person who commits a tort.
– ORIGIN C17: from OFr. *tort-fesor*, from *tort* 'wrong' and *fesor* 'doer'.

**torticollis** /ˌtɔːtɪˈkɒlɪs/ ● n. Medicine a condition in which the head becomes persistently turned to one side, often associated with painful muscle spasms.
– ORIGIN C19: mod. L., from L. *tortus* 'crooked, twisted' + *collum* 'neck'.

**tortilla** /tɔːˈtiːjə/ ● n. **1** (in Mexican cookery) a thin, flat maize pancake, typically eaten with a savoury filling. **2** (in Spanish cookery) a thick omelette containing potato and other vegetables.
– ORIGIN Sp., dimin. of *torta* 'cake'.

**tortious** /ˈtɔːʃəs/ ● adj. Law constituting a tort; wrongful.
– DERIVATIVES **tortiously** adv.
– ORIGIN ME (orig. in the sense 'injurious'): from Anglo-Norman Fr. *torcious*, from the stem of *torcion* 'extortion, violence', from late L. *tortio(n-)* (see **TORSION**).

**tortoise** /ˈtɔːtəs, -tɔɪz/ ● n. **1** a slow-moving land reptile of warm climates, enclosed in a scaly or leathery domed shell into which it can retract its head and legs. [Family Testudinidae: many species.] **2** a testudo.
– ORIGIN ME *tortu*, *tortuce*: from OFr. *tortue* and Sp. *tortuga*, both from med. L. *tortuca*, of uncertain origin.

**tortoiseshell** ● n. **1** the semi-transparent mottled yellow and brown shell of certain turtles, typically used to make jewellery or ornaments. ➤ a synthetic imitation of this. **2** a domestic cat with markings resembling tortoiseshell. **3** a butterfly with mottled orange, yellow, and black markings. [*Aglais urticae* (**small tortoiseshell**) and other species.]

**tortrix** /ˈtɔːtrɪks/ ● n. (pl. **tortrices** /-trɪsiːz/) a small moth whose caterpillars live inside rolled leaves. [Family Tortricidae: many species.]
– DERIVATIVES **tortricid** n. & adj.
– ORIGIN C18: mod. L., fem. of L. *tortor* 'twister'.

**tortuous** /ˈtɔːtʃʊəs, -jʊəs/ ● adj. **1** full of twists and turns. **2** excessively lengthy and complex.
– DERIVATIVES **tortuosity** n. (pl. **-ies**). **tortuously** adv. **tortuousness** n.
– ORIGIN ME: via OFr. from L. *tortuosus*, from *tortus* 'twisting, a twist', from L. *torquere* 'to twist'.

**torture** ● n. **1** the action or practice of inflicting severe pain as a punishment or a forcible means of persuasion. **2** great suffering or anxiety. ● v. subject to torture.
– DERIVATIVES **torturer** n.
– ORIGIN ME: via Fr. from late L. *tortura* 'twisting, torment', from L. *torquere* 'to twist'.

**torturous** ● adj. characterized by pain or suffering.
– DERIVATIVES **torturously** adv.
– ORIGIN C15: from Anglo-Norman Fr., from *torture* 'torture'.

**torula** /ˈtɒruːlə, -(j)ʊlə/ ● n. (pl. **torulae** /-liː/) **1** a yeast used in medicine and as a food additive. [*Candida utilis.*] **2** a yeast-like fungus composed of chains of rounded cells. [Genus *Torula.*]
– ORIGIN mod. L., dimin. of L. *torus* 'swelling, bolster'.

**torus** /ˈtɔːrəs/ ● n. (pl. **tori** /-rʌɪ/ or **toruses**) **1** Geometry a surface or solid resembling a ring doughnut, formed by rotating a closed curve about a line which lies in the same plane but does not intersect it. **2** a ring-shaped object or chamber. **3** Architecture a large convex moulding, semicircular in cross section, especially as the lowest part of the base of a column. **4** Anatomy a ridge of bone or muscle. **5** Botany the receptacle of a flower.
– ORIGIN C16: from L., lit. 'swelling, round moulding'.

**Tory** ● n. (pl. **-ies**) **1** a member or supporter of the British Conservative Party. **2** a member of the English political party opposing the exclusion of James II from the succession and, later, of the British parliamentary party supporting the established religious and political order until the emergence of the Conservative Party in the 1830s. **3** US a colonist who supported the British side during the American Revolution.
– DERIVATIVES **Toryism** n.
– ORIGIN C17 (first used of Irish peasants dispossessed by English settlers and living as robbers, and extended to other marauders, especially in the Scottish Highlands): prob. from Ir. *toraidhe* 'outlaw, highwayman'.

**tosa** /ˈtəʊsə/ ● n. a dog of a breed of mastiff originally kept for dogfighting.
– ORIGIN 1940s: from *Tosa*, the name of a former province in Japan.

**tosh**[1] ● n. Brit. informal rubbish; nonsense.
– ORIGIN C19: of unknown origin.

**tosh**[2] ● n. Brit. informal used as a casual form of address,

especially to an unknown person.
– ORIGIN 1950s: of unknown origin.

**Tosk** /tɒsk/ ● **n.** (pl. same or **Tosks**) **1** a member of one of the main ethnic groups of Albania, living chiefly in the south of the country. Compare with **GHEG**. **2** the dialect of Albanian spoken by this people.
– ORIGIN from Albanian *Toskë*.

**toss** ● **v. 1** throw lightly or casually. ➤(of a horse) throw (a rider) off its back. ➤throw (a coin) into the air so as to make a choice, based on which side of the coin faces uppermost when it lands. **2** move or cause to move from side to side or back and forth. ➤jerk (one's head or hair) sharply backwards. ➤shake or turn (food) in a liquid, so as to coat it lightly. **3** (**toss something off**) drink something rapidly or all at once. ➤produce something rapidly or without thought or effort. **4** (**toss oneself/someone off** or **toss off**) Brit. vulgar slang masturbate. ● **n.** an act of tossing.
– PHRASES **give** (or **care**) **a toss** [usu. with neg.] Brit. informal care at all. **take a toss** fall off a horse. **toss one's cookies** N. Amer. informal vomit.
– ORIGIN C16: of unknown origin.

**tosser** ● **n.** Brit. vulgar slang a person who masturbates (used as a term of abuse).

**tosspot** ● **n.** informal a habitual drinker (also used as a general term of abuse).

**toss-up** ● **n.** informal **1** the tossing of a coin to make a choice. **2** a situation in which any of two or more outcomes or options is equally possible.

**tostada** /tɒˈstɑːdə/ (also **tostado** /tɒˈstɑːdəʊ/) ● **n.** (pl. **tostadas** or **tostados**) a Mexican deep-fried maize flour pancake topped with a seasoned mixture of beans, mincemeat, and vegetables.
– ORIGIN Sp., lit. 'toasted', past part. of *tostar*.

**tostone** /tɒˈstəʊneɪ/ ● **n.** a Mexican dish of fried plantain, typically served with a dip.
– ORIGIN from Sp.

**tot**[1] ● **n. 1** a very young child. **2** chiefly Brit. a small drink of spirits.
– ORIGIN C18 (orig. dial.): of unknown origin.

**tot**[2] ● **v.** (**totted**, **totting**) (**tot something up**) chiefly Brit. **1** add up numbers or amounts. **2** accumulate something over time.
– ORIGIN C18: from archaic *tot* 'set of figures to be added up', abbrev. of **TOTAL** or of L. *totum* 'the whole'.

**tot**[3] ● **v.** (**totted**, **totting**) [usu. as noun **totting**] Brit. informal salvage saleable items from dustbins or rubbish heaps.
– DERIVATIVES **totter** n.
– ORIGIN C19: from sl. *tot* 'bone', of unknown origin.

**total** ● **adj. 1** comprising the whole number or amount. **2** complete; absolute. ● **n.** a total number or amount. ● **v.** (**totalled**, **totalling**; US **totaled**, **totaling**) **1** amount in number to. ➤find the total of. **2** informal, chiefly N. Amer. destroy or kill.
– DERIVATIVES **totalization** (also **-isation**) n. **totalize** (also **-ise**) v. **totally** adv.
– ORIGIN ME: via OFr. from med. L. *totalis*, from *totum* 'the whole', neut. of L. *totus* 'whole'.

**total eclipse** ● **n.** an eclipse in which the whole of the disc of the sun or moon is obscured.

**total heat** ● **n.** another term for **ENTHALPY**.

**total internal reflection** ● **n.** Physics the complete reflection of light (without refraction), occurring at an interface with a less dense medium when the angle of incidence exceeds the critical angle.

**totalitarian** /ˌtəʊtalɪˈtɛːrɪən, tə(ʊ)ˌtalɪ-/ ● **adj.** of or relating to a centralized and dictatorial system of government requiring complete subservience to the state. ● **n.** a person advocating such a system.
– DERIVATIVES **totalitarianism** n.

**totality** ● **n. 1** the whole of something. **2** Astronomy the moment or duration of total obscuration of the sun or moon during an eclipse.

**totalizator** (also **totalisator** or **totalizer**) ● **n. 1** a device showing the number and amount of bets staked on a race, to facilitate the division of the total among those backing the winner. **2** another term for **TOTE**[1].

**Total Quality Management** ● **n.** a system of management based on the principle that every member of staff must be committed to maintaining high standards.

**total war** ● **n.** a war which is unrestricted in terms of the weapons used, the territory or combatants involved, or the objectives pursued.

**tote**[1] ● **n.** (**the tote**) informal a system of betting based on the use of the totalizator, in which dividends are calculated according to the amount staked rather than odds offered.

**tote**[2] ● **v.** informal, chiefly N. Amer. carry.
– DERIVATIVES **-toter** n.
– ORIGIN C17: prob. of dial. origin.

**tote bag** ● **n.** a large bag for carrying a number of items.

**totem** /ˈtəʊtəm/ ● **n.** a natural object or animal believed by a particular society to have spiritual significance and adopted by it as an emblem.
– DERIVATIVES **totemic** /-ˈtɛmɪk/ adj. **totemism** n. **totemist** n. **totemistic** adj.
– ORIGIN C18: from Ojibwa *nindoodem* 'my totem'.

**totem pole** ● **n. 1** a pole on which totems are hung or on which the images of totems are carved. **2** chiefly N. Amer. a hierarchy.

**t'other** /ˈtʌðə/ (also **tother**) ● **adj. & pron.** dialect or humorous the other.
– PHRASES **tell t'other from which** Brit. humorous tell one from the other.
– ORIGIN ME *the tother*, wrong division of *thet other* 'the other'.

**totipotent** /təʊˈtɪpət(ə)nt/ ● **adj.** Biology (of an immature or stem cell) capable of giving rise to any cell type or (of a blastomere) a complete embryo.
– ORIGIN C20: from L. *totus* 'whole' + **POTENT**[1].

**totter** ● **v. 1** move in an unsteady way. **2** [usu. as adj. **tottering**] (of a building) shake or rock as if about to collapse. **3** be insecure or about to collapse. ● **n.** a tottering gait.
– DERIVATIVES **totterer** n. **tottery** adj.
– ORIGIN ME: from MDu. *touteren* 'to swing' (the original sense in Engl.).

**totting-up** ● **n.** Brit. the accumulation of penalty points on a driving licence, a certain number in a fixed period leading to disqualification.

**totty** ● **n.** Brit. informal girls or women collectively regarded as sexually desirable.
– ORIGIN C19: sl. word from **TOT**[1].

**toucan** /ˈtuːk(ə)n/ ● **n.** a tropical American fruit-eating bird with a massive bill and typically brightly coloured plumage. [Genera *Ramphastos* and *Andigena*: several species.]
– ORIGIN C16: via Fr. and Port. from Tupi *tucan*, imitative of its call.

**touch** ● **v. 1** come into or be in contact with. ➤come or bring into mutual contact. ➤bring one's hand or another part of one's body into contact with. ➤strike (a ball) lightly in a specified direction. **2** harm or interfere with. ➤take some of (a store, especially of money) for use. ➤[usu. with neg.] consume (food or drink). **3** have an effect on. ➤informal reach (a specified level or amount). ➤[usu. with neg.] informal approach in excellence. **4** (often **be touched**) produce feelings of affection, gratitude, or sympathy in. **5** [with neg.] have any dealings with: *he took jobs that nobody else would touch.* **6** [as adj. **touched**] informal slightly mad. **7** (**touch someone for**) informal ask someone for (money) as a loan or gift. **8** (**touch something in**) chiefly Art lightly mark in details with a brush or pencil. ● **n. 1** an act of touching. ➤a musician's manner of playing keys or strings or the manner in which an instrument's keys or strings respond to being played. ➤a light stroke with a pen, pencil, etc. **2** the faculty of perception through physical contact, especially with the fingers. **3** a small amount. **4** a distinctive detail or feature. **5** a distinctive manner or method of dealing with something. ➤an ability to deal with something successfully. **6** Rugby & Soccer the area beyond the sidelines, out of play. **7** Bell-ringing a series of changes shorter than a peal. **8** archaic a test of worth or character.
– PHRASES **in touch 1** in or into communication. **2** possessing up-to-date knowledge. **lose touch 1** cease to be

in communication. **2** cease to be informed. **out of touch** lacking up-to-date knowledge or awareness. **to the touch** when touched. **touch bottom** be at the lowest or worst point. **touch of nature** a display of human feeling with which others sympathize (based on a misinterpretation of Shakespeare's *Troilus and Cressida* III iii. 169). **touch of the sun 1** a slight attack of sunstroke. **2** some time spent in the sunlight.

– PHRASAL VERBS **touch at** (of a ship) call briefly at (a port). **touch down 1** Rugby touch the ground with the ball behind the opponents' goal line, scoring a try. **2** American Football score six points by being in possession of the ball behind the opponents' goal line. **3** (of an aircraft or spacecraft) land. **touch something off 1** cause something to ignite or explode by touching it with a match. ➤ cause something to happen suddenly. **2** (of a racehorse) defeat another horse in a race by a short margin. **touch on** (or **upon**) **1** deal briefly with (a subject). **2** come near to being. **touch someone up** Brit. informal caress someone without their consent for sexual pleasure. **touch something up** make small improvements to something.

– DERIVATIVES **touchable** adj.

– ORIGIN ME: the verb from OFr. *tochier*, prob. from a Romance word of imitative origin; the noun orig. from OFr. *touche*, later (in certain senses) directly from the verb.

**touch-and-go** ● adj. (of an outcome) possible but very uncertain.

**touchback** ● n. American Football a ball downed behind one's own goal.

**touchdown** ● n. **1** the moment at which an aircraft or part of a spacecraft touches down. **2** Rugby an act of touching down. **3** American Football a six-point score made by touching down.

**touché** /tuːˈʃeɪ/ ● exclam. **1** (in fencing) used to acknowledge a hit by one's opponent. **2** used to acknowledge a good or clever point made at one's expense.

– ORIGIN Fr., lit. 'touched', past part. of *toucher*.

**toucher** ● n. (in bowls) a wood that touches the jack.

**touch football** ● n. a form of American football in which a ball-carrier is downed by touching instead of tackling.

**touch hole** ● n. a small hole in early firearms through which the charge is ignited.

**touching** ● adj. arousing strong emotion; moving. ● prep. concerning.

– DERIVATIVES **touchingly** adv. **touchingness** n.

**touch-in-goal** ● n. Rugby the area at the corner of the field bounded by continuations of the touchline and the goal line.

**touch judge** ● n. Rugby a linesman.

**touchline** ● n. Rugby & Soccer the boundary line on each side of the field.

**touch mark** ● n. an official manufacturer's mark on items made from pewter.

**touch-me-not** ● n. a yellow-flowered plant of the balsam family, whose ripe seed capsules open explosively when touched. [*Impatiens noli-tangere*.]

**touch needles** ● pl. n. a set of needles of gold or silver alloy of known compositions, used in testing other alloys on a touchstone.

**touch pad** ● n. a computer input device in the form of a small panel containing different touch-sensitive areas.

**touchpaper** ● n. a strip of paper impregnated with nitre, for setting light to fireworks or gunpowder.

**touch screen** ● n. a display device which allows the user to interact with a computer by touching areas on the screen.

**touchstone** ● n. **1** a piece of fine-grained dark schist or jasper formerly used for testing alloys of gold by observing the colour of the mark which they made on it. **2** a standard or criterion.

**touch-tone** ● adj. denoting push-button telephones generating tones to dial rather than pulses.

**touch-type** ● v. [often as noun **touch-typing**] type using all of one's fingers and without looking at the keys.

– DERIVATIVES **touch-typist** n.

**touchwood** ● n. archaic readily flammable wood used as tinder, especially when softened by fungi.

**touchy** ● adj. (**-ier**, **-iest**) **1** quick to take offence; oversensitive. **2** (of a situation or issue) requiring careful handling.

– DERIVATIVES **touchily** adv. **touchiness** n.

– ORIGIN C17: perh. an alt. of **TETCHY**, influenced by **TOUCH**.

**touchy-feely** ● adj. informal, often derogatory **1** openly expressing affection or other emotions, especially through physical contact. **2** characteristic of or relating to such behaviour.

**tough** ● adj. **1** strong enough to withstand wear and tear. ➤ (of food, especially meat) difficult to cut or chew. **2** able to endure hardship, adversity, or pain. **3** strict and uncompromising. **4** involving considerable difficulty or hardship. **5** rough or violent. **6** used to express a lack of sympathy: *if you don't like it, tough.* ● n. informal a rough and violent man.

– PHRASES **tough it out** informal endure a period of hardship or difficulty. **tough shit** (or **titty**) vulgar slang used to express a lack of sympathy.

– DERIVATIVES **toughish** adj. **toughly** adv. **toughness** n.

– ORIGIN OE *tōh*, of Gmc origin.

**toughen** ● v. make or become tough.

– DERIVATIVES **toughener** n.

**toughie** ● n. informal **1** a person who is tough and determined. **2** a difficult problem or question.

**tough love** ● n. **1** promotion of a person's welfare by enforcing certain constraints on them or requiring them to take responsibility for their actions. **2** N. Amer. a political policy designed to encourage self-help by restricting state benefits.

**tough-minded** ● adj. strong, realistic, and unsentimental.

– DERIVATIVES **tough-mindedness** n.

**toupee** /ˈtuːpeɪ/ (also **toupet** /ˈtuːpeɪ, ˈtuːpɪt/) ● n. a small wig or artificial hairpiece worn to cover a bald spot.

– ORIGIN C18: *toupee*, alt. of Fr. *toupet* 'hair-tuft'; ult. rel. to **TOP**[1].

**tour** ● n. **1** a journey for pleasure in which several different places are visited. **2** a short trip to or through a place in order to view or inspect something. **3** a journey made by performers or a sports team, in which they perform or play in several different places. **4** (also **tour of duty**) a spell of duty on military or diplomatic service. ● v. make a tour of. ➤ take (a performer, production, etc.) on tour.

– ORIGIN ME (also denoting a circular movement): from OFr., 'turn', via L. from Gk *tornos* 'lathe'.

**touraco** ● n. variant spelling of **TURACO**.

**tour de force** /ˌtʊə də ˈfɔːs/ ● n. (pl. **tours de force** pronunc. same) a performance or achievement that has been accomplished with great skill.

– ORIGIN Fr., lit. 'feat of strength'.

**tour d'horizon** /ˌtʊə dɒrɪˈzɒ̃, French tuʀ dɔʀizɔ̃/ ● n. (pl. **tours d'horizon** pronunc. same) a broad general survey or summary of an argument or event.

– ORIGIN Fr., lit. 'tour of the horizon'.

**tour en l'air** /ˌtʊə ɒ̃ lɛː/ ● n. (pl. **tours en l'air** pronunc. same) Ballet a movement in which a dancer jumps straight upwards and completes at least one full revolution before landing.

– ORIGIN Fr., lit. 'turn in the air'.

**tourer** ● n. a car, caravan, or bicycle designed for touring.

**Tourette's syndrome** /tʊˈrɛts/ ● n. Medicine a neurological disorder characterized by involuntary tics and vocalizations and often the compulsive utterance of obscenities.

– ORIGIN C19: named after the Fr. neurologist Gilles de la *Tourette*.

**touring car** ● n. a car with room for passengers and luggage.

**tourism** ● n. the commercial organization and operation of holidays and visits to places of interest.

**tourist** ● n. **1** a person who travels for pleasure. **2** a member of a touring sports team. ● v. rare travel as a tourist.

– DERIVATIVES **touristic** adj. **touristically** adv.

**tourist class** ● **n.** the cheapest accommodation or seating in a ship, aircraft, or hotel.

**touristy** ● **adj.** informal, often derogatory relating to, appealing to, or visited by tourists.

**tourmaline** /ˈtʊəməlɪn, -liːn/ ● **n.** a brittle grey or black mineral consisting of a boron aluminosilicate, with piezoelectric and polarizing properties.
– ORIGIN C18: from Fr., based on Sinhalese *tōramalli* 'carnelian'.

**tournament** ● **n.** **1** a series of contests between a number of competitors, competing for an overall prize. **2** a medieval sporting event in which knights jousted with blunted weapons for a prize. **3** a modern event involving display of military techniques and exercises.
– ORIGIN ME: from Anglo-Norman Fr. vars of OFr. *torneiement*, from *torneier* (see TOURNEY).

**tournedos** /ˈtʊənədəʊ/ ● **n.** (pl. same /-dəʊz/) a small round thick cut from a fillet of beef.
– ORIGIN Fr., from *tourner* 'to turn' + *dos* 'back'.

**tourney** /ˈtʊəni, ˈtəːni/ ● **n.** (pl. **-eys**) a medieval joust. ● **v.** (**-eys**, **-eyed**) take part in a tourney.
– ORIGIN ME: from OFr. *tornei* (n.), *torneier* (v.), based on L. *tornus* 'a turn'.

**tourniquet** /ˈtʊənɪkeɪ, ˈtɔː-/ ● **n.** a device for stopping the flow of blood through an artery, typically by compressing a limb with a cord or tight bandage.
– ORIGIN C17: from Fr., prob. from OFr. *tournicle* 'coat of mail', influenced by *tourner* 'to turn'.

**tour operator** ● **n.** a travel agent specializing in package holidays.

**tousle** /ˈtaʊz(ə)l/ ● **v.** [usu. as adj. **tousled**] make (something, especially a person's hair) untidy.
– ORIGIN ME: frequentative of dial. *touse* 'handle roughly', of Gmc origin; cf. TUSSLE.

**tout**[1] /taʊt/ ● **v.** **1** attempt to sell (something), typically by a direct or persistent approach. **2** attempt to persuade people of the merits of. **3** Brit. sell (a ticket) for a popular event at a price higher than the official one. **4** N. Amer. offer racing tips for a share of any resulting winnings. **5** chiefly Brit. spy out the movements and condition of (a racehorse in training) to gain information for use when betting. ● **n.** **1** (also **ticket tout**) Brit. a person who buys up tickets for an event to resell them at a profit. **2** a person who touts. **3** Irish & Scottish informal an informer.
– DERIVATIVES **touter** n.
– ORIGIN ME *tute* 'look out', of Gmc origin.

**tout**[2] /tuː, French tu/ ● **det.** used before the name of a city to refer to its high society or people of importance: *tout Washington*.
– ORIGIN Fr., suggested by *le tout Paris* 'all (of) Paris'.

**tout court** /tuː ˈkʊə, French tu kuʀ/ ● **adv.** briefly; simply.
– ORIGIN Fr., lit. 'very short'.

**tout de suite** /ˌtuː də ˈswiːt, French tu d(ə) sɥit/ ● **adv.** at once.
– ORIGIN Fr., lit. 'quite in sequence'.

**tovarish** /tɒˈvɑːrɪʃ/ (also **tovarich**) ● **n.** (in the former USSR) a comrade (often used as a form of address).
– ORIGIN from Russ. *tovarishch*, from Turkic.

**TOW** ● **abbrev.** tube-launched, optically guided, wire-guided (missile).

**tow**[1] ● **v.** use a vehicle or boat to pull (another vehicle or boat) along. ● **n.** an act of towing.
– PHRASES **in tow** **1** (also **on tow**) being towed. **2** accompanying or following someone.
– DERIVATIVES **towable** adj. **towage** n.
– ORIGIN OE *togian* 'draw, drag', of Gmc origin; rel. to TUG.

**tow**[2] ● **n.** **1** the coarse and broken part of flax or hemp prepared for spinning. **2** a bundle of untwisted natural or man-made fibres.
– DERIVATIVES **towy** adj.
– ORIGIN OE (recorded in *towcræft* 'spinning'), of Gmc origin.

**toward** ● **prep.** /təˈwɔːd, twɔːd, tɔːd/ variant of TOWARDS. ● **adj.** /ˈtəʊəd/ archaic going on.
– ORIGIN OE *tōweard* (see TO, -WARD).

**towards** /təˈwɔːdz, twɔːdz, ˈtɔːdz/ (chiefly N. Amer. also **toward**) ● **prep.** **1** in the direction of. **2** getting nearer to (a time or goal). **3** in relation to. **4** contributing to the cost of.
– ORIGIN OE *tōweardes* (see TO, -WARD).

**tow bar** ● **n.** a bar fitted to the back of a vehicle, used in towing a trailer or caravan.

**tow-coloured** ● **adj.** (of hair) very light blonde.

**towel** ● **n.** a piece of thick absorbent cloth or paper used for drying. ● **v.** (**towelled**, **towelling**; US **toweled**, **toweling**) **1** dry with a towel. **2** informal, chiefly Austral./NZ thrash or beat.
– ORIGIN ME: from OFr. *toaille*, of Gmc origin.

**towelling** (US **toweling**) ● **n.** thick absorbent cloth, typically cotton with uncut loops, used for towels and bathrobes.

**tower** ● **n.** **1** a tall, narrow building, either free-standing or forming part of a building such as a church or castle. **2** a tall structure that houses machinery, operators, etc. **3** a tall structure used as a receptacle or for storage. ● **v.** **1** rise to or reach a great height. **2** (of a bird) soar up to a great height, especially (of a falcon) so as to be able to swoop down on prey. **3** [as adj. **towering**] very important or influential. **4** [as adj. **towering**] very intense: *a towering rage*.
– DERIVATIVES **towered** adj. (chiefly poetic/literary). **towery** adj. (poetic/literary).
– ORIGIN OE *torr*, reinforced in ME by OFr. *tour*, from L. *turris*, from Gk.

**tower block** ● **n.** Brit. a tall modern building containing numerous floors of offices or flats.

**tower of silence** ● **n.** a tall open-topped structure on which Parsees traditionally place and leave exposed the body of someone who has died.

**tow-headed** ● **adj.** having tow-coloured or untidy hair.
– DERIVATIVES **tow-head** n.

**towhee** /ˈtəʊ(h)iː, ˈtaʊ-/ ● **n.** a North American songbird of the bunting family, typically secretive in behaviour. [Genus *Pipilo*: several species.]
– ORIGIN C18: imitative of the call of some towhees.

**towline** ● **n.** a tow rope.

**town** ● **n.** **1** a built-up area with a name, defined boundaries, and local government, that is larger than a village and generally smaller than a city. ➤ Brit. dated the chief city or town of a region. **2** the central part of a neighbourhood, with its business or shopping area. **3** densely populated areas, especially as contrasted with the country or suburbs. **4** the permanent residents of a university town. Often contrasted with GOWN. **5** N. Amer. another term for TOWNSHIP (in sense 3).
– PHRASES **go to town** informal do something thoroughly or enthusiastically. **on the town** informal enjoying the nightlife of a city or town.
– DERIVATIVES **townish** adj. **townlet** n. **townward** adj. & adv. **townwards** adv.
– ORIGIN OE *tūn* 'enclosed piece of land, homestead, village', of Gmc origin.

**town car** ● **n.** US a limousine.

**town clerk** ● **n.** **1** N. Amer. a public official in charge of the records of a town. **2** (in the UK, until 1974) the secretary and legal adviser of a town corporation.

**town council** ● **n.** (especially in the UK) the elected governing body in a municipality.
– DERIVATIVES **town councillor** n.

**town crier** ● **n.** historical a person employed to make public announcements in the streets.

**townee** ● **n.** variant spelling of TOWNIE.

**tow net** ● **n.** Biology a dragnet that is towed behind a boat to collect specimens.

**town gas** ● **n.** Brit., chiefly historical coal gas.

**town hall** ● **n.** a building used for the administration of local government.

**town house** ● **n.** **1** a tall, narrow traditional terrace house, generally having three or more floors. ➤ a modern two- or three-storey house built as one of a row of similar houses. **2** an urban residence of a person owning another property in the country. **3** archaic a town hall.

**townie** (also **townee**) ● **n.** informal a person who lives in a town (used especially with reference to their supposed lack of familiarity with rural affairs).

**townland** ● n. (especially in Ireland) a territorial division of land; a township.

**town major** ● n. historical the chief executive officer in a garrison town or fortress.

**town mayor** ● n. Brit. the chairperson of a town council.

**town meeting** ● n. US a meeting of the voters of a town for the transaction of public business.

**town planning** ● n. the planning and control of the construction, growth, and development of a town or other urban area.
– DERIVATIVES **town planner** n.

**townscape** ● n. an urban landscape.

**township** ● n. **1** (in South Africa) a suburb or city of predominantly black occupation, formerly officially designated for black occupation by apartheid legislation. **2** S. African a new area being developed for residential or industrial use by speculators. **3** N. Amer. a division of a county with some corporate powers. ➤a district six miles square. **4** Brit. historical a manor or parish as a territorial division. ➤a small town or village forming part of a large parish. **5** Austral./NZ a small town.
– ORIGIN OE *tūnscipe* 'the inhabitants of a village' (see TOWN, -SHIP).

**townsite** ● n. N. Amer. a tract of land set apart by legal authority to be occupied by a town and usually surveyed and laid out with streets.

**townsman** (or **townswoman**) ● n. (pl. **-men** or **-women**) a person living in a particular town or city.

**townspeople** (also **townsfolk**) ● pl. n. the people living in a particular town or city.

**towpath** ● n. a path beside a river or canal, originally used as a pathway for horses towing barges.

**towplane** ● n. an aircraft that tows gliders.

**tow rope** ● n. a rope, cable, etc. used in towing.

**toxaemia** /tɒk'siːmɪə/ (US **toxemia**) ● n. Medicine **1** blood poisoning by toxins from a local bacterial infection. **2** (also **toxaemia of pregnancy**) pre-eclampsia.
– DERIVATIVES **toxaemic** adj.
– ORIGIN C19: from TOXI- + -AEMIA.

**toxaphene** /'tɒksəfiːn/ ● n. a synthetic amber waxy solid with an odour of chlorine and camphor, used as an insecticide.
– ORIGIN 1940s: from TOXIN + (*cam*)*phene*, a related terpene.

**toxi-** ● comb. form representing TOXIC or TOXIN.

**toxic** /'tɒksɪk/ ● adj. poisonous. ➤of, relating to, or caused by poison. ● n. (**toxics**) poisonous substances.
– DERIVATIVES **toxically** adv. **toxicity** n.
– ORIGIN C17: from med. L. *toxicus* 'poisoned', from L. *toxicum* 'poison'.

**toxicant** /'tɒksɪk(ə)nt/ ● n. a toxic substance introduced into the environment, e.g. a pesticide.
– ORIGIN C19: var. of INTOXICANT, differentiated in sense.

**toxico-** ● comb. form equivalent to TOXI-.
– ORIGIN from Gk *toxicon* 'poison'.

**toxicology** /ˌtɒksɪ'kɒlədʒi/ ● n. the branch of science concerned with the nature, effects, and detection of poisons.
– DERIVATIVES **toxicological** adj. **toxicologically** adv. **toxicologist** n.

**toxic shock syndrome** ● n. acute septicaemia in women, typically caused by bacterial infection from a retained tampon or IUD.

**toxigenic** /ˌtɒksɪ'dʒɛnɪk/ ● adj. (especially of a bacterium) producing a toxin or toxic effect.
– DERIVATIVES **toxigenicity** n.

**toxin** /'tɒksɪn/ ● n. a poison produced by a microorganism or other organism and acting as an antigen in the body.
– ORIGIN C19: from TOXIC + -IN[1].

**toxo-** ● comb. form equivalent to TOXI-.

**toxocara** /ˌtɒksə'kɑːrə/ ● n. a nematode worm which is a parasite of dogs, cats, and other animals and can be transmitted to humans. [Genus *Toxocara*.]
– DERIVATIVES **toxocariasis** n.
– ORIGIN mod. L., from TOXO- + Gk *kara* 'head'.

**toxoid** ● n. Medicine a chemically modified toxin from a pathogenic micro-organism, which is no longer toxic but is still antigenic and can be used as a vaccine.

**toxophilite** /tɒk'sɒfɪlʌɪt/ rare ● n. a student or lover of archery. ● adj. of or relating to archers and archery.
– DERIVATIVES **toxophily** n.
– ORIGIN C18: from *Toxophilus* (a name invented by the Engl. scholar and writer Roger Ascham, used as the title of his treatise on archery (1545), from Gk *toxon* 'bow' + *-philos* 'loving') + -ITE[1].

**toxoplasmosis** /ˌtɒksəʊplaz'məʊsɪs/ ● n. Medicine a disease caused by a parasitic protozoan, transmitted chiefly through undercooked meat, soil, or in cat faeces.
– ORIGIN 1930s: from *Toxoplasma* (genus name) + -OSIS.

**toy** ● n. **1** an object for a child to play with, typically a model or miniature replica of something. ➤a gadget or machine regarded as providing amusement for an adult. **2** [as modifier] denoting a diminutive breed or variety of dog. ● v. (**toy with**) **1** consider casually or indecisively. ➤treat (someone) in a superficially amorous way. **2** move or handle absent-mindedly or nervously. ➤eat or drink in an unenthusiastic or restrained way.
– DERIVATIVES **toylike** adj.
– ORIGIN ME (orig. denoting a funny story or remark): of unknown origin.

**toy boy** ● n. Brit. informal a male lover who is much younger than his partner.

**toyi-toyi** /'tɔɪtɔɪ/ S. African ● n. (pl. **toyi-toyis**) a dance step characterized by high-stepping movements, typically performed at protest gatherings or marches. ● v. (**toyi-toyis**, **toyi-toyied**, **toyi-toying** or **toyi-toyiing**) perform such a dance.
– ORIGIN Ndebele and Shona.

**toytown** ● adj. **1** resembling a model of a town in being seemingly in miniature. **2** having no real value or substance.

**Tpr** ● abbrev. Trooper.

**TQM** ● abbrev. Total Quality Management.

**TR** ● abbrev. Turkey (international vehicle registration).

**trabeation** /ˌtreɪbɪ'eɪʃ(ə)n/ ● n. the use of beams in architectural construction, rather than arches or vaulting.
– DERIVATIVES **trabeated** /'treɪbɪətɪd/ adj.
– ORIGIN C16 (denoting a horizontal beam): formed irregularly from L. *trabs, trab-* 'beam, timber' + -ATION.

**trabecula** /trə'bɛkjʊlə/ ● n. (pl. **trabeculae** /-liː/) **1** Anatomy each of a series of partitions formed by bands or columns of connective tissue, especially in cancellous bone. **2** Botany a rod-like structure, e.g. a strand of sterile tissue dividing the cavity in a sporangium.
– DERIVATIVES **trabecular** adj. **trabeculate** /-lət/ adj.
– ORIGIN C19: from L., dimin. of *trabs* 'beam, timber'.

**tracasseries** /trə'kas(ə)rɪz/ ● pl. n. archaic petty quarrels or annoyances.
– ORIGIN Fr., from *tracasser* 'to bustle or fuss'.

**trace**[1] ● v. **1** find by investigation. ➤find or describe the origin or development of. **2** follow the course or position of with one's eye, mind, or finger. **3** copy (a drawing, map, or design) by drawing over its lines on a superimposed piece of transparent paper. ➤draw (a pattern or line). **4** give an outline of. ● n. **1** a mark, object, or other indication of the existence or passing of something. ➤a physical change in the brain associated with a memory. **2** a very small quantity. ➤a barely discernible indication: *a trace of a smile.* **3** a line or pattern corresponding to something which is being recorded or measured. ➤the projection or intersection of a curve on or with a plane. **4** a procedure to trace something, such as the place from which a telephone call was made. **5** Mathematics the sum of the elements in the principle diagonal of a square matrix. **6** W. Indian & N. Amer. a path or track.
– DERIVATIVES **traceability** n. **traceable** adj. **traceless** adj.
– ORIGIN ME: from OFr. *trace* (n.), *tracier* (v.), based on L. *tractus* (see TRACT[1]).

**trace**[2] ● n. each of the two side straps, chains, or ropes by which a horse is attached to a vehicle that it is pulling.

– PHRASES **kick over the traces** become insubordinate or reckless.
– ORIGIN ME: from OFr. *trais*, pl. of *trait* (see **TRAIT**).

**trace element** • n. a chemical element present or required only in minute amounts.

**trace fossil** • n. Geology a fossil of a footprint, trail, or other trace of an animal, rather than of the animal itself.

**tracer** • n. **1** a bullet or shell whose course is made visible by a trail of flames or smoke, used to assist in aiming. **2** a substance introduced into a system so that its subsequent distribution can be followed from its colour, radioactivity, or other distinctive property. **3** a device which transmits a signal and so can be located when attached to a moving vehicle or other object.

**tracery** • n. (pl. **-ies**) **1** Architecture ornamental stone openwork, typically in the upper part of a Gothic window. **2** a delicate branching pattern.
– DERIVATIVES **traceried** adj.

**trachea** /trəˈkiːə, ˈtreɪkɪə/ • n. (pl. **tracheae** /-ˈkiːiː/ or **tracheas**) **1** Anatomy the membranous tube, reinforced by rings of cartilage, conveying air between the larynx and the bronchial tubes; the windpipe. **2** Entomology an air passage in the body of an insect. **3** Botany a duct or vessel in a plant.
– DERIVATIVES **tracheal** /ˈtreɪkɪəl/ adj. **tracheate** /ˈtreɪkɪeɪt/ adj.
– ORIGIN ME: from med. L., from late L. *trachia*, from Gk *trakheia* (*artēria*) 'rough (artery)'.

**tracheo-** /trəˈkiːəʊ, ˈtrakɪəʊ, ˈtreɪkɪəʊ/ • comb. form relating to the trachea: *tracheotomy*.

**tracheotomy** /ˌtrakɪˈɒtəmi/ (also **tracheostomy** /-ˈɒstəmi/) • n. (pl. **-ies**) Medicine an incision in the windpipe made to relieve an obstruction to breathing.

**tracheotomy tube** • n. a breathing tube inserted into a tracheotomy.

**trachoma** /trəˈkəʊmə/ • n. a contagious bacterial infection of the eye, causing inflamed granulation on the inner surface of the lids.
– DERIVATIVES **trachomatous** /-ˈkəʊmətəs, -ˈkɒmətəs/ adj.
– ORIGIN C17: from Gk *trakhōma* 'roughness'.

**trachyte** /ˈtreɪkʌɪt, ˈtrakʌɪt/ • n. Geology a grey fine-grained volcanic rock consisting largely of alkali feldspar.
– ORIGIN C19 (orig. denoting a volcanic rock with a gritty surface): from Gk *trakhus* 'rough' or *trakhutēs* 'roughness'.

**trachytic** /trəˈkɪtɪk/ • adj. Geology relating to or denoting a rock texture (characteristic of trachyte) in which crystals show parallel alignment due to liquid flow.

**tracing** • n. **1** a copy of a drawing, map, etc. made by tracing. **2** a faint or delicate mark or pattern. **3** another term for **TRACE**[1] (in sense 3).

**track**[1] • n. **1** a rough path or minor road. **2** a prepared course or circuit for racing. **3** a mark or line of marks left by a person, animal, or vehicle in passing. ➤the course followed by someone or something. **4** a continuous line of rails on a railway. **5** a strip or rail along which something (e.g. a curtain) may be moved. **6** a continuous articulated metal band around the wheels of a heavy vehicle such as a tank, facilitating movement over rough or soft ground. **7** Electronics a continuous line of conductive material on a printed circuit board, connecting parts of a circuit. **8** a section of a record, compact disc, or cassette tape containing one song or piece of music. [orig. denoting a groove on a gramophone record.] ➤a lengthwise strip of magnetic tape containing one sequence of signals. **9** the transverse distance between a vehicle's wheels. **10** US term for **STREAM** (in sense 3). • v. **1** follow the course or movements of. ➤(**track someone/thing down**) find someone or something after a thorough or difficult search. ➤follow a particular course. ➤(of a stylus) follow (a groove in a record). ➤(of a film or television camera) move in relation to the subject being filmed. [with ref. to early filming when a camera was mobile by means of a track.] **2** (of wheels) run so that the back ones are exactly in the track of the front ones. **3** Electronics (of a tunable circuit or component) vary in frequency in the same way as another circuit or component. **4** (**track something up**) N. Amer. leave a trail of dirty footprints on a surface. ➤(**track something in**) N. Amer. leave a trail of dirt, debris, or snow from one's feet. **5** (**track** (**square**) **with**) Austral. informal carry on a romantic or sexual relationship with.
– PHRASES **keep** (or **lose**) **track of** keep (or fail to keep) fully aware of or informed about. **make tracks** (**for**) informal leave (for a place). **off the track** departing from the right course of thinking or behaviour. **on the right** (or **wrong**) **track** following a course likely to result in success (or failure). **on track** following a course likely to achieve what is required. **stop** (or **be stopped**) **in one's tracks** informal be brought to a sudden and complete halt. **the wrong side of the tracks** informal a poor or less prestigious part of town. [with ref. to the railway tracks of American towns, once serving as a line of demarcation between rich and poor quarters.]
– DERIVATIVES **trackage** n. (N. Amer.). **trackless** adj.
– ORIGIN C15: the noun from OFr. *trac*, perh. from Low Ger. or Du. *trek* 'draught, drawing'; the verb from Fr. *traquer* or directly from the noun.

**track**[2] • v. tow (a canoe) along a waterway from the bank.
– ORIGIN C18: appar. from Du. *trekken* 'to pull or travel'; the change in the vowel was due to assoc. with **TRACK**[1].

**trackball** (also **tracker ball**) • n. a small ball set in a holder that can be rotated by hand to move a cursor on a computer screen.

**trackbed** • n. the foundation structure on which railway tracks are laid.

**tracker** • n. **1** a person who tracks. **2** a connecting rod in the mechanism of an organ.

**track events** • pl. n. athletic events that take place on a running track. Compare with **FIELD EVENTS**.

**tracking** • n. **1** Electronics the maintenance of a constant difference in frequency between connected circuits or components. **2** the formation of an electrically conducting path over the surface of an insulator. **3** US the streaming of school pupils. **4** the alignment of the wheels of a vehicle.

**tracking station** • n. a place from which the movements of missiles, aircraft, or satellites are tracked.

**tracklayer** • n. **1** a tractor or other vehicle equipped with continuous tracks. **2** N. Amer. a trackman.

**tracklement** • n. Brit. rare a savoury jelly, served with meat.
– ORIGIN 1950s: of unknown origin.

**trackman** • n. (pl. **-men**) a person employed in laying and maintaining railway track.

**track record** • n. the past achievements or performance of a person, organization, or product.

**track rod** • n. a rod that connects the two front wheels of a motor vehicle and transmits the steering action from the steering column to the wheels.

**track shoe** • n. a running shoe.

**tracksuit** • n. a loose, warm outfit consisting of a sweatshirt and trousers, worn when exercising or as casual wear.

**trackway** • n. a path formed by the repeated treading of people or animals.

**tract**[1] • n. **1** a large area of land. **2** poetic/literary an indefinitely large extent. **3** a major passage in the body or other continuous elongated anatomical structure.
– ORIGIN ME (in the sense 'duration or course (of time)'): from L. *tractus* 'drawing, draught', from *trahere* 'draw, pull'.

**tract**[2] • n. a short treatise in pamphlet form, typically on a religious subject.
– ORIGIN ME, appar. an abbrev. of L. *tractatus* (see **TRACTATE**).

**tract**[3] • n. (in the Roman Catholic Church) an anthem of Scriptural verses formerly replacing the alleluia in certain penitential and requiem Masses.
– ORIGIN ME: from med. L. *tractus* (*cantus*) 'drawn-out (song)', past part. of L. *trahere* 'draw'.

**tractable** • adj. **1** easy to control or influence. **2** (of a situation or problem) easy to deal with.

– DERIVATIVES **tractability** n. **tractably** adv.
– ORIGIN C16: from L. *tractabilis*, from *tractare* (see **TRACTATE**).

**Tractarianism** /trak'tɛːrɪənɪz(ə)m/ ● **n.** a Christian movement founded in Oxford in 1833, seeking to restore traditional Catholic teachings and ceremonial within the Church of England.
– DERIVATIVES **Tractarian** adj. & n.
– ORIGIN C19: from *Tracts for the Times*, the title of a series of pamphlets published in Oxford 1833–41, which set out the doctrines on which the movement was based.

**tractate** /'trakteɪt/ ● **n.** formal a treatise.
– ORIGIN C15: from L. *tractatus*, from *tractare* 'to handle'.

**traction** ● **n. 1** the action of pulling a thing along a surface. ➤ the motive power used for pulling, especially on a railway. **2** Medicine the application of a sustained pull on a limb or muscle, especially in order to maintain the position of a fractured bone or to correct a deformity. **3** the grip of a tyre on a road or a wheel on a rail.
– ORIGIN ME: from Fr., or from med. L. *tractio(n-)*, from L. *trahere* 'draw, pull'.

**traction engine** ● **n.** a steam or diesel-powered road vehicle used (especially formerly) for pulling very heavy loads.

**tractive** ● **adj.** relating to or denoting power exerted in pulling, especially by a vehicle or other machine.

**tractor** ● **n.** a powerful motor vehicle with large rear wheels, used chiefly on farms for hauling equipment and trailers.
– ORIGIN C18 (in the general sense 'someone or something that pulls'): from L., from *tract-*, *trahere* 'pull'.

**tractor beam** ● **n.** (in science fiction) a beam of energy that can be used to move objects such as spaceships or hold them stationary.

**trad** informal ● **adj.** (especially of music) traditional. ● **n.** traditional jazz or folk music.

**trade** ● **n. 1** the buying and selling of goods and services. ➤ a business of a particular kind. **2** a job requiring manual skills and special training. ➤ (**the trade**) [treated as sing. or pl.] the people engaged in a particular area of business. **3** dated, chiefly derogatory the practice of making one's living in business, as opposed to in a profession or from unearned income. **4** a trade wind. **5** N. Amer. (in sport) a transfer; an exchange. ● **v. 1** buy and sell goods and services. ➤ buy or sell (a particular item or product). ➤ (especially of shares or currency) be bought and sold at a specified price. **2** exchange, typically as a commercial transaction. ➤ (**trade something in**) exchange a used article in part payment for another. ➤ (**trade something off**) exchange something of value, especially as part of a compromise. ➤ N. Amer. transfer (a player) to another club or team. **3** (**trade on**) take advantage of.
– DERIVATIVES **tradable** (or **tradeable**) adj. **trading** n.
– ORIGIN ME: from Mid. Low Ger., lit. 'track', of W. Gmc origin; rel. to **TREAD**.

**Trade Board** ● **n.** Brit. historical a statutory body with members from workers and management, set up to settle disputes and regulate conditions of employment in certain industries.

**trade book** ● **n.** a book published by a commercial publisher and intended for general readership.

**trade deficit** ● **n.** the amount by which the cost of a country's imports exceeds the value of its exports.

**trade discount** ● **n.** a discount on a retail price allowed or agreed between traders or to a retailer by a wholesaler.

**traded option** ● **n.** an option on a stock exchange or futures exchange which can itself be bought and sold.

**trade edition** ● **n.** an edition of a book intended for general sale rather than for book clubs or specialist suppliers.

**trade gap** ● **n.** another term for **TRADE DEFICIT**.

**trade-last** ● **n.** US dated a compliment from a third person that is relayed to the person complimented in exchange for a similarly relayed compliment.

**trademark** ● **n. 1** a symbol, word, or words legally registered or established by use as representing a company or product. **2** a distinctive characteristic or object. ● **v.** [usu. as adj. **trademarked**] provide with a trademark.

**trade name** ● **n. 1** a name that has the status of a trademark. **2** a name by which something is known in a particular trade or profession.

**trade plates** ● **pl. n.** Brit. temporary number plates used by car dealers or manufacturers on unlicensed cars.

**trade price** ● **n.** the price paid for goods by a retailer to a manufacturer or wholesaler.

**trader** ● **n. 1** a person who trades goods, currency, or shares. **2** a merchant ship.

**tradescantia** /ˌtradɪ'skantɪə/ ● **n.** an American plant with triangular three-petalled flowers, often grown as a house plant. [Genus *Tradescantia*.]
– ORIGIN mod. L., named in honour of the Engl. botanist John *Tradescant* (1570–1638).

**tradesman** ● **n.** (pl. **-men**) a person engaged in trading or a trade, typically on a relatively small scale.

**trade surplus** ● **n.** the amount by which the value of a country's exports exceeds the cost of its imports.

**trade union** (Brit. also **trades union**) ● **n.** an organized association of workers in a trade, group of trades, or profession, formed to protect and further their rights and interests.
– DERIVATIVES **trade unionism** n. **trade unionist** n.

**trade-weighted** ● **adj.** (especially of exchange rates) weighted according to the importance of the trade with the various countries involved.

**trade wind** ● **n.** a wind blowing steadily towards the equator from the north-east in the northern hemisphere or the south-east in the southern hemisphere, especially at sea.
– ORIGIN C17: from the phr. *blow trade* 'blow steadily'; because of the importance of these winds to navigation, an erroneous connection was made between the word *trade* and 'commerce'.

**trading estate** ● **n.** Brit. a specially designed industrial and commercial area.

**trading post** ● **n.** a store or small settlement established for trading, typically in a remote place.

**trading stamp** ● **n.** a stamp given by some stores to a customer according to the amount spent, and exchangeable in the appropriate number for various articles.

**tradition** ● **n. 1** the transmission of customs or beliefs from generation to generation, or the fact of being so passed on. ➤ a long-established custom or belief passed on in this way. **2** an artistic or literary method or style established by an artist, writer, or movement, and subsequently followed by others. **3** Theology (in Christianity) doctrine not explicit in the Bible but held to derive from the oral teaching of Christ and the Apostles. ➤ (in Judaism) an ordinance of the oral law not in the Torah but held to have been given by God to Moses. ➤ (in Islam) a saying or act ascribed to the Prophet but not recorded in the Koran. See **HADITH**.
– DERIVATIVES **traditionary** adj. **traditionist** n. **traditionless** adj.
– ORIGIN ME: from OFr. *tradicion*, or from L. *traditio(n-)*, from *tradere* 'deliver, betray', from *trans-* 'across' + *dare* 'give'.

**traditional** ● **adj. 1** of, relating to, or following tradition. **2** (of jazz) in the style of the early 20th century.
– DERIVATIVES **traditionally** adv.

**traditionalism** ● **n. 1** the upholding of tradition, especially so as to resist change. **2** chiefly historical the theory that all moral and religious truth comes from divine revelation passed on by tradition, human reason being incapable of attaining it.
– DERIVATIVES **traditionalist** n. & adj. **traditionalistic** adj.

**traduce** /trə'djuːs/ ● **v.** speak badly of or tell lies about.
– DERIVATIVES **traducement** n. **traducer** n.
– ORIGIN C16: from L. *traducere* 'lead in front of others, expose to ridicule'.

**traffic** ● **n. 1** vehicles moving on a public highway. **2** the movement of ships or aircraft. **3** the commercial transportation of goods or passengers. **4** the messages or signals transmitted through a communications system. **5** the action of trafficking. **6** archaic dealings or communication between people. ● **v.** (**trafficked**, **trafficking**) deal

or trade in something illegal.
– DERIVATIVES **trafficker** n. **trafficless** adj.
– ORIGIN C16: from Fr. *traffique*, Sp. *tráfico*, or Ital. *traffico*, of unknown origin.

**trafficator** /ˈtrafɪkeɪtə/ ● n. Brit. an obsolete kind of signalling device on the side of a motor vehicle, having the form of a small extendable illuminated pointer.
– ORIGIN 1930s: blend of **TRAFFIC** and **INDICATOR**.

**traffic calming** ● n. the deliberate slowing of traffic in residential areas, by building road humps or other obstructions.
– ORIGIN 1980s: translation of Ger. *Verkehrsberuhigung*.

**traffic circle** ● n. North American term for **ROUNDABOUT** (in sense 1).

**traffic island** ● n. a small raised area in the middle of a road which provides a safe place for pedestrians to stand and marks a division between two streams of traffic.

**traffic jam** ● n. a line or lines of traffic at or virtually at a standstill.

**traffic lights** (also **traffic light** or **traffic signal**) ● pl. n. a set of automatically operated coloured lights for controlling traffic at road junctions, pedestrian crossings, and roundabouts.

**traffic pattern** ● n. chiefly N. Amer. a pattern in the air above an airport of permitted lanes for aircraft to follow after take-off or prior to landing.

**traffic warden** ● n. Brit. a uniformed official who locates and reports on infringements of parking regulations.

**tragacanth** /ˈtragəkanθ/ (also **gum tragacanth**) ● n. a white or reddish gum obtained from a plant (*Astragalus gummifer*), used in the food, textile, and pharmaceutical industries.
– ORIGIN C16: from Fr. *tragacante*, via L. from Gk *tragakantha* (name of the source plant, lit. 'goat's thorn').

**tragedian** /trəˈdʒiːdɪən/ ● n. 1 (fem. **tragedienne** /trəˌdʒiːdɪˈɛn/) a tragic actor or actress. 2 a writer of tragedies.

**tragedy** ● n. (pl. **-ies**) 1 an event causing great suffering, destruction, and distress. 2 a serious play with an unhappy ending, especially one concerning the downfall of the protagonist.
– ORIGIN ME: from OFr. *tragedie*, via L. from Gk *tragōidia*, appar. from *tragos* 'goat' (the reason remains unexplained) + *ōidē* 'song, ode'.

**tragic** ● adj. 1 extremely distressing or sad. ➤suffering extreme distress or sadness. 2 of or relating to tragedy in a literary work.
– DERIVATIVES **tragical** adj. **tragically** adv.
– ORIGIN C16: from Fr. *tragique*, via L. from Gk *tragikos*, from *tragos* 'goat', but assoc. with *tragōidia* (see **TRAGEDY**).

**tragic flaw** ● n. less technical term for **HAMARTIA**.

**tragic irony** ● n. see **IRONY**[1].

**tragicomedy** /ˌtradʒɪˈkɒmɪdi/ ● n. (pl. **-ies**) a play or novel containing elements of both comedy and tragedy.
– DERIVATIVES **tragicomic** adj. **tragicomically** adv.
– ORIGIN C16: from Fr. *tragicomédie* or Ital. *tragicomedia*, based on L. *tragicocomoedia*, from *tragicus* (see **TRAGIC**) + *comoedia* (see **COMEDY**).

**tragopan** /ˈtragəpan/ ● n. an Asian pheasant, the male of which has fleshy horns on its head. [Genus *Tragopan*: several species.]
– ORIGIN mod. L., from Gk, the name of a horned bird, from *tragos* 'goat' + the name of the Gk god *Pan*.

**tragus** /ˈtreɪgəs/ ● n. (pl. **tragi** /ˈtreɪgʌɪ, ˈtreɪdʒʌɪ/) Anatomy & Zoology a prominence on the inner side of the external ear, in front of and partly closing the passage to the organs of hearing.
– ORIGIN C17: from late L., via L. from Gk *tragos* 'goat' (with ref. to the characteristic tuft of hair resembling a goat's beard).

**trahison des clercs** /ˌtrɑːizɒ̃ deɪ ˈklɛː, French traizɔ̃ de klɛr/ ● n. poetic/literary a betrayal of intellectual, artistic, or moral standards by writers, academics, or artists.
– ORIGIN Fr., lit. 'treason of the scholars', the title of a book by Julien Benda (1927).

**trail** ● n. 1 a mark or a series of signs or objects left behind by the passage of someone or something. ➤a track or scent used in following someone or hunting an animal. 2 a long thin part stretching behind or hanging down from something. 3 a beaten path through rough country. 4 a route planned or followed for a particular purpose: *the tourist trail*. 5 the rear end of a gun carriage, resting or sliding on the ground when the gun is unlimbered. ● v. 1 draw or be drawn along behind. ➤(of a plant) grow along the ground or so as to hang down. 2 walk or move slowly or wearily. ➤(of the voice or a speaker) fade gradually before stopping. ➤be losing to an opponent in a game or contest. 3 follow the trail of. 4 advertise with a trailer. 5 apply (slip) through a nozzle or spout to decorate ceramic ware.
– PHRASES **at the trail** Military with a rifle hanging balanced in one hand and (in Britain) parallel to the ground. **trail arms** Military let a rifle hang in such a way. **trail one's coat** deliberately provoke a quarrel or fight.
– ORIGIN ME: from OFr. *traillier* 'to tow', or Mid. Low Ger. *treilen* 'haul (a boat)', based on L. *tragula* 'dragnet', from *trahere* 'to pull'.

**trail bike** ● n. a light motorcycle for use in rough terrain.

**trailblazer** ● n. 1 a person who makes a new track through wild country. 2 an innovator.
– DERIVATIVES **trailblazing** n. & adj.

**trailer** ● n. 1 an unpowered vehicle towed by another. ➤the rear section of an articulated truck. ➤N. Amer. a caravan. 2 an extract from a film or programme used for advance advertising. 3 a trailing plant. ● v. 1 advertise with a trailer. 2 transport by trailer.

**trailer park** ● n. 1 N. Amer. a caravan site. 2 [as modifier] US lacking refinement, taste, or quality: *a trailer-park floozy*.

**trailer truck** ● n. US an articulated truck.

**trailing arbutus** ● n. a creeping North American plant of the heather family, with leathery evergreen leaves and clusters of pink or white flowers. [*Epigaea repens*.]

**trailing edge** ● n. 1 the rear edge of a moving body, especially an aircraft wing or propeller blade. 2 Electronics the part of a pulse in which the amplitude diminishes.

**trailing wheel** ● n. a wheel on a railway locomotive or other vehicle that is not given direct motive power.

**trail mix** ● n. a mixture of dried fruit and nuts eaten as a snack food.

**train** ● v. 1 teach (a person or animal) a particular skill or type of behaviour through regular practice and instruction. ➤be taught in such a way. 2 make or become physically fit through a course of exercise and diet. 3 (**train something on**) point or aim something at. 4 cause (a plant) to grow in a particular direction or into a required shape. 5 dated go by train. 6 archaic entice. ● n. 1 a series of railway carriages or wagons moved as a unit by a locomotive or by integral motors. 2 a number of vehicles or pack animals moving in a line. ➤a retinue of attendants accompanying an important person. 3 a series of connected events, thoughts, etc. 4 a long piece of trailing material attached to the back of a formal dress or robe. 5 a series of gears or other connected parts in machinery. 6 a trail of gunpowder for firing an explosive charge.
– PHRASES **in train** in progress. **in someone/thing's train** following behind someone or something. **in** (or **out of**) **training** undergoing (or no longer undergoing) physical training for a sporting event. ➤physically fit (or unfit) as a result of this.
– DERIVATIVES **trainability** n. **trainable** adj. **training** n. **trainload** n.
– ORIGIN ME (as a noun in the sense 'delay'): from OFr. *train* (masc.), *traine* (fem.), from *trahiner* (v.), from L. *trahere* 'pull, draw'.

**trainband** ● n. historical a division of civilian soldiers in London and other areas, especially in the Stuart period.

**trainee** ● n. a person undergoing training for a particular job or profession.
– DERIVATIVES **traineeship** n.

**trainer** ● n. 1 a person who trains people or animals. ➤informal an aircraft or simulator used to train pilots. 2 Brit. a soft shoe suitable for sports or casual wear.

**training college** ● n. (in the UK) a college where people, especially prospective teachers, are trained.

**training shoe** ● n. another term for **TRAINER** (in sense 2).

**train mile** ● n. one mile travelled by one train, as a unit of traffic.

**train oil** ● n. chiefly historical oil obtained from the blubber of a whale, especially the right whale.
– ORIGIN C16: from obs. *train* 'train oil', from Mid. Low Ger. *trän*, MDu. *traen*, lit. 'tear' (because it was extracted in droplets).

**train shed** ● n. a large structure providing a shelter over the tracks and platforms of a railway station.

**trainspotter** ● n. Brit. **1** a person who collects locomotive numbers as a hobby. **2** often derogatory a person who obsessively studies the minutiae of any minority interest or specialized hobby.
– DERIVATIVES **trainspotting** n.

**traipse** /treɪps/ ● v. walk or move wearily, reluctantly, or aimlessly. ● n. **1** a tedious or tiring walk. **2** archaic a slovenly woman.
– ORIGIN C16: of unknown origin.

**trait** /treɪ, treɪt/ ● n. a distinguishing quality or characteristic. ➤a genetically determined characteristic.
– ORIGIN C16 (an early sense was 'stroke of the pen or pencil in a picture'): from Fr., from L. *tractus* (see **TRACT**[1]).

**traitor** ● n. a person who betrays their country, a cause, etc.
– DERIVATIVES **traitorous** adj. **traitorously** adv.
– ORIGIN ME: from OFr. *traitour*, from L. *traditor*, from *tradere* 'hand over'.

**trajectory** /trəˈdʒɛkt(ə)ri, ˈtradʒɪkt(ə)ri/ ● n. (pl. **-ies**) **1** the path described by a projectile flying or an object moving under the action of given forces. **2** Geometry a curve or surface cutting a family of curves or surfaces at a constant angle.
– ORIGIN C17: from mod. L. *trajectoria* (fem.), from L. *traject-*, *traicere* 'throw across'.

**Trakehner** /traˈkeɪnə/ ● n. a saddle horse of a light breed first developed at the Trakehnen stud near Kaliningrad in Russia.
– ORIGIN C20: from Ger.

**tra la** ● exclam. chiefly ironic expressing joy or gaiety.
– ORIGIN C19: imitative of a fanfare or of the refrain of a song.

**tram** (also **tramcar**) ● n. **1** Brit. a passenger vehicle powered by electricity conveyed by overhead cables, and running on rails laid in a public road. **2** historical a low four-wheeled cart or barrow used in coal mines.
– ORIGIN C16: from Mid. Low Ger. and MDu. *trame* 'beam, barrow shaft'.

**Traminer** /trəˈmiːnə/ ● n. a variety of white wine grape grown chiefly in Germany and Alsace. ➤a white wine with a perfumed bouquet made from this grape.
– ORIGIN named after the Ital. village *Termeno*.

**tramlines** ● pl. n. Brit. **1** rails for a tramcar. **2** informal a pair of parallel lines at the sides of a tennis court or at the side or back of a badminton court.

**trammel** /ˈtram(ə)l/ ● n. **1** (**trammels**) poetic/literary restrictions or impediments to freedom of action. **2** (also **trammel net**) a three-layered net, designed so that a pocket forms when fish attempt to swim through, thus trapping them. **3** an instrument consisting of a board with two grooves intersecting at right angles, in which the two ends of a beam compass can slide to draw an ellipse. **4** US a hook in a fireplace for a kettle. ● v. (**trammelled**, **trammelling**; US **trammeled**, **trammeling**) constrain or impede.
– ORIGIN ME: from OFr. *tramail*, from a med. L. var. of *trimaculum*, perh. from L. *tri-* 'three' + *macula* 'mesh'.

**tramontana** /ˌtramɒnˈtɑːnə/ ● n. a cold north wind blowing in Italy or the adjoining regions of the Adriatic and Mediterranean.
– ORIGIN Ital., 'north wind, Pole Star' (see **TRAMONTANE**).

**tramontane** /trəˈmɒnteɪn/ ● adj. rare of, relating to, or living on the other side of mountains, especially the Alps as seen from Italy. ● n. **1** another term for **TRAMONTANA**. **2** archaic a tramontane person.
– ORIGIN ME (as a noun denoting the Pole Star): from Ital. *tramontana* 'Pole Star, north wind', *tramontani* 'people living beyond the Alps', from L. *transmontanus* 'beyond the mountains'.

**tramp** ● v. **1** walk heavily or noisily. **2** walk wearily or reluctantly over a long distance. ● n. **1** an itinerant homeless person who lives by begging or doing casual work. **2** the sound of heavy steps. **3** a long walk. **4** a cargo vessel running between many different ports rather than sailing a fixed route. **5** informal, chiefly N. Amer. a promiscuous woman. **6** a metal plate protecting the sole of a boot used for digging.
– DERIVATIVES **tramper** n. **trampish** adj.
– ORIGIN ME: prob. of Low Ger. origin.

**trample** ● v. **1** tread on and crush. **2** (**trample on/upon/over**) treat with contempt. ● n. poetic/literary an act or sound of trampling.
– DERIVATIVES **trampler** n.
– ORIGIN ME: frequentative of **TRAMP**.

**trampoline** /ˈtrampəliːn/ ● n. a strong fabric sheet connected by springs to a frame, used as a springboard and landing area in doing acrobatic or gymnastic exercises. ● v. [usu. as noun **trampolining**] use a trampoline.
– DERIVATIVES **trampolinist** n.
– ORIGIN C18: from Ital. *trampolino*, from *trampoli* 'stilts'.

**tram road** ● n. historical a road with wooden, stone, or metal tracks for wheels, used by wagons in mining districts.

**tram silk** ● n. double silk thread used for the weft of some velvets and silks.
– ORIGIN C17: *tram* from Fr. *trame* 'weft', from L. *trama*.

**tramway** ● n. **1** Brit. a set of rails for a tram. ➤a tram system. **2** historical a tram road.

**trance** /trɑːns/ ● n. **1** a half-conscious state characterized by an absence of response to external stimuli, typically as induced by hypnosis or entered by a medium. **2** a state of abstraction. **3** (also **trance music**) a type of electronic dance music characterized by hypnotic rhythms. ● v. poetic/literary put into a trance.
– DERIVATIVES **trance-like** adj.
– ORIGIN ME: from OFr. *transir* 'depart, fall into a trance', from L. *transire* 'go across'.

**tranche** /trɑːnʃ/ ● n. a portion, especially of money.
– ORIGIN C15: from OFr., lit. 'slice'.

**trank** ● n. informal a tranquillizing drug.

**tranny** (also **trannie**) ● n. (pl. **-ies**) informal **1** chiefly Brit. a transistor radio. **2** a photographic transparency. **3** N. Amer. the transmission in a motor vehicle. **4** a transvestite.

**tranquil** ● adj. free from disturbance; calm.
– DERIVATIVES **tranquillity** (also **tranquility**) n. **tranquilly** adv.
– ORIGIN ME: from Fr. *tranquille* or L. *tranquillus*.

**tranquillize** (also **-ise**; US **tranquilize**) ● v. [usu. as adj. **tranquillizing**] (of a drug) have a calming or sedative effect on. ➤administer such a drug to.
– DERIVATIVES **tranquillizer** n.

**trans-** /trans, trɑːns, -nz/ ● prefix **1** across; beyond: *transcontinental*. ➤on or to the other side of: *transatlantic*. **2** through: *transonic*. ➤into another state or place: *translate*. ➤transcending: *transfinite*. **3** Chemistry (usu. ***trans-***) denoting molecules in which two particular atoms or groups lie on opposite sides of a given plane, in particular denoting an isomer in which substituents at opposite ends of a carbon–carbon double bond are also on opposite sides of the bond: trans-*1,2-dichloroethene*.
– ORIGIN from L. *trans* 'across'.

**transaction** ● n. **1** an instance of buying or selling. ➤the action of conducting business. **2** an exchange or interaction between people. **3** (**transactions**) published reports of proceedings at the meetings of a learned society. **4** an input message to a computer system dealt with as a single unit of work.
– DERIVATIVES **transact** v. **transactional** adj. **transactionally** adv. **transactor** n.
– ORIGIN ME (as a term in Roman Law): from late L. *transactio(n-)*, from *transigere* 'drive through'.

**transactional analysis** ● n. a system of popular psychology based on the idea that behaviour reflects an interchange between parental, adult, and childlike aspects of personality.

**transalpine** • **adj.** **1** of, relating to, or in the area beyond the Alps, especially as viewed from Italy. **2** crossing the Alps.
– ORIGIN C16: from L. *transalpinus*, from *trans-* 'across' + *alpinus* (see **ALPINE**).

**transatlantic** • **adj.** **1** crossing the Atlantic. **2** concerning countries on both sides of the Atlantic, typically Britain and the US. **3** of, relating to, or situated on the other side of the Atlantic; Brit. American; N. Amer. British or European.

**transaxle** • **n.** an integral driving axle and differential gear in a motor vehicle.

**transceiver** • **n.** a combined radio transmitter and receiver.

**transcend** • **v.** **1** be or go beyond the range or limits of. **2** surpass.
– ORIGIN ME: from OFr. *transcendre* or L. *transcendere*, from *trans-* 'across' + *scandere* 'climb'.

**transcendent** • **adj.** **1** transcending normal or physical human experience. ➤(of God) existing apart from and not subject to the limitations of the material universe. Often contrasted with **IMMANENT**. **2** (in scholastic philosophy) higher than or not included in any of Aristotle's ten categories. **3** (in Kantian philosophy) not realizable in experience.
– DERIVATIVES **transcendence** n. **transcendency** n. **transcendently** adv.

**transcendental** • **adj.** **1** of or relating to a spiritual realm. ➤relating to or denoting Transcendentalism. **2** (in Kantian philosophy) presupposed in and necessary to experience; a priori. **3** Mathematics (of a quantity or function) not capable of being produced by the algebraical operations of addition, multiplication, and involution, or the inverse operations.
– DERIVATIVES **transcendentalize** (also **-ise**) v. **transcendentally** adv.

**transcendentalism** • **n.** **1** (**Transcendentalism**) a 19th-century idealistic philosophical and social movement influenced by romanticism, Platonism, and Kantian philosophy, which taught that divinity pervades all nature and humanity. **2** a system developed by Immanuel Kant, based on the idea that, in order to understand the nature of reality, one must first analyse the reasoning process which governs the nature of experience.
– DERIVATIVES **transcendentalist** n. & adj.

**Transcendental Meditation** • **n.** (trademark in the US) a technique for detaching oneself from anxiety and promoting harmony and self-realization by meditation and repetition of a mantra.

**transcontinental** • **adj.** crossing or extending across a continent or continents. • **n.** Canadian a transcontinental railway or train.
– DERIVATIVES **transcontinentally** adv.

**transcribe** • **v.** **1** put (thoughts, speech, or data) into written or printed form. **2** transliterate (foreign characters) or write or type out (shorthand, notes, etc.) into ordinary characters or full sentences. **3** arrange (a piece of music) for a different instrument, voice, etc. **4** Biochemistry synthesize (RNA) using a template of existing DNA (or vice versa), so that the genetic information is copied.
– DERIVATIVES **transcriber** n.
– ORIGIN C16: from L. *transcribere*, from *trans-* 'across' + *scribere* 'write'.

**transcript** • **n.** **1** a written or printed version of material originally presented in another medium. **2** Biochemistry a length of RNA or DNA that has been transcribed. **3** N. Amer. an official record of a student's work and grades.
– DERIVATIVES **transcriptive** adj.
– ORIGIN ME: from OFr. *transcrit*, from L. *transcriptum*, neut. past part. of *transcribere* (see **TRANSCRIBE**).

**transcriptase** /tran'skrɪpteɪz, trɑːn-/ • **n.** Biochemistry an enzyme which catalyses the formation of RNA from a DNA template, or (**reverse transcriptase**), the formation of DNA from an RNA template.

**transcription** • **n.** **1** a transcript. **2** the action or process of transcribing. **3** a piece of music transcribed for a different instrument, voice, etc. **4** a form in which a speech sound or a foreign character is represented.
– DERIVATIVES **transcriptional** adj. **transcriptionally** adv. **transcriptionist** n. (N. Amer.)

**transcutaneous** /ˌtranzkjʊ'teɪnɪəs, ˌtrɑːnz-, -ns-/ • **adj.** existing, applied, or measured across the depth of the skin.

**transdermal** /ˌtranz'dəːməl, trɑːnz, -ns-/ • **adj.** relating to or denoting the application of a medicine or drug through the skin, especially by means of an adhesive patch.

**transducer** /tranz'djuːsə, trɑːnz-, -ns-/ • **n.** a device that converts variations in a physical quantity, such as pressure or brightness, into an electrical signal, or vice versa.
– DERIVATIVES **transduce** v. **transduction** n.
– ORIGIN 1920s: from L. *transducere* 'lead across' + **-ER**[1].

**transect** technical • **v.** cut across or make a transverse section in. • **n.** a straight line or narrow cross section along which observations or measurements are made.
– DERIVATIVES **transection** n.
– ORIGIN C17: from **TRANS-** + L. *sect-*, *secare* 'divide by cutting'.

**transept** /'transɛpt, 'trɑːn-/ • **n.** (in a cross-shaped church) either of the two parts forming the arms of the cross shape, projecting at right angles from the nave.
– DERIVATIVES **transeptal** adj.
– ORIGIN C16: from mod. L. *transeptum* (see **TRANS-**, **SEPTUM**).

**transexual** • **adj.** & **n.** variant spelling of **TRANSSEXUAL**.

**transfect** /tranz'fɛkt, trɑːnz-, -ns-/ • **v.** Microbiology infect (a cell) with free nucleic acid. ➤introduce (genetic material) in this way.
– DERIVATIVES **transfectant** n. **transfection** n.
– ORIGIN 1960s: from **TRANS-** + **INFECT**, or a blend of **TRANSFER** and **INFECT**.

**transfer** • **v.** (**transferred**, **transferring**) **1** move from one place to another. **2** move or cause to move to another department, occupation, etc. ➤redirect (a telephone call) to a new line or extension. **3** change to another place, route, or means of transport during a journey. **4** make over the possession of (property, a right, or a responsibility) to another. **5** [usu. as adj. **transferred**] change (the sense of a word or phrase) by extension or metaphor. • **n.** **1** an act of transferring. **2** Brit. a small coloured picture or design on paper, which can be transferred to another surface by being pressed or heated. **3** N. Amer. a ticket allowing a passenger to change from one public transport vehicle to another as part of a single journey.
– DERIVATIVES **transferability** n. **transferable** adj. **transferee** n. **transferor** n. (chiefly Law). **transferral** n. **transferrer** n.
– ORIGIN ME: from Fr. *transférer* or L. *transferre*, from *trans-* 'across' + *ferre* 'to bear'.

**transference** /'transf(ə)r(ə)ns, 'trɑːns-, -nz-/ • **n.** **1** the action of transferring or the process of being transferred. **2** Psychoanalysis the redirection of emotions originally felt in childhood.

**transfer fee** • **n.** Brit. a fee paid by one soccer or rugby club to another for the transfer of a player.

**transfer payment** • **n.** Economics a payment by a government not made in exchange for goods or services, such as a benefit payment or subsidy.

**transferrin** /trans'fɛrɪn, trɑːns-, -nz-/ • **n.** Biochemistry a protein which transports iron in blood serum.
– ORIGIN 1940s: from **TRANS-** + L. *ferrum* 'iron' + **-IN**[1].

**transfer RNA** • **n.** Biochemistry a folded form of RNA which transports amino acids from the cytoplasm of a cell to a ribosome.

**transfiguration** • **n.** **1** a complete transformation into a more beautiful or spiritual state. **2** (**the Transfiguration**) Christ's appearance in radiant glory to three of his disciples (Matthew 17:2 and Mark 9:2–3). ➤the Church festival commemorating this, held on 6 August.

**transfigure** • **v.** (usu. **be transfigured**) transform into something more beautiful or spiritual.
– ORIGIN ME: from OFr. *transfigurer* or L. *transfigurare*,

from *trans-* 'across' + *figura* 'figure'.

**transfinite** ● **adj.** Mathematics denoting a number corresponding to an infinite set in the way that a natural number counts members of a finite set.

**transfix** ● **v. 1** (usu. **be transfixed**) make motionless with horror, wonder, or astonishment. **2** pierce with a sharp implement or weapon.
– DERIVATIVES **transfixion** n.
– ORIGIN C16: from L. *transfix-*, *transfigere* 'pierce through'.

**transform** ● **v.** subject to or undergo transformation. ➤change the voltage of (an electric current) by electromagnetic induction. ● **n.** Mathematics & Linguistics the product of a transformation. ➤a rule for making a transformation.
– DERIVATIVES **transformable** adj. **transformative** adj.
– ORIGIN ME: from OFr. *transformer* or L. *transformare* (see **TRANS-**, **FORM**).

**transformation** ● **n. 1** a marked change in nature, form, or appearance. **2** Mathematics & Logic a process by which a figure, expression, etc. is converted into another one of similar value. **3** Linguistics a process by which an element in the underlying logical deep structure of a sentence is converted to an element in the surface structure. **4** Biology the genetic alteration of a cell by introduction of extraneous DNA, especially by a plasmid.
– DERIVATIVES **transformational** adj. **transformationally** adv.

**transformational grammar** ● **n.** Linguistics grammar which describes a language in terms of transformations applied to an underlying deep structure in order to generate the surface structure of sentences which can actually occur.

**transformer** ● **n.** a device for changing the voltage of an alternating current by electromagnetic induction.

**transform fault** ● **n.** Geology a strike-slip fault occurring at the boundary between two plates of the earth's crust.

**transfuse** ● **v. 1** Medicine transfer (blood or its components) from one person or animal to another. ➤inject (liquid) into a blood vessel to replace lost fluid. **2** permeate or infuse.
– DERIVATIVES **transfusion** n.
– ORIGIN ME: from L. *transfus-*, *transfundere* 'pour from one container to another'.

**transgender** (also **transgendered**) ● **adj.** transsexual.

**transgenic** /tranz'dʒɛnɪk, trɑːnz-, -ns-/ ● **adj.** Biology containing genetic material into which DNA from a different organism has been artificially introduced.
– DERIVATIVES **transgenics** pl. n.
– ORIGIN 1980s: from **TRANS-** + **GENE** + **-IC**.

**transglobal** ● **adj.** (of an expedition, enterprise, or network) moving or extending across or round the world.

**transgress** ● **v. 1** go beyond the limits set by (a moral principle, standard, law, etc.). **2** Geology (of the sea) spread over (an area of land).
– DERIVATIVES **transgression** n. **transgressive** adj. **transgressor** n.
– ORIGIN C15 (earlier (ME) as *transgression*): from OFr. *transgresser* or L. *transgress-*, *transgredi* 'step across'.

**tranship** ● **v.** variant spelling of **TRANS-SHIP**.

**transhumance** /tranz'hjuːməns, trɑːnz-, -ns-/ ● **n.** the action or practice of moving livestock seasonally from one grazing ground to another, typically to lowlands in winter and highlands in summer.
– DERIVATIVES **transhumant** adj.
– ORIGIN C20: from Fr., from *transhumer*, based on L. *trans-* 'across' + *humus* 'ground'.

**transient** /'transɪənt, 'trɑːns-, -nz-/ ● **adj. 1** lasting only for a short time. **2** staying or working in a place for a short time only. ● **n. 1** a transient person. **2** a momentary variation in current, voltage, or frequency.
– DERIVATIVES **transience** n. **transiency** n. **transiently** adv.
– ORIGIN C16: from L. *transient-*, *transire* 'go across'.

**transilluminate** ● **v.** pass strong light through (an organ or part of the body) in order to detect disease or abnormality.
– DERIVATIVES **transillumination** n.

**transire** /tran'zʌɪə, trɑː-, -s-, -ʌɪri/ ● **n.** (in the UK) a customs document on which a ship's cargo is listed, issued to prove that the goods on it have come from a home port rather than an overseas one.
– ORIGIN C16: from L. *transire* 'go across'.

**transistor** ● **n. 1** a semiconductor device with three connections, capable of amplification and rectification. **2** (also **transistor radio**) a portable radio using circuits containing transistors.
– DERIVATIVES **transistorization** (also **-isation**) n. **transistorize** (also **-ise**) v.
– ORIGIN 1940s: from **TRANSFER** + **RESISTOR**, on the pattern of words such as *varistor*.

**transit** ● **n. 1** the carrying of people or things from one place to another. ➤N. Amer. the conveyance of passengers on public transport. **2** an act of passing through or across a place. ➤Astronomy the passage of a planet across the face of the sun, or of a moon across the face of a planet. ● **v.** (**transited**, **transiting**) pass across or through.
– ORIGIN ME: from L. *transitus*, from *transire* 'go across'.

**transit circle** (also **transit instrument**) ● **n.** another term for **MERIDIAN CIRCLE**.

**transition** ● **n. 1** the process of changing from one state or condition to another. ➤a period of such change. **2** Music a momentary modulation.
– DERIVATIVES **transitional** adj. **transitionally** adv. **transitionary** adj.
– ORIGIN C16: from Fr., or from L. *transitio(n-)*, from *transire* 'go across'.

**transition metal** (also **transition element**) ● **n.** Chemistry any of the set of metallic elements occupying a central block in the periodic table, e.g. iron, manganese, chromium, and copper.

**transitive** /'transɪtɪv, 'trɑːns-, -nz-/ ● **adj. 1** Grammar (of a verb or a sense or use of a verb) able to take a direct object (expressed or implied), e.g. *saw* in *he saw the donkey*. The opposite of **INTRANSITIVE**. **2** Logic & Mathematics (of a relation) such that, if it applies between successive members of a sequence, it must also apply between any two members taken in order.
– DERIVATIVES **transitively** adv. **transitiveness** n. **transitivity** n.
– ORIGIN C16 (in the sense 'transitory'): from late L. *transitivus*, from *transit-* (see **TRANSIT**).

**transitory** /'transɪt(ə)ri, 'trɑːns-, -nz-/ ● **adj.** not permanent; short-lived.
– DERIVATIVES **transitorily** adv. **transitoriness** n.
– ORIGIN ME: from OFr. *transitoire*, from Christian L. *transitorius*, from *transit-* (see **TRANSIT**).

**transit visa** ● **n.** a visa allowing its holder to pass through a country only, not to stay there.

**translate** /trans'leɪt, trɑːns-, -nz-/ ● **v. 1** express the sense of (words or text) in another language. ➤be expressed or be capable of being expressed in another language. **2** (**translate into** or **translate something into**) be converted or convert something into (another form or medium). ➤Biology convert (a sequence of nucleotides in messenger RNA) to an amino-acid sequence during protein synthesis. **3** move from one place or condition to another. ➤formal move (a bishop or, in Scotland, a minister) to another see or pastoral charge. **4** Physics & Mathematics cause to undergo translation.
– DERIVATIVES **translatability** n. **translatable** adj.
– ORIGIN ME: from L. *translat-*, *transferre* (see **TRANSFER**).

**translation** ● **n. 1** the action or process of translating. **2** a text or word that is translated. **3** formal or technical the process of moving something from one place to another. ➤Physics & Mathematics movement of a body such that every point moves in the same direction and over the same distance, without any rotation, reflection, or change in size.
– DERIVATIVES **translational** adj. **translationally** adv.

**translator** ● **n. 1** a person who translates from one language into another. **2** a program that translates from one programming language into another.

**transliterate** ● **v.** (usu. **be transliterated**) write or print (a letter or word) using the closest corresponding

letters of a different alphabet or language.
– DERIVATIVES **transliteration** n. **transliterator** n.
– ORIGIN C19: from **TRANS-** + L. *littera* 'letter' + **-ATE**[3].

**translocate** • v. chiefly technical move from one place to another.
– DERIVATIVES **translocation** n.

**translucent** /trans'lu:s(ə)nt, trɑ:ns-, -nz-/ • adj. allowing light to pass through partially; semi-transparent.
– DERIVATIVES **translucence** n. **translucency** n. **translucently** adv.
– ORIGIN C16: from L. *translucent-*, *translucere* 'shine through'.

**translunar** /tranz'lu:nə, trɑ:nz-, -ns-/ • adj. relating to or denoting the trajectory of a spacecraft travelling between the earth and the moon.

**transmarine** /ˌtranzmə'ri:n, ˌtrɑ:nz-, -ns-/ • adj. dated **1** situated or originating overseas. **2** crossing the sea.
– ORIGIN C16: from L. *transmarinus*, from *trans-* 'across' + *marinus* 'marine'.

**transmigrant** • n. rare a person passing through a country or region in the course of emigrating to another.

**transmigrate** • v. **1** (of the soul) pass into a different body after death. **2** rare migrate.
– DERIVATIVES **transmigration** n. **transmigrator** n. **transmigratory** adj.
– ORIGIN ME: from L. *transmigrat-*, *transmigrare* (see **TRANS-**, **MIGRATE**).

**transmission** • n. **1** the action or process of transmitting or the state of being transmitted. **2** a programme or signal that is transmitted. **3** the mechanism by which power is transmitted from an engine to the axle in a motor vehicle.
– ORIGIN C17: from L. *transmissio* (see **TRANS-**, **MISSION**).

**transmission line** • n. a conductor or conductors carrying electricity over large distances with minimum losses.

**transmit** • v. (**transmitted**, **transmitting**) **1** cause to pass on from one place or person to another. ➤ communicate (an idea or emotion). **2** broadcast or send out (an electrical signal or a radio or television programme). **3** allow (heat, light, etc.) to pass through a medium.
– DERIVATIVES **transmissibility** n. (chiefly Medicine). **transmissible** adj. (chiefly Medicine). **transmissive** adj. **transmissivity** n. (pl. **-ies**) (Physics). **transmittable** adj. **transmittal** n.
– ORIGIN ME: from L. *transmittere*, from *trans-* 'across' + *mittere* 'send'.

**transmittance** • n. Physics the ratio of the light energy falling on a body to that transmitted through it.

**transmitter** • n. **1** a device or installation used to generate and transmit electromagnetic waves carrying messages or signals, especially those of radio or television. **2** short for **NEUROTRANSMITTER**.

**transmogrify** /tranz'mɒgrɪfʌɪ, trɑ:nz-, -ns-/ • v. (**-ies**, **-ied**) (usu. **be transmogrified**) chiefly humorous transform in a surprising or magical manner.
– DERIVATIVES **transmogrification** n.
– ORIGIN C17: of unknown origin.

**transmontane** /tranz'mɒnteɪn, trɑ:nz-, -mɒn'teɪn, -ns-/ • adj. another term for **TRAMONTANE**.

**transmutation** /tranzmju:'teɪʃ(ə)n, trɑ:nz-, -ns-/ • n. the action of transmuting or the state of being transmuted. ➤ the changing of one chemical element into another, either by a nuclear process or as a supposed operation in alchemy.
– DERIVATIVES **transmutational** adj. **transmutationist** n.

**transmute** /tranz'mju:t, trɑ:nz-, -ns-/ • v. change in form, nature, or substance. ➤ subject (an element) to transmutation.
– DERIVATIVES **transmutability** n. **transmutable** adj. **transmutative** adj. **transmuter** n.
– ORIGIN ME: from L. *transmutare*, from *trans-* 'across' + *mutare* 'to change'.

**transnational** • adj. extending or operating across national boundaries. • n. a multinational company.
– DERIVATIVES **transnationalism** n. **transnationally** adv.

**transoceanic** • adj. **1** crossing an ocean. **2** coming from or situated beyond an ocean.

**transom** /'trans(ə)m/ • n. **1** the flat surface forming the stern of a boat. ➤ a horizontal beam reinforcing the stern of a boat. **2** a strengthening crossbar, in particular one set above a window or door. Compare with **MULLION**. **3** US term for **TRANSOM WINDOW**.
– PHRASES **over the transom** N. Amer. informal unsolicited.
– DERIVATIVES **transomed** adj.
– ORIGIN ME (earlier as *traversayn*): from OFr. *traversin*, from *traverser* (see **TRAVERSE**).

**transom window** • n. a window set above the transom of a door or larger window.

**transonic** /tran'sɒnɪk, trɑ:n-/ (also **trans-sonic**) • adj. denoting or relating to speeds close to that of sound.

**trans-Pacific** • adj. **1** crossing the Pacific. **2** of or relating to an area beyond the Pacific.

**transparence** • n. rare term for **TRANSPARENCY** (in sense 1).

**transparency** • n. (pl. **-ies**) **1** the condition of being transparent. **2** a positive transparent photograph printed on plastic or glass, and viewed using a slide projector.

**transparent** /tran'spar(ə)nt, trɑ:n-, -'spɛ:-/ • adj. **1** allowing light to pass through so that objects behind can be distinctly seen. **2** obvious or evident. **3** open to public scrutiny. **4** Physics transmitting heat or other radiation without distortion. **5** Computing (of a process) functioning without the user being aware of its presence.
– DERIVATIVES **transparently** adv.
– ORIGIN ME: from OFr., from med. L. *transparent-*, *transparere* 'shine through'.

**transpersonal** • adj. of, denoting, or dealing with states of consciousness beyond the limits of personal identity.

**transpire** • v. **1** (usu. **it transpires**) come to be known; prove to be so. **2** happen. **3** Botany (of a plant or leaf) give off water vapour through the stomata.
– DERIVATIVES **transpiration** n.
– ORIGIN ME: from Fr. *transpirer* or med. L. *transpirare*, from L. *trans-* 'through' + *spirare* 'breathe'.

**transplant** • v. /trans'plɑ:nt, trɑ:ns-, -nz-/ **1** transfer to another place or situation. ➤ replant (a plant) in another place. **2** take (living tissue or an organ) and implant it in another part of the body or in another body. • n. /'transplɑ:nt, 'trɑ:ns-, -nz-/ **1** an operation in which an organ or tissue is transplanted. **2** a person or thing that has been transplanted.
– DERIVATIVES **transplantable** /-'plɑ:ntəb(ə)l/ adj. **transplantation** /-'teɪʃ(ə)n/ n. **transplanter** /-'plɑ:ntə/ n.
– ORIGIN ME: from late L. *transplantare*, from L. *trans-* 'across' + *plantare* 'to plant'.

**transponder** /tran'spɒndə, trɑ:n-/ • n. a device for receiving a radio signal and automatically transmitting a different signal.
– ORIGIN 1940s: blend of **TRANSMIT** and **RESPOND**, + **-ER**[1].

**transpontine** /trans'pɒntʌɪn, trɑ:ns-, -nz-/ • adj. dated on or from the other side of an ocean, in particular the Atlantic as viewed from Britain; American.
– ORIGIN C19: from **TRANS-** + L. *pontus* 'sea' + **-INE**[1].

**transport** • v. **1** take or carry from one place to another by means of a vehicle, aircraft, or ship. ➤ historical send (a convict) to a penal colony. **2** (usu. **be transported**) overwhelm with a strong emotion, especially joy. • n. **1** a system or means of transporting. ➤ the action of transporting or the state of being transported. ➤ a large vehicle, ship, or aircraft for carrying troops or stores. ➤ historical a convict who was transported to a penal colony. **2** (**transports**) overwhelmingly strong emotions.
– DERIVATIVES **transportation** n.
– ORIGIN ME: from OFr. *transporter* or L. *transportare* 'carry across'.

**transportable** • adj. **1** able to be carried or moved. **2** historical (of an offender or an offence) punishable by transporting to a penal colony. • n. a large portable computer or telephone.
– DERIVATIVES **transportability** n.

**transport cafe** • n. Brit. a roadside cafe for drivers of haulage vehicles.

**transporter** • n. a large vehicle used to carry heavy objects, e.g. cars.

**transpose** • v. **1** cause to exchange places. **2** transfer to

a different place or context. ➤write or play (music) in a different key from the original. ● **n.** Mathematics a matrix obtained from a given matrix by interchanging rows and columns.
– DERIVATIVES **transposable** adj. **transposal** n. **transposer** n. **transposition** n. **transpositional** adv.
– ORIGIN ME (also in the sense 'transform'): from OFr. *transposer*, from *trans-* 'across' + *poser* 'to place'.

**transposing instrument** ● **n.** an orchestral instrument for which parts are written in a different key from that in which they sound, e.g. the clarinet.

**transposon** /trans'pəʊzɒn, trɑːns-, -nz-/ ● **n.** Genetics a segment of bacterial DNA that can be translocated as a whole between chromosomal, phage, and plasmid DNA.
– ORIGIN 1970s: from *transposition* + **-ON**.

**transputer** /trans'pjuːtə, trɑːns-, -nz-/ ● **n.** a microprocessor with integral memory designed for parallel processing.
– ORIGIN 1970s: blend of **TRANSISTOR** and **COMPUTER**.

**transsexual** (also **transexual**) ● **n.** a person born with the physical characteristics of one sex who emotionally and psychologically feels that they belong to the opposite sex. ● **adj.** of or relating to such a person.
– DERIVATIVES **transsexualism** n. **transsexuality** n.

**trans-ship** (also **tranship**) ● **v.** (**-shipped**, **-shipping**) transfer (cargo) from one ship or other form of transport to another.
– DERIVATIVES **trans-shipment** n.

**trans-sonic** ● **adj.** variant spelling of **TRANSONIC**.

**transubstantiate** /ˌtransəb'stanʃɪeɪt, ˌtrɑːn-, -sɪ-/ ● **v. 1** Christian Theology convert (the substance of the Eucharistic elements) into the body and blood of Christ at consecration. **2** formal change the form or substance of into something different.
– ORIGIN ME: from med. L. *transubstantiat-*, *transubstantiare* 'change in substance'.

**transubstantiation** ● **n.** Christian Theology the doctrine that the substance of the Eucharistic elements is converted into the body and blood of Christ at consecration, only the appearances of bread and wine still remaining. Compare with **CONSUBSTANTIATION**.

**transude** /tran'sjuːd, trɑːn-/ ● **v.** archaic discharge gradually through pores in a membrane.
– DERIVATIVES **transudate** n. **transudation** n.
– ORIGIN C17: from Fr. *transsuder*, from L. *trans-* 'across' + L. *sudare* 'to sweat'.

**transuranic** /ˌtransjʊ'ranɪk, ˌtrɑːns-, -nz-/ ● **adj.** Chemistry (of an element) having a higher atomic number than uranium (92).

**Transvaal daisy** ● **n.** a South African gerbera, grown for its large brightly coloured daisy-like flowers. [*Gerbera jamesonii.*]

**transvalue** ● **v.** (**transvalues**, **transvalued**, **transvaluing**) represent (an idea, custom, or quality) differently so as to cause revaluation.
– DERIVATIVES **transvaluation** n.

**transversal** /tranz'vəːs(ə)l, trɑːnz-, -ns-/ Geometry ● **adj.** (of a line) cutting a system of lines. ● **n.** a transversal line.
– DERIVATIVES **transversality** n. **transversally** adv.
– ORIGIN ME, in sense 'transverse': from med. L. *transversalis.*

**transverse** /tranz'vəːs, trɑːnz-, -ns-/ ● **adj.** situated or extending across something.
– DERIVATIVES **transversely** adv.
– ORIGIN ME: from L. *transversus*, *transvertere* 'turn across'.

**transverse flute** ● **n.** a flute which is held horizontally when played.

**transverse magnet** ● **n.** a magnet with poles at the sides and not the ends.

**transverse wave** ● **n.** Physics a wave vibrating at right angles to the direction of propagation.

**transvestite** ● **n.** a person, typically a man, who derives pleasure from dressing in clothes considered appropriate to the opposite sex.
– DERIVATIVES **transvestism** n. **transvestist** n. (dated). **transvestitism** n.
– ORIGIN 1920s: from Ger. *Transvestit*, from L. *trans-* 'across' + *vestire* 'clothe'.

**Transylvanian** /ˌtransɪl'veɪnɪən/ ● **adj.** of or relating to Transylvania, a large region of NW Romania.

**trap**[1] ● **n. 1** a device or enclosure designed to catch and retain animals. **2** an unpleasant situation from which it is hard to escape. ➤a trick betraying someone into acting contrary to their interests or intentions. **3** a container or device used to collect a specified thing. ➤a curve in the waste pipe from a bath, basin, or toilet that is always full of liquid to prevent the upward passage of gases. **4** a bunker or other hollow on a golf course. **5** the compartment from which a greyhound is released at the start of a race. **6** a device for hurling an object such as a clay pigeon into the air to be shot at. ➤historical (in the game of trapball) the shoe-shaped device that is hit with a bat to send the ball into the air. **7** chiefly historical a light, two-wheeled carriage pulled by a horse or pony. **8** informal a person's mouth: *keep your trap shut!* **9** informal a percussion instrument in a jazz band. ● **v.** (**trapped**, **trapping**) **1** catch (an animal) in a trap. **2** prevent from escaping. ➤catch (something) somewhere so that it cannot be freed. **3** trick into doing something.
– DERIVATIVES **trap-like** adj.
– ORIGIN OE *træppe* (in *coltetræppe* 'Christ's thorn'); rel. to MDu. *trappe* and med. L. *trappa*, of uncertain origin.

**trap**[2] ● **v.** (**trapped**, **trapping**) [usu. as adj. **trapped**] archaic put trappings on (a horse).
– ORIGIN ME: from the obs. noun *trap* 'trappings', from OFr. *drap* 'drape'.

**trap**[3] (also **traprock**) ● **n.** N. Amer. basalt or a similar dark, fine-grained igneous rock.
– ORIGIN C18: from Swed. *trapp*, from *trappa* 'stair' (because of the often stair-like appearance of its outcroppings).

**trapball** ● **n.** historical a game in which the player used a bat to hit a trap (see **TRAP**[1] sense 6) to send a ball into the air and then to hit the ball itself.

**trapdoor** ● **n. 1** a hinged or removable panel in a floor, ceiling, or roof. **2** a feature of a computer program which allows surreptitious unauthorized access.

**trapdoor spider** ● **n.** a spider which lives in a burrow with a hinged cover like a trapdoor. [Family Ctenizidae.] ➤Austral. a funnel-web spider.

**trapes** ● **v. & n.** archaic spelling of **TRAIPSE**.

**trapeze** ● **n. 1** (also **flying trapeze**) a horizontal bar hanging by two ropes and free to swing, used by acrobats in a circus. **2** Sailing a harness attached by a cable to a dinghy's mast, enabling a sailor to balance the boat by leaning out backwards over the windward side.
– ORIGIN C19: from Fr. *trapèze*, from late L. *trapezium* (see **TRAPEZIUM**).

**trapezium** /trə'piːzɪəm/ ● **n.** (pl. **trapezia** /-zɪə/ or **trapeziums**) Geometry, Brit. a quadrilateral with one pair of sides parallel. ➤N. Amer. a quadrilateral with no sides parallel.
– ORIGIN C16: via late L. from Gk *trapezion*, from *trapeza* 'table'.

**trapezius** /trə'piːzɪəs/ ● **n.** (pl. **trapezii** /-zɪʌɪ/) Anatomy either of a pair of large triangular muscles extending over the back of the neck and shoulders and moving the head and shoulder blade.
– ORIGIN C18: from mod. L., from Gk *trapezion* 'trapezium' (because of the shape formed by the muscles).

**trapezoid** /'trapɪzɔɪd, trə'piːzɔɪd/ ● **n.** Geometry, Brit. a quadrilateral with no sides parallel. ➤N. Amer. a quadrilateral with one pair of sides parallel.
– DERIVATIVES **trapezoidal** adj.
– ORIGIN C18: from mod. L. *trapezoides*, from late Gk *trapezoeidēs*, from *trapeza* (see **TRAPEZIUM**).

**trapper** ● **n.** a person who traps wild animals, especially for their fur.

**trappings** ● **pl. n. 1** the visible signs or objects associated with a particular situation or role: *I had the trappings of success.* **2** a horse's ornamental harness.
– ORIGIN ME: derivative of **TRAP**[2].

**Trappist** ● **adj.** relating to or denoting a branch of the

Cistercian order of monks noted for an austere rule including a vow of silence. ● **n.** a member of this order.
– ORIGIN C19: from Fr. *trappiste*, from *La Trappe* in Normandy, where the order was founded.

**traprock** ● **n.** see TRAP[3].

**traps** ● **pl. n.** informal personal belongings; baggage.
– ORIGIN C19: perh. a contr. of TRAPPINGS.

**trap shooting** ● **n.** the sport of shooting at clay pigeons released from a spring trap.
– DERIVATIVES **trap shooter** n.

**trash** ● **n.** chiefly N. Amer. **1** waste material; refuse. **2** worthless writing, art, etc. **3** a person or people regarded as being of very low social standing. **4** W. Indian the leaves, tops, and crushed stems of sugar cane, used as fuel. ● **v. 1** informal, chiefly N. Amer. wreck or destroy. **2** informal, chiefly N. Amer. criticize severely. **3** [as adj. **trashed**] informal intoxicated with alcohol or drugs. **4** strip (sugar canes) of their outer leaves to ripen them faster.
– DERIVATIVES **trashily** adv. **trashiness** n. **trashy** adj. (**-ier, -iest**).
– ORIGIN ME: of unknown origin.

**trash can** ● **n.** N. Amer. a dustbin.

**trash talk** US informal ● **n.** insulting or boastful speech intended to demoralize, intimidate, or humiliate. ● **v.** (**trash-talk**) use such speech.
– DERIVATIVES **trash talker** n.

**trass** ● **n.** a light-coloured variety of volcanic ash resembling pozzolana, used in making water-resistant cement.
– ORIGIN C18: from Du. *tras*, Ger. *Trass*, based on L. *terra* 'earth'.

**trattoria** /ˌtratəˈriːə/ ● **n.** an Italian restaurant.
– ORIGIN from Ital.

**trauma** /ˈtrɔːmə, ˈtraʊmə/ ● **n.** (pl. **traumas** or **traumata** /-mətə/) **1** a deeply distressing experience. **2** Medicine physical injury. **3** emotional shock following a stressful event.
– DERIVATIVES **traumatic** adj. **traumatically** adv. **traumatization** (also **-isation**) n. **traumatize** (also **-ise**) v.
– ORIGIN C17: from Gk, lit. 'wound'.

**traumatism** ● **n.** chiefly technical a traumatic effect or condition.

**travail** /ˈtraveɪl/ poetic/literary ● **n.** (also **travails**) painful or laborious effort. ➤labour pains. ● **v.** undergo such effort.
– ORIGIN ME: via OFr. from med. L. *trepalium* 'instrument of torture', from L. *tres* 'three' + *palus* 'stake'.

**travel** ● **v.** (**travelled, travelling**; US also **traveled, traveling**) **1** make a journey. ➤journey along (a road) or through (a region). **2** move or go. ➤informal (especially of a vehicle) move quickly. **3** withstand a journey without impairment. ● **n. 1** the action of travelling. ➤(**travels**) journeys, especially abroad. ➤[as modifier] (of a device) sufficiently compact for use when travelling. **2** the range, rate, or mode of motion of a part of a machine.
– ORIGIN ME: var. of TRAVAIL and orig. in the same sense.

**travel agency** (also **travel bureau**) ● **n.** an agency that makes the necessary arrangements for travellers.
– DERIVATIVES **travel agent** n.

**travelator** /ˈtravəleɪtə/ (also **travolator**) ● **n.** a moving walkway, typically at an airport.
– ORIGIN 1950s: from TRAVEL, suggested by ESCALATOR.

**travelled** /ˈtrav(ə)ld/ ● **adj. 1** having travelled to many places. **2** used by people travelling.

**traveller** (US also **traveler**) ● **n. 1** a person who is travelling or who often travels. **2** a gypsy. **3** (also **New Age traveller**) a person who holds New Age values and leads an itinerant and unconventional lifestyle. **4** Austral. an itinerant worker.

**traveller's cheque** ● **n.** a cheque for a fixed amount that may be cashed or used in payment abroad after endorsement by the holder's signature.

**traveller's joy** ● **n.** a tall scrambling wild clematis with small fragrant flowers and tufts of grey hairs around the seeds. [*Clematis vitalba*.]

**traveller's tale** ● **n.** a story about the unusual characteristics or customs of a foreign country, regarded as exaggerated or untrue.

**travelling crane** ● **n.** a crane able to move on rails, especially along an overhead support.

**travelling salesman** ● **n.** a representative of a firm who visits businesses to show samples and gain orders.

**travelling scholarship** ● **n.** a scholarship given to enable the holder to travel for study or research.

**travelling wave** ● **n.** Physics a wave in which the positions of maximum and minimum amplitude travel through the medium.

**travelogue** ● **n.** a film, book, or illustrated lecture about a person's travels.
– ORIGIN C20: from TRAVEL, on the pattern of *monologue*.

**travel-sick** ● **adj.** suffering from nausea caused by the motion of a moving vehicle, boat, or aircraft.
– DERIVATIVES **travel-sickness** n.

**traverse** /ˈtravəs, trəˈvəːs/ ● **v. 1** travel or extend across or through. ➤cross a rock face by means of a series of sideways movements from one practicable line of ascent or descent to another. ➤ski diagonally across (a slope), losing only a little height. **2** move back and forth or sideways. ➤turn (a large gun or other device on a pivot) to face a different direction. **3** Law deny (an allegation) in pleading. ➤archaic oppose or thwart (a plan). ● **n. 1** an act of traversing. ➤a zigzag course taken by a ship because winds or currents prevent it from sailing directly. **2** a part of a structure that extends or is fixed across something. ➤a gallery extending from side to side of a church or other building. **3** a mechanism enabling a large gun to be traversed. ➤the sideways movement of a part in a machine. **4** a single line of survey, usually plotted from compass bearings and chained or paced distances between angular points. **5** Military a pair of right-angled bends incorporated in a trench to avoid enfilading fire.
– DERIVATIVES **traversable** adj. **traversal** n. **traverser** n.
– ORIGIN ME: from OFr. *traverser*, from late L. *traversare*; the noun is from OFr. *travers* (masc.), *traverse* (fem.), partly based on *traverser*.

**travertine** /ˈtravətɪn/ ● **n.** white or light-coloured calcareous rock deposited from mineral springs, used in building.
– ORIGIN C18: from Ital. *travertino, tivertino*, from L. *tiburtinus* 'of Tibur' (now Tivoli, near Rome).

**travesty** /ˈtravɪsti/ ● **n.** (pl. **-ies**) an absurd or grotesque misrepresentation. ● **v.** (**-ies, -ied**) represent in such a way.
– ORIGIN C17 (as an adj. in the sense 'dressed to appear ridiculous'): from Fr. *travesti, travestir* 'disguise'.

**travois** /trəˈvɔɪ/ ● **n.** (pl. same /-ˈvɔɪz/) a V-shaped frame of poles pulled by a horse, formerly used by North American Indians to carry goods.
– ORIGIN C19: alt. of synonymous *travail*, from Fr.

**travolator** ● **n.** variant spelling of TRAVELATOR.

**trawl** ● **v. 1** fish or catch with a trawl net or seine. **2** search thoroughly. ● **n. 1** an act of trawling. **2** (also **trawl net**) a large wide-mouthed fishing net dragged by a boat along the bottom of the sea or a lake. **3** (also **trawl line**) N. Amer. a long sea-fishing line along which are tied buoys supporting baited hooks on short lines.
– ORIGIN C16: prob. from MDu. *traghelen* 'to drag'.

**trawler** ● **n.** a fishing boat used for trawling.

**tray** ● **n.** a flat, shallow container with a raised rim, typically used for carrying or holding things.
– DERIVATIVES **trayful** n. (pl. **-fuls**).
– ORIGIN OE *trīg*, from the Gmc base of TREE.

**trayf** /treɪf/ ● **adj.** another term for TREFA.

**treacherous** ● **adj. 1** guilty of or involving betrayal or deception. **2** (of ground, water, conditions, etc.) having hidden or unpredictable dangers.
– DERIVATIVES **treacherously** adv. **treacherousness** n. **treachery** n.
– ORIGIN ME: from OFr. *trecherous*, from *trecheor* 'a cheat', from *trechier* 'to cheat'.

**treacle** ● **n.** chiefly Brit. molasses. ➤golden syrup.
– DERIVATIVES **treacly** adj.
– ORIGIN ME (orig. denoting an antidote against venom): from OFr. *triacle*, via L. from Gk *thēriakē* 'antidote against venom', fem. of *thēriakos* (adj.), from *thērion* 'wild beast'.

**tread** • v. (past **trod**; past part. **trodden** or **trod**) **1** walk in a specified way. ➤walk on or along. **2** press down or crush with the feet. • n. **1** a manner or the sound of walking. **2** (also **tread board**) the top surface of a step or stair. **3** the thick moulded part of a vehicle tyre that grips the road. ➤the part of a wheel that touches the ground or rail. **4** the part of the sole of a shoe that rests on the ground. **5** the upper surface of a railway track, in contact with the wheels.
– PHRASES **tread** (or **step**) **on someone's toes** offend someone by encroaching on their area of responsibility. **tread water 1** maintain an upright position in deep water by moving the feet with a walking movement and the hands with a downward circular motion. **2** fail to make progress.
– DERIVATIVES **treader** n.
– ORIGIN OE *tredan*, of W. Gmc origin.

**treadle** /'trɛd(ə)l/ • n. a lever worked by the foot and imparting motion to a machine. • v. operate by a treadle.
– ORIGIN OE *tredel* 'stair, step' (see **TREAD**).

**treadmill** • n. **1** a large wheel turned by the weight of people or animals treading on steps fitted into its inner surface, formerly used to drive machinery. **2** a device used for exercise consisting of a continuous moving belt on which to walk or run. **3** a job or situation that is tiring, boring, or unpleasant.

**treadwheel** • n. another term for **TREADMILL** (sense 1).

**treason** • n. **1** (also **high treason**) the crime of betraying one's country, especially by attempting to kill or overthrow the sovereign or government. **2** (**petty treason**) historical the crime of murdering a master or husband.
– DERIVATIVES **treasonable** adj. **treasonably** adv. **treasonous** adj.
– ORIGIN ME: from Anglo-Norman Fr. *treisoun*, from L. *traditio(n-)*, from *tradere* 'hand over'.

**treasure** • n. **1** a quantity of precious metals, gems, or other valuable objects. ➤a very valuable object. **2** informal a much loved or highly valued person. • v. **1** keep carefully (a valuable or valued item). **2** value highly.
– ORIGIN ME: from OFr. *tresor*, based on Gk *thēsauros* (see **THESAURUS**).

**treasure hunt** • n. a game in which players search for hidden objects by following a trail of clues.

**treasurer** • n. a person appointed to administer or manage the financial assets and liabilities of a society, company, etc. ➤(also **Lord Treasurer** or **Lord High Treasurer**) Brit. historical the head of the Exchequer.
– DERIVATIVES **treasurership** n.

**treasure trove** • n. **1** English Law (abolished in 1996) valuables of unknown ownership that are found hidden and declared the property of the Crown. **2** a hidden store of valuable or delightful things.
– ORIGIN ME: from Anglo-Norman Fr. *tresor trové*, lit. 'found treasure'.

**treasury** • n. (pl. **-ies**) **1** the funds or revenue of a state, institution, or society. ➤(**Treasury**) (in some countries) the government department responsible for the overall management of the economy. **2** a place where treasure is stored. **3** a collection of valuable or delightful things.
– ORIGIN ME: from OFr. *tresorie* (see **TREASURE**).

**Treasury bench** • n. (in the UK) the front bench in the House of Commons occupied by the Prime Minister, the Chancellor of the Exchequer, and other members of the government.

**Treasury bill** • n. a short-dated UK or US government security, yielding no interest but issued at a discount on its redemption price.

**Treasury note** • n. US & historical a note issued by the Treasury for use as currency.

**treat** • v. **1** behave towards or deal with in a certain way. ➤present or discuss (a subject). **2** give medical care or attention to. **3** apply a process or a substance to. **4** (**treat someone to**) provide someone with (food, drink, or entertainment) at one's expense. ➤(**treat oneself**) do or have something very pleasurable. **5** (usu. **treat with**) negotiate terms. • n. **1** a surprise gift, event, etc. that gives great pleasure. **2** (**one's treat**) an act of treating someone to something.
– PHRASES —— **a treat** Brit. informal doing something specified very well: *their tactics worked a treat.* ➤(**look a treat**) look attractive.
– DERIVATIVES **treatable** adj. **treater** n.
– ORIGIN ME: from OFr. *traitier*, from L. *tractare* 'handle', frequentative of *trahere* 'draw, pull'.

**treatise** /'tri:tɪs, -ɪz/ • n. a written work dealing formally and systematically with a subject.
– ORIGIN ME: from Anglo-Norman Fr. *tretis*, from OFr. *traitier* (see **TREAT**).

**treatment** • n. **1** the process or manner of treating someone or something in a certain way. ➤the presentation or discussion of a subject. **2** medical care for an illness or injury. **3** the use of a substance or process to preserve or give particular properties to something. **4** (**the full treatment**) informal used to indicate that something is done enthusiastically or vigorously.

**treaty** • n. (pl. **-ies**) a formally concluded and ratified agreement between states.
– ORIGIN ME: from OFr. *traite*, from L. *tractatus* (see **TRACTATE**).

**treaty port** • n. a port bound by treaty to be open to foreign trade, especially in 19th and early 20th-century China and Japan.

**Trebbiano** /ˌtrɛbɪ'ɑːnəʊ/ • n. a variety of wine grape cultivated in Italy and elsewhere. ➤a wine made from this grape.
– ORIGIN Ital., from the name of the River *Trebbia*, in northern Italy.

**treble**[1] • adj. **1** consisting of three parts. **2** multiplied or occurring three times. • predet. three times as much or as many. • n. **1** Brit. three sporting victories or championships in the same season, event, etc. **2** Darts a hit on the narrow ring enclosed by the two middle circles of a dartboard, scoring treble. **3** Brit. a system of betting in which the winnings and stake from the first bet are transferred to a second and then (if successful) to a third. **4** a thing which is three times larger than usual or is made up of three parts. • pron. an amount which is three times as large as usual. • v. make or become treble.
– ORIGIN ME: via OFr. from L. *triplus* (see **TRIPLE**).

**treble**[2] • n. **1** a high-pitched voice, especially a boy's singing voice. **2** [as modifier] denoting a relatively high-pitched member of a family of instruments. ➤(also **treble bell**) the smallest and highest-pitched bell of a ring or set. **3** the high-frequency output of a radio or audio system, corresponding to the treble in music.
– ORIGIN ME: from **TREBLE**[1], because it was the highest part in a three-part contrapuntal composition.

**treble chance** • n. Brit. a form of football pool in which different numbers of points are awarded for a draw, an away win, and a home win.

**treble clef** • n. Music a clef placing G above middle C on the second-lowest line of the stave.

**trebly** • adj. (of sound, especially recorded music) having too much treble. • adv. three times as much.

**trebuchet** /'trɛbjʊʃɛt, -bəʃɛt/ • n. a machine used in medieval siege warfare for hurling large missiles.
– ORIGIN ME: from OFr., from *trebucher* 'overthrow'.

**trecento** /treɪ'tʃɛntəʊ/ • n. (**the trecento**) the 14th century as a period of Italian art, architecture, or literature.
– ORIGIN Ital., lit. '300', shortened from *milletrecento* '1300', used with ref. to the years 1300–99.

**tree** • n. **1** a woody perennial plant typically with a single stem or trunk growing to a considerable height and bearing lateral branches. **2** a wooden structure or part of a structure. ➤archaic or poetic/literary the cross on which Christ was crucified. ➤archaic a gibbet. **3** (also **tree diagram**) a diagram with a structure of branching connecting lines, representing different processes and relationships. • v. (**trees**, **treed**, **treeing**) **1** N. Amer. force (a hunted animal) to take refuge in a tree. **2** informal, chiefly US force into a difficult situation.
– PHRASES **out of one's tree** informal, chiefly N. Amer. crazy. **up a tree** informal, chiefly N. Amer. in a difficult situation without escape.
– DERIVATIVES **treeless** adj. **treelessness** n. **tree-like** adj.

– ORIGIN OE *trēow, trēo*: from Gmc.

**tree calf** • n. calfskin stained with a tree-like design and used in bookbinding.

**treecreeper** • n. a small songbird with drab plumage which creeps about on the trunks of trees to search for insects. [*Certhia familiaris* and related species.]

**tree fern** • n. a large palm-like fern with a trunk-like stem. [*Cyathea, Dicksonia*, and other genera.]

**tree frog** • n. an arboreal frog that has long toes with adhesive disks and is typically small and brightly coloured. [Families Hylidae and Rhacophoridae: many species.]

**tree heath** • n. a white-flowered shrub of the heather family, with woody nodules that are used to make briar pipes. [*Erica arborea*.]

**treehopper** • n. a tree-dwelling jumping bug that lives chiefly in the tropics. [Family Membracidae: numerous species.]

**tree house** • n. a structure built in the branches of a tree for children to play in.

**tree-hugger** • n. informal, chiefly derogatory an environmental campaigner (used in reference to the practice of embracing a tree to prevent it from being felled).

– DERIVATIVES **tree-hugging** n.

**treeline** • n. **1** the altitude above which no trees grow on a mountain. **2** (in high northern (or southern) latitudes) the line north (or south) of which no trees grow.

**tree mallow** • n. a tall woody-stemmed mallow of coastal regions. [*Lavatera arborea*.]

**treen** • n. [treated as pl.] small domestic wooden antiques.

– ORIGIN OE *trēowen* 'wooden' (see **TREE**, **-EN**[2]).

**treenail** (also **trenail** or US **trunnel**) • n. a hard wooden pin used for fastening timbers together.

**tree of heaven** • n. a tall, fast-growing Chinese tree, cultivated as an ornamental and shade tree. [*Ailanthus altissima*.]

**tree of knowledge** (also **tree of knowledge of good and evil**) • n. (in the Bible) the tree in the Garden of Eden bearing the forbidden fruit which Adam and Eve disobediently ate (Gen. 2:9, 3).

**tree of life** • n. **1** (**Tree of Life**) (in the Bible) a tree in the Garden of Eden whose fruit imparts eternal life (Gen. 3:22–24). **2** the thuja or arbor vitae.

**tree pie** • n. a long-tailed tree-dwelling Asian crow, with blackish or brown and grey plumage. [*Dendrocitta* and other genera.]

– ORIGIN C19: *pie* from **PIE**[2].

**tree ring** • n. each of a number of concentric rings in the cross section of a tree trunk, representing a single year's growth.

**tree shrew** • n. a small squirrel-like insectivorous mammal with a pointed snout, native to SE Asia. [*Tupaia* and other genera.]

**tree surgeon** • n. a person who prunes and treats old or damaged trees in order to preserve them.

– DERIVATIVES **tree surgery** n.

**tree toad** • n. another term for **TREE FROG**.

**tree tomato** • n. another term for **TAMARILLO**.

**treetop** • n. (usu. **treetops**) the uppermost part of a tree.

**trefa** /'treɪfə/ (also **trifa** or **trayf**) • adj. (of food) not satisfying the requirements of Jewish law.

– ORIGIN C19: from Heb. *ṭĕrēpāh* 'the flesh of an animal torn or mauled'.

**trefid** /'trɛfɪd/ • adj. variant spelling of **TRIFID** (in sense 2).

**trefoil** /'trɛfɔɪl, 'triːfɔɪl/ • n. **1** a small plant with yellow flowers and three-lobed cloverlike leaves. [Genera *Trifolium* and *Lotus*: several species.] **2** architectural tracery in the form of three rounded lobes like a clover leaf. **3** a thing having three parts, or a set of three.

– DERIVATIVES **trefoiled** adj.

– ORIGIN ME: from Anglo-Norman Fr. *trifoil*, from L. *trifolium*, from *tri-* 'three' + *folium* 'leaf'.

**trehalose** /'triːhələʊs, trɪ'hɑːləʊs, -z/ • n. Chemistry a sugar of the disaccharide class produced by some fungi, yeasts, and similar organisms.

– ORIGIN C19: from *trehala* (from Turk., denoting a sweet substance derived from insect cocoons) + **-OSE**[2].

**trek** • n. a long arduous journey, especially one made on foot. ➤ S. African a leg or stage of a journey. • v. (**trekked, trekking**) go on a trek. ➤ historical, chiefly S. African migrate or journey by ox-wagon. ➤ S. African (of an ox) draw a vehicle or pull a load.

– DERIVATIVES **trekker** n.

– ORIGIN C19: from S. Afr. Du. *trek* (n.), *trekken* (v.) 'pull, travel'.

**Trekkie** • n. (pl. **-ies**) informal a fan of the US science-fiction television programme *Star Trek*.

**trellis** • n. a framework of light wooden or metal bars used as a support for trees or creepers. • v. (**trellised, trellising**) [usu. as adj. **trellised**] provide or support with a trellis.

– ORIGIN ME (denoting any latticed screen): from OFr. *trelis*, from L. *trilix* 'three-ply', from *tri-* 'three' + *licium* 'warp thread'.

**Trematoda** /ˌtrɛmə'təʊdə/ • pl. n. Zoology a class of flatworms that comprises those flukes that are internal parasites.

– DERIVATIVES **trematode** /'trɛmətəʊd/ n.

– ORIGIN mod. L., from Gk *trēmatōdēs* 'perforated', from *trēma* 'hole'.

**tremble** • v. shake involuntarily, typically as a result of anxiety, excitement, or frailty. ➤ be in a state of extreme apprehension. ➤ (of a thing) shake or quiver slightly. • n. **1** a trembling feeling, movement, or sound. **2** (**the trembles**) informal a physical or emotional condition marked by trembling.

– PHRASES **all of a tremble** informal extremely agitated or excited.

– DERIVATIVES **trembling** adj. **tremblingly** adv. **trembly** adj. (**-ier, -iest**) (informal).

– ORIGIN ME: from OFr. *trembler*, from med. L. *tremulare*, from L. *tremulus* (see **TREMULOUS**).

**trembler** • n. Brit. an automatic vibrator for making and breaking an electric circuit.

**trembling poplar** • n. the European aspen.

**tremendous** • adj. **1** very great in amount, scale, or intensity. ➤ archaic inspiring awe or dread. **2** informal extremely good or impressive; excellent.

– DERIVATIVES **tremendously** adv. **tremendousness** n.

– ORIGIN C17: from L. *tremendus* (gerundive of *tremere* 'tremble') + **-OUS**.

**tremolando** /ˌtrɛmə'landəʊ/ • n. (pl. **tremolandi**) Music another term for **TREMOLO**.

– ORIGIN Ital., lit. 'trembling'.

**tremolite** /'trɛm(ə)lʌɪt/ • n. a white to grey amphibole mineral which occurs widely in igneous rocks and is characteristic of metamorphosed dolomitic limestones.

– ORIGIN C18: from *Tremola* Valley, Switzerland, + **-ITE**[1].

**tremolo** • n. (pl. **-os**) Music a wavering effect in singing or playing some musical instruments. ➤ (also **tremolo arm**) a lever on an electric guitar used to produce such an effect.

– ORIGIN C18: from Ital.

**tremor** • n. **1** an involuntary quivering movement. ➤ (also **earth tremor**) a slight earthquake. **2** a sudden feeling of fear or excitement. • v. undergo a tremor or tremors.

– ORIGIN C17: from L. *tremor*, from *tremere* 'to tremble'.

**tremulous** /'trɛmjʊləs/ • adj. shaking or quivering slightly. ➤ timid; nervous.

– DERIVATIVES **tremulously** adv. **tremulousness** n.

– ORIGIN C17: from L. *tremulus* (from *tremere* 'tremble') + **-OUS**.

**trenail** • n. variant spelling of **TREENAIL**.

**trench** • n. **1** a long, narrow ditch. ➤ a ditch of this type dug by troops to provide shelter from enemy fire. **2** (also **ocean trench**) a long, narrow, deep depression in the ocean bed, typically running parallel to a plate boundary and marking a subduction zone. • v. **1** dig a trench or trenches in. ➤ turn over the earth of (a field or garden) by digging a succession of adjoining ditches. **2** (**trench on/upon**) archaic border closely on; encroach upon.

– ORIGIN ME (in the senses 'track cut through a wood' and

'sever by cutting'): from OFr. *trenche* (n.), *trenchier* (v.), based on L. *truncare* (see **TRUNCATE**).

**trenchant** /ˈtrɛn(t)ʃ(ə)nt/ • **adj. 1** vigorous or incisive in expression or style. **2** archaic or poetic/literary (of a weapon or tool) having a sharp edge.
– DERIVATIVES **trenchancy** n. **trenchantly** adv.
– ORIGIN ME: from OFr., lit. 'cutting', pres. part. of *trenchier* (see **TRENCH**).

**trench coat** • **n. 1** a loose belted, double-breasted raincoat in a military style. **2** a lined or padded waterproof coat worn by soldiers.

**trencher**[1] • **n. 1** historical a wooden plate or platter. **2** old-fashioned term for **MORTAR BOARD** (in sense 1).
– ORIGIN ME: from Anglo-Norman Fr. *trenchour*, from OFr. *trenchier* (see **TRENCH**).

**trencher**[2] • **n.** a machine or attachment used in digging trenches.

**trencherman** • **n.** (pl. **-men**) humorous a person who eats heartily or in a specified manner.

**trench fever** • **n.** a highly contagious rickettsial disease transmitted by lice, that infested soldiers in the trenches in the First World War.

**trench foot** • **n.** a painful condition of the feet caused by long immersion in cold water or mud and marked by blackening and death of surface tissue.

**trench mortar** • **n.** a light simple mortar designed to propel a bomb into enemy trenches.

**trench mouth** • **n.** ulcerative gingivitis.

**trench warfare** • **n.** a type of combat in which opposing troops fight from trenches facing each other.

**trend** • **n. 1** a general direction in which something is developing or changing. **2** a fashion. • **v.** (especially of a geographical feature) bend or turn away in a specified direction. ➤chiefly N. Amer. change or develop in a general direction.
– ORIGIN OE *trendan* 'revolve, rotate', of Gmc origin; cf. **TRUNDLE**.

**trendify** • **v.** informal, chiefly derogatory make fashionable.

**trendsetter** • **n.** a person who leads the way in fashion or ideas.
– DERIVATIVES **trendsetting** adj.

**trendy** informal • **adj.** (**-ier**, **-iest**) very fashionable or up to date. • **n.** (pl. **-ies**) a person of this type.
– DERIVATIVES **trendily** adv. **trendiness** n.

**trente et quarante** /ˌtrɒ̃teɪkaˈrɒ̃t, French trɑ̃tekaʀɑ̃t/ • **n.** a gambling game in which cards are turned up on a table marked with red and black diamonds.
– ORIGIN Fr., lit. 'thirty and forty', these being winning and losing numbers respectively in the game.

**trepan** /trɪˈpan/ • **n. 1** chiefly historical a trephine (hole saw) used by surgeons for perforating the skull. **2** a borer for sinking shafts. • **v.** (**trepanned**, **trepanning**) perforate (a person's skull) with a trepan.
– DERIVATIVES **trepanation** /ˌtrɛpəˈneɪʃ(ə)n/ n.
– ORIGIN ME: the noun via med. L. from Gk *trupanon*, from *trupan* 'to bore', from *trupē* 'hole'; the verb from OFr. *trepaner*.

**trepang** /trɪˈpaŋ/ • **n.** another term for **BÊCHE-DE-MER** (in sense 1).
– ORIGIN C18: from Malay *teripang*.

**trephine** /trɪˈfʌɪn, -ˈfiːn/ • **n.** a hole saw used in surgery to remove a circle of tissue or bone. • **v.** operate on with a trephine.
– DERIVATIVES **trephination** /ˌtrɛfɪˈneɪʃ(ə)n/ n.
– ORIGIN C17: from L. *tres fines* 'three ends', appar. influenced by **TREPAN**.

**trepidation** • **n. 1** a feeling of fear or agitation about something that may happen. **2** archaic trembling motion.
– ORIGIN C15: from L. *trepidatio(n-)*, from *trepidare* 'be agitated, tremble'.

**treponeme** /ˈtrɛpəniːm/ (also **treponema** /-ə/) • **n.** a spirochaete bacterium of a genus (*Treponema*) including the causal agents of syphilis and yaws.
– DERIVATIVES **treponemal** adj.
– ORIGIN C20: from mod. L. *Treponema*, from Gk *trepein* 'to turn' + *nēma* 'thread'.

**trespass** • **v. 1** enter someone's land or property without their permission. ➤(**trespass on**) make unfair claims on or take advantage of (something). **2** (**trespass against**) archaic or poetic/literary commit an offence against (a person or a set of rules). • **n. 1** Law entry to a person's land or property without their permission. **2** archaic or poetic/literary a sin; an offence.
– DERIVATIVES **trespasser** n.
– ORIGIN ME: from OFr. *trespasser* 'pass over, trespass', *trespas* 'passing across', from med. L. *transpassare* (see **TRANS-**, **PASS**[1]).

**tress** • **n.** a long lock of a woman's hair. • **v.** archaic arrange (a person's hair) into long locks.
– DERIVATIVES **-tressed** adj. **tressy** adj.
– ORIGIN ME: from OFr. *tresse*, perh. based on Gk *trikha* 'threefold'.

**tressure** /ˈtrɛʃə, ˈtrɛs(j)ʊə/ • **n. 1** Heraldry a thin border inset from the edge of a shield, narrower than an orle and usually borne double. **2** an ornamental enclosure formerly found on some coins.
– ORIGIN ME (denoting a ribbon or band for the hair): from OFr. *tressour* (see **TRESS**).

**trestle** • **n. 1** a framework consisting of a horizontal beam supported by two pairs of sloping legs, used in pairs to support a flat surface such as a table top. **2** (also **trestlework**) an open braced framework used to support an elevated structure such as a bridge. **3** (also **trestle-tree**) each of a pair of horizontal pieces on a sailing ship's lower mast supporting the topmast.
– ORIGIN ME: from OFr. *trestel*, based on L. *transtrum* 'beam'.

**trestle table** • **n.** a table consisting of a board or boards laid on trestles.

**tret** /trɛt/ • **n.** historical an allowance of extra weight made to purchasers of certain goods to compensate for waste during transportation.
– ORIGIN C15: from an OFr. var. of *trait* (see **TRAIT**).

**trevally** /trɪˈvali/ • **n.** (pl. **-ies**) a marine sporting fish of the Indo-Pacific. [*Caranx* and other genera: several species.]
– ORIGIN C19: prob. an alt. of *cavally* 'horse mackerel', from Sp. *caballo* 'horse'.

**trews** /truːz/ • **pl. n.** chiefly Brit. trousers. ➤close-fitting tartan trousers worn by certain Scottish regiments.
– ORIGIN C16: from Ir. *triús*, Sc. Gaelic *triubhas* (sing.); cf. **TROUSERS**.

**trey** /treɪ/ • **n.** (pl. **-eys**) **1** a playing card or dice with three spots. **2** Basketball a shot scoring three points.
– ORIGIN ME: from OFr. *trei* 'three', from L. *tres*.

**TRH** • **abbrev. 1** Their Royal Highnesses. **2** Biochemistry thyrotropin-releasing hormone.

**tri-** /trʌɪ/ • **comb. form** three; having three: *triathlon*. ➤Chemistry (in names of compounds) containing three atoms or groups of a specified kind: *trichloroethane*.
– ORIGIN from L. and Gk, from L. *tres*, Gk *treis* 'three'.

**triable** /ˈtrʌɪəb(ə)l/ • **adj.** Law (of an offence or case) liable to a judicial trial.

**triac** /ˈtrʌɪak/ • **n.** Electronics a three-electrode semiconductor device that will conduct in either direction when triggered by a positive or negative signal at the gate electrode.
– ORIGIN 1960s: from **TRIODE** + **AC** (short for *alternating current*).

**triacetate** /trʌɪˈasɪteɪt/ (also **cellulose triacetate**) • **n.** a form of cellulose acetate containing three acetate groups per glucose monomer, used as a basis for man-made fibres.

**triad** /ˈtrʌɪad/ • **n. 1** a group or set of three connected people or things. ➤a chord of three musical notes, consisting of a given note with the third and fifth above it. ➤a Welsh form of literary composition with an arrangement of subjects or statements in groups of three. **2** a Chinese secret society involved in organized crime. ➤a member of such a society.
– DERIVATIVES **triadic** adj.
– ORIGIN C16: from Fr. *triade*, or via late L. from Gk *trias*, *triad-*, from *treis* 'three'.

**triage** /ˈtrʌɪɪdʒ/ • **n. 1** the action of sorting according to quality. **2** Medicine the assignment of degrees of urgency to

wounds or illnesses to decide the order of treatment of a large number of patients.
– ORIGIN C18: from Fr., from *trier* 'separate out'.

**trial** • n. **1** a formal examination of evidence in order to decide guilt in a case of criminal or civil proceedings. **2** a test of performance, qualities, or suitability. ➤ a sports match to test the ability of players eligible for selection to a team. ➤ a test of individual ability on a motorcycle. ➤ (**trials**) an event in which horses or dogs compete or perform. **3** something that tests a person's endurance or forbearance. • v. (**trialled**, **trialling**; US **trialed**, **trialing**) **1** test (something) to assess its suitability or performance. **2** (of a horse or dog) compete in trials.
– PHRASES **on trial 1** being tried in a court of law. **2** undergoing tests or scrutiny. **trial and error** the process of experimenting with various methods until one finds the most successful.
– ORIGIN ME: from Anglo-Norman Fr., or from med. L. *triallum*.

**trial balance** • n. a statement of all debits and credits in a double-entry account book, with any disagreement indicating an error.

**trial balloon** • n. a tentative measure taken or statement made to see how a new policy will be received.

**trial court** • n. chiefly N. Amer. a court of law where cases are first tried, as opposed to an appeal court.

**trialist** (Brit. also **triallist**) • n. a person who participates in a sports trial or a trial of a new product.

**trial lawyer** • n. N. Amer. a lawyer who practises in a trial court.

**trialogue** • n. a dialogue between three people.
– ORIGIN C16: formed irregularly from **TRI-** + **DIALOGUE** (the prefix *di-* misinterpreted as 'two').

**trial run** • n. a preliminary test of a new system or product.

**triangle** • n. **1** a plane figure with three straight sides and three angles. **2** something in the form of a triangle. ➤ N. Amer. a drawing instrument in the form of a right-angled triangle. ➤ (**triangles**) historical a frame of three halberds joined at the top to which a soldier was bound for flogging. **3** a musical instrument consisting of a steel rod bent into a triangle, sounded with a rod. **4** an emotional relationship involving a couple and a third person with whom one of them is involved. **5** a small brownish moth of oak and beech woods. [*Heterogenea asella*.]
– ORIGIN ME: from OFr. *triangle* or L. *triangulum*, neut. of *triangulus* (see **TRI-**, **ANGLE**[1]).

**triangle of forces** • n. Physics a triangle whose sides represent in magnitude and direction three forces in equilibrium.

**triangular** • adj. shaped like a triangle. ➤ involving three people or parties. ➤ (of a pyramid) having a three-sided base.
– DERIVATIVES **triangularity** n. **triangularly** adv.

**triangular number** • n. any of the series of numbers (1, 3, 6, 10, 15, etc.) obtained by continued summation of the natural numbers 1, 2, 3, 4, 5, etc.

**triangular trade** • n. a multilateral system of trading in which a country pays for its imports from one country by its exports to another.

**triangulate** • v. /trʌɪˈaŋgjʊleɪt/ **1** divide (an area) into triangles for surveying purposes. ➤ measure and map (an area) by the use of triangles with a known base length and base angles. ➤ determine (a height, distance, or location) in this way. **2** form into a triangle or triangles.

**triangulation** • n. **1** (in surveying) the tracing and measurement of a series or network of triangles in order to determine the distances and relative positions of points spread over a territory or region. **2** formation of or division into triangles.

**triangulation point** • n. another term for **TRIG POINT**.

**Triassic** /trʌɪˈasɪk/ • adj. Geology relating to or denoting the earliest period of the Mesozoic era (between the Permian and Jurassic periods, about 245 to 208 million years ago), a time when the first dinosaurs, ammonites, and primitive mammals appeared.
– ORIGIN C19: from late L. *trias* (see **TRIAD**), because the strata are divisible into three groups, + **-IC**.

**triathlon** /trʌɪˈaθlɒn, -lən/ • n. an athletic contest consisting of three different events, typically swimming, cycling, and long-distance running.
– DERIVATIVES **triathlete** n.
– ORIGIN 1970s: from **TRI-**, on the pattern of *decathlon*.

**triatomic** /ˌtrʌɪəˈtɒmɪk/ • adj. Chemistry consisting of three atoms.

**triaxial** /trʌɪˈaksɪəl/ • adj. having or relating to three axes, especially in mechanical or astronomical contexts.

**triazine** /ˈtrʌɪəziːn, trʌɪˈaziːn, -zɪn/ • n. Chemistry a compound whose molecule contains an unsaturated ring of three carbon and three nitrogen atoms.

**tribade** /ˈtrɪbəd/ • n. rare a lesbian.
– DERIVATIVES **tribadism** n.
– ORIGIN C17: from Fr. *tribade*, or via L. from Gk *tribas*, from *tribein* 'to rub'.

**tribal** • adj. of or characteristic of a tribe or tribes. ➤ chiefly derogatory characterized by a tendency to form groups or by strong group loyalty. • n. (**tribals**) members of tribal communities, especially in the Indian subcontinent.
– DERIVATIVES **tribalism** n. **tribalist** n. **tribalistic** adj. **tribally** adv.

**tribasic** /trʌɪˈbeɪsɪk/ • adj. Chemistry (of an acid) having three replaceable hydrogen atoms.

**tribe** • n. **1** a social division in a traditional society consisting of linked families or communities with a common culture and dialect. ➤ (in ancient Rome) each of several (originally three) political divisions. ➤ derogatory a distinctive close-knit social or political group. ➤ (**tribes**) informal large numbers of people. **2** Biology a taxonomic category that ranks above genus and below family or subfamily.
– ORIGIN ME: from OFr. *tribu* or L. *tribus* (sing. and pl.); perh. rel. to *tri-* 'three' and referring to the three divisions of the early people of Rome.

**USAGE tribe**

In historical contexts, the word **tribe** is unexceptionable (*the area was inhabited by Slavic tribes*). However, in contemporary contexts, used to refer to traditional societies today, use of the word can be problematic, associated, as it is, with past attitudes of white colonialists towards so-called primitive or uncivilized peoples. For this reason, it is generally preferable to use alternative terms such as **community** or **people**.

**tribesman** (or **tribeswoman**) • n. (pl. **-men**, **-women**) a member of a tribe in a traditional society.

**triblet** /ˈtrɪblɪt/ • n. a cylindrical rod used for forging nuts, tubes, and other rounded metallic objects.
– ORIGIN C17: from Fr. *triboulet*, of unknown origin.

**tribo-** /ˈtrʌɪbəʊ, ˈtrɪbəʊ/ • comb. form relating to friction: *triboelectricity*.
– ORIGIN from Gk *tribos* 'rubbing'.

**triboelectricity** • n. electric charge generated by friction.

**tribology** /trʌɪˈbɒlədʒi/ • n. the branch of science and technology concerned with surfaces in relative motion, as in bearings.
– DERIVATIVES **tribological** adj. **tribologist** n.

**triboluminescence** • n. the emission of light from a substance caused by rubbing, scratching, or similar frictional contact.
– DERIVATIVES **triboluminescent** adj.

**tribometer** /trʌɪˈbɒmɪtə/ • n. an instrument for measuring friction in sliding.

**tribrach** /ˈtrʌɪbrak, ˈtrɪ-/ • n. Prosody a metrical foot of three short or unstressed syllables.
– DERIVATIVES **tribrachic** /-ˈbrakɪk/ adj.
– ORIGIN C16: via L. from Gk *tribrakhus*, from *tri-* 'three' + *brakhus* 'short'.

**tribulation** /ˌtrɪbjʊˈleɪʃ(ə)n/ • n. a state of great trouble or suffering. ➤ a cause of this.
– ORIGIN ME: via OFr. from eccles. L. *tribulatio(n-)*, from L. *tribulare* 'press, oppress', based on *terere* 'rub'.

**tribunal** /trʌɪˈbjuːn(ə)l, trɪ-/ • n. **1** Brit. a body established to settle certain types of dispute. **2** a court of justice. **3** a seat or bench for a judge or judges.

– ORIGIN ME: from OFr., or from L. *tribunal* 'raised platform provided for magistrate's seats', from *tribunus* (see **TRIBUNE**[1]).

**tribune**[1] • **n. 1** (also **tribune of the people**) an official in ancient Rome chosen by the plebeians to protect their interests. ➤(also **military tribune**) a Roman legionary officer. **2** a popular leader; a champion of the people.
– DERIVATIVES **tribunate** n. **tribuneship** n.
– ORIGIN ME: from L. *tribunus*, lit. 'head of a tribe', from *tribus* 'tribe'.

**tribune**[2] • **n. 1** an apse in a basilica. **2** a dais, rostrum, or other raised area, especially in a church.
– ORIGIN C17 (denoting the principal room in an Ital. mansion): via Fr. from Ital., from med. L. *tribuna*, alt. of L. *tribunal* (see **TRIBUNAL**).

**tributary** /ˈtrɪbjʊt(ə)ri/ • **n.** (pl. **-ies**) **1** a river or stream flowing into a larger river or lake. **2** historical a person or state that pays tribute to another state or ruler.
– ORIGIN ME: from L. *tributarius*, from *tributum* (see **TRIBUTE**).

**tribute** • **n. 1** an act, statement, or gift that is intended to show gratitude, respect, or admiration. ➤something resulting from and indicating the worth of something else: *his victory was a tribute to his persistence.* **2** historical payment made periodically by one state or ruler to another, especially as a sign of dependence. **3** historical a proportion of ore or its equivalent, paid to a miner for his work, or to the owner or lessor of a mine.
– ORIGIN ME: from L. *tributum*, neut. past part. (used as n.) of *tribuere* 'assign' (orig. 'divide between tribes'), from *tribus* 'tribe'.

**tricameral** /trʌɪˈkam(ə)r(ə)l/ • **adj.** (in South Africa 1983–94) of or denoting the system whereby the legislature consisted of three ethnically based houses.

**tricar** /ˈtrʌɪkɑː/ • **n.** Brit. dated a three-wheeled motor car.

**tricast** /ˈtrʌɪkɑːst/ • **n.** Brit. a bet in which the first three horses in a race are forecast in the correct order.
– ORIGIN 1970s: from **TRI-** + **FORECAST**.

**trice** /trʌɪs/ • **n.** (in phr. **in a trice**) in a moment; very quickly.
– ORIGIN ME *trice* 'a tug', figuratively 'an instant', from MDu. *trīsen* 'pull sharply', rel. to *trīse* 'pulley'.

**tricentenary** • **n.** (pl. **-ies**) another term for **TERCENTENARY**.
– DERIVATIVES **tricentennial** adj. & n.

**triceps** /ˈtrʌɪsɛps/ • **n.** (pl. same) Anatomy any of several muscles having three points of attachment at one end, particularly (also **triceps brachii** /ˈbreɪkɪʌɪ/) the large muscle at the back of the upper arm.
– ORIGIN C16: from L., lit. 'three-headed', from *tri-* 'three' + *-ceps* (from *caput* 'head').

**triceratops** /trʌɪˈsɛrətɒps/ • **n.** a large quadrupedal herbivorous dinosaur living at the end of the Cretaceous period, having a massive head with two large horns, a smaller horn on the beaked snout, and a bony frill above the neck.
– ORIGIN mod. L., from Gk *trikeratos* 'three-horned' + *ōps* 'face'.

**trichiasis** /ˌtrɪkɪˈeɪsɪs, trɪˈkʌɪəsɪs/ • **n.** Medicine ingrowth or introversion of the eyelashes.
– ORIGIN C17: via late L. from Gk *trikhiasis*, from *trikhian* 'be hairy'.

**trichina** /ˈtrɪkɪnə, trɪˈkʌɪnə/ • **n.** (pl. **trichinae** /-niː/) a parasitic nematode worm of humans and other mammals, the adults of which live in the small intestine. [Genus *Trichinella*.]
– ORIGIN C19: from mod. L. (former genus name), from Gk *trikhinos* 'of hair'.

**trichinosis** /ˌtrɪkɪˈnəʊsɪs/ • **n.** a disease caused by trichinae, typically from infected meat, characterized by digestive disturbance, fever, and muscular rigidity.

**trichloroethane** /ˌtrʌɪklɔːrəʊˈiːθeɪn, -klɒr-/ • **n.** Chemistry a colourless non-flammable volatile liquid, used as a solvent and cleaner.

**trichlorophenol** /ˌtrʌɪklɔːrə(ʊ)ˈfiːnɒl, -klɒr-/ • **n.** Chemistry a synthetic crystalline compound used as an insecticide and preservative and in the synthesis of pesticides.

**tricho-** /ˈtrɪkəʊ, ˈtrʌɪkəʊ/ • **comb. form** of or relating to hair: *trichology*.
– ORIGIN from Gk *thrix*, *trikhos* 'hair'.

**trichology** /trɪˈkɒlədʒi/ • **n.** the branch of medical and cosmetic study and practice concerned with the hair and scalp.
– DERIVATIVES **trichological** adj. **trichologist** n.

**trichome** /ˈtrʌɪkəʊm, ˈtrɪ-/ • **n.** Botany a small hair or other outgrowth from the epidermis of a plant, typically unicellular and glandular.
– ORIGIN C19: from Gk *trikhōma*, from *trikhoun* 'cover with hair'.

**trichomonad** /ˌtrɪkə(ʊ)ˈmɒnad/ • **n.** Zoology & Medicine a parasitic protozoan of an order (Trichomonadida) with four to six flagella, infesting the urogenital or digestive system.
– DERIVATIVES **trichomonal** adj.
– ORIGIN C19: from mod. L. *Trichomonadida*, from Gk *thrix*, *trikh-* 'hair' + *monas*, *monad-* 'unit'.

**trichomoniasis** /ˌtrɪkə(ʊ)məˈnʌɪəsɪs/ • **n.** Medicine infection with parasitic trichomonads.

**Trichoptera** /trʌɪˈkɒpt(ə)rə/ • **pl. n.** Entomology an order of insects that comprises the caddis flies.
– DERIVATIVES **trichopteran** n. & adj.
– ORIGIN mod. L., from **TRICHO-** + *pteron* 'wing'.

**trichotomy** /trʌɪˈkɒtəmi, trɪ-/ • **n.** (pl. **-ies**) a division into three categories.
– DERIVATIVES **trichotomous** adj.
– ORIGIN C17: from Gk *trikha* 'threefold', on the pattern of *dichotomy*.

**trichroic** /trʌɪˈkrəʊɪk/ • **adj.** Crystallography (of a crystal) appearing with different colours when viewed along the three crystallographic directions.
– DERIVATIVES **trichroism** /ˈtrʌɪkrəʊɪz(ə)m/ n.
– ORIGIN C19: from Gk *trikhroos* (from *tri-* 'three' + *khrōs* 'colour') + **-IC**.

**trichromatic** /ˌtrʌɪkrəˈmatɪk/ • **adj. 1** having or using three colours. **2** having normal colour vision, which is sensitive to all three primary colours.
– DERIVATIVES **trichromatism** n.

**trick** • **n. 1** a cunning or skilful act or scheme intended to deceive or outwit someone. ➤a mischievous practical joke. ➤a skilful act performed for entertainment. ➤an illusion: *a trick of the light.* ➤[as modifier] intended to mystify or create an illusion: *a trick question.* ➤[as modifier] N. Amer. liable to fail; defective: *a trick knee.* **2** a peculiar or characteristic habit or mannerism. **3** (in bridge, whist, etc.) a sequence of cards forming a single round of play. **4** informal a prostitute's client. **5** a sailor's turn at the helm, usually lasting for two or four hours. • **v. 1** deceive or outwit with cunning or skill. ➤(**trick someone into/out of**) deceive someone into doing or parting with. **2** (**trick someone out/up**) dress or decorate someone in an elaborate or showy way. **3** Heraldry sketch (a coat of arms) in outline, with the colours indicated by letters or signs.
– PHRASES **do the trick** informal achieve the required result. **how's tricks?** informal how are you? **trick or treat** chiefly N. Amer. a children's custom of calling at houses at Halloween with the threat of pranks if they are not given a small gift. **tricks of the trade** special ingenious techniques used in a profession or craft. **turn a trick** informal (of a prostitute) have a session with a client. **up to one's (old) tricks** informal misbehaving in a characteristic way.
– DERIVATIVES **tricker** n. **trickery** n. **trickish** adj. (dated).
– ORIGIN ME: from an OFr. dial. var. of *triche*, from *trichier* 'deceive', of unknown origin.

**trick cyclist** • **n.** Brit. humorous a psychiatrist.

**trickle** • **v. 1** (of a liquid) flow in a small stream. **2** (**trickle down**) (of wealth) gradually benefit the poorest as a result of the increasing wealth of the richest. **3** come or go slowly or gradually. • **n. 1** a small flow of liquid. **2** a small group or number of people or things moving slowly.
– ORIGIN ME: imitative.

**trickle charger** • **n.** an electrical charger for batteries that works at a steady slow rate from the mains.

**trickster** • **n.** a person who cheats or deceives people.

**tricksy** • **adj.** (**-ier**, **-iest**) clever in an ingenious or deceptive way. ➤(of a person) playful or mischievous.
– DERIVATIVES **tricksily** adv. **tricksiness** n.

**tricky** • **adj.** (**-ier**, **-iest**) **1** requiring care and skill because difficult or awkward. **2** deceitful, crafty, or skilful.
– DERIVATIVES **trickily** adv. **trickiness** n.

**triclinic** /trʌɪˈklɪnɪk/ • **adj.** denoting a crystal system with three unequal oblique axes.
– ORIGIN C19: from Gk **TRI-** + *-clinic*, on the pattern of *monoclinic*.

**triclinium** /trʌɪˈklɪnɪəm, trɪ-, -ˈklʌɪn-/ • **n.** (pl. **triclinia** /-nɪə/) a dining table with couches along three sides, used in ancient Rome. ➤a room containing such a table.
– ORIGIN L., from Gk *triklinion*, from *tri-* 'three' + *klinē* 'couch'.

**tricolour** /ˈtrɪkələ, ˈtrʌɪkʌlə/ (US **tricolor**) • **n.** a flag with three bands or blocks of different colours, especially the French national flag with equal upright bands of blue, white, and red. • **adj.** (also **tricoloured**) having three colours.

**tricorne** /ˈtrʌɪkɔːn/ (also **tricorn**) • **adj.** (of a hat) having a brim turned up on three sides. • **n.** a tricorne hat.
– ORIGIN C19: from Fr. *tricorne* or L. *tricornis*, from *tri-* 'three' + *cornu* 'horn'.

**tricot** /ˈtrɪkəʊ, ˈtriː-/ • **n.** a fine knitted fabric made of a natural or man-made fibre.
– ORIGIN C18: from Fr., lit. 'knitting', from *tricoter* 'to knit'.

**tric-trac** • **n.** historical a form of backgammon.
– ORIGIN C17: from Fr., from the clicking sound made by the game pieces.

**tricuspid** /trʌɪˈkʌspɪd/ • **adj.** **1** denoting a tooth with three cusps or points. **2** relating to or denoting a valve formed of three triangular segments, particularly that between the right atrium and ventricle of the heart.
– ORIGIN C17: from **TRI-** + L. *cuspis, cuspid-* 'cusp'.

**tricycle** • **n.** a vehicle similar to a bicycle, but having three wheels, two at the back and one at the front. ➤a three-wheeled motor vehicle for a disabled driver. • **v.** [often as noun **tricycling**] ride on a tricycle.
– DERIVATIVES **tricyclist** n.

**tricyclic** /trʌɪˈsʌɪklɪk/ • **adj.** Chemistry having three rings of atoms in its molecule. • **n.** Medicine any of a class of antidepressant drugs having molecules with three fused rings.

**tridactyl** /trʌɪˈdaktɪl/ • **adj.** Zoology having three toes or fingers.
– DERIVATIVES **tridactyly** n.
– ORIGIN C19: from **TRI-** + Gk *daktulos* 'finger'.

**trident** • **n.** a three-pronged spear, especially as an attribute of Poseidon (Neptune) or Britannia.
– ORIGIN ME: from L. *trident-*, from *tri-* 'three' + *dens, dent-* 'tooth'.

**Tridentine** /trɪˈdɛntʌɪn, trʌɪ-/ • **adj.** of or relating to the Council of Trent (1545–63), especially as the basis of Roman Catholic doctrine.
– ORIGIN from med. L. *Tridentinus*, from *Tridentum* 'Trent'.

**Tridentine mass** • **n.** the Latin Eucharistic liturgy used by the Roman Catholic Church from 1570 to 1964.

**triduum** /ˈtrɪdjʊəm, ˈtrʌɪ-/ • **n.** (especially in the Roman Catholic Church) a period of three days' observance, specifically Maundy Thursday, Good Friday, and Holy Saturday.
– ORIGIN L., from *tri-* 'three' + *dies* 'day'.

**tridymite** /ˈtrɪdɪmʌɪt/ • **n.** a high-temperature form of quartz found as thin hexagonal crystals in some igneous rocks and stony meteorites.
– ORIGIN C19: from Ger. *Tridymit*, from Gk *tridumos* 'threefold', because it occurs in groups of three crystals.

**tried** past and past participle of **TRY**.

**triene** /ˈtrʌɪiːn/ • **n.** Chemistry an unsaturated hydrocarbon containing three double bonds between carbon atoms.

**triennial** /trʌɪˈɛnɪəl/ • **adj.** lasting for or recurring every three years. • **n.** a visitation of an Anglican diocese by its bishop every three years.
– DERIVATIVES **triennially** adv.
– ORIGIN C16: from late L. *triennis* (from L. *tri-* 'three' + *annus* 'year') + **-AL**.

**triennium** /trʌɪˈɛnɪəm/ • **n.** (pl. **triennia** /-nɪə/ or **trienniums**) a period of three years.
– ORIGIN C19: from L., from *tri-* 'three' + *annum* 'year'.

**trier** • **n.** **1** a person who always makes an effort, however unsuccessful they may be. **2** a person or body responsible for trying a judicial case.

**trifa** /ˈtrʌɪfə/ • **adj.** another term for **TREFA**.

**trifacial nerves** /trʌɪˈfeɪʃ(ə)l/ • **pl. n.** another term for **TRIGEMINAL NERVES**.

**trifecta** /trʌɪˈfɛktə/ • **n.** N. Amer. & Austral./NZ a bet in which the person betting correctly forecasts the first three finishers in the correct order.
– ORIGIN 1970s: from **TRI-** + **PERFECTA**.

**trifid** /ˈtrʌɪfɪd/ • **adj.** **1** chiefly Biology partly or wholly split into three divisions or lobes. **2** (also **trefid**) (of an antique spoon) with three notches splitting the end of the handle.
– ORIGIN C18: from L. *trifidus*, from *tri-* 'three' + *fid-, findere* 'split, divide'.

**trifle** • **n.** **1** a thing of little value or importance. ➤a small amount. **2** Brit. a cold dessert of sponge cake and fruit covered with layers of custard, jelly, and cream. • **v.** **1** (**trifle with**) treat without seriousness or respect. **2** archaic talk or act frivolously.
– DERIVATIVES **trifler** n.
– ORIGIN ME: noun from OFr. *trufle*, by-form of *trufe* 'deceit'; verb from OFr. *truffler* 'mock, deceive'.

**trifling** • **adj.** unimportant or trivial.
– DERIVATIVES **triflingly** adv.

**trifocal** • **adj.** (of a pair of glasses) having lenses with three parts with different focal lengths. • **n.** (**trifocals**) a pair of trifocal glasses.

**trifoliate** /trʌɪˈfəʊlɪət/ • **adj.** (of a compound leaf) having three leaflets.

**triforium** /trʌɪˈfɔːrɪəm/ • **n.** (pl. **triforia** /-rɪə/) a gallery or arcade above the arches of the nave, choir, and transepts of a church.
– ORIGIN C18: from Anglo-Latin, of unknown origin.

**triform** • **adj.** technical composed of three parts.

**trifurcate** • **v.** /ˈtrʌɪfəkeɪt/ divide into three branches or forks. • **adj.** /-ˈfəːkət/ divided in this way.
– DERIVATIVES **trifurcation** n.
– ORIGIN C19: from L. *trifurcus* 'three-forked' (from *tri-* 'three' + *furca* 'fork') + **-ATE**[2].

**trig**[1] • **n.** informal trigonometry.

**trig**[2] US or archaic • **adj.** neat and smart in appearance. • **v.** (**trigged**, **trigging**) make neat and smart.
– ORIGIN ME: from ON *tryggr*; rel. to **TRUE**.

**trigamous** /ˈtrɪɡəməs/ • **adj.** having three wives or husbands at the same time.
– DERIVATIVES **trigamist** n. **trigamy** n.
– ORIGIN C19 (earlier (C17) as *trigamist* and *trigamy*): from Gk *trigamos* (from *tri-* 'three' + *gamos* 'marriage') + **-OUS**.

**trigeminal nerves** /trʌɪˈdʒɛmɪn(ə)l/ • **pl. n.** Anatomy the pair of large cranial nerves supplying the front part of the head.

**trigeminal neuralgia** • **n.** Medicine neuralgia involving one or more of the branches of the trigeminal nerves.

**trigeminus** /trʌɪˈdʒɛmɪnəs/ • **n.** (pl. **trigemini** /-nʌɪ/) Anatomy each of the trigeminal nerves.
– ORIGIN C19: from L., lit. 'three born at the same birth', extended to mean 'threefold'.

**trigger** • **n.** **1** a device that releases a spring or catch and so sets off a mechanism, especially in order to fire a gun. **2** an event that causes something to happen. • **v.** **1** cause (a device) to function. **2** cause to happen or exist.
– DERIVATIVES **triggered** adj.
– ORIGIN C17: from dial. *tricker*, from Du. *trekker*, from *trekken* 'to pull'.

**trigger finger** • **n.** **1** the forefinger of the right hand, used to pull the trigger of a gun. **2** Medicine a defect in a tendon causing a finger to jerk or snap straight when the hand is extended.

**triggerfish** • **n.** (pl. same or **-fishes**) a tropical marine fish with a large dorsal spine which can be erected and locked into place. [Family Balistidae: numerous species.]

**trigger-happy** ● **adj.** apt to fire a gun or take other drastic action on the slightest provocation.

**trigger point** ● **n. 1** a circumstance or situation which causes an event to occur. **2** Physiology & Medicine a sensitive area of the body, stimulation or irritation of which causes a specific effect in another part.

**triglyceride** /trʌɪˈglɪsərʌɪd/ ● **n.** Chemistry an ester formed from glycerol and three fatty acid groups, e.g. the main constituents of natural fats and oils.

**triglyph** /ˈtrʌɪglɪf/ ● **n.** Architecture a tablet in a Doric frieze with three vertical grooves alternating with metopes.
– DERIVATIVES **triglyphic** adj.
– ORIGIN C16: via L. from Gk *trigluphos*, from *tri-* 'three' + *gluphē* 'carving'.

**trigon** /ˈtrʌɪgɒn/ ● **n. 1** an ancient triangular lyre or harp. **2** a triangular cutting region formed by three cusps on an upper molar tooth. **3** archaic a triangle.
– ORIGIN C17 (earlier (C16) as *trigonal*): via L. from Gk *trigōnon*, neut. of *trigōnos* 'three-cornered'.

**trigonal** /ˈtrɪg(ə)n(ə)l/ ● **adj. 1** triangular. ➤ chiefly Biology triangular in cross section. **2** denoting a crystal system with three equal axes separated by equal angles that are not right angles.
– DERIVATIVES **trigonally** adv.

**trigonometry** /ˌtrɪgəˈnɒmɪtri/ ● **n.** the branch of mathematics concerned with the relations of the sides and angles of triangles and with the relevant functions of any angles.
– DERIVATIVES **trigonometric** /-nəˈmɛtrɪk/ adj. **trigonometrical** adj.
– ORIGIN C17: from mod. L. *trigonometria* (see **TRIGON**, **-METRY**).

**trig point** ● **n.** Brit. a reference point on high ground used in surveying, typically marked by a small pillar.

**trigram** /ˈtrʌɪgram/ ● **n. 1** a trigraph. **2** each of the eight figures formed of three parallel lines that combine to form the sixty-four hexagrams of the I Ching.

**trigraph** /ˈtrʌɪgrɑːf/ ● **n.** a group of three letters representing one sound, for example German *sch-*.

**trihedron** /trʌɪˈhiːdrən, -ˈhɛdrən/ ● **n.** (pl. **trihedra** /-drə/ or **trihedrons**) a solid figure having three sides or faces (in addition to the base or ends).
– DERIVATIVES **trihedral** adj. & n.
– ORIGIN C19 (earlier (C18) as *trihedral*): from **TRI-** + **-HEDRON**.

**trihydric** /trʌɪˈhʌɪdrɪk/ ● **adj.** Chemistry (of an alcohol) containing three hydroxyl groups.

**trike** ● **n.** informal **1** a tricycle. **2** a kind of ultralight aircraft.

**trilateral** ● **adj.** shared by or involving three parties. ➤ Geometry of, on, or with three sides. ● **n.** a triangle.

**trilby** ● **n.** (pl. **-ies**) chiefly Brit. a soft felt hat with a narrow brim and indented crown.
– DERIVATIVES **trilbied** adj.
– ORIGIN C19: from the name of George du Maurier's novel *Trilby* (1894), in the stage version of which such a hat was worn.

**trilinear** ● **adj.** Mathematics of or having three lines.

**trilingual** ● **adj.** speaking three languages fluently. ➤ written or conducted in three languages.
– DERIVATIVES **trilingualism** n.

**trilithon** /trʌɪˈlɪθ(ə)n/ (also **trilith** /ˈtrʌɪlɪθ/) ● **n.** Archaeology a megalithic structure consisting of two upright stones and a third across the top as a lintel.
– ORIGIN C18: from Gk, from *tri-* 'three' + *lithos* 'stone'.

**trill** ● **n.** a quavering or vibratory sound, especially a rapid alternation of sung or played notes. ➤ the pronunciation of a consonant, especially *r*, with rapid vibration of the tongue against the hard or soft palate or the uvula. ● **v.** produce a quavering or warbling sound; sing or pronounce with a trill.
– DERIVATIVES **triller** n.
– ORIGIN C17: from Ital. *trillo* (n.), *trillare* (v.).

**trillion** ● **cardinal number** (pl. **trillions** or (with numeral or quantifying word) same) **1** (**a/one trillion**) a million million (1,000,000,000,000 or $10^{12}$). ➤ dated, chiefly Brit. a million million million (1,000,000,000,000,000,000 or $10^{18}$). **2** (**trillions**) informal a very large number or amount.
– DERIVATIVES **trillionth** ordinal number.
– ORIGIN C17: from Fr., from *million*, by substitution of the prefix *tri-* 'three' for the initial letters.

**trillium** /ˈtrɪlɪəm/ ● **n.** a plant with a solitary three-petalled flower above a whorl of three leaves. [Genus *Trillium*.]
– ORIGIN mod. L., appar. an alt. of Swed. *trilling* 'triplet'.

**trilobite** /ˈtrʌɪlə(ʊ)bʌɪt, ˈtrɪ-/ ● **n.** a fossil marine arthropod of the Palaeozoic era, with a segmented hindpart divided longitudinally into three lobes.
– ORIGIN C19: from mod. L. *Trilobites*, from Gk *tri-* 'three' + *lobos* 'lobe'.

**trilogy** ● **n.** (pl. **-ies**) a group of three related novels, plays, films, etc. ➤ (in ancient Greece) a series of three tragedies performed one after the other.

**trim** ● **v.** (**trimmed**, **trimming**) **1** make (something) neat by cutting away irregular or unwanted parts. ➤ cut off (irregular or unwanted parts). ➤ reduce the size, amount, or number of. **2** decorate (something), especially along its edges. **3** adjust (a sail) to take advantage of the wind. ➤ adjust the balance of (a ship or aircraft), by rearranging its cargo or using its controls. **4** adapt one's views to the prevailing political trends for personal advancement. **5** informal, dated get the better of or cheat. **6** informal, dated rebuke angrily. ● **n. 1** additional decoration, especially along the edges. ➤ the upholstery or interior lining of a car. **2** an act of trimming. **3** the state of being in good order. **4** the degree to which an aircraft can be maintained at a constant altitude. **5** the way in which a ship floats in the water, especially in relation to the fore-and-aft line. ● **adj.** (**trimmer**, **trimmest**) neat and smart; in good order.
– PHRASES **in trim 1** slim and fit. **2** Nautical in good order. **trim one's sails** (**to the wind**) make changes to suit one's new circumstances.
– DERIVATIVES **trimly** adv. **trimness** n.
– ORIGIN OE *trymman*, *trymian* 'make firm, arrange'.

**trimaran** /ˈtrʌɪməran/ ● **n.** a yacht with three hulls in parallel.
– ORIGIN 1940s: from **TRI-** + **CATAMARAN**.

**trimer** /ˈtrʌɪmə/ ● **n.** Chemistry a polymer comprising three monomer units.
– DERIVATIVES **trimeric** adj.

**trimerous** /ˈtrɪm(ə)rəs, ˈtrʌɪ-/ ● **adj.** Botany & Zoology having parts arranged in groups of three. ➤ consisting of three joints or parts.

**trimester** /trʌɪˈmɛstə/ ● **n. 1** a period of three months, especially as a division of the duration of pregnancy. **2** N. Amer. each of the three terms in an academic year.
– DERIVATIVES **trimestral** adj. **trimestrial** adj.
– ORIGIN C19: from Fr. *trimestre*, from L. *trimestris*, from *tri-* 'three' + *mensis* 'month'.

**trimeter** /ˈtrɪmɪtə, ˈtrʌɪ-/ ● **n.** Prosody a line of verse consisting of three metrical feet.
– DERIVATIVES **trimetric** adj. **trimetrical** adj.

**trimmer** ● **n. 1** a person or implement that trims. **2** (also **trimmer joist**) Architecture a crosspiece fixed between full-length joists to form part of the frame of an opening in a floor or roof. **3** a small capacitor or other component used to tune a circuit such as a radio set. **4** Austral./NZ informal an excellent or outstanding person or thing.

**trimming** ● **n. 1** (**trimmings**) small pieces trimmed off. **2** decoration, especially for clothing. ➤ (**the trimmings**) informal the traditional accompaniments to something.

**trimpot** ● **n.** a small potentiometer used to make small adjustments to the value of resistance or voltage in an electronic circuit.

**trim tab** (also **trimming tab**) ● **n.** Aeronautics an adjustable tab or aerofoil attached to a control surface, used to trim an aircraft in flight.

**trine** /trʌɪn/ ● **n.** Astrology an aspect of 120° (one third of a circle).
– ORIGIN ME (in the sense 'made up of three parts'): from OFr. *trin(e)*, from L. *trinus* 'threefold'.

**Trini** /ˈtrɪni/ ● **n.** W. Indian a Trinidadian.

**Trinidadian** /ˌtrɪnɪˈdeɪdɪən, -ˈdadɪən/ ● **n.** a native or inhabitant of the Caribbean island of Trinidad. ● **adj.** of or relating to Trinidad.

**Trinitarian** /ˌtrɪnɪˈtɛːrɪən/ ● **adj.** of or relating to belief in the doctrine of the Trinity. ● **n.** a person who believes in the doctrine of the Trinity.
– DERIVATIVES **Trinitarianism** n.

**trinitrotoluene** /trʌɪˌnʌɪtrəʊˈtɒljʊiːn/ ● **n.** fuller form of **TNT**.

**trinity** ● **n.** (pl. **-ies**) **1** (**the Trinity** or **the Holy Trinity**) the three persons of the Christian Godhead; Father, Son, and Holy Spirit. **2** a group of three people or things.
– ORIGIN ME: from OFr. *trinite*, from L. *trinitas* 'triad', from *trinus* (see **TRINE**).

**Trinity Brethren** ● **pl. n.** (in the UK) the members of Trinity House, an association responsible for the licensing of ships' pilots and the construction and maintenance of buoys and lighthouses.

**Trinity Sunday** ● **n.** the next Sunday after Pentecost.

**Trinity term** ● **n.** Brit. (in some universities) the term beginning after Easter.

**trinket** ● **n.** a small ornament or item of jewellery that is of little value.
– DERIVATIVES **trinketry** n.
– ORIGIN C16: of unknown origin.

**trinomial** /trʌɪˈnəʊmɪəl/ ● **adj. 1** (of an algebraic expression) consisting of three terms. **2** Biology (of a taxonomic name) consisting of three terms where the first is the name of the genus, the second that of the species, and the third that of the subspecies or variety. ● **n.** a trinomial expression or taxonomic name.
– ORIGIN C17: from **TRI-**, on the pattern of *binomial*.

**trio** ● **n.** (pl. **-os**) a set or group of three. ➤ a group of three musicians. ➤ a composition written for three musicians. ➤ the central section of a minuet, scherzo, or march. ➤ (in piquet) a set of three aces, kings, queens, jacks, or tens held in one hand.
– ORIGIN C18: from Ital., from L. *tres* 'three'.

**triode** /ˈtrʌɪəʊd/ ● **n.** a thermionic valve having three electrodes. ➤ a semiconductor rectifier having three connections.
– ORIGIN C20: from **TRI-** + **ELECTRODE**.

**triolet** /ˈtriːə(ʊ)lɛt, ˈtrʌɪəlɛt/ ● **n.** a poem of eight lines, typically of eight syllables each, rhyming *abaaabab* and so structured that the first line recurs as the fourth and seventh and the second as the eighth.
– ORIGIN C17: from Fr.

**triose** /ˈtrʌɪəʊz, -s/ ● **n.** Chemistry any of a group of monosaccharide sugars whose molecules contain three carbon atoms.

**trioxide** ● **n.** Chemistry an oxide containing three atoms of oxygen in its molecule or empirical formula.

**trip** ● **v.** (**tripped**, **tripping**) **1** catch one's foot on something and stumble or fall. ➤ (**trip up**) make a mistake. **2** walk, run, or dance with quick light steps. **3** activate (a mechanism), especially by contact with a switch. ➤ (of part of an electric circuit) disconnect automatically as a safety measure. **4** Nautical release and raise (an anchor) from the seabed by means of a cable. ➤ turn (a yard or other object) from a horizontal to a vertical position for lowering. **5** informal experience hallucinations induced by taking a psychedelic drug, especially LSD. **6** go on a short journey. ● **n. 1** a journey or excursion, especially for pleasure. **2** an instance of tripping or falling. ➤ a mistake. **3** informal a hallucinatory experience caused by taking a psychedelic drug. ➤ an exciting or stimulating experience. ➤ a self-indulgent attitude or activity: *a power trip*. **4** a device that trips a mechanism, circuit, etc. **5** archaic a light, lively movement of a person's feet.
– PHRASES **trip the light fantastic** humorous dance. [from 'Trip it as you go On the light fantastic toe' (Milton's *L'Allegro*).]
– ORIGIN ME: from OFr. *triper*, from MDu. *trippen* 'to skip, hop'.

**tripartite** /trʌɪˈpɑːtʌɪt/ ● **adj.** consisting of three parts. ➤ shared by or involving three parties.
– DERIVATIVES **tripartitely** adv. **tripartition** n.

**tripe** ● **n. 1** the first or second stomach of a cow or other ruminant used as food. **2** informal nonsense; rubbish.
– ORIGIN ME: from OFr., of unknown origin.

**trip hammer** ● **n.** a large, heavy pivoted hammer used in forging.

**trip hop** ● **n.** a style of dance music combining elements of hip hop and dub reggae with softer sounds.

**triphthong** /ˈtrɪfθɒŋ/ ● **n.** a union of three vowels (letters or sounds) pronounced in one syllable (as in *fire*). ➤ three written vowel characters representing the sound of a single vowel (as in b*eau*).
– DERIVATIVES **triphthongal** adj.
– ORIGIN C16: from Fr. *triphtongue*.

**Tripitaka** /trɪˈpɪtəkə/ ● **n.** the sacred canon of Theravada Buddhism, written in the Pali language.
– ORIGIN from Sanskrit *tripiṭaka*, lit. 'the three baskets or collections'.

**triplane** ● **n.** an early type of aircraft with three pairs of wings, one above the other.

**triple** ● **adj. 1** consisting of or involving three parts, things, or people. **2** having three times the usual size, quality, or strength. ● **predet.** three times as much or as many. ● **n. 1** a thing that is three times as large as usual or is made up of three parts. **2** (**triples**) a sporting contest in which each side has three players. **3** (**triples**) Bell-ringing a system of change-ringing using seven bells, with three pairs changing places each time. **4** Baseball a hit which enables the batter to reach third base. ● **v.** make or become three times as much or as many.
– DERIVATIVES **triply** adv.
– ORIGIN ME: from OFr., or from L. *triplus*, from Gk *triplous*.

**triple acrostic** ● **n.** an acrostic in which the first, middle, and last letters of each line form hidden words.

**triple bond** ● **n.** Chemistry a chemical bond in which three pairs of electrons are shared between two atoms.

**triple crown** ● **n. 1** (**Triple Crown**) an award or honour for winning a group of three important events in a sport. **2** the papal tiara.

**triple harp** ● **n.** a large harp without pedals, and with three rows of strings, the middle row providing sharps and flats.

**triple jump** ● **n. 1** an athletic event in which competitors attempt to jump as far as possible by performing a hop, a step, and a jump from a running start. **2** Skating a jump in which the skater makes three full turns while in the air. ● **v.** (**triple-jump**) perform a triple jump.
– DERIVATIVES **triple jumper** n.

**triple play** ● **n.** Baseball a defensive play in which three runners are put out.

**triple point** ● **n.** Chemistry the temperature and pressure at which the solid, liquid, and vapour phases of a pure substance can coexist in equilibrium.

**triple rhyme** ● **n.** a rhyme involving three syllables.

**triplet** ● **n. 1** one of three children or animals born at the same birth. **2** Music a group of three equal notes to be performed in the time of two or four. **3** a set of three rhyming lines of verse. **4** technical a group of three similar things, e.g. lines in a spectrum.
– ORIGIN C17: from **TRIPLE**, on the pattern of *doublet*.

**triplet code** ● **n.** Biology the genetic code in which a sequence of three nucleotides on a DNA or RNA molecule codes for a specific amino acid in protein synthesis.

**triple time** ● **n.** musical time with three beats to the bar.

**triple tonguing** ● **n.** Music a technique in which alternate movements of the tongue are made to facilitate rapid playing of a wind instrument.

**triplex** /ˈtrɪplɛks/ ● **n. 1** (**Triplex**) Brit. trademark toughened or laminated safety glass, used especially for car windows. **2** N. Amer. a building divided into three self-contained residences. **3** Biochemistry a triple-stranded polynucleotide molecule. ● **v.** (**be triplexed**) (of electrical equipment or systems) be provided or fitted in triplicate so as to ensure reliability.
– ORIGIN C17: from L., 'threefold', from *tri-* 'three' + *plicare* 'to fold'.

**triplicate** ● **adj.** /ˈtrɪplɪkət/ existing in three copies or ex-

amples. ● n. /ˈtrɪplɪkət/ archaic a thing which is part of a set of three copies or corresponding parts. ● v. /ˈtrɪplɪkeɪt/ make three copies of. ➤ multiply by three.
– DERIVATIVES **triplication** /-ˈkeɪʃ(ə)n/ n. **triplicity** /trɪˈplɪsɪti/ n.
– ORIGIN ME: from L. *triplicat-*, *triplicare* 'make three', from *triplex*, *triplic-* (see **TRIPLEX**).

**triploid** /ˈtrɪplɔɪd/ ● adj. Genetics (of a cell or nucleus) containing three homologous sets of chromosomes.
– DERIVATIVES **triploidy** n.

**tripmeter** ● n. a vehicle instrument that can be set to record the distance of individual journeys.

**tripod** /ˈtrʌɪpɒd/ ● n. **1** a three-legged stand for supporting a camera or other apparatus. **2** archaic a stool, table, or cauldron resting on three legs. ➤ historical the bronze altar at Delphi on which a priestess sat to utter oracles.
– DERIVATIVES **tripodal** /ˈtrɪpəd(ə)l/ adj.
– ORIGIN C17: via L. from Gk *tripod-*, *tripous*, from *tri-* 'three' + *pod-*, *pous* 'foot'.

**tripoli** /ˈtrɪpəli/ ● n. another term for **ROTTENSTONE**.
– ORIGIN C17: from Fr., from *Tripoli* in Libya or the Lebanon.

**tripos** /ˈtrʌɪpɒs/ ● n. the final honours examination for a BA degree at Cambridge University.
– ORIGIN C16: alt. of L. *tripus* 'tripod', with ref. to the stool on which a designated graduate sat to deliver a satirical speech at the degree ceremony.

**trippant** /ˈtrɪp(ə)nt/ ● adj. Heraldry (of a stag or deer) represented as walking.
– ORIGIN C17: from OFr., lit. 'walking or springing lightly', pres. part. of *tripper*.

**tripper** ● n. Brit. informal a person who goes on a pleasure trip or excursion.

**trippy** ● adj. (**-ier**, **-iest**) informal resembling or inducing the hallucinatory effect produced by a psychedelic drug.

**triptych** /ˈtrɪptɪk/ ● n. a picture or carving on three panels, typically hinged together vertically and used as an altarpiece. ➤ a set of three associated artistic, literary, or musical works.
– ORIGIN C18 (denoting a set of three writing tablets hinged or tied together): from **TRI-**, on the pattern of *diptych*.

**triptyque** /trɪpˈtiːk/ ● n. dated a customs permit serving as a passport for a motor vehicle.
– ORIGIN C20: from Fr., lit. 'triptych' (because orig. the document had three sections).

**tripwire** ● n. a wire that is stretched close to the ground and activates a trap, explosion, or alarm when disturbed.

**triquetra** /trʌɪˈkwɛtrə, -ˈkwiːtrə/ ● n. (pl. **triquetrae** /-triː/) a symmetrical triangular ornament of three interlaced arcs used on metalwork and stone crosses.
– ORIGIN C16: from L., fem. of *triquetrus* 'three-cornered'.

**triquetral** (also **triquetral bone**) ● n. Anatomy a carpal bone on the outside of the wrist, articulating with the lunate, hamate, and pisiform bones.
– ORIGIN C17: from L. *triquetrus* 'three-cornered' + **-AL**.

**trireme** /ˈtrʌɪriːm/ ● n. an ancient Greek or Roman war galley with three banks of oars.
– ORIGIN from L. *triremis*, from *tri-* 'three' + *remus* 'oar'.

**trisaccharide** /trʌɪˈsakərʌɪd/ ● n. Chemistry any of the class of sugars whose molecules contain three monosaccharide molecules.

**Trisagion** /trɪˈsagɪən, -ˈseɪgɪən/ ● n. a hymn, especially in the Orthodox Church, with a triple invocation of God as holy.
– ORIGIN ME: from Gk, neut. of *trisagios*, from *tris* 'three times' + *hagios* 'holy'.

**trisect** /trʌɪˈsɛkt/ ● v. divide into three parts.
– DERIVATIVES **trisection** n. **trisector** n.
– ORIGIN C17: from **TRI-** + L. *sect-*, *secare* 'divide, cut'.

**trishaw** /ˈtrʌɪʃɔː/ ● n. a light three-wheeled vehicle with pedals, used in the Far East.
– ORIGIN 1940s: from **TRI-** + **RICKSHAW**.

**triskaidekaphobia** /ˌtrɪskʌɪdɛkəˈfəʊbɪə/ ● n. extreme superstition regarding the number thirteen.
– ORIGIN C20: from Gk *treiskaideka* 'thirteen' + **-PHOBIA**.

**triskelion** /trɪˈskɛlɪən/ ● n. a Celtic symbol consisting of three legs or lines radiating from a centre.
– ORIGIN C19: from **TRI-** + Gk *skelos* 'leg'.

**trismus** /ˈtrɪzməs/ ● n. Medicine spasm of the jaw muscles, causing the mouth to remain tightly closed, typically as a symptom of tetanus; lockjaw.
– ORIGIN C17: from mod. L., from Gk *trismos* 'a scream, grinding'.

**trisomy** /ˈtrɪsəmi/ ● n. Medicine a condition in which an extra copy of a chromosome is present in the cell nuclei, causing developmental abnormalities.
– ORIGIN 1930s: from **TRI-** + **-SOME**[3].

**trisomy-21** ● n. Medicine the most common form of Down's syndrome, caused by an extra copy of chromosome number 21.

**tristesse** /trɪˈstɛs/ ● n. poetic/literary a state of melancholy sadness.
– ORIGIN from Fr.

**trisyllable** /trʌɪˈsɪləb(ə)l/ ● n. a word or metrical foot of three syllables.
– DERIVATIVES **trisyllabic** adj.

**tritagonist** /trʌɪˈtag(ə)nɪst, trɪ-/ ● n. the person who is third in importance, after the protagonist and deuteragonist, in an ancient Greek drama.
– ORIGIN C19: from Gk *tritagōnistēs*, from *tritos* 'third' + *agōnistēs* 'actor'.

**tritanope** /ˈtrɪtənəʊp/ ● n. a person suffering from tritanopia.

**tritanopia** /ˌtrɪtəˈnəʊpɪə/ ● n. a rare form of colour blindness resulting from insensitivity to blue light, causing confusion of greens and blues. Compare with **PROTANOPIA**, **DEUTERANOPIA**.
– ORIGIN C20: from Gk *tritos* 'third' (referring to blue as the third colour in the spectrum) + **AN-**[1] + **-OPIA**.

**trite** ● adj. (of a remark or idea) lacking originality or freshness; dull on account of overuse.
– DERIVATIVES **tritely** adv. **triteness** n.
– ORIGIN C16: from L. *tritus*, past part. of *terere* 'to rub'.

**tritheism** /ˈtrʌɪˌθiːɪz(ə)m/ ● n. (in Christian theology) belief in the three persons of the Trinity as three distinct gods.
– DERIVATIVES **tritheist** n.

**tritiated** /ˈtrɪtɪeɪtɪd/ ● adj. Chemistry denoting a compound in which the ordinary isotope of hydrogen has been replaced with tritium.
– DERIVATIVES **tritiation** n.

**triticale** /ˌtrɪtɪˈkeɪli/ ● n. a hybrid cereal produced by crossing wheat and rye, grown as a fodder crop.
– ORIGIN 1950s: mod. L., from a blend of the genus names *Triticum* 'wheat' and *Secale* 'rye'.

**tritium** /ˈtrɪtɪəm/ ● n. Chemistry a radioactive isotope of hydrogen with a mass approximately three times that of the usual isotope. (Symbol: **T**)
– ORIGIN 1930s: from mod. L., from Gk *tritos* 'third'.

**trito-** /ˈtrɪtəʊ, ˈtrʌɪtəʊ/ ● comb. form third.
– ORIGIN from Gk *tritos* 'third'.

**triton**[1] ● n. **1** Greek Mythology a minor sea god or merman represented as a man with a fish's tail and carrying a trident and shell-trumpet. **2** a marine mollusc with a tall spiral shell with a large aperture. [Genus *Charonia*.]

**triton**[2] ● n. a nucleus of a tritium atom, consisting of a proton and two neutrons.

**tritone** ● n. Music an interval of three whole tones (an augmented fourth), as between C and F sharp.

**triturate** /ˈtrɪtjʊreɪt/ ● v. technical grind to a fine powder. ➤ chew or grind (food) thoroughly.
– DERIVATIVES **trituration** n. **triturator** n.
– ORIGIN C18: from L. *triturat-* '(of corn) threshed', from *tritura* 'rubbing' (from the verb *terere*).

**triumph** ● n. **1** a great victory or achievement. ➤ the state of being victorious or successful. ➤ joy or satisfaction resulting from a success or victory. ➤ a highly successful example: *the arrest was a triumph of international co-operation.* **2** the processional entry of a victorious general into ancient Rome. ● v. **1** achieve a triumph. ➤ rejoice or exult at a triumph. **2** (of a Roman general) ride into ancient Rome after a victory.
– DERIVATIVES **triumphal** adj.
– ORIGIN ME: from OFr. *triumphe* (n.), from L. *triump(h)us*,

prob. from Gk *thriambos* 'hymn to Bacchus'.

**triumphalism** • **n.** excessive exultation over one's success or achievements.
– DERIVATIVES **triumphalist** adj. & n.

**triumphant** • **adj.** having won a battle or contest; victorious. ➤jubilant after a victory or achievement.
– DERIVATIVES **triumphantly** adv.

**triumvir** /trʌɪˈʌmvə, ˈtrʌɪəmvə/ • **n.** (pl. **triumvirs** or **triumviri** /-rʌɪ/) (in ancient Rome) each of three public officers jointly responsible for overseeing any of the administrative departments.
– DERIVATIVES **triumviral** adj.
– ORIGIN L., orig. as *triumviri* (pl.), back-form. from *trium virorum* 'of three men', genitive of *tres viri*.

**triumvirate** /trʌɪˈʌmvɪrət/ • **n. 1** a group of three powerful or notable people or things. ➤(in ancient Rome) a group of three men holding power. **2** the office of triumvir in ancient Rome.

**triune** /ˈtrʌɪjuːn/ • **adj.** (especially with reference to the Trinity) consisting of three in one.
– DERIVATIVES **triunity** n. (pl. **-ies**).
– ORIGIN C17: from **TRI-** + L. *unus* 'one'.

**trivalent** /trʌɪˈveɪl(ə)nt/ • **adj.** Chemistry having a valency of three.

**trivet** • **n.** an iron tripod placed over a fire for a cooking pot or kettle to stand on. ➤an iron bracket designed to hook on to bars of a grate for a similar purpose.
– ORIGIN ME: appar. from L. *tripes, triped-* 'three-legged', from *tri-* 'three' + *pes, ped-* 'foot'.

**trivia** • **pl. n.** unimportant details or pieces of information.
– ORIGIN C20: from mod. L., pl. of *trivium* (see **TRIVIUM**), influenced by **TRIVIAL**.

**trivial** • **adj. 1** of little value or importance. **2** Mathematics denoting a subgroup that either contains only the identity element or is identical with the given group.
– DERIVATIVES **triviality** n. (pl. **-ies**). **trivially** adv.
– ORIGIN ME (in the sense 'belonging to the trivium'): from med. L. *trivialis*, from L. *trivium* (see **TRIVIUM**).

**trivialize** (also **-ise**) • **v.** make (something) seem less important or complex than it really is.
– DERIVATIVES **trivialization** n.

**trivial name** • **n. 1** chiefly Chemistry a name that is in general use although not part of systematic nomenclature. **2** chiefly Zoology another term for **SPECIFIC EPITHET**.

**trivium** /ˈtrɪvɪəm/ • **n.** historical an introductory course at a medieval university involving the study of grammar, rhetoric, and logic. Compare with **QUADRIVIUM**.
– ORIGIN C19: from L., lit. 'place where three roads meet'.

**-trix** • **suffix** (pl. **-trices** /trɪˈsiːz, ˈtrʌɪsiːz/ or **-trixes**) (chiefly in legal terms) forming feminine agent nouns corresponding to masculine nouns ending in *-tor* (such as *executrix* corresponding to *executor*).
– ORIGIN from L.

**tRNA** • **abbrev.** Biology transfer RNA.

**trocar** /ˈtrəʊkɑː/ • **n.** a surgical instrument with a three-sided cutting point enclosed in a tube, used for withdrawing fluid from a body cavity.
– ORIGIN C18: from Fr. *trocart, trois-quarts*, from *trois* 'three' + *carre* 'side, face of an instrument'.

**trochaic** /trə(ʊ)ˈkeɪɪk/ Prosody • **adj.** consisting of or featuring trochees. • **n.** (**trochaics**) trochaic verse.

**trochal disc** • **n.** Zoology each of two projections below the neck of the femur (thigh bone) to which muscles are attached.
– ORIGIN C19: *trochal* from Gk *trokhos* 'wheel' + **-AL**.

**trochanter** /trəˈkantə/ • **n. 1** Anatomy any of a number of bony protuberances by which muscles are attached to the upper part of the thigh bone. **2** Entomology the small second segment of the leg of an insect, between the coxa and the femur.
– ORIGIN C17: from Fr., from Gk *trokhantēr*, from *trekhein* 'to run'.

**trochee** /ˈtrəʊkiː/ • **n.** Prosody a foot consisting of one long or stressed syllable followed by one short or unstressed syllable.
– ORIGIN C16: via L. from Gk *trokhaios* (*pous*) 'running (foot)', from *trekhein* 'to run'.

**trochlea** /ˈtrɒklɪə/ • **n.** (pl. **trochleae** /-lɪiː/) Anatomy a structure resembling or acting like a pulley, such as the groove at the lower end of the humerus forming part of the elbow joint.
– DERIVATIVES **trochlear** adj.
– ORIGIN C17: L., 'pulley'.

**trochlear nerves** • **pl. n.** Anatomy the pair of cranial nerves supplying the superior oblique muscle of the eyeballs.

**trochoid** /ˈtrəʊkɔɪd/ • **adj. 1** Anatomy denoting a joint in which one element rotates on its own axis (e.g. the atlas vertebra). **2** Geometry denoting a curve traced by a point on a radius of a circle rotating along a straight line or another circle. **3** Zoology (of a mollusc shell) conical with a flat base. • **n. 1** a trochoid curve. **2** a trochoid joint.
– DERIVATIVES **trochoidal** adj.
– ORIGIN C18: from Gk *trokhoeidēs* 'wheel-like', from *trokhos* 'wheel'.

**troctolite** /ˈtrɒktə(ʊ)lʌɪt/ • **n.** Geology a form of gabbro typically having a spotted appearance likened to a trout's back.
– ORIGIN C19: from Ger. *Troklotit*, from Gk *trōktēs*, a marine fish (taken to be 'trout').

**trod** past and past participle of **TREAD**.

**trodden** past participle of **TREAD**.

**trog**[1] • **n.** Brit. informal a person regarded as contemptible or socially inferior.
– ORIGIN 1950s: abbrev. of **TROGLODYTE**.

**trog**[2] • **v.** (**trogged, trogging**) Brit. informal walk heavily or laboriously; trudge.
– ORIGIN 1980s: perh. a blend of **TRUDGE, SLOG, TROLL**[2], and **JOG**.

**troglodyte** /ˈtrɒglədʌɪt/ • **n. 1** a cave-dweller, especially a primitive or prehistoric one. **2** a person who is deliberately ignorant or old-fashioned.
– DERIVATIVES **troglodytic** /-ˈdɪtɪk/ adj. **troglodytism** n.
– ORIGIN C15: via L. from Gk *trōglodutēs*, alt. of the name of an Ethiopian people, influenced by *trōglē* 'hole'.

**trogon** /ˈtrəʊgɒn/ • **n.** a long-tailed brightly coloured bird of tropical American forests. [Family Trogonidae: many species.]
– ORIGIN C18: from mod. L., from Gk *trōgōn*, from *trōgein* 'gnaw'.

**troika** /ˈtrɔɪkə/ • **n. 1** a Russian vehicle pulled by a team of three horses abreast. ➤a team of three horses for such a vehicle. **2** a group of three people working together, especially as administrators or managers.
– ORIGIN Russ., from *troe* 'set of three'.

**troilism** /ˈtrɔɪlɪz(ə)m/ • **n.** sexual activity involving three participants.
– ORIGIN 1950s: perh. based on Fr. *trois* 'three'.

**Trojan** • **n.** a native or inhabitant of ancient Troy in Asia Minor. • **adj.** of or relating to Troy.
– PHRASES **work like a Trojan** work extremely hard.

**Trojan Horse** • **n.** something intended to undermine or secretly overthrow an enemy or opponent. ➤Computing a program designed to breach the security of a computer system while ostensibly performing some innocuous function.
– ORIGIN from the hollow wooden statue of a horse in which the ancient Greeks are said to have concealed themselves in order to enter Troy.

**troll**[1] /trəʊl, trɒl/ • **n.** (in folklore) an ugly cave-dwelling being depicted as either a giant or a dwarf.
– ORIGIN ME (in the sense 'witch'): from ON and Swed. *troll*, Dan. *trold*.

**troll**[2] /trəʊl, trɒl/ • **v. 1** fish by trailing a baited line along behind a boat. ➤search for something. **2** chiefly Brit. walk; stroll. **3** sing (something) in a happy and carefree way. **4** [usu. as noun **trolling**] Computing, informal send (an email message or Internet posting) intended to provoke a response by containing errors. • **n.** an act or instance of trolling. ➤a line or bait used in such fishing.
– DERIVATIVES **troller** n.
– ORIGIN ME (in the sense 'stroll, roll'): of uncertain origin; cf. OFr. *troller* 'wander in search of game' and Mid. High Ger. *trollen* 'stroll'.

**trolley** • **n.** (pl. **-eys**) **1** Brit. a large wheeled metal basket or

frame used for transporting heavy or unwieldy items such as luggage or supermarket purchases. ➤a small table on wheels or castors, used especially to convey food and drink. **2** (also **trolley wheel**) a wheel attached to a pole, used for collecting current from an overhead electric wire to drive a tram. **3** short for **TROLLEYBUS** or **TROLLEY CAR**.
– PHRASES **off one's trolley** Brit. informal mad; insane.
– ORIGIN C19: of dial. origin, perh. from **TROLL**².

**trolleybus** ● n. a bus powered by electricity obtained from overhead wires by means of a trolley wheel.

**trolley car** ● n. US a tram powered by electricity obtained from overhead wires by means of a trolley wheel.

**trollius** /'trɒlɪəs/ ● n. (pl. same) a plant of a genus that comprises the globeflowers. [Genus *Trollius*.]
– ORIGIN mod. L., appar. representing Ger. *Trollblume* 'globeflower', from the stem of *trollen* 'to roll' (because of the globular flowers).

**trollop** ● n. dated or humorous a sexually disreputable or promiscuous woman.
– ORIGIN C17: perh. rel. to **TRULL**.

**trombone** ● n. a large brass wind instrument having an extendable slide with which different notes are made.
– DERIVATIVES **trombonist** n.
– ORIGIN C18: from Fr. or Ital., from Ital. *tromba* 'trumpet'.

**trommel** /'trɒm(ə)l/ ● n. Mining a rotating cylindrical sieve or screen used for washing and sorting pieces of ore or coal.
– ORIGIN C19: from Ger., lit. 'drum'.

**tromp** ● v. N. Amer. informal **1** trudge or tramp. **2** trample.
– ORIGIN C19: alt. of **TRAMP**.

**trompe l'œil** /ˌtrɒmp 'lɔɪ, French trɔ̃p lœj/ ● n. (pl. **trompe l'œils** pronunc. same) visual illusion in art, especially as used to trick the eye into perceiving a painted detail as a three-dimensional object. ➤a painting or design intended to create such an illusion.
– ORIGIN Fr., lit. 'deceives the eye'.

**-tron** ● suffix Physics **1** denoting a subatomic particle: *positron*. **2** denoting a particle accelerator: *cyclotron*. **3** denoting a thermionic valve: *ignitron*.
– ORIGIN from *(elec)tron*.

**trona** /'trəʊnə/ ● n. a grey mineral consisting of hydrated sodium carbonate and bicarbonate, found as an evaporite.
– ORIGIN C18: from Swed., from Arab. *naṭrūn* (see **NATRON**).

**tronc** /trɒŋk/ ● n. (in a hotel or restaurant) a common fund into which tips and service charges are paid for distribution to the staff.
– ORIGIN 1920s: from Fr., lit. 'collecting box'.

**troop** ● n. **1** (**troops**) soldiers or armed forces. **2** a cavalry unit commanded by a captain. ➤a unit of artillery and armoured formation. ➤a group of three or more Scout patrols. **3** a group of people or animals of a particular kind. ● v. (of a group of people) come or go together or in large numbers.
– PHRASES **troop the colour** Brit. perform the ceremony of parading a regiment's flag along ranks of soldiers.
– ORIGIN C16: from Fr. *troupe*, back-form. from *troupeau*, dimin. of med. L. *troppus* 'flock', prob. of Gmc origin.

**troop carrier** ● n. a large aircraft or armoured vehicle designed for transporting troops.

**trooper** ● n. **1** a private soldier in a cavalry or armoured unit. ➤a cavalry horse. ➤chiefly Brit. a ship used for transporting troops. **2** Austral./NZ & US a mounted police officer. ➤US a state police officer.
– PHRASES **swear like a trooper** swear a great deal.

**troopship** ● n. a ship for transporting troops.

**tropaeolum** /trə(ʊ)'piːələm/ ● n. a Central and South American trailing or climbing plant of a genus that includes the nasturtium and the canary creeper. [Genus *Tropaeolum*.]
– ORIGIN mod. L., from L. *tropaeum* 'trophy', because of the resemblance of the flower and leaf to a helmet and shield.

**trope** /trəʊp/ ● n. a figurative or metaphorical use of a word or expression.
– ORIGIN C16: via L. from Gk *tropos* 'turn, way, trope', from *trepein* 'to turn'.

**trophic** /'trəʊfɪk, 'trɒfɪk/ ● adj. **1** Ecology of or relating to feeding and nutrition. **2** (also **tropic**) Physiology (of a hormone or its effect) stimulating the activity of another endocrine gland.
– ORIGIN C19: from Gk *trophikos*, from *trophē* 'nourishment', from *trephein* 'nourish'.

**-trophic** ● comb. form **1** relating to nutrition: *oligotrophic*. **2** relating to maintenance or regulation of a bodily organ or function, especially by a hormone: *gonadotrophic*.
– DERIVATIVES **-trophism** comb. form in corresponding nouns. **-trophy** comb. form in corresponding nouns.
– ORIGIN from Gk *trophikos*, from *trophē* 'nourishment'.

**tropho-** ● comb. form relating to nourishment: *trophoblast*.
– ORIGIN from Gk *trophē* 'nourishment'.

**trophoblast** /'trɒfə(ʊ)blast, 'trəʊf-/ ● n. Embryology a layer of tissue on the outside of a mammalian blastula, supplying the embryo with nourishment and later forming the major part of the placenta.
– DERIVATIVES **trophoblastic** adj.

**trophy** ● n. (pl. **-ies**) **1** a cup or other decorative object awarded as a prize for a victory or success. ➤a souvenir of an achievement, especially a head of an animal taken when hunting. **2** (in ancient Greece or Rome) the weapons of a defeated army set up as a memorial of victory.
– ORIGIN C15: from Fr. *trophée*, via L. from Gk *tropaion*, from *tropē* 'a rout'.

**trophy wife** ● n. informal, derogatory a young, attractive wife regarded as a status symbol for an older man.

**tropic**¹ /'trɒpɪk/ ● n. **1** the parallel of latitude 23°26′ north (**tropic of Cancer**) or south (**tropic of Capricorn**) of the equator. **2** (**the tropics**) the region between the tropics of Cancer and Capricorn. **3** Astronomy each of two corresponding circles on the celestial sphere where the sun appears to turn after reaching its greatest declination, marking the northern and southern limits of the ecliptic. ● adj. tropical.
– ORIGIN ME: via L. from Gk *tropikos*, from *tropē* 'turning', from *trepein* 'to turn'.

**tropic**² /'trəʊpɪk/ ● adj. **1** Biology relating to, consisting of, or exhibiting tropism. **2** Physiology variant spelling of **TROPHIC**.

**-tropic** ● comb. form **1** turning towards: *heliotropic*. **2** affecting: *psychotropic*. **3** (especially in names of hormones) equivalent to **-TROPHIC**.
– ORIGIN from Gk *tropē* 'turn, turning'.

**tropical** ● adj. **1** of, typical of, or peculiar to the tropics. ➤very hot and humid. **2** archaic of or involving a trope; figurative.
– DERIVATIVES **tropically** adv.

**tropical storm** (also **tropical cyclone**) ● n. a localized, very intense low-pressure wind system, forming over tropical oceans and with winds of hurricane force.

**tropical year** ● n. another term for **SOLAR YEAR**.

**tropicbird** ● n. a tropical seabird with mainly white plumage and very long central tail feathers. [Genus *Phaethon*: three species.]

**tropism** /'trəʊpɪz(ə)m, 'trɒp-/ ● n. Biology the turning of all or part of an organism in response to an external stimulus.
– ORIGIN C19: from Gk *tropos* 'turning' + **-ISM**.

**tropology** /trə'pɒlədʒi/ ● n. **1** the figurative use of language. **2** Christian Theology the figurative interpretation of the scriptures as a source of moral guidance.
– DERIVATIVES **tropological** adj.
– ORIGIN ME: via late L. from Gk *tropologia*, from *tropos* (see **TROPE**).

**tropopause** /'trɒpə(ʊ)pɔːz, 'trəʊp-/ ● n. the interface between the troposphere and the stratosphere.
– ORIGIN C20: from Gk *tropos* 'turning' + **PAUSE**.

**troposphere** /'trɒpə(ʊ)sfɪə, 'trəʊp-/ ● n. the lowest region of the atmosphere, extending from the earth's surface to a height of about 6–10 km (the lower boundary of the stratosphere).

– DERIVATIVES **tropospheric** adj.
– ORIGIN C20: from Gk *tropos* 'turning' + **SPHERE**.

**troppo**[1] /ˈtrɒpəʊ/ ● **adv.** Music too much; excessively.
– ORIGIN from Ital.

**troppo**[2] /ˈtrɒpəʊ/ ● **adj.** Austral./NZ informal mentally disturbed, supposedly as a result of spending too much time in a tropical climate.
– ORIGIN 1940s: from **TROPIC**[1] + **-O**.

**Trot** ● **n.** informal, chiefly derogatory a Trotskyist or supporter of extreme left-wing views.

**trot** ● **v.** (**trotted**, **trotting**) **1** (of a horse or other quadruped) proceed at a pace faster than a walk, lifting each diagonal pair of legs alternately. ➤(**trot something out**) cause a horse to trot to show its paces. **2** (of a person) run at a moderate pace with short steps. ➤informal go or walk briskly. **3** (**trot something out**) informal produce the same account that has been produced many times before. ● **n.** **1** a trotting pace. ➤an act or period of trotting. **2** (**the trots**) informal diarrhoea. **3** informal, chiefly Austral./NZ a period of luck of a specified kind.
– PHRASES **on the trot** informal **1** Brit. in succession. **2** continually busy.
– ORIGIN ME: from OFr. *trot* (n.), *troter* (v.), from med. L. *trottare*, of Gmc origin.

**troth** /trəʊθ, trɒθ/ ● **n.** **1** archaic or formal faith or loyalty when pledged in a solemn agreement or undertaking. **2** archaic truth.
– PHRASES **pledge** (or **plight**) **one's troth** make a solemn pledge of commitment or loyalty, especially in marriage.
– ORIGIN ME: var. of **TRUTH**.

**Trotskyism** ● **n.** the political or economic principles of the Russian revolutionary Leon Trotsky (1879–1940), especially the theory that socialism should be established throughout the world by continuing revolution.
– DERIVATIVES **Trotskyist** n. & adj. **Trotskyite** n. & adj. (derogatory).

**trotter** ● **n.** **1** a horse bred or trained for the sport of trotting. **2** a pig's foot.

**trotting** ● **n.** racing for trotting horses pulling a two-wheeled vehicle (a sulky) and driver.

**troubadour** /ˈtruːbədɔː/ ● **n.** a French medieval lyric poet composing and singing in Provençal, especially on the theme of courtly love. ➤a poet who writes verse to music.
– ORIGIN Fr., from Provençal *trobador*, from *trobar* 'find, invent, compose in verse'.

**trouble** ● **n.** **1** difficulty or problems. ➤malfunction; failure to work properly. ➤effort or exertion. ➤a cause of worry or inconvenience. ➤(often in phr. **in trouble**) a situation in which one is liable to incur punishment or blame. **2** public unrest or disorder. ● **v.** cause distress, pain, or inconvenience to. ➤[as adj. **troubled**] showing or experiencing problems or anxiety. ➤(**trouble about/over/with**) be distressed or anxious about. ➤(**trouble to do something**) make the effort required to do something.
– PHRASES **ask for trouble** informal act in a way that is likely to incur problems or difficulties. **look for trouble** informal behave in a way that is likely to provoke an argument or fight. **trouble and strife** Brit. rhyming slang wife.
– DERIVATIVES **troubler** n.
– ORIGIN ME: from OFr. *truble* (n.), *trubler* (v.), based on L. *turbidus* (see **TURBID**).

**troublemaker** ● **n.** a person who habitually causes trouble, especially by inciting others to defy those in authority.
– DERIVATIVES **troublemaking** n. & adj.

**troubleshoot** ● **v.** [usu. as noun **troubleshooting**] analyse and solve problems for an organization. ➤trace and correct faults in a mechanical or electronic system.
– DERIVATIVES **troubleshooter** n.

**troublesome** ● **adj.** causing difficulty or annoyance.
– DERIVATIVES **troublesomely** adv. **troublesomeness** n.

**trouble spot** ● **n.** a place where difficulties or conflict regularly occur.

**troublous** ● **adj.** archaic or poetic/literary full of troubles.

**trough** ● **n.** **1** a long, narrow open container for animals to eat or drink out of. ➤a similar container, e.g. one for growing plants. **2** a channel used to convey a liquid. ➤a long hollow in the earth's surface. **3** an elongated region of low barometric pressure. **4** a hollow between two wave crests in the sea. **5** a region around the minimum on a curve of variation of a quantity. ➤a point of low activity or achievement.
– ORIGIN OE *trog*, of Gmc origin; rel. to **TREE**.

**trounce** ● **v.** defeat heavily in a contest. ➤rebuke or punish severely.
– DERIVATIVES **trouncer** n.
– ORIGIN C16 (also in the sense 'afflict'): of unknown origin.

**troupe** ● **n.** a group of dancers, actors, or other entertainers who tour to different venues.
– ORIGIN C19: from Fr., lit. 'troop'.

**trouper** ● **n.** **1** an actor or other entertainer, typically one with long experience. **2** a reliable and uncomplaining person.

**trouser** ● **n.** [as modifier] relating to trousers. ● **v.** Brit. informal receive or take for oneself; pocket.

**trousers** ● **pl. n.** an outer garment covering the body from the waist to the ankles, with a separate part for each leg.
– PHRASES **catch someone with their trousers down** see ***catch someone with their pants down*** at **PANTS**. **wear the trousers** informal be the dominant partner in a relationship.
– DERIVATIVES **trousered** adj.
– ORIGIN C17: from archaic *trouse* (sing.) from Ir. *triús* and Sc. Gaelic *triubhas* (see **TREWS**), on the pattern of *drawers*.

**trouser suit** ● **n.** Brit. a pair of trousers and a matching jacket worn by women.

**trousseau** /ˈtruːsəʊ/ ● **n.** (pl. **trousseaux** or **trousseaus** /-səʊz/) the clothes, linen, and other belongings collected by a bride for her marriage.
– ORIGIN C19: from Fr., dimin. of *trousse* 'bundle'.

**trout** ● **n.** (pl. same or **trouts**) an edible fish of the salmon family, chiefly inhabiting fresh water. [*Salmo trutta* (**brown trout**, **sea trout**) and other species.] ● **v.** [as noun **trouting**] fishing for trout.
– PHRASES **old trout** informal an annoying or bad-tempered old person, especially a woman.
– ORIGIN OE *truht*, from late L. *tructa*, based on Gk *trōgein* 'gnaw'.

**trouvaille** /ˈtruːvʌɪ/ ● **n.** a lucky find.
– ORIGIN Fr., from *trouver* 'find'.

**trouvère** /truːˈvɛː/ ● **n.** a medieval epic poet in northern France.
– ORIGIN from OFr. *trovere*, from *trover* 'to find'; cf. **TROUBADOUR**.

**trove** ● **n.** a store of valuable or delightful things.
– ORIGIN C19: from **TREASURE TROVE**.

**trover** ● **n.** Law common-law action to recover the value of personal property that has been wrongfully disposed of by another person.
– ORIGIN C16: from an Anglo-Norman Fr. noun use of OFr. *trover* 'to find'.

**trow** /trəʊ/ ● **v.** archaic think or believe.
– ORIGIN OE *trūwian*, *trēowian* 'to trust'; rel. to **TRUCE**.

**trowel** ● **n.** **1** a small hand-held tool with a flat, pointed blade, used to apply and spread mortar or plaster. **2** a small hand-held tool with a curved scoop for lifting plants or earth. ● **v.** (**trowelled**, **trowelling**; US **troweled**, **troweling**) apply or spread with or as if with a trowel.
– ORIGIN ME: from OFr. *truele*, from med. L. *truella*, alt. of L. *trulla* 'scoop'.

**troy** (also **troy weight**) ● **n.** a system of weights used mainly for precious metals and gems, with a pound of 12 ounces or 5,760 grains. Compare with **AVOIRDUPOIS**.
– ORIGIN ME: from a weight used at the fair of *Troyes* in France.

**truant** ● **n.** a pupil who stays away from school without leave or explanation. ● **adj.** wandering; straying: *her truant husband.* ● **v.** (also **play truant**) (of a pupil) stay away from school without leave or explanation.
– DERIVATIVES **truancy** n.

– ORIGIN ME (denoting a person begging through choice rather than necessity): from OFr., prob. ult. of Celtic origin.

**truce** ● n. an agreement between enemies to stop fighting for a certain time.
– ORIGIN ME *trewes*, *trues* (pl.), from OE *trēowa*, pl. of *trēow* 'belief, trust', of Gmc origin; rel. to TRUE.

**truck**[1] ● n. **1** a large road vehicle, used for carrying goods, materials, or troops. ➤ Brit. a railway vehicle for carrying freight, especially a small open one. ➤ a low flat-topped trolley used for moving heavy items. **2** a railway bogie. ➤ each of two axle units on a skateboard, to which the wheels are attached. **3** a wooden disc at the top of a ship's mast or flagstaff, with holes for halyards to slide through. ● v. chiefly N. Amer. **1** convey by truck. **2** informal go or proceed in a casual or leisurely way.
– DERIVATIVES **truckage** n. **truckload** n.
– ORIGIN ME (denoting a solid wooden wheel): perh. short for TRUCKLE[1] in the sense 'wheel, pulley'.

**truck**[2] ● n. **1** archaic barter. ➤ chiefly historical the payment of workers in kind or with vouchers rather than money. **2** chiefly archaic small wares. ➤ informal odds and ends. **3** N. Amer. market-garden produce, especially vegetables. ● v. archaic barter or exchange.
– PHRASES **have** (or **want**) **no truck with** avoid or wish to avoid dealings or association with.
– ORIGIN ME: prob. from OFr., of unknown origin; cf. med. L. *trocare*.

**trucker** ● n. a long-distance truck driver.

**truckle**[1] ● n. a small barrel-shaped cheese, especially cheddar.
– ORIGIN ME (denoting a wheel or pulley): from Anglo-Norman Fr. *trocle*, from L. *trochlea* 'sheaf of a pulley'.

**truckle**[2] ● v. (usu. **truckle to**) submit or behave obsequiously.
– DERIVATIVES **truckler** n.
– ORIGIN C17: figuratively, from TRUCKLE BED; an earlier use of the verb was in the sense *sleep in a truckle bed*.

**truckle bed** ● n. chiefly Brit. a low bed on wheels that can be stored under a larger bed.
– ORIGIN ME: from TRUCKLE[1] in the sense 'wheel' + BED.

**truck stop** ● n. N. Amer. a transport cafe.

**truculent** /ˈtrʌkjʊl(ə)nt/ ● adj. eager or quick to argue or fight; aggressively defiant.
– DERIVATIVES **truculence** n. **truculently** adv.
– ORIGIN C16: from L. *truculentus*, from *trux*, *truc-* 'fierce'.

**trudge** ● v. walk slowly and with heavy steps, typically because of exhaustion or harsh conditions. ● n. a difficult or laborious walk.
– DERIVATIVES **trudger** n.
– ORIGIN C16: of unknown origin.

**trudgen** /ˈtrʌdʒ(ə)n/ ● n. a swimming stroke like the crawl with a scissors movement of the legs.
– ORIGIN C19: named after the Engl. swimmer John *Trudgen*.

**true** ● adj. (**truer**, **truest**) **1** in accordance with fact or reality. ➤ rightly or strictly so called; genuine: *true love*. ➤ real or actual. **2** accurate or exact. ➤ (of a note) exactly in tune. ➤ (of a compass bearing) measured relative to true north. ➤ correctly positioned or aligned; upright or level. **3** loyal or faithful. ➤ (**true to**) accurately conforming to (a standard or expectation). **4** chiefly archaic honest: *all good men and true*. ● v. (**trues**, **trued**, **truing** or **trueing**) bring into the exact shape or position required.
– PHRASES **come true** actually happen or become the case. **out of** (**the**) **true** not in the correct or exact shape or alignment. **true to form** (or **type**) being or behaving as expected. **true to life** accurately representing real events or objects.
– DERIVATIVES **trueness** n.
– ORIGIN OE *trēowe*, *trȳwe* 'steadfast, loyal'; rel. to TRUCE.

**true bill** ● n. US Law a bill of indictment found by a grand jury to be supported by sufficient evidence to justify the hearing of a case.

**true-blue** ● adj. **1** N. Amer. extremely loyal or orthodox. **2** Brit. staunchly loyal to the Conservative Party.

**true-born** ● adj. of a specified kind by birth; genuine.

**true-love knot** ● n. a kind of knot with interlacing bows on each side, symbolizing the bonds of love.

**true north** ● n. north according to the earth's axis, not magnetic north.

**true rib** ● n. a rib which is attached directly to the breastbone.

**truffle** ● n. **1** a strong-smelling underground fungus that resembles a rough-skinned potato, considered a culinary delicacy. [Family Tuberaceae.] **2** a soft sweet made of a chocolate mixture, typically flavoured with rum and covered with cocoa. ● v. [as noun **truffling**] hunting for truffles.
– ORIGIN C16: prob. via Du. from obs. Fr. *truffle*, perh. based on L. *tubera*, pl. of *tuber* 'hump, swelling'.

**truffled** ● adj. (of food) cooked, garnished, or stuffed with truffles.

**trug** ● n. Brit. a shallow oblong basket made of strips of wood, traditionally used for carrying garden flowers and produce.
– ORIGIN ME (denoting a basin): perh. a dial. var. of TROUGH.

**truism** ● n. **1** a statement that is obviously true and says nothing new or interesting. **2** Logic a proposition that states nothing beyond what is implied by any of its terms.
– DERIVATIVES **truistic** /-ˈɪstɪk/ adj.

**truite au bleu** /ˌtrwiːt əʊ ˈbləː/ ● n. a dish consisting of trout cooked with vinegar, which turns the fish blue.
– ORIGIN Fr., lit. 'trout in the blue'.

**trull** /trʌl/ ● n. archaic a prostitute.
– ORIGIN C16: from Ger. *Trulle*.

**truly** ● adv. **1** in a truthful way. **2** to the fullest degree; genuinely or properly. ➤ absolutely or completely. **3** in actual fact; really. **4** archaic loyally or faithfully.
– PHRASES **yours truly** used as a formula for ending a letter. ➤ humorous used to refer to oneself.

**trumeau** /truːˈməʊ/ ● n. (pl. **trumeaux** /-ˈməʊz/) a section of wall or a pillar between two openings, especially a pillar dividing a large doorway in a church.
– ORIGIN C19: from Fr., lit. 'calf of the leg'.

**trump**[1] ● n. **1** (in bridge, whist, etc.) a playing card of the suit chosen to rank above the others, which can win a trick where a card of a different suit has been led. ➤ (**trumps**) the suit having this rank in a particular hand. ➤ (in a tarot pack) any of a special suit of twenty-two cards depicting symbolic figures and scenes. **2** a valuable resource that may be used, especially as a surprise, to gain an advantage. **3** informal, dated a helpful or admirable person. **4** Austral./NZ informal a person in authority. ● v. **1** play a trump on (a card of another suit). **2** beat by saying or doing something better. **3** (**trump something up**) invent a false accusation or excuse.
– PHRASES **come** (or **turn**) **up trumps** informal, chiefly Brit. have a better performance or outcome than expected. ➤ be especially generous or helpful.
– ORIGIN C16: alt. of TRIUMPH, once used in card games in the same sense.

**trump**[2] ● n. archaic a trumpet or a trumpet blast.
– ORIGIN ME: from OFr. *trompe*, of Gmc origin; prob. imitative.

**trumpery** archaic ● n. (pl. **-ies**) articles, practices, or beliefs of superficial appeal but little real value or worth. ● adj. showy but worthless; delusive.
– ORIGIN ME (denoting trickery): from OFr. *tromperie*, from *tromper* 'deceive'.

**trumpet** ● n. **1** a brass musical instrument with a flared bell and a bright, penetrating tone. ➤ an organ stop with a quality resembling that of a trumpet. **2** something shaped like a trumpet, especially the tubular corona of a daffodil flower. **3** the loud cry of an elephant. ● v. (**trumpeted**, **trumpeting**) **1** play a trumpet. **2** (of an elephant) make its characteristic loud cry. **3** proclaim widely or loudly.
– PHRASES **blow one's** (**own**) **trumpet** talk openly and boastfully about one's achievements.
– ORIGIN ME: from OFr. *trompette*, dimin. of *trompe* (see TRUMP[2]).

**trumpeter** ● n. **1** a person who plays a trumpet, especially a soldier who gives signals with a trumpet. **2** a large gregarious ground-dwelling bird of tropical South American forests, with mainly black plumage and loud trumpeting calls. [Genus *Psophia*: three species.] **3** a pigeon of a domestic breed that makes a trumpet-like sound.

**trumpeter swan** ● **n.** a large migratory swan with a black and yellow bill and a honking call, breeding in northern North America. [*Cygnus buccinator*.]

**trumpet major** ● **n.** the chief trumpeter of a cavalry regiment, typically a principal musician in a regimental band.

**trumpet vine** (also **trumpet creeper**) ● **n.** a climbing shrub with orange or red trumpet-shaped flowers, cultivated as an ornamental. [*Campsis radicans* (N. America) and *C. grandiflora* (China).]

**truncal** ● **adj.** Medicine of or affecting the trunk of the body, or of a nerve.

**truncate** ● **v.** /trʌŋˈkeɪt, ˈtrʌŋ-/ [often as adj. **truncated**] shorten by cutting off the top or the end. ● **adj.** /ˈtrʌŋkeɪt/ Botany & Zoology (of a leaf, feather, etc.) ending abruptly as if truncated.
– DERIVATIVES **truncation** n.
– ORIGIN C15 (earlier (ME) as *truncation*): from L. *truncat-*, *truncare* 'maim'.

**truncheon** /ˈtrʌn(t)ʃ(ə)n/ ● **n.** chiefly Brit. **1** a short thick stick carried as a weapon by a police officer. **2** a staff or baton acting as a symbol of authority, especially that used by the Earl Marshal.
– ORIGIN ME (denoting a piece broken off, also a cudgel): from OFr. *tronchon* 'stump', based on L. *truncus* 'trunk'.

**trundle** ● **v.** move slowly and unevenly on or as if on wheels. ● **n.** an act of trundling.
– ORIGIN C16 (denoting a small wheel or roller): rel. to obs. or dial. *trendle, trindle* 'revolve'; rel. to **TREND**.

**trundle bed** ● **n.** chiefly N. Amer. a truckle bed.

**trunk** ● **n. 1** the main woody stem of a tree as distinct from its branches and roots. ➤ the main part of an artery, nerve, or other structure from which smaller branches arise. **2** a person's or animal's body apart from the limbs and head. **3** the elongated, prehensile nose of an elephant. **4** a large box with a hinged lid for storing or transporting clothes and other articles. **5** N. Amer. the boot of a motor car. **6** [as modifier] of or relating to the main routes of a transport or communication network: *a trunk road.*
– DERIVATIVES **trunkful** n. (pl. **-fuls**). **trunking** n. **trunkless** adj.
– ORIGIN ME: from OFr. *tronc*, from L. *truncus*.

**trunk call** ● **n.** dated, chiefly Brit. a long-distance telephone call made within the same country.

**trunkfish** ● **n.** (pl. same or **-fishes**) another term for **BOXFISH**.

**trunking** ● **n. 1** a system of shafts or conduits for cables or ventilation. **2** the use or arrangement of trunk lines.

**trunks** ● **pl. n.** men's shorts, worn especially for swimming or boxing.

**trunnel** /ˈtrʌn(ə)l/ ● **n.** US variant spelling of **TREENAIL**.

**trunnion** /ˈtrʌnjən/ ● **n.** a pin or pivot forming one of a pair on which something is supported.
– ORIGIN C17: from Fr. *trognon* 'core, tree trunk'.

**truss** ● **n. 1** a framework of rafters, posts, and struts which supports a roof, bridge, or other structure. **2** a surgical appliance worn to support a hernia, typically a padded belt. **3** a large projection of stone or timber, typically one supporting a cornice. **4** Brit., chiefly historical a bundle of old hay (56 lb), new hay (60 lb), or straw (36 lb). **5** a compact cluster of flowers or fruit growing on one stalk. **6** Sailing a heavy metal ring securing the lower yards to a mast. ● **v. 1** tie up the wings and legs of (a chicken or other bird) before cooking. ➤ bind or tie up tightly. **2** [usu. as adj. **trussed**] support with a truss or trusses.
– DERIVATIVES **trusser** n.
– ORIGIN ME: from OFr. *trusse* (n.), *trusser* 'pack up, bind in', based on late L. *tors-*, *torquere* 'twist'.

**trust** ● **n. 1** firm belief in someone or something. ➤ acceptance of the truth of a statement without evidence or investigation. **2** the state of being responsible for someone or something: *a man in a position of trust.* **3** Law an arrangement whereby a person (a trustee) is made the nominal owner of property to be held or used for the benefit of one or more others. **4** a body of trustees. ➤ an organization or company managed by trustees. ➤ US dated a large company that has or attempts to gain monopolistic control of a market. **5** W. Indian or archaic commercial credit. **6** poetic/literary a hope or expectation. ● **v. 1** believe in the reliability, truth, ability, or strength of. ➤ (**trust someone with**) have the confidence to allow someone to have, use, or look after. ➤ (**trust someone/thing to**) commit someone or something to the safe keeping of. ➤ (**trust to**) place reliance on (luck, fate, etc.). **2** have confidence; hope (used as a polite formula): *I trust that you have enjoyed this book.* **3** archaic allow credit to.
– PHRASES **trust someone to ——** it is characteristic or predictable for someone to act in the specified way.
– DERIVATIVES **trustable** adj. **trusted** adj. **truster** n. **trustful** adj. **trustfully** adv. **trustfulness** n.
– ORIGIN ME: from ON *traust*, from *traustr* 'strong'; the verb from ON *treysta*.

**Trustafarian** /trʌstəˈfɛːrɪən/ ● **n.** Brit. informal a rich young person who adopts an ethnic lifestyle and lives in a non-affluent urban area.
– ORIGIN 1990s: blend of **TRUST FUND** and **RASTAFARIAN**.

**trustbuster** ● **n.** informal, chiefly US a person or agency employed to enforce antitrust legislation.

**trust company** ● **n.** a company formed to act as a trustee or to deal with trusts.

**trust deed** ● **n.** Law a deed of conveyance creating and setting out the conditions of a trust.

**trustee** ● **n. 1** Law an individual or member of a board given powers of administration of property in trust with a legal obligation to administer it solely for the purposes specified. **2** a state made responsible for the government of an area by the United Nations.
– DERIVATIVES **trusteeship** n.

**trustee in bankruptcy** ● **n.** Law a person taking administrative responsibility for the financial affairs of a bankrupt.

**trust fund** ● **n.** a fund consisting of assets belonging to a trust, held by the trustees for the beneficiaries.

**trusting** ● **adj.** showing trust in or tending to trust others; not suspicious.
– DERIVATIVES **trustingly** adv. **trustingness** n.

**trust territory** ● **n.** a territory under the trusteeship of the United Nations or of a state designated by them.

**trustworthy** ● **adj.** able to be relied on as honest, truthful, or reliable.
– DERIVATIVES **trustworthily** adv. **trustworthiness** n.

**trusty** ● **adj.** (**-ier, -iest**) archaic or humorous reliable or faithful: *their trusty steeds.* ● **n.** (pl. **-ies**) a prisoner who is given special privileges or responsibilities in return for good behaviour.
– DERIVATIVES **trustily** adv. **trustiness** n.

**truth** ● **n.** (pl. **truths** /truːðz, truːθs/) the quality or state of being true. ➤ (also **the truth**) that which is true as opposed to false. ➤ a fact or belief that is accepted as true.
– PHRASES **in truth** really; in fact. **to tell the truth** (or **truth to tell** or **if truth be told**) to be frank.
– ORIGIN OE *trīewth, trēowth* 'faithfulness, constancy' (see **TRUE, -TH²**).

**truth condition** ● **n.** Logic the condition under which a given proposition is true. ➤ a statement of this condition, sometimes taken to be the meaning of the proposition.

**truth drug** ● **n.** a drug supposedly able to induce a state in which a person answers questions truthfully.

**truthful** ● **adj. 1** telling or expressing the truth; honest. **2** (of a representation) true to life.
– DERIVATIVES **truthfully** adv. **truthfulness** n.

**truth function** ● **n.** Logic a function whose truth value is dependent on the truth value of its arguments.

**truth table** ● **n.** Logic **1** a diagram in rows showing how the truth or falsity of a proposition varies with that of its components. **2** Electronics a similar diagram of the outputs from all possible combinations of input.

**truth value** ● **n.** Logic the attribute assigned to a proposition in respect of its truth or falsehood, which in classical logic has only two possible values (true or false).

**try** ● v. (**-ies**, **-ied**) **1** make an attempt or effort to do something. ➤(also **try something out**) test (something new or different) in order to see if it is suitable, effective, or pleasant. ➤attempt to operate (a device), open (a door), contact (someone), etc.: *I tried the doors, but they were locked.* ➤(**try something on**) put on an item of clothing to see if it fits or suits one. **2** make severe demands on: *Mary tried everyone's patience to the limit.* **3** subject (someone) to trial. ➤investigate and decide (a case or issue) in a formal trial. **4** smooth (wood) with a plane. **5** extract (oil or fat) by heating. ● n. (pl. **-ies**) **1** an effort to accomplish something; an attempt. ➤an act of testing something new or different. **2** Rugby an act of touching the ball down behind the opposing goal line, scoring points and entitling the scoring side to a kick at goal. ➤American Football an attempt to score an extra point after a touchdown.
– PHRASES **tried and tested** (or **true**) having proved effective or reliable before. **try one's hand at** attempt to do for the first time. **try it on** Brit. informal deliberately test or attempt to deceive or seduce someone.
– ORIGIN ME: from OFr. *trier* 'sift', of unknown origin.

**trying** ● adj. difficult or annoying; hard to endure: *it had been a very trying day.*
– DERIVATIVES **tryingly** adv.

**trying plane** ● n. a long, heavy plane used in smoothing the edges of roughly planed wood.

**trypan blue** ● n. a diazo dye used as a biological stain due to its absorption by macrophages of the reticuloendothelial system.
– ORIGIN C20: *trypan* from TRYPANOSOME.

**trypanosome** /ˈtrɪp(ə)nəsəʊm, trɪˈpanə-/ ● n. Medicine & Zoology a single-celled parasitic protozoan with a trailing flagellum, infesting the blood. [Genus *Trypanosoma*.]
– ORIGIN C20: from Gk *trupanon* 'borer' + -SOME[3].

**trypanosomiasis** /ˌtrɪp(ə)nə(ʊ)-, trɪˌpanə(ʊ)sə(ʊ)ˈmʌɪəsɪs/ ● n. Medicine a tropical disease caused by trypanosomes, especially sleeping sickness or Chagas' disease.

**trypsin** /ˈtrɪpsɪn/ ● n. a digestive enzyme which breaks down proteins in the small intestine, secreted by the pancreas as trypsinogen.
– DERIVATIVES **tryptic** adj.
– ORIGIN C19: from Gk *tripsis* 'friction', from *tribein* 'to rub' (because it was first obtained by rubbing down the pancreas with glycerine), + -IN[1].

**trypsinogen** /trɪpˈsɪnədʒ(ə)n/ ● n. Biochemistry an inactive substance secreted by the pancreas, from which the digestive enzyme trypsin is formed.

**tryptophan** /ˈtrɪptəfan/ ● n. Biochemistry an amino acid which is a constituent of most proteins and is an essential nutrient in the diet of vertebrates.
– ORIGIN C19: from *tryptic* 'relating to trypsin' + Gk *phainein* 'appear'.

**trysail** /ˈtrʌɪs(ə)l/ ● n. a small strong fore-and-aft sail set on the mainmast or other mast of a sailing vessel in heavy weather.

**try square** ● n. an implement used to check and mark right angles in constructional work.

**tryst** /trɪst/ poetic/literary ● n. a private, romantic rendezvous between lovers. ● v. keep or arrange a tryst.
– DERIVATIVES **tryster** n.
– ORIGIN ME: var. of obs. *trist* 'an appointed place in hunting', from Fr. *triste* or med. L. *trista*.

**tsar** /zɑː, tsɑː/ (also **czar** or **tzar**) ● n. **1** an emperor of Russia before 1917. ➤a South Slav ruler in former times, especially one reigning over Serbia in the 14th century. **2** a person with great power in a particular area: *America's new drug tsar.*
– DERIVATIVES **tsardom** n. **tsarism** n. **tsarist** n. & adj.
– ORIGIN from Russ. *tsar'*, representing L. *Caesar*.

**tsarevich** /ˈzɑːrɪvɪtʃ, ˈtsɑː-, -ˈrjeɪ-/ (also **czarevich** or **tzarevich**) ● n. historical the eldest son of a Russian tsar.
– ORIGIN Russ., lit. 'son of a tsar'.

**tsarina** /zɑːˈriːnə, tsɑː-/ (also **czarina** or **tzarina**) ● n. historical an empress of Russia before 1917.
– ORIGIN via Ital. and Sp. from Ger. *Czarin*, *Zarin*, fem. of *Czar*, *Zar*.

**tsatske** /ˈtsɒtskə/ ● n. variant spelling of TCHOTCHKE.

**tsessebi** /tsɛˈseɪbi/ (also **tsessebe**) ● n. a topi (antelope) of a race found mainly in southern Africa.
– ORIGIN C19: from Setswana.

**tsetse** /ˈtsɛtsi, ˈtɛtsi/ (also **tsetse fly**) ● n. an African bloodsucking fly which transmits sleeping sickness and other diseases. [Genus *Glossina*.]
– ORIGIN C19: from Setswana.

**TSgt** ● abbrev. Technical Sergeant.

**TSH** ● abbrev. thyroid-stimulating hormone.

**T-shirt** (also **tee shirt**) ● n. a short-sleeved casual top, having the shape of a T when spread out flat.

**tsimmes** /ˈtsɪməs/ (also **tzimmes** or **tzimmis**) ● n. (pl. same) **1** a Jewish stew of sweetened vegetables. **2** a fuss or muddle.
– ORIGIN from Yiddish.

**Tsimshian** /ˈtʃɪmʃɪən/ ● n. (pl. same) **1** a member of an American Indian people of the northern Pacific coast. **2** the Penutian language of this people. ● adj. of or relating to this people or their language.
– ORIGIN from Tsimshian *ĉamsián*, lit. 'inside the Skeena River'.

**tsk tsk** /t(ə)sk t(ə)sk/ ● exclam. expressing disapproval or annoyance.
– ORIGIN 1940s: imitative.

**Tsonga** /ˈtsɒŋgə/ ● n. (pl. same or **Tsongas**) **1** a member of a people living in Transvaal, southern Mozambique, and southern Zimbabwe. **2** the Bantu language of this people.
– ORIGIN a local name, from either Tsonga or Zulu.

**tsotsi** /ˈtsɒtsi/ ● n. (pl. **tsotsis**) S. African a young black urban criminal.
– ORIGIN said to be a Sotho corruption of ZOOT SUIT, with ref. to the flashy clothes orig. assoc. with tsotsis.

**tsp** ● abbrev. (pl. same or **tsps**) teaspoonful.

**T-square** ● n. a T-shaped instrument for drawing or testing right angles.

**TSR** ● abbrev. Computing terminate and stay resident, denoting a type of program that remains in the memory of a microcomputer after it has finished running.

**TSS** ● abbrev. toxic shock syndrome.

**tsuba** /ˈtsuːba/ ● n. (pl. same or **tsubas**) a Japanese sword guard.
– ORIGIN from Japanese.

**tsubo** /ˈtsuːbəʊ/ ● n. (pl. same or **-os**) **1** a Japanese unit of area equal to approximately 3.31 sq. metres (3.95 sq. yards). **2** (in complementary medicine) a point on the face or body to which pressure or other stimulation is applied during treatment.
– ORIGIN from Japanese.

**tsunami** /tsuːˈnɑːmi/ ● n. (pl. same or **tsunamis**) a long high sea wave caused by an earthquake or other disturbance.
– ORIGIN C19: from Japanese, from *tsu* 'harbour' + *nami* 'wave'.

**tsutsugamushi disease** /ˌtsuːtsuːgəˈmʊʃi/ ● n. another term for SCRUB TYPHUS.
– ORIGIN C20: *tsutsugamushi*, from the Japanese name of the mite which transmits the disease.

**Tswana** /ˈtswɑːnə/ ● n. (pl. same, **Tswanas**, or **Batswana**) **1** a member of a southern African people living in Botswana, South Africa, and neighbouring areas. **2** the language of this people, also called Setswana.
– ORIGIN stem of Setswana *moTswana*, pl. *baTswana*.

**TT** ● abbrev. **1** teetotal or teetotaller. **2** Tourist Trophy. **3** tuberculin-tested.

**TTL** ● abbrev. **1** Electronics transistor transistor logic, a widely used technology for making integrated circuits. **2** Photography (of a camera focusing system) through-the-lens.

**TU** ● abbrev. Trade Union.

**Tu.** ● abbrev. Tuesday.

**Tuareg** /ˈtwɑːrɛg/ ● n. (pl. same or **Tuaregs**) a member of a Berber people of the western and central Sahara.
– ORIGIN the name in Berber.

**tuatara** /ˌtuːəˈtɑːrə, ˌtjuː-/ ● n. a burrowing lizard-like reptile with a crest of soft spines, now confined to some small islands off New Zealand. [*Sphenodon punctatum*.]

– ORIGIN C19: from Maori, from *tua* 'on the back' + *tara* 'spine'.

**tub** • n. **1** a low, wide, open container with a flat bottom used for holding liquids, growing plants, etc. ➤ a similar small plastic or cardboard container for food. ➤ informal, chiefly N. Amer. a bath. ➤ Mining a container for conveying ore, coal, etc. **2** informal, derogatory a short, broad boat that handles awkwardly. • v. (**tubbed**, **tubbing**) **1** plant or put in a tub. **2** Brit. informal have a bath.
– DERIVATIVES **tubbable** adj. (informal) **tubful** n. (pl. **-fuls**).
– ORIGIN ME: prob. of Low Ger. or Du. origin; cf. Mid. Low Ger., MDu. *tubbe*.

**tuba** • n. a large brass wind instrument of bass pitch, with three to six valves and a broad bell facing upwards.
– ORIGIN C19: via Ital. from L., 'trumpet'.

**tubal** • adj. of, relating to, or occurring in a tube, especially the Fallopian tubes: *tubal ligation*.

**tubby** • adj. (**-ier**, **-iest**) **1** informal (of a person) short and rather fat. **2** (of a sound) lacking resonance; dull.
– DERIVATIVES **tubbiness** n.

**tube** • n. **1** a long, hollow cylinder used for conveying or holding liquids or gases. ➤ a flexible metal or plastic container sealed at one end and having a cap at the other. ➤ material forming tubes; tubing. **2** Anatomy, Zoology, & Botany a hollow cylindrical organ or structure in an animal or plant. ➤ (**tubes**) informal a woman's Fallopian tubes. **3** Brit. informal (**the tube**) the underground railway system in London. ➤ a train running on this system. **4** a sealed container, typically of glass and either evacuated or filled with gas, containing two electrodes between which an electric current can be made to flow. ➤ a cathode ray tube, especially in a television set. ➤ N. Amer. a thermionic valve. **5** (**the tube**) N. Amer. informal television. **6** (in surfing) the hollow curve under the crest of a breaking wave. **7** informal a cigarette. **8** Austral. informal a can of beer. • v. **1** [usu. as adj. **tubed**] provide with a tube or tubes. **2** convey in a tube.
– PHRASES **go down the tube** (or **tubes**) informal be completely lost or wasted; fail utterly.
– DERIVATIVES **tubeless** adj.
– ORIGIN C17: from Fr. *tube* or L. *tubus*.

**tubectomy** • n. (pl. **-ies**) another term for **SALPINGECTOMY**.

**tube foot** • n. Zoology (in an echinoderm) each of a large number of small flexible hollow appendages protruding through the ambulacra, used either for locomotion or for collecting food.

**tuber** • n. **1** a much thickened underground part of a stem or rhizome, e.g. in the potato, serving as a food reserve and bearing buds from which new plants arise. ➤ a thickened fleshy root, e.g. of the dahlia. **2** Anatomy a rounded swelling or protuberant part.
– ORIGIN C17: from L., lit. 'hump, swelling'.

**tubercle** /'tju:bək(ə)l/ • n. **1** Anatomy, Zoology, & Botany a small rounded projection or protuberance, especially on a bone or on the surface of an animal or plant. **2** Medicine a small nodular lesion in the lungs or other tissues, characteristic of tuberculosis.
– DERIVATIVES **tuberculate** /-'bə:kjʊlət/ adj.
– ORIGIN C16: from L. *tuberculum*, dimin. of *tuber* (see **TUBER**).

**tubercle bacillus** • n. the bacterium that causes tuberculosis. [*Mycobacterium tuberculosis*.]

**tubercular** /tjʊ'bə:kjʊlə/ • adj. **1** Medicine of, relating to, or affected with tuberculosis. **2** Biology & Medicine having or covered with tubercles. • n. a person with tuberculosis.

**tuberculation** /tjʊˌbə:kjʊ'leɪʃ(ə)n/ • n. chiefly Biology the formation or presence of tubercles.

**tuberculin** /tjʊ'bə:kjʊlɪn/ • n. a sterile protein extract from cultures of tubercle bacillus, used to test for tuberculosis.
– ORIGIN C19: from L. *tuberculum* (see **TUBERCLE**) + **-IN**[1].

**tuberculin-tested** • adj. (of milk) certified free from tuberculosis.

**tuberculoid** /tjʊ'bə:kjʊlɔɪd/ • adj. Medicine **1** resembling tuberculosis. **2** relating to or denoting the milder of the two principal forms of leprosy, marked by few, well-defined lesions similar to those of tuberculosis. Compare with **LEPROMATOUS**.

**tuberculosis** /tjʊˌbə:kjʊ'ləʊsɪs/ • n. an infectious bacterial disease characterized by the growth of nodules (tubercles) in the tissues, especially the lungs.
– ORIGIN C19: mod. L., from L. *tuberculum* (see **TUBERCLE**) + **-OSIS**.

**tuberculous** /tjʊ'bə:kjʊləs/ • adj. another term for **TUBERCULAR**.

**tuberose** /'tju:bərəʊz/ • n. a Mexican plant with heavily scented white waxy flowers and a bulb-like base, formerly cultivated as a flavouring for chocolate. [*Polianthes tuberosa*.] • adj. variant spelling of **TUBEROUS**.
– ORIGIN C17: the noun from L. *tuberosa*, fem. of *tuberosus* 'with protuberances'.

**tuberous** /'tju:b(ə)rəs/ (also **tuberose** /'tju:b(ə)rəʊs/) • adj. **1** Botany resembling, forming, or having a tuber or tubers. **2** Medicine characterized by or affected by rounded swellings.
– DERIVATIVES **tuberosity** /-'rɒsɪti/ n.

**tube worm** • n. a fan worm or other marine worm which lives in a tube-like structure.

**tubicolous** /tju:'bɪkələs/ • adj. Zoology (of a marine worm) living in a tube.

**tubifex** /'tju:bɪfɛks/ • n. a small red annelid worm that lives in fresh water, partly buried in the mud. [Genus *Tubifex*.]
– ORIGIN mod. L., from L. *tubus* 'tube' + *-fex* from *facere* 'make'.

**tubing** • n. **1** a length or lengths of material in tubular form. **2** N. Amer. the leisure activity of riding on water or snow on a large inflated inner tube.

**tub-thumping** informal, derogatory • adj. expressing opinions in a loud and violent or dramatic manner. • n. the expression of opinions in such a way.
– DERIVATIVES **tub-thumper** n.

**tubular** • adj. **1** long, round, and hollow like a tube. ➤ made from a tube or tubes. **2** Medicine of or involving tubules or other tube-shaped structures. • n. short for **TUBULAR TYRE**.
– ORIGIN C17: from L. *tubulus* 'small tube' + **-AR**[1].

**tubular bells** • pl. n. an orchestral instrument consisting of a row of vertically suspended metal tubes struck with a mallet.

**tubular tyre** • n. a completely enclosed tyre cemented on to the wheel rim, used on racing bicycles.

**tubule** /'tju:bju:l/ • n. **1** a minute tube, especially as an anatomical structure. **2** Anatomy each of the long, fine, convoluted tubules conveying urine from the glomeruli to the renal pelvis in the vertebrate kidney.
– ORIGIN C17: from L. *tubulus*, dimin. of *tubus* 'tube'.

**tubulin** /'tju:bjʊlɪn/ • n. Biochemistry a protein that is the main constituent of the microtubules of living cells.
– ORIGIN 1960s: from **TUBULE** + **-IN**[1].

**TUC** • abbrev. (in the UK) Trades Union Congress.

**tuck** • v. **1** push, fold, or turn under or between two surfaces or into a confined space. ➤ (**tuck something away**) store something in a secure place. ➤ (**tuck someone in/up**) settle someone in bed by pulling the edges of the bedclothes firmly under the mattress. **2** make a flattened, stitched fold in (a garment or material), to improve the fit or for decoration. **3** (**tuck in/into**) informal eat food heartily. • n. **1** a flattened, stitched fold in a garment or material. ➤ informal a surgical operation which involves removing a fold of flesh or fat. **2** Brit. informal food eaten by children at school as a snack. **3** (also **tuck position**) (in diving, gymnastics, downhill skiing, etc.) a position with the knees bent and held close to the chest.
– DERIVATIVES **tucking** n.
– ORIGIN OE *tūcian* 'to punish, ill-treat', of W. Gmc origin.

**tuckahoe** /'tʌkəhəʊ/ • n. a root or other underground plant part formerly eaten by North American Indians.
– ORIGIN C17: from Virginia Algonquian *tockawhoughe*.

**tucker** • n. **1** Austral./NZ informal food. **2** historical a piece of lace or linen worn on a bodice or as an insert at the front of a low-cut dress. • v. N. Amer. informal exhaust; wear out.

**tucket** • n. archaic a flourish on a trumpet.
– ORIGIN C16: from obs. *tuck* 'beat (a drum)', from ONorth.

Fr. *toquer*, from the base of **TOUCH**.

**tuck-point** ● v. point (brickwork) with coloured mortar so as to have a narrow groove which is filled with fine white lime putty allowed to project slightly.

**tuco-tuco** /ˈtuːkəʊˌtuːkəʊ/ ● n. (pl. **-os**) a burrowing rat-like rodent native to South America. [Genus *Ctenomys*: numerous species.]
– ORIGIN C19: imitative of the call of some species.

**'tude** ● n. N. Amer. informal short for **ATTITUDE**.

**-tude** ● suffix forming abstract nouns such as *beatitude*, *solitude*.
– ORIGIN from Fr. *-tude*, from L. *-tudo*.

**Tudor** ● adj. **1** of or relating to the English royal dynasty which held the throne from the accession of Henry VII in 1485 until the death of Elizabeth I in 1603. **2** of or denoting the prevalent architectural style of the Tudor period, characterized by half-timbering. ● n. a member of this dynasty.

**Tudor rose** ● n. a stylized figure of a rose used in architectural decoration in the Tudor period, especially a combination of the red and white roses of Lancaster and York.

**Tues.** (also **Tue.**) ● abbrev. Tuesday.

**Tuesday** ● n. the day of the week before Wednesday and following Monday. ● adv. chiefly N. Amer. on Tuesday. ➤(**Tuesdays**) on Tuesdays; each Tuesday.
– ORIGIN OE *Tīwesdœg*, named after the Gmc god *Tīw* (assoc. with Mars); translation of L. *dies Marti* 'day of Mars'.

**tufa** /ˈt(j)uːfə/ ● n. **1** a porous rock composed of calcium carbonate and formed by precipitation from water, e.g. around mineral springs. **2** another term for **TUFF**.
– DERIVATIVES **tufaceous** /-ˈfeɪʃəs/ adj.
– ORIGIN C18: from Ital., var. of *tufo* (see **TUFF**).

**tuff** /tʌf/ ● n. a light, porous rock formed by consolidation of volcanic ash.
– DERIVATIVES **tuffaceous** /-ˈfeɪʃəs/ adj.
– ORIGIN C16: via Fr. from Ital. *tufo*, from late L. *tofus*, L. *tophus* (see **TOPHUS**).

**tuffet** ● n. **1** a tuft or clump. **2** a footstool or low seat.
– ORIGIN C16: alt. of **TUFT**.

**tuft** ● n. a bunch of threads, grass, or hair, held or growing together at the base. ➤Anatomy & Zoology a bunch of small blood vessels or other small anatomical structures. ● v. **1** provide with a tuft or tufts. **2** Needlework strengthen (upholstery) by passing a cluster of threads through the material, so making depressions at regular intervals.
– DERIVATIVES **tufted** adj. **tufty** adj.
– ORIGIN ME: prob. from OFr. *tofe*, of unknown origin.

**tufted duck** ● n. a freshwater diving duck with a drooping crest, the male having mainly black and white plumage. [*Aythya fuligula*.]

**tug** ● v. (**tugged**, **tugging**) **1** pull (something) hard or suddenly. **2** tow (a ship) by means of a tug or tugs. ● n. **1** a hard or sudden pull. **2** (also **tugboat**) a small, powerful boat used for towing larger boats and ships, especially in harbour. ➤an aircraft towing a glider. **3** a loop from a horse's saddle which supports a shaft or trace.
– DERIVATIVES **tugger** n.
– ORIGIN ME: from the base of **TOW**[1].

**tug of war** ● n. a contest in which two teams pull at opposite ends of a rope until one drags the other over a central line.

**tugrik** /ˈtuːgriːk/ ● n. (pl. same or **tugriks**) the basic monetary unit of Mongolia, equal to 100 mongos.
– ORIGIN from Mongolian.

**tui** /ˈtuːi/ ● n. a large New Zealand honeyeater with glossy blackish plumage and two white tufts at the throat. [*Prosthemadura novaeseelandiae*.]
– ORIGIN C19: from Maori.

**Tuinal** /ˈt(j)uːɪnal, -nəl/ ● n. trademark a sedative and hypnotic drug composed of two barbiturates.

**tuition** ● n. teaching or instruction, especially of individuals or small groups. ➤N. Amer. a fee charged for this.
– DERIVATIVES **tuitional** adj.
– ORIGIN ME (in the sense 'custody, care'): via OFr. from L. *tuitio(n-)*, from *tueri* 'to watch, guard'.

**tularaemia** /ˌt(j)uːləˈriːmɪə/ (US **tularemia**) ● n. a severe infectious disease of animals which is transmissible to humans, caused by a bacterium (*Pasteurella tularense*) and characterized by ulcers, fever, and loss of weight.
– DERIVATIVES **tularaemic** adj.
– ORIGIN 1920s: mod. L., from *Tulare*, the county in California where it was first observed.

**tule** /ˈtuːli/ ● n. US a clubrush that is abundant in marshy areas of California. [*Scirpus acutus* and *S. validus*.]
– ORIGIN C19: via Sp. from Nahuatl *tullin*.

**tulip** ● n. a bulbous spring-flowering plant of the lily family, with boldly coloured cup-shaped flowers. [Genus *Tulipa*: numerous complex hybrids.]
– ORIGIN C16: from Fr. *tulipe*, via Turk. from Pers. *dulband* 'turban', from the shape of the expanded flower.

**tulip tree** ● n. **1** a deciduous North American tree which has large distinctively lobed leaves and insignificant tulip-like flowers. [*Liriodendron tulipifera*.] **2** informal term for **MAGNOLIA** (in sense 1).

**tulipwood** ● n. the ornamental wood of the tulip tree, or a similar wood from another tree (especially *Harpullia pendula* of Australia).

**tulle** /t(j)uːl/ ● n. a soft, fine net material, used for making veils and dresses.
– ORIGIN C19: from *Tulle*, a town in SW France.

**tulp** /təːlp/ ● n. S. African an African plant of the iris family, which is grown for its showy flowers but is toxic to livestock. [Genera *Homeria* and *Moraea*: several species.]
– ORIGIN C19: from Afrik., from Du.

**tulsi** /ˈtʊlsiː/ ● n. a kind of basil which is cultivated by Hindus as a sacred plant. [*Ocimum sanctum*.]
– ORIGIN from Hindi *tulsī*.

**tum** ● n. informal a person's stomach or abdomen.

**tumble** ● v. **1** fall suddenly, clumsily, or headlong. ➤perform acrobatic feats, typically handsprings and somersaults. **2** decrease rapidly in amount or value. **3** dry in a tumble-dryer. **4** rumple; disarrange. **5** informal have sexual intercourse with. **6** (**tumble to**) informal come to understand; realize: *he's tumbled to the fact that he was deceived*. **7** clean (castings, gemstones, etc.) in a tumbling barrel. ● n. **1** an instance of tumbling. **2** an untidy or confused arrangement or state. **3** a handspring or other acrobatic feat. **4** US informal a friendly sign of recognition or interest.
– ORIGIN ME (also in the sense 'dance with contortions'): from Mid. Low Ger. *tummelen*; cf. OE *tumbian* 'to dance'; prob. influenced by OFr. *tomber* 'to fall'.

**tumblebug** ● n. N. Amer. a dung beetle that rolls balls of dung along the ground.

**tumbledown** ● adj. falling or fallen into ruin; dilapidated.

**tumble-dryer** ● n. a machine that dries washed clothes by spinning them in hot air inside a rotating drum.
– DERIVATIVES **tumble-dry** v. (**-dries**, **-dried**).

**tumblehome** ● n. the inward slope of the upper part of a boat's sides.

**tumbler** ● n. **1** a drinking glass with straight sides and no handle or stem. [formerly having a rounded bottom so as not to stand upright.] **2** an acrobat. **3** another term for **TUMBLE-DRYER**. **4** a pivoted piece in a lock that holds the bolt until lifted by a key. ➤a notched pivoted plate in a gunlock. **5** an electrical switch worked by pushing a small sprung lever. **6** a tumbling barrel.

**tumbleweed** ● n. N. Amer. & Austral./NZ a plant of arid regions which breaks off near the ground in late summer, forming light globular masses blown about by the wind. [Several species in the genera *Salsola* and *Amaranthus*.]

**tumbling barrel** ● n. a revolving device containing an abrasive substance, in which castings, gemstones, or other hard objects can be cleaned by friction.

**tumbril** /ˈtʌmbr(ə)l, -brɪl/ (also **tumbrel**) ● n. historical an open cart that tilted backwards to empty out its load, in particular one used to convey prisoners to the guillotine during the French Revolution.
– ORIGIN ME (orig. denoting a type of cucking-stool): from OFr. *tomberel*, from *tomber* 'to fall'.

**tumefy** /ˈtjuːmɪfʌɪ/ ● v. (**-ies**, **-ied**) become swollen.
– DERIVATIVES **tumefaction** n.
– ORIGIN C16 (earlier (ME) as *tumefaction*): from Fr. *tuméfier*, from L. *tumefacere*, from *tumere* 'to swell'.

**tumescent** /tjʊˈmɛs(ə)nt/ ● **adj.** swollen or becoming swollen.
– DERIVATIVES **tumescence** n. **tumescently** adv.
– ORIGIN C19: from L. *tumescent-*, *tumescere* 'begin to swell', from *tumere* 'to swell'.

**tumid** /ˈtjuːmɪd/ ● **adj. 1** (of a part of the body) swollen or bulging. **2** pompous or bombastic: *tumid oratory.*
– DERIVATIVES **tumidity** n. **tumidly** adv.
– ORIGIN C16: from L. *tumidus*, from *tumere* 'to swell'.

**tummy** ● **n.** (pl. **-ies**) informal a person's stomach or abdomen.
– ORIGIN C19: child's pronunc. of **STOMACH**.

**tummy button** ● **n.** informal a person's navel.

**tumorigenesis** /ˌtjuːmərɪˈdʒɛnɪsɪs/ ● **n.** the formation of a tumour or tumours.

**tumorigenic** /ˌtjuːmərɪˈdʒɛnɪk/ ● **adj.** tending to form tumours.
– DERIVATIVES **tumorigenicity** n.

**tumour** (US **tumor**) ● **n.** a swelling of a part of the body, generally without inflammation, caused by an abnormal growth of tissue, whether benign or malignant.
– DERIVATIVES **tumorous** adj.
– ORIGIN ME: from L. *tumor*, from *tumere* 'to swell'.

**tump** /tʌmp/ ● **n.** chiefly dialect a small rounded hill or clump.
– ORIGIN C16: of unknown origin.

**tumpline** /ˈtʌmplʌɪn/ ● **n.** N. Amer. a sling for carrying a load on the back, with a strap passing round the forehead.
– ORIGIN C18: based on Algonquian *(mat)tump* + **LINE**[1].

**tumult** ● **n. 1** a loud, confused noise, as caused by a large mass of people. **2** confusion or disorder.
– ORIGIN ME: from OFr. *tumulte* or L. *tumultus*.

**tumultuous** /tjʊˈmʌltjʊəs/ ● **adj. 1** very loud or uproarious. **2** excited, confused, or disorderly.
– DERIVATIVES **tumultuously** adv. **tumultuousness** n.

**tumulus** /ˈtjuːmjʊləs/ ● **n.** (pl. **tumuli** /-lʌɪ, -liː/) an ancient burial mound; a barrow.
– ORIGIN ME: from L.; rel. to *tumere* 'swell'.

**tun** ● **n. 1** a large beer or wine cask. ➤a brewer's fermenting-vat. **2** an imperial measure of capacity, equal to 4 hogsheads. ● **v.** (**tunned**, **tunning**) archaic store (wine or drink) in a tun.
– ORIGIN OE *tunne*, from med. L. *tunna*, prob. of Gaulish origin.

**tuna**[1] ● **n.** (pl. same or **tunas**) a large and active predatory schooling fish of warm seas, extensively fished commercially. [*Thunnus* and other genera: several species.]
– ORIGIN C19: from Amer. Sp., from Sp. *atún* 'tunny'.

**tuna**[2] ● **n.** N. Amer. a prickly pear cactus that produces an edible fruit, widely cultivated in Mexico. [*Opuntia tuna* and related species.]
– ORIGIN C16: via Sp. from Taino.

**tundish** /ˈtʌndɪʃ/ ● **n.** Brit. a broad open container or large funnel with one or more holes at the bottom, used especially in plumbing or metal-founding.

**tundra** /ˈtʌndrə/ ● **n.** a vast, flat, treeless Arctic region of Europe, Asia, and North America in which the subsoil is permanently frozen.
– ORIGIN C16: from Lappish.

**tundra swan** ● **n.** an Arctic-breeding migratory swan with a yellow and black bill, with two subspecies (Bewick's swan and whistling swan). [*Cygnus columbianus*.]

**tune** ● **n.** a melody, especially one which characterizes a certain piece of music. ● **v. 1** adjust (a musical instrument) to the correct or uniform pitch. **2** adjust (a receiver circuit such as a radio or television) to the frequency of the required signal. ➤(**tune in**) watch or listen to a television or radio broadcast. **3** adjust (an engine) or balance (mechanical parts) in order that they run smoothly and efficiently. **4** adjust or adapt to a particular purpose or situation. ➤(**tune into**) become sensitive to. ➤(**tune out**) informal stop listening or paying attention.
– PHRASES **in** (or **out of**) **tune 1** with correct (or incorrect) pitch or intonation. **2** (of a motor engine) properly (or poorly) adjusted. **3** in (or not in) agreement or harmony. **to the tune of** informal amounting to or involving: *he was in debt to the tune of forty thousand pounds.*
– DERIVATIVES **tunable** (also **tuneable**) adj. **tuning** n.
– ORIGIN ME: unexplained alt. of **TONE**.

**tuneful** ● **adj.** having a pleasing tune; melodious.
– DERIVATIVES **tunefully** adv. **tunefulness** n.

**tuneless** ● **adj.** not pleasing to listen to; unmelodious.
– DERIVATIVES **tunelessly** adv. **tunelessness** n.

**tuner** ● **n. 1** a person who tunes musical instruments, especially pianos. **2** an electronic device used for tuning. **3** a separate unit for detecting and preamplifying a programme signal and supplying it to an audio amplifier.

**tunesmith** ● **n.** informal a composer of popular music or songs.

**tung oil** ● **n.** an oil obtained from the seeds of a SE Asian tree (genus *Aleurites*), used as a drying agent in inks, paints, and varnishes.
– ORIGIN C19: from Chin.

**tungstate** /ˈtʌŋsteɪt/ ● **n.** Chemistry a salt in which the anion contains both tungsten and oxygen.
– ORIGIN C19: from **TUNGSTEN** + **-ATE**[1].

**tungsten** /ˈtʌŋst(ə)n/ ● **n.** the chemical element of atomic number 74, a hard steel-grey metal with a very high melting point (3410°C), used to make electric light filaments. (Symbol: **W**)
– ORIGIN C18: from Swed., from *tung* 'heavy' + *sten* 'stone'.

**tungsten carbide** ● **n.** a very hard grey compound made by reaction of tungsten and carbon at high temperatures, used in making engineering dies, cutting and drilling tools, etc.

**tungstite** /ˈtʌŋstʌɪt/ ● **n.** a yellow mineral consisting of hydrated tungsten oxide, typically occurring as a powdery coating on tungsten ores.
– ORIGIN C19: from **TUNGSTEN** + **-ITE**[1].

**Tungus** /ˈtʊŋʊs, tʊŋˈguːs/ ● **n.** (pl. same) **1** a member of the northern Evenki people of Siberia. **2** older term for **EVENKI** (the language).
– ORIGIN the name in Yakut.

**Tungusic** /tʊŋˈguːsɪk/ ● **n.** a small family of Altaic languages of Siberia and northern China.

**tunic** ● **n. 1** a loose sleeveless garment reaching to the thigh or knees. ➤a gymslip. **2** a close-fitting short coat worn as part of a uniform. **3** Biology & Anatomy an integument or membrane enclosing or lining an organ or part. ➤Botany any of the concentric layers of a plant bulb, e.g. an onion.
– ORIGIN OE, from OFr. *tunique* or L. *tunica*.

**tunica** /ˈtjuːnɪkə/ ● **n.** (pl. **tunicae** /-kiː/) **1** Anatomy a membranous sheath enveloping or lining an organ. **2** Botany the outer layer of cells at the apex of a growing shoot.
– ORIGIN C17: from L., lit. 'tunic'.

**tunicate** /ˈtjuːnɪkət, -keɪt/ ● **n.** Zoology a marine invertebrate of a group which includes the sea squirts and salps, with a rubbery or hard outer coat. [Subphylum Urochordata.] ● **adj.** (also **tunicated**) Botany (of a plant bulb, e.g. an onion) having concentric layers.

**tunicle** /ˈtjuːnɪk(ə)l/ ● **n.** a short liturgical vestment which is traditionally worn over the alb by a subdeacon at celebrations of the Mass.
– ORIGIN ME: from OFr. *tunicle* or L. *tunicula*, dimin. of *tunica*.

**tuning fork** ● **n.** a two-pronged steel device used for tuning instruments, which vibrates when struck to give a note of specific pitch.

**tuning peg** ● **n.** any of the pegs in the neck of a stringed musical instrument, which can be turned to adjust the tension of the strings and so tune the instrument.

**Tunisian** /tjuːˈnɪzɪən/ ● **n.** a native or inhabitant of Tunisia. ● **adj.** of or relating to Tunisia.

**tunnel** ● **n. 1** an artificial underground passage, as built through a hill or under a building or by a burrowing animal. **2** a polytunnel. ● **v.** (**tunnelled**, **tunnelling**; US **tunneled**, **tunneling**) **1** dig or force a passage underground or through something. **2** Physics (of a particle) pass through a potential barrier.
– DERIVATIVES **tunneller** n.
– ORIGIN ME (in the senses 'tunnel-shaped net' and 'flue of

a chimney'): from OFr. *tonel*, dimin. of *tonne* 'cask'.

**tunnel diode** ● **n.** Electronics a two-terminal semiconductor diode using tunnelling electrons to perform high-speed switching operations.

**tunnel vision** ● **n. 1** defective sight in which objects cannot be properly seen if not close to the centre of the field of view. **2** informal the tendency to focus exclusively on a single or limited objective or view.

**tunny** (also **tunny fish**) ● **n.** (pl. same or **-ies**) a tuna, especially the bluefin.
– ORIGIN C16: from Fr. *thon*, via L. from Gk *thunnos*.

**tup** /tʌp/ ● **n.** chiefly Brit. a ram. ● **v.** (**tupped**, **tupping**) **1** chiefly Brit. (of a ram) copulate with (a ewe). **2** N. English informal headbutt in a fight.
– DERIVATIVES **tupping** n.
– ORIGIN ME: of unknown origin.

**tupelo** /ˈt(j)uːpɪləʊ/ ● **n.** (pl. **-os**) a North American or Asian tree of damp and swampy habitats, which yields useful wood. [*Nyssa sylvatica* and related species.]
– ORIGIN C18: from Creek, from *ito* 'tree' + *opilwa* 'swamp'.

**Tupi** /ˈtuːpi/ ● **n.** (pl. same or **Tupis**) **1** a member of a group of American Indian peoples of the Amazon valley. **2** any of the languages of these peoples.
– DERIVATIVES **Tupian** adj.
– ORIGIN a local name.

**Tupi-Guarani** ● **n.** a South American Indian language family whose principal members are Guarani and the Tupian languages.

**tuppence** ● **n.** Brit. variant spelling of **TWOPENCE**.

**tuppenny** ● **adj.** Brit. variant spelling of **TWOPENNY**.

**Tupperware** /ˈtʌpəwɛː/ ● **n.** trademark a range of plastic containers used chiefly for storing food.
– ORIGIN 1950s: from *Tupper*, the name of the Amer. manufacturer, + **WARE**[1].

**tuque** /tuːk/ ● **n.** Canadian a close-fitting knitted stocking cap.
– ORIGIN Canad. Fr. form of **TOQUE**.

**turaco** /ˈtʊərəkəʊ/ (also **touraco**) ● **n.** (pl. **-os**) a fruit-eating African bird with brightly coloured plumage, a prominent crest, and a long tail. [*Tauraco* and other genera: several species.]
– ORIGIN C18: from Fr. *touraco*, from a W. Afr. word.

**Turanian** /tjʊˈreɪnɪən/ ● **adj.** dated relating to or denoting the languages of central Asia, particularly those of the Uralic and Altaic families, or the peoples that speak them.
– ORIGIN C18: from Pers. *Tūrān*, the region beyond the Oxus, + **-IAN**.

**turban** ● **n.** a man's headdress, consisting of a long length of material wound round a cap or the head, worn especially by Muslims and Sikhs.
– DERIVATIVES **turbaned** (also **turbanned**) adj.
– ORIGIN C16: via Fr. from Turk. *tülbent*, from Pers. *dulband*.

**turbary** /ˈtəːb(ə)ri/ ● **n.** (in full **common of turbary**) (pl. **-ies**) Brit. the legal right to cut turf or peat for fuel on common ground or on another person's ground. ➤a place where turf or peat is dug or cut.
– ORIGIN ME: from Anglo-Norman Fr. *turberie*, from OFr. *tourbe* 'turf'.

**turbid** /ˈtəːbɪd/ ● **adj. 1** (of a liquid) cloudy, opaque, or thick with suspended matter. **2** turbulent; confused.
– DERIVATIVES **turbidity** n. **turbidly** adv. **turbidness** n.
– ORIGIN ME: from L. *turbidus*, from *turba* 'a crowd, a disturbance'.

**turbidimeter** /ˌtəːbɪˈdɪmɪtə/ ● **n.** an instrument for measuring the turbidity of a liquid suspension.
– DERIVATIVES **turbidimetric** adj. **turbidimetry** n.

**turbidite** /ˈtəːbɪdʌɪt/ ● **n.** Geology a sediment or rock deposited by a turbidity current.
– DERIVATIVES **turbiditic** adj.
– ORIGIN 1950s: from *turbidity* (see **TURBID**) + **-ITE**[1].

**turbidity current** ● **n.** an underwater current flowing swiftly down owing to the weight of sediment it carries.

**turbinal** /ˈtəːbɪn(ə)l/ ● **n.** Anatomy & Zoology each of three thin curved shelves of bone in the sides of the nasal cavity, covered in mucous membrane.
– ORIGIN C16 (in the sense 'top-shaped'): from L. *turbo, turbin-* 'spinning top' + **-AL**.

**turbinate** /ˈtəːbɪnət/ ● **adj.** chiefly Zoology (especially of a shell) shaped like a spinning top. ➤Anatomy relating to or denoting the turbinals. ● **n.** Anatomy another term for **TURBINAL**.
– ORIGIN C17: from L. *turbinatus*, from *turbo, turbin-* (see **TURBINE**).

**turbine** /ˈtəːbʌɪn, -ɪn/ ● **n.** a machine for producing continuous power in which a wheel or rotor, typically fitted with vanes, is made to revolve by a fast-moving flow of water, steam, gas, air, or other fluid.
– ORIGIN C19: from Fr., from L. *turbo, turbin-* 'spinning top, whirl'.

**turbit** /ˈtəːbɪt/ ● **n.** a stoutly built pigeon of a domestic breed with a neck frill and short beak.
– ORIGIN C17: appar. from L. *turbo* 'spinning top', from its shape.

**turbo** /ˈtəːbəʊ/ ● **n.** (pl. **-os**) short for **TURBOCHARGER**.

**turbo-** ● **comb. form** having or driven by a turbine: *turboshaft*.

**turbocharge** ● **v.** [usu. as adj. **turbocharged**] equip with a turbocharger.

**turbocharger** ● **n.** a supercharger driven by a turbine powered by the engine's exhaust gases.

**turbofan** ● **n.** a jet engine in which a turbine-driven fan provides additional thrust.

**turbojet** ● **n.** a jet engine in which the jet gases also operate a turbine-driven compressor for compressing the air drawn into the engine.

**turboprop** ● **n.** a jet engine in which a turbine is used to drive a propeller.

**turboshaft** ● **n.** a gas turbine engine in which the turbine drives a shaft other than a propeller shaft.

**turbot** ● **n.** (pl. same or **turbots**) a flatfish of inshore waters, which has large bony tubercles on the body and is prized as food. [*Scophthalmus maximus* (Europe) and other species.]
– ORIGIN ME: from OFr., of Scand. origin.

**turbulent** /ˈtəːbjʊl(ə)nt/ ● **adj. 1** disorderly or confused; not calm or controlled. **2** technical relating to or denoting irregular and disordered flow of fluids.
– DERIVATIVES **turbulence** n. **turbulently** adv.
– ORIGIN ME: from L. *turbulentus* 'full of commotion', from *turba* 'crowd'.

**Turco** /ˈtəːkəʊ/ ● **n.** (pl. **-os**) historical an Algerian soldier in the French army.
– ORIGIN C19: from Sp., Port., and Ital., lit. 'Turk'.

**Turco-** (also **Turko-**) ● **comb. form** Turkish or relating to Turkey; Turkish and ...: *Turco-Tartar.*

**Turcoman** ● **n.** variant spelling of **TURKOMAN**.

**turd** ● **n.** vulgar slang **1** a lump of excrement. **2** an obnoxious or contemptible person.
– ORIGIN OE *tord*, of Gmc origin.

**tureen** /tjʊˈriːn, tə-/ ● **n.** a deep covered dish from which soup is served.
– ORIGIN C18: alt. of earlier *terrine*, from Fr. *terrine* (see **TERRINE**), fem. of OFr. *terrin* 'earthen', based on L. *terra* 'earth'.

**turf** ● **n.** (pl. **turfs** or **turves**) **1** grass and the surface layer of earth held together by its roots. ➤a piece of such grass and earth cut from the ground. **2** (**the turf**) horse racing or racecourses generally. **3** informal an area regarded as someone's territory; a sphere of influence or activity: *he did not like poachers on his turf.* ● **v. 1** informal, chiefly Brit. force to leave somewhere: *they were turfed off the bus.* **2** cover with turf.
– DERIVATIVES **turfy** adj.
– ORIGIN OE, of Gmc origin.

**turf accountant** ● **n.** Brit. formal a bookmaker.

**turfman** ● **n.** (pl. **-men**) chiefly US a devotee of horse racing.

**turgescent** /təːˈdʒɛs(ə)nt/ ● **adj.** chiefly technical becoming or seeming swollen or distended.
– DERIVATIVES **turgescence** n.
– ORIGIN C18: from L. *turgescent-*, *turgescere* 'begin to

swell', from *turgere* 'to swell'.

**turgid** /ˈtəːdʒɪd/ ● **adj.** **1** swollen and distended or congested. **2** (of language or style) tediously pompous or bombastic.
– DERIVATIVES **turgidity** n. **turgidly** adv.
– ORIGIN C17: from L. *turgidus*, from *turgere* 'to swell'.

**turgor** /ˈtəːɡə/ ● **n.** chiefly Botany a state of turgidity and resulting rigidity of cells or tissues.
– ORIGIN C19: from late L., from *turgere* 'to swell'.

**Turing machine** ● **n.** a mathematical model of a hypothetical computing machine which can use a predefined set of rules to determine a result from a set of input variables.
– ORIGIN named after the Engl. mathematician Alan *Turing* (1912–54).

**Turing test** ● **n.** a series of questions used as a test for intelligence in a computer.

**turion** /ˈt(j)ʊərɪən/ ● **n.** Botany (in some aquatic plants) a wintering bud which becomes detached and remains dormant at the bottom of the water.
– ORIGIN C18: from Fr., from L. *turio(n-)* 'a shoot'.

**Turk** ● **n.** **1** a native or national of Turkey, or a person of Turkish descent. **2** historical a member of any of the ancient peoples who spoke Turkic languages, including the Seljuks and Ottomans.
– ORIGIN ME: via OFr. from Turk. *türk*.

**Turkana** /təːˈkɑːnə/ ● **n.** (pl. same) **1** a member of an East African people living between Lake Turkana and the Nile. **2** the Nilotic language of the Turkana.
– ORIGIN a local name.

**turkey** ● **n.** (pl. **-eys**) **1** a large mainly domesticated game bird native to North America, having a bald head and (in the male) red wattles. [*Meleagris gallopavo*.] **2** informal, chiefly N. Amer. something that is extremely unsuccessful, especially a play or film. **3** a stupid or inept person.
– PHRASES **talk turkey** N. Amer. informal discuss frankly and openly.
– ORIGIN C16: short for **TURKEYCOCK** or *turkeyhen*, orig. applied to the guineafowl (which was imported through Turkey), and then erroneously to the Amer. bird.

**turkey buzzard** ● **n.** North American term for **TURKEY VULTURE**.

**turkeycock** ● **n.** a male turkey.

**turkey oak** ● **n.** a southern European oak with a domed spreading crown and acorn cups with long outward-pointing scales. [*Quercus cerris*.]

**Turkey red** ● **n.** a scarlet textile dye obtained from madder or alizarin.

**turkey trot** ● **n.** a kind of ballroom dance to ragtime music, popular in the early 20th century.

**turkey vulture** ● **n.** a common American vulture with black plumage and a bare red head. [*Cathartes aura*.]

**Turkic** /ˈtəːkɪk/ ● **adj.** relating to or denoting a large group of Altaic languages of western and central Asia, including Turkish, Azerbaijani, Uighur, and Tatar. ● **n.** the Turkic languages collectively.

**Turkish** ● **n.** the language of Turkey, a Turkic language written with the Roman alphabet. ● **adj.** of or relating to Turkey or the Turks or their language.

**Turkish bath** ● **n.** a cleansing or relaxing treatment that involves sitting in a room filled with very hot air or steam, followed by washing and massage. ➤ a building or room where such a treatment is available.

**Turkish coffee** ● **n.** very strong black coffee served with the fine grounds in it.

**Turkish delight** ● **n.** a sweet consisting of flavoured gelatin coated in icing sugar.

**Turkish slipper** ● **n.** a soft heelless slipper with a turned-up toe.

**Turkish Van** ● **n.** a cat of a long-haired breed, with a white body, auburn markings on the head and tail, and light orange eyes.
– ORIGIN 1960s: named after the town of *Van*, Turkey.

**Turkmen** /ˈtəːkmən/ ● **n.** (pl. same or **Turkmens**) **1** a member of a group of Turkic peoples inhabiting the region east of the Caspian Sea and south of the Aral Sea. **2** the Turkic language of these peoples.
– ORIGIN from Pers. *turkmān*, from Turk. *türkmen*; also influenced by Russ. *turkmen*.

**Turko-** ● **comb. form** variant spelling of **TURCO-**.

**Turkoman** /ˈtəːkə(ʊ)mən/ (also **Turcoman**) ● **n.** (pl. **Turkomans**) **1** another term for **TURKMEN**. **2** a kind of large, soft, richly coloured rug made by the Turkmens.
– ORIGIN C17: from med. L. *Turcomannus*, Fr. *turcoman*, from Pers. *turkmān* (see **TURKMEN**).

**Turk's cap lily** ● **n.** another term for **MARTAGON LILY**.

**Turk's head** ● **n.** an ornamental knot resembling a turban in shape, made in the end of a rope to form a stopper.

**turlough** /ˈtʊələʊx/ ● **n.** (in Ireland) a low-lying area on limestone which becomes flooded with groundwater in wet weather.
– ORIGIN C17: from Ir. *turloch*, from *tur* 'dry' + *loch* 'lake'.

**turmeric** /ˈtəːmərɪk/ ● **n.** **1** a bright yellow aromatic powder obtained from the rhizome of a plant, used for flavouring and colouring in Asian cookery and formerly as a fabric dye. **2** the Asian plant of the ginger family from which this is obtained. [*Curcuma longa*.]
– ORIGIN ME (earlier as *tarmaret*): perh. from Fr. *terre mérite* and mod. L. *terra merita*, lit. 'deserving earth'.

**turmoil** ● **n.** a state of great disturbance, confusion, or uncertainty.
– ORIGIN C16: of unknown origin.

**turn** ● **v.** **1** move or cause to move in a circular direction wholly or partly around an axis. ➤ move or cause to move into a different position, especially so as to face the opposite direction. ➤ change or cause to change direction. ➤ (of the tide) change from flood to ebb or vice versa. ➤ pass round (the flank or defensive lines of an army) so as to attack from the side or rear. ➤ twist or sprain (an ankle). ➤ archaic bend back (the edge of a blade) so as to make it blunt. **2** change or cause to change in nature, state, form, or colour; make or become. ➤ (of leaves) change colour in the autumn. ➤ (with reference to milk) make or become sour. ➤ make or become nauseated: *the smell would turn the strongest stomach.* **3** (**turn to**) start doing or becoming involved with. ➤ go to for help or information. ➤ have recourse to: *he turned to drink and drugs for solace.* **4** shape on a lathe. **5** give a graceful or elegant form to. **6** make (a profit). ● **n.** **1** an act of turning. ➤ a bend or curve in a road, path, river, etc. ➤ a place where a road meets or branches off another; a turning. ➤ Cricket deviation in the direction of the ball when bouncing off the pitch. ➤ one round in a coil of rope or other material. **2** a development or change in circumstances. ➤ a time when one period of time ends and another begins. ➤ (**the turn**) the beginning of the second nine holes of a round of golf. **3** an opportunity or obligation to do something that comes successively to each of a number of people. **4** a short walk or ride. **5** informal a shock. ➤ a brief feeling or experience of illness: *he's had another of his funny turns.* **6** the difference between the buying and selling price of stocks or other financial products. ➤ a profit made from such a difference. **7** Music a melodic ornament consisting of the principal note with those above and below it. **8** a short performance, especially one of a number given by different performers.
– PHRASES **at every turn** on every occasion; continually. **by turns** alternately. **do someone a good** (or **bad**) **turn** do something that is helpful (or unhelpful) for someone. **in turn** in succession; one after the other. **on the turn** at a turning point; in a state of change. **out of turn** at a time when it is inappropriate or not one's turn. **take turns** (or **take it in turns**) (of two or more people) do something alternately or in succession. **to a turn** to exactly the right degree: *beefburgers done to a turn.* **turn and turn about** chiefly Brit. one after another; in succession. **turn of mind** a particular way of thinking. **turn of speed** the ability to go fast when necessary. **turn something over in one's mind** think about or consider something thoroughly. **turn tail** informal turn round and run away.
– PHRASAL VERBS **turn against** (or **turn someone against**) become (or cause someone to become) hostile towards. **turn someone away** refuse admittance to someone. **turn someone/thing down 1** reject an offer

or application of something or from someone. **2** (**turn something down**) adjust a control on an electrical device to reduce the volume, heat, etc. **turn in** informal go to bed in the evening. **turn someone/thing in** hand someone or something over to the authorities. **turn off** leave one road in order to join another. **turn someone off** informal cause someone to feel bored or repelled. **turn something off** stop the operation of something by means of a tap, switch, or button. **turn on 1** suddenly attack: *he turned on her with cold savagery.* **2** have as the main focus. **turn someone on** informal excite or stimulate someone, especially sexually. **turn something on** start the operation of something by means of a tap, switch, or button. **turn out 1** prove to be the case. **2** go somewhere in order to attend a meeting, vote, play in a game, etc. **turn someone out 1** eject or expel someone from a place. **2** Military call a guard from the guardroom. **3** (**be turned out**) be dressed in the manner specified. **turn something out 1** extinguish an electric light. **2** produce something. **3** empty something, especially one's pockets. **turn over 1** (of an engine) start or continue to run properly. **2** (of a business) have a turnover of. **turn someone/thing over** change or transfer custody or control of someone or something. **turn something round** (or **around**) reverse the previously poor performance of something. **turn up 1** be found, especially by chance. **2** put in an appearance; arrive. **turn something up 1** increase the volume or strength of sound, heat, etc. by turning a knob or switch on a device. **2** reveal or discover something. **3** shorten a garment by raising the hem.
– DERIVATIVES **turner** n.
– ORIGIN OE *tyrnan, turnian* (v.), from L. *tornare*, from *tornus* 'lathe', from Gk *tornos* 'lathe, circular movement'; prob. reinforced in ME by OFr. *turner.*

**turnabout** • n. a sudden and complete change of policy, opinion, etc.

**turnaround** (also **turnround**) • n. **1** an abrupt or unexpected change. **2** the process of completing or the time needed to complete a task. **3** N. Amer. a space for vehicles to turn round in.

**turnbuckle** • n. a coupling with internal screw threads used to connect two rods, lengths of boat's rigging, etc. lengthwise or to regulate their length or tension.

**turncoat** • n. a person who deserts one party or cause in order to join an opposing one.

**Turner's syndrome** • n. Medicine a genetic defect in which affected women have only one X chromosome, causing developmental abnormalities and infertility.
– ORIGIN 1940s: named after the Amer. physician Henry Hubert *Turner.*

**turnery** • n. the action or skill of turning objects on a lathe. ➤objects made on a lathe.

**turning** • n. **1** a place where a road branches off another. **2** the action or skill of using a lathe. ➤(**turnings**) shavings of wood resulting from turning wood on a lathe.

**turning circle** • n. the smallest circle in which a vehicle or vessel can turn without reversing.

**turnip** • n. **1** a round root with white or cream flesh which is eaten as a vegetable and also has edible leaves. **2** the European plant of the cabbage family which produces this root. [*Brassica rapa.*]
– DERIVATIVES **turnipy** adj.
– ORIGIN C16: first element of unknown origin + **NEEP**.

**turnkey** • n. (pl. **-eys**) archaic a jailer. • adj. of or involving a complete product or service ready for immediate use.

**turn-off** • n. **1** a junction at which a road branches off. **2** informal a person or thing causing one to feel bored or repelled.

**turn-on** • n. informal a person or thing that causes one to feel excited or sexually aroused.

**turnout** • n. **1** the number of people attending or taking part in an event. **2** N. Amer. a road or rail junction. ➤N. Amer. a widened place in a road for cars to pass each other or park temporarily. **3** a carriage and horse or horses.

**turnover** • n. **1** the amount of money taken by a business in a particular period. **2** the rate at which employees leave a workforce and are replaced. ➤the rate at which goods are sold and replaced in a shop. **3** a small pie made by folding a piece of pastry over on itself to enclose a filling. **4** N. Amer. (in a game) a loss of possession of the ball.

**turnpike** • n. **1** historical a toll gate. ➤a road on which a toll was collected. ➤US a motorway on which a toll is charged. **2** historical a spiked barrier fixed in or across a road as a defence against sudden attack.

**turnround** • n. another term for **TURNAROUND**.

**turnsole** • n. a Mediterranean plant whose flowers are said to turn with the sun, and from which a blue or purple dye was formerly obtained. [*Chrozophora tinctoria.*]
– ORIGIN ME: from OFr. *tournesole*, based on L. *tornare* (see **TURN**) + *sol* 'sun'.

**turnspit** • n. historical a servant (or small dog running on a treadmill) whose job was to turn a spit on which meat was roasting.

**turnstile** • n. a mechanical gate consisting of revolving horizontal arms fixed to a vertical post, allowing only one person at a time to pass through.

**turnstone** • n. a small short-billed sandpiper noted for turning over stones to find small animals. [Genus *Arenaria*: two species.]

**turntable** • n. **1** a circular revolving plate supporting a gramophone record as it is played. **2** a circular revolving platform for turning a railway locomotive.

**turn-up** • n. Brit. **1** the end of a trouser leg folded upwards on the outside. **2** informal an unusual or unexpected event.

**turpentine** /ˈtəːp(ə)ntʌɪn/ • n. **1** (also **crude** or **gum turpentine**) an oleoresin secreted by certain pines and other trees and distilled to make rosin and oil of turpentine. **2** (also **oil of turpentine**) a volatile pungent oil distilled from this, used in mixing paints and varnishes and in liniment. • v. apply turpentine to.
– ORIGIN ME: from OFr. *ter(e)bentine*, from L. *ter(e)binthina (resina)* '(resin) of the terebinth'.

**turpitude** /ˈtəːpɪtjuːd/ • n. formal depravity; wickedness.
– ORIGIN C15: from Fr., or from L. *turpitudo*, from *turpis* 'disgraceful, base'.

**turps** • n. informal turpentine.
– ORIGIN C19: abbrev.

**turquoise** /ˈtəːkwɔɪz, -kwɑːz/ • n. **1** a semi-precious stone, typically opaque and of a greenish-blue or sky-blue colour, consisting of a hydrated phosphate of copper and aluminium. **2** a greenish-blue colour.
– ORIGIN ME: from OFr. *turqueise* 'Turkish (stone)'.

**turret** • n. **1** a small tower at the corner of a building or wall, especially of a castle. **2** an armoured tower, typically one that revolves, for a gun and gunners in a ship, aircraft, fort, or tank. **3** a rotating holder for tools, especially on a lathe.
– DERIVATIVES **turreted** adj.
– ORIGIN ME: from OFr. *tourete*, dimin. of *tour* 'tower'.

**turret lathe** • n. another term for **CAPSTAN LATHE**.

**turret shell** • n. a mollusc with a long, slender, pointed spiral shell, typically brightly coloured and living in tropical seas. [*Turitella* and other genera.]

**turtle** • n. **1** a marine or freshwater reptile with a bony or leathery shell and flippers or webbed toes. [Many species in the order Chelonia.] ➤the flesh of a sea turtle, used chiefly for soup. **2** Computing a directional cursor in a computer graphics system which can be instructed to move around a screen.
– PHRASES **turn turtle** (chiefly of a boat) turn upside down.
– ORIGIN C16: appar. an alt. of Fr. *tortue* (see **TORTOISE**).

**turtle dove** • n. a small dove with a soft purring call, noted for the apparent affection shown for its mate. [*Streptopelia turtur* and related species.]
– ORIGIN ME: *turtle* from OE *turtla, turtle* 'turtle dove' (from L. *turtur*, of imitative origin).

**turtle grass** • n. a submerged marine flowering plant found in the Caribbean, with long grass-like leaves. [*Thalassia testudinum.*]

**turtleneck** • n. Brit. a high, round, close-fitting neck on a knitted garment. ➤North American term for **POLO**

NECK.

**turves** plural form of TURF.

**Tuscan** /'tʌskən/ • adj. **1** of or relating to Tuscany, its inhabitants, or the dialect of Italian spoken there. **2** relating to or denoting a classical order of architecture resembling the Doric but lacking all ornamentation. • n. **1** a native or inhabitant of Tuscany. **2** the Tuscan dialect. **3** the Tuscan order of architecture.
– ORIGIN ME (denoting an Etruscan): via Fr. from L. *Tuscanus*, from *Tuscus* 'an Etruscan'.

**Tuscarora** /ˌtʌskə'rɔːrə/ • n. (pl. same or **Tuscaroras**) **1** an American Indian people forming part of the Iroquois confederacy. **2** the extinct Iroquoian language of this people.
– ORIGIN the name in Iroquois.

**tush**[1] /tʌʃ/ • exclam. archaic or humorous expressing disapproval, impatience, or dismissal.
– ORIGIN natural utterance: first recorded in ME.

**tush**[2] /tʌʃ/ • n. a long pointed tooth, in particular a canine tooth of a male horse.
– ORIGIN OE *tusc* (cf. TUSK).

**tush**[3] /tʊʃ/ • n. informal, chiefly N. Amer. a person's buttocks.
– ORIGIN 1960s (as *tushy*): from Yiddish *tokhes*, from Heb. *taḥat* 'beneath'.

**tushy** /'tʊʃi/ • n. (pl. **-ies**) another term for TUSH[3].

**tusk** • n. **1** a long, pointed tooth, especially one which protrudes from the closed mouth, as in the elephant, walrus, or wild boar. **2** a long, tapering object or projection.
– DERIVATIVES **tusked** adj. **tusky** adj. (poetic/literary).
– ORIGIN OE *tux*, var. of *tusc* (cf. TUSH[2]).

**tusker** • n. an elephant or wild boar with well-developed tusks.

**tusk shell** • n. a burrowing mollusc with a slender tusk-shaped shell which is open at both ends. [*Dentalium* and other genera, class Scaphopoda.]

**tussah** /'tʌsə/ • n. variant form of TUSSORE.

**tussie-mussie** /'tʌsɪmʌsi/ • n. (pl. **-ies**) a small bunch of flowers or aromatic herbs.
– ORIGIN ME: of unknown origin.

**tussive** /'tʌsɪv/ • adj. Medicine relating to coughing.
– ORIGIN C19: from L. *tussis* 'a cough' + -IVE.

**tussle** • n. a vigorous struggle or scuffle. • v. engage in a tussle.
– ORIGIN ME: perh. a dimin. of dial. *touse* 'handle roughly' (see TOUSLE).

**tussock** /'tʌsək/ • n. a dense clump or tuft of grass.
– DERIVATIVES **tussocky** adj.
– ORIGIN C16: perh. an alt. of dial. *tusk* 'tuft', of unknown origin.

**tussock grass** • n. a coarse grass which grows in tussocks. [*Deschampsia cespitosa* and other species.]

**tussock moth** • n. a woodland moth whose adults and brightly coloured caterpillars both bear tufts of irritant hairs. [Family Lymantriidae: many species.]

**tussore** /'tʌsɔː, 'tʌsə/ (also **tussah**) • n. coarse silk from the larvae of the tussore moth and related species.
– ORIGIN C16: from Hindi *tasar*, from Sanskrit *tasara* 'shuttle'.

**tussore moth** • n. a silk moth that is sometimes kept in India and China, with caterpillars that yield a strong but coarse brown silk. [*Antheraea mylitta*.]

**tut** • exclam. & v. short for TUT-TUT.

**tutee** /tjuː'tiː/ • n. a student or pupil of a tutor.

**tutelage** /'tjuːtɪlɪdʒ/ • n. **1** protection of or authority over someone or something; guardianship. **2** instruction; tuition.
– DERIVATIVES **tutelary** adj.
– ORIGIN C17: from L. *tutela* 'keeping', (from *tut-*, *tueri* 'watch') + -AGE.

**tutor** • n. **1** a private teacher, typically one who teaches a single pupil or a very small group. ➤chiefly Brit. a university or college teacher responsible for assigned students. ➤US an assistant lecturer in a college or university. **2** Brit. a book of instruction in a particular subject. • v. act as a tutor to. ➤work as a tutor.
– DERIVATIVES **tutorage** n. **tutorship** n.
– ORIGIN ME: from OFr. *tutour* or L. *tutor*, from *tueri* 'to watch, guard'.

**tutorial** • n. a period of tuition given by a university or college tutor. ➤an account or explanation of a subject, intended for private study. • adj. of or relating to a tutor or a tutor's tuition.

**tutsan** /'tʌts(ə)n/ • n. a St John's wort with large aromatic leaves and a berry-like fruit, formerly used medicinally. [*Hypericum androsaemum*.]
– ORIGIN ME: from Anglo-Norman Fr. *tutsaine* 'all wholesome'.

**Tutsi** /'tʊtsi/ • n. (pl. same or **Tutsis**) a member of a people forming a minority of the population of Rwanda and Burundi.
– ORIGIN a local name. See also WATUSI.

**tutti** /'tʊti/ • adv. & adj. Music with all voices or instruments together.
– ORIGIN Ital., pl. of *tutto* 'all', from L. *totus*.

**tutti-frutti** /ˌtuːtɪ'fruːti/ • n. (pl. **tutti-fruttis**) a type of ice cream or confectionery containing mixed fruits.
– ORIGIN Ital., lit. 'all fruits'.

**tut-tut** (also **tut**) • exclam. expressing disapproval or annoyance. • v. (**tut-tutted**, **tut-tutting**) make such an exclamation.
– ORIGIN C16: natural utterance.

**tutu**[1] /'tuːtuː/ • n. a female ballet dancer's costume consisting of a bodice and an attached skirt incorporating numerous layers of fabric, this being either short and stiff and projecting horizontally from the waist (the **classical tutu**) or long, soft, and bell-shaped (the **romantic tutu**).
– ORIGIN C20: from Fr., child's alt. of *cucu*, informal dimin. of *cul* 'buttocks'.

**tutu**[2] /'tuːtuː/ • n. a New Zealand shrub which bears poisonous purplish-black berries. [*Coriaria arborea*.]
– ORIGIN C19: from Maori.

**Tuvaluan** /ˌtuːvə'luːən, tuː'vɑːlʊən/ • n. **1** a native or inhabitant of Tuvalu, a country made up of a number of islands in the SW Pacific. **2** the Austronesian language of Tuvalu. • adj. of or relating to Tuvalu or its language.

**tu-whit tu-whoo** • n. a stylized representation of the cry of the tawny owl.
– ORIGIN C16: imitative.

**tux** • n. informal, chiefly N. Amer. a tuxedo.

**tuxedo** /tʌk'siːdəʊ/ • n. (pl. **-os** or **-oes**) chiefly N. Amer. a man's dinner jacket. ➤a formal evening suit including such a jacket.
– DERIVATIVES **tuxedoed** adj.
– ORIGIN C19: from *Tuxedo* Park, the site of a country club in New York.

**tuyère** /twiː'jɛː, tuː-/ • n. a nozzle through which air is forced into a smelter, furnace, or forge.
– ORIGIN C18: Fr., from *tuyau* 'pipe'.

**TV** • abbrev. television.

**TVA** • abbrev. (in the US) Tennessee Valley Authority.

**TV dinner** • n. a prepared pre-packed meal that only requires heating before it is ready to eat.

**TVEI** • abbrev. (in the UK) Technical and Vocational Educational Initiative.

**TVP** • abbrev. trademark textured vegetable protein.

**Twa** /twɑː/ • n. (pl. same or **Twas**) a member of a pygmy people inhabiting parts of Burundi, Rwanda, and Zaire (Democratic Republic of Congo).
– ORIGIN a local word meaning 'foreigner, outsider'.

**twaddle** informal • n. trivial or foolish speech or writing. • v. archaic talk or write in a trivial or foolish way.
– DERIVATIVES **twaddler** n.
– ORIGIN C18: alt. of earlier *twattle*, of unknown origin.

**twain** • cardinal number archaic term for TWO: *he split it in twain* | *never the twain shall meet*.
– ORIGIN OE *twegen*, masc. of *twā* (see TWO).

**twaite shad** /tweɪt/ • n. a shad (fish) with a deep blue back and silvery sides. [*Alosa fallax*.]
– ORIGIN C17 (as *twaite*): of unknown origin.

**twang** • n. **1** a strong ringing sound such as that made by the plucked string of a musical instrument or a released bowstring. **2** a distinctive nasal pronunciation characteristic of the speech of an individual or region. • v. **1** make

or cause to make a twang. **2** utter with a twang.
– DERIVATIVES **twangy** adj.
– ORIGIN C16: imitative.

**'twas** ● contr. archaic or poetic/literary it was.

**twat** /twɒt, twat/ ● n. vulgar slang **1** a woman's genitals. **2** a person regarded as stupid or obnoxious. ● v. Brit. informal hit; punch.
– ORIGIN C17: of unknown origin.

**twayblade** ● n. an orchid with a slender spike of greenish or brownish flowers and a single pair of broad leaves near the base. [*Listera ovata* and related species.]
– ORIGIN C16: from *tway* (var. of **TWAIN**) + **BLADE**, translating L. *bifolium*.

**tweak** ● v. **1** twist or pull with a small but sharp movement. **2** informal improve by making fine adjustments. ● n. **1** an act of tweaking. **2** informal a fine adjustment.
– ORIGIN C17: prob. an alt. of dial. *twick* 'pull sharply'; rel. to **TWITCH**.

**twee** ● adj. (**tweer**, **tweest**) Brit. excessively or affectedly quaint, pretty, or sentimental.
– DERIVATIVES **tweely** adv. **tweeness** n.
– ORIGIN C20: representing a child's pronunc. of **SWEET**.

**tweed** ● n. a rough-surfaced woollen cloth, typically of mixed flecked colours, originally produced in Scotland. ➤(**tweeds**) clothes made of tweed.
– ORIGIN C19: orig. a misreading of *tweel*, Scots form of **TWILL**, influenced by assoc. with the river *Tweed*.

**tweedy** ● adj. (**-ier**, **-iest**) **1** made of tweed cloth. **2** informal of a robust conservative or rural character.
– DERIVATIVES **tweedily** adv. **tweediness** n.

**'tween** ● contr. archaic or poetic/literary between.

**'tween decks** ● pl. n. Nautical the space between the decks of a ship.

**tweenager** (also **tweenie**) ● n. informal a child between the ages of about 10 and 14.

**tweeny** ● n. (pl. **-ies**) archaic, informal a maid who assisted both the cook and the housemaid.
– ORIGIN C19: from *between-maid*, a servant assisting two others.

**tweet** (also **tweet tweet**) ● n. the chirp of a small or young bird. ● v. make a chirping noise.
– ORIGIN C19: imitative.

**tweeter** ● n. a loudspeaker designed to reproduce high frequencies.

**tweeze** ● v. pluck or pull with or as if with tweezers.
– ORIGIN 1930s: back-form. from **TWEEZERS**.

**tweezers** ● pl. n. (also **a pair of tweezers**) a small instrument like a pair of pincers for plucking out hairs and picking up small objects.
– ORIGIN C17: extended form of obs. *tweeze* 'case of surgical instruments', shortening of *etweese*, anglicized pl. of **ETUI**.

**twelfth** /twɛlfθ/ ● ordinal number **1** constituting number twelve in a sequence; 12th. **2** (**a twelfth/one twelfth**) each of twelve equal parts into which something is or may be divided. **3** Music an interval or chord spanning an octave and a fifth in the diatonic scale, or a note separated from another by this interval. **4** (**the (Glorious) Twelfth**) (in the UK) 12 August, the day on which the grouse-shooting season begins.
– DERIVATIVES **twelfthly** adv. **twelvefold** adj. & adv.

**twelfth man** ● n. Cricket a player acting as a reserve in a game.

**Twelfth Night** ● n. 6 January, the feast of the Epiphany. ➤strictly, the evening of 5 January, formerly the twelfth and last day of Christmas festivities.

**twelve** ● cardinal number **1** equivalent to the product of three and four; two more than ten; 12. (Roman numeral: **xii** or **XII**.) **2** (**the Twelve**) the twelve Apostles. **3** (**12**) Brit. (of a film) classified as suitable for people of 12 years and over.
– ORIGIN OE *twelf(e)*, from the base of **TWO** + a second element (prob. expressing the sense 'left over'); of Gmc origin; cf. **ELEVEN**.

**twelvemo** ● n. another term for **DUODECIMO**.

**twelvemonth** ● n. archaic a year.

**twelve-note** (also **twelve-tone**) ● adj. denoting a system of musical composition using the twelve chromatic notes of the octave on an equal basis without dependence on a key system, a technique central to serialism.

**twelve-step** ● adj. denoting or relating to a process of recovery from an addiction by following a twelve-stage programme, especially one devised or similar to that devised by Alcoholics Anonymous. ● v. [often as noun **twelve-stepping**] (of an addict) undergo such a programme.
– DERIVATIVES **twelve-stepper** n.

**twenty** ● cardinal number (pl. **-ies**) the number equivalent to the product of two and ten; ten less than thirty; 20. (Roman numeral: **xx** or **XX**.)
– DERIVATIVES **twentieth** ordinal number. **twentyfold** adj. & adv.
– ORIGIN OE *twentig*, from the base of **TWO** + **-TY**[2].

**twenty-four-hour clock** ● n. a method of measuring the time in hours from one to twenty-four, rather than from one to twelve.

**24-7** (also **24/7**) ● adv. informal, chiefly N. Amer. twenty-four hours a day, seven days a week; all the time.

**twenty-one** ● n. the card game blackjack or pontoon.

**twenty-twenty** (also **20/20**) ● adj. denoting vision of normal acuity.
– ORIGIN with ref. to the fraction for normal visual acuity in eyesight tests.

**'twere** ● contr. archaic or poetic/literary it were.

**twerp** ● n. informal a silly or annoying person.
– ORIGIN C19: of unknown origin.

**Twi** /twiː, tʃwiː/ ● n. (pl. same or **Twis**) **1** a member of an Akan-speaking people of Ghana. **2** another term for **AKAN** (the language).
– ORIGIN the name in Akan.

**twibill** /ˈtwʌɪbɪl/ ● n. archaic a double-bladed battleaxe.
– ORIGIN OE *twibile*, from *twi-* 'double' + **BILL**[3].

**twice** ● adv. **1** two times. **2** double in degree or quantity.
– ORIGIN OE *twiges*, from the base of **TWO** + **-S**[3]; cf. **ONCE**.

**twiddle** ● v. play or fiddle with, typically in a purposeless or nervous way. ➤archaic turn or move in a twirling way. ● n. **1** an act of twiddling. **2** a rapid or intricate series of musical notes.
– PHRASES **twiddle one's thumbs** have nothing to do.
– DERIVATIVES **twiddler** n. **twiddly** adj.
– ORIGIN C16 (in the sense 'trifle'): appar. imitative, combining *twirl* or *twist* with *fiddle*.

**twig**[1] ● n. a slender woody shoot growing from a branch or stem of a tree or shrub. ➤Anatomy a small branch of a blood vessel or nerve.
– DERIVATIVES **twigged** adj. **twiggy** adj.
– ORIGIN OE *twigge*, of Gmc origin; rel. to **TWAIN** and **TWO**.

**twig**[2] ● v. (**twigged**, **twigging**) **1** Brit. informal come to understand or realize something. **2** archaic perceive.
– ORIGIN C18: of unknown origin.

**twilight** /ˈtwʌɪlʌɪt/ ● n. **1** the soft glowing light from the sky when the sun is below the horizon, caused by the reflection of the sun's rays from the atmosphere. **2** a period or state of obscurity or gradual decline: *the twilight of his career.*
– ORIGIN ME: from OE *twi-* 'two' (prob. here used in sense 'half-') + **LIGHT**[1].

**twilight sleep** ● n. Medicine a state of partial narcosis or stupor without total loss of consciousness, in particular a state induced by an injection of morphine and scopolamine.

**twilight zone** ● n. **1** an area or state characterized by being undefined, ambiguous, or intermediate, especially one showing decline. ➤an urban area in a state of dilapidation or decline. **2** the lowest level of the ocean to which light can penetrate.

**twilit** (also **twilighted**) ● adj. dimly illuminated by or as if by twilight.

**twill** ● n. a fabric so woven as to have a surface of diagonal parallel ridges.
– DERIVATIVES **twilled** adj.
– ORIGIN ME: from a var. of obs. *twilly*, from OE *twi-* 'two'.

**'twill** ● contr. archaic or poetic/literary it will.

**twin** ● n. **1** one of two children or animals born at the

same birth. **2** something containing or consisting of two matching or corresponding parts. ● **adj. 1** forming or being one of a twin. **2** forming a matching or closely connected pair. **3** (of a crystal) twinned. ● **v.** (**twinned**, **twinning**) **1** link; combine. ➤ Brit. link (a town or district) with another in a different country, for the purposes of cultural exchange. **2** [as adj. **twinned**] (of a crystal) that is a composite consisting of two (or more) parts which are reversed in orientation with respect to each other.
– DERIVATIVES **twinned** adj. **twinning** n.
– ORIGIN OE *twinn* 'double', from *twi-* 'two'; rel. to ON *tvinnr*.

**twin bed** ● **n.** one of a pair of matching single beds in a room.
– DERIVATIVES **twin-bedded** adj.

**twine** ● **n.** strong thread or string consisting of strands of hemp or cotton twisted together. ● **v.** wind or cause to wind round something.
– DERIVATIVES **twiner** n.
– ORIGIN OE *twīn* 'thread, linen', from the Gmc base of *twi-* 'two' (with ref. to the number of strands).

**twinflower** ● **n.** a slender evergreen trailing plant with pairs of very small trumpet-shaped pink flowers in the leaf axils, native to northern coniferous woodland. [*Linnaea borealis*.]

**twinge** ● **n. 1** a sudden, sharp localized pain. **2** a brief, sharp pang of emotion. ● **v.** (**twingeing** or **twinging**) (of a part of the body) suffer a twinge.
– ORIGIN OE *twengan* 'pinch, wring', of Gmc origin.

**twinkie** ● **n.** (pl. **-ies**) US **1** trademark a small finger-shaped sponge cake with a white synthetic cream filling. **2** informal, derogatory a homosexual or effeminate man.
– ORIGIN C20: prob. rel. to TWINKLE.

**twinkle** ● **v. 1** (of a star or light) shine with a gleam that changes constantly from bright to faint. ➤ (of a person's eyes) sparkle, especially with amusement. **2** move lightly and rapidly. ● **n.** a twinkling sparkle or gleam.
– PHRASES **in a twinkling** (**of an eye**) in an instant.
– DERIVATIVES **twinkler** n. **twinkly** adj.
– ORIGIN OE *twinclian* (v.), of Gmc origin.

**twinkle-toed** ● **adj.** informal nimble and quick on one's feet.
– DERIVATIVES **twinkletoes** n.

**twin-lens reflex** ● **n.** [as modifier] denoting a camera having two identical sets of lenses, either for taking stereoscopic pictures or with one forming an image for viewing and the other an image to be photographed.

**twin-screw** ● **adj.** (of a ship) having two propellers on separate shafts with opposite twists.

**twinset** ● **n.** chiefly Brit. a woman's matching cardigan and jumper.

**twin-tub** ● **n.** a type of washing machine having two top-loading drums, one for washing and the other for spin-drying.

**twirl** ● **v.** spin quickly and lightly round. ● **n.** an act of twirling. ➤ a spiralling or swirling shape, especially a flourish made with a pen.
– DERIVATIVES **twirler** n. **twirly** adj.
– ORIGIN C16: prob. an alt. (by assoc. with WHIRL) of *tirl*, a var. of archaic *trill* 'twiddle, spin'.

**twist** ● **v. 1** form into a bent, curled, or distorted shape. ➤ turn or bend round or into a different direction. ➤ force or be forced out of the natural position by a twisting action: *he twisted his ankle playing tennis*. **2** rotate or cause to rotate around something that remains stationary; turn. ➤ move or cause to move around each other; interlace. ➤ take or have a winding course. **3** distort or misrepresent the meaning of. ➤ [as adj. **twisted**] (of a personality or behaviour) unpleasantly or unhealthily abnormal. **4** dance the twist. **5** Brit. informal cheat; defraud. **6** (in pontoon) request, deal, or be dealt a card face upwards. ● **n. 1** an act or instance of twisting. **2** a thing with a spiral shape. ➤ Brit. a paper packet with twisted ends. ➤ a small quantity of tobacco, sugar, etc., wrapped in such a packet. **3** force producing twisting; torque. ➤ forward motion combined with rotation about an axis. ➤ the rifling in the bore of a gun. **4** an unexpected, normally unwelcome, development of events. ➤ a new treatment or outlook: *she takes conventional subjects and gives them a twist*. ➤ Brit. informal a swindle. **5** a fine strong thread consisting of twisted fibres. **6** Brit. a drink consisting of two ingredients mixed together. **7** a carpet with a tightly curled pile. **8** (**the twist**) a dance with a twisting movement of the body, popular in the 1960s.
– PHRASES **round the twist** Brit. informal crazy. **twist someone's arm** informal forcefully persuade someone to do something that they are reluctant to do. **twist in the wind** be left in a state of suspense or uncertainty.
– DERIVATIVES **twisty** adj.
– ORIGIN OE, of Gmc origin; prob. from the base of TWIN and TWINE.

**twister** ● **n. 1** Brit. informal a swindler; a dishonest person. **2** N. Amer. a tornado.

**twit**[1] ● **n.** informal, chiefly Brit. a silly or foolish person.
– DERIVATIVES **twittish** adj.
– ORIGIN 1930s (orig. dial., in the sense 'tale-bearer'): perh. from TWIT[2].

**twit**[2] ● **v.** (**twitted**, **twitting**) informal tease, especially good-humouredly.
– ORIGIN OE *ætwītan* 'reproach with', from *æt* 'at' + *wītan* 'to blame'.

**twitch** ● **v. 1** make or cause to make a short, sudden jerking movement. **2** use a twitch to subdue (a horse). ● **n. 1** a twitching movement. **2** a pang: *he felt a twitch of annoyance*. **3** a small noose attached to a stick, which may be twisted around the upper lip or ear of a horse to subdue it during veterinary procedures.
– ORIGIN ME: of Gmc origin; rel. to OE *twiccian* 'to pluck, pull sharply'.

**twitcher** ● **n.** Brit. informal a birdwatcher devoted to spotting rare birds.

**twitch grass** ● **n.** couch grass.
– ORIGIN C16: alt. of QUITCH.

**twitchy** ● **adj.** (**-ier**, **-iest**) **1** informal nervous. **2** given to twitching.

**twite** /twʌɪt/ ● **n.** a moorland finch with streaky brown plumage and a pink rump. [*Acanthis flavirostris*.]
– ORIGIN C16: imitative of its call.

**twitter** ● **v. 1** (of a bird) make a series of light tremulous sounds. **2** talk rapidly in a nervous or trivial way. ● **n. 1** a twittering sound. **2** trivial talk.
– PHRASES **in** (or **of**) **a twitter** informal in a state of agitation or excitement.
– DERIVATIVES **twitterer** n. **twittery** adj.
– ORIGIN ME: imitative.

**'twixt** ● **contr.** betwixt.

**twizzle** informal or dialect ● **v.** spin or cause to spin around. ● **n.** a twisting or spinning movement.
– ORIGIN C18: prob. imitative, influenced by TWIST.

**two** ● **cardinal number** equivalent to the sum of one and one; one less than three; 2. (Roman numeral: **ii** or **II**.)
– PHRASES **put two and two together** draw an obvious conclusion from what is known or evident. **that makes two of us** informal that is true of me also. **two by two** (or **two and two**) side by side in pairs. **two can play at that game** informal used to assert that one is equally capable of copying another's strategy, to their disadvantage. **two's company, three's a crowd** two people, especially lovers, should be left alone together.
– DERIVATIVES **twofold** adj. & adv.
– ORIGIN OE *twā* (fem. and neut.) of Gmc origin.

**two-bit** ● **adj.** N. Amer. informal insignificant, cheap, or worthless.

**two-by-four** ● **n. 1** a length of wood with a rectangular cross section nominally two inches by four inches. **2** W. Indian & US a small or insignificant thing, typically a building.

**twoc** /twɒk/ ● **v.** (**twocced**, **twoccing**) Brit. informal steal (a car).
– DERIVATIVES **twoccer** n.
– ORIGIN 1990s (orig. police sl.): acronym from *taken without owner's consent*.

**two-cycle** ● **adj.** another term for TWO-STROKE.

**two-dimensional** ● **adj. 1** having or appearing to have length and breadth but no depth. **2** lacking depth; superficial.

– DERIVATIVES **two-dimensionality** n. **two-dimensionally** adv.
**two-faced** ● adj. insincere and deceitful.
**two-fisted** ● adj. N. Amer. informal tough, aggressive, or vigorous.
**two-hander** ● n. a play for two actors.
**two-horse** ● adj. (of a race or other contest) in which only two of the participants are likely winners.
**twoness** ● n. the fact or state of being two; duality.
**twopence** /ˈtʌp(ə)ns/ (also **tuppence**) ● n. Brit. **1** the sum of two pence, especially before decimalization (1971). **2** [with neg.] informal anything at all: *he didn't care twopence.*
**twopenn'orth** /tuːˈpɛnəθ/ ● n. **1** an amount that is worth or costs twopence. **2** a paltry or insignificant amount.
– PHRASES **add** (or **put in**) **one's twopenn'orth** informal contribute one's opinion.
**twopenny** /ˈtʌp(ə)ni/ (also **tuppenny**) ● adj. Brit. costing two pence, especially before decimalization (1971).
**twopenny-halfpenny** ● adj. Brit. informal insignificant or worthless.
**two-phase** ● adj. relating to or denoting an electricity supply using two separate alternating components with phases differing by half a period.
**two-piece** ● adj. consisting of two matching items. ● n. a two-piece suit.
**two shot** ● n. a cinema or television shot of two people together.
**twosome** ● n. a set of two people or things.
**two-step** ● n. **1** a round dance with a sliding step in march or polka time. **2** another term for **GARAGE** (in sense 4).
**two-stroke** ● adj. denoting an internal-combustion engine having its power cycle completed in one up-and-down movement of the piston.
**two-time** ● v. informal be unfaithful to (a lover or spouse).
– DERIVATIVES **two-timer** n.
**'twould** ● contr. archaic it would.
**two-up** ● n. (in Australia and New Zealand) a gambling game in which two coins are tossed in the air and bets are laid as to whether both will fall heads or tails uppermost.
**two-up two-down** ● n. Brit. informal a house with two reception rooms downstairs and two bedrooms upstairs.
**two-way** ● adj. **1** involving movement or communication in opposite directions. **2** (of a switch) permitting a current to be switched on or off from either of two points.
– PHRASES **two-way street** a situation involving mutual or reciprocal action or obligation.
**two-way mirror** ● n. a panel of glass that can be seen through from one side and is a mirror on the other.
**two-wheeler** ● n. a bicycle or motorcycle.
**TX** ● abbrev. Texas (in official postal use).
**-ty**[1] ● suffix forming nouns denoting quality or condition such as *beauty.*
– ORIGIN via OFr. from L. *-tas, -tat-.*
**-ty**[2] ● suffix denoting specified groups of ten: *forty.*
– ORIGIN OE *-tig.*
**tychism** /ˈtʌɪkɪz(ə)m/ ● n. Philosophy the doctrine that account must be taken of the element of chance in reasoning or explanation of the universe.
– ORIGIN C19: from Gk *tukhē* 'chance' + **-ISM**.
**tycoon** /tʌɪˈkuːn/ ● n. **1** a wealthy, powerful person in business or industry. **2** a title applied by foreigners to the shogun of Japan in power between 1857 and 1868.
– ORIGIN C19: from Japanese *taikun* 'great lord'.
**tying** present participle of **TIE**.
**tyke** (also **tike**) ● n. **1** informal a small child, especially a mischievous one. **2** dated, chiefly Brit. an unpleasant or coarse man. **3** a dog, especially a mongrel. **4** (also **Yorkshire tyke**) Brit. informal a person from Yorkshire. **5** Austral./NZ informal, derogatory a Roman Catholic. [C20: alt. of **TAIG**.]
– ORIGIN ME: from ON *tík* 'bitch'.
**Tylenol** /ˈθʌɪlənɒl/ ● n. chiefly N. Amer. trademark for **PARACETAMOL**.
**tympan** /ˈtɪmpən/ ● n. **1** (in letterpress printing) a layer of packing placed between the platen and the paper to be printed to equalize the pressure over the whole forme. **2** Architecture another term for **TYMPANUM**.
– ORIGIN C16: from Fr. *tympan* or L. *tympanum* (see **TYMPANUM**).
**tympana** plural form of **TYMPANUM**.
**tympani** ● pl. n. variant spelling of **TIMPANI**.
**tympanic** /tɪmˈpanɪk/ ● adj. **1** Anatomy of, relating to, or having a tympanum. **2** resembling or acting like a drumhead.
**tympanites** /ˌtɪmpəˈnʌɪtiːz/ ● n. Medicine swelling of the abdomen with air or gas.
– DERIVATIVES **tympanitic** adj.
– ORIGIN ME: via late L. from Gk *tumpanitēs*, from *tumpanon* (see **TYMPANUM**).
**tympanum** /ˈtɪmpənəm/ ● n. (pl. **tympanums** or **tympana** /-nə/) **1** Anatomy & Zoology the membrane forming part of the organ of hearing, which vibrates in response to sound waves; the eardrum. **2** Architecture a vertical recessed triangular space forming the centre of a pediment or over a door.
– DERIVATIVES **tympanic** adj.
– ORIGIN C17: via L. from Gk *tumpanon* 'drum'.
**tympany** /ˈtɪmpəni/ ● n. another term for **TYMPANITES** (used especially in veterinary medicine).
– ORIGIN C16: from Gk *tumpanias*, from *tumpanon* (see **TYMPANUM**).
**Tynwald** /ˈtɪnw(ə)ld/ ● n. the parliament of the Isle of Man.
– ORIGIN from ON *thing-vǫllr* 'place of assembly', from *thing* 'assembly' + *vǫllr* 'field'.
**type** ● n. **1** a category of people or things having common characteristics. ➤ a person or thing considered as a representative of such a category. ➤ informal a person of a specified character or nature: *two sporty types in tracksuits.* ➤ Linguistics an abstract category or class of linguistic item or unit. Contrasted with **TOKEN**. **2** a person or thing symbolizing or exemplifying the defining characteristics of something. **3** printed characters or letters. ➤ a piece of metal with a raised letter or character on its upper surface, for use in letterpress printing. ➤ such pieces collectively. **4** a design on either side of a medal or coin. **5** Theology a foreshadowing in the Old Testament of a person or event of the Christian dispensation. ● v. **1** write using a typewriter or computer. **2** Medicine determine the type to which (a person or their blood or tissue) belongs.
– PHRASES **in type** Printing composed and ready for printing.
– DERIVATIVES **typal** adj. (rare). **typing** n.
– ORIGIN C15: from Fr., or from L. *typus*, from Gk *tupos* 'impression, figure, type'.
**-type** ● suffix (forming adjectives) that is a certain type: *a champagne-type fizzy wine.*
**Type A** ● n. a personality type characterized by ambition, impatience, and competitiveness, and thought to be susceptible to stress and heart disease.
**type approval** ● n. official confirmation from a government or other body that a manufactured item meets required specifications.
**Type B** ● n. a personality type characterized as easygoing and thought to have low susceptibility to stress.
**typecast** ● v. (past and past part. **-cast**) (usu. **be typecast**) **1** cast (an actor or actress) repeatedly in the same type of role, as a result of the appropriateness of their appearance or previous success in such roles. **2** regard as fitting a stereotype.
**typeface** ● n. Printing a particular design of type.
**type founder** ● n. Printing a designer and maker of metal type.
– DERIVATIVES **type foundry** n.
**type metal** ● n. Printing an alloy of lead, tin, and antimony, used for casting type.
**typescript** ● n. a typed copy of a text.
**typeset** ● v. (**-setting**; past and past part. **-set**) arrange or generate the type for (text to be printed).
– DERIVATIVES **typesetter** n. **typesetting** n.
**type site** ● n. Archaeology a site where objects or materials regarded as typical of a particular period are found.

**type specimen** • **n.** Botany & Zoology the specimen, or each of a set of specimens, on which the description and name of a new species is based. See also **HOLOTYPE**, **SYNTYPE**.

**typewriter** • **n.** an electric, electronic, or manual machine with keys for producing print-like characters.
– DERIVATIVES **typewriting** n. **typewritten** adj.

**typhlitis** /tɪ'flʌɪtɪs/ • **n.** Medicine inflammation of the caecum.
– DERIVATIVES **typhlitic** adj.
– ORIGIN C19: mod. L., from Gk *tuphlon* 'caecum or blind gut' + **-ITIS**.

**typhoid** (also **typhoid fever**) • **n.** an infectious bacterial fever with an eruption of red spots on the chest and abdomen and severe intestinal irritation.
– DERIVATIVES **typhoidal** adj.
– ORIGIN C19: from **TYPHUS** + **-OID**.

**Typhoid Mary** • **n.** (pl. **Typhoid Marys**) informal a transmitter of undesirable opinions or attitudes.
– ORIGIN the nickname of *Mary* Mallon (died 1938), an Irish-born cook who transmitted typhoid in the US.

**typhoon** /tʌɪ'fuːn/ • **n.** a tropical storm in the region of the Indian or western Pacific oceans.
– DERIVATIVES **typhonic** adj.
– ORIGIN C16: partly via Port. from Arab. *ṭūfān*; reinforced by Chin. dial. *tai fung* 'big wind'.

**typhus** /'tʌɪfəs/ • **n.** an infectious disease caused by rickettsiae, characterized by a purple rash, headaches, fever, and usually delirium.
– DERIVATIVES **typhous** adj.
– ORIGIN C17: mod. L., from Gk *tuphos* 'smoke, stupor'.

**typical** • **adj.** **1** having the distinctive qualities of a particular type. ➤characteristic of a particular person or thing. **2** symbolic: *the pit is typical of hell.*
– DERIVATIVES **typicality** /-'kalɪti/ n. **typically** adv.
– ORIGIN C17: from med. L. *typicalis*, via L. from Gk *tupikos*, from *tupos* (see **TYPE**).

**typify** • **v.** (**-ies**, **-ied**) be typical of.
– DERIVATIVES **typification** n. **typifier** n.

**typist** • **n.** a person skilled in typing, especially one who is employed for this purpose.

**typo** /'tʌɪpəʊ/ • **n.** (pl. **-os**) informal a typographical error.

**typography** /tʌɪ'pɒgrəfi/ • **n.** **1** the art or process of setting and arranging types and printing from them. **2** the style and appearance of printed matter.
– DERIVATIVES **typographer** n. **typographic** adj. **typographical** adj. **typographically** adv.
– ORIGIN C17: from Fr. *typographie* or mod. L. *typographia* (see **TYPE**, **-GRAPHY**).

**typology** • **n.** (pl. **-ies**) **1** a classification according to general type, especially in archaeology, psychology, or the social sciences. **2** the study and interpretation of types and symbols, originally especially in the Bible.
– DERIVATIVES **typological** /-ə'lɒdʒɪk(ə)l/ adj. **typologist** n.
– ORIGIN C19: from Gk *tupos* 'type' + **-LOGY**.

**tyramine** /'tʌɪrəmiːn/ • **n.** Biochemistry a compound in cheese and other foods which in some circumstances can cause high blood pressure.
– ORIGIN C20: from *tyr(osine)* + **AMINE**.

**tyrannicide** /tɪ'ranɪsʌɪd, tʌɪ-/ • **n.** the killing of a tyrant. ➤the killer of a tyrant.
– DERIVATIVES **tyrannicidal** adj.
– ORIGIN C17: from Fr., from L. *tyrannicida* 'killer of a tyrant').

**tyrannosaur** /tɪ'ranəsɔː, tʌɪ-/ (also **tyrannosaurus** /tɪˌranə'sɔːrəs/) • **n.** a very large carnivorous dinosaur of the late Cretaceous period, with powerful jaws and small claw-like front legs.
– ORIGIN mod. L. *Tyrannosaurus*, from Gk *turannos* 'tyrant' + *sauros* 'lizard'.

**tyranny** • **n.** (pl. **-ies**) **1** cruel and oppressive government or rule. ➤a state under such rule. **2** cruel and arbitrary exercise of power or control. **3** (especially in ancient Greece) rule by a tyrant.
– DERIVATIVES **tyrannical** adj. **tyrannically** adv. **tyrannize** (also **-ise**) v. **tyrannous** adj. **tyrannously** adv.
– ORIGIN ME: from OFr. *tyrannie*, from late L. *tyrannia*, from L. *turannus* (see **TYRANT**).

**tyrant** /'tʌɪr(ə)nt/ • **n.** **1** a cruel and oppressive ruler. **2** a person exercising power or control in a cruel and arbitrary way. **3** (especially in ancient Greece) a ruler who seized absolute power without legal right.
– ORIGIN ME: from OFr., via L. from Gk *turannos*.

**tyrant flycatcher** • **n.** a flycatcher of a large family (Tyrannidae) including all American species.
– ORIGIN C18: so named because of their aggressive behaviour towards other birds.

**tyre** (US **tire**) • **n.** **1** a rubber covering, typically inflated or surrounding an inflated inner tube, placed round a wheel to form a soft contact with the road. **2** a strengthening band of metal fitted around the rim of a wheel, especially of a railway vehicle.
– ORIGIN C15: perh. a var. of archaic *tire*, shortening of **ATTIRE** (because the tyre was the 'clothing' of the wheel).

**tyre gauge** • **n.** a portable pressure gauge for measuring the air pressure in a tyre.

**Tyrian** /'tɪrɪən/ • **n.** a native or inhabitant of Tyre, an ancient Phoenician city and port on the Mediterranean (now a port in southern Lebanon). • **adj.** of or relating to Tyre.

**Tyrian purple** • **n.** see **PURPLE**.

**tyro** /'tʌɪrəʊ/ (also **tiro**) • **n.** (pl. **-os**) a beginner or novice.
– ORIGIN ME: from L. *tiro*, med. L. *tyro* 'recruit'.

**Tyrolean** /ˌtɪrə'liːən/ (also **Tyrolese** /ˌtɪrə'liːz/) • **n.** a native or inhabitant of the Tyrol, an Alpine region of western Austria and northern Italy. • **adj.** of or relating to the Tyrol.

**tyrosine** /'tʌɪrəsiːn/ • **n.** Biochemistry an amino acid found in most proteins and important in the synthesis of some hormones.
– ORIGIN C19: formed irregularly from Gk *turos* 'cheese' + **-INE**[4].

**Tyrrhene** /'tɪriːn/ • **adj.** & **n.** archaic term for **ETRUSCAN**.
– ORIGIN ME: from L. *Tyrrhenus* 'Etruscan'.

**Tyrrhenian** /tɪ'riːnɪən/ • **adj.** **1** relating to or denoting the Tyrrhenian Sea or the surrounding region. **2** archaic Etruscan. • **n.** archaic an Etruscan.

**tzar** • **n.** variant spelling of **TSAR**.

**tzarevich** • **n.** variant spelling of **TSAREVICH**.

**tzarina** • **n.** variant spelling of **TSARINA**.

**tzatziki** /tsat'siːki/ • **n.** a Greek side dish of yogurt with cucumber, garlic, and often mint.
– ORIGIN from mod. Gk.

**tzedakah** /tsɛ'dɒka/ • **n.** (among Jewish people) charitable giving, regarded as a moral obligation.
– ORIGIN from Heb. *ṣĕḏāqāh* 'righteousness'.

**Tzeltal** /tsɛl'tɑːl, 'tsɛltɑːl; s-/ • **n.** (pl. same or **Tzeltals**) **1** a member of an American Indian people inhabiting parts of southern Mexico. **2** the Mayan language of this people.
– ORIGIN Sp. name of one of the three regions of the Mexican state of *Chiapas*, of uncertain origin.

**tzigane** /tsɪ'gɑːn/ • **n.** (pl. same or **tziganes**) a Hungarian gypsy.
– ORIGIN C18: from Fr., from Hungarian *c(z)igány*.

**tzimmes** (also **tzimmis**) • **n.** variant spelling of **TSIMMES**.

**T-zone** • **n.** the central part of a person's face, including the forehead, nose, and chin.
– ORIGIN *T* designating the shape of the area defined.

**Tzotzil** /'tsəʊtsɪl, tsəʊt'sɪl, s-/ • **n.** (pl. same or **Tzotzils**) **1** a member of an American Indian people inhabiting parts of southern Mexico. **2** the Mayan language of this people.
– ORIGIN the name in Tzotzil.

**U**[1] /juː/ (also **u**) ● **n.** (pl. **Us** or **U's**) **1** the twenty-first letter of the alphabet. **2** denoting the next after T in a set of items, categories, etc.

**U**[2] /juː/ ● **abbrev. 1** (in names of sports clubs) United. **2** Brit. universal (denoting films classified as suitable without restriction). **3** Uruguay (international vehicle registration). ● **symb.** the chemical element uranium.

**U**[3] /juː/ ● **adj.** informal, chiefly Brit. (of language or social behaviour) characteristic of or appropriate to the upper social classes.
– ORIGIN abbrev. of **UPPER CLASS**; coined in 1954 by Alan S. C. Ross, professor of linguistics, and popularized by Nancy Mitford's *Noblesse Oblige* (1956).

**U**[4] /uː/ ● **n.** a Burmese title of respect before a man's name, equivalent to Mr.

**u** ● **symb.** [in combination] micro- ($10^{-6}$). [substituted for **MU**.]

**UAE** ● **abbrev.** United Arab Emirates.

**UB40** ● **n.** (in the UK) a card issued to a person registered as unemployed.

**ubac** /ˈjuːbak/ ● **n.** Geography a mountain slope which receives little sunshine. Compare with **ADRET**.
– ORIGIN 1930s: from Fr., appar. from L. *opacus* 'shady'.

**U-bend** ● **n.** a section of a pipe, in particular of a waste pipe, shaped like a U.

**Übermensch** /ˈuːbəˌmɛnʃ/ ● **n.** the ideal superior man of the future who could rise above conventional Christian morality to create and impose his own values, originally described by Nietzsche in *Thus Spake Zarathustra* (1883–5).
– ORIGIN Ger., lit. 'superhuman person'.

**ubiety** /juːˈbʌɪɪti/ ● **n.** poetic/literary the condition of being in a definite place.
– ORIGIN C17: from med. L. *ubietas*, from L. *ubi* 'where'.

**-ubility** ● **suffix** forming nouns from or corresponding to adjectives ending in *-uble* (such as *solubility* from *soluble*).

**ubiquinone** /juːˈbɪkwɪnəʊn/ ● **n.** Biochemistry a compound of the quinone class which acts as an electron-transfer agent in cell respiration.
– ORIGIN 1950s: blend of **UBIQUITOUS** and **QUINONE**.

**ubiquitarian** /juːˌbɪkwɪˈtɛːrɪən/ Christian Theology ● **n.** a person, typically a Lutheran, who believes that Christ is present everywhere at all times. ● **adj.** relating to or believing in such a doctrine.
– DERIVATIVES **ubiquitarianism** n.
– ORIGIN C17: from mod. L. *ubiquitarius* (from L. *ubique* 'everywhere') + **-AN**.

**ubiquitin** /juːˈbɪkwɪtɪn/ ● **n.** Biochemistry a polypeptide found in living cells, involved in degrading defective and superfluous proteins.
– ORIGIN 1970s: from **UBIQUITOUS** + **-IN**[1].

**ubiquitous** /juːˈbɪkwɪtəs/ ● **adj.** present, appearing, or found everywhere.
– DERIVATIVES **ubiquitously** adv. **ubiquitousness** n. **ubiquity** n.
– ORIGIN C19: from mod. L. *ubiquitas* (from L. *ubique* 'everywhere') + **-OUS**.

**-uble** ● **suffix** (forming adjectives) able to: *voluble*. ➤ able to be: *soluble*.
– DERIVATIVES **-ubly** suffix forming corresponding adverbs.
– ORIGIN from Fr., from L. *-ubilis*.

**U-boat** ● **n.** a German submarine of the First or Second World War.
– ORIGIN from Ger. *U-boot*, abbrev. of *Unterseeboot* 'undersea boat'.

**UBR** ● **abbrev.** uniform business rate (a tax on business property in England and Wales).

**UC** ● **abbrev.** University College.

**u.c.** ● **abbrev.** upper case.

**UCAS** /ˈjuːkas/ ● **abbrev.** (in the UK) Universities and Colleges Admissions Service.

**UDA** ● **abbrev.** Ulster Defence Association (a Loyalist paramilitary organization).

**udal** /ˈjuːd(ə)l/ ● **n.** Law a kind of freehold tenure based on uninterrupted possession, formerly practised in northern Europe and still in use in Orkney and Shetland.
– ORIGIN C15: from ON *othal* 'property held by inheritance'.

**UDC** ● **abbrev. 1** (in the UK) Urban Development Corporation. **2** historical (in the UK) Urban District Council.

**udder** ● **n.** the mammary gland of female cattle, sheep, goats, horses, and related ungulates, hanging near the hind legs as a bag-like organ with two or more teats.
– DERIVATIVES **-uddered** adj.
– ORIGIN OE *ūder*, of W. Gmc origin.

**UDI** ● **abbrev.** unilateral declaration of independence.

**udon** /ˈuːdɒn/ ● **n.** (in Japanese cookery) large noodles made from wheat flour.
– ORIGIN from Japanese.

**UDR** ● **abbrev.** Ulster Defence Regiment.

**UEFA** /juːˈiːfə, -ˈeɪfə/ ● **abbrev.** Union of European Football Associations.

**UF** ● **abbrev.** urea-formaldehyde.

**UFO** ● **n.** (pl. **UFOs**) a mysterious object seen in the sky for which it is claimed no orthodox scientific explanation can be found, popularly said to be vehicles carrying extraterrestrials.
– DERIVATIVES **ufological** adj. **ufologist** n. **ufology** n.
– ORIGIN 1950s: acronym from *unidentified flying object*.

**Ugandan** /juːˈgandən/ ● **n.** a native or inhabitant of Uganda. ● **adj.** of or relating to Uganda.

**Ugaritic** /ˌjuːgəˈrɪtɪk/ ● **n.** a pre-Phoenician Semitic language written in a distinctive cuneiform alphabet, spoken by the people of Ugarit, an ancient port and Bronze Age trading city in northern Syria. ● **adj.** of or relating to this language.

**ugh** ● **exclam.** informal used to express disgust or horror.

**Ugli fruit** /ˈʌgli/ ● **n.** (pl. same) trademark a mottled green and yellow citrus fruit which is a hybrid of a grapefruit and tangerine.
– ORIGIN 1930s: *ugli*, alt. of **UGLY**.

**ugly** ● **adj.** (**-ier**, **-iest**) **1** unpleasant or repulsive in appearance. **2** hostile or threatening; likely to involve unpleasantness.
– DERIVATIVES **uglification** n. **uglify** v. **uglily** adv. **ugliness** n.
– ORIGIN ME: from ON *uggligr* 'to be dreaded', from *ugga* 'to dread'.

**ugly American** ● **n.** informal, chiefly US an American who behaves offensively when abroad.

**ugly duckling** ● **n.** a person who turns out to be beautiful or talented against all expectations.
– ORIGIN from the title of one of Hans Christian Andersen's fairy tales, in which the 'ugly duckling' becomes a swan.

**Ugrian** /ˈuːgrɪən, ˈjuː-/ ● **adj.** another term for **UGRIC**.

**Ugric** /ˈuːgrɪk, ˈjuː-/ ● **adj.** relating to or denoting a branch of the Finno-Ugric language family including only Hungarian and the Ob-Ugric languages.
– ORIGIN from Russ. *ugry* (the name of a people dwelling

east of the Urals) + **-IC**.

**uh** • **exclam.** used to represent a sound made to express hesitation or enquiry.

**UHF** • **abbrev.** ultra-high frequency.

**uh-huh** • **exclam.** used to express assent or as a non-committal response.
– ORIGIN 1920s: imitative.

**uhlan** /ˈuːlɑːn, ˈjuː-, ʊˈlɑːn/ • **n.** historical (in various European armies) a cavalryman armed with a lance.
– ORIGIN C18: via Fr. and Ger. from Polish *(h)ulan*, from Turk. *oğlan* 'youth, servant'.

**uh-oh** • **exclam.** used to express alarm or dismay.

**UHT** • **abbrev.** ultra heat treated (a process typically used to extend the shelf life of milk).

**uh-uh** • **exclam.** used to express a negative response.

**Uighur** /ˈwiːɡə/ (also **Uigur**, **Uygur**) • **n.** **1** a member of a Turkic people of NW China. **2** the Turkic language of this people.
– ORIGIN the name in Uighur.

**uillean pipes** /ˈɪlɪn, ˈɪlən/ • **pl. n.** Irish bagpipes played using bellows worked by the elbow, and having three extra pipes on which chords can be played.
– ORIGIN C20: from Ir. *píob uilleann*, lit. 'pipe of the elbow'.

**ujamaa** /ˌʊdʒaˈmɑː/ • **n.** (in Tanzania) a socialist system of self-help village cooperatives, established in the 1960s.
– ORIGIN Kiswahili, lit. 'brotherhood'.

**UK** • **abbrev.** United Kingdom.

**UKAEA** • **abbrev.** United Kingdom Atomic Energy Authority.

**ukase** /juːˈkeɪz/ • **n.** **1** (in tsarist Russia) a decree with the force of law. **2** an arbitrary or peremptory command.
– ORIGIN from Russ. *ukaz* 'ordinance, edict', from *ukazat'* 'show, decree'.

**ukiyo-e** /uːˌkiːjəʊˈeɪ/ • **n.** a school of Japanese art depicting subjects from everyday life, dominant in the 17th–19th centuries.
– ORIGIN Japanese, from *ukiyo* 'fleeting world' + *e* 'picture'.

**Ukrainian** • **n.** **1** a native or national of Ukraine, or a person of Ukrainian descent. **2** the Eastern Slavic language of Ukraine. • **adj.** of or relating to Ukraine, its people, or their language.

**ukulele** /ˌjuːkəˈleɪli/ • **n.** a small four-stringed guitar of Hawaiian origin.
– ORIGIN C19: from Hawaiian, lit. 'jumping flea'.

**ulama** • **n.** variant spelling of **ULEMA**.

**-ular** • **suffix** forming adjectives, sometimes corresponding to nouns ending in *-ule* (such as *pustular*), but often without diminutive force (as in *granular*).
– DERIVATIVES **-ularity** suffix forming corresponding nouns.
– ORIGIN from L. *-ularis*.

**ulcer** • **n.** an open sore on an external or internal surface of the body, caused by a break in the skin or mucous membrane which fails to heal.
– DERIVATIVES **ulcered** adj. **ulcerous** adj.
– ORIGIN ME: from L. *ulcus, ulcer-*.

**ulcerate** • **v.** develop into or become affected by an ulcer.
– DERIVATIVES **ulceration** n. **ulcerative** adj.

**-ule** • **suffix** forming diminutive nouns such as *capsule*.
– ORIGIN from L. *-ulus, -ula, -ulum*.

**ulema** /ˈʊləmə, ˈuːlɪmə, ˌuːləˈmɑː/ (also **ulama**) • **n.** **1** [treated as sing. or pl.] a body of Muslim scholars recognized as expert in Islamic sacred law and theology. **2** a member of such a body.
– ORIGIN from Arab. *'ulamā'*, pl. of *'ālim* 'learned', from *'alima* 'know'.

**-ulent** • **suffix** (forming adjectives) full of: *fraudulent*.
– DERIVATIVES **-ulence** suffix forming corresponding nouns.
– ORIGIN from L. *-ulentus*.

**ullage** /ˈʌlɪdʒ/ • **n.** **1** the amount by which a container falls short of being full. **2** loss of liquid by evaporation or leakage.
– ORIGIN ME: from Anglo-Norman Fr. *ulliage*, from OFr. *euillier* 'fill up', based on L. *oculus* 'eye' (with ref. to a container's bunghole).

**ulna** /ˈʌlnə/ • **n.** (pl. **ulnae** /-niː/ or **ulnas**) Anatomy & Zoology a bone of the forearm or forelimb, in humans the thinner and longer of the two.
– DERIVATIVES **ulnar** adj.
– ORIGIN ME (denoting the humerus): from L.; rel. to **ELL**.

**U-lock** • **n.** another term for **D-LOCK**.

**-ulous** • **suffix** forming adjectives such as *incredulous*.
– ORIGIN from L. *-ulosus, -ulus*.

**ulster** • **n.** a man's long, loose overcoat of rough cloth, typically with a belt at the back.
– ORIGIN C19: from *Ulster* in Ireland, where it was orig. sold.

**Ulsterman** (or **Ulsterwoman**) • **n.** (pl. **-men** or **-women**) a native or inhabitant of Northern Ireland or Ulster.

**ult.** • **abbrev.** **1** ultimate. **2** ultimo.

**ulterior** • **adj.** **1** other than what is obvious or admitted: *she had some ulterior motive in coming.* **2** beyond what is immediate or present.
– ORIGIN C17: from L., lit. 'further, more distant'.

**ultimata** plural form of **ULTIMATUM**.

**ultimate** • **adj.** **1** being or happening at the end of a process. **2** being the best or most extreme example of its kind: *the ultimate accolade.* **3** basic or fundamental. **4** Physics denoting the maximum possible strength or resistance beyond which an object breaks. • **n.** **1** (**the ultimate**) the best achievable or imaginable of its kind: *the ultimate in luxury.* **2** a final or fundamental fact or principle.
– DERIVATIVES **ultimacy** n. (pl. **-ies**). **ultimately** adv.
– ORIGIN C17: from late L. *ultimatus*, past part. of *ultimare* 'come to an end'.

**ultima Thule** • **n.** a distant unknown region; the extreme limit of travel and discovery.
– ORIGIN L., lit. 'furthest Thule', a country to the north of Britain (prob. Norway), believed by ancient Greeks and Romans to be the northernmost part of the world.

**ultimatum** • **n.** (pl. **ultimatums** or **ultimata** /-tə/) a final demand or statement of terms, the rejection of which will result in retaliation or a breakdown in relations.
– ORIGIN C18: from L., neut. past part. of *ultimare* 'come to an end'.

**ultimo** /ˈʌltɪməʊ/ • **adj.** [postpos.] dated of last month.
– ORIGIN from L. *ultimo mense* 'in the last month'.

**ultisol** /ˈʌltɪsɒl/ • **n.** Soil Science a highly weathered leached reddish acid soil with a clay-rich B horizon, occurring in warm, humid climates.
– ORIGIN 1960s: from **ULTIMATE** + L. *solum* 'soil'.

**ultra** informal • **n.** an extremist. • **adv.** very.
– ORIGIN C19: an independent usage of **ULTRA-**, orig. as an abbrev. of Fr. *ultra-royaliste*.

**ultra-** • **prefix** **1** beyond; on the other side of: *ultramontane.* **2** extreme; to an extreme degree: *ultramicroscopic*.
– ORIGIN from L. *ultra* 'beyond'.

**ultracentrifuge** • **n.** a very fast centrifuge used to precipitate or separate large biological molecules.
– DERIVATIVES **ultracentrifugation** n.

**ultradian** /ʌlˈtreɪdɪən/ • **adj.** Physiology recurring more than once a day (but less than once an hour). Compare with **INFRADIAN**.
– ORIGIN 1960s: from **ULTRA-** 'beyond' on the pattern of *circadian*.

**ultrafiltration** • **n.** filtration using a medium fine enough to retain colloidal particles, viruses, or large molecules.

**ultra-high frequency** (abbrev.: **UHF**) • **n.** a radio frequency in the range 300 to 3,000 MHz.

**ultraism** • **n.** rare extremism.

**ultramafic** /ˌʌltrəˈmafɪk/ • **adj.** Geology relating to or denoting igneous rocks composed chiefly of mafic minerals.

**ultramarine** • **n.** a brilliant deep blue pigment originally obtained from lapis lazuli, and now made from pow-

dered fired clay, sodium carbonate, sulphur, and resin. ● **adj.** archaic situated beyond the sea.
– ORIGIN C16 (as adj.): from med. L. *ultramarinus* 'beyond the sea'; the name of the pigment is from obs. Ital. *(azzurro) oltramarino*, lit. '(azure) from overseas' (because the lapis lazuli was imported).

**ultramicroscope** ● **n.** an optical microscope used to detect very small particles by observing light scattered from them.

**ultramicroscopic** ● **adj.** too small to be seen by an ordinary optical microscope. ➤ of or relating to an ultramicroscope.

**ultramontane** /ˌʌltrəˈmɒnteɪn/ ● **adj.** **1** advocating supreme papal authority in matters of faith and discipline. Compare with **GALLICAN**. **2** situated on the other side of the Alps from the point of view of the speaker. ● **n.** an advocate of supreme papal authority.
– DERIVATIVES **ultramontanism** n.
– ORIGIN C16 (denoting a representative of the Roman Catholic Church north of the Alps): from med. L. *ultramontanus*, from L. *ultra* 'beyond' + *mons, mont-* 'mountain'.

**ultramundane** /ˌʌltrəˈmʌndeɪn/ ● **adj.** poetic/literary existing outside the known world or the universe.
– ORIGIN C17: from late L. *ultramundanus*, from *ultra* 'beyond' + *mundanus* (from *mundus* 'world').

**ultrasonic** ● **adj.** of or involving sound waves with a frequency above the upper limit of human hearing.
– DERIVATIVES **ultrasonically** adv.

**ultrasonics** ● **pl. n.** **1** [treated as sing.] the science and application of ultrasonic waves. **2** [treated as sing. or pl.] ultrasound.

**ultrasonography** /ˌʌltrəsəˈnɒgrəfi/ ● **n.** Medicine a technique using echoes of ultrasound pulses to delineate objects or areas of different density in the body.
– DERIVATIVES **ultrasonographic** adj.

**ultrasound** ● **n.** sound or other vibrations having an ultrasonic frequency, particularly as used in medical imaging.

**ultrastructure** ● **n.** Biology fine structure that can only be seen with an electron microscope.

**ultraviolet** ● **n.** electromagnetic radiation having a wavelength just shorter than that of violet light but longer than that of X-rays. ● **adj.** of or denoting such radiation.

**ultra vires** /ˌʌltrə ˈvʌɪriːz, ˌʊltrɑː ˈviːreɪz/ ● **adj. & adv.** Law beyond one's legal power or authority.
– ORIGIN L., lit. 'beyond the powers'.

**ulu** /ˈuːluː/ ● **n.** (pl. **ulus**) an Eskimo woman's short-handled knife with a broad crescent-shaped blade.
– ORIGIN from Inuit.

**ululate** /ˈjuːljʊleɪt, ˈʌl-/ ● **v.** howl or wail, typically to express grief.
– DERIVATIVES **ululant** adj. **ululation** n.
– ORIGIN C17: from L. *ululat-*, *ululare* 'howl, shriek', of imitative origin.

**um** ● **exclam.** expressing hesitation or a pause in speech.

**-um** ● **suffix** variant spelling of **-IUM** (in sense 2).

**Umbanda** /ʊmˈbandə/ ● **n.** a Brazilian folk religion combining elements of macumba, Roman Catholicism, and South American Indian practices.
– ORIGIN from Port.

**umbel** /ˈʌmb(ə)l/ ● **n.** Botany a flower cluster in which stalks of nearly equal length spring from a common centre and form a flat or curved surface, characteristic of the parsley family.
– DERIVATIVES **umbellate** adj.
– ORIGIN C16: from obs. Fr. *umbelle* or L. *umbella* 'sunshade'.

**umbellifer** /ʌmˈbɛlɪfə/ ● **n.** Botany a plant of the parsley family (Umbelliferae).
– DERIVATIVES **umbelliferous** adj.
– ORIGIN C18: from obs. Fr. *umbellifère*, from L. *umbella* 'parasol' + *-fer* 'bearing'.

**umber** /ˈʌmbə/ ● **n.** a natural pigment resembling but darker than ochre, normally dark yellowish-brown in colour (**raw umber**) or dark brown when roasted (**burnt umber**).
– ORIGIN C16: from Fr. *(terre d')ombre* or Ital. *(terra di) ombra*, lit. '(earth of) shadow'.

**umbilical** /ʌmˈbɪlɪk(ə)l, ˌʌmbɪˈlʌɪk(ə)l/ ● **adj.** **1** relating to or affecting the navel or umbilical cord. **2** extremely close; inseparable. **3** (of a pipe or cable) connecting someone or something to a source of essential supplies. ● **n.** short for **UMBILICAL CORD**.
– DERIVATIVES **umbilically** adv.
– ORIGIN C16: from Fr. *ombilical*, or based on L. *umbilicus* (see **UMBILICUS**).

**umbilical cord** ● **n.** **1** a flexible cord-like structure containing blood vessels, attaching a fetus to the placenta during gestation. **2** a flexible cable, pipe, or other line carrying essential services or supplies.

**umbilicate** /ʌmˈbɪlɪkət/ ● **adj.** Zoology & Botany having an umbilicus or central depression.

**umbilicus** /ʌmˈbɪlɪkəs, ˌʌmbɪˈlʌɪkəs/ ● **n.** (pl. **umbilici** /-sʌɪ/ or **umbilicuses**) **1** Anatomy the navel. **2** Zoology a central depression or hole in the whorl of some gastropod molluscs and many ammonites. **3** Zoology a hole at each end of the hollow shaft of a feather.
– ORIGIN C17: from L.: rel. to Gk *omphalos*, also to **NAVEL**.

**umbles** ● **pl. n.** variant spelling of **NUMBLES**.

**umbo** /ˈʌmbəʊ/ ● **n.** (pl. **umbones** /-ˈbəʊniːz/ or **umbos**) **1** historical the central boss of a shield. **2** Biology a central swelling or protuberance.
– DERIVATIVES **umbonal** adj. **umbonate** adj.
– ORIGIN C18: from L., 'shield boss'.

**umbra** /ˈʌmbrə/ ● **n.** (pl. **umbras** or **umbrae** /-briː/) **1** the fully shaded inner region of a shadow cast by an opaque object, especially the area on the earth or moon experiencing totality in an eclipse. **2** Astronomy the dark central part of a sunspot.
– DERIVATIVES **umbral** adj.
– ORIGIN C16 (denoting a phantom or ghost): from L., lit. 'shade'.

**umbrage** /ˈʌmbrɪdʒ/ ● **n.** **1** offence or annoyance. **2** archaic shade or shadow, especially as cast by trees.
– DERIVATIVES **umbrageous** adj.
– ORIGIN ME (an early sense was 'shadowy outline', giving rise to 'ground for suspicion', whence sense 1): from OFr., from L. *umbra* 'shadow'.

**umbrella** ● **n.** **1** a device consisting of a circular fabric canopy on a folding metal frame supported by a central rod, used as protection against rain. **2** a protecting force or influence. ➤ a screen of fighter aircraft or anti-aircraft artillery. **3** [usu. as modifier] a thing that includes or contains many different parts: *an umbrella organization.* **4** Zoology the gelatinous disc of a jellyfish, which it contracts and expands to move through the water.
– DERIVATIVES **umbrellaed** adj.
– ORIGIN C17: from Ital. *ombrella*, dimin. of *ombra* 'shade'.

**umbrellabird** ● **n.** a large black tropical American cotinga with a radiating crest and long wattles. [Genus *Cephalopterus*: three species.]

**umbrella fund** ● **n.** an offshore investment fund which invests only in other investment funds.

**umbrella pine** ● **n.** **1** another term for **STONE PINE**. **2** a tall Japanese conifer with leaves growing in umbrella-like whorls. [*Sciadopitys verticillata*.]

**umbrella plant** ● **n.** a tropical sedge with stiff green stems terminating in a whorl of arching green bracts, often grown as a house plant. [*Cyperus involucratus*.]

**umbrella tree** ● **n.** a plant with leaves or leaflets arranged in umbrella-like whorls. [*Schefflera actinophylla* (Australia) and *Magnolia tripetala* (N. America).]

**Umbrian** ● **n.** **1** a native or inhabitant of Umbria, a region of central Italy, especially in pre-Roman times. **2** an extinct Italic language of central Italy. ● **adj.** of or relating to Umbria, its people, or their languages.

**umbriferous** /ʌmˈbrɪf(ə)rəs/ ● **adj.** poetic/literary providing shade.
– ORIGIN C17: from L. *umbrifer* + **-OUS**.

**umiak** /ˈuːmɪak/ ● **n.** an Eskimo open boat made of wood and skin, traditionally rowed by women.
– ORIGIN from Inuit *umiaq*.

**umlaut** /ˈʊmlaʊt/ Linguistics ● **n.** **1** a mark (¨) used over a

vowel, especially in German, to indicate a different vowel quality. **2** the process in Germanic languages by which the quality of a vowel was altered in certain phonetic contexts. ● **v.** modify with an umlaut.
– ORIGIN C19: from Ger. *Umlaut*, from *um* 'about' + *Laut* 'sound'.
**umma** /'ʊmə/ (also **ummah**) ● **n.** the whole community of Muslims bound together by ties of religion.
– ORIGIN Arab., lit. 'people, community'.
**ump** ● **n.** informal, chiefly N. Amer. an umpire.
**umph** ● **n.** variant spelling of **OOMPH**.
**umpire** ● **n. 1** (in certain sports) an official who watches a game or match closely to enforce the rules and arbitrate on matters arising from the play. **2** a person chosen to arbitrate between contending parties. ● **v.** act as an umpire. ➤act as umpire in (a game or match).
– DERIVATIVES **umpirage** n. **umpireship** n.
– ORIGIN ME (orig. as *noumpere*): from OFr. *nonper* 'not equal'; the *n* was lost by wrong division of *a noumpere*.
**umpteen** ● **cardinal number** informal indefinitely many.
– DERIVATIVES **umpteenth** ordinal number.
– ORIGIN C20: humorous formation based on **-TEEN**.
**UMTS** ● **abbrev.** Universal Mobile Telephone System.
**umu** /'ʊmʊ/ ● **n.** a Maori oven consisting of a hollow in the earth in which food is cooked on heated stones.
– ORIGIN from Maori.
**UN** ● **abbrev.** United Nations.
**un-**[1] ● **prefix 1** (added to adjectives, participles, and their derivatives) denoting the absence of a quality or state; not: *unacademic*. ➤the reverse of: *unselfish*. **2** (added to nouns) a lack of: *untruth*.
– ORIGIN OE, of Gmc origin.
**un-**[2] ● **prefix** added to verbs: **1** denoting the reversal or cancellation of an action or state: *unsettle*. **2** denoting deprivation, separation, or reduction to a lesser state: *unmask*. ➤denoting release: *unhand*.
– ORIGIN OE *un-*, *on-*, of Gmc origin.
**'un** ● **contr.** informal one.
**UNA** ● **abbrev.** United Nations Association.
**unabashed** ● **adj.** not embarrassed, disconcerted, or ashamed.
– DERIVATIVES **unabashedly** adv.
**unabated** ● **adj.** without any reduction in intensity or strength.
– DERIVATIVES **unabatedly** adv.
**unable** ● **adj.** lacking the skill, means, or opportunity to do something.
**unabridged** ● **adj.** (of a text) not cut or shortened.
**unaccented** ● **adj.** having no accent, stress, or emphasis.
**unacceptable** ● **adj.** not satisfactory or allowable.
– DERIVATIVES **unacceptability** n. **unacceptably** adv.
**unaccompanied** ● **adj. 1** having no companion or escort. **2** without instrumental accompaniment. **3** without something occurring at the same time.
**unaccountable** ● **adj. 1** unable to be explained. **2** not responsible for or required to justify consequences.
– DERIVATIVES **unaccountability** n. **unaccountably** adv.
**unaccounted** ● **adj.** (**unaccounted for**) not taken into consideration or explained.
**unaccustomed** ● **adj. 1** not customary; unusual. **2** (**unaccustomed to**) not familiar with or used to.
– DERIVATIVES **unaccustomedly** adv.
**unacknowledged** ● **adj. 1** existing or having taken place but not accepted or admitted to. **2** deserving but not receiving recognition.
**una corda** /ˌuːnə 'kɔːdə/ ● **adv. & adj.** Music using the soft pedal on a piano.
– ORIGIN Ital., lit. 'one string'.
**unacquainted** ● **adj. 1** (**unacquainted with**) having no experience of or familiarity with. **2** not having met before.
**unadjusted** ● **adj.** (especially of statistics) not adjusted or refined.
**unadopted** ● **adj.** Brit. (of a road) not taken over for maintenance by a local authority.
**unadulterated** ● **adj. 1** complete; utter. **2** having no inferior added substances.
**unadventurous** ● **adj.** not offering, involving, or eager for new or stimulating things.
– DERIVATIVES **unadventurously** adv.
**unadvisable** ● **adj.** another term for **INADVISABLE**.
**unadvisedly** ● **adv.** in an unwise or rash manner.
**unaesthetic** ● **adj. 1** not visually pleasing. **2** not motivated by aesthetic principles.
**unaffected** ● **adj. 1** feeling or showing no effects. **2** sincere and genuine.
– DERIVATIVES **unaffectedly** adv. **unaffectedness** n.
**unaffiliated** ● **adj.** not officially attached to or connected with an organization.
**unaffordable** ● **adj.** too expensive to be afforded by the average person.
**unafraid** ● **adj.** feeling no fear.
**unaided** ● **adj.** needing or having no assistance.
**unalienable** ● **adj.** another term for **INALIENABLE**.
**unaligned** ● **adj. 1** not placed or arranged in a straight line or in correct relative positions. **2** not allied with or supporting an organization or cause.
**unalike** ● **adj.** differing from each other.
**unalloyed** ● **adj. 1** (of metal) not alloyed. **2** complete and unreserved.
**unalterable** ● **adj.** not able to be changed.
– DERIVATIVES **unalterableness** n. **unalterably** adv.
**unaltered** ● **adj.** remaining the same.
**unambiguous** ● **adj.** without ambiguity.
– DERIVATIVES **unambiguity** n. **unambiguously** adv.
**unambitious** ● **adj. 1** not motivated by a strong desire to succeed. **2** not involving anything new, exciting, or demanding.
– DERIVATIVES **unambitiously** adv. **unambitiousness** n.
**un-American** ● **adj. 1** not in accordance with American characteristics. **2** US, chiefly historical contrary to the interests of the US and therefore treasonable.
– DERIVATIVES **un-Americanism** n.
**unanalysable** (US **unanalyzable**) ● **adj.** not able to be explained or interpreted through methodical examination.
**unaneled** /ˌʌnə'niːld/ ● **adj.** archaic having died without receiving extreme unction.
**Unani** /juː'nɑːni/ ● **n.** a system of medicine practised in parts of India, thought to be derived via medieval Muslim physicians from Byzantine Greece.
– ORIGIN from Arab. *Yūnānī* 'Greek'.
**unanimous** /juː'nanɪməs/ ● **adj. 1** fully in agreement. **2** (of an opinion, decision, or vote) held or carried by everyone involved.
– DERIVATIVES **unanimity** /ˌjuːnə'nɪmɪti/ n. **unanimously** adv.
– ORIGIN C17: from L. *unanimus* (from *unus* 'one' + *animus* 'mind') + **-ous**.
**unannounced** ● **adj. 1** not publicized. **2** without warning; unexpected.
**unanswerable** ● **adj. 1** unable to be answered. **2** unable to be refuted.
– DERIVATIVES **unanswerably** adv.
**unanswered** ● **adj.** not answered or responded to.
**unapologetic** ● **adj.** not acknowledging or expressing regret.
– DERIVATIVES **unapologetically** adv.
**unappealable** ● **adj.** Law (of a case or ruling) not able to be referred to a higher court for review.
**unappealing** ● **adj.** not inviting or attractive.
– DERIVATIVES **unappealingly** adv.
**unappetizing** (also **-ising**) ● **adj.** not inviting or attractive.
– DERIVATIVES **unappetizingly** adv.
**unappreciated** ● **adj.** not fully understood, recognized, or valued.
**unappreciative** ● **adj.** not fully understanding or recognizing something.
**unapprehended** ● **adj. 1** not perceived or understood. **2** not arrested.
**unapproachable** ● **adj. 1** not welcoming or friendly.

2 archaic (of a place) remote and inaccessible.
– DERIVATIVES **unapproachability** n. **unapproachably** adv.

**unapproved** • adj. not officially accepted or sanctioned.

**unapt** • adj. not appropriate in the circumstances.
– DERIVATIVES **unaptly** adv. **unaptness** n.

**unarguable** • adj. **1** not open to disagreement; certain. **2** not able to be argued.
– DERIVATIVES **unarguably** adv.

**unarmed** • adj. not equipped with or carrying weapons.

**unary** /ˈjuːnəri/ • adj. Mathematics consisting of or involving a single component or element.

**unashamed** • adj. feeling or showing no guilt or embarrassment.
– DERIVATIVES **unashamedly** adv. **unashamedness** n.

**unasked** • adj. **1** (of a question) not asked. **2** (often **unasked for**) not requested or sought.

**unassailable** • adj. unable to be attacked, questioned, or defeated.
– DERIVATIVES **unassailability** n. **unassailably** adv.

**unassertive** • adj. not having or showing a confident and forceful personality.
– DERIVATIVES **unassertively** adv. **unassertiveness** n.

**unassisted** • adj. not helped by anyone or anything.

**unassociated** • adj. not connected or associated.

**unassuming** • adj. not pretentious or arrogant.
– DERIVATIVES **unassumingly** adv. **unassumingness** n.

**unattached** • adj. **1** not working for or belonging to a particular organization. **2** without a spouse or established lover.

**unattainable** • adj. not able to be reached or achieved.
– DERIVATIVES **unattainableness** n. **unattainably** adv.

**unattended** • adj. **1** not dealt with. **2** not looked after.

**unattractive** • adj. not pleasing, appealing, or inviting.
– DERIVATIVES **unattractively** adv. **unattractiveness** n.

**unattributed** • adj. (of a quotation, story, or work of art) of unknown or unpublished provenance.
– DERIVATIVES **unattributable** adj. **unattributably** adv.

**unauthorized** (also **-ised**) • adj. not having official permission or approval.

**unavailable** • adj. **1** not at someone's disposal. **2** not free to do something.
– DERIVATIVES **unavailability** n.

**unavailing** • adj. achieving little or nothing.
– DERIVATIVES **unavailingly** adv.

**unavoidable** • adj. not able to be avoided or prevented; inevitable.
– DERIVATIVES **unavoidability** n. **unavoidably** adv.

**unavowed** • adj. not openly declared.

**unaware** • adj. having no knowledge of a situation or fact. • adv. variant of UNAWARES.
– DERIVATIVES **unawareness** n.

**unawares** (also **unaware**) • adv. so as to surprise.
– ORIGIN C16: from UNAWARE + -S³.

**unbacked** • adj. **1** having no material or moral support. **2** (of a horse) having no backers in a race. **3** having no backing layer.

**unbalance** • v. **1** upset the balance of. **2** [often as adj. **unbalanced**] upset the mental equilibrium of; derange. **3** [as adj. **unbalanced**] treating aspects of something unequally; partial. • n. a lack of balance or stability.

**unbearable** • adj. not able to be endured or tolerated.
– DERIVATIVES **unbearableness** n. **unbearably** adv.

**unbeatable** • adj. **1** not able to be surpassed or defeated. **2** extremely good.

**unbeaten** • adj. not defeated or surpassed. ➤ Cricket (of a batsman) not out in his or her side's innings.

**unbecoming** • adj. **1** (especially of clothing) not flattering. **2** not fitting; unseemly.
– DERIVATIVES **unbecomingly** adv. **unbecomingness** n.

**unbeknown** (also **unbeknownst**) • adj. (**unbeknown to**) without the knowledge of.
– ORIGIN C17: from UN-¹ + archaic *beknown* 'known'.

**unbelief** • n. lack of religious belief.
– DERIVATIVES **unbeliever** n. **unbelieving** adj. **unbelievingly** adv.

**unbelievable** • adj. **1** unlikely to be true. **2** extraordinary.
– DERIVATIVES **unbelievability** n. **unbelievably** adv.

**unbelted** • adj. **1** without a belt. **2** not wearing a vehicle seat belt.

**unbend** • v. (past and past part. **unbent**) **1** straighten. **2** become less reserved, formal, or strict. **3** Sailing unfasten (sails) from yards and stays. ➤ untie (a rope) or cast (a cable) loose.

**unbending** • adj. austere and inflexible.
– DERIVATIVES **unbendingly** adv. **unbendingness** n.

**unbiased** (also **unbiassed**) • adj. showing no prejudice; impartial.

**unbidden** • adj. **1** without having been invited. **2** arising without conscious effort.

**unbirthday** • n. humorous any day except one's birthday.
– ORIGIN 1871: coined by Lewis Carroll in *Through the Looking Glass*.

**unbleached** • adj. (especially of paper, cloth, or flour) not bleached.

**unblind** • v. conduct (a test or experiment) in such a way that it is not blind.

**unblock** • v. **1** remove an obstruction from. **2** Bridge play in such a way that (a long suit) becomes established.

**unblown** • adj. informal (of a vehicle or its engine) not provided with a turbocharger.

**unblushing** • adj. not feeling or showing embarrassment or shame.
– DERIVATIVES **unblushingly** adv.

**unbolt** • v. open by drawing back a bolt.

**unborn** • adj. (of a baby) not yet born.

**unbosom** • v. archaic disclose (one's thoughts or secrets). ➤ (**unbosom oneself**) unburden oneself.

**unbound** • adj. **1** not bound or restricted. **2** (of printed sheets) not bound together. ➤ (of a bound book) not provided with a permanent cover.

**unbounded** • adj. having no limits.
– DERIVATIVES **unboundedly** adv. **unboundedness** n.

**unbowed** • adj. not having submitted to pressure, demands, or accusations.

**unbranded** • adj. **1** (of a product) not bearing a brand name. **2** (of livestock) not branded with the owner's mark.

**unbreachable** • adj. not able to be breached or overcome.

**unbreakable** • adj. not liable to break or able to be broken.

**unbreathable** • adj. (of air) not fit or pleasant to breathe.

**unbridgeable** • adj. (of a gap or difference) not able to be bridged or made less significant.

**unbridled** • adj. uncontrolled; unconstrained.

**unbroken** • adj. **1** not broken; intact. **2** not interrupted. **3** not surpassed. **4** (of a horse) not broken in.
– DERIVATIVES **unbrokenly** adv. **unbrokenness** n.

**unbuckle** • v. unfasten the buckle of.

**unbuild** • v. (past and past part. **unbuilt**) **1** demolish or destroy. **2** [as adj. **unbuilt**] (of buildings or land) not yet built or built on.

**unbundle** • v. **1** market or charge for (items or services) separately rather than as part of a package. **2** split (a company or conglomerate) into its constituent businesses, especially prior to selling them off.
– DERIVATIVES **unbundler** n.

**unburden** • v. relieve of a burden. ➤ (**unburden oneself**) be relieved of a cause of anxiety or distress through confiding in someone.

**unburnt** (also **unburned**) • adj. **1** not damaged or destroyed by fire. **2** (especially of bricks) not exposed to heat in a kiln.

**unbutton** • v. **1** unfasten the buttons of. **2** informal relax and become less inhibited.

**uncalled** • adj. **1** not summoned or invited. **2** (**uncalled for**) undesirable and unnecessary.

**uncanny** • adj. (**-ier**, **-iest**) strange or mysterious.

– DERIVATIVES **uncannily** adv. **uncanniness** n.
– ORIGIN C16 (orig. Scots in the sense 'relating to the occult, malicious'): from **UN-**[1] + **CANNY**.

**uncap** • v. (**uncapped**, **uncapping**) **1** remove the cap from. **2** remove a limit from (a price, rate, etc.).

**uncapped** • adj. chiefly Brit. (of a player) never having been chosen as a member of a national sports team.

**uncared** • adj. (**uncared for**) not looked after properly.

**uncaring** • adj. **1** not displaying sympathy or concern for others. **2** not interested; unconcerned.
– DERIVATIVES **uncaringly** adv.

**unceasing** • adj. not ceasing; continuous.
– DERIVATIVES **unceasingly** adv.

**unceremonious** • adj. discourteous; abrupt.
– DERIVATIVES **unceremoniously** adv. **unceremoniousness** n.

**uncertain** • adj. **1** not known, reliable, or definite. **2** not completely confident or sure.
– PHRASES **in no uncertain terms** clearly and forcefully.
– DERIVATIVES **uncertainly** adv. **uncertainty** n. (pl. **-ies**).

**uncertainty principle** • n. Physics the principle, stated by Werner Heisenberg, that the momentum and position of a particle cannot both be precisely determined at the same time.

**unchallengeable** • adj. not able to be disputed, opposed, or defeated.
– DERIVATIVES **unchallengeably** adv.

**unchallenged** • adj. **1** not disputed, opposed, or defeated. **2** not called on to prove one's identity.

**unchallenging** • adj. not presenting a challenge.

**unchancy** • adj. (**-ier**, **-iest**) chiefly Scottish unlucky, inauspicious, or dangerous.

**unchangeable** • adj. not liable to variation or able to be altered.
– DERIVATIVES **unchangeability** n. **unchangeableness** n. **unchangeably** adv.

**unchanged** • adj. not changed; unaltered.

**unchanging** • adj. remaining the same.
– DERIVATIVES **unchangingly** adv.

**uncharacteristic** • adj. not typical of a particular person or thing.
– DERIVATIVES **uncharacteristically** adv.

**uncharged** • adj. **1** not accused of an offence under the law. **2** not carrying an electric charge. **3** not charged to a particular account.

**uncharismatic** • adj. lacking charisma.

**uncharitable** • adj. unkind or unsympathetic to others.
– DERIVATIVES **uncharitableness** n. **uncharitably** adv.

**uncharted** • adj. (of an area of land or sea) not mapped or surveyed.

**unchartered** • adj. not having a charter or written constitution.

**unchaste** • adj. relating to or engaging in sexual activity, especially of an illicit or extramarital nature.
– DERIVATIVES **unchastely** adv. **unchastity** n.

**unchastened** • adj. not chastened by a reproof or misfortune.

**unchecked** • adj. (of something undesirable) not controlled or restrained.

**unchivalrous** • adj. (of a man) discourteous, especially towards women.
– DERIVATIVES **unchivalrously** adv.

**unchristian** • adj. not in accordance with the teachings of Christianity. ➤ ungenerous or unfair.
– DERIVATIVES **unchristianly** adv.

**unchurch** • v. **1** officially exclude (someone) from participation in the Christian sacraments; excommunicate. **2** deprive (a building) of its status as a church.

**unchurched** • adj. not belonging to or connected with a Church.

**uncial** /ˈʌnsɪəl, -ʃ(ə)l/ • adj. **1** of or written in a majuscule script with rounded separated letters which is found in European manuscripts of the 4th–8th centuries and from which modern capital letters are derived. **2** rare of or relating to an inch or an ounce. • n. an uncial letter, script, or manuscript.
– ORIGIN C17: from L. *uncialis*, from *uncia* 'inch' (in sense 1 from *unciales litterae* 'uncial letters').

**unciform** /ˈʌnsɪfɔːm/ • adj. another term for **UNCINATE**. ➤ dated denoting the hamate bone of the wrist.

**uncinate** /ˈʌnsɪnət, -eɪt/ • adj. chiefly Anatomy having a hooked shape.
– ORIGIN C18: from L. *uncinatus*, from *uncinus* 'hook'.

**uncircumcised** • adj. **1** (of a boy or man) not circumcised. **2** archaic irreligious or heathen.
– DERIVATIVES **uncircumcision** n.

**uncivil** • adj. discourteous; impolite.
– DERIVATIVES **uncivilly** adv.

**uncivilized** (also **-ised**) • adj. **1** not socially or culturally advanced. **2** impolite; bad-mannered.

**unclad** • adj. **1** unclothed; naked. **2** not provided with cladding.

**unclaimed** • adj. not having been claimed.

**unclasp** • v. **1** unfasten (a clasp or similar device). **2** release the grip of.

**unclassifiable** • adj. not able to be classified.

**unclassified** • adj. **1** not classified. ➤ Brit. (of a road) not classified according to the overall system of road numbering. **2** Brit. denoting a university degree without honours. ➤ (of a grade in an examination) denoting a fail.

**uncle** • n. **1** the brother of one's father or mother or the husband of one's aunt. ➤ informal an unrelated adult male friend of a child. **2** archaic, informal a pawnbroker.
– PHRASES **cry** (or **say**) **uncle** N. Amer. informal surrender or admit defeat.
– ORIGIN ME: from OFr. *oncle*, from late L. *aunculus*, alt. of L. *avunculus* (see **AVUNCULAR**).

**-uncle** • suffix forming chiefly diminutive nouns: *carbuncle*.
– ORIGIN from OFr. *-oncle*, *-uncle*, or from L. *-unculus*, a special form of *-ulus*.

**unclean** • adj. **1** dirty. **2** immoral. **3** ritually impure and unfit for use or consumption. ➤ (in biblical use, of a spirit) evil.
– DERIVATIVES **uncleanness** n.

**uncleanliness** • n. the state of being dirty.

**uncleanly** • adj. archaic unclean.

**unclear** • adj. **1** not easy to see, hear, or understand. **2** not obvious, definite, or certain.
– DERIVATIVES **unclearly** adv. **unclearness** n.

**uncleared** • adj. **1** (of a cheque) not having passed through a clearing house and been paid into the payee's account. **2** (of land) not cleared of vegetation.

**unclench** • v. release (a clenched part of the body).

**Uncle Sam** • n. a personification of the federal government or citizens of the US.
– ORIGIN C19: said to have arisen as a facetious expansion of the letters US.

**Uncle Tom** • n. derogatory, chiefly N. Amer. a black man considered to be excessively obedient or servile.
– ORIGIN 1920s: from the name of the hero of H. B. Stowe's *Uncle Tom's Cabin* (1852).

**unclimbed** • adj. (of a mountain or rock face) not previously climbed.
– DERIVATIVES **unclimbable** adj.

**uncloak** • v. poetic/literary uncover; reveal.

**unclog** • v. (**unclogged**, **unclogging**) remove accumulated matter from.

**unclothed** • adj. wearing no clothes; naked.

**unclouded** • adj. **1** (of the sky) not dark or overcast. **2** not troubled or spoiled by anything.

**uncluttered** • adj. not cluttered by too many objects or elements.

**unco** /ˈʌŋkə/ Scottish • adj. unusual or remarkable. • adv. remarkably; very. • n. (pl. **-os**) **1** a stranger. **2** (**uncos**) news.
– ORIGIN ME: alt. of **UNCOUTH**.

**uncoil** • v. straighten from a coiled or curled position.

**uncoloured** (US **uncolored**) • adj. **1** having no colour; neutral in colour. **2** not influenced, especially in a negative way.

**uncombed** ● **adj.** (of a person's hair) not combed.

**uncomely** ● **adj.** archaic or humorous (especially of a woman) not attractive. ➤ archaic not agreeable or suitable.

**uncomfortable** ● **adj.** not physically comfortable. ➤ uneasy or awkward.
– DERIVATIVES **uncomfortableness** n. **uncomfortably** adv.

**uncommercial** ● **adj.** not making, intended to make, or allowing a profit.

**uncommon** ● **adj.** out of the ordinary; unusual. ➤ remarkably great: *an uncommon amount of noise.* ● **adv.** archaic remarkably.
– DERIVATIVES **uncommonly** adv. **uncommonness** n.

**uncommunicative** ● **adj.** unwilling to talk or impart information.
– DERIVATIVES **uncommunicatively** adv. **uncommunicativeness** n.

**uncompetitive** ● **adj.** not competitive or marked by fair competition.
– DERIVATIVES **uncompetitively** adv. **uncompetitiveness** n.

**uncomplaining** ● **adj.** not complaining; stoical.
– DERIVATIVES **uncomplainingly** adv.

**uncomplicated** ● **adj.** simple or straightforward.
– DERIVATIVES **uncomplicatedly** adv. **uncomplicatedness** n.

**uncomplimentary** ● **adj.** not complimentary; negative or insulting.

**uncomprehending** ● **adj.** unable to comprehend something.
– DERIVATIVES **uncomprehendingly** adv.

**uncompromising** ● **adj.** unwilling to make concessions; resolute. ➤ harsh or relentless.
– DERIVATIVES **uncompromisingly** adv. **uncompromisingness** n.

**unconcealed** ● **adj.** (especially of an emotion) not concealed; obvious.

**unconcern** ● **n.** a lack of worry or interest.
– DERIVATIVES **unconcerned** adj. **unconcernedly** adv.

**unconditional** ● **adj.** not subject to any conditions.
– DERIVATIVES **unconditionality** n. **unconditionally** adv.

**unconditioned** ● **adj. 1** unconditional. **2** relating to or denoting instinctive reflexes or other behaviour not formed or influenced by conditioning or learning. **3** not subjected to a conditioning process.

**unconfident** ● **adj.** not confident; hesitant.
– DERIVATIVES **unconfidently** adv.

**unconfined** ● **adj. 1** not confined to a limited space. **2** (of joy or excitement) very great.

**unconfirmed** ● **adj.** not confirmed as to truth or validity.

**unconformable** ● **adj.** Geology (of rock strata in contact) marking a discontinuity in the geological record, and typically not having the same direction of stratification.
– DERIVATIVES **uncomformably** adv.

**unconformity** ● **n.** Geology a surface of contact between two groups of unconformable strata. ➤ the condition of being unconformable.

**uncongenial** ● **adj. 1** (of a person) not friendly or pleasant to be with. **2** unsuitable and therefore unlikely to promote success or well-being.

**unconnected** ● **adj.** not joined together or to something else. ➤ not associated or linked in a sequence.
– DERIVATIVES **unconnectedly** adv. **unconnectedness** n.

**unconquerable** ● **adj.** not conquerable: *unconquerable pride.*
– DERIVATIVES **unconquerably** adv. **unconquered** adj.

**unconscionable** /ʌnˈkɒnʃ(ə)nəb(ə)l/ ● **adj.** not right or reasonable. ➤ unreasonably excessive: *they had to wait an unconscionable time.*
– DERIVATIVES **unconscionably** adv.
– ORIGIN C16: from **UN-**[1] + obs. *conscionable*, from **CONSCIENCE** (interpreted as a pl.) + **-ABLE**.

**unconscious** ● **adj. 1** not awake and aware of and responding to one's environment. **2** done or existing without one realizing. **3** (**unconscious of**) unaware of. ● **n.** (**the unconscious**) the part of the mind which is inaccessible to the conscious mind but which affects behaviour and emotions.
– DERIVATIVES **unconsciously** adv. **unconsciousness** n.

**unconsecrated** ● **adj.** not consecrated.

**unconsidered** ● **adj. 1** disregarded and unappreciated. **2** not thought about in advance; rash.

**unconsolable** ● **adj.** inconsolable.
– DERIVATIVES **unconsolably** adv.

**unconstitutional** ● **adj.** not in accordance with the political constitution or with procedural rules.
– DERIVATIVES **unconstitutionality** n. **unconstitutionally** adv.

**unconstrained** ● **adj.** not restricted or limited.
– DERIVATIVES **unconstrainedly** adv.

**unconstructed** ● **adj.** chiefly N. Amer. (of a garment) unstructured.

**unconsummated** ● **adj.** (of a marriage) not having been consummated.

**uncontainable** ● **adj.** (especially of an emotion) very strong.

**uncontaminated** ● **adj.** not contaminated.

**uncontentious** ● **adj.** not contentious.

**uncontested** ● **adj.** not contested.
– DERIVATIVES **uncontestedly** adv.

**uncontrived** ● **adj.** not artificially created. ➤ not appearing artificial.

**uncontrollable** ● **adj.** not controllable.
– DERIVATIVES **uncontrollableness** n. **uncontrollably** adv.

**uncontrolled** ● **adj.** not controlled.
– DERIVATIVES **uncontrolledly** adv.

**uncontroversial** ● **adj.** not controversial; avoiding controversy.
– DERIVATIVES **uncontroversially** adv.

**uncontroverted** ● **adj.** of which the truth or validity is not disputed.

**unconventional** ● **adj.** not based on or conforming to what is generally done or believed.
– DERIVATIVES **unconventionality** n. **unconventionally** adv.

**unconvinced** ● **adj.** not certain that something is true or can be relied on.

**unconvincing** ● **adj.** failing to convince or impress.
– DERIVATIVES **unconvincingly** adv.

**uncooked** ● **adj.** not cooked; raw.

**uncool** ● **adj.** informal not fashionable or impressive.

**uncooperative** ● **adj.** unwilling to help others or do what they ask.
– DERIVATIVES **uncooperatively** adv.

**uncoordinated** ● **adj. 1** badly organized. **2** (of a person or their movements) clumsy.

**uncork** ● **v. 1** pull the cork out of. **2** N. Amer. informal (in a game or sport) deliver (a kick, throw, or punch).

**uncorroborated** ● **adj.** not corroborated or confirmed by evidence.

**uncountable** ● **adj.** too many to be counted.
– DERIVATIVES **uncountability** n. **uncountably** adv.

**uncountable noun** (also **uncount noun**) ● **n.** another term for **MASS NOUN**.

**uncounted** ● **adj.** not counted. ➤ very numerous.

**uncouple** ● **v.** disconnect or become disconnected. ➤ release (hunting dogs) from being fastened together in couples.

**uncouth** ● **adj. 1** lacking good manners, refinement, or grace. **2** archaic (of a place) uncomfortable because of remoteness or poor conditions.
– DERIVATIVES **uncouthly** adv. **uncouthness** n.
– ORIGIN OE *uncūth* 'unknown', from **UN-**[1] + *cūth* (past part. of *cunnan* 'know, be able').

**uncovenanted** ● **adj.** not bound by or in accordance with a covenant or agreement.

**uncover** ● **v. 1** remove a cover or covering from. ➤ discover (something previously secret or unknown). **2** archaic remove one's hat, especially as a mark of respect.

**uncritical** ● **adj.** not expressing criticism or using one's critical faculties. ➤ not in accordance with the principles

of critical analysis.
– DERIVATIVES **uncritically** adv.

**uncross** • v. move (something) back from a crossed position.

**uncrossed** • adj. Brit. (of a cheque) not crossed.

**uncrowded** • adj. not crowded.

**uncrowned** • adj. not formally crowned as a monarch.

**uncrushable** • adj. (of a fabric) resistant to creasing.

**UNCSTD** • abbrev. United Nations Conference on Science and Technology for Development.

**UNCTAD** /ˈʌŋ(k)tad/ • abbrev. United Nations Conference on Trade and Development.

**unction** /ˈʌŋ(k)ʃ(ə)n/ • n. **1** formal the action of anointing someone with oil or ointment as a religious rite or as a symbol of investiture as a monarch. ➤the oil or ointment so used. ➤short for **EXTREME UNCTION**. **2** archaic treatment with a medicinal oil or ointment. ➤an ointment. **3** a fervent manner of expression apparently arising from deep emotion, especially when assumed.
– ORIGIN ME: from L. *unctio(n-)*, from *unguere* 'anoint'.

**unctuous** /ˈʌŋ(k)tjʊəs/ • adj. **1** excessively flattering or ingratiating. **2** having a greasy or soapy feel.
– DERIVATIVES **unctuously** adv. **unctuousness** n.
– ORIGIN ME (in the sense 'greasy'): from med. L. *unctuosus*, from L. *unctus* 'anointing', from *unguere* 'anoint'.

**uncultivated** • adj. **1** (of land) not used for growing crops. **2** (of a person) not highly educated.

**uncultured** • adj. not characterized by good taste, manners, or education.

**uncured** • adj. not preserved by salting, drying, or smoking.

**uncurl** • v. straighten from a curled position.

**uncut** • adj. not cut. ➤(of a text, film, etc.) complete; unabridged. ➤(of a stone, especially a diamond) not shaped by cutting. ➤chiefly historical (of a book) with the edges of its pages not slit open or trimmed off. ➤(of fabric) having its pile loops intact. ➤(of alcohol or a drug) not diluted or adulterated.

**undamaged** • adj. not harmed or damaged.

**undated** • adj. not provided or marked with a date.

**undaunted** • adj. not intimidated or discouraged by difficulty, danger, or disappointment.
– DERIVATIVES **undauntedly** adv. **undauntedness** n.

**undead** • adj. (of a fictional being, especially a vampire) technically dead but still animate.

**undecagon** /ʌnˈdɛkəg(ə)n/ • n. another term for **HENDECAGON**.
– ORIGIN C18: formed irregularly from L. *undecim* 'eleven', on the pattern of *decagon*.

**undeceive** • v. tell (someone) that an idea or belief is mistaken.

**undecidable** • adj. not able to be firmly established or refuted. ➤Logic (of a proposition or theorem) not able to be proved or disproved.
– DERIVATIVES **undecidability** n.

**undecided** • adj. not having made a decision; uncertain. ➤not settled or resolved.
– DERIVATIVES **undecidedly** adv.

**undecipherable** • adj. (of speech or writing) not able to be read or understood.

**undee** /ˈʌndeɪ/ • adj. variant spelling of **UNDY**.

**undefeated** • adj. not defeated.

**undefended** • adj. not defended.

**undefined** • adj. not clear or defined.
– DERIVATIVES **undefinable** adj. **undefinably** adv.

**undemanding** • adj. (especially of a task) not demanding.

**undemocratic** • adj. not relating or according to democratic principles.
– DERIVATIVES **undemocratically** adv.

**undemonstrative** • adj. not tending to express feelings, especially of affection, openly.
– DERIVATIVES **undemonstratively** adv. **undemonstrativeness** n.

**undeniable** • adj. unable to be denied or disputed.
– DERIVATIVES **undeniably** adv.

**under** • prep. **1** extending or directly below. ➤below or behind so as to cover or protect. ➤planted with. **2** at a lower level, layer, or grade than. **3** expressing submission or subordination. ➤as provided for by the rules of; in accordance with. ➤used to express grouping or classification. **4** lower than (a specified amount, rate, or norm). **5** undergoing (a process). • adv. **1** extending or directly below something. **2** affected by an anaesthetic; unconscious.
– PHRASES **under way 1** (of a boat) moving through the water. **2** having started and making progress.
– DERIVATIVES **undermost** adj.
– ORIGIN OE, of Gmc origin.

**under-** • prefix **1** below; beneath: *undercover.* ➤lower in status; subordinate: *undersecretary.* **2** insufficiently; incompletely: *undernourished.*

**underachieve** • v. do less well than is expected, especially in school work.
– DERIVATIVES **underachievement** n. **underachiever** n.

**underact** • v. act a part in a play or film in an overly restrained or unemotional way.

**under age** • adj. too young to engage legally in a particular activity, especially drinking alcohol or having sex.

**underarm** • adj. & adv. (of a throw or stroke in sport) made with the arm or hand below shoulder level. • n. a person's armpit.

**underbelly** • n. (pl. **-ies**) **1** the soft underside or abdomen of an animal. **2** an area vulnerable to attack. **3** a hidden unpleasant or criminal part of society.

**underbid** • v. (**-bidding**; past and past part. **-bid**) **1** (in an auction) make a bid lower than another. **2** Bridge make a lower bid on (one's hand) than its strength warrants. • n. a bid that is lower than another or than is justified.
– DERIVATIVES **underbidder** n.

**underbite** • n. the projection of the lower teeth beyond the upper.

**underbody** • n. (pl. **-ies**) the underside of a road vehicle, ship, or animal's body.

**underbred** • adj. dated ill-mannered; rude.

**underbridge** • n. a bridge spanning an opening under a railway or road.

**underbrush** • n. N. Amer. undergrowth in a forest.

**undercapitalize** (also **-ise**) • v. provide (a company) with insufficient capital to achieve desired results.
– DERIVATIVES **undercapitalization** n.

**undercarriage** • n. **1** a wheeled structure beneath an aircraft which supports the aircraft on the ground. **2** the supporting frame under the body of a vehicle.

**undercast** • v. (past and past part. **-cast**) allocate the parts in (a play or film) to insufficiently skilled actors.

**undercharge** • v. **1** charge (someone) a price or amount that is too low. **2** give less than the proper charge to (an electric battery).

**underclass** • n. the lowest social stratum in a country or community, consisting of the poor and unemployed.

**undercliff** • n. a terrace or lower cliff formed by a landslip.

**underclothes** • pl. n. clothes worn under others next to the skin.
– DERIVATIVES **underclothing** n.

**undercoat** • n. **1** a layer of paint applied after the primer and before the topcoat. **2** an animal's underfur or down. • v. apply a coat of undercoat to.

**undercook** • v. [usu. as adj. **undercooked**] cook (something) insufficiently.

**undercover** • adj. & adv. involving secret work for investigation or espionage: *an undercover operation.*

**undercroft** • n. the crypt of a church.
– ORIGIN ME: from **UNDER-** + the rare term *croft* 'crypt', from MDu. *crofte* 'cave', from L. *crypta*.

**undercurrent** • n. **1** a current of water below the surface and moving in a different direction from any surface current. **2** an underlying feeling or influence.

**undercut** • v. (**-cutting**; past and past part. **-cut**) **1** offer goods or services at a lower price than (a competitor). **2** cut or wear away the part under (something, especially a cliff). ➤ weaken; undermine. ➤ cut away material to leave (a carved design) in relief. **3** Tennis strike (a ball) with backspin so that it rises high in the air. ● **n. 1** a space formed by the removal or absence of material from the lower part of something. ➤ N. Amer. a notch cut in a tree trunk to guide its fall when felled. **2** Brit. the underside of a sirloin of beef.

**underdetermine** ● **v.** account for (a theory or phenomenon) with less than the amount of evidence needed for proof or certainty.
– DERIVATIVES **underdetermination** n.

**underdeveloped** ● **adj.** not fully developed. ➤ (of a country or region) not advanced economically.
– DERIVATIVES **underdevelopment** n.

**underdog** ● **n.** a competitor thought to have little chance of winning a fight or contest. ➤ a person who has little status in society.

**underdone** ● **adj.** (of food) insufficiently cooked.

**underdress** ● **v.** (also **be underdressed**) dress too plainly or too informally for a particular occasion.

**underemphasize** (also **-ise**) ● **v.** place insufficient emphasis on.
– DERIVATIVES **underemphasis** n.

**underemployed** ● **adj.** not having sufficient or sufficiently demanding paid work.
– DERIVATIVES **underemployment** n.

**underestimate** ● **v.** estimate (something) to be smaller or less important than it really is. ➤ regard (someone) as less capable than they really are. ● **n.** an estimate that is too low.
– DERIVATIVES **underestimation** n.

**underexpose** ● **v.** Photography expose (film) for too short a time.
– DERIVATIVES **underexposure** n.

**underfed** ● **adj.** insufficiently fed or nourished.

**underfelt** ● **n.** Brit. felt laid under a carpet for protection or support.

**underflow** ● **n. 1** an undercurrent. ➤ a horizontal flow of water through the ground. **2** Computing the generation of a number that is too small to be represented in the device meant to store it.

**underfoot** ● **adv. 1** under one's feet; on the ground. **2** constantly present and in one's way.

**underframe** ● **n. 1** the substructure of a motor vehicle or railway carriage. **2** the supporting frame of a chair seat or table top.

**underfund** ● **v.** provide with insufficient funding.
– DERIVATIVES **underfunding** n.

**underfur** ● **n.** an inner layer of short, fine fur or down underlying an animal's outer fur.

**undergarment** ● **n.** an article of underclothing.

**undergird** ● **v. 1** secure or fasten from the underside, especially by a rope or chain passed underneath. **2** formal provide support or a firm basis for.

**underglaze** ● **n.** colour or decoration applied to pottery before the glaze is applied.

**undergo** ● **v.** (**-goes**; past **-went**; past part. **-gone**) experience or be subjected to (something unpleasant or arduous).
– ORIGIN OE *undergān* 'undermine' (see **UNDER-**, **GO**[1]).

**undergrad** ● **n.** informal an undergraduate.

**undergraduate** ● **n.** a student at a university who has not yet taken a first degree.

**underground** ● **adj. & adv. 1** beneath the surface of the ground. **2** in secrecy or hiding, especially as a result of carrying out subversive political activities. **3** seeking to explore alternative forms of lifestyle or artistic expression; radical and experimental. ● **n. 1** Brit. an underground railway, especially the one in London. **2** a group or movement organized secretly to work against an existing regime. **3** a group or movement seeking to explore alternative forms of lifestyle or artistic expression.

**underground economy** ● **n.** North American term for **BLACK ECONOMY**.

**undergrowth** ● **n.** a dense growth of shrubs and other plants, especially under trees.

**underhand** (also **underhanded**) ● **adj. 1** acting or done in a secret or dishonest way. **2** underarm. ➤ with the palm of the hand upward or outward.
– DERIVATIVES **underhandedly** adv.

**underhung** ● **adj.** another term for **UNDERSHOT** (in sense 2).

**underinsured** ● **adj.** having inadequate insurance cover.
– DERIVATIVES **underinsurance** n.

**underlay**[1] ● **v.** (past and past part. **-laid**) place something under (something else), especially to support or raise it. ● **n. 1** material laid under a carpet for protection or support. **2** Music the manner in which the words are fitted to the notes of a piece of vocal music.

**underlay**[2] past tense of **UNDERLIE**.

**underlease** ● **n. & v.** another term for **SUBLET**.

**underlet** ● **v.** (**-letting**; past and past part. **-let**) another term for **SUBLET**.

**underlever** ● **n.** a lever behind the trigger guard on a rifle.

**underlie** ● **v.** (**-lying**; past **-lay**; past part. **-lain**) **1** lie or be situated under. **2** [often as adj. **underlying**] be the cause or basis of.

**underline** ● **v. 1** draw a line under (a word or phrase) to give emphasis or indicate special type. **2** emphasize. ● **n. 1** a line drawn under a word or phrase. **2** the line of the lower part of an animal's body.

**underlinen** ● **n.** archaic underclothes.

**underling** ● **n.** chiefly derogatory a subordinate.

**underlip** ● **n.** the lower lip of a person or animal.

**underlying** present participle of **UNDERLIE**.

**underman** ● **v.** (**-manned**, **-manning**) fail to provide with enough workers or crew.

**undermanager** ● **n.** a manager who is subordinate to another manager.

**undermentioned** ● **adj.** Brit. mentioned at a later place in a book or document.

**undermine** ● **v. 1** erode the base or foundation of (a rock formation). ➤ dig or excavate beneath (a building or fortification) so as to make it collapse. **2** damage or weaken, especially gradually or insidiously.
– DERIVATIVES **underminer** n.

**underneath** ● **prep. & adv. 1** situated directly below. **2** so as to be concealed by. ➤ partly or wholly concealed by (a garment). ● **n.** the part or side facing towards the ground; the underside.
– ORIGIN OE *underneothan*; cf. **BENEATH**.

**undernourished** ● **adj.** having insufficient food for good health and condition.
– DERIVATIVES **undernourishment** n.

**underpaid** past and past participle of **UNDERPAY**.

**underpants** ● **pl. n.** an undergarment, especially for men or boys, covering the lower part of the body and having two holes for the legs.

**underpart** ● **n.** a lower part or portion. ➤ (**underparts**) the underside of an animal's body.

**underpass** ● **n.** a road or pedestrian tunnel passing under another road or a railway.

**underpay** ● **v.** (past and past part. **-paid**) pay too little to (someone) or for (something).
– DERIVATIVES **underpayment** n.

**underperform** ● **v.** perform less well than expected.
– DERIVATIVES **underperformance** n.

**underpin** ● **v.** (**-pinned**, **-pinning**) **1** support (a building or other structure) from below by laying a solid foundation or substituting stronger for weaker materials. **2** support, justify, or form the basis for.
– DERIVATIVES **underpinning** n.

**underplant** ● **v.** plant or cultivate the ground around (a tall plant) with smaller plants.

**underplay** ● **v. 1** perform (a role or part) in a restrained way. **2** represent (something) as being less important than it really is.

**underpopulated** ● **adj.** having an insufficient or very small population.
– DERIVATIVES **underpopulation** n.

**underpowered** ● **adj.** lacking sufficient mechanical,

electrical, or other power.

**underprice** ● **v.** sell or offer at too low a price.

**underprivileged** ● **adj.** not enjoying the same rights or standard of living as the majority of the population.

**underproduce** ● **v. 1** produce less of (a commodity) than is wanted or needed. **2** [often as adj. **underproduced**] record or produce (a song or film) in such a basic way that it appears rough or unfinished.

– DERIVATIVES **underproduction** n.

**underproof** ● **adj.** containing less alcohol than proof spirit does.

**underprop** ● **v.** (**-propped**, **-propping**) archaic support, especially with a prop.

**underrate** ● **v.** [often as adj. **underrated**] underestimate the extent, value, or importance of.

**under-represent** ● **v.** provide with insufficient or inadequate representation.

– DERIVATIVES **under-representation** n.

**under-resourced** ● **adj.** provided with insufficient resources.

– DERIVATIVES **under-resourcing** n.

**undersaturated** ● **adj.** technical falling short of being saturated with a particular constituent.

– DERIVATIVES **undersaturation** n.

**underscore** ● **v.** another term for **UNDERLINE**. ● **n.** another term for **UNDERLINE** (in sense 1).

**undersea** ● **adj.** relating to or situated below the sea or the surface of the sea.

**underseal** chiefly Brit. ● **v.** coat (the underpart of a motor vehicle) with waterproof material as protection against rust. ● **n.** waterproof coating used in this way.

**undersecretary** ● **n.** (pl. **-ies**) **1** (in the UK) a junior minister or senior civil servant. **2** (in the US) the principal assistant to a member of the cabinet.

**undersell** ● **v.** (past and past part. **-sold**) **1** sell something at a lower price than (a competitor). **2** promote or rate (something) insufficiently.

**undersexed** ● **adj.** having unusually weak sexual desires.

**undersheriff** ● **n.** a deputy sheriff.

**undershirt** ● **n.** chiefly N. Amer. an undergarment worn under a shirt; a vest.

**undershoot** ● **v.** (past and past part. **-shot**) **1** (of an aircraft) land short of (the runway). **2** fall short of (a point or target).

**undershorts** ● **pl. n.** chiefly N. Amer. underpants.

**undershot** past and past participle of **UNDERSHOOT**. ● **adj. 1** (of a waterwheel) turned by water flowing under it. **2** denoting a lower jaw which projects beyond the upper jaw.

**underside** ● **n.** the bottom or lower side or surface of something.

**undersigned** formal ● **adj.** appending one's signature to the document in question. ● **n.** (**the undersigned**) the signatory or co-signatories to the document in question.

**undersized** (also **undersize**) ● **adj.** of less than the usual size.

**underskirt** ● **n.** a skirt worn under another; a petticoat.

**underslung** ● **adj.** suspended from the underside of something. ➤(of a vehicle chassis) hanging lower than the axles.

**undersoil** ● **n.** subsoil.

**undersold** past and past participle of **UNDERSELL**.

**undersow** ● **v.** (past part. **-sown**) sow (a later-growing crop) on land already seeded with another crop.

**underspend** ● **v.** (past and past part. **-spent**) spend too little or less than has been planned. ● **n.** an act of underspending.

**understaff** ● **v.** provide (an organization) with too few members of staff to operate effectively.

– DERIVATIVES **understaffing** n.

**understand** ● **v.** (past and past part. **-stood**) **1** perceive the intended meaning of (words, a language, or a speaker). ➤perceive the significance, explanation, or cause of. ➤interpret or view in a particular way. **2** infer from information received: *I understand you're at art school.* ➤supply (a missing word, phrase, or idea) mentally. ➤assume to be the case; take for granted.

– DERIVATIVES **understander** n.

– ORIGIN OE *understandan* (see **UNDER-**, **STAND**).

**understandable** ● **adj. 1** able to be understood. **2** to be expected; natural, reasonable, or forgivable.

– DERIVATIVES **understandability** n. **understandably** adv.

**understanding** ● **n. 1** the ability to understand something; comprehension. ➤the power of abstract thought; intellect. ➤an individual's perception or judgement of a situation. **2** sympathetic awareness or tolerance. **3** an informal or unspoken agreement or arrangement. ● **adj. 1** sympathetically aware of other people's feelings; tolerant and forgiving. **2** archaic having insight or good judgement.

– DERIVATIVES **understandingly** adv.

**understate** ● **v.** describe or represent (something) as being smaller or less significant than it really is.

– DERIVATIVES **understatement** n. **understater** n.

**understated** ● **adj.** presented or expressed in a subtle and effective way.

– DERIVATIVES **understatedly** adv.

**understeer** ● **v.** (of a motor vehicle) have a tendency to turn less sharply than is intended. ● **n.** the tendency of a vehicle to turn in such a way.

**understood** past and past participle of **UNDERSTAND**.

**understorey** ● **n.** (pl. **-eys**) Ecology a layer of vegetation beneath the main canopy of a forest.

**understrapper** ● **n.** informal, dated an assistant or junior official.

**understudy** ● **n.** (pl. **-ies**) an actor who learns another's role in order to be able to act in their absence. ● **v.** (**-ies**, **-ied**) study (a role or actor) as an understudy.

**undersubscribed** ● **adj. 1** (of a course or event) having more places available than applications. **2** (of a share issue) having fewer applications for shares than there are shares available.

**underswell** ● **n.** an undercurrent.

**undertake** ● **v.** (past **-took**; past part. **-taken**) **1** commit oneself to and begin (an enterprise or responsibility); take on. **2** formally guarantee, pledge, or promise.

**undertaker** ● **n.** a person whose business is preparing dead bodies for burial or cremation and making arrangements for funerals.

**undertaking** ● **n. 1** a formal pledge or promise to do something. ➤a task that is taken on; an enterprise. **2** a company or business. **3** the management of funerals as a profession.

**undertenant** ● **n.** a subtenant.

– DERIVATIVES **undertenancy** n. (pl. **-ies**).

**underthings** ● **pl. n.** underclothes.

**underthrust** ● **v.** (past and past part. **-thrust**) Geology force (a body of rock) beneath another formation.

**undertint** ● **n.** a subdued or delicate tint.

**undertone** ● **n. 1** a subdued or muted tone of sound or colour. **2** an underlying quality or feeling.

**undertook** past participle of **UNDERTAKE**.

**undertow** ● **n.** another term for **UNDERCURRENT**.

**undertrick** ● **n.** Bridge a trick by which the declarer falls short of his or her contract.

**underuse** /ʌndə'ju:z/ ● **v.** [usu. as adj. **underused**] use (something) below the optimum level. ● **n.** /ʌndə'ju:s/ insufficient use.

**underutilize** (also **-ise**) ● **v.** underuse.

– DERIVATIVES **underutilization** n.

**undervalue** ● **v.** (**-values**, **-valued**, **-valuing**) [often as adj. **undervalued**] **1** rate insufficiently highly; fail to appreciate. **2** underestimate the financial value of.

– DERIVATIVES **undervaluation** n.

**undervest** ● **n.** a vest worn as an undergarment.

**underwater** ● **adj. & adv.** situated or occurring beneath the surface of the water.

**underwear** ● **n.** clothing worn under other clothes next to the skin.

**underweight** ● **adj. 1** below a weight considered normal or desirable. **2** Finance having insufficient investment in a particular area. ● **v.** apply too little weight to. ● **n.** insufficient weight.

**underwent** past of **UNDERGO**.

**underwhelm** ● **v.** humorous fail to impress or make a positive impact on.
– ORIGIN 1950s: suggested by **OVERWHELM**.

**underwing** ● **n.** **1** the hindwing of an insect, especially when it is normally hidden by a forewing. ➤ used in names of noctuid moths with drab forewings and brightly coloured hindwings, e.g. **yellow underwing**. **2** the underside of a bird's wing.

**underwire** ● **n.** a semicircular wire support stitched under each cup of a bra.
– DERIVATIVES **underwired** adj.

**underwood** ● **n.** small trees and shrubs growing beneath taller timber trees.

**underwork** ● **v.** [usu. as adj. **underworked**] impose too little work on (someone).

**underworld** ● **n.** **1** the world of criminals or of organized crime. **2** the mythical abode of the dead, imagined as being under the earth.

**underwrite** ● **v.** (past **-wrote**; past part. **-written**) **1** sign and accept liability under (an insurance policy). ➤ accept (a liability or risk) in this way. **2** undertake to finance or otherwise support or guarantee. **3** engage to buy all the unsold shares in (an issue of new shares). **4** archaic write below something else.
– DERIVATIVES **underwriter** n.

**undescended** ● **adj.** Medicine (of a testicle) remaining in the abdomen instead of descending normally into the scrotum.

**undeserved** ● **adj.** not warranted, merited, or earned.
– DERIVATIVES **undeservedly** adv.

**undeserving** ● **adj.** not deserving or worthy of something positive, especially help or praise.
– DERIVATIVES **undeservingly** adv.

**undesigned** ● **adj.** unintended.
– DERIVATIVES **undesignedly** adv.

**undesirable** ● **adj.** not wanted or desirable because harmful, objectionable, or unpleasant. ● **n.** a person considered to be objectionable in some way.
– DERIVATIVES **undesirability** n. **undesirableness** n. **undesirably** adv.

**undesired** ● **adj.** (especially of an act or consequence) not wanted or desired.

**undesirous** ● **adj.** (usu. **undesirous of**) formal not wanting or wishing something.

**undetectable** ● **adj.** not able to be detected.
– DERIVATIVES **undetectability** n. **undetectably** adv.

**undetected** ● **adj.** not detected or discovered.

**undetermined** ● **adj.** not authoritatively decided or settled.

**undeterred** ● **adj.** persevering despite setbacks.

**undeveloped** ● **adj.** not having developed or been developed.

**undeviating** ● **adj.** showing no deviation; constant and steady.
– DERIVATIVES **undeviatingly** adv.

**undiagnosed** ● **adj.** not diagnosed or having been subject to diagnosis.

**undid** past of **UNDO**.

**undies** ● **pl. n.** informal articles of underwear.

**undifferenced** ● **adj.** Heraldry (of arms) not made distinct by a mark of difference.

**undifferentiated** ● **adj.** not different or differentiated.

**undigested** ● **adj.** **1** (of food) not digested. **2** not having been properly understood or assimilated.

**undignified** ● **adj.** appearing foolish and unseemly; lacking in dignity.

**undiluted** ● **adj.** **1** (of a liquid) not diluted. **2** not moderated or weakened in any way.

**undiminished** ● **adj.** not diminished, reduced, or lessened.

**undine** /ˈʌndiːn/ ● **n.** a female spirit or nymph imagined as inhabiting water.
– ORIGIN C19: from mod. L. *undina* (a word invented by the C16 Swiss physician Paracelsus), from L. *unda* 'a wave'.

**undiplomatic** ● **adj.** insensitive and tactless.
– DERIVATIVES **undiplomatically** adv.

**undirected** ● **adj.** without a coherent plan or purpose.

**undiscerning** ● **adj.** lacking judgement, insight, or taste.

**undischarged** ● **adj.** (especially of a bankrupt) not discharged.

**undisciplined** ● **adj.** lacking in discipline; uncontrolled in behaviour or manner.

**undisclosed** ● **adj.** not revealed or made known.

**undiscovered** ● **adj.** not discovered.

**undiscriminating** ● **adj.** lacking good judgement or taste.

**undiscussed** ● **adj.** not discussed.

**undisguised** ● **adj.** (of a feeling) not disguised or concealed; open.
– DERIVATIVES **undisguisedly** adv.

**undismayed** ● **adj.** not dismayed or discouraged by a setback.

**undisputed** ● **adj.** not disputed or called in question; accepted.

**undistinguishable** ● **adj.** indistinguishable.

**undistinguished** ● **adj.** lacking distinction; unexceptional.

**undistorted** ● **adj.** not distorted.

**undistributed** ● **adj.** not distributed.

**undistributed middle** ● **n.** Logic a fallacy arising from the failure of the middle term of a syllogism to refer to all the members of a class in at least one premise.

**undisturbed** ● **adj.** not disturbed.

**undivided** ● **adj.** **1** not divided, separated, or broken into parts. **2** devoted completely to one object: *my undivided attention.*

**undo** ● **v.** (**undoes**; past **undid**; past part. **undone**) **1** unfasten, untie, or loosen. **2** cancel or reverse the effects or results of (a previous action or measure). **3** formal cause the downfall or ruin of.

**undocumented** ● **adj.** **1** not recorded in or proved by documents. **2** N. Amer. not having the appropriate legal document or licence.

**undoing** ● **n.** a person's ruin or downfall. ➤ the cause of such ruin or downfall: *complacency was to be their undoing.*

**undomesticated** ● **adj.** **1** (of an animal) not tamed. **2** not accustomed to domestic tasks.

**undone** ● **adj.** **1** not tied or fastened. **2** not done or finished. **3** formal or humorous ruined by a disastrous setback.

**undoubted** ● **adj.** not questioned or doubted by anyone.
– DERIVATIVES **undoubtable** adj. **undoubtably** adv. **undoubtedly** adv.

**UNDP** ● **abbrev.** United Nations Development Programme.

**undrained** ● **adj.** not emptied of water; not drained.

**undramatic** ● **adj.** **1** lacking the qualities expected in drama. **2** unexciting.

**undraped** ● **adj.** not covered with cloth or drapery. ➤ (of a model or subject in art) naked.

**undreamed** /ʌnˈdriːmd, -ˈdrɛmt/ (Brit. also **undreamt** /ʌnˈdrɛmt/) ● **adj.** (**undreamed of**) not previously thought to be possible: *undreamed-of success.*

**undress** ● **v.** (also **get undressed**) take off one's clothes. ➤ take the clothes off (someone else). ● **n.** **1** the state of being naked or only partially clothed. **2** Military ordinary clothing or uniform, as opposed to that worn on ceremonial occasions (full dress).

**undressed** ● **adj.** **1** wearing no clothes; naked. **2** not treated, processed, or prepared for use. **3** (of food) not having a dressing.

**undrinkable** ● **adj.** not fit to be drunk because of impurity or poor quality.

**UNDRO** ● **abbrev.** United Nations Disaster Relief Office.

**undue** ● **adj.** unwarranted or inappropriate because excessive or disproportionate.
– DERIVATIVES **unduly** adv.

**undue influence** ● n. Law influence by which a person is induced to act otherwise than by their own free will or without adequate attention to the consequences.

**undulant** /ˈʌndjʊl(ə)nt/ ● adj. undulating.

**undulant fever** ● n. brucellosis in humans.
– ORIGIN C19: so named because of the intermittent fever associated with the disease.

**undulate** ● v. /ˈʌndjʊleɪt/ move with a smooth wave-like motion. ➤[usu. as adj. **undulating**] have a wavy form or outline. ● adj. /ˈʌndjʊlət/ Botany & Zoology having a wavy surface or edge.
– DERIVATIVES **undulately** adv. **undulation** n. **undulatory** adj.
– ORIGIN C17: from late L. *undulatus*, from L. *unda* 'a wave'.

**undutiful** ● adj. not respectful or obedient.
– DERIVATIVES **undutifully** adv. **undutifulness** n.

**undy** /ˈʌndi/ (also **undee**) ● adj. Heraldry another term for **WAVY**.

**undyed** ● adj. (of fabric) not dyed; of its natural colour.

**undying** ● adj. (especially of an emotion) lasting forever.
– DERIVATIVES **undyingly** adv.

**unearned** ● adj. not earned or deserved.

**unearned income** ● n. income from investments rather than from work.

**unearned increment** ● n. an increase in the value of land or property without labour or expenditure on the part of the owner.

**unearth** ● v. **1** find in the ground by digging. ➤discover by investigation or searching. **2** drive (an animal, especially a fox) out of a hole or burrow.

**unearthly** ● adj. **1** unnatural or mysterious, especially in a disturbing way. **2** informal unreasonably early or inconvenient: *an unearthly hour.*
– DERIVATIVES **unearthliness** n.

**unease** ● n. anxiety or discontent.

**uneasy** ● adj. (**-ier**, **-iest**) causing or feeling anxiety; troubled or uncomfortable.
– DERIVATIVES **uneasily** adv. **uneasiness** n.

**uneatable** ● adj. not fit to be eaten.

**uneaten** ● adj. not eaten.

**uneconomic** ● adj. not profitable or making efficient use of resources.

**uneconomical** ● adj. wasteful of money or other resources; not economical.
– DERIVATIVES **uneconomically** adv.

**unedifying** ● adj. distasteful; unpleasant: *the unedifying sight of two squabbling politicians.*
– DERIVATIVES **unedifyingly** adv.

**unedited** ● adj. (of material for publication or broadcasting) not edited.

**uneducated** ● adj. poorly educated.
– DERIVATIVES **uneducable** adj.

**unelectable** ● adj. very likely to be defeated at an election.

**unelected** ● adj. (of an official) not elected.

**unembarrassed** ● adj. not feeling or showing embarrassment.

**unembellished** ● adj. not embellished or decorated.

**unemotional** ● adj. not having or showing strong feelings.
– DERIVATIVES **unemotionally** adv.

**unemphatic** ● adj. not emphatic.
– DERIVATIVES **unemphatically** adv.

**unemployable** ● adj. not able or likely to get paid employment because of a lack of skills or qualifications.
– DERIVATIVES **unemployability** n.

**unemployed** ● adj. **1** without a paid job but available to work. **2** (of a thing) not in use.

**unemployment** ● n. the state of being unemployed. ➤the number or proportion of unemployed people.

**unemployment benefit** ● n. payment made by the state or a trade union to an unemployed person.

**unenclosed** ● adj. (especially of land) not enclosed.

**unencumbered** ● adj. not having any burden or impediment. ➤free of debt or other financial liability.

**unending** ● adj. having or seeming to have no end. ➤countless or continual: *unending demands.*
– DERIVATIVES **unendingly** adv. **unendingness** n.

**unendowed** ● adj. not endowed, especially by donated funds.

**unendurable** ● adj. not able to be tolerated or endured.
– DERIVATIVES **unendurably** adv.

**unenforceable** ● adj. (especially of an obligation or law) impossible to enforce.

**un-English** ● adj. not characteristic of English people or the English language.

**unenlightened** ● adj. not enlightened in outlook.
– DERIVATIVES **unenlightening** adj. **unenlightenment** n.

**unentangle** ● v. another term for **DISENTANGLE**.

**unenterprising** ● adj. lacking initiative or entrepreneurial ability.

**unenthusiastic** ● adj. not having or showing enthusiasm.
– DERIVATIVES **unenthusiastically** adv.

**unenviable** ● adj. difficult, undesirable, or unpleasant.
– DERIVATIVES **unenviably** adv. **unenvied** adj.

**UNEP** ● abbrev. United Nations Environment Programme.

**unequal** ● adj. **1** not equal in quantity, size, or value. ➤not fair, evenly balanced, or having equal advantage. **2** (usu. **unequal to**) not having the ability or resources to meet a challenge.
– DERIVATIVES **unequally** adv.

**unequalled** (US **unequaled**) ● adj. superior to all others in performance or extent.

**unequipped** ● adj. not equipped with the necessary items or skills.

**unequivocal** ● adj. leaving no doubt; unambiguous.
– DERIVATIVES **unequivocally** adv. **unequivocalness** n.

**unerring** ● adj. always right or accurate.
– DERIVATIVES **unerringly** adv. **unerringness** n.

**unescapable** ● adj. unable to be avoided or denied.

**UNESCO** /juːˈnɛskəʊ/ ● abbrev. United Nations Educational, Scientific, and Cultural Organization.

**unescorted** ● adj. not escorted, especially for protection or security.

**unessential** ● adj. inessential.

**unethical** ● adj. not morally correct.
– DERIVATIVES **unethically** adv.

**uneven** ● adj. **1** not level or smooth. **2** not regular, consistent, or equal. ➤(of a contest) not equally balanced.
– DERIVATIVES **unevenly** adv. **unevenness** n.

**uneven bars** ● pl. n. North American term for **ASYMMETRIC BARS**.

**uneventful** ● adj. not marked by interesting or exciting events.
– DERIVATIVES **uneventfully** adv. **uneventfulness** n.

**unexamined** ● adj. not investigated or examined.

**unexampled** ● adj. formal having no precedent or parallel.

**unexceptionable** ● adj. not open to objection, but not particularly new or exciting.
– DERIVATIVES **unexceptionableness** n. **unexceptionably** adv.

**unexceptional** ● adj. not out of the ordinary; usual.
– DERIVATIVES **unexceptionally** adv.

**unexcitable** ● adj. not easily excited.
– DERIVATIVES **unexcitability** n.

**unexciting** ● adj. not exciting; dull.

**unexercised** ● adj. **1** not made use of or put into practice. **2** (of a person) not taking exercise; unfit.

**unexpected** ● adj. not expected or regarded as likely to happen.
– DERIVATIVES **unexpectedly** adv. **unexpectedness** n.

**unexpired** ● adj. (of an agreement or period of time) not yet having come to an end.

**unexplained** ● adj. not made clear or accounted for.
– DERIVATIVES **unexplainable** adj. **unexplainably** adv.

**unexploded** ● adj. (of a bomb or other explosive device) not having exploded.

**unexploited** ● adj. (of resources) not used to maximum

benefit.

**unexplored** • adj. not explored, investigated, or evaluated.

**unexposed** • adj. not exposed. ➤(**unexposed to**) not introduced to or acquainted with.

**unexpressed** • adj. **1** (of a thought or feeling) not communicated or made known. **2** Genetics (of a gene) not appearing in a phenotype.

**unexpurgated** • adj. (of a text) complete and containing all the original material; not censored.

**unfading** • adj. not losing brightness, vitality, or strength.
– DERIVATIVES **unfadingly** adv.

**unfailing** • adj. **1** without error. **2** reliable or constant.
– DERIVATIVES **unfailingly** adv. **unfailingness** n.

**unfair** • adj. not based on or showing fairness; unjust. ➤contrary to the rules of a game.
– DERIVATIVES **unfairly** adv. **unfairness** n.

**unfaithful** • adj. not faithful; disloyal. ➤engaging in sexual relations with a person other than one's lover or spouse.
– DERIVATIVES **unfaithfully** adv. **unfaithfulness** n.

**unfaltering** • adj. not faltering; steady or resolute.
– DERIVATIVES **unfalteringly** adv.

**unfamiliar** • adj. **1** not known or recognized; uncharacteristic. **2** (**unfamiliar with**) not having knowledge or experience of.
– DERIVATIVES **unfamiliarity** n.

**unfancied** • adj. not considered likely to win.

**unfashionable** • adj. not fashionable or popular.
– DERIVATIVES **unfashionableness** n. **unfashionably** adv.

**unfasten** • v. open the fastening of; undo.

**unfathomable** • adj. **1** incapable of being fully explored or understood. **2** impossible to measure the depth or extent of.
– DERIVATIVES **unfathomableness** n. **unfathomably** adv. **unfathomed** adj.

**unfavourable** (US **unfavorable**) • adj. **1** expressing lack of approval or support. **2** adverse; inauspicious.
– DERIVATIVES **unfavourableness** n. **unfavourably** adv.

**unfazed** • adj. informal not disconcerted or perturbed.

**unfeasible** • adj. inconvenient or impractical.
– DERIVATIVES **unfeasibility** n. **unfeasibly** adv.

**unfeeling** • adj. **1** unsympathetic, harsh, or callous. **2** lacking physical sensation.
– DERIVATIVES **unfeelingly** adv. **unfeelingness** n.

**unfeigned** • adj. genuine; sincere.
– DERIVATIVES **unfeignedly** adv.

**unfeminine** • adj. lacking feminine qualities.
– DERIVATIVES **unfemininity** n.

**unfenced** • adj. not provided with fences.

**unfermented** • adj. not fermented.

**unfertilized** (also **-ised**) • adj. not fertilized.

**unfetter** • v. [usu. as adj. **unfettered**] release from restraint or inhibition.

**unfilled** • adj. not filled; vacant or empty.

**unfiltered** • adj. **1** not filtered. **2** not provided with a filter.

**unfinished** • adj. not finished; incomplete. ➤not having been given an attractive surface appearance in manufacture.

**unfit** • adj. **1** unsuitable or inadequate for something. **2** not in good physical condition, especially through lack of regular exercise. • v. (**unfitted**, **unfitting**) archaic make unsuitable; disqualify.
– DERIVATIVES **unfitly** adv. **unfitness** n.

**unfitted** • adj. **1** unfit for something. **2** (of furniture, linen, etc.) not fitted.

**unfitting** • adj. unsuitable or unbecoming.
– DERIVATIVES **unfittingly** adv.

**unfixed** • adj. **1** unfastened; loose. **2** uncertain or variable.
– DERIVATIVES **unfix** v.

**unflagging** • adj. tireless; persistent.
– DERIVATIVES **unflaggingly** adv.

**unflappable** • adj. informal calm in a crisis.
– DERIVATIVES **unflappability** n. **unflappably** adv.

**unflattering** • adj. not flattering.
– DERIVATIVES **unflatteringly** adv.

**unfledged** • adj. not yet fledged. ➤inexperienced; youthful.

**unfleshed** • adj. chiefly poetic/literary not covered with flesh.

**unflinching** • adj. not afraid or hesitant.
– DERIVATIVES **unflinchingly** adv.

**unfocused** (also **unfocussed**) • adj. **1** not focused; out of focus. **2** without a specific aim or direction.

**unfold** • v. **1** open or spread out from a folded position. **2** make or become revealed or disclosed.
– DERIVATIVES **unfoldment** n. (US).

**unforced** • adj. **1** produced naturally and without effort. **2** not compelled.
– DERIVATIVES **unforcedly** adv.

**unforeseen** • adj. not anticipated or predicted.
– DERIVATIVES **unforeseeable** adj.

**unforgettable** • adj. highly memorable.
– DERIVATIVES **unforgettably** adv.

**unforgivable** • adj. so bad as to be unable to be forgiven or excused.
– DERIVATIVES **unforgivably** adv.

**unforgiven** • adj. not forgiven.

**unforgiving** • adj. **1** not willing to forgive or excuse faults. **2** (of conditions) harsh; hostile.
– DERIVATIVES **unforgivingly** adv. **unforgivingness** n.

**unformed** • adj. **1** without a definite form. **2** not fully developed.

**unforthcoming** • adj. **1** not willing to divulge information. **2** not available when needed.

**unfortunate** • adj. **1** having bad fortune; unlucky. ➤inauspicious. **2** regrettable or inappropriate. • n. a person who suffers bad fortune.
– DERIVATIVES **unfortunately** adv.

**unfounded** • adj. having no foundation or basis in fact.
– DERIVATIVES **unfoundedly** adv. **unfoundedness** n.

**UNFPA** • abbrev. United Nations Fund for Population Activities.

**unfree** • adj. deprived or devoid of liberty.
– DERIVATIVES **unfreedom** n.

**unfreeze** • v. (past **unfroze**; past part. **unfrozen**) **1** thaw. **2** remove restrictions on the use of (an asset).

**unfrequented** • adj. visited only rarely.

**unfriended** • adj. poetic/literary without friends.

**unfriendly** • adj. (**-ier**, **-iest**) not friendly.
– DERIVATIVES **unfriendliness** n.

**unfrock** • v. another term for DEFROCK.

**unfroze** past of UNFREEZE.

**unfrozen** past participle of UNFREEZE.

**unfulfilled** • adj. not fulfilled.
– DERIVATIVES **unfulfillable** adj. **unfulfilling** adj.

**unfunded** • adj. **1** not receiving funds; not having a fund. **2** (of a debt) repayable on demand; not funded.

**unfunny** • adj. (**-ier**, **-iest**) (especially of something intended to be funny) not amusing.
– DERIVATIVES **unfunnily** adv. **unfunniness** n.

**unfurl** • v. make or become spread out from a furled state.

**unfurnished** • adj. **1** without furniture. **2** archaic not supplied.

**ungainly** • adj. clumsy; awkward.
– DERIVATIVES **ungainliness** n.
– ORIGIN C17: from UN-[1] + obs. *gainly* 'graceful', based on ON *gegn* 'straight'.

**ungeared** • adj. **1** not having gears. **2** (of a company) having no debt.

**ungenerous** • adj. not generous; mean.
– DERIVATIVES **ungenerously** adv. **ungenerousness** n.

**ungentle** • adj. not gentle; rough.
– DERIVATIVES **ungentleness** n. **ungently** adv.

**ungentlemanly** • adj. not appropriate to or behaving like a gentleman.
– DERIVATIVES **ungentlemanliness** n.

**unget-at-able** • adj. informal inaccessible.

**ungird** • v. archaic release or take off by undoing a belt or girth.

**ungiving** • adj. **1** cold or stubborn towards other people. **2** not pliable; stiff.

**unglazed** • adj. not glazed.

**unglued** • adj. **1** not or no longer stuck. **2** informal confused and emotionally strained.

**ungodly** • adj. **1** irreligious or immoral. **2** informal unreasonably early or inconvenient.
– DERIVATIVES **ungodliness** n.

**ungovernable** • adj. impossible to control or govern.
– DERIVATIVES **ungovernability** n. **ungovernably** adv.

**ungraceful** • adj. lacking in grace; clumsy.
– DERIVATIVES **ungracefully** adv. **ungracefulness** n.

**ungracious** • adj. not gracious.
– DERIVATIVES **ungraciously** adv. **ungraciousness** n.

**ungrammatical** • adj. not conforming to grammatical rules.
– DERIVATIVES **ungrammaticality** n. (pl. **-ies**). **ungrammatically** adv. **ungrammaticalness** n.

**ungrateful** • adj. not feeling or showing gratitude.
– DERIVATIVES **ungratefully** adv. **ungratefulness** n.

**ungreen** • adj. not environmentally green.

**ungrounded** • adj. **1** groundless. **2** not electrically earthed. **3** (**ungrounded in**) not properly instructed or proficient in.

**ungual** /ˈʌŋgw(ə)l/ • adj. Zoology & Medicine of or relating to a nail, hoof, or claw.
– ORIGIN C19: from L. *unguis* 'nail' + **-AL**.

**unguarded** • adj. **1** without protection or a guard. **2** not well considered; careless.
– DERIVATIVES **unguard** v. **unguardedly** adv. **unguardedness** n.

**unguent** /ˈʌŋgwənt/ • n. a soft greasy or viscous substance used as ointment or for lubrication.
– ORIGIN ME: from L. *unguentum*, from *unguere* 'anoint'.

**unguiculate** /ʌŋˈgwɪkjʊlət/ • adj. **1** Zoology having one or more nails or claws. **2** Botany (of a petal) having a narrow stalk-like base.
– ORIGIN C19: from mod. L. *unguiculatus*, from L. *unguiculus* 'fingernail, toenail', dimin. of *unguis* 'nail'.

**ungulate** /ˈʌŋgjʊlət, -leɪt/ • n. Zoology a hoofed mammal. See **ARTIODACTYLA**, **PERISSODACTYLA**.
– ORIGIN C19: from late L. *ungulatus*, from L. *ungula* 'hoof'.

**unhand** • v. archaic or humorous release from one's grasp.

**unhandy** • adj. **1** not easy to handle or manage. **2** not skilful in using the hands.
– DERIVATIVES **unhandily** adv. **unhandiness** n.

**unhappy** • adj. (**-ier**, **-iest**) not happy. ➤ unfortunate.
– DERIVATIVES **unhappily** adv. **unhappiness** n.

**unharmed** • adj. not harmed; uninjured.

**unharness** • v. remove a harness from.

**unhasp** • v. archaic unfasten.

**unhatched** • adj. not yet hatched.

**UNHCR** • abbrev. United Nations High Commission for Refugees.

**unhealthful** • adj. harmful to health.
– DERIVATIVES **unhealthfulness** n.

**unhealthy** • adj. (**-ier**, **-iest**) in poor health. ➤ not conducive to health.
– DERIVATIVES **unhealthily** adv. **unhealthiness** n.

**unheard** • adj. **1** not heard or listened to. **2** (**unheard of**) previously unknown.

**unheated** • adj. not heated.

**unhedged** • adj. **1** not bounded by a hedge. **2** not protected against loss by other dealings.

**unheeded** • adj. heard or noticed but disregarded.

**unheeding** • adj. not paying attention.
– DERIVATIVES **unheedingly** adv.

**unhelpful** • adj. not helpful.
– DERIVATIVES **unhelpfully** adv. **unhelpfulness** n.

**unheralded** • adj. not previously announced, expected, or recognized.

**unhesitating** • adj. without doubt or hesitation.
– DERIVATIVES **unhesitatingly** adv.

**unhinge** • v. **1** [usu. as adj. **unhinged**] make mentally unbalanced. ➤ throw into disorder. **2** take (a door) off its hinges.

**unhistorical** • adj. not in accordance with history or historical analysis.
– DERIVATIVES **unhistoric** adj. **unhistorically** adv.

**unhitch** • v. unhook or unfasten.

**unholy** • adj. (**-ier**, **-iest**) sinful; wicked. ➤ unnatural and potentially harmful: *an unholy alliance*. ➤ informal dreadful (used for emphasis).
– DERIVATIVES **unholiness** n.

**unhook** • v. unfasten or detach (something held by a hook).

**unhoped** • adj. (**unhoped for**) exceeding hope or expectation.

**unhorse** • v. drag or cause to fall from a horse.

**unhoused** • adj. having no accommodation or shelter.

**unhung** • adj. not hanging or hung.

**unhurried** • adj. moving, acting, or taking place without haste or urgency.
– DERIVATIVES **unhurriedly** adv.

**unhurt** • adj. not hurt or harmed.

**unhygienic** • adj. not hygienic.
– DERIVATIVES **unhygienically** adv.

**unhyphenated** • adj. not written with a hyphen.

**uni** • n. (pl. **unis**) informal university.

**uni-** • comb. form one; having or consisting of one: *unicycle*.
– ORIGIN from L. *unus* 'one'.

**Uniate** /ˈjuːnɪeɪt/ (also **Uniat**) • adj. of or denoting a Christian community in eastern Europe or the Near East acknowledging papal supremacy but with its own liturgy. • n. a member of a Uniate community.
– ORIGIN C19: from Russ. *uniat*, from *uniya*, from L. *unio* (see **UNION**).

**uniaxial** /ˌjuːnɪˈaksɪəl/ • adj. having or relating to a single axis.
– DERIVATIVES **uniaxially** adv.

**unicameral** /ˌjuːnɪˈkam(ə)r(ə)l/ • adj. (of a legislative body) having a single legislative chamber.
– ORIGIN C19: from **UNI-** + L. *camera* 'chamber' + **-AL**.

**UNICEF** /ˈjuːnɪsɛf/ • abbrev. United Nations Children's (originally International Children's Emergency) Fund.

**unicellular** • adj. Biology consisting of a single cell.

**unicity** /juːˈnɪsɪti/ • n. rare the fact of being or consisting of one.

**unicolour** (also **unicoloured**) (US **-color** or **-colored**) • adj. of one colour.

**unicorn** • n. **1** a mythical animal represented as a horse with a single straight horn projecting from its forehead. ➤ a heraldic representation of this, with a twisted horn, a deer's feet, a goat's beard, and a lion's tail. **2** historical a team of three horses arranged two abreast with one leading.
– ORIGIN ME: via OFr. from L. *unicornis*, from *uni-* 'single' + *cornu* 'horn', translating Gk *monokerōs*.

**unicorn fish** • n. **1** a fish with a horn-like projection on the head. [Genus *Naso* (Indo-Pacific).] **2** a crestfish with a forward-pointing dorsal fin. [*Lophotes fiskii*.]

**unicursal** /ˌjuːnɪˈkəːs(ə)l/ • adj. Mathematics denoting a closed curve which can be drawn in a single movement.
– ORIGIN C19: from **UNI-** + L. *cursus* 'course' + **-AL**.

**unicuspid** • adj. having one cusp or point. • n. a tooth with a single cusp, especially a canine tooth.

**unicycle** • n. a cycle with a single wheel, chiefly used by acrobats.
– DERIVATIVES **unicyclist** n.

**unidea'd** • adj. archaic having no ideas.

**unidentifiable** • adj. unable to be identified.

**unidentified** • adj. not recognized or identified.

**unidimensional** • adj. having one dimension.

**unidiomatic** • adj. not using or containing expressions natural to a native speaker of a language.

**unidirectional** • adj. moving or operating in a single direction.
– DERIVATIVES **unidirectionality** n. **unidirectionally** adv.

**UNIDO** /juːˈniːdəʊ/ • **abbrev.** United Nations Industrial Development Organization.
**uniface** • **adj.** (of a coin or medallion) having one side blank.
**unification** • **n.** the process of being united.
– DERIVATIVES **unificatory** adj.
**Unification Church** • **n.** an evangelistic religious and political organization founded in 1954 in Korea by Sun Myung Moon.
**unified field theory** • **n.** Physics a theory that describes two or more of the four interactions (electromagnetic, gravitational, weak, and strong) previously described by separate theories.
**uniflow** • **adj.** involving flow in one direction, especially of steam or waste gases in an engine's cylinder.
**uniform** • **adj.** not varying; the same in all cases and at all times. • **n. 1** the distinctive clothing worn by members of the same organization or body or by children attending certain schools. ➤ informal, chiefly N. Amer. a police officer wearing a uniform. **2** a code word representing the letter U, used in radio communication. • **v.** make uniform.
– DERIVATIVES **uniformed** adj. **uniformity** n. **uniformly** adv.
– ORIGIN C16: from Fr. *uniforme* or L. *uniformis* (see **UNI-**, **FORM**).
**uniformitarianism** • **n.** Geology the theory that changes in the earth's crust during geological history have resulted from the action of continuous and uniform processes. Often contrasted with **CATASTROPHISM**.
– DERIVATIVES **uniformitarian** adj. & n.
**unify** /ˈjuːnɪfʌɪ/ • **v.** (**-ies**, **-ied**) make or become united or uniform.
– DERIVATIVES **unifier** n.
– ORIGIN C16: from Fr. *unifier* or late L. *unificare*.
**unilateral** • **adj. 1** performed by or affecting only one person, group, etc. **2** relating to or affecting only one side of an organ, the body, etc.
– DERIVATIVES **unilateralism** n. **unilateralist** n. & adj. **unilaterally** adv.
**unilingual** • **adj.** another term for **MONOLINGUAL**.
– DERIVATIVES **unilingualism** n.
**unilocular** /ˌjuːnɪˈlɒkjʊlə/ • **adj.** Botany & Zoology having only one loculus or cavity; single-chambered.
**unimaginable** • **adj.** impossible to imagine or comprehend.
– DERIVATIVES **unimaginably** adv.
**unimaginative** • **adj.** not using or displaying imagination; stolid and somewhat dull.
– DERIVATIVES **unimaginatively** adv. **unimaginativeness** n.
**unimodal** • **adj.** having or involving one mode.
**unimolecular** • **adj.** Chemistry consisting of or involving a single molecule.
**unimpaired** • **adj.** not weakened or damaged.
**unimpeachable** • **adj.** beyond reproach.
– DERIVATIVES **unimpeachably** adv.
**unimpeded** • **adj.** not obstructed or hindered.
**unimportant** • **adj.** lacking in importance.
– DERIVATIVES **unimportance** n.
**unimpressed** • **adj.** not impressed.
**unimpressive** • **adj.** not impressive.
– DERIVATIVES **unimpressively** adv. **unimpressiveness** n.
**unimproved** • **adj.** not improved. ➤ (of land) not cleared or cultivated.
**unincorporated** • **adj. 1** not formed into a legal corporation. **2** not included as part of a whole.
**uninflected** • **adj.** not varied by inflection.
**uninfluenced** • **adj.** not influenced.
**uninformative** • **adj.** not providing useful or interesting information.
**uninformed** • **adj.** lacking awareness or understanding of the facts.
**uninhabitable** • **adj.** unsuitable for living in.
**uninhabited** • **adj.** without inhabitants.
**uninhibited** • **adj.** expressing oneself or acting without restraint.
– DERIVATIVES **uninhibitedly** adv. **uninhibitedness** n.
**uninitiated** • **adj.** without special knowledge or experience.
**uninjured** • **adj.** not harmed or damaged.
**uninspired** • **adj. 1** unimaginative; dull. **2** not filled with excitement.
**uninspiring** • **adj.** not producing excitement or interest.
– DERIVATIVES **uninspiringly** adv.
**uninsurable** • **adj.** not eligible for insurance cover.
**uninsured** • **adj.** not covered by insurance.
**unintelligent** • **adj.** lacking intelligence.
– DERIVATIVES **unintelligence** n. **unintelligently** adv.
**unintelligible** • **adj.** impossible to understand.
– DERIVATIVES **unintelligibility** n. **unintelligibly** adv.
**unintended** • **adj.** not planned or meant.
**unintentional** • **adj.** not done on purpose.
– DERIVATIVES **unintentionally** adv.
**uninterested** • **adj.** not interested or concerned.
– DERIVATIVES **uninterestedly** adv. **uninterestedness** n.

**USAGE** uninterested

On the meaning and use of **uninterested** and **disinterested**, see **DISINTERESTED**.

**uninteresting** • **adj.** not interesting.
– DERIVATIVES **uninterestingly** adv. **uninterestingness** n.
**uninterrupted** • **adj. 1** continuous. **2** unobstructed.
– DERIVATIVES **uninterruptedly** adv.
**uninterruptible** • **adj.** not able to be interrupted.
**uninventive** • **adj.** not inventive.
– DERIVATIVES **uninventively** adv. **uninventiveness** n.
**uninvited** • **adj.** arriving or acting without invitation.
– DERIVATIVES **uninvitedly** adv.
**uninviting** • **adj.** not attractive; unpleasant.
– DERIVATIVES **uninvitingly** adv.
**uninvolved** • **adj.** not involved.
**union** • **n. 1** the action or fact of uniting or being united. ➤ a state of harmony or agreement. ➤ marriage; sexual coupling. ➤ (**the Union**) historical the uniting of the English and Scottish crowns in 1603, of the English and Scottish parliaments in 1707, or of the parliaments of Great Britain and Ireland in 1801. **2** a club, society, or association formed by people with a common interest or purpose, especially a trade union. **3** (also **Union**) a political unit consisting of a number of states or provinces with the same central government, especially the US or the UK. ➤ (**the Union**) the northern states of the US in the American Civil War. **4** Brit. historical a number of parishes consolidated for administering the Poor Laws. ➤ a workhouse set up by such a group of parishes. **5** Mathematics the set that comprises all the elements (and no others) contained in any of two or more given sets. **6** a joint or coupling for pipes. **7** a part of a flag with an emblem symbolizing national union, normally in the upper corner next to the staff. **8** a fabric made of different yarns, typically cotton and linen or silk.
– ORIGIN ME: from OFr., or from eccles. L. *unio(n-)* 'unity', from L. *unus* 'one'.
**union catalogue** • **n.** a list of the combined holdings of several libraries.
**Union flag** • **n.** another term for **UNION JACK** (in sense 1).
**unionist** • **n. 1** a member of a trade union. **2** (**Unionist**) a person in Northern Ireland in favour of union with Great Britain. ➤ historical a member of a British political party supporting maintenance of the parliamentary union between Great Britain and Ireland. ➤ historical a person who opposed secession during the American Civil War of 1861–5.
– DERIVATIVES **unionism** n. **unionistic** adj.
**unionize** (also **-ise**) • **v.** become or cause to become members of a trade union.
– DERIVATIVES **unionization** n.
**unionized** (also **-ised**) • **adj.** belonging to, or having

workers belonging to, a trade union.

**Union Jack** ● n. **1** the national flag of the United Kingdom, formed by combining the flags of St George, St Andrew, and St Patrick. **2** (**union jack**) (in the US) a jack consisting of the union from the national flag.

**union suit** ● n. N. Amer. dated an all-in-one undergarment.

**uniparous** /juːˈnɪp(ə)rəs/ ● adj. chiefly Zoology producing a single young at a birth.
– ORIGIN C17: from mod. L. *uniparus* (from L. *uni-* 'one' + *-parus* 'bearing') + **-OUS**.

**uniplanar** ● adj. lying in one plane.

**unipod** /ˈjuːnɪpɒd/ ● n. a one-legged support for a camera.
– ORIGIN 1930s: from **UNI-**, suggested by **TRIPOD**.

**unipolar** ● adj. having or relating to a single pole or extremity. ➤(of psychiatric illness) characterized by either depressive or manic episodes but not both. ➤(of a nerve cell) having one axon. ➤Electronics (of a transistor or other device) using either negative or positive charge carriers but not both.
– DERIVATIVES **unipolarity** /-ˈlarɪti/ n.

**unique** ● adj. being the only one of its kind; unlike anything else. ➤(**unique to**) belonging or connected to (one particular person, group, or place). ➤remarkable or unusual.
– DERIVATIVES **uniquely** adv. **uniqueness** n.
– ORIGIN C17: from Fr., from L. *unicus*, from *unus* 'one'.

**uniserial** ● adj. Botany & Zoology arranged in or consisting of one series or row.

**unisex** ● adj. designed to be suitable for both sexes.

**unisexual** ● adj. of one sex. ➤Botany having either stamens or pistils but not both.
– DERIVATIVES **unisexuality** n. **unisexually** adv.

**UNISON** ● n. (in the UK) a trade union representing employees in the health service and public sector.

**unison** /ˈjuːnɪs(ə)n/ ● n. **1** simultaneous action or utterance. **2** Music a coincidence in pitch of sounds or notes. ● adj. performed in unison.
– DERIVATIVES **unisonous** adj.
– ORIGIN ME: from OFr., or from late L. *unisonus*, from L. *uni-* 'one' + *sonus* 'sound'.

**unison string** ● n. Music a string tuned to the same pitch (or to a pitch an octave higher) as another string and meant to be sounded with it.

**unit** ● n. **1** an individual thing or person regarded as single and complete; each of the individual components making up a larger whole. ➤a device or part with a specified function. ➤a self-contained or distinct section of a building or group of buildings. ➤a subdivision of a larger military grouping. ➤a self-contained part of an educational course. ➤a single manufactured item. **2** a standard quantity in terms of which other quantities may be expressed. **3** one as a number or quantity.
– DERIVATIVES **unitize** (also **-ise**) v.
– ORIGIN C16: from L. *unus*, prob. suggested by **DIGIT**.

**UNITAR** /juːˈniːtɑː/ ● abbrev. United Nations Institute for Training and Research.

**unitard** /ˈjuːnɪtɑːd/ ● n. a tight-fitting one-piece garment covering the whole body.
– ORIGIN 1960s: from **UNI-** + **LEOTARD**.

**Unitarian** /ˌjuːnɪˈtɛːrɪən/ Christian Theology ● adj. of or relating to belief in the unity of God and rejection of the doctrine of the Trinity. ● n. a Christian holding this belief.
– DERIVATIVES **Unitarianism** n.
– ORIGIN C17: from mod. L. *unitarius* (from L. *unitas* 'unity') + **-AN**.

**unitary** /ˈjuːnɪt(ə)ri/ ● adj. **1** single; uniform. ➤of or denoting a system of government or organization in which the powers of constituent parts are vested in a central body. **2** of or relating to a unit or units.
– DERIVATIVES **unitarily** adv. **unitarist** n. **unitarity** /-ˈtarɪti/ n.

**unitary authority** (also **unitary council**) ● n. (chiefly in the UK) a division of local government established in place of a two-tier system of local councils.

**unit cell** ● n. Crystallography the smallest group of atoms from which an entire crystal can be built up by repetition.

**unite** ● v. come or bring together for a common purpose or to form a whole. ➤archaic join in marriage.
– DERIVATIVES **united** adj. **unitedly** adv. **unitive** adj.
– ORIGIN ME: from L. *unit-*, *unire* 'join together', from *unus* 'one'.

**unitholder** ● n. chiefly Brit. a person with an investment in a unit trust.

**unit trust** ● n. Brit. a trust managing a portfolio of stock exchange securities, in which small investors can buy units.

**unity** ● n. (pl. **-ies**) **1** the state of being united or forming a whole. ➤a thing forming a complex whole. **2** Mathematics the number one. **3** a dramatic principle requiring limitation of the supposed time of a drama to that occupied in acting it or to a single day (**unity of time**), use of one scene throughout (**unity of place**), or concentration on a single plot (**unity of action**).
– ORIGIN ME: from OFr. *unite*, from L. *unitas*, from *unus* 'one'.

**Univ.** ● abbrev. University.

**univalent** ● adj. **1** /juːˈnɪvəl(ə)nt/ Biology (of a chromosome) remaining unpaired during meiosis. **2** /ˌjuːnɪˈveɪl(ə)nt/ Chemistry another term for **MONOVALENT**. ● n. /juːˈnɪvəl(ə)nt/ Biology a univalent chromosome.

**univalve** Zoology ● adj. having one valve or shell. ● n. a univalve mollusc; a gastropod.

**universal** ● adj. of, affecting, or done by all people or things in the world or in a particular group; applicable to all cases. ➤Logic denoting a proposition in which something is asserted of all of a class. Contrasted with **PARTICULAR**. ● n. **1** Logic a universal proposition. **2** Philosophy a term or concept of general application. ➤a nature or essence signified by a general term.
– DERIVATIVES **universality** n. **universally** adv.
– ORIGIN ME: from OFr., or from L. *universalis*, from *universus* (see **UNIVERSE**).

**universal compass** ● n. a pair of compasses with legs that can be extended for large circles.

**universal donor** ● n. a person of blood group O, who can in theory donate blood to recipients of any ABO blood group.

**universal indicator** ● n. Chemistry a mixture of dyes that changes colour gradually over a range of pH and is used to test for acids and alkalis.

**universalist** ● n. **1** Christian Theology a person who believes that all humankind will eventually be saved. **2** a person advocating concern for everyone without regard to national or sectional allegiances.
– DERIVATIVES **universalism** n. **universalistic** adj.

**universalize** (also **-ise**) ● v. make universal.
– DERIVATIVES **universalizability** n. **universalization** n.

**universal joint** ● n. a joint which can transmit rotary power by a shaft at any selected angle.

**universal product code** ● n. a bar code.

**universal recipient** ● n. a person of blood group AB, who can in theory receive donated blood of any ABO blood group.

**universal suffrage** ● n. the right of all adults (with minor exceptions) to vote in political elections.

**Universal Time** ● n. Greenwich Mean Time, as used internationally.

**universe** ● n. **1** all existing matter and space considered as a whole; the cosmos. **2** a particular sphere of activity or experience.
– ORIGIN ME: from OFr. *univers* or L. *universum*, neut. of *universus* 'combined into one, whole', from *uni-* 'one' + *versus* 'turned'.

**university** ● n. (pl. **-ies**) a high-level educational institution in which students study for degrees and academic research is done.
– ORIGIN ME: from OFr. *universite*, from L. *universitas* 'the whole', in late L. 'guild', from *universus* (see **UNIVERSE**).

**univocal** /ˌjuːnɪˈvəʊk(ə)l, juːˈnɪvək(ə)l/ ● adj. Philosophy & Linguistics having only one possible meaning; unambiguous.
– DERIVATIVES **univocality** n. **univocally** adv.

**unjoined** • **adj.** not joined together.
**unjointed** • **adj.** lacking a joint or joints; consisting of a single piece.
**unjust** • **adj.** not just; unfair.
– DERIVATIVES **unjustly** adv. **unjustness** n.
**unjustifiable** • **adj.** impossible to justify.
– DERIVATIVES **unjustifiably** adv.
**unjustified** • **adj.** not justified.
**unkempt** /ʌnˈkɛm(p)t/ • **adj.** untidy or dishevelled.
– DERIVATIVES **unkemptly** adv. **unkemptness** n.
– ORIGIN ME: from **UN-**[1] + *kempt* 'combed' (past part. of archaic *kemb*, rel. to **COMB**).
**unkept** • **adj.** **1** (of an undertaking) not honoured. **2** not tidy or cared for.
**unkind** • **adj.** inconsiderate and harsh.
– DERIVATIVES **unkindly** adv. **unkindness** n.
**unking** • **v.** archaic remove (a monarch) from power.
**unkink** • **v.** make or become straight.
**unknowable** • **adj.** not able to be known.
– DERIVATIVES **unknowability** n.
**unknowing** • **adj.** not knowing or aware. • **n.** poetic/literary ignorance.
– DERIVATIVES **unknowingly** adv. **unknowingness** n.
**unknown** • **adj.** not known or familiar. • **n.** an unknown person or thing. ➤Mathematics an unknown quantity or variable.
– PHRASES **unknown to** without the knowledge of.
– DERIVATIVES **unknownness** n.
**unknown quantity** • **n.** a person or thing whose nature, value, or significance is not known or knowable.
**Unknown Soldier** (also **Unknown Warrior**) • **n.** an unidentified representative member of a country's armed forces killed in war, buried with special honours in a national memorial.
**unlabelled** (US **unlabeled**) • **adj.** without a label.
**unlace** • **v.** undo the laces of.
**unlade** /ʌnˈleɪd/ • **v.** archaic unload (a ship or cargo).
**unladen** • **adj.** not carrying a load.
**unladylike** • **adj.** not appropriate to or behaving like a lady.
**unlaid**[1] • **adj.** not laid.
**unlaid**[2] past and past participle of **UNLAY**.
**unlamented** • **adj.** not mourned or regretted.
**unlash** • **v.** unfasten (something securely tied down).
**unlatch** • **v.** unfasten the latch of.
**unlawful** • **adj.** not conforming to or permitted by the law or rules.
– DERIVATIVES **unlawfully** adv. **unlawfulness** n.
**unlay** • **v.** (past and past part. **unlaid**) Nautical untwist (a rope) into separate strands.
**unleaded** • **adj.** **1** (especially of petrol) without added lead. **2** not covered, weighted, or framed with lead. **3** Printing not spaced with leads.
**unlearn** • **v.** (past and past part. **unlearned** or **unlearnt**) aim to discard (something learned) from one's memory.
**unlearned**[1] /ʌnˈləːnd, -ˈləːnɪd/ • **adj.** not well educated.
– DERIVATIVES **unlearnedly** adv.
**unlearned**[2] /ʌnˈləːnd/ (also **unlearnt** /-ˈləːnt/) • **adj.** not having been learned.
**unleash** • **v.** release from a leash or restraint.
**unleavened** • **adj.** made without yeast or other raising agent.
**unless** • **conj.** except when; if not.
– ORIGIN ME: from **ON** or **IN** (assimilated through lack of stress to **UN-**[1]) + **LESS**.
**unlettered** • **adj.** poorly educated or illiterate.
**unlicensed** • **adj.** not having an official licence, especially (chiefly Brit.) for the sale of alcoholic liquor.
**unlike** • **prep.** different from; not like. ➤in contrast to. ➤uncharacteristic of. • **adj.** dissimilar or different from each other. ➤(**unlike to/from**) archaic different from.
– DERIVATIVES **unlikeness** n.
– ORIGIN ME: perh. orig. an alt. of ON *úlíkr*; cf. OE *ungelīc*.
**unlikely** • **adj.** (**-ier**, **-iest**) not likely; improbable.
– DERIVATIVES **unlikelihood** n. **unlikeliness** n.
**unlimber** • **v.** detach (a gun) from its limber. ➤chiefly US unpack or unfasten ready for use.
**unlimited** • **adj.** not limited or restricted; infinite.
– DERIVATIVES **unlimitedly** adv. **unlimitedness** n.
**unlined**[1] • **adj.** not marked with lines or wrinkles.
**unlined**[2] • **adj.** without a lining.
**unlink** • **v.** make no longer connected.
**unlisted** • **adj.** not included on a list, especially of stock exchange prices or telephone numbers.
**unlit** • **adj.** **1** not provided with lighting. **2** not having been lit.
**unlivable** • **adj.** uninhabitable.
**unlived-in** • **adj.** not appearing to be inhabited or used.
**unload** • **v.** **1** remove a load from. ➤remove (goods) from a vehicle, ship, etc. **2** informal get rid of (something unwanted). ➤chiefly N. Amer. give expression to (oppressive thoughts). **3** remove (ammunition) from a gun or (film) from a camera.
– DERIVATIVES **unloader** n.
**unlock** • **v.** **1** undo the lock of (something) using a key. **2** make (something) available.
**unlooked** • **adj.** (**unlooked for**) unexpected.
**unloose** • **v.** undo; let free.
**unloosen** • **v.** another term for **UNLOOSE**.
**unloved** • **adj.** loved by no one.
**unlovely** • **adj.** not attractive; ugly.
– DERIVATIVES **unloveliness** n.
**unlucky** • **adj.** (**-ier**, **-iest**) having, bringing, or resulting from bad luck.
– DERIVATIVES **unluckily** adv. **unluckiness** n.
**unmade** • **adj.** **1** (of a bed) not arranged tidily ready for sleeping in. **2** Brit. (of a road) without a hard, smooth surface.
**unmake** • **v.** (past and past part. **unmade**) reverse or undo the making of; annul or destroy.
**unman** • **v.** (**unmanned**, **unmanning**) poetic/literary deprive of manly qualities such as self-control or courage.
**unmanageable** • **adj.** difficult or impossible to manage or control.
– DERIVATIVES **unmanageableness** n. **unmanageably** adv.
**unmanly** • **adj.** not manly.
– DERIVATIVES **unmanliness** n.
**unmanned** • **adj.** not having or needing a crew or staff.
**unmannerly** • **adj.** not well mannered.
– DERIVATIVES **unmannerliness** n.
**unmarked** • **adj.** **1** not marked. **2** not noticed.
**unmarried** • **adj.** not married; single.
**unmask** • **v.** expose the true character of.
– DERIVATIVES **unmasker** n.
**unmatched** • **adj.** not matched or equalled.
**unmeasurable** • **adj.** not able to be measured objectively.
– DERIVATIVES **unmeasurably** adv.
**unmeasured** • **adj.** **1** not having been measured. **2** chiefly poetic/literary limitless.
**unmelodious** • **adj.** not melodious; discordant.
– DERIVATIVES **unmelodiously** adv.
**unmentionable** • **adj.** too embarrassing, offensive, or shocking to be spoken about. • **n.** chiefly humorous an unmentionable thing.
– DERIVATIVES **unmentionability** n. **unmentionableness** n. **unmentionably** adv.
**unmerciful** • **adj.** showing no mercy.
– DERIVATIVES **unmercifully** adv. **unmercifulness** n.
**unmerited** • **adj.** not deserved or merited.
**unmetalled** • **adj.** Brit. (of a road) not having a hard surface.
**unmethodical** • **adj.** not orderly and systematic.
– DERIVATIVES **unmethodically** adv.
**unmetrical** • **adj.** not composed in or using metre.
**unmindful** • **adj.** (**unmindful of**) not conscious or aware of.
– DERIVATIVES **unmindfully** adv. **unmindfulness** n.

**unmissable** ● adj. that should not or cannot be missed.

**unmistakable** (also **unmistakeable**) ● adj. not able to be mistaken for anything else.
– DERIVATIVES **unmistakability** n. **unmistakably** adv.

**unmitigated** ● adj. absolute; unqualified.
– DERIVATIVES **unmitigatedly** adv.

**unmixed** ● adj. not mixed.

**unmodulated** ● adj. not modulated.

**unmoor** ● v. release the moorings of.

**unmoral** ● adj. not concerned with morality.
– DERIVATIVES **unmorality** n.

**unmotivated** ● adj. **1** not motivated. **2** without apparent motive.

**unmoved** ● adj. **1** not affected by emotion or excitement. **2** not changed in purpose or position.
– DERIVATIVES **unmovable** (also **unmoveable**) adj.

**unmoving** ● adj. **1** not moving; still. **2** not stirring any emotion.

**unmuffle** ● v. free from something that muffles or conceals.

**unmurmuring** ● adj. poetic/literary not complaining.
– DERIVATIVES **unmurmuringly** adv.

**unmusical** ● adj. **1** not pleasing to the ear. **2** unskilled in or indifferent to music.
– DERIVATIVES **unmusicality** n. **unmusically** adv. **unmusicalness** n.

**unmuzzle** ● v. **1** remove a muzzle from. **2** allow freedom of expression to.

**unnameable** (also **unnamable**) ● adj. unmentionable.

**unnatural** ● adj. **1** contrary to nature; abnormal. **2** affected; not spontaneous.
– DERIVATIVES **unnaturally** adv. **unnaturalness** n.

**unnavigable** ● adj. not able to be sailed on by ships or boats.
– DERIVATIVES **unnavigability** n.

**unnecessary** ● adj. not necessary; more than is necessary. ● n. (**unnecessaries**) unnecessary things.
– DERIVATIVES **unnecessarily** adv. **unnecessariness** n.

**unnerve** ● v. deprive of courage or confidence.
– DERIVATIVES **unnerving** adj. **unnervingly** adv.

**unnoticeable** ● adj. not easily observed or noticed.
– DERIVATIVES **unnoticeably** adv.

**unnoticed** ● adj. not noticed.

**unnumbered** ● adj. **1** not assigned a number. **2** not counted; countless.

**unobliging** ● adj. not helpful or cooperative.

**unobserved** ● adj. not observed; unseen.

**unobstructed** ● adj. not obstructed.

**unobtainable** ● adj. not able to be obtained.

**unobtrusive** ● adj. not conspicuous or attracting attention.
– DERIVATIVES **unobtrusively** adv. **unobtrusiveness** n.

**unoccupied** ● adj. not occupied.

**unofficial** ● adj. not officially authorized or confirmed.
– DERIVATIVES **unofficially** adv.

**unopened** ● adj. not opened.

**unopposed** ● adj. not opposed; unchallenged.

**unorganized** (also **-ised**) ● adj. **1** not organized. **2** not unionized.

**unoriginal** ● adj. lacking originality; derivative.
– DERIVATIVES **unoriginality** n. **unoriginally** adv.

**unorthodox** ● adj. contrary to what is usual, traditional, or accepted; not orthodox.
– DERIVATIVES **unorthodoxly** adv. **unorthodoxy** n.

**unostentatious** ● adj. not ostentatious.
– DERIVATIVES **unostentatiously** adv. **unostentatiousness** n.

**unowned** ● adj. **1** not having an owner. **2** not admitted to; unacknowledged.

**unpack** ● v. **1** open and remove the contents of (a suitcase or container). ➤ remove from a packed container. **2** analyse into component elements. ➤ Computing convert (compressed data).
– DERIVATIVES **unpacker** n.

**unpaid** ● adj. **1** (of a debt) not yet paid. **2** (of work or leave) undertaken without payment. ➤ (of a person) not receiving payment for work done.

**unpaired** ● adj. **1** not arranged in pairs. **2** not forming one of a pair.

**unpalatable** ● adj. **1** not pleasant to taste. **2** difficult to put up with or accept.
– DERIVATIVES **unpalatability** n. **unpalatably** adv.

**unparalleled** ● adj. having no parallel or equal; exceptional.

**unpardonable** ● adj. (of a fault or offence) unforgivable.
– DERIVATIVES **unpardonableness** n. **unpardonably** adv.

**unparliamentary** ● adj. (especially of language) contrary to the rules or procedures of parliament.

**unpasteurized** (also **-ised**) ● adj. not pasteurized.

**unpatriotic** ● adj. not patriotic.
– DERIVATIVES **unpatriotically** adv.

**unpaved** ● adj. lacking a metalled or paved surface.

**unpeg** ● v. (**unpegged**, **unpegging**) **1** unfasten by the removal of pegs. **2** cease to maintain a fixed relationship between (a currency) and another currency.

**unpeople** ● v. [usu. as adj. **unpeopled**] empty of people; depopulate.

**unperson** ● n. (pl. **-persons**) a person whose name or existence is officially denied or ignored.

**unperturbed** ● adj. not perturbed or concerned.
– DERIVATIVES **unperturbedly** adv.

**unpick** ● v. **1** undo the sewing of (stitches or a garment). **2** carefully break down and analyse the different elements of (something), especially in order to find faults.

**unpin** ● v. (**unpinned**, **unpinning**) unfasten or detach by removing a pin or pins.

**unpitying** ● adj. not feeling or showing pity.
– DERIVATIVES **unpityingly** adv.

**unplaceable** ● adj. not able to be placed or classified.

**unplaced** ● adj. **1** not having or assigned to a specific place. **2** chiefly Horse Racing not one of the first three (sometimes four) to finish in a race.

**unplanned** ● adj. not planned.

**unplayable** ● adj. **1** not able to be played or played on. **2** (of music) too difficult or bad to perform.
– DERIVATIVES **unplayably** adv.

**unpleasant** ● adj. not pleasant; disagreeable.
– DERIVATIVES **unpleasantly** adv.

**unpleasantness** ● n. **1** the state or quality of being unpleasant. **2** bad feeling or quarrelling between people.

**unploughed** (US **unplowed**) ● adj. **1** (of land) not having been ploughed. **2** N. Amer. not cleared of snow by a snowplough.

**unplug** ● v. (**unplugged**, **unplugging**) **1** disconnect (an electrical device) by removing its plug from a socket. **2** remove an obstacle or blockage from.

**unplugged** ● adj. trademark (of pop or rock music) performed or recorded with acoustic rather than electrically amplified instruments.

**unplumbed** ● adj. **1** not provided with plumbing. **2** not fully explored or understood.
– DERIVATIVES **unplumbable** adj.

**unpointed** ● adj. **1** (of brickwork) not pointed. **2** (of a Semitic language) written without dots or strokes to indicate vowels or distinguish consonants.

**unpolished** ● adj. **1** not having a polished surface. **2** (of a work) not polished.

**unpolled** ● adj. **1** (of a voter) not having voted, or registered to vote, at an election. ➤ (of a vote) not cast at or registered for an election. **2** (of a person) not included in an opinion poll.

**unpopular** ● adj. not liked or popular.
– DERIVATIVES **unpopularity** n.

**unpopulated** ● adj. **1** without inhabitants. **2** (of a printed circuit board) having no components fitted.

**unpowered** ● adj. having no fuel-burning source of power for propulsion.

**unpractical** ● adj. another term for **IMPRACTICAL** (in sense 1).
– DERIVATIVES **unpracticality** n.

**unpractised** (US **unpracticed**) ● **adj.** **1** not trained or experienced. **2** not often done before.

**unprecedented** /ʌnˈprɛsɪdɛntɪd/ ● **adj.** never done or known before.

– DERIVATIVES **unprecedentedly** adv.

**unpredictable** ● **adj.** not able to be predicted; changeable.

– DERIVATIVES **unpredictability** n. **unpredictably** adv.

**unprejudiced** ● **adj.** without prejudice; unbiased.

**unpremeditated** ● **adj.** not thought out or planned beforehand.

– DERIVATIVES **unpremeditatedly** adv.

**unprepared** ● **adj.** **1** not ready or able to deal with something. **2** (of a thing) not made ready for use.

– DERIVATIVES **unpreparedness** n.

**unprepossessing** ● **adj.** not attractive or appealing to the eye.

**unpressurized** (also **-ised**) ● **adj.** (of a gas or its container) not having raised pressure that is produced or maintained artificially. ➤(of an aircraft cabin) not having normal atmospheric pressure maintained at a high altitude.

**unpretending** ● **adj.** archaic not pretentious or false.

**unpretentious** ● **adj.** not pretentious; modest.

– DERIVATIVES **unpretentiously** adv. **unpretentiousness** n.

**unprincipled** ● **adj.** not acting in accordance with moral principles.

**unprintable** ● **adj.** (of words, comments, or thoughts) too offensive or shocking to be published.

– DERIVATIVES **unprintably** adv.

**unproblematic** ● **adj.** not constituting or presenting a problem or difficulty.

– DERIVATIVES **unproblematical** adj. **unproblematically** adv.

**unprocessed** ● **adj.** not processed.

**unproductive** ● **adj.** **1** not producing or able to produce large amounts of goods, crops, etc. **2** not achieving much; not very useful.

– DERIVATIVES **unproductively** adv. **unproductiveness** n.

**unprofessional** ● **adj.** below or contrary to the standards expected in a particular profession.

– DERIVATIVES **unprofessionalism** n. **unprofessionally** adv.

**unprofitable** ● **adj.** not yielding a profit. ➤not beneficial or useful.

– DERIVATIVES **unprofitability** n. **unprofitably** adv.

**unpromising** ● **adj.** not giving hope of future success or good results.

– DERIVATIVES **unpromisingly** adv.

**unprompted** ● **adj.** without being prompted.

**unpronounceable** ● **adj.** too difficult to pronounce.

– DERIVATIVES **unpronounceably** adv.

**unprotected** ● **adj.** **1** not protected or kept safe from harm. **2** (of sexual intercourse) performed without a condom.

**unproven** /ʌnˈpruːv(ə)n, -ˈprəʊ-/ (also **unproved** /-ˈpruːvd/) ● **adj.** not demonstrated by evidence or argument as true or existing. ➤not tried and tested.

**unprovided** ● **adj.** not provided. ➤(**unprovided for**) without sufficient money to cover the cost of living.

**unprovoked** ● **adj.** (of an attack, crime, etc.) not directly provoked.

**unpublished** ● **adj.** (of a work) not published. ➤(of an author) having no writings published.

– DERIVATIVES **unpublishable** adj.

**unpunished** ● **adj.** (of an offence or offender) not receiving any punishment or penalty.

**unputdownable** ● **adj.** informal (of a book) so engrossing that one cannot stop reading it.

**unqualified** ● **adj.** **1** not having the necessary qualifications or requirements. **2** without reservation or limitation; total: *an unqualified success.*

– DERIVATIVES **unqualifiedly** adv.

**unquantifiable** ● **adj.** impossible to express or measure in terms of quantity.

**unquenchable** ● **adj.** not able to be quenched.

– DERIVATIVES **unquenchably** adv.

**unquestionable** ● **adj.** not able to be disputed or doubted.

– DERIVATIVES **unquestionability** n. **unquestionably** adv.

**unquestioned** ● **adj.** **1** not disputed or doubted; certain. **2** accepted without question: *an unquestioned assumption.* **3** not subjected to questioning.

– DERIVATIVES **unquestioning** adj. **unquestioningly** adv.

**unquiet** ● **adj.** restless; unable to be still. ➤anxious.

– DERIVATIVES **unquietly** adv. **unquietness** n.

**unquote** ● **v.** (in phr. **quote —— unquote**) see **QUOTE**.

**unquoted** ● **adj.** not quoted or listed on a stock exchange.

**unrated** ● **adj.** not having received a rating. ➤US (of a film) not allocated an official classification, typically because regarded as unsuitable for general release.

**unravel** ● **v.** (**unravelled**, **unravelling**; US **unraveled**, **unraveling**) **1** undo (twisted, knitted, or woven threads); unwind. ➤become undone. **2** investigate and solve (a mystery or puzzle). **3** begin to fail or collapse.

**unreachable** ● **adj.** unable to be reached or contacted.

– DERIVATIVES **unreachableness** n. **unreachably** adv.

**unreactive** ● **adj.** having little tendency to react chemically.

**unread** ● **adj.** not having been read. ➤archaic (of a person) not well read.

**unreadable** ● **adj.** **1** not clear enough to read; illegible. **2** too dull or difficult to be worth reading.

– DERIVATIVES **unreadability** n. **unreadably** adv.

**unready** ● **adj.** **1** not ready or prepared. **2** archaic slow to act; hesitant.

– DERIVATIVES **unreadiness** n.

**unreal** ● **adj.** **1** imaginary; not seeming real. **2** unrealistic. **3** informal, chiefly N. Amer. incredible; amazing.

– DERIVATIVES **unreality** n. **unreally** adv.

**unrealistic** ● **adj.** not realistic.

– DERIVATIVES **unrealistically** adv.

**unrealized** (also **-ised**) ● **adj.** **1** not achieved or created. **2** not converted into money: *unrealized property assets.*

**unreason** ● **n.** irrationality; lack of reasonable thought.

**unreasonable** ● **adj.** **1** not guided by or based on good sense. **2** beyond the limits of acceptability.

– DERIVATIVES **unreasonableness** n. **unreasonably** adv.

**unreasoning** ● **adj.** not guided by or based on reason.

– DERIVATIVES **unreasoned** adj. **unreasoningly** adv.

**unreceptive** ● **adj.** not receptive.

**unreciprocated** ● **adj.** not reciprocated; unrequited.

**unreclaimed** ● **adj.** (especially of land) not reclaimed.

**unrecognizable** (also **-isable**) ● **adj.** not able to be recognized.

– DERIVATIVES **unrecognizably** adv.

**unrecognized** (also **-ised**) ● **adj.** **1** not identified from previous encounters or knowledge. **2** not acknowledged as valid; not officially recognized.

**unreconciled** ● **adj.** not reconciled.

**unreconstructed** ● **adj.** **1** not reconciled or converted to the current political theory or movement: *unreconstructed Communists.* **2** not rebuilt.

**unrecorded** ● **adj.** not recorded.

– DERIVATIVES **unrecordable** adj.

**unredeemed** ● **adj.** not redeemed.

**unreel** ● **v.** **1** unwind. **2** (of a film) wind from one reel to another during projection.

**unrefined** ● **adj.** **1** not processed to remove impurities. **2** not elegant or cultured.

**unregenerate** /ˌʌnrɪˈdʒɛn(ə)rət/ ● **adj.** not reforming or showing repentance; obstinately wrong or bad.

– DERIVATIVES **unregeneracy** n. **unregenerately** adv.

**unregistered** ● **adj.** not officially recognized and recorded.

**unregulated** ● **adj.** not controlled or supervised by regulations or laws.

**unrehearsed** ● **adj.** not rehearsed.

**unrelated** ● **adj.** not related.

– DERIVATIVES **unrelatedness** n.

**unreleased** ● **adj.** (especially of a film or recording) not released.

**unrelenting** ● adj. not yielding in strength, severity, or determination.
– DERIVATIVES **unrelentingly** adv. **unrelentingness** n.

**unreliable** ● adj. not able to be relied upon.
– DERIVATIVES **unreliability** n. **unreliably** adv.

**unrelieved** ● adj. **1** lacking variation or change; monotonous. **2** not provided with relief; not aided or assisted.
– DERIVATIVES **unrelievedly** adv.

**unremarkable** ● adj. not particularly interesting or surprising.
– DERIVATIVES **unremarkably** adv.

**unremarked** ● adj. not remarked upon; unnoticed.

**unremitting** ● adj. never relaxing or slackening.
– DERIVATIVES **unremittingly** adv. **unremittingness** n.

**unremunerative** ● adj. bringing little or no profit or income.
– DERIVATIVES **unremuneratively** adv.

**unrepeatable** ● adj. **1** not able to be repeated. **2** too offensive or shocking to be said again.
– DERIVATIVES **unrepeatability** n.

**unrepentant** ● adj. showing no regret for one's wrongdoings.
– DERIVATIVES **unrepentantly** adv.

**unreported** ● adj. not reported.

**unrepresentative** ● adj. not typical of a class, group, or body of opinion.
– DERIVATIVES **unrepresentativeness** n.

**unrequited** ● adj. (of a feeling, especially love) not returned or rewarded.
– DERIVATIVES **unrequitedly** adv. **unrequitedness** n.

**unreserve** ● n. archaic lack of reserve; frankness.

**unreserved** ● adj. **1** without reservations; complete. **2** frank and open. **3** not set apart or booked in advance.
– DERIVATIVES **unreservedly** adv. **unreservedness** n.

**unresolved** ● adj. (of a problem, dispute, etc.) not resolved.
– DERIVATIVES **unresolvedly** /-vɪdli/ adv. **unresolvedness** n.

**unresponsive** ● adj. not responsive.
– DERIVATIVES **unresponsively** adv. **unresponsiveness** n.

**unrest** ● n. a state of rebellious dissatisfaction and agitation in a group of people: *civil unrest*. ➤a state of uneasiness or disturbance.

**unrestrained** ● adj. not restrained or restricted.
– DERIVATIVES **unrestrainedly** adv. **unrestrainedness** n.

**unrestricted** ● adj. not limited or restricted.
– DERIVATIVES **unrestrictedly** adv.

**unrewarding** ● adj. not rewarding or satisfying.

**unripe** ● adj. not ripe.
– DERIVATIVES **unripeness** n.

**unrivalled** (US **unrivaled**) ● adj. surpassing all others.

**unroll** ● v. open or cause to open out from a rolled-up state.

**unromantic** ● adj. not romantic.
– DERIVATIVES **unromantically** adv.

**unrope** ● v. Climbing detach oneself from a rope.

**unrounded** ● adj. Phonetics (of a vowel) pronounced with the lips not rounded.

**unruffled** ● adj. not disordered or disturbed. ➤(of a person) not agitated; calm.

**unruly** ● adj. (**-ier**, **-iest**) disorderly and disruptive; difficult to control.
– DERIVATIVES **unruliness** n.
– ORIGIN ME: from **UN-**[1] + archaic *ruly* 'disciplined; orderly' (from **RULE**).

**UNRWA** ● abbrev. United Nations Relief and Works Agency.

**unsaddle** ● v. remove the saddle from. ➤dislodge from a saddle.

**unsafe** ● adj. **1** not safe; dangerous. **2** Law (of a verdict or conviction) not based on reliable evidence and likely to constitute a miscarriage of justice. **3** denoting sexual activity in which precautions are not taken to reduce the risk of spreading sexually transmitted diseases, especially Aids.
– DERIVATIVES **unsafely** adv. **unsafeness** n.

**unsaid** past and past participle of **UNSAY**. ● adj. not said or uttered.

**unsaleable** (also **unsalable**) ● adj. not able to be sold.
– DERIVATIVES **unsaleability** n.

**unsalted** ● adj. not salted.

**unsanitary** ● adj. not sanitary.

**unsatisfactory** ● adj. **1** unacceptable because poor or not good enough. **2** Law another term for **UNSAFE**.
– DERIVATIVES **unsatisfactorily** adv. **unsatisfactoriness** n.

**unsatisfied** ● adj. not satisfied.

**unsatisfying** ● adj. not satisfying.
– DERIVATIVES **unsatisfyingly** adv.

**unsaturated** ● adj. Chemistry (of organic molecules) having carbon–carbon double or triple bonds and therefore not containing the greatest possible number of hydrogen atoms.
– DERIVATIVES **unsaturation** n.

**unsaved** ● adj. not saved, in particular (in Christian use) not having had one's soul saved from damnation.

**unsavoury** (US **unsavory**) ● adj. **1** disagreeable to taste, smell, or look at. **2** objectionable; disreputable.
– DERIVATIVES **unsavourily** adv. **unsavouriness** n.

**unsay** ● v. (past and past part. **unsaid**) withdraw or retract (a statement).

**unsayable** ● adj. not able to be said, especially because considered too controversial or offensive.

**unscarred** ● adj. not scarred or damaged.

**unscathed** ● adj. without suffering any injury, damage, or harm.

**unscented** ● adj. not scented.

**unscheduled** ● adj. not scheduled.

**unschooled** ● adj. **1** lacking schooling or training. ➤uncontrolled; undisciplined. **2** not affected; natural and spontaneous.

**unscientific** ● adj. **1** not in accordance with scientific principles or methodology. **2** lacking knowledge of or interest in science.
– DERIVATIVES **unscientifically** adv.

**unscramble** ● v. restore or convert to an intelligible or readable state.
– DERIVATIVES **unscrambler** n.

**unscreened** ● adj. **1** not subjected to screening. **2** not shown or broadcast. **3** not provided with a screen.

**unscrew** ● v. (with reference to a screw, lid, etc.) unfasten or be unfastened by twisting.

**unscripted** ● adj. said or delivered without a prepared script; impromptu.

**unscrupulous** ● adj. without moral scruples.
– DERIVATIVES **unscrupulously** adv. **unscrupulousness** n.

**unseal** ● v. remove or break the seal of.

**unsealed** ● adj. not sealed. ➤chiefly Austral./NZ (of a road) not surfaced with bitumen or a similar substance.

**unseasonable** ● adj. **1** (of weather) unusual for the time of year. **2** untimely; inopportune.
– DERIVATIVES **unseasonableness** n. **unseasonably** adv.

**unseasonal** ● adj. (especially of weather) unusual or inappropriate for the time of year.

**unseasoned** ● adj. **1** (of food) not flavoured with salt, pepper, or other spices. **2** (of timber) not treated or matured. **3** (of a person) inexperienced.

**unseat** ● v. **1** cause to fall from a saddle or seat. **2** remove from a position of power or authority.

**unsecured** ● adj. **1** (of a loan) made without an asset given as security. ➤(of a creditor) having made such a loan. **2** not made secure or safe.

**unseeded** ● adj. **1** (chiefly of a competitor in a sports tournament) not seeded. **2** without seeds; not sown with seeds.

**unseeing** ● adj. with one's eyes open but without noticing or seeing anything.
– DERIVATIVES **unseeingly** adv.

**unseemly** ● **adj.** **1** (of behaviour or actions) not proper or appropriate. **2** archaic unattractive.
– DERIVATIVES **unseemliness** n.

**unseen** ● **adj.** **1** not seen or noticed. **2** chiefly Brit. (of a passage for translation in an examination) not previously read or prepared. ● **n.** Brit. an unseen passage for translation.

**unselfconscious** ● **adj.** without self-consciousness; not shy or embarrassed.
– DERIVATIVES **unselfconsciously** adv. **unselfconsciousness** n.

**unselfish** ● **adj.** not selfish.
– DERIVATIVES **unselfishly** adv. **unselfishness** n.

**unsentimental** ● **adj.** not displaying or influenced by sentimental feelings.
– DERIVATIVES **unsentimentally** adv.

**unserious** ● **adj.** not serious; light-hearted.

**unserved** ● **adj.** **1** not attended to or catered for. **2** (of a female animal) not mated with a male.

**unserviceable** ● **adj.** not in working order; unfit for use.
– DERIVATIVES **unserviceability** n.

**unsettle** ● **v.** cause to be anxious or uneasy; disturb.
– DERIVATIVES **unsettlement** n. **unsettling** adj. **unsettlingly** adv.

**unsettled** ● **adj.** **1** lacking stability; changeable or liable to change. ➤agitated; uneasy. **2** not yet resolved. ➤(of a bill) not yet paid. **3** (of an area) having no settlers or inhabitants.
– DERIVATIVES **unsettledness** n.

**unsex** ● **v.** deprive of gender, sexuality, or the characteristic attributes of one or other sex.

**unshackle** ● **v.** release from shackles or other restraints.

**unshakeable** (also **unshakable**) ● **adj.** (of a belief, feeling, etc.) firm and unable to be changed or disputed.
– DERIVATIVES **unshakeability** n. **unshakeably** adv.

**unshaken** ● **adj.** steadfast and unwavering.
– DERIVATIVES **unshakenly** adv.

**unshaven** ● **adj.** not having shaved or been shaved.

**unsheathe** ● **v.** draw or pull out (a knife or similar weapon) from a sheath.

**unshed** ● **adj.** (of tears) welling in a person's eyes but not falling.

**unshelled** ● **adj.** not extracted from its shell.

**unship** ● **v.** (**unshipped**, **unshipping**) chiefly Nautical **1** remove (an oar, mast, or other object) from a fixed or regular position. **2** unload (a cargo) from a ship or boat.

**unshockable** ● **adj.** impossible to shock.
– DERIVATIVES **unshockability** n.

**unshorn** ● **adj.** (of hair or wool) not cut or shorn.

**unsighted** ● **adj.** **1** lacking the power of sight. **2** (especially in sport) prevented from having a clear view. ➤not seen.

**unsightly** ● **adj.** unpleasant to look at; ugly.
– DERIVATIVES **unsightliness** n.

**unsigned** ● **adj.** **1** not bearing a person's signature. ➤not having signed a contract of employment. **2** Mathematics & Computing not having a plus or minus sign, or a bit representing this.

**unsinkable** ● **adj.** (of a ship or boat) unable to be sunk.
– DERIVATIVES **unsinkability** n.

**unsized** ● **adj.** (of fabric, paper, or a wall) not treated with size.

**unskilful** (also chiefly US **unskillful**) ● **adj.** not having or showing skill.
– DERIVATIVES **unskilfully** adv. **unskilfulness** n.

**unskilled** ● **adj.** not having or requiring special skill or training.

**unsling** ● **v.** (past and past part. **unslung**) remove from a position of being slung or suspended.

**unsmiling** ● **adj.** not smiling; serious or unfriendly.
– DERIVATIVES **unsmilingly** adv. **unsmilingness** n.

**unsmoked** ● **adj.** **1** (of meat or fish) not cured by exposure to smoke. **2** (of tobacco or a cigarette) not having been smoked.

**unsnap** ● **v.** (**unsnapped**, **unsnapping**) unfasten or open with a brisk movement and a sharp sound.

**unsociable** ● **adj.** not making an effort to behave sociably. ➤not conducive to friendly social relations.
– DERIVATIVES **unsociability** n. **unsociableness** n. **unsociably** adv.

**unsocial** ● **adj.** **1** (of the hours of work of a job) falling outside the normal working day and thus socially inconvenient. **2** antisocial.
– DERIVATIVES **unsocially** adv.

**unsold** ● **adj.** (of an item) not sold.

**unsolicited** ● **adj.** not asked for; given or done voluntarily: *unsolicited junk mail.*
– DERIVATIVES **unsolicitedly** adv.

**unsolved** ● **adj.** not solved.

**unsophisticated** ● **adj.** **1** lacking refined worldly knowledge or tastes. **2** not complicated or highly developed; basic.
– DERIVATIVES **unsophisticatedly** adv. **unsophisticatedness** n. **unsophistication** n.

**unsorted** ● **adj.** not sorted or arranged.

**unsound** ● **adj.** **1** not safe or robust; in poor condition. ➤injured, ill, or diseased. **2** not based on sound evidence or reasoning; unreliable or unacceptable. ➤(of a person) not competent, reliable, or holding acceptable views.
– DERIVATIVES **unsoundly** adv. **unsoundness** n.

**unsparing** ● **adj.** **1** merciless; severe. **2** given freely and generously.
– DERIVATIVES **unsparingly** adv. **unsparingness** n.

**unspeakable** ● **adj.** not able to be expressed in words. ➤too bad or horrific to express in words.
– DERIVATIVES **unspeakableness** n. **unspeakably** adv.

**unspecialized** (also **-ised**) ● **adj.** not specialized.

**unspecific** ● **adj.** not specific; vague.

**unspecified** ● **adj.** not stated clearly or exactly.

**unspectacular** ● **adj.** not spectacular; unremarkable.
– DERIVATIVES **unspectacularly** adv.

**unspoilt** (also **unspoiled**) ● **adj.** not spoilt, in particular (of a place) not marred by development.

**unspoken** ● **adj.** not expressed in speech; tacit.

**unspool** ● **v.** **1** unwind from or as if from a spool. **2** (of a film) be screened.

**unsporting** ● **adj.** not fair or sportsmanlike.
– DERIVATIVES **unsportingly** adv.

**unsportsmanlike** ● **adj.** unsporting.

**unsprung** ● **adj.** not provided with springs.

**unstable** ● **adj.** (**-er**, **-est**) **1** prone to change or collapse; not stable. **2** prone to psychiatric problems or sudden changes of mood.
– DERIVATIVES **unstableness** n. **unstably** adv.

**unstained** ● **adj.** not stained.

**unstated** ● **adj.** not stated or declared.

**unsteady** ● **adj.** (**-ier**, **-iest**) **1** liable to fall or shake; not firm. **2** not uniform or regular.
– DERIVATIVES **unsteadily** adv. **unsteadiness** n.

**unstep** ● **v.** (**unstepped**, **unstepping**) Nautical detach (a mast) from its step.

**unstick** ● **v.** (past and past part. **unstuck**) **1** cause to become no longer stuck together. **2** Brit. informal (of an aircraft) take off.
– PHRASES **come** (or **get**) **unstuck** informal fail.

**unstinting** ● **adj.** given or giving without restraint; unsparing.
– DERIVATIVES **unstinted** adj. **unstintingly** adv.

**unstop** ● **v.** (**unstopped**, **unstopping**) free from obstruction. ➤remove the stopper from.

**unstoppable** ● **adj.** impossible to stop or prevent.
– DERIVATIVES **unstoppability** n. **unstoppably** adv.

**unstopper** ● **v.** remove the stopper from (a container).

**unstressed** ● **adj.** **1** Phonetics (of a syllable) not pronounced with stress. **2** not subjected to stress.

**unstring** ● **v.** (past and past part. **unstrung**) **1** [usu. as adj. **unstrung**] unnerve: *a mind unstrung by loneliness.* **2** remove or relax the string or strings of. **3** remove from a string.

**unstructured** ● **adj.** without formal organization or

structure. ➤(of a garment) made with little or no interfacing or other material which would give definition to its shape.

**unstuck** past and past participle of **UNSTICK**.

**unstudied** • adj. not laboured or artificial; natural.
– DERIVATIVES **unstudiedly** adv.

**unstuffy** • adj. **1** friendly, informal, and approachable. **2** having fresh air or ventilation.

**unsubstantial** • adj. having little or no solidity, reality, or factual basis.
– DERIVATIVES **unsubstantiality** n. **unsubstantially** adv.

**unsubstantiated** • adj. not supported or proven by evidence.

**unsubtle** • adj. not subtle; obvious; clumsy.
– DERIVATIVES **unsubtly** adv.

**unsuccessful** • adj. not successful.
– DERIVATIVES **unsuccessfully** adv. **unsuccessfulness** n.

**unsuitable** • adj. not fitting or appropriate.
– DERIVATIVES **unsuitability** n. **unsuitableness** n. **unsuitably** adv.

**unsuited** • adj. not right or appropriate.

**unsullied** • adj. not spoiled or made impure.

**unsung** • adj. not celebrated or praised: *unsung heroes of the industrial revolution.*

**unsupervised** • adj. not done or acting under supervision.

**unsupportable** • adj. insupportable.
– DERIVATIVES **unsupportably** adv.

**unsupported** • adj. **1** not supported. ➤Computing (of a program, device, etc.) not having assistance for the user available from a manufacturer or system manager. **2** not borne out by evidence or facts.

**unsure** • adj. **1** lacking confidence. **2** not fixed or certain.
– DERIVATIVES **unsurely** adv. **unsureness** n.

**unsurfaced** • adj. (of a road or path) not provided with a durable upper layer.

**unsurpassable** • adj. not able to be surpassed.
– DERIVATIVES **unsurpassably** adv.

**unsurpassed** • adj. better or greater than any other.

**unsurprising** • adj. not unexpected and so not causing surprise.
– DERIVATIVES **unsurprisingly** adv.

**unsuspected** • adj. **1** not known or thought to exist; not imagined as possible. **2** not regarded with suspicion.
– DERIVATIVES **unsuspectedly** adv.

**unsuspecting** • adj. not aware of the presence of danger; feeling no suspicion.
– DERIVATIVES **unsuspectingly** adv.

**unsustainable** • adj. **1** not able to be sustained. ➤Ecology upsetting the ecological balance by depleting natural resources. **2** not able to be upheld or defended.
– DERIVATIVES **unsustainably** adv.

**unswayed** • adj. not influenced or affected.

**unsweetened** • adj. (of food or drink) without added sugar or sweetener.

**unswerving** • adj. not changing or becoming weaker.
– DERIVATIVES **unswervingly** adv.

**unsworn** • adj. Law (of testimony or evidence) not given under oath.

**unsymmetrical** • adj. not symmetrical; asymmetrical.
– DERIVATIVES **unsymmetrically** adv.

**unsympathetic** • adj. **1** not sympathetic. ➤not showing approval of an idea or action. **2** not likeable.
– DERIVATIVES **unsympathetically** adv.

**unsystematic** • adj. not done or acting according to a fixed plan or system; unmethodical.
– DERIVATIVES **unsystematically** adv.

**untack** • v. remove the saddle and bridle from (a horse).

**untainted** • adj. not contaminated, polluted, or tainted.

**untameable** (also **untamable**) • adj. not capable of being tamed or controlled.

**untamed** • adj. not tamed or controlled. ➤(of land) wild or uncultivated: *the untamed wilderness.*

**untangle** • v. **1** free from tangles. **2** free from complications or confusion.

**untanned** • adj. **1** not converted into leather by tanning. **2** not tanned by exposure to the sun.

**untapped** • adj. (of a resource) not yet exploited or used.

**untarnished** • adj. **1** not tarnished. **2** not spoiled or ruined.

**untasted** • adj. (of food or drink) not sampled or tested for flavour.

**untaught** • adj. not having been taught or educated. ➤not acquired by teaching; natural or spontaneous.

**unteachable** • adj. (of a pupil or skill) unable to be taught.

**untempered** • adj. **1** not moderated or lessened. **2** (of a material) not brought to the proper hardness or consistency.

**untenable** • adj. not able to be maintained or defended against attack or objection.
– DERIVATIVES **untenability** n. **untenably** adv.

**untended** • adj. not cared for or looked after; neglected.

**untenured** • adj. (of a college teacher or post) without tenure.

**Untermensch** /ˈʊntəmɛn(t)ʃ, German ˈʊntɐmɛnʃ/ • n. (pl. **Untermenschen** /-mɛn(t)ʃ(ə)n, German -mɛnʃn/) a person considered racially or socially inferior.
– ORIGIN Ger., lit. 'underperson'.

**untested** • adj. not subjected to testing; unproven.
– DERIVATIVES **untestable** adj.

**unthaw** • v. N. Amer. melt or thaw.

**unthinkable** • adj. too unlikely or undesirable to be considered a possibility.
– DERIVATIVES **unthinkability** n. **unthinkably** adv.

**unthinking** • adj. without proper consideration.
– DERIVATIVES **unthinkingly** adv. **unthinkingness** n.

**unthought** • adj. (**unthought of**) not imagined or dreamed of.

**unthread** • v. **1** remove the thread from (a needle). **2** undo; unravel.

**unthreatening** • adj. not threatening.

**untidy** • adj. (**-ier, -iest**) not arranged tidily. ➤(of a person) not inclined to be neat.
– DERIVATIVES **untidily** adv. **untidiness** n.

**untie** • v. (**untying**) undo or unfasten (something tied).

**untied** • adj. **1** not fastened or knotted. **2** (of an international loan or aid) given without special conditions.

**until** • prep. & conj. up to (the point in time or the event mentioned).
– ORIGIN ME: from ON *und* 'as far as' + **TILL**[1] (the sense thus duplicated).

**untimely** • adj. happening or done at an unsuitable time; inappropriate. ➤(of a death or end) happening too soon or sooner than normal. • adv. archaic at a time that is unsuitable or premature.
– DERIVATIVES **untimeliness** n.

**untiring** • adj. continuing at the same rate without loss of vigour.
– DERIVATIVES **untiringly** adv.

**untitled** • adj. **1** (of a book or other work) having no title. **2** not having a title indicating high social or official rank.

**unto** • prep. **1** archaic term for **TO**. **2** archaic term for **UNTIL**.
– ORIGIN ME: from **UNTIL**, with **TO** replacing **TILL**[1] (in its northern dial. meaning 'to').

**untold** • adj. **1** too much or too many to be counted; indescribable: *thieves caused untold damage.* **2** not narrated or recounted.
– ORIGIN OE *unteald* 'not counted' (see **UN-**[1], **TOLD**).

**untouchable** • adj. **1** not able to be touched or affected. **2** unable to be matched or rivalled. **3** of or belonging to the lowest-caste Hindu group or the people outside the caste system. • n. a member of the lowest-caste Hindu group, with whom contact is traditionally held to defile members of higher castes.
– DERIVATIVES **untouchability** n.

**USAGE** untouchable

In senses relating to the traditional Hindu caste system, the term **untouchable** and the social restrictions accompanying it were declared illegal in the constitution of India in 1949 and of Pakistan in 1953. The official term today is **scheduled caste**.

**untouched** • adj. **1** not handled, used, or tasted. ➤(of a subject) not treated or discussed. **2** not affected, changed, or damaged in any way.

**untoward** • adj. unexpected and inappropriate or adverse.
– DERIVATIVES **untowardly** adv. **untowardness** n.

**untraceable** • adj. unable to be found or traced.
– DERIVATIVES **untraceably** adv.

**untracked** • adj. (of land) not previously traversed; without tracks.
– PHRASES **get untracked** US get into one's stride or find good form.

**untrained** • adj. not having been trained.
– DERIVATIVES **untrainable** adj.

**untrammelled** (US also **untrammeled**) • adj. not restricted or hampered.

**untransferable** • adj. not able to be transferred to another place, occupation, or person.

**untranslatable** /ˌʌntransˈleɪtəb(ə)l, ˌʌntrɑːns-, -z-/ • adj. not able to be translated.
– DERIVATIVES **untranslatability** n.

**untravelled** (US also **untraveled**) • adj. **1** not having travelled much. **2** (of a road or region) not journeyed along or through.

**untreatable** • adj. for whom or which no medical care is available or possible.

**untreated** • adj. **1** not given treatment. **2** not treated by the use of a chemical, physical, or biological agent: *untreated sewage*.

**untried** • adj. **1** not yet tested; inexperienced. **2** Law (of an accused person) not yet subjected to a trial in court.

**untrodden** • adj. not having been walked on.

**untroubled** • adj. not troubled.

**untrue** • adj. **1** false or incorrect. **2** not faithful or loyal. **3** not upright or level.
– DERIVATIVES **untruly** adv.

**untrustworthy** • adj. unable to be trusted.
– DERIVATIVES **untrustworthiness** n.

**untruth** • n. (pl. **untruths**) **1** a lie. **2** the quality of being false.

**untruthful** • adj. not truthful.
– DERIVATIVES **untruthfully** adv. **untruthfulness** n.

**untuck** • v. free from being tucked in or up.

**untuned** • adj. not tuned or in tune.

**unturned** • adj. not turned.

**untutored** • adj. not formally taught.

**untwine** • v. make or become unwound or untwisted.

**untwist** • v. open or cause to open from a twisted position.

**untying** present participle of **UNTIE**.

**untypical** • adj. unusual.
– DERIVATIVES **untypically** adv.

**unusable** • adj. not fit to be used.

**unused** • adj. **1** not used. **2** (**unused to**) not accustomed to.

**unusual** • adj. **1** not habitually or commonly done or occurring. **2** remarkable; exceptional.
– DERIVATIVES **unusually** adv. **unusualness** n.

**unutterable** • adj. too great or awful to describe.
– DERIVATIVES **unutterably** adv.

**unuttered** • adj. not spoken or expressed.

**unvalued** • adj. not valued.

**unvaried** • adj. not varied.

**unvarnished** • adj. **1** not varnished. **2** plain and straightforward.

**unvarying** • adj. not varying.
– DERIVATIVES **unvaryingly** adv. **unvaryingness** n.

**unveil** • v. **1** remove a veil or covering from. **2** show or announce publicly for the first time.

**unventilated** • adj. not ventilated.

**unverifiable** • adj. unable to be verified.

**unverified** • adj. not verified.

**unversed** • adj. (**unversed in**) not versed in.

**unviable** • adj. not viable.
– DERIVATIVES **unviability** n.

**unvisited** • adj. not visited.

**unvitiated** /ʌnˈvɪʃɪeɪtɪd/ • adj. archaic not corrupted.

**unvoiced** • adj. **1** unuttered. **2** Phonetics (of a speech sound) uttered without vibration of the vocal cords.

**unwaged** • adj. chiefly Brit. unemployed or doing unpaid work. ➤(of work) unpaid.

**unwalled** • adj. without walls.

**unwanted** • adj. not wanted.

**unwarned** • adj. not warned.

**unwarrantable** • adj. unjustifiable.
– DERIVATIVES **unwarrantably** adv.

**unwarranted** • adj. not warranted.

**unwary** • adj. not cautious.
– DERIVATIVES **unwarily** adv. **unwariness** n.

**unwashed** • adj. not washed.
– PHRASES **the (great) unwashed** derogatory the multitude of ordinary people.

**unwatchable** • adj. disturbing or uninteresting to watch.

**unwatched** • adj. not watched.

**unwavering** • adj. not wavering.
– DERIVATIVES **unwaveringly** adv.

**unweaned** • adj. not weaned.

**unwearable** • adj. not fit to be worn.

**unwearied** • adj. not wearied.
– DERIVATIVES **unweariedly** adv.

**unwearying** • adj. never tiring or slackening.
– DERIVATIVES **unwearyingly** adv.

**unwed** (also **unwedded**) • adj. not married.
– DERIVATIVES **unweddedness** n.

**unweight** • v. remove the weight from (a ski or skateboard) to make a turn more easily.
– ORIGIN 1930s: back-form. from **UNWEIGHTED**.

**unweighted** • adj. not weighted.

**unwelcome** • adj. not welcome.
– DERIVATIVES **unwelcomely** adv. **unwelcomeness** n.

**unwelcoming** • adj. inhospitable.

**unwell** • adj. ill.

**unwept** • adj. chiefly poetic/literary not mourned or lamented.

**unwhipped** • adj. Brit. (of an MP or vote) not subject to a party whip.

**unwholesome** • adj. not wholesome.
– DERIVATIVES **unwholesomely** adv. **unwholesomeness** n.

**unwieldy** • adj. (**-ier, -iest**) hard to move or manage because of its size, shape, or weight.
– DERIVATIVES **unwieldily** adv. **unwieldiness** n.
– ORIGIN ME (in the sense 'lacking strength, infirm'): from **UN-**[1] + **WIELDY** (in the obs. sense 'active').

**unwilling** • adj. not willing.
– DERIVATIVES **unwillingly** adv. **unwillingness** n.

**unwind** • v. (past and past part. **unwound**) **1** undo or be undone after winding or being wound. **2** relax.

**unwinking** • adj. (of a stare or light) unwavering.
– DERIVATIVES **unwinkingly** adv.

**unwinnable** • adj. not winnable.

**unwisdom** • n. folly.

**unwise** • adj. foolish.
– DERIVATIVES **unwisely** adv.
– ORIGIN OE *unwīs* (see **UN-**[1], **WISE**[1]).

**unwished** • adj. not wished for.

**unwitting** • adj. **1** not aware of the full facts: *an unwitting accomplice*. **2** unintentional.
– DERIVATIVES **unwittingly** adv. **unwittingness** n.
– ORIGIN OE *unwitende* 'not knowing or realizing' (see **UN-**[1], **WIT**[2]).

**unwomanly** • adj. not womanly.

– DERIVATIVES **unwomanliness** n.

**unwonted** /ʌn'wəʊntɪd/ ● **adj.** unaccustomed or unusual.

– DERIVATIVES **unwontedly** adv. **unwontedness** n.

**unwooded** ● **adj. 1** having few trees. **2** (of a wine) not stored in a wooden cask.

**unworkable** ● **adj. 1** impractical. **2** (of a material) not able to be worked.

– DERIVATIVES **unworkability** n. **unworkably** adv.

**unworked** ● **adj.** not cultivated, mined, or carved.

**unworkmanlike** ● **adj.** badly done or made.

**unworldly** ● **adj. 1** having little awareness of the realities of life. **2** not seeming to belong to this world.

– DERIVATIVES **unworldliness** n.

**unworn** ● **adj.** not worn.

**unworried** ● **adj.** not worried.

**unworthy** ● **adj.** (**-ier**, **-iest**) not worthy.

– DERIVATIVES **unworthily** adv. **unworthiness** n.

**unwound**[1] ● **adj.** (of a clock or watch) not wound or wound up.

**unwound**[2] past and past participle of **UNWIND**.

**unwounded** ● **adj.** not wounded.

**unwrap** ● **v.** (**unwrapped**, **unwrapping**) remove the wrapping from.

**unwrinkled** ● **adj.** not wrinkled.

**unwritable** ● **adj.** not able to be written.

**unwritten** ● **adj. 1** not written. **2** (especially of a law) resting originally on custom or judicial decision rather than on statute.

**unyielding** ● **adj.** not yielding.

– DERIVATIVES **unyieldingly** adv. **unyieldingness** n.

**unyoke** ● **v. 1** release (animals) from a yoke. **2** archaic cease work.

**unzip** ● **v.** (**unzipped**, **unzipping**) **1** unfasten the zip of. **2** Computing decompress (a compressed file).

**up** ● **adv. 1** towards a higher place or position. ➤ to or at a place perceived as higher: *a walk up to the shops.* ➤ (of the sun) visible in the sky. ➤ towards the north. ➤ Brit. towards or in the capital or a major city. ➤ Brit. at or to a university, especially Oxford or Cambridge. **2** (often **up and about**) out of bed. **3** to the place where someone is. **4** at or to a higher level or value. ➤ winning by a specified margin. **5** into the desired or a proper condition. ➤ so as to be finished or closed. **6** into a happy mood. **7** in a publicly visible place. **8** (of sailing) against the current or the wind. ➤ (of a ship's helm) moved round to windward. **9** Baseball at bat. **10** (**up with** ——) expressing support for a person or thing. ● **prep. 1** from a lower to a higher point of. **2** from one end to another of (a street or other area). **3** informal at or to (a place). ● **adj. 1** directed or moving towards a higher place or position. ➤ denoting trains travelling towards the main terminus. **2** (of the road) being repaired. **3** (of a jockey) in the saddle. **4** cheerful. **5** (of a computer system) working properly. **6** at an end. **7** Physics denoting a flavour of quark having a charge of +⅔. ● **n.** informal a period of good fortune. ● **v.** (**upped**, **upping**) **1** (**up and do something**) informal do something abruptly or boldly. **2** increase (a level or amount). **3** lift up.

– PHRASES **it is all up with** informal it is the end or there is no hope for. **on the up and up** informal **1** Brit. steadily improving. **2** chiefly N. Amer. honest; sincere. **something is up** informal something unusual or undesirable is happening. **up against** close to or touching. ➤ informal confronted with. **up and doing** active. **up and down** in various places throughout. **up and running** functioning. **up before** appearing for a hearing in the presence of (a judge, magistrate, etc.). **up for 1** available for. **2** due or being considered for. **3** informal ready to take part in. **up hill and down dale** all over the place. **up on** well informed about. **up to 1** as far as. ➤ (also **up until**) until. **2** indicating a maximum amount. **3** [with neg. or in questions] good enough for. **4** capable of. **5** the duty or choice of. **6** informal occupied with. **up top** Brit. informal in the way of intelligence. **up yours** vulgar slang expressing contemptuous defiance or rejection. **what's up?** informal what is going on? ➤ what is the matter?

– ORIGIN OE *up(p)*, *uppe*, of Gmc origin.

**up-** ● **prefix 1** (added to verbs and their derivatives) upwards: *upturned.* ➤ to a more recent time: *update.* **2** (added to nouns) denoting motion up: *uphill.* **3** (added to nouns) higher: *upland.* ➤ increased: *up-tempo.*

**up-anchor** ● **v.** (of a ship) weigh anchor.

**up-and-coming** ● **adj.** likely to become successful.

– DERIVATIVES **up-and-comer** n.

**up-and-over** ● **adj.** (of a door) opened by being raised and pushed back into a horizontal position.

**up-and-under** ● **n.** Rugby a high kick allowing time for teammates to reach the point where the ball will come down.

**Upanishad** /u:'panɪʃad/ ● **n.** each of a series of Hindu sacred treatises written in Sanskrit and expounding the Vedas.

– ORIGIN from Sanskrit, lit. 'sitting near (i.e. at the feet of a master)', from *upa* 'near' + *ni-ṣad* 'sit down'.

**upas** /'ju:pəs/ ● **n. 1** a tropical Asian tree with poisonous milky sap. [*Antiaris toxicaria.*] **2** (in folklore) a Javanese tree alleged to poison its surroundings.

– ORIGIN C18: from Malay (*pohun*) *upas* 'poison'.

**upbeat** ● **n.** (in music) an unaccented beat preceding an accented beat. ● **adj.** informal cheerful; optimistic.

**upbraid** ● **v.** scold or reproach.

– ORIGIN OE *upbrēdan* 'allege as a basis for censure', based on **BRAID** in the obs. sense 'brandish'.

**upbringing** ● **n.** the treatment and instruction received from one's parents throughout childhood.

– ORIGIN C15: from obs. *upbring* 'to rear' (see **UP-**, **BRING**).

**upcast** ● **n.** (also **upcast shaft**) a shaft through which air leaves a mine. ● **v.** (past and past part. **-cast**) cast upward.

**upchuck** ● **v. & n.** N. Amer. informal vomit.

**upcoming** ● **adj.** forthcoming.

**upcountry** ● **adv. & adj.** inland.

**update** ● **v.** /ʌp'deɪt/ **1** make more modern. **2** give the latest information to. ● **n.** /'ʌpdeɪt/ an act of updating or an updated version.

– DERIVATIVES **updatable** adj. (Computing).

**updraught** (US **updraft**) ● **n.** an upward current of air.

**upend** ● **v.** set or turn on its end or upside down.

**upfield** ● **adv. 1** (in sport) in or to a position nearer to the opponents' end of a field. **2** Physics in a direction corresponding to increasing field strength.

**upfront** informal ● **adv.** (usu. **up front**) **1** at the front; in front. **2** (of a payment) in advance. ● **adj. 1** bold and frank. **2** (of a payment) made in advance. **3** chiefly N. Amer. front or most prominent.

**upgrade** ● **v.** raise to a higher standard or rank. ● **n.** an act of upgrading or an upgraded version.

– PHRASES **on the upgrade** improving.

– DERIVATIVES **upgradeability** (also **upgradability**) n. **upgradeable** (also **upgradable**) adj.

**upgrowth** ● **n.** the process or result of growing upwards. ➤ an upward growth.

**upheaval** ● **n. 1** a violent or sudden change or disruption. **2** an upward displacement of part of the earth's crust.

**upheave** ● **v.** poetic/literary heave or lift up.

**uphill** ● **adv.** towards the top of a slope. ● **adj. 1** sloping upwards. **2** difficult: *an uphill struggle.* ● **n.** an upward slope.

**uphold** ● **v.** (past and past part. **-held**) confirm or support. ➤ maintain (a custom or practice).

– DERIVATIVES **upholder** n.

**upholster** /ʌp'həʊlstə, -'hɒl-/ ● **v.** provide (furniture) with a soft, padded covering. ➤ cover the walls or furniture in (a room) with textiles.

– ORIGIN C19: back-form. from **UPHOLSTERER**.

**upholsterer** ● **n.** a person who upholsters furniture.

– ORIGIN C17: from the obs. noun *upholster* (from **UPHOLD** in the obs. sense 'keep in repair') + **-STER**.

**upholstery** ● **n. 1** soft, padded textile used to upholster furniture. **2** the art or practice of upholstering.

**upkeep** ● **n.** the process of keeping something in good condition. ➤ the cost of this or of supporting a person.

**upland** • n. (also **uplands**) an area of high or hilly land.

**uplift** • v. **1** [usu. as adj. **uplifted**] raise. **2** (**be uplifted**) (of an island, mountain, etc.) be created by an upward movement of the earth's surface. **3** [usu. as adj. **uplifting**] elevate morally or spiritually. • n. **1** an act of uplifting. **2** support from a garment, especially for a woman's bust. **3** a morally or spiritually uplifting influence.
– DERIVATIVES **uplifter** n.

**uplighter** (also **uplight**) • n. a lamp designed to throw light upwards.
– DERIVATIVES **uplighting** n.

**uplink** • n. a communications link to a satellite. • v. provide with or send by such a link.

**upload** Computing • v. transfer (data) to a larger computer system. • n. the action or process of uploading.

**upmarket** • adj. & adv. chiefly Brit. towards or relating to the more expensive or affluent sector of the market.

**upmost** • adj. uppermost.

**upon** • prep. more formal term for **ON**.
– ORIGIN ME: from **UP** + **ON**, suggested by ON *upp á*.

**upper**[1] • adj. **1** situated above another part. ➤ higher in position or status. ➤ (often **Upper**) Geology & Archaeology denoting a younger (and hence typically shallower) part of a stratigraphic or archaeological division: *the Upper Palaeolithic.* **2** situated on higher ground. **3** [in place names] situated to the north. • n. the part of a boot or shoe above the sole.
– PHRASES **have** (or **gain**) **the upper hand** have (or gain) an advantage or control. **on one's uppers** informal extremely short of money. **the upper crust** informal the upper classes.
– ORIGIN ME: from the adj. **UP** + **-ER**[2].

**upper**[2] • n. informal a stimulating drug, especially amphetamine.
– ORIGIN 1960s: from the verb **UP** + **-ER**[1].

**upper case** • n. capital letters.
– ORIGIN referring orig. to two type cases positioned on an angled stand, the case containing the capital letters being higher.

**upper chamber** • n. another term for **UPPER HOUSE**.

**upper class** • n. [treated as sing. or pl.] the social group with the highest status, especially the aristocracy. • adj. of, relating to, or characteristic of the upper class.

**upperclassman** • n. (pl. **-men**) US a junior or senior in high school or college.

**uppercut** • n. **1** a punch delivered with an upwards motion and the arm bent. **2** Baseball an upward batting stroke.

**upper house** • n. the higher house in a bicameral parliament or similar legislature. ➤ (**the Upper House**) (in the UK) the House of Lords.

**uppermost** • adj. (also **upmost**) highest in place, rank, or importance. • adv. at or to the uppermost position.

**upper regions** • pl. n. archaic or poetic/literary the sky or heaven.

**upper school** • n. **1** a secondary school for children aged from about fourteen upwards. **2** the section of a school comprising or catering for the older pupils.

**upper works** • pl. n. the parts of a fully laden ship above water.

**uppish** • adj. informal arrogantly self-assertive.
– DERIVATIVES **uppishly** adv. **uppishness** n.

**uppity** • adj. informal self-important.
– ORIGIN C19: a fanciful formation from **UP**.

**upraise** • v. raise to a higher level.

**uprate** • v. **1** increase the value of. **2** improve the performance of.

**upright** • adj. **1** vertical; erect. ➤ (of a piano) having vertical strings. **2** greater in height than breadth. **3** strictly honourable or honest. • adv. in or into an upright position. • n. **1** a vertical post, structure, or line. **2** an upright piano.
– DERIVATIVES **uprightly** adv. **uprightness** n.
– ORIGIN OE *upriht*, of Gmc origin; see **UP**, **RIGHT**.

**uprise** • v. (past **-rose**; past part. **-risen**) archaic or poetic/literary rise up.

**uprising** • n. an act of resistance or rebellion.

**upriver** • adv. & adj. towards or situated at a point nearer the source of a river.

**uproar** • n. a loud and impassioned noise or disturbance. ➤ a public expression of outrage.
– ORIGIN C16: from MDu. *uproer*, from *op* 'up' + *roer* 'confusion', assoc. with **ROAR**.

**uproarious** • adj. **1** characterized by or provoking loud noise or uproar. **2** very funny.
– DERIVATIVES **uproariously** adv. **uproariousness** n.

**uproot** • v. **1** pull (a plant, tree, etc.) out of the ground. **2** move (someone) from their home or a familiar location. **3** eradicate.
– DERIVATIVES **uprooter** n.

**uprose** past of **UPRISE**.

**uprush** • n. a sudden upward surge or flow.

**UPS** • abbrev. Computing uninterruptible power supply.

**ups-a-daisy** • exclam. variant spelling of **UPSY-DAISY**.

**upscale** • adj. & adv. N. Amer. upmarket.

**upset** • v. /ʌpˈsɛt/ (**-setting**; past and past part. **-set**) **1** make unhappy, disappointed, or worried. **2** knock over. **3** disrupt. ➤ disturb the digestion of (a person's stomach). **4** [often as noun **upsetting**] shorten and thicken the end or edge of (a metal bar, wheel rim, or other object). • n. /ˈʌpsɛt/ **1** a state of being upset. **2** an unexpected result or situation. • adj. **1** /ʌpˈsɛt/ unhappy, disappointed, or worried. **2** /ˈʌpsɛt/ (of a person's stomach) having disturbed digestion.
– DERIVATIVES **upsetter** n. **upsetting** adj. **upsettingly** adv.

**upset price** • n. a reserve price in an auction.

**upshift** • v. **1** change to a higher gear. **2** increase. • n. **1** a change to a higher gear. **2** an increase.

**upshot** • n. the eventual outcome or conclusion.

**upside** • n. **1** the positive aspect of something. **2** a rise in share prices.

**upside down** • adv. & adj. **1** with the upper part where the lower part should be. **2** in or into total disorder.
– ORIGIN ME: orig. *up so down*, perh. in the sense 'up as if down'.

**upside-down cake** • n. a sponge cake baked over a layer of fruit in syrup and inverted for serving.

**upsides** • adv. (especially in horse racing) alongside. ➤ (**upsides with**) archaic even or equal with.
– ORIGIN C18: from **UPSIDE** in the sense 'upper part' + the adverbial suffix *-s*.

**upsilon** /ʌpˈsʌɪlən, juːp-, ˈʊpsɪlɒn, ˈjuːp-/ • n. the twentieth letter of the Greek alphabet (Υ, υ), transliterated as 'u' or (chiefly in English words derived through Latin) as 'y'.
– ORIGIN Gk, lit. 'slender U', from *psilos* 'slender', referring to the need to distinguish upsilon from the diphthong *oi*: in late Gk the two had the same pronunc.

**upsize** • v. chiefly N. Amer. increase or cause to increase in size or complexity.

**upslope** • n. an upward slope. • adv. & adj. at or towards a higher point on a slope.

**upstage** • adv. & adj. **1** at or towards the back of a stage. **2** [as adj.] informal, dated aloof. • v. **1** divert attention from (someone) towards oneself. **2** (of an actor) move towards the back of a stage to make (another actor) face away from the audience.

**upstairs** • adv. on or to an upper floor. • adj. (also **upstair**) situated on an upper floor. • n. an upper floor.

**upstand** • n. an upright structure or object.

**upstanding** • adj. **1** respectable. **2** erect. **3** (of an animal) strong and healthy.

**upstart** • n. **1** derogatory a person who has risen suddenly to prominence, especially one who behaves arrogantly. **2** Gymnastics a series of movements by which a gymnast swings to a position supported by their arms above a bar, especially at the start of a routine.

**upstate** US • adj. & adv. of, in, or to a part of a state remote from its large cities, especially the northern part. • n. an upstate area.
– DERIVATIVES **upstater** n.

**upstream** ● **adv. & adj.** situated or moving in the direction opposite to that in which a stream or river flows.

**upstroke** ● **n.** an upwards stroke.

**upsurge** ● **n.** an increase.

**upswept** ● **adj.** curved, sloping, or directed upwards. ➤(of the hair) brushed upwards and off the face.

**upswing** ● **n.** an upward trend.

**upsy-daisy** (also **ups-a-daisy**, **oops-a-daisy**) ● **exclam.** expressing encouragement to a child who has fallen or is being lifted.
– ORIGIN C19: alt. of earlier *up-a-daisy*; cf. **LACKADAISICAL**.

**uptake** ● **n.** the action of taking up or making use of something.
– PHRASES **be quick** (or **slow**) **on the uptake** informal be quick (or slow) to understand something.

**uptempo** ● **adj. & adv.** Music played with a fast or increased tempo.

**upthrow** ● **v.** (past **-threw**; past part. **-thrown**) Geology displace upwards.

**upthrust** ● **n. 1** Physics the upward force that a fluid exerts on a body floating in it. **2** Geology the upward movement of part of the earth's surface. ● **v.** [usu. as adj. **upthrust**] thrust upwards.

**uptick** ● **n.** N. Amer. a small increase.

**uptight** ● **adj.** informal nervously tense or angry.

**uptime** ● **n.** time during which a machine, especially a computer, is in operation.

**up to date** ● **adj.** incorporating or aware of the latest developments and trends.

**uptown** chiefly N. Amer. ● **adj. & adv.** of, in, or into the residential area of a town or city. ➤[as adj.] of or characteristic of an affluent area or people. ● **n.** an uptown area.
– DERIVATIVES **uptowner** n.

**upturn** ● **n.** an improvement or upward trend. ● **v.** [usu. as adj. **upturned**] turn upwards or upside down.

**UPU** ● **abbrev.** Universal Postal Union.

**uPVC** ● **abbrev.** unplasticized polyvinyl chloride, a rigid form of PVC used for pipework and window frames.

**upward** ● **adv.** (also **upwards**) towards a higher point or level. ● **adj.** moving or leading towards a higher point or level.
– PHRASES **upwards** (or **upward**) **of** more than.
– DERIVATIVES **upwardly** adv.

**upwarp** ● **n.** Geology a broad elevated area of the earth's surface.

**upwelling** ● **n.** a rising up of seawater, magma, or other liquid. ● **adj.** (especially of emotion) building up.

**upwind** /ʌp'wɪnd/ ● **adv. & adj.** into the wind.

**ur-** /ʊə/ ● **comb. form** primitive; original; earliest: *urtext*.
– ORIGIN from Ger.

**uracil** /'jʊərəsɪl/ ● **n.** Biochemistry a compound found in living tissue as a constituent base of RNA (and replaced by thymine in DNA).
– ORIGIN C19: from *ur*(*ea*) + *ac*(*etic*) + **-IL**.

**uraemia** /jʊ'ri:mɪə/ (US **uremia**) ● **n.** Medicine a raised level in the blood of urea and other nitrogenous waste compounds.
– DERIVATIVES **uraemic** adj.
– ORIGIN C19: mod. L., from Gk *ouron* 'urine' + *haima* 'blood'.

**uraeus** /jʊ'ri:əs/ ● **n.** (pl. **uraei** /jʊ'ri:ʌɪ/) a sacred serpent as an emblem of supreme power, represented on the headdresses of ancient Egyptian deities and sovereigns.
– ORIGIN C19: mod. L., from Gk *ouraios*, representing the Egyptian word for 'cobra'.

**Ural-Altaic** ● **adj.** relating to or denoting a hypothetical language group formerly proposed to include the Uralic and Altaic languages.

**Uralic** /jʊ'ralɪk/ ● **adj. 1** relating to or denoting a family of languages comprising the Finno-Ugric and Samoyedic groups. **2** of or relating to the Ural Mountains or surrounding areas. ● **n.** the Uralic languages collectively.

**uraninite** /jʊ'ranɪnʌɪt/ ● **n.** a black, grey, or brown mineral consisting mainly of uranium dioxide.

**uranium** /jʊ'reɪnɪəm/ ● **n.** the chemical element of atomic number 92, a grey dense radioactive metal used as a fuel in nuclear reactors. (Symbol: **U**)
– ORIGIN C18: mod. L., from **URANUS**.

**urano-**[1] /'jʊər(ə)nəʊ/ ● **comb. form** relating to the heavens: *uranography*.
– ORIGIN from Gk *ouranos* 'heavens, sky'.

**urano-**[2] /'jʊər(ə)nəʊ/ ● **comb. form** representing **URANIUM**.

**uranography** /,jʊərə'nɒgrəfi/ ● **n.** archaic the branch of astronomy concerned with describing and mapping the stars.
– DERIVATIVES **uranographer** n. **uranographic** adj.

**Uranus** /'jʊərənəs, jʊ'reɪnəs/ ● **n.** a planet of the solar system, seventh in order from the sun.

**urban** ● **adj.** of or relating to a town or city.
– DERIVATIVES **urbanism** n. **urbanist** n. **urbanization** (also **-isation**) n. **urbanize** (also **-ise**) v.
– ORIGIN C17: from L. *urbanus*, from *urbs*, *urb-* 'city'.

**urban district** ● **n.** Brit. historical a group of urban communities governed by an elected council.

**urbane** /ə:'beɪn/ ● **adj.** (especially of a man) suave, courteous, and refined.
– DERIVATIVES **urbanely** adv.
– ORIGIN C16 (in the sense 'urban'): from Fr. *urbain* or L. *urbanus* (see **URBAN**).

**urbanite** ● **n.** informal a town or city dweller.

**urbanity** ● **n. 1** an urbane quality. **2** urban life.

**urban myth** (also chiefly N. Amer. **urban legend**) ● **n.** an entertaining story or piece of information of uncertain origin that is circulated as though true.

**urban renewal** ● **n.** the redevelopment of slum areas in a large city.

**urbs** /ə:bz/ ● **n.** chiefly poetic/literary the city.
– ORIGIN from L.

**URC** ● **abbrev.** United Reformed Church.

**urchin** /'ə:tʃɪn/ ● **n. 1** a mischievous child, especially a raggedly dressed one. **2** archaic a goblin. **3** chiefly dialect a hedgehog. **4** short for **SEA URCHIN**.
– ORIGIN ME *hirchon*, *urchon* 'hedgehog', from ONorth. Fr. *herichon*, based on L. *hericius* 'hedgehog'.

**Urdu** /'ʊədu:, 'ə:du:/ ● **n.** an Indic language closely related to Hindi.
– ORIGIN from Pers. (*zabān-i-*)*urdū* '(language of the) camp' (because it developed as a lingua franca after the Muslim invasions between the occupying armies and the people of Delhi), *urdū* being from Turkic *ordu* (see **HORDE**).

**-ure** ● **suffix** forming nouns: **1** denoting an action, process, or result: *closure*. **2** denoting an office or function: *judicature*. **3** denoting a collective: *legislature*.
– ORIGIN from OFr. *-ure*, from L. *-ura*.

**urea** /jʊ'ri:ə, 'jʊərɪə/ ● **n.** Biochemistry a colourless crystalline compound which is the main nitrogenous breakdown product of protein metabolism in mammals and is excreted in urine.
– ORIGIN C19: mod. L., from Fr. *urée*, from Gk *ouron* 'urine'.

**uremia** ● **n.** US spelling of **URAEMIA**.

**ureter** /jʊ'ri:tə, 'jʊərɪtə/ ● **n.** the duct by which urine passes from the kidney to the bladder or cloaca.
– DERIVATIVES **ureteral** adj. **ureteric** /jʊərɪ'tɛrɪk/ adj.
– ORIGIN C16: from Fr. *uretère* or mod. L. *ureter*, from Gk *ourētēr*, from *ourein* 'urinate'.

**urethane** /'jʊərɪθeɪn, jʊ'rɛθeɪn/ ● **n. 1** Chemistry ethyl carbamate, a synthetic crystalline compound used to make pesticides and fungicides. **2** short for **POLYURETHANE**.
– ORIGIN C19: from Fr. *uréthane* (see **UREA**, **ETHANE**).

**urethra** /jʊ'ri:θrə/ ● **n.** Anatomy & Zoology the duct by which urine is conveyed out of the body, and which in male vertebrates also conveys semen.
– DERIVATIVES **urethral** adj.
– ORIGIN C17: from late L., from Gk *ourēthra*, from *ourein* 'urinate'.

**urethritis** /,jʊri:'θrʌɪtɪs/ ● **n.** Medicine inflammation of the urethra.

**urge** ● **v.** encourage or entreat earnestly to do something. ➤strongly recommend. ➤encourage to move more quickly. ➤(**urge someone on**) encourage someone to

continue. ● n. a strong desire or impulse.
– ORIGIN C16: from L. *urgere* 'press, drive'.

**urgent** ● adj. **1** requiring immediate action or attention. **2** earnest and insistent.
– DERIVATIVES **urgency** n. **urgently** adv.
– ORIGIN C15: from OFr., from L. *urgent-* 'pressing, driving', from *urgere* (see **URGE**).

**urger** /ˈəːdʒə/ ● n. Austral. informal **1** a tipster. **2** a racketeer.

**-uria** ● comb. form in nouns denoting that a substance is present in the urine, especially in excess: *glycosuria*.
– ORIGIN mod. L., from Gk *-ouria*, from *ouron* 'urine'.

**uric acid** ● n. Biochemistry an almost insoluble nitrogenous compound which is the main excretory product of birds, reptiles, and insects.
– DERIVATIVES **urate** n.
– ORIGIN C19: from Fr. *urique*, from *urine* (see **URINE**).

**uridine** /ˈjʊərɪdiːn/ ● n. Biochemistry a nucleoside consisting of uracil combined with ribose.

**urinal** /jʊˈrʌɪn(ə)l, ˈjʊərɪn(ə)l/ ● n. a receptacle into which men may urinate, typically attached to the wall in a public toilet.

**urinalysis** /ˌjʊərɪˈnalɪsɪs/ ● n. (pl. **urinalyses** /-siːz/) Medicine analysis of urine by physical, chemical, and microscopical means.

**urinary** ● adj. of or relating to urine. ➤ relating to or denoting the organs, structures, and ducts in which urine is produced and discharged.

**urinate** ● v. discharge urine.
– DERIVATIVES **urination** n.
– ORIGIN C16: from med. L. *urinat-*, *urinare* 'urinate'.

**urine** /ˈjʊərɪn, -rʌɪn/ ● n. a pale yellowish fluid stored in the bladder and discharged through the urethra, consisting of excess water and substances removed from the blood by the kidneys.
– ORIGIN ME: via OFr. from L. *urina*.

**URL** ● abbrev. Computing uniform (or universal) resource locator, the address of a World Wide Web page.

**urn** ● n. **1** a tall, rounded vase with a stem and base, especially one for storing a cremated person's ashes. **2** a large metal container with a tap, in which tea or coffee is made and kept hot. ● v. archaic place in an urn.
– ORIGIN ME: from L. *urna*; rel. to *urceus* 'pitcher'.

**uro-**[1] ● comb. form of or relating to urine or the urinary organs: *urogenital*.
– ORIGIN from Gk *ouron* 'urine'.

**uro-**[2] ● comb. form Zoology relating to a tail or the caudal region: *urodele*.
– ORIGIN from Gk *oura* 'tail'.

**uroboros** /ˌjʊərə(ʊ)ˈbɒrəs/ (also **ouroboros**) ● n. a circular depiction of a snake or dragon swallowing its tail, symbolizing wholeness or infinity.
– DERIVATIVES **uroboric** adj.
– ORIGIN 1940s: from Gk (*drakōn*) *ouroboros* '(snake) devouring its tail'.

**Urochordata** /ˌjʊərə(ʊ)kɔːˈdeɪtə/ ● pl. n. Zoology a subphylum of chordate animals comprising the tunicates.
– DERIVATIVES **urochordate** n. & adj.
– ORIGIN mod. L., from **URO-**[2] + **CHORDATA**.

**Urodela** /ˌjʊərə(ʊ)ˈdiːlə/ ● pl. n. Zoology an order of amphibians comprising the newts and salamanders.
– DERIVATIVES **urodele** /ˈjʊərə(ʊ)diːl/ n. & adj.
– ORIGIN mod. L., from **URO-**[2] 'tail' + Gk *dēlos* 'evident'.

**urogenital** ● adj. relating to or denoting both the urinary and genital organs.

**urology** /jʊˈrɒlədʒi/ ● n. the branch of medicine concerned with the urinary system.
– DERIVATIVES **urologic** adj. **urological** adj. **urologist** n.

**uropygium** /ˌjʊərə(ʊ)ˈpɪdʒɪəm/ ● n. Zoology the rump of a bird.
– DERIVATIVES **uropygial** adj.
– ORIGIN C18: via med. L. from Gk *ouropugion*.

**uroscopy** /jʊˈrɒskəpi/ ● n. Medicine, historical the diagnostic examination of urine by simple inspection.

**ursine** /ˈəːsʌɪn, -ɪn/ ● adj. of, relating to, or resembling bears.
– ORIGIN C16: from L. *ursinus*, from *ursus* 'bear'.

**Ursuline** /ˈəːsjʊlʌɪn, -lɪn/ ● n. a nun of an order founded in northern Italy in 1535 for nursing the sick and teaching girls. ● adj. of or relating to this order.
– ORIGIN from St *Ursula*, the founder's patron saint, + **-INE**[1].

**urtext** /ˈuːətɛkst/ ● n. (pl. **urtexte** /-tə/) an original or the earliest version of a text.

**urticaria** /ˌəːtɪˈkɛːrɪə/ ● n. Medicine a rash of round, red weals on the skin which itch intensely, caused by an allergic reaction.
– ORIGIN C18: mod. L., from L. *urtica* 'nettle'.

**urticate** /ˈəːtɪkeɪt/ ● v. sting or prickle like a burn from a nettle.
– DERIVATIVES **urtication** n.
– ORIGIN C19 (earlier (C17) as *urtication*): from med. L. *urticat-*, *urticare* 'to sting', from L. *urtica* (see **URTICARIA**).

**Uruguayan** /ˌjʊərəˈgwʌɪən, Spanish uruˈɣwajən/ ● n. a native or inhabitant of Uruguay. ● adj. of or relating to Uruguay.

**US** ● abbrev. **1** Brit. undersecretary. **2** United States. **3** Brit. informal unserviceable.

**us** ● pron. [first person pl.] **1** used by a speaker to refer to himself or herself and one or more others as the object of a verb or preposition. ➤ used after the verb 'to be' and after 'than' or 'as'. ➤ N. Amer. informal to or for ourselves. **2** informal me.
– ORIGIN OE *ūs*, accusative and dative of **WE**, of Gmc origin.

**USA** ● abbrev. **1** United States of America. **2** United States Army.

**usable** (also **useable**) ● adj. able to be used.
– DERIVATIVES **usability** n.

**USAF** ● abbrev. United States Air Force.

**usage** ● n. **1** the action of using something or the fact of being used. **2** habitual or customary practice.

**usance** /ˈjuːz(ə)ns/ ● n. archaic **1** usage. **2** the time allowed for the payment of foreign bills of exchange.
– ORIGIN ME: from OFr., from the base of *user* 'to use'.

**USB** ● abbrev. Computing universal serial bus.

**USD** ● abbrev. United States dollar(s).

**use** ● v. /juːz/ **1** take, hold, or deploy as a means of accomplishing or achieving something. ➤ (**use something up**) consume or expend the whole of something. ➤ informal take (an illegal drug). **2** treat in a particular way. ➤ exploit unfairly. ➤ (**be used up**) informal (of a person) be worn out. **3** (**one could use**) informal one would like or benefit from. **4** /juːst/ (**used to**) did repeatedly or existed in the past. **5** /juːst/ (**be/get used to**) be or become familiar with through experience. ● n. /juːs/ **1** the action of using or state of being used. ➤ the ability or power to exercise or manipulate something: *he lost the use of his legs*. ➤ a purpose for or way in which something can be used. **2** value; advantage. **3** Law, historical the benefit or profit of lands, especially lands in the possession of another who holds them solely for the beneficiary. **4** the characteristic ritual and liturgy of a Church or diocese.
– PHRASES **have no use for** informal dislike or be impatient with. **make use of** benefit from. **use and wont** formal established custom. **use someone's name** cite someone as an authority or reference.
– ORIGIN ME: the noun from OFr. *us*, from L. *usus*, from *uti* 'to use'; the verb from OFr. *user*, based on L. *uti*.

**useable** ● adj. variant spelling of **USABLE**.

**use-by date** ● n. chiefly Brit. the recommended date by which a perishable product should be used or consumed.

**used** /juːzd/ ● adj. having already been used. ➤ secondhand.

**useful** ● adj. **1** able to be used for a practical purpose or in several ways. **2** informal very able or competent.
– PHRASES **make oneself useful** do something that is of some value or benefit.
– DERIVATIVES **usefully** adv. **usefulness** n.

**useful load** ● n. the load carried by an aircraft in addition to its own weight.

**useless** ● adj. **1** serving no purpose. **2** informal having little ability or skill.
– DERIVATIVES **uselessly** adv. **uselessness** n.

**Usenet** ● **n.** Computing an Internet service consisting of thousands of newsgroups.

**user** ● **n. 1** a person who uses or operates something. **2** a person who exploits others. **3** Law the continued use or enjoyment of a right.

**user-friendly** ● **adj.** easy to use or understand.
– DERIVATIVES **user-friendliness** n.

**usher** ● **n. 1** a person who shows people to their seats in a theatre or cinema or at a wedding. **2** Brit. a person employed to walk before a person of high rank on special occasions. **3** an official in a law court who swears in jurors and witnesses and keeps order. **4** archaic an assistant teacher. ● **v.** show or guide somewhere.
– ORIGIN ME (denoting a doorkeeper): from Anglo-Norman Fr. *usser*, from med. L. *ustiarius*, from L. *ostiarius*, from *ostium* 'door'.

**usherette** ● **n.** a woman who shows people to their seats in a cinema or theatre.

**USN** ● **abbrev.** United States Navy.

**Usonian** /juːˈsəʊnɪən/ ● **adj. 1** of or relating to the United States. **2** denoting inexpensive flat-roofed buildings designed in the 1930s by the architect Frank Lloyd Wright. ● **n. 1** a native or inhabitant of the United States. **2** a Usonian house.

**usquebaugh** /ˈʌskwɪbɔː/ ● **n.** chiefly Irish & Scottish whisky.
– ORIGIN C16: from Ir. and Sc. Gaelic *uisge beatha* 'water of life'; cf. **WHISKY**.

**USS** ● **abbrev.** United States Ship.

**USSR** ● **abbrev.** historical Union of Soviet Socialist Republics.

**usual** ● **adj.** habitually or typically occurring or done. ● **n.** (**the/one's usual**) informal the drink someone habitually prefers. ➤the thing which is typically done or present.
– DERIVATIVES **usually** adv. **usualness** n.
– ORIGIN ME: from OFr., or from late L. *usualis*, from L. *usus* (see **USE**).

**usucaption** /ˌjuːzjʊˈkapʃ(ə)n/ (also **usucapion** /ˌjuːzjʊˈkeɪpɪən/) ● **n.** Roman Law, chiefly historical the acquisition of a title or right to property by uninterrupted and undisputed possession for a prescribed term.
– ORIGIN C17: from med. L. *usucaptio(n-)*, from *usucapere* 'acquire by prescription'.

**usufruct** /ˈjuːzjʊfrʌkt/ ● **n.** Roman Law the right to enjoy the use of another's property short of the destruction or waste of its substance.
– DERIVATIVES **usufructuary** adj. & n.
– ORIGIN C17: from med. L. *usufructus*, from L. *usus (et) fructus* 'use (and) enjoyment'.

**usurer** /ˈjuːʒ(ə)rə/ ● **n.** a person who lends money at unreasonably high rates of interest.
– ORIGIN ME: from Anglo-Norman Fr., from OFr. *usure*, from L. *usura* (see **USURY**).

**usurious** /juːˈʒʊərɪəs, juːˈzj-/ ● **adj.** of or relating to usury.
– DERIVATIVES **usuriously** adv.

**usurp** /jʊˈzəːp, jʊˈsəːp/ ● **v. 1** take (a position of power) illegally or by force. ➤supplant. **2** (**usurp on/upon**) archaic encroach or infringe upon.
– DERIVATIVES **usurpation** /ˌjuːzəˈpeɪʃ(ə)n, ˌjuːs-/ n. **usurper** n.
– ORIGIN ME: from OFr. *usurper*, from L. *usurpare* 'seize for use'.

**usury** /ˈjuːʒ(ə)ri/ ● **n.** the practice of lending money at unreasonably high rates of interest. ➤archaic interest at such rates.
– ORIGIN ME: from Anglo-Norman Fr. *usurie*, or from med. L. *usuria*, from L. *usura*, from *usus* (see **USE**).

**UT** ● **abbrev. 1** Universal Time. **2** Utah (in official postal use).

**Utahan** /ˈjuːtɔːən, -tɑːən/ ● **n.** a native or inhabitant of the US state of Utah. ● **adj.** of or relating to Utah.

**UTC** ● **abbrev.** Universal Time Coordinated.

**Utd** ● **abbrev.** United (in names of soccer teams).

**Ute** /juːt/ ● **n.** (pl. same or **Utes**) **1** a member of an American Indian people living chiefly in Colorado, Utah, and New Mexico. **2** the Uto-Aztecan language of this people.
– ORIGIN from Sp. *Yuta*; cf. **PAIUTE**.

**ute** /juːt/ ● **n.** N. Amer. & Austral./NZ informal a utility vehicle.

**utensil** ● **n.** a tool or container, especially for household use.
– ORIGIN ME: from OFr. *utensile*, from med. L., neut. of L. *utensilis* 'usable', from *uti* (see **USE**).

**uteri** plural form of **UTERUS**.

**uterine** /ˈjuːtərɪn, -ʌɪn/ ● **adj. 1** of or relating to the uterus. **2** having the same mother but not the same father.
– ORIGIN ME: from **UTERUS** + **-INE**[1]; sense 2 from late L. *uterinus*.

**uterus** ● **n.** (pl. **uteri** /-rʌɪ/) the womb.
– ORIGIN from L.

**utile**[1] /ˈjuːtʌɪl/ ● **adj.** rare useful.
– ORIGIN C15: via OFr. from L. *utilis*, from *uti* 'to use'.

**utile**[2] /ˈjuːtɪli/ ● **n.** a large tropical African hardwood tree with wood used as a substitute for mahogany. [*Entandrophragma utile*.]
– ORIGIN 1950s: mod. L., specific epithet (see above), from L. *utilis* 'useful'.

**utilitarian** /jʊˌtɪlɪˈtɛːrɪən/ ● **adj. 1** useful or practical rather than attractive. **2** Philosophy of, relating to, or adhering to utilitarianism. ● **n.** Philosophy an adherent of utilitarianism.

**utilitarianism** ● **n.** the doctrine that actions are right if they are useful or for the benefit of a majority. ➤the doctrine that the greatest happiness of the greatest number should be the guiding principle of conduct.

**utility** ● **n.** (pl. **-ies**) **1** the state of being useful, profitable, or beneficial. ➤(in game theory or economics) the value of that which is sought to be maximized in any situation involving a choice. **2** a public utility. **3** Computing a utility program. ● **adj. 1** useful, especially through having several functions. **2** functional rather than attractive.
– ORIGIN ME: from OFr. *utilite*, from L. *utilitas*, from *utilis* 'useful'.

**utility knife** ● **n.** a Stanley knife.

**utility pole** ● **n.** N. Amer. a telegraph pole.

**utility program** ● **n.** Computing a program for carrying out a routine function.

**utility room** ● **n.** a room with appliances for washing and other domestic work.

**utility vehicle** (also **utility truck**) ● **n.** a truck having low sides and used for small loads.

**utilize** (also **-ise**) ● **v.** make practical and effective use of.
– DERIVATIVES **utilizable** adj. **utilization** n. **utilizer** n.
– ORIGIN C19: from Fr. *utiliser*, from Ital. *utilizzare*, from *utile* (see **UTILE**[1]).

**-ution** ● **suffix** (forming nouns) equivalent to **-ATION** (as in *solution*).
– ORIGIN via Fr. from L. *-utio(n-)*.

**utmost** ● **adj.** most extreme; greatest. ● **n.** (**the utmost**) the greatest or most extreme extent or amount.
– PHRASES **do one's utmost** do the most that one is able.
– ORIGIN OE *ūt(e)mest* 'outermost' (see **OUT**, **-MOST**).

**Uto-Aztecan** /ˌjuːtəʊˈaztɛk(ə)n/ ● **n.** a language family of Central America and western North America. ● **adj.** relating to or denoting this family.

**Utopia** /juːˈtəʊpɪə/ ● **n.** an imagined perfect place or state of things.
– ORIGIN the title of a book (1516) by Sir Thomas More, based on Gk *ou* 'not' + *topos* 'place'.

**utopian** ● **adj.** idealistic. ● **n.** an idealistic reformer.
– DERIVATIVES **utopianism** n.

**utricle** /ˈjuːtrɪk(ə)l/ ● **n. 1** a small cell, sac, or bladder-like protuberance in an animal or plant. **2** (also **utriculus** /juːˈtrɪkjʊləs/) the larger of the two fluid-filled sacs forming part of the labyrinth of the inner ear. Compare with **SACCULE**.
– DERIVATIVES **utricular** /juːˈtrɪkjʊlə/ adj.
– ORIGIN C18: from Fr. *utricule* or L. *utriculus*, dimin. of *uter* 'leather bag'.

**utter**[1] ● **adj.** complete; absolute: *utter amazement*.
– DERIVATIVES **utterly** adv.
– ORIGIN OE *ūtera*, *ūttra* 'outer', compar. of *ūt* 'out'; cf. **OUTER**.

**utter**[2] ● **v.** **1** make (a sound) or say (something). **2** Law put (forged money) into circulation.
– DERIVATIVES **utterable** adj. **utterer** n.
– ORIGIN ME: from MDu. *ūteren* 'speak, make known, give currency to (coins)'.

**utterance** ● **n.** a word, statement, or sound uttered. ➤the action of uttering. ➤Linguistics an uninterrupted chain of speech or writing.

**uttermost** ● **adj. & n.** another term for **UTMOST**.

**U-turn** ● **n.** **1** the turning of a vehicle in a U-shaped course so as to face the opposite way. **2** a reversal of policy.

**UV** ● **abbrev.** ultraviolet.

**UVA** ● **abbrev.** ultraviolet radiation of relatively long wavelengths.

**UVB** ● **abbrev.** ultraviolet radiation of relatively short wavelengths.

**UVC** ● **abbrev.** ultraviolet radiation of very short wavelengths, which does not penetrate the earth's ozone layer.

**uvea** /'ju:vɪə/ ● **n.** the pigmented layer of the eye, comprising the iris, choroid, and ciliary body.
– DERIVATIVES **uveal** adj. **uveitis** n.
– ORIGIN ME: from med. L., from L. *uva* 'grape'.

**uvula** /'ju:vjʊlə/ ● **n.** (pl. **uvulae** /-li:/) Anatomy a fleshy extension at the back of the soft palate which hangs above the throat.
– ORIGIN ME: from late L., dimin. of L. *uva* 'grape'.

**uvular** /'ju:vjʊlə/ ● **adj.** **1** Phonetics articulated with the back of the tongue and the uvula, as *r* in French. **2** Anatomy of or relating to the uvula. ● **n.** Phonetics a uvular consonant.

**uxorial** /ʌk'sɔ:rɪəl/ ● **adj.** of or relating to a wife.
– ORIGIN C19: from L. *uxor* 'wife' + **-IAL**.

**uxoricide** /ʌk'sɔ:rɪsʌɪd/ ● **n.** the killing of one's wife. ➤a man who kills his wife.
– DERIVATIVES **uxoricidal** adj.
– ORIGIN C19: from L. *uxor* 'wife' + **-CIDE**.

**uxorilocal** /ˌʌksɒrɪ'ləʊk(ə)l/ ● **adj.** another term for **MATRILOCAL**.
– ORIGIN 1930s: from L. *uxorius* 'of a wife' (from *uxor* 'wife') + **LOCAL**.

**uxorious** /ʌk'sɔ:rɪəs/ ● **adj.** showing great or excessive fondness for one's wife.
– DERIVATIVES **uxoriously** adv. **uxoriousness** n.
– ORIGIN C16: from L. *uxoriosus*, from *uxor* 'wife'.

**Uygur** ● **n. & adj.** variant spelling of **UIGHUR**.

**Uzbek** /'ʊzbɛk, 'ʌz-/ ● **n.** **1** a member of a Turkic people living mainly in Uzbekistan. ➤a native or national of Uzbekistan. **2** the Turkic language of Uzbekistan.
– ORIGIN the name in Uzbek.

**Uzi** /'u:zi/ ● **n.** a type of sub-machine gun.
– ORIGIN 1950s: from *Uziel* Gal, the Israeli army officer who designed it.

# V v

**V**[1] (also **v**) ● **n.** (pl. **Vs** or **V's**) **1** the twenty-second letter of the alphabet. **2** denoting the next after U in a set of items, categories, etc. **3** the Roman numeral for five. **4** [as modifier] denoting an internal-combustion engine with a number of cylinders arranged in two rows at an angle to each other.

**V**[2] ● **abbrev. 1** Vatican City (international vehicle registration). **2** volt(s). ● **symb. 1** the chemical element vanadium. **2** voltage or potential difference. **3** (in mathematical formulae) volume.

**v** ● **abbrev. 1** Grammar verb. **2** verse. **3** verso. **4** versus. **5** very. **6** (in textual references) vide. ● **symb.** velocity.

**V-1** ● **n.** a small bomb powered by a simple jet engine, used by the Germans in the Second World War.
– ORIGIN abbrev. of Ger. *Vergeltungswaffe* 'reprisal weapon'.

**V-2** ● **n.** a rocket-powered flying bomb used by the Germans in the Second World War.
– ORIGIN see **V-1**.

**VA** ● **abbrev. 1** (in the UK) Order of Victoria and Albert. **2** (in the US) Veterans' Administration. **3** Vicar Apostolic. **4** Vice Admiral. **5** Virginia (in official postal use).

**Va** ● **abbrev.** Virginia.

**vac** ● **n.** Brit. informal **1** a vacation. **2** a vacuum cleaner.

**vacancy** ● **n.** (pl. **-ies**) **1** an unoccupied position or job. **2** an available room in a hotel, guest house, etc. **3** empty space. **4** lack of intelligence or understanding.

**vacant** ● **adj. 1** not occupied; empty. ➤(of a position) not filled. **2** showing no intelligence or interest.
– DERIVATIVES **vacantly** adv.
– ORIGIN ME: from OFr., or from L. *vacant-*, *vacare* 'remain empty'.

**vacant possession** ● **n.** Brit. ownership of a property on completion of a sale, any previous occupant having moved out.

**vacate** /veɪˈkeɪt, vəˈkeɪt/ ● **v. 1** leave (a place). ➤give up (a position or job). **2** Law cancel or annul (a judgement, contract, or charge).
– ORIGIN C17 (earlier (ME) as *vacation*): from L. *vacat-*, *vacare* 'leave empty'.

**vacation** ● **n. 1** a holiday period between terms in universities and law courts. ➤chiefly N. Amer. a holiday. **2** the action of vacating. ● **v.** chiefly N. Amer. take a holiday.
– DERIVATIVES **vacationer** n. **vacationist** n.

**vacationland** ● **n.** N. Amer. an area with attractions for holidaymakers.

**vaccinate** /ˈvaksɪneɪt/ ● **v.** treat with a vaccine to produce immunity against a disease.
– DERIVATIVES **vaccination** n. **vaccinator** n.

**vaccine** /ˈvaksiːn, -ɪn/ ● **n. 1** Medicine an antigenic preparation used to stimulate the production of antibodies and provide immunity against a disease. **2** Computing a program that detects computer viruses and prevents them from operating.
– ORIGIN C18: from L. *vaccinus*, from *vacca* 'cow' (because of the early use of the cowpox virus against smallpox).

**vaccinia** /vakˈsɪnɪə/ ● **n.** Medicine cowpox or the virus causing it.
– ORIGIN C19: mod. L., from L. *vaccinus* (see **VACCINE**).

**vacillate** /ˈvasɪleɪt/ ● **v.** waver between different opinions or actions.
– DERIVATIVES **vacillation** n. **vacillator** n.
– ORIGIN C16 (in the sense 'sway unsteadily'): from L. *vacillat-*, *vacillare* 'sway'.

**vacua** plural form of **VACUUM**.

**vacuole** /ˈvakjʊəʊl/ ● **n.** Biology a space or vesicle within the cytoplasm of a cell, enclosed by a membrane and typically containing fluid.
– DERIVATIVES **vacuolar** /ˈvakjʊələ/ adj. **vacuolation** n.
– ORIGIN C19: from Fr., dimin. of L. *vacuus* 'empty'.

**vacuous** /ˈvakjʊəs/ ● **adj. 1** showing a lack of thought or intelligence. **2** archaic empty.
– DERIVATIVES **vacuity** /vəˈkjuːɪti/ n. **vacuously** adv. **vacuousness** n.
– ORIGIN C17: from L. *vacuus* 'empty' + **-ous**.

**vacuum** /ˈvakjʊəm/ ● **n.** (pl. **vacuums** or **vacua** /-jʊə/) **1** a space entirely devoid of matter. ➤a space or container from which the air has been completely or partly removed. **2** a gap left by the loss or departure of someone or something important. **3** (pl. **vacuums**) informal a vacuum cleaner. ● **v.** informal clean with a vacuum cleaner.
– PHRASES **in a vacuum** in isolation from the normal context.
– ORIGIN C16: mod. L., neut. of L. *vacuus* 'empty'.

**vacuum brake** ● **n.** a railway vehicle brake operated by changes in pressure in a pipe which is kept exhausted of air.

**vacuum cleaner** ● **n.** an electrical apparatus that collects dust from floors and other surfaces by means of suction.
– DERIVATIVES **vacuum-clean** v.

**vacuum flask** ● **n.** chiefly Brit. a container that keeps a substance hot or cold by means of a double wall enclosing a vacuum.

**vacuum gauge** ● **n.** a gauge for testing pressure after the production of a vacuum.

**vacuum-pack** ● **v.** seal (a product) in a pack or wrapping with the air removed. ● **n.** (**vacuum pack**) a pack of this kind.

**vacuum tube** ● **n.** a sealed glass tube containing a near-vacuum which allows the free passage of electric current.

**VAD** ● **abbrev.** historical Voluntary Aid Detachment.

**vada** /ˈvɑːdə/ (also **wada**) ● **n.** an Indian dish consisting of a ball made from ground lentils and deep-fried.
– ORIGIN from Hindi *vaḍā*.

**vade mecum** /ˌvɑːdi ˈmeɪkəm, ˌveɪdi ˈmiːkəm/ ● **n.** a handbook or guide kept constantly at hand.
– ORIGIN C17: mod. L., lit. 'go with me'.

**vadose** /ˈveɪdəʊs/ ● **adj.** Geology relating to or denoting underground water in the zone above the water table. Compare with **PHREATIC**.
– ORIGIN C19: from L. *vadosus*, from *vadum* 'shallow expanse of water'.

**vagabond** ● **n. 1** a vagrant. **2** informal, dated a rogue. ● **adj.** having no settled home. ● **v.** archaic wander about as or like a vagabond.
– DERIVATIVES **vagabondage** n.
– ORIGIN ME: from OFr., or from L. *vagabundus*, from *vagari* 'wander'.

**vagal** ● **adj.** of or relating to the vagus nerve.

**vagarious** /vəˈgɛːrɪəs/ ● **adj.** rare erratic and unpredictable.

**vagary** /ˈveɪg(ə)ri/ ● **n.** (pl. **-ies**) an unexpected and inexplicable change.
– ORIGIN C16: from L. *vagari* 'wander'.

**vagi** plural form of **VAGUS**.

**vagina** /vəˈdʒʌɪnə/ ● **n.** (pl. **vaginas** or **vaginae** /-niː/) **1** the muscular tube leading from the vulva to the cervix in women and most female mammals. **2** Botany a sheath

formed round a stem by the base of a leaf.
– DERIVATIVES **vaginal** adj.
– ORIGIN C17: from L., lit. 'sheath, scabbard'.

**vaginismus** /ˌvadʒɪˈnɪzməs/ ● **n.** painful spasmodic contraction of the vagina in response to physical contact or pressure, especially in sexual intercourse.
– ORIGIN C19: mod. L., from L. *vagina* (see **VAGINA**).

**vaginitis** /ˌvadʒɪˈnʌɪtɪs/ ● **n.** inflammation of the vagina.

**vagotomy** /veɪˈgɒtəmi/ ● **n.** (pl. **-ies**) the surgical operation of cutting a vagus nerve, typically to reduce gastric secretion.
– DERIVATIVES **vagotomized** adj.

**vagrant** /ˈveɪgr(ə)nt/ ● **n. 1** a person without a home or job. ➤ archaic a wanderer. **2** Ornithology a bird that has strayed from its usual range or migratory route. ● **adj.** of, relating to, or living like a vagrant; wandering. ➤ poetic/literary unpredictable or inconstant.
– DERIVATIVES **vagrancy** n. **vagrantly** adv.
– ORIGIN ME: from Anglo-Norman Fr. *vagarant* 'wandering about', from *vagrer*.

**vague** ● **adj.** of uncertain or indefinite character or meaning. ➤ imprecise in thought or expression.
– DERIVATIVES **vaguely** adv. **vagueness** n. **vaguish** adj.
– ORIGIN C16: from Fr., or from L. *vagus* 'wandering, uncertain'.

**vagus** /ˈveɪgəs/ ● **n.** (pl. **vagi** /-dʒʌɪ, -gʌɪ/) Anatomy each of the pair of cranial nerves supplying the heart, lungs, and other organs of the chest and abdomen.
– ORIGIN C19: from L. (see **VAGUE**).

**vail** /veɪl/ ● **v.** archaic take off or lower (one's hat or crown) as a token of respect or submission. ➤ take off one's hat or otherwise show respect or submission.
– ORIGIN ME: shortening of obs. *avale*, from OFr. *avaler* 'to lower', from *a val* 'down' (lit. 'in the valley').

**vain** ● **adj. 1** having or showing an excessively high opinion of one's appearance or abilities. **2** useless. ➤ having no meaning or likelihood of fulfilment: *a vain boast*.
– PHRASES **in vain** without success. **take someone's name in vain** use someone's name in a way that shows a lack of respect.
– DERIVATIVES **vainly** adv.
– ORIGIN ME: via OFr. from L. *vanus* 'empty, without substance'.

**vainglory** ● **n.** poetic/literary excessive vanity.
– DERIVATIVES **vainglorious** adj. **vaingloriously** adv. **vaingloriousness** n.
– ORIGIN ME: suggested by OFr. *vaine gloire*, L. *vana gloria*.

**vair** /vɛː/ ● **n. 1** fur obtained from a variety of red squirrel, used in the 13th and 14th centuries as a trimming or lining for garments. **2** Heraldry fur represented by interlocking rows of blue and white shield-shaped or bell-shaped figures.
– ORIGIN ME: via OFr. from L. *varius* (see **VARIOUS**).

**vairy** /ˈvɛːri/ ● **adj.** Heraldry resembling vair, typically in other colours.

**Vaisya** /ˈvʌɪsjə, -ʃjə/ (also **Vaishya**) ● **n.** a member of the third of the four Hindu castes, comprising merchants and farmers.
– ORIGIN from Sanskrit *vaiśya* 'peasant, labourer'.

**valance** /ˈval(ə)ns/ (also **valence**) ● **n.** a length of decorative drapery attached to the canopy or frame of a bed to screen the structure or space beneath it. ➤ a sheet with a gathered border designed to hang down over the mattress and sides of a bed. ➤ a length of decorative drapery screening the curtain fittings above a window.
– DERIVATIVES **valanced** adj.
– ORIGIN ME: perh. Anglo-Norman Fr., from a shortened form of OFr. *avaler* (see **VAIL**).

**vale**[1] /veɪl/ ● **n.** poetic/literary (except in place names) a valley.
– PHRASES **vale of tears** poetic/literary the world as a scene of trouble or sorrow.
– ORIGIN ME: from OFr. *val*, from L. *vallis*, *valles*.

**vale**[2] /ˈvɑːleɪ/ archaic ● **exclam.** farewell. ● **n.** a farewell.
– ORIGIN L., lit. 'be well!, be strong!', imper. of *valere*.

**valediction** /ˌvalɪˈdɪkʃ(ə)n/ ● **n.** the action of saying farewell. ➤ a farewell.
– ORIGIN C17: based on L. *vale* 'goodbye' + *dicere* 'to say', on the pattern of *benediction*.

**valedictorian** /ˌvalɪdɪkˈtɔːrɪən/ ● **n.** (in North America) a student who delivers the valedictory at a graduation ceremony.

**valedictory** /ˌvalɪˈdɪkt(ə)ri/ ● **adj.** serving as a farewell. ● **n.** (pl. **-ies**) a farewell address.

**valence**[1] /ˈveɪl(ə)ns/ ● **n.** Chemistry another term for **VALENCY**.

**valence**[2] ● **n.** variant spelling of **VALANCE**.

**Valenciennes** /ˌvalɒ̃ˈsjɛn/ ● **n.** a type of bobbin lace.
– ORIGIN named after a town in NE France, where it was made in the 17th and 18th cents.

**valency** /ˈveɪl(ə)nsi/ ● **n.** (pl. **-ies**) Chemistry, chiefly Brit. the combining power of an element, especially as measured by the number of hydrogen atoms it can displace or combine with.
– ORIGIN C17: from late L. *valentia* 'power, competence'.

**valentine** ● **n.** a card sent, often anonymously, on St Valentine's Day (14 February) to a person one loves or is attracted to. ➤ a person to whom one sends such a card.
– ORIGIN ME: from OFr. *Valentin*, from L. *Valentinus*, the name of two saints.

**valerian** /vəˈlɪərɪən/ ● **n. 1** a plant bearing clusters of small pink, red, or white flowers. [*Valeriana officinalis*, *Centranthus ruber* (**red valerian**), and other species.] **2** a sedative drug obtained from a valerian root.
– ORIGIN ME: from OFr. *valeriane*, from med. L. *valeriana* (*herba*), appar. the fem. of *Valerianus* 'of Valerius' (a personal name).

**valeric acid** /vəˈlɛrɪk, -ˈlɪərɪk/ ● **n.** Chemistry a liquid fatty acid present in various plant oils, used in making perfumes.
– DERIVATIVES **valerate** n.
– ORIGIN C19: *valeric* from **VALERIAN** + **-IC**.

**valet** /ˈvalɪt, ˈvaleɪ/ ● **n. 1** a man's personal male attendant, responsible for his clothes and appearance. ➤ a hotel employee performing such duties for guests. **2** a person employed to clean or park cars. ● **v.** (**valeted**, **valeting**) **1** act as a valet to. ➤ work as a valet. **2** clean (a car).
– ORIGIN C15: from Fr.; rel. to **VASSAL**.

**valeta** ● **n.** variant spelling of **VELETA**.

**valetudinarian** /ˌvalɪtjuːdɪˈnɛːrɪən/ ● **n.** a person who is unduly anxious about their health. ➤ a person in poor health. ● **adj.** showing undue concern about one's health. ➤ in poor health.
– DERIVATIVES **valetudinarianism** n.
– ORIGIN C18: from L. *valetudinarius* 'in ill health'.

**valetudinary** /ˌvalɪˈtjuːdɪn(ə)ri/ ● **adj. & n.** (pl. **-ies**) another term for **VALETUDINARIAN**.

**valgus** /ˈvalgəs/ ● **n.** Medicine a deformity involving oblique displacement of part of a limb away from the midline. Compare with **VARUS**.
– ORIGIN C19: from L., lit. 'knock-kneed'.

**Valhalla** /valˈhalə/ ● **n.** Scandinavian Mythology a palace in which heroes killed in battle feasted for eternity.
– ORIGIN mod. L., from ON *Valhǫll*, from *valr* 'the slain' + *hǫll* 'hall'.

**valiant** ● **adj.** showing courage or determination.
– DERIVATIVES **valiantly** adv.
– ORIGIN ME: from OFr. *vailant*, based on L. *valere* 'be strong'.

**valid** ● **adj. 1** actually supporting the intended point or claim: *a valid criticism*. **2** executed in compliance with the law. ➤ legally or officially acceptable.
– DERIVATIVES **validity** n. **validly** adv.
– ORIGIN C16: from Fr. *valide* or L. *validus* 'strong'.

**validate** ● **v.** check or prove the validity of. ➤ confirm. ➤ make or declare legally valid.
– DERIVATIVES **validation** n.

**valine** /ˈveɪliːn/ ● **n.** Biochemistry an amino acid which is an essential nutrient in the diet.
– ORIGIN C20: from *val(eric acid)* + **-INE**[4].

**valise** /vəˈliːz/ ● **n.** a small travelling bag or suitcase.
– ORIGIN C17: from Fr., from Ital. *valigia*; cf. med. L. *valesia*, of unknown origin.

**Valium** /ˈvalɪəm/ ● **n.** trademark for **DIAZEPAM**.
– ORIGIN 1960s: of unknown origin.

**Valkyrie** /valˈkɪəri, ˈvalkɪri/ ● **n.** Scandinavian Mythology each of Odin's twelve handmaids who conducted slain warriors of their choice to Valhalla.
– ORIGIN from ON *Valkyrja*, lit. 'chooser of the slain', from *valr* 'the slain' + *kyrja* 'chooser'.

**vallecula** /vaˈlɛkjʊlə/ ● **n.** (pl. **valleculae** /-liː/) Anatomy & Botany a groove or furrow.
– DERIVATIVES **vallecular** adj.
– ORIGIN C19: from a late L. var. of L. *vallicula*, dimin. of L. *vallis* 'valley'.

**valley** ● **n.** (pl. **-eys**) **1** a low area between hills or mountains, typically with a river or stream flowing through it. **2** Architecture an internal angle formed by the intersecting planes of a roof, or by the slope of a roof and a wall.
– ORIGIN ME: from OFr. *valee*, based on L. *vallis*, *valles*; cf. **VALE**[1].

**vallum** /ˈvaləm/ ● **n.** (in ancient Rome) a defensive wall, rampart, or stockade.
– ORIGIN L., collective from *vallus* 'stake, palisade'.

**valonia** /vaˈləʊnɪə/ ● **n.** the acorn cups of an evergreen oak (*Quercus macrolepis*), which yield a black dye and are used in tanning.
– ORIGIN C18: from Ital. *vallonia*, based on Gk *balanos* 'acorn'.

**valor** ● **n.** US spelling of **VALOUR**.

**valorize** /ˈvalərʌɪz/ (also **-ise**) ● **v.** give or ascribe value or validity to. ➤ artificially raise or fix the price or value of.
– DERIVATIVES **valorization** n.
– ORIGIN 1920s: back-form. from *valorization* (from Fr. *valorisation*, from *valeur* 'value').

**valour** (US **valor**) ● **n.** courage in the face of danger, especially in battle.
– DERIVATIVES **valorous** adj.
– ORIGIN ME: via OFr. from late L. *valor*, from *valere* 'be strong'.

**valproic acid** /valˈprəʊɪk/ ● **n.** Chemistry a synthetic crystalline compound used in the treatment of epilepsy.
– DERIVATIVES **valproate** n.
– ORIGIN 1970s: from *val(eric)* (see **VALERIC ACID**) + *pro(pyl)* + **-IC**.

**Valsalva manoeuvre** /valˈsalvə/ ● **n.** Medicine the action of attempting to exhale with the nostrils and mouth, or the glottis, closed, serving to increase pressure in the middle ear and the chest or equalize pressure in the ears.
– ORIGIN C19: named after the Ital. anatomist Antonio M. *Valsalva*.

**valse** /vals, vɔːls/ ● **n.** (pl. pronounced same) French term for **WALTZ**.
– ORIGIN C18: via Fr. from Ger. *Walzer*.

**valuable** ● **adj.** worth a great deal of money. ➤ extremely useful or important. ● **n.** (**valuables**) valuable things, especially small items of personal property.
– DERIVATIVES **valuably** adv.

**valuation** ● **n.** an estimation of something's worth, especially one carried out by a professional valuer. ➤ the monetary worth estimated.
– DERIVATIVES **valuate** v. (chiefly N. Amer.).

**valuator** ● **n.** archaic a valuer.

**value** ● **n. 1** the regard that something is held to deserve; importance or worth. ➤ material or monetary worth. ➤ the worth of something compared to its price: *at £12.50 it is good value*. **2** (**values**) principles or standards of behaviour. **3** the numerical amount denoted by an algebraic term; a magnitude, quantity, or number. **4** Music the relative duration of the sound signified by a note. **5** Linguistics the meaning of a word or other linguistic unit. ➤ the sound represented by a letter or symbol. **6** (in art) the relative degree of lightness or darkness of a colour. ● **v.** (**values, valued, valuing**) **1** estimate the value of. **2** consider to be important or beneficial.
– DERIVATIVES **valueless** adj. **valuelessness** n. **valuer** n.
– ORIGIN ME: from OFr., fem. past part. of *valoir* 'be worth', from L. *valere*.

**value added** ● **n.** Economics the amount by which the value of an article is increased at each stage of its production, exclusive of initial costs. ● **adj. 1** (of goods) having added features for which the buyer is prepared to pay extra. **2** (of a company) offering specialized or extended services.

**value added tax** ● **n.** a tax on the amount by which the value of an article has been increased at each stage of its production or distribution.

**value judgement** ● **n.** an assessment of something as good or bad in terms of one's standards or priorities.

**valuta** /vəˈljuːtə, -ˈluː-/ ● **n.** foreign currency. ➤ the value of one currency against another.
– ORIGIN C19: from Ital., lit. 'value'.

**valvate** /ˈvalveɪt/ ● **adj.** Botany (of sepals or other parts) having adjacent edges abutting rather than overlapping. Compare with **IMBRICATE**.

**valve** ● **n. 1** a device for controlling the passage of fluid through a pipe or duct, especially an automatic device allowing movement in one direction only. **2** a cylindrical mechanism to vary the effective length of the tube in a brass musical instrument. **3** Anatomy & Zoology a membranous fold in an organ or vessel which allows blood or other fluid to flow in one direction. **4** Zoology each of the halves of the hinged shell of a bivalve mollusc or brachiopod. **5** Botany each of the halves or sections into which a dry fruit dehisces.
– DERIVATIVES **valved** adj. **valveless** adj.
– ORIGIN ME (denoting a leaf of a folding or double door): from L. *valva*.

**valve gear** ● **n.** the mechanism that controls the opening and closing of the cylinder valves in a steam engine or internal-combustion engine.

**valvular** ● **adj.** relating to, having, or acting as a valve or valves.

**valvulitis** /ˌvalvjʊˈlʌɪtɪs/ ● **n.** Medicine inflammation of the valves of the heart.

**vambrace** /ˈvambreɪs/ ● **n.** historical a piece of armour for the arm, especially the forearm.
– ORIGIN ME: from an Anglo-Norman Fr. shortening of OFr. *avantbras*, from *avant* 'before' + *bras* 'arm'; cf. **VAMPLATE**.

**vamoose** /vəˈmuːs/ ● **v.** informal depart hurriedly.
– ORIGIN C19: from Sp. *vamos* 'let us go'.

**vamp**[1] ● **n. 1** the upper front part of a boot or shoe. **2** (in jazz and popular music) a short, simple introductory passage, usually repeated several times until otherwise instructed. ● **v. 1** repeat a short, simple passage of music. **2** (**vamp something up**) informal repair or improve something. **3** attach a new upper to (a boot or shoe).
– ORIGIN ME (denoting the foot of a stocking, later something patched or improvised): shortening of OFr. *avantpie*, from *avant* 'before' + *pie* 'foot'.

**vamp**[2] informal ● **n.** a woman who uses sexual attraction to exploit men. ● **v.** blatantly set out to attract (a man).
– DERIVATIVES **vampish** adj. **vampishly** adv. **vampishness** n. **vampy** adj.
– ORIGIN C20: abbrev. of **VAMPIRE**.

**vampire** /ˈvampʌɪə/ ● **n. 1** (in folklore) a corpse supposed to leave its grave at night to drink the blood of the living. ➤ a person who exploits others ruthlessly. **2** a small bat that feeds on blood by piercing the skin with its incisor teeth, found mainly in tropical America. [*Desmodus rotundus* and other species.] **3** (also **vampire trap**) Theatre a small spring trapdoor used for sudden disappearances from a stage.
– DERIVATIVES **vampiric** /-ˈpɪrɪk/ adj. **vampirism** n.
– ORIGIN C18: from Fr., from Hungarian *vampir*, perh. from Turk. *uber* 'witch'.

**vamplate** /ˈvampleɪt/ ● **n.** historical a circular plate on a spear or lance designed to protect the hand.
– ORIGIN ME: from Anglo-Norman Fr. *vauntplate*, from *avant* 'before' + *plate* 'thin plate'; cf. **VAMBRACE**.

**van**[1] ● **n.** a covered motor vehicle used for transporting goods or people. ➤ Brit. a railway carriage for conveying luggage, mail, etc. ➤ Brit. a caravan.
– ORIGIN C19: shortening of **CARAVAN**.

**van**[2] ● **n.** (**the van**) **1** the foremost part of a company of people, especially the foremost division of an advancing

military force. **2** the forefront.
– ORIGIN C17: abbrev. of **VANGUARD**.

**van[3]** ● **n.** **1** archaic a winnowing fan. **2** archaic or poetic/literary a bird's wing.
– ORIGIN ME: dial. var. of **FAN[1]**, prob. reinforced by OFr. *van* or L. *vannus*.

**van[4]** ● **n.** Brit. Tennis informal term for **ADVANTAGE**.

**vanadate** /ˈvanədeɪt/ ● **n.** Chemistry a salt in which the anion contains both vanadium and oxygen.

**vanadium** /vəˈneɪdɪəm/ ● **n.** the chemical element of atomic number 23, a hard grey metal used to make alloy steels. (Symbol: **V**)
– ORIGIN C19: mod. L., from ON *Vanadis* (a name of the Scand. goddess Freyja).

**Van Allen belt** ● **n.** each of two regions of intense radiation partly surrounding the earth at heights of several thousand kilometres.
– ORIGIN C20: named after the Amer. physicist J. A. *Van Allen*.

**vancomycin** /ˌvaŋkəˈmʌɪsɪn/ ● **n.** Medicine a bacterial antibiotic used against resistant strains of streptococcus and staphylococcus.
– ORIGIN 1950s: from *vanco-* (of unknown origin) + **-MYCIN**.

**V. & A.** ● **abbrev.** Victoria and Albert Museum.

**vandal** ● **n.** **1** a person who deliberately destroys or damages public or private property. **2** (**Vandal**) a member of a Germanic people that ravaged Gaul, Spain, Rome, and North Africa in the 4th–5th centuries.
– DERIVATIVES **vandalism** n. **vandalistic** adj. **vandalistically** adv.
– ORIGIN from L. *Vandalus*, of Gmc origin.

**vandalize** (also **-ise**) ● **v.** deliberately destroy or damage (property).

**Van de Graaff generator** /ˌvan də ˈgrɑːf/ ● **n.** Physics an electrostatic generator having a vertical endless belt which transfers charge to a large insulated metal dome, where a high voltage is produced.
– ORIGIN C20: named after the Amer. physicist R. J. *Van de Graaf*.

**van der Waals forces** /ˌvan də ˈwɑːlz, ˈvɑːlz/ ● **pl. n.** Chemistry weak, short-range electrostatic attractive forces between uncharged molecules, arising from the interaction of permanent or transient electric dipole moments.
– ORIGIN C19: named after the Du. physicist Johannes *van der Waals*.

**Vandyke** /vanˈdʌɪk/ ● **n.** **1** a broad lace or linen collar with an edge deeply cut into large points, fashionable in the 18th century. **2** (also **Vandyke beard**) a neat pointed beard.
– ORIGIN C18: named after the C17 Flemish painter Sir Anthony *Van Dyck*, whose portraits freq. depict such styles.

**Vandyke brown** ● **n.** a deep rich brown.

**vane** ● **n.** **1** a broad blade attached to a rotating axis or wheel which pushes or is pushed by wind or water, forming part of a device such as a windmill, propeller, or turbine. ➤ a weathervane. **2** a projecting surface designed to guide the motion of a projectile, e.g. a feather on an arrow. **3** the flat part on either side of the shaft of a feather.
– DERIVATIVES **vaned** adj.
– ORIGIN ME: dial. var. of obs. *fane* 'banner', of Gmc origin.

**vang** /vaŋ/ ● **n.** Sailing **1** each of two guy ropes running from the end of a gaff to the deck. **2** (also **boom vang**) a fitting used to pull a boat's boom down and help control the shape of the sail.
– ORIGIN C18: var. of obs. *fang*, denoting a gripping device, from ON *fang* 'grasp'; cf. **FANG**.

**vanguard** ● **n.** **1** the foremost part of an advancing army or naval force. **2** a group of people leading the way in new developments or ideas. ➤ a position at the forefront of developments or ideas.
– ORIGIN ME shortening of OFr. *avan(t)garde*, from *avant* 'before' + *garde* 'guard'.

**vanilla** ● **n.** **1** a substance obtained from vanilla pods or produced artificially and used to flavour sweet foods or to impart a fragrant scent to cosmetic preparations. **2** a tropical climbing orchid with fragrant flowers and long pod-like fruit. [*Vanilla planifolia* and related species.] ● **adj.** informal having no special or extra features.
– ORIGIN C17: from Sp. *vainilla* 'pod', dimin. of *vaina* 'sheath, pod', from L. *vagina* 'sheath'.

**vanillin** ● **n.** Chemistry a fragrant compound which is the essential constituent of vanilla.

**vanish** ● **v.** **1** disappear suddenly and completely. ➤ gradually cease to exist. **2** Mathematics become zero.
– DERIVATIVES **vanishing** adj. & n. **vanishingly** adv.
– ORIGIN ME: shortening of OFr. *e(s)vaniss-*, lengthened stem of *e(s)vanir*, from L. *evanescere* 'die away'.

**vanishing cream** ● **n.** dated a cream or ointment that leaves no visible trace when rubbed into the skin.

**vanishing point** ● **n.** **1** the point at which receding parallel lines viewed in perspective appear to converge. **2** the point at which something that has been growing smaller or increasingly faint disappears altogether.

**vanitas** /ˈvanɪtɑːs/ ● **n.** a still-life painting of a 17th-century Dutch genre containing symbols of death or change as a reminder of their inevitability.
– ORIGIN L., lit. 'vanity'.

**Vanitory unit** /ˈvanɪt(ə)ri/ ● **n.** trademark a vanity unit.
– ORIGIN 1950s: *Vanitory* from **VANITY**, on the pattern of *lavatory*.

**vanity** ● **n.** (pl. **-ies**) **1** excessive pride in or admiration of one's own appearance or achievements. ➤ [as modifier] denoting a company publishing works at the author's expense. **2** the quality of being worthless or futile. **3** N. Amer. a dressing table.
– ORIGIN ME: from OFr. *vanite*, from L. *vanitas*, from *vanus* (see **VAIN**).

**vanity case** ● **n.** a small case fitted with a mirror and compartments for make-up.

**vanity mirror** ● **n.** a small mirror used for applying make-up, especially one fitted in a motor vehicle.

**vanity plate** ● **n.** N. Amer. a vehicle licence plate bearing a distinctive or personalized combination of letters or numbers.

**vanity table** ● **n.** a dressing table.

**vanity unit** ● **n.** a unit consisting of a washbasin set into a flat top with cupboards beneath.

**vanquish** /ˈvaŋkwɪʃ/ ● **v.** defeat thoroughly.
– DERIVATIVES **vanquishable** adj. **vanquisher** n.
– ORIGIN ME: from OFr. *vencus*, *venquis* (past part. and past tense of *veintre*), *vainquiss-* (lengthened stem of *vainquir*), from L. *vincere* 'conquer'.

**vantage** /ˈvɑːntɪdʒ/ ● **n.** (usu. **vantage point**) a place or position affording a good view.
– ORIGIN ME: from Anglo-Norman Fr., shortening of OFr. *avantage* 'advantage'.

**Vanuatuan** /ˌvanuːˈɑːtuːən/ ● **n.** a native or inhabitant of Vanuatu, a country in the SW Pacific. ● **adj.** of or relating to Vanuatu.

**vapid** /ˈvapɪd/ ● **adj.** offering nothing that is stimulating or challenging.
– DERIVATIVES **vapidity** n. **vapidly** adv.
– ORIGIN C17 (orig. in sense 'lacking in flavour'): from L. *vapidus*.

**vapor** ● **n.** US spelling of **VAPOUR**.

**vaporetto** /ˌvapəˈrɛtəʊ/ ● **n.** (pl. **vaporetti** /-ti/ or **vaporettos**) (in Venice) a canal boat for public transport.
– ORIGIN Ital., dimin. of *vapore* 'steam', from L. *vapor*.

**vaporize** (also **-ise**) ● **v.** convert or be converted into vapour.
– DERIVATIVES **vaporable** adj. **vaporizable** adj. **vaporization** n.

**vaporizer** ● **n.** a device that generates a vapour, especially for medicinal inhalation.

**vapour** (US **vapor**) ● **n.** **1** a substance diffused or suspended in the air. ➤ Physics a gaseous substance that can be liquefied by pressure alone. Compare with **GAS**. **2** (**the vapours**) dated a sudden feeling of faintness or nervousness or a state of depression. ● **v.** talk in a vacuous, boastful, or pompous way.
– DERIVATIVES **vaporous** adj. **vaporousness** n. **vapourish**

adj. (archaic). **vapoury** adj.
– ORIGIN ME: from OFr., or from L. *vapor* 'steam, heat'.

**vapour density** • n. Chemistry the density of a particular gas or vapour relative to that of hydrogen at the same pressure and temperature.

**vapourer moth** • n. a day-flying tussock moth, the female of which is wingless. [Genus *Orgyia*: several species.]

**vapour pressure** • n. Chemistry the pressure of a vapour in contact with its liquid or solid form.

**vapour trail** • n. a trail of condensed water from an aircraft or rocket at high altitude, seen as a white streak against the sky.

**vapourware** • n. Computing, informal software or hardware that has been advertised but is not yet available to buy.

**vaquero** /və'kɛːrəʊ/ • n. (pl. **-os**) (in Spanish-speaking parts of the USA) a cowboy; a cattle driver.
– ORIGIN Sp., from *vaca* 'cow'.

**VAR** • abbrev. **1** value-added reseller. **2** value at risk.

**var.** • abbrev. variety.

**varactor** /və'raktə/ • n. a semiconductor diode with a capacitance dependent on the applied voltage.
– ORIGIN 1950s: from elements of *variable reactor*.

**Varangian** /və'randʒɪən/ • n. a member of the bands of Scandinavians who travelled into Russia in the 9th and 10th centuries and traditionally established the Rurik dynasty. • adj. of or relating to the Varangians.
– ORIGIN from med. L. *Varangus* (a name ult. from ON, prob. based on *vár* 'pledge') + **-IAN**.

**vardo** /'vɑːdəʊ/ (also **varda** /'vɑːdə/) • n. (pl. **vardos** or **vardas**) a gypsy caravan.
– ORIGIN C19: from Romany.

**varec** /'varɛk/ • n. seaweed, especially kelp.
– ORIGIN C17: from Fr. *varec(h)*, from ON; rel. to **WRECK**.

**vari-** • comb. form various: *variform*.
– ORIGIN from L. *varius*.

**variable** • adj. **1** not consistent or having a fixed pattern; liable to vary. ➤ Mathematics (of a quantity) able to assume different numerical values. ➤ Botany & Zoology (of a species) liable to deviate from the typical colour or form, or to occur in different colours or forms. **2** able to be changed or adapted. ➤ (of a gear) designed to give varying ratios or speeds. • n. a variable element, feature, or quantity. ➤ Astronomy a star whose brightness changes (regularly or irregularly). ➤ (**variables**) the region of light, variable winds to the north of the NE trade winds or (in the southern hemisphere) between the SE trade winds and the westerlies.
– DERIVATIVES **variability** n. **variableness** n. **variably** adv.

**variable-geometry** • adj. denoting a swing-wing aircraft.

**variance** • n. **1** (usu. in phr. **at variance with**) the fact or quality of being different or inconsistent. ➤ the state of disagreeing or quarrelling. ➤ chiefly Law a discrepancy between two statements or documents. **2** US Law an official dispensation from a rule or regulation. **3** Statistics a quantity equal to the square of the standard deviation.

**variant** • n. a form or version that varies from other forms of the same thing or from a standard.

**variate** /'vɛːrɪət/ • n. Statistics a quantity having a numerical value for each member of a group, especially one whose values occur according to a frequency distribution.

**variation** • n. **1** a change or slight difference in condition, amount, or level. ➤ (also **magnetic variation**) the angular difference between true north and magnetic north at a particular place. **2** a different or distinct form or version. ➤ Music a new but still recognizable version of a theme. ➤ Ballet a solo dance as part of a performance.
– DERIVATIVES **variational** adj.

**variationist** • n. a person who studies variations in usage among different speakers of the same language.

**variceal** /ˌvarɪ'siːəl/ • adj. Zoology & Medicine relating to or involving a varix.

**varicella** /ˌvarɪ'sɛlə/ • n. Medicine technical term for **CHICKENPOX**. ➤ (also **varicella zoster**) a herpesvirus that causes chickenpox and shingles; herpes zoster.
– ORIGIN C18: mod. L., irregular dimin. of **VARIOLA**.

**varices** plural form of **VARIX**.

**varicocele** /'varɪkə(ʊ)ˌsiːl/ • n. Medicine a mass of varicose veins in the spermatic cord.
– ORIGIN C18: from L. *varix, varic-* 'dilated vein' + **-CELE**.

**varicoloured** /'vɛːrɪˌkʌləd/ (US **varicolored**) • adj. consisting of several different colours.

**varicose** /'varɪkəʊs, -kəs, -z/ • adj. affected by a condition causing the swelling and tortuous lengthening of veins, most often in the legs.
– DERIVATIVES **varicosed** adj. **varicosity** n.
– ORIGIN ME: from L. *varicosus*, from *varix* (see **VARIX**).

**varied** • adj. incorporating a number of different types or elements; showing variation or variety.
– DERIVATIVES **variedly** adv.

**variegated** /'vɛːrɪgeɪtɪd, 'vɛːrɪə-/ • adj. exhibiting different colours, especially as irregular patches or streaks.
– DERIVATIVES **variegation** /-'geɪʃ(ə)n/ n.
– ORIGIN C17: from L. *variegat-*, *variegare* 'make varied'.

**varietal** /və'rʌɪət(ə)l/ • adj. **1** (of a wine or grape) made from or belonging to a single specified variety of grape. **2** chiefly Botany & Zoology of, forming, or characteristic of a variety. • n. a varietal wine.
– DERIVATIVES **varietally** adv.

**varietist** /və'rʌɪətɪst/ • n. dated a person who enjoys sexual variety.

**variety** • n. (pl. **-ies**) **1** the quality or state of being different or diverse. **2** (**a variety of**) a number of things of the same general class that are distinct in character or quality. ➤ a thing which differs in some way from others of the same general class; a type. ➤ Biology a subspecies or cultivar. **3** a form of entertainment consisting of a series of different types of act, such as singing, dancing, and comedy.
– ORIGIN C15: from Fr. *variété* or L. *varietas*, from *varius* (see **VARIOUS**).

**variety meats** • pl. n. N. Amer. offal.

**variety store** • n. N. Amer. a small shop selling a wide range of inexpensive items.

**varifocal** /ˌvɛːrɪ'fəʊk(ə)l/ • adj. denoting a lens that allows an infinite number of focusing distances for near, intermediate, and far vision. • n. (**varifocals**) varifocal glasses.

**variform** /'vɛːrɪfɔːm/ • adj. (of a group of things) differing from one another in form. ➤ (of a single thing or a mass) consisting of a variety of forms or things.

**variola** /və'rʌɪələ/ • n. Medicine technical term for **SMALLPOX**.
– DERIVATIVES **variolar** adj. **variolous** adj. (archaic).
– ORIGIN C18: from med. L., lit. 'pustule, pock'.

**varioloid** /'vɛːrɪəlɔɪd/ Medicine • adj. resembling smallpox. • n. a mild form of smallpox affecting people who have already had the disease or have been vaccinated against it.

**variometer** /ˌvɛːrɪ'ɒmɪtə/ • n. **1** a device for indicating an aircraft's rate of climb or descent. **2** a device whose total inductance can be varied. **3** an instrument for measuring variations in the earth's magnetic field.

**variorum** /ˌvɛːrɪ'ɔːrəm/ • adj. (of an edition of an author's works) having notes by various editors or commentators. ➤ including variant readings from manuscripts or earlier editions. • n. a variorum edition.
– ORIGIN C18: genitive pl. of *varius* 'diverse', from L. *editio cum notis variorum* 'edition with notes by various (commentators)'.

**various** • adj. different from one another; of different kinds or sorts. ➤ having or showing different properties or qualities. • det. & pron. more than one; individual and separate: *various people arrived late*.
– DERIVATIVES **variously** adv. **variousness** n.
– ORIGIN ME: from L. *varius* 'changing, diverse' + **-OUS**.

**varistor** /vɛː'rɪstə, və-/ • n. a semiconductor diode with resistance dependent on the applied voltage.
– ORIGIN 1930s: contr. of *varying resistor*.

**varix** /'vɛːrɪks/ • n. (pl. **varices** /'varɪsiːz/) **1** Medicine a varicose vein. **2** Zoology each of the ridges on the shell of a

gastropod mollusc, marking a former position of the aperture.
– ORIGIN ME: from L.

**varlet** /'vɑːlɪt/ ● **n.** **1** archaic an unprincipled rogue. **2** historical an attendant or servant.
– DERIVATIVES **varletry** n.
– ORIGIN ME: from OFr., var. of *valet* (see **VALET**).

**varmint** /'vɑːmɪnt/ ● **n.** N. Amer. informal or dialect a troublesome or mischievous person or wild animal.
– ORIGIN C16: alt. of **VERMIN**.

**varna** /'vɑːnə/ ● **n.** each of the four Hindu castes, Brahman, Kshatriya, Vaisya, and Sudra.
– ORIGIN Sanskrit, lit. 'colour, class'.

**varnish** ● **n.** **1** a substance consisting of resin dissolved in a liquid, applied to wood to give a hard, clear, shiny surface when dry. **2** archaic an external or superficial appearance: *an outward varnish of civilization.* ● **v.** apply varnish to.
– DERIVATIVES **varnisher** n.
– ORIGIN ME: from OFr. *vernis*, from med. L. *veronix* 'fragrant resin, sandarac' or med. Gk *berenikē*, prob. from *Berenice*, a town in Cyrenaica.

**varroa** /'varəʊə/ ● **n.** a microscopic mite which is a debilitating parasite of the honeybee. [*Varroa jacobsoni.*]
– ORIGIN 1970s: mod. L., from the name of the Roman writer *Varro* (with ref. to his work on bee-keeping) + **-A**[1].

**varsity** ● **n.** (pl. **-ies**) Brit. dated or S. African university. ➤ [usu. as modifier] chiefly N. Amer. a sports team representing a university or college.
– ORIGIN C17: shortening of **UNIVERSITY**, reflecting an archaic pronunc.

**varus** /'vɛːrəs/ ● **n.** Medicine a deformity involving oblique displacement of part of a limb towards the midline. Compare with **VALGUS**.
– ORIGIN C19: from L., lit. 'bent, crooked'.

**varve** /vɑːv/ ● **n.** Geology a pair of thin layers of clay and silt of contrasting colour and texture which represent the deposit of a single year (summer and winter) in a lake.
– DERIVATIVES **varved** adj.
– ORIGIN C20; from Swed. *varv* 'layer'.

**vary** ● **v.** (**-ies**, **-ied**) **1** differ in size, degree, or nature from something else of the same general class. **2** change from one form or state to another. ➤ modify or change (something) to make it less uniform.
– DERIVATIVES **varying** adj. **varyingly** adv.
– ORIGIN ME: from OFr. *varier* or L. *variare*, from *varius* 'diverse'.

**vas** /vas/ ● **n.** (pl. **vasa** /'veɪsə/) Anatomy a vessel or duct.
– DERIVATIVES **vasal** /'veɪs(ə)l/ adj.
– ORIGIN C16: from L., lit. 'vessel'.

**vascular** /'vaskjʊlə/ ● **adj.** relating to or denoting the system of vessels for carrying blood or (in plants) sap, water, and nutrients.
– DERIVATIVES **vascularity** /-'larɪti/ n. **vascularization** (also **-isation**) n. **vascularize** (also **-ise**) v.
– ORIGIN C17: from mod. L. *vascularis*, from L. *vasculum* (see **VASCULUM**).

**vascular bundle** ● **n.** Botany a strand of conducting vessels in the stem or leaves of a plant, typically with phloem on the outside and xylem on the inside.

**vascular plants** ● **pl. n.** plants with vascular tissue, i.e. flowering plants, conifers, cycads, ferns, horsetails, and clubmosses.

**vasculature** /'vaskjʊlətʃə/ ● **n.** Anatomy the vascular system of a part of the body and its arrangement.

**vasculitis** /ˌvaskjʊ'lʌɪtɪs/ ● **n.** (pl. **vasculitides** /-'lʌɪtɪdiːz/) Medicine inflammation of a blood vessel or blood vessels.
– DERIVATIVES **vasculitic** /-'lɪtɪk/ adj.

**vasculum** /'vaskjʊləm/ ● **n.** (pl. **vascula** /-lə/) Botany a collecting box for plants, typically a flattened cylindrical metal case with a lengthwise opening.
– ORIGIN C18: from L., dimin. of *vas* 'vessel'.

**vas deferens** /'dɛfərɛnz/ ● **n.** (pl. **vasa deferentia** /ˌdɛfə'rɛnʃɪə/) Anatomy the duct which conveys sperm from the testicle to the urethra.
– ORIGIN C16: from **VAS** + L. *deferens* 'carrying away', pres. part. of *deferre*.

**vase** ● **n.** a decorative container without handles, typically made of glass or china and used as an ornament or for displaying cut flowers.
– ORIGIN ME: from Fr., from L. *vas* 'vessel'.

**vasectomy** /və'sɛktəmi/ ● **n.** (pl. **-ies**) the surgical cutting and sealing of part of each vas deferens, especially as a means of sterilization.
– DERIVATIVES **vasectomize** (also **-ise**) v.

**vaseline** /'vasɪliːn/ ● **n.** trademark a type of petroleum jelly used as an ointment and lubricant.
– ORIGIN C19: formed irregularly from Ger. *Wasser* + Gk *elaion* 'oil' + **-INE**[4].

**vaso-** /'veɪzəʊ/ ● **comb. form** of or relating to a vessel or vessels, especially blood vessels: *vasoconstriction.*
– ORIGIN from L. *vas* 'vessel'.

**vasoactive** ● **adj.** Physiology affecting the diameter of blood vessels (and hence blood pressure).

**vasoconstriction** ● **n.** the constriction of blood vessels, which increases blood pressure.
– DERIVATIVES **vasoconstrictive** adj. **vasoconstrictor** n.

**vasodilation** (also **vasodilatation** /-ˌdʌɪleɪ'teɪʃ(ə)n/) ● **n.** the dilatation of blood vessels, which decreases blood pressure.
– DERIVATIVES **vasodilator** n. **vasodilatory** adj.

**vasomotor** ● **adj.** causing or relating to the constriction or dilatation of blood vessels.

**vasopressin** /ˌveɪzəʊ'prɛsɪn/ ● **n.** Biochemistry a pituitary hormone which promotes water retention by the kidneys and increased blood pressure.

**vasopressor** /veɪzəʊ'prɛsə/ ● **n.** Medicine a drug or other agent which causes constriction of blood vessels.

**vassal** /'vas(ə)l/ ● **n.** **1** historical a holder of land by feudal tenure on conditions of homage and allegiance. **2** a person or country in a subordinate position to another.
– DERIVATIVES **vassalage** n.
– ORIGIN ME: via OFr. from med. L. *vassallus* 'retainer', of Celtic origin.

**vast** ● **adj.** of very great extent or quantity; immense. ● **n.** archaic an immense space.
– DERIVATIVES **vastly** adv. **vastness** n.
– ORIGIN ME: from L. *vastus* 'void, immense'.

**vastation** /va'steɪʃ(ə)n/ ● **n.** archaic or poetic/literary **1** violent or drastic purification or purging. **2** devastation.
– ORIGIN C16: from L. *vastatio(n-)*, from *vastare* 'lay waste'.

**VAT** ● **abbrev.** value added tax.

**vat** ● **n.** a large tank or tub used to hold liquid. ● **v.** (**vatted**, **vatting**) place or treat in a vat.
– ORIGIN ME: southern and western dial. var. of obs. *fat* 'container', of Gmc origin.

**vat dye** ● **n.** an insoluble dye that is applied to a fabric in a reducing bath which converts it to a soluble form, the colour being obtained on subsequent oxidation.

**vatic** /'vatɪk/ ● **adj.** poetic/literary predicting what will happen in the future.
– ORIGIN C17: from L. *vates* 'prophet' + **-IC**.

**Vatican** ● **n.** the palace and official residence of the Pope in Rome.

**vaticinate** /va'tɪsɪneɪt/ ● **v.** rare foretell the future.
– DERIVATIVES **vaticinal** adj. **vaticination** n. **vaticinator** n. **vaticinatory** adj.
– ORIGIN C17: from L. *vaticinat-*, *vaticinari* 'prophesy'.

**vatu** /'vatuː/ ● **n.** (pl. same) the basic monetary unit of Vanuatu, equal to 100 centimes.
– ORIGIN from Bislama.

**vaudeville** /'vɔːdəvɪl, 'vəʊd-/ ● **n.** **1** a type of entertainment popular in the early 20th century, featuring a mixture of musical and comedy acts. ➤ a stage play on a trivial theme with songs. **2** archaic a satirical or topical song.
– DERIVATIVES **vaudevillian** adj. & n.
– ORIGIN C18: from Fr., earlier *vau de ville* (or *vire*), appar. denoting songs composed by Olivier Basselin, a C15 fuller born in *Vau de Vire* in Normandy.

**Vaudois**[1] /'vəʊdwɑː/ ● **n.** (pl. same) **1** a native of Vaud in Switzerland. **2** the French dialect spoken in this region.

● **adj.** of or relating to Vaud, its people, or their dialect.

**Vaudois²** /ˈvəʊdwɑː/ ● **n.** (pl. same) historical a member of the Waldenses religious sect. ● **adj.** of or relating to the Waldenses.
– ORIGIN C16: Fr., representing med. L. *Valdensis* (see **WALDENSES**).

**vault¹** /vɔːlt/ ● **n. 1** a roof in the form of an arch or a series of arches, typical of churches and other large, formal buildings. **2** a large room or chamber used for storage, especially an underground one. ➤ a secure room in a bank in which valuables are stored. ➤ a chamber beneath a church or in a graveyard used for burials. **3** Anatomy the arched roof of a cavity, especially that of the skull. ● **v.** [usu. as adj. **vaulted**] provide with or form into an arched roof.
– ORIGIN ME: from OFr. *voute*, based on L. *volvere* 'to roll'.

**vault²** /vɔːlt/ ● **v.** leap or spring while supporting or propelling oneself with the hands or a pole. ● **n.** an act of vaulting.
– DERIVATIVES **vaulter** n.
– ORIGIN C16: from OFr. *volter* 'to turn (a horse), gambol'.

**vaulting** ● **n.** ornamental work in a vaulted roof or ceiling.

**vaulting horse** ● **n.** a padded wooden block used for vaulting over by gymnasts and athletes.

**vaunt** /vɔːnt/ ● **v.** [usu. as adj. **vaunted**] boast about or praise (something), especially excessively. ● **n.** archaic a boast.
– DERIVATIVES **vaunter** n. **vaunting** adj. **vauntingly** adv.
– ORIGIN ME: the noun a shortening of obs. *avaunt* 'boasting, a boast'; the verb from OFr. *vanter*, from late L. *vantare*, based on L. *vanus* 'vain, empty'.

**vavasory** /ˈvavəs(ə)ri/ ● **n.** (pl. **-ies**) historical the estate of a vavasour.

**vavasour** /ˈvavəsʊə/ ● **n.** historical a vassal owing allegiance to a great lord and having other vassals under him.
– ORIGIN ME: from OFr. *vavas(s)our*, from med. L. *vavassor*, perh. from *vassus vassorum* 'vassal of vassals'.

**VC** ● **abbrev. 1** Vice-Chairman. **2** Vice Chancellor. **3** Vice-Consul. **4** Victoria Cross.

**V-chip** ● **n.** a computer chip installed in a television receiver that can be programmed to block violent or sexually explicit material.

**VCR** ● **abbrev.** video cassette recorder.

**VD** ● **abbrev.** venereal disease.

**VDU** ● **abbrev.** visual display unit.

**'ve** ● **abbrev.** informal have.

**veal** ● **n.** the flesh of a calf, used as food.
– ORIGIN ME: from Anglo-Norman Fr. *ve(e)l*, from L. *vitellus*, dimin. of *vitulus* 'calf'.

**vector** /ˈvɛktə/ ● **n. 1** Mathematics & Physics a quantity having direction as well as magnitude, especially as determining the position of one point in space relative to another. **2** an organism that transmits a particular disease or parasite from one animal or plant to another. ➤ Genetics a bacteriophage or plasmid which transfers genetic material into a cell. **3** a course to be taken by an aircraft. ● **v.** direct (an aircraft in flight) to a desired point.
– DERIVATIVES **vectorial** /-ˈtɔːrɪəl/ adj. **vectorially** adv. **vectorization** (also **-isation**) n. **vectorize** (also **-ise**) v.
– ORIGIN C19: from L., lit. 'carrier'.

**vector product** ● **n.** Mathematics the product of two vectors which is itself a vector at right angles to both the original vectors and equal to the product of their magnitudes and the sine of the angle between them (written as $\mathbf{a} \times \mathbf{b}$).

**VED** ● **abbrev.** vehicle excise duty.

**Veda** /ˈveɪdə, ˈviːdə/ ● **n.** [treated as sing. or pl.] the most ancient Hindu scriptures, in particular the Rig Veda, Sama Veda, Yajur Veda, and Atharva Veda.
– ORIGIN Sanskrit, lit. '(sacred) knowledge'.

**Vedanta** /vɪˈdɑːntə, -ˈdaː-, vɛ-/ ● **n.** a Hindu philosophy based on the doctrine of the Upanishads, especially in its monistic form.
– DERIVATIVES **Vedantic** adj. **Vedantist** n.
– ORIGIN from Sanskrit *vedānta*, from *veda* (see **VEDA**) + *anta* 'end'.

**VE day** ● **n.** the day (8 May) marking the Allied victory in Europe in 1945.
– ORIGIN abbrev. of *Victory in Europe*.

**Vedda** /ˈvɛdə/ ● **n.** a member of an aboriginal people inhabiting the forests of Sri Lanka.
– ORIGIN from Sinhalese *vaddā* 'hunter'.

**vedette** /vɪˈdɛt/ ● **n. 1** historical a mounted sentry positioned beyond an army's outposts to observe the movements of the enemy. **2** informal, chiefly N. Amer. a star of the entertainment world.
– ORIGIN C17: from Fr., lit. 'scout'.

**Vedic** /ˈveɪdɪk, ˈviː-/ ● **n.** the language of the Vedas, an early form of Sanskrit. ● **adj.** of or relating to the Veda or Vedas.

**vee** ● **n.** something shaped like the letter V.

**veejay** ● **n.** informal, chiefly N. Amer. a person who introduces and plays popular music videos.
– ORIGIN 1980s: representing a pronunc. of *VJ*, short for *video jockey*, on the pattern of *deejay*.

**veena** /ˈviːnə/ (also **vina**) ● **n.** an Indian stringed instrument, with four main and three auxiliary strings.
– ORIGIN from Sanskrit *vīṇā*.

**veep** ● **n.** N. Amer. informal vice-president.
– ORIGIN 1940s: from the initials *VP*.

**veer¹** ● **v. 1** change direction suddenly. ➤ suddenly change in opinion, subject, etc. **2** (of the wind) change direction clockwise around the points of the compass. The opposite of **BACK**. ● **n.** a sudden change of direction.
– ORIGIN C16: from Fr. *virer*, perh. from an alt. of L. *gyrare* (see **GYRATE**).

**veer²** ● **v.** Nautical, dated slacken or let out (a rope or cable) in a controlled way.
– ORIGIN ME: from MDu. *vieren*.

**veery** /ˈvɪəri/ ● **n.** a North American woodland thrush with a brown back and speckled breast. [*Catharus fuscescens*.]
– ORIGIN C19: perh. imitative.

**veg¹** /vɛdʒ/ ● **n.** (pl. same) Brit. informal a vegetable or vegetables.

**veg²** /vɛdʒ/ ● **v.** (**vegges**, **vegging**, **vegged**) (often **veg out**) informal relax to the point of complete inertia; vegetate.

**vega** /ˈveɪɡə/ ● **n.** (in Spain and Spanish America) a large grassy plain or valley.
– ORIGIN from Sp. and Catalan.

**vegan** ● **n.** a person who does not eat or use animal products.
– ORIGIN 1940s: from **VEGETARIAN** + **-AN**.

**Vegeburger** ● **n.** trademark for **VEGGIE BURGER**.

**Vegemite** /ˈvɛdʒɪmʌɪt/ ● **n.** Austral./NZ trademark a type of savoury spread made from concentrated yeast extract.
– ORIGIN 1920s: from **VEGETABLE**, on the pattern of *marmite*.

**vegetable** /ˈvɛdʒtəb(ə)l, ˈvɛdʒɪtə-/ ● **n. 1** a plant or part of a plant used as food. **2** informal, derogatory a person who is incapable of normal mental or physical activity, especially through brain damage. ➤ a person with a dull or inactive life.
– ORIGIN ME (in the sense 'growing as a plant'): from OFr., or from late L. *vegetabilis* 'animating', from L. *vegetare* (see **VEGETATE**).

**vegetable ivory** ● **n.** a hard white material obtained from the endosperm of the ivory nut.

**vegetable oil** ● **n.** an oil derived from plants, e.g. olive oil or sunflower oil.

**vegetable oyster** ● **n.** the edible root of salsify, the taste of which is said to resemble that of oysters.

**vegetable spaghetti** ● **n.** Brit. an edible squash of a variety with slightly stringy flesh which when cooked has a texture and appearance like that of spaghetti.

**vegetable sponge** ● **n.** another term for **LOOFAH**.

**vegetable tallow** ● **n.** vegetable fat used as tallow.

**vegetal** /ˈvɛdʒɪt(ə)l/ ● **adj. 1** formal of or relating to plants. **2** Biology denoting the pole or extremity of an embryo containing the less active cytoplasm. The opposite of **ANIMAL**.

– ORIGIN ME: from med. L. *vegetalis*, from L. *vegetare* 'animate'.

**vegetarian** ● **n.** a person who does not eat meat for moral, religious, or health reasons. ● **adj.** eating or including no meat.
– DERIVATIVES **vegetarianism** n.

**vegetate** ● **v. 1** live or spend a period of time in a dull, inactive, unchallenging way. **2** dated (of a plant or seed) grow or sprout.
– ORIGIN C17 (earlier (ME) in *vegetative*): from L. *vegetat-*, *vegetare* 'enliven'.

**vegetated** ● **adj.** covered with vegetation or plant life.

**vegetation** ● **n.** plants collectively, especially those found in a particular area or habitat.
– DERIVATIVES **vegetational** adj.

**vegetative** /ˈvɛdʒɪtətɪv, -teɪtɪv/ ● **adj. 1** Biology relating to or denoting reproduction or propagation achieved by asexual means, either naturally or artificially. **2** of or relating to vegetation or the growth of plants. **3** Medicine alive but comatose and without apparent brain activity or responsiveness.
– DERIVATIVES **vegetatively** adv. **vegetativeness** n.

**veggie** (also **vegie**) ● **n. & adj.** informal another term for **VEGETARIAN** or **VEGETABLE**.

**veggie burger** (also trademark **Vegeburger**) ● **n.** a savoury cake resembling a hamburger but made with vegetable protein or soya instead of meat.

**vehement** /ˈviːɪm(ə)nt/ ● **adj.** showing strong feeling; forceful, passionate, or intense.
– DERIVATIVES **vehemence** n. **vehemently** adv.
– ORIGIN ME (describing intense pain or high temperature): from Fr. *véhément* or L. *vehement-* 'impetuous, violent', perh. from an unrecorded adjective meaning 'deprived of mind', influenced by *vehere* 'carry'.

**vehicle** ● **n. 1** a thing used for transporting people or goods on land, e.g. a car, truck, or cart. **2** a means of expressing, embodying, or fulfilling something. ➤a substance that facilitates the use of a drug, pigment, or other material mixed with it. ➤a film, programme, song, etc., intended to display the leading performer to the best advantage.
– DERIVATIVES **vehicular** /vɪˈhɪkjʊlə/ adj.
– ORIGIN C17: from Fr. *véhicule* or L. *vehiculum*, from *vehere* 'carry'.

**veil** ● **n. 1** a piece of fine material worn to protect or conceal the face. ➤a piece of fabric forming part of a nun's headdress, resting on the head and shoulders. **2** a thing that conceals, disguises, or obscures: *an eerie veil of mist.* **3** (in Jewish antiquity) the piece of precious cloth separating the sanctuary from the body of the Temple or the Tabernacle. **4** Botany a membrane which is attached to the immature fruiting body of some toadstools and ruptures in the course of development. ● **v.** cover with or as though with a veil. ➤[usu. as adj. **veiled**] partially conceal, disguise, or obscure: *a thinly veiled threat.*
– PHRASES **draw a veil over** avoid discussing or calling attention to (something embarrassing or unpleasant). **take the veil** become a nun.
– DERIVATIVES **veiling** n. **veilless** adj.
– ORIGIN ME: from Anglo-Norman Fr. *veil(e)*, from L. *vela*, pl. of *velum* (see **VELUM**).

**vein** ● **n. 1** any of the tubes forming part of the circulation system by which blood is conveyed from all parts of the body towards the heart. ➤(in general use) a blood vessel. **2** (in plants) a slender rib running through a leaf, typically dividing or branching, and containing vascular tissue. ➤(in insects) a hollow rib forming part of the supporting framework of a wing. **3** a streak or stripe of a different colour in wood, marble, cheese, etc. ➤a fracture in rock containing a deposit of minerals or ore. ➤a source of a specified quality or other abstract resource: *a rich vein of satire.* **4** a distinctive quality, style, or tendency: *he closes his article in a humorous vein.*
– DERIVATIVES **veined** adj. **veining** n. **veinless** adj. **veinlet** n. **vein-like** adj. & adv. **veiny** adj. (**-ier**, **-iest**).
– ORIGIN ME: from OFr. *veine*, from L. *vena*.

**veinous** ● **adj.** having prominent or noticeable veins.

**veinstone** ● **n.** another term for **GANGUE**.

**vela** plural form of **VELUM**.

**velamen** /vɪˈleɪmən/ ● **n.** (pl. **velamina** /-mɪnə/) Botany an outer layer of empty cells in the aerial roots of epiphytic orchids and aroids.
– ORIGIN C19: from L., from *velare* 'to cover'.

**velar** /ˈviːlə/ ● **adj. 1** of or relating to a veil or velum. **2** Phonetics (of a speech sound) pronounced with the back of the tongue near the soft palate, as in *k* and *g* in English. ● **n.** a velar sound.
– DERIVATIVES **velarization** /ˌviːlərʌɪˈzeɪʃ(ə)n/ (also **-isation**) n. **velarize** (also **-ise**) v.
– ORIGIN C18: from L. *velaris*, from *velum* (see **VELUM**).

**velarium** /vɪˈlɛːrɪəm/ ● **n.** (pl. **velaria** /-rɪə/) **1** a large awning used in ancient Rome to shelter an amphitheatre. **2** an inner ceiling used to improve acoustics in a theatre.
– ORIGIN from L.

**Velcro** /ˈvɛlkrəʊ/ ● **n.** trademark a fastener consisting of two strips of thin plastic sheet, one covered with tiny loops and the other with tiny flexible hooks, which adhere when pressed together.
– DERIVATIVES **Velcroed** adj.
– ORIGIN 1960s: from Fr. *velours croché* 'hooked velvet'.

**veld** /vɛlt/ (also **veldt**) ● **n.** open, uncultivated country or grassland in southern Africa.
– ORIGIN Afrik., from Du., lit. 'field'.

**veldskoen** /ˈfɛltskʊn, ˈfɛls-/ ● **n. 1** a strong suede or leather shoe or boot. **2** [as modifier] S. African conservative or reactionary.
– ORIGIN Afrik., lit. 'field shoe'.

**veleta** /vəˈliːtə/ (also **valeta**) ● **n.** a ballroom dance in triple time, faster than a waltz and with partners side by side.
– ORIGIN C20: from Sp., lit. 'weathervane'.

**veliger** /ˈviːlɪdʒə/ ● **n.** Zoology the final larval stage of certain molluscs, having two ciliated flaps for swimming and feeding.
– ORIGIN C19: from **VELUM** + L. *-ger* 'bearing'.

**velleity** /vɛˈliːɪti/ ● **n.** (pl. **-ies**) formal a wish or inclination not strong enough to lead to action.
– ORIGIN C17: from med. L. *velleitas*, from L. *velle* 'to wish'.

**vellum** /ˈvɛləm/ ● **n.** fine parchment made originally from the skin of a calf.
– ORIGIN ME: from OFr. *velin*, from *veel* (see **VEAL**).

**velocimeter** /ˌvɛlə(ʊ)ˈsɪmɪtə/ ● **n.** an instrument for measuring velocity.
– DERIVATIVES **velocimetry** n.

**velocipede** /vɪˈlɒsɪpiːd/ ● **n. 1** historical an early form of bicycle propelled by working pedals on cranks fitted to the front axle. **2** US a child's tricycle.
– DERIVATIVES **velocipedist** n.
– ORIGIN C19: from Fr. *vélocipède*, from L. *velox*, *veloc-* 'swift' + *pes*, *ped-* 'foot'.

**velociraptor** /vɪˌlɒsɪˈraptə/ ● **n.** a small dromaeosaurid dinosaur of the late Cretaceous period.
– ORIGIN mod. L., from L. *velox*, *veloc-* 'swift' + **RAPTOR**.

**velocity** /vɪˈlɒsɪti/ ● **n.** (pl. **-ies**) the speed of something in a given direction. ➤(in general use) speed.
– ORIGIN ME: from Fr. *vélocité* or L. *velocitas*, from *velox*, *veloc-* 'swift'.

**velodrome** /ˈvɛlədrəʊm/ ● **n.** a cycle-racing track with steeply banked curves.
– ORIGIN C19: from Fr. *vélodrome*, from *vélo* 'bicycle' + *-drome* (see **-DROME**).

**velour** /vəˈlʊə/ (also **velours**) ● **n.** a plush woven fabric resembling velvet, chiefly used for soft furnishings and hats.
– ORIGIN C18: from Fr. *velours* 'velvet'.

**velouté** /vəˈluːteɪ/ ● **n.** a sauce made from a roux of butter and flour with chicken, veal, or pork stock.
– ORIGIN Fr., lit. 'velvety'.

**velum** /ˈviːləm/ ● **n.** (pl. **vela** /-lə/) **1** Zoology a membrane, typically bordering a cavity, especially in certain molluscs, medusae, and other invertebrates. **2** Botany the veil of a toadstool. **3** Anatomy the soft palate.
– ORIGIN C18: from L., lit. 'sail, curtain, covering, veil'.

**velvet** ● **n. 1** a closely woven fabric of silk, cotton, or

nylon with a thick short pile on one side. **2** soft downy skin that covers a deer's antler while it is growing.
– DERIVATIVES **velveted** adj. **velvety** adj.
– ORIGIN ME: from OFr. *veluotte*, from *velu* 'velvety', from med. L. *villutus*, from L. *villus* 'tuft, down'.

**velvet ant** • n. a velvety-bodied hymenopterous insect whose larvae parasitize bees and wasps. [Family Mutillidae: numerous species.]

**velveteen** • n. a cotton fabric with a pile resembling velvet.

**velvet worm** • n. a tropical terrestrial invertebrate with a soft worm-like body and stumpy legs. [Phylum Onychophorac.]

**Ven.** • abbrev. Venerable (as the title of an archdeacon).

**vena cava** /ˌviːnə ˈkeɪvə/ • n. (pl. **venae cavae** /-niː -viː/) each of two large veins carrying deoxygenated blood into the heart.
– ORIGIN C16: from L., lit. 'hollow vein'.

**venal** /ˈviːn(ə)l/ • adj. showing or motivated by susceptibility to bribery.
– DERIVATIVES **venality** n. **venally** adv.
– ORIGIN C17 (in the sense 'available for purchase'): from L. *venalis*, from *venum* 'thing for sale'.

**venation** /vɪˈneɪʃ(ə)n/ • n. Biology the arrangement of veins in a leaf or in an insect's wing. ➤ the system of venous blood vessels in an animal.
– DERIVATIVES **venational** adj.
– ORIGIN C17: from L. *vena* 'vein' + **-ATION**.

**vend** • v. **1** offer (small items) for sale, especially from a slot machine. **2** Law or formal sell.
– DERIVATIVES **vendible** adj.
– ORIGIN C17 (earlier (C16) in *vendor*): from Fr. *vendre* or L. *vendere* 'sell'.

**Venda** /ˈvɛndə/ • n. (pl. same or **Vendas**) **1** a member of a people living in Northern Transvaal and southern Zimbabwe. **2** the Bantu language of this people.
– ORIGIN from the stem of Venda *Muvenda* (in sense 1), *Tshivenda* (in sense 2).

**vendace** /ˈvɛndɪs/ • n. an edible whitefish found in lakes in northern Europe. [*Coregonus albula*.]
– ORIGIN C18: from obs. Fr. *vendese*, from a base rel. to Welsh *gwyn* 'white'.

**vendetta** /vɛnˈdɛtə/ • n. **1** a blood feud in which the family of a murdered person seeks vengeance on the murderer or the murderer's family. **2** a prolonged bitter quarrel with or campaign against someone.
– ORIGIN C19: from Ital., from L. *vindicta* 'vengeance'.

**vendeuse** /vɒ̃ˈdəːz, French vɑ̃døz/ • n. a saleswoman, especially one in a fashionable dress shop.
– ORIGIN from Fr.

**vending machine** • n. a machine that dispenses small articles when a coin or token is inserted.

**vendor** (US also **vender**) • n. **1** a person or company offering something for sale, especially a trader in the street. **2** Law the seller in a sale, especially of property.

**vendue** /vɛnˈdjuː/ • n. US & W. Indian a public auction.
– ORIGIN C17: via Du. from Fr. dial. *vendue* 'sale'.

**veneer** /vɪˈnɪə/ • n. **1** a thin decorative covering of fine wood applied to a coarser wood or other material. ➤ a layer of wood used to make plywood. **2** an attractive appearance that covers or disguises true nature or feelings. • v. [usu. as adj. **veneered**] cover with a veneer.
– DERIVATIVES **veneering** n.
– ORIGIN C18 (orig. as *fineer*): from Ger. *furni(e)ren*, from OFr. *fournir* 'furnish'.

**venepuncture** /ˈvɛnɪˌpʌŋ(k)tʃə, ˈviːnɪ-/ (chiefly N. Amer. also **venipuncture**) • n. the puncture of a vein to withdraw a blood sample or for an intravenous injection.
– ORIGIN 1920s: from L. *vena* 'vein' + **PUNCTURE**.

**venerable** • adj. **1** accorded great respect because of age, wisdom, or character. **2** (in the Anglican Church) a title given to an archdeacon. **3** (in the Roman Catholic Church) a title given to a deceased person who has attained a certain degree of sanctity but has not been fully beatified or canonized.
– DERIVATIVES **venerability** n. **venerableness** n. **venerably** adv.
– ORIGIN ME: from OFr., or from L. *venerabilis*, from *venerari* (see **VENERATE**).

**venerate** /ˈvɛnəreɪt/ • v. regard with great respect.
– DERIVATIVES **veneration** n. **venerator** n.
– ORIGIN C17 (earlier (ME) as *veneration*): from L. *venerat-*, *venerari* 'adore, revere'.

**venereal** /vɪˈnɪərɪəl/ • adj. **1** of or relating to venereal disease. **2** formal of or relating to sexual desire or sexual intercourse.
– DERIVATIVES **venereally** adv.
– ORIGIN ME: from L. *venereus* (from *venus*, *vener-* 'sexual love') + **-AL**.

**venereal disease** • n. a disease contracted by sexual intercourse with a person already infected.

**venereology** /vɪˌnɪərɪˈɒlədʒi/ • n. the branch of medicine concerned with venereal diseases.
– DERIVATIVES **venereological** adj. **venereologist** n.

**venery**[1] /ˈvɛn(ə)ri/ • n. archaic sexual indulgence.
– ORIGIN ME: from med. L. *veneria*, from *venus*, *vener-* 'sexual love'.

**venery**[2] /ˈvɛn(ə)ri/ • n. archaic hunting.
– ORIGIN ME: from OFr. *venerie*, from *vener* 'to hunt', from L. *venari*.

**venesection** /ˌvɛnɪˈsɛkʃ(ə)n, ˈvɛnɪ-/ • n. another term for **PHLEBOTOMY**.
– ORIGIN C17: from med. L. *venae sectio(n-)* 'cutting of a vein'.

**Venetian** • adj. of or relating to Venice or its people. • n. a native or citizen of Venice.

**venetian blind** • n. a window blind consisting of horizontal slats which can be pivoted to control the amount of light that passes through.

**Venetian red** • n. a reddish-brown pigment consisting of ferric oxide.

**Venetian window** • n. a window with three separate openings, the central one being arched and taller than the others.

**Venezuelan** /ˌvɛnɪˈzweɪlən, Spanish beneˈswelan, -θwelan/ • n. a native or inhabitant of Venezuela. • adj. of or relating to Venezuela.

**vengeance** /ˈvɛn(d)ʒ(ə)ns/ • n. punishment inflicted or retribution exacted for an injury or wrong.
– PHRASES **with a vengeance** with great intensity.
– ORIGIN ME: from OFr., from *venger* 'avenge'.

**vengeful** • adj. seeking to harm someone in return for a perceived injury.
– DERIVATIVES **vengefully** adv. **vengefulness** n.
– ORIGIN C16: from obs. *venge* 'avenge' (see **VENGEANCE**), on the pattern of *revengeful*.

**venial** /ˈviːnɪəl/ • adj. Christian Theology denoting a sin that is not regarded as depriving the soul of divine grace. Often contrasted with **MORTAL**. ➤ (of a fault or offence) slight and pardonable.
– DERIVATIVES **veniality** /-ˈalɪti/ n. **venially** adv.
– ORIGIN ME: via OFr. from late L. *venialis*, from *venia* 'forgiveness'.

**venipuncture** • n. chiefly N. Amer. variant spelling of **VENEPUNCTURE**.

**venison** /ˈvɛnɪs(ə)n, ˈvɛnɪz(ə)n/ • n. meat from a deer.
– ORIGIN ME: from OFr. *veneso(u)n*, from L. *venatio(n-)* 'hunting', from *venari* 'to hunt'.

**Venite** /vɪˈnʌɪti, vɪˈniːti, -teɪ/ • n. Psalm 95 used as a canticle in Christian liturgy, chiefly at matins.
– ORIGIN L., lit. 'come ye', the first word of the psalm.

**Venn diagram** • n. a diagram representing mathematical or logical sets as circles, common elements of the sets being represented by intersections of the circles.
– ORIGIN C20: named after the Engl. logician John *Venn*.

**vennel** /ˈvɛn(ə)l/ • n. chiefly Scottish an alley.
– ORIGIN ME: from OFr. *venele*, from med. L. *venella*, dimin. of L. *vena* 'vein'.

**venom** • n. **1** poisonous fluid secreted by animals such as snakes and scorpions and typically injected into prey or aggressors by biting or stinging. **2** extreme malice, bitterness, or aggression.
– DERIVATIVES **venomed** adj.
– ORIGIN ME: from OFr. *venim*, var. of *venin*, from an alt. of L. *venenum* 'poison'.

**venomous** /ˈvɛnəməs/ ● **adj.** **1** secreting or capable of injecting venom. **2** very malicious, bitter, or aggressive.
– DERIVATIVES **venomously** adv. **venomousness** n.

**venous** /ˈviːnəs/ ● **adj.** of a vein or the veins.
– DERIVATIVES **venosity** /vɪˈnɒsɪti/ n. **venously** adv.
– ORIGIN C17: from L. *venosus* 'having many veins', from *vena* 'vein'.

**vent**[1] ● **n.** **1** an opening that allows air, gas, or liquid to pass out of or into a confined space. ➤the opening of a volcano, through which lava and other materials are emitted. ➤chiefly Scottish a flue of a chimney. **2** (usu. in phr. **give vent to**) release or expression of a strong emotion, energy, etc. **3** the anus of a lower animal such as a fish, serving for both excretion and reproduction. **4** historical the touch hole of a gun. ● **v.** **1** give free expression to (a strong emotion). **2** discharge (air, gas, or liquid) through an outlet. ➤provide with an outlet for air, gas, or liquid. ➤permit air to enter (a beer cask).
– DERIVATIVES **vented** adj. **ventless** adj.
– ORIGIN ME: partly from Fr. *vent* 'wind', from L. *ventus*, reinforced by Fr. *évent*, from *éventer* 'expose to air'.

**vent**[2] ● **n.** a slit in a garment, especially one in the lower edge of the back of a coat through the seam.
– ORIGIN ME: alt. of dial. *fent*, from OFr. *fente* 'slit', based on L. *findere* 'cleave'.

**ventiduct** /ˈvɛntɪdʌkt/ ● **n.** Architecture an air passage, especially one for ventilation.
– ORIGIN C17: from L. *ventus* 'wind' + *ductus* 'duct'.

**ventifact** /ˈvɛntɪfakt/ ● **n.** Geology a stone shaped by the erosive action of wind-blown sand.
– ORIGIN C20: from L. *ventus* 'wind' + *fact-*, *facere* 'make'.

**ventil** /ˈvɛntɪl/ ● **n.** Music **1** a valve in a wind instrument. **2** a shutter for regulating the airflow in an organ.
– ORIGIN C19: from Ger., from Ital. *ventile*, from med. L. *ventile* 'sluice', from L. *ventus* 'wind'.

**ventilate** ● **v.** **1** cause air to enter and circulate freely in (a room or building). **2** discuss (an opinion or issue) in public. **3** Medicine subject to artificial respiration. **4** informal kill by shooting. **5** archaic oxygenate (the blood).
– DERIVATIVES **ventilation** n.
– ORIGIN ME (in the sense 'winnow, scatter'): from L. *ventilat-*, *ventilare* 'blow, winnow', from *ventus* 'wind'.

**ventilator** ● **n.** **1** an appliance or aperture for ventilating a room or other space. **2** Medicine an appliance for artificial respiration; a respirator.
– DERIVATIVES **ventilatory** adj.

**Ventolin** /ˈvɛntəlɪn/ ● **n.** trademark for **SALBUTAMOL**.
– ORIGIN 1960s: perh. from **VENTILATE** + **-OL** + **-IN**[1].

**ventouse** /ˈvɛntuːs/ ● **n.** Medicine a cup-shaped suction device applied to the baby's head to assist the birth.
– ORIGIN 1960s: from Fr., lit. 'cupping-glass', based on L. *ventus* 'wind'.

**ventral** ● **adj.** Anatomy, Zoology, & Botany on or relating to the underside of an animal or plant; abdominal. Compare with **DORSAL**.
– DERIVATIVES **ventrally** adv.
– ORIGIN ME: from L. *venter*, *ventr-* 'belly' + **-AL**.

**ventral fin** ● **n.** Zoology another term for **PELVIC FIN**.

**ventre à terre** /ˌvɒ̃tr(ə) ɑː ˈtɛː, French vɑ̃tʀ a tɛʀ/ ● **adv.** (especially of a horse) at full speed.
– ORIGIN Fr., lit. '(with) belly to the ground'.

**ventricle** /ˈvɛntrɪk(ə)l/ ● **n.** Anatomy **1** each of the two larger and lower cavities of the heart. **2** each of four connected fluid-filled cavities in the centre of the brain.
– DERIVATIVES **ventricular** /-ˈtrɪkjʊlə/ adj.
– ORIGIN ME: from L. *ventriculus*, dimin. of *venter* 'belly'.

**ventriloquist** /vɛnˈtrɪləkwɪst/ ● **n.** an entertainer who makes their voice seem to come from a dummy of a person or animal.
– DERIVATIVES **ventriloquial** /ˌvɛntrɪˈləʊkwɪəl/ adj. **ventriloquism** n. **ventriloquize** (also **-ise**) v. **ventriloquy** n.
– ORIGIN C17: from mod. L. *ventriloquium* (from L. *venter* 'belly' + *loqui* 'speak') + **-IST**.

**venture** ● **n.** a risky or daring journey or undertaking. ➤a business enterprise involving considerable risk. ● **v.** undertake a risky or daring journey or course of action. ➤expose to the risk of loss.
– DERIVATIVES **venturer** n.
– ORIGIN ME: shortening of **ADVENTURE**.

**venture capital** ● **n.** capital invested in a project in which there is a substantial element of risk.
– DERIVATIVES **venture capitalist** n.

**Venture Scout** ● **n.** a member of the Scout Association aged between 16 and 20.

**venturesome** ● **adj.** willing to take risks or embark on difficult or unusual courses of action.
– DERIVATIVES **venturesomely** adv. **venturesomeness** n.

**venturi** /vɛnˈtjʊəri/ ● **n.** (pl. **venturis**) a short piece of narrow tube between wider sections for measuring flow rate or exerting suction.
– ORIGIN C19: named after the Ital. physicist Giovanni B. *Venturi*.

**venue** /ˈvɛnjuː/ ● **n.** **1** the place where something happens, especially an event such as a concert or sports event. **2** English Law the county or district within which a criminal or civil case must be heard.
– ORIGIN C16 (denoting a thrust or bout in fencing; also in the legal sense): from OFr., lit. 'a coming', fem. past part. of *venir* 'come'.

**venule** /ˈvɛnjuːl/ ● **n.** Anatomy a very small vein, especially one collecting blood from the capillaries.
– ORIGIN C19: from L. *venula*, dimin. of *vena* 'vein'.

**Venus** ● **n.** a planet of the solar system, second in order from the sun and the brightest object in the sky after the sun and moon.
– DERIVATIVES **Venusian** /vɪˈnjuːzɪən/ adj. & n.

**Venus flytrap** ● **n.** a small carnivorous bog plant with hinged leaves that spring shut on and digest insects which land on them. [*Dionaea muscipula*.]

**venus shell** (also chiefly US **venus clam**) ● **n.** a burrowing marine bivalve mollusc having a rounded shell with clearly defined growth lines. [*Venus* and other genera.]

**Venus's looking glass** ● **n.** a blue-flowered bellflower whose shiny brown seeds inside their open capsule supposedly resemble looking glasses. [*Legousia hybrida* (Europe) and *Triodanis perfoliata* (N. America).]

**veracious** /vəˈreɪʃəs/ ● **adj.** formal speaking or representing the truth.
– DERIVATIVES **veraciously** adv. **veraciousness** n.
– ORIGIN C17: from L. *verax*, *verac-* (from *verus* 'true') + **-IOUS**.

**veracity** /vəˈrasɪti/ ● **n.** conformity to facts; accuracy. ➤habitual truthfulness.

**veranda** (also **verandah**) ● **n.** **1** a roofed platform along the outside of a house, level with the ground floor. **2** Austral./NZ a roof over the pavement in front of a shop.
– DERIVATIVES **verandaed** adj.
– ORIGIN C18: from Hindi *varaṇḍā*, from Port. *varanda* 'railing, balustrade'.

**veratrine** /ˈvɛrətriːn, -ɪn/ ● **n.** Chemistry a poisonous substance consisting of a mixture of alkaloids which occurs in the seeds of sabadilla and related plants.
– ORIGIN C19: from Fr. *vératrine*, from L. *veratrum* 'hellebore'.

**verb** ● **n.** Grammar a word used to describe an action, state, or occurrence, and forming the main part of the predicate of a sentence, such as *hear*, *become*, or *happen*.
– DERIVATIVES **verbless** adj.
– ORIGIN ME: from OFr. *verbe* or L. *verbum* 'word, verb'.

**verbal** ● **adj.** **1** relating to or in the form of words. **2** spoken rather than written; oral. ➤informal tending to talk a lot. **3** Grammar relating to or derived from a verb. ● **n.** **1** Grammar a word or words functioning as a verb. ➤a verbal noun. **2** (also **verbals**) Brit. informal abuse; insults. **3** (also **verbals**) Brit. informal a verbal statement containing a damaging admission alleged to have been made to the police, offered as evidence by the prosecution. ● **v.** (**verballed**, **verballing**) Brit. informal attribute a damaging statement to (a suspect), especially dishonestly.
– DERIVATIVES **verbally** adv.

**verbalism** ● **n.** **1** concentration on forms of expression rather than content. ➤excessive or empty use of language. **2** a verbal expression.
– DERIVATIVES **verbalist** n. **verbalistic** adj.

**verbalize** (also **-ise**) ● **v.** **1** express in words, especially

by speaking aloud. **2** speak at length and with little real content. **3** make (a word, especially a noun) into a verb.
– DERIVATIVES **verbalizable** adj. **verbalization** n. **verbalizer** n.

**verbal noun** ● n. Grammar a noun formed as an inflection of a verb and partly sharing its constructions, such as *smoking* in *smoking is forbidden*.

**verbascum** /vəːˈbaskəm/ ● n. a plant of a genus that comprises the mulleins. [Genus *Verbascum*.]
– ORIGIN mod. L., from L., lit. 'mullein'.

**verbatim** /vəːˈbeɪtɪm/ ● adv. & adj. in exactly the same words as were used originally.
– ORIGIN C15: from med. L., from L. *verbum* 'word'.

**verbena** /vəːˈbiːnə/ ● n. a chiefly American ornamental plant with heads of bright showy flowers. [Genus *Verbena*.]
– ORIGIN mod. L., from L., lit. 'sacred bough', in med. L. 'vervain'.

**verbiage** /ˈvəːbɪɪdʒ/ ● n. excessively lengthy or technical speech or writing.
– ORIGIN C18: from Fr., from obs. *verbeier* 'to chatter'.

**verbose** /vəːˈbəʊs/ ● adj. using or expressed in more words than are needed.
– DERIVATIVES **verbosely** adv. **verbosity** n.
– ORIGIN C17: from L. *verbosus*, from *verbum* 'word'.

**verboten** /vəˈbəʊt(ə)n, German fɛɐˈboːtn/ ● adj. forbidden by an authority.
– ORIGIN from Ger.

**verb phrase** ● n. Grammar the part of a sentence containing the verb and any direct or indirect object, but not the subject.

**verdant** /ˈvəːd(ə)nt/ ● adj. green with grass or other lush vegetation.
– DERIVATIVES **verdancy** n. **verdantly** adv.
– ORIGIN C16: perh. from OFr. *verdeant*, pres. part. of *verdoier* 'be green'.

**verd-antique** /ˌvəːdanˈtiːk/ ● n. **1** a green ornamental marble consisting of serpentine with calcite and dolomite. **2** verdigris on ancient bronze or copper. **3** a green form of porphyry.
– ORIGIN C18: from obs. Fr., lit. 'antique green'.

**Verdelho** /vəːˈdɛljuː, -ljəʊ/ ● n. (pl. **-os**) a white grape grown originally in Madeira. ➤ a medium Madeira made from this grape.
– ORIGIN from Port.

**verderer** /ˈvəːd(ə)rə/ ● n. Brit. a judicial officer of a royal forest.
– ORIGIN C16: from Anglo-Norman Fr., based on L. *viridis* 'green'.

**verdict** ● n. **1** a decision on an issue of fact in a civil or criminal case or an inquest. **2** an opinion or judgement.
– ORIGIN ME: from Anglo-Norman Fr. *verdit*, from OFr. *veir* 'true' (from L. *verus*) + *dit* (from L. *dictum* 'saying').

**verdigris** /ˈvəːdɪgriː, -griːs/ ● n. a bright bluish-green encrustation or patina formed on copper or brass by atmospheric oxidation.
– ORIGIN ME: from OFr. *verte-gres*, earlier *vert de Grece* 'green of Greece'.

**verdure** /ˈvəːdjə, -jʊə/ ● n. lush green vegetation.
– DERIVATIVES **verdured** adj. **verdurous** adj.
– ORIGIN ME: via Fr. from OFr. *verd* 'green'.

**verge**[1] ● n. **1** an edge or border. ➤ Brit. a grass edging by the side of a road or path. ➤ Architecture an edge of tiles projecting over a gable. **2** an extreme limit beyond which something specified will happen: *I was on the verge of tears*. ● v. (**verge on**) be very close or similar to.
– ORIGIN ME: via OFr. from L. *virga* 'rod'.

**verge**[2] ● n. a wand or rod carried before a bishop or dean as an emblem of office.
– ORIGIN ME: from L. *virga* 'rod'.

**verge**[3] ● v. incline in a certain direction or towards a particular state.
– ORIGIN C17 (in the sense 'descend (to the horizon)'): from L. *vergere* 'to bend, incline'.

**vergence** ● n. **1** Physiology the simultaneous movement of the pupils of the eyes towards or away from one another during focusing. **2** Geology the direction in which a fold is inclined or overturned.
– ORIGIN 1980s: common element of *convergence* and *divergence*.

**verger** ● n. **1** an official in a church who acts as a caretaker and attendant. **2** an officer who carries a rod before a bishop or dean as a symbol of office.
– DERIVATIVES **vergership** n.
– ORIGIN ME: from Anglo-Norman Fr. (see **VERGE**[2]).

**Vergilian** ● adj. variant spelling of **VIRGILIAN**.

**verglas** /ˈvɛːglɑː/ ● n. a thin coating of ice or frozen rain on an exposed surface.
– ORIGIN C19: Fr., from *verre* 'glass' + *glas* (now *glace*) 'ice'.

**veridical** /vɪˈrɪdɪk(ə)l/ ● adj. formal truthful or coinciding with reality.
– DERIVATIVES **veridicality** n. **veridically** adv.
– ORIGIN C17: from L. *veridicus* (from *verus* 'true' + *dicere* 'say') + **-AL**.

**veriest** ● adj. archaic used to emphasize a description: *everyone but the veriest greenhorn knows by now*.
– ORIGIN C16: superlative of **VERY**.

**verification** ● n. the process of verifying. ➤ Philosophy the establishment by empirical means of the validity of a proposition. ➤ the process of ensuring that procedures laid down in weapons limitation agreements are followed.

**verify** /ˈvɛrɪfʌɪ/ ● v. (**-ies**, **-ied**) **1** make sure or demonstrate that (something) is true, accurate, or justified. **2** Law swear to or support (a statement) by affidavit.
– DERIVATIVES **verifiable** adj. **verifiably** adv. **verifier** n.
– ORIGIN ME: from OFr. *verifier*, from med. L. *verificare*, from *verus* 'true'.

**verily** ● adv. archaic truly; certainly.
– ORIGIN ME: from **VERY** + **-LY**[2], suggested by OFr. *verrai(e)ment*.

**verisimilitude** /ˌvɛrɪsɪˈmɪlɪtjuːd/ ● n. the appearance of being true or real.
– DERIVATIVES **verisimilar** adj.
– ORIGIN C17: from L. *verisimilitudo*, from *verisimilis* 'probable', from *veri* (genitive of *verus* 'true') + *similis* 'like'.

**verismo** /vɛˈrɪzməʊ/ ● n. realism in the arts (especially with reference to late 19th-century Italian opera).
– ORIGIN from Ital.

**veristic** /vɪəˈrɪstɪk/ ● adj. (of art or literature) extremely or strictly naturalistic.
– DERIVATIVES **verism** n. **verist** n. & adj.
– ORIGIN C19: from L. *verum* (neut.) 'true' or Ital. *vero* 'true' + **-IST** + **-IC**.

**veritable** ● adj. genuine; actual; properly so called (used to qualify a metaphor): *a veritable price explosion*.
– DERIVATIVES **veritably** adv.
– ORIGIN ME (in senses 'true' and 'truthful'): from OFr., from *verite* (see **VERITY**).

**vérité** /ˈvɛrɪteɪ, French veʀite/ ● n. a genre of film and television emphasizing realism and naturalism.
– ORIGIN Fr., lit. 'truth'.

**verity** ● n. (pl. **-ies**) a true principle or belief, especially one of fundamental importance: *the eternal verities*. ➤ truth.
– ORIGIN ME: from OFr. *verite*, from L. *veritas*, from *verus* 'true'.

**verjuice** /ˈvəːdʒuːs/ ● n. a sour juice obtained especially from crab apples or unripe grapes.
– ORIGIN ME: from OFr. *vertjus*, from *vert* 'green' + *jus* 'juice'.

**verkrampte** /fɛːˈkramptə/ (also **verkramp** /fɛːˈkramp/) ● adj. S. African conservative or reactionary.
– DERIVATIVES **verkramptheid** n.
– ORIGIN Afrik., lit. 'narrow, cramped'.

**verligte** /fɛːˈlɪxtə/ (also **verlig**) ● adj. S. African progressive or enlightened.
– DERIVATIVES **verligtheid** n.
– ORIGIN Afrik., lit. 'enlightened'.

**vermeil** /ˈvəːmeɪl, -mɪl/ ● n. **1** gilded silver or bronze. **2** poetic/literary vermilion.
– ORIGIN ME: from OFr. (see **VERMILION**).

**vermi-** ● comb. form of or relating to a worm or worms, especially parasitic ones: *vermiform*.
– ORIGIN from L. *vermis* 'worm'.

**vermian** /ˈvəːmɪən/ ● **adj.** poetic/literary relating to or resembling a worm; worm-like.

**vermicelli** /ˌvəːmɪˈtʃɛli, ˌvɛːm-, -ˈsɛli/ ● **pl. n.** **1** pasta made in long slender threads. **2** Brit. shreds of chocolate used to decorate cakes.
– ORIGIN Ital., pl. of *vermicello*, dimin. of *verme* 'worm'.

**vermicide** /ˈvəːmɪsʌɪd/ ● **n.** a substance that is poisonous to worms.

**vermicular** /vəˈmɪkjʊlə/ ● **adj.** **1** like a worm in form or movement; vermiform. **2** relating to or caused by intestinal worms.
– ORIGIN C17: from med. L. *vermicularis*, from L. *vermiculus*, dimin. of *vermis* 'worm'.

**vermiculate** /vəˈmɪkjʊlət/ ● **adj.** another term for **VERMICULAR** or **VERMICULATED**.

**vermiculated** ● **adj.** **1** marked with sinuous or wavy lines. **2** archaic worm-eaten.

**vermiculite** /vəˈmɪkjʊlʌɪt/ ● **n.** a yellow or brown mineral found as an alteration product of mica and other minerals, used for insulation or as a moisture-retentive medium for growing plants.
– ORIGIN C19: from L. *vermiculari* 'be full of worms' (because on expansion due to heat, it shoots out forms resembling small worms) + **-ITE**[1].

**vermiform** ● **adj.** chiefly Zoology or Anatomy resembling or having the form of a worm.

**vermifuge** /ˈvəːmɪfjuːdʒ/ ● **n.** Medicine an anthelmintic medicine.

**vermilion** /vəˈmɪljən/ (also **vermillion**) ● **n.** a brilliant red pigment made from mercury sulphide (cinnabar). ➤ a brilliant red colour.
– ORIGIN ME: from OFr. *vermeillon*, from *vermeil*, from L. *vermiculus*, dimin. of *vermis* 'worm'.

**vermin** ● **n.** [treated as pl.] **1** wild mammals and birds which are harmful to crops, farm animals, or game, or which carry disease. ➤ parasitic worms or insects. **2** very unpleasant and destructive people.
– DERIVATIVES **verminous** adj.
– ORIGIN ME: from OFr., based on L. *vermis* 'worm'.

**verminate** ● **v.** [usu. as adj. **verminating**] archaic breed or become infested with vermin.
– DERIVATIVES **vermination** n.

**Vermonter** /vəˈmɒntə/ ● **n.** a native or inhabitant of the US state of Vermont.

**vermouth** /ˈvəːməθ, vəˈmuːθ/ ● **n.** a red or white wine flavoured with aromatic herbs, chiefly drunk mixed with gin.
– ORIGIN from Fr. *vermout*, from Ger. *Wermut* 'wormwood'.

**vernacular** /vəˈnakjʊlə/ ● **n.** **1** the language or dialect spoken by the ordinary people of a country or region. ➤ informal the specialized terminology of a group or activity. **2** vernacular architecture. ● **adj.** **1** spoken as or using one's mother tongue rather than a second language. **2** (of architecture) concerned with domestic and functional rather than monumental buildings.
– DERIVATIVES **vernacularism** n. **vernacularity** n. **vernacularize** (also **-ise**) v. **vernacularly** adv.
– ORIGIN C17: from L. *vernaculus* 'domestic, native' + **-AR**[1].

**vernal** /ˈvəːn(ə)l/ ● **adj.** of, in, or appropriate to spring.
– DERIVATIVES **vernally** adv.
– ORIGIN C16: from L. *vernalis*, from *vernus* 'of the spring', from *ver* 'spring'.

**vernal equinox** ● **n.** **1** the spring equinox. **2** Astronomy another term for ***First Point of Aries*** (see **ARIES**).

**vernal grass** (also **sweet vernal grass**) ● **n.** a sweet-scented grass which is sometimes grown as a meadow or hay grass. [*Anthoxanthum odoratum*.]

**vernalization** (also **-isation**) ● **n.** the cooling of seed during germination in order to accelerate flowering when it is planted.
– DERIVATIVES **vernalize** (also **-ise**) v.

**vernation** /vəːˈneɪʃ(ə)n/ ● **n.** Botany the arrangement of bud scales or young leaves in a leaf bud before it opens. Compare with **AESTIVATION**.
– ORIGIN C18: from mod. L. *vernatio(n-)*, from L. *vernare* 'to grow (as in the spring)'.

**vernicle** /ˈvəːnɪk(ə)l/ ● **n.** another term for **VERONICA** (in sense 2).
– ORIGIN ME: from OFr., alt. of *vernique*, from med. L. *veronica*.

**vernier** /ˈvəːnɪə/ ● **n.** a small movable graduated scale for obtaining fractional parts of subdivisions on a fixed main scale of a barometer, sextant, or other measuring instrument.
– ORIGIN C18: named after Pierre *Vernier* (1580–1637), Fr. mathematician.

**vernier engine** ● **n.** a thruster on a spacecraft.

**vernissage** /ˌvɛːnɪˈsɑːʒ/ ● **n.** (pl. pronounced same) a private view of paintings before public exhibition.
– ORIGIN Fr., lit. 'varnishing', orig. referring to the day prior to an exhibition when artists were allowed to retouch and varnish hung work.

**vernix** /ˈvəːnɪks/ ● **n.** a greasy deposit covering the skin of a baby at birth.
– ORIGIN C16: from med. L., var. of *veronix* (see **VARNISH**).

**veronal** /ˈvɛrən(ə)l/ ● **n.** another term for **BARBITONE**.
– ORIGIN C20: from Ger., from *Verona* in Italy + **-AL**.

**veronica** ● **n.** **1** a herbaceous plant of north temperate regions, typically with upright stems bearing narrow pointed leaves and spikes of blue or purple flowers. [Genus *Veronica*: many species, including the speedwells.] **2** a cloth supposedly impressed with an image of Christ's face. **3** the movement of a matador's cape away from a charging bull.
– ORIGIN C16: from med. L., from the given name *Veronica*; sense 2 with ref. to St *Veronica*, who offered her headcloth to Christ on the way to Calvary, to wipe his face.

**veronique** /ˌvɛrəˈniːk/ ● **adj.** [postpos.] denoting a dish, typically of fish or chicken, prepared or garnished with grapes.
– ORIGIN from the Fr. given name *Véronique*.

**verruca** /vəˈruːkə/ ● **n.** (pl. **verrucae** /-kiː, -siː/ or **verrucas**) a contagious wart on the sole of the foot. ➤ (in medical use) a wart of any kind.
– DERIVATIVES **verrucose** /ˈvɛrʊkəʊz, vəˈruː-/ adj. **verrucous** /ˈvɛrʊkəs, vəˈruː-/ adj.
– ORIGIN ME: from L.

**versal** /ˈvəːs(ə)l/ ● **n.** a style of ornate capital letter used to start a verse or paragraph in a manuscript.
– ORIGIN C19: from L. *vers-* 'turned' + **-AL**, influenced by **VERSE**.

**versant** /ˈvəːs(ə)nt/ ● **n.** a region of land sloping in one general direction.
– ORIGIN C19: from Fr., pres. part. (used as n.) of *verser* 'tilt over'.

**versatile** ● **adj.** **1** able to adapt or be adapted to many different functions or activities. **2** archaic changeable; inconstant.
– DERIVATIVES **versatilely** adv. **versatility** n.
– ORIGIN C17: from Fr., or from L. *versatilis*, from *versat-*, *versare* 'turn about, revolve'.

**verse** ● **n.** **1** writing arranged with a metrical rhythm. ➤ archaic a line of poetry. **2** a group of lines that form a unit in a poem or song. **3** each of the short numbered divisions of a chapter in the Bible or other scripture. **4** a versicle. ➤ a passage in an anthem for a soloist or a small group of voices. ● **v.** archaic speak in or compose verse.
– DERIVATIVES **verselet** n.
– ORIGIN OE *fers*, from L. *versus* 'a turn of the plough, a furrow, a line of writing', from *vertere* 'to turn'; reinforced in ME by OFr. *vers*.

**versed** ● **adj.** (**versed in**) experienced or skilled in; knowledgeable about.
– ORIGIN C17: from Fr. *versé* or L. *versatus*, past part. of *versari* 'be engaged in'.

**versed sine** ● **n.** **1** Mathematics unity minus cosine. **2** Architecture the rise of an arch of a bridge.

**verset** /ˈvəːsɪt/ ● **n.** Music a short prelude or interlude for organ.

**versicle** /ˈvəːsɪk(ə)l/ ● **n.** a short sentence said or sung by the minister in a church service, to which the congregation gives a response.

**versicoloured** /ˈvəːsɪˌkʌləd/ (US **versicolored**) ● **adj.** archaic **1** changing from one colour to another in different

lights. **2** variegated.
– ORIGIN C18: from L. *versicolor* (from *versus* 'turned' + *color* 'colour') + **-ED**[2].

**versify** • v. (**-ies, -ied**) turn into or express in verse.
– DERIVATIVES **versification** n. **versifier** n.

**versin** /ˈvəːsɪn, -sʌɪn/ (also **versine**) • n. Mathematics short for **VERSED SINE**.

**version** • n. **1** a particular form of something differing in certain respects from an earlier form or from other forms of the same type of thing. ➤ an account of a matter from a particular person's point of view. **2** Medicine the manual turning of a fetus in the womb to make delivery easier.
– DERIVATIVES **versional** adj.
– ORIGIN ME (in the sense 'translation'): from Fr., or from med. L. *versio(n-)*, from L. *vertere* 'to turn'.

**vers libre** /vɛː ˈliːbr(ə), French vɛʀ libʀ/ • n. another term for **FREE VERSE**.
– ORIGIN from Fr.

**verso** /ˈvəːsəʊ/ • n. (pl. **-os**) **1** a left-hand page of an open book, or the back of a loose document. Contrasted with **RECTO**. **2** the reverse of something such as a coin or painting.
– ORIGIN C19: from L. *verso (folio)* 'on the turned (leaf)'.

**verst** /vəːst/ • n. a Russian measure of length, about 1.1 km (0.66 mile).
– ORIGIN from Russ. *versta*.

**versus** • prep. (especially in sporting and legal use) against. ➤ as opposed to; in contrast to.
– ORIGIN ME: from a med. L. use of L. *versus* 'towards'.

**vert** /vəːt/ • n. green, as a heraldic tincture.
– ORIGIN ME: via OFr. from L. *viridis* 'green'.

**vertebra** /ˈvəːtɪbrə/ • n. (pl. **vertebrae** /-breɪ, -briː/) each of the series of small bones forming the backbone.
– DERIVATIVES **vertebral** adj.
– ORIGIN C17: from L., from *vertere* 'to turn'.

**vertebrate** /ˈvəːtɪbrət/ • n. an animal of a large group (subphylum Vertebrata) distinguished by the possession of a backbone or spinal column, including mammals, birds, reptiles, amphibians, and fishes. Compare with **INVERTEBRATE**. • adj. of or relating to the vertebrates.
– ORIGIN C19: from L. *vertebratus* 'jointed', from *vertebra* (see **VERTEBRA**).

**vertex** /ˈvəːtɛks/ • n. (pl. **vertices** /-tɪsiːz/ or **vertexes**) **1** the highest point; the top or apex. **2** Geometry each angular point of a polygon, polyhedron, or other figure. ➤ a meeting point of two lines that form an angle. **3** Anatomy the crown of the head.
– ORIGIN ME: from L., 'whirlpool, crown of a head, vertex', from *vertere* 'to turn'.

**vertical** • adj. **1** at right angles to a horizontal plane; having the top directly above the bottom. **2** archaic at the zenith or the highest point. **3** Anatomy relating to the crown of the head. **4** involving or passing through all the different levels of a hierarchy or progression. • n. **1** a vertical line or plane. **2** an upright structure.
– DERIVATIVES **verticality** n. **verticalize** (also **-ise**) v. **vertically** adv.
– ORIGIN C16 (in the sense 'directly overhead'): from Fr., or from late L. *verticalis*, from *vertex* (see **VERTEX**).

**vertical angles** • pl. n. Mathematics each of the pairs of opposite angles made by two intersecting lines.

**vertical stabilizer** • n. US an aircraft's tail fin.

**vertical thinking** • n. chiefly Brit. the solving of problems using conventional logical processes, as opposed to lateral thinking.

**verticillium** /ˌvəːtɪˈsɪlɪəm/ • n. a fungus causing wilt in plants. [Genus *Verticillium*.]
– ORIGIN mod. L., from L. *verticillus* 'whorl of a spindle'.

**vertiginous** /vəːˈtɪdʒɪnəs/ • adj. causing vertigo, especially by being extremely high or steep. ➤ relating to or affected by vertigo.
– DERIVATIVES **vertiginously** adv.

**vertigo** /ˈvəːtɪgəʊ/ • n. a sensation of whirling and loss of balance, caused by looking down from a great height or by disease affecting the inner ear or the vestibular nerve.
– ORIGIN ME: from L., 'whirling', from *vertere* 'to turn'.

**vertisol** /ˈvəːtɪsɒl/ • n. Soil Science a clayey soil with little organic matter, found in regions with distinct wet and dry seasons.
– ORIGIN 1960s: from **VERTICAL** + L. *solum* 'soil'.

**vertu** • n. variant spelling of **VIRTU**.

**vervain** /ˈvəːveɪn/ • n. a herbaceous plant with small blue, white, or purple flowers, used in herbal medicine. [*Verbena officinalis*.]
– ORIGIN ME: from OFr. *verveine*, from L. *verbena* (see **VERBENA**).

**verve** • n. vigour, spirit, and style.
– ORIGIN C17 (denoting special talent in writing): from Fr., 'vigour', earlier 'form of expression'.

**vervet monkey** /ˈvəːvɪt/ • n. a common African monkey with greenish-brown upper parts and a black face. [*Cercopithecus aethiops*.]
– ORIGIN C19: from Fr., of unknown origin.

**very** • adv. in a high degree. ➤ [with superlative or **own**] without qualification: *the very best quality*. • adj. **1** actual; precise: *his very words*. ➤ archaic real; genuine. **2** emphasizing an extreme point in time or space. **3** with no addition; mere.
– PHRASES **not very 1** in a low degree. **2** far from being. **very good** (or **well**) an expression of consent.
– ORIGIN ME: from OFr. *verai*, based on L. *verus* 'true'.

**Very light** /ˈvɛri, ˈvɪəri/ • n. a flare fired into the air from a pistol for signalling or for temporary illumination.
– ORIGIN C20: named after the Amer. naval officer Edward W. *Very*.

**Very Reverend** • adj. a title given to a dean in the Anglican Church.

**Vesak** /ˈvɛsak/ (also **Wesak** or **Visākha**) • n. the most important Buddhist festival, commemorating the birth, enlightenment, and death of the Buddha.
– ORIGIN Sinhalese *vesak*, via Pali from Sanskrit *vaiśākha*, denoting the month April–May.

**vesical** /ˈvɛsɪk(ə)l, ˈviː-/ • adj. Anatomy & Medicine relating to or affecting the urinary bladder.
– ORIGIN C18: from L. *vesica* 'bladder' + **-AL**.

**vesicant** /ˈvɛsɪkənt, ˈviː-/ • adj. tending to cause blistering. • n. an agent that causes blistering.
– ORIGIN ME: from late L. *vesicant-*, *vesicare* 'form pustules', from *vesica* 'bladder'.

**vesica piscis** /ˌvɛsɪkə ˈpɪskɪs, ˈviː-/ • n. (pl. **vesicae** /ˈvɛsɪkiː, ˈviː-/) a pointed oval figure used as an architectural feature and as an aureole enclosing figures such as Christ or the Virgin Mary in medieval art.
– ORIGIN L., lit. 'fish's bladder'.

**vesicate** /ˈvɛsɪkeɪt, ˈviː-/ • v. chiefly Medicine blister.
– DERIVATIVES **vesication** n. **vesicatory** adj. & n.
– ORIGIN C17: from late L. *vesicat-* 'having pustules', from *vesica* 'bladder'.

**vesicle** /ˈvɛsɪk(ə)l, ˈviː-/ • n. **1** Anatomy & Zoology a small fluid-filled sac or cyst within the body. ➤ Medicine a blister full of clear fluid. **2** Botany an air-filled swelling in a seaweed or other plant. **3** Geology a small cavity in volcanic rock, produced by gas bubbles.
– DERIVATIVES **vesicular** adj. **vesiculated** adj. **vesiculation** n.
– ORIGIN C16: from Fr. *vésicule* or L. *vesicula*, dimin. of *vesica* 'bladder'.

**vesper** • n. **1** evening prayer. **2** archaic evening.
– ORIGIN ME: from L. *vesper* 'evening (star)'.

**vespers** • n. a service of evening prayer in the Divine Office of the Western Christian Church (sometimes said earlier in the day). ➤ a service of evening prayer in other churches.
– ORIGIN C15: from OFr. *vespres* 'evensong', from L. *vesperas*, on the pattern of *matutinas* 'matins'.

**vespertilionid** /ˌvɛspətɪlɪˈɒnɪd/ • n. Zoology a bat of a large family (Vespertilionidae) that includes most of the typical insectivorous bats of northern temperate regions.
– ORIGIN C19: from mod. L. *Vespertilionidae* (pl.), from L. *vespertilio* 'bat'.

**vespertine** /ˈvɛspətʌɪn, -tɪn/ • adj. technical or poetic/literary of or relating to the evening.
– ORIGIN ME: from L. *vespertinus*, from *vesper* 'evening'.

**vessel** ● **n.** **1** a ship or large boat. **2** a hollow container used to hold liquid. **3** Anatomy & Zoology a duct or canal conveying blood or other fluid. ➤ Botany any of the tubular structures in the vascular system of a plant, serving to conduct water and nutrients from the root. **4** (chiefly in biblical use) a person regarded as embodying a particular quality: *she was inherently the weaker vessel.*
– ORIGIN ME: from Anglo-Norman Fr. *vessel(e)*, from late L. *vascellum*, dimin. of *vas* 'vessel'.

**vest** ● **n.** **1** Brit. an undergarment worn on the upper part of the body, typically having no sleeves. **2** a similar garment worn for a particular purpose: *a bulletproof vest.* **3** N. Amer. & Austral. a waistcoat or sleeveless jacket. ● **v.** **1** (**vest something in**) confer or bestow power, property, etc. on: *executive power is vested in the President.* ➤ (usu. **be vested with**) give (someone) the legal right to power, property, etc. **2** put on vestments. ➤ poetic/literary dress.
– PHRASES **play** (or **keep**) **one's cards close to one's vest** see **CHEST**.
– ORIGIN ME: the verb from OFr. *vestu* 'clothed', past part. of *vestir*, from L. *vestire*; the noun from Fr. *veste*, via Ital. from L. *vestis* 'garment'.

**vesta** ● **n.** chiefly historical a short wooden or wax match.
– ORIGIN C19: from the name of *Vesta*, the Roman goddess of the hearth.

**vestal** ● **adj.** **1** of or relating to the Roman goddess Vesta. **2** poetic/literary chaste; pure. ● **n.** a vestal virgin. ➤ poetic/literary a chaste woman, especially a nun.

**vestal virgin** ● **n.** (in ancient Rome) a virgin consecrated to the goddess Vesta and vowed to chastity.

**vested interest** ● **n.** **1** Law an interest (usually in land or money held in trust) recognized as belonging to a particular person. **2** a personal stake in an undertaking or state of affairs, especially one with an expectation of financial gain.

**vestee** ● **n.** North American term for **WAISTCOAT**.

**vestiary** /ˈvɛstɪəri/ ● **adj.** poetic/literary of or relating to dress. ● **n.** (pl. **-ies**) a room in a monastery in which clothes are kept.
– ORIGIN ME (denoting a vestry): from OFr. *vestiarie*, from L. *vestiarium* (see **VESTRY**).

**vestibule** /ˈvɛstɪbjuːl/ ● **n.** **1** an antechamber or hall just inside the outer door of a building. **2** Anatomy a chamber or channel opening into another, especially in the inner ear.
– DERIVATIVES **vestibular** adj. (Anatomy). **vestibuled** adj.
– ORIGIN C17 (denoting the space in front of the main entrance of a Roman or Greek building): from Fr., or from L. *vestibulum* 'entrance court'.

**vestibulocochlear nerves** /vɛˌstɪbjʊləʊˈkɒklɪə/ ● **pl. n.** Anatomy the pair of cranial nerves transmitting impulses from the ears to the brain.

**vestibulo-ocular reflex** /vɛˌstɪbjʊləʊˈɒkjʊlə/ ● **n.** the reflex by which the direction of the eyes remains constant when the head is moved.

**vestige** /ˈvɛstɪdʒ/ ● **n.** **1** a trace of something. ➤ the smallest amount. **2** Biology a vestigial part or organ.
– ORIGIN ME: from Fr., from L. *vestigium* 'footprint'.

**vestigial** /vɛˈstɪdʒɪəl, -dʒ(ə)l/ ● **adj.** **1** forming a very small remnant of something that was once greater or more noticeable. **2** Biology (of an organ or part of the body) degenerate, rudimentary, or atrophied, having become functionless in the course of evolution.
– DERIVATIVES **vestigially** adv.

**vestimentary** /ˌvɛstɪˈmɛnt(ə)ri/ ● **adj.** formal of or relating to clothing or dress.
– ORIGIN C19: from L. *vestimentum* 'clothing' + **-ARY**[1].

**vestiture** /ˈvɛstɪtjə, -tʃə/ ● **n.** archaic clothing.
– ORIGIN C19: based on L. *vestire* 'clothe'.

**vestment** ● **n.** a chasuble or other robe worn by the clergy or choristers during services. ➤ archaic a garment, especially a ceremonial or official robe.
– ORIGIN ME: from OFr. *vestiment*, from L. *vestimentum*, from *vestire* (see **VEST**).

**vest-pocket** ● **adj.** N. Amer. small enough to fit into a pocket.

**vestry** ● **n.** (pl. **-ies**) a room in or attached to a church, used as an office and for changing into ceremonial vestments. ➤ a meeting of parishioners, originally in a vestry, for the conduct of parochial business.
– DERIVATIVES **vestryman** n.
– ORIGIN ME: prob. from an Anglo-Norman Fr. alt. of OFr. *vestiarie*, from L. *vestiarium*.

**vesture** ● **n.** poetic/literary clothing.
– ORIGIN ME: from OFr., based on L. *vestire* 'clothe'.

**vet**[1] ● **n.** a veterinary surgeon. ● **v.** (**vetted**, **vetting**) make a careful and critical examination of (someone, especially of a person prior to employment).
– ORIGIN C19: abbrev. of **VETERINARY** or **VETERINARIAN**.

**vet**[2] ● **n.** N. Amer. informal a veteran.

**vetch** ● **n.** a leguminous plant with purple, pink, or yellow flowers, some kinds of which are cultivated for silage or fodder. [*Vicia sativa* and other species.]
– ORIGIN ME: from Anglo-Norman Fr. *veche*, from L. *vicia*.

**vetchling** ● **n.** a widely distributed plant related to the vetches, typically having fewer leaflets. [Genus *Lathyrus*.]

**veteran** ● **n.** **1** a person who has had long experience in a particular field. **2** an ex-serviceman or -servicewoman.
– ORIGIN C16: from Fr. *vétéran* or L. *veteranus*, from *vetus* 'old'.

**veteran car** ● **n.** Brit. an old style or model of car, specifically one made before 1919 or (strictly) before 1905. Compare with **VINTAGE CAR**.

**Veterans Day** ● **n.** (in the US) the anniversary of the end of the First World War (11 November), honouring US veterans and victims of all wars.

**veterinarian** /ˌvɛt(ə)rɪˈnɛːrɪən/ ● **n.** North American term for **VETERINARY SURGEON**.

**veterinary** /ˈvɛt(ə)rɪn(ə)ri, ˈvɛt(ə)nri/ ● **adj.** of or relating to the diseases, injuries, and treatment of farm and domestic animals.
– ORIGIN C18: from L. *veterinarius*, from *veterinae* 'cattle'.

**veterinary surgeon** ● **n.** Brit. a person qualified to treat diseased or injured animals.

**vetiver** /ˈvɛtɪvə/ (also **vetivert**) ● **n.** a fragrant extract or essential oil obtained from the root of an Indian grass (*Vetiveria zizanioides*), used in perfumery and aromatherapy.
– ORIGIN C19: from Fr. *vétiver*, from Tamil *veṭṭivēr*, from *vēr* 'root'.

**veto** /ˈviːtəʊ/ ● **n.** (pl. **-oes**) a constitutional right to reject a decision or proposal made by a law-making body. ➤ any prohibition. ● **v.** (**-oes**, **-oed**) exercise a veto against. ➤ refuse to accept or allow.
– DERIVATIVES **vetoer** n.
– ORIGIN C17: from L., lit. 'I forbid', used by Roman tribunes of the people when opposing measures of the Senate.

**vex** ● **v.** cause to feel annoyed or worried. ● **adj.** chiefly W. Indian angry; annoyed.
– DERIVATIVES **vexation** n. **vexer** n. **vexing** adj. **vexingly** adv.
– ORIGIN ME: from OFr. *vexer*, from L. *vexare* 'shake, disturb'.

**vexatious** ● **adj.** **1** causing annoyance or worry. **2** Law (of an action) brought without sufficient grounds for winning, purely to cause annoyance to the defendant.
– DERIVATIVES **vexatiously** adv. **vexatiousness** n.

**vexed** ● **adj.** **1** difficult and much debated; problematic. **2** annoyed or worried.
– DERIVATIVES **vexedly** adv.

**vexillology** /ˌvɛksɪˈlɒlədʒi/ ● **n.** the study of flags.
– DERIVATIVES **vexillological** adj. **vexillologist** n.
– ORIGIN 1950s: from L. *vexillum* 'flag' + **-LOGY**.

**vexillum** /vɛkˈsɪləm/ ● **n.** (pl. **vexilla** /-lə/) **1** a standard, flag, or banner, especially of the Roman military. **2** Botany the large upright petal of a sweet pea or related flower. **3** Ornithology the vane of a feather.
– ORIGIN C18: from L., 'flag, banner'.

**VFR** ● **abbrev.** visual flight rules (used under conditions of good visibility).

**VG** ● **abbrev.** **1** very good. **2** Vicar General.

**VGA** ● **abbrev.** videographics array, a standard for defining colour display screens for computers.

**vgc** • **abbrev.** very good condition.

**VHF** • **abbrev.** very high frequency.

**VHS** • **abbrev.** trademark video home system (as used by domestic video recorders).

**VI** • **abbrev.** Virgin Islands.

**via** • **prep.** travelling through (a place) en route to a destination. ➤by way of; through. ➤by means of.
– ORIGIN C18: from L., ablative of *via* 'way, road'.

**viable** /'vʌɪəb(ə)l/ • **adj. 1** capable of working successfully; feasible. **2** Biology (of a plant, animal, or cell) capable of surviving or living successfully. ➤Botany (of a seed or spore) able to germinate. ➤Medicine (of a fetus or unborn child) able to live after birth.
– DERIVATIVES **viability** n. **viably** adv.
– ORIGIN C19: from Fr., from *vie* 'life'.

**viaduct** • **n.** a long bridge-like structure, typically a series of arches, carrying a road or railway across a valley or other low ground.
– ORIGIN C19: from L. *via* 'way', on the pattern of *aqueduct*.

**Viagra** /vʌɪ'agrə/ • **n.** trademark a synthetic compound used to enhance male potency.
– ORIGIN 1990s: appar. a blend of *virility* and the name *Niagara*.

**vial** /'vʌɪəl/ • **n.** a small container used especially for holding liquid medicines.
– ORIGIN ME: alt. of **PHIAL**.

**via media** /'mi:dɪə, 'mɛdɪə/ • **n.** formal a middle way or compromise between extremes.
– ORIGIN from L.

**viand** /'vʌɪənd/ • **n.** archaic an item of food.
– ORIGIN ME: from OFr. *viande* 'food', from an alt. of L. *vivenda*, neut. pl. gerundive of *vivere* 'to live'.

**via negativa** /ˌnɛgə'ti:və/ • **n.** Theology a way of describing something by saying what it is not.
– ORIGIN L., lit. 'negative path'.

**viatical settlement** /vʌɪ'atɪk(ə)l/ • **n.** an arrangement whereby a person with a terminal illness sells their life insurance policy to a third party, in order to benefit from the proceeds while alive.
– ORIGIN 1990s: *viatical* from L. *viaticus* 'relating to a journey or departing' + **-AL**.

**viaticum** /vʌɪ'atɪkəm/ • **n.** (pl. **viatica** /-kə/) **1** the Eucharist as given to a person near or in danger of death. **2** archaic a supply of provisions or allowance of money for a journey.
– ORIGIN C16: from L., neut. of *viaticus*, from *via* 'road'.

**vibe** • **n.** informal **1** the atmosphere or aura of a person or place as communicated to and felt by others. **2** (**vibes**) short for **VIBRAPHONE**.

**vibist** /'vʌɪbɪst/ • **n.** a musician who plays the vibraphone.

**vibrant** • **adj. 1** full of energy and enthusiasm. ➤(of colour or sound) bold and strong. **2** quivering; pulsating.
– DERIVATIVES **vibrancy** n. **vibrantly** adv.
– ORIGIN C17: from L. *vibrant-* 'shaking to and fro', from *vibrare* (see **VIBRATE**).

**vibraphone** /'vʌɪbrəfəʊn/ • **n.** a musical percussion instrument with a double row of tuned metal bars, each above a tubular resonator containing a motor-driven rotating vane, giving a vibrato effect.
– DERIVATIVES **vibraphonist** n.
– ORIGIN 1920s: from **VIBRATO** + **-PHONE**.

**vibrate** • **v. 1** move or cause to move with small movements rapidly to and fro. **2** (of a sound) resonate.
– DERIVATIVES **vibrating** adj.
– ORIGIN ME: from L. *vibrat-*, *vibrare* 'move to and fro'.

**vibratile** /'vʌɪbrətʌɪl/ • **adj.** Biology (of cilia, flagella, or other small appendages) capable of or characterized by oscillatory motion.

**vibration** • **n. 1** an instance of vibrating. ➤Physics an oscillation of the parts of a fluid or an elastic solid whose equilibrium has been disturbed or of an electromagnetic wave. **2** (**vibrations**) informal a person's emotional state, the atmosphere of a place, or the associations of an object, as communicated to and felt by others.
– DERIVATIVES **vibrational** adj.

**vibrato** /vɪ'brɑ:təʊ/ • **n.** Music a rapid, slight variation in pitch in singing or playing some musical instruments, producing a stronger or richer tone.
– ORIGIN C19: Ital., past part. of *vibrare* 'vibrate'.

**vibrator** • **n.** a device that vibrates or causes vibration. ➤a vibrating device used for massage or sexual stimulation.
– DERIVATIVES **vibratory** adj.

**vibrio** /'vɪbrɪəʊ, 'vʌɪ-/ • **n.** (pl. **-os**) Medicine a water-borne bacterium of curved, rod-like shape, belonging to a group including the causative agent of cholera. [*Vibrio* and related genera.]
– ORIGIN mod. L., from L. *vibrare* 'vibrate'.

**vibrissae** /vʌɪ'brɪsi:/ • **pl. n.** Zoology long stiff hairs growing around the mouth or elsewhere on the face of many mammals; whiskers. ➤Ornithology coarse bristle-like feathers growing around the gape of certain insectivorous birds that catch insects in flight.
– ORIGIN C17: from L., lit. 'nostril hairs'.

**viburnum** /vɪ'bə:nəm, vʌɪ-/ • **n.** a shrub or small tree of temperate and warm regions, typically bearing flat or rounded clusters of small white flowers. [Genus *Viburnum*: many species.]
– ORIGIN mod. L., from L., 'wayfaring tree'.

**Vic.** • **abbrev.** Victoria.

**vicar** • **n. 1** (in the Church of England) an incumbent of a parish where tithes formerly passed to a chapter or religious house or layman. ➤(in other Anglican Churches) a member of the clergy deputizing for another. ➤(in the Roman Catholic Church) a representative or deputy of a bishop. ➤(in the US Episcopal Church) a clergyman in charge of a chapel. **2** a cleric or choir member appointed to sing certain parts of a cathedral service.
– DERIVATIVES **vicarship** n.
– ORIGIN ME: via Anglo-Norman Fr. from OFr. *vicaire*, from L. *vicarius* 'substitute', from *vic-* 'change, place' (cf. **VICE**³).

**vicarage** • **n.** the residence of a vicar. ➤historical the benefice or living of a vicar.

**vicar apostolic** • **n. 1** a Roman Catholic missionary. **2** a titular bishop.

**vicar general** • **n.** (pl. **vicars general**) an official serving as a deputy or representative of a bishop or archbishop.

**vicarial** /vɪ'kɛ:rɪəl, vʌɪ-/ • **adj.** archaic of or relating to a vicar.

**vicariate** /vɪ'kɛ:rɪət, vʌɪ-/ • **n.** the office or authority of a vicar. ➤a church or parish ministered to by a vicar.

**vicarious** /vɪ'kɛ:rɪəs, vʌɪ-/ • **adj. 1** experienced in the imagination through the feelings or actions of another person: *vicarious pleasure*. **2** acting or done for another.
– DERIVATIVES **vicariously** adv. **vicariousness** n.
– ORIGIN C17: from L. *vicarius* (see **VICAR**) + **-OUS**.

**vice**¹ /vʌɪs/ • **n. 1** immoral or wicked behaviour. ➤criminal activities involving prostitution, pornography, or drugs. ➤an immoral or wicked personal characteristic. ➤a weakness of character; a bad habit. **2** (also **stable vice**) a bad or neurotic habit of stabled horses, typically arising as a result of boredom.
– DERIVATIVES **viceless** adj.
– ORIGIN ME: via OFr. from L. *vitium*.

**vice**² /vʌɪs/ (US **vise**) • **n.** a metal tool with movable jaws which are used to hold an object firmly in place while work is done on it.
– DERIVATIVES **vice-like** adj.
– ORIGIN ME (denoting a screw or winch): from OFr. *vis*, from L. *vitis* 'vine'.

**vice**³ /'vʌɪsi/ • **prep.** as a substitute for.
– ORIGIN L., ablative of *vic-* 'change'.

**vice-** • **comb. form** next in rank to (typically denoting capacity to deputize for): *vice-president*.
– ORIGIN from L. *vice* 'in place of'.

**vice admiral** • **n.** a high rank of naval officer, above rear admiral and below admiral.

**vice chamberlain** • **n.** a deputy chamberlain, especially (in the UK) the deputy of the Lord Chamberlain.

**vice chancellor** • **n.** a deputy chancellor, especially one of a British university who discharges most of its administrative duties.

**vicegerent** /vʌɪsˈdʒɪər(ə)nt, -ˈdʒɛ-/ • **n.** formal a person exercising delegated power on behalf of a sovereign or ruler. ➤a person regarded as an earthly representative of God, especially the Pope.
– DERIVATIVES **vicegerency** n. (pl. **-ies**).
– ORIGIN C16: from med. L. *vicegerent-* '(person) holding office', from L. *vic-* 'office, place, turn' + *gerere* 'carry on, hold'.

**vice-president** • **n.** an official or executive ranking below and deputizing for a president.
– DERIVATIVES **vice-presidency** n. (pl. **-ies**). **vice-presidential** adj.

**viceregal** • **adj.** of or relating to a viceroy.

**vicereine** /ˈvʌɪsreɪn/ • **n.** the wife of a viceroy, or a female viceroy.
– ORIGIN C19: Fr., from *vice-* 'in place of' + *reine* 'queen'.

**viceroy** /ˈvʌɪsrɔɪ/ • **n.** a ruler exercising authority in a colony on behalf of a sovereign.
– DERIVATIVES **viceroyal** adj. **viceroyship** n.
– ORIGIN C16: from archaic Fr., from *vice-* 'in place of' + *roi* 'king'.

**viceroyalty** • **n.** (pl. **-ies**) the office, position, or authority of a viceroy. ➤a territory governed by a viceroy.

**vice versa** /ˌvʌɪs ˈvəːsə, vʌɪsə/ • **adv.** with the main items in the preceding statement the other way round.
– ORIGIN C17: from L., lit. 'in-turned position'.

**vichyssoise** /ˌviːʃiːˈswɑːz/ • **n.** a soup made with potatoes, leeks, and cream and typically served chilled.
– ORIGIN Fr. (fem.) 'of *Vichy*', a town in central France.

**vicinage** /ˈvɪsɪnɪdʒ/ • **n.** chiefly N. Amer. another term for **VICINITY**.
– ORIGIN ME: from OFr. *vis(e)nage*, from an alt. of L. *vicinus* 'neighbour'.

**vicinal** /ˈvɪsɪn(ə)l, vɪˈsʌɪn(ə)l/ • **adj. 1** neighbouring; adjacent. **2** Chemistry relating to or denoting substituents attached to adjacent atoms in a ring or chain.
– ORIGIN C17: from Fr., or from L. *vicinalis*, from *vicinus* 'neighbour'.

**vicinity** • **n.** (pl. **-ies**) the area near or surrounding a particular place. ➤archaic proximity.
– ORIGIN C16: from L. *vicinitas*, from *vicinus* 'neighbour'.

**vicious** • **adj. 1** cruel or violent. ➤(of an animal) wild and dangerous. **2** poetic/literary immoral. **3** archaic (of language or a line of reasoning) imperfect; defective.
– DERIVATIVES **viciously** adv. **viciousness** n.
– ORIGIN ME: from OFr. *vicious* or L. *vitiosus*, from *vitium* 'vice'.

**vicious circle** • **n.** a sequence of reciprocal cause and effect in which two or more elements intensify and aggravate each other, leading inexorably to a worsening of the situation.

**vicissitude** /vɪˈsɪsɪtjuːd, vʌɪ-/ • **n. 1** a change of circumstances or fortune, typically for the worse. **2** poetic/literary alternation between opposite or contrasting things.
– DERIVATIVES **vicissitudinous** /-ˈtjuːdɪnəs/ adj.
– ORIGIN C17: from Fr., or from L. *vicissitudo*, from *vicissim* 'by turns', from *vic-* 'turn, change'.

**vicomte** /ˈviːkɔ̃t, ˈviːkɒmt, French vikɔ̃t/ • **n.** (pl. pronounced same) a French nobleman corresponding in rank to a British or Irish viscount.
– ORIGIN from Fr.

**vicomtesse** /ˌvikɔ̃ˈtɛs, ˌviːkɒnˈtɛs, French vikɒmtɛs/ • **n.** (pl. pronounced same) a French noblewoman corresponding in rank to a British or Irish viscountess.
– ORIGIN from Fr.

**victim** • **n. 1** a person harmed, injured, or killed as a result of a crime, accident, etc. **2** an animal or person killed as a religious sacrifice.
– PHRASES **fall victim to** be hurt, killed, or destroyed by.
– ORIGIN C15: from L. *victima*.

**victimize** (also **-ise**) • **v.** single (someone) out for cruel or unjust treatment.
– DERIVATIVES **victimization** n. **victimizer** n.

**victimless** • **adj.** (of a crime) in which there is no injured party.

**victimology** • **n.** (pl. **-ies**) the study of the victims of crime and the psychological effects on them.

**victor** • **n. 1** a person who defeats an enemy or opponent in a battle, game, or competition. **2** a code word representing the letter V, used in radio communication.
– ORIGIN ME: from Anglo-Norman Fr. *victo(u)r* or L. *victor*, from *vincere* 'conquer'.

**victoria** /vɪkˈtɔːrɪə/ • **n.** historical a light four-wheeled horse-drawn carriage with a collapsible hood, seats for two passengers, and an elevated driver's seat in front.
– ORIGIN C19: named after Queen *Victoria*.

**Victoria Day** • **n.** (in Canada) the Monday preceding May 24, observed as a national holiday to commemorate the birthday of Queen Victoria.

**Victoria lily** • **n.** a tropical South American water lily which has gigantic floating leaves with raised sides. [Genus *Victoria*: two species.]

**Victorian** • **adj.** of or relating to the reign of Queen Victoria (1837–1901). ➤of or relating to the attitudes and values associated with this period, especially those of prudishness and high moral tone. • **n.** a person who lived during the Victorian period.
– DERIVATIVES **Victorianism** n.

**Victoriana** • **pl. n.** articles, especially collectors' items, from the Victorian period.

**Victoria plum** • **n.** Brit. a plum of a large red dessert variety.

**Victoria sandwich** (also **Victoria sponge**) • **n.** Brit. a cake consisting of two layers of sponge with a jam filling.

**victorious** • **adj.** having won a victory; triumphant. ➤of or characterized by victory.
– DERIVATIVES **victoriously** adv. **victoriousness** n.

**victor ludorum** /luːˈdɔːrəm/ • **n.** Brit. a boy or man who is the overall champion in a sports competition.
– ORIGIN L., lit. 'victor of the games'.

**victory** • **n.** (pl. **-ies**) an act of defeating an enemy or opponent in a battle, game, or competition.
– ORIGIN ME: from Anglo-Norman Fr. *victorie*, from L. *victoria*.

**victory roll** • **n.** a roll performed by an aircraft as a sign of triumph, as after a successful mission.

**victrix** /ˈvɪktrɪks/ • **n.** (pl. **victrices** /-trɪsiːz/) rare a female victor or champion.
– ORIGIN L., fem. of *victor* (see **VICTOR**).

**victual** /ˈvɪt(ə)l/ dated • **n.** (**victuals**) food or provisions. • **v.** (**victualled**, **victualling**; US **victualed**, **victualing**) **1** provide with food or other stores. **2** eat.
– ORIGIN ME: from OFr. *vitaille*, from late L. *victualia*, neut. pl. of L. *victualis*, from *victus* 'food'; the pronunc. still represents the early spelling *vittel*.

**victualler** /ˈvɪt(ə)lə/ (US **victualer**) • **n. 1** Brit. a person who is licensed to sell alcoholic liquor. **2** dated a person providing or selling food or other provisions. ➤a ship providing supplies for troops or other ships.

**vicuña** /vɪˈkjuːnjə, -kuː-, vɪˈkuːnə/ • **n. 1** a wild relative of the llama, inhabiting mountainous regions of South America and valued for its fine silky wool. [*Vicugna vicugna*.] **2** cloth made from this wool.
– ORIGIN C17: from Sp., from Quechua.

**vicus** /ˈvʌɪkəs, ˈviːkəs/ • **n.** (pl. **vici** /ˈvʌɪkiː, ˈviːkiː/) the smallest unit of ancient Roman municipal administration.
– ORIGIN L., lit. 'group of dwellings'.

**vid** • **n.** informal short for **VIDEO**.

**vide** /ˈvɪdeɪ, ˈviː-, ˈvʌɪdi/ • **v.** see; consult (used as an instruction in a text to refer the reader elsewhere).
– ORIGIN L., 'see!', imper. of *videre*.

**videlicet** /vɪˈdɛlɪsɛt, vʌɪ-, -kɛt/ • **adv.** more formal term for **VIZ**.
– ORIGIN L., from *videre* 'to see' + *licet* 'it is permissible'.

**video** • **n.** (pl. **-os**) the system of recording, reproducing, or broadcasting moving visual images on or from videotape. ➤a film or other recording on videotape. ➤a video cassette. ➤Brit. a video recorder. • **v.** (**-oes**, **-oed**) film or make a video recording of.
– ORIGIN 1930s: from L. *videre* 'to see', on the pattern of

*audio.*

**videoconference** • n. an arrangement in which television sets linked to telephone lines are used to enable a group of people in different locations to communicate with each other in sound and vision.
– DERIVATIVES **videoconferencing** n.

**videodisc** • n. a CD-ROM or other disc used to store visual images.

**video frequency** • n. a frequency in the range used for video signals in television.

**video game** • n. a game played by electronically manipulating images produced by a computer program on a television screen or monitor.

**videographics** • pl. n. [also treated as sing.] visual images produced using computer technology.

**videography** • n. the process or art of making video films.
– DERIVATIVES **videographer** n.

**video jockey** • n. a person who introduces and plays music videos on television.

**video-on-demand** • n. a system in which viewers choose their own filmed entertainment, by means of a PC or interactive TV system.

**videophile** • n. an enthusiast for or devotee of video recordings or video technology.

**videophone** • n. a telephone device transmitting and receiving a visual image as well as sound.

**VideoPlus** • n. trademark a system for identifying broadcast television programmes by a numerical code which can be input into a video recorder in order to preset recording.

**video recorder** • n. a device which, when linked to a television set, can be used for recording on and playing videotapes.
– DERIVATIVES **video recording** n.

**videotape** • n. magnetic tape for recording and reproducing visual images and sound. ➤a video cassette. • v. record on video.

**vie** /vʌɪ/ • v. (**vying**) compete eagerly with others in order to do or achieve something.
– ORIGIN C16: prob. a shortening of obs. *envy*, via OFr. from L. *invitare* 'challenge'.

**vielle** /vɪˈɛl/ • n. a hurdy-gurdy.
– ORIGIN C18: from Fr., from OFr. *viele* (see **VIOL**).

**Vienna sausage** • n. a small frankfurter made of pork, beef, or veal.

**Viennese** /vɪəˈniːz/ • n. a native or inhabitant of Vienna. • adj. of or relating to Vienna.

**Viennese waltz** • n. a waltz characterized by a slight anticipation of the second beat of the bar.

**Vietcong** /vjɛtˈkɒŋ/ • n. the Communist guerrilla force in Vietnam which fought the South Vietnamese government forces 1954–75 and opposed the South Vietnam and US forces in the Vietnam War.
– ORIGIN Vietnamese, lit. 'Vietnamese Communist'.

**Vietnamese** • n. (pl. same) **1** a native or national of Vietnam, or a person of Vietnamese descent. **2** the language of Vietnam, which probably belongs to the Mon-Khmer group. • adj. of or relating to Vietnam, its people, or their language.

**Vietnamese pot-bellied pig** • n. a pig of a small, dark breed with short legs and a large stomach, sometimes kept as a pet.

**vieux jeu** /vjəː ˈʒəː, French vjø ʒø/ • adj. old-fashioned; hackneyed.
– ORIGIN Fr., lit. 'old game'.

**view** • n. **1** vision or sight, as from a particular position. ➤a sight or prospect from a particular position, typically an appealing one. **2** a particular way of regarding something; an attitude or opinion. **3** an inspection of things for sale by prospective purchasers, especially of works of art. • v. **1** look at or inspect. ➤inspect (a house or other property) with the prospect of buying or renting. ➤watch on television. **2** regard in a particular light or with a particular attitude. **3** Hunting see (a fox) break cover.
– PHRASES **in full view** clearly visible. **in view 1** visible. **2** in one's mind or as one's aim. **in view of** because or as a result of. **on view** being shown or exhibited to the public. **with a view to** with the hope or intention of.
– DERIVATIVES **viewable** adj. **viewing** n. **viewless** adj.
– ORIGIN ME: from Anglo-Norman Fr. *vieue*, fem. past part. of *veoir* 'see', from L. *videre*.

**viewer** • n. **1** a person who views something. **2** a device for looking at film transparencies or similar photographic images.

**viewership** • n. [treated as sing. or pl.] the audience for a particular television programme or channel.

**viewfinder** • n. a device on a camera showing the field of view of the lens, used in framing and focusing the picture.

**viewgraph** • n. a graph or other data produced as a transparency for projection on to a screen or for transmission during a teleconference.

**view halloo** • n. a shout given by a hunter on seeing a fox break cover.

**viewpoint** • n. **1** a position affording a good view. **2** a point of view; an opinion.

**viewport** • n. **1** a window in a spacecraft or in the conning tower of an oil rig. **2** Computing a framed area on a display screen for viewing information.

**VIFF** /vɪf/ Aeronautics, informal • n. a technique used by a vertical take-off aircraft to change direction abruptly by altering the direction of thrust of the aircraft's jet engines. • v. change direction in such a way.
– ORIGIN 1970s: acronym from *vectoring in forward flight*.

**vig** • n. short for **VIGORISH**.

**viga** /ˈviːɡə/ • n. US a rough-hewn roof timber, especially in an adobe building.
– ORIGIN from Sp.

**vigesimal** /vɪˈdʒɛsɪm(ə)l, vʌɪ-/ • adj. rare relating to or based on the number twenty.
– ORIGIN C17: from L. *vigesimus* (from *viginti* 'twenty') + **-AL**.

**vigil** /ˈvɪdʒɪl/ • n. **1** a period of staying awake during the time usually spent asleep, especially to keep watch or pray. **2** (in the Christian Church) the eve of a festival or holy day as an occasion of religious observance. ➤(**vigils**) nocturnal devotions.
– ORIGIN ME: via OFr. from L. *vigilia*, from *vigil* 'awake'.

**vigilance committee** • n. US a group of vigilantes.

**vigilant** • adj. keeping careful watch for possible danger or difficulties.
– DERIVATIVES **vigilance** n. **vigilantly** adv.
– ORIGIN C15: from L. *vigilant-*, *vigilare* 'keep awake'.

**vigilante** /ˌvɪdʒɪˈlanti/ • n. a member of a self-appointed group of people who undertake law enforcement in their community without legal authority, typically because the legal agencies are thought to be inadequate.
– DERIVATIVES **vigilantism** n.
– ORIGIN C19: from Sp., lit. 'vigilant'.

**vigneron** /ˈviːnjərɒ̃, French viɲ(ə)ʀɔ̃/ • n. a person who cultivates grapes for winemaking.
– ORIGIN Fr., from *vigne* 'vine'.

**vignette** /viːˈnjɛt, vɪ-/ • n. **1** a brief evocative description, account, or episode. **2** a small illustration or portrait photograph which fades into its background without a definite border. ➤a small ornamental design in a book or carving, typically based on foliage. • v. portray in the style of a vignette. ➤produce (a photograph) with softened or fading edges.
– DERIVATIVES **vignettist** n.
– ORIGIN ME (also denoting a carved representation of a vine): from Fr., dimin. of *vigne* 'vine'.

**vigor** • n. US spelling of **VIGOUR**.

**vigorish** • n. US informal **1** an excessive rate of interest on a loan. **2** the percentage deducted from a gambler's winnings by the organizers of a game.
– ORIGIN C20: prob. from Yiddish, from Russ. *vyigrysh* 'gain, winnings'.

**vigoro** /ˈvɪɡ(ə)rəʊ/ • n. an Australian team ball game combining elements of cricket and baseball, traditionally played by women.
– ORIGIN 1930s: appar. from **VIGOROUS**.

**vigorous** • adj. **1** strong, healthy, and full of energy.

➤characterized by or involving physical strength, effort, or energy. **2** (of language) forceful.
– DERIVATIVES **vigorously** adv. **vigorousness** n.

**vigour** (US **vigor**) ● **n.** physical strength and good health. ➤effort, energy, and enthusiasm. ➤strong, healthy growth of a plant.
– DERIVATIVES **vigourless** adj.
– ORIGIN ME: from OFr., from L. *vigor*, from *vigere* 'be lively'.

**vihuela** /vɪ'(h)weɪlə/ ● **n.** a type of early Spanish stringed musical instrument.
– ORIGIN C19: Sp.

**Viking** /'vʌɪkɪŋ/ ● **n.** any of the Scandinavian seafaring pirates and traders who raided and settled in many parts of NW Europe in the 8th–11th centuries.
– ORIGIN from ON *víkingr*, from *vík* 'creek' or OE *wīc* 'camp, dwelling place'.

**vilayet** /vɪ'lɑːjɛt/ ● **n.** (in Turkey, and formerly in the Ottoman Empire) a major administrative district.
– ORIGIN Turk., from Arab. *wilāya(t)* 'government, administrative district'.

**vile** ● **adj. 1** extremely unpleasant. **2** morally bad; wicked. **3** archaic of little worth or value.
– DERIVATIVES **vilely** adv. **vileness** n.
– ORIGIN ME: via OFr. from L. *vilis* 'cheap, base'.

**vilify** /'vɪlɪfʌɪ/ ● **v.** (**-ies**, **-ied**) speak or write about in an abusively disparaging manner.
– DERIVATIVES **vilification** /-fɪ'keɪʃ(ə)n/ n. **vilifier** n.
– ORIGIN ME (in the sense 'lower in value'): from late L. *vilificare*, from L. *vilis* (see **VILE**).

**villa** ● **n. 1** (especially in continental Europe) a large country residence in its own grounds. ➤Brit. a detached or semi-detached house in a residential district. ➤a rented holiday home abroad. **2** (in Roman times) a large country house, having an estate and consisting of buildings arranged around a courtyard.
– ORIGIN C17: from Ital., from L.

**village** ● **n. 1** a group of houses situated in a rural area, larger than a hamlet and smaller than a town. ➤a self-contained district or community within a town or city: *the Olympic village*. ➤N. Amer. a small municipality with limited corporate powers. **2** Austral./NZ a select suburban shopping centre.
– DERIVATIVES **villager** n. **villagey** adj.
– ORIGIN ME: from OFr., from L. *villa* 'country house'.

**villain** /'vɪlən/ ● **n. 1** a wicked person or a person guilty of a crime. ➤(in a play or novel) a character whose evil actions or motives are important to the plot. **2** archaic variant spelling of **VILLEIN**.
– DERIVATIVES **villainous** adj. **villainously** adv. **villainousness** n. **villainy** n.
– ORIGIN ME (in the sense 'a rustic'): from OFr. *vilein*, based on L. *villa* (see **VILLA**).

**villancico** /ˌviːjan'siːkəʊ/ ● **n.** (pl. **-os** /-əʊz/) a form of Spanish and Portuguese song with short stanzas and a refrain.
– ORIGIN Sp., dimin. of *villano* 'peasant'.

**villanella** /ˌvɪlə'nɛlə/ ● **n.** (pl. **villanelle** /ˌvɪlə'nɛleɪ/ or **villanellas**) a form of Italian part song originating in Naples, in rustic style with a vigorous rhythm.
– ORIGIN Ital., fem. of *villanello* 'rural'.

**villanelle** /ˌvɪlə'nɛl/ ● **n.** a pastoral or lyrical poem of nineteen lines, with only two rhymes throughout, and some lines repeated.
– ORIGIN C19: from Fr., from Ital. *villanella* (see **VILLANELLA**).

**-ville** ● **comb. form** informal used in fictitious place names with reference to a particular quality: *dullsville*.
– ORIGIN from Fr. *ville* 'town'.

**villein** /'vɪlən, -eɪn/ ● **n.** (in medieval England) a feudal tenant entirely subject to a lord or manor to whom he paid dues and services in return for land.
– ORIGIN ME: var. of **VILLAIN**.

**villeinage** /'vɪlənɪdʒ, -leɪn-/ ● **n.** historical the tenure or status of a villein.

**villi** plural form of **VILLUS**.

**villus** /'vɪləs/ ● **n.** (pl. **villi** /-lʌɪ, -liː/) Anatomy any of numerous minute elongated projections set closely together on a surface, especially in the absorbent lining of the small intestine.
– DERIVATIVES **villous** adj.
– ORIGIN C18: from L., lit. 'shaggy hair'.

**vim** ● **n.** informal energy; enthusiasm.
– ORIGIN C19 (orig. US): perh. from L., accusative of *vis* 'energy'.

**VIN** ● **abbrev.** vehicle identification number.

**vina** ● **n.** variant spelling of **VEENA**.

**vinaceous** /vʌɪ'neɪʃəs/ ● **adj.** of the colour of red wine.
– ORIGIN C17: from L. *vinaceus* (from *vinum* 'wine') + **-OUS**.

**vinaigrette** /ˌvɪnɪ'grɛt, ˌvɪneɪ-/ ● **n. 1** salad dressing of oil, wine vinegar, and seasoning. **2** historical a small ornamental bottle for holding smelling salts.
– ORIGIN Fr., dimin. of *vinaigre* 'vinegar'.

**vinca** /'vɪŋkə/ ● **n.** another term for **PERIWINKLE**[1].
– ORIGIN 1930s: from mod. L. *Vinca* (genus name), from late L. *pervinca* (see **PERIWINKLE**[1]).

**vincible** /'vɪnsɪb(ə)l/ ● **adj.** poetic/literary able to be overcome or conquered.
– DERIVATIVES **vincibility** n.
– ORIGIN C16: from L. *vincibilis*, from *vincere* 'to overcome'.

**vinculum** /'vɪŋkjʊləm/ ● **n.** (pl. **vincula** /-lə/) **1** Anatomy a connecting band of tissue, such as that attaching a flexor tendon to the bone of a finger or toe. **2** Mathematics a horizontal line drawn over a group of terms in a mathematical expression to indicate that they are to be operated on as a single entity by the preceding or following operator.
– DERIVATIVES **vincular** adj.
– ORIGIN C17 (in the sense 'bond, tie'): from L., lit. 'bond'.

**vindaloo** /ˌvɪndə'luː/ ● **n.** a very hot Indian curry made with meat or fish.
– ORIGIN prob. from Port. *vin d'alho* 'wine and garlic (sauce)', from *vinho* 'wine' + *alho* 'garlic'.

**vindicate** /'vɪndɪkeɪt/ ● **v.** clear of blame or suspicion; show to be right or justified.
– DERIVATIVES **vindicable** adj. **vindication** n. **vindicator** n. **vindicatory** adj.
– ORIGIN C16 (in the sense 'deliver, rescue'): from L. *vindicat-*, *vindicare* 'claim, avenge'.

**vindictive** /vɪn'dɪktɪv/ ● **adj.** having or showing a strong or unreasoning desire for revenge.
– DERIVATIVES **vindictively** adv. **vindictiveness** n.
– ORIGIN C17: from L. *vindicta* 'vengeance' + **-IVE**.

**vine** ● **n. 1** a climbing or trailing woody-stemmed plant related to the grapevine. [*Vitis* and other genera.] ➤used in names of climbing or trailing plants of other families, e.g. **Russian vine**. **2** the slender stem of a trailing or climbing plant.
– DERIVATIVES **viny** adj.
– ORIGIN ME: from OFr., from L. *vinea* 'vineyard, vine', from *vinum* 'wine'.

**vine dresser** ● **n.** a person who prunes, trains, and cultivates vines.

**vinegar** ● **n. 1** a sour-tasting liquid containing acetic acid, obtained by fermenting dilute alcoholic liquids, typically wine, cider, or beer, and used as a condiment or for pickling. **2** sourness or peevishness of behaviour.
– DERIVATIVES **vinegarish** adj. **vinegary** adj.
– ORIGIN ME: from OFr. *vyn egre*, based on L. *vinum* 'wine' + *acer* 'sour'.

**vinery** ● **n.** (pl. **-ies**) a greenhouse for grapevines. ➤a vineyard.

**vineyard** ● **n.** a plantation of grapevines, typically producing grapes used in winemaking.

**vingt-et-un** /ˌvãteɪ'əːn, French vɛ̃teœ̃/ ● **n.** the card game pontoon or blackjack.
– ORIGIN Fr., lit. 'twenty-one'.

**vinho verde** /ˌviːnəʊ 'vɛːdi/ ● **n.** a young Portuguese wine, not allowed to mature.
– ORIGIN Port., lit. 'green wine'.

**vini-** ● **comb. form** of or relating to wine: *viniculture*.
– ORIGIN from L. *vinum* 'wine'.

**viniculture** /ˈvɪnɪˌkʌltʃə/ ● **n.** the cultivation of grapevines for winemaking.
– DERIVATIVES **vinicultural** adj. **viniculturist** n.

**vinification** /ˌvɪnɪfɪˈkeɪʃ(ə)n/ ● **n.** the conversion of grape juice or other vegetable extract into wine by fermentation.
– DERIVATIVES **vinify** v. (**-ies**, **-ied**).

**vining** /ˈvʌɪnɪŋ/ ● **n.** the separation of leguminous crops from their vines and pods. ● **adj.** (of a plant) having climbing or trailing woody stems like a vine.

**vino** /ˈviːnəʊ/ ● **n.** (pl. **-os**) informal, chiefly Brit. wine, especially that which is cheap or of inferior quality.
– ORIGIN Sp. and Ital., 'wine'.

**vin ordinaire** /vã ˌɔːdɪˈnɛː, French vɛ̃ ɔʀdinɛʀ/ ● **n.** (pl. **vins ordinaires**) cheap table wine for everyday use.
– ORIGIN Fr., lit. 'ordinary wine'.

**vinous** /ˈvʌɪnəs/ ● **adj.** of, resembling, or associated with wine. ➤ of the reddish colour of wine.
– DERIVATIVES **vinosity** n. **vinously** adv.
– ORIGIN ME: from L. *vinum* 'wine' + **-OUS**.

**vintage** ● **n.** **1** the year or place in which wine, especially wine of high quality, was produced. ➤ a wine of high quality made from the crop of a single identified district in a good year. ➤ the harvesting of grapes for winemaking. ➤ the grapes or wine of a particular season. **2** the time that something was produced. ● **adj.** **1** referring to vintage wine. **2** denoting something from the past of high quality: *a vintage Sherlock Holmes adventure.*
– ORIGIN ME: alt. (influenced by **VINTNER**) of earlier *vendage*, from OFr. *vendange*, from L. *vindemia* (from *vinum* 'wine' + *demere* 'remove').

**vintage car** ● **n.** Brit. an old style or model of car, specifically one made between 1919 and 1930. Compare with **VETERAN CAR**.

**vintager** ● **n.** a person who harvests grapes.

**vintner** /ˈvɪntnə/ ● **n.** a wine merchant.
– ORIGIN ME: via Anglo-Latin from OFr. *vinetier*, from med. L. *vinetarius*, from L. *vinetum* 'vineyard'.

**vinyl** /ˈvʌɪn(ə)l/ ● **n.** **1** synthetic resin or plastic based on polyvinyl chloride, used e.g. for wallpaper and emulsion paint and formerly for gramophone records. **2** /also ˈvʌɪnʌɪl, -nɪl/ [as modifier] Chemistry of or denoting the unsaturated hydrocarbon radical $-CH=CH_2$, derived from ethylene: *vinyl chloride.*
– ORIGIN C19: from L. *vinum* 'wine' (suggested by the relationship of ethylene to ethyl alcohol) + **-YL**.

**viol** /ˈvʌɪəl/ ● **n.** a musical instrument of the Renaissance and baroque periods, typically six-stringed, held vertically and played with a bow.
– ORIGIN C15: from OFr. *viele*, from Provençal *viola*.

**viola**[1] /vɪˈəʊlə/ ● **n.** an instrument of the violin family, larger than the violin and tuned a fifth lower.
– ORIGIN C18: from Ital. and Sp.; cf. **VIOL**.

**viola**[2] /ˈvʌɪələ/ ● **n.** a plant of a genus that includes the pansies and violets. [Genus *Viola*: many species.]
– ORIGIN mod. L., from L., lit. 'violet'.

**violaceous** /ˌvʌɪəˈleɪʃəs/ ● **adj.** **1** of a violet colour. **2** Botany referring to plants of the violet family (Violaceae).
– ORIGIN C17: from L. *violaceus* (from *viola* 'violet') + **-OUS**.

**viola da braccio** /vɪˌəʊlə da ˈbrɑːtʃɪəʊ/ ● **n.** an early musical instrument of the violin family (as distinct from a viol), specifically one corresponding to the modern viola.
– ORIGIN Ital., lit. 'viol for the arm'.

**viola da gamba** /ˈgambə/ (also **viol da gamba**) ● **n.** a viol, specifically a bass viol (corresponding to the modern cello).
– ORIGIN Ital., lit. 'viol for the leg'.

**viola d'amore** /da'mɔːreɪ/ ● **n.** a sweet-toned 18th-century musical instrument similar to a viola.
– ORIGIN Ital., lit. 'viol of love'.

**violate** ● **v.** **1** break or fail to comply with (a rule or formal agreement). **2** treat with disrespect. **3** rape or sexually assault.
– DERIVATIVES **violable** adj. (rare). **violation** n. **violator** n.
– ORIGIN ME: from L. *violat-*, *violare* 'treat violently'.

**violence** ● **n.** behaviour involving physical force intended to hurt, damage, or kill. ➤ strength of emotion or an unpleasant or destructive natural force.

**violent** ● **adj.** **1** using or involving violence. **2** very intense, forceful, or powerful: *violent dislike.*
– DERIVATIVES **violently** adv.
– ORIGIN ME: via OFr. from L. *violent-* 'violent'.

**violet** ● **n.** **1** a small plant typically with purple, blue, or white five-petalled flowers. [Many species in the genus *Viola*, family Violaceae.] ➤ used in names of unrelated plants with similar flowers, e.g. **African violet**. **2** a bluish-purple colour seen at the end of the spectrum opposite red.
– ORIGIN ME: from OFr. *violette*, dimin. of *viole*, from L. *viola* 'violet'.

**violin** ● **n.** a stringed musical instrument of treble pitch, having four strings and a body narrowed at the middle and with two f-shaped soundholes, played with a horsehair bow.
– DERIVATIVES **violinist** n.
– ORIGIN C16: from Ital. *violino*, dimin. of *viola* (see **VIOLA**[1]).

**violist** ● **n.** **1** /vɪˈəʊlɪst/ a viola player. **2** /ˈvʌɪəlɪst/ a viol player.

**violoncello** /ˌvʌɪələnˈtʃɛləʊ, ˌviːə-/ ● **n.** formal term for **CELLO**.
– DERIVATIVES **violoncellist** n.
– ORIGIN C18: Ital., dimin. of *violone* (see **VIOLONE**).

**violone** /vɪəˈləʊneɪ, -ni/ ● **n.** an early form of double bass, especially a large bass viol.
– ORIGIN Ital., augmentative of *viola* (see **VIOLA**[1]).

**VIP** ● **abbrev.** **1** Biochemistry vasoactive intestinal polypeptide (or peptide), a substance which acts as a neurotransmitter. **2** very important person.

**vipassana** /vɪˈpasənə/ ● **n.** (in Theravada Buddhism) meditation involving concentration on the body, or the insight which this provides.
– ORIGIN Pali, lit. 'inward vision'.

**viper** /ˈvʌɪpə/ ● **n.** **1** a venomous snake with large hinged fangs, typically with dark patterns on a lighter background. [*Vipera berus* (the adder) and other species, family Viperidae.] **2** a spiteful or treacherous person.
– DERIVATIVES **viperine** /-rʌɪn/ adj. **viperish** adj. **viperous** adj.
– ORIGIN C16: from Fr. *vipère* or L. *vipera*, from *vivus* 'alive' + *parere* 'bring forth' (with ref. to the former belief that vipers bore live young).

**viper's bugloss** ● **n.** a bristly plant of the borage family, with pink buds which open to blue flowers, formerly used in the treatment of snake bites. [*Echium vulgare.*]

**viraemia** /vʌɪˈriːmɪə/ (also **viremia**) ● **n.** Medicine the presence of viruses in the blood.
– DERIVATIVES **viraemic** adj.
– ORIGIN 1940s: from **VIRUS** + **-AEMIA**.

**virago** /vɪˈrɑːgəʊ, -ˈreɪgəʊ/ ● **n.** (pl. **-os** or **-oes**) **1** a domineering, violent, or bad-tempered woman. **2** archaic a woman of masculine strength or spirit.
– ORIGIN OE (used as the name given by Adam to Eve, following the Vulgate), from L. 'heroic woman, female warrior', from *vir* 'man'.

**viral** /ˈvʌɪr(ə)l/ ● **adj.** of the nature of, caused by, or relating to a virus or viruses.
– DERIVATIVES **virally** adv.

**viral marketing** ● **n.** a marketing technique whereby information about a company's goods or services is passed electronically from one Internet user to another.
– ORIGIN from the idea of the information being passed on like a computer virus.

**virement** /ˈvʌɪəm(ə)nt, ˈvɪəmɒ̃/ ● **n.** Brit. Finance the process of transferring items from one financial account to another.
– ORIGIN C20: from Fr., from *virer* 'to turn'.

**viremia** ● **n.** variant spelling of **VIRAEMIA**.

**vireo** /ˈvɪrɪəʊ/ ● **n.** (pl. **-os**) a small American warbler-like songbird, typically green or grey with yellow or white underparts. [Family Vireonidae: several species.]
– ORIGIN C19: from L., perh. denoting a greenfinch.

**virescent** /vɪˈrɛs(ə)nt/ ● **adj.** poetic/literary greenish.
– DERIVATIVES **virescence** n. **virescently** adv.
– ORIGIN C19: from L. *virescent-* 'turning green'.

**virga** /ˈvəːɡə/ ● **n.** (pl. **virgae** /ˈvəːɡiː/) Meteorology a mass of streaks of rain appearing to hang under a cloud and evaporating before reaching the ground.
– ORIGIN 1940s: from L., lit. 'rod, stripe'.

**virgate** /ˈvəːɡət/ ● **n.** Brit. historical a varying measure of land, typically 30 acres.
– ORIGIN C17: from L. *virgatus*, from *virga* 'rod'.

**Virgilian** /vəˈdʒɪlɪən/ (also **Vergilian**) ● **adj.** of, relating to, or in the style of the Roman poet Virgil (70–19 BC) or his works.

**virgin** ● **n. 1** a person, typically a woman, who has never had sexual intercourse. ➤(**the Virgin**) the Virgin Mary. **2** a person who is naive or inexperienced in a particular context: *a political virgin*. **3** Entomology a female insect that produces eggs without being fertilized. ● **adj. 1** being, relating to, or appropriate for a virgin. **2** not yet used or exploited: *acres of virgin forest*. ➤(of wool) not yet, or only once, spun or woven. ➤(of olive oil) obtained from the first pressing of olives. ➤(of metal) made from ore by smelting.
– ORIGIN ME: from OFr. *virgine*, from L. *virgo*, *virgin-*.

**virginal** ● **adj.** of, relating to, or appropriate for a virgin. ● **n.** an early spinet with the strings parallel to the keyboard, popular in 16th- and 17th-century houses.
– DERIVATIVES **virginalist** n. **virginally** adv.
– ORIGIN ME: from OFr., or from L. *virginalis*, from *virgo* 'young woman'; the instrument was perh. so called because it was usually played by young women.

**virgin birth** ● **n. 1** (**the Virgin Birth**) the doctrine of Christ's birth from a mother, Mary, who was a virgin. **2** Zoology parthenogenesis.

**Virginia** ● **n.** a type of tobacco grown and manufactured in Virginia.

**Virginia creeper** ● **n.** a North American vine which is chiefly cultivated for its red autumn foliage. [*Parthenocissus quinquefolia* and other species.]

**Virginian** ● **n.** a native or inhabitant of the US states of Virginia or West Virginia. ● **adj.** of or relating to Virginia or West Virginia.

**Virginia reel** ● **n.** a lively North American country dance performed by a number of couples facing each other in parallel lines.

**virginity** ● **n. 1** the state of being a virgin. **2** the state of being innocent or inexperienced in a particular context.

**Virgo** /ˈvəːɡəʊ/ ● **n. 1** Astronomy a large constellation (the Virgin), said to represent a maiden or goddess associated with the harvest. **2** Astrology the sixth sign of the zodiac, which the sun enters about 23 August.
– DERIVATIVES **Virgoan** n. & adj.
– ORIGIN from L.

**virgo intacta** /ˌvəːɡəʊ ɪnˈtaktə/ ● **n.** chiefly Law a girl or woman who has never had sexual intercourse, originally a virgin whose hymen is intact.
– ORIGIN L., lit. 'untouched virgin'.

**virgule** /ˈvəːɡjuːl/ ● **n.** another term for **SLASH** (in sense 3).
– ORIGIN C19: from Fr., lit. 'comma'.

**viridescent** /ˌvɪrɪˈdɛs(ə)nt/ ● **adj.** greenish or becoming green.
– DERIVATIVES **viridescence** n.
– ORIGIN C19: from late L. *viridescent-*, *viridescere* 'become green'.

**viridian** /vɪˈrɪdɪən/ ● **n.** a bluish-green pigment consisting of hydrated chromium hydroxide.
– ORIGIN C19: from L. *viridis* 'green' + **-IAN**.

**virile** ● **adj.** (of a man) having strength, energy, and a strong sex drive. ➤vigorous, strong, and manly.
– DERIVATIVES **virility** n.
– ORIGIN C15 (in the sense 'characteristic of a man'): from Fr. *viril* or L. *virilis*, from *vir* 'man'.

**virilization** /ˌvɪrɪlʌɪˈzeɪʃ(ə)n/ (also **-isation**) ● **n.** Medicine the development in a female (or precociously in a boy) of male physical characteristics (such as body hair, deep voice, etc.), typically as a result of excess androgen production.
– DERIVATIVES **virilism** n.

**virilocal** /ˌvɪrɪˈləʊk(ə)l/ ● **adj.** another term for **PATRILOCAL**.
– ORIGIN 1940s: from L. *virilis* 'of a man' + **LOCAL**.

**viroid** /ˈvʌɪrɔɪd/ ● **n.** Microbiology an infectious entity affecting plants, smaller than a virus and consisting only of nucleic acid without a protein coat.

**virology** /vʌɪˈrɒlədʒi/ ● **n.** the branch of science concerned with the study of viruses.
– DERIVATIVES **virological** adj. **virologically** adv. **virologist** n.

**virtu** /vəːˈt(j)uː/ (also **vertu**) ● **n. 1** knowledge of or expertise in the fine arts. **2** curios or objets d'art collectively.
– PHRASES **article** (or **object**) **of virtu** an article that is interesting because of its antiquity, beauty, quality of workmanship, etc.
– ORIGIN C18: from Ital. *virtù* 'virtue'; the var. *vertu* is an alt., as if from Fr.

**virtual** /ˈvəːtjʊəl/ ● **adj. 1** almost or nearly as described, but not completely or according to strict definition. **2** Computing not physically existing as such but made by software to appear to do so. **3** Optics relating to the points at which rays would meet if produced backwards: *a virtual image*. **4** Mechanics relating to or denoting infinitesimal displacements of a point in a system.
– DERIVATIVES **virtuality** /-jʊˈalɪti/ n.
– ORIGIN ME (also in the sense 'possessing certain virtues'): from med. L. *virtualis*, from L. *virtus* 'virtue'.

**virtually** ● **adv. 1** nearly; almost. **2** Computing by means of virtual reality techniques.

**virtual memory** (also **virtual storage**) ● **n.** Computing memory that appears to exist as main storage although most of it is supported by data held in secondary storage.

**virtual reality** ● **n.** Computing the computer-generated simulation of a three-dimensional image or environment that can be interacted with in a seemingly real or physical way by using special electronic equipment.

**virtue** /ˈvəːtjuː, -tʃuː/ ● **n. 1** behaviour showing high moral standards. ➤a quality considered morally good or desirable. ➤a good or useful quality of a thing. **2** archaic virginity or chastity.
– PHRASES **by** (or **in**) **virtue of** because or as a result of. **make a virtue of** derive benefit or advantage from submitting to (something unwelcome).
– DERIVATIVES **virtueless** adj.
– ORIGIN ME: from OFr. *vertu*, from L. *virtus* 'valour, merit, moral perfection', from *vir* 'man'.

**virtuoso** /ˌvəːtjʊˈəʊzəʊ, -səʊ/ ● **n.** (pl. **virtuosi** /-si/ or **virtuosos**) **1** a person highly skilled in music or another artistic pursuit. **2** a person with a special knowledge of or interest in works of art or curios.
– DERIVATIVES **virtuosic** adj. **virtuosity** n.
– ORIGIN C17: from Ital., lit. 'learned, skilful'.

**virtuous** ● **adj. 1** having or showing high moral standards. **2** archaic (especially of a woman) chaste.
– DERIVATIVES **virtuously** adv. **virtuousness** n.

**virtuous circle** ● **n.** a recurring cycle of events, the result of each one being to increase the beneficial effect of the next.

**virulent** /ˈvɪrʊl(ə)nt, ˈvɪrjʊ-/ ● **adj. 1** (of a disease or poison) extremely severe or harmful in its effects. ➤(of a pathogen, especially a virus) highly infective. **2** bitterly hostile.
– DERIVATIVES **virulence** n. **virulently** adv.
– ORIGIN ME (orig. describing a poisoned wound): from L. *virulentus*, from *virus* (see **VIRUS**).

**virus** /ˈvʌɪrəs/ ● **n. 1** a submicroscopic infective particle, typically consisting of nucleic acid coated in protein, which is able to multiply within the cells of a host organism. ➤informal an infection or disease caused by such an agent. **2** (also **computer virus**) a piece of code surreptitiously introduced into a system in order to corrupt it or destroy data.
– ORIGIN ME (denoting snake venom): from L., lit. 'slimy liquid, poison'.

**Vis.** ● **abbrev.** Viscount.

**visa** /ˈviːzə/ ● **n.** an endorsement on a passport indicating that the holder is allowed to enter, leave, or stay for a specified period of time in a country.

– ORIGIN C19: via Fr. from L. *visa*, past part. of *videre* 'to see'.

**visage** /ˈvɪzɪdʒ/ ● **n.** poetic/literary a person's face, with reference to the form of the features. ➤a person's facial expression.
– DERIVATIVES **visaged** adj.
– ORIGIN ME: via OFr. from L. *visus* 'sight', from *videre* 'to see'.

**Visākha** /vɪˈsɑːkə/ ● **n.** variant of **VESAK**.

**vis-à-vis** /ˌviːzɑːˈviː, French vizavi/ ● **prep. 1** in relation to. **2** as compared with; as opposed to. ● **adv.** archaic in a position facing a specified or implied subject. ● **n.** (pl. same) a person or thing occupying a corresponding position to that of another; a counterpart.
– ORIGIN C18: Fr., lit. 'face to face', from OFr. *vis* 'face'.

**Visc.** ● **abbrev.** Viscount.

**viscacha** /vɪˈskatʃə/ ● **n.** a large South American burrowing rodent of the chinchilla family, sometimes hunted for its fur and flesh. [Genera *Lagidium* and *Lagostomus*: four species.]
– ORIGIN C17: via Sp. from Quechua *(h)uiscacha*.

**viscera** /ˈvɪs(ə)rə/ ● **pl. n.** (sing. **viscus**) the internal organs in the main cavities of the body, especially those in the abdomen, e.g. the intestines.
– ORIGIN C17: from L., pl. of *viscus*.

**visceral** ● **adj. 1** of or relating to the viscera. **2** relating to deep inward feelings rather than to the intellect.
– DERIVATIVES **viscerally** adv.

**viscid** /ˈvɪsɪd/ ● **adj.** glutinous; sticky.
– DERIVATIVES **viscidity** n.
– ORIGIN C17: from late L. *viscidus*, from L. *viscum* 'birdlime'.

**viscoelasticity** /ˌvɪskəʊɛlaˈstɪsɪti, -iːla-, -ɪla-/ ● **n.** Physics the property of a substance of exhibiting both elastic and viscous behaviour.
– DERIVATIVES **viscoelastic** adj.

**viscometer** /vɪsˈkɒmɪtə/ ● **n.** an instrument for measuring the viscosity of liquids.
– DERIVATIVES **viscometric** adj. **viscometrically** adv. **viscometry** n.

**viscose** /ˈvɪskəʊz, -kəʊs/ ● **n. 1** a viscous orange-brown solution obtained by treating cellulose with sodium hydroxide and carbon disulphide, used as the basis of manufacturing rayon and transparent cellulose film. **2** rayon fabric or fibre made from this.
– ORIGIN C19: from late L. *viscosus*, from L. *viscus* 'birdlime'.

**viscosity** /vɪˈskɒsɪti/ ● **n.** (pl. **-ies**) the state of being viscous. ➤a quantity expressing the magnitude of internal friction in a fluid, as measured by the force per unit area resisting uniform flow.

**viscount** /ˈvʌɪkaʊnt/ ● **n.** a British nobleman ranking above a baron and below an earl.
– DERIVATIVES **viscountcy** n.
– ORIGIN ME: from OFr. *visconte*, from med. L. *vicecomes*, *vicecomit-* (see **VICE-**, **COUNT**[2]).

**viscountess** /ˈvʌɪkaʊntɪs/ ● **n.** the wife or widow of a viscount, or a woman holding the rank of viscount in her own right.

**viscounty** (also **viscountcy**) ● **n.** the land under the authority of a particular viscount.

**viscous** /ˈvɪskəs/ ● **adj.** having a thick, sticky consistency between solid and liquid; having a high viscosity.
– DERIVATIVES **viscously** adv. **viscousness** n.
– ORIGIN ME: from Anglo-Norman Fr. *viscous* or late L. *viscosus*, from L. *viscum* 'birdlime'.

**viscus** /ˈvɪskəs/ singular form of **VISCERA**.
– ORIGIN from L.

**vise** ● **n.** US spelling of **VICE**[2].

**visibility** ● **n.** the state of being able to see or be seen. ➤the distance one can see as determined by light and weather conditions.

**visible** ● **adj. 1** able to be seen. ➤Physics (of light) within the range of wavelengths to which the eye is sensitive. ➤able to be perceived or noticed easily. ➤in a position of public prominence. **2** of or relating to imports or exports of tangible commodities. ● **n.** (**visibles**) visible imports or exports.
– DERIVATIVES **visibleness** n. **visibly** adv.
– ORIGIN ME: from OFr., or from L. *visibilis*, from *videre* 'to see'.

**Visigoth** /ˈvɪzɪgɒθ/ ● **n.** a member of the branch of the Goths who invaded the Roman Empire between the 3rd and 5th centuries AD and ruled much of Spain until overthrown by the Moors in 711.
– DERIVATIVES **Visigothic** adj.
– ORIGIN from late L. *Visigothus*, the first element possibly meaning 'west' (cf. **OSTROGOTH**).

**vision** ● **n. 1** the faculty or state of being able to see. **2** the ability to think about or plan the future with imagination or wisdom. ➤a mental image of what the future will or could be like. **3** an experience of seeing something in a dream or trance, or as a supernatural apparition. ➤a person or sight of unusual beauty. ● **v.** imagine; envision.
– DERIVATIVES **visional** adj. **visionless** adj.
– ORIGIN ME: via OFr. from L. *visio(n-)*, from *videre* 'to see'.

**visionary** ● **adj. 1** thinking about or planning the future with imagination or wisdom. **2** of or relating to supernatural visions or visions in a dream or trance. **3** archaic existing only in the imagination. ➤(of a scheme or idea) not practical. ● **n.** (pl. **-ies**) a visionary person.
– DERIVATIVES **visionariness** n.

**visit** ● **v.** (**visited**, **visiting**) **1** go to see and spend some time with (someone) socially or as a guest. ➤go to see and spend some time in (a place) as a tourist or guest. ➤go to see for any specific purpose, such as to receive or give professional advice. **2** (usu. **be visited**) (with reference to something harmful or unpleasant) inflict or be inflicted on someone. ➤archaic punish. **3** N. Amer. informal chat. **4** (of God) come to in order to bring comfort or salvation. ● **n. 1** an act of visiting. ➤a temporary stay at a place. **2** N. Amer. an informal conversation.
– DERIVATIVES **visitable** adj. **visiting** adj.
– ORIGIN ME: from OFr. *visiter* or L. *visitare* 'go to see'.

**visitant** ● **n. 1** chiefly poetic/literary a supernatural being; an apparition. **2** archaic a visitor or guest. **3** Ornithology a visitor. ● **adj.** archaic or poetic/literary paying a visit.

**visitation** ● **n. 1** the appearance of a divine or supernatural being. **2** (in Church use) an official visit of inspection, especially one by a bishop. ➤a pastoral or charitable visit. **3** US Law a divorced person's right to spend time with their children in the custody of a former spouse. **4** US a gathering with the family of a deceased person before the funeral. **5** a disaster or difficulty regarded as a divine punishment. **6** (**the Visitation**) the visit of the Virgin Mary to Elizabeth related in Luke 1:39–56.

**visiting card** ● **n.** Brit. a card bearing a person's name and address, sent or left in lieu of a formal visit.

**visiting fireman** ● **n.** N. Amer. informal a visitor who is accorded special attention on account of being an important figure, extravagant spender, etc.

**visitor** ● **n. 1** a person visiting a person or place, especially socially or as a tourist. **2** Ornithology a migratory bird present in a locality for only part of the year.

**visitorial** ● **adj.** of or relating to an official visitor or visitation.

**vis medicatrix naturae** /vɪs mɛdɪˌkeɪtrɪks ˈnatʃərʌɪ/ ● **n.** the body's natural ability to heal itself.
– ORIGIN L., 'the healing power of nature'.

**visor** /ˈvʌɪzə/ (also **vizor**) ● **n. 1** a movable part of a helmet that can be pulled down to cover the face. **2** a screen for protecting the eyes from unwanted light, especially one at the top of a vehicle windscreen. **3** N. Amer. a stiff peak at the front of a cap. **4** historical a mask.
– DERIVATIVES **visored** adj.
– ORIGIN ME: from Anglo-Norman Fr. *viser*, from OFr. *vis* 'face', from L. *visus* (see **VISAGE**).

**vista** ● **n. 1** a pleasing view, especially one seen through a long, narrow opening. **2** a mental view of an imagined future event or situation: *vistas of freedom seemed to open ahead of him.*
– ORIGIN C17: from Ital., lit. 'view'.

**visual** /ˈvɪʒjʊəl, -zj-/ ● **adj.** of or relating to seeing or sight. ● **n.** a picture, piece of film, or display used to illustrate or accompany something.
– DERIVATIVES **visuality** n. **visually** adv.
– ORIGIN ME (orig. describing a supposed beam proceeding from the eye and making vision possible): from late L. *visualis*, from L. *visus* 'sight', from *videre* 'to see'.

**visual angle** ● **n.** Optics the angle formed at the eye by rays from the extremities of an object viewed.

**visual display unit** ● **n.** Computing, chiefly Brit. a device for displaying input signals as characters on a screen, typically incorporating a keyboard.

**visualize** (also **-ise**) ● **v. 1** form a mental image of; imagine. **2** make visible to the eye.
– DERIVATIVES **visualizable** adj. **visualization** n.

**visual purple** ● **n.** a purplish-red light-sensitive pigment present in the retinas of humans and many other animal groups.

**visuospatial** /ˌvɪʒjʊəʊˈspeɪʃ(ə)l, -zj-/ ● **adj.** Psychology relating to or denoting the visual perception of the spatial relationships of objects.

**vital** ● **adj. 1** absolutely necessary; essential. ➤ indispensable to the continuance of life: *the vital organs.* **2** full of energy; lively. **3** archaic fatal. ● **n.** (**vitals**) the body's important internal organs.
– DERIVATIVES **vitally** adv.
– ORIGIN ME: via OFr. from L. *vitalis*, from *vita* 'life'.

**vital capacity** ● **n.** the greatest volume of air that can be expelled from the lungs after taking the deepest possible breath.

**vital force** ● **n.** the energy or spirit which animates living creatures.

**vitalism** ● **n.** the theory that the origin and phenomena of life are dependent on a force or principle distinct from purely chemical or physical forces.
– DERIVATIVES **vitalist** n. & adj. **vitalistic** adj.

**vitality** ● **n. 1** the state of being strong and active; energy. **2** the power giving continuance of life, present in all living things.

**vitalize** /ˈvʌɪt(ə)lʌɪz/ (also **-ise**) ● **v.** give strength and energy to.
– DERIVATIVES **vitalization** n.

**vital signs** ● **pl. n.** clinical measurements, specifically pulse rate, temperature, respiration rate, and blood pressure, that indicate the state of a patient's essential body functions.

**vital statistics** ● **pl. n. 1** quantitative data concerning the population, such as the number of births, marriages, and deaths. **2** informal the measurements of a woman's bust, waist, and hips.

**vitamin** /ˈvɪtəmɪn, ˈvʌɪt-/ ● **n.** any of a group of organic compounds which are essential for normal growth and nutrition and are required in small quantities in the diet because they cannot be synthesized by the body.
– ORIGIN C20: from L. *vita* 'life' + **AMINE**, because vitamins were orig. thought to contain an amino acid.

**vitamin A** ● **n.** another term for **RETINOL**.

**vitamin B** ● **n.** any of a group of substances essential for the working of certain enzymes in the body, including thiamine (**vitamin $B_1$**), riboflavin (**vitamin $B_2$**), pyridoxine (**vitamin $B_6$**), and cyanocobalamin (**vitamin $B_{12}$**).

**vitamin C** ● **n.** another term for **ASCORBIC ACID**.

**vitamin D** ● **n.** any of a group of compounds found in liver and fish oils, essential for the absorption of calcium and including calciferol (**vitamin $D_2$**) and cholecalciferol (**vitamin $D_3$**).

**vitamin E** ● **n.** another term for **TOCOPHEROL**.

**vitamin H** ● **n.** chiefly N. Amer. another term for **BIOTIN**.

**vitaminize** (also **-ise**) ● **v.** add vitamins to (food).

**vitamin K** ● **n.** any of a group of compounds found mainly in green leaves and essential for the blood-clotting process, including phylloquinone (**vitamin $K_1$**) and menaquinone (**vitamin $K_2$**).

**vitamin M** ● **n.** chiefly N. Amer. another term for **FOLIC ACID**.

**vitamin P** ● **n.** chiefly US the bioflavonoids, regarded collectively as a vitamin.

**vitelli** plural form of **VITELLUS**.

**vitellin** /vɪˈtɛlɪn, vʌɪ-/ ● **n.** Biochemistry the chief protein constituent of egg yolk.
– ORIGIN C19: from **VITELLUS** + **-IN**[1].

**vitelline** /vɪˈtɛlʌɪn, vʌɪ-, -lɪn/ ● **adj.** Zoology & Embryology of or relating to the yolk (or yolk sac) of an egg or embryo, or to yolk-producing organs.
– ORIGIN ME: from med. L. *vitellinus*, from *vitellus* (see **VITELLUS**).

**vitelline membrane** ● **n.** Embryology a transparent membrane surrounding and secreted by the fertilized ovum, preventing the entry of further spermatozoa.

**vitellus** /vɪˈtɛləs, vʌɪ-/ ● **n.** (pl. **vitelli** /-lʌɪ, -liː/) Embryology the yolk of an egg or ovum.
– ORIGIN C18: from L., lit. 'yolk'.

**vitiate** /ˈvɪʃɪeɪt/ ● **v.** formal spoil or impair the quality or efficiency of. ➤ destroy or impair the legal validity of.
– DERIVATIVES **vitiation** n. **vitiator** n.
– ORIGIN C16: from L. *vitiat-*, *vitiare* 'impair'.

**viticulture** /ˈvɪtɪˌkʌltʃə/ ● **n.** the cultivation of grapevines. ➤ the study of grape cultivation.
– DERIVATIVES **viticultural** adj. **viticulturist** n.
– ORIGIN C19: from L. *vitis* 'vine' + **CULTURE**.

**vitiligo** /ˌvɪtɪˈlʌɪgəʊ/ ● **n.** Medicine a condition in which the pigment is lost from areas of the skin, causing whitish patches.
– ORIGIN C16: from L., lit. 'tetter'.

**vitreous** /ˈvɪtrɪəs/ ● **adj.** like glass in appearance or physical properties. ➤ (of a substance) derived from or containing glass.
– DERIVATIVES **vitreousness** n.
– ORIGIN ME: from L. *vitreus* (from *vitrum* 'glass') + **-OUS**.

**vitreous humour** ● **n.** the transparent jelly-like tissue filling the eyeball behind the lens.

**vitriform** /ˈvɪtrɪfɔːm/ ● **adj.** having the form or appearance of glass.

**vitrify** /ˈvɪtrɪfʌɪ/ ● **v.** (**-ies**, **-ied**) (often **be vitrified**) convert into glass or a glass-like substance, typically by exposure to heat.
– DERIVATIVES **vitrifaction** /-ˈfakʃ(ə)n/ n. **vitrifiable** adj. **vitrification** /-fɪˈkeɪʃ(ə)n/ n.
– ORIGIN ME: from Fr. *vitrifier* or based on L. *vitrum* 'glass'.

**vitrine** /ˈvɪtriːn/ ● **n.** a glass display case.
– ORIGIN Fr., from *vitre* 'glass pane'.

**vitriol** /ˈvɪtrɪəl/ ● **n. 1** archaic or poetic/literary sulphuric acid. ➤ in names of metallic sulphates, e.g. **blue vitriol** (copper sulphate) and **green vitriol** (ferrous sulphate). **2** extreme bitterness or malice.
– DERIVATIVES **vitriolic** adj. **vitriolically** adv.
– ORIGIN ME (denoting the sulphate of various metals): from OFr., or from med. L. *vitriolum*, from L. *vitrum* 'glass'.

**vitta** /ˈvɪtə/ ● **n.** (pl. **vittae** /ˈvɪtiː/) Zoology a band or stripe of colour.
– ORIGIN C19: from L., lit. 'band, chaplet'.

**vittle** ● **n.** archaic variant spelling of **VICTUAL**.

**vituperate** /vɪˈtjuːpəreɪt, vʌɪ-/ ● **v.** archaic blame or insult in strong or violent language.
– DERIVATIVES **vituperator** n.
– ORIGIN C16 (earlier (ME) as *vituperation*): from L. *vituperat-*, *vituperare* 'censure, disparage'.

**vituperation** ● **n.** bitter and abusive language.

**vituperative** /vɪˈtjuːp(ə)rətɪv, vʌɪ-/ ● **adj.** bitter and abusive.

**viva**[1] /ˈvʌɪvə/ Brit. ● **n.** an oral examination, typically for an academic qualification. ● **v.** (**vivas**, **vivaed** /-vəd/ or **viva'd**, **vivaing**) subject to a viva.
– ORIGIN abbrev. of **VIVA VOCE**.

**viva**[2] /ˈviːvə/ ● **exclam.** long live! (used to express acclaim or support).
– ORIGIN from Ital.

**vivace** /vɪˈvɑːtʃeɪ/ ● **adv. & adj.** Music in a lively and brisk manner.
– ORIGIN Ital., 'brisk, lively'.

**vivacious** /vɪˈveɪʃəs, vʌɪ-/ ● **adj.** (especially of a woman or child) attractively lively and animated.
– DERIVATIVES **vivaciously** adv. **vivaciousness** n. **vivacity** n.

– ORIGIN C17: from L. *vivax, vivac-* 'lively, vigorous' + **-IOUS**.

**vivarium** /vʌɪ'vɛːrɪəm, vɪ-/ ● **n.** (pl. **vivaria** /-rɪə/) an enclosure or structure used for keeping animals under semi-natural conditions for observation or study or as pets; an aquarium or terrarium.
– ORIGIN C17: from L., lit. 'warren, fish pond'.

**viva voce** /ˌvʌɪvə 'vəʊtʃeɪ, 'vəʊtʃi/ ● **adj.** (especially of an examination) oral rather than written. ● **adv.** orally rather than in writing. ● **n.** Brit. full form of **VIVA**[1].
– ORIGIN C16: from med. L., lit. 'with the living voice'.

**viverrid** /vɪ'vɛrɪd, vʌɪ-/ ● **n.** Zoology a mammal of the civet family (Viverridae).
– ORIGIN C20: from mod. L. *Viverridae*, from L. *viverra* 'ferret'.

**vivers** /'vʌɪvəz/ ● **pl. n.** Scottish, chiefly poetic/literary food; provisions.
– ORIGIN C16: from Fr. *vivres*, from *vivre* 'to live'.

**vivid** ● **adj.** **1** producing powerful feelings or strong, clear images in the mind: *a vivid description.* **2** (of a colour) intensely deep or bright. **3** archaic lively and vigorous.
– DERIVATIVES **vividly** adv. **vividness** n.
– ORIGIN C17: from L. *vividus*, from *vivere* 'to live'.

**vivify** /'vɪvɪfʌɪ/ ● **v.** (**-ies**, **-ied**) enliven or animate.
– DERIVATIVES **vivification** /-fɪ'keɪʃ(ə)n/ n.
– ORIGIN ME: from Fr. *vivifier*, from late L. *vivificare*, from L. *vivus* 'living', from *vivere* 'to live'.

**viviparous** /vɪ'vɪp(ə)rəs, vʌɪ-/ ● **adj.** **1** Zoology (of an animal) bringing forth live young which have developed inside the body of the parent. Compare with **OVIPAROUS** and **OVOVIVIPAROUS**. **2** Botany (of a plant) reproducing from buds which form plantlets while still attached to the parent plant, or from seeds which germinate within the fruit.
– DERIVATIVES **viviparity** /ˌvɪvɪ'parɪti/ n. **viviparously** adv.
– ORIGIN C17: from L. *viviparus* (from *vivus* 'alive' + *-parus* 'bearing') + **-OUS**.

**vivisection** ● **n.** **1** the practice of performing operations on live animals for the purpose of experimentation or scientific research (used by those opposed to such work). **2** ruthlessly sharp and detailed criticism or analysis.
– DERIVATIVES **vivisect** v. **vivisectionist** n. & adj. **vivisector** n.
– ORIGIN C18: from L. *vivus* 'living', on the pattern of *dissection*.

**vixen** ● **n.** **1** a female fox. **2** a spiteful or quarrelsome woman.
– DERIVATIVES **vixenish** adj.
– ORIGIN ME *fixen*, perh. from OE *fyxen* 'of a fox'.

**Viyella** /vʌɪ'ɛlə/ ● **n.** trademark a fabric made from a twilled mixture of cotton and wool.
– ORIGIN C19: from *Via Gellia*, a valley in Derbyshire.

**viz.** ● **adv.** namely; in other words (used to introduce a gloss or explanation).
– ORIGIN abbrev. of **VIDELICET**, *z* being a med. L. symbol for *-et*.

**vizard** /'vɪzəd/ ● **n.** archaic a mask or disguise.
– ORIGIN C16: alt. of **VISOR**.

**vizier** /vɪ'zɪə, 'vɪzɪə/ ● **n.** historical a high official in some Muslim countries, especially in Turkey under Ottoman rule.
– DERIVATIVES **vizierate** /-rət/ n. **vizierial** /vɪ'zɪərɪəl/ adj. **viziership** n.
– ORIGIN C16: via Turk. from Arab. *wazīr* 'caliph's chief counsellor'.

**vizor** ● **n.** variant spelling of **VISOR**.

**vizsla** /'vɪʒlə/ ● **n.** a dog of a breed of golden-brown pointer with large drooping ears.
– ORIGIN 1940s: named after the town of *Vizsla* in Hungary.

**VJ** ● **abbrev.** video jockey.

**VJ day** ● **n.** the day (15 August) in 1945 on which Japan ceased fighting in the Second World War, or the day (2 September) when Japan formally surrendered.
– ORIGIN *VJ*, abbrev. of *Victory over Japan*.

**Vlach** /vlak/ ● **n.** a member of the indigenous population of Romania and Moldova.
– ORIGIN from a Slavic word meaning 'foreigner', from a Gmc word rel. to OE *Wœlisc* (see **WELSH**).

**vlei** /fleɪ, vlʌɪ/ ● **n.** S. African a shallow natural pool of water or area of marshy ground.
– ORIGIN Afrik., from Du. *vallei* 'valley'.

**VLF** ● **abbrev.** very low frequency (denoting radio waves of frequency 3–30 kHz and wavelength 10–100 km).

**VLSI** ● **abbrev.** Electronics very large-scale integration.

**VN** ● **abbrev.** Vietnam (international vehicle registration).

**V-neck** ● **n.** a neckline having straight sides meeting at a point to form a V-shape.
– DERIVATIVES **V-necked** adj.

**VO** ● **abbrev.** (in the UK) Royal Victorian Order.

**vocable** /'vəʊkəb(ə)l/ ● **n.** a word, especially with reference to form rather than meaning.
– ORIGIN ME (denoting a name): from Fr., or from L. *vocabulum*, from *vocare* 'call'.

**vocabulary** ● **n.** (pl. **-ies**) **1** the body of words used in a particular language or in a particular sphere. ➤the body of words known to an individual person. ➤a list of difficult or foreign words with an explanation of their meanings. **2** a range of artistic or stylistic forms or techniques.
– ORIGIN C16: from med. L. *vocabularius*, from L. *vocabulum* (see **VOCABLE**).

**vocal** ● **adj.** **1** of or relating to the human voice. ➤Anatomy used in the production of speech sounds. **2** expressing opinions or feelings freely or loudly. **3** (of music) consisting of or incorporating singing. ● **n.** **1** (also **vocals**) a musical performance involving singing. **2** a part of a piece of music that is sung.
– DERIVATIVES **vocality** n. **vocally** adv.
– ORIGIN ME: from L. *vocalis*, from *vox, voc-* (see **VOICE**).

**vocal cords** (also **vocal folds**) ● **pl. n.** folds of the membranous lining of the larynx which form a slit within the glottis and whose edges vibrate in the airstream to produce the voice.

**vocalese** /ˌvəʊkə'liːz/ ● **n.** a style of singing in which singers put words to jazz tunes or solos.

**vocalic** /və(ʊ)'kalɪk/ ● **adj.** Phonetics of, relating to, or consisting of a vowel or vowels.

**vocalise** /ˌvəʊkə'liːz, 'vəʊkəliːz/ ● **n.** Music a singing exercise using individual syllables or vowel sounds to develop flexibility and control of pitch and tone. ➤a vocal passage consisting of a melody without words.

**vocalism** ● **n.** **1** the use of the voice or vocal organs in speech or singing. **2** Phonetics a vowel sound or articulation. ➤a system of vowels used in a given language.

**vocalist** ● **n.** a singer, especially in jazz or popular music.

**vocalize** /'vəʊk(ə)lʌɪz/ (also **-ise**) ● **v.** **1** utter (a sound or word). ➤express (something) with words. ➤Music sing with several notes to one vowel. **2** Phonetics change (a consonant) to a semivowel or vowel. **3** write (a language such as Hebrew) with vowel points.
– DERIVATIVES **vocalization** n. **vocalizer** n.

**vocation** /və(ʊ)'keɪʃ(ə)n/ ● **n.** **1** a strong feeling of suitability for a particular career or occupation. **2** a person's employment or main occupation, especially one requiring dedication. ➤a trade or profession.
– ORIGIN ME: from OFr., or from L. *vocatio(n-)*, from *vocare* 'to call'.

**vocational** ● **adj.** of or relating to an occupation or employment. ➤(of education or training) directed at a particular occupation and its skills.
– DERIVATIVES **vocationalism** n. **vocationalize** (also **-ise**) v. **vocationally** adv.

**vocative** /'vɒkətɪv/ Grammar ● **adj.** relating to or denoting a case of nouns, pronouns, and adjectives used in addressing or invoking a person or thing. ● **n.** a word in the vocative case.
– ORIGIN ME: from OFr. *vocatif, -ive* or L. *vocativus*, from *vocare* 'to call'.

**vociferate** /və(ʊ)'sɪfəreɪt/ ● **v.** shout, complain, or argue loudly or vehemently.
– DERIVATIVES **vociferant** adj. **vociferation** n.
– ORIGIN C16: from L. *vociferat-, vociferari* 'exclaim'.

**vociferous** ● **adj.** vehement or clamorous.
– DERIVATIVES **vociferously** adv. **vociferousness** n.

**vocoder** /vəʊˈkəʊdə/ ● **n.** a synthesizer that produces sounds from an analysis of speech input.
– ORIGIN 1930s: from **VOICE** + **CODE** + **-ER**[1].

**VOD** ● **abbrev.** video-on-demand.

**vodka** /ˈvɒdkə/ ● **n.** an alcoholic spirit of Russian origin made by distillation of rye, wheat, or potatoes.
– ORIGIN Russ., dimin. of *voda* 'water'.

**vodun** /ˈvəʊduːn/ ● **n.** another term for **VOODOO**.
– ORIGIN Fon, 'fetish'.

**voe** /vəʊ/ ● **n.** a small bay or creek in Orkney or Shetland.
– ORIGIN C17: from Norw. *våg*, from ON *vágr*.

**vogue** ● **n.** (often in phr. **in/out of vogue**) the prevailing fashion or style at a particular time.
– DERIVATIVES **voguish** adj.
– ORIGIN C16: from Fr., from Ital. *voga* 'rowing, fashion'.

**voice** ● **n. 1** the sound produced in a person's larynx and uttered through the mouth, as speech or song. ➤the ability to speak or sing. ➤vocal condition for singing or speaking: *the soprano is in good voice.* **2** Music the range of pitch or type of tone with which a person sings, such as soprano or tenor. ➤a vocal part in a composition. ➤a constituent part in a fugue. ➤each of the notes or sounds able to be produced simultaneously by a musical instrument, especially an electronic one. **3** an opinion or attitude, or a means or agency by which it is expressed: *a dissenting voice.* **4** Phonetics sound uttered with resonance of the vocal cords (used in the pronunciation of vowels and certain consonants). **5** Grammar a form or set of forms of a verb showing the relation of the subject to the action. ● **v. 1** express in words. **2** [usu. as adj. **voiced**] Phonetics utter (a speech sound) with resonance of the vocal cords. **3** Music regulate the tone quality of (organ pipes).
– DERIVATIVES **-voiced** adj. **voiceful** adj. (poetic/literary). **voicer** n.
– ORIGIN ME: from OFr. *vois*, from L. *vox*, *voc-*.

**voice box** ● **n.** the larynx.

**voiceless** ● **adj. 1** lacking a voice; mute; speechless. **2** Phonetics (of a speech sound) uttered without resonance of the vocal cords.
– DERIVATIVES **voicelessly** adv. **voicelessness** n.

**voicemail** ● **n.** a centralized electronic system which can store messages from telephone callers.

**voice-over** ● **n.** a piece of narration in a film or broadcast not accompanied by an image of the speaker. ● **v.** narrate (spoken material) in this way.

**voiceprint** ● **n.** a visual record of speech, analysed with respect to frequency, duration, and amplitude.

**void** /vɔɪd/ ● **adj. 1** not valid or legally binding. ➤(of speech or action) ineffectual; useless. **2** completely empty. ➤(**void of**) free from; lacking. ➤formal (of an office or position) vacant. **3** (in bridge and whist) having been dealt no cards in a particular suit. ● **n. 1** a completely empty space. ➤an unfilled space in a wall, building, or structure. **2** (in bridge and whist) a suit in which a player is dealt no cards. ● **v. 1** chiefly N. Amer. declare to be not valid or legally binding. **2** discharge or drain away (water, gases, etc.). ➤chiefly Medicine excrete (waste matter). ➤[usu. as adj. **voided**] empty or evacuate (a container or space).
– DERIVATIVES **voidable** adj. **voidness** n.
– ORIGIN ME (in the sense 'unoccupied'): from a dial. var. of OFr. *vuide*; rel. to L. *vacare* 'vacate'; the verb partly a shortening of **AVOID**, reinforced by OFr. *voider*.

**voidance** ● **n. 1** the action or state of voiding or being voided. **2** chiefly Law an annulment of a contract. **3** Christian Church a vacancy in a benefice.

**voided** ● **adj.** Heraldry (of a bearing) having the central area cut away so as to show the field.

**voila** /vwʌˈlɑː/ ● **exclam.** there it is; there you are.
– ORIGIN Fr. *voilà*.

**voile** /vɔɪl, vwɑːl/ ● **n.** a thin, semi-transparent fabric of cotton, wool, or silk.
– ORIGIN C19: Fr., lit. 'veil'.

**vol.** ● **abbrev.** volume.

**volant** /ˈvəʊlənt/ ● **adj. 1** Zoology able to fly or glide. **2** Heraldry represented as flying.
– ORIGIN C16 (as a military term in the sense 'capable of rapid movement'): from Fr., lit. 'flying', pres. part. of *voler* 'to fly'.

**Volapük** /ˈvɒləˌp(j)uːk/ ● **n.** an artificial language devised in 1879 for universal use by a German cleric, Johann M. Schleyer, and based on extremely modified forms of words from English and Romance languages, with complex inflections.
– ORIGIN from *vol* representing Engl. *world* + *-a-* (as a connective) + *pük* representing Engl. *speak* or *speech*.

**volar** /ˈvəʊlə/ ● **adj.** Anatomy relating to the palm of the hand or the sole of the foot.
– ORIGIN C19: from L. *vola* 'hollow of hand or foot' + **-AR**[1].

**volatile** /ˈvɒlətʌɪl/ ● **adj. 1** (of a substance) easily evaporated at normal temperatures. **2** liable to change rapidly and unpredictably, especially for the worse. ➤liable to display rapid changes of emotion. **3** (of a computer's memory) retaining data only as long as there is a power supply connected. ● **n.** a volatile substance.
– DERIVATIVES **volatility** n. **volatilizable** (also **-isable**) adj. **volatilization** (also **-isation**) n. **volatilize** (also **-ise**) v.
– ORIGIN ME (in the senses 'creature that flies', 'birds'): from OFr. *volatil* or L. *volatilis*, from *volare* 'to fly'.

**volatile oil** ● **n.** another term for **ESSENTIAL OIL**.

**vol-au-vent** /ˈvɒlə(ʊ)vɒ̃/ ● **n.** a small round case of puff pastry filled with a savoury mixture.
– ORIGIN Fr., lit. 'flight in the wind'.

**volcanic** ● **adj. 1** relating to or produced by a volcano or volcanoes. **2** (of a feeling or emotion) bursting out or liable to burst out violently.
– DERIVATIVES **volcanically** adv.

**volcanic glass** ● **n.** another term for **OBSIDIAN**.

**volcanicity** ● **n.** another term for **VOLCANISM**.

**volcanism** /ˈvɒlkənɪz(ə)m/ (also **vulcanism**) ● **n.** Geology volcanic activity or phenomena.

**volcano** ● **n.** (pl. **-oes** or **-os**) a mountain or hill having a crater or vent through which lava, rock fragments, hot vapour, and gas are or have been erupted from the earth's crust.
– ORIGIN C17: from Ital., from L. *Volcanus* 'Vulcan', the Roman god of fire.

**volcanology** /ˌvɒlkəˈnɒlədʒi/ (also **vulcanology**) ● **n.** the scientific study of volcanoes.
– DERIVATIVES **volcanological** adj. **volcanologist** n.

**vole** ● **n.** a small mouse-like rodent with a rounded muzzle. [Subfamily Microtinae: numerous species.]
– ORIGIN C19 (orig. *vole-mouse*): from Norw. *voll(mus)* 'field (mouse)'.

**volet** /ˈvɒleɪ/ ● **n.** a panel or wing of a triptych.
– ORIGIN C19: from Fr., lit. 'shutter'.

**volition** /vəˈlɪʃ(ə)n/ ● **n.** (often in phr. **of one's own volition**) the faculty or power of using one's will.
– DERIVATIVES **volitional** adj. **volitionally** adv. **volitive** adj. (formal or technical).
– ORIGIN C17: from Fr., or from med. L. *volitio(n-)*, from *volo* 'I wish'.

**volk** /fɒlk/ ● **n.** (pl. **volke**) **1** S. African a nation or people, in particular the Afrikaner people. **2** the German people (with reference to Nazi ideology).
– ORIGIN from Du., Afrik., and Ger.

**Völkerwanderung** /ˈfəːlkəˌvɑːndərʊŋ, German ˈfœlkɐˌvandərʊŋ/ ● **n.** a migration of peoples, especially that of Germanic and Slavic peoples into Europe from the 2nd to the 11th centuries.
– ORIGIN Ger., from *Völker* 'nations' + *Wanderung* 'migration'.

**volley** ● **n.** (pl. **-eys**) **1** a number of bullets, arrows, or other projectiles discharged at one time. ➤a series of utterances directed at someone in quick succession. **2** (in sport, especially tennis or soccer) a strike or kick of the ball made before it touches the ground. ● **v.** (**-eys**, **-eyed**) **1** strike or kick (the ball) before it touches the ground. **2** utter or discharge in quick succession.
– DERIVATIVES **volleyer** n.
– ORIGIN C16: from Fr. *volée*, based on L. *volare* 'to fly'.

**volleyball** ● **n.** a game for two teams in which a large ball is hit by hand over a high net, the aim being to score points by making the ball reach the ground on the opponent's side of the court.

**volplane** /ˈvɒlpleɪn/ Aeronautics ● **n.** a controlled dive at a

steep angle, especially by an aircraft with the engine shut off. ● v. (of an aircraft) make such a dive.
– ORIGIN C20: from Fr. *vol plané*, lit. 'glided flight'.

**vols** ● abbrev. volumes.

**Volscian** /ˈvɒlʃ(ə)n/ ● n. a member of an ancient Italic people absorbed into Rome in the 4th century BC. ● adj. of or relating to the Volscians.
– ORIGIN from L. *Volsci* (the name of the people) + **-AN**.

**volt**[1] /vəʊlt, vɒlt/ (abbrev.: **V**) ● n. the SI unit of electromotive force, the difference of potential that would carry one ampere of current against one ohm resistance.
– ORIGIN C19: named after the Ital. physicist Alessandro *Volta*.

**volt**[2] /vɒlt, vəʊlt/ ● n. variant spelling of **VOLTE**. ● v. Fencing make a quick movement to avoid a thrust.
– ORIGIN C17: from Fr. *volter* (see **VOLTE**).

**voltage** ● n. an electromotive force or potential difference expressed in volts.

**voltaic** /vɒlˈteɪɪk/ ● adj. of or relating to electricity produced by chemical action in a primary battery; galvanic.

**volte** /vɒlt, vəʊlt/ (also **volt**) ● n. **1** Fencing a sudden quick movement to escape a thrust, especially a swing of the rear leg to turn the body sideways. **2** Riding a movement in which a horse describes a circle.
– ORIGIN C17: from Fr., from Ital. *volta* 'a turn'.

**volte-face** /vɒltˈfas, -ˈfɑːs/ ● n. **1** an act of turning round so as to face in the opposite direction. **2** an abrupt and complete reversal of attitude, opinion, or position.
– ORIGIN C19: from Fr., from Ital. *voltafaccia*, based on L. *volvere* 'to roll' + *facies* 'appearance, face'.

**voltmeter** ● n. an instrument for measuring electric potential in volts.

**voluble** /ˈvɒljʊb(ə)l/ ● adj. speaking or spoken incessantly and fluently.
– DERIVATIVES **volubility** n. **volubleness** n. **volubly** adv.
– ORIGIN ME (in senses 'rotating about an axis' and 'tending to change'): from Fr., or from L. *volubilis*, from *volvere* 'to roll'.

**volume** ● n. **1** a book forming part of a work or series. ➤a single book or a bound collection of printed sheets. ➤a consecutive sequence of issues of a periodical. ➤historical a parchment or papyrus scroll. **2** the amount of space occupied by a substance or object or enclosed within a container. ➤the amount or quantity of something, especially when great. ➤fullness or expansive thickness. **3** quantity or power of sound; degree of loudness.
– ORIGIN ME: from OFr. *volum(e)*, from L. *volumen*, *volumin-* 'a roll', from *volvere* 'to roll'.

**volumetric** /ˌvɒljʊˈmɛtrɪk/ ● adj. of or relating to the measurement of volume.
– DERIVATIVES **volumetrically** adv.

**voluminous** /vəˈljuːmɪnəs/ ● adj. **1** (of clothing or drapery) loose and ample. **2** (of writing) very lengthy and full.
– DERIVATIVES **voluminously** adv. **voluminousness** n.
– ORIGIN C17: partly from late L. *voluminosus* 'having many coils', partly from L. *volumen* (see **VOLUME**).

**volumize** (also **-ise**) ● v. give volume or body to (hair).
– DERIVATIVES **volumizer** n.

**voluntarism** ● n. **1** the principle of relying on voluntary action. ➤historical the principle that the Church or schools should be independent of the state and supported by voluntary contributions. **2** Philosophy the doctrine that the will is a fundamental or dominant factor in the individual or the universe.
– DERIVATIVES **voluntarist** n. & adj.

**voluntary** ● adj. **1** done, given, or acting of one's own free will. ➤Physiology under the conscious control of the brain. **2** working or done without payment. ➤Law (of a conveyance or disposition) made without return in money or other consideration. ● n. (pl. **-ies**) **1** an organ solo played before, during, or after a church service. ➤historical a piece of music performed extempore or composed in a free style. **2** (in a competition) a special performance left to the performer's choice.
– DERIVATIVES **voluntarily** adv. **voluntariness** n.
– ORIGIN ME: from OFr. *volontaire* or L. *voluntarius*, from *voluntas* 'will'.

**voluntary-aided** ● adj. (in the UK) denoting a voluntary school funded mainly by the local authority.

**voluntary-controlled** ● adj. (in the UK) denoting a voluntary school fully funded by the local authority.

**voluntaryism** /ˈvɒlənt(ə)rɪˌɪz(ə)m/ ● n. less common term for **VOLUNTARISM** (in sense 1).
– DERIVATIVES **voluntaryist** n.

**voluntary school** ● n. (in the UK) a school which, though not established by the local education authority, is funded mainly or entirely by it, and which typically encourages a particular set of religious beliefs.

**voluntary simplicity** ● n. a philosophy or way of life that rejects materialism, characterized by minimal consumption and environmental responsibility.

**volunteer** ● n. **1** a person who freely offers to do something. ➤a person who freely enrols for military service rather than being conscripted. **2** a person who works for an organization without being paid. **3** a plant that has not been deliberately planted. **4** Law a person to whom a voluntary conveyance or deposition is made. ● v. **1** freely offer to do something. ➤freely enrol for military service rather than being conscripted. ➤commit (someone) to an undertaking without consulting them. **2** say or suggest something without being asked. **3** work for an organization without being paid.
– ORIGIN C16 (as n.): from Fr. *volontaire* 'voluntary'.

**volunteerism** ● n. chiefly N. Amer. the use or involvement of volunteer labour, especially in community services.

**voluptuary** /vəˈlʌptjʊəri/ ● n. (pl. **-ies**) a person devoted to luxury and sensual pleasure. ● adj. concerned with luxury and sensual pleasure.
– ORIGIN C17: from L. *volupt(u)arius*, from *voluptas* 'pleasure'.

**voluptuous** /vəˈlʌptjʊəs/ ● adj. **1** relating to or characterized by luxury or sensual pleasure. **2** (of a woman) curvaceous and sexually attractive.
– DERIVATIVES **voluptuously** adv. **voluptuousness** n.
– ORIGIN ME: from OFr. *voluptueux* or L. *voluptuosus*, from *voluptas* 'pleasure'.

**volute** /vəˈl(j)uːt/ ● n. **1** Architecture a spiral scroll characteristic of Ionic capitals and also used in Corinthian and composite capitals. **2** a deep-water marine mollusc with a colourful thick spiral shell. [*Voluta* and other genera.] ● adj. forming a spiral curve or curves.
– DERIVATIVES **voluted** adj.
– ORIGIN C16: from Fr., or from L. *voluta*, fem. past part. of *volvere* 'to roll'.

**volution** ● n. **1** poetic/literary a rolling or revolving motion. **2** a single turn of a spiral or coil.
– ORIGIN C15: from late L. *volutio(n-)*, from L. *volut-*, *volvere* 'to roll'.

**volvox** /ˈvɒlvɒks/ ● n. Biology a green single-celled aquatic organism which forms minute free-swimming spherical colonies. [Genus *Volvox*.]
– ORIGIN mod. L., from L. *volvere* 'to roll'.

**volvulus** /ˈvɒlvjʊləs/ ● n. (pl. **volvuli** /ˈvɒlvjʊlʌɪ, -liː/ or **volvuluses**) Medicine an obstruction caused by twisting of the stomach or intestine.
– ORIGIN C17: mod. or med. L., from L. *volvere* 'to roll'.

**vomer** /ˈvəʊmə/ ● n. Anatomy the small thin bone separating the left and right nasal cavities in humans and most vertebrates.
– ORIGIN C18: from L., lit. 'ploughshare' (because of the shape).

**vomit** ● v. (**vomited**, **vomiting**) eject matter from the stomach through the mouth. ➤emit in an uncontrolled stream or flow. ● n. **1** matter vomited from the stomach. **2** archaic an emetic.
– DERIVATIVES **vomiter** n.
– ORIGIN ME: from OFr. *vomite* (n.) or L. *vomitus*, from *vomere* 'to vomit'.

**vomitorium** /ˌvɒmɪˈtɔːrɪəm/ ● n. (pl. **vomitoria** /-rɪə/) **1** an entrance or exit passage in an ancient Roman amphitheatre or theatre. **2** a place in which the ancient Romans are supposed to have vomited during feasts to make room for more food.
– ORIGIN from L.

**vomitory** /ˈvɒmɪt(ə)ri/ ● adj. rare relating to or inducing vomiting. ● n. (pl. **-ies**) another term for **VOMITORIUM** (in

## Word *Formation*

**-vorous** 'feeding on a specified food', from Latin *vorare* 'to devour'

➤ Commonest **-vorous** words:

| | | |
|---|---|---|
| carnivorous | feeding on flesh | L. *caro, carn-* 'flesh' |
| frugivorous | feeding on fruit | L. *frux, frug-* 'fruit' |
| graminivorous | feeding on grass | L. *gramen, gramin-* 'grass' |
| herbivorous | feeding on plants | L. *herba* 'green crops, herb' |
| insectivorous | feeding on insects | based on INSECT |
| nectarivorous | feeding on nectar | based on NECTAR |
| omnivorous | feeding on both plants and animals | L. *omnis* 'all' |
| piscivorous | feeding on fish | L. *piscis* 'fish' |

➤ Rarer **-vorous** words:

| | | |
|---|---|---|
| baccivorous | feeding on berries | L. *bacca* 'berry' |
| hominivorous | feeding on human beings | L. *homin-, hominem* 'man' |
| lignivorous | feeding on wood | L. *lignum* 'wood' |
| mellivorous | feeding on honey | L. *mell-, mel* 'honey' |
| merdivorous | feeding on dung | OFr. *merde* 'dung' |
| ovivorous | feeding on eggs | L. *ovum* 'egg' |
| sanguivorous | feeding on blood | L. *sanguis* 'blood' |

➤ Related words:

-vore forming nouns, as ***carnivore*** 'a person or animal that eats meat'

sense 1).

**vomitous** ● **adj.** chiefly N. Amer. nauseating.

**vomitus** /'vɒmɪtəs/ ● **n.** chiefly Medicine matter that has been vomited.
– ORIGIN C20: from L.

**voodoo** ● **n.** a black religious cult practised in the Caribbean and the southern US, combining elements of Roman Catholic ritual with traditional African rites and characterized by sorcery and spirit possession.
– DERIVATIVES **voodooism** n. **voodooist** n.
– ORIGIN C19: from Louisiana Fr., from Kwa *vodũ*.

**Voortrekker** /'fʊəˌtrɛkə/ ● **n.** S. African **1** historical a member of a group of Dutch-speaking people who migrated from the Cape Colony in the 1830s. **2** a member of an Afrikaner youth movement similar to the Boy Scouts and Girl Guides.
– ORIGIN Afrik., from Du. *voor* 'fore' + *trekken* 'to travel'.

**voracious** /və'reɪʃəs/ ● **adj. 1** wanting or devouring great quantities of food. **2** eagerly consuming something: *voracious reading.*
– DERIVATIVES **voraciously** adv. **voraciousness** n. **voracity** n.
– ORIGIN C17: from L. *vorax, vorac-* (from *vorare* 'devour') + **-IOUS**.

**-vorous** /v(ə)rəs/ ● **comb. form** feeding on a specified food: *carnivorous.* See word-formation panel.
– DERIVATIVES **-vora** /v(ə)rə/ comb. form in names of groups. **-vore** /vɔː/ comb. form in names of individuals.
– ORIGIN from L. *-vorus* (from *vorare* 'devour') + **-OUS**.

**vortal** ● **n.** an Internet site that provides a directory of links to information related to a particular industry.
– ORIGIN from *vertical industry,* an industry specializing in a narrow range of goods and services + **PORTAL**[1].

**vortex** /'vɔːtɛks/ ● **n.** (pl. **vortexes** or **vortices** /-tɪsiːz/) a whirling mass, especially a whirlpool or whirlwind.
– DERIVATIVES **vortical** adj. **vortically** adv. **vorticity** /vɔː'tɪsɪti/ n. **vorticose** adj. **vorticular** /vɔː'tɪkjʊlə/ adj.
– ORIGIN C17: from L. *vortex, vortic-*, lit. 'eddy', var. of **VERTEX**.

**vorticella** /ˌvɔːtɪ'sɛlə/ ● **n.** Zoology a sedentary, single-celled aquatic animal with a contractile stalk and a bell-shaped body bearing a ring of cilia. [Genus *Vorticella*.]
– ORIGIN C18: mod. L., dimin. of L. *vortex, vortic-* 'eddy'.

**Vorticism** /'vɔːtɪsɪsm/ ● **n.** a British artistic movement of 1914–15 influenced by cubism and futurism.
– DERIVATIVES **Vorticist** n. & adj.
– ORIGIN from L. *vortex, vortic-* 'eddy' + **-IST**.

**votary** /'vəʊt(ə)ri/ ● **n.** (pl. **-ies**) **1** a person, e.g. a monk or nun, who has made vows of dedication to religious service. **2** a devoted follower, adherent, or advocate.
– DERIVATIVES **votarist** n.
– ORIGIN C16: from L. *vot-, vovere* 'vow' + **-ARY**[1].

**vote** ● **n.** a formal indication of a choice between two or more candidates or courses of action, expressed typically through a ballot or a show of hands. ➤an act of voting. ➤(**the vote**) the right to indicate a choice in an election. ● **v. 1** give or register a vote. ➤grant or confer by vote. **2** informal express a wish or suggestion.
– PHRASES **vote of (no) confidence** a vote showing that a majority continues to support (or no longer supports) the policy of a leader or governing body. **vote with one's feet** informal indicate an opinion by being present or absent or by some other course of action.
– DERIVATIVES **voteless** adj. **voter** n.
– ORIGIN ME: from L. *votum* 'a vow, wish', from *vovere* 'to vow'.

**votive** ● **adj.** offered or consecrated in fulfilment of a vow.
– ORIGIN C16: from L. *votivus*, from *votum* (see **VOTE**).

**votive Mass** ● **n.** (in the Roman Catholic Church) a Mass celebrated for a special purpose or occasion.

**vouch** ● **v.** (**vouch for**) assert or confirm the truth or accuracy of. ➤confirm the identity or good character of.
– ORIGIN ME (in the sense 'summon (a person) to court to prove title to property'): from OFr. *voucher* 'summon', based on L. *vocare* 'to call'.

**voucher** /'vaʊtʃə/ ● **n.** a small printed piece of paper that entitles the holder to a discount, or that may be exchanged for goods or services. ➤a receipt.

**vouchsafe** ● **v.** give, grant, or disclose in a gracious or condescending manner.
– ORIGIN ME: orig. as the phr. *vouch* something *safe* on someone, i.e. 'warrant the secure conferment of'.

**voussoir** /'vuːswɑː/ ● **n.** Architecture a wedge-shaped or tapered stone used to construct an arch.
– ORIGIN C18: via Fr. from pop. L. *volsorium*, based on L. *volvere* 'to roll'.

**Vouvray** /'vuːvreɪ, French vuvʀe/ ● **n.** dry white wine produced in the Vouvray district of the Loire Valley.

**vow** ● **n.** a solemn promise. ➤(**vows**) a set of such promises committing one to a prescribed role or course of action, especially marriage or a monastic career. ● **v. 1** solemnly promise to do something. **2** archaic dedicate to someone or something, especially a deity.

– ORIGIN ME: from OFr. *vou*, from L. *votum* (see **VOTE**); the verb is from OFr. *vouer.*

**vowel** ● **n.** a speech sound which is produced by comparatively open configuration of the vocal tract and which is capable of forming a syllable. ➤a letter representing such a sound.
– DERIVATIVES **vowelled** (US **voweled**) adj. **vowelless** adj. **vowelly** adj.
– ORIGIN ME: from OFr. *vouel*, from L. *vocalis* (*littera*) 'vocal (letter)'.

**vowel gradation** ● **n.** another term for **ABLAUT**.

**vowelize** (also **-ise**) ● **v.** supply (something such as a Hebrew or shorthand text) with vowel points or signs representing vowels.

**vowel point** ● **n.** each of a set of marks indicating vowels in writing phonetically explicit text in Semitic languages such as Hebrew and Arabic.

**vowel shift** ● **n.** a phonetic change in a vowel or vowels. ➤(**the Great Vowel Shift**) a series of changes between medieval and modern English affecting the long vowels of the standard language.

**vox angelica** /ˌvɒks anˈdʒɛlɪkə/ ● **n.** a soft stop on an organ or harmonium which is tuned slightly sharp to produce a tremolo effect.
– ORIGIN C19: from late L., lit. 'angelic voice'.

**vox humana** /hjuːˈmɑːnə/ ● **n.** an organ stop with a tone supposedly resembling the human voice.
– ORIGIN C18: from L., lit. 'human voice'.

**vox pop** ● **n.** Brit. informal popular opinion as represented by informal comments from members of the public.
– ORIGIN 1960s: abbrev. of **VOX POPULI**.

**vox populi** /ˈpɒpjʊliː, -lʌɪ/ ● **n.** the opinions or beliefs of the majority.
– ORIGIN C16: from L., lit. 'the people's voice'.

**voyage** ● **n.** a long journey involving travel by sea or in space. ● **v.** go on a voyage. ➤archaic sail over or along (a sea or river).
– DERIVATIVES **voyageable** adj. (archaic). **voyager** n.
– ORIGIN ME: from OFr. *voiage*, from L. *viaticum* 'provisions for a journey'.

**voyageur** /ˌvwʌjəˈʒəː, ˌvɔɪə-/ ● **n.** historical (in Canada) a boatman employed to transport goods and passengers to and from fur-trading posts.
– ORIGIN Fr., lit. 'voyager'.

**voyeur** /vwʌˈjəː, vɔɪ-/ ● **n. 1** a person who gains sexual pleasure from watching others when they are naked or engaged in sexual activity. **2** a person who enjoys seeing the pain or distress of others.
– DERIVATIVES **voyeurism** n. **voyeuristic** adj. **voyeuristically** adv.
– ORIGIN C20: from Fr., from *voir* 'see'.

**VP** ● **abbrev.** Vice-President.

**VPL** ● **abbrev.** informal visible panty line.

**VR** ● **abbrev. 1** Queen Victoria. [abbrev. of L. *Victoria Regina.*] **2** variant reading. **3** virtual reality.

**VRML** ● **abbrev.** Computing virtual reality modelling language.

**vroom** informal ● **v.** (of a vehicle or its engine) make a roaring sound when travelling or running at high speed. ● **n.** the roaring sound of an engine or motor vehicle.
– ORIGIN 1960s: imitative.

**VS** ● **abbrev.** Veterinary Surgeon.

**vs** ● **abbrev.** versus.

**V-sign** ● **n. 1** Brit. a sign resembling the letter V made with the first two fingers pointing up and the back of the hand facing outwards, used as a gesture of abuse or contempt. **2** a similar sign made with the palm of the hand facing outwards, used as a symbol or gesture of victory.

**VSO** ● **abbrev.** Voluntary Service Overseas.

**VSOP** ● **abbrev.** Very Special Old Pale, a kind of brandy.

**VT** ● **abbrev.** Vermont (in official postal use).

**Vt** ● **abbrev.** Vermont.

**VTO** ● **abbrev.** vertical take-off.

**VTOL** ● **abbrev.** vertical take-off and landing.

**VTR** ● **abbrev.** videotape recorder.

**vug** /vʌg/ ● **n.** Geology a cavity in rock, lined with mineral crystals.
– DERIVATIVES **vuggy** adj. **vugular** adj.
– ORIGIN C19: from Cornish *vooga.*

**Vulcanian** /vʌlˈkeɪnɪən/ ● **adj.** Geology relating to or denoting a type of volcanic eruption marked by periodic explosive events.
– ORIGIN C20: from *Vulcano*, the name of a volcano in the Lipari Islands, Italy, + **-IAN**.

**vulcanism** /ˈvʌlkənɪz(ə)m/ ● **n.** variant spelling of **VOLCANISM**.

**vulcanite** /ˈvʌlkənʌɪt/ ● **n.** hard black vulcanized rubber.
– ORIGIN C19: from *Vulcan*, the Roman god of fire, + **-ITE**[1].

**vulcanize** /ˈvʌlkənʌɪz/ (also **-ise**) ● **v.** harden (rubber or rubber-like material) by treating it with sulphur at a high temperature.
– DERIVATIVES **vulcanizable** adj. **vulcanization** n. **vulcanizer** n.

**vulcanology** ● **n.** variant spelling of **VOLCANOLOGY**.

**vulgar** ● **adj. 1** lacking sophistication or good taste. ➤making explicit reference to sex or bodily functions. **2** dated characteristic of or belonging to ordinary people.
– DERIVATIVES **vulgarity** n. (pl. **-ies**). **vulgarly** adv.
– ORIGIN ME: from L. *vulgaris*, from *vulgus* 'common people'.

**vulgar fraction** ● **n.** Brit. a fraction expressed by numerator and denominator, not decimally.

**vulgarian** /vʌlˈgɛːrɪən/ ● **n.** an unrefined person, especially one with newly acquired power or wealth.

**vulgarism** ● **n. 1** a word or expression that is considered vulgar. **2** archaic an instance of rude or offensive behaviour.

**vulgarize** (also **-ise**) ● **v. 1** make less refined. **2** make commonplace or less subtle or complex.
– DERIVATIVES **vulgarization** n.

**vulgar Latin** ● **n.** informal Latin of classical times.

**vulgar tongue** ● **n.** the national or vernacular language of a people (especially as contrasted with Latin).

**Vulgate** /ˈvʌlgeɪt, -gət/ ● **n. 1** the principal Latin version of the Bible, the official text for the Roman Catholic Church. **2** (**vulgate**) formal common or colloquial speech.
– ORIGIN from L. *vulgata* (*editio(n-)*) '(edition) prepared for the public', fem. past part. of *vulgare*, from *vulgus* 'common people'.

**vulnerable** ● **adj. 1** exposed to being attacked or harmed, either physically or emotionally. **2** Bridge (of a partnership) liable to higher penalties, either by convention or through having won one game towards a rubber.
– DERIVATIVES **vulnerability** n. (pl. **-ies**). **vulnerableness** n. **vulnerably** adv.
– ORIGIN C17: from late L. *vulnerabilis*, from L. *vulnerare* 'to wound'.

**vulnerary** /ˈvʌln(ə)rəri/ archaic ● **adj.** used in the healing of wounds. ● **n.** (pl. **-ies**) a medicine of this kind.
– ORIGIN C16: from L. *vulnerarius*, from *vulnus* 'wound'.

**vulpine** /ˈvʌlpʌɪn/ ● **adj.** of, relating to, or reminiscent of a fox or foxes.
– ORIGIN C17: from L. *vulpinus*, from *vulpes* 'fox'.

**vulture** /ˈvʌltʃə/ ● **n. 1** a large bird of prey feeding chiefly on carrion, with the head and neck more or less bare of feathers. [Several species in the families Accipitridae (Old World) and Cathartidae (New World).] **2** a contemptible person who preys on or exploits others.
– DERIVATIVES **vulturine** /-rʌɪn/ adj. **vulturish** adj. **vulturous** adj.
– ORIGIN ME: from Anglo-Norman Fr. *vultur*, from L. *vulturius.*

**vulva** /ˈvʌlvə/ ● **n.** the female external genitals. ➤Zoology the external opening of the vagina or reproductive tract in a female mammal or nematode.
– DERIVATIVES **vulval** adj. **vulvar** adj.
– ORIGIN ME: from L., lit. 'womb'.

**vulvitis** /vʌlˈvʌɪtɪs/ ● **n.** Medicine inflammation of the vulva.

**vv.** ● **abbrev. 1** verses. **2** volumes.

**vying** present participle of **VIE**.

**W**[1] (also **w**) ● **n.** (pl. **Ws** or **W's**) **1** the twenty-third letter of the alphabet. **2** denoting the next after V in a set of items, categories, etc.

**W**[2] ● **abbrev. 1** (in tables of sports results) games won. **2** watt(s). **3** West or Western. **4** Cricket (on scorecards) wicket(s). **5** women's (clothes size). ● **symb.** the chemical element tungsten. [from mod. L. *wolframium*.]

**w** ● **abbrev. 1** weight. **2** Cricket (on scorecards) wide(s). **3** with.

**WA** ● **abbrev. 1** Washington (State) (in official postal use). **2** Western Australia.

**Waaf** /waf/ ● **n.** historical (in the UK) a member of the Women's Auxiliary Air Force (1939–48).
– ORIGIN acronym.

**wabbit** /ˈwabɪt/ ● **adj.** Scottish exhausted or slightly unwell.
– ORIGIN C19: of unknown origin.

**WAC** ● **abbrev.** (in the US) Women's Army Corps.

**wack**[1] ● **n.** Brit. informal used as a familiar term of address, chiefly in Liverpool.
– ORIGIN 1960s: perh. from *wacker* 'a Liverpudlian', of unknown origin.

**wack**[2] US informal ● **n. 1** a crazy or eccentric person. **2** worthless or stupid ideas or work; rubbish. ● **adj.** bad; inferior.
– ORIGIN 1930s: prob. a back-form. from **WACKY**.

**wacke** /ˈwakə/ ● **n.** Geology a sandstone of which the mud matrix in which the grains are embedded amounts to between 15 and 75 per cent of the mass.
– ORIGIN C19: from Ger., from Mid. High Ger. *wacke* 'large stone'.

**wacked** ● **adj.** variant spelling of **WHACKED**.

**wacko** (also **whacko**) informal, chiefly N. Amer. ● **adj.** mad; insane. ● **n.** (pl. **-os** or **-oes**) a crazy person.
– ORIGIN 1970s: from **WACKY** + **-O**.

**wacky** (also **whacky**) ● **adj.** (**-ier**, **-iest**) informal funny or amusing in a slightly odd or peculiar way.
– DERIVATIVES **wackily** adv. **wackiness** n.
– ORIGIN C19 (orig. dial.): from **WHACK** + **-Y**[1].

**wacky baccy** ● **n.** Brit. informal cannabis.

**wad** /wɒd/ ● **n. 1** a lump or bundle of a soft material, as used for padding, stuffing, or wiping. ➤ chiefly historical a disc of felt or another material used to keep powder or shot in place in a gun barrel. **2** a bundle of paper, banknotes, or documents. ➤ informal a large amount of something, especially money. **3** Brit., chiefly military slang a bun, cake, sandwich, or other piece of food. ● **v.** (**wadded**, **wadding**) [usu. as adj. **wadded**] **1** compress (a soft material) into a wad. **2** line, stuff, or stop with soft material.
– DERIVATIVES **wadding** n.
– ORIGIN C16: perh. rel. to Du. *watten*, Fr. *ouate* 'padding, cotton wool'.

**wada** ● **n.** variant spelling of **VADA**.

**waddle** ● **v.** walk with short steps and a clumsy swaying motion. ● **n.** a waddling gait.
– DERIVATIVES **waddler** n.
– ORIGIN C16: perh. a frequentative of **WADE**.

**waddy** /ˈwɒdi/ ● **n.** (pl. **-ies**) **1** an Australian Aboriginal's war club. **2** Austral./NZ a club or stick, especially a walking stick.
– ORIGIN from Dharuk *wadi* 'tree, stick, club'.

**wade** ● **v. 1** walk through a liquid or viscous substance. **2** (**wade through**) read laboriously through (a long piece of writing). **3** (**wade in/into**) informal attack, intervene, or become involved in a vigorous or forceful way. ● **n.** an act of wading.
– DERIVATIVES **wadable** (also **wadeable**) adj.
– ORIGIN OE *wadan* 'move onward', also 'penetrate', from a Gmc word meaning 'go (through)'.

**Wade–Giles** ● **n.** a system of romanized spelling for transliterating Chinese, largely superseded by Pinyin.
– ORIGIN named after Sir T. F. *Wade* (1818–95) and H. A. *Giles* (1845–1935), professors of Chinese at Cambridge, who devised it.

**wader** ● **n. 1** a sandpiper, plover, or other wading bird. **2** (**waders**) high waterproof boots, used by anglers.

**wadi** /ˈwɑːdi, ˈwɒdi/ (also **wady**) ● **n.** (pl. **wadis** or **wadies**) (in Arabic-speaking countries) a valley, ravine, or channel that is dry except in the rainy season.
– ORIGIN C17: from Arab. *wādī*.

**wading pool** ● **n.** North American term for **PADDLING POOL**.

**WAF** ● **abbrev.** (in the US) Women in the Air Force.

**wafer** ● **n. 1** a very thin light, crisp sweet biscuit. **2** a thin disc of unleavened bread used in the Eucharist. **3** a disc of red paper stuck on a legal document as a seal. ➤ historical a small disc of dried paste formerly used for fastening letters or holding papers together. **4** Electronics a very thin slice of a semiconductor crystal used as the substrate for solid-state circuitry.
– DERIVATIVES **wafery** adj.
– ORIGIN ME: from an Anglo-Norman Fr. var. of OFr. *gaufre* (see **GOFFER**), from Mid. Low Ger. *wāfel* 'waffle'; cf. **WAFFLE**[2].

**wafer-thin** ● **adj. & adv.** very thin or thinly.

**Waffen SS** /ˈvaf(ə)n/ ● **n.** the combat units of the SS in Nazi Germany.
– ORIGIN Ger. *Waffen* 'armed'.

**waffle**[1] informal ● **v. 1** chiefly Brit. speak or write at length in a vague or trivial manner. **2** N. Amer. fail to make up one's mind. ● **n. 1** chiefly Brit. lengthy but vague or trivial talk or writing. **2** US a failure to make up one's mind.
– DERIVATIVES **waffler** n. **waffly** adj.
– ORIGIN C17 (orig. in the sense 'yap, yelp'): frequentative of dial. *waff* 'yelp', of imitative origin.

**waffle**[2] ● **n.** a small crisp batter cake, baked in a waffle iron and eaten hot with butter or syrup.
– ORIGIN C18: from Du. *wafel*; cf. **WAFER** and **GOFFER**.

**waffle iron** ● **n.** a utensil for baking waffles, consisting of two shallow metal pans hinged together.

**waft** /wɒft, wɑːft/ ● **v.** pass easily or gently through the air. ● **n. 1** a gentle movement of air. ➤ a scent carried in the air. **2** (also **weft**) Nautical, historical a knotted ensign or garment displayed by a ship as a signal.
– ORIGIN C16 (in the sense 'escort (a ship)'): back-form. from obs. *wafter* 'armed convoy vessel', from Low Ger., Du. *wachten* 'to guard'; sense 2 perh. rel. to Scots and northern *waff* 'a signal or wave', a var. of **WAVE**.

**WAG** ● **abbrev.** Gambia (international vehicle registration).
– ORIGIN from *West Africa Gambia*.

**wag**[1] ● **v.** (**wagged**, **wagging**) (especially with reference to an animal's tail) move rapidly to and fro. ● **n.** a wagging movement.
– ORIGIN ME: from the Gmc base of OE *wagian* 'to sway'.

**wag**[2] ● **n.** informal **1** a person who makes facetious jokes. **2** Austral./NZ informal a truant.
– ORIGIN C16 (denoting a young man or mischievous boy): prob. from obs. *waghalter* 'person likely to be hanged'.

**wage** ● **n.** (also **wages**) **1** a fixed regular payment for work, typically paid on a daily or weekly basis.

➤(**wages**) Economics the part of total production that is the return to labour as earned income as distinct from the remuneration received by capital as unearned income. **2** the result or effect of doing something wrong or unwise: *the wages of sin.* ● **v.** carry on (a war or campaign).
– DERIVATIVES **waged** adj.
– ORIGIN ME: from Anglo-Norman Fr. and ONorth. Fr., of Gmc origin; rel. to **GAGE**[1] and **WED**.

**wager** ● **n. & v.** more formal term for **BET**.
– ORIGIN ME (also in the sense 'solemn pledge'): from Anglo-Norman Fr. *wageure*, from *wager* 'to wage'.

**wager of battle** ● **n.** historical a form of trial by which someone's guilt or innocence was decided by personal combat between the parties or their champions.

**wager of law** ● **n.** historical a form of trial in which the defendant was required to produce witnesses who would swear to his or her innocence.

**wage slave** ● **n.** informal a person who is wholly dependent on income from employment.
– DERIVATIVES **wage slavery** n.

**waggery** ● **n.** (pl. **-ies**) informal, dated jocular behaviour or remarks.

**waggish** ● **adj.** informal humorous, playful, or facetious.
– DERIVATIVES **waggishly** adv. **waggishness** n.

**waggle** ● **v.** informal move with short quick movements from side to side or up and down. ➤swing (a golf club) loosely to and fro over the ball before playing a shot. ● **n.** an act of waggling.
– DERIVATIVES **waggler** n. **waggly** adj.
– ORIGIN C16: frequentative of **WAG**[1].

**Wagnerian** /vɑːɡˈnɪərɪən/ ● **adj.** relating to the German composer Richard Wagner (1813–83). ● **n.** an admirer or follower of Wagner.

**Wagner tuba** ● **n.** a brass instrument combining features of the tuba and the French horn and first used in Wagner's *Der Ring des Nibelungen*.

**wagon** (Brit. also **waggon**) ● **n. 1** a vehicle, especially a horse-drawn one, for transporting goods. ➤a light covered horse-drawn vehicle as used by early settlers in North America. ➤chiefly N. Amer. a wheeled cart or hut used as a food stall. **2** Brit. a railway freight vehicle; a truck.
– PHRASES **on the wagon** informal teetotal.
– DERIVATIVES **wagonload** n.
– ORIGIN C15: from Du. *wagen*; rel. to **WAIN**.

**wagoner** (Brit. also **waggoner**) ● **n.** the driver of a horse-drawn wagon.

**wagonette** (Brit. also **waggonette**) ● **n.** a four-wheeled horse-drawn pleasure vehicle with facing side seats and one or two seats arranged crosswise in front.

**wagon-lit** /ˌvaɡɔ̃ˈliː, French vaɡɔ̃li/ ● **n.** (pl. **wagons-lits** pronunc. same) a sleeping car on a train in continental Europe.
– ORIGIN Fr., from *wagon* 'railway coach' + *lit* 'bed'.

**wagon-roof** (also **wagon-vault**) ● **n.** another term for **BARREL VAULT**.

**wagon train** ● **n.** historical a convoy or train of covered horse-drawn wagons, as used by pioneers or settlers in North America.

**wagtail** ● **n.** a slender songbird with a long tail that is frequently wagged up and down. [*Motacilla alba* (**pied wagtail**) and other species.]

**Wahhabi** /wəˈhɑːbi/ (also **Wahabi**) ● **n.** (pl. **Wahabis**) a member of a strictly orthodox Sunni Muslim sect, the predominant religious force in Saudi Arabia.
– DERIVATIVES **Wahhabism** n.
– ORIGIN named after the founder, Muhammad ibn Abd al-*Wahhab* (1703–92).

**wahine** /wɑːˈhiːni/ ● **n.** NZ a Maori woman or wife.
– ORIGIN from Maori.

**wahoo**[1] /wɑːˈhuː/ ● **n. 1** (also **wahoo elm**) a North American elm which yields useful wood. [*Ulmus alata*.] **2** a North American spindle tree. [Genus *Euonymus*: two species.]
– ORIGIN sense 1 perh. from Gk *ahá-hwa* 'walnut'; sense 2 from Dakota.

**wahoo**[2] /wɑːˈhuː/ ● **n.** a large predatory tropical marine fish of the mackerel family, prized as a game fish. [*Acanthocybium solanderi*.]
– ORIGIN C20: of unknown origin.

**wahoo**[3] /wɑːˈhuː/ ● **exclam.** N. Amer. another way of saying **YAHOO**[2].

**wah-wah** (also **wa-wa**) ● **n.** a musical effect achieved on brass instruments by alternately applying and removing a mute and on an electric guitar by use of a pedal. ➤a pedal for producing such an effect on an electric guitar.
– ORIGIN 1920s: imitative.

**waiata** /ˈwʌɪətə/ ● **n.** a Maori song.
– ORIGIN from Maori.

**waif** ● **n.** a homeless and helpless person, especially a neglected or abandoned child.
– DERIVATIVES **waifish** adj.
– ORIGIN ME (in *waif and stray*, denoting a piece of property found and, if unclaimed, falling to the lord of the manor): from an Anglo-Norman Fr. var. of ONorth. Fr. *gaif*, prob. of Scand. origin.

**wail** ● **n.** a prolonged high-pitched cry of pain, grief, or anger. ➤a sound resembling this. ● **v. 1** give or utter a wail. **2** poetic/literary manifest or feel deep sorrow for; lament.
– DERIVATIVES **wailer** n. **wailful** adj. (poetic/literary). **wailing** n. & adj. **wailingly** adv.
– ORIGIN ME: from ON; rel. to **WOE**.

**wain** ● **n.** archaic a wagon or cart.
– ORIGIN OE *wæg(e)n*, of Gmc origin; rel. to **WAY** and **WEIGH**[1].

**wainscot** /ˈweɪnskɒt/ ● **n. 1** an area of wooden panelling on the lower part of the walls of a room. **2** historical fine imported oak, as used for such panelling. **3** a drab yellowish to brown-coloured moth. [*Mythimna* and other genera: several species.] ● **v.** (**wainscoted**, **wainscoting** or **wainscotted**, **wainscotting**) line (a room or wall) with wooden panelling.
– DERIVATIVES **wainscoting** (also **wainscotting**) n.
– ORIGIN ME: from Mid. Low Ger. *wagenschot*, appar. from *wagen* 'wagon' + *schot*, prob. meaning 'partition'.

**wainwright** ● **n.** historical a wagon-builder.

**waist** ● **n. 1** the part of the human body below the ribs and above the hips. **2** a narrow part in the middle of something, e.g. a violin, hourglass, etc. ➤the middle part of a ship, between the forecastle and the quarterdeck. **3** US a blouse or bodice.
– DERIVATIVES **waisted** adj. **waistless** adj.
– ORIGIN ME: appar. representing an OE word from the Gmc root of **WAX**[2].

**waistband** ● **n.** a strip of cloth encircling the waist, attached to a skirt or a pair of trousers.

**waist cloth** ● **n.** a loincloth.

**waistcoat** /ˈweɪs(t)kəʊt, ˈwɛskɪt/ ● **n.** Brit. a close-fitting waist-length garment with no sleeves or collar and buttoning down the front, worn typically by men over a shirt and under a jacket.

**waistline** ● **n.** the measurement around a person's body at the waist. ➤the part of a garment that is shaped or constructed to fit at or near the waist.

**wait** ● **v. 1** stay where one is or delay action until a particular time or occurrence. ➤be delayed or deferred. ➤informal defer (a meal) until a person's arrival. ➤[usu. as noun **waiting**] park a vehicle for a short time at the side of a road. **2** (**wait on/upon**) act as an attendant to. ➤archaic pay a respectful visit to. **3** act as a waiter or waitress. ● **n. 1** a period of waiting. **2** (**waits**) Brit. archaic street singers of Christmas carols. ➤historical official bands of musicians maintained by a city or town.
– PHRASES **in wait** watching for an enemy or potential victim and preparing to attack them. **you wait** used to convey a threat, warning, or promise.
– ORIGIN ME: from ONorth. Fr. *waitier*, of Gmc origin; rel. to **WAKE**[1].

**wait-a-bit** ● **n.** chiefly S. African an acacia or other bush with hooked thorns that catch the clothing.

**waiter** ● **n. 1** a man whose job is to serve customers at their tables in a restaurant. **2** a person who waits for a time, event, or opportunity. **3** a small tray; a salver.

**waiting list** (N. Amer. **wait list**) ● **n.** a list of people waiting for something, especially housing or admission to a hospital or school.

**waiting room** • **n.** a room for people waiting to see a medical practitioner or to catch a bus or train.

**waitperson** • **n.** chiefly N. Amer. a waiter or waitress.

**waitress** • **n.** a woman whose job is to serve customers at their tables in a restaurant.
– DERIVATIVES **waitressing** n.

**waitron** • **n.** US a waiter or waitress.

**wait staff** • **n.** N. Amer. a waiter or waitress or waiters and waitresses collectively.

**waive** • **v.** refrain from insisting on or applying (a right or claim).
– ORIGIN ME (orig. as a legal term relating to removal of the protection of the law): from an Anglo-Norman Fr. var. of OFr. *gaiver* 'allow to become a waif, abandon'.

**waiver** • **n.** an act or instance of waiving a right or claim. ➤a document recording this.

**Wakamba** /wa'kambə/ plural form of **KAMBA**.

**wakame** /'wakameɪ/ • **n.** an edible brown seaweed used in Chinese and Japanese cookery. [*Undaria pinnitafida*.]
– ORIGIN from Japanese.

**Wakashan** /wa'kaʃ(ə)n/ • **n.** a small family of almost extinct American Indian languages of the northern Pacific coast, including Kwakiutl and Nootka.
– ORIGIN from Nootka *waukash* 'good' + **-AN**.

**wake**[1] • **v.** (past **woke** or US, dialect, or archaic **waked**; past part. **woken** or US, dialect, or archaic **waked**) **1** (often **wake up**) emerge or cause to emerge from a state of sleep; stop sleeping. ➤(**wake up to**) become alert to or aware of. ➤cause to stir or come to life. **2** chiefly Irish or N. Amer. dialect hold a vigil beside (someone who has died). • **n. 1** a watch or vigil held beside the body of someone who has died. ➤(especially in Ireland) a party held after a funeral. **2** (**wakes**) [treated as sing.] an annual festival and holiday in some parts of northern England. [prob. from ON *vaka*.]
– PHRASES **be a wake-up** Austral./NZ informal be fully alert or aware.
– DERIVATIVES **waker** n.
– ORIGIN OE (recorded only in the past tense *wōc*), also partly from the weak verb *wacian* 'remain awake, hold a vigil', of Gmc origin; cf. **WATCH**.

**wake**[2] • **n.** a trail of disturbed water or air left by the passage of a ship or aircraft.
– PHRASES **in the wake of** following as a consequence or result.
– ORIGIN C15: prob. via Mid. Low Ger. from ON *vǫk*, *vaka* 'hole or opening in ice'.

**wakeboarding** • **n.** the sport of riding on a short, wide board resembling a surfboard while being towed behind a motor boat.
– DERIVATIVES **wakeboard** n.

**wakeful** • **adj.** unable or not needing to sleep. ➤alert and vigilant.
– DERIVATIVES **wakefully** adv. **wakefulness** n.

**waken** • **v.** wake from sleep.
– ORIGIN OE *wæcnan* 'be aroused', of Gmc origin.

**wake-robin** • **n. 1** Brit. another term for **CUCKOO PINT**. **2** N. Amer. another term for **TRILLIUM**.

**wakizashi** /ˌwakɪ'zaʃi/ • **n.** (pl. same) a Japanese sword shorter than a katana.
– ORIGIN Japanese, from *waki* 'side' + *sasu* 'wear at one's side'.

**WAL** • **abbrev.** Sierra Leone (international vehicle registration).
– ORIGIN from *West Africa Leone*.

**Waldenses** /wɒl'dɛnsiːz/ • **pl. n.** a puritan religious sect originating in southern France.
– DERIVATIVES **Waldensian** adj. & n.
– ORIGIN named after the founder, Peter *Valdes* (d.1205).

**waldo** /'wɔːldəʊ/ • **n.** (pl. **-oes**) a remote-controlled device for handling objects.
– ORIGIN 1940s: named after *Waldo* F. Jones, a fictional inventor described by the science-fiction writer Robert Heinlein.

**Waldorf salad** /'wɔːldɔːf/ • **n.** a salad made from apples, walnuts, celery, and mayonnaise.
– ORIGIN named after the *Waldorf*-Astoria Hotel in New York, where it was first served.

**wale** • **n. 1** a ridge on a textured woven fabric such as corduroy. **2** Nautical a horizontal wooden strip fitted as strengthening to a boat's side. **3** a horizontal band around a woven basket.
– ORIGIN OE *walu* 'stripe, weal'.

**wale knot** (also **wall knot**) • **n.** a knot made at the end of a rope by intertwining strands.

**walk** • **v. 1** move at a regular and fairly slow pace by lifting and setting down each foot in turn. ➤travel over (a route or area) on foot. ➤(of a quadruped) proceed with the slowest gait, always having at least two feet on the ground at once. ➤informal (of a thing) go missing or be stolen. ➤Cricket (of a batsman) leave the field without waiting to be given out by the umpire. ➤N. Amer. informal abandon a job or commitment. ➤N. Amer. informal be released from suspicion or from a charge. **2** guide, accompany, or escort (someone) on foot. ➤take (a dog) out for exercise. ➤train and look after (a hound puppy). **3** archaic live or conduct oneself in a specified way. **4** Baseball reach first base automatically after not hitting at four balls pitched outside the strike zone. • **n. 1** an excursion or act of travelling on foot. **2** an unhurried rate of movement on foot. ➤the slowest gait of an animal. **3** a route for recreational walking. ➤a path. ➤chiefly Brit. the round followed by a postman. **4** a part of a forest under one keeper. **5** chiefly Brit. a farm where a hound puppy is trained.
– PHRASES **walking encyclopedia** (also **walking dictionary**) informal a person with an impressive knowledge of facts or words. **walk it** informal achieve a victory easily. **walk of life** the position within society that someone holds. **walk on eggshells** be extremely cautious about one's words or actions. **walk one's talk** chiefly N. Amer. suit one's actions to one's words. **walk the wards** dated gain experience as a clinical medical student. **win in a walk** N. Amer. win without effort or competition.
– PHRASAL VERBS **walk (all) over** informal treat in a thoughtless, disrespectful, and exploitative manner. ➤defeat easily. **walk away** casually or irresponsibly abandon an involvement or responsibility. **walk off with** (or **away with**) informal **1** steal. **2** win. **walk out 1** depart suddenly or angrily. ➤go on strike. **2** Brit. informal, dated go for walks in courtship.
– DERIVATIVES **walkable** adj.
– ORIGIN OE *wealcan* 'roll, toss', also 'wander', of Gmc origin.

**walkabout** • **n. 1** chiefly Brit. an informal stroll among a crowd conducted by an important visitor. **2** (often in phr. **go walkabout**) Austral. a journey on foot undertaken by an Australian Aboriginal in order to live in the traditional manner.

**walkathon** • **n.** informal a long-distance walk organized as a fund-raising event.
– ORIGIN 1930s: from **WALK**, on the pattern of *marathon*.

**walker** • **n. 1** a person who walks. **2** a device for helping a baby learn to walk, consisting of a harness set into a frame on wheels. **3** short for **WALKING FRAME**.

**walkies** • **n.** informal a spell of walking with a dog.
– PHRASES **go walkies** go missing, especially as a result of theft.

**walkie-talkie** • **n.** a portable two-way radio.

**walk-in** • **adj.** (of a storage area) large enough to walk into.

**walking bass** • **n.** Music a bass part in 4/4 time in which a note is played on each beat of the bar, typically moving up and down the scale in small steps.

**walking frame** • **n.** Brit. a frame used by disabled or infirm people for support while walking.

**walking papers** • **pl. n.** informal, chiefly N. Amer. notice of dismissal from a job.

**walking stick** • **n. 1** a stick with a curved handle used for support when walking. **2** (also **walking-stick insect**) North American term for **STICK INSECT**.

**walking wounded** • **pl. n.** people who have been injured in a battle or major accident but who are still able to walk.

**Walkman** • n. (pl. **Walkmans** or **Walkmen**) trademark a type of personal stereo.

**walk-on** • adj. denoting or having a small non-speaking part in a play or film.

**walkout** • n. a sudden angry departure, especially as a protest or strike.

**walkover** • n. an easy victory.

**walk-through** • n. **1** an undemanding task or lacklustre performance. **2** a rough rehearsal of a play or film.

**walk-up** • n. N. Amer. a building allowing access to the upper floors by stairs only.

**walkway** • n. a raised passageway in a building, or a wide path in a park or garden.

**wall** • n. **1** a continuous vertical brick or stone structure that encloses or divides an area of land. ➤a side of a building or room. **2** a protective or restrictive barrier likened to a wall: *a wall of silence.* **3** Soccer a line of defenders forming a barrier against a free kick taken near the penalty area. **4** Anatomy & Zoology the membranous outer layer or lining of an organ or cavity. **5** Mining the rock enclosing a lode or seam. **6** another term for **WALL BROWN**. • v. enclose within walls. ➤**(wall something up)** block or seal a place by building a wall. ➤**(wall someone in/up)** confine someone in a restricted or sealed place.
– PHRASES **drive someone up the wall** informal make someone very irritated or angry. **go to the wall** informal (of a business) fail; go out of business. **hit the wall** (of an athlete) experience a sudden loss of energy in a long race. **off the wall** N. Amer. informal **1** eccentric or unconventional. **2** angry. **3** (of an accusation) without basis or foundation. **wall-to-wall** (of a carpet) fitted to cover an entire floor. ➤ informal very numerous or plentiful.
– DERIVATIVES **walling** n.
– ORIGIN OE, from L. *vallum* 'rampart', from *vallus* 'stake'.

**wallaby** • n. (pl. **-ies**) **1** an Australasian marsupial similar to but smaller than a kangaroo. [Numerous species in the family Macropodidae.] **2** (**the Wallabies**) informal the Australian international rugby union team.
– ORIGIN C19: from Dharuk *walabi* or *waliba*.

**Wallace's line** • n. Zoology a hypothetical line marking the boundary between the Oriental and Australian zoogeographical regions.
– ORIGIN proposed by the Engl. naturalist Alfred Russel *Wallace* (1823–1913).

**Wallachian** /wɒˈleɪkɪən/ • n. a native or inhabitant of Wallachia, a former principality of SE Europe. • adj. of or relating to Wallachia.

**wallah** /ˈwɒlə/ • n. Indian or informal a person of a specified kind or having a specified role.
– ORIGIN from the Hindi suffix *-vālā* 'doer' (commonly interpreted in the sense 'fellow'), from Sanskrit *pālaka* 'keeper'.

**wallaroo** /ˌwɒləˈruː/ • n. a large stocky kangaroo of hilly country. [*Macropus robustus*.]
– ORIGIN C19: from Dharuk *walaru*.

**wall bar** • n. Brit. each of a set of parallel horizontal bars attached to the wall of a gymnasium, on which exercises are performed.

**wallboard** • n. chiefly N. Amer. a type of board made from wood pulp and plaster, used for covering walls and ceilings.

**wall brown** • n. a brown butterfly with orange markings on the wings. [*Lasiommata megera*.]

**wallchart** • n. a chart for display on a wall as a teaching aid or source of information.

**wallcreeper** • n. a grey and red bird related to the nuthatches, living among rocks. [*Tichodroma muraria*.]

**wall cress** • n. another term for **ARABIS**.

**wallet** • n. **1** a pocket-sized, flat, folding holder for money and plastic cards. **2** archaic a bag for holding provisions when travelling.
– ORIGIN ME: prob. via Anglo-Norman Fr. from a Gmc word rel. to **WELL**[2].

**wall eye** • n. **1** an eye squinting outwards. **2** an eye with a streaked or opaque white iris. **3** (**walleye**) a North American pikeperch with large, opaque silvery eyes. [*Stizostedion vitreum*.]
– DERIVATIVES **wall-eyed** adj.
– ORIGIN C16: back-form. from earlier *wall-eyed*, from ON *vagleygr*; rel. to Icelandic *vagl* 'film over the eye'.

**wallflower** • n. **1** a southern European plant with fragrant flowers that bloom in early spring. [*Cheiranthus cheiri*.] **2** informal a shy or excluded person at a dance or party, especially a girl without a partner.

**wall knot** • n. another term for **WALE KNOT**.

**Wall of Death** • n. a fairground sideshow in which a motorcyclist rides around the inside walls of a vertical cylinder.

**Walloon** /wɒˈluːn/ • n. **1** a member of a people who speak a French dialect and live in southern and eastern Belgium and neighbouring parts of France. Compare with **FLEMING**. **2** the French dialect spoken by this people.
– ORIGIN from Fr. *Wallon*, from med. L. *Wallo(n-)*, from the same Gmc origin as **WELSH**.

**wallop** informal • v. (**walloped**, **walloping**) **1** strike or hit very hard. ➤heavily defeat (an opponent). **2** [as adj. **walloping**] strikingly large. • n. **1** a heavy blow or punch. ➤chiefly N. Amer. potent effect. **2** Brit. alcoholic drink, especially beer.
– DERIVATIVES **walloping** n.
– ORIGIN ME (denoting a horse's gallop): from ONorth. Fr. *walop* (n.), *waloper* (v.), perh. from a Gmc phr. meaning 'run well', from the bases of **WELL**[1] and **LEAP**; cf. **GALLOP**.

**walloper** • n. informal **1** a strikingly large person or thing. **2** Austral. a policeman.

**wallow** • v. **1** roll about or lie in mud or water. ➤(of a boat or aircraft) roll from side to side. **2** (**wallow in**) indulge without restraint in (something pleasurable). • n. **1** an act of wallowing. **2** an area of mud or shallow water where mammals go to wallow.
– DERIVATIVES **wallower** n.
– ORIGIN OE *walwian* 'to roll about', of Gmc origin.

**wall painting** • n. a painting made directly on a wall, such as a fresco or mural.

**wallpaper** • n. **1** paper pasted in strips over the walls of a room to provide a decorative or textured surface. **2** something, especially music, providing a bland or unvaried background. **3** Computing an optional background pattern or picture on a screen. • v. apply wallpaper to (a wall or room).

**wall pass** • n. Soccer a short pass to a teammate who immediately returns it; a one-two.

**wall pepper** • n. the yellow stonecrop.

**wall plate** • n. a timber laid horizontally in or on a wall as a support for a girder, rafter, or joist.

**wall rocket** • n. a yellow-flowered plant which resembles mustard and emits a foul smell when crushed. [*Diplotaxis muralis*.]

**wall rue** • n. a small delicate spleenwort (fern) which resembles rue, growing on walls and rocks. [*Asplenium ruta-muraria*.]

**wall tent** • n. N. Amer. a frame tent.

**wally** • n. (pl. **-ies**) Brit. informal a silly or inept person.
– ORIGIN 1960s: perh. a shortened form of the given name *Walter*: the use possibly arose from an incident at a 1960s pop festival when a *Wally* became separated from his companions, his name being taken up as a chant by the crowd following numerous loudspeaker announcements.

**walnut** • n. **1** an edible wrinkled nut enclosed by a hard shell, produced inside a green fruit. **2** the tree which produces this nut, with compound leaves and valuable ornamental wood. [*Juglans regia* and related species.]
– ORIGIN OE *walh-hnutu*, from a Gmc compound meaning 'foreign nut'.

**Walpurgis night** /valˈpʊəgɪs/ • n. (in German folklore) the night of April 30 (May Day's eve), when witches meet on the Brocken mountain and hold revels with the Devil.
– ORIGIN from Ger. *Walpurgisnacht*: named after St *Walburga*, whose feast day coincided with an ancient pagan festival.

**walrus** • n. a large gregarious marine mammal related to the eared seals, having two large downward-pointing

tusks and found in the Arctic Ocean. [*Odobenus rosmarus*.]
– ORIGIN C18: prob. from Du. *walrus*, perh. by an inversion of elements (influenced by *walvis* 'whale-fish') of ON *hrosshvalr* 'horse-whale'.

**walrus moustache** ● n. a long, thick, drooping moustache.

**waltz** /wɔːl(t)s, wɒl-/ ● n. a dance in triple time performed by a couple, who turn rhythmically round and round as they progress around the dance floor. ➤a piece of music written for or in the style of this dance. ● v. **1** dance a waltz. **2** move or act lightly, casually, or inconsiderately: *you can't just waltz in and expect to make a mark*.
– ORIGIN C18: from Ger. *Walzer*, from *walzen* 'revolve'.

**waltzer** ● n. **1** a person who dances the waltz. **2** a fairground ride in which cars spin round as they are carried round an undulating track.

**Wampanoag** /ˌwɑːmpəˈnəʊəg/ ● n. (pl. same or **Wampanoags**) a member of a confederacy of American Indian peoples of SE Massachusetts.
– ORIGIN Narragansett, lit. 'easterners'.

**wampum** /ˈwɒmpəm/ ● n. historical a quantity of small cylindrical beads made by North American Indians from shells, strung together and worn as a decorative belt or used as money.
– ORIGIN from Algonquian *wampumpeag*, from *wap* 'white' + *umpe* 'string' + the pl. suffix *-ag*.

**WAN** ● abbrev. **1** Computing wide area network. **2** Nigeria (international vehicle registration). [from *West Africa Nigeria*.]

**wan** /wɒn/ ● adj. (of a person) pale and giving the impression of illness or exhaustion. ➤(of light) pale; weak. ➤(of a smile) weak; strained.
– DERIVATIVES **wanly** adv. **wanness** /ˈwɒnnɪs/ n.
– ORIGIN OE *wann* 'dark, black', of unknown origin.

**wand** ● n. **1** a stick or rod thought to have magic properties, used in casting spells or performing tricks. **2** a slender staff or rod, especially one held as a symbol of office. ➤informal a conductor's baton. **3** (**wands**) one of the suits in some tarot packs, corresponding to batons in others. **4** a hand-held electronic device passed over a bar code to read the encoded data.
– ORIGIN ME: from ON *vǫndr*, prob. of Gmc origin and rel. to **WEND** and **WIND**[2].

**wander** ● v. walk or move in a leisurely, casual, or aimless way. ➤move slowly away from a fixed point or place. ➤move slowly through or over (a place or area). ● n. an act or instance of wandering.
– DERIVATIVES **wanderer** n.
– ORIGIN OE *wandrian*, of W. Gmc origin; rel. to **WEND** and **WIND**[2].

**wandering Jew** ● n. **1** a legendary person said to have been condemned by Christ to wander the earth until the second advent. **2** a trailing tradescantia with striped leaves suffused with purple. [*Tradescantia albiflora* and *T. pendula*.]

**wanderlust** ● n. a strong desire to travel.
– ORIGIN C20: from Ger. *Wanderlust*.

**wane**[1] ● v. **1** (of the moon) have a progressively smaller part of its visible surface illuminated, so that it appears to decrease in size. **2** become weaker.
– PHRASES **on the wane** becoming weaker or less vigorous.
– ORIGIN OE *wanian* 'lessen', of Gmc origin; rel. to L. *vanus* 'vain'.

**wane**[2] ● n. the amount by which a plank or log is bevelled or falls short of a squared shape.
– DERIVATIVES **waney** adj.
– ORIGIN C17: from **WANE**[1].

**wangle** informal ● v. obtain (something desired) by persuading others to comply or by manipulating events. ● n. an instance of obtaining something in such a way.
– DERIVATIVES **wangler** n.
– ORIGIN C19 (first recorded as printers' sl.): of unknown origin; perh. based on **WAGGLE**.

**wank** Brit. vulgar slang ● v. masturbate. ● n. an act of masturbating.
– ORIGIN 1940s: of unknown origin.

**Wankel engine** /ˈwaŋk(ə)l, ˈvaŋ-/ ● n. a rotary internal-combustion engine in which a curvilinear, triangular, eccentrically pivoted piston rotates in an elliptical chamber, forming three combustion spaces that vary in volume as it turns.
– ORIGIN 1960s: named after the Ger. engineer Felix *Wankel*.

**wanker** ● n. Brit. vulgar slang a stupid or contemptible person.

**wanna** ● contr. informal want to; want a.

**wannabe** /ˈwɒnəbi/ ● n. informal, derogatory a person who tries to be like someone else or to fit in with a particular group of people.

**want** ● v. **1** have a desire to possess or do (something); wish for. ➤wish to speak to (someone). ➤desire (someone) sexually. **2** (**be wanted**) (of a suspected criminal) be sought by the police. **3** informal, chiefly Brit. (of a thing) require to be attended to: *the wheel wants greasing*. ➤ought to, should, or need to do something. **4** (often **want for**) chiefly archaic lack or be short of something desirable or essential. ● n. **1** chiefly archaic lack or deficiency. ➤poverty. **2** a desire for something.
– ORIGIN ME: the noun from ON *vant*, neut. of *vanr* 'lacking'; the verb from ON *vanta* 'be lacking'.

**wanting** ● adj. lacking in something required, necessary, or usual. ➤informal deficient in intelligence.

**wanton** ● adj. **1** (of a cruel or violent action) deliberate and unprovoked. **2** sexually immodest or promiscuous. **3** poetic/literary growing profusely; luxuriant. ➤lively; playful. ● n. archaic a sexually immodest or promiscuous woman. ● v. archaic or poetic/literary **1** play; frolic. **2** behave in a sexually immodest or promiscuous way.
– DERIVATIVES **wantonly** adv. **wantonness** n.
– ORIGIN ME *wantowen* 'rebellious, lacking discipline', from *wan-* 'badly' + OE *togen* 'trained' (rel. to **TEAM** and **TOW**[1]).

**WAP** ● abbrev. Wireless Application Protocol, a set of protocols enabling mobile phones and other radio devices to be connected to the Internet.

**wapentake** /ˈwɒp(ə)nteɪk, ˈwap-/ ● n. historical a subdivision of certain northern and midland English counties, corresponding to a hundred in other counties.
– ORIGIN OE *wǣpen(ge)tæc*, from ON *vápnatak*, from *vápn* 'weapon' + *taka* 'take', perh. with ref. to voting in an assembly by a show of weapons.

**wapiti** /ˈwɒpɪti/ ● n. (pl. **wapitis**) a red deer of a large North American subspecies.
– ORIGIN C19: from Shawnee, lit. 'white rump'.

**War.** ● abbrev. Warwickshire.

**war** ● n. a state of armed conflict between different nations, states, or armed groups. ➤a state of competition, conflict, or hostility: *a price war*. ➤a sustained campaign against something undesirable: *a war on drugs*. ● v. (**warred**, **warring**) engage in a war.
– PHRASES **be in the wars** humorous (especially of a child) be hurt or injured. **war clouds** a threatening situation of instability in international relations.
– ORIGIN OE *werre*, from an Anglo-Norman Fr. var. of OFr. *guerre*, from a Gmc base shared by **WORSE**.

**waratah** /ˈwɔːrətɑː, ˌwɒrəˈtɑː/ ● n. an Australian shrub which bears slender leathery leaves and clusters of crimson flowers. [*Telopea speciosissima* and related species.]
– ORIGIN C18: from Dharuk *warata*.

**war baby** ● n. a child born in wartime, especially one fathered illegitimately by a serviceman.

**warble**[1] ● v. (of a bird) sing softly and with a succession of constantly changing notes. ➤(of a person) sing in a trilling or quavering voice. ● n. a warbling sound or utterance.
– ORIGIN ME (as a noun in the sense 'melody'): from ONorth. Fr. *werble* (n.), *werbler* (v.), of Gmc origin; rel. to **WHIRL**.

**warble**[2] ● n. a swelling or abscess beneath the skin on the back of cattle, horses, and other mammals, caused by the presence of the larva of a warble fly. ➤the larva causing this.
– ORIGIN ME: of uncertain origin.

**warble fly** ● n. a large fly whose parasitic larvae infest the skin of cattle, horses, etc. [*Hypoderma bovis* and related species.]

**warbler** ● **n.** **1** a small, active songbird, typically living in trees and bushes and having a warbling song. [Many species, chiefly in the families Sylviidae (Old World), Parulidae (N. America), and Acanthizidae (Australasia).] **2** informal a person who sings in a trilling or quavering voice.

**warby** ● **adj.** Austral. informal shabby or decrepit.
– ORIGIN 1920s: prob. from *warb* 'larva of the warble fly' + **-Y**[1].

**war chest** ● **n.** a reserve of funds used for fighting a war.

**war crime** ● **n.** an action carried out during the conduct of a war that violates accepted international rules of war.
– DERIVATIVES **war criminal** n.

**war cry** ● **n.** a call made to rally soldiers for battle or to gather together participants in a campaign.

**ward** ● **n.** **1** a room in a hospital, typically one allocated to a particular type of patient. **2** an administrative division of a city or borough, typically represented by a councillor or councillors. **3** a child or young person under the care and control of a guardian appointed by their parents or a court. ➤archaic guardianship. **4** any of the internal ridges or bars in a lock which prevent the turning of any key without corresponding grooves. ➤the corresponding grooves in the bit of a key. **5** historical an area of ground enclosed by the encircling walls of a fortress or castle. **6** archaic the action of keeping a lookout for danger. ● **v.** **1** (**ward someone/thing off**) prevent someone or something from harming or affecting one. **2** archaic guard; protect.
– DERIVATIVES **wardship** n.
– ORIGIN OE *weard*, *weardian* 'keep safe, guard', of Gmc origin; reinforced in ME by ONorth. Fr. *warde* (n.), *warder* (v.) 'guard'.

**-ward** (also **-wards**) ● **suffix** **1** (usu. **-wards**) (forming adverbs) towards the specified place or direction: *homewards*. **2** (usu. **-ward**) (forming adjectives) turned or tending towards: *upward*.
– ORIGIN OE *-weard*, from a Gmc base meaning 'turn'.

**war dance** ● **n.** a ceremonial dance performed before a battle or to celebrate victory.

**warden** ● **n.** **1** a person responsible for the supervision of a particular place or procedure. **2** Brit. the head of certain schools, colleges, or other institutions. **3** chiefly N. Amer. a prison governor.
– DERIVATIVES **wardenship** n.
– ORIGIN ME: from Anglo-Norman Fr. and ONorth. Fr. *wardein*, var. of OFr. *guarden* 'guardian'.

**warder** ● **n.** (fem. **wardress**) chiefly Brit. a prison guard.
– ORIGIN ME (denoting a watchman or sentinel): from Anglo-Norman Fr. *wardere*, from ONorth. Fr. *warder* 'to guard'.

**ward heeler** ● **n.** US informal, chiefly derogatory a person who assists in a political party's campaign by canvassing votes and performing menial tasks.

**ward of court** ● **n.** a child or young person for whom a guardian has been appointed by the Court of Chancery or who has become directly subject to the authority of that court.

**wardrobe** ● **n.** **1** a large, tall cupboard in which clothes may be hung or stored. **2** a person's entire collection of clothes. **3** the costume department or costumes of a theatre or film company. **4** a department of a royal or noble household in charge of clothing.
– ORIGIN ME (in the sense 'private chamber'): from ONorth. Fr. *warderobe*, var. of OFr. *garderobe* (see **GARDEROBE**).

**wardrobe trunk** ● **n.** chiefly N. Amer. a trunk fitted with rails and shelves for use as a travelling wardrobe.

**wardroom** ● **n.** a commissioned officers' mess on board a warship.

**-wards** ● **suffix** variant spelling of **-WARD**.

**ware**[1] /wɛː/ ● **n.** **1** pottery, typically that of a specified type. ➤manufactured articles of a specified type. **2** (**wares**) articles offered for sale.
– ORIGIN OE *waru* 'commodities', of Gmc origin, perh. the same word as Scots *ware* 'cautiousness', with the sense 'object of care'; rel. to **WARE**[3].

**ware**[2] /wɛː/ (also **'ware**) ● **v.** beware (used as a warning cry).
– ORIGIN OE *warian* 'be on one's guard', from a Gmc base meaning 'observe, take care'.

**ware**[3] /wɛː/ ● **adj.** archaic aware.
– ORIGIN OE *wær*, from the Gmc base of **WARE**[2].

**warehouse** /ˈwɛːhaʊs/ ● **n.** **1** a large building where raw materials or manufactured goods may be stored. **2** a large wholesale or retail store. ● **v.** /also -haʊz/ **1** store (goods) in a warehouse. ➤place (imported goods) in a bonded warehouse pending the payment of import duty. **2** N. Amer. informal place (a prisoner or a psychiatric patient) in a large institution offering unsatisfactory care.
– DERIVATIVES **warehousing** n.

**warehouse party** ● **n.** a large public party with dancing, typically organized without official permission.

**warfare** ● **n.** engagement in or the state of war.

**warfarin** /ˈwɔːfərɪn/ ● **n.** a water-soluble compound with anticoagulant properties, used as a rat poison and in the treatment of thrombosis.
– ORIGIN 1950s: from the initial letters of *Wisconsin Alumni Research Foundation* + *-arin* on the pattern of *coumarin*.

**war game** ● **n.** **1** a military exercise carried out to test or improve tactical expertise. **2** a simulated military conflict carried out as a game or exercise in personal development. ● **v.** (**war-game**) N. Amer. engage in (a campaign or course of action) using the strategies of a war game.
– DERIVATIVES **war-gamer** n. **war gaming** n.

**war grave** ● **n.** a grave of a member of the armed forces who has died on active service, especially one in a special cemetery.

**warhead** ● **n.** the explosive head of a missile, torpedo, or similar weapon.

**Warholian** /wɔːˈhəʊlɪən/ ● **adj.** of or characteristic of the work of the American artist Andy Warhol (*c.*1928–87).

**warhorse** ● **n.** informal a veteran soldier, politician, sports player, etc. who has fought many campaigns or contests.

**warlike** ● **adj.** **1** disposed towards or threatening war; hostile. **2** directed towards or prepared for war.

**war loan** ● **n.** stock issued by the British government to raise funds at a time of war.

**warlock** ● **n.** a man who practises witchcraft.
– ORIGIN OE *wǣrloga* 'traitor, scoundrel, monster', also 'the Devil', from *wǣr* 'covenant' + an element rel. to *lēogan* 'belie, deny'.

**warlord** ● **n.** a military commander, especially an aggressive regional commander with individual autonomy.

**warm** ● **adj.** **1** of or at a fairly or comfortably high temperature. **2** (of clothes or coverings) made of a material that helps the body to retain heat. **3** having or showing enthusiasm, affection, or kindness. **4** (of a colour) containing red, yellow, or orange tones. **5** (of a scent or trail) fresh; strong. ➤(in children's games) close to finding or guessing what is sought. **6** archaic characterized by lively or heated disagreement. **7** archaic sexually explicit or titillating. ● **v.** **1** make or become warm. **2** (**warm up** or **down**) prepare for (or recover from) strenuous physical exertion by doing gentle stretches and exercises. **3** (**warm up**) (of an engine or electrical appliance) reach a temperature high enough to allow it to operate efficiently. ➤become livelier or more animated. **4** (**warm to/towards** or N. Amer. **warm up to/towards**) become more interested in or enthusiastic about. ➤(**warm someone up** or US **over**) amuse or entertain an audience or crowd so as to make them more receptive to the main act. ● **n.** **1** (**the warm**) a warm place or area. **2** an act of warming.
– DERIVATIVES **warmer** n. **warmish** adj. **warmly** adv. **warmness** n.
– ORIGIN OE *wearm* (adj.), *werman*, *wearmian* (v.), of Gmc origin.

**warmblood** ● **n.** a horse of a breed that is a cross between an Arab or similar breed and another breed of the draught or pony type.

**warm-blooded** ● **adj.** **1** denoting animals (chiefly mam-

mals and birds) which maintain a constant body temperature by their metabolism; homeothermic. **2** ardent; passionate.
– DERIVATIVES **warm-bloodedness** n.

**warm-hearted** ● adj. sympathetic and kind.
– DERIVATIVES **warm-heartedly** adv. **warm-heartedness** n.

**warming pan** ● n. historical a wide, flat brass pan on a long handle, filled with hot coals and used for warming a bed.

**warmonger** /ˈwɔːmʌŋgə/ ● n. a person who seeks to bring about or promote war.
– DERIVATIVES **warmongering** n. & adj.

**warmth** ● n. **1** the quality, state, or sensation of being warm. **2** enthusiasm, affection, or kindness. **3** intensity of emotion.

**warm-ups** ● pl. n. N. Amer. a garment worn during light exercise or training; a tracksuit.

**warn** ● v. **1** inform of a possible danger, problem, etc. ➤(**warn someone off**) order someone to keep away or to refrain from doing something. **2** give cautionary advice about actions or conduct to.
– PHRASES **warn someone off the course** Horse Racing prohibit someone who has broken the laws of the Jockey Club from riding or running horses at meetings under the Jockey Club's jurisdiction.
– DERIVATIVES **warner** n.
– ORIGIN OE *war(e)nian*, *wearnian*, from a W. Gmc base meaning 'be cautious'; cf. WARE[3].

**warning** ● n. **1** a statement or event that warns or serves as a cautionary example. **2** cautionary advice. **3** advance notice.
– DERIVATIVES **warningly** adv.

**warning coloration** ● n. Zoology conspicuous colouring that warns a predator that an animal is unpalatable or poisonous.

**warning track** ● n. Baseball a strip around the outside of the outfield which warns approaching fielders of the proximity of a wall.

**warp** ● v. **1** become or cause to become bent or twisted out of shape, typically from the action of heat or damp. **2** make abnormal; distort. **3** (with reference to a ship) move or be moved along by hauling on a rope attached to a stationary object ashore. **4** arrange (yarn) so as to form the warp of a piece of cloth. **5** cover (land) with a deposit of alluvial soil by flooding. ● n. **1** a distortion or twist in shape. **2** the lengthwise threads on a loom over and under which the weft threads are passed to make cloth. **3** a rope attached at one end to a fixed point and used for moving or mooring a ship. **4** archaic alluvial sediment.
– DERIVATIVES **warpage** n. **warper** n.
– ORIGIN OE (early senses included 'throw' and 'hit') *weorpan* (v.), *wearp* (n.), of Gmc origin.

**warpaint** ● n. **1** paint traditionally used to decorate the face and body before battle, especially by North American Indians. **2** informal elaborate or excessive make-up.

**warpath** ● n. (in phr. **on the warpath**) in an angry and aggressive state.
– ORIGIN with ref. to Amer. Indians heading towards a battle with an enemy.

**war pension** ● n. a pension paid to someone who is disabled or bereaved by war.

**warplane** ● n. an aircraft designed and equipped to engage in air combat or to drop bombs.

**warragal** ● n. & adj. variant spelling of WARRIGAL.

**warrant** ● n. **1** an official authorization enabling the police or some other body to make an arrest, search premises, etc. **2** a document entitling the holder to receive goods, money, or services. **3** Finance a negotiable security allowing the holder to buy shares at a specified price at or before some future date. **4** justification or authority. **5** an official certificate of appointment issued to an officer of lower rank than a commissioned officer. ● v. **1** justify or necessitate. **2** officially affirm or guarantee.
– PHRASES **I** (or **I'll**) **warrant (you)** dated no doubt.
– DERIVATIVES **warrantable** adj. **warrantableness** n. **warrantably** adv. **warranter** n.
– ORIGIN ME (in the senses 'protector', 'safeguard', and 'protect from danger'): from vars of OFr. *guarant* (n.), *guarantir* (v.), of Gmc origin; cf. GUARANTEE.

**warrant card** ● n. a document of authorization and identification carried by a police officer.

**warrant officer** ● n. a rank of officer in the army, RAF, or US navy, below the commissioned officers and above the NCOs.

**warranty** ● n. (pl. **-ies**) **1** a written guarantee, issued to the purchaser of an article by its manufacturer, promising to repair or replace it if necessary within a specified period. **2** an engagement by an insured party that certain statements are true or that certain conditions shall be fulfilled, the breach of it invalidating the policy.
– DERIVATIVES **warrantee** n. **warrantor** n.
– ORIGIN ME (as a legal term denoting a covenant annexed to a conveyance of property, in which the vendor affirmed the security of the title): from Anglo-Norman Fr. *warantie*, var. of *garantie* (see GUARANTY).

**warren** ● n. **1** (also **rabbit warren**) a network of interconnecting rabbit burrows. **2** a densely populated or labyrinthine building or district. **3** Brit. historical an enclosed piece of land set aside for breeding game, especially rabbits.
– ORIGIN ME: from an Anglo-Norman Fr. and ONorth. Fr. var. of OFr. *garenne* 'game park', of Gaulish origin.

**warrigal** /ˈwɒrɪg(ə)l/ (also **warragal**) Austral. ● n. **1** a dingo dog. **2** a wild or untamed horse. **3** another term for MYALL (in sense 2). ● adj. wild.
– ORIGIN from Dharuk *warrigal* 'wild dingo'.

**warrior** ● n. (especially in former times) a brave or experienced soldier or fighter.
– ORIGIN ME: from ONorth. Fr. *werreior*, var. of OFr. *guerreior*, from *guerreier* 'make war', from *guerre* 'war'.

**warship** ● n. a ship equipped with weapons and designed to take part in warfare at sea.

**wart** ● n. **1** a small, hard, benign growth on the skin, caused by a virus. **2** any rounded excrescence on the skin of an animal or the surface of a plant. **3** informal an obnoxious person.
– PHRASES **warts and all** informal including faults or unattractive qualities.
– DERIVATIVES **warty** adj.
– ORIGIN OE *wearte*, of Gmc origin.

**wart disease** ● n. a fungal disease of potatoes which produces warty outgrowths on the tubers.

**warthog** ● n. an African wild pig with a large head, warty lumps on the face, and curved tusks. [*Phacochoerus aethiopicus*.]

**wartime** ● n. a period during which a war is taking place.

**war-torn** ● adj. (of a place) racked or devastated by war.

**wary** ● adj. (**-ier**, **-iest**) cautious about possible dangers or problems.
– DERIVATIVES **warily** adv. **wariness** n.
– ORIGIN C15: from WARE[3] + -Y[1].

**was** first and third person singular past of BE.

**wasabi** /wəˈsɑːbi/ ● n. a Japanese plant with a thick green root which tastes like strong horseradish and is used in cookery, especially in powder or paste form as an accompaniment to raw fish. [*Eutrema wasabi*.]
– ORIGIN C20: from Japanese.

**Wash.** ● abbrev. Washington.

**wash** ● v. **1** clean with water and, typically, soap or detergent. ➤remove (a stain or dirt) in this way. ➤(of fabric, a garment, or dye) withstand cleaning to a specified degree without shrinking or fading. ➤do one's laundry. **2** (of flowing water) carry or move in a particular direction. ➤be carried by flowing water. ➤sift metallic particles from (earth or gravel) by running water through it. **3** (**wash over**) occur all around without greatly affecting. **4** poetic/literary wet or moisten. **5** brush with a thin coat of dilute paint or ink. ➤(**wash something with**) coat inferior metal with (a film of gold or silver from a solution). **6** [with neg.] informal seem convincing or genuine. ● n. **1** an act of washing or an instance of being washed. ➤a quantity of clothes needing to be or just having been washed. **2** the water or air disturbed by a moving boat or aircraft. ➤the breaking of waves on a shore. **3** a medicinal or cleansing solution. **4** a thin coating of paint or metal. **5** silt or gravel carried by water and deposited as sediment. ➤a sandbank exposed only at low tide. **6** malt fermenting in preparation for distillation. **7** N. Amer. informal a situation or result that is of no benefit to either of two opposing sides.

– PHRASES **come out in the wash** informal be resolved eventually. **wash one's dirty linen** (or **laundry**) **in public** informal discuss one's personal affairs in public. **wash one's hands** euphemistic go to the toilet. **wash one's hands of** disclaim responsibility for. [orig. with biblical allusion to Matt. 27:24.]

– PHRASAL VERBS **wash out** (or **wash someone out**) N. Amer. be excluded (or exclude someone) from a course or position after a failure to meet the required standards. **wash something out 1** (usu. **be washed out**) cause an event to be postponed or cancelled because of rain. **2** (of a flood or downpour) make a breach in a road. **wash up 1** (also **wash something up**) chiefly Brit. clean crockery and cutlery after use. **2** N. Amer. clean one's hands and face.

– DERIVATIVES **washability** n. **washable** adj.

– ORIGIN OE *wæscan* (v.), of Gmc origin; rel. to WATER.

**washbag** • n. Brit. a toilet bag.

**washbasin** • n. a basin, typically fixed to a wall or on a pedestal, used for washing one's hands and face.

**washboard** • n. **1** a board made of ridged wood or a sheet of corrugated zinc, against which clothes are scrubbed during washing. ➤a similar board played as a percussion instrument by scraping. **2** N. Amer. a worn, uneven road surface. **3** [as modifier] denoting a man's stomach that is lean and has well-defined muscles.

**washcloth** • n. N. Amer. a facecloth.

**washed out** • adj. **1** faded by or as if by repeated washing. **2** pale and tired.

**washed-up** • adj. informal no longer effective or successful.

**washer** • n. **1** a person or device that washes. **2** Austral. a facecloth. **3** a small flat ring fixed between two joining surfaces or between a nut and bolt to spread the pressure or act as a spacer.

**washer-dryer** • n. a washing machine with an inbuilt tumble-dryer.

**washerwoman** • n. (pl. **-women**) a woman whose occupation is washing clothes.

**washeteria** • n. another term for LAUNDERETTE.

– ORIGIN 1950s: from WASH, on the pattern of *cafeteria*.

**washing** • n. a quantity of clothes, bedlinen, etc. that is to be washed or has just been washed.

**washing machine** • n. a machine for washing clothes, bedlinen, etc.

**washing powder** • n. chiefly Brit. powdered detergent for washing laundry.

**washing soda** • n. sodium carbonate, used dissolved in water for washing and cleaning.

**Washingtonian** • n. a native or inhabitant of the US state or city of Washington. • adj. of or relating to Washington.

**washing-up** • n. Brit. crockery, cutlery, and other kitchen utensils that are to be washed.

**washland** • n. land that is periodically flooded by a river or stream.

**wash leather** • n. dated chamois or a similar leather.

**washout** • n. **1** informal a disappointing failure. **2** a breach in a road or railway track caused by flooding. **3** Geology a channel cut into a sedimentary deposit by rushing water and filled with younger material. **4** Medicine the removal of material from the body by washing with a fluid or by allowing it to be eliminated over a period.

**washrag** • n. US term for FACECLOTH.

**washroom** • n. N. Amer. a room with washing and toilet facilities.

**washstand** • n. chiefly historical a piece of furniture designed to hold a jug, bowl, or basin for washing one's hands and face.

**washtub** • n. a large metal tub for washing laundry.

**wash-up** • n. informal a debrief or follow-up discussion.

**washy** • adj. (**-ier**, **-iest**) **1** archaic (of food or drink) too watery. **2** archaic insipid. **3** (of a colour) having a faded look.

– DERIVATIVES **washiness** n.

**wasn't** • contr. was not.

**Wasp** • n. N. Amer. an upper- or middle-class American white Protestant, regarded as a member of the most powerful social group.

– DERIVATIVES **Waspish** adj. **Waspy** adj.

– ORIGIN 1960s: from *white Anglo-Saxon Protestant*.

**wasp** • n. **1** a social insect with a narrow-waisted, typically black and yellow striped body, which carries a sting and builds elaborate nests from wood pulp. [*Vespula*, *Polistes*, and other genera.] **2** a hymenopterous insect of a large group resembling the social wasps in appearance and either solitary or parasitic in habits.

– ORIGIN OE *wæfs*, *wæps*, *wæsp*, of W. Gmc origin; perh. rel. to WEAVE[1] (from the web-like form of its nest).

**waspie** • n. (pl. **-ies**) a woman's corset or belt designed to accentuate a slender waist.

– ORIGIN 1950s: dimin. of *wasp* from WASP WAIST.

**waspish** • adj. sharply irritable.

– DERIVATIVES **waspishly** adv. **waspishness** n.

**wasp waist** • n. a very narrow waist, especially one that is tightly corseted.

– DERIVATIVES **wasp-waisted** adj.

**wassail** /ˈwɒseɪl, ˈwɒs(ə)l, ˈwa-/ archaic • n. **1** spiced ale or mulled wine drunk during celebrations for Twelfth Night and Christmas Eve. **2** lively festivities involving the drinking of much alcohol. • v. **1** make merry with much alcohol. **2** [usu. as noun **wassailing**] go from house to house at Christmas singing carols.

– DERIVATIVES **wassailer** n.

– ORIGIN ME *wæs hæil* 'be in (good) health!': from ON *ves heill* (cf. HAIL[2]).

**wassail bowl** (also **wassail cup**) • n. a large bowl in which wassail was made and from which it was dispensed for the drinking of toasts.

**wast** /wɒst, wəst/ archaic or dialect second person singular past of BE.

**wastage** • n. **1** the action or process of wasting. ➤an amount wasted. **2** (also **natural wastage**) the reduction in the size of a workforce as a result of voluntary resignation or retirement rather than enforced redundancy. ➤the number of people leaving a job or further educational establishment before they have completed their training or education.

**waste** • v. **1** use carelessly, extravagantly, or to no purpose. **2** (usu. **be wasted on**) expend on an unappreciative recipient: *small talk was wasted on him.* **3** fail to make full or good use of. **4** (often **waste away**) become progressively weaker and more emaciated. **5** poetic/literary lay waste to. **6** N. Amer. informal kill or severely injure. **7** [as adj. **wasted**] informal under the influence of alcohol or illegal drugs. **8** poetic/literary (of time) pass away. • adj. **1** eliminated or discarded as no longer useful or required. **2** (of an area of land, typically an urban one) not used, cultivated, or built on. • n. **1** an act or instance of wasting. **2** unusable or unwanted material. **3** a large area of barren, typically uninhabited land. **4** Law damage to an estate caused by an act or by neglect, especially by a life-tenant.

– PHRASES **go to waste** be wasted. **lay waste to** (or **lay something (to) waste**) completely destroy. **waste of space** informal a person perceived as useless.

– ORIGIN ME: from ONorth. Fr. *wast(e)* (n.), *waster* (v.), based on L. *vastus* 'unoccupied, uncultivated'.

**waste-disposal unit** (also **waste disposer**) • n. an electrically operated device fitted to the waste pipe of a kitchen sink for grinding up food waste.

**wasteful** • adj. using or expending something carelessly, extravagantly, or to no purpose.

– DERIVATIVES **wastefully** adv. **wastefulness** n.

**wastegate** • n. a device in a turbocharger which regulates the pressure at which exhaust gases pass to the turbine by opening or closing a vent to the exterior.

**wasteland** • n. a barren or empty area of land.

**waste pipe** • n. a pipe carrying waste water, such as

that from a sink or bath, to a drain.

**waster** ● n. **1** a wasteful person or thing. **2** informal a person who does little or nothing of value. **3** a discarded piece of defective pottery.

**wastrel** /ˈweɪstr(ə)l/ ● n. poetic/literary a wasteful or worthless person.
– ORIGIN C16 (denoting a strip of waste land): from **WASTE** + **-REL**.

**watch** ● v. **1** look at attentively. ➤keep under careful or protective observation. ➤(**watch for**) look out for. **2** exercise care, caution, or restraint about. ➤[usu. in imper.] (**watch out**) be careful. **3** maintain an interest in. **4** archaic remain awake for the purpose of religious observance. ● n. **1** a small timepiece worn typically on a strap on one's wrist. **2** an act or instance of watching. ➤a period of vigil, typically during the night. **3** a fixed period of duty on a ship, usually lasting four hours. ➤(also **starboard** or **port watch**) the officers and crew on duty during one such period. ➤a shift worked by firefighters or police officers. **4** (also **night watch**) historical a watchman or group of watchmen who patrolled and guarded the streets of a town at night.
– PHRASES **be on the watch** be on the alert for danger or trouble. **keep watch** stay on the lookout for danger or trouble. **watch one's** (or **someone's**) **back** protect oneself (or someone else) against danger from an unexpected quarter. **the watches of the night** poetic/literary waking hours during the night.
– DERIVATIVES **watcher** n.
– ORIGIN OE *wæcce* 'watchfulness', *wæccende* 'remaining awake'; rel. to **WAKE**[1].

**watchable** ● adj. moderately enjoyable to watch.
– DERIVATIVES **watchability** n.

**watch cap** ● n. chiefly N. Amer. a close-fitting knitted cap of a kind worn by sailors in cold weather.

**watch chain** ● n. a metal chain securing a pocket watch.

**Watch Committee** ● n. historical (in the UK) the committee of a county borough council dealing with policing and public lighting.

**watchdog** ● n. **1** a dog kept to guard private property. **2** a person or group that monitors the practices of companies providing a particular service or utility. ● v. (**-dogged**, **-dogging**) maintain surveillance over.

**watchfire** ● n. a fire maintained during the night as a signal or for the use of someone who is on watch.

**watchful** ● adj. **1** alert and vigilant. **2** archaic wakeful.
– DERIVATIVES **watchfully** adv. **watchfulness** n.

**watch glass** ● n. **1** Brit. a glass disc covering the dial of a watch. **2** a concave glass disc used in a laboratory to hold material for use in experiments.

**watching brief** ● n. **1** Brit. Law a brief held by a barrister to follow a case on behalf of a client who is not directly involved. **2** an interest in a proceeding in which one is not directly concerned.

**watchmaker** ● n. a person who makes and repairs watches and clocks.
– DERIVATIVES **watchmaking** n.

**watchman** ● n. (pl. **-men**) **1** a man employed to look after an empty building, especially at night. **2** historical a member of a night watch.

**watchnight** ● n. a religious service held on New Year's Eve or Christmas Eve.

**watch spring** ● n. a mainspring in a watch.

**watchtower** ● n. a tower built to create an elevated observation point.

**watchword** ● n. **1** a word or phrase expressing a core aim or belief. **2** archaic a military password.

**water** ● n. **1** the liquid which forms the seas, lakes, rivers, and rain and is the basis of the fluids of living organisms. [Chemical formula: $H_2O$.] ➤one of the four elements in ancient and medieval philosophy and in astrology. ➤(**the waters**) the water of a mineral spring as used medicinally. ➤a solution of a specified substance in water: *ammonia water.* ➤urine. ➤(**waters**) amniotic fluid, especially as discharged shortly before birth. **2** (**the water**) a stretch of water, such as a river, sea, or lake. ➤the surface of this. ➤[as modifier] found in, on, or near the water. ➤(**waters**) an area of sea regarded as under the jurisdiction of a particular country. **3** the quality of transparency and brilliance shown by a diamond or other gem. **4** Finance capital stock which represents a book value greater than the true assets of a company. ● v. **1** pour water over (a plant or an area of ground). ➤give a drink of water to (an animal). ➤take a fresh supply of water on board (a ship or steam train). **2** (of the eyes or mouth) produce tears or saliva. **3** dilute (a drink, typically an alcoholic one) with water. ➤(**water something down**) make something less forceful or controversial by changing or leaving out certain details. **4** (of a river) flow through (an area). **5** Finance increase (a company's debt, or nominal capital) by the issue of new shares without a corresponding addition to assets.
– PHRASES **like water** in great quantities. **make water** (of a ship or boat) take in water through a leak. **of the first water 1** (of a diamond or pearl) of the greatest brilliance and transparency. **2** referring to a person or thing unsurpassed of their kind: *she was a bore of the first water.* **under water** submerged; flooded. **the water of life** whisky. **water on the brain** informal hydrocephalus. **water under the bridge** (or N. Amer. **water over the dam**) past events that are over and done with.
– DERIVATIVES **waterer** n. **waterless** adj.
– ORIGIN OE *wæter* (n.), *wæterian* (v.), of Gmc origin.

**water bailiff** ● n. Brit. **1** an official who enforces fishing laws. **2** historical a customs officer at a port.

**water-based** ● adj. **1** (of a substance or solution) using or having water as a medium or main ingredient. **2** (of a sporting activity) carried out on water.

**water bear** ● n. a minute animal with a short body and four pairs of stubby legs, living in fresh water. [Phylum Tardigrada.]

**waterbed** ● n. a bed with a water-filled rubber or plastic mattress.

**waterbird** ● n. a bird that frequents water, especially one that habitually wades or swims in fresh water.

**water birth** ● n. a birth in which the mother spends the final stages of labour in a birthing pool.

**water biscuit** ● n. a thin, crisp unsweetened biscuit made from flour and water.

**water blinks** ● n. see **BLINKS**.

**water bloom** ● n. another term for **BLOOM**[1] (in sense 5).

**water boatman** ● n. a predatory aquatic bug that swims on its back using its long back legs as oars. [Family Notonectidae.]

**water-borne** ● adj. **1** transported by water. **2** (of a disease) communicated or propagated by water.

**waterbrash** ● n. a sudden flow of saliva associated with indigestion.
– ORIGIN C19: from **WATER** + dial. *brash* 'eruption of fluid from the stomach'.

**waterbuck** ● n. a large African antelope occurring near rivers and lakes in the savannah. [*Kobus ellipsiprymnus.*]

**water buffalo** ● n. a large black buffalo with heavy swept-back horns, used as a beast of burden throughout the tropics. [*Bubalus bubalus* (domesticated) and *B. arnee* (its wild ancestor).]

**water butt** ● n. a large barrel used for catching and storing rainwater.

**water calla** ● n. another term for **BOG ARUM**.

**water cannon** ● n. a device that ejects a powerful jet of water, typically used to disperse a crowd.

**water chestnut** ● n. **1** the crisp, white-fleshed tuber of a tropical aquatic sedge, used in oriental cookery. ➤the sedge which yields this tuber. [*Eleocharis tuberosa.*] **2** (also **water caltrop**) an aquatic plant with small white flowers, producing an edible rounded seed with projecting horns. [*Trapa natans.*]

**water clock** ● n. historical a clock that used the flow of water to measure time.

**water closet** ● n. dated a flush toilet.

**watercolour** (US **watercolor**) ● n. **1** artists' paint made

with a water-soluble binder, and thinned with water rather than oil. **2** a picture painted with watercolours. **3** the art of painting with watercolours.
– DERIVATIVES **watercolourist** n.

**water cooler** • n. a dispenser of cooled drinking water, typically used in offices and other places of work.

**watercourse** • n. **1** a brook, stream, or artificially constructed water channel. **2** the bed along which this flows.

**watercress** • n. a cress which grows in running water and whose pungent leaves are used in salad. [*Nasturtium officinale*.]

**water cure** • n. chiefly historical a session of treatment by hydropathy.

**water diviner** • n. Brit. a person who searches for underground water by using a dowsing rod.

**water drum** • n. **1** a West African instrument played by striking a bowl or gourd floating upside down in a pail of water. **2** an American Indian drum partly filled with water to adjust the pitch and timbre.

**watered silk** • n. silk that has been treated in such a way as to give it a wavy lustrous finish.

**waterfall** • n. a cascade of water falling from a height, formed when a river or stream flows over a precipice or steep incline.

**water flea** • n. another term for **DAPHNIA**.

**Waterford glass** • n. fine clear, colourless flint glassware first manufactured in Waterford in Ireland in the 18th and 19th centuries.

**waterfowl** • pl. n. ducks, geese, or other large aquatic birds, especially when regarded as game.

**waterfront** • n. a part of a town or city alongside a body of water.

**water gas** • n. a fuel gas consisting mainly of carbon monoxide and hydrogen, made by passing steam over incandescent coke.

**watergate** • n. a gate of a town or castle opening on to a lake, river, or sea.

**water glass** • n. **1** a solution of sodium or potassium silicate which solidifies on exposure to air, used for preserving eggs and hardening artificial stone. **2** a tube with a glass bottom, for observing beneath the surface of water.

**water hammer** • n. a knocking noise in a water pipe that occurs when a tap is turned off briskly.

**water hemlock** • n. another term for **COWBANE**.

**waterhen** • n. a moorhen or similar bird.

**waterhole** • n. a depression in which water collects, typically one at which animals drink.

**water hyacinth** • n. a free-floating tropical American water plant, widely introduced as an ornamental and in some places a serious weed of waterways. [*Eichhornia crassipes*.]

**water ice** • n. a frozen dessert consisting of fruit juice or purée in a sugar syrup.

**watering can** • n. a portable water container with a long spout and a detachable perforated cap, used for watering plants.

**watering hole** • n. **1** a waterhole from which animals regularly drink. **2** informal a pub or bar.

**watering place** • n. **1** a watering hole. **2** a spa or seaside resort.

**water jacket** • n. a casing containing water placed around something to protect it from extremes of temperature.
– DERIVATIVES **water-jacketed** adj.

**water jump** • n. an obstacle in a jumping competition or steeplechase, where a horse must jump over or into water.

**water level** • n. **1** the height reached by a body of water. **2** another term for **WATER TABLE**.

**water lily** • n. an ornamental aquatic plant with large round floating leaves and large, typically cup-shaped, floating flowers. [Family Nymphaeaceae: many species.]

**waterline** • n. **1** the level normally reached by the water on the side of a ship. **2** a line on a shore, riverbank, etc. marking the level reached by the sea or a river. **3** a linear watermark in paper.

**waterlogged** • adj. saturated with or full of water.
– ORIGIN C18: past part. of the verb *waterlog* 'make (a ship) unmanageable by flooding', from **WATER** + **LOG**[1].

**Waterloo** /ˌwɔːtəˈluː/ • n. (usu. **meet one's Waterloo**) a decisive defeat or failure.
– ORIGIN *Waterloo*, a village in what is now Belgium, site of a battle in 1815 in which Napoleon was finally defeated.

**water main** • n. the main pipe in a water supply system.

**waterman** • n. (pl. **-men**) a boatman. ➤ an oarsman who has attained a particular level of knowledge or skill.

**watermark** • n. a faint design made in some paper during manufacture that is visible when held against the light and typically identifies the maker. • v. mark with such a design.

**water meadow** • n. a meadow that is periodically flooded by a stream or river.

**water measurer** • n. a long, thin aquatic bug which walks slowly on the surface film of water. [Genus *Hydrometra*: several species.]

**watermelon** • n. the large melon-like fruit of an African plant (*Citrullus lanatus*), with smooth green skin, red pulp, and watery juice.

**watermill** • n. a mill worked by a waterwheel.

**water moccasin** • n. another term for **COTTONMOUTH**.

**water nymph** • n. (in folklore and classical mythology) a nymph inhabiting or presiding over water, especially a naiad or nereid.

**water of crystallization** • n. Chemistry water molecules forming an essential part of the crystal structure of some compounds.

**water opossum** • n. another term for **YAPOK**.

**water ouzel** • n. dialect term for **DIPPER** (in sense 1).

**water pepper** • n. an aquatic plant of the dock family with peppery-tasting leaves and irritant sap. [*Polygonum hydropiper* and related species.]

**water pipe** • n. a pipe for smoking tobacco, cannabis, etc., that draws the smoke along a tube through water to cool it.

**water pistol** • n. a toy pistol that shoots a jet of water.

**waterplane** • n. the horizontal plane which passes through a floating ship on a level with the waterline.

**water polo** • n. a seven-a-side game played by swimmers in a pool, with a ball like a football that is thrown into the opponents' net.

**water power** • n. power that is derived from the weight or motion of water, used as a force to drive machinery.
– DERIVATIVES **water-powered** adj.

**waterproof** • adj. impervious to water. • n. Brit. a waterproof garment. • v. make waterproof.
– DERIVATIVES **waterproofer** n. **waterproofness** n.

**water purslane** • n. a creeping plant of damp places and bare ground. [*Lythrum portula*.]

**water rail** • n. a secretive rail inhabiting reedbeds, with a squealing call. [*Rallus aquaticus*.]

**water rat** • n. **1** a large semiaquatic rat-like rodent. [*Hydromys* (Australasia) and other genera.] **2** Brit. another term for **WATER VOLE**.

**water-repellent** • adj. having or denoting a finish or coating that is not easily penetrated by water.

**water-resistant** • adj. able to resist the penetration of water to some degree but not entirely.
– DERIVATIVES **water-resistance** n.

**water scorpion** • n. a predatory water bug with grasping forelegs. [Family Nepidae.]

**watershed** • n. **1** an area or ridge of land that separates waters flowing to different rivers, basins, or seas. **2** an event or period marking a turning point in a state of affairs. **3** Brit. the time after which programmes that are regarded as unsuitable for children are broadcast on television.

– ORIGIN C19: from **WATER** + *shed* in the sense 'ridge of high ground', suggested by Ger. *Wasserscheide*.

**water shoot** ● n. a vigorous but unproductive shoot from the trunk, main branch, or root of a tree.

**waterside** ● n. the area adjoining a sea, lake, or river.

**waterski** ● n. (pl. **-skis**) each of a pair of skis enabling the wearer to skim the surface of the water when towed by a motor boat. ● v. travel on waterskis.
– DERIVATIVES **waterskier** n.

**water slide** ● n. a slide into a swimming pool, typically flowing with water and incorporating a number of twists and turns.

**water softener** ● n. a device or substance that softens hard water by removing certain minerals.

**water soldier** ● n. an aquatic plant with slender leaves in submerged rosettes that rise to the surface to flower. [*Stratiotes aloides*.]

**water splash** ● n. Brit. a water-filled dip in a road.

**water sports** ● pl. n. **1** sports that are carried out on water, such as waterskiing and windsurfing. **2** informal sexual activity involving urination.

**waterspout** ● n. a rotating column of water and spray formed by a whirlwind occurring over the sea or other body of water.

**water stone** ● n. a whetstone used with water rather than oil.

**water strider** ● n. North American term for **POND SKATER**.

**water table** ● n. the level below which the ground is saturated with water.

**waterthrush** ● n. a thrush-like North American warbler found near woodland streams and swamps. [Genus *Seiurus*: two species.]

**watertight** ● adj. **1** closely sealed, fastened, or fitted so as to prevent the passage of water. **2** (of an argument or account) unable to be disputed or questioned.

**water torture** ● n. a form of torture in which the victim is exposed to the incessant dripping of water on the head or to the sound of dripping.

**water tower** ● n. a tower supporting an elevated water tank, whose height creates the pressure required to distribute the water through a piped system.

**water vole** ● n. a large semiaquatic vole which excavates burrows in the banks of rivers. [*Arvicola terrestris* (Europe) and other species.]

**waterway** ● n. **1** a river, canal, or other route for travel by water. **2** a channel at the outer edge of a deck of a boat that allows water to run off.

**waterweed** ● n. vegetation growing in water, typically with inconspicuous flowers.

**waterwheel** ● n. a large wheel driven by flowing water, used to work machinery or to raise water to a higher level.

**water wings** ● pl. n. inflated floats fixed to the arms of someone learning to swim to give increased buoyancy.

**water witch** (also **water-witcher**) ● n. US a water diviner.
– DERIVATIVES **water witching** n.

**waterworks** ● pl. n. **1** [treated as sing.] an establishment for managing a water supply. **2** informal the shedding of tears. **3** Brit. euphemistic, humorous the urinary system.

**watery** ● adj. **1** consisting of, containing, or resembling water. ➤(of food or drink) thin or tasteless as a result of containing too much water. **2** weak; pale.
– DERIVATIVES **wateriness** n.
– ORIGIN OE *wæterig* (see **WATER**, **-Y**[1]).

**Watsu** ● n. trademark a form of shiatsu massage that takes place in water.
– ORIGIN a blend of **WATER** + **SHIATSU**.

**watt** (abbrev.: **W**) ● n. the SI unit of power, equivalent to one joule per second, corresponding to the rate of energy in an electric circuit where the potential difference is one volt and the current one ampere.
– ORIGIN C19: named after the Sc. engineer James *Watt*.

**wattage** ● n. an amount of electrical power expressed in watts. ➤the operating power of an electrical appliance expressed in watts.

**watt-hour** ● n. a measure of electrical energy equivalent to a power consumption of one watt for one hour.

**wattle**[1] /ˈwɒt(ə)l/ ● n. **1** a material for making fences, walls, etc., consisting of rods or stakes interlaced with twigs or branches. **2** an Australian acacia with long pliant branches and cream, yellow, or golden flowers. [*Acacia pycnatha* (**golden wattle**, Australia's national emblem) and related species.] ● v. make, enclose, or fill up with wattle.
– ORIGIN OE *watul*, of unknown origin.

**wattle**[2] /ˈwɒt(ə)l/ ● n. a coloured fleshy lobe hanging from the head or neck of the turkey and some other birds.
– DERIVATIVES **wattled** adj.
– ORIGIN C16: of unknown origin.

**wattle and daub** ● n. a material formerly or traditionally used in building walls, consisting of wattle covered with mud or clay.

**wattlebird** ● n. **1** an Australian honeyeater with a wattle hanging from each cheek. [Genera *Anthochaera* and *Melidectes*.] **2** a New Zealand songbird with wattles hanging from the base of the bill. [Family Callaeidae.]

**wattmeter** ● n. a meter for measuring electric power in watts.

**Watusi** /wəˈtuːsi/ (also **Watutsi** /wəˈtʊtsi/) ● n. **1** [treated as pl.] the Tutsi people collectively (now dated in English use). **2** an energetic dance popular in the 1960s.
– ORIGIN a local name, from the pl. prefix *wa-* + **TUTSI**.

**waul** /wɔːl/ ● v. give a loud plaintive cry like that of a cat.
– ORIGIN C16: imitative.

**wave** ● v. **1** move one's hand to and fro in greeting or as a signal. ➤move (one's hand or arm, or something held in one's hand) to and fro. ➤(**wave someone/thing down**) wave one's hand to stop a driver or vehicle. **2** move to and fro with a swaying motion while remaining fixed to one point. **3** style (hair) so that it curls slightly. ➤(of hair) grow with a slight curl. **4** (**wave something aside**) dismiss something as unnecessary or irrelevant. ● n. **1** a ridge of water curling into an arched form and breaking on the shore or between two depressions in open water. ➤(**the waves**) poetic/literary the sea. **2** a sudden occurrence of or increase in a specified phenomenon or emotion. **3** a gesture or signal made by waving one's hand. **4** a slightly curling lock of hair. ➤a tendency to curl in a person's hair. **5** Physics a periodic disturbance of the particles of a substance which may be propagated without net movement of the particles, as in the passage of undulating motion or sound. ➤a single curve in the course of this motion. ➤a similar variation of an electromagnetic field in the propagation of light or other radiation.
– PHRASES **make waves** informal **1** create a significant impression. **2** cause trouble.
– DERIVATIVES **waveless** adj.
– ORIGIN OE *wafian* (v.), from the Gmc base of **WAVER**; the noun by alt. (influenced by the verb) of ME *wawe* '(sea) wave'.

**waveband** ● n. a range of wavelengths between two given limits, used in radio transmission.

**wave equation** ● n. Mathematics a differential equation expressing the properties of motion in waves.

**waveform** ● n. Physics a curve showing the shape of a wave at a given time.

**wavefront** ● n. Physics a surface containing points affected in the same way by a wave at a given time.

**wave function** ● n. Physics a function that satisfies a wave equation and describes the properties of a wave.

**waveguide** ● n. a metal tube or other device confining and conveying microwaves.

**wavelength** /ˈweɪvlɛŋθ, -lɛŋkθ/ ● n. **1** Physics the distance between successive crests of a wave, especially as a distinctive feature of sound, light, radio waves, etc. **2** a person's way of thinking when communicated to another: *we* *weren't on the same wavelength.*

**wavelet** • **n.** a small wave.

**wave mechanics** • **pl. n.** [treated as sing.] Physics a method of analysis of the behaviour of atomic phenomena with particles represented by wave equations.

**wave number** • **n.** Physics the number of waves in a unit distance.

**waver** • **v. 1** move quiveringly; flicker. **2** begin to weaken; falter. **3** be irresolute.
– DERIVATIVES **waverer** n. **wavering** n. & adj. **waveringly** adv. **wavery** adj.
– ORIGIN ME: from ON *vafra* 'flicker', of Gmc origin; cf. **WAVE**.

**WAVES** • **pl. n.** the women's section of the US Navy.
– ORIGIN acronym from *Women Appointed* (later *Accepted*) *for Volunteer Emergency Service.*

**wavetable** • **n.** Computing a file or memory device containing data that represents a sound.

**wave theory** • **n.** Physics, historical the theory that light is propagated by a wave motion imparted to the ether by the molecular vibrations of the radiant body.

**wave train** • **n.** a group of waves of equal or similar wavelengths travelling in the same direction.

**wavicle** /ˈweɪvɪk(ə)l/ • **n.** Physics an entity having characteristic properties of both waves and particles.
– ORIGIN 1920s: blend of **WAVE** and **PARTICLE**.

**wavy** • **adj.** (**-ier**, **-iest**) having or consisting of a series of wave-like curves. ➤Heraldry divided or edged with a line formed of alternating shallow curves.
– DERIVATIVES **wavily** adv. **waviness** n.

**wa-wa** • **n.** variant spelling of **WAH-WAH**.

**wax**[1] • **n. 1** beeswax. ➤a white translucent material obtained by bleaching and purifying this, used to make candles and polishes. ➤any similar viscous substance, especially a lipid or hydrocarbon. **2** informal used in reference to gramophone records. • **v. 1** polish or treat with wax. ➤remove hair from (a part of the body) by applying wax and then peeling it off with the hairs. **2** informal make a recording of.
– DERIVATIVES **waxer** n. **waxing** n.
– ORIGIN OE *wæx*, *weax*, of Gmc origin.

**wax**[2] • **v. 1** (of the moon) have a progressively larger part of its visible surface illuminated, so that it appears to increase in size. **2** poetic/literary become larger or stronger. **3** speak or write in the specified manner: *they waxed lyrical about the old days.*
– ORIGIN OE *weaxan*, of Gmc origin.

**wax**[3] • **n.** Brit. informal, dated a fit of anger.
– ORIGIN C19: origin uncertain; perh. from phrs such as *wax angry.*

**waxberry** • **n.** a bayberry or other shrub with berries that have a waxy coating.

**waxbill** • **n.** a small finch-like songbird, typically brightly coloured and with a red bill that resembles sealing wax in colour. [Family Estrildidae: several species.]

**waxcloth** (also **waxed cloth**) • **n. 1** cloth that has been treated with wax to make it waterproof. **2** another term for **OILCLOTH**.

**waxed jacket** • **n.** an outdoor jacket made of a waxed waterproof fabric.

**waxed paper** • **n.** paper treated with wax to make it waterproof or greaseproof.

**waxen** • **adj. 1** having a smooth, pale, translucent surface like that of wax. **2** archaic or poetic/literary made of wax.

**wax moth** • **n.** a brownish moth whose larvae live damagingly in beehives, feeding on beeswax. [*Galleria mellonella* and other species.]

**wax myrtle** • **n.** another term for **BAYBERRY**.

**waxpod** • **n.** a dwarf French bean of a variety with yellow, stringless pods.

**wax resist** • **n.** a process similar to batik used in pottery and printing.

**waxwing** • **n.** a crested songbird, mainly pinkish-brown and with bright red tips to some wing feathers. [Genus *Bombycilla*: three species.]

**waxwork** • **n.** a lifelike dummy modelled in wax. ➤(**waxworks**) [treated as sing.] an exhibition of waxworks.

**waxy**[1] • **adj.** (**-ier**, **-iest**) resembling wax in consistency or appearance.
– DERIVATIVES **waxily** adv. **waxiness** n.

**waxy**[2] • **adj.** (**-ier**, **-iest**) Brit. informal, dated angry; bad-tempered.

**way** /weɪ/ • **n. 1** a method, style, or manner of doing something. ➤the typical manner in which someone behaves or in which something happens. ➤formal or Scottish a person's occupation or line of business. **2** [in place names] a road, track, path, or street. ➤a route or means taken in order to reach, enter, or leave a place. ➤the route along which someone or something is travelling or would travel if unobstructed. ➤a specified direction. ➤(**one's way**) used with a verb and adverbial phrase to intensify the force of an action or to denote movement or progress. ➤forward motion or momentum of a ship or boat through water. **3** the distance in space or time between two points. **4** informal a particular area or locality. **5** a particular aspect. **6** a specified condition or state. **7** (**ways**) parts into which something divides or is divided. **8** (**ways**) a sloping structure down which a new ship is launched. • **adv.** informal at or to a considerable distance or extent (used before an adverb or preposition for emphasis). ➤chiefly N. Amer. much. ➤really (used for emphasis). [shortening of **AWAY**.]
– PHRASES **across** (Brit. also **over**) **the way** nearby, especially on the opposite side of the street. **by the way** incidentally. **by way of 1** via. **2** as a form of. **3** by means of. **come one's way** happen or become available to one. **get** (or **have**) **one's** (**own**) **way** get or do what one wants in spite of opposition. **give way 1** yield. **2** (of a support or structure) be unable to carry a load or withstand a force and collapse or break. **3** allow someone or something to be or go first. **4** (**give way to**) be replaced or superseded by. **5** (of rowers) row hard. **go all** (or **the whole**) **way** informal have full sexual intercourse with someone. **go out of one's way** make a special effort to do something. **go one's own way** act independently or as one wishes, especially against contrary advice. **go one's way 1** (of events, circumstances, etc.) be favourable to one. **2** leave. **go someone's way** travel in the same direction as someone. **have it your** (**own**) **way** [in imper.] informal used to indicate grudging acceptance of something said or proposed, even though one is in disagreement with it. **have a way with** have a particular talent for dealing with or ability in. **have a way with one** have a charming and persuasive manner. **have one's way with** humorous have sexual intercourse with (someone) (typically implying that it is against their wishes). **in a way** (or **in some ways** or **in one way**) to a certain extent. **in someone/thing's** (**own**) **way** if regarded from a particular standpoint appropriate to that person or thing. **in no way** not at all. **keep** (or **stay**) **out of someone's way** avoid someone. **lead the way** go first along a route to show someone the way. ➤be a pioneer. **look the other way** deliberately avoid seeing or noticing someone or something. **one way and another** taking most aspects or considerations into account. **one way or the other** (or **one way and another**) used to indicate that something is the case for any of various reasons. ➤by some means. ➤whichever of two given alternatives is the case. **on the** (or **its**) **way** about to arrive or happen. ➤informal (of a child) conceived but not yet born. **on the** (or **one's**) **way out 1** informal going out of fashion or favour. **2** informal dying. **the other way round** (or **around**; Brit. also **about**) in the opposite position or direction. ➤the opposite of what is expected or supposed. **out of the way 1** (of a place) remote. **2** dealt with or finished. ➤(of a person) no longer an obstacle to someone's plans. **3** [usu. with neg.] unusual or exceptional. **that way** euphemistic homosexual. **way back** (US also **way back when**) informal long ago. **the way of the Cross 1** the journey of Jesus to the place of his crucifixion. **2** the suffering and self-sacrifice of a Christian. **the way of the world** the manner in which people typically behave or things typically happen. **ways and means** the

methods and resources for achieving something. **way to go** N. Amer. informal used to express pleasure, approval, or excitement.
– ORIGIN OE *weg*, of Gmc origin, from a base meaning 'move, carry'.

**-way** • suffix equivalent to **-WAYS**.

**wayang** /'wɑːjaŋ/ • n. **1** (in Indonesia and Malaysia) a theatrical performance employing puppets or human dancers. **2** (also **wayang kulit**) a Javanese and Balinese shadow puppet play.
– ORIGIN from Javanese.

**waybill** • n. a list of passengers or goods being carried on a vehicle.

**wayfarer** • n. poetic/literary a person who travels on foot.
– DERIVATIVES **wayfaring** n.

**wayfaring tree** • n. a white-flowered shrub which has berries turning from green through red to black. [*Viburnum lantana*.]

**waylay** • v. (past and past part. **waylaid**) intercept in order to attack. ➤ intercept and detain with questions, conversation, etc.
– DERIVATIVES **waylayer** n.

**way leave** • n. a right of way granted by a landowner for payment and typically for purposes such as the erection of telegraph wires.

**waymark** • n. (also **waymarker**) a sign forming one of a series used to mark out a footpath or similar route. • v. identify (a route) with a waymark.

**way-out** • adj. informal unconventional or avant-garde.

**waypoint** • n. **1** a stopping place on a journey. **2** the computer-checked coordinates of each stage of a flight or sea journey.

**-ways** • suffix forming adjectives and adverbs of direction or manner: *lengthways*. Compare with **-WISE**.

**wayside** • n. the edge of a road.
– PHRASES **fall by the wayside** fail to persist in an undertaking. [with biblical allusion to Luke 8:5.]

**wayside pulpit** • n. a board placed outside a place of worship, displaying a religious text or maxim.

**way station** • n. N. Amer. **1** a waypoint on a journey. **2** a minor station on a railway.

**wayward** • adj. self-willed and unpredictable; perverse.
– DERIVATIVES **waywardly** adv. **waywardness** n.
– ORIGIN ME: shortening of obs. *awayward* 'turned away'.

**wayzgoose** /'weɪzguːs/ • n. (pl. **wayzgooses**) Brit. historical an annual summer dinner or outing held by a printing house for its employees.
– ORIGIN C18 (orig. as *waygoose*): of unknown origin.

**wazir** /wə'zɪə/ • n. another term for **VIZIER**.

**wazoo** /wə'zuː/ • n. US informal a person's buttocks or anus.
– PHRASES **up** (or **out**) **the wazoo** in great quantities.
– ORIGIN C20: of unknown origin.

**wazzock** /'wazək/ • n. Brit. informal a stupid person.
– ORIGIN 1980s: of unknown origin.

**Wb** • abbrev. weber(s).

**WBA** • abbrev. World Boxing Association.

**WBC** • abbrev. World Boxing Council.

**W boson** • n. another term for **W PARTICLE**.

**WC** • abbrev. Brit. water closet.

**WCC** • abbrev. World Council of Churches.

**we** • pron. [first person pl.] **1** used by a speaker to refer to himself or herself and one or more other people considered together or regarded as in the same category. ➤ people in general. **2** used in formal contexts for or by a royal person, or by a writer, to refer to himself or herself. **3** you (used condescendingly).
– ORIGIN OE, of Gmc origin.

**WEA** • abbrev. (in the UK) Workers' Educational Association.

**weak** • adj. **1** lacking physical strength and energy. **2** liable to break or give way under pressure. ➤ not convincing or forceful. ➤ not secure, stable, or firmly established. ➤ (of prices or a market) having a downward tendency. **3** lacking power, influence, or ability. **4** lacking intensity. ➤ (of a liquid or solution) heavily diluted. ➤ (of features) not strongly marked. ➤ (of a syllable) unstressed. **5** Grammar denoting a class of verbs in Germanic languages that form the past tense and past participle by addition of a suffix (in English, typically *-ed*).
– PHRASES **the weaker sex** [treated as sing. or pl.] dated women regarded collectively. **weak at the knees** helpless with emotion.
– DERIVATIVES **weakish** adj.
– ORIGIN OE *wāc* 'pliant', 'of little worth', 'not steadfast', reinforced in ME by ON *veikr*, from a Gmc base meaning 'yield, give way'.

**weaken** • v. make or become weak.
– DERIVATIVES **weakener** n.

**weak ending** • n. Prosody an unstressed syllable in a place at the end of a line of verse that normally receives a stress.

**weakfish** • n. (pl. same or **-fishes**) a large slender-bodied edible marine fish of the east coast of North America. [*Cynoscion regalis*.]
– ORIGIN C18: from obs. Du. *weekvisch*, from *week* 'soft' + *visch* 'fish'.

**weak interaction** (also **weak force**) • n. Physics a short-range interaction between particles which is very much weaker than the electromagnetic and the strong interactions and conserves neither strangeness, parity, nor isospin.

**weak-kneed** • adj. **1** weak and shaky from fear or excitement. **2** lacking in resolve or courage.

**weakling** • n. a weak person or animal.

**weakly** • adv. in a weak manner. • adj. (**-ier**, **-iest**) weak or sickly.
– DERIVATIVES **weakliness** n.

**weakness** • n. **1** the state of being weak. **2** a disadvantage or fault. **3** a person or thing that one is unable to resist. ➤ (**weakness for**) a self-indulgent liking for.

**weak sister** • n. N. Amer. informal a weak member of a group.

**weal**[1] /wiːl/ (also chiefly Medicine **wheal**) • n. a red, swollen mark left on flesh by a blow or pressure. ➤ Medicine a temporarily raised and reddened area of skin, usually accompanied by itching. • v. mark with a weal.
– ORIGIN C19: var. of **WALE**, influenced by obs. *wheal* 'suppurate'.

**weal**[2] /wiːl/ • n. formal that which is best for someone or something: *guardians of the public weal*.
– ORIGIN OE *wela* 'wealth, well-being', of W. Gmc origin; rel. to **WELL**[1].

**Weald clay** • n. Geology a series of clays, sandstones, limestones, and ironstones forming the upper part of the Wealden strata.

**Wealden** /'wiːld(ə)n/ • adj. Brit. of or relating to the Weald, a formerly wooded district including parts of Kent, Surrey, and East Sussex. ➤ Geology denoting a series of Lower Cretaceous sedimentary deposits best exemplified in the Weald.
– ORIGIN OE, var. of *wald* (see **WOLD**) + **-EN**[2].

**wealth** • n. **1** an abundance of valuable possessions or money. ➤ the state of being rich. **2** an abundance or profusion of something desirable: *a wealth of information*. **3** archaic well-being.
– ORIGIN ME *welthe*, from **WELL**[1] or **WEAL**[2], on the pattern of *health*.

**wealth tax** • n. a tax levied on personal capital.

**wealthy** • adj. (**-ier**, **-iest**) having a great deal of money, resources, or assets; rich.
– DERIVATIVES **wealthily** adv.

**wean**[1] • v. **1** accustom (an infant or other young mammal) to food other than its mother's milk. **2** (often **wean someone off**) make (someone) give up a habit or addiction. **3** (**be weaned on**) be strongly influenced by (something) from an early age.
– ORIGIN OE *wenian*, of Gmc origin.

**wean**[2] • n. Scottish & N. English a young child.
– ORIGIN C17: contr. of *wee ane* 'little one'.

**weaner** • n. a calf, lamb, or pig weaned during the current year.

**weanling** • n. a newly weaned animal.

**weapon** • n. **1** a thing designed or used for inflicting

bodily harm or physical damage. **2** a means of gaining an advantage or defending oneself.
– DERIVATIVES **weaponed** adj. **weaponless** adj. **weaponry** n.
– ORIGIN OE *wǣp(e)n*, of Gmc origin.

**wear**[1] • v. (past **wore**; past part. **worn** /wɔːn/) **1** have on one's body or a part of one's body as clothing, decoration, or protection. **2** exhibit or present (a particular facial expression or appearance). **3** undergo or cause to undergo damage or destruction by friction or use. ➤form (a hole, path, etc.) in this way. **4** withstand continued use to a specified degree: *the fabric wears well wash after wash.* **5** (**wear off**) lose effectiveness or intensity. **6** (**wear someone/thing down**) overcome someone or something by persistence. **7** (**wear someone/thing out**) exhaust someone or something. ➤[as adj. **wearing**] mentally or physically tiring. **8** [usu. with neg.] Brit. informal tolerate or accept. **9** (**wear on**) (of time) pass slowly or tediously. **10** (of a ship) fly (a flag). • n. **1** the action of wearing or the state of being worn. **2** clothing suitable for a particular purpose or of a particular type: *evening wear.* **3** damage sustained from continuous use. ➤the capacity for withstanding such damage.
– PHRASES **wear thin** gradually dwindle or be used up.
– DERIVATIVES **wearability** n. **wearable** adj. **wearer** n. **wearingly** adv.
– ORIGIN OE *werian*, of Gmc origin.

**wear**[2] • v. (past and past part. **wore**) Sailing bring (a ship) about by turning its head away from the wind.
– ORIGIN C17: of unknown origin.

**weary** • adj. (**-ier**, **-iest**) **1** tired. ➤causing tiredness. **2** (often **weary of**) reluctant to experience any more of. • v. (**-ies**, **-ied**) **1** make weary. **2** (**weary of**) grow tired of. **3** chiefly Scottish fret.
– DERIVATIVES **weariless** adj. **wearily** adv. **weariness** n. **wearisome** adj. **wearisomely** adv. **wearisomeness** n. **wearying** adj. **wearyingly** adv.
– ORIGIN OE *wērig*, *wǣrig*, of W. Gmc origin.

**weasel** • n. **1** a small slender carnivorous mammal related to, but smaller than, the stoat. [*Mustela nivalis* and other species.] ➤Irish term for **STOAT**. **2** informal a deceitful or treacherous person. • v. (**weaselled**, **weaselling**; US **weaseled**, **weaseling**) **1** achieve through cunning or deceit. **2** chiefly N. Amer. behave or talk evasively.
– DERIVATIVES **weaselly** adj.
– ORIGIN OE *wesle*, *wesule*, of W. Gmc origin.

**weasel-faced** • adj. having a face with unattractively thin, sharp features.

**weasel words** • pl. n. statements that are intentionally ambiguous or misleading.

**weather** • n. **1** the state of the atmosphere at a place and time as regards temperature, wind, rain, etc. **2** [as modifier] windward. Contrasted with **LEE**. • v. **1** wear away or change in form or appearance by long exposure to the weather. ➤(of rock or other material) be worn away or altered by such processes. **2** come safely through. **3** make (boards or tiles) overlap downwards to keep out rain. ➤(in building) slope or bevel (a surface) to throw off rain. **4** Sailing (of a ship) get to the windward of (a cape). **5** [usu. as noun **weathering**] Falconry allow (a hawk) to spend a period perched in the open air.
– PHRASES **keep a weather eye on** be watchful for developments. **make heavy weather of** informal have unnecessary difficulty in dealing with (a task or problem). [from the naut. phr. *make good* or *bad weather of it*, referring to a ship in a storm.] **under the weather** informal slightly unwell or depressed.
– ORIGIN OE *weder*, of Gmc origin.

**weather balloon** • n. a balloon equipped with meteorological apparatus which is sent into the atmosphere to provide information about the weather.

**weather-beaten** • adj. damaged, worn, or tanned by exposure to the weather.

**weatherboard** chiefly Brit. • n. **1** a sloping board attached to the bottom of an outside door to keep out the rain. **2** each of a series of horizontal boards nailed to outside walls with edges overlapping to keep out the rain. • v. fit with weatherboards.
– DERIVATIVES **weatherboarding** n.

**weatherbound** • adj. prevented by bad weather from travelling or proceeding with a course of action.

**weathercock** • n. a weathervane in the form of a cockerel. • v. (of a boat or aircraft) tend to turn to head into the wind.

**weather glass** • n. dated a barometer.

**weather helm** • n. Nautical a tendency in a sailing ship to head into the wind if the tiller is released.

**weather house** • n. a toy hygroscope in the form of a small house with figures of a man and woman standing in two porches, the man coming out in wet weather and the woman in dry.

**weatherly** • adj. Sailing (of a boat) able to sail close to the wind without drifting to leeward.
– DERIVATIVES **weatherliness** n.

**weatherman** (or **weatherwoman**) • n. (pl. **-men** or **-women**) a person who broadcasts a description and forecast of weather conditions.

**weather station** • n. an observation post where weather conditions and meteorological data are observed and recorded.

**weatherstrip** • n. a strip of rubber, metal, or other material used to seal the edges of a door or window against rain and wind. • v. (**-stripped**, **-stripping**) apply such a strip to.
– DERIVATIVES **weatherstripping** n.

**weather tile** • n. each of a series of overlapping tiles used to cover a wall.

**weathervane** • n. a revolving pointer to show the direction of the wind.

**weave**[1] • v. (past **wove**; past part. **woven** or **wove**) **1** form (fabric) by interlacing long threads passing in one direction with others at a right angle to them. ➤[usu. as noun **weaving**] make fabric in this way, typically with a loom. **2** make (basketwork or a wreath) by interlacing rods or flowers. **3** (**weave something into**) make interconnected elements into (a story). • n. a particular style or manner in which fabric is woven.
– ORIGIN OE *wefan*, of Gmc origin.

**weave**[2] • v. **1** move from side to side to progress around obstructions. **2** (of a horse) repeatedly swing the head and forepart of the body from side to side.
– PHRASES **get weaving** Brit. informal set briskly to work.
– ORIGIN C16: prob. from ON *veifa* 'to wave, brandish'.

**weaver** • n. **1** a person who weaves fabric. **2** (also **weaver bird**) a finch-like songbird of tropical Africa and Asia, related to the sparrows and building elaborately woven nests. [Family Ploceidae: numerous species.]

**weaver's knot** • n. a sheet bend used for joining threads in weaving.

**web** • n. **1** a network of fine threads constructed by a spider from fluid secreted by its spinnerets, used to catch its prey. **2** a complex system of interconnected elements. ➤(**the Web**) short for **WORLD WIDE WEB**. **3** a membrane between the toes of a swimming bird or other aquatic animal. **4** a thin flat part connecting thicker or more solid parts in machinery. **5** a roll of paper used in a continuous printing process. ➤the endless wire mesh in a machine on which such paper is made. **6** a piece of woven fabric. • v. (**webbed**, **webbing**) cover with a web.
– ORIGIN OE *web(b)* 'woven fabric', of Gmc origin; rel. to **WEAVE**[1].

**webbed** • adj. **1** (of an animal's feet) having the toes connected by a web. ➤Medicine (of fingers or toes) abnormally united by a fold of skin. **2** (of a band of material) made from webbing or similar fabric.

**webbing** • n. **1** strong, closely woven fabric used chiefly for making straps and belts and for supporting the seats of upholstered chairs. **2** the part of a baseball glove between the thumb and forefinger.

**webcam** (also **Webcam**) • n. (trademark in the US) a video camera connected to a computer connected to the Internet, so that its images can be seen by Internet users.

**webcast** • n. a live video broadcast of an event transmitted across the Internet.
– DERIVATIVES **webcasting** n.

**weber** /ˈveɪbə/ (abbrev.: **Wb**) • n. the SI unit of magnetic

flux, sufficient to cause an electromotive force of one volt in a circuit of one turn when generated or removed in one second.
– ORIGIN C19: named after the Ger. physicist W. E. *Weber*.

**weblog** • n. a personal website, on which an individual or group of users record opinions, links to other sites, etc. on a regular basis.
– DERIVATIVES **weblogger** n.

**webmaster** • n. Computing a person who is responsible for a particular server on the World Wide Web.

**web offset** • n. offset printing on continuous paper fed from a reel.

**web page** • n. Computing a hypertext document accessible via the World Wide Web.

**web site** • n. Computing a location connected to the Internet that maintains one or more web pages.

**web wheel** • n. a wheel with a plate instead of spokes, or one with rim, spokes, and centre made in one piece, as in the balance wheel of a clock or watch.

**webwork** • n. a network of links or connecting pieces.

**webworm** • n. N. Amer. a caterpillar which spins a web in which to rest or feed.

**Wed.** • abbrev. Wednesday.

**wed** • v. (**wedding**; past and past part. **wedded** or **wed**) **1** formal or poetic/literary marry. ➤ give or join in marriage. ➤ [as adj. **wedded**] of or concerning marriage. **2** combine (two desirable factors or qualities). **3** (**be wedded to**) be entirely devoted to (an activity, belief, etc.).
– ORIGIN OE *weddian*, from the Gmc base of Scots *wed* 'a pledge'; rel. to **GAGE**[1].

**we'd** • contr. **1** we had. **2** we should or we would.

**wedding** • n. a marriage ceremony, especially one including the associated celebrations.

**wedding band** • n. chiefly N. Amer. a wedding ring.

**wedding breakfast** • n. Brit. a celebratory meal eaten just after a wedding by the couple and their guests.

**wedding cake** • n. **1** a rich iced cake, typically in two or more tiers, served at a wedding reception. **2** [as modifier] denoting a very ornate building.

**wedding march** • n. a piece of march music played at the entrance of the bride or the exit of the couple at a wedding.

**wedding ring** • n. a ring worn by a married person, given to them by their spouse at their wedding.

**wedge**[1] • n. **1** a piece of wood, metal, etc. with a thick end that tapers to a thin edge, that is driven between two objects or parts of an object to secure or separate them. **2** a wedge-shaped thing or piece. ➤ a golf club with a low, angled face for maximum loft. **3** a shoe with a fairly high heel forming a solid block with the sole. • v. **1** fix in position using a wedge. **2** force into a narrow space.
– PHRASES **drive a wedge between** cause a breach between. **the thin end of the wedge** informal an action of little intrinsic importance that is likely to lead to more serious developments.
– ORIGIN OE *wecg* (n.), of Gmc origin.

**wedge**[2] • v. prepare (pottery clay) for use by cutting, kneading, and throwing down to homogenize it and remove air pockets.
– ORIGIN C17: of unknown origin.

**wedge-shaped** • adj. **1** (of a solid object) tapering to a thin edge at one end. **2** (of a plane shape) V-shaped.

**wedgie** • n. informal a shoe with a wedged heel.

**Wedgwood** /ˈwɛdʒwʊd/ • n. **1** trademark ceramic ware made by the English potter Josiah Wedgwood (1730–95) and his successors, especially a kind of powder-blue stoneware with white embossed cameos. **2** a powder-blue colour characteristic of this stoneware.

**wedlock** • n. the state of being married.
– PHRASES **born in** (or **out of**) **wedlock** born of married (or unmarried) parents.
– ORIGIN OE *wedlāc* 'marriage vow', from *wed* 'pledge' + the suffix *-lāc* (denoting action).

**Wednesday** • n. the day of the week before Thursday and following Tuesday. • adv. chiefly N. Amer. on Wednesday. ➤ (**Wednesdays**) on Wednesdays; each Wednesday.
– ORIGIN OE *Wōdnesdæg*, named after the Germanic god *Odin*; translation of late L. *Mercurii dies*.

**Weds.** • abbrev. Wednesday.

**wee**[1] • adj. (**weer**, **weest**) chiefly Scottish little.
– ORIGIN ME (orig. a noun use in Scots, usu. as *a little wee* 'a little bit'): from OE *wēg(e)* (see **WEY**).

**wee**[2] informal, chiefly Brit. • n. an act of urinating. ➤ urine. • v. (**wees**, **weed**) urinate.
– ORIGIN 1930s: imitative.

**weed** • n. **1** a wild plant growing where it is not wanted and in competition with cultivated plants. **2** informal cannabis. ➤ (**the weed**) informal tobacco. **3** informal a weak or skinny person. **4** informal a leggy, loosely built horse. • v. **1** remove weeds from. **2** (**weed something out**) remove unwanted items or members from something.
– DERIVATIVES **weeder** n. **weedless** adj.
– ORIGIN OE *wēod* (n.), *wēodian* (v.), of unknown origin.

**weedgrown** • adj. overgrown with weeds.

**weedkiller** • n. a substance used to destroy weeds.

**weeds** • pl. n. short for **WIDOW'S WEEDS**.

**weed whacker** • n. US an electrically powered grass trimmer with a rapidly rotating nylon cutting cord.

**weedy** • adj. (**-ier**, **-iest**) **1** containing or covered with many weeds. **2** informal thin and puny.
– DERIVATIVES **weediness** n.

**Wee Free** • n. a member of the minority group nicknamed the **Wee Free Kirk** which stood apart from the Free Church of Scotland when the majority amalgamated with the United Presbyterian Church to form the United Free Church in 1900.

**weejuns** /ˈwiːdʒənz/ • pl. n. trademark, chiefly US moccasin-style casual shoes.
– ORIGIN 1950s: a fanciful formation.

**week** • n. **1** a period of seven days. ➤ the period of seven days generally reckoned from and to midnight on Saturday night. ➤ chiefly Brit. (preceded by a specified day) a week after (that day). **2** the five days from Monday to Friday, or the time spent working during this period.
– ORIGIN OE *wice*, of Gmc origin, from a base prob. meaning 'sequence, series'.

**weekday** • n. a day of the week other than Sunday or Saturday.

**weekend** • n. Saturday and Sunday. • v. informal spend a weekend somewhere.

**weekender** • n. **1** a person who spends weekends away from their main home. **2** Austral. informal a holiday cottage. **3** a small pleasure boat.

**weekly** • adj. done, produced, or occurring once a week. • adv. once a week. • n. (pl. **-ies**) a newspaper or periodical issued every week.

**ween** • v. archaic think or suppose.
– ORIGIN OE *wēnan*, of Gmc origin; rel. to **WISH**.

**weenie** • n. another term for **WIENER**.

**weeny** • adj. (**-ier**, **-iest**) informal tiny.
– ORIGIN C18: from **WEE**[1], on the pattern of *tiny*; cf. **TEENY**.

**weep** • v. (past and past part. **wept**) **1** shed tears. ➤ archaic mourn for; shed tears over. **2** exude liquid. **3** [as adj. **weeping**] used in names of tree and shrub varieties with drooping branches, e.g. **weeping cherry**. • n. a fit or spell of shedding tears.
– DERIVATIVES **weeping** n. & adj. **weepingly** adv.
– ORIGIN OE *wēpan* (v.), of Gmc origin, prob. imitative.

**weeper** • n. **1** a person who weeps. ➤ historical a hired mourner at a funeral. ➤ a small image of a mourner on a monument. **2** (**weepers**) historical mourning clothes, in particular a man's crape hatband or a widow's black crape veil and white cuffs.

**weepie** (also **weepy**) • n. (pl. **-ies**) informal a sentimental or emotional film, novel, or song.

**weeping willow** • n. a willow with trailing branches and foliage reaching down to the ground. [*Salix* × *chrysocoma* and related species and hybrids.]

**weepy** • adj. (**-ier**, **-iest**) informal tearful; inclined to weep. ➤ sentimental. • n. variant spelling of **WEEPIE**.
– DERIVATIVES **weepily** adv. **weepiness** n.

**weever** • n. a small fish with venomous dorsal spines, typically burying itself in the sand. [Family Trachinidae: several species.]

– ORIGIN C17: perh. a transferred use of OFr. *wivre* 'serpent, dragon', from L. *vipera* 'viper'.

**weevil** /ˈwiːv(ə)l, ˈwiːvɪl/ ● **n.** a small beetle with an elongated snout, several kinds of which are pests of crops or stored foodstuffs. [Curculionidae and other families: many species.]
– DERIVATIVES **weevily** adj.
– ORIGIN OE *wifel* 'beetle', from a Gmc base meaning 'move briskly'.

**wee-wee** informal, chiefly Brit. ● **n.** a child's word for urine. ● **v.** urinate.
– ORIGIN 1930s: imitative.

**w.e.f.** ● **abbrev.** Brit. with effect from.

**weft¹** ● **n.** (in weaving) the crosswise threads that are passed over and under the warp threads on a loom to make cloth.
– ORIGIN OE *weft(a)*, of Gmc origin; rel. to **WEAVE¹**.

**weft²** ● **n.** variant spelling of **WAFT** (in sense 2).

**Wehrmacht** /ˈvɛːrmɑːxt, German ˈveːɐmaxt/ ● **n.** the German armed forces from 1921 to 1945.
– ORIGIN Ger., lit. 'defensive force'.

**weigela** /wʌɪˈdʒiːlə/ ● **n.** an ornamental Asian flowering shrub with pink, red, or yellow flowers. [*Weigela florida* and related species.]
– ORIGIN C19: mod. L., named after the Ger. physician Christian E. *Weigel*.

**weigh¹** ● **v. 1** find out how heavy (someone or something) is. ➤have a specified weight. ➤balance in the hands to assess the weight of. ➤(**weigh something out**) measure and take out a portion of a particular weight. ➤(**weigh someone down**) be heavy and cumbersome or oppressive to someone. ➤(**weigh on**) be depressing or burdensome to. ➤(**weigh in**) (of a boxer or jockey) be officially weighed before or after a contest. ➤(**weigh out**) (of a jockey) be weighed before a race. **2** (often **weigh something up/against**) assess the nature or importance of. ➤(often **weigh against**) influence a decision or action. **3** (**weigh in**) informal make a forceful contribution to a competition or argument. ➤(**weigh into**) join in or attack forcefully or enthusiastically.
– PHRASES **weigh anchor** Nautical take up the anchor when ready to sail.
– DERIVATIVES **weighable** adj. **weigher** n.
– ORIGIN OE *wegan*, of Gmc origin.

**weigh²** ● **n.** (in phr. **under weigh**) Nautical another way of saying ***under way*** (see **UNDER**).
– ORIGIN C18: from an erroneous assoc. with *weigh anchor* (see **WEIGH¹**).

**weighbridge** ● **n.** a machine for weighing vehicles, set into the ground to be driven on to.

**weigh-in** ● **n.** an official weighing, e.g. of boxers before a fight.

**weight** ● **n. 1** a body's relative mass or the quantity of matter contained by it, giving rise to a downward force; heaviness. ➤Physics the force exerted on the mass of a body by a gravitational field. ➤the quality of being heavy. ➤a unit or system of units used for expressing how much something weighs. **2** a piece of metal known to weigh a definite amount and used on scales to determine how heavy something is. ➤a heavy object, especially one being lifted or carried or used as a counterpoise in a mechanism. ➤(**weights**) heavy blocks or discs used in weightlifting or weight training. **3** the surface density of cloth, used as a measure of its quality. **4** ability to influence decisions or actions. ➤the importance attached to something. **5** a feeling of oppression or pressure: *a weight on one's mind.* **6** Statistics a factor associated with one of a set of numerical quantities, used to represent its importance relative to the other members of the set. ● **v. 1** hold (something) down by placing a heavy object on top of it. **2** attach importance or value to. ➤plan or arrange so as to give someone or something an advantage. **3** Statistics multiply the components of (an average) by factors to take account of their importance. **4** assign a handicap weight to (a horse). **5** treat (a fabric) with a mineral to make it seem thicker and heavier.
– PHRASES **be worth one's weight in gold** be exceedingly useful or helpful. **throw one's weight about** (or **around**) informal be unpleasantly self-assertive.
– ORIGIN OE *(ge)wiht*, of Gmc origin; form influenced by **WEIGH¹**.

**weighting** ● **n. 1** allowance or adjustment made to take account of special circumstances or compensate for a distorting factor. **2** Brit. additional wages or salary paid to allow for a higher cost of living in a particular area.

**weightless** ● **adj.** (of a body, especially in an orbiting spacecraft) not apparently acted on by gravity.
– DERIVATIVES **weightlessly** adv. **weightlessness** n.

**weightlifting** ● **n.** the sport or activity of lifting barbells or other heavy weights.
– DERIVATIVES **weightlifter** n.

**weight training** ● **n.** physical training that involves lifting weights.

**weight-watcher** ● **n.** a person who is on a diet in order to lose weight.
– DERIVATIVES **weight-watching** n. & adj.

**weighty** ● **adj.** (**-ier, -iest**) **1** weighing a great deal; heavy. **2** very serious and important. ➤very influential.
– DERIVATIVES **weightily** adv. **weightiness** n.

**Weil's disease** /vʌɪlz/ ● **n.** a severe form of leptospirosis transmitted by rats via contaminated water.
– ORIGIN C19: named after the Ger. physician H. Adolf *Weil*.

**Weimaraner** /ˈvʌɪməˌrɑːnə, ˈwʌɪ-/ ● **n.** a dog of a thin-coated, typically grey breed of pointer used as a gun dog.
– ORIGIN 1940s: from Ger., from *Weimar* in Germany, where the breed was developed.

**weir** ● **n. 1** a low dam built across a river to raise the level of water upstream or regulate its flow. **2** an enclosure of stakes set in a stream as a trap for fish.
– ORIGIN OE *wer*, from *werian* 'dam up'.

**weird** ● **adj. 1** suggesting something supernatural; uncanny. ➤informal very strange; bizarre. **2** archaic connected with fate. ● **n.** archaic, chiefly Scottish a person's destiny. ● **v.** (**weird someone out**) N. Amer. informal induce a sense of disbelief or alienation in someone.
– DERIVATIVES **weirdly** adv. **weirdness** n.
– ORIGIN OE *wyrd* 'destiny', of Gmc origin.

**weirdo** ● **n.** (pl. **-os**) informal a strange or eccentric person.

**Weisswurst** /ˈvʌɪsvəːst/ (also **weisswurst**) ● **n.** whitish German sausage made chiefly of veal.
– ORIGIN Ger., lit. 'white sausage'.

**weka** /ˈwɛkə/ ● **n.** a large flightless New Zealand rail. [*Gallirallus australis*.]
– ORIGIN C19: from Maori, imitative of its cry.

**welch** /wɛltʃ/ ● **v.** variant spelling of **WELSH**.

**welcome** ● **n.** an instance or manner of greeting someone. ➤a pleased or approving reaction. ● **exclam.** used to greet someone in a glad or friendly way. ● **v. 1** greet (someone arriving) in a glad, polite, or friendly way. **2** be glad to receive or hear of: *the decision was widely welcomed.* ● **adj. 1** (of a guest or new arrival) gladly received. **2** very pleasing because much needed or desired. **3** allowed or invited to do a specified thing: *you are welcome to join in.* ➤(**welcome to**) used to indicate relief at relinquishing something to another: *you're welcome to it!*
– DERIVATIVES **welcomely** adv. **welcomeness** n. **welcomer** n. **welcoming** n. & adj. **welcomingly** adv.
– ORIGIN OE *wilcuma* 'a person whose coming is pleasing', *wilcumian* (v.), from *wil-* 'desire, pleasure' + *cuman* 'come'; change to *wel-* influenced by OFr. *bien venu* or ON *velkominn*.

**weld¹** ● **v. 1** join together (metal parts) by heating the surfaces to the point of melting and pressing or hammering them together. ➤forge (an article) by such means. **2** cause to combine and form a whole. ● **n.** a welded joint.
– DERIVATIVES **weldability** n. **weldable** adj. **welder** n.
– ORIGIN C16 (in the sense 'become united'): alt. (prob. influenced by the past part.) of **WELL²** in the obs. sense 'melt or weld (heated metal)'.

**weld²** ● **n.** a plant related to mignonette, yielding a yellow dye. [*Reseda luteola*.]
– ORIGIN ME: rel. to Du. *wouw*, perh. also to **WOLD**.

**welfare** ● **n. 1** the health, happiness, and fortunes of a person or group. **2** action or procedure designed to pro-

mote the basic physical and material well-being of people in need. ➤ chiefly N. Amer. financial support given for this purpose.
– ORIGIN ME: from **WELL**[1] + **FARE**.

**welfare state** ● n. a system whereby the state undertakes to protect the health and well-being of its citizens, especially those in need, by means of grants, pensions, and other benefits.

**welfare to work** ● n. (in the UK) a government policy of encouraging unemployed people to find a job, for example by making a payment to their new employers.

**welfarism** ● n. the principles or policies associated with a welfare state.
– DERIVATIVES **welfarist** n. & adj.

**welkin** /ˈwɛlkɪn/ ● n. poetic/literary the sky or heaven.
– ORIGIN OE *wolcen* 'cloud, sky', of W. Gmc origin.

**well**[1] ● adv. (**better**, **best**) **1** in a good or satisfactory way. ➤ in a condition of prosperity or comfort. ➤ archaic luckily; opportunely: *hail fellow, well met.* **2** in a thorough manner. ➤ to a great extent or degree; very much. ➤ Brit. informal very; extremely: *he was well out of order.* **3** very probably; in all likelihood. ➤ without difficulty. ➤ with good reason. ● adj. (**better**, **best**) **1** in good health; free or recovered from illness. ➤ in a satisfactory state or position. **2** sensible; advisable. ● exclam. used to express surprise, anger, resignation, etc., or when pausing in speech.
– PHRASES **as well 1** in addition; too. **2** (**as well** or **just as well**) with equal reason or an equally good result. ➤ sensible, appropriate, or desirable. **be well out of** Brit. informal be fortunate to be no longer involved in. **be well up on** (or **in**) know a great deal about. **leave** (or **let**) **well** (N. Amer. **enough**) **alone** refrain from interfering with or trying to improve something. **very well** used to express agreement or understanding. **well and truly** completely.
– DERIVATIVES **wellness** n.
– ORIGIN OE *wel(l)*, of Gmc origin; prob. rel. to the verb **WILL**[1].

**USAGE** well

The adverb **well** is often used in combination with past participles to form adjectival compounds. The general stylistic principle for hyphenation is that if the adjectival compound is placed attributively (i.e. before the noun), it should be hyphenated (*a well-intentioned remark*) but that if it is placed predicatively (i.e. standing alone after the verb), it should not be hyphenated (*her remarks were well intentioned*). In this dictionary, the unhyphenated form is generally the only one given.

**well**[2] ● n. **1** a shaft sunk into the ground to obtain water, oil, or gas. ➤ a depression made to hold liquid. **2** a plentiful source or supply: *a deep well of sympathy.* **3** an enclosed space in the middle of a building, giving room for stairs or a lift or allowing light or ventilation. **4** Brit. the place in a law court where the clerks and ushers sit. **5** Physics a region of minimum potential. **6** archaic a water spring or fountain. ● v. (often **well up**) (of a liquid) rise up to the surface and spill or be about to spill. ➤ (of an emotion) arise and become more intense.
– ORIGIN OE *wella*, of Gmc origin.

**we'll** ● contr. we shall; we will.

**well advised** ● adj. sensible; wise.

**well appointed** ● adj. (of a building or room) having a high standard of equipment or furnishing.

**well-being** ● n. the state of being comfortable, healthy, or happy.

**well covered** ● adj. Brit. informal slightly plump.

**well deck** ● n. an open space on the main deck of a ship, lying at a lower level between the forecastle and poop.

**well disposed** ● adj. having a positive, sympathetic, or friendly attitude.

**well done** ● adj. **1** carried out successfully or satisfactorily. **2** (of food) thoroughly cooked. ● exclam. used to express congratulation or approval.

**well dressing** ● n. the ancient custom of decorating wells with flowers at Whitsuntide, especially in Derbyshire.

**well earned** ● adj. fully merited or deserved.

**well endowed** ● adj. having plentiful supplies of a resource. ➤ informal, humorous (of a man) having large genitals. ➤ informal, humorous (of a woman) large-breasted.

**well favoured** (US **well favored**) ● adj. having special advantages, especially good looks.

**well head** ● n. **1** the place where a spring comes out of the ground. **2** the structure over a well.

**well-heeled** ● adj. informal wealthy.

**well hung** ● adj. informal, humorous (of a man) having large genitals.

**wellie** ● n. variant spelling of **WELLY**.

**wellington** (also **wellington boot**) ● n. chiefly Brit. a knee-length waterproof rubber or plastic boot.
– ORIGIN C19: named after the Brit. soldier and Prime Minister the 1st Duke of *Wellington*.

**wellingtonia** /ˌwɛlɪŋˈtəʊnɪə/ ● n. the giant redwood.
– ORIGIN C19: mod. L., from the former binomial *Wellingtonia gigantea*.

**well knit** ● adj. (of a person) strongly and compactly built.

**well known** ● adj. known widely or thoroughly.

**well made** ● adj. **1** strongly or skilfully constructed. **2** (of a person) having a sturdy build.

**well meaning** (also **well meant**) ● adj. having good intentions but not necessarily the desired effect.

**well-nigh** ● adv. chiefly poetic/literary almost.

**well off** ● adj. wealthy. ➤ in a favourable situation or circumstances.

**well oiled** ● adj. **1** operating smoothly. **2** informal drunk.

**well pleased** ● adj. highly gratified or satisfied.

**well preserved** ● adj. (of an old person) showing little sign of ageing.

**well rounded** ● adj. **1** having a pleasing curved shape. ➤ (of a person) plump. **2** having a mature personality and varied interests.

**well set** ● adj. firmly established; solidly fixed or arranged. ➤ (also **well set-up**) (of a person) strongly built.

**well spent** ● adj. (of money or time) usefully or profitably expended.

**well spoken** ● adj. speaking in an educated and refined manner.

**wellspring** ● n. poetic/literary **1** a well head of a spring. **2** an abundant source of something.

**well thumbed** ● adj. (of a book) having been read often and bearing marks of frequent handling.

**well-to-do** ● adj. wealthy; prosperous.

**well travelled** ● adj. **1** (of a person) having travelled widely. **2** (of a route) much frequented by travellers.

**well tried** ● adj. having been used often and therefore known to be reliable.

**well trodden** ● adj. much frequented by travellers.

**well turned** ● adj. **1** (of a phrase or compliment) elegantly expressed. **2** (of a woman's ankle or leg) attractively shaped.

**well upholstered** ● adj. humorous (of a person) fat.

**well-wisher** ● n. a person who desires happiness or success for another, or who expresses such a desire.

**well worn** ● adj. showing the signs of extensive use or wear. ➤ (of a phrase or idea) used or repeated so often that it no longer has interest or significance.

**welly** (also **wellie**) ● n. (pl. **-ies**) Brit. informal **1** short for **WELLINGTON**. **2** power or vigour.

**wels** /wɛls, vɛls/ ● n. a very large freshwater catfish found from central Europe to central Asia. [*Silurus glanis*.]
– ORIGIN C19: from Ger. *Wels*.

**Welsh** ● n. the Celtic language of Wales. ● adj. of or relating to Wales, its people, or their language.
– DERIVATIVES **Welshman** n. **Welshness** n. **Welshwoman** n.
– ORIGIN OE *Welisc*, *Wælisc*, from a Gmc word meaning 'foreigner', from L. *Volcae*, the name of a Celtic people.

**welsh** (also **welch**) ● v. (**welsh on**) fail to honour (a debt or obligation).
– DERIVATIVES **welsher** n.

– ORIGIN C19: of unknown origin.

**Welsh dresser** • n. a piece of wooden furniture with cupboards and drawers in the lower part and open shelves in the upper part.

**Welsh harp** • n. another term for **TRIPLE HARP**.

**Welsh onion** • n. an Asian onion that forms clusters of slender bulbs which resemble spring onions. [*Allium fistulosum*.]
– ORIGIN C18 (as *Welch onion*): *Welsh* from Ger. *welsch* 'foreign'.

**Welsh rarebit** (also **Welsh rabbit**) • n. another term for **RAREBIT**.

**Welsh terrier** • n. a stocky, rough-coated, typically black-and-tan terrier of a breed with a square muzzle and drop ears.

**welt** • n. **1** a leather rim round the edge of the upper of a shoe, to which the sole is attached. ➤ a ribbed, reinforced, or decorative border of a garment or pocket. **2** a weal. **3** a heavy blow. • v. **1** provide with a welt. **2** strike hard and heavily. **3** develop a weal.
– ORIGIN ME: of unknown origin.

**Weltanschauung** /ˈvɛltˌanʃaʊʊŋ, German ˈvɛltˌanʃaʊʊŋ/ • n. (pl. **Weltanschauungen** /-(ə)n/) a particular philosophy or view of life; a world view.
– ORIGIN Ger., from *Welt* 'world' + *Anschauung* 'perception'.

**welter** • v. poetic/literary **1** move in a turbulent fashion. **2** lie steeped in blood. • n. a large number of items in no order; a confused mass. ➤ a state of general disorder.
– ORIGIN ME (in the sense 'writhe, wallow'): from MDu., Mid. Low Ger. *welteren*.

**welterweight** • n. a weight in boxing and other sports intermediate between lightweight and middleweight.
– ORIGIN C19: *welter* of unknown origin.

**Weltschmerz** /ˈvɛltˌʃmɛːts, German ˈvɛltˌʃmɛrts/ • n. a feeling of melancholy and world-weariness.
– ORIGIN Ger., from *Welt* 'world' + *Schmerz* 'pain'.

**wen**[1] • n. **1** a boil or other swelling or growth on the skin, especially a sebaceous cyst. **2** archaic a very large or overcrowded city.
– ORIGIN OE *wen(n)*, of unknown origin; cf. Low Ger. *wehne* 'tumour, wart'.

**wen**[2] (also **wyn**) • n. a runic letter, used in Old and Middle English, later replaced by *w*.
– ORIGIN OE, lit. 'joy'; so named because it is the first letter of this word.

**wench** /wɛn(t)ʃ/ • n. **1** archaic or humorous a girl or young woman. **2** archaic a prostitute. • v. archaic (of a man) consort with prostitutes.
– DERIVATIVES **wencher** n.
– ORIGIN ME: abbrev. of obs. *wenchel* 'child, servant, prostitute'; perh. rel. to OE *wancol* 'unsteady, inconstant'.

**Wend** /wɛnd/ • n. another term for **SORB**.
– DERIVATIVES **Wendish** n. & adj.
– ORIGIN from Ger. *Wende*, of unknown origin.

**wend** • v. (**wend one's way**) go slowly or by an indirect route.
– ORIGIN OE *wendan* 'to turn, depart', of Gmc origin; rel. to **WIND**[2].

**wendigo** /ˈwɛndɪgəʊ/ • n. variant spelling of **WINDIGO**.

**Wendy house** • n. Brit. a toy house large enough for children to play in.
– ORIGIN named after the house built around *Wendy* in J. M. Barrie's play *Peter Pan*.

**Wensleydale** /ˈwɛnzlɪdeɪl/ • n. **1** a type of white cheese with a crumbly texture. **2** a sheep of a breed with long wool.
– ORIGIN named after *Wensleydale* in Yorkshire.

**went** past of **GO**[1].

**wentletrap** /ˈwɛnt(ə)ltrap/ • n. a marine mollusc with a tall spiral shell of many whorls. [*Clathrus clathrus* and other species.]
– ORIGIN C18: from Du. *wenteltrap*, lit. 'winding stair'.

**wept** past and past participle of **WEEP**.

**were** second person singular past, plural past, and past subjunctive of **BE**.

**we're** • contr. we are.

**weren't** • contr. were not.

**werewolf** /ˈwɛːwʊlf, ˈwɪə-, ˈwəː-/ • n. (pl. **werewolves**) (in folklore) a person who periodically changes into a wolf, typically when there is a full moon.
– ORIGIN OE *werewulf*; the first element has usu. been identified with OE *wer* 'man'.

**wert** /wəːt/ archaic second person singular past of **BE**.

**Wesak** /ˈvɛsak/ • n. variant spelling of **VESAK**.

**Wesleyan** • adj. relating to or denoting the teachings of the English preacher John Wesley (1703–91) or the main branch of the Methodist Church which he founded. • n. a follower of Wesley or adherent of the main Methodist tradition.
– DERIVATIVES **Wesleyanism** n.

**west** • n. (usu. **the west**) **1** the direction towards the point of the horizon where the sun sets at the equinoxes, on the left-hand side of a person facing north. **2** the west of a country, region, or town. ➤ (**the West**) Europe and North America seen in contrast to other civilizations. ➤ (**the West**) historical the non-Communist states of Europe and North America. • adj. **1** lying towards, near, or facing the west. **2** (of a wind) blowing from the west. • adv. to or towards the west.
– PHRASES **go west** Brit. informal be killed or lost.
– DERIVATIVES **westbound** adj. & adv.
– ORIGIN OE, of Gmc origin.

**westering** • adj. poetic/literary (especially of the sun) nearing the west.
– ORIGIN C17: from the literary verb *wester*, from **WEST**.

**westerly** • adj. & adv. **1** in a westward position or direction. **2** (of a wind) blowing from the west. • n. a wind blowing from the west. ➤ (**westerlies**) the belt of prevailing westerly winds in medium latitudes in the southern hemisphere.

**western** • adj. **1** situated in, directed towards, or facing the west. **2** (usu. **Western**) living in, coming from, or characteristic of the west, in particular Europe and North America. • n. a film or novel about cowboys in western North America.
– DERIVATIVES **westernmost** adj.

**Western blot** • n. Biochemistry an adaptation of the Southern blot procedure, used to identify specific amino-acid sequences in proteins.
– ORIGIN suggested by **SOUTHERN BLOT**.

**Western Church** • n. the part of the Christian Church originating in the Western Roman Empire, including the Roman Catholic, Anglican, Lutheran, and Reformed Churches.

**westerner** • n. a native or inhabitant of the west of a particular region or country.

**westernize** (also **-ise**) • v. bring or come under the influence of the cultural, economic, or political systems of Europe and North America.
– DERIVATIVES **westernization** n. **westernizer** n.

**Western saddle** • n. a saddle with a deep seat, high pommel and cantle, and broad stirrups.

**western swing** • n. a style of country music influenced by jazz, popular in the 1930s.

**West Germanic** • n. the western group of Germanic languages, comprising High and Low German, Dutch, Frisian, and English. • adj. of or relating to West Germanic.

**West Highland terrier** • n. a dog of a small, short-legged breed of terrier with a white coat and erect ears and tail.

**West Indian** • n. a native or national of the West Indies, or a person of West Indian descent. • adj. of or relating to the West Indies or its people.

**westing** • n. **1** distance travelled or measured westward, especially at sea. **2** a figure or line representing westward distance on a map.

**west-north-west** • n. the direction or compass point midway between west and north-west.

**Westphalian** /wɛstˈfeɪlɪən/ • n. a native or inhabitant of Westphalia, a former province of NW Germany. • adj. of or relating to Westphalia.

**West Saxon** • n. **1** a native or inhabitant of the Anglo-

Saxon kingdom of Wessex. **2** the dialect of Old English used by the West Saxons.

**west-south-west** ● **n.** the direction or compass point midway between west and south-west.

**westward** ● **adj.** towards the west. ● **adv.** (also **westwards**) in a westerly direction. ● **n.** (**the westward**) a direction or region towards the west.
– DERIVATIVES **westwardly** adj. & adv.

**wet** ● **adj.** (**wetter**, **wettest**) **1** covered or saturated with liquid. ➤(of the weather) rainy. ➤involving the use of water or liquid. **2** (of paint, ink, etc.) not yet having dried or hardened. **3** Brit. informal lacking forcefulness or strength of character; feeble. **4** informal (of an area) allowing the free sale of alcoholic drink. ● **v.** (**wetting**; past and past part. **wet** or **wetted**) cover or touch with liquid. ➤(especially of a baby or young child) urinate in or on. ➤(**wet oneself**) urinate involuntarily. ➤dialect infuse (tea) by pouring on boiling water. ● **n.** **1** liquid that makes something damp. ➤(**the wet**) rainy weather. ➤Brit. informal a drink. **2** Brit. informal a feeble person. **3** Brit. a Conservative politician (especially in the 1980s) with liberal tendencies. **4** US a person opposed to the prohibition of alcohol.
– PHRASES **all wet** N. Amer. completely wrong. **wet the baby's head** Brit. informal celebrate a baby's birth with a drink. **wet behind the ears** informal lacking experience; immature. **wet one's whistle** informal have a drink.
– DERIVATIVES **wetly** adv. **wetness** n. **wettable** adj. **wettish** adj.
– ORIGIN OE *wǣt* (adj. and n.), *wǣtan* (v.); rel. to **WATER**.

**weta** /ˈwɛtə/ ● **n.** a large brown wingless insect with wood-boring larvae, found only in New Zealand. [Family Stenopelmatidae.]
– ORIGIN C19: from Maori.

**wetback** ● **n.** US informal, derogatory a Mexican who is an illegal immigrant to the US.
– ORIGIN 1920s: so named from the practice of swimming the Rio Grande to reach the US.

**wet bar** ● **n.** N. Amer. a bar or counter in the home for serving alcoholic drinks.

**wet blanket** ● **n.** informal a person who spoils other people's enjoyment with their disapproving or unenthusiastic manner.

**wet bulb** ● **n.** a thermometer bulb enclosed in wetted material so that it is cooled by evaporation, as used in a psychrometer.

**wet dock** ● **n.** a dock in which water is maintained at a level at which a ship is able to float.

**wet dream** ● **n.** an erotic dream that causes involuntary ejaculation of semen.

**wet fish** ● **n.** fresh fish, as opposed to fish which has been frozen, cooked, or dried.

**wet fly** ● **n.** an artificial fishing fly designed to sink below the surface of the water.

**wether** /ˈwɛðə/ ● **n.** a castrated ram.
– ORIGIN OE, of Gmc origin.

**wetland** ● **n.** (also **wetlands**) swampy or marshy land.

**wet lease** ● **n.** an arrangement for the hire of an aircraft with a flight crew and sometimes fuel.

**wet look** ● **n.** a shiny appearance possessed by a clothing fabric or achieved by applying gel to the hair.

**wet nurse** ● **n.** chiefly historical a woman employed to suckle another woman's child. ● **v.** (**wet-nurse**) act as a wet nurse to. ➤informal look after (someone) as though they were a helpless infant.

**wet pack** ● **n.** **1** a session of hydrotherapy in which the body is wrapped in wet cloth. **2** a washbag.

**wet plate** ● **n.** Photography a sensitized collodion plate exposed in the camera while the collodion is moist.

**wet rot** ● **n.** a brown fungus causing decay in moist timber. [*Coniophora puteana* and other species.]

**wetsuit** ● **n.** a close-fitting rubber garment covering the entire body, worn for warmth in water sports or diving.

**wetting agent** ● **n.** a chemical added to a liquid to reduce its surface tension and make it more effective in spreading over and penetrating surfaces.

**wetware** ● **n.** human brain cells viewed as counterparts of computer systems.

**WEU** ● **abbrev.** Western European Union.

**we've** ● **contr.** we have.

**wey** /weɪ/ ● **n.** a former unit of weight or volume varying with different kinds of goods, e.g. 3 cwt. of cheese.
– ORIGIN OE *wǣg(e)*, *wēg(e)* 'balance, weight', of Gmc origin; rel. to **WEIGH**[1].

**w.f.** ● **abbrev.** Printing wrong fount.

**WFTU** ● **abbrev.** World Federation of Trade Unions.

**Wg Cdr** ● **abbrev.** Wing Commander.

**whack** informal ● **v.** **1** strike forcefully with a sharp blow. ➤defeat heavily. ➤place or insert roughly or carelessly. **2** N. Amer. murder. **3** (**whack off**) vulgar slang masturbate. ● **n.** **1** a sharp or resounding blow. **2** a try or attempt. **3** Brit. a specified share of or contribution to something.
– PHRASES **out of whack** chiefly N. Amer. & Austral./NZ not working. **top** (or **full**) **whack** chiefly Brit. the maximum price or rate.
– DERIVATIVES **whacker** n.
– ORIGIN C18: imitative, or perh. an alt. of **THWACK**.

**whacked** (also **whacked out** or **wacked**) ● **adj.** informal **1** chiefly Brit. completely exhausted. **2** chiefly N. Amer. under the influence of drugs.

**whacking** ● **adj.** Brit. informal very large.

**whacko**[1] ● **exclam.** Brit. informal, dated used to express delight and enthusiasm.
– ORIGIN 1940s: from **WHACK** + **-O**.

**whacko**[2] ● **adj.** & **n.** (pl. **-os**) variant spelling of **WACKO**.

**whacky** ● **adj.** variant spelling of **WACKY**.

**whale**[1] ● **n.** (pl. same or **whales**) a very large marine mammal with a horizontal tail fin and a blowhole on top of the head for breathing. [Order Cetacea.]
– PHRASES **a whale of a ——** informal an exceedingly good example of something. **have a whale of a time** informal enjoy oneself very much.
– ORIGIN OE *hwæl*, of Gmc origin.

**whale**[2] ● **v.** informal, chiefly N. Amer. beat; hit.
– ORIGIN C18: var. of **WALE**.

**whaleback** ● **n.** something shaped like a whale's back, especially an arched structure over the bow or stern part of a steamer's deck, or a large elongated hill.

**whaleboat** ● **n.** a long manoeuvrable rowing boat with a bow at each end, formerly used in whaling.

**whalebone** ● **n.** an elastic horny substance which grows in a series of thin parallel plates in the upper jaw of some whales and is used by them to strain plankton from the seawater; baleen. ➤strips of this substance, formerly used as stays in corsets and dresses.

**whalebone whale** ● **n.** another term for **BALEEN WHALE**.

**whale oil** ● **n.** oil obtained from the blubber of a whale, formerly used in oil lamps or for making soap.

**whaler** ● **n.** **1** a whaling ship. ➤a seaman engaged in whaling. **2** (usu. **whaler shark**) a large, slender-bodied shark of inshore waters. [*Carcharhinus brachyurus* (Australia) and related species.] **3** Austral. informal a tramp.

**whale shark** ● **n.** a very large tropical shark which feeds chiefly on plankton, the largest known fish. [*Rhincodon typus*.]

**whaling** ● **n.** the practice or industry of hunting and killing whales for their oil, meat, or whalebone.

**wham** informal ● **exclam.** used to express the sound of a forcible impact or the idea of a sudden and dramatic occurrence. ● **v.** (**whammed**, **whamming**) strike something forcefully.

**whammy** ● **n.** (pl. **-ies**) informal **1** an event with a powerful and unpleasant effect; a blow. **2** chiefly US an evil or unlucky influence.
– ORIGIN 1940s: from **WHAM** + **-Y**[1].

**whang** informal ● **v.** strike, throw, or hit heavily and loudly. ● **n.** a noisy blow.

**whap** ● **v.** (**whapped**, **whapping**) & **n.** chiefly N. Amer. variant spelling of **WHOP**.

**whare** /ˈwɒri/ ● **n.** a Maori hut or house.
– ORIGIN from Maori.

**wharf** /wɔːf/ ● **n.** (pl. **wharves** or **wharfs**) a level quayside area to which a ship may be moored to load and unload.

– ORIGIN OE *hwearf*, of Gmc origin.

**wharfage** ● n. accommodation provided at a wharf for the loading, unloading, or storage of goods. ➤ payment made for such accommodation.

**wharfie** ● n. Austral./NZ informal a dock labourer.

**wharfinger** /ˈwɔːfɪn(d)ʒə/ ● n. an owner or keeper of a wharf.

– ORIGIN ME: from **WHARFAGE** + **-ER**[1].

**wharves** plural form of **WHARF**.

**what** ● pron. & det. **1** asking for information specifying something. ➤ [as pron.] asking for repetition of something not heard or confirmation of something not understood. **2** [as pron.] the thing or things that. **3** whatever. **4** used to emphasize something surprising or remarkable. ● interrog. adv. **1** to what extent? **2** informal, dated used for emphasis or to invite agreement: *poor show, what?*

– PHRASES **and** (or **or**) **what have you** informal and/or anything else similar. **and what not** informal and other similar things. **what about ——? 1** used when asking for information or an opinion. **2** used to make a suggestion. **what-d'you-call-it** (or **what's-its name**) informal used as a substitute for a name not recalled. **what for?** informal for what reason? **what if ——? 1** what would result if ——? **2** what does it matter if ——? **what is more** and as an additional point; moreover. **what of ——?** what is the news concerning ——? **what of it?** why should that be considered significant? **what's-his** (or **-its**) **-name** another term for ***what-d'you-call-it***. **what's what** informal what is useful or important. **what with** because of.

– ORIGIN OE *hwæt*, of Gmc origin.

**whatever** ● rel. pron. & det. used to emphasize a lack of restriction in referring to any thing, no matter what. ● interrog. pron. used for emphasis instead of 'what' in questions. ● adv. **1** [with neg.] at all; of any kind. **2** informal no matter what happens.

**whatnot** ● n. **1** informal used to refer to an unidentified item or items having something in common with items already named. **2** a stand with shelves for small objects.

**whatsit** ● n. informal a person or thing whose name one cannot recall, does not know, or does not wish to specify.

**whatso** ● pron. & det. archaic whatever.

**whatsoever** ● adv. [with neg.] at all. ● det. & pron. archaic whatever.

**whaup** /(h)wɔːp/ ● n. chiefly Scottish another term for **CURLEW**.

– ORIGIN C16: imitative of its cry.

**wheal** ● n. variant spelling of **WEAL**[1].

**wheat** ● n. a cereal widely grown in temperate countries, the grain of which is ground to make flour for bread, pasta, etc. [*Triticum aestivum* and related species.]

– ORIGIN OE *hwǣte* of Gmc origin; rel. to **WHITE**.

**wheatear** ● n. a songbird with black and grey, buff, or white plumage and a white rump. [*Oenanthe oenanthe* and related species.]

– ORIGIN C16: appar. from **WHITE** (assimilated to **WHEAT**) + **ARSE** (assimilated to **EAR**[2]).

**wheaten** ● adj. made of wheat.

**wheaten terrier** ● n. a terrier of a breed with a soft, wavy pale golden coat.

**wheatgerm** ● n. a nutritious foodstuff of a dry floury consistency consisting of the extracted embryos of grains of wheat.

**wheatgrass** ● n. another term for **COUCH**[2].

**wheatmeal** ● n. flour made from wheat from which some of the bran and germ has been removed.

**Wheatstone bridge** ● n. a device for measuring an unknown resistance by combining it in a circuit with known resistances and equalizing the potential at two points.

– ORIGIN C19: named after the Engl. physicist Sir Charles *Wheatstone*.

**whee** ● exclam. used to express delight or excitement.

**wheech** /hwiːx, hwiːk/ ● v. Scottish **1** snatch or remove quickly. **2** rush; dash.

– ORIGIN C19: symbolic.

**wheedle** ● v. employ endearments or flattery to persuade someone to do something.

– DERIVATIVES **wheedler** n. **wheedling** adj. **wheedlingly** adv.

– ORIGIN C17: perh. from Ger. *wedeln* 'cringe, fawn'.

**wheel** ● n. **1** a circular object that revolves on an axle, fixed below a vehicle to enable it to move over the ground or forming part of a machine. **2** something resembling a wheel or having a wheel as its essential part. ➤ a steering wheel. ➤ a device with a revolving disc or drum used in various games of chance. ➤ a cheese made in the form of a shallow disc. **3** (**wheels**) informal a car. **4** an instance of wheeling; a turn or rotation. **5** a set of short lines concluding the stanza of a poem. ● v. **1** push or pull (a vehicle with wheels). ➤ carry in or on a vehicle with wheels. ➤ (**wheel something in/on/out**) informal produce something that is unimpressive because it has been frequently seen or heard before. **2** fly or turn in a wide circle or curve. ➤ turn round quickly to face another way.

– PHRASES **on wheels 1** travelling by car or cycle. **2** Brit. informal smoothly. **wheel and deal** engage in commercial or political scheming, especially unscrupulously. **the wheel of Fortune** the wheel which the deity Fortune is fabled to turn as a symbol of random luck or change. **wheels within wheels** secret or indirect influences affecting a complex situation.

– DERIVATIVES **wheeled** adj. **wheelless** adj.

– ORIGIN OE *hwēol* (n.), of Gmc origin.

**wheelback** ● adj. (of a chair) having a back incorporating the design of a wheel.

**wheelbarrow** ● n. a small cart with a single wheel at the front and two supporting legs and two handles at the rear, used for carrying loads in building or gardening.

**wheelbase** ● n. the distance between the front and rear axles of a vehicle.

**wheelchair** ● n. a mobile wheeled chair for an invalid or disabled person.

**wheel clamp** ● n. a device for immobilizing an unlawfully parked car. ● v. (**wheel-clamp**) clamp (a car) with such a device.

**wheeler** ● n. **1** [in combination] a vehicle having a specified number of wheels. **2** a wheelwright. **3** a horse harnessed next to the wheels of a cart and behind a leading horse.

**wheeler-dealer** (also **wheeler and dealer**) ● n. a person who engages in commercial or political scheming.

– DERIVATIVES **wheeler-dealing** n.

**wheelhouse** ● n. a shelter for the person at the wheel of a boat or ship.

**wheelie** ● n. informal a trick or manoeuvre whereby a bicycle or motorcycle is ridden for a short distance with the front wheel raised off the ground.

**wheelie bin** (also **wheely bin**) ● n. Brit. informal a large refuse bin set on wheels.

**wheel lock** ● n. historical a kind of gunlock having a steel wheel that rubbed against a flint. ➤ a gun having such a gunlock.

**wheelman** ● n. (pl. **-men**) chiefly N. Amer. **1** a person who steers a boat or drives a car, especially a getaway car. **2** informal a cyclist.

**wheelsman** ● n. (pl. **-men**) N. Amer. a person who steers a ship or boat.

**wheelspin** ● n. rotation of a vehicle's wheels without traction.

**wheelwright** ● n. chiefly historical a person who makes or repairs wooden wheels.

**wheely bin** ● n. variant spelling of **WHEELIE BIN**.

**wheen** /wiːn/ ● n. Scottish a considerable number or amount.

– ORIGIN ME: from OE *hwēne* 'in some degree'.

**wheesht** /wiːʃt/ ● exclam. variant of **WHISHT**.

**wheeze** ● v. breathe with a whistling or rattling sound in the chest, as a result of obstruction in the air passages. ➤ (of a device) make an irregular rattling or spluttering sound. ● n. **1** a sound of a person wheezing. **2** Brit. informal a clever or amusing scheme or trick.

– DERIVATIVES **wheezer** n. **wheezily** adv. **wheeziness** n. **wheezing** adj. **wheezingly** adv. **wheezy** adj.

– ORIGIN ME: prob. from ON *hvæsa* 'to hiss'.

**whelk**[1] ● **n.** a predatory marine mollusc with a heavy pointed spiral shell. [Family Buccinidae.]
– ORIGIN OE *wioloc*, *weoloc*, of unknown origin; spelling perh. influenced by **WHELK**[2].

**whelk**[2] ● **n.** archaic a pimple.
– ORIGIN OE *hwylca*, rel. to *hwelian* 'suppurate'.

**whelm** /wɛlm/ archaic or poetic/literary ● **v.** engulf, submerge, or bury. ● **n.** a surge of water.
– ORIGIN ME: representing an OE form parallel to *hwelfan* 'overturn (a vessel)'.

**whelp** ● **n.** chiefly archaic **1** a puppy. ➤ a cub. **2** derogatory a boy or young man. **3** (**whelps**) a set of projections on the barrel of a capstan or windlass. ● **v.** give birth to (a puppy).
– ORIGIN OE *hwelp* (n.), of Gmc origin.

**when** ● **interrog. adv. 1** at what time. ➤ how soon. **2** in what circumstances. ● **rel. adv.** at which time or in which situation. ● **conj. 1** at or during the time that. ➤ at any time that; whenever. **2** after which; and just then. **3** in view of the fact that; considering that. **4** although; whereas.
– ORIGIN OE *hwanne*, *hwenne*; of Gmc origin.

**whence** (also **from whence**) formal or archaic ● **interrog. adv.** from what place or source. ● **rel. adv.** from which; from where. ➤ to the place from which. ➤ as a consequence of which.
– ORIGIN ME *whennes*, from earlier *whenne* (from OE *hwanon*, of Gmc origin) + **-s**[3] (later respelled *-ce*).

**USAGE** whence

Strictly speaking, **whence** means 'from what place'. Thus, use of the preposition **from** is redundant and its use is considered incorrect by some. It is very common, though (occurring in more than 20 per cent of citations for **whence** in the British National Corpus), and has been used by reputable writers since the 14th century. It is now broadly accepted in standard English.

**whencesoever** ● **rel. adv.** formal or archaic from whatever place or source.

**whenever** ● **conj.** at whatever time; on whatever occasion. ➤ every time that. ● **interrog. adv.** used for emphasis instead of 'when' in questions.

**whensoever** ● **conj. & adv.** formal word for **WHENEVER**.

**where** ● **interrog. adv.** in or to what place or position. ➤ in what direction or respect. ● **rel. adv. 1** at, in, or to which. **2** the place or situation in which. ➤ in or to a place or situation in which. ➤ in or to any place in which.
– ORIGIN OE *hwǣr*, of Gmc origin.

**whereabouts** ● **interrog. adv.** where or approximately where. ● **n.** [treated as sing. or pl.] the place where someone or something is.

**whereafter** ● **rel. adv.** formal after which.

**whereas** ● **conj.** in contrast or comparison with the fact that. ➤ taking into consideration the fact that.

**whereat** ● **rel. adv. & conj.** archaic or formal at which.

**whereby** ● **rel. adv.** by which.

**wherefore** archaic ● **interrog. adv.** for what reason. ● **rel. adv. & conj.** as a result of which.

**wherefrom** ● **rel. adv.** archaic from which or from where.

**wherein** ● **adv.** formal **1** in which. **2** in what place or respect?

**whereof** /wɛːrˈɒv/ ● **rel. adv.** formal of what or which.

**whereon** ● **rel. adv.** archaic on which.

**wheresoever** ● **adv. & conj.** formal word for **WHEREVER**.

**whereto** /wɛːˈtuː/ ● **rel. adv.** archaic or formal to which.

**whereupon** ● **conj.** immediately after which.

**wherever** ● **rel. adv.** in or to whatever place. ● **interrog. adv.** used for emphasis instead of 'where' in questions. ● **conj.** in every case when.

**wherewith** ● **rel. adv.** formal or archaic with or by which.

**wherewithal** ● **n.** the money or other resources needed for a particular purpose: *they lacked the wherewithal to pay.*

**wherry** /ˈwɛri/ ● **n.** (pl. **-ies**) a light rowing boat used chiefly for carrying passengers. ➤ Brit. a large light barge.
– DERIVATIVES **wherryman** n. (pl. **-men**).
– ORIGIN ME: of unknown origin.

**whet** /wɛt/ ● **v.** (**whetted**, **whetting**) **1** sharpen the blade of (a tool or weapon). **2** excite or stimulate (someone's desire, interest, or appetite). ● **n.** archaic a thing that stimulates appetite or desire.
– DERIVATIVES **whetter** n. (rare).
– ORIGIN OE *hwettan*, of Gmc origin, based on an adjective meaning 'sharp'.

**whether** ● **conj.** expressing a doubt or choice between alternatives. ➤ expressing an enquiry or investigation. ➤ indicating that a statement applies whichever of the alternatives mentioned is the case.
– PHRASES **whether or no 1** whether or not. **2** archaic in any case.
– ORIGIN OE *hwæther*, *hwether*, of Gmc origin.

**whetstone** ● **n.** a fine-grained stone used for sharpening cutting tools.

**whew** /hwjuː, fjuː/ ● **exclam.** used to express surprise, relief, or a feeling of being very hot or tired.
– ORIGIN ME: imitative; cf. **PHEW**.

**whey** /weɪ/ ● **n.** the watery part of milk that remains after the formation of curds.
– ORIGIN OE *hwæg*, *hweg*, of Gmc origin.

**whey-faced** ● **adj.** (of a person) pale, especially as a result of ill health, shock, or fear.

**which** ● **interrog. pron. & det.** asking for information specifying one or more people or things from a definite set. ● **rel. pron. & det.** used referring to something previously mentioned when introducing a clause giving further information.
– ORIGIN OE *hwilc*, from the Gmc bases of **WHO** and **ALIKE**.

**whichaway** US informal or dialect ● **interrog. adv. 1** in which direction? **2** how? ● **rel. adv.** however.
– PHRASES **every whichaway** in a disorderly fashion.

**whichever** ● **rel. det. & pron.** used to emphasize a lack of restriction in selecting one of a definite set of alternatives. ➤ regardless of which.

**whichsoever** ● **det. & pron.** archaic whichever.

**whicker** ● **v.** (of a horse) give a soft breathy whinny. ● **n.** a sound of this type.
– ORIGIN C17 (in the sense 'to snigger, titter'): imitative.

**whidah** ● **n.** archaic spelling of **WHYDAH**.

**whiff**[1] ● **n. 1** a smell that is smelt only briefly or faintly. ➤ Brit. informal an unpleasant smell. **2** a trace or hint of something bad or exciting: *a whiff of danger.* **3** a puff or breath of air or smoke. **4** N. Amer. informal an unsuccessful attempt to hit a ball. ● **v. 1** get a brief or faint smell of. ➤ Brit. informal give off an unpleasant smell. **2** N. Amer. informal try unsuccessfully to hit a ball.
– DERIVATIVES **whiffy** adj. (**-ier**, **-iest**) (Brit. informal).
– ORIGIN C16: imitative.

**whiff**[2] ● **n.** another term for **MEGRIM**[2].
– ORIGIN C18: perh. from **WHIFF**[1].

**whiffle** ● **v.** (of the wind) blow lightly in a specified direction. ➤ blow or move with a puff of air. ● **n.** a slight movement of air.
– ORIGIN C16: frequentative (v.), dimin. (n.) of **WHIFF**[1].

**whiffletree** ● **n.** N. Amer. a swingletree.
– ORIGIN C19: var. of **WHIPPLETREE**.

**Whig** ● **n. 1** a member of the British reforming party that sought the supremacy of Parliament, succeeded in the 19th century by the Liberal Party. **2** a supporter of the American Revolution. ➤ a member of a 19th-century American political party succeeded by the Republicans. **3** a 17th-century Scottish Presbyterian.
– DERIVATIVES **Whiggery** n. **Whiggish** adj. **Whiggism** n.
– ORIGIN prob. a shortening of Scots *whiggamore*, the nickname of C17 Sc. rebels, from *whig* 'to drive' + **MARE**[1].

**while** ● **n. 1** (**a while**) a period of time. ➤ for some time. **2** (**the while**) at the same time; meanwhile. ➤ poetic/literary during the time that. ● **conj. 1** at the same time as. **2** whereas (indicating a contrast). ➤ although. ● **rel. adv.** during which. ● **v.** (**while time away**) pass time in a leisurely manner. ● **prep.** N. English until.
– PHRASES **worth while** (or **worth one's while**) worth the

time or effort spent.
– ORIGIN OE *hwīl* 'period of time', of Gmc origin; the conjunction is an abbrev. of OE *thā hwīle the* 'the while that'.

**whiles** ● conj. archaic form of **WHILE**.
– ORIGIN ME: orig. in adverbs such as *somewhiles* 'formerly', *otherwhiles* 'at times'.

**whilom** /ˈwʌɪləm/ archaic ● adv. formerly. ● adj. former.
– ORIGIN OE *hwīlum* 'at times', dative pl. of *hwīl* (see **WHILE**).

**whilst** ● conj. & rel. adv. chiefly Brit. while.
– ORIGIN ME: from **WHILES** + *-t* as in **AGAINST**.

**whim** ● n. **1** a sudden desire or change of mind, especially one that is unusual or unexplained. **2** archaic a windlass for raising ore or water from a mine.
– ORIGIN C17: of unknown origin.

**whimbrel** /ˈwɪmbr(ə)l/ ● n. a small migratory curlew with a striped crown and a trilling call. [*Numenius phaeopus*.]
– ORIGIN C16: from **WHIMPER** or synonymous dial. *whimp* (imitative of the bird's call) + **-REL**.

**whimper** ● v. make a series of low, feeble sounds expressive of fear, pain, or discontent. ● n. a whimpering sound.
– DERIVATIVES **whimperer** n. **whimpering** adj. **whimperingly** adv.
– ORIGIN C16: from dial. *whimp* 'to whimper', of imitative origin.

**whimsical** ● adj. **1** playfully quaint or fanciful, especially in an appealing and amusing way. **2** acting or behaving in a capricious manner.
– DERIVATIVES **whimsicality** n. **whimsically** adv.

**whimsy** (also **whimsey**) ● n. (pl. **-ies** or **-eys**) **1** playfully quaint or fanciful behaviour or humour. ➤ a thing that is fanciful or odd. **2** a whim.
– ORIGIN C17 (in the sense 'caprice'): prob. based on **WHIM-WHAM**.

**whim-wham** ● n. archaic **1** a quaint and decorative object; a trinket. **2** a whim.
– ORIGIN C16: fanciful reduplication.

**whin**[1] ● n. chiefly N. English furze; gorse.
– ORIGIN ME: prob. of Scand. origin.

**whin**[2] (also **whinstone**) ● n. Brit. hard, dark basaltic rock.
– ORIGIN ME: of unknown origin.

**whinchat** /ˈwɪntʃat/ ● n. a small songbird related to the stonechat, with a brown back and orange-buff underparts. [*Saxicola rubetra*.]
– ORIGIN C17: from **WHIN**[1] + **CHAT**[2].

**whine** ● n. **1** a long, high-pitched complaining cry. ➤ a long, high-pitched unpleasant sound. **2** a feeble or petulant complaint. ● v. **1** give or make a whine. **2** complain in a feeble or petulant way.
– DERIVATIVES **whiner** n. **whining** adj. **whiningly** adv. **whiny** adj.
– ORIGIN OE *hwīnan* 'whistle through the air', rel. to **WHINGE**.

**whinge** Brit. informal ● v. (**whingeing**) complain persistently and peevishly. ● n. an act of whingeing.
– DERIVATIVES **whingeing** adj. **whingeingly** adv. **whinger** n. **whingy** adj.
– ORIGIN OE *hwinsian*, of Gmc origin; cf. **WHINE**.

**whinny** ● n. (pl. **-ies**) a gentle, high-pitched neigh. ● v. (**-ies, -ied**) (of a horse) make such a sound.
– ORIGIN ME: imitative.

**whinstone** ● n. another term for **WHIN**[2].

**whip** ● n. **1** a strip of leather or length of cord fastened to a handle, used for beating a person or urging on an animal. **2** an official of a political party appointed to maintain parliamentary discipline among its members, especially so as to ensure attendance and voting in debates. ➤ Brit. a written notice from such an official requesting attendance for voting. ➤ (**the whip**) Brit. party membership of a Member of Parliament. **3** a dessert made from cream or eggs beaten into a light fluffy mass. **4** a violent striking or beating movement. **5** short for **WHIPPER-IN**. **6** a slender, unbranched shoot or plant. **7** N. Amer. a scythe for cutting specified crops. **8** a rope-and-pulley hoisting apparatus. ● v. (**whipped, whipping**) **1** beat with a whip. ➤ (of a flexible object or rain or wind) strike or beat violently. ➤ informal defeat heavily in a sporting contest. ➤ (**whip someone up**) deliberately excite or provoke someone. ➤ (**whip something up**) stimulate a particular feeling in someone. **2** move or take out fast or suddenly. ➤ (**whip something up**) make or prepare something, especially food, very quickly. **3** beat (cream, eggs, or other food) into a froth. **4** Brit. informal steal. **5** (**whip in**) Hunting act as whipper-in. **6** bind with spirally wound twine. ➤ sew or gather with overcast stitches. **7** [as adj. **whipped**] N. Amer. informal worn out; exhausted.
– PHRASES **the whip hand** a position of power or control.
– DERIVATIVES **whip-like** adj. **whipper** n. **whipping** n.
– ORIGIN ME: prob. from Mid. Low Ger. and MDu. *wippen* 'swing, leap, dance', from a Gmc base meaning 'move quickly'.

**whip aerial** (also **whip antenna**) ● n. an aerial in the form of a long flexible wire or rod.

**whipbird** ● n. a long-tailed Australian songbird of the logrunner family, with a call like the crack of a whip. [Genus *Psophodes*: two species.]

**whipcord** ● n. **1** thin, tough, tightly twisted cord used for making the flexible end part of whips. **2** a closely woven ribbed worsted fabric, used for making garments such as jodhpurs.

**whip graft** ● n. (in horticulture) a simple graft in which both stock and scion are cut diagonally.

**whiplash** ● n. **1** the lashing action of a whip. ➤ the flexible part of a whip. **2** injury caused by a severe jerk to the head, typically in a motor accident. ● v. jerk suddenly.

**whipless** ● adj. Brit. (of an MP) having formally relinquished, or been deprived of, party membership.

**whip pan** ● n. a camera panning movement fast enough to give a blurred picture. ● v. (**whip-pan**) pan quickly to give a blurred picture.

**whipper-in** ● n. (pl. **whippers-in**) a huntsman's assistant who brings straying hounds back into the pack.

**whippersnapper** ● n. informal a young and inexperienced person who is presumptuous or overconfident.
– ORIGIN C17: perh. representing *whipsnapper*, expressing noise and unimportance.

**whippet** ● n. a dog of a small slender breed originally produced as a cross between the greyhound and the terrier or spaniel, bred for racing.
– ORIGIN C17: partly from obs. *whippet* 'move briskly'.

**whipping boy** ● n. a person who is blamed or punished for the faults or incompetence of others.
– ORIGIN C17: orig. denoting a boy educated with a young prince and punished instead of him.

**whipping post** ● n. historical a post to which offenders were tied to be whipped as a public punishment.

**whippletree** /ˈwɪp(ə)ltriː/ ● n. archaic term for **SWINGLETREE**.
– ORIGIN C18: appar. from **WHIP** + **TREE**.

**whippoorwill** /ˈwɪpəwɪl/ ● n. a North and Central American nightjar with a distinctive call. [*Caprimulgus vociferus*.]
– ORIGIN C18: imitative of its call.

**whippy** ● adj. flexible; springy.
– DERIVATIVES **whippiness** n.

**whip-round** ● n. Brit. informal a collection of contributions of money for a particular purpose.

**whipsaw** ● n. a saw with a narrow blade and a handle at both ends, used typically by two people. ● v. (past part. **-sawn** or **-sawed**) N. Amer. **1** cut with a whipsaw. **2** informal subject to two difficult situations or opposing pressures at the same time. **3** informal cheat or exploit.

**whip scorpion** ● n. a scorpion-like arachnid with a long slender tail. [Order Uropygi.]

**whip snake** ● n. a slender, fast-moving snake. [*Coluber viridiflavus* (Eurasia), *Desmansia psammophis* (Australia, venomous), and other species.]

**whipstitch** ● n. an overcast stitch.

**whipworm** ● n. a parasitic nematode worm with a slender anterior part, especially one that infests the intestines of domestic animals. [Genus *Trichuris*.]

**whir** ● n. & v. variant spelling of **WHIRR**.

**whirl** ● v. move or cause to move rapidly round and round. ➤ move rapidly. ➤ (of the head or mind) seem to spin round. ● n. **1** a rapid movement round and round. **2** frantic activity: *the mad social whirl.* **3** a sweet or biscuit with a spiral shape: *a hazelnut whirl.*
– PHRASES **give something a whirl** informal give something a try. **in a whirl** in a state of confusion.
– DERIVATIVES **whirler** n. **whirling** adj. **whirlingly** adv.
– ORIGIN ME: the verb prob. from ON *hvirfla* 'turn about'; the noun partly from Mid. Low Ger., MDu. *wervel* 'spindle', or from ON *hvirfill* 'circle', from a Gmc base meaning 'rotate'.

**whirligig** ● n. **1** a toy that spins round, e.g. a top or windmill. **2** another term for **ROUNDABOUT** (in sense 2). **3** (also **whirligig beetle**) a small black water beetle which typically swims rapidly in circles on the surface. [Family Gyrinidae.]
– ORIGIN ME: from **WHIRL** + obs. *gig* 'toy for whipping'.

**whirlpool** ● n. **1** a quickly rotating mass of water in a river or sea into which objects may be drawn. **2** (also **whirlpool bath**) a heated pool in which hot aerated water is continuously circulated.

**whirlwind** ● n. **1** a column of air moving rapidly round and round in a cylindrical or funnel shape. **2** a very energetic or tumultuous person or process: *a whirlwind of activity.* ➤ [as modifier] very rapid and unexpected: *a whirlwind romance.*
– PHRASES (**sow the wind and**) **reap the whirlwind** suffer serious consequences as a result of one's actions. [with biblical allusion to Hos. 8:7.]

**whirlybird** ● n. informal, chiefly N. Amer. a helicopter.

**whirr** (also **whir**) ● v. (**whirred**, **whirring**) (of something rapidly rotating or moving to and fro) make a low, continuous, regular sound. ● n. a whirring sound.
– ORIGIN ME: prob. of Scand. origin; cf. **WHIRL**.

**whisht** /(h)wɪʃt/ (also **wheesht**, **whist**) ● exclam. chiefly Scottish & Irish hush!
– PHRASES **hold one's whisht** keep silent.
– ORIGIN natural exclam.: first recorded in Engl. in C16.

**whisk** ● v. **1** move or take suddenly, quickly, and lightly. **2** beat (a substance, especially cream or eggs) with a light, rapid movement. ● n. **1** a utensil for whipping eggs or cream. **2** a bunch of grass, twigs, or bristles for flicking away dust or flies. **3** a brief, rapid action or movement.
– ORIGIN ME: of Scand. origin.

**whisker** ● n. **1** a long projecting hair or bristle growing from the face or snout of an animal such as a cat. ➤ (**whiskers**) the hair growing on a man's face, especially on his cheeks. **2** (**a whisker**) informal a very small amount. **3** a single crystal of a material in the form of a filament with no dislocations.
– PHRASES **have** (or **have grown**) **whiskers** informal (especially of a story) be very old.
– DERIVATIVES **whiskered** adj. **whiskery** adj.
– ORIGIN ME (orig. denoting a bundle of feathers, twigs, etc., used for whisking): from **WHISK** + **-ER**[1].

**whisky** ● n. (pl. **-ies**) **1** (also Irish & US **whiskey**) a spirit distilled from malted grain, especially barley or rye. **2** (**whiskey**) a code word representing the letter W, used in radio communication.
– ORIGIN C18: abbrev. of obs. *whiskybae*, var. of **USQUEBAUGH**.

**whisky mac** ● n. a drink consisting of whisky and ginger wine mixed in equal amounts.

**whisky sour** ● n. a drink consisting of whisky mixed with lemon or lime juice.

**whisper** ● v. speak very softly using one's breath rather than one's throat. ➤ poetic/literary rustle or murmur softly. ➤ (**be whispered**) be rumoured. ● n. **1** a whispered word or phrase, or a whispering tone of voice. ➤ poetic/literary a soft rustling or murmuring sound. ➤ a rumour or piece of gossip. **2** a slight trace; a hint: *a whisper of interest.*
– DERIVATIVES **whisperer** n. **whispery** adj.
– ORIGIN OE *hwisprian*, of Gmc origin, from the imitative base of **WHISTLE**.

**whispering campaign** ● n. a systematic circulation of a rumour, especially in order to damage someone's reputation.

**whispering gallery** ● n. a gallery or dome with acoustic properties such that a faint sound may be heard round its entire circumference.

**whist**[1] /wɪst/ ● n. a card game, usually for two pairs of players, in which points are scored according to the number of tricks won.
– ORIGIN C17 (earlier as *whisk*): perh. from **WHISK** (with ref. to whisking away the tricks); perh. assoc. with **WHIST**[2].

**whist**[2] /(h)wɪst/ ● exclam. variant spelling of **WHISHT**.

**whistle** ● n. **1** a clear, high-pitched sound made by forcing breath through a small hole between partly closed lips, or between one's teeth. ➤ any similar sound. **2** an instrument used to produce such a sound, especially for giving a signal. **3** Brit. informal a suit. [from rhyming sl. *whistle and flute.*] ● v. **1** emit or produce a whistle. ➤ produce (a tune) in such a way. ➤ move rapidly through the air or a narrow opening with a whistling sound. **2** blow a whistle. **3** (**whistle for**) wish for or expect (something) in vain.
– PHRASES **blow the whistle on** informal bring (an illicit activity) to an end by informing on the person responsible. (**as**) **clean as a whistle** extremely clean or clear. **whistle something down the wind 1** let go or abandon something. **2** archaic turn a trained hawk loose by casting it off with the wind. **whistle in the dark** pretend to be unafraid.
– DERIVATIVES **whistler** n.
– ORIGIN OE *(h)wistlian* (v.), *(h)wistle* (n.), of Gmc origin; imitative.

**whistle-blower** ● n. informal a person who informs on someone engaged in an illicit activity.
– DERIVATIVES **whistle-blowing** n. & adj.

**whistle-stop** ● adj. very fast and with only brief pauses: *a whistle-stop tour.* ● n. N. Amer. a small unimportant town on a railway.

**whistling swan** ● n. a bird of the North American race of the tundra swan. [*Cygnus columbianus columbianus.*]

**Whit** ● n. short for **WHITSUNTIDE**.

**whit** ● n. a very small part or amount.
– PHRASES **every whit** wholly. **not a whit** not at all.
– ORIGIN ME: appar. an alt. of obs. *wight* 'small amount'.

**white** ● adj. **1** of the colour of milk or fresh snow, due to the reflection of all visible rays of light. ➤ very pale. ➤ Brit. (of coffee or tea) served with milk or cream. ➤ (of food such as bread or rice) light in colour through having been refined. **2** relating to or denoting a human group having light-coloured skin, especially of European ancestry. **3** morally or spiritually pure. **4** (of wine) made from white grapes, or dark grapes with the skins removed, and having a yellowish colour. **5** (**White**) historical counter-revolutionary or reactionary. ● n. **1** white colour or pigment. ➤ (also **whites**) white clothes or material. **2** (**White**) the player of the white pieces in chess or draughts. **3** the visible pale part of the eyeball around the iris. **4** the outer part (white when cooked) which surrounds the yolk of an egg; the albumen. **5** a member of a light-skinned people. **6** a white or cream butterfly. [*Pieris brassicae* (**large white**), *P. rapae* (**small white**, both crop pests), and other species.] ● v. **1** (usu. **white something out**) turn (something) white. ➤ obliterate (a mistake) with white correction fluid. **2** (**white out**) lose colour vision as a prelude to losing consciousness.
– PHRASES **bleed someone/thing white** drain of wealth or resources. **whited sepulchre** poetic/literary a hypocrite. [with biblical allusion to Matt 23:27.]
– DERIVATIVES **whitely** adv. **whiten** v. **whitener** n. **whiteness** n. **whitish** adj.
– ORIGIN OE *hwīt*, of Gmc origin; rel. to **WHEAT**.

**white admiral** ● n. a butterfly with dark brown wings bearing a broad white band. [*Ladoga camilla* (Europe) and other species.]

**white ant** ● n. another term for **TERMITE**.

**white arsenic** ● n. arsenic trioxide, an extremely toxic soluble white solid.

**whitebait** ● n. the small silvery-white young of herrings, sprats, and similar marine fish as food.

**whitebeam** ● n. a tree related to the rowan, with red

berries and hairy oval leaves that are white underneath. [*Sorbus aria*.]

**white belt** • n. a white belt worn by a beginner in judo or karate.

**whiteboard** • n. a wipeable board with a white surface used for teaching or presentations.

**white-bread** • adj. N. Amer. informal bland and unchallenging in a way thought characteristic of the white middle classes.

**white cell** • n. less technical term for LEUCOCYTE.

**white Christmas** • n. a Christmas during which there is snow on the ground.

**white-collar** • adj. of or relating to the work done or people who work in an office or other professional environment.

**white currant** • n. a cultivated variety of redcurrant with pale edible berries.

**white dwarf** • n. Astronomy a small, very dense star that is typically the size of a planet.

**white elephant** • n. a possession that is useless or troublesome, especially one that is expensive to maintain or difficult to dispose of.
– ORIGIN from the story that the kings of Siam gifted such animals to courtiers they disliked, in order to ruin the recipient by the great expense incurred in maintaining the animal.

**white ensign** • n. a white flag carrying a St George's cross with the Union Jack in the top corner next to the flagstaff, flown by the Royal Navy and the Royal Yacht Squadron.

**white-eye** • n. a small songbird with a ring of white feathers around the eye. [*Zosterops* and other genera.]

**whiteface** • n. **1** white stage make-up. **2** chiefly N. Amer. a Hereford cow or bull.

**white feather** • n. a white feather given to someone as a sign that they are considered a coward.
– ORIGIN C18: with ref. to a white feather in the tail of a game bird, being a mark of bad breeding.

**whitefish** • n. (pl. same or **-fishes**) a mainly freshwater fish of the salmon family, widely used as food. [*Coregonus* and other genera: several species.]

**white fish** • n. fish with pale flesh, such as cod, plaice, and haddock. Compare with RED FISH.

**white flag** • n. a white flag or cloth used as a symbol of surrender, truce, or a desire to parley.

**whitefly** • n. (pl. same or **-flies**) a minute winged bug covered with powdery white wax, damaging plants by feeding on sap and coating them with honeydew. [Family Aleyrodidae: many species.]

**white gold** • n. a silver-coloured alloy of gold with nickel, platinum, or another metal.

**white goods** • pl. n. **1** large domestic electrical goods such as refrigerators and washing machines. Compare with BROWN GOODS. **2** archaic domestic linen.

**whitehead** • n. **1** informal a pale or white-topped pustule on the skin. **2** a small New Zealand songbird with a white head and underparts. [*Mohoua albicilla*.]

**white heat** • n. the temperature or state of something that is so hot that it emits white light.

**white hole** • n. a hypothetical opposite of a black hole, from which matter and energy emerge.

**white hope** (also **great white hope**) • n. a person expected to bring much success to a team or organization.

**white horses** • pl. n. white-crested waves at sea.

**white-hot** • adj. so hot as to glow white.

**white information** • n. positive information about a person's creditworthiness.

**white knight** • n. a person or thing that comes to someone's aid. ➤ a person or company making an acceptable counter offer for a company facing a hostile takeover bid.

**white-knuckle** • adj. causing fear or nervous excitement: *a white-knuckle ride.*
– ORIGIN 1970s: with ref. to the effect caused by gripping tightly to steady oneself.

**white-label** • adj. denoting a musical recording for which the printed commercial label is not yet available, issued with a plain white label before general release for promotional purposes.

**white land** • n. open land not designated for development or change of use, or on which development is not allowed.

**white lead** • n. a white pigment consisting of a mixture of lead carbonate and lead hydroxide.

**white lie** • n. a harmless lie told to avoid hurting someone's feelings.

**white light** • n. apparently colourless light containing all the wavelengths of the visible spectrum at equal intensity (such as ordinary daylight).

**white lightning** • n. N. Amer. illicit home-made whiskey, typically colourless and distilled from corn.

**white lime** • n. whitewash.

**white list** • n. informal a list of people or products viewed with approval.

**white magic** • n. magic used only for good purposes.

**white matter** • n. the paler tissue of the brain and spinal cord, consisting mainly of nerve fibres with their myelin sheaths.

**white meat** • n. pale meat such as poultry, veal, and rabbit.

**white metal** • n. a white or silvery alloy, especially a tin-based alloy used for the surfaces of bearings.

**white mouse** • n. an albino form of the house mouse.

**white night** • n. **1** a sleepless night. [translating Fr. *nuit blanche*.] **2** a night when it is never properly dark, as in high latitudes in summer.

**white noise** • n. Physics noise containing many frequencies with equal intensities.

**white-out** • n. **1** a dense blizzard. ➤ a weather condition in which the features and horizon of snow-covered country are indistinguishable due to uniform light diffusion. **2** white correction fluid for covering typing mistakes.

**White Paper** • n. (in the UK) a government report giving information or proposals on an issue.

**white park cattle** • pl. n. white cattle with dark ears and muzzles, belonging to an ancient semi-wild breed kept in certain parks in Britain.

**white pointer** • n. another term for GREAT WHITE SHARK.

**white poplar** • n. a poplar with lobed leaves that are white underneath and grey-green above. [*Populus alba*.]

**white pudding** • n. a kind of sausage made of oatmeal and suet.

**white rose** • n. the emblem of Yorkshire or the House of York.

**White Russian** • n. **1** a Belorussian. **2** an opponent of the Bolsheviks during the Russian Civil War. • adj. of or relating to White Russians.

**white sauce** • n. a sauce consisting of flour blended and cooked with butter and milk or stock.

**white shark** • n. see GREAT WHITE SHARK.

**white-shoe** • adj. US informal denoting a law firm or other company run by members of the Wasp elite and regarded as conservative.
– ORIGIN with ref. to the white shoes fashionable among Ivy League college students in the 1950s.

**white slave** • n. a woman tricked or forced into prostitution in a foreign country.
– DERIVATIVES **white slaver** n. **white slavery** n.

**whitesmith** • n. a person who makes articles out of metal, especially tin.
– ORIGIN ME: from WHITE (denoting 'white iron', i.e. tin) + SMITH.

**white spirit** • n. Brit. a volatile colourless liquid distilled from petroleum, used as a paint thinner and solvent.

**whitethorn** • n. the hawthorn.

**whitethroat** • n. a migratory warbler with a grey head and white throat. [*Sylvia communis* and related species.]

**white tie** • n. a white bow tie worn by men as part of full evening dress. ➤ full evening dress.

**white trash** • n. N. Amer. derogatory poor white people, especially those living in the southern US.

**white-van man** ● **n.** Brit. informal an aggressive male driver of a delivery or workman's van (typically white in colour).

**white vitriol** ● **n.** archaic crystalline zinc sulphate.

**whitewall** ● **n. 1** a tyre with a white stripe round the outside, or a white side wall. **2** [as modifier] N. Amer. denoting a haircut in which the sides of the head are shaved and the top and back are left longer.

**whitewash** ● **n. 1** a solution of lime and water or of whiting, size, and water, used for painting walls white. **2** a deliberate concealment of someone's mistakes or faults. **3** a victory by the same side in every game of a series. ● **v. 1** paint with whitewash. **2** conceal (mistakes or faults). **3** defeat with a whitewash.
– DERIVATIVES **whitewashed** adj. **whitewasher** n.

**white water** ● **n.** a fast shallow stretch of water in a river.

**white wedding** ● **n.** Brit. a traditional wedding at which the bride wears a formal white dress.

**white whale** ● **n.** another term for **BELUGA** (in sense 1).

**white witch** ● **n.** a practitioner of witchcraft for altruistic purposes.

**whitewood** ● **n.** light-coloured wood, especially when made up into furniture and ready for staining, varnishing, or painting.

**whitework** ● **n.** embroidery worked in white thread on a white ground.

**whitey** ● **n.** (pl. **-eys**) informal, derogatory a white person. ● **adj.** with a whitish tinge.

**whither** archaic or poetic/literary ● **interrog. adv.** to what place or state. ➤what is the likely future of. ● **rel. adv.** to which (with reference to a place). ➤to whatever place.
– ORIGIN OE *hwider*, from the Gmc base of **WHICH**; cf. **HITHER** and **THITHER**.

**whithersoever** ● **rel. adv.** archaic wherever.

**whiting**[1] ● **n.** (pl. same) a slender-bodied marine fish with edible white flesh. [*Merlangius merlangus* (cod family, shallow European waters), and other species.]
– ORIGIN ME: from MDu. *wijting*, from *wijt* 'white'.

**whiting**[2] ● **n.** ground chalk used for purposes such as whitewashing and cleaning metal plate.

**whitleather** ● **n.** leather that has been dressed with alum and salt so as to retain its natural colour.
– ORIGIN ME: from **WHITE** + **LEATHER**.

**whitlow** /ˈwɪtləʊ/ ● **n.** an abscess in the soft tissue near a fingernail or toenail.
– ORIGIN ME (also as *whitflaw*, *-flow*), appar. from **WHITE** + **FLAW**[1] in the sense 'crack', but perh. rel. to Du. *fijt* 'whitlow'.

**whitlow grass** ● **n.** a dwarf plant with small white flowers, formerly believed to cure whitlows. [*Erophila verna* and related species.]

**Whitsun** /ˈwɪts(ə)n/ ● **n.** Whitsuntide.
– ORIGIN ME: from **WHIT SUNDAY**.

**Whit Sunday** ● **n.** the seventh Sunday after Easter, a Christian festival commemorating the descent of the Holy Spirit at Pentecost (Acts 2).
– ORIGIN OE *Hwīta Sunnandæg*, lit. 'white Sunday', prob. with ref. to the white robes of those newly baptized at Pentecost.

**Whitsuntide** /ˈwɪts(ə)ntʌɪd/ ● **n.** the weekend or week including Whit Sunday.

**whittle** ● **v. 1** carve (wood) by repeatedly cutting small slices from it. ➤make by whittling. **2** (**whittle something away/down**) reduce something by degrees.
– ORIGIN C16: from dial. *whittle* 'knife'.

**Whitworth** ● **n.** [as modifier] denoting a standard series of screw threads in imperial sizes.
– ORIGIN C19: from the name of the Engl. engineer Sir Joseph *Whitworth*.

**whiz-bang** (also **whizz-bang**) informal ● **n. 1** (especially during the First World War) a low-velocity shell. **2** chiefly N. Amer. a resounding success. ● **adj.** chiefly N. Amer. impressively lively and fast-paced.

**whizz** (also **whiz**) ● **v.** (**whizzed**, **whizzing**) **1** move quickly through the air with a whistling or whooshing sound. ➤move or cause to move or go fast. ➤(**whizz through**) do or deal with quickly. **2** informal urinate. ● **n. 1** a whizzing sound. **2** informal a fast movement or brief journey. **3** (also **wiz**) informal a person who is extremely clever at something. [C20: influenced by **WIZARD**.] **4** informal an act of urinating. **5** Brit. informal amphetamines.
– DERIVATIVES **whizzy** adj.
– ORIGIN C16: imitative.

**whizz-kid** (also **whiz-kid**) ● **n.** informal a young person who is very successful or highly skilled.

**whizzo** (also **wizzo**) ● **adj.** informal excellent.

**WHO** ● **abbrev.** World Health Organization.

**who** ● **pron. 1** [interrog. pron.] what or which person or people. **2** [rel. pron.] introducing a clause giving further information about a person or people previously mentioned. ➤archaic the person that; whoever.
– ORIGIN OE *hwā*, of Gmc origin.

> **USAGE** who
>
> According to formal grammar, **who** forms the subjective case, while **whom** forms the objective case and so should be used in object position in a sentence. In modern English there are many speakers who rarely use **whom** at all, employing **who** in all contexts; today this use is broadly accepted in standard English.

**whoa** /wəʊ/ (also **wo**) ● **exclam.** used as a command to a horse to stop or slow down.
– ORIGIN ME: var. of **HO**[1].

**who'd** ● **contr. 1** who had. **2** who would.

**whodunnit** (US **whodunit**) ● **n.** informal a story or play about a murder in which the identity of the murderer is not revealed until the end.
– ORIGIN 1930s: from *who done it?*, non-standard form of *who did it?*

**whoever** ● **rel. pron.** the person or people who; any person who. ➤regardless of who. ● **interrog. pron.** used for emphasis instead of 'who' in questions.

**whole** ● **adj. 1** complete; entire. ➤emphasizing a large extent or number: *a whole range of issues.* **2** in an unbroken or undamaged state. ➤with no part removed. ● **n. 1** a thing that is complete in itself. **2** (**the whole**) all of something. ● **adv.** informal emphasizing the novelty or distinctness of something: *a whole new meaning.*
– PHRASES **as a whole** in general. **in whole** entirely or fully. **on the whole** taking everything into account; in general. **the whole nine yards** informal, chiefly N. Amer. everything possible or available.
– DERIVATIVES **wholeness** n.
– ORIGIN OE *hāl*, of Gmc origin; rel. to **HAIL**[2].

**whole cloth** ● **n.** cloth of the full size as manufactured, as distinguished from a piece cut off for a garment or other item.
– PHRASES **out of (the) whole cloth** N. Amer. informal totally false.

**wholefood** ● **n.** (also **wholefoods**) Brit. food that has been minimally processed and is free from additives.

**wholehearted** ● **adj.** completely sincere and committed.
– DERIVATIVES **wholeheartedly** adv. **wholeheartedness** n.

**whole-life** ● **adj.** relating to or denoting a life insurance policy that may be realized only on the death of the person insured.

**wholemeal** ● **adj.** Brit. denoting flour or bread made from wholewheat, including the husk.

**whole note** ● **n.** Music, chiefly N. Amer. a semibreve.

**whole number** ● **n.** a number without fractions; an integer.

**wholesale** ● **n.** the selling of goods in large quantities to be retailed by others. ● **adv. 1** being sold in such a way. **2** on a large scale. ● **adj.** done on a large scale; extensive. ● **v.** sell (goods) wholesale.
– DERIVATIVES **wholesaler** n.
– ORIGIN ME: orig. as *by whole sale* 'in large quantities'.

**wholescale** ● **adj.** another term for **WHOLESALE**.

**wholesome** ● **adj.** conducive to or suggestive of good health and physical well-being. ➤conducive to or promoting moral well-being.

– DERIVATIVES **wholesomely** adv. **wholesomeness** n.
– ORIGIN ME: prob. already in OE (see **WHOLE**, **-SOME**[1]).

**whole step** ● n. Music an interval of a (whole) tone.

**whole-tone scale** ● n. Music a scale consisting entirely of intervals of a tone, with no semitones.

**wholewheat** ● n. whole grains of wheat including the husk.

**wholly** /ˈhəʊlli, ˈhəʊli/ ● adv. entirely; fully.
– ORIGIN ME: prob. already in OE (see **WHOLE**, **-LY**[2]).

**whom** ● pron. used instead of 'who' as the object of a verb or preposition.

**USAGE** whom

On the use of **who** and **whom**, see **WHO**.

**whomever** ● pron. chiefly formal used instead of 'whoever' as the object of a verb or preposition.

**whomp** /wɒmp/ informal ● v. **1** strike heavily; thump. **2** (**whomp something up**) N. Amer. produce something quickly. ● n. a thump.
– ORIGIN 1920s: imitative.

**whomso** ● pron. archaic used instead of 'whoso' as the object of a verb or preposition.

**whomsoever** ● rel. pron. formal used instead of 'whosoever' as the object of a verb or preposition.

**whoomph** /wʊm(p)f/ (also **whoomp** /wʊmp/) ● n. a loud muffled sound.
– ORIGIN 1950s: imitative.

**whoop** /huːp, wuːp/ ● n. **1** a loud cry of joy or excitement. **2** a long rasping indrawn breath. **3** (in motorcycling or cycling) a bump or dip on an off-road track. ● v. give or make a whoop.
– PHRASES **whoop it up** informal enjoy oneself or celebrate unrestrainedly. ➤ N. Amer. create a stir.
– ORIGIN ME: prob. imitative.

**whoopee** informal ● exclam. /wʊˈpiː/ expressing wild excitement or joy. ● n. /ˈwʊpi/ wild revelry.
– PHRASES **make whoopee 1** celebrate wildly. **2** have sexual intercourse.

**whoopee cushion** ● n. a rubber cushion that makes a sound like the breaking of wind when someone sits on it.

**whooper** /ˈhuːpə, ˈw-/ ● n. a large migratory swan with a black and yellow bill and a loud trumpeting call, breeding in northern Eurasia and Greenland. [*Cygnus cygnus*.]

**whooping cough** /ˈhuːpɪŋ/ ● n. a contagious bacterial disease chiefly affecting children, characterized by convulsive coughs followed by a whoop.

**whooping crane** /ˈhuːpɪŋ, ˈw-/ ● n. a large mainly white crane with a trumpeting call, breeding in central Canada and now endangered. [*Grus americana*.]

**whoops** (also **whoops-a-daisy**) ● exclam. informal expressing mild dismay.
– ORIGIN 1920s: prob. an alt. of **UPSY-DAISY**; cf. **OOPS**.

**whoosh** /wʊʃ, wuːʃ/ (also **woosh**) ● v. move or cause to move quickly or suddenly and with a rushing sound. ● n. a whooshing movement. ● exclam. used to express such a movement or sound.
– DERIVATIVES **whooshing** adj.
– ORIGIN C19: imitative.

**whop** /wɒp/ (chiefly N. Amer. also **whap**) informal ● v. (**whopped**, **whopping**) hit hard. ● n. a heavy blow or its sound. ➤ the regular pulsing sound of a helicopter rotor.
– ORIGIN ME: var. of dial. *wap* 'strike', of unknown origin.

**whopper** ● n. informal **1** a thing that is extremely large. **2** a gross or blatant lie.

**whopping** ● adj. informal extremely large.

**whore** ● n. derogatory a prostitute or promiscuous woman. ● v. work as a prostitute. ➤ use the services of prostitutes. ➤ debase oneself by doing something for unworthy motives.
– DERIVATIVES **whoredom** n. **whoring** adj. & n. **whorish** adj. **whorishly** adv. **whorishness** n.
– ORIGIN OE *hōre*, of Gmc origin.

**whorehouse** ● n. informal a brothel.

**whoremonger** (also **whoremaster**) ● n. archaic a person who has dealings with prostitutes.

**whoreson** /ˈhɔːs(ə)n/ ● n. archaic a despicable person.
– ORIGIN ME: from **WHORE** + **SON**, suggested by Anglo-Norman Fr. *fiz a putain*.

**whorl** /wɔːl, wəːl/ ● n. **1** Zoology each of the convolutions in the shell of a gastropod or ammonoid mollusc. **2** Botany a set of leaves, flowers, or branches springing from the stem at the same level and encircling it. ➤ Botany (in a flower) each of the sets of organs, especially the petals and sepals, arranged concentrically round the receptacle. **3** a complete circle in a fingerprint. **4** chiefly historical a small wheel or pulley in a spinning wheel, spinning machine, or spindle. ● v. poetic/literary spiral or move in a twisted or convoluted fashion.
– DERIVATIVES **whorled** adj.
– ORIGIN ME (denoting a small flywheel): appar. a var. of **WHIRL**, influenced by OE *wharve* 'whorl of a spindle'.

**whortleberry** /ˈwəːt(ə)l,b(ə)ri, -ˈbɛri/ ● n. a bilberry.
– ORIGIN C16: dial. var. of ME *hurtleberry*, of unknown origin.

**who's** ● contr. **1** who is. **2** who has.

**whose** ● interrog. possess. det. & pron. belonging to or associated with which person. ● rel. possess. det. of whom or which.
– ORIGIN OE *hwæs*, genitive of *hwā* 'who' and *hwæt* 'what'.

**whosesoever** ● rel. pron. & det. formal whoever's.

**whosever** ● rel. pron. & det. belonging to or associated with whichever person; whoever's.

**whoso** ● pron. archaic term for **WHOEVER**.
– ORIGIN ME: shortening OE *swā hwā swā* 'so who so'.

**whosoever** ● pron. formal term for **WHOEVER**.

**who's who** ● n. a list or directory of facts about notable people.

**whump** /wʌmp, wʊmp/ ● n. a dull thud. ● v. make a whump. ➤ strike heavily.
– ORIGIN C19: imitative.

**whup** /wʌp/ ● v. (**whupped**, **whupping**) informal, chiefly N. Amer. beat; thrash.
– ORIGIN C19: var. of **WHIP**.

**why** ● interrog. adv. for what reason or purpose. ● rel. adv. (with reference to a reason) on account of which; for which. ➤ the reason for which. ● exclam. **1** expressing surprise or indignation. **2** used to add emphasis to a response. ● n. (pl. **whys**) a reason or explanation.
– ORIGIN OE *hwī*, *hwȳ* 'by what cause', instrumental case of *hwæt* 'what', of Gmc origin.

**whydah** /ˈwɪdə/ (also **whyda**) ● n. **1** an African weaver bird, the male of which has a black back and a very long black tail used in display flight. [Genus *Vidua*: several species.] **2** another term for **WIDOWBIRD**.
– ORIGIN C18 (orig. *widow-bird*): alt. by assoc. with *Whidah* (now Ouidah), a town in Benin.

**WI** ● abbrev. **1** West Indies. **2** Wisconsin (in official postal use). **3** Brit. Women's Institute.

**wibble** ● v. informal **1** another term for **WOBBLE**. **2** Brit. speak or write at length.
– DERIVATIVES **wibbly** adj.
– ORIGIN C19: independent usage of the first element of the reduplication *wibble-wobble*; sense 2 is perh. a different word and influenced by **DRIVEL**.

**Wicca** /ˈwɪkə/ ● n. the religious cult of modern witchcraft.
– DERIVATIVES **Wiccan** adj. & n.
– ORIGIN representing OE *wicca* 'witch'.

**wick**[1] ● n. **1** a strip of porous material up which liquid fuel is drawn by capillary action to the flame in a candle, lamp, or lighter. **2** Medicine a gauze strip inserted in a wound to drain it. ● v. absorb or draw off (liquid) by capillary action.
– PHRASES **dip one's wick** vulgar slang (of a man) have sexual intercourse. **get on someone's wick** Brit. informal annoy someone.
– ORIGIN OE *wēoce*, of W. Gmc origin.

**wick**[2] ● n. **1** [in place names] a town, hamlet, or district. **2** dialect a dairy farm.
– ORIGIN OE *wīc* 'dwelling place', prob. based on L. *vicus* 'street, village'.

**wick**[3] ● adj. N. English quick; lively.

– ORIGIN C18: var. of **QUICK**.

**wicked** ● adj. (**-er, -est**) **1** evil or morally wrong. **2** playfully mischievous. **3** informal excellent; wonderful.
– DERIVATIVES **wickedly** adv. **wickedness** n.
– ORIGIN ME: prob. from OE *wicca* 'witch' + **-ED**[1].

**wicker** ● n. pliable twigs, typically of willow, plaited or woven to make items such as furniture and baskets.
– DERIVATIVES **wickerwork** n.
– ORIGIN ME: of Scand. origin; cf. Swed. *viker* 'willow'.

**wicket** ● n. **1** Cricket each of the sets of three stumps with two bails across the top at either end of the pitch, defended by a batsman. ➤the prepared strip of ground between these two sets of stumps. ➤the dismissal of a batsman. **2** a small door or gate, especially one beside or in a larger one. ➤N. Amer. an opening in a door or wall. **3** N. Amer. a croquet hoop.
– PHRASES **at the wicket** Cricket **1** batting. **2** by the wicketkeeper. **a sticky wicket 1** Cricket a pitch that has been drying after rain and is difficult to bat on. **2** informal a tricky or awkward situation.
– ORIGIN ME: from Anglo-Norman Fr. and ONorth. Fr. *wiket*; origin uncertain, usu. referred to the Gmc root of ON *vīkja* 'to turn, move'.

**wicketkeeper** ● n. Cricket a fielder stationed close behind a batsman's wicket.
– DERIVATIVES **wicketkeeping** n.

**wickiup** /ˈwɪkɪʌp/ ● n. an American Indian hut consisting of an oval frame covered with brushwood or grass.
– ORIGIN from Algonquian.

**widdershins** /ˈwɪdəʃɪnz/ (also **withershins**) ● adv. chiefly Scottish in a direction contrary to the sun's course (or anticlockwise), considered as unlucky.
– ORIGIN C16: from Mid. Low Ger. *weddersins*, from Mid. High Ger. *widersinnes*, from *wider* 'against' + *sin* 'direction'; the second element was assoc. with Scots *sin* 'sun'.

**widdle** informal ● v. urinate. ● n. an act of urinating. ➤urine.
– ORIGIN 1950s: alt. of **PIDDLE**.

**wide** ● adj. (**wider, widest**) **1** of great or more than average width. ➤(after a measurement and in questions) from side to side. ➤open to the full extent: *wide eyes.* **2** including a great variety of people or things. ➤spread among a large number or over a large area: *wider share ownership.* ➤[in combination] extending over the whole of: *industry-wide.* **3** at a considerable or specified distance from a point or mark. ➤(especially in football) at or near the side of the field. ● adv. **1** to the full extent. **2** far from a particular point or mark. ➤(especially in football) at or near the side of the field. ● n. (also **wide ball**) Cricket a ball that is judged to be too wide of the stumps for the batsman to play.
– PHRASES **wide awake** fully awake. **wide of the mark** a long way from an intended target. ➤inaccurate. **wide open 1** (of a contest) of which the outcome is not predictable. **2** vulnerable to attack.
– DERIVATIVES **widely** adv. **wideness** n. **widish** adj.
– ORIGIN OE *wīd* 'spacious, extensive', *wīde* 'over a large area', of Gmc origin.

**wide-angle** ● adj. (of a lens) having a short focal length and hence a field covering a wide angle.

**wide area network** ● n. a computer network in which the computers connected may be far apart, generally having a radius of more than 1 km.

**wideawake** ● n. a soft felt hat with a low crown and wide brim.
– ORIGIN C19: punningly so named, because the hat does not have a nap.

**widebody** ● adj. (also **wide-bodied**) **1** denoting a jet airliner with a wide fuselage. **2** chiefly US denoting a tennis racket with a wide head. ● n. (pl. **-ies**) a widebody aircraft or tennis racket.

**wide boy** ● n. Brit. informal a man involved in petty criminal activities.

**wide-eyed** ● adj. **1** having one's eyes wide open in amazement. **2** inexperienced; innocent.

**widen** ● v. make or become wider.
– DERIVATIVES **widener** n.

**wideout** ● n. American Football a wide receiver.

**wide receiver** ● n. American Football an offensive player positioned away from the line, used primarily as a pass receiver.

**widescreen** ● adj. denoting a screen or a format used with a screen presenting a wide field of vision in relation to height.

**widespread** ● adj. spread among a large number or over a large area.

**widgeon** ● n. variant spelling of **WIGEON**.

**widger** /ˈwɪdʒə/ ● n. a spatula used in gardening to transplant seedlings.
– ORIGIN 1950s: a word from a nonsense definition used in a series of memory tests.

**widget** /ˈwɪdʒɪt/ ● n. informal a small gadget or mechanical device. ➤Computing a component of a user interface with a particular function.
– ORIGIN 1930s (orig. US): perh. an alt. of **GADGET**.

**widow** ● n. **1** a woman who has lost her husband by death and has not married again. ➤humorous a woman whose husband is often away participating in a specified sport or activity: *a golf widow.* **2** Printing a last word or short last line of a paragraph falling at the top of a page or column. ● v. (**be widowed**) become a widow or widower.
– ORIGIN OE *widewe*, from an Indo-Eur. root meaning 'be empty'.

**widowbird** ● n. **1** an African weaver bird, the male of which has mainly black plumage and typically a long tail used in leaping displays. [Genus *Euplectes*: several species.] **2** another term for **WHYDAH**.

**widower** ● n. a man who has lost his wife by death and has not married again.

**widowhood** ● n. the state or period of being a widow or widower.

**widow's cruse** ● n. an apparently small supply that proves inexhaustible.
– ORIGIN with biblical allusion to 1 Kings 17:10–16.

**widow's mite** ● n. a small monetary contribution from someone who is poor.
– ORIGIN with biblical allusion to Mark 12:43.

**widow's peak** ● n. a V-shaped growth of hair towards the centre of the forehead.

**widow's walk** ● n. N. Amer. a railed or balustraded platform built on a roof in early New England houses, providing an unimpeded view of the sea.
– ORIGIN 1930s: with ref. to its use as a viewpoint for return of a seafaring husband.

**widow's weeds** ● pl. n. black clothes worn by a widow in mourning.
– ORIGIN C18 (earlier as *mourning weeds*): *weeds* (obs. in the general sense 'garments') is from OE *wǣd(e)*, of Gmc origin.

**width** /wɪtθ, wɪdθ/ ● n. **1** the measurement or extent of something from side to side; the lesser of two or the least of three dimensions of a body. ➤a piece of something at its full extent from side to side. **2** wide range or extent.
– ORIGIN C17: from **WIDE** + **-TH**[2], on the pattern of *breadth* (replacing *wideness*).

**widthways** (also **widthwise**) ● adv. in a direction parallel with a thing's width.

**wield** ● v. **1** hold and use (a weapon or tool). **2** have and be able to use (power or influence).
– DERIVATIVES **wielder** n.
– ORIGIN OE *wealdan*, *wieldan* 'govern, subdue, direct', of Gmc origin.

**wieldy** ● adj. (**-ier, -iest**) easily controlled or handled.
– ORIGIN C16: back-form. from **UNWIELDY**.

**wiener** /ˈwiːnə/ (also informal **weenie, wienie** /ˈwiːni/) ● n. N. Amer. **1** a frankfurter or similar sausage. **2** vulgar slang a man's penis. **3** informal a stupid or contemptible person.
– ORIGIN C20: abbrev. of Ger. *Wienerwurst* 'Vienna sausage'.

**Wiener schnitzel** ● n. a thin slice of veal that is breaded and fried.
– ORIGIN from Ger., lit. 'Vienna cutlet'.

**wife** • n. (pl. **wives**) a married woman considered in relation to her husband. ➤ archaic or dialect a woman, especially an old or uneducated one.
– DERIVATIVES **wifehood** n. **wifeless** adj. **wifeliness** n. **wifely** adj.
– ORIGIN OE *wīf* 'woman', of Gmc origin.

**wife-swapping** • n. informal the practice within a group of married couples of exchanging sexual partners on a casual basis.

**wifie** • n. (pl. **-ies**) Scottish a woman.
– ORIGIN C18: dimin. of **WIFE**.

**wig**[1] • n. a covering for the head made of real or artificial hair.
– DERIVATIVES **wigged** adj. **wigless** adj.
– ORIGIN C17: shortening of **PERIWIG**.

**wig**[2] • v. (**wigged**, **wigging**) informal **1** Brit. dated rebuke severely. **2** (**wig out**) chiefly N. Amer. become deliriously excited.
– DERIVATIVES **wigging** n.
– ORIGIN C19: appar. from **WIG**[1], perh. from **BIGWIG** and assoc. with a rebuke given by a person in authority.

**wigeon** /'wɪdʒ(ə)n/ (also **widgeon**) • n. a dabbling duck with mainly reddish-brown and grey plumage, the male having a whistling call. [*Anas penelope* (Eurasia) and *A. americana* (N. America).]
– ORIGIN C16: perh. of imitative origin and suggested by **PIGEON**[1].

**wiggle** • v. move or cause to move with short movements up and down or from side to side. • n. a wiggling movement.
– DERIVATIVES **wiggler** n. **wiggly** adj. (**-ier**, **-iest**).
– ORIGIN ME: from Mid. Low Ger. and MDu. *wiggelen* (frequentative).

**wiggy** • adj. (**-ier**, **-iest**) informal, chiefly N. Amer. emotionally uncontrolled or weird.
– ORIGIN 1960s: from *wig out* (see **WIG**[2]).

**wight** • n. **1** archaic or dialect a person of a specified kind: *an unlucky wight*. **2** poetic/literary a spirit or ghost.
– ORIGIN OE *wiht* 'thing, creature', of Gmc origin.

**wigwag** • v. (**wigwagged**, **wigwagging**) N. Amer. informal **1** move to and fro. **2** signal by waving something.
– ORIGIN C16: reduplication of **WAG**[1].

**wigwam** • n. a dome-shaped or conical dwelling made by fastening mats, skins, or bark over a framework of poles (as used formerly by some North American Indian peoples).
– ORIGIN C17: from Ojibwa *wigwaum*, Algonquian *wikiwam* 'their house'.

**wilco** • exclam. expressing compliance or agreement (used in radio communication).
– ORIGIN 1940s (orig. in military use): abbrev. of *will comply*.

**wild** • adj. **1** (of animals or plants) living or growing in the natural environment; not domesticated or cultivated. ➤ (of people) not civilized; barbarous. ➤ (of scenery or a region) desolate-looking. **2** uncontrolled; unrestrained. ➤ haphazard: *a wild guess*. ➤ informal very enthusiastic or excited. ➤ informal very angry. ➤ (of looks, appearance, etc.) indicating distraction. • n. (**the wild**) a natural state or uncultivated or uninhabited region. ➤ (**the wilds**) a remote area.
– PHRASES **run wild** grow or behave without restraint or discipline. **wild and woolly** uncouth or rough.
– DERIVATIVES **wildish** adj. **wildly** adv. **wildness** n.
– ORIGIN OE *wilde*, of Gmc origin.

**wild arum** • n. another term for **CUCKOO PINT**.

**wild card** • n. **1** a playing card that can have any value, suit, colour, or other property in a game at the discretion of the player holding it. **2** a person or thing whose qualities are uncertain. **3** Computing a character that will match any character or sequence of characters in a search. **4** an opportunity to enter a sports competition without taking part in qualifying matches or being ranked at a particular level. ➤ a player or team given such an opportunity.

**wildcat** • n. **1** a small Eurasian and African cat, typically grey with black markings and a bushy tail, believed to be the ancestor of the domestic cat. [*Felis silvestris*.] ➤ a bobcat or other small felid. **2** a hot-tempered or ferocious person. **3** an exploratory oil well. • adj. **1** (of a strike) sudden and unofficial. **2** commercially unsound or risky. • v. US prospect for oil.
– DERIVATIVES **wildcatter** n.

**wild cherry** • n. another term for **GEAN**.

**wildcraft** US • v. gather (herbs, plants, and fungi) from the wild. • n. the action or practice of wildcrafting.

**wild dog** • n. a hunting dog, dhole, dingo, or other wild member of the dog family.

**wild duck** • n. another term for **MALLARD**.

**wildebeest** /'wɪldəbiːst, 'vɪ-/ • n. (pl. same or **wildebeests**) another term for **GNU**.
– ORIGIN C19: from Afrik., lit. 'wild beast'.

**wilder** /'wɪldə/ • v. archaic lead or drive astray. ➤ bewilder.
– ORIGIN C17: origin uncertain; perh. based on **WILDERNESS**.

**wilderness** • n. **1** an uncultivated, uninhabited, and inhospitable region. ➤ a neglected or abandoned area. **2** a position of disfavour.
– PHRASES **a voice in the wilderness** an unheeded advocate of reform (see Matt. 3:3 etc.).
– ORIGIN OE *wildēornes* 'land inhabited only by wild animals', from *wild dēor* 'wild deer' + **-NESS**.

**wildfire** • n. **1** historical a highly flammable liquid used in warfare. **2** less common term for **WILL-O'-THE-WISP**.
– PHRASES **spread like wildfire** spread with great speed.

**wildfowl** • pl. n. game birds, especially aquatic ones; waterfowl.

**wild garlic** • n. another term for **RAMSONS**.

**wild ginger** • n. a North American plant with an aromatic root which is used as a ginger substitute. [*Asarum canadense*.]

**wild goose chase** • n. a foolish and hopeless search for or pursuit of something unattainable.

**wild hyacinth** • n. another term for **BLUEBELL** (in sense 1).

**wilding**[1] /'wʌɪldɪŋ/ • n. US informal violent rampage.
– ORIGIN 1980s: from the adjective **WILD** + **-ING**[1].

**wilding**[2] /'wʌɪldɪŋ/ (also **wildling** /-lɪŋ/) • n. a wild plant, especially an apple tree descended from cultivated varieties, or its fruit.
– ORIGIN C16: from the adjective **WILD** + **-ING**[3].

**wildlife** • n. the native fauna (and sometimes flora) of a region.

**wild mustard** • n. charlock or a related wild plant.

**wild oat** • n. a grass which is related to the cultivated oat and is found as a weed of other cereals. [*Avena fatua*.]
– PHRASES **sow one's wild oats** see **OAT**.

**wild pitch** Baseball • n. a pitch which is not hit by the batter and cannot be stopped by the catcher, enabling a base runner to advance. • v. (**wild-pitch**) enable (a base runner) to advance by making such a pitch.

**wild rice** • n. a tall aquatic American grass with edible grains, related to rice. [*Zizania aquatica*.]

**wild silk** • n. coarse silk produced by wild silkworms, especially tussore.

**wild type** • n. Genetics a strain, gene, or characteristic which prevails among individuals in natural conditions, as distinct from an atypical mutant type.

**wile** • n. a devious or cunning stratagem. • v. archaic lure; entice.
– ORIGIN ME: perh. from an ON word rel. to *vél* 'craft'.

**wilful** (US also **willful**) • adj. **1** intentional; deliberate. **2** stubborn and determined.
– DERIVATIVES **wilfully** adv. **wilfulness** n.
– ORIGIN ME: from the noun **WILL**[2] + **-FUL**.

**wilga** /'wɪlgə/ • n. a small white-flowering Australian tree which is resistant to drought and a valuable source of fodder. [*Geijera parviflora*.]
– ORIGIN C19: from Wiradhuri *wilgar*.

**will**[1] • modal v. (3rd sing. present **will**; past **would**) **1** expressing the future tense. ➤ expressing a strong intention or assertion about the future. **2** expressing inevitable events. **3** expressing a request. ➤ expressing desire, consent, or willingness. **4** expressing facts about ability or capacity. **5** expressing habitual behaviour. **6** expressing probabil-

ity or expectation about something in the present.
– ORIGIN OE *wyllan*, of Gmc origin.

**will²** ● n. **1** the faculty by which a person decides on and initiates action. ➤(also **will power**) control or restraint deliberately exerted. ➤a desire or intention. **2** a legal document containing instructions for the disposition of one's money and property after one's death. ● v. **1** chiefly formal or poetic/literary intend or desire to happen. ➤bring about by the exercise of mental powers. **2** (**will something to**) bequeath something to. ➤leave specified instructions in one's will.
– PHRASES **at will** at whatever time or in whatever way one pleases. **have a will of one's own** have a wilful character. **with the best will in the world** however good one's intentions. **with a will** energetically and resolutely.
– DERIVATIVES **-willed** adj. **willer** n.
– ORIGIN OE *willa* (n.), *willian* (v.), of Gmc origin; rel. to **WILL¹** and the adverb **WELL¹**.

**willet** /ˈwɪlɪt/ ● n. (pl. same or **willets**) a large North American sandpiper. [*Catoptrophorus semipalmatus*.]
– ORIGIN C19: imitative of its call, *pill-will-willet*.

**willful** ● adj. US variant spelling of **WILFUL**.

**Williams** ● n. a dessert pear of an early green variety.
– ORIGIN C19: named after its first distributor in England.

**willie** ● n. variant spelling of **WILLY**.

**willies** ● pl. n. (**the willies**) informal a strong feeling of nervous discomfort: *the room gave him the willies*.
– ORIGIN C19 (orig. US): of unknown origin.

**willie wagtail** (also **willy wagtail**) ● n. **1** a common Australian monarch flycatcher with striking black and white plumage. [*Rhipidura leucophrys*.] **2** Brit. informal the pied wagtail.

**willing** ● adj. ready, eager, or prepared to do something. ➤given or done readily.
– DERIVATIVES **willingly** adv. **willingness** n.

**williwaw** /ˈwɪlɪwɔː/ ● n. a sudden violent squall blowing offshore from a mountainous coast.
– ORIGIN C19: of unknown origin.

**will-o'-the-wisp** ● n. **1** a phosphorescent light seen hovering or floating at night on marshy ground, thought to result from the combustion of natural gases. **2** a person or thing that is difficult or impossible to reach or catch.
– ORIGIN C17: orig. as *Will with the wisp*, the sense of *wisp* being 'handful of (lighted) hay'.

**willow** ● n. a tree or shrub of temperate climate which typically grows near water, has narrow leaves and pliant branches yielding osiers and wood, and bears catkins. [Genus *Salix*: many species.]
– ORIGIN OE *welig*, of Gmc origin.

**willow grouse** ● n. a Eurasian and North American grouse of which the red grouse is a distinct subspecies. [*Lagopus lagopus*.]

**willowherb** ● n. a plant with long narrow leaves and pink or pale purple flowers. [*Epilobium* and related genera: many species.]

**willow pattern** ● n. a conventional design in pottery featuring a Chinese scene depicted in blue on white, typically including figures on a bridge, a willow tree, and birds.

**willow ptarmigan** ● n. North American term for **WILLOW GROUSE**.

**willow warbler** ● n. a small migratory warbler with mainly drab plumage and a tuneful song. [*Phylloscopus trochilus* and related species.]

**willowware** ● n. chiefly US pottery with a willow-pattern design.

**willow wren** ● n. Brit. another term for **WILLOW WARBLER**.

**willowy** ● adj. **1** bordered, shaded, or covered by willows. **2** (of a person) tall, slim, and lithe.

**will power** ● n. see **WILL²** (sense 1).

**willy** (also **willie**) ● n. (pl. **-ies**) Brit. informal a penis.
– ORIGIN C20: familiar form of the given name *William*.

**willy-nilly** ● adv. **1** whether one likes it or not. **2** without direction or planning; haphazardly.
– ORIGIN C17: later spelling of *will I, nill I* 'I am willing, I am unwilling'.

**willy wagtail** ● n. variant spelling of **WILLIE WAGTAIL**.

**willy-willy** ● n. (pl. **-ies**) Austral. a whirlwind or dust storm.
– ORIGIN from Yindjibarndi (an Aborig. lang. of western Australia).

**Wilms' tumour** /wɪlmz, vɪlmz/ ● n. a malignant tumour of the kidney, of a type that occurs in young children.
– ORIGIN C20: named after the Ger. surgeon Max *Wilms*.

**wilt¹** ● v. **1** (of a plant) become limp through loss of water, heat, or disease; droop. ➤(of a person) lose one's energy or vigour. **2** leave (mown grass or a forage crop) in the open to dry partially before being collected for silage. ● n. any of a number of fungal or bacterial diseases of plants characterized by wilting of the foliage.
– ORIGIN C17 (orig. dial.): perh. an alt. of dial. *welk* 'lose freshness', of Low Ger. origin.

**wilt²** archaic second person singular of **WILL¹**.

**Wilton** ● n. a woven carpet with a velvet pile.
– ORIGIN C18: from *Wilton*, a town in southern England noted for the manufacture of carpets.

**Wilts.** ● abbrev. Wiltshire.

**wily** /ˈwʌɪli/ ● adj. (**-ier**, **-iest**) skilled at gaining an advantage, especially deceitfully.
– DERIVATIVES **wilily** adv. **wiliness** n.

**wimmin** ● pl. n. non-standard spelling of 'women' adopted by some feminists to avoid the word ending *-men*.

**WIMP¹** ● n. Computing a set of software features and hardware devices designed to simplify or demystify computing operations for the user.
– ORIGIN 1980s: acronym from *windows, icons, mice, and pull-down menus* (*or pointers*).

**WIMP²** ● n. Physics a hypothetical heavy subatomic particle postulated as a constituent of dark matter.
– ORIGIN 1980s: acronym from *weakly interacting massive particle*.

**wimp** informal ● n. a weak and cowardly person. ● v. (**wimp out**) withdraw from something in a cowardly way.
– DERIVATIVES **wimpish** adj. **wimpishly** adv. **wimpishness** n. **wimpy** adj.
– ORIGIN 1920s: origin uncertain, perh. from **WHIMPER**.

**wimple** ● n. a cloth headdress covering the head, neck, and sides of the face, formerly worn by women and still by some nuns.
– DERIVATIVES **wimpled** adj.
– ORIGIN OE *wimpel*, of Gmc origin.

**Wimshurst machine** /ˈwɪmzhəːst/ ● n. a device for generating an electric charge by turning glass discs in opposite directions.
– ORIGIN C19: named after the Engl. engineer James *Wimshurst*.

**win** ● v. (**winning**; past and past part. **won**) **1** be successful or victorious in (a contest or conflict). **2** acquire as a result of a contest, conflict, etc. ➤gain (someone's attention, support, or love). ➤(**win someone over**) gain the support or favour of someone. **3** (**win out/through**) manage to succeed or achieve something by effort. ➤archaic manage to reach (a place) by effort. **4** obtain (ore) from a mine. **5** dry (hay) by exposure to the air. ● n. a victory, especially in a game or contest.
– PHRASES **win the day** be victorious. **win** (or **earn**) **one's spurs** historical gain a knighthood by an act of bravery. ➤informal gain one's first distinction or honours.
– DERIVATIVES **winless** adj. **winnable** adj.
– ORIGIN OE *winnan* 'strive, contend' also 'subdue and take possession of, acquire', of Gmc origin.

**wince¹** ● v. give a slight involuntary grimace or flinch due to pain or distress. ● n. an instance of wincing.
– DERIVATIVES **wincer** n. **wincing** adj. **wincingly** adv.
– ORIGIN ME: from an Anglo-Norman Fr. var. of OFr. *guenchir* 'turn aside'.

**wince²** ● n. Brit. a roller for moving textile fabric through a dyeing vat.
– ORIGIN C17: var. of **WINCH**.

**wincey** ● n. (pl. **-eys**) Brit. a strong, lightweight twilled fabric, typically made of wool with cotton or linen.
– ORIGIN C19: appar. an alt. of *woolsey* in **LINSEY-WOOLSEY**.

**winceyette** /ˌwɪnsɪˈɛt/ ● n. Brit. a lightweight napped flannelette, used especially for nightclothes.

**winch** ● n. **1** a hauling or lifting device consisting of a rope or chain winding around a horizontal rotating drum, turned by a crank or by motor. ➤ Brit. the reel of a fishing rod. **2** the crank of a wheel or axle. **3** another term for **WINCE**[2]. ● v. hoist or haul with a winch.
– DERIVATIVES **wincher** n.
– ORIGIN OE *wince* 'reel, pulley', of Gmc origin; rel. to **WINK**.

**Winchester** /ˈwɪntʃɪstə/ ● n. **1** (also **Winchester rifle**) trademark a breech-loading side-action repeating rifle. **2** (also **Winchester disk** or **drive**) Computing a disk drive in a sealed unit containing a high-capacity hard disk and the read-write heads.
– ORIGIN sense 1 named after the American rifle manufacturer Oliver F. *Winchester*; sense 2 so named because its original numerical designation corresponded to the calibre of the rifle.

**winchester** ● n. Brit. a large cylindrical bottle for liquids.
– ORIGIN C18: orig. applied to containers holding a bushel, gallon, or quart, according to an obsolete system of measurement with standards kept at *Winchester* in southern England.

**wind**[1] /wɪnd/ ● n. **1** the perceptible natural movement of the air, especially in the form of a current blowing from a particular direction. ➤ the rush of air caused by a fast-moving body. **2** breath as needed in physical exertion, speech, playing an instrument, etc. **3** Brit. air swallowed while eating or gas generated in the stomach and intestines by digestion. **4** meaningless talk. **5** (also **winds**) [treated as sing. or pl.] wind or woodwind instruments forming a band or section of an orchestra. **6** a scent carried by the wind, indicating the proximity of an animal or person. ● v. **1** cause to have difficulty breathing because of exertion or a blow to the stomach. **2** Brit. make (a baby) bring up wind after feeding by patting its back. **3** detect the scent of. **4** /wʌɪnd/ (past and past part. **winded** or **wound** /waʊnd/) poetic/literary sound (a bugle or call) by blowing.
– PHRASES **before the wind** Sailing with the wind blowing from astern. **get wind of** informal hear a rumour of. **off the wind** Sailing with the wind on the quarter. **on a wind** Sailing against a wind on either bow. **put** (or **have**) **the wind up** Brit. informal alarm or frighten (or be alarmed or frightened). **sail close to** (or **near**) **the wind 1** sail as nearly against the wind as is consistent with using its force. **2** informal verge on indecency, dishonesty, or disaster. **take the wind out of someone's sails** frustrate someone by anticipating an action or remark. **to the wind (s)** (or **the four winds**) in all directions. [from 'And fear of death deliver to the winds' (Milton's *Paradise Lost*).]
– DERIVATIVES **windless** adj.
– ORIGIN OE, of Gmc origin.

**wind**[2] /wʌɪnd/ ● v. (past and past part. **wound** /waʊnd/) **1** move in or take a twisting or spiral course. **2** pass (something) around a thing or person so as to encircle or enfold them. ➤ (with reference to a length of something) twist or be twisted around itself or a core. **3** make (a clock or clockwork device) operate by turning a key or handle. ➤ turn (a key or handle) repeatedly. **4** move (an audio or video tape or a film) back or forwards to a desired point. **5** hoist or draw with a windlass, winch, etc. ● n. **1** a twist or turn in a course. **2** a single turn made when winding.
– PHRASAL VERBS **wind down 1** (of a clockwork mechanism) gradually lose power. **2** informal relax. **3** (also **wind something down**) draw or bring gradually to a close. **wind up** informal end up in a specified state, situation, or place. **wind someone up** Brit. informal tease or irritate someone. **wind something up 1** arrange the affairs of and dissolve a company. **2** gradually bring an activity to a conclusion. **3** informal increase the tension or power of something.
– ORIGIN OE *windan* 'go rapidly', 'twine', of Gmc origin; rel. to **WANDER** and **WEND**.

**windage** ● n. the air resistance of a moving object or the force of the wind on a stationary object. ➤ the effect of the wind in deflecting a missile.

**windbag** ● n. informal a person who talks a lot but says little of any value.
– DERIVATIVES **windbaggery** n.

**windbound** ● adj. (of a ship) unable to sail because of extreme or contrary winds.

**windbreak** ● n. a row of trees, wall, or screen providing shelter from the wind.

**windbreaker** ● n. US trademark a windcheater.

**windburn** ● n. reddening and soreness of the skin caused by prolonged exposure to the wind.
– DERIVATIVES **windburned** (also **windburnt**) adj.

**windcheater** ● n. chiefly Brit. a wind-resistant jacket with a close-fitting neck, waistband, and cuffs.

**wind chill** ● n. the cooling effect of wind on a surface.

**wind chimes** ● pl. n. small decorative pieces of glass or metal suspended from a frame, typically hung near a door or window so as to tinkle in the draught.

**winder** /ˈwʌɪndə/ ● n. a device or mechanism for winding something, especially a watch, clock, or camera film.

**windfall** ● n. **1** an apple or other fruit blown from a tree by the wind. **2** a piece of unexpected good fortune, especially a legacy.

**windfall tax** (also **windfall profits tax**) ● n. a tax levied on an unexpectedly large profit, especially one regarded to be excessive or unfairly obtained.

**wind farm** ● n. an area containing a group of energy-producing windmills or wind turbines.

**windflower** ● n. an anemone.

**wind gap** ● n. a valley cut through a ridge by a river which no longer flows through the valley.

**wind gauge** ● n. an anemometer.

**windhover** ● n. dialect a kestrel.

**windigo** /ˈwɪndɪɡəʊ/ (also **wendigo**) ● n. (pl. **-os** or **-oes**) (in the folklore of the northern Algonquian Indians) a person transformed into a monster by eating human flesh.
– ORIGIN from Ojibwa *wintiko*.

**winding** /ˈwʌɪndɪŋ/ ● n. **1** a twisting movement or course. **2** a thing that winds or is wound round something. ➤ a coil of conducting wire in an electric motor, generator, etc. ● adj. having a twisting or spiral course.

**winding sheet** ● n. a shroud.

**wind instrument** ● n. a musical instrument in which sound is produced by the vibration of air. ➤ a woodwind instrument as distinct from a brass instrument.

**windjammer** ● n. **1** historical a merchant sailing ship. **2** US a windcheater.

**windlass** ● n. a winch, especially one on a ship or in a harbour. ● v. haul or lift with a windlass.
– ORIGIN ME: prob. an alt. of obs. *windas*, via Anglo-Norman Fr. from ON *vindáss*, lit. 'winding pole'.

**wind load** (also **wind loading**) ● n. Engineering the force on a structure arising from the impact of wind on it.

**wind machine** ● n. **1** a machine used in the theatre or in film-making for producing a blast of air or imitating the sound of wind. **2** a wind-driven turbine.

**windmill** ● n. **1** a building with sails or vanes that turn in the wind and generate power to grind corn into flour. ➤ a similar structure used to generate electricity or draw water. **2** Brit. a toy consisting of a stick with curved vanes attached that turn in the wind. **3** a propeller, especially one on an autogiro. ● v. **1** move (one's arms) in a manner suggestive of the sails of a windmill. **2** (of a propeller, rotor, or aircraft) spin unpowered.
– PHRASES **fling** (or **throw**) **one's cap over the windmill(s)** dated act recklessly or unconventionally.

**window** ● n. **1** an opening in a wall or roof, fitted with glass in a frame to admit light or air and allow people to see out. ➤ an opening through which customers are served in a bank, ticket office, etc. ➤ a space behind the window of a shop where goods are displayed. **2** a transparent panel in an envelope to show an address. **3** Computing a framed area on a display screen for viewing information. ➤ (**Windows**) [treated as sing.] trademark a GUI operating system for personal computers. **4** (**window on/into/to**) a means of observing and learning about. **5** an interval or opportunity for action. **6** Physics a range of

electromagnetic wavelengths for which a medium (especially the atmosphere) is transparent. **7** strips of metal foil dispersed in the air to obstruct radar detection. [military code word.]
– PHRASES **go out (of) the window** informal (of a plan or behaviour) be abandoned or cease to exist. **windows of the soul** the eyes.
– DERIVATIVES **windowed** adj. **windowless** adj.
– ORIGIN ME: from ON *vindauga*, from *vindr* 'wind' + *auga* 'eye'.

**window box** • n. a long narrow box in which flowers and other plants are grown on an outside windowsill.

**window dressing** • n. **1** the arrangement of an attractive display in a shop window. **2** an adroit but superficial or misleading presentation of something.

**window frame** • n. a frame holding the glass of a window.

**windowing** • n. Computing the use of windows for the simultaneous display of more than one item on a screen.

**window ledge** • n. a window sill.

**windowpane** • n. **1** a pane of glass in a window. **2** a sand dab or similar flatfish.

**window seat** • n. **1** a seat below a window, especially one in a bay or alcove. **2** a seat next to a window in an aircraft or train.

**window-shop** • v. look at the goods in shop windows, especially without intending to buy.
– DERIVATIVES **window-shopper** n.

**window sill** • n. a ledge or sill forming the bottom part of a window.

**window tax** • n. Brit. a tax on windows and similar openings that was abolished in 1851.

**windpipe** • n. the trachea.

**wind rose** • n. a diagram showing the relative frequency of wind directions at a place.

**windrow** • n. **1** a long line of raked hay, corn sheaves, or peats drying in the wind. **2** N. Amer. a line of material heaped up by the wind.

**windsail** • n. historical a long tube or funnel of sailcloth conveying air to the lower parts of a ship.

**windscreen** • n. Brit. a glass screen at the front of a motor vehicle.

**windscreen wiper** • n. Brit. a device for keeping a windscreen clear of rain, typically with a rubber blade on an arm that moves in an arc.

**wind shear** • n. variation in wind velocity along a direction at right angles to the wind's direction, tending to exert a turning force.

**windshield** • n. N. Amer. a windscreen.

**windsock** • n. a light, flexible cylinder or cone mounted on a mast to show the direction and strength of the wind, especially at an airfield.

**Windsor chair** • n. a wooden dining chair with a semicircular back supported by upright rods.

**Windsor knot** • n. a large, loose triangular knot in a tie, produced by making extra turns when tying.

**wind sprint** • n. Athletics an exercise involving moving from a walk or slow run to a faster run and repeatedly reversing the process.

**windstorm** • n. chiefly N. Amer. a gale.

**windsurfer** • n. **1** a person who takes part in windsurfing. **2** (trademark in the US) a sailboard.

**windsurfing** • n. the sport of riding on water on a sailboard.
– DERIVATIVES **windsurf** v.

**windswept** • adj. exposed to strong winds. ➤untidy after being exposed to the wind.

**wind tunnel** • n. a tunnel-like apparatus for producing an airstream past models of aircraft, buildings, etc., in order to investigate flow or the effect of wind on the full-size object.

**wind-up** • n. **1** Brit. informal an attempt to tease or irritate someone. **2** an act of concluding something. **3** Baseball the motions of a pitcher preparing to pitch the ball.

**windward** • adj. & adv. facing the wind or on the side facing the wind. Contrasted with **LEEWARD**. • n. the side from which the wind is blowing.
– PHRASES **to windward of** dated in an advantageous position relative to.

**windy**[1] /ˈwɪndi/ • adj. (**-ier**, **-iest**) **1** marked by or exposed to strong winds. **2** Brit. suffering from, marked by, or causing wind in the alimentary canal. **3** informal using or expressed in words of little substance. **4** Brit. informal nervous or anxious.
– DERIVATIVES **windily** adv. **windiness** n.

**windy**[2] /ˈwʌɪndi/ • adj. (of a road or river) following a winding course.

**wine**[1] • n. **1** an alcoholic drink made from fermented grape juice. ➤a fermented alcoholic drink made from other fruits or plants. **2** short for **WINE RED**. • v. (**wine and dine someone**) entertain someone with drinks and a meal. ➤take part in such entertainment.
– DERIVATIVES **winey** (also **winy**) adj.
– ORIGIN OE *wīn*, of Gmc origin, based on L. *vinum*.

**wine**[2] • v. W. Indian dance with gyratory movements of the pelvis.
– ORIGIN from **WIND**[2], influenced by **TWINE**.

**wine bar** • n. a bar or small restaurant where wine is the main drink available.

**wineberry** • n. **1** a bristly shrub native to China and Japan, producing scarlet berries used in cookery. [*Rubus phoenicolasius*.] **2** the fruit of this bush. **3** another term for **MAKO**[2].

**winebibber** • n. archaic or poetic/literary a drunkard.
– DERIVATIVES **winebibbing** n. & adj.

**wine bottle** • n. a glass bottle for wine, the standard size holding 75 cl or 26⅔ fl. oz.

**wine box** • n. a square carton of wine with a dispensing tap.

**wine cellar** • n. a cellar for storing wine. ➤a stock of wine.

**wine glass** • n. a glass with a stem and foot, used for drinking wine.
– DERIVATIVES **wineglassful** n. (pl. **-fuls**).

**winegrower** • n. a grower of grapes for wine.

**wine gum** • n. a small coloured fruit-flavoured sweet made with gelatin.

**wine list** • n. a list of the wines available in a restaurant.

**winemaker** • n. a producer of wine.
– DERIVATIVES **winemaking** n.

**wine red** • n. a dark red colour like that of red wine.

**winery** • n. (pl. **-ies**) an establishment where wine is made.

**wineskin** • n. an animal skin sewn up and used to hold wine.

**wine tasting** • n. judging the quality of wine by tasting it. ➤an occasion for this.
– DERIVATIVES **wine taster** n.

**wine vinegar** • n. vinegar made from wine rather than malt.

**wing** • n. **1** a modified forelimb or other appendage enabling a bird, bat, insect, or other creature to fly. **2** a rigid horizontal structure projecting from both sides of an aircraft and supporting it in the air. ➤(**wings**) a pilot's badge representing a pair of wings. **3** Brit. a raised part of the body of a vehicle above the wheel. **4** a part of a large building, especially one that projects from the main part. **5** Anatomy a lateral part or projection of an organ or structure. ➤Botany a thin membranous appendage of a fruit or seed dispersed by the wind. **6** a group within an organization having particular views or a particular function. **7** (**the wings**) the sides of a theatre stage out of view of the audience. **8** the part of a soccer, rugby, or hockey field close to the sidelines. ➤(also **wing forward**) an attacking player positioned near the sidelines. **9** a flank of a battle array. **10** an air force unit of several squadrons or groups. • v. **1** fly or move quickly, as if flying. ➤archaic enable to fly or move rapidly. **2** shoot (a bird) in the wing, so as to prevent flight. ➤wound superficially, especially in the arm or shoulder. **3** (**wing it**) informal speak or act without preparation.
– PHRASES **in the wings** ready for use or action at the ap-

propriate time. **on the wing** (of a bird) in flight. **on a wing and a prayer** with only the slightest chance of success. **spread** (or **stretch** or **try**) **one's wings** extend one's activities and interests. **take wing** fly away. **under one's wing** in or into one's protective care.

– DERIVATIVES **winged** adj. **wingless** adj. **winglet** n. **winglike** adj.

– ORIGIN ME (orig. in the pl.): from ON *vængir*, pl. of *vængr*; sense 3 of the verb was orig. theatrical sl. meaning 'to play a role without properly knowing the text' (by relying on a prompter in the wings or by studying in the wings between scenes).

**wing back** • n. Soccer a player in a wide position on the field, taking part both in attack and defence.

**wingbeat** • n. one complete set of motions of a wing in flying.

**wing case** • n. each of a pair of modified toughened forewings covering the functional wings of a beetle or other insect.

**wing chair** • n. an armchair with side pieces projecting forwards from a high back.

**wing collar** • n. a high stiff shirt collar with turned-down corners.

**wing commander** • n. a rank of RAF officer, above squadron leader and below group captain.

**wingding** • n. informal, chiefly N. Amer. a lively event or party.

– ORIGIN 1920s (meaning 'spasm, seizure', especially one due to drug-taking): of unknown origin.

**winged words** • pl. n. poetic/literary highly apposite or significant words.

**winger** • n. **1** an attacking player on the wing in soccer, hockey, etc. **2** [in combination] a member of a specified political wing: *a Tory right-winger.*

**wing forward** • n. see WING (sense 8).

**wing half** • n. Soccer, dated a halfback positioned towards the right or left wing.

**wingman** • n. (pl. **-men**) **1** a pilot whose aircraft is positioned behind and outside the leading aircraft in a formation. **2** another term for WINGER (in sense 1).

**wing mirror** • n. a rear-view mirror projecting from the side of a vehicle.

**wing nut** • n. **1** a nut with a pair of projections for the fingers to turn it on a screw. **2** an Asian tree producing characteristic broad-winged nutlets. [Genus *Pterocarya*.]

**wingover** • n. a manoeuvre in which an aircraft turns at the top of a steep climb and flies back along its original path.

**wing sail** • n. a rigid structure similar to an aircraft wing fixed vertically on a boat to provide thrust.

**wingspan** (also **wingspread**) • n. the maximum extent across the wings of an aircraft, bird, etc., measured from tip to tip.

**wingstroke** • n. a wingbeat.

**wing tip** (also **wingtip shoe**) • n. N. Amer. a shoe with a toecap having a backward extending point and curving sides, resembling the shape of a wing.

**wing walking** • n. acrobatic stunts performed on the wings of an airborne aircraft.

– DERIVATIVES **wing walker** n.

**wink** • v. **1** close and open one eye quickly, typically as a signal of affection or greeting or to convey a message. **2** shine or flash intermittently. **3** (**wink at**) pretend not to notice (something bad). • n. an act of winking.

– PHRASES **as easy as winking** informal very easy or easily. **in the wink of an eye** (or **in a wink**) very quickly. **not sleep** (or **get**) **a wink** (or **not get a wink of sleep**) not sleep at all.

– ORIGIN OE *wincian* 'close the eyes', of Gmc origin; rel. to WINCE[1].

**winkle** • n. **1** a small herbivorous shore-dwelling mollusc with a spiral shell. [*Littorina littorea* and other species.] **2** informal a penis. • v. (**winkle something out**) chiefly Brit. extract or obtain something with difficulty.

– DERIVATIVES **winkler** n.

– ORIGIN C16: shortening of PERIWINKLE[2].

**winkle-picker** • n. Brit. informal a shoe with a long pointed toe, popular in the 1950s.

**Winnebago** /ˌwɪnəˈbeɪɡəʊ/ • n. (pl. same or **-os**) **1** a member of an American Indian people formerly living in eastern Wisconsin. **2** the Siouan language of this people. **3** (pl. **-os**) US trademark a motor vehicle with living accommodation for long-distance travelling or camping.

– ORIGIN Algonquian, lit. 'person of the dirty water', referring to the muddy Fox River.

**winner** /ˈwɪnə/ • n. a person or thing that wins. ➤informal a successful or highly promising thing.

**winning** /ˈwɪnɪŋ/ • adj. **1** gaining, resulting in, or relating to victory. **2** attractive; endearing. • n. (**winnings**) money won, especially by gambling.

– DERIVATIVES **winningly** adv.

**winningest** • adj. N. Amer. informal having achieved the most success.

**winning post** • n. a post marking the end of a race.

**winnow** • v. **1** blow air through (grain) in order to remove the chaff. ➤remove (chaff) from grain. **2** examine in order to identify the most valuable or useful elements. ➤identify (a valuable or useful element). **3** poetic/literary (of the wind) blow. **4** (of a bird) fan (the air) with its wings.

– DERIVATIVES **winnower** n.

– ORIGIN OE *windwian*, from *wind* (see WIND[1]).

**wino** • n. (pl. **-os**) informal a person who drinks excessive amounts of cheap wine or other alcohol.

**winsome** • adj. attractive or appealing.

– DERIVATIVES **winsomely** adv. **winsomeness** n.

– ORIGIN OE *wynsum*, from *wyn* 'joy' + -SOME[1].

**winter** • n. **1** the coldest season of the year, after autumn and before spring. ➤Astronomy the period from the winter solstice to the vernal equinox. **2** (**winters**) poetic/literary years. • adj. **1** (of fruit) ripening late in the year. **2** (of crops) sown in autumn for harvesting the following year. • v. **1** spend the winter in a particular place. **2** keep or feed (plants or cattle) during winter.

– DERIVATIVES **winterer** n. **winterless** adj. **winterly** adj.

– ORIGIN OE, of Gmc origin; prob. rel. to WET.

**winter aconite** • n. see ACONITE (sense 2).

**winterberry** • n. (pl. **-ies**) a North American holly with toothed, non-prickly leaves. [*Ilex verticillata* and related species.]

**winter cress** • n. a bitter-tasting cress of north temperate regions. [*Barbarea vulgaris* and other species.]

**winter garden** • n. **1** a garden of plants, such as evergreens, that flourish in winter. **2** a conservatory in which flowers and other non-hardy plants are grown in winter.

**wintergreen** • n. **1** a low-growing plant of acid soils, with spikes of white bell-shaped flowers. [*Pyrola* and other genera.] **2** the checkerberry or a related American shrub whose leaves produce oil. **3** (also **oil of wintergreen**) a pungent oil obtained from these plants or from the bark of a birch (*Betula lenta*), used medicinally and as a flavouring.

– ORIGIN C16: the plants so named because they remain green in winter.

**winter heliotrope** • n. a plant of the daisy family producing fragrant lilac flowers in winter. [*Petasites fragrans*.]

**winterize** (also **-ise**) • v. (usu. **be winterized**) chiefly N. Amer. adapt or prepare for use in cold weather.

– DERIVATIVES **winterization** n.

**Winter Olympics** • pl. n. an international contest of winter sports held every four years at a two-year interval from the Olympic games.

**winter sports** • pl. n. sports performed on snow or ice.

**winter squash** • n. a squash of a variety with a hard rind, able to be stored.

**wintersweet** • n. a Chinese shrub which produces heavily scented yellow flowers in winter before the leaves appear. [*Chimonanthus praecox*.]

**winter-tide** • n. poetic/literary wintertime.

**wintertime** /ˈwɪntətʌɪm/ • n. the season or period of winter.

**wintry** (also **wintery**) • adj. (**-ier, -iest**) characteristic of winter, especially in being very cold or bleak.

– DERIVATIVES **wintrily** adv. **wintriness** n.

**win-win** • adj. of or denoting a situation in which each party benefits.

**WIP** • abbrev. work in progress.

**wipe** • v. **1** clean or dry by rubbing with a cloth or one's hand. ➤remove (dirt or moisture) in this way. **2** spread (liquid) over a surface by rubbing. **3** (often **wipe something out**) remove or eliminate completely. ➤erase (data) from a magnetic medium. **4** pass (a swipe card) over an electronic reader. ➤pass (a light pen) over a bar code. **5** Austral./NZ informal reject or dismiss. • n. **1** an act of wiping. **2** an absorbent disposable cleaning cloth. **3** a cinematographic effect in which an existing picture seems to be wiped out by a new one.

– PHRASES **wipe someone's eye** Brit. informal, dated get the better of someone. **wipe the floor with** informal inflict a humiliating defeat on. **wipe the slate clean** make a fresh start.

– PHRASAL VERBS **wipe something off** subtract an amount from a value or debt. **wipe out** informal be capsized by a wave while surfing. ➤N. Amer. fall over or off a vehicle. **wipe someone out 1** kill a large number of people. **2** ruin someone financially. **3** informal exhaust or intoxicate someone.

– DERIVATIVES **wipeable** adj.

– ORIGIN OE *wīpian*, of Gmc origin; rel. to **WHIP**.

**wipe-out** • n. informal **1** an instance of complete destruction. **2** a fall from a surfboard. **3** the obliteration of one radio signal by another.

**wiper** • n. **1** a windscreen wiper. **2** an electrical contact which moves across a surface. **3** a cam or tappet.

**WIPO** • abbrev. World Intellectual Property Organization.

**Wiradhuri** /wɪ'radʒəri/ • n. an extinct Aboriginal language of SE Australia.

– ORIGIN Aborig., appar. from a Wiradhuri word for 'no', *wirai* (contrasted with related langs).

**wire** • n. **1** metal drawn out into a thin flexible thread or rod. ➤a length or quantity of wire used for fencing, to carry an electric current, etc. **2** a concealed electronic listening device. **3** informal a telegram or cablegram. • v. **1** install electric circuits or wires in. **2** provide, fasten, or reinforce with wire. **3** informal, chiefly N. Amer. send a telegram or cablegram to. ➤send (money) to (someone) by such means. **4** snare with wire. **5** Croquet obstruct (a ball, shot, or player) by a hoop.

– PHRASES **by wire** by telegraph. **down to the wire** informal until the very last minute. **under the wire** N. Amer. informal just in time.

– DERIVATIVES **wirer** n.

– ORIGIN OE *wīr*; of Gmc origin, prob. from the base of L. *viere* 'plait, weave'.

**wire brush** • n. a brush with tough wire bristles for cleaning hard surfaces. ➤a brush with wire strands, used on cymbals to produce a soft metallic sound. • v. (**wire-brush**) clean with a wire brush.

**wired** • adj. informal **1** making use of computers and information technology to transfer or receive information. **2** nervous, tense, or edgy. ➤intoxicated by drugs or alcohol.

**wire-draw** • v. (past **-drew**; past part. **-drawn**) **1** [often as noun **wire-drawing**] draw out (metal) into wire. **2** [often as adj. **wire-drawn**] archaic refine (an argument or idea) in such a way that it becomes forced.

– DERIVATIVES **wire-drawer** n.

**wire fraud** • n. chiefly US fraud involving the use of telecommunications or information technology.

**wire gauge** • n. a gauge for measuring the diameter of wire. ➤any of a series of standard sizes of wire.

**wire grass** • n. chiefly N. Amer. & Austral. grass with tough wiry stems.

**wire-haired** • adj. (especially of a dog breed) having wiry hair.

**wireless** • n. dated, chiefly Brit. **1** (also **wireless set**) a radio receiving set. **2** broadcasting or telegraphy using radio signals. • adj. lacking or not requiring wires.

**wireline** • n. **1** a telegraph or telephone wire. **2** (in the oil industry) a cable for lowering and raising tools and other equipment in a well shaft.

**wireman** • n. (pl. **-men**) **1** chiefly US an installer or repairer of electric wiring. **2** a journalist working for a news agency.

**wirepuller** • n. N. Amer. informal a politician or other person who exerts control or influence from behind the scenes.

– DERIVATIVES **wirepulling** n.

**wire rope** • n. a length of rope made from wires twisted together as strands.

**wire service** • n. N. Amer. a news agency that supplies syndicated news by teleprinter or other electronic means to newspapers, radio, and television stations.

**wire stripper** • n. a tool for removing the insulation from electric wires.

**wiretapping** • n. the practice of tapping a telephone line to monitor conversations secretly.

– DERIVATIVES **wiretap** n. & v. **wiretapper** n.

**wire-walker** • n. an acrobat who walks along and performs feats on a tightrope.

**wire wheel** • n. a wheel on a car, especially a sports car, having narrow metal spokes.

**wire wool** • n. Brit. another term for **STEEL WOOL**.

**wireworm** • n. the worm-like larva of a click beetle, which feeds on roots and can cause damage to crops.

**wiring** • n. **1** a system of wires providing electric circuits for a device or building. **2** informal the connections of the nervous system or brain, especially as determining behaviour.

**wiry** • adj. (**-ier**, **-iest**) **1** resembling wire in form and texture. **2** lean, tough, and sinewy.

– DERIVATIVES **wirily** adv. **wiriness** n.

**Wis.** • abbrev. Wisconsin.

**wis** • v. (**wisses**, **wissed**, **wissing**) archaic know well.

– ORIGIN C16: orig. in *I wis*, alt. of the obs. adverb *iwis* 'certainly', erroneously interpreted as 'I know' (assoc. with *wist*, past tense of **WIT²**).

**Wisconsinite** /wɪs'kɒnsɪnʌɪt/ • n. a native or inhabitant of the US state of Wisconsin.

**Wisd.** • abbrev. (in biblical references) Wisdom of Solomon (Apocrypha).

**wisdom** • n. **1** the quality of being wise. **2** the body of knowledge and experience that develops within a specified society or period.

– PHRASES **in someone's wisdom** used ironically to suggest that an action is ill-judged: *in their wisdom they decided to dispense with him.*

**wisdom tooth** • n. each of the four hindmost molars in humans, which usually appear at about the age of twenty.

**wise¹** • adj. **1** having or showing experience, knowledge, and good judgement. **2** (**wise to**) informal aware of, especially so as to know how to act. • v. (**wise up**) informal become alert or aware.

– PHRASES **be wise after the event** understand and assess something only after its implications have become obvious.

– DERIVATIVES **wisely** adv.

– ORIGIN OE *wīs*, of Gmc origin; rel. to **WIT²**.

**wise²** • n. archaic manner, way, or extent.

– PHRASES **in no wise** not at all.

– ORIGIN OE *wīse*, of Gmc origin; rel. to **WIT²**.

**-wise** • suffix **1** forming adjectives and adverbs of manner or respect such as *clockwise*. Compare with **-WAYS**. **2** informal with respect to: *price-wise*.

**wiseacre** /'wʌɪzeɪkə/ • n. a person with an affectation of wisdom or knowledge.

– ORIGIN C16: from MDu. *wijsseggher* 'soothsayer', prob. from the Gmc base of **WIT²**.

**wisecrack** informal • n. a witty remark or joke. • v. make a wisecrack.

– DERIVATIVES **wisecracker** n.

**wise guy** • n. informal **1** a person who makes sarcastic or insolent remarks so as to demonstrate their cleverness. **2** US a member of the Mafia.

**wise man** • n. a man versed in magic, witchcraft, or astrology.

**wisenheimer** /'wʌɪz(ə)n,hʌɪmə/ • n. US informal a wiseacre.

– ORIGIN C20: from **WISE**[1] + the suffix *-(n)heimer* found in surnames such as *Oppenheimer.*

**wisent** /ˈwiːz(ə)nt/ ● **n.** the European bison. See **BISON**.

– ORIGIN C19: from Ger.; rel. to **BISON**.

**wise woman** ● **n.** chiefly historical a woman knowledgeable in herbal healing, magic charms, or other traditional lore.

**wish** ● **v. 1** desire something that cannot or probably will not happen. **2** want to do something. ➤ask (someone) to do something or that (something) be done. **3** express a hope that (someone) has (happiness, success, etc). ➤(**wish something on**) [with neg.] hope that something unpleasant will happen to. ● **n. 1** a desire or hope, or an expression of this. ➤(**wishes**) an expression of a hope for someone's happiness, success, or welfare. **2** a thing wished for.

– DERIVATIVES **-wisher** n.

– ORIGIN OE *wȳscan*, of Gmc origin; rel. to **WEEN** and **WONT**.

**wishbone** ● **n. 1** a forked bone (the furcula) between the neck and breast of a bird, especially one from a cooked bird which, when broken by two people, entitles the holder of the longer portion to make a wish. **2** a forked element in the suspension of a motor vehicle or aircraft, typically attached to a wheel at one end with the two arms hinged to the chassis. **3** Sailing a boom in two halves which curve outwards around a sail and meet aft of it.

**wishful** ● **adj. 1** having or expressing a wish for something to happen. **2** based on impractical wishes rather than facts: *wishful thinking.*

– DERIVATIVES **wishfully** adv. **wishfulness** n.

**wish-fulfilment** ● **n.** the satisfying of wishes or desires in dreams or fantasies.

**wishing well** ● **n.** a well into which one drops a coin and makes a wish.

**wish-wash** ● **n.** informal **1** a weak drink. **2** insipid or sentimental talk or writing.

– ORIGIN C18: reduplication of **WASH**.

**wishy-washy** ● **adj. 1** (of drink or soup) weak or thin. **2** feeble or insipid.

– ORIGIN C18: reduplication of **WASHY**.

**wisp** ● **n. 1** a small thin bunch, strand, or amount of something. **2** a small thin person.

– DERIVATIVES **wispily** adv. **wispiness** n. **wispy** adj. (**-ier**, **-iest**).

– ORIGIN ME: origin uncertain.

**wist** past and past participle of **WIT**[2].

**wisteria** /wɪˈstɪərɪə/ (also **wistaria** /-ˈstɛːrɪə/) ● **n.** a climbing shrub of east Asia and North America, with hanging clusters of pale bluish-lilac flowers. [Genus *Wisteria*: several species.]

– ORIGIN mod. L., named after Caspar *Wistar* (or *Wister*) (1761–1818), Amer. anatomist.

**wistful** ● **adj.** having or showing a feeling of vague or regretful longing.

– DERIVATIVES **wistfully** adv. **wistfulness** n.

– ORIGIN C17: appar. from obs. *wistly* 'intently', influenced by **WISHFUL**.

**wit**[1] ● **n. 1** (also **wits**) the capacity for inventive thought and quick understanding; keen intelligence. **2** a natural aptitude for using words and ideas in a quick and inventive way to create humour. **3** a person with this aptitude.

– PHRASES **be at one's wits' end** be completely at a loss as to what to do. **be frightened** (or **scared**) **out of one's wits** be extremely frightened. **gather** (or **collect**) **one's wits** allow oneself to think calmly and clearly in a demanding situation. **have** (or **keep**) **one's wits about one** be constantly alert. **live by one's wits** earn money by clever and sometimes dishonest means, having no regular employment.

– DERIVATIVES **-witted** adj. **wittily** adv. **wittiness** n. **witty** adj. (**-ier**, **-iest**).

– ORIGIN OE *wit(t)*, *gewit(t)*, denoting the mind as the seat of consciousness, of Gmc origin; rel. to **WIT**[2].

**wit**[2] ● **v.** (**wot**, **witting**; past and past part. **wist**) **1** archaic know. **2** (**to wit**) that is to say.

– ORIGIN OE *witan*, of Gmc origin.

**witan** /ˈwɪtən/ ● **n.** another term for **WITENAGEMOT**.

– ORIGIN representing the OE pl. of *wita* 'wise man'.

**witch** ● **n. 1** a woman thought to have evil magic powers. **2** a follower or practitioner of modern witchcraft. **3** informal an ugly or unpleasant old woman. **4** a fascinatingly attractive girl or woman. **5** an edible North Atlantic flatfish. [*Glyptocephalus cynoglossus.*] ● **v. 1** cast an evil spell on. **2** (of a girl or woman) enchant (a man).

– DERIVATIVES **witchlike** adj. **witchy** adj.

– ORIGIN OE *wicca* (masc.), *wicce* (fem.), *wiccian* (v.).

**witchcraft** ● **n.** the practice of magic, especially the use of spells and the invocation of evil spirits. See also **WICCA**.

**witch doctor** ● **n.** a tribal magician credited with powers of healing, divination, and protection against the magic of others.

**witch elm** ● **n.** variant spelling of **WYCH ELM**.

**witchery** ● **n. 1** the practice of magic. **2** bewitching quality or power.

**witches' broom** ● **n.** dense twiggy growth in a tree caused by infection with fungus (especially rusts), mites, or viruses.

**witches' sabbath** ● **n.** see **SABBATH** (sense 2).

**witchetty** /ˈwɪtʃɪti/ (also **witchetty grub**) ● **n.** (pl. **-ies**) a large whitish wood-eating larva of a beetle or moth, eaten as food by some Aboriginals.

– ORIGIN from Adnyamathanha *wityu* 'hooked stick (for extracting grubs)' + *varti* 'grub'.

**witch grass** ● **n. 1** couch grass. **2** (also **old witch grass**) a tough creeping North American grass that can become an invasive weed. [*Panicum capillare.*]

**witch hazel** (also **wych hazel**) ● **n. 1** a shrub with fragrant yellow flowers. [*Hamamelis virginiana* (N. America) and other species.] **2** an astringent lotion made from the bark and leaves of this plant.

– ORIGIN C16: *witch*, var. of *wych* (see **WYCH ELM**).

**witch-hunt** ● **n.** a campaign directed against a person or group holding views considered unorthodox or a threat to society.

– DERIVATIVES **witch-hunting** n.

**witching hour** ● **n.** midnight, regarded as the time when witches are supposedly active.

– ORIGIN with allusion to *the witching time of night* from Shakespeare's *Hamlet* (III. ii. 377).

**witchweed** ● **n.** a small parasitic plant which attaches itself to the roots of maize, sugar, and other plants. [Genus *Striga*.]

**witenagemot** /ˈwɪt(ə)nəgɪˌməʊt/ ● **n.** an Anglo-Saxon national assembly that met to advise the king.

– ORIGIN OE, from *witena*, genitive pl. of *wita* 'wise man' + *gemōt* 'meeting' (cf. **MOOT**).

**with** ● **prep. 1** accompanied by. ➤in the same direction as. **2** possessing; having. **3** indicating the instrument used to perform an action or the material used for a purpose. **4** in opposition to. **5** indicating the manner or attitude in which a person does something. **6** indicating responsibility. **7** in relation to. **8** employed by. ➤using the services of. **9** affected by (a particular fact or condition). ➤indicating the cause of an action or condition. **10** indicating separation or removal from something.

– PHRASES **away** (or **off** or **out** etc.) **with!** take or send away, in, out, etc. **be with someone** informal follow someone's meaning. **with it** informal **1** up to date or fashionable. **2** [usu. with neg.] alert and comprehending. **3** in addition. **with that** at that point.

– ORIGIN OE, prob. a shortening of a Gmc preposition rel. to obs. Engl. *wither* 'adverse, opposite'.

**withal** /wɪˈðɔːl/ archaic ● **adv. 1** in addition. **2** nevertheless. ● **prep.** with.

– ORIGIN ME: orig. as *with all*.

**withdraw** ● **v.** (past **-drew**; past part. **-drawn**) **1** remove or take away. ➤take (money) out of an account. **2** take back; discontinue or retract. **3** leave or cause to leave a place, especially a war zone. ➤cease to participate in an activity or be a member of a team or organization. **4** depart to another place in search of quiet or privacy. ➤retreat from social contact. **5** cease to take an addictive drug.

– DERIVATIVES **withdrawal** n.

– ORIGIN ME: from the prefix *with-* 'away' + **DRAW**.

**withdrawing room** ● n. archaic term for DRAWING ROOM.

**withdrawn** past participle of WITHDRAW. ● adj. unusually shy or reserved.

**withe** /wɪθ, wɪð, wʌɪð/ ● n. variant spelling of WITHY.

**wither** ● v. **1** (of a plant) become dry and shrivelled. **2** become shrunken or wrinkled from age or disease. ➤ fall into decay or decline. **3** mortify with a scornful look or manner. ➤ [as adj. **withering**] scornful.
– DERIVATIVES **witheringly** adv.
– ORIGIN ME: appar. a var. of WEATHER.

**withers** ● pl. n. the highest part of a horse's back, lying at the base of the neck above the shoulders.
– ORIGIN C16: appar. a reduced form of *widersome*, from obs. *wither-* 'against' (as the part that resists the strain of the collar) + a second element of obscure origin.

**withershins** /ˈwɪðəʃɪnz/ ● adv. variant spelling of WIDDERSHINS.

**withhold** ● v. (past and past part. **-held**) **1** refuse to give (something due to or desired by another). **2** suppress or restrain (an emotion or reaction).
– DERIVATIVES **withholder** n.
– ORIGIN ME: from the prefix *with-* 'away' + HOLD[1].

**withholding tax** ● n. a tax levied by some countries on interest or dividends paid to a person resident outside that country.

**within** ● prep. **1** inside. ➤ inside the range of. ➤ inside the bounds set by. **2** not further off than (a particular distance). **3** occurring inside (a particular period of time). ● adv. **1** inside; indoors. **2** internally or inwardly.
– ORIGIN OE *withinnan* 'on the inside'.

**without** ● prep. **1** not accompanied by or having the use of. **2** in which the action mentioned does not happen. **3** archaic or poetic/literary outside. ● adv. archaic or poetic/literary outside. ● conj. archaic or dialect **1** without it being the case that. **2** unless.
– ORIGIN OE *withūtan* 'on the outside'.

**with-profits** ● adj. Brit. (of an insurance policy) allowing the holder to receive a share of the profits made by the company, typically in the form of a bonus.

**withstand** ● v. (past and past part. **-stood**) **1** remain undamaged or unaffected by. **2** offer strong resistance or opposition to.
– DERIVATIVES **withstander** n.
– ORIGIN OE *withstandan*, from the prefix *with-* 'against' + STAND.

**withy** /ˈwɪði/ (also **withe**) ● n. (pl. **withies** or **withes**) **1** a tough flexible branch of an osier or other willow, used for tying, binding, or basketry. **2** another term for OSIER.
– ORIGIN OE *wīthig*, of Gmc origin.

**witless** ● adj. foolish; stupid.
– DERIVATIVES **witlessly** adv. **witlessness** n.

**witling** ● n. archaic, chiefly derogatory a person who considers themselves to be witty.

**witloof** /ˈwɪtluːf/ ● n. chicory of a broad-leaved variety grown for blanching.
– ORIGIN C19: from Du., lit. 'white leaf'.

**witness** ● n. **1** a person who sees an event take place. **2** a person giving sworn testimony to a court of law or the police. **3** a person who is present at the signing of a document and signs it themselves to confirm this. **4** evidence; proof. ➤ open profession of one's religious faith through words or actions. ● v. **1** be a witness to. **2** be the place, period, etc. in which (a particular event) takes place. **3** (**witness to**) give or serve as evidence of. ➤ openly profess one's religious faith in.
– ORIGIN OE *witnes* (see WIT[1], -NESS).

**witness box** (N. Amer. **witness stand**) ● n. Law the place in a court where a witness stands to give evidence.

**witter** ● v. (usu. **witter on**) Brit. informal speak at length about trivial matters.
– ORIGIN C19 (orig. Scots and dial.): prob. imitative.

**witticism** ● n. a witty remark.
– ORIGIN 1677: coined by John Dryden from *witty*, on the pattern of *criticism*.

**witting** ● adj. **1** deliberate. **2** aware of the full facts.
– DERIVATIVES **wittingly** adv.
– ORIGIN ME: from WIT[2] + -ING[2].

**wivern** ● n. archaic spelling of WYVERN.

**wives** plural form of WIFE.

**wiz** ● n. variant spelling of WHIZZ (in sense 3).

**wizard** ● n. **1** a man who has magical powers, especially in legends and fairy tales. **2** a person who is very skilled in a particular field or activity. **3** Computing a software tool that operates automatically to guide a user through a particular process. ● adj. Brit. informal, dated excellent.
– DERIVATIVES **wizardly** adj.
– ORIGIN ME (in the sense 'philosopher, sage'): from WISE[1] + -ARD.

**wizardry** ● n. **1** the art or practice of magic. **2** great skill in a particular field or activity. ➤ the product of such skill: *hi-tech wizardry*.

**wizened** /ˈwɪz(ə)nd/ ● adj. shrivelled or wrinkled with age.
– ORIGIN C16: past part. of archaic *wizen* 'shrivel', of Gmc origin.

**wizzo** ● adj. variant spelling of WHIZZO.

**wk** ● abbrev. week.

**WLTM** ● abbrev. would like to meet.

**Wm** ● abbrev. William.

**WMO** ● abbrev. World Meteorological Organization.

**WNW** ● abbrev. west-north-west.

**WO** ● abbrev. Warrant Officer.

**wo** ● exclam. variant spelling of WHOA.

**woad** /wəʊd/ ● n. **1** a yellow-flowered plant whose leaves were formerly used to make blue dye. [*Isatis tinctoria*.] **2** the dye obtained from this plant, now superseded by synthetic products.
– ORIGIN OE *wād*, of Gmc origin.

**wobbegong** /ˈwɒbɪgɒŋ/ ● n. a brown Australian carpet shark with pale markings. [*Orectolobus maculatus*.]
– ORIGIN C19: prob. from a New South Wales Aborig. lang.

**wobble** ● v. move unsteadily from side to side. ➤ (of the voice) tremble. ➤ waver between different courses of action. ● n. a wobbling movement or sound.
– ORIGIN C17 (orig. as *wabble*): of Gmc origin; rel. to WAVE.

**wobble-board** ● n. Austral. a piece of fibreboard used as a musical instrument, producing a low, rhythmic booming sound when flexed.

**wobbler** ● n. **1** a person or thing that wobbles. ➤ (in angling) a lure that wobbles and does not spin. **2** another term for WOBBLY.

**Wobbly** ● n. informal a member of the Industrial Workers of the World, a former radical US labour movement.
– ORIGIN C20: of unknown origin.

**wobbly** ● adj. (**-ier**, **-iest**) **1** tending to wobble. ➤ weak and unsteady from illness, tiredness, or anxiety. **2** uncertain or insecure. ● n. Brit. informal a fit of temper or panic: *I drove off and threw a wobbly*.
– DERIVATIVES **wobbliness** n.

**wodge** ● n. Brit. informal a large piece or amount.
– ORIGIN C19: alt. of WEDGE[1].

**woe** ● n. poetic/literary **1** great sorrow or distress. **2** (**woes**) troubles.
– PHRASES **woe betide someone** (or **woe to someone**) humorous a person will be in trouble if they do a specified thing. **woe is me!** humorous an exclamation of sorrow or distress.
– ORIGIN natural exclamation of lament: recorded as *wā* in OE and found in several Gmc langs.

**woebegone** /ˈwəʊbɪgɒn/ ● adj. sad or miserable in appearance.
– ORIGIN ME: from WOE + *begone* 'surrounded' (past part. of obs. *bego* 'go around, beset').

**woeful** ● adj. **1** full of sorrow; miserable. **2** deplorable.
– DERIVATIVES **woefully** adv. **woefulness** n.

**wog**[1] ● n. Brit. informal, offensive a person who is not white.
– ORIGIN 1920s: of unknown origin.

**wog**[2] ● n. Austral. informal a minor illness or infection.
– ORIGIN 1930s: of unknown origin.

**woggle** ● n. a loop or ring of leather or cord through which the ends of a Scout's neckerchief are threaded.
– ORIGIN 1930s: of unknown origin.

**wok** • **n.** a bowl-shaped frying pan used in Chinese cookery.
– ORIGIN Chin. (Cantonese dial.).

**woke** past of **WAKE**[1].

**woken** past participle of **WAKE**[1].

**wold** /wəʊld/ • **n.** (especially in British place names) a piece of high, open, uncultivated land or moor.
– ORIGIN OE *wald* 'wooded upland', of Gmc origin.

**wolf** • **n.** (pl. **wolves**) **1** a carnivorous mammal which is the largest member of the dog family, living and hunting in packs. [*Canis lupus*.] ➤ used in names of similar or related mammals, e.g. **Tasmanian wolf**. **2** a rapacious or ferocious person. ➤ informal a man who habitually seduces women. **3** an out-of-tune effect produced when playing particular notes or intervals on a musical instrument, caused either by the instrument's construction or by divergence from equal temperament. • **v.** (usu. **wolf something down**) devour (food) greedily.
– PHRASES **cry wolf** raise repeated false alarms, so that a real cry for help is ignored. [with allusion to the fable of the shepherd boy who deluded people with false cries of 'Wolf!'] **hold** (or **have**) **a wolf by the ears** be in a precarious position. **keep the wolf from the door** have enough money to avert hunger or destitution. **throw someone to the wolves** sacrifice someone so as to avert trouble for oneself. **a wolf in sheep's clothing** a person who appears friendly but is really hostile. [with biblical allusion to Matt. 7:15.]
– DERIVATIVES **wolfish** adj. **wolfishly** adv. **wolf-like** adj.
– ORIGIN OE *wulf*, of Gmc origin.

**Wolf Cub** • **n.** chiefly Brit. former term for ***Cub Scout*** (see **CUB** sense 2).

**wolf fish** • **n.** a large long-bodied marine fish with a long-based dorsal fin and sharp teeth. [*Anarhichas lupus* and other species.]

**wolfhound** • **n.** a dog of a large breed originally used to hunt wolves.

**wolfram** /ˈwʊlfrəm/ • **n.** tungsten or its ore, especially as a commercial commodity.
– ORIGIN C18: from Ger., perh. from *Wolf* 'wolf' + Mid. High Ger. *rām* 'soot', prob. orig. a pejorative miners' term referring to the ore's inferiority to tin.

**wolframite** • **n.** a black or brown mineral consisting of a tungstate of iron and manganese.

**wolfsbane** /ˈwʊlfsbeɪn/ • **n.** a northern aconite with yellow or purple flowers. [*Aconitum lycoctonum* and related species.]

**wolf spider** • **n.** a fast-moving ground spider which runs after and springs on its prey. [Family Lycosidae.]

**wolf whistle** • **n.** a whistle with a rising and falling pitch, used to express sexual attraction or admiration. • **v.** (**wolf-whistle**) whistle in such a way at.

**wollastonite** /ˈwʊləstənʌɪt/ • **n.** a white or greyish mineral consisting of calcium silicate, used as a source of rock wool.
– ORIGIN C19: named after the Engl. chemist William Hyde *Wollaston* + **-ITE**[1].

**Wolof** /ˈwəʊlɒf/ • **n.** (pl. same or **Wolofs**) **1** a member of a people living in Senegal and Gambia. **2** the Niger–Congo language of this people.
– ORIGIN the name in Wolof.

**wolverine** /ˈwʊlvəriːn/ • **n.** a heavily built short-legged carnivorous mammal of northern tundra and forests. [*Gulo gulo*.]
– ORIGIN C16 (orig. as *wolvering*): formed obscurely from *wolv-*, pl. stem of **WOLF**.

**wolves** plural form of **WOLF**.

**woman** • **n.** (pl. **women**) **1** an adult human female. **2** a female worker or employee. ➤ a female domestic help. **3** a wife or lover.
– PHRASES **the little woman** a condescending way of referring to one's wife. **woman of letters** a female scholar or author. **woman of the streets** euphemistic, dated a prostitute. **woman to woman** in a direct and frank way between two women.
– DERIVATIVES **womanless** adj. **womanlike** adj. **womanliness** n. **womanly** adj.
– ORIGIN OE *wīfmon*, *-man* (see **WIFE**, **MAN**), a formation peculiar to Engl., the ancient word being **WIFE**.

**-woman** • **comb. form 1** in nouns denoting a female of a specified nationality or origin: *Englishwoman*. **2** in nouns denoting a woman belonging to a specified group or having a specified occupation or role: *laywoman* | *oarswoman*.

**womanhood** • **n. 1** the state or condition of being a woman. **2** women considered collectively. **3** the qualities traditionally associated with women.

**womanish** • **adj.** derogatory **1** suitable for or characteristic of a woman. **2** (of a man) effeminate.
– DERIVATIVES **womanishly** adv. **womanishness** n.

**womanism** • **n.** (especially among black women) a form of feminism that acknowledges women's natural contribution to society.
– DERIVATIVES **womanist** n.

**womanize** (also **-ise**) • **v.** [usu. as noun **womanizing**] (of a man) enter into numerous casual sexual relationships with women.
– DERIVATIVES **womanizer** n.

**womankind** • **n.** women considered collectively.

**woman of the bedchamber** • **n.** (in the UK) a female attendant to the queen or queen mother, ranking in the royal household below lady of the bedchamber.

**womb** • **n.** the organ in the lower body of a woman or female mammal where offspring are conceived and in which they gestate before birth; the uterus.
– ORIGIN OE *wamb*, *womb*, of Gmc origin.

**wombat** /ˈwɒmbat/ • **n.** a burrowing plant-eating Australian marsupial which resembles a small bear with short legs. [*Vombatus ursinus* and other species.]
– ORIGIN C18: from Dharuk.

**women** plural form of **WOMAN**.

**womenfolk** • **pl. n.** a group of women considered collectively.

**women's lib** • **n.** informal short for **WOMEN'S LIBERATION**.
– DERIVATIVES **women's libber** n.

**women's liberation** • **n.** the liberation of women from inequalities and subservient status in relation to men, and from attitudes causing these (now generally replaced by the term *feminism*).

**women's movement** • **n.** a broad movement campaigning for women's liberation and rights.

**women's rights** • **pl. n.** rights that promote a position of legal and social equality of women with men.

**women's studies** • **pl. n.** [usu. treated as sing.] academic courses which focus on the roles, experiences, and achievements of women.

**women's work** • **n.** work traditionally undertaken by women, especially domestic tasks such as cooking and child rearing.

**womyn** /ˈwɪmɪn/ • **pl. n.** non-standard spelling of 'women' adopted by some feminists in order to avoid the word ending in *-men*.

**won**[1] past and past participle of **WIN**.

**won**[2] /wɒn/ • **n.** (pl. same) the basic monetary unit of North and South Korea, equal to 100 jun in North Korea and 100 jeon in South Korea.
– ORIGIN from Korean *wǒn*.

**wonder** • **n. 1** a feeling of surprise and admiration, caused by something beautiful, unexpected, or unfamiliar. **2** a person or thing that causes such a feeling. ➤ [as modifier] having remarkable properties or abilities. • **v. 1** feel curious; desire to know. ➤ used to express a polite question or request. **2** feel doubt. **3** feel wonder.
– PHRASES **I shouldn't wonder** informal I think it likely. **no** (or **little** or **small**) **wonder** it is not surprising. **nine days'** (or **seven-day** or **one-day**) **wonder** something that attracts great interest for a short while but is then forgotten. **wonders will never cease** often ironic an exclamation of surprise and pleasure. **work** (or **do**) **wonders** have a very beneficial effect.
– DERIVATIVES **wonderer** n. **wondering** adj. **wonderingly** adv.
– ORIGIN OE *wundor* (n.), *wundrian* (v.), of Gmc origin.

**wonderful** • **adj.** extremely good, pleasant, or remarkable.

– DERIVATIVES **wonderfully** adv. **wonderfulness** n.

**wonderland** • n. a place full of wonderful things.

**wonderment** • n. a state of awed admiration or respect.

**wondrous** • adj. poetic/literary inspiring wonder. • adv. archaic wonderfully.
– DERIVATIVES **wondrously** adv. **wondrousness** n.
– ORIGIN C15: alt. of obs. *wonders* (adj. and adv.), genitive of WONDER, on the pattern of *marvellous*.

**wonga** /ˈwɒŋgə, ˈvɒŋgə/ • n. Brit. informal money.
– ORIGIN C20: perh. from Romany *wongar* 'coal', also 'money'.

**wonk** • n. N. Amer. informal, derogatory **1** a studious or hardworking person. ➤(often **policy wonk**) a person who takes an excessive interest in minor details of political policy. **2** nautical slang an incompetent or inexperienced sailor, especially a naval cadet.
– ORIGIN 1920s: of unknown origin.

**wonky** • adj. (**-ier, -iest**) informal **1** crooked; askew. **2** unsteady or faulty.
– DERIVATIVES **wonkily** adv. **wonkiness** n.
– ORIGIN C20: fanciful formation.

**wont** /wəʊnt/ • adj. archaic or poetic/literary accustomed: *he was wont to arise at 5.30.* • n. (**one's wont**) formal or humorous one's customary behaviour. • v. (3rd sing. present **wonts** or **wont**; past and past part. **wont** or **wonted**) archaic make or become accustomed.
– ORIGIN OE *gewunod*, past part. of *wunian*, 'dwell, be accustomed', of Gmc origin.

**won't** • contr. will not.

**wonted** /ˈwəʊntɪd/ • adj. archaic or poetic/literary usual.
– ORIGIN ME: from WONT.

**wonton** /wɒnˈtɒn/ • n. (in Chinese cookery) a small round dumpling with a savoury filling, served in soup.
– ORIGIN from Chin. (Cantonese dial.) *wān t'ān*.

**woo** • v. (**woos, wooed**) **1** try to gain the love of (a woman). **2** seek the support or custom of.
– DERIVATIVES **wooable** adj. **wooer** n.
– ORIGIN OE *wōgian, āwōgian*, of unknown origin.

**wood** • n. **1** the hard fibrous material forming the main substance of the trunk or branches of a tree or shrub, used for fuel or timber. ➤(**the wood**) wooden barrels used for storing alcoholic drinks. ➤a golf club with a wooden or other head that is relatively broad from face to back. ➤another term for BOWL² (in sense 1). **2** (also **woods**) a small forest.
– PHRASES **be unable to see the wood** (or N. Amer. **the forest**) **for the trees** fail to grasp the main issue because of over-attention to details. **out of the wood** (or **woods**) [usu. with neg.] out of danger or difficulty. **touch** (or chiefly N. Amer. **knock on**) **wood** touch something wooden to ward off bad luck.
– DERIVATIVES **woodless** adj.
– ORIGIN OE *wudu*, from Gmc.

**wood alcohol** • n. crude methanol made by distillation from wood.

**wood anemone** • n. a spring-flowering anemone with pink-tinged white flowers, growing in woodland and shady places. [*Anemone nemorosa*.]

**wood avens** • n. a yellow-flowered plant favouring damp shady habitats. [*Geum urbanum*.]

**woodbine** • n. **1** Brit. the common honeysuckle. **2** N. Amer. Virginia creeper.

**woodblock** • n. **1** a block of wood from which woodcut prints are made. **2** a hollow wooden block used as a percussion instrument.

**woodchat shrike** • n. a black and white shrike with a chestnut head, native to southern Europe, North Africa, and the Middle East. [*Lanius senator*.]

**woodchip** (also **woodchip paper**) • n. chiefly Brit. wallpaper with woodchips embedded in it to give a grainy surface texture.

**woodchuck** • n. a North American marmot with a heavy body and short legs. [*Marmota monax*.]
– ORIGIN C17: alt. (by assoc. with WOOD) of an Amer. Indian name.

**woodcock** • n. (pl. same) a long-billed woodland bird of the sandpiper family, with brown plumage. [*Scolopax rusticola* (Eurasia) and related species.]

**woodcraft** • n. chiefly N. Amer. **1** skill in woodwork. **2** knowledge of woodland, especially with reference to outdoor pursuits.

**woodcut** • n. a print of a type made from a design cut in relief in a block of wood, formerly used for book illustrations.

**woodcutter** • n. **1** a person who cuts down wood, especially for fuel. **2** a person who makes woodcuts.
– DERIVATIVES **woodcutting** n.

**wood duck** • n. a tree-nesting North American duck, the male of which has brightly coloured plumage. [*Aix sponsa*.]

**wooded** • adj. (of land) covered with woods.

**wooden** • adj. **1** made of wood. ➤like or characteristic of wood: *a dull wooden sound.* **2** stiff and awkward.
– DERIVATIVES **woodenly** adv. **woodenness** n.

**wood engraving** • n. **1** a print made from a finely detailed design cut into the end grain of a block of wood. **2** the technique of making such prints.
– DERIVATIVES **wood engraver** n.

**wooden-head** • n. informal a stupid person.
– DERIVATIVES **wooden-headed** adj. **wooden-headedness** n.

**wooden spoon** • n. chiefly Brit. a real or imaginary prize awarded to the person who is last in a race or competition.
– ORIGIN orig. a spoon given to the candidate coming last in the Cambridge mathematical tripos.

**woodentop** • n. Brit. informal, derogatory **1** a uniformed policeman. **2** a soldier belonging to the Guards.

**wood fibre** • n. fibre obtained from wood and used especially in the manufacture of paper.

**woodgrain** • adj. denoting a surface or finish imitating the grain pattern of wood.

**woodland** • n. (also **woodlands**) land covered with trees.
– DERIVATIVES **woodlander** n.

**woodlark** • n. a small lark with a short tail and melodious song, frequenting open ground with scattered trees. [*Lullula arborea*.]

**woodlouse** • n. (pl. **woodlice**) a small terrestrial crustacean with a greyish segmented body which it is able to roll into a ball. [*Oniscus* and other genera.]

**woodman** • n. (pl. **-men**) dated a forester or woodcutter.

**wood mouse** • n. a common dark brown mouse with a long tail and large eyes. [*Apodemus sylvaticus* and related species.]

**woodnote** • n. poetic/literary a natural and untrained musical note or song resembling that of a bird.

**wood nymph** • n. **1** (in folklore and classical mythology) a dryad or hamadryad. **2** a brown American butterfly with eyespots on its wings. [Genus *Cercyonis*.]

**woodpecker** • n. a bird with a strong bill and a stiff tail, typically pecking at tree trunks to find insects and drumming on dead wood. [Family Picidae: many species.]

**wood pigeon** • n. a common large pigeon, mainly grey with white patches forming a ring round its neck. [*Columba palumbus*.]

**woodpile** • n. a stack of wood stored for fuel.

**wood pulp** • n. wood fibre reduced chemically or mechanically to pulp and used in the manufacture of paper.

**woodrat** • n. a rat-like rodent that accumulates a mound of sticks and debris at the nest hole, native to North and Central America. [*Neotoma* and other genera: many species.]

**woodruff** (also **sweet woodruff**) • n. a white-flowered plant with sweet-scented leaves used to flavour drinks and in perfumery. [*Galium odoratum*.]
– ORIGIN OE *wudurofe*, from *wudu* 'wood' + an element of unknown meaning.

**woodrush** • n. a grass-like plant with long flat leaves fringed with long hairs. [Genus *Luzula*: many species.]

**wood sage** • n. a yellow-flowered plant of the mint family, growing in dry shady places. [*Teucrium scorodonia*.]
**woodscrew** • n. a tapering metal screw with a sharp point.
**woodshed** • n. a shed where firewood is stored.
– PHRASES **something nasty in the woodshed** Brit. informal a shocking or distasteful thing that has been kept secret. [from the novel *Cold Comfort Farm* by Stella Gibbons (1933).] **take someone to the woodshed** N. Amer. informal, dated reprove or punish someone.
**woodsman** • n. (pl. **-men**) a forester, hunter, or woodcutter.
**wood sorrel** • n. a woodland plant with clover-like leaves and pink or white flowers. [*Oxalis acetosella*.]
**wood spirit** • n. another term for WOOD ALCOHOL.
**wood stain** • n. a commercially produced substance for colouring wood.
**woodsy** • adj. N. Amer. of, relating to, or characteristic of wood or woodland.
**woodturning** • n. the activity of shaping wood with a lathe.
– DERIVATIVES **woodturner** n.
**wood warbler** • n. **1** a yellow-breasted warbler found in woodland, with a trilling song. [*Phylloscopus sibilatrix*.] **2** any of the North American warblers. [Family Parulidae.]
**woodwasp** • n. a large wasp-like sawfly with a long egg-laying tube which deposits its eggs in the trunks of trees. [Family Siricidae: several species.]
**woodwind** • n. [treated as sing. or pl.] wind instruments other than brass instruments forming a section of an orchestra, including flutes, oboes, clarinets, and bassoons.
**wood wool** • n. Brit. a mass of fine soft wood shavings, used as a packing material.
**woodwork** • n. **1** the wooden parts of a building or other structure. **2** Brit. the activity or skill of making things from wood.
– PHRASES **come out of the woodwork** (of an unpleasant person or thing) emerge from obscurity.
– DERIVATIVES **woodworker** n. **woodworking** n.
**woodworm** • n. **1** the wood-boring larva of the furniture beetle. **2** the damaged condition of wood resulting from infestation with this larva.
**woody** • adj. (**-ier**, **-iest**) **1** covered with trees. **2** made of, resembling, or suggestive of wood.
– DERIVATIVES **woodiness** n.
**woodyard** • n. a yard where wood is chopped or stored.
**woody nightshade** • n. a climbing plant with purple flowers and poisonous red berry-like fruit. [*Solanum dulcamara*.]
**woof[1]** /wʊf/ • n. the barking sound made by a dog. • v. **1** bark. **2** US black slang say something boastfully or aggressively. **3** informal consume (food) ravenously.
– ORIGIN C19: imitative.
**woof[2]** /wu:f/ • n. another term for WEFT[1].
– ORIGIN OE *ōwef*, a compound from the base of WEAVE[1]; ME *oof* later became *woof* by assoc. with WARP.
**woofer** /ˈwu:fə, ˈwʊfə/ • n. a loudspeaker designed to reproduce low frequencies.
**woofter** /ˈwʊftə, ˈwu:ftə/ • n. Brit. informal, derogatory an effeminate or homosexual man.
– ORIGIN 1970s: alt. of POOFTER.
**wool** • n. the fine soft curly or wavy hair forming the coat of a sheep, goat, or similar animal, especially when shorn and made into cloth or yarn. ➤ the soft underfur or down of some other mammals. ➤ a metal or mineral made into a mass of fine fibres: *lead wool*.
– PHRASES **pull the wool over someone's eyes** deceive someone.
– DERIVATIVES **wool-like** adj.
– ORIGIN OE *wull*, of Gmc origin.
**wool-gathering** • n. indulgence in aimless thought.
– DERIVATIVES **wool-gather** v.
**wool grower** • n. a breeder of sheep for wool.
**woollen** (US **woolen**) • adj. made wholly or partly of wool. • n. (**woollens**) woollen garments.
**woolly** • adj. (**-ier**, **-iest**) **1** made of wool. ➤ (of an animal or plant) covered with wool or hair resembling wool. ➤ resembling wool in texture or appearance. **2** vague or confused: *woolly thinking*. **3** (of a sound) indistinct or distorted. • n. (pl. **-ies**) informal **1** chiefly Brit. a woollen garment, especially a pullover. **2** Austral./NZ a sheep.
– DERIVATIVES **woolliness** n.
**woolly bear** • n. **1** a large hairy caterpillar, especially that of a tiger moth. **2** the small hairy larva of a carpet beetle or museum beetle.
**woolman** • n. (pl. **-men**) chiefly historical a wool merchant.
**woolpack** • n. historical a bale of wool.
**Woolsack** • n. **1** (in the UK) the Lord Chancellor's wool-stuffed seat in the House of Lords. **2** (**the woolsack**) the position of Lord Chancellor.
**woolshed** • n. Austral./NZ a large shed for shearing and baling wool.
**wool-sorters' disease** • n. a form of anthrax in humans causing pneumonia.
**wool-stapler** • n. archaic a person who buys wool from a producer, grades it, and sells it to a manufacturer.
**wool work** • n. needlework executed in wool on a canvas foundation.
**woomera** /ˈwu:m(ə)rə/ • n. Austral. an Aboriginal stick used to throw a dart or spear more forcibly.
– ORIGIN from Dharuk *wamara*.
**woomph** /wu:mf, wʊmf/ • adv. & exclam. used to imitate a sound like that of a sudden blow or impact accompanied by an expulsion of air.
**Woop Woop** /ˈwʊp wʊp/ • n. Austral./NZ informal a humorous name for a remote outback town or district.
– ORIGIN 1920s: mock Aborig.
**woosh** • v., n., & exclam. variant spelling of WHOOSH.
**woozy** • adj. (**-ier**, **-iest**) informal unsteady, dizzy, or dazed.
– DERIVATIVES **woozily** adv. **wooziness** n.
– ORIGIN C19: of unknown origin.
**wop** • n. offensive an Italian or other southern European.
– ORIGIN C20 (orig. US): origin uncertain, perh. from Ital. *guappo* 'bold, showy'.
**Worcester** /ˈwʊstə/ (also **Royal Worcester**) • n. trademark porcelain made at Worcester in England since 1751.
**Worcester sauce** (also **Worcestershire sauce**) • n. a pungent sauce containing soy sauce and vinegar, first made in Worcester.
**Worcs.** • abbrev. Worcestershire.
**word** • n. **1** a single distinct meaningful element of speech or writing, used to form sentences with others. **2** a remark or statement. ➤ [with neg.] (**a word**) even the smallest amount of something spoken or written: *don't believe a word*. ➤ (**words**) angry talk. ➤ (**the word**) a command, slogan, or signal. **3** speech as distinct from action. **4** (**one's word**) a person's account of the truth, especially when it differs from that of another person. ➤ a promise or assurance. **5** (**words**) the text of a play, opera, or other performed piece. **6** news. **7** a basic unit of data in a computer, typically 16 or 32 bits long. • v. **1** express in particular words. **2** (**word up**) [as imper.] black English listen.
– PHRASES **at a word** as soon as requested. **be as good as one's word** do what one has promised. **have a word** speak briefly to someone. **have a word in someone's ear** speak to someone privately and discreetly. **in other words** that is to say. **in so many words** [often with neg.] precisely in the way mentioned. **in a word** briefly. **a man** (or **woman**) **of his** (or **her**) **word** a person who keeps their promises. **on** (or **upon**) **my word** an exclamation of surprise or emphasis. **put words into someone's mouth 1** inaccurately report what someone has said. **2** prompt someone to say something inadvertently. **take someone at their word** interpret a person's words literally. **take the words out of someone's mouth** say what someone else was about to say. **take someone's word** (**for it**) believe what someone says or writes without checking for oneself. **too —— for words** informal extremely ——. **waste words** talk in vain. **the Word** (**of God**) **1** the Bible, or a part of it. **2** Jesus Christ (see LOGOS). **word for word** in exactly the same or, when translated, exactly equivalent words. **word of honour** a solemn promise. **word of mouth** spoken communication

as a means of transmitting information. **the word on the street** informal a current rumour or piece of information. **a word to the wise** a hint or brief explanation given, that being all that is required.
– DERIVATIVES **wordage** n. **wordless** adj. **wordlessly** adv. **wordlessness** n.
– ORIGIN OE, of Gmc origin.

**word association** • n. the spontaneous production of other words in response to a given word, especially as a technique in psychiatric evaluation.

**word blindness** • n. less technical term for **ALEXIA**, or (less accurately) for **DYSLEXIA**.

**wordbook** • n. a study book containing lists of words and meanings or other related information.

**word break** (also **word division**) • n. Printing a point at which a word is split between two lines of text by means of a hyphen.

**word class** • n. a category of words of similar form or function; a part of speech.

**word deafness** • n. an inability to identify spoken words, resulting from a brain defect.

**wording** • n. the words used to express something; the way in which something is expressed.

**word-perfect** • adj. (of an actor or speaker) knowing one's part or speech by heart.

**wordplay** • n. the witty exploitation of the meanings and ambiguities of words.

**word problem** • n. Mathematics the problem of determining whether two different products are equal, or two sequences of operations are equivalent.

**word processor** • n. a purpose-built computer or program for storing, manipulating, and formatting text entered from a keyboard and providing a printout.
– DERIVATIVES **word-process** v. **word-processing** n.

**word salad** • n. Psychiatry a form of speech indicative of advanced schizophrenia, in which random words and phrases are mixed together unintelligibly.

**wordsearch** • n. a puzzle consisting of letters arranged in a grid, containing several hidden words written in any direction.

**wordsmith** • n. a skilled user of words.

**word square** • n. a puzzle requiring the discovery of a set of words of equal length written one under another to read the same down as across, e.g. *too old ode*.

**wordy** • adj. (**-ier**, **-iest**) **1** using or expressed in too many words. **2** archaic consisting of words.
– DERIVATIVES **wordily** adv. **wordiness** n.

**wore**[1] past of **WEAR**[1].

**wore**[2] past and past participle of **WEAR**[2].

**work** • n. **1** activity involving mental or physical effort done in order to achieve a result. **2** such activity as a means of earning income. ➤W. Indian a job. **3** a task or tasks to be undertaken. ➤the materials for this. ➤(**works**) Theology good or moral deeds. **4** a thing or things done or made; the result of an action. ➤(**works**) the complete artistic production of a particular author, composer, or artist. **5** (**works**) [treated as sing.] chiefly Brit. a place where industrial or manufacturing processes are carried out. **6** (**works**) chiefly Brit. operations of building or repair. **7** Military a defensive structure. **8** (**works**) the mechanism of a clock or other machine. **9** Physics the exertion of force overcoming resistance or producing molecular change. **10** (**the works**) informal everything needed, desired, or expected. • v. (past and past part. **worked** or archaic **wrought**) **1** do work, especially as one's job. ➤have a job. ➤set to or keep at work. **2** (of a machine or system) function, especially properly or effectively. ➤(with reference to a machine) be or cause to be in operation. **3** have the desired result. ➤bring about. ➤campaign. ➤(**work on/upon**) exert influence on. **4** bring (a material or mixture) to a desired shape or consistency. ➤(**work in**) produce articles or pictures using (a particular material or medium). ➤produce (an article or design) using a specified material or sewing stitch. ➤cultivate (land) or extract materials from (a mine or quarry). **5** move or cause to move gradually or with difficulty into another position. ➤(of a person's features) move violently or convulsively. **6** bring into a specified emotional state: *Harold had worked himself into a rage.* **7** Sailing make progress to windward, with repeated tacking.
– PHRASES **give someone the works** informal **1** tell someone everything. **2** treat someone harshly or violently. **have one's work cut out** be faced with a hard or lengthy task. **in the works** chiefly N. Amer. being planned, worked on, or produced. **work to rule** chiefly Brit. follow official working rules and hours exactly in order to reduce output and efficiency, especially as a form of industrial action. **work one's passage** pay for one's journey on a ship with work instead of money.
– PHRASAL VERBS **work something in** try to include something. **work something off 1** discharge a debt by working. **2** reduce or eliminate something by activity. **work out 1** be capable of being solved. **2** develop in a good or specified way. **3** engage in vigorous physical exercise. **work out at** be calculated at. **work someone out** understand someone's character. **work something out 1** solve something. **2** plan something in detail. **work someone over** informal beat someone up. **work up to** proceed gradually towards (something more advanced). **work someone up** (often **get worked up**) gradually bring someone, especially oneself, to a state of intense excitement, anger, or anxiety. **work something up 1** develop or improve something gradually. **2** develop by activity or effort.
– DERIVATIVES **workless** adj.
– ORIGIN OE *weorc* (n.), *wyrcan* (v.), of Gmc origin.

**-work** • comb. form **1** denoting things or parts made of a specified material or with specified tools: *silverwork*. **2** denoting a mechanism or structure of a specified kind: *clockwork*. **3** denoting ornamentation of a specified kind, or articles having such ornamentation: *knotwork*.

**workable** • adj. **1** able to be worked. **2** capable of producing the desired result.
– DERIVATIVES **workability** n. **workably** adv.

**workaday** • adj. not unusual or interesting; ordinary.

**workaholic** • n. informal a person who compulsively works excessively hard for unusually long hours.
– DERIVATIVES **workaholism** n.

**workaround** • n. Computing a method for overcoming a problem or limitation in a program or system.

**workbench** • n. a bench at which carpentry or other mechanical or practical work is done.

**workbook** • n. a student's book containing instruction and exercises relating to a particular subject.

**work camp** • n. a camp at which community work is done, especially by young volunteers.

**workday** • n. a day on which one works.

**worker** • n. **1** a person who works. ➤informal a person who works hard. **2** a neuter or undeveloped female bee, wasp, ant, etc., large numbers of which perform the basic work of a colony. **3** a person who achieves a specified thing: *a worker of miracles.*

**worker priest** • n. a Roman Catholic or Anglican priest who engages part-time in secular work.

**work ethic** • n. another term for **PROTESTANT ETHIC**.

**work experience** • n. short-term experience of employment, arranged for older pupils by schools.

**workfare** • n. a welfare system which requires some work or attendance for training from those receiving benefits.
– ORIGIN 1960s: from **WORK** + *(wel)fare.*

**workforce** • n. [treated as sing. or pl.] the people engaged in or available for work, either in an area or in a particular firm or industry.

**work-harden** • v. [often as noun **work-hardening**] Metallurgy toughen (a metal) as a result of cold-working.

**workhorse** • n. a person or machine that works hard and reliably over a long period.

**workhouse** • n. **1** historical (in the UK) a public institution in which the destitute of a parish received board and lodging in return for work. **2** US a prison in which petty offenders are expected to work.

**working** • adj. **1** having paid employment. ➤engaged in manual labour. ➤(of an animal) used in farming, hunting, or for guard duties. **2** functioning or able to function.

➤(of parts of a machine) moving and causing a machine to operate. **3** good enough as the basis for work or argument and likely to be developed or improved later: *a working title.* ● **n. 1** a mine or a part of a mine from which minerals are being extracted. **2** (**workings**) the way in which a machine, organization, or system operates. ➤the record of the successive calculations made in solving a mathematical problem. **3** a scheduled duty or trip performed by a locomotive, bus, etc.

**working capital** ● **n.** Finance the capital of a business which is used in its day-to-day trading operations, calculated as the current assets minus the current liabilities.

**working class** ● **n.** [treated as sing. or pl.] the social group consisting of people who are employed for wages, especially in manual or industrial work. ● **adj.** of or relating to the working class.

**working drawing** ● **n.** a scale drawing which serves as a guide for the construction or manufacture of something.

**working girl** ● **n.** informal, euphemistic a prostitute.

**working party** (also **working group**) ● **n.** Brit. a group appointed to study and report on a particular question and make recommendations.

**workload** ● **n.** the amount of work to be done by someone or something.

**workman** ● **n.** (pl. **-men**) **1** a man employed to do manual labour. **2** a person who works in a specified way.

**workmanlike** ● **adj.** showing efficient competence.

**workmanship** ● **n.** the degree of skill with which a product is made or a job done.

**workmate** ● **n.** chiefly Brit. a colleague.

**work of art** ● **n.** a creative product with strong imaginative or aesthetic appeal.

**workout** ● **n.** a session of vigorous physical exercise.

**workpeople** ● **pl. n.** Brit. people in paid employment, especially in manual or industrial labour.

**work permit** ● **n.** an official document giving a foreigner permission to take a job in a country.

**workpiece** ● **n.** an object being worked on with a tool or machine.

**workplace** ● **n.** a place where people work.

**work rate** ● **n.** the amount of energy that is expended in sport or physical exercise.

**work release** ● **n.** leave of absence from prison by day enabling a prisoner to continue in normal employment.

**workroom** ● **n.** a room for working in.

**works council** ● **n.** chiefly Brit. a group of employees representing a workforce in discussions with their employers.

**worksheet** ● **n. 1** a paper listing questions or tasks for students. **2** a record of work done or in progress.

**workshop** ● **n. 1** a room or building in which goods are manufactured or repaired. **2** a meeting at which a group engages in intensive discussion and activity on a particular subject or project.

**work-shy** ● **adj.** disinclined to work.

**worksite** ● **n.** an area where work takes place.

**workspace** ● **n. 1** an area rented or sold for commercial purposes. **2** Computing a memory storage facility for temporary use.

**workstation** ● **n. 1** a desktop computer terminal, typically networked and more powerful than a personal computer. **2** an area where work of a particular nature is carried out, such as a location on an assembly line.

**worktop** ● **n.** Brit. a flat surface for working on, especially in a kitchen.

**workweek** ● **n.** N. Amer. the total number of hours or days worked in a week.

**world** ● **n. 1** (**the world**) the earth with all its countries and peoples. ➤all of the people on the earth. **2** a region or group of countries: *the English-speaking world.* **3** human and social interaction. ➤(**one's world**) a person's life and activities. **4** all that belongs to a particular historical period or sphere of activity. **5** secular or material matters as opposed to spiritual ones. ➤a stage of human life, either mortal or after death. **6** another planet like the earth.

– PHRASES **the best of both** (or **all possible**) **worlds** the benefits of widely differing situations, enjoyed at the same time. **bring someone into the world** give birth to or assist at the birth of someone. —— **in the world** used to express astonishment or disbelief in questions: *what in the world are they doing?* **man** (or **woman**) **of the world** a person who is experienced in the ways of sophisticated society. **not do something for the world** not do something whatever the inducement. **out of this world** informal extremely enjoyable or impressive. **think the world of** have a very high regard for. **the world and his wife** Brit. informal everybody. **the world, the flesh, and the devil** all forms of temptation to sin. **a** (or **the**) **world of** a very great deal of.

– ORIGIN OE *w(e)oruld*, from a Gmc compound meaning 'age of man'.

**world-beater** ● **n.** a person or thing that is better than all others in its field.

**world-class** ● **adj.** of or among the best in the world.

**World Cup** ● **n.** a competition between teams from several countries in a sport, in particular an international soccer tournament held every four years.

**world English** ● **n.** the English language including all of its regional varieties, such as North American, Australian, and South African English.

**world fair** (also **world's fair**) ● **n.** an international exhibition of the industrial, scientific, technological, and artistic achievements of the participating nations.

**world-famous** ● **adj.** known throughout the world.

**World Heritage Site** ● **n.** a natural or man-made site or structure recognized as being of outstanding international importance and as deserving special protection.

**world line** ● **n.** Physics a curve in space–time joining the positions of a particle throughout its existence.

**worldling** ● **n.** a worldly person.

**worldly** ● **adj.** (**-ier**, **-iest**) **1** of or concerned with material affairs rather than spiritual ones. **2** experienced and sophisticated.

– PHRASES **worldly goods** (or **possessions** or **wealth**) everything that someone owns.

– DERIVATIVES **worldliness** n.

**worldly-wise** ● **adj.** having sufficient experience not to be easily shocked or deceived.

**world music** ● **n.** music from the developing world incorporating traditional and/or popular elements.

**world order** ● **n.** a set of arrangements established internationally for preserving global political stability.

**world power** ● **n.** a country that has significant influence in international affairs.

**world-ranking** ● **adj.** among the best in the world.

**world's fair** ● **n.** variant form of **WORLD FAIR**.

**world-shaking** ● **adj.** very important; momentous.

**world view** ● **n.** a particular philosophy of life or conception of the world.

**world war** ● **n.** a war involving many large nations in all different parts of the world, especially the wars of 1914–18 and 1939–45.

**world-weary** ● **adj.** bored with or cynical about life.

– DERIVATIVES **world-weariness** n.

**worldwide** ● **adj.** extending or applicable throughout the world. ● **adv.** throughout the world.

**World Wide Web** ● **n.** Computing an extensive information system on the Internet providing facilities for documents to be connected to other documents by hypertext links.

**WORM** ● **abbrev.** Computing write-once read-many.

**worm** ● **n. 1** an earthworm or other creeping or burrowing invertebrate animal having a long slender soft body and no limbs. [Annelida, Nematoda (roundworms), Platyhelminthes (flatworms), and other phyla.] ➤(**worms**) intestinal or other internal parasites. ➤used in names of long slender insect larvae and other creatures, e.g. **army worm**, **slow-worm**. **2** a maggot regarded as eating dead bodies buried in the ground. **3** informal a weak or despicable person. **4** the threaded cylin-

der in a worm gear. **5** the coiled pipe of a still in which the vapour is cooled and condensed. **6** Computing a self-replicating program able to propagate itself across a network, typically having a detrimental effect. ● **v. 1** move by crawling or wriggling. **2** (**worm one's way into**) insinuate one's way into. **3** (**worm something out of**) obtain information from by cunning persistence. **4** treat (an animal) with a preparation designed to expel parasitic worms. **5** Nautical, archaic make (a rope) smooth by winding thread between the strands.
– DERIVATIVES **worm-like** adj.
– ORIGIN OE *wyrm* (n.), of Gmc origin.

**worm cast** (also **worm casting**) ● **n.** a convoluted mass of soil, mud, or sand thrown up at the surface by a burrowing worm.

**worm-charming** ● **n.** the sport of enticing worms from their burrows.
– DERIVATIVES **worm-charmer** n.

**worm-eaten** ● **adj.** (of wood) full of holes made by woodworm.

**wormer** ● **n.** a substance used to worm animals.

**wormery** ● **n.** (pl. **-ies**) a container in which worms are kept for study or bred, especially for fishing bait.

**worm-fishing** ● **n.** angling with worms for bait.

**worm gear** ● **n.** a mechanical arrangement consisting of a toothed wheel worked by a short revolving cylinder (worm) bearing a screw thread.

**wormhole** ● **n. 1** a hole made by a burrowing insect larva or worm in wood, fruit, etc. **2** Physics a hypothetical connection between widely separated regions of space-time.

**worm lizard** ● **n.** a subterranean burrowing reptile resembling an earthworm, being blind, apparently segmented, and typically without limbs. [Suborder Amphisbaenia: numerous species.]

**wormseed** ● **n.** a plant whose seeds have anthelmintic properties. [*Artemisia cina* (Turkestan, source of santonica) and *Chenopodium ambrosioides* (N. America).]

**worm's-eye view** ● **n.** a view as seen from below or from a humble position.

**wormwheel** ● **n.** the wheel of a worm gear.

**wormwood** ● **n. 1** a woody shrub with a bitter aromatic taste, used as an ingredient of vermouth and absinthe and in medicine. [*Artemisia absinthium* (Eurasia) and related species.] **2** bitterness or grief, or a source of this.
– ORIGIN OE *wermōd*, assoc. with **WORM** and **WOOD**; cf. **VERMOUTH**.

**wormy** ● **adj.** (**-ier**, **-iest**) **1** full of worms; worm-eaten. **2** informal weak or despicable.
– DERIVATIVES **worminess** n.

**worn** past participle of **WEAR**[1]. ● **adj. 1** suffering from wear. **2** very tired.

**worn out** ● **adj. 1** exhausted. **2** worn to the point of being no longer usable.

**worriment** ● **n.** US archaic or humorous term for **WORRY**.

**worrisome** ● **adj.** chiefly N. Amer. causing anxiety or concern.
– DERIVATIVES **worrisomely** adv.

**worrit** /ˈwʌrɪt/ ● **v.** (**worrited**, **worriting**) & **n.** Brit. archaic another term for **WORRY**.
– ORIGIN C18: appar. an alt. of **WORRY**.

**worry** ● **v.** (**-ies**, **-ied**) **1** feel or cause to feel troubled over actual or potential difficulties. ➤ [as adj. **worried**] expressing anxiety. **2** annoy or disturb. **3** (of a dog or other carnivorous animal) tear at or pull about with the teeth. ➤ (of a dog) chase and attack (livestock, especially sheep). **4** (**worry at**) pull at or fiddle with repeatedly. **5** (**worry something out**) discover or devise a solution by persistent thought. ● **n.** (pl. **-ies**) the state of being worried. ➤ a source of anxiety.
– DERIVATIVES **worriedly** adv. **worrier** n. **worrying** adj. **worryingly** adv.
– ORIGIN OE *wyrgan* 'strangle', of W. Gmc origin.

**worry beads** ● **pl. n.** a string of beads that one fingers so as to calm oneself.

**worryguts** ● **n.** informal a person who tends to worry unduly; a habitual worrier.

**worrywart** ● **n.** North American term for **WORRYGUTS**.

**wors** /vɔːs/ ● **n.** S. African sausage.
– ORIGIN Afrik., from Du. *worst* 'sausage'.

**worse** ● **adj. 1** of poorer quality or lower standard. ➤ more serious, severe, or evil. **2** more ill or unhappy. ● **adv. 1** less well. **2** more seriously or severely. ● **n.** a worse event or circumstance. ➤ (**the worse**) a worse condition.
– PHRASES **none the worse for** not adversely affected by. **or worse** or as an even worse unspecified alternative. **the worse for drink** rather drunk. **the worse for wear** informal **1** worn. **2** feeling rather unwell, especially as a result of drinking too much alcohol. **worse off** less fortunate or prosperous.
– ORIGIN OE *wyrsa*, *wiersa* (adj.), *wiers* (adv.), of Gmc origin; rel. to **WAR**.

**worsen** ● **v.** make or become worse.

**worship** ● **n. 1** the feeling or expression of reverence and adoration for a deity. ➤ religious rites and ceremonies. **2** great admiration or devotion. **3** (**His/Your Worship**) chiefly Brit. a title of respect used chiefly to or of a magistrate or mayor. **4** archaic honour given in recognition of merit. ● **v.** (**worshipped**, **worshipping**; US also **worshiped**, **worshiping**) **1** show reverence and adoration for (a deity). **2** feel great admiration or devotion for.
– DERIVATIVES **worshipper** n.
– ORIGIN OE *weorthscipe* 'worthiness, acknowledgement of worth' (see **WORTH**, **-SHIP**).

**worshipful** ● **adj. 1** feeling or showing reverence and admiration. **2** (**Worshipful**) Brit. a title given to justices of the peace and to certain old companies or their officers.
– DERIVATIVES **worshipfully** adv. **worshipfulness** n.

**worst** ● **adj.** of the poorest quality or the lowest standard. ➤ most severe or serious. ● **adv. 1** most severely or seriously. **2** least well. ● **n.** the worst event or circumstance. ➤ the worst part or stage of something. ● **v.** (usu. **be worsted**) get the better of.
– PHRASES **at its** (or **someone's**) **worst** in the worst state possible. **at worst** (or **the worst**) in the worst possible case. **do one's worst** do as much damage as one can (often expressing defiance). **get** (or **have**) **the worst of it** suffer the most. **if the worst comes to the worst** if the most serious or difficult circumstances arise.
– ORIGIN OE *wierresta*, *wyrresta* (adj.), *wierst*, *wyrst* (adv.), of Gmc origin; rel. to **WORSE**.

**worsted** /ˈwʊstɪd/ ● **n.** a fine smooth yarn spun from combed long-staple wool. ➤ fabric made from such yarn, having a close-textured surface with no nap.
– ORIGIN ME: from *Worstead*, the name of a parish in Norfolk, England.

**wort** /wəːt/ ● **n. 1** [in combination] used in names of plants and herbs, especially those used formerly as food or medicinally, e.g. **butterwort**. See word-formation panel. ➤ archaic such a plant or herb. **2** the sweet infusion of ground malt or other grain before fermentation, used to produce beer and distilled malt liquors.
– ORIGIN OE *wyrt*, of Gmc origin; rel. to **ROOT**[1].

**worth** ● **adj. 1** equivalent in value to the sum or item specified. ➤ having income or property amounting to a specified sum. **2** deserving to be treated or regarded in the way specified. ● **n. 1** the value or merit of someone or something. ➤ an amount of a commodity equivalent to a specified sum of money. **2** the amount that could be achieved or produced in a specified time.
– PHRASES **for all one is worth** informal as energetically or enthusiastically as one can. **for what it is worth** used when offering a suggestion or opinion without making a claim as to its validity.
– ORIGIN OE *w(e)orth* (adj. and n.), of Gmc origin.

**worthless** ● **adj. 1** having no real value or use. **2** having no good qualities.
– DERIVATIVES **worthlessly** adv. **worthlessness** n.

**worthwhile** ● **adj.** worth the time, money, or effort spent.
– DERIVATIVES **worthwhileness** n.

**worthy** ● **adj.** (**-ier**, **-iest**) **1** (often **worthy of**) deserving. ➤ good enough; suitable. **2** deserving effort, attention, or

## Word *Formation*

**-wort** used in names of herbs and plants, especially those with medicinal uses, from Old English *wyrt*

| | |
|---|---|
| barrenwort | a creeping plant, formerly thought to cause infertility |
| birthwort | a climbing plant, formerly used as an aid to childbirth and to induce abortion |
| butterwort | an insectivorous bog plant, reputed to be able to keep cows in milk |
| figwort | a herbaceous plant, originally denoting a different plant which was used as treatment for piles (from the obsolete term *fig* 'piles') |
| fleawort | a plant reputed to drive away fleas |
| gypsywort | a plant of the mint family, reputed to have been used by gypsies to stain the skin brown |
| honewort | a plant of the parsley family, believed to be a remedy for swelling (from the obsolete term *hone* 'swelling') |
| lungwort | a plant with white-spotted leaves said to resemble a diseased lung |
| milkwort | a plant reputed to increase a mother's milk production |
| moneywort | a trailing evergreen plant with round glossy leaves resembling coins in shape |
| motherwort | a plant of the mint family, used to treat gynaecological disorders |
| mugwort | a plant reputed to drive away midges (OE *mycg(e)*) |
| ragwort | a plant with yellow flowers and ragged leaves |
| rupturewort | a plant of the pink family, formerly believed to cure hernia |
| St John's wort | a herbaceous plant, some species of which flower near the feast day of St John the Baptist (24 June) |
| sneezewort | a plant related to the yarrow, which can induce sneezing |
| soapwort | a plant whose leaves were formerly used to make soap |
| stitchwort | a plant formerly believed to cure a stitch in the side |
| woundwort | a plant resembling a dead-nettle, formerly used in treating wounds |

respect. **3** showing good intent but lacking in humour or imagination. ● **n.** (pl. **-ies**) often humorous a person important in a particular sphere: *local worthies.*
– DERIVATIVES **worthily** adv. **worthiness** n.

**-worthy** ● **comb. form 1** deserving of a specified thing: *newsworthy.* **2** suitable for a specified thing: *roadworthy.*

**wot** present of **WIT**[2].

**wotcha** (also **wotcher**) ● **exclam.** Brit. informal used as a friendly or humorous greeting.
– ORIGIN C19: corruption of *what cheer?*

**would** ● **modal v.** (3rd sing. present **would**) **1** past of **WILL**[1], in various senses. **2** (expressing the conditional mood) indicating the consequence of an imagined event. ➤(**I would**) used to give advice. **3** expressing a desire. ➤expressing consent. **4** expressing a polite request. **5** expressing a conjecture or opinion. **6** poetic/literary expressing a wish or regret.
– ORIGIN OE *wolde*, past of *wyllan* (see **WILL**[1]).

**would-be** ● **adj.** often derogatory desiring or aspiring to be a specified type of person.

**wouldn't** ● **contr.** would not.

**wouldst** archaic second person singular of **WOULD**.

**Woulfe bottle** /wʊlf/ ● **n.** Chemistry a glass bottle with two or more necks, used for passing gases through liquids.
– ORIGIN C19: named after the Engl. chemist Peter *Woulfe.*

**wound**[1] /wuːnd/ ● **n. 1** an injury to living tissue caused by a cut, blow, or other impact. **2** an injury to a person's feelings or reputation. ● **v.** inflict a wound on.
– DERIVATIVES **wounding** n. & adj. **woundingly** adv. **woundless** adj.
– ORIGIN OE *wund* (n.), *wundian* (v.), of Gmc origin.

**wound**[2] past and past participle of **WIND**[2].

**woundwort** ● **n.** a hairy purple-flowered plant resembling a dead-nettle, formerly used in the treatment of wounds. [Genus *Stachys*: several species.]

**wove** past of **WEAVE**[1].

**woven** past participle of **WEAVE**[1].

**wove paper** ● **n.** paper made on a wire-gauze mesh so as to have a uniform unlined surface. Compare with **LAID PAPER**.
– ORIGIN C19: *wove*, var. of **WOVEN**.

**wow**[1] informal ● **exclam.** (also **wowee**) expressing astonishment or admiration. ● **n.** a sensational success. ● **v.** impress and excite greatly.
– ORIGIN C16: natural exclamation; first recorded in Scots.

**wow**[2] ● **n.** Electronics slow pitch fluctuation in sound reproduction, perceptible in long notes. Compare with **FLUTTER** (in sense 4).
– ORIGIN C20: imitative.

**wowser** /ˈwaʊzə/ ● **n.** Austral./NZ informal **1** a puritanical person. **2** a teetotaller.
– ORIGIN C19: of obscure origin.

**WP** ● **abbrev.** word processing or word processor.

**w.p.** ● **abbrev.** weather permitting.

**W particle** ● **n.** Physics a heavy charged elementary particle considered to transmit the weak interaction between other particles.
– ORIGIN *W*, the initial letter of *weak.*

**WPC** ● **abbrev.** (in the UK) woman police constable.

**wpm** ● **abbrev.** words per minute (used after a number to indicate typing speed).

**WRAC** ● **abbrev.** Women's Royal Army Corps (in the UK, until 1993).

**wrack**[1] ● **v.** variant spelling of **RACK**[1], **RACK**[4].

**wrack**[2] ● **n.** a coarse brown seaweed which grows on the shoreline, often with air bladders providing buoyancy. [Several species belonging to *Fucus* and other genera.]
– ORIGIN C16: appar. from **WRACK**[4]; cf. **VAREC**.

**wrack**[3] (also **rack**) ● **n.** a mass of high, thick, fast-moving cloud.
– ORIGIN ME: var. of **RACK**[6].

**wrack**[4] ● **n.** archaic or dialect a shipwreck. ➤wreckage.
– ORIGIN ME: from MDu. *wrak*; rel. to **WREAK** and **WRECK**.

**WRAF** ● **abbrev.** (in the UK) Women's Royal Air Force (until 1994).

**wraith** /reɪθ/ ● **n. 1** a ghost or ghostly image of someone, especially one seen shortly before or after their death. **2** poetic/literary a wisp or faint trace.
– DERIVATIVES **wraith-like** adj.
– ORIGIN C16 (orig. Scots): of unknown origin.

**wrangle** ● **n.** a long and complicated dispute or argument. ● **v. 1** engage in a wrangle. **2** N. Amer. round up or take charge of (livestock).
– ORIGIN ME: cf. Low Ger. *wrangeln*, frequentative of *wrangen* 'to struggle'; rel. to **WRING**.

**wrangler** ● **n. 1** N. Amer. a person in charge of horses or other livestock on a ranch. **2** a person engaging in a wrangle.

**wrap** ● **v.** (**wrapped**, **wrapping**) **1** cover or enclose in

paper or soft material. ➤arrange (paper or soft material) round something, as a covering or for warmth or protection. ➤place around so as to encircle. **2** Computing cause (a word or unit of text) to be carried over to a new line automatically. ➤(of a word or unit or text) be carried over in such a way. **3** informal finish filming or recording. ● **n. 1** a loose outer garment or piece of material. ➤(also **wrap-around**) [as modifier] (of a garment) worn wrapped round the body so that the edges overlap: *a wrap skirt.* **2** paper or material used for wrapping. **3** informal the end of a session of filming or recording. **4** Brit. informal a small packet of a powdered illegal drug. **5** a tortilla wrapped around a cold filling, eaten as a sandwich.
– PHRASES **under wraps** kept secret.
– PHRASAL VERBS **wrap up 1** (also **wrap someone up**) put on (or dress someone in) warm clothes. **2** Brit. informal be quiet; stop talking. **3** (**wrapped up**) engrossed or absorbed to the exclusion of other things. **wrap something up 1** complete or conclude a meeting or other process. **2** win a game or competition.
– DERIVATIVES **wrapping** n.
– ORIGIN ME: of unknown origin.

**wrapped** ● **adj.** Austral. informal overjoyed; delighted.
– ORIGIN 1960s: blend of *wrapped* (*up*) 'engrossed' and **RAPT**.

**wrapper** ● **n. 1** a piece of paper or other material used for wrapping something, especially something sold or for sale. ➤the dust jacket of a book. **2** chiefly N. Amer. a loose robe or gown. **3** chiefly N. Amer. a tobacco leaf of superior quality enclosing a cigar.

**wrasse** /ras/ ● **n.** (pl. same or **wrasses**) a marine fish with thick lips and strong teeth, typically brightly coloured. [Family Labridae: numerous species.]
– ORIGIN C17: from Cornish *wrah*; rel. to Welsh *gwrach*, lit. 'old woman'.

**wrath** /rɒθ, rɔːθ/ ● **n.** extreme anger.
– ORIGIN OE *wrǣththu*, from *wrāth* (see **WROTH**).

**wrathful** ● **adj.** poetic/literary full of or characterized by intense anger.
– DERIVATIVES **wrathfully** adv. **wrathfulness** n.

**wrathy** ● **adj.** N. Amer. informal, dated wrathful.

**wreak** ● **v. 1** cause (a large amount of damage or harm). **2** inflict (vengeance). ➤archaic avenge (a wronged person).
– DERIVATIVES **wreaker** n.
– ORIGIN OE *wrecan* 'drive (out), avenge', of Gmc origin; cf. **WRACK**[4], **WRECK**, and **WRETCH**.

**wreath** ● **n.** (pl. **wreaths** /riːðz, riːθs/) **1** an arrangement of flowers, leaves, or stems fastened in a ring and used for decoration or for laying on a grave. **2** a curl or ring of smoke or cloud.
– ORIGIN OE *writha*, rel. to **WRITHE**.

**wreathe** /riːð/ ● **v. 1** (usu. **be wreathed**) envelop, surround, or encircle. ➤poetic/literary twist or entwine round or over something. ➤(of smoke) move with a curling motion. **2** form (flowers, leaves, or stems) into a wreath.
– ORIGIN C16: partly a back-form. from archaic *wrethen*, past part. of **WRITHE**, reinforced by **WREATH**.

**wreck** ● **n. 1** the destruction of a ship at sea; a shipwreck. ➤a ship destroyed in such a way. ➤Law goods brought ashore by the sea from a wreck. **2** a building, vehicle, etc. that has been destroyed or badly damaged. ➤N. Amer. a road or rail crash. **3** a person whose physical or mental health or strength has failed: *an emotional wreck.* ● **v. 1** (usu. **be wrecked**) cause the destruction of (a ship) by sinking or breaking up. ➤[as noun **wrecking**] chiefly historical the practice of destroying a ship in order to steal the cargo. ➤archaic suffer or undergo shipwreck. **2** destroy or severely damage. ➤spoil completely: *the eye injury wrecked his chances.* **3** [usu. as noun **wrecking**] chiefly N. Amer. engage in breaking up badly damaged vehicles or demolishing old buildings to obtain usable spares or scrap.
– ORIGIN ME: from Anglo-Norman Fr. *wrec*, from the base of ON *reka* 'to drive'; rel. to **WREAK**.

**wreckage** ● **n.** the remains of something that has been badly damaged or destroyed.

**wrecked** ● **adj.** informal **1** exhausted. **2** drunk.

**wrecker** ● **n. 1** a person or thing that wrecks or destroys something. ➤chiefly N. Amer. a person who breaks up damaged vehicles or demolishes old buildings to obtain usable spares or scrap. **2** N. Amer. a recovery vehicle.

**wreckfish** ● **n.** (pl. same or **-fishes**) a large heavy-bodied fish of warm Atlantic waters, the young of which are often found near driftwood or wreckage. [*Polyprion americanus*.]

**wrecking ball** ● **n.** a heavy metal ball swung from a crane into a building to demolish it.

**Wren** ● **n.** (in the UK) a member of the former Women's Royal Naval Service.
– ORIGIN C20: from the abbrev. **WRNS**.

**wren** ● **n.** a very small short-winged songbird with a cocked tail. [*Troglodytes troglodytes*.] ➤any of numerous small songbirds of the same family (Troglodytidae) or of unrelated families.
– ORIGIN OE *wrenna*, of Gmc origin.

**wrench** ● **n. 1** a sudden violent twist or pull. **2** a feeling of abrupt pain and distress caused by one's own or another's departure. **3** an adjustable tool like a spanner, used for gripping and turning nuts or bolts. **4** Mechanics a combination of a couple with a force along its axis. ● **v. 1** pull or twist suddenly and violently. ➤injure (a part of the body) as a result of a sudden twisting movement. **2** turn or adjust with a wrench. **3** archaic distort to fit a particular theory or interpretation.
– ORIGIN OE *wrencan* 'twist', of unknown origin.

**wrentit** ● **n.** a long-tailed North American songbird with dark plumage, the only American member of the babbler family. [*Chamaea fasciata*.]

**wrest** /rɛst/ ● **v. 1** forcibly pull from a person's grasp. ➤take (power or control) after considerable effort or resistance. **2** archaic distort the meaning or interpretation of. ● **n.** archaic a key for tuning a harp or piano.
– ORIGIN OE *wrǣstan* 'twist, tighten', of Gmc origin; rel. to **WRIST**.

**wrestle** ● **v. 1** take part in a fight that involves close grappling with one's opponent, either as sport or in earnest. ➤force into a particular position in such a way. ➤extract or manipulate (an object) with difficulty and some physical effort. **2** struggle with a difficulty or problem. ● **n. 1** a wrestling bout or contest. **2** a hard struggle.
– DERIVATIVES **wrestler** n. **wrestling** n.
– ORIGIN OE, frequentative of *wrǣstan* 'wrest'.

**wrest pin** ● **n.** a pin to which the strings of a piano or harpsichord are attached.

**wrest plank** (also **wrest block**) ● **n.** the part of a piano or harpsichord holding the wrest pins.

**wretch** ● **n.** an unfortunate person. ➤informal a contemptible person.
– ORIGIN OE *wrecca* (also in the sense 'banished person'), of W. Gmc origin.

**wretched** ● **adj.** (**-er, -est**) **1** in a very unhappy or unfortunate state; miserable. **2** used to express anger or annoyance: *she disliked the wretched man intensely.*
– DERIVATIVES **wretchedly** adv. **wretchedness** n.
– ORIGIN ME: formed irregularly from **WRETCH** + **-ED**[1].

**wriggle** ● **v. 1** twist and turn with quick writhing movements. ➤move with wriggling movements. **2** (**wriggle out of**) avoid by devious means. ● **n.** a wriggling movement.
– DERIVATIVES **wriggler** n. **wriggly** adj.
– ORIGIN C15: from Mid. Low Ger. *wriggelen*, frequentative of *wriggen* 'twist, turn'.

**wright** ● **n.** archaic (except in combination) a maker or builder: *playwright* | *shipwright.* See word-formation panel.
– ORIGIN OE *wryhta*, *wyrhta*, of W. Gmc origin; rel. to **WORK**.

**wring** ● **v.** (past and past part. **wrung** /rʌŋ/) **1** squeeze and twist to force liquid from. ➤extract (liquid) in this way. **2** break (an animal's neck) by twisting forcibly. ➤squeeze (someone's hand) tightly. **3** (often **wring something from/out of**) obtain with difficulty or effort. **4** cause great pain or distress to: *the letter wrung her heart.* ● **n.** an act of wringing.
– PHRASES **wring one's hands** clasp and twist one's hands together as a gesture of distress or despair.
– ORIGIN OE *wringan* (v.), of W. Gmc origin; rel. to

## Word *Formation*

### -wright 'a maker or builder'

The word ***wright*** comes from Old English *wryhta*, and was in general use until the 19th century, also with the specific sense of 'a carpenter'. In modern use it appears only in combination (earliest recorded dates shown):

| | | |
|---|---|---|
| cartwright | a person who makes carts | 15th century (York Mystery Plays) |
| millwright | a person who builds or maintains mills | 15th century |
| playwright | a person who writes plays | 17th century (in the *Workes* of Ben Jonson) |
| ploughwright | a person who makes ploughs | 13th century |
| shipwright | a shipbuilder | 11th century |
| wainwright | a person who makes wagons | 11th century (from the archaic term *wain* 'wagon') |
| wheelwright | a person who makes wooden wheels | 13th century |

WRONG.

**wringer** ● n. a device for wringing water from wet clothes or other objects.

**wringing** ● adj. extremely wet; soaked.

**wrinkle** ● n. **1** a slight line or fold, especially in fabric or the skin of the face. **2** informal a clever innovation, or useful piece of information or advice. ● v. [often as adj. **wrinkled**] make or become wrinkled.
– ORIGIN ME: origin obscure, possibly a back-form. from the OE past part. *gewrinclod* 'sinuous'.

**wrinkly** ● adj. (**-ier**, **-iest**) having many wrinkles. ● n. (also **wrinklie**) (pl. **-ies**) Brit. informal, derogatory an old person.

**wrist** ● n. **1** the joint connecting the hand with the forearm. ➤ the equivalent joint (the carpal joint) in the foreleg of a quadruped or the wing of a bird. **2** (also **wrist pin**) (in a machine) a stud projecting from a crank as an attachment for a connecting rod.
– ORIGIN OE, of Gmc origin, prob. from the base of WRITHE.

**wristband** ● n. a band worn round the wrist, especially for identity purposes or as a sweatband.

**wrist-drop** ● n. paralysis of the muscles which normally raise the hand at the wrist and extend the fingers.

**wristlet** ● n. a band or bracelet worn on the wrist.

**wristwatch** ● n. a watch worn on a strap round the wrist.

**wristy** ● adj. Cricket & Tennis (of a stroke) performed using a pronounced movement of the wrist.

**writ**[1] ● n. **1** a form of written command in the name of a court or other legal authority to do or abstain from doing a specified act. ➤ (**one's writ**) one's power to enforce compliance or submission. **2** archaic a piece or body of writing.
– ORIGIN OE, from the Gmc base of WRITE.

**writ**[2] ● v. archaic past participle of WRITE.
– PHRASES **writ large** in an obvious or exaggerated form.

**write** ● v. (past **wrote**; past part. **written**) **1** mark (letters, words, or other symbols) on a surface, with a pen, pencil, or similar implement. ➤ have learnt and have the ability to do this: *he couldn't read or write.* ➤ fill out or complete in writing. ➤ (**write something up**) write a full or formal account of something. ➤ Canadian & S. African take (an exam or test). **2** write in a cursive hand, as opposed to printing individual letters. **3** write and send (a letter) to someone. ➤ chiefly N. Amer. write and send a letter to (someone). **4** compose (a text or work) in writing. ➤ compose (a musical work). ➤ archaic describe in writing. **5** Computing enter (data) into a specified storage medium or location in store. **6** underwrite (an insurance policy).
– PHRASES **be written all over one's face** informal be obvious from one's expression. **(and) that's all she wrote** N. Amer. informal there is nothing more to be said.
– PHRASAL VERBS **write something down** reduce the nominal value of stock or goods. **write someone in** chiefly US (when voting) add the name of someone not on the original list of candidates and vote for them. **write something off 1** (**write someone/thing off**) dismiss someone or something as insignificant. **2** cancel the record of a bad debt; acknowledge the failure to recover an asset. **3** Brit. damage a vehicle so badly that it cannot be repaired or is not worth repairing.
– DERIVATIVES **writable** adj. (chiefly Computing).
– ORIGIN OE *wrītan* 'score, form (letters) by carving, write', of Gmc origin.

**write-back** ● n. Finance the process of restoring to profit a provision for bad or doubtful debts previously made against profits and no longer required.

**write-down** ● n. Finance a reduction in the estimated or nominal value of an asset.

**write-in** ● n. US a vote cast for an unlisted candidate by writing their name on a ballot paper.

**write-off** ● n. **1** a vehicle, aircraft, etc. that is too badly damaged to be repaired. **2** a worthless or ineffectual person or thing. **3** Finance a cancellation from an account of a bad debt or worthless asset.

**write-protect** ● v. Computing protect (a disk) from accidental writing or erasure.

**writer** ● n. **1** a person who has written a particular text. ➤ a person who writes books or articles as a regular occupation. ➤ Brit. historical a scribe. **2** Computing a device that writes data to a storage medium. **3** Brit. archaic a clerk, especially in the navy or in government offices.
– PHRASES **writer's block** the condition of being unable to think of what to write or how to proceed with writing. **writer's cramp** pain or stiffness in the hand caused by excessive writing.

**writerly** ● adj. of or characteristic of a professional author. ➤ consciously literary.

**writer to the Signet** ● n. historical (in Scotland) a senior solicitor conducting cases in the Court of Session.

**write-up** ● n. a newspaper article giving the author's opinion of a recent event, performance, or product.

**writhe** /rʌɪð/ ● v. twist or squirm in pain or as if in pain.
– ORIGIN OE *wrīthan* 'make into coils, plait', of Gmc origin.

**writhen** /ˈrɪð(ə)n/ (also **wrythen**) ● adj. **1** poetic/literary twisted or contorted out of normal shape. **2** (of antique glass or silver) having spirally twisted ornamentation.
– ORIGIN OE, archaic past part. of WRITHE.

**writing** ● n. **1** the activity or skill of writing. **2** written work, especially with regard to its style or quality. ➤ (**writings**) books or other written works. **3** a sequence of letters or symbols forming coherent words. ➤ handwriting.
– PHRASES **in writing** in written form. **the writing** (or N. Amer. **handwriting**) **is on the wall** there are clear signs that something unpleasant or unwelcome is going to happen. [with biblical allusion to Dan. 5:5, 25–8.]

**writing paper** ● n. paper of good quality used for writing letters by hand.

**writ of execution** ● n. Law a judicial order that a judgement be enforced.

**written** past participle of WRITE.

**WRNS** ● abbrev. historical (in the UK) Women's Royal Naval Service.

**wrong** ● adj. **1** not correct or true. ➤mistaken. **2** unjust, dishonest, or immoral. **3** in a bad or abnormal condition; amiss. ● adv. in an unsuitable or undesirable manner or direction. ➤with an incorrect result. ● n. an unjust, dishonest, or immoral action. ● v. act unjustly or dishonestly towards. ➤mistakenly attribute bad motives to; misrepresent.
– PHRASES **get someone wrong** misunderstand someone, especially by falsely imputing malice. **get (hold of) the wrong end of the stick** misunderstand something. **in the wrong** responsible for a mistake or offence.
– DERIVATIVES **wronger** n. **wrongly** adv. **wrongness** n.
– ORIGIN OE *wrang*, from ON *rangr* 'awry, unjust'; rel. to **WRING**.

**wrongdoing** ● n. illegal or dishonest behaviour.
– DERIVATIVES **wrongdoer** n.

**wrong-foot** ● v. Brit. **1** (in a game) play so as to catch (an opponent) off balance. **2** place in a difficult or embarrassing situation by saying or doing something unexpected.

**wrongful** ● adj. (of an act) not fair, just, or legal.
– DERIVATIVES **wrongfully** adv. **wrongfulness** n.

**wrong-headed** ● adj. having or showing bad judgement; misguided.
– DERIVATIVES **wrong-headedly** adv. **wrong-headedness** n.

**wrong side** ● n. the reverse side of something.
– PHRASES **on the wrong side of 1** out of favour with. **2** somewhat more than (a specified age). **wrong side out** inside out.

**wrong'un** ● n. Brit. informal a person of bad character.
– ORIGIN C19: contr. of *wrong one*.

**wrot** /rɒt/ ● n. timber with one or more surfaces planed smooth.
– ORIGIN 1930s: alt. of **WROUGHT**.

**wrote** past tense of **WRITE**.

**wroth** /rəʊθ, rɒθ/ ● adj. archaic angry.
– ORIGIN OE *wrāth*, of Gmc origin; rel. to **WRITHE**.

**wrought** /rɔːt/ ● adj. **1** (of metals) beaten out or shaped by hammering. **2** [in combination] made or fashioned in the specified way: *well-wrought*. **3** (**wrought up**) upset and anxious.
– ORIGIN ME: archaic past and past part. of **WORK**.

**wrought iron** ● n. a tough malleable form of iron suitable for forging or rolling rather than casting, obtained by puddling pig iron while molten.

**wrung** past and past participle of **WRING**.

**WRVS** ● abbrev. (in the UK) Women's Royal Voluntary Service.

**wry** /rʌɪ/ ● adj. (**wryer, wryest** or **wrier, wriest**) **1** using or expressing dry, especially mocking, humour. **2** (of a person's face or features) twisted into an expression of disgust, disappointment, or annoyance. **3** bending or twisted to one side.
– DERIVATIVES **wryly** adv. **wryness** n.
– ORIGIN C16 (in the sense 'contorted'): from OE *wrīgian* 'tend, incline', in ME 'deviate, swerve, contort'.

**wrybill** ● n. a small New Zealand plover with grey and white plumage and a bill that bends to the right. [*Anarhynchus frontalis*.]

**wryneck** ● n. **1** a bird of the woodpecker family, with brown plumage and a habit of twisting its head backwards. [*Jynx torquilla*.] **2** another term for **TORTICOLLIS**.

**wrythen** ● adj. variant spelling of **WRITHEN**.

**WSW** ● abbrev. west-south-west.

**wt** ● abbrev. weight.

**WTO** ● abbrev. World Trade Organization.

**Wu** /wuː/ ● n. a dialect of Chinese spoken in Jiangsu and Zhejiang provinces and the city of Shanghai.
– ORIGIN the name in Chin.

**Wunderkammer** /ˈvʊndəˌkamə, German ˈvʊndɐˌkamɐ/ ● n. (pl. **Wunderkammern** /-ˌkaməːn, German -ˌkamɐn/) a place where a collection of curiosities and rarities is exhibited.
– ORIGIN Ger., lit. 'wonder chamber'.

**wunderkind** /ˈvʊndəkɪnd/ ● n. (pl. **wunderkinds** or **wunderkinder** /-kɪndə/) a person who achieves great success when relatively young.
– ORIGIN C19: from Ger., from *Wunder* 'wonder' + *Kind* 'child'.

**Wurlitzer** /ˈwəːlɪtsə/ ● n. trademark a large pipe organ or electric organ, especially one formerly used in cinemas.
– ORIGIN named after the Amer. instrument-maker Rudolf *Wurlitzer* (1831–1914).

**wurst** /vəːst, vʊəst, w-/ ● n. German or Austrian sausage.
– ORIGIN from Ger. *Wurst*.

**wushu** /wuːˈʃuː/ ● n. the Chinese martial arts.
– ORIGIN from Chin. *wǔshù*, from *wǔ* 'military' + *shù* 'art'.

**wuss** /wʊs/ ● n. informal, chiefly N. Amer. a weak or ineffectual person.
– DERIVATIVES **wussy** n. (pl. **-ies**) & adj.
– ORIGIN 1980s: of unknown origin.

**WV** ● abbrev. West Virginia (in official postal use).

**W. Va** ● abbrev. West Virginia.

**WWI** ● abbrev. World War I.

**WWII** ● abbrev. World War II.

**WWF** ● abbrev. **1** World Wide Fund for Nature. **2** World Wrestling Federation.

**WWW** ● abbrev. World Wide Web.

**WY** ● abbrev. Wyoming (in official postal use).

**Wyandot** /ˈwʌɪəndɒt/ (also **Wyandotte**) ● n. **1** a member of an American Indian people now living mainly in Oklahoma and Quebec. **2** the extinct Iroquoian language of this people. **3** (**Wyandotte**) a domestic chicken of a medium-sized American breed.
– ORIGIN C18: from Fr. *Ouendat*, from Huron *Wendat*.

**wych elm** /wɪtʃ/ (also **witch elm**) ● n. a European elm with large rough leaves, chiefly growing in woodland or near flowing water. [*Ulmus glabra*.]
– ORIGIN C17: *wych*, used in names of trees with pliant branches, from OE *wic(e)*, appar. from a Gmc root meaning 'bend'.

**wych hazel** ● n. variant spelling of **WITCH HAZEL**.

**Wykehamist** /ˈwɪkəmɪst/ ● n. a past or present pupil of Winchester College.
– ORIGIN C18: from mod. L. *Wykehamista*, from the name of William of *Wykeham* (1324–1404), founder of the college.

**wyn** /wɪn/ ● n. variant spelling of **WEN**[2].

**wynd** /wʌɪnd/ ● n. [chiefly in place names] Scottish & N. English a narrow street or alley.
– ORIGIN ME: appar. from the verb **WIND**[2].

**Wyo.** ● abbrev. Wyoming.

**Wyomingite** /wʌɪˈəʊmɪŋʌɪt/ ● n. a native or inhabitant of the US state of Wyoming.

**WYSIWYG** /ˈwɪzɪwɪg/ (also **wysiwyg**) ● adj. Computing denoting the representation of text on-screen in a form exactly corresponding to its appearance on a printout.
– ORIGIN 1980s: acronym from *what you see is what you get*.

**wyvern** /ˈwʌɪv(ə)n/ ● n. Heraldry a winged two-legged dragon with a barbed tail.
– ORIGIN ME (denoting a viper): from OFr. *wivre*, from L. *vipera*.

**X**[1] (also **x**) ● **n.** (pl. **Xs** or **X's**) **1** the twenty-fourth letter of the alphabet. **2** denoting the next after W in a set of items, categories, etc. **3** denoting an unknown or unspecified person or thing. **4** (usu. ***x***) the first unknown quantity in an algebraic expression. ➤ denoting the principal or horizontal axis in a system of coordinates. **5** a cross-shaped written symbol, used: ➤ to indicate a position on a map. ➤ to indicate an incorrect answer. ➤ to symbolize a kiss. ➤ to indicate one's vote on a ballot paper. **6** the Roman numeral for ten.

**X**[2] ● **symb.** films classified as suitable for adults only (replaced in the UK in 1983 by *18*, and in the US in 1990 by *NC-17*).

**-x** ● **suffix** forming the plural of many nouns ending in *-u* taken from French: *tableaux*.
– ORIGIN from Fr.

**X-acto knife** /ɪɡ'zaktəʊ/ ● **n.** N. Amer. trademark a utility knife with a very sharp replaceable blade.
– ORIGIN 1940s: respelling of **EXACT**, + **-O**.

**Xanadu** /'zanədu:/ ● **n.** (pl. **Xanadus**) an imaginary wonderful place.
– ORIGIN alt. of *Shang-tu*, an ancient city in SE Mongolia, as portrayed in Coleridge's poem *Kubla Khan* (1816).

**Xanax** /'zanaks/ ● **n.** trademark for **ALPRAZOLAM**.

**xanthine** /'zanθi:n/ ● **n.** Biochemistry a crystalline compound formed in the metabolic breakdown of nucleic acids and related to caffeine and other alkaloids.
– ORIGIN C19: from *xanthic* (from Gk *xanthos* 'yellow') + **-INE**[4].

**xanthoma** /zan'θəʊmə/ ● **n.** (pl. **xanthomas** or **xanthomata** /-mətə/) Medicine an irregular yellow patch or nodule on the skin, caused by deposition of lipids.
– ORIGIN C19: from Gk *xanthos* 'yellow' + **-OMA**.

**xanthophyll** /'zanθə(ʊ)fɪl/ ● **n.** Biochemistry a yellow or brown carotenoid plant pigment which causes the autumn colours of leaves.
– ORIGIN C19: from Gk *xanthos* 'yellow' + *phullon* 'leaf'.

**X chromosome** ● **n.** Genetics (in humans and other mammals) a sex chromosome, two of which are normally present in female cells (designated XX) and only one in male cells (designated XY). Compare with **Y CHROMOSOME**.

**xd** ● **abbrev.** ex dividend.

**Xe** ● **symb.** the chemical element xenon.

**xebec** /'zi:bɛk/ (also **zebec**) ● **n.** historical a small three-masted Mediterranean sailing ship with lateen and square sails.
– ORIGIN C18: alt. of Fr. *chebec*, via Ital. from Arab. *šabbāk*.

**Xenical** /'zɛnɪk(ə)l/ ● **n.** trademark a synthetic drug which blocks pancreatic enzymes involved in the digestion of fats, used to treat obesity.
– ORIGIN C20: of unknown origin.

**xeno-** ● **comb. form 1** relating to a foreigner or foreigners: *xenophobia*. **2** other; different in origin: *xenograft*.
– ORIGIN from Gk *xenos* 'stranger', (adj.) 'strange'.

**xenobiotic** /ˌzɛnə(ʊ)bʌɪ'ɒtɪk/ ● **adj.** relating to or denoting a substance that is foreign to the body or to an ecological system. ● **n.** a substance of this kind.

**xenocryst** /'zɛnə(ʊ)krɪst/ ● **n.** Geology a crystal in an igneous rock which is not derived from the original magma.
– DERIVATIVES **xenocrystic** adj.
– ORIGIN C19: from **XENO-** + **CRYSTAL**.

**xenogamy** /zɛ'nɒɡəmi/ ● **n.** Botany fertilization of a flower by pollen from a flower on a genetically different plant. Compare with **GEITONOGAMY**.
– DERIVATIVES **xenogamous** adj.
– ORIGIN C19: from **XENO-** + Gk *gamos* 'marriage'.

**xenogeneic** /ˌzɛnə(ʊ)dʒɪ'ni:ɪk, -'neɪɪk/ ● **adj.** Physiology relating to or denoting immunologically incompatible tissues which belong to individuals of different species.
– ORIGIN 1960s: from **XENO-** + Gk *genea* 'race, stock' + **-IC**.

**xenograft** ● **n.** a tissue graft or organ transplant from a donor of a different species from the recipient.

**xenolith** /'zɛnə(ʊ)lɪθ/ ● **n.** Geology a piece of rock within an igneous mass which is not derived from the original magma but has been introduced from elsewhere, especially the surrounding country rock.
– DERIVATIVES **xenolithic** adj.

**xenology** /ˌzɛn'ɒlədʒi/ ● **n.** (chiefly in science fiction) the scientific study of alien biology, cultures, etc.
– DERIVATIVES **xenologist** n.

**xenon** /'zɛnɒn, 'zi:-/ ● **n.** the chemical element of atomic number 54, a member of the noble gas series, obtained by distillation of liquid air and used in some specialized electric lamps. (Symbol: **Xe**)
– ORIGIN C19: from Gk, neut. of *xenos* 'strange'.

**xenophobia** ● **n.** intense or irrational dislike or fear of people from other countries.
– DERIVATIVES **xenophobe** n. **xenophobic** adj.

**Xenopus** /'zɛnəpəs/ ● **n.** the African clawed toad, used in embryological research and formerly in pregnancy testing as it produces eggs in response to substances in the urine of a pregnant woman. [*Xenopus laevis*.]
– ORIGIN C19: mod. L., from **XENO-** + Gk *pous* 'foot'.

**xenotransplantation** ● **n.** the process of grafting or transplanting organs or tissues between members of different species.
– DERIVATIVES **xenotransplant** n.

**xeric** /'zɪərɪk, 'zɛ-/ ● **adj.** Ecology containing little moisture; very dry. Compare with **HYDRIC** and **MESIC**[1].
– ORIGIN 1920s: from **XERO-** + **-IC**.

**xeriscape** /'zɪərɪskeɪp, 'zɛ-/ ● **n.** chiefly N. Amer. a style of landscape design requiring little or no irrigation or other maintenance, used in arid regions.
– DERIVATIVES **xeriscaping** n.

**xero-** /'zɪərəʊ, 'zɛrəʊ/ ● **comb. form** dry: *xerophyte*.
– ORIGIN from Gk *xēros* 'dry'.

**xeroderma** /ˌzɪərə(ʊ)'də:mə, ˌzɛ-/ ● **n.** any of various diseases characterized by extreme dryness of the skin, especially a mild form of ichthyosis.
– ORIGIN C19: mod. L., from **XERO-** + Gk *derma* 'skin'.

**xerography** ● **n.** a dry copying process in which powder adheres to parts of a surface remaining electrically charged after being exposed to light from an image of the document to be copied.
– DERIVATIVES **xerographic** adj. **xerographically** adv.

**xerophilous** /zɪə'rɒfɪləs, zɛ-/ ● **adj.** Botany & Zoology (of a plant or animal) adapted to a dry climate or habitat.
– DERIVATIVES **xerophile** n.

**xerophthalmia** /ˌzɪərɒf'θalmɪə, ˌzɛ-/ ● **n.** Medicine abnormal dryness of the conjunctiva and cornea of the eye, typically associated with vitamin A deficiency.

**xerophyte** /'zɪərə(ʊ)fʌɪt, 'zɛ-/ ● **n.** Botany a plant which needs very little water.
– DERIVATIVES **xerophytic** adj.

**Xerox** /'zɪərɒks, 'zɛ-/ ● **n.** trademark a xerographic copying process. ➤ a copy made using such a process. ● **v.** (**xerox**) copy (a document) by such a process.
– ORIGIN 1950s: an invented name, based on **XEROGRAPHY**.

**x-height** ● **n.** the height of a lower-case x, considered characteristic of a given typeface or script.

**Xhosa** /'kəʊsə, 'kɔːsə/ ● **n.** (pl. same or **Xhosas**) **1** a member of a South African people traditionally living in the Eastern Cape Province. **2** the Bantu language of this people.
– ORIGIN from the stem of Xhosa *umXhosa*.

**xi** /ksʌɪ, gzʌɪ, sʌɪ, zʌɪ/ ● **n.** the fourteenth letter of the Greek alphabet (Ξ, ξ), transliterated as 'x'.
– ORIGIN from Gk.

**Xiang** /ʃiː'aŋ/ (also **Hsiang**) ● **n.** a dialect of Chinese spoken mainly in Hunan province.

**-xion** ● **suffix** forming nouns such as *fluxion*.
– ORIGIN from L. participial stems (see also **-ION**).

**xiphisternum** /ˌzɪfɪ'stəːnəm/ ● **n.** Anatomy another term for **XIPHOID PROCESS**.
– ORIGIN C19: from Gk *xiphos* 'sword' + **STERNUM**.

**xiphoid process** /'zɪfɔɪd/ (also **xiphoid cartilage**) ● **n.** Anatomy the cartilaginous section at the lower end of the sternum, not attached to any ribs.
– ORIGIN C18: from Gk *xiphoeidēs*, from *xiphos* 'sword'.

**XL** ● **abbrev.** extra large (as a clothes size).

**Xmas** /'krɪsməs, 'ɛksməs/ ● **n.** informal term for **CHRISTMAS**.
– ORIGIN *X* representing the initial chi of Gk *Khristos* 'Christ'.

**XML** ● **abbrev.** Extensible Mark-up Language.

**XMS** ● **abbrev.** Computing extended memory system.

**xoanon** /'zəʊənɒn/ ● **n.** (pl. **xoana** /-nə/) (in ancient Greece) a primitive wooden image of a deity.
– ORIGIN C18: from Gk; rel. to *xein* 'carve'.

**XOR** ● **n.** Electronics exclusive OR (a Boolean operator).

**X-rated** ● **adj.** pornographic or indecent. ➤(formerly) denoting a film given an X classification.

**X-ray** ● **n.** **1** an electromagnetic wave of very short wavelength (between ultraviolet and gamma rays), able to pass through many materials opaque to light. ➤[as modifier] informal denoting an apparent or supposed faculty for seeing beyond an outward form: *X-ray eyes.* **2** a photograph or other image of the internal structure of an object, especially a part of the body, produced by passing X-rays through the object. **3** a code word representing the letter X, used in radio communication. ● **v.** photograph or examine with X-rays.
– ORIGIN translation of Ger. *X-Strahlen* (pl.), from *X-* (because, when discovered in 1895, the nature of the rays was unknown) + *Strahl* 'ray'.

**X-ray astronomy** ● **n.** the branch of astronomy concerned with the detection and measurement of high-energy electromagnetic radiation emitted by celestial objects.

**X-ray crystallography** ● **n.** the study of crystals and their structure by means of the diffraction of X-rays by the regularly spaced atoms of crystalline materials.

**X-ray fish** ● **n.** a small almost transparent freshwater fish with an opaque body cavity, native to South America. [*Pristella riddlei.*]

**X-ray tube** ● **n.** Physics a device for generating X-rays by accelerating electrons to high energies and causing them to strike a metal target from which the X-rays are emitted.

**xu** /suː/ ● **n.** (pl. same) a monetary unit of Vietnam, equal to one hundredth of a dong.
– ORIGIN Vietnamese, from Fr. *sou*.

**xylem** /'zʌɪləm/ ● **n.** Botany the vascular tissue in plants which conducts water and dissolved nutrients upwards from the root and also helps to form the woody element in the stem.
– ORIGIN C19: from Gk *xulon* 'wood' + the passive suffix *-ēma*.

**xylene** /'zʌɪliːn/ ● **n.** Chemistry a volatile liquid hydrocarbon obtained by distilling wood, coal tar, or petroleum, used in fuels and solvents and in chemical synthesis.
– ORIGIN C19: from **XYLO-** + **-ENE**.

**xylo-** /'zʌɪləʊ/ ● **comb. form** of or relating to wood: *xylophone.*
– ORIGIN from Gk *xulon* 'wood'.

**xylophagous** /zʌɪ'lɒfəgəs/ ● **adj.** Zoology feeding on or boring into wood.

**xylophone** ● **n.** a musical instrument played by striking a row of wooden bars of graduated length with small beaters.
– DERIVATIVES **xylophonic** adj. **xylophonist** n. /zʌɪ'lɒfənɪst/.
– ORIGIN C19: from **XYLO-** + **-PHONE**.

**xylose** /'zʌɪləʊz, -s/ ● **n.** Chemistry a sugar of the pentose class which occurs widely in plants, especially as a component of hemicelluloses.

**Y**[1] (also **y**) ● **n.** (pl. **Ys** or **Y's**) **1** the twenty-fifth letter of the alphabet. **2** denoting the next after X in a set of items, categories, etc. **3** denoting an unknown or unspecified person or thing (coming second after 'x'). **4** (usu. ***y***) the second unknown quantity in an algebraic expression, usually the dependent variable. ➤denoting the secondary or vertical axis in a system of coordinates.

**Y**[2] ● **abbrev. 1** yen. **2** N. Amer. informal a YMCA or YWCA hostel. ● **symb.** the chemical element yttrium.

**y** ● **abbrev.** year(s).

**-y**[1] ● **suffix** forming adjectives: **1** (from nouns and adjectives) full of; having the quality of: *messy.* ➤with depreciatory reference: *boozy.* **2** (from verbs) apt to: *sticky.*
– ORIGIN OE *-ig*, of Gmc origin.

**-y**[2] (also **-ey** or **-ie**) ● **suffix** forming diminutive nouns, pet names, etc.: *aunty.* ➤forming verbs: *shinny.*
– ORIGIN ME: orig. Scots.

**-y**[3] ● **suffix** forming nouns: **1** denoting a state or quality: *jealousy.* **2** denoting an action or its result: *victory.*
– ORIGIN from Fr. *-ie*, from L. *-ia*, *-ium*, or Gk *-eia*, *-ia*.

**Y2K** ● **abbrev.** year 2000 (with reference to the millennium bug).

**yaar** /jɑː/ ● **n.** Indian informal a friendly form of address.
– ORIGIN via Hindi from Arab. *yar.*

**yabber** ● **v.** informal chatter.
– ORIGIN prob. from Wuywurung (an Aborig. lang.).

**yabby** (also **yabbie**) ● **n.** (pl. **-ies**) Austral. a small freshwater crayfish. [*Charax destructor* and related species.] ➤another term for **NIPPER** (in sense 4).
– ORIGIN C19: from Wemba-wemba (an Aborig. lang.).

**YAC** ● **abbrev.** Biology yeast artificial chromosome.

**yacht** /jɒt/ ● **n.** a medium-sized sailing boat equipped for cruising or racing. ➤a powered boat equipped for cruising. ● **v.** race or cruise in a yacht.
– DERIVATIVES **yachting** n.
– ORIGIN C16: from early mod. Du. *jaghte*, from *jaghtschip* 'fast pirate ship', from *jag(h)t* 'hunting' + *schip* 'ship'.

**yachtie** ● **n.** informal a person who sails yachts.

**yachtsman** ● **n.** (pl. **-men**) a man who sails yachts.

**yack** ● **n. & v.** variant spelling of **YAK**[2].

**yacker** ● **n.** variant spelling of **YAKKA**.

**yackety-yak** ● **n. & v.** another term for **YAK**[2].
– ORIGIN 1950s: imitative.

**yagé** /ˈjɑːʒeɪ/ ● **n.** another term for **AYAHUASCA**.
– ORIGIN 1920s: from Amer. Sp.

**Yagi antenna** /ˈjɑːgi/ (also **Yagi aerial**) ● **n.** a highly directional narrowband radio aerial made of several short rods mounted across an insulating support.
– ORIGIN 1940s: named after the Japanese engineer Hidetsugu *Yagi.*

**yah**[1] ● **exclam.** yes (used in representations of upper-class speech). ● **n.** Brit. informal an upper-class person.

**yah**[2] ● **exclam.** expressing derision.
– ORIGIN C17: natural exclamation.

**yahoo**[1] /ˈjɑːhuː, jəˈhuː/ ● **n.** informal a rude, coarse, or brutish person.
– ORIGIN C18: from the name of an imaginary race in Jonathan Swift's *Gulliver's Travels* (1726).

**yahoo**[2] /jɑːˈhuː, ja-/ ● **exclam.** expressing great joy or excitement.
– ORIGIN C20: natural exclamation.

**yahrzeit** /ˈjɑːtsʌɪt/ ● **n.** (among Jews) the anniversary of the death of a close relative, at which special candles are lit.
– ORIGIN C19: Yiddish, lit. 'anniversary time'.

**Yahweh** /ˈjɑːweɪ/ (also **Yahveh** /-veɪ/) ● **n.** a form of the Hebrew name of God used in the Bible.
– ORIGIN from Heb. *YHWH* with added vowels; cf. **JEHOVAH**.

**Yajur Veda** /ˌjʌdʒʊə ˈveɪdə, -ˈviːdə/ ● **n.** one of the four Vedas, used in the sacrificial ritual.
– ORIGIN from Sanskrit *yajus* 'sacrificial formula' and **VEDA**.

**yak**[1] ● **n.** a large ox with shaggy hair, humped shoulders, and large horns, used in Tibet as a pack animal and for its milk, meat, and hide. [*Bos grunniens* (domesticated) and *B. mutus* (its wild ancestor).]
– ORIGIN C18: from Tibetan *gyag.*

**yak**[2] (also **yack**) informal ● **n.** a trivial or unduly persistent conversation. ● **v.** (**yakked**, **yakking**) talk at length about trivial or boring subjects.
– ORIGIN 1950s: imitative.

**yakitori** /ˌjakɪˈtɔːri/ ● **n.** a Japanese dish of chicken pieces grilled on a skewer.
– ORIGIN Japanese, from *yaki* 'grilling, toasting' + *tori* 'bird'.

**yakka** /ˈjakə/ (also **yacker**) ● **n.** Austral./NZ informal work.
– ORIGIN from Jagara (an Aborig. lang.) *yaga* 'to work'.

**Yakut** /jaˈkʊt/ ● **n.** (pl. same or **Yakuts**) **1** a member of an indigenous people of northern Siberia. **2** the Turkic language of this people.
– ORIGIN via Russ. from Yakut.

**yakuza** /jəˈkuːzə/ ● **n.** (pl. same) (**the Yakuza**) a powerful Japanese criminal organization. ➤a member of this organization; a Japanese gangster or racketeer.
– ORIGIN Japanese, from *ya* 'eight' + *ku* 'nine' + *za* 'three', referring to the worst hand in a gambling game.

**Yale** ● **n.** trademark a type of lock with a latch bolt and a flat key with a serrated edge.
– ORIGIN C19: named after the Amer. locksmith Linus *Yale* Jr.

**yam** ● **n. 1** the edible starchy tuber of a climbing plant, widely distributed in tropical and subtropical countries. **2** the plant which yields this tuber. [Genus *Dioscorea*: many species.] **3** N. Amer. a sweet potato.
– ORIGIN C16: from Port. *inhame* or obs. Sp. *iñame*, prob. of W. Afr. origin.

**yam bean** ● **n.** a Central American climbing plant of the pea family, long cultivated for its edible tubers. [*Pachyrhizus erosus.*]

**yammer** informal ● **n.** loud and sustained noise. ● **v. 1** talk loudly and incessantly. **2** make a loud, incessant noise.
– DERIVATIVES **yammerer** n.
– ORIGIN ME (as a verb meaning 'lament, cry out'): alt. of earlier *yomer*, from OE *geōmrian* 'to lament'.

**yang** ● **n.** (in Chinese philosophy) the active male principle of the universe, characterized as male and creative and associated with heaven, heat, and light. Contrasted with **YIN**.
– ORIGIN from Chin. *yáng* 'male genitals', 'sun', 'positive'.

**Yank** ● **n.** informal **1** often derogatory an American. **2** US another term for **YANKEE** (in sense 2).

**yank** informal ● **v.** pull with a jerk. ● **n.** a sudden hard pull.
– ORIGIN C18 (as a Scots word in the sense 'sudden sharp blow'): of unknown origin.

**Yankee** ● **n.** informal **1** often derogatory an American. **2** US an inhabitant of New England or one of the northern states. ➤historical a Federal soldier in the Civil War. **3** a bet on four or more horses to win (or be placed) in different races. **4** (also **Yankee jib**) Sailing a large jib set forward of

a staysail in light winds. **5** used in radio communication as a code word representing the letter Y.
– ORIGIN C18: origin uncertain; recorded in the late 17th cent. as a nickname; perh. from Du. *Janke*, dimin. of *Jan* 'John'.

**Yanomami** /ˈjanə,mɑːmi/ (also **Yanomamö** /-ˌmɑːməʊ/) ● n. (pl. same) **1** a member of an American Indian people living in the forests of southern Venezuela and northern Brazil. **2** either of the two related languages of this people.
– ORIGIN the name in Yanomami, lit. 'people'.

**Yanqui** /ˈjaŋki/ ● n. variant spelling of **YANKEE**, as used in Latin American contexts.

**yantra** /ˈjantrə/ ● n. a geometrical diagram, or any object, used as an aid to meditation in tantric worship.
– ORIGIN Sanskrit, lit. 'device for holding'.

**Yao** /jaʊ/ ● n. (pl. same) **1** a member of a mountain-dwelling people of the Guangxi, Hunan, Yunnan, Guangdong, and Guizhou provinces of China. **2** the language of this people.
– ORIGIN from Chin. *Yáo*, lit. 'precious jade'.

**yap** ● v. (**yapped**, **yapping**) **1** give a sharp, shrill bark. **2** informal talk at length in an irritating manner. ● n. a sharp, shrill bark.
– DERIVATIVES **yapper** n. **yappy** adj. (informal).
– ORIGIN C17: imitative.

**yapok** /ˈjapɒk/ ● n. a semiaquatic carnivorous opossum with dark-banded grey fur and webbed hind feet, native to tropical America. [*Chironectes minimus*.]
– ORIGIN C19: from *Oyapock*, the name of a north Brazilian river.

**Yaqui** /ˈjaki/ ● n. (pl. same or **Yaquis**) **1** a member of an American Indian people of NW Mexico and Arizona. **2** the Uto-Aztecan language of this people.
– ORIGIN Sp., from earlier *Hiaquis*, from Yaqui *Hiaki*.

**yarak** /ˈjarak/ ● n. (in phr. **in yarak**) (of a trained hawk) fit and in a proper condition for hunting.
– ORIGIN C19: perh. from Pers. *yārakī* 'strength, ability' or from Turk. *yarağ* 'readiness'.

**yarborough** /ˈjɑːb(ə)rə/ ● n. (in bridge or whist) a hand with no card above a nine.
– ORIGIN C20: named after an Earl of *Yarborough*, said to have bet 1,000 to 1 against its occurrence.

**yard**[1] ● n. **1** (abbrev.: **yd**) a unit of linear measure equal to 3 feet (0.9144 metre). ➤ a square or cubic yard, especially of sand or other building materials. **2** a cylindrical spar, tapering to each end, slung across a ship's mast for a sail to hang from. **3** US informal one hundred dollars.
– PHRASES **by the yard** in large numbers or quantities.
– ORIGIN OE *gerd*, of W. Gmc origin.

**yard**[2] ● n. **1** chiefly Brit. a piece of uncultivated ground adjoining a building, typically one enclosed by walls. ➤ an area of land used for a particular purpose or business: *a builder's yard*. **2** N. Amer. the garden of a house. **3** W. Indian a house and the land attached. ➤ a residential compound comprising a number of small rented dwellings around a shared open area. ➤ S. African a plot of land accommodating a number of rooms let out as living space. **4** (**Yard**) (among expatriate Jamaicans) home; Jamaica. ● v. **1** N. Amer. store or transport (wood) in or to a timber yard. **2** put (farm animals) into an enclosure.
– ORIGIN OE *geard* 'building, home, region', from a Gmc base rel. to **GARDEN** and **ORCHARD**.

**yardage** ● n. **1** a distance or length measured in yards. **2** archaic the use of a yard for storage or the keeping of animals, or payment for such use.

**yardarm** ● n. the outer extremity of a ship's yard.

**yardbird** ● n. US informal **1** a new military recruit, especially one assigned to menial tasks. **2** a convict.
– ORIGIN 1940s: perh. suggested by **JAILBIRD**.

**Yardie** /ˈjɑːdi/ informal ● n. **1** (among Jamaicans) a fellow Jamaican. **2** (in the UK) a member of a Jamaican or West Indian gang of criminals.
– ORIGIN 1980s: from Jamaican Engl., lit. 'house, home'.

**yardman** ● n. (pl. **-men**) **1** a person working in a railway or timber yard. **2** US a person who does various outdoor jobs.

**yard of ale** ● n. Brit. the amount of beer (typically two to three pints) held by a narrow glass about a yard high.

**yard sale** ● n. N. Amer. a sale of miscellaneous second-hand items held in the grounds of a private house.

**yardstick** ● n. **1** a measuring rod a yard long. **2** a standard used for comparison.

**yare** /jɛː/ ● adj. US (of a ship) moving lightly and easily; easily manageable.
– ORIGIN OE *gearu* 'prepared, ready', of Gmc origin.

**yarmulke** /ˈjɑːmʊlkə/ (also **yarmulka**) ● n. a skullcap worn in public by Orthodox Jewish men or during prayer by other Jewish men.
– ORIGIN C20: from Yiddish *yarmolke*.

**yarn** ● n. **1** spun thread used for knitting, weaving, or sewing. **2** informal a long or rambling story, especially one that is implausible. ➤ Austral./NZ a chat. ● v. informal tell a yarn. ➤ Austral./NZ chat; talk.
– ORIGIN OE *gearn*; of Gmc origin.

**yarraman** /ˈjarəmən/ ● n. (pl. **yarramans** or **yarramen** /-mɛn/) Austral. a horse.
– ORIGIN prob. from an Aborig. root meaning 'teeth'.

**yarran** /ˈjarən/ ● n. a small Australian acacia with durable scented wood. [*Acacia omalophylla*.]
– ORIGIN C19: from Kamilaroi (and rel. langs) *yarraan*.

**yarrow** ● n. a plant with feathery leaves and heads of small white or pale pink aromatic flowers, used in herbal medicine. [*Achillea millefolium*.]
– ORIGIN OE *gearwe*, of W. Gmc origin.

**yashmak** /ˈjaʃmak/ ● n. a veil concealing all of the face except the eyes, worn by some Muslim women in public.
– ORIGIN C19: via Arab. from Turk.

**yatra** /ˈjɑːtrɑː/ ● n. Indian a procession or pilgrimage, especially one with a religious purpose.
– ORIGIN from Sanskrit *yātrā* 'journey', from *yā* 'go'.

**yatter** informal ● v. talk incessantly; chatter. ● n. incessant talk.
– ORIGIN C19: imitative.

**yaupon** /ˈjɔːpɒn/ ● n. a North American holly, the leaves of which have emetic properties and were formerly used as a tea by American Indians. [*Ilex vomitoria*.]
– ORIGIN C18: a N. Amer. Ind. word.

**yaw** ● v. (of a moving ship or aircraft) twist or oscillate about a vertical axis. ● n. twisting or oscillation of a moving ship or aircraft about a vertical axis.
– ORIGIN C16: of unknown origin.

**yawl** ● n. **1** a two-masted fore-and-aft-rigged sailing boat with the mizzenmast stepped far aft so that the mizzen boom overhangs the stern. **2** historical a ship's jolly boat with four or six oars.
– ORIGIN C16: from Mid. Low Ger. *jolle* or Du. *jol*, of unknown origin; cf. **JOLLY**[2].

**yawn** ● v. **1** involuntarily open one's mouth wide and inhale deeply due to tiredness or boredom. **2** [usu. as adj. **yawning**] be wide open: *a yawning chasm*. ● n. **1** an act of yawning. **2** informal a boring or tedious thing or event.
– DERIVATIVES **yawningly** adv.
– ORIGIN OE *geonian*, of Gmc origin.

**yawp** ● n. **1** a harsh or hoarse cry or yelp. **2** N. Amer. foolish or noisy talk. ● v. **1** shout or exclaim hoarsely. **2** N. Amer. talk foolishly or noisily.
– DERIVATIVES **yawper** n.
– ORIGIN ME: imitative.

**yaws** ● pl. n. [treated as sing.] a contagious tropical disease caused by a bacterium that enters skin abrasions and causes small crusted lesions which may develop into deep ulcers.
– ORIGIN C17: prob. from Carib *yaya*.

**yay** /jeɪ/ (also **yea**) ● adv. informal, chiefly N. Amer. **1** (with measurements) so; to this extent: *I knew him when he was yay big*. **2** to a considerable degree; much.
– ORIGIN 1960s: prob. a var. of **YEA**.

**Yb** ● symb. the chemical element ytterbium.

**Y chromosome** ● n. Genetics (in humans and other mammals) a sex chromosome which is normally present only in male cells, which are designated XY. Compare with **X CHROMOSOME**.

**yclept** /ɪˈklɛpt/ ● adj. archaic or humorous by the name of.

– ORIGIN OE *gecleopod*, past part. of *cleopian* 'call', of Gmc origin.

**yd** • abbrev. yard (measure).

**ye**[1] • pron. [second person pl.] archaic or dialect plural form of **THOU**[1].
– ORIGIN OE *gē*, of Gmc origin.

**ye**[2] • det. pseudo-archaic term for **THE**.
– ORIGIN from a misunderstanding of ME þ (see **THORN**), which could be written as y, so that *the* could be written *ye*; it was never, however, pronounced as 'ye'.

**yea** archaic or formal • adv. yes. • n. an affirmative answer. ➤(in the US Congress) an affirmative vote or voter.
– ORIGIN OE *gēa*, *gē*, of Gmc origin.

**yeah** (also **yeh**) • exclam. & n. informal non-standard spelling of **YES**.

**yean** /jiːn/ • v. archaic (of a sheep or goat) give birth to (a lamb or kid).
– ORIGIN ME: perh. representing an OE verb rel. to *ēanian* 'to lamb'.

**year** /jɪə, jəː/ • n. **1** the time taken by the earth to make one revolution around the sun. **2** (also **calendar year** or **civil year**) the period of 365 days (or 366 days in leap years) starting from the first of January, used for reckoning time in ordinary affairs. ➤a period of the same length as this starting at a different point. ➤a similar period used for reckoning time according to other calendars. **3** (**one's years**) one's age or time of life. **4** (**years**) informal a very long time. **5** a set of students grouped together as being of roughly similar ages.
– PHRASES **in the year of grace** (or **Our Lord**) —— in the year —— AD. [*year of grace* from med. L. *anno gratiae*, used by chroniclers.] **a year and a day** the period specified in some legal matters to ensure the completion of a full year. **year in, year out** continuously or repeatedly over a period of years.
– ORIGIN OE *gē(a)r*, of Gmc origin.

**yearbook** • n. an annual publication giving current information about and listing events of the previous year. ➤N. Amer. an annual publication of the graduating class in a school or university, giving photographs of students and details of school activities in the previous year.

**yearling** • n. an animal of a year old, or in its second year. ➤a racehorse in the calendar year after its year of foaling. • adj. **1** having lived or existed for a year. **2** Finance denoting a bond which is redeemable after one year.

**yearly** • adj. & adv. happening or produced once a year or every year.

**yearn** /jəːn/ • v. **1** have an intense feeling of loss and longing for something. **2** archaic be filled with compassion or warm feeling.
– DERIVATIVES **yearner** n. **yearning** n. **yearningly** adv.
– ORIGIN OE *giernan*, from a Gmc base meaning 'eager'.

**year-on-year** • adj. (of figures, prices, etc.) as compared with the corresponding ones from a year earlier.

**year-round** • adj. happening or continuing throughout the year.

**yeast** • n. **1** a microscopic single-celled fungus capable of converting sugar into alcohol and carbon dioxide. [*Saccharomyces cerevisiae* (**brewer's yeast**) and related species.] ➤a greyish-yellow preparation of this obtained chiefly from fermented beer, used as a fermenting agent, to raise bread dough, and as a food supplement. **2** Biology any unicellular fungus that reproduces vegetatively by budding or fission, e.g. candida.
– ORIGIN OE, of Gmc origin.

**yeasty** • adj. (**-ier**, **-iest**) **1** of, resembling, or containing yeast. **2** turbulent or restless.
– DERIVATIVES **yeastily** adv. **yeastiness** n.

**yeehaw** (also **yeehah**) • exclam. N. Amer. an expression of enthusiasm or exuberance, typically associated with cowboys of the southern US.
– ORIGIN C20: natural exclamation.

**yegg** • n. N. Amer. informal a burglar or safe-breaker.
– ORIGIN C20: of unknown origin.

**yell** • n. **1** a loud, sharp cry, especially of pain, surprise, or delight. **2** N. Amer. an organized rhythmic cheer, especially one used to support a sports team. **3** (**a yell**) Brit. informal, dated an amusing person or thing. • v. shout in a loud or piercing way.
– ORIGIN OE *g(i)ellan* (v.), of Gmc origin.

**yellow** • adj. **1** of the colour between green and orange in the spectrum, a primary subtractive colour complementary to blue; coloured like ripe lemons or egg yolks. **2** offensive having a yellowish or olive skin (as used to describe Chinese or Japanese people). **3** denoting a warning of danger which is thought to be near but not actually imminent. **4** informal cowardly. ➤archaic showing jealousy or suspicion. **5** (of a book or newspaper) unscrupulously sensational. • n. **1** yellow colour or pigment. **2** used in names of yellow butterflies and moths, e.g. **clouded yellow**. **3** (**yellows**) any of a number of plant diseases in which the leaves turn yellow, typically caused by viruses and transmitted by insects. • v. become a yellow colour, especially with age.
– PHRASES **the yellow peril** offensive the political or military threat regarded as being posed by the Chinese or by the peoples of SE Asia.
– DERIVATIVES **yellowed** adj. **yellowing** adj. **yellowish** adj. **yellowness** n. **yellowy** adj.
– ORIGIN OE *geolu*, *geolo*, of W. Gmc origin; rel. to **GOLD**.

**yellowback** • n. historical a cheap novel in a yellow board binding.

**yellow-belly** • n. informal **1** a coward. **2** any of a number of animals with yellow underparts.
– DERIVATIVES **yellow-bellied** adj.

**yellow bile** • n. historical another term for **CHOLER**.

**yellowcake** • n. impure uranium oxide obtained during processing of uranium ore.
– ORIGIN 1950s; so named because it is obtained as a yellow precipitate.

**yellow card** • n. (especially in soccer) a yellow card shown by the referee to a player being cautioned. • v. (**yellow-card**) (of the referee) show a yellow card to.

**yellow dog** • n. N. Amer. informal a contemptible person or thing.

**yellow fever** • n. a tropical virus disease transmitted by mosquitoes, which affects the liver and kidneys, causing fever and jaundice, and is often fatal.

**yellowfin** • n. a widely distributed, commercially important tuna that has yellow anal and dorsal fins. [*Thunnus albacares*.]

**yellow flag** • n. **1** a ship's yellow or quarantine flag, used to indicate the presence or absence of disease aboard. **2** Motor Racing a yellow flag used to signal to drivers that there is a hazard ahead. **3** see **FLAG**[3].

**yellowhammer** • n. a common Eurasian bunting, the male of which has a yellow head, neck, and breast. [*Emberiza citrinella*.]
– ORIGIN C16: *-hammer* is perh. from OE *amore* (a kind of bird), perh. conflated with *hama* 'feathers'.

**yellow jack** • n. archaic term for **YELLOW FEVER**.

**yellow jacket** • n. N. Amer. informal a wasp or hornet.

**yellow jersey** • n. (in a cycling race involving stages) a yellow jersey worn each day by the rider who is ahead on time over the whole race, and presented to the rider with the shortest overall time at the finish of the race.

**yellowlegs** • n. a migratory sandpiper that resembles the greenshank but has yellowish legs, breeding in northern Canada. [Genus *Tringa*: two species.]

**yellow metal** • n. a form of brass containing about 60 parts copper and 40 parts zinc, with a little lead.

**Yellow Pages** • pl. n. (trademark in the UK) a telephone directory printed on yellow paper and listing businesses and other organizations according to the goods or services they offer.

**yellow poplar** • n. North American term for **TULIP TREE**.

**yellow rattle** • n. a partly parasitic yellow-flowered plant whose ripe seeds are shed into a pouch which rattles when shaken. [*Rhinanthus minor*.]

**yellowtail** • n. (pl. same or **yellowtails**) an amberjack or other marine fish with yellow on the tail.

**yellow underwing** • n. a moth with hindwings that are yellow with a black terminal band. [*Noctua pronuba* and other species.]

**yelp** ● n. a short sharp cry, especially of pain or alarm. ● v. utter a yelp or yelps.
– DERIVATIVES **yelper** n.
– ORIGIN OE *g(i)elpan* (v.) 'to boast', later 'cry with a loud voice', from a Gmc imitative base.

**Yemeni** /ˈjɛməni/ ● n. a native or inhabitant of Yemen. ● adj. of or relating to Yemen.

**Yemenite** ● n. another term for **YEMENI**. ➤a Jew who was, or whose ancestors were, formerly resident in Yemen. ● adj. of or relating to Yemeni Arabs or Jews.

**yen**[1] ● n. (pl. same) the basic monetary unit of Japan.
– ORIGIN from Japanese *en* 'round'.

**yen**[2] informal ● n. a longing or yearning. ● v. (**yenned**, **yenning**) feel a longing or yearning.
– ORIGIN C19 (in the sense 'craving for a drug'): from Chin. *yăn*.

**yenta** /ˈyɛntə/ ● n. N. Amer. informal a female gossip and busybody.
– ORIGIN 1920s: Yiddish, orig. a given name.

**yeoman** /ˈjəʊmən/ ● n. (pl. **-men**) **1** historical a man holding a small landed estate; a freeholder. ➤a person qualified for jury duties, electoral rights, etc. by virtue of possessing free land. **2** historical a servant in a royal or noble household, ranking between a sergeant and a groom or a squire and a page. **3** Brit. a member of the yeomanry force. **4** (also **yeoman of signals**) (in the Royal and other Commonwealth navies) a petty officer concerned with signalling. ➤a petty officer in the US navy performing clerical duties on board ship.
– PHRASES **yeoman service** efficient help.
– DERIVATIVES **yeomanly** adj.
– ORIGIN ME: prob. from **YOUNG** + **MAN**.

**Yeoman of the Guard** ● n. a member of the British sovereign's bodyguard (now having only ceremonial duties).

**yeomanry** ● n. [treated as sing. or pl.] historical a body of yeomen, or yeomen collectively. ➤(in Britain) a volunteer cavalry force raised from the yeomanry (1794–1908).

**Yeoman Usher** ● n. (in the UK) the deputy of Black Rod.

**Yeoman Warder** ● n. a warder at the Tower of London.

**-yer** ● suffix variant spelling of **-IER** (as in *lawyer*).

**yerba** /ˈjəːbə/ ● n. another term for **MATÉ**.
– ORIGIN C19: from Sp., lit. 'herb'.

**yerba buena** /ˈbweɪnə/ ● n. a trailing aromatic herb related to savory and native to the western US, with whitish or lilac flowers. [*Satureja douglasii.*]
– ORIGIN C19: from Sp., lit. 'good herb'.

**yes** ● exclam. **1** used to give an affirmative response. **2** responding to someone addressing one or attracting one's attention. **3** questioning a remark. **4** expressing delight. ● n. (pl. **yeses** or **yesses**) an affirmative answer, decision, or vote.
– ORIGIN OE *gēse*, *gīse*, prob. from an unrecorded phr. meaning 'may it be so'.

**yeshiva** /jəˈʃiːvə/ ● n. an Orthodox Jewish college or seminary.
– ORIGIN from Heb. *yĕšīḇāh*.

**yes-man** ● n. (pl. **-men**) informal a person who always agrees with their superiors.

**yessir** /ˈjɛsə, jɛsˈsəː/ ● exclam. informal expressing assent, especially to a superior. ➤N. Amer. expressing emphatic affirmation.
– ORIGIN C20: alt. of *yes sir*.

**yester-** ● comb. form poetic/literary or archaic of yesterday: *yestereve*.
– ORIGIN OE *geostran*, of Gmc origin.

**yesterday** ● adv. on the day before today. ➤in the recent past. ● n. the day before today. ➤the recent past.
– ORIGIN OE *giestran dæg* (see **YESTER-**, **DAY**).

**yesteryear** ● n. poetic/literary last year or the recent past.

**yet** ● adv. **1** up until the present or a specified or implied time; by now or then. ➤[with neg.] as soon as the present or a specified or implied time. ➤from now into the future for a specified length of time. ➤referring to something that will or may happen in the future: *I'll find her yet.* **2** still; even (emphasizing increase or repetition). **3** nevertheless; in spite of that. ● conj. but at the same time; but nevertheless.
– PHRASES **nor yet** and also not.
– ORIGIN OE *gīet(a)*, of unknown origin.

**yeti** /ˈjɛti/ ● n. a large hairy manlike creature said to live in the highest part of the Himalayas.
– ORIGIN 1930s: from Tibetan *yeh-teh* 'little manlike animal'.

**yew** ● n. a coniferous tree with poisonous red berry-like fruit and dense, springy wood. [*Taxus baccata* and related species.]
– ORIGIN OE *īw*, *ēow*, of Gmc origin.

**Y-fronts** ● pl. n. Brit. trademark men's or boys' underpants with a branching seam at the front in the shape of an upside-down Y.

**YHA** ● abbrev. (in the UK) Youth Hostels Association.

**Yid** ● n. informal, offensive a Jew.
– ORIGIN C19: back-form. from **YIDDISH**.

**Yiddish** /ˈjɪdɪʃ/ ● n. a language used by Jews in or from central and eastern Europe, originally a German dialect with words from Hebrew and several modern languages. ● adj. of or relating to this language.
– DERIVATIVES **Yiddisher** n.
– ORIGIN C19: from Yiddish *yidish* (*daytsh*) 'Jewish (German)'.

**Yiddishism** ● n. **1** a Yiddish word or idiom. **2** advocacy of Yiddish culture.
– DERIVATIVES **Yiddishist** n.

**yield** ● v. **1** produce or provide (a natural, agricultural, or industrial product). ➤produce or deliver (a result or gain). ➤generate (a specified financial return). **2** give way to demands or pressure; submit. ➤relinquish possession of. ➤concede (a point of dispute). ➤give way to other traffic. **3** (of a mass or structure) give way under force or pressure. ● n. an amount or result yielded.
– DERIVATIVES **yielder** n. **yielding** adj. **yieldingly** adv.
– ORIGIN OE *g(i)eldan* 'pay, repay', of Gmc origin.

**yield point** ● n. Physics the stress beyond which a material becomes plastic.

**yield strength** ● n. Physics (in materials without a well-defined yield point) the stress at which a specific amount of plastic deformation is produced.

**yikes** ● exclam. informal expressing shock and alarm, for humorous effect.
– ORIGIN 1970s: of unknown origin; cf. **YOICKS**.

**yin** ● n. (in Chinese philosophy) the passive female principle of the universe, characterized as female and sustaining and associated with earth, dark, and cold. Contrasted with **YANG**.
– ORIGIN from Chin. *yīn* 'feminine', 'moon', 'shade'.

**yip** /jɪp/ ● n. a short, sharp cry or yelp, especially of excitement or delight. ● v. (**yipped**, **yipping**) give a yip.
– ORIGIN C20 (orig. US): imitative.

**yippee** ● exclam. expressing wild excitement or delight.
– ORIGIN natural exclamation: first recorded in Amer. Engl. in the 1920s.

**yippie** ● n. (pl. **-ies**) a member of a group of young politically active hippies, originally in the US.
– ORIGIN 1960s: acronym from *Youth International Party* + the suffix *-ie*, suggested by **HIPPY**[1].

**yips** ● pl. n. (**the yips**) informal extreme nervousness causing a golfer to miss easy putts.
– ORIGIN C20: of unknown origin.

**Yizkor** /ˈjɪzkə/ ● n. (pl. same or **Yizkors**) a memorial service held by Jews on certain holy days for deceased relatives or martyrs.
– ORIGIN from Heb. *yizkōr*, lit. 'may (God) remember'.

**-yl** ● suffix Chemistry forming names of radicals: *phenyl*.
– ORIGIN from Gk *hulē* 'wood, material'.

**ylang-ylang** /ˌiːlaŋˈiːlaŋ/ (also **ilang-ilang**) ● n. **1** a sweet-scented essential oil obtained from the flowers of a tropical tree, used in perfumery and aromatherapy. **2** the yellow-flowered tree, native to Malaya and the Philippines, from which this oil is obtained. [*Cananga odorata.*]
– ORIGIN C19: from Tagalog *ilang-ilang*.

**ylem** /ˈiːlɛm/ ● **n.** Astronomy (in the big bang theory) the primordial matter of the universe, originally conceived as composed of neutrons at high temperature and density.
– ORIGIN 1940s: from late L. *hylem* (accusative) 'matter'.

**YMCA** ● **abbrev.** Young Men's Christian Association.

**-yne** ● **suffix** Chemistry forming names of unsaturated compounds containing a triple bond: *ethyne*.
– ORIGIN alt. of **-INE**[4].

**yo** ● **exclam.** informal used to greet someone, attract their attention, or express excitement.
– ORIGIN natural exclamation: first recorded in ME.

**yob** ● **n.** Brit. informal a rude and loutish young man.
– DERIVATIVES **yobbery** n. **yobbish** adj. **yobbishly** adv. **yobbishness** n. **yobby** adj.
– ORIGIN C19: back sl. for **BOY**.

**yobbo** ● **n.** (pl. **-os** or **-oes**) Brit. informal a yob.

**yock** (also **yok**) ● **n.** US informal a hearty laugh.
– ORIGIN 1930s (theatrical sl.): prob. imitative.

**yocto-** /ˈjɒktəʊ/ ● **comb. form** denoting a factor of $10^{-24}$: *yoctojoule*.
– ORIGIN adapted from **OCTO-**, on the pattern of combining forms such as *peta-* and *exa-*.

**yod** /jɒd/ ● **n. 1** the tenth and smallest letter of the Hebrew alphabet. **2** Phonetics the semivowel or glide /j/.
– ORIGIN from Heb. *yōḏ*; rel. to *yaḏ* 'hand'.

**yodel** /ˈjəʊd(ə)l/ ● **v.** (**yodelled**, **yodelling**; US **yodeled**, **yodeling**) practise a form of singing or calling marked by rapid alternation between the normal voice and falsetto. ● **n.** a song or call delivered in such a way.
– DERIVATIVES **yodeller** n.
– ORIGIN C19: from Ger. *jodeln*.

**yoga** ● **n.** a Hindu spiritual and ascetic discipline, a part of which, including breath control, simple meditation, and the adoption of specific bodily postures, is widely practised for health and relaxation.
– DERIVATIVES **yogic** adj.
– ORIGIN Sanskrit, lit. 'union'.

**yogh** /jɒg/ ● **n.** a Middle English letter (ȝ) used mainly where modern English has *gh* and *y*.
– ORIGIN ME: of unknown origin.

**yogi** ● **n.** (pl. **yogis**) a person who is proficient in yoga.
– ORIGIN from Sanskrit *yogī*, from *yoga* (see **YOGA**).

**yogic flying** ● **n.** a technique of Transcendental Meditation involving thrusting oneself off the ground while in the lotus position.

**yogurt** /ˈjɒgət, ˈjəʊ-/ (also **yoghurt** or **yoghourt**) ● **n.** a semi-solid sourish food prepared from milk fermented by added bacteria.
– ORIGIN C17: from Turk. *yoğurt*.

**yo-heave-ho** ● **exclam. & n.** another term for **HEAVE-HO**.

**yohimbe** /jəʊˈhɪmbeɪ/ ● **n.** a tropical West African tree from which the drug yohimbine is obtained. [*Pausinystalia johimbe*.]
– ORIGIN C19: a local word.

**yohimbine** /jəʊˈhɪmbiːn/ ● **n.** Chemistry a toxic compound obtained from the yohimbe tree, used in the treatment of impotence.

**yo-ho** ● **exclam. 1** dated used to attract attention. **2** (also **yo-ho-ho**) Nautical, archaic a seaman's chant used while hauling ropes.

**yoicks** /jɔɪks/ ● **exclam.** used by fox-hunters to urge on the hounds.
– ORIGIN C18: of unknown origin.

**yok** ● **n.** variant spelling of **YOCK**.

**yoke** ● **n. 1** a wooden crosspiece that is fastened over the necks of two animals and attached to a plough or cart that they pull in unison. ➤(pl. same or **yokes**) a pair of yoked animals. ➤archaic the amount of land that one pair of oxen could plough in a day. ➤something that represents a bond between two parties: *the yoke of marriage*. **2** a frame fitting over the neck and shoulders of a person, used for carrying pails or baskets. ➤something that is regarded as oppressive or burdensome. **3** a part of a garment that fits over the shoulders and to which the main part of the garment is attached. **4** a crosspiece similar to a yoke, such as the crossbar of a rudder. **5** (in ancient Rome) an arch of three spears under which a defeated army was made to march. ● **v.** put a yoke on; couple or attach with or to a yoke.
– ORIGIN OE *geoc* (n.), *geocian* (v.), of Gmc origin.

**yokel** ● **n.** an unsophisticated country person.
– ORIGIN C19: perh. figuratively from dial. *yokel* 'green woodpecker'.

**yokozuna** /ˌjəʊkəˈzuːnə/ ● **n.** (pl. same) a grand champion sumo wrestler.
– ORIGIN Japanese, from *yoko* 'crosswise' + *tsuna* 'rope' (orig. denoting a belt presented to the champion).

**yolk** /jəʊk/ ● **n.** the yellow internal part of a bird's egg, which is rich in protein and fat and nourishes the developing embryo. ➤Zoology the corresponding part in the ovum or larva of all egg-laying vertebrates and many invertebrates.
– DERIVATIVES **yolked** adj. **yolkless** adj. **yolky** adj.
– ORIGIN OE *geol(o)ca*, from *geolu* 'yellow'.

**yolk sac** ● **n.** Zoology a membranous sac containing yolk attached to the embryos of reptiles and birds and the larvae of some fishes.

**Yom Kippur** /jɒm ˈkɪpə, kɪˈpʊə/ ● **n.** the most solemn religious fast of the Jewish year, the last of the ten days of penitence that begin with Rosh Hashana (the Jewish New Year).
– ORIGIN from Heb.

**yomp** Brit. informal ● **v.** (of a soldier) march with heavy equipment over difficult terrain. ● **n.** a march of such a kind.
– ORIGIN 1980s: of unknown origin.

**yon** poetic/literary or dialect ● **det. & adv.** yonder; that. ● **pron.** yonder person or thing.
– ORIGIN OE *geon*, of Gmc origin.

**yonder** archaic or dialect ● **adv.** at some distance in the direction indicated; over there. ● **det.** that or those (referring to something situated at a distance). ● **n.** (**the yonder**) the far distance.
– ORIGIN ME: of Gmc origin; rel. to **YON**.

**yoni** /ˈjəʊni/ ● **n.** (pl. **yonis**) Hinduism the vulva, regarded as a symbol of divine procreative energy and conventionally represented by a circular stone.
– ORIGIN Sanskrit, lit. 'source, womb, female genitals'.

**yonks** ● **pl. n.** Brit. informal a very long time.
– ORIGIN 1960s: origin unknown; perh. rel. to *donkey's years* (see **DONKEY**).

**yoo-hoo** ● **exclam.** a call to attract attention.
– ORIGIN natural exclamation: first recorded in Engl. in the 1920s.

**yore** ● **n.** (in phr. **of yore**) poetic/literary of former times or long ago.
– ORIGIN OE *geāra*, *geāre*, of unknown origin.

**york** ● **v.** Cricket (of a bowler) bowl out (a batsman) with a ball that pitches under the bat.
– ORIGIN C19: back-form. from **YORKER**.

**yorker** ● **n.** Cricket a ball bowled so that it pitches immediately under the bat.
– ORIGIN prob. from *York*, suggesting its introduction by Yorkshire players.

**Yorkist** ● **n.** a follower of the House of York in the Wars of the Roses. ● **adj.** of or relating to the House of York.

**Yorks.** ● **abbrev.** Yorkshire.

**Yorkshire fog** ● **n.** a common pasture grass with soft downy leaves. [*Holcus lanatus*.]
– ORIGIN C19: *fog* from **FOG**[2].

**Yorkshireman** (or **Yorkshirewoman**) ● **n.** (pl. **-men** or **-women**) a native or inhabitant of Yorkshire.

**Yorkshire pudding** ● **n.** a baked batter pudding typically eaten with roast beef.

**Yorkshire terrier** ● **n.** a dog of a small long-haired blue-grey and tan breed of terrier.

**Yoruba** /ˈjɒrʊbə/ ● **n.** (pl. same or **Yorubas**) **1** a member of an African people of SW Nigeria and Benin. **2** the Kwa language of this people.
– ORIGIN the name in Yoruba.

**yotta-** /ˈjɒtə/ ● **comb. form** denoting a factor of $10^{24}$: *yottameter*.
– ORIGIN appar. adapted from Ital. *otto* 'eight' (see also

**YOCTO-**).

**you** • pron. [second person sing. or pl.] **1** used to refer to the person or people that the speaker is addressing. ➤used to refer to the person being addressed together with other people regarded in the same class. **2** used to refer to any person in general.
– PHRASES **you and yours** you together with your family and close friends.
– ORIGIN OE *ēow*, accusative and dative of *gē* (see **YE**[1]), of W. Gmc origin.

**you'd** • contr. **1** you had. **2** you would.

**you'll** • contr. you will; you shall.

**young** • adj. (**-er**, **-est**) having lived or existed for only a short time; not far advanced in life. ➤relating to, characteristic of, or consisting of young people. • n. [treated as pl.] young children or animals; offspring.
– DERIVATIVES **youngish** adj.
– ORIGIN OE *g(e)ong*, of Gmc origin.

**young offender** • n. Law (in the UK) a criminal between 14 and 17 years of age.

**youngberry** • n. (pl. **-ies**) a bramble of a variety which bears large edible reddish-black fruit, believed to be a hybrid of the dewberry.
– ORIGIN 1920s: named after the Amer. horticulturalist B. M. *Young*.

**young gun** • n. informal an assertive and self-confident young man.

**youngling** • n. poetic/literary a young person or animal.

**Young's modulus** • n. Physics a measure of elasticity, equal to the ratio of the stress acting on a substance to the strain produced.
– ORIGIN C19: named after the Engl. physicist Thomas *Young*.

**youngster** • n. a child, young person, or young animal.

**Young Turk** • n. **1** a member of a revolutionary party in the Ottoman Empire in the late 19th and early 20th centuries. **2** a young person eager for radical change to the established order.

**younker** /ˈjʌŋkə/ • n. dated a youngster.
– ORIGIN C16: from MDu. *jonckher*, from *jonc* 'young' + *hēre* 'lord'; cf. **JUNKER**.

**your** /jɔː, jʊə/ • possess. det. **1** belonging to or associated with the person or people that the speaker is addressing. **2** belonging to or associated with any person in general. **3** (**Your**) used when addressing the holder of certain titles.
– ORIGIN OE *ēower*, genitive of *gē* (see **YE**[1]), of Gmc origin.

**you're** /jɔː, jə, jʊə/ • contr. you are.

**yours** • possess. pron. used to refer to something belonging to or associated with the person or people that the speaker is addressing.

**yourself** • pron. [second person sing.] (pl. **yourselves**) **1** used as the object of a verb or preposition when this is the same as the subject of the clause and the subject is the person or people being addressed. **2** [emphatic] you personally.

**youse** /juːz/ (also **yous**) • pron. dialect you (usually more than one person).

**youth** • n. (pl. **youths**) **1** the period between childhood and adult age. ➤the qualities of vigour, freshness, immaturity, etc. associated with being young. **2** [treated as sing. or pl.] young people. ➤a young man.
– ORIGIN OE *geoguth*, of Gmc origin; rel. to **YOUNG**.

**youth club** (also **youth centre**) • n. a place or organization providing leisure activities for young people.

**youthful** • adj. young or seeming young. ➤characteristic of young people.
– DERIVATIVES **youthfully** adv. **youthfulness** n.

**youth hostel** • n. a place providing cheap accommodation, aimed mainly at young people on holiday. • v. (**youth-hostel**) travel around, sleeping in youth hostels.
– DERIVATIVES **youth-hosteller** n.

**you've** • contr. you have.

**yowl** /jaʊl/ • n. a loud wailing cry of pain or distress. • v. make such a cry.
– ORIGIN ME: imitative.

**yo-yo** (trademark in the UK) • n. (pl. **-os**) **1** a toy consisting of a pair of joined discs with a deep groove between them in which string is attached and wound, which can be spun alternately downward and upward by its weight and momentum as the string unwinds and rewinds. ➤a thing that repeatedly falls and rises again. **2** informal, chiefly N. Amer. a stupid, insane, or unpredictable person. • v. (**-oes**, **-oed**) move up and down repeatedly; fluctuate.
– ORIGIN 1915: prob. ult. from a lang. of the Philippines.

**yr** • abbrev. **1** year or years. **2** younger. **3** your.

**yrs** • abbrev. **1** years. **2** yours (as a formula ending a letter).

**YT** • abbrev. Yukon Territory (in official postal use).

**YTS** • abbrev. Youth Training Scheme.

**ytterbium** /ɪˈtəːbɪəm/ • n. the chemical element of atomic number 70, a silvery-white metal of the lanthanide series. (Symbol: **Yb**)
– ORIGIN C19: mod. L., from *Ytterby* in Sweden, where minerals containing several rare-earth elements were found; cf. **ERBIUM**, **TERBIUM**, **YTTRIUM**.

**yttrium** /ˈɪtrɪəm/ • n. the chemical element of atomic number 39, a greyish-white metal resembling the rare-earth elements. (Symbol: **Y**)
– ORIGIN C19: mod. L., from *Ytterby* (see **YTTERBIUM**).

**yuan** /jʊˈɑːn/ • n. (pl. same) the basic monetary unit of China, equal to 10 jiao or 100 fen.
– ORIGIN Chin., lit. 'round'; cf. **YEN**[1].

**yuca** /ˈjuːkə/ • n. chiefly US another term for **CASSAVA**.
– ORIGIN C16: from Carib; cf. **YUCCA**.

**yucca** /ˈjʌkə/ • n. a plant of the agave family with sword-like leaves and spikes of white bell-shaped flowers, native to warm regions of the US and Mexico. [Genus *Yucca*: many species.]
– ORIGIN C17: var. of **YUCA**.

**yuck** (also **yuk**) informal • exclam. used to express strong distaste or disgust. • n. something messy or disgusting.
– DERIVATIVES **yucky** (also **yukky**) adj.
– ORIGIN 1960s (orig. US): imitative.

**Yugoslav** /ˈjuːgə(ʊ)slɑːv, ˌjuːgə(ʊ)ˈslɑːv/ • n. a native or national of Yugoslavia, or a person of Yugoslav descent.
– DERIVATIVES **Yugoslavian** n. & adj.
– ORIGIN from Austrian Ger. *Jugoslav*, from Serbo-Croat *jug* 'south' + **SLAV**.

**yukata** /jʊˈkata/ • n. (pl. same or **yukatas**) a light cotton kimono.
– ORIGIN Japanese, from *yu* 'hot water' (because orig. worn after a bath) + *kata(bira)* 'light kimono'.

**Yule** (also **Yuletide**) • n. archaic term for **CHRISTMAS**.
– ORIGIN OE *gēol(a)*; cf. ON *jól*, orig. applied to a heathen festival lasting twelve days.

**yule log** • n. a large log traditionally burnt in the hearth on Christmas Eve. ➤a log-shaped chocolate cake eaten at Christmas.

**yummy** • adj. (**-ier**, **-iest**) informal delicious.

**yum-yum** • exclam. informal used to express pleasure at eating delicious food.
– ORIGIN C19: imitative.

**Yupik** /ˈjuːpɪk/ • n. (pl. same or **Yupiks**) **1** a member of an Eskimo people of Siberia, the Aleutian Islands, and Alaska. **2** any of the languages of this people, a division of the Eskimo-Aleut family.
– ORIGIN from Alaskan Yupik *Yup'ik* 'real person'.

**yuppie** (also **yuppy**) • n. (pl. **-ies**) informal, derogatory a well-paid young middle-class professional working in a city.
– DERIVATIVES **yuppiedom** n. **yuppification** n. **yuppify** v.
– ORIGIN 1980s: elaboration of the acronym from *young urban professional*.

**yuppie flu** • n. informal derogatory term for **CHRONIC FATIGUE SYNDROME**.

**yurt** /jʊət, jəːt/ • n. a circular tent of felt or skins used by nomads in Mongolia, Siberia, and Turkey.
– ORIGIN from Russ. *yurta*, via Fr. or Ger. from Turkic *jurt*.

**YV** • abbrev. Venezuela (international vehicle registration).

**YWCA** • abbrev. Young Women's Christian Association.

# Zz

**Z**[1] /zɛd, US ziː/ (also **z**) ● **n.** (pl. **Zs** or **Z's**) **1** the twenty-sixth letter of the alphabet. **2** denoting the next after Y in a set of items, categories, etc. **3** (usu. **z**) the third unknown quantity in an algebraic expression. ➤denoting the third axis in a three-dimensional system of coordinates. **4** used in repeated form to represent buzzing or snoring.
– PHRASES **catch some** (or **a few**) **Zs** informal, chiefly N. Amer. get some sleep.

**Z**[2] ● **abbrev.** Zambia (international vehicle registration). ● **symb.** Chemistry atomic number.

**ZA** ● **abbrev.** South Africa (international vehicle registration).
– ORIGIN from Afrik. *Zuid Afrika.*

**zabaglione** /ˌzabaˈljəʊni/ ● **n.** an Italian dessert made of whipped egg yolks, sugar, and Marsala wine.
– ORIGIN from Ital.

**zaffre** /ˈzafə/ (also **zaffer**) ● **n.** impure cobalt oxide, formerly used to make smalt and blue enamels.
– ORIGIN C17: from Ital. *zaffera* or Fr. *safre.*

**zaftig** /ˈzaftɪg/ (also **zoftig**) ● **adj.** N. Amer. informal (of a woman) having a full, rounded figure; curvaceous.
– ORIGIN 1930s: Yiddish, from Ger. *saftig* 'juicy'.

**zag** ● **n.** a sharp change of direction in a zigzag course. ● **v.** (**zagged, zagging**) make a zag.
– ORIGIN C18: shortening of ZIGZAG.

**zaibatsu** /zʌɪˈbatsuː/ ● **n.** (pl. same) a large Japanese business conglomerate.
– ORIGIN Japanese, from *zai* 'wealth' + *batsu* 'clique'.

**zaire** /zʌɪˈɪə/ ● **n.** (pl. same) the basic monetary unit of Zaire (Democratic Republic of Congo), equal to 100 makuta.

**Zairean** /zʌɪˈɪərɪən/ (also **Zairian**) ● **n.** a native or inhabitant of Zaire (Democratic Republic of Congo). ● **adj.** of or relating to Zaire.

**zakat** /zəˈkɑːt/ ● **n.** obligatory payment made annually under Islamic law and used for charitable and religious purposes.
– ORIGIN via Pers. and Urdu from Arab. *zakā(t)* 'almsgiving'.

**Zambian** /ˈzambɪən/ ● **n.** a native or inhabitant of Zambia. ● **adj.** of or relating to Zambia.

**zamindar** /zəˈmiːndɑː/ (also **zemindar**) ● **n.** Indian, historical a landowner who leased land to tenant farmers.
– ORIGIN via Urdu from Pers. *zamīndār*, from *zamīn* 'land' + *-dār* 'holder'.

**zamindari** /zəˈmiːndəri, ˌzəmiːnˈdɑːri/ (also **zemindari**) ● **n.** Indian, historical the system under which zamindars held land.
– ORIGIN from Urdu.

**Zande** /ˈzandi/ (also **Azande**) ● **n.** (pl. same or **Azande** /aˈzandi/) **1** a member of a central African people. **2** the Niger-Congo language of this people.
– ORIGIN the name in Zande.

**zander** /ˈzandə/ ● **n.** (pl. same) a large predatory freshwater perch native to northern and central Europe. [*Stizostedion lucioperca.*]
– ORIGIN C19: from Ger. *Zander.*

**Zantac** /ˈzantak/ ● **n.** trademark for RANITIDINE.
– ORIGIN C20: prob. from *Z-* + ANTACID.

**ZANU** (also **ZANU-PF**) ● **abbrev.** Zimbabwe African National Union (Patriotic Front).

**zany** ● **adj.** (**-ier, -iest**) amusingly unconventional and idiosyncratic. ● **n. 1** a zany person. **2** historical a comic performer partnering a clown, whom he imitated in an amusing way.
– DERIVATIVES **zanily** adv. **zaniness** n.
– ORIGIN C16: from Fr. *zani* or Ital. *zan(n)i*, Venetian form of *Gianni, Giovanni* 'John', stock name of the servants acting as clowns in the commedia dell'arte.

**zap** informal ● **v.** (**zapped, zapping**) **1** destroy or obliterate. **2** move or propel suddenly and rapidly. ➤use a remote control to change television channels, operate a video recorder, etc. ● **n.** a sudden burst of energy or sound, or other sudden dramatic event.
– DERIVATIVES **zapper** n. **zappy** adj.
– ORIGIN 1920s (orig. US): imitative.

**zapateado** /zaˌpatɪˈɑːdəʊ/ ● **n.** (pl. **-os**) a flamenco dance with rhythmic stamping of the feet.
– ORIGIN C19: Sp., from *zapato* 'shoe'.

**Zapotec** /ˈzapətɛk/ ● **n.** (pl. same or **Zapotecs**) **1** a member of an American Indian people of southern Mexico. **2** the language of this people.
– ORIGIN from Sp. *zapoteco*, from Nahuatl *tzapoteca* (pl.) 'people of the place of the sapodilla'.

**ZAPU** /ˈzɑːpuː/ ● **abbrev.** Zimbabwe African People's Union.

**zariba** /zəˈriːbə/ (also **zareba**) ● **n.** (in Sudan and neighbouring countries) a thorn fence fortifying a camp or village.
– ORIGIN from Arab. *zarība* 'cattle pen'.

**zarzuela** /θɑːˈθweɪlə, Spanish θarˈθwela, sarˈswela/ ● **n. 1** a traditional Spanish form of musical comedy. **2** a Spanish dish of seafood cooked in a rich sauce.
– ORIGIN Sp., appar. from a place name.

**zax** ● **n.** variant spelling of SAX[2].

**zazen** /zɑːˈzɛn/ ● **n.** Zen meditation.
– ORIGIN Japanese, from *za* 'sitting' + *zen* (see ZEN).

**Z boson** ● **n.** another term for **Z** PARTICLE.

**zeal** /ziːl/ ● **n.** great energy or enthusiasm for a cause or objective.
– ORIGIN ME: via eccles. L. from Gk *zēlos.*

**zealot** /ˈzɛlət/ ● **n. 1** a fanatical and uncompromising follower of a religion or policy. **2** (**Zealot**) a member of an ancient Jewish sect aiming at a world Jewish theocracy and resisting the Romans until AD 70.
– DERIVATIVES **zealotry** n.
– ORIGIN C16: via eccles. L. from Gk *zēlōtēs*, from *zēloun* 'be jealous', from *zēlos* (see ZEAL).

**zealous** /ˈzɛləs/ ● **adj.** having or showing zeal.
– DERIVATIVES **zealously** adv. **zealousness** n.

**zebec** ● **n.** variant spelling of XEBEC.

**zebra** /ˈzɛbrə, ˈziːbrə/ ● **n.** an African wild horse with black-and-white stripes and an erect mane. [*Equus burchellii* and other species.]
– ORIGIN C17: from Ital., Sp., or Port., orig. in the sense 'wild ass', perh. ult. from L. *equiferus*, from *equus* 'horse' + *ferus* 'wild'.

**zebra crossing** ● **n.** Brit. a pedestrian street crossing marked with broad white stripes.

**zebra finch** ● **n.** a small Australian waxbill with a black and white striped face. [*Poephila guttata.*]

**zebra mussel** ● **n.** a small freshwater bivalve mollusc with zigzag markings on the shell. [*Dreissena polymorpha.*]

**zebu** /ˈziːbuː/ ● **n.** an ox of a humped breed originally domesticated in India.
– ORIGIN C18: from Fr. *zébu*, of unknown origin.

**Zech.** ● **abbrev.** Zechariah (in biblical references).

**zedoary** /ˈzɛdəʊəri/ ● **n.** an Indian plant related to turmeric, with an aromatic rhizome. [*Curcuma zedoaria.*]

➤ a ginger-like substance made from this rhizome.
– ORIGIN ME: from med. L. *zedoarium*, from Pers. *zadwār*.

**Zeeman effect** /ˈziːmən, ˈzeɪ-/ ● **n.** Physics the splitting of a spectrum line into several components by a magnetic field.
– ORIGIN C19: named after the Du. physicist Pieter *Zeeman*.

**zeera** ● **n.** variant spelling of **JEERA**.

**zein** /ˈziːɪn/ ● **n.** Biochemistry the principal protein of maize.
– ORIGIN C19: from mod. L. *Zea* (genus name of maize) + **-IN**¹.

**zeitgeist** /ˈzʌɪtɡʌɪst/ ● **n.** the defining spirit or mood of a particular period of history.
– ORIGIN C19: from Ger. *Zeitgeist*, from *Zeit* 'time' + *Geist* 'spirit'.

**Zen** ● **n.** a Japanese school of Mahayana Buddhism emphasizing the value of meditation and intuition.
– ORIGIN Japanese, lit. 'meditation', from Chin. *chán* 'quietude', from Sanskrit *dhyāna* 'meditation'.

**zenana** /zɪˈnɑːnə/ ● **n.** (in India and Iran) the part of a house for the seclusion of women.
– ORIGIN from Pers. and Urdu *zanānah*, from *zan* 'woman'.

**Zend-Avesta** ● **n.** the Zoroastrian sacred writings, comprising the Avesta (the text) and the Zend (the commentary).
– ORIGIN *Zend* from Pers. *zand* 'interpretation'.

**Zener cards** /ˈziːnə/ ● **pl. n.** cards bearing symbols, used in ESP research.
– ORIGIN 1930s: named after the Amer. psychologist Karl E. *Zener*.

**Zener diode** /ˈziːnə/ ● **n.** Electronics a semiconductor diode in which at a critical reverse voltage a large reverse current can flow.
– ORIGIN 1950s: named after the Amer. physicist Clarence M. *Zener*.

**zenith** /ˈzɛnɪθ/ ● **n. 1** the point in the sky directly overhead. The opposite of **NADIR**. **2** the highest point in the sky reached by a given celestial object. **3** the time at which something is most powerful or successful.
– DERIVATIVES **zenithal** adj.
– ORIGIN ME: from OFr. or med. L. *cenit*, based on Arab. *samt* (*ar-ra's*) 'path (over the head)'.

**zenithal projection** ● **n.** a map projection in which a part of the globe is projected on to a plane tangential to the centre of the part, showing the correct directions of all points from the centre.

**zeolite** /ˈziːəlʌɪt/ ● **n.** any of a large group of minerals consisting of hydrated aluminosilicates, used as cation exchangers and molecular sieves.
– DERIVATIVES **zeolitic** /-ˈlɪtɪk/ adj.
– ORIGIN C18: from Swed. and Ger. *zeolit*, from Gk *zein* 'to boil' + **-LITE** (from their characteristic swelling when heated).

**Zeph.** ● **abbrev.** Zephaniah (in biblical references).

**zephyr** /ˈzɛfə/ ● **n. 1** poetic/literary a soft gentle breeze. **2** historical a fine cotton gingham. ➤ a very light article of clothing.
– ORIGIN OE *zefferus*, denoting a personification of the west wind, via L. from Gk *zephuros*.

**Zeppelin** /ˈzɛp(ə)lɪn/ ● **n.** historical a large German dirigible airship of the early 20th century.
– ORIGIN named after Ferdinand, Count von *Zeppelin*, Ger. airship pioneer.

**zepto-** /ˈzɛptəʊ/ ● **comb. form** denoting a factor of $10^{-21}$: *zeptosecond*.
– ORIGIN adapted from **SEPTI-**, on the pattern of combining forms such as *peta-* and *exa-*.

**zero** /ˈzɪərəʊ/ ● **cardinal number** (pl. **-os**) the figure 0; nought; nothing. ➤ a temperature of 0°C (32°F), marking the freezing point of water. ➤ informal a worthless or insignificant person. ● **v.** (**-oes**, **-oed**) **1** adjust (an instrument) to zero. **2** set the sights of (a gun) for firing. ➤ (**zero in on**) take aim at or focus attention on.
– ORIGIN C17: from Fr. *zéro* or Ital. *zero*, via Old Sp. from Arab. *ṣifr* 'cipher'.

**zero-based** ● **adj.** Finance (of budgeting) in which items are costed anew rather than related to previous figures.

**zero-coupon bond** ● **n.** a bond issued at a deep discount but paying no interest.

**zero hour** ● **n.** the time at which a military or other operation is set to begin.

**zero-sum** ● **adj.** denoting a game or situation in which whatever is gained by one side is lost by the other.

**zeroth** /ˈzɪərəʊθ/ ● **adj.** chiefly Physics & Mathematics immediately preceding what is regarded as first in a series.
– ORIGIN C19: from **ZERO** + **-TH**¹.

**zero tolerance** ● **n.** strict enforcement of the law regarding any form of anti-social behaviour.

**zest** ● **n. 1** great enthusiasm and energy. ➤ excitement or piquancy. **2** the outer coloured part of the peel of citrus fruit, used as flavouring.
– DERIVATIVES **zestful** adj. **zestfully** adv. **zestfulness** n. **zesty** adj.
– ORIGIN C15: from Fr. *zeste* 'orange or lemon peel', of unknown origin.

**zester** ● **n.** a kitchen utensil for scraping or peeling zest from citrus fruit.

**zeta** /ˈziːtə/ ● **n.** the sixth letter of the Greek alphabet (Z, ζ), transliterated as 'z'.
– ORIGIN from Gk.

**zetetic** /zɪˈtɛtɪk/ ● **adj.** rare proceeding by inquiry.
– ORIGIN C17: from Gk *zētētikos*, from *zētein* 'seek'.

**zetta-** /ˈzɛtə/ ● **comb. form** denoting a factor of $10^{21}$: *zettahertz*.
– ORIGIN appar. adapted from Ital. *sette* 'seven'.

**zeugma** /ˈzjuːɡmə/ ● **n.** a figure of speech in which a word applies to two others in different senses (e.g. *John and his driving licence expired last week*).
– DERIVATIVES **zeugmatic** adj.
– ORIGIN ME: via L. from Gk, from *zeugnunai* 'to yoke'.

**zho** ● **n.** variant spelling of **DZO**.

**zidovudine** /zɪˈdɒvjʊdiːn, -ˈdəʊ-/ ● **n.** Medicine an antiviral drug used to slow the growth of HIV infection in the body.
– ORIGIN 1980s; arbitrary alt. of **AZIDOTHYMIDINE**.

**ZIF socket** ● **n.** a socket for electronic devices that is designed not to damage them during insertion.
– ORIGIN C20: acronym from *zero insertion force*.

**zig** ● **n.** a sharp change of direction in a zigzag course. ● **v.** (**zigged**, **zigging**) make a zig.
– ORIGIN 1960s: shortening of **ZIGZAG**.

**ziggurat** /ˈzɪɡʊrat/ ● **n.** (in ancient Mesopotamia) a rectangular stepped tower.
– ORIGIN from Akkadian *ziqqurratu*.

**zigzag** ● **n.** a line or course having abrupt alternate right and left turns. ➤ a turn on such a course. ● **adj. & adv.** veering to right and left alternately. ● **v.** (**zigzagged**, **zigzagging**) take a zigzag course.
– ORIGIN C18: from Fr., from Ger. *Zickzack*, first applied to fortifications.

**zilch** /zɪltʃ/ informal, chiefly N. Amer. ● **pron.** nothing. ● **det.** not any; no.
– ORIGIN 1960s: origin uncertain; perh. from a Mr *Zilch*, a character in the 1930s magazine *Ballyhoo*.

**zilla** /ˈzɪlə/ ● **n.** an administrative district in India, containing several parganas.
– ORIGIN from Pers. and Urdu *żila*' 'division'.

**zillion** ● **cardinal number** informal an extremely large number of people or things.
– DERIVATIVES **zillionaire** n. **zillionth** ordinal number.
– ORIGIN 1940s: from *Z* (perh. as a symbol of an unknown quantity) + **MILLION**.

**Zimbabwean** /zɪmˈbɑːbwɪən, -weɪən/ ● **n.** a native or inhabitant of Zimbabwe. ● **adj.** of or relating to Zimbabwe.

**Zimmer** /ˈzɪmə/ (also **Zimmer frame**) ● **n.** trademark a kind of walking frame.
– ORIGIN 1950s: from *Zimmer* Orthopaedic Limited, the name of the manufacturer.

**zinc** ● **n.** the chemical element of atomic number 30, a silvery-white metal which is a constituent of brass and is used for galvanizing iron and steel. (Symbol: **Zn**) ➤ galvanized iron or steel. ● **v.** (**zinced** /ˈzɪŋ(k)t/) coat with zinc.
– ORIGIN C17: from Ger. *Zink*, of unknown origin.

**zinc blende** • n. another term for **SPHALERITE**.

**zinco** • n. (pl. **-os**) an etched letterpress printing plate made of zinc.

**zinc ointment** • n. ointment containing zinc oxide, used for various skin conditions.

**zinc white** • n. a white pigment consisting of zinc oxide.

**'zine** • n. informal a magazine, especially a fanzine.

**Zinfandel** /'zɪnfand(ə)l/ • n. a variety of wine grape grown in California. ➤ a red or blush wine made from this grape.
– ORIGIN C19: of unknown origin.

**zing** informal • n. energy, enthusiasm, or liveliness. • v. move swiftly. ➤ N. Amer. criticize sharply.
– DERIVATIVES **zingy** adj.
– ORIGIN C20: imitative.

**zinger** • n. informal, chiefly N. Amer. an outstanding person or thing.

**zinnia** /'zɪnɪə/ • n. an American plant of the daisy family, cultivated for its bright showy flowers. [Genus *Zinnia*.]
– ORIGIN mod. L., named after the C18 Ger. physician and botanist Johann G. *Zinn*.

**Zion** /'zʌɪən/ (also **Sion**) • n. **1** the hill of Jerusalem on which the city of David was built. ➤ the Jewish people or religion. **2** (in Christian thought) the heavenly city or kingdom of heaven. ➤ the Christian Church. **3** a Nonconformist chapel.
– ORIGIN OE, from eccles. L. *Sion*, from Heb. *ṣīyōn*.

**Zionism** /'zʌɪənɪz(ə)m/ • n. a movement for the development and protection of a Jewish nation in Israel.
– DERIVATIVES **Zionist** n. & adj.

**zip** • n. **1** chiefly Brit. a fastener consisting of two flexible strips of metal or plastic with interlocking projections closed or opened by pulling a slide along them. **2** informal energy; vigour. • pron. N. Amer. informal nothing at all. • v. (**zipped**, **zipping**) **1** fasten with a zip. **2** informal move or propel at high speed. **3** Computing compress (a file) so that it takes up less space.
– ORIGIN C19: imitative.

**zip code** (also **ZIP code**) • n. US a postal code consisting of five or nine digits.
– ORIGIN 1960s: acronym from *zone improvement plan*.

**zip gun** • n. N. Amer. informal a cheap home-made or makeshift gun.

**zipless** • adj. informal (of a sexual encounter) brief, uncomplicated, and passionate.
– ORIGIN 1970s: coined by the US author Erica Jong.

**ziplock** (also trademark **Ziploc**) • adj. denoting a plastic bag with strips along the opening that can be pressed together to reseal it.

**zipper** chiefly N. Amer. • n. a zip fastener. • v. fasten with a zipper.

**zippo** • pron. N. Amer. informal zip; nothing.

**zippy** • adj. (**-ier**, **-iest**) informal bright, fresh, or lively. ➤ speedy.
– DERIVATIVES **zippily** adv. **zippiness** n.

**zip-up** • adj. chiefly Brit. fastened with a zip.

**zircon** /'zəːk(ə)n/ • n. a mineral consisting of zirconium silicate, typically brown but sometimes in translucent forms of gem quality.
– ORIGIN C18: from Ger. *Zirkon*.

**zirconia** /zəː'kəʊnɪə/ • n. zirconium dioxide, a white solid used in ceramic glazes and refractory coatings. [$ZrO_2$.]
– ORIGIN C18: from **ZIRCON** + **-IA**[1].

**zirconium** /zəː'kəʊnɪəm/ • n. the chemical element of atomic number 40, a hard silver-grey metal. (Symbol: **Zr**)
– ORIGIN C19: mod. L., from **ZIRCON**.

**zit** • n. informal, chiefly N. Amer. a spot on the skin.
– ORIGIN 1960s: of unknown origin.

**zither** /'zɪðə/ • n. a musical instrument consisting of a flat wooden soundbox with numerous strings stretched across it, placed horizontally and played with the fingers and a plectrum.
– DERIVATIVES **zitherist** n.
– ORIGIN C19: from Ger., from L. *cithara* (see **CITTERN**).

**ziti** /'ziːti/ • pl. n. pasta in the form of tubes resembling large macaroni.
– ORIGIN from Ital.

**zizz** informal, chiefly Brit. • n. a whizzing or buzzing sound. • v. make such a sound.
– ORIGIN C19: imitative.

**zloty** /'zlɒti/ • n. (pl. same, **zlotys**, or **zloties**) the basic monetary unit of Poland, equal to 100 groszy.
– ORIGIN Polish, lit. 'golden'.

**Zn** • symb. the chemical element zinc.

**zodiac** /'zəʊdɪak/ • n. a belt of the heavens within about 8° of the ecliptic, including all apparent positions of the sun, moon, and planets and divided by astrologers into twelve equal divisions or signs.
– DERIVATIVES **zodiacal** /zə(ʊ)'dʌɪək(ə)l/ adj.
– ORIGIN ME: from OFr. *zodiaque*, via L. from Gk *zōidiakos*, from *zōidion* 'sculptured animal figure', dimin. of *zōion* 'animal'.

**zodiacal light** • n. Astronomy a faint elongated cone of light sometimes seen in the night sky, extending from the horizon along the ecliptic.

**zoetrope** /'zəʊɪtrəʊp/ • n. a cylinder with a series of pictures on the inner surface that, when viewed through slits with the cylinder rotating, give an impression of continuous motion.
– ORIGIN C19: formed irregularly from Gk *zōē* 'life' + *-tropos* 'turning'.

**zoftig** /'zɒftɪg/ • adj. N. Amer. variant spelling of **ZAFTIG**.

**Zohar** /'zəʊhɑː/ • n. the chief text of the Jewish Kabbalah, presented as an allegorical or mystical interpretation of the Pentateuch.
– ORIGIN from Heb. *zōhar*, lit. 'light, splendour'.

**zombie** • n. **1** a corpse supposedly revived by witchcraft, especially in certain African and Caribbean religions. **2** informal a lifeless, apathetic, or completely unresponsive person.
– DERIVATIVES **zombify** v.
– ORIGIN C19: of W. Afr. origin; cf. Kikongo *zumbi* 'fetish'.

**zona pellucida** /ˌzəʊnə pɪ'luːsɪdə/ • n. (pl. **zonae pellucidae** /ˌzəʊniː pɪ'luːsɪdiː/) Anatomy & Zoology the thick transparent membrane surrounding a mammalian ovum before implantation.
– ORIGIN C19: from L., lit. 'pellucid girdle'.

**zonation** /zəʊ'neɪʃ(ə)n/ • n. distribution in or division into distinct zones.

**zone** • n. **1** an area distinguished on the basis of a particular characteristic, use, restriction, etc. ➤ (also **time zone**) a range of longitudes where a common standard time is used. **2** archaic a belt or girdle. **3** chiefly Botany & Zoology an encircling band or stripe of distinctive colour, texture, etc. • v. **1** divide into or assign to zones. **2** archaic encircle as or with a band or stripe. **3** (**zone out**) N. Amer. informal fall asleep or lose concentration.
– DERIVATIVES **zonal** adj. **zonally** adv.
– ORIGIN ME: from Fr., or from L. *zona* 'girdle', from Gk *zōnē*.

**zoned** • adj. **1** divided into zones. **2** chiefly Botany & Zoology marked with zones. **3** US informal under the influence of drugs or alcohol. [1970s: blend of **ZONKED** and **STONED**.]

**zone plate** • n. a glass plate marked out into concentric rings alternately transparent and opaque, used like a lens to focus light.

**zone refining** • n. a method of purifying a crystalline solid by causing a narrow molten zone to travel slowly along a rod to one end, at which impurities become concentrated.

**zone therapy** • n. a system of alternative medicine in which different parts of the feet or hands are associated with different parts of the body.

**zonk** • v. informal **1** hit or strike heavily. **2** (usu. **zonk out**) fall suddenly and heavily asleep.
– ORIGIN 1940s: imitative.

**zonked** • adj. informal under the influence of drugs or alcohol.

**zoo** • n. an establishment which keeps wild animals for study, conservation, or display to the public.
– ORIGIN C19: abbrev. of **ZOOLOGICAL GARDEN**, orig. applied specifically to that of Regent's Park, London.

**zoo-** ● **comb. form** of animals; relating to animal life: *zoogeography.*
– ORIGIN from Gk *zōion* 'animal'.

**zoogeography** /ˌzuːə(ʊ)dʒɪˈɒɡrəfi, ˌzəʊə(ʊ)-, ˌzuːdʒɪ-/ ● **n.** the branch of zoology concerned with the geographical distribution of animals.
– DERIVATIVES **zoogeographer** n. **zoogeographic** adj. **zoogeographical** adj. **zoogeographically** adv.

**zooid** /ˈzuːɔɪd, ˈzəʊ-, ˈzuːɪd/ ● **n.** Zoology an animal arising from another by budding or division, especially each of the individuals which make up a colonial organism.
– DERIVATIVES **zooidal** /zuːˈɔɪd(ə)l, zəʊ-, ˈzuːɪd(ə)l/ adj.
– ORIGIN C19: from **zoo-** + **-OID**.

**zookeeper** ● **n.** an animal attendant employed in a zoo.

**zoolatry** /zuːˈɒlətri, zəʊ-/ ● **n.** rare the worship of animals.

**zoological garden** ● **n.** dated a zoo.

**zoology** /zuːˈɒlədʒi, zəʊ-/ ● **n.** the scientific study of the behaviour, structure, physiology, classification, and distribution of animals. ➤the animal life of a particular region or geological period.
– DERIVATIVES **zoological** adj. **zoologically** adv. **zoologist** n.

**zoom** ● **v. 1** (especially of a car or aircraft) move or travel very quickly. **2** (of a camera) change smoothly from a long shot to a close-up or vice versa. ● **n.** the action of a camera zooming. ➤short for **ZOOM LENS**.
– ORIGIN C19: imitative.

**zoom lens** ● **n.** a lens allowing a camera to zoom by varying the focal length.

**zoomorphic** /ˌzuːə(ʊ)ˈmɔːfɪk, ˌzəʊə(ʊ)-, zuːˈmɔːfɪk/ ● **adj.** having or representing animal forms or gods of animal form.
– DERIVATIVES **zoomorphism** n.
– ORIGIN C19: from **zoo-** + Gk *morphē* 'form' + **-IC**.

**zoonosis** /ˌzuːəˈnəʊsɪs, ˌzəʊə-/ ● **n.** (pl. **zoonoses** /-siːz/) Medicine any disease which can be transmitted to humans from animals.
– DERIVATIVES **zoonotic** adj.
– ORIGIN C19: from **zoo-** + Gk *nosos* 'disease'.

**zoophyte** /ˈzuːəfʌɪt, ˈzəʊə-, ˈzuːfʌɪt/ ● **n.** Zoology, dated a plant-like animal, especially a coral, sea anemone, sponge, or sea lily.

**zooplankton** /ˈzuːə(ʊ)ˌplaŋ(k)t(ə)n, ˈzəʊə(ʊ)-, ˈzuːplaŋ(k)t(ə)n/ ● **n.** Biology plankton consisting of small animals.

**zoospore** /ˈzuːəspɔː, ˈzəʊə-, ˈzuːspɔː/ ● **n.** Biology a spore of certain algae, fungi, etc., capable of swimming by means of a flagellum.

**zoot suit** ● **n.** a man's suit characterized by a long loose jacket with padded shoulders and high-waisted tapering trousers, popular in the 1940s.
– ORIGIN 1940s: rhyming formation on **SUIT**.

**zooxanthella** /ˌzəʊəzanˈθɛlə/ ● **n.** (pl. **zooxanthellae** /-liː/) Biology a yellowish-brown symbiotic dinoflagellate present in the cytoplasm of many marine invertebrates.
– DERIVATIVES **zooxanthellate** adj.
– ORIGIN C19: mod. L., from **zoo-** + Gk *xanthos* 'yellow' + the dimin. suffix *-ella*.

**zorbing** /ˈzɔːbɪŋ/ ● **n.** a sport in which a participant is secured inside an inner capsule in a large, transparent ball which is then rolled along the ground or down hills.
– ORIGIN 1990s: invented word from *zorb* (the name of the ball used in this activity) + **-ING**[1].

**zori** /ˈzɔːri, ˈzɒri/ ● **n.** (pl. **zoris**) a traditional Japanese flip-flop, originally with a straw sole.
– ORIGIN from Japanese.

**zorilla** /zɒˈrɪlə/ ● **n.** a skunk-like black and white carnivorous mammal inhabiting arid regions of southern Africa. [*Ictonyx striatus.*]
– ORIGIN C18: via Fr. from Sp. *zorrilla*, dimin. of *zorro* 'fox'.

**Zoroastrianism** /ˌzɒrəʊˈastrɪəˌnɪz(ə)m/ ● **n.** a monotheistic pre-Islamic religion of ancient Persia founded by the prophet Zoroaster (Zarathustra) in the 6th century BC.
– DERIVATIVES **Zoroastrian** adj. & n.

**Zouave** /zuːˈɑːv, zwɑːv/ ● **n. 1** a member of a French light-infantry corps, originally formed of Algerians and long retaining an oriental uniform. **2** (**zouaves**) women's trousers with wide tops, tapering to a narrow ankle.
– ORIGIN C19: from Fr., from Kabyle *Zouaoua*, the name of a tribe.

**zouk** /zuːk/ ● **n.** an exuberant style of popular music combining Caribbean and Western elements.
– ORIGIN 1970s: Guadeloupian Creole, lit. 'to party'.

**zounds** /zaʊndz/ ● **exclam.** archaic or humorous expressing surprise or indignation.
– ORIGIN C16: contr. from (*God*)*'s wounds.*

**Z particle** ● **n.** Physics a heavy uncharged particle believed to transmit the weak interaction between other particles.

**Zr** ● **symb.** the chemical element zirconium.

**ZRE** ● **abbrev.** Zaire (international vehicle registration).

**zucchetto** /tsʊˈkɛtəʊ/ ● **n.** (pl. **-os**) a Roman Catholic cleric's skullcap: black for a priest, purple for a bishop, red for a cardinal, and white for the Pope.
– ORIGIN C19: from Ital. *zucchetta*, dimin. of *zucca* 'gourd, head'.

**zucchini** /zʊˈkiːni/ ● **n.** (pl. same or **zucchinis**) chiefly N. Amer. a courgette.
– ORIGIN Ital., pl. of *zucchino*, dimin. of *zucca* 'gourd'.

**zugzwang** /ˈzʌɡzwaŋ, ˈzuːɡ-/ ● **n.** Chess a situation in which the obligation to make a move is a serious disadvantage.
– ORIGIN C20: from Ger. *Zug* 'move' + *Zwang* 'compulsion'.

**Zulu** /ˈzuːluː/ ● **n. 1** a member of a South African people living mainly in KwaZulu/Natal province. **2** the Bantu language of this people. **3** a code word representing the letter Z, used in radio communication.
– ORIGIN from the stem of Zulu *umZulu* (pl. *amaZulu*).

**Zuni** /ˈzuːni/ (also **Zuñi** /ˈzuːɲi/) ● **n.** (pl. same or **Zunis**) **1** a member of a Pueblo Indian people of western New Mexico. **2** the language of this people.

**ZW** ● **abbrev.** Zimbabwe (international vehicle registration).

**zwitterion** /ˈzwɪtərʌɪən, ˈtsvɪ-/ ● **n.** Chemistry an ion having separate positively and negatively charged groups.
– DERIVATIVES **zwitterionic** adj.
– ORIGIN C20: from Ger., from *Zwitter* 'a hybrid' + *Ion* 'ion'.

**Zyban** /ˈzʌɪban/ ● **n.** trademark an antidepressant drug used to relieve nicotine withdrawal symptoms.
– ORIGIN an invented word.

**zydeco** /ˈzʌɪdɪkəʊ/ ● **n.** a kind of black American dance music originally from southern Louisiana, typically featuring accordion and guitar.
– ORIGIN 1960s: Louisiana Creole, possibly from Fr. *les haricots* in a dance-tune title.

**zygo-** ● **comb. form** relating to joining or pairing: *zygodactyl.*
– ORIGIN from Gk *zugon* 'yoke'.

**zygodactyl** /ˌzʌɪɡə(ʊ)ˈdaktɪl, zɪɡ-/ ● **adj.** Ornithology having two toes pointing forward and two backward.
– DERIVATIVES **zygodactyly** n.

**zygoma** /zʌɪˈɡəʊmə, zɪɡ-/ ● **n.** (pl. **zygomata** /-tə/) Anatomy the bony arch of the cheek formed by connection of the zygomatic and temporal bones.
– DERIVATIVES **zygomatic** adj.
– ORIGIN C17: from Gk *zugōma*, from *zugon* 'yoke'.

**zygomatic bone** ● **n.** Anatomy the bone forming the prominent part of the cheek and the outer side of the eye socket.

**zygomorphic** /ˌzʌɪɡə(ʊ)ˈmɔːfɪk, ˌzɪɡ-/ ● **adj.** Botany (of a flower) bilaterally symmetrical, as in a snapdragon. Compare with **ACTINOMORPHIC**.
– DERIVATIVES **zygomorphy** n.

**Zygoptera** /zʌɪˈɡɒptərə/ ● **pl. n.** Entomology a suborder of insects which comprises the damselflies.
– DERIVATIVES **zygopteran** n. & adj.
– ORIGIN mod. L., from Gk *zugon* 'yoke' + *pteron* 'wing'.

**zygote** /ˈzʌɪɡəʊt/ ● **n.** Biology a cell resulting from the fusion of two gametes.
– DERIVATIVES **zygotic** /-ˈɡɒtɪk/ adj.

– ORIGIN C19: from Gk *zugōtos* 'yoked', from *zugoun* 'to yoke'.

**zygotene** /ˈzʌɪɡə(ʊ)tiːn/ ● **n.** Biology the second stage of the prophase of meiosis, following leptotene, during which homologous chromosomes begin to pair.

**zymase** /ˈzʌɪmeɪz/ ● **n.** Biochemistry a mixture of enzymes obtained from yeast which promote alcoholic fermentation.

– ORIGIN C19: from Fr., from Gk *zumē* 'leaven'.

**zymo-** /ˈzʌɪməʊ/ (also **zym-** before a vowel) ● **comb. form** relating to enzymes or fermentation: *zymogen.*

– ORIGIN from Gk *zumē* 'leaven'.

**zymogen** /ˈzʌɪmə(ʊ)dʒ(ə)n/ ● **n.** Biochemistry an inactive substance which is converted into an enzyme when activated by another enzyme.

**zymotic** ● **adj.** Medicine, historical relating to or denoting contagious disease regarded as developing after infection, like the fermenting of yeast.

**zymurgy** /ˈzʌɪməːdʒi/ ● **n.** the study or practice of fermentation in brewing, winemaking, or distilling.

– ORIGIN C19: from Gk *zumē* 'leaven', on the pattern of *metallurgy.*

# Contents

# Appendix 1: Countries of the world

| Country | Adjective/noun | Capital | Currency unit | Abbreviation (Olympics) |
|---|---|---|---|---|
| **Afghanistan** | Afghan | Kabul | afghani = 100 puls | AFG |
| **Albania** | Albanian | Tirana | lek = 100 qindarka | ALB |
| **Algeria** | Algerian | Algiers | dinar = 100 centimes | ALG |
| **America** (*see* **United States of America**) | | | | |
| **Andorra** | Andorran | Andorra la Vella | French franc, Spanish peseta | AND |
| **Angola** | Angolan | Luanda | kwanza = 100 lwei | ANG |
| **Antigua and Barbuda** | Antiguan, Barbudan | St John's | dollar = 100 cents | ANT |
| **Argentina** | Argentinian | Buenos Aires | peso = 10,000 australes | ARG |
| **Armenia** | Armenian | Yerevan | dram = 100 luma | ARM |
| **Australia** | Australian | Canberra | dollar = 100 cents | AUS |
| **Austria** | Austrian | Vienna | schilling = 100 groschen | AUT |
| **Azerbaijan** | Azerbaijani | Baku | manat = 100 gopik | AZE |
| **Bahamas** | Bahamian | Nassau | dollar = 100 cents | BAH |
| **Bahrain** | Bahraini | Manama | dinar = 1,000 fils | BRN |
| **Bangladesh** | Bangladeshi | Dhaka | taka = 100 poisha | BAN |
| **Barbados** | Barbadian | Bridgetown | dollar = 100 cents | BAR |
| **Belarus** | Belorussian *or* Byelorussian | Minsk | Belorussian rouble | BLR |
| **Belgium** | Belgian | Brussels | franc = 100 centimes | BEL |
| **Belize** | Belizian | Belmopan | dollar = 100 cents | BIZ |
| **Benin** | Beninese | Porto Novo | African franc | BEN |
| **Bhutan** | Bhutanese | Thimphu | ngultrum = 100 chetrum, Indian rupee | BHU |
| **Bolivia** | Bolivian | La Paz | boliviano = 100 centavos | BOL |
| **Bosnia-Herzegovina** | Bosnian | Sarajevo | dinar = 100 paras | BIH |
| **Botswana** | Botswanan/Tswana | Gaborone | pula = 100 thebe | BOT |
| **Brazil** | Brazilian | Brasilia | real = 100 centavos | BRA |
| **Brunei** | Bruneian | Bandar Seri Begawan | dollar = 100 sen | BRU |
| **Bulgaria** | Bulgarian | Sofia | lev = 100 stotinki | BUL |
| **Burkina Faso** | Burkinese | Ouagadougou | African franc | BUR |
| **Burma** (officially called **Myanmar**) | Burmese | Rangoon | kyat = 100 pyas | MYA |
| **Burundi** | Burundian | Bujumbura | franc = 100 centimes | BDI |
| **Cambodia** | Cambodian | Phnom Penh | riel = 100 sen | CAM |
| **Cameroon** | Cameroonian | Yaoundé | African franc | CMR |
| **Canada** | Canadian | Ottawa | dollar = 100 cents | CAN |
| **Cape Verde Islands** | Cape Verdean | Praia | escudo = 100 centavos | CPV |
| **Central African Republic** | – | Bangui | African franc | CAF |
| **Chad** | Chadian | N'Djamena | African franc | CHA |
| **Chile** | Chilean | Santiago | peso = 100 centavos | CHI |
| **China** | Chinese | Beijing | yuan = 10 jiao *or* 100 fen | CHN |
| **Colombia** | Colombian | Bogotá | peso = 100 centavos | COL |
| **Comoros** | Comoran | Moroni | African franc | COM |
| **Congo** | Congolese | Brazzaville | African franc | CGO |
| **Congo, Democratic Republic of (Zaire)** | Congolese | Kinshasa | Congolese franc | COD |

| Country | Adjective/noun | Capital | Currency unit | Abbreviation (Olympics) |
|---|---|---|---|---|
| **Costa Rica** | Costa Rican | San José | colón = 100 centimos | CRC |
| **Croatia** | Croat *or* Croatian | Zagreb | kuna = 100 lipa | CRO |
| **Cuba** | Cuban | Havana | peso = 100 centavos | CUB |
| **Cyprus** | Cypriot | Nicosia | pound = 100 cents | CYP |
| **Czech Republic** | Czech | Prague | koruna = 100 haleru | CZE |
| **Denmark** | Danish/Dane | Copenhagen | krone = 100 øre | DEN |
| **Djibouti** | Djiboutian | Djibouti | franc = 100 centimes | DJI |
| **Dominica** | Dominican | Roseau | dollar = 100 cents | DMA |
| **Dominican Republic** | Dominican | Santo Domingo | peso = 100 centavos | DOM |
| **Ecuador** | Ecuadorean | Quito | sucre = 100 centavos | ECU |
| **Egypt** | Egyptian | Cairo | pound = 100 piastres *or* 1,000 milliemes | EGY |
| **El Salvador** | Salvadorean | San Salvador | colón = 100 centavos | ESA |
| **Equatorial Guinea** | Equatorial Guinean | Malabo | African franc | GEQ |
| **Eritrea** | Eritrean | Asmara | Ethiopian birr | ERI |
| **Estonia** | Estonian | Tallinn | kroon = 100 sents | EST |
| **Ethiopia** | Ethiopian | Addis Ababa | birr = 100 cents | ETH |
| **Fiji** | Fijian | Suva | dollar = 100 cents | FIJ |
| **Finland** | Finn | Helsinki | markka = 100 penniä | FIN |
| **France** | French | Paris | franc = 100 centimes | FRA |
| **Gabon** | Gabonese | Libreville | African franc | GAB |
| **Gambia, the** | Gambian | Banjul | dalasi = 100 butut | GAM |
| **Georgia** | Georgian | Tbilisi | lari = 100 tetri | GEO |
| **Germany** | German | Berlin | Deutschmark =100 pfennig | GER |
| **Ghana** | Ghanaian | Accra | cedi = 100 pesewas | GHA |
| **Greece** | Greek | Athens | drachma = 100 leptae | GRE |
| **Grenada** | Grenadian | St George's | dollar = 100 cents | GRN |
| **Guatemala** | Guatemalan | Guatemala City | quetzal = 100 centavos | GUA |
| **Guinea** | Guinean | Conakry | franc = 100 centimes | GUI |
| **Guinea-Bissau** | – | Bissau | peso = 100 centavos | GBS |
| **Guyana** | Guyanese | Georgetown | dollar = 100 cents | GUY |
| **Haiti** | Haitian | Port-au-Prince | gourde = 100 centimes | HAI |
| **Holland** (*see* **Netherlands**) | | | | |
| **Honduras** | Honduran | Tegucigalpa | lempira = 100 centavos | HON |
| **Hungary** | Hungarian | Budapest | forint = 100 filler | HUN |
| **Iceland** | Icelandic/Icelander | Reykjavik | krona = 100 aurar | ISL |
| **India** | Indian | New Delhi | rupee = 100 paisa | IND |
| **Indonesia** | Indonesian | Djakarta | rupiah = 100 sen | INA |
| **Iran** | Iranian | Tehran | rial = 100 dinars | IRI |
| **Iraq** | Iraqi | Baghdad | dinar = 1,000 fils | IRQ |
| **Ireland, Republic of** | Irish | Dublin | pound (punt) = 100 pence | IRL |
| **Israel** | Israeli | Jerusalem | shekel = 100 agora | ISR |
| **Italy** | Italian | Rome | lira = 100 centesemi | ITA |
| **Ivory Coast** | Ivorian | Yamoussoukro | African franc | CIV |
| **Jamaica** | Jamaican | Kingston | dollar = 100 cents | JAM |
| **Japan** | Japanese | Tokyo | yen = 100 sen | JPN |
| **Jordan** | Jordanian | Amman | dinar = 1,000 fils | JOR |
| **Kazakhstan** | Kazakh | Astana | tenge = 100 teins | KAZ |
| **Kenya** | Kenyan | Nairobi | shilling = 100 cents | KEN |
| **Kiribati** | – | Bairiki | dollar = 100 cents | |
| **Kuwait** | Kuwaiti | Kuwait City | dinar = 1,000 fils | KUW |
| **Kyrgyzstan** | Kyrgyz | Bishkek | som = 100 tiyin | KGZ |

| Country | Adjective/noun | Capital | Currency unit | Abbreviation (Olympics) |
|---|---|---|---|---|
| **Laos** | Laotian | Vientiane | kip = 100 ats | LAO |
| **Latvia** | Latvian | Riga | lat = 100 santims | LAT |
| **Lebanon** | Lebanese | Beirut | pound = 100 piastres | LIB |
| **Lesotho** | Lesothan/Mosotho, *pl.* Basotho | Maseru | loti = 100 lisente | LES |
| **Liberia** | Liberian | Monrovia | dollar = 100 cents | LBR |
| **Libya** | Libyan | Tripoli | dinar = 1,000 dirhams | LBA |
| **Liechtenstein** | –/Liechtensteiner | Vaduz | franc = 100 centimes | LIE |
| **Lithuania** | Lithuanian | Vilnius | litas = 100 centas | LTU |
| **Luxembourg** | –/Luxembourger | Luxembourg | franc = 100 centimes | LUX |
| **Macedonia** | Macedonian | Skopje | denar | MKD |
| **Madagascar** | Malagasay *or* Madagascan | Antananarivo | franc malgache = 100 centimes | MAD |
| **Malawi** | Malawian | Lilongwe | kwacha = 100 tambala | MAW |
| **Malaysia** | Malaysian | Kuala Lumpur | dollar (ringgit) = 100 sen | MAS |
| **Maldives** | Maldivian | Male | rufiyaa = 100 laris | MDV |
| **Mali** | Malian | Bamuko | African franc | MLI |
| **Malta** | Maltese | Valletta | lira = 100 cents | MLT |
| **Marshall Islands** | Marshallese | Majuro | US dollar | |
| **Mauritania** | Mauritanian | Nouakchott | ouguiya = 5 khoums | MTN |
| **Mauritius** | Mauritian | Port Louis | rupee = 100 cents | MRI |
| **Mexico** | Mexican | Mexico City | peso = 100 centavos | MEX |
| **Micronesia, Federated States of** | Micronesian | Kolonia | US dollar | FSM |
| **Moldova** | Moldovan | Chişinău | leu = 100 bani | MDA |
| **Monaco** | Monégasque *or* Monacan | – | franc = 100 centimes | MON |
| **Mongolia** | Mongolian | Ulan Bator | tugrik = 100 mongos | MGL |
| **Montenegro** (*see* **Yugoslavia**) | | | | |
| **Morocco** | Moroccan | Rabat | dirham = 100 centimes | MAR |
| **Mozambique** | Mozambican | Maputo | metical = 100 centavos | MOZ |
| **Myanmar** (*see* **Burma**) | | | | |
| **Namibia** | Namibian | Windhoek | rand = 100 cents | NAM |
| **Nauru** | Nauruan | – | Australian dollar | NRU |
| **Nepal** | Nepalese | Kathmandu | rupee = 100 paisa | NEP |
| **Netherlands, the** | Dutch | Amsterdam | guilder = 100 cents | NED |
| **New Zealand** | –/New Zealander | Wellington | dollar = 100 cents | NZL |
| **Nicaragua** | Nicaraguan | Managua | cordoba = 100 centavos | NCA |
| **Niger** | Nigerien | Niamey | African franc | NIG |
| **Nigeria** | Nigerian | Abuja | naira = 100 kobo | NGR |
| **North Korea** | North Korean | Pyongyang | won = 100 jun | PRK |
| **Norway** | Norwegian | Oslo | krone = 100 øre | NOR |
| **Oman** | Omani | Muscat | rial = 1,000 baiza | OMA |
| **Pakistan** | Pakistani | Islamabad | rupee = 100 paisa | PAK |
| **Panama** | Panamanian | Panama City | balboa = 100 centésimos | PAN |
| **Papua New Guinea** | Papua New Guinean *or* Guinean | Port Moresby | kina = 100 toea | PNG |
| **Paraguay** | Paraguayan | Asunción | guarani = 100 centimos | PAR |
| **Peru** | Peruvian | Lima | nuevo sol = 100 cents | PER |
| **Philippines** | Filipino *or* Philippine | Manila | peso = 100 centavos | PHI |
| **Poland** | Polish/Pole | Warsaw | zloty = 100 groszy | POL |
| **Portugal** | Portuguese | Lisbon | escudo = 100 centavos | POR |
| **Qatar** | Qatari | Doha | riyal = 100 dirhams | QAT |
| **Romania** | Romanian | Bucharest | leu = 100 bani | ROM |
| **Russia** | Russian | Moscow | rouble = 100 copecks | RUS |
| **Rwanda** | Rwandan | Kigali | franc = 100 centimes | RWA |

| Country | Adjective/noun | Capital | Currency unit | Abbreviation (Olympics) |
|---|---|---|---|---|
| **St Kitts and Nevis** | – | Basseterre | dollar = 100 cents | SKN |
| **St Lucia** | St Lucian | Castries | dollar = 100 cents | LCA |
| **St Vincent and the Grenadines** | Vincentian, Grenadian | Kingstown | dollar = 100 cents | VIN |
| **Samoa** | Samoan | Apia | tala = 100 sene | SAM |
| **San Marino** | – | San Marino | Italian lira | SMR |
| **São Tomé and Príncipe** | – | São Tomé | dobra = 100 centavos | STP |
| **Saudi Arabia** | Saudi Arabian *or* Saudi | Riyadh | riyal = 20 qursh *or* 100 halalas | KSA |
| **Senegal** | Senegalese | Dakar | African franc | SEN |
| **Serbia** (*see* **Yugoslavia**) | | | | |
| **Seychelles, the** | Seychellois | Victoria | rupee = 100 cents | SEY |
| **Sierra Leone** | Sierra Leonean | Freetown | leone = 100 cents | SLE |
| **Singapore** | Singaporean | Singapore | dollar = 100 cents | SIN |
| **Slovakia** | Slovak | Bratislava | koruna = 100 haleru | SVK |
| **Slovenia** | Slovene *or* Slovenian | Ljubljana | tolar = 100 stotins | SLO |
| **Solomon Islands** | –/Solomon Islander | Honiara | dollar = 100 cents | SOL |
| **Somalia** | Somali | Mogadishu | shilling = 100 cents | SOM |
| **South Africa** | South African | Pretoria | rand = 100 cents | RSA |
| **South Korea** | South Korean | Seoul | won = 100 jeon | KOR |
| **Spain** | Spanish/Spaniard | Madrid | peseta = 100 centimos | ESP |
| **Sri Lanka** | Sri Lankan | Colombo | rupee = 100 cents | SRI |
| **Sudan** | Sudanese | Khartoum | dinar = 10 pounds | SUD |
| **Suriname** | Surinamese | Paramaribo | guilder = 100 cents | SUR |
| **Swaziland** | Swazi | Mbabane | lilangeni = 100 cents | SWZ |
| **Sweden** | Swedish/Swede | Stockholm | krona = 100 öre | SWE |
| **Switzerland** | Swiss | Berne | franc = 100 centimes | SUI |
| **Syria** | Syrian | Damascus | pound = 100 piastres | SYR |
| **Taiwan** | Taiwanese | Taipei | New Taiwan dollar = 100 cents | TPE |
| **Tajikistan** | Tajik *or* Tadjik | Dushanbe | Russian rouble | TJK |
| **Tanzania** | Tanzanian | Dodoma | shilling = 100 cents | TAN |
| **Thailand** | Thai | Bangkok | baht = 100 satangs | THA |
| **Togo** | Togolese | Lomé | African franc | TOG |
| **Tonga** | Tongan | Nuku'alofa | pa'anga = 100 seniti | TGA |
| **Trinidad and Tobago** | Trinidadian, Tobagonian | Port-of-Spain | dollar = 100 cents | TRI |
| **Tunisia** | Tunisian | Tunis | dinar = 1,000 milliemes | TUN |
| **Turkey** | Turkish/Turk | Ankara | lira = 100 kurus | TUR |
| **Turkmenistan** | Turkmen *or* Turkoman | Ashgabat | manat = 100 tenge | TKM |
| **Tuvalu** | Tuvaluan | Funafuti | dollar = 100 cents | |
| **Uganda** | Ugandan | Kampala | shilling = 100 cents | UGA |
| **Ukraine** | Ukrainian | Kiev | hryvna = 100 kopiykas | UKR |
| **United Arab Emirates** | – | Abu Dhabi | dirham = 100 fils | UAE |
| **United Kingdom** | British/Briton | London | pound = 100 pence | GBR |
| **United States of America** | American | Washington, DC | dollar = 100 cents | USA |
| **Uruguay** | Uruguayan | Montevideo | peso = 100 centésimos | URU |
| **Uzbekistan** | Uzbek | Tashkent | som | UZB |
| **Vanuatu** | Vanuatuan | Vila | vatu = 100 centimes | VAN |
| **Vatican City** | – | – | Italian lira | |
| **Venezuela** | Venezuelan | Caracas | bolivar = 100 centimos | VEN |
| **Vietnam** | Vietnamese | Hanoi | dong= 10 hao *or* 100 xu | VIE |
| **Yemen** | Yemeni | Sana'a | riyal = 100 fils | YEM |
| **Yugoslavia** (**Montenegro**, **Serbia**) | Yugoslav (Montenegrin, Serbian) | Belgrade | dinar = 100 paras | YUG |
| **Zaire** (*see* **Congo, Democratic Republic of**) | | | | |
| **Zambia** | Zambian | Lusaka | kwacha = 100 ngwee | ZAM |
| **Zimbabwe** | Zimbabwean | Harare | dollar = 100 cents | ZIM |

# Appendix 2: Alphabets, accents, and punctuation marks

## Arabic

| Alone | Final | Medial | Initial | | |
|---|---|---|---|---|---|
| ا | ـا | | | 'alif | ' |
| ب | ـب | ـبـ | بـ | bā' | b |
| ت | ـت | ـتـ | تـ | tā' | t |
| ث | ـث | ـثـ | ثـ | thā' | th |
| ج | ـج | ـجـ | جـ | jīm | j |
| ح | ـح | ـحـ | حـ | ḥā' | ḥ |
| خ | ـخ | ـخـ | خـ | khā' | kh |
| د | ـد | | | dāl | d |
| ذ | ـذ | | | dhāl | dh |
| ر | ـر | | | rā' | r |
| ز | ـز | | | zāy | z |
| س | ـس | ـسـ | سـ | sīn | s |
| ش | ـش | ـشـ | شـ | shīn | sh |
| ص | ـص | ـصـ | صـ | ṣād | ṣ |
| ض | ـض | ـضـ | ضـ | ḍād | ḍ |
| ط | ـط | ـطـ | طـ | ṭā' | ṭ |
| ظ | ـظ | ـظـ | ظـ | ẓā' | ẓ |
| ع | ـع | ـعـ | عـ | 'ayn | ' |
| غ | ـغ | ـغـ | غـ | ghayn | gh |
| ف | ـف | ـفـ | فـ | fā' | f |
| ق | ـق | ـقـ | قـ | qāf | q |
| ك | ـك | ـكـ | كـ | kāf | k |
| ل | ـل | ـلـ | لـ | lām | l |
| م | / | ـمـ | مـ | mīm | m |
| ن | ـن | ـنـ | نـ | nūn | n |
| ه | ـه | ـهـ | هـ | hā' | h |
| و | ـو | | | wāw | w |
| ى | ـى | ـيـ | يـ | yā' | y |

## Hebrew

| | | | |
|---|---|---|---|
| א | | 'aleph | ' |
| ב | | beth | b, bh |
| ג | | gimel | g, gh |
| ד | | daleth | d, dh |
| ה | | he | h |
| ו | | waw | w |
| ז | | zayin | z |
| ח | | ḥeth | ḥ |
| ט | | ṭeth | ṭ |
| י | | yodh | y |
| כ | ך | kaph | k, kh |
| ל | | lamedh | l |
| מ | ם | mem | m |
| נ | ן | nun | n |
| ס | | samekh | s |
| ע | | 'ayin | ' |
| פ | ף | pe | p, ph |
| צ | ץ | ṣadhe | ṣ |
| ק | | qoph | q |
| ר | | resh | r |
| שׂ | | śin | ś |
| שׁ | | shin | sh |
| ת | | taw | t, th |

## Greek

| | | |
|---|---|---|
| *Α α* | alpha | a |
| *Β β* | beta | b |
| *Γ γ* | gamma | g |
| *Δ δ* | delta | d |
| *Ε ε* | epsilon | e |
| *Ζ ζ* | zeta | z |
| *Η η* | eta | ē |
| *Φ θ* | theta | th |
| *Ι ι* | iota | i |
| *Κ κ* | kappa | k |
| *Λ λ* | lambda | l |
| *Μ μ* | mu | m |
| *Ν ν* | nu | n |
| *Ξ ξ* | xi | x |
| *Ο ο* | omicron | o |
| *Π π* | pi | p |
| *Ρ ρ* | rho | r, rh |
| *Σ σ ς* | sigma | s |
| *Τ τ* | tau | t |
| *Υ υ* | upsilon | u |
| *Φ φ* | phi | ph |
| *Χ χ* | chi | kh |
| *Ψ ψ* | psi | ps |
| *Ω ω* | omega | ō |

## Russian

| | |
|---|---|
| А а | a |
| Б б | b |
| В в | v |
| Г г | g |
| Д д | d |
| Е е | e, ye |
| Ё / | yo |
| Ж ж | zh |
| З з | z |
| И и | i |
| Й й | ĭ |
| К к | k |
| Л л | l |
| М м | m |
| Н н | n |
| О о | o |
| П п | p |
| Р р | r |
| С с | s |
| Т т | t |
| У у | u |
| Ф ф | f |
| Х х | kh |
| Ц ц | ts |
| Ч ч | ch |
| Ш ш | sh |
| Щ щ | shch |
| Ъ ъ ('hard sign') | " |
| Ы ы | y |
| Ь ь ('soft sign') | ' |
| Э э | e |
| Ю ю | yu |
| Я я | ya |

## Punctuation marks

( ) brackets, parentheses

< > angle brackets

[ ] square brackets

{ brace

• bullet

† dagger, obelisk

‡ double dagger/diesis

* asterisk/star

/ solidus/oblique/slash/virgule

§ section

~ swung dash

... ellipsis/suspension points

¶ paragraph

## Accents & diacritical marks

´ é acute

° å bolle

˘ ŭ breve

¸ ç cedilla

ˆ ê circumflex

¨ ö umlaut/diaeresis

` è grave

ˇ č háček

¯ ō macron

/ ø streg

˜ ñ tilde

## Phonetic alphabet

**A** Alpha
**B** Bravo
**C** Charlie
**D** Delta
**E** Echo
**F** Foxtrot
**G** Golf
**H** Hotel
**I** India
**J** Juliet
**K** Kilo
**L** Lima
**M** Mike
**N** November
**O** Oscar
**P** Papa
**Q** Quebec
**R** Romeo
**S** Sierra
**T** Tango
**U** Uniform
**V** Victor
**W** Whisky
**X** X-ray
**Y** Yankee
**Z** Zulu

# Appendix 3: Weights and measures

## British and American, with metric equivalents

### Linear measure

| | |
|---|---|
| 1 inch | = 25.4 millimetres exactly |
| 1 foot = 12 inches | = 0.3048 metre exactly |
| 1 yard = 3 feet | = 0.9144 metre exactly |
| 1 (statute) mile = 1,760 yards | = 1.609 kilometres |
| 1 int. nautical mile = 1.150779 miles | = 1.852 kilometres exactly |

### Square measure

| | |
|---|---|
| 1 square inch | = 6.45 sq. centimetres |
| 1 square foot = 144 sq. in. | = 9.29 sq. decimetres |
| 1 square yard = 9 sq. ft | = 0.836 sq. metre |
| 1 acre = 4,840 sq. yd | = 0.405 hectare |
| 1 square mile = 640 acres | = 259 hectares |

### Cubic measure

| | |
|---|---|
| 1 cubic inch | = 16.4 cu. centimetres |
| 1 cubic foot = 1,728 cu. in. | = 0.0283 cu. metre |
| 1 cubic yard = 27 cu. ft | = 0.765 cu. metre |

### Capacity measure

| | |
|---|---|
| British | |
| 1 fluid oz = 1.7339 cu. in. | = 0.0284 litre |
| 1 gill = 5 fluid oz | = 0.1421 litre |
| 1 pint = 20 fluid oz = 34.68 cu. in. | = 0.568 litre |
| 1 quart = 2 pints | = 1.136 litres |
| 1 gallon = 4 quarts | = 4.546 litres |
| 1 peck = 2 gallons | = 9.092 litres |
| 1 bushel = 4 pecks | = 36.4 litres |
| American dry | |
| 1 pint = 33.60 cu. in. | = 0.550 litre |
| 1 quart = 2 pints | = 1.101 litres |
| 1 peck = 8 quarts | = 8.81 litres |
| 1 bushel = 4 pecks | = 35.3 litres |
| American liquid | |
| 1 pint = 16 fluid oz = 28.88 cu. in. | = 0.473 litre |
| 1 quart = 2 pints | = 0.946 litre |
| 1 gallon = 4 quarts | = 3.785 litres |

### Avoirdupois weight

| | |
|---|---|
| 1 grain | = 0.065 gram |
| 1 dram | = 1.772 grams |
| 1 ounce = 16 drams | = 28.35 grams |
| 1 pound = 16 ounces = 7,000 grains | = 0.4536 kilogram (0.4535923 exactly) |
| 1 stone = 14 pounds | = 6.35 kilograms |
| 1 hundredweight = 112 pounds | = 50.80 kilograms |
| 1 short ton = 2,000 pounds | = 0.907 tonne |
| 1 (long) ton = 20 hundredweight | = 1.016 tonnes |

## Metric, with British equivalents

### Linear measure

| | |
|---|---|
| 1 millimetre | = 0.039 inch |
| 1 centimetre = 10 mm | = 0.394 inch |
| 1 decimetre = 10 cm | = 3.94 inches |
| 1 metre = 100 cm | = 1.094 yards |
| 1 kilometre = 1,000 m | = 0.6214 mile |

### Square measure

| | |
|---|---|
| 1 square centimetre | = 0.155 sq. inch |
| 1 square metre = 10,000 sq. cm | = 1.196 sq. yards |
| 1 are = 100 square metres | = 119.6 sq. yards |
| 1 hectare = 100 ares | = 2.471 acres |
| 1 square kilometre = 100 hectares | = 0.386 sq. mile |

### Cubic measure

| | |
|---|---|
| 1 cubic centimetre | = 0.061 cu. inch |
| 1 cubic metre = 1,000,000 cu. cm | = 1.308 cu. yards |

### Capacity measure

| | |
|---|---|
| 1 millilitre | = 0.002 pint (British) |
| 1 centilitre = 10 ml | = 0.018 pint |
| 1 decilitre = 10 cl | = 0.176 pint |
| 1 litre = 1000 ml | = 1.76 pints |
| 1 decalitre = 10 l | = 2.20 gallons |
| 1 hectolitre = 100 l | = 2.75 bushels |
| 1 kilolitre = 1,000 l | = 3.44 quarters |

### Weight

| | |
|---|---|
| 1 milligram | = 0.015 grain |
| 1 centigram = 10 mg | = 0.154 grain |
| 1 decigram = 100 mg | = 1.543 grains |
| 1 gram = 1000 mg | = 15.43 grains |
| 1 decagram = 10 g | = 5.64 drams |
| 1 hectogram = 100 g | = 3.527 ounces |
| 1 kilogram = 1,000 g | = 2.205 pounds |
| 1 tonne (metric ton) = 1,000 kg | = 0.984 (long) ton |

# Temperature

**Fahrenheit** water boils (under standard conditions) at 212° and freezes at 32°.

**Celsius or Centigrade** water boils at 100° and freezes at 0°.

**Kelvin** water boils at 373.15 K and freezes at 273.15 K.

*To convert Centigrade into Fahrenheit:*
multiply by 9, divide by 5, and add 32.

*To convert Fahrenheit into Centigrade:*
subtract 32, multiply by 5, and divide by 9.

*To convert Centigrade into Kelvin:*
add 273.15.

| °F | °C |
|---|---|
| −40 | −40 |
| −10 | −23 |
| 0 | −18 |
| 10 | −12 |
| 20 | −7 |
| 30 | −1 |
| 40 | 4 |
| 50 | 10 |
| 60 | 16 |
| 70 | 21 |
| 80 | 27 |
| 90 | 32 |
| 100 | 38 |
| | *(approx.)* |

| °C | °F |
|---|---|
| −40 | −40 |
| −10 | 14 |
| 0 | 32 |
| 10 | 50 |
| 20 | 68 |
| 30 | 86 |
| 40 | 104 |
| 50 | 122 |
| 60 | 140 |
| 70 | 158 |
| 80 | 176 |
| 90 | 194 |
| 100 | 212 |
| | *(exact)* |

# The metric prefixes

| | Abbreviations | Factors |
|---|---|---|
| deca- | da | 10 |
| hecto- | h | $10^2$ |
| kilo- | k | $10^3$ |
| mega- | M | $10^6$ |
| giga- | G | $10^9$ |
| tera- | T | $10^{12}$ |
| peta- | P | $10^{15}$ |
| exa- | E | $10^{18}$ |
| deci- | d | $10^{-1}$ |
| centi- | c | $10^{-2}$ |
| milli- | m | $10^{-3}$ |
| micro- | μ | $10^{-6}$ |
| nano- | n | $10^{-9}$ |
| pico- | p | $10^{-12}$ |
| femto- | f | $10^{-15}$ |
| atto- | a | $10^{-18}$ |

Pronunciations and derivations of these are given at their alphabetical places in the dictionary. They may be applied to any units of the metric system: hectogram (abbr. hg) = 100 grams; kilowatt (abbr. kW) = 1,000 watts; megahertz (MHz) = 1 million hertz; centimetre (cm) = 1/100 metre; microvolt (μV) = one millionth of a volt; picofarad (pF) = $10^{-12}$ farad, and are sometimes applied to other units (megabit, microinch).

# Power notation

This expresses concisely any power of 10 (any number that is formed by multiplying or dividing ten by itself), and is sometimes used in the dictionary.

$10^2$ (ten squared) = 10 × 10 = 100
$10^3$ (ten cubed) = 10 × 10 × 10 = 1,000
$10^4$ = 10 × 10 × 10 × 10 = 10,000
$10^{10}$ = 10,000,000,000 (1 followed by ten noughts)
$10^{-2} = 1/10^2$ = 1/100 = 0.01
$10^{-10} = 1/10^{10}$ = 1/10,000,000,000
$6.2 \times 10^3$ = 6,200
$4.7 \times 10^{-2}$ = 0.047

# SI units

### *Base units*

| Physical quantity | Name | Abbreviation or symbol |
|---|---|---|
| length | metre | m |
| mass | kilogram | kg |
| time | second | s |
| electric current | ampere | A |
| temperature | kelvin | K |
| amount of substance | mole | mol |
| luminous intensity | candela | cd |

### *Supplementary units*

| Physical quantity | Name | Abbreviation or symbol |
|---|---|---|
| plane angle | radian | rad |
| solid angle | steradian | sr |

### *Derived units with special names*

| Physical quantity | Name | Abbreviation or symbol |
|---|---|---|
| frequency | hertz | Hz |
| energy | joule | J |
| force | newton | N |
| power | watt | W |
| pressure | pascal | Pa |
| electric charge | coulomb | C |
| electromotive force | volt | V |
| electric resistance | ohm | Ω |
| electric conductance | siemens | S |
| electric capacitance | farad | F |
| magnetic flux | weber | Wb |
| inductance | henry | H |
| magnetic flux density | tesla | T |
| luminous flux | lumen | lm |
| illumination | lux | lx |

# *Appendix 4: Terms for groups of animals etc.*

Terms marked * belong to 15th-century lists of 'proper terms', notably that in the *Book of St Albans* attributed to Dame Juliana Barnes (1486). Many of these are fanciful or humorous terms which probably never had any real currency, but have been taken up by Joseph Strutt in *Sports and Pastimes of England* (1801) and by other antiquarian writers.

a *shrewdness of **apes**
a herd or *pace of **asses**
a *cete of **badgers**
a *sloth or *sleuth of **bears**
a hive of **bees**; a swarm, drift, or bike of **bees**
a flock, flight, (*dial.*) parcel, pod, *fleet, or *dissimulation of (small) **birds**; a volary of **birds** in an aviary
a sounder of **wild boar**
a *blush of **boys**
a herd or gang of **buffalo**
a *clowder or *glaring of **cats**; a *dowt (= ?do-out) or *destruction of **wild cats**
a herd, drove, (*dial.*) drift, or (*US* & *Austral.*) mob of **cattle**
a brood, (*dial.*) cletch or clutch, or *peep of **chickens**
a *chattering or *clattering of **choughs**
a *drunkship of **cobblers**
a *rag or *rake of **colts**
a *hastiness of **cooks**
a *covert of **coots**
a herd of **cranes**
a litter of **cubs**
a herd of **curlew**
a *cowardice of **curs**
a herd or mob of **deer**
a pack or kennel of **dogs**
a trip of **dotterel**
a flight, *dole, or *piteousness of **doves**
a raft, bunch, or *paddling of **ducks** on water; a team of **wild ducks** in flight
a fling of **dunlins**
a herd of **elephants**
a herd or (*US*) gang of **elk**
a *business of **ferrets**
a charm or *chirm of **finches**
a shoal of **fish**; a run of **fish** in motion
a cloud of **flies**
a *stalk of **foresters**
a *skulk of **foxes**
a gaggle or (in the air) a skein, team, or wedge of **geese**
a herd of **giraffes**
a flock, herd, or (*dial.*) trip of **goats**
a pack or covey of **grouse**
a *husk or *down of **hares**
a cast of **hawks** let fly
an *observance of **hermits**
a *siege of **herons**
a stud or *haras of (breeding) **horses**; (*dial.*) a team of **horses**
a kennel, pack, cry, or *mute of **hounds**
a flight or swarm of **insects**
a mob or troop of **kangaroos**
a kindle of **kittens**
a bevy of **ladies**
a *desert of **lapwing**
an *exaltation or bevy of **larks**
a *leap of **leopards**
a pride of **lions**
a *tiding of **magpies**
a *sord or *sute (= suit) of **mallard**
a *richesse of **martens**
a *faith of **merchants**
a *labour of **moles**
a troop of **monkeys**
a *barren of **mules**
a *watch of **nightingales**
a *superfluity of **nuns**
a covey of **partridges**
a *muster of **peacocks**
a *malapertness (= impertinence) of **pedlars**
a rookery of **penguins**
a head or (*dial.*) nye of **pheasants**
a kit of **pigeons** flying together
a herd of **pigs**
a stand, wing, or *congregation of **plovers**
a rush or flight of **pochards**
a herd, pod, or school of **porpoises**
a *pity of **prisoners**
a covey of **ptarmigan**
a litter of **pups**
a bevy or drift of **quail**
a string of **racehorses**
an *unkindness of **ravens**
a bevy of **roe deer**
a parliament or *building of **rooks**
a hill of **ruffs**
a herd or rookery of **seals**; a pod of **seals**
a flock, herd, (*dial.*) drift or trip, or (*Austral.*) mob of **sheep**
a *dopping of **sheldrake**
a wisp or *walk of **snipe**
a *host of **sparrows**
a *murmuration of **starlings**
a flight of **swallows**
a game or herd of **swans**; a wedge of **swans** in the air
a herd of **swine**; a *sounder of tame **swine**, a *drift of **wild swine**
a *glozing (= fawning) of **taverners**
a *spring of **teal**
a bunch or knob of **waterfowl**
a school, herd, or gam of **whales**; a pod of **whales**; a grind of **bottle-nosed whales**
a company or trip of **wigeon**
a bunch, trip, or plump of **wildfowl**; a knob (less than 30) of **wildfowl**
a pack or *rout of **wolves**
a gaggle of **women** (*derog.*)
a *fall of **woodcock**
a herd of **wrens**

# *Appendix 5: Proofreading marks*

Proofreading symbols generally in use have been strongly influenced by the British Standard's Institution's BS 5261 Part 2: 1976 and supplements. Traditional or alternative symbols are still found, especially abroad; the most common are included here.

| Instruction | Textual mark | Marginal mark |
|---|---|---|
| Correction is concluded | None | / |
| Insert in text the matter indicated in the margin | ⋏ | New matter followed by |
| Insert additional matter identified by a letter in a diamond | ⋏ Followed by, e.g. ◇A | The relevant section of the copy should be supplied with the corresponding letter marked on it in a diamond, e.g. ◇A |
| Delete | / through character(s) or ⊢—⊣ through words to be deleted | ₰ or ₰ |
| Close up and delete space between characters or words | linking ⁀‿ characters | ⁀‿/ |
| Delete and close up | / through character or ⊢—⊣ through characters, e.g. character character | ₰ or ₰ |
| Substitute character or substitute part of one or more word(s) | / through character or ⊢—⊣ through word(s) | New character or new word(s) followed by / |
| Substitute or insert full point or decimal point | / or ⋏ through character where required | ⊙/ or · |
| Substitute or insert colon | / or ⋏ through character where required | (:)/ or : |
| Substitute or insert semicolon | / or ⋏ through character where required | ;/ or ; |
| Substitute or insert comma | / or ⋏ through character where required | ,/ or , or ; |
| Substitute or insert solidus (oblique) | / or ⋏ through character where required | (/) |
| Substitute or insert character in superior (superscript) position | / or ⋏ through character where required | ⋎ or V under character e.g. $\overset{2}{\curlyvee}$ or |
| Substitute or insert character in inferior (subscript) position | / or ⋏ through character where required | ⋏ or ∧ over character e.g. $\underset{2}{\curlywedge}$ |
| Substitute or insert opening or closing parenthesis, square bracket, or curly brace | / or ⋏ through character where required | ( / ) or ( / ), [ / ], or { / } |
| Substitute or insert hyphen | / or ⋏ through character where required | ⊢-⊣ / or = or |
| Substitute or insert rule | / or ⋏ through character, e.g. 2 em | Give the size of rule in marginal mark ⊢1 em⊣ |
| Set in or change to bold type | ~~~ under character(s) to be set or changed | (bold) or or ~~~ |
| Set in or change to bold italic type | ~~~ under character(s) to be set or changed | (bold ital) or or |
| Set in or change to italic | — under character(s) to be set or changed | (ital) or |
| Change italic to upright (roman) type | Encircle character(s) to be changed | (rom) or |
| Set in or change to capital letters | ≡ under character(s) to be set or changed | (cap) or ≡ |
| Change capital letters to lower-case letters | Encircle character(s) to be changed | (lc) or ≢ |
| Spell out number or abbreviation | Encircle matter to be changed (38pp.) | (sp) |
| Set in or change to small capital letters | = under character(s) to be set or changed | (sc) or (s.cap) or = |
| Set in or change to capital letters for initial letters and small capital letters for the rest of the word(s) | ≡ under initial letters and = under rest of the word(s) | ≡ where space does not permit textual marks, encircle the affected area instead |

| Instruction | Textual mark | Marginal mark |
|---|---|---|
| Change small capital letters to lower-case letters | Encircle character(s) to be changed | (lc) or ≠ |
| Start new paragraph | ⎯⎾ | (NP) or ⎯⎾ or ¶ |
| Run on (no new paragraph) | ⮐ | ⊋ or ⊋ |
| Transpose characters or words | ⊔⊓ between characters or words, numbered when necessary | (trs) or (tr) or ⊔⊓ |
| Transpose lines | ⎾⏌ | (trs) or (tr) or ⎾⏌ |
| Invert type | Encircle character to be inverted | ↻ |
| Transpose a number of lines | ——— ③<br>——— ②<br>——— ① | To be used when the sequence cannot be clearly indicated otherwise. Rules extend from the margin into the text, with each line to be transplanted numbered in the correct sequence |
| Centre | [ ] or [ enclosing matter to be centred ] | |
| Insert space between characters | \| between characters affected | Y or # |
| Insert space between words | Y between words affected | Y or (more#) |
| Reduce space between characters | \| between characters affected | ⊤ or (less#) |
| Reduce space between words | ⊤ between words affected | ⊤ |
| Equalize space between characters or words | \| between characters or words affected | X or (eq#) |
| Close up to normal interlinear spacing | ( each side of column linking lines ) | |
| Insert space between lines or paragraphs | —( or )— | The marginal mark extends between the lines of text. Give the size of the space to be inserted if necessary |
| Reduce space between lines or paragraphs | ←— or —→ | The marginal mark extends between the lines of text. Give the amount by which the space is to be reduced if necessary |
| Take over character(s), word(s), or line to next line, column, or page | ⌈⎯⎯⎯ | The textual mark surrounds the matter to be taken over and extends into the margin |
| Take back character(s), word(s), or line to previous line, column, or page | ⎯⎯⎯⌉ | The textual mark surrounds the matter to be taken back and extends into the margin |
| Insert or substitute em space, en space, or thin space | □ (em), ⊠ (en), ǂ or ҁ (thin) | □ (em), ⊠ (en), ǂ or ҁ (thin) |
| Indent | ⊏ | ⊏ |
| Cancel indent | ⊢⊏ | ⊐ |
| Move matter specified distance to the right | ⊏ enclosing matter to be moved to the right ⊐→\| | ⊏ |
| Move matter specified distance to the left | ⊢⊏ enclosing matter to be the left ⊐ | ⊐ |
| Correct vertical alignment | \|\| | \|\| or (align) |
| Correct horizontal alignment | Single line above and below misaligned matter, e.g. misaligned | = or (align) |
| Correction made in error. Leave unchanged | under characters to remain - - - - - - - | (✓) or (stet) |
| Remove extraneous mark(s) or replace damaged character(s) | Encircle mark(s) to be removed or character(s) to be changed | × |
| Wrong font. Replace by character(s) of correct font | Encircle character(s) to be changed | (×) or (wf) |
| Refer to appropriate authority anything of doubtful accuracy | Encircle word(s) affected | (?) |

**Note:**
All instructions to the typesetter should be circled as shown above, e.g. (align) (stet) Otherwise they can be mistakenly inserted into the text.

# Appendix 6: Games and puzzles wordbuilder

Players of word games may be at an advantage if they have access to a supply of short or lexically unusual words. Two-letter words, words containing a *q* not followed by a *u*, and words beginning with *x* can be particularly useful and a wide selection is included in the following lists. Proper names and abbreviations which are not pronounced as they are spelt (such as *Dr* or *Mr*) are excluded from the lists as most word games do not regard these as valid items.

## Two-letter words

**aa** rough cindery lava
**ab** an abdominal muscle
**ad** an advertisement
**ag** (S. African) expressing various emotions, e.g. irritation, grief, or pleasure
**ah** expressing surprise, sympathy, pleasure, etc.
**ai** the three-toed sloth
**am** the present tense of 'be'
**an** a form of the indefinite article
**as** used to convey relative extent or degree
**at** expressing location or time
**aw** expressing mild protest, entreaty, etc.
**ba** (in Egyptian mythology) the soul
**be** exist
**bi** bisexual
**bo** a kind of fig tree
**by** beside
**da** one's father
**DJ** a disc jockey
**do** perform (an action)
**dy** a type of sediment
**eh** seeking explanation or agreement
**El** an elevated railway or section of railway
**em** a measuring unit in printing
**en** a measuring unit in printing
**er** expressing doubt or hesitation
**ex** a former spouse or partner
**fa** a musical note
**Ga** a member of a people living in Ghana
**GI** a soldier in the US army
**go** move or travel
**ha** expressing surprise, triumph, etc.
**he** a male person or animal previously mentioned
**hi** used as a greeting
**ho** expressing surprise, triumph, etc.
**id** a part of the mind
**if** introducing a conditional clause
**in** within
**io** a North American moth
**is** the present tense of 'be'
**it** a thing previously mentioned
**ja** (S. African) yes
**jo** (Scottish, old use) a sweetheart
**Ju** used to designate a kind of Chinese pottery
**ka** (in Egyptian mythology) the spirit
**ki** a plant of the lily family
**KO** a knockout in boxing match
**la** a musical note
**li** a Chinese unit of distance
**lo** (old use) used to draw attention to something
**ma** one's mother
**MD** (Brit.) a managing director
**me** the objective case of 'I'
**mi** a musical note
**mo** a moment
**MP** a Member of Parliament
**mu** the 12th letter of the Greek alphabet
**my** belonging to me
**no** not any
**nu** the 13th letter of the Greek alphabet
**ob** a type of gene
**od** a power once thought to pervade the natural world
**of** belonging to
**og** (Australian, old use) a shilling
**oh** expressing surprise, anger, disappointment, etc.
**oi** used to attract attention
**OK** used to express assent, agreement, etc.
**om** a mystic syllable which constitutes a sacred mantra
**on** supported by or covering
**op** an operation
**or** used to link alternatives
**os** a bone
**ou** a Hawaiian bird
**ow** expressing pain
**ox** a cow or bull
**oy** = oi
**Oz** Australia
**pa** one's father
**pi** the 16th letter of the Greek alphabet
**po** a chamber pot
**qi** (in Chinese philosophy) the life force

| | |
|---|---|
| **ra** | (in Norway and Sweden) a moraine |
| **re** | a musical note |
| **ri** | a Japanese unit of length |
| **se** | a Chinese musical instrument |
| **si** | = te |
| **so** | therefore |
| **ta** | thank you |
| **te** | a musical note |
| **ti** | = te |
| **TV** | (a) television |
| **uh** | expressing hesitation |
| **um** | expressing hesitation |
| **up** | towards a higher position |
| **us** | the objective case of 'we' |
| **Wa** | a member of a people living on the borders of China and Burma |
| **we** | oneself and others |
| **Wu** | a dialect of Chinese |
| **xi** | the 14th letter of Greek alphabet |
| **xu** | a monetary unit of Vietnam |
| **ye** | (old use) the plural form of 'thou' |
| **Yi** | a people living in parts of China |
| **yo** | used as a greeting |
| **yu** | an ancient Chinese wine container |

## Words with a q not followed by a u

| | |
|---|---|
| **qadi** | a Muslim judge |
| **qanat** | an irrigation tunnel |
| **qasida** | an Arabic or Persian poem |
| **qawwal** | a qawwali singer |
| **qawwali** | Muslim devotional music |
| **qi** | (in Chinese philosophy) the life force |
| **qibla** | the direction towards Mecca |
| **qigong** | a Chinese system of physical exercises |
| **qin** | a Chinese musical instrument |
| **qintar** | a monetary unit of Albania |
| **qiviut** | wool from the musk ox |
| **qwerty** | the standard layout of typewriters and keyboards |
| **tariqa** | the Sufi method of spiritual learning |

## Words beginning with x

| | |
|---|---|
| **xanthan** | a polysaccharide |
| **xanthate** | a chemical compound |
| **xanthene** | a chemical compound |
| **xanthic** | yellowish |
| **xanthin** | a yellow colouring matter |
| **xanthine** | a biochemical compound |
| **xanthoma** | a yellow patch on the skin |
| **xebec** | a sailing ship |
| **xeme** | a fork-tailed gull |
| **xenia** | gifts to a guest or guests |
| **xenial** | relating to hospitality |
| **xenon** | a noble gas |
| **xeric** | very dry |
| **xeroma** | abnormal dryness of a body part |
| **xerox** | to photocopy |
| **Xhosa** | a South African people or their language |
| **xi** | the 14th letter of the Greek alphabet |
| **xiphoid** | sword-shaped |
| **Xmas** | Christmas |
| **xoanon** | a wooden image of a god |
| **xography** | a photographic process |
| **xu** | a monetary unit of Vietnam |
| **xylan** | a compound found in wood |
| **xylary** | of or relating to xylem |
| **xylem** | plant tissue |
| **xylene** | a liquid hydrocarbon |
| **xylite** | a volatile liquid |
| **xylol** | = xylene |
| **xylose** | a plant sugar |
| **xyrid** | a sedge-like herb |
| **xyster** | a surgical instrument |
| **xyston** | an ancient Greek spear |
| **xystus** | an ancient Greek portico |

# Appendix 7: SMS (electronic text messaging)

SMS stands for Short Message (or Messaging) Service and is the name given to the system that enables mobile phone users to send and receive text messages. On most mobile phone networks each text message is restricted to about 150 characters, so abbreviations are used to allow maximum use to be made of this limited space. Apart from this, the increasing popularity of SMS stems from the fact that messages are quick to write and can be a source of entertainment to both sender and receiver: the same kind of language is becoming quite standard in emails and conversations in Internet chat rooms.

The basic principles governing the abbreviations are quite simple. Certain words or syllables can be represented by letters or numbers that sound the same but take up less space. For example, the letter 'C' sounds the same as the word 'see' (or 'sea', for that matter), while 'U' sounds the same as 'you', and the number '8' can be substituted wherever the sound /-ayt/ occurs in a word. So, 'see you later' can be abbreviated to *CUL8R*, to which the response might be *GR8*. Another way of shortening words is simply to omit certain letters, especially vowels. So, 'message' becomes *MSG*, 'please' becomes *PLS*, and 'speak' becomes *SPK*. But the majority of SMS abbreviations are derived from the initial letters of familar fixed phrases, like *FYI* 'for your information', or *TTYL* 'talk to you later'. Some of these can look puzzlingly obscure when first encountered, but regular exposure soon breeds familiarity.

A further feature of SMS is its use of 'emoticons', representations of facial expressions which can be formed with keyboard or keypad characters and which are intended as a quick, amusing way of conveying the sender's feelings or intended tone, from **:-)** for happiness, to **:~(** for disgruntlement or confusion. Characters can be used to create other 'message pictures': for example, **:-X** means 'my lips are sealed'. Some of the more established and respectable emoticons are included in the table.

Many SMS abbreviations are rapidly attaining the status of accepted conventions familiar to most users of the 'language', and listed below is a wide selection of the most commonly used vocabulary. Some of the principles of SMS are already spreading into the general language, so that, for example, abbreviations such as *B2B* ('business to business') and *SME* ('small to medium-sized enterprise') are now standard. But it is a method of communication that can be endlessly exploited and developed by individuals or small groups to create a kind of personal language that will remain opaque to the uninitiated: this will doubtless serve to increase its popularity.

## Glossary of SMS abbreviations

**@** at
**ADN** any day now
**AFAIK** as far as I know
**ATB** all the best
**B** be
**BBL** be back late(r)
**BCNU** be seeing you
**BFN** bye for now
**B4** before
**BRB** be right back
**BTW** by the way
**BWD** backward
**C** see
**CU** see you
**CUL8R** see you later
**F2F** face to face
**F2T** free to talk
**FWD** forward
**FWIW** for what it's worth
**FYI** for your information
**GAL** get a life
**GR8** great
**HAND** have a nice day
**H8** hate
**HTH** hope this helps
**IC** I see
**ILUVU** I love you
**IMHO** in my humble opinion
**IMO** in my opinion
**IOW** in other words
**JIC** just in case
**JK** just kidding
**KIT** keep in touch
**KWIM** know what I mean?
**L8** late
**L8R** later
**LOL** lots of luck/laughing out loud
**MOB** mobile
**MSG** message
**MYOB** mind your own business
**NE** any
**NE1** anyone
**NO1** no one
**OIC** oh, I see
**OTOH** on the other hand
**PCM** please call me
**PLS** please
**PPL** people
**R** are
**RU** are you
**RUOK** are you okay?
**SIT** stay in touch
**SOM1** someone

| | | | | | |
|---|---|---|---|---|---|
| **SPK** | speak | **WERV U BIN** | where have you been? | **YR** | your |
| **THKQ** | thank you | **W/** | with | **1** | one |
| **TTYL** | talk to you later | **WKND** | weekend | **2** | to, too |
| **TX** | thanks | **WOT** | what | **2DAY** | today |
| **U** | you | **WU** | what's up? | **2MORO** | tomorrow |
| **UR** | you are | **X** | kiss | **2NITE** | tonight |
| **WAN2** | want to | **XLNT** | excellent | **3SUM** | threesome |
| **WAN2TLK** | want to talk? | **XOXOX** | hugs and kisses | **4** | for |

### *Emoticons*

| | | | |
|---|---|---|---|
| **:-)** | I'm happy (a smiley) | **:-P** | I'm sticking my tongue out |
| **:~(** | I'm unhappy | **:-D** | I'm laughing |
| **:-X** | My lips are sealed | **:´-(** | I'm crying |
| **:-Q** | I don't understand | **:-/** | I'm sceptical |
| **;-)** | I'm winking | **:-o** | I'm surprised |
| **X=** | Fingers crossed | | |

# Appendix 8: Guide to good English

## 1. Parts of speech

In this section the traditional names are used for parts of speech (*noun, verb, adjective, adverb, pronoun, conjunction*, and *preposition*). Two other terms are sometimes used in describing grammar. One is *modifier*, which means any word that modifies the meaning of another word (usually a noun). It is broader in scope than 'adjective' and includes, for example, *table* in *table lamp* as well as *bright* in *a bright lamp* or *the lamp was bright*. The other is *determiner*, which means any word such as *a, the, this, those*, and *every* which you put before a noun to show how you are using the noun (as in *a fire, the fire, this fire, those fires*, and *every fire*).

### Nouns

A noun is a word that names something: a person (*woman, boy, Frances*), a thing (*building, tree*), or an idea (*birth, happiness*). A common noun names things generally, whereas a proper noun names a particular person, place, or thing when there is only one example. Collective nouns, such as *audience, family, generation, government, team*, are nouns which refer to groups of people or things. They can be treated as singular or plural: see the section on **AGREEMENT**.

#### *Proper nouns*

Proper nouns are normally spelled with a capital initial letter and refer to persons or things of which there is only one example (*Asia, Ark Royal, Dickens*). The term is sometimes understood more broadly to include geographical and ethnic designations such as *American* and *Ashanti*, which behave like common nouns, for example in allowing the forms *an American* and *the Ashanti*. Some genuinely proper names can also behave like common nouns in certain uses, for example *a fine Picasso* (= a painting by Picasso) and *three Picassos* (plural), *another Callas* (= a singer comparable to Callas). In these uses it is usual to retain the capital initial letter.

#### *Verbal nouns*

A verbal noun (also called a gerund) is a form of a verb ending with *-ing* that acts as a noun, for example *smoking* in the phrase no smoking and in the sentence Smoking annoys people. It should be distinguished from *smoking* used as an adjective (a smoking fire) and as the present participle of the verb (The man was smoking).

Because a verbal noun is a part of a verb as well as being a noun, it keeps some of the characteristics of verbs in its grammatical behaviour; for example the forms They objected to me swearing (non-possessive) and They objected to my swearing (possessive) are both established in ordinary usage, although the second, in which swearing is treated as a full noun, is often preferred in more formal writing. In current use, certain patterns are clear:

The possessive is the more normal choice when the word preceding the *-ing* form is a personal name or a noun denoting a person:

> She did not know what to think about Richard's constantly leaving her in the lurch.
>
> I was now counting on my father's being able to make some provision somehow.

When the noun is non-personal or in the plural, the possessive is not normally used:

> They turned a blind eye to toffee apples going missing.
>
> Then we had our old conversation about the house being haunted.

With personal pronouns, usage varies between the possessive and non-possessive, the possessive being more usual at the start of a sentence:

> His being so capable was the only pleasant thing about the whole dreadful day.
>
> Fancy him minding that you went to the Summer Exhibition.

With indefinite pronouns the possessive sounds less natural, and a non-possessive form is more usual:

> ☑ He didn't think for a time of anyone clawing at his back.
>
> ? There are many sound reasons, then, for everyone's wanting to join in this new Gold Rush.

You can also use an infinitive with *to* as a verbal noun (To err is human, to forgive divine), and choice between this and an *-ing* form is largely a matter of idiom. For example, you *hope to do something* but you *think of doing something, have a fondness for doing something*, and *have an aversion to doing something*. You need to be careful not to confuse these patterns, especially when more than one is used in the same sentence.

#### *Related nouns and verbs*

Some words exist as both nouns and verbs, in some cases with no difference in the form and pronunciation (e.g. *insult, master, score*) and in others with differences of form (e.g. *cloth / clothe*, *half* / *halve*, *licence* / *license*) or pronunciation (usually stress, with the noun stressed on the first syllable and the verb on the second, e.g. *conduct*, *record*, *transfer*). Some nouns have affected the pronunciation of their corresponding verbs, so that (for example) *decrease* and *export* are increasingly heard with a stress on the first rather than the second syllable as verbs as well as nouns. Conversely, and more controversially, some nouns are now heard stressed on the first syllable when the traditional pronunciation has been a second-syllable stress as both noun and verb (e.g. *dispute*).

## Verbs

A verb is a word that describes an action (*go*, *sit*, *put*) or state (*be*, *become*, *live*) and is normally an essential element in a clause or sentence. A verb is classified as transitive when the action affects a person or thing called the object (We lit a fire), and as intransitive when there is no object (She smiled).

### *Using the correct tense*

Tense is the location in time of the state or action expressed by a verb. English verbs properly have only two tenses, the present (*I am*) and the past (*I was*). The future is formed with *shall* or *will*, other forms of the past are formed with auxiliary verbs (*I have been* / *I was being*), and the past perfect is formed with the past tense of *have* (*I had been*).

The tense used mostly corresponds to actual time, apart from conventional uses such as the so-called 'historic present', used for dramatic effect in narratives (as in George gets up and walks over to the window), and the future used in polite requests (as in Will that be all for now?).

However, choice of tense (called 'sequence of tenses') becomes more complex in reported speech. If a simple statement such as I'm afraid I haven't finished is put into indirect speech by means of a reporting verb such as *said*, *thought*, etc., the tense of the reported action changes in accordance with the time perspective of the speaker: He said he was afraid he hadn't finished.

The tense of the reported verb can stay the same if the time relative to the speaker is the same as that relative to the person reported: She likes beans can be converted either to She said she liked beans or to She said she likes beans, and I won't be here tomorrow can be converted either to I said I wouldn't be here tomorrow or to I said I won't be here tomorrow.

#### shall *and* will

With *I* and *we*, *shall* should be used to form the simple future tense (expressing a prediction of a future action), while *will* is used to express an intention to do something:

☑ I shall be late for work.

☑ We will not tolerate this rudeness.

With *you*, *he*, *she*, *it*, and *they*, the situation is reversed; simple future action is expressed with *will*, while *shall* expresses an intention or command:

☑ He will be late for work.

☑ You shall join us or die!

In speech, these distinctions are often not observed. Contractions like *I'll* and *she'll* are commonly used, and strong determination is more likely to be conveyed by intonation than by strictly correct syntax.

#### should *and* would

The situation is similar with *should* and *would*. Strictly speaking *should* is used with *I* and *we*, while *would* is used with *you*, *he*, *she*, *it*, and *they*:

☑ I should be grateful if you would let me know.

☑ You didn't say you would be late.

In practice, however, it is normal to use *would* instead of *should* in reported speech and conditional clauses, such as I said I would be late. In speech the distinction is also often obscured through the use of the contracted forms *I'd*, *we'd*, etc.

### *Active and passive*

Verbs can be either active, in which the subject is the person or thing performing the action (as in France beat Brazil in the final), or passive, in which the subject undergoes the action (Brazil were beaten by France). In the passive voice verbs are usually formed with *be*, and the subject is expressed as an agent introduced by the preposition *by*.

Other forms of the passive include:

- impersonal constructions with *it*:

  It is believed that no action should be taken.

  It is felt that your complaint arises from a misunderstanding.

This is a style found in official documents and reports, which usually seek to avoid the personal responsibility that is implied by the active voice (We feel that your complaint arises from a misunderstanding). It is not suitable for ordinary writing and speaking.

- other verbs besides *be* can be used to form so-called 'semi-passives' (as in He got changed, They seem bothered). Here *changed* and *bothered* are behaving almost more like adjectives.
- double passive. This awkward construction occurs with verbs such as *attempt*, *begin*, *desire*, *endeavour*, *propose*, *threaten*, and others involving constructions with a passive infinitive:

[?] The order was attempted to be carried out.

Avoid this construction when there is no corresponding active form (☒ They attempted the order to be carried out). Use a fully active construction instead:

☑ They attempted to carry out the order.

In some cases the sentence can be rephrased,

for example:

☑ There was an attempt to carry out the order.

Other verbs, such as *expect*, *intend*, and *order*, which are grammatically more versatile, will allow a double passive construction. For example, we can say:

☑ They ordered the deserters to be shot.

and therefore a double passive form is allowed:

☑ The deserters were ordered to be shot.

### Subjunctive

The subjunctive is a special form (or mood) of a verb expressing a wish or possibility instead of fact. It has a limited role in English:

It was suggested he wait till the next morning.

Fundamentalist Islam ... decrees that men and women be strictly segregated.

In these sentences, the verbs *wait* (in the first) and *be* (in the second) are in the subjunctive; the ordinary forms (called the indicative) would be *waits* and *are*.

There are other typical uses of the subjunctive:

- after *if* (or *as if*, *as though*, *unless*) in hypothetical conditions:

  Each was required to undertake that if it were chosen it would place work here.

- *be* or *were* at the beginning of a clause with the subject following:

  Were I to get drunk, it would help me in the fight.

  All books, be they fiction or non-fiction, should provide entertainment in some form or other.

- in certain fixed expressions and phrases, e.g. *be that as it may*, *come what may*, *perish the thought*, *so be it*, and others.

In most cases, an alternative construction (e.g. with *should* or *might*) can also be used:

It was suggested that he should wait till the next morning.

In negative constructions, *not* (or *never* etc.) is normally placed before the subjunctive verb:

Again he insisted that you not be followed.

### Participles

There are two kinds of participle in English: the present participle ending with *-ing* as in We are going, and the past participle ending with *-d* or *-ed* for many verbs and with *-t* or *-en* or some other form for others, as in Have you decided?, New houses are being built, and It's not broken.

Participles are often used to introduce subordinate clauses that are attached to other words in a sentence, e.g.

Her mother, opening the door quietly, came into the room.

Hearing a noise I went out to look.

Born in Rochdale, he spent most of his life in the area.

Participles at the beginning of a sentence, as in the last two examples, are acceptable grammatically but when overdone can produce a poor style, especially when the clause they introduce bears little relation to the main one:

[?] Being blind from birth, she became a teacher and travelled widely.

A worse stylistic error occurs with so-called 'unattached', 'misrelated', or 'dangling' participles, when the participle does not refer to the noun to which it is attached, normally the subject of the sentence:

☒ Recently converted into apartments, I passed by the house where I grew up.

Grammatically, this sentence implies that the writer has recently been converted into apartments. Here is another example:

☒ Driving near home recently, a thick pall of smoke turned out to be a bungalow well alight.

Although everyone knows what these two examples mean, unattached participles can distract and sometimes mislead the reader, and are best avoided.

Certain participles, such as *considering*, *assuming*, *excepting*, *given*, *provided*, *seeing*, *speaking* (*of*), etc., have virtually become prepositions or conjunctions in their own right, and their use in a grammatically free role is now standard:

☑ 'Speaking of money,' said Beryl, 'do you mind my asking what you did with yours?'

## Adjectives and adverbs

### Position

Most adjectives can be used in two positions: either before the noun they describe, where they are called 'attributive', as in a black cat and a gloomy outlook, or after a verb such as *be*, *become*, *grow*, *look*, or *seem*, where they are called 'predicative', as in the cat was black and the prospect looks gloomy. A few adjectives used to denote status stand immediately after the noun and are called 'postpositive', as in *the body politic* and *the president elect*. You will find information about these later in this section.

Some adjectives are nearly always used in the predicative position and cannot stand before a noun (e.g. *afraid*). Others by contrast are found in the attributive position, either always (e.g. *main* as in the main reason, *mere* as in This is mere repetition) or in certain meanings (e.g. *big* as in He is a big eater, *whole* as in Have you told the whole truth?).

In these last examples, the adjective can only be made predicative by repeating the noun or by using the pronoun *one*:

The truth I have told is the whole truth.

This reason is the main one.

Other adjectives that have been restricted in the past are now becoming more mobile; for example, *aware* and *ill* are increasingly heard in the attributive position, as in a highly aware person and an ill woman.

### *Comparatives and superlatives*

An adjective has three forms, called a positive (or absolute), e.g. *hot*, *splendid*, a comparative, e.g. *hotter*, *more splendid*, and a superlative, e.g. *hottest*, *most splendid*.

Adjectives of one syllable and some adjectives of two syllables can form their comparative and superlative forms by adding *-er* and *-est*, sometimes with a change of spelling such as *y* to *i* (*soft*, *softer*, *softest*; *happy*, *happier*, *happiest*). Adjectives of more than two syllables are normally preceded by *more* or *most* instead of changing their form (*more frightening*; *most remarkable*).

Some adjectives (such as *dead*, *infinite*, and *unique*) have an all-or-nothing kind of meaning and cannot logically be qualified by *more* or *most*. These are called 'absolute' or 'non-gradable' adjectives. They are not normally used in comparative or superlative forms and cannot be qualified by adverbs that intensify or moderate such as *fairly*, *largely*, *more*, *rather*, or *very*.

There are exceptions to this rule, but these are normally obvious special cases:

> All animals are equal but some animals are more equal than others.
>
> His profile is most utterly perfect.

Absolute adjectives can be regularly qualified by adverbs that denote an extreme or completeness, such as *absolutely*, *completely*, and *utterly*, since these are consistent with the absolute nature of the adjectives concerned:

> ☑ The ghosts made the place utterly impossible.

In this sentence, *utterly impossible* is acceptable, and so is *completely* or *absolutely impossible*, but *fairly* or *rather impossible* is much less so, except conversationally.

### *Adjectives following a noun*

In many fixed standard expressions, adjectives denoting status are placed immediately after the nouns they describe, e.g. in *court martial*, *heir apparent*, *poet laureate*, *president elect*, *situations vacant*, and *the village proper*. In other cases, an adjective follows a noun as a matter of sentence structure rather than peculiarity of expression:

> The waiter picked up our dirty glasses in his fingertips, his eyes impassive.

### *Adjectives used as adverbs*

Some adjectives have corresponding adverbs that are identical, e.g. *fast*, *late*, *straight*, and the type *monthly*, *weekly*, etc. So you can say He left in the late afternoon or He left late in the afternoon (*lately* has a different meaning).

In other cases, adjectives are used as adverbs only informally, often in fixed expressions such as *come clean* and *hold tight*. To these we can add *real* and *sure*, which are characteristic of informal North American speech (That was real nice and I sure liked seeing you) and are also found in non-standard and dialect use in Britain.

### *Position of adverbs*

The position of adverbs in phrases and clauses follows fairly clear rules, i.e. they normally come between the subject and its verb, or between an auxiliary verb and a main verb:

> She dutifully observes all its quaint rules.
>
> Roosevelt's financial policy was roundly criticised in 1933.

But for emphasis, or when the adverb belongs closely to what follows the main verb, it comes after the verb and before a following adverbial phrase:

> There is little chance that the student will function effectively after he returns home.
>
> They aim to set each subject briefly in context.

### *Sentence adverbs*

Some adverbs (such as *clearly*, *happily*, *hopefully*, *thankfully*, *unhappily*) refer to a whole statement, and form a comment associated more closely with the speaker or writer than with what is said. In this role they are called 'sentence adverbs'. This use can be seen by comparing the use of *unhappily* as an ordinary adverb of manner (She went unhappily to bed) with its use as a sentence adverb (She was, unhappily, too ill to leave the house). Sentence adverbs often stand at the beginning of the sentence:

> Clearly, we will have to think again.

Sentence adverbs are well established in English, although the use of *thankfully* and (in particular) *hopefully* can arouse controversy:

> [?] All that lay before a young lady of breeding were duty to parents and hopefully a good marriage.
>
> [?] It was five o'clock by the time he reached the house, which was thankfully empty.

The reason for this appears to be that unlike other adverbs such as *clearly* and *happily*, *thankfully* and *hopefully* do not correspond to an equivalent phrase such as 'as is clear' (or 'it is clear that') or 'as is a happy circumstance' (or 'it is a happy circumstance that'). Although this objection is artificial, and such use is now very familiar, be aware that some people may take exception to these words, especially in written or formal contexts.

## Pronouns

A pronoun is a word such as *I*, *we*, *they*, *me*, *you*, *them*, etc., and other forms such as the possessive *hers* and *theirs* and the reflexive *myself* and *themselves*. They are used to refer to (and take the place of) a noun or noun phrase that has already been mentioned or is known, especially in order to avoid repetition, as in the sentence When she saw her husband again, she wanted to hit him.

When a pronoun refers back to a person or thing previously named, it is important that the gap is not so large that the reader or hearer might have difficulty relating the two, and that ambiguity is avoided when more than one person might be referred to, as in the following exchange in a play (where the ambiguity is deliberate):

> SEPTIMUS: Geometry, Hobbes assures us in the Leviathan, is the only science God has been pleased to bestow on mankind.
> LADY CROOM: And what does he mean by it?
> SEPTIMUS: Mr Hobbes or God?
> (Tom Stoppard)

### *Reflexive pronouns*

Reflexive pronouns are the type formed with *-self*, e.g. *myself*, *herself*, and *ourselves*, used in sentences in which the subject of the verb and the object are the same person or thing, as in We enjoyed ourselves and Make yourself at home.

A problem occurs when a reflexive pronoun refers back to a singular noun or pronoun of unknown or irrelevant gender:

> ? Take the case of someone who is still too young to look after themselves.

The use of the plural form *themselves* is the solution that is often used in ordinary speaking and writing, and it is generally acceptable.

In more precise writing, and in cases where the individuality of the person referred to is significant, the more cumbersome (and traditional) alternative is:

> ☑ Take the case of a person who is still too young to look after himself or herself.

This is a particular instance of a problem discussed further in the section on **AGREEMENT**.

## Conjunctions

A conjunction is a word such as *and*, *because*, *but*, *for*, *if*, *or*, and *when*, used to connect words, phrases, clauses, and sentences.

There are some conjunctions that are used in British English but not in American English:

- *now* (Now the tourist season's starting it's better to have someone there, like a caretaker)
- *and nor* (His septic tank did not work, and nor did most others in the village)
- *but nor* (I am not a trained architect but nor was Sir Edwin Lutyens).

On the use of *and* and *but* at the beginning of a sentence, see the section on **SENTENCES**.

### and/or

*And/or* is a formula indicating that the items connected by it can be taken either together or as alternatives. Its principal uses are in legal and other formal documents, but in general use it is often clumsy:

> The Press has rather plumped for the scholar as writer, and/or as bibliophile.

A more comfortable way of expressing the same idea is to use *X or Y or both*, and in some cases *or* by itself will do.

### but

*But* is both a preposition and a conjunction:

> Everyone seems to know but me.

(preposition, equivalent to 'except for')

> Everyone seems to know but I don't.

(conjunction, equivalent to 'except that')

Confusion between these overlapping roles can cause uncertainty about whether to say:

> Everyone but she can see the answer.
> *or* Everyone but her can see the answer.

Usage varies on this point, but here are some guidelines:

- when the phrase introduced by *but* is associated with the subject of the sentence, treat the pronoun as a subject form (i.e. No one saw him but I) and when the phrase is associated with the object, treat it like an object (i.e. I saw no one but him).
- when the association is not as clear-cut, the case of the pronoun is determined by the position of the *but*-phrase in the sentence: when the *but*-phrase is in the subject area, treat the pronoun as a subject form (i.e. Everyone but she can see the answer) and when the *but*-phrase is in the object area treat the pronoun as an object (Everyone can see the answer but her).
- usage is unstable when the verb is intransitive: Everyone knows but her is somewhat more natural than Everyone knows but she.

### for

As a conjunction *for* overlaps with *because* and *since*. It is generally more formal in effect, but it suffers from two limitations:

- it normally comes at the beginning of a phrase, following a main clause:

> He picked his way down carefully, step by step, for the steps were narrow.

- it is normally preceded by a comma, except occasionally when the sentence is short:

> It was gloomy and damp, for the sun could hardly shine through the tops of the trees.
> He did not cry any more for it did not help.

## Prepositions

A preposition is a word such as *after*, *in*, *to*, and *with*, which usually stands before a noun or pronoun and establishes the way it relates to what has gone before (The man on the platform, They came after dinner, and What did you do it for?).

The superstition that a preposition should always precede the word it governs and should not end a sentence (as in the last example given) seems to have developed from an observation of the 17th-century poet John Dryden, although Dryden himself did not always follow the rule in his own prose. It is not based on a real appreciation of the structure of English, which regularly separates words that are grammatically related.

There are cases when it is either impossible or not natural to organise the sentence in a way that avoids a final preposition:

- in relative clauses and questions featuring verbs with linked adverbs or prepositions:

  What did Marion think she was up to?

  They must be convinced of the commitment they are taking on.

  Budget cuts themselves are not damaging: the damage depends on where the cuts are coming from.

- in passive constructions:

  The dress had not even been paid for.

- in short sentences including an infinitive with *to* or a verbal noun:

  There are a couple of things I want to talk to you about.

  It was my dancing he objected to.

# 2. Inflection

## Basic rules

Inflection is the process by which words (principally nouns, verbs, adjectives, and adverbs) change their form, especially their ending, in accordance with their grammatical role in a sentence. The typical patterns of inflection in English are as follows:

- nouns add *-s* or *-es* to form plurals (*book, books*; *church, churches*)
- verbs add *-s* or *-es*, *-ed*, and *-ing* to form third-person present-tense forms (*change, changes*; *want, wants*), past tenses (*changed*; *wanted*), past participles (*changed*; *wanted*), and present participles (*changing*; *wanting*)
- adjectives and adverbs add *-er* and *-est* to form their comparative and superlative forms, sometimes also changing the stem (the main part of the word) as in *funnier, funniest*.

Some words that end in a vowel or a single consonant, or that have certain other features of spelling in the stem, can cause uncertainty in their inflections (e.g. *shellac, shellacked*; *samba, sambaed* or *samba'ed*).

Some verbs, called strong verbs, form tenses by changing their stem (*throw, threw, thrown*); and others are completely irregular (*have, had, had*; *go, went, gone*).

A verb ending in a double consonant usually has the following inflections:

- the past and past participle form *-ed* (as in *filled*)
- the present participle form *-ing* (as in *filling*)
- the adjective form *-able* (as in *fillable*) and its derived forms *-ably* and *-ability*
- the agent form *-er* (denoting a person or thing that does the action, as in *filler*).

Verbs of one syllable ending in a single consonant double the consonant when adding any of the suffixes given above: *beg, begged, begging*; *clap, clapped, clapping*; *rub, rubbed, rubbing*. (An exception is the verb *bus*, which has forms *bused, busing*.)

When the final consonant is *w, x*, or *y* this is not doubled: *tow, towed, towing*; *vex, vexed, vexing*; *toy, toyed, toying*.

When the final consonant is preceded by more than one vowel (other than *u* in *qu*), the consonant is not normally doubled: *boil, boiled, boiling*; *clean, cleaned, cleaning*.

Verbs of more than one syllable ending in a single consonant double the consonant when the stress (i.e. the natural emphasis used in pronouncing it) is placed on the final syllable: *allot, allotted, allotting*; *begin, beginning*; *occur, occurred, occurring*.

When the final consonant is *w, x*, or *y* this is again not doubled: *guffaw, guffawed, guffawing*; *relax, relaxed, relaxing*; *array, arrayed, arraying*.

Verbs that do not have their stress on the final syllable do not double the consonant unless it is an *l*: *audit, audited, auditing*; *gallop, galloped, galloping*; *offer, offered, offering*.

Exceptions in British English are: *input, inputting*; *output, outputting*; *kidnap, kidnapped, kidnapping*; *worship, worshipped, worshipping*. (In American English the forms are usually *kidnaped, kidnaping* and *worshiped, worshiping*.)

Verbs ending in *-l* normally double the *l* in British English regardless of where the stress occurs in the word: *annul, annulled, annulling*; *enrol, enrolled, enrolling*; *grovel, grovelled, grovelling, groveller*; *travel, travelled, travelling, traveller*. In American English the final *l* only doubles when the stress is on the final syllable (as in *annul* and *enrol* but not *grovel* and *travel*), and the basic form of the verb is sometimes spelled with *-ll* as well (as in *enroll, fulfill*, and *instill*).

Exceptions in British English are: *appeal, appealed, appealing*; *conceal, concealed, concealing*; *reveal, revealed, revealing*; *parallel, paralleled, paralleling*.

The verb *focus* also sometimes has the forms *focussed, focussing*; but the forms recommended here are *focused, focusing*.

## Verbs: dropping final silent e

Verbs drop a final silent *e* when the suffix begins with a vowel (as in *blue, bluish*; *brave, bravest*; *continue, continuous*; *queue, queued*). But a final *e* is usually retained in *ageing*, to preserve the soft sound of the *g* in *changeable* (but not in *changing*), *twingeing*, and *whingeing*, and in *dyeing* (from *dye*), *singeing* (from *singe*), and *swingeing*, to distinguish these from the corresponding forms *dying* (from *die*), *singing* (from *sing*), and *swinging* (from *swing*).

## More about plurals of nouns

English nouns normally form their plurals by adding *-s*, or *-es* if the singular form ends in *-s*, *-x*, *-z*, *-sh*, or soft *-ch* (as in *church* but not *loch*).

Words ending in *-y* form plurals with *-ies* (*policy*, *policies*) unless the ending is *-ey* in which case the plural form is normally *-eys* (*valley*, *valleys*); an exception is *money*, which has two plural forms *moneys* and *monies* in the meaning 'sums of money'.

Difficulties occur mainly when the singular form is unusual and does not allow you to use the normal rules or when the word is of foreign origin (or both).

Nouns ending in *-f* and *-fe* form plurals sometimes with *-fes*, sometimes *-ves*, and occasionally both *-fes* and *-ves* (in some cases with a difference in meaning). Many of these words also have corresponding verbs:

| noun | -fs plural | -ves plural | verb form |
|---|---|---|---|
| calf | | calves | calve, calved |
| dwarf | dwarfs | dwarves | dwarf, dwarfed |
| elf | | elves | |
| half | | halves | halve, halved |
| handkerchief | handkerchiefs | | |
| hoof | hoofs | hooves | hoof, hoofed |
| knife | | knives | knife, knifed |
| leaf | | leaves | leaf, leafed |
| life | | lives | live, lived |
| loaf | | loaves | loaf, loafed |
| oaf | oafs | | |
| proof | proofs | | prove, proved |
| roof | roofs | rooves | roof, roofed |
| scarf | scarfs | scarves | |
| self | | selves | |
| sheaf | | sheaves | sheave, sheaved |
| shelf | | shelves | shelve, shelved |
| thief | | thieves | thieve, thieved |
| turf | turfs | turves | turf, turfed |
| wharf | wharfs | wharves | |
| wife | | wives | |
| wolf | | wolves | wolf, wolfed |

The following tables list other plural forms that cause difficulties of various kinds.

### Irregular plurals

| singular | plural | singular | plural |
|---|---|---|---|
| child | children | man | men |
| foot | feet | mouse | mice |
| goose | geese | tooth | teeth |
| louse | lice | woman | women |

### Animal names the same in the plural

| singular | plural | singular | plural |
|---|---|---|---|
| bison | bison | salmon | salmon |
| cod | cod | sheep | sheep |
| deer | deer | squid | squid |
| grouse | grouse | swine | swine |

### Nouns only having a plural form: tools

| | | | |
|---|---|---|---|
| bellows | gallows | pliers | tongs |
| binoculars | glasses | scissors | tweezers |
| clippers | goggles | shears | |
| forceps | pincers | spectacles (= glasses) | |

### Nouns only having a plural form: articles of clothing

| | | | |
|---|---|---|---|
| braces | jeans | pyjamas | suspenders |
| breeches | knickers | (US pajamas) | tights |
| briefs | leggings | shorts | trousers |
| flannels | pants | slacks | |

### Compound nouns

| singular | plural |
|---|---|
| Attorney-General | Attorneys-General |
| brother-in-law | brothers-in-law |
| commander-in-chief | commanders-in-chief |
| court martial | courts martial* |
| daughter-in-law | daughters-in-law |
| father-in-law | fathers-in-law |
| Governor-General | Governors-General |

| singular | plural |
|---|---|
| lay-by | lay-bys |
| man-of war | men-of-war |
| mother-in-law | mothers-in-law |
| passer-by | passers-by |
| Poet Laureate | Poets Laureate* |
| sister-in-law | sisters-in-law |
| son-in-law | sons-in-law |

*The forms court martials and Poet Laureates are also used.

## Nouns ending in -o

Plurals of nouns ending in *-o* cause difficulty in English because there are few convenient rules for choosing between *-os* (as in *ratios*) and *-oes* (as in *heroes*). But here are some guidelines:

- when a vowel (usually *i* or *e*) precedes the final *-o*, the plural is normally *-os* (*trios*, *videos*), probably because of the bizarre look of *-ioes* etc.
- names of animals and plants normally form plurals with *-oes* (*buffaloes*, *tomatoes*).
- words that are shortenings of other words invariably form plurals with *-os* (*demos*, *hippos*).
- words introduced from foreign languages, especially recently, form plurals with *-os* (*boleros*, *placebos*).
- words of many syllables tend to have *-os* plurals (*aficionados*, *manifestos*).
- proper names used allusively, i.e. to refer to

people of a certain type or character, form plurals with *-os* (*Neros*, *Romeos*).

In other cases practice varies quite unpredictably: we refer to *kilos* and *pianos*, *dominoes* and *vetoes*. With some words things are not settled, e.g. both *mementoes* and *mementos* are widely used.

## Nouns: Latin plurals

Plurals of Latin words used in English are formed according to the rules either of Latin (*apex*, *apices*; *stratum*, *strata*) or of English (*gymnasium*, *gymnasiums*; *arena*, *arenas*). Often more than one form is in use, sometimes with a usage distinction (*appendix*, *appendices* or *appendixes*; *formula*, *formulae* or *formulas*) and sometimes with no clear distinction (*cactus*, *cacti* or *cactuses*).

Words ending in *-is* usually follow the original Latin form (*basis*, *bases*; *crisis*, *crises*) because they sound best that way, and the same rule operates in other cases (*nucleus*, *nuclei*). A more alien form is the plural *-mata* of words ending in *-ma* in the singular (*carcinoma*, *carcinomata*; *stigma*, *stigmata*).

Some Latinate nouns ending in *-us* cannot form plurals in *-i* for technical reasons: *hiatus* (a fourth-declension noun in Latin whose plural is the same, *hiatus*), *ignoramus* (a first-person plural verb in Latin, not a noun), *octopus* (a Romanised form of a Greek word *octopous*), *vade mecum* (*cum* being a preposition meaning 'with'): their English plurals are *hiatuses*, *ignoramuses*, *octopuses*, and *vade mecums*.

## Adjectives and adverbs: comparatives and superlatives

### Adjectives

Adjectives that form comparatives and superlatives using *-er* and *-est* in preference to (or as well as) *more* and *most* are:

- words of one syllable (e.g. *fast*, *hard*, *rich*, *wise*). Words of one syllable ending in a single consonant double the consonant when it is preceded by a single vowel (*glad*, *gladder*, *gladdest*; *hot*, *hotter*, *hottest*) but not when it is preceded by more than one vowel (*clean*, *cleaner*, *cleanest*; *loud*, *louder*, *loudest*).
- words of two syllables ending in *-y* and *-ly* (e.g. *angry*, *early*, *happy*, *holy*, *likely*, *lively*) and corresponding *un-* forms when these exist (e.g. *unhappy*, *unlikely*). Words ending in *-y* change the *y* to *i* (e.g. *angrier*, *earliest*).
- words of two syllables ending in *-le* (e.g. *able*, *humble*, *noble*, *simple*).
- words of two syllables ending in *-ow* (e.g. *mellow*, *narrow*, *shallow*).
- some words of two syllables ending in *-er* (e.g. *bitter*, *clever*, *slender*, *tender*, but not *eager*). In some cases only the *-est* form is used (e.g. *bitterest* but *more bitter*).
- some words of two syllables pronounced with the stress on the second syllable (e.g. *polite*, *profound*, but not *antique*, *bizarre*, *secure*, and others).
- other words of two syllables that do not belong to any classifiable group (e.g. *common*, *cruel*, *pleasant*, *quiet*); some words can take *-er* and *-est* although the forms sound somewhat less natural (e.g. *awkward*, *crooked*).

Words of two syllables ending in *-l* double the *l* (e.g. *cruel*, *crueller*, *cruellest*); words ending in other consonants do not double them.

Adjectives of three or more syllables need to use forms with *more* and *most* (*more beautiful*, *most interesting*, etc.).

### Adverbs

Adverbs that take *-er* and *-est* in preference to (or as well as) *more* and *most* are:

- adverbs that are not formed with *-ly* but are identical in form to corresponding adjectives (e.g. *runs faster*, *hits hardest*, *hold it tighter*).
- some independent adverbs (e.g. *often* and *soon*).

Adverbs ending in *-ly* formed from adjectives (e.g. *richly*, *softly*, *wisely*) generally do not have *-er* and *-est* forms but appear as *more softly*, *most wisely*, etc.

# 3. Sentences

A sentence is a group of words that makes complete sense, contains a main verb, and when written begins with a capital letter and ends with a full stop (or the equivalent such as a question mark or an exclamation mark). Some groups of words vary from these rules and are still normally regarded as sentences, for example answers to questions: 'Could you close the window?' 'Sure.'

There are three basic kinds of sentence:

- a simple sentence normally contains one statement:

  The train should be here soon.

- a compound sentence contains more than one statement, normally joined by a conjunction such as *and* or *but*:

  I have looked at the evidence and I have to say it is not sufficient.

  He was at the meeting but said very little.

- a complex sentence contains a main clause and one or more subordinate clauses, such as a conditional clause beginning with *if* or a relative clause introduced by *which* or *who*:

The story would make headlines if it ever became public.

This is a matter which the lawyers will have to resolve.

## Getting words in the right order

The normal order of the key elements of an English sentence is subject - verb - object or complement (if any) - adverb or adverb phrase (if any):

Kate had seen a large grey rat in the cellar.

The boys always went to the cinema on Tuesday.

However, the order is sometimes changed by a process called 'inversion':

Here comes the train.

'Hey,' shouted the woman.

Each of these elements can consist of a single word or a group of words. Because English has so few inflections (word endings that change a word's grammatical role), the order of words is an essential part of meaning; change the order and you often change the meaning.

There are more detailed rules of word order that we normally follow without thinking (for example, an adverb phrase referring to place normally comes before one referring to time, as with *to the cinema* and *on Tuesday* in the example above).

Normal sentence order is often reversed in questions, except when the question begins with an interrogative word such as *who* and *what*:

Did Thomas remember to take his passport?

Was your father there?

Who said that?

Indirect questions should follow the word order of statements and should not be followed by a question mark. For example, it is non-standard to say:

☒ I asked them what did they want to do?

☒ Tell me how old are you?

The correct forms are:

☑ I asked them what they wanted to do.

☑ Tell me how old you are.

Sometimes a word or phrase that normally occurs later in the sentence is brought to the beginning for emphasis:

On Tuesday we went to London.

Suddenly the door flew open.

Great literature this is not.

## Relative clauses: using words like *who* and *when*

A relative clause is one connected to a main clause by a relative pronoun or adjective such as *who* or *whom*, *which*, *whose*, or *that*, or by a relative adverb such as *when* and *where*. (These words, apart from *that*, are collectively called *wh*-words, and a *wh*- word means any of these.) Most problems with this kind of clause are to do with the choice between *that* and a *wh*- word, principally *which*, *who*, or *whom*. For much of the time *that* is interchangeable with any of these words, and it is the more usual choice, especially in relation to *which*, in everyday writing and conversation:

She held out the hand that was hurt.

*or* She held out the hand which was hurt.

The man who had spoken to us then walked in.

*or* The man that had spoken to us then walked in.

There are two types of relative clause, called 'restrictive' and 'non-restrictive'. A restrictive clause gives essential information about a noun or noun phrase that comes before. In the sentence above, 'the hand' is defined as 'the one that (or which) was hurt'. By contrast, in the sentence She held out her hand, which I clasped in both of mine, the information in the relative clause introduced by *which* is extra information that could be left out without affecting the structure or meaning of the sentence. This type is called a non-restrictive clause. A restrictive clause can be introduced by *that*, *which*, *who*, or *whose* and is not normally preceded by a comma, whereas a non-restrictive clause is normally introduced by *which*, *who*, or *whose* (and not usually *that*), and is preceded by a comma.

A non-restrictive clause introduced by a *wh*-word can apply to a whole clause and not just the preceding noun or noun phrase:

The sun came out, which was nice.

Sometimes *that* is more idiomatic than *which*, for example when the construction is based on an impersonal *it* or an indefinite pronoun such as *anything*:

There is something that I forgot to mention.

Is there anything that you want?

*That* is also more usual when *which* already occurs earlier in the sentence in another role, for example as an interrogative word:

Which is the one that you want?

(In all these types involving a preference for *that*, leaving out the relative word altogether is common: see **ELLIPSIS** below. But use of *which* in any of these sentences would be unnatural.)

## Leaving words out: ellipsis

In some sentences, a verb and other words can be left out when they can be understood from what has gone before or comes later in the sentence. This process is called *ellipsis*:

It had been a good party. An unforgettable party, actually. And still was.

Here, there is ellipsis of *it had been* in the second sentence and of *it* in the third. Ellipsis happens most often in conversation in expressions such as Told you so (= I told you so) and Sounds fine to me (= It or that sounds fine to me), and also occurs in all kinds of spoken and written English. This practice is standard in informal English.

Other common types of ellipsis are that of the subject of a verb (I just pick up wood in a leisurely way, stack it, and slowly rake the bark into heaps), and the verb itself after *to* (Knowledge didn't really advance, it only seemed to) or after an auxiliary verb (We must and will rectify the situation).

You can use ellipsis when the words left out can reasonably be supplied by the hearer or reader from the rest of the sentence without causing confusion. Ellipsis is less satisfactory, and in some cases not possible, when the omitted word does not have the same form and function as it does where it is present in the sentence:

> ⍰ Our officials ought to manage things better than they have been.

(The word to be supplied is *managed*, not *manage*.)

> ☒ No state has or can adopt such measures.

(The word to be supplied is *adopted*, not *adopt*.)

> ☒ The budget must be equal or greater than the total cost of supplying the product.

(The word *equal* should be followed by *to* and not *than*.)

Cases where the number (singular or plural) changes should also be avoided:

> ⍰ The ringleader was hanged and his followers imprisoned.

(The word needed before 'imprisoned' is *were*, not *was*.)

The relative pronoun *that* or *which* is routinely left out informally, especially when a final preposition refers back:

> It reminded him of the house he used to live in.

The verb *be* is often omitted, especially in informal English, in cases such as

> They are sorry for what they did and anxious to make amends.
>
> We're leaving now and catching the nine o'clock train.

But when *be* is used as an auxiliary verb and as a linking verb in the same sentence, it must be repeated because its role is different:

> The bill was overtaken by the election and its postponement was welcome.

## Ambiguity

When words have more than one meaning it is not always clear which meaning is intended in a particular statement. For example, if someone says to you that you should 'check your speed', this could mean either 'reduce your speed' or 'look and see what your speed is', because the verb *check* has both these key meanings.

Some forms of sentence structure and word order can also lead to more than one meaning being possible. This situation, called ambiguity, is normally unintentional, although ambiguity is sometimes used deliberately, for example in advertising. In speech, ambiguity is often avoided by the rise and fall of the voice as you speak. In writing, the context will often make the right meaning clear, but not always.

Typical ambiguities in everyday language usually involve:

- the association of a word or phrase with the wrong part of the sentence in so-called 'misrelated constructions':

  > ⍰ The council plans to notify parents whose children are affected by post.

  (where *by post* should be placed after *notify*)

  > ⍰ The claims were regarded as mere posturing by the management.

  (where *by the management* should be placed after *regarded*)

- the unclear application of a negative, especially in statements of intention or reason:

  > ⍰ She did not go out to water the plants.

  (which can mean either that she did not go out at all, or that she did go out but not to water the plants)

- lack of clarity about how far a modifying word applies:

  > ⍰ The boy was wearing old jeans and trainers.

  (in which it is unclear whether the jeans and trainers were old or just the jeans)

- words or expressions that have more than one meaning or function:

  > ⍰ Visiting friends can be tiresome.
  >
  > ⍰ The Minister appealed to her supporters.

- a pronoun with wrong or unclear reference:

  > ⍰ If the children don't like their toys, get rid of them.

The normal position of intensifying or emphasising adverbs, such as *even*, *usually*, and in particular *only*, is between the subject and its verb, or after an auxiliary verb such as *has* and *are*, although the words they refer to often occur later in the sentence:

> ☑ The company has even admitted that it was negligent.
>
> ☑ In those days, you only applied to one college.

In written English, these adverbs are sometimes placed close to the actual words they refer to, especially when another modifying word occurs in their normal position, and in contexts, such as legal language, in which precision is more important than a pleasing style:

> ☑ The public interest is properly served only where companies pursue the traditional goal of maximising profit.

## Beginning sentences with *and* and *but*

It is not wrong to begin a sentence with a conjunction such as *and* or *but*. The practice is common in literature and can be effective:

ARTHUR: Must you with hot irons burn out both mine eyes?
HUBERT: Young boy, I must.
ARTHUR: And will you?
HUBERT: And I will.
(Shakespeare, *King John*)

It is also used for other rhetorical purposes, especially to denote surprise (And are you really going?) and sometimes just to introduce an improvised afterthought (I'm going to swim. And don't you dare watch).

## Negatives and double negatives

A repeated negative of the type He never did no harm to no one is incorrect to the point of being regarded as illiterate in current English. However, it surprises many people, who regard double negatives as self-evidently wrong, that they were once regarded as reinforcing each other and were an integral feature of standard English, found in Chaucer, Shakespeare, and other writers up to the 17th century. For some reason the logic then changed, and a sequence of negatives came to be regarded as cancelling each other out.

By contrast, a double negative is acceptable when it is used with intentional cancelling effect as a figure of speech, as in It has not gone unnoticed (= It most certainly has been noticed).

Double negatives also occur, especially in speech, in uses of the type You can't not go (= you cannot consider not going, i.e. you have to go), in which *not go* is effectively a single idea expressed in a verb phrase.

# 4. Agreement

When we use words together in sentences, we often have to change their form so that they produce the right grammar and meaning. In the sentence John wants me to give you these flowers, *wants* is the form of the verb *want* that agrees with its subject *John* and *give* is the form that goes with *to*. The word *these* is a plural form to agree with its noun *flowers*, and the pronoun *me* is in the first person because it refers to the speaker. This process of making words fit the context of sentences is called 'agreement'.

For most of the time we apply the rules of agreement instinctively, but problems can arise. Sometimes words have special meanings that do not seem to correspond to their grammatical form. When we mix words about with other words in sentences we can easily lose mental track and link the wrong words together, especially in conversation when we have less time to think.

In some sentences, especially longer ones, the subject can be singular but separated from its verb by other words that happen to be in the plural. This can lead you to put the verb in the plural as well, and this is incorrect:

☒ The consequence of long periods of inactivity or situations in which patients cannot look after themselves are often quite severe and long-lasting.

Here, the string of plural nouns coming before the main verb *are* has caused the writer to lose sight of the real subject of the sentence, which is *consequence*. To make this sentence correct, we have three choices: to change *consequence* to *consequences*, to change *are* to *is*, or to recast the sentence more simply, e.g.:

☑ Long periods of inactivity or situations in which patients cannot look after themselves can often have quite severe and long-lasting consequences.

## Agreement within phrases

### *Awkward phrases*

Some expressions can cause uncertainty because they are grammatically ambiguous or combine seemingly contradictory roles, for example phrases such as *more than one* and *either or both*:

More than one dealer has shown an interest in the painting.

The meaning is clearly plural, but the grammar remains singular because *one* is closer to the verb as well as being the dominant word in its phrase (we could not say More than one dealer have shown an interest in the painting).

[?] The purchaser gets a licence to use either or both products.

Here there is a problem of agreement with the following noun, because *either* calls for the singular form *product* whereas *both* calls for the plural form *products*; *both* wins out because it is closer to the noun. Usually a better solution is to adjust or recast the sentence to avoid the problem altogether:

☑ The purchaser gets a licence to use either or both of the products.

We find a similar problem with *one or more*:

[?] To qualify you must be responsible for one or more children aged under 16.

Again a small adjustment gets round the difficulty:

☑ To qualify you must be responsible for at least one child under 16.

### *Compound subjects*

Two nouns joined by *and* are normally treated as plural:

Speed and accuracy are top of the list.

His mum and dad are meeting him at the station.

But when the two nouns form a phrase that can be regarded as a single unit, they are sometimes (or, when the unity is very strong, always) treated as singular even when one of them is plural:

Fish and chips is my favourite meal.

This Romeo and Juliet is the best I have seen.

This practice can extend to concepts that are distinct in themselves but are regarded as a single item in a particular sentence:

[?] The hurt and disbelief of parents' friends and families is already quite real.

[?] The extent and severity of drug use in the city has been a severe shock.

When a singular noun forming the subject of a sentence is followed by an additional element tagged on by means of a phrase such as *as well as*, *accompanied by*, or *together with*, the following verb should be singular and not plural, since the singular noun is by itself the true subject:

The little girl, together with her friend Kerry, was busy filling her bucket with sand.

(but note The little girl and her friend Kerry were busy filling their buckets with sand.)

Your booking form, accompanied by a cheque or card details, needs to reach us by the end of January.

## Singular and plural

Another kind of problem is the mismatch between a word's form and its meaning. Here are some typical cases:

### *Singular nouns treated as plural*

Some nouns are singular in form but are used with a verb that can be either singular or plural, or in some cases only plural. The commonest of these are the collective nouns which stand for a group or collection of people or things, such as *audience*, *committee*, *crew*, *family*, *generation*, *government*, *group*, *jury*, *team*, and many others.

The general rule with words like these is to treat them as singular when the emphasis is on the group as a whole and as plural when the emphasis is on the individuals that form the group. The choice affects the form of the following verb and any pronouns such as *he*, *she*, *they*, or *their* that are used to refer to the noun:

(*singular*) Each succeeding generation of gallery visitors finds it easier to recognise Cubist subject-matter.

A group of four young men in overalls was standing close to him.

(*plural*) The jury retired at the end of the day to consider their verdict.

A handful of bathers were bobbing about in the waves.

Collective nouns representing a large or indeterminate number of people, such as *government*, *mob*, and *staff*, are treated in British English as either singular or plural with little effective difference, but in American English the singular is always used:

The government is / are under increasing pressure to deal with the backlog of asylum seekers.

When there is a choice, the important point is to avoid a mixture of singular and plural forms:

[x] The committee has decided to postpone their decision.

Names of countries often behave like collective nouns, and can be followed by plural verbs, when they denote the people or representatives of the country:

Germany continue to defend their policy on food imports.

France play Brazil in the final on Saturday.

Some collective nouns are fully plural, taking plural verbs and being used with plural determiners such as *these* and *many*:

Many people agree that some form of control is needed.

By and large the police do a good job.

### *Plural nouns treated as singular*

Other nouns are plural in form but are treated as singular, either always or in some meanings. Chief among these are the names of branches of knowledge or science, such as *acoustics* and *mathematics*, activities such as *billiards* and *gymnastics*, and diseases such as *measles*:

Acoustics is taught as part of the extended course.

The plural noun *acoustics* is equivalent to the singular expression *the subject of acoustics*; but note the plural agreement in The cathedral's acoustics are spectacularly good for this kind of music, where *acoustics* has a different meaning that is physical rather than conceptual.

The figures show that measles is on the increase.

Here, *measles* is equivalent to the notional subject *disease* or *illness*. In more casual conversation, this pattern extends to other plurals:

If he bought a small chips, he'd have enough for some chocolate too.

(where a word such as *bag* or *portion* is the notional subject).

Other plural nouns, such as *data*, *media*, and *agenda*, are now commonly treated as singular. Depending on their meaning, they are either countable nouns, which can be used with *a* or *an* and have plural forms, e.g. *agendas*, or mass nouns, which do not have a plural form but are used in the singular with words such as *this* and *much*:

The media has lost interest in the subject.

This data is in a form that can be used by other institutions.

The Prime Minister has set himself a formidable agenda.

Some plural words adopted unchanged from other languages, such as *spaghetti* and *graffiti*, develop singular meanings:

The furniture had been damaged and graffiti was daubed on the walls.

There are also words, such as *means*, that are

plural in form but can function as singular (even to the extent that you can say *a means*) or plural depending on the words used with them:

(*singular*) Complaints are valuable as a means of identifying where improvements can be made.

(*plural*) Various means are being sought to revive public interest in the scheme.

### *Subjects and objects*

People often wonder what to do when the subject of the verb *be* is singular and the part that follows the verb (the complement) is plural. The answer is that the verb should generally agree with its subject, regardless of what comes after the verb:

The only traffic is ox-carts and bicycles.

There is usually no problem when the reverse situation occurs, with the subject in the plural and the complement in the singular:

These huge biographies are usually a mistake nowadays.

When the subject is a singular collective noun, the verb may be in the plural, following the usual pattern with such nouns:

Its prey are other small animals.

When the subject is the relative pronoun *what*, the verb is singular:

What I'm really interested in is the objects in this house.

## Indefinite pronouns

Pronouns such as *each*, *either*, *neither*, and *none* are called indefinite pronouns. When used on their own like a noun, they can vary between singular and plural depending on whether the emphasis is on the individuals or on the collection or group as a whole:

(*singular*) Either is preferable to muddling through with neither.

Neither the chairman nor the chief executive is planning any dramatic gestures.

None of them has had enough practical experience to run the company.

(*plural*) They each carry several newspapers.

Neither his mother nor his father earn much money now.

None of the staff were aware of the ransom demand.

Like all pronouns these words (apart from *none*) can also come before nouns, as in *each person* and *neither house*. In this role they are classed, like *every*, as determiners, and they are then always singular:

Each party has members in the Federal National Assembly.

Neither suggestion is the right one.

### *Plural pronouns used in the singular*

You may sometimes be unsure about what possessive word (*his*, *her*, etc.) to put in the place indicated by the question mark in the example that follows:

Every student should hand in ? assignment by Tuesday.

Here, *every* can stand for a male or female person with correspondingly different forms of possessive word. The safest option is to put *his or her*:

Every student should hand in his or her assignment by Tuesday.

But this can be awkward, especially when the sentence continues for some time with repeated references back to the original subject. In cases like this it is now acceptable to use a plural form of pronoun to refer back to an indefinite pronoun, so as to avoid having to specify gender at all when this is unknown or irrelevant:

Every student should hand in their assignment by Tuesday.

This is a great deal neater, and is supported historically: the use of *they* and *their* in this way used to be common in English until people took against it in the 19th century, along with other grammatical superstitions that arose then. But there is an alternative that gets round the problem altogether, by putting the whole sentence in the plural:

All students should hand in their assignments by Tuesday.

This option is worth remembering, but you have to keep the sentence in the singular when you use singular indefinite pronouns such as *anyone* or *somebody*:

☑ Does anyone want their tea now?

### **either ... or ...** ***and*** **neither ... nor ...**

A problem arises when one of the alternatives in an *either ... or ...* or *neither ... nor ...* construction is singular and the other plural. Here, the normal choice is to make the verb agree with the one closer to it:

☑ Either the twins or their mother is responsible for this.

But often a better solution is to recast the sentence to avoid the problem:

☑ Either the twins are responsible for this or their mother is.

A mixture of persons normally has to be resolved by this kind of rephrasing:

[?] Neither you nor I am / are / is the right person.

is better as

☑ You are not the right person, and neither am I.

(or ... and nor am I.)

## Personal pronouns

It's a tiny bit boring, between you and me.

*I*, *we*, *he*, *she*, and *they* are subjective pronouns, which act as the subjects of verbs, while *me*, *us*, *him*, *her*, and *them* are objective, acting as the objects of verbs and prepositions. In the sentence above, therefore, *me* is correct, since the preposition *between* refers to both *you* and *me* and *I* has to be the subject of a sentence. The same applies to other prepositions used in this way (such as *for* and *with*):

> The boys are coming with Gavin and me.

After the verb *be* it is more natural and usual to use *me*, *us*, *him*, *her*, or *they* (the objective pronouns), although what follows *be* is not an object but a complement:

> I said it was only me.
>
> That's us sitting on the bench.
>
> Is it them you wanted to see?

The subjective forms (*I*, *we*, *he*, *she*, or *they*) are not wrong but often sound stilted, especially the first-person forms *I* and *we*:

> ⍰ I said it was only I.
>
> ⍰ That's we sitting on the bench.

It is however usual to use the subjective forms when a relative clause (introduced by *who* or *that*) follows:

> ☑ It was I who did it.

(It was me who did it, and especially ⍰ It was me that did it, are much more informal in tone.)

## 5. Punctuation

The purpose of punctuation is to make writing clear. Bad punctuation is like a badly laid out timetable: the information may be correct but the way it is organised can clarify or obscure it. Like other aspects of language, punctuation has changed over the centuries; modern practice was influenced by the development of printing in the 15th and 16th centuries, which had the effect of standardising a practice that before then had been haphazard and unreliable.

There are several ways in which punctuation makes writing clearer:

- it can clarify the structure of continuous writing (full stop, comma, colon, semicolon, and brackets).
- it can indicate words that form something other than a statement (question mark, exclamation mark, quotation marks).
- it can show how words relate to each other (apostrophe, hyphen).
- it can indicate that a group of letters is an abbreviation (full stop) or that letters are missing (apostrophe).

### Full stop

The principal use of the full stop (also called point, full point, and period) is to mark the end of a sentence that is a statement:

> Bernard went over to the bookcase and took down an atlas.

This applies to sentences when they are not complete statements or contain ellipsis, as in the opening of Dickens's *Bleak House*:

> London. Michaelmas term lately over, and the Lord Chancellor sitting in Lincoln's Hall. Implacable November weather.

If the sentence is a question or exclamation, the mark used is the question mark or exclamation mark, which include a full stop in their forms (see further on the **QUESTION MARK** and **EXCLAMATION MARK** below).

### Comma

The role of the comma is to give detail to the structure of sentences and to make their meaning clear by marking off words that either do or do not belong together. It usually represents the natural breaks and pauses that you make in speech, and operates at phrase level and word level:

**at phrase level** You should use a comma to mark off parts of a sentence that are separated by conjunctions (*and*, *but*, *yet*, etc.). This is especially important when there is a change or repetition of the subject:

> Attempts to block him failed, and he went ahead on 23 June.
>
> Mokosh could foretell the future, and she could change herself into any form she pleased.

The use of a comma in these cases is especially important when the sentence is a long one:

> Readings are taken at points on a grid marked out on the ground, and the results are usually plotted in the form of computer-drawn diagrams.

(It may be preferable to use two sentences here.)

It is not normally correct to join the clauses of a compound sentence without a conjunction:

> ☒ His was the last house, the road ended with him.

(In this sentence, the comma should either be replaced by a semicolon, or retained and followed by *and*.)

It is also incorrect to separate a subject from its verb with a single comma:

> ☒ Those with the lowest incomes and no other means, should get the most support.

(Remove the comma.)

A comma also separates parts of a sentence that balance or complement each other, and can introduce direct speech, especially in continuation of dialogue:

> Parliament is not dissolved, only prorogued.
>
> He was getting better, but not as fast as his doctor wished.
>
> Then Laura said, 'Do you mean that?'

An important function of the comma is to prevent ambiguity or momentary misunderstanding:

> A hundred feet below, the woman in the red dress was gazing up at them.
>
> Mr Hogg said that he had shot, himself, as a small boy.

Commas are used in pairs to separate elements in a sentence that are asides or not part of the main statement:

All history, of course, is the history of wars.

By then, however, it was very close to being dark.

It is important to remember *both* the commas in cases like this. Using only one can be worse than none at all:

☒ By then, however it was very close to being dark.

Commas are also used to separate a relative clause (one beginning with *which*, *who*, *whom*, or *whose*) when this is adding extra information and could be removed from the sentence without changing the meaning or producing nonsense:

The money, which totals more than half a million, comes from three anonymous donors.

But they are not used when the clause begins with *which* or *that* and is essential to the meaning by identifying a person or thing just mentioned:

What have you done with the money that I gave you?

A single comma sometimes follows adverbs (such as *already*, *moreover*, and *yesterday*), phrases, and subordinate clauses that come at the beginning of a sentence:

Moreover, they had lied about where they had been.

Next morning, the air glittered and the palm tree stood upright in the sun.

When the sun began to sink, she could take the riverside walk to the hotel and join her friends.

In all these cases and many others this comma is optional, but one or more is always needed with *however* when it means 'by contrast' or 'on the other hand':

However, a good deal of discretion is left in the hands of area managers.

**at word level** A comma is used to separate adjectives having the same range of reference coming before a noun:

a cold, damp, badly heated room

a ruthless, manipulative person

The comma can be replaced by *and* between a pair of adjectives to make a stronger effect:

a ruthless and manipulative person

The comma is omitted when the adjectives have a different range of reference (for example, size and colour) or when the last adjective has a closer relation to the noun:

his baggy green jacket

a distinguished foreign politician

a dear little baby

Commas are used to separate items in a list or sequence:

The visitors were given tea, scones, and cake.

The comma before *and* is regarded by many people as unnecessary and left out; this dictionary always includes one. There are cases where the final comma is essential for clarity (for example, where one of the items in the list is a pair joined by *and*), and sometimes not having one produces ambiguity:

☑ For breakfast they wanted tea, toast and marmalade, and eggs.

☒ I would like to thank my parents, Anne Smith and God.

Leave out the comma between nouns that occur together in the same grammatical role in a sentence (called apposition):

My friend Judge Peters was not at home.

Her daughter Mary became a nurse.

But use one when the noun is a piece of extra information that could be removed from the sentence without any noticeable effect on the meaning:

His father, Humphrey V. Roe, was not so fortunate.

## Semicolon

The semicolon is the punctuation mark that causes most trouble in ordinary writing, and it is the one least noticeable if you skim the pages of a modern novel. But if you use it carefully, it can be extremely helpful.

Its main role is to mark a grammatical separation that is stronger in effect than a comma but less strong than a full stop. Normally the two parts of a sentence divided by a semicolon balance each other, as distinct from leading from one to the other (in which case a colon is usually more suitable, as explained below):

The sky grew bright with sunset; the earth glowed, and his face also with its own light.

Honey looked up and glared; the man scurried away.

You can also use it as a stronger division in a sentence that already contains commas:

What has crippled me? Was it my grandmother, frowning on my childish affection and turning it to formality and cold courtesy; or my timid, fearful mother, in awe of everyone including, finally, me; or was it my wife's infidelities, or my own?

## Colon

The colon tends to be used much more in formal print than in everyday writing. Whereas a semicolon links two balanced statements, a colon leads from the first statement to the second. Typically it links a general or introductory statement to an example, a cause to an effect, or a premise to a conclusion. (In many cases a conjunction such as 'so' or 'for example' could be introduced between the two halves.)

He was being made to feel more part of the family: the children kissed him goodnight, like a third parent.

I feel angry: do I look angry?

You also use a colon to introduce a list:

The price includes the following: travel to London, flight to Venice, hotel accommodation, and excursions.

A colon can sometimes give more emphasis or drama to a statement in direct speech:

> Dobson told them: 'He has been arrested.'

In American English, a colon follows the initial greeting in a letter (Dear Ms Jones:), where in British English you would normally use a comma.

## Brackets

The brackets you will use most often in writing are round brackets or parentheses ( ).

You use round brackets:

- to show explanations and additional comment:

> She let herself plan out what she would say, what her tone could be (easy but serious), how much need she could show (fatigue, strained loyalty).
>
> A verbal noun (also called a gerund) is a form of a verb ending in -ing.

- to show optional words, implying doubt or caution about them:

> There are many (apparent) difficulties.

- to give references and statistical information:

> a brass-rubbing of Sir Toby and Lady Falconer (*c*.1428)
>
> If music be the food of love (Shakespeare, *Twelfth Night*)

Square brackets [ ] are mostly used in formal printing. Their main use is to enclose extra information provided, often by someone other than the writer of the surrounding text, such as an editor, to clarify an obscure point or identity:

> When Charles had spoken to Henry, he [Henry] withdrew graciously.

## Dash

In formal printing there are two types of dash: the en-rule (–) and the longer em-rule (—). Most word-processing programs are able to distinguish the two lengths of rule, but in ordinary writing no distinction is usually made. In printing, the en-rule has certain special uses (e.g. to mark a range of numbers, as in pages 34–6), whereas the em-rule is the one corresponding to the dash in general use.

The principal uses of the dash are:

- a single dash is used to introduce an explanation or expansion of what comes before it:

> It is a kind of irony of history that I should write about the French Revolution in the very country where it has had the least impact—I mean England, of course.

- a pair of dashes is used to indicate asides and parentheses, forming a more distinct break than commas would:

> Helen has only seen her father once in her adult life and—until her flight from Grassdale—her brother is a virtual stranger to her.

## Question mark

The main use of the question mark (?) is to indicate a direct question:

> Are they leaving tomorrow?
>
> What time is it?

You can sometimes use it even when the question is put in the form of a statement:

> They told you that?
>
> Surely it's the same one?
>
> I wonder if you can help me?

You should not use a question mark in indirect questions in which the question is reported rather than expressed (He asked what time it was), but you should use it in tag questions of the kind She's much taller now, isn't she?.

A question mark is conventionally placed before a word about which there is some doubt, e.g. uncertain locations on maps and uncertain dates (Thomas Tallis, ?1505–85).

## Exclamation mark

An exclamation mark (!) shows in writing what you would normally say loudly or strongly in speech, to attract attention or to tell someone what to do. You will most often use it:

- to mark a command or warning:

> Go to your room!
>
> Be careful!

- to indicate the expression of a strong feeling of absurdity, surprise, approval, dislike, regret, etc., especially after *how* or *what*:

> How awful!
>
> Aren't they odd!

- to express a wish or a feeling of regret:

> I'd love to come!
>
> If only I had known!

- in speech, to indicate someone calling out or shouting:

> Outside Edith's house, someone knocked. 'Edith!'
>
> 'You're only shielding her.' 'Shielding her!' His voice rose to a shriek.

The exclamation mark also occurs quite often in literature, especially in poetry, to express a strong feeling or idea:

> O, weep for Adonais! (Shelley)
>
> Ah! parted lips and little pearly teeth, Wide eyes, snub noses, shorts, divided skirts! (Betjeman)

In ordinary writing, you do not often need to use the exclamation mark in this way. Avoid using it just to add a false sense of drama or sensation to writing that is otherwise routine or unexciting.

## Quotation marks

The main use of quotation marks (also called inverted commas) is to indicate direct speech and quotations. In writing it is common to use double quotation marks (" "), and in printing practice varies between the double and single style (' '). Single marks are more often used in Britain and double marks in America. The guidelines that follow reflect practice in British English, with indications of any variations in American English.

In direct speech and quotations, the closing quotation mark normally comes after a final full stop, and after any other punctuation that forms part of the quotation, such as an exclamation mark:

> Christie nodded her head as she said, 'A fine proposal this is, I must say.'
>
> Then they shouted, 'Watch out!'

When the quoted speech is followed or interrupted by a reporting verb such as *say*, *shout*, etc., the punctuation that divides the sentence is put inside the quotation marks:

> 'No,' he said, slamming the suitcase shut.
>
> 'You must have read my mind,' she said, 'a good strong cup of tea is just what I need.'

If a quoted word or phrase comes at the end of a sentence or coincides with a comma, the punctuation that belongs to the sentence as a whole is placed outside the quotation marks:

> What is a 'gigabyte'?
>
> No one should 'follow a multitude to do evil', as the Scripture says.

In American English, however, it is usual to place quotation marks outside the sentence punctuation (and note the more characteristic double quotation marks):

> No one should "follow a multitude to do evil," as the Scripture says.

When a quotation occurs within a quotation, the inner quotation is put in double quotation marks if the main quotation is in single marks (or vice versa, especially in American practice):

> 'Have you any idea,' he asked, 'what a "gigabyte" is?' (British)
>
> "Have you any idea," he asked, "what a 'gigabyte' is?" (American)

## Apostrophe

The principal role of the apostrophe is to indicate a possessive, as in Tessa's house and the town's mayor. For its conventional role to indicate omitted letters, see below.

Singular nouns form the possessive by adding *'s* (the dog's barks = one dog), and plural nouns ending in *s* add an apostrophe after the *s* (the dogs' barks = more than one dog).

When a plural noun ends in a letter other than *s*, the possessive is formed by adding *'s*: the children's games, the oxen's hoofs, etc.

Beware of the so-called 'grocers' apostrophe', an apostrophe wrongly applied to an ordinary plural, particularly in words ending in *-o* but also in quite harmless words such as *apples* and *pears* (e.g. ☒ pear's 30p a pound ).

Beware also of confusing the possessive *whose* with *who's*, which is a contraction of *who is* (e.g. ☒ Who's turn is it?).

There is a problem with names ending in *-s*, because of the awkward sound that can result. Practice varies, but the best course is to add *'s* to names that end in *s* when you would pronounce the resulting form with an extra *s* in speech (e.g. *Charles's*, *Dickens's*, *Thomas's*, *The Times's*); and omit *'s* when the name is normally pronounced without the extra *s* (e.g. *Bridges'*, *Connors'*, *Mars'*, *Herodotus'*). With French names ending in (silent) *-s* or *-x*, add *'s* (e.g. *Dumas's*, *le Roux's*) and pronounce the modified word with a final *-z*.

An apostrophe should not be used in the pronouns *hers*, *its*, *ours*, *yours*, and *theirs*:

> ☑ a friend of yours
>
> ☒ a friend of your's

Be careful to distinguish *its* from *it's*. *Its* (no apostrophe) is a possessive meaning 'belonging to it', whereas *it's* (with an apostrophe) is a contraction meaning 'it is':

> ☑ Give the cat its dinner.
>
> ☒ Give the cat it's dinner.
>
> ☑ It's hard to know where to start.
>
> ☑ It's been raining.

An apostrophe is no longer normally used in the plural of abbreviated forms (e.g. several MPs were standing around), although it is used in the possessive (e.g. the BBC's decision to go ahead with the broadcast). It is used in plurals when clarity calls for it, e.g. dot your i's and cross your t's. The apostrophe is also rapidly disappearing in company names and other commercial uses, e.g. *Barclays Bank*, *Citizens Advice Bureau*.

Another important use of the apostrophe is to mark contractions such as *I'll*, *they've*, *couldn't*, and *she's*, and informally also in contractions involving nouns (e.g. The joke's on them).

The apostrophe is no longer needed in words that were originally shortened forms but are now treated as words in their own right, e.g. *cello*, *flu*, *phone*, and *plane*. Other words retain them in their spelling, usually in the middle of words rather than at the beginning, e.g. *fo'c'sle*, *ne'er-do-well*, *o'er*, *rock 'n' roll*.

## Hyphen

In print, a hyphen is half the length of a dash, but in writing there is often little noticeable difference. While the dash has the purpose of separating words and groups of words, the hyphen is meant to link words and parts of words (apart from its use as a printing convention to split a word at the end of a line). Although the use of hyphens is very variable in English, the following guidelines reflect generally agreed principles.

As a so-called 'spelling hyphen', the hyphen is used to join two or more words so as to form a single word (often called a compound word), e.g. *free-for-all*, *multi-ethnic*, and *right-handed*, and words having a grammatical relationship which form a compound, e.g. *dive-bomb* (based on 'to bomb by making a dive'), *load-bearing* (based on 'bearing a load'), *punch-drunk* (based on 'drunk from a punch'). Straightforward noun compounds are now much more often spelt either as two words (*boiling point, credit card, focus group, garden party*) or as one, even when this involves a collision of consonants, which used to be a reason for putting in the hyphen (*database, earring, breaststroke, radioisotope*). However, there are two cases in which a compound spelt as two words is made into a hyphened form or a one-word form:

- when a verb phrase such as *hold up* or *kick back* is made into a noun (*hold-up, kick-back*).
- when a noun compound is made into a verb (e.g. *a date stamp* but *to date-stamp*).

A hyphen is often used:

- to join a prefix ending in a vowel (such as *co-* and *neo-*) to another word (e.g. *co-opt, neo-Impressionism*), although one-word forms are becoming more usual (*cooperate, neoclassical*).
- to avoid ambiguity by separating a prefix from the main word, e.g. to distinguish *re-cover* (= provide with a new cover) from *recover* and *re-sign* (= sign again) from *resign*.
- to join a prefix to a name or designation, e.g. *anti-Christian, ex-husband*. There is no satisfactory way of dealing with the type *ex-Prime Minister*, in which the second element is itself a compound, except to rely on the tendency of readers to use their knowledge of the world to choose the natural meaning. A second hyphen, e.g. *ex-Prime-Minister*, is not standard.
- to stand for a common second element in all but the last word of a list, e.g. two-, three-, or fourfold.
- to clarify meanings in groups of words which might otherwise be unclear or ambiguous:

  The library is reducing its purchase of hard-covered books.

  Twenty-odd people came to the meeting.

  There will be special classes for French-speaking children.

You should also use a hyphen to clarify the meaning of a compound that is normally spelled as separate words, when it is used before a noun: an up-to-date record but the record is up to date.

But there is no need to insert a hyphen between an adverb ending in *-ly* and an adjective qualified by it, even when they come before the noun: a highly competitive market, recently published material. When the adverb does not end in *-ly*, however, a hyphen is normally required to make the meaning clear: a well-known woman, an ill-defined topic.

## Other uses of punctuation

### *Abbreviations (full stop)*

Abbreviations are increasingly spelled without full stops when they are made up of all capital letters (*AGM, NNE, TUC*) or a mixture of capital and small letters (*BSc, Ms*). But full stops are more usual when the abbreviation is made up entirely of small letters, because in this form they are less immediately recognisable as abbreviations rather than words (*a.o.b., p.m., t.b.a.*). Shortenings, or abbreviations consisting of the first few letters of words, are usually spelled with a final full point (*co., Oct., cert.*), but those where the abbreviation ends with the last letter of the word tend not to be (*Dr, Dept*).

If an abbreviation with a full stop comes at the end of a sentence, another full stop is not added when the full stop of the abbreviation is the last character: Bring your own pens, pencils, rulers, etc. but Bring your own things (pens, pencils, rulers, etc.).

### *Number markers*

Full stops are routinely used between units of money (£11.99, $27.50), before decimals (10.5%), and between hours and minutes (10.30 a.m.; American English uses a colon as in 10:30 a.m.).

Commas are used in numbers of four or more figures, to separate each group of three consecutive figures starting from the right (e.g. 14,236,681). Omit the comma when giving house numbers in addresses (44 High Street), and in dates (27 July 2001).

# 6. Spelling

## Changes in spelling

Before the invention of printing in the 15th century, English and other European languages had no regularity of spelling and usage was largely based on personal preference. At first the development of printed books added to the problem, with printers (many of them not English) using different spellings of the same word even in the same passage of text. For example, Caxton—the first English printer—spelled *book* as *booke* and *boke* within a few lines of each other. Even people's names were not spelled consistently (*Shakespeare*, for example, appeared as *Shakspere, Shakespear*, etc.). It was not until the 17th century, when the first dictionaries were written, that some order was brought to bear on this chaos.

Many words, therefore, have changed their spelling over centuries of use. Words derived from French that we spell with *-re* at the end (e.g. *theatre* and *lustre*) used to be spelled with the ending *-er*, and these forms (e.g. *theater* and *luster*) have survived in American English. There have been dozens of ways of spelling the word *through* (including *thourth, thurght*, and *thorght*), all now obsolete. If you look at letters written in the 18th century, you will find people writing *teaze* for *tease* and *happyness* for *happiness*, and signing themselves *your dutifull daughter*. *Duty* itself has had many forms, including *deuty*, *dewite*, and *dewtie*.

Even now, English is full of irregularities of spelling. The same sounds can be written in different ways (such as -oo- in *moon*, *threw*, *through*, and *lute*), and the same group of letters can stand for different sounds (such as *-ough* in *bough*, *though*, *through*, *enough*, and *cough*). Various proposals have been made over the years for reforms (some dating back to the 16th century) that would make spelling more straightforward for the benefit of native speakers and foreign learners alike. Among the most famous proposals were those of Isaac Pitman (the inventor of shorthand) and the playwright George Bernard Shaw, who left money in his will to finance the development of a new alphabet that could more consistently reflect the ways in which words are pronounced.

There are two serious problems with all these proposals for reforming the alphabet. First, there is the question of managing the change and getting people to use the new system. Second, English is pronounced in different accents, and so the question arises of which accent should provide the model on which the reformed alphabet is based. There are other difficulties: for example, which spelling to adopt when more than one is available for a particular sound (e.g. *ou* as in *count* or *ow* as in *cow*), and the objection that phonetic spelling would obscure word origins and connections, especially in groups of words in which the stress pattern changes, e.g. *adore*, *adoration* and *nation*, *national*. In any case, no machinery for reform exists, and it is unlikely that significant change can be achieved except by the weight of ordinary usage.

A major cause of confusion is the exceptional tolerance English has for different spellings of the same word. This works in unpredictable ways, so that *banister*, *bannister* and *judgement*, *judgment* are all permitted spellings whereas *accomodation* is not a permitted variant of *accommodation* nor *millenium* of *millennium*, even though these rejected forms are very common.

## Difficult spellings

The tables following give examples of some of the most commonly misspelled and confused words. Systematic problems occur in words belonging to a certain type (e.g. the formation of nouns from verbs ending in *-edge*, such as *acknowledgement* and *judgement*) and in the inflection of words (e.g. the plural of nouns ending in *-o* such as *potato* and *solo*, and the *-ed* and *-ing* forms of verbs such as *benefit* and *unravel*). Some of these difficulties have been addressed in the section on **INFLECTION**.

The best-known spelling rule is 'i before e except after c'. This is generally valid when the combination is pronounced -ee-, as in *believe*, *brief*, *fiend*, *hygiene*, *niece*, *priest*, *siege*, and in *ceiling*, *deceive*, *conceit*, *receipt*, *receive*. There are exceptions: *caffeine*, *codeine*, *protein* (all formed from elements ending in *-e* followed by *-in* or *-ine*); *plebeian*, and *seize*.

The rule is not valid when the syllable is pronounced in other ways, as in *beige*, *freight*, *neighbour*, *sleigh*, *veil*, *vein*, and *weigh* (all pronounced as in *lake*), in *eiderdown*, *feisty*, *height*, *heist*, *kaleidoscope*, and *sleight* (all pronounced as in *like*), and in words in which the *i* and *e* are pronounced as separate vowels, e.g. *holier*, *occupier*.

### *Different spellings, related meaning, different parts of speech*

| word 1 | part of speech | word 2 | part of speech |
|---|---|---|---|
| **annexe** | noun | **annex** | verb |
| **dependant** | noun | **dependent** | adjective |
| **envelope** | noun | **envelop** | verb |
| **licence** | noun | **license** | verb |
| **practice** | noun | **practise** | verb |
| **thief** | noun | **thieve** | verb |
| **wreath** | noun | **wreathe** | verb |

## Frequently misspelled words

| word | comment |
|---|---|
| **accommodate, accommodation, etc.** | two *c*s, two *m*s |
| **acquaint, acquire, etc.** | *acq-* |
| **ageing** | preferred to *aging* |
| **aggressive, aggression, etc.** | two *g*s, two *s*'s |
| **appal** | two *p*s, one *l*; American also *appall* |
| **appalling** | two *p*s, two *l*s |
| **artefact** | *arte-* preferred to *arti-* |
| **attach** | not *-atch* |
| **besiege** | *i* before *e* |
| **biased** | preferred to *biassed* |
| **commemorate** | two *m*s followed by one *m* |
| **committee** | two *m*s, two *t*s |
| **consensus** | not *-census* |
| **desperate** | *-per-* not *-par-* |
| **detach** | not *-atch* |
| **disappear** | one *s*, two *p*s |
| **disappoint** | one *s*, two *p*s |
| **ecstasy** | ends *-asy* |
| **eighth** | two *h*s |
| **embarrass, embarrassment, etc.** | two *r*s, two *s*'s |
| **enthral** | one *l* |
| **fulfil** | one final *l*; American also *fulfill* |
| **gauge** | *-au-* not *-ua-* |
| **guarantee** | *-ua-* not *-au-* |
| **guard, guardian, etc.** | *-ua-* not *-au-* |
| **harass, harassment, etc.** | one *r*, two *s*'s |
| **hygienic** | *i* before *e* |

| word | comment |
|---|---|
| **independent** | ends *-ent*, noun and adjective |
| **install** | two *l*s |
| **instalment** | one *l*; American *installment* |
| **itinerary** | ends *-erary* |
| **judgement** | *-dge-* preferred form |
| **manoeuvre** | *-oeu-*; American *maneuver* |
| **medieval** | *-ev-* preferred to *-aev-* |
| **Mediterranean** | one *t*, two *r*s |
| **memento** | *mem-* not *mom-* |
| **millennium** | two *l*s, two *n*s |
| **millionaire** | two *l*s, one *n* |
| **miniature** | *-ia-* in second syllable |
| **minuscule** | not *-iscule* |
| **mischievous** | not *-ievious* |
| **misspell** | two *s*'s |
| **necessary** | one *c*, two *s*'s |
| **niece** | *i* before *e* |
| **occurrence** | two *c*s, two *r*s |
| **parliament** | *-ia-* in second syllable |
| **privilege** | ends *-ilege* |
| **questionnaire** | two *n*s |
| **receive** | *e* before *i* |
| **recommend** | one *c*, two *m*s |
| **rhythm** | begins *rh-* |
| **seize** | *e* before *i* |
| **separate** | *-par-* not *-per-* |
| **siege** | *i* before *e* |
| **sieve** | *i* before *e* |
| **skilful** | single *l*s; American also *skillful* |
| **supersede** | not *-cede* |
| **suppress** | not *sur-*, two *p*s |
| **surprise** | begins *sur-* |
| **threshold** | one *h* |
| **unwieldy** | not *-wieldly* |
| **wilful** | single *l*s |
| **withhold** | two *h*s |

## 7. Capital letters

Capital letters mark special uses of words. They emphasise a significant point in writing, especially the beginning of a sentence, and distinguish special kinds of words, for example proper names. They also occur in some abbreviations.

You should always use a capital letter:

- to begin a new sentence, or a quotation within a sentence.
- at the start of proper names and personal names (*New York*, *Alison*, *Churchill*).
- in certain special cases, e.g. the personal pronoun *I* and the exclamation *O*.

Beyond these elementary rules, practice and usage is not consistent. The following is based on a consensus of practice in British English. Capital letters are used for:

- prefixes and titles forming part of names referring to one person: *the Duke of Wellington*, *Sir Bob Geldof*, *Her Majesty the Queen*, *Queen Elizabeth the Queen Mother*, *His Excellency the American Ambassador*. When the reference is general, i.e. to many such people, a capital is not used: every king of England from William I to Richard II (where *king* is a common noun like *monarch* or *sovereign*).
- titles of office-holders when these refer to a particular holder: I have an appointment with the Mayor and He was appointed Bishop of Durham; but not when the reference is general or descriptive: He wanted to be a bishop and When I become mayor.
- recognised and official place-names: *Northern Ireland* (but *northern England*, which is simply descriptive), *Western Australia*, *South Africa*, *New England*, *the Straits of Gibraltar*, *Plymouth Sound*, *London Road* (when it is an address; but Take the London road, i.e. the road to London, when it is descriptive).
- compass directions when these are abbreviated (*N*, *NNE*, *SW*) or when denoting a recognised region (prosperity in the South).
- names of peoples and languages and derived words directly relating to them (*Irishman*, *German*, *Swahili*).
- names of months and days (*July*, *Tuesday*, *Christmas Day*, *the Annunciation*).
- names of events and periods of time: *the Bronze Age*, *the Middle Ages*, *the Renaissance*, *the First World War* (but *the 1914–18 war* is generally regarded as descriptive).
- names of institutions, when these are regarded as identifying rather than describing: *Christianity*, *Buddhism*, *Islam*, *Marxism*, *the (Roman) Catholic Church*, *the House of Lords*.
- names of ships and vehicles: *Cutty Sark*, *HMS Dreadnought*, *the US bomber Enola Gay*: see next section. Note also *a Boeing*, *a Renault*, which are trademarks.
- words referring to the deity of a religion (*God*, *Father*, *Allah*, *Almighty*), although the use of capitals in possessive words (as in in His name) is no longer common.

Abbreviations and initialisms are usually spelled with capitals, whether they refer to institutions or are more generic (*BBC*, *MPs*); but acronyms, which are pronounced like words and tend to behave like words, often become wholly or partly lower-case (*Nato*, *radar*, *Aids*).

### *Words derived from proper names*

You should use a capital letter when the word still has a direct reference to the original name: *Christian* (noun and adjective), *Machiavellian*, *Shakespearian*. But a small initial is used when the reference is remote or indirect: *arabic letters*, *french windows*, *mackintosh*, *wellington boot*; and when the sense is an attribute or quality suggested by the proper name: *chauvinistic*, *titanic*.

# Frequently confused words

## *Different spellings, same or close pronunciation, different meanings*

| word 1 | meaning | word 2 | meaning |
|---|---|---|---|
| **aural** | relating to the ears and hearing | **oral** | relating to the mouth and speaking |
| **breach** | a gap or break, make a break | **breech** | part of a gun or cannon |
| **canvas** | material for tents and sails | **canvass** | seek opinions or solicit votes |
| **chord** | a group of notes in music | **cord** | string or rope |
| **complacent** | smug and self-satisfied | **complaisant** | willing to please |
| **complement** | addition that completes, add in a way that improves | **compliment** | expression of praise, express praise for |
| **council** | advisory or administrative body | **counsel** | adviser, barrister in court, give professional advice |
| **desert** | waterless area of sand (stress on first syllable), abandon (stress on second syllable) | **dessert** | sweet course of meal (stress on second syllable) |
| **discreet** | circumspect | **discrete** | distinct |
| **draft** | preliminary sketch etc. | **draught** | air current, quantity of liquid |
| **draw** | make a picture of, to pull, have an equal score | **drawer** | a compartment in a desk or chest |
| **ensure** | make sure | **insure** | take out insurance on |
| **faint** | hard to see or hear | **feint** | a pretended blow, to make a pretended blow, denoting paper with faint lines |
| **flair** | a natural ability | **flare** | a burst of flame or light, give a sudden light, become angry |
| **forbear (verb)** | desist from | **forebear (noun)** | ancestor |
| **forego** | go before | **forgo** | go without |
| **forever** | continually | **for ever** | eternally |
| **grisly** | causing revulsion | **grizzly** | as in *grizzly bear* |
| **hoard** | store of valuables | **horde** | large group of people (usually unwelcome) |
| **its** | possessive word, as in *the cat licked its paws* | **it's** | = it is or it has |
| **loath** | reluctant or unwilling | **loathe** | dislike greatly |
| **naught** | chiefly in *come to naught* and *set at naught* | **nought** | the digit 0, nothing |
| **naval** | relating to a navy | **navel** | umbilicus |
| **ordinance** | an authoritative order | **ordnance** | mounted guns, military stores |
| **palate** | roof of the mouth, sense of taste | **palette** | artist's mixing board |
| **principal** | first or main, chief person | **principle** | basis of belief or action |
| **shear** | cut wool off, cut | **sheer** | swerve or avoid, utter or complete (as in *sheer delight*) |
| **stationary** | not moving | **stationery** | writing materials |
| **storey** | part of a building on one level | **story** | account of imaginary events |
| **straight** | extending without a curve or bend | **strait** | narrow passage of water |
| **who's** | = who is | **whose** | possessive word, as in *whose house is this?* |

Verbs follow the same rule: *Americanize, Romanize*, but *bowdlerize, galvanize, pasteurize*. The guide in this area is the extent to which the name on which the word is based is present in the meaning used, as it clearly is with *Shakespearian* but not with *titanic* (which many people use without knowing about the mythological Titans from which the word is derived).

## 8. Italics

Italics are *a style of sloping type, like this*, and are used in printing for a number of special purposes (in ordinary writing you can underline words instead).

The principal uses of italics are:

- for titles of books, plays, longer poems, films, works of art, etc.: *Harry Potter and the Philosopher's Stone, A Midsummer Night's Dream, Paradise Lost, Four Weddings and a Funeral, The Laughing Cavalier*.
- for names of newspapers, magazines, and journals: *The Daily Express, Reader's Digest, Cosmopolitan*.
- for names of ships and vehicles: *Ark Royal, Concorde*.
- to denote foreign words and phrases that are not yet regarded as English: *echt, film noir, joie de vivre, magnum opus*. This practice is becoming less common, and many dictionaries (including this one) print them in ordinary roman type.
- to show emphasis: 'Oh, come on, it can't be *that* bad.'

## 9. What words mean

### Changes of meaning

Words change their meanings even in relatively short periods of time. Some words change so drastically that they come to mean virtually the opposite of their original meaning, for example *nice*. You can still talk about a *nice distinction* (meaning 'a fine or subtle one') as well as a *nice day*, a *nice dinner*, a *nice rest*, and all sorts of things that are pleasant or enjoyable. And you may be surprised to know that the earliest meaning of *nice*, no longer used, was 'foolish' or 'stupid'.

Words develop whole new areas of meaning. For example, *check* has three core meanings: the meaning in chess, 'to threaten your opponent's king' (which is one of the earliest meanings of the word), the meaning 'to restrain' (All these distractions did not check their progress too much) and the meaning 'to verify' which is now the most common (Her father went to check that the door was locked). The verb *start* has two core meanings: 'to jump in surprise' (The old woman started at the noise) and 'to begin' (We will start the work next week).

Some words even change back to earlier meanings: a famous and troublesome example is provided by the pair *disinterested* and *uninterested*, which for several centuries have swapped two meanings based on different meanings of the word *interest*: 'not have any interest', i.e. 'not curious or wishing to know more', and 'not having an interest', i.e. 'not being involved' or 'impartial'.

In current usage *uninterested* has the first of these meanings:

> Paul showed her his work but she seemed uninterested.

and *disinterested* has the second meaning:

> A solicitor's ability to give disinterested advice is a fundamental element of his or her relationship with you, the client.

Most people now consider it wrong to use *disinterested* to mean 'not interested':

> ☒ He'd been so disinterested in her progress during six years of primary school that he'd only ever visited the school once.

When a word is no longer needed or useful it will either disappear or develop a new and more useful meaning. The verb *decimate* is a case in point: it is no longer needed in its original meaning 'to kill every tenth person' (usually as a military punishment) and has developed a new meaning, 'to kill in large numbers':

> ? Henry decided to lead what remained of his army, decimated by illness contracted at the siege, to Calais.

It has even produced a figurative meaning in which no physical killing or destruction takes place at all:

> ? Some matches were cancelled and attendances at those that went ahead were decimated.

#### *Weakened meanings*

There is a group of adjectives, such as *dreadful* and *terrific*, with basic meanings that are rooted in very strong feelings and emotions (in these cases, *dread* and *terror*). Some are used to describe something good or enjoyable and others to describe something bad or unpleasant:

- (bad) *awful, diabolical, dreadful, frightful, terrible*
- (good) *fabulous, fantastic, incredible, marvellous, terrific, tremendous*

Nowadays, a *fantastic film* is more likely to mean 'a very good or enjoyable film' than 'a film based on fantasy' (which is the original meaning of *fantastic*), and an *awful experience* is more likely to mean 'a very unpleasant experience' than 'an experience that gives you a feeling of awe or wonder' (which is the original meaning of *awful*). Words like these lose their power with use, and *awful* has gone a stage further in expressions such as *an awful lot* or *an awful shame*:

[?] The introduction of council tax is going to hurt an awful lot of people and there is no point in pretending otherwise.

The corresponding adverbs (such as *awfully*, *dreadfully*, and *incredibly*) have weakened in meaning to little more than 'extremely' or 'very':

[?] Once they were out of the building and had time to recover, they realised they had been incredibly lucky.

The result of this weakening of meaning is that such words no longer make much impact. They are all right in everyday conversation, and it would be difficult to avoid them. But if you want to sound convincing and make a real impression, you should use other words, such as *excellent*, *remarkable*, *spectacular*, *outstanding*, *exceptional*, *extraordinary*, *momentous*, or *phenomenal*.

If you need a strengthening adverb, you will often find that a simpler word such as *extremely*, *exceedingly*, *exceptionally*, or sometimes, as with feelings, *intensely* or *acutely*, will be more effective:

☑ Once they were out of the building and had time to recover, they realised they had been extremely lucky.

### *Special meanings*

Some words with special or semi-technical meanings, such as *dilemma* and *alibi*, tend to develop more general meanings that not everyone accepts or likes. Strictly speaking, a *dilemma* is a difficult choice or predicament involving two possibilities:

☑ The authority faces the familiar dilemma of cutting public services or increasing local taxes.

Avoid the word if you simply mean 'problem' or 'difficulty':

☒ The dilemma arose because the doctor coming from outside the area could not get there until 6.30, and the crematorium mortuary closed at 4.30.

An *alibi* is a legal term for evidence of where an accused person was at the time of a crime:

☑ Joseph had done nothing about contacting his old friend until he needed an alibi for the night of the murder.

Again, avoid the word if you simply mean 'excuse' or 'pretext':

☒ Other politically imposed demands, such as the requirement to keep prices down, provide management with a plausible alibi for failing to meet their targets.

The table below shows some other words that have controversial meanings and need care in use.

| word | main meaning | controversial meaning |
|---|---|---|
| **aggravate** | to make worse | to annoy |
| **alibi** | evidence that a person was elsewhere | an excuse or pretext |
| **anticipate** | to forestall or prevent | to expect |
| **crescendo** | an increasing noise or excitement | a climax |
| **decimate** | to kill one in ten of | to kill or destroy a large proportion of |
| **dilemma** | a difficult choice between two or more alternatives | a problem |
| **feasible** | able to be done | likely or probable |
| **fulsome** | excessive, cloying (praise) | extravagant (praise) |
| **ironic** | showing irony | strange, paradoxical |
| **majority** | the larger or largest number (*the majority of people*) | the largest part (*the majority of the time*) |
| **obscene** | indecent, tending to deprave | offensive or outrageous (*obscene salary increases*) |
| **pristine** | in its original condition | completely clean, spotless |
| **transpire** | to come to be known, to emerge | to happen |

## Confusable meanings

The table overleaf shows many more words that are commonly confused, with a summary of their main meanings.

Pairs of words that are close in both form and meaning are the most likely to be confused. For example, *fortuitous* means 'happening by chance' and *fortunate* means 'happening by good chance'. *Regrettable* means 'to be regretted' and *regretful* means 'having regrets'; they are often confused especially in their adverb forms *regrettably* and *regretfully*. *Prevaricate* means 'to be evasive' and *procrastinate* means 'to put off action', and the two meanings overlap in a way that makes it possible to use either of them in many contexts although their precise meanings are different.

## Tautology

Tautology is the repetition of the same idea or meaning in a phrase or sentence, as in *a free gift* (all gifts are free), *a new innovation*, and *to return again*. Some tautologies are contained within a small group of words such as a noun phrase (e.g. *future prospects*, *past history*, *no other alternative*, *the general consensus*). This kind of tautology is common, especially in the rapid flow of speech, and some have become idiomatic (such as *free gift* and *past history*).

Others occur in the way sentences are put together:

☒ The activities of the club are not limited only to golf.

☒ There is no need for undue haste.

The words *only* and *undue* can be dropped from their sentence without any loss of sense because their meanings are contained in other words. This kind of tautology is not good style and you should avoid it, especially in writing.

## Euphemism

A euphemism is a milder or vaguer word or phrase used in place of one that might seem too harsh or embarrassing in a particular context. The commonest subjects for euphemism are bodily functions (*to relieve yourself*), sexual activity (*to make love*), death (*to pass away*), economics (*downsizing*), and violence (*to do away with*).

We all need to resort to this kind of language in order to respect people's sensitivities, and our own. But there are two kinds of euphemisms that are questionable:

- euphemisms that blur the meaning or cause confusion (e.g. *cloakroom* for *lavatory*).
- euphemisms that attempt to show unpleasant activities in a more positive light (e.g. *ethnic cleansing* for the wholesale killing of peoples).

Some euphemisms have become official clichés, e.g. *helping the police with their inquiries* (= under interrogation and imminent arrest), or are only suitable as jokes, e.g. *tired and emotional* (= drunk).

## Synonyms and antonyms

Synonyms are words that are identical or close in meaning, such as the pair *close* and *shut*, or the trio *begin*, *start*, and *commence*. English is rich in synonyms, often because words entered it from other languages (especially Old Norse during the Viking raids of the 9th and 10th centuries and French after the Norman Conquest in 1066), and failed to drive out those already in use. For example, *close* is a Middle English (13th-century) word derived from Old French, and joined the existing Old English word *shut*. Because French was the language of government in England after the Norman Conquest, some of the words taken from French are more formal than their Old English counterparts, for example, *commence* instead of *begin*, or *purchase* instead of *buy*.

Other pairs of words have their own special areas of use; for example, *kill* is a general word whereas *slay* is literary or rhetorical, and *little* implies an affection or intimacy not present in the more neutral word *small* (compare *a little child* and *a small child*). *Baby* is a general word for a newborn child, *infant* has a special meaning, and *neonate* is used chiefly in medical contexts.

Many words are loosely described as synonyms although their meanings are close rather than identical, and they are not always used in identical ways (e.g. *entreat* and *implore*, *leave* and *depart*). Other words are more restricted in use than the words they might replace. For example, *enquire* and *request* are considered to be synonyms of *ask*, but their effect is more formal and they are not always interchangeable even for the same general meaning:

☑ Kate went to ask what happened next.

☑ Kate went to enquire what happened next.

☑ I'll go and ask them to stop.

☑ I'll go and request them to stop.

☑ The headteacher asked the mayor if he would give the prizes.

☒ The headteacher requested the mayor if he would give the prizes.

? The headteacher requested the mayor to give the prizes.

The second of the last three sentences is ungrammatical, and the third, with its grammar corrected, does not convey the meaning of the original wording.

Synonyms are most useful as more exact or descriptive alternatives for very generalised words. The following sentences all contain the adjective *nice*, which is one of the most overworked words in English:

He wished her a nice time in Paris.

We are hoping tomorrow will be a nice day.

Frank always seems such a nice man.

Instead of *nice* in the three sentences you can say:

He wished her an enjoyable (or agreeable or pleasant) time in Paris.

We are hoping tomorrow will be a fine (or sunny or warm or pleasant) day.

Frank always seems such a likeable (or kind or generous or pleasant) man.

Notice that *pleasant* is possible in all three sentences. It is often an improvement on *nice* but because it too is so versatile it is liable to be overused just as *nice* is.

Other synonyms are not really equivalents at all but are special kinds of a more general word. There is no synonym for the word *bed* (in its furniture meaning): words like *berth*, *bunk*, *divan*, and *futon* are not alternatives for the word *bed* but types of bed, and you can only use them when you mean that particular type (and even then you will be changing the emphasis). There is no synonym for *sing*: words like *chant*, *croon*, and *warble* mean particular kinds of singing but not singing in general.

Antonyms are words that are opposite in meaning, such as *allow* and *forbid*, *alive* and *dead*. Compared with synonyms, there are far fewer antonyms in language, because not all words allow opposite meaning (even *give* and *take* are

# Commonly confused pairs of words

| word 1 | meaning | word 2 | meaning |
|---|---|---|---|
| **adherence** | (to belief etc.) | **adhesion** | sticking |
| **adverse** | unfavourable | **averse** | opposed |
| **affect** | cause a change in | **effect** | bring about |
| **alternate** | one after another | **alternative** | available instead |
| **ambiguous** | (statements etc.) | **ambivalent** | (feelings etc.) |
| **amend** | change | **emend** | alter (a text etc.) |
| **amoral** | having no moral sense | **immoral** | not conforming to moral standards |
| **appraise** | assess the quality of | **apprise** | inform |
| **avoid** | keep away from | **evade** | avoid by guile |
| **biannual** | twice a year | **biennial** | every two years |
| **censor** | act as censor of | **censure** | criticise harshly |
| **climactic** | forming a climax | **climatic** | relating to climate |
| **compose** | constitute | **comprise** | consist of |
| **continual** | happening constantly or repeatedly | **continuous** | going on without a break |
| **credible** | believable | **credulous** | too ready to believe |
| **decided** | unquestionable | **decisive** | conclusive, unfaltering |
| **definite** | clear and distinct | **definitive** | decisive, authoritative |
| **defuse** | remove the fuse from, reduce tension in | **diffuse** | spread out, not clear or concise |
| **deprecate** | disapprove of | **depreciate** | lower in value |
| **discomfit** | disconcert | **discomfort** | make uneasy |
| **disinterested** | impartial | **uninterested** | not interested |
| **enormity** | extreme seriousness, grave crime | **enormousness** | great size or scale |
| **especially** | in particular, above all | **specially** | for a special purpose |
| **exceptionable** | open to objection | **exceptional** | unusually good |
| **flaunt** | display ostentatiously | **flout** | disregard (rules etc.) |
| **fortuitous** | happening by chance | **fortunate** | happening by good chance, lucky |
| **flounder** | (of a person) struggle or be in confusion | **founder** | (of an undertaking) fail or come to nothing |
| **gourmand** | glutton | **gourmet** | food connoisseur |
| **illegal** | against the law | **illicit** | not allowed |
| **imply** | suggest strongly | **infer** | deduce or conclude |
| **impracticable** | not able to be done | **impractical** | not practical |
| **incredible** | not believable | **incredulous** | unwilling to believe |
| **ingenious** | well thought out | **ingenuous** | innocent, honest |
| **intense** | extreme in force or degree | **intensive** | thorough or concentrated |
| **interment** | burial | **internment** | being interned |
| **loose** | not fixed; unfasten or relax | **lose** | be deprived of or no longer have |
| **luxuriant** | lush | **luxurious** | comfortable and rich |
| **masterful** | powerful, domineering | **masterly** | highly skilful |
| **militate** | have force (against) | **mitigate** | make less severe |
| **observance** | keeping a law or custom etc. | **observation** | perception, remark |
| **occupant** | person in a vehicle etc. | **occupier** | person living in a property |
| **official** | having authorized status etc. | **officious** | aggressive in asserting authority |
| **perquisite** | special right or privilege | **prerequisite** | (something) needed in advance |
| **perspicacious** | having a ready understanding, perceptive | **perspicuous** | clearly expressed |
| **pitiable** | deserving pity | **pitiful** | causing pity, contemptible |
| **practicable** | able to be done | **practical** | effective or realistic, (of a person) skilled at manual tasks |
| **precipitate** | headlong | **precipitous** | abruptly steep |
| **prescribe** | recommend with authority, issue a prescription | **proscribe** | forbid or condemn |
| **prevaricate** | act evasively | **procrastinate** | defer action |
| **purposely** | intentionally | **purposefully** | resolutely |
| **refute** | prove to be false | **repudiate** | reject or disown |
| **regrettable** | causing regret, undesirable | **regretful** | feeling regret |
| **sensual** | gratifying the body sexually | **sensuous** | gratifying the senses as distinct from the intellect |
| **sociable** | friendly and willing to mix with people | **social** | relating to society |
| **titillate** | excite pleasantly | **titivate** | adorn or smarten |
| **tortuous** | twisting, devious | **torturous** | causing torture, tormenting |
| **triumphal** | done or made to celebrate a victory | **triumphant** | victorious, jubilant after a victory |
| **turbid** | (of a liquid) cloudy; confused | **turgid** | swollen or congested, tediously pompous |
| **unsociable** | not willing to mix with people | **unsocial** | socially inconvenient |
| **venal** | open to bribery, corrupt | **venial** | (of a sin) minor |

only approximately opposite, and in some contexts are not opposite at all). Obviously concrete nouns such as *bed* and *floor* cannot have opposites, nor can classifying words such as *circular* and *German*.

# 10. Formal and informal language

## Written and spoken English

The different contexts and levels of formality in which English is used are called registers. At a broad level English, like all languages, varies from the formal and technical to the informal and casual. Register also takes account of the various types of communication, such as conversation, informal writing, journalism and broadcasting, and formal writing including essays, speeches, and academic books. In conversation, for example, use of the personal pronouns *I* and *you* is relatively high, contractions such as *I've*, *you're*, and *don't* predominate over the fuller forms, and colloquial and slang words occur regularly. In more formal writing, colloquialisms are uncommon, the indefinite personal pronoun *one* is more likely to be used than the less formal *you*, *upon* is likely to be used as well as *on*, and more formal words such as *ascertain* and *desirous* are likely to occur.

## Slang and informal language

The term *slang* is first recorded in the 1750s, shortly after the publication of Samuel Johnson's *Dictionary of the English Language* in 1755 (in which the disapproving term 'low word' is used instead). But the existence of words that are highly informal or are associated with a particular social group or occupation is much older, and this type of vocabulary has been commented on, usually unfavourably, for centuries.

Modern dictionaries tend to use the label 'informal' for vocabulary that would once have been termed 'slang', using 'slang' for the informal vocabulary of particular groups of people, for example military slang. In general, informal vocabulary typically includes extensions of meanings of established words and especially idioms and phrases (e.g. *to do in* = to kill), shortenings of words (e.g. *fab* from *fabulous* and *cred* from *credibility*), compound formations (e.g. *airhead* and *couch potato*), and blends (e.g. *ginormous* from *gigantic* and *enormous*), as well as special processes such as rhyming slang (e.g. *butcher's* = butcher's hook = look) and back slang, in which words are reversed (e.g. *yob* = boy).

Much informal vocabulary is short-lived, and relatively few words and uses pass into standard English. Exceptions include *bogus*, *clever*, *flog*, *joke*, *prim*, *rogue*, *sheer* (as in *sheer joy*), *snob*, and *tip* (meaning a gratuity), which were all classed by Samuel Johnson as 'low words'. Conversely some words that were once standard have passed into vulgar slang (e.g. *arse*, *shit*, and *tit*).

## Choosing the right level of formality

Each mode of writing and speaking calls for its own different kind of language. In the most formal register, a machine might be said to be *malfunctioning*; in a neutral or everyday register it will be described as *not working*, and at the informal extreme it will be said to be *bust* or *kaput*. Formal words are usual in instructions and notices: *alight* (from a bus or train), *conveyance* (for *vehicle*), *enquire* (rather than *ask*), *notify* (rather than *tell*), and *select* (rather than *choose*). In more general contexts, *purchase* is more formal than *buy*, *edifice* than *building*, *endeavour* than *try*, and *purloin* than *steal*. The language of technical writing has its own terminology; for example, *gravid*, meaning pregnant, occurs only in medicine and biology. Most of these formal words can be turned on their heads and made to look affected or silly in trivial or jocular use (Do you really live in this edifice?).

No one style of vocabulary and grammar is superior to another; it is their appropriateness to the occasion that matters.